Who's Who Among American High School Students®

Honoring Tomorrow's Leaders Today®

1989-90

Twenty-fourth Annual Edition

Volume XV

Educational Communications, Inc.

California, Guam/American Samoa, Hawaii

Students are listed alphabetically within the state where they attend school.

Students featured in this volume attended school in the states listed above.

© Copyright 1990

Educational Communications, Inc.
721 N. McKinley Road
Lake Forest, Illinois 60045

Printed in U.S.A.

Vol. I	ISBN 0-930315-84-7
Vol. II	ISBN 0-930315-85-5
Vol. III	ISBN 0-930315-86-3
Vol. IV	ISBN 0-930315-87-1
Vol. V	ISBN 0-930315-88-X
Vol. VI	ISBN 0-930315-89-8
Vol. VII	ISBN 0-930315-90-1
Vol. VIII	ISBN 0-930315-91-X
Vol. IX	ISBN 0-930315-92-8
Vol. X	ISBN 0-930315-93-6
Vol. XI	ISBN 0-930315-94-4
Vol. XII	ISBN 0-930315-95-2
Vol. XIII	ISBN 0-930315-96-0
Vol. XIV	ISBN 0-930315-97-9
Vol. XV	ISBN 0-930315-98-7
15 Volume Set	ISBN 0-930315-83-9

Table of Contents

Publisher's Corner

Education-The Weapon to Win the Next War*

To the students being honored in this publication I would like to offer my congratulations and best wishes for continued success. Fortunately, most of you have already demonstrated that you're capable of succeeding by working hard, not by wishing hard. And, from where I sit, it's going to take a lot of hard work from everyone to succeed individually and nationally as the 90's roll into high gear.

As peace breaks out all over the world (with a few obvious exceptions) and the cold war winds down to a surprisingly wonderful conclusion, we are entering a new era where the major battles will be fought on the economic front and the most effective weapon will be improved education. In order to win or even just hold our own economically, we are going to have to do much better educationally. You already know this and you and the other students listed in this book are not the problem. What you need to do, however, is use your leadership skills to make certain that the quality and quantity of education is improved dramatically in your community, your school(s) and ultimately throughout our country.

Today our adversaries are no longer communists, they are competitors. Our warriors need to be well-armed with knowledge, skills, and expertise instead of guns, planes and tanks. Even though the threat of a nuclear holocaust may be greatly reduced, the pain and suffering we might endure if we lose this economic war could cause a slow and terrible death and the disappearance of a way of life we have all valued and cherished.

Almost 50 years ago our nation mobilized and unified to defeat our enemies who sought to control the world. Today, we need the same resolve to make every classroom a factory of knowledge, every teacher a dedicated and demanding drill instructor and every student a highly trained, motivated and educated soldier.

It is wonderful that the students being honored in this book have performed so well. I don't want to minimize the significance or importance of your achievements. I do want to emphasize that all of you must insist that all current and future students have the tools to perform and contribute to our society in a more substantial manner than presently exists. The alternatives are unacceptable.

* *This article went to press before the Iraqi invasion of Kuwait.*

Who's Who Review

A Summary of the Objectives, Programs, Policies for Who's Who Among American High School Students®

Since 1967, WHO'S WHO AMONG AMERICAN HIGH SCHOOL STUDENTS® has been committed to honoring outstanding students for their achievements in academics, athletics, school and community service. Our first edition recognized 13,500 students from 4,000 high schools; the current, 24th edition, published in fifteen regional volumes, honors 684,243 high school students representing approximately 18,000 of the 22,000 public, private and parochial high schools nationwide.

As our program has grown, we have expanded the scope and depth of the services and benefits provided for listed students. Policies and procedures have been refined in response to the needs of the schools and youth organizations who share our objectives.

During the past several years, we have hosted over 90 day-long reviews with key education association executives to exchange ideas and perspectives regarding our standards and services. The growth, acceptance and preeminence of WHO'S WHO AMONG AMERICAN HIGH SCHOOL STUDENTS® as the leading student recognition publication in the nation, can be attributed to the involvement of educators in the policy-making areas of our programs.

Most importantly, we must acknowledge the contributions of our Committee on Ethics, Standards and Practices, a group of distinguished educators representing secondary and post-secondary education. The committee was created in 1979 to formalize standards for our program which could be used as a guide for all student recognition programs. These standards are distributed to 80,000 high school principals, guidance counselors and other faculty members each year.

The standards developed by the committee have been used as a model by several education associations who have created their own guidelines for evaluating student recognition programs on a uniform basis. WHO'S WHO is proud of its well-documented leadership role in promoting standards and ethics for all student recognition programs.

The committee meets each year and reviews literature, policies, programs, and services. They bring a perspective to the company which assures students and school administrators that WHO'S WHO policies and programs are in compliance and compatible with the standards and objectives of the educational community.

Major Policies and Procedures

Free Book Program:
Guarantees extensive recognition through wide circulation

WHO'S WHO sponsors the largest Free Book Program of any publisher in any field. The book is automatically sent free to all participating high schools and youth organizations and offered free to all 7,500 libraries and 3,000 colleges and universities. Up to 15,000 complimentary copies are distributed each year.

The major purposes of this extensive free distribution system are to provide meaningful, national recognition for listed students among institutions traditionally concerned with student achievement, and to make it convenient and easy for these students to view their published biography without purchasing the book.

For students who cannot locate an inspection copy of the book in their community, a listing of libraries within their state which received the most current edition is available upon request.

The recognition and reference purpose(s) of WHO'S WHO AMONG AMERICAN HIGH SCHOOL STUDENTS® have been acknowledged in the favorable review of the publication by the Reference and Subscription Books Reviews Committee of the American Library Association (Booklist, 3/1/82).

Financial Policies:
Legitimate honors do not cost the recipient money

There are no financial requirements whatsoever contingent upon recognition in WHO'S WHO AMONG AMERICAN HIGH SCHOOL STUDENTS® The vast majority of students featured in all past editions have not purchased the book, but have received the recognition they have earned and deserve.

For those students who do purchase the publication or any related award insignia, satisfaction is guaranteed. Refunds are always issued on request.

Nominating Procedures:
Representation from all areas of student achievement

Each year, all 22,000 public, private and parochial high schools are invited to nominate students who have achieved a "B" grade point average or better and demonstrated leadership in academics, athletics or extracurricular activities. Occasionally, students with slightly under a "B" average have been included when their achievements in non-academic areas were meritorious. Schools are requested to limit selections to 15 percent of their eligible students. Most nominate less.

Approximately 14,500 high schools participate in our program by nominating students. An additional 5,000-7,500 schools are represented by their outstanding students as a result of nominations received from bona fide youth organizations, churches with organized youth activities, scholarship agencies and civic and service groups. Many of our nation's major youth groups participate in our program by nominating their student leaders.

Editing:
Maintains the integrity of the honor

Occasionally, nominators recommend students who are not qualified for recognition. When these students receive our literature and forms, there may be confusion concerning our standards and criteria. When biography forms are submitted for publication, they are all reviewed and edited to monitor compliance with our high standards. In the past 14 years, 285,141 students were disqualified by our editors because they did not meet our standards, including over 75,000 students who ordered the publication. More than $1,803,553 in orders was returned to these students. Our standards are never compromised by the profit motive. (Auditor's verification available upon request.)

Verification of Data:
A continuous safety check on the effectiveness of our procedures

To monitor the accuracy and integrity of data submitted by students, a nationally respected accounting firm conducts annual, independent audits of published biographical data. Previous audits reveal that up to 95.5 percent of the data published was substantially accurate. (Complete studies available upon request.)

Programs, Services and Benefits for Students

Scholarship Awards:
From $4,000 in 1968 to
$100,000 annually since 1982

The Educational Communications Scholarship Foundation®, a not-for-profit organization funded by the publishing company, sponsors three scholarship award programs which award over $100,000 in scholarships each year. $1,200,000 has been funded to date.

Through the general high school program, 65 awards of $1,000 each are awarded to students by a committee of extremely dedicated educators on the basis of grade point average, class rank, test scores, activities, an essay and financial need. An additional $15,000 in scholarships is funded through grants to youth organizations. For students already in college, $25,000 in scholarships is awarded through THE NATIONAL DEAN'S LIST® Program.

The Educational Communications Scholarship Foundation's programs represent one of the 10 largest scholarship programs funded by a single private sector organization. The Foundation is listed in numerous directories on financial aid and scholarships.

Teachers Nomination Program:
The best teachers in America
selected by the best students™

All students listed in WHO'S WHO are given the opportunity to nominate a limited number of their former teachers from grades K-12 for special recognition in our publication, WHO'S WHO AMONG AMERICA'S TEACHERS™. Thus, students acknowledge those teachers who have contributed significantly to their success and growth.

Grants-in-Aid:
Financial support for organizations
who work with or for students

Since 1975, we have funded grants to youth and educational organizations to support their student programs and scholarships. A brief summary of grants issued or committed to date, totalling approximately $410,700 appears in this review.

The College Referral Service (CRS)®:
Links students with colleges

WHO'S WHO students receive a catalog listing all 3,000 colleges and universities. They may complete a form indicating which institutions they wish us to notify of their honorary award. This service links interested students with colleges and universities.

Although most selective colleges rely almost exclusively on grade point average, class rank and test scores for admissions decisions, several hundred colleges have indicated that the CRS and the publication are valuable reference sources in their recruitment programs. (Surveys from colleges available for inspection.)

Annual Survey of High Achievers™:
The views of student leaders are
as important as their achievements

Since 1969, we have polled the attitudes and opinions of WHO'S WHO students on timely issues. This study provides students with a collective voice otherwise not available to them. A summary of the poll is sent to leaders in government, education and the press.

Each year, survey results are widely reported in the press and have been utilized in academic studies and research indicating the educational value of this program.

College-Bound Digest®:
What students need to know

A compilation of articles written by prominent educators covering twenty various topics of interest to college-bound students, i.e., financial aid opportunities, the advantages of large schools, small schools, achievement test usage and preparation and numerous other appropriate articles. The Digest appears in the introductory section of WHO'S WHO and is available free to 20,000 high school guidance offices and 3,000 college admissions offices.

Local Newspaper Publicity:
Additional recognition for honor
students

Consistent with our primary purpose of providing recognition for meritorious students, we routinely provide over 2,000 newspapers nationwide with rosters of their local students featured in the publication with appropriate background information. (Students must authorize this release.)

Who's Who Student Profile

Statistics from 1990 Edition

General Listing

Total Number of students • 684,243

Seniors • 137,568

Juniors • 261,925

Sophomores • 205,288

Freshmen • 79,462

Who's Who Students as Percentage of 12,000,000 High School Students Enrolled Nationwide • 6%

Females • 63%

Males • 37%

Academics

Grade Point Average (%)

"A+/A" • 54%

"B+/B" • 46%

"B-" • less than 1%

Local Honor Roll • 480,362

National Honor Society • 137,723

Valedictorian/Salutatorian • 7,994

Leadership Activities/Clubs

Student Council • 96,687

Boys State/Girls State • 28,626

Senior Class Officers • 26,238

Junior Class Officers • 48,726

Sophomore Class Officers • 58,502

Freshman Class Officers • 59,793

Key Club • 40,030

Major Vocational Organizations

4-H • 42,713

Junior Achievement • 20,494

Future Farmers of America • 25,377

Distributive Education Clubs of America • 8,617

Business Professionals of America • 10,980

Athletics

Basketball • 134,263

Track • 100,839

Cheerleading/Pom Pon • 74,775

Football • 68,358

Volleyball • 61,043

Baseball • 45,708

Soccer • 43,168

Tennis • 41,160

Cross Country • 32,949

Wrestling • 17,775

Music/Performing Arts

Orchestra/Band • 164,041

Chorus • 107,858

Drama • 63,341

School Play/Stage Crew • 93,987

Miscellaneous

Church/Temple Activities • 264,637

Yearbook • 80,204

School Paper • 57,661

Students Against Driving Drunk • 96,686

Community Worker • 60,785

Fellowship of Christian Athletes • 42,123

Also from ECI

The National Dean's List®

The thirteenth edition of THE NATIONAL DEAN'S LIST® recognizes 110,000 outstanding students representing 2,500 colleges and universities. Most students were selected by their respective deans or registrars because of their academic achievements. This year, $25,000 in scholarships was distributed to twenty-five students who each received $1,000. For 1990-91, a minimum of $25,000 in scholarships will again be awarded.

Who's Who Among America's Teachers™

The first edition of WHO'S WHO AMONG AMERICA'S TEACHERS™ was published in October 1990 and lists 24,500 teachers from grades K-12. All teachers recognized were nominated by at least one student listed in either WHO'S WHO AMONG AMERICAN HIGH SCHOOL STUDENTS® or THE NATIONAL DEAN'S LIST®.

Memberships

Educational Communications, Inc. or its publisher is a member of the following organizations:

American Association of Higher Education

American Association of School Administrators

American Library Association

American School Counselors Association

Business Professionals of America, National Business Advisory Council

Chicago Metropolitan Better Business Bureau

Distributive Education Clubs of America, National Advisory Board

Educational Press Association

Future Farmers of America, Executive Sponsor

Illinois Association of College Admissions Counselors

National Association of Financial Aid Administrators

National School Public Relations Association

Grants to Youth and Educational Organizations*

American Association for Gifted Children - $2,000, 1 Grant
To sponsor a conference for educators concerning: "The Gifted Child, The Family and the Community."

American Children's Television Festival - $2,000, 1 Grant
To promote excellence in television programming for children.

American Council on the Teaching of Foreign Language - $500, 1 Grant
To support the general goals and objectives in the field of foreign language.

American Legion Auxiliary Girls Nation - $27,500, 12 Grants
Scholarships for Vice President and Outstanding Senator of program where students participate in mock government structure.

American Legion Boys Nation - $33,500, 13 Grants
Scholarships for President and Vice President of program where students learn about government through participation.

Animal Welfare Institute - $1,582, 2 Grants
For biology textbook on experiments which do not involve cruelty towards animals. Second grant to fund convention booth equipment.

Black United Fund - $5,000, 1 Grant
Scholarships for Black students, selected by BUF Committee.

Business Professionals of America - $50,000, 14 Grants
ECI serves on the National Business Advisory Council, sponsors scholarships and support services.

Colorado Forum of Educational Leaders - $1,000, 1 Grant
To fund a series of quarterly activities regarding the educational successes of Colorado Schools.

Contemporary-Family Life Curriculum - $1,500, 1 Grant
Funded formal grant request, resulting in $100,000 grant from government to test this contemporary curriculum.

Distributive Education Clubs of America (DECA) - $50,000, 16 Grants
ECI serves on the National Advisory Board, sponsors scholarships and support services.

Earthwatch - $3,000, 3 Grants
Scholarships for students conducting scientific expeditions with scientists, researchers.

Education Roundtable - $5,000, 1 Grant
To fund the creation of a committee of representatives from government, education, private industry and the general public to support and improve education in America.

Fellowship of Christian Athletes - $12,800, 5 Grants
Scholarships for coaches' conferences concerning spiritual, professional and family growth.

Joint Council on Economic Education - $10,000, 3 Grants
Funds ongoing economic education program for students and educators from elementary school to college level.

Junior Achievement - $13,000, 8 Grants
Scholarship for the winner of the WHO'S WHO Essay Contest.

Junior Classical League - $6,000, 6 Grants
Scholarship to the outstanding member selected by this organization.

Junior Engineering Technical Society - $11,600, 6 Grants
Annual Scholarship award and support services.

*As of September 30, 1990

Bill Kurtis, Former host of the "CBS Morning News", interviews WHO'S WHO Spokesteens Stephanie Woolwich, Long Beach, NJ and Alex Tachmes, Miami Beach, FL

A group of 12 WHO'S WHO Spokesteens appear with host Pat Robertson (center) on the popular TV magazine program, "700 Club" (CBN) to present teen leaders' views on American's future in a special 7 part, 8 hour debate.

WHO'S WHO sponsors scholarships for the president and vice president of the American Legion Boy's Nation program (l to r) Renard Francois, 1989 Vice President; Doug Mory, Conference Chairman; Thomas C. Workman, 1989 President.

Grants to Youth and Educational Organizations*

Key Club International - $5,000, 5 Grants
For two scholarships of $500 each for two outstanding Key Clubbers.

Law and Economic Center, University of Miami Law School - $4,500, 1 Grant
Funded study on use of media to effectively communicate economic issues and policies to general public.

Lester Benz Memorial Fund - $1,000, 1 Grant
To the School of Journalism and Mass Communications, University of Iowa in honor of an original and valuable member of our Scholarship Committee, and former Executive Director of the Quill and Scroll Society.

Miss American Co-Ed - $4,500, 7 Grants
Scholarship for Academic Achievement Award.

Miss Teenage America Scholarship Program - $33,000, 8 Grants
Scholarship for student selected as Miss Teenage America; previously funded four $1,000 awards for semifinalists.

Modern Miss - $2,500, 5 Grants
Scholarship for the National Academic Winner

Modern Music Masters - $4,500, 2 Grants
For chapter expansion program of this national music honor society, high school level.

Mu Alpha Theta - $10,700, 4 Grants
Scholarships for outstanding math students.

National Cheerleaders Association - $7,100, 8 Grants
Scholarships for winners of state drill team contests.

National Exchange Club - $3,500, 2 grants
Grant to fund a scholarship for the Student of the Year.

National Federation for Catholic Youth Ministry - $1,500, 1 Grant
Scholarship for student leaders

National Forensic League - $11,000, 6 Grants
Scholarships of $1,000 each to winners of the National Debate Team.

National Foundation for Advancement in the Arts - $7,000, 7 Grants
For general support of the Arts, Recognition and Talent Search Program of this Foundation.

National 4-H Council - $20,000, 8 Grants
Grants are used for scholarships for outstanding 4-H students.

National Future Farmers of America (FFA) - $33,000, 14 Grants
Grants are used for scholarships for outstanding FFA students.

National Society of Professional Engineers - $1,000, 1 Grant
Grant used for scholarships for outstanding NSPE students.

Performing & Visual Arts Society (PAVAS) - $4,000, 2 Grants
To conduct expansion program for high school chapters.

The President's Committee on the Employment of the Handicapped - $6,000, 6 Grants
Scholarship for the winner of the President's Committee National Poster contest, high school division.

Quill and Scroll Society - $13,000, 9 Grants
For one scholarship of $1,000.

Soroptimist International of the Americas, Inc. - $3,000, 3 Grants
Scholarship for organization's Youth Citizenship Award Winner.

Special Olympics, Inc. - $1,000, 1 Grant
Scholarship for outstanding student volunteer.

*As of September 30, 1990

On the NBC "Today Show," former host Tom Brokow (center) interviews Who's Who Spokesteens (left) Burnell Newsome, Hazelhurst, MS, Amy Krentzman, Deerfield Beach, FL, Tari Marshall, ECI Representative, and Mike McGriff, Chicago, IL.

David Hartman, former host of ABC's "Good Morning America" (right) interviewed Who's Who Spokesteen Shannin Mealiffe from LaCanada High School, LaCanada, CA (second from left) with two authorities on teen suicide.

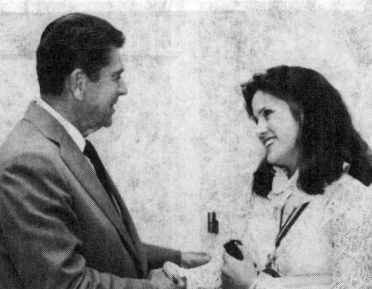

Former President Reagan greets Miss Teenage America, Amy Sue Brenkacz. Who's Who sponsors a $5,000 scholarship for Miss Teenage America and listed Amy Sue in the publication.

Standards for Who's Who Among American High School Students® and Other Recognition Programs and Societies

Our company's adherence to the standards listed below has been attested to by an independent public accounting firm. A copy of their report is available upon request. Copies of the standards/guidelines adopted by other education associations are also available upon request.

1.Nominations will be from established organizations that work with and for the benefit of high school-aged youth. Under no circumstances will recommendations be accepted from students, their parents or solicited from standard commercial lists.

2.Criteria for students to be selected will be clearly defined and reflect high personal achievement.

3.Listing in "Who's Who" will not require purchase of any items or payments of any fees.

4.Additional programs and services which are available to those listed in "Who's Who" at cost to the students, will be clearly described in the literature provided.

5.A refund policy will be clearly stated in all literature.

6.Nominators will be able to recommend students without releasing confidential data or fear of having confidential data released by program sponsors.

7.Student information will be confidential and will not be released except where authorized by the student.

8.Home addresses will not be published in the book or made public in any way.

9.Under no circumstances will "Who's Who" sell student information or lists.

10.The publisher will describe, disseminate and verify the methods employed to assure national/regional recognition to students listed.

11.The publisher will respond to all inquiries, complaints and requests for relevant background information.

12.The basis of the scholarship program competition will be defined. Number and amount of awards will be stated, lists of previous winners will be available. Finalist selection process and funding method will be clearly defined. Employees or their relatives will not be eligible for scholarships.

13.There will be an advisory council (external to the organization) to review and make recommendations regarding the policies, procedures and evaluation process of the "Who's Who" programs.

14.The publisher will set forth in writing and make publicly known the policies and procedures it follows in the implementation of these standards.

Members of the Committee on Ethics, Standards and Practices

Dr. Wesley Apker
Executive Director
Association of
    California School
    Administrators
Sacramento, CA

Adrienne Y. Bailey
Deputy Superintendent
    for Instructional
    Services
Chicago Public Schools
Chicago, IL

James T. Barry
Assoc. Vice President
    for University
    Relations
St. Ambrose University
Davenport, IA

Dr. Harold Crosby
Regents Professor
University of West
    Florida
Pensacola, FL

Dr. S. Norman Feingold
President
National Career &
    Counseling Services
Washington, D.C.

Charles R. Hilston
Executive Director
Association of
    Wisconsin School
    Administrators
Madison, WI

Dr. John Lucy
Superintendent
District 128
Palos Heights, IL

Dr. Paul Masem
Superintendent of
    Schools
Alexandria City Public
    Schools
Alexandria, VA

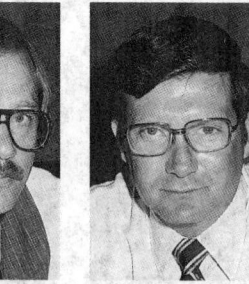

Dr. Edward J. Rachford
Superintendent
Homewood-Flossmoor
    Community HS
Flossmoor, IL

Dr. Vincent Reed
Vice President for
    Communications
The Washington Post
Washington, DC

The Educational Communications Scholarship Foundation®

During the 1989-90 academic year, approximately 20,000 students competed for scholarship awards sponsored by the Educational Communications Scholarship Foundation® which is funded by the publishing company. Students competed by completing an application which requested data regarding aptitude test scores, grade point average, extracurricular activities, work experience and general background information. Semifinalists were selected based on careful examination of all this information and were then requested to provide information regarding financial need. In addition, semifinalists were asked to write an essay from which the Scholarship Awards Committee attempted to evaluate the overall maturity of the students.

Sixty-five winners were selected and a total of $65,000 was awarded. Over $1,200,000 has been distributed through the Foundation to date.

Educational Communications Scholarship Foundation Committee members meet to select 65 scholarship winners. Each winner receives a $1,000 award.

The 1989-90 Scholarship Winners

Maria Adelina Aguirre
Flagstaff High School
Flagstaff, AZ
University of Arizona
Tucson, AZ

Laura Becker
Winnebago Lutheran Acad.
Fond du Lac, WI
Dr. Martin Luther College
New Ulm, MN

Robin Christine Clark
Marquette High School
Bellevue, IA
Yale University
New Haven, CT

Richard Alan Conn
Mary Fuller Frazier Mem. HS
Dawson, PA
University of Pittsburgh
Pittsburgh, PA

Keri Lynn Dawson
Hickory High School
Hickory, NC
University of North Carolina
Chapel Hill, NC

James Harold Ballowe, Jr.
Duluth High School
Duluth, GA
Vanderbilt University
Nashville, TN

Scott Brown
The Lakeside School
Eufaula, AL
Georgia Tech
Atlanta, GA

Susan L. Clark
Churchill High School
Eugene, OR
Pepperdine University
Malibu, CA

Justin Corvino
Easton Area High School
Martin's Creek, PA
Mass. Inst. of Technology
Cambridge, MA

Long Van Dinh
Robert E. Lee High School
Jacksonville, FL
Jacksonville University
Jacksonville, FL

Gregory A. Becerra
East Chicago Central HS
East Chicago, IN
Berklee College of Music
Boston, MA

Stephen Robert Castile
Lane Technical High School
Chicago, IL
Princeton University
Princeton, NJ

Robert Keith Clinton
Palisade High School
Palisade, CO
Greenville College
Greenville, IL

Christopher William Dahl
Roundup High School
Roundup, MT
Stanford University
Stanford, CA

Cara Eleshuk
Green River High School
Green River, WY
Western Wyo. Comm. Coll.
Rock Springs, WY

The 1989-90 Scholarship Winners

Andrew Espinoza
Muleshoe High School
Muleshoe, TX
Texas Tech University
Lubbock, TX

Chet W. Hammill
Big Sky High School
Missoula, MT
University of Illinois
Urbana, IL

Michelle Iva Hlubinka
Fountain Valley High School
Fountain Valley, CA
Yale University
New Haven, CT

Susan M. Huitink
Oskaloosa Senior HS
Oskaloosa, IA
Northwestern College
Orange City, IA

Joseph H. Karlin
George Washington HS
Philadelphia, PA
Mass. Inst. of Technology
Cambridge, MA

Michael David Fowler
Stromsburg Public HS
Stromsburg, NE
University of Nebraska
Lincoln, NE

Thomas W. Harman
Waccamaw Academy
Conway, SC
University of South Carolina
Columbia, SC

Tien T. Hoang
Sacramento High School
Sacramento, CA
University of California
Berkeley, CA

Thomas Lee Hutchison
Division Avenue High School
Levittown, NY
Yale University
New Haven, CT

Jewel Dale Lambert, Jr.
NW Rankin Attendance Ctr.
Brandon, MS
University of Miami
Coral Gables, FL

Gary Joseph Freitas
Stonington High School
Pawcatuck, CT
Yale University
New Haven, CT

Stephanie Jean Hart
Clarkdale High School
Meridian, MS
Univ. of Southern Mississippi
Hattiesburg, MS

Rodney Jerome Hobbs
Central High
Memphis, TN
University of Virginia
Charlottesville, VA

Kristen Nicole Jaax
Clear Lake High School
Houston, TX
Stanford University
Stanford, CA

James C. Lee
Dixie High School
Dammeron Valley, UT
Brigham Young University
Provo, UT

Kristin Gunnerson
Edison High School
Huntington Beach, CA
University of California
Los Angeles, CA

Ryan Hayden
Kettle Falls High School
Kettle Falls, WA
Whitman College
Walla Walla, WA

Chong Min Hong
Jenks High School
Jenks, OK
Harvard University
Cambridge, MA

Robert James Jensen
Evanston High School
Evanston, WY
Brigham Young University
Provo, UT

Todd A. Lewis
Norris High School
Roca, NE
University of Nebraska
Lincoln, NE

Catherine Hall
Salmon River Central
Bombay, NY
Macalester College
St. Paul, MN

Elizabeth Hernandez
Maria Vazquez de Umpierre
Bayamon, PR
Col. Univ. Tecn. de Bayamon
Bayamon, PR

James A. Hornsten
Chisago Lakes Senior HS
Lindstrom, MN
College of St. Thomas
St. Paul, MN

Shauna Leialoha Kanekoa
Maui High School
Kahului, HI
Brigham Young University
Provo, UT

Kanika A.M. Magee
Benjamin Franklin HS
Fort Lauderdale, FL
Howard University
Washington, DC

The 1989-90 Scholarship Winners

Sheila Macael Marmon
Cate School
Los Angeles, CA
Princeton University
Princeton, NJ

Sarinda Newell
Mendocino Community HS
Mendocino, CA
Mass. Inst. of Technology
Cambridge, MA

Jennefer Allyn Russo
West Windsor-Plainsboro HS
Princeton Junction, NJ
Cornell University
Ithaca, NY

Christopher David Spruell
Haralson County HS
Felton, GA
Georgia Inst. of Technology
Atlanta, GA

Craig A. VanZante
Pella Community HS
Otley, IA
Iowa State University
Ames, IA

Colleen Marshall
Highlands High School
N. Highlands, CA
Boston University
Boston, MA

Steven J. O'Berski
Interlochen Arts Academy
Goodrich, MI
The University of Michigan
Ann Arbor, MI

Michael Scott Scheschuk
J. Frank Dobie High School
Houston, TX
University of Texas
Austin, TX

Brian David Stark
Prairie High School
Cedar Rapids, IA
Stanford University
Stanford, CA

Ruth Wagnon
LaSalle High School
Olla, LA
Louisiana College
Pineville, LA

Tom George Matzakos
Aurora Central High School
Aurora, CO
University of Colorado
Boulder, CO

Jeffrey C. Olson, Jr.
Fenwick High School
River Forest, IL
Mass. Inst. of Technology
Cambridge, MA

Stacy Shor
Chamberlain High School
Tampa, FL
University of Florida
Gainesville, FL

Anna Marie Thompson
Eau Gallie High School
Melbourne, FL
Cornell University
Ithaca, NY

Jane S. Wey
Huntington Beach HS
Huntington Beach, CA
Harvard University
Cambridge, MA

Jeff M. McCombs
Laguna Hills High School
Laguna Hills, CA
Univ. of Southern California
Los Angeles, CA

Julie Pfaff
Pius XI High School
Milwaukee, WI
Marquette University
Milwaukee, WI

Julie Ellen Smith
Jackson Christian School
Humboldt, TN
Tennessee Tech. Univ.
Cookeville, TN

Thanh Thi-Dieu Tran
Sidney Lanier High School
Montgomery, AL
Cornell University
Ithaca, NY

Heidi Michelle Whigham
Atlantic Comm. High School
Boynton Beach, FL
University of Florida
Gainesville, FL

Lik Mui
San Leandro High School
San Leandro, CA
Mass. Inst. of Technology
Cambridge, MA

Maria Christina Rojas
Norman High School
Norman, OK
Brown University
Providence, RI

Cole Spainhour
Captain Shreve High School
Shreveport, LA
Cornell University
Ithaca, NY

Joel Trotter
Morrison Academy
Richmond, VA
University of Virginia
Charlottesville, VA

Daniel William Wood
Milford High School
Milford, OH
University of Toledo
Toledo, OH

College-Bound Digest®

As a public service to the 96 percent of WHO'S WHO students who will continue their education after graduation from high school, we have invited a group of distinguished educators to use our publication as a forum to inform and assist students through the articles in this section.

While we do not presume that these articles contain "everything you need to know" about preparing for college, we believe you will find they will be helpful in learning "some of the things you need to know."

We wish to acknowledge the special contribution of Robert McLendon, Dean of Admissions, Brevard College, Brevard, North Carolina, who was instrumental in selecting appropriate topics and authors for this section.

Getting the most from your high school counselor

By James Warfield

Your high school counselor's job is to help you. Your job is to get to know your counselor so that he/she can help you in an effective manner. Helping your counselor help you requires open and frank discussions regarding your goals and personal plans. Your high school counselor should:

- know your abilities;
- know your goals;
- recommend academic course selections;
- recommend which college entrance test to take;
- recommend colleges that meet your criteria;
- help you focus your ideas;
- and most importantly, make you think.

Recommendations should be based upon your academic abilities and goals. This is a critical issue because the appropriateness of this advice is determined by the consistency between your aspirations and aptitudes. Verifying the accuracy of your self-perceptions is important in order to avoid sudden surprises caused by false hopes or unrealistic expectations. The reason why your counselor exists is to help you become everything you are capable of within a realistic framework.

For many students, the college selection process begins with the PSAT, taken in the fall of the junior year. Your counselor should advise you which of the college entrance tests to take, SAT, ACT, ACH and AP, and when to take them. The type of college you apply to will determine which tests to take. The quality of the college, or the quality of your own academic program, and whether or not you plan to apply Early Decision, will determine when you should take such tests. Many juniors don't know to which schools they'd like to apply, so advance planning is necessary in order to maintain open options.

Finding the right college will require you to know yourself, your likes and dislikes. In what kind of environment do you see yourself being most comfortable? Can you picture yourself at a small college or a mid-size or large university setting? Do you want a school to be in a rural community, a suburb or to be in an urban environment? Do you want to be in a different geographic part of the country, or is being close to home important to you? What are some of your academic areas of interest? What kind of extracurricular offering do you want to participate in? As you answer these questions, the attributes of your ideal college will become more clear. Through discussion with your counselor you'll be able to assess your needs, and more clearly focus your perceptions of yourself and of the schools you will be researching.

Your counselor should help generate a list of colleges that meet your requirements by drawing upon his/her own wealth of knowledge or utilizing the many reference materials available.

Many counselors have access to computers that will provide a list of colleges for you to investigate, once you have determined the characteristics you are looking for. If the guidance office does not have a computer, the same information can be obtained from the commercially published reference books that are available through your counselor or library. After generating a list of perhaps twelve to twenty schools, your research really begins.

Resource books provide a wealth of statistical and narrative descriptions on virtually every college. The counseling office is likely to have college catalogs as well as files on each college containing brochures, view books and leaflets of the various academic and extracurricular offerings available at that particular school. Although college catalogs are boring reading material, information relating to admission procedures and requirements, course offerings and requirements for each of the academic majors are outlined. In addition, course prerequisites and methods of exempting yourself from some prerequisites are also indicated. As your research continues, you'll be able to eliminate schools and determine some colleges in which you are seriously interested.

Many high schools set up procedures whereby students may meet with representatives from colleges to obtain more information or answer individual questions. These representatives may be the Director of Admissions, admissions officers, or personnel hired to represent the college. Of course, the more you know about the college before talking with the college representative, the more value they will be to you. Some colleges require an interview either by the representative, an alumnus, or by an admissions officer. Your counselor should help you determine if an interview is necessary in your situation.

Campus visits are the most effective means to determine if the college is right for you. When to visit is a matter of individual taste or need. A school you casually visit during a summer vacation will serve a different purpose, and have different flavor, than a visit made in the fall after you have applied. It is also difficult to compare schools that are on break from those in session. Keep in mind that as you visit more schools your observational skills will become more sophisticated and your reflections of each will be altered. It may be more prudent to visit only those schools to which you have been accepted, after you have received all your admissions decisions.

As you narrow your choice of colleges, your counselor should review with you the possibilities of acceptance or rejection at each. At least one of your choices should be a safety choice, one in which you are almost guaranteed of being admitted.

After the list of colleges to which you are going to apply has been determined, it is your responsibility to obtain the application and meet deadline dates. Many colleges require a counselor's recommendation or a Secondary School Reference. Some require additional recommendations from specific teachers. Establish application procedures with your counselor so that he/she, the teacher, and school have adequate time to do their part in order to meet your deadline dates. If you are required to write an essay or personal statement, discuss this with your counselor. These discussions serve several purposes: help you generate ideas and narrow topics that you wish to write about; provide you with suggestions that will enhance your applications; and provide the counselor with insights that will compliment your application.

It is your responsibility to file your applications on time, see that your test scores are sent to the admissions office, and file the financial aid applications. Your counselor will help you determine which scores to send, which financial aid form is required and how to fulfill these requirements.

Finding, selecting and applying to the colleges that are right for you is a long and studied process. It involves a lot of letter-writing, telephoning, research, weighing alternatives, and just plain old thinking. It's a decision-making process that requires questioning, information gathering, evaluation of the information and more questioning. This cycle is often repeated in order to make effective decisions. The better the decision-making process the more likely your college experience will be successful.

Jim Warfield is Director of Pupil Personnel at Lake Forest High School, Lake Forest, Illinois. Jim is currently President of Suburban Chicago Directors of Guidance Association, involved and active in a number of professional organizations, and past member of the National Advisory Council for the Educational Records Bureau, Wellesley, Massachusetts.

The use of the SAT at selective colleges

By Dr. Judith G. Bainbridge

For many students the numbers — from 200 to 800 on the verbal and on the quantitative sections of the College Board examination — seem to be the voice of doom; for others, they announce the possibility of admission into the nation's most selective colleges. But just how important, really, are those scores, and how will college admissions committees interpret them?

It is important to remember that the SAT (or ACT) is only one part of your total record. Your rank in your high school class, your grades, extracurricular activities which show leadership potential, and your recommendations are all

extremely important. In addition, some colleges will consider your geographic location (it may be easier for the valedictorian of a South Dakota high school to enter Harvard than for the top student in a Connecticut prep school), your relationship with alumni, your religious preference at some denominational colleges, and the success of other graduates from your school at the institution.

Colleges treat scores, grades, rank, activities and recommendations in a variety of ways, but very few use arbitrary cut-off scores to determine acceptance. Every selective college or university attempts to select a class which will be successful (they don't want you to flunk out after your first year). Students who are admitted are those who they can predict will do well; and admissions staff experience with standardized tests suggests that certain levels of achievement can be predicted with a fair degree of accuracy when used in conjunction with the high school record.

Often the total score on the SAT is less important than the individual score on either the verbal or the quantitative aptitude section. While colleges and universities may publish their average SAT as a combination, many liberal arts colleges believe that the verbal score is a particularly good indicator of ability, and many technically-oriented engineering programs will be impressed with a very good quantitative score. A pre-engineering student with an 1150 SAT may be a very good candidate if his scores are 450 on the verbal section and 700 in the quantitative area; he might be substantially less impressive with 650/500.

One of the problems that many students confront when they first look at their scores is a sinking feeling that their numbers do not match their high school achievement level. The 'A' student who is third in her class and barely makes a 450/450 on the SAT is

disappointed for days afterwards. It is important, however, to understand what your scores mean. The national average on the verbal section of the SAT is 427; on the mathematics section it is 467. Clearly, many college bound students will have a total score under 900. Many colleges and most state universities have average scores at this level or below it; more selective institutions will have average scores that are substantially higher, but even among these colleges there will be a number of students whose scores range from 900 to 1,000, but whose grades and rank indicate a strong chance of success.

But how can you explain or understand an average score when you have been an excellent student? It may be that you had a bad day (or a bad night before); a headache, too little sleep, a testing environment that is too hot or too cold may cause your scores to be less than your best. It may be that the scores are an accurate indicator of your aptitude and that you are a high achiever. Or it may mean that your grades have been inflated and that you have not been challenged by teachers or peers. One way that you can determine if it was just the specific test day is to compare your scores on the SAT with your PSAT. If you scored, for example, 48/50 on the PSAT and have a combined total on the SAT of from 970 to 1020 your test is probably valid. If, on the other hand, your PSAT was 55/58 and you scored 1020 on the SAT, you probably should plan to retake the examination to see if the second time might show real improvement.

In addition to the "bad day" low score there are other reasons that good students do not do well on standardized tests. It may be that they panic under time pressure, that they are unfamiliar with national tests and the testing environment, or that their skills and abilities cannot be shown on

such tests. Really creative students, those with talents in the arts, and those who work very slowly through a problem, analyzing as they go, are sometimes at a disadvantage. If you fall in one of these categories, it is especially useful for a teacher whose recommendation you have requested be asked to discuss your other strengths in an admissions letter.

Some students retake the SAT two or three times to see if they can improve their overall scores, and it is important to realize that scores will vary slightly every time you take a Scholastic Aptitude Test. A variation of 30 points in either direction is normal; more than 50 points, unusual. How worthwhile is it to retake the SAT if your scores are under the average published by the college of your choice? Some schools, like Furman, acccept your best scores from each section. Others may average your test results. It is probably true that you can improve your quantitative score with tutoring over several months; improving verbal scores is more difficult. You should remember, however, that while selective colleges have many high-scoring students, their *average* SAT is just that; there have been many others whose scores are under the average but who have the proven achievement to be admitted.

Suppose, however, that you are very interested in an institution which indicates an average SAT of 1275, your score is 1050, but your parents are alumni, you graduated in the top 10% of your class, and you have been an outstanding high school leader. Academically you would be in the bottom quarter of your class, yet you may well be admitted because of your parents and your activities. Should you attend such a college? Will you be able to compete at a level comfortable for you with students whose high school backgrounds may be substantially superior? Are you ready to make a number of "C's" or to study harder and longer than your roommates?

You should consider, too, that very high scores do not necessarily mean admission to the college of your choice. Several years ago a young man with an SAT score of 1440 applied to a selective Southeastern liberal arts college. He had graduated in the lower half of his high school class and although he had been involved in some extracurricular activities, he also had been a discipline problem in high school. After substantial discussion, he was not admitted, but the college admissions office was interested enough to trace his career several years later. He had flunked out of two other colleges. SAT scores indicate aptitude — the ability to learn — not achievement. They do not show the desire to learn, the ambition to succeed or the perseverance necessary for academic excellence. College admissions officers are aware of these facts and they will read your entire application with an awareness that you are more than a score on a computer printout.

Dr. Judith G. Bainbridge is the Director of Educational Services at Furman University, Greenville, South Carolina. She has authored various articles for the Journal of College Placement and is a former columnist for the Charlotte Observer.

Tips on taking the SAT...to the victor belongs the spoils

By Suzanne Money

Consider these words: "Victim," "Victor". Finding them sequentially in the dictionary recently prompted the theme for this article.

According to the American Heritage dictionary, a victim is "one who is harmed by or made to suffer by an act." One of the steps in the process of being admitted to college is the taking of a college admissions test. Many students feel they are a victim in this experience, but STOP right there! There are numerous activities that cost nothing, and can improve your comfort level going into the testing experience. Perhaps it will even be to the point of claiming yourself as the victor... that is, "one who is the winner of a struggle."

First, read, read, read! A recent survey caught my attention because it gave average outside reading times for 5th graders scoring in the 90th percentile in reading. Would you believe the first group read for 5-6 minutes a day in outside reading, excluding assignments from school? The 90th percentile group read 15-20 minutes per day outside school.

There's a much greater reward in reading than the potential improvement of your scores. Reading can take you to Kathmandu or Timbuktu, inside your brain, or inside the double helix, for that matter. It can stretch your imagination and your understanding in so many ways

beyond the images of a television screen. I'm not knocking TV. I'm encouraging you to take charge of your life in productive ways. Remember those 5th graders...think what you could do on a consistent basis with a half an hour a day of quality reading.

While you read, develop your own vocabulary. Be curious. If you run across an unfamiliar word, try to define it from context and then check it out in a dictionary. Read *All the King's Men* and develop your own vocabulary as one English teacher in Atlanta requires of his students. Challenge crossword puzzles, brain teasers, and word power exercises, while waiting in your orthodontist's office. Think beyond English class. Consider, for example, the word, "symmetry". You'll find it in art, biology, mathematics. If you encounter that word in all three disciplines and understand its usage, it's yours!

Secondly, think, think, think. Remember that you are in control of your learning. There is no quick fix. You have to organize your assignments, be persistent and challenge those you cannot conquer the first time through. Figure out in math if there is another method of solving a problem. If so, try it out with your instructor. This is the "what if" and most teachers love for a student to offer alternative solutions. If you are asked to memorize a math formula, question in your mind how you are going to use it. Take a logic course or computer programming.

Thirdly, study, study, study. Pick up the free College Board test preparation publications in your guidance office and spend some time studying the test taking tips, particularly the guessing strategy, then take the practice test. If you are in the 10th or 11th grade, begin with the Preliminary Scholastic Aptitude Student Bulletin, available in late September or early October in your counseling office.

Remember that 15-20 minutes in outside reading mentioned earlier? Why not try it for one week on that booklet. Next action, take the PSAT/NMSQT in late October. Then you can graduate to the *Taking the SAT*, available in your counseling office, and surprise yourself with a knowledge of the format and content of the test before you sit for the SAT.

The SAT is not the end all, nor is it the enemy. It is a common measure of the ability to do freshman-level work in college. When your score arrives in that admissions office, it does not jump off the page with a thumbs up or thumbs down signal to the admissions committee. It is discussed in conjunction with grades, weight of courses taken, needs of the institution, and other pertinent information provided.

Challenge yourself with the best courses available at your school; take charge of your outside reading; energetically participate in class, keeping the teacher on his/her toes; and commit to knowing the format and content of the PSAT/ NMSQT and SAT. That makes a winner and that can be you!

Suzanne Money has been in education for nineteen years, ten as a high school guidance counselor and nine with the College Board office in Atlanta, Georgia.

Can you prepare for the SAT?

By Stanley H. Kaplan

Can you prepare for the SAT? Of course you can. In fact, more than 64 years after the debut of the SAT in 1926, the question has become a non-issue. In the last several decades, a major study by the Federal Trade Commission and independent surveys at high schools through the country have proved conclusively that the right kind of test preparation does indeed improve performance on this crucial test. In fact, thousands of students like you have scored improvements of 200, 250, 300 points or more after completing our program.

The question you and your parents are asking today is not WHETHER, but HOW you should prepare for the SAT. The answer, naturally, depends on your individual temperament and needs. My firm has been in the business of test preparation for more than a half century, but I'd be the last to suggest that everyone requires formal SAT review. However, I'm the first to suggest that most do!

Some students do very well with self-study. IF you decide to "go it alone," there are many materials available at book stores, including practice tests released by the College Board and simulated exams in SAT review texts. There's no denying that taking these tests and famil-iarizing yourself with basic question types can help "demystify" the SAT.

But most students want more. Commitment to a regular class schedule and reassurance provided by a skilled, enthusias-tic teacher go a long way toward easing test anxiety. It's a big help to know that you can ask questions and get individual help, even an encouraging word, when you need it!

Which is why school sponsored and commercial preparation courses, as well as private tutoring, have become so popular. The Stanley H. Kaplan Educational Center graduates more than 25,000 students each year, thanks to the fact that our program includes not only a thorough review of the math and

verbal skills tested by the SAT, but also a solid grounding in what I call "testmanship."

"Testmanship" can make the difference between a mediocre performance and an outstanding one, between a student who knows the material but is still overwhelmed by anxiety and one who is prepared and confident. The SAT, after all, is a different kind of test, framed by testmakers with particular goals in mind. It is not — as the misnomer, Scholastic Aptitude Test, implies — a test of innate ability. Rather it is designed to measure what you have learned in and out of school and your ability to handle that knowledge in new and challenging ways. Any student who sits for the test armed with that knowledge PLUS strategies that reflect the testmaker's thinking, including time budgeting formulas, guessing techniques and a solid understanding of the test's structure, is bound to have a competitive edge.

So how can you be sure the preparation method you choose will be right for you? That it will provide proven test-taking techniques as well as the essential math and verbal review that must go with it? If you decide that you stand to gain from structured SAT prepara-tion, the following guidelines should help you select a legitimate program that will maximize your test potential:

1. Weekend cram courses are of little value. Lessons should be held weekly so you have time to study and practice what's been learned in class.

2. Classes should be small; 10 to 20 students is the optimum size. Of course, individual help should be available if you need it.

3. There must be opportunity to make up missed lessons. Certainly, you shouldn't give up studying for an important exam at school to attend an SAT class. Nor should illness

prevent you from getting the full benefit of a class session.

4. Any program you choose should have a permanent location where you can get extra study materials or talk with someone knowledgeable and supportive. Beware of fly-by-night courses that advertise box numbers, hold classes in rented rooms and then silently steal away when the program ends!

5. You should have the opportu-nity to continue your SAT studies if you choose to take the test a second time. (Re-member, you can retake the SAT as often as you want. Most schools accept the highest reported score.)

6. The better programs offer scholarship assistance if you cannot afford to pay for their course.

7. Be suspicious of fast talk designed to corral students. Inflated, undocumented score claims, for example, have little bearing on whether a particular course will benefit you. "Guarantees" with lots of small print may make it im-possible for you to qualify. (At our Centers, students can retake or extend their studies for any reason whatsoever, regardless of their score.)

8. Most important, you should check out a program with previous enrollees. Their ex-perience can speak volumes about the quality of teaching, the adequacy of study materials, and the range of score improvement achieved.

Please remember that, despite the scare tactics of some prep courses, the SAT is NOT the most important test you'll ever take. It is only one of many criteria used by admissions offices to judge your college ap-plication. Certainly, your grade point average weighs more heavily in most admissions formulas than your SAT score.

Remember, too, that the SAT

can be prepared for even before you open a review text, choose a tutor, or enroll in a prep course. You can start right now, by reading as much as you can — newspapers, magazines, best-sellers — anything that catches your eye and holds your interest! The more you read, the more your vocabulary and your ability to integrate ideas will improve. And that, of course, means a higher SAT verbal score.

What about math? The place to start is with your work at school. Begin now to start attacking problems instead of memorizing them. Try to reason things through and discover the why as well as the what. It will make you a more creative thinker — one who thinks like the SAT! Best of luck on the SAT and all the other tests you'll be facing through your life!

Stanley H. Kaplan is Chairman and Chief Executive Officer of the Stanley H. Kaplan Educational Center Ltd., the nation's largest test preparation specialist. Kaplan has been featured in numerous publications, including Time, Newsweek, The New York Times, and The Wall Street Journal, and has guested on many radio and television programs. He has been invited to speak at meetings of the College Board and high school advisory organizations, as well as to testify at federal and state legislative hearings as an acknowl-edged expert on test preparation.

Searching for student financial aids

By S. Norman Feingold and Marie Feingold

In this article, we suggest practical steps for students and parents to follow for obtaining information about the twenty-four billion dollars ($24,000,000,000) of student financial aid that is annually awarded.

We can not overemphasize that a great deal of time and concentrated effort is required: to search for financial aid; to write for application materials; to effectively fill out application forms; to obtain references; and to mail all the required materials well before the deadline date.

The twenty steps below will increase the likelihood of your receiving the student financial aid you seek.

1. Start Early

The high school student should begin the search as early as possible in the sophomore year. The out-of-school student of any age should start the financial aid search as far in advance of applying for college admission as is possible. Some financial aid application deadline dates are a year prior to announcement of recipients.

Many scholarships for high school graduates require that the student take the Scholastic Aptitude Test or the Preliminary SAT or the ACT. The National Merit Scholarship competition starts the beginning of the junior year in high school. Many organizations use the NMSC results for the selection of recipients, and this includes some companies which award scholarships to employees' children. Some colleges select student aid recipients from National Merit competitors.

2. Set up a Student Financial Aid File

As early as the tenth grade, develop your own collection of materials about scholarships, loans, work study, and prepaid plans for which you may be eligible. Small local newspapers all over the United States contain a great deal of information about scholarships and loans for which local students may apply. Many times these local funds cannot be found in national directories.

In sections 3 through 6 are suggestions for materials that you should read at your school or library. Those publications which are free or of nominal cost may be obtained for your own student aid file.

3. Federal Publications

A. *The Student Guide: Five Federal Financial Aid Programs.* Student Guide, Dept. 511T, Consumer Information Center, Pueblo, CO 81009, FREE, published annually. The 1991-92 edition will be available January 1991. It contains a list with names, addresses and telephone numbers of sources of information on guaranteed student loans, PLUS loans, SLS loans, and state student aid. Terms are defined, procedures are outlined, and name changes of programs are provided.
B. *Federal Benefits for Veterans and Dependents, VA Fact Sheet IS-1*, Superintendent of Documents, U.S. Government Printing Office, Washington, DC, 20402, $2.25 prepaid is published annually in January and provides details of educational assistance for veterans, their spouses, and their children.
C. *U.S. Department of Defense.* Each of the services has a number of programs to assist its members in obtaining college degrees. Reserve Officers Training is not the only program. To obtain information about the various programs, contact the recruiting office of each of the services in your area. Addresses and telephone numbers are available in the telephone book, either in the white pages under the heading United States Government, Recruiting, or in the special government blue pages in large city directories.
D. *U.S. Department of Health and Human Services.* Information about programs for students enrolled in health professions may be obtained from the Health Resources and Service Administrations, Bureau of Health Professions, 5600 Fishers Lane, Rockville, MD 20857.
E. *U.S. Department of Interior.* Members of Indian tribes, which have established their own Grants and Loans Programs for the higher education of their members, obtain information from their tribal headquarters or the Bureau of Indian Affairs, Washington, DC 20240. Indians who are members of a tribal group that is being served by the Bureau of Indian Affairs, write to BIA, Office of Education Programs, MS 3512, Code 522, 18th and C Street, NW, Washington, DC 20240.

If you are having difficulty locating information about Federal financial assistance for training and education, write to your local Congressman or Senator at either his local office or at his Washington DC office in the House of Representatives or Senate office buildings.

4. Non-Governmental Publications

A. *Need a Lift?*, $2.00 prepaid is published each September by the American Legion, National Emblem Sales, P.O. Box 1050, Indianapolis, IN 46202. Sources of financial aid are categorized as those specifically for veterans and their dependents, and those available to all students, which makes this publication valuable to non-veteran families as well as to veterans' families. The Table of State Educational Benefits for Veterans and Their Dependents is particularly helpful.
B. *The College Financial Aid Emergency Kit 1989-90 Edition*, by Joyce Lain Kennedy and Dr. Herm Davis, $4.50 prepaid, Sun Features Inc., Box 368, Cardiff, CA 92007 is upbeat with helpful details not usually found in student financial aid publication.
C. *Scholarships, Fellowships and Loans*, by S. Norman Feingold and Marie Feingold. Gale Research, Inc., 835 Penobscot Building, Detroit, MI 48226 is now the publisher of these books. These books contain detailed information about scholarships, fellowships, loans, and grants that are not awarded by the institutions which recipients attend. They are available at public libraries, university and college libraries and financial aid offices, and high school guidance or career planning offices.
D. *Student Aid Newsletter: Fellowships, Grants, Awards, Loans and Scholarships,* Bellman Publishing Company, P.O. Box 34937, Bethesda, MD 20817, $37.50/year is a quarterly newsletter about financial aid for education and training for traditional and non-traditional students.
E. *Financial Aid for Students with Disabilities*, Heath Resource Center, The National Clearing House on Post-secondary Education for Handicapped Individuals, One Dupont Circle, NW, Suite 670, Washington, DC 20036-1193 provides information about how to handle the special expenses of these students as well as about the funds available especially for them.

5. State Publications

Most if not all states publish

booklets or flyers about the student financial aid programs they administer.

States also publish material on scholarships for special groups such as veterans, policemen, prison guards, firemen and their dependents. It is likely that the state scholarship agency can give you the name and address you need.

Your guidance counselor or public librarian will know how to obtain copies of state directories of local financial aids, or they will have copies for you to read.

6. Local Publications (City and County)

Many communities have a listing of student aids that are available to their residents. Your counselor and librarian can direct you to them.

7. Know the ethnic, religious, and place origins of your family

A fairly large amount of student financial aid is awarded by private organizations to persons of specific origins and religions. Consult the book *Scholarships, Fellowships and Loans.*

8. Know for whom your parents or guardian work.

Some corporations and labor unions provide awards for their employees and members respectively. Have your parents speak to the personnel department of the company and the steward of the labor union for details. Company and union newspapers and magazines are good sources for keeping abreast of these financial aids.

9. Know the names and addresses of organizations of which your parents or guardian are members

They may have student financial aid for members' children.

10. As soon as practical for you, try to determine a field of interest and hobby

Some aids are given for majoring or studying certain subjects or having engaged in specific activities. Entries in *Scholarships, Fellowships and Loans* are

indexed by vocational goals as well as alphabetically.

11. Enter Contests

There are many different kinds of contests. The American Beekeeping Federations, Inc., 11637 NW 39th Avenue, Gainesville, FL 32606, for example, sponsored a 1988 essay on "The Talking Honey Bees" for active 4-H members.

12. Get your own work experience

Students who have been caddies or delivered newspapers or work in other capacities are often eligible for scholarship competitions.

The company for which you work may provide tuition refunds which cover a part or all of course fees. Generally the course must be related to your work, and permission must be obtained.

13. Consider scholarship loans

In areas of work in which there are manpower shortages, it is possible to convert a loan to a scholarship by working in a given geographic area or in a specific subject matter field.

14. Loans to parents and loans or scholarships to children of employees or to residents of service areas

They may be administered by businesses, foundations, banks, or non-profit corporations. Pacific Gas and Electric, for example, awards scholarships to high school seniors who live in or attend high school in areas served by it.

15. Attend cooperative or workstudy schools

Earnings will cover much if not all of the tuition and living expenses of students enrolled in cooperative education programs. In the "typical" co-op program, students alternate semesters of study and supervised paid work. Information is available at no cost from the National Commission for Cooperative Education, 360 Huntington Avenue, Boston, MA 02115.

16. Apprenticeship training

In the skilled trades, this is the way to learn and earn. Details are available from the following four sources: State Bureau of Apprenticeships and Training (one office is located in each state capital); local and state employment offices; in a number of states, a state apprenticeship council; and the U.S. Department of Labor, Bureau of Apprenticeship and Training, 200 Constitution Avenue NW Washington, DC 20210.

17. Teachers, principals, ministers, lawyers bankers, business people, counselors may know of

individuals who anonymously assist deserving individuals to obtain the training and education they are seeking.

They are also often aware of funds about which there is little or no publicity.

Usually there is less competition for local student aid funds than there is for national ones.

18. The financial aid office of the institution you wish to attend or are attending

Many funds are administered by the schools themselves, and you must let the financial aid office know of your need for assistance. Many schools and universities publish a directory of their student aids; they are usually free.

19. Answer all letters and application forms with great care

Be certain that you have answered every question. Many funds screen out applicants who do not answer all the questions. For those not applicable, write N/A. If at all possible, type; be certain of accuracy and neatness. Meet all deadline dates.

You need enough time to edit your answer several times. The quality of essays, when they are required, is an important screening device.

Be certain to give references and schools you've attended enough time to submit their materials on time. Also be certain to remind them of deadline dates.

If you try each one of the methods described above and have ability and potential, you have a good chance of getting student aid. A study by the authors shows that with students of equal ability, the ones who applied to more resources were more successful in obtaining assistance. You may get a scholarship on your second try from the same fund.

Good luck. Don't let the lack of money deter you from seeking further education and training. Your post-secondary education can open up rewarding careers to which you otherwise would not have access.

Dr. S. Norman Feingold is President, National Career and Counseling Services, Washington, DC; Honorary National Director of B'nai B'rith Career and Counseling Services; Past President American Association for Counseling and Development; and the author of many publications including the eight volumes of Scholarships, Fellowships and Loans. Marie Feingold, formerly a securities analyst and rehabilitation counselor, is co-author of volumes 6, 7, and 8. She is executive editor of Student Aid Newsletter: Fellowships, Grants, Awards, Loans and Scholarships.

Tough questions to ask any admissions officer

By Robert G. McLendon

As a college admissions officer for the past eighteen years, it is clear to me that today's prospective students are carefully comparing colleges and striving to learn all they can about the colleges to which they apply. The age group of 18 to 24 year olds is declining in the United States, and this is creating a type of "buyer's market" in the market place of higher education.

In order to assure yourself that your expectations of a college are met, you, the student consumer, need not hesitate to ask admissions officers some "tough questions." This article will offer you a few suggestions of some tough questions that I hope will help you make the right choice when selecting a college.

Academic Questions

1. How many students in last year's freshman class returned for their sophomore year?

2. What percent of the freshman class obtained a 2.00 (C) average or above last year?

3. If accepted, will you tell me my predicted freshman grade-point average? Many colleges use a mathematical formula based on studies of currently enrolled students to predict an applicant's freshman grade average.

4. What is the college's procedure for class placement? This is especially important in the areas of English and mathematics because freshmen often vary significantly in their ability to handle these important academic skills.

5. What procedure is used to assign a faculty advisor when the student is undecided as to the major area of study?

6. What type of additional academic services does your college offer at no additional cost to the student (e.g., tutoring, career or personal counseling, study-skills workshops, improving reading speed, etc.)?

7. How effective is your college's honor code? What is the penalty for cheating?

Social Questions

1. What is the average age of your student body and what percent resides on campus?

Many colleges today have a large and increasing population of commuting part-time adult students and a dwindling enrollment of 17 to 18 year old full-time, degree-seeking students residing on campus.

2. Is your college a "suitcase college" on the weekends? If not, what are some typical weekend activities for students on your campus?

3. What procedure is used to select roommates if no preference is listed?

4. What are some of the causes of students being suspended or dismissed from your college? Is there a system of appeal for those who have been dismissed?

5. How can a prospective student arrange a campus visit? Clearly the best possible way to evaluate a college socially is to plan a visit to the campus. When you visit, try not to be shy. After your talk and tour with the admissions officer, walk around by yourself and informally ask students their opinions. A good place to chat with students is in the college's student center or at the dining hall.

6. What are some of the rules and regulations that govern residence hall life? Are there co-educational residence halls?

Financial Questions

1. What percent of your students received financial aid based on financial need?

2. What percent of your students received scholarships based on academic ability?

3. What percent of a typical financial aid offer is in the form of a loan?

4. How much did your college increase cost (room, board, tuition, and fees) from last year to current year?

5. If an accepted student must submit a room deposit, when is the deposit due, and when is it refundable? The deposit should be refundable in full up to May 1, if the college or university is a member of the National Associa-

tion of College Admissions Counselors.

6. If my family demonstrates a financial need on the FAF or FFS forms, what percent of the established need will typically be awarded? When can I expect to receive an official financial aid award letter?

The distinguishing quality of any person is the quality of the mind, and the college you select will have a long-lasting impact on your career and life. I realize that you are painfully aware of the need to make the right college choice because most high school students realize that the college years are often the most productive stage of life. Knowing what questions to ask an admissions officer is an important part of this decision-making process. Most admissions officers want you to ask "tough questions" because if you make the wrong choice we, too, have failed in our job.

Bob McLendon is Dean of Admissions at Brevard College, Brevard, North Carolina. He served on the Admissions Practices Committee of the National Association of College Admissions Counselors and has been Chairman of the Admissions Practices Committee of the Southern Association of College Admissions Counselors. He is a past member of the Executive Board of SACAC and past President of the Carolinas Association of Collegiate Registrars and Admissions Officers.

Common mistakes students make in selecting a college

By William B. Stephens, Jr.

The process of choosing a college can be a rewarding, worthwhile

experience or it can be an endless, frustrating series of mistakes. Those mistakes are common and are usually the result of inadequate research and preparation — both characteristics you will need as a successful college student. The selection of a college is a good place to begin developing those virtues.

Begin the process with a series of questions. Am I most interested in a small, medium, or large college? Do I want to stay close to home or go away? What will be my major? Does the college have a broad curriculum if my major is undecided? How academically competitive do I want my college to be? What are the costs? Is financial aid available? Which extracurricular activities are the most important to me? When these questions are satisfactorily answered, it is time to begin the next stage.

Research is of primary importance in selecting a college. Do not make the mistake of choosing a college simply because your friends go there. List priorities. Be willing to invest time and effort in investigating colleges which share these priorities.

In writing to colleges for information, be neat, concise, and accurate in providing information about yourself. Many students forget to include the address to which the college should send material. Also include your high school graduation date, the high school you attend, your anticipated major (if that has been decided), and any pertinent information regarding grades and test scores. Decisions are made about students on the basis of their initial contact with the college. Do not be careless in this important decision.

There are numerous publications which are helpful in gathering information. These publications may be located in school and public libraries, bookstores, and guidance offices. Many are cross-referenced according to majors offered, geographic locations, costs, and sizes. Once familiar with college publications, the task of choosing a college becomes an easier one. Do not make the mistake of floundering with too many college options.

Your school guidance office can offer an abundance of information. Among the many contributions of guidance counselors is the provision of data concerning financial aid, college representatives scheduled to visit the school and/or vicinity, College Fairs, and testing for college entrance. In addition, most schools provide counseling to help students choose colleges compatible with their scholastic aptitudes, personality, financial means, and extracurricular interests. Often these guidance resources are not tapped, yet they can be among the most beneficial that you could explore.

Do not neglect the value of contacting alumni, college representatives, and currently enrolled students. Alumni can provide firsthand accounts of life at college while representatives will have the current facts about admissions requirements, new majors offered, scholarships, sports, and campus activities. Students who are currently enrolled in a particular college can provide additional insight into the actual experiences you can expect at the institution.

It is important that you visit the colleges which are your first preferences. Never will catalogs, counseling, or recommendations from alumni replace an actual visit to the campus. Much can be learned from sitting in on a few classes, walking through dormitories, and talking to faculty and staff. It is extremely risky to choose a college without personal observation.

Many colleges have orientation programs to acquaint students and their parents with the facilities and various aspects of student and faculty involvement. Investigate the colleges being considered to discover their plans for orientation

programs. Do not fail to be present at the programs in which you are most interested.

Since the cost of attending college can be one of the greatest factors determining your choice, the possibility of obtaining financial aid is to be taken into careful consideration. Watch for the deadlines in applying for financial assistance, and have the appropriate forms completed well in advance. If financial aid is offered, be certain to compare the amount of aid offered and the total cost of attending that particular college. Remember that the matter of final importance is in determining the amount which has to be paid by you and your family.

College preparations should begin in the ninth grade. Solid academic courses (usually beyond the minimum required for high school graduation) should be completed each year. Four years of English is normally expected. Most colleges expect a student to complete at least three years of math, including two years of algebra and one of geometry. Although requirements vary from college to college, it is generally advantageous to have a sound background in biology, chemistry, physics, history, and a foreign language.

High schools administer PSAT, SAT, and ACT exams to juniors and seniors. It is wise to plan to take a College Board exam more than once. As these exams take four to six weeks to be graded, you should allow plenty of time so as not to delay the application process. Your score on a college board exam will further indicate the type of college to attend. Colleges vary considerably in their College Board score requirements.

By October of your senior year, choices should be narrowed to two or three prospective colleges. You should be aware of all admission requirements for each institution considered. Do not delay the application process until after Christmas. Many colleges begin

waiting lists very soon after the beginning of each new year. Your application and all required documents should be on file by November 1 at each college considered. Do not expect high schools to send transcripts or teachers to send recommendations the day the request is made. Allow a couple of weeks for these items to be completed and mailed to the college.

Incomplete or illegible applications will greatly diminish the opportunity for rapid processing. These types of delays can mean the difference between being able to attend your first choice of colleges and having to wait another full academic year to enroll.

College-bound students should never hesitate to ask questions. Begin early and be organized. Parental involvement is essential in choosing a college that will meet the need of you and your family. Diligent research and careful planning are the keys to the prevention of the most common mistakes made by college applicants today.

Bill Stephens is Director of Admissions at Florida Southern College, Lakeland, Florida and has worked in the Admissions field for seventeen years. Stephens is a member of the National Association of Admissions Counselors, the Southern Association of Admissions Counselors, the American Association of Collegiate Admissions and Registrar Officers, and the Southern and Florida Associations of Collegiate Admissions and Registrars Officers.

The advantages and pitfalls of advanced placement and credit by examination for the freshman year of college

By Carl D. Lockman

I think we all agree that gifted young people need help in order to recognize their potential role in society. Through advanced placement and credit by examination programs, secondary school systems and universities alike are making a bona fide effort to encourage the development of academic talent, thus helping students to better understand their contributions to society and self.

Perhaps an explanation of the main difference between advanced placement and credit by examination is appropriate at this point. Both programs serve the purpose of awarding the student college course credit for acceptable scores on examinations. However, the Advanced Placement Program is a function of the College Entrance Examination Board. It is a formally structured program of instruction culminating in an examination. Institutions also may give departmental examinations which may be referred to as advanced placement. Credit by examination may or may not be a formally structured program. The College Level Examination Program (CLEP) is an example of the former, through which a student can receive credit for non-traditional (learning outside the classroom) educational experiences by presenting satisfactory scores on examinations.

All programs designed to award credit at the university level have advantages that are worth the student's consideration. Credit programs complement conventional instruction by allowing students to begin academic study at a level appropriate to their experience. They require students to demonstrate that they have achieved at a level equal to college experience. By being given this opportunity, the student can save both time and money.

A second advantage is that studies indicate that advanced placement continues throughout the undergraduate years. Quantitatively and qualitatively the student benefits. Course credit granted through advanced placement generally allows for increased hours to be completed in a four-year program, much of which may be completed at the junior level and above. This certainly allows for greater flexibility and versatility in designing one's curriculum. Somewhat the opposite has shown up in the early studies of CLEP credit. Students with CLEP credit tend to graduate earlier. However, this still permits the student the advantages of having saved money and time and allows the opportunity to move into graduate studies at an earlier date. The challenge for the student is brought to the front when he/she is placed into courses recognizing achievement when his/her ability surpasses basic proficiency level courses.

Another advantage to the participation in and the receiving of credit through these programs is the quality of instruction associated with advanced placement. Generally speaking, it is safe to say that some of the best secondary instructors are asked to conduct the advanced

courses. These instructors will stretch to stay ahead of these bright students who comprise the classes. Also, students in these programs not only benefit from the quality of instruction, but from the fact that most schools set up programs by drawing on the experiences of other school systems. In effect, students are being exposed to highly researched programs that have been trial tested for years by many systems.

A closer look at these programs reveals additional advantages. Many advanced placement programs borrow lectures, lab facilities, and equipment from local businesses and universities to accelerate their programs. Schools sometimes pool courses to give a wider curriculum offering. Credit programs allow secondary schools and colleges to articulate their programs, thus helping to bridge the curriculum gap that has been prevalent for years. In bridging this gap the student with an outstanding background can be recognized.

The advantages far outweigh the disadvantages when studying advanced placement and credit by examination programs. Two negative comments might be made at this point. There is always the possibility that students entering these programs do not have a thorough understanding of the extra demands that will be placed on them. Remember that the courses offered in the secondary schools are rigorous college-level courses, which in turn will demand more effort on the student's part. It is not a bad idea either that parents be made aware of what is to be expected of students involved in advanced placement programs and of those having received credit by examination.

Secondly, uninformed secondary and college personnel cause very definite problems. After a student has participated in an advanced placement program

or has the experience to achieve credit through examination, it is imperative that the secondary counselors advise students and their parents of colleges that have established policies that would meet the needs of the student. I can think of few things more disappointing than for a student to miss the opportunity to have more flexibility in his courses and to avoid repetition. The other fears are that the college officials may not have required faculty members in the subject areas covered by the tests to review the examinations and that the procedures and practices of the college regarding credit have not been carefully studied. As you can see, such omissions by the institution in establishing policies could lead to improper credit and, even worse, improper placement in courses "over the head" of the student.

In conclusion, whether a student goes through the CEEB Advanced Placement Program, participates in the institution's own advanced placement program by taking department examinations, or receives credit for life experiences, the importance of the programs is that they are attempts to equate classroom and/or non-classroom experience to college-level learning. The programs are models of learning closely conforming with college courses. Placement and credit programs are relatively new opportunities which each year seem to become more and more accepted by the academic communities. These are ways to recognize the individual differences in students, an attempt to confront the age-long problems of recognizing the variety of experiences students bring to college, and a breaking from the tradition that all students need to enroll in core curricula.

For students with exceptional learning experiences and/or intellectual talents, advanced placement and credit by examination programs are recom-

mended. The rewards for such accomplishments are great.

Carl D. Lockman is Associate Director of Admissions at Georgia Institute of Technology, Atlanta, Georgia. Lockman served on the Admissions Practices Committee of the Southern Association for College Admissions Counselors and is a member of the American and Georgia Associations of Collegiate Registrars and Admissions Officers. He was appointed to the Governor's committee to study recruitment techniques, is a former board member of the Middle Georgia Drug Council and a charter consultant for Probe Choice in the state of Georgia.

The academic and social benefits of large American universities

By James C. Blackburn

There is no type of collegiate experience which is most appropriate for all students. The purpose(s) of this essay are to identify and discuss the academic and social benefits of large universities. In almost every state in the union, there is at least one large university whose enrollment exceeds 10,000 persons. More than a score of states have within their borders, universities enrolling more than 35,000 students. There are several community colleges whose enrollments meet the criterion of having 10,000+ enrollments. Those institutions are not included within the scope of this essay.

A substantial number of large universities are state-supported. However, more than a few large universities are private institutions of high education. Such universities are more common in the more populous regions of the nation, e.g., the East Coast, upper Midwest, and California. The tuition prices of large universities vary from nominal charges to $15,000 per year. It is, therefore, possible to select a large university from any price range. Some of America's most expensive and least costly institutions can be classified as large universities.

Large universities are located in large cities such as New York, Boston, and Los Angeles, as well as in small towns, e.g., Bloomington, Indiana and Tuscaloosa, Alabama. The selectivity of admission to large universities is also quite varied. Some universities admit as few as one in five of its applicants. Other moderately large institutions offer admission to more than 90% of their applicant pools.

In short, the diversity between and among large universities makes it possible for almost every student who desires to attend such an institution. Enrollment at a large university is not the private privilege of any socio-economic or intellectual sub-segment of American society. That being the case, there must be some good reasons for matriculation at and graduation from a large university.

There are academic benefits which apply to each size and type of college or university. The academic benefits of enrolling at a large university are especially striking.

Few freshmen actually complete the academic major which they begin. At a large university, the available academic majors often number in the hundreds, not dozens. If a student changes his or her major or career choice, the large university is most likely to be able to accommodate that change.

As a result of the "knowledge explosion," many undergraduate curricula now require extensive equipment and large library resources. Because of their graduate and professional schools, large universities tend to offer more sophisticated laboratory equipment and libraries of considerable size. So called "economics of scale" seems likely to perpetuate this circumstance. At a large university, undergraduates often compete with others for these resources. The point is that the equipment and libraries are available.

For most students, postgraduate employment is a major reason for college enrollment. Large universities typically offer a multiplicity of services designed to help students in the identification and pursuit of career options. Selecting a career and finding a job are not often easy; it may be well to get as much help as possible.

There is an additional "job search" benefit to holding a degree from a large university. Most such institutions are well known on at least a regional basis. Assuming the reputation of a given institution is good, the employer or graduate school may be more impressed if they are familiar with an applicant's university.

Each type and size of college and university has academic benefits to offer. Only a few of the academic benefits of the large university have been addressed here. There are other benefits related to the academic learning environment of each large university. Academic learning is clearly the primary reason for the existence of colleges and universities. It would be foolish to suggest that all of the benefits of college attendance happen inside the classroom, laboratory, and library. Many of the non-academic benefits of college attendance are social in nature. It is well that those benefits be discussed.

The typical ages of college attendance (18-22) constitute an important period of intellectual and social development. It is important that these changes take place in the most nearly appropriate environment possible. Intellectual development is obviously an academic enterprise. Social development, which is more than just dating, parties, and football games, happens throughout the campus environment. As with the academic areas, each type of college or university has social benefits to offer prospective students. The social benefits of large universities are significant; those benefits should be considered carefully by aspiring freshmen.

It is reasonable to state that larger universities offer more student activities and more varied opportunities to associate with other students. In fact, many freshmen who enroll at the largest university find themselves inundated with opportunities for social involvement, community service, etc. It may be difficult to select the activities, clubs and personal associations which are most appropriate for individual students.

The variety of opportunities for student involvement at a large university are often more impressive than the sheer number of such involvements, activities, clubs, etc. Many larger universities offer organizations which cater to a plethora of interest ranging from handicrafts to hang gliding. There are often religious organizations for many faiths and deonominations. The opportunities for policitical involvement are often wide ranging. From the most serious of religious or political convictions to the desire for big or small parties, large universities can frequently provide activities which meet the needs of all their students.

As universities grow, the size of the student services staffs also grow. With regard to academics, this growth in student services results in improved opportunities for career identification and job seeking. In the arena of social development, this growth means more opportunities for personal counseling and other activities which are designed to help a person to improve their social awareness and skills.

A final social benefit of large universities has to do with one's classmates. Because of their size, large universities often enroll students whose backgrounds present a wide variety of experiences, values, and perspectives. Exceptions to this rule do exist, but it is generally true that one's classmates at a large university will be less homogeneous than might be the case at smaller colleges and universities.

There is an important social benefit in this lack of sameness among a student's classmates. Most students will study, work, and live out their lives in a world composed of a huge variety of persons. Our society has become more pluralistic in recent years. It seems, therefore, likely that there is a good in being able to live and work with a wide variety of persons. College is an excellent place to gain experience in dealing with people whose backgrounds and perspectives may be different from your own. Large universities offer many opportunities for such experiences.

By way of the above, it is hoped the nature(s) and benefits of large universities may be better understood by qualified prospective students. The more important points of this essay are that American higher education is quite varied and that no type of colleges or universities is inherently superior to any other type or types. Each student must make his or her own decisions about the appropriateness of small colleges, community colleges, church affiliated colleges, and large universities. This writer's bias for large universities should be obvious. Huge varieties of academic and social opportunities are available at large universities. Those varieties serve to make such institutions an excellent choice for many aspiring freshmen. Large universities, although varied themselves, are not for everyone. They do present very appropriate choices for many prospective students.

Jim Blackbrun is Director of Admissions and Records at California State University, Fullerton, California, and has been involved in the college admissions process for over 20 years. He has published several papers and over 20 book reviews concerning admissions issues. Blackburn is a frequent speaker on topics relating to college admissions and higher education in general.

The academic and social advantages of a private church-related college or university

By A. Mitchell Faulkner

Many educators in recent days are concerned that moral and ethical matters have been so largely excluded from the educational experience. Under the influence of a technology expanding beyond all expectations, the demands placed upon most professions, including the social and natural sciences, have worked to exclude serious consideration of moral and ethical concerns inseparably bound up in that expanding technology.

But the assumption that our complex society can be safely led by technicians untrained in the making of serious ethical decisions affecting our corporate well being is totally unacceptable to any thinking person.

As Bruce Haywood has written in The Chronicle of Higher Education, "too many of our colleges and universities have been vocational schools... Whereas once they offered our children avenues to a larger sense of their humanity, they now direct them to the market place. Instead of seeing themselves enlarged under the influence of great minds and grand ideas, students find themselves shrunken to fit the narrowing door of the graduate school or tailored to a job description. It is time for our colleges and universities to talk again about the worth of a free life, time while we are still able to distinguish between the training of young people and their education."(1/8/79)

Young people are not born with moral and ethical convictions. They are learned in the educational process, if learned at all, by precept and by example, by being in the presence of people with convictions. Healthy self-identity, says Lloyd Averill, emerges out of an environment which has convictional distinctiveness, in which the maturing self has access to a range of clear and competing values where the competition serves to sharpen and enliven the options rather than to subjugate or obliterate them.

A subtle but pervasive element emerging in our day is what Archibald MacLeish has called the diminution of man, the "long diminishment of value put upon the idea of man" in our society. Why has this happened now at the moment of our greatest intellectual triumphs, our never equalled technological mastery, our electronic miracles? "Man was a wonder to Sophocles when he could only sail and ride horseback and plow; now that he knows the whole of modern science he is a wonder to no one," says MacLeish.

At least part of this loss of the humane is cause by the knowledge explosion, the sheer weight of information in the print and electronic media, so that man despairs of any cognitive wholeness and surrenders ever increasing areas of knowledge to a vast array of experts.

Earl McGrath, former Commissioner of Education, says on the other hand, that this vast array of facts and theories need to be collated and evaluated within the framework of philosophic convictions and religious beliefs in order for the wisdom of the ages to again invest dehumanizing facts with meaning for man.

One further point of definition needs stating. Our sense of community has well nigh been lost, and every social philosopher recognizes the need to restore it. What is at stake here, says John Gardner, is the individual's sense of responsibility for something beyond the self. The "me" generation threatens the cohesiveness of our social fabric, and a spirit of concern and caring is virtually impossible to sustain in a vast, impersonal society.

All of the above points directly to the purpose of the church-related liberal arts college. The essence of the liberal arts is the passion for man, the development of the humane values in literature, philosophy, history, and religion; and the great ideas of the race, such as truth, justice, love, beauty, honor, and wisdom are precisely the vehicles through which the deepest purposes of religion are served. Religion is only secondarily a matter of creeds and rituals. At its heart it is a matter of meaning, and this meaning is conveyed most effectively through the wisdom of the ages, the liberal arts.

Education is more than a learned set of mental exercises, the ability to respond properly to fixed mental inquiries. A computer does this admirably. To be fully human is to add to this a capacity for imagination, the ability to feel reverence and awe in the presence of mystery, a capacity for caring and compassion, and appreciation for the mixed grandeur and misery of the human experience. These represent the uniquely human accomplishment and point the direction for the church-related liberal arts college.

Further, the church-related college, usually smaller, offers a community in which students have more opportunity to learn through experience the interpersonal skills so necessary to effective participation in today's society. The development of the whole person involves taking responsibility for the care of the community, its governance, its social life, its ethical and moral tone, its operative effectiveness. A broad participation in all aspects of the campus community should mark the church-related college.

Students are not uniformly at the same place in their development, and ought not to be coerced to march lock step through some standardized program. The undergraduate program, through flexibility made possible by forms of governance and individual care, ought to allow as much as possible for diversity of interest and differences in development as the student progresses. A college ought to find ways to encourage each student to develop to the fullest potential his individual gifts and educational aspirations. A student's goals ought to be headed by the desire not only to master the curriculum but to develop himself. The church-related college will seek to aid this through the total experience, intellectual, social, cultural and religious.

The church-related college, if dedicated to the full human development of its students, will retain a healthy respect for the vocational skills. In order to fully be, a person must be able to do. Life cannot be divorced from work, and a healthy self identity depends in part upon the ability to make some significant contribution to society. Thus the great truths of the liberal arts must be brought to focus and a point of service through competency in a chosen area of the world's work, where one may serve and fully live.

After all, as Montaigne said a long time ago, the purpose of education is not to make a scholar but a man.

A. Mitchell Faulkner is the former Executive Director, Council for Higher Education, Western North Carolina Conference, the United Methodist Church. He was on the Board of Trustees for Pfeiffer, Greensboro, High Point and Brevard colleges, and was a member of many education associations including the North Carolina Association of Independent Colleges and Universities, Secretary, S.E. Jurisdictional Commission on Higher Education.

Advantage of attending a state university

By Stanley Z. Koplik

For most students and their families, the cost of a four-year college education is an important consideration, and for this reason alone, many choose state colleges and universities. These institutions are usually considerably less expensive than private institutions and in many cases provide students with the option of living at home while pursuing a degree.

State scholarship programs are frequently available providing monetary incentives even to those who attend state institutions. Some families appreciate the opportunity of utilizing a system they continue to support with their tax dollars. But state universities are a wise choice for the college bound for many reasons other than simply economics. For young people growing toward independence, the proximity of the state college or university to parents, friends and home community can provide the firm base of support students need as they adjust to the academic, social and emotional pressures of a more demanding way of life.

High school graduates seeking to continue their education in an atmosphere of intellectual challenge and academic diversity should also look to the state universities and colleges. With a wide range of courses and curricula from which to choose, state institutions of high education provide a solid grounding in most fields from vocational and technical training to liberal arts and professional education. No longer stereotyped as teacher training schools, state colleges and universities now emphasize engineering, computer technology, business and sciences, as well as teacher education and the humanities.

As a first step for those seeking professional careers, state institutions offer programs in such fields as medicine, dentistry, law and architecture. Virtually any area of academic interest can be satisfied through state college programs. At the University of Kansas, for example, there are 112 degree programs offered; the University of Missouri offers approximately 125. Other states offer an equally broad array of programs. With outstanding faculties in many disciplines, and national reputations in many areas, state institutions have developed into comprehensive universities where intellectual inquiry and academic excellence flourish.

A large number of state colleges and universities are equipped with fine research facilities and outstanding libraries providing unlimited opportunities for questioning and stimulating creative minds. In some areas the most complete and comprehensive library in the state thrives on the campus of the state university, while inter-library loan systems enhance access of all state residents to study and research materials.

For those who are concerned about "being lost in the crowd," state higher education systems usually provide a variety of campus sizes ranging from the very small school with 1-2,000 students to the "mega-campus" with a student population of 25,000 or more. Attendance at a small campus does not imply inferior educational quality or diminished services. Excellent instruction, stimulating classroom discussion and challenging extracurricular activities can be found on all state college campuses regardless of size.

Providing an integrated educational program with a maximum of flexibility is the goal of many state systems. To facilitate student choice, states such as Kansas and Missouri have developed clear articulation or transfer agreements with junior college for a senior institution. Many junior college graduates enter four-year institutions as juniors with legitimate class standing.

Continuous attendance at college or university is ideal for those pursuing a degree but it is not always possible. When attendance must be interrupted many state universities provide cooperative extension programs and programs of continuing education for those who cannot attend classes full-time on campus. State higher education institutions also use sophisticated telecommunications systems to bring the university and its courses to the most outlying areas of the state.

The college years are, for many, a time to develop relationships which will provide a source of friendships and professional contacts for a lifetime. Attending college in one's home state increases opportunities to establish such long-lasting relationships and to be woven more fully into the fabric of state life.

Young people are increasingly aware of significant roles they will play in the social, political and economic life of this country. A college education in the state in which they are most likely to live can provide students with early involvement in the complexities of state activity. Increasingly, states are encouraging participation by student government groups in legislative activities. Some states, including Kansas, have authorized the appointment of a Student Advisory Committee to the Board of Regents, thus ensuring direct student participation in the decision making process.

State universities have long been known for athletic as well as academic excellence, and this continues to be true. On many campuses, intramural sports along with intercollegiate sports enable large numbers of students to develop athletic prowess. As early responders to the growing need for quality in women's athletics, state universities provide equal opportunity in such sports as basketball, volleyball, swimming and tennis. Large multi-purpose buildings springing up on many campuses indicate a dedication of state institutions to physical development and the cultural development of both campus and community. In some areas, the state college campus is the site of important cultural events, bringing lecturers, exhibits and the performing arts to an entire region. Attention must be given to the academic interest, the scholastic ability and the social and emotional maturity of the student as well as to the range of curricula, quality of instruction and extracurricular activities of the institution. A close examination of state university systems in the United States will indicate that there is virtually around every corner a quality institution of high education solidly grounded in academics and attuned to the social and cultural needs of both students and community. State colleges and universities are a vital link in the network of public educational services and as such, merit serious consideration by the college bound.

Stanley Z. Koplik is Executive Director of the Kansas Board of Regents, the governing body of public higher education in Kansas. Prior to assuming his current duties, Koplik served as Commissioner of Higher Education for the State of Missouri, where he directed activities of the Coordinating Board for Higher Education.

The liberal arts advantage

By Dr. Julia M. McNamara

What does it mean to be a "liberal arts" college in an age when so much emphasis is placed on specialized career training?

The mission of the College is to assist students in becoming the best possible citizens of the planet. These are not idle words spoken only at commencement, but something we really believe. By being initiated into the process of liberating themselves — freeing their minds from the shackles of ignorance, and unlocking their minds from their own prejudices and personal problems — students can face the world armed with the truth. Veritas. Any college worthy of the name should have veritas included in its motto.

In other words, the mission of the College is to seek truth in all its form. To seek truth can be a rather painful process. Indeed, I would surmise if a student sailed through College in four years without ever having experience conflict, without ever having his or her assumptions and values challenged, then no growth nor education occurred.

Do parents have the right to ask: "What kind of job can my child get after graduation?" Of course, but students looking for purely vocational or pre-professional training probably do not belong at a liberal arts college. Students who would use us that way would miss the raison d'etre of the college experience.

The more rapidly society and technology change, the more valuable a liberal arts background becomes. "Facts" are quickly outmoded; how to think and communicate never go out of fashion. Tara O'Rourke, a 1988 graduate of Albertus Magnus college, was offered a high-power job with a New York corporation. It took quite a bit of chutzpah on her part to even ask for the job, having majored in English. But she was offered the position.

There is a lot of talk about the Japanese educational system, compared to the American. It works, in a narrow sense, but it is not a good model for America. They cram students full of facts and teach them what to think, not how to think. The one advantage is the Japanese achieve 99% literacy, whereas we allow those who choose illiteracy to do so.

A liberal education offers one choices, just as one, as a moral being, will be faced with choices in the "real" world. For example, in the American liberal tradition, a citizen has the right and the responsibility to speak out publicly and to act on one's beliefs in service of the greater society. We are educating students for leadership by giving them the necessary tools and habits of mind.

As learned as we might be, much of life remains a mystery, and the acceptance of that fact is a hallmark of the liberally educated mind.

Dr. Julia McNamara is President of Albertus Magnus College in New Haven, Connecticut. President McNamara received her master's degree from Middlebury College and her Ph.D. from Yale University. She also earned a Fulbright Fellowship for advanced French study in Paris and a University Fellowship for study at Yale.

Opportunities at independent research universities

By F. Gregory Campbell

The diversity in American higher education is one of the greatest glories of our culture. No where else in the world does a prospective student enjoy such a wide range of choice. Public or private, large or small, urban or rural, secular or religiously oriented — American universities and colleges vary so greatly that any student should be able to find an institution seemingly tailor-made for that individual.

The major independent research universities constitute an important segment of American higher education. Frequently, they are considered primarily graduate or professional centers, and it is true that many students would be well advised to spend their undergraduate years elsewhere. But those universities typically possess vital undergraduate colleges offering a highly stimulating intellectual and extracurricular environment. For the right kind of student there is no better place.

In academic circles, the independent research universities enjoy an extraordinary reputation. That image depends on the quality of the faculty, and research is normally the means by which a scholar is evaluated. No one has yet devised a reliable method of measuring, comparing, and publicizing good teachers across the country. Good researchers are easy to spot, however, for they publish their discoveries for their colleagues around the world to evaluate. The research universities boast outstanding faculties containing highly innovative scholars with world-wide reputations.

But do they - or can they - teach? In ideal circumstances, the answer is yes. A standard view is that teachers are best when they continue to discover knowledge in their respective fields of scholarship. Conversely, the challenge of sharing their discoveries with critical young minds makes researchers better as a result of their also being teachers. Clearly, this ideal is not always realized. No university can guarantee that its most recent Nobel-prize winner will be teaching freshman chemistry, but such does happen.

The hope of learning from such scholars lures top-notch students to the research universities. Indeed, those institutions would have to do very little in order to produce outstanding graduates. Most college students quickly discover that they learn as much, or more, from their fellow students as from their professors. In as much as the research universities serve as a meeting point for many bright young people, much of the intellectual stimulation on the campuses is provided by the students themselves. Compatibility with others who take their studies seriously is an essential prerequisite for prospective students.

But college life cannot be all work and pressure. There have been persistent efforts over the past fifteen years or so to reduce intellectual competition among students. Professorial complaints about "grade inflation" reflect the fact that it is much easier for a student to stay in the universities than to get into them to begin with. The drop-out rate is low, the failure rate even lower.

The learning experience extends beyond classrooms, libraries, and laboratories, and cannot be measured by grades alone. Extracurricular opportunities for learning and growth are central to a college experience. Most of the independent research universities seek to encourage informal association between professors and students. Professors may be encouraged to eat meals regularly with students in the dining halls. Leaders in public affairs or the arts and sciences may be invited to the campuses in order to engage in informal meetings with students. How does one measure the worth to a pre-law student of a breakfast conversation with a Supreme Court justice?

The independent research universities almost never appear on the list of major NCAA powers in football or basketball. Their teams normally compete at a lower level. But their programs do offer opportunities to participate in intercollegiate athletics to many young men and women who could not make the teams of the major powers. In addition, the intramural programs typically attract the vast majority of students on campus. The schools do not figure prominently in the sports pages, but the student communities are active and vigorous.

The undergraduate colleges within the independent research

universities are normally quite small. Whereas they enroll more students than a typical liberal arts college, they have many fewer students than the state universities. That size both provides a critical mass for a wide variety of activities and allows for a sense of community and personal identity in a manageable environment.

The student bodies themselves are quite diverse. Admissions officers try hard to insure a nationally representative student body — including students from various regions of the country, diverse ethnic groups, and economic levels. There is also a significant number of foreign students. This intimate exposure to differences among people is a key element in the growth to adulthood.

The kind of education that is offered in the independent research universities is expensive, and tuition levels are high. Yet, since the 1960's, those institutions have tried to provide sufficient amounts of aid to enable students to matriculate regardless of financial need. It is an open question whether that policy can be maintained, even formally, in a more difficult economic environment.

The concept of a "University College" is the most apt way of thinking about undergraduate programs in an independent research university. Students find a relatively small college with a distinct identity of its own. Yet that colleges lives within a much larger institution possessing resources available for undergraduates to exploit. Those "University Colleges" are not appropriate for everyone, and there are many other excellent institutions from which to choose. But, when the match is right, a "University College" can offer gifted and serious young people opportunities seldom found elsewhere.

Formerly at the University of Chicago, Mr. Campbell is now the President of

Carthage College. He is an historian specializing in international relations and Central and Eastern European History.

Major decisions: choosing the right college major

By Dr. Donald Quirk

Under the best of circumstances, choosing a college major is not easy, and a number of conditions often complicate the task. First of all, most freshmen are surprised to learn that college is significantly different from their previous school experience and that the nature of most major fields differs considerably from courses offered in high school. So, to major in history because you are good at memorizing dates, names and battles or to choose accountancy because you enjoyed a high school book-keeping or "accounting" course is likely to lead to dissatisfaction. Secondly, well-intentioned but naive "advisors," often as not, ignore *your* interests, skills or ambitions. Blindly following Dad's suggestion to "study law so you can get rich like Uncle Zeke" nearly guarantees a mismatch. Finally, many young people find themselves in the midst of personal change and discovery. Making a commitment that may affect the rest of your life at a time when your dreams change more often than the blue-light special at K mart can leave the hardiest person paralyzed by fear.

Adding to the pressure felt by many students are the expecta-

tions of those around them that everyone beginning college should have already decided what he or she intends to study. Even colleges -- often unintentionally -- add to the pressure: applications usually require a student to select from a list of intended majors. Typically, a college will list 30 to 100 major choices; in the list -- usually appearing last -- comes the choice, "undecided". It comes as little surprise that many students feel that they are somehow defective if they have not yet made up their minds.

Now, there are some students who "always wanted to study medicine" and a good number of others who have given a great deal of time to their selection of a major, but the hard truth of the matter is that many students -- including those who have declared a major -- really don't know what they want to study. This is evidenced by a national statistic showing that nearly four out of five college students eventually change their major at least once.

So what's a person to do?

Don't Worry

If you're beginning college and you're unsure about what you want to study, you probably don't have to make a choice quite yet. While a few technical and scientific fields have highly structured curricula that require that beginning courses be taken immediately, most students can delay major decisions for one or even two years without disastrous consequences. For colleges -- unlike trade schools -- require students to study subjects that provide a breadth of knowledge outside the major. Usually described as general education courses, these courses include selections in the arts, the natural and social sciences and the humanities. Typically, they represent a third to a half of the total course requirement for graduation and they provide an opportunity to experiment, to get a taste of a range of fields.

"Know Thyself"

Get to know more about what fits you. Remember, you are not choosing a major for Uncle Zeke; you're choosing one for yourself, so the place to begin is with yourself, your personality, your interests, your abilities, your values and your goals. Choosing a major -- like any significant personal decision -- requires you to think through some important questions about yourself. What has my previous experience prepared me to do? How can I connect the knowledge and skills that I've already developed with a course of study? What areas that I've studied in the past were interesting to me? What college majors capitalize on that interest? How do my personal and career goals connect with my selection of a major?

Avoid Career Planning "Tunnel Vision"

Be broad-minded when thinking about a major that matches your career plan. Many students recognize that choosing a major is closely linked to choosing a career but are confused into believing that only management majors can hope to become business executives or only "pre-law" students can hope to become lawyers. The fact of the matter is that there are many majors that lead to these or a number of other career goals. Increasingly, firms have shown that they value the analytical thinking, communication and research skills developed by students in the liberal arts by hiring graduates from philosophy, English, sociology and a variety of other non-vocational majors.

Find Help

There are a large number of tools -- books, interest inventories, aptitude tests, values and goals assessments -- that can help you find a major that fits. A number of self-help books, like

Richard Bolles' *What Color is Your Parachute*, provide a guided tour through the process of choosing a field of study and a career. Interest inventories, like the Kuder or the Strong-Campbell, help you match your interests with those of people in a variety of professions. Computerized self-assessments like Discover, developed by ACT, or SIGI, from the College Board, lead your through a systematic process of self-exploration that leads to some potential matches. High school counselors or college advising or career planning offices can help you put these and a number of other resources to work for you.

In addition, a growing number of colleges have programs and services to help students develop an academic plan. Some of these include academic advising programs, special courses for undecided students, and career planning workshops and counseling services to name a few. In recent years, more and more colleges have also developed freshman seminars. Designed to help new students make the transition to college life, these seminars often include the related topics of choosing a major field and choosing a career.

But probably the most effective resources are people. Find someone you can trust -- a good high school guidance counselor, a sympathetic college advisor, an accessible faculty member, or a knowledgeable career planning counselor in your college. They can help you begin the process. With a little help and and some persistence, you'll find that major decisions do not have to be major problems.

Dr. Quirk, former Director of Assessment and Advisement at DePaul University, is now Director of Assessment at Northeastern Illinois University. He has had extensive experience directing advising programs for new freshmen and has developed programs and courses to help new freshmen make the difficult

transition to college. He holds degrees in English and English Education from the University of Illinois, Urbana-Champaign.

Surviving the freshman year experience

By John N. Gardner

I hope you will read this once you get beyond the first line: it's about a very important yet sort of grim subject, namely, **survival**. This is not necessarily a modern day college freshman version of "survival of the fittest," but nevertheless, your survival. I write to you out of my concern that we lose far too many college freshmen, lose them in the sense that they drop out or flunk out of the first year and many never return. As a matter of fact, from baccalaureate level institutions, we lose about 25% in the first year alone. Our nation cannot continue to afford this unacceptable attrition rate. I write because I want you to survive the freshman year and to graduate.

Why should you listen to me? Because I have been teaching college freshmen for 24 years and because I am what the *New York Times* has called the Dean of Freshman Happiness (which was a cute term they gave me because of my nearly two decades of work to enhance what has become known as The Freshman Year Experience in American higher education); because I have a child of my own in college and I have directed a special course at my University, a so-called freshman seminar, entitled University 101, the purpose of which is to help

freshmen survive the first year. We have been very successful in doing just that: freshmen who take my course are much more likely to become sophomores.

My school is just one of several thousand institutions which have developed special courses to make future freshmen like you even more successful. Therefore, it would seem sensible that in selecting a college you need to find one that is "freshman friendly." You need to find out to what extent they have devoted significant resources to the care and feeding of freshmen. What about freshman class size and who teaches the freshmen: real faculty or graduate teaching assistants? What kind of emphasis do they place on freshman advisement and career planning? How much time and resources do they devote to freshman orientation? What kind of special activities do they have in freshman residence halls? Many colleges have developed special courses to help freshmen make a successful adjustment to higher education. In fact, over 2,000 of them have done so. Is the college you're considering one of those? If not, I'd think twice before attending.

In this brief essay, It's appropriate for me to share some of the things I have learned that seem to make a difference as to whether or not freshmen are successful in the first year and literally survive it and go on to become sophomores. So I want to offer you some advice. This is based on 18 years of research at my university on what are the characteristics of students who survive the freshman year as compared to those who don't. Based on that type of study, I offer you the following advice:

1. Go to class. In my 24 years of teaching, I have rarely ever failed a student who attended class. As Woody Allen said, "ninety-five percent of success is showing up."

2. In America, there is no free lunch. You have to work hard. Specifically, you have to work harder than you did in high school. For example, you need to spend two to three hours out of class studying for every hour of the week you spend in class. And that's really not as much as it sounds, particularly compared to the real world. Let's say you have a fifteen hour class schedule and you spend two hours a week for every hour inside class. That means you spend 30 hours a week studying and 15 in class. That's 45 hours a week. None of you are going to make it in the big time world after college in only a 45 hour work week.

3. Play hard. College is not meant to be all work. You need to relax and have some kind of balance in your life.

4. Participation. Participate in all the orientation activities that your college offers both for no academic credit and for academic credit. That means if your college offers a freshman seminar/freshman orientation course as an elective, take it. All the evidence across the country suggests that students who participate in these elective courses have a higher probability of becoming sophomores.

5. Live on campus. Years of research has shown that students who live on campus have a higher survival rate.

6. Choose your friends wisely. You are likely to become just like them. Winners select winners. Losers select losers.

7. Get help early. Don't wait until late in the semester. There is no stigma to seeking assistance. Remember, you're paying the salaries of the college employees and you have a right to ask them for help.

8. Develop a relationship with that very special person, your academic advisor. If you don't have one initially who seems to show an interest in you and whom you feel you can relate to comfortably, ask for another one.

9. During the first semester, find a "significant other." This is the phrase coined by the famous psychologist Carl Rogers that describes a very special adult person and relationship. Research has shown that college students who find at least one significant adult during the freshman year are much more likely to survive.

10. Identify outstanding upper class students after whose behaviors you can pattern your own behaviors.

11. Join a group that is some kind of legitimate group that is sponsored by the college. Research has shown that students who join groups have much higher survival rates. At most colleges, there are a large number of groups consisting of people like you with similar interests that you can join.

12. Get involved. That means, do things on your college campus in addition to going to class. For example, not only join a group but attend plays, concerts, lectures, etc. The research shows that the more time you invest in activities on campus other than simply going to class, the more likely you are to survive the freshman year.

13. Get career planning early. many freshmen may think they know what they want to major in but have really inappropriately chosen a major for which they are not suited. On the other hand, many freshmen have not decided on a major. Regardless of whether you have or not, visit your campus career planning center; take a battery of vocational aptitude tests; sign up for computer assisted interactive guidance and career planning; and most importantly, see a career planning specialist to discuss your individual needs and characteristics.

14. Most colleges today provide a tremendous array of helping services and resources. Use them. Remember that you pay the salaries of those people who provide them and there is no stigma to accepting assistance. For example, use a personal counseling center. It's free and confidentially trained counseling professionals deal with the normal adjustment problems of college life. That doesn't mean that you are "sick" if you accept assistance.

15. Learn college study skills. Most high school students have not learned the kind of study skills they need to do well in college. Virtually all colleges have study skills centers where trained professionals are on duty to help you develop the skills you need. Ask your professor in each course what study skills are particularly useful and appropriate for that individual course. As a college freshman, once I learned study skills such as lecture notetaking, there wasn't hardly a course that I couldn't "smash," i.e., receive a high grade.

There are lots of sources of advice in college, some of it from the least appropriate individuals, so accept advice carefully. In spite of that caveat I hope that you'll give mine more than a moment's consideration. If you have questions or concerns about how to survive the freshman year, I would welcome a letter or a phone call from you. You can write me at the University of South Carolina or call me at (803) 777-7695. You are going to find that whatever college you choose, there are lots of faculty and administrators like me who really have a special interest in college freshmen like you. So I bid you a special welcome and best wishes.

John Gardner is the Vice Chancellor for University Campus and Continuing Education at the University of South Carolina, the Director of University 101 and a Professor of Library and Information Sciences. He has a B.A. in Social Sciences from Marietta College, Marietta, OH and a M.A. in American Studies from Purdue University.

The two-year experience

By Dr. Jacob C. Martinson, Jr.

It is a difficult adjustment for a student to go from a high school, sometimes a small high school at that, directly into a multi-complex university often with thousands and thousands of other students. Are the majority of high school graduates equipped for this kind of transition? The answer, of course, if that some are, and some are not. There is an alternative approach.

There is a wide range of academic programs available among two-year colleges today. There are many accredited institutions which offer outstanding two-year terminal programs in areas such as business arts, computer science, and medical arts. This article, however, will focus on the two-year colleges that are designed to prepare the students for continuation at a four-year college or university. It will address the belief that, in many cases, the pursuit of the baccalaureate degree is greatly enhanced by "The Two-Year Experience."

When it comes to the role of a college education in career

performance, an academically recognized two-year college can provide the essential foundations of undergraduate training often better than the best universities. After all, it doesn't take an expert to see that faculty qualifications are not that different from one center of learning to another. For example, a survey of the educational credentials of faculty members at good two-year colleges reveals that they have received their graduate training at the finest colleges and universities in the country.

The advantages of getting a good start at a two-year college are numerous. I will cite some reasons why a two-year college program should be considered.

1. Access to the Faculty

A faculty member ordinarily does not choose to teach at a two-year college unless he/she is specifically dedicated to teaching. Those faculty members who are interested in publishing or research usually go to the multi-complex universities where much of their undergraduate teaching responsibilities are delegated to graduate assistants. Classes in two-year colleges are generally taught by first-line faculty members.

Students have a right to expect some time with their professors who have spent many hours embodying much of the knowledge in which the students are interested. In the small two-year colleges, the opportunity is provided to know professors on a one-to-one basis. It is not uncommon to observe ballgames between faculty and students, or for faculty to invite students to their homes for refreshments.

2. A Good Beginning

The first two years of college are probably the most important of a student's college career. With the exception of kindergarten and first grade, they are all-important to the pursuance of formal education. Statistics show that when a student does well in an academically sound two-year college, he/she seldom does poorly academically anywhere else. A good start can make the difference.

3. Budget Appropriations

Many multi-complex universities give the "lion's share" of the funds to the upper-level undergraduate courses and to the graduate programs. Two-year colleges, on the other hand, give their entire budget to those critical first two undergraduate years.

4. Less Expense to the Student

One can attend a fine two-year college with a superb academic reputation for less than one can attend most universities. The community colleges are less expensive to the student, but even the private residential two-year colleges are relatively inexpensive. Of course, if commuting is possible, the expense is even less. Since the private college also wants to serve the surrounding community, special scholarships to commuting area residents are offered by some colleges.

5. Opportunities for Leadership and Participation

The freshmen and sophomores at a two-year college will have no junior and seniors to compete with in extra-curricular activities for campus leadership roles, team sport participation, and faculty time. The individual has an opportunity to become involved more quickly and more deeply in the total life of the college. Where else could a student be a representative to the college committees and the Board of Trustees at the age of 18? In short, there is no "sophomore slump" in the two-year college.

6. Vocational Future

The two-year college can enrich one's vocational future. The fact is that too many college graduates today are ignorant of the English language, history, science, and math. Many are deficient in their ability to get along with others and in that all-important skill of communication. One need only watch a nationally televised athletic event to observe the inability of some students from the so-called "prestigious" centers of learning to speak proper English. This is not to imply that the two-year college student will consistently perform any better; however, at good two-year colleges, there is a concerted effort to start wherever a student is academically and teach him/her to read and write effectively. For example, some of the better two-year colleges have three or four different levels of beginning English. The same is true of math. These schools place great emphasis on English and math with the conviction that if one can read and write and add and subtract, one has the educational foundation to function in the world. The hallmark of the best two-year colleges is that of toughness with caring. Such colleges encourage the formulation of long-range educational goals and positive views on how education can assist one in meeting vocational objectives. Obviously, there are some limitations to the depth to which one can pursue objectives in a two-year setting, but the seeds are planted and the incentives aroused.

7. The Best of Both Worlds

A student can have the best of the two-year and the four-year educational systems. During those critical first two years of college, a fine two-year school can provide an excellent academic program and curriculum, caring faculty members, and a concerned college community, all of which prepare the student to transfer to the larger college or university.

There are those in educational circles who would have one believe that transferring is dangerous to one's educational future. In most cases this belief is unfounded. On the contrary, it is sometimes easier to get into the best four-year schools after a two-year Associate of Arts/Science/Fine Arts degree than to apply right out of high school. Academic credits from a good, academically sound, two-year college are accepted by most of the finest universities. In fact, transfer students are not only accepted, they are actively recruited because of the natural attrition in the senior colleges and universities after the first and second years. Also, some students perform better in a two-year college than they did in high school; therefore, these students are more likely to have their application accepted when they leave the two-year college than when they graduated from high school. Further, there are certain rights and responsibilities which are uniquely applicable to the transferring student. A statement of these rights and responsibilities has been approved by the NACAC (National Association of College Admissions Counselors) in 1980 and revised in 1982.

In conclusion, today's two-year college generally offers a university-parallel curriculum. It is nearly always designed for the brilliant as well as the average student. The task is to successfully meet and challenge each student where he/she is academically despite varying aptitudes, dispositions, and outlooks.

The two-year college experience is not for everyone, but it certainly fills a need. It is a good place to start in higher educational pursuits — a good place to begin on the way toward the baccalaureate degree.

Dr. Martinson is President of High Point College, a four-year liberal arts institution located in High Point, North Carolina. Prior to this position, he served as President of Andrew College in Cuthbert, Georgia and Brevard College, Brevard, North Carolina each of which are two-year institutions. He holds degrees from Huntingdon College, Duke University, and Vanderbilt University. While at High Point College, he has served as

President of the North Carolina Friends of Higher Education and is a Trustee of the Independent College Fund of North Carolina as well as an elected Board member of the National Association of Schools and Colleges of the United Methodist Church. Born of Norwegian-American lineage, he is an honorary member of the American-Scandinavian Foundation.

The value of a liberal arts education

By Dr. David Maxwell

We are in the midst of a crisis that threatens the very fabric of higher education in America today, and that endangers the quality of education that we all desire for our children. The crisis centers on the relationship between undergraduate education and the so-called "real world": What are we preparing our students for? The resolution of this crisis has serious implications for the undergraduate curriculum, for the nature of the demands placed on our students by the institutions, by their parents and by themselves — and profound consequences for the continuing health and vitality of our nation.

A liberal education has always been measured in terms of its relevance to society's needs, and there is no reason that it should not continue to be; the notion of utility is firmly ingrained in our national character. The crisis to which I refer lies in the determination of precisely what those needs are, for it is in those "needs" that we express the relationship between education and the "real world."

I have witnessed a trend in American College students that I find particularly disturbing. An increasingly large number of students are demanding what they term "relevance" in their studies. Clearly, I feel that liberal education has profound relevance to the "real world," but these students have a definition of that term that is different from mine. By "relevance," they often mean professional training, training not just for the future, but for jobs. With an entirely justifiable concern for their future economic well-being, they are making — I am afraid — a terrible and potentially devastating error of logic.

Although few of our students would accept the state of our "reality" as ideal, many are allowing the priorities of that reality — as expressed in economic terms — to dictate the priorities of their education. They are mistaking financial reward, prestige, and excitement for genuine intellectual interest. Many, I fear, view the undergraduate experience as a "credentialling" process, rather than as an education that will make them productive, fulfilled adults. I am not suggesting that our students do not have neither genuine intellectual curiosity nor the thirst for pure knowledge, for they have ample supplies of both. But they are subject to enormous pressure from the outside: the fear that the field in which they are truly interested will not provide them with a comfortable income; the fear that their parents (often professionals themselves) will not approve of their interests; the fear that their ambitions are not sufficiently "prestigious" in the eyes of their peers. These are all very real fears and pressure that must be recognized as valid, but they have two important — and destructive — consequences. It is my sense that many of our students go on to careers in the so-called "professions" with very little idea of what these professions entail and, what is worse,

they have tailored their entire undergraduate education to fit what they feel is appropriate preparation for those professions.

We are engaging in the process of creating many unhappy adults as such students grow up to find that they have no real intellectual investment in the occupation toward which they have aspired since they were teenagers. Having focused their education at an early stage, with the mistaken impression that you have to major in economics to go into business, in political science to enter law school, or in biology to be a physician, they will be plagued with the gnawing feeling that they have missed something — but without knowing quite what it was that they have missed.

Furthermore, the misplaced emphasis on grades caused by the intense competition for professional schools discourages many students from their natural inclination to question, to challenge, to experiment, to take risks. Rather than risk the uncharted waters of their own ideas and their own imagination, many students choose the safe route of repeating what they've heard and read as they write their examinations and papers.

Clearly, it is our responsibility to find ways to encourage our students to follow their natural inclinations, to resist the pressures — we must make it clear to them that, as teachers, we will reward initiative, originality, and risk-taking. Perhaps most important is that we must convince them that it is precisely these skills that are the most "pre-professional," that no business ever grew without developing original ideas, that every physician must take calculated risks daily, and that the practice of law rests on the principle of challenge to ideas.

Most people with professional aspirations hope to advance beyond entry-level positions into managerial or executive roles;

positions in which they can assume responsibility, control, and authority and positions in which they can implement their own visions. It is precisely these roles that demand breadth of education — not only in subject matter, but breadth in the range of personal and intellectual skills that the student acquires in his/her studies.

There is growing evidence that the "real world" is taking notice of the correlation between liberal arts skills and the professions. For the past twenty-nine years, AT&T has been conducting longitudinal studies of its managers, correlating field of undergraduate major to career advancement and managerial skills. The AT&T study showed clearly that those with non-technical majors (humanities and the social sciences) were "clearly superior in administrative and interpersonal skills." (Robert E. Beck, The Liberal Arts Major in Bell System Management [Washington, D.C.: 1981], pp. 6, 8). Significantly, "Nearly half of the humanities and social science majors were considered to have potential for middle management, compared to only thirty-one percent of the business majors..." (p.12) Within eight years of employment, the average management level of humanities and social science majors was significantly higher than that of other groups. As the author of the Bell report states: "One overall conclusion from these data is that there is no need for liberal arts majors to lack confidence in approaching business careers." (p.13) It is interesting to note that this affirmation of the professional value of a liberal education comes from the experience of one of the world's largest high-tech corporations!

I am not presenting this evidence to argue that those who genuinely love engineering and the sciences should not pursue them, for their love is the best reason to enter those fields. Rather, the evidence presents a powerful argument for those whose interest lie elsewhere to follow their interest without fearing that their skills and knowledge will not be needed.

Not long ago, I had a meeting with several people who work in admissions at the Harvard Business School. We discussed the criteria for evaluating applicants, and they stressed that the single most important criterion was academic excellence at a respected, selective institution. Certainly, a few courses in economics and a familiarity with mathematics were an advantage, but the field of undergraduate major was not significant. As do the law and medical schools, they stress breadth of excellence and potential ability as reflected in the quality of the student's educational experience. It is significant that at Harvard, like many of the nation's best business schools, ninety-seven percent of their admitted applicants have had at least one year of full-time work experience before applying.

It should be clear from what I've said that liberal education is valued in certain segments of the "real world," and that there is often no correlation between choice of major and choice of career. Therefore we must encourage our students to spend their first year or more exploring, taking courses in a broad range of fields; courses in which they suspect they might be interested because they sound fascinating, courses in subjects that they know nothing about.

They should talk with the teachers, their advisors, their deans, their fellow students, with their parents, with other adults. In this process of exploration — if they are allowed to explore without pressure — they will find something in which they are genuinely fascinated. Pursuit of that fascination will lead them

not only to sophisticated knowledge of a particular field, but to the development of intellectual and personal skills that will enable them to survive, happily and productively, as adults. The fascination will lead them to accept challenges, exercise their creativity, to take risks in the name of learning, to find out what they are good at and what to avoid, to be critical rather than accepting, and to be pathfinders rather than followers. It will also lead them, the evidence suggests, to a career that will allow them to use what they've learned in the broadest sense; one which they will find rewarding, interesting and challenging. To put it simply, they should decide who they want to be when they grow up, not just what they want to be.

David Maxwell is President of Whitman College in the State of Washington. Formerly the Dean of Undergraduate Studies and Director of the Program in Russian at Tufts University, he has been teaching Russian literature and language for nineteen years and in 1979 was the recipient of the Lillian Leibner Award for Distinguished Teaching and Advising. A Fulbright Fellow in Moscow in 1970-71, President Maxwell is the author of numerous scholarly articles on Russian literature. He is active in a number of organizations concerned with liberal arts education, is a member of the American Council on Education Commission on International Education, and in 1990 chaired the Soviet-American Human Rights Conference in Seattle, Washington.

Preparing for a career in the arts

By Dr. William Banchs

Although the notion that there is no future in a career in the arts is still espoused by many, the number and quality of opportunities in the arts has dramatically increased in the past ten years. Many colleges and universities are responding to this trend, by greatly expanding their programs in the arts (dance, music, theater, visual arts and writing) for developing performers, creative artists, arts educators and arts administrators. In addition, there are many course offerings in the arts for those students less determined to pursue a career in the arts, but who also desire further training and experience.

Many young people are able to combine their artistic and academic skills in preparation for the demands of being an artist. A combination of skills is also necessary for careers in the management of artists or arts organization.

If you are seriously considering further training and education in dance, music, theater, visual arts or writing, you should be aware of a program designed to assist young artists. Arts Recognition and Talents Search (ARTS) of the National Foundation for Advancement in the Arts is a national program to recognize and support excellence in the arts. Over 5,000 high school seniors from every state participate in ARTS every year.

Applications received from aspiring young artists include a video tape of performances in

dance and theater, an audio tape of solo music performance, a slide portfolio for visual artists and a portfolio of manuscripts by writers.

Each year, high school seniors with ability in the arts register for the ARTS program by these two dates: the regular registration deadline on June 1 (as a junior), and the late registration deadline on October 1 (as a senior).

The decisions of a panel of expert judges in each art field are made solely on the basis of the artistic content of the student's application packets. No other criteria, such as grades or academic standing, have any bearing on their decisions.

As a result of these evaluations, applicants are granted one of four award levels: Level I consisting of $3,000, Level II consisting of $1,500, Level III consisting of $500, and Honorable Mention consisting of $100. In addition, through NFAA's Scholarship List Service, all applicants and award winners are recruited by leading colleges, universities and professional arts organization and offered in excess of three million dollars in scholarships and internships.

The Foundation recommends their top artistic talent to the Presidential Scholars Commission each year and twenty are selected as Presidential Scholars in the Arts. These young artists are presented in concert at the John F. Kennedy Center for the Performing Arts and at an exhibit at the National Museum of American Art, Smithsonian Institution. In addition, all the Presidential Scholars are honored by the President of the United States at a ceremony in the White House. These events are all part of National Recognition Week which takes place in Washington, DC in June of every year.

If you aspire to a creative career, you need to be realistic about your talent, for that is what is most important in getting a job in the arts or establishing a reputation. Practical experience outside of the school environment — with local theaters, music and dance groups, galleries and community newspapers — can give you an extra edge. Even the most talented artists must be willing to spend years of their lives mastering their skills. It is never too early to develop that necessary dedication and commitment to your art.

Dr. William Banchs is Vice President, Programs, for the National Foundation for Advancement in the Arts.

Guide to guides for high school students

Reprinted with permission from the "Chronicle of Higher Education."

The Best Buys in College Education, by Edward B. Fiske (Times Books; 393 pages). Mr. Fiske, the education editor of the New York Times, has published his Selective Guide to Colleges singe 1982. He recently released Best Buys, which lists 200 colleges — both public and private — that are identified as particularly good values. The institutions range from Pratt Institute ($10,088 tuition) to Cooper Union ($300). Included are statistics (including admissions and financial-aid figures), and essays describing what Mr. Fiske calls "the academic and social climate" of the institutions.

The Insider's Guide to the Colleges, by the staff of the Yale Daily News (St. Martin's Press, 568 pages). "Obviously," the editors say in their preface, "it's impossible to capture the full scope and breadth of any institution in two or three pages of text." The editors of the Yale Daily News — and student correspondents on more than 150 campuses — offer readers, according to the book's cover, an

account of "what...colleges are really like."

The brief descriptive sections tend to give colleges labels, provide a sweeping sense of the atmosphere, and describe campus social life. The book also provides an introduction to college "trends in the Eighties" and includes lists of colleges in categories such as "liberal arts colleges with an emphasis on pre-professionalism," and "colleges de-emphasizing varsity sports."

100 Top Colleges, by John McClintock (John Wiley & Sons, Inc; 225 pages). In addition to its statistical descriptions of what it calls "America's best" institutions, 100 Top Colleges suggests a systematic method for selecting a college. By answering a series of multiple-choice questions and plugging the answers into boxes, students may narrow their choice of institutions to conform to the qualities they value. "Choosing a college may never become a strictly scientific process," writes Mr. McClintock, "but it can be rational." The profiles of institutions rely heavily on statistics of all kinds, including ratings for "personal life," "mix of students," and "student motivation."

Rugg's Recommendations on the Colleges, by Frederick E. Rugg (Whitebrook Books; 65 pages). Mr. Rugg, a high-school guidance counselor, organizes his book by academic majors, from agriculture to zoology. In each section, the book recommends several colleges whose departments are felt to be among the best in the country. Within majors, the lists are divided into three categories: "most selective," "very selective," and "selective." Information about the colleges was obtained primarily through random interviews with students and others affiliated with institutions, according to the book.

"I even did weird things like interview the scorer and timer at

the halftime of a basketball game at Williams College," Mr. Rugg writes. "We ended up discussing the classics department there (small, but good)." Mr. Rugg rates William's classics department among the best in the nation.

Lisa Birnbach's College Book, by Lisa Birnbach (Ballantine Book; 515 pages). Lake Forest College has the best salad bar of any college. The most promiscuous students are at Boston University. Connoisseurs of such information will find plenty of it in Ms. Birnbach's book, which describes student life at 186 colleges. "This is the inside scoop," writes Ms. Birnbach, "the juicy stuff you can only learn by visiting the campuses, by going to school there. This is the real thing." Entries place little emphasis on statistics and list such categories as "best professors," "gay situation," and "best thing about school."

The Public Ivys: A Guide to America's Best Public Undergraduate Colleges and Universities, by Richard Moll (Viking, 289 pages) "Even the parents with ready cash are wondering if Olde Ivy is worth two or three times the price of a thoroughly respectable public institution," Mr. Moll writes. His book contains lengthy narrative and statistical descriptions of 17 public institutions he says are comparable to Ivy League universities. Mr. Moll chose the 17 based on admissions selectivity, "quality" of "undergraduate experience," institutions' financial resources, and prestige.

America's Lowest Cost Colleges, by Nicholas A. Ross (Freundlich Books; 253 pages). North Carolina residents will be delighted to learn that, according to Mr. Ross's book, 13 institutions in their state charge $150 or less for one year's tuition. Californians have more reason to celebrate: 36 colleges are identified here as charging $100.

"This book was written," Mr.

Ross writes, "because too many parents have been forced to sacrifice for their children's education...Worst of all, too many young people have decided not to go to college, because they think they can't afford it." The book includes brief descriptions of more than 700 colleges with annual tuitions of less than $1,500.

The College Handbook, 1985-86 (College Entrance Examination Board; 1,900 pages). The College Board's guide is filled with facts and figures that answer any basic question a prospective student might have about more than 3,000 institutions: number of students, a description of the location ("city," "small town," etc.), major fields of study, and special programs. It also gives a brief "class profile" and statistics on the number of applicants admitted from the most recent pool. The introduction offers students advice on how to choose a college.

Selective Guide to Colleges, by Edward B. Fiske (Times Books; 482 pages). "If you are wondering whether to consider a particular college," Mr. Fiske writes, "it is logical to seek out friends or acquaintances who go there and ask what it's like. What we have done is exactly this..." Mr. Fiske has written brief, general descriptions of what the book calls "the 275 colleges you are most likely to consider." The descriptions tend to emphasize various components of student life, as well as the academic reputations of institutions. In addition to the narrative descriptions, Mr. Fiske rates three qualities — "Academics," "Social Life," and "Quality of Life," on a subjective one-to-five scale.

General Catalogs

Barron's Guide to the Two-Year Colleges (Barron's Education Series, Inc.; volume one: 319 pages; volume two: 282 pages). The first volume of this two-volume set lists facilities, costs, programs and admissions requirements of more than 1,500 two-year institutions. Using charts, the second volume identifies institutions offering programs in five general categories: business and commerce; communications, media, and public services; health services; agricultural and environmental management; engineering and technologies. It also provides a separate list of institutions offering liberal-arts programs.

Barron's Profiles of American Colleges (Barron's Educational Series, Inc.; 1,151 pages). In addition to providing statistical information — including median SAT scores, student-faculty ratio and tuition costs — Barron's ranks each college on a scale from "most competitive" to "non-competitive." The book's introduction says the rankings are determined by a combination of the institution's rate of acceptance and the average high-school grade-point average and median SAT scores of students who are accepted.

Comparative Guide to American Colleges, by James Cass and Max Birnbaum (Harper & Row; 706 pages). While it includes many of the statistical laundry lists of other fact-filled guides, Cass and Birnbaum's book also throws in an introductory paragraph giving a general description of each institution. Each entry also includes sections on "academic environment," "religious orientation," and "campus life" and information on the proportion of degrees conferred in various departments. Like Barron's, the book uses what it calls a "selectivity index," rating institutions with competitive admissions from "selective" to "among the most selective in the country."

Lovejoy's College Guide, edited by Charles Straughn and Barbarasue Lovejoy Straughn (Monarch Press; 604 pages).

Listing more than 2,500 colleges and universities, Lovejoy's is concise and informative but offers less statistical material than do some of the other catalogues. Its descriptions are much briefer than those in most of the other guides, such as Barron's and Cass and Birnbaum.

Peterson's Competitive Colleges, Karen C. Hegener, editor (Peterson's Guides; 358 pages). In its fourth edition, it includes one-page profiles of 301 "selective" institutions — those whose students do well on standardized tests and which consistently have more applicants who meet entrance standards than are admitted. The book contains lists of the colleges and universities by cost, size, religious affiliation, and other factors. It also includes one-paragraph profiles of selective arts colleges and conservatories.

Peterson's Four-Year Colleges , Andrea E. Lehman, editor (Peterson's Guides; 2,237 pages). In a volume larger than the Manhattan telephone directory, Peterson's, which is updated annually, provides general information about more than 3,000 institutions. It also includes a section of two-page "messages from the colleges," profiles provided by the institutions that each pay $895 for the space. In addition, the book provides a chart with a state-by-state breakdown of colleges, listing of institutions organized by majors offered, difficulty of admission, and costs.

Lovejoy's Concise College Guide, edited by Charles Straughn and Barbarasue Lovejoy Straughn (Monarch Press; 375 pages). "The criteria used for the selection of the 370 institutions are varied to include the most diverse selection of schools for you to choose from," says the introduction. The book never explains these criteria, but the editors seem to have included

the most selective institutions. The descriptions of the colleges are slightly abbreviated selections from the larger Lovejoy's, including information on enrollment, cost, academic majors, and student life.

Specialized Guides

Who Offers Part-Time Degree Programs? edited by Karen C. Hegener (Peterson's Guides, 417 pages). The listings include more than 2,500 institutions offering part-time undergraduate and graduate degree programs. The guide also includes separate directories of colleges with evening, summer, and weekend programs.

The Black Student's Guide to Colleges, edited by Barry Beckham (Beckham House Publishers, 495 pages). Mr. Beckham, a professor of English at Brown University, writes in his introduction that he wishes to provide information "in both objective and subjective terms" to help black students choose among colleges. Each campus profile is based on information supplied by the institutions and by five of its students, whose individual statements are often noted. In narrative form, the book provides details on topics including race relations, support services, cultural opportunities, and black organizations.

Everywoman's Guide to Colleges and Universities, edited by Florence Howe, Suzanne Howard, and Mary Jo Boehm Strauss (Feminist Press; 412 pages). For each of the 600 colleges it evaluates, *Everywoman's Guide* provides a ranking — on a three-star scale — for each of several categories: "students," "faculty," "administrators," "woman and the curriculum," and "woman and athletics." An introduction notes that these are areas of "special importance." In narrative form, each entry provides additional material under such headings as "policies to ensure fairness to women," "women in leadership

positions," and "special services and programs for women."

A Guide to Colleges for Learning Disabled Students, edited by Mary Ann Liscio (Academic Press, Inc.; 490 pages). In addition to some basic information about admissions requirements and tuition, each entry lists services for learning disabled students, "modifications to the traditional learning environment" (including such details as tape recorders provided to tape lectures, and "longer time to complete exams"), and a person on campus for learning-disabled students to contact.

Learning a new role

By Paul and Ann Krouse

Most literature directed to parents of college-bound students focuses on financial matters, an area of great interest and concern to most of us. Yet there are other roles besides bankrolls which require attention and involvement. Some are obvious and others more subtle. Having just completed the college admissions process with our eldest daughter, my wife and I would like to share our experiences and views.

Be involved.
Selecting a college is just one more experience in the parenting process with the usual mixture of risks, rewards, joys, and uncertainties. You will find yourself pouring over directories, college catalogs, counselor recommendations, applications, and financial aid forms. The more you do together, the less tedious the tasks and the more enlightening the process becomes. We found

ourselves engaged in a very productive cycle which started with counselor/student meetings. From this counselor-to-parent shuttle which was repeated several times over a period of a few weeks, our daughter developed a list of six or seven college choices. We visited several of her college choices on a 4-day car trip and ultimately she selected a college which happily accepted her. Waiting for the acceptance letter was agonizing, receiving it was joyous. The family celebration which followed was memorable.

Our experiences were undoubtedly quite common. The subtleties merit equal awareness.

Listen to your child.

Most of us have our own preferences of where we would like our children to go to school, but we've had our chance(s) and now it's their turn. Certainly your guidance, opinions, and views are important. You may have some inflexible requirements which your child must be responsive to such as financial limitations. Nevertheless, it is imperative that you listen to your child's preferences and to the best of your ability and with your best judgement encourage your child to fulfill his or her dreams, not yours.

Be patient and "tune-in."

The separation between child and family is beginning and it impacts on everyone involved in different ways and at different times. So much of the college admissions process requires that the children initiate action which will cause separation that there is frequently a reluctance to complete a task which can easily be misinterpreted as laziness or irresponsibility. An application may remain untouched, an essay delayed, a conference postponed. You must "tune-in" to your child's emotions and try to determine when he or she is being lax and when normal

anxieties are rising to the surface, slowing down progress. Try to be patient, guide instead of push, and acknowledge your mutual feelings instead of hiding them. The closer the family is, the more pronounced these experiences may be.

Respect your child's privacy.

Social gatherings will undoubtedly bring you into contact with other parents of college-bound students and the plans and experiences of your children will become timely topics of conversation. Sharing experiences with other parents can be mutually beneficial. But, revealing your child's exact SAT scores, GPA, class rank and similar information is an invasion of privacy. If your child wants to announce this information to friends, relatives or other parents, that's his or her business and choice — not yours. Certainly you wouldn't want your child publicizing your income or other personal information to outsiders. Similarly, your child probably would prefer that some aspect of this process remain within the family. You will be amazed at what remarkable bad taste some parents exhibit in discussing their children's experiences.

Shop carefully.

As adults, you are undoubtedly a more experienced and sophisticated shopper than your child and your experience can be significant as your child shops for a college. Most colleges are very ethical and professional in their recruitment practices, but remember they are "selling." At college fairs, admissions officers can be persuasive, which is not to their discredit. College catalogs can be slick and attractive, which is also understandable and acceptable. But remember, most colleges are selling a package that can cost $5,000 to $15,000 per year or $20,00 to $60,000 over four

years. They need from 100 to 1,000 new students each year to keep their doors open. That's not an indictment of their motives, but simply a representation of their realities. Read between the lines and beyond the pretty pictures. Don't hesitate to confer with your child's counselors about the choices and options available — counselors are generally objective and committed to service the student, not a particular institution. When you visit campuses, allow enough time to wander on your own after your formal tour, usually conducted by the admissions office. Walk into the library, dormitories, student union and even classrooms, if possible. Talk to students around the campus and observe as much as you can. Virtually all college admissions officials will encourage such "investigations" on your part since they don't want your child to make a mistake and stay for one year or less any more than you do.

Naturally, each family's experiences will be a little different. The process is not very scientific yet, in spite of computerbanks, search services, video presentations, etc. Like looking for a house, there is more emotion in the process than some are ready to acknowledge. Nevertheless, as we look back, it was another enjoyable family experience where the rewards far outweigh the risks.

Paul and Ann Krouse are the publishers of WHO'S WHO AMONG AMERICAN HIGH SCHOOL STUDENTS and the parents of four delightful children. This article was written shortly after they completed the college selection/admissions process for the first time with their eldest daughter, Amy, who entered the freshman class at Tufts University in the fall of 1983. Since then, Beth followed at the University of Illinois, class of 1989; Joe at the University of Michigan, class of 1993; and Katie at Indiana University, class of 1994. WHEW!

Glossary of Abbreviations

Acad Academic
Acpl Chr Acappella Choir
AFS American Field Service
Am Leg Boys St American Legion Boys State
Am Leg Aux Girls St American Legion Auxiliary Girls State
Assoc Association
Aud/Vis Audio-Visual
Awd Award

Badmtn Badminton
Bsbl Baseball
Bsktbl Basketball
Bus Business
Bwlng Bowling

C of C Awd Chamber of Commerce Award
Camp Fr Inc Camp Fire, Inc.
CAP Civil Air Patrol
Capt Captain
Cheerldng Cheerleading
Chrmn Chairman
Cit Awd Citizenship Award
Clb Club
Cmnty Wkr Community Worker
Co-Capt Co-Captain
Co-Ed Co-Editor
Coach Actv Coaching Activities
Crs Cntry Cross Country

DAR Awd Daughters of the American Revolution Award
DECA Distributive Education Clubs of America
Dnfth Awd Danforth (I Dare You) Award

Drm & Bgl Drum and Bugle Corps
Drm Mjr(t) Drum Major(ette)
Ed Editor
Ed-Chief Editor-in-Chief
FBLA Future Business Leaders of America
FCA Fellowship of Christian Athletes
FFA Future Farmers of America
FHA Future Homemakers of America
Fit Fitness
Fld Hcky Field Hockey
FNA Future Nurses of America
FTA Future Teachers of America
Ftbl Football

GAA Girls Athletic Association
Gov Hon Prg Awd Governors Honor Program Award
Gym Gymnastics
Hist Historian
Hon Honor
Hosp Aide Hospital Aide
Ice Hcky Ice Hockey
Indus Industrial
Intnl Clb International Club
Intrml Intramural
JA Junior Achievement
JC Awd Jaycees Award
JCL Junior Classical League
JETS Awd Junior Engineering Technical Society Award

JP Sousa Awd John Philip Sousa Award
Jr NHS Junior National Honor Society
JV Junior Varsity
L Letter
Lbrn Librarian
Lcrss Lacrosse
Lion Award Lions Club Award
Lit Mag Literary Magazine

Mgr(s) Manager(s)
Mrchg Band Marching Band

NCTE Awd National Council of Teachers of English Award
NEDT National Educational Development Test Award
NFL National Forensic League
NHS National Honor Society
Ntl National
Nwsp Newspaper

Off Officer
Opt Clb Awd Optimist Club Award
Orch Orchestra

PAVAS Performing and Visual Arts Society
Phtg Photographer
Pres President
Prfct Atten Awd Perfect Attendance Award
Profs Professionals
Rep Representative
Rptr Reporter
ROTC Reserve Officer Training Corps

S.A.D.D. Students Against Driving Drunk
Sal Salutatorian
SAR Awd Sons of the American Revolution Award
Schol Scholarship
Scrkpr Scorekeeper
Sec Secretary
SF Semifinalist
Sftbl Softball
Socr Soccer
Sprt Ed Sports Editor
Stat Statistician
St Schlr State Scholar
Stf Staff
Stu Cncl Student Council
Swmmng Swimming
Symp Band Symphonic Band

Tm Team
Thesps Thespians
Trea, Treas Treasurer
Trk Track
Twrlr Twirler

V, Var Varsity
Val Valedictorian
VICA Vocational Industrial Clubs of America
Vllybl Volleyball
Voice Dem Awd Voice of Democracy Award
VP Vice President

Wrstlng Wrestling
Wt Lftg Weight Lifting

Yrbk Yearbook

Sample Biographical Sketch

This sample is presented to familiarize the reader with the format of the biographical listings. Students are identified by name, school, home city and state. In order to protect the privacy and integrity of all students, home addresses are not published.

Key

1 Name
2 High School
3 Home, City and State
4 Year in School*
5 Class Rank (when given)
6 Accomplishments
7 Future Plans

1 WOLK, BARNET D.; **2** Normandy Isle H.S.; **3** Miami, FL; **4** (4); **5** 10-350; **6** Pres Stu Cncl; VP Sr Cls; Ftbl; 4-H; NHS; Cit Awd; Am Leg Awd; **7** Harvard University; Biochemist

* 1 = Freshman   2 = Sophomore   3 = Junior   4 = Senior

STUDENT BIOGRAPHIES

CALIFORNIA

AABEL, JENNIFER; Abraham Lincoln HS; San Francisco, CA; (2); Acpl Chr; VP Stu Cncl; Var Swmmng; Hon Roll; Soph Clb; Outdoors Clb; UC Davis; Cardiology.

AALA, BETH; Elk Grove HS; Sacramento, CA; (2); 11/500; SADD; Rep Frsh Cls; Off Soph Cls; Pres Jr Cls; JV Cheerldng; Powder Puff Ftbl; High Hon Roll; Pres Acad Fit Awd; CASC Hstrn 88-89; Advertising Mgr.

AALA, LIZA; Elk Grove HS; Sacramento, CA; (3); 27/550; Drill Tm; Yrbk; Pres Frsh Cls; Pres Sr Cls; Stu Cncl; Powder Puff Ftbl; Hon Roll; Notre Dame; Anesthslgy.

AANERUD, AARON M; Gompers Secondary HS; San Diego, CA; (2); Chess Clb; Church Yth Grp; Hon Roll; UCSD.

AARNES, TURI KENNA; Glen A Wilson HS; Hacienda Hts, CA; (3); Pres Science Clb; Spanish Clb; SADD; Band; Drm Mjr(t); Mrchg Band; JV Var Swmmng; Aerospace Engrng.

AARONSON, BRANDI; Leland HS; San Jose, CA; (3); Key Clb; SADD; Stu Cncl; Cheerldng; Pom Pon; Teacher.

AASDO, NOEL; Tulare Union HS; Pixley, CA; (3); 30/500; Spanish Clb; Sci.

ABAD, MICHELLE C; Serra HS; San Diego, CA; (4); Intnl Clb; Office Aide; SADD; Cit Awd; Hon Roll; Prfct Atten Awd; Advnc Via Indvdl Determination Cert Of Awd; Pblc Rltns.

ABAD, RAMIRO; Sacred Heart Cathedral Prep; Daly City, CA; (1); Church Choir; School Musical; School Play; Stage Crew; Ftbl; Wt Lftg; Pres Acad Fit Awd; U HI; Med.

ABADAJOS, STEPHANIE; Arroyo Grande HS; Grover City, CA; (1); 331/580; SADD; Socr; Sftbl; AYSO Mid Fldr, Fullback Soccr; City Sftbl Pitchr All Star; AYSO Soccr Natls; Cal Poly; Chiroprctr.

ABADIA, CLAUDIA; Arroyo HS; San Leandro, CA; (3).

ABAGON, FREDDIE M; Samuel F B Morse HS; San Diego, CA; (2); Hon Roll; Ambssdr Coll Bible C Crs; Hmwrk Consistency Awd 89-90; ROPS Bus Info Sys; UCSD; Med Tech.

ABAKAN, STEPHEN; Santa Monica HS; Santa Monica, CA; (4); Church Yth Grp; FBLA; Math Tm; Scholastic Bowl; Service Clb; Band; Church Choir; High Hon Roll; NHS; Pres Acad Fit Awd; UCLA Cncl For Adv Stds; UCLA; CPA.

ABALOS, JAY W; Mojave HS; California City, CA; (3); 5/101; Teachers Aide; Band; Mrchg Band; Pep Band; JV Bsbl; Hon Roll; San Diego ST U; Bus.

ABALOS JR, MELENCIO A; Lemoore Union HS; Lemoore, CA; (3); 8/293; Art Clb; Church Yth Grp; FCA; Office Aide; Science Clb; Spanish Clb; SADD; Var Crs Cntry; Var Tennis; Var Trk; Envrnmntl Clb; Comp Engrng.

ABAN, GEORGE T; Dana Hills HS; Laguna Niguel, CA; (1); Bsktbl; Hon Roll; U CA Berkeley; Aerontcl Engrng.

ABANO, GUIA; Mercy HS; S San Francisco, CA; (4); 10/110; Church Yth Grp; Cmnty Wkr; GAA; Rep Jr Cls; Sec Treas Sr Cls; Var Socr; High Hon Roll; Hon Roll; NHS; Spanish NHS; Patty Jean Ryan Art Schlrshp; Physcs.

ABARO, RONALD C; Glendale Adventist Acad; Glendale, CA; (2); 16/50; Aud/Vis; Church Yth Grp; Teachers Aide; Band; Sprts Med.

ABASTA, ELIZABETH; California HS; Whittier, CA; (3); SADD; Chorus; Sci Awd; U San Diego; Comp Prgmr.

ABASTO, ERICK O; Mission Viejo HS; Mission Viejo, CA; (2); Church Yth Grp; Computer Clb; French Clb; Math Tm; SADD; Bsktbl; Diving; Swmmng.

ABBAS, CHERYN R; El Cajon Valley HS; El Cajon, CA; (1); Church Yth Grp; GAA; SADD; School Play; Var Socr; Var Sftbl; Adv Via Indvdl Determination; AZ ST U; Arch.

ABBAS, LEANNE; Highland HS; Bakersfield, CA; (3); Church Yth Grp; FCA; Pep Clb; VP Sr Cls; Var JV Cheerldng; JV Swmmng; Hon Roll; Chrldng Ltrmn; Nrsng.

ABBATE, ANGELIQUE L; Paraclete HS; Palmdale, CA; (2); Church Yth Grp; Dance Clb; High Hon Roll; Hon Roll; Asst Dnc Tchr; Phys Thrpst.

ABBATE, CATHERINE M; Modoc HS; Likely, CA; (3); 11/71; Am Leg Aux Girls St; Pres VP 4-H; Pres Sr Cls; Sec Stu Cncl; Var Sftbl; Var JV Vllybl; High Hon Roll; Pres Schlr; Letterman Clb; Office Aide; Hugh O'brien Yth Ldrshp Cnfrnc Ambssdr; UCC Yth Cmp Cnclr; Habitat Humanity Vlntr; Elem Ed.

ABBEY, LAURA K; Montgomery HS; Santa Rosa, CA; (3); Am Leg Aux Girls St; VP Church Yth Grp; Pep Clb; Ed Yrbk; Rep Jr Cls; Pres Sr Cls; Rep Stu Cncl; Capt Cheerldng; Var Socr; Hon Roll; Psych.

ABBOTT, GALEN A; Marin Acad; Mill Valley, CA; (3); Boy Scts; Chorus; Jazz Band; School Play; Phtg Yrbk; Treas Sr Cls; JV Var Socr; Var Capt Swmmng; Hon Roll.

ABBOTT, HEATHER; Yosemite HS; Oakhurst, CA; (3); 26/174; French Clb; Office Aide; Teachers Aide; Stat Bsktbl; Hon Roll; Bus Admin.

ABBOTT, LAURA; Bonita Vista HS; Bonita, CA; (4); Intnl Clb; Nwsp; Cit Awd; Hon Roll; Southwestern JC; Jrnlsm.

ABBOTT, ROBERT C; Bonita Vista HS; Bonita, CA; (2); 1/600; Dance Clb; Letterman Clb; Model UN; Varsity Clb; Chorus; Swing Chorus; Variety Show; Pres Frsh Cls; Pres Soph Cls; Off Jr Cls; Outstndng Associated Stu Body Activity Awd; Presdntl Phys Ftnss Awd.

ABBOTT, SUSAN; Elsinore HS; Lk Elsinore, CA; (4); 27/475; Church Yth Grp; Dance Clb; FBLA; Girl Scts; ROTC; Cheerldng; Hon Roll; Amer Lgn Schlstc Awd 88; Acad Decthln 89; U Of CA Santa Barbara; Intl Rl.

ABDALA, ELYCIA M; St Pats-St Vincent HS; Vallejo, CA; (2); Var Bsktbl; JV Sftbl; Var Vllybl.

ABDELSAYED, CHERIN A; Culver City HS; Culver City, CA; (3); Church Yth Grp; Girl Scts; Yrbk; Gym; Trk; Hon Roll; Prfct Atten Awd; Med.

ABDOLCADER, SOLEH; Phillip & Sala Burton HS; San Francisco, CA; (3); Computer Clb; French Clb; Math Clb; ROTC; Color Guard; Yrbk; Socr; High Hon Roll; Bus/Hstry; Amer Lgn Mdl Awd; UC Berkeley.

ABDOUN, OLA; Sunset HS; Hayward, CA; (2); French Clb; FTA; Girl Scts; Math Clb; Office Aide; Science Clb; Service Clb; SADD; Teachers Aide; Band; Mount Eden; Engl.

ABE, TRISHA M; Mater Dei HS; Fountain Valley, CA; (1); JV Socr; Var Tennis; Hon Roll; CSF; Stu Of Mnth; 2nd Tm All Cnty Tennis; UC Coll; Psych.

ABED, MICHAEL; American HS; Fremont, CA; (4); 37/305; Debate Tm; Bsktbl; Socr; High Hon Roll; Hon Roll; San Jose ST U; Phrmcy.

ABEGAZE, BANCH; Banch Abegaze HS; Bakersfield, CA; (2); Dance Clb; Drama Clb; Intnl Clb; NFL; Pep Clb; Variety Show; Off Stu Cncl; Bsktbl; Tennis; Hon Roll; Santa Barbara; Jrnlsm Acctng.

ABEL, HEIDI I; Santa Rosa HS; Santa Rosa, CA; (3); 40/640; Boy Scts; Church Yth Grp; French Clb; Hosp Aide; Ski Clb; Rptr Yrbk; Var L Tennis; JV Trk; Hon Roll; NHS; Safe Rides Scheduler 89-90, Pres 90-91; Ten Most Dedicated Plyr; CA Schlrshp Fed; Law.

ABEL, JANE M; Corning Union HS; Corning, CA; (3); Treas Sec Drama Clb; Treas 4-H; GAA; Girl Scts; Intnl Clb; Science Clb; Church Choir; Flag Corp; School Musical; School Play; Davis; Phys Thrpy.

ABELEDO, AMI; Victory Christian HS; Carlsbad, CA; (4); 1/10; Church Yth Grp; Key Clb; Teachers Aide; Yrbk; Sec Treas Frsh Cls; VP Soph Cls; Sec Treas Sr Cls; High Hon Roll; Prfct Atten Awd; Acad All American; Redlands; Bilingual Educ.

ABELLA, CLAIRE N; Pasadena HS; Altadena, CA; (3); 67/425; Church Yth Grp; Key Clb; Spanish Clb; Acpl Chr; School Musical; Capt Pom Pon; Hon Roll; CSF; Ldrshp Clb; Acad Decthln Team; U San Diego; Acctng.

ABELLAR, RONALD C; St Joseph Notre Dame HS; Union City, CA; (3); Rep Am Leg Boys St; Boy Scts; Church Yth Grp; Cmnty Wkr; Dance Clb; Intnl Clb; Teachers Aide; Varsity Clb; Rptr Nwsp; Yrbk; K Of C Columbian Squires; Natl Schlrshp Fed; Commnty Awds Schlrshp; Social Justice Clb; Dentistry.

ABELLO, LOURDES L; Woodside HS; Redwood City, CA; (2); Drama Clb; Thesps; School Musical; School Play; VP Frsh Cls; Pres Soph Cls; JV Pom Pon; French Hon Soc; Hon Roll; CSF; Brd Of Studs Affairs; Stu Affrmtv Action Early Outrch Prgm; Bus Adm.

ABELS, KRISTINE L; Dana Hills HS; Laguna Niguel, CA; (1); Latin Clb; High Hon Roll; Pedatric Nrsng.

ABELS, TRACY; Dos Pueblos HS; Goleta, CA; (4); 1/303; Cmnty Wkr; Debate Tm; VP 4-H; Math Clb; Science Clb; Sec Speech Tm; Pres SADD; School Play; Treas Stu Cncl; Var Swmmng; U Of PA Bk Awd; Golden St Schlr; 89 Amer Horse Show Assn Mdl Fnlst; Cornell U; Intl Law.

ABELSON, RACHEL H; El Cerrito HS; El Cerrito, CA; (2); Acpl Chr; Flag Corp; Orch; School Musical; Ed Lit Mag; Swmmng; Hon Roll; Berkely U; Law.

ABERCROMBIE, JONATHAN M; Highlands HS; Sacramento, CA; (3); French Clb; JV Ftbl; Powder Puff Ftbl; JV Trk; Cit Awd; High Hon Roll; Pres Acad Fit Awd; Aviation.

ABERG, KRISTINA; Grossmont HS; La Mesa, CA; (4); 2/371; Am Leg Aux Girls St; Hosp Aide; Pep Clb; Ski Clb; SADD; Ed Nwsp; Rep Jr Cls; Sec Stu Cncl; Var Cheerldng; Hon Roll; UCLA.

ABERNATHY, LA TASHA R; Crenshaw HS; Los Angeles, CA; (2); Aud/Vis; Church Yth Grp; Hon Roll; Hstry/Math Teacher.

ABERNATHY, MICHAEL J; Sonora Union HS; Sonora, CA; (2); 11/336; Science Clb; Spanish Clb; Var L Bsbl; JV Capt Bsktbl; JV Capt Ftbl; High Hon Roll; Ftbl JV Passing Rcrd 1,083 Yrd 20 Td's; Bsktbl All-Star Tm To TX Tech U.

ABERSOLD, GLENN A; Porterville HS; Porterville, CA; (4); VP FBLA; Letterman Clb; Sprt Ed Nwsp; Ftbl; Capt Var Swmmng; Hon Roll; Rotary Awd; Rotary Clb Schlrshp 90; Acad Ltr 90; Waterpolo Capt 88-89; Vrsty Swmmng MVP, & Capt 88-90; CA ST U Sacramento; Bus Admin.

ABEYRATNE, PRIYAN L; Magnolia HS; Anaheim, CA; (1); Church Yth Grp; High Hon Roll; Hon Roll.

ABEYTA, MARGIE L; Corning Union HS; Corning, CA; (3); Church Yth Grp; GAA; Off Jr Cls; Vllybl; Prom Cmmtte; Heald Coll; Legal Secy.

ABEYTA, PAUL N; John Swett HS; Rodeo, CA; (2); Science Clb; JV Bsktbl; Hon Roll; Engrg.

ABI-NADER, MICHELLE L; Casa Roble Fundamental HS; Orangevale, CA; (2); 37/461; Church Yth Grp; Spanish Clb; SADD; Cit Awd; Hon Roll; Piano; UCSB.

ABIERA, RON E; Santa Clara HS; Oxnard, CA; (2); Bsktbl; Ftbl; High Hon Roll; Hon Roll; NHS; Pres Acad Fit Awd; CSF CA Schlrshp Fed; US Naval Acad; Engrng.

ABLES, DELISSA; Washington Prep HS; Los Angeles, CA; (4); 9/565; Service Clb; Speech Tm; Drill Tm; Hon Roll; Tlnt Srch; Yng Black Schlrs; UCLA; Microbio.

ABLES, ERIKA L; Livermore HS; Livermore, CA; (3); Art Clb; Treas 4-H; German Clb; Intnl Clb; Model UN; Ski Clb; Nwsp; 4-H Awd; Hon Roll; CAL Poly; Graphic Design.

ABLOG, ELYMARIE P; Homestead HS; Sunnyvale, CA; (1); Drill Tm; Bus.

ABLOLA, HOWELL N; University City HS; San Diego, CA; (3); Treas Church Yth Grp; Var Wrstlng; Kiwanis Awd; Prfct Atten Awd; Pres Acad Fit Awd; MVP/Mst Dedicated-Wrstlng; U CA-SAN Diego.

ABNEY, JACQUELINE; Will C Wood HS; Sacramento, CA; (1); Church Yth Grp; Girl Scts; Intnl Clb; Band; Mrchg Band; Pep Band; Nwsp; Sftbl; Vllybl; Hon Roll; U CA-DAVIS; Criminal Law.

ABNEY, JOEL C; Faith Christian HS; Yuba City, CA; (3); Church Yth Grp; Rep Frsh Cls; Var L Bsktbl; Var Capt Socr; High Hon Roll; West Point; Engrng.

ABNEY, JOSEPH J; Montclair HS; Ontario, CA; (3); Computer Clb; Intrml Bsktbl; Cit Awd; Hon Roll; Prfct Atten Awd; U Of La Verne; Pre Dntl.

ABO, BRANDON K; Edison HS; Huntington Beach, CA; (2); Boy Scts; Model UN; Intrml Var Ftbl; Intrml Vllybl; Intrml Var Wt Lftg; Huntington Bch Sr Cty Yth Cncl; VP Sangha Teens Orange Cty Buddhist Chrch; Anesthesiologist.

ABOS, YVETTE; Westminster HS; Westminster, CA; (2); German Clb; Library Aide; Speech Tm; Bsbl; Hon Roll; Philosophy.

ABOU LAHOUD, NADA F; Louisville HS; West Hills, CA; (3); 1/65; Cmnty Wkr; Pres FHA; GAA; Office Aide; Teachers Aide; Stage Crew; Rptr Nwsp; Sec Jr Cls; JV Tennis; Hon Roll; Accptd UCLS HS Schlrs Prgrm; UCLA; Bus.

ABOVSKY, IRENE; George Washington HS; San Francisco, CA; (2); Debate Tm; Speech Tm; High Hon Roll; Hon Roll; UCLA; Sci.

ABRACEN, MICHELE; Taft HS; Woodland Hills, CA; (4); 42/560; Office Aide; Drill Tm; Var Cheerldng; High Hon Roll; Pres Acad Fit Awd; Golden St Awd Geom; Dept Span I & II Awd; CSF; Berkeley; Poltcl Sci.

ABRAHAM, AIDA; Eisenhour HS; Rialto, CA; (1); Church Yth Grp; Band; Church Choir; Intrml Bsktbl; Intrml Swmmng; Intrml Tennis; Hon Roll; Prfct Atten Awd.

ABRAHAM, ANGELA V; Edison HS; Huntington Beach, CA; (4); Pres Dance Clb; Teachers Aide; School Play; Ftbl Statistics Mgr 4 Yrs; Dance Golden Key Mdlln Wnnr; Best All Rnd Dancer 4 Yrs; Best Choreographer; OCC; Dancing.

ABRAHAM, JASON R; Laguna Beach HS; Laguna Beach, CA; (2); French Clb; Model UN; Science Clb; Teachers Aide; JV Bsbl; JV Bsktbl; JV Ftbl; Intrml Wt Lftg; US Amt Bsbl Team In USSR 90; Safe Rides; Med.

ABRAHAMSON, CARRIE L; Vintage HS; Reno, NV; (2); Orch; Envrnmntl Club; Humane Soc Club; Psych.

ABRAHAMSON, KENNETH A; Pinole Valley HS; Pinole, CA; (1); Hon Roll; History.

ABRAHIM, ABBEY M; Hilltop HS; Chula Vista, CA; (4); Mgr Nwsp; Mem Humnties Club; Awd Being Lftm Mem CA Schlrshp Fed; SW Coll.

ABRAHIM-YOURI, NEBONEED; Turlock HS; Turlock, CA; (2); NFL; Science Clb; Speech Tm; Lit Mag; JV Tennis; Hon Roll; Aerospc Engrng.

ABRAJANO, ANNE G; Westmoor HS; Daly City, CA; (4); Hon Roll; Acad Achvt-Engl 86-87; Schl Recogntn-Golden St Exam 87; U CA-BERKELEY; Chem.

ABRAMS, ASHLY A; Antelope Valley HS; Lancaster, CA; (2); JV Sftbl.

ABRAMS, SAMANTHA L; Vanden HS; Travis Afb, CA; (3); 15/150; Varsity Clb; Ed Nwsp; Pres Frsh Cls; Pres Soph Cls; Var Bsktbl; Capt Cheerldng; Capt Sftbl; Var Tennis; High Hon Roll; NHS; Quill & Scroll; Outstndng JR Artist; U Southern CA; Engr.

ABRAMSON, DENA M; Los Amigos HS; Fountain Valley, CA; (2); 47/374; French Clb; German Clb; Key Clb; Rep Pep Clb; Sec Chorus; School Musical; Variety Show; Off Soph Cls; Hon Roll; Gate Music; Garden Grove Unified Schl Dist Hnr Choir; Comm.

ABREGO, RICARDO; Sierra Vista HS; Baldwin Park, CA; (1); French Clb; Varsity Clb; Pres Frsh Cls; Crs Cntry; Trk; Wrstlng; Hon Roll; Spanish NHS; Real Est.

ABREU, CLAUDIO; Southwest HS; San Diego, CA; (2); Outstndng ESL Stu; Mecha Clb.

ABRIL, FRANK A; Hemet HS; Hemet, CA; (3); Yrbk; Var L Bsbl; Crs Cntry; JV Trk; Art Assn Of Fontana-Painting; Drftng-Mech & Arch; Arch.

ABRIS, DONALD M; Simi Valley HS; Simi Valley, CA; (3); 180/666; UCLA; Engrng.

ABRONSON, LOUIS S; Beverly Hills HS; Beverly Hills, CA; (4); 2/500; Thesps; Chorus; Jazz Band; Mrchg Band; School Musical; School Play; Mdrgl Singers Bass Sctn Ldr; NYU; Prfrmng Arts.

ABRUZZI, DANIEL E; Palm Springs HS; Palm Springs, CA; (3); L Capt Swmmng; Vrsty/Lttr Water Polo; Engr.

ABSHER, JENNIFER A; San Benito HS; Hollister, CA; (3); Church Yth Grp; Cmnty Wkr; School Play; Hon Roll; UC Santa Cruz; Behvrl Sci.

ABSHIRE, ED D; Village Christian Schls; Los Angeles, CA; (2); Chess Clb; Office Aide; JV Bsbl; Score Keeper; CSF; Elec & Comp; USAFA; Pilot.

ABSOOD, NADER S; Riverbank HS; Modesto, CA; (1); French Clb; Letterman Clb; Science Clb; Tennis; High Hon Roll; Rep Frsh Cls; Float Cmmtte; UCSF; Opthmlgy.

ABSTON- SACKS, TANYA L; Monte Vista HS; Alamo, CA; (2); 51/440; Art Clb; Church Yth Grp; Ski Clb; Varsity Clb; Var Socr; Var Swmmng; Var Trk; High Hon Roll; Hon Roll; Pres Acad Fit Awd; Athlte Wk Vlly Tms; Dist Lvl Sccr 2nd Wstrn Rgnl Play; Piano; UCLA.

ABU-NASSAR, SAMI G; St Ignatius HS; San Francisco, CA; (3); Cmnty Wkr; Library Aide; Stat Bsktbl; Mgr(s); Hon Roll; U Of San Francisco; Health Care.

ABUAN, ROWENA D; Bishop Amat Memorial HS; Duarte, CA; (1); Church Yth Grp; Hosp Aide; High Hon Roll; Prfct Atten Awd; Studies Piano; Musical Teachers Assn Of CA; Cert Of Mrt S CA Beach Fstvl; Branch Honors Rctl.

ABULARACH, SARA; Etiwanda HS; Rancho Cucamonga, CA; (4); Church Yth Grp; Intnl Clb; Library Aide; Office Aide; Spanish Clb; Teachers Aide; Pres Jr Cls; VP Stu Cncl; Fld Hcky; Vllybl; Psych; Forgn Corresp.

ABUYEN, ANTHONY C; Delano HS; Delano, CA; (2); Mgr(s); Tennis; Prfct Atten Awd; Drafting.

ACAMPORA, TINA F; Bishop O'dowd HS; Oakland, CA; (2); Ski Clb; Hiking & Horseback Riding Clubs; UC-DAVIS; Hotel/Bus Admin.

ACANTILADO, MARC; Franklin JR HS; Vallejo, CA; (2); Science Clb; Teachers Aide; Hon Roll; Sci Outstndg Stu 89-90; Engineering.

ACAY, MICHAEL R; Lowell HS; San Francisco, CA; (2); Office Aide; Science Clb; Sftbl Clb; UC Berkeley; Civil Engrng.

ACCAD, ELIE; St Monica Catholic HS; Los Angeles, CA; (4); Chess Clb; French Clb; Socr; High Hon Roll; Bk Of Amer Achvmnt Awd In Math; US Air Force Recruiting Svc Awd In Math & Sci; Stu Of Mnth; U Of S CA; Aerospace Engr.

ACCAD, LARA; St Monica Catholic HS; Los Angeles, CA; (3); Pres French Clb; Key Clb; Teachers Aide; Chorus; Socr; High Hon Roll; NHS; CSF VP/Pres; Reading Club; Stu Of Mnth/Soc Stud & Math; Pediatrician.

ACCARDO, JOSEPH; Bishop O'dowd HS; Castro Valley, CA; (2); Church Yth Grp; Cmnty Wkr; Ski Clb; Orch; Socr; High Hon Roll.

ACETO, ALAN; John A Rowland HS; Rowland Hgts, CA; (3); Church Yth Grp; Var Bsbl; Var Ftbl; Hon Roll; Arch.

ACEUEDO, CLAUDIA G; South San Francisco HS; S San Francisco, CA; (2); JV Sftbl.

ACEVEDO, ANDREA; Hawthorne HS; Hawthorne, CA; (4); 5/488; Key Clb; Pres Model UN; Quiz Bowl; Nwsp; Hon Roll; Pres Acad Fit Awd; CSF; Acad Dcthln Tres; Bnk America Sci Awd; Pan-Amer Clb Pres; UCLA.

ACEVEDO, HUGO C; Rio Mesa HS; Oxnard, CA; (3); Var Ftbl; Hon Roll; Prfct Atten Awd; CSF; Super Spartan Awd.

ACEVEDO, MICHELLE; Bishop Amat Memorial HS; West Covina, CA; (4); 49/392; Church Yth Grp; Color Guard; School Play; Stu Cncl; Hon Roll; Pres Acad Fit Awd; Wrk Exprnce Awd; Natl Hispanic Schlrshp; Cal ST U; Spch Path.

ACEVEDO, SONIA; Baldwin Park HS; Baldwin Park, CA; (4); Pres FBLA; Sec Spanish Clb; Hon Roll; CA ST Fullerton; Comp.

ACEVES, ENRIQUE; Gonzales HS; Soledad, CA; (2); JV Bsktbl; Var Crs Cntry; Var Trk; High Hon Roll; Prfct Atten Awd; Med.

ACEVES JR, JOSE; Arvin HS; Lamont, CA; (2); Drama Clb; Spanish Clb; JV Ftbl; Var Wrstlng; High Hon Roll; Hon Roll; Masonic Awd; Prfct Atten Awd; Pres Acad Fit Awd; CA ST U Bakersfield.

ACEVES, SONIA; Venice HS; Los Angeles, CA; (2); Spanish Clb; SADD; Teachers Aide; Orch; School Play; Nwsp; Yrbk; Lit Mag; Off Frsh Cls; Sftbl; Indian Ed Pgm; UCLA; Med.

ACEVES, VERONICA Y; Ramona Convent Secondary Schl; Alhambra, CA; (3); French Clb; GAA; Model UN; VP Jr Cls; Stu Cncl; Var Swmmng; Hon Roll; NHS.

ACEVES, VERONIKA; Bishop Amat HS; La Puente, CA; (1); Church Yth Grp; Spanish Clb; High Hon Roll; Jr NHS; Spanish NHS; Engl Lit.

ACHONDOA, FRANCIS L; Bellarmine College Prep; Santa Clara, CA; (3); 75/300; Cmnty Wkr; Service Clb; Intrml Mgr Bsktbl; Intrml Mgr Sftbl; Bus Admin.

ACKENBACK, RUBEN F; East Bakersfield HS; Bakersfield, CA; (1); Church Yth Grp; JV Bsbl; JV Bsktbl; Var Score Keeper; Art.

ACKER, HEATHER A; Redlands HS; Redlands, CA; (2); Chorus; Hon Roll; Pres Acad Fit Awd; Friday Night Live; Commnctns.

ACKERMAN, CAMERON T; Nevada Union HS; Nevada City, CA; (2); 1/535; Science Clb; Rep Frsh Cls; JV Capt Bsktbl; Var Tennis; Cit Awd; High Hon Roll; FCA; Pres Acad Fit Awd; Sal; Stu Mnth-NV Union.

ACKERMAN, DAVID J; Oakdale HS; Oakdale, CA; (3); 2/350; Boy Scts; Chess Clb; Cmnty Wkr; Debate Tm; Drama Clb; Letterman Clb; Math Tm; Quiz Bowl; Science Clb; Ski Clb; Vrsty Soccer Team MVP & All League; UC Berkeley; Bus.

ACKERMAN, JOSH T; Nevada Union HS; Nevada City, CA; (1); 1/589; Bsktbl; Tennis; High Hon Roll; Hon Roll; Prfct Atten Awd.

ACKERMAN, MARSHALL WARREN; Rio Lindo Acad; Sebastopol, CA; (4); Church Yth Grp; Acpl Chr; Chorus; School Play; Pacif Union Coll; Theology.

ACKERMAN, REBECCA D; Live Oak/West HS; Morgan Hill, CA; (3); Debate Tm; Drama Clb; French Clb; Science Clb; Service Clb; Speech Tm; Thesps; Chorus; School Musical; School Play; Amnsty Intl; Theatre.

ACKLEY, ANGELA K; Red Bluff Union HS; Red Bluff, CA; (2); 36/422; Church Yth Grp; FCA; JA; Key Clb; Letterman Clb; Spanish Clb; SADD; Church Choir; Stu Cncl; JV Bsktbl; CA Chrch Of God Yth VP; Sacramento ST U; Med.

ACOSTA, BONNIE; Montebello HS; Montebello, CA; (1); French Clb; Math Tm; Cit Awd; Hon Roll; Sci Comp & Alg Clubs.

ACOSTA, CHRISTINA; Fresno HS; Fresno, CA; (4); 61/400; SADD; Var Capt Cheerldng; Hon Roll; Stu Cncl; Fresno City Coll; Paralgl.

ACOSTA, CHRISTINA D; Notre Dame HS; Riverside, CA; (1); 4/165; High Hon Roll; Semi Fnlst Natl Poetry Cont; Creatv Wrtng.

ACOSTA, EVELYN; Venice HS; Los Angeles, CA; (2); Church Yth Grp; Letterman Clb; Teachers Aide; Yrbk; Stat Mgr(s); JV L Vllybl; Hon Roll; CSF; Athenians; Photo Clb; UCLA; Psycht.

ACOSTA JR, FRANK LUGO; Don Bosco Technical Inst; Montebello, CA; (1); 20/244; Crs Cntry; Hon Roll; NHS; Stanford; Med.

ACOSTA, JOE; Redwood HS; Visalin, CA; (3); German Clb; SADD; Rptr Nwsp; Capt Bsktbl; Capt Golf; 2nd All Vly Sprts Wmns Press Awd Jrnlsm; Glf WYL League Chmp 88-89; Area Chmp 88; Vly Chmp 88-89; AZ ST; Cmmnctn.

ACOSTA, LUIS J; Monache HS; Tulare, CA; (3); Church Yth Grp; 4-H Awd; High Hon Roll; Hon Roll; Prfct Atten Awd; Allstate Schlr Of Wk; Sci Hnrs-Bio & Math; Comp Sci.

ACOSTA, MARIA R; Bell HS; Maywood, CA; (4); 20/600; Sec Stu Cncl; JV Sftbl; Svc Above Self Awd Bell-Maywood Rotary Clb; CA Schlrshp Fed Sealbearer; Jr Sr Cabinet; Loyola Marymount U; Elem Ed.

ACOSTA, MARISOL; St Genevieve HS; Sun Valley, CA; (2); Harvard U; Lawyer.

ACOSTA, PETRA B; Wasco Union HS; Wasco, CA; (2); Church Yth Grp; Math Clb; Chorus; Rep Frsh Cls; Mgr Soph Cls; High Hon Roll; Prfct Atten Awd; Wasco Cmnty Schlrshp Awd; Hnr Soc; CSF; UCLA; Lawyer.

ACOSTA, RACHEL; Alemany HS; Sepulveda, CA; (2); Drill Tm; Yrbk; Hon Roll; NHS; Asian Clb; CSF; UC Berkley; Med.

ACOSTA, RAMONA R; John F Kennedy HS; Buena Park, CA; (1); Church Yth Grp; Chorus; Church Choir; School Musical; Hon Roll; Pres Acad Fit Awd; Vet.

ACOSTA, RICHARD M; Edison HS; Huntington Bch, CA; (3); Church Yth Grp; Cmnty Wkr; Model UN; Var JV Bsktbl; Acadmc Dcthln; Yth In Govt.

ACOSTA, SANDRA; Carson HS; Carson, CA; (2); Church Yth Grp; Latin Clb; Teachers Aide; Chorus; School Play; Cit Awd; Hon Roll; Prfct Atten Awd; CA ST Long Bch; Acctng.

ACOSTA, SOCORRO; Stagg HS; Stockton, CA; (1); High Hon Roll; UC Davis Early Outreach Pgm; Stanislaus U.

ACOSTA, TERESA L; Orosi HS; Orosi, CA; (2); Drama Clb; FHA; Band; Church Choir; Mrchg Band; Pep Band; Hon Roll; 1st Runner Up Cutler Latin Amer Clb; Fresno ST U; Pub Admin.

ACOSTA, TONI C; Los Banos HS; Los Banos, CA; (2); Latin Clb; Stat Bsktbl; Hon Roll; TX ST U; Law.

ACOSTA, YECENIA; John Glenn HS; Norwalk, CA; (3); Church Yth Grp; Dance Clb; French Clb; Church Choir; Wt Lftg; Cit Awd; Hon Roll.

ACQUARO, PAOLA; Academy Of Our Lady Of Peace; San Diego, CA; (4); 12/130; Art Clb; Hosp Aide; Teachers Aide; School Musical; High Hon Roll; Hon Roll; CSF; Religious Stds & Math Analysis Awds 90; U San Diego; Pediatrician.

ACQUISTAPACE, CHRISTINA L; Willow Glen HS; San Jose, CA; (2); JV Sftbl; Hon Roll; Pres Acad Fit Awd; U Of CA; Comp Sci.

ACREE, CHRISTINA M; Skyline HS; Oakland, CA; (3); Computer Clb; ROTC; Teachers Aide; Varsity Clb; Drill Tm; Mgr(s); Score Keeper; Vllybl; High Hon Roll; Hon Roll; Sons Of Amer Revolution; Cnslr Of Hearing Impaired Camp; Genetic Engrng.

ACREE, KARENA J; Alameda HS; Alameda, CA; (3); Pres Church Yth Grp; Drama Clb; Spanish Clb; Teachers Aide; Church Choir; High Hon Roll; Hon Roll; Latinos Unidos Club; U CA LA; Pol Sci.

ACUFF, ANDREA L; Marysville HS; Marysville, CA; (1); Spanish Clb; Treas Frsh Cls; Stat Bsktbl; Intrml Powder Puff Ftbl; Hon Roll; Chico ST; Psycht.

ACUNA, ALVARO; Calexico HS; Calexico, CA; (3); Key Clb; Office Aide; Hon Roll; CSF; MECA Club; Migrant Club; Prom Cmmtte; Active Clss Mem; Arch.

ACUNA, ANA M; Eisenhower HS; Bloomington, CA; (2); Hon Roll; Teacher.

ACUNA, DEBORAH V; Channel Islands HS; Oxnard, CA; (3); JV Vllybl; High Hon Roll; Hon Roll; Prfct Atten Awd; Athlte Schlr 89; Asian Amer Clb 87-88; CSF; UCLA; Med Sci.

ACUNA, GEORGE; Palo Verde HS; Blythe, CA; (3); 17/263; Letterman Clb; Teachers Aide; JV Var Ftbl; Var Trk; Wt Lftg; High Hon Roll; Desert Vly Leag Ftbl.

ACUNA, LISA A; Arcadia HS; Arcadia, CA; (3); 343/649; Art Clb; Church Yth Grp; Dance Clb; Girl Scts; Pep Clb; Ski Clb; Teachers Aide; Chorus; Nwsp; Yrbk; Commendations In World Hstry & Schl Spirit; Prin Hnr Rl; U Of CA Irvine; Med.

ACUNA, SOFIA; Coachella Valley HS; Indio, CA; (3); Math Clb; JV Var Bsktbl; JV Var Sftbl; JV Var Vllybl; Hon Roll; Prfct Atten Awd; OR; Accntng.

ADAIR, BEKKI A; Edison HS; Huntington Beach, CA; (1); Church Yth Grp; Girl Scts; Quiz Bowl; Scholastic Bowl; Teachers Aide; Acpl Chr; Chorus; Church Choir; Lit Mag; Hon Roll; Pegasus Poetry Cont Semi-Fnlst; Orange Cty Acad Decathlon; Teacher.

ADAIR, BRIAN; Warren HS; Downey, CA; (4); 18/465; Computer Clb; Debate Tm; FBLA; VP Key Clb; Scholastic Bowl; Hon Roll; Pres Acad Fit Awd; Cert Of Acad Mrt; Acad Ltr; CSF Sealbearer 4 Yrs; CSULB; Bio.

ADAIR, KATHERINE G; Foothill SR HS; Sacramento, CA; (1); Hon Roll; 4.0 GPA; Phys Ftns & Hme Ec Achvt Awds; OR ST U; Pedtrcn.

ADAM, IAN J; Huntington Beach HS; Huntington Beach, CA; (3); Var Crs Cntry; Var Socr; Var Trk; Var Vllybl; Hon Roll; Sports Med.

ADAM, JOY C; Sunny Hills HS; Fullerton, CA; (2); 143/463; Church Yth Grp; Cmnty Wkr; Drama Clb; German Clb; Church Choir; School Musical; Stage Crew; Variety Show; High Hon Roll; Hon Roll; Dance Prod; Piano & Choreography; Brigham Young U; Psych.

ADAM, MELINDA C; California HS; San Ramon, CA; (4); Church Yth Grp; SADD; Stage Crew; JV Var Swmmng; High Hon Roll; Hon Roll; Fshn Clb; Diablo Valley Coll; Child Devlp.

ADAME, ELIZABETH M; Bishop Montgomery HS; Wilmington, CA; (2); Drill Tm; Air Force Acad; Astronaut.

ADAMIEC, DAVID C; Center For Independent Studies; Concord, CA; (3); Church Yth Grp; French Clb; German Clb; Teachers Aide; Diablo Valley Coll; Med.

ADAMS II, ALAN A; Bellarmine College Prep; Rochester, NY; (4); 160/350; Church Yth Grp; Cmnty Wkr; Drama Clb; Service Clb; Teachers Aide; Ftbl; Yth Grp/Bellarmine Retreat Ldr; St John Fisher Coll; Mortg Brkr.

ADAMS, ANGELA M; East Union HS; Manteca, CA; (1); 6/450; High Hon Roll; UCLA.

ADAMS, BRAD; Fontana HS; Fontana, CA; (2); Varsity Clb; Wrstlng; Psych.

ADAMS, CATHERINE A; Covina HS; Covina, CA; (2); Church Yth Grp; French Clb; JCL; Latin Clb; Model UN; Hon Roll; CA Schlrshp Fed; U CA Berkeley; Art Hstry Ed.

ADAMS, CATHERINE S; Yucaipa HS; Yucaipa, CA; (2); 68/441; Church Yth Grp; FTA; Spanish Clb; Mgr Yrbk; Hon Roll; Prfct Atten Awd; Natl Young Ldrs Conf Congrssnl Schlr; Bio.

ADAMS, CYNTHIA; Valley HS; Sacramento, CA; (4); Spanish Clb; Var Mgr(s); Var Powder Puff Ftbl; Var Trk; High Hon Roll; Hon Roll; Afro Amer Stu Union; CSF; VICA Drftng Clb; UCD Outreach; San Diego ST U.

ADAMS, DAVID A; Rio Lindo Acad; Anderson, CA; (4); 1/94; French Clb; Ski Clb; Band; Chorus; VP Stu Cncl; JV Bsktbl; Var Ftbl; Var Golf; Var Sftbl; Var Vllybl; Pacific Union Coll; Bus Admin.

ADAMS, DENISE L; Orange HS; Orange, CA; (3); Church Yth Grp; Chorus; Church Choir; Cit Awd; Hon Roll; Rotary Awd; Rancho Santiago; Bus.

ADAMS, GINA L; Valley Christian HS; Lakewood, CA; (2); Church Yth Grp; GAA; Band; Mrchg Band; Pep Band; JV Bsktbl; Hon Roll; NHS; Law.

ADAMS, HELANE; Madison HS; San Diego, CA; (4); 66/368; Church Yth Grp; Hosp Aide; NFL; Treas Soph Cls; Treas Jr Cls; Powder Puff Ftbl; Trk; Hon Roll; Pres Acad Fit Awd; Outstnand Achvt Co Wide Subj A Write-Off 90; U Of CA-SAN Diego; Psych.

ADAMS, JAMES M; El Cajon SR HS; El Cajon, CA; (4); Pres Computer Clb; VP FBLA; Sec Math Clb; SADD; Rptr Yrbk; VP Stu Cncl; Intrml Bsktbl; Stat Ftbl; Cit Awd; Gov Hon Prg Awd; UCLA; Bus.

ADAMS, JAMIE D; Mira Mesa HS; San Diego, CA; (2); 36/797; Office Aide; Pres Acad Fit Awd; Mtn Bkng; Bodybrdng.

ADAMS, JANICE D; Modesto HS; Modesto, CA; (3); Hist FBLA; Orch; Score Keeper; Stat Sftbl; Legal Assnt.

ADAMS, JENNIFER; Dublin HS; Dublin, CA; (3); 3/200; Church Yth Grp; Dance Clb; French Clb; Hosp Aide; SADD; Color Guard; JV Swmmng; High Hon Roll; Peer Cnslng Pres; Russian Exch Stu; Pre Med.

ADAMS, JEREMY E; Tulare Union HS; Tulare, CA; (4); Capt Church Yth Grp; Church Yth Grp; Computer Clb; Drama Clb; SADD; Golf; Hon Roll; Eagle Scout; BYU; Cmptr Sci.

ADAMS, KATE; Del Campo HS; Citrus Heights, CA; (2); Band; Flag Corp; Mrchg Band; Var Swmmng; All Star Sftbl Team; Law.

ADAMS, KATHLEEN M; South Pasadena HS; Pasadena, CA; (3); Church Yth Grp; Cmnty Wkr; Debate Tm; Drama Clb; Hosp Aide; Ski Clb; SADD; Teachers Aide; Nwsp; Mgr(s); Law Office Adm Asst; Peer Cnslng Conf; Staff Writer Schl Nwsppr; Jrnlsm.

ADAMS, KATIE; San Dieguito HS; Carlsbad, CA; (3); Aud/Vis; Debate Tm; 4-H; Hosp Aide; Library Aide; Office Aide; Pep Clb; Ski Clb; Teachers Aide; Band.

ADAMS, KHIRA L; York HS; Aptos, CA; (4); Key Clb; Math Clb; Ski Clb; Stu Cncl; Crs Cntry; Fld Hcky; Trk; High Hon Roll; Ntl Merit Schol; Physics Awd 89; Math Awd 90; Gen Excel Awd 90; Harvard; Engrng.

ADAMS, KIMBERLY K; Corona HS; Corona, CA; (2); 11/425; Church Yth Grp; Office Aide; Chorus; Cit Awd; High Hon Roll; CSF Membership 1 Smstr; Hnrs 1st Yr Alg Gldn ST Exam; Psych.

ADAMS, KRISTIE; San Marino HS; San Gabriel, CA; (2); AFS; Church Yth Grp; Cmnty Wkr; Dance Clb; English Clb; GAA; Intnl Clb; Latin Clb; Pep Clb; SADD.

ADAMS, KRISTINA L; Coalinga Unified HS; Coalinga, CA; (4); AFS; Red Cross Aide; Teachers Aide; Band; Yrbk; Bsktbl; Cheerldng; Crs Cntry; Trk; Wt Lftg; Miss Coalinga CA; Work Restaurant & Day Care Ctr; Babysitting; W Hills JC; Teacher.

ADAMS, MARK; Templeton HS; Paso Robles, CA; (3); Key Clb; Band; Jazz Band; Pres Frsh Cls; Pres Stu Cncl; Var Bsbl; Var Ftbl; Letterman Clb; Varsity Clb; Pep Band; Creatv Wrtng Cont 1st Pl Clss Div; Mjr Hugo Hrrcn Spprt Dr Chrmn; Bus.

ADAMS, MARK D; Servite HS; Placentia, CA; (2); JV Var Bsbl; Intrml Ftbl; Stanford U; Law.

ADAMS, MARY BETH; South Tahoe HS; South Lake Tahoe, CA; (3); 19/211; Aud/Vis; Church Yth Grp; Key Clb; SADD; Band; School Musical; Var Tennis; Cmnty Wkr; Drama Clb; Pep Band; CA Tech; Elec Engrng.

ADAMS, MONIQUE; Pasadena HS; Pasadena, CA; (3); Church Yth Grp; Drama Clb; Girl Scts; Acpl Chr; Chorus; Church Choir; Drill Tm; School Play; Cngrssnl Schlr; CA Natl Yng Ldrs Conf; Court Stonagrapher.

ADAMS, NATALIE; Santiago HS; Garden Grove, CA; (2); Drama Clb; School Play; Stu Cncl; Vllybl; Hon Roll; JV Chrldr; ASB Ldrshp; CA ST Fullerton; Jrnlsm.

ADAMS, PHILIP H; South San Francisco HS; South San Francis, CA; (2); Cmnty Wkr; SADD; Nwsp; Var Bsktbl; Prfct Atten Awd; Math Engrng Sci Achvt Awd; Commnctns.

ADAMS, RYAN; Tulelake HS; Tulelake, CA; (2); Church Yth Grp; Chorus; Church Choir; School Musical; School Play; Variety Show; Bsktbl; Cit Awd; High Hon Roll; Hon Roll; Amercnsm Essay Awd 3rd Pl; Missionary Cncrt Tour In Europe; Music.

ADAMS, RYAN L; Fairfield HS; Fairfield, CA; (3); 40/445; Boy Scts; Church Yth Grp; JV Var Crs Cntry; JV Socr; JV Var Trk; ST Qualifier Cross-Cnty Var; Won Lg Mt Cross Cnty W/Schl Rcrd; Schl Rcd Mile Track Var; Brigham Young U; Elec Engrng.

ADAMS, SABRINA; West HS; Bakersfield, CA; (2); Dance Clb; Hosp Aide; Band; Mrchg Band; Pep Band; Var Cheerldng; Cit Awd; Hon Roll; Kiwanis Awd; Prfct Atten Awd; Vlntr; Spellman U; Med.

ADAMS, SEAN A; George Washington Prep HS; Los Angeles, CA; (2); MLK Peace March; Spec Interest Illustration & Creative Writing; Pratt Inst; Freelnc Cartoonist.

ADAMS, SHAUN C; John F Kennedy HS; Granada Hills, CA; (3); Church Yth Grp; Computer Clb; French Clb; Cit Awd; Hon Roll; UCLA; Math.

ADAMS, STACEY L; Turlock HS; Turlock, CA; (3); 96/600; AFS; Church Yth Grp; Key Clb; NFL; Speech Tm; Teachers Aide; JV Score Keeper; JV Sftbl; JV Var Vllybl; Hon Roll; Phrmcy.

ADAMS, STEFFNEE D; Buena HS; Ventura, CA; (3); 62/488; Church Yth Grp; Color Guard; Humanities Club; CSF; Acad Ltr; Sci.

ADAMS, STEPHEN E; Liberty Union HS; Oakley, CA; (1); Boy Scts; Church Yth Grp; Quiz Bowl; JV Trk; Pres Acad Fit Awd; BYU; PE Tchr.

ADAMS, TAMARA A; Ukiah HS; Ukiah, CA; (4); 88/450; Church Yth Grp; Drama Clb; FBLA; SADD; Band; Chorus; Mrchg Band; School Musical; School Play; Swing Chorus; Comp Litrcy Awd; Cert St Phys Ftng Tstng; Sonoma ST U; Gospel Music.

ADAMS, TIMOTHY D; Poway HS; Poway, CA; (1); Church Yth Grp; Drama Clb; JV Crs Cntry; JV Trk; JV Wrstlng; High Hon Roll; Outstndng Stu 89-90; A-Team; Pilot.

ADAMS, WILLIE L; Mc Clymonds HS; Oakland, CA; (3); Chorus; Rptr Nwsp; Yrbk; Pres Frsh Cls; Pres Jr Cls; Pres Sr Cls; JV Swmmng; Hon Roll; Radio/Tv.

ADAMS, YOHANNA M; Pasadena HS; Pasadena, CA; (3); Church Yth Grp; Dance Clb; Drama Clb; Girl Scts; Office Aide; Acpl Chr; Chorus; Church Choir; Drill Tm; School Play; Ct Stngrphr.

ADAMS-EL, TARIQ-BILAL S; Mojave HS; California City, CA; (2); Chess Clb; Band; Mrchg Band; Pep Band; High Hon Roll; Hon Roll; Soph Prince 89-90; Acad Decathalon; MIT; Aerospace Engrng.

ADAMSON, DWIGHT; Faith Christian HS; Yuba City, CA; (2); Church Yth Grp; High Hon Roll; NW Div Royal Ranger Of Yr 89; Sr Guide Out-Post 229 N CA & NV Dist; CSF; MWA Club Wnnr Ldrshp Awd.

ADAMSON, HEATHER; Corcoran HS; Corcoran, CA; (2); Pres Church Yth Grp; Church Choir; Rptr Nwsp; Yrbk; JV Cheerldng; High Hon Roll; Pres Acad Fit Awd; CSF; Acad Boosters Club; Brigham Young U; Cmmnctns.

ADAMSON III, RUSS E; San Rafael HS; San Rafael, CA; (3); 6/230; Aud/Vis; Boy Scts; Drama Clb; French Clb; Band; Orch; Pep Band; School Musical; School Play; Stage Crew; Stus For Envrnmntl Awareness; Tai Chi Clb; CSF; Arch.

ADAMZADEH, SHARLET; Turlock HS; Turlock, CA; (1); Church Yth Grp; Hosp Aide; Office Aide; Hon Roll; Assyrian Clb; AACCOT Yth Grp; CA ST U-Stanislaus; Med.

ADAN, SANDRA; Palo Verde HS; Blythe, CA; (3); 10/263; Spanish Clb; Hon Roll; Spanish NHS; CSF; CA U Riverside; Bus.

ADCOCK, AMINAH; Fremont HS; Oakland, CA; (2); Dance Clb; Math Tm; Speech Tm; Chorus; Church Choir; Cit Awd.

ADDIS, APRIL; Community Christian HS; Bakersfield, CA; (4); Church Yth Grp; Teachers Aide; Chorus; Nwsp; Stu Cncl; Trk; Vllybl; Hon Roll; Kiwanis Awd; Opt Clb Awd; Chpln At Schl; Chrstn Schlrs; Stu Gvrnmnt; San Jaquin Vly Coll; Dntl Assis.

ADDISON, MONICKIE S; San Gorgonio HS; Highland, CA; (3); Pep Clb; Teachers Aide; Chorus; Stu Cncl; JV Var Cheerldng; Powder Puff Ftbl; Cit Awd; Hon Roll; Pres Acad Fit Awd; Black Stu Union Pres; Bus.

ADDOTTA, ALICE M; Whittier Christian HS; Fullerton, CA; (2); 1/182; Church Yth Grp; Cheerldng; High Hnr Rll; CA Schlstc Fdr; Notre Dame; Law.

ADELIZZI, JIM F; Francis Parker HS; San Diego, CA; (4); 2/60; Intnl Clb; Key Clb; Math Tm; Service Clb; SADD; Sprt Ed Nwsp; Pres Sr Cls; Stu Cncl; Var Capt Bsbl; Var L Ftbl; Outstndng Athlete 90 Natl Ftbl Leaque Hall Fame; Harvard Bk Awd Outstndng Stu Cls, Math, Sci Awd; Dartmouth.

ADELSBACH, TERRY; Yosemite HS; Ahwahnee, CA; (2); Cmnty Wkr; FFA; Letterman Clb; Varsity Clb; Crs Cntry; Socr; U CA San Diego; Marine Bio.

ADENWALA, SABEEN; Armijo HS; Fairfield, CA; (2); Teachers Aide; Cit Awd; ABA; Elem.

ADETOYE, ANTHONY A; Fontana HS; Fontana, CA; (4); Drama Clb; VICA; School Play; Stage Crew; JV Trk; Cit Awd; Hon Roll; Hm Econ Clbs.

ADIAO, MICHAEL N; James Logan HS; Union City, CA; (3); 84/832; Church Yth Grp; Ed Yrbk; CSU Long Beach; Electrcl Engr.

ADINATA, HARRY; Ontario HS; Ontario, CA; (3); Church Yth Grp; Teachers Aide; Band; Chorus; Treas Frsh Cls; VP Soph Cls; Hon Roll; Prfct Atten Awd; Bus.

ADKINS, DEBRA S; Bellflower HS; Bellflower, CA; (3); 132/276; Church Yth Grp; Quiz Bowl; Thesps; Chorus; Mrchg Band; School Musical; Stage Crew; Hon Roll; Communication.

ADKINS, JAMES; El Sereno HS; Citrus Heights, CA; (4); Elks Awd; Hon Roll; Prfct Atten Awd; Pres Acad Fit Awd; Val; Inst Of Govt Affairs & U Of CA Davis Cert Of Merit Essay Comptn; Challenge Magzn Hnrbl Mntn; American River Coll; Hist Tchr.

ADKINS, PAMELA A; Rosemead HS; Rosemead, CA; (4); 20/380; Church Yth Grp; Cmnty Wkr; FCA; Capt GAA; Service Clb; Teachers Aide; VP Frsh Cls; VP Soph Cls; Pres Sr Cls; Rep Stu Cncl; U Of Sthrn CA; Bio Sci.

ADKINS, TONISA B; Victor Valley HS; Victorville, CA; (3); Teachers Aide; Capt Drill Tm; Mrchg Band; Stat Trk; Indr Capt Drill Team 90; Most Imprvd Drill Team Mem 89; Photo.

ADLAWAN, ARLYNN; Notre Dame HS; Salinas, CA; (4); 10/92; Church Yth Grp; Hosp Aide; Pep Clb; Var JV Cheerldng; Var Pom Pon; High Hon Roll; NHS; CSF Life Member; Bank Of America Cert In Math; Ballet Tap Jazz & Piano; CA Polytechnic ST; Civil Engr.

ADLER, AARON J; California HS; Whittier, CA; (2); 1/500; JV Crs Cntry; JV Trk; Hon Roll; Acad Deca; Blue Gold Soc Stu; Pres Finance Clb; USC; Chem.

ADLER, HILARY; Palo Alto SR HS; Palo Alto, CA; (2); Church Yth Grp; Key Clb; Rptr Nwsp; Stu Cncl; JV Tennis; JV Trk; High Hon Roll; Hon Roll; Encmcs.

ADLER, JESSICA D; California HS; Whittier, CA; (2); Latin Clb; JV Tennis; JV Trk; Hon Roll; Int Desgn.

ADLOF, BYRDIE M; Royal HS; Simi Valley, CA; (3); 235/600; Church Yth Grp; Office Aide; Yrbk; Artist; Art.

ADRIAN, DONNELL; Tusti HS; Tustin, CA; (4); Swmmng; Wt Lftg; Wrstlng; Surfing; Triathalona; Irvine Valley Coll; Psych.

ADRIAN, LEIGH; Banning HS; Banning, CA; (2); Church Yth Grp; Drama Clb; Letterman Clb; Model UN; Pep Clb; Spanish Clb; Varsity Clb; Band; Color Guard; Orch; CSF Awd; Span II Hnr Awd; Advncd Engl II Awd; Scholar Athl Awd; Acad Lttr Awd; UCLA; Law.

ADRIANO, JANET L; Immaculate Heart HS; Los Angeles, CA; (3); 34/125; Cmnty Wkr; GAA; Math Clb; Science Clb; Service Clb; Yrbk; JV Intrml Vllybl; CLA Yth Grp; CA U; Nrsng.

ADRIANZEN, DANISE; Sweetwater HS; National City, CA; (2); 34/589; Teachers Aide; Stage Crew; Variety Show; Ed Nwsp; Ed Yrbk; Sec Frsh Cls; Sec Soph Cls; Var Capt Socr; Cit Awd; Hon Roll; FBLA FL; Best Persnlty & Bggst Smile Hall Of Fame; Swthrts Qn 88-89; Psych.

ADRIATICO, ELVIE R; Monterey HS; Monterey, CA; (2); Spanish Clb; Chorus; JV Crs Cntry; Cit Awd; High Hon Roll; Hon Roll; NHS; Prfct Atten Awd; Pres Acad Fit Awd; Coach San Diego Recreatn Dept After Schl; Math.

ADRIATICO JR, JOEL U; Pater Noster HS; Glendale, CA; (1).

ADRIATICO, MARIEJOY E; St Joseph HS; Artesia, CA; (3); Hosp Aide; Ed Yrbk; Hon Roll; NEDT Awd; Hnrs Clss Math; Yrbk Photogrphr; CSF; Pol Sci.

ADRIATICO, RONALD; Chaminade College Prep; Bell Canyon, CA; (3); Boy Scts; Hosp Aide; Letterman Clb; Bsktbl; Mgr(s); JV Var Vllybl; Cit Awd; High Hon Roll; Hon Roll; NHS; Vlybl MVP; Hosptl & Vlybl Coach Vlntr; UCLA; Gyn/Ob.

ADRID, AMARA A; Serra HS; San Diego, CA; (2); 36/460; Church Yth Grp; FTA; Key Clb; JV Fld Hcky; JV Var Mgr(s); Stat Socr; Mgr Trk; Hon Roll; Prfct Atten Awd; Hnrs Smnrs Pgm; Teen Cnnctn; Acadmc Leag; Acctng.

ADUNA, KATHERINE; Bloomington HS; Bloomington, CA; (2); Hon Roll; Modeling.

ADVENTO, MAIDA; Montgomery HS; San Diego, CA; (4); 32/410; Church Yth Grp; Cmnty Wkr; Drama Clb; JA; Pep Clb; Service Clb; Band; Church Choir; Drll Tm; Flag Corp; Drll Team World Chmpns; Jrnlsm Awd; Schlrshp Awd; San Diego ST U; Nrsg.

ADVIENTO, LEILANI R; Encinal HS; Alameda, CA; (1); ROTC; Band; Mrchg Band; Orch; Pep Band; NSOA Orch Awd; Honor Roll; Music.

AFAGA, MICHAEL W; Fred C Beyer HS; Modesto, CA; (3); Dance Clb; Cit Awd; Hon Roll; Prfct Atten; Art Awd Postr Constutnl Gala 88-89; Arch Engrng.

AFENIR, RACHEL M; Bell HS; Bell, CA; (3); Hon Roll; Comp Production; Comp Sci.

AFFLECK, JOHN J; Serrano HS; Baldy Mesa, CA; (4); Off Boy Scts; Sec FFA; Office Aide; Rep Teachers Aide; Chorus; Var Ftbl; Hon Roll; FFA St & Forest Mngmnt Awd; Phelan Fire Station Schlrshp; Crafton Hills; Frstry.

AFGHAN, ASHKAN; Fullerton Union HS; Fullerton, CA; (3); Fullerton Coll; Orthodontics.

AFGHANI, GREGORY H; Capistrano Valley HS; Mission Viejo, CA; (3); Rptr Nwsp; UCLA; Pre Law.

AFIUNE, MAGALY; California HS; Whittier, CA; (2); French Clb; Hon Roll; Prfct Atten Awd; Acad Decathlon; Top 100 Stu Pgm; CSF; Whittier Coll; Bus Exec.

AFRA, ROBERT; Santa Monica HS; Santa Monica, CA; (4); VP JA; Ski Clb; Pres Temple Yth Grp; Orch; Ed Nwsp; Ed Yrbk; Ed Lit Mag; Rep Frsh Cls; Rep Soph Cls; Rep Jr Cls; Rep Sr Cls; Med Vlntr; Med.

AGAMAITE, DAVID M; Pacifica HS; Garden Grove, CA; (1); Bsbl; Ftbl; Bst Dfns Plyr Bsbl Tm; Cptn Cyprss Pny Lg All Str Tm; AZ ST; Psychlgy.

AGAMAO, CAROLYN F; North Salinas HS; Salinas, CA; (3); Spanish Clb; Var Crs Cntry; Var Capt Fld Hcky; Var Capt Sftbl; Tennis; Wt Lftg; High Hon Roll; Pres Acad Fit Awd.

AGARWAL, JAY S; Sunny Hills HS; Buena Park, CA; (2); 11/450; Rptr FBLA; Intnl Clb; High Hon Roll; Stanford; Phy.

AGATEP, KATHRINA L; Westmoor HS; Daly City, CA; (2); French Clb; High Hon Roll; Hon Roll; Prfct Atten Awd; U CA-SAN Francisco; Dentistry.

AGATON, KATHLEEN; Arosary HS; Yorba Linda, CA; (3); NFL; Spanish Clb; Speech Tm; Varsity Clb; Nwsp; Off Frsh Cls; Off Soph Cls; Bsktbl; Trk; High Hon Roll; Ampus Mnstry Rtrt Tm; JR Stsmn Amrca; Hugs Not Drgs.

AGAZARYAN, ALINA; Burbank HS; Burbank, CA; (2); Stat Teachers Aide; Drill Tm; Mgr(s); Hon Roll; Pres Acad Fit Awd; Z-Clb; Acad Games; Peer Ldrshp; Acad Dcthln; CJSF; UCLA; Med.

AGDA, CHRISTINA C; Moivache HS; Poplar, CA; (3); Church Yth Grp; Cmnty Wkr; Debate Tm; Service Clb; Treas SADD; Ed Nwsp; Rep Frsh Cls; Cit Awd; High Hon Roll; Hon Roll; Rotary Intl; CSF; FNL; STOPP; Ed.

AGEE, KELLI; Montgomery HS; San Diego, CA; (4); 3/400; Pep Clb; SADD; Band; Mrchg Band; Stu Cncl; Cit Awd; Hon Roll; NHS; Pres Acad Fit Awd; Deprtmntl Awd Span & Sci; Outstndng Schlr Trphy; ASB Designated Service Plaque; U Of Redlands; Med.

AGEPOGU, ESTHER P; Mayfield SR HS; Pasadena, CA; (2); AFS; Office Aide; Hon Roll; 2 Dimnsnl Art Cnsrvtry; CSF.

AGIA, BASSAM; University City HS; San Diego, CA; (2); SADD; Teachers Aide; Rptr Nwsp; JV Var Crs Cntry; JV Var Trk; JV Var Wrstlng; High Hon Roll; Hon Roll; Prfct Atten Awd; Fri Night Live; Golden St Exam Honors.

AGLIPAY, CHLEORA L; Notre Dame HS; San Jose, CA; (4); Cmnty Wkr; Hosp Aide; Intnl Clb; Library Aide; Pep Clb; Chorus; Pres Frsh Cls; Rep Soph Cls; Pres Jr Cls; Pres Stu Cncl; Pres Filipino Amer Yth Assn; Yth Recgntn Awd; Yth Congrssnl Schlr Of WA DC 1990; San Jose ST U; Pre Med.

AGLIPAY, ERNEST L; Bellarmine HS; San Jose, CA; (1); Cmnty Wkr; Intnl Clb; Service Clb; SADD; Rep Frsh Cls; Sftbl; Mayors Yth Conf Blue Rbn Dlgt 89; Xmas In The Park San Jose Chrmn; Karate; Bellarmine Coll Pre; Intl Law.

AGLUBAT, MELISSA E; John A Rowland HS; Rowland Heights, CA; (2); Church Yth Grp; GAA; Science Clb; Varsity Clb; Ed Yrbk; Pres Soph Cls; Var Socr; Var Tennis; Var Trk; Hon Roll; Sierra Leg Hnrb Mntn Vrsty Sccr; Cmmssnr Of Pblcty; UDSB; Corp Lawyer.

AGNEW, STEPHANIE S; Antelope Valley HS; Lancaster, CA; (3); 28/631; Church Yth Grp; German Clb; Ed Lit Mag; Rep Soph Cls; Rep Jr Cls; Hon Roll; CSF/CA Assctd Stu Body Rptr & Hstrn; Gftd & Tlntd Educ Pgm; Jrnlsm.

AGNITSCH, TONY A; Pinole Valley HS; Rodeo, CA; (3); Wt Lftg; Hon Roll; Prfct Atten Awd; Summer Pre Coll Prgm.

AGOJO, YVETTE MARIE B; Nogales HS; Walnut, CA; (1); Dance Clb; Hon Roll; CSF; Med.

AGRAWAL, RAKA; Monterey HS; Monterey, CA; (1); Model UN; JV Fld Hcky; JV Trk; High Hon Roll.

AGREDANO, YOLANDA Z; Yerba Buena HS; San Jose, CA; (2); Church Yth Grp; Math Tm; Varsity Clb; Variety Show; Var Socr; High Hon Roll; Pre-Engrng Magnet Pgm; MESA Clb; NHS/Csf Clbs; JETS Clb; Princpl Hnrs Awds; Hnr Achvt Awds; Stanford U; Pediatrics.

AGUAYO, RAUL; Sierra Vista HS; Baldwin Park, CA; (1); Church Yth Grp; Ftbl; Wt Lftg; High Hon Roll; Hon Roll; Amateur Guitarist; Intrst In Cmptrs; Cal Poly Pomona; Cmptr Prgrmng.

AGUBA, ERIC C; Pittsburg HS; Pittsburg, CA; (3); 53/335; Church Yth Grp; Cmnty Wkr; French Clb; FBLA; Letterman Clb; Pep Clb; Ski Clb; SADD; Rep Sr Cls; Tennis; GSE Schlr 89; Bus.

AGUERO, CYNTHIA A; Louisville HS; Simi Valley, CA; (1); Art Clb; Church Yth Grp; Cmnty Wkr; Drama Clb; School Play; High Hon Roll; CSF; Harvard HS Frgn Lang Comptn Excllnc Awds Spnsh I & Alg I Advncd; Harvard U; Pediatrician.

AGUIAR, ANN M; Amos Alonzo Stagg HS; Stockton, CA; (4); 1/305; Church Yth Grp; Cmnty Wkr; Hosp Aide; Treas Speech Tm; Thesps; Cheerldng; Cit Awd; DAR Awd; Pres Acad Fit Awd; Val; Westinghouse Sci Talent Search Semi-Fnlst; Gold Medal Essay CA Acadc Decathlon 89; U Of Pacific; Biochem.

AGUIAR, COURTNEY; St Francis HS; Lincoln, CA; (1); SADD; Hist Soph Cls; High Hon Roll; Prfct Atten Awd.

AGUILA, NORA M; Pomona HS; Pomona, CA; (3); Cert Mst Outstndng Stu, Hnr Rl Hnrbl Mntn, Completion Of Adolescent Pregnancy Prevention Course; Psych.

AGUILA, RAUL; Baldwin Park HS; Baldwin Pk, CA; (2); Chess Clb; Church Yth Grp; Band; JV Bsbl; JV Bsktbl; Hon Roll.

AGUILA, VERONICA N; Paraclete HS; Palmdale, CA; (3); Church Yth Grp; Hosp Aide; Var Socr; Hon Roll; Prncpls Lst; A V Coll; Med.

AGUILAR, ALBERT A; Colton HS; Colton, CA; (2); JV Var Crs Cntry; JV Var Trk; Hon Roll; Boxing; Cmmnty Svc.

AGUILAR, ALEJANDRA; Modesto HS; Modesto, CA; (2); Cit Awd; Hon Roll; Prfct Atten Awd; Sacramento ST.

AGUILAR, ALICIA CRISTINA S; Westmoor HS; Daly City, CA; (2); Church Yth Grp; Band; Hon Roll; St Schlr; Nrsng.

AGUILAR, ANCELI; Balboa HS; San Francisco, CA; (3); ROTC; Mrchg Band; Hon Roll; Pilipino & Asian Amer Club; Sn Frnsco ST U; Acctg.

AGUILAR, ANDRES; Culver City HS; Culver City, CA; (2); JV Var Wrstlng; Hon Roll; UC San Diego; Marine Bio.

AGUILAR, ANITA; Lemoore HS; Lemoore, CA; (4); 10/290; Church Yth Grp; Drama Clb; Sec English Clb; FBLA; Letterman Clb; Office Aide; Pep Clb; Red Cross Aide; Spanish Clb; Pres SADD; CSF; Sci Con; Academic Dcthln; U Sthrn CA; Bus.

AGUILAR, ANTHONY; St Paul HS; Montebello, CA; (3); 40/300; Cmnty Wkr; Hon Roll; NHS; Spanish NHS; CSF; UCLA; Law.

AGUILAR, CYNTHIA; Mt Pleasant HS; San Jose, CA; (4); Church Yth Grp; Office Aide; Teachers Aide; Heald Bus Coll; Legal Sec.

AGUILAR, DEBORAH; Bishop Amat Memorial HS; West Covina, CA; (3); Flag Corp; JV Sftbl; Pep Sqd; San Diego ST; Jrnlsm.

AGUILAR, DIANA; Livingston HS; Livingston, CA; (4); Am Leg Aux Girls St; Church Yth Grp; SADD; Teachers Aide; Phtg Yrbk; Rep Frsh Cls; Sec Sr Cls; Treas Stu Cncl; Stat Bsktbl; Powder Puff Ftbl; 1st Annual Kiwanis Sftbl All Star Game 90; JR Winter Hmcng Atten; Modesto JC; Elem Teacher.

AGUILAR, EDWARD PHILIP; Saddleback HS; Santa Ana, CA; (3); VP Spanish Clb; Var L Ftbl; JV Trk; Wt Lftg; CSF; MESA Pres; Schlr Athl Vrsty Ftbl; Acad Ltr 2 Yr; Biomedcl Engr.

AGUILAR, FRANK; Arlington HS; Riverside, CA; (2); Socr; Prfct Atten Awd; Outstndng Achvt Awd GPA 3.0 Or Abv; Cert Achvt Visual Arts; U Of CA Riverside.

AGUILAR, HAZEL SANTOS; Peoples HS; Vallejo, CA; (3); JA; Pres Spanish Clb; Drill Tm; Sec Stu Cncl; Cit Awd; High Hon Roll; Hon Roll; SAC ST; Accntng.

AGUILAR, JULIETTE; St Francis HS; Mountain View, CA; (4); English Clb; Pep Clb; Service Clb; Var Cheerldng; Var Pom Pon; High Hon Roll; Hon Roll; Ntl Merit SF; UC Davis; Psych.

AGUILAR, LIZA M; St Paul HS; Whittier, CA; (3); JCL; Latin Clb; Pep Clb; Var Pom Pon; Hon Roll.

AGUILAR, LOURDES E; William Workman HS; Valinda, CA; (2); 6/323; Intnl Clb; Var Tennis; Hon Roll; CSF; Schl Schlr.

AGUILAR, MARIA CECILIA; San Diego HS/Writing Acad; San Diego, CA; (3); Drama Clb; Teachers Aide; Rptr Nwsp; Cit Awd; High Hon Roll; NHS; Ntl Merit Schol; Prfct Atten Awd; Pres Schlr; Wrtng Awd; Publctn Shor Story Schl Mag; Pres Clb Clio; Pomona Coll; Writer.

AGUILAR, MARIBEL; Lindsay HS; Strathmore, CA; (2); Letterman Clb; Spanish Clb; SADD; Var Bsktbl; Var Capt Sftbl; Var Vllybl; Wt Lftg; Hon Roll; Fresno ST U; Phys Ed.

AGUILAR, MARTHA Y; San Gabriel HS; Rosemead, CA; (2); Spanish Clb; JV Bsktbl; JV Crs Cntry; JV Mgr(s); Cit Awd; Hon Roll; Prfct Atten Awd; USC; Arch.

AGUILAR, MICHAEL A; Don Bosco Tech; Whittier, CA; (3); Am Leg Boys St; Church Yth Grp; Dance Clb; Rep Frsh Cls; Pres Soph Cls; Pres Jr Cls; JV Crs Cntry; JV Var Socr; Hon Roll; Law.

AGUILAR, NORMA A; Gonzales Union HS; Soledad, CA; (2); Church Yth Grp; GAA; Church Choir; Capt JV Vllybl; High Hon Roll; CSF; Bio.

AGUILAR, OSCAR G; Corona HS; Corona, CA; (1); Drama Clb; School Play; Variety Show; Lit Mag; Cit Awd; Poetrys Gldn Poet Awd; Jrnlsm.

AGUILAR, PATRICIA; Tracy Joint Union HS; Stockton, CA; (2); 36/489; 4-H; Spanish Clb; 4-H Awd; Hon Roll; Pedtrcn.

AGUILAR, ROBERTO; Southwest HS; San Diego, CA; (2); Socr; Sftbl; Prfct Atten Awd; San Diego ST U; Engr.

AGUILAR, ROBIN D; George Washington HS; San Francisco, CA; (2); Cmnty Wkr; Dance Clb; Drama Clb; Girl Scts; Pep Clb; School Musical; Variety Show; Lit Mag; Cheerldng; Hon Roll; Peer Resource Ctr; Prtnrshp Pre-Coll Acad; Amsty Intl; UCLA; Aerosp Engrng.

AGUILAR, SARA; Rio Mesa HS; Oxnard, CA; (4); Teachers Aide; Hon Roll; Oxnard Chamber Of Commerce Awd; Rio Mesa Mecha Clb Schlrshp; CA Poly San Luis Obispo; Econ.

AGUILAR, VERONICA; 7-Day Advantist Acad; Santa Maria, CA; (1); 2/15; Church Yth Grp; Band; Chorus; Church Choir; School Musical; VP Pres Frsh Cls; Bsktbl; Vllybl; Scholastic Achvmnt Awrd; Vlly View Adv Acad; Dentist Bus.

AGUILAR, VERONICA; Southwest HS; San Diego, CA; (2); Church Yth Grp; Teachers Aide; Var Soph Cls; Cit Awd; Hon Roll; Prfct Atten Awd; Pres Acad Fit Awd; Pres Schlr; Mdl For Schlr; Play Tennis; French; UCSD; Fash Dsgnr.

AGUILAR, YADHIRA G; Sacred Heart Of Jesus HS; Los Angeles, CA; (2); 6/128; Dance Clb; Hosp Aide; Quiz Bowl; High Hon Roll; NHS; CSF; LAC; Nrsng.

AGUILAR, YESENIA E; Chula Vista HS; Chula Vista, CA; (3); 21/535; Church Yth Grp; French Clb; Latin Clb; Cit Awd; Prfct Atten Awd; Elua Lima Karate-Orange Belt; Arch.

AGUILERA, CAROLINA; Tranquillity Union HS; Cantua Creek, CA; (3); Aud/Vis; Teachers Aide; JV Var Vllybl; U CA Riverside; Bus.

AGUILERA, JEANNIE L; East Bakersfield HS; Bakersfield, CA; (1); Church Yth Grp; Var Trk; Bakersfield Coll; Reg Nurse.

AGUILERA, MIGUEL; Alisal HS; Salinas, CA; (2); Art Clb; Computer Clb; Dance Clb; Drama Clb; FBLA; Library Aide; Scholastic Bowl; Off Frsh Cls; Crs Cntry; Socr; Bus.

AGUILERA, SYLVIA; Lindsay HS; Strathmore, CA; (3); Art Clb; French Clb; Office Aide; Spanish Clb; Yrbk; Friday Night Live; CA Poly; Comp Tech.

AGUILLON, MARIA G; Our Lady Of Loretto-Bishop Conaty; Los Angeles, CA; (4); 16/80; Pres Art Clb; Bus Profs of Am; Drama Clb; FBLA; Intnl Clb; Library Aide; School Play; Stat Bsktbl; Hon Roll; NHS; Bnk Of Amer Achvt Awd In Sci; Mclstr Coll; Spnsh.

AGUILO, DAVID A; Canyon Springs HS; Moreno Valley, CA; (2); Drama Clb; Pres Thesps; Jazz Band; Capt Mrchg Band; School Musical; School Play; Stage Crew; High Hon Roll; Cinematography.

AGUINALDO, CATHERINE; Bonita Vista HS; Bonita, CA; (2); Rep Model UN; Pep Clb; Teachers Aide; Rptr Nwsp; Lit Mag; Cit Awd; Hon Roll; Prfct Atten Awd; Mst Imprvd Stu Awd Chem; Harvard; Law.

AGUINID, MARCELLO JOHN; Providence HS; Burbank, CA; (2); Letterman Clb; Varsity Clb; Stat Bsktbl; Var Crs Cntry; Mgr(s); Score Keeper; Var Trk; Hon Roll; Loyola Marymount; Astronaut.

AGUINIGA, BRANDY D; Mt Whitney HS; Visalia, CA; (3); FBLA; Campus Life; County Sheriff Explrs-Lt; Law.

AGUIRRE, CHRISTINA; Tehachapi HS; Tehachapi, CA; (1); French Clb; Cit Awd; Hon Roll.

AGUIRRE, CRISTINA; Roosevelt HS; Fresno, CA; (1); Spanish Clb; Var Crs Cntry; Var Trk; Stanford; Ped.

AGUIRRE, CYNTHIA; Davis HS; Modesto, CA; (4); 18/442; Church Yth Grp; GAA; Letterman Clb; Office Aide; Spanish Clb; SADD; Teachers Aide; Varsity Clb; Var Bsktbl; Var Sftbl; Yth Ldrshp Awd For Ldrshp In Hispanic; Prin Awd; Staneslaus U; Bio.

AGUIRRE, CYNTHIA E; Edison Computech HS; Fresno, CA; (1); Band; Mrchg Band; Cit Awd; High Hon Roll; Music Tchr.

AGUIRRE, FRANCISCO JAVIER; Central Union HS; El Centro, CA; (1); 42/665; Boy Scts; Nwsp; Yrbk; Crs Cntry; Trk; Wt Lftg; Cit Awd; High Hon Roll; Hon Roll; Pres Acad Fit Awd; Eagle Sct; UCSD; Chirprctr.

AGUIRRE, JASON W; Richard Gahr HS; Cerritos, CA; (3); Capt Debate Tm; Latin Clb; NFL; Speech Tm; High Hon Roll; Hon Roll; CSF; Berkeley; Comp Sci.

AGUIRRE, JEANNETTE; Warren HS; Downey, CA; (2); Church Yth Grp; Cit Awd; Prfct Atten Awd; Law.

AGUIRRE, JENNIFER M; El Toro HS; El Toro, CA; (2); Church Yth Grp; GAA; Key Clb; Service Clb; Score Keeper; JV Trk; JV Vllybl; Cit Awd; High Hon Roll; Hon Roll; Girls Leag Clb; Chrch Yth Cncl; Clb Vlybl; Dntstry.

AGUIRRE, JOSE N; Garfield HS; Los Angeles, CA; (3); ROTC; High Hon Roll; Hon Roll; Pres Acad Fit Awd; Amer Legn Schl Awd; Runnr L A Marathon V 90; Aerospace Engrng.

AGUIRRE, LAURA R; Nathaniel Narbonne HS; Torrance, CA; (2); Math Clb; Hon Roll; Prfct Atten Awd; PAL Clb; Eclgy Clb.

AGUIRRE, MAGDALENA; Palo Verde HS; Blythe, CA; (3); 33/263; Spanish Clb; Hon Roll.

AGUIRRE, MARTHA B; Lynwood HS; Lynwood, CA; (3); 30/864; Letterman Clb; Math Clb; Math Tm; Band; Drm Mjr(t); Pres Mrchg Band; Pep Band; Yrbk; Treas Stu Cncl; Jr NHS; USC; Arch.

AGUIRRE, MICHAEL C; San Pedro HS; San Pedro, CA; (3); Spanish Clb; Teachers Aide; JV Var Bsbl; JV Bsktbl; JV Ftbl; Hon Roll; Elec.

AGUIRRE, NANCY; Don Antonio Lugo HS; Chino, CA; (1); Drama Clb; Science Clb; Stu Cncl; Sftbl; Vllybl; UCLA; Law.

AGUIRRE, OSCAR M; Cajon HS; San Bernardino, CA; (3); Aud/Vis; Spanish Clb; Stage Crew; Off Jr Cls; Socr.

AGUIRRE, RAPHI S; Gahr HS; Cerritos, CA; (3); Church Yth Grp; Spanish Clb; Band; Mrchg Band; Hon Roll; Psych.

AGUIRRE, RENE A; Walnut HS; West Covina, CA; (2); Intrml Bsbl; Intrml Bsktbl; JV Ftbl; Wt Lftg; Engr.

AGUIRRE, SONIA; Richard Gahr HS; Norwalk, CA; (1); 99/439; VP Drama Clb; School Play; Hon Roll; Blue & Gold Awd For Bst Actrss; Prfssnl Actrss.

AGUIRRE, TINAH; Calexico HS; Calexico, CA; (1); Hon Roll; U CA San Diego.

AGUNDES, JONATHAN; Mercy HS; Red Bluff, CA; (4); Church Yth Grp; Key Clb; SADD; Varsity Clb; JV Var Bsktbl; Var Golf; Hon Roll; Chico ST; Engrng.

AGUNDEZ, EDWARD; Southwest HS; San Diego, CA; (2); Art Clb; Drama Clb; Science Clb; Band; Jazz Band; Pep Band; Ftbl; Vllybl; Wt Lftg; Cit Awd; Harvard Law Schl; Crmnl Law.

AGUON JR, FRANK S; Silver Valley HS; Fort Irwin, CA; (2); Pres Frsh Cls; JV Var Bsbl; JV Bsktbl; Var Crs Cntry; JV Ftbl; Cit Awd; High Hon Roll; Hon Roll; UCLA; Math.

AGUSTIN, JIMMY J; Whitney HS; Cerritos, CA; (1); Boy Scts; Church Yth Grp; Band; Mrchg Band; Orch; High Hon Roll; Prin Hnr Roll; CA Jr Schlrshp Fed; CA Inst Of Tech; Techncl Field.

AGUSTIN, RAMSES M; Dr James T Hogan SR HS; Vallejo, CA; (4); 2/400; VP Chess Clb; Computer Clb; Math Clb; Spanish Clb; Yrbk; Treas Stu Cncl; Bausch & Lomb Sci Awd; Ntl Merit SF; Prfct Atten Awd; Acad Decathlon Team; Pftct Score Golden ST Exam; Xerox Awd Humanities Soc Stds; UC-BERKELEY; Mech Engr.

AGY, CINDY M; Cerritos HS; Norwalk, CA; (1); Church Yth Grp; French Clb; Science Clb; Japanese Natl Hnr Soc; CSF.

AH HING, PATRICK LAIESE; Rosemead HS; Rosemead, CA; (2); Pres Frsh Cls; Bsktbl; Ftbl; Trk; Wt Lftg.

AHARONI, ILAN; Carlsbad HS; Carlsbad, CA; (3); 1/390; AFS; Key Clb; Math Tm; Pep Clb; Quiz Bowl; SADD; Temple Yth Grp; Var L Swmmng; High Hon Roll; Waterpolo Var Ltr; CSF; Rotry Yth Ldrshp Awds; Golden St Math Awd; Doctor.

AHART, GREG; Lincoln HS; Lincoln, CA; (4); 10/150; Pres 4-H; FFA; Band; Jazz Band; Pep Band; 4-H Awd; Hon Roll; Comm Coll; Hstry.

AHDOUT, SAMY; Calabasas HS; Woodland Hills, CA; (2); Debate Tm; Var Bsktbl; Var Wt Lftg.

AHEDO, NOEL; Tulare Union HS; Pixley, CA; (2); 30/500; Spanish Clb; Sci.

AHERN, LIAM; Sacramento Waldorf Schl; Carmichael, CA; (2); Chorus; Orch; School Musical; Prof & Amat Theatre; Intrlchn Ctr Arts Natl Music Comp; Law.

AHLBERG, ERIK T; Bear River HS; Auburn, CA; (2); FFA; Off Frsh Cls; Var JV Bsktbl; Var Capt Golf; Hon Roll; Masonic Awd; Pres Acad Fit Awd; MVP Jr Var B-Ball Tm 90; MVP Var Golf 89-90; UCLA; Airline Industry.

AHLEFELD, JIMMY C; Hueneme HS; Oxnard, CA; (4); Church Yth Grp; Office Aide; Chorus; Mgr Ftbl; Mgr Sftbl; Amer Red Cross CPR/1st Aid Cert; Lampbearers; Bus Dept Hnr; Oxnard Coll; Firefighter.

AHLERS, LORI; Livermore HS; Livermore, CA; (2); FFA; JV Score Keeper; High Hon Roll; Wrstlng Stat Grl; Intr Dsgn.

AHLES, KELLY M; Lindhurst HS; Marysville, CA; (2); Church Yth Grp; GAA; Varsity Clb; Band; Mrchg Band; Rep Stu Cncl; JV Bsktbl; JV Var Sftbl; JV Vllybl; High Hon Roll; VP Friday Night Live; Stanford; Elect Engrng.

AHLSTRAND, MELANIE M; California HS; Whittier, CA; (4); 57/367; Church Yth Grp; Cmnty Wkr; Dance Clb; Drama Clb; FBLA; Hosp Aide; Letterman Clb; Pep Clb; Varsity Clb; Off Soph Cls; Southern CA Coll; Mrktng.

AHMAD, RIHANA; Sutter HS; Yuba City, CA; (2); 4-H; FBLA; Science Clb; JV Bsktbl; Stat Vllybl; 4-H Awd; Hon Roll; Gldn St Exam Schl Rcgntn.

AHMADI, KIANOUSH; Costa Mesa HS; Costa Mesa, CA; (4); Math Clb; Math Tm; Pres Acad Fit Awd; UCI; Elec Engrng.

AHMADI, REZA E; University HS; Irvine, CA; (2); French Clb; Band; Ftbl; Wt Lftg; Wrstlng; Cit Awd; Hon Roll; Prfct Atten Awd; Medicine.

AHMED, AMIR; Stagg HS; Stockton, CA; (1); High Hon Roll; Pharmacy.

AHMED, HADIA T; Fontana HS; Fontana, CA; (3); High Hon Roll; Cal Poly; Bus.

AHMED, NEHAD R; Magnolia HS; Anaheim, CA; (2); Church Yth Grp; Nwsp; High Hon Roll; Hon Roll; NHS; CA Schlrshp Fed; Grls Leag; Cls Cabnt; U Of CA Irvine; Mdcn.

AHMED, OMAR; Irvine HS; Irvine, CA; (2); Chess Clb; Cmnty Wkr; Key Clb; Math Clb; Scholastic Bowl; Science Clb; Hon Roll; Jr NHS; NHS; Sci Olympd Team Rgnl St; AMER Chemcl Society Team; Harvard; Med.

AHMED, SONELA; Santa Barbara HS; Santa Barbara, CA; (3); 1/470; Cmnty Wkr; Debate Tm; Scholastic Bowl; High Hon Roll; Val; SADD; Ecology Clb; Accelerated Study Stu; Tutor; Wellesley Bk Awd Outstndng Acad Achvt & Ldrshp; Pre-Med.

AHN, CARRIE; Flintridge Preparatary Schl; Duarte, CA; (3); Sec Church Yth Grp; Hosp Aide; Sec Key Clb; Service Clb; Spanish Clb; Chorus; Church Choir; Orch; School Musical; Variety Show; Sun Schl Tchr; Flute/Piano Awds; Peer Cnslr; U CA-BERKELEY; Psych.

AHN, DANIEL H; West HS; Torrance, CA; (1); Treas Church Yth Grp; Capt FCA; Intnl Clb; Service Clb; Spanish Clb; Church Choir; Score Keeper; Trk; Wt Lftg; Cit Awd; West Point.

AHN, JASON C; Corona HS; Corona, CA; (3); Elect Engrng.

AHN, JOHN YOUNG; Poway HS; Poway, CA; (4); 29/728; Church Yth Grp; Chorus; Church Choir; JV Tennis; NHS; Gldn St Exam-Algb & Geom Hgh Hnrs; CA Schlrshp Fed; U Of AZ; Elec Engrng.

AHN, PIUS S; Alameda HS; Alameda, CA; (2); Church Yth Grp; Science Clb; Teachers Aide; Chorus; VP Soph Cls; Tennis; High Hon Roll; Cal Poly; Chem.

AHN, SUNYOUNG; Westlake Schl For Girls; Northridge, CA; (2); Art Clb; Church Yth Grp; Cmnty Wkr; French Clb; Var JV Trk; Hstry.

AHN, TONY S; Whitney HS; Cerritos, CA; (2); JA; Key Clb; JV Var Bsktbl; JV Var Tennis; High Hon Roll; Hon Roll; JV Water Polo; Key Clb Convention MP; Stanford; Bus.

AHO, CHRISTINE M; Huntington Beach HS; Huntington Bch, CA; (4); German Clb; Yrbk; Lit Mag; Hon Roll; Outstndng Achvt Awds German & Bio Sci; Towers Awds Engl Compstn & Soc Sci; PTSA Scholar & Pres Hnrs; Humboldt ST U; Wildlife Mgmt.

AHRENS, DAVID L; Buena HS; Ventura, CA; (4); Boy Scts; Pres Church Yth Grp; Pep Clb; Band; Jazz Band; Mrchg Band; Orch; Pep Band; School Musical; Trk; Bank Amer Fine Arts Achvt Awd; Prfrmnc W/Brass Trio; CA ST U Northridge; Music.

AHRENS, GEORGE; Monte Vista HS; Spring Valley, CA; (3); 60/373; Teachers Aide; Treas Frsh Cls; Var Ftbl; Var Trk; Var Wt Lftg; Hon Roll; Achvt Cert; Athl Awd; USC.

AHRENS, SARA E; Mayfair HS; Lakewood, CA; (2); Teachers Aide; High Hon Roll; Math Dept Awd; Clb Sccr Tm.

AHROLD, DENISE S; Don Antonio Lugo HS; Chino, CA; (3); Sec French Clb; SADD; Teachers Aide; Powder Puff Ftbl; Trk; High Hon Roll; Pres Acad Fit Awd; Cls Of 91 Club; CA ST Fullerton; Social Svc.

AHUMADA, CYNTHIA; Norwalk HS; Norwalk, CA; (4); Church Yth Grp; Key Clb; Model UN; Service Clb; Band; Drill Tm; Treas Bus Profs of Am; Pres Jr Cls; Pres Sr Cls; Rep Stu Cncl; Cypress Coll; Law.

AHUMADA, JOSE A; North Monter County HS; Castroville, CA; (1); Hon Roll; ASB Clb; Doctor.

AICHELE, AMANDA A; Pioneer HS; San Jose, CA; (2); Var Swmmng; High Hon Roll; Hon Roll; CSF.

AIESE, IAELI C; Grant Joint Union HS; Sacramento, CA; (3); Church Yth Grp; Intnl Clb; Chorus; Church Choir; Nwsp; Yrbk; Vllybl; U HI; Ecnmcs.

AIHARA, YOSHIE; Southwestern Acad; Pasadena, CA; (1); Church Yth Grp; Yrbk; Bsktbl; Vllybl; High Hon Roll; Gold Awd; CIF Awd; Deptmntl Awds; Law.

AIKEN, SPENCER A; Temecula Valley HS; Temecula, CA; (2); JV Bsbl; JV Bsktbl; JV Ftbl; Sports Med.

AINSLIE, JAMES A; Atwater HS; Atwater, CA; (2); Boy Scts; VP Church Yth Grp; German Clb; Var Swmmng; Hon Roll; Prfct Atten Awd; JV Waterpolo; Engr.

AIONO, UFIAU M; Carson HS; Torrance, CA; (2); Library Aide; ROTC; Band; Mrchg Band; Orch; Hon Roll; UCLA; Pdtrcs.

AITCHISON, JORDAN M; The Thacher Schl; Leucadia, CA; (2); AFS; Hosp Aide; Rptr Nwsp; Var Crs Cntry; Var Trk; High Hon Roll; Hon Roll; Pres Acad Fit Awd; CSF; Torey Pines Music Hnrs Sco; Physcn.

AITKEN, AMY; Sonora HS; Sonora, CA; (3); 1/293; Cmnty Wkr; Pep Clb; Science Clb; Spanish Clb; SADD; Band; Drm Mjr(t); Mrchg Band; Orch; School Musical; All Amer Perfmnc Team 89-90; GSE Geom Awd 88; Schl Hnr Guard 90; Deaf Educ.

AITKEN, ERIC D; Sonora HS; Sonora, CA; (4); 35/279; Am Leg Boys St; Cmnty Wkr; Pres Letterman Clb; Science Clb; Service Clb; Spanish Clb; Varsity Clb; VP Jr Cls; JV Bsbl; Var Capt Bsktbl; Acad Decathlon Team; VOL All Flag Player Of Yr Bsktbl; Modesto Bee & Stockton Record All Star Bsktbl; U Redlands; Commercial Pilot.

AITKENS, CHRIS; Bellarmine Jefferson HS; Thousand Oaks, CA; (2); Church Yth Grp; Pep Clb; Rep Frsh Cls; Stu Cncl; JV Bsktbl; Golf; Trk; Hon Roll; UCLA; Dentist.

AIWAZZI, JENNIFER; John F Kennedy HS; Buena Park, CA; (4); Stage Crew; NHS; Real Estate Office Receptnst; Cypress Coll; Real Estate Brkr.

AJA, ROSEMARY; Hemet HS; Hemet, CA; (2); 2/700; Key Clb; Spanish Clb; Elks Awd; Hon Roll; Prfct Atten Awd; Chicano-Latino Yth Ldrshp Conf; CSF; Interact Clb.

AJAYI, OLUKEMI; Menlo-Atherton HS; Redwood City, CA; (3); Am Leg Aux Girls St; Pres Key Clb; Jazz Band; School Musical; School Play; Rptr Nwsp; Stu Cncl; Capt Var Cheerldng; Hon Roll; Natl Achvt Schlr; Stu Advsry Cncl Schl Brd Rep; Commissioner Inter Cultural Relations; USC.

AKAKI, DANELLE K; Del Mar HS; San Jose, CA; (1); Hosp Aide; Rptr Yrbk; Rep Frsh Cls; Var Sftbl; JV Vllybl; High Hon Roll; Outstndng Frshmn Yr; MVP Vlybl JV; Rookie Of Yr Sftbl Vrsty; Stanford; Neurosrgn.

AKBAR, MARYAM; Poly HS; Riverside, CA; (3); Dance Clb; Drama Clb; Intnl Clb; Teachers Aide; Hon Roll; Golden St Schlrs Algebra 89; Girls Lg Publicity Commissioner; Stu Of Month World His; U Riverside CA; Bio.

AKBAR, SALEEMAH E; Narbonne Math/Science Magnet HS; Los Angeles, CA; (3); Cmnty Wkr; FBLA; Hosp Aide; Pep Clb; Mrchg Band; School Musical; School Play; VP Frsh Cls; Cit Awd; Hon Roll; Schltc All-Amer; Los Angeles Cty Miss Teen Pgnt; Spelman Coll; Med.

AKERS, MARGARET F; Norte Vista HS; Pomona, CA; (1); Church Yth Grp; French Clb; Hon Roll; PAL; FNL Drnk Drvng Pgm; UCLA; Jrnlsm.

AKERS, MICHELE; Charter Oak HS; Covina, CA; (2); 10/375; Cmnty Wkr; Dance Clb; Stage Crew; Treas Frsh Cls; Off Soph Cls; Cheerldng; High Hon Roll; NHS; Pres Acad Fit Awd; Rotary Awd; Natl Conf Christians & Jews Schlrshp; DARE Pgm; Acting.

AKESSON, HAYLEE K; St Genevieve HS; Sherman Oaks, CA; (3); Hon Roll; Outstndng Sociology & Geom Awds; UCLA; Grammer Sch Educ.

AKEY, STEPHANIE; Fremont Christian Schl; Newark, CA; (4); French Clb; Letterman Clb; Varsity Clb; Chorus; Church Choir; School Musical; Capt Var Tennis; High Hon Roll; ACSI Musicl Cmmnd Prfrmnc; Fremont Cltrl Arts Cncl Shwcs Gst Solo/Duet; Biola U; Vcl Prfrmnc.

AKHZAR, LILA S; Terra Linda HS; San Rafael, CA; (3); Stu Scl Respnsblty.

AKIN, SALAME S; Miramonte HS; Orinda, CA; (3); 118/175; Church Yth Grp; Cmnty Wkr; Spanish Clb; Chorus; Rptr Ed Nwsp; Hnrs Span; Ailanthus; Schl Nwspr Feature Editor Next Yr 90-91; UCSD; Jrnlsm.

AKINS, AMY M; Bishop Montgomery HS; San Pedro, CA; (2); JV Bsktbl; High Hon Roll; Hon Roll; Amnsty Intl; Piano; Sci.

AKINS, ERIC M; Las Plumas HS; Oroville, CA; (2); Letterman Clb; VP Pres VICA; Socr; Tennis; Wt Lftg; Gld Medal Reg 1 VICA Skl Olympcs Intro Drftng; Slvr Medal St VICA Skl Olympcs Intro Drftng; Arch Drftng.

AKINS, LAMONT D; Fairfield HS; Fairfield, CA; (1); Church Yth Grp; Cmnty Wkr; Rptr Nwsp; Mgr Yrbk; Off Soph Cls; Stu Cncl; JV Trk; Hon Roll; Jr NHS; NHS; ; Jrnlsm.

AKINS, RUTH E; Los Gatos HS; Campbell, CA; (2); Church Yth Grp; Cmnty Wkr; Chorus; Church Choir; School Musical; Hon Roll; Dghtr Of Yr Awd; Stanford U; Mech Engr.

AKINS, SHELLEY L; Victor Valley HS; Victorville, CA; (3); Church Yth Grp; Office Aide; ROTC; Ski Clb; Chorus; Church Choir; Swmmng; Wt Lftg; Hon Roll; St Schlr; PEOPLE Pgm; Point Loma Nazarene Coll; Psych.

AKISKALIAN, KAREN J; San Marcos HS; Santa Barbara, CA; (3); 156/380; Church Yth Grp; Cmnty Wkr; Girl Scts; Nwsp; JV Swmmng; Prfct Atten Awd; Dance; Silver Awd; Santa Barbara City Coll; Dsgn.

AKIYAMA, JANIS A; La Mirada HS; La Mirada, CA; (2); Key Clb; NFL; Bsktbl; Tennis; Trk; High Hon Roll; Hon Roll; Nrsng.

AKMAL, AAMIR; Whitney HS; Cerritos, CA; (2); 25/300; JA; Berkely; Phys.

AKMAL, HAMAAD B; Hiram W Johnson-West Campus HS; Sacramento, CA; (2); 20/186; Intrml Ice Hcky; JV Socr; Hon Roll; UC Davis; Med Schl.

AKPAN, ENEFIOK SOLOMON; South San Francisco HS; South San Francis, CA; (3); Math Clb; Science Clb; Chrmn Service Clb; SADD; Bsktbl; Trk; Hon Roll; Actv CA Schlrshp Fdr; Block Lttr For Acad Achvmnt; Ldrshp Cnfrnc.

AKRE, JOHN S; Terra Nova HS; Pacifica, CA; (2); Varsity Clb; Bsbl; Bsktbl; Ftbl; Wt Lftg; Hon Roll.

AKRE, JONATHAN; Sonoma Valley HS; Sonoma, CA; (4); 1/285; Am Leg Boys St; Service Clb; Var L Bsbl; Var L Bsktbl; High Hon Roll; Peer Cnslr; U Of CA; Engnrng.

AL-MOUSAWI, NAHRAIN; Rosary HS; Yorba Linda, CA; (3); Cmnty Wkr; French Clb; Hosp Aide; High Hon Roll; Bus.

AL-SHAMKHANI, ZAINAB; Valhalla HS; El Cajon, CA; (3); Church Yth Grp; French Clb; French Hon Soc; Arch.

ALACAR, GRACIELLE GATINGA; Louisville HS; Agoura Hills, CA; (1); Church Yth Grp; Science Clb; Chorus; Drill Tm; Trk; Hon Roll; Pres Acad Fit Awd; Pdtrcs.

ALACAR, HELEN T; Roosevelt HS; Fresno, CA; (3); 135/500; SADD; Chorus; Vllybl; Cit Awd; UC Davis; Bus.

ALACIO, EDWARD I; Chaffey HS; Ontario, CA; (3); High Hon Roll; Hon Roll; NHS; CSF; Mech Engrng.

ALAGHA, HOUMAN; Mission Viejo HS; Mission Viejo, CA; (3); Computer Clb; VP German Clb; Key Clb; JV Crs Cntry; Intrml Trk; Hon Roll; ROP Classes; Pres Of Herbie Club; Comps.

ALAIMO, PAOLA; Norte Vista HS; Riverside, CA; (1); FFA; Letterman Clb; Varsity Clb; Var Swmmng; High Hon Roll; Hon Roll; Parlimentary Procedure Awd; CA U; Pediatrician.

ALAM, SARAH M; Mt Diablo HS; Concord, CA; (2); Dance Clb; English Clb; Library Aide; Office Aide; Teachers Aide; Chorus; Bsktbl; Socr; Sftbl; Tennis.

ALAM, WAHAJIA M; Mt Diablo HS; Concord, CA; (3); Art Clb; FCA; FBLA; Teachers Aide; Tennis; Vllybl; Cit Awd; High Hon Roll; Hon Roll.

ALAMARI, ANWAR; Arvin HS; Arvin, CA; (3); Teachers Aide; High Hon Roll; Hon Roll; Achvmt Awd; Multiple Yr Awd.

ALAMEDA, TERESA M; East Union HS; Manteca, CA; (2); Rptr Nwsp; Hon Roll; Acad Ltr; Delta Coll; Rdlgc Tech.

ALAN, NALA ANA A; San Fernando HS; Arleta, CA; (2); Band; Mrchg Band; Ed Yrbk; Cit Awd; Hon Roll; Prfct Atten Awd; Pres Acad Fit Awd; UC Santa Barbara; Chem Engr.

ALANDY, ETHEL R; Dr James J Hogan HS; Vallejo, CA; (3); Drama Clb; French Clb; Spanish Clb; Band; Ed Nwsp; Ntl Merit SF; Band; CA ST U; Nrsng.

ALANIS, ARACELY; Etiwanda HS; Rancho Cucamonga, CA; (2); Hon Roll; Hmwrk, Ltr K & C Clubs; CSF; USC; Intntl Bus.

ALANIS, MARISOL; Mission HS; San Gabriel, CA; (2); 40/108; Cmnty Wkr; Drama Clb; French Clb; Rptr FBLA; Math Clb; Science Clb; Yrbk; Hon Roll; Cert Merit Frnch; USC; Cmmnctns.

ALANIS, VIOLET; Bassett HS; La Puente, CA; (2); FBLA; Bsktbl; Vllybl; Hon Roll; Los Angeles Coll Of Chiroprctc.

ALANIZ, JENNIFER; Serrano HS; Phelan, CA; (4); Church Yth Grp; FBLA; Drill Tm; High Hon Roll; Hon Roll; Coach Little League; Business Administration.

ALANIZ, MARY ANN; Lindsay HS; Exeter, CA; (3); Church Yth Grp; Spanish Clb; Teachers Aide; Cit Awd; Hon Roll; Mecha Clb; Acad Ltr Jacket; Santa Barbara; Sci Engrng.

ALANIZ, ROSA; Holtville HS; Holtville, CA; (3); 4/110; Church Yth Grp; VP SADD; Teachers Aide; Band; Drm Mjr(t); Mrchg Band; Pep Band; Treas Jr Cls; JV Sftbl; Hon Roll; Gldn ST Exam Hnrs Rcpt; CSF 87-90; Dir Awd.

ALAPA JR, CLIFFORD K; Rancho Cotate HS; Rohnert Park, CA; (3); Cmnty Wkr; JV Var Ftbl; High Hon Roll; Hon Roll; NHS; Hnrs Geomtry; Physics.

ALAPAG, GUENEVERE M; Bellarmine-Jefferson HS; Los Angeles, CA; (4); Pep Clb; Acpl Chr; Chorus; Church Choir; School Musical; Stage Crew; Variety Show; Phtg Yrbk; Stu Cncl; JV Cheerldng; San Diego ST U; Jrnlsm.

ALAPIZCO, LIZZY; Azusa HS; Azusa, CA; (2); Pep Clb; JV Capt Cheerldng; Pom Pon; Hon Roll; Bus.

ALARCON, ANGIE; Arroyo HS; El Monte, CA; (2); Church Yth Grp; Key Clb; Pep Clb; Cheerldng; Hon Roll; Psychlgy.

ALARCON, CRIS; San Pasqual HS; Yuma, AZ; (2); Chess Clb; Church Yth Grp; Cmnty Wkr; Spanish Clb; High Hon Roll; Hon Roll; Arch Engrng.

ALARCON, DANIEL; San Pasqual Valley United Schl; Winterhaven, CA; (2); Var Wrstlng; High Hon Roll; Hon Roll; Prfct Atten Awd; Technical Engr.

ALARCON, LYNN A; St Paul HS; Pico Rivera, CA; (3); French Clb; Red Cross Aide; Spanish Clb; High Hon Roll; Hon Roll; NHS; Spanish NHS; CSF; Mrch For Hunger; USC; Psych.

ALARCON, MARIA; San Dimas HS; San Dimas, CA; (3); Girl Scts; JV Capt Socr; Hon Roll; Saint Singers; CSF; Hnr Guard 90; Ed.

ALARCON, MARICAR; Sacred Heart Cathedral Prep; Daly City, CA; (3); Church Yth Grp; Science Clb; Spanish Clb; Teachers Aide; Varsity Clb; Phtg Yrbk; Frsh Cls; Treas Soph Cls; Rep Jr Cls; Stu Cncl; Hnr Scty CSF; Star Students Against Racism; UCLA; Bus.

ALARCON, MONICA; Locke HS; Gardena, CA; (3); Spanish Clb; BROADCASTER.

ALARCON, RICK; Dos Palos HS; Dos Palos, CA; (3); JV Var Bsbl; JV Bsktbl; JV Var Ftbl; 1st Tm All Leag Ftbl; Fresno ST.

ALARCON, VERONICA; Andrew Hill HS; San Jose, CA; (3); Teachers Aide; JV Sftbl; JV Vllybl; Hon Roll; MESA; Tutr Jose Valdes Mth Prjct; San Jose ST U; Comp Engr.

ALAS, CHARISSA M; Whitney HS; Cerritos, CA; (3); Drama Clb; Key Clb; School Play; Variety Show; Rptr Nwsp; Yrbk; High Hon Roll; Club Kaibigan Dance Troupe; U CA Los Angeles; Bus Admin.

ALAVAREN, BONI MAY; S San Francisco HS; South San Francis, CA; (3); Church Yth Grp; Treas French Clb; Math Clb; Science Clb; Church Choir; Hon Roll; Hstry Day CA 90 2nd Pl Media Ind; St Assmbly Cert Rcgntn/Senate Resolution St; Cngrssnl Rec Hist Day; CA ST U; Forensic.

ALAVI, SHARIQ S; Live Oak HS; Morgan Hill, CA; (3); 105/504; Ftbl; Trk; Wt Lftg; Hon Roll; Prfct Atten Awd; Pre-Med.

ALBA, ADRIANA H; Los Amigos HS; Santa Ana, CA; (3); Latin Clb; Library Aide; Teachers Aide; Bsbl; Hon Roll; Acctng.

ALBA, CRISTINA G; Baldwin Park HS; Baldwin Park, CA; (2); Hon Roll; Kywntts Clb Treas; Hnr Soc; Chld Cr.

ALBA, IVAN; Morse HS; San Diego, CA; (4); Church Yth Grp; French Hon Soc; JETS Awd; NHS; Prfct Atten Awd; Tutoring Clb Pres; Karate Clb Pres; ATA Blackbelt; UC Riverside; Math Prof.

ALBA, MARIA H; Santa Ana HS; Tustin, CA; (3); Orch; Vllybl; Hon Roll; Vol Wrk Convalescent Wstrn Med Ctr/Bart Let, Law Offices Brewer & Brewer; CA ST U; Bus.

ALBA, MARICELA; Mcfarland HS; Mcfarland, CA; (4); 9/107; FHA; ROTC; VICA; Band; Var Cheerldng; Var Trk; Hon Roll; Pres Acad Fit Awd; CA ST U Bkrsfield; Bus Admin.

ALBA, REGINA M; Chino HS; Ontario, CA; (3); Ski Clb; Band; Color Guard; Mrchg Band; Variety Show; Powder Puff Ftbl; Socr; Cit Awd; Silver Spur Award For Business Department; Business.

ALBAN, BLAKE; Marina HS; Huntington Bch, CA; (3); 1/650; Cmnty Wkr; Key Clb; Temple Yth Grp; Ed Nwsp; Treas Jr Cls; Capt Golf; JV Wrstlng; High Hon Roll; Ntl Merit Ltr; Jewish Yng Ldrs Sprst Awd; Schlr Athlete Awd; 1st Tm Mock Trial.

ALBANO, MARIANNE; Granger JR HS; San Diego, CA; (1); 1/268; Math Tm; Ed Nwsp; Yrbk; Vllybl; High Hon Roll; Hon Roll; Prfct Atten Awd; Assctd Stu Body Treas; Bus Mgmt.

ALBARRAN, NANCY; Mark Koppel HS; Fontana, CA; (3); Pep Clb; Sec Varsity Clb; Rep Frsh Cls; Rep Soph Cls; JV Var Bsktbl; Var Cheerldng; Capt Powder Puff Ftbl; Var Capt Sftbl; Prfct Atten Awd; Most Imprvd Vrsty Sftbl Team; Tri Hi Y; Schl Admin.

ALBARRAN, ROBERTO; Mark Keppel HS; Fontana, CA; (2); Church Yth Grp; JV Bsbl; Var Score Keeper; JV Wt Lftg; Cit Awd; Hon Roll; Pres Acad Fit Awd; UC Berkley; Bus Admin.

ALBERGA, KAREN F; Rubidoux HS; Riverside, CA; (4); 30/550; AFS; Girl Scts; Hosp Aide; Model UN; Pres Spanish Clb; SADD; Teachers Aide; L Mgr(s); Powder Puff Ftbl; JV Vllybl; UCR; Phys Thrpy.

ALBEROLA, JUAN; Liberty Union HS; Antioch, CA; (3); Golden St Exam Hnrs; Uc Berkeley; Art.

ALBERS, HILARY A; St Margarets Episcopal Schl; San Clemente, CA; (2); Cmnty Wkr; VP Jr Cls; Var L Bsktbl; Var L Sftbl; Var L Vllybl; High Hon Roll; NHS; Span III Awd; Mod European Hstry Awd; Balboa Isle Yacht Clb-Vice Commodore; Female Athlete Of Yr 90; Annapolis; Hstry Ed.

ALBERS, KAREN; University Of San Diego HS; San Diego, CA; (2); SADD; Stat JV Ftbl; Stat Var Sftbl; High Hon Roll; Hon Roll; CSF; Safe Rides; Outdoor Wilderness Experience Clb; UCLA; Pediatrics.

ALBERT, LARRY L; James Lick HS; San Jose, CA; (3); 15/300; Chess Clb; Drama Clb; French Clb; Letterman Clb; Math Clb; Math Tm; Science Clb; Ski Clb; Varsity Clb; Phtg Nwsp; Rugby Team Capt; 1st Team All Lg Ftbl; 1st League Wrstlng; Berkeley; Chem.

ALBERT, SHARHONDA; Lincoln Prep HS; San Diego, CA; (2); Dance Clb; Yrbk; OH ST; Bus Law.

ALBERT, TAMMERA E; Bishop Amat Memorial HS; Glendora, CA; (2); Church Yth Grp; French Clb; Drill Tm; Hon Roll; CA ST Fullerton; Psych.

ALBERTO, GAYLE BETH; Sacred Heart Of Mary HS; Montebello, CA; (3); GAA; Pep Clb; School Musical; School Play; Pres Jr Cls; Var JV Cheerldng; NHS; Assoc Stu Body Pres 90-91; CSF; Mthr Butler Assn; Stanford U; Med.

ALBINO, JENNY I; Pittsburg HS; Pittsburg, CA; (3); Church Yth Grp; Teachers Aide; Temple Yth Grp; Church Choir; Nwsp; Cit Awd; Hon Roll; Acadc Achvt Awd; Los Medanos Coll; Comp Prgrmmg.

ALBISTEGUI, ELLEN M; Santa Monica HS; Santa Monica, CA; (4); Dance Clb; Chorus; Pres Lit Mag; Hon Roll; Ntl Merit Ltr; Sthrn CA HS Hnr Choir; Gldn St Exam Geom Hnrs.

ALBO, NICOLE J; North Tahoe HS; Tahoe City, CA; (3); 14/60; Band; Jazz Band; Pep Band; Var Powder Puff Ftbl; Var Sftbl; JV Var Vllybl; Hon Roll; JAMM; CSF; Alpine Ski Tm.

ALBOVIAS, JENNIFER G; Bishop Amat Memorial HS; West Covina, CA; (2); GAA; School Play; Stage Crew; Bsktbl; Sftbl; Hon Roll; CSF; Wrk Experience Prog; Cert Of Rcgntn Spnch II; Med.

ALBRECHT, ROBYN; Santa Ynez Valley Union HS; Buellton, CA; (3); Church Yth Grp; Office Aide; Pep Clb; SADD; Varsity Clb; Yrbk; JV Var Cheerldng; Var Score Keeper; JV Tennis; Prfct Atten Awd; Yng Womn Yr Phys Ftns Wnnr; Mst Dedcts JV Chrldr; Biola U; Elem Educ.

ALBRECHT, WENDY M; Orange Lutheran HS; Orange, CA; (2); 7/138; Band; Church Choir; Jazz Band; Pep Band; Var JV Bsktbl; Var L Tennis; Hon Roll.

ALBRIGHT III, HARRIS B; Mt Whitney HS; Visalia, CA; (2); Drama Clb; Thesps; School Play; JV Socr; Rotary Awd; Intl Thspn Soc; Rtry Intl Paul Harris Fllw; UC San Diego; Bus.

ALBRIGHT, JUSTIN; Saint Paul HS; Hacienda Hghts, CA; (4); 11/280; Rep Sr Cls; Stat Bsktbl; Var Golf; Hon Roll; Rotary Awd; Natl Hnr Soc; CA Schlrshp Fed; Comp Sci Awd 2 Yrs; A P Calculus A B Exam 4; CA Polytech U Pomona; Engrng.

ALBU, GABRIELA; Warren HS; Downey, CA; (2); Schlrshp Club CSF; Arch.

ALBURQUERQUE, JULIA R; James Logan HS; Union City, CA; (3); Intnl Clb; Spanish Clb; Hon Roll; Comp Engr.

ALCAIDE, ADRIAN; Tulare Union HS; Earlimart, CA; (3); 25/350; Math Tm; VICA; Pres Jr Cls; Treas Stu Cncl; JV Tennis; Hon Roll; K Red; Cal Poly; Math.

ALCALA, DAVID; Davis SR HS; Davis, CA; (4); 40/364; Q&S; Spanish Clb; Varsity Clb; Orch; School Musical; Var Tennis; JV Vllybl; Hon Roll; Ntl Merit SF; Pres Acad Fit Awd; Hnr Orch; Natl Hwy Sfty Cmpgn.

ALCALA, NATHAN; Don Antonio Lugo HS; Chino, CA; (3); Var Socr; Cit Awd; Hon Roll; Cmnty Sccr; U Of Fullerton; Jrnlsm.

ALCALA, ROSALVA; Garfield HS; Los Angeles, CA; (3); JA; Letterman Clb; Office Aide; Service Clb; Teachers Aide; Varsity Clb; Powder Puff Ftbl; Swmmng; Cit Awd; Athltc Awd; Ltr; Nrsng.

ALCALAN, ELITA L; St Joseph Notre Dame HS; Oakland, CA; (3); Band; Sftbl; Hon Roll; NHS; Spanish NHS; USC; Guidnc Cnslr.

ALCALAY, VIVIAN S; Westlake HS; Pacific Palisades, CA; (2); Art Clb; Intnl Clb; Letterman Clb; Diving; Swmmng; Trk.

ALCANTAR, CYNTHIA; Bonita Vista HS; Chula Vista, CA; (3); Acpl Chr; Chorus; Cit Awd; Hon Roll; Prfct Atten Awd; Soph Stu Cncl; SDSU; Child Psych.

ALCANTAR, KATHRYN I; Lowell HS; San Francisco, CA; (2); Church Yth Grp; Cmnty Wkr; Latin Clb; Service Clb; VP Soph Cls; Rep Stu Cncl; JV Bsktbl; JV Trk; CA Schlrshp Fed; U Of CA; Psych.

ALCANTAR, MIGUEL A; Alta Loma HS; Alta Loma, CA; (2); Band; Mrchg Band; Bus.

ALCANTAR, RANDY; John Glenn HS; Norwalk, CA; (3); ROTC; Mech Engr.

ALCANTARA, AGNES K; Bishop Montgomery HS; Carson, CA; (4); 25/358; Band; Mrchg Band; Hon Roll; Magna Cum Laude Grdtd; CSF Lftm; Bk Of America Achvmnt Awd Frgn Lng; U Of CA Los Angeles; Psych.

ALCANTARA, MAYEN O; Mayfield SR Schl; Pasadena, CA; (3); Scholastic Bowl; Spanish Clb; Stage Crew; Pres NHS; Ntl Merit SF; CSF Pres; Chrstn Action Mvmnt; Engrng.

ALCARAZ, ERIC; Gonzales HS; Soledad, CA; (4); 17/189; Computer Clb; Math Tm; Science Clb; Spanish Clb; School Play; Var Trk; CSF; Comp Engrng.

ALCARAZ, LISA JAN; Chaminade College Prep; Granada Hills, CA; (4); 1/203; Cmnty Wkr; Key Clb; NFL; Sec Treas Speech Tm; Chorus; Drill Tm; Nwsp; Lit Mag; VP Stu Cncl; NHS; CA Schlrshp Fed; Bnk Amer Achvt Awd Sci & Math; Vlntr Srv Awd; VAMC Smmr Yth Pgm; U Of CA San Diego; Bio Engrng.

ALCARAZ, MA ELENA; Saddleback HS; Santa Ana, CA; (4); French Clb; Office Aide; Q&S; SADD; Ed Yrbk; U De Morelia; Dentistry.

ALCAUSIN, DARLEEN; Montgomery HS; San Diego, CA; (3); 9/552; Chorus; Variety Show; Rep Soph Cls; Rep Jr Cls; Cit Awd; High Hon Roll; Hon Roll; Prfct Atten Awd; Pacific Asian Clb 89-90; Cncssns For Culture Nght 90; Teen Aide Vlntr 88-89; SDSU; Advrtsng.

ALCAYAGA, NICOLE; Sonoma Valley HS; Sonoma, CA; (2); Gldn St Exam Recgntn; US Navy.

ALCAZAR, ADRIANA F; Analy HS; Sebastopol, CA; (2); 8/246; French Clb; Chorus; Intrml JV Bsktbl; JV Vllybl; Hon Roll; Coll Bound Pgm; CSF; N Coast Section CIF.

ALCAZAR, EDUARDO; Los Altos HS; Hacienda Hgts, CA; (3); Ftbl; High Hon Roll; Prfct Atten Awd; Engrng Elec Or Industrial.

ALCAZAR, JOSUE U; Rio Mesa HS; Somis, CA; (3); #120 In Class; Church Yth Grp; Dance Clb; Pres Jr Cls; Rep Sr Cls; Rep Stu Cncl; Intrml JV Bsbl; Intrml Ftbl; JV Var Score Keeper; JV Var Wrstlng; Opt Clb Awd; Boys St 90; Occidental; Psych.

ALCID, GERALDINE A; Valley HS; Sacramento, CA; (2); 1/470; SADD; Ed Yrbk; JV Sftbl; High Hon Roll; Hon Roll; GATE; CSF; Berkeley; Bus.

ALCOCER, LUCINA E; Orangewood Acad; Lakewood, CA; (4); Chorus; Yrbk; Loma Linda U Riverside; Psych.

ALCORDO, CAROLYN; Cypress HS; Cypress, CA; (3); Office Aide; Pep Clb; Ski Clb; Cheerldng; Hon Roll; NHS; Prfct Atten Awd; Soroptomist Clb; U CA San Diego; Child Educ.

ALCORN, STEPHANIE; G Washington Preparatory HS; Los Angeles, CA; (3); Pep Clb; Acpl Chr; Swmmng; Emprss Club; Med.

ALDAZ, MARK A; San Leandro HS; San Leandro, CA; (3); 48/362; Spanish Clb; Teachers Aide; Band; Hon Roll; Aerosp Eng.

ALDEA, MARIA ALMA U; Lowell HS; San Francisco, CA; (2); Church Yth Grp; ROTC; Chorus; Church Choir; Color Guard; Drill Tm; School Musical; Rep Pres Frsh Cls; Rep Soph Cls; Med.

ALDEGUER, JAQUELYN; George Washington HS; San Francisco, CA; (2); French Clb; Speech Tm; Teachers Aide; Stu Cncl; Gym; Cit Awd; High Hon Roll; Hon Roll; CSF; All-City Gym; UCD; CPA.

ALDER, AMBER; Oxnard HS; Oxnard, CA; (1); 7/300; High Hon Roll; CSF.

ALDERINK, AMANDA L; El Dorado HS; Placerville, CA; (3); Science Clb; Band; Mrchg Band; Nwsp; Yrbk; Var L Swmmng; High Hon Roll; NHS; Ntl Merit Ltr; CSF; AP Class Achvt; Marine Bio.

ALDERMAN, DERRICK; Cardinal Newman HS; Cotati, CA; (2); Stage Crew; Yrbk; High Hon Roll; Hon Roll.

ALDERSON, JENNIFER; Lincoln HS; Vallecito, CA; (4); 32/513; Church Choir; Mrchg Band; Orch; Lit Mag; Mgr Crs Cntry; Hon Roll; Advncd Plcmnt Engl; Columbia CC; Bus Mgmt.

ALDON, JOYCE; Hamilton HS; Los Angeles, CA; (3); Dance Clb; Girl Scts; Math Tm; Science Clb; Drill Tm; High Hon Roll; Hon Roll; UCLA; Pedtrcs.

ALDRETE, ALMA C; Monte Vista HS; Spring Valley, CA; (3); 110/373; L Chorus; Show Choir; 1st Yr Alg Awd 88; San Diego ST U; Interior Decor.

ALDRETE, MARIA; Edison HS; Fresno, CA; (1); Church Yth Grp; MECHA 4-H; Edison; Peds.

ALDRICH, CHRISTY N; Norte Vista HS; Riverside, CA; (3); 64/350; Girl Scts; VP Spanish Clb; Pres Band; Pres Mrchg Band; Pres Pep Band; Hon Roll; Mst Vlbl Wdwn 88-90; Mst Dedctd Bnd Stu 90; Cottey; Music Tchr.

ALDRICH, HEIDI L; Eisenhower HS; Rialto, CA; (3); Church Yth Grp; Cmnty Wkr; Hosp Aide; Var Swmmng; High Hon Roll; Pres Acad Fit Awd; Leadership Cls; Rainbow For Girls Worthy Advisor; Nrsng.

ALDRICH, ROGER J; Del Campo HS; Fair Oaks, CA; (3); 32/449; Varsity Clb; Variety Show; Rep Frsh Cls; Bsktbl; Diving; Ftbl; Socr; Trk; Vllybl; Wt Lftg; AAA Awd; Schlr Athl Awd; Phys Ther.

ALDRIDGE, MICHELIN A; San Pasqual HS; Escondido, CA; (4); 41/355; Church Yth Grp; Pep Clb; Rep Soph Cls; Rep Jr Cls; Rep Sr Cls; Rep Stu Cncl; Powder Puff Ftbl; DAR Awd; Hon Roll; Kiwanis Awd; CA Inst Of Tech; Genetic Engr.

ALDRIDGE, SARAH; South Pasadena HS; South Pasadena, CA; (2); Drama Clb; German Clb; Hon Roll; Peace Club; UCLA; Psych.

ALDRIGHETTI, TOMMI J; Fontana HS; Fontana, CA; (3); FBLA; Teachers Aide; High Hon Roll; Hon Roll; Pres Acad Fit Awd; Daisey Chain Mem; CPA.

ALEATE JR, CAESAR D; Garden Grove HS; Garden Grove, CA; (3); Art Clb; Yrbk; Wrstlng; GATE Pgm; Art.

ALEGRE, ALETHEA; Gonzales HS; Chualar, CA; (2); GAA; JV Bsktbl; JV Sftbl; Hon Roll; Prfct Atten Awd; Tchr.

ALEJANDRINO, JEREMY M; Chino HS; Chino, CA; (2); Drama Clb; Thesps; School Musical; School Play; Variety Show; Lit Mag; Socr; High Hon Roll; Drama Imprv & Silvr Spur Awds; Wrtng Celebrtn; Tchr.

ALEJANDRO, MARIA; James Lick HS; San Jose, CA; (3); Office Aide; Teachers Aide; Color Guard; Cheerldng; Trk; Hon Roll; Mexican Amer Yth Orgnztn; Chrldng Cmptns; UCSB; Acting.

ALEMAN JR, FRANK J; Wasco Union HS; Fresno, CA; (4); JV Var Crs Cntry; JV Ftbl; JV Socr; JV Trk; USA/Abf Amateur Boxer; Stu Of Boxing Hstry; Fresno ST U.

ALEMAN, MARITZA; Manual Arts HS; Los Angeles, CA; (2); Church Yth Grp; High Hon Roll; Dominguez Hill Coll; Tchr.

ALEMAN, RONALD M; Westmoor HS; Daly City, CA; (2); Church Yth Grp; Letterman Clb; School Play; VP Frsh Cls; JV Bsktbl; Var JV Ftbl; JV Trk; Pro Athl; San Francisco ST; Mech Engrng.

ALEMANIA, DANIEL; Fresno Christian HS; Fresno, CA; (3); Church Yth Grp; Service Clb; Band; Mrchg Band; Sec Jr Cls; Var L Ftbl; Var Socr.

ALEMANIA, ELENA T; Fresno Christian HS; Fresno, CA; (2); Off Church Yth Grp; Drama Clb; Church Choir; School Musical; School Play; Variety Show; High Hon Roll; Drama Mary Poppins Awd; Awds Engl, Span, Bible; Evangelistic Ministry Tm In Mexicali; Actress.

ALEXANDER, ALLEN; Madera HS; Madera, CA; (4); Am Leg Boys St; Boy Scts; Science Clb; Hon Roll; Ntl Merit Ltr; Pres Acad Fit Awd; Egl Sct; Exchng Clb By Mth; Tp 10 Awd; U Of CA Davis; Aerntcl Engr.

ALEXANDER, ANGELA; Lodi HS; Lodi, CA; (4); Drama Clb; FCA; VP FHA; Library Aide; Teachers Aide; School Play; Crs Cntry; Cit Awd; Hon Roll; Badminton; Sacramento ST U; Psych.

ALEXANDER, APRIL; Torrey Pines HS; Rancho Santa Fe, CA; (2); 55/503; Church Yth Grp; Cmnty Wkr; Church Choir; Rptr Nwsp; Pres Frsh Cls; JV Fld Hcky; Stat Ftbl; Elks Awd; Hon Roll; Pres Acad Fit Awd; Music; Stanford; Econ.

ALEXANDER, BRANDON R; Poly HS; Riverside, CA; (2); Church Yth Grp; JA; Var Swmmng; Hon Roll; Cert Mrt Piano Achvt; Med.

ALEXANDER, BRANDYE; Lincoln HS; Lincoln, CA; (3); 5/130; Am Leg Aux Girls St; Treas FBLA; Pres Spanish Clb; Rptr Nwsp; Sec Treas Soph Cls; Pres Sr Cls; Treas Stu Cncl; Capt Cheerldng; Pres Acad Fit Awd; HOBY Fndtn Ambssdr; Aloha Bwl Chrldr 89; Acad Decthln Tm; Jrnlsm.

ALEXANDER, BRIAN K; Bishop Montgomery HS; Los Angeles, CA; (2); Church Yth Grp; Var Ftbl; Trk; Wt Lftg; Tchrs Awd Alge; Black Cult Clb; U South CA; Bus.

ALEXANDER, CAROLYN J; Marymount HS; Los Angeles, CA; (2); Cmnty Wkr; Hosp Aide; Science Clb; SADD; Rep Frsh Cls; VP Jr Cls; Bsktbl; Crs Cntry; Swmmng; CSF; Amnesty Intl; UCLA; Med.

ALEXANDER, CHARLOTTE R; Taft HS; Woodland Hills, CA; (2); Art Clb; Church Yth Grp; Dance Clb; Drama Clb; Acpl Chr; Drill Tm; Sec Soph Cls; L Pom Pon; Hon Roll; Arch.

ALEXANDER, CHAUNCEY I; St Patricks-St Vincent HS; Vallejo, CA; (3); Church Choir; Yrbk; Cit Awd; High Hon Roll; Hon Roll; Cal Davis; Psych.

ALEXANDER, DANIEL; Willows HS; Willows, CA; (3); Church Yth Grp; Key Clb; Letterman Clb; SADD; Varsity Clb; Pres Frsh Cls; Rep Stu Cncl; JV Bsktbl; JV Var Ftbl; Var Tennis; Cngrsnl Yth Ldrsh Cncl; Acadc Achvt Awd.

ALEXANDER, DAVID; Righetti HS; Orcutt, CA; (1); Church Yth Grp; Church Choir; High Hon Roll; Aerospace Engr.

ALEXANDER, ERIN; Novato HS; Novato, CA; (3); French Clb; Key Clb; Ed Lit Mag; Pres Frsh Cls; VP Stu Cncl; Var Cheerldng; Var Diving; Var Tennis; Hon Roll; Pres Acad Fit Awd; Creative Wrtng.

ALEXANDER, EVERETT C; La Jolla Country Day Schl; San Diego, CA; (2); Church Yth Grp; Cmnty Wkr; SADD; School Musical; School Play; Pres Frsh Cls; Pres Soph Cls; Var L Bsktbl; JV Ftbl; Var L Trk; HOBY Fnd Ldrshp Sem; 5 Piano Concert; Jack Jill Am Inc; Georgetown; Pol Sci.

ALEXANDER, GREGORY H; Cajon HS; San Bernardino, CA; (2); Band; Church Choir; Drm Mjr(t); Jazz Band; Mrchg Band; Orch; Pep Band; School Musical; Bsktbl; Ftbl; Blue Belt Martial Arts; King Of Mt Calvary Missionary Baptist Church; Med.

ALEXANDER, HEATHER C; Vallejo SR HS; Vallejo, CA; (3); Church Yth Grp; Office Aide; SADD; PETA.

ALEXANDER, JENNIFER L; St Anthony HS; Long Beach, CA; (4); Cmnty Wkr; Treas GAA; Letterman Clb; Capt Var Socr; Capt Var Sftbl; Var Vllybl; High Hon Roll; NHS.

ALEXANDER, KAREN L; Manteca HS; Manteca, CA; (2); 49/420; Key Clb; SADD; Band; Jazz Band; Mrchg Band; Pep Band; Treas Stu Cncl; JV Vllybl; High Hon Roll; Hon Roll; Acad Dcthln; Jrnlst.

ALEXANDER, KRISTA; Monte Vista HS; Alamo, CA; (2); Teachers Aide; Chorus; Capt Drill Tm; Capt Mrchg Band; Hon Roll; Hstry Awd; Cal Poly; Arch.

ALEXANDER, MARK A; Brawley Union HS; Brawley, CA; (1); Math Tm; Ftbl; Hon Roll.

ALEXANDER, MARQUEZ L; George Washington HS; San Francisco, CA; (3); Cmnty Wkr; Chorus; Var Ftbl; Var Wt Lftg; Hon Roll; Pop Warner Ftbl Lge; Merit Awd Rcgntn SYEP 8alpha Kappa Alpha Cert Of Merit Schlrshp-Ctznshp 87; San Jose ST; Comp Sci.

ALEXANDER, MICHELLE L; University City HS; San Diego, CA; (3); Church Yth Grp; Cmnty Wkr; Dance Clb; Drama Clb; Spanish Clb; School Play; Cit Awd; Hon Roll; Outstndng Achvt Awd Hstry; VP Orgnztn Nature Consrvtn.

ALEXANDER, NICOLE; Palm Desert HS; Palm Desert, CA; (2); Drama Clb; French Clb; Science Clb; Temple Yth Grp; School Play; Ed Nwsp; Ed Yrbk; Hon Roll; Val; Aztec Actn Nws Anchr Wmn; Yale; Jrnlsm.

ALEXANDER, SHARON L; Lower Lake HS; Clearlake, CA; (2); #14 In Class; Drama Clb; Chorus; School Play; Rep Soph Cls; Vllybl; Hon Roll; Friday Night Live; Nels 88; Music; Psych.

ALEXANDER, STEPHANIE M; Vallejo SR HS; Mare Island, CA; (2); French Clb; Hon Roll; Photo; Sci; Omp; Accntng.

ALEXANDER, WALTER L; Arlington HS; Riverside, CA; (3); Teachers Aide; Chorus; JV Bsktbl; Var L Ftbl; Var Trk; Var Wt Lftg; Road Rnnr 4x100 Relay St Chmpn; OR ST U.

ALEXANDRIA, ALYSHA A; Tulare Union HS; Tulare, CA; (3); NFL; School Play; Var Crs Cntry; Var Trk; Phys Ed.

ALEXANIAN, JULIE R; Bullard HS; Fresno, CA; (1); Church Yth Grp; FCA; French Clb; Intnl Clb; Key Clb; SADD; High Hon Roll; Prfct Atten Awd; Pres Acad Fit Awd; PSAT Frshmn; UC Berkely; Pedtrcs.

ALEXOVICS, ANIKO; Culver City HS; Culver City, CA; (2); Church Yth Grp; Off Frsh Cls; Off Soph Cls; Pres Jr Cls; French Hon Soc; Student League; Special Education.

ALFANO, ANGELA M; Huntington Beach HS; Huntington Beach, CA; (2); Church Yth Grp; Girl Scts; Red Cross Aide; School Musical; Score Keeper; Stat Wrstlng; Yth Grp Mssn Trps Brooklyn NY; Natl Cmptn Fn Art Fstv-Drma; UCLA; Cmnctns.

ALFARO, ELVIRA; Independence HS; San Jose, CA; (2); Spanish Clb; Hon Roll; Chicano Latino Clb; VCO Prgm.

ALFARO, ESPERANZA M; Pittsburg HS; Pittsburg, CA; (1); Prfct Atten Awd; Acad Excllnc Awd; Psych.

ALFARO, GLORIA; Orestimba HS; Newman, CA; (4); 13/54; Church Yth Grp; Drama Clb; Pep Clb; Pres Spanish Clb; Band; School Musical; Yrbk; Treas Frsh Cls; Treas Jr Cls; Hon Roll; Mirgrant Parent Advsry Cmmtte Secy; Migrnt Educ Schlrshp; Bank Amer Cert Engl 2nd Lang; CSU Stanislaus; Liberal Stds.

ALFARO, HILDA V; John Glen HS; Norwalk, CA; (2); 9/400; Church Yth Grp; French Clb; GAA; Letterman Clb; Varsity Clb; Var Bsktbl; Var Sftbl; JV Vllybl; Cit Awd; French Hon Soc.

ALFARO, JO ANNE; Bonita Vista HS; Chula Vista, CA; (2); Library Aide; Pep Clb; Speech Tm; Rptr Nwsp; Yrbk; JV Tennis; Hon Roll; Pres Acad Fit Awd; Ofcr SEA; Brdmembr & Vlntr PTSA; CSF; UCSD; Med.

ALFARO, MARIBEL; Calistoga HS; Calistoga, CA; (3); Bus Profs of Am; Chess Clb; Computer Clb; Debate Tm; FBLA; Hosp Aide; Latin Clb; Spanish Clb; VICA; Nwsp.

ALFELOR, RAYMOND J; Bellarmine College Prep; San Jose, CA; (2); Church Yth Grp; Cmnty Wkr; Service Clb; Yrbk; Ltr Of Commendation; UCLA; Biochem.

ALFEROS, NORIFE F; Vallejo SR HS; Vallejo, CA; (3); Church Yth Grp; FHA; Teachers Aide; Ed Yrbk; Ed Lit Mag; Treas Stu Cncl; JV Sftbl; Hon Roll; Jr NHS; Prfct Atten Awd; Ldrshp Cls; UC Davis; Med.

ALFIDI, TONY J; Cordova SR HS; Rancho Cordova, CA; (3); 15/480; Boy Scts; VP FBLA; Key Clb; Math Tm; Model UN; Var L Socr; High Hon Roll; Hon Roll; Jr NHS; Ntl Merit SF; CSF; Key, Octagon Clb; Optimists & Masons Essay Wnnr; Bus Mgmnt.

ALFILER, LAURIE; Santa Clara HS; Santa Clara, CA; (3); Church Yth Grp; French Clb; Chorus; Church Choir; Flag Corp; Mrchg Band; Var Sftbl; Chrch Yth Grp; 1st Prz Illustratn Robert Frost Poem Cont; San Jose ST; Advrtsng.

ALFONSI, MARIE A; Ramona HS; Ramona, CA; (3); 27/280; Dance Clb; Drama Clb; French Clb; Teachers Aide; Chorus; School Musical; School Play; Variety Show; French Hon Soc; High Hon Roll; Amnesty Intl Ofcr; Earth Clb; Animal Rights Grp; Theatre Arts.

ALFONSO, DANIEL J; Aragon HS; San Mateo, CA; (2); Computer Clb; Office Aide; Teachers Aide; Stage Crew; Crs Cntry; Mgr(s).

ALFORD, KIMBERLY D; Rubidoux HS; Riverside, CA; (4); Church Yth Grp; Dance Clb; Office Aide; Teachers Aide; Varsity Clb; Capt Cheerldng; Var JV Pom Pon; San Diego ST.

ALFORD, KRISTIN M; Foothill HS; Santa Ana, CA; (3); 36/328; Church Yth Grp; Cmnty Wkr; English Clb; Hosp Aide; VP Spanish Clb; JV Sftbl; JV Vllybl; Hon Roll.

ALFRED, TRACEY D; Fairfield HS; Suisun City, CA; (2); Art Clb; Dance Clb; Art.

ALGARIN, TIFFANY; Herbert Hoover HS; San Diego, CA; (3); Var Socr; Var Sftbl; Var Vllybl; Fundraising/Finances Commsnr Amnsty Interrntl Clb; UCSD; Psych.

ALGER, ODEN; Hemet HS; Idyllwild, CA; (4); 31/500; Am Leg Boys St; VP FBLA; Pres Service Clb; JV Trk; Cit Awd; High Hon Roll; Pres Acad Fit Awd; San Jose ST U; Aerospace Engr.

ALGER, WAYNE R; Vanden HS; Vacaville, CA; (4); Church Yth Grp; Latin Clb; Capt Var Bsbl; JV Bsktbl; JV Var Ftbl; High Hon Roll; Hon Roll; Pres Acad Fit Awd; ALL-SCAL Bsbl; All County Bsbl Team 90; U CA Davis; Engrng.

ALGER-ALVES, MELISSA; Valley HS; Sacramento, CA; (4); 68/440; Treas GAA; Teachers Aide; Varsity Clb; Sprt Ed Yrbk; Off Frsh Cls; Off Soph Cls; Off Jr Cls; Pres Stu Cncl; Powder Puff Ftbl; Capt Var Sftbl; Outstndng Stu Of Yr, Sr; Sftbl Silver Viking; UC Santa Cruz; Sociology.

ALGNAY, JOYCE L; Bonita Vista HS; Chula Vista, CA; (3); 27/559; Church Yth Grp; Model UN; Pep Clb; Teachers Aide; Yrbk; Rep Soph Cls; Rep Jr Cls; JV Bsktbl; Cit Awd; Hon Roll; Bst Scl/Bhvrl Sci Stu & Outstndng Acad Achvt Awds; JV Girls Mst Imprvd Plyr 87-88; UC Los Angeles; Med.

ALGRA, JOSHUA L; Arroyo Grande HS; Arroyo Grande, CA; (3); Church Yth Grp; German Clb; Key Clb; Teachers Aide; Yrbk; Off Sr Cls; Bsktbl; Golf; Vllybl; High Hon Roll; Hon Roll; Golf Schlrshp; UCSB; Med.

ALHAMBRA, ANGEL; Bellarmine Jefferson HS; Los Angeles, CA; (3); 3/160; Church Yth Grp; Cmnty Wkr; Math Clb; Red Cross Aide; Science Clb; Spanish Clb; Church Choir; Rep Soph Cls; Rep Jr Cls; Var Cheerldng; CSF Secy, Outstndng Cmnty Svc Awd.

ALHART, JENNIFER L; Lompoc HS; Lompoc, CA; (2); Church Yth Grp; Band; Jazz Band; Mrchg Band; Pep Band; Prfct Atten Awd; Poem Publ In Poetic Voices Of Amer 90; Early Chldhd Studies.

ALI, HESHMAT M; Warren HS; Downey, CA; (2); FBLA; L Swmmng; Pres Acad Fit Awd; Debate Clb; Mosque Yth Grp; UCLA; Med.

ALI, IRFAN B; Santa Monica HS; Santa Monica, CA; (3); Boy Scts; Math Clb; Tennis; Vllybl; CA Poly ST U; Aero Engrng.

ALI, KAMILAH S; Moreno Valley HS; Moreno Valley, CA; (3); 24/520; Var L Crs Cntry; Var L Socr; Var L Trk; High Hon Roll; NHS; Black Stu Union Pres; CA Schlstc Federation; Political Sci.

ALI, KARRAR AUSSAIN; Moorpark HS; Moorpark, CA; (4); 7/208; Orch; Intrml Bsktbl; JV Socr; Var Intrml Tennis; High Hon Roll; Hon Roll; Jr NHS; Lion Awd; NHS; Spcl Spnsh Rcgntn Awd; Enterprise Awd-Outstndng Acad Achvt; CSF; Med.

ALI, MOHAMMED A; Westmoor HS; Daly City, CA; (2); Boy Scts; Band; Jazz Band; Auto Tech.

ALIAGA, PAOLA F; Notre Dame Academy Girls HS; Inglewood, CA; (4); Cmnty Wkr; Service Clb; Cit Awd; Hon Roll; Pres Acad Fit Awd; Acad Decthln; UC Davis; Poltcl Sci.

ALIAGA, ROSSIO S; College Park HS; Pleasant Hill, CA; (3); #3 In Class; Hosp Aide.

ALIBERTE, NICOLE S; La Reina HS; Westlake Village, CA; (2); Drama Clb; Thesps; Chorus; School Musical; School Play; Variety Show; Rptr Nwsp; Cit Awd; Hon Roll; Glee Club VP; CSF; 1000 Oaks Teen Ctr Advsry Cmmtte; Psych.

ALICEA, OLGA M T; Lincoln HS; Stockton, CA; (4); Art Clb; Aud/Vis; Church Yth Grp; Cmnty Wkr; Dance Clb; Debate Tm; Hosp Aide; SADD; Powder Puff Ftbl; Swmmng; Sci Camp Cnslr Piano Voice Karate Stu Writer; Psych.

ALILAIN, DARLENE; Southwest HS; San Diego, CA; (2); 24/673; SADD; Var Tennis; Hon Roll; Prfct Atten Awd; CA Schlrshp Fdrtn; Acad Dcthln; Schl Cncssns-Swrd & Shld; Engrng.

ALIM, RINA D; La Reina HS; Westlake Village, CA; (2); 5/91; Teachers Aide; Cit Awd; High Hon Roll; CSF; Skirball Inst Amer Values Awd; Arch.

ALIMAGNO, MARION D; San Diego Acad; Spring Valley, CA; (3); Church Yth Grp; Teachers Aide; Band; Cit Awd; High Hon Roll; Hon Roll; Prfct Atten Awd; Pres Acad Fit Awd.

ALINDOGAN, REVERIE-MARIE T; Mayfield SR Schl; Burbank, CA; (3); Hon Roll; Bio & Geom Excllnc Awd; Medicine.

ALITA, ADRIAN D; Del Mar HS; Campbell, CA; (3); 15/267; Church Yth Grp; Office Aide; Chorus; School Musical; Var Crs Cntry; Var Trk; Var Wrstlng; Outstndng Prfrmnc Mock Trial Comptn; Best Supporting Actor Sch Musical; Outstndng Soph Awd 90; Math.

ALJIBURY, HALIM; Edison Computech HS; Fresno, CA; (3); VP Chess Clb; German Clb; Stat Ftbl; Var L Golf; High Hon Roll; JETS Awd; Odyssey Of Mind; CA Schlrshp Fed; Historian Jr Mets; Chem.

ALKER, AMY; Westlake HS; Thousand Oaks, CA; (2); Church Yth Grp; Dance Clb; Stat Ftbl; JV Socr; Cit Awd; Hon Roll; Pres Acad Fit Awd; Interact; CA Schlrshp Foundation; UCSB; Astronomy/Oceanography.

ALLAS, ROGER; Whitney HS; Cerritos, CA; (2); Var L Trk; High Hon Roll; Pres Acad Fit Awd; CSF; Golden ST Exam Geometry Hghst Hnrs; CA Inst Of Tech; Engr.

ALLAVESEN, FELICIANO PALOMAR; John Burroughs HS; Burbank, CA; (3); Var Gym; Var Socr; Wt Lftg; Stanford U; Lwyr.

ALLBRITTON, RICHARD E; Selma HS; Selma, CA; (1); Church Yth Grp; French Clb; Ftbl; Wt Lftg; Fresno ST; Drftng.

ALLBROOKS, JASMINE; O'farrel SCPA HS; San Diego, CA; (3); 7/143; Dance Clb; GAA; Girl Scts; Letterman Clb; Math Clb; Model UN; Varsity Clb; Variety Show; Yrbk; Off Sr Cls; Coca Cola Fshn Clb; SADD Clb; UCLA; Dancer.

ALLCORN, SHERRY MENDES; San Rafael HS; San Rafael, CA; (1); Church Yth Grp; JV Bsktbl; Var Sftbl; Var Tennis; Bsktbl MVP; 1st Tm All Leag Sftbl; CIF Schlr Athl; UCLA; Sports Med.

ALLEE, BRIDGET M; Live Oak HS; Live Oak, CA; (3); Drama Clb; School Play; Ed Nwsp; Yrbk; Co-Capt VP Cheerldng; Var Trk; High Hon Roll; Hon Roll; Hgh Hnrs GSE Math; Camp Cnslr Woodleaf Natrlst Camp; Yng Writers Clb; Jrnslm.

ALLEMAN, JULIE L; Milpitas HS; Milpitas, CA; (2); Church Yth Grp; Intnl Clb; Teachers Aide; Chorus; Church Choir; School Musical; Hon Roll; Pres Acad Fit Awd; Sci.

ALLEMAN, KELLIE L; Corona HS; Corona, CA; (1); Church Yth Grp; GAA; Mgr(s); Socr; High Hon Roll; Hon Roll; CSF; Pres Acad Fit Awd; Schlr-Athl Lttr Awd; Real Est.

ALLEN, ANGELEE M; Miramonte HS; Canyon, CA; (3); Mgr Nwsp; Yrbk; Var Crs Cntry; JV Trk; Hon Roll; Hrs Bck Rdng; Dns Lst; CSF; Intl Bus & Fnc.

ALLEN, CASSANDRA; Rincon Valley Christian HS; Santa Rosa, CA; (3); Church Yth Grp; Chorus; Off Jr Cls; Stu Cncl; Co-Capt Cheerldng; Sftbl; Vllybl; UCLA; Bus Admin.

ALLEN, CATHERINE A; Whitney HS; Cerritos, CA; (2); Band; Mrchg Band; Stu Cncl; Cit Awd; Hon Roll; CSF, Med Club, Wind Instr Ensmbl Mem; Med.

ALLEN, CHARESE L; Hayward HS; Hayward, CA; (2); Art Clb; Church Yth Grp; Sec Debate Tm; German Clb; Acpl Chr; Stage Crew; Off Soph Cls; Tennis; Hon Roll; Badminton; CA Schlrshp Fed; Ec.

ALLEN, CHRIS J; Lodi HS; Stockton, CA; (2); 31/587; Boy Scts; Church Yth Grp; Ski Clb; Intrml Ftbl; High Hon Roll; Eagle Sct; BYU; Engrng.

ALLEN, CHRISTINA; Bolsa Grande HS; Garden Grove, CA; (2); 43/377; Orch; High Hon Roll; Hon Roll; Grls Leag Board; Outdoors Clb VP; Yth Ldrshp For Action; Berkeley CA U; Geophysics.

ALLEN JR, DAVID; Andrew P Hill HS; San Jose, CA; (3); Boy Scts; JV Bsbl; JV Bsktbl; JV Crs Cntry; Penn ST; Automotive.

ALLEN, DIANA H; Salinas HS; Salinas, CA; (3); Church Yth Grp; Sec GAA; Church Choir; Yrbk; JV Bsktbl; Powder Puff Ftbl; Var L Tennis; Var L Trk; High Hon Roll; Hon Roll; CSF; Chmpns Clb; Fine Arts.

ALLEN, DONETTA M; Mt Pleasant HS; San Jose, CA; (1); Church Yth Grp; Band; Church Choir; Pep Band; Var L Swmmng; High Hon Roll; CSF.

ALLEN, ELIZABETH C; La Reina HS; Thousand Oaks, CA; (3); GAA; Letterman Clb; Varsity Clb; Phtg Yrbk; L Var Socr; Stat Sftbl; L Var Tennis; Cit Awd; Hon Roll.

ALLEN, ERICA M; Gardena HS; Gardena, CA; (2); JA; Office Aide; Pep Clb; Band; Drill Tm; Mrchg Band; Cit Awd; Hon Roll; Magnet Clss Sprtmnshp Awd/Trphy 88-89; Private Ballet Dance Lssns 4 Yrs; Brothrhd/Sistrhd Club HS; Berkeley U Of CA; Math.

ALLEN, ERICA M; Tulare Union HS; Tulare, CA; (3); Church Yth Grp; Band; Church Choir; Mrchg Band; JV Var Tennis; JV Var Vllybl; Hon Roll; MVP Fresh Vlybl; All Star Church Vllybl Team; All Am Hall Of Fame Music; Point Loma Nazarene; Phys Ed.

ALLEN, ERIKA L; Roseville HS; Rocklin, CA; (2); Drama Clb; Sec French Clb; German Clb; Science Clb; SADD; VP Soph Cls; Hon Roll; NHS; Amnsty Intl Pres; VP Cls; Marine Bio.

ALLEN, ERYN L; San Benito HS; Hollister, CA; (3); 33/407; Am Leg Aux Girls St; Church Yth Grp; Drama Clb; French Clb; Pep Clb; Science Clb; Color Guard; Stage Crew; Off Pep Band; Off Soph Cls; CSF Sec; Drama Awd; Rotary Yth Ldr; Bio.

ALLEN, FONTAINE S; San Marcos HS; San Marcos, CA; (1); Dance Clb; Var Trk; Hon Roll; U Of CA; Psych.

ALLEN, HEATHER L; Pasadena HS; Sierra Madre, CA; (4); 5/350; Girl Scts; Acpl Chr; Church Choir; Mrchg Band; Orch; School Musical; DAR Awd; Prfct Atten Awd; Sal; CSF Sealbearer; Pasadena City Coll; Humanities.

ALLEN, HOLLY J; Helix HS; La Mesa, CA; (4); Church Yth Grp; Drama Clb; Key Clb; Pep Clb; Science Clb; Speech Tm; School Play; Yrbk; Stu Cncl; Old Globe Theatre Awd; Westmont Coll; Cmmnctns.

ALLEN, IAN; Carlmont HS; Belmont, CA; (2); Aud/Vis; Model UN; Office Aide; Teachers Aide; Rptr Nwsp; Rep Stu Cncl; JV Ftbl; JV Trk; Pres Acad Fit Awd; Acad Dcthln; Intrct Clb; 2nd Pl Schl Essy Cont; Trck Awd; Ski, Sail, Surf; Naval Acad; Law.

ALLEN, JACQUIE Y; Ontario HS; Ontario, CA; (3); Math Clb; Office Aide; Cit Awd; Hon Roll; Prfct Atten Awd; Pres Acad Fit Awd; Cert Spcl Mrt Exclinc Essay Compstn; Black Stu Union; MIT.

ALLEN, JAMES; Cerritos HS; Cerritos, CA; (3); 54/550; Boy Scts; Sec Church Yth Grp; Spanish Clb; Teachers Aide; JV Socr; Var Trk; High Hon Roll; Hon Roll; Eagle Scout Awd BSA; USAFA; USAF Officer.

ALLEN, JAMES F; Arroyo Grande HS; Nipomo, CA; (3); 222/405; JV Bsbl; Var Golf; Hancock JC; Bus Accntng.

ALLEN, JANE C; Pinole Valley HS; Pinole, CA; (3); Church Yth Grp; Debate Tm; French Clb; NFL; Yrbk; L Var Trk; L Var Vllybl; YMCA Yth & Govt Mdl Legislature & Ct; Rcvd Best News/Media Reporter Awd; Chrmn City Pinole Yth Cmmssn; Environmental Law.

ALLEN, JANE R; Manual Arts HS; Los Angeles, CA; (2); High Hon Roll; Hon Roll; UCLA Partnrshp Pgm; UCLA; Acctng.

ALLEN, JASON; Clovis West HS; Fresno, CA; (4); Pres FBLA; Science Clb; SADD; Varsity Clb; Ed Yrbk; Var Crs Cntry; Var Trk; JV Wrstlng; Pres Acad Fit Awd; Exchng Club Yth Of Mnth; Fresno Pacific Coll; Ecology.

ALLEN, JEFF; Gompers Secondary HS; San Diego, CA; (3); Chess Clb; Church Yth Grp; Office Aide; Hon Roll; NHS; Cert Of Awd Spnsh; Engl Hnrbl Merit; UCSD; Med.

ALLEN, JEFFREY ANDREW; Diamond Bar HS; Diamond Bar, CA; (4); 24/460; French Clb; Key Clb; Science Clb; Rep Jr Cls; Rep Sr Cls; Intrml Bsbl; Intrml Bsktbl; JV Ftbl; Var Capt Socr; Var Capt Trk; Sccr Clb; UC Irvine; Scl Ecology.

ALLEN, JENNIFER; Capistrano Valley Christian HS; Dana Point, CA; (2); 1/50; Dance Clb; Drama Clb; School Play; High Hon Roll; Blng To Ensmbl At Laguna Moulton Yth Thtr; Actrss.

ALLEN, JENNIFER L; Sacramento Country Day Schl; Sacramento, CA; (2); Dance Clb; School Play; Ed Yrbk; Var Cheerldng; Var Vllybl; Hon Roll; Ntl Merit Schol; Piano; Awd Exclnc In Span.

ALLEN, JENNIFER R; Irvine HS; Irvine, CA; (2); Church Yth Grp; Dance Clb; Drama Clb; Chorus; School Musical; School Play; Stu Cncl; Hon Roll; Marketing.

ALLEN, JEREMIAH L; Mayfair HS; Bellflower, CA; (2); Church Yth Grp; Band; Jazz Band; Orch; Pep Band; High Hon Roll; Hon Roll; Prfct Atten Awd; Law.

ALLEN, JOHN M; Brea-Olinda HS; Brea, CA; (2); 60/300; JV Bsbl; Hon Roll; CA Schlrshp Fdr; Bsktbl; Acad Awd Of Achvmnt; Cal ST Fullerton; Bus Mngmnt.

ALLEN, JULEE; Lindsay HS; Lindsay, CA; (1); Church Yth Grp; Drama Clb; GAA; SADD; Rep Frsh Cls; Rep Soph Cls; Cit Awd; Hon Roll; Prfct Atten Awd; Pres Acad Fit Awd; Cal Poly; Radio/T V Brdcstng.

ALLEN, JUSTIN; Livingston HS; Livingston, CA; (1); French Clb; FFA; Band; Jazz Band; Mrchg Band; JV Tennis; Wt Lftg; JV Wrstlng; High Hon Roll; Hon Roll; Stanford.

ALLEN, KARYN L; Hanford Joint Union HS; Hanford, CA; (3); 32/487; Band; Mrchg Band; Pep Band; JV Crs Cntry; Hon Roll; UC Davis; Biochem.

ALLEN, KEVIN H; Woodbridge HS; Irvine, CA; (4); Church Yth Grp; JA; Teachers Aide; JV Bsbl; Intrml Bsktbl; Hon Roll; Pres Acad Fit Awd; Biola U Hnr Mrt Schlrshp; Woodbridge HS Schlrshp; Biola U; Chrstn Educ.

ALLEN, LA TRICE; Nogales HS; West Covina, CA; (1); Harvard; Law.

ALLEN III, LADELL; Pomona HS; Pomona, CA; (3); 58/279; Chess Clb; MESA Club; AZ ST; Aerospace Engr.

ALLEN, LISHA M; Phillip & Sala Burton HS; San Francisco, CA; (3); Church Yth Grp; Cmnty Wkr; Debate Tm; Girl Scts; Speech Tm; Church Choir; Drill Tm; School Musical; Rptr Nwsp; Hon Roll; Clark U; Public Speaking.

ALLEN, MARC C; Charter Oak HS; Glendora, CA; (4); 43/337; Boy Scts; French Clb; Letterman Clb; SADD; Varsity Clb; Stage Crew; Ed Yrbk; Capt Swmmng; Capt Wrstlng; Water Polo Capt; Los Angeles Coll Chiropractic.

ALLEN, MARCIA; La Sierra Acad; Riverside, CA; (2); Chorus; Phtg Yrbk; Sec Soph Cls; JV Bsktbl; Score Keeper; High Hon Roll; Hon Roll; NHS; Howard; Med.

ALLEN, MATTHEW D; San Gorgonio HS; Highland, CA; (3); Church Yth Grp; Speech Tm; Hon Roll; GATE Stu; Mck Trl Tm.

ALLEN, MERIDETH; Los Alamizos HS; Los Alamitos, CA; (3); Church Yth Grp; Drama Clb; French Clb; SADD; Chorus; Variety Show; Hon Roll; USC.

ALLEN, MICHAEL J; Bellarmine College Prep; San Carlos, CA; (2); #1 In Class; Church Yth Grp; Cmnty Wkr; Debate Tm; Latin Clb; Library Aide; NFL; Speech Tm; Nwsp; Stat Bsktbl; Gen Excel Awd 89-90; Engr.

ALLEN, MIKE J; Helix HS; La Mesa, CA; (3); 105/449; Var Ftbl; Grossmont JC.

ALLEN JR, NEWELL GENE; Rosemead HS; Temple City, CA; (3); Church Yth Grp; Computer Clb; Dance Clb; FCA; FBLA; Letterman Clb; ROTC; SADD; Varsity Clb; Bsbl; New Encounter; Friday Night Live; Comptr Rop; Foods Coop; Santa Bar; Comp.

ALLEN, RACHEL; Livermore HS; Livermore, CA; (2); Band; Mrchg Band; JV Swmmng; Hon Roll; Jazz Dancing Performing; State Coll; Court Reporting.

ALLEN, REAGAN M; Monterey HS; Monterey, CA; (2); Church Yth Grp; Girl Scts; Library Aide; Spanish Clb; Acpl Chr; Chorus; Drill Tm; Flag Corp; School Play; Variety Show; 3rd Pl Photo Awd SC Assn; 3rd Pl Photo Awd GA Assn Chrstn Schls; Charm Assocs Schl; Fshn.

ALLEN, REGINA D; Luther Burbank HS; Sacramento, CA; (3); Church Yth Grp; Teachers Aide; Chorus; Church Choir; School Musical; Bsktbl; Wt Lftg; Hon Roll; Schlsp Awd Eng; Spllg Awd; Music Entrtnmt.

ALLEN, RYAN J; Santa Clara HS; Santa Clara, CA; (1); JV Trk; JV Wrstlng; Orthopedics.

ALLEN, SHARON E; Redwood HS; Visalia, CA; (1); Church Yth Grp; Band; Mrchg Band; Pep Band; Pres Frsh Cls; Var Trk; Vllybl; ASB Strng Cmmttee Mem; San Diego ST; Englsh.

ALLEN, SHEINA D; Point Loma HS; San Diego, CA; (4); Church Yth Grp; Drill Tm; Hon Roll; EMOJA Unity Clb; Treas; San Diego City Coll; Nrs.

ALLEN, TYE W; La Seirra HS; Riverside, CA; (1); Chorus; JV Bsktbl; JV Ftbl; JV Trk; Wt Lftg; Hon Roll; Trck CA ST Champ; Bsktbl Team 1st Pl; Music; UCLA.

ALLENBAUGH, RANDY B; Foothill HS; Bakersfield, CA; (3); Letterman Clb; Office Aide; Teachers Aide; Varsity Clb; Ftbl; Wt Lftg; Wrstlng; Hon Roll; Bst Non-Sr Lnmn Ftbl Awd; Cmmrcl Arln Plt.

ALLENDORF, MICHELLE L; Clear Lake HS; Upper Lake, CA; (3); 3/86; Drama Clb; School Musical; School Play; Variety Show; VP Soph Cls; Rep Stu Cncl; Tennis; High Hon Roll; CSF; Rotary Yth Ldrshp Awd Camp; Founded Environmental Awareness Group; Rhetoric.

ALLENSWORTH, DAVE; Sierra HS; Coarsegold, CA; (2); Aud/Vis; Church Yth Grp; Cmnty Wkr; Computer Clb; Red Cross Aide; ROTC; Spanish Clb; Band; Color Guard; Wrstlng; US Sea Cadet Corps; Phy.

ALLENSWORTH, GREG D; Rio Linda HS; Sacramento, CA; (2); Quiz Bowl; Scholastic Bowl; Spanish Clb; Hon Roll; Prfct Atten Awd; Golden St Exam Hnrs Awd; Berkely U CA; Elec Engr.

ALLES, JENNI L; Trinity HS; Weaverville, CA; (1); FFA; Ski Clb; JV Bsktbl; JV Sftbl; Hon Roll; Shasta; Hortcltr.

ALLES, ROCHELLE; San Joaquin Memorial HS; Fresno, CA; (2); GAA; Math Clb; VP Service Clb; Spanish Clb; JV Bsktbl; JV Cheerldng; JV Powder Puff Ftbl; Var Score Keeper; JV Vllybl; High Hon Roll; UC Santa Barbara; Math.

ALLETT, BRIAN; Vallejo SR HS; Vallejo, CA; (3); Var JV Wrstlng; Hon Roll; NHS; Comp Sci.

ALLEY, KRISTEN D; Roseville HS; Rocklin, CA; (1); Church Yth Grp; Spanish Clb; Pres Soph Cls; JV Bsktbl; JV Sftbl; JV Vllybl; Hon Roll; MVP Volleyball; MVP Basketball; MVP Softball; Ucla; Stanford; Science.

ALLFREE, HELEN; San Gorgonio HS; Highland, CA; (3); Hosp Aide; Key Clb; Library Aide; Science Clb; Teachers Aide; Cit Awd; Hon Roll; Bio Clb; ACES; CA ST U; Nrsng.

ALLGEIER, LOUIE; Fontana HS; Fontana, CA; (2); Var Socr; Prfct Atten Awd; UCLA.

ALLGIER, CHRISTINE Y; Victory Christian HS; Sacramento, CA; (3); Church Yth Grp; Pep Clb; School Play; Sec Stu Cncl; Cheerldng; Vllybl; High Hon Roll; Schltc All-Amer Schlr Directory 88; Honor Society; Work At Burger King; Masters Coll; Ed.

ALLINGHAM, WILLIAM C; Grossmont HS; La Mesa, CA; (3); 44/385; L Trk; Hon Roll; NHS; Sftbl, Vllybl & Martial Arts; SDSU; Bus Mgmt.

ALLINGTON, TODD R; Bishop O'dowd HS; Alameda, CA; (3); Church Yth Grp; Chorus; Var Capt Crs Cntry; JV Var Socr; Var Trk; High Hon Roll; Outstndg Stu 87-88; Campus Ministry Team; Cross Cntry All Leag 89.

ALLIS, KATRINA; Coastal Christian Schl; Arroyo Grande, CA; (1); Church Yth Grp; Drama Clb; Office Aide; Church Choir; Yrbk; JV Cheerldng; Score Keeper; Life Bbl Coll; Law.

ALLISON, BECKY; Del Mar HS; San Jose, CA; (3); GAA; Girl Scts; Key Clb; Teachers Aide; Varsity Clb; Stat Bsbl; Var JV Fld Hcky; Var Socr; Var Trk; High Hon Roll; Stu Athltc Trnr; Fresno ST; Athltc Trng.

ALLISON, ERIC; Bel-Air Prep HS; Los Angeles, CA; (2); Church Yth Grp; English Clb; Spanish Clb; Stu Cncl; Var Bsbl; Var Bsktbl; Cit Awd; Hon Roll; Most Promisng Athlt 89-90; Bel Air Bsktbl Tm; CIF Southrn Sect Trnmnt Bsktbl; Fld Trip To WA DC; LSU; Lwyr.

ALLISON, LORY C; Point Loma HS; San Diego, CA; (3); 215/430; Hosp Aide; Office Aide; Speech Tm; Chorus; Yrbk; Rep Frsh Cls; Rep Stu Cncl; JV Intrml Bsktbl; Var JV Mgr(s); JV Socr; Part Time Model; USD; Law.

ALLOR, JASON M; Ramona HS; Riverside, CA; (2); Band; Mrchg Band; Orch; Pep Band; School Musical; Lamar U; Engrng.

ALLOWAY, LARK; Heritage Christian HS; Villa Park, CA; (4); 2/12; Church Yth Grp; Speech Tm; VP Frsh Cls; VP Soph Cls; VP Jr Cls; VP Sr Cls; Var Co-Capt Cheerldng; High Hon Roll; ACSI Outstndng Chrstn HS Stu Awd; Physics Clb; 1st Pl ACSI Dram Int Spch Meet; Liberty U; Comm.

ALLOWAY, ROSS; Heritage Christian HS; Villa Park, CA; (1); 2/15; Church Yth Grp; Ski Clb; Bsktbl; Hon Roll; Archery & Photogrphy Awds.

ALLOWAY, STEPHANIE R; Edison HS; Huntington Beach, CA; (3); Church Yth Grp; Teachers Aide; Vllybl; Cit Awd; HS Teacher.

ALLREAD, TOM M; Sutter Union HS; Live Oak, CA; (2); Art Clb; Intnl Clb; Letterman Clb; Bsbl; Bsktbl; Ftbl; Wt Lftg; High Hon Roll; Hon Roll; Pres Acad Fit Awd; MVP Bsbl 90; Most Imprvd Ftbl 89; Golden St Math Exams; U CA; Math.

ALLRED, AMY; Upland HS; Upland, CA; (4); 12/650; Pres Sec Church Yth Grp; Chorus; Church Choir; Rep Stu Cncl; Capt Cheerldng; Powder Puff Ftbl; High Hon Roll; Opt Clb Awd; Pres Acad Fit Awd; ASB Pep Comm Stu Govt; CSF Sec; Brigham Young U; Elem Educ.

ALLRED, JULIE NICHOLLE; Perris Lake HS; Perris, CA; (2); #4 In Class; FBLA; Key Clb; Office Aide; Teachers Aide; Color Guard; Nwsp; Cheerldng; Sftbl; High Hon Roll; Chrldng Sqd Capt; Bus Admin.

ALLRED, MICHAEL J; North HS; Bakersfield, CA; (4); 50/400; JA; Ski Clb; Teachers Aide; Hon Roll; Spanish NHS; Active Teens Against Comm Crime; Kern Co Sheriff Dept Explorer; Bakersfield Coll; Law Enf.

ALLRED, WADE A; Pinole Valley HS; Hercules, CA; (3); Band; Jazz Band; Mrchg Band; Pep Band; JV Var Ftbl; Var Trk; Hnr Band; Hnr Orch.

ALLSPAW, TRACY; Reseda HS; Reseda, CA; (4); Drama Clb; Pep Clb; Teachers Aide; Thesps; Drill Tm; School Play; VP Stu Cncl; Bank Of Amer Achvt Cert; Pierce Coll; Anthropology.

ALLYN JR, RICHARD D; Vista HS; Vista, CA; (4); 2/400; Am Leg Boys St; Aud/Vis; Cmnty Wkr; Pres Debate Tm; Scholastic Bowl; Pres Speech Tm; Stu Cncl; Elks Awd; High Hon Roll; Kiwanis Awd; CSF VP; Yale U; Law.

ALMADER, JUAN C; Lincoln HS; Los Angeles, CA; (2); Ftbl; Wt Lftg; UCLA; Law Enfrcmnt.

ALMAGUER, PATRICIA D; Mayfield SR Schl; Pasadena, CA; (3); Library Aide; Pres Spanish Clb; Sec SADD; Teachers Aide; School Play; Pres Stu Cncl; Bausch & Lomb Sci Awd; High Hon Roll; NHS; Xerox Awd; VP CSF & Natl Hnr Soc 89-91; Bio.

ALMAJAN, ARIANA M; La Jolla Country Day Schl; San Diego, CA; (2); Math Tm; Spanish Clb; Chorus; School Musical; Lit Mag; Hon Roll; Spanish NHS; 1st Pl Penwomns Soc Fictn Wrtng Cntst; Space Camp.

ALMAJANO, MARILYN; Delano HS; Earlimart, CA; (3); Key Clb; High Hon Roll; Hon Roll; Prfct Atten Awd; UFO 2 Yrs; UCLA; Pre Law.

ALMALEL, OLIVIA; Hillcrest Christian Schl; Northridge, CA; (2); 1/23; Church Yth Grp; Teachers Aide; VP Stu Cncl; JV Score Keeper; JV Sftbl; JV Vllybl; Hon Roll; Bus Mngmnt.

ALMAND, CHRIS; Pittsburg HS; Pittsburg, CA; (1); Boy Scts; Band; Mrchg Band; High Hon Roll; Hon Roll.

ALMANZAN, CELIA; Arroyo HS; Temple City, CA; (4); AFS; Key Clb; Letterman Clb; Ed Yrbk; Hon Roll; Treas Stu Cncl; Var Sftbl; Var Capt Trk; UC Irvine.

ALMARAZ, NORMA; Wilson Woodrow HS; Montebello, CA; (3); Dance Clb; French Clb; Varsity Clb; Bsktbl; Cheerldng; Crs Cntry; Trk; Hon Roll; UC Irvine; Med.

ALMAZAN, JULIET G; Torrey Pines HS; San Diego, CA; (3); 43/457; Church Yth Grp; JV Var Bsktbl; High Hon Roll; CA Shclrshp Fed Mem; Schlr Athlete Awd; Bio.

ALMAZOL, SARAH L; Santa Clara HS; Santa Clara, CA; (2); Church Yth Grp; Drama Clb; Pep Clb; Spanish Clb; Chorus; School Musical; School Play; Variety Show; Hon Roll; Ofcr Amnsty Intl; Theatr Arts.

ALMEDA, GENEL H; Valley HS; Sacramento, CA; (3); Church Yth Grp; Dance Clb; Treas Sr Cls; Intrml Mgr Cheerldng; JV Mgr(s); Powder Puff Ftbl; Hon Roll; Blck Stu Union Club; U Of San Diego; Chld Psych.

ALMER, MARISABEL; Immaculate Heart HS; Los Angeles, CA; (3); GAA; Math Clb; Science Clb; Mgr Bsktbl; Var Vllybl; High Hon Roll; CA Schlrshp Fed; Bio Awd; Envrnmntl Bio.

ALMIRANTEARENA, JOSEPH R; Chino HS; Chino, CA; (3); Band; Mrchg Band; Pep Band; Cit Awd; Hon Roll; Prfct Atten Awd; Pres Acad Fit Awd; Dance.

ALMODOVA, ALEXANDER J; Mojave HS; California City, CA; (3); Teachers Aide; Hon Roll; Pres Acad Fit Awd; Mock Trial Team; Acadmc Dcthln Team; Loyola Marymount U; Sci Educ.

ALMODOVAR, LISA M; Victor Valley HS; Victorville, CA; (4); Church Yth Grp; Office Aide; Spanish Clb; Hon Roll; Spanish NHS; Black Stu Union; San Francisco ST U; Ecolgy.

ALMOND, ANDRE D; Crenshaw HS; Los Angeles, CA; (4); Chess Clb; Church Yth Grp; Drama Clb; FFA; ROTC; Teachers Aide; Band; Chorus; Mrchg Band; Diving; Howard U; Comm.

ALMQUIST, BRENDA J; El Camino HS; Daly City, CA; (3); Teachers Aide; High Hon Roll; Hon Roll; San Francisco ST U; Sci.

ALON, EDDIE E; William Howard Taft HS; Tarzana, CA; (2); Cmnty Wkr; Library Aide; Red Cross Aide; Rep Hist Service Clb; Capt JV Tennis; Cit Awd; High Hon Roll; Hon Roll; CSF 88-90; Knighs & Ladies Svc Club Hstrn; UC; Bus.

ALONSO, ALONSO; Calipatria HS; Calipatria, CA; (2); FHA; Math Tm; Spanish Clb; SADD; JV Bsbl; JV Bsktbl; Hon Roll; Friday Night Live; Acctng.

ALONSO, AMY D; River City HS; W Sacramento, CA; (2); 4/225; SADD; JV Stat Bsktbl; JV Sftbl; High Hon Roll; Hon Roll; MESA; CSF.

ALONSO, CHRIS A; Miramonte HS; Orinda, CA; (1); Boy Scts; NFL; Spanish Clb; Wrstlng.

ALONSO, DULCE PALOMA; South West HS; San Diego, CA; (2); Teachers Aide; Cit Awd; High Hon Roll; Hon Roll; Pres Acad Fit Awd; Bus.

ALONSO, JOSEFINA; St Joseph HS; Downey, CA; (4); 9/174; Cmnty Wkr; Drama Clb; Key Clb; VP Treas Spanish Clb; Off Frsh Cls; High Hon Roll; Prfct Atten Awd; Pres Acad Fit Awd; Pres Schlr; Pres Schlr & Presdntl Schlrshp; CSF; Bank Of Amer Frgn Lang Awd; CA ST U Flltrtn; Spanish Prof.

ALONSO, MARCOS H; Don Bosco Technical Inst; Whittier, CA; (3); Cmnty Wkr; JV Crs Cntry; Wt Lftg; Hon Roll; Play Guitar & Organ; Med.

ALONSO, MARIA; Manual Arts HS; Los Angeles, CA; (4); 3/430; Service Clb; Off Jr Cls; Var Cheerldng; High Hon Roll; Hon Roll; Prfct Atten Awd; CSF Treas; MESA; UCLA.

ALONZO, DAVE C; San Benito HS; Hollister, CA; (4); Letterman Clb; Varsity Clb; Var Bsbl; Var Bsktbl; Var Ftbl; Wt Lftg; Hon Roll; Fresno ST; Sports Med.

ALONZO, EILEEN JANE; Samuel F B Morse HS; National City, CA; (4); 29/583; Hosp Aide; Library Aide; SADD; Teachers Aide; Chorus; High Hon Roll; Hon Roll; Pres Acad Fit Awd; Sci Olympiad; Recgntn Of Outstndng Accmplshmnt & Prfrmnc; CSF; Pt Loma Nazarene Clg; Nrsng.

ALONZO, JUDY P; Woodrow Wilson HS; San Francisco, CA; (3); Church Yth Grp; Cmnty Wkr; Computer Clb; FBLA; Hosp Aide; Office Aide; Teachers Aide; Chorus; Church Choir; Rep Frsh Cls; Speaker Of House Awd; Doyle & Mc Clusthen Jr Law Explorer; Comp Clb; IHSP Mst Likely To Succeed; CA ST; Law.

ALONZO, KARLA; San Gabriel HS; Rosemead, CA; (1); Cit Awd; Hon Roll; Arch.

ALONZO, MONICA G; Redwood HS; Visalia, CA; (2); Church Yth Grp; Cmnty Wkr; Band; Church Choir; Mrchg Band; Rep Stu Cncl; Hon Roll; Jr NHS; MECHA Clb Treas; Bus.

ALONZO, PERLA S; Alameda HS; Alameda, CA; (1); Spanish Clb; CA Schltc Fed; Stanford U.

ALPAY, EMILY F; Bishop Amat HS; West Covina, CA; (1); Drama Clb; VP L Socr; VP L Trk; High Hon Roll.

ALPER, SCOTT D; Marina HS; Huntington Bch, CA; (4); 48/484; Boy Scts; Band; Jazz Band; Mrchg Band; Orch; Pep Band; School Musical; School Play; High Hon Roll; Hon Roll; Sthrn CA Jazz Hnrs Band, Twice; IMC Pres,HS Band Orgnztn; USC; Jazz Guitarist.

ALQUITELA, CYNTHIA B; Baldwin Park HS; Chino Hills, CA; (3); Letterman Clb; Pep Clb; Teachers Aide; Varsity Clb; Intrml JV Cheerldng; Var L Fld Hcky; Var L Sftbl; Var Capt Vllybl; Hon Roll; LAC; Nurse.

ALSTAD, DENNIS B; Oakdale HS; Oakdale, CA; (2); Church Yth Grp; SADD; JV Bsbl; JV Bsktbl; Hon Roll; Prfct Atten Awd; Math.

ALSTON, KA SHONDA M; Mt Diablo HS; W Pittsburg, CA; (2); Church Yth Grp; Dance Clb; FBLA; SADD; Church Choir; Nwsp; VP Jr Cls; Cit Awd; High Hon Roll; Spanish NHS; UC Berkely Prtnrshp Pgm; Saturday Coll; Awd Cmpltn Evnglsm 101; UC Berkeley; Law.

ALSUP, REBECCA; Christian HS; San Diego, CA; (3); 1/100; Church Yth Grp; Key Clb; SADD; Band; Chorus; Mrchg Band; Orch; Bsktbl; Elks Awd; Hon Roll; CSF VP; CBDA All St Hnr Band.

ALSUP, TAMMY L; Victor Valley HS; Victorville, CA; (2); Church Yth Grp; Cheerldng; David Lipscomb U; Educ.

ALT, CARTER; Bullard HS; Fresno, CA; (1); Church Yth Grp; Letterman Clb; Intrml L Bsktbl; Wt Lftg; Hon Roll; Med.

ALTAMAR, DIANA T; Ramona Convent Secondary Schl; Alhambra, CA; (3); Church Yth Grp; Cmnty Wkr; Dance Clb; Debate Tm; French Clb; JA; Model UN; Acpl Chr; Church Choir; School Play; Eclgy Clb Rep; Euchrstc Minstr; Thrpy.

ALTAMERO, KIM R; Luther Burbank HS; Sacramento, CA; (4); Hon Roll; Cert Mrt Coll Headstart; Indstrl Desgn.

ALTAMIRANO, MARTHA; Roosevelt HS; Los Angeles, CA; (3); Key Clb; SADD; Drill Tm; Ed Yrbk; Hist Sr Cls; Cit Awd; High Hon Roll; Hon Roll; Prfct Atten Awd; Hmnts Prgrm; Coll Core Curr; Cornell U; Arch.

ALTHOF, KURT C; Trinity HS; Weaverville, CA; (2); German Clb; Ski Clb; Rep Soph Cls; Var Bsbl; JV Capt Bsktbl; JV Ftbl; Intrml Gym; Intrml Socr; Intrml Swmmng; JV Trk; Phys Thrpy.

ALTI, JAMELLE L; Bakersfield HS; Bakersfield, CA; (2); Church Yth Grp; Cmnty Wkr; JA; Lit Mag; Hosp Play Grp Vlntr; Plus Pgm Vlntr; Church Tchr Pgm Vlntr; Envrnmntl Sci.

ALTMAN, ELISA M; Sunny Hills HS; Fullerton, CA; (4); 1/400; Cmnty Wkr; Pres Spanish Clb; Temple Yth Grp; School Musical; JV Crs Cntry; High Hon Roll; Masonic Awd; Pres NHS; Ntl Merit SF; Rotary Awd; Extensive Invlmnt Comm Theater; Acad Decateam 3 Yrs; Teachers Aide Temple Sunday Schl; Social Sci.

ALTMYER, MICHELLE; Upland HS; Alta Loma, CA; (3); Pres Sec Church Yth Grp; Pres Frsh Cls; JV Var Cheerldng; JV Var Cheerldng; Cit Awd; High Hon Roll; Hon Roll; Kiwanis Awd; Pres Acad Fit Awd; Graphic Arts.

ALTO, HAYWARD M; Ukiahi HS; Ukiah, CA; (3); Boy Scts; Church Yth Grp; Cmnty Wkr; French Clb; Letterman Clb; Quiz Bowl; Scholastic Bowl; Speech Tm; Teachers Aide; Color Guard; Eagle Sct 90; Mst Imspirational Crss Cntry 89-90; St Marys; Frgn Svc.

ALTON, JULIE LYNN; Buena HS; Ventura, CA; (4); 4/475; Pres Church Yth Grp; SADD; Pres Acad Fit Awd; CSF-GOLD Seal Bearer; Trustees Schlrshp BYU; Natl Mrt Commended Stu; BYU; Econ.

ALUMBAUGH, LARISSA D; Las Lomas HS; Walnut Creek, CA; (3); VP French Clb; JV Tennis; Frgn Lang; Rotary Clb Spnsrd Trip UC Davis Freedom & Ldrshp Day; Elem Educ.

ALUMBAUGH, LETICIA V; Las Lomas HS; Walnut Creek, CA; (1); JV Swmmng; Fri Nght Live; Club Agnst Drnk Drvng; Upcmng Schl Yr Will Be Jng Frnch Club; Coll; Sci.

ALUMNO, CLIFFORD S; Jefferson HS; Daly City, CA; (4); 3/257; Model UN; Pres Science Clb; Band; Mrchg Band; Ed Nwsp; Tennis; High Hon Roll; Pres Acad Fit Awd; CSF Treas; Gldn ST Exm Hgh Hnrs Alg, Geom; UC Davis; Comp Sci.

ALUR, MAHESH N; Santa Teresa HS; San Jose, CA; (2); Chess Clb; Computer Clb; French Clb; VP JA; Model UN; Hon Roll; No 2 Badmntn Tm; Frnds Of Open Space; CSF; UC Berkeley; Comp Sci.

ALVARADO, ALFONSO J; Palo Verde HS; Blythe, CA; (3); Dance Clb; Varsity Clb; Bsbl; Bsktbl; Crs Cntry; ITT; Comp Pgmng.

ALVARADO, ALICE L; Oxnard HS; Oxnard, CA; (2); Church Yth Grp; Color Guard; Mrchg Band; U S CA; Lab Phy.

ALVARADO, ANNA; St Anthony HS; Carson, CA; (1); SADD; High Hon Roll.

ALVARADO, CARRIE A; Weed HS; Weed, CA; (4); 3/43; Church Yth Grp; Teachers Aide; Chorus; Pres Acad Fit Awd; Sal; CA Schltc Fed; Acad Dcthln; Cougar Rally Squad; Bank Of Amer Cert Math; Frank Bascom Schlrhsp; Coll Of Siskiyous; Ed.

ALVARADO, CELESTE D; Indio HS; Indio, CA; (1); Treas French Clb; Band; Mrchg Band; Lit Mag; Cit Awd; High Hon Roll; Hon Roll; Pres Acad Fit Awd; CSF; Optimae For Creative Writing-Trophy; Proj Pursuit-Gftd/Tlntd; Future Ldrs Of Amer Schlrshp; Sci.

ALVARADO, DANIEL; St Michaels Prep; Norwalk, CA; (3); School Play; Stage Crew; Ed Nwsp; Yrbk; Pres Soph Cls; Hon Roll; NHS; Orange Cnty Acad Dcthln.

ALVARADO, DARIUS A; Bolsa Grande HS; Garden Grove, CA; (4); 420/3000; Computer Clb; FCA; FBLA; Intnl Clb; Speech Tm; Chorus; Church Choir; School Musical; School Play; Stage Crew; CLC; Comp Pgm.

ALVARADO, DAWN P; Anderson Union HS; Palo Cedro, CA; (2); Debate Tm; FFA; Sphmr FFA Chptr Sctry; JR Yr FFA Chptr Pres 1990-91; CA Poly; Ag Bus.

ALVARADO, FRANK A; John H Glenn HS; Norwalk, CA; (4); 80/380; Church Yth Grp; Office Aide; Teachers Aide; Thesps; Stage Crew; Golf; Elks Awd; Hon Roll; Prfct Atten Awd; Southern CA Edison Co Edctnl Grant; Norwalk La Mirada Cncl PTA & CA Schl Emplyees Assn Schlrshps; De Vry Inst; Electronics.

ALVARADO, JOE; Kingsburg HS; Kingsburg, CA; (2); 5/32; Latin Clb; Crs Cntry; Socr; Trk; Hon Roll; Phy.

ALVARADO, JOSE; University HS; Los Angeles, CA; (2); Hon Roll; Prfct Atten Awd; Pilot.

ALVARADO, JUAN; Garey HS; Pomona, CA; (4); #100 In Class; Computer Clb; Debate Tm; JA; Math Tm; Scholastic Bowl; Science Clb; Mrchg Band; Ntl Merit SF; UCLA; Comp Sci.

ALVARADO, JUANITA; Modesto HS; Modesto, CA; (2); Hon Roll; Greenpeace Club; Amer Diabetes Assn; UCLA; Psych.

ALVARADO, ORILIA; Dinuba Joint Union HS; Dinuba, CA; (2); Band; Mrchg Band; Swmmng; Hon Roll; Med.

ALVARADO, RAUL PRADO; Dinuba Joint Union HS; Dinuba, CA; (3); Am Leg Boys St; Church Yth Grp; Cmnty Wkr; FFA; Office Aide; Pres Stu Cncl; Score Keeper; Cit Awd; Hon Roll; Prfct Atten Awd; CA Hwy Patrol.

ALVARADO, SABRINA; Whittier Christian HS; Pico Rivera, CA; (4); Church Yth Grp; Cmnty Wkr; Drama Clb; Office Aide; Ski Clb; Spanish Clb; Teachers Aide; School Play; Yrbk; Rep Frsh Cls; Westmont Coll; Poli Sci.

ALVARADO, SANDRA; Modoc HS; Alturas, CA; (3); 19/77; Powder Puff Ftbl; Hon Roll; Amer Indian Yth Ldrshp Conf; CA Acad Decathlon; Explorations In Creativity II; Marine Bio.

ALVARADO, SUSANA; Coachela Valley HS; Thermal, CA; (3); Computer Clb; Spanish Clb; Swmmng; Vllybl; High Hon Roll; Hon Roll; Comp Pgmr.

ALVARADO, SYLVIA; South Gate HS; South Gate, CA; (3); Computer Clb; Dance Clb; Pep Clb; Teachers Aide; Drill Tm; Off Jr Cls; Swmmng; Hon Roll.

ALVARADO, TERESA; Escondido HS; San Marcos, CA; (3); Spanish Clb; Hon Roll; Certs Schlstc Achvt Superior Effrt Cl S & Excel Effrt/Attitude; Cert Awd, Achvt; Cert Achvt Excptnl; Astronomy.

ALVARADO, VANESSA C; Mission HS; San Francisco, CA; (4); Dance Clb; French Clb; Spanish Clb; JV Cheerldng; Hon Roll; Dance; Frgn Lang; Trvl; Fshn Inst; Cosmetics.

ALVARENGA, MAYRA C; Canoga Park HS; Los Angeles, CA; (4); Church Yth Grp; Debate Tm; Drama Clb; VP French Clb; Pres Latin Clb; Capt Drill Tm; Ed Nwsp; Rep Frsh Cls; Rep Soph Cls; Rep Jr Cls; Vanguard Schlrshp; Close-Up Trip To Washington DC 89-90; Bst Stu Frgn Lang 90; Bk Amer Awd 90; USC; Bus Admin.

ALVAREZ, AILEEN; Chaminade College Prep; West Hills, CA; (2); Hosp Aide; Cheerldng; High Hon Roll; Outstndng Prfrmnc Hstry Awd; CSF; Loyola Marymount U.

ALVAREZ, ARTURO A; Mojave HS; Mojave, CA; (3); Bsbl; Bsktbl; Ftbl; Vllybl; UCLA.

ALVAREZ, AUDREY; Holy Family HS; Los Angeles, CA; (1); Art Clb; Church Yth Grp; Scl Action Clb; Law.

ALVAREZ, AURORA V; Sweetwater HS; National City, CA; (2); Pep Clb; Ski Clb; Spanish Clb; Drill Tm; Ed Nwsp; Ed Yrbk; Treas Frsh Cls; JV Vllybl; Cit Awd; Hon Roll; Std Cncl; U Of CA Los Angeles; Acting.

ALVAREZ, BONI B; Carlmont HS; Palo Alto, CA; (2); 69/268; Math Clb; School Musical; School Play; Ed Yrbk; Off Soph Cls; VP Jr Cls; Lion Awd; Amnsty Intl; CA Schlrshp Fed; Asian Amer Club; Pre Law.

ALVAREZ, CONSUELO; Gardena HS; Gardena, CA; (3); Aud/Vis; Cmnty Wkr; Pres French Clb; FTA; JA; Sec Office Aide; Sec Teachers Aide; School Musical; Variety Show; Ed Nwsp; Vlntr; Drug & Alcohol Abuse Prevention Task Force; Brthrhd/Sistrhd Natl Conf Chrstns/Jews; AZ ST U; Jrnlsm.

ALVAREZ, CORINA; Chula Vista HS; San Ysidro, CA; (2); 69/605; Pres Church Yth Grp; Cmnty Wkr; Latin Clb; Pep Clb; CSF; SDSU; Intl Reltns.

ALVAREZ, CYNTHIA; Montebello HS; Los Angeles, CA; (1); Band; Chorus; Church Choir; Mrchg Band; Pep Band; Ballet; USC; Bus Adm.

ALVAREZ, CYNTHIA S; Vallejo SR HS; Vallejo, CA; (2); Office Aide; Teachers Aide; Hon Roll; Jr NHS; NHS; Acad Exclince Cert; Acad Awds; UC Berkeley; Optometry.

ALVAREZ, DAVID R; Pius X HS; South Gate, CA; (4); Boy Scts; Church Yth Grp; Latin Clb; Letterman Clb; Math Clb; Varsity Clb; Crs Cntry; Ftbl; Socr; Trk; U Of Sthrn CA; Dntst.

ALVAREZ JR, EFRAIN; Santa Ana HS; Santa Ana, CA; (3); High Hon Roll; Hon Roll; Rancho Santiago Coll; Fire Fght.

ALVAREZ, ELIANA; Eisenhower HS; Rialto, CA; (2); Dance Clb; Drama Clb; FTA; Latin Clb; Spanish Clb; Speech Tm; Teachers Aide; School Play; Stage Crew; Off Soph Cls; Spanish Clb; UCLA; Teacher.

ALVAREZ, EVA I; Saint Michaels HS; Los Angeles, CA; (2); Spanish Clb; Flag Corp; High Hon Roll; Hon Roll; Acad Decthln; Crmnl Lawyer.

ALVAREZ, FABIOLA; El Rancho HS; Pico Rivera, CA; (2); ROTC; Hon Roll; Prfct Atten Awd; CSF Clb; UC Partners.

ALVAREZ, ISMAEL; Calexico HS; Calexico, CA; (2); Jr Statesman Of Amer; IVC; Law Enforcement.

ALVAREZ, JACQUELINE; Baldwin Park HS; Baldwin Park, CA; (4); Church Yth Grp; GAA; Key Clb; Science Clb; Spanish Clb; Treas Jr Cls; Rep Stu Cncl; Capt Var Sftbl; Var Tennis; Hon Roll; Schlr Ath For Baldwin Pk HS; Schlr Ath For Army Rsrvs; U La Verne; Ecnmcs.

ALVAREZ, JAIME; Mt Diablo HS; Concord, CA; (2); Church Yth Grp; English Clb; Hosp Aide; Latin Clb; Math Clb; Math Tm; Spanish Clb; Mrchg Band; School Play; Off Soph Cls; Concord Coll; Lawyer.

ALVAREZ, JANET; Fontana HS; Rialto, CA; (4); 79/794; Church Yth Grp; Spanish Clb; Color Guard; Drill Tm; Mgr(s); Cit Awd; Hon Roll; Prfct Atten Awd; CSF; Acad Achvt Mdls; Acctng II Cert; CA ST San Brnrdno; Acctng.

ALVAREZ, JENNIFER D; Indio HS; Indio, CA; (1); Color Guard; Flag Corp; Hon Roll; Story Wrtng; Early Outreach Stu; UC Riverside; Med.

ALVAREZ, JERRY J; William Workman HS; Valinda, CA; (2); Band; Mrchg Band; Hon Roll; Sctn Of Yr Awd Band; USC; Music.

ALVAREZ, JESSE S; Abraham Lincoln HS; San Francisco, CA; (2); Church Yth Grp; JV Bsbl; JV Ftbl.

ALVAREZ, JOHNNY M; Sunset HS; Hayward, CA; (1); Var Bsbl; JV Ftbl; Hon Roll; Babe Ruth Bsbl; Boys & Girls Club Bsktbl Team.

ALVAREZ, JOSE I; Notre Dame HS; Corona, CA; (1); Bsbl; Socr.

ALVAREZ, KATRINA I; Whittier Christian HS; Whittier, CA; (3); 4-H; Var Sftbl; UCLA; Med.

ALVAREZ, LEWIS; Arvin HS; Bakersfield, CA; (1); Intrml Bsktbl; Pro Bsktbl.

ALVAREZ, MAGDALENA; Moreau HS; San Leandro, CA; (4); Church Yth Grp; Cmnty Wkr; JV Cheerldng; L Var Pom Pon; Cit Awd; Hon Roll; Hiking & Yth Endng Hunger Clbs; UC Davis; Childrn.

ALVAREZ, MANUEL R; Bell HS; Bell, CA; (3); Church Yth Grp; Pres French Clb; Pres Key Clb; Church Choir; School Play; Variety Show; Yth In Govt-Assmbly Man; Jnr St Of Amer-Metro Dist Supv; Govt.

ALVAREZ, MARCO A; Castle Park HS; Chula Vista, CA; (3); French Clb; Lit Mag; CSF Clb & MECHA Clb; UC Berkeley; Elec Engr.

ALVAREZ, MARIA L; Calexico HS; Calexico, CA; (3); Spanish Clb; S Clb VP; Law.

ALVAREZ, MARINA; Calexico HS; Calexico, CA; (2); Imperial Valley Coll.

ALVAREZ, MARYBEL; Calexico HS; Calexico, CA; (2); Church Yth Grp; Cmnty Wkr; Hosp Aide; Key Clb; Church Choir; VP Frsh Cls; VP Soph Cls; Rep Stu Cncl; JV Sftbl; JV Capt Vllybl; SDSU; Biling Exec Secy.

ALVAREZ, MONICA L; Calexico HS; Calexico, CA; (1); Church Yth Grp; 4-H; Girl Scts; Pep Clb; Drill Tm; Flag Corp; Hon Roll; Clb Avid, Pep Clb Secy; RN.

ALVAREZ, PATRICIA; Modesto HS; Modesto, CA; (1); Chess Clb; Church Yth Grp; Cmnty Wkr; Church Choir; Careing Of Small Chldrn, Play Piano; CSU Stanislaus; Psych.

ALVAREZ, RICARDO; Arvin HS; Lamont, CA; (3); Bus Profs of Am; Computer Clb; English Clb; French Clb; FBLA; Science Clb; Spanish Clb; SADD; Var Bsbl; Var Ftbl; Bio.

ALVAREZ, ROCIO; Savanna HS; Anaheim, CA; (2); Latin Clb; Doctor.

ALVAREZ, ROSY; San Lorenzo HS; San Leandro, CA; (4); Intnl Clb; Yrbk; Ed Lit Mag; High Hon Roll; Minorty Ldrshp VP; Peer Conflct Mgmt; Girls Clb Mentorshp Pgm; UC Berkeley.

ALVAREZ, SERGIO A; Azusa HS; Azusa, CA; (3); 31/175; Bausch & Lomb Sci Awd; NHS; Cal Poly Pomona; Engrng.

ALVAREZ, TAMI MARIE; Carlsbad HS; Carlsbad, CA; (4); Chorus; Swmmng; Cit Awd; Pres Acad Fit Awd; Rotar Mrt Awd; HS Success Connection; Rutherford Awd Outstndng Achvt Physic 90; Palomar Coll; Cmmrcl Dsgn.

ALVAREZ, VANESSA K; Skyline HS; Oakland, CA; (2); Boy Scts; Hosp Aide; Intnl Clb; Band; Lit Mag; Socr; L Trk; High Hon Roll; Hon Roll; Val; CSF; Intl Clb-VP; Stanford U; Plastic Srgn.

ALVAREZ, VERONICA; Pasadena HS; Pasadena, CA; (2); Spanish Clb; Hon Roll; CA Schlrshp Fed; Math Engrng Sci Achvt; Math.

ALVEAR, CARLA J; Pacifica HS; Cypress, CA; (3); 48/260; Spanish Clb; Nwsp; Pres Jr Cls; VP Stu Cncl; Hon Roll; Vet.

ALVERDI, TINA M; Fillmore HS; Fillmore, CA; (1); Church Yth Grp; JV Bsktbl; Var Sftbl; Cit Awd; Hon Roll; Pres Acad Fit Awd.

ALVES, BOBBY L; Selma HS; Selma, CA; (2); Boy Scts; FFA; FFA; Fresno ST; Grape Frmr.

ALVES, CARRIE; Richard Gahr HS; Artesia, CA; (3); 58/460; Spanish Clb; Teachers Aide; Powder Puff Ftbl; High Hon Roll; CSF; Century 2000 Scl Stds Club; Outstndng & Dedicated Svc Awd Spnsh Club.

ALVES, DAVID T; Fred C Beyer HS; Modesto, CA; (3); Teachers Aide; Hon Roll; Prfct Atten Awd; Arch.

ALVES, JEANNA M; Atwater HS; Winton, CA; (3); Church Yth Grp; FFA; Stat Wrstlng; Hon Roll; Shw Beef Cattl, Sheep For FFA; Ag.

ALVES, JOE M; Orestimba HS; Newman, CA; (2); Hon Roll; Prfct Atten Awd.

ALVES, JOHN; James Lick HS; San Jose, CA; (4); 46/250; Church Yth Grp; Math Tm; Band; Color Guard; Jazz Band; Mrchg Band; Pep Band; School Musical; JV Ftbl; Var Golf; Radio.

ALVES, LEE; Tulare Union HS; Tipton, CA; (1); FFA; Score Keeper; Little League Sprts Announcr & Scorekpr; Sequoias Coll; Commnctns.

ALVES, SUZANA M; Mt Pleasant HS; San Jose, CA; (4); French Clb; FBLA; Teachers Aide; Phtg Yrbk; Hon Roll; San Jose ST.

ALVIDREZ, MARC E; University HS; Irvine, CA; (3); 180/551; Sec Debate Tm; Key Clb; NFL; Sec Speech Tm; Lit Mag; JV Crs Cntry; JV Trk; Hon Roll; Laureat Awd Mdlln Awd Acad Excl.

ALVIS, CYNTHIA M; Tracy HS; Tracy, CA; (2); High Hon Roll; Tutor; CA Schlrshp Fed.

ALVITE, ELAINE M; James Logan HS; Union City, CA; (3); 27/790; Church Yth Grp; Key Clb; Capt Color Guard; Mrchg Band; Stat Ftbl; Powder Puff Ftbl; JV Sftbl; Hon Roll; Baton Corp Sr Capt; Psych.

ALVIZURES, CECILIA E; El Rancho HS; Pico Rivera, CA; (4); 10/560; Computer Clb; French Clb; Intnl Clb; Spanish Clb; Cit Awd; High Hon Roll; Hon Roll; Prfct Atten Awd; 1st Pl Essay Cont; Rio Honko Coll; Teach.

ALZNAUER, ISABEL L; Glendora HS; Glendora, CA; (4); Ed Yrbk; Treas Stu Cncl; Kiwanis Awd; Pres Acad Fit Awd; CSF; TAMS Clb; Citrus Coll; Psych.

AMA III, GEORGE; Pinole Valley HS; Hercules, CA; (1); Boy Scts; Church Yth Grp; Red Cross Aide; Acpl Chr; Band; Chorus; Church Choir; Rep Frsh Cls; Ftbl; High Hon Roll; Brigham Young U; OB/Gyn.

AMADO, ARLINDA; St Genevieve HS; Arleta, CA; (3); Church Yth Grp; French Clb; Letterman Clb; Varsity Clb; Drill Tm; Rep Nwsp; Ed Yrbk; JV Bsktbl; VP Var Sftbl; Poetry; Cmmnctns.

AMADO, MOR; Lowell HS; San Francisco, CA; (3); Cmnty Wkr; School Play; Israeli Culture Club; Dentistry.

AMADO, TRACY D; Oak Grove HS; San Jose, CA; (3); Drama Clb; Chorus; School Musical; School Play; Stage Crew; Swing Chorus; Var Socr; Var Vllybl; San Jose City Coll.

AMADOR, CAROL A; La Habra HS; La Habra, CA; (2); Sec Drama Clb; Speech Tm; School Play; Stage Crew; Prfrmng Arts.

AMADOR, GLORIA MARIA; Glendale HS; Glendale, CA; (2); Service Clb; Teachers Aide; Flag Corp; Orch; Ed Yrbk; Var Crs Cntry; Var Trk; Cit Awd; Hon Roll; Pres Acad Fit Awd; Golden St Exam-Alg Hnrs; Squad Ldr-Tall Flags 89-90; L A Crss Cntry Chmpnshps-2nd Pl 89-90; CA Tech; Aerospace Engr.

AMADOR, HUMBERTO; Castle Park HS; Chula Vista, CA; (3); Drama Clb; Speech Tm; Thesps; School Play; Bsktbl; Crs Cntry; Ftbl; Tennis; UCLA; Police Ofcr.

AMADOR, MICHELE; Livingston HS; Livingston, CA; (1); Hon Roll; Prfct Atten Awd; Secy.

AMADOR, NELLY; Glendale HS; Glendale, CA; (3); 18/696; Church Yth Grp; Computer Clb; GAA; Hosp Aide; Service Clb; Speech Tm; Flag Corp; Orch; JV Co-Capt Bsktbl; Cit Awd; Dist Symph; High Tall Flags-Capt 89-90; Bio.

AMADOR, PABLO; Gonzales JR HS; Gonzales, CA; (1); Off Frsh Cls; Socr; Hon Roll.

AMADOR, RAPUNZEL JOAN R; Jefferson HS; Vallejo, CA; (4); 3/263; Pres Art Clb; Church Yth Grp; Cmnty Wkr; Dance Clb; GAA; Hosp Aide; Model UN; VP Science Clb; VP Service Clb; Band; Bnk Amer Achvmnt Awd Fnlst Appld Arts; San Mateo Tms Nwspr Cntst Awd 3rd Feature Stry; Cal Poly; Archtctl Engr.

AMADOR, RYAN J; Santa Monica HS; Brentwood, CA; (3); Band; Mrchg Band; High Hon Roll; NHS; Heal The Bay; Cngrssnl Schlr; Yng Ldrs Conf; Bio Chem.

AMAN, JENNIFER M; Amos Alonzo Stagg HS; Stockton, CA; (2); Dance Clb; Variety Show; Hon Roll; Jr NHS; NHS; Prfct Atten Awd; CA Schlrshp Fed 90-91; Jrnlsm.

AMAR, KAVITA; Beverly Hills HS; Beverly Hills, CA; (3); French Clb; Ed Nwsp; Ed Lit Mag; Rep Frsh Cls; Powder Puff Ftbl; French Hon Soc; Hon Roll; Ntl Merit SF; VP CA Schlrhsp Fed; Wnnr Coll Book Prz Brd Of Govnrs; Otstndng Bio Stu Awd; Awds Of Excllnc.

AMARAL, ERIN; Orestimba HS; Crow Landing, CA; (2); SADD; Bsktbl; Sftbl; Vllybl; Hon Roll; CSF; Stanislaus ST U.

AMARAL, KAREN E; American HS; Fremont, CA; (3); 1/350; Spanish Clb; VP SADD; Off Jr Cls; Stat Bsbl; Stat Bsktbl; High Hon Roll; Hon Roll; Sci Mdl & Spnsh Mrt Hnr Awds; Peer Cnslng; Math Teacher.

AMARAL, NANCY; Hanford Joint Union HS; Hanford, CA; (1); Acpl Chr; Chorus; Cmmrcl Arts.

AMARO, KENDRA; California HS; San Ramon, CA; (3); Ski Clb; Teachers Aide; Treas Soph Cls; Pres Jr Cls; Stu Cncl; Var Capt Cheerldng; Powder Puff Ftbl; Var Swmmng; JV Vllybl; High Hon Roll; Scrtry Interact; Acad Lttr; Gldn ST Exam Geo W/Hnrs; CA Poly; Bus Admin.

AMARO, SERGIO; Bell Gardens HS; Bell Gardens, CA; (2); Art Clb; French Clb; Yrbk; CSF & MECHA Clbs; ASB Pblc Rltns; Art.

AMASH, ROSALINDA; Saddleback HS; Santa Ana, CA; (2); Office Aide; High Hon Roll; Schl Top 5 Medal; Mdlng Classes; UCI; Psych.

AMASON JR, STEVE ROGER; Hueneme HS; Oxnard, CA; (3); Key Clb; Library Aide; Perfect Attendence; Oxnard Coll; Music Teacher.

AMATH, NORA K; Andrew Hill HS; San Jose, CA; (1); Hon Roll; UC Santa Cruz; Pediatrc Nrsng.

AMATO, DONNA DENISE; San Jose HS Acad; San Jose, CA; (2); Library Aide; Rptr Nwsp; Cit Awd; Jrnlsm; Accntnt.

AMAYA, DIANA M; Fred C Beyer HS; Modesto, CA; (1); Church Yth Grp; Temple Yth Grp; Hon Roll.

AMAYA, DORIAN; Central Union HS; Heber, CA; (3); Church Yth Grp; Teachers Aide; Chorus; Swing Chorus; Stu Cncl; Cheerldng; Spanish NHS; Imperial Valley Coll; Scndry Ed.

AMAYA, GREG R; Mission Viejo HS; Mission Viejo, CA; (4); Capt Bsktbl; Score Keeper; Capt Vllybl; NHS; Prfct Atten Awd; Pres Acad Fit Awd; US Army Reserve Schlr Athl Awd; Athl Of Yr Awd; Saferiders; U Of CA Irvine; Econ.

AMAYA, LOURDES; Bishop Amat HS; Chino, CA; (3); Hon Roll; CA ST Fullerton; Bus.

AMAYA, PATSY; San Fernando HS; San Fernando, CA; (3); Math Clb; Church Choir; Rptr Nwsp; Rptr Lit Mag; Var Tennis; Hon Roll; NHS; Art Clb; Church Yth Grp; French Clb; Top 10 Mail-In Cont Jrnlsm; Schl Sci Fair Hnrbl Mntn; Acad Decthln, Penthln; CSF Secy; NHS Treas; USC; Engrng.

AMBAS, JENNIFER; Ontario HS; Ontario, CA; (2); French Clb; Key Clb; Drill Tm; Cit Awd; High Hon Roll; Hon Roll; CSF.

AMBAYON, AARONMARK S; Mission San Jose HS; Fremont, CA; (3); Church Yth Grp; French Clb; Intnl Clb; Science Clb; Spanish Clb; SADD; Hon Roll; Filipino Clb Gen Rep; Var Badminton; Buck Sing Choy Lay Fut Kung Fu; U CA Berkeley; Pre Med.

AMBRIZ, GABRIELLA M; Nogales HS; West Covina, CA; (3); Acpl Chr; Band; Chorus; Church Choir; Jazz Band; Mrchg Band; Orch; Pep Band; Variety Show; JV Sftbl; Outstndg Marcher; Most Imprv Sftbl Player; UCLA; Psychtry.

AMBROSE, JASON S; Chadwick HS; Manhattan Beach, CA; (4); Speech Tm; School Play; Stage Crew; JV Var Bsktbl; Var Capt Ftbl; Intrml Wt Lftg; Hon Roll; Ntl Merit SF; Pres Spanish NHS; NCTE Wrtng Cmptn; Cum Laude Soc; Cmmnty Svc.

AMBROSE, JOSEPH A; Don Antonio Lugo HS; Chino, CA; (2); 3/800; Drama Clb; Thesps; School Play; High Hon Roll; Hon Roll; Biblical Stds, Lang; Pastoral.

AMBROSE, PAMELA J; Homestead HS; Sunnyvale, CA; (3); Church Yth Grp; Child Education Business.

AMBROSE, STEVE E; Channel Islands HS; Oxnard, CA; (4); 10/475; Letterman Clb; Scholastic Bowl; Science Clb; High Hon Roll; Prfct Atten Awd; CA Schlrshp Fed 4 Yrs; Mock Trial Tm 90; Asian Amer Clb 86-89; Bio Clb 87-88; Elec Engrng.

AMBROSINI, JENNIFER; Kerman HS; Fresno, CA; (2); 34/225; FFA; Letterman Clb; Office Aide; SADD; Cheerldng; Pom Pon; Swmmng; Prfct Atten Awd; Ldrshp; Prom Cmmtte; Fresno ST; Sports Med.

AMBROSIO, CHRISTINE; Bishop Amat Memorial HS; West Covina, CA; (4); 29/400; Cmnty Wkr; Math Clb; Teachers Aide; Ed Yrbk; Stu Cncl; High Hon Roll; NHS; Christn Svc Awds.

AMBROZAK, STEFFIE M; St Joseph HS; Santa Maria, CA; (3); 12/145; JV Bsktbl; Var Capt Crs Cntry; Var Capt Trk; Hon Roll; MVP Var Track 90; MVP Var Crss Cntry 89.

AMBROZEVICIUS, ISELA L; Pasadena HS; Pasadena, CA; (4); Church Yth Grp; Office Aide; Teachers Aide; Color Guard; Drill Tm; Flag Corp; Mrchg Band; Hon Roll; Pasadena City Coll; Bus Admin.

AMBROZICH, JANET F; Bishop Amat HS; Temple City, CA; (3); Pep Clb; Red Cross Aide; Teachers Aide; Co-Capt Drill Tm; Var Pom Pon; Powder Puff Ftbl; Work Experience Pgm; Bus.

AMBUSKI, REBECCA A; Chino HS; Chino, CA; (2); Drama Clb; Thesps; School Musical; School Play; Stage Crew; Hon Roll; CA ST Fullerton; Actress.

AMENDOLA, TARA L; Bullard HS; Fresno, CA; (1); French Clb; Key Clb; SADD; JV Socr; Tennis; Cit Awd; High Hon Roll; Masonic Awd; CSF; Hons Alg Golden St Ex Awd; Outstndng Sci Awd; Stanford; Bus.

AMENDOLA, THOMAS M; Carlmont HS; Belmont, CA; (3); Bsbl; Crs Cntry; Trk; Bus.

AMENTASTRO, MONICA L; Serrano HS; Phelan, CA; (3); Church Yth Grp; Drama Clb; Office Aide; SADD; Chorus; School Play; Stat Sftbl; High Hon Roll; Hon Roll; Flght Attendnt.

AMERLAN, KELLY A; Santa Rosa HS; Santa Rosa, CA; (4); Church Yth Grp; Key Clb; Teachers Aide; Chorus; Drill Tm; School Musical; Var L Cheerldng; Hon Roll; NHS; Variety Show; Gldn St Xmntn Awds; Santa Rosa JC.

AMERSI, AMIN F; Santa Monica HS; Santa Monica, CA; (3); VP Church Yth Grp; Treas French Clb; Sec FBLA; Sec Intnl Clb; High Hon Roll; Hon Roll; Tennis; UCLA; Econ.

AMERSON, LESLEY A; Lemoore HS; Stratford, CA; (3); 38/300; 4-H; FHA; Spanish Clb; JV Vllybl; Hon Roll; Accntng.

AMESBUTR, VARATORN; Chino HS; Ontario, CA; (2); Var Tennis; Hon Roll; Prfct Atten Awd; Var Badminton; UC-IRVINE; Engrng.

AMEZCUA, DANIA; Downtown Business Magnet HS; South Gate, CA; (3); Art Clb; Computer Clb; Latin Clb; Acad Dcthln Tm; USC; Civil Eng.

AMEZCUA, JUAN R; Bell HS; Maywood, CA; (4); Boy Scts; Chess Clb; Cmnty Wkr; Debate Tm; French Clb; Math Tm; Quiz Bowl; CSU Dominguez Hills; Chem.

AMEZCUA, NORMA IVONNE; Coachella Valley HS; Thermal, CA; (2); Sec Church Yth Grp; Church Choir; Var Gym; OH U; Chld Psych.

AMEZCUA, PATRICIA; Roosevelt HS; Los Angeles, CA; (3); 10/39; Aud/Vis; Debate Tm; FCA; Key Clb; Science Clb; SADD; Hon Roll; Animal Shelter Aide; CA Poly Pomona; Animal Sci.

AMICAY, SHANNON M; Los Amigos HS; Fountain Valley, CA; (3); Science Clb; Ski Clb; JV Vllybl; Hon Roll; Trvl Clb; Long Beach ST; Engr.

AMICK III, ALBERT J; Madera HS; Madera, CA; (2); Intrml JV Socr; Cal-Poly; Arch.

AMIGON, ARISTEO; Gardena HS; Gardena, CA; (2); Band; Church Choir; Prfct Atten Awd; Translator.

AMILHUSSIN, ZAHEED M; Flintridge Prep; Glendale, CA; (3); Debate Tm; JCL; Latin Clb; Band; Bsktbl; Hon Roll; UCSD.

AMINI, PEDRAM; Grossmont HS; La Mesa, CA; (1); Spanish Clb; Hon Roll; Outstndng Span Stu; Stanford; Biochem.

AMIRFAR, SAM; Leland HS; San Jose, CA; (4); 1/363; Cmnty Wkr; French Clb; Intnl Clb; JA; Library Aide; Math Tm; Teachers Aide; High Hon Roll; Pres Acad Fit Awd; Stanford U.

AMIRI, HEDY; Campolindo HS; Moraga, CA; (4); Dance Clb; High Hon Roll; Prfct Atten Awd; Pres Acad Fit Awd; Soc Wmn Engrs High Hnrs; Vienna Morgan Meml Concrto Schlrshp 1st Pl; CSF; UC Berkeley; Biochem.

AMIRIAN, NICOLE; Montclair College Prep; Hidden Hills, CA; (1); French Clb; Girl Scts; Chorus; School Play; Yrbk; Var JV Cheerldng; Gym; Pom Pon; Sftbl; Tennis; Fshn Dsgnr.

AMISCARAY, ROWENA T; Trabuco Hills HS; Mission Viejo, CA; (2); Dance Clb; Pep Clb; Spanish Clb; Swmmng; Hon Roll; Prfct Atten Awd; Pres Acad Fit Awd; Athl Awd, Acad Achvt Awd 89-90.

AMMANN, TANYA; International Studies Acad HS; San Francisco, CA; (4); 5/82; Church Yth Grp; Intnl Clb; Teachers Aide; Yrbk; High Hon Roll; Hon Roll; Sal; Intrnshp Prgm; Lang Awd Frnch; Bnk Of Amer Achvt Awd-Soc Stud; U Of San Francisco; Intl Bus.

AMMARI, RAJA S; University HS; Irvine, CA; (4); 50/500; Treas French Clb; Varsity Clb; Var Capt Socr; Intrml Tennis; French Hon Soc; High Hon Roll; Hon Roll; NHS; Lareate Awd Engl; St Hnrs Geom & Alg; Rigrs Course Stdy Awd; U Of CA Los Angeles; Law.

AMMENDOLIA, TINA M; Oakmont HS; Roseville, CA; (4); Church Yth Grp; French Clb; Service Clb; Hon Roll; NHS; Ntl Merit Ltr; Glbl Impct; Amnsty Intl.

AMMERMAN, MIKLE J; El Camino HS; Oceanside, CA; (2); Intrml Bsbl; JV Bsktbl; JV Ftbl; Intrml Tennis; Hon Roll; USC; Bus.

AMO, ROGELINE; Mt Pleasant HS; San Jose, CA; (1); Asian Club; Reading; San Jose ST U; Jrnlsm.

AMODO, KENNETH S; East Union HS; French Camp, CA; (1); 12/440; Hon Roll; Prfct Atten Awd; JV Bsktbl; JV Ftbl; Phillippine Stu Alliance Clb; Mst Outstndng Athl Awd; Arch.

AMOG, GERARDO A; Sunset HS; Fremont, CA; (3); Art Clb; ROTC; Hon Roll; Falcon Pride Award; Karate Training; Drawing; Navy.

AMOH, DAVID; La Quinta HS; Westminster, CA; (2); Var Socr; JV Trk.

AMOR, HANNAH A; Los Altos HS; Hacienda Hts, CA; (3); Color Guard; JV Vllybl; Hon Roll.

AMOREN, CHRISTETA R; Fairfield HS; Suisun City, CA; (1); Church Yth Grp; High Hon Roll; Hon Roll; Prfct Atten Awd; UC Davis; Orthondontist.

AMORES, CHARITO S; Galileo HS; San Francisco, CA; (4); Service Clb; Acpl Chr; Hon Roll; Orgnztn Filipino Ed Schlr; 2nd Pl Wnnr Galileos Crtv Wrtngs; Fnlst KPIX Chnl 5 Reprtr Of Day Cntst; San Francisco CC; Nrs.

AMORIM, VICTOR M; Don Bosco Technical Inst; Monterey Park, CA; (4); Letterman Clb; Ski Clb; Band; Church Choir; Mrchg Band; Pep Band; Yrbk; Hon Roll; NHS; Right Stuff Awd; 2nd Place Biology Awd; Big Brother Prgrm; Aerospace Engnrng.

AMORIM, VITOR; Don Bosco Technical Inst; Monterey Park, CA; (4); Letterman Clb; Ski Clb; Band; Mrchg Band; Yrbk; Hon Roll; NHS; Prfct Atten Awd; US Space Acad Right Stuff Awd; Aerospace Engrng.

AMOS, BRYAN; Mt Whitney HS; Visalia, CA; (3); Church Yth Grp; Key Clb; Math Clb; Band; Drm Mjr(t); Jazz Band; Mrchg Band; Crs Cntry; Socr; Baylor U; Aerospc Engrng.

AMOS, JONATHAN M; Desert HS; N Edwards, CA; (2); Boy Scts; Capt Math Tm; Band; Mrchg Band; Treas Frsh Cls; High Hon Roll; CSF; Engrng.

AMPARANO, MYLA R; Garfield HS; Los Angeles, CA; (3); Chess Clb; Teachers Aide; School Play; Lit Mag; High Hon Roll; Hon Roll; Law.

AMPON, RODERICK D; North Salinas HS; Salinas, CA; (4); High Hon Roll; Hon Roll; Rcvd Cert Microcomp Bus Application Cls; High Hnr Rl; Hartnell Coll; Comp Sci.

AMPOSTA, GRACELYN G; Don Antonio Lugo HS; China Hills, CA; (3); Acpl Chr; Off Frsh Cls; VP Soph Cls; Vllybl; Hon Roll; Bst Soc Stud, Prctcl Art, Chrstn Dctrn; UCLA; Nrsng.

AMRHEIN, KARL S; Turlock HS; Turlock, CA; (3); AFS; Science Clb; JV Var Swmmng; Wt Lftg; Bicycle Racing CA Fresh Cycling Team; Weight Training Turlock Fitness Club; Photo Hobby; UC Santa Cruz; Bio.

AMRHEIN, NEIL T; Oak Ridge HS; El Dorado Hills, CA; (3); 7/264; Am Leg Boys St; Math Tm; SADD; Rep Soph Cls; Var Bsbl; Var Bsktbl; High Hon Roll; CSF; Acad Ltr; Outstnd Algebra II Math Stu; Outstnd Wrld Hist Stu; Hgh Hnrs GSL Geo Awd 88; Aerospc Engrng.

AMRHEIN, TIMOTHY J; Turlock HS; Turlock, CA; (3); AFS; Am Leg Boys St; Boy Scts; Chess Clb; Church Yth Grp; Debate Tm; Drama Clb; Key Clb; NFL; Science Clb; PTSA Pres; Stu Mnth; 34th Pl Ntl Spch Trnmnt; Young Rep Pres; 5th Pl ST Speech Trnmnt; Reed Coll; Pltcl Sci.

AMRINE, HEATHER M; Apple Valley HS; Apple Valley, CA; (2); Church Yth Grp; Cmnty Wkr; Spanish Clb; Church Choir; Sec Frsh Cls; VP Soph Cls; High Hon Roll; Pep Clb; Rep Stu Cncl; Drug Use Is Life Abuse; Sheriffs Stu Advsry Cncl; Hmcmng Princess; Fnlst Facefinders Wrld Model Search; U CA; Corp Law.

AMRO, TANYA L; Clovis HS; Clovis, CA; (3); Debate Tm; Latin Clb; NFL; Office Aide; Science Clb; Speech Tm; Band; Mrchg Band; Orch; Hon Roll; 4 Sems CSF; Passed CA HS Proficiency Exm; U Of CA; Sports Med.

AMSBARY, LAURIE J; San Pasqual HS; Escondido, CA; (4); 5/355; Am Leg Aux Girls St; Church Yth Grp; Sec Treas French Clb; Stu Cncl; Var Mgr(s); Var Powder Puff Ftbl; JV Sftbl; JV Vllybl; Pres Acad Fit Awd; Parents Clb Schlrshp; Tandy Technlgy Awd Wnnr; Presdntl Schlr Baylor U; Baylor U; Engl.

AMUNDSON, DUSTY; Lakewood HS; Lakewood, CA; (2); VP Pres Debate Tm; Drama Clb; Girl Scts; JA; Office Aide; Pep Clb; Speech Tm; SADD; Teachers Aide; Drill Tm; Deabate Awd; Drama Best Actress; Stu Body Pres; UCLA; Med.

AMY, GUAN; International Studies Acad; San Francisco, CA; (4); Teachers Aide; Sftbl; Hon Roll; San Franisco ST U; Accntng.

AN, IRIS; Andrew Hill HS; San Jose, CA; (2); DECA; Math Clb; Math Tm; Acpl Chr; High Hon Roll; Hon Roll; CSF; Badmntn; UC Davis; Med.

AN, JEE YOUNG; Glendale HS; Glendale, CA; (3); Church Yth Grp; Hosp Aide; Teachers Aide; Acpl Chr; UC School; Accntng.

AN, SOK C; Sierra Vista HS; Baldwin Park, CA; (3); Chess Clb; JCL; Latin Clb; JV Bsktbl; Hon Roll; Prfct Atten Awd.

AN, TEA; Pioneer HS; San Jose, CA; (3); 10/392; Pres Church Yth Grp; Computer Clb; Math Clb; Band; JV Ftbl; High Hon Roll; Hon Roll; Pres Acad Fit Awd; Guitar Perf Music Band; Gldn St Exam Hnr Alg & Geom; Personal Rsrch Religion & Philosphy; UC Berkeley; Comp Sci.

ANACAYA, CALVIN; Orangewood Adventist Acad; Bellflower, CA; (4); Church Yth Grp; FCA; Spanish Clb; Teachers Aide; Varsity Clb; Capt Bsktbl; Capt Ftbl; Var Sftbl; Var Vllybl; Hon Roll; La Sierra Coll; Pre-Med.

ANACAYA, MARGIE; Orangewood Adventist Acad; Bellflower, CA; (3); Church Yth Grp; Drama Clb; Rptr Nwsp; Pres Jr Cls; Var Stat Bsktbl; Var Ftbl; Var Sftbl; Var Vllybl; Rep Frsh Cls; Medicine.

ANAGNOSON, STEPHANIE M; Dos Pueblos HS; Goleta, CA; (4); Pres Debate Tm; Pres French Clb; Pres Intnl Clb; Quiz Bowl; Acpl Chr; Sec VP Jr NHS; Ntl Merit SF; Smith Coll.

ANAGNOSTOPOULOS, ANDREAS H; La Jolla Country Day Schl; Del Mar, CA; (2); Church Yth Grp; Math Tm; Chorus; School Musical; High Hon Roll; ASMA, AHSMA, Sigma Cont Math Awds; Cal Poly Math Cont; Sci.

ANAND, AMBIKA; Homestead HS; Sunnyvale, CA; (4); 1/367; Debate Tm; NFL; Pres Service Clb; Speech Tm; Teachers Aide; Ed Nwsp; NHS; Ntl Merit SF; Pres Acad Fit Awd; Mst Insprtnl Bdmntn Plyr; Mck Trl.

ANAND, RONALD R; Serra HS; South San Francis, CA; (2); Cmnty Wkr; Math Clb; High Hon Roll; Hon Roll; Play Bsbl City Leag; Trivia Club; CSF; Photo Club; Anglers Club; Natl Yth Ldrshp Awd; Engrng.

ANAYA, JASON A; North Salinas HS; Salinas, CA; (2); Spanish Clb; JV Bsbl; JV Ftbl; JV Socr; Hon Roll.

ANAYA, SANDRA Y; Los Banos HS; Los Banos, CA; (3); Dance Clb; 4-H; GAA; Girl Scts; Latin Clb; Math Clb; Office Aide; Science Clb; Spanish Clb; Teachers Aide; Stanislaus ST; Child Dvlpmnt.

ANCHETA, ANDREW I; Saint Ignatius College Prep; Daly City, CA; (4); Cmnty Wkr; Hosp Aide; Band; Jazz Band; Orch; Pep Band; School Musical; UC Davis; Comp Sci.

ANCHONDO, JERRY; Imperial HS; Imperial, CA; (4); 1/95; Church Yth Grp; 4-H; FFA; Math Tm; Speech Tm; Teachers Aide; Nwsp; Yrbk; Ftbl; Golf; US Hstry Awd; Alt Boys St; US Naval Acad; Aerospc Engrng.

ANCONA, PALMIRA M; Tomales HS; Occidental, CA; (3); Hon Roll; Graphic Dsgn Art.

ANCTIL, CHRISTOPHER M; Bishop Amat Memorial HS; West Covina, CA; (2); Pres French Clb; Hon Roll; NEDT Awd; Sign Lang Awd; Stry Publshd Schl Anthology; Tchr.

ANDALIS, ALEX; Montgomery HS; San Diego, CA; (3); 1/419; Band; Mrchg Band; Rptr Nwsp; Treas Frsh Cls; JV Ftbl; Var Trk; JV Vllybl; DAR Awd; Pres Acad Fit Awd; Presdntl Acad Ftnss Awd; High Hnrs Algebra, Geom Golden St Exam.

ANDALON, ANDREA; Ontario HS; Altaloma, CA; (2); French Clb; Office Aide; Drill Tm; Rptr Nwsp; Hon Roll; CSF.

ANDALON, BELIA V; Warren HS; Downey, CA; (3); Art Clb; JA; VP SADD; JV Sftbl; Stu Recogntn Awd; Grphc Arts.

ANDAM, ERIC A; Daniel Murphy Catholic HS; Los Angeles, CA; (3); 5/80; Church Yth Grp; Quiz Bowl; Scholastic Bowl; Teachers Aide; Rep Frsh Cls; Rep Soph Cls; Hon Roll; Ntl Merit Schol; Med Technlgst.

ANDAM, ERROL A; Daniel Murphy HS; Los Angeles, CA; (2); 1/90; Church Yth Grp; Dance Clb; Scholastic Bowl; Teachers Aide; Variety Show; Pres Frsh Cls; Pres Soph Cls; JV Crs Cntry; Score Keeper; High Hon Roll; Pharmacy.

ANDARGATCHEW, DAGMAWI; Dublin HS; Dublin, CA; (3); 17/170; Intnl Clb; Varsity Clb; JV Bsktbl; Var Trk; High Hon Roll; Hon Roll; Cert Acad Excllnce Gldn St Exam Alg I & Geom; Cert Hnr Rcgntn Outstndng Achvt Acad & Schlrshp; UCLA; Engrng.

ANDAYA, MICHELLE G; Pittsburg HS; Pittsburg, CA; (2); Band; Flag Corp; Mrchg Band; Orch; School Play; Stage Crew; Var Socr; Hon Roll; Prfrmng Arts Club VP; Gldn St Exam Alg Schl Rcgntn Awd; UCLA; Bus Mgmt.

ANDERS, CHARLENE; Righetti HS; Santa Maria, CA; (3); 8/365; Church Yth Grp; German Clb; Band; Mrchg Band; Orch; Var Swmmng; Hon Roll; JV Waterpolo; Acadc Ltr; Jnr Statesmn Of Amer.

ANDERS, KENNETH D; Newark Memorial HS; Newark, CA; (3); German Clb; VP SADD; Nwsp; Treas Sr Cls; Var Capt Socr; High Hon Roll; Hon Roll; NHS; Pres Acad Fit Awd; Interact Clb; CA N Olympic Dvlpmnt St Tm Sccr.

ANDERSEN, ERIK; Canyon HS; Anaheim, CA; (4); German Clb; Letterman Clb; Math Clb; Scholastic Bowl; Mrchg Band; Orch; Off Jr Cls; Treas Sr Cls; Bsktbl; Var Ftbl; UCLA; Philosphy.

ANDERSEN, JASON J; Adolfo Camarillo HS; Camarillo, CA; (2); JV Bsbl; Hon Roll; Weight Lifting; Hunting; Fishing; Hiking; USAF Acad; Aviation.

ANDERSEN, JEFF A; Rancho Cotate HS; Rohnert Park, CA; (3); French Clb; Envrnmntl Club; Somona ST U; Math.

ANDERSEN, JULIE; Kingsburg HS; Kingsburg, CA; (3); Dance Clb; Off English Clb; Mu Alpha Theta; Pres Frsh Cls; Rep Soph Cls; Var Capt Bsktbl; Var Vllybl; Wt Lftg; High Hon Roll; Rotary Awd; Rtrys Cmp Ryl; CSF; Acad Awd 89-90; Psych.

ANDERSEN, KRISTIN; Lincoln HS; Stockton, CA; (3); 70/564; Hosp Aide; Mu Alpha Theta; Ski Clb; Spanish Clb; SADD; Var Crs Cntry; Var Trk; Hon Roll; Pres Acad Fit Awd; Politcal Clb VP; Engrng.

ANDERSEN, NEIL A; Redondo Union HS; Hermosa Beach, CA; (4); 25/389; Church Yth Grp; Key Clb; Ed Yrbk; JV Bsbl; JV Var Socr; Cit Awd; Hon Roll; Pres Acad Fit Awd; Sccr Best Defensive Jr Var & Var; CA Schlrshp Fed; Engl Teachers Awd; Long Beach ST; Bus Admin.

ANDERSEN, RACHELLE; Grace Davis HS; Modesto, CA; (2); Key Clb; VP Soph Cls; JV Cheerldng; Var Trk; UCLA; Advrtsmnt.

ANDERSEN, RODNEY A; Village Christian HS; Burbank, CA; (4); 2/120; Church Yth Grp; Math Clb; Mu Alpha Theta; Nwsp; VP Jr Cls; Rep Stu Cncl; L Capt Bsktbl; JV Ftbl; JV Socr; Sal; UC Los Angeles.

ANDERSEN, WAYNE P; Mission Viejo HS; Mission Viejo, CA; (1); 63/455; Church Yth Grp; Hon Roll.

ANDERSON, ALEXIS; Novato HS; Novato, CA; (2); Acpl Chr; Chorus; Church Choir; School Musical; School Play; Hon Roll; Super CA Music Edctrs Assoc Solo/Ensmble Fstvl; Nurse.

ANDERSON, AMBER; South Bay Lutheran HS; Los Angeles, CA; (4); Hosp Aide; Teachers Aide; Band; Yrbk; Score Keeper; Hon Roll; Bsktbl Stat; Cal ST Northridge; Dental.

ANDERSON, AMY; Mt Whitney HS; Visalia, CA; (4); Var AFS; Am Leg Aux Girls St; Church Yth Grp; Drama Clb; Math Clb; School Play; Yrbk; High Hon Roll; Pres Acad Fit Awd; Yth & Govt; UC Davis; Envrnmntl Stds.

ANDERSON, AMY C; Foothill HS; Santa Ana, CA; (4); Art Clb; English Clb; Hosp Aide; Office Aide; Science Clb; Swmmng; Hon Roll; Cnty Art Awd; UC Santa Cruz; Law.

ANDERSON, AMY MAURINE; San Marcos HS; Solvang, CA; (4); 12/303; Sec Church Yth Grp; Cmnty Wkr; Drill Tm; School Musical; Ed Yrbk; Cit Awd; High Hon Roll; Ntl Merit Ltr; Pres Acad Fit Awd; Rotary Awd; Northwestern U.

ANDERSON, ANDREA; Bullard HS; Fresno, CA; (2); ROTC; SADD; Teachers Aide; Chorus; Yrbk; Off Soph Cls; Bsbl; Bsktbl; Trk; Vllybl; Law.

ANDERSON, ANGELA Y; Kennedy HS; Richmond, CA; (3); Church Yth Grp; 4-H; ROTC; Teachers Aide; Chorus; Church Choir; Drill Tm; Yrbk; Var JV Sftbl; Jst Sy No Clb.

ANDERSON, APRYL D; St Francis HS; Sunnyvale, CA; (1); 159/388; SADD; JV Cheerldng; Hon Roll; Prfct Atten Awd; Notre Dame; Law.

ANDERSON, ARPI; Lowell HS; San Francisco, CA; (4); 32/620; Band; Jazz Band; Pres Orch; Ntl Merit Ltr; Pres Acad Fit Awd; CSF; Bk Of Amer Achvmt Cert Music; San Fran Symphony Yth Orch; Schlrshp Stu SFCM Prep Dept; U Of CA Los Angeles; Music.

ANDERSON, ASENIA T; Fremont Christian HS; Newark, CA; (3); Drama Clb; Quiz Bowl; Teachers Aide; Stage Crew; Bsktbl; Tennis; High Hon Roll; Hon Roll; Ntl Merit Ltr; U CA Coll; Phrmcy.

ANDERSON, AVELLE; Grant HS; Sacramento, CA; (3); Church Yth Grp; Debate Tm; Science Clb; Spanish Clb; Speech Tm; Teachers Aide; Church Choir; Off Frsh Cls; High Hon Roll; Hon Roll; UC Davis Early Outreach Prtnrshp; MESA; GSU Hgh Ability 90; Gramblin ST U; Bus Acctg.

ANDERSON, BOB; Pacifica HS; Garden Grove, CA; (4); 11/285; Am Leg Boys St; Off Church Yth Grp; Pep Clb; Pres Stu Cncl; Var Bsbl; Var Capt Ftbl; Var Socr; Wt Lftg; Elks Awd; High Hon Roll; WASC Cmmtte Head; Mariner Of Mnth; Most Worthy Mariner; U Of CA Santa Barb; Bus Mgmt.

ANDERSON, BRETT D; Montgomery HS; Santa Rosa, CA; (3); FBLA; Hon Roll; Accntng.

ANDERSON, BRITT; Francis W Parker HS; San Diego, CA; (2); Chorus; School Musical; School Play; Ed Yrbk; Pres Soph Cls; Hon Roll; Safe Rides Pgm; Latin Hnr Soc; Duke U; Bus Admin.

ANDERSON, BRITTANIE D; Pinole Valley HS; Pinole, CA; (3); Church Yth Grp; Dance Clb; NFL; Teachers Aide; High Hon Roll; Hon Roll; Kiwanis Awd; Azusa Pacific; Psych.

ANDERSON, CARLY; Foothill HS Santa Ana, CA; (3); 19/328; Church Yth Grp; Math Clb; JV Crs Cntry; Var L Trk; JV Vllybl; High Hon Roll; 3rd Pl Orange Cnty Engr & Sci Fair Envrnmntl Div; 3 Yr Top Scholar 4.0 GPA; Awd Of Excl Tech Ed Engr; Engr.

ANDERSON, CAROLYN T; Ontario HS; Ontario, CA; (3); Church Yth Grp; Cmnty Wkr; Key Clb; Office Aide; Spanish Clb; Teachers Aide; Church Choir; Trk; Hon Roll; Score Keeper; Azusa Pacific U; Cmmnctns.

ANDERSON, CHARLES; Desert Christian HS; Palmdale, CA; (1); Church Yth Grp; English Clb; JA; Math Clb; Science Clb; Spanish Clb; Cit Awd; Hon Roll; UCLA; Anstslgst.

ANDERSON, CHRISTINA B; Hilltop HS; Chula Vista, CA; (2); Natl Beta Clb; Spanish Clb; Speech Tm; Hon Roll; Renaissance Club; Outstndng Achvt Awd; Gen Dynamics Club; Engl FLAGS Awd Outstndng Achvt; Crt Rprtr.

ANDERSON, CHRISTOPHER; Bishop Amat Memorial HS; Rowland Hts, CA; (4); 69/400; Teachers Aide; Pres Band; Mrchg Band; School Musical; Hon Roll; Ntl Merit Ltr; Natl Hspnc Schlr Awds Pgm; Natl Sci Olympd Chem & US Hstry; Bio Chemst.

ANDERSON, CRAIG W; Foothill HS; Santa Ana, CA; (3); Church Yth Grp; German Clb; Key Clb; Crs Cntry; Var L Trk; Wt Lftg; High Hon Roll; CSF Seal Bearer; German Hnr Soc; Safe Rides; Dentistry.

ANDERSON, DAVID; Holtville HS; Holtville, CA; (4); 3/110; Chess Clb; Church Yth Grp; FCA; Math Clb; Quiz Bowl; Teachers Aide; Varsity Clb; Band; Chorus; Jazz Band; Presidents & Chorus Schlrshps; Coll Band CA Grant; All League Bsktbl; Azusa Pacific U; Phys Educ.

ANDERSON, DAVID B; Imperial HS; Duarte, CA; (2); Church Yth Grp; Chorus; School Musical; Intrml Bsktbl; Intrml Vllybl; Wt Lftg; Cit Awd; High Hon Roll; Hon Roll; Geom Awd; Presdntl Phys Ftnss Awd; Embry-Riddle U; Aeronautic Sci.

ANDERSON, DAVID W; Pacifica HS; Garden Grove, CA; (2); Off Church Yth Grp; Drama Clb; Var L Bsbl; JV Capt Ftbl; Wt Lftg; Hon Roll; CSF; Acctng.

ANDERSON, DEANNA M; Eisenhower HS; Rialto, CA; (2); Band; Chorus; Vllybl; Trmpt; Law.

ANDERSON, DENA B; Lincoln HS; Stockton, CA; (3); 43/550; Drama Clb; Teachers Aide; Thesps; School Play; Stage Crew; High Hon Roll; Hon Roll; Delta JC; Frgn Lang.

ANDERSON, DENNIS; Edison HS; Costa Mesa, CA; (3); Church Yth Grp; JA; Var Ftbl; Var Trk; Wt Lftg; Acad Booster Clb Awd-Math Dept; 1st Team All Sunset Leag-Defnsv End-Vrsty Ftbl; Schlrs-In-Training; Phys Therapy.

ANDERSON, DERON G; Yosemite Union HS; Oakhurst, CA; (2); Am Leg Boys St; Church Yth Grp; Ski Clb; Bsbl; Bsktbl; Score Keeper; Hon Roll; Ad.

ANDERSON, DEVANIE M; Yreka HS; Yreka, CA; (4); 14/142; Church Yth Grp; Cmnty Wkr; Debate Tm; Spanish Clb; Speech Tm; Band; Jazz Band; Mrchg Band; Orch; Pep Band; Voctnl Arts Publc Spkng 1st Pl; Humboldt ST U; Jrnlsm.

ANDERSON, ERIC C; Palo Verde HS; Blythe, CA; (4); Drama Clb; 4-H; FFA; Hon Roll; Mck Trl; St Frmr Dgree; Cal Poly Pomona; Vet Med.

ANDERSON, ERICA L; Victorvalley HS; Victorville, CA; (3); Church Yth Grp; Cmnty Wkr; FTA; Var Capt Bsktbl; Var Trk; JV Vllybl; Hon Roll; Black Stu Union; NAACP; Cal ST San Berdo; Chld Dvlpmnt.

ANDERSON, ERRIN E; Bullard HS; Fresno, CA; (1); Cmnty Wkr; French Clb; Key Clb; SADD; High Hon Roll; CSF; Cmnty Natl Asstnce Leagues Guild; Stanford; Bio.

ANDERSON, GAISHA M; Washington Prep HS; Los Angeles, CA; (3); Pres Church Yth Grp; Girl Scts; Pep Clb; Rep Soph Cls; Rep Jr Cls; Prfct Atten Awd; Marthonians Clb; Chrch Usher Brd Yth Pres; Tuskeegee; Child Dev.

ANDERSON, GUY W; Dos Palos HS; Dos Palos, CA; (2); Nwsp; Tennis; San Francisco Acad Art; Adv.

ANDERSON, HARLEAN; College Park HS; Pleasant Hill, CA; (3); 39/288; French Clb; Latin Clb; Varsity Clb; Var L Tennis; Hon Roll; Schlr Athl 88-89; Golden St Exam 1st Yr Alg Hgh Hnrs, Geom Hnrs; Embry-Riddle; Aerontcl Sci.

ANDERSON, HEATHER G; Sylmar HS; Sylmar, CA; (3); Church Yth Grp; FFA; Key Clb; SADD; High Hon Roll; Hon Roll; Piano; Chorus; Gymnstcs; Girl Scouts; Bus.

ANDERSON, HEATHER L; Clovis HS; Clovis, CA; (3); 57/670; FCA; Chorus; Sec Frsh Cls; JV Bsktbl; Var Trk; JV Var Vllybl; Hon Roll; Fresno Cnty Yng Wmn Of Yr 90; Vlybl For Sierra Pacific VB Clb All League, All Tourn; Bus.

ANDERSON, HEATHER L; Ofarrell Schl Of Crtv & Prfrmn Arts; San Diego, CA; (1); 12/235; Cmnty Wkr; Lit Mag; JV Bsktbl; JV Vllybl; High Hon Roll; CSF; Vlntr Mayor Maureen O'connor Soviet Arts Fest & Intl Frndshp Clb & Booster HS Clb; Vet.

ANDERSON, HOLLY E; O'farrell SCPA; San Diego, CA; (2); 1/151; Dance Clb; Drama Clb; School Musical; School Play; Stage Crew; Variety Show; Ed Lit Mag; High Hon Roll; Hon Roll; Pres Acad Fit Awd; Choreographer Modern Dance; Env & Peace Movements; UC-SANTA Cruz; Env Stds.

ANDERSON, INGRID A.; Lincoln HS; Stockton, CA; (3); 79/538; Church Yth Grp; Latin Clb; Mu Alpha Theta; Teachers Aide; Drill Tm; Flag Corp; Crs Cntry; Trk; Hon Roll; Jobs Dghtrs Bethel 277; UCSD; Bio Sci.

ANDERSON, JAMES D; Victory Christian Schls; Carmichael, CA; (2); Church Yth Grp; Pep Clb; Science Clb; Chorus; School Play; Pres Frsh Cls; Var Bsbl; Var JV Bsktbl; Hon Roll; Point Coma Nazerne Coll; Med.

ANDERSON, JARED R; Victor Valley HS; Victorville, CA; (2); Ftbl; Trk; Wt Lftg; Hon Roll; Prfct Atten Awd; Pres Acad Fit Awd.

ANDERSON, JASON; San Diego HS; San Diego, CA; (3); Cmnty Wkr; Intnl Clb; Model UN; Spanish Clb; Rep Soph Cls; Rep Jr Cls; Rep Sr Cls; Var JV Bsktbl; JV Crs Cntry; Var Capt Trk; Exchange Student Mexico/Soviet Union; Sci Fair Finalist; Record Holder Decathlonbaccalaureate; Webster U; Intl Law, Foreign Sv.

ANDERSON, JASON C; Fred C Beyer HS; Modesto, CA; (3); Var Ftbl; Var Trk; Hon Roll; Modesto JC; Forestry.

ANDERSON, JASON E; Pleasant Valley SR HS; Chico, CA; (4); Am Leg Boys St; Pres Church Yth Grp; Letterman Clb; Co-Ed Nwsp; Ed Yrbk; Treas Frsh Cls; Pres Jr Cls; Pres Stu Cncl; JV Bsktbl; Var Trk; U Of Notre Dame; Bus.

ANDERSON, JEFFREY; San Ramon Valley HS; Danville, CA; (1); Band; Mrchg Band; Orch; Pep Band; School Play; Georgetown; Criminal Law.

ANDERSON, JEFFRY R; Huntington Beach HS; Huntington Bch, CA; (3); Boy Scts; Diving; Hon Roll; Surf Team; UCSB; Aerospace Engr.

ANDERSON, JELANI A; Hayward HS; Hayward, CA; (3); Church Yth Grp; ROTC; Band; Drill Tm; Orch; JV Bsbl; JV Var Bsktbl; Var Ftbl; Tm Cptn JV Bsktbl Tm; Aviation.

ANDERSON, JENNA M; San Leandro HS; San Leandro, CA; (2); Ski Clb; VP Frsh Cls; JV Var Vllybl; Hon Roll; Moorpark U; Anml Trnr.

ANDERSON, JENNIFER L; Serrano HS; Wrightwood, CA; (3); Pres Church Yth Grp; Chorus; Church Choir; Crs Cntry; Trk; Hon Roll; Pres Acad Fit Awd; Ricks Coll; Nrsng.

ANDERSON, JENNIFER M; Sonora Union HS; Sonora, CA; (3); #16 In Class; Church Yth Grp; French Clb; Girl Scts; Band; Jazz Band; Mrchg Band; Pep Band; School Musical; Hon Roll; Bethany Coll; Yth Ministries.

ANDERSON, JENNIFER R; Village Christian Schls; Burbank, CA; (3); Teachers Aide; Yrbk; Mgr Ftbl; Powder Puff Ftbl; Stat Sftbl; Stat Trk; CSF; Ltrgirls Clbc; Accntng.

ANDERSON II, JOEL M; Chaffey HS; Ontario, CA; (3); Stu Cncl; Bsbl; Capt Bsktbl; Ftbl; High Hon Roll; Prfct Atten Awd; MVP Bsktbl; Best Offnsv Plyr Bsktbl; Set 3 Pnt Recrd Schl Bsktbl; UNLV; Prof Bsktbll.

ANDERSON, JOHANNA; Arcata HS; Arcata, CA; (1); VP Frsh Cls; Top 10 Frosh; Humboldt ST U; Archlgy.

ANDERSON, JOHN C; P U C Preparatory Schl; Angwin, CA; (2); Church Yth Grp; Ski Clb; Band; Pres Soph Cls; VP Stu Cncl; Var Intrml Bsktbl; Var Intrml Ftbl; Var Intrml Sftbl; Intrml Vllybl; Woodwind Quintet; String Quartet; Pacific Union Coll; Med.

ANDERSON, JONATHAN D; Live Oak HS; Live Oak, CA; (2); Computer Clb; Spanish Clb; Variety Show; Pres Frsh Cls; Pres Soph Cls; Pres Jr Cls; Bsktbl; Ftbl; Trk; High Hon Roll.

ANDERSON, KARI; Dublin HS; Dublin, CA; (3); 29/158; Sec Girl Scts; JV Bsktbl; Var Trk; Hon Roll; Law.

ANDERSON, KARRIE A; Temecula Valley HS; Temecula, CA; (3); Church Yth Grp; Drama Clb; Teachers Aide; Yrbk; JV Var Bsktbl; JV Var Sftbl; JV Vllybl; Cit Awd; Hon Roll; 1st Aid Asst; Patriotic Pgm; Mrt Awd 2 Yrs; Tchng.

ANDERSON, KATE EDEN; Sonoma Valley HS; Sonoma, CA; (3); AFS; Church Yth Grp; Powder Puff Ftbl; JV Var Sftbl.

ANDERSON, KELLY O; Oakmont HS; Roseville, CA; (2); Pres Church Yth Grp; Dance Clb; Drill Tm; Hon Roll; Active W/Church Actvts; Scorekeeper Ltl Leag Bsbl; Sacramento ST; Educ.

ANDERSON, KEN E; La Habra HS; Whittier, CA; (3); Science Clb; Teachers Aide; High Hon Roll; Hon Roll; Cal Poly Pomona; Engr.

ANDERSON, KENTON L; Cordova SR HS; Rancho Cordova, CA; (3); Boy Scts; Church Yth Grp; FBLA; Model UN; Band; Pep Band; Swmmng; Wrstlng; NHS; Srfng; Water Skiing; UC Santa Cruz; Marine Biolgst.

ANDERSON, KEONI C; Eisenhower HS; Rialto, CA; (3); Church Yth Grp; Hon Roll; Stu Of Mnth 1990; Math.

ANDERSON, KEVIN; Kerman HS; Kerman, CA; (3); 17/130; Aud/Vis; Debate Tm; FTA; German Clb; Letterman Clb; Math Tm; Quiz Bowl; Science Clb; Service Clb; Band; Rotary Ldrshp Camp; City Srvce/Recrtn Cncl Stu Cmssnr; Cal Poly San Luis Obispo; Mech.

ANDERSON, KIMBERLY S; Alta Loma HS; Alta Loma, CA; (3); Dance Clb; French Clb; Pep Clb; Off Jr Cls; Stu Cncl; Cheerldng; Score Keeper; Cit Awd; High Hon Roll; Rotary Awd; UCLA; Frnch Prfssr.

ANDERSON, KRISHNA K; Pius X HS; Compton, CA; (3); 15/180; GAA; Chorus; Bsktbl; Capt Trk; Hon Roll; PAHA; Prom Comm Pblcity; Howard U; Obstetrcn.

ANDERSON, KRISTI; Carondelet HS; Antioch, CA; (3); Church Yth Grp; Dance Clb; Drama Clb; Pep Clb; SADD; School Musical; Cheerldng; Pom Pon; Powder Puff Ftbl; Hon Roll; USTA St, Wstrn Rgnl Chmpn Twrlr 90; Religious Stds Awd 90; St Chmpn Dancer 90; U Of The Pacific; Paralegal.

ANDERSON, KRISTI; Norte Vista HS; Riverside, CA; (2); Dance Clb; Pep Clb; Pres Frsh Cls; Rep Soph Cls; Off Jr Cls; Cheerldng; Trk; Hon Roll; Hist Day Pgm; UCLA; Law.

ANDERSON, KRISTIN E; Irvine HS; Irvine, CA; (3); Dance Clb; Drama Clb; Capt Pep Clb; SADD; Yrbk; Off Frsh Cls; Off Sr Cls; Var Capt Cheerldng; Stat Wrstlng; Diving; Orange Coast Coll.

ANDERSON, KRISTINA; Cajon HS; San Bernardino, CA; (3); Church Yth Grp; SADD; Hon Roll; Prfct Atten Awd; Eng.

ANDERSON, KRYSTIN L; Woodcrest Christian HS; Sun City, CA; (3); Pres Church Yth Grp; Teachers Aide; Band; Chorus; Rep Jr Cls; VP Sr Cls; Stat Bsbl; Var Sftbl; Var Vllybl; High Hon Roll; Biola U; Psych.

ANDERSON, KURT; Kerman HS; Kerman, CA; (3); 13/133; German Clb; Letterman Clb; Math Tm; Office Aide; Scholastic Bowl; Science Clb; Teachers Aide; School Play; Variety Show; Treas Frsh Cls; Ldrshp Pride Awd; Odyssey Of The Mind 2nd Pl; Zone Fnlst; Yth Summit Teens In Action Facilitator 90; U Of CA; Psych.

ANDERSON, LAURA C; Central Union HS; El Centro, CA; (1); Sec Hosp Aide; Flag Corp; Hon Roll; CSF.

ANDERSON, LINDA; Leuzinger HS; Gardena, CA; (4); Spanish Clb; Band; Chorus; Mrchg Band; VP Of Jobs For Amer Grads; Dntstry.

ANDERSON, LISA A; Redwood HS; Visalia, CA; (3); JCL; Latin Clb; Var Socr; Var Sftbl; Hon Roll; Sccr Awd 1st WYL RHS Chmps Sccr; U Of Davis; Pre-Med.

ANDERSON, LISA K; Sacramento HS; Sacramento, CA; (2); 1/500; L Co-Capt Swmmng; Hon Roll; Rectnl Swmmng & Soccer.

ANDERSON, MARCI DEANN; Glen A Wilson HS; Hacienda Heights, CA; (4); Library Aide; Teachers Aide; VP Drill Tm; Pres Acad Fit Awd; Most Outstanding JR Drill Team/Highest GPA 88-89; CADTD All Star 89-90; Lg Military Lg Dance Med; Cal St Fullerton; Bus Mgmt.

ANDERSON, MARK B; University HS; Irvine, CA; (2); 90/500; JCL; Teachers Aide; Swmmng; Hon Roll; Acad Decathlon; Water Polo; Med.

ANDERSON, MARK K; Mt Carmel HS; San Diego, CA; (1); Acad League Quiz Bowl; Knights Of Columbus Good Ctzn Awd; Rancho Bernardo Smmr Bsktbll JV Tm; Med.

ANDERSON, MARTIA; North Valley Christian Schl; Anderson, CA; (4); 2/10; Church Yth Grp; Teachers Aide; Church Choir; School Play; Sec Jr Cls; Pres Sr Cls; JV Var Sftbl; JV Var Vllybl; High Hon Roll; Pres Acad Fit Awd; Sunday Schl Teacher; Awana Ldr; Freedoms Song; Shasta Bible Coll; Missionary.

ANDERSON, MARYANN M; Valley HS; Sacramento, CA; (4); 97/435; Church Yth Grp; Pres Dance Clb; FTA; Pres Varsity Clb; Yrbk; Stu Cncl; Capt Cheerldng; Capt Gym; Elks Awd; Prfct Atten Awd; Hghst Grad Awd Silver Viking; CA ST U; Lbrl Studs.

ANDERSON, MAURINE; San Marcos HS; Solvang, CA; (4); 12/300; Cmnty Wkr; Co-Capt Drill Tm; School Musical; Ed Yrbk; Cit Awd; High Hon Roll; Ntl Merit Ltr; Pres Acad Fit Awd; Rotary Awd; CSF Sealbearer Life Mem; Northwestern U; Econ.

ANDERSON, MELE; Hilmar JR/Sr HS; Hilmar, CA; (1); 5/140; AFS; Art Clb; Church Yth Grp; Drama Clb; Pep Clb; SADD; Yrbk; JV Cheerldng; JV Sftbl; Pres Acad Fit Awd; Frgn Lang Clb.

ANDERSON, MELISSA; Torrey Pines HS; Del Mar, CA; (4); 30/400; Dance Clb; French Clb; SADD; Co-Capt Drill Tm; Off Sr Cls; Pepsi Ldrshp Stu Of Yr 90; Miss Drill Tm Intl Japan; WASC Stu Comm Chrprsn; U Of CA Los Angeles; Pol Sci.

ANDERSON, MICHAEL D; Casa Roble HS; Orangevale, CA; (2); 3/461; French Clb; Science Clb; Tennis; High Hon Roll; NHS; Gold Card 4 Times In Renaissance Pgm; Engl, Span, Fr.

ANDERSON, MICHAEL G; Hamilton Union HS; Hamilton City, CA; (3); 4-H; FFA; SADD; Band; Var Bsbl; JV Var Bsktbl; Score Keeper; Var Trk; Hon Roll; Asst Coach-Little League; Math.

ANDERSON, MICHAEL T; Chino HS; Chino, CA; (3); Science Clb; Ski Clb; Spanish Clb; JV Var Bsbl; JV Var Bsktbl; High Hon Roll; Hon Roll; Prfct Atten Awd; Pres Schlr; CA ST U Fullerton; Bus.

ANDERSON, NICOLE; Winters HS; Winters, CA; (2); FFA; JV Bsktbl; JV Vllybl; Hon Roll.

ANDERSON, PAGE R; Hiram Johnson HS; Sacramento, CA; (4); Church Yth Grp; Cmnty Wkr; Teachers Aide; Church Choir; JV Socr; Hon Roll; Tchng.

ANDERSON, PAMELA; Sonora HS; Sonora, CA; (4); 20/275; Am Leg Aux Girls St; Church Yth Grp; Ski Clb; Spanish Clb; Pres Frsh Cls; VP Stu Cncl; Elks Awd; Opt Clb Awd; Acad Decathlon De-Athlete; CSF; Surgeon.

ANDERSON, PATRICIA C; O'farrell Schl; San Diego, CA; (1); #1 In Class; Church Yth Grp; High Hon Roll; Jr NHS; Prfct Atten Awd; Pres Acad Fit Awd; Pres CJHS; Dance Club, Jazz; Coca-Cola Fashion Club; Pediatrician.

ANDERSON, PHILIP B; King City HS; King City, CA; (2); Church Yth Grp; SADD; Hon Roll; Golden St Exam High Hnrs; Commercl Clb; Friday Night Live.

ANDERSON, RAE D; Arlington HS; Riverside, CA; (2); 30/530; Dance Clb; Drama Clb; Thesps; School Musical; School Play; Stage Crew; Hon Roll; NHS; Advsry Cnsl; Stu Mth Socl Stud; Acad Dcthln Tm 90-91; Arlington; Chem Engr.

ANDERSON, REBECCA L; San Pasqual HS; Escondido, CA; (2); Church Yth Grp; Cmnty Wkr; GAA; Hosp Aide; Pep Clb; JV Tennis; High Hon Roll; Hon Roll; Prfct Atten Awd; Rotary Awd; Jr Var Tnns GPA Awd, Ltr; Hnr Awd Golden St Exam In Alg; U Of CA; Dsgn.

ANDERSON, RIO; South Fork HS; Redway, CA; (3); Cmnty Wkr; Drama Clb; Varsity Clb; Bsktbl; Var JV Crs Cntry; Socr; Trk; Hon Roll; Kiwanis Awd; Humbolt ST; Road Runner.

ANDERSON, ROBERT H; Foothill HS; Santa Ana, CA; (2); Ftbl; JV Socr; Skaetboarding; UC San Diego; Math.

ANDERSON, ROLEENA Y; Roosevelt The School Of The Arts; Selma, CA; (2); Dance Clb; Drama Clb; Chorus; JR LARCS.

ANDERSON, SEAN C; Mira Loma HS; Sacramento, CA; (1); 19/283; Math Clb; Math Tm; Science Clb; Socr; Trk; Elks Awd; Hon Roll; Lion Awd; Sci Olympied Tm; Sch Rep CAL ST U Chemcl Instr Course; Teaching Asst Acad Talent Srch 90; Bus.

ANDERSON, SHAD; Coast Christian HS; Torrance, CA; (3); Rep Jr Cls; Var Bsktbl; High Hon Roll; Art.

ANDERSON, SILVIA; Bishop Montgomery HS; Lomita, CA; (3); Church Yth Grp; Cmnty Wkr; Dance Clb; Intnl Clb; Letterman Clb; Office Aide; Red Cross Aide; Service Clb; SADD; Teachers Aide; Dance Team; Drill Team; Color Guard; Flag Team; Band Seamstress; Rifle Line; Marymoung.

ANDERSON, STEVEN M; Oroville HS; Oroville, CA; (4); 1/189; Am Leg Boys St; Boy Scts; Band; Drm Mjr(t); Treas Jr Cls; Pres Sr Cls; Var Socr; JV Tennis; Eagle Scout; UC Davis; Cvl Engrng.

ANDERSON, SUSAN R; Analy HS; Sebastopol, CA; (3); 1/234; Church Yth Grp; High Hon Roll; Pres Acad Fit Awd.

ANDERSON, T JASON; Bishop O'dowd HS; Alameda, CA; (2); Math Clb; Math Tm; Stage Crew; JV Var Swmmng; High Hon Roll; NEDT Awd; Peace Grp; Amesty Intl; CA Schlrshp Fed.

ANDERSON, TAMARA C; Oakmont HS; Roseville, CA; (2); Drama Clb; Ski Clb; Hon Roll; American River JC; Arch.

ANDERSON, TANYA R; Piedmont HS; Piedmont, CA; (3); Church Yth Grp; Acpl Chr; Chorus; Orch; School Musical; Variety Show; Cheerldng; Command Perfrmnc Awd CMEA; Interact Club Div Of Rotary Pres; Musical Theatre.

ANDERSON, TARA L; Willits HS; Willits, CA; (2); Church Yth Grp; Church Choir; Cit Awd; Hon Roll; Refree Yth Sccr; BYU.

ANDERSON, TE-NICHA K; Oakland Technical HS; Oakland, CA; (2); Church Yth Grp; Cmnty Wkr; ROTC; Teachers Aide; Acpl Chr; Church Choir; School Musical; School Play; Stage Crew; Hon Roll; MESA; Incentive Awd; Columbia U; Bus Admin.

ANDERSON, TEMERA L; Highlands HS; Sacramento, CA; (3); Cmnty Wkr; Chorus; School Musical; JV Cheerldng; Capt Pom Pon; Var Trk; Hon Roll; Dance Tchr; Davis; Psych.

ANDERSON, TIFFANY L; Paramount HS; Paramount, CA; (1); Mrchg Band; Hon Roll; Tchr.

ANDERSON, TIFFANY L; Richard Gahr HS; Cerritos, CA; (3); 61/408; Girl Scts; Hosp Aide; Pep Clb; Band; Drm Mjr(t); Var Cheerldng; Powder Puff Ftbl; Score Keeper; Var Capt Tennis; Music Awd; Mst Artstc Ic Sktr; Mst Imrpvd All Arnd Tennis Plyr; U Of CO; Physcn.

ANDERSON, TOM R; Santa Barbara HS; Santa Barbara, CA; (3); Church Yth Grp; Cmnty Wkr; Key Clb; Library Aide; Science Clb; Ski Clb; SADD; Varsity Clb; JV Var Bsbl; JV Bsktbl; JV Vrsty Water Polo; Santa Cruz Bk Schlrshp Awd Hist; Med.

ANDERSON, TORI R; San Dieguito HS; Encinitas, CA; (2); Girl Scts; Hosp Aide; Drill Tm; School Play; Ed Lit Mag; Var Cheerldng; JV Fld Hcky; High Hon Roll; Hon Roll; Prfct Atten Awd; CSF; Bus.

ANDERSON, TRACEY J; James Lick HS; San Jose, CA; (3); Cmnty Wkr; Debate Tm; Pep Clb; Speech Tm; Flag Corp; Nwsp; Rep Stu Cncl; Bsktbl; Hon Roll; Death Valley Field Stds Pgm; CA Symposium On Politics/Govt; San Jose Rotary Camp Enterprise Schlrshp; UC Davis; Vet.

ANDERSON, TRAN; Mt Diablo HS; W Pittsburg, CA; (3); Bus Profs of Am; Church Yth Grp; JA; JCL; Scholastic Bowl; Ski Clb; Varsity Clb; Chorus; School Musical; Swing Chorus; Ping Pong; UC Davis; Elec Engr.

ANDERSON, VALERIE P; El Toro HS; El Toro, CA; (4); Pres Cmnty Wkr; Band; Chorus; Mrchg Band; School Musical; Hon Roll; Natl Schl Choral Awd; John Phillip Sousa Awd-Band; Vocal Music Stu Of Mnth; Azusa Pacific U; Music Ed.

ANDERSON, VINCENT H; Adolfo Camarillo HS; Camarillo, CA; (2); Boy Scts; Church Yth Grp; JV Socr; Var Vllybl; High Hon Roll; Spanish Achvmnt Arwd; CA Poly Tech; Arch.

ANDERTON, ROXANN L; Clovis West HS; Clovis, CA; (3); FBLA; Intnl Clb; Ski Clb; High Hon Roll; Hon Roll; UC Santa Barbara; Bus.

ANDO, TRACI; Sanger HS; Fresno, CA; (3); Pep Clb; Science Clb; Spanish Clb; Color Guard; Rptr Nwsp; Yrbk; Rep Frsh Cls; Stu Cncl; Var Pom Pon; High Hon Roll; World Baton Twirling Chmpn 90; CA Schlrshp Fed; Asian Clb; Mech Engrng.

ANDOLINA, LISA MARIE; Foothill HS; Sacramento, CA; (3); SADD; Teachers Aide; School Play; Powder Puff Ftbl; Swmmng; Davis; Law.

ANDRADE, ALLEN T; Live Oak HS; Morgan Hill, CA; (3); 53/300; Var Bsbl; Pres Acad Fit Awd; Construction.

ANDRADE, ALMA; Southwest HS; San Ysidro, CA; (2); Office Aide; Teachers Aide; Cit Awd; High Hon Roll; Schlrshp Medal; Elem Tchr.

ANDRADE, ALMA R; Santiago HS; Santa Ana, CA; (2); French Clb; GAA; Spanish Clb; Acpl Chr; Chorus; School Musical; Off Soph Cls; Fld Hcky; Sftbl; Capt Vllybl; MVP Offns Sftbl; Capt Vllybl Tm; USC; Arch.

ANDRADE, ANNA; Dos Palos HS; Firebaugh, CA; (2); Spanish Clb; SADD; Medcl.

ANDRADE, ANTHONY C; Independence HS; San Jose, CA; (3); Pres Latin Clb; VP Stu Cncl; Crs Cntry; Hon Roll; U & Coll Opprtnty Rep; Early Acadmc Outreach Pgm; Santa Clara; Law.

ANDRADE, CHRISTOPHER M; La Sierra HS; Riverside, CA; (1); Var Swmmng; Hon Roll; Stanford; Marine Bio.

ANDRADE, CINDY; Turlock Christian HS; Hughson, CA; (3); Church Yth Grp; Teachers Aide; Church Choir; Mrchg Band; Pres Frsh Cls; Rep Stu Cncl; Var JV Cheerldng; High Hon Roll.

ANDRADE, COURTNEY E; Esperanza HS; Banning, CA; (2); Church Yth Grp; Cmnty Wkr; Computer Clb; Library Aide; Office Aide; Teachers Aide; Chorus; Powder Puff Ftbl; Cit Awd; Hon Roll; UCLA; Bus Comp.

ANDRADE, DANIEL; Garfield HS; Los Angeles, CA; (2); Prfct Atten Awd; Math.

ANDRADE, DARLENE I; Don Antonio Lugo HS; Ontario, CA; (3); Spanish Clb; Hon Roll; Wrtng Shrt Strs; Boston U; Commnctns.

ANDRADE, DIANE M; Oakdale HS; Oakdale, CA; (2); Drama Clb; SADD; School Play; Fri Night Live; Stanislaus; Actress.

ANDRADE, ELIZABETH; Oakdale HS; Oakdale, CA; (2); CSF; Stanislaus ST; Bus Mgmt.

ANDRADE, GEORGINA; Corcoran HS; Corcoran, CA; (4); 6/116; Church Yth Grp; Science Clb; SADD; Teachers Aide; Varsity Clb; Band; Mrchg Band; Orch; Pep Band; Rep Frsh Cls; Wrld Ptry Achvd Gldn Pt Awd; Hnrb Mntn & Awd Of Mrt; Scripps Coll; Prnt Brdcst Media.

ANDRADE, ISAAC F; Sierra Vista HS; Baldwin Park, CA; (1); Band; Mrchg Band; School Musical; Capt Intrml Bsktbl; Intrml Ftbl; Var Score Keeper; Hon Roll.

ANDRADE, KATHLEEN; Orestimba HS; Newman, CA; (2); Church Yth Grp; 4-H; Girl Scts; Pep Clb; SADD; Color Guard; Stu Cncl; Capt JV Cheerldng; JV Vllybl; 4-H Awd; Mst Insprtnl Plyr Vllybl.

ANDRADE, LENISE N; Eagle Rock HS; Alhambra, CA; (4); Capt Pep Clb; VP Sec SADD; Sec Thesps; School Play; Stage Crew; Ed Nwsp; Yrbk; Stu Cncl; Pres Acad Fit Awd; Hotchkiss Summer Theatre Pgm Schlrshp; NYU; Acting.

ANDRADE, LOURDES; Carpinteria HS; Carpinteria, CA; (2); 49/169; Cmnty Wkr; Library Aide; Flag Corp; Nwsp; Phtg Yrbk; JV Capt Bsktbl; JV Capt Vllybl; Cinco De Mayo Queen; Clb Unidos Pres.

ANDRADE, LUCIA H; Santiago HS; Santa Ana, CA; (2); French Clb; Teachers Aide; Color Guard; Mrchg Band; Var Trk; Hon Roll; Grls Leag; UC Santa Barbara; Elem Ed.

ANDRADE, NORMA; Amos Alonzo Stagg HS; Stockton, CA; (3); Bsktbl; Crs Cntry; Powder Puff Ftbl; Trk; High Hon Roll; Prfct Atten Awd; 89 Crs Cntry; MVP Trphy 89 Trck; 90 Trck Mst Insprtnl; Cert Invlvd Cmnty Schl Actvts; UC Davis; Lawyer.

ANDRADE, NORMAS A; St Paul HS; Whittier, CA; (3); Spanish Clb; Bsktbl; Sftbl; Vllybl; Hon Roll; Jr NHS; NHS; Spanish NHS; Cpa Accntnt.

ANDRADE, RUBEN; Le Grand HS; Le Grand, CA; (2); Cmnty Wkr; Bsktbl; Ftbl; MVP Bsktbl; U Of AZ; Tchr.

ANDRADE, SHAWN M; Woodland HS; Woodland, CA; (2); Capt Aud/Vis; Capt Library Aide; Teachers Aide; Intrml Ftbl; Intrml Trk; Hon Roll; Prfct Atten Awd; Pres Acad Fit Awd; Bwlng Pres Of Trnmnt Cmmtte; Amer Lgn Awd; Friday Night Live; U CA Santa Cruz; Engl.

ANDRADE, SYLVIA; Bell HS; Maywood, CA; (3); Pep Clb; High Hon Roll; CSF; Golden Eagle Acad Prtnrshp Pgm; Usc; Pedtrcn.

ANDRADE, TRINI M; Brawley Union HS; Brawley, CA; (3); Dance Clb; FTA; Library Aide; Flag Corp; Powder Puff Ftbl; Hon Roll; Prfct Atten Awd; UC San Diego; Child Psych.

ANDRADE, VERONICA; Senior HS; Bell Gardens, CA; (3); Rptr Yrbk; MECHA Clb; Gins Leag; CA ST Long Beach; Trvl Agnt.

ANDRAKA, VALERIE T; Sierra Vista HS; Baldwin Park, CA; (1); Band; Jazz Band; Mrchg Band; Pep Band; Bsktbl; Var Trk; Hon Roll; UCLA; Med.

ANDRE, CHERI; Chino HS; Chino, CA; (3); Spanish Clb; Teachers Aide; Chorus; JV Bsktbl; JV Sftbl; Var Trk; JV Var Vllybl; Hon Roll; Prfct Atten Awd; Ivy Chain; UCSD; Theatre Drama.

ANDRE, JENNIFER C; Louisville HS; Woodland Hills, CA; (3); 15/65; Dance Clb; Drama Clb; School Musical; Rptr Nwsp; Treas Stu Cncl; Cheerldng; Hon Roll; NHS; St Schlr; Mock Trl.

ANDRE, NICOLE M; Pinole Valley HS; Hercules, CA; (2); Computer Clb; French Clb; SADD; Masonic Awd; Hnrd Qn Intl Order Of Jobs Dghtrs & JR Cls Indpndnt Offcr; Orthodontics.

ANDRE, ROGER A; Sacramento HS; Sacramento, CA; (4); 38/400; French Clb; FFA; Letterman Clb; Pep Clb; Teachers Aide; Band; Mrchg Band; Capt Swmmng; Cit Awd; High Hon Roll; Drctrs Awd Prtcptn, Achvt Mrchng Band; Dept Awd US Hstry Hnrs; Dept Awd Music; UCLA; Aerontcl Engrng.

ANDREACCHI, KRISTEN A; Ramona HS; Ramona, CA; (3); Drama Clb; FBLA; FHA; Girl Scts; Science Clb; SADD; Golf; Sftbl; Cit Awd; Hon Roll; Wrkng At Pre Schl; Taking Coll Night Courses Chld Dev; Palomar Jr Coll; Teacher.

ANDREAS, REBECCA; Lee Vining HS; Lee Vining, CA; (2); Office Aide; Sec Frsh Cls; Rep Soph Cls; JV Bsktbl; JV Ftbl; JV Powder Puff Ftbl; JV Sftbl; JV Vllybl; Cit Awd; Hon Roll.

ANDREJKO, CHRIS D; Bellarmine HS; San Jose, CA; (2); Latin Clb; Teachers Aide; Math.

ANDREONI, JULEE; Casa Roble HS; Orangevale, CA; (3); French Clb; Drill Tm; Cheerldng; Hon Roll; All Star Chrldr At UCA Cmptn Camp; CSUS; Nutritional Sci.

ANDREOTTI, ELISSA J; Bishop O'dowd HS; Castro Valley, CA; (2); Var Cheerldng; Hon Roll; Swm Tm; Psych.

ANDREOZZI, MARK; Westminster HS; Westminster, CA; (2); JV Bsbl; Var Wrstlng; UCLA; Arch Engr.

ANDRES, ALICE D; Ontario HS; Ontario, CA; (2); Band; Hon Roll; Prfct Atten Awd; Asian Clb Sec; USC; Med.

ANDRES, KELLY; Bishop Amat HS; W Covina, CA; (3); Drama Clb; Hosp Aide; Stage Crew; Var Capt Socr; NHS.

ANDRES, LIZZA N; Santa Clara HS; Oxnard, CA; (4); Debate Tm; French Clb; Office Aide; Speech Tm; Varsity Clb; Variety Show; Mgr Yrbk; Pres Sr Cls; Rep Stu Cncl; Hon Roll; Asst Promotions Mgr; Intern At Mjr Recrd Label; CA Lutheran U; Commnctns.

ANDRESKI, CINDY; Livermore HS; Livermore, CA; (3); Church Yth Grp; Pep Clb; SADD; Capt Var Cheerldng; Var Pom Pon; Stat Wrstlng; Hon Roll; Mst Imprvd JV Chrldr 89; Mst Inspiratnl Chrldr 90; CA ST U; Elem Ed.

ANDRESON, JENNIFER L; Mater Dei HS; Newport Beach, CA; (2); GAA; Chorus; Vllybl; Cit Awd; French Hon Soc; Scripps Coll; Archeology.

ANDREU, JOSEPH B; Glendale HS; Glendale, CA; (3); Spanish Clb; Acpl Chr; Church Choir; High Hon Roll; Hon Roll; NHS; Harvey Mudd U; Electrncs Engr.

ANDREWS, ALESHA; Rio Mesa HS; Camarillo, CA; (4); 25/374; Pres Church Yth Grp; FCA; Hosp Aide; Scholastic Bowl; School Play; VP Sr Cls; Chrmn Stu Cncl; High Hon Roll; CSF; 100% Life Sealbearer; Mock Trial Team; U CA San Diego; Medcl.

ANDREWS, ANTOINE; Miracle Baptist Christian Schl; Carson, CA; (1); Church Yth Grp; Cit Awd; Hon Roll; Prfct Atten Awd; Cal Tech Coll; Comp.

ANDREWS, CARLY K; Clovis West HS; Fresno, CA; (1); Church Yth Grp; Drama Clb; FCA; Ski Clb; Speech Tm; SADD; Color Guard; Stage Crew; Treas Frsh Cls; Var Diving; Friday Night Live.

ANDREWS, CARRIE; San Clemente HS; San Juan Capistra, CA; (1); German Clb; Pep Clb; Capt Bsktbl; JV Cheerldng; Var Pom Pon; Hon Roll; Stu Of Mnth German & Social Sci; San Diego ST; Adv Mgr.

ANDREWS, DAVID; Fairfield HS; Fairfield, CA; (4); Church Yth Grp; Drama Clb; FCA; Ed Yrbk; Rep Frsh Cls; Pres Jr Cls; Off Jr Cls; Off Sr Cls; Powder Puff Ftbl; Socr; HOBY Fndtn; U AZ; Bus.

ANDREWS, FRANCHESKA; La Reina HS; Wlv, CA; (4); 13/85; Church Yth Grp; GAA; VP JA; Letterman Clb; Service Clb; Var Capt Cheerldng; Cit Awd; Hon Roll; UCSB; Bus Econ.

ANDREWS, JASON W; Riverdale HS; Laton, CA; (2); Church Yth Grp; FFA; Math Tm; JV Bsktbl; JV Var Ftbl; Var Trk; Acad Achvt Awds.

ANDREWS, JEFFREY; Highland SR HS; North Highlands, CA; (3); JV Crs Cntry; JV Var Trk; Hon Roll; Prfct Atten Awd; Bus.

ANDREWS, JENNIFER; Apple Valley SR HS; Apple Valley, CA; (4); Church Yth Grp; French Clb; Sec Letterman Clb; Jazz Band; Pres Soph Cls; Capt L Crs Cntry; Capt Var Socr; Capt Var Trk; Hon Roll; Pres Acad Fit Awd; CSF; CIF Trk Fnlst; HS Female Athl Of Yr; CSU Northridge; Sprts Med.

ANDREWS, JENNIFER M; Edison HS; Huntington Beach, CA; (2); Church Yth Grp; Girl Scts; Ski Clb; Swmmng; Vllybl; Hon Roll; Most Vlbl Player Vllybl 89; Qlfd For CIF Swimming 89-90.

ANDREWS, JOHN; Valencia HS; Montebello, CA; (1); Hon Roll; UC Riverside; Crmnl Sci.

ANDREWS, JOHN M; Redondo Union HS; Redondo Beach, CA; (4); 17/389; Key Clb; Ski Clb; Teachers Aide; Nwsp; Var Capt Vllybl; Cit Awd; High Hon Roll; Hon Roll; Kiwanis Awd; Pres Acad Fit Awd; Schlr Athlete Awrd; Leader For A Day Conv Part; Ivy Chain Jr Hnr Grd; CA ST U; Lawyer.

ANDREWS, KIM; Banning HS; Banning, CA; (3); 44/182; Church Yth Grp; French Clb; Letterman Clb; Pep Clb; Varsity Clb; Var L Cheerldng; Var L Swmmng; High Hon Roll; Jr NHS; French Outstndng Acvht Awd; Soc Stud Outstndng Achvt Awd; CSF; Teacher.

ANDREWS, KRISTIL A; Mira Loma HS; Carmichael, CA; (3); Drama Clb; Chorus; School Play; Intrml Trk; Hon Roll; Prfct Atten Awd; Civic Theater; Actress.

ANDREWS, LISA M; Mater Dei HS; Tustin, CA; (3); Church Yth Grp; Cmnty Wkr; Drama Clb; Hosp Aide; Rep Soph Cls; Hon Roll; Jr NHS; NHS; Jr Statesman Of Amer; CA ST Fullerton; Lawyer.

ANDREWS, LISA MICHELLE LAUREN; San Marcos HS; Santa Barbara, CA; (3); Debate Tm; Key Clb; NFL; Pep Clb; Speech Tm; SADD; Teachers Aide; School Musical; L Var Cheerldng; L Var Tennis; Yng Wmn Or Yr 90; Physcl Ftns Awd; Extnsv Ballet Trng; UCLA; Pshcy.

ANDREWS, LISA R; Westminster HS; Westminster, CA; (4); 88/414; Church Yth Grp; French Clb; Girl Scts; Key Clb; Service Clb; SADD; Band; Jazz Band; Mrchg Band; Orch; Schlrs Trng U Of CA Irvine; UCLA; City Planner.

ANDREWS, NICOLE K; Whittier Christian HS; Fullerton, CA; (3); 9/200; Speech Tm; Thesps; Chorus; School Musical; School Play; Stage Crew; Rep Frsh Cls; Rep Soph Cls; Var Cheerldng; Lion Awd; Pedal Harpist; Chrch Yth Grp; Drama Play Director; Commnctns.

ANDREWS, PAMELA D; Clearlake HS; Lakeport, CA; (3); 4-H; Teachers Aide; Bsktbl; Cheerldng; Hon Roll; Prfct Atten Awd; Ftbl Season Mascot; Peer Cnslng; U CA-DAVIS; Psycht.

ANDREWS, SHARON; Del Campo HS; Citrus Heights, CA; (3); 5/450; Church Yth Grp; Spanish Clb; Teachers Aide; Yrbk; NHS; Ntl Merit Ltr; Opt Clb Awd; Stu Reachng Out Pres; CSF Sec; Pediatrics.

ANDREWS, STEPHANIE R; Antioch HS; Antioch, CA; (2); Teachers Aide; Varsity Clb; Var Sftbl; Var Vllybl; Hon Roll; Most Vlbl Offnsv Girls Vllybl; Most Vlbl Girls Vrsty Sftbl; Coaches Awd Girls Bsktbl; Psych.

ANDRION, ELIZABETH; Cerritos HS; Cerritos, CA; (4); Church Yth Grp; Cmnty Wkr; JA; Key Clb; SADD; Nwsp; Rep Jr Cls; JV Sftbl; High Hon Roll; NHS; Corp Law.

ANDRUS, JARED; Grossmont HS; El Cajon, CA; (2); Dance Clb; JA; Key Clb; School Play; Pres Soph Cls; Capt JV Ftbl; Score Keeper; Capt Var Vllybl; Hon Roll; Pres Acad Fit Awd.

ANDRUS, JENNIFER L; Lemoore HS; Lemoore, CA; (3); SADD; Teachers Aide; Photogrphy Clb; Crmnlgy.

ANDRUS, VICTORIA A; Samuel F B Morse HS; San Diego, CA; (2); 1/764; Science Clb; Var Crs Cntry; Var Trk; Hon Roll; Prfct Atten Awd; Mst Insprtnl Crs Cntry; CSF.

ANDRY, DAVID B; East Union HS; Manteca, CA; (2); 13/425; Church Yth Grp; JV Bsbl; JV Ftbl; Var Swmmng; JV Wt Lftg; Cit Awd; Hon Roll; Prfct Atten Awd; Pres Acad Fit Awd; CSF; Sci.

ANDUJO, MICHELE M; Sacred Heart Of Jesus HS; Los Angeles, CA; (4); GAA; JA; VP Letterman Clb; Sec Soph Cls; Stu Cncl; Stat Bsktbl; Mgr(s); Var Vllybl; NHS; Pres Acad Fit Awd; Bank Of Amer Achvt Awd Fld Math; U Of S CA.

ANG, ROBERT J; Don Bosco Tech; Montebello, CA; (3); 3/250; Church Yth Grp; Intrml Bsktbl; Cit Awd; Hon Roll; NHS; Ntl Merit Ltr; NEDT Awd; Intramural Sports; Music; Math Awd.

ANG, VENUS S; Bonita Vista HS; Coronado, CA; (4); Church Yth Grp; Pep Clb; Chorus; School Musical; Nwsp; Yrbk; Lit Mag; Most Insprtnl, Outstndng Rookie, Most Lkly To Succeed & Most Valuable Mem Music Mchne; Cal Poly; Engrng.

ANGEL, CLAUDIA M; Pasadena HS; Pasadena, CA; (3); French Clb; Off Jr Cls; Stat Socr; JV Vllybl; Hon Roll; Prfct Atten Awd; CSF; Greenpeace; Z Clb Correspndng Sec; UCLA; Pediatrics.

ANGEL, VENICE M; Chula Vista HS; San Diego, CA; (2); Red Cross Aide; Teachers Aide; Stage Crew; Socr; Swmmng; Trk; Vllybl; Teacher/Bio.

ANGELES, ANA M; Bell HS; Bell Gardens, CA; (4); Church Yth Grp; Teachers Aide; Church Choir; School Musical; Diving; Prfct Atten Awd; Outstndg Math Student; Outstndg ESL Student; Cal ST Long Bch; Ed Spanish.

ANGELES, CRUZ JOEL; University HS; Riverside, CA; (2); VP JCL; Teachers Aide; Varsity Clb; Rep Frsh Cls; Rep Jr Cls; Rep Stu Cncl; Ftbl; Trk; High Hon Roll; Hon Roll; Clean Campus Clb; Dance Cmmttee; UCLA; Bus.

ANGELES, DARREN V; Henry Gunn HS; Palo Alto, CA; (2); Church Yth Grp; JA; SADD; Cit Awd; Arch.

ANGELES, JAIME; Sanger HS; Fresno, CA; (3); Church Yth Grp; FCA; Science Clb; Spanish Clb; Var Crs Cntry; Var Trk; Var Wrstlng; Hi-Y Clb; Fresno ST; Med.

ANGELES, MARY ANNE M; Dr James Hogan SR HS; Vallejo, CA; (4); 29/400; Church Yth Grp; Computer Clb; Teachers Aide; Band; Chorus; Church Choir; JV Tennis; Cit Awd; High Hon Roll; Hon Roll; Fine Arts; Piano; Solano CC; Engr.

ANGELES, MINERVA PANGANIBAN; Montgomery HS; San Diego, CA; (3); Church Yth Grp; Teachers Aide; Chorus; Church Choir; Cit Awd; Hon Roll; Prfct Atten Awd; Yth Choir Organist; Jr Choir; Bihhi VP; SDSU; Cmptr Systems Analyst.

ANGELES, SALVIA MARIE B; Pinole Valley HS; Hercules, CA; (2); Computer Clb; French Clb; SADD; Co-Ed Lit Mag; Gym; Hon Roll; AFS; CSF; Amnesty Intl; UC Davis; Acctng.

ANGELINO, DEANNA L; Notre Dame HS; Gilroy, CA; (3); 10/60; Church Yth Grp; Hosp Aide; Scholastic Bowl; SADD; Church Choir; Rptr Yrbk; Sec Soph Cls; High Hon Roll; Hon Roll; Associated Stu Body Commissioner Of Activies; CSF; Fashion Merch.

ANGELITO, RANDY C; Encinal HS; Pittsburg, CA; (1); 48/279; Band; Mrchg Band; Pep Band; Hon Roll; UC Berkeley.

ANGELITO, ROBERT S; Pittsburg HS; Pittsburg, CA; (4); 2/283; Key Clb; Mu Alpha Theta; Science Clb; Bsktbl; Var Tennis; Cit Awd; High Hon Roll; Prfct Atten Awd; Sal; Acad Decathlon; Yth Educator; CSF; U CA Berkeley; Human Bio.

ANGELO, PAUL D; Thomas Downey HS; Modesto, CA; (4); Art Clb; SADD; Teachers Aide; Stage Crew; Tennis; Cit Awd; Hon Roll; Downey Achvt Awd 89; ITT; Comp Tech.

ANGELONI, LISA M; La Canada HS; La Canada-Flint, CA; (3); 1/250; Cmnty Wkr; Hosp Aide; Intnl Clb; Key Clb; Math Clb; Mu Alpha Theta; Science Clb; Spanish Clb; Off Jr Cls; NHS; CA Schlrshp Fed; Bio.

ANGELOPOULOS, CRYSTAL L; Notre Dame HS; Riverside, CA; (1); #8 In Class; Church Yth Grp; Var Cheerldng; High Hon Roll; Ms Tn Photognc Pgnt.

ANGELSEA, PETER; Santa Cruz HS; Santa Cruz, CA; (3); French Clb; Spanish Clb; Speech Tm; Rptr Nwsp; Swmmng; Hon Roll; U Of CA.

ANGER, SILKE; North HS; West Germany; (4); Hon Roll; Exchange Stu; Bio.

ANGHESOM, DEBORAH D; La Habra HS; La Habra, CA; (2); 34/388; Powder Puff Ftbl; High Hon Roll; Prfct Atten Awd; UC Los Angeles; Med.

ANGLE, CHRIS; Calvary Baptist Schl; Suisun, CA; (3); Church Yth Grp; Var Bsktbl; Var Socr; Var Sftbl; Cit Awd; Hon Roll; 1st Pl Chess, 2nd Pl Hist, Geog; 1st Pl Chess, 3rd Pl Hist, Geog; Geom Awd.

ANGLIN, TONYA L; Tehachapi HS; Tehachapi, CA; (2); Church Yth Grp; Pep Clb; Rep Soph Cls; Rep Stu Cncl; Var Cheerldng; Var L Trk; Hon Roll; Spcl Awds Math; Pepperdine Law Schl; Law.

ANGSUMALIKUL, JANNY; San Gabriel Acad; Alhambra, CA; (4); Church Yth Grp; Teachers Aide; Chorus; Bsktbl; Tennis; Vllybl; NHS; Prfct Atten Awd; Cello Recgntn Awd; Outstndng Contrbtn Awd; Med.

ANGSUPANICH, KAHN; Clear Lake HS; Lakeport, CA; (3); 1/77; Am Leg Boys St; Pres Computer Clb; SADD; Band; Var Tennis; High Hon Roll; Cngrsnl Schlr; Acad Excl Awd Geom; Tp 5 Pct Math-Bus ASVAB; Dr.

ANGUIANDO, CARLOS; Junipero Serra HS; Los Angeles, CA; (2); Boy Scts; Church Yth Grp; Latin Clb; Spanish Clb; Color Guard; JV Bsbl; Var Socr; Var Vllybl; Cit Awd; Hon Roll; Elect.

ANGUIANO, JENNIFER; Gladstone HS; Azusa, CA; (3); Church Yth Grp; Ski Clb; SADD; Band; Jazz Band; Mrchg Band; Pep Band; Swmmng; Tennis; Hon Roll.

ANGUIANO, MARIA; Oxnard HS; Oxnard, CA; (4); 6/441; Church Yth Grp; Cmnty Wkr; Math Clb; Quiz Bowl; Scholastic Bowl; Science Clb; Service Clb; Spanish Clb; SADD; Teachers Aide; Oxnard Safe Rides; SYETP Achvt Awd; Stanford U; Med.

ANGUIANO, MILDRED; Montebello HS; Montebello, CA; (2); Acpl Chr; Chorus; Color Guard; Psych.

ANGUIANO, NANCY; Montebello HS; Montebello, CA; (1); Band; Chorus; Mrchg Band; Med.

ANGULO, ADRIAN; Sunny Hills HS; Fullerton, CA; (2); French Clb; FBLA; JA; Stu Cncl; JV Crs Cntry; JV Socr; Emery Riddle; Aeron Engr.

ANGULO, ANTHONY M; Elk Grove HS; Elk Grove, CA; (3); 171/650; MESA; UC Davis; Bio.

ANGULO, FRANCISCO; Sweetwater HS; National City, CA; (2); JV Socr; High Hon Roll; Gifted & Talented Ed Prgm; Lawyer.

ANGULO, JANEL J; Notre Dame HS; San Jose, CA; (3); Drama Clb; Pep Clb; SADD; JV Cheerldng; Var Crs Cntry; High Hon Roll; Hon Roll; CA Schlrshp Fed; UCLA; Brdcst Jrnlsm.

ANGULO, OCTAVIO; Ernest Righetti HS; Guadalupe, CA; (4); Debate Tm; JA; Teachers Aide; Rep Stu Cncl; Socr; Wt Lftg; Elks Awd; Hon Roll; Upwrd Bnd Pgm; Outreach Pgm; Guadalupe Rec Awd; CA Polytech ST U; Ind Tech.

ANGULO, ROBERTO; Sweetwater HS; National City, CA; (2); FBLA; Science Clb; Off Frsh Cls; Cit Awd; High Hon Roll; Hon Roll; Prfct Atten Awd; Hstry & Engl Awds; UCSD; Aviation.

ANICO, ANTHONY R; Hueneme HS; Oxnard, CA; (4); 2/333; FBLA; Key Clb; Quiz Bowl; Scholastic Bowl; SADD; Teachers Aide; Chorus; School Play; High Hon Roll; Jr NHS; Elec Engrng.

ANISHCHENKO, OLEG ALEC; Capuchino HS; San Bruno, CA; (2); Church Yth Grp; Wghtlftng MHC; CSM; Camer Engr.

ANIVERSARIO, CHRISTINA L; Edison HS; Huntington Beach, CA; (2); Teachers Aide; Hon Roll.

ANKUNDING, WENDY C; Enterprise HS; Palo Cedro, CA; (3); Office Aide; Rep Soph Cls; Var Cheerldng; Var Swmmng; High Hon Roll; Altrnte Grls St; Recrtnl Gymnstcs; Trip To France; Chem.

ANN, LY; Milpitas HS; Milpitas, CA; (3); 24/487; Chess Clb; Computer Clb; JA; Math Tm; Spanish Clb; JV Vllybl; Hon Roll; Jr NHS; NHS; GATE; Chns Clb; CSF; UC Davis; Pre-Med.

ANNABI, ISSA N; Bonita HS; La Verne, CA; (4); English Clb; SADD; High Hon Roll; Hon Roll; Lion Awd; Ntl Merit Schol; Pres Acad Fit Awd; Advncd Plcmnt Hnrs Pgm; LA Cnty Awd Cmnty Invlmnt; CSU Fullerton; Bus.

ANNIE, SU; Mark Keppel HS; Monterey Park, CA; (4); #2 In Class; Cmnty Wkr; Key Clb; Math Clb; Science Clb; Service Clb; Bausch & Lomb Sci Awd; Cit Awd; High Hon Roll; Hon Roll; Kiwanis Awd; Leos Club; Crown & Sceptre; Girls Leag; UCLA; Biochem.

ANSARI, ANEESAH Z; Richard Gehr HS; Carson, CA; (3); Cmnty Wkr; Hosp Aide; Teachers Aide; School Play; Hon Roll; Prfmrd Several Musical Prdctns-Featured Top Dncr; El Camino CC.

ANSELL, ANGELA L; Mayfield SR Schl; Glendale, CA; (3); Church Yth Grp; Teachers Aide; Hon Roll; NHS; Amnsty Intl; Engl Profssr.

ANSELMO, MARK J; Bullard HS; Fresno, CA; (2); Boy Scts; Ski Clb; Band; Jazz Band; Mrchg Band; Pep Band; School Musical; Fresno ST Coll; Bus.

ANSLEY, JANET; Chatsworth HS; Canoga Park, CA; (4); Church Yth Grp; Dance Clb; Drama Clb; Pep Clb; Ski Clb; SADD; Thesps; Drill Tm; School Musical; School Play; CA ST U Northridge; Chld Dev.

ANSLEY, SIERRA D; Albany HS; Albany, CA; (3); Pres AFS; School Musical; Ed Lit Mag; Var Crs Cntry; Var Trk; Hon Roll; Science Clb; Orch; Stat Wrstlng; YMCA Yth Gov Secy Delg; Bay Area Wind Symp; People To People; Intl Stud.

ANSON, ADRIANA J; Anaheim HS; Anaheim, CA; (3); Church Yth Grp; French Clb; Teachers Aide; Church Choir; Cit Awd; Hon Roll; Chrch Yth Drama/Prdctns; Elem Ed.

ANTAYA, MONICA; Clovis HS; Fresno, CA; (3); SADD; Hon Roll; Fresno ST.

ANTENORCRUZ, CHARLENE A; Providence HS; Burbank, CA; (2); Sec Intnl Clb; Model UN; Pep Clb; Pres Art Clb; Sec Treas Frsh Cls; VP Soph Cls; Med Tech.

ANTER, GARY; South Tahoe HS; So Lake Tahoe, CA; (3); Debate Tm; JA; Ski Clb; Band; Sec Jr Cls; Tennis; Trk; High Hon Roll; Pres Acad Fit Awd; Alpine Ski Tm.

ANTHENIEN, CATHERINE V; Bishop O'dowd HS; Oakland, CA; (2); Cal ST Hayward; Arch.

ANTHONY, IAN J; Santa Clara HS; Oxnard, CA; (3); 50/150; Varsity Clb; Rep Jr Cls; Var Crs Cntry; Var Socr; Hon Roll; Outstndng Stu Awd Math 89-90; Outstndng Stu Of Yr Schlrshp; Sccr Best Offensive Plyr, 1st Tm Leag; Arch.

ANTHONY, JENNIFER C; Milpitas HS; Milpitas, CA; (1); ROTC; Color Guard; VP Frsh Cls; Cit Awd; High Hon Roll; Amnesty Intl; Ldrshp Recogntn Awd.

ANTHONY, JOSEPH H; Barstow HS; Barstow, CA; (1); Church Yth Grp; Hon Roll; USC; Law.

ANTHONY, RAQUEL N; John W North HS; Riverside, CA; (2); 173/353; FTA; Office Aide; Color Guard; Hon Roll; NY U; Socl Wrk.

ANTIC, MICHELLE L; Monte Vista HS; Danville, CA; (2); 40/450; SADD; Teachers Aide; Rep Stu Cncl; Hon Roll; Piano; Tnns Tm Blackhawn Tnns Clb; Acad Dcthln; Bus.

ANTIGUA, BEVERLY H; James Logan HS; Union City, CA; (3); 200/900; Computer Clb; Intnl Clb; Math Clb; Ed Yrbk; UC Berkeley Prtnrshp Pgm, Pre-Coll Acad, Saturday Coll; Badminton Tm; Coll Clb; Asian Clb; Trvl Clb; Comp Engr.

ANTILLON, ROSEMARY; Montclair HS; Montclair, CA; (3); Letterman Clb; Teachers Aide; Varsity Clb; JV Socr; Var Sftbl; Elks Awd; CA Schl Crt Rprtng; Crt Rprtr.

ANTOINE JR, RICHARD; Moreno Valley HS; Moreno Valley, CA; (3); 3/450; VP Key Clb; Pep Clb; VP Science Clb; Stu Cncl; Var Ftbl; Var Socr; High Hon Roll; NHS; Rotary Awd; CSF; U Of MI; Bus Admin.

ANTOLA, JESSICA C; Marymount HS; Los Angeles, CA; (2); Art Clb; Pres Cmnty Wkr; Letterman Clb; Science Clb; Ski Clb; Varsity Clb; Rep Jr Cls; Var L Tennis; JV L Trk; High Hon Roll; AP Hstry Frnch Art & Hnrs Engl; CA Schlrshp Fed; Art Of Mnth & Yr; Art.

ANTOLINEZ, EVA; Laguna Beach HS; Laguna Beach, CA; (4); 9/175; Pres German Clb; Model UN; Band; Capt Drill Tm; Ed Nwsp; Var Cheerldng; High Hon Roll; J P Sousa Hnr Band 1st Clrnt; CSF Sl Br; Acad Dcthln Tm-Ec Wnnr; Domona Coll; Intl Rltns.

ANTONELLI, TODD A; Simi Valley HS; Simi Valley, CA; (3); Teachers Aide; Chorus; School Musical; School Play; Socr; Sccr Coach; CA Luthern U; Schl Psych.

ANTONIAN, MAGDALENA M; North Hollywood HS; N Hollywood, CA; (4); Dance Clb; French Clb; Office Aide; Acpl Chr; Chorus; Off Soph Cls; Off Jr Cls; Off Sr Cls; Stu Cncl; Figure Sktng; Cmnty Svc; Occptnl Ctr Educ; Trade Tech Coll; Fshn Dsgn.

ANTONICO, JOSE L; Buena HS; Ventura, CA; (1).

ANTONIO, EZRA-ALICIA D; El Camino HS; Daly City, CA; (3); Hosp Aide; Treas Intnl Clb; Math Tm; Pres Service Clb; Teachers Aide; Thesps; School Musical; Phtg Co-Ed Nwsp; Cit Awd; High Hon Roll; Lrng Lab Peer Tutor; CSF; Vrsty Badminton Team; BSE Geom H Hons; UC Davis; Pre Med.

ANTONIO, JORGE S; Calexico HS; Calexico, CA; (1); Dentist.

ANTONIO, MARK; Pinole Valley HS; Hercules, CA; (1); AFS; French Clb; Teachers Aide; Hon Roll; CSF; Friday Night Live; UC Davis; Med.

ANTONIO, ORLANDO M; Daniel Murphy Catholic HS; Los Angeles, CA; (3); Bsktbl; Hon Roll; UCLA; Psych.

ANTONIO, RHODORA; El Camino HS; Daly City, CA; (4); Math Tm; Teachers Aide; Var L Gym; Var Mgr(s); Var Capt Tennis; Hnrs Grad S San Francisco Cmmnty Schlrshp Assn; CSF; San Jose ST U; Intl Bus.

ANTONIO, ROSALIE A; St Joseph HS; Cerritos, CA; (2); Cmnty Wkr; Variety Show; Hon Roll; NEDT Awd; Prfct Atten Awd; CA Schlrshp Fed; CPA.

ANTONIO, TERESA B; Armijo HS; Fairfield, CA; (2); Church Yth Grp; Office Aide; Teachers Aide; Church Choir; Hon Roll; Bus.

ANTONOPOULOS, JASON R; Simi Valley HS; Simi Valley, CA; (3); 66/675; Var Bsktbl; Hon Roll; NHS; Pres Acad Fit Awd; Schlr Athlte Awd; Accntnt.

ANTONUCCI, KATRINA; El Cajon Valley HS; El Cajon, CA; (3); Church Yth Grp; Letterman Clb; Teachers Aide; Chorus; Church Choir; Drill Tm; Flag Corp; Semi Fnlst 2 Poetry Cont; Biola U; Marine Bio.

ANTONUCCIO, JENNIFER; University HS; Irvine, CA; (2); Church Yth Grp; French Clb; SADD; Varsity Clb; Fld Hcky; Trk; Hon Roll; Japan Smmr Exchng Pgm; Mst Insprtnl Vrsty Fld Hcky Awd.

ANTONY, MICHELLE M; Ramona HS; Ramona, CA; (3); 62/280; Church Yth Grp; Teachers Aide; Kiwanis Awd; Peer Cnslr; Campus Life Yth Ldr; Hmcmng Float Cmmtte; San Diego ST U; Visual Prsntn.

ANTONYSHYN, KEITH; Trabuco Hills HS; Coto De Caza, CA; (2); #2 In Class; Quiz Bowl; Spanish Clb; High Hon Roll; NHS.

ANTUNA, MARIA R; Indio HS; Indio, CA; (2); Color Guard; UC Santa Cruz; Fmly Cnslr.

ANTUNOVICH, DAWN T; Alverno HS; Temple City, CA; (2); Church Yth Grp.

ANTWINE, TELICIA P; Canyon Springs HS; Moreno Valley, CA; (2); Cmnty Wkr; FBLA; Intnl Clb; Library Aide; Church Choir; Sec Soph Cls; High Hon Roll; NHS; Prfct Atten Awd; CA Schlrshp Fed; Elem Ed.

ANULAO, KATHLEEN J; Alverno HS; Los Angeles, CA; (3); Model UN; Pep Clb; Chorus; Lit Mag; Sec Frsh Cls; Pres Soph Cls; Sec Jr Cls; Var Cheerldng; Peer Counseling.

ANVAR, BEHZAD; Edison HS; Huntington Beach, CA; (2); Computer Clb; FBLA; Key Clb; Science Clb; Ski Clb; Cit Awd; Hon Roll; Piano; UCI; Sci.

ANZALDO, MARIA; Woodrow Wilson HS; Los Angeles, CA; (3); Church Yth Grp; Dance Clb; Hosp Aide; Hon Roll; JETS Awd; CSF Clb; MESA Clb; Future Nrs Clb; Engrng.

ANZOATEGUI, MARK R; Diamond Bar HS; Moreno Valley, CA; (4); Chorus; Var Bsktbl; Cit Awd; High Hon Roll; Hon Roll; Amer Lgn Axlrys Amercnsm Essy Cont 5th Pl; Outstndng Sci Awd; U Of Sound Arts; Music Prodcr.

AOCHI, NANCY; Oak Grove HS; San Jose, CA; (4); 5/489; Hosp Aide; Treas Key Clb; Q&S; Nwsp; Off Soph Cls; Pres Jr Cls; Var Capt Crs Cntry; High Hon Roll; VP NHS; Pres Acad Fit Awd; CA Schlrshp Fdrtn Pres; Walt Disney Wrlds Drmrs & Doers CA Semifnlst; UC Davis; Biolgcl Sci.

AOKI, AGNES; Yoicota HS; Apo San Francisco, CA; (3); 1/102; Mu Alpha Theta; Quiz Bowl; Yrbk; Treas Soph Cls; JV Fld Hcky; Var Trk; Var Vllybl; High Hon Roll; NHS; Rnbw Grls; Vet.

AOKI, ALEXANDER; Yokota HS; APO San Francisc, CA; (2); 17/145; French Clb; Math Clb; Mu Alpha Theta; Varsity Clb; Var Ftbl; Var Socr; High Hon Roll; Hon Roll; NHS; Pres Acad Fit Awd; Med.

AOKI, ALYSSA; Culver City HS; Culver City, CA; (4); Capt Pep Clb; Pres Varsity Clb; Stage Crew; Off Frsh Cls; Off Soph Cls; Off Jr Cls; Off Sr Cls; Var Capt Cheerldng; Co-Ed Trk; High Hon Roll; Stu Leg Pres; UCLA.

AOKI, STACY M; Woodland HS; Woodland, CA; (3); Key Clb; Rptr Nwsp; Rep Frsh Cls; Intrml JV Bsktbl; Intrml JV Sftbl; Intrml JV Vllybl; Hon Roll; VP Jr NHS; NHS; Prfct Atten Awd; HEROES Awd; Sprts Phys Thrpy.

AOKI, STEPHANIE; North Torrance HS; Torrance, CA; (1); Church Yth Grp; FBLA; Spanish Clb; Color Guard; Cit Awd; Hon Roll; FBLA Southern Sctn Conf 1st Pl Keyboard Applctns; UCLA; Pediatrics.

AOUN, LARA G; Palmdale HS; Little Rock, CA; (2); #11 In Class; Church Yth Grp; Hon Roll; GATE Acad; Wrtng Jrnlsm.

AOYAMA, JENNIFER M; Davis SR HS; Davis, CA; (3); Art Clb; Cmnty Wkr; Key Clb; Office Aide; Pep Clb; Ski Clb; SADD; Teachers Aide; Temple Yth Grp; Yrbk; Vrsty Badmttn; Bsktbl Scorekpr/JV Mgr; CA Poly San Luis Obispo; Bus.

APAHIDEAN, IAIELA; Magnolia HS; Anaheim, CA; (3); 25/315; Church Yth Grp; Rep Intnl Clb; Treas Service Clb; Teachers Aide; Church Choir; Orch; Cit Awd; Hon Roll; Rep NHS; Prfct Atten Awd; Interest Math; Sci 88-89; Stu Of Yr German 87-89; Davis; Elec Engr.

APAHIDEAN, OLIMPIU; Savanna HS; Anaheim, CA; (3); Church Yth Grp; FBLA; Intnl Clb; Key Clb; Church Choir; Mrchg Band; Pep Band; High Hon Roll; NHS; Ldrshp Acad; CA Schlrshp Fed; Aerospace Engrng.

APALATEA, JANEEN M; Turlock HS; Turlock, CA; (3); 6/600; Church Yth Grp; Drama Clb; Key Clb; Math Tm; NFL; Speech Tm; Teachers Aide; Mgr(s); Score Keeper; Stat Socr; Intract Clbs Amer Treas; PTSA Awd Span; Advncd Math; Hnrs Bio; Hnrs US Hist; Pre-Calc.

APALIT, CELESTINA B; Sweetwater Union HS; National City, CA; (2); Drama Clb; Intnl Clb; SADD; Church Choir; School Play; Cit Awd; Hon Roll; Pilipino-Awd; Essay Cntst Horizon 88; Vlntry Work For Eldry; UCSD; RN.

APARICIO, ANNA M; Bishop Amat Memorial HS; Baldwin Park, CA; (2); Sec French Clb; Hon Roll; Fri Night Live; Spcl Olympcs Vlntr; Photo Club; Psych.

APARICIO, ARACELI; J Eugene Mc Ateer HS; San Francisco, CA; (2); Rptr Nwsp; Intrml Mgr Wt Lftg; Yale U; Crmnl Law.

APARICIO, HEYDI K; Glendale Adventist Acad; Los Angeles, CA; (1); 36/90; Church Yth Grp; Dance Clb; Drama Clb; FCA; Chorus; Church Choir; Stu Cncl; Intrml Diving; Intrml Swmmng; Var Vllybl; Piano; Drawing; Loma Linda U; Ped.

APARICIO, MARIBELLA; Fillmore HS; Fillmore, CA; (2); Church Yth Grp; Var L Crs Cntry; Var L Trk; Pres Acad Fit Awd; Chrch Cls Pres; BYU; Psych.

APEPE, ACE R; Don Lugo HS; Chino Hills, CA; (2); Jazz Band; Cit Awd; Hon Roll; Sal; Spllng B Cont Wnnr 88; Comp Analyst.

APILADO, ANTHONY C; Cantwell HS; Montebello, CA; (3); Art Clb; Cmnty Wkr; Science Clb; Teachers Aide; Rep Nwsp; Rep Yrbk; VP Stu Cncl; Var Bsktbl; Intrml Vllybl; Hon Roll; Bus.

APILADO, DARRELL M; Cabrillo HS; Vandenberg Afb, CA; (2); Spanish Clb; JV Bsbl; JV Var Socr; Hon Roll; Prfct Atten Awd; CSF; Goldn St Exam Hnrs Awd Alg 89; Asian-Pacific Amer Assn 90; UC Santa Barbara; Chem Engr.

APODACA, JOY M; Dos Palos HS; Dos Palos, CA; (3); FHA; SADD; Teachers Aide; Sec Treas Frsh Cls; JV Bsktbl; JV Var Sftbl; JV Var Vllybl; High Hon Roll; Hon Roll; NHS; Spirit Ldrs Clb; CSF.

APODACA, YVONNE M; Warren HS; Downey, CA; (3); Pep Clb; Drill Tm; Nwsp; Cheerldng; Powder Puff Ftbl; Swmmng; USC; Jrnlsm.

APOSTOLOV, VASSIL A; Chaffey HS; Cucamonga, CA; (2); Hon Roll; Intl Bus.

APP, CHRISTOPHER Z; Napa Valley HS; Napa, CA; (1); Intrml Ftbl; JV Trk; Wt Lftg; High Hon Roll; Prfct Atten Awd; Bstl; Yrbk; Ski & Danc Clb; Stanford U; Chrgrphr.

APPEL, MIKE; Hilmar JR SR HS; Hilmar, CA; (4); Church Yth Grp; Drama Clb; Cheerldng; Ftbl; Trk; Cit Awd; Hon Roll; Acadmc Dec $300.00 Awd; Cal Grant A&B Recipnt; Crmnl Just.

APPELBAUM, JEFF F; Rio Americano HS; Carmichael, CA; (4); 38/263; Cmnty Wkr; SADD; Temple Yth Grp; JV Var Ftbl; Cit Awd; High Hon Roll; Pres Acad Fit Awd; United Synagogue Yth; Cinematography.

APPELGREN, CHRISTOPHER; South Fork HS; Miranda, CA; (3); Art Clb; Drama Clb; SADD; School Play; Ed Nwsp; High Hon Roll; Rotary Awd; Creatr & Edtr-Altrntv Magzn; Amnesty Intl Pres; Actng.

APPERSON, WENDY R; North Bakersfield HS; Bakersfield, CA; (3); Church Yth Grp; FCA; Teachers Aide; Acpl Chr; Chorus; Var Crs Cntry; Var Trk; Hon Roll; NHS; CA Schlrshp Fed; CSUB; Ed.

APPLEBAUM, SCOTT L; Oxnard HS; Oxnard, CA; (2); French Clb; JV Crs Cntry; JV Trk; High Hon Roll; USCF Cyclist; Engrng.

APPLEGARTH, SHANNON L; Taft Union HS; Taft, CA; (3); 91/200; Church Yth Grp; Ski Clb; Chorus; Yrbk; Hon Roll; Pres Acad Fit Awd; Pacific Union Coll.

APPLEGATE, APRIL A; Arcata HS; Arcata, CA; (2); Drama Clb; German Clb; Stage Crew; High Hon Roll; Hon Roll; U CA Davis; Med.

APPLEGATE, DEBORAH L; Milpitas HS; Milpitas, CA; (3); 67/487; Cmnty Wkr; Drama Clb; Band; Mrchg Band; School Musical; School Play; Stage Crew; Mgr(s); Score Keeper; JV Vllybl; Amnesty Intl Clb; Eclgy Clb; Santa Clara U; Pre-Med.

APPLEGATE, DIANE YVONNE; Desert Christian HS; Indio, CA; (4); 1/3; Church Yth Grp; Hosp Aide; Model UN; Teachers Aide; Chorus; Yrbk; Pres Jr Cls; Pres Sr Cls; Stu Cncl; JV Sftbl; ACSI Dstgshd Chrstn HS Stu 88-89; Teen Missions Intl Poalnd 89 & New Zealand 90; The Masters Coll; Nrsg.

APPLEGATE, TRACI D; Coalinga HS; Coalinga, CA; (2); VP FFA; Bsktbl; Sftbl; Hon Roll; Fresno ST U; Ag.

APPLEN, HEATHER D; Cajon HS; San Bernardino, CA; (1); Pep Clb; Varsity Clb; Capt Cheerldng; JV Sftbl; Schlrshp/Ldrshp Awds Engl, World Geogrphy.

APPLETON, STACI R; Sanger HS; Sanger, CA; (2); Drama Clb; Office Aide; Teachers Aide; Band; Color Guard; Jazz Band; Mrchg Band; Pep Band; School Play; Stage Crew; Improv Team; Drama.

APPLEWHITE-SHEPARD, DANITA; Sierra Vista HS; Baldwin Park, CA; (3); Church Yth Grp; Teachers Aide; Rep Stu Cncl; Sftbl; Cit Awd; Prfct Atten Awd; Pres Schlr; Chapman Coll; Poli Sci.

APPLING, ERIN; Adolfo Camarillo HS; Camarillo, CA; (2); Church Yth Grp; Drama Clb; Church Choir; School Play; JV Capt Cheerldng; Hon Roll; Oxnard Dist Hnr Roll.

APPRILL, MARY S; Paraclete HS; Lancaster, CA; (2); Church Yth Grp; Cmnty Wkr; Drama Clb; SADD; Church Choir; JV Bsktbl; JV Cheerldng; Powder Puff Ftbl; JV Vllybl; Sign Lang; Intl Law.

APRA, DENISE K; Branham HS; San Jose, CA; (2); 30/277; 4-H; SADD; JV Tennis; Hon Roll; Pres & Co Fndr Bay Area Mdl Horse Clb; Enjoy Showing Horses & Cmptng Dressage; Vrsty Bdmttn Team; San Jose St U; Advrtsng.

APRILE, BRYAN; Fred C Beyer HS; Modesto, CA; (4); 80/506; Math Tm; Science Clb; Acpl Chr; Band; Chorus; Jazz Band; Mrchg Band; Pep Band; School Musical; Hon Roll; St Hnr Choir; CSF; Rose-Holman Inst Tech; Math.

AQUILAR, FERNANDO C; Livingston HS; Livingston, CA; (3); Art Clb; French Clb; Rep Stu Cncl; Hon Roll; Prfct Atten Awd; Sec Of SCORE Clb; FIDM; Inter Dsgn.

AQUILAR, RONNY; Lynwood HS; Lynwood, CA; (2); Debate Tm; ROTC; Ftbl; Wt Lftg.

AQUILINO, NOELLE; Louisville HS; Woodland Hills, CA; (1); Church Yth Grp; Science Clb; Chorus; School Musical; School Play; Stu Cncl; Tennis; Hon Roll; Psych.

AQUILINO, STACY; Marin Catholic HS; Novato, CA; (4); 15/200; Rep Soph Cls; Var Capt Cheerldng; Var Capt Socr; Hon Roll; VP NHS; Snow & Water Skiing; Vrsty Socr All League; CA Schrlshp Fed Life Mem; 100 Hrs Cmnty Svc; K Of C; Santa Clara U.

AQUINO, ALICIA; La Quinta HS; Westminster, CA; (2); 32/342; SADD; Cit Awd; Hon Roll; Pres Acad Fit Awd; Silver Aztec; UC Berkeley; Genetics.

AQUINO, CHRISTINA A; John A Rowland HS; Rowland Heights, CA; (2); Acpl Chr; Chorus; School Musical; Stat Bsktbl; Stat Swmmng; JV Vllybl; Cit Awd; Hon Roll; Prfct Atten Awd; Choral Music Awd.

AQUINO, GERRY; East Union HS; Lathrop, CA; (2); Hon Roll; Prfct Atten Awd.

AQUINO, MARITZA; Bishop Amat Memorial HS; La Puente, CA; (3); Spanish Clb; Natl Span Exam Awd; Slvr Screen Clb; Comm Art.

AQUINO, NOVELYN; Lincoln HS; Stockton, CA; (3); Church Yth Grp; Cmnty Wkr; Pep Clb; Sec Aud/Vis; Drill Tm; Flag Corp; Pep Band; Yrbk; Var Cheerldng; Var Pom Pon; Princpls Awd; Fash Desgnr.

AQUINO, VERONICA C; Calexico HS; Calexico, CA; (1); Church Yth Grp; Drama Clb; FCA; GAA; SADD; Var Crs Cntry; Var Trk; Cit Awd; High Hon Roll; Pres Acad Fit Awd; UC Irvine; Ed.

AQUIRRE, MAGDALENA; Palo Verde HS; Blythe, CA; (3); 10/260; Spanish Clb.

ARABE, ARMI; Garey HS; Pomona, CA; (3); Sec Soph Cls; Sec Jr Cls; Cheerldng; Tennis; Trk; High Hon Roll; NHS; Pres Acad Fit Awd; Keywanetts; CSF; UCLA; Bus.

ARAGON, ALICIA M; West Covina HS; West Covina, CA; (1); Am Leg Aux Girls St; Chorus; Modeling; USC; Fine Arts.

ARAGON, ELIZA G; Pomona Adventist JR Acad; Ontario, CA; (1); 2/15; Church Yth Grp; Girl Scts; Teachers Aide; Band; Off Frsh Cls; Hon Roll; Prfct Atten Awd; Algebra Awd; Med.

ARAGON, GERALDINE; Antioch SR HS; Antioch, CA; (4); 3/585; Art Clb; Debate Tm; Spanish Clb; Swmmng; High Hon Roll; Hon Roll; CSF Clb-Two Awds; Engl Learning Awd; U CA-DAVIS; Med.

ARAGON, KATHY J; North Monterey County HS; Salinas, CA; (4); Outstndng Achvt Cert Engl, US Hstry, Art; Org 2 Fshn Shows 89-90; FIDM; Visual Presentation.

ARAGON, RACHEL; Buena HS; Santa Paula, CA; (1); Mgr(s); JV Vllybl; Writing Poetry; Psych.

ARAGON, RUBEN R; Downey HS; South Gate, CA; (2); Church Yth Grp; Drama Clb; Latin Clb; Intrml Ftbl; UCLA; Comp Sci.

ARAGONES, GINA MARIA; Southwest HS; San Diego, CA; (3); 52/553; Intnl Clb; Key Clb; Pep Clb; Teachers Aide; CSF; GATE; UCSD; Comp Prog.

ARAIZA, CLAUDIA V; Mountain View HS; El Monte, CA; (1); Drill Tm; Flag Corp; Trk; Cit Awd; Comp Prgmr.

ARAIZA, GUS M; Hemet HS; Hemet, CA; (3); JV Ftbl; Chrprtctr.

ARAIZA, JENNIFER J; Central Union HS; El Centro, CA; (4); Church Yth Grp; Pep Clb; SADD; Sftbl; Cit Awd; Mat Mds Capt; San Diego ST U; Lbrl Stud.

ARAKAKI, LISA A; Schurr HS; Montebello, CA; (4); 4/580; Key Clb; SADD; Sec Mrchg Band; Ed Nwsp; Rep Soph Cls; Sec Sr Cls; Hon Roll; NHS; Ntl Merit SF; Clsscl Japnese Dncng; CSF Secy; Mock Trl; Lwyr.

ARAKELIAN, WENDY L; John Glenn HS; Norwalk, CA; (2); Church Yth Grp; German Clb; Hon Roll; Teacher.

ARAM, JESSICA R; Glendale HS; Burbank, CA; (4); 150/690; Pep Clb; Spanish Clb; Drill Tm; Variety Show; Yrbk; JV Bsktbl; Var Cheerldng; Score Keeper; Hon Roll; St Schlr; Glendale Safe Rides; Law Explorers; Persian Assn Of U Women Schlrshp; News Press Essay Cont 3rd Pl; Cal ST Northridge; Poltcl Sci.

ARAMBEL, STELLA R; Chino HS; Chino, CA; (3); Girl Scts; Ski Clb; Hon Roll; Ntl Merit Ltr; Vocational Cert In Comp Applctns & Comp Oprtns In Small Bus; Bio Sci.

ARAMBUL, MIGUEL D; Buena Park HS; Anaheim, CA; (3); 124/407; Church Yth Grp; Science Clb; JV Ftbl; Var Trk; Var Capt Wrstlng; Hon Roll; Boxing; Pre-Med.

ARAMBULA, BLANCA E; Bell Gardens HS; Bell Gardens, CA; (4); French Clb; SADD; Band; Mrchg Band; Phtg Nwsp; Powder Puff Ftbl; Var Tennis; Cit Awd; Hon Roll; Pres Acad Fit Awd; Qlty Inn, Bell Grdns Front Desk; Played Flute 7 Yrs; Mock Trial; Pre-Med.

ARAMBULA, CORINA E; Nogales HS; La Puente, CA; (2); Chorus; Hon Roll; Prfct Atten Awd; Spnsh Hnrs; USC; Bus.

ARAMBULO, JAYJAY; Chaminade College Prep; Chatsworth, CA; (2); Church Yth Grp; Ftbl; Wt Lftg; High Hon Roll; Hon Roll; Pres Acad Fit Awd; Outstndg Achvt Awds 88-89 & 89-90; Med.

ARANAS, JONATHAN B; Lakewood HS; Long Beach, CA; (3); 57/720; Church Yth Grp; Math Tm; Band; JV Var Tennis; L Vllybl; Kiwanis Awd; VP NHS; Prfct Atten Awd; Jr CSF; Vrsty & JV Water Polo; UC Irvine; Elec Engrng.

ARANAS, RYAN D; Sacred Heart Cathedral Prep; San Francisco, CA; (2); Cmnty Wkr; Science Clb; Service Clb; Varsity Clb; JV Var Tennis; High Hon Roll; Hon Roll; CSF.

ARANCIBIA, DENISE V; Westlake HS; Westlake Village, CA; (2); SADD; Drill Tm; Variety Show; Acting; Bsktbl; Vllybl; UCLA; Acting.

ARANDA, CANDEE ROSE A; Sunset HS; Hayward, CA; (3); 10/290; VP Jr Cls; Sec Stu Cncl; Var Tennis; Hon Roll; Tnns Coachs & MVP Awds; Samuel Meritt; Nrsng.

ARANDA, CONNIE; Selma HS; Selma, CA; (1); Sectry.

ARANDA, FRANK; Leuzingr HS; Hawthorne, CA; (3); Office Aide; Teachers Aide; Cit Awd; Hon Roll; La Raza Clb; El Camino Coll; Auto Tech.

ARANDA, FRANK; Santa Maria HS; Santa Maria, CA; (2); 5/527; CSF; Upward Bound Pgm; Achvd 1st 4.0 GPA 89-90 Schl Yr.

ARANDA, MIGUEL A; Leffingwell Christian HS; Norwalk, CA; (3); 3/60; Church Yth Grp; Drama Clb; Math Tm; Church Choir; School Play; High Hon Roll; Pres Acad Fit Awd; AYSO Soccer; Arch.

ARANDA, VELMA L; Colton HS; Colton, CA; (4); Treas AFS; Hist Key Clb; VP Frsh Cls; Pres Soph Cls; Rep Jr Cls; Rep Sr Cls; Rep Stu Cncl; Mgr Bsktbl; Hon Roll; Jr NHS; HOBY; Parent Teacher Stu Assn Historian; U CA Riverside; Bus Admin.

ARANGO, MARIBEL; Chula Vista HS; Chula Vista, CA; (3); 43/493; Church Yth Grp; Red Cross Aide; Scholastic Bowl; Stu Cncl; Opt Clb Awd; Peer Cnslng; Jr Stsmn Of Amer-Sec & Treas; CA Schlstc Fed-VP; Psych.

ARANTE, RICHARD J; James Logan HS; Union City, CA; (3); Church Yth Grp; FCA; Letterman Clb; Varsity Clb; Band; Mrchg Band; Orch; Pep Band; JV Var Bsbl; Prfct Atten Awd; Pre-Med.

ARANYAWAT, VIATANAPONG B; Cerritos HS; Cerritos, CA; (1); Model UN; Var Wrstlng; UCLA.

ARAQUISTAIN, KIMBERLY; Amos Alonzo Stagg SR HS; Stockton, CA; (2); School Musical; Perfct Atten; Accntnt.

ARASMITH, HEATHER J; Simi Valley HS; Simi Valley, CA; (4); 30/728; VP Art Clb; Church Yth Grp; French Clb; Tennis; Trk; Cit Awd; Hon Roll; Jr NHS; CSF; Art Center Schlrshps; Illustration.

ARASTOOZADEH, NAZANIN; Rio Americano HS; Sacramento, CA; (4); 30/259; Debate Tm; French Clb; Intnl Clb; Latin Clb; Temple Yth Grp; Variety Show; Nwsp; Crs Cntry; Score Keeper; Trk; Lndscp Arch.

ARATOUNIANS, ANI B; Holy Martyrs Ferrahian HS; Reseda, CA; (4); 3/53; Office Aide; Chorus; Nwsp; Var Bsktbl; Var Vllybl; Cit Awd; High Hon Roll; Hon Roll; Ntl Merit Schol; Pres Acad Fit Awd; CSUN; Bus.

ARAU, MATTHEW R; Rio Americano HS; Sacramento, CA; (3); 8/300; Debate Tm; French Clb; VP Key Clb; Band; Jazz Band; Pep Band; Var Crs Cntry; Var Trk; Ntl Merit Ltr; Rotary Awd; Dixieland Band Ldr; Jazz Combo Ldr; Acadmc Ltr; CSF; Social Stds.

ARAUJO, ERICKA; El Cajon Valley HS; El Cajon, CA; (2); Drama Clb; Teachers Aide; Var Fld Hcky; JV Score Keeper; Var Socr; Var Trk; JV Vllybl; Flight Attendant.

ARAUJO, MARIA; Rosary HS; Placentia, CA; (4); #17 In Class; Church Yth Grp; Sec French Clb; Science Clb; Var Trk; JV Vllybl; High Hon Roll; Hon Roll; NHS; NEDT Awd; Prfct Atten Awd; CA ST U Fullerton; Intl Bus.

ARAUJO, MARTHA A; El Toro HS; El Toro, CA; (4); Cmnty Wkr; Key Clb; Office Aide; Service Clb; Teachers Aide; Cit Awd; Hon Roll; UC Irvine; Bio Sci.

ARAUJO, NANCY; Francis Polytechnic HS; Arleta, CA; (3); Cmnty Wkr; Treas Debate Tm; Drama Clb; French Clb; Pep Clb; Pres Spanish Clb; Pres SADD; Drill Tm; Rep Soph Cls; Off Jr Cls; Pepperdine; Law.

ARAUJO, TINA; Independence HS; San Jose, CA; (2); Chorus; Var Cheerldng; Hayward ST; Psych.

ARAULLO, FRANCIS; Bellarmine Col Prep; Belmont, CA; (4); 38/308; Library Aide; Math Clb; Science Clb; Hon Roll; Ntl Merit Schol; Pres Acad Fit Awd; UC San Diego; Elec Engrng.

ARAUTO, JACKIE M; Polytechnic HS; Arleta, CA; (2); Spanish Clb; Drill Tm; VP Stu Cncl; Var Trk; Hon Roll; College Readiness Pgm/Future Schlrs Pgm CSUN; CA Jr Schlrshp Fed.

ARAVJO, ROGELIO L; Merced Union HS; Merced, CA; (3); Math Clb; Spanish Clb; Hon Roll; Prfct Atten Awd; GMI; Electrncs Engr.

ARAYA, KIDISTI; Hoover HS; San Diego, CA; (2); French Clb; Hon Roll; PTSA Fndrs Day Awd Cert Of Merit; Frnch Achvt Awd; Harvard U; Law.

ARAYATA, MARISSA; Castle Park HS; Chula Vista, CA; (4); 1/320; Cmnty Wkr; Hosp Aide; Lit Mag; Off Frsh Cls; Off Soph Cls; Off Jr Cls; Off Sr Cls; Stu Cncl; DAR Awd; High Hon Roll; Tandy Technology Schlr; Amer-Asian Clb VP; UCSD; Psych.

ARAZA, ELVIRA; Vallejo SR HS; Vallejo, CA; (3); Letterman Clb; Model UN; Teachers Aide; Varsity Clb; Tennis; High Hon Roll; Hon Roll; Jr NHS; NHS; Ldrshp Cls; Tutoring; UC Davis; Comp Sci.

ARBAGEY, JULIE A; St Francis HS; Los Altos, CA; (3); Drama Clb; Service Clb; SADD; Thesps; Chorus; Church Choir; School Musical; Variety Show; Co-Ed Nwsp; Rptr Yrbk; Cmmnty & Prof Musical Theatre; Respect Life; Asst Leag Of Santa Clara; Santa Clara U; Criminal Law.

ARBALLO, COREY T; El Rancho HS; Pico Rivera, CA; (4); Varsity Clb; Jazz Band; VP Mrchg Band; Var Crs Cntry; Capt Powder Puff Ftbl; Var Trk; Var Wt Lftg; Water Polo V; Coed Capers; Outstndng Sr; Mt San Antonio; Music Engrng.

ARBALLO, NATALIE B; Madera HS; Madera, CA; (2); Church Yth Grp; Cmnty Wkr; Drama Clb; GAA; Letterman Clb; Ski Clb; SADD; Teachers Aide; Thesps; Varsity Clb; UCLA; Bus Law.

ARBANASIN, JOHN; Lodi HS; Lodi, CA; (4); Art Clb; Treas Drama Clb; Off German Clb; Science Clb; High Hon Roll; Masonic Awd; Stu Of Mnth Sept 89; U CA Davis.

ARBAUGH, JOSHUA A; Eureka HS; Eureka, CA; (3); Drama Clb; School Play; Gym; Hon Roll; Engl.

ARBIZU, SANDRA; Manual Arts CIP HS; Los Angeles, CA; (4); Drama Clb; Varsity Clb; Band; Chorus; School Musical; Stu Cncl; Var Tennis; Cit Awd; Hon Roll; Prfct Atten Awd; MVP Girls Tennis Tm; Joiners & Yng Schlrs Pgm At UCSB; 2nd Pl Wnnr Sci Fr; U Of PA; Econ.

ARBOLEDA, ZARA A; Notre Dame HS; San Mateo, CA; (3); Sec Math Clb; Teachers Aide; School Musical; Nwsp; Lit Mag; VP Soph Cls; Rep Jr Cls; Pres Sr Cls; Rep Stu Cncl; Var Trk; Law.

ARCE, TRACY M; Covina HS; Covina, CA; (2); Sec French Clb; Band; Drill Tm; JV Stat Score Keeper; Swmmng; Sccr West Covina Yth Sccr; Obstrcn.

ARCE, WILLIAM; Los Angeles HS; Los Angeles, CA; (3); #27 In Class; Computer Clb; Red Cross Aide; Service Clb; Spanish Clb; Rptr Nwsp; Stu Cncl; Var Socr; Var Swmmng; JV Vllybl; Hon Roll; Bus Admin.

ARCEO, GAIUS; Southwest HS; San Diego, CA; (3); Church Yth Grp; Library Aide; Intrml Vllybl; Cit Awd; Hon Roll; Prfct Atten Awd.

ARCEO, NICK; Encina HS; Sacramento, CA; (3); Art Clb; Lit Mag; JV Crs Cntry; JV Trk; JV Wrstlng; Hon Roll; Student Of The Month In Industrial Arts; Regnl Occupational Prog In Commrcl Art; Principal Honor Roll; Art Major/Commercial Artist.

ARCEO, PETER S; Santa Clara HS; Oxnard, CA; (3); 10/170; French Clb; Golf; NHS; Prfct Atten Awd; Typing Awd; Wght Lftng Clb; Engrng.

ARCHER, REGINA R; Portola JR & SR HS; Portola, CA; (2); Chess Clb; Cmnty Wkr; Girl Scts; Teachers Aide; Rptr Nwsp; Sec Frsh Cls; Treas Soph Cls; JV Crs Cntry; Intrml Sftbl; JV Trk; U CA Davis; Child Psych.

ARCHER, RYAN; Hesperia Christian HS; Hesperia, CA; (3); 4/32; Church Yth Grp; Drama Clb; Letterman Clb; Quiz Bowl; School Play; Rep Sr Cls; Var Bsbl; JV Var Bsktbl; Var Ftbl; High Hon Roll; Point Loma; Bus.

ARCHER-KLINTWORTH, STEPHANIE D; El Toro HS; El Toro, CA; (4); Church Yth Grp; Office Aide; Teachers Aide; High Hon Roll; Intl Order Jobs Dghtrs Past Hnrd Qn; 7th Pl Cnty Acctng Cmptn; CA ST Fullerton; Acctng.

ARCHEY, RACHEL L; Lincoln HS; San Francisco, CA; (3); Dance Clb; Red Cross Aide; ROTC; SADD; Drill Tm; Cheerldng; Bell ST; Nrsng.

ARCHOUNIANI, ARA H; International Studies Acad; San Francisco, CA; (3); Cmnty Wkr; German Clb; Capt Socr; High Hon Roll; Hon Roll; Acad Decathlon; Close Up; UCSF Vlntr; Quiz Master; U CA Davis; Med.

ARCHULETA, FRANKIE; Salinas HS; Salinas, CA; (4); Dance Clb; Drama Clb; SADD; School Play; Rep Frsh Cls; Rep Sr Cls; Cheerldng; Gym; Powder Puff Ftbl; Score Keeper; Hartnell JC; Bus.

ARCHULETA, NERISSA; Palo Verde HS; Blythe, CA; (2); Church Yth Grp; Drama Clb; Pep Clb; Flag Corp; Off Soph Cls; Golf; Hon Roll; NHS; Ntl Merit Ltr; Rotary Awd; Cal Poly Pmna; Psych.

ARCHULETA, PATRICK A; Point Arena HS; Point Arena, CA; (2); Church Yth Grp; Library Aide; Hon Roll; Lion Awd; Marine Bio.

ARCIA, ROVIL P; St Ignatius Coll Prep; Daly City, CA; (3); 27/251; Hosp Aide; Science Clb; Hon Roll; CA Schlrshp Fed; St Ignatius Bwlng Tm & Christian Lfe Cmmnty.

ARCINAS, REGINA L; Salinas HS; Salinas, CA; (4); Church Yth Grp; Hist FBLA; Office Aide; Spanish Clb; Teachers Aide; Band; Mrchg Band; Pep Band; Hon Roll.

ARCINIEGA, ELICIA M; Don Lugo HS; Chino, CA; (3); Office Aide; Teachers Aide; JV Sftbl; Hon Roll; Golden Cnqust Awd Sci; Bus.

ARCINIEGA, JULIO A; Southwest HS; San Ysidro, CA; (3); Stdnt Mnth; UCSD; Arch.

ARCULARIUS, BRET L; Bishop Union HS; Bishop, CA; (3); 4-H; FFA; JV Var Bsktbl; JV Ftbl; Socr; 4-H Awd; Hon Roll; Rchr.

ARDOHAIN, LISA; Washington Union HS; Fresno, CA; (3); FBLA; Intnl Clb; Band; Nwsp; Yrbk; VP Frsh Cls; Bsktbl; Trk; Vllybl; Hon Roll; Girls Bsktbl Defensive Plyr 89-90; Girls Bsktbl All League Offensive & Defensive 89-90.

AREAS, MIRYAM P; Ygnacio Valley HS; Pittsburg, CA; (4); 87/360; Pres Church Yth Grp; Pres French Clb; Spanish Clb; Teachers Aide; Church Choir; JV Vllybl; Bank Of Amer Cert; Forgn Lang Ygnacio Vly Dept Awds; Prin Outstndng Stu Achvt Awd; San Francisco ST U; Intl Reltn.

ARECHIGA, CASSANDRA; Calvary Chapel HS; Midway City, CA; (2); Church Yth Grp; Var Sftbl; Var Vllybl; Hon Roll.

AREF, MICHAEL; Torrey Pines HS; Solana Beach, CA; (1); Hon Roll; Pres Acad Fit Awd; Brown Belt-Vechi Ryu Karate; Fencing.

ARELLANO, ALICIA; Nogales HS; La Puente, CA; (3); Teachers Aide; Wt Lftg; Scrtry.

ARELLANO, ANABEL; Paramount HS; Paramount, CA; (2); 5/700; French Clb; Var L Tennis; French Hon Soc; High Hon Roll; Prfct Atten Awd.

ARELLANO, ANGELICA; Montclair HS; Ontario, CA; (2); Computer Clb; Dance Clb; Math Tm; Teachers Aide; Yrbk; Off Soph Cls; Bsbl; Bsktbl; Sftbl; Swmmng; Art; Typing; Cooking; Montclair High; Cosmotologist.

ARELLANO, BESS; Encinal HS; Alameda, CA; (4); 9/210; Sec Pres FBLA; Office Aide; Treas Spanish Clb; Band; Chorus; Var Tennis; Hon Roll; Philippine Tradtnl Folk Dancng; Playing Piano; 2nd Prz CA Voctnl Educ Olympics For Wrd Procssng; UC Berkeley; Bus.

ARELLANO, EFREN; Alisal HS; Salinas, CA; (3); Teachers Aide; JV Var Ftbl; Cit Awd; High Hon Roll; Hon Roll.

ARELLANO, ESMERALDA; Paramount HS; Paramount, CA; (4); 5/470; French Clb; Letterman Clb; Var L Tennis; French Hon Soc; High Hon Roll; Ntl Merit Ltr; Pres Acad Fit Awd; CSF; Coll Clb; Loyola Marymount U; Bus.

ARELLANO, GIOVANNY M; Pioneer HS; Whittier, CA; (4); Teachers Aide; Var Socr; Rio Hound JC; Sci.

ARELLANO, ISELA R; Arvin HS; Arvin, CA; (2); Latin Clb; Spanish Clb; Church Choir; Swing Chorus; Hon Roll; Aerobics; Cinemtgrphy.

ARELLANO, JAKKIE C; Manteca HS; Manteca, CA; (3); 37/358; Ed Yrbk; Stat Socr; Var Trk; Stat Wt Lftg; Hon Roll; Organize Fund Raisers Cls; Var Ltr Track Freshman Yr; Chico ST; Sec Math Teacher.

ARELLANO, JAVIER; Valley HS; Santa Ana, CA; (1); Engr.

ARELLANO, JERRY L; Balboa HS; San Francisco, CA; (2); MESA Prgrm.

ARELLANO, JOANNE M; Montgomery HS; San Diego, CA; (2); 66/474; Band; Flag Corp; Rep Soph Cls; Stu Cncl; Pep Clb; Phtg Yrbk; JV Vllybl; Conticore; CA Schlrshp Fed; San Diego ST U; Advrtsng.

ARELLANO, JOSE A; Santa Ana HS; Orange, CA; (2); Pres Art Clb; Science Clb; Cit Awd; Hon Roll; Japanese; USC; Bus.

ARELLANO, JOSE L; Washington Prep; Los Angeles, CA; (2); Band; Jazz Band; Mrchg Band; Hon Roll; Ntl Merit Schol; USC; Engrng.

ARELLANO, JOY; Ontario HS; Ontario, CA; (2); Drama Clb; Teachers Aide; School Musical; School Play; Score Keeper; JV Vllybl; Wt Lftg; Pres Acad Fit Awd; Fshn Industry.

ARELLANO, JUAN R; Roosevelt HS; Los Angeles, CA; (3); JV Bsbl; Cit Awd; High Hon Roll; ITT; Electrncs.

ARELLANO, LOURDES M; Roosevelt HS; Los Angeles, CA; (2); Ed Yrbk; Hon Roll; Coll Core Curriclm; CSULA; Scl Workr.

ARELLANO, LUIS E; Winters HS; Winters, CA; (2).

ARELLANO, MYRA; Bishop Amat HS; Diamond Bar, CA; (3); High Hon Roll; Sal; Filipino Am Yth Grp Of Diamond Bar; Qn Of Pesce Rosary Grp Yth Clb; Wrkng Part Time Family Bus; Med.

ARELLANO, PATRICIA E; Bell Gardens HS; Bell Gardens, CA; (3); Treas French Clb; Rptr Nwsp; Cit Awd; Hon Roll; Girls League; CSF Sec; Engl Tchr.

ARELLANO, PATTI M; Riverbank HS; Riverbank, CA; (2); Church Yth Grp; Church Choir; Hon Roll; Fshn Dsgn.

ARELLANO, ROCIO; Roosevelt HS; Los Angeles, CA; (3); Key Clb; Service Clb; Drill Tm; Yrbk; Rep Frsh Cls; Rep Stu Cncl; Var Score Keeper; Hon Roll; Mecha Advanced Placement Club; Mariposa Awd Of Rmt; Pres Awd; Cal St Northridge; Bus Mgmt.

ARENA, ALBERT; Capichino HS; San Bruno, CA; (3); Math Clb; Capt Math Tm; School Play; Ed Lit Mag; Rep Sr Cls; Hon Roll; Lion Awd; Franklin; Lwyr.

ARENAS JR, ANTENOR D; Saint Ignatius HS; Daly City, CA; (2); French Clb; Office Aide; Science Clb; Service Clb; Hon Roll; CA Schlrshp Fed; Asian Stu Coalition; Bus.

ARENAS, AUDREY; Bishop Amat HS; Ontario, CA; (2); French Clb; Swmmng; Hon Roll; Silver Screen & Photogrph Clbs; Med.

ARENAS, PAMELA C; Lowell HS; San Francisco, CA; (3); ROTC; Drill Tm; Variety Show; Filipino Amer Club; Registry Rep; U Of CA San Francisco; Dental.

ARENAS, YOLANDA A; John O'connell HS; San Francisco, CA; (4); Church Yth Grp; Cmnty Wkr; Yrbk; Treas Stu Cncl; Mgr(s); Cit Awd; High Hon Roll; Hon Roll; Bank Of Amer Achvt Awd-Fld Of Librl Arts; San Francisco ST; Mech Engrng.

AREND, SEAN; Yucaipa HS; Calimesa, CA; (3); 7/350; Key Clb; Letterman Clb; Spanish Clb; Var Bsbl; Var Ftbl; Var Wrstlng; High Hon Roll; Outstndng Wrstlr Awd 90; Mst Imprvd V Bsbl Plyr Awd 90; Smmr Scientific Smnr; US Air Force Acad; Engrng.

ARENTZ, LISA ANN; Fontana HS; Fontana, CA; (2); Church Yth Grp; Cmnty Wkr; Dance Clb; Chorus; Cit Awd; Hon Roll; Campus Life; Interior Dsgn.

AREVALO, ALEX; Theodore Roosevelt HS; Los Angeles, CA; (3); Drama Clb; French Clb; Service Clb; Ski Clb; School Play; French Hon Soc; Hon Roll; Earthday Clb; Acad Decathlon Tm; Korean Clb; NYU; Engl.

AREVALO, BLANCA R; St Monica HS; Venice, CA; (3); Church Yth Grp; Var Socr; Co-Capt JV Sftbl; CSF; 1st Hnrs; Air Force Acad; Police Offcr.

AREVALO, DOMINGO; San Benito HS; Hollister, CA; (1); Art Clb; French Clb; Library Aide; Stage Crew; Crs Cntry; Trk; Wt Lftg; Wrstlng; Hon Roll; Phys Ed Teacher.

AREVALO, RENE A; Montebello HS; Montebello, CA; (2); Trk; Hon Roll; Congrssnl Schlr Rep CA Natl Yng Ldrs Conf; UCLA.

AREVALO, SUSANA; Eagle Rock HS; Los Angeles, CA; (3); Teachers Aide; L Crs Cntry; L Trk; Hon Roll; Pres Acad Fit Awd; Outstndng Schlrshp Awd Indus Arts; CA Jr Schlrshp Fed Hnr Awd; Medallion Awd Indus Educ.

AREVALOS, MARIA; Southwest HS; San Ysidro, CA; (2); Church Yth Grp; Spanish Clb; Hon Roll; Folkloric Dance; AVID; MECHA Club; Fshn Des.

ARGANDONA, ALEENA; Schurr HS; Monterey Park, CA; (3); Drama Clb; Key Clb; Acpl Chr; Chorus; Capt L Flag Corp; School Musical; Stu Cncl; Hon Roll; Cal ST Long Beach; Actng.

ARGAO, CAROL; Brea Olinda HS; Brea, CA; (3); 14/290; Cmnty Wkr; Sec GAA; Pres Intnl Clb; Var L Crs Cntry; Var L Trk; NHS; Pres Acad Fit Awd; Pres & Dist Govnr Interact Clb; CSF; USN Acad; Astronaut.

ARGOSINO, FERNANDO T; John A Rowland HS; Walnut, CA; (2); Intnl Clb; Science Clb; VP Jr Cls; Var Wrstlng; High Hon Roll; Hon Roll; Pres Acad Fit Awd; Nmrs Awds In Anmtn; Dsgn.

ARGUELLES, MARTI C; Corona HS; Corona, CA; (2); 13/473; GAA; Library Aide; Office Aide; Science Clb; Rep Stu Cncl; Var Cheerldng; Var Crs Cntry; Capt JV Socr; Var Trk; Hon Roll; Gymnstcs.

ARGUELLO, MICHELLE C; Madera HS; Madera, CA; (3); Church Yth Grp; JA; SADD; Teachers Aide; Chorus; School Play; Treas Frsh Cls; High Hon Roll; Hon Roll; Stu Of Mnth April 90; Math Achvt Awds 87-89; Typing Achvt Awds 87-88; USC; Dentist.

ARGUETA, YESENIA; Liberty Union HS; Brentwood, CA; (3); 26/339; Church Yth Grp; Latin Clb; Office Aide; Hon Roll; CA Schlstc Fed; Bus.

ARGUIJO, ARTURO A; Channel Islands HS; Oxnard, CA; (3); VICA; High Hon Roll; Hon Roll; Prfct Atten Awd; Cal Poly; Civil Engrng.

ARGUMANIZ, ARACELY; Sacred Heart HS; Los Angeles, CA; (3); 12/100; Library Aide; School Play; Treas Sr Cls; VP Stu Cncl; Hon Roll; NHS; Prfct Atten Awd; Typing Awd; Mat Tutor; Natl Span Exam Awds; CCD Teacher; CA Poly Pomona; Arch.

ARIAS, ADRIANA; Coalinga HS; Coalinga, CA; (2); Dermatologist.

ARIAS JR, CARLOS; Nogales HS; West Covina, CA; (3); Letterman Clb; Varsity Clb; Band; Mrchg Band; Var L Swmmng; Intrml Vllybl; Hon Roll; Prfct Atten Awd; Water Polo Var Let & Capt; Bus.

ARIAS, CHRISTINA M; Patrick Henry/Francis Parker HS; San Diego, CA; (2); 1/530; Scrkpr NFL; Speech Tm; JV Score Keeper; JV Vllybl; High Hon Roll; Jr NHS; Lion Awd; Opt Clb Awd; Pres Acad Fit Awd; Schl Schlrshp; Astronomy Club Pres; Physics.

ARIAS, GISELLE; Bishop Amat HS; West Covina, CA; (3); Spanish Clb; Drill Tm; Var Cheerldng; 1st Pl Natl Span Exam; U Of CA Los Angeles; Poltc Sci.

ARIAS, HECTOR A; Fontana HS; Fontana, CA; (2); JV Socr; JV Wt Lftg; Acctng.

ARIAS, IRENE; Bell Gardens HS; Bell Gardens, CA; (4); 22/500; Church Yth Grp; Cmnty Wkr; FTA; Treas SADD; Teachers Aide; Ed Yrbk; Lit Mag; Rep Stu Cncl; High Hon Roll; CSF; Whittier Coll; Poltcl Sci.

ARIAS, JOSE A; Glendale Adventist Acad; Los Angeles, CA; (3); Church Yth Grp; FCA; Teachers Aide; Band; Church Choir; Jazz Band; Mrchg Band; Crs Cntry; Ftbl; Mgr(s); Adventist Yth Grp Ldr; Pacific Union Coll; Hstry.

ARIAS, LETICIA; Pasadena HS; Pasadena, CA; (2); Spanish Clb; Hon Roll; Badmntn Tm; MESA; CSF; Engr.

ARIAS, LUIS F; Pasadena HS; Pasadena, CA; (3); JV Var Socr; CSF; Latin Amer Stu Assn; Constitutional Rights Fndtn.

ARIAS, LUZ C; Regina Caeli HS; Compton, CA; (3); Cmnty Wkr; Chorus; School Play; Cit Awd; High Hon Roll; Hon Roll; NHS; CCD; Untd Culture Clb; Schl Awd Hghst Avg Jr Cls; Bus.

ARIAS, MICHAEL A; Santa Clara HS; Oxnard, CA; (2); Church Yth Grp; JV Bsbl; JV Bsktbl; JV Ftbl; Hon Roll; NHS; Law.

ARIAS, NYDIA L; Fontana HS; Fontana, CA; (3); Spanish Clb; JV Vllybl; Hon Roll; Hnr Clb Pres; U La Verne; Bus.

ARIAS, STAR; Rialto JR HS; Rialto, CA; (1); Girl Scts; Office Aide; Teachers Aide; School Play; Variety Show; Rep Frsh Cls; Stu Cncl; Cheerldng; Gym; High Hon Roll; Lttr R Clb; Ldrshp Cls; GATE Cls; OH ST U; Law.

ARIAS, YESELI; Riverbank HS; Riverbank, CA; (3); Church Yth Grp; Rep Frsh Cls; Sec Soph Cls; Sec Jr Cls; Treas Sr Cls; Rep Stu Cncl; Var Tennis; Var Trk; Var Vllybl; Cit Awd; CSF CA Schltc Fed; Schlr Athlete; Standiford; Med.

ARIAS, ZIMPRICIO; Compton HS; Compton, CA; (3); Cmnty Wkr; Drm Mjr(t); Yrbk; Off Sr Cls; Wt Lftg; Lion Awd.

ARIAZ, SHEILA E; South HS; Bakersfield, CA; (3); Teachers Aide; Band; Mrchg Band; Pep Band; Swmmng; Hon Roll; Cmps Lf; Yth For Chrst; CA ST U Fllrtn; Chld Psych.

ARIYOSHI, ERIC Y; Berkeley HS; Berkeley, CA; (3); Ski Clb; Rptr Nwsp; Stu Cncl; Var Swmmng; Var Wrstlng; Hon Roll; Water Polo; Falconry; Jr Statesmn Amer; UCLA; Bus.

ARKO, BETH A; University City HS; San Diego, CA; (3); AFS; Aud/Vis; Church Yth Grp; Cmnty Wkr; Dance Clb; German Clb; SADD; Orch; Yrbk; Var JV Swmmng; Yng Art Exhib & Awds 88; UCSD Airbrshng Crs; USC; Arch.

ARLOTTI, KEITH; Cajon HS; San Bernardino, CA; (2); Ftbl; Cit Awd; High Hon Roll; Jr NHS; CA Schlrshp Fndtn; Music.

ARLOTTO, LORI M; Loretto HS; El Dorado Hills, CA; (4); 5/53; Debate Tm; JA; Science Clb; Speech Tm; Nwsp; Ed Yrbk; Lit Mag; VP Soph Cls; Pres Jr Cls; French Hon Soc; Natl Cncl Tchrs Engls Awd Wrtng; Print Jrnlsm.

ARLUCK, JACK A; Livermore HS; Livermore, CA; (1); Boy Scts; Band; High Hon Roll; Hon Roll; Bus Profs of Am; Eagle Scout Rank Attained 90; Order Of Arrow Boy Scts; Eng.

ARMANTROUT, CRISTY; Downey HS; Downey, CA; (1); Church Yth Grp; SADD; Church Choir; Mrchg Band; Cheerldng; Cit Awd; Kiwanis Awd; Pres Acad Fit Awd; UCLA; Med.

ARMAS, MICHELE F; Atwater HS; Merced, CA; (2); Rptr FFA; Hon Roll; Cal Poly; Genetic Engrng.

ARMENDARIZ, BIG JOHN; Garces Memorial HS; Delano, CA; (4); Church Yth Grp; Office Aide; Church Choir; Yrbk; Bsbl; Swmmng; Hon Roll; Mst Inspriational Swmmr For 2 Yrs Awd; Mst Inspriational Bsebl Awd; CSF; Bakersfield Coll; Bus Mgmt.

ARMENDARIZ, CESAR; Rosemead HS; Rosemead, CA; (4); 8/398; Am Leg Boys St; Teachers Aide; Pres Frsh Cls; Pres Soph Cls; Pres Jr Cls; Var Ftbl; Trk; Wt Lftg; Hon Roll; Kiwanis Awd; CSF Pres; Sr Hall Fame Awd; Yth Opprtnts Fndnt Excptnl Schlr Awd; U Of South CA; Bus Admin.

ARMENDARIZ, ROSA L; Saint Bonaventure HS; Camarillo, CA; (2); Church Yth Grp; NFL; Speech Tm; Pre-Coll Acad; Lector Spnsh, Engl Chrch Svcs; Mime Grp; Child Psych.

ARMENIAN, GARIN; Holy Martyrs HS; Tarzana, CA; (3); 2/65; Church Yth Grp; Cmnty Wkr; Dance Clb; Var Trk; Hon Roll; Poetry Cont Przs; Mem CSF; Cmnty Work Awd; Writer.

ARMENTA, ERICA; San Dimas HS; San Dimas, CA; (2); Intrct Clb; Peer Cnslr; Azusa Pacific U; Bus.

ARMENTA, ROBERT P; North Salinas HS; Salinas, CA; (3); Spanish Clb; Var Bsbl; Ftbl; Wt Lftg; Cal ST Berkeley; Bus.

ARMENTROUT, NATHAN R; Paraclete HS; Lancaster, CA; (2); JA; Key Clb; Bsktbl; High Hon Roll; Pres Schlr; Mechanical Design Technology.

ARMI, THERESIA; Golden West HS; Visalia, CA; (1); Band; Mrchg Band; Pep Band; Sftbl; Hon Roll; Outstndng Band Stu Of Yr; Winter Circuit Percussion Grp; Tulare/Kings Cnty Hnr Band; UCLA; Music.

ARMIJO, ANITA; John F Kennedy HS; La Palma, CA; (4); Church Yth Grp; Computer Clb; Pep Clb; Varsity Clb; Chorus; School Musical; Cheerldng; Hon Roll; Orange Co HS Arts; CSF; Psych.

ARMIJO, KARRIE L; Ontario HS; Ontario, CA; (3); GAA; Spanish Clb; Varsity Clb; Var L Socr; Var L Sftbl; High Hon Roll; Hon Roll; NHS; Prfct Atten Awd; Pres Schlr; CSF; GATE; Vrsty Sftbl Coachs Awd & Rookie Yr; Med.

ARMIJO, LORRAINE; San Gabriel Mission HS; Los Angeles, CA; (2); FBLA; GAA; Spanish Clb; Hon Roll; Mission Hnr Rl; Fine Arts Clb; Mission Mrt; Loyola Marymount; Engrng.

ARMINTIA, ARNEL D; Point Loma HS; San Diego, CA; (3); 158/431; Off ROTC; Color Guard; Prfct Atten Awd; Natl Sjrnrs Awd; Natl Soc Sons Amer Revltn, Brnz ROTC Mdl; Ldrshp Acad Grad & Mini OCS Grad; Aerontcl Engrng.

ARMITAGE, JOHN; Sonoma Valley HS; Sonoma, CA; (4); 34/277; Letterman Clb; Varsity Clb; JV Bsbl; JV Bsktbl; JV Capt Ftbl; Capt Vllybl; Var Capt Wrstlng; High Hon Roll; Hon Roll; CA Schltc Fdrtn; Chem Engr.

ARMOUR, MELANIE A; Sacred Heart HS; Los Angeles, CA; (3); Hosp Aide; Library Aide; Service Clb; School Play; Sec Frsh Cls; VP Soph Cls; Co-Capt Pom Pon; High Hon Roll; NHS; CA Schlrshp Fed; Liturgy Clb; Med.

ARMOUR, RAYLENE S; Sacred Heart HS; Los Angeles, CA; (2); Cmnty Wkr; Library Aide; Service Clb; Lit Mag; Treas Frsh Cls; Var Cheerldng; Var Pom Pon; Hon Roll; NHS; Liturgical Ministry; Med.

ARMOUR, WENDI; Helix HS; Lemon Grove, CA; (4); 81/367; Church Yth Grp; FTA; SADD; Yrbk; VP Sr Cls; Rep Stu Cncl; Highland League; UCSD; Psych.

ARMSTEAD, TAUNYA C; Canyon Springs HS; Moreno Valley, CA; (3); SADD; Acpl Chr; Capt Drill Tm; Swing Chorus; Sec Jr Cls; Cit Awd; High Hon Roll; Hon Roll; Archtctr.

ARMSTRONG, ALLAN W; Bullard HS; Fresno, CA; (1); Ski Clb; Wrstlng; Water Polo; Surfing; Mtn Biking; Sci.

ARMSTRONG, ANETTE J; Pasadena HS; Pasadena, CA; (3); Art Clb; Pep Clb; Red Cross Aide; JV Cheerldng; Hon Roll; Black Stu Union; Brdcst News T V Clb; Bus.

ARMSTRONG, CARRIE E; Merced HS; Merced, CA; (3); Sec Drama Clb; French Clb; Teachers Aide; Thesps; Band; Chorus; Mrchg Band; School Musical; Hon Roll; Masonic Awd; All St Hnr Choir; Past Worthy Advsr Rainbow; Past Divsnl De Molay Swthrt; UOP; Commnctns.

ARMSTRONG, CASSANDRA S; Homestead HS; Cupertino, CA; (3); Baylor U; Med.

ARMSTRONG, CHAD P; Highlands HS; N Highlands, CA; (2); Church Yth Grp; French Clb; Ski Clb; Phtg Yrbk; JV Socr; Cit Awd; Hon Roll; Awd Most Outstndng Male Soph Cls Phys Ed; MVP Sccr JV Tm; WA ST U; Law.

ARMSTRONG, CHARLOTTE D; Rio Lindo Adventist Acad; Burney, CA; (2); Teachers Aide; Chorus; Church Choir; Treas Frsh Cls; Bsbl; Powder Puff Ftbl; Score Keeper; Sftbl; Swmmng; Vllybl; Pacific Union Coll; Bus.

ARMSTRONG, CHERYL; El Cajon Valley HS; El Cajon, CA; (4); 3/438; Church Yth Grp; Ed Yrbk; Hon Roll; Rotary Awd; UC Irving; Physical Thrpst.

ARMSTRONG, DANIELLE; Long Beach Polytechnic HS; Longbeach, CA; (2); French Clb; Office Aide; Drill Tm; Variety Show; JV Capt Cheerldng; Sftbl; Hon Roll; Pres Acad Fit Awd; St Schlr; Hosp & Lib Volunteer; Young Black Schlrs Club; Black Onyx Club; S CA Schlr 3 Yrs; Howard U; Ed.

ARMSTRONG, DANIELLE; St Anthony HS; Long Beach, CA; (2); Church Yth Grp; Cmnty Wkr; Drama Clb; Spanish Clb; School Musical; VP Frsh Cls; Hon Roll; Campus Ministry Tm 88-90; Bus Mgmt.

ARMSTRONG, GREGORY; Calvary Chaple HS; Laguna Beach, CA; (2); Ski Clb; Hon Roll; Skikmbrd Team; Beach Vllybl; Scuba Dvng; CA Poly San Luis Obispo; Arch.

ARMSTRONG, JEFFREY D; San Bernardino HS; San Bernardino, CA; (2); Computer Clb; Cit Awd; Prfct Atten Awd; Army.

ARMSTRONG, KATE; Millikan JR HS; Sherman Oaks, CA; (4); Cmnty Wkr; Service Clb; Cit Awd; Hon Roll; Historical Pk Volunteer; Mock Trial Team; Sci.

ARMSTRONG, MARK A; Clayton Valley HS; Concord, CA; (3); Boy Scts; Church Yth Grp; Letterman Clb; Science Clb; Varsity Clb; Trk; Hon Roll; Prfct Atten Awd; Friday Night Live; Lindsey Museum Vlntr 4 Yrs.

ARMSTRONG, MICHELLE J; Live Oak HS; Morgan Hill, CA; (3); Art Clb; Debate Tm; Drama Clb; Library Aide; Speech Tm; SADD; Acpl Chr; Chorus; School Musical; Variety Show; Jrnlsm.

ARMSTRONG, MIKE; Red Bluff HS; Red Bluff, CA; (1); Church Yth Grp; Yrbk; Bsbl; Bsktbl; Hon Roll.

ARMSTRONG, PATRICIA L; Bloomington HS; Bloomington, CA; (2); 4/203; Church Yth Grp; Band; Mrchg Band; Pep Band; Stat Bsbl; JV Sftbl; High Hon Roll; Friday Night Live VP; BYU; Law.

ARMSTRONG, SHANNAN L; Roseville HS; Roseville, CA; (2); Church Yth Grp; Dance Clb; Drill Tm; Swmmng; Hon Roll; Dntl Hygnst.

ARMSTRONG, SHELBI; Modoc HS; Alturas, CA; (2); Church Yth Grp; Drama Clb; 4-H; FFA; Office Aide; Pep Clb; Pres Spanish Clb; Teachers Aide; School Play; Stu Cncl; Marine Bio.

ARMSTRONG, STEVEN T; Merced HS; Merced, CA; (3); Aud/Vis; Church Yth Grp; 4-H; FFA; Bsbl; Socr; Trk; Wt Lftg; Wrstlng; Martial Arts; Navy Seal.

ARMSTRONG, TAMARA; Skyline HS; Oakland, CA; (1); Sec Office Aide; Teachers Aide; Variety Show; Cit Awd; Comp Sci.

ARNAIZ, KRISTI; Helix HS; Santee, CA; (4); 100/400; FTA; Letterman Clb; Pep Clb; Speech Tm; SADD; Rep Frsh Cls; Rep Soph Cls; Rep Jr Cls; Rep Sr Cls; Rep Stu Cncl; Hnrb Mntn Gldn St Exam; San Diego ST U; Tchr.

ARNALL, JULIANNE L; Coronado HS; Coronado, CA; (3); 1/150; Thesps; School Play; Pres Frsh Cls; Crs Cntry; Bausch & Lomb Sci Awd; NHS; Ntl Merit Ltr; Opt Clb Awd; Pres Acad Fit Awd; Rotary Awd; 4 Plays Lamps Players Theatre; Acting.

ARNAS, BURAK E; El Camino HS; Sacramento, CA; (3); 107/366; Art Clb; French Clb; Library Aide; Band; Mrchg Band; Treas Sr Cls; Var L Swmmng; MVP Swmmng 5 Schl Records; Stu/Athl Of Mnth Awd; Ltrmn; Arch.

ARNDT, WENDY M; San Gorgonio HS; San Bernardino, CA; (3); Schlr Awd.

ARNETT, CRAIG D; Rio Vista HS; Rio Vista, CA; (3); AFS; Aud/Vis; Drama Clb; Science Clb; Spanish Clb; Rptr Nwsp; Yrbk; JV Tennis; High Hon Roll; Hon Roll; Friday Night Live, CA Schlrshp Fed Mem; Delta Coll; Engrg.

ARNETT, SHERMAN; Antioch SR HS; Antioch, CA; (2); Church Yth Grp; Rptr Nwsp; Score Keeper; Tennis; Hon Roll; San Francisco ST; Comm.

ARNFELD, REBECCA J; Wm S Hart HS; Newhall, CA; (3); Drama Clb; School Play; Stage Crew; Photography.

ARNO, MEGAN; Dunsmuir HS; Dunsmuir, CA; (2); 3/35; VP Church Yth Grp; Rep Stu Cncl; JV Bsktbl; Var Cheerldng; Tennis; Trk; JV Vllybl; High Hon Roll; CSF; Pacific Luthern U; Ed.

ARNOLD, DERRICK G; Clear Lake HS; Lakeport, CA; (3); Am Leg Boys St; Boy Scts; Drama Clb; Scholastic Bowl; Jazz Band; School Musical; School Play; JV Bsbl; JV Var Ftbl; Var Trk; UC; Gntcs.

ARNOLD, JAMES L; Orange Glen HS; Escondido, CA; (3); 75/458; Church Yth Grp; Computer Clb; Off ROTC; Color Guard; Drill Tm; Hon Roll; NHS; Awds Navy League US & Daedalian Fndtn; Cmptr Prgmmng; UCSD; Elec Engr.

ARNOLD, JEFFREY; Kings Christian HS; Hanford, CA; (4); 4/12; Pep Clb; Cit Awd; Hon Roll; CSF; Cls Ctzn Awd; Bst Actor Awd.

ARNOLD, JOSHUA; San Gorgonio HS; San Bernardino, CA; (4); 50/400; Boy Scts; Church Yth Grp; Letterman Clb; Var Swmmng; Wrstlng; High Hon Roll; Hon Roll; Var Waterplo 3 Yrs Lttrmn; CA ST U; History Teacher.

ARNOLD, KEVIN L; Carlmont HS; Belmont, CA; (2); Church Yth Grp; Latin Clb; School Play; JV Ftbl; JV Wt Lftg; High Hon Roll; Hon Roll; CSF; Amnsty Intl; Astrphyscst.

ARNOLD, KRISTIN G; Hemet HS; Hemet, CA; (3); 40/475; Key Clb; Flag Corp; Cheerldng; Socr; Trk; High Hon Roll; Congrssnl Schlr; 90 Hnr Grad; San Diego ST U; Ed.

ARNOLD, LA TONYA R; Stagg HS; Stockton, CA; (3); Drama Clb; Spanish Clb; Chorus; Variety Show; Stu Cncl; Var Cheerldng; High Hon Roll; Hon Roll; Jr NHS; NHS; Mgr Of Jenkins, Assocs Acctng Firm; Yale U; Engl Lit.

ARNOLD, MARC D; Antioch HS; Pittsburg, CA; (2); Church Yth Grp; Letterman Clb; Math Tm; Band; Mrchg Band; School Play; Var Ftbl; JV Socr; JV Trk; Var Wt Lftg; Ap Calculus As Jr; Mrchng Band.

ARNOLD, MATTHEW P; Moorpark HS; Moorpark, CA; (2); Var Crs Cntry; Var Trk; Cit Awd; High Hon Roll; Sunday Sch Teacher; Yth Group Leader; Summer Cnslr; UC Davis; Doctor.

ARNOLD, SPENCER H; Central Union HS; El Centro, CA; (1); Boy Scts; Church Yth Grp; Band; Mrchg Band; Pep Band; High Hon Roll; Hon Roll; Eagle Scout.

ARNOLD, TRACI; Woodland HS; Woodland, CA; (2); Cmnty Wkr; Band; Color Guard; Flag Corp; Mrchg Band; Trk; Hon Roll; Physics.

ARNOLD, WENDELL C; The Athenian Schl; Fremont, CA; (2); Computer Clb; Band; School Play; Var L Tennis; Wt Lftg; Hon Roll; Prfct Atten Awd; Cmmty Svc Act; Campus Cleanup; Math.

ARNS, WILLIAM; Sweetwater HS; National City, CA; (3); 81/429; Boy Scts; Church Yth Grp; French Clb; Spanish Clb; Teachers Aide; Socr; Wt Lftg; Cit Awd; Hon Roll; Pres Acad Fit Awd; Bicycling; Photography; Engrng.

ARO, MARGARET; Chino HS; Ontario, CA; (2); Church Yth Grp; Treas Drama Clb; Science Clb; Church Choir; Variety Show; Rptr Nwsp; VP Jr Cls; Cit Awd; Hon Roll; Pres Acad Fit Awd; Sunday Schl Tchr; CA Schlrshp Fed; Broadcast Jrnlsm.

ARONCHICK, DAVID M; Tustin HS; Santa Ana, CA; (2); Church Yth Grp; Debate Tm; French Clb; VP JA; Key Clb; Math Tm; Quiz Bowl; Science Clb; Speech Tm; Off Jr Cls; HOBY Rnnr Up; Mem OCAD 1989-90; Yale; Anesthslgst.

ARONE, MICHAEL P; West HS; Bakersfield, CA; (1); Band; Mrchg Band; JV Bsbl; JV Bsktbl; Hon Roll.

ARONEN, CHAD; Poway HS; Poway, CA; (3); Varsity Clb; Var L Swmmng; High Hon Roll; Hon Roll; NHS; Water Polo Capt; Schlr Athlete Awd 88-89.

ARORA, SHALINI; Ygnacio Valley HS; Walnut Creek, CA; (4); Cmnty Wkr; Drama Clb; Treas Sec French Clb; German Clb; Hosp Aide; Pres VP Key Clb; Model UN; Service Clb; Teachers Aide; Nwsp; Natl Yth Ldrshp Awd; Hnrs Cncl & Schl Ldrshp Awds; UC-SANTA Barbara; Psych.

ARPRAYOON, V KAROL; San Gabriel Mission HS; Rosemead, CA; (2); 35/118; Hon Roll; CSF; Comp; Music; Hstry; Aerosp Engrng.

ARRACHE, JENEEN; West HS; Bakersfield, CA; (3); 10/500; Am Leg Aux Girls St; Cmnty Wkr; School Play; Rptr Yrbk; Pres Soph Cls; Rep Jr Cls; Stu Cncl; Var Cheerldng; Powder Puff Ftbl; Vllybl; Wings For Life Clb; CSF; Interact Commnty Service; Bus.

ARRAIGA, MARCELA; Hawthorne HS; Lennox, CA; (2); Dance Clb; Variety Show; Spnsh Hnrs; Elem Drill Team Asst; USC; Law.

ARRAMBIDE, NOE; Sunset HS; Hayward, CA; (3); JV Var Bsbl; High Hon Roll; Hon Roll; Prfct Atten Awd.

ARREAGA, CHRIS; Southwest HS; San Diego, CA; (3); 58/498; Church Yth Grp; Office Aide; Teachers Aide; Band; Jazz Band; Pep Band; JV Ftbl; Music Technlgy Ensmb; UCSD; Engr.

ARRECHE, JEANETTE MARJORIE; Surprise Valley HS; Cedarville, CA; (4); 5/17; Pres GAA; Library Aide; Nwsp; Ed Yrbk; Pres Sr Cls; Treas Stu Cncl; Var Capt Bsktbl; Var Capt Vllybl; DAR Awd; Hon Roll; Acad Decthln; Bus.

ARREDONDO, ARLENE; Moore JR HS; Redlands, CA; (1); Library Aide; Pep Clb; Teachers Aide; Capt Cheerldng; Trk; Hon Roll; Rotary Awd; Hnrs Golden St Exam Alg; CSF.

ARREDONDO, JOSE; San Benito HS; Hollister, CA; (2); 10/300; Latin Clb; Rep Jr Cls; VP Socr; Var Trk; Pres Acad Fit Awd; Water Polo Tm; Comm Club; Cal Poly; Engrng.

ARREGUIN, ARLENE; Santa Ana HS; Santa Ana, CA; (3); Hon Roll; Rancho Santiago Coll; Bus.

ARREOLA, AMY; Westminster HS; Westminster, CA; (2); Church Yth Grp; Letterman Clb; Spanish Clb; Varsity Clb; Chorus; Crs Cntry; Trk; Interact Club; Jrnlsm.

ARREOLA, ELIZABETH; San Gabriel HS; Rosemead, CA; (1); Church Yth Grp; Varsity Clb; Band; Crs Cntry; Trk; Hon Roll; MASA Club; Speical Interests-Dance Sing Workout Swim Play Soccer And Volleyball; USC; Doctor.

ARREOLA, JOSE J; King City HS; Greenfield, CA; (3); FFA; JV Bsbl; JV Ftbl; Cit Awd; High Hon Roll; Hon Roll; Prfct Atten Awd; Rotary Awd; Cal Poly; Bus Intl.

ARREOLA, SHEYLA; Central Union HS; El Centro, CA; (2); Church Yth Grp; Bsktbl; Hon Roll; Prfct Atten Awd; Santa Barbara Coll; Real Est.

ARRIADA, ROSEMARY; El Camino HS; Daly City, CA; (4); GAA; Service Clb; Var Trk; Var Vllybl; High Hon Roll; Hon Roll; Pres Acad Fit Awd; Cntrl Coast Sctn Outstndng Schlstc Accmplshmnt; Los Angeles CA U; Intl Bus.

ARRIAGA, SHELLEY M; Golden West HS; Exeter, CA; (2); Stat Bsbl; JV Crs Cntry; Score Keeper; JV Socr; Hon Roll; UC Davis; Pharmacy.

ARRIETA, MARILUCY; Chino HS; Chino, CA; (3); 73/565; Church Yth Grp; Cmnty Wkr; 4-H; Ski Clb; JV Mgr(s); Powder Puff Ftbl; Hon Roll; Prfct Atten Awd; Rotary Awd; Nrsng.

ARRIETA, SANDRA; Westmoor HS; San Francisco, CA; (3); GAA; SADD; Band; Rep Frsh Cls; Cheerldng; Pom Pon; Trk; High Hon Roll; Hon Roll; Sal; Exchng Stu Spain; Frgn Lang; San Francisco ST U; Bus Admin.

ARRINGTON, ERIK; Van Nuys Math/Science Magnet HS; Sepulveda, CA; (4); 17/534; Chess Clb; Rep Frsh Cls; Var Crs Cntry; Var Swmmng; Var Trk; NHS; Ntl Merit SF; Prfct Atten Awd; Bridge Clb Pres; Jr Statesmn Amer; Elctrcl Engr.

ARRIOLA, SHEILA R; St Joseph HS; Long Beach, CA; (2); 13/196; Church Yth Grp; GAA; Hosp Aide; School Play; Rep Frsh Cls; JV Socr; Var Swmmng; Hon Roll; 2 Yr Cnfrmtn Process; CSF; Bus.

ARRIZON, OLIVIA; Bolsa Grande HS; Garden Grove, CA; (2); 104/377; Bsktbl Jr Var Or Var; Fshn Dsgnr.

ARROYO, BARBARA A; Irvine HS; Irvine, CA; (4); Dance Clb; Drama Clb; Pep Clb; Band; Mrchg Band; Variety Show; Capt Cheerldng; Cit Awd; Hon Roll; UC Santa Cruz; Commnctns.

ARROYO, CARMEN; Sweetwater HS; National City, CA; (2); Church Yth Grp; Cit Awd; Migrant Educ Pgm; 2 Cert Achvt; 3 Cert Hnr; Best Pathfinder Awd & 3 Cert; City Coll; Nurse.

ARROYO, DINORA; El Rancho HS; Pico Rivera, CA; (1); Church Yth Grp; Debate Tm; Vllybl; Stanford U; Econ.

ARROYO, GREGORY; Don Bosco Technical Inst; Montebello, CA; (2); 18/250; Church Yth Grp; Cmnty Wkr; Nwsp; Bsbl; Bsktbl; NHS; Museum Research Apprenticeship Pgm; MVP Bsbl; Stanford; Psych.

ARROYO, NICOLE; Los Alamitos HS; Seal Beach, CA; (3); Math Tm; Ski Clb; Spanish Clb; Stage Crew; Var Capt Crs Cntry; Var Trk; Cit Awd; Hon Roll; Prfct Atten Awd; Golden St Exam Hnrs; All Leag; UCLA; Physcl Thrpy.

ARROYO, SYLVIA; Oxnard HS; Oxnard, CA; (2); 122/604; Cit Awd; Awd Of B Pnt Avrg; Arch.

ARRUDA, LEAH; Cabrillo HS; Acushnet, MA; (4); 22/225; SADD; Ed Nwsp; Mgr(s); JV Swmmng; High Hon Roll; Hon Roll; Pres Acad Fit Awd; CSF; Bnk America Commnctns Awd; Bridgewater ST Coll; Jrnlsm.

ARSENEAULT, DENISE M; Saugus HS; Saugus, CA; (4); Sec FBLA; Varsity Clb; Nwsp; Lit Mag; Bsktbl; L Swmmng; Var Tennis; Wrstlng; Hon Roll; Voice Dem Awd; Intl Order Of Rainbow Girls; Athl Of Month, Athltc Acad Awd; Cape Awd For Frnch & Fine Arts; U Of Puget Sound; Med.

ARSHI, ARSHAN ALI; Rancho Cotate HS; Rohnert Park, CA; (3); Cmnty Wkr; French Clb; Hosp Aide; Socr; Vllybl; Wt Lftg; High Hon Roll; Hon Roll; NHS; Prfct Atten Awd; CSF; JSA; Hist Clb; Harvard; Law.

ARTEAGA, ARLENA; Mira Loma HS; Orangevale, CA; (4); 48/256; Acad Presndntl Fitness Awd 90; American River; Hstry.

ARTEAGA, GLORIA; Rio Mesa HS; Fillmore, CA; (3); Fashion Dsgn.

ARTEAGA, MERCEDES; Leuzinger HS; Inglewood, CA; (3); El Camino Coll; Elem Teacher.

ARTECHE, HEIDI J; Whittier Christian HS; Downey, CA; (3); Church Yth Grp; Trk; High Hon Roll; St Schlr; CA Schltc Fed 3 Yrs; Orange Cnty Acad Decthln 2 Yrs; UCLA; Pre-Med.

ARTHUR, CHRISTY; Walnut HS; Walnut, CA; (3); 53/487; Church Yth Grp; Cmnty Wkr; Dance Clb; 4-H; German Clb; Key Clb; Pep Clb; Service Clb; Ski Clb; SADD; Most Dctd Sngldr; 1st Pl Sci Fair; Brigham Young U; Ed.

ARTIAGA, CORINE A; Kerman HS; Kerman, CA; (2); FFA; SADD; Color Guard; JV Sftbl; Hon Roll; Fresno Police Acad; Police Ofcr.

ARTILES, GREGORY; Paso Robles HS; Paso Robles, CA; (4); 1/250; Computer Clb; Treas Science Clb; Bausch & Lomb Sci Awd; High Hon Roll; Hon Roll; Ntl Merit Schol; Rotary Awd; UC Berkeley; Bio Engrng.

ARTINIAN, TANYA A; San Dieguito HS; Carlsbad, CA; (2); Girl Scts; Teachers Aide; Hon Roll; Ecology Club; CSF; U San Diego; Chem.

ARTINO, AMY; Ramona HS; Riverside, CA; (1); 97/582; Dance Clb; Chorus; Pediatrcn.

ARUIL, JOAQUIN P; Point Loma HS; San Diego, CA; (3); Church Yth Grp; Cmnty Wkr; Prfct Atten Awd; San Diego ST U.

ARVETIS, TOM A; Serra HS; San Mateo, CA; (2); Letterman Clb; Ski Clb; Speech Tm; Varsity Clb; School Play; Nwsp; Crs Cntry; Trk; Wrstlng; Gov Hon Prg Awd; Broadcst Jrnlsm.

ARVIZU, KARIN RENEE; East Bakersfield HS; Bakersfield, CA; (4); Hosp Aide; SADD; VICA; Chorus; Church Choir; Bakersfield Coll; Day Care Ed.

ARVIZU, YESENIA; Mountain View HS; El Monte, CA; (3); Church Yth Grp; Cit Awd; High Hon Roll; Hon Roll; CA ST Long Bch; Rsprtry Thrpy.

ARYAN, EYAD H; Fountain Valley HS; Fountain Valley, CA; (2); Church Yth Grp; Cmnty Wkr; French Clb; Intrml Socr; JV Trk; Lion Awd; Masonic Awd; Pres Acad Fit Awd; Med.

ARZAGA, JESSICA S; Sweetwater HS; National City, CA; (3); Dance Clb; Model UN; Hon Roll; SDSU; Real Estate.

ARZATE, IRMA; Savanna HS; Anaheim, CA; (3); Church Yth Grp; Teachers Aide; Var Socr; Cit Awd; Prncpls Acad Awd-Sccr; Coaches Awd 89-90; Barbizon Mdlng Schl Grad; MECHA Clb-VP; Math/Span Achvt Awd; Ed.

ARZOLA, ELIZABETH G; Rubidoux HS; Riverside, CA; (2); French Clb; Pep Clb; Teachers Aide; Varsity Clb; Rep Frsh Cls; Rep Soph Cls; Rep Jr Cls; JV Var Cheerldng; UC Riverside; Commnctns.

ASADULLAH, EFURU F; King Drew Medical Magnet HS; Los Angeles, CA; (3); Computer Clb; Intnl Clb; JCL; Latin Clb; Math Tm; School Play; Variety Show; JV Bsktbl; High Hon Roll; Hon Roll; African Stu Allnc; U Southern CA; Obstrcn.

ASAI, ATHENA A; Bret Harte HS; Avery, CA; (2); Cmnty Wkr; Dance Clb; GAA; Pep Clb; SADD; JV Vllybl; Hon Roll; Davis U; Pysch.

ASAI, MASANORI; Rowland HS; Rowland Heights, CA; (2); Hon Roll; UCSB; Drftng.

ASAKI, KAROLYN A; El Toro HS; Lake Forest Keys, CA; (4); Boy Scts; Band; Jazz Band; Mrchg Band; Orch; High Hon Roll; Hon Roll; Pres Acad Fit Awd; Bk Amer Cert Wnnr Music; Frseno ST; Math.

ASANTEWA, TIA; Milpitas HS; San Jose, CA; (4); 50/500; Sec Church Yth Grp; Cmnty Wkr; JA; Church Choir; Rep Jr Cls; Rep Cmnty Wkr; High Hon Roll; Office Aide; Thesps; Rep Frsh Cls; Black Stu Union VP; Mesa Clb; Mock Trial Clb; UCLA; Bus Mgmt.

ASARO, MATTHEW I; Casa Grande HS; Petaluma, CA; (2); French Clb; Ftbl; Hon Roll; Mech Engrng.

ASAVASOPON, PAUL; Temple City HS; Temple City, CA; (2); Trk; UCLA; Med.

ASBELL, RICK; Manteca HS; Manteca, CA; (3); 26/410; Letterman Clb; Var Bsktbl; Var Capt Ftbl; Var Capt Trk; Cit Awd; Hon Roll; Phys Educ.

ASCENCIO, CLAUDIA; Estancia HS; Costa Mesa, CA; (3); Latin Clb; Pep Clb; Spanish Clb; Pres Jr Cls; Pres Sr Cls; Crs Cntry; Mecha & Creatve Wrtng Clbs; Safe & Sober Gradtn; Orange Coast Coll; Teacher.

ASCHBACHER, APRIL; Fortuna HS; Rio Dell, CA; (3); Church Yth Grp; Hosp Aide; Teachers Aide; Church Choir; RN.

ASCHENBRENNER, HEIDI; Brethren HS; Los Alamitos, CA; (4); 1/69; Church Yth Grp; Math Tm; Acpl Chr; VP Soph Cls; Sec Sr Cls; Rep Stu Cncl; Var Capt Cheerldng; Hon Roll; Opt Clb Awd; Val; Campus Life; Scty Women Engrs Awd; Math.

ASCHENBRENNER, KATRINA; Mendocino HS; Ft Bragg, CA; (4); Art Clb; French Clb; FBLA; Office Aide; Ski Clb; Spanish Clb; Yrbk; Hon Roll; NHS; Van Assen Moura Awd; U Sweden; Lang.

ASCHER, ADAM A; Will C Wood HS; Vacaville, CA; (1); Treas FBLA; Band; Jazz Band; Mrchg Band; Pep Band; High Hon Roll; Hon Roll; Kiwanis Awd; Prfct Atten Awd; UC Davis; Arch.

ASCUNSION, NICHOLE; Notre Dame HS; Santa Clara, CA; (2); Intnl Clb; CSF Tutr; Outstndng Achvt Engl, Geom, Bio, Rlgn; Bus Admin.

ASDEL, ROBYN L; Ventura HS; Ventura, CA; (4); Church Yth Grp; JA; Rep Stu Cncl; High Hon Roll; U Southern CA; Dental Hygiene.

ASELTINE, LISA; Marina HS; Huntington Bch, CA; (3); AFS; Church Yth Grp; Service Clb; Capt Color Guard; Ed Nwsp; High Hon Roll; Hon Roll; Chinese Club; U Of Puget Sound; Journalism.

ASENCIO, SCOTT; William C Overfelt HS; San Jose, CA; (4); Computer Clb; Math Clb; Math Tm; Pep Clb; Science Clb; Teachers Aide; Varsity Clb; Ed Nwsp; Ed Yrbk; Ed Lit Mag; Boys Clbs Of Amer St Yth Of Yr; Sect Edtr CSPA Gld Crwn; 3rd Pl Oil Derrick MESA St Cmptn; CSU Northridge; Jrnlsm.

ASENJO, JUAN C; Thomas Downey HS; Modesto, CA; (2); 1/517; Pres Chess Clb; VP Key Clb; Math Tm; Teachers Aide; Var Swmmng; Cit Awd; Hon Roll; Sci Olympiad Tm 1st Pl 90; Sigma Xi Sci Rsrch Soc Awd Outstndng Achvt In HS Sci; Med.

ASGARZADIE, FARBOD; King/Drew Med Mag HS; Los Angeles, CA; (3); English Clb; Intnl Clb; JCL; Latin Clb; Pres Math Clb; Math Tm; Science Clb; School Play; Yrbk; Sftbl; Stanford Pre Med.

ASGUR, ANJUM; Sacramento HS; Sacramento, CA; (2); 161/500; Key Clb; School Play; Stage Crew; Variety Show; Wt Lftg; Hon Roll; NHS; Pres Acad Fit Awd; Media Awd; Cmnctns.

ASHBY, DIANNE E; Pioneer HS; San Jose, CA; (4); 47/264; Church Yth Grp; German Clb; Teachers Aide; Orch; Hon Roll; JV Sftbl; Music Cncl Rep; CSF; CA Lutheran U; Teacher.

ASHBY, KARYN; Abraham Lincoln HS; San Jose, CA; (3); 45/385; Church Yth Grp; GAA; Office Aide; Spanish Clb; Teachers Aide; Varsity Clb; Ed Yrbk; Rep Stu Cncl; Var Sftbl; Hon Roll; CA Lutheran U; Jrnlst.

ASHBY-WALLACE, KARLA; Junipero Serra HS; San Diego, CA; (4); 82/425; JA; Model UN; VP Varsity Clb; Stu Cncl; Var Bsktbl; Var Cheerldng; Stat Ftbl; JV Sftbl; Var Trk; Hon Roll; Xionos Yth Grp Natl Chptr Phi Delta Kappa; U Of Southern CA; Bus Fin.

ASHCRAFT, ALISON N; Laguna Hills HS; Laguna Hills, CA; (2); Church Yth Grp; Cmnty Wkr; Drama Clb; SADD; Pres Acad Fit Awd; Natl Charity League; U NV Las Vegas; Hotel Mgmt.

ASHCRAFT, PAIGE J; Orange Glen HS; Escondido, CA; (4); Church Yth Grp; DECA; German Clb; Hon Roll; Dnc; Ricks Coll; Bus.

ASHFORD, DANA L; Riverdale HS; Five Points, CA; (2); 5/135; Treas Var GAA; Pep Clb; Science Clb; Ski Clb; SADD; Treas Frsh Cls; Var L Cheerldng; Var L Sftbl; Var L Vllybl; High Hon Roll; Gottschalks Hi-Debs.

ASHFORD, KRISTEN; Los Alamitos HS; Cypress, CA; (3); Church Yth Grp; Cmnty Wkr; Service Clb; Ski Clb; Varsity Clb; Var Gym; Hon Roll; St Schlr; Safe Rides Amnesty Intl Poetry Club CSF Yth Ctr Achletic Excllnc Awd; Bio Engrng.

ASHLAND, ARON W; Alhambra HS; Martinez, CA; (3); 8/205; Church Yth Grp; Office Aide; School Play; Var L Socr; Var L Swmmng; Var L Trk; High Hon Roll; Hon Roll; Pres Acad Fit Awd; Cmmnty Sccr; Golf; Clrcl Wrk Dntl Offc; Chem Engr.

ASHLEY, CAROLE; Bonita Vista HS; Bonita, CA; (4); 21/521; DAR Awd; Elks Awd; Swmmng; Prfct Atten Awd; Church Yth Grp; Chorus; Pep Clb; Office Aide; Opt Clb Awd; CA Schlrshp Fed Treas; Mst Imprvd Swmmr Awd; Outstndng 1st Yr Frnch Stu; Harding U; Elem Educ.

ASHLEY, ERIC; Pinole Valley HS; Pinole, CA; (1); Cmnty Wkr; UC-BERKLEY; Accntnt.

ASHLEY, KRISTINA L; North Hollywood HS; North Hollywood, CA; (3); French Clb; Acpl Chr; VP Chorus; Church Choir; Lbrn Swing Chorus; Cit Awd; High Hon Roll; Hon Roll; Ntl Merit SF; Prfct Atten Awd; CSF; Pomona Coll; Jrnlsm.

ASHLEY III, LEO; St Bernards HS; Gardena, CA; (3); Am Leg Boys St; Church Yth Grp; Treas Frsh Cls; Off Soph Cls; Off Jr Cls; JV Var Bsbl; Var Bsktbl; High Hon Roll; Hon Roll; NHS; CA Schlrshp Fdrtn; Parish Altr Svr; Bus Mgmt.

ASHLEY, LISA D; Warren HS; Downey, CA; (3); Church Yth Grp; Chorus; Church Choir; Abilene Christian U; Psych.

ASHRAF, MADEEHA S; Madera HS; Madera, CA; (1); Intnl Clb; SADD; High Hon Roll; Hon Roll; CA Schlstc Fed; Psych.

ASHTON, CAREY L; Los Amigos HS; Fountain Valley, CA; (1); Church Yth Grp; Hosp Aide; CA U; Attorney.

ASHTON, MICHELLE A; Beaumont HS; Beaumont, CA; (1); Church Yth Grp; French Clb; Pep Clb; Treas Frsh Cls; Sec Soph Cls; Cheerldng; Hon Roll; Psych.

ASHURY, NATHAN E; Galileo HS; San Francisco, CA; (4); VP JA; Pres Model UN; Capt ROTC; Hon Roll; San Fran Police Actvts Leag Law Enfrcmnt Pgm; Police Force.

ASHWORTH, BRITIN; Mayfield SR HS; South Pasadena, CA; (3); Hosp Aide; Spanish Clb; SADD; School Musical; School Play; Ed Nwsp; VP Stu Cncl; Var Pom Pon; Hon Roll; NHS.

ASIMOVIC, ROBERT; James Madison HS; San Diego, CA; (3); 19/349; Drama Clb; School Musical; School Play; Stage Crew; Variety Show; Hon Roll; Natyl Yng Ldrs Conf.

ASISTIN, ERIC L; Bullard HS; Fresno, CA; (2); #54 In Class; Ski Clb; JV Capt Vllybl; Modeling Composition 89-90; Fashion Dsgn.

ASKIN, FLETCHER W; Clovis West HS; Clovis, CA; (3); Trk; Hon Roll; Fresno ST; Engrng.

ASLAMI, MONICA S; Saddleback HS; Santa Ana, CA; (1); Am Leg Aux Girls St; Rptr Yrbk; CSF; UCLA; Pre-Med.

ASLANIAN, KARINNEH; Ferrahian HS; Granada Hills, CA; (3); 7/65; Var Bsbl; Var Crs Cntry; Var Socr; Var Sftbl; Var Trk; Var Vllybl; High Hon Roll; Hon Roll; Ntl Merit Schol; AP Bio Hnrs; Hnrs Chem & Engl; Armenian Politcal/Athletic Organizations; UCLA; Law.

ASMAR, DALE R; Grossmont HS; El Cajon, CA; (4); Church Yth Grp; SADD; Teachers Aide; Swmmng; Cit Awd; Girls Leag; Fshn Show Model; Spnsh Clb; Spnsh Awd; U Of San Diego; Bus Admin.

ASMAR, JENNIFER; Kearny Stephen Watts HS; San Diego, CA; (4); 36/297; Library Aide; Pep Clb; Speech Tm; Teachers Aide; Rep Sr Cls; Cheerldng; Gym; Trk; Wt Lftg; Med.

ASOO, BEVERLY; C K Mc Clatchy HS; Sacramento, CA; (2); 1/549; French Clb; JV Cheerldng; High Hon Roll; CSF; Amensty Intl; Arch Engr.

ASPELL, JASON C; San Dieguito HS; Encinitas, CA; (2); German Clb; Key Clb; Quiz Bowl; Science Clb; Hon Roll; Engrng.

ASPREY, JENNA M; Manteca HS; Manteca, CA; (2); 56/420; Rptr FFA; SADD; JV Socr; Hon Roll; NHS; Hrs Trng/Shwng; UC Davis; Vet Med.

ASSADI, CAMRON S; Irvine HS; Irvine, CA; (3); Drama Clb; French Clb; Ski Clb; Speech Tm; VP SADD; School Play; Phtg Yrbk; Var Swmmng; Surf Clb; Med.

ASSELIN, STEWART; Clovis HS; Clovis, CA; (3); High Hon Roll; Ecology Club; Infrml Target Shtng; CA ST U Fresno.

ASSELSTINE, JASON N; Arroyo Grande HS; Santa Maria, CA; (2); Church Yth Grp; FCA; SADD; Band; Mrchg Band; Pep Band; Wrstlng; Hon Roll; Pres Acad Fit Awd; Chrch Musicals, Dramas; Athlete Of Wk 89; San Luis Obispo Paper; Mnstry.

ASSEMI, REZA; Bullard HS; Fresno, CA; (1); German Clb; Hon Roll; Bsbl Card Clb; CSF; SADD; Bus.

ASSINI, ANTHONY; San Gorgonio HS; Highland, CA; (3); Church Yth Grp; Office Aide; Teachers Aide; Arch.

AST, STEPHANIE L; Atascadero HS; Creston, CA; (1); Hon Roll; NHS; Astronomy.

ASTARABADI, LEMIA; University HS; Irvine, CA; (2); Church Yth Grp; French Clb; GAA; Trk; Vllybl; Hon Roll; CA Jr Vlybl Clb; Orange County Vlybl Clb; Girls Lg Cmmssn & Social Chrmn.

ASTIN, RICHARD A; Glendora HS; Glendora, CA; (4); Boy Scts; VP German Clb; Pres Key Clb; Math Clb; Hon Roll; Badminton; CSU Northridge; Engrng.

ASTORGA, GRACE F; De Anza HS; Richmond, CA; (3); Church Yth Grp; French Clb; Tennis; Trk; Hon Roll; Bio Olympiad Fnlst; Friday Night Live; UC Berkeley; Psych.

ASTORGA, OLGA L; San Marcos HS; Santa Barbara, CA; (2); Boy Scts; Cmnty Wkr; Hosp Aide; Red Cross Aide; Off Jr Cls; Swmmng; Tennis; Vllybl; Cit Awd; Hon Roll; Cmnty Service Awd 200 Hrs; Registered Nurse.

ASTORGA, YESENIA S; Regina Caeli HS; Compton, CA; (2); Spanish Clb; Rep Frsh Cls; High Hon Roll; Hon Roll; Med.

ASTORGA, YESENIA-LIZETTE C; Foothill HS; Tustin, CA; (3); Teachers Aide; Chorus; School Musical; School Play; Rancho Santiago Coll; Cosmtlgy.

ATALLAH, AMIRA; Davis SR HS; Davis, CA; (4); 1/365; Pres Spanish Clb; Pep Band; Ed Nwsp; High Hon Roll; Ntl Merit SF; U CA Davis; Bus.

ATANACIO, SHELENE; El Camino HS; Daly City, CA; (2); Church Yth Grp; Variety Show; Mgr Crs Cntry; Corp Law.

ATCHISON, CASEY D; El Cajon Valley HS; El Cajon, CA; (2); #52 In Class; Church Yth Grp; VP Jr Cls; JV Trk; Human Power Vehicle Team; Skating, Surfing, Biking, Motor Biking, Jet Skiing, Body Boarding; UCSD; Arch.

ATEBAR, SHAH A; Mira Loma HS; Sacramento, CA; (3); French Clb; Teachers Aide; Socr; Hon Roll; UC Davis; Pre Med.

ATENCIO, AIMEE A; El Rancho HS; Pico Rivera, CA; (4); 28/600; German Clb; School Musical; Swing Chorus; Variety Show; Var Swmmng; Smfnlst Natl Hspnc Schlrs; Bank Of Amer Cert Wnnr Music; Boston U; Phys Thrpy.

ATENGCO, ANNA P; Pinole Valley HS; Hercules, CA; (3); Church Yth Grp; Pep Clb; Nrsng.

ATENGCO JR, REYNALDO M; Pinole Valley HS; Hercules, CA; (2); Band; Nrsng.

ATHERTON, ELISA N; North HS; Bakersfield, CA; (1); Dance Clb; Color Guard; Hon Roll; GATE Phys Sci & Engl; Adv Math Pgm; US Santa Barbara; Arch Engr..

ATHYAL, VIDUSH P; John Marshall Fundamental HS; Pasadena, CA; (3); Debate Tm; Pres Key Clb; Science Clb; Speech Tm; Chorus; Stu Cncl; Var Trk; Bausch & Lomb Sci Awd; NHS; Church Yth Grp; CSF; Friday Nite Live Clb; Acad Decathlon Team; Pre Med.

ATIANZAR, MELONNIE D; Palm Springs HS; Palm Springs, CA; (3); Hosp Aide; Spanish Clb; Sftbl; Badmntn; UNLV; Pre-Law.

ATIENZA, ELY; Los Alamitos HS; Los Alamitos, CA; (3); 1/500; Science Clb; Spanish Clb; Hon Roll; Eclgy Club; Intrct Club; CSF; Engrg.

ATIENZA, MARIE C; La Reina HS; Agoura Hills, CA; (4); 7/81; Rep Drama Clb; Hosp Aide; NFL; Service Clb; Speech Tm; Teachers Aide; Mgr Stage Crew; Rep Frsh Cls; Sec Jr Cls; Sec Sr Cls; CSF; Parent Cncl Serv Awd; Bank Of Am Achvt Awd Frgn Lang; U CA San Diego; Biochem.

ATIENZA, SHARON; San Diego Acad; San Diego, CA; (4); Band; Chorus; Yrbk; Off Jr Cls; Pres Sr Cls; Var Sftbl; Pres NHS; Ntl Merit SF; Pres Acad Fit Awd; Presdntl Acad Schlrshp; Southern CA Coll; Bio.

ATILANO, JOHN; Orosi HS; Orosi, CA; (2); 3/150; Drama Clb; Spanish Clb; Band; Mrchg Band; School Play; Ftbl; High Hon Roll; Hon Roll; CSF; Mck Trl Tm.

ATIQEE, JAMILA; Mount Eden HS; Hayward, CA; (3); Cmnty Wkr; SADD; VICA; School Play; Variety Show; Hon Roll.

ATKINS, AMY L; Hesperia HS; Hesperia, CA; (3); Pres Church Yth Grp; Church Choir; Rptr Nwsp; Var Trk; High Hon Roll; Prfct Atten Awd; Vllybl & Bsktbl Chrch Yth Tm; BYU; Nurse.

ATKINS, ANDREA; El Capitan HS; Lakeside, CA; (4); 1/450; Math Clb; Math Tm; Scholastic Bowl; Var Swmmng; Cit Awd; Hon Roll; Ntl Merit SF; Prfct Atten Awd; Pres Acad Fit Awd; Val; Wtr Polo; Chem Engr.

ATKINS, HEATHER; Antelope Valley HS; Lancaster, CA; (3); Dance Clb; Drama Clb; Spanish Clb; Stat Sftbl; Art Clb; Acctng.

ATKINS, JENNIFER A; San Ramon Valley HS; Danville, CA; (4); 17/400; Sec Drama Clb; Key Clb; SADD; Teachers Aide; School Musical; School Play; Stage Crew; Rep Stu Cncl; Dist Schl Brd Stu Rep; Bst Char Actrss Awd; Prncpl Schlr Prfrmn Awds GPA; Loyola Marymount; Theatre Arts.

ATKINS, JULIE; Westmont HS; Campbell, CA; (2); Church Yth Grp; Drama Clb; Acpl Chr; Chorus; Church Choir; School Musical; Powder Puff Ftbl; Sftbl; Tennis; Juliard; Music.

ATKINS, QUIXOTE D; Skyline HS; Oakland, CA; (2); 1/600; Church Yth Grp; Chorus; Church Choir; Jazz Band; Pep Band; School Musical; Rep Frsh Cls; Off Soph Cls; Natl NAACP ACT-SO Cmptn 3rd Pl Orgnl Essay Wrtg; Human Rel Awd; Obstrtcn.

ATKINS, ZEMIA A; St Bernard Catholic HS; Los Angeles, CA; (3); 45/333; Church Yth Grp; Cmnty Wkr; Hosp Aide; Red Cross Aide; Pres Thesps; Chorus; School Musical; School Play; Cit Awd; Hon Roll; UCLA; Med.

ATKINSON, BRIAN D; Camarillo HS; Camarillo, CA; (3); 158/450; Church Yth Grp; Letterman Clb; Spanish Clb; SADD; Var Swmmng; Chistman Decortng Cont 2 1st Pl Home, 2nd Pl Home & 1st Pl Neighbrhd; Accntng.

ATKINSON, CARISA K; Grant HS; Sacramento, CA; (1); Spanish Clb; Yrbk; Grant Coll; House Interior.

ATKINSON, JAMIE E; Apple Valley SR HS; Apple Valley, CA; (2); 20/740; Church Yth Grp; German Clb; Math Tm; Mrchg Band; High Hon Roll; Hon Roll; CSF; Golden ST Exam/Geom Hnrs.

ATKINSON, KAREN; St Rose Acad; San Francisco, CA; (4); 2/90; Off Church Yth Grp; Sec GAA; Ed Nwsp; L Socr; High Hon Roll; NHS; Ntl Merit Ltr; Pres Acad Fit Awd; Sal; Pep Clb; St Dominic Awd; CSF; UCLA; Soc Sci.

ATKINSON, KRISSY A; Potter Valley HS; Potter Valley, CA; (4); 1/40; Band; Mrchg Band; Pep Band; JV Var Bsktbl; Var Sftbl; JV Var Vllybl; Lion Awd; Val; North Coast Sect CIF Scholar Athlete; US Natl Math Awd; Bank Of Amer Awd/Math-Science; UC Santa Cruz; Mathematics.

ATKINSON, NATHAN S; Paso Robles HS; Paso Robles, CA; (1); Art.

ATKINSON, SHAUNA; Westchester HS; Los Angeles, CA; (2); Model UN; Teachers Aide; Crs Cntry; JV Sftbl; Trk; Hon Roll; Psych.

ATKISSION, COLLEEN; Edison HS; Fresno, CA; (1); 6/32; Ski Clb; Hon Roll; CSF; UC Berkeley; Bus.

ATO, GLADYS; Turlock HS; Turlock, CA; (1); 31/625; Church Yth Grp; Dance Clb; Key Clb; Pep Clb; Speech Tm; Co-Capt Cheerldng; JV Swmmng; Hon Roll; Opt Clb Awd; Water Polo; MIT; Arch.

ATONDO, CHRISTINE A; Los Amigos HS; Fountain Valley, CA; (2); 43/357; Drama Clb; Thesps; Capt Color Guard; Mrchg Band; School Musical; School Play; Var Swmmng; Hon Roll; Jr NHS; NHS; CSF; USC; Ped.

ATTUBATO, CHERYL L; Novato HS; Novato, CA; (3); Church Yth Grp; Office Aide; Spanish Clb; SADD; Teachers Aide; Pres Frsh Cls; Stu Cncl; Swmmng; Hon Roll; Water Polo; Sports Psych.

ATWAL, MANWINDER; Tranquillity HS; San Joaquin, CA; (4); 1/120; Office Aide; Science Clb; Ski Clb; Rptr Nwsp; Pres Frsh Cls; VP Pres Stu Cncl; Var L Bsktbl; Cit Awd; High Hon Roll; Val; Stu Of Yr, Qtr; CSF; San Luis Olaspo; Mech Engrng.

ATWELL, JERRY; Mc Farland HS; Mc Farland, CA; (3); Church Yth Grp; Band; Jazz Band; Mrchg Band; Pep Band; Pres Frsh Cls; Var Bsktbl; Hon Roll; Prfct Atten Awd; Bakersfield JC; Med.

ATWELL, MELANIE; Arlington HS; Riverside, CA; (3); 20/437; Church Yth Grp; Cmnty Wkr; FBLA; Teachers Aide; Tennis; High Hon Roll; CSF Offcr Treas; Youth To Youth Stu; Private Tutor Math & Alg; UCR; MD.

ATWOOD, JO ANN C; Chula Vista HS; San Diego, CA; (3); 9/600; Office Aide; Flag Corp; Lit Mag; Off Soph Cls; Off Jr Cls; Off Sr Cls; Stu Cncl; Var Stat Socr; JV Vllybl; Masonic Awd; CSF; SPEAK; Basics Gftd Pgm; Schl Creatv & Prfrmng Arts Art Maj; U Of CA; Art.

AU, ANDREA Y; Whitney HS; Cerritos, CA; (2); 1/180; French Clb; JA; Key Clb; VP Am Leg Aux Girls St; Co-Ed Nwsp; Ed Lit Mag; Co-Ed Jr Cls; High Hon Roll; ABC Dist Yth Orch; CSF.

AU, CUONG V; Mark Keppel HS; Monterey Park, CA; (3); Chess Clb; Math Clb; Office Aide; High Hon Roll; Hon Roll; Prfct Atten Awd; Perf Art-Chinese Zither; Med.

AU, SANDRA B; Mission HS; San Francisco, CA; (3); Hon Roll; Amer Red Cross Volunteer; Chinese Schl Marching Band; San Jose U.

AU, VAN; Mark Keppel HS; Rosemead, CA; (2); FBLA; Off Soph Cls; Tennis; High Hon Roll; Hon Roll; Jr NHS; Prfct Atten Awd; Pres Acad Fit Awd; Bus.

AU, VINH; Rosemead HS; W Covina, CA; (2); Key Clb; Badminton; UCLA; Bus.

AU-YEUNG, EUNICE W; International Studies Acad; San Francisco, CA; (2); Cmnty Wkr; High Hon Roll; Japanese Club; California Scholarship Federation; Hotel Management.

AUBERT, JENNIFER L; Loretto HS; Sacramento, CA; (2); Church Yth Grp; SADD; Ed Yrbk; Stu Cncl; Trk; Vllybl; Hon Roll; Safe Rides Outstndng Stu; Fri Night Live Pblcty Coord & Outstndng Stu; Elem Sch Vlybl Coach; CSF; Notre Dame; Psych.

AUCHARD, BRIAN; Bullard HS; Fresno, CA; (4); 1/420; Boy Scts; Debate Tm; FBLA; German Clb; Intnl Clb; Letterman Clb; Treas Math Clb; Math Tm; Model UN; NFL; NBA & Robert Bryd Schlrshp; Munster Germny Exchng Stu & Exchng Boy Of Mnth; Harvey Mudd Coll; Engr.

AUCKLAND, ALEX; Granite Hills HS; El Cajon, CA; (4); 1/433; VP Drama Clb; Treas Chorus; Church Choir; School Musical; School Play; JV L Bsktbl; JV L Crs Cntry; Socr; Val; Natl Cncl Tchrs Englsh Wrtng Awd; UCSD; Drama.

AUDA, KRISTEN S; Pomona HS; Pomona, CA; (2); French Clb; Teachers Aide; Color Guard; Flag Corp; Hon Roll; U Southern CA; Nrsng.

AUER, ADAM P; Rim Of The World HS; Crestline, CA; (3); 16/256; Church Yth Grp; Model UN; Pres Pep Clb; Chorus; School Play; Pres Stu Cncl; Var Bsktbl; JV Socr; Hon Roll; NHS; Sci.

AUERBACH, SHANETT M; Hesperia HS; Hesperia, CA; (1); Church Yth Grp; Key Clb; Model UN; University Clb; Phys Thrpst.

AUFDERMAUR, KAREN A; East Union HS; Manteca, CA; (4); 57/280; Teachers Aide; Var L Bsktbl; Var Capt Vllybl; Hon Roll; Hmcmng Queen 89-90; Delta JC; :Crt Rprtr.

AUGSTIN, MICHELLE A; Riverside Poly HS; Riverside, CA; (2); 40/459; Church Yth Grp; Cmnty Wkr; Girl Scts; Key Clb; SADD; Band; Mrchg Band; Pep Band; Yrbk; Cit Awd; Corp Atty.

AUGSUTINE, CARLA; George Washington Preparatory HS; Los Angeles, CA; (3); Church Choir; Gym; Tennis; Trk; Cit Awd; Hon Roll.

AUGUST, KELLY; Lemoore HS; Hanford, CA; (3); Church Yth Grp; Treas Pep Clb; Stu Cncl; Capt Cheerldng; Hon Roll; CA Schlrshp Fed; Worthy Advsr Rainbow Girls; Fresno ST U; Educ.

AUGUSTIN, CHAD M; Woodland HS; Woodland, CA; (2); Church Yth Grp; Quiz Bowl; Ski Clb; SADD; Pres Soph Cls; Rep Stu Cncl; Intrml Bsbl; Intrml Ftbl; Wt Lftg; Var L Wrstlng; Mst Val Wrstlr; Mst Val Defnsve Ftbl Plyr.

AUGUSTINE, ANGELINA; Bishop O'dowd HS; Oakland, CA; (2); Cmnty Wkr; Dance Clb; Drama Clb; Hosp Aide; Varsity Clb; School Musical; School Play; Stage Crew; Rptr Nwsp; Cheerldng; CSF Clb; Hiking & Bio; Jack & Jill Clb; Stanford; Orthpdc Srgn.

AUGUSTINE, DAVID P; Hayward HS; Hayward, CA; (2); 7/273; Art Clb; Boy Scts; Cmnty Wkr; French Clb; German Clb; Acpl Chr; Jazz Band; Mrchg Band; Treas Stu Cncl; Crs Cntry; Sci Fair Awd Wnnr.

AUGUSTINE, JASON L; El Dorado HS; Placentia, CA; (3); 36/317; Church Yth Grp; Drama Clb; JV Capt Bsbl; JV Wrstlng; Hon Roll; NHS; Ecology Club; U Of CA San Diego; Bio.

AUGUSTINE, KIMARI; St Michaels HS; Los Angeles, CA; (1); JV Trk; Hon Roll; CA St Northridge; Pdtrc Nrsng.

AUGUSTINE, LESLEY; Point Loma HS; San Diego, CA; (1); Var Vllybl; Hon Roll; U CA Berkeley; Medcl.

AUGUSTINE, RAJ M; Saint Monica HS; Los Angeles, CA; (2); 1/200; Church Yth Grp; High Hon Roll; CSF; Spnsh Lang Tutor; Harvard; Med.

AUGUSTINE, RHONDA; St Michaels HS; L A, CA; (4); FBLA; Pep Clb; Teachers Aide; Variety Show; Var Cheerldng; Var Pom Pon; Var Trk; CA ST U; Communication.

AUGUSTYN, BEN L; John Marshall Fundamental HS; Pasadena, CA; (4); 26/150; Chess Clb; Math Clb; Tennis; Cit Awd; DAR Awd; Hon Roll; VP NHS; Pres Acad Fit Awd; CSF Treas; Acad Decthln Dist & Cnty 3rd Ecnmcs, 4th Engl; Boston U; Archaeology.

AUJLA, INDER P; Sunset HS; Hayward, CA; (1); Cit Awd; Hon Roll; Prfct Atten Awd; UC Berkeley.

AULAKH, RUPINDER; Washington Union HS; Fresno, CA; (3); Hon Roll; Algebra 2 Trig Stu Of Yr; Top 30 JRS List; Reg Nurse.

AUNG, KYAW Z; Pittsburg HS; Pittsburg, CA; (4); Science Clb; School Musical; Socr; Wt Lftg; Wrstlng; Los Medanos Coll; Engrng.

AURAND, CATHY; Corcoran HS; Corcoran, CA; (1); Church Yth Grp; Cmnty Wkr; Pep Clb; Church Choir; JV Cheerldng; JV Tennis; Hon Roll.

AUREUS, AMY M; International Studies Acad; San Francisco, CA; (3); Gereonthlgy.

AURORA, NAVEEN S; El Toro HS; El Toro, CA; (2); JV Wrstlng; High Hon Roll; Pres Acad Fit Awd; Arch.

AUSMUS, JODY W; Hesperia HS; Hesperia, CA; (2); 26/800; Cmnty Wkr; JA; Letterman Clb; Math Tm; Spanish Clb; Bsbl; Wt Lftg; High Hon Roll; Hon Roll; JETS Awd; UC Irvine; Mech Engr.

AUSONIO, TIRZAH; Mira Mesa HS; San Diego, CA; (2); Science Clb; Teachers Aide; NHS; THOT, Teens Hlpng Other Teens Hotline; CSF; Psych.

AUST, ERIN M; Fortuna HS; Fortuna, CA; (3); Am Leg Aux Girls St; SADD; Rep Frsh Cls; Rep Soph Cls; Pres Sr Cls; Cheerldng; Powder Puff Ftbl; Hon Roll; NHS Treas; CSF; FFAD; Peer Cnslr; Wmns Lgue Sccr; Humboldt ST; Acctng.

AUSTIN, AMANDA; Fred C Beyer HS; Modesto, CA; (3); German Clb; NFL; Speech Tm; Ed Yrbk; Rep Jr Cls; JV Mgr(s); Swmmng; Trk; Hon Roll; HOBY; Conclr Trng Amer Diabetes Assoc Camp; Srptmst Clb; Nutritional Sci.

AUSTIN, BRANDY; Washington Union HS; Kosse, TX; (2); Art Clb; FFA; Cit Awd; Hon Roll; Cmptrs.

AUSTIN, JENNIFER L; Grossmont HS; El Cajon, CA; (3); 21/430; Drama Clb; JA; Key Clb; Pep Clb; Chorus; School Musical; School Play; Variety Show; Off Frsh Cls; Stu Cncl; Dance Comptn Awds; Prfssnl & Cmmnty Theatre; Theatre.

AUSTIN, JOSH D; Tustin HS; Tustin, CA; (2); French Clb; JA; Science Clb; Hon Roll; CSF; UCLA.

AUSTIN, KATINA M; Dos Palos HS; Dos Palos, CA; (3); 1/140; FCA; Pres GAA; Mrchg Band; Yrbk; VP Stu Cncl; Var Capt Bsktbl; Var Sftbl; Var Trk; Var JV Vllybl; Hon Roll; Medicine.

AUSTIN, LACI; Yosemite HS; Coarsegold, CA; (2); Office Aide; VP Frsh Cls; Pres Soph Cls; JV Bsktbl; Socr; Var Tennis; Hon Roll; UC Santa Barbara; Marine Bio.

AUSTIN, LISA M; Castle Park HS; Chula Vista, CA; (4); 45/328; Service Clb; Band; Mrchg Band; Pep Band; Stat Bsktbl; Elem Schl Tchr.

AUSTIN, LISSA M; Norco HS; Norco, CA; (4); 34/405; Art Clb; Bus Profs of Am; Dance Clb; Drama Clb; French Clb; FBLA; FHA; Key Clb; Letterman Clb; Pep Clb; Merit & 1st Pl His Day Cont Cert Awd; Prom Ct 90; UC Irvine; Merch Mktg.

AUSTIN, MAPRI; A A Stagg HS; Stockton, CA; (2); Church Yth Grp; Dance Clb; English Clb; Teachers Aide; Church Choir; Bsktbl; Trk; Grambling U; Comp Analyst.

AUSTIN, MATTHEW M; El Camino Real HS; Woodland Hills, CA; (2); Var L Wrstlng; High Hon Roll; Hon Roll; Math Tutor; UC San Diego; Law.

AUSTIN, MICHELE A; Hogan HS; Vallejo, CA; (3); Church Yth Grp; Pep Clb; SADD; Church Choir; Rep Stu Cncl; Hon Roll; Afro Amer Stu Union Rep; Langston U; Med.

AUSTIN, MICHELLE; Arvin HS; Arvin, CA; (2); Church Yth Grp; Hon Roll; Cyrntcs.

AUSTIN, MONIQUE A; San Jose HS Acad; San Jose, CA; (3); GAA; Teachers Aide; Varsity Clb; Drill Tm; Rep Jr Cls; Cheerldng; Pom Pon; Score Keeper; Socr; Sftbl; MVP; Crmnl Law.

AUSTIN, SHANNON L; St Joseph HS; Garden Grove, CA; (2); Church Yth Grp; Cmnty Wkr; Debate Tm; GAA; Girl Scts; Hosp Aide; SADD; Chorus; VP Jr Cls; Var Socr; Garden Grove Clb Sccr; Los Alamitos Clb Sccr; Spec Olympcs 90; Berkeley; Poltcl Sci.

AUSTIN, STACEY LEANNE; Clovis West HS; Fresno, CA; (2); Church Yth Grp; Ski Clb; SADD; Cheerldng; Score Keeper; Hon Roll; Mst Insprtnl Chr Awd 89-90; CSF Clb; Fresno ST.

AUSTIN, STEPHANIE M; Irvine HS; Irvine, CA; (3); 167/589; Dance Clb; Teachers Aide; Heritage Awd; Englsh.

AUSTIN, TINA M; Santa Ana HS; Santa Ana, CA; (2); Office Aide; Church Choir; School Play; Variety Show; Var Trk; Prfct Atten Awd; Bio Med Club; Comm Of Assmblies 90-91; Howard U; Med.

AVAKIAN, TODD ADAM; Bullard HS; Fresno, CA; (4); 100/480; Church Yth Grp; Pres Cmnty Wkr; Drama Clb; FCA; Key Clb; SADD; Varsity Clb; School Play; Off Frsh Cls; Off Soph Cls; Waterpolo Vrsty; U Of CA Los Angeles; Psych.

AVALOS, GUADALUPE; Saddleback HS; Santa Ana, CA; (3); Hispnc Socty; Girls Leag; U Of CA Irvine; Educ.

AVALOS, JESUS FRANCISCO; Bell Gardens HS; Norwalk, CA; (4); Am Leg Boys St; Church Yth Grp; Debate Tm; FCA; Scholastic Bowl; Speech Tm; VP Stu Cncl; Ftbl; Var Capt Wrstlng; Hon Roll; Natl Hspnc Schlrshp Sm Fnlst; V Wrstlng 2 X MVP 2 X Leag Chmp; CA Interschlstc Fed Chmpn; CSF Pres; Norwich U; Psych.

AVALOS, JOHN; Bassett HS; La Puente, CA; (3); JV Bsktbl.

AVALOS, MARCELLA; Corcoran HS; Corcoran, CA; (1); Band; Color Guard; JV Cheerldng.

AVALOS, YOLANDA; Sramuel F B Morse HS; San Diego, CA; (2); Cit Awd; Art Awds; Athletic Tchr.

AVANCE, QUINTA R; Eisenhower HS; Rialto, CA; (4); German Clb; Rptr Nwsp; Socr; High Hon Roll; Hon Roll; Eisenhowers On Cite Wrtng Celebration 1st Pl; CSUSB Wrtng Cmptn Hnrb Mntn; Forestry.

AVANCENA, ELLEN LOUISE O; Carson HS; Carson, CA; (3); 1/500; Intnl Clb; Teachers Aide; Orch; Cit Awd; High Hon Roll; Hon Roll; Prfct Atten Awd; Pres Acad Fit Awd; All Yr Outstndng Engl Achvt; Filipino Club; Plaque Of Excllnc In Math; UCLA; Law.

AVANSINO, KAREN; Linden HS; Linden, CA; (4); 2/110; Yrbk; Stu Cncl; 4-H Awd; NHS; Rep Rotary Awd; Sal; Church Yth Grp; Pres 4-H; Pres FHA; Math Tm; Bank Of Amer Liberal Arts Awd; Jostens Fnlst; Xerox Humanities/Scl Sci Awd; Regnl FHA VP; Ctznshp Awd; St Marys; Bio.

AVANTES, LORENA; Eagle Rock HS; Los Angeles, CA; (2); Church Yth Grp; Cmnty Wkr; Office Aide; Pep Clb; Teachers Aide; Cit Awd; Prfct Atten Awd; Stu To Stu Interaction Pgm; Marines.

AVANZINO, GUSTAVO; El Camino HS; S San Francisco, CA; (4); Am Leg Boys St; Church Yth Grp; Math Tm; Teachers Aide; Var JV Bsbl; JV Bsktbl; Mgr(s); Hon Roll; Pres Acad Fit Awd; Golden St Geomtry Honors Awd; Close-Up; San Jose ST U; Bus Admn.

AVEDISSIAN, ALAN S; Bellarmine-Jefferson HS; Burbank, CA; (3); 11/130; 4-H; Spanish Clb; Tennis; High Hon Roll; Treas VP NHS; Outstndng Svc Awd; 1st Pl Chrstms Story Cont; Mst Imprvd Tnns; Awd Kng Wk Fstvl Essy Cont; Math/Sci Clb; Stanford; Bus.

AVELAR, CARLOS; Birmingham HS; Sepulveda, CA; (2); Teachers Aide; Sprt Ed Nwsp; JV Capt Bsktbl; JV Trk; Hon Roll; TV Tech Dir.

AVELAR, ELIZABETH; Lakewood HS; Long Beach, CA; (3); Art Clb; Teachers Aide; High Hon Roll; Hon Roll; Comp.

AVELAR, LUZ M; John A Rowland HS; Rowland Heights, CA; (2); Church Yth Grp; Church Choir; Drill Tm; Yrbk; LACC; Mdlng.

AVELAR, VANESSA; La Mirada HS; La Mirada, CA; (2); Church Yth Grp; Drama Clb; Treas Key Clb; Latin Clb; NFL; Sec Spanish Clb; Speech Tm; Thesps; School Play; Stage Crew; Poems Published; Schl Play Awd; Civil Law.

AVELLINO, CHRISTOPHER A; University Of S D; Encinitas, CA; (2); Ski Clb; Nwsp; Off Soph Cls; Stu Cncl; Ftbl; Wt Lftg; Hon Roll; Christian Ministry; Medcl Explorer.

AVENDANA, PRISCILLA; Central Union HS; El Centro, CA; (3); 132/535; Mgr(s); Trk; Jrnlsm.

AVENDANO, JACQUELINNE G; Mc Farland HS; Mc Farland, CA; (3); Church Yth Grp; FTA; Band; Chorus; Church Choir; Mrchg Band; Pep Band; Hon Roll; Cert Hnr Outstndng Achvmnt Engl 11 & US Hstry; U Of Bakersfield; Sclgy.

AVENDANO, RACHEL ANN; Hemet HS; Hemet, CA; (4); Latin Clb; Pep Clb; SADD; JV Bsktbl; JV Var Mgr(s); Var Powder Puff Ftbl; JV Var Score Keeper; High Hon Roll; Hon Roll; Natl Hispanic Schlr Awd Semi Fnslt; CSF; U CA Snta Barbara; Bus.

AVERBUCK, ALEXIS G; Skyline HS; Oakland, CA; (4); 6/562; Pres Treas AFS; Church Yth Grp; Cmnty Wkr; Drama Clb; Pres Treas Intnl Clb; SADD; Thesps; Stage Crew; Rep Frsh Cls; Rep Jr Cls; Natl Comm Tchrs Eng Wrtng Awd; CSF Treas; Accelerated Enrlmnt UC Berkeley; Intl Stds.

AVERBUCK, RACHEL S; Skyline HS; Monte Rio, CA; (2); AFS; Intnl Clb; Capt Ski Clb; Ed Lit Mag; Cit Awd; High Hon Roll; Badminton; Junior Statesmen Of America; Calif Scholarship Federation; Banana Specialist.

AVERSA, ADAM J; Yucca Valley HS; Yucca Valley, CA; (2); Band; Mrchg Band; Pep Band; JV Var Ftbl; Var L Swmmng; JV L Wrstlng; Hon Roll; Annapolis; Aeronautics.

AVERY, BLUEWATER; Sacramento HS; Sacramento, CA; (4); Art Clb; Lit Mag; Oakland Coll Schlrshp; CA Summer Schl Of Arts Awd; Published Writings; Oklnd Coll Of Arts/Crfts; Art.

AVERY, BRIAN; San Marcos HS; Santa Barbara, CA; (3); JV Ftbl; Var Golf; UCLA; Stuntmn.

AVERY, BRYAN P; Bellarmine College Prep; San Jose, CA; (3); Cmnty Wkr; Pep Clb; SADD; Teachers Aide; Rptr Nwsp; Stu Cncl; Bsktbl; Intrml Ftbl; Intrml Sftbl; Intrml Vllybl; Jack & Jill Of Amer Sec; Black Stu Union; Med.

AVERY, JACOB W; San Diego HS; San Diego, CA; (3); 10/415; Aud/Vis; Drama Clb; Speech Tm; School Play; Ntl Merit Ltr; Nmntd Cngrssnl Yth Ldrshp Cncl; 1st Plc Cty Wide Essy Cntst Tianomen Square; 3rd Plc ST Poetry Cntst; Berkeley; PHD.

AVERY, JANNEA M; Notre Dame HS; Millbrae, CA; (3); Cmnty Wkr; Teachers Aide; School Play; Stage Crew; Rep Jr Cls; Mgr(s); High Hon Roll; Hon Roll; CSF; SCI Stu Vol; Santa Clara U; Law.

AVERY, LIBBY A; Trinity HS; Weaverville, CA; (1); Drama Clb; Ski Clb; Chorus; Hon Roll; Cnslng-Disabld.

AVERY, LIBRA J; Immaculate Heart HS; Los Angeles, CA; (4); 1/125; Cmnty Wkr; Math Clb; Mu Alpha Theta; Science Clb; Nwsp; High Hon Roll; Hon Roll; NEDT Awd; Natl Merit Schlrshp Cmmnd Black Stud; UC Berkeley.

AVERY, MIKEL J; Monterey HS; Monterey, CA; (3); Science Clb; Ed Yrbk; Lit Mag; Rep Frsh Cls; JV Ftbl; Var Trk; High Hon Roll; Ldrshp & Tech Cnfrnce Mdl Tech Exhbtr; Vet Of Wrld Wars Ldrshp Cnfrnce; CA Maritime Acad.

AVILA, ALBERT D; Chaffey HS; Clovis, NM; (3); Church Yth Grp; Library Aide; Band; Church Choir; Mrchg Band; Pep Band; Arch.

AVILA, ALMA; King City HS; Greenfield, CA; (3); Church Yth Grp; Teachers Aide; High Hon Roll; Hon Roll; Acad Achvt Awd; Bus.

AVILA, ANNEMARIE; San Gabriel Mission HS; Temple City, CA; (2); Church Yth Grp; Chorus; Swmmng; Hon Roll; Nrsng.

AVILA, ANTOINETTE T; San Gabriel Mission HS; Temple City, CA; (3); Drama Clb; Tchng.

AVILA, ARMANDO; Fremont HS; Oakland, CA; (2); ROTC; Rep Frsh Cls; Rep Stu Cncl; Cit Awd; High Hon Roll; Hon Roll; Meida Acad Awds; Gras In 92 With High Hnrs; Astrnmy.

AVILA, DAVID C; Beaumont HS; Beaumont, CA; (1); Math Clb; JV Ftbl; JV Trk; Cit Awd; CA ST Santa Barbara; Acting.

AVILA, DEBBIE F; Tulare Union HS; Tulare, CA; (2); 21/435; Church Yth Grp; Drama Clb; Ed Nwsp; Rep Frsh Cls; Off Soph Cls; High Hon Roll; Schl Svc Awd; Mock Trial; Ldrshp Cls; Hmcmng Chrmn; Friday Night Live Treas VP Pres; UCLA; Law.

AVILA, ERIKA V; Mission HS; Los Angeles, CA; (3); French Clb; FBLA; Sec GAA; Library Aide; Sec Frsh Cls; Sec Sr Cls; Var Bsbl; Var Bsktbl; Var Vllybl; Hon Roll; LIFE; UNLV; Interior Dsgn.

AVILA, JEFFRY E; St Genevieves HS; Arleta, CA; (3); Art Clb; Boy Scts; Chorus; Church Choir; Ftbl; Vllybl; Wt Lftg.

AVILA, JUAN E; Firebaugh HS; Firebaugh, CA; (1); Church Yth Grp; Debate Tm; FFA; Latin Clb; Spanish Clb; Church Choir; Rep Yrbk; Rep Stu Cncl; Crs Cntry; Socr; Fresno ST U; Engr.

AVILA, KATIE G; Lemoore HS; Lemoore, CA; (2); Dance Clb; GAA; Member Lemoore Dance Workshop; Received Lemoore High Felix Award For Sculpture; USC Davis.

AVILA, LELENA A; Sacramento Country Day Schl; Sacramento, CA; (3); Dance Clb; Drama Clb; School Play; Stage Crew; Yrbk; Var Sftbl; Var Trk; Var Vllybl; Hon Roll; Score Keeper; Malacoff Diggings 4th Grade Trip Chaperone; U Of CA; Bus.

AVILA, MARLENE C; Hilmar JR/Sr HS; Stevinson, CA; (3); Office Aide; Var Sftbl; Cit Awd; High Hon Roll; Hon Roll; CA ST Stanislaus; Elem Tchg.

AVILA, SONIA L; Tulare Western HS; Tulare, CA; (3); English Clb; Band; Mrchg Band; Cert Articulation Typing; Acad Bstrs Cert Cmmndtn; Hispanic Yth Ldrshp Acad Excllnc; Fresno ST U; Phrmcy.

AVILAN, ALETHYA T; Castlemont HS; Oakland, CA; (2); Spanish Clb; Cit Awd; High Hon Roll; Prfct Atten Awd; Val; MESA Club; Engrng.

AVILES, ANN MARIE L; Independence HS; San Jose, CA; (4); Cmnty Wkr; Church Choir; Mrchg Band; Orch; Pres Frsh Cls; Sec Soph Cls; Pres Jr Cls; Pres Sr Cls; NHS; Vrsty Ltr Badmntn; San Jose ST U; Poly Sci.

AVILES, NORCA; Fontana HS; Fontana, CA; (3); Office Aide; ROTC; Teachers Aide; Color Guard; Hon Roll; Law.

AVINA, LAURA A; Lynwood HS; Lynwood, CA; (1); Church Yth Grp; Church Choir; Cit Awd; U LA Verne; Engr.

AVINA, RUBEN; Montgomery HS; San Diego, CA; (4); 99/411; Cmnty Wkr; FBLA; JA; SADD; Ed Nwsp; Stu Cncl; Var Ftbl; JV Trk; MESA; MECHA; U CA San Diego; Engrng.

AVITIA JR, HUMBERTO; Oakland HS; Oakland, CA; (2); German Clb; Teachers Aide; JV Bsbl; JV Sftbl; U Of Sthrn CA.

AVITIA, MARIA A; Costa Mesa HS; Costa Mesa, CA; (3); 23/231; Spanish Clb; High Hon Roll; Geom Golden St Exam High Hnrs; CSF; Sci.

AVITSIAN, EDWIN; Glendale Adventist Academy; Glendale, CA; (3); 12/62; Boy Scts; Letterman Clb; JV Bsktbl; Var Socr; NHS; UCLA; Aerospc Engrng.

AVRIL, MICHELLE; Crescenta Valley HS; Montrose, CA; (3); Dance Clb; Drama Clb; Hosp Aide; Key Clb; Math Clb; Mu Alpha Theta; Pep Clb; Spanish Clb; Drill Tm; School Play; CSF; Stanford; Corp Lawyer.

AWAYAN, WILMER; Saint Joseph Notre Dame HS; Alameda, CA; (4); Church Yth Grp; Computer Clb; Dance Clb; Intnl Clb; Math Clb; Science Clb; Ski Clb; Tennis; Hon Roll; NHS; U Of Pacific; Engrng.

AXCELL, TERESA; Adolfo Camarillo HS; Somis, CA; (4); French Clb; SADD; High Hon Roll; Hon Roll; Pres Acad Fit Awd; GATE Pgm; Interact Clb; Moorpark; Psycht.

AXELRAD, JOSH B; Viewpoint Schl; Woodland Hills, CA; (2); Cmnty Wkr; Drama Clb; Chorus; School Play; Phtg Yrbk; Treas Stu Cncl; Bsktbl; Mgr(s); High Hon Roll; Theatre Arts.

AXTELL, JEFF S; Sacramento HS; Sacramento, CA; (2); Church Yth Grp; Letterman Clb; Yrbk; Treas Soph Cls; JV Ftbl; Var Tennis; JV Trk; Mst Vlble Rnng Back Ftbl, Mst Tackls Defnse; Sac ST Coll; Phys Thrpst.

AYAD, GIHAN S; Burbank HS; Burbank, CA; (3); Art Clb; Cmnty Wkr; Computer Clb; Debate Tm; FBLA; Red Cross Aide; Teachers Aide; Church Choir; Stat Bsbl; L Bsktbl; Hghst Acad Achvt Rdng Lb; Stu Of Wk For Cmmdbl Ctznshp & Effrts 87; Lttr Of Cmmndtn Exclnt Wrk; Loyola Marymont U; Bus.

AYALA, BLANCA C; La Puente HS; La Puente, CA; (1); Library Aide; Yrbk; Cit Awd.

AYALA, CARMEN; Channel Island HS; Oxnard, CA; (3); Computer Clb; Dance Clb; Drama Clb; Math Clb; Off Jr Cls; Channel Island; Accntng.

AYALA, CHRISTOPHER; Cantwell HS; Alhambra, CA; (2); Var Bsktbl; Var Crs Cntry; JV Trk; UCLA; Acctng.

AYALA, DELIA; Delta HS; Courtland, CA; (3); Cmnty Wkr; FHA; Spanish Clb; Off Jr Cls; Fridy Nght Live; Lit.

AYALA, EDWIN A; Daniel Murphy Catholic HS; Los Angeles, CA; (3); 26/79; Letterman Clb; Service Clb; Sprt Ed Nwsp; Sprt Ed Yrbk; Off Frsh Cls; VP Soph Cls; Sec Jr Cls; Off Sr Cls; Var Co-Capt Socr; JV Trk; Campus Minstry; Law Enfrcmnt.

AYALA, JEANETTE; North Hollywood HS; North Hollywood, CA; (3); Church Yth Grp; Wt Lftg; Hon Roll; Prfct Atten Awd; CA Jr Schlrshp Fed; Jr Beta; Fullfillment Fund Org; UCLA; Bus Admin.

AYALA, LOUIS; Cantwell HS; Alhambra, CA; (3); Letterman Clb; Var Ftbl; JV Socr; JV Trk; Intrml Wt Lftg; High Hon Roll; NHS; After Schl Job; Bus.

AYALA, MARIO; Garfield HS; Los Angeles, CA; (2); Crs Cntry; Ftbl; Trk.

AYALA, MARTHA; Indio HS; Indio, CA; (1); NFL; Teachers Aide; School Play; Bsktbl; Vllybl; Cit Awd; High Hon Roll; Hon Roll; Pres Acad Fit Awd.

AYALA, NANCY; San Gabriel HS; Rosemead, CA; (2); Dance Clb; Drama Clb; Office Aide; SADD; School Play; Bsktbl; Sftbl; Cit Awd; Hon Roll; Prfct Atten Awd; U Of Southern CA; Bus.

AYALA, RAFAEL P; Napa HS; Napa, CA; (2); Latin Clb; Spanish Clb; Cit Awd; Hon Roll; Art Awds; Police Cadets; Sacramento ST; Arch.

AYALA, RICHARD; Don Bosco Technical Inst; El Monte, CA; (3); German Clb; Var Bsbl; Hon Roll; JETS Awd; CA Poly; Arch.

AYALA, ROBYN; Folsom HS; Folsom, CA; (3); Flag Corp; Hon Roll; BYU HI.

AYALA, TAWNYA L; Cabrillo HS; Lompoc, CA; (4); 7/220; Sec Church Yth Grp; FBLA; Spanish Clb; Var Co-Capt Bsktbl; JV Trk; Var Capt Vllybl; Elks Awd; High Hon Roll; Pres Acad Fit Awd; CA Schlrshp Fed Life Sec; Loyola Marymount U; Accntng.

AYALA, VERONICA; Strathmore Union HS; Strathmore, CA; (1); Spanish Clb; Wt Lftg; Cit Awd; High Hon Roll; Hon Roll; Prfct Atten Awd; Pres Acad Fit Awd.

AYARS, VANNESSA M; St Joseph Notre Dame HS; Alameda, CA; (3); Chorus; School Musical; School Play; Variety Show; Cheerldng; Gym; Pom Pon; Sftbl; Cit Awd; High Hon Roll; Ice Skatng; Trvlng; Booige Brdng; Swmmng; Gardening; Animals Care & Brdng; Child Dev.

AYCOCK, TINA L; San Dieguito HS; Encinitas, CA; (2); 61/615; Dance Clb; Drama Clb; School Play; Variety Show; DAR Awd; High Hon Roll; Hon Roll; Masonic Awd; Pres Acad Fit Awd; St Schlr; Prfrmd San Francisco Ballet Co; Numrs Piano Awds; Cnty Sci Fair 1st Pl Physics; Engrng.

AYE, DEBORAH; William S Hart HS; Valencia, CA; (4); 2/480; Church Yth Grp; Cmnty Wkr; French Clb; VP Math Clb; Math Tm; Mu Alpha Theta; Science Clb; SADD; Church Choir; Nwsp; Bio; Physcl Thrpy.

AYELE, MEWOSEGNA F; Santa Clara HS; Santa Clara, CA; (3); Cmnty Wkr; Intnl Clb; Model UN; Yrbk; Off Sr Cls; Crs Cntry; Socr; Tennis; Trk; Vllybl; Stanford U; Engrng.

AYER, LOREN; Christian HS; La Mesa, CA; (4); 4/90; Church Yth Grp; Yrbk; Pres Frsh Cls; VP Soph Cls; Pres Jr Cls; Pres Stu Cncl; Var Capt Crs Cntry; JV Var Ftbl; VP Capt Golf; Var Capt Socr; Wake Forest U; Law.

AYERS, CYNDI; Dinuba Union HS; Dinuba, CA; (3); 2/200; Church Yth Grp; Chorus; VP Frsh Cls; Rep Stu Cncl; Stat Bsbl; Var Swmmng; JV Vllybl; Hon Roll; Rotary Awd; Cngrssnl Yth Ldrshp Cncl; Vocal Perfmnc.

AYERS, KELLY; El Camino Real HS; West Hills, CA; (3); Church Yth Grp; SADD; Chorus; Drill Tm; Rep Frsh Cls; Rep Soph Cls; Rep Jr Cls; Cheerldng; Powder Puff Ftbl; House Of Rep; UC Santa Barbara; Drama.

AYERS, LESLIE; Sonoma Valley HS; Fair Oaks, CA; (4); 2/275; Ed Yrbk; VP Sr Cls; Powder Puff Ftbl; High Hon Roll; Sal; U CA Davis; Eng.

AYERS, LISA L; Ramona HS; Ramona, CA; (3); 34/280; Dance Clb; Treas 4-H; FBLA; Teachers Aide; Stat Bsktbl; 4-H Awd; Hon Roll; Dance Cncrt; Peer Cnslng; Peer Tutor.

AYERS, NICHELE L; Hogan SR HS; Vallejo, CA; (4); Church Yth Grp; Drama Clb; French Clb; Church Choir; School Play; Rep Stu Cncl; Var Tennis; Var JV Vllybl; Jr NHS; Ntl Merit Ltr; Vallejo Yth Cnsrvtry Drama Grp; Acad Decathalon; Interact Clb; Cmmnctns.

AYLESWORTH, KRISTIN M; Santa Barbara HS; Santa Barbara, CA; (2); Church Yth Grp; 4-H; Acpl Chr; Band; Chorus; Mrchg Band; 4-H Awd; Mallet Line Southern CA #1; Oberlin; Music.

AYON, LORENA; George Washington Prep HS; Los Angeles, CA; (2); Math Clb; Science Clb; High Hon Roll; Hon Roll; Yth Cmnty Svc Clb Chrmn; JROTC JR Rsrv Offcr Trng Corps; Peer Cnslng; Educ.

AYRAMDJIAN, NATACHA L; Eugene J Mc Ateer HS; San Francisco, CA; (2); ROTC; Chorus; School Musical; School Play; Variety Show; High Hon Roll; San Francisco ST; Vocal Music.

AYRES, JENNIFER; Los Alamitos HS; Seal Beach, CA; (4); Church Yth Grp; Dance Clb; Intnl Clb; Chorus; Church Choir; Drill Tm; Variety Show; Mexico City MO Wrk; Inner City Wrk W/Hmelss; Orangewood Chldrns Hme Vol; Phys Thrpy.

AYRES, MIKE; River City HS; W Sacremento, CA; (2); Varsity Clb; Bsbl; Bsktbl; Swmmng; Prfct Atten Awd; MVP JV 89-90; Mrt Roll; Sports.

AYROMLOU, REYHANEH; Arcadia HS; Temple City, CA; (2); 130/605; French Clb; Library Aide; Ski Clb; Teachers Aide; Var Trk; Cit Awd; Hon Roll; Prfct Atten Awd; Pres Acad Fit Awd; Octagon Clb; UCLA; Engrng.

AYYAD, HASSAN A; Watsonville HS; Watsonville, CA; (4); 54/570; Dance Clb; Drama Clb; Math Clb; Hon Roll; San Jose ST; Dentstry.

AZAR, TAREK; Coast Christian HS; Redondo Beach, CA; (1); Teachers Aide; Var Bsbl; Var Bsktbl; Var Ftbl; Harvard; Arch.

AZELTON, JIM T; Folsom HS; Folsom, CA; (3); Model UN; Band; Mrchg Band; Var Ftbl; Hon Roll; Aviation.

AZENON, ENRIQUE; Brea Olinda HS; Brea, CA; (3); 52/290; Hosp Aide; Intnl Clb; Key Clb; Letterman Clb; Crs Cntry; Trk; Hon Roll; Rotary Awd; Bst Effrt & Mst Imprvd Awds Vrsty Crss Cntry; Engr.

AZERBEGI, RENEE; Miramonte HS; Orinda, CA; (1); Church Yth Grp; French Clb; JV Bsktbl; High Hon Roll; Hon Roll; Pres Acad Fit Awd; Accelerated Geometry; Stanford.

AZERKAN, YASEMIN; Atascadero HS; Templeton, CA; (3); Art Clb; Church Yth Grp; Computer Clb; FBLA; Office Aide; Spanish Clb; Teachers Aide; Chorus; Flag Corp; Rep Stu Cncl; CA Poly Tech; Bus Adm.

AZEVEDO, ANTHONY A; Montgomery HS; Santa Rosa, CA; (2); Boy Scts; Church Yth Grp; JA; Spanish Clb; SADD; Jr NHS; Pres Acad Fit Awd; Spanish NHS; Whiz Kid; Vlntr.

AZEVEDO, CHRISTINA; Beyer HS; Ceres, CA; (1); Church Yth Grp; Dance Clb; Drama Clb; Cheerldng; Gym; Sftbl; Hon Roll; Masonic Awd; Aiming A Awd; Friday Nite Live; Marine Bio.

AZEVEDO, GENE C; Antioch HS; Antioch, CA; (2); Letterman Clb; Varsity Clb; Var Tennis; Hon Roll; Pres Acad Fit Awd; Babe Ruth Bsbl & Bowlng Lgu; Math.

AZEVEDO, GREG S; Hanford Union HS; Hanford, CA; (3); 4-H; FFA; Teachers Aide; 4-H Awd; FFA CA St Chmpnshp, 1st High Indvdl Awds; All Terrain Vehicle Racer; Cal Poly; Ag Mech.

AZIZ, NATALI; Turlock HS; Turlock, CA; (4); 1/535; AFS; Art Clb; Cmnty Wkr; Hosp Aide; Key Clb; Math Tm; NFL; Scholastic Bowl; Speech Tm; Orch; B Of A Achvt Awd Wnn Math/Sci; 4th Expstry Spkng Nation; Robert C Byrd Hnr Schlr; U Of CA Davis; Biolgcl Sci.

AZIZ, SHENIZ; Loara HS; Anaheim, CA; (2); Color Guard; Flag Corp; Hon Roll; GATE Clb; CSF; UC Verkely; Dentistry.

AZIZADAH, TAMIM; Savanna HS; Anaheim, CA; (3); Key Clb; Ed Lit Mag; Off Jr Cls; Crs Cntry; Ftbl; Trk; High Hon Roll; Hon Roll; Jr NHS; Opt Clb Awd; Private Ind Cncl Orange Cty-Participant Of Month; Rensselear Mdl For Sci & Math; Natl Yth Ldrshp Awd; Cal Tech; Elec Eng.

AZNARAN, VANESSA E; Abraham Lincoln HS; San Jose, CA; (2); 57/231; Church Yth Grp; Library Aide; Office Aide; Spanish Clb; Var Bsktbl; JV Sftbl; Var Vllybl; Pres Acad Fit Awd; San Jose ST U; Arch Engr.

AZOD, ARMIN; Etiwanda HS; Cucamonga, CA; (2); Chess Clb; French Clb; Intnl Clb; Socr; Orthopedic Surgeon.

AZPARREN, JEREMY; West HS; Bakersfield, CA; (2); Ski Clb; JV Ftbl; JV Wrstlng; Hon Roll; UCLA; Marine Bio.

AZPEITIA, JASON D; Mater Dei HS; West Covina, CA; (1); ROTC; Trk; Naval Acad; Pilot.

AZRILYAR, STANLEY; University HS; Los Angeles, CA; (2); Hosp Aide; Office Aide; Bsktbl; Gym; Wt Lftg; Med.

AZURDIA, RICHARD E; Crenshaw HS; Los Angeles, CA; (2); Office Aide; Science Clb; Yrbk; Ftbl; Wt Lftg; Cit Awd; Hon Roll; Ntl Merit Ltr; CIA.

BABA, EDDIE JOHN; Turlock HS; Turlock, CA; (2); 82/500; UC Davis; Pediatrician.

BABA, HIROKAZU; Torrey Pines HS; San Diego, CA; (3); 10/30; Swmmng; Frgn Lang Span, Ger; Tokyo U Japan; Frgn Lang.

BABAKHANI, KAROLIN; John F Kennedy HS; Granada Hills, CA; (3); Dance Clb; Key Clb; SADD; Teachers Aide; Jazz Band; Off Jr Cls; Hon Roll; Awd Credit Cnslr Cls; Prfct Attndnce; ESL Hnrs Awd; Cesun; Accntnt.

BABAO, NARRISON N; Samuel F B Morse HS; San Diego, CA; (3); 111/641; Library Aide; ROTC; Science Clb; SADD; Cit Awd; Hon Roll; Jr NHS; Prfct Atten Awd; Pres Acad Fit Awd; G Q Club 89-90; Invent Amer Awd 90; Sci.

BABAO, TONYA J; Nevada Union HS; Penn Valley, CA; (1); Church Yth Grp; Girl Scts; Hosp Aide; Chorus; JV Trk; High Hon Roll; Girl Sct Slvr Awd.

BABB, JOSEPH W; Corning Union HS; Corning, CA; (3); 1/120; Intnl Clb; JV Var Tennis; Var Trk; Hon Roll; Astrophysics.

BABB, KIMBERLEY A; Santa Monica HS; Santa Monica, CA; (3); Drama Clb; French Clb; Chorus; Church Choir; School Musical; School Play; Stage Crew; Swmmng; NHS; Rotary Awd; UCLA; Psych.

BABBITT, DECY F; Chino HS; Chino, CA; (2); Band; Color Guard; Flag Corp; Jazz Band; Mrchg Band; Pep Band; Cit Awd; Prfct Atten Awd; Yth Band; Drumline Circuit 5th Pl; 1st Pl Mallets Soloist; Riverside CC; Music.

BABCOCK, ANNA R; Oak Ridge HS; Cameron Park, CA; (1); Pres Church Yth Grp; Church Choir; Variety Show; Hon Roll; CA Schlrshp Fed; Numerous Dance Troupes; Brigham Young U; Dance.

BABCOCK, GLYNIS S; Mount Shasta HS; Mount Shasta, CA; (2); French Clb; Yrbk; High Hon Roll.

BABCOCK, KATHY A; Fort Bragg HS; Fort Bragg, CA; (2); 4-H; Varsity Clb; JV Capt Bsktbl; JV Var Vllybl; 4-H Awd; Mst Imprvd JV Bsktbl; Rodeo Qn; Tn Ldr Awd Wnnr 4-H; Sacramento ST; Bus.

BABCOCK, ROBERT; Moorpark HS; Moorpark, CA; (2); Church Yth Grp; Computer Clb; Office Aide; Ski Clb; Ftbl; Wt Lftg; Wrstlng; High Hon Roll; Air Force Acad; Bus.

BABCOCK, STACEY; Highlands HS; North Highlands, CA; (3); Church Yth Grp; Church Choir; School Musical; Cit Awd; Hon Roll; Prfct Atten Awd; Sci & Bio Awds; Multnomah Schl Bible; Vet Asst.

BABELLA, ANTHONY; Thomas Downey HS; Modesto, CA; (4); 12/452; Var Socr; Cit Awd; Pres Acad Fit Awd; Bnk America Acad Awd Comp; Modesto JC; Engrng.

BABER, RACHEL A; Turlock Union HS; Turlock, CA; (2); 53/480; German Clb; Temple Yth Grp; Church Choir; Hon Roll; Biola U; Elem Ed.

BABIC, JENNIFER I; Mission Viejo HS; Mission Viejo, CA; (1); 30/449; Church Yth Grp; Dance Clb; French Clb; Girl Scts; Color Guard; High Hon Roll; Baton Twirler; Ice Skater; CSF; U TX Austin; Engr.

BABINEAU, BROOKE E; Hawthorne HS; Hawthorne, CA; (2); Teachers Aide; Off Soph Cls; Stat Bsbl; Score Keeper; Hon Roll; Gldn St Exam Al Hnrs Awd; Alg Tutor.

BABIONE, JULIE A; Poway HS; Poway, CA; (2); Church Yth Grp; Drama Clb; Teachers Aide; School Play; Stage Crew; Sftbl; High Hon Roll; Courtesy Clerk; Poway Schltc Achvt Awd; Play Bsktbl.

BABULA, JARED J; Montgomery HS; Santa Rosa, CA; (4); JA; Cit Awd; High Hon Roll; Hon Roll; Schlr Athl Awd; Interact Club; Boys Club Sprtsmnshp Awd; Sonoma ST.

BABULA, JOELLE D; Montgomery HS; Santa Rosa, CA; (2); Art Clb; GAA; Letterman Clb; Spanish Clb; Varsity Clb; Var Bsktbl; Var Trk; Var Vllybl; Cit Awd; Hon Roll; Brdcst Jrnlsm.

BAC, ALBA D; Artesia HS; Hawaiian Gardens, CA; (3); Church Yth Grp; Teachers Aide; Hon Roll; GATE Sem; Tutor ESL Stu; Physician.

BACA, BLANCA E; George Washington Prep HS; Los Angeles, CA; (2); Mesa Clb; Latino Cmmssn Hispanic Clb; UCLA; Scndry Hstry Ed.

BACA, CARMEN C; Notre Dame HS; Rialto, CA; (1); 13/165; Spanish Clb; Yrbk; Swmmng; High Hon Roll; Religion Awd; AZ ST U; Jrnlsm.

BACA, EMIGDIO; Manual Arts HS; Los Angeles, CA; (2); Var Bsbl; Hon Roll; Prfct Atten Awd; Engr.

BACA III, GILBERT; San Pasqual HS; Escondido, CA; (2); 207/409; Letterman Clb; Science Clb; SADD; Jazz Band; Mrchg Band; Rep Frsh Cls; Rep Stu Cncl; Var Swmmng; Hon Roll; Water Polo JV; U Of Southern CA; Dentist.

BACA, GLORIA J; Downey HS; Downey, CA; (3); Hon Roll; Artst; Cllctn Of Poetry & Short Stories; Doctor.

BACA, JENNIFER E; Bishop Amat HS; West Covina, CA; (2); Drama Clb; Trk; Vllybl; Hon Roll; NHS; Prfct Atten Awd; Spcl Olympcs Coach; CA Schlrshp Fed; Psych.

BACA, LEONCIO A; Gladstone HS; Azusa, CA; (3); Letterman Clb; Ftbl; Arch.

BACA, MARTA; Irvine HS; Irvine, CA; (3); Church Yth Grp; Drama Clb; Key Clb; Pep Clb; Band; Rep Frsh Cls; VP Soph Cls; Capt Bsktbl; L Sftbl; Gov Hon Prg Awd; Presdntl Ldrshp Awd; HOBY Ldrshp Conf.

BACA JR, RICHARD E; Ribet Acad; Glendale, CA; (2); Pres Church Yth Grp; Drama Clb; SADD; Church Choir; School Musical; Phtg Nwsp; Socr; Tennis; SADD Cntst Photo Spcl Awd; Natl Piano Plyng Audtns Awd; Mixed Dbls Tnns Chmpns 90; UCLA; Pre Med.

BACANI, JENNIFER D; Tustin HS; Tustin, CA; (2); Cmnty Wkr; Hosp Aide; Hon Roll; Golden St Exam Hnrs In Geom; Acad Achvt Awd.

BACCUS, CARL J; Boron HS; N Edwards, CA; (3); Office Aide; Science Clb; Var Crs Cntry; Var Trk; Hon Roll; Freestyle Bike Riding.

BACH, DUC; John Marshall Fund HS; Pasadena, CA; (1); Science Clb; Hon Roll; Pres Acad Fit Awd; U Of Southern CA.

BACHE, RYAN J; Palmdale HS; Agua Dulce, CA; (2); 19/813; Cmnty Wkr; Pres 4-H; Trk; 4-H Awd; Hon Roll; St Schlr; Photo Best Of Div Awd Antelope Vly Fair 89; UCLA; Bus Law.

BACHMAN, AMY B; Monteray Bay Acad; Astoria, OR; (1); Church Yth Grp; Model UN; Office Aide; Intrml Bsktbl; Intrml Swmmng; Intrml Vllybl; Cit Awd; High Hon Roll; Prfct Atten Awd; Pacific Union Coll; Elem Tchr.

BACHMAN, BRITTANY; Fred C Beyer HS; Modesto, CA; (3); Church Yth Grp; German Clb; Band; Jazz Band; Mrchg Band; Orch; Pep Band; Cheerldng; Hon Roll.

BACHMAN, SARA; Foothill HS; Santa Ana, CA; (1); Debate Tm; Girl Scts; Hosp Aide; Latin Clb; Office Aide; Science Clb; Temple Yth Grp; Flag Corp; Mrchg Band; Cit Awd; UC Davis; Vet.

BACHO, JOENILA J; Selma HS; Selma, CA; (3); Hon Roll; CA ST U Of Fresno.

BACHRACH, ELEANOR B; Gunn HS; Palo Alto, CA; (4); 5/300; Pres Spanish Clb; Fld Hcky; School Play; Off Sr Cls; JV Gym; JV Capt Swmmng; Ntl Merit SF; Spanish NHS; Bio.

BACHWICK, AMY; Palm Springs HS; Palm Springs, CA; (2); Church Yth Grp; Cmnty Wkr; Teachers Aide; Chorus; Cheerldng; High Hon Roll.

BACIGALUPI, MATT T; Burlingame HS; Burlingame, CA; (2); French Clb; Band; Mrchg Band; Pep Band; Ftbl; Trk; Wt Lftg; YADA.

BACK, DEBRA L; La Canada HS; La Canada Flintri, CA; (3); 17/240; Church Yth Grp; Cmnty Wkr; Dance Clb; Math Clb; Mu Alpha Theta; Pep Clb; Red Cross Aide; Flag Corp; Variety Show; Rep Frsh Cls; CSF; U Of CA.

BACK, STEVEN; Francis W Parker HS; La Jolla, CA; (2); Math Tm; Treas Service Clb; Ed Yrbk; Var Tennis; High Hon Roll; Excaliber, Mt W/Prspctve Stu & Parents To Schl; Dr.

BACKER, BARBARA A; Bishop O'dowd HS; Oakland, CA; (2); Hosp Aide; Math Clb; Orch; High Hon Roll.

BACKER, MELISSA K; Clovis West HS; Fresno, CA; (3); Church Yth Grp; FCA; Intnl Clb; Letterman Clb; Office Aide; JV Var Fld Hcky; Var Capt Swmmng; Hon Roll; St Rnnr Up Fld Hockey Tm 88; Swmmng St Qualifier 88-89; Vly Chmpn Swmmng Tm 90.

BACKLIN, JEREMY; El Toro HS; El Toro, CA; (2); Cmnty Wkr; Key Clb; JV Tennis; Cit Awd; High Hon Roll; Hon Roll; Pres Acad Fit Awd; ASB VP; Indian Guide; Pepperdine.

BACOCH, MICHAELE; Big Pine HS; Big Pine, CA; (1); 1/15; Am Leg Aux Girls St; Treas Frsh Cls; Treas Soph Cls; VP Jr Cls; Treas Sr Cls; Pres VP Stu Cncl; Sftbl; Vllybl; Pres Acad Fit Awd; Val; CSF 100% Awd; Mck Trl; NASA; Westminster Coll; Sci.

BACON, DENNIS A; San Jacinto HS; San Jacinto, CA; (3); 1/200; Am Leg Boys St; Church Yth Grp; Letterman Clb; Spanish Clb; Varsity Clb; Band; Bsbl; Bsktbl; Ftbl; High Hon Roll; Valley Teen Task Force; Stanford U; Math.

BACON, JENNIFER; Apple Valley HS; Rancho Murieta, CA; (3); 135/469; Math Clb; Math Tm; Office Aide; SADD; Gym; Hon Roll; Merchent Maritimea Cad; Bus.

BACON, KIMBERLY M; Calvary Chapel HS; Garden Grove, CA; (2); Church Yth Grp; Bsktbl; Taught Bible Study; SCC; Child Psych.

BACON, TRACI L; Ponderosa HS; Shingle Springs, CA; (1); Church Yth Grp; Cmnty Wkr; 4-H; French Clb; Rptr Nwsp; 4-H Awd; High Hon Roll; Library Sci.

BACTAD, CHRISTOPHER; Vallejo SR HS; Suisun, CA; (2); JV Bsbl; JV Bsktbl; JV Tennis; Hon Roll; Prfct Atten Awd; CSF; Civil Engr.

BACUS, MELANIO M; Woodland HS; Woodland, CA; (2); Church Yth Grp; SADD; JV Ftbl; JV Golf; UCLA Loma Linda; Med.

BADAL, MICHELLE; Willow Glen HS; San Jose, CA; (2); 15/469; Church Yth Grp; Intnl Clb; SADD; Yrbk; Hon Roll; NHS; Bdmntn; CA Schlstc Fed CSF; Sprt Awd Cert Tm Lg Chmpshp Bdmtn; Block Awd Vrsty Bdmtn; San Jose ST U; Engrng.

BADANI, NIKITA V; Mission San Jose HS; Fremont, CA; (4); 8/361; Girl Scts; Hosp Aide; VP Treas Spanish Clb; Ed Nwsp; NHS; Ntl Merit SF; CA Schlstc Fed; Leo Clb Sec; Pr Cnslng; Comp Engrng.

BADENHOPE, JAY; Gompers Secondary HS; San Diego, CA; (4); 38/100; German Clb; School Play; Phtg Nwsp; Pres Soph Cls; Ntl Merit Ltr; Bicentennial Constitution 88-89 3rd In Nat, 1st St, 89-90 1st St, 4th Nat; Acad Leag 1st City/2nd Cnt; UCLA; Bus.

BADER, LUCAS J; Edison HS; Huntington Beach, CA; (1); Bsbl; Ftbl; Socr; Wt Lftg; Coaches Awd-Sccr; Captn Awd-Bsbl.

BADER, NICOLE ELIZABETH; San Ramon Valley HS; Danville, CA; (3); Speech Tm; School Play; Trk; High Hon Roll; UCSB; Law.

BADERTSCHER, MELISSA; Roseville HS; Roseville, CA; (2); Church Yth Grp; Band; Jazz Band; Mrchg Band; Orch; Sftbl; Arch.

BADHAN, PWANDIP K; Turlock HS; Turlock, CA; (2); 34/600; Stanislaus U; Med.

BADILLO, DAVID; Canyon HS; Newhall, CA; (3); 22/501; School Musical; Hon Roll; Spanish NHS; CA Schlstc Fed; Bus.

BADILLO, JOSE G; Independence HS; San Jose, CA; (3); Teachers Aide; Bsbl; Socr; Pres Acad Fit Awd; Jr Athlete Of Yr Indpndce, CCS Sccr; 3rd Team All-Cntry CCS Sccr; Bus.

BADKOOBEHI, HEDIEH; Poway HS; San Diego, CA; (4); 22/728; Sec Key Clb; Latin Clb; NFL; School Play; Variety Show; High Hon Roll; Kiwanis Awd; NHS; CSF; Peer Counselor; U AZ; Psych.

BADKOUBEI, YASAMAN; Glendale HS; Glendale, CA; (4); Church Yth Grp; Rep Sr Cls; Prfct Atten Awd; Ice Sktng Clb; Grls Clb; Glendale Coll Schlrs Pgm; UCLA.

BADRA, MARIO; Alameda HS; Hazelwood, MO; (2); 58/260; Drama Clb; Acpl Chr; Chorus; School Musical; School Play; Theatre.

BADUA, RUSSELL; Rancho Alamitos HS; Garden Grove, CA; (3); Cngrssnl Yth Ldrshp Cncl; Kung Fu Green Belt; Law.

BAE, CRISTINA; Mark Keppel HS; Glendale, CA; (3); Dance Clb; Sec Debate Tm; FBLA; Math Clb; Sec NFL; Chorus; Cit Awd; Pol Sci.

BAE, JUDY S; Loma Linda Acad; Redlands, CA; (2); Teachers Aide; Chorus; Ed Nwsp; Pres Frsh Cls; Treas Stu Cncl; Hon Roll; NHS; Pres Acad Fit Awd; Medcl Clb; Bd Of Trstees Awd; Med.

BAE, JULIE; Whtiney HS; Cerritos, CA; (3); JA; Key Clb; Latin Clb; Teachers Aide; Color Guard; Flag Corp; Hon Roll; CSF; Prom Cmmtte; UC.

BAECKE, MIKE J; Red Bluff Union HS; Red Bluff, CA; (1); 13/455; Var Socr; CSF; Engrng.

BAEDER, REBECCA R; Mayfair HS; Lakewood, CA; (1); Church Yth Grp; Cmnty Wkr; Chorus; High Hon Roll; Prfct Atten Awd; Pres Acad Fit Awd; Rec Sccr.

BAELLY, PAUL W; Redlands HS; Redlands, CA; (2); Cmnty Wkr; Hosp Aide; Key Clb; NFL; Speech Tm; School Play; Intrml Ftbl; Cit Awd; High Hon Roll; Hon Roll; Law.

BAER, GREG E; Arcata HS; Bayside, CA; (1); 4-H; French Clb; JV Bsktbl; Var Golf; French Hon Soc; 4-H Awd; High Hon Roll; Hon Roll; Pilot.

BAEZ, GABRIEL; Schurr HS; Montebello, CA; (4); JV Bsbl; Hon Roll; Prfct Atten Awd; UCLA; Bio.

BAEZ, HEATHER A; Mayfield SR HS; Arcadia, CA; (2); AFS; Church Yth Grp; Drama Clb; Ski Clb; Spanish Clb; SADD; School Play; Stage Crew; Hon Roll; Lw.

BAEZA, JUANITA; Hemet HS; Hemet, CA; (3); Church Yth Grp; 4-H; Teachers Aide; Temple Yth Grp; CA ST-SAN Bernardino; Acctng.

BAEZA, PATRICIA; Delano HS; Earlimart, CA; (3); Cit Awd; Hon Roll; Prfct Atten Awd; MESA; Police Offcr.

BAEZA, PATRICIA P; Whittier Christian HS; Rowland Hts, CA; (4); 9/179; Church Yth Grp; Band; Chorus; Church Choir; School Musical; Var L Tennis; JV Trk; NHS; Hnrs Clsses; Arch.

BAFFUNNO, ANN MARIE; Los Banos HS; Los Banos, CA; (1); 4-H; High Hon Roll; CA Schlrshp Fed.

BAGALSO, MARY GRACE; Upland HS; Upland, CA; (3); Pres Varsity Clb; Stu Cncl; Var Capt Bsktbl; Var Capt Trk; Var Capt Vllybl; Pres Acad Fit Awd; 2nd Team All-Bsln Lg Bsktbll; 1st Team All-Bsln Lg Vllybll; Mst Insprtnl Vllybll; Med.

BAGBY, NICOLE; Bullard HS; Fresno, CA; (1); Dance Clb; Drama Clb; German Clb; Key Clb; Pep Clb; Ski Clb; SADD; School Musical; JV Cheerldng; High Hon Roll; Southern Mthdst U Of TX; Bus.

BAGGALEY, BRENDA; Mt Whitney HS; Visalia, CA; (3); 1/322; Church Yth Grp; Math Clb; Math Tm; Band; Mrchg Band; Pep Band; Var Socr; High Hon Roll; NEDT Awd.

BAGGALEY, JOHN; Mt Whitney HS; Visalia, CA; (1); 1/462; Art Clb; Chess Clb; Church Yth Grp; Math Clb; Math Tm; Science Clb; Band; Mrchg Band; JV Swmmng; Water Polo; Engrng.

BAGGARLY, ANDY; Damien HS; Upland, CA; (1); 1/318; Chess Clb; Debate Tm; NFL; Speech Tm; Off Frsh Cls; DAR Awd; Hon Roll; Pres Acad Fit Awd; Syracuse U; Cmmnctns.

BAGGERLY, JAMES R; Chula Vista HS; Chula Vista, CA; (3); 54/493; Church Yth Grp; Letterman Clb; Var Ftbl; JV Var Trk; Golden St Exam Hnrs; San Diego Unions All Acad Tm For Ftbl; Engrng.

BAGGETT, CHRISSI L; Dos Palos HS; Dos Palos, CA; (1); Cmnty Wkr; Library Aide; SADD; Band; Drm Mjr(t); Mrchg Band; VP Frsh Cls; VP Soph Cls; Hon Roll; CSF; AFS; MercedJC; Psych.

BAGHERIAN, ELHAM; Novato HS; Novato, CA; (2); French Clb; Key Clb; Service Clb; Spanish Clb; SADD; Treas Lit Mag; JV Vllybl; Var Tennis; High Hon Roll; Hon Roll; Interact Club; CA Polytech; Arch.

BAGHOOMIAN, CAROLIN; Holy Martyrs Ferrahian HS; Encino, CA; (2); Girl Scts; Hosp Aide; Library Aide; Teachers Aide; Band; School Musical; Cit Awd; Hon Roll; Prfct Atten Awd; Ballet 10 Yrs; Dntstry.

BAGIS, MARISTELLE JOY; Moreau HS; Fremont, CA; (4); Church Yth Grp; Hosp Aide; JA; Office Aide; SADD; Teachers Aide; Varsity Clb; Variety Show; Stat Bsktbl; Var Cheerldng; CA ST U; Aerospace Engr.

BAGLEY, CHRISTIAN A; Don Lugo HS; Chino, CA; (3); Debate Tm; FFA; Ski Clb; SADD; Varsity Clb; VICA; Cit Awd; High Hon Roll; Kiwanis Awd; Parl Prcdr 5th ST; Pblc Spkng 5th ST; Cal ST Fresno; Ed.

BAGLEY, MARCUS A; La Quinta HS; Westminster, CA; (3); 27/333; Church Yth Grp; Key Clb; SADD; Teachers Aide; Band; Drm Mjr(t); Jazz Band; Mrchg Band; Orch; Pep Band; Frgn Stds-U Of Nice-France; U CA-BERKELEY; Law.

BAGOON, SAMUEL H; Bella Vista HS; Citrus Hts, CA; (1); FBLA; School Musical; Nwsp; Outstndng FBLA Mem Yr; U Of CA Davis; Doc.

BAGUIOSO, BILLY V; Channel Islands HS; Oxnard, CA; (2); High Hon Roll; Hon Roll; SDSU; Bus.

BAGWILL, PATTI D; Serrano HS; Phelan, CA; (3); Church Yth Grp; Cmnty Wkr; Drama Clb; Letterman Clb; Speech Tm; School Play; Bsktbl; Cheerldng; Gym; Hon Roll; Comptv Cheer Grp; Sign Lang; Victor Valley JC; Lang.

BAHADORI, BAHAREH; Savanna HS; Buena Park, CA; (3); 6/314; Am Leg Aux Girls St; Hosp Aide; Key Clb; Pep Clb; Ed Nwsp; Sec Soph Cls; Rep Stu Cncl; Var JV Tennis; French Hon Soc; High Hon Roll; Stu Of Mnth Awd; PTSA Cert Of Commendation; Cert Of Grd Kanku Karate Assoc; U Of CA; Phy.

BAHAR, TANISHA L; Bonita HS; La Verne, CA; (2); Dance Clb; Drama Clb; School Play; Var Bsktbl; Var Vllybl; High Hon Roll; Exect Womens Intl Schlrshp Awd; Most Improved Player Vllybl; Stu Of Month 87-88-89; Corporate Law.

BAHENA, MARIA ESTHER; Abraham Lincoln HS; Los Angeles, CA; (2); Church Yth Grp; Cmnty Wkr; Chorus; Gym; High Hon Roll; Prfct Atten Awd; Doctor.

BAHMANI, TEYMY; Poway HS; San Diego, CA; (3); 2/800; FBLA; German Clb; Model UN; JV Crs Cntry; JV Capt Socr; JV Trk; Intrml Wrstlng; High Hon Roll; NHS; Rotary Awd; Outstndng Soph Of Yr Awd 89; Coach-Sccr Team-Yng Kids Div V CYSA Sccr; Stanford U; Bus.

BAHR, PETER RILEY; Rio Linda HS; Sacramento, CA; (4); 7/350; L Church Yth Grp; Cmnty Wkr; Science Clb; Speech Tm; High Hon Roll; Pres Acad Fit Awd; Supt Schlr; Air Force ROTC Schlrshp; Fndr & Ldr Of 100 Strong Campus Prayer Grp; U Of Southern CA; Cvl Engrng.

BAI, CYNTHIA Y; Victor Valley HS; Victorville, CA; (2); Key Clb; Hon Roll; CSF.

BAILDON, SHERRI LOUISE; Poway HS; Poway, CA; (4); 5/725; AFS; Girl Scts; Teachers Aide; Band; Mrchg Band; High Hon Roll; Kiwanis Awd; NHS; Stdy Abrd Spain; Tchr.

BAILEY, ADAM S; North HS; Bakersfield, CA; (2); Boy Scts; Church Yth Grp; Spanish Clb; Teachers Aide; Bsktbl; Cit Awd; High Hon Roll; Hon Roll; NHS; Pres Schlr; BYU.

BAILEY, AHBRA C; Robert A Millikan HS; Long Beach, CA; (3); Church Yth Grp; Teachers Aide; Treas Mrchg Band; Orch; School Musical; Hon Roll; NHS; Yng Gftd & Black Awd; Medal Of Merit Fnlst US His; NCTE Wrtg Contest; Journ.

BAILEY, ANGI G; Enterprise HS; Redding, CA; (2); Teachers Aide; Off Soph Cls; Rep Stu Cncl; JV L Cheerldng; Gym; Hon Roll; Chico ST; Engl Tchr.

BAILEY, APRIL D; Eisenhower HS; Rialto, CA; (4); Mgr(s); High Hon Roll; Hon Roll; Outstndng Achvt Wrd Prcssng; Cert Of Excllnc In Vctnl Educ; Cert Of Comp Advncd Sls & Merch; CA ST; Bus Admin.

BAILEY, APRIL N; Bishop Amat Memorial HS; Los Angeles, CA; (1); Church Yth Grp; Drill Tm; Hon Roll; Spellman Coll; Pediatrician.

BAILEY, BRENDAN; Taft Union HS; Taft, CA; (4); 3/100; Am Leg Boys St; Aud/Vis; Church Yth Grp; Key Clb; Letterman Clb; Varsity Clb; Yrbk; Stu Cncl; Var JV Bsktbl; Var JV Crs Cntry; Boys St; CA ST Bakersfield.

BAILEY, BRENNAN M; Tomales HS; Petaluma, CA; (3); Pres Soph Cls; Treas Jr Cls; JV Var Bsbl; Var Bsktbl; JV Var Ftbl; Var Score Keeper; Var Wt Lftg; Bus.

BAILEY, BRIAN C; Pasadena HS; Pasadena, CA; (3); Ski Clb; Spanish Clb; Treas Frsh Cls; Treas Soph Cls; Treas Jr Cls; Stu Cncl; Bsbl; Var Socr; Swmmng; Wtr Polo; S CA Ldrshp Cnfrnc; Grnpc & Srf Clb.

BAILEY, CHELSEA A; Palo Alto SR HS; Palo Alto, CA; (2); French Clb; Key Clb; Band; Mrchg Band; Nwsp; Tennis; Rachel Austin Frnch Awd; Sci Awd; Poltcl Sci.

BAILEY, CHERIL; Santa Ynez Valley HS; Santa Ynez, CA; (4); Church Yth Grp; Office Aide; Teachers Aide; Cheerldng; Diving; Gym; Swmmng; Spirit Of Jr Miss; Homcmng Duchess; Santa Barbara City Coll.

BAILEY, CONNIE; Mother Lode Christian HS; Tuolumne, CA; (2); Church Yth Grp; 4-H; Library Aide; Band; Score Keeper; Stat Sftbl; JV Vllybl; Prfct Atten Awd; Church Mscl; Elem Ed.

BAILEY, DAVID J; Mission Viejo HS; Mission Viejo, CA; (4); Church Yth Grp; FCA; Letterman Clb; Spanish Clb; Varsity Clb; JV Var Bsktbl; Var Ftbl; Trk; JV Var Vllybl; Var Wt Lftg; S Coast League Champn Ftbl 89; S Coast League Champn Bsktbl 90; Laguna Hills Tourney Champ 90; USC; Pltcl Sci.

BAILEY, EDDI R; Mission Viejo HS; Mission Viejo, CA; (1); Church Yth Grp; Cmnty Wkr; GAA; Service Clb; Trk; Girls Leag.

BAILEY, ELENA A; Bishop O'dowd HS; Oakland, CA; (2); Drama Clb; Girl Scts; Hosp Aide; Church Choir; Orch; School Musical; Stage Crew; Rep Soph Cls; Rep Stu Cncl; High Hon Roll; Med.

BAILEY, ELIZABETH L; Pinole Valley HS; Pinole, CA; (2); Cmnty Wkr; Teachers Aide; High Hon Roll; Hon Roll; Law.

BAILEY, ERIC; Yosemite HS; Coarsegold, CA; (3); Boy Scts; Band; Jazz Band; Golf; Var Tennis; High Hon Roll; Goldn Sst Schlr; Arch.

BAILEY, ERIKA; Moore JR HS; Redlands, CA; (2); School Play; Cheerldng; Schl & Cnty Spelling Bee; Schl & Dist Sci Fair.

BAILEY, FRED E; Modoc HS; Alturas, CA; (2); 4-H; FFA; Office Aide; Sec Frsh Cls; Ftbl; FFA Jnr Show Brd; Military.

BAILEY, JAMES A; Corona HS; Corona, CA; (2); Teachers Aide; Lit Mag; Hon Roll; Prfct Atten Awd; Pres Acad Fit Awd; Comp.

BAILEY, JENNIFER G; Woodland HS; Woodland, CA; (3); Pres Church Yth Grp; Treas Drama Clb; Var Pres FHA; Treas Thesps; Var Pres Acpl Chr; Church Choir; School Musical; School Play; Score Keeper; High Hon Roll; HERO Awd; Clthng Str Mdl; 1st Aid, CPR Cert/Cmnty Aide; Mdcl.

BAILEY, JOSEPH W; John Marshall HS; Altadena, CA; (3); Latin Clb; Office Aide; Cit Awd; Opt Clb Awd; Stage Crew; Var Capt Ftbl; Var Trk; Var Capt Wt Lftg; Excptnl Achvt CA Interschlstc Fed; Ortrcl Cont Cert; U Of CA L A; Neurpthlgy.

BAILEY, KARI L; Redwood HS; Visalia, CA; (3); Pep Clb; Speech Tm; Intrml Cheerldng; Var Pom Pon; JV Var Socr; Intrml JV Swmmng; Hon Roll; JV Boy Waterpolo; Var Grls Waterpolo; Acad Ltr; UC Santa Barbara; Psych.

BAILEY, MELISSA; Lincoln Preparatory HS; San Diego, CA; (3); VP AFS; Pres French Clb; Girl Scts; ROTC; Science Clb; Rep Stu Cncl; Var Tennis; Hon Roll; MESA; Upwrd Bnd UC San Diego; Medcl Rsrch.

BAILEY, PAUL R; Pater Noster HS; Glendale, CA; (3); #7 In Class; Church Yth Grp; Cmnty Wkr; Drama Clb; School Play; Stage Crew; Ed Nwsp; Sec Stu Cncl; Ftbl; Hon Roll; Cal Tech; Astrophysics.

BAILEY, STEPHANIE R; Morningside HS; Inglewood, CA; (2); Art Clb; FCA; Varsity Clb; Score Keeper; Var Sftbl; Cit Awd; Hon Roll; Pres Acad Fit Awd; UCLA Tri Mntrp Pgm; UC Davis; Vet Med.

BAIN, TIM; Colfax HS; Weimar, CA; (2); Church Yth Grp; JV Ftbl; JV Trk; JV Wt Lftg; Pres Acad Fit Awd; Presdntl Phys Ftnss Awd; Sierra JC; Chef.

BAIN, TIMOTHY D; Trabuco Hills HS; Mission Viejo, CA; (1); 21/350; JV Bsbl; JV Ftbl; JV Wt Lftg; High Hon Roll; Hon Roll; Stanford.

BAINS, HARINDER S; Yuba City HS; Yuba City, CA; (2); JA; Spanish Clb; Temple Yth Grp; High Hon Roll; Hon Roll; NHS; UC Davis; Engr.

BAINS, MANJIT S; Kerman HS; Kerman, CA; (2); 13/170; Math Tm; Teachers Aide; Rptr Yrbk; JV Bsktbl; Stat Score Keeper; Hon Roll; Prfct Atten Awd; CSF; U CA San Francisco; Phrmcy.

BAINS, RUPINDER K; James Logan HS; Union City, CA; (3); Hon Roll; Mem CSF Club; UC Davis; Pharmacist.

BAIR, AMBER; Vacaville HS; Vacaville, CA; (3); 1/500; Church Yth Grp; Science Clb; Var Capt Bsktbl; Var Trk; Var L Vllybl; High Hon Roll; Pres Jr NHS; NHS; Amer Leg Aux Grls St Alt; Yale Bk Awd; Jr Vldctrn; Cellular Bio.

BAIRD, DAWN M; Moore HS; Canby, CA; (3); 6/60; Am Leg Aux Girls St; Teachers Aide; Hon Roll; CA Schlrshp Fed; Aviation Club, Sec, Treas; Uc Davis; Pre-Vet Med.

BAIRD, JENNIFER; Palm Desert HS; Palm Desert, CA; (4); 7/289; Co-Capt Dance Clb; Girl Scts; High Hon Roll; Jr NHS; Stu Of Month; CA Schlstc Fdrtn; Jr Statesman Of Amer; Jr Hnr Escort; Top Achvr Awd; UC San Diego; Psych.

BAIRD, MAX; Calvary Baptist HS; Montclair, CA; (1); High Hon Roll; Hon Roll; Medical.

BAIRD, MICHELLE L; La Sierra HS; Murrieta, CA; (2); 19/461; Church Yth Grp; Teachers Aide; Band; Jazz Band; Mrchg Band; Pep Band; Cit Awd; High Hon Roll; Hon Roll; Prfct Atten Awd; CA Schlrshp Fed; Amer Hstry Teacher.

BAIRD JR, RONALD D; Lompoc HS; Lompoc, CA; (3).

BAIRES, MARC A; Serra HS; San Bruno, CA; (2); Band; Jazz Band; Pep Band; JV Ftbl; Wrstlng; High Hon Roll; Hon Roll; 2 Yrs Natl Music Guild; Great Books Reading Clb; UC Davis; Vet.

BAJAJ, GURPREET S; Antelope Valley HS; Lancaster, CA; (3); Cmnty Wkr; German Clb; Intnl Clb; Letterman Clb; Math Clb; Math Tm; Science Clb; Service Clb; Teachers Aide; Rptr Yrbk; Cal St Sacramento Hstry Day Fnlst; Sci Olympiad; Physics Day Cmptn; UCLA; Med.

BAJPAI, JOTIKA A; Monterey HS; Monterey, CA; (3); French Clb; Sec FBLA; Hosp Aide; Teachers Aide; Hon Roll; Med.

BAK, MIKE; Fairfield HS; Fairfield, CA; (3); Boy Scts; Church Yth Grp; French Clb; Rep Sec Frsh Cls; Sec Soph Cls; Rep Jr Cls; Stu Cncl; JV Var Crs Cntry; JV Var Trk; French Hon Soc; Europe Trp 89; Egl Sct; Engrng.

BAK-BOYCHUK, LAURA; Miraleste HS; Ranchos Palos Ver, CA; (3); Church Yth Grp; Cmnty Wkr; GAA; Model UN; Service Clb; Spanish Clb; Var Tennis; Pres Acad Fit Awd; Pres Schlr; Comptv Trnmt Tnns Plyr; Soroptmist Svc Club.

BAKCHT, MIRIAM; La Jolla HS; La Jolla, CA; (3); Dance Clb; Service Clb; Pres Spanish Clb; Temple Yth Grp; Ed Yrbk; Off Frsh Cls; Stu Cncl; Cheerldng; High Hon Roll; Jr NHS; Hstry Fr 1st & 2nd Pl; Bus.

BAKEER, AKILAH; Dorsey HS; Los Angeles, CA; (4); #51 In Class; Mgr(s); Stat Trk; Prairie View A&M Alumni Assn Stu Achvt Awd 2 Yrs; San Diego ST; Bus Admin.

BAKER, AMY; Glen A Wilson HS; Hacienda Heights, CA; (2); Library Aide; Chorus; Drill Tm; School Musical; Variety Show; Performing Arts.

BAKER, ANTOINETTE R; C K Mc Clatchy HS; Sacramento, CA; (2); Church Yth Grp; Dance Clb; SADD; Bsbl; Bsktbl; Cit Awd; Hon Roll; Berkeley.

BAKER II, BOBBY L; Granada HS; Livermore, CA; (4); 130/350; Cmnty Wkr; Spanish Clb; Varsity Clb; Band; Church Choir; Var Capt Bsktbl; Var Capt Ftbl; Tennis; Wt Lftg; Hon Roll; Grambling ST U; Bus Admin.

BAKER, CAROL A; Ontario HS; Ontario, CA; (3); Dance Clb; Variety Show; Rptr Nwsp; Hon Roll; GATE Pgm; UCLA; Law.

BAKER, CHAD J; California HS; Whittier, CA; (3); 12/500; Am Leg Boys St; Cmnty Wkr; Letterman Clb; Service Clb; Ski Clb; SADD; Varsity Clb; Rep Soph Cls; Pres Jr Cls; Rep Stu Cncl; ASB; CSF:Inter Clb Cncl; Stu Congress; Yth To Yth; Bus Mgmt.

BAKER, CHRISTOPHER M; Santa Clara HS; Oxnard, CA; (3); 82/142; Hon Roll; Math.

BAKER, COLLEEN M; Orange Lutheran HS; Santa Ana, CA; (2); 30/120; Hosp Aide; Pep Clb; Cmnty Wkr; Var Cheerldng; Var Pom Pon; Tap Orange Cty Acad Deca; Jazz; Ice Skating Comptn Figure; Ballet; Hosp Svc Vol; Modeling; USC; Pre-Med.

BAKER, DARAYL L; Mc Clymonds HS; Oakland, CA; (3); VP Church Yth Grp; Band; Church Choir; Rptr Nwsp; Phtg Yrbk; Var Crs Cntry; Var Trk; JV Wt Lftg; Hon Roll; Bowling; Outstndng Stu, Sunday Schl Yth Div; 3.00 & Better GPA; Howard U; Architect.

BAKER, DIANNE; Berkeley HS; Berkeley, CA; (4); Pres Art Clb; Debate Tm; Nwsp; Yrbk; Lit Mag; JV Tennis; Hon Roll; Schlstc Art Awd; African Stu Assn; NAACP Act-So Natl Photo; San Francisco Art Inst; Photo.

BAKER, DUSTIN; Casa Roble HS; Citrus Heights, CA; (2); Church Yth Grp; Drama Clb; Spanish Clb; SADD; Church Choir; Intrml JV Ftbl; Intrml Trk; Intrml JV Wt Lftg; Cit Awd; Hon Roll; Chrch Sftbl; Chrch Yth Prjcts Vlntr; UCLA; Medcl.

BAKER, EMILY M; Ventura HS; Ventura, CA; (3); 25/431; Church Yth Grp; SADD; Thesps; School Play; Phtg Nwsp; Phtg Yrbk; Swmmng; UC Brkly; Envrmntl Stds.

BAKER, GLORY L; Palmdale HS; Littlerock, CA; (3); 40/675; Cit Awd; Hon Roll.

BAKER, HEATHER L; Warren HS; Downey, CA; (2); Golden St Exam; Jobs Daughters; Northrup U; Aerospace Eng.

BAKER, HOLLY M; Ramona HS; Ramona, CA; (2); Dance Clb; Sec Key Clb; SADD; Variety Show; Cit Awd; Stu Mnth Hnrs Engl & World Civilztn; U CA; Law.

BAKER, JASON; North HS; Bakersfield, CA; (2); Hon Roll; Pres Acad Fit Awd; Sheriff.

BAKER, JASON K; Dana Hills HS; Dana Point, CA; (2); Vllybl; Bio Awd 88; Med.

BAKER, JENNIFER; Los Alamitos HS; Los Alamitos, CA; (3); Math Tm; Spanish Clb; JV Sftbl; JV Vllybl; Hon Roll; Intract Clb; Atty.

BAKER, JENNIFER A; Brea Olinda HS; Brea, CA; (1); Peds.

BAKER, JENNIFER L; Escondido Adventist Acad; Escondido, CA; (4); Teachers Aide; Lit Mag; Sec Frsh Cls; Sec Soph Cls; Pres Sr Cls; Treas Stu Cncl; Gym; Cit Awd; Hon Roll; Pres Acad Fit Awd; Awd Gov Cls, Work Expernce; UCSD; Art.

BAKER, JOHN BENJAMIN; Claremont HS; Claremont, CA; (4); Computer Clb; Key Clb; Nwsp; Yrbk; Var Swmmng; High Hon Roll; Hon Roll; Ntl Merit SF; Pres Acad Fit Awd; Acad Decathlon Team; CSF Cmssnr; U CA Santa Cruz.

BAKER, JOHN M; Turlock HS; Denair, CA; (2); 11/500; AFS; French Clb; NFL; Science Clb; Speech Tm; Treas VICA; Rptr Nwsp; Ntl Merit SF; Rotary Awd; CSF; 1st Pl Goethe Inst Cntst Talk A Mile In German 90; CA Inst Tech; Biotech.

BAKER, JONI L; Viejo HS; Mission Viejo, CA; (4); 75/450; Acpl Chr; Lbrn Chorus; Color Guard; Orch; Elks Awd; High Hon Roll; Kiwanis Awd; Pres Acad Fit Awd; Sec Pres Church Yth Grp; Elsie Parry Music Appreciation Awd; Mst Outstndng Rifle; BYU.

BAKER, JOSHUA D; Modoc HS; Alturas, CA; (2); 2/65; Boy Scts; Drama Clb; Letterman Clb; Speech Tm; Varsity Clb; School Play; High Hon Roll; Rotary Awd; JV L Bsktbl; JV L Ftbl; Cty Juvnl Justc Cmmssn; CSF; Law.

BAKER, KATHLEEN; Notre Dame HS; Riverside, CA; (1); 32/165; Hon Roll; Friday Night Live; UCLA.

BAKER, KATRINA M; Armijo HS; Fairfield, CA; (3); Office Aide; Bsktbl; Vllybl; High Hon Roll; Hon Roll.

BAKER, LAURA; Royal HS; Simi Valley, CA; (4); Church Yth Grp; Acpl Chr; Chorus; Church Choir; Variety Show; Hon Roll; Pres Acad Fit Awd; CSUN; Music.

BAKER, LAURA E; Santa Rosa HS; Santa Rosa, CA; (4); 1/473; Sec Frsh Cls; VP Bsktbl; JV Mgr(s); Var JV Vllybl; Hon Roll; Masonic Awd; Rotary Awd; Sal; Bus Admin.

BAKER, LAUREEN KELLY; Hesperia HS; Hesperia, CA; (2); Church Yth Grp; 4-H; SADD; Var L Crs Cntry; Var L Trk; Cit Awd; Hon Roll; Schlr Athl Achvt Awd; Most Outstndng Spanish II Stu; Bus Law.

BAKER, MARIA P; Covina HS; Covina, CA; (3); VP 4-H; FFA; Red Cross Aide; SADD; Teachers Aide; Rep Jr Cls; Var Capt Swmmng; 4-H Awd; Pres Acad Fit Awd; Swimmer Of Yr 90; Stu In Govt; Alcyonians Service Clb; CA Poly Pomont; Vet Asstnt.

BAKER, MARY ANN; Valhalla HS; El Cajon, CA; (4); 131/412; Art Clb; Church Yth Grp; Intnl Clb; Key Clb; Library Aide; Office Aide; Spanish Clb; SADD; Teachers Aide; Chorus; Schl Prayer Grp-Pres; Church Yth Choir-Sec; San Diego ST; Deaf Ed.

BAKER, MATTHEW J; Winters HS; Winters, CA; (2); 1/102; Boy Scts; Pres Church Yth Grp; FFA; SADD; JV Bsbl; JV Bsktbl; JV Ftbl; JV Socr; JV Trk; High Hon Roll; CA Schlstc Fed; Brigham Young Y; Engr.

BAKER, MICHELLE B; Villanova Preparatory HS; Camarillo, CA; (4); 3/43; Church Yth Grp; Dance Clb; School Play; Yrbk; High Hon Roll; Hon Roll; NHS; Sal; CA Gold Seal Bearer; UCSB; Bus.

BAKER, MIKE S; Fort Bragg HS; Fort Bragg, CA; (3); 11/119; Boy Scts; Math Tm; JV Var Bsktbl; JV Var Ftbl; NHS; Sacramento State; Engineer.

BAKER, MITCHELL K; Abraham Lincoln HS; San Jose, CA; (4); Dance Clb; Drama Clb; VP Latin Clb; Teachers Aide; Thesps; Acpl Chr; Chorus; School Musical; School Play; Stage Crew.

BAKER, NICHOLE K; Rio Lindo Adventist Acad; Chico, CA; (2); Church Yth Grp; Ski Clb; Acpl Chr; Chorus; Orch; VP Frsh Cls; VP Soph Cls; Stu Cncl; Golf; Intrml Powder Puff Ftbl; Pacific Union Coll; Attrny.

BAKER, REBEKAH A; Yucaipa HS; Yucaipa, CA; (3); Church Yth Grp; Spanish Clb; Nwsp; Thunderword Edtr-In-Chief; Yucaipa-Caumesa Nws Mirror Intern; Jrnlst.

BAKER, SHANA K; Perris HS; Moreno Valley, CA; (4); 10/375; FBLA; High Hon Roll; Hon Roll; Riverside CC Schlrshp Awd; 88 Natl Awd Wnnr; Acad Ltr; Riverside CC; CPA.

BAKER, SIAN; Laguna Hills HS; Laguna Hills, CA; (3); 24/300; French Clb; Key Clb; Math Clb; Model UN; Band; Orch; Swmmng; Hon Roll; Acad Dcthln Tm.

BAKER, STACY; Etiwanda HS; Rancho Cucamonga, CA; (2); Church Yth Grp; Cmnty Wkr; Dance Clb; JA; Pep Clb; Varsity Clb; Var Swmmng; Stat Wrstlng; Hon Roll; Acadmc Athl Awd; U Of San Diego; Marine Bio.

BAKER, TIFFANY; Ventura HS; Ventura, CA; (4); Cmnty Wkr; Drama Clb; Intnl Clb; Pep Clb; SADD; Thesps; School Play; Stage Crew; Variety Show; Ed Yrbk; Bank Of Am Achvt Awd Drama; Mss Am Co-Ed Pgnt Fnlst; CA ST U Northridge; Film Dir.

BAKER, TIMOTHY M; Jesuit HS; Fair Oaks, CA; (4); 1/174; Cmnty Wkr; Church Choir; School Musical; Ed Nwsp; Off Jr Cls; Off Sr Cls; Var Tennis; Hon Roll; Ntl Merit SF; Kenpo Karate-Blck Blt; Clscl Piano For 11 Yrs.

BAKER, VERA E; Sacred Heart Cathedral HS; San Francisco, CA; (1); Band; Var Sftbl; Hon Roll; Stu Together Agnst Racism STAR; Cntrl Coast Sectn CIF Schlstc Achvt Awd Prog.

BAKER-CUMPOY, KERI L; Roseville HS; Roseville, CA; (3); Dance Clb; Teachers Aide; Ed Nwsp; Hon Roll; Stu Trainer-Ftbl/Bsktbl/Bsbl/Sccr/Trck; Humboldt ST; Investgtv Jrnlst.

BAKHSHANDEHPOUR, SAM; Laguna Hills HS; Laguna Hills, CA; (1); French Clb; Key Clb; Bsktbl; Cit Awd; High Hon Roll; Hon Roll; Jr NHS; NHS; Harvard Bus Coll; Bus.

BAKHTARI, ARASH; Mira Costa HS; Manhattan Beach, CA; (2); Scholastic Bowl; Var Tennis; Cit Awd; Gov Hon Prg Awd; Hon Roll; Prfct Atten Awd; Pres Acad Fit Awd; Frgn Lang & Boys Tnns Outstndng Achvt; Schlr Athlt Awd; Med.

BAKHTIARI, MANIJEH; Lycee Francais De L A HS; Studio City, CA; (2); Debate Tm; Nwsp; Yrbk; Sftbl; Tennis; Hon Roll; Presdntl Phys Ftnss Awd; Debate Clb VP; Yale Jrnlsm.

BAKKER, MEIKA; Turlock Christian HS; Turlock, CA; (2); Church Yth Grp; Drama Clb; Teachers Aide; Band; Chorus; Church Choir; School Play; Cheerldng; High Hon Roll; Sec Frsh Cls; Acctnt.

BAKKER, SHEILA; Modesto HS; Modesto, CA; (1); FHA; Hon Roll; UC Davis; Vet.

BALA, ERIC T; Seaside HS; Seaside, CA; (4); French Clb; FBLA; Teachers Aide; Sprt Ed Nwsp; Rep Stu Cncl; Bsbl; Ftbl; Trk; High Hon Roll; Hon Roll; Schl Bld Drv; FNL Clb; MPC; History.

BALAA, DANIA; Norco SR HS; Corona, CA; (2); 32/404; Model UN; Spanish Clb; Teachers Aide; Cit Awd; Hon Roll; Medcnl Bio; Swng Crafts; Tennis; Ped.

BALABANIAN, MARLENE; Pasadena HS; Pasadena, CA; (2); Church Yth Grp; FCA; French Clb; Church Choir; Swmmng; Vllybl; Hon Roll; Bus Admin.

BALAGTAS, GLENN; Woodrow Wilson HS; San Francisco, CA; (3); Art Clb; Aud/Vis; Boy Scts; JA; Science Clb; Church Choir; Drm Mjr(t); Bsbl; Diving; Swmmng; Nrsng.

BALAGTAS, NONA; Phillip & Sara Burton Academic HS; San Francisco, CA; (4); #22 In Class; ROTC; Teachers Aide; Lit Mag; High Hon Roll; Hon Roll; Med.

BALAJADIA, GRACE C; West Covina HS; W Covina, CA; (4); 2/450; Computer Clb; Math Tm; Spanish Clb; High Hon Roll; Ntl Merit Ltr; Pres Acad Fit Awd; Sal; Golden St Exam Geom High Hnrs; Cal Poly U Pomona; Comp Sci.

BALANCIO, LEILANI G; John A Rowland HS; Rowland Heights, CA; (3); Cmnty Wkr; GAA; Science Clb; Spanish Clb; Hon Roll; Prfct Atten Awd; Wn Dance Schlrs; Piano; Bus.

BALANE, ALEXIS; Southwest HS; San Diego, CA; (3); 5/498; Science Clb; Teachers Aide; Var Tennis; Hon Roll; Prfct Atten Awd; Arch.

BALANGON, ALBERT A; Gompers Secondary Schl; San Diego, CA; (1); Church Yth Grp; Cmnty Wkr; Cartooning; USNA; Aero Engrng.

BALANI, RANIAG L; William Howard Taft HS; Canoga Park, CA; (3); Letterman Clb; Ski Clb; Varsity Clb; Phtg Nwsp; Ed Yrbk; Phtg Lit Mag; L Var Ftbl; L Var Trk; Var Wt Lftg; High Hon Roll; Blck Blt Aikido; Asst Instr Aikido; CSF; U CA Los Angeles; Sprts Med.

BALANON, SYNYA; Vanden HS; Vacaville, CA; (3); 1/150; Science Clb; Spanish Clb; SADD; Band; VP Stu Cncl; Var Crs Cntry; Var Socr; Var Tennis; High Hon Roll; U C Davis; Med.

BALBIN, JOHN M; Mt Pleasant HS; San Jose, CA; (1); Chess Clb; Church Choir; Cit Awd; Hon Roll; Prfct Atten Awd; Stanford U; Engrng.

BALBUENA, CARRIE; Summerville HS; Sonora, CA; (2); 1/135; Church Yth Grp; Spanish Clb; Teachers Aide; Band; Chorus; Mrchg Band; Pep Band; School Musical; School Play; VP Jr Cls; Camp Royal 90; U CA-SANTA Barbara; Med.

BALCACERES, EDWIN ALFREDO; Polytechnic HS; Panorama City, CA; (3); Teachers Aide; Nwsp; Hon Roll; Prfct Atten Awd; Bus Ed Mrt Awd; Bus Dept Awd Of Svc; Elect.

BALCENA, ERIKA A; Lompoc HS; Lompoc, CA; (4); 125/287; Letterman Clb; Office Aide; Pep Clb; Varsity Clb; Band; Flag Corp; Mrchg Band; Pep Band; Cheerldng; Sftbl; Flower Fstvl Qn; Chico ST; Reg Nrs.

BALCHUS, HOLLY J; Elk Grove HS; Elk Grove, CA; (1); Church Yth Grp; Var Gym; Hon Roll; Delta Leag Var Gymnastics All Round Chmpn; CA Schlrshp Fed; Med.

BALCOS, ELNA A; Mayfair HS; Lakewood, CA; (3); 12/300; English Clb; JA; Tennis; High Hon Roll; Hon Roll; Prfct Atten Awd; Stat JV Bsktbl; Engl Lit Clb; Long Beach ST; Nrsng.

BALDAR, ARZHANG; Canyon HS; Anaheim, CA; (1); Stu Cncl; Wt Lftg; Wrstlng; Orange Cnty Acadmc Decathlon.

BALDENEGRO, MARTHA; Roosevelt HS; Los Angeles, CA; (3); Teachers Aide; Band; Mrchg Band; Orch; School Play; Hon Roll; Accntng.

BALDERAS, ELIZABETH; St Joseph HS; Downey, CA; (3); Church Yth Grp; Dance Clb; Pep Clb; Spanish Clb; SADD; Varsity Clb; Var Cheerldng; Hon Roll; UC Irvine; Obstetrician.

BALDERRAMA, KIMBERLY; Rosary HS; Brea, CA; (3); Church Yth Grp; Debate Tm; French Clb; Science Clb; Pres Frsh Cls; Sec Stu Cncl; Hon Roll; CSF; U Notre Dame; Aerosp Engrng.

BALDONADO, JAIME B; Mayfair HS; Bellflower, CA; (3); Cmnty Wkr; Hon Roll; Prfct Atten Awd; Deans & Princpls List; UCLA; Nrsng.

BALDONADO, SHANNON K; Lowell HS; San Francisco, CA; (2); 250/750; Church Yth Grp; Cmnty Wkr; French Clb; JV Var Mgr(s); Var Swmmng; Amnesty Internation Club; Big Brother/Big Sister Org; Travel; Coll.

BALDWIN, AMY S; Dublin HS; Dublin, CA; (3); 32/175; JA; Teachers Aide; Var Mgr(s); Var Powder Puff Ftbl; Var Score Keeper; Var Vllybl; Hon Roll; Recvd Acad Achvt Awd.

BALDWIN, CANDICE; Redwood HS; Visalia, CA; (3); 1/363; Church Yth Grp; German Clb; Math Tm; SADD; Varsity Clb; Chorus; School Musical; Var Capt Socr; High Hon Roll; Jr NHS; Biola U; Math.

BALDWIN, CHARLIE ANNE; Glendora HS; Glendora, CA; (3); Vllybl; High Hon Roll; Hon Roll; Spnsh, Bible, World Hstry Acad Awds; Pt Loma U; Pshych.

BALDWIN, DEBORAH; Elsinore HS; Elsinore, CA; (4); 31/325; Thesps; School Play; Yrbk; Stu Cncl; JV Cheerldng; Var Capt Socr; Cit Awd; Hon Roll; Stu Schl Board Rep; Outstndng Srvc; Riverside City Coll; Ed Tchr.

BALDWIN, JASON T; Bellarmine College Prep; San Jose, CA; (3); Church Yth Grp; Cmnty Wkr; SADD; Intrml Vllybl; Santa Clara U; Law.

BALDWIN, JENNIFER L; Aptos HS; Aptos, CA; (2); Pres Church Yth Grp; GAA; Church Choir; School Musical; School Play; Nwsp; Hon Roll; Piano; High Hnrs Golden ST Exam Gmtry; Brigham Young U.

BALDWIN, MARK P; Edison Computech HS; Fresno, CA; (2); Debate Tm; NFL; Speech Tm; JV Tennis; Opt Clb Awd; Jr Statesmn America.

BALDWIN, MATTHEW C; Escondido HS; Escondido, CA; (3); JV Crs Cntry; Var Bsktbl; JV Ftbl; JV Swmmng; High Hon Roll; Hon Roll; Rotary Awd; Golden ST Exam Geom High Hnrs; Golden ST Exam Alg Hnrs; Spec Interest Woodworking; Math.

BALDWIN, MICHAEL D; Montclair HS; Montclair, CA; (3); 6/421; Ski Clb; Band; Mrchg Band; High Hon Roll; Prfct Atten Awd; Vrsty Acad Ltr 89 & 90; Hgh Scorer-Natl Latin Exam 90; Math.

BALDWIN, MICHAEL S; Escondido HS; Escondido, CA; (3); 38/382; Boy Scts; Letterman Clb; Science Clb; JV Capt Bsktbl; Var Swmmng; High Hon Roll; Hon Roll; Var Water Polo Capt; Water Polo All Leag HM; Acad Dcthln; JV Acad Leag; Ron Packards Amer Govt Smnr; Sci.

BALDWIN, NATYLIE; Sunset HS; Hayward, CA; (2); School Play; Hon Roll.

BALDWIN, SARAH K; Whitney HS; Cerritos, CA; (3); Church Yth Grp; Service Clb; Chorus; Bsktbl; Swmmng; Vllybl; NHS; Long Bch Rowing Assn 90; CA Jr Rowing Chmpn Eights.

BALDWIN, SHERI L; Beaumont HS; Beaumont, CA; (1); Pep Clb; Hon Roll; Advrtsng.

BALDWIN, SHON L; Redwood HS; Visalia, CA; (1); Church Yth Grp; German Clb; Math Clb; Math Tm; Teachers Aide; Orch; Golf; Socr; High Hon Roll; Pres Acad Fit Awd; U CA.

BALDWIN, SUSAN M; Bishop O'dowd HS; Castro Valley, CA; (2); L Var Socr; L Var Sftbl; Hon Roll; CSF; Russian Pen Pals Clb.

BALENBIN, LILLIAN; El Camino HS; Daly City, CA; (3); Office Aide; JV Bsktbl; Hon Roll; Asian Club; Hotel Mgmt.

BALESTERI, ADAM J; Monterey HS; Monterey, CA; (3); Drama Clb; FTA; SADD; Teachers Aide; Lit Mag; Swmmng; Hon Roll; Teachers Aid; San Jose; Elem Ed.

BALESTRERI, MONICA D; Notre Dame HS; San Carlos, CA; (2); Church Yth Grp; Debate Tm; Cit Awd; Hon Roll; Pres Acad Fit Awd; Jr Stsmn Amer Assmblywmn; Sprt Club Awd; Aquacades; Exec Cncl Hostess Clb; UC San Diego; Crm Law.

BALESTRIERI, JULIANA M; Notre Dame HS; Belmont, CA; (3); Church Yth Grp; Debate Tm; Teachers Aide; Milliard Fillmore Trivia, Hostess & Cultural Awareness Clubs; Psych.

BALIKIAN, SEVAG; Pasadena HS; Pasadena, CA; (2); Art Clb; French Clb; Intnl Clb; Math Clb; Swmmng; Tennis; Chrch Yth Grp & Bsktbl Team; U CA; Finance.

BALINGIT, CHRISTINE R; Sacred Heart-Cathedral HS; Rodeo, CA; (1); Hon Roll; San Francisco ST; Math/Acctng.

BALINGIT, PETER P; Pioneer HS; Whittier, CA; (4); 1/318; Pres Key Clb; Rptr Nwsp; Ed Lit Mag; Off Sr Cls; Rep Stu Cncl; JV Crs Cntry; JV Trk; Kiwanis Awd; Ntl Merit Ltr; Intl Smmr Schl Cambrdg U England; Mst Outstndng Stdt 87-89; NCTE Wrtg Awd; Med.

BALINGIT, ROSE E; Castle Park HS; Chula Vista, CA; (3); 19/422; Prfct Atten Awd; Christian Club Amer-Asian Club Interact; Psych.

BALINGIT, ROSELLE A; Castle Park HS; Chula Vista, CA; (4); 17/328; Cmnty Wkr; French Clb; German Clb; Hosp Aide; Service Clb; Rep Soph Cls; Rep Stu Cncl; Schlstc Al-Amer; CA Schlrshp Fdrtn; UCSD; Bio.

BALKIAN, ARA; Hoover HS; Glendale, CA; (3); FCA; Letterman Clb; Var Capt Ftbl; Wt Lftg; Scl Sci Stu Of Yr; Bio.

BALKON, CHARLES C; Bellarmine College Prep; San Jose, CA; (2); Boy Scts; Chess Clb; Computer Clb; Model UN; Aerosp Explorer Post 757-Exec Offcr; Comp Sci.

BALL, CARISA L; Valhalla HS; El Cajon, CA; (3); Church Yth Grp; Chorus; Church Choir; Variety Show; Var Trk; Hon Roll; Young Women Cls Pres; CSF; Campcrafter Adventurer Awd; BYU; Nrsng.

BALL, DAVID ANDREW; Analy HS; Rohnert Park, CA; (4); DECA; Crs Cntry; Socr; Auto Shp; USN; Military.

BALL, DAVID M; Bonita Vista HS; Bonita, CA; (3); VP Church Yth Grp; Cmnty Wkr; Model UN; Intrml Bsktbl; Var Swmmng; Cit Awd; High Hon Roll; Hon Roll; Pres Acad Fit Awd; Vrsty Water Polo; Task Force; Engrng.

BALL, GURMAIL; Tranquillity Union HS; Caruthers, CA; (3); Computer Clb; French Clb; FBLA; Science Clb; Spanish Clb; VP Frsh Cls; Rep Soph Cls; Rep Jr Cls; Var Bsktbl; JV Ftbl; India Club Vp; Mecha Club; Fresno ST; Bus.

BALL, JAMIE M; Laguna Hills HS; Laguna Hills, CA; (3); Drama Clb; Rep French Clb; SADD; JV Sftbl; JV Tennis; High Hon Roll; Hon Roll; Stanford U; Law.

BALL, MARTIN; Pleasant Valley HS; Chico, CA; (4); Debate Tm; Drama Clb; French Clb; SADD; Stage Crew; Ed Lit Mag; High Hon Roll; Kiwanis Awd; Lion Awd; Pres Acad Fit Awd; Occidental.

BALL, MERAE CHRISTY; Del Oro HS; Loomis, CA; (3); 51/266; Sec GAA; Intrml Mgr Bsktbl; Intrml Mgr Sftbl; Intrml Mgr Vllybl; Cit Awd; Hon Roll; Prfct Atten Awd; Rgnl Occptnl Pgm; Cum Laude Acadmc Dstnctn; UC Davis; Vet Med.

BALL, SHAUN E; Golden West HS; Visalia, CA; (2); Math Clb; Math Tm; Teachers Aide; JV Bsbl; JV Bsktbl; Hon Roll; Golden ST Exam Geom Hnrs; Engrng.

BALL, STEPHANIE R; Marina HS; Huntington Beach, CA; (3); Church Yth Grp; Drama Clb; Thesps; School Musical; School Play; Stage Crew; Hon Roll; ROP Pre Sch Aide; Peer Asstnts League; Golden West; Law.

BALLANCE, DENNIS W; Arcadia HS; Arcadia, CA; (3); 10/639; Art Clb; Boy Scts; Cmnty Wkr; French Clb; Math Clb; Science Clb; DAR Awd; High Hon Roll; NHS; Pres Acad Fit Awd; Eagle Scout; LA Espiscopal Diocese Yth Rep; CA Gldn St Awds, Hgh Hnrs Algebra & Geo Exams; Vet Med.

BALLARD, ALAN D; Tehachapi HS; Tehachapi, CA; (4); Church Yth Grp; Chorus; Ed Lit Mag; High Hon Roll; Gld Music, Bk Of Amer Achvt Awd; Bear Valley Sprngs Twn Frm Schlrshp; Bakersfield Coll; Art.

BALLARD, ALICE D; Lindsay HS; Lindsay, CA; (1); Church Yth Grp; FBLA; Key Clb; SADD; Vllybl; Friday Night Live; Natural Helpers; Cal Poly SLO; Bus.

BALLARD, BRIAN C; Vacaville HS; Vacaville, CA; (3); Church Yth Grp; Cmnty Wkr; FCA; Var Bsbl; JV Bsktbl; High Hon Roll; Hon Roll; CSU Chico; Accounting.

BALLARD, CELESTE; San Bernardino HS; San Bndo, CA; (2); Chorus; Cert Of Recognition GPA; College; Computer.

BALLARD, DAWNA I; Eisenhower HS; Rialto, CA; (4); Pres Church Yth Grp; Cmnty Wkr; Drama Clb; FBLA; Speech Tm; Stu Cncl; Hon Roll; Martin Luther King Awd New Hope Miss Bapt Church 89; Pres Blck Stu Union; ASB Spkr Hse Rep; Howard U; Communications.

BALLARD, RICHARD; Narbonne HS; Harbor City, CA; (2); Boy Scts; FCA; French Clb; Key Clb; Letterman Clb; Math Clb; Varsity Clb; School Play; Variety Show; Var Bsktbl; Golf, Chess, Swmmr; MI U; Math.

BALLARD, THERESA M; Ponole Valley HS; Hercules, CA; (1); Church Yth Grp; Office Aide; Spanish Clb; Teachers Aide; Vllybl; Hon Roll; NHS; Counselors Offc Aid 2 Yrs; Basic Life Support CPR; Solano CC; Paramedic.

BALLECER, LEILANI S; Workman HS; West Covina, CA; (2); Church Yth Grp; Intnl Clb; JA; Key Clb; Sec Soph Cls; Bsktbl; Vllybl; Wt Lftg; Cit Awd; Hon Roll; Tchrs Aid CCD Prgm At Church; Med.

BALLESTER, CARLOS R; Salesian HS; Bell, CA; (3); 3/90; Debate Tm; Drama Clb; Letterman Clb; Scholastic Bowl; School Musical; School Play; Rptr Nwsp; Rep Stu Cncl; Bsktbl; Score Keeper; U Of CA Berkeley; Cvl Engr.

BALLESTEROS, AMALIO D; Fontana HS; Fontana, CA; (3); Art Clb; French Clb; Math Clb; Science Clb; Off Jr Cls; JV Bsbl; Var Wt Lftg; Cit Awd; French Hon Soc; High Hon Roll; Future Sci Of Amer Awd; Arch Engrng.

BALLESTEROS, AMPARO; Rim Of The World HS; Crestline, CA; (3); Dance Clb; Spanish Clb.

BALLESTEROS, AZDIO C; Bellarmine College Prep; San Jose, CA; (1).

BALLEZA, MARK; American HS; Fremont, CA; (3); Bsbl; Bsktbl; Arts.

BALLI, SERGIO A; Sanger HS; Sanger, CA; (2); Model UN; Ski Clb; Var Swmmng; Aquatics Clb; Med.

BALLINGER, KIMBERLY; Pioneer Baptist HS; Long Beach, CA; (2); Church Yth Grp; Teachers Aide; Bsktbl; Cheerldng; Sftbl; Vllybl; Expree Leag Vllybl Hnrb Mntn & Dachs Awd, 2nd Tm Bsktbl, 1st Tm & Spark Plub Awd Sftbl; Elem Educ.

BALLINGER, RUSTY D; Mira Loma HS; Sacramento, CA; (4); Art Clb; Chess Clb; Pres Drama Clb; Science Clb; Thesps; School Play; Rptr Nwsp; Rptr Yrbk; Ed Lit Mag; Rep Stu Cncl.

BALLOTTI, CHRISTINA J; Torrance HS; Torrance, CA; (3); 103/414; French Clb; Band; Mrchg Band; Pep Band; Concert Band; Nrsng.

BALMACEDA, LIBY; Bell Gardens HS; Bell Gardens, CA; (3); French Clb; Quiz Bowl; SADD; Ed Nwsp; Powder Puff Ftbl; Var Tennis; Cit Awd; French Hon Soc; High Hon Roll; Hon Roll; Mock Trl; Sci Bowl; SR Clb; Pre Law.

BALOGH, MICHELLE M; Canyon Springs HS; Riverside, CA; (3); FBLA; SADD; Teachers Aide; Trk; High Hon Roll; Prfct Atten Awd; Spcl Olympcs Vlntr; OH ST U; Cnslr.

BALON, JENNIFER G; St Rose Acad; Daly City, CA; (3); Cmnty Wkr; GAA; Spanish Clb; Yrbk; Lit Mag; Var L Bsktbl; Var L Vllybl; High Hon Roll; NHS; CSF; Jnr Statesmn Amer; JV Bsktbl MVP; CA ST Polytechnic; Arch.

BALONEY, AARON EDWARD; Bellarmine College Prep; Milpitas, CA; (3); 74/300; Computer Clb; Sec Intnl Clb; Letterman Clb; Service Clb; Teachers Aide; Varsity Clb; Ed Nwsp; Stat JV Bsktbl; Var Crs Cntry; Var Mgr(s); People To People Stu Ambssdr.

BALOUN, KAREL M; Bellarmine College Prep; Campbell, CA; (4); VP Bus Profs of Am; Debate Tm; Pres Math Clb; NFL; Science Clb; Speech Tm; Nwsp; Intrml Mgr Bsktbl; Intrml Mgr Sftbl; Lion Awd; Macalaster Coll; Physics.

BALSAMO, EDWARD J; Irvine HS; Irvine, CA; (2); 45/565; Cmnty Wkr; JA; Rep Frsh Cls; Rep Soph Cls; JV Bsbl; JV Socr; Hon Roll; Pres Schlr; Scrd 1230 As Soph SAT; Stanford U; Orthodontstry.

BALSKE, MICHELLE L; Clovis HS; Fresno, CA; (3); Co-Ed Nwsp; High Hon Roll; Hon Roll; VP & Pres Sign Lang Clb; CA Schlrhsp Fed; Fresno ST U; Psych.

BALSLEY, BRIAN D; Thousand Oaks HS; Thousand Oaks, CA; (3); Boy Scts; Var Tennis; Eagle Scout.

BALTAZAR, DOMINIC; Harvard Schl; Culvercity, CA; (2); Church Yth Grp; Debate Tm; Library Aide; NFL; Office Aide; Speech Tm; Intrml Fld Hcky; Intrml Ftbl; Intrml Vllybl.

BALTAZAR, MARIA T; Victor Valley HS; Los Angeles, CA; (3); 144/416; Spanish Clb; Crs Cntry; Trk; George Murphy Frgn Lang Excllnc Awd; Deptmntl Commndtn Frgn Lang Awd; Translator.

BALTER, TAMARA L; Yucca Valley HS; Morongo Valley, CA; (1); Girl Scts; Band; Mrchg Band; Hon Roll; USC; Psychiatrist.

BALTES, DANIEL R; Servite HS; Orange, CA; (3); Church Yth Grp; Debate Tm; Ski Clb; Intrml Bsktbl; JV Trk; Bicycling, Water Ski, Tnns, Golf; Arch.

BALTHROP-LEWIS, AMARA; Lowell HS; Tallahassee, FL; (2); Latin Clb; Science Clb; Chorus; High Hon Roll; Hon Roll; Schlrshp Bllt Schl NY 89; Schlrshp Bllt Schl San Francsisco 89-91; Schlrshp Schl Amer Bllt 90-91.

BALUCAN, JENNIFER P; Whitney HS; Cerritos, CA; (3); Band; Mrchg Band; Yrbk; High Hon Roll; NHS; Pilipino Clb Kaibigan Pres, VP, Historian; Jr Hnr Guard; CSF; Bio.

BALUYUT, ROWENA C; Notre Dame HS; Salinas, CA; (3); Cmnty Wkr; FBLA; VP Science Clb; Teachers Aide; Chorus; Sec Jr Cls; VP Sr Cls; Stu Cncl; High Hon Roll; NHS; Monterey Co Mthltc Cont & Spllng Bees; CSF; Sec Amnesty Intl; Stanford U; Sci Res.

BAMFORD, BILL; San Lorenzo HS; San Lorenzo, CA; (2); 4/200; VP Treas FBLA; Treas Frsh Cls; Bsktbl; Capt L Crs Cntry; L Trk; High Hon Roll; Big Bros/Big Sis Club Vp; San Jose ST U; Engr.

BAMFORD, MIKE L; Apple Valley HS; Apple Valley, CA; (2); Boy Scts; Church Yth Grp; SADD; Band; Mrchg Band; Hon Roll; Eagle Scout.

BANACH, KRISTIN E; Poway HS; Poway, CA; (1); Key Clb; Band; Mrchg Band; School Musical; Hon Roll; NHS.

BANAS, BRIDGET E; Dixon HS; Dixon, CA; (3); 1/160; Treas AFS; Am Leg Aux Girls St; Cmnty Wkr; Sec Intnl Clb; Varsity Clb; Rep Jr Cls; Treas Sr Cls; Rep Stu Cncl; JV Bsktbl; Var L Crs Cntry; Red Rbbn Wk; CSF.

BANCHI, ANGELA GAIL; Cypress HS; Cypress, CA; (4); Church Yth Grp; Pep Clb; Capt Color Guard; Flag Corp; Jr NHS; Mock Trial Team; Campus Bible Study; Envrnmntl Club; Stu Of Mnth Photo; San Francisco ST U; Photo.

BANDA, ANITA M; Fred C Beyer HS; Modesto, CA; (1); Church Yth Grp; Cmnty Wkr; Church Choir; Color Guard; Hon Roll; U CA Davis; Bus Admin.

BANDA, CRISANTA; Santa Ana HS; Santa Ana, CA; (2); Achvt Awds; UCLA; Math.

BANDA, MARIBEL C; San Benito HS; Hollister, CA; (2); Church Yth Grp; Cmnty Wkr; FBLA; Teachers Aide; Stage Crew; Cit Awd; Prfct Atten Awd; Smmr Inst Ldrshp & Comp Awrnss; Mexican Amer Politcl Asso; Movimierto Estudiantil Chicano De Atzlan; Law.

BANDAK, LOUIE F; Western HS; Stanton, CA; (4); Spanish Clb; Teachers Aide; Cit Awd; Hon Roll; CSF; CA ST U Long Beach; Comp Sci.

BANDSMA, JENNIFER; Oakdale HS; Oakdale, CA; (3); Church Yth Grp; Dance Clb; Drama Clb; Science Clb; Ski Clb; School Play; Sec Soph Cls; JV Cheerldng; JV Var Swmmng; High Hon Roll; Bus.

BANDUCCI, FRANCESCA B; Dixon HS; Dixon, CA; (1); FFA; SADD; Off Frsh Cls; Tennis; Cit Awd; Hon Roll; Lion Awd; March Of Dimes Walk A Thon; Harvard U; Corp Law.

BANDUCCI, STEFAN S; Rio Americano HS; Carmichael, CA; (3); 12/290; Cmnty Wkr; French Clb; Sec NFL; Science Clb; Ski Clb; Speech Tm; High Hon Roll; Natl Yth Ldrshp Cncl Congrssnl Schlr; Stu Tutor.

BANDY, ANGELA NICOLE; Alhambra HS; Martinez, CA; (4); 9/219; Rptr Nwsp; Yrbk; Lit Mag; Stu Cncl; Capt Var Cheerldng; Lion Awd; Ntl Merit SF; Peer Cnslr; Yth Educ; CSF-TREAS; Day Care Ctr.

BANDY, DANIEL W; Fred C Beyer HS; Modesto, CA; (3); Cmnty Wkr; Drama Clb; JA; Key Clb; Varsity Clb; School Play; Stage Crew; Rep Stu Cncl; JV Bsbl; JV Socr; Acad All-Conf Team Track; Outstndng Ctznshp 89-90; Jr Olympic Alpine Ski Team; USNA; Arch.

BANE, LESLIE; Amador HS; Pine Grove, CA; (3); Pres VP 4-H; JV Var Cheerldng; Var Capt Tennis; 4-H Awd; Rep High Hon Roll; Lion Awd; Val; VP Sr Cls; Rep Jr Cls; Rep Stu Cncl; Bnk Amer Schlrshp Awd; Native Sons Gldn West Spch Wnnr; Bus Admin.

BANERJEE, SANCHITA; Moreau HS; Fremont, CA; (4); 32/300; Cmnty Wkr; Math Clb; SADD; Rptr Nwsp; Intrml Powder Puff Ftbl; High Hon Roll; NHS; Pres Acad Fit Awd; CSF; UC Davis.

BANERJEE, SHELLEY; Chula Vista HS; Chula Vista, CA; (3); 12/493; Cmnty Wkr; Treas French Clb; Hosp Aide; Math Tm; SADD; Teachers Aide; Var Crs Cntry; Var Swmmng; Var Tennis; Var Trk; CSF Treas 89-90, Pres 90-91; Neurology.

BANET-RUMMELL, LASHEL; Tri-City Christian HS; Oceanside, CA; (3); Church Yth Grp; Library Aide; Pep Clb; Chorus; Yrbk; Var Bsktbl; Var Cheerldng; High Hon Roll; Nurse.

BANG, PHAN; Mountain View HS; El Monte, CA; (2).

BANG, STEPHEN T; Villa Park HS; Villa Park, CA; (2); Hon Roll; Keybrd & Piano; Arch.

BANG, WON; Eagle Rock HS; Los Angeles, CA; (4); 1/336; Off Am Leg Boys St; Boy Scts; English Clb; Key Clb; Science Clb; Ski Clb; Variety Show; Treas Jr Cls; Treas Sr Cls; Stu Cncl; St Sci Olympiad Gold Mdl 87, Silver Mdl 89, 3 Gold Mdls 90; Six Flags Magic Mtn Physics Cont 2 Golds; CA Tech; Engrng.

BANG-ROSE, CHARITY E; Faith Christian HS; Wheatland, CA; (3); 4-H; Hosp Aide; Yuba Coll; Lbrl Arts.

BANGA, ALANA; Antioch HS; Antioch, CA; (3); Church Yth Grp; Office Aide; Teachers Aide; Fashion Design.

BANGALAN, DESIREE; Samuel F B Morse HS; San Diego, CA; (2); Office Aide; ROTC; Color Guard; Drill Tm; Cit Awd; Hon Roll; Jr NHS; Prfct Atten Awd; ROTC Outstndng 1st Yr Cadet; Yth Phys Ftnss; San Diego ST U; Pharmacy.

BANGERTER, DEBBIE; La Habra HS; Whittier, CA; (2); Treas Key Clb; Band; Mrchg Band; Orch; Pep Band; Stu Leag; Acad Dcthln; Law.

BANGLOY, ERIC M; East Bakersfield HS; Bakersfield, CA; (2); Church Yth Grp; German Clb; Intrml Ftbl; Intrml Trk; High Hon Roll; Hon Roll; CSF; US Naval Acad; Math.

BANGS, ELIZABETH T; Sunny Hills HS; Fullerton, CA; (1); Church Yth Grp; Library Aide; Swmmng; High Hon Roll; Kiwanis Awd; Rotary Awd; Natl Chartiy League Fullerton Chapter; St Andrews Episcoal Church Acolyte; Mng Editor 90 SHHS Accolad; Law.

BANGSUND, KEVIN W; North Salinas HS; Salinas, CA; (3); Chess Clb; Church Yth Grp; Computer Clb; Science Clb; High Hon Roll; Prfct Atten Awd; Pres Acad Fit Awd; Columbia Chrstn Coll; Marne Bio.

BANH, CAU; Mark Keppel HS; Rosemead, CA; (3); Prfct Atten Awd; Los Angeles Cnty, Rop, Cert Achvt, Course Comp Applcnt Gld, Office Occupation Grade A; UCLA; Dentist.

BANH, HIEN D; Cupertino HS; San Jose, CA; (3); French Clb; VP JA; Service Clb; Stu Cncl; Swmmng; Capt Tennis; French Hon Soc; Jr NHS; CA Poly; Airline Pilot.

BANH, JENNIFER; Cupertino HS; San Jose, CA; (2); Varsity Clb; Band; Nwsp; Yrbk; Stu Cncl; Bsktbl; Trk; Vllybl; Interact Clb; Altruette Clb; UCSD; Nrsng.

BANH, MEIU DUNG; Hoover HS; San Diego, CA; (4); Hon Roll; NHS; Grossmont Coll.

BANH, THUC DUNG; Hoover HS; San Diego, CA; (4); Hon Roll; NHS; Grossmont Coll; Accntnt.

BANH, VIRGINIA N; Schurr HS; Monterey Park, CA; (2); Cmnty Wkr; Hosp Aide; Intnl Clb; Math Clb; SADD; Prfct Attndnc; Hnrs Golden St Exam Geom; Tutor Of Yr CA Schlrshp Fed; CO U; Med.

BANH, YEN; Oakland HS; Oakland, CA; (2); Hon Roll.

BANKAR, REENA; Poway HS; Poway, CA; (1); Pep Clb; English Clb.

BANKHEAD, ADRIAN C; University HS; Los Angeles, CA; (3); Aud/Vis; Boy Scts; Church Yth Grp; Dance Clb; Amnsty Intl; Acad Decath; Carnegie Mellon.

BANKS, BRAD S; Victor Valley HS; Victorville, CA; (2); 6/325; Key Clb; Ftbl; Var Tennis; High Hon Roll; UC Berkeley; Engrng.

BANKS, DAWN; Grace M Davis HS; Modesto, CA; (2); French Clb; Hosp Aide; Hon Roll; Prfrmd In Mdrn Dance Cncrt; MJC; Psych.

BANKS, EDWARD; Phillip And Sala Burton Acad HS; San Francisco, CA; (3); Art Clb; Cmnty Wkr; Debate Tm; French Clb; Chorus; Rep Frsh Cls; Rep Soph Cls; Rep Jr Cls; Rep Stu Cncl; Cit Awd; Finance.

BANKS JR, HEROD P; Silver Valley HS; Fort Irwin, CA; (2); Red Cross Aide; Spanish Clb; JV Bsktbl; JV Capt Ftbl; Hon Roll; U Of NC; Elec Engrng.

BANKS, MICHELLE LISETTE; Central Union HS; El Centro, CA; (2); 47/660; Library Aide; Office Aide; Teachers Aide; Treas Soph Cls; Cit Awd; Hon Roll; GATE 89-90; Eng GATE; Wrld Hstry GATE; Legal Secy.

BANKS, MITZIE M; Bret Harte Union HS; Angels Camp, CA; (2); Var L Bsktbl; Stat Ftbl; Hon Roll; Adv Piano; Elem Ed.

BANKS, NZINGHA; Canyon Springs HS; Moreno Valley, CA; (2); Church Yth Grp; Dance Clb; Drama Clb; ROTC; SADD; Band; Drill Tm; Yrbk; Cheerldng; Cit Awd.

BANKS, SHRONDA; Washington Prep HS; Los Angeles, CA; (4); 47/600; Math Tm; Hon Roll; Prfct Atten Awd; MESA; SR Senate; CA ST; Bus.

BANKS, TIMOTHY J; Mission Viejo HS; Mission Viejo, CA; (3); Church Yth Grp; FCA; Key Clb; Teachers Aide; Yrbk; Var Socr; Var Tennis; UC-SAN Francisco; Phy Ther.

BANNA, RHONDA M; Torrey Pines HS; San Diego, CA; (3); Office Aide; Church Choir; JV Sftbl; USD; Idol Psych.

BANNAI, HIDEJIRO A; San Marino HS; San Marino, CA; (4); FBLA; Latin Clb; Letterman Clb; Ski Clb; Capt Varsity Clb; Var Swmmng; Var Wt Lftg; Stu Yr Awd ROP; Natl Rnkd Skier & Vrsty Water Polo Plyr; Japanese Schl; CO U Boulder; Bus.

BANNER, KELLY M; Paraclete HS; Palmdale, CA; (3); 25/121; High Hon Roll; Hon Roll; NM Highlands U; Chem.

BANNISTER, RAND; Antelope Valley HS; Palmdale, CA; (2); Boy Scts; Teachers Aide; Water Skiing; BMX Racing; Photo; Navy; Electrncs.

BANNISTER, STACY; Fontana HS; Fontana, CA; (4); 82/792; Acpl Chr; Drill Tm; School Musical; Hon Roll; Pres Acad Fit Awd; CSF Sealbearer; Acadmc Gold & Slvr Mdlst; Z Club; CA ST San Bernardino; Nrsng.

BANS, JASON; Christian Community Acad; San Jose, CA; (2); 1/6; Rep Soph Cls; Bsbl; Bsktbl; Socr; Cit Awd; High Hon Roll; Pilot.

BANTILAN, EMILY J; Eisenhower HS; Rialto, CA; (2); Band; Mrchg Band; Pep Band; Nrsng.

BANTOLINO, MARIA DOLORES; Skyline HS; Oakland, CA; (4); 84/541; ROTC; Drill Tm; Stu Cncl; DAR Awd; Hon Roll; Cert Recgntn Golden St Schlr 88; Filipino Clb Pres; Rifle Tm Capt; Brigade 5-2 Security Office ROTC; CA Poly; Comp Engrng.

BANTZ, KELLY; Edison HS; Huntington Beach, CA; (2); Church Yth Grp; Off Drill Tm; Mrchg Band; Hon Roll; San Diego ST U; Commnctns.

BANUELOS, CRIS D; Tulare Western HS; Tulare, CA; (3); Letterman Clb; Model UN; Science Clb; Spanish Clb; Var Crs Cntry; Var Capt Trk; Var Wrstlng; Hon Roll; CSF VP; Physics Engr.

BANUELOS, DANIEL A; Channel Island HS; Oxnard, CA; (4); Teachers Aide; JV Var Crs Cntry; Wt Lftg; Hon Roll; Geom Gldn St Schlr Awd; Elec Engrng.

BANUELOS, EVA; Gonzalez Union HS; Soledad, CA; (2); GAA; Acpl Chr; Chorus; Church Choir; Off Jr Cls; Sftbl; Vllybl; Wt Lftg; Hon Roll; Prfct Atten Awd; UCLA.

BANUELOS, JOSE L; Roosevelt HS; Los Angeles, CA; (3); Church Yth Grp; Socr; High Hon Roll; Hon Roll; NHS; Prfct Atten Awd; Auto Mech.

BANUELOS, MARGARITA; Dos Palos HS; Dos Palos, CA; (3); Church Yth Grp; FBLA; Rep FHA; Math Clb; Science Clb; SADD; Off Jr Cls; Off Sr Cls; JV Bsktbl; Var Crs Cntry; Pres Mo Eo Cho A; CSF 3 Yrs; BSU; Fresno ST U; Bus Admin.

BANUELOS, MARGARITA; Pasadena HS; Pasadena, CA; (3); French Clb; Service Clb; Hon Roll; Ltn Amer Stu Assn; Photo Clb.

BANUELOS, RAFAEL G; Pasadena HS; Pasadena, CA; (3); Pasadena City Coll; Car Uphlstr.

BANUELOS, TERESA G; Pasadena HS; Pasadena, CA; (4); 33/433; Church Yth Grp; Q&S; Treas Spanish Clb; Drill Tm; Flag Corp; Yrbk; Hon Roll; Prom Cmmttee; CSF; Photo Clb; Watterson Coll; Travel.

BANUELOS, VICTOR M; Southwest HS; San Diego, CA; (3); Cit Awd; Hon Roll; Pres Acad Fit Awd; UCSD; Phy.

BAO, THUY NGUYEN; Hoover HS; San Diego, CA; (3); 3/365; Drama Clb; Intnl Clb; Key Clb; Library Aide; Math Clb; Cit Awd; High Hon Roll; Hon Roll; NHS; Prfct Atten Awd; Top Mark; Jr Chain; Hgh Schlrhp Awd; Goldn St Exm Alg & Geom; Outstndng Math Stu; Top 10 Badmntn; CSF; UCSD; Cosmtlgy.

BAPTISTA, BARTHOLOMEW LEANDRO Z; San Lorenzo HS; Hayward, CA; (4); 39/215; Church Yth Grp; Intnl Clb; Rptr Yrbk; Sec Capt Lit Mag; Co-Capt L Cheerldng; Capt L Gym; Var Trk; Hon Roll; Mnrty Ldrshp Clb; U Of CA Prtnrshp Prgrm; UC Santa Barbar; Pltcl Sci.

BAPTISTA, CHERYL; St Patrick-St Vincent HS; Vallejo, CA; (3); Letterman Clb; Pep Clb; Teachers Aide; Varsity Clb; Church Choir; Var Cheerldng; High Hon Roll; Hon Roll; CA Schlrshp Fdrtn; U San Francisco; Bus Admin.

BAPTISTA, SHANE J; Calaveras HS; Wallace, CA; (2); 7/236; VICA; JV Trk; Var JV Wrstlng; High Hon Roll; Hon Roll; Pres Acad Fit Awd.

BAQUERO, MARI A; Alameda HS; Alameda, CA; (1); Dance Clb; Variety Show.

BAR-COHEN, YANIV; Los Alamitos HS; Seal Beach, CA; (4); Math Tm; Model UN; Ski Clb; Temple Yth Grp; JV Tennis; Hon Roll; Kiwanis Awd; Pres Acad Fit Awd; Kiwanis Bowl; Interact Clb; Bnk Amer Math & Sci Plaque Wnnr; Johns Hopkins U; Med.

BARADARAN, YAS; Novato HS; Novato, CA; (1); Spanish Clb; Band; Mrchg Band; Hon Roll; Prfct Atten Awd; Novato Gymnstcs Tm; Golden St Xm Hi Hnrs; CA Music Educ Assn Superior Rtg; UC Berkeley; Math Engrng.

BARAG, TALIA; Taft HS; Woodland Hills, CA; (2); Teachers Aide; Temple Yth Grp; Swmmng; Hon Roll; UCLA; Jrnlsm.

BARAHONA, FLORA A; Andrew P Hill HS; San Jose, CA; (2); Latin Amer Stu Org; Upward Bound Pgm; CIT Cnslr Santa Clara U; Partnrshp Pgm U Of CA Berkeley; Bus.

BARAJAS, ADELINA; Sweetwater HS; National City, CA; (2); 34/589; Model UN; Spanish Clb; Teachers Aide; Socr; Vllybl.

BARAJAS, DIANA L; Rio Linda SR HS; Rio Linda, CA; (3); Art Clb; FBLA; Sec Latin Clb; Mgr Office Aide; VP Spanish Clb; SADD; Stage Crew; Yrbk; Rep Stu Cncl; Prfct Atten Awd; Stu Rching Out; Fri Night Live; Math Engrng Sci Achvrs; Parsons Schl Dsgn; Mktng.

BARAJAS, GUADALUPE; Petaluma HS; Petaluma, CA; (3); 52/267; Teachers Aide; JV Var Sftbl; Cit Awd; Hon Roll; Bus.

BARAJAS, JOSE; Cathedral HS; Los Angeles, CA; (3); Computer Clb; Library Aide; Math Clb; Science Clb; Sec Frsh Cls; JV Crs Cntry; JV Var Socr; JV Var Tennis; JV Trk; Hon Roll; St Marys Coll; Math Teacher.

BARAJAS, JUAN; Fontana HS; Fontana, CA; (2); VICA; Hon Roll; Accntng.

BARAJAS, MELINDA; San Gabriel HS; San Gabriel, CA; (3); Pres JA; Pep Clb; Spanish Clb; Treas VICA; JV L Sftbl; Tutor Alg; Hon Men San Gabriel Hghs Sci Fair; Coach Vllybllbsktbll Coach Chrldng Drll Tm T-Bll; Loyola Marymont U; Law.

BARAJAS, NORMA H; Washington Union HS; Fresno, CA; (3); #6 In Class; FBLA; FTA; Club Amistad; Teenage Cnslr.

BARAJAS, ROD; Mater Dei HS; Anaheim, CA; (2); Art Clb; Aud/Vis; Church Yth Grp; Cmnty Wkr; Computer Clb; Debate Tm; Drama Clb; Model UN; Off ROTC; Ski Clb; HS TV Prodctn Unit VP; Stus Offrng Spprt; Juilliard; Drama.

BARAJAS, SUSANA; Ramona HS; Ramona, CA; (2); 13/826; Dance Clb; French Clb; FBLA; Latin Clb; SADD; Cit Awd; Kiwanis Awd; Mdlng With STATUS Intl Tlnt Ntwrk; 8 Stu Of Qrtr Awds; UCSD; Social Wrkr.

BARAJAS, VERONICA M; Delano HS; Earlimart, CA; (4); FHA; Library Aide; Office Aide; Hon Roll; Coll Of The Sequoias; Optmtry.

BARANEK, RANDY J; Delta HS; Courtland, CA; (4); 6/60; Boy Scts; Church Yth Grp; Cmnty Wkr; Pres 4-H; Pres FFA; Pres Letterman Clb; Pep Clb; Red Cross Aide; Ski Clb; Teachers Aide; Eagle Sct Boy Scts; Fresno ST; Ag Bus.

BARANGAN, LORNA C; Nogales HS; W Covina, CA; (3); Church Yth Grp; Cmnty Wkr; Science Clb; Acpl Chr; Chorus; Church Choir; Variety Show; Lit Mag; Rep Stu Cncl; Hon Roll; CA Schlrshp Fed 3yrs; Wnnr Martin Luther King Jr Local Essay Cont; Piano; Singing; Psych; Running; Cyclng; UC Irving.

BARANOV, JENNIFER; Patrick Henry HS; San Diego, CA; (4); Model UN; Spanish Clb; Ed Lit Mag; Hon Roll; Jr NHS; Deptmntl Eng & Comp Pol & Economic Systems; CSF; De Witt Bisbee Williams Schlrshp; SDSU; Teacher.

BARAUSKAS, TANYA M; La Mirada HS; La Mirada, CA; (2); Debate Tm; Drama Clb; Hosp Aide; NFL; Speech Tm; Flag Corp; JV Tennis; Var Trk; High Hon Roll; CSF.

BARAUSKAS, TARA J; La Mirada HS; La Mirada, CA; (4); 17/332; Drama Clb; FBLA; Girl Scts; Chorus; JV Crs Cntry; Var Trk; High Hon Roll; NHS; Grad Highest Hnrs; Folk Dncng Group; CSULB.

BARAY, MICHELE-RAE; Bishop Amat Memorial HS; Chino, CA; (3); Debate Tm; Speech Tm; Band; Church Choir; Color Guard; Jazz Band; Mrchg Band; Pep Band; Hon Roll; UC Santa Cruz; Music.

BARB, JENNIFER A; Mission HS; San Francisco, CA; (4); Teachers Aide; Chorus; School Musical; Var Capt Bsktbl; Crs Cntry; Trk; Hon Roll; Blck Stu Union; San Francisco ST; Radio.

BARBA, DORA M; Santa Monica HS; Santa Monica, CA; (3); Cmnty Wkr; Teachers Aide; Hon Roll; Mecha Clb; UCLA Partnrshp.

BARBA, EDUARDO; Daniel Murphy HS; Los Angeles, CA; (3); 14/90; Latin Clb; Letterman Clb; Var L Bsktbl; Var Mgr(s); Var Stat Trk; Frosh Most Imprvd Bsktbl; Cham All Tour Jv; La Salle All Tour Var; SDSU; Marine Bio.

BARBA, FERNANDO; St Genevieve HS; Arleta, CA; (2); Letterman Clb; Var Bsbl; JV Bsktbl; Var Ftbl; Wt Lftg; Hon Roll; Ftbl All Leag; Notre Dame U; Law.

BARBA, JUDITH; Regina Caeli HS; Compton, CA; (3); Spanish Clb; Chorus; Rep Frsh Cls; Travel Tourism.

BARBA, OSCAR; Southwest HS; San Diego, CA; (2); Math Tm; Teachers Aide; Varsity Clb; Socr; Cit Awd; Hon Roll; Pres Schlr; Arch.

BARBEAU, SHARI L; Mills HS; Millbrae, CA; (3); Hosp Aide; JV Var Mgr(s); JV Sftbl; JV Var Swmmng; Acad Achvmnt 88-90; Sftbl, Sv Swmmng & Vrsy Swmmng Lttrs; Nrsng.

BARBEE, LISA; Don Antonio Lugo HS; Chino Hills, CA; (3); Church Yth Grp; Dance Clb; Q&S; Teachers Aide; Drill Tm; Variety Show; Ed Nwsp; Hon Roll; Outstndng Schlrshp-Ctznshp Awd; UCSD; Psych.

BARBEE, STEVEN K; Testimonial Christian Schl; Los Angeles, CA; (1); Art Clb; Dance Clb; English Clb; ROTC; School Play; Yrbk; Bsbl; Bsktbl; Ftbl; Trk.

BARBEIRO, ALISHA; Willows HS; Artois, CA; (1); Pep Clb; SADD; Cheerldng; Hon Roll; Chld Psych.

BARBER, AMY; Lutheran HS; Yorba Linda, CA; (3); Teachers Aide; Church Choir; Var Cheerldng; Var Pom Pon; Hon Roll; Dance, Water & Snow Skng; Parks & Rec Vlntr.

BARBER, CELIA; Herbert Hoover HS; Glendale, CA; (3); Church Yth Grp; Cmnty Wkr; VP Spanish Clb; SADD; Drill Tm; Pres Frsh Cls; Var Cheerldng; Var Sftbl; Var Capt Tennis; Hon Roll; American Legion Award; GI UOHA Award; Served On Glendale Youth Comm As Sec & VP; Glendale Safe Rides; NSC; Law.

BARBER, HEATHER M; Montgomery HS; Kenwood, CA; (3); Am Leg Aux Girls St; Treas Spanish Clb; VICA; Mrchg Band; Orch; Phtg Ed Yrbk; Treas Frsh Cls; Hist Sr Cls; Stu Cncl; Var Bsktbl; Outstndnd Female Stu Of Yr Awd For Distinction Spam, Wrld Hstry; Arch.

BARBER, J SCOTT; Silver Valley HS; Newberry Spgs, CA; (4); 11/67; Cmnty Wkr; Pres 4-H; Letterman Clb; Varsity Clb; Rptr Nwsp; Rptr Lit Mag; JV Var Ftbl; JV Var Wt Lftg; 4-H Awd; Hon Roll; Natl Soc Range Mgnt Yth Forum Paper Prsntatn; Outstndng Sr Sci Stu 90; Rsrv Champ 4-H Mrktbeef; CA Poly San Lusi Obispo; Vet.

BARBER, JAMES SCOTT; Silver Valley HS; Newberry Spgs, CA; (4); 11/65; Cmnty Wkr; 4-H; Letterman Clb; Science Clb; Varsity Clb; Rptr Nwsp; Var L Ftbl; Wt Lftg; Elks Awd; 4-H Awd; Scty Range Mgmt HS Paper Pres 1st US; Outstndng SR Sci Stu 90; Hstry Club Civil War Re Enactments; CA Poly San Luis Obispo; Vet.

BARBER, LOUREN B; Vallejo SR HS; Vallejo, CA; (3); Church Yth Grp; Band; Mrchg Band; Hon Roll; Prfct Atten Awd; Outstndng Band Stu Awd.

BARBER, MICHELLE L; Fontana HS; Fontana, CA; (2); Orch; Yrbk; CA Achvt Tst Scr 99 Pct Rdng; Engl Tchr.

BARBER, SARAH N; Carlmont HS; Half Moon Bay, CA; (3); Skiing; CFS; UC.

BARBER, STACIE; Whittier Christian HS; Fullerton, CA; (2); 23/186; Church Yth Grp; Drama Clb; School Play; Stage Crew; Cit Awd; High Hon Roll; Hon Roll; Stanford; Corp Atty.

BARBERA, JACQUELINE; Mayfair HS; Bellflower, CA; (3); Cmnty Wkr; Hosp Aide; Office Aide; Cheerldng; Pom Pon; Cit Awd; Gov Hon Prg Awd; Hon Roll; Opt Clb Awd; Church Yth Grp; 10th Grd Art Drwngs Displayed At Cty Hall; Grafic Art Dsgn Art.

BARBERI, MONICA L; St Paul HS; Whittier, CA; (3); 132/265; Girl Scts; Hosp Aide; Chorus; JV Trk; March 4 Hunger; Chrstn Svc Rep; Med.

BARBICH, LAURA A; El Camino HS; Carmichael, CA; (3); 4-H; Office Aide; Teachers Aide; Work Raleys; Accntnt.

BARBIERI, PAIGE; Herbert Slater JR HS; Santa Rosa, CA; (2); Art Clb; Drama Clb; Pep Clb; Spanish Clb; Drill Tm; Cheerldng; Hon Roll.

BARBONI, MICHAEL P; Upland HS; Upland, CA; (2); 42/900; Band; Jazz Band; Mrchg Band; Trk; Hon Roll; Harvey Mudd; Elec Engrng.

BARBOSA, PAUL; Seaside HS; Fort Ord, CA; (2); Church Yth Grp; JV Ftbl; JV Socr; Var Wt Lftg; Peer Cnslr; Friday Night Live; San Diego ST U; Photojrnlst.

BARBOUR, JUSTINA L; Cajon HS; San Bernardino, CA; (3); Teachers Aide; Rptr Ed Nwsp; Phtg Yrbk; JV Sftbl; JV Var Tennis; JV Vllybl; Cit Awd; San Diego ST; Cosmetologist.

BARBOZA, ANDREA LYNN; Castle Park HS; Chula Vista, CA; (3); 372/422; Church Yth Grp; Pep Clb; Cit Awd; Prfct Atten Awd; Oral Roberts U; Dr.

BARCELATA, STACEE; Canyon HS; Anaheim Hills, CA; (3); Church Yth Grp; Cmnty Wkr; Dance Clb; JCL; Latin Clb; Pep Clb; Ski Clb; Spanish Clb; School Musical; Stu Cncl; Rgnl & Natl Rllr Sktng Champ; Dance Chrgrphy; Cncl Mem Accrdtn Cmmtte; Arspc/Arntcl Engr.

BARCELON, MYLENE B; Lowell HS; San Francisco, CA; (2); Intnl Clb; Latin Clb; Red Cross Aide; Cert Cmpltn Schl Mural; Fashn.

BARCELON, ROSALINDA P; South San Francisco SR HS; South San Francis, CA; (2); Cmnty Wkr; FBLA; JV Tennis; Hon Roll; San Francisco ST U; Bus.

BARCENAS, ARTURO; Tustin HS; Tustin, CA; (1); Church Yth Grp; Key Clb; Band; Mrchg Band; Ftbl; Wt Lftg; JV Wrstlng; US Naval Sea Cdts/Navy League Pres Awd; Cdt Of Yr; Gftd/Hnr Prgm.

BARCENAS, IRENE M; River City SR HS; West Sacramento, CA; (3); Creative Wrtng; Merit Roll; Metaphysics; Berkley; Genetics.

BARCIA, KARLA V; Fairfield HS; Suisun City, CA; (3); Church Yth Grp; Rptr Nwsp; French Hon Soc; Hon Roll; Law.

BARCIA, RAQUEL D; Fairfield HS; Fairfield, CA; (4); 151/524; Church Yth Grp; Cmnty Wkr; French Clb; Teachers Aide; Color Guard; Flag Corp; Ed Nwsp; Rep Sr Cls; Rep Stu Cncl; Capt Powder Puff Ftbl; CA St Employees Assn Ch 302 Schlrshp; U CA Hayward; Crmnl Jstc.

BARCOHANA, MICHAEL; Sherman Oaks Ctr For Enriched Students; Tarzana, CA; (3); French Clb; Spanish Clb; Varsity Clb; Var Tennis; Tnns Capt City Leag Chmps 90; U Of CA Los Angeles; Law.

BARCUS, MARINA L; Rincon Valley Christian HS; Sebastopol, CA; (2); Color Guard; Var Bsktbl; JV Vllybl; Cit Awd; Educ.

BARD, MELINDA J; L A Baptist HS; Sepulveda, CA; (3); Church Yth Grp; Var Pep Clb; Chorus; Church Choir; School Musical; Yrbk; Cheerldng; Gym; Powder Puff Ftbl; Sftbl; CA ST Univ Northridge; Psych.

BARDACKE, JAIME; Watsonville HS; Watsonville, CA; (1); 1/762; Pep Clb; Rep Frsh Cls; Cheerldng; Trk; High Hon Roll; Hon Roll; CSF; Gymnstcs.

BARDALES, TOM; Indio HS; Indio, CA; (3); 84/605; Varsity Clb; Var L Bsktbl; Var L Crs Cntry; Var L Tennis; Hon Roll; Prfct Atten Awd; All League Bsktbl Tm; Dfnsv Player Of Yr 89-90; San Jose ST; Med Tech.

BARDON, MARNA KAY; Tri-City Christian HS; Encinitas, CA; (4); 5/16; Church Yth Grp; Teachers Aide; Sec Rep Jr Cls; Sec Treas Sr Cls; Var Capt Bsktbl; Var Score Keeper; Var Capt Vllybl; Cit Awd; High Hon Roll; Bob Jones U; Criminal Justice.

BAREH, MAGDY; Hesperia HS; Apple Valley, CA; (3); Church Yth Grp; Cmnty Wkr; Debate Tm; Key Clb; Off ROTC; Science Clb; Spanish Clb; Speech Tm; Rep Jr Cls; High Hon Roll; 2nd Pl Wnnr Dist Sci Fair; MOWW Monterey Ldrshp Conf; Mech Engrng.

BAREILLES, SANDY M; St Bernard HS; Eureka, CA; (2); Church Yth Grp; Cmnty Wkr; JV Bsktbl; Var Cheerldng; JV Vllybl; Cit Awd; Hon Roll; Translator.

BARELA, AMY; Gladstone HS; Azusa, CA; (4); 18/190; Church Yth Grp; GAA; JV Var Sftbl; Var Capt Tennis; High Hon Roll; Hon Roll; NHS; Prfct Atten Awd; CA Schlrshp Fed; Azusa Pacific U; Bus.

BARELA, FLORA; Kingsburg HS; Kingsburg, CA; (2); FFA; Spanish Clb; SADD; Bsktbl; Trk; Hon Roll; Treas Jr Cls; Bsktbl Coaches Awd; FFA Chptr Farmer; Greenhand Ofcr; Berkley U; Law.

BARELA, JEANNE; La Sierra HS; Riverside, CA; (4); 4/370; VP French Clb; Math Clb; Science Clb; Flag Corp; Stat Trk; High Hon Roll; Ntl Merit SF; Gldn St Exam Hnrs Geo; Ca Schlstc Fed Treas; CA ST U Pomona; Engrng.

BARELLI, MARIA E; Immaculate Heart HS; Los Angeles, CA; (3); 28/112; Drama Clb; Girl Scts; Thesps; Chorus; School Musical; School Play; Hon Roll; Close-Up; CSF; History.

BARESE, DANIELLE; Yosemite HS; Coarsegold, CA; (3); 2/174; Ski Clb; Spanish Clb; Teachers Aide; Band; Jazz Band; Stage Crew; Var L Sftbl; High Hon Roll; St Schlr; CSF; U Of Pacific; Orthodontics.

BARFIELD, DAMON; Far West HS; Oakland, CA; (4); 8/24; Pep Clb; School Musical; Rptr Nwsp; Rptr Yrbk; Promise Schlrshp Awd; Lang Arts Awd; Songwrtg & Music Prodctn; CA ST Hayward; Music.

BARFIELD, JENNY; Rincon Valley Christian HS; Santa Rosa, CA; (2); Church Yth Grp; Band; Drm Mjr(t); Mrchg Band; Pep Band; Rep Frsh Cls; Sftbl; Vllybl; Cit Awd; High Hon Roll; Natl Artistic Figure Skating 87; Med.

BARFIELD, KIM A; Lynwood HS; Lynwood, CA; (3); Church Yth Grp; GAA; Teachers Aide; Church Choir; Var Bsktbl; Var Trk; Var Vllybl; Press Telegrm Dream Tm; 2nd Tm CIF & Athlt Of Mnth; Times Awd Iron Woman Of Lynwood; Track MVP; Teacher.

BARGAS, PATRICIA ANN; Tulare Western HS; Tulare, CA; (3); 23/224; Church Yth Grp; Hosp Aide; Spanish Clb; Teachers Aide; Band; Color Guard; Var Tennis; Hon Roll; CS; Mexican-Amer Poltcl Assoc Acad Awd; Fresno ST U; Crmnl Psych.

BARGER, MARY ANNE; Summerville HS; Sonora, CA; (3); Cmnty Wkr; FCA; ROTC; Teachers Aide; Var Capt Bsktbl; JV Var Sftbl; Var Vllybl; DAR Awd; Hon Roll; Kiwanis Awd; AFJROTC.

BARGIEL, WENDY A; El Toro HS; El Toro, CA; (4); Debate Tm; Pep Clb; SADD; School Play; Treas Sr Cls; Cheerldng; Pom Pon; Hon Roll; Teen Model Main Pl Plaza-Volunteer Showcase & Fshn Shows; Choc Hosp Volunteer; Miss CA Teen Unltd 88; AZ ST U; Bus.

BARGUERO, GAVIN P; Casa Grande HS; Petaluma, CA; (2); 50/250; Computer Clb; Spanish Clb; JV Bsktbl; JV Socr; Hon Roll; Stu Of Month.

BARHUM, HATEM M; American HS; Fremont, CA; (3); 24/310; Teachers Aide; Hon Roll; Spanish NHS; Alg Golden St Exam Awd; Golden Globe; Stu Of Month Awd 90.

BARI, AUSAF A; Salinas HS; Salinas, CA; (4); English Clb; Hosp Aide; VP Pres Science Clb; Teachers Aide; Band; Pep Band; Nwsp; High Hon Roll; Ntl Merit Ltr; Rotary Awd; Natl Sci Tlnt Search Hnrs; Cnty Sci Fr 1 St Pl Zoology; UCLA; Med.

BARI, NADIA O; Saint Francis HS; Mountain View, CA; (4); 6/350; Cmnty Wkr; English Clb; GAA; Letterman Clb; Service Clb; SADD; Varsity Clb; JV Var Socr; JV Tennis; High Hon Roll; Berkeley Bach Fstvl; Tandy Schlrshp; GTE Schlrshp; Soup Kitchen Wrkr; Stanford U; Pol Sci.

BARIA, ARIEL M; Lowell HS; San Francisco, CA; (3); Aud/Vis; Red Cross Aide; Chorus; School Musical; Filipino-Amer Clb; Nrsng.

BARIAMIS, JASON M; Taft HS; Woodland Hills, CA; (2); Drama Clb; French Clb; Trk; Ice Hcky; Leag Bsbl; Law.

BARIL, WILMA N; Chula Vista HS; San Diego, CA; (3); 33/493; Dance Clb; Pep Clb; Variety Show; Sec Frsh Cls; Sec Soph Cls; Sec Jr Cls; Capt Cheerldng; Cit Awd; Hon Roll; Masonic Awd; Outstndng Dance Stu Awd; Gldn Schlrshp Awd; Gldn Ctznshp Awd; San Diego ST U; Elem Educ.

BARILE, DAVID T; Woodside HS; Redwood City, CA; (3); Boy Scts; Church Yth Grp; Nwsp; Yrbk; Pres Acad Fit Awd; St Schlr; Waterpolo Jv, 2 Times Vrsty; Scout Ldrshp ; Snow Skiing, Srfng, Cmptr Grphcs, Video, Cartooning; UCLA; Art.

BARIMAN, BORA A; Pacific Grove HS; Pacific Grove, CA; (4); Debate Tm; Drama Clb; Orch; School Play; Yrbk; JV Var Socr; Var High Hon Roll; Ntl Merit SF; Hon Roll; NFL; Internshp CA Assemblyman Sam Farr; Chrmn Monterey Co Yth For Bush; Govt.

BARISDALE, MICHELLE M; Gahr HS; Cerritos, CA; (2); 15/490; Var Bsktbl; Var Capt Crs Cntry; Var Trk; Hon Roll; Sccr Indoor Sccr MVP Track Crss Cntry; Athl Of Mnth Wk & Yr; Envrnmntl Clb; Bus Sci.

BARIZO, CHARMAINE; Glendale Adventist Acad; Tujunga, CA; (1); 1/62; Church Yth Grp; Office Aide; Band; Chorus; Rptr Nwsp; Yrbk; Intrml Vllybl; High Hon Roll; Chorale; UCLA.

BARIZO, JERRY C; San Diego Acad; San Diego, CA; (1); Aud/Vis; Church Yth Grp; Chorus; Church Choir; Color Guard; Drill Tm; Hon Roll; Pres Acad Fit Awd.

BARKA, KRISTEN A; Simi Valley HS; Simi Valley, CA; (2); 141/754; Hosp Aide; Office Aide; Teachers Aide; Var Tennis; Schlr Athl Awd-Var Ten; Vlntr Wrk W/Handcppd Chldrn; Ten Dbls Girls Chmpn; Loyola Marymount; Lawyr.

BARKAN, LIANA; Cajon HS; San Bndo, CA; (4); 6/365; Cmnty Wkr; Debate Tm; French Clb; Temple Yth Grp; Varsity Clb; Swmmng; Tennis; High Hon Roll; Hon Roll; NHS; Physics.

BARKER, DENNIS A; Strathmore HS; Porterville, CA; (3); 41/77; Teachers Aide; Var Socr; Var Tennis; High Hon Roll; Hon Roll; Unconformed-A Clb; Bakersfield U; Engl Tchr.

BARKER, JASON C; Poway HS; Poway, CA; (1); Ftbl; Outstndng Frosh; Outstndng Frosh Wrstlr.

BARKER, JASON T; Atascadero HS; Atascadero, CA; (2); Church Yth Grp; Office Aide; Teachers Aide; High Hon Roll; Hon Roll; Rodeo 90-91:Space Acad April 90; L A Schl Chiropractic; Chrprctc.

BARKER, KAREN L; Trabuco Hills HS; Mission Viejo, CA; (3); Church Yth Grp; Dance Clb; Spanish Clb; SADD; Crs Cntry; Score Keeper; Trk; Hon Roll; Jr NHS; Kiwanis Awd; Distngshd Schlr-Sci/Engl/Soc Sci; U Of HI; Bus Mgmt.

BARKER, KAREN M; Portola JR SR HS; Portola, CA; (3); Church Yth Grp; Letterman Clb; Ski Clb; Spanish Clb; Church Choir; Swing Chorus; Cheerldng; Tennis; Hon Roll; Prfct Atten Awd; Ski Rcng Team Slalom St Finals Qlfr; Word Prcssng.

BARKER, KELDA L; Dos Palos HS; Dos Palos, CA; (3); AFS; Church Yth Grp; FHA; Pep Clb; SADD; Band; Mrchg Band; Orch; Pep Band; Merced JC; Fine Arts.

BARKER, LORI M; Castle Park HS; Chula Vista, CA; (3); 26/422; Spanish Clb; Speech Tm; Band; Mrchg Band; Pep Band; Var Sftbl; Computers.

BARKER, MIKI; Placer HS; Lincoln, CA; (3); Church Yth Grp; Powder Puff Ftbl; Tennis; St Marys.

BARKER, ROSHON S; Castlemont HS; Oakland, CA; (2); Sec Church Yth Grp; Sec Hosp Aide; Var ROTC; Drill Tm; Hon Roll; NHS; Prfct Atten Awd; Cert Rcgntn & Commndatn; Medcl.

BARKER, SANDRA L; Tulare Union HS; Tulare, CA; (3); 21/401; Church Yth Grp; Co-Ed Yrbk; Hon Roll; Jrnlsm.

BARKER, TABITHA L; Mission San Jose HS; Fremont, CA; (1); 93/466; High Hon Roll; Bus Owner.

BARKHORDAR, SOHRAB; Lincoln HS; Stockton, CA; (4); French Clb; FBLA; Science Clb; Teachers Aide; Ftbl; Socr; Tennis; High Hon Roll; Hon Roll; Prfct Atten Awd; UC Santa Cruz; Bio.

BARKLEY, ANGALA; Arlington HS; Riverside, CA; (2); Church Yth Grp; Drama Clb; Letterman Clb; SADD; Thesps; School Musical; School Play; Stage Crew; Variety Show; Yrbk; Equus Awd Wnng Spprtng Role In Play, 1st Pl In SCETA; Piano Lssns For 6 Yrs; Acting.

BARKLOW, LAUREL R; San Lorenzo HS; San Lorenzo, CA; (2); Cmnty Wkr; Drama Clb; Stage Crew; Hon Roll; Trophy Outstndng Achvt Tech Theatre; Stu Of Day Twice 89-90; Atten Chabot Coll For Kids Drama Wrkshp; Chabot CC; Stage Mgr.

BARKMAN, JAY S; Mater Dei HS; Santa Ana, CA; (1); ROTC; Ski Clb; ROTC Drill Tm; Famous Guitarist.

BARKSDALE, DENISE M; Desert JR/Sr HS; Edwards, CA; (3); 4/100; Sec Church Yth Grp; Drama Clb; FBLA; Math Tm; Church Choir; School Play; Rep Stu Cncl; High Hon Roll; Hon Roll; VP Jr NHS; Bk Of America Achvt Awd Field Sci; Cert Hnr Phy & Bio Sci; Kern Cty Amercn Heart Assn Awd; Vet Med.

BARLE, MOLLY A; Mayfield SR Schl; North Hollywood, CA; (2); Hon Roll; Phy.

BARLETT, DOUGLAS; Arlington HS; Riverside, CA; (4); 5/370; Cmnty Wkr; Pres Drama Clb; Pep Clb; Scholastic Bowl; Pres Thesps; School Musical; School Play; Stage Crew; Lit Mag; Stu Cncl; Mock Trl; Acad Dcthln; CA Schlrshp Fed Life Mem; U Of CA Berkeley; Bus Admin.

BARLOW, ADAM; Wm S Hart HS; Newhall, CA; (4); #40 In Class; Boy Scts; FBLA; Pres Letterman Clb; Mu Alpha Theta; Yrbk; JV Bsbl; JV Var Ftbl; JV Var Trk; JV Var Wt Lftg; Natl Ftbl Foundation; Hall Of Fame Schlr-Atlete; CA Poly San Louis Obispo; Engr.

BARLOW, CHRISTOPHER P; Richard Gahr HS; Norwalk, CA; (3); JV Capt Bsbl; Hon Roll; AZ ST; Ed.

BARLOW, ERICA S; Tokay HS; Stockton, CA; (1); 2/850; Church Yth Grp; FCA; Swmmng; Japanese Clb VP Sec Treas; PRO; Vet.

BARLOW, MARIANNE; John F Kennedy HS; Granada Hills, CA; (2); Pres Church Yth Grp; Key Clb; SADD; Drill Tm; Lit Mag; Hon Roll; Co-Crtr & Sec Of Cnsrvtn Clb; Chld Psych.

BARNARD, SWEETHING; Far West HS; Oakland, CA; (4); 6/24; Aud/Vis; Dance Clb; Drama Clb; English Clb; Spanish Clb; Teachers Aide; Nwsp; Yrbk; High Hon Roll; Tchng Chldrn With Lrning Hndcps-8 Yrs; Bi-Lingual Tutoring-2 Yrs; Taek Won Do-Korean Martial Arts; U C Berkeley; Genetic Engrng.

BARNAS, MONICA R; Apple Valley HS; Apple Valley, CA; (1); Acpl Chr; Chorus; School Play; Swing Chorus; Variety Show; High Hon Roll; Ntl Merit Ltr; 1st Rnnr Up Most Outstndng Fresh Choir Dept; Sect Ldr; Drama.

BARNEDO, M JENNIFER; Armona Union Acad; Hanford, CA; (2); Church Yth Grp; Drama Clb; Spanish Clb; Teachers Aide; Band; Chorus; Ed Nwsp; Capt Vllybl; Soc VP Stu Bdy; Med.

BARNEDO, M JOY; Armona Union Acad; Hanford, CA; (4); 1/10; Drama Clb; Hosp Aide; Office Aide; Band; Rptr Nwsp; Ed Yrbk; Sec Sr Cls; Vllybl; High Hon Roll; Prfct Atten Awd; Pacific Union Coll; Acctg.

BARNES, CONNIE; San Marin HS; Novato, CA; (3); Church Yth Grp; Hosp Aide; SADD; Band; Diving; Hon Roll; Davis; Nutrition.

BARNES, CRAIG; Calvary Chapel HS; Westminster, CA; (2); 1/83; Chess Clb; Ski Clb; Teachers Aide; Wt Lftg; Hon Roll; FVHS Hnrs Cmmssn; Cal Poly U; Engrng.

BARNES, DAVID K; Bakersfield HS; Bakersfield, CA; (3); 34/712; Church Yth Grp; Capt Debate Tm; Key Clb; NFL; Science Clb; Ski Clb; Co-Capt Speech Tm; JV Crs Cntry; Intrml Ftbl; Var Trk; CA Yng Rep.

BARNES, DAVID P; Salinas HS; Salinas, CA; (3); Cmnty Wkr; Computer Clb; Frgn Exchange Stu; Vlntr Work; Cal Polytechnical U; Arch Dsgn.

BARNES, DHIA R; Skyline HS; Oakland, CA; (3); Church Yth Grp; Debate Tm; Girl Scts; JA; Key Clb; Office Aide; SADD; Teachers Aide; Rep Stu Cncl; Var Bsktbl; John Brown Anti-Klan Assoc Volunteer; Black Student Union; Volunteer In Various Soup Kitchens & SPCA.

BARNES, DON E; Fairfield HS; Fairfield, CA; (3); German Clb; Concordia Coll; Bus.

BARNES, JARED F; Roseville HS; Rocklin, CA; (3); 2/400; Boy Scts; German Clb; Science Clb; Ski Clb; Spanish Clb; JV Var Socr; Var L Swmmng; Bausch & Lomb Sci Awd; High Hon Roll; NHS.

BARNES, KOBIE P; Clovis HS; Clovis, CA; (1); Church Yth Grp; Library Aide; Math Tm; Pep Clb; Band; Mrchg Band; Cheerldng; Score Keeper; Tennis; Hon Roll; UCLA; Real Estate.

BARNES, KYLE; Casa Roble Fundamental HS; Citrus Heights, CA; (3); 57/390; Church Yth Grp; Cmnty Wkr; 4-H; French Clb; Off Frsh Cls; Rep Pres Soph Cls; Pres Jr Cls; Stu Cncl; L Socr; 4-H Awd; CSF; Dist Stu Grad Comm; Rep SJUSD Budget Forum; Law.

BARNES, LARECE J; St Michaels Catholic Girls HS; Los Angeles, CA; (3); Library Aide; Office Aide; Quiz Bowl; Teachers Aide; Church Choir; High Hon Roll; Hon Roll; Dentistry.

BARNES, LIZABETH A; Notre Dame Academy Girls HS; Mar Vista, CA; (3); Cmnty Wkr; GAA; Latin Clb; Spanish Clb; SADD; Var Score Keeper; Var Sftbl; JV Vllybl; Cit Awd; Hon Roll; Loyola Marymount U; Marine Bio.

BARNES, MATTHEW T; Cordova HS; Sacramento, CA; (3); Boy Scts; Model UN; Chorus; School Musical; High Hon Roll; NHS; Advncd Chmbr Choir; Mens Ensmbl Chorus; CSF; CA St Hnr Choir; Vocal Music.

BARNES, MIKE S; Garden Grove HS; Garden Grove, CA; (1); Boy Scts; Church Yth Grp; OR ST U.

BARNES, NOELLE V; Southern Cal Christian HS; Chino, CA; (3); Church Yth Grp; Drama Clb; Office Aide; Teachers Aide; Chorus; School Musical; School Play; Stu Cncl; Hon Roll; Sngr.

BARNES, PATRICK M; Trabuca Hills HS; Mission Viejo, CA; (1); Spanish Clb; Rep Frsh Cls; JV Bsktbl; Capt Ftbl; JV Golf; Traveling Club Bsktbl Orange Crush Orange Cnty.

BARNES, RANDY T; Andrew Hill HS; San Jose, CA; (3); Church Yth Grp; Cmnty Wkr; Band; Chorus; Jazz Band; Mrchg Band; Orch; Pep Band; Speical Achievement In Band Award; San Diego St U; Musician.

BARNES, SHAWN H; Sanger HS; Sanger, CA; (3); Spanish Clb; Var Bsktbl; JV Trk; Bicycling, Road Cycling; Fresno ST U; Elec Engrng.

BARNES, STACEY G; Whittier Christian HS; Whittier, CA; (2); Church Yth Grp; Church Choir; JV Bsktbl; Var L Trk; JV Vllybl; Oasis Singing Grp.

BARNES, STEPHANIE M; Locke HS; Los Angeles, CA; (3); Church Yth Grp; FHA; ROTC; Jazz Band; Mrchg Band; Off Jr Cls; Bsktbl; Hon Roll; Prfct Atten Awd; Cert Awd FBLA; Cert Awd GPA Genesis Prgm; Cal ST Domingez Hills; Bus.

BARNES, TRESSIA C; Canyon HS; Attadena, CA; (3); Chorus; School Play; Nwsp; Phsy Sci Awd; Creative Wrtng Awd; Chorus Awd; Pasadena City Coll; Chld Psych.

BARNETT, AARON L; Lemoore HS; Lemoore, CA; (2); FCA; Bsktbl; Co-Capt JV Crs Cntry; Co-Capt JV Ftbl; JV Var Trk; Wt Lftg; REACH.

BARNETT, CARISSA J; Sonora HS; Groveland, CA; (2); 11/400; Church Yth Grp; Drama Clb; School Musical; School Play; Tennis; High Hon Roll; Hon Roll; Stu For Future Envrnmntlst Grp; Chsn Recgnzd CA St Arts Schlrs CSSA Theater; Gate Hons Prog; Theater.

BARNETT, CARLI K; San Dieguito HS; Olivenhain, CA; (2); 4-H; VP Frsh Cls; Cit Awd; Pres Acad Fit Awd; Natl Chrty Lge; UCLA; Bus.

BARNETT, CHAD L; Imperial HS; Pasadena, CA; (3); Cmnty Wkr; German Clb; Speech Tm; Varsity Clb; Pres Jr Cls; Var L Bsbl; Var L Bsktbl; Var L Sftbl; Var L Vllybl; Sign Lang-Interp; Prom Cmmttee-Head; Bus Admin.

BARNETT, HEATHER L; San Gorgonio HS; Highland, CA; (3); VP AFS; French Clb; Model UN; Service Clb; Speech Tm; Treas Soph Cls; JV Tennis; Pol Sci.

BARNETT, JENNIFER C; Hemet HS; Hemet, CA; (3); 124/475; Church Yth Grp; L Acpl Chr; Chorus; Church Choir; High Hon Roll; Hon Roll; CA Lgsltr Assmbly Cert Rcgntn Geom Gldn St Schlrs 89; Rgstrd Nrsng.

BARNETT, KATE; Tamalpais HS; Mill Valley, CA; (4); 39/241; Art Clb; Drama Clb; Teachers Aide; School Play; Stage Crew; Variety Show; High Hon Roll; Hon Roll; Drama Achvt Awd; Ed Bode Eng Awd; Mem Ensemble Theatre Co; UC-SANTA Barbara; Elem Tchr.

BARNETT, PAMELA J; Mariposa HS; Mariposa, CA; (3); Mgr(s); Med.

BARNETT, SCOTT C; Sonora HS; La Habra, CA; (2); 20/350; Church Yth Grp; Ski Clb; Temple Yth Grp; L Var Bsbl; L Capt Socr; Pres Acad Fit Awd; Sal; CSF; UCLA.

BARNETT, TOM A; Bonita Vista HS; Chula Vista, CA; (2); 20/575; Pres Soph Cls; JV Ftbl; JV Socr; JV Trk; Cit Awd; High Hon Roll; Athlt Of Yr, Coca Cola Schl Svc Awd & ASB Cmmsnr Of Sales At Bonita Vista JR HS.

BARNETT, WILLIAM; Bellarmine Jefferson HS; Glendale, CA; (1); Church Yth Grp; Cmnty Wkr; JV L Bsbl; JV L Bsktbl; JV L Ftbl; Mst Imprvd Bsbl, Bsktbl; Altar Boy Server; Parish Rectory Wrkr; UCLA; Arch.

BARNETT-CORTEZ, ANDREA; Bassett HS; La Puente, CA; (3); 11/200; Frnd & Frnd; Comm Svc; Samuel Merrit Nrsng; Nrsng.

BARNETT-GUARDALABENE, LINDA A; Rio Americano HS; Sacramento, CA; (3); 111/290; Service Clb; SADD; Band; Pep Band; JV Var Bsktbl; JV Var Sftbl; Stu Rchng Out; Friday Night Live; Jr Statesmen Amer; UC Berkley; Pre Natal Doctor.

BARNEY, CHALOE R; Nevada Union HS; Grass Valley, CA; (3); 132/551; Church Yth Grp; 4-H; SADD; Teachers Aide; Rep Stu Cncl; Hon Roll; Educ.

BARNEY, MONICA; Henry T Gunderson HS; San Jose, CA; (3); Rep Stu Cncl; JV Cheerldng; JV Fld Hcky; JV Socr; L Var Trk; Hon Roll; U Southern CA; Chem.

BARNEY, SHANEE I; John F Kennedy HS; Sacramento, CA; (2); 528/559; Drama Clb; Off Frsh Cls; Off Soph Cls; Off Stu Cncl; Cit Awd; Hon Roll; Act; Write Poems Essays & Different Affairs; Mc George Or Stanford U; Law.

BARNHART, TARA; Poway HS; Poway, CA; (3); Science Clb; Varsity Clb; Var Capt Crs Cntry; Score Keeper; Var L Trk; Hon Roll; NHS; Env Aware Club; Amnesty Intl; Outstndng Grl 88-89; Bio.

BARNHART, TONJA RENEE; Desert Christian HS; Indio, CA; (3); 2/9; Church Yth Grp; Letterman Clb; Teachers Aide; Phtg Yrbk; Stat Bsktbl; Score Keeper; Var L Sftbl; Var L Vllybl; Cit Awd; Hon Roll; Indio Pathfinders Teen Cnslr; Pacific Union Coll; Psych.

BARNHORST, KILEY A; The Bishops Schl; San Diego, CA; (4); AFS; Service Clb; SADD; Varsity Clb; Yrbk; Off Sr Cls; Var JV Sftbl; Var JV Tennis; Ntl Merit SF; Pres Acad Fit Awd; Perf Dance Grp; MADCAPS; Photo; Intl Bus.

BARNICA, EDITH CRUZ; South San Francisco HS; S San Francisco, CA; (3); Bus Profs of Am; Cmnty Wkr; FBLA; Intnl Clb; Latin Clb; Spanish Clb; Teachers Aide; Hon Roll; Acad Excllnce Awd Engl 90; 3rd Pl Bus Competncy Accntng; Library Vlntr; Coll San Mateo; Intl Acctnt.

BARNTHOUSE, STEVE R; Palmdale HS; Palmdale, CA; (2); Psych.

BARNUM, DAVIA; Mesa Verde HS; Citrus Heights, CA; (2); Church Yth Grp; Church Choir; Rptr Nwsp; Hon Roll; Friday Night Live Clb.

BARNWELL, JAMES; Compton HS; Compton, CA; (1); ROTC; JV Bsbl; JV Ftbl; Prof Bsbl.

BARON, DANA L; Torrey Pines HS; San Diego, CA; (4); Drama Clb; Thesps; Nwsp; High Hon Roll; Hnrs-Sealbearer For CA Schlrshp Fed; Active Prtcpnt In Amateur & Prof Theater; Semi-Prof Dance Co; Cmnctns.

BARON, HELEN; Rosary HS; Fullerton, CA; (2); NFL; Speech Tm; School Play; Var Socr; JV Swmmng; Intrml Vllybl; Cit Awd; High Hon Roll; Kiwanis Awd; NHS; U Of CA Irvine; Sci.

BARON, JENNIFER M; Torrey Pines HS; San Diego, CA; (3); 17/457; SADD; Rptr Nwsp; Ed Yrbk; Gym; High Hon Roll; Hon Roll; Jazz, Tap & Ballet Dance.

BARONE, JOHN; Christian Brothers HS; Sacramento, CA; (4); 1/126; Church Yth Grp; Computer Clb; Math Clb; Math Tm; Lit Mag; Sec Stu Cncl; Var L Tennis; Cit Awd; Elks Awd; High Hon Roll; Air Force Math And Science Award; Bank Of America Science Award; MA Inst Tech; Computer Science.

BARQUERO, GAVIN P; Casa Grande HS; Petaluma, CA; (2); 52/255; Cmnty Wkr; Computer Clb; Spanish Clb; JV Bsktbl; JV Socr; UNLV; Bus.

BARQUERO, OSCAR A; Montebello HS; Montebello, CA; (2); Acpl Chr; Chorus; Socr; Swmmng; Cit Awd; Med Doctor.

BARR, CHERISE; Atascadero HS; Atascadero, CA; (1); VP 4-H; FFA; Capt JV Cheerldng; 4-H Awd; Hon Roll; Odyssey Racing; Fashion & Dsgn 1st Pl Ladies Lead.

BARR, CHRISTIE; Katella HS; Anaheim, CA; (2); Church Yth Grp; Pep Clb; Thesps; Chorus; Cheerldng; High Hon Roll; Hon Roll; Long Beach ST; Nurse.

BARR, DANIELLE; Castle Park HS; Chula Vista, CA; (2); 40/474; French Clb; Band; Mrchg Band; Pep Band; Hon Roll; San Diego Yth Prep Wind Ensmbl; Music.

BARR, GABRIEL M; El Molino HS; Forestville, CA; (3); French Clb; Speech Tm; High Hon Roll; Dist Art Show 2nd Pl; Yth For Environmental Solutions; Physics.

BARR, KERSTIN M; Andrew Hill HS; San Jose, CA; (2); VP Church Yth Grp; Cmnty Wkr; Var Cheerldng; Var Swmmng; Hon Roll; NHS; Supreme Court Justice; Peer Cnslng; Mock Trial; Soph Hnrs Engl Stu Of Yr; Med.

BARR, STEPHANIE A; Willow Glen HS; San Jose, CA; (1); L Swmmng; Hon Roll; Swim San Jose Aquatics Team; Musicals At Cmnty Ctrs; Art Classes At Art Studio.

BARR, TRAVIS; Westminster HS; Westminster, CA; (4); 116/411; Band; Jazz Band; Mrchg Band; Orch; Pep Band; 2 Yrs In Hnr Band; Annual Royal Banquet Cert Wnr Music-Instrmntl; Golden West JC; Bus.

BARRAGAN, DAN; Saugus HS; Valencia, CA; (3); 7/456; Var Bsktbl; NHS; Bus Awd; Ucla; Elect Engrng.

BARRAGAN, ED S; Oak Ridge HS; Folsom, CA; (3); 3/261; Math Tm; Hon Roll; Outstndng Stu Awd 87-88.

BARRAGAN, GUADALUPE; Saddleback HS; Santa Ana, CA; (2); Science Clb; Color Guard; Orch; VP Soph Cls; Rancho Santiago Coll Math Tutor; CSF; Pediatrician.

BARRAGAN, IMELDA; Notre Dame HS; Menlo Park, CA; (2); French Clb; Teachers Aide; Hon Roll; Tutor Chldrn Reading; Doctor.

BARRAGAN, MARIA T; John F Kennedy HS; Cypress, CA; (2); Cmnty Wkr; Computer Clb; FBLA; Bsktbl; Crs Cntry; Var Trk; Hon Roll; Citizen Bee; Sch Rcgntn For Gldn St Exam Alg I; MIT; Sci.

BARRAGAN, NOEMI A; Pasadena HS; Pasadena, CA; (2); Drill Tm; Flag Corp; Hon Roll; CA Schlrshp Fed; Math Engrng Sci Achvt; UCLA; Teacher.

BARRAGAN, SILVIA; Clayton Valley HS; Concord, CA; (4); Church Yth Grp; Dance Clb; Latin Clb; Spanish Clb; Teachers Aide; Church Choir; Yrbk; Off Sr Cls; Crs Cntry; Socr; Gynclgst.

BARRAGAN, SONIA J; Alisal HS; Salinas, CA; (3); 1/250; Cmnty Wkr; Math Clb; Math Tm; Cit Awd; High Hon Roll; CSF; Partnership Pgm; Acad Decathlon; Comp Engrng.

BARRALES, JORGE; Bassett HS; La Puente, CA; (2); Cit Awd; Hon Roll; Jr NHS.

BARRANGO, CHRIS W; Sequoia HS; Redwood City, CA; (2); JV Bsbl; JV Bsktbl; JV Ftbl; Boy Block S Club.

BARRAZA, ALBERTO; Brawley Union HS; Brawley, CA; (2); Hon Roll; Prfct Atten Awd; Migrant Clb; CSF; Ldrshp Cls; OB.

BARRAZA, DEBORAH; Banning HS; Banning, CA; (2); French Clb; Model UN; Rep Stu Cncl; Var Tennis; Var Trk; Cit Awd; High Hon Roll; Hon Roll; Acad Achvt Awd Engl; UCLA; Fshn Dsgn.

BARRAZA, GREGORY; Bakersfield HS; Bakersfield, CA; (3); #725 In Class; Var Ftbl; Var Wt Lftg; Hon Roll; Elect Engrng.

BARRAZA, HUMBERTO G; Bishop Amat Memorial HS; West Covina, CA; (3); Spanish Clb; Bsktbl; Hon Roll; NHS; CSF; Pepperdine U; Psych.

BARREDO, MARISSA M; Culver City HS; Culver City, CA; (2); Church Yth Grp; Spanish Clb; Off Soph Cls; Cit Awd; High Hon Roll; Hon Roll; Loyola Marymount; Law.

BARREIRO, CARLOS G; Mission Bay HS; San Diego, CA; (2); 124/380; JV Ftbl; JV Trk; Wt Lftg; Hon Roll; Jr NHS; Pres Acad Fit Awd.

BARRELL, LORI A; Glendale HS; Glendale, CA; (4); Church Yth Grp; Rptr Q&S; Sec Spanish Clb; Teachers Aide; Acpl Chr; School Musical; Rptr Nwsp; Rep Sr Cls; Sec Stu Cncl; Bsktbl; Cert Svc Sch Acapella Choir; Prom Ct 1st Rnnr Up; Most Insprtnl Singer; Glendale Coll; Psychlgy.

BARRERA, JUAN A; East Union HS; Manteca, CA; (1); Var L Wrstlng; AZ ST U; Phy Educ.

BARRERA, MARICELA; Francis Polytechnic HS; Sun Valley, CA; (3); Cmnty Wkr; Dance Clb; Pep Clb; SADD; Hon Roll; Prfct Atten Awd.

BARRERA, MINERVA Z; Sweet Water Union HS; National City, CA; (1); Cit Awd; Hon Roll; Prfct Atten Awd; UCSD; Comp Engr.

BARRERA, YVONNE J; La Puente HS; La Puente, CA; (3); Sec Stu Cncl; JV Bsktbl; JV Score Keeper; Var Trk; Cit Awd; Hon Roll; SIGMA; CSF Clb.

BARRERAS, ABLE A; Benjamin Franklin HS; Los Angeles, CA; (2); Computer Clb; Dance Clb; Math Clb; SADD; Teachers Aide; Bsbl; High Hon Roll; Hon Roll; Prfct Atten Awd; Hmn Rghts Clb; Comp Pgmr.

BARRERAS, JOSEPH; Palo Verde HS; Blythe, CA; (3); School Play; Hon Roll.

BARRETO, KATHERINE I; Louisville HS; Northridge, CA; (3); 17/64; Art Clb; Church Yth Grp; GAA; JV Sftbl; Vllybl; High Hon Roll; Jr NHS; NHS; CSF; Pre-Med.

BARRETT, BRAD A; Santa Barbara HS; Santa Barbara, CA; (2); 3/450; Church Yth Grp; Math Tm; Model UN; High Hon Roll; Golden ST Geom & Alg High Hnrs.

BARRETT, CAROL; Montgomery HS; Santa Rosa, CA; (4); Treas Key Clb; Math Clb; Science Clb; Spanish Clb; Drill Tm; Capt Cheerldng; High Hon Roll; UC Berkeley; Elec Engrng.

BARRETT, CATHY A; George Washington HS; San Francisco, CA; (3); Rep Sr Cls; Mgr(s); Hon Roll; Anaconda Club; Green Earth Organization; Amnesty International; U Of San Fran; Child Psych/Dev.

BARRETT, JEANE M; Capistrano Valley HS; Mission Viejo, CA; (4); Cmnty Wkr; Var Capt Swmmng; Pres Acad Fit Awd; Rotary Awd; Val; LA Cnty Lfgrd; CA Poly; Archtctl Engr.

BARRETT, MELANIE K; Encina HS; Sacramento, CA; (2); 22/221; Spanish Clb; Band; Mrchg Band; Rep Frsh Cls; JV Socr; Cit Awd; Hon Roll; Member Of Stu Reaching Out; Member Of Friday Night Live; Ran For Jr Class Tres In 89-90 And Won; Harvard U; Phycology.

BARRETT, SHANE T; Canyon Springs HS; Moreno Valley, CA; (3); Church Yth Grp; Office Aide; Mrchg Band; Hon Roll; TV Prdctn.

BARRETT, SHELLY; Rancho Alamitos HS; Garden Grove, CA; (1); Church Yth Grp; Cmnty Wkr; Office Aide; Pep Clb; Teachers Aide; Church Choir; Rep Stu Cncl; Cheerldng; Gym; Score Keeper; Skid Row Feeding The Hmlss; Lwyr.

BARRETT, TRICIA; Newport Christian HS; Westminster, CA; (4); Ski Clb; School Play; Rep Frsh Cls; Rep Jr Cls; Var Cheerldng; Var Sftbl; Hon Roll; NEDT Awd; Hmcmng Ct SR Prncss; Chapman Coll; Bio.

BARRICELLA, LESLEY C; Mission Viejo HS; Mission Viejo, CA; (3); Am Leg Aux Girls St; GAA; Model UN; Pres Soph Cls; Stu Cncl; Capt JV Tennis; Trk; UC Santa Barbara.

BARRICK, KERI A; Hemet HS; San Jacinto, CA; (2); Dance Clb; Cit Awd; High Hon Roll; Hon Roll; Law.

BARRIE, JENNIFER J; Bishop Montgomery HS; Torrance, CA; (3); 4/400; Letterman Clb; Service Clb; Stage Crew; JV Var Bsktbl; Hon Roll; NHS; CSF; Bus.

BARRIGA, CARMEN; Madera HS; Madera, CA; (2); Mrchg Band; Cit Awd; High Hon Roll; CA Schlrshp Fed; Gftd/Tlntd Ed; Mexican-Amer Clb; Intl Law.

BARRIGA, MONICA R; University HS; Santa Monica, CA; (4); Church Yth Grp; Key Clb; Speech Tm; Drill Tm; Treas Frsh Cls; VP Soph Cls; Tennis; Art Stu; Art Ctr Coll Of Dsgn; Advr Dsgn.

BARRINGER, CHANNING K; Vallejo HS; Vallejo, CA; (4); 410/460; Pres French Clb; Teachers Aide; Pres Sr Cls; Capt Bsbl; Capt Ftbl; Outstndng Stu Cncl; Marine Corps Ldrshp Awd; Army Reserve Natl Schlr/Athl Awd; Morehouse Coll; Poltcl Sci.

BARRINGER, JULIE E; Sutter Union HS; Sutter, CA; (3); 4/75; Drama Clb; VP FBLA; Pres GAA; Letterman Clb; Teachers Aide; Pres Frsh Cls; Pres Stu Cncl; Var Capt Bsktbl; Var Sftbl; Trk; Walt Disneys Dreamers & Doers Hnrbl Mntn; Yng Rpblcns Club; Teens With Purpose; CSU Fresno; Bus Admin.

BARRINGTON, FAITH; Fall River HS; Fall River, CA; (2); FFA; Var Cheerldng; Var Sftbl; High Hon Roll; CSF; Am Leg Aux Math Awd.

BARRINGTON, TIMOTHY E; Norwalk HS; Norwalk, CA; (2); Church Yth Grp; Cmnty Wkr; Hon Roll; Pres Acad Fit Awd; U Southern CA; Commrcl Art.

BARRIOS, CAROLINA; Canoga Park HS; Los Angeles, CA; (1); Hosp Aide; Nrsng.

BARRIOS, GEORGE; Rim Of The World HS; Rim Forest, CA; (3); 11/26; French Clb; Library Aide; Varsity Clb; Var Bsbl; Var Ftbl; Prfct Atten Awd.

BARRIOS, JASON; Valley Christian HS; Long Beach, CA; (2); Church Yth Grp; Varsity Clb; Crs Cntry; Socr; Trk; Cal ST Long Beach; Physcn.

BARRIOS, JOANNE M; St Genevieve HS; Studio City, CA; (3); Church Yth Grp; Dance Clb; French Clb; Pep Clb; Drill Tm; School Play; Var Cheerldng; JV Sftbl; Hon Roll; Business.

BARRIOS, KENNETH M; Servite HS; Cerritos, CA; (3); Letterman Clb; Varsity Clb; Var Ftbl; Var Trk; Var Wt Lftg; Hon Roll; Prfct Atten Awd; Cngrsnl Schlr; Engr.

BARRIOS, RICHARD M; Bishop Amat Memorial HS; La Puente, CA; (2); SADD; Intrml Trk; Paint Ball Plyr.

BARRIOS, ROBERT; Rim Of The World HS; Rim Forest, CA; (4); 50/250; Var Bsbl; Capt Var Ftbl; Var Wt Lftg.

BARRIOS, ROBERTO A; John Muir HS; Pasadena, CA; (3); Math Clb; Red Cross Aide; ROTC; Science Clb; Drill Tm; Crs Cntry; Socr; Cit Awd; Hon Roll.

BARRIOS, RUTH; Manual Arts HS; Los Angeles, CA; (3); Bus Profs of Am; Computer Clb; French Clb; Girl Scts; Science Clb; VICA; Nwsp; Cheerldng; Swmmng.

BARRIOS, VICKY; El Rancho HS; Pico Rivera, CA; (2); French Clb; Teachers Aide; High Hon Roll; Hon Roll; Nesa Clb; CSF; Migrnt Ed.

BARRIOS, VICTOR F; Saint Ignatius HS; San Francisco, CA; (2); French Clb; Hon Roll; Video Yrbk; CA Schlrshp Fed; Stanford; Bus.

BARRIS, BRANDI L; Cordova SR HS; Rancho Cordova, CA; (3); 76/547; Key Clb; Model UN; Band; Orch; Pep Band; Rep Soph Cls; Pres Sr Cls; Var Capt Crs Cntry; Socr; Var Trk; Acad Decthln Tm 1st Yr Schlstc, 2nd Yr Hnrs; Raise/Trn Horse; St Marys; Marine Bio.

BARROETA, DIANA L; Central Union HS; El Centro, CA; (2); 1/600; Dance Clb; Drill Tm; JV Cheerldng; JV Swmmng; Rotary Awd; Sci,GATE Engl Hnrs 89-90; Interact Clb; CSF Secy; Stanford U; Medcl Sci.

BARRON, CARLOS C; Galt HS; Galt, CA; (2); Intnl Clb; Latin Clb; Yrbk; JV Wrstlng; Hon Roll; Out Reach Prog UC Davis; USC; Bus.

BARRON, CATALINA P; Woodrow Wilson HS; Long Beach, CA; (3); Church Yth Grp; Teachers Aide; Chorus; Orch; Cit Awd; Prfct Atten Awd; Deca Club; Unided Latin Amrca Clb; Cmptr Prgrmr.

BARRON, KIRSTEN; Golden West HS; Visalia, CA; (1); Church Yth Grp; Dance Clb; German Clb; Intnl Clb; Orch; High Hon Roll; Hon Roll; CA Schlstc Fed; Acad Ltr; Tulare Cnty Womens Symphony Guild Music Schlrshp; UC Irvine; Dance.

BARRON, NIKKI; Orangewood Adventist Acad; Fullerton, CA; (2); 3/30; Drama Clb; Acpl Chr; Color Guard; Drill Tm; School Play; Variety Show; Bsktbl; Ftbl; Hon Roll; Loma Linda U; Pediatrcn.

BARRON, SANDRA; San Gabriel Mission HS; Los Angeles, CA; (3); Drama Clb; GAA; Hon Roll; Mssn Mrt; Cmnty Svc; Lawyr.

BARROSO, LILLIAN; John Marshall HS; Los Angeles, CA; (3); Office Aide; Teachers Aide; Drill Tm; Gym; Prfct Atten Awd; Drill Team Squad Ldr; Cal ST Los Angeles; Fshn Advrt.

BARROW, KARLA R; Western Christian HS; Covina, CA; (4); Church Yth Grp; Hosp Aide; Service Clb; Teachers Aide; Rep Jr Cls; Var Trk; JV Vllybl; High Hon Roll; Ntl Merit SF; CA Schlrshp Fed.

BARRY, BETSY D; Chester JR-SR HS; Chester, CA; (2); 6/51; French Clb; Yrbk; VP Soph Cls; Pres Jr Cls; Tennis; Vllybl; High Hon Roll; Hon Roll; HOBY Ambssdr; Cal Poly San Luis Obispo; Pltcl.

BARRY, DONETTE E; Santiago HS; Santa Ana, CA; (2); 14/538; French Clb.

BARRY, GEOFF G; Grossmont HS; La Mesa, CA; (3); Church Yth Grp; Var Swmmng; JV Wrstlng; Fluent Spanish; Advanced Piano; Engrng.

BARRY, HEATHER LEE; Irvine HS; Irvine, CA; (3); 105/525; Off Dance Clb; Office Aide; Teachers Aide; Variety Show; Off Sr Cls; Stu Cncl; JV Crs Cntry; Var Capt Pom Pon; Hon Roll; Natl Ptry Assn Gldn Poet Awd; CA St Chmpn Chrldng 89; Unvrsl Dnc Assn Al-Str Tm Trps London; UC; Vet Med.

BARRY, RENO D; Yucca Valley HS; Morongo Valley, CA; (3); 1/200; Treas FBLA; Pres Math Clb; Quiz Bowl; High Hon Roll; Prfct Atten Awd; Math Stu Of Yr 89-90; University Club Pres; U CA Riverside; Chem.

BARRY II, ROBERT N; Paraclete HS; Lancaster, CA; (3); Key Clb; Service Clb; Rep Stu Cncl; High Hon Roll; Hon Roll; Ntl Merit Ltr; Achvt Awds Hnrs Engl III, Alg, Chem, US Hstry & Comp Sci; Physcs.

BARSANTI, SCOTT; Fortuna Union HS; Rio Dell, CA; (3); Am Leg Boys St; Computer Clb; SADD; JV Golf; Var Wrstlng; Pre-Law.

BARSON III, LARRY; Ganesha HS; Diamond Bar, CA; (3); Math Clb; Ski Clb; Hon Roll; MESA Orgnztn; U Of CA Riverside Early Outreach Pgm; UC Riverside; Bus.

BARSTOW, EMILY A; Bonita Vista HS; Chula Vista, CA; (2); Cmnty Wkr; Model UN; Pep Clb; Variety Show; Nwsp; Yrbk; Cheerldng; Cit Awd; Hon Roll; The Friendly Follies; GATE Pgm; Dncng; Singng; Brdcst Nws.

BART-PLANGE, MARGARET E; Etiwanda HS; Alta Loma, CA; (3); Cmnty Wkr; French Clb; GAA; Office Aide; Cit Awd; High Hon Roll; Hon Roll; NHS; Prfct Atten Awd; JV Var Bsktbl; Cngrssnl Yth Ldrsp Cncl; CA Interschlstc Fed; Plaq Recgntn Schl Rcrd Discus; UCLA; Accntnt.

BARTA, TAMMIE M; Temple City HS; San Gabriel, CA; (2); UCLA; Arch.

BARTCH, SHANNON N; St Bernard HS; Los Angeles, CA; (2); Intnl Clb; Ski Clb; Yrbk; Socr; Sftbl; Vllybl; High Hon Roll; NHS; Piano; CSF; Vllybl Clb; CA Poly Tech; Arch.

BARTEK, DOMINIC C; 29 Palms HS; Wahoo, NE; (2); 1/206; Church Yth Grp; Debate Tm; Treas French Clb; Quiz Bowl; Science Clb; Masonic Awd; Prfct Atten Awd; Acolyte Of Yr Blessed Sacrament Parish; Engr.

BARTELL, SCOTT M; Rio Americano HS; Gold Rvr, CA; (3); 18/290; Church Yth Grp; Latin Clb; Math Clb; Math Tm; Pres Science Clb; Treas Acpl Chr; Church Choir; Var L Crs Cntry; High Hon Roll; Ntl Merit Ltr; Yo-Yo Clb-Pres; Congrssnl Schlr; 90 CA Poly Math Cont-8th Pl; Engrng.

BARTELLS, KATE; Cope JR HS; Redlands, CA; (1); Church Yth Grp; Rep Frsh Cls; Capt Cheerldng; Trk; Cit Awd; Hon Roll; NHS; Prfct Atten Awd; Rotary Awd; Chrch Yth Camp Jr Cnslr; UC Davis; Vet Med.

BARTELS, SAMUEL G; Chula Vista HS; Chula Vista, CA; (3); 32/535; Chess Clb; Computer Clb; JA; Library Aide; Scholastic Bowl; Teachers Aide; Socr; Swmmng; Tennis; Trk; Golden St Exam Acad Excllnc Awd; San Diego Tribune Athl & Acad Cert; Coll Ready Writers Project; AZ ST U; Arch.

BARTER, WENDY R; Hesperia HS; Victorville, CA; (3); Church Yth Grp; Spanish Clb; SADD; Mgr(s); Pres Tennis; Trk; Hon Roll; Schlr Athl Achvt Awd; St Fnlst Miss US Teen Pageant & Schlrshp Awd; Comp Anaylist.

BARTH, MELISSA D; Fred C Beyer HS; Modesto, CA; (3); Church Yth Grp; Teachers Aide; Hon Roll; 1st Pl 3 Times YABA Bowling League; Modesto JC; Chld Dvlpmnt.

BARTHEL, JASON P; Lompoc HS; Lompoc, CA; (3); Am Leg Boys St; FBLA; Letterman Clb; Var Bsbl; JV Bsktbl; Var Ftbl; Cit Awd; High Hon Roll; Prfct Atten Awd; Engl Achvt Awd 2 Yrs; Schlr Athl Awd 2 Yrs; CSF; CA Poly; Comp Sci.

BARTHOLOMEW, JAMAICA; The Bishops Schl; San Diego, CA; (4); Church Yth Grp; Cmnty Wkr; French Clb; Office Aide; Teachers Aide; Lit Mag; Hon Roll; Kiwanis Awd; Rotary Awd; Cornell Clg; Tchng.

BARTHOLOMEW, MARY; Yosemite Union HS; Oakhurst, CA; (4); Church Yth Grp; Drama Clb; VP Pres FBLA; Treas FHA; Library Aide; Scholastic Bowl; Yrbk; Lit Mag; High Hon Roll; Hon Roll; Hnrd Queen Jobs Daughters; State Awds Photgrphy.

BARTLETT, EDWIN; Washington Prep; Los Angeles, CA; (4); Computer Clb; Debate Tm; Drama Clb; Letterman Clb; Science Clb; Varsity Clb; Nwsp; Trk; Wt Lftg; Big Brother; ND ST U; Microbio.

BARTLETT, IAN J; Trabuco Hills HS; San Juan Capstrno, CA; (1); Church Yth Grp; JV Bsbl; JV Socr.

BARTLETT, MARK; Casa Roble HS; Orangevale, CA; (2); 20/540; High Hon Roll; Hon Roll; Prfct Atten Awd; Berkely; Mrn Bio.

BARTLETT-PALACIO, JENNIFER; Delta HS; Marysville, CA; (3); VP FHA; Letterman Clb; Chorus; School Play; JV Bsktbl; JV Var Cheerldng; Stat Ftbl; Intrml Powder Puff Ftbl; JV Var Trk; Hon Roll; Psych.

BARTOLE, SHANNON; O'farrell SCPA; San Diego, CA; (1); 13/125; Church Yth Grp; Hon Roll.

BARTOLINI, ALBERT; Sonora HS; Fullerton, CA; (3); Pres FBLA; Ski Clb; Teachers Aide; Nwsp; Stu Cncl; Ftbl; Trk; Hon Roll; Most Insprtnl Awd Trk; CIF Trk; UCLA.

BARTOLOME, CANDICE; Eagle Rock HS; Los Angeles, CA; (3); Sec Church Yth Grp; Pres VP Chorus; Ed Nwsp; Yrbk; Sec Frsh Cls; Off Jr Cls; Cheerldng; Hon Roll; Pres Acad Fit Awd; Crmnl Lawyer.

BARTON, DAWN M; Paraclete HS; Palmdale, CA; (3); 21/111; Church Yth Grp; Stage Crew; High Hon Roll; Hon Roll; Ntl Merit Ltr; CSF; UC Los Angeles; Child Psych.

BARTON, JILL; Newport Harbor HS; Newport Beach, CA; (4); 45/365; Church Yth Grp; Pres French Clb; GAA; Key Clb; Pep Clb; Capt Var Cheerldng; JV Socr; Capt Var Trk; Hon Roll; Reach Amer Pres/Treas; UC Santa Barbara; Law.

BARTON, MICHELE; Folsom HS; Folsom, CA; (3); Church Yth Grp; Model UN; Office Aide; Pep Clb; Science Clb; SADD; Teachers Aide; Nwsp; Hist Frsh Cls; JV Bsktbl; UC Sn Dgo; Lic Nrs.

BARTONI, DANIELLE L; Willow Glenn HS; San Jose, CA; (3); 28/539; Pep Clb; Quiz Bowl; Science Clb; SADD; Ed Yrbk; Treas Jr Cls; JV Pom Pon; JV Swmmng; High Hon Roll; NHS; Schlrshp Jnr Statsmn Fndtn.

BARTOSH MEDINA, MELISSA; Trabuco Hills HS; Orange, CA; (4); Art Clb; Dance Clb; Drama Clb; Chorus; School Musical; School Play; Stage Crew; Variety Show; Fld Hcky; Swmmng; Distngshd Schlr; Macy Awd Drams; Pony Awd Drama; Dixie Awd Drama; Yth Expo Art; Saddle Back Coll; Theater Arts.

BARTSCH, ELLI D; Clovis HS; Fresno, CA; (3); Church Yth Grp; Debate Tm; FCA; German Clb; NFL; Office Aide; Ski Clb; Varsity Clb; Rep Frsh Cls; Var Swmmng; Lifeguard & Swim Coach; Fresno ST; Ed.

BARTU, SANDY M; Santa Cruz HS; Santa Cruz, CA; (3); Church Yth Grp; Cmnty Wkr; Hosp Aide; Pres Key Clb; Ski Clb; Spanish Clb; Band; Jazz Band; Mrchg Band; Pep Band; Bus.

BARTZ, JASON R; Pioneer HS; San Jose, CA; (1); Debate Tm; Math Tm; Spanish Clb; Nwsp; JV Tennis; High Hon Roll; Hon Roll; Pres Acad Fit Awd; Hnrs On Gldn St Exam 1st Yr Alg; Stanford.

BARTZ, JASON S; Ramona HS; Ramona, CA; (2); Church Yth Grp; Sec VICA; JV Ftbl; JV Trk; SDSU; Crmnlgy.

BARTZ, JODY; West Valley Christian HS; Canoga Park, CA; (4); 2/8; Church Yth Grp; Drama Clb; Teachers Aide; Yrbk; Pres Sr Cls; VP Stu Cncl; Var Capt Cheerldng; Var L Vllybl; Hon Roll; Sal; Dstngshd Chrstn Stu 87-89; 1st Tm Al-Leag CIF Vllybl 88 & 89; The Masters Coll; Bus.

BARTZ, KRISTA K; Santa Barbara HS; Santa Barbara, CA; (4); 6/473; Church Yth Grp; Cmnty Wkr; Dance Clb; Orch; Vllybl; Elks Awd; High Hon Roll; Gov Art Gala; CA Arts Schlr 87-89; Natl Sci Essy Awd; Eclgy Clb Earth Dy Plng Chr; CSF Sealbearer; Oberlin Conservatory; Piano.

BARTZ, LAURA C; Patrick Henry HS; San Diego, CA; (3); 80/528; Church Yth Grp; Cmnty Wkr; Hosp Aide; Acpl Chr; Hon Roll; JETS Awd; Jr NHS; Gtr San Diego Sci Fair Winner; St Sci Fair; Assn Prof Sci Awd; Media Awd Winner; U CA; Ed.

BARTZ, TODD S; Pioneer HS; San Jose, CA; (2); Church Yth Grp; JV Bsktbl; High Hon Roll; Hon Roll; Stanford.

BARUT, MARGIE S; East Union HS; Lathrop, CA; (2); Church Yth Grp; French Clb; Vllybl; Prfct Atten Awd; Asian Clb; CA Schlrshp Fed; Delta Coll; Nrsng.

BARUT, VILMA M; Palm Springs HS; Palm Springs, CA; (3); Dance Clb; Teachers Aide; Drill Tm; Hon Roll; CA ST Long Beach; Bus.

BASA, NICOLE; Mt Eden HS; Hayward, CA; (2); 1/380; Church Yth Grp; Dance Clb; Varsity Clb; Chorus; Orch; VP Frsh Cls; Pres Soph Cls; Var Tennis; Hon Roll; Pres Acad Fit Awd; CA Schlrshp Fed; S Alameda Cnty Yth Orch; Harvard; Law.

BASBAS, JENNIFER E; Lowell HS; San Francisco, CA; (2); Chess Clb; Cmnty Wkr; German Clb; Hosp Aide; Latin Clb; Office Aide; Science Clb; SADD; Arch.

BASCARA, DANIEL; Archbishop Riordan HS; Daly City, CA; (4); 6/177; Cmnty Wkr; Drama Clb; Band; Orch; Pep Band; School Musical; Pres Sr Cls; High Hon Roll; Hon Roll; Stu Cncl; LIFE; Kairos.

BASCO, ALEXANDER; South San Francisco HS; South San Francis, CA; (2); Math Clb; Color Guard; Bsbl; Tennis; Hon Roll; Pianst; Photo Clb; Columbian Squires; CA Tech; Arch.

BASCO, MARIA A; Bishop Amat Mem HS; Walnut, CA; (2); Dance Clb; Cit Awd; High Hon Roll; Hon Roll; NHS; U Of CA Irvine; Pre-Med.

BASCONCILLO, CHRIS; San Fernando Valley Acad; Sepulveda, CA; (2); 2/20; Acpl Chr; Chorus; Church Choir; School Musical; Pres Frsh Cls; Pres Soph Cls; Hon Roll; Assoc Stu Body Scrtry Pblcty; Photo Club; Chrch Bell Chrs; Loma Linda U; Med.

BASCOS, ARTEMIO; Sacred Heart Prep; East Palo Alto, CA; (3); Sec Treas Church Yth Grp; VP Sr Cls; JV Capt Bsktbl; Tennis; Hon Roll; Med.

BASE, HOWARD C; Pater Noster HS; Los Angeles, CA; (3); 3/40; Chess Clb; Math Clb; Yrbk; JV Bsbl; High Hon Roll; NHS; Bus.

BASH, CHRIS L; Bloomington HS; Bloomington, CA; (2); French Clb; High Hon Roll; Prin Hnr Rl; USC; Phy.

BASH, CINDY L; Morro Bay HS; Los Osos, CA; (4); 10/226; Key Clb; SADD; Chorus; Church Choir; Swing Chorus; JV Var Bsktbl; JV Var Sftbl; JV Var Tennis; High Hon Roll; Pres Acad Fit Awd; Cal Poly San Luis Obispo; Comp.

BASHO, SHRUTI; Armijo HS; Fairfield, CA; (3); AFS; Sec Key Clb; Ski Clb; Sec Sr Cls; JV Crs Cntry; JV Tennis; High Hon Roll; Varsty Badmntn; CSF Secy; Davis U; Opthlmlgy.

BASILA, CARRIE S; Madera HS; Madera, CA; (1); Intnl Clb; VP Treas Frsh Cls; JV Trk; High Hon Roll; Trk Vrsty Ltr; Dfns Law.

BASILE, DANIELA O; Louisville HS; Calabasas, CA; (2); 1/106; Chorus; Chrstn Svcs; CSF; LMU; Med.

BASILE, MARA E; Santa Barbara HS; Santa Barbara, CA; (2); 135/450; ROTC; Trk; High Hon Roll; Hon Roll; Prfct Atten Awd; Rcvd Ftnss Awds; Intrstd Ballet-Stud 10 Yrs.

BASINAL, GREG N; Grace Davis HS; Modesto, CA; (1); JV Ftbl; JV Trk; Hon Roll; Law Enforcmnt.

BASINGER, CHAD R; Poway HS; San Diego, CA; (4); 8/728; SADD; Varsity Clb; Rep Stu Cncl; JV Bsktbl; Var Capt Tennis; Intrml Wt Lftg; Hon Roll; Kiwanis Awd; NHS; Interact; CSF; UCLA; Sales.

BASKERVILLE, JACQUELINE; St Anthonys HS; Compton, CA; (1); Church Choir; Drill Tm; Howard U; Attorney.

BASNETT, BOBBY G; Santa Ynez HS; Buellton, CA; (3); SADD; Teachers Aide; Band; Jazz Band; Mrchg Band; Pep Band; Var L Ftbl; Ntwrk For Drug Free Yth; Alan Hancock; Sheriff.

BASQUIN, ASHLEY; Moorpark HS; Moorpark, CA; (2); Cmnty Wkr; Cheerldng; High Hon Roll; Jr NHS; Miss Teen Channel Islands Prin 90; VP JR Brd Of Dirs LA Figure Skating Clb; Stanford U; Ortho Surgeon.

BASRA, INDERPAL; Fred C Beyer HS; Modesto, CA; (4); Cmnty Wkr; Computer Clb; Debate Tm; FBLA; Pres Sec Hosp Aide; NFL; Sec Science Clb; Sec Spanish Clb; Speech Tm; SADD; U Of CA Davis; Pre-Med.

BASS, JAMES L; Riverdale HS; Riverdale, CA; (2); VP Soph Cls; Bsbl; Ftbl; Military.

BASS, JULIE E; Irvine HS; Irvine, CA; (3); Ski Clb; Teachers Aide; Yrbk; Hist Stu Cncl; Cheerldng; Diving; Horse Riding & Training; Ranch Mgmt.

BASS, LAURA; Santiago HS; Garden Grove, CA; (2); Art Clb; JV Bsktbl; JV Sftbl; High Hon Roll; Laguna Arts Fest; Acadmc Dec; CSF; USC.

BASS, VICTORIA; Hamilton HS; Rohnert Park, CA; (4); Am Leg Aux Girls St; Spanish Clb; Pres SADD; Stu Cncl; Capt Var Bsktbl; Stat Var Sftbl; Var JV Trk; Capt Var Vllybl; Elks Awd; Hon Roll; Upward Bound Pgm & Step To Coll CSU Chico; CSU Sonoma; Law.

BASSETT, ERIC A; Bella Vista HS; Fair Oaks, CA; (3); 40/423; Ski Clb; Spanish Clb; SADD; Sec Jr Cls; Pres Stu Cncl; Var Socr; Tennis; Hon Roll; Pres Acad Fit Awd; League Soccer & Tnns.

BASSETT, JANA; Archbishop Mitty HS; San Jose, CA; (4); 7/215; Cmnty Wkr; French Clb; Math Tm; Red Cross Aide; Ski Clb; Teachers Aide; Stat Bsktbl; JV Crs Cntry; High Hon Roll; NHS; Slsprsn, Pacesttr & Key Carrier Gap; Math, Engl, Frnch & High GPA Awds; Skiing; UCLA; Civil Engr.

BASSETT, KAYE C; Rio Americano HS; Carmichael, CA; (3); 24/290; Cmnty Wkr; Service Clb; Spanish Clb; SADD; Drill Tm; Stage Crew; High Hon Roll; JV Socr; CA Schlrshp Fed; Acad Ltr Awd; Apollo Awd; Brdcst Jrnlsm.

BASSETT, PAULA; Fremont HS; Sunnyvale, CA; (3); Cmnty Wkr; Pres Service Clb; Drill Tm; Stu Cncl; Rotary Awd; GATE Pres & Dist Sec; Mst Dedicated On Drill Tm 89-90; San Jose CA; Phy Therapy.

BASSI, JOSH; Temecula Valley HS; Temecula, CA; (3); ROTC; Var Ftbl; Var Trk; Var Wrstlng; Hon Roll; USC; Accntng.

BASSIG, NIELMA; St Anthony HS; Long Beach, CA; (2); School Play; VP Frsh Cls; Sec Jr Cls; Var Capt Cheerldng; Hon Roll; NHS; California Scholarship Federation; Fishing Club; Ucla; Business Law.

BASSO, CUBBY U; Downey HS; Bellflower, CA; (3); Boy Scts; Church Yth Grp; SADD; Band; Mrchg Band; Var Cheerldng; Var Swmmng; Pres Acad Fit Awd; Vrsty Wtr Polo; CSF Slbearer; Gldn St Exm Hgh Hnrs.

BASTON, CHRISTOPHER J; Leuzinger HS; Lawndale, CA; (1); Chorus; Cit Awd; Hon Roll; US Marine Corps Aviation; Flight Engr.

BASU, RUPA; Woodbridge HS; Irvine, CA; (4); Cmnty Wkr; Pres Intnl Clb; SADD; Band; Treas Drill Tm; Yrbk; High Hon Roll; NHS; Pres Acad Fit Awd; Rotary Awd; UC San Diego.

BASUINO, ERIN K; Novato HS; Novato, CA; (2); Church Yth Grp; Drama Clb; French Clb; School Musical; School Play; Stage Crew; JV Cheerldng; Var Swmmng; JV Tennis; High Hon Roll; Exchange Stu France 1990; Synchronized Swmmr; Skier; UC Berkeley; Genetic Engr.

BATAC, KATHLEEN G; Poway HS; Poway, CA; (2); Church Yth Grp; Cmnty Wkr; Key Clb; Sec Soph Cls; Sec Jr Cls; Stat Bsbl; Hon Roll; Golden St Exam Geom & Alg Hnrs; Peer Cnlsr; Law.

BATACAN, CATHERINE B; Reedley HS; Reedley, CA; (4); 19/329; Church Yth Grp; Cmnty Wkr; FCA; French Clb; German Clb; Intnl Clb; Service Clb; Teachers Aide; Ed Yrbk; Treas Jr Cls; Drm Grl 90; Cal Poly San Luis Obispo.

BATANGAN, ELEANOR B; Milpitas HS; Milpitas, CA; (3); 59/487; Spanish Clb; JV Swmmng; UC Davis; Engrng.

BATARSE, RODOLFO; Poway HS; San Diego, CA; (3); 3/761; Church Yth Grp; Cmnty Wkr; Key Clb; French Hon Soc; High Hon Roll; NHS; CSF; 5-6th Grdrs Bsktbl Coach; Yth Bsktbl; Bio.

BATCHAN, CELESSA T; Valley View HS; Riverside, CA; (3); Spanish Clb; Var Bsktbl; Var Trk; Cit Awd; Hon Roll; Pres Acad Fit Awd; BSU VP; Interact; Spellman; Pedtrcn.

BATE, JENNIFER P; Burlingame HS; Redwood City, CA; (4); 30/270; French Clb; Hosp Aide; Service Clb; Teachers Aide; Var Swmmng; Hon Roll; Pres Acad Fit Awd; CSF; Psych.

BATEMAN, JASON; Chaminade College Prep; Northridge, CA; (4); Church Yth Grp; Cmnty Wkr; VP Treas French Clb; Model UN; Scholastic Bowl; VP SADD; Treas Thesps; Swmmng; Trk; Gov Hon Prg Awd; St Marys Coll CA; Bus Econ.

BATES, ANNETTE R; Hilltop HS; Chula Vista, CA; (2); 125/529; Chorus; Cit Awd; Hon Roll; Frgn Lang & Global Stds; Outstndng Atten; Spanish Excllnc Awd; Southwestern Coll; Mltry Nurse.

BATES, ANNIE M; Burney JR/Sr HS; Burney, CA; (1); School Musical; Hon Roll; Achvt Engl Awd; Achvt Music Awd; 1st Pl Poem; Tchr.

BATES, CHRIS G; Tustin HS; Tustin, CA; (2); 20/600; Cmnty Wkr; Debate Tm; Letterman Clb; Thesps; School Play; Stu Cncl; JV Crs Cntry; St Schlr; Orange Cnty Acad Decathln; Forum Human Rltns; Harvard; Med.

BATES, CONNIE H; Santa Teresa HS; San Jose, CA; (2); Church Yth Grp; Science Clb; Spanish Clb; SADD; Bsktbl; Hon Roll; Pres Acad Fit Awd; Lcl Swm Tm; BYU.

BATES, CURTIS L; John Muir HS; Altadena, CA; (3); 23/400; Pres VP Key Clb; Church Choir; Drm Mjr(t); Jazz Band; Mrchg Band; Orch; Pep Band; Rep Jr Cls; Var L Trk; Leag Champn Hgh Jump 88-89; Choir Bay Yr Pasadena Boys Choir 87; Aerospace.

BATES, DAN P; El Camino HS; Oceanside, CA; (3); 50/364; SADD; Teachers Aide; Yrbk; JV Bsbl; Hon Roll; Prfct Atten Awd; Var Photographic Awds 1988-90; Brooks Inst; Phorography.

BATES, DEVIN; Cardinal Newman HS; Rohnert Park, CA; (1); Church Yth Grp; Cmnty Wkr; Service Clb; Lit Mag; Ice Hcky-Goalie Nor-Cal Hcky Leag; Clsscl & Blues Guitar; Reading; Hockey.

BATES, JEFFREY; Porterville HS; Porterville, CA; (3); Church Yth Grp; Bsbl; Hon Roll; Boys State Nominee; Leadership Conference; Water Polo Captain; Fresno ST U; Architect.

BATES, KEVIN L; Irvine HS; Irvine, CA; (4); 20/575; Debate Tm; Key Clb; Math Tm; Ski Clb; Spanish Clb; Speech Tm; Rep Frsh Cls; Rep Jr Cls; JV Bsbl; JV Crs Cntry; Cmptitv Alpine Skier-5th Pl Statewd Race UT 89; U Of CA San Diego; Lwyr.

BATES, MARJORIE; Wasco Union HS; Wasco, CA; (3); 101/200; Pres Church Yth Grp; Pep Clb; Band; Pep Band; Rep Frsh Cls; Sec Soph Cls; Sec Jr Cls; Sec Stu Cncl; Var Cheerldng; JV Powder Puff Ftbl; CA Schlstc Fdrtn; Brigham Young U; Med Fld.

BATES, MATT J; Kingsburg HS; Kingsburg, CA; (2); Band; Jazz Band; Mrchg Band; Pep Band; Cnty Hnr Band; Acad Lttr; Musician.

BATES, MICHELLE L; Acalanes HS; Lafayette, CA; (3); 45/260; Cmnty Wkr; Hosp Aide; SADD; Teachers Aide; Varsity Clb; Powder Puff Ftbl; Score Keeper; Var Sftbl; Hon Roll; CSF; Pedtrcn.

BATES, PETER JOHN; Torrey Pines HS; Del Mar, CA; (2); 55/503; JV Bsktbl; JV Vllybl; Hon Roll; CSF; Vtd Mst Imprtnt Ply Bkstlbl & Bllybl Tms; Duke; Law.

BATES, RACHEL; San Bernardino HS; San Bernardino, CA; (2); 6/580; Key Clb; SADD; Ed Yrbk; Rep Jr Cls; High Hon Roll; Prfct Atten Awd; UC Berkeley; Marketing.

BATES, RADD N; Fallbrook Union HS; Fallbrook, CA; (4); Church Yth Grp; Letterman Clb; Scholastic Bowl; Teachers Aide; Sec Frsh Cls; Treas Soph Cls; Sec Stu Cncl; Bsktbl; Ftbl; High Hon Roll; Pepperdine U; Poltcl Sci.

BATES, REBECCA N; Oroville HS; Oroville, CA; (1); L Var Socr; L JV Sftbl; L JV Tennis.

BATES, SHERRI; Orange HS; Orange, CA; (4); Pep Clb; Phtg Yrbk; JV Cheerldng; Cit Awd; High Hon Roll; Hon Roll; Prfct Atten Awd; Dubere; CSF; JV Chrldr Yr Awd; UCI; Vet.

BATES, SUNJIA; George Washington Prep; Los Angeles, CA; (4); Rptr Church Yth Grp; Cmnty Wkr; Pep Clb; Spanish Clb; Speech Tm; Chorus; Church Choir; Capt Drill Tm; Nwsp; Yrbk; Dare Cert; Pr Cnslr; CASC; Snr Snate; Yng Blck Schlrs; UCLA Prtnrshp; ICC Pres; Brdcst Jrnlsm.

BATES, TRACI L; Tracy HS; Tracy, CA; (4); 74/350; Church Yth Grp; Drama Clb; Intnl Clb; Math Clb; Hist SADD; Teachers Aide; Band; Chorus; Church Choir; Jazz Band; Church Ministry Schlrshp; Schlrshp From Traey Miniserial Assn; Bethany Bible Coll; Teaching.

BATHE, KARRIE; Madera HS; Madera, CA; (4); 35/450; Church Yth Grp; Pep Clb; SADD; Teachers Aide; Band; Color Guard; Drill Tm; Mrchg Band; Rep Frsh Cls; Rep Soph Cls; Fshn & Bridal Show Model; U San Luis Obispo; RN.

BATHKE, ERIKA L; Rio Mesa HS; Camarillo, CA; (4); 10/365; Treas Church Yth Grp; Drama Clb; Treas German Clb; School Play; Ed Yrbk; Capt Swmmng; NHS; Opt Clb Awd; Pres Acad Fit Awd; Mock Trial Team; UC San Diego; Engrng.

BATIN, MIMI; Orangewood Acad; Cerritos, CA; (4); FCA; Hosp Aide; Chorus; Ed Yrbk; Pres Jr Cls; Pres Stu Cncl; Cheerldng; Gym; Vllybl; Ntl Merit Schol; Nrtl Mrt; Bnk America Sci Awd; Pre-Med.

BATISTA, LISETTE M; Village Christian HS; Glendale, CA; (3); Church Yth Grp; Drama Clb; Spanish Clb; Teachers Aide; Powder Puff Ftbl; Mdrn Dance 8 Yrs; UCSB.

BATISTE, DEATRA P; El Cerrito HS; Richmond, CA; (4); Library Aide; Office Aide; Teachers Aide; Rep Jr Cls; Hon Roll; ROP; Comp Prgmr.

BATISTE, STEPHANIE L; Westlake School For Girls; Los Angeles, CA; (4); Var Cmnty Wkr; French Clb; Letterman Clb; School Play; Lit Mag; Rep Stu Cncl; Var L Bsktbl; Hon Roll; Cltrl Awrns Club Pres; Robinson Essay Cont 1st Pl; Awd Outstndg Cmmnty Svc.

BATMAN, CHRISTINA L; Norte Vista HS; Riverside, CA; (1); High Hon Roll; Hon Roll; GATE; Vet.

BATONG, ABRAHAM B; Monterey Bay Acad; Milpitas, CA; (3); Band; Hon Roll; Comp Engr.

BATOYON, DEREK S; Gomers/Mira Mesa HS; San Diego, CA; (2); Lbrn Crs Cntry; JV Trk; Hon Roll.

BATSON, ERIN C; Palmdale HS; Palmdale, CA; (3); Teachers Aide; Bsktbl; Var Powder Puff Ftbl; Var Trk; Typing Awd; U TX El Paso; Obstetrician.

BATT, INGRID R; Fontana HS; Fontana, CA; (2); Church Yth Grp; GAA; Latin Clb; Drill Tm; Variety Show; Bsktbl; Cheerldng; Socr; Sftbl; Vllybl; Lawyer.

BATTAGLIA, ADRIA I; Foothill HS; Pleasanton, CA; (3); French Clb; Teachers Aide; Capt Band; Capt Color Guard; Capt Drill Tm; Flag Corp; Mrchg Band; Ed Nwsp; Pleasntn Piano Cmptn 1st Pl Duet 4th Pl Solo; U CA Berkeley; Psych.

BATTCHER, LAURA J; Pacific Grove HS; Pacific Grove, CA; (3); AFS; Church Yth Grp; Sec Band; Jazz Band; Mrchg Band; Orch; Pep Band; Var Vllybl; High Hon Roll; Outstndng Musician; CSF.

BATTEN, KIT; Chaminade College Prep; Woodland Hills, CA; (2); Art Clb; Church Yth Grp; French Clb; Hosp Aide; Cheerldng; Jr NHS; NHS; Hstry Clb; CSF; Pre-Med.

BATTEN, WILLIAM W; Cajon HS; San Bernardino, CA; (3); Arch Draftr.

BATTENFIELD, HEATHER L; Grossmont HS; La Mesa, CA; (2); 12/400; Church Yth Grp; Cmnty Wkr; Dance Clb; French Clb; Church Choir; Rptr Phtg Yrbk; High Hon Roll; High Hnrs Golden ST Alg Exam 89; Outstndg Frnch Stu 89; Stu Of Handbell Choir; Teaching.

BATTERSON, CHRISTIE S; Antelope Valley HS; Lancaster, CA; (4); 29/488; Church Yth Grp; French Clb; Service Clb; Teachers Aide; Off Jr Cls; Off Sr Cls; Var Socr; Sftbl; High Hon Roll; Hon Roll; CA Scholastic Fed-Gold Grad/Life Mem; Bank Of Am Cert Of Excllc; Womens Club Of Lancaster Schlrshp; Elem Education.

BATTLES, HEATHER J; O'farrell Schl Creatv Prfrmg Arts; San Diego, CA; (1); 9/380; Art Clb; Church Yth Grp; Dance Clb; French Clb; Hon Roll; Educ.

BATTO, JEANNIE L; Vintage HS; Napa, CA; (2); Cmnty Wkr; Hist Pres 4-H; Band; Chorus; Mrchg Band; Stage Crew; Phtg Yrbk; Cit Awd; Jr NHS; Intl Ordr Of Rainbow Girls Charity, Hope, Faith, Treas, Oter OD Svr, Confndtl Obsrvr, Rlgn & Nature; USAF Acad; Airlines Pilot.

BATTS, JUSTINE P; El Cajon Valley HS; El Cajon, CA; (2); 187/431; Church Yth Grp; Dance Clb; Key Clb; SADD; School Musical; JV Bsktbl; JV Cheerldng; JV Sftbl; Snowball Princess; Newscaster; Jrnlsm.

BATTY, JOHN R; Chino HS; Ontario, CA; (2); Boy Scts; Spanish Clb; Var L Ftbl; BYU; Law.

BATY, JERRY V; Panorama Christian Schl; Yucaipa, CA; (3); 1/5; Art Clb; Chess Clb; Church Yth Grp; Drama Clb; German Clb; Rptr Nwsp; Rptr Yrbk; Var L Bsbl; Cit Awd; Hon Roll; Abilene Christian U; Comp Pgmng.

BATY, SCOTT S; Delta HS; Courtland, CA; (2); FFA; Pres Frsh Cls; VP Soph Cls; JV Bsbl; JV Ftbl; JV Trk; Hon Roll.

BAUER, KAREN; Fairfield HS; Fairfield, CA; (4); Church Yth Grp; German Clb; Teachers Aide; Exchng Stu To Japan; Congrssnl Page; Chrstn Ldrshp Camp; Holy Names Coll; Intl Affairs.

BAUER, PAUL J; Bullard HS; Fresno, CA; (2); 45/500; FCA; SADD; Var Bsbl; Var Ftbl; Wt Lftg; High Hon Roll; CSF; Vrsty Ftbl Schlr/Athl Awd 89-90; Bsbl MVP 89; CA ST U Fresno; Law.

BAUER, SEAN L; Mt Diablo HS; W Pittsburg, CA; (3); Teachers Aide; JV Var Bsbl; JV Ftbl; Intrml Powder Puff Ftbl; Intrml Sftbl; JV Trk; Intrml Wt Lftg; High Hon Roll; Hon Roll; Pres Acad Fit Awd; As Jr Maintained 4.17 GPA While Exclng In JV & Var Sports/Ftbl & Bsbl; Pre-Med.

BAUER, TRAVIS A; Cleveland HS; Northridge, CA; (3); Church Yth Grp; Cmnty Wkr; Hosp Aide; Library Aide; Teachers Aide; VICA; High Hon Roll; Hon Roll; 2nd Pl Photo Cntst.

BAUGH, JASON; Carpinteria HS; Carpinteria, CA; (4); Cmnty Wkr; FFA; Varsity Clb; Bsbl; Ftbl; Trk; Hon Roll; Kiwanis Awd; Church Yth Grp; Teachers Aide; Santa Barbara CC; Envrmntl Stu.

BAUGH, VALERIE; Yuba City HS; Yuba City, CA; (2); Church Yth Grp; Drama Clb; Key Clb; Acpl Chr; School Musical; School Play; Variety Show; Stat Ftbl; Hon Roll; Rtng II At Chico Small & Solo/Ensmbl Fstvl 90; Theater.

BAUGHER, SHANNON MARIE; Etiwanda HS; Alta Loma, CA; (3); 13/850; Church Yth Grp; Chorus; Var Crs Cntry; Var Trk; High Hon Roll; Kiwanis Awd; CSF; Gldn St Exam Alg I & Geom Hnrs; U Of CA Riverside; Tchr.

BAUGHMAN, ADAM T; Oxnard HS; Oxnard, CA; (3); 5/650; Am Leg Boys St; Boy Scts; Church Yth Grp; Stu Cncl; JV Ftbl; JV Socr; Var Trk; High Hon Roll; Hon Roll; Jr NHS; Engrng.

BAUGHMAN, MICHELLE; Casa Roble HS; Orangevale, CA; (2); AFS; VP Treas German Clb; Orch; School Play; VP Jr Cls; Var Crs Cntry; Var Swmmng; Cit Awd; Hon Roll; BYU; Poltcl Sci.

BAUGHN, HEATHER; Oak Hill Schl; Thousand Oaks, CA; (2); Church Yth Grp; Drama Clb; School Play; Stage Crew; Rep Soph Cls; Intrml Sftbl; Intrml Vllybl.

BAUGUS, SHAWN E; Ceres HS; Ceres, CA; (4); Intnl Clb; Key Clb; Model UN; Office Aide; Service Clb; Teachers Aide; High Hon Roll; Hon Roll; Pres Acad Fit Awd; Var Bsbl.

BAULEKE, JACKIE M; Ventura HS; Ventura, CA; (4); 3/420; Church Yth Grp; Cmnty Wkr; English Clb; GAA; Pep Clb; SADD; Capt L Socr; Stat Swmmng; Trk; JV Var Vllybl; Hmecmng Princess; Hall Fame Wnnr; Girl 1st Qtr; CIF Schlr Athlt; Soc Wmn Engrs Awd; 4 Yr Acad Vrsty Ltr; UCLA; Psych.

BAULKMAN, TERIKA; Southwest HS; San Ysidro, CA; (2); Cit Awd; UCSD; Law.

BAUM, ANYA J; Berkeley HS; Berkeley, CA; (4); Office Aide; Var L Sftbl; High Hon Roll; Ntl Merit SF; Smith Coll.

BAUM, CHRIS J; Nranham HS; San Jose, CA; (2); 1/300; Crs Cntry; Socr; Tennis; Hon Roll; MA; Engl.

BAUM, KATRINA; San Gorgonio HS; Highland, CA; (3); 14/440; GAA; Letterman Clb; Pep Clb; Service Clb; Treas Spanish Clb; SADD; Cheerldng; Pom Pon; Powder Puff Ftbl; Score Keeper; Mock Trial; Outstndng Attorney Awd; CSF Treas & Pres; Berkeley; Crmnl Law.

BAUM, KELLY C; Sutter Union HS; Sutter, CA; (2); 11/75; Drama Clb; Sec Pres 4-H; Intnl Clb; Science Clb; School Play; Stage Crew; Variety Show; Mgr Yrbk; Bsktbl; Trk; CA ST U; Phy Sci.

BAUMAN, ADAM M; Trabuco Hills HS; Mission Viejo, CA; (2); 1/410; Boy Scts; Church Yth Grp; Cmnty Wkr; Math Tm; Scholastic Bowl; Spanish Clb; Phtg Yrbk; JV Capt Bsktbl; High Hon Roll; NHS; Golden St Exam Alg I, Geom Hgh Hnrs; Bsktbl Coaches Awd, Schlr Athl; 4.67 GPA Hnrs & A P Cls; US Air Force Acad; Engrng.

BAUMAN, JASON N; Newbury Park Acad; Northridge, CA; (3); Church Yth Grp; Ski Clb; Varsity Clb; Chorus; School Musical; School Play; Variety Show; Pres Jr Cls; Bsbl; Bsktbl; Pacific Union Coll; Orthdntst.

BAUMAN, PHILIP; Fred C Beyer HS; Modesto, CA; (4); 15/506; Church Yth Grp; French Clb; Math Clb; Church Choir; Yrbk; Cit Awd; Hon Roll; Prfct Atten Awd; CSF; Patriot Awd Frgn Lang; Boys St Finalist; Fresno ST; Bio.

BAUMANN, CHERYL L; Colton HS; Colton, CA; (2); Var Trk; Humboldt St; Mrn Bio.

BAUMANN, KIP A; Lompoc HS; Lompoc, CA; (3); 8/284; Am Leg Boys St; Letterman Clb; Math Tm; SADD; Varsity Clb; Var L Socr; Var L Tennis; Cit Awd; High Hon Roll; Math.

BAUMGARTEN, KRISTIN A; Edison HS; Huntington Beach, CA; (3); Model UN; Teachers Aide; JV Crs Cntry; JV Trk; High Hon Roll; Balboa Yacht Clb Rcng Tm & Jr Offcr; Coaches Awd JV Trck 90; Offcr Jobs Dghtrs; Lawyer.

BAUMGARTNER JR, GARY L; Fontana HS; Brandon, MS; (3); Letterman Clb; Teachers Aide; Varsity Clb; VICA; Intrml Bsktbl; Var Ftbl; Hon Roll; OH ST U; Elect.

BAUMGARTNER, JIM R; Cajon HS; San Bernardino, CA; (2); Boy Scts; Pres Band; Pres Mrchg Band; Pres Pep Band; Cit Awd; High Hon Roll; Jr NHS; NHS; Rotary Awd; Rtry Lfe Schlrshp; US Air Force Acad; Mltry Pol.

BAUN, GLEN K; Mission Viejo HS; Trabuco Canyon, CA; (2); Boy Scts; German Clb; Trk; Hon Roll; Eagle Sct; Hnr Ctzn Orng Cnty; CSF; Pol Sci.

BAUNGARTNER, NICOLLE A; Santa Clara HS; Oxnard, CA; (3); Letterman Clb; Var Bsktbl; Var Swmmng; Hon Roll; CA Poly Pomona; Psych.

BAUONGKHOUN, BOUASOUTH; Clairemont HS; San Diego, CA; (2); 38/254; Dance Clb; School Musical; VP Soph Cls; Bsktbl; Ftbl; Socr; Vllybl; Wt Lftg; Wrstlng; Hon Roll; UCSD; Electrnc.

BAURIEDEL, GABRIEL Q; Henry S Gunn SR HS; Palo Alto, CA; (4); Drama Clb; Quiz Bowl; Thesps; Orch; School Play; JV Crs Cntry; JV Trk; Harpsichordist Palo Alto Chmbr Orchstr; Prfmd Amer Cnsrvtry Theatre; Toured Australia W/Orchstra 88 89; Actor.

BAURLAND, CHRISTOPHER M; Valencia HS; Placentia, CA; (2); Boy Scts; FFA; Swmmng; Water Polo; Naval Acad.

BAURMANN, HEIDI M; Corona HS; Corona, CA; (2); 69/468; Church Yth Grp; Science Clb; Band; JV Sftbl; Hon Roll; Pres Acad Fit Awd; Acctg.

BAUTISTA, ALLISON; Holy Family HS; Glendale, CA; (3); VP Church Yth Grp; Hosp Aide; Office Aide; Chorus; Ed Yrbk; Pres Frsh Cls; Sec Soph Cls; Rep Stu Cncl; JV Vllybl; NEDT Awd; Psych.

BAUTISTA, CHRISTIANNE; Elk Grove HS; Elk Grove, CA; (1); FFA; Chorus; Drill Tm; Hon Roll; Acad Achvmnt Awd; CA Schlrshp Fed; Phy.

BAUTISTA, DEVIN M; Del Oro HS; Loomis, CA; (2); 20/280; JV Ftbl; JV Wt Lftg; Hon Roll; Law.

BAUTISTA, DULCE R; Sweetwater HS; National City, CA; (4); 20/396; DECA; VP French Clb; Sec FBLA; Pres Science Clb; Sec SADD; Chorus; Ed Lit Mag; JV Vllybl; Hon Roll; JETS Awd; Chrch Chr; Stu Cncl Sec; Vllybll Mgr; Pepperdine U; Engl.

BAUTISTA, EFFIE L; Moreau HS; Hayward, CA; (4); Church Yth Grp; Cmnty Wkr; Drama Clb; Math Clb; Math Tm; Teachers Aide; School Play; High Hon Roll; Hon Roll; NHS; Grad Cum Laude 90; Humana Schlrshp; CA ST Hayward; Nrsng.

BAUTISTA, ERICA; Watsonville HS; Watsonville, CA; (1); Stu Cncl; Cheerldng; Hon Roll; Class Treas 90-91; Pom Pon Girl; Dance.

BAUTISTA, JANELLE; Eisenhower HS; Rialto, CA; (4); 40/610; Church Yth Grp; Sec Frsh Cls; Stu Cncl; Var Sftbl; Var Trk; Var Vllybl; High Hon Roll; Treas NHS; Pres Acad Fit Awd; San Diego ST U; Criminal Jstc.

BAUTISTA, JEFF M; Bellarmine-Jefferson HS; Los Angeles, CA; (2); Boy Scts; Church Yth Grp; Math Clb; Science Clb; Spanish Clb; Vllybl; High Hon Roll; NHS; San Louis Obispo; Architecture.

BAUTISTA, JENNIFER V; Redwood Christian HS; Memphis, TN; (2); Church Yth Grp; Chorus; Hon Roll; 1st Pl Assn Chrstn Schls Intl HS Speech Mt; Nrsng.

BAUTISTA, JESUS A; Kearny HS; San Diego, CA; (2); 150/378; Church Yth Grp; Cmnty Wkr; German Clb; Library Aide; ROTC; Color Guard; Drill Tm; Swmmng; Southern CA HSROTC Invitatnl Drill Team & Color Grd; Accntng.

BAUTISTA, JOAQUIN S; Indio HS; Indio, CA; (3); 166/443; Teachers Aide; JV Crs Cntry; Var Trk; Indio Compact Job Clb; Coll Of Desert; Bus Admin.

BAUTISTA, JOCELYN Q; Fairfield HS; Suisun City, CA; (3); Sec Treas Art Clb; German Clb; Red Cross Aide; Service Clb; SADD; Band; Rep Sr Cls; Tennis; Hon Roll; NHS; Med Explr Club VP; UC Davis; Psych.

BAUTISTA, JOSEPH LAUENGCO; Don Bosco Technical Inst; Upland, CA; (2); Chess Clb; Computer Clb; Bsktbl; Hon Roll; NHS; NEDT Awd; CA Polytechnic Inst; Chem Engr.

BAUTISTA, JOYCE E; Bonita Vista HS; Bonita, CA; (3); Art Clb; Debate Tm; Var Quiz Bowl; Ed Nwsp; Var Fld Hcky; Cit Awd; High Hon Roll; Hon Roll; Pres Acad Fit Awd; Prs Of Amnesty Intl Grp; Acad Vrsty Ltr; Mst Enthstc Nwspr; Phlsphy Clb; CSF; Intr-Clb Cncl; Intl Rltns.

BAUTISTA, JUAN F; Rosemead HS; Baldwin Park, CA; (3); Art Clb; Latin Clb; Hon Roll; Police Dept Explorer Sct; CSF; Cal ST; Paralegal.

BAUTISTA, MARIA; Saddleback HS; Santa Ana, CA; (3); French Clb; CA ST Fullerton.

BAUTISTA, MINERVA; Anaheim HS; Anaheim, CA; (3); CSF; Mexican Amer Engrng Soc; U Prep Prgm; CA ST Fullerton; Bus.

BAUTISTA, N MONICA; Huntington Park HS; Huntington Park, CA; (2); Church Yth Grp; Dance Clb; Office Aide; Teachers Aide; Church Choir; Swmmng; Undrcvr Cop.

BAUTISTA, NORA R; Indio HS; Indio, CA; (3) Church Yth Grp; Key Clb; Chorus; Yth Cnslr; Linguist.

BAUTISTA, PATRICIA; Fullerton HS; Anaheim, CA; (2); FBLA; FFA; Lions Clb Schlrshp; Emrgng Ldrs Awd.

BAUTISTA, RAYMOND; Sacred Heart Cathedral HS; Daly City, CA; (1); UC Davis; Med.

BAUTISTA, ROGER; San Gabriel Acad; Montebello, CA; (3); Teachers Aide; Band; Treas Frsh Cls; Rep Soph Cls; Pres Jr Cls; Intrml Socr; Intrml Sftbl; Capt Vllybl; NHS.

BAUTISTA, ROSA E; Magnolia HS; Stanton, CA; (1); Spanish Clb; Bsktbl; Ftbl; Golf; Socr; Sftbl; Tennis; Comp Prog.

BAUTISTA, STEPHANIE C; Notre Dame HS; San Jose, CA; (3); Church Yth Grp; Cmnty Wkr; Hosp Aide; Intnl Clb; Church Choir; Var Bsktbl; Cheerldng; Hon Roll; Yth Smmr Sprts Prog Sftbl & Vlybl; San Jose ST U; Engr.

BAUTISTA, VIVIAN M; St Joseph HS; Paramount, CA; (3); 16/180; Cmnty Wkr; Drama Clb; Treas Spanish Clb; Church Choir; High Hon Roll; Candy Striper Charter Suburban Of Paramount; Volunteer At Paramount Chateau Convalescent Hm; Commnctns.

BAUTISTA, WINZELLA; Southwest HS; San Diego, CA; (4); 24/498; JA; Key Clb; SADD; Rptr Nwsp; Church Yth Grp; Pep Clb; Teachers Aide; Variety Show; Hon Roll; Pres Acad Fit Awd; Associated Stu Bdy Sec; CA Schlrshp Fed; U Of CA San Diego; Elec Engrng.

BAUZON, ERNEST I; Gladstone HS; Azusa, CA; (3); 15/200; VP Frsh Cls; VP Soph Cls; Var Bsktbl; Var Ftbl; Var Tennis; Var Trk; Hon Roll; NHS; CSF.

BAUZON, MARIA CARMEN I; Gladstone HS; Azusa, CA; (4); 2/198; Dance Clb; Intnl Clb; Spanish Clb; Rptr Nwsp; Pres Capt Frsh Cls; Pres Capt Soph Cls; Capt Jr Cls; Intrml Cheerldng; Intrml Trk; High Hon Roll; Sci Fair Outstndng Awd 87-88; CSF-SEAL Bearer; CA ST Polytech U-Pomona; Bus.

BAVTISTA, DAVID B; Nogales HS; West Covina, CA; (2); Chess Clb; Science Clb; Teachers Aide; Yrbk; JV Tennis; High Hon Roll; Hon Roll; NHS; Prfct Atten Awd; Pres Acad Fit Awd; Future Cook Of Amer; CA Poly; Restaurant Mgmt.

BAXLEY, DENISE M; Nevada Union HS; Nevada City, CA; (3); 59/593; Girl Scts; Hosp Aide; School Play; VP Soph Cls; Rep Stu Cncl; Crs Cntry; Powder Puff Ftbl; Var Socr; Hon Roll; Law.

BAXTER, BRIAN C; Del Campo HS; Carmichael, CA; (4); 5/429; Chess Clb; Math Tm; Elks Awd; High Hon Roll; Pres Acad Fit Awd; Val; Bank Of America Achvmt Awd Sci; U CA Davis; Chem.

BAXTER, CHRISTOPHER A; Lemoore HS; Lemoore, CA; (4); 37/286; English Clb; Hon Roll; Acad Dcthln 7 Gold Medals Cty Cmptn; Fresno ST U; Elec Engrg.

BAXTER, DESTINY T; East Bakersfield HS; Bakersfield, CA; (2); Church Yth Grp; Drama Clb; FCA; Library Aide; SADD; Teachers Aide; Chorus; Hon Roll; Peer Cnslng; Hlth Careers Acad; Stanford:Medcl.

BAXTER, MELISSA; Clovis HS; Clovis, CA; (2); Church Yth Grp; Band; Mrchg Band; School Musical; Angelo TX U; Bus.

BAXTER, NATASHA L; Norco SR HS; Norco, CA; (2); Art Clb; Pep Clb; Varsity Clb; Yrbk; Cheerldng; Swmmng; Hon Roll; Pres Acad Fit Awd; Tax Accntnt.

BAXTER, STACEY A; Sierra Joint Union HS; Madera, CA; (3); Teachers Aide; Yrbk; Diving; Sftbl; Tennis; Girls Leag; Fri Night Live; Psych.

BAY, J KIRSTEN; Nevada Union HS; Nevada City, CA; (3); 123/530; Intnl Clb; Model UN; Var L Tennis; Cit Awd; High Hon Roll; Vrsty Ski Tm Ltr/Hgh Pt JV Scorer; CSF; Shakespeare Clb Pub Dir/Outstndng Stu; U Of FL; Intl Law.

BAYBARZ, SHAUNA; Lodi Acad; Lodi, CA; (1); Church Yth Grp; Ski Clb; Band; Chorus; VP Frsh Cls; Intrml Bsktbl; Intrml Powder Puff Ftbl; Intrml Vllybl; High Hon Roll; Natl Phys Ftns Awd; Pacific Union Coll.

BAYHI, AMY C; Capistrano Valley HS; Mission Viejo, CA; (4); FBLA; Pres Acad Fit Awd; CSF; Saddleback Coll Wrtg Cntst 2nd Pl; AP Lit Tst 5; AP Comp Test 3; Bus.

BAYLESS, ALICIA NICOELE; Manteca HS; Manteca, CA; (3); 5/358; VP Pep Clb; SADD; Var Trk; High Hon Roll; Hon Roll; CA Schlrshp Fed; Friday Night Live.

BAYLESS, JENIFER N; Nogales HS; West Covina, CA; (3); Dance Clb; Acpl Chr; Chorus; Variety Show; Cit Awd; High Hon Roll; Hon Roll; Wrk Exprnc Stu Yr; Bus.

BAYLEY, RUSSELL R; Albany HS; Albany, CA; (2); Band; Jazz Band; Mrchg Band; Pep Band; Bus.

BAYNES, JASON C; Encina HS; Sacramento, CA; (3); French Clb; Scholastic Bowl; Band; Orch; Ed Lit Mag; Var JV Bsktbl; Ftbl; High Hon Roll; Opt Clb Awd; Music Camp At U Of Pacific Outstndng Mscn; CA Poly SLO; Arntcl Engrng.

BAYOR II, ZSOLT I; Redlands JR Acad; Loma Linda, CA; (2); Aud/Vis; Chess Clb; Computer Clb; Debate Tm; Math Tm; Band; Chorus; Ed Phtg Yrbk; JV Bsbl; JV Fld Hcky; Editor, Engr Media Ministries; Loma Linda Acad; Law.

BAYS, BRYAN D; Clovis HS; Clovis, CA; (3); Church Yth Grp; Latin Clb; Chorus; Hon Roll; Wrkd Wold Water Adventures 3 Yrs, Kay Bee Toys 2 Yrs; Cal ST U; Ped.

BAYSAC, FATIMA S; Lowell HS; San Francisco, CA; (2); Debate Tm; NFL; Sec VP Red Cross Aide; SADD; Drill Tm; Rep Frsh Cls; Rep Soph Cls; Brd Schl Cmmnty Svc Rep; Pre-Med Clb; Gldn St Exm Alg Hnrs; VP Big Brother/Sister Org; Bio.

BAZA, DEAN M; Vallejo SR HS; Vallejo, CA; (2); Church Yth Grp; Wrstlng; High Hon Roll; UC Berkeley; Mech Drwng.

BAZAN, CLAUDIA G; Notre Dame HS; Salinas, CA; (2); Cmnty Wkr; Library Aide; Teachers Aide; Chorus; Vllybl; Hon Roll; TX A&M; Med.

BAZAN, LINA E; Tracy HS; Lathrop, CA; (2); 47/483; Var Trk; JV Vllybl; Hon Roll; CSF; Psycht.

BAZAN, PHIL PATRICK; Loyola HS; Whittier, CA; (2); Cmnty Wkr; Debate Tm; Spanish Clb; Speech Tm; JV Trk; Hon Roll; NHS; Spanish NHS; Vars Hnrs & A P Classes; Loyola Marymount U; Atty.

BAZGAN, ION C; Acalanes HS; Lafayette, CA; (4); Trk; UC Davis; Statistics.

BAZYOUROS, CHRISTOPHER; Bishop Amat Memorial HS; Azusa, CA; (3); Church Yth Grp; English Clb; High Hon Roll; NHS; Jrnlsm.

BAZZINI, BETTINA; Carlmont HS; Belmont, CA; (2); Bsktbl; Pom Pon; Socr; Vllybl; Hon Roll; CSF; Dntl Hygn.

BEACH, DEVON R; Capistrano Valley HS; Mission Viejo, CA; (3); Cmnty Wkr; Pep Clb; Teachers Aide; Temple Yth Grp; Varsity Clb; Stat Bsktbl; Capt Socr; JV Sftbl; Most Inspirational Soccer; U Southern CA; Dntl Hygnst.

BEACH, RUTH M; Escondido Adventist Acad; Fallbrook, CA; (3); Church Yth Grp; Dance Clb; Spanish Clb; Acpl Chr; Chorus; JV Capt Gym; JV Socr; Var Vllybl; Cit Awd; Hon Roll.

BEACHAM, LEILANI B; Bullard HS; Fresno, CA; (2); Teachers Aide; Rptr Nwsp; PETA; Film Clb; Wn 2 Art Cont; Dir.

BEACOM, JEAN J; Grace M Davis HS; Modesto, CA; (3); Church Yth Grp; Cmnty Wkr; FCA; Pep Clb; Red Cross Aide; Teachers Aide; Stu Cncl; JV Bsktbl; Var Cheerldng; JV Powder Puff Ftbl; Yng Dmcrts; Rd Crss Amer Clb; Frsno ST; Crmnlgy.

BEAGLES, GINA M; Washington HS; Fremont, CA; (2); Drama Clb; Pep Clb; School Play; Sec Soph Cls; JV Cheerldng; CSF; Goldn St Exam Alg Hnrs; Accntnt.

BEAHAN, ALISON K; Bella Vista HS; Fair Oaks, CA; (1); AFS; SADD; JV Swmmng; Synchrnzd Swmmng; WA DC Through Grl Scts For 75th Clbrtn; Accntng.

BEAIRD, BENJAMIN JAY; Oak Hill HS; Van Nuys, CA; (4); Aud/Vis; Chess Clb; Cmnty Wkr; Computer Clb; Drama Clb; Letterman Clb; Teachers Aide; School Play; Variety Show; Off Sr Cls; Brooks Inst; Cinematgrphy.

BEAKLEY, TRACEY; Rio Mesa HS; Camarillo, CA; (3); FCA; Varsity Clb; Stu Cncl; Var Cheerldng; Hon Roll; UOP; Psych.

BEAL, BENJAMIN J; Hesperia HS; Hesperia, CA; (4); Cmnty Wkr; Variety Show; Var Capt Bsktbl; Intrml Capt Ftbl; Var Mgr(s); Var Capt Trk; High Hon Roll; Exchange Clb Yth Of Month; Yth Bsktbl Coach; Bsktbll Coaches Awd 90; Track & Fld Seth Machen Awd 90; Cal ST Bakerfield; Bus Educ.

BEAL, CAROL A; Folsom HS; Folsom, CA; (3); Church Yth Grp; 4-H; Intnl Clb; Library Aide; Ski Clb; SADD; Chorus; Flag Corp; Mrchg Band; Hon Roll; Safe Rides For FNL; Elem Ed.

BEAL, EMILY M; Castro Valley HS; Castro Valley, CA; (3); 2/371; Off Church Yth Grp; Sec Spanish Clb; Acpl Chr; Chorus; School Musical; School Play; High Hon Roll; Hon Roll; Pres Acad Fit Awd; Interact Clb; New Trojans Clb Co-Pres; Madrigals Chr; Insprtn Clb.

BEAL, JENNIFER; Coast Joint Union HS; San Simeon, CA; (4); 3/63; Am Leg Aux Girls St; Church Yth Grp; Office Aide; SADD; Sec Treas Soph Cls; Sec Stu Cncl; Stat Ftbl; Var L Tennis; Elks Awd; Hon Roll; Specl Olympcs; Sr Who Made A Difference; Bank Of Am Awd Soc Stud; Cuesta Coll; Envrnmntl Sci.

BEALER, CHRIS S; Chaffey HS; Upland, CA; (4); 31/350; Church Yth Grp; High Hon Roll; U AZ; Nuclear Engrng.

BEALESSIO, SALLY; Garces Memorial HS; Bakersfield, CA; (1); Cmnty Wkr; Ski Clb; Thesps; Lit Mag; Bsktbl; High Hon Roll.

BEALS, JAYME; Sonoma Valley HS; Sonoma, CA; (3); 39/282; 4-H; SADD; JV Var Cheerldng; JV Sftbl; High Hon Roll; Hon Roll; Interact.

BEAM, JOEL C; West HS; Bakersfield, CA; (2); VP Ski Clb; Band; Mrchg Band; Stat Bsbl; JV Trk; NHS.

BEAMAN, AUDREY A; Skyline HS; Oakland, CA; (3); ROTC; Band; Pep Band; Variety Show; Rptr Nwsp; Cheerldng; Hon Roll; Pres Acad Fit Awd; Law Explorers Post; Law.

BEAMER, JENNIE L; San Marcos HS; San Marcos, CA; (3); Pep Clb; Teachers Aide; Sec Sr Cls; Stu Cncl; Stat Bsktbl; Var Cheerldng; Var Pom Pon; Var Score Keeper; JV Socr; Var Sftbl; Palomar Coll; Educ.

BEAN, JENI LIANE; San Clemente HS; San Clemente, CA; (4); Pres Church Yth Grp; Cmnty Wkr; Dance Clb; Drama Clb; Teachers Aide; Band; Chorus; Church Choir; Mrchg Band; School Musical; Miss Orange Cty Teen USA 88; Star Tomorrow San Diego Metro St Teen Qn 87; U Tulsa; Theatre.

BEAN, KRISTA L; Livermore HS; Livermore, CA; (3); 53/418; Hon Roll; Prfct Atten Awd; Pres Acad Fit Awd; CA ST U Hayward; Eng.

BEAN, LISA; Shasta HS; Redding, CA; (4); Model UN; Varsity Clb; Band; Drm Mjr(t); Mrchg Band; Pep Band; School Musical; Lit Mag; Var Diving; Var Capt Vllybl; San Diego ST U; Poltcl Sci.

BEAN, SHAWNNA; Corning Union HS; Corning, CA; (4); GAA; Intnl Clb; Science Clb; Band; Yrbk; Sec Sr Cls; Cheerldng; Fld Hcky; Powder Puff Ftbl; Trk; Bethany Bible Coll; Chld Dev.

BEANAN, SHIRLEY M; Bella Vista HS; Citrus Heights, CA; (2); 14/201; Pres Church Yth Grp; School Musical; School Play; Variety Show; Off Jr Cls; Stu Cncl; Pres Acad Fit Awd; Rotary Awd; Youngest New Mem Acad Decathlon Team 90-91; Miss Tonga 90-Youngest; Capt Winning Sect Lds Vllybl; Postsecondary Ed/Linguist.

BEAR, LIANE E; A A Stagg HS; Stockton, CA; (2); Church Yth Grp; Hosp Aide; Key Clb; Teachers Aide; School Musical; Variety Show; Pres Frsh Cls; Off Soph Cls; Rep Stu Cncl; JV Var Cheerldng; All-Acad Team 89 & 90; Sci Camp Cnslr; Diabetes Assn, Big Bro/Big Sis & Spcl Olympcs Vlntr; Bus.

BEARCE, SARAH; Point Loma HS; San Diego, CA; (1); 35/499; Girl Scts; Spanish Clb; Hon Roll; Advncmnt Via Individual Dev; Bilingual Magnet Pgm; U CA Berkeley; Span Ed.

BEARD, KATIE A; Edison HS; Huntington Beach, CA; (3); Church Yth Grp; JA; Model UN; Stu Cncl; Var Fld Hcky; Var Tennis; Tnns Athl Mnth; Elem Educ.

BEARD, KRISTA D; Whittier Christian HS; Yorba Linda, CA; (4); 18/169; Church Yth Grp; Pep Clb; Yrbk; Var Trk; NHS; CA Schlstc Fed.

BEARD, RYAN C; Cajon HS; San Bernardino, CA; (1); 1/873; Church Yth Grp; JV Tennis; VP Rotary Awd; Hnrs On Golden St Exam Algebra; Aerontcl Engrng.

BEARDEN, JODI G; Clovis West HS; Fresno, CA; (2); Debate Tm; NFL; Service Clb; SADD; CSF.

BEAS, FLAVIO; Liberty Union HS; Brentwood, CA; (3); 14/405; Dance Clb; French Clb; Intnl Clb; Spanish Clb; Acpl Chr; Variety Show; Hon Roll; Prfct Atten Awd; UC Davis; Art.

BEASLEY, DOUGLASS; Roseville HS; Rocklin, CA; (2); 5/400; Church Yth Grp; French Clb; Band; Mrchg Band; Pep Band; Crs Cntry; Trk; High Hon Roll; NHS; Mexico Outreach Thrgh Azusa Pacific U 89 & 90; Chico ST U; Engl.

BEASLEY, SONYA A; Eisenhower HS; Rialto, CA; (4); Office Aide; Teachers Aide; Brotner & Sister United BSU; CA ST-LONG Beach; Comp Sci.

BEASON, MICHAEL W; Tulare Union HS; Tulare, CA; (3); Church Yth Grp; Drama Clb; JA; Science Clb; SADD; Teachers Aide; Variety Show; Rep Soph Cls; Rep Jr Cls; JV Var Socr; UCLA; Mssnry.

BEATON, STEPHANIE A; Oxnard Union HS; Port Hueneme, CA; (3); Drama Clb; Hosp Aide; SADD; Hon Roll; Prfct Atten Awd; World Wide Talent Agency; Northridge; Acting.

BEATTIE, MARGARET J; Clayton Valley HS; Clayton, CA; (2); FBLA; SADD; High Hon Roll; Hon Roll; CA Schlstc Fed; Amer MENSA; Diablo Valley Coll; Commnctns.

BEATTY, DAVID A; Robert A Millikan HS; Long Beach, CA; (3); Church Yth Grp; Band; Church Choir; Stage Crew; Bsbl; Bsktbl; Trk; Cit Awd; Hon Roll; Pres Acad Fit Awd; Ldr Organizer & Promoter Of Ultimate Sacrifice Christian Rock Bnd; Prsnl Mgr For Sackett Lndscpe Co; ST Coll; Music.

BEAUCHAMP, AWILDA JUDITH; Fontana HS; Fontana, CA; (3); 127/950; Church Yth Grp; Drama Clb; Math Tm; Hist Thesps; Chorus; Flag Corp; Stage Crew; Stat Bsbl; Cit Awd; High Hon Roll; CSF; Outstndng Hstry Awd 88.

BEAUCHAMP, KIM; Village Christian Schl; Sun Valley, CA; (2); Church Yth Grp; English Clb; Mu Alpha Theta; Spanish Clb; Teachers Aide; Drill Tm; School Play; Rep Frsh Cls; Rep Stu Cncl; Stat Bsktbl; CSF; Law.

BEAUCHAMP, MARY GRACE P; Santa Clara HS; Oxnard, CA; (4); 16/177; Am Leg Aux Girls St; Variety Show; Rep Stu Cncl; Cit Awd; High Hon Roll; NHS; Cmnty Wkr; Drama Clb; Science Clb; CSF; Bank Of Amer Field Of Engl Awd; Shakespeare Clb; U OH Steubenville; Elem Ed.

BEAUDETTE, BRIAN S; Chaffey HS; Ontario, CA; (3); Office Aide; Ftbl; L JV Swmmng; Hon Roll; EMT.

BEAUER, CLINT L; Canyon HS; Canyon Country, CA; (4); 50/470; Capt Bsktbl; Capt Ftbl; Trk; Hon Roll; US Army Rsrve Natl Schlr Athl; Golden League Trk 400 M Chmpn; UN Reno; Phys Thrpy.

BEAUJEAN, DESIREE L; Rubidoux HS; Riverside, CA; (4); 21/578; Drama Clb; Acpl Chr; Ed Nwsp; Off Jr Cls; High Hon Roll; Pres Acad Fit Awd; Prm Cmmtte; UCR; Bus.

BEAULIEU, MICHELLE; Marin Acad; Fairfax, CA; (4); Cmnty Wkr; Drama Clb; English Clb; Math Clb; Science Clb; Teachers Aide; Chorus; School Musical; School Play; Stage Crew; Danielle Plumb Zumbron Outdoor Ldrshp Awd; Carleton Coll.

BEAUMONT, JEFF N; La Habra HS; La Habra, CA; (3); Aud/Vis; Church Yth Grp; Science Clb; Band; Mrchg Band; Orch; Pep Band; School Play; Stage Crew; Variety Show; Drumline; OCAD; Cal Poly-Pomona; Elec Engrng.

BEAUMONT, JENNIE; Righetti HS; Santa Maria, CA; (2); Church Yth Grp; Drama Clb; NFL; Speech Tm; JV Cheerldng; Gym; Stu Congress; Spch Trophies & Awds; Chrldng Ribbons; U Of San Diego; Advrtsmnt.

BEAUMONT, MIKE N; La Habra HS; La Habra, CA; (4); 14/380; Cmnty Wkr; Key Clb; Quiz Bowl; Science Clb; Pres Acad Fit Awd; Golden State Exam; Phys Sci.

BEAUREGARD, JOSEPH; Encinal HS; Alameda, CA; (4); 6/222; Letterman Clb; ROTC; Teachers Aide; Varsity Clb; Band; Color Guard; Drill Tm; Var Ftbl; JV Var Socr; Var Bausch & Lomb Sci Awd; MVP JV Sccr; U Of CA Berkeley; Engr.

BEAVER, AMY C; Ceres HS; Modesto, CA; (3); 1/300; AFS; Cmnty Wkr; SADD; Rptr Nwsp; Pres Stu Cncl; Var L Bsktbl; Score Keeper; Var L Swmmng; Var L Vllybl; Hon Roll; Camp Royal; Ca Schrlshp Fed; Bus.

BEAVER, CAREN; Moorpark HS; Moorpark, CA; (3); 4/210; Band; Mrchg Band; Crs Cntry; Trk; Stat Wrstlng; High Hon Roll; CSF; Med.

BEAVER, CINDY M; Ukiah HS; Ukiah, CA; (1); 41/625; 4-H; Color Guard; Drill Tm; 4-H Awd; Redwood Empire Quarter Horse & Amer Quarter Horse Assns; Cal Poly; Animal Sci.

BEAVER, KEVIN J; Mesa Verde HS; Citrus Heights, CA; (2); Var L Bsbl; L Hon Roll; Pro Bsbl.

BEAVER, KRISTA A; John North HS; Riverside, CA; (3); 10/374; Church Yth Grp; Drama Clb; Letterman Clb; Quiz Bowl; Band; Church Choir; Mrchg Band; Pep Band; School Musical; School Play; All Southern CA Hnr Band 88-90; John Philip Sousa Hnr Band 89-90; Chem.

BEAVER, NICOLE M; Ukiah Unified HS; Willits, CA; (3); French Clb; School Musical; Phtg Rptr Nwsp; JV Vllybl; Past Hnrd Queen-Intl Ordr Of Jobs Dghtr Bethl #106; 1st Pl Cty Cmptn-Pblc Spkng; Penn ST; Bio.

BEAVERS, ERIN M; Cordova HS; Rancho Cordova, CA; (3); Church Yth Grp; Key Clb; Model UN; SADD; Orch; Rep Frsh Cls; Rep Soph Cls; Rep Jr Cls; Rep Sr Cls; JV Bsktbl; Campfire Boys & Girls; USS Swmmng Tm; San Francisco ST; Psych.

BEAVERS, JAMIE R; Brawley Union HS; Brawley, CA; (3); Treas Church Yth Grp; FBLA; Math Tm; High Hon Roll; CSF; Bus.

BEBAWI, JIHAN; St Monica Catholic HS; Los Angeles, CA; (2); Church Yth Grp; Cmnty Wkr; English Clb; French Clb; Chorus; Church Choir; Rptr Nwsp; Pres Soph Cls; Hon Roll; NHS; Outstndng Ldrshp Awd; Med.

BEBB, CHRISTINE; Notre Dame Acad; Culver City, CA; (4); 5/120; Sftbl; Dance Clb; French Clb; Girl Scts; VP SADD; Trk; Elks Awd; Hon Roll; NHS; Ntl Merit Schol; CA Schlrshp Fed; Schlstc All Amer 88; Silver Ldrshp Awd; Marian Awd; UC San Diego; Aerospace Engrng.

BEBOUX, CYNTHIA L; Carlmont HS; Redwood City, CA; (3); Church Yth Grp; Cmnty Wkr; Key Clb; Teachers Aide; Hon Roll; Notre Dame; Psych.

BECERRA, ANA E; Canyon HS; Canyon Country, CA; (2); French Clb; Hon Roll; Word Proc.

BECERRA, BRAD L; Kingsburg HS; Kingsburg, CA; (1); Church Yth Grp; FFA; Hon Roll; Envrnmtl Clb; Meat Jdg Team; Air Force Acad; Pilot.

BECERRA, DAVID; Southwest HS; San Ysidro, CA; (2); Key Clb; Intrml Bsktbl; JV Trk; Var Cit Awd; Hon Roll; Outstndng Engl Stu; UCSD; Educ.

BECERRA, JOEY M; Chaffey HS; Ontario, CA; (1); Church Yth Grp; Rep Frsh Cls; Var Swmmng; High Hon Roll; CSF; Physics.

BECERRA, LAURA I; Paramount HS; Paramount, CA; (2); UCLA; Psych.

BECERRA, LOUIE; Pomona HS; Pomona, CA; (3); Letterman Clb; Varsity Clb; Var Ftbl; Var Capt Trk; Var Wt Lftg; Prfct Atten Awd; MECHA; USC; Poli Sci.

BECERRA, REENA A; Merced North Campus HS; Merced, CA; (3); Office Aide; Science Clb; Spanish Clb; Hon Roll; Prfct Atten Awd; Marine Bio.

BECERRA, STEPHANIE; Chaffey HS; Ontario, CA; (3); 15/400; Church Yth Grp; Cmnty Wkr; Office Aide; Gym; Powder Puff Ftbl; High Hon Roll; Snow Skiing; Camp Counselor; Cngrssnl Yth Ldrshp Cncl; Law.

BECERRA, VERONICA; Ramona Convent HS; Montebello, CA; (3); Hosp Aide; Spanish Clb; Chrmn Stu Cncl; Var Swmmng; Loyola Marymount.

BECERRA, VILMER; Channel Islands HS; Oxnard, CA; (1); Art Clb; Bsbl; Prfct Atten Awd; UCSC; Law.

BECERRIL, ALMA D; Palo Verde HS; Blythe, CA; (4); 26/130; Pres Church Yth Grp; Sec Latin Clb; Pep Clb; Spanish Clb; Chorus; Flag Corp; High Hon Roll; Palo Verde Cmmnty JC; Scl Work.

BECHAR, RANI; Canyon Springs HS; Moreno Valley, CA; (3); Hosp Aide; Intnl Clb; Teachers Aide; Hon Roll; U Of CA; Envrnmntl Toxicology.

BECHTEL, MATT; Damien HS; Rancho Cucamonga, CA; (2); 69/268; Debate Tm; Speech Tm; Chorus; Off Frsh Cls; JV Bsbl; JV Capt Ftbl; Hon Roll; U Of Southern CA.

BECHTEL, RICHARD; Armijo HS; Fairfield, CA; (3); AFS; Key Clb; Hon Roll; Prfct Atten Awd; 1st Dgr Blck Blt Karate; Asian-Amrcn Clb; CSF; Pre-Med.

BECHTLE, TARINA G; Armijo HS; Suisun City, CA; (4); AFS; Church Yth Grp; SADD; Treas Band; Chorus; Color Guard; Jazz Band; Mrchg Band; Orch; Pep Band; Solano CC; Chrprctc.

BECHTOL, CHRISTOPHER P; Napa HS; Napa, CA; (2); Var L Crs Cntry; Var Capt Trk; Hon Roll; UC Santa Barbara; Hstry.

BECHTOL, MICHAEL J; Napa HS; Napa, CA; (1); Capt L Bsktbl; L Ftbl; L Trk; High Hon Roll; Bus Skls Awd; Stanford.

BECK, ANN M; North Salinas HS; Salinas, CA; (2); FFA; Teachers Aide; High Hon Roll; Hon Roll; FFA Awds; Santa Cruz Co JR Fairbrd.

BECK, BRENDA S; Fontana HS; Fontana, CA; (2); Ski Clb; Co-Capt Drill Tm; School Play; Hist Stu Cncl; JV Cheerldng; Pom Pon; Hon Roll.

BECK, BRYAN; Sonora HS; Sonora, CA; (3); Church Yth Grp; Teachers Aide; JV Bsktbl; High Hon Roll; Hon Roll; Pres Acad Fit Awd.

BECK, CARMELA; Academy Of Our Lady Of Peace; San Diego, CA; (1); Church Yth Grp; Latin Clb; Spanish Clb; School Musical; Sec Frsh Cls; Crs Cntry; Socr; Hon Roll; NHS; U Of CA Berkeley; Lawyer.

BECK, CAROLINE E; Vista HS; Vista, CA; (3); 13/400; Pep Clb; Teachers Aide; Var JV Bsktbl; JV Crs Cntry; Var JV Fld Hcky; Var JV Sftbl; High Hon Roll; Amer Cancer Soc Rsrch Salk Inst; U Of CA San Diego; Med.

BECK, CARRIE E; Tustin HS; Tustin, CA; (2); Hosp Aide; Sec Frsh Cls; Soph Cls; Pres Jr Cls; JV Pom Pon; JV Tennis; Hon Roll.

BECK, CRYSTAL Y; Viewpoint Schl; Agoura Hills, CA; (3); Drama Clb; Office Aide; Service Clb; Chorus; School Play; Ed Yrbk; Lit Mag; VP Frsh Cls; Pres VP Stu Cncl; Mgr(s); Spch.

BECK, DANIEL A; San Marcos HS; Santa Barbara, CA; (2); Boy Scts; Church Yth Grp; VP German Clb; Hon Roll; Phy.

BECK, ERIC S; Villa Park HS; Orange, CA; (2); Rptr Nwsp; JV Crs Cntry; Hon Roll; Prfct Atten Awd; Orange Cnty Acad Decathlon Tm; Hstry.

BECK, GENA R; Modesto HS; Modesto, CA; (1); Drama Clb; German Clb; Davis; Zoology.

BECK, JENNIFER A; Redlands HS; Redlands, CA; (4); 60/861; Mgr Nwsp; Intrml Sftbl; Pres Acad Fit Awd; CSF; Daisy Chn; Kimberly Jr Hosptly Cmmssnr; San Diego ST U; Bus Admin.

BECK, JENNIFER C; Tulare Union HS; Earlimart, CA; (3); 106/500; Teachers Aide; Band; Mrchg Band; Hon Roll; Prfct Atten Awd; All Amer Hall Of Fame Band Hnrs; Coll Of Sequois; Music.

BECK, JENNIFER E; Thomas Downey HS; Modesto, CA; (3); AFS; Church Yth Grp; Cmnty Wkr; Debate Tm; Drama Clb; French Clb; Key Clb; NFL; Pep Clb; Speech Tm; Rtry Intl Camp Royal; Intl Rel.

BECK, JUSTIN M; Glendora HS; Glendora, CA; (4); 50/430; Boy Scts; Church Yth Grp; Debate Tm; Key Clb; Speech Tm; Church Choir; Hon Roll; People To People Org Stu Ambssdr; Brigham Young U; Real Est Inv.

BECK, JUSTIN R; Riverside Poly HS; Riverside, CA; (3); 4/300; FBLA; Key Clb; Quiz Bowl; Nwsp; JV Tennis; High Hon Roll; Spanish NHS; Mock Trial 5th Pl ST Comp; Rensselaer Mdl Outstndng Math & Sci; Natl Acad Champ; Engrng.

BECK, KASI D; Tulare Union HS; Tulare, CA; (2); Church Yth Grp; Dance Clb; Drama Clb; Pep Clb; Speech Tm; Band; Church Choir; Mrchg Band; Pep Band; School Play; Hi-Debs; Miss Tulare Pgnt Entrnmnt Singer 89-91; Sch Rcgntn Gldn St Exam & CSF.

BECK, KATHLEEN M; Edison HS; Huntington Beach, CA; (2); Church Yth Grp; Hosp Aide; Hon Roll; Pres Acad Fit Awd; Aide Chrstn Elem Schl; 1st Chrstn Church Huntington Bch Yth Grp; Cal ST Fullerton; Elem Ed.

BECK, KELLY L; Moreno Valley HS; Moreno Valley, CA; (3); 54/520; Yrbk; Lit Mag; High Hon Roll; Bowling Leag; Library Aide; Sci.

BECK, KIMBERLEE J; Fontana HS; Fontana, CA; (2); Office Aide; Mrchg Band; Rep Stu Cncl; Var Bsktbl; Hon Roll; Hnr Club; Comm.

BECK, KRISTY M; Mayfair HS; Lakewood, CA; (3); GAA; Pep Clb; Varsity Clb; Intrml Cheerldng; JV Var Sftbl; JV Var Vllybl; Hon Roll; 1st Tm All Leag Sftbl; Chiropractics.

BECK, LOREN H; Woodbridge HS; Irvine, CA; (3); VP JA; JV Var Bsktbl; JV Ftbl; Var Golf; Intrml Vllybl; Boys/Girls Clb Bsktbl Coach; Pepperdine U; Bus Admin.

BECK, MARLENE; Hoopa HS; Willow Creek, CA; (3); Cit Awd; High Hon Roll; Hon Roll; CA Schlrshp Fed; Jrnlsm.

BECK, MELISSA; Polytechnic HS; Arleta, CA; (3); Yrbk; CSUN; Comp Sci.

BECK, MELISSA; South Lake Tahoe HS; South Lake Tahoe, CA; (4); Computer Clb; VP Math Clb; Band; Pep Band; Powder Puff Ftbl; ROP Television Prdctn Tech Dir; Phrmcy.

BECK, RACHEL H; O Farrell SCPA HS; San Diego, CA; (3); #1 In Class; Quiz Bowl; School Play; Stage Crew; High Hon Roll; Poltcl Sci.

BECK, RAYMOND D; Durham HS; Durham, CA; (2); Church Yth Grp; Cmnty Wkr; Letterman Clb; VP Ski Clb; Yrbk; Rep Soph Cls; Stu Cncl; Var Bsbl; Var JV Bsktbl; JV Capt Ftbl; Gftd & Tlntd Educ; CSF; Bsktbl Congrss Intl Smmr Prep Trmnt; Commnctns.

BECK, SHANNON; St Francis HS; Los Altos, CA; (3); SADD; School Musical; JV Var Cheerldng; JV Gym; High Hon Roll; Hon Roll; BYU; Psych.

BECK, SHAUNA; Chester JR SR HS; Chester, CA; (4); 17/55; Library Aide; Teachers Aide; Temple Yth Grp; Rep Nwsp; Phtg Yrbk; VP Cheerldng; VP JV Powder Puff Ftbl; Sec JV Trk; Sec Wrstlng; High Hon Roll; Lassen Coll; Bus Admin.

BECK, SHIRA F; Concord HS; Beverly Hills, CA; (4); Sonoma ST U; Psych.

BECK, STEPHANI D; Winters HS; Winters, CA; (2); Church Yth Grp; Library Aide; SADD; Hon Roll; Friday Night Live; Life Bible Coll.

BECK, TASHA C.; Millikan HS; Long Beach, CA; (4); 150/694; Church Yth Grp; Drama Clb; ROTC; Band; L Drill Tm; L Bsktbl; Prfct Atten Awd; Jazz Band; Mrchg Band; School Musical; Phys Ftnss Medal; Medallion Awd Wnnr; Persnl Apprnc Trphs; Long Beach City Coll; Bus.

BECK, TRACY K; Bret Harte HS; Vallecito, CA; (2); FFA; Pep Clb; Ski Clb; Cheerldng; Pom Pon; Hon Roll; FFA Grnhnd VP, Chptr VP 89, 90; FFA Natl Cnvntn Trip Top Pnt Wnnr; Cal Poly; Tchr.

BECKA, MICHELLE; Woodbridge HS; Irvine, CA; (4); 68/379; Church Yth Grp; Cmnty Wkr; Dance Clb; Pep Clb; Ski Clb; Chorus; Drill Tm; Cheerldng; High Hon Roll; Pres Acad Fit Awd; CSF; Natl Chrty Leag; Grls Leag; AZ ST U.

BECKER, BRIAN J; Garden Grove HS; Garden Grove, CA; (3); 23/336; High Hon Roll; Hon Roll.

BECKER, BROOKE E; Woodside HS; Redwood City, CA; (2); 73/391; Church Yth Grp; Cmnty Wkr; St Schlr; UCLA; Bus Admin.

BECKER, KELLIE A; Louisville HS; Woodland Hills, CA; (3); Art Clb; Dance Clb; FHA; Chorus; School Musical; School Play; Stu Cncl; Hon Roll; U CA; Tchr.

BECKER, LISA; Oak Park HS; Agoura Hills, CA; (1); #8 In Class; Key Clb; JV Sftbl; JV Vllybl; Hon Roll; Piano; Peer Cnslng; OH ST U.

BECKER, MOLLY; Skyline HS; Oakland, CA; (2); Church Yth Grp; Debate Tm; Chorus; Rptr Phtg Nwsp; Rptr Phtg Yrbk; Ed Lit Mag; Cheerldng; Pres Acad Fit Awd; Peer Cnslng; Princeton; Bus.

BECKER, STEFAN; Orange Glen HS; Escondido, CA; (4); Art Clb; Dance Clb; Drama Clb; German Clb; Thesps; Chorus; Drama Dept Apprctn Awd; Juilliard Schl; Drama.

BECKER, TRACY; Lower Lake HS; Clearlake, CA; (3); 2/200; Church Yth Grp; SADD; VP Jr Cls; Cheerldng; High Hon Roll; Sal; CSF; UC Davis; Vet Sci.

BECKER, TRACY L; Lower Lake HS; Soulsbyville, CA; (3); 2/300; Am Leg Aux Girls St; Church Yth Grp; VP Jr Cls; Cheerldng; Pom Pon; High Hon Roll; Outstndng Stu Orgnztn; UC Davis; Vet Sci.

BECKERLEG, NICOLE; Foothill HS; Pleasanton, CA; (3); Ski Clb; Spanish Clb; Teachers Aide; High Hon Roll; Hon Roll; Spcl Hnrs Bio; Envrnmntlst Clb; CSULB; Ed/Lang.

BECKERS, STEVEN; Ocean View HS; Solvang, CA; (3); German Clb; JV Crs Cntry; JV Trk; Mba.

BECKETT, ROBERT J; Casa Grande HS; Petaluma, CA; (3); Hon Roll; NHS; Ntl Merit Ltr; Escllnt Achvt Awd In Chem; Jr Eng; Sacram St U; Adv Major.

BECKETT, SARAH; Branham HS; San Jose, CA; (1); Pep Band; Capt Cheerldng; SDSU; Obstetrician.

BECKHAM, CRISTIN T; Mountain View HS; Mountain View, CA; (3); 44/346; Rep Church Yth Grp; Dance Clb; Pres Girl Scts; Red Cross Aide; Rep Band; Color Guard; Mrchg Band; Orch; Pep Band; Var Socr; Grl Sct Gld Ldrshp Awd; 1 Of 8 Grl Scts Trvld To Norway Stu Exch; Brdcst Jrnlsm.

BECKHAM, DIDI; Chula Vista HS; San Ysidro, CA; (2); Aud/Vis; Dance Clb; Flag Corp; Mrchg Band; Stage Crew; Cit Awd; Stage Tech; Dnc Cls; Nrsng.

BECKHAM II, JACK MARLIN; North HS; Bakersfield, CA; (2); Boy Scts; Church Yth Grp; ROTC; Teachers Aide; Temple Yth Grp; Drill Tm; Hon Roll; BYU; Engl Ed.

BECKHART, CHRISTINA A; Modesto HS; Ceres, CA; (3); Girl Scts; Pep Clb; Swmmng; Girls Var Water Polo; Modesto JC; Sci.

BECKLEY, CASEY ANN; Bishop Montgomery HS; Redondo Beach, CA; (2); Hon Roll; Campus Mnstry; CA Schlrshp Fdrtn; Job-Ins Agncy; Finance.

BECKMAN, JACOB H; Chula Vista Schl; San Diego, CA; (1); 1/216; Church Yth Grp; Library Aide; Math Tm; Scholastic Bowl; Hon Roll; Pres Acad Fit Awd; High Hnrs-Golden St Exam Geom; CSF Mem; Jr Statesmen Of America Mem; Bio.

BECKMANN, BIANCA G; Norte Vista HS; Riverside, CA; (4); 29/281; Church Yth Grp; Dance Clb; French Clb; Office Aide; Variety Show; Cit Awd; High Hon Roll; Hon Roll; 6th Grade Camp Cnslr; Riverside CC; Lang.

BECKNER, AMY; West Valley Christian HS; Woodland Hills, CA; (4); 2/8; Church Yth Grp; Drama Clb; Speech Tm; Church Choir; School Play; Variety Show; Sec Stu Cncl; Vllybl; High Hon Roll; Val; Pacific Chrstn Coll; Psych.

BECKSTEAD, AMY L; College Park HS; Martinez, CA; (1); Church Yth Grp; Church Choir; Rptr Nwsp; Bsktbl; JV Sftbl; Cit Awd; Hon Roll; Prfct Atten Awd; Pres Of Church Yth Group; Babysit; Voice Lessons; Brigham Young U.

BECKWITH, MARCO MING; Mills HS; Hillsborough, CA; (2); Boy Scts; Cmnty Wkr; Ski Clb; High Honors Golden State Exams Algebra; School Recognition Golden State Geometry; Skiing; UC Davis; Biochemistry.

BECKWITH, TARO J; La Quinta HS; Westminster, CA; (4); Boy Scts; Cmnty Wkr; German Clb; Treas Key Clb; Latin Clb; L Var Crs Cntry; L Var Swmmng; NHS; Water Polo; UC San Diego; Psych.

BECRIS, NICK P; Leffingwell Christian HS; La Mirada, CA; (3); JV Bsktbl; Outstdng Eng III; CA U Irvne; Med.

BEDAYN, BRIANNA; Berean Christian HS; Danville, CA; (2); Church Yth Grp; Sec Treas Soph Cls; JV Cheerldng; High Hon Roll; Pres Schlr; Piano Stu.

BEDERIO, MARIE J; Beaumont HS; Banning, CA; (4); 1/139; Church Chior; Stat Bsktbl; Var L Crs Cntry; Var L Trk; NHS; Ntl Merit Ltr; Pres Acad Fit Awd; Val; Sch Site Cncl Sec; Bsktbl Hmcmng Queen; Biola U; General Studies.

BEDFORD, CHRISSY M; Ponderosa HS; Rescue, CA; (3); 4-H; French Clb; Teachers Aide; School Play; Var Sftbl; 4-H Awd; Interior Decor.

BEDFORD, JENNIFER R; Rancho Cotate HS; Rohnert Park, CA; (3); 8/400; Dance Clb; Drama Clb; Thesps; School Play; Stage Crew; High Hon Roll; Hon Roll; NHS; Smmr 90 Stu Exchng Pgm; Secy/Treas Drama Clb; Katherine Wheeler Dancer; Comp Engrng.

BEDFORD, KURTIS L; Sherman Oaks Ctr For Enriche Studies; Reseda, CA; (3); Cmnty Wkr; Debate Tm; Letterman Clb; NFL; Speech Tm; School Play; Stage Crew; Ftbl; Trk; Wt Lftg; Thtr.

BEDFORD, NICOLLE A; Lincoln HS; Stockton, CA; (3); Hosp Aide; Library Aide; Teachers Aide; Chorus; Swmmng; Hon Roll; Spec Olymps; Ordr Fainbow; Delta JC; Librarian.

BEDFORD, VANESSA; Mills JR HS; Rancho Cordova, CA; (1); Girl Scts; Science Clb; Chorus; Orch; Rep Frsh Cls; Rep Stu Cncl; Bsktbl; Cheerldng; Swmmng; High Hon Roll; Spelman Coll; Engl Lit.

BEDGOOD, BILL; William S Hart HS; Valencia, CA; (2); JV Bsbl; JV Bsktbl; Coll Schlrshp Fund; Acad Excllnc Awd Golden St Exam Geom With Hnrs; Comp Sci.

BEDI, STEPHANIE M; San Dimas HS; San Dimas, CA; (2); GAA; Var Bsktbl; Var Trk; Var Vllybl; High Hon Roll; Hon Roll; Pres Acad Fit Awd; ASB Treas; UCLA; Sprts Med.

BEDNAR, JOBY SETH; San Rafael HS; San Rafael, CA; (2); Chess Clb; Church Yth Grp; Computer Clb; German Clb; CSF; Golden St Exam Geom Hgh Hnrs; Prof Art Shwngs; CA Tech; Psych.

BEDOLLO, KARINA; Arvin HS; Arvin, CA; (1); Computer Clb; Math Clb; Science Clb; JV Bsbl; JV Sftbl; JV Vllybl; Hon Roll; UCLA; Lawyer.

BEDROSIAN, BRIAN; Clovis HS; Sanger, CA; (3); Drama Clb; Spanish Clb; High Hon Roll; CSF; Bus.

BEDROSIAN, MICHELLE L; San Marino HS; San Marino, CA; (4); 16/252; Church Yth Grp; Cmnty Wkr; Dance Clb; Math Clb; Science Clb; Service Clb; Ski Clb; Teachers Aide; School Play; Stu Cncl; Jr Advsry Bd; Stu Comm For Accreditation; CARE Cnslr; U S CA; Frnsc Psych.

BEDROSIAN, PATRICIA ANTOINETTE; Marina HS; Huntington Beach, CA; (3); 91/500; Latin Clb; Office Aide; Science Clb; Service Clb; Stage Crew; Stage Crew; Intrml Trk; Hon Roll; Jr NHS; Polaris Clb Pres 1989-90 & Treas 1990-91; JR Aux Mem 1989-90 & Secy; Dominican Coll; Med.

BEE, ALICIA D; Bonita Vista HS; Bonita, CA; (2); Church Yth Grp; Drama Clb; Model UN; Office Aide; Cit Awd; Psych.

BEE, LEE; Grace M Davis HS; Modesto, CA; (2); FBLA; Key Clb; VICA; Treas Stu Cncl; JV Swmmng; Cit Awd; Hon Roll; St Schlr; 1st Pl Bus Math Cntrl CA FBLA Conf; Hgh Hnr Golden St Math Exam; Schl Pursuit Of Excllnc Awd; Stanford U; Med.

BEEBE, MARGARET L; East Union HS; Manteca, CA; (1); 12/439; Church Yth Grp; Swmmng; High Hon Roll; Education.

BEECHICK, BEN A; El Dorado HS; Pollock Pines, CA; (4); Church Yth Grp; Library Aide; Math Tm; VP Science Clb; Var Bsktbl; Var Crs Cntry; Var Trk; Pres Acad Fit Awd; Hnrs Entrance Westmont Coll; Bank Of America Math Achvmt Awd; Westmont Coll; Cmptr Sci.

BEECKMAN, JEANNIE; Liberty Union HS; Byron, CA; (2); VP 4-H; Letterman Clb; Band; Chorus; JV Bsbl; Stat Trk; JV Vllybl; Hon Roll; Accntng.

BEEDON, TRICIA A; South Pasadena HS; South Pasadena, CA; (2); SADD; Law Clb; Histry.

BEEDY, TRAVIS D; Chino HS; Chino, CA; (3); Teachers Aide; Band; High Hon Roll; Hon Roll; JV Badmntn; Cal Poly Pomona; Aerontcs.

BEEMAN, DAWN M; Victor Valley HS; Victorville, CA; (1); Drill Tm; San Bernardino Cnty Shrffs Explr Scts; Amer Rd Crss Vlntr; Atty.

BEEMAN, JENNA R; Porterville HS; Springville, CA; (3); Church Yth Grp; Chorus; Church Choir; Hon Roll; Bethany Bible Coll; Psych.

BEER, SARAH S; Alta Loma HS; Rancho Cucamonga, CA; (4); 52/420; Church Yth Grp; Mrchg Band; JV Swmmng; High Hon Roll; Hon Roll; Azusa Pacific U; Pre-Med.

BEERMAN, DAVID A; Carmel HS; Carmel, CA; (3); Rep Frsh Cls; VP Soph Cls; VP Stu Cncl; JV Var Ftbl; Var Trk; DAR Awd; High Hon Roll; Pres Acad Fit Awd; CSF; Engrng.

BEERS, CINDY; Poway HS; Poway, CA; (4); Varsity Clb; Stat Bsktbl; Var Capt Trk; JV Capt Vllybl; Cit Awd; Miramar Coll; Fire Fighter.

BEERS, ELIZABETH L; Chino HS; Chino, CA; (3); 10/610; Church Yth Grp; Teachers Aide; Varsity Clb; Var Bsktbl; High Hon Roll; All League, Vly, Cty, CIF Bsktbl Plyr; Slvrspr Acad Awd; Med.

BEERS, EMILY L; Chino HS; Chino, CA; (4); 20/609; Church Yth Grp; Cmnty Wkr; Treas FHA; Office Aide; Teachers Aide; JV Var Bsktbl; JV Vllybl; High Hon Roll; Hon Roll; St Schlr; Fresno ST U; Physcl Thrpy.

BEERS, JULIE A; Lompoc HS; Lompoc, CA; (4); Church Yth Grp; Dance Clb; FFA; Sec FTA; Letterman Clb; Pep Clb; Drill Tm; Stu Cncl; Var L Cheerldng; Var Swmmng; Slvr St Emblm Awd; ,Th St Flrcltre; Chico ST; Liberal Stds.

BEERY, MARIANNA D; La Habra HS; Whittier, CA; (3); Drama Clb; Pep Clb; Teachers Aide; Chorus; School Play; Stage Crew; Variety Show; Nwsp; Cit Awd; High Hon Roll.

BEESLEY, CHENOA A; Monrovia HS; Monrovia, CA; (4); Var Crs Cntry; Var Socr; Var Trk; Brigham Young U; MBA.

BEESON, J C; Santa Monica HS; Santa Monica, CA; (2); Band; Mrchg Band; Pep Band; Var L Trk; Hon Roll; Jr NHS; Prfct Atten Awd; Pres Acad Fit Awd; JV Trk MVP Awd 90; Arch.

BEETSCHEN, BARBI J; Rim Of The World HS; Crestline, CA; (3); 25/259; Aud/Vis; Computer Clb; Dance Clb; Spanish Clb; Teachers Aide; Color Guard; Flag Corp; Prfct Atten Awd; Tlcmmnctns.

BEGAY, WINIFRED; Oceanside HS; Oceanside, CA; (3); Cmnty Wkr; Rptr Nwsp; Sec Frsh Cls; Cit Awd; Hon Roll.

BEGIN, KRISTINE E; Calvary Christian HS; Ridgecrest, CA; (4); 1/8; Church Yth Grp; Drama Clb; Pep Clb; Ski Clb; Nwsp; Ed Yrbk; Rep Sr Cls; Stu Cncl; JV Var Bsktbl; Var Cheerldng; Sngldng Squad; Advncd Bible Cls; Coll Weight Trning Cls.

BEGINES, GRISELDA P; Santa Clara HS; Santa Clara, CA; (2); Service Clb; Spanish Clb; Socr; Hnrs Engl; Stat Girl Wrstlng Tm; CSF; Wilderness Adventures Clb; Stanford; Law.

BEGLEY, JASON S; Bellarmine Jefferson HS; Burbank, CA; (4); 4/112; Quiz Bowl; Off Sr Cls; Var Capt Ftbl; Vllybl; Hon Roll; NHS; Surfing; Bk Of Amer Sci Scholar; Ntl Ftbl Fed Schlr/Athl; UCLA; Med.

BEHAN, SEAN; Bonita Vista HS; Chula Vista, CA; (4); 67/521; Treas Church Yth Grp; Key Clb; Model UN; JV Var Ftbl; Cit Awd; High Hon Roll; Hon Roll; Var Ftbl; Var Socr; Hgh Hnrs Geo; Trib All Acad Tm; CA U Sn Dgo; Crimnlgy.

BEHLENDORF, BRIAN E; La Canada HS; La Canada Flintri, CA; (3); 7/200; Aud/Vis; Chess Clb; Intnl Clb; Key Clb; Math Clb; Scholastic Bowl; Spanish Clb; Nwsp; Treas Frsh Cls; Var Crs Cntry; Dir Space Explrtn Post 509; Annl Space Set Cmptn; Prod Video Yrbk For Sch Sold 80; Disc Jockey; Sci.

BEHMER, JENNIFER; Victor Valley HS; Victorville, CA; (4); 32/420; Cmnty Wkr; Model UN; Pep Clb; Teachers Aide; Varsity Clb; Var L Cheerldng; High Hon Roll; Hon Roll; Tchr.

BEHNAM, GINE B; Gladstone HS; Azusa, CA; (4); French Clb; High Hon Roll; Karate Green Blt; Citrus Coll; Htl Mgr.

BEHNKEN, TIMOTHY V; Orange Lutheran HS; Mission Viejo, CA; (2); Church Yth Grp; Band; Stage Crew; U Of CA Irvine; Physcn.

BEHRMANN, STACY L; Etiwanda HS; Alta Loma, CA; (4); 123/521; Church Yth Grp; Ed Yrbk; Rep Stu Cncl; Var Capt Bsktbl; Var Capt Sftbl; Hon Roll; ASB Presidents Award; Service Award-50 Hrs Of Service To Staff/Students And School; Northern AZ U; Communitactions.

BEHUNIN, JONATHAN RAY; Fountain Valley HS; Westminster, CA; (2); Boy Scts; Church Yth Grp; Jazz Band; Mrchg Band; Orch; Rep Soph Cls; JV Trk; JV Wrstlng; High Hon Roll; Pres Acad Fit Awd; BYU; Aviation.

BEHYMER, GABRIEL D; Summerville Union HS; Tuolumne, CA; (3); French Clb; Spanish Clb; Band; Color Guard; Jazz Band; Mrchg Band; Var L Socr; Hon Roll; Gldn St Exam Acad Excel Awd Hnrs In Algebra & Hgh Hnrs In Geo; 6 Wks Smmr Live In Lussac, France; Aerospc.

BEIER, JEFF S; William S Hart HS; Newhall, CA; (2); Church Yth Grp; FBLA; SADD; Rptr Soph Cls; JV Bsbl; JV Bsktbl; JV Ftbl; Powder Puff Ftbl; CSF CA Schlrshp Fed; Cls Rep Orient Incmng Frsh; Med.

BEIG, ABDUL-JABBAR; Mount Whitney HS; Visalia, CA; (4); 17/373; Treas Art Clb; Pres Church Yth Grp; VP Computer Clb; Debate Tm; Math Clb; NFL; L Crs Cntry; L Trk; AFS; VP Chess Clb; CSF; Musum Yth Of N Amer Exec Cmmtte 88-90; U CA Berkeley; Chem.

BEIMER, CHRISTINE M; Mission Viejo HS; Mission Viejo, CA; (3); Church Yth Grp; Dance Clb; Key Clb; Model UN; Office Aide; Pep Clb; Acpl Chr; Chorus; Church Choir; School Musical; Child Psych.

BEJAR, MARIA G; Anaheim HS; Anaheim, CA; (3); Debate Tm; German Clb; Hon Roll; UP Stu; Santa Monica Coll; Paralegal.

BEJJANI, SALMA; Arlington HS; Riverside, CA; (3); 4/437; Sec Treas Church Yth Grp; Church Choir; High Hon Roll; Loma Linda U; Pre-Med.

BELANGER, CHRISTY J; St Patricks/St Vincents HS; Suisun, CA; (1); Church Yth Grp; French Clb; Church Choir; Pres Frsh Cls; Var Bsbl; Var Cheerldng; Med.

BELCHER, MARCIA; Lemoore HS; Lemoore, CA; (3); Office Aide; Red Cross Aide; SADD; Teachers Aide; Flag Corp; Score Keeper; Cit Awd; Hon Roll; Vol Work, Snackbars, Ftbl Games; Nrsng.

BELD, BRIAN R; Mt Whitney HS; Visalia, CA; (1); Orch; JV Socr; JV Tennis; Hon Roll; CA Schlrshp Fed; Acad Ltr.

BELDING, JESSALYNN ANN; Bear River HS; Grass Valley, CA; (4); 6/150; Science Clb; Sec Treas Yrbk; Rep Frsh Cls; Rep Soph Cls; Rep Jr Cls; Var Capt Sftbl; Cit Awd; High Hon Roll; CSF; Principals Lttr Awd; U Denver CO; Med.

BELDON, KATHLEEN; Tamalpais HS; Mill Valley, CA; (3); SADD; Acpl Chr; Chorus; Rptr Nwsp; Cheerldng; Gym; Sftbl; Vllybl; High Hon Roll; Teachers Aide; Impct Tm; Acctg.

BELEN, MARCEL; Saint Anthony HS; Long Beach, CA; (2); Boy Scts; JV Var Ftbl; JV Trk; High Hon Roll; Hon Roll; Prfct Atten Awd; Chrstn Svc Veterans; World Hist Wad; Hnrs Cls Prgm Geomtry & Bio; Cal ST Fulerton; Cmptr Prgm.

BELEN, RAMONETTE; Downey HS; Downey, CA; (3); 89/610; Art Clb; Spanish Clb; Teachers Aide; Var JV Tennis; Cit Awd; Prfct Atten Awd; UCLA; Jrnlsm.

BELENKY, DIANA S; George Washington HS; San Francisco, CA; (3); Cmnty Wkr; Drama Clb; Temple Yth Grp; School Play; Variety Show; Hon Roll; Cnclr 2 Yrs & Vice Chmn Of Bd Bnei Akiva, Jewish Yth Group; SFSU; Med Illustrator.

BELENSON, ELIZABETH J; Mountain View Acad; San Francisco, CA; (3); Office Aide; Spanish Clb; Chorus; Church Choir; Ed Yrbk; Pres Soph Cls; Sftbl; Cit Awd; Hon Roll; San Francisco ST U; Law.

BELIGAN, CHRISTINE M; Notre Dame Acad; Los Angeles, CA; (3); Dance Clb; Debate Tm; Drama Clb; English Clb; French Clb; Model UN; Pep Clb; SADD; Teachers Aide; Drill Tm; Usc; Poly Sci.

BELISLE, TRISK E; Vacaville HS; Vacaville, CA; (3); Boy Scts; Scholastic Bowl; School Play; Trk; Hon Roll; CA ST U; Arch Engr.

BELL, ALFONZO M; Balboa HS; San Francisco, CA; (2); Off Soph Cls; Bsktbl; Ftbl; Cit Awd; Hon Roll; Black Stu Union; 100 Bucs Srvce Soc; Notre Dame; Bus.

BELL, ANNA-MARIE L; Cajon HS; San Bernardino, CA; (3); Church Yth Grp; Hon Roll; Hsptl Vlntr Wrk; Nrsng.

BELL, BENJAMIN L; Vacaville HS; Vacaville, CA; (4); Boy Scts; Pres Church Yth Grp; Varsity Clb; Band; JV Bsbl; Var Ftbl; Var Wrstlng; High Hon Roll; NHS; UC Davis; Sprts Med.

BELL, CARRIE E; Bullard HS; Fresno, CA; (1); Cmnty Wkr; English Clb; Key Clb; NFL; Ski Clb; SADD; Lit Mag; Rep Pep Band; Rep Stu Cncl; High Hon Roll; CSF; GATE; U Of CA; Psych.

BELL, CHARISSA L; Los Alamitos HS; Stanton, CA; (4); Teachers Aide; Chorus; Hon Roll; Grmn Amer Prtnrshp Pgm; Cypress Coll; Arch.

BELL, CHRIS J; Casa Robles HS; Citrus Heights, CA; (2); AFS; 4-H; Stage Crew; DECA; High Hon Roll; Hon Roll; NHS; U CA; Corp Law.

BELL, DAMON AMIRI; Morse HS; San Diego, CA; (4); 121/600; Church Yth Grp; Chorus; Church Choir; Lit Mag; Trk; Cit Awd; Hon Roll; Masonic Awd; Alpha Phi Alpha Acad Excllnc Pgm; San Diego Metro Schlrshp Recpnt; LIVE Inc Bk Schlrshp; Clark Atlant U; Clncl Psych.

BELL, DEBBIE M; West HS; Bakersfield, CA; (3); 38/438; Library Aide; Office Aide; Spanish Clb; Teachers Aide; Chorus; School Musical; Swing Chorus; Hon Roll; Spanish NHS; Law.

BELL, DEBRA L; Grace Davis HS; Salida, CA; (3); Bus Profs of Am; Office Aide; Red Cross Aide; Teachers Aide; Acpl Chr; Chorus; Powder Puff Ftbl; Sftbl; Vllybl; Hon Roll; U Of Southern CA; Med.

BELL, DHANNA M; Bloomington HS; Bloomington, CA; (4); Church Yth Grp; Drama Clb; Thesps; School Musical; School Play; Ed Nwsp; Ed Lit Mag; Rep Stu Cncl; Var Capt Cheerldng; High Hon Roll; CA Gftd & Tlntd Pgm; CA St Smmr Schl For Arts Grad 89; Theatre Arts Ltr; Ldrshp Cls; Howard U; Engl.

BELL, EDWARD C; Santa Paula Union HS; Santa Paula, CA; (1).

BELL, ERICA K; Torrey Pines HS; Del Mar, CA; (3); 109/457; JV Fld Hcky.

BELL, ERIN L; Bakersfield HS; Bakersfield, CA; (3); Church Yth Grp; Debate Tm; NFL; Service Clb; Speech Tm; Orch; School Musical; Phtg Ed Lit Mag; Hon Roll.

BELL, GYLA; Western HS; Buena Park, CA; (4); Art Clb; Church Yth Grp; Capt GAA; Pep Clb; Service Clb; SADD; Varsity Clb; Powder Puff Ftbl; Var Capt Socr; Var Capt Vllybl; Phys Thrpy.

BELL, HEATHER; Apple Valley HS; Lucerne Valley, CA; (3); Cmnty Wkr; FHA; Spanish Clb; VP Frsh Cls; VP Soph Cls; Var Sftbl; Var Vllybl; High Hon Roll; Vlntr In Spcl Olympcs; Ed.

BELL, HEATHER M; Liberty Union HS; Brentwood, CA; (2); 4-H; Girl Scts; Band; Jazz Band; Mrchg Band; Pep Band; Var L Swmmng; Hon Roll; St Schlr; Eng Spkng Unions Shakespr Cmptn Semi-Fnlst; Zoology.

BELL, JEANNIE R; Rim HS; Rimforest, CA; (2); Office Aide; Yrbk; Var Socr; Hon Roll; Prfct Atten Awd; Pres Acad Fit Awd; Police Explorer; AK; Marine Bio.

BELL, JENNIFER L; El Toro HS; El Toro, CA; (2); Girl Scts; Red Cross Aide; Acpl Chr; School Musical; Variety Show; Hon Roll; Red Cross Ldrshp Dev Center Delegate 1989, Staff 1990; GSA Silver Awd 1989; Teacher.

BELL, JENNIFER M; El Monte HS; El Monte, CA; (2); Church Yth Grp; German Clb; Hosp Aide; Band; Chorus; Church Choir; Mrchg Band; Pep Band; Cit Awd; High Hon Roll; Certfd Lifeguard; Yth Secy & Treas; Choir Secy & Treas; Doc.

BELL, KATHY A; East Nicolaus HS; Rio Oso, CA; (2); 12/55; Letterman Clb; Office Aide; Ski Clb; SADD; Teachers Aide; Var Bsktbl; JV Trk; Vllybl; Hon Roll; Pres Acad Fit Awd.

BELL, KEMBA; Lynwood Adventist Acad; Cerritos, CA; (4); 3/37; Aud/Vis; Church Yth Grp; GAA; Spanish Clb; Quiz Bowl; Scholastic Bowl; Teachers Aide; Varsity Clb; Church Choir; Nwsp; Oakwood Coll; Acctng.

BELL, KENA L; Gretchen A Whitney HS; Cerritos, CA; (4); Key Clb; Teachers Aide; Co-Ed Yrbk; Rep Frsh Cls; Rep Soph Cls; Rep Jr Cls; JV Cheerldng; Kiwanis Awd; Prom Comm; UC Berkeley.

BELL, KEYLA; Santa Monica HS; Santa Monica, CA; (2); Church Yth Grp; Church Choir; Stu Cncl; Bsktbl; Sftbl; UCLA; Law.

BELL, KIANDA K; Skyline HS; Oakland, CA; (2); Boy Scts; Church Yth Grp; Jazz Band; Yrbk; Var Tennis; Wt Lftg; Wrstlng; Cornell Med Schl; Sprts Med.

BELL, KRIS; Maxwell HS; Maxwell, CA; (2); FBLA; FFA; Band; Pres Soph Cls; Rep Stu Cncl; Var JV Bsktbl; Cheerldng; JV Vllybl; High Hon Roll; Pres Acad Fit Awd.

BELL, KRISTIN; Brethren JR/Sr HS; Long Beach, CA; (1); Pep Clb; Cheerldng; High Hon Roll; Opt Clb Awd.

BELL, MATT M; Tomales HS; Tomales, CA; (3); FFA; Letterman Clb; Ski Clb; SADD; Teachers Aide; JV Var Bsbl; Var Capt Bsktbl; Hon Roll.

BELL, MELISSA; Tulare Union HS; Tulare, CA; (2); #5 In Class; Church Yth Grp; Band; Mrchg Band; Hon Roll; CA Schlstc Fed; Brigham Young U.

BELL, MICHELLE; Fred C Beyer HS; Modesto, CA; (3); Math Clb; Pep Clb; Ski Clb; Rptr Nwsp; Rep Frsh Cls; Pres Soph Cls; Score Keeper; Hon Roll; Secy CSF; Pre-Med.

BELL, MICHELLE; West Shores HS; Salton City, CA; (4); Drama Clb; Key Clb; Office Aide; Teachers Aide; School Musical; School Play; Stage Crew; Yrbk; Var Cheerldng; Var Sftbl; Chrldng Awd Outstndng Prtcptn & Mst Sprtd; Sftbl Mst Insrptnl; Stu Spkr Awd Lions Clb; Prncpls Awd; Design.

BELL, PENNY J; Oakdale HS; Oakdale, CA; (2); Hon Roll; CSF; U San Diego; Acctg.

BELL, POLLY A; Apple Valley HS; Lucerne Valley, CA; (1); Church Yth Grp; Hon Roll; Desert Aquatics Swm Tn; BYU; Accntng.

BELL, RALPH; Woodcrest Christian HS; Moreno Valley, CA; (3); Var Bsbl; Var Vllybl; Cal ST Fullerton; Bus Mgmt.

BELL, RICARDO D; Pasadena HS; Altadena, CA; (3); Wt Lftg; UCLA; Arch.

BELL, RODNEY J; Mt Carmel HS; San Diego, CA; (3); Wt Lftg; JV Wrstlng.

BELL, STACY; Upper Lake HS; Upper Lake, CA; (3); 6/38; Office Aide; Pep Clb; Spanish Clb; SADD; Band; Nwsp; Yrbk; Sec Frsh Cls; Sec Soph Cls; Sec Jr Cls; Real Est.

BELL, TAMMIE L; L A Baptist HS; Granada Hills, CA; (3); Church Yth Grp; Chorus; Church Choir; Drill Tm; Var Sftbl; JV Vllybl; Hon Roll; 2nd Tm All Leag; 1st Tm Elem Sftbl; Teach Windsrfng; Purple Belt Karate; CSUN; Cinema.

BELL, TERESA Y; Rowland HS; Rowland Hts, CA; (4); Teachers Aide; School Play; Rep Stu Cncl; Cit Awd; High Hon Roll; Hon Roll; Prfct Atten Awd; Drama I Awrd; Outstndng Achvt Intrmdt Drama; Prncpls Hnr Roll; Cal Grant Awrd From Govnr Grade Pt Avrg; CC; Theater Arts/Acting.

BELL, WENDY A; Casa Roble HS; Orangevale, CA; (3); Church Yth Grp; SADD; Cit Awd; Water & Snow Skiing; Qtr Midget Car Racing; American River; Chld Psych.

BELLACERA, ALTHEA D; Dixon HS; Dixon, CA; (2); Boy Scts; Cmnty Wkr; Office Aide; Pep Clb; Color Guard; Sec Frsh Cls; Rep Stu Cncl; Var Cheerldng; Var Pom Pon; JV Var Sftbl; Dixon Police Cadet; UN Legacy Intnl Youth Camp; Dixon Tribune Production Artist.

BELLAMY, RENO F; Huntington Beach HS; Huntington Beach, CA; (2); Varsity Clb; JV Ftbl; JV Trk; JV Wt Lftg; Cit Awd; Hon Roll; Notre Dame U; Bus.

BELLANDE, REGINALD; Whittier Christian HS; La Habra, CA; (3); 19/200; Varsity Clb; Band; Chorus; Var Ftbl; JV Var Socr; Tennis; High Hon Roll; Hon Roll; Engrng.

BELLEAU, WILL J; Sacramento Adventist Acad; Carmichael, CA; (2); Church Yth Grp; Spanish Clb; Teachers Aide; Band; Chorus; Drill Tm; NHS; Pacific Union Coll; Arch.

BELLEVILLE, NANCY N; Mater Dei HS; Santa Ana, CA; (2); French Clb; Rep Frsh Cls; Gym; French Hon Soc; High Hon Roll; Pres Acad Fit Awd; I Teach Piano And Gymnastic; Coach Cheerleading; I Am Getting A Pilots License & Fly As A Hobby; Ucsb; Pilot.

BELLINGHAM, KERRY L; Clayton Valley HS; Concord, CA; (4); 13/458; Letterman Clb; Pres Science Clb; Service Clb; Lit Mag; Var L Crs Cntry; Var L Swmmng; Var L Trk; Ntl Merit SF; Sec Amnesty Intl; UC Santa Cruz; Engl Prof.

BELLINGHAUSEN, NICHOLE ANNE; College Park HS; Martinez, CA; (4); JV Cheerldng; Wt Lftg; High Hon Roll; Hon Roll; Diablo Valley Coll; Busi.

BELLINIS, DEBBIE R; Mayfair HS; Lakewood, CA; (2); Church Yth Grp; Cmnty Wkr; Hosp Aide; SADD; Band; Mrchg Band; High Hon Roll; Hon Roll; Peer Cnslr; Sociology.

BELLO, JOSE; Grossmont HS; La Mesa, CA; (4); 78/371; Church Yth Grp; Intnl Clb; JA; Key Clb; Speech Tm; SADD; Varsity Clb; Rep Jr Cls; Var Crs Cntry; JV Socr; Tribune Achvt Cert; Outstndng Achvt Spanish; Bio.

BELLO, ROEL; Damien HS; West Covina, CA; (3); 20/222; Letterman Clb; Chorus; Trk; Hon Roll; Baseline League High Jump Champ 89; UCLA; Gen Practician.

BELLOMY, LAURA M; Cajon HS; Devore, CA; (1); Ed Lit Mag; Var Crs Cntry; Natl Chrty League.

BELLONI, CAROLYN M; Fortuna Union HS; Fortuna, CA; (3); Pres Church Yth Grp; SADD; School Play; Ed Yrbk; High Hon Roll; Hon Roll; NHS; Free From Alcohol & Drugs Bd Mem; CSF; Interact Club; Bus Cmmnctns.

BELMARES, ANA; Montebello HS; Montebello, CA; (1); Office Aide; Chorus; Spanish NHS; Choir Awds; Hnr Soc; Comp Prgmr.

BELMONT, TOBI M; Mesa Verde HS; Citrus Heights, CA; (2); Church Yth Grp; English Clb; Variety Show; Swmmng; High Hon Roll; Bst Tchr Drctd Scn San Juan Ply Fstvl; Bst Actrss 90; Acad Excllnc Ltr, Awd, Pin; Sacramento ST; Lit.

BELMONTOZ, LETICIA; Fontana HS; Fontana, CA; (2); Hon Roll; Prfct Atten Awd; CSF.

BELOCH, SUJIN; Liberty Union HS; Oakley, CA; (4); Model UN; Office Aide; Teachers Aide; Hon Roll; Santa Clara U; Graphic Dsgn.

BELOTE, ELIZABETH; Redlands HS; Redlands, CA; (2); Cmnty Wkr; FHA; Pep Clb; Ski Clb; Spanish Clb; SADD; Socr; Swmmng; Tennis; Trk; UC Santa Cruz; Sci.

BELSER, CHRISTINE K; Las Plumas HS; Oroville, CA; (4); French Clb; Butte Coll; CPA.

BELT, JEFFREY RYAN; Tehachapi HS; Tehachapi, CA; (4); 1/160; Boy Scts; Church Yth Grp; Computer Clb; Math Tm; Jazz Band; Mrchg Band; Rep Stu Cncl; Var Tennis; Var Wrstlng; Sal; BYU; Bio-Medcl.

BELTER, AMY; Aquinas HS; San Bernadino, CA; (2); Capt Cheerldng; High Hon Roll; Aquinas Pro Merita Awd 90; Marine Bio.

BELTRAN, ETHEL; Samuel F B Morse HS; San Diego, CA; (4); FHA; Church Choir; Drill Tm; Ed Nwsp; Yrbk; Var Cheerldng; Hon Roll; Jr NHS; Pres Acad Fit Awd; U Of CA San Diego; Med.

BELTRAN, GABRIELA; Moreno Valley HS; Moreno Valley, CA; (3); Church Choir; Kindergarden Teacher.

BELTRAN, IVETTE A; Warren HS; Downey, CA; (2); Pep Clb; Pep Band; UC Davis; Vet.

BELTRAN, JAIME M; Sonoma Valley HS; Sonoma, CA; (3); Cmnty Wkr; Latin Clb; Band; Socr; Marine Corp; Police Ofcr.

BELTRAN, JORGE L; Highlands HS; N Highlands, CA; (3); Hon Roll.

BELTRAN, LUIS A; Theodore Roosevelt HS; Los Angeles, CA; (3); Rptr Nwsp; Var Ftbl; Powder Puff Ftbl; Wt Lftg; Santa Barbara; Pilot.

BELTRAN, LYDIA M; Sierra Vista HS; Baldwin Park, CA; (1); Band; Mrchg Band; Pep Band; JV Bsktbl; Hon Roll; Band Letter; U Of Redlands; Music Dir.

BELTRAN, MAYRA; Moreno Valley HS; Moreno Valley, CA; (2); Church Choir; High Hon Roll; Doctor.

BELTRAN, MONICA; Hesperia HS; Hesperia, CA; (2); French Clb; SADD; Hon Roll; Stu Trainer.

BELTRANENA, JORGE R; South San Francisco HS; South San Francis, CA; (3); Stu Fo Mnth Frgn Lang 89; Stu Of Mnth US Hstry 90; San Mateo JC; Engrng.

BEMIS, NICOLE; Woodbridge HS; Irvine, CA; (4); Teachers Aide; Varsity Clb; Pres Band; Drm Mjr(t); Pres Jazz Band; Pres Mrchg Band; Pres Orch; Pres Pep Band; Capt Var Trk; Ntl Merit Schol; CA ST U Long Beach; Orthdntst.

BEMIS, PAUL A; Riverdale Joint Union HS; Riverdale, CA; (2); Boy Scts; Church Yth Grp; JV Bsktbl; JV Mgr(s); High Hon Roll; Hon Roll; Fresno ST U; Lab Tech.

BEN-ROOHI, MOSHE; Laguna Hills HS; Laguna Hills, CA; (2); French Clb; Socr; Wt Lftg.

BENADOM, ROXANNE; Royal HS; Simi Valley, CA; (4); Co-Capt Dance Clb; VP Girl Scts; Co-Capt Drill Tm; Mrchg Band; School Musical; School Play; Variety Show; Ed Yrbk; Rep Frsh Cls; Rep Soph Cls; Engl Dept Hghst Hnrs Schl; Hgh Lassie Yr Hghst Hnr Drill Tm; Mst Dedicated Drill Tm Mem; Moorpark; MA Educ.

BENAQUISTO, ERIK H; Santa Cruz HS; Santa Cruz, CA; (1); JV Ftbl.

BENARAW, ARNALDO; Bishop Amat HS; West Covina, CA; (4); 5/400; Math Clb; Hon Roll; Prfct Atten Awd; 1st Hnrs Math; CA Schlrshp Fdrtn; 2nd Hnrs Frnch II; Med.

BENATAR, TODD R; San Ramon HS; Danville, CA; (2); Varsity Clb; JV Bsbl; Var L Bsktbl; High Hon Roll; Little Leag-Challngr Handicapped Div-Jr Coach; Bsktbl Camp-Jr Coach.

BENAVIDES, MIKE S; Irvine HS; Irvine, CA; (1); Boy Scts; Church Yth Grp; Band; Mrchg Band; Pep Band; Vllybl; Hon Roll; Pres Acad Fit Awd; AYSO Soccer Referee; Law.

BENAVIDEZ, STEPHANIE A; St Paul HS; Santa Fe Springs, CA; (3); Church Yth Grp; Cmnty Wkr; Hosp Aide; JCL; Latin Clb; Pep Clb; Var Pres Cheerldng; Trk; Hon Roll; NHS; USC; Psych.

BENAZA, KATHLEEN R; Bishop Montgomery HS; Hawthorne, CA; (2); Hon Roll; CSF; Asian Culture Clb; UCLA; Med.

BENBOW, JOSHUA; Arvin HS; Bakersfield, CA; (2); High Hon Roll; CSF; Elect Engrng.

BENCAR, MICHELE L; Washington Union HS; Fresno, CA; (2); FCA; French Clb; Var Tennis; Hon Roll; Frnch Awd; Engl Prep Awd; CSF; Stanford U; Vet Med.

BENCAR, YVONNE M; Washington Union HS; Fresno, CA; (3); FCA; FBLA; Office Aide; SADD; Color Guard; Rptr Nwsp; Var Tennis; Am Hstry Acad Awd.

BENCE, NEIL F; Clovis HS; Clovis, CA; (3); Science Clb; Band; Mrchg Band; High Hon Roll; Hon Roll; Ecology Clb; Cycling; Rock Climbing; Backpacking; Ecology; Geology.

BENCH, CINDY A; Rim Of The World HS; Rimforest, CA; (3); 34/259; Church Yth Grp; Girl Scts; Letterman Clb; Hon Roll; Pres Acad Fit Awd; Phtg Nwsp; Rep Frsh Cls; Rep Soph Cls; Rep Jr Cls; Stat Socr; Photo For Nwspr; Riverside Vllybl Clb; Photo.

BENCH, CLOVER; Lincoln HS; San Jose, CA; (2); 14/375; Church Yth Grp; VP 4-H; Pres FFA; Sec Latin Clb; Varsity Clb; Color Guard; Ed Nwsp; Rep Stu Cncl; Diving; Score Keeper; Meriel Kilfoil Schlrshp; CA Jr Schltc Fndtn Mdl; UC Davis; Vet Med.

BENCIVENGA, MARIO; Fontana HS; Fontana, CA; (2); Teachers Aide; Crs Cntry; Trk; Hon Roll; Prfct Atten Awd; UCLA; Law.

BENCIVENGO, BRIAN M; Clovis West HS; Fresno, CA; (2); Church Yth Grp; Surfing; Diving; Bio; Scripps; Marine Bio.

BENDANA, LIZETH; Brethren Christian HS; Cypress, CA; (3); 20/56; Am Leg Aux Girls St; Church Yth Grp; Var Tennis; JV Vllybl; Hstry/Tchr.

BENDECK, ERIN; Ernest Righetti HS; Santa Maria, CA; (1); Church Yth Grp; Church Choir; High Hon Roll; Hon Roll; Pres Acad Fit Awd; Pacfc Consrvtry Prfrmng Arts; Jrnlsm.

BENDER, JEFFREY M; Grossmont HS; La Mesa, CA; (1); Letterman Clb; Math Tm; Spanish Clb; Varsity Clb; Stu Cncl; JV L Bsktbl; JV L Swmmng; Var L Vllybl; High Hon Roll; JV Ltrmn Water Polo; Engr.

BENDER, MICHAEL C; San Gabriel HS; San Gabriel, CA; (1); Boy Scts; Chess Clb; Debate Tm; Hosp Aide; Key Clb; SADD; Chorus; Church Choir; Bsktbl; Var Swmmng; Hnr Awd BSA; Phy.

BENDER, MICHAEL P; Cleveland HS; Reseda, CA; (3); Cmnty Wkr; VICA; Hon Roll; Outstndng Vlntr Svc Awd Kidsville USA 88; FL Inst Tech; Arch.

BENDER, SARAH J; Hesperia HS; Hesperia, CA; (4); Drama Clb; French Clb; Thesps; Chorus; School Play; Rptr Nwsp; Ed Lit Mag; High Hon Roll; Hrd-Wrkg Drama Stu 89-90; Show Choir; UC Irvine; Thtr Arts.

BENDER JR, STEPHEN G; Mission San Jose HS; Fremont, CA; (2); Boy Scts; Pep Clb; Chorus; School Musical; School Play; Swing Chorus; Variety Show; Off Frsh Cls; Stu Cncl; Socr; Sngng & Dancng Grp; 1st Strng Goalkppr City Sccr; Play Piano; Princeton; Eng Prfssr.

BENEDETTI, MICHAEL W; Tulare Western HS; Tulare, CA; (4); 1/231; Church Yth Grp; 4-H; Scholastic Bowl; VP Soph Cls; School Play; Pres Soph Cls; Pres Jr Cls; Pres Sr Cls; Pres Stu Cncl; Bsktbl; Vrsty Waterpolo Cptn; UC Davis; Engrng.

BENEDICT, ADRIENNE; Moreau HS; Union City, CA; (2); Church Yth Grp; Ski Clb; SADD; JV Cheerldng; Gym; Var Trk; Hon Roll; UCLA.

BENEDICT, BRENDA M; Elk Grove HS; Wilton, CA; (4); Chrmn Church Yth Grp; Pres VP 4-H; Science Clb; Treas Speech Tm; Off Soph Cls; Stu Cncl; L Swmmng; 4-H Awd; Hon Roll; HOBY; Mst Imprvd Swimmer; Homcmng/Powder Puff Ftbl/Effctv Schls/WASC Planning Cmmttees; SCIONS Clb; U Of S CA; Cmmnctns.

BENEDICT, BRIAN D; Alhambra HS; Martinez, CA; (2); Var Socr; Hon Roll; Biking; Civil Air Patrol; UC Berkely; Engr.

BENEDICT, DIANA M; Grossmont HS; El Cajon, CA; (1); Art Clb; Spanish Clb; Teachers Aide; Hon Roll; Spanish Outstndng Achvt; UCSD; Pediatrician.

BENEDICT, HAROLD M; James Logan HS; Union City, CA; (3); Art Clb; French Clb; Ski Clb; Nwsp; Crs Cntry; Swmmng; Hon Roll; Prfct Atten Awd; Yng Athrs Faire Awd; Pre-Coll Acad Berkeley Awd; Jrnlsm.

BENEFIELD, ROBERT; Savanna HS; Buena Park, CA; (4); 8/286; JA; Letterman Clb; Pep Clb; Science Clb; Service Clb; Teachers Aide; Varsity Clb; Variety Show; Ed Nwsp; Rep Jr Cls; Mgr, Disc Jcky HS Radio Sta; All Orange Leag Track; GATE; U Of CA Los Angls; Aeroscp Eng.

BENESCH, JON D; Monterey HS; Pacific Grove, CA; (4); Aud/Vis; Acpl Chr; Band; Jazz Band; Mrchg Band; Yrbk; Var Crs Cntry; JV Socr; Var JV Swmmng; JV Wrstlng; Only Awd Div Satire/Comdy Video CA Stu Media Fstvl; Cert Outstndng Acad Excllnce Apri 88; Music; U Of CA Los Angeles.

BENEUX, JENNIFER A; Hesperia HS; Hesperia, CA; (2); Church Yth Grp; Cmnty Wkr; ROTC; Drill Tm; High Hon Roll; Sound Technician; Survival Games; Engrng.

BENFIELD, AMY L; Red Bluff Union HS; Red Bluff, CA; (4); 9/300; Church Yth Grp; SADD; Band; Drm Mjr(t); Mrchg Band; School Musical; Variety Show; High Hon Roll; CSF Pres 89-90; Christ Coll Irvine; Scl Wrk.

BENFIELD, KIMBERLY A; Red Bluff Union HS; Red Bluff, CA; (4); 11/275; Church Yth Grp; Dance Clb; Mu Alpha Theta; Pres SADD; Mrchg Band; Rep Soph Cls; Rep Jr Cls; Treas Sr Cls; Stu Cncl; Powder Puff Ftbl; Friday Night Live Publcty Ofcr & Pres; CSF; Kiwanis Camp Cnslr; Shasta Coll; Acctng.

BENGEL, CYNTHIA; Edison Computech HS; Fresno, CA; (4); 30/228; Office Aide; Orch; L Swmmng; Hon Roll; CSF Highest Honor & Life Mem; Envir Awareness Club Mem; Society For High Adventure Mem; Cal Poly-San Luis Obispo; Cmptr.

BENGS, ALICIA R; Mills HS; Millbrae, CA; (4); 56/256; Church Yth Grp; English Clb; Teachers Aide; Stage Crew; Var L Swmmng; Lion Awd; Pres Acad Fit Awd; Mills-Peninsula Hospitals Auxiliary Schlrshp; San Francisco ST; Nrsng.

BENIGNI, MAURA A; Hemet HS; Hemet, CA; (2); Eng Prof.

BENIGNO, ANTHONY O; Westmoor HS; Daly City, CA; (3); Band; Jazz Band; Pep Band; Rep Sr Cls; Tennis; Music.

BENISEK, ALISSA; Claremont HS; Claremont, CA; (3); Drama Clb; Teachers Aide; Drill Tm; Stage Crew; JV Var Cheerldng; VP Pom Pon; Lions Clb Stu Vstr To Austria 89; People To People Stu Ambssdr To Russia 90; Art.

BENITEZ, ADRIANA; Sweetwater HS; National City, CA; (1).

BENITEZ, EDGAR; East Union HS; French Camp, CA; (2); Spanish Clb; SADD; Plan Mech.

BENITEZ, MARISSA; St Rose Acad; Pacifica, CA; (3); Church Yth Grp; GAA; Spanish Clb; School Musical; Lit Mag; JV Bsktbl; JV Vllybl; Cit Awd; Hon Roll; UC Santa Barbara; Resort Mgmt.

BENITEZ, MARK A; St Ignatius College Prep; Pacifica, CA; (3); Cmnty Wkr; VP Band; VP Jazz Band; VP Orch; School Musical; Intrml Bsktbl; JV Var Ftbl; Intrml Sftbl; Vllybl; High Hon Roll; Asian Stus Coalition 86-90; CSF-LIFE Member; Cmmnty/Filipino Bsktbl Leags; UCLA.

BENITEZ, MICHAEL; Sierra Vista HS; Baldwin Park, CA; (4); Speech Tm; Rep Stu Cncl; Var Tennis; High Hon Roll; Opt Clb Awd; Cal Poly Pomona; Comp Sci.

BENITEZ, NORMA A; Buena Park HS; Fullerton, CA; (3); Cmnty Wkr; French Clb; Intnl Clb; Spanish Clb; French Hon Soc; High Hon Roll; Hon Roll; Prfct Atten Awd; Prins Hnr Roll; CA Schlrshp Fed; Prt-Tme Stu Cstdn, Ace Tllr Security Pcfc Bnk; Claremont; Accntng.

BENITEZ, RIZALDY; Nogales HS; West Covina, CA; (3); Library Aide; Teachers Aide; Hon Roll; Bus.

BENITEZ, ROBERT; St Bernards HS; Hawthorne, CA; (3); Art Clb; Latin Clb; Spanish Clb; Off Jr Cls; Socr; Cit Awd; Cls Rep; Art Dept Awd; CA ST Northridge; Phy.

BENITEZ, SADY; Mt Diablo HS; W Pittsburg, CA; (1); Hon Roll; Vet.

BENJAMIN, DORE; Templeton HS; Paso Robles, CA; (1); Church Yth Grp; Spanish Clb; Sec Frsh Cls; Vllybl; Hon Roll; Pres Acad Fit Awd; Marine Bio.

BENJAMIN, JENNIFER L; Mayfair HS; Bellflower, CA; (1); Drama Clb; Thesps; Stage Crew; Treas Frsh Cls; Stu Cncl; Hon Roll; Vet.

BENJAMIN, JIM A; Enterprise HS; Palo Cedro, CA; (3); 4/18; Church Yth Grp; FBLA; Math Clb; Mu Alpha Theta; Band; Jazz Band; Mrchg Band; Pep Band; School Musical; Variety Show; Dixieland Band; Music Educators Assn; Shasta Coll; Mech Engr.

BENJAMIN, MICHAEL A; Inglewood HS; Inglewood, CA; (3); Aud/Vis; Church Yth Grp; Cmnty Wkr; Dance Clb; FCA; French Clb; JA; Math Tm; Spanish Clb; SADD; Bus Mgmt.

BENJAMIN, QURINA S; La Habra HS; La Habra Heights, CA; (2); Drama Clb; Key Clb; Science Clb; Stage Crew; Gov Hon Prg Awd; Hon Roll; Pres Acad Fit Awd; Jehovash Witness; Equestrian Water Sking; U Las Vegas; Envrnmntl Engr.

BENJAMIN, RAMON; Franklin JR HS; Vallejo, CA; (1); Church Yth Grp; Band; Mrchg Band; Hon Roll; Military.

BENNAGE, CATHERINE R; Redlands SR HS; Redlands, CA; (3); 90/907; Art Clb; Cmnty Wkr; Pep Clb; Red Cross Aide; Variety Show; JV Capt Cheerldng; High Hon Roll; Hon Roll; St Fnlst Miss US Teen CA Pgnt; PRAISE Awd; Russian Stu Ambssdr; Boston U; Jrnlsm.

BENNER, ARTHUR B; Diamond Bar HS; Diamond Bar, CA; (3); 141/500; Spanish Clb; Varsity Clb; Var Ftbl; JV Trk; Var Wt Lftg; Hon Roll.

BENNER, JAMIE L; Summerville HS; Tuolumne, CA; (3); Church Yth Grp; Spanish Clb; JV Var Crs Cntry; JV Var Trk; Hon Roll; Acad Decthln; Stu Of Yr; Bear Bwl.

BENNETT, AARON M; Rim Of The World HS; Crestline, CA; (3); Spanish Clb; Intrml Diving; Intrml Swmmng; JV Wrstlng; French Hon Soc; Hon Roll; Prfct Atten Awd; Sci.

BENNETT, ALISSA C; Lincoln HS; Stockton, CA; (2); 74/568; Church Yth Grp; L Crs Cntry; L Trk; Hon Roll; Prfct Atten Awd; CSF; Outstndng Achvt Spnsh I, II; Clncl Pthlgst.

BENNETT, AMEE M; Redwood HS; Visalia, CA; (3); 76/364; Church Yth Grp; Hosp Aide; Office Aide; Teachers Aide; Bsktbl; Swmmng; Pres Acad Fit Awd; Archlgy.

BENNETT, ASTRID; Pius X HS; Huntington Park, CA; (3); Cmnty Wkr; Math Clb; Mu Alpha Theta; Hon Roll; Interact, Hispanic & Biomed Clbs; CSF; Campus Ministry Natl Hnrs Soc; Cardiologist.

BENNETT, BILL G; Orange Glen HS; Escondido, CA; (3); 51/659; Boy Scts; Church Yth Grp; German Clb; Band; Jazz Band; L Mrchg Band; Orch; Pep Band; Yrbk; Var L Tennis; Drums Across CA; CA Schlrshp Fed; U CA Santa Barbara.

BENNETT, BRAD K; Alta Loma HS; Alta Loma, CA; (3); Boy Scts; Church Yth Grp; Letterman Clb; Treas Soph Cls; VP Jr Cls; Pres Sr Cls; JV Var Bsktbl; High Hon Roll; Hon Roll; Rotary Awd; Badmntn JV & V; BYU; Arch Engrng.

BENNETT, CAMILLE; San Gabriel Acad; Fontana, CA; (4); Church Yth Grp; Teachers Aide; Chorus; Church Choir; Intrml Vllybl; Prfct Atten Awd; Flr Hckry; CYB; Amdntn; Loma Linda U; Educ.

BENNETT, CARRIE; Mt Whitney HS; Visalia, CA; (2); FFA; Pres Soph Cls; Var L Swmmng; Hon Roll; Vly Fnls Swmng 6th Pl; Chptr Farmr Deg; Ride & Show Hrs; UC Davis; Vet.

BENNETT, CHARLTON W; Hesperia HS; Hesperia, CA; (4); Capt Socr; Hon Roll; US Army Rsrv Natl Schlr/Athlt Awd; All-League Soccer Hnrs Mstng Insprtnl & Coaches Awd 89-90; Cal ST U.

BENNETT, CHRIS P; Chino HS; Ontario, CA; (2); Photo, Jewelery, Electrncs Class; UC Barkley; Engrng.

BENNETT, CHRISTINE; Harbor HS; Santa Cruz, CA; (4); Teachers Aide; Cheerldng; High Hon Roll; Hon Roll; Pres Acad Fit Awd; Bus Ldr; Wrk Exp Schlrshp; Comp Cnsltnt.

BENNETT, DANA M; Rio Mesa HS; Oxnard, CA; (4); 74/359; Bus Profs of Am; Church Yth Grp; FBLA; Swmmng; Hon Roll; Ventura Coll; Travel Agent.

BENNETT, JAMES G; Temple City HS; Arcadia, CA; (2); JV Swmmng; Cit Awd; High Hon Roll; NHS; Eagle Sct; UCLA; Medcl.

BENNETT, JAMES J; Alta Loma HS; Rancho Cucamonga, CA; (2); Ski Clb; Trk; Hon Roll; Prfct Atten Awd; Doctor.

BENNETT, JENNIFER K; St Paul HS; Fullerton, CA; (3); Cmnty Wkr; FTA; JA; Library Aide; Office Aide; Service Clb; SADD; Teachers Aide; Rptr Nwsp; Vllybl; Cmnty Svcs Vlntr; U CA Fullerton; Bus.

BENNETT, JOSHUA; Hoover HS; San Diego, CA; (1); Aud/Vis; Church Yth Grp; Letterman Clb; Varsity Clb; Var L Socr; Hon Roll; UCSD; Bio Chem.

BENNETT, KATE; Lodi Acad; Woodbridge, CA; (1); Church Yth Grp; Ski Clb; Teachers Aide; Band; Chorus; Pres Frsh Cls; Pacific Union Coll; Bio.

BENNETT, KIMBERLY J; San Luis Obispo HS; San Luis Obispo, CA; (2); Church Yth Grp; Key Clb; Pep Clb; Ski Clb; SADD; Rptr Nwsp; Rep Stu Cncl; Var Cheerldng; Capt Powder Puff Ftbl; Var Trk; Amer Inst Aerontcs & Astrontcs; Spirit Comssnr For Assocd Stu Bdy 91; Bus.

BENNETT, KIRSTEN L; Laguna Beach HS; Laguna Beach, CA; (2); Office Aide; Teachers Aide; Chorus; Cheerldng; Cit Awd; Hon Roll; Jazz Dancng 6 Yrs; Princpls Awd Engl; Phys Thrpy.

BENNETT, MARALINA; Yosemite HS; Oakhurst, CA; (2); Drama Clb; Pres Service Clb; SADD; School Play; Hon Roll; UC Sn Dgo; Pedtrcs.

BENNETT, MICHELLE; Louisville HS; Chatsworth, CA; (2); Church Yth Grp; Dance Clb; GAA; Hosp Aide; Sftbl; Trk; Vllybl; Hon Roll; Prfct Atten Awd; Prncpls Acad Schlrshp 89; Piano.

BENNETT, MYSTI; Chino HS; Chino, CA; (3); FHA; Cmnty Wkr; Pep Clb; Rptr Nwsp; Var Crs Cntry; Bus Mgmt.

BENNETT, PATRICIA O; Manual Arts HS; Los Angeles, CA; (4); Sec Church Yth Grp; Rptr Nwsp; Sec Stu Cncl; Crs Cntry; Trk; Vllybl; Hon Roll; CA ST U Northridge; Flm Prod.

BENNETT, PATRICK A; Sutter Union HS; Yuba City, CA; (3); Drama Clb; Science Clb; Teachers Aide; School Play; Stage Crew; Variety Show; Wt Lftg; Yuba Coll; Elec.

BENNETT, STACY R; Gardena HS; Gardena, CA; (2); Sec Library Aide; Spanish Clb; Acpl Chr; Chorus; Ed Lit Mag; Treas Stu Cncl; Cit Awd; Hon Roll; Interact Club; Gardena Libr Assn Club; Occidental; Jrnlsm.

BENNETT, SUZANNE R; Montgomery HS; Santa Rosa, CA; (3); Art Clb; Cmnty Wkr; French Clb; German Clb; Teachers Aide; Ed Yrbk; Swmmng; High Hon Roll; Hon Roll; Pres Acad Fit Awd; German Lang Schl; UC Berkley; Frgn Lang.

BENNETT, TERRI A; Woodlake Union HS; Woodlake, CA; (4); 4/130; Sec GAA; Key Clb; Pep Clb; SADD; Sprt Ed Phtg Yrbk; Var L Bsktbl; Var Capt Sftbl; L Var Vllybl; Hon Roll; Rotary Awd; Schlrshp GPA; Bank Amer Achvt Awd, Plqu Wnnr; Appld Arts; CIF Schlr Athlt; Coll Sequoias; Tchr.

BENNETT, TISHA N; Dixon HS; Dixon, CA; (2); AFS; Intnl Clb; Drill Tm; JV Crs Cntry; Var Pom Pon; JV Tennis; Hon Roll; NHS; Clss Fnd Rsrs; UC-DAVIS; Med.

BENNETT, WILLIAM A; Aragon HS; San Mateo, CA; (3); Church Yth Grp; Cmnty Wkr; SADD; Ed Nwsp; Off Jr Cls; Rep Stu Cncl; Hon Roll; Ntl Merit Ltr; Cmpgn Steerng Comm Ted Lempert St Assmbly 90; Rep San Mateo Yth Advsry Cncl; Corp Mgmt.

BENNIE, MIKE; Orangewood Adventist Acad; Anaheim, CA; (3); 1/25; Church Yth Grp; Drama Clb; FCA; Spanish Clb; Nwsp; VP Jr Cls; Var Ftbl; Ntl Merit Ltr; Handbell Choir; Engl.

BENNING, JEFF M; Casa Roble HS; Citrus Heights, CA; (4); 93/325; Boy Scts; Ed Nwsp; Hon Roll; Story Publshd Orangevale News 90; Brigham Young U; Jrnlsm.

BENNIT, KIMBERLY A; Redlands JR Acad; Rialto, CA; (2); Church Yth Grp; Chorus; Hon Roll; Wrld Hstry Best All Arnd Stu Awd; Music Prfcncy Awd; Loma Linda Acad; Marine Oceangr.

BENOIT, ARTHUR R; Will E Wood HS; Vacaville, CA; (2); OR ST; Comp Sci.

BENOIT, CARL E; Quincy JR/Sr HS; Quincy, CA; (3); Crs Cntry; Phys Thrpy.

BENON, CHARLENE; Beyer HS; Modesto, CA; (2); Speech Tm; Rep Frsh Cls; Capt Cheerldng; Hon Roll; UCLA; Actress.

BENSHOOF, TERRA D; Vacaville HS; Vacaville, CA; (3); Church Yth Grp; GAA; Teachers Aide; L Bsktbl; Cit Awd; Hon Roll; Jr NHS; Prfct Atten Awd; Stanford U; Ed.

BENSON, AMY; Calabasas HS; Calabasas, CA; (3); 11/244; Cmnty Wkr; Debate Tm; School Play; Ed Nwsp; Ed Lit Mag; Pres Sr Cls; Stu Cncl; Var Bsktbl; Var Crs Cntry; Var Socr; Amigos De Las Americas Vlntr In Dominican Republic.

BENSON, BRIAN R; River City HS; W Sacramento, CA; (2); 1/250; VP French Clb; Key Clb; Ski Clb; SADD; Thesps; Band; Pep Band; School Musical; School Play; Rep Frsh Cls; Fri Night Live Clb; Mock Trial; U CA-DAVIS; Pediatrcs.

BENSON, DORSHAY; Saint Monica HS; Los Angeles, CA; (3); Church Yth Grp; Cmnty Wkr; Pep Clb; Teachers Aide; Chorus; Church Choir; School Musical; School Play; Var Cheerldng; High Hon Roll; CSF; Loyola Marymount U; Prfrmng Art.

BENSON, JAMES V; Central Valley HS; Central Valley, CA; (3); 2/350; Am Leg Boys St; Quiz Bowl; VP Soph Cls; Pres Jr Cls; VP Sr Cls; JV Bsbl; JV Var Bsktbl; JV Ftbl; Var Tennis; Hon Roll; CSF.

BENSON, JEFFERY; Cajon HS; San Bernardino, CA; (3); 40/463; Church Yth Grp; Cmnty Wkr; Computer Clb; Key Clb; Teachers Aide; High Hon Roll; Hon Roll; Outstndng Vlntr Of Yr 89; Schlrshp In Math Awd; Cal Poly Pomona; Aerontcl Engr.

BENSON, JENNIFER L; Brawley HS; Brawley, CA; (2); 1/350; Church Yth Grp; Math Tm; SADD; Church Choir; High Hon Roll; Psych.

BENSON, KIMBERLY L; Tehachapi HS; Tehachapi, CA; (3); Church Yth Grp; Debate Tm; Drama Clb; Key Clb; Office Aide; Teachers Aide; Varsity Clb; Chorus; Powder Puff Ftbl; Socr; USC; Engl.

BENSON, KINDY L; Pacific Grove HS; Pacific Grove, CA; (4); Church Yth Grp; Sec Key Clb; Teachers Aide; School Musical; Lit Mag; Trk; Vllybl; High Hon Roll; Pres Acad Fit Awd; Drama Awd; Arch Schlrshp To CA Poly Smmr Wkshp; Dsgn.

BENSON, LATREACE J; Montclair HS; Ontario, CA; (1); Church Yth Grp; Dance Clb; Treas Soph Cls; JV Bsktbl; Trk; Hon Roll; Pres Acad Fit Awd; Top Female Athl; Harvard; Bus.

BENSON, LINDA; Liberty Union HS; Brentwood, CA; (3); Letterman Clb; Office Aide; Band; Color Guard; Var Crs Cntry; Var Trk; Hon Roll; CA Schlrshp Fdrtn; Sci Tchr Aide; Wildlf.

BENSON, MANDY R; La Sierra HS; Riverside, CA; (1); Temple Yth Grp; Prfct Atten Awd; Child Psych.

BENSON, MICHAEL W; Apple Valley HS; Apple Valley, CA; (3); Math.

BENSON, SINIA S; La Puente HS; La Puente, CA; (2); Drama Clb; Band; Chorus; Mrchg Band; School Play; Prfrmng Arts.

BENSTON, ELIZABETH; Bakersfield HS; Bakersfield, CA; (3); German Clb; JA; Orch; Rptr Nwsp; Lit Mag; Var JV Crs Cntry; High Hon Roll; Hon Roll; Pres Acad Fit Awd; Private Violin Lessons; Command Performance Violine; Hnrs & A P Classes; Bryn Mawr; Engl.

BENTLEY, AMY; Lower Lake HS; Lower Lake, CA; (1); 1/150; Treas Frsh Cls; Var Sftbl; High Hon Roll; Prfct Atten Awd; Fri Night Live Sober & Drug Free; CSF; Outstndng Stu Orgnztn; U Of CA; Structural Engr.

BENTLEY, CAMERON; Winters HS; Winters, CA; (2); Art Clb; FFA; Ski Clb.

BENTLEY, CLAYTON W; Winters HS; Winters, CA; (2); FFA; Ski Clb; JV Bsbl.

BENTLEY, EILEEN S; Buena Park HS; Buena Park, CA; (1); Dance Clb; JV Cheerldng; Hon Roll.

BENTLEY, JULIANNE N; Central Catholic HS; Empire, CA; (3); 4/57; Art Clb; Cmnty Wkr; French Clb; Intnl Clb; JV Powder Puff Ftbl; Cit Awd; Hon Roll; NHS; Acad Decathlon Team; CSF.

BENTLEY, JULIE M; Kern Valley HS; Kernville, CA; (1); Rptr 4-H; Pep Clb; SADD; Score Keeper; 4-H Awd; Hon Roll; Fri Nght Lv Co-Chrprsn Pblcty; Tchr.

BENTLEY, KARIE S; Big Pine HS; Big Pine, CA; (2); Ski Clb; Spanish Clb; VP Soph Cls; VP Stu Cncl; Mock Trial; Psych.

BENTO, RAYMOND A; Pasadena HS; Pasadena, CA; (3); Cmnty Wkr; JA; Letterman Clb; ROTC; Cit Awd; DAR Awd; Sons Of Amer Rvltn; Phys Ftnss, Armed Drill Team, Mini-Boot Cmp Awds; US Marine Corp; Dog Trnr.

BENTON, CINDY M; Palm Springs HS; Cathedral City, CA; (3); Church Yth Grp; Debate Tm; Pres Drama Clb; School Musical; School Play; Stage Crew; French Hon Soc; Hon Roll; Pres Acad Fit Awd; UCSD; Law.

BENTSON, HEIDI C; Mt Shasta HS; Mount Shasta, CA; (2); Church Yth Grp; Chorus; JV Trk; Hon Roll; U CA Davis; Orthodontist.

BENTZ, MOLLY; Modesto HS; Modesto, CA; (2); Sec FFA; Humboldt ST; Frstry.

BENTZ, SHARMAINE L; San Gorgonio HS; San Bernardino, CA; (3); Drama Clb; English Clb; Model UN; NFL; ROTC; Thesps; School Play; Stage Crew; Sci.

BENYUSKA, MICHELLE; Sacramento HS; Sacramento, CA; (3); 135/342; Dance Clb; Girl Scts; Orch; School Musical; Rptr Yrbk; Capt Var Cheerldng; Var JV Swmmng; Benefit Multiple Sclerosis 87-90; 97 KROY Chrldr; Modeling; Japanese Lang; Dance.

BENZ, JENNIFER A; Hemet HS; Hemet, CA; (3); 21/597; Church Yth Grp; Spanish Clb; JV Vllybl; High Hon Roll; Hon Roll; CSF; UC Santa Barbara; Comp Prgmr.

BENZ, MICHELLE M; Shasta HS; Redding, CA; (4); 30/340; Church Yth Grp; Hosp Aide; Ed Phtg Yrbk; Gym; Socr; Sftbl; Swmmng; High Hon Roll; Pres Acad Fit Awd; Rotary Awd; CSU Sacramento; Chld Dvlpmnt.

BENZA, CHAD J; Carpintevia HS; Carpinteria, CA; (2); 98/161; Cmnty Wkr; Spanish Clb; JV Ftbl; UCLA; Real Est Brkr.

BENZON, LORAINE T; Whitney HS; Cerritos, CA; (2); Church Yth Grp; Sec Key Clb; Band; Mgr Mrchg Band; Orch; Ed Yrbk; Hist Soph Cls; Off Jr Cls; JV Co-Capt Bsktbl; Cit Awd; Certified Peer Counselor; Cultural & Modern Dance; CSF; Acad Pentathlon Silver Medal; Engrng.

BER, FRANCES; George Washington HS; San Francisco, CA; (2); Pep Clb; Cheerldng; Hon Roll; Tutoring; Peer Cnslng; U SANTA Barbara; Marine Bio.

BERAN, MICHAEL A; Bonita HS; La Verne, CA; (1); Boy Scts; Intrml Bsktbl; Hon Roll.

BERBARI, LUIS CARLOS; Burbank HS; Burbank, CA; (4); 120/429; Spanish Clb; Capt Socr; Stu Mnth Word Processing; Athl Of Mnth; ROP Rep Of Bus; Faculty Excllnc Awd; CA ST Bakersfield; Rstrnt Mgr.

BERBER, ERNESTO; Ramona HS; Jacksonville, AR; (2); Church Yth Grp; Ftbl; Wt Lftg; Prfct Atten Awd; Outstndng GPA; Riverside CC; Ftbl.

BERCH, CHRIS; Damien HS; Alta Loma, CA; (2); 90/270; Ski Clb; JV Tennis; DAR Awd; Tennis Clb; Cal Poly San Luis Obispo; Engr.

BERCIAN, ROSA; Compton SR HS; Compton, CA; (3); ROTC; Socr; Tech Eng.

BERCUTT, LARRY D; Harvard Schl; Beverly Hills, CA; (4); 1/135; Debate Tm; Var Swmmng; Hon Roll; Ntl Merit SF; Spanish NHS; Var Water Polo; Admissions Ofcr.

BERDUGO, MAYRA; Pius X HS; Compton, CA; (2); Math Clb; Chorus; Hon Roll.

BERDY, ALEXANDER G; Whitney HS; Cerritos, CA; (4); Cmnty Wkr; Treas FBLA; Hosp Aide; JA; Key Clb; L Letterman Clb; Service Clb; Ski Clb; Spanish Clb; Varsity Clb; Water Polo, Var Lttr; Med Club; U Of CA Irvine; Med.

BEREAL, MARIEA L; Pasadena HS; Altadena, CA; (4); Church Yth Grp; Cmnty Wkr; JA; Library Aide; Office Aide; Acpl Chr; Chorus; Church Choir; School Musical; School Play; Chrch Music; Music.

BEREJIKLIAN, TALAR; Holy Martyrs HS; Reseda, CA; (2); JV Crs Cntry; JV Trk; Golden Poet Awd; CSUV; Optomtrst.

BERENGIAN, ANDEREE R; Edison HS; Huntington Beach, CA; (3); Debate Tm; French Clb; FBLA; Key Clb; Model UN; Spanish Clb; SADD; Trk; High Hon Roll; Hon Roll; Med.

BERES, DOLLY; Burlingame HS; Burlingame, CA; (2); Church Yth Grp; Drama Clb; Spanish Clb; Yrbk; JV Cheerldng; High Hon Roll; CA Schltc Fed; USA Spirit Assoc; Tutor; Natl Fnlst JC Penney/17 Magzn Mdlng Cont; Bus.

BERG, AUDREY M; Capital Christian Schl; Citrus Heights, CA; (3); Church Yth Grp; Drama Clb; Pep Clb; Spanish Clb; SADD; Band; Mrchg Band; Pep Band; Var Swmmng; Hon Roll; Pwrs Advncd Mdlng Stu Grad; USA Cmptn Swmmr; UC Davis; Psych.

BERG, GRETCHEN C; Oakmont HS; Roseville, CA; (1); Hosp Aide; Ski Clb; Hon Roll; Piano; Bus.

BERG, JEAN M; Redlands HS; Redlands, CA; (2); Church Yth Grp; Teachers Aide; Stat Socr; Hon Roll; Swim Instrctr/Lifeguard Coach Redlands Fmly YMCA; U San Diego; Bus Acctng.

BERG, KIM K; Orange Lutheran HS; Orange, CA; (2); Ski Clb; Psych.

BERG, TRISHA C; Chino HS; Ontario, CA; (3); Drama Clb; Science Clb; Ski Clb; JV Socr; High Hon Roll; Hon Roll; CA Poly; Tchr.

BERGADO, RUBYLYN; John W North HS; Riverside, CA; (2); Cmnty Wkr; Pep Clb; Teachers Aide; Varsity Clb; Yrbk; Sec Soph Cls; Cheerldng; Pom Pon; Hon Roll; Prfct Atten Awd; Art Awd; Harvard; Law.

BERGANTZ, NAOMI; Lodi HS; Lodi, CA; (3); 255/518; Chrmn Drama Clb; Key Clb; School Play; Swmmng; High Hon Roll; Hon Roll; Stu Ambssdr Pgm Russia; Hmcmng Parade; UCLA; Advrtsng.

BERGDORF, LISA C; Esperanza HS; Yorba Linda, CA; (4); 13/485; Drama Clb; VP Sec German Clb; Pres VP Girl Scts; Thesps; Pres Acpl Chr; School Musical; Stage Crew; High Hon Roll; Acad Awd; Dir Awd-Choir; Family Bus.

BERGE, SHANNON R; Carmel HS; Carmel, CA; (3); Art Clb; English Clb; Service Clb; Teachers Aide; Variety Show; Yrbk; High Hon Roll; Hon Roll; Rotary Awd; Envrnmntl Awrnss Grp SMART; Humboldt ST U; Art.

BERGE, SUSAN L; Bishop O'dowd HS; Oakland, CA; (2); Art Clb; Church Yth Grp; Nwsp; High Hon Roll; CSF; Engl.

BERGEMAN, FELICIA A; Notre Dame Acad; Inglewood, CA; (3); Drama Clb; SADD; Cit Awd; Soc Actvst; Cmptr Sci.

BERGEN, SKYE; Bret Harte HS; Murphy's, CA; (3); Aud/Vis; Church Yth Grp; Cmnty Wkr; Pep Clb; Drill Tm; Phtg Rptr Yrbk; Cheerldng; Pom Pon; Vllybl; Hon Roll; Rainbow Girls Cmmnty Svc Intl Order; Pepperdine; Linquist/Diplomatic.

BERGENTY, LYNETTE; Louisville HS; Northridge, CA; (3); Church Yth Grp; GAA; Ski Clb; SADD; Ed Yrbk; Sec Soph Cls; Sec Sr Cls; Var JV Crs Cntry; Var JV Trk; Loyola Marymount U; Bus.

BERGER, ARLENE; Chatsworth HS; Chatsworth, CA; (4); 63/550; Hosp Aide; Temple Yth Grp; Capt Drill Tm; Nwsp; Hon Roll; Prfct Atten Awd; Rotary Awd; Octagom Clb; Daily News Jrnlsm Awd; CA Schlrshp Fed; U Of CA Santa Barbara.

BERGER, MARILYN A; Immaculate Heart HS; Los Angeles, CA; (3); Cmnty Wkr; Drama Clb; GAA; Math Clb; Mu Alpha Theta; Science Clb; Spanish Clb; Var Crs Cntry; Var JV Swmmng; Critics Choice-Stu Cncl; Bus.

BERGER, RACHEL; El Camino Real HS; West Hills, CA; (3); Cmnty Wkr; GAA; SADD; Temple Yth Grp; JV Bsktbl; L Capt Vllybl; Hon Roll; Prfct Atten Awd; Ldrshp Smnr.

BERGERON, HEATHER A; Edison HS; Huntington Beach, CA; (3); Intl Ordr Of Jobs Daughters.

BERGERON, KRISTINA; Roseville HS; Penryn, CA; (4); Teachers Aide; School Musical; Variety Show; JV Var Gym; Hon Roll; Pres Acad Fit Awd; Sierra Coll; Comp.

BERGERON, VALERIE; San Pasqual HS; Escondido, CA; (3); French Clb; Var Crs Cntry; Var Trk; Med.

BERGHOLZ, CHERYL V; Napa HS; Napa, CA; (1); 35/400; Chorus; Hon Roll; CA U San Diego; Marine Bio.

BERGLUND, ANGELA L; Westlake HS; Thousand Oaks, CA; (4); Church Yth Grp; JA; Teachers Aide; Stat Bsktbl; Hon Roll; Photo; Allan Hancock CC; Crmnlgy.

BERGMAN, ANTHONY J; Whittier Christian HS; Whittier, CA; (4); Church Yth Grp; Cmnty Wkr; Crs Cntry; Socr; Trk; Azusa Pacific U; Bus.

BERGMAN, KORY J; Edward C Reed HS; Sparks, NV; (1); 124/408; Pep Clb; Orch; Jrnlsm.

BERGMAN, LORRETTA M; Templeton HS; Paso Robles, CA; (1); Hon Roll; 1st Pl Immgntv Wrtng Cont 90; Cert Excllnc-San Luis Obispo Cty Wrtng Cont.

BERGMAN, SARA; Brethren HS; Signal Hill, CA; (3); Art Clb; Church Yth Grp; Office Aide; Pep Clb; Teachers Aide; Flag Corp; JV Bsktbl; Var Cheerldng; High Hon Roll; Hon Roll; Chrch Vlybll; Excel Singng; Engl.

BERGQUIST, SEAN P; Henry M Gunn HS; Palo Alto, CA; (2); JV Socr; JV Swmmng; Awds Bio & Art, Top Stu Cls; Awd GSE Alg; Engrng.

BERGREN, DOUGLAS R; Concord HS; Concord, CA; (3); Church Yth Grp; Teachers Aide; Hon Roll; CSB; Bus.

BERGREN, JOSHUA C; Anaheim HS; Anaheim, CA; (3); Office Aide; Mgr Yrbk; Relgious Svc; Ldrs Of Tomorrow-Photo Display Awd.

BERGSTROM, ANN L; Arcata HS; Arcata, CA; (2); Spanish Clb; Cit Awd; Hon Roll; Humbolt ST U.

BERGSTROM, SERENA D; Trinity HS; Junction City, CA; (3); Church Yth Grp; Cmnty Wkr; Drama Clb; Intnl Clb; SADD; Ed Nwsp; Yrbk; VP Jr Cls; Rep Stu Cncl; Score Keeper; Natl Wrtng Awd; Dance Cls-Jazz; Tennis; Cmnctns.

BERGSTROM, TROY; Santa Teresa HS; San Jose, CA; (1); Aud/Vis; Boy Scts; Science Clb; Service Clb; SADD; Varsity Clb; Ed Yrbk; Var L Ftbl; Powder Puff Ftbl; Intrml Vllybl; Eagle Sct; NESA Schlshp Awd; Humboldt ST U; Wldlf Mgmt.

BERGULA, ARNIE; Poway HS; Poway, CA; (2); Teachers Aide; Cit Awd; High Hon Roll; Hon Roll; Weight Training Awd; Aeronautical Engrng.

BERHANE, LIDIA; J Eugene Mc Ateer HS; San Francisco, CA; (4); Debate Tm; Teachers Aide; Swmmng; Vllybl; Hon Roll; Bus Adm.

BERJIKLY, ARTIN; El Camino Real HS; West Hills, CA; (3); Church Yth Grp; Teachers Aide; Off Frsh Cls; Off Soph Cls; Off Jr Cls; Sec Stu Cncl; Var L Socr; JV L Trk; Hon Roll; CSF; Jr Statesmn Of Am; Advncd Placemnt-US Hstry/Engl/Calculus; UCLA; Med.

BERJIS, AMIR; Palisades HS; Los Angeles, CA; (3); Drama Clb; JA; Math Tm; Science Clb; Cit Awd; High Hon Roll; Jr NHS; NHS; Prfct Atten Awd; Pres Acad Fit Awd; UCLA; Med.

BERKE, DAVID R; El Toro HS; Laguna Niguel, CA; (4); 100/550; Cmnty Wkr; Debate Tm; Key Clb; Intrml Bsbl; JV Tennis; High Hon Roll; Hon Roll; Civil Air Patrol; Aero Clb Flyng Lessons; Cal ST Fullerton; US Marine.

BERKE, TARA; Livermoore HS; Pleasanton, CA; (1); Drama Clb; Band; Mrchg Band; School Musical; Stage Crew; Tennis; High Hon Roll; Hon Roll; Santa Barbara; Music.

BERKHEIMER, WENDY L; Yucaipa HS; Angelus Oaks, CA; (1); Hosp Aide; Intrml Var Vllybl; Prfct Atten Awd; MVP Vlybl; Loma Linda U.

BERKLEY JR, JOSEPH L; Twentynine Palms HS; Twentynine Palms, CA; (3); Mrchg Band; San Bernardino Cty Hnr Mscn; Hi Dsrt Hnr Band; CC Jazz Band; Cal ST Hayward; Music.

BERLOGAR, ALLISON L; Napa HS; Napa, CA; (1); 59/400; Church Yth Grp; Key Clb; SADD; Var Bsktbl; JV Vllybl; JV Wt Lftg; Cit Awd; Hon Roll; NHS; Art Awd.

BERLOW, PAMELA S; Mission College Prep; San Luis Obispo, CA; (3); 4-H; Letterman Clb; Service Clb; Teachers Aide; Varsity Clb; Chorus; Pres Jr Cls; Stu Cncl; L Capt Bsktbl; JV Crs Cntry.

BERLS, CHARLES ERIK; Bellarmine College Prep; San Jose, CA; (3); 122/300; Boy Scts; Pres Computer Clb; Treas Science Clb; Teachers Aide; Lit Mag; Var Wrstlng; People To People; Intl Stu Ambsdr Prgm 90; Serra Clb; Alter Server Awd; BSA Order Of Arrow; Comp Sci.

BERMAN, CASEY B; Lowell HS; San Francisco, CA; (2); Temple Yth Grp; Ed Nwsp; JV Capt Bsbl; Bsktbl Jewish Yth Athletic Leag; Wrk Prt Time-Lifeguard.

BERMAN, JOEL; Brethren HS; Signal Hill, CA; (1); 13/105; Letterman Clb; Speech Tm; Varsity Clb; Bsktbl; Crs Cntry; Tennis; Wt Lftg; High Hon Roll; CSF; UCLA; Doctor.

BERMAN, RUSSELL T; Fountain Valley HS; Fountain Valley, CA; (2); JA; Red Cross Aide; Science Clb; Band; Jazz Band; Pep Band; School Musical; Off Soph Cls; High Hon Roll; CSF; Bike Club; Aircraft Engr.

BERMEA, JOAQUIN; Firebaugh HS; Firebaugh, CA; (1); FFA; Spanish Clb; Bsbl; Bsktbl; Ftbl; Wt Lftg; Hon Roll; Syracuse U; Bus Mgmt.

BERMEJO, LETICIA M; Bell Gardens HS; Belle Gardens, CA; (2); Science Clb; Prfct Atten Awd; U S CA; Sci Ed.

BERMUDEZ, BERNADETTE; Woodbridge HS; Irvine, CA; (2); Chorus; Drill Tm; School Musical; Hon Roll; UC Irvine; Sociology.

BERMUDEZ, CANDICE T; Mountain View HS; El Monte, CA; (3); Office Aide; USC; Lawyer.

BERMUDEZ, CARLA; Moreau HS; Fremont, CA; (3); Cmnty Wkr; JV Swmmng; High Hon Roll; Hon Roll; Princpls Hnr Roll; Graphic Dsgn.

BERMUDEZ, MARISELA; North Salinas HS; Salinas, CA; (4); 53/350; Church Yth Grp; English Clb; Key Clb; Science Clb; Teachers Aide; High Hon Roll; Hon Roll; Rotary Awd; Stu Yr 88-89; Hartrell; Bus Admin.

BERMUDEZ, RENE; Castle Park HS; Chula Vista, CA; (4); 53/328; JV Var Ftbl; JV Var Wrstlng; U Miami; Acctng.

BERMUDEZ, ROSALIA; Los Angeles County HS For The Arts; North Hollywood, CA; (4); Art Clb; French Clb; Science Clb; Stage Crew; Lit Mag; Various Art Shows; Yth Ending Hunger; Amnesty Intl; LA Stu Coalition; Art.

BERNA, PEBBLES R; Madera HS; Madera, CA; (3); Church Yth Grp; Dance Clb; Drama Clb; FBLA; JA; Science Clb; SADD; Crs Cntry; Wt Lftg; Cit Awd; Algebra I Awd; 3 Ctznshp Awds; Typing I Awd; Typing II Awd; PE Awd; Fresno ST; Bus Law.

BERNABE, WENDY C; Cajon HS; San Bernardino, CA; (1); 1/25; Ed Nwsp; Ed Yrbk; Rep Stu Cncl; Cit Awd; Hon Roll; Prfct Atten Awd; Schlrshp Awds Engl & Span; Principals Hnr Rl; CA Jr Schlstc Fed Awd; Ed.

BERNAL, DAN C; St Anthony HS; Carson, CA; (2); CA Poly Pamona; Arch.

BERNAL, JAZMIN; Antelope Valley HS; Pearblossom, CA; (2); Church Yth Grp; Dance Clb; Office Aide; SADD; Off Soph Cls; Stu Cncl; Trk; Hon Roll; Lwyr.

BERNAL, JENNA; Monte Vista Christian HS; Watsonville, CA; (4); 48/87; Stu Cncl; JV Score Keeper; JV Vllybl; NHS; Cal Poly San Louis; Hm Econ.

BERNAL, JOANN L; Fowler HS; Fresno, CA; (4); 34/60; Church Yth Grp; Drama Clb; Library Aide; Pep Clb; Spanish Clb; SADD; Flag Corp; Nwsp; Yrbk; Var Sftbl; U Of CA Davis.

BERNAL, MARIA; Modesto Christian HS; Modesto, CA; (3); Church Yth Grp; Chorus; Church Choir; Bsktbl; Sftbl; Letterman Clb; Pep Clb; Teachers Aide; Varsity Clb; Yrbk; UC Berkeley; Pre-Law.

BERNAL, VICTORIA; Nogales HS; Rowland Hts, CA; (4); Drill Tm; Yrbk; Olympians Clb; Whittier Coll; Bus Admin.

BERNAL, YOLANDA S; Valencia HS; Placentia, CA; (3); Sec Math Clb; Spanish Clb; Yrbk; Spnsh Merit Awd; Ed.

BERNARD, JAMIE S; Notre Dame HS; Moreno Valley, CA; (1); JV Ftbl; JV Socr; Hon Roll; Math.

BERNARD, NERISHA A; Venice HS; Venice, CA; (1); Intrml Crs Cntry; Vrs Awds Realstc Sktchs & Collages; Actvst Hlpng Statewd Ognzntn Defnd Initiative Prcss.

BERNARDI, GREGORY M; Modesto HS; Modesto, CA; (2); VP 4-H; Treas FFA; Teachers Aide; Golf; 4-H Awd; Outdoor Actvts; Gardng; UC Davis; Agronomy.

BERNARDIN, AARON S; Ocean View HS; Huntington Bch, CA; (4); 12/460; Chrmn Debate Tm; Key Clb; Math Clb; Chrmn Model UN; Sec Speech Tm; JV Swmmng; Hon Roll; CSF Bd Mbr Schlrshp; PTSA Schlrshp; Stu Mnth; Dstngshd Schlr Rcgntn; U CA Irvine.

BERNARDIN, LINDSEY; Ocean View HS; Huntington Beach, CA; (1); Model UN; Swmmng.

BERNARDINO, ADRIAN C; Fairfield HS; Suisun City, CA; (2); JV Ftbl; Hon Roll; Engrng.

BERNARDINO, RHEA B; San Gabriel Mission HS; El Monte, CA; (3); Drama Clb; French Clb; FBLA; Math Clb; Science Clb; Off Soph Cls; Hon Roll; Prfct Atten Awd; 3 Yrs Hnrs Engl; Child Psych.

BERNARDO, EDEL MAR A; Clayton Valley HS; Concord, CA; (3); Band; Jazz Band; Mrchg Band; Pep Band; Var Capt Tennis; Hon Roll; Jr NHS; Prfct Atten Awd.

BERNARDO, ENRICO J; St Francis HS; Glendale, CA; (2); Math Clb; Mu Alpha Theta; Pep Clb; Spanish Clb; Orch; Ed Yrbk; Pres Frsh Cls; Var Tennis; Hon Roll; NHS; CSF; Med.

BERNARDO, JOY GRACE; Lowell HS; San Francisco, CA; (3); Intnl Clb; Red Cross Aide; SADD; UC Partnership Pgm.

BERNARDO, RAINIER; Southwest HS; San Diego, CA; (3); Yrbk; Trk; Wt Lftg; Prfct Atten Awd; San Diego-Tijuana Intl Hstry Fair 3rd Pl Wnnr; Elect Engr.

BERNARDO, STACEY; Ceres HS; Ceres, CA; (1); FBLA; Sec Soph Cls; JV Cheerldng; JV Crs Cntry; JV Pom Pon; Var Trk; Hon Roll; Stanislaus ST; Law.

BERNARDO, STACY; Ernest Righetti HS; Santa Maria, CA; (4); 50/370; Hosp Aide; JA; Office Aide; Teachers Aide; Ed Rptr Nwsp; Phtg Yrbk; Treas Soph Cls; Treas Jr Cls; Treas Sr Cls; Stu Cncl; Deans List 87 & 90; Allan Hancock Coll; Accntng.

BERNARDS, BRIGETTE; Canyon HS; Canyon Country, CA; (3); 13/501; Church Yth Grp; Drama Clb; School Play; VP Stu Cncl; Hon Roll; NHS; Spanish NHS; CSF; Chrch Vlybl & Sftbl Team; Brigham Young U; Pediatrics.

BERNATH, EVA T; Fontana HS; Fontana, CA; (3); Cmnty Wkr; Drama Clb; Ski Clb; Teachers Aide; Vllybl; Hon Roll; NHS; Zonta Clb.

BERNDT, SUZANNE; Village Christian Schls; Sunland, CA; (4); 6/117; Cmnty Wkr; English Clb; Math Clb; Sec Mu Alpha Theta; Spanish Clb; Nwsp; Yrbk; Mgr Ftbl; Powder Puff Ftbl; Var Sftbl; Miss Sunland-Tujunga; Arspc Engrng.

BERNHARD, NICOLE; Fairfield HS; Fairfield, CA; (3); Pres Church Yth Grp; Cmnty Wkr; Debate Tm; Hosp Aide; JA; NFL; Pres Frsh Cls; Pres Soph Cls; Off Jr Cls; Stu Cncl; Piano Lssns; Dance Clss; Med.

BERNHARDT, CHAD J; Alameda HS; Alameda, CA; (4); 179/321; Chorus; Variety Show; Var JV Bsbl; JV Bsktbl; Var Ftbl; Bsbl MVP Both; Ohlone Coll.

BERNHEIM, ALICE J; Davis SR HS; Davis, CA; (2); 1/373; German Clb; Band; Pep Band; Bsktbl; Socr; Tennis; Pres Acad Fit Awd; Bio.

BERNS, JASON D; La Canada HS; La Canada Flintri, CA; (3); 50/250; Church Yth Grp; Math Clb; Mu Alpha Theta; Var Capt Bsktbl; Var Tennis; John Wooden Bsktbl Awd; Schlr-Athl Awd Bsktbl & Tnns.

BERNSTEIN, ARON R; San Ramon Valley HS; Danville, CA; (2); Hon Roll; Mt Diablo Astrnmcl Society; UC Berkeley; Astrphyscst.

BERNSTEIN, DAVID T; Bellarmine College Prep; Saratoga, CA; (3); Church Yth Grp; Debate Tm; NFL; Service Clb; Speech Tm; Nwsp; Yrbk; Hs Of Reps Page 90; U CA Berkley; Med.

BERNSTEIN, ERAN Y; Granada Hills HS; Northridge, CA; (2); Pres Computer Clb; Pres School Musical; VP Jwsh Frtrnty; UCLA; Bus.

BERNSTEIN, JESSICA E; Fremont HS; Sunnyvale, CA; (4); Cmnty Wkr; Debate Tm; Speech Tm; School Musical; School Play; Ed Nwsp; Stu Cncl; JV Tennis; JV Trk; Hon Roll; Engl, Jrnlsm Red-Wht Awd; CA Schlrshp Soc; UC Santa Barbara; Cmnctns.

BERNSTEIN, MICHELLE M; Alta Loma HS; Rancho Cucamonga, CA; (1); Church Yth Grp; Hosp Aide; High Hon Roll; Prfct Atten Awd; Nurse.

BERNSTEIN, TASHA L; Downey HS; Downey, CA; (3); French Clb; Service Clb; Ski Clb; Teachers Aide; Temple Yth Grp; Ed Nwsp; JV Var Swmmng; Hon Roll; Assisteens Downey, Treas; PTA Stu Recgntn Awd; CSF; Pepperdine; Jrnlsm.

BERNTSEN, RICHARD; Bellarmine College Prep; San Jose, CA; (3); 62/300; Letterman Clb; Varsity Clb; Var Ftbl; Var Wt Lftg; Block B; TX Chrstn U; Orthdntst.

BERQUAM, PAUL R; Rio Linda HS; N Highlands, CA; (3); Boy Scts; Chess Clb; French Clb; Hon Roll; NHS; Pres Acad Fit Awd; Martial Arts; Blck Blt; Cmptr Sci.

BERRENS, MELISSA J; Modesto Christian HS; Ripon, CA; (3); Church Yth Grp; Cmnty Wkr; Pep Clb; Phtg Ed Yrbk; Cheerldng; Gym; Swmmng; Hon Roll; Poltcl Sci.

BERRIDGE, JAMILA A; Whitney HS; Cerritos, CA; (1); Dance Clb; Drama Clb; Key Clb; Band; High Hon Roll; CJSF; 1st Pl Showstopper Natl Dance Cmptn; U CA; Law.

BERRIOS, CLAUDIA J; J Eugene Mc Ateer HS; San Francisco, CA; (3); Art Clb; Spanish Clb; School Play; Costume Designer.

BERRY, BRANDI DEANNA; Western HS; Anaheim, CA; (4); Cmnty Wkr; Drama Clb; School Play; Trk; Hon Roll; NHS; Animal Rights; Theatre Arts.

BERRY, BRENDA; Jordan HS; Long Beach, CA; (1); Church Yth Grp; Drill Tm; Orch; High Hon Roll; Medcl.

BERRY, CRYSTAL R; George Washington HS; San Francisco, CA; (4); 56/610; Church Yth Grp; Dance Clb; NFL; Speech Tm; Teachers Aide; Cit Awd; High Hon Roll; Black Stu Union Treas; VIP Clb; Howard U; Commnctns.

BERRY, DEBORAH A; Grant HS; Sacramento, CA; (3); Drama Clb; Rptr Nwsp; Yrbk; Hon Roll; UCLA; Actress.

BERRY, ERIKA; Anderson Union HS; Anderson, CA; (2); Acpl Chr; Chorus; Trk; Nrsng.

BERRY, HEATHER M; Thousand Oaks HS; Thousand Oaks, CA; (4); SADD; Band; Mrchg Band; Orch; School Musical; Yrbk; U Of CA Los Angeles; Law.

BERRY, JENNA; Yuba City HS; Yuba City, CA; (3); 21/600; Am Leg Aux Girls St; 4-H; Office Aide; Pep Clb; SADD; Off Yrbk; Stu Cncl; Cheerldng; 4-H Awd; High Hon Roll; Friends Intl; CSF; Hugh O Brian Schlrshp Outstndng Soph Ldr; Pres Clssrm; U CA Davis; Vet Sci.

BERRY, JENNIFER; Bishop Amat Memorial HS; Azusa, CA; (3); Drama Clb; Ed Yrbk; High Hon Roll; Hon Roll; Jr NHS; Occidental Clg.

BERRY, JENNIFER J; Hemet HS; Hemet, CA; (3); 33/600; Cmnty Wkr; Rep Sr Cls; Cit Awd; High Hon Roll; Hon Roll; Ntl Merit Ltr; CSF; Law.

BERRY, LISA; Campolindo HS; Moraga, CA; (3); Church Yth Grp; GAA; Spanish Clb; SADD; Acpl Chr; School Musical; Var Socr; JV Swmmng; Var Trk; Hon Roll.

BERRY, MAYA M; Davis SR HS; Davis, CA; (2); Girl Scts; Intnl Clb; Varsity Clb; Swmmng; HS Sectn & Delta League Chmpnshp Swim Team.

BERRY, RHONDA K; Weed HS; Weed, CA; (3); Am Leg Aux Girls St; Teachers Aide; Sftbl; Intr Decrtr.

BERRY, SHANLEY; Herlong HS; Doyle, CA; (4); 1/30; Cmnty Wkr; FBLA; Variety Show; Lit Mag; Pres Frsh Cls; Pres Soph Cls; Pres Stu Cncl; Stat Var Bsktbl; Capt Var Cheerldng; Var Sftbl; HOBY Ambsdr; Dsnys Doers & Drmrs Awd; CA ST U Sonoma; Elem Ed.

BERRY, SUZANNE M; California HS; Whittier, CA; (2); 1/482; Church Yth Grp; Hosp Aide; Swing Chorus; Var Crs Cntry; JV Var Trk; Kiwanis Awd; Golden State Exam Algebra; California High Schl Top 100; California Scholastic Federation; College; Business.

BERRY, TERRI; Pasadena HS; Pasadena, CA; (1); JA; Office Aide; Band; Drill Tm; Yrbk; Cheerldng; Cit Awd; Prfct Atten Awd; Awds For Chrldng,Music & Hstry; USC; Doctor.

BERRYHILL, LAURA M; Mira Mesa HS; San Diego, CA; (2); Drama Clb; French Clb; School Play; Stage Crew; JV Socr; JV Trk; Drmtc Arts; U Of CA; Marine Bio.

BERRYMAN, AARON R; St Bernard HS; Culver City, CA; (3); 31/357; Letterman Clb; Off Frsh Cls; Bsktbl; Var Capt Ftbl; Var L Trk; Hon Roll; NHS; All Amer Schlr; Cmnty Arct Awd; Pre-Law.

BERRYMAN, JOHN; Palmdale HS; Palmdale, CA; (3); Office Aide; Spanish Clb; Teachers Aide; Var Swmmng; Cit Awd; Prfct Atten Awd; Pres Acad Fit Awd.

BERRYMAN, KATHERINE D; Thousand Oaks HS; Thousand Oaks, CA; (2); German Clb; JA; JCL; Latin Clb; JV Trk; Pilot.

BERSHEE, MICHAEL B; Serrano HS; Wrightwood, CA; (1); FFA; Letterman Clb; JV L Bsbl; JV L Ftbl; Wt Lftg; Hon Roll; Junior Varsity Baseball Booster Club Award.

BERTELSEN, DEREK M; Saint Ignatius HS; Ross, CA; (2); Church Yth Grp; JV Tennis; Hon Roll; Mst Insprtnl Plyr Tnns Tm.

BERTELSEN, TRACY A; Montclair HS; Ontario, CA; (3); Church Yth Grp; Teachers Aide; Band; Mrchg Band; Orch; Pep Band; Hon Roll; Prfct Atten Awd; John Phillip Souza Awd; Phychthrpst.

BERTOK, RHONDA J; Highlands HS; North Highlands, CA; (3); Pres Church Yth Grp; Library Aide; Teachers Aide; Church Choir; Hon Roll; Prfct Atten Awd; Ricks Coll.

BERTOLERO, CHRISTINE M; Monte Vista HS; San Ramon, CA; (4); 85/418; Church Yth Grp; Teachers Aide; Band; Chorus; Drill Tm; Mrchg Band; Orch; Pep Band; Yrbk; High Hon Roll; U Of Pacific; Music Ed.

BERTOLI, TROY P; San Pasqual Acad; Perris, CA; (4); Church Yth Grp; Cmnty Wkr; Pres Soph Cls; Pres Jr Cls; Pres Stu Cncl; Capt Ftbl; Capt Gym; Intrml Socr; Intrml Sftbl; Intrml Swmmng; Physcal Ftnss Awd; 4 Yr Clb; 1st Pl In Schl Triathelon; Rvrside Cmnty Coll; Arch Engr.

BERTOLUCCI, MARIO; Carmel HS; Carmel, CA; (3); Bsbl; Ftbl; Socr; Hon Roll; Capt Ftbl Jr; Capt Sccr Jr & Soph; Contracting.

BERTRAM, KEELY; Yosemite HS; Oakhurst, CA; (3); 4/174; Drama Clb; Library Aide; Science Clb; Teachers Aide; Flag Corp; Stat Ftbl; Var Sftbl; Cit Awd; High Hon Roll; 9th Vlntr Knnl Aide At Vet Offc; Vet.

BERTRAM II, RICHARD L; Clovis HS; Clovis, CA; (3); Cmnty Wkr; French Clb; Office Aide; SADD; Teachers Aide; Vlntr Lcl Muscular Dystrophy Assn Office; US Intl San Diego; Scl Studies.

BERTRAM, RICKEY L; Arlington HS; Riverside, CA; (3); Boy Scts; Church Yth Grp; Lit Mag; Yth To Yth; Arch Clb; Med Rsrch.

BERTRAND, JENNIFER; Grace Davis HS; Modesto, CA; (3); Church Yth Grp; Letterman Clb; Var Bsktbl; Powder Puff Ftbl; Var JV Sftbl; Psych.

BERUMEN, DIANA; Mt View HS; El Monte, CA; (2); Science Clb; JV Tennis; High Hon Roll; Hon Roll; Prfct Atten Awd; Vrsty Badmntn; CSF; U Of CA Riverside; Med.

BERWIND, ANDREA E; Shasto HS; Redding, CA; (3); Am Leg Aux Girls St; Church Yth Grp; Drama Clb; Model UN; School Play; Stage Crew; JV Bsktbl; Sftbl; JV Trk; JV Intrml Vllybl; Ecology Club; Foreign Affairs.

BESAW, MICHELLE B; Bishop O'dowd HS; Castro Valley, CA; (2); Church Yth Grp; Pres 4-H; GAA; Ski Clb; Varsity Clb; Var Bsktbl; JV Crs Cntry; 4-H Awd; Hon Roll; Wstrn Pleasure Shw Hrs Trnr; Santa Barbara ST U; Mktng.

BESHEARS, RACHEL P; Paso Robles HS; Paso Robles, CA; (1); Church Yth Grp; FHA; Hon Roll.

BESKE, HEATH M; Lutheran HS; Orange, CA; (2); Ski Clb; JV Ftbl; JV Socr; Var Tennis; Surf Clb; Drexel; Bus.

BESS, LILLI JOI-TASHA; St Michaels HS; Inglewood, CA; (4); FBLA; GAA; Ed Yrbk; Rep Stu Cncl; Var Bsktbl; Var Vllybl; Hon Roll; NHS; Xerox Awd Soc Sci & Hmnties U Rochester NY; Cert Merit Hghst Hnr Sci & Math Soc Of Wmn Engrs; U Rochester; Comp Sci.

BESSER, GEORGE S; St Francis HS; Mountain View, CA; (4); Service Clb; JV Crs Cntry; JV Var Trk; High Hon Roll; NHS; Ntl Merit Ltr; Maxima Cum Laude Grad; UC Davis Chandellors Schlr; UC Davis; Phys Thrpy.

BESSIRE, AUTUMN; Pinole Valley HS; Richmond, CA; (2); Letterman Clb; Band; Color Guard; Drill Tm; Flag Corp; Mrchg Band; Pep Band; School Play; Stage Crew.

BEST, CHRISTINA M; Modesto HS; Modesto, CA; (4); 81/450; Dance Clb; Ski Clb; Chorus; School Musical; Ed Yrbk; Rep Stu Cncl; JV Var Cheerldng; Swmmng; Hon Roll; Hi-Deb Modeling; Rally Clb; U CA-DAVIS; Vet.

BEST, MELISSA B; Monte Vista HS; Danville, CA; (3); 76/356; Office Aide; Pep Clb; SADD; Teachers Aide; Chorus; Cit Awd; Hon Roll; Blackhawk Cntry Club Learning Merch/Mktg; Asst Organize, Plan, Decorate, Carry Out Functions; CA U Davis; Bus.

BEST, MICHELE J; Cordova SR HS; Rancho Cordova, CA; (3); Model UN; Teachers Aide; High Hon Roll; Hon Roll; Jr NHS; NHS; Ntrl Hlprs Scty; Schlstc Amer; Bus.

BESTER, JANET K; Cornelia Connelly Schl; La Palma, CA; (3); Girl Scts; Science Clb; Rptr Nwsp; Rep Stu Cncl; L Var Socr; Var Trk; High Hon Roll; NHS; Ntl Merit Ltr; Pres Acad Fit Awd; Library Clb-VP; Chrstn Action Rep.

BESTUL, MICHELLE; Prospect HS; San Jose, CA; (2); Pres Church Yth Grp; Piano; Lttrng Bdmntn; Babysttng; W Valley Coll; Teacher.

BESWICK, ROBERT; Westen Christian HS; La Verne, CA; (4); 6/100; Church Yth Grp; Pres Model UN; High Hon Roll; NHS; Ntl Merit SF; Rotary Awd; SEOS, Stu Explrtn & Dvlpmnt Of Space Club Pres; Martial Arts, Green Blt Karate; Astro Physics.

BETANCOURT, ANDRES; Le Grand Union HS; Planada, CA; (3); Church Yth Grp; Letterman Clb; Teachers Aide; JV Var Ftbl; Wt Lftg; Math.

BETANCOURT, DEBBIE; Roosevelt HS; Los Angeles, CA; (2); Art Clb; Computer Clb; Girl Scts; School Play; Bsktbl; Tennis; UCLA.

BETANCOURT, MARTIN; San Fernando Magnet HS; N Hollywood, CA; (3); Church Yth Grp; Science Clb; Off Jr Cls; JV Ftbl; Hon Roll; MESA; Sci Club; Magnet Monents.

BETANCOURT, STEVEN; Brawley Union HS; Brawley, CA; (3); Church Yth Grp; Teachers Aide; Varsity Clb; School Play; Pres Frsh Cls; Pres Jr Cls; Var Bsbl; Var Ftbl; Var Wt Lftg; Lion Awd; Stu Of Mnth Nov 89; UC Santa Barbara; Crmnl Jstc.

BETANCUR, STEPHANIE M; Rubidoux HS; Riverside, CA; (4); Church Yth Grp; Var Pom Pon; VP Of New Visions.

BETANZOS, DAVID J; Dana Hills HS; Laguna Beach, CA; (2); Chess Clb; Computer Clb; Letterman Clb; Varsity Clb; Jazz Band; Pep Band; Nwsp; Yrbk; Lit Mag; Stu Cncl; V Water Polo; Berkeley; Arch.

BETCHER, JENNIFER; Ambassador Baptist HS; Rialto, CA; (4); Church Yth Grp; FCA; GAA; Office Aide; Chorus; Church Choir; Nwsp; Ed Yrbk; Rep Soph Cls; VP Jr Cls; Vrs Sport Awds; Writing Awds; Chrch Reptr; Writing.

BETH, SAM R; Escondido HS; San Marcos, CA; (3); Stage Crew; Cert Merit For Strong Imprvmnt; Palona; Crtnst.

BETTENCOURT, ANDREA; Tulare Western HS; Tulare, CA; (3); Church Yth Grp; FFA; Office Aide; Cheerldng; Score Keeper; Swmmng; Tennis; Hon Roll; Cal Poly San Luis Opispo; Bus.

BETTENCOURT, ANGELA M; Tulare Union HS; Tipton, CA; (2); Church Yth Grp; Pep Clb; Rep Soph Cls; Var Cheerldng; Var Trk; Hon Roll; Prfct Atten Awd; LUSO Amer Fraternal Federation; Hnrs Hstry; Stu Cncl Debate Rep; Loyola Marymount U; Broadcastng.

BETTENCOURT, BRIAN; East Union HS; Manteca, CA; (2); 19/350; Bsbl; Bsktbl; Ftbl; Wt Lftg; Hon Roll; Prfct Atten Awd; Babe Ruth Bsbl All Stars & MVP; Drafting.

BETTENCOURT, DANIELLE R; East Union HS; Manteca, CA; (1); Var Trk; UCLA; Law.

BETTENCOURT, FRANK; Hanford Joint Union HS; Hanford, CA; (2); 4-H; FFA; 4-H Awd; High Hon Roll; Hon Roll; Outstndng Exhbtr Cnty Fair; Chptr Rprtr FFA Club; CA Polytechnic; Dairy Prod Sci.

BETTENCOURT, JANELLE L; Thomas Downey HS; Modesto, CA; (3); Church Yth Grp; SADD; Chorus; Church Choir; JV Var Crs Cntry; Var Trk; Hon Roll; CSF; Weber ST U; Nrsng.

BETTENCOURT, JOHN M; Sonora Union HS; Sonora, CA; (3); 59/263; Teachers Aide; JV Ftbl; Var JV Socr; AFROTC; Phlsphy.

BETTENCOURT, KAMA L; Hanford Union HS; Hanford, CA; (4); FBLA; Office Aide; Fresno City Coll; Bus Admin.

BETTENCOURT, MANDY M; Atwater HS; Winton, CA; (3); Var Sftbl; Var Vllybl; High Hon Roll; City Leag Sftbl; Writing Poetry; Bio.

BETTENCOURT, MARIA J; James Lick HS; San Jose, CA; (1); Comp Prgrmmng.

BETTENCOURT, PAT J; Turlock HS; Ceres, CA; (2); 154/400; Church Yth Grp; Rptr 4-H; Rptr Yrbk; 4-H Awd; CA Jr Holstein Assn; Bus Mgmt.

BETTERS, SAMANTHA L; Chula Vista HS; Imperial Beach, CA; (3); 39/493; Church Yth Grp; Pep Clb; Swmmng; Vllybl; Cit Awd; Dance Cls CA Ballet.

BETTES, LAURIE A; East Nicolaus HS; Pleasant Grove, CA; (2); Church Yth Grp; SADD; Ed Yrbk; Stu Cncl; Capt JV Bsktbl; Var Sftbl; Capt JV Vllybl; Hon Roll; Prfct Atten Awd; Dentist.

BETTIS, GABRIEL M; Cordova HS; Rancho Cordova, CA; (2); Church Yth Grp; German Clb; Model UN; Color Guard; Drill Tm; Cit Awd; Hon Roll; Jr NHS; Civil Air Patrol; Law.

BETTIS, GINA M; Yreka HS; Yreka, CA; (3); 20/175; Church Yth Grp; Quiz Bowl; Ski Clb; Spanish Clb; SADD; Band; Mrchg Band; Pep Band; JV Var Bsktbl; Intrml Powder Puff Ftbl; CSF; Sprts Med.

BETTS, BROOKE; Tustin HS; Tustin, CA; (2); AFS; JV Var Sftbl; Var Vllybl; Hon Roll; Sftbl MVP; Gldn ST Exam Hnrs Geo.

BEVERAGE, LISA; San Jacinto HS; Hemet, CA; (1); Pep Clb; San Diego ST U; Attrny.

BEVIEN, ROSAAN J; George Washington HS; San Francisco, CA; (2); Drama Clb; French Clb; Thesps; Varsity Clb; School Play; Rep Stu Cncl; JV Bsbl; Var Ftbl; JV Swmmng; JV Trk; San Diego ST U; Aeronaut Engr.

BEVILAQUA, RICHENE; Palisades HS; Pacific Palisades, CA; (4); 40/445; Debate Tm; Sec JA; Ski Clb; SADD; Chorus; JV Vllybl; Hon Roll; NHS; CA St Fair Wnnr Indstrl Educ.

BEYER, ALICE E; Granite Hills HS; Alpine, CA; (2); Art Clb; Drama Clb; 4-H; French Clb; Library Aide; Office Aide; Ski Clb; Teachers Aide; Band; Chorus; 3rd Pl Ice Sktng Comptn; U Of CA San Diego; Bus.

BEYER, LEZLIE; Mc Farland HS; Delano, CA; (3); 1/115; FBLA; Letterman Clb; Math Clb; Math Tm; SADD; Teachers Aide; Yrbk; Rep Stu Cncl; JV Var Cheerldng; Var Tennis; Acamdc Dcthln Team Slvr Medal For Essay; Mock Trial Team; Stu Brd Mem; Engrng.

BEYKE, SCOTT R; Quincy JR/Sr HS; Quincy, CA; (3); FFA; Socr; Vet.

BEYLER, NATHAN L; Fontana HS; Fontana, CA; (2); Church Yth Grp; Dance Clb; Letterman Clb; Ski Clb; L Swmmng; Pres Acad Fit Awd.

BEYLERIAN, PAOLA; Whittier Christian HS; Whittier, CA; (4); 21/180; Church Yth Grp; Drama Clb; French Clb; Girl Scts; Red Cross Aide; Ski Clb; Tennis; Trk; High Hon Roll; Investments Clb; CSF 87-89; MVP Ten; Intl Law.

BEYSCHAU, ANDREA; Oakmont HS; Roseville, CA; (3); 22/437; Drama Clb; Color Guard; Drill Tm; Trk; High Hon Roll; Hon Roll; CSF; Medcl.

BHAKTA, BINA; Gompers Secondary HS; San Diego, CA; (4); 5/101; Debate Tm; Hosp Aide; Key Clb; Scholastic Bowl; Treas Frsh Cls; Rep Soph Cls; Rep Jr Cls; Var Sftbl; Var Vllybl; Hon Roll; Greater San Diego Sci/ Engrng Fair Ind Pl 88 & 89; UC San Diego; Biophysics.

BHAKTA, CHHAYA; Saddleback HS; Santa Ana, CA; (4); 32/525; Band; Mrchg Band; Pep Band; Ed Yrbk; Swmmng; Tennis; Prfct Atten Awd; CSF; Ob.

BHAKTA, DHARMENDRA; St Paul HS; Los Angeles, CA; (3); 54/343; Varsity Clb; JV Var Vllybl; Hon Roll; NHS; Mrch For Hunger; U Of S CA; Phrmcy.

BHAKTA, MANISH; PV HS; Blythe, CA; (3); Hon Roll; Prfct Atten Awd; Pharm.

BHAKTA, RAKESH S; Culver City HS; Los Angeles, CA; (3); Cmnty Wkr; Teachers Aide; Tennis; Vllybl; Wt Lftg; Cit Awd; Hon Roll; Prfct Atten Awd; Cal Poly San Luis Obispo; Engr.

BHAKTA, RITA; Gompers Secondary HS; San Diego, CA; (1); 1/433; Scholastic Bowl; Intrml Vllybl; High Hon Roll; Treas Jr NHS; Spanish Class Award; Mahatma Gandhi Essay Contest Winner; Indian Cultural Dance Participant.

BHAN, NALINI; South San Francisco HS; S San Francisco, CA; (3); 3/30; San Francisco ST; Sys Analyst.

BHATIA, TARANJEET K; Richmond HS; San Pablo, CA; (2); Comp Operator.

BHATNAGAR, TANYA; Bishop Amat HS; Pomona, CA; (4); 8/400; Math Clb; Stu Cncl; Hon Roll; NHS; CA Acad Decathlon; CSF; Comp Engr.

BHATTI, NAVEENPAL S; Mission San Jose HS; Fremont, CA; (3); Computer Clb; Debate Tm; French Clb; Hosp Aide; Math Clb; Math Tm; NFL; Science Clb; Ski Clb; Speech Tm; Vlnt WA Hosp; Hnrs Golden St Exam Alg, Geom; Scuba Dvr; Cardiovsclr Srgn.

BHAWAN, SANDHYA D; Modesto HS; Modesto, CA; (3); Dance Clb; Math Clb; Model UN; Chorus; Rep Stu Cncl; Investigation.

BHIMANI, MEENESH A; Piedmont HS; Piedmont, CA; (3); Math Clb; Math Tm; Model UN; Spanish Clb; JV Bsbl; Var JV Socr; Ntl Merit Ltr; Med.

BHOOPAT, MITCH; Westminster HS; Westminster, CA; (3); 4/500; JCL; Latin Clb; JV Bsbl; Var Socr; CSF; Rotary Club Awd; Sports For Undrstndng Exch Stu; Med.

BIAGIOTTI, EDWARD J; Tustin HS; Tustin, CA; (2); Bus Profs of Am; Church Yth Grp; French Clb; JA; Math Clb; Var Ftbl; JV Wrstlng; High Hon Roll; Pres Acad Fit Awd; CSF; Top 25 Of Cls.

BIAGTAN, LOUELLA; Edison HS; Stockton, CA; (4); 21/400; Hosp Aide; Orch; Ed Yrbk; Stat Swmmng; Var Tennis; Hon Roll; Pres Sec NHS; CSF Secy; Sci Olympiad Team; Keywanettes; San Joaquin Delta Coll; Bio Sci.

BIANCHI, AMBER; Canyon HS; Canyon Country, CA; (1); Church Yth Grp; Cmnty Wkr; Girl Scts; Pep Clb; Church Choir; Cheerldng; DAR Awd; Hon Roll; Music Award Winning Compositions; X Country/Track; Writing Awds; Avid Reader; Westmont; Writing Short Stories.

BIANCHI, JENNIFER; Central Catholic HS; Manteca, CA; (2); 9/65; Art Clb; Cmnty Wkr; Ski Clb; Spanish Clb; VP Frsh Cls; Pres Soph Cls; JV Cheerldng; Var L Socr; JV Sftbl; High Hon Roll; CSF; 3rd Pl Schl Sci Fair; HOBY Ldrshp Awd.

BIANCHINI, DIANA M; Mills HS; San Bruno, CA; (2); Church Yth Grp; Cmnty Wkr; JA; Teachers Aide; Orch; Stu Cncl; Bsktbl; Gym; Mgr(s); Score Keeper; UC San Diego; Bio.

BIANDO, MARNIE F.; John Swett HS; Hercules, CA; (2); 1/123; Sec Science Clb; Sec Treas SADD; Drm Mjr(t); Rptr Nwsp; Treas Jr Cls; JV Bsktbl; JV Cheerldng; Var Pom Pon; JV Vllybl; High Hon Roll; CSF Secy; Educ.

BIASON, CHERRY ANNE G; Eagle Rock HS; Los Angeles, CA; (3); Key Clb; Science Clb; Chorus; Drill Tm; Ed Yrbk; Off Frsh Cls; Hon Roll; Prfct Atten Awd; Chmbr Sngrs; Hds Acrss Cmps; CSF; Rpbrs 89-90; Law.

BIBB, MATTHEW L; Bullard HS; Fresno, CA; (2); Intnl Clb; SADD; HS Sci Olympiad Team; Golden St Exam Algebra & Geom High Hnrs; CSF; Elem Educ.

BIBBS, MIALEEKA; Bloomington HS; Rialto, CA; (3); #1 In Class; Am Leg Aux Girls St; Drill Tm; Nwsp; Stu Cncl; JV Cheerldng; Var Capt Pom Pon; High Hon Roll; Jr NHS; NHS; Pres Acad Fit Awd; Ms Black Teen CA; Swans Deb; CSF; UCLA; Med.

BIBEL, SARA A; Berkeley HS; Berkeley, CA; (3); French Clb; Ed Nwsp; Ed Lit Mag; NHS; Cert Mrt Soc Womn Engrs; Bk Awd Smtih Coll; Excllnce Yth 1st Pl Creatv Wrtng; Chldrs Exprss Edtr; CSF.

BIBELHEIWER, ERIK D; Nevada Union HS; Nevada City, CA; (3); 36/551; Church Yth Grp; Hon Roll; Sci.

BIBLE, RAMIKA; St Michaels HS; Los Angeles, CA; (3); Cmnty Wkr; Variety Show; Cheerldng; Hon Roll; Intl Gold Teen Pgnt Cnst Mdlng 89; Phrmcst.

BIBLE, RONDE L; Lassen HS; Susanville, CA; (3); FFA; Library Aide; Chorus; JV Var Bsktbl; Stat Ftbl; JV Var Powder Puff Ftbl; Var Trk; High Hon Roll; Hon Roll; CSF; Phys Thrpy.

BIBLER, CHRIS S; Hoover HS; Fresno, CA; (3); French Clb; Letterman Clb; Science Clb; Ski Clb; Varsity Clb; Var L Bsbl; Var L Ftbl; High Hon Roll; Pres Acad Fit Awd; Gldn St Geom Awd; Bus Mgmt.

BIBLER, STACIE; Sunny Hills HS; Fullerton, CA; (4); Cmnty Wkr; Dance Clb; Pep Clb; Varsity Clb; Rep Frsh Cls; Rep Jr Cls; Rep Sr Cls; Stu Cncl; Var Cheerldng; Var Diving; Spcl Olympics Volunteer; Hrdles Leag Champn; San Luis Obispo; Phys Thrpy Ed.

BICERA, MICHELLE M; Nogales HS; Walnut, CA; (3); Teachers Aide; Church Choir; Hon Roll; UC Riverside; Bio.

BICK, MAYER; Yeshiva University Of Los Angeles; Los Angeles, CA; (4); 1/29; Chess Clb; Debate Tm; Pres English Clb; Ed Nwsp; Ed Yrbk; Var Bsbl; Intrml JV Bsktbl; NHS; Ntl Merit SF; Lg Pres Rotisserie Bsbll; Writer.

BICKERT, MARTA A; El Toro HS; El Toro, CA; (3); 19/512; German Clb; Orch; Var Capt Bsktbl; Var Sftbl; Var Vllybl; High Hon Roll; Kiwanis Awd; NHS; Pres Acad Fit Awd; Keywanettes; CA Schlrshp Fed; Phys Thrpy.

BICKFORD, TARA D; Prospect HS; Campbell, CA; (1); 55/225; Church Yth Grp; Teachers Aide; Band; Color Guard; Drm Mjr(t); Flag Corp; Mrchg Band; Powder Puff Ftbl; Score Keeper; JV Sftbl; Teacher.

BICKHAM, MELISSA D; Apple Valley HS; Apple Valley, CA; (4); Church Yth Grp; Drama Clb; French Clb; Chorus; Church Choir; School Play; Crs Cntry; Hon Roll; Pres Acad Fit Awd; CA Schlrshp Fed Lftm; Bible Quizzing & From Drama Clb Schlrshp; Pres Schlrshp Point Loma Naz Coll; Pt Loma Nazarene Coll; Ed.

BICKLEY, COLIN H; Oak Park HS; Agoura Hills, CA; (1); Church Yth Grp; Thesps; School Musical; School Play; JV Ftbl; JV Socr; Var Tennis; USC; Film Prdctn.

BICKLEY, JAMI D; Tustin HS; Tustin, CA; (1); JV Socr; Var L Trk; Hon Roll; Bst Offnsv Plyr; JV Sccr Team; Mst Outstndg Dist Rnnr V Track Team.

BICKNELL, DIANE; Lone Pine HS; Wickenberg, AZ; (1); Cmnty Wkr; Dance Clb; Ski Clb; Varsity Clb; Cheerldng; High Hon Roll; CFS; Secy.

BIDDISON, NICOLE H; Arroyo Grande HS; Arroyo Grande, CA; (2); 21/625; AFS; Church Yth Grp; Church Choir; VP Frsh Cls; JV Var Score Keeper; JV Sftbl; High Hon Roll; Hon Roll; Pres Acad Fit Awd; Stu Tutor; Point Loma Nazarene; Sec Ed.

BIDDLE, CHRISTY L; Turlock HS; Turlock, CA; (4); Church Yth Grp; VP Band; Church Choir; VP Mrchg Band; Sunday Sch Tchr; Bank Of Amer Music Awd; CA ST U Stanislaus; Elem Tchr.

BIDILA, DENISA; Downey HS; Downey, CA; (4); Church Yth Grp; Cmnty Wkr; Library Aide; Office Aide; CSU Long Beach.

BIDINIAN, ARLINE O; Pasadena HS; Pasadena, CA; (2); Bsktbl; Hon Roll; Armenian & CSF Clubs.

BIDWAL, INDERPREET; Livingston HS; Livingston, CA; (3); Hon Roll; Stanislaus U; Sec.

BIDWELL, DEBBIE M; College Park HS; Concord, CA; (2); Church Yth Grp; Cmnty Wkr; Model UN; Band; Jazz Band; Mrchg Band; Swmmng; High Hon Roll; William K Holt Sci Schlrshp; CA Schlrshp Fed; USF; Med.

BIDWELL, SARAH; Big Valley HS; Bieber, CA; (4); 1/22; Church Yth Grp; Speech Tm; Pres SADD; School Play; Pres Sr Cls; Cheerldng; High Hon Roll; Kiwanis Awd; Val; Voice Dem Awd; 2nd Pl Vocational Educ Olympics; CSU Chico; Elem Educ.

BIE, LARRY R; South San Francisco HS; South San Francis, CA; (2); Church Yth Grp; Computer Clb; French Clb; FBLA; Math Clb; Math Tm; JV Trk; High Hon Roll; 1st Pl Natl Math Leag Alg II 89-90; CSF; Concerned Stu Clb; Asian Amer Clb.

BIEGERT, BRIAN; Capistrano Valley Christian HS; Sa J Capistrano, CA; (3); Church Yth Grp; Var L Bsbl; Var JV Ftbl; Var L Socr; High Hon Roll; JV Bsbl Mst Insprtnl Plyr; JV Ftbl Coaches Awd; Vrsty Ftbl Mst Imsprtnl Plyr, Offnsv Plyr Of Yr.

BIELECKI, NICHOLAS M; Gilroy HS; Gilroy, CA; (1); JV Ftbl; JV Trk; Wt Lftg; Pres Acad Fit Awd; CSF; Amer Leg Schltc Mdl; UCLA; Med.

BIERICH, STEPHANIE N; Mission Viejo HS; Laguna Hills, CA; (2); 34/439; JV Swmmng; JV Vllybl; CSF; Acad Achvt Awd; Spnsh Mrt Cert; Berkeley; Med.

BIERNACKI, KRISTI M; Sonora Union HS; Jamestown, CA; (2); Bus.

BIERNACKI, PETER; Arcadia HS; Arcadia, CA; (4); 112/651; Am Leg Boys St; Church Yth Grp; Pres Service Clb; Capt Varsity Clb; Rep Stu Cncl; Var Capt Swmmng; Hon Roll; NHS; Rotary Awd; Alumni Assn-Dr Richard Cordano Schlrshp; Ewport Sailng Clb; 13th Annl Rotary I Ntl Wrld Affrs Semnr; U Of CA-IRVINE; Phys Sci.

BIESECKER, LORI; Mc Kinleyville HS; Arcata, CA; (4); Drama Clb; 4-H; Stage Crew; Hon Roll; Humboldt ST U.

BIGBY, TIFFANY L; John Muir HS; Altadena, CA; (3); Church Yth Grp; Debate Tm; VP Drama Clb; Key Clb; Speech Tm; Drill Tm; Rep Stu Cncl; Cheerldng; Pom Pon; Score Keeper; ACSI Cheer Cmp; 1st Pl Spch Meet; Spelman Coll; Frnsc Sci.

BIGELOW, CARA E; Dublin HS; Dublin, CA; (3); 12/156; Church Yth Grp; Service Clb; Teachers Aide; JV Bsktbl; JV Sftbl; High Hon Roll; Hon Roll; Psych.

BIGELOW, KATY; Bret Harte HS; Murphys, CA; (1); AFS; Church Yth Grp; Cmnty Wkr; Ski Clb; Chorus; Tennis; High Hon Roll; Hon Roll; CSF.

BIGELOW, MARGARET I; Westwood HS; Westwood, CA; (2); FHA; Girl Scts; Band; Mrchg Band; Bsktbl; Sftbl; Vllybl; Hon Roll; Peer Pgm; Ar Frc; Intr Dcrtr.

BIGELOW, NICHOLAS W; La Serna HS; Whittier, CA; (2); 1/450; Boy Scts; Church Yth Grp; JCL; SADD; JV Bsbl; JV Bsktbl; VP L Crs Cntry; High Hon Roll; NHS; Eagle Scout; Piano; CSF.

BIGGS, RICK L; Apple Valley SR HS; Apple Valley, CA; (3); VP FBLA; Trk; Med.

BIGGS, SAMUEL J; Marysville HS; Marysville, CA; (1); Art Clb; 4-H; Band; Mrchg Band; JV Bsbl; Stat Bsktbl; Ftbl; Hon Roll.

BIGGS, TRICIA; Pioneer HS; San Jose, CA; (1); Church Yth Grp; Cmnty Wkr; Service Clb; Spanish Clb; Yrbk; Rep Frsh Cls; Pres Soph Cls; Var Socr; Var Trk; Elks Awd; Mayors Yth Conf; CSF; Art.

BIGHAM, GENEVA G; Trona HS; Trona, CA; (2); 9/40; 4-H; JV Tennis; Mgr Vllybl; 4-H Awd; Attrny.

BIGLANG-AWA, VAN ERIC; Liberty Union HS; Oakley, CA; (3); French Clb; Nwsp; High Hon Roll; CSF; U Of CA Berkeley; Mech Engrng.

BIGLER, AZRAEL E; School Of The Arts; San Francisco, CA; (3); Thesps; Chorus; School Musical; School Play; Variety Show; Hon Roll; Young Peoples Musical Theater; Webster U; Theater.

BIGLIETTI, DEBORAH; Canyon HS; Canyon Country, CA; (3); 22/550; French Clb; ROTC; Color Guard; School Musical; Swing Chorus; High Hon Roll; NHS; Martial Arts/Recieve Black Belt In 6 Mnths; Taekwondo; VFW Awd & Schlstc Excell Awd; U Of Tampa; Pre-Law.

BIGNELL, GAYLIN; Maranatha HS; Arcadia, CA; (2); Church Yth Grp; Service Clb; Teachers Aide; Flag Corp; High Hon Roll; Hon Roll; CSF.

BIHN, MICHELE C; San Pedro HS; San Pedro, CA; (3); Band; Drill Tm; School Musical; VP Frsh Cls.

BIJOR, SHIPRA K; Mission San Jose HS; Fremont, CA; (2); Debate Tm; Speech Tm; Chorus; School Musical; Swing Chorus; Stu Cncl; Dance; UCLA; Law.

BIKUL, NEVIN L; Branham HS; San Jose, CA; (1); School Play; Swmmng; Hon Roll; Part Time Job; San Jose ST U; Radio Brdcstng.

BILBERRY, RON E; Nevada Union HS; Grass Valley, CA; (4); SADD; Teachers Aide; Var Capt Bsbl; Var L Socr; Hon Roll; Santa Rosa JC; Lw Enfrcmnt.

BILBREY, JULIE J; Warren HS; Downey, CA; (3); 52/350; Var Sftbl; Hon Roll; Prfct Atten Awd; San Gabriel Valley Leag 2nd Team-All Leag Sftbl 89-90.

BILBREY, SHANON; Bonita Vista HS; Bonita, CA; (1); Church Yth Grp; Dance Clb; Pep Clb; Ski Clb; SADD; Cheerldng; Cit Awd; Avid Pres.

BILEY, MONICA L; Las Plumas HS; Oroville, CA; (1); Church Yth Grp; Hon Roll; Pres Acad Fit Awd; Registered Nrsng.

BILICIC, JACK; San Pedro HS; San Pedro, CA; (3); Acad All-Stars; Bus Accntng.

BILKOO, PAREENA; Marysville HS; Marysville, CA; (1); Letterman Clb; JV Bsbl; High Hon Roll; Hon Roll; Mst Insprtnl Plyr-Bsktbl; Alt GATE Rep; Stanford U; Medcl Doctor.

BILKOO, PERRY S; Marysville HS; Marysville, CA; (3); 35/130; Cmnty Wkr; Debate Tm; Letterman Clb; Speech Tm; Socr; Tennis; Trk; High Hon Roll; Hon Roll; Lion Awd; Lions Clb Speech Cont Awd; Debate Trnmt 1st Pl Wnnr, 3rd Pl Trphy; Bus Admin.

BILL, LEMKE E; Canyon HS; Canyon Country, CA; (3); Ftbl; Law Enfrcmnt.

BILLAN, AMARJIT; Tranquillity Union HS; Cantua Creek, CA; (3); 31/250; Bus Profs of Am; Intnl Clb; SADD; Teachers Aide; Yrbk; Hon Roll; Stu Of Qrtr; Hrn Roll; Fresno STU; Bus Accntnt.

BILLER, JENNIFER LYNN; Montclair HS; Ontario, CA; (3); Pres Sec Church Yth Grp; Cmnty Wkr; Band; Chorus; Mrchg Band; Stat Tennis; High Hon Roll; Hon Roll; Alg II Math Awd; Advncd Alg III, Trig & Geom Awd; Outstndng Engl Awds 88 & 90; Outstndng Music Awd; Cal Poly Pomona; Animal Husband.

BILLETER, DARRON M; Acalanes HS; Lafayette, CA; (4); Boy Scts; Church Yth Grp; VP Drama Clb; Letterman Clb; Acpl Chr; Chorus; School Play; Treas Stu Cncl; Var L Bsktbl; Brigham Young U.

BILLIET, ROD A; Bret Harte HS; Angels Camp, CA; (3); Art Clb; Ski Clb; Varsity Clb; Var Bsktbl; Var Trk; High Hon Roll; Art Inst FL; Commrcl Art.

BILLINGSLEY, JOHN W; Bishop O'dowd HS; Bartlesville, OK; (2); Cmnty Wkr; ROTC; Ski Clb; Rptr Nwsp; Pres Frsh Cls; JV L Ftbl; JV L Socr; JV L Swmmng; High Hon Roll; Hon Roll; Tae Kwon Do 2nd Degree Black Belt; Harvard; Law.

BILLMAN, ANGE; North Hollywood HS; North Hollywood, CA; (3); Church Yth Grp; Debate Tm; Drama Clb; Spanish Clb; Speech Tm; Drill Tm; Var Cheerldng; Powder Puff Ftbl; High Hon Roll; Pres Acad Fit Awd.

BILLMAN, MICHAEL; Clovis West HS; Fresno, CA; (3); Boy Scts; Crs Cntry; Fresno U; Med.

BILLOO, ABDULNASIR; Chaffey HS; Rancho Cucamonga, CA; (3); Key Clb; Spanish Clb; High Hon Roll; Hon Roll; CSF; Interact; Friday Night Live; Matls Sci.

BILLOW, KRISTIN L; College Park HS; Pleasant Hill, CA; (3); Cmnty Wkr; German Clb; Rep Soph Cls; Sec Stu Cncl; Swmmng; Vllybl; High Hon Roll; Hon Roll; Aids Educ Cmmtte; Hnrbl Mntns Art Work; UC Davis; Law.

BILLS, CYBIL L; Channel Islands HS; Oxnard, CA; (2); Cmnty Wkr; UCLA; Sci.

BILSKI, CHRISTOPHER R; Casa Role Fundamental HS; Citrus Heights, CA; (2); 10/461; AFS; Church Yth Grp; Spanish Clb; Cit Awd; High Hon Roll; CSF.

BINDER, DAVID M; Bonita HS; La Verne, CA; (2); 1/350; Ed Nwsp; Ed Yrbk; Mgr(s); High Hon Roll; JV Bdmntn; CTY; 4th Pl Acad Olympiad, Acad Decath; Treas CSF; Math.

BINFORD, SUSANNE R; North HS; Bakersfield, CA; (4); Dance Clb; Debate Tm; Sec Drama Clb; French Clb; Pres Pep Clb; Ski Clb; School Play; Nwsp; Yrbk; NHS; UC Riverside; Bio-Med Sci.

BINGAMAN, SHERI R; Fontana HS; Rialto, CA; (2); 110/1200; Church Yth Grp; Girl Scts; Scholastic Bowl; Acpl Chr; Band; Church Choir; Mrchg Band; Orch; School Musical; Swing Chorus; CSF; Campus Life; Azusa Pacific U; Music.

BINGHAM, CORBIN J; Fall River HS; Fall River Mills, CA; (2); Art Clb; Boy Scts; Church Yth Grp; Pep Clb; Ski Clb; Lit Mag; Bsbl; Bsktbl; Ftbl; Trk; Ricks Coll.

BINGHAM, FREDDIE R; East Bakersfield HS; Bakersfield, CA; (2); Library Aide; High Hon Roll; JV Bsbl; NFL; Hghst GPA Bsbl Awd; CSF; Bio Sci.

BINGHAM, SHERRIE A; Antioch HS; Antioch, CA; (3); 51/634; Church Yth Grp; Cmnty Wkr; Pres Key Clb; Letterman Clb; Spanish Clb; Church Choir; Jazz Band; Orch; School Musical; School Play; Stu Amb Soviet Un 90; Ed.

BINION, PAUL C; Milpitas HS; Milpitas, CA; (2); Church Yth Grp; JV Crs Cntry; De Anza Coll; Bus Mgmt.

BINNEWEG, ANNA M; North Tahoe HS; Tahoe City, CA; (1); 19/120; JA; Ski Clb; Teachers Aide; Band; Jazz Band; School Musical; Crs Cntry; Sftbl; High Hon Roll; Spanish NHS; Stanford U; Tchr.

BINNING, PETER; Caruthers Union HS; Caruthers, CA; (3); Computer Clb; French Clb; VP FBLA; Letterman Clb; Math Clb; SADD; JV Bsktbl; Var Mgr(s); Var Tennis; Outstndng Frshmn Of Yr; Most Imprvd Tennis; Most Inspirational Bsktbl; Fresno ST U; Elec Engr.

BINTOCAN, ALEJO N; Oak Grove HS; San Jose, CA; (3); Math Clb; Engrng.

BIPPUS, MARISA T; Western Christian HS; La Verne, CA; (4); Church Yth Grp; French Clb; Pep Clb; Ski Clb; Teachers Aide; Cheerldng; Trk; Vllybl; Cit Awd; Hon Roll; Hnrs Bible; Been In Two Movies, Los Angeles Magazine Sept 90; Stage Name Maeisa Myles; UC Irvine; Psych.

BIR, NATASHA DINKER; Mt Pleasant HS; San Jose, CA; (2); 1/467; SADD; Thesps; Band; School Musical; JV Vllybl; High Hon Roll; St Schlr; JR Stsmn Amer; Vrsty Bdmntn; Hlpng Hands Cmmnty Svc Grp Fndr & Ldr; Stanford; Doc.

BIR, SAMISH; Mount Pleasant HS; San Jose, CA; (3); 34/439; Computer Clb; Math Clb; Thesps; School Play; Stage Crew; Tennis; NHS; Pres Acad Fit Awd; Engr.

BIRCH, CHRISTIAN W; Etna HS; Etna, CA; (4); 3/62; Church Yth Grp; Math Clb; Ski Clb; Teachers Aide; Varsity Clb; Band; Capt Bsktbl; Capt Tennis; Elks Awd; High Hon Roll; Westmont Coll; Phys Ed.

BIRCHLER, LARA N; University City HS; San Diego, CA; (3); Dance Clb; Model UN; Treas Pep Clb; Pres SADD; School Play; Lit Mag; Treas Frsh Cls; Var Sftbl; High Hon Roll; Pres Acad Fit Awd; Golden St Exam Geom High Hnrs; U CA.

BIRD, AMANDA MARIE; Reedley HS; Reedley, CA; (3); 12/310; Computer Clb; Debate Tm; Drama Clb; French Clb; Service Clb; Speech Tm; School Play; JV Sftbl; Hon Roll; Beginning Piano Lssns & Recitals; Cnty Employee At Branch Libraries; 2 Frnscs Vrsty Awds.

BIRD, AMBER M; Manteca HS; Manteca, CA; (2); 7/430; Church Yth Grp; Drama Clb; SADD; Thesps; Church Choir; School Play; Stage Crew; Variety Show; High Hon Roll; Chuch Yth Grp Ldr; MIT; Math.

BIRD, CHRISTOPHER B; Ponderosa HS; Placerville, CA; (1); JV Crs Cntry; Var L Swmmng; Hon Roll; Prfct Atten Awd; Arch.

BIRD, JOSEPH D; Del Campo HS; Carmichael, CA; (2); 35/450; Boy Scts; Church Yth Grp; French Clb; FBLA; Quiz Bowl; SADD; Acpl Chr; Chorus; Church Choir; Rep Stu Cncl; Galena Street East Prfmng Ambssdrs At World Expo Brisbane Australia 88 USA Rep; Brigham Young U.

BIRD, RYAN L; Savanna HS; Buena Park, CA; (3); Boy Scts; Drama Clb; Spanish Clb; Stage Crew; Variety Show; Pres Frsh Cls; Rep Soph Cls; Rep Jr Cls; Pres Stu Cncl; JV Socr; BYU; Bus.

BIRD, STACY L; Hayward HS; Castro Valley, CA; (2); 20/274; Church Yth Grp; Cmnty Wkr; Dance Clb; Spanish Clb; Band; Mrchg Band; High Hon Roll; Hon Roll; Chabot Coll; Vet Med.

BIRDSONG, JENNIFER K; Palo Verde HS; Blythe, CA; (3); Church Yth Grp; Drama Clb; 4-H; FFA; Pep Clb; Teachers Aide; Chorus; 4-H Awd; Hon Roll; FFA Chapter Sweetheart 89-90; Cal ST.

BIRKEY, SIMON; Maranatha HS; Pasadena, CA; (2); Drama Clb; Teachers Aide; Stage Crew; CSF; Med.

BIRKHIMER, JOHN; Liberty Union HS; Byron, CA; (3); Pres VP Church Yth Grp; VP 4-H; JV Ftbl; Var Trk; Wt Lftg; 4-H Awd; Hon Roll; CSF; Close Up; CIF Schlr Athlte Awd; Pilot.

BIRKINSHAW, JULIE JEAN; Apple Valley HS; Apple Valley, CA; (1); 54/462; FFA; Letterman Clb; Pep Clb; Spanish Clb; Varsity Clb; Var L Socr; Cit Awd; Hon Roll; Pres Acad Fit Awd; Stu Of Mnth Oct 89; Athl Awd 87-88, 88-89, 89-90; CIF Achvt Awd 90; Cal Poly Pomona; Bus.

BIRLA, RADHA; Tracy HS; Tracy, CA; (3); FHA; Spanish Clb; Rep Stu Cncl; JV Bsktbl; Var Trk; Hon Roll; Prfct Atten Awd; UCLA; Bus Leader.

BIRMINGHAM, SARAH J; Thomas Downey HS; Modesto, CA; (2); Library Aide; NFL; Speech Tm; Swmmng; CSF; Mck Trl Tm; Acad All Conf Tm.

BIRMINGHAM, TODD K; Bishop Union HS; Bishop, CA; (3); Am Leg Boys St; Band; Pres Stu Cncl; JV Ftbl; Trk; Hon Roll; Mock Trial; Stu Bdy Pres; UCLA; Med.

BIRNIE, TATE A; Analy HS; Sebastopol, CA; (2); 1/260; Math Clb; Service Clb; Rptr Nwsp; Lit Mag; Rep Stu Cncl; JV Bsktbl; Var Swmmng; High Hon Roll; Outstndng Math & Spanish Stu; Stu Of Month; Athl Of Month.

BIS, RICHARD P; John F Kennedy HS; San Pablo, CA; (1); JV Bsbl; Hon Roll; Outstndng Achvt Wrld Hstry; Stanford U; Lawyer.

BISCARRA, ESTHER; Westmoor HS; Daly City, CA; (3); Church Yth Grp; GAA; Hosp Aide; SADD; Teachers Aide; Var Cheerldng; JV Vllybl; Hon Roll; UC Davis; Med.

BISCHOFF, JOLENE; Archbishop Mitty HS; Cupertino, CA; (3); 32/255; Art Clb; Cmnty Wkr; SADD; Teachers Aide; JV Fld Hcky; Intrml Powder Puff Ftbl; Var Trk; High Hon Roll; Hon Roll; NHS; Envrmntlst Clb; 1stpl Parent Stu Directory Covr Cont.

BISCHOFF, SHANNON L; Oakmont HS; Roseville, CA; (2); Church Yth Grp; Cmnty Wkr; Drama Clb; Hosp Aide; Latin Clb; Service Clb; SADD; Teachers Aide; Chorus; Church Choir; Spnsh I Viking Pride Awd; U Of CA San Diego; Bus.

BISHO, JASON BRAUN; Mira Loma HS; Sacramento, CA; (3); Boy Scts; ROTC; SADD; Swmmng; UC Davis; Natl Frst Rngr.

BISHOP, JEFF; Capistrano Valley Christian HS; Laguna Beach, CA; (3); Church Yth Grp; JV Var Bsbl; Intrml JV Bsktbl; JV Var Ftbl; High Hon Roll; Prfct Atten Awd; Pres Acad Fit Awd; Schlstc Lttr.

BISHOP, JENNIFER; Lompoc HS; Lompoc, CA; (2); 44/344; 4-H; Band; Flag Corp; Hon Roll; Schl Of Ballet; Cal ST-POMONIA; Htl/Rest Mgt.

BISHOP, JENNIFER A; Mountain View HS; Los Altos, CA; (4); Church Yth Grp; Dance Clb; Drama Clb; French Clb; Pep Clb; Service Clb; Thesps; Acpl Chr; Chorus; Church Choir; Gardening; Community Theatre; Antiques; Needlepoint; U Of Oregon; History.

BISHOP, KATHY M; Barstow HS; Barstow, CA; (2); Library Aide; VP Frsh Cls; Var Trk; Cit Awd; High Hon Roll; Hon Roll; Wn Desert Heritage Wrtng Cont 2nd Pl Poetry; Sccr Trnmnt; Duke U; Bus.

BISHOP, KIMBERLY D; Tranquility Union HS; Tranquillity, CA; (3); Church Yth Grp; 4-H; Letterman Clb; Pep Clb; Science Clb; Ski Clb; Teachers Aide; Yrbk; VP Soph Cls; Rep Stu Cncl; San Diego ST U; Bus.

BISHOP, KYLE; Loyalton HS; Loyalton, CA; (1); Drama Clb; Ski Clb; Spanish Clb; Rptr Nwsp; Ed Yrbk; VP Soph Cls; Cheerldng; Vllybl; High Hon Roll; Hon Roll; Long Beach ST; Sports Med.

BISHOP, LE ANN; Escondido HS; San Marcos, CA; (3); Key Clb; Teachers Aide; Rep Nwsp; Yrbk; JV Swmmng; Hon Roll; Geom Awd; Nrsng.

BISHOP, MARY K; Manteca HS; Manteca, CA; (4); 14/300; Cmnty Wkr; NFL; SADD; Teachers Aide; Color Guard; Flag Corp; JV Var Bsktbl; Var Trk; Mgr Vllybl; High Hon Roll; Delta JC; Med.

BISHOP, MELANIE A; Sherman E Burroughs HS; Ridgecrest, CA; (4); Art Clb; Church Yth Grp; Key Clb; Pep Clb; Ski Clb; Teachers Aide; Church Choir; Rptr Nwsp; VP Frsh Cls; Rep Jr Cls; Art Excllnce Awd; Techncl Mentor Pgm Comp Aide Naval Weapons Ctr; BYU; Grphc Dsgn.

BISHOP, RYAN DEAN; Irvine HS; Irvine, CA; (1); Bsbl; Pres Acad Fit Awd; U CA Irvine; Art.

BISHOP, SOMMER JOANNA; John F Kennedy HS; Corona, CA; (1); Church Yth Grp; Letterman Clb; Pep Clb; Off Frsh Cls; Cheerldng; JV Socr; Var L Swmmng; NHS; Grn Pce; Lfgrd Trng; Snta Brbra U; Marine Bio.

BISHOP, YASMIN; Hanford Joint Union HS; Hanford, CA; (3); 1/411; Church Yth Grp; Drama Clb; School Play; High Hon Roll; Pres Acad Fit Awd; UCSB; Anthropology.

BISPO, POLLY A; Clovis HS; Fresno, CA; (1); Church Yth Grp; Var Debate Tm; NFL; Speech Tm; Hon Roll; Ntl Merit Ltr; CA Schlrshp Fed; Sociology.

BISSELL, BRIAN T; Redwood Christian Schools Schls; San Leandro, CA; (2); 3/59; Aud/Vis; Office Aide; Chorus; School Musical; Mgr Yrbk; Treas Frsh Cls; Treas Soph Cls; Mgr(s); Hon Roll; Treas Jr Cls; CSF; Booster Clb-Chrmn/Mgr; People- People Stu Ambssdr To N Europe; Dir/Coordntr-Bay Chrstn Trck Meet; Law.

BISSELL, MATTHEW A; Berkeley HS; Berkeley, CA; (3); JV Var Bsbl; JV Var Ftbl; Engr.

BISTROW, CARI; Agoura HS; Agoura Hills, CA; (2); 17/469; Hosp Aide; Pep Clb; Spanish Clb; Rep Stu Cncl; Cheerldng; Cit Awd; Hon Roll; Pres Acad Fit Awd.

BITER, CINDY L; Arvin HS; Bakersfield, CA; (2); Drama Clb; Ski Clb; School Play; Off Soph Cls; Stu Cncl; Sftbl; Vllybl; Hon Roll; Fine Arts Awd; Gate Eng & Bio; Santa Barbara JC; Psych.

BITON, CHARLOTTE A; Bishop Amat HS; Diamond Bar, CA; (3); Drill Tm; Stu Cncl; Powder Puff Ftbl; Hon Roll; NHS; Prfct Atten Awd; Amer Hstry.

BITTE, RACHEL E; Fortuna HS; Carlotta, CA; (2); Church Yth Grp; Cmnty Wkr; Acpl Chr; Rep Soph Cls; Rep Jr Cls; Crs Cntry; Trk; High Hon Roll; Hon Roll; NHS; Girls Frshmn PE Awd; U Of CA; Phy Thrpy.

BITTER, KIRK P; Kerman HS; Kerman, CA; (4); 1/120; Treas Church Yth Grp; Pres 4-H; FTA; German Clb; Letterman Clb; Math Tm; Model UN; Scholastic Bowl; SADD; Band; Army Rsrvs Schlr/Ath Awd; Astrlgy Club Pres; CA Poly; Mech Engrng.

BITTNER, JAMES A; Newark Memorial HS; Newark, CA; (3); 38/355; Teachers Aide; Hon Roll; 1st Yr Alg Golden St Exm Hnrs Awd; Alameda Cnty Fr 3rd Awd Arch Dsgn; San Jose ST; Civil Engr.

BJAANES, ANNELISE P; Rim Of The World HS; Running Springs, CA; (2); 33/352; Church Yth Grp; Letterman Clb; Model UN; Spanish Clb; Rptr Nwsp; JV Bsktbl; JV Var Tennis; Hon Roll; NHS; CSF VP; Stu Action Comm Chm; JR St Of Amer Dist Supvr; Poly Sci.

BJARNASON, DEBORAH; Turlock HS; Turlock, CA; (3); #3 In Class; Church Yth Grp; Key Clb; NFL; Service Clb; Speech Tm; Band; Church Choir; Mrchg Band; Pep Band; Hon Roll; Geom Golden St Exam Hnrs; Brigham Young U; Sec Educ.

BJELLAND, ANDREW A; Don Antonio Lugo HS; Chino, CA; (3); 12/700; Boy Scts; Teachers Aide; Socr; High Hon Roll; Hon Roll; Pres Acad Fit Awd; CSF; BYU; Poltcs.

BJERRE, TORBEN; Clear Lake HS; Lakeport, CA; (3); Letterman Clb; Yrbk; Var Trk; Hon Roll; Prfct Atten Awd; Frgn Exchng Stu From Denmark; 3rd Pl Photo Awds Voc-Ed Fair; Lang.

BJORK, JEFF E; Los Angeles Baptist HS; West Hills, CA; (3); Church Yth Grp; Varsity Clb; Stu Cncl; Var L Socr; Hon Roll; Stu Bdy Pres; Surf Clb; Chrstn Srvc Brgde; U Of CA Santa Barbara; Lwyr.

BJORKLUND, ERICA L; Villa Park HS; Villa Park, CA; (3); Church Yth Grp; French Clb; Key Clb; Bus.

BLACHLY, BOBBIE J; Mc Kinleyville HS; Mckinleyville, CA; (2); Church Yth Grp; Dance Clb; Drama Clb; FBLA; Pep Clb; SADD; Band; Chorus; Church Choir; Rptr Nwsp; Tutr Mntly-Physcly Dsabld Kds; Cmp Cnclr; UC Davis; Lwyr.

BLACK, AMY ANN; Point Loma HS; San Diego, CA; (3); Science Clb; Stu Cncl; Hon Roll; People For Environment And Peace; Interact Club; Univ; Physical Therapists.

BLACK, BROOKE M; Imperial HS; Pasadena, CA; (3); Church Yth Grp; English Clb; Speech Tm; Varsity Clb; Chorus; School Musical; Nwsp; Yrbk; Sec Jr Cls; Var L Ftbl; Church Yth Vllybl Capt, Chrldng; Aerontcs.

BLACK, CANDACE; American HS; Fremont, CA; (3); Pep Clb; Spanish Clb; Teachers Aide; Flag Corp; Ed Nwsp; JV Stat Bsktbl; Score Keeper; Gov Hon Prg Awd; High Hon Roll; Hon Roll; Young Journalist Of Amer Awd; Editors Choice Awd U Of Pacific Journlsm Acad; San Diego ST; Mag Journlst.

BLACK, CAROL M; Owens Valley HS; Independence, CA; (2); 1/13; Drama Clb; Letterman Clb; Sec Spanish Clb; Speech Tm; Nwsp; Yrbk; Sec Frsh Cls; Off Soph Cls; Sec Stu Cncl; Drama Clb; Mock Trial Tm; U Of CA Davis; Animal Hsbndry.

BLACK, COREY; Canyon Springs HS; Moreno Valley, CA; (4); Library Aide; SADD; Mgr(s); Trk; High Hon Roll; Hon Roll; Ntl Merit Ltr; Mst Promising Chld Care Stu Awd; CA ST U-Hayward; Scl Sci.

BLACK, COY J; Hart HS; Valencia, CA; (3); Var L Golf; Hon Roll; Wk Vista Valencia Glf Course; Bus Mgmt.

BLACK, DAWN; San Diego HS; San Diego, CA; (3); Church Yth Grp; GAA; Varsity Clb; Yrbk; VP Sr Cls; Var Bsktbl; Var Mgr(s); Var Score Keeper; Var Socr; Var Trk; 1st Team All Lge Soccer & Track; 1st Team All CIF Soccer; MVP Vllybl; Med.

BLACK, DUSTIN L; North Salinas HS; Salinas, CA; (2); Pres Drama Clb; Thesps; School Play; Stage Crew; Variety Show; Crs Cntry; Var Swmmng; JV Trk; High Hon Roll; Hon Roll.

BLACK, E DOMINIC; Bishop Amat Memorial HS; Valinda, CA; (3); VP Aud/Vis; Cmnty Wkr; Drama Clb; School Musical; School Play; Pres Frsh Cls; Pres Soph Cls; Pres Sr Cls; Stu Cncl; JV Wrstlng; CSF; Shipoopi Awd For Most Dedicated Cast Mem.

BLACK, ELIZABETH L; Miramonte HS; Orinda, CA; (3); 18/180; Drama Clb; JCL; Latin Clb; Office Aide; Acpl Chr; Chorus; School Musical; School Play; Natl Latin Exam Slvr Mdl Maxima Cum Laude; UC Riverside; Elem Tchr.

BLACK, JADAH K; Porterville HS; Porterville, CA; (4); Art Clb; Church Yth Grp; Dance Clb; Drama Clb; 4-H; GAA; Office Aide; Science Clb; VP SADD; Teachers Aide; Stu Mnth; Drama Stu Dir; Fresno ST U; Psych.

BLACK, JEREMY K; Oakmont HS; Roseville, CA; (2); Church Yth Grp; Wt Lftg; Hon Roll; Pres Acad Fit Awd; Natl Chmpn Bible Quiz; Elec Engr.

BLACK, JOHN; Amos Alnzo Stagg HS; Stockton, CA; (2); Church Yth Grp; Cmnty Wkr; Debate Tm; Key Clb; SADD; JV Bsbl; JV Ftbl; Var Wrstlng; Hon Roll; NHS; Speech Tm; Ntl Forn Lg; CSUS; Ed.

BLACK, KRISTINA; Taft Union HS; Taft, CA; (1); 1/250; AFS; Key Clb; Letterman Clb; Math Clb; Service Clb; SADD; Cheerldng; Crs Cntry; Swmmng; Hon Roll; Mst Insprtnl Chrldr; Pre-Med.

BLACK, KRISTINA L; Ontario Christian HS; Rancho Cucamonga, CA; (3); 18/69; Church Yth Grp; Office Aide; Variety Show; Hon Roll; Stu Ldr Chrch Yth Grp; Penn ST; Psych.

BLACK, KRISTINA NICOLE; Clovis West HS; Clovis, CA; (4); French Clb; German Clb; Intnl Clb; Key Clb; Teachers Aide; Ntl Merit Ltr; Pres Acad Fit Awd; JETS Awd; Jr Engrng Technel Soc Awd AP Cmpstn, Frnch, Frnch Lit, US Hstry, Amer Govt; CSF; 1360 SAT Score; Occidental Coll; Intl Reltns.

BLACK, MARY P; Redwood HS; Visalia, CA; (4); Spanish Clb; Teachers Aide; Rptr Nwsp; Var Swmmng; Jrnslm Schlrshp Ron Einstross Memrl Fund; Cal Poly; Brdcst Jrnlsm.

BLACK, SHAWN A; Lakewood HS; Long Beach, CA; (3); English Clb; Intnl Clb; Spanish Clb; Outstndng Stu Wrtr 89; Jr Statesman Fndtn Delg 90; 8 & 9 Yr Old Sftbl Team Asst Coach 90; CA ST U Long Beach; Lbrl Arts.

BLACK, SYLVIA L; Palo Verde Valley HS; Blythe, CA; (2); 18/289; Church Yth Grp; Rptr Nwsp; Hon Roll; H3ward U; Pedtrcs.

BLACK, TRISHA M; Paramount HS; Fontana, CA; (1); Church Yth Grp; Band; Mrchg Band; Hon Roll; Math Educ.

BLACKBURN, DEIRDRE O; Concord HS; Concord, CA; (3); SADD; Ntrtn.

BLACKBURN, JOSHUA C; Rubidoux HS; Riverside, CA; (4); FBLA; JA; Teachers Aide; Cit Awd; Hon Roll; Prfct Atten Awd; UCLA; Phy.

BLACKBURN, KIMBERLY J; Palo Verde HS; Ehrenberg, AZ; (3); Church Yth Grp; Girl Scts; School Play; Swmmng; Cit Awd; Prfct Atten Awd; Stu Month Engl III.

BLACKBURN, KIMYON; Washington Prep HS; Los Angeles, CA; (3); Drill Tm; Sftbl; Hon Roll; Marthonian Clb.

BLACKBURN, MICHELLE L; Atascadero HS; Atascadero, CA; (4); 12/270; Key Clb; Teachers Aide; Cit Awd; High Hon Roll; Pres Acad Fit Awd; Pacific Coast Qurtr Hrs Jrnl Top 10 Yth; 4 Rgstr Of Merits Qurtr Hrs Assn; Chem.

BLACKBURN, REBEKAH D; Monache HS; Porterville, CA; (3); Art Clb; Pres Church Yth Grp; Cmnty Wkr; FBLA; Teachers Aide; Varsity Clb; Band; Chorus; Church Choir; Mrchg Band; Outstndng Bus Stu; Brigham Young U; Bus.

BLACKBURN, TANYA DALE; Fairfield HS; Fairfield, CA; (2); Girl Scts; Teachers Aide; Nwsp; JV Var Bsktbl; Cit Awd; Sparrowgrass Poetry Forum Publshd Poet; U Of CA; Engl.

BLACKFORD, LESLEY; El Segundo HS; El Segundo, CA; (4); 11/147; AFS; Pres Church Yth Grp; Hist French Clb; Key Clb; Office Aide; Sec Pres Science Clb; Band; Capt Color Guard; Capt Flag Corp; Stu Cncl; Humboldt ST U; Wildlife Mgt.

BLACKHAM, REBECCA A; Huntington Beach HS; Huntington Bch, CA; (3); Church Yth Grp; Spanish Clb; L Var Fld Hcky; JV Vllybl; Varsity Lettered In Badminton; HBHS Toweer Awards In History Physical Sci & Biological Science; Brigham Young U; Biology.

BLACKHAM, TEISHI N; Merced HS; Merced, CA; (2); Pres Church Yth Grp; Color Guard; Flag Corp; Mrchg Band; Hon Roll; Jr NHS; Dir Actvtys-Kewanettes; CSF; Brigham Young U; Tchr.

BLACKKETTER, JESSICA A; Immanuel Christian HS; Ridgecrest, CA; (4); 1/14; Church Yth Grp; Church Choir; Sec Treas Stu Cncl; Var Capt Bsktbl; Cheerldng; Var Sftbl; Var Capt Vllybl; High Hon Roll; Val; Bnk Of Amer Achvt Awd Liberal Arts 90; Cal Poly San Luis Obispo; Engr.

BLACKMAN, DAVID O; Desert HS; Burkburnett, TX; (2); Office Aide; Cit Awd; Psych.

BLACKMAN, JEANA M; Branham HS; San Jose, CA; (2); 1/277; Church Yth Grp; French Clb; SADD; Chorus; School Musical; Stage Crew; JV Swmmng; High Hon Roll; CSF Jr Ofcr; Theater.

BLACKMAN, STACY L; Golden West HS; Visalia, CA; (1); Church Yth Grp; FFA; Hosp Aide; SADD; Band; Mrchg Band; BYU; Sci.

BLACKMER, NICOLE; Upland HS; Upland, CA; (3); 71/692; Cmnty Wkr; Dance Clb; Hosp Aide; Pep Clb; Red Cross Aide; Drill Tm; Cheerldng; Church Yth Grp; Powder Puff Ftbl; Hon Roll; Natl Chrty Leag; UCLA; Pedtrcn.

BLACKMON, JENNIFER; Mt Whitney HS; Visalia, CA; (2); Church Yth Grp; Key Clb; Pep Clb; Spanish Clb; SADD; Church Choir; Rep Frsh Cls; Rep Soph Cls; Vllybl; Hon Roll; Sftbl Tm; Cathlc Dghtrs Amer; Coach Little Leag Bsbl Tm; Bus.

BLACKMORE, BRADLEY C; Sonora HS; Jamestown, CA; (4); 26/254; Ski Clb; Band; Jazz Band; Mrchg Band; Pep Band; High Hon Roll; Hon Roll; Outstndng Phys Sci Stu 89-90; Pearl Segrestrom Memorial Schlrshp; Chem.

BLACKMORE, LEE S; Escalon HS; Farmington, CA; (2); 12/131; Boy Scts; Church Yth Grp; Treas German Clb; VP Key Clb; Hon Roll; Prfct Atten Awd; Pres Acad Fit Awd; Chef.

BLACKSTOCK, MICHELLE; Chico SR HS; Chico, CA; (4); Pep Clb; School Play; Rep Stu Cncl; JV Bsktbl; Intrml Mgr Cheerldng; Lion Awd; UC Santa Barbara; Bio.

BLACKWELDER, JENNIFER A; Ukiah HS; Ukiah, CA; (4); 44/450; Church Yth Grp; Cmnty Wkr; SADD; Phtg Nwsp; Ed Yrbk; Rep Stu Cncl; JV Crs Cntry; Var L Tennis; Hon Roll; Pres Acad Fit Awd; St Marys Coll Of Moraga; Psych.

BLACKWELL, JENNIFER J; Simi Valley HS; Simi Valley, CA; (2); Drama Clb; Pep Clb; JV Bsktbl; JV Crs Cntry; JV Trk; Hon Roll; UCSD; Dntstry.

BLACKWELL, JOHN; Lemoore HS; Lemoore, CA; (2); Hosp Aide; JV Ftbl; JV Trk; JV Capt Wrstlng; Cit Awd; Hon Roll; Wrestling Booster Clb; Communion Cls; Med.

BLACKWELL, SCOTT; Brethren HS; Lakewood, CA; (2); 1/90; Church Yth Grp; Math Tm; Band; Drm Mjr(t); Mrchg Band; Pep Band; Pres Stu Cncl; Var Bsbl; High Hon Roll; Hon Roll; Biola.

BLACKWOOD, MARITESS; Cajon HS; San Bernardino, CA; (2); Drama Clb; Intnl Clb; Chorus; School Play; Wt Lftg; Awd Excllnc Chrl Music Clnc; Cert Rcgntn-Wrld Hstry, Cncrt Choir, Wrld Geog, Bio; Acad Ltr Choir, Drma; Nrsng.

BLAGG, CARI R; Oakdale HS; Waterford, CA; (3); 4/250; AFS; Pres Church Yth Grp; Debate Tm; Drama Clb; Math Tm; Speech Tm; School Play; Powder Puff Ftbl; Swmmng; Vllybl; Assoc Yth Cncl-Music Ofcr; Jrny Clb-Pres; Ed.

BLAGG, JILL E; Sanger HS; Sanger, CA; (2); FCA; GAA; Bsktbl; Score Keeper; Swmmng; High Hon Roll.

BLAGRAVE, JAMES D; Castle Park HS; Chula Vista, CA; (3); Drama Clb; Speech Tm; Thesps; School Play; Stage Crew; Var Ftbl; Opt Clb Awd; Law.

BLAHA, MICHELLE; Paraclete HS; Lancaster, CA; (4); 35/130; Am Leg Aux Girls St; Drama Clb; Key Clb; Nwsp; Ed Yrbk; Stu Cncl; JV Var Cheerldng; Hon Roll; Zonta Club Pres; CSF; UC Riverside; Bus.

BLAIR, CAS S; Upper Lake HS; Lucerne, CA; (2); 3/70; Var Bsbl; JV Bsktbl; JV Ftbl; JV Trk; High Hon Roll; Hon Roll; Pres Schlr; Jr Statesmn; UCSC; Prelaw.

BLAIR III, THOMAS B; Poway HS; Poway, CA; (2).

BLAIR, TIFFANY A; Westlake HS; Westlake Village, CA; (2); 120/400; Church Yth Grp; Rep Frsh Cls; Crs Cntry; Trk; Hon Roll; Greenpeace; Mst Imprvd Hurdler; Cmmnctn Arts.

BLAKE, CAROLEE L; Hayward HS; Castro Valley, CA; (4); 7/210; Church Yth Grp; Cmnty Wkr; Sec French Clb; Office Aide; SADD; Band; Church Choir; Mgr Nwsp; Lit Mag; Rep Frsh Cls; CSF; Black & Gold Character & Ldrshp Awd; Cal ST Hayward.

BLAKE, HEATHER L C; Los Alamitos HS; Cypress, CA; (4); Pres Debate Tm; Letterman Clb; Q&S; Pres Speech Tm; SADD; Chorus; School Play; Stage Crew; Yrbk; Trk; OCHSA Rep Co Stu Director/Actress; JR Honor Guard; U CA Snta Cruz; Dsny Imgnrng.

BLAKE, JENNIFER A; Thousand Oaks HS; Thousand Oaks, CA; (2); Art Clb; Cmnty Wkr; Spanish Clb; School Musical; Swmmng; Tennis; UCLA; Law.

BLAKE, JONATHAN V; Pinole Valley HS; Pinole, CA; (2); Drama Clb; Teachers Aide; School Musical; School Play; Var Ftbl; JV Trk; JV Wt Lftg; Hon Roll; Pres Acad Fit Awd; CA U.

BLAKE, LEAH; Fall River HS; Burney, CA; (4); Art Clb; FFA; Teachers Aide; Acpl Chr; Chorus; Stage Crew; Swing Chorus; Variety Show; Ed Nwsp; Hon Roll; Art Cert; Hmecnmcs Medl; Artstry Dsply.

BLAKE, LISA A; Foothill HS; Santa Ana, CA; (3); Cmnty Wkr; Girl Scts; Yrbk; High Hon Roll; St Schlr; Stu For Greenpeace; Jr Statesmen Amer; CSF; Bio.

BLAKE, MARK P; Santa Margarita HS; San Juan Capistra, CA; (3); 42/235; Cmnty Wkr; Nwsp; Stu Cncl; VP L Bsbl; JV Bsktbl; JV Crs Cntry; Hon Roll; NHS; Prfct Atten Awd; 2nd Tm All-Olympic Lg Bsbl 89; Cmmssnr Athletics 88-89; Comm.

BLAKE, NOELLE F; Fort Bragg HS; Fort Bragg, CA; (3); FBLA; SADD; Teachers Aide; Chorus; NHS; Cmmnty Theatre; Humboldt ST U; Bus Mgmt.

BLAKE, SAMANTHA L; Royal HS; Simi Valley, CA; (3); #44 In Class; Church Yth Grp; Pres Band; Jazz Band; Mrchg Band; Orch; Pep Band; Sprt Ed Nwsp; Stu Cncl; Var Capt Bsktbl; Var L Sftbl; Instrmntl Mscn Of Yr 88-89; Ovrll Oustndng JR Musician; Most Imprvd Plyr On Vrsty Bsktbl & Trk Tm; CA St Fullerton; Music.

BLAKE, SHERRY; El Camino HS; Oceanside, CA; (3); Dance Clb; French Clb; SADD; Teachers Aide; Var JV Cheerldng; Var Capt Gym; Sftbl; Cit Awd; Hon Roll; Pop Warner Coach Chrldng; Bwlng Leag Jr Pres; Bus Mgmt.

BLAKELEY, MATTHEW P; Modesto Christian HS; Modesto, CA; (3); Drama Clb; Teachers Aide; Chorus; School Musical; Sec Frsh Cls; L Capt Bsktbl; JV Ftbl; L Var Trk; Hon Roll; Slam/Jam All Star 2 Yrs; Bus.

BLAKELY, KEISHA L; Clovis West HS; Fresno, CA; (3); Church Yth Grp; Drama Clb; Hosp Aide; NFL; Speech Tm; Yrbk; Lit Mag; High Hon Roll; Hon Roll; CSF; UC Davis; Vet Med.

BLAKEMORE, TANYA; Redlands HS; Redlands, CA; (2); 364/1376; Sec Church Yth Grp; Cmnty Wkr; Drama Clb; French Clb; Key Clb; Thesps; Treas Chorus; Church Choir; School Play; Variety Show; San Diego ST U; Bus Adm.

BLAKESLEE, CAROLYN R; Savanna HS; Anaheim, CA; (3); Teachers Aide; Chorus; UCLA; Nrsng.

BLAMES, ALEXEY S; S Calif Christian HS; West Covina, CA; (2); Church Yth Grp; VP Jr Cls; JV Bsbl; JV Bsktbl; JV Crs Cntry; Anti Drug Drama; Bus Adm.

BLAMEY, CAMERYN; Rio Americano HS; Sacramento, CA; (4); 65/290; Aud/Vis; Cmnty Wkr; Dance Clb; Pep Clb; SADD; Chorus; Variety Show; VP JV Cheerldng; VP Pom Pon; 1st Chrldng Comp Best Of Show 89; Apollo Awd Excl Cmmnctns Pub Spkng 88; Inter-Local Rcrdng Studio 90; U CA Santa Barbara; Cmmnctns.

BLANCAFLOR, PAMELA S; Duncan Poly Tech; Fresno, CA; (1); Church Yth Grp; ROTC; Drill Tm; Orch; Friday Night Live; Air Force ROTC Vlybl Tm; CA ST U Fresno; Chld Psych.

BLANCARTE, STEPHANIE A; Mills HS; Millbrae, CA; (3); Cmnty Wkr; Nwsp; Cheerldng; Hon Roll; Coll Of San Mateo; Cnslg.

BLANCHARD, LYNN R; Patrick Henry HS; San Diego, CA; (2); 104/530; Church Yth Grp; Office Aide; Dnc Tm; Interior Dsgnr.

BLANCHARD, THOMAS L; South Pasadena HS; South Pasadena, CA; (4); 6/317; Boy Scts; Pres Latin Clb; Band; VP Sr Cls; JV L Swmmng; Ntl Merit Schol; Acad Dcthln; CSF; Tnage Mutant Ninja Turtles Clb; UCLA.

BLANCHE, HEATHER N; La Canada HS; La Canada-Flint, CA; (3); Church Yth Grp; Key Clb; Yrbk; Off Jr Cls; Off Sr Cls; Stu Cncl; Capt Powder Puff Ftbl; JV Sftbl; Var Capt Tennis; NHS; Prom Cmmssnr; Actvts Dir; Scoville Tupper Awd; All Area Sftbl Team Abroad Russia Sweden & Finland; Law.

BLANCHETTE, DAWN M; Tehachapi HS; Tehachapi, CA; (1); Church Yth Grp; FFA; Band; Church Choir; Hon Roll; Azuza Coll; Music.

BLANCHETTE, GABRIEL M; San Dieguito HS; Carlsbad, CA; (2); Hon Roll.

BLANCHETTE, GABRIEL SINGH; Santa Cruz HS; Santa Cruz, CA; (1); Natl Beta Clb; Ftbl; Wt Lftg; Hon Roll; Pres Acad Fit Awd; Undr Grad Awd Geom.

BLANCO, ABE A; Independence HS; San Jose, CA; (1); Church Yth Grp; Church Choir; JV Ftbl; JV Trk; Hon Roll; UCLA; Engr.

BLANCO, CHRISTINA M; Bellarmine Jefferson HS; Burbank, CA; (2); Cmnty Wkr; Spanish Clb; JV Tennis; Hon Roll; Hnr Rbn For GPA; SNT Brbr Coll.

BLANCO, ERIN M; Edison HS; Huntington Bch, CA; (3); Ski Clb; Spanish Clb; Lit Mag; Var Socr; Var Capt Vllybl; Achvt Awd Engl & Spansh; Golden Key Awd Medlln Girls Athltcs.

BLANCO, JUANITA G; Grossmont HS; El Cajon, CA; (2); French Clb; Mrchg Band; Orch; Pep Band; School Musical; Rptr Nwsp; Var L Trk; Hon Roll; CSF; Acad Decthln; Johns Hopkins U; Surgeon.

BLANCO, KATHERINA R; Chula Vista HS; National City, CA; (2); 16/605; Hosp Aide; Co-Capt Pep Clb; Cit Awd; High Hon Roll; Prfct Atten Awd; Asian Clb 2 Yrs; Swords & Shields; Assn Stu Body Comssnr Of Dance; Med.

BLANCO, LESLIE; George Washington Prep HS; Los Angeles, CA; (3); Computer Clb; Dance Clb; Math Clb; Variety Show; Treas Frsh Cls; Var Bsktbl; Var Sftbl; Var Vllybl; Hon Roll; Engrng.

BLANCO, MARIA V; Morningside HS; Inglewood, CA; (1); El Camino; Doc.

BLANCO, TERESA R; Ernest Righetti HS; Santa Maria, CA; (4); 42/368; Teachers Aide; Var Tennis; Hon Roll; U Exploration Clb; Interact Clb Cmnty Servce; Stu Wanting Envrnmntl Hrmny Clb; Allan Hancock JC; Nrsng.

BLAND, EMMA K; Lowell HS; San Francisco, CA; (2); Boy Scts; French Clb; Orch; Var Gym; CSF; Natl Frnch Cntst; Shrt Stry Clb; Gldn St Exam-Alg; U Of CA At Davis; Vet Med.

BLAND, JAMES E; Desert HS; Edwards, CA; (3); Var Bsbl; Var Ftbl; Cit Awd; Hon Roll; Prfct Atten Awd; Pres Acad Fit Awd; Voice Dem Awd; UN Omaha; Sprts Med.

BLAND, JENNIFER D; Ponderosa HS; Placerville, CA; (4); 70/250; French Clb; Teachers Aide; Band; Color Guard; Drill Tm; Flag Corp; Mrchg Band; Hon Roll; CRC Placerville.

BLAND, KEITH R; Victorville HS; Victorville, CA; (2); Boy Scts.

BLAND, SHARI; Armijo HS; Suisun City, CA; (3); AFS; Art Clb; DECA; JV Capt Cheerldng; Cit Awd; High Hon Roll; NHS; Prfct Atten Awd; Cmmrcl Art.

BLAND, T J; Damien HS; Pomona, CA; (2); 81/269; High Hon Roll; Hon Roll; Pres Acad Fit Awd; Bowling Clb League; Fishing Clb; Cal Poly; Architect.

BLANDA, REBECCA J; Glendora HS; Glendora, CA; (4); 17/375; Art Clb; Pres Church Yth Grp; Speech Tm; SADD; Chorus; Var L Fld Hcky; Stat Swmmng; Hon Roll; CSF; Hnr Grad & Usher Honorary Sch Banquet; BYU; Psych.

BLANDA, WENDY; Rosary HS; Orange, CA; (4); 10/135; Church Yth Grp; Debate Tm; NFL; Ski Clb; Speech Tm; Lit Mag; Stu Cncl; Bausch & Lomb Sci Awd; High Hon Roll; NHS; Mock Trial; JSA; Rsrch.

BLANDING, JOY; Los Gatos HS; San Jose, CA; (4); Cmnty Wkr; French Clb; Sftbl; Peer Counseling; Amnesty International; W Valley.

BLANDON, OSMAN F; Hawthorne HS; Inglewood, CA; (4); Mech.

BLANGSTED, SARAH L; Atascadero HS; Atascadero, CA; (1); JV Bsktbl; Var Tennis; JV Trk; Hon Roll; Acctng.

BLANK, LAURA E; The Bishops Schl; Rancho Santa Fe, CA; (4); Cmnty Wkr; Spanish Clb; SADD; Acpl Chr; Chorus; Nwsp; Phtg Yrbk; Off Jr Cls; Off Sr Cls; JV Vllybl; Wellesley Coll.

BLANK, RICHARD A; Cordova HS; Rancho Cordova, CA; (4); 20/50; Drama Clb; VP German Clb; Model UN; Church Choir; School Play; Stage Crew; Rep Sr Cls; Var Socr; High Hon Roll; Hon Roll; Physcs.

BLANKENSHIP, KELLY; Garden Grove HS; Santa Ana, CA; (4); 8/352; GAA; Pep Clb; Spanish Clb; SADD; Phtg Nwsp; Stu Cncl; Var Trk; Var Capt Vllybl; DAR Awd; Elks Awd; Girls Lgu Pres; 1st Team All Trnmnt Vlybl; Hnrbl Mntn All Lgu Vlybl; CSF; Southern CA U; Pblc Admnstr.

BLANKENSHIP, KELLY; Lincoln HS; Stockton, CA; (3); #1 In Class; Intnl Clb; Mu Alpha Theta; Service Clb; Spanish Clb; Band; Mrchg Band; High Hon Roll; CSF; Smmr Exch Norway; Med.

BLANKENSHIP, KRISTI; Madera HS; Madera, CA; (2); 17/693; Church Yth Grp; Rptr FBLA; Sec Treas Hosp Aide; Band; Flag Corp; Mrchg Band; Pep Band; High Hon Roll; Fresno Bee Teen Tempo Press Corps; Top Twenty In Class Awd; SCU; Jrnlsm.

BLANKENSHIP, MICHELLE; Moreno Valley HS; Moreno Valley, CA; (4); 41/400; Church Yth Grp; High Hon Roll; Hon Roll; Princpls List Awd; Spcl Acad Ltr-Supt; Dntl Asst.

BLANKENSHIP, TIFFANY; Calvary Chapel HS; Mission Viejo, CA; (2); Dance Clb; Pep Clb; Ski Clb; Spanish Clb; Var Cheerldng; Var Pom Pon; Pres Acad Fit Awd; Pepperdine; Photo.

BLANKINSHIP, ANDREA L; St Patrick HS; Vallejo, CA; (1); 18/175; Computer Clb; GAA; Letterman Clb; Rep Stu Cncl; L JV Bsktbl; L Var Sftbl; High Hon Roll; Prfct Atten Awd; Pres Acad Fit Awd; All Leag Var Sftbl; UC Davis; Pre-Law.

BLANNING, BRIAN; Village Christian HS; Tujunga, CA; (3); 8/123; Church Yth Grp; Rep English Clb; Math Clb; Mu Alpha Theta; Ed Yrbk; JV Crs Cntry; Var L Trk; Cmmssnr La County Cmmsn Yth; CSF; Law.

BLAS, ANTHONY J; Mission Bay HS; San Diego, CA; (4); 10/340; Aud/Vis; Church Yth Grp; Pres Letterman Clb; Ftbl; Trk; High Hon Roll; Lion Awd; Pres Schlr; Rotary Awd; U Of Puget Sound; Liberal Arts.

BLAS, MARLENE; Sweetwater HS; National City, CA; (4); 46/460; FBLA; Speech Tm; Teachers Aide; Chorus; Var Tennis; Hon Roll; NHS; Idntfctn Mrchng Unit; Dept Str Mdl; Bus Adm.

BLASER, SUMMER; Vallejo SR HS; Vallejo, CA; (4); Dance Clb; Drama Clb; Acpl Chr; Drill Tm; School Musical; School Play; Variety Show; Var Pom Pon; French Clb; Office Aide; Miss Natl Teen Pgnt St Fnlst; Dance.

BLASETTI, ANN M; Chino HS; Chino Hills, CA; (2); Church Yth Grp; Drama Clb; FHA; Library Aide; Science Clb; Hon Roll; Slvr Spur Wrld Cvlztns; UCLA.

BLASINGHAM, JANE; Capistrano Valley Christian Schl; Dana Point, CA; (1); Chrstn Charctr Awd; The Masters Coll; Home Ec.

BLASINGHAM, LAURA; Capostrano Valley Christian HS; Dana Point, CA; (2); High Hon Roll; Hon Roll; Laguna Moulton Plyhs Yth Ensmbl; Vol Commnty Lbry; CSF; Mst Acadc Fresh Cls; Masters Coll; Hist Prof.

BLASS, MIGUEL; Abraham Lincoln HS; San Diego, CA; (3); 16/254; AFS; French Clb; Library Aide; Science Clb; Crs Cntry; Socr; High Hon Roll; Hon Roll; Rotry Yth Ldrshp Awds; CSF; Upward Bound; Bio.

BLATARIC, JASON D; Mayfair HS; Bellflower, CA; (1); JA; JV Golf; Hon Roll; U Of CA Snta Brbra; Hlcptr Plt.

BLATT, STEVEN JAY; Del Oro HS; Loomis, CA; (4); 6/250; Teachers Aide; Var Tennis; High Hon Roll; Hon Roll; NHS; Ntl Merit Schol; Prfct Atten Awd; Pres Acad Fit Awd; Rotary Awd; Acad Decathlon; Rgnts Schlrshp; Lorene Logner Keena Schlrshp; UC Berkeley; Econ.

BLATTER, LISA; Monte Vista HS; Alamo, CA; (4); Pres Church Yth Grp; Dance Clb; Ski Clb; Teachers Aide; Variety Show; Rep Soph Cls; Rep Jr Cls; Sec Stu Cncl; Var Cheerldng; Powder Puff Ftbl; BYU.

BLAUFUSS, MAIJA; Westwood HS; Westwood, CA; (1); 2/30; Church Yth Grp; Spanish Clb; Speech Tm; Band; Mrchg Band; JV Bsktbl; Var Trk; Wt Lftg; High Hon Roll; Hon Roll; Skiing; UC Berkley; Child Psych.

BLAUVELT, ROCHELLE N; Sweetwater HS; National City, CA; (2); Teachers Aide; Stage Crew; Hon Roll; Acdmc Leag; Zoo.

BLAZE, ALLISON E; Rim Of The World HS; Blue Jay, CA; (1); Church Yth Grp; German Clb; Spanish Clb; Rptr Yrbk; Cit Awd; Prfct Atten Awd; Piano.

BLAZER, ABBIE; Mt Carmel HS; San Diego, CA; (3); Drama Clb; Key Clb; Color Guard; Flag Corp; Prfct Atten Awd; CSF; Ecology Clb; UC Santa Cruz; Marine Bio.

BLAZIC, MIROSLAV; Diamond Bar HS; Diamond Bar, CA; (2); 1/496; High Hon Roll; Hon Roll; Elec Engr.

BLEASE, JENNIFER L; Homestead HS; Sunnyvale, CA; (1); Stage Crew; Hon Roll.

BLEDSOE, BERT; Yosemite HS; Coarsegold, CA; (3); Church Yth Grp; Drama Clb; Key Clb; ROTC; Ski Clb; Band; Color Guard; Treas Soph Cls; Pres Stu Cncl; JV Ftbl; Cmmnctns.

BLEDSOE, BRENDA; Pasadena HS; Altadena, CA; (2); Dance Clb; Math Clb; Mgr(s); Trk; Hon Roll; CSF; Blck Stu Union.

BLEDSOE, DERICK; George Washington Prep HS; Los Angeles, CA; (3); Var Bsbl; High Hon Roll; Hon Roll; MESA Assn 89-90; Yng Gftd & Blck Awd 90; Engrng.

BLEECKER, FELICIA N; Irvine HS; Irvine, CA; (2); Hosp Aide; Key Clb; Ski Clb; Chorus; School Play; Lit Mag; Pres/Fndr Actvsts Poltcl Awrns; Acad Hrtge Awd Wnnr Frnch & Hstry; HOBY Ambsdr & ILS Sm Fnlst; Law.

BLEESS, JAMES; Ukiah HS; Hopland, CA; (2); 2/554; Chess Clb; Stage Crew; Trk; High Hon Roll; Lawrence Hall Of Sci & Soc Issues Symposium; Liver Fluke Rsrch Team; Ukiah Fencing Team; Sci.

BLEIJENBERG, CLAUDETTE; John Muir HS; Altadena, CA; (4); 18/365; Dance Clb; VP French Clb; Ed Lit Mag; Sec Sr Cls; Hon Roll; ROP; Cal Poly San Luis Obispo; Arch.

BLEIWEISS, AMIT X; Homestead HS; Sunnyvale, CA; (1); JV Bsktbl; Graphics Desgn.

BLESSING, MARIA L; Chula Vista HS; San Diego, CA; (3); 1/535; Library Aide; Co-Ed Nwsp; Yrbk; Lit Mag; JV Socr; JV Sftbl; Prfct Atten Awd; CA Schlrshp Fed; Cert Outstndng Achvt-Cnty-Wd Sbjct A Wrt-Off; Sword-Shld.

BLEVINS, BRANDON K; Whittier Christian HS; Whittier, CA; (3); Church Yth Grp; Rep Jr Cls; Rep Stu Cncl; Bsktbl; Vllybl; Bus.

BLEVINS, EDWIN A; Vallejo SR HS; Vallejo, CA; (2); SADD; JV Ftbl; Hon Roll; Prfct Atten Awd; Pres Acad Fit Awd; William K Holt Sci Schlrshp Prog 89; Natl Sci Olympd Awd; CSF; Engr.

BLEVINS, KIMBERLY A; East Union HS; Manteca, CA; (2); 60/411; Church Yth Grp; Cmnty Wkr; Dance Clb; Church Choir; Color Guard; Drill Tm; Flag Corp; Trk; Guardsman Awd Hgst Hnr Guard; Band Colorgurd Clb; Guard Cptn; Stanford; Bus.

BLEVINS, STACI; Santa Monica HS; Santa Monica, CA; (3); Teachers Aide; Rptr Nwsp; Natl Achvt Schlrshp Pgm; Jrnlsm.

BLEWETT, ANNE G; Mount Pleasant HS; San Jose, CA; (4); 24/390; French Clb; High Hon Roll; NHS; CA Schlrshp Fdrtn; Otstndng Achvmnt Sci; Otstndng JR Artst; Natl Cncl Tchrs Englsh Wrtng Awd.

BLEWETT, TIM J; Mt Pleasant HS; San Jose, CA; (1); Boy Scts; High Hon Roll; CSF; Aviation Club; Engrng.

BLEWITT, LISA A; Arroyo Grande HS; Grover City, CA; (2); 1/625; SADD; Stage Crew; Tennis; High Hon Roll; Hon Roll; Masonic Awd; Intl Ord Rainbow Girls; CSF; Stu Recogntn Awd Bus Dept; Cmptr Sci.

BLIAYA, MOUATOU G; La Quinta HS; Santa Ana, CA; (4); Hon Roll; NSC; Comp Sci.

BLICKLE, KENDRA G; Del Campo HS; Fair Oaks, CA; (3); 26/446; School Play; Rptr Yrbk; Pres Jr Cls; Pres Stu Cncl; Stat Ftbl; CSF Svc Awd; Site Cncl Secy; Del Campo Rowdy Rooters Secy; Poli Sci.

BLINCO, STEPHENIE; Arlington HS; Riverside, CA; (3); 144/460; Church Yth Grp; Yrbk; Crs Cntry; Gym; Socr; Trk; Hon Roll.

BLINN, JENNIFER; St Marys HS; Stockton, CA; (4); 12/160; Am Leg Aux Girls St; Key Clb; Letterman Clb; Sprt Ed Yrbk; Sec Stu Cncl; Var L Sftbl; Var L Vllybl; High Hon Roll; Pres Acad Fit Awd; Girls Cabinet; CSF; Rec Clb; U AZ; Phys Thrpst.

BLINT, VICTORIA C; Oak Park HS; Agoura, CA; (1); 2/125; GAA; Key Clb; Letterman Clb; Temple Yth Grp; Varsity Clb; Stu Cncl; Var Socr; Var Sftbl; Var Tennis; High Hon Roll; Advncd Peer Cnslng; UC Berkeley; Med.

BLISS, HEATHER J; Paraclete HS; Palmdale, CA; (3); Key Clb; Letterman Clb; Varsity Clb; Crs Cntry; Trk; High Hon Roll; Hon Roll; Gymnstcs; Med.

BLISS, JOHN PAUL; Ukiah HS; Ukiah, CA; (2); 3/554; Orch; VP Soph Cls; JV Bsbl; High Hon Roll; CSF; Lawrence Hall Of Sci, Socl Issues Sympsm 88-89; Bio.

BLISS, KAREN E; Huntington Beach HS; Huntington Beach, CA; (2); Band; Mrchg Band; Orch; Pep Band; School Musical; Hon Roll; U Of ND; Aviatn.

BLISS, KRISTINE E; South Valley HS; Ukiah, CA; (4); 2/70; Boy Scts; Cmnty Wkr; Office Aide; Teachers Aide; Rep Frsh Cls; Rep Sr Cls; Rep Stu Cncl; Sal; Safe Rides; PG&E Schlrshp; Earned Bank Teller Cert 210 Hrs; Mendocino CC; Elem Educ.

BLISS, REGAN C; Yucaipa HS; Yucaipa, CA; (2); Aud/Vis; Church Yth Grp; Office Aide; Church Choir; Mgr Ftbl; Mgr Socr; Atten Hnrs 2 Yrs; Commnctns.

BLISS, SERENA; Hanford Joint Union HS; Hanford, CA; (1); FBLA; Treas FHA; Hon Roll; Frgn Exch Clb; CSF; Acad Lttr Awd; Med.

BLISS, SHERRI; Mira Costa HS; Manhattan Beach, CA; (4); 62/367; Sec Thesps; Drill Tm; School Musical; School Play; Sec Jr Cls; Stu Cncl; Hon Roll; Pres Acad Fit Awd; Hmcmng Queen; Honor Roll; CSF; U Of San Diego; Comm.

BLITZER, MARA; Palo Alto HS; Palo Alto, CA; (2); Key Clb; Temple Yth Grp; Rachel Austin Awd Engl; Amnesty Intl; CSF.

BLOCH, ALAN; Tulelake HS; Tulelake, CA; (2); 2/35; FBLA; VP Soph Cls; JV Bsktbl; High Hon Roll; Hon Roll; CSF; Bus Adm.

BLOCH, REBECCA; Berkeley HS; Berkeley, CA; (2); Aud/Vis; Hosp Aide; Hon Roll; Med.

BLOCHER, MATT D; Orange Luthern HS; Villa Park, CA; (3); Ski Clb; JV Ftbl; JV Socr; Var Trk; Vlybl; Scuba Dvng Openwater 2 & Speclty Cert; Snowbrdng; UCI; Engrng.

BLOCK, ADAM F; The Head Royce Schl; Berkeley, CA; (4); Cmnty Wkr; Spanish Clb; Yrbk; Sec Soph Cls; Off Sr Cls; Mgr(s); Swmmng; High Hon Roll; Hon Roll; Ntl Merit SF; Pol Sci.

BLOCK, ARLANA M; Hogan SR HS; Vallejo, CA; (3); Church Yth Grp; French Clb; Office Aide; Spanish Clb; Church Choir; Drill Tm; Rep Sr Cls; JV Pom Pon; Hon Roll; Clark-Atlanta U; Poltcl Sci.

BLOCK, DAVID D; Lindsay HS; Lindsay, CA; (2); Office Aide; Spanish Clb; Bsktbl; Golf; Score Keeper; Vllybl; Wt Lftg; High Hon Roll; Hon Roll; Acad Ltr 89-90; Coll Of Sequoias.

BLOCK, MARTHA R; Apple Valley HS; Apple Valley, CA; (1); High Hon Roll; Hon Roll; Long Beach ST; Tchr.

BLOCK, MATTHEW S; Sequoia HS; San Carlos, CA; (1); 1/450; JV Socr; High Hon Roll; Pres Acad Fit Awd; CSF; Med.

BLODGET, EMILY; La Reina HS; Camarillo, CA; (3); GAA; Hosp Aide; Letterman Clb; Service Clb; Ed Yrbk; Sec Frsh Cls; Rep Sr Cls; Stat Sftbl; JV Var Tennis; Cit Awd; Natl Chrty Leag Ticktockers; CSF.

BLODGETT, LAUREL E; San Luis Obispo HS; Shell Beach, CA; (2); 30/300; Church Yth Grp; Intnl Clb; Chorus; Powder Puff Ftbl; Var Sftbl; JV Var Vllybl; High Hon Roll; Prfct Atten Awd; Pres Acad Fit Awd; Med.

BLODGETT, MATT J; Bret Harte HS; Copperopolis, CA; (2); JV L Bsbl; JV L Bsktbl; Var L Ftbl; Hon Roll; Sacramento ST U.

BLODGETT, MICHELLE; Mtn View HS; Mountain View, CA; (2); Cmnty Wkr; Dance Clb; Band; Chorus; Color Guard; Mrchg Band; High Hon Roll; Hon Roll; Music Cncl-Publicity Mgr; Pediatrics.

BLODGETT, WALLY; Tokay HS; Lodi, CA; (3); Pres Treas 4-H; Treas Band; Jazz Band; Mrchg Band; Orch; Pep Band; JV Trk; 4-H Awd; Italian Clb; Intl Pblc Svc.

BLOMERKAMP, RUTH; Turlock Christian HS; Turlock, CA; (4); 6/28; Church Yth Grp; Hosp Aide; Band; Chorus; Church Choir; Mrchg Band; Pep Band; School Musical; Pres Soph Cls; Stu Cncl; CA Schlrshp Fed; Biola U; Mssnry Nurse Prctnr.

BLOMGREN, AMBER L; Workman HS; La Puente, CA; (3); Intnl Clb; Key Clb; SADD; Teachers Aide; Nwsp; Powder Puff Ftbl; Sftbl; Hon Roll; Friend To Friend VP; Hugs Not Drugs; CA ST Fullerton; Engrng.

BLOMQUIST, AUGUSTA A; Red Bluff Union HS; Mineral, CA; (3); Key Clb; Ski Clb; SADD; Teachers Aide; Yrbk; Pres Jr Cls; JV Wt Lftg; Hon Roll; Steering Committe; ASB Bkpr; Spirit Princess; Ski Tm; Chico U; RN.

BLOMQUIST, DEREK R; Clayton Valley HS; Clayton, CA; (3); Art Clb; Letterman Clb; SADD; Teachers Aide; Varsity Clb; Intrml Bsbl; Var Capt Crs Cntry; Var Socr; Var Trk; Clb Soccer; UCLA.

BLOMQUIST, NILS W; Del Campo HS; Fair Oaks, CA; (3); 10/470; SADD; Variety Show; JV Var Ftbl; JV Trk; JV Var Vllybl; Hon Roll; Val; Video Yrbk; Arch.

BLOODWORTH, MICHAEL; Palisades HS; Los Angeles, CA; (4); Service Clb; Teachers Aide; JV Bsbl; Var Capt Bsktbl; Hon Roll; All Amer Bsktbl; CA ST Fullerton; Bus Mgmt.

BLOOM, AMY; El Camino Real HS; Bell Cyn, CA; (3); Temple Yth Grp; Drill Tm; Stu Cncl; Cheerldng; Powder Puff Ftbl; Jr Stateman Of Amer; Cls Steering Cmmttes; House Of Reps.

BLOOM, BETSY A; Mater Dei HS; Anaheim, CA; (2); German Clb; GAA; JV Capt Bsktbl; JV Crs Cntry; Var L Trk; Hon Roll; Cal Poly Pomona; Animal Sci.

BLOOM, CLENN; Tri City Christian HS; Oceanside, CA; (2); 5/17; Church Choir; School Play; Stat Bsktbl; High Hon Roll; UCLA; Med.

BLOOM, GREGG; Canyon HS; Anaheim Hills, CA; (3); Key Clb; Math Clb; Mu Alpha Theta; Scholastic Bowl; Band; Jazz Band; Mrchg Band; Orch; Pep Band; Variety Show; Wrk Jngl Crs Disneyland; Won Rgnl Tlnt Shw Rock & Roll Band Jim; Lrng Rssn Bttr Tdys Soc; U Of CA; Bus.

BLOOM, HOLLY; Novato HS; Novato, CA; (2); Wt Lftg; Hon Roll; JV Diving; Var Swmmng; Var Tennis; High Hon Roll; Phys Thrpy.

BLOOM, MINDY R; Monte Vista HS; Spring Valley, CA; (2); 14/422; Art Clb; Church Yth Grp; French Clb; Chorus; Church Choir; Hon Roll; Church Camps Cnslr; Piano; Artist; Biola U; Artist.

BLOOM, RYAN; University HS; Los Angeles, CA; (3); Math Tm; Office Aide; Quiz Bowl; Scholastic Bowl; Stu Cncl; High Hon Roll; Hon Roll; Hnrs Alg Gldn St Exam; High Hnrs Geo Gldn St Exam; Cert Of Awd 4.0 GPA Span; Arch.

BLOOMFIELD, JANALYN; Ganesha HS; Diamond Bar, CA; (3); Church Yth Grp; FCA; Treas Jr Cls; VP Stu Cncl; Var Socr; Var Sftbl; Var Vllybl; Ntl Merit SF; Rotary Awd; UC Berkeley; Pre-Law.

BLOOMQUIST, FRANCES; La Canada HS; La Canada-Flint R, CA; (2); Church Yth Grp; Dance Clb; FTA; Hosp Aide; Intnl Clb; Pep Clb; Spanish Clb; Teachers Aide; Chorus; Rep Frsh Cls; Fshn Dsgn; Chrldng; Dncng; Dance.

BLOOMQUIST, KRISTEN; Coronado HS; Coronado, CA; (3); Art Clb; Church Yth Grp; Cmnty Wkr; Drama Clb; VP French Clb; Girl Scts; Hosp Aide; Key Clb; Model UN; Service Clb; Tuto Inner City Homelss Chldrn; Vlntr Retiremnt Home; Play Piano; Educ.

BLOSSER, JUDY A; Mt Diablo HS; Pittsburg, CA; (2); Cmnty Wkr; Hosp Aide; JV Capt Vllybl; High Hon Roll; HS Red Devil Trophy Vlybl Awd; HS Cert Hm Ec Outstndng Promotion Article; UC Davis; Chld Devlpmnt.

BLOUT, MIKEL; Santa Ynez HS; Santa Ynez, CA; (3); Church Yth Grp; Cmnty Wkr; Dance Clb; German Clb; Library Aide; Model UN; Office Aide; Pep Clb; SADD; Temple Yth Grp; Wellesly; Cardiac Srgn.

BLOWER, MARCI A; Lincoln HS; Stockton, CA; (3); 44/538; Church Yth Grp; Cmnty Wkr; French Clb; SADD; Ed Nwsp; French Hon Soc; High Hon Roll; Pres Acad Fit Awd; Rotary Smr Xchng Stu; Gldn St Xm Math Awd.

BLUE, JODI; Boron HS; Boron, CA; (3); 10/50; ROTC; Teachers Aide; Band; Drill Tm; Bsktbl; Sftbl; Vllybl; Hon Roll; NHS; CSF; Perfrmng Arts Awd 89; AV Coll; X-Ray Tech.

BLUE, TREY; Folsom HS; Folsom, CA; (4); 14/209; Debate Tm; Letterman Clb; Model UN; Treas Stu Cncl; JV Var Bsbl; JV Var Ftbl; Cit Awd; Elks Awd; Hon Roll; Lion Awd; UC Davis; Engrng.

BLUM, BRADLEY M; Fontana HS; Fontana, CA; (3); Drama Clb; Spanish Clb; Crs Cntry; Trk; Cit Awd; Hon Roll; UCR; Bus Admin.

BLUM, CARRIE R; La Jolla Country Day Schl; San Diego, CA; (2); Cmnty Wkr; Hosp Aide; Spanish Clb; SADD; Phtg Yrbk; JV Tennis; Hon Roll; Cmnty Svc Exec Bd; Social Worker.

BLUMBERG, CHRIS D; Cajon HS; San Bernardino, CA; (3); 62/439; JV Var Crs Cntry; JV Var Trk; Martial Arts; Temple Yth Grp; UCLA; Vet.

BLUMBERG, DAVID M; Granada Hills HS; Northridge, CA; (2); Bus Profs of Am; FBLA; Math Clb; Office Aide; Ski Clb; Teachers Aide; Rep Stu Cncl; Hon Roll; NHS.

BLUMENTHAL, HOLLY A; Santa Clara HS; Saratoga, CA; (4); 1/380; Cmnty Wkr; Math Clb; Pres Service Clb; Pres Band; Mrchg Band; Orch; DAR Awd; Ntl Merit SF; Val; Role Plyng Clb; Gntc Rsrch.

BLUMER, MOLLY E; University HS; Irvine, CA; (3); Cmnty Wkr; French Clb; Ski Clb; SADD; Teachers Aide; Stage Crew; Lit Mag; Off Jr Cls; Cheerldng; Cit Awd; Amnesty Intl Stu Of Month 90; Envrnmntl Awareness Clb Pres; Stu Advsry Brd Of Educ; Recycling Cmmtte; Art Mgmt.

BLUNK, SHERRY L; Grant Union HS; Sacramento, CA; (3); German Clb; Pep Clb; Quiz Bowl; Scholastic Bowl; Science Clb; Teachers Aide; Band; Mrchg Band; Pep Band; Ed Yrbk; MESA Pres; CSF Mngr; FNL; Pre-Med Biomed Engrng.

BLUNT, ALLEN R; Junipero Serra HS; San Diego, CA; (3); Spanish Clb; JV Capt Ftbl; Capt Wt Lftg; Hon Roll; Pres Acad Fit Awd; San Diego ST U; Bus.

BLUNT, ERIN D; San Pasqual HS; Escondido, CA; (2); Church Yth Grp; Pep Clb; Church Choir; Variety Show; Stu Cncl; Var Crs Cntry; JV Var Socr; Var Trk; Cit Awd; Hon Roll.

BOADO, CHRISTINE D; James Logan HS; Union City, CA; (3); Cmnty Wkr; FBLA; FTA; Library Aide; Science Clb; Ski Clb; Teachers Aide; Band; Mrchg Band; Pep Band; UCSF; Pre-Med.

BOARD, PRINCE L; Canyon HS; Canyon Country, CA; (4); 55/500; Dance Clb; Spanish Clb; Band; Jazz Band; Mrchg Band; Orch; Pep Band; Nwsp; Lit Mag; Rep Frsh Cls; Jazz Fstvl Awrds; Principals Awrd; Louis Armstron Jazz Awrd; Msc Schlrshp To SDSU; J P Sousa Awrd; San Diego ST U; Music.

BOARDMAN, NICOLE A; Yosemite Union HS; Oakhurst, CA; (3); Key Clb; Rptr Phtg Yrbk; Gym; Mgr(s); Swmmng; Cit Awd; High Hon Roll; Hon Roll; Fresno City; Ins.

BOAS, MELISSA; Dublin HS; Dublin, CA; (3); 9/210; French Clb; Treas Jr Cls; Gov Hon Prg Awd; High Hon Roll; Hon Roll; CSF; Acad Boosters Clb.

BOAZ, CATHRIN A; Skyline HS; Oakland, CA; (2); Church Yth Grp; Hosp Aide; Science Clb; Church Choir; Orch; School Musical; Cheerldng; Hon Roll; Med.

BOAZ, MEGHAN; Monache HS; Porterville, CA; (3); Am Leg Aux Girls St; Mrchg Band; Nwsp; Stu Cncl; Cheerldng; Tennis; Cit Awd; High Hon Roll; Rotary Awd; Art Clb; Porterville Yth Soroptmst Awd; Stanford; Law.

BOBADILLA, ANDY; Victor Valley HS; Victorville, CA; (3); Church Yth Grp; Key Clb; Church Choir; Mrchg Band; Rep Sr Cls; Cit Awd; Hon Roll; Sr Clss Cmmttee; Musich Synthsis.

BOBADILLA, JOYCE; Pittsburg HS; Pittsburg, CA; (1); FBLA; Science Clb; Yrbk; Stu Cncl; Socr; Stanford; Bus.

BOBBITT, AMY NICHELLE; Bakersfield HS; Bakersfield, CA; (4); 83/670; Dance Clb; 4-H; Spanish Clb; Cheerldng; Pom Pon; 4-H Awd; High Hon Roll; Hon Roll; 4-H Pres; JR HS Chrldng Coach; CA ST U; Ed.

BOBBY, R M; Canyon Springs HS; Moreno Valley, CA; (2); JV Crs Cntry; JV Sftbl; Intrml Vllybl; Hon Roll; Teens Agnst Drugs Clb; Sprt Clb; Visual Arts; U Of Southern CA; Prod Movies.

BOBE, AMY; Fremont Christian HS; Fremont, CA; (1); Church Yth Grp; Ski Clb; JV Var Bsktbl.

BOBILA, LALAINE E; George Washington HS; San Francisco, CA; (2); Church Yth Grp; School Musical; Variety Show; Tennis; Cit Awd; High Hon Roll; Hon Roll; Prncpls Cabinet; Schl Rep; Golden St Exam Geom; U Of CA San Francisco; Nrs.

BOBITA, JENNIFER; Grossmont HS; El Cajon, CA; (4); 15/350; French Clb; Intnl Clb; L Var Tennis; High Hon Roll; Pres Acad Fit Awd; CSF; Girls League; San Diego Cnty Women Engr Assn Awd; U CA San Diego; Sec Educ.

BOBO, LARISSA R; Edison HS; Fresno, CA; (2); Church Yth Grp; Cmnty Wkr; FTA; JV Sftbl; Cit Awd; Hon Roll.

BOBST, TIFFANY; Forest Lake HS; Auburn, CA; (2); Church Yth Grp; Chorus; Bsktbl; Sftbl; Trk; Vllybl; Hon Roll; Pres Acad Fit Awd; MVP Vlybl; Point Loma Nazarene Coll.

BOCHUM, MEGAN; Para Clete HS; Lancaster, CA; (3); Pres Key Clb; Yrbk; VP Jr Cls; High Hon Roll; CSF; Mktg.

BOCK, SUSANNE R; Burlingame HS; San Bruno, CA; (3); Debate Tm; German Clb; JA; Red Cross Aide; Service Clb; Ski Clb; JV Var Tennis; JV Var Trk; Hon Roll; 1st To Re-Start Jr Ski Patrol Pgm At Squaw Valley; Fluent In German Lang; German Exchange Pgm; UC Davis; Nursing.

BOCK, TONIA R; Norte Vista HS; Riverside, CA; (3); 1/298; FBLA; Yrbk; High Hon Roll; Prfct Atten Awd; Comp.

BOCKELMAN, ALIX; San Pedro HS; San Pedro, CA; (4); 2/522; Church Yth Grp; Cmnty Wkr; Pep Clb; Service Clb; Drill Tm; School Play; Stage Crew; Rep Frsh Cls; JV Var Cheerldng; High Hon Roll; CSF; Tandy Schlr; YMCA CA Modl Legsltve/Crt Pgm; UC Berkeley; Civil Engrng.

BODDULA, CHETHAN R; Brea Olinda HS; Brea, CA; (2); 3/344; Pres VP Intnl Clb; Speech Tm; Var JV Tennis; High Hon Roll; UC Irvine Pre Coll Smmr Pgm; Interact Clb; WALKAMERICA; Hist Day Cmptn 1st Cnty, 2nd St; UC; Dr.

BODEN, DAWN A; Granite Hills HS; El Cajon, CA; (2); Church Yth Grp; Cmnty Wkr; Debate Tm; SADD; Chorus; Stage Crew; Rptr Nwsp; Trk; Vllybl; Wt Lftg; Peer Cnslr; UCSD; Scl Svc.

BODENBENDER, MICHAEL R; Morro Bay HS; Baywood Pk, CA; (3); 111/250; Cmnty Wkr; Drama Clb; French Clb; JA; SADD; Pres Varsity Clb; Chorus; Variety Show; Var Capt Swmmng; Hon Roll; Vrsty Swmmng Coaches Awd; San Luis Obispo; Emrgncy Med.

BODENHAMER, LORI J; Mira Loma HS; Sacramento, CA; (2); 4/297; Art Clb; Math Clb; Math Tm; JV Sftbl; Cit Awd; High Hon Roll; CA Schlrshp Fndtn; People-People Stu Ambassador Pgm, Frndshp Caravan Soviet Union; Intl Rltns.

BODENSTEIN, MICHAEL; Montclair College Prep; Van Nuys, CA; (4); 10/80; Art Clb; Computer Clb; JA; Office Aide; Science Clb; Spanish Clb; Teachers Aide; Nwsp; Lit Mag; Off Frsh Cls; UCLA; Bus Admn.

BODIE, KATIE A; Del Oro HS; Loomis, CA; (3); 43/266; Art Clb; Cmnty Wkr; SADD; Teachers Aide; Yrbk; Jrnlsm.

BODILY, ANGELA; El Modena HS; Corona, CA; (4); 2/385; Church Yth Grp; Key Clb; Pep Clb; Phtg Nwsp; Cheerldng; Var Pom Pon; High Hon Roll; NHS; Sal; Mock Trial; Grls Lg Hstrn; U CA San Diego.

BODINE, ANDREW; Merced HS; Merced, CA; (4); Am Leg Boys St; Church Yth Grp; Band; Church Choir; Jazz Band; Mrchg Band; Orch; Pep Band; Bsktbl; High Hon Roll; Mech Engrng.

BODO, JOHN E; Bellarmine HS; Los Altos, CA; (2); Computer Clb; Debate Tm; Latin Clb; NFL; Swmmng; JSA; Water Polo; Cal Poly.

BOE, ANNA K; Napa HS; Napa, CA; (2); Church Yth Grp; Chorus; Church Choir; Swmmng; High Hon Roll; Hon Roll; Acad Block/Patch/Pin; BYU; Math.

BOEDEKER, DION M; Trabuco Hills HS; Mission Viejo, CA; (2); Spanish Clb; JV Bsktbl; Hon Roll; KS U; Lndscp Arch.

BOEHLE, CHRISTINE N; Notre Dame Acad; Los Angeles, CA; (3); 25/126; Capt Varsity Clb; Var Bsktbl; Var Capt Vllybl; Hon Roll; NHS; All Amer Jr Olympics OH; MVP Arcadia Trnment & Marlborough Invit 89; Law.

BOEHLE, DANIEL L; Mater Dei HS; Garden Grove, CA; (4); Church Yth Grp; ROTC; JV Var Bsktbl; High Hon Roll; NHS; Ntl Merit Ltr; Pres Acad Fit Awd; Pres Schlr; Loyola Marymount U; Comp Sci.

BOEHLE, MICHELLE; Mater Dei HS; Garden Grove, CA; (3); Dance Clb; Drama Clb; GAA; Girl Scts; Pep Clb; Stage Crew; Sec Rep Stu Cncl; JV Bsktbl; JV Crs Cntry; Var Capt Pom Pon; Loyola Marymount; Psych.

BOEHM, MICHELE M; Oakmont HS; Roseville, CA; (4); 80/350; Drama Clb; Hosp Aide; Service Clb; Pres SADD; Drill Tm; School Play; Yrbk; Stu Cncl; VP Cheerldng; VP Gym; CA Scholastic Federation; Skiing; Art; U C Irvine.

BOEHME, JESSICA R; Portola JR/Sr HS; Portola, CA; (1); Church Yth Grp; Cmnty Wkr; Hosp Aide; Letterman Clb; Pep Clb; Ski Clb; Spanish Clb; Varsity Clb; Variety Show; VP Frsh Cls; Yth To Yth Clb; Commnctn.

BOEHME, MICHAEL E; Turlock HS; Turlock, CA; (2); Boy Scts; Church Yth Grp; Rotary Awd; BYU; Arch.

BOENZI, APRIL L; Paraclete HS; Lancaster, CA; (2); Key Clb; Office Aide; SADD; Cit Awd; Hon Roll; Z-Clb; Spcl Ed Aide; Chld Psych.

BOESCH, CONNIE L; Cordova SR HS; Rancho Cordova, CA; (4); Church Yth Grp; Pep Clb; Yrbk; Off Frsh Cls; High Hon Roll; Hon Roll; Opt Clb Awd; Pres Acad Fit Awd; Yng Wmns Awrd Chrch Jesus Christ; Acadmc Achvmnt US Hstry; Top 10% Grdtng Clss; BYU; Tchng Deaf Chldrn.

BOESCH, JASON B; Atwater HS; Winton, CA; (3); FCA; Stu Cncl; Var L Bsbl; Var L Bsktbl; Var L Ftbl; Hon Roll; Bus Mgmt.

BOESTERLING, YVONNE; San Ramon Valley HS; Danville, CA; (1); Church Yth Grp; Girl Scts; Orch; Piano 3 Cert Of Mrt Hnrs.

BOEVING, BETTY ANN; Monte Vista HS; Danville, CA; (1); Cmnty Wkr; GAA; Stu Cncl; Var Bsktbl; Var Sftbl; Var Vllybl; Cit Awd; High Hon Roll; Jr NHS; Natl Chrty Leag; EBAL All Leag Bsktbl Team; Kiwanis Clb Wnnr; Schlstc Awd; Stanford; Med.

BOGDANOFF, DEBRA A; La Mirada HS; La Mirada, CA; (2); Band; Mrchg Band; High Hon Roll; Prfct Atten Awd; AYSO Referee/Plyr; Hi Hnrs Gldn St Alg Exam; CSF; PTSA.

BOGDANOVICH, JOSEPHINE MARIE; El Monte HS; El Monte, CA; (4); Cmnty Wkr; Office Aide; Service Clb; Rptr Nwsp; Co-Ed Lit Mag; JV Tennis; High Hon Roll; Pres Acad Fit Awd; Ca Shclrshp Fed Life Memb; Soroptomist Clb Awd; B Of A Awd For Liberal Arts; UC Santa Cruz; Devl Psy.

BOGE, DAVID T; Redwood Christian HS; San Leandro, CA; (2); Church Yth Grp; Library Aide; Office Aide; Spanish Clb; Teachers Aide; Varsity Clb; Stu Cncl; Bsbl; Bsktbl; Score Keeper; YMCA Yth Camp Cnslr; SL Recrtn Dept Playground Ldr Vlntr; UCLA; Polc Ofcr.

BOGERT, GEORGIANNA C; Calvary Chapel HS; Costa Mesa, CA; (2); Church Yth Grp; Letterman Clb; Yrbk; Score Keeper; Var Sftbl; Var Vllybl; Hon Roll; Pres Acad Fit Awd; MVP Sftbl Pitchr.

BOGETTI, TAMARA E; Tracy Joint Union HS; Tracy, CA; (2); 21/522; Art Clb; Church Yth Grp; Debate Tm; 4-H; French Clb; NFL; Speech Tm; SADD; Lit Mag; Treas Frsh Cls; Chrmn Leo Club; Acad Block T 4.0 GPA; CSF; Bio-Med Artist.

BOGGES, CHRIS R; Indio HS; Indio, CA; (1); Cit Awd; Hon Roll; Soarng Clb; Aviation.

BOGGS, RYAN; Capital Christian HS; Orangevale, CA; (3); Var Bsbl; Var Bsktbl; High Hon Roll; Azusa Pac U; Bus Admin.

BOGHOSIAN, DARREN N; Bullard HS; Fresno, CA; (1); Key Clb; NFL; Ski Clb; SADD; Var L Tennis; CSF; Schlr Athl Awd; UCLA.

BOGHOSSIAN, HILARY LYNN; Bear River HS; Grass Valley, CA; (2); Spanish Clb; SADD; Ed Lit Mag; Var L Tennis; Var Capt Vllybl; Cit Awd; High Hon Roll; Hon Roll; Opt Clb Awd; Prfct Atten Awd; Vlybl Clb USVBA Tm; Chico ST; Tchng.

BOGLE, RHONDA D; Monache HS; Porterville, CA; (3); Church Yth Grp; Cmnty Wkr; Mrchg Band; Rptr Nwsp; Bible Quiz Tm 3rd Sectl Div; Piano Lessns; Lwyr.

BOHANNA, PAUL; Tomales HS; Point Reyes Stati, CA; (3); Letterman Clb; Ski Clb; Varsity Clb; JV Var Bsbl; JV Bsktbl; Var Capt Ftbl; Wt Lftg; Prfct Atten Awd; Rep Frsh Cls; Rep Soph Cls; Mst Imprvd Bsktbl & Bsbl; Coachs Awd Ftbl; Arch.

BOHANNON, LARRY; Carson HS; Compton, CA; (2); Church Yth Grp; Band; Church Choir; Ftbl; Trk; Gftd Artistc Ablts; U Of Las Vegas NV; Crmnl Law.

BOHN, KATRINA E; San Clemente HS; San Juan Capistra, CA; (2); German Clb; Girl Scts; Varsity Clb; Socr; Trk; Vllybl; Hon Roll; Pres Acad Fit Awd; Poseiden Awd.

BOHN, KISI; Ramona HS; Pamona, CA; (4); 9/256; Teachers Aide; Var Gym; High Hon Roll; Exchng Stu To Spain 1988-89; Eqestrn; U CA San Diego; Ed.

BOHN, REBEKAH L; Gardena HS; Gardena, CA; (2); Church Yth Grp; Spanish Clb; Church Choir; Orch; School Musical; Hon Roll; Honors Classes; Early Morning Seminary Stu; Brigham Young U; Psychlgy.

BOHNENSTIEHL, MICHELLE L; Victory Christian Schl; North Highlands, CA; (2); Church Yth Grp; Teachers Aide; Var Bsktbl; Var Vllybl; Hon Roll; Bus Admin.

BOHORGUEZ, MILDRED; Jefferson HS; Daly City, CA; (4); 64/250; Art Clb; Church Yth Grp; Latin Clb; Pep Clb; Science Clb; Church Choir; Rptr Nwsp; Var Capt Cheerldng; Hon Roll; Stu Of Dist Awd, Stu Of Month Awd 89; San Francisco ST U.

BOIK, PAULA L; Fresno Christian HS; Fresno, CA; (4); 1/65; VP Church Yth Grp; Band; Chorus; Color Guard; Flag Corp; Mrchg Band; Tennis; Pres Acad Fit Awd; Val; Teachers Aide; CSF VP; Fresno Pacific Coll; Sociology.

BOIVIN, LYNN; Santa Margarita Catholic HS; El Toro, CA; (1); Church Yth Grp; JV Capt Cheerldng; High Hon Roll; Hon Roll; CSF Club; Fshn Design.

BOJORQUEZ, BRIDGET D; Village Christian HS; Sun Valley, CA; (3); Drama Clb; Letterman Clb; Spanish Clb; JV L Bsktbl; Var L Crs Cntry; Var L Trk; Missions Club; Mrktng.

BOJORQUEZ, MICHAEL V; Woodland HS; Woodland, CA; (4); SADD; Band; Mrchg Band; Pep Band; Off Frsh Cls; Stu Cncl; Intrml JV Bsbl; JV Ftbl; Hon Roll; Jr NHS; PG&E James B Black Schlrshp Awd; MESA; Babe Ruth Schlrshp Awd; WA ST; Arch.

BOLA, RASHPALL S; Livingston HS; Delhi, CA; (2); High Hon Roll; Pres Acad Fit Awd.

BOLA, SUKHVINDER; Livingston HS; Delhi, CA; (1); Hon Roll; CSF Mem; Law.

BOLAND, AMANDA; Delano HS; Delano, CA; (4); 6/255; Drama Clb; Letterman Clb; Scholastic Bowl; School Musical; Yrbk; VP Soph Cls; Cheerldng; Golf; High Hon Roll; NHS; UC Santa Barbara; Sociology.

BOLAND, PATRICIA A; Mater Dei HS; Huntington Beach, CA; (1); Church Yth Grp; Rep Frsh Cls; Rep Stu Cncl; Stat Score Keeper; JV Sftbl; JV Vllybl; Med.

BOLANDAR, JENNY A; Madera HS; Madera, CA; (2); Church Yth Grp; FHA; Rep Frsh Cls; Rep Soph Cls; JV Capt Bsktbl; JV Swmmng; Ernd Advncd Lfsvng; Brigham Young U; Engl Tchr.

BOLANDER-ZIMMERMAN, KIM R; Prospect HS; San Jose, CA; (1); Church Yth Grp; Church Choir; Hon Roll; Ballet Stu San Jose Dance Theater Acad Dance; Juried Art Shw Santa Clara Cnty Fr; Writing.

BOLANDS, MARTHA E; Downey HS; Downey, CA; (2); Church Yth Grp; Cmnty Wkr; Key Clb; Service Clb; Spanish Clb; Church Choir; School Play; Cit Awd; Kiwanis Awd; Prfct Atten Awd; 89 Bst Actrss Awd; Keywannettes Clb Cmnty Ldr; Chrch Choir Directr; Cal Poly Pomona; Engl Prfssr.

BOLANOS, DELMY; Saddleback HS; Santa Ana, CA; (2); French Clb; JV Crs Cntry; Var JV Trk; CSF; Paris Clb; Law.

BOLANOS, DENNIS; Duarte HS; San Diego, CA; (3); Art Clb; Aud/Vis; Drama Clb; Varsity Clb; Band; Jazz Band; School Musical; JV Bsktbl; Var Capt Tennis; Elec Dsgn.

BOLANOS, LIDA X; La Puente HS; La Puente, CA; (3); GAA; Latin Clb; JV Bsktbl; Cit Awd; Hon Roll; Prfct Atten Awd; Cert Achvt; Comp Pgmng.

BOLANOS, PATRICIA; Alisal HS; Salinas, CA; (2); FBLA; Teachers Aide; High Hon Roll; Hon Roll; Biling GATE; Mech Clb; UC Santa Cruz; Hstry.

BOLANOS, SYLVIA; Sacred Heart Of Mary HS; Los Angeles, CA; (3); GAA; Pres Frsh Cls; Pres Soph Cls; VP Jr Cls; Sec Treas Sr Cls; Stu Cncl; Var Sftbl; High Hon Roll; Hon Roll; NHS; Cum Laude Hnrs; UCLA; Pediatrics.

BOLDEN, DENA S L; Caruthers Union HS; Fresno, CA; (3); 18/87; Rep Church Yth Grp; FHA; Math Clb; Teachers Aide; Band; Mrchg Band; Sec Stu Cncl; Cheerldng; Hon Roll; Golden St Exam-Geom-Hnrs Awd; Nazarene World Mission Soc-Sec; Miss Am Coed-St Fnlst; Pt Loma Nazarene Coll; Soc Sci.

BOLDEN, KAREENA; Shafter HS; Bakersfield, CA; (4); Pep Clb; SADD; Acpl Chr; Chorus; Color Guard; Mrchg Band; Pep Band; Variety Show; Prfct Atten Awd; Prfrmd Cruise Shp To Mexico Wn 1st Pl; Bakersfield Coll; Psych.

BOLDEN, MICHAEL A; Valley HS; Sacramento, CA; (4); Church Yth Grp; Varsity Clb; Band; Color Guard; Drill Tm; Mrchg Band; Var Ftbl; Intrml Wt Lftg; Hon Roll; Ntl Merit Ltr; Mst Outstndng Frnch II Stu; Frnch Hnr Society; Prctc Plyr 2 Weeks Vrsty Ftbl; CA ST U Sacramento; Bus.

BOLDEN, VAUGHNYA; Pioneer SR HS; San Jose, CA; (1); Church Yth Grp; Gardan Clb; Chorus; Church Choir; Tutor; Stanford; Defns Attrny.

BOLDING, KASSANDRA; Oakridge HS; El Dorado Hills, CA; (2); Cmnty Wkr; FCA; Letterman Clb; Math Tm; Office Aide; Spanish Clb; VP Jr Cls; Stu Cncl; Cit Awd; High Hon Roll; ST Balance Beam Champ CA Advncd Optnl Level 89; U CA San Diego; Optometry.

BOLDON, KEITH; Los Alamitos HS; Seal Beach, CA; (3); Rep Soph Cls; VP Jr Cls; Stu Cncl; Var Capt Bsktbl; Var Trk; Hon Roll; UCLA; Invstmnt Bnkng.

BOLDUC, MICHELLE L; San Jacinto HS; San Jacinto, CA; (1); Church Yth Grp; Band; Church Choir; Mrchg Band; Pep Band.

BOLE, BRITTANY JANE; California HS; San Ramon, CA; (3); Church Yth Grp; Service Clb; Teachers Aide; Stat Bsktbl; Var Crs Cntry; Var Trk; Hon Roll; Pres Acad Fit Awd; San Ramon Valley Bus/Ed Round Table Photogrphy; BYU; Elem Ed.

BOLEN, TISNA M; Hueneme HS; Port Hueneme, CA; (4); Debate Tm; Pep Clb; SADD; Chorus; JV L Socr; JV Sftbl; Hon Roll; Campus Leag; Jr Statesmen; Mock Trial; US Navy; Frgn Lang.

BOLES, JASON K; Temecula Valley HS; Temecula, CA; (2); 73/500; Letterman Clb; Varsity Clb; JV Var Ftbl; JV Var Trk; Wt Lftg; Wrstlng; Hon Roll.

BOLGER, MIKE; Bonita Vista HS; Bonita, CA; (3); 15/559; Key Clb; Hon Roll; Outstndng Acad Awd; Prncpls Honor Roll.

BOLIN, DERRICK J; Chula Vista HS; Chula Vista, CA; (2); 315/558; Library Aide; Office Aide; Teachers Aide; JV Ftbl; JV Var Wrstlng; Sheldon Jackson Coll; Vet.

BOLINE, KIRSTEN N; California HS; Whittier, CA; (3); Drama Clb; Pep Clb; Varsity Clb; School Musical; Rep Jr Cls; Treas Stu Cncl; Var Cheerldng; Var Swmmng; Var Trk; Ntl Merit Ltr; Pre-Med.

BOLING, CHAD R; Hanford Union HS; Hanford, CA; (2); Church Yth Grp; JV Crs Cntry; JV Trk; Hon Roll; Acctng/CPA.

BOLIVAR, LUPE D; La Puente HS; La Puente, CA; (2); Teachers Aide; Hon Roll; Fshn Design.

BOLLA, DIXIE L; Galt Joint HS; Galt, CA; (3); Library Aide; Office Aide; Teachers Aide; Hon Roll; Pediatric Nrsng.

BOLLA, JOHN A; Irvington HS; Fremont, CA; (3); Teachers Aide; High Hon Roll; Hon Roll; Prfct Atten Awd; Accntng.

BOLLA, STACY; Dublin HS; Dublin, CA; (2); 10/224; Color Guard; Ed Nwsp; Treas Soph Cls; Var Bsktbl; High Hon Roll; HOBY; CSF; Acad Ltr.

BOLLOW, MICHAEL J; Venice HS; Marina Del Rey, CA; (3); Pres Church Yth Grp; Var Socr; Intrml Wt Lftg; Crnrssnl Schlr Rep CA At The Natl Yng Ldrs Conf; UCLA; Psych.

BOLOUR, ASHKAN; St Joseph HS; Santa Maria, CA; (3); 17/150; JA; Letterman Clb; Math Tm; Ski Clb; L Var Ftbl; Var Trk; L Capt Wrstlng; Hon Roll; Pres Acad Fit Awd; Surfing; UCSB; Bus.

BOLSTAD, DARREN C; Clayton Valley HS; Concord, CA; (2); Model UN; Var L Trk; Cit Awd; Hon Roll; Physic.

BOLT, JEREMY L; Abraham Lincoln HS; San Jose, CA; (4); 82/260; Latin Clb; Ski Clb; Band; Jazz Band; Mrchg Band; Orch; Pep Band; School Musical; Variety Show; Var Tennis; San Jose Symphony Yth Orch; CA All-St Hnr Band; Santa Clara Cnty Hnr Band; Music.

BOLTAS, DENISE K; Royal HS; Simi Valley, CA; (3); 8/600; Key Clb; Yrbk; Stu Cncl; Cheerldng; Sftbl; High Hon Roll; NHS; Simi Vly Yth Cncl; Jr Stsmn Amer Secy; CA Schlrshp Fed; Sci.

BOLTER, MICHAEL; Canoga Park HS; Canoga Pk, CA; (1); Boy Scts; French Clb; ROTC; U Of AZ; Comp Prgmr.

BOLTON, KIMI; Palm Desert HS; Palm Springs, CA; (1); Hosp Aide; Var Tennis; Hon Roll; Natl Charity Leag; Law.

BOLTON, LISA; Helix HS; La Mesa, CA; (3); 53/330; Dance Clb; FTA; Teachers Aide; Chorus; Church Choir; Variety Show; JV Bsktbl; Var Cheerldng; JV Gym; Hon Roll; Wnn Natl Anthem Cont; Brdcst Jrnlsm.

BOMAN, KRISTINA; Grace M Davis HS; Albuquerque, NM; (3); Band; Capt Color Guard; Pres Acad Fit Awd; U Of NE Albq; Bus Admin.

BONALOS, JENNIFER; East Union HS; Lathrop, CA; (2); 1/411; French Clb; JV Vllybl; High Hon Roll; Prfct Atten Awd; Asian Clb-Rep; CSF; UC Santa Barbara; Bus Econ.

BONAR, LISA D; Foothill HS; Santa Ana, CA; (3); Church Yth Grp; 4-H; Key Clb; Spanish Clb; 4-H Awd; High Hon Roll; Cngrssnl Schlr Rep CA; CA Schlrshp Fdr; Smmr Chldrn Mnstry Tm.

BONAR, NICOLE M; The Bishops Schl; San Diego, CA; (3); Cmnty Wkr; Girl Scts; Spanish Clb; Speech Tm; Varsity Clb; Chorus; Var Capt Tennis.

BONATO, MARIKO L; Apple Valley HS; Apple Valley, CA; (2); Key Clb; Pep Clb; Spanish Clb; JV Capt Cheerldng; Var Pom Pon; High Hon Roll; Hon Roll; JR Statesmen Of Amer; Med.

BONAWITZ, JOHN C; El Camino Fundamental HS; North Highlands, CA; (3); 106/366; French Clb; VP Ski Clb; Yrbk; US Santa Barbara; Real Est.

BONCANEGRA, VICTOR H; Imperial HS; Pomona, CA; (3); Church Yth Grp; Dance Clb; Speech Tm; VP Soph Cls; JV Bsktbl; JV Trk; JV Vllybl; Hon Roll; Prfct Atten Awd; Elctrnc Engr.

BOND, DELIA; Etiwanda HS; Cucamonga, CA; (4); Am Leg Aux Girls St; Church Yth Grp; Spanish Clb; Yrbk; Sec Treas Jr Cls; Trk; High Hon Roll; Prfct Atten Awd; Rotary Awd; CA Polytech U; Mech Engrng.

BOND, MARTIN J; St Joseph Notre Dame HS; Oakland, CA; (3); 10/100; Am Leg Boys St; JV Bsktbl; High Hon Roll; NHS; CSF.

BOND, MICHAEL B; Palmdale HS; Palmdale, CA; (2); 1/800; JV Bsbl; Hon Roll; Stu Of Wk; CSF Stu; Golden St Exam Alg I Hnr; USAF Acad; AF Pilot.

BOND, MICHAEL E; Hoover HS; Fresno, CA; (3); Church Yth Grp; CA Schlrshp Fed.

BOND, SUSAN M; San Gabriel Mission HS; Alhambra, CA; (3); Church Yth Grp; Pres Drama Clb; French Clb; Girl Scts; Chorus; School Musical; School Play; Stage Crew; Off Soph Cls; Hon Roll; Grl Sct Gld, Slvr Awd; Peer Cnslr; CIT; Psych.

BONDA, VICTOR M; Escalon HS; Farmington, CA; (3); 9/180; Key Clb; Latin Clb; Math Clb; Spanish Clb; Teachers Aide; JV Var Crs Cntry; JV Var Trk; JV Var Wt Lftg; JV Var Wrstlng; High Hon Roll; MVP; Sacramento U; Phys Therapist.

BONDAR, VICTORIA; Los Angeles County HS For The Arts; Woodland Hills, CA; (3); Cmnty Wkr; Debate Tm; Drama Clb; Speech Tm; School Musical; School Play; Stage Crew; Variety Show; Var Bsktbl; Hon Roll; Hnr Artist Growth; Hnr Achvt Lit & Crtcsm; Athltc Awd Grls Vrsty Bsktbl; Theatre Arts.

BONDOC, CRISTILIE B; Montgomery HS; San Diego, CA; (2); Chorus; Yrbk; Cit Awd; Hon Roll; Prfct Atten Awd.

BONDURANT, BETH; Bakersfield HS; Bakersfield, CA; (3); Boy Scts; German Clb; Science Clb; Orch; Hon Roll; Horse Riding; Anml Sci.

BONE, DANIELLE N; Gilroy HS; Gilroy, CA; (4); 20/400; 4-H; Letterman Clb; SADD; School Musical; Powder Puff Ftbl; JV Var Socr; JV Vllybl; High Hon Roll; Santa Clara Cnty Yth Hall Fame Fnlst; CA Schlrshp Fed Offcr; Acad Excllnc; Prncpls List; U Of CA Santa Barbara.

BONE, DARLENE; Desert Christian HS; Redlands, CA; (1); Church Yth Grp; Drama Clb; Band; Chorus; High Hon Roll; Hillcrest Intl Sch Irian; Psych.

BONE, JASON C; Monte Vista HS; Alamo, CA; (3); Boy Scts; Computer Clb; Teachers Aide; Band; Jazz Band; Mrchg Band; JV Socr; Var L Trk; Mst Outstndng Musician Band Awd.

BONE, SARA; El Toro HS; El Toro, CA; (4); 1/570; Debate Tm; French Clb; Key Clb; Speech Tm; Bsktbl; Tennis; Trk; High Hon Roll; JETS Awd; Pres Acad Fit Awd; Tp 10 Schlr Athlts ST Of CA; Cnty Prep Class Schlr Athlt Of Yr; US Army Resrv Natl Schlr Athlt Awd; Dartmouth Coll; Law.

BONEA, JARED; Bellarmine College Prep; San Jose, CA; (3); Boy Scts; Church Yth Grp; Service Clb; Cheerldng; Wrstlng; Mountaineering; Rock Clmbng; Backpacking; UC Berkeley; Biologcl Engr.

BONES, RYAN M; Downey HS; Downey, CA; (2); Boy Scts; Church Yth Grp; Key Clb; Trk; Hon Roll; CSULB; Pilot.

BONES, SHANDRA; Fortuna Union HS; Rio Dell, CA; (2); 25/212; Girl Scts; SADD; JV Var Cheerldng; Score Keeper; Cit Awd; Pres Of Grappelettes; Commnctns.

BONESTEEL, CHRIS P; Simi Valley HS; Simi Valley, CA; (2); Aud/Vis; Rep Church Yth Grp; Cmnty Wkr; Drama Clb; Thesps; Band; Jazz Band; School Play; Stage Crew; Stat Ftbl; Cmmnty Svc Rec Awd; Delg Natl Luth Yth Gathrng 89; Arch.

BONFIGLIO, TINA-MARIE; San Marcos HS; San Marcos, CA; (3); Key Clb; Teachers Aide; Var Hon Roll; CA Schlrshp Fdrtn; Psychlgy.

BONFOEY, MARYA T; Fontana HS; Fontana, CA; (3); Office Aide; Teachers Aide; Intrml Mgr Socr; Trk; High Hon Roll; Hon Roll; Z Clb; Comp Sci.

BONGATO, ARIEL; Fremont HS; Sunnyvale, CA; (3).

BONHAM, JUDY L; Sanger HS; Sanger, CA; (3); Church Yth Grp; Cmnty Wkr; Hosp Aide; Ricks Coll; Ed.

BONHAM, LAURA E; Clovis HS; Clovis, CA; (1); Drama Clb; Girl Scts; SADD; Bsktbl; JV Score Keeper; JV Tennis; Hon Roll; Pres Acad Fit Awd; Soph Cls Soc Cmmssnr 90-91; JV Chrldr 90-91; Ldrshp Clss 93; Drama Stage 71; UC Santa Cruz; Int Dsgn.

BONIFACIO, ANTHONY C; St Lgnaus HS; Daly City, CA; (2); Cmnty Wkr; French Clb; JV Var Vllybl; Asian Stu Coalition; Stanford U; Bus.

BONILLA, ALMA L; Indio HS; Indio, CA; (1); Drama Clb; Spanish Clb; Color Guard; Loma Linda U; Pediatrics.

BONILLA, ANGELA; Huntington Beach HS; Huntington Beach, CA; (4); 27/457; Pres Church Yth Grp; Red Cross Aide; Flag Corp; High Hon Roll; Semi-Fnlst Ntl Hspnc Schlr Awds Prgm; Brghm Yng U Schlrshp; Brghm Yng U; Ed.

BONILLA, BENECITO; Delta HS; Walnut Grove, CA; (3); Off Jr Cls; Lion Awd; ESL.

BONILLA, CARLOS A; Atascadero HS; Atascadero, CA; (3); JV Socr; Med.

BONILLA, DENISE; Ygnacio Valley HS; Concord, CA; (2); Church Yth Grp; Cmnty Wkr; Dance Clb; Drama Clb; Key Clb; Red Cross Aide; Spanish Clb; Teachers Aide; Thesps; Acpl Chr; NCA Natl Chrldng Chmps 89-90; NCA Natl & Rgnl Pompon Chmps 89-90; Cnflct Mgmt Yth Edctr Drg Awrnss; Chico ST; Psych.

BONILLA, DIANA I; Louisville HS; Reseda, CA; (2); Church Yth Grp; GAA; Chorus; School Musical; JV Swmmng; JV Vllybl; CSF; Engl Awd; 15th Annual Los Ninos Walkathon; UCLA; Med.

BONILLA, ELVIA; San Clemente HS; San Clemente, CA; (1); Yrbk; Off Frsh Cls; Saddleback; Counseling.

BONILLA, ERIC M; Valley Christian HS; Norwalk, CA; (2); Church Yth Grp; Var L Crs Cntry; Stat Socr; JV Trk; Hon Roll; Coaches Awd Crss Cntry; Sprtsmnshp Awd JR Vrsty Trck; AZ ST; Arch.

BONILLA, IRMA; Pasadena HS; Pasadena, CA; (2); Latin Clb; Office Aide; Science Clb; Spanish Clb; Drill Tm; Bsktbl; Cheerldng; Gym; Pom Pon; Swmmng; Stanford; Law.

BONILLA, JESSICA; Huntington Bch HS; Ferndale, WA; (2); Color Guard; Variety Show; Sec Soph Cls; Hon Roll; Recd Mdln Hstns Acad Achvt In Tower Awd Crmny; BYU.

BONILLA, JOIE R; Chula Vista HS; San Diego, CA; (3); Church Yth Grp; Drama Clb; Thesps; Church Choir; School Play; Stage Crew; Off Frsh Cls; Sec Sr Cls; Var Sftbl; JV Var Vllybl; Invlvd In Sftbl; Trvlng Sftbl Team Plcd 4th ASA Champ 89; Bus.

BONNAR, KACIE D; East Bakersfield HS; Bakersfield, CA; (1); Aud/Vis; Church Yth Grp; Rep Drama Clb; Key Clb; Teachers Aide; Thesps; School Musical; School Play; Stage Crew; Variety Show; Equestrian Engl; UCLA; Dramatics.

BONNELL, APRIL E; Hesperia HS; Hesperia, CA; (2); 105/790; Church Yth Grp; FTA; Office Aide; SADD; Teachers Aide; Band; Mrchg Band; Pep Band; Cit Awd; High Hon Roll; Point Loma Nazarene Coll; Educ.

BONNER, CAPRII; Gompers Secondary HS; San Diego, CA; (1); 88/267; Dance Clb; Church Choir; Yrbk; Cheerldng; Gym; Sftbl; Actng In Play The Wiz; Obst.

BONNER, CHEMITRI V; Downtown HS; Daly City, CA; (3); Chorus; Lit Mag; Hon Roll; Law.

BONNER, CHRISTINA M; Clovis HS; Clovis, CA; (2); Church Yth Grp; Drama Clb; School Musical; JV Socr; Var Tennis; Hon Roll.

BONNER, JENNIFER J; Terra Nova HS; Pacifica, CA; (3); 32/300; Church Yth Grp; Cmnty Wkr; English Clb; 4-H; French Clb; GAA; JA; Letterman Clb; Office Aide; Pep Clb; San Diego U; Pre Law.

BONNER, KAZANDRA J; Junipero Serro HS; San Diego, CA; (4); 19/400; Cmnty Wkr; English Clb; Model UN; Sec Pep Clb; Science Clb; Lit Mag; Sec Soph Cls; Sec Jr Cls; Sec Stu Cncl; Cheerldng; Berkeley Undergrad Schlrshp; UC Berkeley; Microbio.

BONNER, SHANNAH; Walnut HS; Walnut, CA; (2); Sec Drill Tm; High Hon Roll; Hon Roll; Prfct Atten Awd; United Stu Union; UCLA; Med.

BONNETT, CAREN S; San Leandro HS; San Leandro, CA; (2); 62/399; Library Aide; Rep Soph Cls; VP Stu Cncl; Var Swmmng; Hon Roll; Pres Acad Fit Awd; Tchr.

BONNETT, ELIZABETH; Shasta HS; Redding, CA; (4); 10/438; Church Yth Grp; Cmnty Wkr; Model UN; School Play; Ed Yrbk; Stu Cncl; Cit Awd; High Hon Roll; Pres Acad Fit Awd; CSF; CA ST U At Chico; Bus.

BONNEY, MARK; Calvary Chapel HS; Huntington Beach, CA; (3); Am Leg Boys St; Boy Scts; Church Yth Grp; Rptr Yrbk; Rep Jr Cls; JV Bsktbl; L Ftbl; JV Vllybl; HOBY; Aviation.

BONO, JOE S; San Dieguito HS; Encinitas, CA; (2); 30/615; Office Aide; SADD; Varsity Clb; Var Ftbl; Var Trk; Var Wt Lftg; High Hon Roll; Hon Roll; Pres Acad Fit Awd; Pres Schlr; Bus Admin.

BONOCAN, TERESITO; Amos Alonzo Stagg SR HS; Stockton, CA; (4); Hon Roll; U Pacific; Chem.

BONOFIGLIO, JOSEPH A; Gahr HS; Cerritos, CA; (2); 1/450; Church Yth Grp; Spanish Clb; Var Socr; High Hon Roll; Prfct Atten Awd; Val; Tnns Clb; Outstndng Achvt Bio.

BONOT, LORI; Temecula Valley HS; Murrieta, CA; (1); Debate Tm; Cheerldng; High Hon Roll; Prfct Atten Awd; Pep Squad Secr; Yale; News Anchor.

BONSER, HEATHER; El Dorado HS; Placerville, CA; (4); 8/300; Am Leg Aux Girls St; Drama Clb; NFL; Cit Awd; High Hon Roll; NHS; Ntl Merit Schol; Pres Acad Fit Awd; Capt Debate Tm; Math Tm; Acad Decathlon; Sci Club; CSF; U Houston; Bus.

BOOCK, MICHAEL W; Victor Valley HS; Apple Valley, CA; (4); German Clb; JV JV Ftbl; JV JV Wrstlng; Irvine; Comp Aided Drftng.

BOOK, JOANNA E; Santa Clara HS; Oxnard, CA; (4); Mgr(s); Score Keeper; Trk; Stat Vllybl; Hon Roll; NHS; Pres Acad Fit Awd; Ventura Cty Prof Womens Network Mentor Schlrshp 3rd Pl; Santa Clara HS Achvt Awd; Cls Part Awd; CA ST U-Northridge; Corp Law.

BOOKATAUB III, S JOSEPH; Poway HS; San Diego, CA; (3); 215/761; Ski Clb; JV Bsbl; Var Ftbl; Var Wt Lftg; Var Wrstlng; Pres Acad Fit Awd; Cmmnctns.

BOOKER IV, JOHN W; Nogales HS; La Puente, CA; (2); Church Yth Grp; Cmnty Wkr; Library Aide; Math Tm; Office Aide; Pep Clb; Teachers Aide; Band; Mrchg Band; Orch; CPA.

BOOKER, RODNEY E; Ontario HS; Ontario, CA; (3); Ftbl; Coachs Awd; Appeard On Little House On Prairie, Days Of Our Lives, Nmrs Cmmrcls; Morehouse; Med.

BOOKMAN, KEA G; Hart HS; Valencia, CA; (1); Church Yth Grp; JV Cheerldng; Hon Roll; Pres Acad Fit Awd; Masters Coll.

BOOMHOWER, TRACI Y; Bell Jeff HS; Sun Valley, CA; (2); Cmnty Wkr; Teachers Aide; JV Bsktbl; JV Trk; High Hon Roll; Hon Roll; San Diego ST; Marine Bio.

BOONE, AARON J; Villa Park HS; Villa Park, CA; (3); SADD; Varsity Clb; Rep Frsh Cls; Rep Soph Cls; Rep Jr Cls; Var Bsbl; Var Bsktbl; Var Ftbl; Hon Roll; Pres Acad Fit Awd; All Century League Bsbl & Bsktbl; Princpls Hnr Soc; USC; Bsbl.

BOONE, ERIC N; Thomas Downey HS; Modesto, CA; (2); Debate Tm; NFL; Speech Tm; School Play; L Swmmng; Waterpolo; Intl Bus.

BOONE, JEFF M; Winters HS; Vacaville, CA; (2); SADD; JV Trk; Wt Lftg.

BOONE, JERMAINE; Crenshaw HS; Los Angeles, CA; (4); 10/400; Church Yth Grp; Cmnty Wkr; FBLA; FTA; JA; Teachers Aide; School Play; Pres Jr Cls; VP Stu Cncl; JV Bsbl; Morehouse Coll; Cmmnctns.

BOONE, KENYA A; Westlake School For Girls; Los Angeles, CA; (4); Diving; Gym; Video Wrkshp.

BOONE, MELISSA G; Apple Valley HS; Apple Valley, CA; (3); Church Yth Grp; Dance Clb; Teachers Aide; Acpl Chr; Chorus; Variety Show; Hon Roll; Sunday Schl Aide; Doctor.

BOONE, NICOL A; El Toro HS; El Toro, CA; (4); Service Clb; Teachers Aide; Ed Yrbk; Hon Roll; Intl Ordr Of Jobs Dghtrs; Instrnctl Aide Engl; Wrkd With Edtrs Yrbk, 1st Pl Publshng Yrbk; Cal ST Fullerton; Commctns.

BOONE, RACHAEL A; Lincoln HS; Stockton, CA; (4); 83/550; Church Yth Grp; 4-H; German Clb; Math Tm; Office Aide; SADD; Acpl Chr; Chorus; Church Choir; Swmmng; CSU-STANISLAUS; Acctng.

BOONE, ROCHELLE S; Eisenhower HS; Rialto, CA; (3); Church Yth Grp; Speech Tm; Pres Frsh Cls; Rep Soph Cls; Pres Jr Cls; Hon Roll; Pres Acad Fit Awd; Hse Rep Page; Model Congrs; Mock Trl; Lwyr.

BOONJAKUAKUL, JENNI K; El Dorado HS; China Hills, CA; (2); High Hon Roll; CA Schlstc Fed; US Gymnastics Fed; Vet Med.

BOONPENG, ANNOPE; St John Bosco HS; Downey, CA; (3); Computer Clb; French Clb; Varsity Clb; Band; Jazz Band; Mrchg Band; Pep Band; Intrml Trk; Hon Roll; CSULB; Psych.

BOONSOM, VIENGCHAI; Highlands HS; North Highlands, CA; (2); #10 In Class; Socr; Cit Awd; High Hon Roll; Hon Roll; Arch.

BOONYAVONG, DUANGMANY; Modesto HS; Modesto, CA; (3); Hon Roll; Fshn Dsgnr.

BOOT, ANGEL D; Amador HS; Plymouth, CA; (4); 2/139; Office Aide; Teachers Aide; Stat Mgr(s); Score Keeper; Sftbl; Stat Wrstlng; High Hon Roll; Hon Roll; Acad Achvt Plaque; Schlr Of Week; Bank Of Amer Cert Of Achvt; Amer River Coll.

BOOTH, ALLISON J; Torrey Pines HS; San Diego, CA; (4); Pres Frsh Cls; JV Bsktbl; Var Sftbl; Pres NHS; Opt Clb Awd; Pres Acad Fit Awd; Key Clb; Spanish Clb; High Hon Roll; Jr NHS; Natl Bobby Sox Schlrshp 91; 90-91 Cngrssnl Schlr; 89 GSE Awd; 89-91 All League & All Acad Team Sftbl; Law.

BOOTH, CHANNING T; Roosevelt Performing Arts HS; Fresno, CA; (3); 6/600; Cmnty Wkr; Band; Jazz Band; Mrchg Band; Pep Band; School Musical; School Play; Stage Crew; High Hon Roll; Hon Roll; San Joaquin Jazz Fstvl Top Outstndng Soloist 90; Natl Assn Jazz Edctrs Schlrshp; Berklee Schl Schlrshp; CA ST Hayward; Music.

BOOTH, CRYSTAL L; Mission Bay HS; San Diego, CA; (2); 43/380; DECA; JV Sftbl; JV Vllybl; Cit Awd; Hon Roll; Bus.

BOOTH, JANA L; Covina HS; Covina, CA; (2); French Clb; Library Aide; USC; Law Acctng.

BOOTH, MINDY G; A A Stagg SR HS; Stockton, CA; (1); Church Yth Grp; High Hon Roll; CSF; Pediatrician.

BOOTH, SHELLY L; A A Stagg HS; Stockton, CA; (3); Church Yth Grp; Key Clb; Pep Clb; Spanish Clb; Teachers Aide; JV Cheerldng; High Hon Roll; NHS; Orgnzd Eating Disorder Pgm At Schl; UC, Davis; Chld Psych.

BOOTHBY, DOUG; Sierra HS; Tollhouse, CA; (4); 20/175; Office Aide; SADD; Teachers Aide; Nwsp; Yrbk; Treas Stu Cncl; High Hon Roll; Hon Roll; NHS; Ntl Merit Ltr; CA Schlrshp Fdrtn; Fresno St U; Law.

BOOZELL, JEFFREY N; Palm Springs HS; Rancho Mirage, CA; (3); 10/750; French Clb; Pres Jr Cls; Off Sr Cls; JV Bsbl; High Hon Roll; Jr Statesman Of Amer; CSF; Pepperdine Southern CA Yth Ctznshp Seminar 90; Engrng.

BOPARAI, NANAK S; Mission San Jose HS; Fremont, CA; (3); Boy Scts; Church Yth Grp; Science Clb; Variety Show.

BOQUIREN, CHELLYN C; Mira Mesa HS; San Diego, CA; (2); Church Yth Grp; Cmnty Wkr; French Clb; Pres Soph Cls; Rep Jr Cls; Rep Stu Cncl; Hon Roll; Pres Acad Fit Awd; CSF; Prjct Prevent; Peer Cnslng; Bus Admin.

BORBA, LISA; Antioch HS; Antioch, CA; (4); 12/595; Letterman Clb; Spanish Clb; Varsity Clb; Acpl Chr; Band; Chorus; Jazz Band; Mrchg Band; Orch; Pep Band; Mst Outstndng Musician; Fresno ST; Music Ed.

BORBA, SCOTT V; Redwood HS; Visalia, CA; (3); Cmnty Wkr; Debate Tm; Drama Clb; Key Clb; Pep Clb; Spanish Clb; Nwsp; Yrbk; Pres Soph Cls; Rep Stu Cncl; UC Davis; Psych.

BORBA, SUSANNE M; Wasco Union HS; Wasco, CA; (2); Church Yth Grp; Cmnty Wkr; Band; Mrchg Band; Pep Band; Rep Soph Cls; JV Sftbl; JV Vllybl; High Hon Roll; Prfct Atten Awd; Hgh Hnr Soc; CSF; UOP Stockton; Pharmacist.

BORBE, MARY GRACE; Bishop Amat HS; La Puente, CA; (4); 33/392; Cmnty Wkr; Flag Corp; Yrbk; High Hon Roll; NHS; CSF; Acad All Amer; Slvr Scrn Clb Pres 89-90; CA Poly Tech U; Arch.

BORBON, CATHERINE G; Ganesha HS; Diamond Bar, CA; (4); 2/230; Hosp Aide; JA; Sec Math Clb; Science Clb; Ed Nwsp; Rep Stu Cncl; Capt Tennis; High Hon Roll; Rotary Awd; Sal; Cal Poly U Pomona; Bus.

BORBON, FLORINDA; Westmoor HS; Daly City, CA; (3); Church Yth Grp; Band; Sftbl; Hon Roll; Filipino-Amer Clb-VP.

BORBON, RENE F; Duarte HS; Duarte, CA; (3); 3/284; Church Yth Grp; Cmnty Wkr; Key Clb; Ed Nwsp; Chrch-Vllybl, Sftbl, & Bsktbl Tms; Chicano-Latino Yth Ldrshp Conf 90; Engrng.

BORCHARD, ANDREA M; North Salinas HS; Salinas, CA; (2); Spanish Clb; Color Guard; Flag Corp; Cheerldng; Elks Awd; High Hon Roll; Hon Roll; Rotary Awd; Outstndng Achvt Physcs Awd; Hnrs Gldn St Exms; Stu Of Yr Awd; Stus Of NSHS Awd; Stanford U; Srgn.

BORCHARDT, JULIA A; Campolindo HS; Moraga, CA; (4); Church Yth Grp; Girl Scts; Rep Stu Cncl; JV Crs Cntry; JV Trk; Hon Roll; Ntl Merit SF; Acadc Dcthln; CA Schlrshp Fed; USNA & USMA Smmr Smnr; Mlclr Bio.

BORDALO, JANE M; Alameda HS; Alameda, CA; (2); 10/275; French Clb; Sec Frsh Cls; Rep Soph Cls; JV Pom Pon; Hon Roll; Bon Voyage Club-An Exch Prog French Stu.

BORDEN, JAMES; Washington Preparatory HS; Los Angeles, CA; (2); Church Yth Grp; Math Clb; Band; Mrchg Band; Swmmng; Hon Roll; NHS; Engrng.

BORDER, JUSTIN; Liberty Union HS; Brentwood, CA; (2); JV Bsbl; JV Capt Bsktbl; JV Capt Ftbl; High Hon Roll; Hon Roll; CA U Los Angeles; Bus.

BORDERS, MIKE D; Mission Bay HS; San Diego, CA; (4); Church Yth Grp; Bus Profs of Am; Ed Nwsp; Var Vllybl; Hon Roll; Schltc Jrnlstc Awd; Humboldt ST U; Jrnlsm.

BORDERS, STEVEN V; Arcata HS; Arcata, CA; (2); Church Yth Grp; Cmnty Wkr; U Of CA Davis; Vet Med.

BORDINARO, LISA C; Redlands HS; Redlands, CA; (3); 178/896; Church Yth Grp; French Clb; Pep Clb; Orch; Cit Awd; High Hon Roll; Hon Roll; Write Poems; UCLA; Acctng.

BORDING, KIRSTEN L; Santa Monica HS; Little Rock, AR; (2); SADD; JV Trk; Hon Roll; Dance; Intl Rltns.

BORDNER, EUNICE L; J E Mc Ateer HS; San Francisco, CA; (3); Teachers Aide; Rep Frsh Cls; Rep Soph Cls; High Hon Roll; Close Up Clb; Med.

BORELLI, SARA YOLANDA; St Joseph Notre Dame HS; Alameda, CA; (4); Cmnty Wkr; GAA; Varsity Clb; Bsktbl; Cheerldng; Score Keeper; Sftbl; Vllybl; NHS; Spnsh.

BORG, GINA; Foothill HS; Pleasanton, CA; (3); English Clb; Lit Mag; High Hon Roll; UC Santa Barbara; Marine Bio.

BORG, MICHAEL A; Santa Teresa HS; San Jose, CA; (2); Drama Clb; Yrbk; Arch.

BORGES, BRIAN; Redwood Christian HS; San Lorenzo, CA; (3); Church Yth Grp; Ski Clb; Spanish Clb; Crs Cntry; Socr; Trk; Vllybl; Pres Acad Fit Awd; Schl Recognition For Golden St Exam Geom; ASVAB Test 80th Precentile; US Hstry Exam 90th Percentile; AZ ST U Tempe; Engrng.

BORGES, CHAD; Armona Union Acad; Hanford, CA; (1); Drama Clb; Band; Chorus; High Hon Roll; Hon Roll.

BORGES, EDUARDO; Loyola HS; Los Angeles, CA; (2); Cmnty Wkr; Intrml Ftbl; Intrml Trk; Wt Lftg; 1st Pl Natl Spanish Exam Amer Assn Of Teachers; Prof Dancer For Ballet Folklorico De Maria Luisa; Psych.

BORGES, ERIK R; Armona Union Acad; Hanford, CA; (2); Drama Clb; Band; Chorus; Nwsp; Off Soph Cls; Bsbl; Vllybl; Bus.

BORGHEI, KARIMEH N; El Camino Real HS; Woodland Hills, CA; (3); Church Yth Grp; Ski Clb; SADD; Chorus; Drill Tm; Stu Cncl; Save Earth Clb; Pierce Coll; Pediatrics.

BORGHESANI, LISSHA LYNN; Roseville HS; Roseville, CA; (3); French Clb; Drill Tm; Hon Roll; Hotel Mgmt.

BORGMAN, TONY L; East Nicolaus HS; Pleasant Grove, CA; (2); 4/45; Church Yth Grp; 4-H; Ski Clb; JV L Trk; 4-H Awd; High Hon Roll; Hon Roll.

BORGOMINI, ERCOLE F; Monterey HS; Monterey, CA; (1); JV Bsbl; Stanford.

BORGSTROM, ERIN E; El Segundo HS; El Segundo, CA; (4); AFS; Church Yth Grp; Science Clb; Stu Cncl; JV Var Socr; JV Sftbl; Girls Soccer Schlrshp; Vrsty Soccer Coaches Awd; UCLA; Engrng.

BORJA, ANGIE A; Chino HS; Chino, CA; (2); Girl Scts; Band; Mrchg Band.

BORJA, ELIZABETH; Mercy HS; San Francisco, CA; (1); Church Yth Grp; Office Aide; Hon Roll; Asian Club.

BORJA, JENNIFER C; Pasadena HS; Pasadena, CA; (2); Hosp Aide; Q&S; Mgr Yrbk; Hon Roll; Badmntn Team JR & Var; CSF; Jrnlsm.

BORJA, ROBERT T; Montgomery HS; San Diego, CA; (4); Church Yth Grp; Pres Band; Drm Mjr(t); Mrchg Band; Stage Crew; Capt Tennis; Peer Mnstry; Cnslrs Aide; CA Bus Ed Assn Acctng Awd; Acctng.

BORJAN, ELAINE M; Napa HS; Napa, CA; (3); Key Clb; SADD; Ed Yrbk; Sacramento ST U; Photogrphy.

BORK, DAVID T; Clovis West HS; Fresno, CA; (4); 78/600; Intnl Clb; Letterman Clb; Ski Clb; Varsity Clb; Nwsp; Crs Cntry; Socr; Trk; Hon Roll; Pres Acad Fit Awd; CA Press Women Sprts Jrnlsm Schlrshp; West Press Schlrshp; UC Santa Barbara.

BORKEY, CARRIE; Tulare Union HS; Tulare, CA; (3); 6/381; Am Leg Aux Girls St; Church Yth Grp; Drama Clb; GAA; Drill Tm; Stu Cncl; High Hon Roll; L Var Bsktbl; JV Sftbl; JV Vllybl; Camp Royal Ldrshp Camp; CA Girls St; Natl Yng Ldrs Conf; Rally Spirit Chairman; UCLA.

BORKEY, DAWNELLE B; Burney HS; Burney, CA; (2); Church Yth Grp; Pep Clb; Band; School Musical; VP Frsh Cls; Treas Soph Cls; JV Var Cheerldng; High Hon Roll; Gldn St Exm 1st Yr Alg W/Hnrs; Yth/Yth Clb; Intl Span Inst Ensenada Mexico; Engrng.

BORN, MONETT; Santa Ynez HS; Solvang, CA; (3); 38/168; AFS; Teachers Aide; VP Jr Cls; VP Stu Cncl; Var L Cheerldng; Var L Socr; JV Capt Tennis; Rotary Awd; KS ST; Aviation.

BORN, NICOLE M; Oceanview HS; FPO San Francisc, CA; (2); Drama Clb; Spanish Clb; Powder Puff Ftbl; Socr; Trk; Vllybl; Hon Roll; Spnsh II & US Hstry Outstndng Acdmcs; Bus.

BORNEMANN, CHANDA; Fairfield HS; Fairfield, CA; (4); Church Yth Grp; Dance Clb; German Clb; Pep Clb; Teachers Aide; Variety Show; Yrbk; Rep Jr Cls; VP Sr Cls; Var Cheerldng; Comptv Gymnast; Fresno ST.

BORNHOLDT, PAIGE ELLEN; Bonita Vista HS; Bonita, CA; (3); Pres Church Yth Grp; Cmnty Wkr; Key Clb; Pep Clb; Chorus; Church Choir; Rep Frsh Cls; JV Capt Cheerldng; High Hon Roll; Hon Roll; San Diego All-Star Chrldr 90; U CA; Bus.

BORNHORST, ERIKA L; Chula Vista HS; Chula Vista, CA; (2); 9/558; Pep Clb; Var Capt Socr; Var L Trk; Var L Vllybl; Cit Awd; Acad Leag; CA Schlstc Fed.

BORO, JENNIFER A; Bullard HS; Fresno, CA; (1); Dance Clb; Key Clb; SADD; Temple Yth Grp; Gov Hon Prg Awd; Hon Roll; Pres Acad Fit Awd; Ballet; UCLA; Fshn Dsgn.

BORRAYO, MARIO; Mountain Empire HS; Potrero, CA; (3); Spanish Clb; Rptr Nwsp; Var Bsbl; Var Bsktbl; Wt Lftg; ROP Awd; Intl Bus.

BORREGO, ANDREA A; St Anthony HS; Long Beach, CA; (3); Church Yth Grp; Red Cross Aide; Intrml Socr; Hon Roll; Music Achvt 4 Cert Mrts; UCLA; Med.

BORRELLI, LISA M; Mt Whitney HS; Visalia, CA; (2); Chorus; JV Vllybl; Hon Roll; CSF; Acad Lttr; Bus Mgmt.

BORRELLI, MICHAEL; Francis W Parker HS; San Diego, CA; (3); Drama Clb; Service Clb; Chorus; School Musical; School Play; Stage Crew; Variety Show; Rep Frsh Cls; Rep Soph Cls; Pres Jr Cls; USC; Actor.

BORRERO, LARA JANE F; Diamond Bar HS; Diamond Bar, CA; (2); Church Yth Grp; Dance Clb; French Clb; Varsity Clb; Bsktbl; Var Tennis; Hon Roll; Pres Acad Fit Awd; Amnsty Intl; Prncpls Lst; Cert Recgntn Cty; JV Tnns Outstndng Sngls & MVP Awd; Ucla.

BORRES, CHRISTIAN; Maricopa Unified HS; Maricopa, CA; (2); 2/50; Spanish Clb; Sec Treas Soph Cls; JV Bsbl; JV Mgr(s); Teenwrk Prtcpnt; CSF Clb; Comp Sci.

BORRETT, SUNSHINE; Redondo Union HS; Redondo Beach, CA; (2); Girl Scts; Service Clb; Spanish Clb; Var Swmmng; Hon Roll; Prfct Atten Awd; Natl Spnsh Exam; Spnsh Awds; CSF; Bio.

BORROMEO, BEVERLY MANUEL; Arvin HS; Arvin, CA; (3); Drama Clb; English Clb; French Clb; Library Aide; Math Clb; Office Aide; Science Clb; Ski Clb; Spanish Clb; SADD; CSF; Acad Hnr Roll Awd; U Of CA Santa Barbara; Math.

BORSTEIN, ROBYN HEATHER; Granada Hills HS; Northridge, CA; (3); Dance Clb; FBLA; Spanish Clb; Teachers Aide; Temple Yth Grp; High Hon Roll; Hon Roll; NHS; Spanish NHS; Acting; Modeling; UCLA; Law.

BORSUK, BETH M; Pittsburg HS; Pittsburg, CA; (2); Cmnty Wkr; Hon Roll; Stu Ldrshp Elects Cmmssnr; USA Travel Clb; Bus Mgt.

BORSUM, JENNIFER A; Carlsbad HS; Carlsbad, CA; (3); ROTC; Ski Clb; Speech Tm; Stage Crew; Hon Roll; Photo; NE London Polytech; Bus Mgmt.

BORTOLI, DARRYL R; Carlmont HS; Belmont, CA; (2); 11/320; Cmnty Wkr; Rep Frsh Cls; JV Bsktbl; Score Keeper; High Hon Roll; Hon Roll; Prfct Atten Awd; Outstndng Math Awds; Accntng.

BORUM, AARON; Fremont Union HS; Sunnyvale, CA; (4); Aud/Vis; Stage Crew; Yrbk; Film Dir.

BOS, URAINA R; Valley Christian HS; Cypress, CA; (3); Church Yth Grp; Drama Clb; Acpl Chr; Chorus; Church Choir; School Musical; Rptr Nwsp; NHS; Ntl Merit Ltr; Classic Muscle Mopar Auto Clb Secy; Long Beach ST; Prfrmng Arts.

BOSCH, ERIC E; Sacred Heart HS; San Francisco, CA; (1); Hon Roll.

BOSCH, JENNIFER L; Oak Ridge HS; El Dorado Hills, CA; (1); GAA; Band; JV Bsktbl; JV Sftbl; JV Vllybl; High Hon Roll; Pres Acad Fit Awd; Stanford U; Bus.

BOSCH, ROCHELLE A; Corona HS; Corona, CA; (2); Pepperdine; Adv.

BOSCHETTI, ANDREA D; Ygnacio Vaney HS; Pleasant Hill, CA; (1); Church Yth Grp; Hist 4-H; French Clb; FBLA; Pep Clb; Chorus; Church Choir; School Musical; JV Cheerldng; Var Swmmng; Intl Mrktng.

BOSCO, MELISSA; Gustine HS; Gustine, CA; (2); 3/82; Church Yth Grp; Sec 4-H; Hist FBLA; Girl Scts; SADD; Church Choir; Pres Frsh Cls; Capt JV Bsktbl; Capt Var Cheerldng; Swmmng; FBLA Cmptn Pub Spkng 1st Pl 90; Lions Clb Wnnr & Zone Fnlst 89 & 90; Spkng Cont 2nd Pl 89 & 90; Georgetown U; Educ.

BOSDIJK, JACQUELINE A; Highlands HS; North Highlands, CA; (2); Church Yth Grp; French Clb; FBLA; SADD; Hon Roll; Prfct Atten Awd; U Pacific; Bus Mgmt.

BOSE, RAJEN; Bishop Amat Memorial HS; West Covina, CA; (3); Letterman Clb; Pres VP Math Tm; Varsity Clb; Treas Lit Mag; Stu Cncl; Var Tennis; High Hon Roll; Treas NHS; Ntl Merit SF; Prfct Atten Awd; CA Schlrshp Fed Treas; Stanford; Med.

BOSHOFF, FENELLA FIKI; Adolfo Camarillo HS; Camarillo, CA; (4); German Clb; Pres Science Clb; SADD; Pres Frsh Cls; Var L Swmmng; Var L Tennis; High Hon Roll; Jr NHS; Opt Clb Awd; Pres Acad Fit Awd; Golden St Xmntns W/Hnrs; Sci Schlstc Achvt Cittn; UC Santa Barbara Rgnts Schlr; Miss Teen Prt Hueneme; UCLA; Med.

BOSI, RACHEL; Rosary HS; Fullerton, CA; (4); 2/135; VP French Clb; Red Cross Aide; Service Clb; Var Bsktbl; Var Sftbl; High Hon Roll; NHS; Pres Acad Fit Awd; Rosary Hnr Stu Of Month; Yth For Understndng Intl Exchng Cert Of Mrt; Schlr-Athl Awd; U Of Puget Sound; Intl Relation.

BOSMA, MATTHEW J; Thomas Downey HS; Modesto, CA; (1); Church Yth Grp; Swmmng; Jr Var Water Polo; Engl Ed.

BOSMAN, JOHN; Redlands HS; Redlands, CA; (4); Boy Scts; Bsbl; JV L Socr; Intrml Wt Lftg; Cit Awd; Hon Roll; Pres Acad Fit Awd; PTA Schlrshp; Cultural Exchng Soccer Team Germany; CSF; U San Diego; Bus.

BOSNIADISE, DEMETRIOS J; Saint Ignatius College Prep; San Francisco, CA; (3); 5/240; Chess Clb; Science Clb; Hon Roll; Bwlng Clb; CSF; Sci.

BOSQUE, SHEILAH; Independence HS; San Jose, CA; (3); Cmnty Wkr; Dance Clb; Science Clb; Teachers Aide; VP Jr Cls; Pres Sr Cls; Var JV Cheerldng; Hon Roll; NHS; Rotary Awd; UCSF; Nrsg.

BOSS, DEVIN; Hamilton HS Academy Of Music; Los Angeles, CA; (4); 104/504; Church Yth Grp; Cmnty Wkr; Service Clb; Band; Orch; School Musical; School Play; Stage Crew; Ind Educ Awd; Amer Legn Awd Ctznshp; Constitutnl Rights Fndtn Awd; CA Inst Of Arts; Stage Mgmt.

BOSS, MELINDA; Montclair HS; Montclair, CA; (3); Church Yth Grp; FHA; Hosp Aide; Library Aide; Teachers Aide; JV Socr; Hon Roll; Outstndng Libry Contrbtns; UC Davis; Vet.

BOSSE, MATTHEW J; Servite HS; Orange, CA; (3); 5/150; Aud/Vis; Boy Scts; Church Yth Grp; Cmnty Wkr; Debate Tm; Office Aide; Quiz Bowl; Scholastic Bowl; Service Clb; Speech Tm; JSA; Corazon; Princeton; Poltcl Sci.

BOSSENBROEK, TRACY L; El Cajon Valley HS; El Cajon, CA; (2); 16/431; Key Clb; Letterman Clb; Stu Cncl; L Var Gym; Hon Roll.

BOSSI, KRISTEN J; Newbury Park HS; Newbury Park, CA; (3); Art Clb; Church Yth Grp; Teachers Aide; Band; Mrchg Band; Powder Puff Ftbl; Hon Roll; Band Ltr Awd; Commercial Art.

BOSTER, CHRIS; Newport Harbor HS; Costa Mesa, CA; (3); Computer Clb; Teachers Aide; Wt Lftg; JV Wrstlng; ROP Cls Data Entry Lotus 1-2-3; UCI; Law.

BOSTICK, STACEY; East Union HS; Ripon, CA; (4); 6/269; Cmnty Wkr; Bsktbl; JV Trk; Wt Lftg; Lion Awd; Humphreys Bus Coll; Bus Mgmt.

BOSTROM, JENNY; Palo Verde HS; Blythe, CA; (2); Var Cheerldng; JV Sftbl; French Hon Soc; Hon Roll; Dancing; Aloha Bowl Half-Time Show 89; U NV Reno; Bus Mgt.

BOSTROM, MICHAEL; San Bernardino HS; San Bernardino, CA; (2); Debate Tm; NFL; Speech Tm; School Play; Hon Roll; Mock Trial Team; Atty.

BOSTROM, VIRGINIA; Palo Verde HS; Blythe, CA; (2); Dance Clb; Drama Clb; Cheerldng; Pom Pon; JV Sftbl; Hon Roll; Prfct Atten Awd; Jazz Dancing; Ice Skating; Camping; U NV Reno; Bus Mgmt.

BOSWELL, ANISSA; Edison HS; Fresno, CA; (4); Church Yth Grp; Cmnty Wkr; Off French Clb; Math Tm; Model UN; Teachers Aide; Var Crs Cntry; Var Swmmng; High Hon Roll; Bicentennial Cmptn Of Constitution 2nd In St; UC Santa Barbara; Marine Bio.

BOSWELL, CYNTHIA C; Lompoc HS; Lompoc, CA; (3); 71/284; Pres Church Yth Grp; Office Aide; Teachers Aide; Hon Roll; Young Women Excllnce Awd; BYU; Child Psych.

BOSWELL, JENNIFER K; Dublin HS; Dublin, CA; (4); 43/158; Church Yth Grp; French Clb; Teachers Aide; Color Guard; School Play; Variety Show; JV Var Swmmng; Hon Roll; Golden St Exam Awd; Hnrs Geom 88; Best Supporting Actress Awd 89; BYU; Math.

BOSWELL, STACEY; Bullard HS; Fresno, CA; (3); 1/500; Church Yth Grp; Cmnty Wkr; English Clb; FCA; SADD; Teachers Aide; Color Guard; School Musical; Ed Lit Mag; Masonic Awd; CSF Mem; Brigham Young U.

BOTELLO, NICOLE Y; St Patrick-St Vincent HS; Vallejo, CA; (2); Hon Roll; CA Schlrshp Fed; Arch, Egyptology; U Of Southern CA; Drctr/Prdcr.

BOTROS, AYMAN S; St John Bosco HS; Bellflower, CA; (2); VP Church Yth Grp; Cmnty Wkr; English Clb; Key Clb; Church Choir; School Play; Rptr Nwsp; Off Jr Cls; Stu Cncl; Bsktbl; CSF; Jr Statesmen Of Amer; UCLA; Teaching.

BOTROS, DAVID; Alhambra HS; Alhambra, CA; (2); Debate Tm; Red Cross Aide; Science Clb; Service Clb; Ski Clb; Crs Cntry; Trk; Disting Achvt Awd; CA Assoc Stu Cncls CASC Sec; UCLA; Bio.

BOTTITA, LISA C; Highlands HS; Sacramento, CA; (1); Church Yth Grp; French Clb; Girl Scts; SADD; Sec Frsh Cls; JV Powder Puff Ftbl; JV Sftbl; Hon Roll; Dist Cncl, Bd; OR ST; Lwyr.

BOTTORFF, REBECCA A; Saddleback HS; Santa Ana, CA; (3); Library Aide; SADD; Teachers Aide; Rptr Nwsp; Prfct Atten Awd; Western ST Coll; Elem Ed.

BOU, RACHANA; Paramount HS; Paramount, CA; (3); 13/402; French Clb; Crs Cntry; Trk; Var Vllybl; Cit Awd; French Hon Soc; Hon Roll; Prfct Atten Awd; CSF; Goldn St Math Exam Schl Rcgntn Geom; UCLA; Med Researchr.

BOU SALMAN, SAMAR; Mills HS; Millbrae, CA; (3); 4-H; Intnl Clb; Office Aide; Outstndng Awd Goldn St Exam; Badmntn; UC Davis; Bus/Hotel Mgmt.

BOUCHARD, CASEY; Lassen HS; Susanville, CA; (2); 5/235; Cmnty Wkr; Letterman Clb; Ski Clb; Spanish Clb; Golf; High Hon Roll; Hon Roll; CA Schltc Fed.

BOUCHARD, JOHN M; Redwood HS; Visalia, CA; (3); French Clb; Capt Var Bsktbl; Var Ftbl; Capt Var Tennis; Var Trk; Hon Roll; Notre Dame; Arch.

BOUCHARD, MATTHEW; Lincoln HS; Stockton, CA; (3); Computer Clb; FBLA; Math Clb; Mu Alpha Theta; VP Science Clb; Thesps; Stage Crew; JV Swmmng; High Hon Roll; CSF; Golden St Math Exam, High Hnrs Alge, Geom; Natl Sci Olympd St Fnlst 2nd, 3rd Circ Lab 88-89; Engrg.

BOUCHARD, MELINDA J; San Diego Acad; National City, CA; (1); Church Yth Grp; Cmnty Wkr; Hosp Aide; Chorus; Var Bsbl; Loma Linda U; Occptnl Thrpy.

BOUCHELION, DOMINIC C; James Logan HS; Union City, CA; (3); Teachers Aide; Bsbl; Var Ftbl; Wt Lftg; Hon Roll; Bsbl Player Of Yr; MVP 90; MVP Ftbl Var; Work Full Time For Father; Hmcmng Jr Prince; Cal-Berkely; Bus.

BOUCHER, DANE M; Tulare Union HS; Tulare, CA; (4); FFA; VP JA; Band; Jazz Band; Mrchg Band; Pep Band; Treas Jr Cls; Stu Cncl; Cit Awd; Hon Roll; ASB Treas; Fri Night Live Pres & Secy; Block T Svc Awd; St High Indvdl FFA Ag Comp Cntst; Coll Of Sequoia; Ag Bus Mgmt.

BOUCHER, DAVE M; Irvine HS; Irvine, CA; (3); 138/512; Var Ftbl; Var Wt Lftg; AZ ST U; Commnctns.

BOUCHER, LAWRENCE E; St Francis HS; La Crescenta, CA; (2); Church Yth Grp; Cmnty Wkr; Computer Clb; Pep Clb; Ski Clb; Teachers Aide; Hon Roll; CSF; 2nd Pl Sci Fair; Cal-Poly San Luis Obispa; Comp.

BOUCHER, MIKE A; Irvine HS; Irvine, CA; (2); 158/553; Ftbl; U Of Southern CA; Bus.

BOUCK, KIMBERLY B; Central Union HS; El Centro, CA; (4); VP Drama Clb; Key Clb; VP Service Clb; Speech Tm; SADD; Stu Cncl; Swmmng; Hon Roll; Imperial Valley JC; Cmmnctns.

BOUDREAU, CHRISTINE RAMOS; California HS; San Ramon, CA; (1); Letterman Clb; Chorus; Co-Capt Cheerldng; Var Crs Cntry; High Hon Roll; U Of CA Santa Barbara; Law.

BOUDREAU, RICHER; Bell HS; Cudahy, CA; (3); French Clb; Hon Roll; Tech Engr.

BOUGHEY, BRANDI S; Chaffey HS; Ontario, CA; (1); Band; Mrchg Band; Hon Roll; Berkeley; Parapsych.

BOUGIE, TIM M; Cajon HS; San Bernardino, CA; (3); Church Yth Grp; Cmnty Wkr; Office Aide; Teachers Aide; Bsbl; Tennis; Vllybl; High Hon Roll; Hon Roll; NHS.

BOUIE, CARMELITA MARIE; El Camino Real HS; Los Angeles, CA; (2); 4-H; Spanish Clb; Cit Awd; Schlrshp Awd.

BOUKIS, HELEN; Skyline HS; Oakland, CA; (3); Pres Sec Church Yth Grp; Church Choir; High Hon Roll; Hon Roll; Pres Acad Fit Awd; Hnrs Golden St Ex Alg, Geo; Marcus Foster Awd.

BOUKNIGHT, RAY; Atwater HS; Winton, CA; (3); JV Ftbl; Hon Roll; Rochester Inst Tech; Engrng.

BOULDING, AARON; Santa Cruz HS; Santa Cruz, CA; (4); Rep Sr Cls; Var Bsktbl; Hon Roll; Santa Barbara CA U; Jrnlsm.

BOULDING, SONJA; Palo Alto HS; Palo Alto, CA; (3); Drill Tm; Var Cheerldng; Cosmetology School; FL A & M U; Business Admin.

BOULET, MICHELLE L; Sir Francis Drake HS; San Anselmo, CA; (4); 5/144; Chorus; Pres Soph Cls; VP Sec Sr Cls; Var Capt Cheerldng; Var Capt Socr; DAR Awd; Pres Acad Fit Awd; Sal; Marin Alumne Panhellenic Assoc Awd Mrt; Bank Amer Plaq Fine Arts; Army Rsrve Natl Schlr/Athlte Awd; UC Davis; Math.

BOULET, RICHARD C; Sir Francis Drake HS; San Anselmo, CA; (3); Am Leg Boys St; Model UN; School Musical; School Play; Variety Show; Var Capt Crs Cntry; JV Var Socr; Var Capt Trk; French Hon Soc; Hon Roll; U Of CO Boulder; Bus.

BOULTON, R JEDEDIAH; Porterville HS; Porterville, CA; (3); 17/352; Am Leg Boys St; Mu Alpha Theta; JV Crs Cntry; JV Capt Socr; Var L Trk; Hon Roll.

BOUMA, JENNIFER A; El Cajon Valley HS; El Cajon, CA; (1); Church Yth Grp; JV Cheerldng; Var Crs Cntry; JV Gym; UCSD; Lwyr.

BOUMA, MANDY J; Valley Christian HS; Cerritos, CA; (2); Church Yth Grp; Band; Church Choir; Mrchg Band; Rptr Yrbk; Sec Soph Cls; JV Capt Bsktbl; JV Vllybl; Hon Roll; NHS; Hmcmng Prncss; Chrch Musical; Calvin; Educ.

BOUNDS, CATHERINE A; Los Angeles Baptist HS; Simi Valley, CA; (3); VP Sr Cls; JV Cheerldng; Var Trk; Stat Vllybl; Hon Roll; Big Brother/Sister Pgm; UCLA; Math.

BOUNLUTAY, NIRA; Edison Computech HS; Fresno, CA; (3); Intnl Clb; Spanish Clb; Hon Roll; CSF; Golden St Math Awd; Med.

BOURCIER, KRISTEN; Armijo HS; Fairfield, CA; (2); Color Guard; JV Cheerldng; Gym; High Hon Roll; Hon Roll; NHS; Horseback Riding; U CA Davis; Ped Nurse.

BOURDE, CHRISTIAN; Petaluma HS; Petaluma, CA; (3); 6/267; French Clb; Science Clb; High Hon Roll; Prfct Atten Awd; Pres Acad Fit Awd; Prin Awd; Concours Natl De Francais Hnrs Awd; Elec Engrng.

BOURDON, CARL R; Norte Vista HS; Riverside, CA; (1); French Clb; ROTC; Hon Roll; U Of Berkley; Marine Zoolgy.

BOURGEOIS, BRIAN R; Orange Glen HS; Escondido, CA; (3); 45/498; Church Yth Grp; JA; Var L Swmmng; Var L Wrstlng; NHS; Pres Acad Fit Awd; Water Polo 1 V Ltr; Bus.

BOURGEOIS, NICOLE; Barstow HS; Barstow, CA; (4); #16 In Class; GAA; Teachers Aide; Band; Mrchg Band; Socr; Sftbl; Hon Roll; GSA Acad Excllnce Awd Alg & Geom; CA ST U; Educ.

BOURIS, AMY; Downey HS; Downey, CA; (3); Cmnty Wkr; French Clb; Sec Math Clb; Science Clb; Service Clb; SADD; Pres Sec Band; Chorus; Pres Sec Mrchg Band; High Hon Roll; PTA Stu Recogntn Awd; Girls St Alt; Frgn Lang Awd-Span; Med.

BOURIS, YANNA; Downey HS; Downey, CA; (3); 1/600; French Clb; Math Clb; Treas Science Clb; VP Service Clb; SADD; Sec Band; Sec Mrchg Band; High Hon Roll; Ntl Merit SF; Stu Recogntn Awd; Outstndng Musician Stu-Twice; 2nd Pl Tlnt Cont; Keywanettes; Engr.

BOURKE, JOYCE E; Colton HS; San Bernardino, CA; (3); Cmnty Wkr; Var Socr; Var Swmmng; Hon Roll; NHS.

BOUS, SARAH J; Galt HS; Galt, CA; (2); Intnl Clb; High Hon Roll; Hon Roll; Hnrs Engl & History; Debate Tm.

BOUSMAN, MATT T; St Joseph HS; Santa Maria, CA; (3); Church Yth Grp; Teachers Aide; Var JV Ftbl; Var Capt Vllybl; JV Ftbl Schlr Athlete; Son City Staff Capt; Youth Mnstry Club.

BOUTTE, BRIAN; American HS; Fremont, CA; (3); Church Yth Grp; Bsktbl; Wt Lftg; JV Wrstlng; Hon Roll; Convstnal Spnsh Achvmnt Awd; VIP Awd.

BOUTWELL, TERI LYNN; Imperial HS; Imperial, CA; (3); Church Yth Grp; FFA; Hon Roll; Vrs Engl Awds; CSF; Naval Acad; Pilot.

BOVE, PAUL M; Bellarmine-Jefferson HS; Burbank, CA; (2); Spanish Clb; JV Capt Bsktbl; JV Ftbl; JV Var Trk; High Hon Roll; NHS; Mem CA Schlstc Fed; Mem Spirit Cmmtte.

BOWDEN, CLINTON; Manteca HS; Manteca, CA; (3); FCA; Ftbl; Trk; Bus.

BOWDEN, MELANY A; Apple Valley HS; Apple Valley, CA; (3); Church Yth Grp; Ski Clb; Band; Mrchg Band; Hon Roll; Devrie; Emergency Med Tech.

BOWDEN, MICHELLE; Banning HS; Banning, CA; (2); Drama Clb; Girl Scts; Model UN; Spanish Clb; Chorus; Color Guard; Mrchg Band; Pres Soph Cls; JV Sftbl; DAR Awd; U Of CA; Sci.

BOWDEN, NITA M; Foothill HS; Bakersfield, CA; (2); 42/356; Teachers Aide; L Var Bsktbl; Hon Roll; UCLA; Ed.

BOWE, DREW; Sonoma Valley HS; Sonoma, CA; (3); Boy Scts; Var Socr; Var Trk; Hon Roll; Eagle Sct 87; Solo Flight Completed In Sngl Engine Aircraft 89.

BOWEN, CASEY; Santa Monica HS; Malibu, CA; (2); SADD; Acpl Chr; Chorus; Off Soph Cls; JV L Cheerldng; Var Trk; Hon Roll; Pres Acad Fit Awd; UCLA; Psycht.

BOWEN, CASSANDRA; Fall River JR SR HS; Fall River Mills, CA; (3); Art Clb; FFA; Hon Roll; JR Hmcmg Prncss 89; Chico ST; Ag.

BOWEN, CLAUDIA; Mt Whitney HS; Visalia, CA; (3); Sec FHA; Office Aide; Teachers Aide; Var JV Vllybl; Hon Roll; U Of Santa Barbara; Pharm.

BOWEN, ERICA A; Mountain Empire HS; Jacumba, CA; (3); Drama Clb; GAA; Letterman Clb; Pep Clb; Spanish Clb; School Play; Stage Crew; Rep Frsh Cls; Rep Soph Cls; Rep Jr Cls; Spansh.

BOWEN, HEATHER R; James Madison SR HS; San Diego, CA; (3); 1/450; Debate Tm; Pres Girl Scts; Latin Clb; Mu Alpha Theta; NFL; VP Science Clb; Speech Tm; Var Powder Puff Ftbl; Var L Tennis; High Hon Roll; Sci Fair Prof Named Best In St Of CA 90; 1st Pl Intl Sci & Engrng Fair; UCSD; Bio Engrng.

BOWEN, JACK B; Coronado HS; Coronado, CA; (3); 10/156; Boy Scts; Church Yth Grp; Off Frsh Cls; Off Soph Cls; Treas Jr Cls; Stu Cncl; JV Bsktbl; Var Lcrss; Socr; Var Swmmng; All Amer Waterpolo Goalie & Natl Jr Team; Med.

BOWEN, LORELEI; Seaside HS; Marina, CA; (3); Church Yth Grp; French Clb; Orch; Var Swmmng; High Hon Roll; UC Davis; Hstry.

BOWEN, MICHAEL A; Atwater HS; Atwater, CA; (2); French Clb.

BOWEN, MICHAEL B; Foothill HS; Bakersfield, CA; (3); 13/358; German Clb; Bsbl; Hon Roll; CSF; CA ST U Fresno; Civ Engr.

BOWEN, MICHELLE; Fall River JR SR HS; Fall River Mills, CA; (4); 6/60; Church Yth Grp; 4-H; Library Aide; Office Aide; Varsity Clb; Capt Var Bsktbl; Var L Sftbl; Hon Roll; Stdt Mnth Sept/Oct 89; Block F Tourn Bsktbl Qn 89; Hmcmg Chrmn 89; CA ST U Chico; Bus.

BOWEN, ROCHELLE L; Paraclete HS; Lancaster, CA; (2); Church Yth Grp; Drama Clb; School Play; Stage Crew; JV Vllybl; Hon Roll; Acting Workshops; Advrtsng.

BOWEN, SHALECE A; Alhambra HS; Martinez, CA; (3); Art Clb; Church Yth Grp; Dance Clb; Spanish Clb; Diving.

BOWEN, SHANE; Poly HS; Riverside, CA; (2); JV Bsbl; Hon Roll; UCSD; Arch.

BOWER, AMY N; Montgomery HS; Santa Rosa, CA; (4); Key Clb; Teachers Aide; School Play; Yrbk; Treas Soph Cls; Stu Cncl; Var Capt Cheerldng; High Hon Roll; Jr NHS; Opt Clb Awd; Princpls Outstndng Schlstc Achvt Awd; CSF-LIFE Mem; U CA-SAN Diego; Biochem.

BOWERMAN, CINDY M; Cloverdale HS; Cloverdale, CA; (1); 1/80; Church Yth Grp; FHA; Band; JV Tennis; Hon Roll; Math Problem Of Wk Solver 89-90; Engrng Course For Women At CA Poly Pomona; UC Davis; Medcl Tech.

BOWERS, BRIDGET; Oroville HS; Oroville, CA; (3); 9/193; Key Clb; Variety Show; Nwsp; High Hon Roll; CSF; Engl Stu Mnth 87-88; Top Ten Of Cls 87-90; Davis; Pre Vet.

BOWERS, JEFFREY A; Oxnard HS; Oxnard, CA; (1); Band; Jazz Band; Mrchg Band; Orch; Lit Mag; Hon Roll; Mock Trial Clb; Stanford U; Arch.

BOWERS, JOLENE; Granite Hills HS; El Cajon, CA; (4); 58/500; Drama Clb; Acpl Chr; Chorus; School Musical; Stu Cncl; Var Cheerldng; Hon Roll; Pres Hnr Choir; Outstndng Musician Awd; Best Major Supporting Actress; Grossmont Clg; Music Ed.

BOWERS, PATRICIA K; University HS; Santa Ana, CA; (3); 18/551; Church Yth Grp; JCL; Acpl Chr; JV Fld Hcky; High Hon Roll; Jr NHS; Ntl Merit Ltr; Math Clb; Science Clb; Church Choir; Pres Newcomers Clb; CSF; Acolyte St Georges Episcopal Chrch; Engr.

BOWERS, RYAN N; Poway HS; Poway, CA; (2); JA; Letterman Clb; SADD; Varsity Clb; Ed Yrbk; Rep Frsh Cls; Var Socr; JV Vllybl; High Hon Roll; Hon Roll; Olympc Dev Sccr Prgm; ST Sccr Champ 89-90; CIF Champ Sccr 90; Hat Trick Tour; Sprts Med.

BOWERS, TAWANDA L; Gardena HS; Los Angeles, CA; (2); Church Yth Grp; Math Clb; Office Aide; Spanish Clb; Church Choir; Off Soph Cls; Bsktbl; Cit Awd; MESA Math Engr Sci Achvt; NCCJ Ntl Conf Christians & Jews; NSF Schlrs Prog Sci Research; Ed.

BOWHAN, EDMOND J; Northview HS; Pomona, CA; (3); Hon Roll; Bowling Awd YABA, St & Natl Trnmnts; Car Restrtn; Citrus Coll; Pro Bowler.

BOWIE, BRIDGET E; Temple City HS; Arcadia, CA; (2); CSI; Congrssnl Schlr; UCSB; Bus.

BOWKER, TOBY; Nevada Union HS; Grass Valley, CA; (3); Boy Scts; Church Yth Grp; Cmnty Wkr; FFA; JV Var Ftbl; Tennis; Cit Awd; Hon Roll; To Be Music JD; Killer Whales & Dolphins; San Diego ST; Train Kllr Whale.

BOWLBY, LAURA L; Rio Lindo Adventist Acad; Fortuna, CA; (3); Church Yth Grp; Cmnty Wkr; Office Aide; Spanish Clb; Drill Tm; Yrbk; Sec Frsh Cls; Cit Awd; Hon Roll; Prfct Atten Awd; Spch Pathology.

BOWLER, BRIAN M; North HS; Bakersfield, CA; (1); Ski Clb; Spanish Clb; Teachers Aide; JV Bsbl; JV Capt Socr; Wt Lftg; Hon Roll; Stanford.

BOWLES, CARA M; Mckinleyville HS; Mckinleyville, CA; (2); Band; Court Rprtr.

BOWLES, DANA; Liberty Union HS; Brentwood, CA; (2); Church Yth Grp; Band; Jazz Band; Mrchg Band; Pres Frsh Cls; JV Score Keeper; Hon Roll; Bus.

BOWLES, MELISSA D; Wasco Union HS; Wasco, CA; (3); Nwsp; Hon Roll; Acad Decathlon; CSF.

BOWLES, VERNON; San Gorgonio HS; Highland, CA; (4); 98/450; Boy Scts; Ntl Merit SF; Harvey Mudd; Comp Sci.

BOWMAN, JASON; Cardinal Newman HS; Santa Rosa, CA; (1); Cmnty Wkr; Nwsp; Bsktbl; Ftbl; Vllybl; Wt Lftg; High Hon Roll; CA U; Sci.

BOWMAN, JENNIFER; Northview HS; Covina, CA; (3); Cmnty Wkr; Dance Clb; Hosp Aide; Pep Clb; Spanish Clb; SADD; Drill Tm; VP Soph Cls; Cheerldng; Pom Pon; UC Riverside; Psych.

BOWMAN, KELLY; Fred C Beyer HS; Modesto, CA; (4); 119/546; Dance Clb; Pep Clb; Ski Clb; SADD; Teachers Aide; Cheerldng; Pom Pon; Hon Roll; Philsphy Clb; San Dieg ST; Child Devlpmnt.

BOWMAN, KRISTEN A; Westminster HS; Westminster, CA; (4); 1/410; Treas French Clb; VP JA; JCL; Pres Sec Latin Clb; Rep Soph Cls; Stu Cncl; Var Fld Hcky; Var Trk; Rotary Awd; Val; Stanford U; Orthopedic Srgry.

BOWMAN, MARINO; San Diego HS; San Diego, CA; (3); 25/300; Church Yth Grp; Church Choir; Bsktbl; Wt Lftg; Hon Roll; Prfct Atten Awd; Upward Bound Pgm; STEP Pgm; Ethnic Awareness, Wrtng, Intermedte Alg Awds; U CA; Engrng.

BOWMAN, MARK A; Hilltop HS; Chula Vista, CA; (4); 182/444; Church Yth Grp; Teachers Aide; Off Soph Cls; JV Crs Cntry; Southwestern; Comp Repair.

BOWMAN, RENAE L; Hemet HS; Winchester, CA; (4); Office Aide; Teachers Aide; Mt San Jacinto Coll; Comp.

BOWMAN, SEAN E; Casa Roble Fundamental HS; Orangevale, CA; (2); 27/461; AFS; Church Yth Grp; Pres German Clb; High Hon Roll; Friday Night Live; Music.

BOWMAN, WENDE M; Canyon HS; Anaheim, CA; (3); Drama Clb; French Clb; SADD; Sec Mrchg Band; School Play; Stage Crew; High Hon Roll; Hon Roll; NHS; Riverside CC; Ed.

BOWN, MISTY; Hogan SR HS; Vallejo, CA; (4); SADD; Teachers Aide; Color Guard; JV Bsktbl; Var Swmmng; JV Tennis; High Hon Roll; Hon Roll; Interact Clb; Unitd Spirit Assn; Solano CC; Mrktng.

BOWSHER, KATHLEEN S; C L Mc Lane HS; Fresno, CA; (4); Church Yth Grp; Cmnty Wkr; Drama Clb; Band; Mrchg Band; Stage Crew; Ntl Merit SF; Pepsi FUSD Awd 89.

BOWYER, DEENA; Mission San Jose HS; Fremont, CA; (4); French Clb; Science Clb; Spanish Clb; Teachers Aide; Phtg Yrbk; Stu Cncl; JV Swmmng; High Hon Roll; NHS; UC Rgnts UC Santa Cuiz; Presdntl Acad Fitness; CA Schlrshp Fed; UC Santa Cruz; Engl Teacher.

BOX, DAVID N; Rim Of The World HS; Cedar Glen, CA; (3); 7/239; Church Yth Grp; Capt Var Crs Cntry; Var Trk; JV Wrstlng; High Hon Roll; NHS; Prfct Atten Awd; Rotary Awd; Exchnge Pgm Japan; Hnrs Japanese; Bio.

BOX, JOE; San Bernardino HS; San Bernardino, CA; (2); German Clb; Hon Roll; Jr NHS; NHS; Phoenix Pgm; Pilot.

BOX, STEPHANIE M; Bear River HS; Auburn, CA; (2); Science Clb; Spanish Clb; Speech Tm; Rptr Nwsp; Yrbk; Stanford U; Intl Bus.

BOYADJIAN, SETA; Rowland HS; Rowland Hts, CA; (1); Church Yth Grp; Church Choir; High Hon Roll.

BOYAJIAN, ANOUSH; Francis Polytechnic HS; N Hollywood, CA; (4); French Clb; Pres Acad Fit Awd; Acad Decathelon; UCLA; Med.

BOYBAL, EDWARD D; Bellflower HS; Bellflower, CA; (2); Bsktbl; High Hon Roll; Hon Roll; Long Beach ST; Arch.

BOYCE, CHARLES K; La Canada HS; La Canada, CA; (3); 34/256; Chess Clb; Key Clb; Math Clb; Science Clb; School Play; Stage Crew; Lit Mag; NHS; Ntl Merit Ltr; Pres Schlr; Fncng No 1 In Cntry; Bio.

BOYCE, KRISTIN M; Abraham Lincoln HS; San Jose, CA; (3); 67/313; Church Yth Grp; Teachers Aide; Band; Church Choir; Mrchg Band; Stage Crew; Hon Roll; 90 CA Arts Schlr Music Compstn; 90 HS Grammy Awd Wnnr Elctrnc Music; Music Thrpy.

BOYD, CHRISTY; Foothill HS; Pleasanton, CA; (3); 4/290; Mrchg Band; VP Soph Cls; Capt Var Crs Cntry; Var Socr; Capt Var Trk; DAR Awd; High Hon Roll; Pres Acad Fit Awd; Bus.

BOYD, DANIELLE M; Grossmont HS; El Cajon, CA; (2); 1/431; Church Yth Grp; Pres Treas German Clb; Girl Scts; Intnl Clb; JV Swmmng; High Hon Roll; Hon Roll; Los Angeles Times/Cathay Pacific Essay Cont Fnlst; Astronaut.

BOYD, ERICA R; Regina Caeli HS; Compton, CA; (3); Church Yth Grp; GAA; Pep Clb; Chorus; Church Choir; Nwsp; Off Jr Cls; Bsktbl; Sftbl; Trk; Phy.

BOYD, ERIN; Fred C Beyer HS; Modesto, CA; (3); German Clb; NFL; Service Clb; Ski Clb; Speech Tm; Rep Soph Cls; Rep Jr Cls; Var Diving; Var Swmmng; Cit Awd; Hnrs Geo Golden St Ex; Girls Waterpolo; CSA; UCLA; Acctng.

BOYD, EVY L; Roseville HS; Rocklin, CA; (4); 136/375; Rgnl Occptn Pgm; Cmmrcl Art.

BOYD, HEATHER M; Calvary Acad; Cedaredge, CO; (2); Church Yth Grp; Teachers Aide; Band; Chorus; Flag Corp; Mrchg Band; School Play; Stat Bsktbl; Mgr(s); Hon Roll; Rstrtn Of Clssc Cars; Elem Ed.

BOYD, JASON R; Fred C Beyer HS; Modesto, CA; (4); 116/506; Var Bsbl; Stat Bsktbl; Var Mgr(s); Cit Awd; Hon Roll; Prfct Atten Awd; Navy; Nuclear Sci.

BOYD, JOHN; Grossmont HS; El Cajon, CA; (4); 68/400; English Clb; German Clb; Math Clb; Hon Roll; Acadc Decathlon; Comp Engrng.

BOYD, KIMBERLY A; Casa Grande HS; Petaluma, CA; (2); JV Capt Cheerldng; UC; Bio.

BOYD, NATALIE M; Alta Loma HS; Cucamonga, CA; (4); 4/444; Office Aide; SADD; Teachers Aide; Acpl Chr; School Play; Off Jr Cls; Off Sr Cls; Mgr(s); High Hon Roll; Cal ST Sn Bernardino; Lib Stds.

BOYD, PENNY; Sacred Heart Prep; Redwood City, CA; (2); Cmnty Wkr; Chorus; Church Choir; School Play; Socr; Hon Roll; Peer Cnslng; Pediatrics.

BOYD, TROY A; Dos Pueblos SR HS; Goleta, CA; (2); Drama Clb; Model UN; SADD; Acpl Chr; School Musical; School Play; Swing Chorus; Variety Show; Stu Cncl; Model CCMT; Waterski Trophies; Julliard; Actr.

BOYDEN, KRIS; Argonaut HS; Jackson, CA; (1); VP AFS; French Clb; Pep Clb; Science Clb; Ski Clb; Cheerldng; Pom Pon; High Hon Roll; CSF; Stanford; Med.

BOYDSTUN, TRACI; Redwood HS; Visalia, CA; (4); Church Yth Grp; Cmnty Wkr; French Clb; SADD; Teachers Aide; Color Guard; Flag Corp; VP Pres Frsh Cls; Cit Awd; French Hon Soc; Schlrshp Native Dghtrs Of Golden West; Intermed Sgn Lang; Coll Of Sequioas; Sgn Lang.

BOYENGER, KRISTINA; Enterprise HS; Palo Cedro, CA; (4); 35/350; Church Yth Grp; Capt Dance Clb; Drama Clb; Pep Clb; Capt Drill Tm; Ed Nwsp; JV Capt Cheerldng; Capt Pom Pon; Intrml Powder Puff Ftbl; Score Keeper; CSF; Ms Shasta Cnty Pgnt 1st Altrnt Schlrshp; UC Davis; Psych.

BOYER, AMANDA M; Enterprise HS; Redding, CA; (2); 72/483; Church Yth Grp; Dance Clb; Office Aide; Acpl Chr; Variety Show; Hon Roll.

BOYER, DAVID R; North Salinas HS; Salinas, CA; (2); Drama Clb; French Clb; FBLA; Intnl Clb; Quiz Bowl; Ski Clb; Spanish Clb; Thesps; High Hon Roll; Hon Roll; Stu Ambssdr To Russian Smmr 90.

BOYER, MARK L; Bonita HS; La Verne, CA; (1); Church Yth Grp; Hon Roll; Prfct Atten Awd.

BOYES, EDWARD A; Nevada Union HS; Grass Valley, CA; (3); JV Swmmng; Var Vllybl; Shakespeare Clb; JV Water Polo Tm; Bus.

BOYES, RYAN K; Mammoth HS; Wrightwood, CA; (3); Ski Clb; JV Ftbl; French Clb; Alpine Skiing Jr Olympics; Sports Psych.

BOYKIN, KALINI N; C K Mc Clatchy HS; Sacramento, CA; (3); 26/426; Sec Treas Key Clb; Math Clb; Math Tm; Science Clb; Spanish Clb; Orch; School Musical; Intrml Powder Puff Ftbl; Hon Roll; Fri Night Live Pres; Civil Engrng.

BOYKINS, GEORGE; Antelope Valley HS; Lancaster, CA; (3); JA; Letterman Clb; SADD; Varsity Clb; Var Bsbl; Var Ftbl; Hon Roll; Law.

BOYLAN, JENNIFER A; Calaveras HS; San Andreas, CA; (3); 4/170; 4-H; Girl Scts; Teachers Aide; Chorus; 4-H Awd; High Hon Roll; Hon Roll; Arch Bishop.

BOYLE, AMANDA; Rosamond HS; Rosamond, CA; (1); Educator.

BOYLE, DELBERT E; Hogan HS; Vallejo, CA; (2); Bsbl; Bsktbl; Hon Roll; CA Tech; Engrng.

BOYLE, MICHAEL S; Poway HS; Poway, CA; (3); 96/761; JV Ftbl; Hon Roll; Poway Teen Cncl Srgnt-At-Arms; UC Berkeley; Biochem Engr.

BOYLES, JEFF G; Fontana HS; Fontana, CA; (3); FBLA; Ski Clb; VP Jr Cls; Pres Stu Cncl; JV Var Ftbl; Var Tennis; High Hon Roll; Pres Acad Fit Awd; Shrff Yth Advsry Grp Drug Use Is Life Abuse; SDSU; Mktng.

BOYLES, SEAN W; Sunset HS; Hayward, CA; (2); 22/286; Band; Mrchg Band; Orch; Pep Band; Hon Roll; Pride Awd Cmmtte; Outstndng Achvta Wds; Graphic Art.

BOYNTON, LAURA E; Fairview Junior Acad; Rialto, CA; (2); Church Yth Grp; Ski Clb; Band; Yrbk; Pres Stu Cncl; Var Bsbl; Bell Choir; Bio Achvt Awd; Loma Linda Acad; Med.

BOYSE, TAMARA L; Fontana HS; Fontana, CA; (2); Church Yth Grp; Band; Drill Tm; Mrchg Band; Pep Band; High Hon Roll; Hon Roll; U CA Riverside; Librl Arts.

BOZARTH, ANGELA J; Taft Union HS; Taft, CA; (4); 9/150; Aud/Vis; Drama Clb; Letterman Clb; School Play; Ed Yrbk; Rep Soph Cls; VP Stu Cncl; Var Cheerldng; High Hon Roll; Pres Acad Fit Awd.

BOZARTH, ERIN M; San Pasqual HS; Escondido, CA; (2); Drama Clb; German Clb; JV Tennis; Hon Roll; Prfct Atten Awd; CSF; Amnsty Intl; UC Davis; Ed.

BOZEMAN, STACY; Etiwanda HS; Fontana, CA; (3); Teachers Aide; Variety Show; Mgr(s); Score Keeper; Trk; Hon Roll; Prfct Atten Awd; MESA; Radiology.

BOZULIC, LARRY; La Sierra HS; Riverside, CA; (2); Jazz Band; Mrchg Band; Pep Band; Hon Roll; Prfct Atten Awd; Pres Acad Fit Awd.

BOZURICH, GARY J; Village Christian Schls; Sunland, CA; (2); Spanish Clb; Orthopedic Med.

BRAA, JOANNA D; Atwater HS; Winton, CA; (2); Church Yth Grp; FCA; SADD; JV Bsktbl; Var Swmmng; High Hon Roll; Waterpolo V; CSF; Accntng.

BRACAMONTE, DEBRA R; River City HS; West Sacramento, CA; (3); 105/215; SADD; Rptr Nwsp; Kiwanis Awd; Data Processing.

BRACCO, CHASE; Grace M Davis HS; Modesto, CA; (4); VP Key Clb; Service Clb; Pres Ski Clb; Rep Soph Cls; VP Sr Cls; VP Stu Cncl; JV Intrml Bsbl; Var L Ftbl; Powder Puff Ftbl; Var L Socr; Spcl Olympcs Worker; Kiwanis Clb Tree Planter; WASC Cmmtee; Modesto JC; Econ.

BRACE, JULIET; Turlock HS; Turlock, CA; (3); Pres Church Yth Grp; Drama Clb; VP Sec Key Clb; Letterman Clb; Speech Tm; Sec Soph Cls; Sec Stu Cncl; JV Var Cheerldng; Diving; Var Capt Pom Pon; Turlocks Young Woman Of Yr 91; Camp Royal; Commnctns.

BRACKEN, DAVID; L A Center For Enriched Studies; Los Angeles, CA; (1); Church Yth Grp; Fncng; UC Santa Cruz; Mrne Bio.

BRACKEN, MICHAEL; L A Center For Enriched Studies; Los Angeles, CA; (4); 21/120; Church Yth Grp; Cmnty Wkr; School Play; Stage Crew; Variety Show; Nwsp; Lit Mag; Cit Awd; High Hon Roll; Hon Roll; Ntl Achvmnt Fnlst.

BRACKETT, JENNIFER C; Tehachapi HS; Tehachapi, CA; (1); Church Yth Grp; FHA; Ski Clb; SADD; Teachers Aide; Bsktbl; Cheerldng; Powder Puff Ftbl; Trk; Vllybl; Interior Dsgn.

BRACKETT, LEIGH T; Coachella Valley HS; Coachella, CA; (3); Office Aide; Rep Sr Cls; Var Gym; Hon Roll; Prfct Atten Awd; UCLA; Fashion.

BRACY, TERINA; Springs Of Living Water Acad; Richardson Spgs, CA; (2); 2/28; Cmnty Wkr; Quiz Bowl; Teachers Aide; Chorus; Church Choir; High Hon Roll; Perfrmng Arts Tm; Kings Kids Perfrmng Arts Tm; Missionary.

BRADBURY, GENEVIEVE; Encina HS; Sacramento, CA; (3); 18/226; Church Yth Grp; Drama Clb; French Clb; Church Choir; School Play; Stage Crew; Lit Mag; Hon Roll; Wn Trphy Bst Actrss Lead Role Ply; Theatrical Arts.

BRADEN, TAMRA D; Fresno Christian HS; Clovis, CA; (2); Church Yth Grp; Hosp Aide; JV Capt Cheerldng; JV Vllybl; High Hon Roll; Bus Mgmt.

BRADFORD, AMY; Rio Mesa HS; Camarillo, CA; (3); 32/369; AFS; Pep Clb; Teachers Aide; Cheerldng; Swmmng; Hon Roll; Acad Merit Exclnce Awd; GATE; Hnrs Pgm; UCSB; Commnctns.

BRADFORD, CHERYL; Palo Verde HS; Blythe, CA; (3); Church Yth Grp; Chorus; Hon Roll; NHS; U AZ; Chld Psych.

BRADFORD, ERIK J; Monterey HS; Seaside, CA; (2); Cmnty Wkr; Debate Tm; Model UN; Ski Clb; Yrbk; Rep Frsh Cls; Rep Soph Cls; Trk; Wrstlng; High Hon Roll; Monterey Bay Aquarium Volunteer; UC Santa Barbara; Marine Bio.

BRADFORD, GARY M; Napa HS; Napa, CA; (3); 30/400; AFS; Church Yth Grp; Intnl Clb; Hon Roll; Bro & Sisters In Christ; Oper Of CompBBS With Christian Theme; Wrk Chrstn Camp; Comp Sci.

BRADFORD, JENNIFER L; Le Grand HS; Le Grand, CA; (2); 1/100; Letterman Clb; Drill Tm; Var L Bsktbl; Var L Sftbl; Var L Vllybl; Lion Awd; CSF; All Lge Sftbl & Coaches Awd 90; Bill Taylor Mem Awd Vllybl 89.

BRADFORD, JULIE; Monte Vista HS; Danville, CA; (4); 23/420; Dance Clb; Ski Clb; Spanish Clb; SADD; Chorus; Rptr Nwsp; Powder Puff Ftbl; Var Trk; NHS; UCLA; Med.

BRADFORD, KONIKA; St Michaels HS; Los Angeles, CA; (1); Cheerldng; Hon Roll; UBC; Law.

BRADFORD, REMEGIA A; Seaside HS; Fort Ord, CA; (2); Orch; Powder Puff Ftbl; Hon Roll; Alg & Music Proficiency; Psycht.

BRADFORD, ROBERT K; Thomas Downey HS; Modesto, CA; (2); Boy Scts; Chess Clb; French Clb; Math Tm; High Hon Roll; Knight Achvt Awd Sci & Frnch.

BRADFORD, RUSSELL; South Tahoe HS; Tahoe Paradise, CA; (3); Pres Debate Tm; Quiz Bowl; Rptr VICA; Hon Roll; CSF; Humboldt ST; English.

BRADFORD, SARA; Thomas Downey HS; Modesto, CA; (3); Church Yth Grp; French Clb; Service Clb; Acpl Chr; Chorus; Church Choir; Orch; High Hon Roll; Acad Exclnce Awd Sci, Engl & Chem; BYU; Elem Schl Teacher.

BRADFORD, TEGAN M; San Luis Obispo SR HS; San Luis Obispo, CA; (1); JV Sftbl; JV Tennis; Hon Roll; Prfct Atten Awd; Amnesty Intl; Astronomy Clb Sec; Sci.

BRADHURST, AMY J; Clovis HS; Fresno, CA; (1); Drama Clb; Cheerldng; Hon Roll; Accntnt.

BRADISON, SUZY L; College Park HS; Pacheco, CA; (3); Office Aide; Teachers Aide; Hon Roll; UC Davis; Animal Husbandry.

BRADLEY, ANGELIQUE; Ambassador Baptist HS; Rialto, CA; (2); Church Yth Grp; Office Aide; Yrbk; Off Soph Cls; Cheerldng; High Hon Roll; Bus Admin.

BRADLEY, BILL P; Clovis West HS; Fresno, CA; (3); Church Yth Grp; Cmnty Wkr; FBLA; Letterman Clb; Teachers Aide; Var L Tennis; Hon Roll; Pres Acad Fit Awd; Bus.

BRADLEY, BRAD VINCENT; O'farrell Schl/Creatv & Prfrmg Arts; San Diego, CA; (4); 18/103; Dance Clb; Drama Clb; English Clb; Acpl Chr; Chorus; School Musical; School Play; Variety Show; Nwsp; High Hon Roll; Bst Dancer; Main Stage Clb-Hghst Hnr; U S CA; Drama.

BRADLEY, DAWN P; Concord HS; Concord, CA; (3); Rep Jr Cls; Cit Awd; Hon Roll; Bus.

BRADLEY, DEBRA L; Gateway Community Schl; Pt Mugu, CA; (4); High Hon Roll; Hon Roll.

BRADLEY, DERRICK; Long Beach Jordan HS; Compton, CA; (1); 2/50; Computer Clb; Teachers Aide; JV Bsbl; JV Ftbl; Cit Awd; Hon Roll; MESA; JETS; Comp Sci/Engr.

BRADLEY, ERIN K; Carondelet HS; Pleasant Hill, CA; (4); 30/180; Church Yth Grp; Capt GAA; Off Frsh Cls; Socr; Var Capt Vllybl; Hon Roll; Treas NHS; CA Interschlstc Fdrtn Schlr/Ath; CSF; Psych.

BRADLEY JR, JAMES CHARLES; Liberty Union HS; Oakley, CA; (2); 3/405; Boy Scts; Pres Chess Clb; Church Yth Grp; Debate Tm; Drama Clb; Sec Intnl Clb; Letterman Clb; NFL; Speech Tm; Teachers Aide; CSF; Acad Dcthln; BYU; Engrng.

BRADLEY, JAMIE C; Dana Hills HS; Dana Point, CA; (3); Clss Cncl; Anml Sci.

BRADLEY, KARYN D; El Dorado HS; Pollock Pines, CA; (3); 25/376; Am Leg Aux Girls St; Church Yth Grp; Pres Science Clb; Service Clb; Teachers Aide; Temple Yth Grp; Band; Drm Mjr(t); Jazz Band; Mrchg Band; Exec Cmmte JR St; Bus Admin.

BRADLEY, LINCJABBAR; Mt Pleasant HS; Milpitas, CA; (4); Boy Scts; Latin Clb; Church Choir; Mgr(s); Latin Clb Treas; Photo Clb; San Jose ST; Engl.

BRADLEY, R MAREN; Arcata HS; Arcata, CA; (2); Church Yth Grp; Drama Clb; NFL; Band; Pep Band; Co-Ed Lit Mag; Cit Awd; Hon Roll; Jr NHS; NHS; CSF Treas & Pres; Northern CA Hnr Band; Schl Bd Ciriculum Advsry Cmmtte; Comm.

BRADLEY, ROBERT; L A Center For Enriched Studies; Sylmar, CA; (4); Church Yth Grp; Cmnty Wkr; Computer Clb; Drama Clb; German Clb; Science Clb; School Play; Ed Nwsp; VP Frsh Cls; Off Sr Cls; S CA Coll; Pastor.

BRADLEY, SARAH J; Monte Vista HS; Spring Valley, CA; (1); Church Yth Grp; Intrml Bsktbl; Intrml Socr; Intrml Vllybl; Cit Awd; Hon Roll.

BRADLEY, SHANNON M; Colfax HS; Colfax, CA; (3); 45/165; Red Cross Aide; Service Clb; Teachers Aide; Flag Corp; JV Crs Cntry; Var Stat Ftbl; JV Sftbl; Var Trk; Hon Roll; Svc Clb Pres; Frgn Lang.

BRADLYN, CAROB D F; Shasta HS; Redding, CA; (2); Church Yth Grp; FHA; Acpl Chr; Chorus; School Musical; School Play; Stage Crew; Hon Roll; Sunshine Generation; Eclgy Clb; Music Educ.

BRADRICK, MICHELE L; Tustin HS; Tustin, CA; (2); Church Yth Grp; German Clb; Science Clb; Band; Jazz Band; Mrchg Band; JV Bsktbl; Hon Roll; Civil Air Patrol Air Force Axlry; Music Dept Awd; Bio.

BRADSHAW, AMIE; St Joseph HS; Lakewood, CA; (3); 15/180; GAA; JV Bsktbl; JV Var Sftbl; JV Capt Vllybl; High Hon Roll; Alg, Rlgn, Phys Sci, Engl, Typng Awds; CSF; MVP, Mst Insprtnl JV Vllybl; MIP JV Sftbl; LB ST; Psych.

BRADSHAW, DESIRAE; Will C Crawford HS; San Diego, CA; (2); French Clb; Trk; Hon Roll; Educ.

BRADSHAW, ELOISE E; Bishop Amat HS; West Covina, CA; (4); 72/392; Pres French Clb; School Play; L Tennis; JV Trk; Hon Roll; Prtcpted Frgn Exchg Hosting Stu & Visiting France; U C Santa Barbara; Engl.

BRADSHAW, PATRICIA; Thousand Oaks HS; Thousand Oaks, CA; (2); 30/554; Church Yth Grp; Spanish Clb; SADD; Color Guard; Flag Corp; Hon Roll; Jr NHS; NHS; Prfct Atten Awd; Archtctr.

BRADSHAW, REGINA A; Fowler HS; Fowler, CA; (3); Latin Clb; Pres Drama Clb; FCA; Spanish Clb; SADD; Ed Yrbk; Treas VP Stu Cncl; Var Bsktbl; Var Vllybl; High Hon Roll; Grls St Cnvnt 90; Md-Yr Yth Cnfrnc CSF; Gottschalks Hi-Deb; Acad Dcthln Vrsty Tm; Pltcl Sci.

BRADY, ALETHEA C; Portola JR SR HS; Blairsden, CA; (3); Church Yth Grp; Dance Clb; 4-H; Office Aide; Teachers Aide; Drill Tm; Swing Chorus; Cheerldng; 4-H Awd; Hon Roll; Sierra JC; Bus Mgt.

BRADY, ANN M; St Francis HS; Sacramento, CA; (4); 18/110; Church Yth Grp; Cmnty Wkr; French Clb; Hosp Aide; Church Choir; High Hon Roll; Pres Acad Fit Awd; CSF; Hstry Day Essay Fnlst; CSU Sacramento; Psych.

BRADY, JAMES D; Alta Loma HS; Alta Loma, CA; (4); 8/438; Church Yth Grp; Cmnty Wkr; VP Math Clb; School Play; Stage Crew; Rptr Nwsp; High Hon Roll; Pres Acad Fit Awd; Acad Dcdthln; CHRIST Clb Treas; CA Poly Pomona; Cvl Engrng.

BRADY, KATRINA; Fremont Christian HS; Union City, CA; (4); 7/43; Church Yth Grp; Drama Clb; Ed Yrbk; L Vllybl; High Hon Roll; NHS; CA Schlrshp Fed; Boy Scts Of Amer Law Post; Biola U; Law.

BRADY, MICHELE M; Castle Park HS; Chula Vista, CA; (3); 21/422; Church Yth Grp; Drama Clb; NFL; Speech Tm; Thesps; School Play; Stage Crew; High Hon Roll; Opt Clb Awd; Pres Acad Fit Awd; Acting.

BRADY, MICHELLE L; Tokay HS; Stockton, CA; (4); 62/614; French Clb; Office Aide; Teachers Aide; High Hon Roll; Hon Roll; Pres Acad Fit Awd; CSF; Tutor; Bus Mgr.

BRADY, SCOTT; L A Baptist HS; Sherman Oaks, CA; (3); Boy Scts; Church Yth Grp; FCA; Office Aide; Teachers Aide; Chorus; Church Choir; School Musical; Var Capt Ftbl; Var Trk; Seabreeze Awd; Big Brthr; Ftbl Team Capt; SUN; Bus.

BRADY, TODD; Golden West HS; Ivanhoe, CA; (2); Boy Scts; Chess Clb; Church Yth Grp; Cmnty Wkr; Hosp Aide; Jazz Band; Mrchg Band; JV Tennis; High Hon Roll; NHS; Band Hnrs, Jr Hall Of Fame; Sci.

BRADY, WILLIAM; Valley View HS; Moreno Valley, CA; (1); Math Tm; Ski Clb; Rep Yrbk; Ftbl; Hon Roll; Top 2 Pct Nation Math 3-R Tstng; Recd A Partcptn & Tm Wrk Bwlng; ITT Voc Schl; Laser Tech.

BRAGA, BERNADETTE M; Andrew P Hill HS; San Jose, CA; (2); Latin Clb; Pres Soph Cls; Rep Stu Cncl; Cheerldng; JV Sftbl; JV Vllybl; Prjct 50 CIT; Santa Clara U.

BRAGG, DANIELLE; Pacific Grove HS; Pacific Grove, CA; (3); 2/130; AFS; Pep Clb; Flag Corp; Yrbk; Var Vllybl; AFS Stu Exchange In France Smmr 90; Ed.

BRAHAM, EUGENA A; Oak Grove HS; San Jose, CA; (3); Church Yth Grp; Cmnty Wkr; Rep FCA; VP JA; Math Clb; Church Choir; Ed Yrbk; Var L Swmmng; Var Trk; Work At YMCA; Humbold ST; Communications.

BRAHMA, BARUNASHISH; Clovis HS; Clovis, CA; (2); 1/617; Cmnty Wkr; Computer Clb; Debate Tm; Pres FBLA; Math Clb; Math Tm; NFL; Science Clb; Spanish Clb; Speech Tm; 3rd Pl CA St FBLA Partnership With Bus Project; 2nd Pl Bus Math; Outstndng Achvmt Ctrl Vly Sci Fair; Mech Eng.

BRAHMA, CHARANJIT; Clovis HS; Clovis, CA; (4); 1/551; Debate Tm; VP Treas Math Clb; Capt Math Tm; Science Clb; Ed Nwsp; Rep Stu Cncl; Tennis; High Hon Roll; JETS Awd; Ntl Merit SF; Acad Decthln Team Awds; Sci & Engr Fair Team; Century III Ldrs Awd; Stanford U; Engr Ed.

BRAIDIC, DEBORAH; Imperial HS; Pacoma, CA; (3); Church Yth Grp; Q&S; Nwsp; Yrbk; Sec Treas Soph Cls; High Hon Roll; Hon Roll; Ntl Merit SF; Intrml Vllybl; Speech Club Secy & Vp; Prom Decorations Cmmte; Yth Ldrshp Pgm; Bus.

BRAILO, STEVE J; Moorpark HS; Moorpark, CA; (3); 30/230; Boy Scts; Church Yth Grp; Intnl Clb; Variety Show; Pres Soph Cls; Pres Jr Cls; VP Sr Cls; Crs Cntry; Socr; Var L Trk; Mem CSF; Grand Prize Wnnr Lip Sync 88-89; Fnniest Act In Lip Sync 89-90; U Of Virgin Islands; Ocnogrphy.

BRAINERD, TIMOTHY R; James Logan HS; Union City, CA; (3); Art Clb; FTA; Math Clb; NFL; School Play; Hon Roll; Prfct Atten Awd; Stu Senator Rep; Tchr.

BRAIO, JOFF C; Rio Americano HS; Sacramento, CA; (4); 40/250; Church Yth Grp; Key Clb; Service Clb; Spanish Clb; JV Var Bsbl; JV Capt Ftbl; Hon Roll; Pres Acad Fit Awd; CSF; U Of S CA; Bio Sci.

BRAKE, STEVEN L; North HS; Torrance, CA; (4); 37/466; Spanish Clb; Teachers Aide; Rep Sr Cls; Stu Cncl; JV Var Bsbl; Cit Awd; Hon Roll; Pres Acad Fit Awd; U CA Irvine; Engrng.

BRAKENSIEK, KARIN L; Del Campo-Fair Oaks HS; Carmichael, CA; (3); Sec Soph Cls; Stat Bsktbl; Hon Roll; Wrtng Awds.

BRALEY, MARK E; Modesto Christian HS; Modesto, CA; (3); 3/40; Church Yth Grp; Letterman Clb; Teachers Aide; Varsity Clb; Pres Stu Cncl; JV Bsbl; JV Bsktbl; Var Capt Ftbl; Capt Var Trk; Wt Lftg.

BRAMBLEY, ROBERT R; Vanden HS; Vacaville, CA; (4); Church Yth Grp; Drama Clb; Spanish Clb; School Play; Var Ftbl; Hon Roll; Law Enfrcmnt Cadet Pgm; Spartan Schl; Aeronautics.

BRAMSTEDT, NICOLE L; Arcadia HS; Arcadia, CA; (3); 115/600; AFS; Art Clb; Cmnty Wkr; VP Hosp Aide; Pres Red Cross Aide; Science Clb; Spanish Clb; L Var Tennis; Var Vllybl; High Hon Roll; Kiowas Honorary Sr Girls Svc Club; Arcadia Red Cross Bd Of Dir Yth Rep; Pediatrics.

BRAMWELL, ELIZABETHE A; Mission Viejo HS; Mission Viejo, CA; (3); Rep Drama Clb; Key Clb; Pres Pep Clb; Treas Thesps; School Play; Stu Cncl; NHS; Smnry VP; Laurel Pres; Grls Camp LIT.

BRANAM, SHERRI L; Paramount HS; South Gate, CA; (2); 9/616; FTA; SADD; High Hon Roll; Lbrl Stud.

BRANCH, ASHANTI D; John C Fremont HS; Oakland, CA; (2); Pres Church Yth Grp; Drama Clb; ROTC; VP Frsh Cls; JV Ftbl; Prfct Atten Awd; MIT; Engrng.

BRANCH, ERIC D; Silver Creek HS; San Jose, CA; (4); 3/415; Chess Clb; Pres Acad Fit Awd; CSF; UC Davis; Engrng.

BRANCH, JENNIFER R; South Fork HS; Phillipsville, CA; (3); 16/70; FHA; Library Aide; High Hon Roll; Hon Roll; SADD; Upward Bound, HSU; Coll Of The Redwoods; Math.

BRANCH, SHANA M; Oxnard HS; Oxnard, CA; (2); 179/604; Church Yth Grp; Sftbl; Stat Trk; Blk Stu Union Mem; Pediatrician.

BRANCH, WILLIAM A; San Rafael HS; San Rafael, CA; (4); Church Yth Grp; Ski Clb; Spanish Clb; SADD; Hon Roll; Equestrian Sprts; US Pony Club; UCLA; Ec.

BRAND, ADAM J; Monterey HS; Monterey, CA; (3); Model UN; Temple Yth Grp; Varsity Clb; Var Tennis; High Hon Roll; NHS; CSF; UNA-USA Mem.

BRANDENBURGER, KARA L; St Francis HS; West Sacramento, CA; (2); Latin Clb; Var Capt Sftbl; JV Capt Vllybl; High Hon Roll; Pres Acad Fit Awd; All Trny Natl Sftbl Tm Stu; Latin Hnr Soc; CSF; Notre Dame U; Arch Engrng.

BRANDES, DEIRDRE E; Torrey Pines HS; San Diego, CA; (4); 15/430; SADD; Varsity Clb; Rep Stu Cncl; Var L Gym; Var Sec Socr; High Hon Roll; Pres Acad Fit Awd; Volun At Animal Clinic; Union Tribune All-Acad Tm Awd; Recvd The Scholar Athlete Awd For Four Years; U Of CA At Davis.

BRANDES, JAMES; Foothill HS; Pleasanton, CA; (4); 1/320; Church Yth Grp; Scholastic Bowl; Science Clb; Service Clb; Pres Sr Cls; Stu Cncl; Var Bsktbl; Bausch & Lomb Sci Awd; High Hon Roll; Ntl Merit Ltr; CSF; UC San Diego; Bio.

BRANDON, BOBBY D; Hanford Union HS; Hanford, CA; (2); Var L Ftbl; JV Wt Lftg; Hon Roll; CSF; Northern AZ U; Phys Thrpy.

BRANDON, JENNIFER; El Dorado HS; Placentia, CA; (3); 28/317; Intnl Clb; Pep Clb; Stu Cncl; Stat Bsktbl; JV Var Cheerldng; High Hon Roll; Law.

BRANDON, JOSH; Paraclete HS; Lancaster, CA; (2); Church Yth Grp; Quiz Bowl; SADD; JV Trk; High Hon Roll; CA ST Schlrshp Fdrtn; UCLA.

BRANDON, KIA N; San Leandro HS; Oakland, CA; (3); 3/30; Bus Profs of Am; Church Yth Grp; Cmnty Wkr; English Clb; JCL; Math Clb; Office Aide; Scholastic Bowl; Teachers Aide; Church Choir; CA ST U Hayward; Physlgy.

BRANDON, MATTHEW; Calaveras HS; Mtn Ranch, CA; (3); AFS; Church Yth Grp; German Clb; Var Band; Var Mrchg Band; Var Orch; Socr; Hon Roll; Capt Of Paintball Team; Cal Poly; Elec Engrng.

BRANDON, ROCHELLE M; Trabuco Hills HS; Trabuco Canyon, CA; (1); Drama Clb; Theatre.

BRANDRUP, KELLI B; El Camino HS; Oceanside, CA; (1); Flag Corp; Yrbk; Sftbl; Cit Awd; City Drill Team; Dance Classes; UCSD; Education.

BRANDT, JESSICA K; William S Hart HS; Newhall, CA; (2); Bus.

BRANDT, NICHOLAS A; Poway HS; Poway, CA; (2); JV Wrstlng; High Hon Roll; Hon Roll; CSF; Teenage Republicans; Physics.

BRANDT, TARCI; Highlands HS; North Highlands, CA; (2); Drama Clb; Chorus; Hon Roll; Wrtg.

BRANNAN, KATIE D; Villanova Preparatory Schl; Ojai, CA; (4); Church Yth Grp; Spanish Clb; Powder Puff Ftbl; Var Socr; Intrml Tennis; Hon Roll; NHS; Pres Acad Fit Awd; Englsh Awd; Ucsb.

BRANNAN, RYAN L; Burney JR SR HS; Burney, CA; (1); Church Yth Grp; FFA; Band; School Musical; Var Bsbl; JV Bsktbl; Socr; Hon Roll; U Of OR; Pharm.

BRANNEN, EMILY A; Chico SR HS; Chico, CA; (4); Cmnty Wkr; Key Clb; Spanish Clb; SADD; School Play; Rptr Nwsp; Lit Mag; Var Cheerldng; Hon Roll; Aud/Vis; Stdst Qtr Acdmc Bio; UCSD; Geriantlgy.

BRANNEN, KIMBERLY K; Calvary Baptist HS; Fairfield, CA; (3); Church Yth Grp; Treas Pep Clb; Church Choir; Rptr Yrbk; Capt Cheerldng; Hon Roll; Prfct Atten Awd; Christian Heritage; Pre-Med.

BRANNIGAN, MIKE J; La Sierra HS; Riverside, CA; (2); Chess Clb; Church Yth Grp; Computer Clb; Debate Tm; French Clb; Math Clb; Math Tm; High Hon Roll; Hon Roll; Prfct Atten Awd; MADD Essay Pblctn; 2nd Pl Inland Cnty Sci Fair; Opened BBS; MIT; Engrng.

BRANNON, ELIZABETH S; Vacaville HS; Vacaville, CA; (3); Church Yth Grp; Cmnty Wkr; Peer Counseling; Psych.

BRANNUM, HEATHER D; Righetti HS; Santa Maria, CA; (2); ASB Cnvntn.

BRANNUM, KERRI L; Clovis HS; Clovis, CA; (2); Church Yth Grp; FCA; FBLA; SADD; Church Choir; Vllybl; Hon Roll; Fresno ST U; Intr Dsgn.

BRANSCUM, KENNETH L; Barstow HS; Barstow, CA; (4); Boy Scts; Teachers Aide; Color Guard; Rptr Nwsp; Hon Roll; Eagle Scout; Enjoy-Bike Riding, Swmmng, Rowing, Canoeing & Going Camping W/Friends; AAI Trade Schl; Advrtsng.

BRANSON, DELICIA; Carson HS; Carson, CA; (4); 57/570; Church Yth Grp; GAA; Mgr Nwsp; Lit Mag; Hon Roll; Pres Acad Fit Awd; Carson Moose Lodge Schlrshp; CA Schlrshp Fdrtn; Howard U; Bus Mgmt.

BRANSON, STACY; Tokay HS; Stockton, CA; (2); Church Yth Grp; Dance Clb; Drama Clb; Thesps; School Play; Variety Show; Cheerldng; Socr; Hon Roll; Pres Acad Fit Awd; Engl Lit.

BRANSTETTER, BRYAN S; Esperanza HS; Placentia, CA; (2); 31/550; Church Yth Grp; Socr; JV Tennis; Cit Awd; High Hon Roll; Top 25 Awd; SUPA; UC Berkeley; Bus.

BRANSTETTER, CRAIG M; Dos Palos HS; Dos Palos, CA; (3); AFS; Am Leg Boys St; Band; Mrchg Band; VP Sr Cls; Stu Cncl; JV Var Bsktbl; JV Var Ftbl; Wt Lftg; High Hon Roll; Bus.

BRANT, BILL J; Serrano HS; Phelan, CA; (1); JV L Golf; Hon Roll; CA Polytech ST U; Arch.

BRANT, JASON C; El Dorado HS; Placentia, CA; (2); 105/363; Church Yth Grp; Band; Church Choir; Mrchg Band; Pep Band; Rep Soph Cls; Hon Roll; Surfing Body Brdng; Water & Jet Skiing; Azusa Pacific Christian; Dntstr.

BRANT, JENNIFER L; St Francis HS; Los Altos, CA; (2); 21/386; Drama Clb; Hosp Aide; SADD; Thesps; School Musical; School Play; Cheerldng; High Hon Roll; Tch Ballet; Art Crtnng, Acrylc & Wtrclrs; Theatre Prfrmng; Frnch, Engl, Math, Bio Hnrs Courses; Stanford U; Pre Med.

BRANT, JENNIFER R; Kingsburg HS; Kingsburg, CA; (3); Hon Roll; Barbizon Mdlng Schl; Kings River Coll; Law.

BRANUM, SCOTT W; Alhambra HS; Martinez, CA; (3); Varsity Clb; Intrml Crs Cntry; JV Ftbl; Var Trk; Hon Roll; Pres Acad Fit Awd; Assoc U Wmns Club Mrt Cert.

BRAR, AMRIT PAL KAUR; East HS; Bakersfield, CA; (3); Church Yth Grp; FCA; FBLA; Teachers Aide; School Play; Bsktbl; Vllybl; Wt Lftg; High Hon Roll; Prfct Atten Awd; Accntnt.

BRAR, BALWINDER; Tranquility Union HS; San Joaquin, CA; (2); Cit Awd; Prfct Atten Awd; Fresno City Coll.

BRAR, HAMDEEP K; Wasco HS; Wasco, CA; (3); Church Yth Grp; Cmnty Wkr; Computer Clb; Debate Tm; FHA; GAA; JA; Math Clb; Math Tm; Varsity Clb; Freedoms Fndtn Awd; CSF; Med.

BRASCH, SAMUEL E; Tamalpais HS; Mill Valley, CA; (2); Spanish Clb; Rep Soph Cls; Pres Jr Cls; Stu Cncl; Var Golf; JV Capt Socr; High Hon Roll; Hnr T; CSF Hnrs Soc.

BRASHEARS, LEA J.; Miramonte HS; Orinda, CA; (3); Dance Clb; Stu Cncl; Cheerldng; Pom Pon; Swmmng; Trk; Cit Awd; Hon Roll; Pres Acad Fit Awd; School Play.

BRASIEL, HEIDI L; Exeter HS; Exeter, CA; (3); Church Yth Grp; FHA; Office Aide; Teachers Aide; Chorus; School Musical; School Play; Variety Show; Crs Cntry; Hon Roll; Guitar; Sequoias Coll.

BRASIL, MARIO; Santa Clara HS; Santa Clara, CA; (2); JV Ftbl; Cit Awd; Hon Roll; Prfct Atten Awd; Law Enfrcmnt.

BRASIL, NANCY P; Kingsburg HS; Kingsburg, CA; (3); Art Clb; Cmnty Wkr; SADD; Teachers Aide; Acpl Chr; Chorus; Church Choir; High Hon Roll; Hon Roll; 5th Lvl Piano Course; Portuguese Cmnty; Pre-Med.

BRASS, GRACE A; Troy HS; Fullerton, CA; (2); 64/334; Art Clb; Boy Scts; Church Yth Grp; Ski Clb; Var Tennis; Cit Awd; DAR Awd; High Hon Roll; Kiwanis Awd; Csf Club; Ib Program; P A L; Troy Tech Program; Cal State; Literature.

BRASSETT, ELIZABETH ANNE; Whittier Christian HS; Fullerton, CA; (3); Church Yth Grp; Cmnty Wkr; Spanish Clb; Drill Tm; School Play; Rep Stu Cncl; Var Capt Cheerldng; Gym; High Hon Roll; CSF; Bus Mgmt.

BRASUELL, ANGELA M; Los Gatos HS; San Jose, CA; (3); Church Yth Grp; Debate Tm; Drama Clb; Teachers Aide; School Musical; JV Crs Cntry; JV Trk; Work SASS; U CA Santa Clara; Law.

BRATAKOS, ARGIRI; Alverno HS; Arcadia, CA; (3); Church Yth Grp; Cmnty Wkr; Pep Clb; Chorus; School Play; Cheerldng; Score Keeper; Swmmng; Tennis; Greek Folk Dncng 90; Maids Of Athena; Green Orthodox Yth Assn; U Of San Francisco; Pre-Med.

BRATCHER, ALLISON; Francis Polytechnic HS; North Hollywood, CA; (4); Am Leg Aux Girls St; Cmnty Wkr; Drama Clb; School Musical; School Play; Variety Show; Pres Jr Cls; Stu Cncl; Hon Roll; Lion Awd; LA Valley Col; Commnctns.

BRATCHER, BRIAN P; Orange Lutheran HS; Santa Ana, CA; (2); FCA; Office Aide; JV Bsbl; JV Bsktbl; Var Ftbl; Wt Lftg.

BRATCHER, MICHELLE; Williams HS; Williams, CA; (1); Band; Mrchg Band; Pep Band; JV Bsktbl; JV Vllybl; Hon Roll; Stanford; Law.

BRATINA, KASSIA L; James Madison HS; San Diego, CA; (4); 54/368; Hon Roll; Psych.

BRATIS, DANIELLE L; Yucaipa HS; Calimesa, CA; (3); 23/375; Key Clb; Letterman Clb; Pep Clb; Spanish Clb; Gym; Powder Puff Ftbl; Var Socr; Var Trk; High Hon Roll; Prfct Atten Awd; Mst Imprvd Trk 88-89; All League Trk 88-90; Bus.

BRATTON, RICKY C; Junipero Serra HS; Los Angeles, CA; (3); 17/35; Church Yth Grp; Varsity Clb; Stu Cncl; Var Ftbl; UCLA; Med.

BRAUCH, MICHAEL D; Bellarmine College Prep; San Jose, CA; (3); Cmnty Wkr; Latin Clb; Service Clb; Ski Clb; Varsity Clb; JV Crs Cntry; Var Wrstlng; Rugby; Jr Olympc Wrstlng; Tutorial Soc; Intrmrl Sports; Bus.

BRAUER, VERONICA A; Castle Park HS; Chula Vista, CA; (1); Avid Pgm; Modeling.

BRAUN, AMANDA K; Galileo HS; San Francisco, CA; (3); Cmnty Wkr; Drama Clb; German Clb; Chorus; Drill Tm; Flag Corp; School Play; Rptr Soph Cls; L Crs Cntry; Var Trk; Acad Decathln Hnrs Grp 90-91; Aerontcl Engnrng.

BRAUN, JENNIFER C; Hemet HS; Idyllwild, CA; (3); 67/570; Church Yth Grp; SADD; Band; Mrchg Band; Pep Band; Mgr(s); Stat Sftbl; Cit Awd; Hon Roll; U Of CA Santa Barbara.

BRAUN, KRISTIN L; College Park HS; Martinez, CA; (2); AFS; VP Model UN; Yrbk; VP Soph Cls; Capt JV Cheerldng; JV Swmmng; High Hon Roll; CSF; Friday Night Live; YMCA Yth & Govt Senator.

BRAUN, SARA; Menlo-Atherton HS; Menlo Park, CA; (4); 55/355; Am Leg Aux Girls St; Cmnty Wkr; Sprt Ed Yrbk; Rep Soph Cls; Rep Jr Cls; VP Sr Cls; Var JV Bsktbl; Var L Swmmng; Cit Awd; Hon Roll; Multi-Cultrl Clb Fndr; Envrnmntl Awareness Clb; Homcmng Qn; UC San Diego; Intl Rltns.

BRAUNING, JUSTIN J; Arcata HS; Arcata, CA; (2); SADD; Var L Bsbl; JV Bsktbl; Hon Roll; All-Star Bsbl Team; All-County Bsbl Team; OR ST; Prfssnl Bsbl.

BRAUNSTEIN, CHRISTOPHER J; Etiwanda HS; Alta Loma, CA; (3); SADD; Amer Hertg Clb; Yrbk Staff 90-91; Friday Night Live; Roses Awd; Advrtsng.

BRAVERMAN, KARIN B; Westlake Schl; Santa Monica, CA; (4); Art Clb; Cmnty Wkr; French Clb; Nwsp; Yrbk; Sec Soph Cls; Var Tennis; Ntl Merit Ltr; U Of PA Alumnai Bk Awd 89; Cmmnty Svc Rcgntn 3 Yrs; Fluent German; Harvard U.

BRAVERMAN, LEE G; Moreno Valley HS; Riverside, CA; (3); Boy Scts; ROTC; Scholastic Bowl; Color Guard; Drill Tm; NHS; Odyssey Of Mind VP; Air Force Acad; Aerosp Engr.

BRAVO, ANGEL M; Fowler HS; Fowler, CA; (3); Teachers Aide; Var Crs Cntry; Var Socr; JV Tennis; JV Trk; Acadmc Awd Art & Span; Fresno ST U; Anim Rsrch.

BRAVO, CARMEN; Strathmore HS; Poplar, CA; (2); Psych.

BRAVO, EARL A; Tulare Western HS; Tulare, CA; (4); Spanish Clb; Band; Jazz Band; Mrchg Band; Orch; Pep Band; Socr; AP Engl & Math; Drumline Capt; COS; Bus Accntng.

BRAVO, FELIPE; Hueneme HS; Oxnard, CA; (2); 89/357; JV Bsbl; Cit Awd; Hon Roll; Prfct Atten Awd; U CA Santa Barbara; Arch.

BRAVO, GEORGE C; Riverbank HS; Riverbank, CA; (2); Engr.

BRAVO, LISA; Carlsbad HS; Carlsbad, CA; (1); Band; Color Guard; Mrchg Band; Pep Band; JV Gym; Medcl.

BRAVO, LUIS A; Dos Palos HS; Dos Palos, CA; (3); Band; Merced Coll; Electrcn.

BRAVO, MARIA Y; Saddleback HS; Santa Ana, CA; (2); Church Yth Grp; FBLA; Chorus; Yrbk; JV Tennis; MESA Awd Wnnr; Advertising Bus Exec.

BRAVO, RYAN L; King City HS; Greenfield, CA; (3); Art Clb; FFA; Chorus; School Musical; Stu Cncl; JV Bsbl; L Capt Ftbl; L Capt Trk; Wt Lftg; High Hon Roll; Ldrshp Cls; Stanford U; Phy Thrpy.

BRAVO, VERONICA; Holy Family HS; Los Angeles, CA; (2); Vet.

BRAWLEY, JODI L; Ukiah HS; Ukiah, CA; (2); Church Yth Grp; Spanish Clb; Varsity Clb; Band; Mrchg Band; Pep Band; Var Capt Crs Cntry; Var Capt Trk.

BRAY, HAZEL; Chula Vista HS; National City, CA; (3); 97/493; Orch; Ed Nwsp; Ed Yrbk; MECHA Pres; San Diego ST U; Psych.

BRAY, KENDRA M; Rim Of The World HS; Running Springs, CA; (3); 1/210; Am Leg Aux Girls St; Church Yth Grp; Debate Tm; Stu Cncl; Capt JV Vllybl; Hon Roll; NHS; CSF.

BRAY, MONICA; Abraham Lincoln HS; San Francisco, CA; (3); Ski Clb; Yrbk; Hon Roll; Law.

BRAY, STEFANI L; Temecula Valley HS; Murrieta, CA; (4); Church Yth Grp; Cmnty Wkr; Acpl Chr; Chorus; Church Choir; Hon Roll; Chrch Pianist 86-90 & Bd Sec 89-90; Cmptn US Cnstn & Bill Of Rghts 90 St Level; Point Loma Mazorene Coll; Psych.

BRAY, TANYA M; Woodrow Wilson HS; San Francisco, CA; (2); Church Yth Grp; Cmnty Wkr; Pres Soph Cls; Var Bsktbl; Var Crs Cntry; Var Trk; Var Vllybl; FBLA; Law.

BRAYNIN, ALAN V; Lowell HS; San Francisco, CA; (3); Computer Clb; Debate Tm; Pres JA; Service Clb; Varsity Clb; Var Socr; NHS; SITE; Bridge Club; Law.

BRAYSHAW, MOLLY; Tokay HS; Stockton, CA; (4); 29/614; Pres French Clb; Scholastic Bowl; Band; Mrchg Band; Orch; Pep Band; School Musical; Cit Awd; High Hon Roll; Hon Roll; All-St Hnr Band; John Philip Sousa Music Awd; Lewis & Clark; Deaf Tchr.

BRAYTON, JAMIE L; Fort Bragg HS; Fort Bragg, CA; (2); 5/166; VP Treas 4-H; Band; Treas Jr Cls; 4-H Awd; High Hon Roll; Hon Roll; Jr NHS; NHS; Redwood Writing Awd Best General Essay; John Rainey Yearwod Schlrshp Awd; Teen Leader Awd Winner 4-H; U CA Davis; Ag Engrng.

BRAYTON, KARI; Antelope Valley HS; Lancaster, CA; (4); Church Yth Grp; Dance Clb; Hosp Aide; Pep Clb; Teachers Aide; Cheerldng; Gym; Hon Roll; Antelope Valley JC; Phys Thrpy.

BRAZEAL, CODY; North Monterey Co HS; Salinas, CA; (2); Wt Lftg; Wrstlng; Cit Awd; High Hon Roll; Skate Brdng; Engrng.

BRAZELTON, CHRISTOPHER M; Ocean View HS; Huntington Beach, CA; (3); 2/17; Boy Scts; Church Yth Grp; Pres Stu Cncl; Var L Bsbl; JV Bsktbl; Capt L Crs Cntry; L Vllybl; Cit Awd; Hon Roll; Pres Acad Fit Awd; Crown Chrstn Leag 89 Double Champ Tennis Tournmnt; CSUF; Arch.

BRAZIER, ANDREW S; Madera HS; Madera, CA; (2); Church Yth Grp; Tennis; Pacific Chrstn Coll.

BRAZIL, JANNA L; Fresno Christian HS; Madera, CA; (2); Church Yth Grp; Pep Clb; Cheerldng; Gym; Pom Pon; Hon Roll; Psych.

BRAZZI, LENOR S; Atascadero HS; Atascadero, CA; (3); Sec Band; Sec Mrchg Band; JV Bsktbl; Capt Powder Puff Ftbl; Var Socr; JV Sftbl; Hon Roll; Law.

BREAM, BRENDAN; Redwood HS; Visalia, CA; (4); Chess Clb; FBLA; Ed Yrbk; VP Sr Cls; Var Capt Bsktbl; Hon Roll; Pres Acad Fit Awd; Humboldt ST U; Env Rsrcs Engr.

BREAUX, CORDELL D; Fremont HS; Sunnyvale, CA; (3); 45/400; Teachers Aide; Hon Roll; CSF; Engrng Drftng Aide; UC Berkeley; Arch.

BREAUX, CRYSTA-LINN; Kern Valley HS; Bodfish, CA; (3); Church Yth Grp; Cmnty Wkr; Drama Clb; Sec FHA; Library Aide; Office Aide; Teachers Aide; School Play; Hon Roll; U CA Santa Cruz; Marine Bio.

BRECHTEL, CHRISTOPHER W; Paso Robles HS; Paso Robles, CA; (2); 1/270; Boy Scts; Varsity Clb; Capt JV Bsktbl; Var Golf; Cit Awd; Elks Awd; High Hon Roll; Rotary Awd; Law.

BREDEAU, SHANE B; Modoc HS; Alturas, CA; (2); JV Bsktbl; Cit Awd; High Hon Roll; Hon Roll; Prfct Atten Awd; Pres Acad Fit Awd; Cert Of Grade Imprvmnt; Acad Awd Cnsmr Ed; Above Avg Achvt Awd TEACH; Elec Engr.

BREDICE, BETH A; Paramount HS; Bellflower, CA; (4); 1/492; Am Leg Aux Girls St; Drama Clb; French Clb; Letterman Clb; Science Clb; Var Capt Swmmng; Bausch & Lomb Sci Awd; Elks Awd; High Hon Roll; Prfct Atten Awd; Bk Of Amer Plaq Wnr Liberal Art; Tandy Outstndng Schlr Math,Sci & Cmptr Sci; Mars Milky Way Awd; IA ST U; Arch.

BREDOW, ROB D; Troy HS; La Habra, CA; (2); 22/300; Aud/Vis; Church Yth Grp; Sec Computer Clb; Speech Tm; Band; Nwsp; NHS; Acadc Decatholon.

BREDWELL, HAL; Bellarmine Prep; San Bruno, CA; (2); Church Yth Grp; JV Golf; Hon Roll; NHS; Bellarmine Irish Club; Libr Asst; Schlrshp Recipient 88-89; BYU; Bus.

BREED, CHARMAYNE; Inner City Christian Acad; Stockton, CA; (1); Church Yth Grp; Church Choir; Off Frsh Cls; Crs Cntry; Hon Roll; Prfct Atten Awd.

BREED, LISA M; Davis SR HS; Davis, CA; (2); Hon Roll; Pres Acad Fit Awd; Amnesty Intl; Violin; Engrng.

BREED, REBECCA L; College Park HS; Pleasant Hill, CA; (3); 20/400; Church Yth Grp; Cmnty Wkr; Drama Clb; Spanish Clb; SADD; Church Choir; School Musical; Sec Jr Cls; JV Swmmng; Hon Roll; Chrch Mission & Svc Trp Mendenhall MS, Mexico & Ecuador; Pediatrican.

BREEDEN, MATTHEW C; Will C Wood HS; Vacaville, CA; (2); Intnl Clb; Teachers Aide; JV Bsbl; JV Bsktbl; High Hon Roll; Hon Roll; Jr NHS; NHS; GATE Clb Pres; UCLA; Law.

BREEDING, JENNIFER A; Torrey Pines HS; San Diego, CA; (4); Church Yth Grp; Intnl Clb; Orch; School Musical; Stu Cncl; Var JV Gym; JV Trk; High Hon Roll; NHS; Volunteer Work-Mexico; Pepperdine U; Premed.

BREEN, SARAH L; Hayward HS; Hayward, CA; (2); 69/274; Church Yth Grp; Cmnty Wkr; Stat Bsktbl; Hon Roll; Piano; Photo; Bio.

BREEN, SASHA; Templeton HS; Templeton, CA; (2); 4/69; Drama Clb; School Play; Rptr Nwsp; Cheerldng; Hon Roll; 3rd Pl Sci Fair; Geology.

BREEN, TRICIA; Bishop Amat HS; Covina, CA; (2); Church Yth Grp; JV Cheerldng; JV Trk; Wt Lftg; Hon Roll; NHS; Pres Acad Fit Awd; Ballet Cls; U Of Southern CA.

BREES, KEAMMEE; Yreka HS; Montague, CA; (4); German Clb; Ski Clb; Var Powder Puff Ftbl; High Hon Roll; Hon Roll; Pres Acad Fit Awd; Rotary Awd; CSF; Astronomy & Horse Clbs; CA ST U Sacramento; Bus Admin.

BREESE, ANDREA L; Hilltop HS; Chula Vista, CA; (2); 42/530; Church Yth Grp; JV Socr; Cit Awd; Hon Roll; Hnrs Courses; Acctng.

BREESE, JENNIFER R; Hilltop HS; Chula Vista, CA; (4); French Clb; Mgr Nwsp; Southwestern Coll; Nrsng.

BREIDERT, JASON R; Palmdale HS; Palmdale, CA; (2); Key Clb; Spanish Clb; JV Swmmng; JV Wrstlng; Hon Roll; Jason Preidert; Arch.

BREILING, STEPHANIE A; St Francis HS; Boulder Creek, CA; (3); Church Yth Grp; Letterman Clb; Service Clb; SADD; Varsity Clb; Powder Puff Ftbl; Var L Swmmng; Trk; High Hon Roll; US Swimming Tm; Bus.

BREITEN JR, ALBERT F; Mt Pleasant HS; San Jose, CA; (2); Proj 50-Santa Clara U; Cnslr In Training-S CA U; Santa Clara U; Bus Mgmt.

BREITKOPF, NICK P; Bishop Montgomery HS; Redondo Beach, CA; (2); Boy Scts; JV Tennis; Cit Awd; Hon Roll; Prfct Atten Awd; R G Canning Outstndng Yth Awd; Military.

BRELSFORD, MISTI; Piner HS; Santa Rosa, CA; (3); Ed Yrbk; JV Cheerldng; High Hon Roll; Hon Roll; Real Est.

BREMBY, DINAH A; Richard Gahr HS; Cerritos, CA; (3); 82/436; FBLA; Teachers Aide; Var Bsktbl; Hon Roll; CSULB; Telecommnctns.

BREMER, STEVEN G; Paraclete HS; Palmdale, CA; (3); 12/31; Church Yth Grp; School Play; Crs Cntry; Hon Roll; Antelope Vly CC; Art.

BREMER, SUZANNE N; Westwood HS; Westwood, CA; (2); Spanish Clb; Acpl Chr; Nwsp; Bsktbl; Sftbl; Vllybl; High Hon Roll; Hon Roll; Chico ST; Pilot.

BRENDE, KIM S; Louisville HS; Woodland Hills, CA; (1); Church Yth Grp; Hosp Aide; Hon Roll; Achvt Awds Span I, Engl I, Relgn I; CSF.

BRENNAN, AANA R; Eureka SR HS; Eureka, CA; (4); 2/300; Hosp Aide; Temple Yth Grp; Orch; School Play; Treas Soph Cls; High Hon Roll; Sal; Ed Lit Mag; CMEA All St Hnr Orchestra 2 Yrs; Natl Cncl Of Tchrs Of Engl Wrtng Awd; Fnlst Natl Schltc Wrtng Cont; UC Berkeley; Anthropology.

BRENNAN, ROBYN E; Poway HS; San Diego, CA; (2); Church Yth Grp; Dance Clb; Letterman Clb; Pep Clb; SADD; Varsity Clb; Yrbk; Stat Ftbl; Var Swmmng; Hon Roll; Friday Night Live Saferides; Conslr Yuth Retreat; Env Club; U C; Kineslgy.

BRENNEISE, JOHN C; Pioneer HS; San Jose, CA; (4); U S Navy DEPS 90; U S Navy; Bus.

BRENNEMAN, AMY J; Berkeley HS; Berkeley, CA; (3); AFS; Cmnty Wkr; GAA; Letterman Clb; Ski Clb; Teachers Aide; Socr; Hon Roll; Wmns Crew Team; Close Up; Pre Med.

BRENNER, CAMERON S; Canyon HS; Santa Clarita, CA; (4); 13/520; Church Yth Grp; Var L Ftbl; High Hon Roll; Pres NHS; Ntl Merit SF; Arspc Engrng.

BRENNER, JOANNE E; Troy HS; Fullerton, CA; (1); Church Yth Grp; Drill Tm; Hon Roll; UC Colorado Springs; Marne Bio.

BRENT, CYNTHIA J; Bakersfield HS; Bakersfield, CA; (3); 16/718; Church Yth Grp; Dance Clb; Hosp Aide; Key Clb; Powder Puff Ftbl; Hon Roll; CSF; UC Davis; Intl Rltns.

BRENT, MICHELLE; East Bakersfield HS; Bakersfield, CA; (3); Church Yth Grp; Cmnty Wkr; Drama Clb; SADD; Thesps; Chorus; School Musical; School Play; Stage Crew; Stu Cncl; Hlth Careers Stu Outstndng Stu Sprg 90; Outstndng Shdwng Stu Soc Wrk 90; Outstndg Stu Field Gerontlgy; Long Beach ST Coll; Phyclgst.

BRENZEL, SETH; Jesuit HS; Sacramento, CA; (4); 4/160; Am Leg Boys St; Teachers Aide; Band; School Musical; School Play; Ed Nwsp; Pres Soph Cls; Var Bsbl; Val; Sacramento Symphny Stu Artst Cncrto Comptn Wnnr; Swarthmore Coll; Music.

BRESCHINI, GORDON R; Salinas HS; Salinas, CA; (4); Church Yth Grp; Cmnty Wkr; Drama Clb; English Clb; VP Thesps; School Play; Var JV Ftbl; Hon Roll; Hnr Thespian; Cert Outstndng Achvt Dramatc Arts; Cal Poly San Luis Obispo; Dsgn.

BRESNIHAN, ROBYN M; Alta Loma HS; Alta Loma, CA; (2); Acpl Chr; Chorus; School Musical; Stage Crew; Sec Jr Cls; High Hon Roll; Hon Roll; Ice Hockey; Acting; Piano.

BRETHOUR, BRANDI N; Saugus HS; Valencia, CA; (2); 18/525; Teachers Aide; School Play; Stage Crew; Stat Bsktbl; Score Keeper; French Hon Soc; High Hon Roll; UC Berkely; Law.

BRETZ, SANDRA DEE; Hemet HS; Hemet, CA; (4); 7/513; Key Clb; Hist Frsh Cls; Treas Soph Cls; Var Capt Socr; Var Vllybl; Cit Awd; High Hon Roll; Lion Awd; NHS; Rotary Awd; Sonoma ST U; Hstry.

BREUER, PETER H; Bishop O'dowd HS; Alameda, CA; (2); Boy Scts; Cmnty Wkr; 3 1st Pl Rbbns & 2 Bst Shw Rbbns Model Bldng; Painting; Aviation.

BREWER, CHARLES; Castle Park HS; Chula Vista, CA; (4); #6 In Class; Am Leg Boys St; Boy Scts; Intnl Clb; Letterman Clb; Quiz Bowl; Varsity Clb; Yrbk; Treas Sr Cls; High Hon Roll; Hon Roll; Fiction Wrtng; UCLA; Comp Analyst.

BREWER, CLINT; Tulelake HS; Tulelake, CA; (3); FFA; Hon Roll; VP FFA; Shasta Coll; Forest Svc.

BREWER, DALE; Capuchino HS; Millbrae, CA; (4); Am Leg Boys St; Sprt Ed Nwsp; Rep Sr Cls; Var L Bsbl; Var L Ftbl; Var Capt Socr; Hon Roll; Pres Acad Fit Awd; Natl Ftbl Hall Fame Schlr Athl; Millbrae Pol Acts Schlrshp; Carl Reyna Spirit Awd; Santa Clara U; Brdcst Jrnlsm.

BREWER, EMILY C; Brea Olinda HS; Brea, CA; (1); Dance Clb; Color Guard; Cheerldng; Cit Awd; High Hon Roll; Jr NHS; UCLA.

BREWER, GAIL; Whitney HS; Cerritos, CA; (2); Church Yth Grp; Dance Clb; Drama Clb; Spanish Clb; Color Guard; Flag Corp; Stage Crew; Rptr Nwsp; Off Soph Cls; Hon Roll.

BREWER, HEIDI S; Academy Of Our Lady Of Peace; San Diego, CA; (1); Art Clb; GAA; Hosp Aide; School Musical; Sec Pres Frsh Cls; VP Soph Cls; JV Bsktbl; High Hon Roll; Pres Acad Fit Awd; Artwk Outstndng Hnrs; Piano; 1st Price Natl Comptn US Schls Won Coll Schlrshp; CA U; Bio.

BREWER, JANET L; El Toro HS; El Toro, CA; (2); 115/557; Treas Girl Scts; Red Cross Aide; Band; Jazz Band; Mrchg Band; Orch; Hon Roll; Bus.

BREWER, KEVIN M; Casa Grande HS; Petaluma, CA; (2); Boy Scts; Church Yth Grp; Cmnty Wkr; JV Bsbl; Intrml Bsktbl; JV Ftbl; Intrml Socr; Intrml Wrstlng; Santa Rosa JC; Psych.

BREWER, LINDA; Hanford Joint Union HS; Hanford, CA; (1); FHA; Hon Roll; Acad Lttr Awd; UCLA.

BREWER, MATTHEW W; Alameda HS; Alameda, CA; (4); 10/325; Boy Scts; Church Yth Grp; Teachers Aide; Jazz Band; Mrchg Band; Pep Band; School Musical; Var Capt Socr; Hon Roll; Skatebrdng; U Of CA; Psych.

BREWER, RONALD D; John F Kennedy HS; Sacramento, CA; (2); Letterman Clb; Var Bsbl; Dentist.

BREWER, WENDY S; Trinity HS; Weaverville, CA; (1); Cit Awd; Hon Roll; Med.

BREWINGTON, DAVID V; Sierra Jt Union HS; Madera, CA; (3); 1/150; Science Clb; JV Bsbl; High Hon Roll; CSF Treas; Natl Hnr Soc Treas Secy & Pres; Gldn St Exam High Hnrs Geom; UC Berkeley; Physics.

BREWSTER, DEANNA; College Park HS; Martinez, CA; (4); Church Yth Grp; German Clb; Teachers Aide; Friday Night Live; UC Santa Barbara.

BREWSTER, JESSICA Y; C K Mc Clathcy HS; Sacramento, CA; (3); Church Yth Grp; Cmnty Wkr; FBLA; Girl Scts; Hosp Aide; Key Clb; Math Clb; Math Tm; Science Clb; Spanish Clb; Bio Awd; Outstndng Orch Stu; Outstndng Mth & Eng Stu; Law.

BREZEL, LAURA E; Santa Cruz HS; Santa Cruz, CA; (2); Drama Clb; Speech Tm; Thesps; Acpl Chr; Chorus; School Musical; School Play; Stage Crew; JV Var Swmmng; Hon Roll; Johns Hopkins U Yth Tlnt Srch; Globl Yth Exchng 1990.

BRIANA, SHINDI; Lindsay HS; Lindsay, CA; (3); Computer Clb; Hosp Aide; Library Aide; Office Aide; SADD; Band; Rptr Nwsp; Rptr Yrbk; High Hon Roll; Hon Roll; Fresno ST U; Law Enfrcmnt.

BRIBIESCAS, RAY J; Tranquillity Union HS; Firebaugh, CA; (3); Band; Jazz Band; Mrchg Band; Pep Band; Phtg Nwsp; JV Wrstlng; Hon Roll; US Marines Corps Resrve; Doctor.

BRICE, JAMI; St Francis HS; Sunnyvale, CA; (4); Church Yth Grp; Pep Clb; Service Clb; Var Cheerldng; High Hon Roll; Earth Sci AwdCSMTLGY; Modeling; San Jose ST U.

BRICE, VIRGINIA L; Whitney HS; Cerritos, CA; (1); Church Yth Grp; Cmnty Wkr; Drama Clb; Church Choir; JV Stat Bsktbl; JV Stat Vllybl; Hon Roll; CA Jr Schlrshp Fed; Chrch Actvts; Ed.

BRICKEEN, MARSHALL A; Hogan SR HS; Vallejo, CA; (3); 1/450; Boy Scts; Chess Clb; Drama Clb; Pres French Clb; German Clb; Pres Key Clb; VP Service Clb; Ski Clb; SADD; Thesps; HOBY; 90 HOBY Soviet Union Ambssdr Exchnge CA Rep; Stanford; Intl Law.

BRICKER, JON B; Tustin HS; Santa Ana, CA; (2); 34/435; AFS; Drama Clb; JA; Thesps; School Play; JV Crs Cntry; JV Trk; Hon Roll; Orange Cnty Acad Dcthln Team; Pilot.

BRIDGE, TAWNY L; Nevada Union HS; Grass Valley, CA; (3); Var Capt Bsktbl; High Hon Roll; Pres Acad Fit Awd; Princpls Awd; Golden St Exam Acad Excllnce; CA Lgsltre Assmbly Cert Rcgntn.

BRIDGERS, COURTNEY A; Dos Pueblos HS; Goleta, CA; (2); Pres Church Yth Grp; Drama Clb; Pep Clb; SADD; Stage Crew; Variety Show; Rep Stu Cncl; JV Cheerldng; JV Trk; Pres Acad Fit Awd; BYU; Film.

BRIDGES, NICOLE L; San Gorgonio HS; Highland, CA; (3); Church Yth Grp; Key Clb; Science Clb; Phtg Yrbk; Stu Cncl; Score Keeper; Hon Roll; Acad Ltr; USC; TV Prdctn.

BRIDGES, SUZY KATHLEEN; West Covina HS; West Covina, CA; (1); Church Yth Grp; GAA; Band; Mrchg Band; Bsktbl; JV Sftbl; High Hon Roll; Hon Roll; Kindergarten Ed.

BRIDGES JR, VERNON LEE; Nevada Union HS; Grass Valley, CA; (3); Church Yth Grp; Temple Yth Grp; Thesps; Varsity Clb; Lit Mag; Bsbl; Capt Bsktbl; Ftbl; Powder Puff Ftbl; Vllybl; Phys Ed/Coach.

BRIDGMAN, DAWN; Western Christian HS; Pomona, CA; (4); Church Yth Grp; Rep Stu Cncl; Var Cheerldng; Hon Roll; Vrsty Chr Sqd 3rd St; 89 Hmcmng Prncs; Outstndng Ldrshp Awd; Mt San Antonio JC; Bus.

BRIDGWOOD, TAMMY C; Arcata HS; Arcata, CA; (2); Drama Clb; VP German Clb; School Musical; Variety Show; Rptr Yrbk; Hon Roll; Prfct Atten Awd.

BRIDWELL, JOSH W; Hilltop HS; Jamul, CA; (4); 35/457; Model UN; Scholastic Bowl; Stu Cncl; Var L Tennis; NHS; Pres Acad Fit Awd; Regent Of Public Relations; U Of S CA; Bus.

BRIEN, JONATHAN E; Athenian HS; San Ramon, CA; (3); Cmnty Wkr; Socr; Swmmng; Safe Rides; Mech Engr.

BRIERLEY, SALLY; Palm Springs HS; Palm Springs, CA; (4); Drama Clb; Treas Pep Clb; Ski Clb; School Musical; Yrbk; Stu Cncl; JV Var Cheerldng; Elks Awd; Hon Roll; Pres Acad Fit Awd; Wldwd Chrs; CA ST U Nrthrdge; Chld Psych.

BRIEVA, ALAN; Bishop Amat Memorial HS; Baldwin Park, CA; (3); Pres Church Yth Grp; Dance Clb; Wrstlng; Barkada Filipino Cltrl Grp; Filipino Rosary Yth Grp; UC Irvine; Accntng.

BRIGGS, DAWN; Valley View HS; Moreno, CA; (1); Art Clb; Church Yth Grp; Computer Clb; Letterman Clb; Quiz Bowl; Chorus; Church Choir; School Play; Variety Show; Vllybl; Outstndg Prfrmnc In Choir Awd; Tutoring Other HS Stus; Performing Arts.

BRIGGS, JANE L; Armijo HS; Suisun, CA; (2); AFS; Letterman Clb; Ski Clb; Var Tennis; Rep Soph Cls; High Hon Roll; Hon Roll; Tnns MVP.

BRIGGS, MICHELE E; Rim Of The World HS; Crest Park, CA; (3); Church Yth Grp; Cmnty Wkr; Quiz Bowl; Teachers Aide; Rep Frsh Cls; Rep Soph Cls; Cit Awd; High Hon Roll; Hon Roll; Prfct Atten Awd; Acad Ltr 90; Writers Conf 89; Visual Arts Fstvl 89; Cnty Fnlst Wrtng Clbrtn 89, 90; St Fnlst Natl Teen; UCR; Commercial Adv.

BRIGGS, SHANNON M; Village Christian HS; Mission Hills, CA; (3); 40/130; Church Yth Grp; English Clb; Math Clb; Rep Stu Cncl; Intrml Powder Puff Ftbl; JV Trk; Prfct Atten Awd; Bowling Leag; Educ.

BRIGGS, TODD M; North HS; Bakersfield, CA; (3); 12/425; Var Golf; Var Capt Socr; High Hon Roll; CA Schlrshp Fed; Engrng.

BRIGGS, WENDY S; John F Kennedy HS; Sacramento, CA; (3); 30/422; Chorus; Swing Chorus; Variety Show; Ed Lit Mag; Hon Roll; NHS; Campfire Boys & Grls; Psych.

BRIJ, NILESH D; Luther Burbank HS; Sacramento, CA; (3); 45/302; Hon Roll; NHS; Prfct Atten Awd; Pilot.

BRIJOVA, DANIELA; Western HS; Anaheim, CA; (3); VP German Clb; Hon Roll; CSF Clb; Clss 91 Clb.

BRIKOVICH, AMANDA; Pinole Valley HS; Pinole, CA; (2); Church Yth Grp; Spanish Clb; Boston U; Pediatrician.

BRILEY, AARON J; Merced HS North; Merced, CA; (2); Var Ftbl; JV Var Wt Lftg; JV Hon Roll; Bus.

BRIMBUELA, MICHELLE; Cerritos HS; Artesia, CA; (3); VP Treas Church Yth Grp; Pep Clb; Science Clb; Spanish Clb; Chorus; JV Cheerldng; Powder Puff Ftbl; Hon Roll; CA Schlrshp Fed; USC; Child Psych.

BRINGGOLD, WILLIAM J; Marysville HS; Yuba City, CA; (1); 6/200; JV L Bsbl; Intrml Bsktbl; Intrml Capt Ftbl; Powder Puff Ftbl; Rotary Awd.

BRINGHURST, DAWN; Fontana HS; Fontana, CA; (3); Am Leg Aux Girls St; Pres Church Yth Grp; Service Clb; Off Soph Cls; Off Jr Cls; VP Stu Cncl; Capt Cheerldng; Sftbl; High Hon Roll; CSF VP & Pres; Brigham Youn U; Nurse.

BRINK, CHRISTOPHER; San Bernardino HS; San Bernardino, CA; (2); 12/367; Debate Tm; Science Clb; Service Clb; Wt Lftg; High Hon Roll; Hon Roll; 1st Pl Inland Empire Sci Fair; Interace Clb; U Of CA; Engrng.

BRINK, KERSTIN; Analy HS; Sebastopol, CA; (4); 20/220; Pres French Clb; Letterman Clb; Teachers Aide; JV Var Tennis; French Hon Soc; High Hon Roll; Pres Acad Fit Awd; Math Awd Outstndng Achvt; CSF Lifetime Mem; CA Schlr Ath; Natl Math League; UC Santa Cruz; Cmptr Engrng.

BRINSON, KATERINA; Alta Loma HS; Cucamonga, CA; (4); 7/520; Acpl Chr; Capt Color Guard; Variety Show; High Hon Roll; Pres Acad Fit Awd; Badmntn JV Cptn, MVP & Vrsty Ltr; Jbs Dghtrs Past Hnrd Qn; Cum Laude Soc; U Of Southern CA; Arch.

BRINTON, HEATHER; Thomas Downey HS; Modesto, CA; (3); Church Yth Grp; Teachers Aide; Acpl Chr; Band; Church Choir; Mrchg Band; Var L Swmmng; Brigham Young U; Engl.

BRION, JOHN N; Village Christian HS; Sun Valley, CA; (2); JV Bsktbl; JV Crs Cntry; Var Trk; Arch.

BRIONES, JENNY G; Casa Roble Fundamental HS; Orangevale, CA; (2); 8/461; Spanish Clb; Var Socr; Cit Awd; High Hon Roll; Cert Recvng Supr Scr Standards Prfcny Tst; Friday Night Live; Ltr Grls Vrsty Sccr.

BRIONES, LAURA M; St Josephs Notre Dame HS; Oakland, CA; (3); JA; Crs Cntry; Swmmng; Trk; JETS Awd; NHS; Lfegrd; San Francisco ST; Nutrition.

BRIONES, SUSAN D; Rosemead HS; Rosemead, CA; (3); New Encounter Club; Med.

BRISBANE, KAREN A; Antioch HS; Antioch, CA; (2); Drama Clb; Hosp Aide; Pep Clb; School Play; Trk; Hon Roll; Antioch Family Fun Center; UC Davis; Med.

BRISBOIS, SUSAN M; Notre Dame HS; San Mateo, CA; (2); Teachers Aide; Var Bsktbl; Hon Roll; Educ.

BRISCOE, CHRISTOPHER P; Los Angeles Baptist HS; Thousand Oaks, CA; (3); Church Yth Grp; English Clb; Hosp Aide; Office Aide; Teachers Aide; Thesps; Varsity Clb; VICA; Chorus; School Play; Psych.

BRISCOE, FORREST S; San Diego HS; San Diego, CA; (3); Church Yth Grp; Cmnty Wkr; Math Tm; Church Choir; VP Jr Cls; Var L Crs Cntry; Var L Trk; High Hon Roll; Ntl Merit Ltr; Rotary Awd.

BRISCOE, HEATHER D; Del Campo HS; Citrus Heights, CA; (3); 122/446; Church Yth Grp; Teachers Aide; Hon Roll; Stu Intrprtr Deaf; Brigham Young U; Elem Ed.

BRISCOE, MONA F; Canyon HS; Monrovia, CA; (3); Church Yth Grp; French Clb; Chorus; Church Choir; School Musical; School Play; Rep Nwsp; Yrbk; Sec Stu Cncl; Vllybl; Cert Of Merit Sci,Spnsh,Photo,Jrnlsm & Stu Of Mnth; Actvts Awd For Chorus,Yrbk & Stu Cncl; CA ST U; Social Work.

BRISCOE-SMITH, ALLEN G; Simi Valley HS; Simi Valley, CA; (3); 6/665; Computer Clb; Office Aide; Ski Clb; Cit Awd; Hon Roll; CSUN; Comp Prgmr.

BRISENO, ALMA; San Fernando HS; San Fernando, CA; (4); Treas French Clb; Rptr FBLA; Science Clb; Ed Yrbk; High Hon Roll; Hon Roll; Prfct Atten Awd; Pres Schlr; MESA; U Of Southern CA; Bus Admin.

BRISENO, FRANK C; Tulare Western HS; Tulare, CA; (3); Model UN; Band; Var Crs Cntry; Var Trk; Var Wrstlng; Hon Roll; Mock Trial; Law.

BRISTOL, JUSTIN; Richard Gahr HS; Norwalk, CA; (4); 22/435; Debate Tm; French Clb; School Musical; School Play; Ftbl; Trk; Wt Lftg; Wrstlng; High Hon Roll; Hon Roll; CF Wrestling; U CA Irvine; Ec.

BRISTOL, PATIENCE M; Apple Valley HS; Apple Valley, CA; (1); Key Clb; Spanish Clb; Rptr Yrbk; High Hon Roll; Hon Roll; CA Schltc Fed; Corp Law.

BRISTOW, MICHELLE R; Lodi HS; Lodi, CA; (3); Church Yth Grp; Band; Church Choir; Drm Mjr(t); Jazz Band; Mrchg Band; Pep Band; Hon Roll; CA Schlrshp Fed; Cert Of Awd Music Theory; Cert Mrt; Branch Hnrs Fstvl; UOP; Piano.

BRITO, JOHN T; Overfelt HS; San Jose, CA; (2); Band; Ftbl; Hon Roll; Prfct Atten Awd; Med.

BRITO, MANUEL; Santa Ana HS; Santa Ana, CA; (2); Computer Clb; Math Clb; Bsktbl; Crs Cntry; Intrml Capt Socr; Jr NHS; Spanish NHS; UCI Partnership Pgm; Future Leaders Of Amer; UCLA; Real Estate.

BRITT, JIMMY A; Inglewood HS; Inglewood, CA; (2); Boy Scts; Church Yth Grp; Band; Church Choir; School Musical; Var Bsktbl; Crs Cntry; Gym; Trk; Cit Awd; Track; Citizenship Award.

BRITT, KATINA D; International Studies Acad; San Francisco, CA; (3); Church Yth Grp; Scholastic Bowl; Bsktbl; Trk; Cit Awd; Hon Roll; UC Berkeley; Law.

BRITT, NAOMI A; Ernest Righetti HS; Santa Maria, CA; (4); 28/349; Var Capt Socr; Var Trk; High Hon Roll; MVP Trk 4 Yrs; Mst Athletic; Stu Athl Of Yr 90; All Northern Leag 1st Tm Sccr; Phys Thrpy.

BRITTAIN, TRICIA L; Red Bluff HS; Red Bluff, CA; (3); Aud/Vis; FCA; Key Clb; Office Aide; Pep Clb; School Musical; Variety Show; Phtg Nwsp; Score Keeper; Trk; Block R B Athltc Club; Steering Cmmtte; CA Polytech SLO; Pltcl Sci.

BRITTIN, TANYA Y; Villa Park HS; Orange, CA; (3); Church Yth Grp; Debate Tm; Sec French Clb; Key Clb; Ski Clb; SADD; Yrbk; Gov Hon Prg Awd; Hon Roll; Jr NHS; Cert Of Merit HS Diploma; Piano Master Class James Barbagallo; Chosn People To People Sci Exch Russia; Stanford; Intl Bus.

BRITTON, RICHARD D; Pinole Valley HS; Pinole, CA; (3); Teachers Aide; Acpl Chr; Swmmng; Waterpolo.

BRITTON, TAMMY S; David Starr Jordan HS; Long Beach, CA; (3); French Clb; Chorus; UCLA; Ed.

BRITTON, TRACEY; Western HS; Anaheim, CA; (4); Am Leg Aux Girls St; Service Clb; Varsity Clb; Treas Stu Cncl; JV Var Cheerldng; High Hon Roll; Hon Roll; Jr NHS; NHS; Youth Spotlight Awd; Stud Yth Cncl; Hugh O'brianyth Fndtn; USC; Bus.

BRIZENDINE, ROBERT; Katella HS; Anaheim, CA; (2); Boy Scts; Cit Awd; Hon Roll; Prfct Atten Awd; PTA Reflections Awd 87 1st Pl Visual Arts Watercolors; Arch.

BRIZIC, JASON A; El Toro HS; El Toro, CA; (3); VP Sr Cls; Var L Ftbl; Var L Trk; Wt Lftg; High Hon Roll; Hon Roll; Civil Air Patrol; Cmptr Sci.

BRIZUELA, ISELA; Morningside HS; Inglewood, CA; (3); Cit Awd; Hon Roll; Loyola Marymount U; Psych.

BRIZUELA, JOSE A; Lynwood HS; Lynwood, CA; (3); Dance Clb; Latin Clb; Bilingual Stu Of Mnth Apr 87-88.

BRIZZI, JOSHUA S; Arlington HS; Riverside, CA; (2); 34/193; Church Yth Grp; Church Choir; School Play; Variety Show; Pres Frsh Cls; JV Bsbl; JV Wrstlng; Cit Awd; Hon Roll; HS Bsbl Team Ivy Leag Chmps & Norti Vista Tourn Chmpns 90; Bsbl Team Capt 89; Stanford.

BROAD, STEVEN E; Lemoore Union HS; Lemoore, CA; (2); Treas Church Yth Grp; Band; Mrchg Band; Pep Band; JV Crs Cntry; JV Socr; JV Tennis; Conserv Clb Treas; Acad Decathlon; U Of CA Santa Barbara; Physics.

BROADBENT, BRIAN P; Mater Dei HS; Anaheim Hills, CA; (2); Church Yth Grp; Ftbl; JV Socr; High Hon Roll; St Schlr; CSF; Notre Dame.

BROADBENT, JO ANN; Palo Verde HS; Blythe, CA; (4); 19/153; Pres Church Yth Grp; Drama Clb; Treas Service Clb; SADD; Yrbk; Stat Wrstlng; Hon Roll; NHS; Elem Schl Tchr.

BROADBENT, SPENCER; Palo Verde HS; Evanston, WY; (2); 1/300; Boy Scts; Church Yth Grp; Drama Clb; Key Clb; School Musical; School Play; Wrstlng; High Hon Roll; NHS; CA Schlrshp Fed Pres; Interact Board Of Directors; Student Body House Of Representatives; Medical Or Physical Doctor.

BROADHEAD, SHERRY; Etiwanda HS; Alta Loma, CA; (2); Pep Clb; Sec Soph Cls; Var Cheerldng; Soph Sec; Bus.

BROADWAY, ELIZABETH; Covenant Christian HS; El Cajon, CA; (2); Church Yth Grp; School Play; Bsktbl; Capt Vllybl; High Hon Roll; Hon Roll; Pres Acad Fit Awd; Schlrshp Awd; Outstndg Chrstn Char Awd; Pres Phy Ftns Awd; Hist.

BROCCHINI, JULIE A; Monterey HS; Monterey, CA; (3); Church Yth Grp; Cmnty Wkr; Model UN; Service Clb; Ski Clb; Teachers Aide; Varsity Clb; Fld Hcky; Stat Ftbl; Powder Puff Ftbl; Parks & Recreation Commission Yth Commisioner; Natural Helper; Math.

BROCHARD, PHILIP T; Skyline HS; Oakland, CA; (2); Church Yth Grp; Intnl Clb; Band; Jazz Band; Orch; Ed Lit Mag; Capt Var Vllybl; Hon Roll; St Schlr.

BROCK, JOHN D; Apple Valley HS; Apple Valley, CA; (2); Church Yth Grp; Key Clb; Spanish Clb; High Hon Roll; Construction Projects In Mexico; U Of CA; Comp.

BROCK, KEITH A; Hanford HS; Hanford, CA; (3); 5/450; Church Yth Grp; FBLA; Office Aide; Teachers Aide; Pres Church Choir; Tennis; High Hon Roll; Ntl Merit Ltr; Stanford; Aerospc Engrng.

BROCK, KEN; Ernest Righetti HS; Santa Maria, CA; (2); French Clb; JV Bsbl; Cit Awd; Hon Roll; Photo Clb; San Diego ST; Sports Med.

BROCK, KRISTINA A; Central Union HS; El Centro, CA; (2); AFS; Church Yth Grp; Debate Tm; Pres 4-H; NFL; Pep Clb; Pres Speech Tm; Drill Tm; Cheerldng; Score Keeper; ASB/Csf Cmmssnr Stu Rep; Tutor For Literacy Vlntrs Amer; GATE Stu; Mock Trial Dfns Atty; Law.

BROCK, NICOLE R; Fred C Beyer HS; Modesto, CA; (3); Church Yth Grp; Church Choir; Hon Roll; U Of The Pacific; Engineering.

BROCKINGTON, ANTHONY J; Edison HS; Stockton, CA; (2); Teachers Aide; Off Frsh Cls; Off Jr Cls; JV Bsbl; JV Capt Socr; JV Trk; Hon Roll; Sci Camp Counselor Mrt Awd; Golden St Exam Geom Recognition Awd; GATE; Comp Engrng.

BROCKMAN, ADAM S; Granada Hills HS; Granada Hills, CA; (2); FHA; Quiz Bowl; Ski Clb; Teachers Aide; Temple Yth Grp; JV Ftbl; JV Swmmng; Cit Awd; High Hon Roll; Hon Roll; UCLA; Corp Lawyer.

BROCKMAN, ALISE M; Trabuco Hills HS; Mission Viejo, CA; (2); 30/415; JV Sftbl; Hon Roll; NHS; St Schlr; High Hnrs Golden St Exam Algebra 1.

BROCKMAN, KIM; Woodrow Wilson HS; Long Beach, CA; (4); 1/800; Office Aide; Pres Soph Cls; Off Jr Cls; Off Sr Cls; Sec Stu Cncl; NHS; Pres Acad Fit Awd; Val; Capt Var Cheerldng; Var Socr; St Sccr Team; Assisteens; Pomona Coll; Intl Relations.

BROCKMAN, TED; Arroyo HS; San Leandro, CA; (4); FBLA; Drm Mjr(t); Jazz Band; Pep Band; Capt Tennis; High Hon Roll; Acad All-Amer; Jr All Amer Hall Of Fame; Bank Of Amer Acad Awd; Cogswell Coll; Music Engr Tech.

BROCKNEY, LISA M; Lincoln HS; Stockton, CA; (3); 60/538; Mu Alpha Theta; Spanish Clb; SADD; Teachers Aide; JV Socr; Stat Wrstlng; Hon Roll; Chem.

BROCKWAY, ALEX; Daniel Murphy HS; Los Angeles, CA; (3); Tennis; Congrssnl Yth Ldrshp Cncl; Math Achvt Awd; Math 1st Hnrs; Engrng.

BRODER, TAMARA; Palm Desert HS; Palm Desert, CA; (4); 4/359; Hosp Aide; Teachers Aide; Var Bsktbl; JV Gym; Pres Var Trk; Hon Roll; Kiwanis Awd; Acad Dcthln 89; MIP Bsktbl 86-89; Bus Admin.

BRODERICK, ALICIA M; Canyon HS; Canyon Country, CA; (2); SADD; Pep Clb; Drill Tm; Hon Roll; Jr NHS; Pres Acad Fit Awd; Amnesty Intl; UCLA; Doctor.

BRODERSON, TAHRA C; College Park HS; Concord, CA; (3); 27/350; Cmnty Wkr; Drama Clb; Pres French Clb; Pep Clb; Service Clb; Teachers Aide; Drill Tm; Lit Mag; Hon Roll; Ntl Merit Ltr; Slctd Phi Delta Kappa Smmr Inst Tchng; Yth Ed For 1989-90; Hnrs Gldn ST Exam Geom; Trinty U; Engl.

BRODERSON, TARA; College Park HS; Concord, CA; (3); 27/300; Art Clb; Cmnty Wkr; Drama Clb; Pres French Clb; Hon Roll; Ntl Merit Ltr; Yth Eductr 89-90; Hnrs Gldn St Exam Geom; Tutor Engl & Frnch; Accptnc Phi Dela Kappas Smmr Inst; Trinity U; Engl.

BRODEUR, TIM P; Placer HS; Auburn, CA; (2); French Clb; Key Clb; JV Crs Cntry; JV Trk; JV Cross Country Ski Team; HS Century Club Top 100 Stus Academically.

BRODHAGEN, BRENT R; Garden Grove HS; Garden Grove, CA; (3); 88/366; Var L Ftbl; Prncpls Hnr Roll; Comp Sci.

BRODIE, DALE R; Buena HS; Ventura, CA; (1); Computer Clb; Phtg Yrbk; High Hon Roll; Hon Roll; UC Santa Barbara; Auto Engr.

BRODIE, RICHARD D; Alta Loma HS; Alta Loma, CA; (2); Band; JV L Ftbl; L Socr; JV Var Wt Lftg; High Hon Roll; Most Valuable Defensive Ftball Player; UCLA.

BRODIE, RUBERT E; Berkeley HS; Berkeley, CA; (4); Cmnty Wkr; Ed Nwsp; Pres Jr Cls; JV Bsbl; JV Ftbl; Yth Pr Cnslr; UC Irvine; Psych.

BRODIE, SHERRY; Del Campo HS; Fair Oaks, CA; (3); 31/450; Pep Clb; Var L Cheerldng; L Diving; NHS; Vet.

BRODOSKI, SHAWN M; South Valley HS; Ukiah, CA; (4); Boy Scts; Band; Med.

BRODY, BRAD A; Rowland HS; Rowland Hts, CA; (4); Boy Scts; Church Yth Grp; Crs Cntry; Mgr(s); Trk; Hon Roll; Gldnst Geom Hnrs & Alg Hi Hnrs; 55 & 56 Classic Chryslers Owner & Driver; Citrus Coll; Auto Body/Paint.

BROGAN, TINA; Hanford HS; Hanford, CA; (3); 7/511; Church Yth Grp; FBLA; Band; Mrchg Band; Pep Band; High Hon Roll; Acad Ltr Awd; Mc Donalds Schlr Awd; Acad Decathlon; Phrmclgy.

BROHARD, JOHN W; Glendale Adventist Acad; Tujunga, CA; (2); 11/53; Letterman Clb; Pres Soph Cls; Off Jr Cls; Var Ftbl; Cit Awd; Hon Roll; NHS; Pres Acad Fit Awd; Walla Walla Coll; Dntst.

BROITMAN, EDWARD M; Granada Hills HS; Northridge, CA; (2); Ski Clb; Varsity Clb; JV Ftbl; Var L Socr; Hon Roll; Pres Acad Fit Awd; UCLA; Law.

BROKAW, DAVID C; Rancho Cotate HS; Rohnert Park, CA; (4); 9/280; Am Leg Boys St; Boy Scts; Church Yth Grp; French Clb; Ski Clb; School Play; Var Golf; High Hon Roll; NHS; U-19 Select Soccer Tm; San Francisco Bay Area Engrs Week Awd; CSF Sealbearer; Cal Poly SLO; Civil Engr.

BROKCMOLLER, KRISTI L; Poway HS; Poway, CA; (2); Orch.

BROMBY, HOLLY; Atascadero HS; Atascadero, CA; (3); Office Aide; SADD; Drill Tm; Hon Roll.

BROMFIELD, TIFFANY C; Point Loma HS; San Diego, CA; (4); Key Clb; School Musical; Stu Cncl; Cheerldng; Rotary Awd; Voice Dem Awd; SFSU; Urban Planner.

BROMLEY, TRENT M; North Tahoe HS; Incline Village, NV; (3); 19/60; JV Bsktbl; JV Ftbl; Hon Roll; Art, Crmcs & Gtr; Music.

BROMMERICH, PAUL W; Lincoln HS; Lincoln, CA; (3); 12/145; JV Ftbl; Var Capt Wrstlng; Hon Roll; Vrsty Wrstlng MVP 89; Stu Of Mnt 89; All Metro Wrstlng Team 90.

BROMSTEAD, SCOTT; Monte Vista HS; Alamo, CA; (3); Cmnty Wkr; Ski Clb; Var Crs Cntry; Var Socr; JV Trk; Hon Roll; Jr NHS; NHS; Pre-Med.

BRONSON, CHRISTOPHER; Woodrow Wilson HS; Signal Hill, CA; (3); Church Yth Grp; Bsbl; Bsktbl; Ftbl; Hon Roll; Prfct Atten Awd; Pres Acad Fit Awd.

BRONSON, LORI; Glen A Wilson HS; Hacienda Hts, CA; (3); 77/426; Church Yth Grp; Cmnty Wkr; Band; Mrchg Band; Hon Roll; Acctg.

BRONSON, SCOTT A; Henry M Gunn SR HS; Palo Alto, CA; (3); Boy Scts; 4-H; Stage Crew; Nwsp; Crs Cntry; Comp.

BROOKE, HEATHER; Folsom HS; Folsom, CA; (3); Model UN; Pep Clb; Acpl Chr; Chorus; School Musical; School Play; Ed Nwsp; Stu Cncl; Cheerldng; High Hon Roll; Peer Tutrng; Peer Cnslng; Hugh O'brian Yth Fndtn; San Diego ST; Brdcst Jrnlsm.

BROOKE, LOUANNE; Folsom HS; Folsom, CA; (2); 6/235; Model UN; Pep Clb; AFS; Yrbk; Pres Frsh Cls; Rep Soph Cls; Cheerldng; Trk; High Hon Roll; Ntrl Hlprs-Peer Cnslng Pgm.

BROOKS, AMY M; Thomas Downey HS; Modesto, CA; (2); Sec Chess Clb; Church Yth Grp; Key Clb; NFL; Speech Tm; Band; Mrchg Band; Sec Jr Cls; JV Crs Cntry; Hon Roll; CA Schlrshp Fed; Brigham Young U; Med.

BROOKS, CHRISTINE J; Roseville HS; Roseville, CA; (1); Church Yth Grp; Drama Clb; Friday Night Live Clb; Acad Mrt Awd; Engl Teacher.

BROOKS, CYNTHEA; Riverdale HS; Riverdale, CA; (4); 2/70; FFA; Sec Letterman Clb; Science Clb; Ski Clb; SADD; Sec Sr Cls; VP Stu Cncl; Capt Bsktbl; Var Tennis; High Hon Roll; Mid Yr Yth Conf Chrmn; Fresno ST.

BROOKS, DAVID A; Healdsburg HS; Windsor, CA; (4); 16/241; Math Tm; SADD; Teachers Aide; Rep Soph Cls; Rep Jr Cls; Var Bsktbl; Var Vllybl; High Hon Roll; Boy Scts; Geom Golden St Exam Hnrs; Outdoor Educ Cnslr; Saferides Pgm; U CA San Diego; Engrng.

BROOKS, DENA R; Saddleback HS; Santa Ana, CA; (2); Spanish Clb; Chorus; Off Soph Cls; Var Bsktbl; Score Keeper; JV Sftbl; JV Vllybl; Schl Mascot-Roadrunner Beep-Beep; BSU; SDSU; Bus Adm.

BROOKS, DONOVAN W; San Bernardino HS; Riverside, CA; (3); 24/472; Var Bsbl; Var Ftbl; Hon Roll; Bus.

BROOKS, JENNIFER A; Pinole Valley HS; Pinole, CA; (2); Teachers Aide; Stage Crew; Hon Roll; Diablo Valley JC; Lawyer.

BROOKS, JEREMY RYAN; Kingsburg HS; Kingsburg, CA; (3); Church Yth Grp; FCA; FFA; Math Clb; Mu Alpha Theta; Spanish Clb; SADD; Treas Jr Cls; Bsktbl; Ftbl; Dfnsv Mst Vlbl Lnmn; Mdcl.

BROOKS, JUSTIN W; Wilcox HS; Sunnyvale, CA; (1); JV Bsbl; JV Bsktbl; Hon Roll; MVP, 1st Team All Leag Bsktbl; 2nd Team All Leag Bsbl; GATE Pgm Stu; UCLA; Engrng.

BROOKS, LAURA; Canyon Springs HS; Moreno Valley, CA; (2); Church Yth Grp; Drama Clb; FBLA; Key Clb; Cheerldng; Swmmng; High Hon Roll; Hon Roll; NHS; U C Irvine; Psycn.

BROOKS, LESLEY A; Point Arena HS; Gualala, CA; (2); Girl Scts; Sec Frsh Cls; Pres Soph Cls; Var Sftbl; JV Capt Vllybl; High Hon Roll; CSF; Elem Schl Tchr.

BROOKS, LESLIE; Upland HS; Upland, CA; (4); 1/600; AFS; Church Yth Grp; Cmnty Wkr; Model UN; Red Cross Aide; High Hon Roll; Hon Roll; Ntl Merit Ltr; Pres Acad Fit Awd; Acad Decthln; Scl Sci, Sci & Ecnmcs Awds; Shakespear On Tour Prfrmng; BYU; Comp Sci.

BROOKS, MAYA A; John Muir HS; Altadena, CA; (2); Church Yth Grp; Cmnty Wkr; Math Clb; Science Clb; Acpl Chr; Band; Church Choir; Mrchg Band; Orch; Pep Band.

BROOKS, MICHAEL C; Etiwanda HS; Rancho Cucamonga, CA; (2); Church Yth Grp; VICA; JV Ftbl; JV Trk; Wt Lftg; High Hon Roll; Hon Roll; Alta Loam Brethren In Christ Church Yth Grp; POMC; GATE; Hnrs Pgm; Arch.

BROOKS, NATALIE; Charter Oak HS; Covina, CA; (3); 50/400; Var Co-Capt Pep Clb; Ski Clb; Off Jr Cls; Var Capt Cheerldng; Hon Roll; Gold Mdlst Figure Staking; Prncpls Hnr Roll; CA Schlrshp Fed; Long Beach ST U; Bus.

BROOKS, OMEGA R; Skyline HS; Oakland, CA; (2); Chorus; School Musical; Rep Frsh Cls; Rep Stu Cncl; Cit Awd; Howard U.

BROOKS, PATRICIA; Hueneme HS; Oxnard, CA; (2); Church Yth Grp; GAA; Chorus; Church Choir; Bsktbl; Mgr(s); Trk.

BROOKS, SARAH; Rubidoux HS; Mira Loma, CA; (3); 6/800; Cmnty Wkr; Pep Clb; Acpl Chr; Rep Frsh Cls; Sec Soph Cls; Sec Jr Cls; Sec Stu Cncl; JV Var Cheerldng; Var Pom Pon; Rotary Awd; Music Clb Sec; Hnr Roll; Assoctd Stu Bdy; Madrigals.

BROOKS, SHANNON R; American HS; Fremont, CA; (3); Drama Clb; Pres 4-H; French Clb; Quiz Bowl; Lit Mag; Hon Roll; ESL Stu Tutor; Schl Plys Makeup Artst; Sci Fair Wnnr; St Marys Coll; Chem.

BROOKS, TONYA R; Edison HS; Huntington Bch, CA; (4); 60/500; Church Yth Grp; Drama Clb; German Clb; Ski Clb; Teachers Aide; Cheerldng; Capt Pom Pon; High Hon Roll; Hon Roll; Pres Acad Fit Awd; Alternate In Alcea Scholarship; Cal Poly San Luis Obispo; Biolg.

BROOM JR, DAVE; Mayfair HS; Bellflower, CA; (1); Art Clb; Boy Scts; Church Yth Grp; JA; School Play; Off Frsh Cls; Intrml Wt Lftg; Cit Awd; Hon Roll; Swmmng, Golf & Actng; Soccer, Vlybl, Sftbl & Track; US Navy; Med.

BROOMALL, TRAVIS T; Morro Bay HS; Los Osos, CA; (3); 71/238; Church Yth Grp; Cmnty Wkr; JV Var Bsktbl; JV Score Keeper; Hon Roll; Srfng, Wrkng; Psychlgy.

BROOME, LIZA; Canyon HS; Canyon Country, CA; (3); Church Yth Grp; Dance Clb; Drama Clb; Pep Clb; Spanish Clb; SADD; Varsity Clb; Drill Tm; School Play; Rep Stu Cncl; Peer Cnslng; Campus After Dark; Psych.

BROST, TRACY; Rosary HS; Yorba Linda, CA; (3); Sec Computer Clb; Science Clb; Band; School Play; High Hon Roll; Mck Trial; CA Schlrshp Fdrtn-CSF; Accntng.

BROTHERS, DAVID; Fontana HS; Fontana, CA; (2); Church Yth Grp; French Clb; Treas Science Clb; Chorus; Church Choir; Yrbk; JV Tennis; Hon Roll; Jr NHS; Goldn ST Exam F/Geomtry; Law.

BROTHERS, KRISTIN; Santa Rosa HS; Santa Rosa, CA; (4); VP JA; VP Key Clb; Pres Spanish Clb; Acpl Chr; Nwsp; Yrbk; Treas Frsh Cls; Treas Soph Cls; Treas Jr Cls; Treas Sr Cls; CSF Lftm Membrshp; Fnlst Press Dmcrts Yth Svc Awds; Saferides; OR U; Jrnlsm.

BROU, ALISA D; Pasadena HS; Pasadena, CA; (4); 43/433; Dance Clb; Office Aide; Ski Clb; Variety Show; Pres Sr Cls; Bsktbl; Mgr(s); Swmmng; Hon Roll; YWCA Second Century Award; LA County Youth Of The Year; Associate Student Body Award; Xavier U; English Attorney.

BROUDY, ABRAHAM; Bonita Vista HS; Chula Vista, CA; (4); 1/522; Key Clb; Variety Show; Ed Yrbk; Pres Stu Cncl; NHS; Pres Acad Fit Awd; Teachers Aide; Hon Roll; Jr NHS; Freedoms Fndtn Vly Forge Prtcpnt; Dartmouth Clg Outstnd Jr Awd; Trinity Clg Music Lndn Exam Pss W/Hnrs; Dr.

BROUGHTON, GARRETT; Fairfield HS; Fairfield, CA; (3); Boy Scts; Chess Clb; French Clb; Var Tennis; French Hon Soc; Hon Roll; Jr NHS; NHS; Prfct Atten Awd; Pres Acad Fit Awd.

BROUILLETTE, AUBRE K; Hemet HS; Idyllwild, CA; (2); Hosp Aide; Chorus; Hon Roll; Bullupu Hnr Awd 88-89; Engl Achvt; Marine Bio.

BROUSSARD, GINA; Mariposa HS; Catheys Valley, CA; (2); JV Var Cheerldng; Hon Roll; Med.

BROUSSARD, MICHAEL D; Pasadena HS; Pasadena, CA; (2); Cmnty Wkr; Sec Debate Tm; Pep Clb; Scholastic Bowl; Sec Speech Tm; Treas Acpl Chr; Treas Chorus; Nwsp; Hon Roll; LA Cnty Sci Fair 2nd Pl Physics Div; Marine Sci.

BROUSSARD, SHANDREA R; Liberty Union HS; Oakley, CA; (1); 48/444; Dance Clb; Debate Tm; Drama Clb; Speech Tm; SADD; Variety Show; Pres Frsh Cls; Rep Stu Cncl; Swmmng; Hon Roll; Brentwood Cmnty Theatre Prfrmnt Arts Acad; Entertainment.

BROUSSEAU, GUY B; Morro Bay HS; Los Osos, CA; (4); 35/244; Boy Scts; Drama Clb; Jazz Band; Var Bsbl; JV Crs Cntry; Wrstlng; Hon Roll; Prfct Atten Awd; Pres Classroom; Cuesta Coll.

BROUWER, KIMBERLY; Sanger HS; Arroyo Grande, CA; (3); 1/350; AFS; Church Yth Grp; Sec VP Computer Clb; Sec Model UN; NFL; ROTC; Science Clb; Off Nwsp; Stu Cncl; Val; Bnk Of Amer Plaque, 3rd Pl Lbrl Arts; Flute Choir/Piano; UC Berkeley; Biolgcl Sci.

BROVELLI, MICHELE L; San Rafael HS; San Rafael, CA; (2); 45/256; Cmnty Wkr; SADD; Var Bsktbl; Var Socr; Var Sftbl; Var Capt Vllybl; First Tm All Lge MCAL; N Cst Sctn CIF Schlr Athlt; Hnrbl Mtn MCAL; MVP Bsktbl; Grls Sprstr Cmp.

BROWER, RAYNA; Riverside Poly HS; Palmdale, CA; (4); Church Yth Grp; Intnl Clb; Key Clb; Service Clb; Hon Roll.

BROWER, ROBERT K; Montgomery HS; Santa Rosa, CA; (3); 45/400; Church Yth Grp; Pep Clb; Science Clb; Treas Sr Cls; Var Capt Cheerldng; Hon Roll; Prfct Atten Awd; Gldn St Exam Geom Hgh Hnrs, Alg Hnrs; UC San Diego; Mech Engrng.

BROWN, ABIGAIL; Torrey Pines HS; Del Mar, CA; (2); 21/503; Office Aide; Sftbl; JV Tennis; High Hon Roll; CSF; Gldn St Exam Math High Hnrs; Comp.

BROWN, AHDAM O; Oaklan Technical HS; Oakland, CA; (3); Church Yth Grp; Var Trk; JV Wrstlng; Hon Roll; U C Davis; Corporate Law.

BROWN, AIMEE L; Warren HS; Downey, CA; (3); Church Yth Grp; Teachers Aide; Chorus; Swing Chorus; Psych.

BROWN, ALANA J; St Pats St Vincents HS; Vallejo, CA; (1); Church Yth Grp; Cmnty Wkr; Drama Clb; Office Aide; Teachers Aide; Chorus; Church Choir; Yrbk; Bsktbl; Hon Roll; Oral Roberts U; Pediatrics.

BROWN, ALEXANDER STEVENSON; Torrey Pines HS; San Diego, CA; (2); Boy Scts; Library Aide; Thesps; Band; Jazz Band; Mrchg Band; Pep Band; School Musical; JV Bsktbl; Hon Roll; UC Davis; Jrnlsm.

BROWN, ALISHIA; Crenshaw HS; Los Angeles, CA; (2); Church Yth Grp; Dance Clb; Model UN; Teachers Aide; Prfct Atten Awd; Mdlng; Mst Achvts; Art.

BROWN, ALLISON J; San Diego HS; Poway, CA; (3); Dance Clb; SADD; Hon Roll; Ballet CA Schl Of Ballet; Modern Dance Palamar Coll; Trips To Tijuana Orphanage; Homeless Work; Soc Work.

BROWN, AMANDA L; Sir Francis Drake HS; Pataluma, CA; (2); Hon Roll; Goldn St Exam Outstndng Prfrmnce/Schl Recgntn 1st Yr Alg; Sonoma ST U CA.

BROWN, AMIE; Beyer HS; Modesto, CA; (2); Drama Clb; Cit Awd; Hon Roll; Teenage Republicans; Sch Plays, Crew & Acting; GATE; Med.

BROWN, AMY; Modesto HS; Modesto, CA; (2); Pep Clb; Score Keeper; Sftbl; Vllybl; High Hon Roll; Hon Roll; Stu Curriculum Cmmtte; CA Schlrshp Fndtn.

BROWN, AMY E; Fresno Christian HS; Fresno, CA; (2); Color Guard; Mrchg Band; JV Tennis; Hon Roll; Barbizon Schl Grad; Fresno St U; Physcl Thrpy.

BROWN, AMY R; Monte Vista HS; Spring Valley, CA; (3); 177/373; Church Yth Grp; Office Aide; Church Choir; Military Corpsman.

BROWN, ARIANA SUDEL; Marymount Schl; Los Angeles, CA; (4); Church Yth Grp; Cmnty Wkr; French Clb; Red Cross Aide; Service Clb; Varsity Clb; Stu Cncl; Bsktbl; Swmmng; Cit Awd; ROTC Stu/Athl Awd; Marymount Alumnae Awd 90; Bank Of Amer Achvt Frgn Lang Awd; Stanford U; Intl Reltns.

BROWN, AUTUMN; Calvary Chapel HS; Santa Ana, CA; (2); Acpl Chr; Color Guard; Stat Bsktbl; Cheerldng; Mgr(s); Score Keeper; Hon Roll; Westmont U; Lit Ed.

BROWN, BONNIE J; Hawthorne HS; Hawthorne, CA; (2); Treas Key Clb; Teachers Aide; High Hon Roll; High Honors Golden St Exam Geom; Doctor.

BROWN, BRIAN; Mc Farland HS; Delano, CA; (4); 40/100; Boy Scts; Church Yth Grp; FFA; Teachers Aide; Bsbl; Crs Cntry; Mgr(s); Tennis; Vllybl; Cit Awd; FFA Officer; Awd Wnr In Vctnl Ag; Bakersfield Coll; Law.

BROWN, BRIANA E; John Marshall Fundamental HS; Altadena, CA; (3); Capt Debate Tm; Pres Drama Clb; Model UN; Capt Speech Tm; Teachers Aide; Church Choir; Stat Bsktbl; Stat Ftbl; Stat Trk; Cit Awd; Spellman Coll; Pltcl Sci.

BROWN, BTAKA T L; Lower Lake HS; Clearlake Oaks, CA; (4); 15/165; JV Am Leg Boys St; Cmnty Wkr; Dance Clb; Drama Clb; JA; Letterman Clb; ROTC; Spanish Clb; Varsity Clb; Chorus; Native Amer Stu Assn Pres 90; Plyr Of Week Bsktbl 90; Plyr Of Game Chmpnshp Ftbl 90; Humbolt ST U; Tchr.

BROWN, CANDICE; St Joseph HS; Downey, CA; (2); 6/196; Cmnty Wkr; GAA; Service Clb; Drill Tm; Variety Show; Var Cheerldng; High Hon Roll; Hon Roll; CSF; Assisteens; Sci/Math Honor Stu; Loyola Marymount U; Medcl.

BROWN, CERI E; University City HS; San Diego, CA; (3); 49/373; Church Yth Grp; Cmnty Wkr; Computer Clb; Math Tm; Science Clb; SADD; High Hon Roll; Ntl Merit SF; Acadmc Dcthln; Acadmc Leag JV; Microbio.

BROWN, CHALON E; Rim Of The World HS; Running Springs, CA; (1); 11/435; Pres Church Yth Grp; Dance Clb; Church Choir; Rep Frsh Cls; JV Vllybl; High Hon Roll; NHS; Schlr Athlete; CA Schlrshp Fed; JR Statesmen Of Amer; Brigham Yng U.

BROWN, CHANDRA R; Mc Clymonds HS; Oakland, CA; (3); AFS; Debate Tm; Intnl Clb; Letterman Clb; Chorus; Nwsp; Rep Frsh Cls; Sec Jr Cls; Sec Stu Cncl; Score Keeper; Natl Assn Negro Bus Prfssnl Wmn Yth Awd; Wiley Manual Law Fndtn Moot Crt Semifnlst; Upward Bound 1st; Stanford; Law.

BROWN, CHARLES A; Servite HS; Seal Beach, CA; (2); 9/160; Service Clb; Phtg Yrbk; NHS; Long Beach Rowing Assn Jr Crew; CSF; Jr Statesman Of Amer; Space Sci.

BROWN, CHIP; San Ramon Valley HS; Danville, CA; (2); Hon Roll; Engrng.

BROWN, CHRISTINA L; Sutter Union HS; Yuba City, CA; (3); FBLA; Cheerldng; Pom Pon; Trk; Friday Night Live; Yuba Coll; Dietican.

BROWN, CHRISTINE D; Tehachapi HS; Tehachapi, CA; (3); Church Yth Grp; Treas FHA; Chorus; Flag Corp; Hon Roll; Poetry Cntst; Santa Cruz; Zoology.

BROWN, CHRISTOPHER JOHN-THOMAS; El Toro HS; El Toro, CA; (2); 30/557; Church Yth Grp; Cmnty Wkr; Drama Clb; Key Clb; School Play; Var Capt Tennis; High Hon Roll; OCAD Mem 2 Yrs; 1st Orange Cnty,4th ST Fnls Hstry Day 90; YMCA Yth/Govt/Model Leg Senator.

BROWN, CHRISTOPHER M; San Gorgonio HS; Highland, CA; (4); 149/550; English Clb; Letterman Clb; Science Clb; Teachers Aide; Var Bsbl; Var Crs Cntry; Var Wrstlng; Hon Roll; 1st Tm All CBL Bsbl; CA ST San Bernardino.

BROWN, CHRISTOPHER R; Burroughs HS; Ridgecrest, CA; (2); Bsbl; Ftbl.

BROWN, CHRISTY; Linden HS; Stockton, CA; (3); 7/155; Am Leg Aux Girls St; Debate Tm; Drama Clb; French Clb; GAA; JA; Letterman Clb; Q&S; Speech Tm; Rptr Nwsp; JSA Stanford Smmr Schl Grad; Pltcl Sci.

BROWN, CLIFTON CRAIG; Ukiah HS; Ukiah, CA; (3); 2/439; Spanish Clb; SADD; Band; Mrchg Band; School Musical; Stage Crew; Treas Soph Cls; Treas Stu Cncl; JV Var Tennis; High Hon Roll; HOBY Ldrshp Smnr; CSF; 1st Chr Flute Band; Stanford U; Chem.

BROWN, COLLEEN D; St Francis HS; Los Altos, CA; (1); SADD; School Musical; JV Diving; Var L Gym; Mgr(s); Stat Socr; Intrml Vllybl; Hon Roll; ACIS; Drama Most Outstndng Newcomer Awd; Outstndng Drama I Stu; Vrsty Gymnastics MVP; Drama.

BROWN, DAMON; St Bernard Catholic HS; Los Angeles, CA; (3); Chess Clb; Hon Roll; UCLA; Elec Eng.

BROWN, DAVID J; Oak Grove HS; San Jose, CA; (2); Cmnty Wkr; Stage Crew; Educ.

BROWN, DAVID T; Trinity HS; Weaverville, CA; (3); 16/100; Church Yth Grp; Hon Roll; Point Loma Nazarene; Bible.

BROWN, DENISE M; Quincy JR SR HS; Quincy, CA; (2); Sec Spanish Clb; Speech Tm; Rep Stu Cncl; Bsktbl; Swmmng; Trk; Vllybl; Cit Awd; High Hon Roll; Pres Acad Fit Awd; CA Schlrshp Fed; Dance Instrctr; UCSD; Med.

BROWN, DENISE M; Tracy HS; Tracy, CA; (2); 58/483; 4-H; Color Guard; Flag Corp; JV Gym; 4-H Awd; High Hon Roll; Hon Roll; CSF; Hiking Club; Elem Tchr.

BROWN, EDDIE; Live Oak HS; Live Oak, CA; (3); 1/90; Teachers Aide; Var Capt Bsbl; JV Var Bsktbl; Var Capt Ftbl; Cit Awd; Gov Hon Prg Awd; High Hon Roll; Hon Roll; Prfct Atten Awd; Pres Acad Fit Awd; Acadmc Excllnc Club Pres; CSF Pres; UCD; Med.

BROWN, ELAYNE; Santa Cruz HS; Santa Cruz, CA; (1); Church Yth Grp; Church Choir; Mrchg Band; Rep Stu Cncl; JV Capt Bsktbl; Score Keeper; JV Sftbl; Var Trk; JV Bsktbl Capt; Var Bsktbl; Stanford U; Chld Psych.

BROWN, ELISABETH R; Livermore HS; Livermore, CA; (3); 1/320; Chorus; School Musical; Pres Frsh Cls; Pres Soph Cls; VP Pres Stu Cncl; Var Socr; Var Tennis; Rotary Awd; Poltcl Sci.

BROWN, ERIC C; Santa Marqurita HS; El Toro, CA; (3); 90/230; Cmnty Wkr; Stu Cncl; JV Bsktbl; Var Ftbl; All League Saftey Football; Team Defensive Player Year; Hnrb Mntn Orange Co Engineering Fair; Naval Academy; Engineering.

BROWN, ERIC H; San Dimas HS; San Dimas, CA; (3); 5/350; Sec VICA; School Play; Hon Roll.

BROWN, ERICA A; Santa Rosa HS; Santa Rosa, CA; (4); Church Yth Grp; Speech Tm; Teachers Aide; Acpl Chr; Chorus; Church Choir; Variety Show; Leopold Wrasse Schlrshp; CA Grnt A; Cal Plytchnc; Fd Sci.

BROWN, ERIN C; Rim Of The World HS; Running Springs, CA; (3); 18/296; Am Leg Aux Girls St; Pres Church Yth Grp; Cmnty Wkr; French Clb; GAA; Letterman Clb; Varsity Clb; Church Choir; Ed Yrbk; Off Frsh Cls; Athletic Schlr; CA Schlrshp Fed Treas; Clb Vllybl; Advrtsng.

BROWN, ERIN M; John F Kennedy HS; Granada Hills, CA; (3); Key Clb; Co-Capt Pep Clb; VP Service Clb; Ski Clb; Rep Frsh Cls; Rep Jr Cls; VP Stu Cncl; Co-Capt Cheerldng; High Hon Roll; Pres Acad Fit Awd; Stanford U; Cmmnctns.

BROWN, EVYONE; Gardena HS; Rialto, CA; (3); School Musical; Stu Cncl; Golf; Cit Awd; Hon Roll.

BROWN, GARY D; Washington HS; Los Angeles, CA; (2); Teachers Aide; Band; School Musical; Stage Crew; Off Jr Cls; Hon Roll; Pres Acad Fit Awd; Music Awd; UCLA; Bus Mgmt.

BROWN, GINA C; Highlands HS; Sacramento, CA; (2); Art Clb; SADD; Nwsp; Yrbk; Cit Awd; Hon Roll; Prfct Atten Awd; Sociology.

BROWN, GREG M; Piedmont HS; Piedmont, CA; (3); Boy Scts; Church Yth Grp; Pres Model UN; Red Cross Aide; Science Clb; JV Var Ftbl; Vrsty Crew.

BROWN, GREGORY SCOTT; Poway HS; San Diego, CA; (4); 45/728; Varsity Clb; Var L Ftbl; Var L Golf; Var L Socr; NHS; St Schlr; CSF; Athltc Awd; U CA Davis; Math.

BROWN, GRETCHEN L; Nevada Union HS; Nevada City, CA; (3); Teachers Aide; JV Var Mgr(s); JV Var Swmmng; Hon Roll; Intl Order Rainbow; San Jose ST U; Chld Dvlpmnt.

BROWN, HEATHER; 29 Palms HS; Twentynine Palm, CA; (4); 2/138; Church Yth Grp; Band; Drm Mjr(t); Mrchg Band; Orch; Stu Cncl; Jr NHS; NHS; Pres Acad Fit Awd; Sal; VA Tech; Engrng.

BROWN, HEATHER; Oakmont HS; Roseville, CA; (1); High Hon Roll.

BROWN, JACQUELINE D; Luther Burbank HS; Sacramento, CA; (1); 141/494; Church Yth Grp; Red Cross Aide; ROTC; Church Choir; Trk; Trck Vrsty Awd-1 ROTC Yr Completion Cert; Study Skills/Productv Advrtsng Awd; Howard; Engr.

BROWN, JAMES C; Corona HS; Corona, CA; (4); 2/561; Boy Scts; High Hon Roll; Ntl Merit Schol; Pres Acad Fit Awd; Sal; CSF; Eagle Sct; Bnk Amer Engl Awd; US Air Force Math & Sci Awd; U Of S CA; Aeronaut Engrng.

BROWN, JAMIE T; Covina HS; West Covina, CA; (3); 1/250; Church Yth Grp; Cmnty Wkr; Model UN; Church Choir; Stu Cncl; High Hon Roll; Intl Mrktng.

BROWN, JAMIESON S; Whittier Christian HS; Whittier, CA; (2); French Clb; Whittier Chrstn Piano Clb Chrmn 89-90; Intl Wnnr Natl Piano Playing Audtns Sectn D 90; U Paris-Sorbonne; Bio Sci.

BROWN, JAMILA F; Santa Maria HS; Santa Maria, CA; (3); 56/467; Church Yth Grp; Church Choir; Powder Puff Ftbl; Black Stu Union; Piano Awd Cert; Pepperdine U; Bus Admin.

BROWN, JASON K; Chaffey HS; Ontario, CA; (1); Art Clb; French Clb; Chorus; Nwsp; Crs Cntry; Trk; Wrstlng; Pres Acad Fit Awd; Judo; Boxing; Psych.

BROWN, JEANETTE E; Trinity HS; Weaverville, CA; (1); 3/100; Church Yth Grp; Vllybl; High Hon Roll; Hon Roll.

BROWN, JEFFREY; San Ramon Valley HS; Danville, CA; (3); 13/435; FBLA; Band; Mrchg Band; High Hon Roll; Princpls Schl Muscn Awd; Pilot License; Outstndng Acad Achvt Awd; Comm Pilot.

BROWN, JEFFREY G; John F Kennedy HS; Granada Hills, CA; (2); Boy Scts; Key Clb; JV Bsbl; JV Ftbl; Surfing; Waterskiing; Eagle Sct; MBA.

BROWN, JENNIE; Nevada Union HS; Penn Valley, CA; (3); FFA; Letterman Clb; Crs Cntry; High Hon Roll; Hon Roll; Dressage.

BROWN, JERAMY W; South HS; Bakersfield, CA; (3); Var Socr; Cit Awd; Hon Roll; UCLA; Eng.

BROWN, JEREMY L; Enterprise HS; Redding, CA; (3); 8/425; Model UN; Mu Alpha Theta; Capt Quiz Bowl; Capt Scholastic Bowl; Capt Science Clb; Ed Yrbk; JV Ftbl; Var L Wrstlng; DAR Awd; High Hon Roll; Sci Olympd Gold Medal; PG&E Stu Semester Bio; Stanford U; Hstry.

BROWN, JESSICA L; Kerman HS; Kerman, CA; (3); 19/289; Church Yth Grp; Color Guard; Flag Corp; Mrchg Band; Yrbk; Hon Roll; Pride Awd Engl II & Colorguard; Simson Coll; Chld Educ.

BROWN, JOHN T; Village Christian HS; Sun Valley, CA; (3); Church Yth Grp; Drama Clb; Science Clb; Spanish Clb; School Play; Bsbl; Bsktbl; Crs Cntry; Trk; Rcrtnl Admin.

BROWN, JULIE A; C K Mc Clatchy HS; Sacramento, CA; (2); Church Yth Grp; Cmnty Wkr; Pres Girl Scts; Key Clb; SADD; Acpl Chr; Drill Tm; School Musical; School Play; Variety Show; Galena St E Prfrmng Prod; Hmnts & Intl Studies Hgh Acad Alt Prgm; Physcl/Socl Psych.

BROWN, KATHERINE; Los Angeles HS; Los Angeles, CA; (3); Church Yth Grp; Cmnty Wkr; Teachers Aide; Band; Rep Jr Cls; Cit Awd; High Hon Roll; Pres Acad Fit Awd; Yng, Gftd & Black Acad Achvt Awd; Peer Acad Ldrshp Pgm; Cert Of Achvt For Ldrshp Abilities; Med.

BROWN, KATHERINE E; El Cajon Valley HS; El Cajon, CA; (2); 82/486; Acpl Chr; Chorus; School Musical; JV Sftbl; Jacksonville ST U; Law.

BROWN, KEISHA; Pius X HS; Los Angeles, CA; (3); Letterman Clb; Chorus; School Musical; School Play; Capt Cheerldng; Powder Puff Ftbl; Score Keeper; Trk; Hon Roll; Church Athl Assn Vllybl; Associated Stu Body; Pan African Heritage; Broadcast Jrnlsm.

BROWN, KEISHA J; Pasadena HS; Altadena, CA; (2); JV Cheerldng; Var Trk; ROP Medcl Asst Trng; Phy.

BROWN, KELLY R; Westmoor HS; Daly City, CA; (2); German Clb; Band; Mrchg Band; High Hon Roll; Prfct Atten Awd; CO; Geologist.

BROWN, KEVIN T; University HS; Irvine, CA; (1); 17/480; Church Yth Grp; Treas Frsh Cls; Crs Cntry; Trk; Hon Roll; Laureate Math Awd.

BROWN, KIMBERLEE M; Petaluma HS; Petaluma, CA; (3); 54/267; Phtg Nwsp; Phtg Yrbk; Stu Spprt Svc; Photo Nwsp; Photo Jrnlsm.

BROWN, KRISTEN; Folsom HS; Rancho Cordova, CA; (4); 19/290; Sec Treas GAA; Intnl Clb; Model UN; Pep Clb; Ski Clb; Band; Mrchg Band; Yrbk; Rep Jr Cls; Var Cheerldng; CSF Secy; UC Santa Barbara; Engrng.

BROWN, LA SHAWN M; Skyline HS; Oakland, CA; (2); Church Yth Grp; Church Choir; Hon Roll; Prfct Atten Awd; Hmmkng Top Schlr Trphy.

BROWN, LA TRECEE A; Morningside HS; Inglewood, CA; (3); Hosp Aide; Rep Stu Cncl; JV Var Cheerldng; JV Trk; Hon Roll; Acad Achvt; Los Angeles Ped Soc; Summe Med Career Pgm; Outdoor Sci Sch; Pre-Med.

BROWN, LAMAR; Fontana HS; Fontana, CA; (2); Var JV Bsktbl; Hon Roll; Consumer Ed Awd; UNLV; Bsktbl.

BROWN, LASHAWN; Skyline HS; Oakland, CA; (2); Art Clb; Church Yth Grp; Teachers Aide; Church Choir; Cit Awd; High Hon Roll; Hon Roll; Prfct Atten Awd; CA ST U Hayward; Comp Sci.

BROWN, LAURA; Rio Mesa HS; Camarillo, CA; (3); Pep Clb; Var Cheerldng; Var Pom Pon; JV Sftbl; Wt Lftg; Hon Roll; Pres Acad Fit Awd; Dance.

BROWN, LEAH L; Eureka HS; Eureka, CA; (2); Church Yth Grp; Cmnty Wkr; Service Clb; Var Cheerldng; JV Trk; Stat Vllybl; Hon Roll; Psych.

BROWN, LESLIE D; Tehachapi HS; Tehachapi, CA; (3); FBLA; Teachers Aide; Hon Roll; Bakersfield Coll; Bus.

BROWN, LISA; Ponderosa HS; Rescue, CA; (2); 50/360; Church Yth Grp; Dance Clb; Drama Clb; Pep Clb; SADD; Church Choir; School Play; JV Cheerldng; JV Var Score Keeper; Opt Clb Awd; Peer Cnslng; UCLA; Psycht.

BROWN, LORA; Fresno Christian HS; Fresno, CA; (3); Letterman Clb; Sec Stu Cncl; Var L Bsktbl; Var Vllybl; Cit Awd; Hon Roll; SCC; Art.

BROWN, LORI; Colusa HS; Colusa, CA; (4); 5/90; Church Yth Grp; FBLA; Band; Chorus; Rep Soph Cls; VP Stu Cncl; JV Var Bsktbl; JV Var Tennis; JV Var Trk; Hon Roll; Bank Of Am Fine Art Fnlst; Semper Fidelis Awd Musical Excl; John Philip Sousa Band Awd; Humboldt ST; Music.

BROWN, LUKE D; Pescadero HS; Pescadero, CA; (2); 1/13; Boy Scts; Church Yth Grp; Teachers Aide; Pres Soph Cls; Rep Stu Cncl; L VP Bsbl; Score Keeper; Hon Roll.

BROWN, MARINA; Mater Dei HS; Anaheim, CA; (3); Cmnty Wkr; Model UN; Pep Clb; Drill Tm; Rep Stu Cncl; Var Pom Pon; Intrml Swmmng; Pres NHS; Advncd Lifesavng, 1st Aid & CPR Certfd; Jr Lifegrd Capt.

BROWN, MARK K; Riverdale HS; Riverdale, CA; (4); FFA; Ftbl; Trk; Fresno ST U; Elect Engr.

BROWN, MARTINIA; Granada Hills HS; Northridge, CA; (3); Office Aide; Teachers Aide; Drill Tm; Treas Frsh Cls; Var JV Cheerldng; Var JV Pom Pon; Cit Awd; Prfct Atten Awd; Susan B Anthony Awd Ldrshp, Schlrshp & Svc; St Cert Gftd; UC Berkeley; Bus Mgmt.

BROWN, MARY; Mount Diablo HS; Pittsburg, CA; (1); French Clb; SADD; Cheerldng; Lawyer.

BROWN, MATT F; San Diego Acad; San Diego, CA; (3); Church Yth Grp; Varsity Clb; Var Intrml Bsktbl; Intrml Ftbl; Intrml Sftbl; Intrml Vllybl; Hon Roll; NHS; Mar Bio.

BROWN, MATTHEW G; St Margarets Episcopal HS; San Juan Capis, CA; (2); Church Yth Grp; Orch; Nwsp; Yrbk; Swmmng; High Hon Roll; Hon Roll; Boy Scts; Service Clb; School Musical; Capts Lvl Lifeguard Intl Jr Guards 89; US Ocean Safety Lifeguard; Instr Orange Coast Ocean Rescue.

BROWN, MATTHEW R; Bellarmine College Prep; Redwood City, CA; (1); Stage Crew; Sci Fctn Club; Wrk Schlrshp Pgm; MIT; Engrng.

BROWN, MEKA; Gardena HS; Gardena, CA; (2); Church Yth Grp; Dance Clb; Teachers Aide; Church Choir; Drill Tm; School Play; Bsktbl; Mgr(s); Trk; Cit Awd; Schlrshp; Harvard U; Bus.

BROWN, MELANIE L; Woodside HS; Redwood City, CA; (3); Rep Frsh Cls; Rep Soph Cls; Rep Jr Cls; Rep Sr Cls; Rep Stu Cncl; High Hon Roll; San Francisco Ballet Stu; San Francisco ST U; Dance.

BROWN, MICHAEL D; Rio Vista HS; Rio Vista, CA; (3); 1/74; VP AFS; Church Yth Grp; FHA; Office Aide; Q&S; Pres Science Clb; Ed Nwsp; Tennis; High Hon Roll; Prfct Atten Awd; Fri Night Live; CSF; Acdmc Dcthln; U Of CA; Comp.

BROWN, MICHAEL K; Laekwood HS; Long Beach, CA; (2); Math Tm; Teachers Aide; CA Schlrshp Fed; Badminton JV; MIT; Biolgcl Sci.

BROWN, MICHAEL WINSTON; Taft HS; Tarzana, CA; (2); VP Chess Clb; Teachers Aide; Temple Yth Grp; Rep Stu Cncl; Hon Roll; CSF; Peer Tutor; Bus.

BROWN, MICHELLE A; Canyon Springs HS; Moreno Valley, CA; (2); Church Yth Grp; Pep Clb; Rep Soph Cls; Cheerldng; High Hon Roll; Pop Warner Chrldng Volunteer Walk; U Of Santa Barbara; Scl Worker.

BROWN, MIKE C; Faith Christian HS; Yuba City, CA; (3); 4/20; Church Yth Grp; Drama Clb; English Clb; Yrbk; Pres Soph Cls; Hon Roll; Prfct Atten Awd; CSF; Stu Of Mnth Awd; Jrnlsm.

BROWN, MINDI; Lodi HS; Lodi, CA; (2); 45/547; Church Yth Grp; Cmnty Wkr; Drama Clb; Chorus; Drill Tm; School Play; Socr; Gov Hon Prg Awd; High Hon Roll; Hon Roll; Miss CA Co-Ed Fnlst; Dsgn T-Shrts; SID; Pre-Law.

BROWN, MITCHELL W; Grossmont HS; La Mesa, CA; (3); 48/385; Letterman Clb; Rptr Nwsp; Rep Jr Cls; Rep Stu Cncl; Var L Ftbl; Powder Puff Ftbl; Var L Socr; JV Tennis; JV Trk; Hon Roll; Econmy.

BROWN, MOLLY E; Santa Rosa HS; Santa Rosa, CA; (2); Church Yth Grp; Drama Clb; JA; Spanish Clb; Chorus; Bsktbl; Trk; Cit Awd; Hon Roll; Prfct Atten Awd; Fencing Lessons; Local Theater; Psych.

BROWN, MONICA; East Bakersfield HS; Bakersfield, CA; (1); Debate Tm; Speech Tm; Rptr Yrbk; Cheerldng; Bakersfield Coll; Marine Bio.

BROWN, MORGAN P; Brea Olinda HS; Brea, CA; (2); 16/344; Cmnty Wkr; Capt Bsktbl; JV Golf; High Hon Roll; Pres Acad Fit Awd; Sprts Card Coll; Fishng; High Hnrs Golden St Exam Geom Test 89; Air Force Acad; Arontcs.

BROWN, NATALIE M; Hoover HS; Fresno, CA; (1); Flag Corp; Trk; Vllybl; High Hon Roll; Med.

BROWN, NATASHA A; Lompoc HS; Lompoc, CA; (3); SADD; Mgr Ftbl; JV Powder Puff Ftbl; Black Stds Clb; Smmr Acad Inst; Alan Hancock Coll; Med.

BROWN, NICOLE; Palm Springs HS; Palm Springs, CA; (4); Church Yth Grp; Cmnty Wkr; Dance Clb; French Clb; GAA; Pep Clb; Ski Clb; Var Gym; Var Pom Pon; Hon Roll; U Of CO; Bio.

BROWN, NIKITA J; Bishop Montgomery HS; Carson, CA; (4); Church Yth Grp; JA; Stat Bsktbl; JV Trk; Var Wt Lftg; Hon Roll; Black Data Prcssng Assocs; Digital Comp & Cafe Pgm; Black Cultrl Clb; UCLA; Engrng.

BROWN, NOELL L; Los Alamitos HS; Los Alamitos, CA; (3); Church Yth Grp; French Clb; FBLA; SADD; Chorus; Cheerldng; Hon Roll; Orange Cnty Arts Mscl Theatre Dept; Stu Rep City Cncl Cmmtte Fine Arts; Outstndng Acadc Achvt Engl Awd; Fine Arts.

BROWN, NOVA M; Skyline HS; Orinda, CA; (3); Office Aide; Acpl Chr; Chorus; Church Choir; School Musical; Swing Chorus; Crs Cntry; Hon Roll.

BROWN, PAMELA L; Edison-Computech HS; Fresno, CA; (1); Church Yth Grp; Band; Mrchg Band; Cheerldng; Hon Roll; Psych.

BROWN, PLEASANCE LA RAE; San Gorgonio HS; San Bernardino, CA; (3); 100/500; Cmnty Wkr; Debate Tm; DECA; Drama Clb; Intnl Clb; JA; Key Clb; Library Aide; Model UN; NFL; Peer Cnslng; Blck Stu Union; Future Blck Teadter Am; Lawyer.

BROWN, RACHEL; Sacramento Country Day Schl; Sacromento, CA; (3); Dance Clb; Phtg Nwsp; Phtg Yrbk; Rep Stu Cncl; Var Cheerldng; High Hon Roll; Spnish Awds 89-90; Acad Talent Srch; Amer Hist Awd 90; Bus.

BROWN, REBECCA; Elk Grove HS; Elk Grove, CA; (2); Color Guard; Students Reaching Out; Drug Free Prgm; Long Beach U; Marine Biologist.

BROWN, RICHARD; Central Union HS; El Centro, CA; (2); Rock Combo; USC; Pedtrcn.

BROWN, RODNEY L; Lindsay HS; Lindsay, CA; (3); Church Yth Grp; Letterman Clb; Spanish Clb; Teachers Aide; Rptr Nwsp; JV Var Bsbl; JV Var Ftbl; Hon Roll; Prfct Atten Awd; All-Lg Rcvr Ftbl All Area Hnrb Mntn; Gldn St Exm Geomtry Hnrs; Comp Sci.

BROWN, ROSEMARY K; Mater Dei HS; Garden Grove, CA; (3); Church Yth Grp; Cmnty Wkr; Hosp Aide; Acpl Chr; Chorus; Church Choir; School Musical; Stage Crew; High Hon Roll; Hon Roll; Student Of The Month; Psychology.

BROWN, RYAN H; Bishop O Dowd HS; Oakland, CA; (3); Ski Clb; Band; Pep Band; JV Var Ftbl; Socr; High Hon Roll; CSF; Black Stu Union; UC Berkeley; Engrng.

BROWN, RYAN M; Santa Clara HS; Oxnard, CA; (2); 16/201; NFL; Spanish Clb; SADD; Sec Soph Cls; JV Crs Cntry; JV Swmmng; JV Trk; High Hon Roll; NHS; Opt Clb Awd; Jr Lifeguard Aide; UCLA; Pediatrician.

BROWN, SAM B; Brawley Union HS; Brawley, CA; (3); 8/320; Am Leg Boys St; Boy Scts; Church Yth Grp; Computer Clb; Debate Tm; Letterman Clb; Math Tm; Ftbl; Wt Lftg; Cit Awd; Eagle Scout; ASB Treas; Bus Admin.

BROWN, SAMANTHA; Mater Dei HS; Fountain Valley, CA; (4); 139/526; Cmnty Wkr; VP Pres Drama Clb; Girl Scts; Pres Spanish Clb; Thesps; School Musical; School Play; Stage Crew; Stu Cncl; Hon Roll; CSF; Natl Hispanic Schlrshp Semifnlst; Drama Clb Awds; Broadcast Commnctns.

BROWN, SARA; Western Christian HS; Azusa, CA; (2); Church Yth Grp; Service Clb; Sec Soph Cls; JV Cheerldng; Score Keeper; Var Trk; High Hon Roll; Azusa Pacific U.

BROWN, SARAH; Mission San Jose HS; Fremont, CA; (2); Pres Church Yth Grp; Hosp Aide; Science Clb; Spanish Clb; Church Choir; JV Sftbl; CA Schlrshp Fed; CA U; Brdcst Nws.

BROWN, SARAH; Red Bluff HS; Red Bluff, CA; (2); Church Yth Grp; Hosp Aide; SADD; School Musical; School Play; Variety Show; Sec Jr Cls; Cheerldng; Steering Comm Fresh & Sophmore; Ballet; Piano.

BROWN, SCOTT S; Santa Cruz HS; Santa Cruz, CA; (3); Church Yth Grp; Letterman Clb; Band; Jazz Band; Mrchg Band; Pep Band; JV Bsktbl; JV Ftbl; JV Golf; Mens Hnr Soc; Bethany Clg.

BROWN, SEAN E; Canyon HS; Canyon Country, CA; (1); Quiz Bowl; Socr; Trk; Hon Roll; Pres Schlr; Santa Clara; Author.

BROWN, SHANNON MARIE; Temecola Valley HS; Murrieta, CA; (4); 37/360; Pep Clb; Drill Tm; Hon Roll; Walk Amer Mrch Of Dimes; UC Riverside; Acctg.

BROWN, SHAROB; Ribet Acad; Altadena, CA; (4); 3/45; Church Yth Grp; Cmnty Wkr; Debate Tm; Drama Clb; Letterman Clb; NFL; Pep Clb; Speech Tm; School Play; Variety Show; Black Stu Union Pres; UCSB; Cmmnctns.

BROWN, SHEILA R; Redlands HS; Redlands, CA; (4); Art Clb; Church Yth Grp; Pep Clb; Hon Roll; Pres Acad Fit Awd; BYU; Commnctns.

BROWN, SHEILA R; Riverdale HS; Riverdale, CA; (2); GAA; Pep Clb; SADD; Stat Bsktbl; Var Sftbl; Var Vllybl; Prfct Atten Awd; Fresno ST; Educ.

BROWN, SHELLEY A; Bishop Amat HS; Temple City, CA; (3); Pep Clb; Drill Tm; Cheerldng; Powder Puff Ftbl; Hon Roll; Comp Sci.

BROWN, STEPHANIE B; Del Oro HS; Loomis, CA; (2); Church Yth Grp; GAA; Chorus; Variety Show; VP Soph Cls; Crs Cntry; Trk; Cit Awd; Hon Roll; Pres Acad Fit Awd; Yng Life; Stu Of Mnth; Child Care; Ed.

BROWN, SUSAN E; Colton HS; Colton, CA; (3); 3/350; Church Yth Grp; Q&S; Church Choir; Ed Nwsp; High Hon Roll; Hon Roll; Jr NHS; NHS; Chrch League Vlybl & Sftbl; UC Riverside; Mass Commnctn.

BROWN, SUZANNE D; Whittier Christian HS; La Habra, CA; (4); Church Yth Grp; School Play; Var L Bsktbl; Stat Ftbl; Powder Puff Ftbl; Capt L Socr; Capt L Sftbl; Var Vllybl; High Hon Roll; US Army Reserve; Natl Schlr Athl Awd; Dstngshd Chrstn HS Stu 89-90; Azusa Pacific U.

BROWN, TAMMIE J; Apple Valley HS; Apple Valley, CA; (2); Drama Clb; Drill Tm; Var Crs Cntry; Var Trk; Cit Awd; Hon Roll; Drill Team Lt; Psych.

BROWN, TARA; Brea-Olinda HS; Brea, CA; (1); Church Yth Grp; Cmnty Wkr; Library Aide; Chorus; Color Guard; School Musical; School Play; Variety Show; Hon Roll; Piano Lessons.

BROWN, TARA L; Mater Dei HS; Fountain Valley, CA; (4); 1/521; VP French Clb; Chorus; School Musical; High Hon Roll; NHS; Prfct Atten Awd; Pres Acad Fit Awd; Fstvl Ballet Theatre; Plcd Grnd Cncours De Francais; Loyola Marymount; Bio.

BROWN, TIM B; San Marcos HS; Santa Barbara, CA; (3); Teachers Aide; Cit Awd; Hon Roll; Nmbr One Clb 88-89; Santa Barbara City; Bus.

BROWN, TODD P; Desert HS; Edwards, CA; (2); Var Bsbl; JV Ftbl; MI Tech U; Engrng.

BROWN, TRACEY L; Bakersfield HS; Bakersfield, CA; (2); 30/785; Church Yth Grp; Cmnty Wkr; Drama Clb; Sec Thesps; School Musical; School Play; Stage Crew; Variety Show; High Hon Roll; Hon Roll; Outstndng Soph 90 Intl Thespian Soc; Youth To Youth 89; Wstrn States Cnfrnc Drug Free Yth; CA ST U; Bus Admin.

BROWN, VERMELLE LONNISHA C; Valley HS; Sacramento, CA; (3); 137/555; Am Leg Aux Girls St; Girl Scts; Red Cross Aide; Ski Clb; SADD; Teachers Aide; Ed Yrbk; Stat Bsktbl; Powder Puff Ftbl; Socr; Kendall Grant 90; MESA; Bsu; Sacramento City JC; Pblc Hlth.

BROWN, WENDY; Fremont Christian HS; Fremont, CA; (4); Ski Clb; Spanish Clb; Chorus; School Musical; Pres Frsh Cls; Stu Cncl; Stat Bsktbl; Var Sftbl; Var Capt Vllybl; Hon Roll; Cmmnd Perf At ACSI Musicale; Duet 2 Yr&quartet 1 Yr; Mst Insprtnl Sftbl & Vb; JR & SR Cl Hc Princess; Azosa Pac U; Pre Law Lawyer.

BROWN, YVONNE CHERISSE; Bishop Montogomery HS; Carson, CA; (4); 40/354; Church Yth Grp; Letterman Clb; Ski Clb; Varsity Clb; Stu Cncl; Bsktbl; Trk; Hon Roll; CA Schlrshp Fed; Cum Laude; UCLA; Pol Sci.

BROWN-SMITH, TRYNISHA D; Washington Prep HS; Los Angeles, CA; (2); Church Yth Grp; Dance Clb; Model UN; Church Choir; Prfct Atten Awd; Criminal Law.

BROWNE, MALIKA M; The Oak Grove Schl; Pasadena, CA; (4); Rptr Nwsp; Ed Yrbk; Rep Frsh Cls; Rep Soph Cls; Ntl Merit Ltr; Semifnlst-Ntl Achvt Schlrshp Cmptn-Outstndng Negro Stu; Extracrrclr Study-Black Engl Vernacular; Engl Tchr.

BROWNE, REBECCA L; Hesperia Christian HS; Hesperia, CA; (3); 5/28; Church Yth Grp; Computer Clb; Girl Scts; Letterman Clb; Office Aide; Spanish Clb; Teachers Aide; Ed Yrbk; Stat Bsbl; Wt Lftg; Sign Lang, Wrkd With Deaf Children.

BROWNFIELD, JIMMY H; Tulare Union HS; Tulare, CA; (2); Church Yth Grp; Archry; Comp; Mth.

BROWNFIELD, KATIE B; Lindsay HS; Lindsay, CA; (1); #4 In Class; Church Yth Grp; Sec 4-H; French Clb; Ski Clb; JV Bsktbl; Var Diving; Powder Puff Ftbl; Var Swmmng; 4-H Awd; High Hon Roll.

BROWNFIELD, MIKE R; Lindsay HS; Lindsay, CA; (2); Church Yth Grp; Cmnty Wkr; Computer Clb; VP 4-H; JA; VP Key Clb; Ski Clb; Var Swmmng; 4-H Awd; Hon Roll; Wtr Polo-Var; Cal Poly SLO; Ag.

BROWNING, AMANDY A; El Cajon Valley HS; El Cajon, CA; (1); Vllybl; Cit Awd; Hon Roll; San Diego ST U; Medicine.

BROWNING, CHRIS M; Hiram W Johnson West Campus; Sacramento, CA; (3); 30/120; VP Church Yth Grp; ROTC; SADD; Drill Tm; Rptr Nwsp; Var Bsbl; JV Intrml Bsktbl; JV Intrml Ftbl; Var Trk; Hon Roll; Med.

BROWNING, CYDNEY; Franklin JR HS; Vallejo, CA; (1); Dance Clb; Office Aide; Service Clb; Teachers Aide; School Musical; Stage Crew; Variety Show; High Hon Roll; Hon Roll; Finest Awd; UC Davis; Math.

BROWNING, JENNIFER J; Los Alamitos HS; Los Alamitos, CA; (3); Church Yth Grp; Cmnty Wkr; Office Aide; Service Clb; Teachers Aide; Band; Chorus; Church Choir; Mrchg Band; School Musical; CSF; Natl Schlr Day; Awd Cert Acad Excllnce; UC Santa Barbara; Lawyer.

BROWNING, LORI; Mira Mesa HS; San Diego, CA; (3); Pres Church Yth Grp; Cmnty Wkr; Rptr FBLA; Hosp Aide; Spanish Clb; School Play; Mgr Nwsp; Var Trk; Pres Acad Fit Awd; San Diego Tribune All Acad Team; Assoc Stu Body Cmssnr Of Hosptlty; Brigham Young U; Commnctns.

BROWNING, SOMMER; Venice HS; Venice, CA; (1); Russian Club; Envrnmntl Engrs.

BROWNLEE, NICOLE C; Barstow HS; Barstow, CA; (3); Church Yth Grp; Cmnty Wkr; Church Choir; Acadmc Imprvmnt Awd; Marine Corp; Med Doc.

BROWNLEE, PATRICIA; Gunderson HS; San Jose, CA; (4); Church Yth Grp; Cmnty Wkr; Drama Clb; Girl Scts; Intnl Clb; JA; Letterman Clb; Library Aide; Spanish Clb; Teachers Aide; San Jose Chldrns Musical Theater, Musicals; San Jose Hstrcl Soc; Vol YMCA Many Smmrs; Westmont Coll; Hstry.

BROYLES, JODY A; Fred C Beyer HS; Modesto, CA; (3); GAA; SADD; Color Guard; Var Bsktbl; Var Trk; Cit Awd; High Hon Roll; NHS; Pres Acad Fit Awd; U C Davis; Psych.

BROYLES, TODD E; Highlands HS; North Highlands, CA; (3); Cmnty Wkr; Red Cross Aide; Ski Clb; SADD; Yrbk; JV Var Ftbl; Var Golf; High Hon Roll; Mech Engrng.

BRUBAKER, TOM J; King City HS; King City, CA; (3); Quiz Bowl; Scholastic Bowl; JV Var Bsktbl; Var Golf; Var Trk; 4-H Awd; High Hon Roll; Hon Roll; Rotary Awd; CPR Cert; Camp Royal 90; 1st Pl Knowledge Bowl; Cal Poly; Landscape Arch.

BRUCE, CHRISTOPHER; Western Christian HS; Claremont, CA; (3); Church Yth Grp; Library Aide; VP Frsh Cls; Off Soph Cls; Var L Bsbl; Var Capt Bsktbl; JV Ftbl; High Hon Roll; Physiolgy.

BRUCE, CYNTHIA A; Skyline HS; Oakland, CA; (3); Teachers Aide; Chorus; Yrbk; Lit Mag; Mgr Mgr(s); JV Sftbl; JV Vllybl; Hon Roll; Yth Endg Hunger; NAACP Yth Cncl; Natl Explrs Post 2028 Law; Poltcl Sci.

BRUCE, ERMILITA; Lowell HS; San Francisco, CA; (2); Office Aide; Teachers Aide; Acpl Chr; Chorus; School Musical; School Play; Rep Stu Cncl; Hon Roll.

BRUCE, JOSHUA W; Santa Cruz HS; Santa Cruz, CA; (3); Boy Scts; Chess Clb; JV Ftbl; JV Tennis; Var Trk; Hon Roll; Pres Acad Fit Awd; People To People Stu Ambssdr Pgm-Friendshp Caravan; Cabrillo Coll; Engr.

BRUCE, KARIN C; Bishop Montgomery HS; Gardena, CA; (3); VP JA; Key Clb; Chorus; School Musical; Rep Soph Cls; Pres Sr Cls; Rep Stu Cncl; Mountaineering Clb; Envrnmntl Awrnss Clb; Fshn Dsgn.

BRUCE, KRISTIE L; Senior HS; Bakersfield, CA; (4); Ski Clb; Teachers Aide; Var Socr; Var Sftbl; Var Vllybl; Hon Roll; NHS; High Schlstc Achvt Schl Emblem; Bakersfield Coll; Dentistry.

BRUCE, MIKELLE; Fresno Christian HS; Fresno, CA; (4); 10/65; Church Yth Grp; Intnl Clb; Letterman Clb; Ed Yrbk; Cheerldng; Cit Awd; High Hon Roll; Pres Acad Fit Awd; Hi-Deb Rep 89-90; CSF; Fresno ST U; Telecmmnctns.

BRUCE, NATALIE; Torrey Pines HS; San Diego, CA; (4); 23/448; AFS; Drill Tm; Ed Yrbk; Hon Roll; CSF Sealbearer; Intl Bus.

BRUCE, STEPHANIE S; Canyon HS; Canyon Country, CA; (2); Church Yth Grp; Teachers Aide; Mgr(s); CSF; Bus.

BRUCE, STEVE C; Pescadero HS; San Gregorio, CA; (2); Teachers Aide; Hon Roll; CSM; Prof Weldr.

BRUCE, TIRZAH D; Fillmore HS; Fillmore, CA; (2); Ski Clb; Phtg Ed Yrbk; Cit Awd; Hon Roll; NEDT Awd; St Schlr; Writer Of Month; Zoology.

BRUCKER, JAMIE; Adolfo Camarillo HS; Camarillo, CA; (2); 89/506; Church Yth Grp; Pep Clb; Sec Soph Cls; JV Cheerldng; Hon Roll; Hmcmng Princess; Schlstc Achvt Awd-Local Sci; Superior Individual Achvt Trophy 89; UCLA; Med.

BRUEBAKER, CHRISTOPHER; Arlington HS; Riverside, CA; (4); Boy Scts; Off ROTC; Color Guard; Drill Tm; School Musical; School Play; Rptr Yrbk; Acad Decathlon Tm; 4 Ltrs; ROTC Sons Amer Revolution Mdl; Mayoral Citation For Cmnty Service.

BRUECKNER, SHANNON L; Bakersfield HS; Bakersfield, CA; (3); 9/718; Cmnty Wkr; NFL; Science Clb; Pres Service Clb; SADD; Stu Cncl; Powder Puff Ftbl; Var L Swmmng; High Hon Roll; Prfct Atten Awd; Envrnmntl Sci.

BRUEGGEMANN, TIFFANY L; Temple City HS; Temple City, CA; (2); Dance Clb; Office Aide; Pep Clb; Stu Cncl; Score Keeper; Hon Roll; Santa Barbara; Modeling.

BRUENSTEINER, MATTHEW M; Davis Ssr HS; Davis, CA; (4); 11/389; Art Clb; Chess Clb; Debate Tm; German Clb; Nwsp; Ntl Merit SF; Var Badminton; Engr.

BRUER, JAMES A; Yosemite HS; Coarsegold, CA; (3); Ski Clb; Var Wrstlng; UC San Francisco; Dentistry.

BRUFF, JULIE A; Bishop O'dowd HS; Oakland, CA; (3); Drama Clb; Ski Clb; Thesps; School Musical; School Play; Stage Crew; Variety Show; Pres Soph Cls; Rep Jr Cls; High Hon Roll; Mst Outstndng Grl 88-89; Wstrn Assn Schls-Coll Stu Cmmtte; Rtrt Tm 89-90; Carnegie Mellon U Smmr Cls; Thtr.

BRUGHELLI, KERRI; Riverdale HS; Riverdale, CA; (2); 1/137; GAA; Science Clb; Ski Clb; Spanish Clb; SADD; Varsity Clb; Pres Stu Cncl; Var Score Keeper; Var Trk; JV Var Vllybl; Acad Achvt Awd-Phys Sci 89, Geo 90; Schl Rcgntn Gldn St Exam, Algbra 89; League Wnnr Grls Trck 89; Santa Clara; Engrng.

BRUHN, DAVID WILLIAM; Don Bosco Tech Inst; Montebello, CA; (2); Dance Clb; Drama Clb; Ski Clb; Band; Mrchg Band; Orch; School Musical; School Play; Rep Frsh Cls; Pres Soph Cls; Acting Mem Screen Actros Guild; Mem Amer Fed Of TV, Radio; Cal Poly; Material Sci.

BRUHN, HEATHER; William S Hart HS; Valencia, CA; (3); 127/480; Church Yth Grp; Cmnty Wkr; Red Cross Aide; SADD; Capt L Cheerldng; Intrml Powder Puff Ftbl; Stat Socr; NHS; Alg & Geom Natl Mrt Math Awds; Engrng.

BRUINS, PETER A; Valley Christian HS; Bellflower, CA; (4); 36/120; Hon Roll; Lion Awd; NHS; Northwestern Coll; Broadcasting.

BRULAND, GREGORY L; Santa Cruz HS; Santa Cruz, CA; (1); 1/300; Letterman Clb; JV Socr; JV Vllybl; High Hon Roll; Tom Hilton Awd; 90 Boys JV Soccer Sprtsmnshsp Awd; Cert Excllnce Outstndng Achvt Lang Arts & Math; Stanford; Jrnlsm.

BRUM, FRANK; Oakdale Joint Union HS; Valley Home, CA; (3); 12/420; SADD; Teachers Aide; Rep Jr Cls; VP Stu Cncl; Capt Bsbl; Var Tennis; Cit Awd; Hon Roll; Pres Schlr; Fashion Dsgn.

BRUM, GENNA M; Riverdale HS; Riverdale, CA; (2); Church Yth Grp; FBLA; GAA; Intnl Clb; Pep Clb; Science Clb; Ski Clb; Spanish Clb; SADD; Church Choir; Med.

BRUMBAUGH, APRIL K; Apple Valley HS; Apple Valley, CA; (3); 124/708; AFS; Church Yth Grp; ROTC; Teachers Aide; L Crs Cntry; L Trk; Hon Roll; Chrstian Clb VP; Chrstn Clb Treas; Point Loma Nazarene; Pre-Med.

BRUMLEY, DAVID R; Gridley HS; Gridley, CA; (3); 5/140; Am Leg Boys St; Church Yth Grp; Cmnty Wkr; Drama Clb; Letterman Clb; Service Clb; Spanish Clb; School Musical; School Play; Variety Show; Swim Team; HOBY Ldrshp Smnr; Acadc Ltr.

BRUMLEY, EGAN M; San Luis Obispo HS; San Luis Obispo, CA; (3); 26/330; Hon Roll; U CA.

BRUMLEY, JULIE A; Sonora HS; Fullerton, CA; (2); Cmnty Wkr; French Clb; Ski Clb; SADD; Var Cheerldng; Powder Puff Ftbl; Var Socr; Var Trk; Hon Roll; Jr NHS; Cmptitive Tap Dancer; USC:Physcl Thrpy.

BRUMMEL, MICHELLE; San Pedro HS; San Pedro, CA; (4); Cmnty Wkr; Quiz Bowl; Stage Crew; Gov Hon Prg Awd; CSU Dominguez Hills.

BRUMMETT, SHELLY L; Santa Ynez Union HS; Buellton, CA; (3); Office Aide; SADD; NM ST U; Teacher.

BRUN, LAURA; Los Alamitas HS; Los Alamitos, CA; (3); Cmnty Wkr; Varsity Clb; Var L Socr; Var L Tennis; Var L Trk; Hon Roll; NHS; Olympc Dev Pgm ST Tm Ntl Camp.

BRUNDAGE, BRENT B; Chino HS; Chino, CA; (3); Band; Jazz Band; Mrchg Band; Pep Band; JV Bsktbl; Intrml Ftbl; Wt Lftg; Hon Roll; Prfct Atten Awd; Santa Ana Winds Yth & San Bernadino Cnty Hnr Band; Mrch In Rose Parade 90; Chsn S CA Yth Ctznshp Smnr; Bus Admin.

BRUNDIGE, JASON R; Monte Vista HS; Spring Valley, CA; (3); 90/373; Band; Drm Mjr(t); Jazz Band; Mrchg Band; Pep Band; School Musical; CA Schlrshp Fed; Musical Prfmnce.

BRUNEAU, ANNA E; Huntington Beach HS; Huntington Beach, CA; (2); Church Yth Grp; JV Sftbl; Hon Roll; MVP Sftbll; Schl Bible Study; Biola; Educ.

BRUNEAU, EMILE G; Willits HS; Willits, CA; (4); 4/120; Am Leg Boys St; VP Crs Cntry; VP Stu Cncl; JV Var Ftbl; JV Var Trk; JV Var Wrstlng; Elks Awd; High Hon Roll; Pres Acad Fit Awd; Rotary Awd; Stanford U; Engrng.

BRUNER, DOTTIE L; Red Bluff Union HS; Red Bluff, CA; (3); 4/300; Church Yth Grp; Key Clb; SADD; Teachers Aide; Church Choir; Hon Roll; CA Schlrshp Fed; John Lyon Reid Memrl Schlrshp; Mc Connell Schlrshp Fndtn; 1st Chrch God Discipleship; Shasta Coll; Elem Ed.

BRUNER, JENNA; South Pasadena HS; South Pasadena, CA; (4); 43/300; Am Leg Aux Girls St; Cmnty Wkr; Hosp Aide; Ed Yrbk; Treas Frsh Cls; Capt Cheerldng; Powder Puff Ftbl; Var Swmmng; High Hon Roll; Cnslr Sthrn CA Ldrshp Camps CASC; 1 Of 25 CA Delegts Slctd Attend Natl Asso Stu Cncls Wstrn Cnfrn; Colgate U; Politcl Sci.

BRUNETTI, KEVIN A; Bishop O'dowd HS; Alameda, CA; (1); Band; Jazz Band; Pep Band; Crs Cntry; Ftbl; Hon Roll; NEDT Awd; UC Santa Cruz; Lit.

BRUNETTI, MICHAEL J; Encinal HS; Alameda, CA; (3); 17/230; French Clb; Band; Var Crs Cntry; Var Trk; High Hon Roll; CSF; Crss Cntry All-League Awd; Spcl Olympcs Vlntr; U CA; Biochem.

BRUNING, SHANNON; Valley View HS; Moreno Valley, CA; (2); 20/321; Art Clb; Color Guard; High Hon Roll; Hon Roll; NHS; Indio Date Fest 1st & 2nd Pl Art Awds; CA Coll; Interior Dsgn.

BRUNKHORST JR, GENE; Grant Joint Union HS; Sacramento, CA; (2); Church Yth Grp; Bsktbl; Mgr(s); Score Keeper.

BRUNNEMER, KRISTIN C; Santa Cruz HS; Santa Cruz, CA; (4); 18/250; Church Yth Grp; Treas Spanish Clb; Acpl Chr; Chorus; Rptr Nwsp; JV Swmmng; High Hon Roll; Hon Roll; Pres Acad Fit Awd; Gamma Chi Sigma; Westmont Coll; Pre-Law.

BRUNNER, ERIN M; Chula Vista HS; Chula Vista, CA; (2); Office Aide; Pep Clb; Ed Nwsp; Co-Ed Yrbk; Pres Soph Cls; Stu Cncl; Cheerldng; Cit Awd; Hon Roll; Masonic Awd; U CA; Law.

BRUNSON, JENNIFER; Bellarmine Jefferson HS; Sunland, CA; (1); Church Yth Grp; Co-Ed Nwsp; Hon Roll; Eng Hnrs; Journlsm.

BRUNSTAD, KRISTI; Antioch HS; Antioch, CA; (1); Chorus; School Musical; School Play; Variety Show; Cheerldng; Hon Roll; Hnrs Choir; BYU; Prfrmng Arts.

BRUNT, WENDY A; Mission Viejo HS; Mission Viejo, CA; (4); 29/432; Church Yth Grp; Band; Lbrn Mrchg Band; Orch; School Musical; JV Trk; Hon Roll; NHS; Pres Acad Fit Awd; Intl Baccalaureate Dip; Ntl Merit Schlr; CSF; U CA-DAVIS; Animal Sci.

BRUNZELL, JEFF R; Granada Hills HS; Granada Hills, CA; (2); Intrml Tennis; Hon Roll; Goldn St Exam High Hnrs Alg & Geom; CJSF; CSU Northridge; Pediatrics.

BRUSATI, ELIZABETH D; Sir Francis Drake HS; San Anselmo, CA; (3); 2/179; Model UN; Band; Jazz Band; Pep Band; Var Crs Cntry; Capt Var Trk; French Hon Soc; High Hon Roll; Hon Roll; Natl Mrt High Scorer; Bio.

BRUSCHKE, CRAIG; Capistrano Valley HS; Mission Viejo, CA; (3); Boy Scts; Church Yth Grp; JV Capt Bsktbl; High Hon Roll; Athl Activity.

BRUSHIA, JENNIFER MARGARET; Oak Ridge HS; El Dorado Hills, CA; (4); 18/235; Cmnty Wkr; FBLA; Intnl Clb; Office Aide; Varsity Clb; Band; Chorus; Var Swmmng; High Hon Roll; Pres Acad Fit Awd; CSUS; Frgn Lang.

BRUSO, BECKY; So Tahoe HS; South Lake Tahoe, CA; (4); 6/210; Cmnty Wkr; Debate Tm; Drama Clb; Key Clb; Letterman Clb; Quiz Bowl; Service Clb; Spanish Clb; Pres SADD; Varsity Clb; Young Woman Of The Month; CA Schlr Federation Life Member; Principals Serv Awd; Graduation Speaker; Advertising.

BRUST, PAUL F; Bellarmine College Prep; San Jose, CA; (3); 47/325; Boy Scts; Church Yth Grp; Cmnty Wkr; Debate Tm; Latin Clb; NFL; Service Clb; Speech Tm; SADD; Varsity Clb; Eagle Sct; JV All Leag Ftbl; Leag Hvywght Chmpn Wrstlng; Economics.

BRUSTER, TAMARA; Mar Vista HS; San Diego, CA; (1); Band; Cit Awd; Hon Roll; BSU; MESA; Psych.

BRUSTIN, CHAD; U S Grant HS; N Hollywood, CA; (4); VICA; JV Var Socr; JV Var Trk; Hon Roll; Kiwanis Awd; Religious/Ed VP W Rgn United Synagogue Yth; U AZ Tucson; Arch.

BRUSZER, BRAD D; Warren HS; South Gate, CA; (1); Church Yth Grp; Church Choir; Ftbl; Wt Lftg; Cit Awd; Peer Cnslng; Electrnc Engr.

BRUTLAG, JACOB D; Shasta HS; Redding, CA; (3); 10/415; Boy Scts; Drama Clb; School Play; Rptr Nwsp; Yrbk; High Hon Roll; Prfct Atten Awd; Cmmnctns.

BRUTOCO, KRIS K; Burlingame HS; Burlingame, CA; (3); Drama Clb; 4-H; Spanish Clb; School Musical; School Play; JV Socr; 4-H Awd; Gov Hon Prg Awd; Hon Roll; Rgn I Resrv Chmpn Engl Pleasure JOTR; IAHA Natl Saddleseat Equitation Semifnlst; Bus.

BRUTON, HEATHER C; Central Union HS; El Centro, CA; (3); Church Yth Grp; Pep Clb; Church Choir; Rptr Nwsp; Phtg Yrbk; Hon Roll; Pres Acad Fit Awd; 3 Day Cmmnty Perspectv Seminar; Jrnlsm.

BRUTON, JENNIFER N; Livermore HS; Livermore, CA; (3); Office Aide; Teachers Aide; Phtg Rptr Nwsp; Hon Roll.

BRUTTIG, ANDREW J; George Washington HS; San Francisco, CA; (2); Church Yth Grp; JV Bsbl; JV Ftbl; JV Golf; Hon Roll; U Of NE.

BRYAN, JEFF; San Benito HS; Hollister, CA; (3); 84/370; Phtg Yrbk; Bsbl; Golf; Hon Roll; Chico ST U; Jrnlsm.

BRYAN, KENNETH L; Chaffey HS; Rancho Cucamonga, CA; (1); 109/756; JV Ftbl; JV Capt Tennis; Var L Wrstlng; Med.

BRYAN, MATT; Bella Vista HS; Fair Oaks, CA; (2); FBLA; Swmmng; 1st Pl FBLA Sctnl Meet Accntng I; 6th Pl FBLA ST Cmptn Accntng; Accntng.

BRYAN, ROBERTA; Oroville HS; Oroville, CA; (3); Intnl Clb; Hon Roll; Heald Business Coll; Acctng.

BRYAN, TANYA; Fairfield HS; Andrews AFB, MD; (3); German Clb; Stage Crew; Rep Frsh Cls; Rep Jr Cls; Var Powder Puff Ftbl; High Hon Roll; Hon Roll; NHS; Conservation Clb; MESA; Biomedcl Engrng.

BRYAN, TANYA; Fairfield HS; Suisun, CA; (3); German Clb; Stage Crew; Rep Frsh Cls; Pres Jr Cls; Var Powder Puff Ftbl; High Hon Roll; NHS; MESA; Bio Engr.

BRYANT, ANNA R; Arvin HS; Lamont, CA; (3); 3/380; Church Yth Grp; Computer Clb; Math Clb; Scholastic Bowl; Ski Clb; Speech Tm; High Hon Roll; Hon Roll; NHS; Spanish NHS; Mck Trl; ASB Rally Cmmssnr; Acad Decthln; Commnctns.

BRYANT, BROOKE L; Orange HS; Garden Grove, CA; (4); Pres GAA; Letterman Clb; Varsity Clb; Var Bsktbl; Var Sftbl; Var Vllybl; High Hon Roll; Hon Roll; Pres Acad Fit Awd; Athlt Yr 90; Bill Hall Awd; Rancho Santiago Coll.

BRYANT, CARISSA D; La Sierra HS; Riverside, CA; (1); Band; Mrchg Band; Pep Band; Crs Cntry; Trk; Air Force.

BRYANT, DARREN; Washington Union HS; Fresno, CA; (3); 1/160; FCA; FBLA; Drm Mjr(t); Mrchg Band; Pres Church Choir; Tennis; High Hon Roll; JETS Awd; CSF; Acad Dcthln; Elec Engrng.

BRYANT, DARYL; Santa Teresa HS; San Jose, CA; (4); Church Yth Grp; Sec Computer Clb; Off Frsh Cls; Off Soph Cls; Off Jr Cls; Off Sr Cls; Var JV Bsktbl; Var JV Ftbl; JV Trk; Philosphy Clb; UC Santa Barbara; Comp Sci.

BRYANT, DAVID ERIC; Ukiah HS; Redwood Valley, CA; (1); Hon Roll; Pres Schlr; Harvard; Law.

BRYANT, DEREK RAY; Washington HS; Los Angeles, CA; (3); Intnl Clb; Teachers Aide; U Southern CA; Med.

BRYANT, ERICA; East Nicolaus HS; Rio Oso, CA; (3); Girl Scts; Office Aide; Pep Clb; SADD; Ed Yrbk; Sec Frsh Cls; Sec Soph Cls; Pres Jr Cls; Stat Bsbl; Stat Bsktbl; Stu Cncl.

BRYANT, ISABELLE A; Saint Anthony HS; Long Beach, CA; (2); Cmnty Wkr; Drama Clb; SADD; Band; Mrchg Band; Pep Band; School Musical; School Play; High Hon Roll; NHS; Ldr Band; Hnr Classes; CSF; USLA.

BRYANT, JOHN; Righetti HS; Santa Maria, CA; (3); 7/354; Church Yth Grp; Rptr Nwsp; JV Bsktbl; Var Swmmng; Cit Awd; High Hon Roll; Pres Acad Fit Awd; CSF; Asstd Stu Body; Water Polo JV, V; AR Acad; Aerontcl Engr.

BRYANT, LISA A; Savanna HS; Anaheim, CA; (2); Pep Clb; Rep Frsh Cls; Rep Soph Cls; Stat Bsktbl; JV Gym; JV Vllybl; High Hon Roll; Hon Roll; CSF; UCLA; Orthodontist.

BRYANT, MARIA; Lindhurst HS; Marysville, CA; (3); SADD; Sec Jr Cls; Rep Stu Cncl; Cit Awd; Hon Roll; CSF; Acad Dcthln; Yuba Cnty Juvnle Jstce Cmssn Stu Cmssnr; Law.

BRYANT, MARLENE Y; Clovis West HS; Clovis, CA; (4); Chess Clb; Cmnty Wkr; Hosp Aide; Office Aide; Ed Nwsp; Lit Mag; High Hon Roll; Hon Roll; Schlrshps/Frtrnty, Hansier Vctnl, Fresno Rtract, PTA, Simurietta Memrl 90; CSU Fresno; Lbrl Stdy.

BRYANT, MARY; Rancho Buena Vista HS; Vista, CA; (4); 13/408; Cmnty Wkr; Key Clb; Office Aide; SADD; Teachers Aide; Color Guard; Drill Tm; Flag Corp; Stu Cncl; Cit Awd; CSF; Palomar CC; Hlth Sci.

BRYANT, MELISSA B; Oakmont HS; Roseville, CA; (1); Band; Jazz Band; Mrchg Band; Pep Band; Var Trk; Hon Roll; NHS; Prfct Atten Awd; Harvard; Art.

BRYANT, MICHELLE L; Hesperia HS; Hesperia, CA; (2); Cmnty Wkr; FFA; Stu Cncl; Var Trk; Var Vllybl; Hon Roll; JV Capt Chess Clb; People To People HS Ambssdr Pgm; UCLA; Sports Thrpy.

BRYANT, TALYA O; Washington Prep HS; Los Angeles, CA; (2); Dance Clb; Drill Tm; Cit Awd; Hon Roll; Prfct Atten Awd.

BRYNING, JENNIFER L; Crawford HS; San Diego, CA; (1); 1/407; Church Yth Grp; Dance Clb; Spanish Clb; Var L Socr; Spanish NHS; Soccer Mst Insprtnl Plyr Awd; Ed.

BRYSON, LISA L; Woodland HS; Woodland, CA; (2); FBLA; Cheerldng; Pom Pon; Hon Roll; U CA Santa Barbara; Psych.

BUBENIK, CHRIS L; Sanger HS; Sanger, CA; (2); Model UN; Science Clb; Chorus; Oxford U London Englnd 90.

BUBLITZ, BECKETT L; Newbury Park HS; Newbury Park, CA; (3); 150/365; Art Clb; Church Yth Grp; Teachers Aide; Powder Puff Ftbl; High Hon Roll; Hon Roll; UCSB; Art/Dsgn.

BUBP, MEGAN C; North HS; Bakersfield, CA; (2); Church Yth Grp; French Clb; Ski Clb; Chorus; Cheerldng; Hon Roll; NHS; BYU; Vet.

BUCACCIO, JULIE S; Poway HS; Poway, CA; (1); Band; Mrchg Band; High Hon Roll.

BUCCIERI III, ALBERT M; Bullard HS; Fresno, CA; (1); Boy Scts; Debate Tm; NFL; Spanish Clb; Bsktbl; Diving; Socr; Tennis; Vllybl; Hon Roll; Naval Aviator.

BUCHANAN, CORAL P; Apple Valley HS; Lucerne Valley, CA; (1); Commrcl Advrtsng.

BUCHANAN, JEFF T; College Park HS; Martinez, CA; (2); Var L Swmmng; Vrsty Swimming MVP 90; Natl Math Leag 2nd Pl Algebr A; MEDICINE.

BUCHANAN, JOHN W; Bullard HS; Fresno, CA; (2); Debate Tm; Key Clb; Ski Clb; SADD; VP Golf; Hon Roll; UC San Diego; Engl.

BUCHANAN, JOSEPH D; San Ramon Valley HS; San Ramon, CA; (3).

BUCHANAN, SHERRI L; Paso Robles HS; Paso Robles, CA; (2); Church Yth Grp; Church Choir; Var L Sftbl; Var L Vllybl; Lion Awd; CA Hstry Day; Vlybl.

BUCHBINDER, DANIEL B; Poway HS; Poway, CA; (3); VP Math Clb; Math Tm; Mu Alpha Theta; VP Band; Jazz Band; Mrchg Band; Nwsp; JV Trk; High Hon Roll; Hon Roll; Worked In Electronics Store 4 Yrs; Enjoy The Sun & Beach & Studying Exotic Cars; Med.

BUCHHOLZ, JASON D; Montgomery HS; Santa Rosa, CA; (2); Socr; JV Wrstlng; Hon Roll; Pres Acad Fit Awd; Soup Ktchn Vlntr; UCSB; Pre-Med.

BUCHOLZ, RICK J; Tulare Union HS; Tulare, CA; (1); FFA; Intrml Mgr Ftbl; Hon Roll; Advertising.

BUCHS, BECKY; Boron SR HS; Boron, CA; (2); Dance Clb; Math Clb; Varsity Clb; Band; Mrchg Band; Treas Frsh Cls; Sec Soph Cls; Cheerldng; Sftbl; Vllybl; Spirit Awd; CPA.

BUCHSBAUM, JESSICA G; Lick-Wilmerding HS; San Francisco, CA; (4); SADD; Teachers Aide; Acpl Chr; Nwsp; Lit Mag; Ntl Merit SF; Rcpnt Harvard Book Prize.

BUCK, CHRISTIE; Lodi HS; Lodi, CA; (3); Debate Tm; 4-H; Key Clb; ROTC; Band; Orch; Pep Band; School Play; Stage Crew; Variety Show; US Army Reserve; Army; Med.

BUCK, JAMI; Placer HS; Auburn, CA; (4); 8/270; Church Yth Grp; Dance Clb; English Clb; Spanish Clb; Chorus; School Musical; Capt Cheerldng; High Hon Roll; Hon Roll; Pres Acad Fit Awd; Brigham Young U; Medicine.

BUCK, MELANIE; Ramona HS; Thornton, CO; (2); Church Yth Grp; Dance Clb; Chorus; Gym; Med Secy.

BUCKELS, CHRISTOPHER; Liberty Christian HS; Fountain Valley, CA; (4); 1/25; Church Yth Grp; Pres Jr Cls; VP Sr Cls; Stu Cncl; Capt Bsbl; Ftbl; Cit Awd; High Hon Roll; Natl Coll Hall Fame Athletic & Acad Awd 90; Coca Cola Prep Fndtn MVP Bsbl 89; USC.

BUCKLEY, JESSICA; Ontario HS; Chino, CA; (2); Drama Clb; School Musical; Stage Crew; Wt Lftg; Sci.

BUCKLEY, LISA; Mojave HS; California City, CA; (3); 2/100; Spanish Clb; Teachers Aide; Band; Mrchg Band; Pep Band; Rptr Nwsp; Yrbk; High Hon Roll; CSF; Arch Dsgn.

BUCKLEY, SHAWN D; Chaffey HS; Ontario, CA; (3); Church Yth Grp; Science Clb; Ftbl; High Hon Roll; Hon Roll; Mech Engrng.

BUCKLEY, STEVE D; Redwood HS; Visalia, CA; (2); Chess Clb; Science Clb; Spanish Clb; Band; Mrchg Band; Pep Band; Golf; JV Wrstlng; Hon Roll; Fresno ST U; CPA.

BUCKLEY, TIM D; Livermore HS; Livermore, CA; (1); Church Yth Grp; Letterman Clb; Mrchg Band; Ftbl; Wt Lftg; High Hon Roll; CA Schlrshp Fed; Green And Gold Club; Athlet Schlr; Academic Achvt; Vet.

BUCKLEY, VALERIE D; Trabuco Hills HS; Mission Viejo, CA; (2); Church Yth Grp; Drama Clb; Spanish Clb; SADD; Church Choir; Pres Acad Fit Awd; Saddleback JC; Elem Ed.

BUCKLEY, WILLIAM F; San Pasqual HS; Escondido, CA; (2); JV L Crs Cntry; Cit Awd; Hon Roll; 24 Hr Relay For Cross Cntry Tm, Ltr Awd Wnnr; Stadium Cleanup Cross Cntry; Frosh Trophy Awd; Comp.

BUCKLY, JEANNE; Paraclete HS; Quartz Hill, CA; (1); Girl Scts; Hosp Aide; SADD; High Hon Roll; Math Awd In Geom; SS Awd In Geo; Svc Awd For Chrstn Svc.

BUCKNER, ANNETT D; Saint Anthony HS; Carson, CA; (3); Cmnty Wkr; DECA; GAA; Letterman Clb; Chorus; Var Vllybl; High Hon Roll; NHS; Prfct Atten Awd; CIF IA Plyr Of Yr 88 & 89; Vrs Sports Awds; All Amer; Med.

BUCKNER, DAVID J; Caruthers Union HS; Caruthers, CA; (3); Boy Scts; Church Yth Grp; Computer Clb; FBLA; Letterman Clb; VP Math Clb; Sec Spanish Clb; Treas Jr Cls; Var Ftbl; Var Tennis; Eagle Sct Prjct; Joining Natl Guard; Brigham Young U; Bus.

BUCKNER, DORIAN; James Lick HS; San Jose, CA; (2); Math Tm; Science Clb; Drill Tm; Fld Hcky; Wt Lftg; Independence; Nurse.

BUCKNER, PAMELA; Junipero Serra HS; San Diego, CA; (3); 52/391; Pres Church Yth Grp; Cmnty Wkr; Letterman Clb; Office Aide; Pep Clb; Teachers Aide; Varsity Clb; Drill Tm; Cheerldng; Hon Roll; Brigham Young U.

BUCKNER, YOLANDA C; Tehachapi HS; Tehachapi, CA; (2); Church Yth Grp; Cmnty Wkr; FFA; Girl Scts; Teachers Aide; Church Choir; School Play; Stage Crew; Girl Scout Silver Awd; Marine Bio.

BUDAYA, ANGELIQUE; Sunny Hills HS; Fullerton, CA; (2); 14/424; Church Yth Grp; Spanish Clb; Vllybl; Cit Awd; High Hon Roll; Acad Ltr; Eng Brz Mdl; Jhns Hpkns; Med.

BUDDING, KELLEY J; Elk Grove HS; Elk Grove, CA; (4); 14/588; Am Leg Aux Girls St; Drama Clb; Speech Tm; Teachers Aide; Stu Cncl; Trk; Hon Roll; Acad Olympics; CSF; Omaha Woodman Outstndng Proficiency US Hstry Awd; Chico ST; Spanish Ed.

BUDESHTSKY, STAN S; Whitney HS; Cerritos, CA; (1); Model UN; Law.

BUDGE, PHILIP J; Clovis HS; Clovis, CA; (3); Boy Scts; Church Yth Grp; German Clb; Math Clb; Math Tm; Var L Swmmng; Hon Roll; Ntl Merit Ltr; Vrsty Water Polo 2 Ltrs; Engrng.

BUDNEY, AMIE JOY; Turlock HS; Turlock, CA; (3); 76/550; AFS; Am Leg Aux Girls St; FBLA; Key Clb; Science Clb; Hon Roll; Amnesty Intl; CSF; Teenline Vol; DARE Spkr; U OF CA Santa Cruz; Psych.

BUDRICK, SUZIE; Sequoia HS; San Carlos, CA; (4); Church Yth Grp; Cmnty Wkr; Dance Clb; Pep Clb; Variety Show; Pres Frsh Cls; VP Jr Cls; Pres Sr Cls; Kiwanis Awd; Rotary Awd; JR & SR Prm Prncss; Plc Offcrs Schlrshp; Hmcmng Qun; Dnc Schlrshp; Westmont Coll; Psych.

BUEHLER, JOHN; Mc Kinleyville HS; Mc Kinleyville, CA; (4); 3/130; Church Yth Grp; Key Clb; Letterman Clb; Teachers Aide; Varsity Clb; Rep Frsh Cls; Rep Soph Cls; Treas Stu Cncl; Capt L Bsktbl; Capt L Ftbl; US Military Acad; Poltcl Sci.

BUEHLER, MARK D; Whittier Christian HS; La Mirada, CA; (4); 11/177; Church Yth Grp; Nwsp; Treas Stu Cncl; JV Bsktbl; Var Socr; JV Vllybl; Cit Awd; High Hon Roll; Jr NHS; NHS; CSF; Bus.

BUEHLER, RANDALL D; University City HS; San Diego, CA; (3); 2/373; Boy Scts; Math Tm; Model UN; Teachers Aide; Ed Nwsp; Var Ftbl; Var Trk; Var Wrstlng; Cit Awd; High Hon Roll; Hnrs Math Cont Tm Hgh Scr, Top 25 Scrs; Amer Math Cmptn Schl Wnnr; CSF; UC Berkeley; Physics.

BUEHLER, STEVE W; Saddleback HS; Santa Ana, CA; (4); Sec Kiwanis Awd; Ed Nwsp; Gold Mdlln Cmptr Stud; Bnk Of Amer Achvt Awd Cmptr Stud; Santa Ana Unified Schl Dist To 90 Acad Awd; Orange Coast Coll; Bus Media.

BUELL, HEATHER G; Eureka SR HS; Eureka, CA; (3); Boy Scts; Church Yth Grp; Dance Clb; Service Clb; Ski Clb; Varsity Clb; Sec Frsh Cls; Sec Soph Cls; Cheerldng; Powder Puff Ftbl; Law.

BUELL, SANDRA E; Artesia HS; Lakewood, CA; (2); Church Yth Grp; Drama Clb; Thesps; School Play; Stage Crew; Score Keeper; Var Swmmng; Cit Awd; Hon Roll; ITT Tech; Comp Tech.

BUENA, EMMALIE; Westmoor HS; Daly City, CA; (2); Church Yth Grp; French Clb; GAA; Church Choir; Var Swmmng; Hon Roll; CSF; Coll Entrance Clb; Gifted & Talented Ed; Med.

BUENAFLOR, CHERRYMAINE; Providence HS; Los Angeles, CA; (2); Dance Clb; Hon Roll; Asian/Pacific Islanders Club Treas; Boston Coll; Accntnt.

BUENALUZ, RUBY BERNADETTE Z; Sierra Vista HS; Baldwin Park, CA; (4); Science Clb; Teachers Aide; Hon Roll; CA ST U Fullerton; Anthrplgy.

BUENAVENTURA, ALLAN; Don Bosco Tech Inst; Whittier, CA; (1); 2/244; Cmnty Wkr; Math Tm; High Hon Roll; Hon Roll; NHS; NEDT Awd; Prfct Atten Awd; Sal; Engrns Day Math Rlys; Hnrs Entrnc Awd 89; Stanford U; Aerospc Engrng.

BUENAVENTURA, ANGELINE R; Holy Family HS; Montebello, CA; (3); Church Yth Grp; Sec Sr Cls; Socl Act Club; Nwsp Club; Miss Montebello Self Dev Pgm; LMU; Bus Admin.

BUENDIA, OLGA; Selma HS; Selma, CA; (3); Church Yth Grp; Teachers Aide; JV Var Bsktbl; Reedlet Coll; Crrctnl Ofcr.

BUENO, TERESA; Hottville HS; Holtville, CA; (3); Hosp Aide; Spanish Clb; Flag Corp; Cit Awd; Prfct Atten Awd; Pdiatrc.

BUENSALIDO, MARK A; St Ignatius College Preparator HS; Benicia, CA; (3); 31/250; Cmnty Wkr; Letterman Clb; Service Clb; Co-Ed Nwsp; Var Capt Swmmng; Hon Roll; Mem Of Marin Pirates Swim Team; Mem Of CA Schlrshp Fed; Sprts Med.

BUENSUCESO, ANN THERESE S; Lynwood HS; Lynwood, CA; (3); #27 In Class; Church Yth Grp; Chorus; Hon Roll; Prfct Atten Awd; GATE; Child Psych.

BUENVIAJE, CARMINIA; North Hollywood HS; North Hollywood, CA; (3); Church Yth Grp; Natl Beta Clb; Spanish Clb; Teachers Aide; Var Vllybl; Cit Awd; High Hon Roll; UCLA Hrns Prgm; CSF; Indstrl Engr.

BUENVIAJE, JANINE D; Lemoore HS; Lemoore, CA; (1); Church Yth Grp; Hon Roll; CSF; Ucla; Astronomy.

BUENVIAJE, JEROME DECASTRO; Sweetwater Union HS; National City, CA; (3); Spanish Clb; Chorus; Var Bsktbl; Hon Roll; Kiwanis Awd; Comp; Debate; San Diego ST U; Comp Sci.

BUERER, JENNIFER P; Modesto Christian HS; Modesto, CA; (3); Church Yth Grp; Chorus; Hon Roll; Bronze Medal Eng; Accntnt.

BUERGER, CHRIS; Saddleback HS; Santa Ana, CA; (4); Chess Clb; Rptr Nwsp; Swmmng; Vllybl; Hon Roll; Step Club; CSF; UC San Diego; Econ.

BUERGLER, CHRISTINE M; Cloverdale HS; Cloverdale, CA; (2); 4-H; JA; Band; Mrchg Band; Sec Frsh Cls; JV Bsktbl; JV Tennis; 4-H Awd; UC-DAVIS; Vet.

BUERGLER, JOHNNY P; Cloverdale HS; Cloverdale, CA; (4); 4/64; Cmnty Wkr; Teachers Aide; Band; Drm Mjr(t); Jazz Band; Mrchg Band; Off Jr Cls; JV Bsbl; JV Bsktbl; JV Var Trk; Cloverdale Jr Citrus Fair Bd & Cloverdale Amer Lgn Gun Club Jrs Pres; Cloverdale 4-H Gun Sfty Asst; OR ST U; Aeronautics.

BUETTNER, TANA M; Victory Christian HS; Sacramento, CA; (2); Var L Bsktbl; Var L Sftbl; Var L Vllybl; High Hon Roll; Hon Roll; Advncd Plcmnt Alg Hnrs Awd; Bus.

BUFALINO, JEANNE; John W North HS; Riverside, CA; (2); Art Clb; Pep Clb; Color Guard; Rep Frsh Cls; Rep Soph Cls; Var JV Cheerldng; Mgr(s); SAVE; Art.

BUFFORD, JAMES T; Artesia HS; Lakewood, CA; (3); Letterman Clb; Teachers Aide; Varsity Clb; Bsbl; Bsktbl; Ftbl; Wt Lftg; High Hon Roll; 1st Team All Lge, All SE Los Angeles Cnty, All Area Team Defensive Tackle; Detective.

BUGARIN, DEBBIE M; Huntington Beach Union HS; Huntington Beach, CA; (2); Church Yth Grp; Spanish Clb; Stu Cncl; Aviation.

BUGARIN, GIL; Southwest HS; San Diego, CA; (3); Office Aide; Science Clb; Cit Awd; Hon Roll.

BUGARIN, JOSE L; Pasadena HS; Pasadena, CA; (3); Drama Clb; Spanish Clb; Pres Jr Cls; Ftbl; Hon Roll; CSF; UCLA; Drama.

BUGARIN, PRECIOUS; East Union HS; Stockton, CA; (2); 8/411; Mrchg Band; School Play; Vllybl; High Hon Roll; Prfct Atten Awd; Asian Club.

BUGARIN, SUSANA; San Fernando HS; Arleta, CA; (3); Science Clb; Yrbk; Sec Stu Cncl; Var Tennis; Cit Awd; Hon Roll; Jr NHS; NHS; Pres Acad Fit Awd.

BUGAYONG, MARITES G; Phillip & Sala Burton Academic HS; San Francisco, CA; (3); French Clb; School Musical; Rptr Nwsp; High Hon Roll; Acad Schlrshp & Mdl Awd; Outstndng Mrt Cert Music Apprctn; UC Berkeley; Pre-Med.

BUGL, LAURA M; Patrick Henry HS; San Diego, CA; (3); Library Aide; Office Aide; Yrbk; Cit Awd; Hon Roll; Jr NHS; NHS; Pres Acad Fit Awd; Bus.

BUGLIONE, JESSE M; Carpinteria HS; Carpinteria, CA; (2); 7/175; Nwsp; JV Ftbl; High Hon Roll; Prfct Atten Awd; Achvt Art Awd; CA Fdrtn Of Chaparral Poets Statewide Cont 3rd Pl; Engl.

BUGSCH, DORI; Clovis HS; Clovis, CA; (4); 16/550; Church Yth Grp; Cmnty Wkr; Dance Clb; Math Clb; Science Clb; Chorus; Stage Crew; Hon Roll; Sal; CSF; Sci Fair Wnnr; Mills Coll; Bio.

BUHLMAN, THERESA M; Northgate HS; Walnut Creek, CA; (3); Am Leg Aux Girls St; Pres Church Yth Grp; Capt GAA; Letterman Clb; Office Aide; SADD; Varsity Clb; Off Sr Cls; Rep Stu Cncl; Capt Var Bsktbl; Asst Rcrd Happening; UCSB; Real Estate Attorney.

BUHRE, YVETTE; Foothill HS; Pleasanton, CA; (4); #23 In Class; Debate Tm; Hosp Aide; Intnl Clb; Service Clb; Spanish Clb; SADD; Varsity Clb; Color Guard; Flag Corp; Lit Mag; Natl Hspnc Schlr Semi-Fnlst; Biomdcl Rsrch Intrnshp Awd; A P Spnsh Awd; Bio.

BUI, AI; Bolsa Grande HS; Westminster, CA; (2); Intrml Bsktbl; Cit Awd; High Hon Roll; Prfct Atten Awd; UCLA; Arch.

BUI, AN TUYET; Washington HS; Fremont, CA; (3); 5/306; Service Clb; High Hon Roll; Lion Awd; Dept Awds Engl, Chem, Frnch; High Hnrs Algebra I 87; Amnesty Intl; Adv Dsgn.

BUI, ANH V; Herbert Hoover HS; Glendale, CA; (4); Key Clb; Pep Clb; Treas Spanish Clb; Rep Stu Cncl; Cheerldng; Intrml Vllybl; High Hon Roll; Hon Roll; Kiwanis Awd; Pres Acad Fit Awd; U Of Southern CA.

BUI, ANN; Mission Bay HS; San Diego, CA; (2); 1/380; French Clb; Library Aide; High Hon Roll; Hon Roll; Vrsty Badminton Tm Lttr; CSF; DECA; Math.

BUI, ANN; Sequoia HS; Redwood, CA; (3); 17/363; Teachers Aide; Nwsp; Yrbk; Rotary Awd; Interact Clb; Asian Club; CSF; Sanford; Med.

BUI, BAO-UYEN K; Santa Teresa HS; San Jose, CA; (3); Chess Clb; Cmnty Wkr; Computer Clb; French Clb; Girl Scts; Intnl Clb; JA; Math Clb; Math Tm; Science Clb; Var Badminton Tm; Yth Club; U CA Berkeley; Med.

BUI, CATHERINE; Foothill HS; Sacramento, CA; (1); Hon Roll; CSF Clb; Key Clb.

BUI, CUONG; Modesto HS; Modesto, CA; (3); Intnl Clb; Math Clb; Hon Roll; U Of Ocean Pacific; Elec Engr.

BUI, DUC T; Downtown Business Magnet HS; Los Angeles, CA; (2); Computer Clb; JV Bsktbl; JV Tennis.

BUI, HIEN; Hoover SR HS; San Diego, CA; (4); Bus Profs of Am; Computer Clb; English Clb; GAA; Office Aide; Stu Cncl; Tennis; Wt Lftg; Cit Awd; JETS Awd; Engr.

BUI, HIEU T; Tustin HS; Tustin, CA; (2); Art Clb; German Clb; Latin Clb; Science Clb; Trk; Vllybl; Wrstlng; Hon Roll; Orng Cnty Acadmc Dcthln; Johns Hopkins U; Med.

BUI, JASMINE-HIEN; Bolsa Grande HS; Garden Grove, CA; (2); 162/846; Church Yth Grp; Hon Roll; CA ST Long Beach; Acctng.

BUI, JERRY T; La Sierra HS; Riverside, CA; (2); 1/500; Hist Drama Clb; Thesps; School Play; Nwsp; Pres Frsh Cls; Pres Jr Cls; Stu Cncl; Var Tennis; High Hon Roll; Pres Acad Fit Awd; MIT; Engr.

BUI, KAREN; Lowell HS; San Francisco, CA; (2); Cmnty Wkr; Dance Clb; Drama Clb; French Clb; Hosp Aide; SADD; Band; Orch; UC Davis; Optometry.

BUI, KIM; Clayton Valley HS; Concord, CA; (4); FBLA; Varsity Clb; Rptr Nwsp; Sec Treas Jr Cls; Sec Treas Sr Cls; Var Capt Cheerldng; Hon Roll; Vlntr John Muir Hosp; Csu Sacramento; Cmnctns.

BUI, MAI; Valley HS; Santa Ana, CA; (1); Hon Roll; Prfct Atten Awd; Acad Awds.

BUI, NGOC; Lakewood HS; Lakewood, CA; (4); 38/757; VP AFS; Art Clb; French Clb; Intnl Clb; Key Clb; Spanish Clb; Var Tennis; High Hon Roll; NHS; VP CA Schlrsp Fed; Pres Tennis Clb; Peer Tutor; U Of CA; Bio Sci Dentistry.

BUI, NGOC H; Rosemead HS; Rosemead, CA; (3); Computer Clb; Pres FBLA; Pres Key Clb; Lit Mag; Off Frsh Cls; Stu Cncl; Hon Roll; CSF; Psych.

BUI, PATRICK THIEN C; Bolsa Grande HS; Garden Grove, CA; (4); 17/340; Boy Scts; Chess Clb; JCL; Key Clb; Science Clb; Cit Awd; Hon Roll; Ntl Merit Ltr; Prfct Atten Awd; Pres Acad Fit Awd; Science Bowl Team; Latin Bowl Team.

BUI, PHAN VINCENT; Carson HS; Carson, CA; (4); Chess Clb; Church Yth Grp; Office Aide; Teachers Aide; Rptr Lit Mag; Rep Frsh Cls; Stu Cncl; Cit Awd; High Hon Roll; Pres Acad Fit Awd; Libr Aide; Svc Club; Prfct Atten Awd; U Of CA Long Beach; Bus Admin.

BUI, PHILIP N; Irvine HS; Irvine, CA; (3); 45/520; Chess Clb; Church Yth Grp; Hosp Aide; Teachers Aide; High Hon Roll; Hon Roll; Golden St Exam Geom Hnrs Awd; UC Irvine; Med.

BUI, PHUONG K; Santiago HS; Santa Ana, CA; (2); Art Clb; French Clb; Off Frsh Cls; Off Soph Cls; Tennis; High Hon Roll; Hon Roll; UCLA; Cvl Engr.

BUI, THANH; Andrew Hill HS; San Jose, CA; (2); 1/30; Math Tm; Bsktbl; Hon Roll; Prfct Atten Awd; Jr Vol At Hosp; UC Davis; Doctor.

BUI, THANH; Carson HS; Carson, CA; (4); Hon Roll; Prfct Atten Awd; Cal ST Dominguez Hill; Elec.

BUI, THANHHOA; South HS; Bakersfield, CA; (4); Chess Clb; Church Yth Grp; Computer Clb; French Clb; JA; Math Clb; Math Tm; Spanish Clb; Teachers Aide; Tennis; U CA-SANTA Barbara; Engr.

BUI, THIEN C; Bolsa Grande HS; Garden Grove, CA; (4); 17/343; Boy Scts; Chess Clb; JCL; Key Clb; Latin Clb; Math Clb; Science Clb; Cit Awd; Hon Roll; Ntl Merit Ltr; Sci Bowl Tm; Latin Bowl Tm; U Of CA; Irvine; Mech Engrn.

BUI, THUAN D; Villa Park HS; Orange, CA; (4); 5/445; Am Leg Boys St; Latin Clb; Var Ftbl; Var Trk; High Hon Roll; NHS; Pres Schlr; UC Berkely; Bus.

BUI, TOAN; Paradise HS; Paradise, CA; (1); Church Yth Grp; Var Tennis; High Hon Roll; Prfct Atten Awd; UC Davis; Bio Chem.

BUI, TRAM; Rosemead HS; Rosemead, CA; (2); Cmnty Wkr; GAA; Treas Key Clb; JV Trk; JV Vllybl; Hon Roll; CA ST-LOS Angeles; Bus Mgmt.

BUI, TUANKHANH A; Andrew Hill HS; San Jose, CA; (3); Evergreen Vly Clg; Elec Engrg.

BUI, TUYETANH; Tustin HS; Tustin, CA; (4); 36/377; GAA; Key Clb; Science Clb; JV Vllybl; High Hon Roll; Hon Roll; Vietnamese Club; CA Schlrshp Fed; Jr Vrsty Athltcs Awd; High Achvt Math; Excllnc In ESL; Orange Cnty Coll; Bio.

BUI, UYEN; Katella HS; Garden Grove, CA; (4); Key Clb; Spanish Clb; High Hon Roll; Hon Roll; Prfct Atten Awd; Pres Acad Fit Awd; Fullerton JC; Optometry.

BUILTEMAN, DANA; Inland Christian Schl; Rialto, CA; (1); Church Yth Grp; Computer Clb; Church Choir; School Musical; Var Cheerldng; L Vllybl; Hon Roll; Cal Poly Pomona; Hotel Mngmnt.

BUITRAGO, DIANE; Bishop Amat Memorial HS; West Covina, CA; (3); Church Yth Grp; Latin Clb; Spanish Clb; CA Schlrshp Fndtn; UCLA; Law.

BUJANDA, BRANDON E; Warren HS; Walnut, CA; (2); AFS; Church Yth Grp; FBLA; Office Aide; Gldn Bear Awd Acctng; Acctng.

BUKENAS, JENNIFER L; Trabuco Hills HS; Rancho Snta Margr, CA; (3); Spanish Clb; Hon Roll; Jr NHS; Pres Acad Fit Awd; Schl Snt; Dstngshd Schlr Awd Phys Ed; Mrtrs Awd Glf, Bdmntn & Pddl Tnns; Med.

BUKSH, MONA K; Wood HS; Vacaville, CA; (2); Art Clb; FHA; Chorus; Typing; Dance; Cosmetology.

BULACAN, JAMIE L; Bishop Montgomery HS; Redondo Beach, CA; (2); Flag Corp; Socr; Trk; Vllybl; Torrance United Soccer Clb; Corp Law.

BULACAN, JAMIELYN; Bishop Montgomery HS; Redondo Beach, CA; (2); Flag Corp; Var Socr; JV Trk; JV Vllybl; Hon Roll; Torrance United Scr Club; Corp Attorney.

BULAHAO, LARRY; Highlands HS; North Highlands, CA; (4); Spanish Clb; Var Trk; Cit Awd; High Hon Roll; Hon Roll; Pres Acad Fit Awd; Comp Sci Acad Achvt; Black Hstry Poster Cont 2nd Pl Wnnr; UC Davis; Elec Engrng.

BULALACAO, EMMARUTH G; Saddleback HS; Irvine, CA; (3); Cmnty Wkr; Drama Clb; FBLA; Hosp Aide; Pres Spanish Clb; SADD; Nwsp; Peers In Contact Pres; Dancer St Joseph Ballet Co; Outstndng Achvtmnt Awd & Acad Ltr Spanish; Boston U; Med.

BULATAO, AURORA G; Encinal HS; Alameda, CA; (3); Sec FBLA; Spanish Clb; Acpl Chr; Comp.

BULL, MICHELE; Marysville HS; Marysville, CA; (2); Dance Clb; Drama Clb; Key Clb; Pep Clb; Ski Clb; SADD; Sec Frsh Cls; Sec Soph Cls; Cheerldng; Tennis; Various Awds In Dancing Throughout US; Coll; Business/Fashion.

BULLARD, HILARY L; Elk Grove HS; Elk Grove, CA; (4); 143/650; Drama Clb; Pep Clb; Teachers Aide; Off Sr Cls; JV Var Swmmng; Piano Plyr; Golf; Swmmng; Sacramento ST; Chel Psych.

BULLARD, MICHAEL S; Palmdale HS; Palmdale, CA; (4); 10/580; Key Clb; Letterman Clb; Off Sr Cls; Var Capt Socr; Var Vllybl; Pres Acad Fit Awd; Investor.

BULLARD, SEAN L; Skyline HS; Oakland, CA; (2); Computer Clb; FBLA; Ski Clb; Varsity Clb; Band; Var Bsktbl; Var Ftbl; High Hon Roll; Hon Roll; Morehouse; Lawyer.

BULLARD, VICTORIA M; Skyline HS; Oakland, CA; (2); Dance Clb; Library Aide; Acpl Chr; Chorus; Church Choir; Orch; School Musical; Stage Crew; Swing Chorus; Boston U; Perfmer.

BULLER, EZRA E; Hemet HS; Mountain Center, CA; (2); JV Bsbl; JV Bsktbl; JV Var Ftbl; Wrstlng; Sci Achvt Awd 89-90; Phys Ed.

BULLIS, TRACI L; Folsom HS; Mather Afb, CA; (4); 8/210; Church Yth Grp; Hosp Aide; Teachers Aide; Band; Church Choir; Mrchg Band; Pep Band; Ed Nwsp; Off Stu Cncl; Pres Jr NHS; VP Friday Nite Live; San Jose ST; Recreation Thrpy.

BULLOCK, JENNIFER A; Enterprise HS; Redding, CA; (3); 12/427; Church Yth Grp; Math Clb; Sec Model UN; Mu Alpha Theta; Quiz Bowl; Intrml Bsktbl; High Hon Roll; Rotary Awd; Sci Olympd; Atten Camp Royal; Intl Club; UC Santa Barbara; Pre Med.

BULLOCK, MATTHEW; Wm S Hart HS; Valencia, CA; (4); Cmnty Wkr; Math Tm; Red Cross Aide; Science Clb; Intrml Bsktbl; Var Ftbl; Var Capt Socr; Var Trk; NHS; Ntl Merit SF; Peer Cnslng; Vet.

BULMER, DONNY; Galt HS; Galt, CA; (3); Speech Tm; Band; Jazz Band; Mrchg Band; Pep Band; School Musical; Wt Lftg; Wrstlng; Hon Roll; Stanford; Pre-Med.

BULONE, DOMINIC P; Irvine HS; Irvine, CA; (3); 80/530; Chess Clb; Church Yth Grp; Office Aide; Swmmng; Wrstlng; High Hon Roll; Hon Roll; Water Polo; Heritage Awd Alg II & Trig; Hnrs Precalc & Math; VIVA Espana Hnrs; Adv Span Hnrs; U CA; Comp.

BULSARA, PRADEEP P; Alhambra HS; Alhambra, CA; (2); Key Clb; Intrml Bsktbl; Pres Acad Fit Awd; Biomedcl Independent Stds Cls; Stanford; Med.

BULURAN, MARICRIS R; Bishop Amat Memorial HS; Baldwin Park, CA; (3); Church Yth Grp; Rep Stu Cncl; High Hon Roll; Hon Roll; NHS; CSF; Photo Club; Bus.

BULURAN, ROBERT C; Pittsburg HS; Pittsburg, CA; (1); Church Yth Grp; Hon Roll; Prfct Atten Awd; CA Poly; Mech Engr.

BUMA, MARGO L; Yucca Valley HS; Yucca Valley, CA; (4); Office Aide; Pep Clb; Pres Frsh Cls; VP Stu Cncl; JV Var Cheerldng; Var Gym; Var Powder Puff Ftbl; Var Tennis; Prom Qn 90; Elem Ed.

BUMAN, MICHAEL D; Hoover HS; Glendale, CA; (3); Church Yth Grp; Red Cross Aide; JV Bsbl; Intrml Bsktbl; Prfct Atten Awd; U MI; Intl Bus.

BUMANGLAG, GERALD; N Salinas HS; Salinas, CA; (3); Church Yth Grp; Hon Roll; Spanish NHS; Avtn.

BUMGARNER, ROBYN A; Tulare Western HS; Tulare, CA; (4); GAA; Letterman Clb; Teachers Aide; Varsity Clb; Rep Frsh Cls; Rep Soph Cls; Rep Jr Cls; Rep Sr Cls; Off Stu Cncl; Var JV Bsktbl; Academic Decathlon; Prom Comm; Kings Riv CC; Physical Therp.

BUMGART, HERBERT R; Central Union HS; El Centro, CA; (3); 73/543; Var Ftbl; Hon Roll; Imperial Valley Coll; Reg Nrs.

BUMPAS, KAREN E; Lemoore Union HS; Lemoore, CA; (3); FFA; SADD; Yrbk; JV Var Bsktbl; JV Var Sftbl; JV Var Vllybl; Hon Roll; Intl Order Of Jobs Daughters; Amer Sftbl Leag; Educ.

BUN, HOURTH; Mark Keppel HS; Las Angeles, CA; (4); Math Clb; Pefect Attendance; Outstndng Stu; Mechanic; Mechanic.

BUN, SOPHAL; Lincoln HS; San Francisco, CA; (2); Coll Prep Cls; City Coll Of San Francisco; Eng.

BUNCAB, IMELDA C; Mira Mesa HS; San Diego, CA; (3); VP Treas Church Yth Grp; Yrbk; VP Stu Cncl; JV Var Cheerldng; Cit Awd; AWE Rcgntn 88; Bus Admin.

BUNCE, KATHLEEN; Capistrono Valley Christian HS; S Laguna, CA; (1); Church Yth Grp; Letterman Clb; Rep Frsh Cls; Var Vllybl; High Hon Roll; Pres Acad Fit Awd.

BUNCH, CHRIS M; Salinas HS; Salinas, CA; (4); Teachers Aide; JV Var Bsbl; JV Var Bsktbl; JV Var Ftbl; High Hon Roll; Hon Roll; Wwahss 88-89 Yr; Mvp Ftbl And Bsktbl; Schlstc Championship Team; Var Bskbl Highest Grade Pt Ave; Hartnell; Physical Therapist.

BUNCH, DUANE E; John Burroughs HS; Burbank, CA; (2); Chess Clb; Church Yth Grp; Office Aide; Band; Jazz Band; Orch; Stage Crew; Variety Show; Phtg Nwsp; Phtg Yrbk; Amer Lgn Awd; Cougar Awd; Starr Awd; U Of Southern CA; Poltcl Sci.

BUNCH, JANE T; Alpaugh HS; Alpaugh, CA; (4); 1/10; Varsity Clb; Pep Band; Sftbl; Vllybl; Hon Roll; Val; VP Church Yth Grp; Pres Soph Cls; Rep Jr Cls; Rep Sr Cls; CA ST Bakersfield.

BUNCH, SHANNON L; Antelope Valley HS; Lancaster, CA; (4); Church Yth Grp; Letterman Clb; Quiz Bowl; Spanish Clb; Church Choir; L Capt Bsktbl; High Hon Roll; Hon Roll; Pres Acad Fit Awd; Bsktbl All League; Chrch Handbell Choir; Paresetter Awd; U C Riverside; Chem.

BUNKER, BROOKE A; Mission Viejo HS; Mission Viejo, CA; (3); Church Yth Grp; Office Aide; Orch; Var Bsktbl; Hon Roll; Elem Educ.

BUNKLEY, NATALIE; Newbridge HS; Los Angeles, CA; (2); Church Yth Grp; Cheerldng; Spellman Coll; Bus.

BUNOAN, HAZEL M; Colton HS; Grand Terrace, CA; (3); Band; Mrchg Band; Orch; Hist Sr Cls; Fld Hcky; Powder Puff Ftbl; Hon Roll; Dentistry.

BUNTEN, THOMAS; Ocean View HS; Huntington Beach, CA; (1); Model UN; Tennis; Yng Repulblcns Clb; US Air Force Acad; Pilot.

BUNTING, GLEN A; Santa Clara HS; Santa Clara, CA; (3); 44/389; Spanish Clb; Var Ftbl; JV Var Wrstlng; Hon Roll; Indstrl Arts Awd; Stu Ambssdr For Ple To Ple; Engr.

BUNTING, JESSIE R; Del Oro HS; Penryn, CA; (3); 44/260; Art Clb; Boy Scts; Science Clb; Band; Jazz Band; Mrchg Band; Pep Band; Var L Crs Cntry; Var L Swmmng; Hon Roll.

BUNYAN, LAURA M; North Hollywood HS; Northridge, CA; (2); Cmnty Wkr; Treas Girl Scts; Service Clb; Band; JV Tennis; Var Trk; High Hon Roll; Pres Schlr; UC Davis; Bio.

BUOT, FREDERICK LANCE G; Hueneme HS; Oxnard, CA; (2); 19/503; High Hon Roll; Masonic Awd; Hnr Rl; Lawyerl.

BURACCHIO, NIKKI N; Fountain Valley HS; Fountain Valley, CA; (2); Church Yth Grp; German Clb; Hon Roll; GATE; U CA-IRVINE; Law.

BURAK, BRIAN; Palm Desert HS; Palm Desert, CA; (3); Church Yth Grp; Ftbl; Swmmng; Hon Roll; Automotv Design.

BURBACK, AMY; Santa Ynez Valley HS; Buellton, CA; (4); Church Yth Grp; Off FBLA; Pep Clb; Spanish Clb; Teachers Aide; Capt Drill Tm; Yrbk; Var Cheerldng; Cit Awd; Hon Roll; Pr Cnslng; Whittier Coll; Psych.

BURBANK, TAMMY K; Corcoran HS; Corcoran, CA; (3); 4/130; Pres Church Yth Grp; FBLA; Letterman Clb; Office Aide; Band; JV Bsktbl; Capt Var Vllybl; High Hon Roll; Hon Roll; Kiwanis Awd; VSF; Acctng.

BURBANO, SONJA; Archbishop Mitty HS; San Jose, CA; (4); 5/210; Hosp Aide; Math Tm; Science Clb; Service Clb; SADD; Teachers Aide; Yrbk; Treas Soph Cls; Var Fld Hcky; JV Socr; Intergenerational Pgm/Crippled Chldrn Soc Volunteer; Duke U; Med.

BURCH, CHRISTOPHER A; Victor Valley HS; Murrieta, CA; (2); JV Bsbl; Stanford; Pro Bsbl.

BURCH, JO D; Apple Valley HS; Apple Valley, CA; (3); Church Yth Grp; Dance Clb; French Clb; Spanish Clb; SADD; Var L Cheerldng; High Hon Roll; Cmnty Wkr; Letterman Clb; Office Aide; 1st Rnnrup Miss Apple Vly 90; UCA All Star Chrldr; Sheriff Stu Advsry Cncl 89; DARE Pgm; Sociology.

BURCH, PAT; Oakmont HS; Roseville, CA; (1); Bsktbl; Var Trk; JV Vllybl; Cit Awd; High Hon Roll; Opt Clb Awd; Prfct Atten Awd; Ltr JV Vlybl, Vrsty Track 4 Mdls; Tutor Mainly Span; Princeton; Atty.

BURCH, RACHEL I; Thomas Downey HS; Modesto, CA; (3); Church Yth Grp; Cmnty Wkr; Drama Clb; Key Clb; Thesps; Chorus; School Musical; School Play; Stage Crew; Swing Chorus; Pres Conservation Clb; Amer Legn Yth Envrnmntl Conf; Project SAFT Vlntr; UC Davis; Humanities.

BURCH, TAWNEE L; Mission Bay HS; San Diego, CA; (3); Church Yth Grp; Cmnty Wkr; Chorus; Stage Crew; Off Sr Cls; Sec Stu Cncl; Var Mgr(s); Var Swmmng; Var Tennis; Cit Awd; Miss TEEN CA Pgnt 90; U CA San Diego; Genetics.

BURCHETT, ANDY A; Downey HS; Downey, CA; (2); FBLA; Capt Bsktbl; Pres Acad Fit Awd; Rcvd Awd Hghst GPA 4.0 On Bsktbl Tm.

BURCHETT, MICHAEL D; Chino HS; Chino, CA; (3); Intnl Clb; Teachers Aide; School Play; Score Keeper; BSU-PRES; CA Poly; Law.

BURCHFIELD, THOMAS D; Santa Clara HS; Oxnard, CA; (3); 15/121; French Clb; Letterman Clb; SADD; Crs Cntry; Trk; NHS; CSF; Cal ST San Luis Obispo; Arch.

BURCIAGA, MIKE J; St Ignatius College Prep; San Francisco, CA; (3); 14/244; Chess Clb; Dance Clb; Spanish Clb; Teachers Aide; JV Bsktbl; Intrml Ftbl; JV Socr; Intrml Tennis; Intrml Vllybl; High Hon Roll; Bwlng; Santa Clara; Engrng.

BURCIAGA, VERONICA; Marshal HS; Los Angeles, CA; (2); Church Yth Grp; Cmnty Wkr; Office Aide; Dancer; Psych.

BURCOMBE, JONATHAN; Avalon HS; Avalon, CA; (2); Church Yth Grp; Golf; Hon Roll; Excllnc In Math; Awana Clbs Intl Ldr.

BURD, HEATHER R; Grossmont HS; El Cajon, CA; (2); 14/429; Teachers Aide; CSF; San Diego ST U; Bus.

BURDEN, JAMES; Palmdale HS; Palmdale, CA; (4); French Clb; Band; Drm Mjr(t); Mrchg Band; Orch; Pep Band; Off Soph Cls; Off Jr Cls; Hon Roll; Associated Stu Body; CA ST U; Music Tchr.

BURDEN, STACI; San Gabriel HS; San Gabriel, CA; (2); Church Yth Grp; French Clb; Service Clb; Teachers Aide; Church Choir; Drill Tm; JV Cheerldng; Pom Pon; Swmmng; Cit Awd; 3rd Pl Amer Leg Awd; Child Psych.

BURDETTE, ANGEL D; Atwater HS; Merced, CA; (3); Church Yth Grp; Teachers Aide; Church Choir; JV Crs Cntry; JV Trk; Hon Roll; Zoologist.

BURDETTE, JOHN A; Durham HS; Durham, CA; (2); Teachers Aide; Var Wrstlng; High Hon Roll; Hon Roll; CA Schlrshp Fed; Acad Block; Camera Crew; Chico ST U; Bus.

BURDICK, ERIN M; Ramona HS; Riverside, CA; (2); 18/422; Church Yth Grp; Letterman Clb; Scholastic Bowl; Thesps; Church Choir; School Play; Stage Crew; Var Swmmng; NHS; Drama.

BURDICK, MORGAN P; Clovis HS; Clovis, CA; (1); FCA; Ski Clb; SADD; Var Bsbl; JV Ftbl; Hon Roll; Fresno ST U; Bus.

BURDICK, ORION N; Mendocino Community HS; Comptche, CA; (2); Drama Clb; School Play; Prdcd, Engrd, Wrote, Prfrmd, Cover & Graphics For 2 Albums; Music.

BURDYSHAW, TYSON; W C Overfelt HS; San Jose, CA; (2); Science Clb; Teachers Aide; Band; School Musical; Ftbl; Swmmng; Wt Lftg; Wrstlng; Cit Awd; Hon Roll; Outstndng Woodshop; Art; San Jose ST; Carpenter.

BURG, MICHAEL; Bishop Amat Memorial HS; Phillips Ranch, CA; (3); Letterman Clb; Ski Clb; Varsity Clb; Stu Cncl; Var L Ftbl; Var L Trk; Var L Wt Lftg; Var L Wrstlng; UCSD; Bus Admin.

BURG, WENDY L; Will C Crawford HS; San Diego, CA; (2); AFS; Spanish Clb; Teachers Aide; Varsity Clb; Flag Corp; Rep Frsh Cls; Rep Soph Cls; Var Socr; Spanish NHS.

BURGE, ERIKA M; Clovis West HS; Fresno, CA; (2); JV Cheerldng; JV Vllybl; Hon Roll; Fresno ST; Med.

BURGE, MATTHEW J; Bellarmine College Prep; Gilroy, CA; (1); Boy Scts; Latin Clb; Ftbl; Intrml Sftbl.

BURGER, CHERYL L; Whittier Christian HS; Fullerton, CA; (4); 9/180; Church Yth Grp; Teachers Aide; Band; Church Choir; Mrchg Band; Pep Band; High Hon Roll; Band Sec; Biola; Comp Sci.

BURGER, CHRISTINE M; Acad Of Our Lady Of Peace; San Diego, CA; (4); Drama Clb; VP Girl Scts; Office Aide; Chorus; Church Choir; School Musical; Spanish NHS; Grl Sct Gld Ldrshp Awd; Bshp Mhr Cthlc Ldrshp Schlrshp; Grl Sct Marian Awd; U CA San Diego; Msc.

BURGESS, CANDACE A; La Habra HS; Whittier, CA; (3); Fullerton JC; Parallegal.

BURGESS, JOE C; Huenene HS; Oxnard, CA; (3); 40/350; Boy Scts; Church Yth Grp; SADD; Band; Church Choir; Jazz Band; Mrchg Band; Pep Band; Hon Roll; Jr NHS; Army Natl Guard Split Trng Pgm Basic Trng 90, Specialized Trng 91; Ventura CC; Pilot.

BURGESS, SCOTT K; Poway HS; San Diego, CA; (2); 28/870; Scholastic Bowl; Spanish Clb; Band; Jazz Band; Mrchg Band; Stage Crew; High Hon Roll; CSF; A Team; Brdcst Cmmnctns.

BURGESS, SEAN; Olympic Valley Schl; Bullhead City, AZ; (4); 2/8; Ski Clb; Yrbk; Off Sr Cls; Capt Socr; Cit Awd; High Hon Roll; Hon Roll; Rck Clmbng; Mountn Bkng; Deans Awd Acad, Athltcs & Socially; U Of CO Boulder; Liberal Arts.

BURGHARDT, MATTHEW A; Servite HS; Anaheim, CA; (3); 63/143; Quiz Bowl; JV Bsbl; JV Ftbl; Cit Awd; W Coast Bass; Bass Anglng Sprtsmn Soc; 5th Pl W Coast Bass Southern Amatr Trnmnt; Marine Biolgst.

BURGHART, JASON D; Rio Lindo Acad; Healdsburg, CA; (3); Aud/Vis; French Clb; Office Aide; Band; Orch; Walla Walla Coll; Commcl Pilot.

BURGIN, ILIANA D; Richard Gahr HS; Cerritos, CA; (1); Church Yth Grp; Model UN; Hon Roll; Blue & Gold Awd Of Excllnc; Fnlst In Miss CA American Teen Pageant; CA ST Long Beach; Bus.

BURGLE, KEITH W; Mission College Prep; Cambria, CA; (3); JV Bsbl; JV Var Bsktbl; JV Ftbl; JV Var Golf; Santa Clara; Bus.

BURGONIO, VICMAR S; Antelope Valley HS; Lancaster, CA; (3); Sec Treas Church Yth Grp; Computer Clb; French Clb; Church Choir; Hon Roll; CSF; U Of CA Los Angeles; Dntstry.

BURGOS, CARMELA M; Orange HS; Orange, CA; (3); Intnl Clb; Key Clb; Library Aide; Tennis; Hon Roll; NHS; CSF; Cultures Action; UCI; Art.

BURIK, BRYAN; Edison HS; Huntington Beach, CA; (4); Art Clb; Ski Clb; Spanish Clb; Teachers Aide; Lit Mag; Socr; Pres Acad Fit Awd; Golden Key Awd-Art; 4th Pl Awd Creatv Arts Mag; Acad Achvt; Long Beach ST; Cmmrcl Art.

BURK, ALICIA K; Oakmont HS; Roseville, CA; (4); 1/400; Pres Church Yth Grp; Chorus; Drill Tm; Rptr Nwsp; Sec Jr Cls; Stu Cncl; Var Cheerldng; L Var Gym; Pres Acad Fit Awd; Val; BYU; Teaching.

BURK, GREGORY; Mc Farland HS; Delano, CA; (3); Church Yth Grp; Letterman Clb; Yrbk; Bsktbl; Trk; Bausch & Lomb Sci Awd; Hon Roll; Comp Prgrmmg; Water Skiing; Jet Skiing; Fresno ST U; Comp Sci.

BURK, WAYNE E; Santa Teresa HS; San Jose, CA; (3); 14/467; Church Yth Grp; Scholastic Bowl; Spanish Clb; Treas SADD; Varsity Clb; Rptr Yrbk; Intrml Bsktbl; Var Intrml Socr; Var Tennis; Intrml Vllybl; Mech Engrng.

BURKART, KRISTIN J; Santa Rosa HS; Santa Rosa, CA; (3); Church Yth Grp; Cmnty Wkr; FFA; School Musical; Stage Crew; Hon Roll; Santa Cruz; Envrnmntl Sci.

BURKE, BRANDON; Monte Vista HS; Spring Valley, CA; (2); 61/422; Jazz Band; Hon Roll; Musician.

BURKE, CASEY; Red Bluff Union HS; Red Bluff, CA; (2); 1/450; French Clb; Key Clb; Cheerldng; High Hon Roll; Kiwanis Awd; Fri Night Live; CSF; Steering Cmmtte; Landscape Arch.

BURKE, CHRISTINA; San Gorgonio HS; Highland, CA; (3); AFS; English Clb; Latin Clb; Pep Clb; Rep Stu Cncl; Var Pom Pon; JV Socr; Zonta Club; Director Of Communications; CA ST; Education.

BURKE, CLAIRE C; Los Gatos HS; Los Gatos, CA; (3); Acpl Chr; Variety Show; JV Sftbl; JV Swmmng; Hon Roll; Badminton V; Envrnmntl Help Clb; Leos Clb; UC Santa Cruz; Art.

BURKE, ERIN C; Canyon Springs HS; Moreno Valley, CA; (3); Office Aide; High Hon Roll; Golden St Exam Hgh Hnrs Geom.

BURKE, JACQUELINE M; Montgomery HS; Santa Rosa, CA; (2); Church Yth Grp; Cmnty Wkr; Office Aide; Spanish Clb; Teachers Aide; YMCA Vlntr Yr Awd Admin Dept; Action Clb; Rincon Valley Union Schl Dist Offce Assistnt; Bus.

BURKE, JENNIFER R; San Gabriel HS; San Gabriel, CA; (1); Church Yth Grp; Intrml Mgr Bsktbl; Hon Roll; Brigham Young U; Animal Sci.

BURKE, MARY K; Serrano HS; Wrightwood, CA; (3); 4/213; Am Leg Aux Girls St; Cmnty Wkr; JA; Model UN; Chorus; Drill Tm; Flag Corp; High Hon Roll; Hon Roll; Mck Trl Awd Outstndg Prfrmnc By Witness; CSF 4 Sems; Span Hnr Soc; Communications.

BURKE, MICHELLE; South Tahoe HS; South Lake Tahoe, CA; (1); Debate Tm; Drama Clb; Girl Scts; School Musical; School Play; JV Cheerldng; Cit Awd; Hon Roll; Pageant Awds Talent, Photo, Cinderella Grl; Bus.

BURKE-ROSS, CHRISTY; Valley Christian HS; San Jose, CA; (3); 7/67; Church Yth Grp; French Clb; Band; Church Choir; Mrchg Band; Pep Band; School Musical; Yrbk; Var Tennis; Var Trk; Biola U; Tchr.

BURKETT, LEXI; Norte Vista HS; Riverside, CA; (3); 63/336; JA; SADD; Varsity Clb; Stat Bsktbl; Score Keeper; JV Sftbl; Var Tennis; Stat Trk; High Hon Roll; Hon Roll; Prom Cmmtte; Tnns Clb Sec; CA Poly Pomona; Acctnt.

BURKHALTER, DANA D; Oak Ridge HS; Cameron Park, CA; (3); 5/244; Church Yth Grp; Speech Tm; Band; Church Choir; Jazz Band; Pep Band; Variety Show; High Hon Roll; Spelling Bee Co Wnnr; Hist Day Co Wnnr; Most Oustndng Jr; CA ST U Sacramento; Psych.

BURKHARDT, MARK R; Winters HS; Winters, CA; (3); Church Yth Grp; Cmnty Wkr; Letterman Clb; Varsity Clb; JV Socr; Var Tennis; High Hon Roll; Hon Roll; Work After Schl C&S True Value; Flying Lessons; Embry-Riddle; Aviation Pilot.

BURKHEAD, MICHELLE; Arvin HS; Lamont, CA; (4); 28/320; Drama Clb; Office Aide; Spanish Clb; SADD; Band; Color Guard; Flag Corp; Mrchg Band; Hon Roll; Spanish NHS; Bakresfield Coll; Math.

BURKHOLDER, JASON D; Nevada Union HS; Grass Valley, CA; (3); 50/535; Church Yth Grp; 4-H; Letterman Clb; Crs Cntry; Socr; Elks Awd; 4-H Awd; Hon Roll; Prfct Atten Awd; Pres Acad Fit Awd; Law.

BURKHOLDER, SHERI L; Capistrano Valley HS; Mission Viejo, CA; (3); Church Yth Grp; Pep Clb; Color Guard; Mrchg Band; Cit Awd; Sunday Sch Tchr; Hstrcl Soc; UC Davis; Elem Ed.

BURKNER, MONICA; Lincoln HS; Stockton, CA; (3); Pres French Clb; SADD; Teachers Aide; Stat Wrstlng; Hon Roll; French II/Iii Hnr Excllnc Cert; Earth Day Cmmtee 90.

BURKS, CARYN W; Alhambra HS; Alhambra, CA; (3); Cmnty Wkr; Service Clb; Band; Drill Tm; Jazz Band; Mrchg Band; CSF; YMCA Svc Grp; Psych.

BURKS, LYNIESE D; Etiwanda HS; Alta Loma, CA; (2); Church Yth Grp; FBLA; JA; Latin Clb; Office Aide; SADD; Chorus; Church Choir; Rep Frsh Cls; Stat Score Keeper; Tlnt Shws/LYP Syncs; Spelman; Law.

BURKS, STEPHANIE K; Monterey HS; Monterey, CA; (3); Church Yth Grp; German Clb; SADD; Other; High Hon Roll; Hon Roll; Bus.

BURLINGAME, BRYAN D; Manteca HS; Manteca, CA; (3); SADD; High Hon Roll; CSF; Gifted & Talented Ed; High Hnrs GSA Algebra; Psych.

BURLISON, JEREMY C; River City HS; West Sacramento, CA; (3); Church Yth Grp; Drama Clb; French Clb; Library Aide; Pep Clb; SADD; Thesps; School Play; Stage Crew; Peer Cnslng; Friday Night Live; Psych.

BURMAN, JOSHUA D; Norta Vista HS; Riverside, CA; (1); Boy Scts; ROTC; Photogrphy.

BURMAN, SIAN K; Notre Dame HS; San Carlos, CA; (3); Church Yth Grp; French Clb; Hosp Aide; Teachers Aide; Cheerldng; Pom Pon; High Hon Roll; Hon Roll; NHS; Ntl Merit Ltr; Frnch Awd; Engrng.

BURMEISTER, ELIZABETH; Rosary HS; Cerritos, CA; (2); Church Yth Grp; French Clb; Ski Clb; School Musical; School Play; Hon Roll; Danube-Swabian Dance Grp Of LA; Culinary Inst Of San Fran; Chef.

BURMEISTER, KATE J; Academy Of Our Lady Of Peace; San Diego, CA; (2); Church Yth Grp; Cmnty Wkr; GAA; Hosp Aide; Library Aide; Teachers Aide; School Musical; Variety Show; Hon Roll; Girls Athl Assn Club Pres; Morality Awd; UCSD; Med.

BURNES, KIMBERLEY D; Bret Harte HS; Angels Camp, CA; (2); FHA; Math Tm; Quiz Bowl; SADD; Band; Sec Frsh Cls; Score Keeper; High Hon Roll; U CA Santa Cruz; Marine Bio.

BURNETT, ALICIA M; John A Rowland HS; Rowland Heights, CA; (2); Church Yth Grp; Acpl Chr; Chorus; Stage Crew; Engl Tchr.

BURNETT, ANDRIA MICHELLE; Armijo HS; Fairfield, CA; (3); Am Leg Aux Girls St; Drama Clb; Teachers Aide; Chorus; School Play; Stage Crew; Adapted/Co-Dir/Prod A Stu Production Of A Christmas Carol; Active & Interested In Doing Plays; Amer Acad Dramatic Arts; Actrss.

BURNETT, BRENT; Newbury Park HS; Newbury Park, CA; (2); Art Clb; Boy Scts; Church Yth Grp; Band; Crs Cntry; Trk; Hon Roll.

BURNETT, CHASIE D; Tulare Union HS; Tulare, CA; (2); 46/461; Church Yth Grp; FFA; Pep Clb; Band; Mrchg Band; Rep Frsh Cls; Cheerldng; Var Socr; Var Swmmng; Hon Roll; CSF; Jrnlsm.

BURNETT, CHRISTINE; San Jacinto HS; San Jacinto, CA; (4); 32/123; French Clb; Pep Clb; Quiz Bowl; Chorus; Hon Roll; Mt San Jacinto Coll; Arch.

BURNETT, DOUGLAS; Fallbrook HS; Fallbrook, CA; (4); Boy Scts; Sec FBLA; Acpl Chr; Chorus; School Musical; Variety Show; Hon Roll; CSU Fullerton; Music.

BURNETT, IAN J; Bret Harte HS; Arnold, CA; (2); Church Yth Grp; Ski Clb; Band; High Hon Roll; Hon Roll; Prfct Atten Awd; Hnrs Golden St Math Ex; Arch.

BURNETT, JAMES P; Hogan SR HS; Vallejo, CA; (3); School Play; Stage Crew; Wrstlng; Gov Hon Prg Awd; High Hon Roll; Hon Roll; NHS; Pres Acad Fit Awd; Attained Chrtr W/Jr Statesman Fndtn Pres; Corp Law.

BURNETT, JAMES R; Mission Viejo HS; Mission Viejo, CA; (1); 70/437; Ftbl; JV Trk; Wrstlng; CSF; Marine Bio.

BURNHAM, MATTHEW; Kingsburg Joint Union HS; Kingsburg, CA; (4); Bsbl; Hon Roll; Fresno ST; Arch Drafting.

BURNISON, ALISON K; College Park HS; Pleasant Hill, CA; (2); Teachers Aide; Chorus; Drill Tm; High Hon Roll; Hon Roll; UC Davis; Law Enfrcmnt.

BURNS, ALLISON; Dos Pueblos HS; Santa Barbara, CA; (3); 31/370; Church Yth Grp; Drama Clb; Pep Clb; Varsity Clb; School Play; Stage Crew; Cheerldng; Vllybl; Sec NHS; Intl Order Rainbow Past Wrthy Advsr; U Of CA; Law.

BURNS, DAVID M; Aptos HS; Aptos, CA; (2); 16/341; Band; Jazz Band; Pep Band; Var Wrstlng; Monterey Jazz Fstvl All Star Big Band; Hnr Jazz Big Band; Hnr Orch; Engrng.

BURNS, DE ANNA J; Paradise HS; Paradise, CA; (3); Teachers Aide; Sftbl; Cit Awd; Hon Roll; Pres Acad Fit Awd; Peer Cnslr 3 Yrs; Butte Coll; Family Cnslr.

BURNS, DIANE; John Burroughs HS; Burbank, CA; (3); Dance Clb; Teachers Aide; Chorus; Hon Roll; Acad Decathlon; Psych.

BURNS, ERIKA D; J Eugene Mc Ateer HS; San Francisco, CA; (2); Var Bsktbl; Cheerldng; Pom Pon; Hon Roll; Princeton; Pre-Med.

BURNS, GREGORY R; Dorsey HS; Los Angeles, CA; (3); Variety Show; Var Ftbl; Var Trk; Hon Roll; Psych.

BURNS, GUENEVERE T; Cajon HS; San Bernardino, CA; (3); Hosp Aide; Spanish Clb; Chorus; School Musical; Yrbk; Var Crs Cntry; High Hon Roll; NHS; Pres Acad Fit Awd; U CA Davis; Nutrition.

BURNS, HEATHER; Kern Valley HS; Lake Isabella, CA; (1); 10/30; Drama Clb; FBLA; FFA; FHA; Pep Clb; Spanish Clb; SADD; Drill Tm; Nwsp; Yrbk; U Of CA Los Angeles; Law.

BURNS, INGE A; Tustin HS; Tustin, CA; (4); 96/398; Church Yth Grp; Drama Clb; Teachers Aide; Thesps; School Play; Stage Crew; Hon Roll; Perf Arts-Num Awds; Drama Dept Awd; Fullerton JC; Acting.

BURNS, JEFFREY; Shafter HS; Bakersfield, CA; (4); 4/190; Church Yth Grp; FCA; 4-H; Key Clb; Letterman Clb; Science Clb; SADD; Teachers Aide; Varsity Clb; Var Ftbl; Bakersfield Coll; Architecture.

BURNS, JENNIFER A; Bishop O'dowd HS; Berkeley, CA; (2); Church Yth Grp; Cmnty Wkr; Debate Tm; Ski Clb; Church Choir; Cheerldng; Pom Pon; Hon Roll; Vlntr Disbld Chldrns Comp Grp; Chld Psych.

BURNS, JENNIFER H; Dana Hills HS; Dana Point, CA; (2); Rep Stu Cncl; JV Socr; L Var Trk; Pres Acad Fit Awd; Marine Bio.

BURNS, JOEY; Torrey Pines HS; Del Mar, CA; (2); Debate Tm; Drama Clb; Ski Clb; Spanish Clb; School Play; Hon Roll.

BURNS, JULIE N; Willow Glen HS; San Jose, CA; (2); SADD; Rep Stu Cncl; Var Crs Cntry; St Marys Coll; Real Estate.

BURNS, JULIE V; Canyon Springs HS; Moreno Valley, CA; (3); Art Clb; Church Yth Grp; VP Sr Cls; Var Capt Crs Cntry; Var L Trk; High Hon Roll; Hon Roll; Coaches Awd Trk; Natl Art Hnrs Soc; MVP Awd Crss Cntry; 1st Pl Indio Date Fstvl Art Cmptn; U CA; Pre-Med.

BURNS, JULIELYNN; Berean Christian HS; Alamo, CA; (3); Church Yth Grp; Teachers Aide; Band; Chorus; School Musical; Treas Stu Cncl; High Hon Roll; CSF; Cedarville Coll; Bus Mgmt.

BURNS, LAURIE A; Alverno HS; San Gabriel, CA; (2); Aud/Vis; Science Clb; Service Clb; Chorus; Off Jr Cls; Hon Roll; Jr NHS; Pres Acad Fit Awd; Sci.

BURNS, MADELINE K; Bishop O'dowd HS; San Leandro, CA; (2); 62/290; GAA; Ski Clb; Stu Cncl; Var L Tennis; High Hon Roll; NEDT Awd; Cmps Mnstry Team.

BURNS, MARY E; Tokay HS; Stockton, CA; (4); FHA; FTA; German Clb; Hon Roll; Schlrshp For Comp Trng Cls; Delta CC.

BURNS, MELISSA; Mc Kinleyville HS; Arcata, CA; (1); JV Cheerldng; Prfct Atten Awd; UC Santa Barbara; Sociology.

BURNS, MICHAEL; Capistrano Valley Christian HS; San Juan Capstrno, CA; (1); Church Yth Grp; Var Socr; Intrml Vllybl; Hon Roll; Pres Acad Fit Awd.

BURNS, RICHARD F; Oakmont HS; Roseville, CA; (3); Boy Scts; Science Clb; Teachers Aide; Academic Decathlon.

BURNS, SHANNON L; Carson HS; Carson, CA; (2); Teachers Aide; VP Tennis; Adv Of Intl Order Of Rainbow For Girls; Acad Awds In Geom, Eng, French II, Health.

BURNS, SHARON R; Rio Lindo Adventist Boarding Acad; Oakland, CA; (3); Church Yth Grp; Chorus; Church Choir; Yrbk; Rep Soph Cls; Prfct Atten Awd; Pres Girls Dnmtry; Adventist Yth Soc VP; Adv Pathfinders; Yale; Law.

BURNS, SHELBY B; Dos Palos Joint Union HS; Dos Palos, CA; (2); AFS; FHA; SADD; Teachers Aide; Band; Chorus; Mrchg Band; Var Cheerldng; Stat Mgr(s); Hon Roll; Merced JC; Wrtr.

BURNS, THOMAS M; Saint Ignatius HS; San Rafael, CA; (3); Boy Scts; Model UN; Service Clb; Yrbk; Vrsty Crew Tm Capt; Chrstn Life Cmmnty Leader; Big Bro.

BURNS, TOM J; J Eugene Mc Ateer HS; Pacifica, CA; (3); Debate Tm; Office Aide; Pep Clb; Q&S; Rep Soph Cls; Hon Roll; CA Schlrshp Fed; Mass Cmmnctns.

BURNS, WILLIAM M; Marysville HS; Oregon House, CA; (3); 1/202; Am Leg Boys St; VP Art Clb; Debate Tm; German Clb; NFL; Speech Tm; Pres Stu Cncl; Var Tennis; High Hon Roll; U CA San Diego; Physics.

BUROW, DAVID A; Grant Union HS; Sacramento, CA; (3); Church Yth Grp; Science Clb; SADD; Band; Jazz Band; Pep Band; Hon Roll; Goldn St Exm Geom Acad Exclince Awd; Arch.

BURR, ERIK; Palmdale HS; Palmdale, CA; (3); 114/644; FFA; Letterman Clb; Band; Mrchg Band; Var L Ftbl; JV Vllybl; Var Wt Lftg; USC; Actor.

BURR, JESSE; Palmdale HS; Palmdale, CA; (3); 141/644; FFA; Hosp Aide; L Ftbl; JV Vllybl; Var Wt Lftg; Greenhand & Chapt Farmer Degree; Acting.

BURR JR, RICKY D; Silver Valley HS; Fort Irwin, CA; (2); Cmnty Wkr; Drama Clb; School Play; Bsbl; Ftbl; Hon Roll; Yth Offcls Assn Soccer & Bsbl; U MN; Forestry.

BURRELL, ADIJA R; Pittsburg HS; Pittsburg, CA; (2); Church Yth Grp; Cmnty Wkr; Variety Show; Treas Frsh Cls; Treas Soph Cls; Stat Bsktbl; Stat Ftbl; Hon Roll; 2nd Contra Costa Cty Historical Day; Pittsburgh Sci Fair; Walk Amer; Stanford U; Med.

BURRELL, AMY L; Las Plumas HS; Oroville, CA; (3); Pep Clb; Cheerldng; High Hon Roll; Hon Roll; Prfct Atten Awd; Pres Acad Fit Awd; Bus.

BURRELL, ANDREA; Rosamond HS; Rosamond, CA; (2); 2/81; Letterman Clb; Office Aide; Science Clb; Spanish Clb; Band; Sec Soph Cls; Var Bsktbl; Var Sftbl; Var Vllybl; Hon Roll; UCLA; Aeronautical Engr.

BURRELL, IAN; La Jolla Country Day Schl; Del Mar, CA; (2); Church Yth Grp; AFS; Math Tm; Model UN; SADD; Lit Mag; JV Bsktbl; JV Trk; Hon Roll; Amer Chhem Socty Comptn 2nd Pl; AHSME Schl Comptn 3rd Pl; Sci.

BURRIS, LEANNE; Central HS; Fresno, CA; (4); Church Yth Grp; Computer Clb; Drama Clb; 4-H; Science Clb; Ski Clb; Spanish Clb; SADD; Sec Frsh Cls; Sec Soph Cls; Friday Night Live; Just Be Cool Clb; Vllybl Clb; Accntng.

BURROUGHS, ALEX M; Upper Lake HS; Upper Lake, CA; (2); JV Bsktbl; JV Ftbl; Hon Roll; Pres Acad Fit Awd; Schlr Athl; Hmcmng Prince; CA U; Law.

BURROUGHS, SCOTT A; Chino HS; Chino, CA; (4); 18/450; Bsktbl; High Hon Roll; Hon Roll; Pres Acad Fit Awd; Trvl Club; Amnsty Intl Club; USAF Acad; Poly Sci.

BURROW, MICHAEL; Washington Union HS; Fresno, CA; (2); Art Clb; FFA; SADD; Wt Lftg; Outstndng Achvt In Art Awd; UCLA; Optometry.

BURROWS, BRIAN D; El Camino HS; Carmichael, CA; (3); 89/366; Letterman Clb; Spanish Clb; SADD; Yrbk; Stat Bsktbl; Stat Ftbl; L Score Keeper; Cit Awd; Hon Roll; Opt Clb Awd; Spec Olympics Mst Vlbl Athl 90; Golf Trnmnt Wnnr 89; Adaptive P E Mst Outsntdng; U Of AL; Phys Thrpy.

BURROWS, MARGARET R; San Benito HS; Hollister, CA; (1); 12/400; GAA; Pep Clb; Church Choir; JV Bsktbl; Var L Crs Cntry; Play & Teach Piano; Church Yth Grp; Brigham Young U.

BURROWS, MICHAEL; Cajon HS; San Bernardino, CA; (2); Church Yth Grp; Pep Band; Var Socr; Trk; Wt Lftg; Hon Roll; NHS; Usc; Med.

BURROWS JR, SHELDON E; Apple Valley HS; Lucerne Valley, CA; (3); 10/708; Chess Clb; Cmnty Wkr; Computer Clb; Key Clb; Math Tm; High Hon Roll; Ntl Merit Ltr; CSF; Jnr Statesman Amer; Harvey Mudd Coll; Math.

BURROWS, TAMARA; Apple Valley HS; Lucerne Valley, CA; (3); Chess Clb; Church Yth Grp; Cmnty Wkr; Computer Clb; Drama Clb; Key Clb; Rptr Nwsp; Hon Roll; Kiwanis Awd; Schlstc Achvt Awd; Animal Rights Actvst; Envrnmntl Stds.

BURROWS, TRACY K; Poway HS; Poway, CA; (2); Model UN; Varsity Clb; Swmmng; Pres Acad Fit Awd; Mst Val Mid Dstnc Swmmr; A-Team; 1st Tm All Leag; UCSB; Jrnlsm.

BURROWS, WYETH E; Santa Barbara HS; Santa Barbara, CA; (2); Church Yth Grp; Pres Frsh Cls; Pres Soph Cls; JV Ftbl; Var Trk; High Hon Roll; Yth Ambssdr Soviet Union Smmr 89; HOBY Ldrshp 90; Come Clean Santa Barbara; Bio.

BURRUSS, MARIE; North HS; Bakersfield, CA; (2); JA; Office Aide; JV Socr; Sftbl; Hon Roll; Karate; Wghtlftng; Hghst Salea JA Co; Accntng.

BURSTEIN, CARI D; El Camino Real HS; Woodland Hills, CA; (2); SADD; Hgh Hnrs Golden St Exam Geom; Cmmnctns.

BURT, JAMIE L; Kingsburg HS; Dinuba, CA; (2); Capt Ftbl; Cit Awd; Auto Mechanics; Restoring Old Cars; College.

BURT, JOANNA M; Irvine HS; Irvine, CA; (3); Letterman Clb; Ski Clb; Varsity Clb; JV Crs Cntry; JV Socr; Var Swmmng; Hon Roll; Prfct Atten Awd; Pres Acad Fit Awd; Natl Charity Society; Summer Swim Team; Northwood Northstars; Astronaut.

BURTLE, CATHERINE M; Yosemite HS; Oakhurst, CA; (2); 16/192; FBLA; Service Clb; SADD; JV Bsktbl; Var Crs Cntry; JV Sftbl; Var Trk; Cit Awd; Hon Roll; MAUI; PRIDE Of CA; Sccr Referee For Mtn Area Yth Sccr; La Verne U; Corp Lawyer.

BURTON, ANDREA H; La Reina HS; Westlake Village, CA; (3); 6/70; Cmnty Wkr; Library Aide; Service Clb; SADD; Teachers Aide; Ed Yrbk; Cit Awd; High Hon Roll; Ntl Merit Ltr; Skirball Essy Cont; U Of CA; Civil Engrng.

BURTON, BILL L; Escondido HS; Escondido, CA; (1); JV Tennis; UCSD; Science.

BURTON, CHRIS L; Lindsay HS; Lindsay, CA; (3); Band; Mrchg Band; School Musical; School Play; Wt Lftg; Cit Awd; Hon Roll; Music.

BURTON, CHRISTINE L; Helix HS; Lemon Grove, CA; (2); Church Choir; Var Bsktbl; JV Crs Cntry; Var Trk; Cvl Engr.

BURTON, DANNY L; Vacaville HS; Vacaville, CA; (3); Church Yth Grp; Teachers Aide; Stage Crew; Var Socr; Hon Roll; Prfct Atten Awd; Bush Cmpgn; Sccr Team Coach.

BURTON, DAWN E; Mojave HS; Mojave, CA; (3); 15/101; Spanish Clb; Rptr Nwsp; Phtg Yrbk; Rep Stu Cncl; Hon Roll; St Schlr; Acad Decath; Mock Trial; Ltry Soc-Treas; Bus Admin.

BURTON, KATHLEEN N; College Park HS; Concord, CA; (3); 25/300; Church Yth Grp; Spanish Clb; Teachers Aide; Church Choir; Treas Sr Cls; Stu Cncl; Var Sftbl; Var Tennis; High Hon Roll; Hon Roll; Sacramento ST; Bus.

BURTON, KIMBRAE A; Seaside HS; Ft Ord, CA; (2); Hosp Aide; School Play; Rptr Nwsp; Rptr Yrbk; High Hon Roll; Hon Roll; Pres Acad Fit Awd; Upwards Bounds Program; College; Journalism.

BURTON, ONEZIA L; Vallejo SR HS; Vallejo, CA; (3); Church Yth Grp; Office Aide; VP Church Choir; Rep Stu Cncl; JV Bsktbl; Var Trk; Hon Roll; Grad Barbizion Modlng Sch; Sch Recog High Score Golden St Exam; Activ Learning Prgm; Spelman Coll; Jrnlsm.

BURTON, SHAMONIQUE R; Paramount HS; Paramount, CA; (3); Aud/Vis; Cmnty Wkr; Hosp Aide; Office Aide; Stage Crew; Lit Mag; Stu Cncl; Cheerldng; Mgr Ftbl; Cit Awd; Coca-Cola Mdlng Clb; San Francisco ST U; Doctor.

BURTON, WILLIAM HENRY; Daniel Murphy HS; Los Angeles, CA; (4); Art Clb; School Musical; School Play; Stage Crew; Phtg Rptr Nwsp; Phtg Rptr Yrbk; Var Swmmng; Var Trk; JV Vllybl; Water Polo Vrsty; Peace Clb, Pres; Jazz Clb, Pres; Phantom Bth Clb; Picaresque Prod; Big Brother Clb; Poltcl Sci.

BUSALACCHI, CARLA; Linden HS; Stockton, CA; (4); 3/125; Church Yth Grp; Cmnty Wkr; Pres VP 4-H; Pres FHA; GAA; Q&S; Rptr Yrbk; Pres Frsh Cls; Off Soph Cls; Sec Stu Cncl; ST Wnr 4h Awds Prgm Spch Dele Chgo; ST Vllybl Team Div III 88-89; UN-RENO.

BUSCAGLIA, MACIE D; Holtville HS; Holtville, CA; (3); FFA; Pep Clb; Teachers Aide; Rep Stu Cncl; Cheerldng; Sftbl; High Hon Roll; Schl Tchng-Elem.

BUSCH, JODI M; Fontana HS; Bloomington, CA; (3); Pep Clb; Ski Clb; Teachers Aide; Treas Jr Cls; Var Cheerldng; Stat Swmmng; Cls Treas; Riverside CC; Ocngrphy.

BUSCH, MELINDA S; Pittsburg HS; Pittsburg, CA; (1); Church Yth Grp; Swmmng; High Hon Roll; Astronaut.

BUSCHKOETTER, RICHARD; El Dorado HS; Fullerton, CA; (3); 1/307; Computer Clb; Science Clb; High Hon Roll; CA Schlrshp Fed; Elec Engr.

BUSE, DAVID; Cajon HS; San Bernardino, CA; (3); #4 In Class; Cmnty Wkr; SADD; Var Socr; JV Tennis; High Hon Roll; NHS; Pres Rotary Awd; CSF; Statesmen Am; Engrng.

BUSEK, JEANNETTE; Redlands HS; Redlands, CA; (4); 25/800; Am Leg Aux Girls St; Church Yth Grp; Letterman Clb; Ed Nwsp; Hosp Aide; Var Crs Cntry; Var Trk; DAR Awd; High Hon Roll; Pres Acad Fit Awd; U Of CA-IRVINE; Poli Sci.

BUSH, AIMEE M; Casa Grande HS; Rohnert Park, CA; (2); 150/295; Bus.

BUSH, BOB; Inland Christian HS; San Bernardino, CA; (4); 2/8; Church Yth Grp; School Musical; Treas Jr Cls; Treas Sr Cls; Treas Stu Cncl; Var L Bsbl; Var L Bsktbl; Var L Crs Cntry; Sal; 5th & 28th Pl St Crss Cntry Chmpnshps 2 Yrs; U Of AZ; Accntng.

BUSH, CECILY F; Washington Prep; Los Angeles, CA; (2); Drama Clb; Teachers Aide; School Play; High Hon Roll; Hon Roll; USC; Psych.

BUSH, CHRISTIE L; San Gorgonio HS; Highland, CA; (4); 73/480; AFS; Church Yth Grp; Aud/Vis; Band; Church Choir; Mrchg Band; Yrbk; Rep Stu Cncl; Var L Swmmng; Alive Clb Pres; UC Irvine; Music.

BUSH, CHRISTINE R; John F Kennedy HS; Sacramento, CA; (2); Drama Clb; German Clb; Color Guard; Orch; School Play; U Of Irvine; Crmnl Justice.

BUSH, DAWN M; Lassen Union HS; Susanville, CA; (3); Ski Clb; Teachers Aide; Yrbk; Stats Track; Humbolt; Wldlife Bio.

BUSH, JEFF J; Newbury Park HS; Newbury Park, CA; (3); Church Yth Grp; Rep Stu Cncl; Var Swmmng; High Hon Roll; Waterpolo-Var; Assoctd Stu Govt; Engrng.

BUSH, SHAWN A; Huntington Beach HS; Huntington Beach, CA; (2); Boy Scts; Teachers Aide; Var Bsbl; Ftbl; San Diego ST; Law.

BUSHEK, JENNIFER A; Laguna Hills HS; Laguna Hills, CA; (1); 4/321; French Clb; Math Clb; SADD; JV Tennis; High Hon Roll; CSF.

BUSKIRK, ALLEN R; Saratoga HS; Saratoga, CA; (1); Boy Scts; Church Yth Grp; Drama Clb; Chorus; Church Choir; School Musical; Hon Roll; Pres Chrch Daily Seminary Cls.

BUSS, LAURIE; Chaminade College Prep; West Hills, CA; (4); Church Yth Grp; Drama Clb; School Play; Off Lit Mag; Swmmng; High Hon Roll; NHS; UCLA; Aerospace Engrng.

BUSSARD, JOSEPH MICHAEL; Bear River HS; Grass Valley, CA; (3); Church Yth Grp; FCA; Yrbk; Bsktbl; Crs Cntry; Trk; Hon Roll; Sprtsmnshp Awd Trck; LA Art Inst; Cartnst.

BUSSARD, REGINA M; Irvington HS; Fremont, CA; (2); Ski Clb; High Hon Roll; Acad Achvt Awds; Hnrs Engl Mdl & Hnrs Phys Sci Cert; Hnrs Bio Mdl, Alg II, Trig Mdl & Wrld Hstry Mdl.

BUSSEE, MICHELLE; Hesperia HS; Hesperia, CA; (4); Art Clb; Church Yth Grp; French Clb; Science Clb; Church Choir; Yrbk; Cit Awd; DAR Awd; High Hon Roll; Hon Roll; Nrsng.

BUSSI, PETER; Cardinal Newman HS; Santa Rosa, CA; (2); Latin Clb; Service Clb; Ski Clb; Treas Soph Cls; JV Socr; Var Tennis.

BUSSIE, JASON A; Gompers Secondary HS; San Diego, CA; (2); Band; Bst Drmmr Awd Wnnr; SDSU; Record Prodcr.

BUSTAMANTE, JUAN A; Kerman HS; Kerman, CA; (4); 4/115; Math Tm; Model UN; Office Aide; Treas Stu Cncl; JV Tennis; DAR Awd; Hon Roll; Pres Acad Fit Awd; CA Schlrshp Fed; Friday Night Live Treas; Principals Awd; CSU Fresno; Bus.

BUSTAMANTE, SANDRA KARIN; Bonita Vista HS; Chula Vista, CA; (1); 82/533; Cit Awd; Gate Hnrs Classes; Intl Baccalaureate; Diploma Of Merit Spanish; Capt PE Sprts Soccer Bsktbl Sftbl; Law.

BUSTINDUI, MANUEL S; Castle Park HS; Chula Vista, CA; (3); 70/422; JV Ftbl; Cit Awd; Prfct Atten Awd; UCSD; Bus Adm.

BUSTOS, ANA-KARINA; Indio HS; Indio, CA; (1); Cit Awd; Hon Roll; Prfct Atten Awd; Math Excllnc; Stu Of Mnth; Air Force Acad.

BUSTOS, ANGELICA G; Sweetwater HS; National City, CA; (2); Cit Awd; Hon Roll; Academic Superbowl; UCSD; Mrktng Mgmt.

BUSTOS, ANGELINA R; Holy Names HS; Richmond, CA; (4); Acpl Chr; Chorus; Ntl Merit SF; Hispanic Merit Semi Finalist; Bio.

BUSTOS, GABRIELA; Sweetwater HS; National City, CA; (2); Southwestern Coll.

BUSTOS, MARGARET A; St Paul HS; Whittier, CA; (3); Hon Roll; Sister Cities Clb.

BUSWELL, ELIZABETH R; Mayfield SR Schl; Pasadena, CA; (2); Church Yth Grp; Dance Clb; Hosp Aide; ROTC; Stage Crew; Variety Show; DAR Awd; High Hon Roll; Psycht.

BUTKOVIC, IVANA; King City HS; King City, CA; (3); Spanish Clb; Hon Roll; Cmmrcl Clb; Hartnell Clg; Bus.

BUTKUS, ALEXANDER GEORGE; Bishop O'dowd HS; Oakland, CA; (4); 20/220; Art Clb; Church Yth Grp; Ski Clb; Band; School Musical; Nwsp; Ed Yrbk; Treas Soph Cls; VP Jr Cls; Sec Stu Cncl; Bk Of Amer Achvt Awd Fine Arts; Anna Costa Mem Awd Creativty; CSF Life; UCLA; Grphc Arts.

BUTLER, BARBARA J; Fountain Valley HS; Fountain Valley, CA; (3); 258/624; Teachers Aide; Star Cert Bus Courses; Bus.

BUTLER, CHAD M; Carlsbad HS; Carlsbad, CA; (2); Church Yth Grp; Teachers Aide; Var Swmmng; Hon Roll; Vrsty Water Polo; Med.

BUTLER, CHRISTINE; Bloomington Christian Schl; Colton, CA; (4); 1/9; Church Yth Grp; Drama Clb; Church Choir; Ed Yrbk; Stu Cncl; Var Cheerldng; Hon Roll; Val; Prncpls Awd; Rev Paul Coxe Awd; Pt Loma Nazarene Coll; Bus Adm.

BUTLER, DAVID J; Calistoga HS; Calistoga, CA; (2); 1/50; Band; Rep Frsh Cls; Pres Soph Cls; Sec Stu Cncl; JV Var Bsbl; JV Capt Bsktbl; JV Capt Ftbl; High Hon Roll; Prfct Atten Awd; Blue Belt Mrtl Art.

BUTLER, DREWKAI L; Bridgemont HS; San Francisco, CA; (3); AFS; Art Clb; Church Yth Grp; Varsity Clb; Church Choir; Var Vllybl; Intrml Wt Lftg; High Hon Roll; Hon Roll; Shirt Dsgnr 3 Yrs In Row; Best Typist Jr Yr; Air Force Pilot.

BUTLER, J PAIGE; Bonita Vista HS; Chula Vista, CA; (2); 108/600; Teachers Aide; JV Var Bsktbl; Var Sftbl; JV Vllybl; Metro League Bsktbl Hnrb Mntn, Sftbl 2nd Team; U TX; Law.

BUTLER, JA-RON; Ambassador Baptist HS; Rialto, CA; (1); Boy Scts; Bsbl; Bsktbl; Ftbl; Cit Awd; High Hon Roll; Hon Roll; USC; Banking.

BUTLER, JASON A; Mt Whitney HS; Visalia, CA; (1); JV Wrstlng; Hon Roll; Spanish NHS; Acad Var Lttrmn; UC Irvine; Vet Med.

BUTLER, JEFF S; Fontana HS; Fontana, CA; (3); 151/1168; Army; Accntng.

BUTLER, JENDAYI A; Barstow HS; Barstow, CA; (2); Church Yth Grp; Cmnty Wkr; GAA; Letterman Clb; Teachers Aide; Church Choir; Bsktbl; Powder Puff Ftbl; Cit Awd; Hon Roll; UNLV; Psych.

BUTLER, JIM D; Pasadena HS; Pasadena, CA; (3); Church Yth Grp; Jazz Band; Music.

BUTLER, JOHN J; King City Joint Union HS; King City, CA; (3); Computer Clb; 4-H; FFA; Teachers Aide; Pres Jr Cls; Ftbl; Trk; Wt Lftg; High Hon Roll; Hon Roll; Honors Achievement In The Golden State Exam In 1st Yr Albegra; Hartwell JR Coll; Engineering.

BUTLER, KERRY S; Sanger HS; Squaw Valley, CA; (2); 4-H; 4-H Awd; Won Many Ribbons Horse At Horseshows; Pres Of 4-H Group; UC Davis; Vet.

BUTLER, KEVIN S; Torrey Pines HS; Solana Beach, CA; (2); Intrml Bsbl; Hon Roll; U Of CA; Psych.

BUTLER, LAURA; San Joaquin Memorial HS; Madera, CA; (4); 7/119; Church Yth Grp; Drama Clb; Science Clb; Service Clb; Spanish Clb; Chorus; School Play; Cheerldng; Pom Pon; Hon Roll; CSF; Engl Awds, Excllnc In Drama; U Southern CA; Exercise Sci.

BUTLER, MARK; Armona Union Acad; Hanford, CA; (3); 1/12; Drama Clb; Band; School Play; Nwsp; Nwsp; Yrbk; VP Soph Cls; Pres Stu Cncl; Vllybl; High Hon Roll; Schlstc All Amer; UCLA; Law.

BUTLER, PAUL J; San Ramon Valley HS; Alamo, CA; (2); JV Crs Cntry; JV Trk.

BUTLER, RIKKI; Orestimba HS; Newman, CA; (1); Pep Clb; Spanish Clb; SADD; Color Guard; Score Keeper; Hon Roll; CSF; UC Santa Barbara.

BUTLER, SHANNON L; Hesperia HS; Hesperia, CA; (3); Church Yth Grp; Pres Spanish Clb; Band; Jazz Band; Mrchg Band; Orch; Pep Band; High Hon Roll; 1st Assmbly Gold Drama Co; Chrch Orch; UC San Bernardino; Prfrmng Art.

BUTMAN, RAYMOND J; Etiwanda HS; Alta Loma, CA; (2); 14/700; Bsktbl; JV Var Crs Cntry; JV Var Tennis; High Hon Roll; Hon Roll; Pres Acad Fit Awd; CSF 89-90; Schlr Athlete-Bsktbl 88-89/Vrsty Cross Country 89; UCLA; Psych.

BUTROS, NANCY; Victor Valley HS; Victorville, CA; (3); Key Clb; Arch.

BUTTACAVOLI, MATTHEW; Pacifica HS; Garden Grv, CA; (3); 5/274; Debate Tm; VP Spanish Clb; Band; Drm Mjr(t); Jazz Band; Mrchg Band; Orch; Ftbl; Var L Tennis; High Hon Roll; Cmmssnr Publcty; Mem CA Schlrshp Fnd; Cngrssnl Schl 90; Distngshd Schlr Hstry, Eng; U CA Irvine; Poltcl Sci.

BUTTERFIELD, JULIE; San Pedro HS; San Pedro, CA; (2); Church Yth Grp; Girl Scts; Math Clb; Teachers Aide; Temple Yth Grp; Band; Chorus; Church Choir; Color Guard; Drill Tm; Bus.

BUTTERFIELD, LESA L; Washington Union HS; Fresno, CA; (4); 7/180; Church Yth Grp; FBLA; Science Clb; Yrbk; Sec Sr Cls; Var Cheerldng; JV Vllybl; Hon Roll; CSF; Fresno City.

BUTTNER, MELISSA M; Ventura HS; Ventura, CA; (3); SADD; Score Keeper; JV Var Socr; Hon Roll; Jobs Dghtrs; Div I Girls Amer Yth Soccer; Clincl Psych.

BUTTON, BRIAN E; Hoover HS; Fresno, CA; (2); Church Yth Grp; Letterman Clb; Spanish Clb; SADD; Varsity Clb; Var Socr; Var Trk; UCLA; Phys Therapist.

BUTTON, JAMES; Lone Pine HS; Lone Pine, CA; (2); Church Yth Grp; Math Tm; Spanish Clb; Rep Soph Cls; Var Bsbl; JV Bsktbl; JV Ftbl; Hon Roll; Stanford.

BUTTRESS, KRISTIN E; Santa Barbara HS; Santa Barbara, CA; (3); 29/472; Church Yth Grp; Cmnty Wkr; Varsity Clb; Var JV Vllybl; Pres Acad Fit Awd; Fri Night Live; Hmlss Shltr Vlntr; Cmmnctns.

BUTTS, ALLISON D; Polytechnic HS; Riverside, CA; (1); Church Yth Grp; GAA; L Var Crs Cntry; Var Trk; High Hon Roll; Young Life; Duke U; Corp Attrny.

BUTTS, TRACY L; Live Oak HS; Morgan Hill, CA; (3); Debate Tm; FBLA; FFA; Pep Clb; Teachers Aide; JV Var Swmmng; High Hon Roll; Hon Roll; Womens Water Polo; Mock Trl Vrsty; CSF; Amnesty Intl; US Santa Cruz; Marine Bio.

BUTTSON, JEREMY A; Huntington Beach HS; Huntington Beach, CA; (1); Crs Cntry; JV Socr; Trk; Alreboin Awd; Crss Cntry Fresh Sunset Leag Chmpn, All Cnty Fresh; Trck 3200 M Chmpn, 2nd 1600 M.

BUTTZ, MELISSA A; Healdsburg HS; Santa Rosa, CA; (4); 32/273; FTA; Teachers Aide; High Hon Roll; Hon Roll; Doyle Schlrshp; Jess Manley HATA Schlrshp; Futr Tchrs Of Amer Ed Sugars Schlrshp; Santa Rosa JC; Elem Schl Tchr.

BUTZKE, TESSA M; Notre Dame Acad; Los Angeles, CA; (3); Drama Clb; Science Clb; Spanish Clb; Lit Mag; High Hon Roll; Hon Roll; NHS; Campus Ministry; UCLA; Pre-Vet Med.

BUU, PHUC; Castle Park HS; Chula Vista, CA; (4); 30/328; Boy Scts; Office Aide; Varsity Clb; JV Var Ftbl; Var Vllybl; San Diego ST U; Aerontcl Engr.

BUU, THAO; Castle Park HS; Chula Vista, CA; (2); JV Trk; JV Vllybl.

BUXMAN, JENNIFER: Moorpark HS; Moorpark, CA; (4); 1/206; Cit Awd; High Hon Roll; Jr NHS; NHS; Pres Acad Fit Awd; Outstndng Bus Stu; CA Schlrshp Fed Treas; Stu Ath Trainer; CA Poly SLO; Comp Engrng.

BUXTON, CHAD L; Andrew Hill HS; San Jose, CA; (1); Lit Mag; L Trk; High Hon Roll; Hon Roll; Pres Acad Fit Awd; Spellout Clb; OM.

BUXTON, DAVID L; Vacaville HS; Vacaville, CA; (3); Game Clb; Golden St Exam High Hnrs; Cartoonist.

BUYS, ANDREW R; Yosemite HS; Coarsegold, CA; (3); Church Yth Grp; Cmnty Wkr; FFA; SADD; Orch; School Play; Invited By Cngrssnl Yth Ldrshp Cncl To Attend Natl Yng Ldrs Conf In Washington DC 90; San Francisco Acad Of Art; Art.

BUZZARD, STEPHANIE; St Francis HS; Sacramento, CA; (2); Church Yth Grp; Cmnty Wkr; Dance Clb; SADD; Chorus; Rep Frsh Cls; Cheerldng; Socr; Hon Roll; Mdlng; Fashion Desgn.

BY, KOLBOT; Hollywood HS; Monterey Park, CA; (4); 8/350; Am Leg Boys St; Chess Clb; Key Clb; Off Soph Cls; Off Jr Cls; Off Sr Cls; Stu Cncl; Tennis; Hon Roll; Lion Awd; USC Smmrs Hnrs Pgm; UCSB.

BYARS, DEANNA J; Oroville HS; Oroville, CA; (3); Drama Clb; Pep Clb; SADD; School Play; Sec Stu Cncl; Var Cheerldng; Hon Roll; Pres Acad Fit Awd; Chico ST U; Teacher.

BYBEE, JEROD B; Oak Ridge HS; El Dorado Hills, CA; (2); Boy Scts; Variety Show; Pres Frsh Cls; JV Capt Bsktbl; JV Capt Ftbl; High Hon Roll; VP Jr NHS; Pres Acad Fit Awd; Perfrmng Galena Street East Singer, Dancer; Stanford; Med.

BYE, JOHN A; Antelope Valley HS; Lancaster, CA; (3); 147/631; Teachers Aide; Cit Awd; Hon Roll; Trade.

BYERLY, DAVID A; Serrano HS; Pinon Hills, CA; (3); 3/213; Church Yth Grp; VP 4-H; FFA; Band; Church Choir; Mrchg Band; Stage Crew; High Hon Roll; Jr Hnr Guard; Sound Tech For Schl Choral Grps; Med.

BYERS, ALEXANDER J; Mira Mesa HS; San Diego, CA; (2); JV Swmmng; Var Wrstlng; Pres Acad Fit Awd; Letterman Clb; Jr Water Polo Capt; Jr Natl & Jr Olympic Water Polo; Aquatics; UCSB.

BYERS, ANDREW; Mira Mesa HS; San Diego, CA; (2); 111/797; Letterman Clb; Off Frsh Cls; Var Swmmng; Pres Acad Fit Awd; Jr Olympic Water Polo; Aquatics Club; UCSB.

BYERS, JULIE; Las Plumas HS; Oroville, CA; (2); Church Yth Grp; Fash Dsgn.

BYERS, MICHELLE L; Independence HS; San Jose, CA; (3); German Clb; Chorus; I-Pride; Golden St Exam Schl Rcgntn Geom & Alg I; Awd Excl Physics; San Jose ST U; Bus.

BYERS, NATALYN; Canyon HS; Santa Clarita, CA; (4); Pres Church Yth Grp; Band; Church Choir; Mrchg Band; Pep Band; High Hon Roll; Hon Roll; NHS; BYU; Vet Med.

BYFORD, JOEL J; Sunset HS; Hayward, CA; (4); 16/248; Church Yth Grp; Church Choir; Mrchg Band; Phtg Yrbk; Rep Jr Cls; Hist Stu Cncl; JV Capt Tennis; Hon Roll; John Philip Sousa Band Awd 90; Bank Of Am Achvt Awd-Fine Arts 90; Falcon Pride Awd 89 & 90; Azusa Pacific U; Math.

BYINGTON, ASHTON B; Fred C Beyer HS; Modesto, CA; (1); Boy Scts; Church Yth Grp; Hon Roll; Med.

BYLOOS, MATTHEW C; Loyola HS; Bell Canyon, CA; (2); Art Clb; Thesps; School Play; Lit Mag; Trk; Wt Lftg; High Hon Roll; Hon Roll; Pres Acad Fit Awd; Loyola Marymount U; Philosophy.

BYLOOS, NOELLE G; Louisville HS; Bell Canyon, CA; (3); Art Clb; Church Yth Grp; Cmnty Wkr; FHA; Nwsp; Hon Roll; NHS; Peer Cnslng; U Of San Francisco.

BYNUM, JAMIE D; Yucca Valley HS; Yucca Valley, CA; (2); Church Yth Grp; JV Var Sftbl; Var Tennis; CA Schltc Fed; Univ Clb; Stanford; Law.

BYNUM, TINA; South HS; Bakersfield, CA; (3); Var Sftbl; Var Vllybl; Hon Roll; MVP Sftbl; Mst Inspirational Vrsty Vllybl.

BYNUM, VIVIAN ANN; St Bernard HS; Inglewood, CA; (3); Church Yth Grp; Pep Clb; VP Jr Cls; Rep Stu Cncl; JV Bsktbl; Cit Awd; High Hon Roll; Hon Roll; Black Cultural Awrnss Clb Treas; Bronze Comitatus Awd; Bsktbl Mst Imprvd Athlt; Clark Atlanta U; Med.

BYOUER, BRENDA K; Lower Lake HS; Lower Lake, CA; (4); 5/120; Church Yth Grp; Letterman Clb; Office Aide; Pep Clb; Vllybl; Cit Awd; High Hon Roll; Cngrssnl Yth Ldrshp Awd; Fri Night Live; Intl Frgn Lang Awd; Schltc All Amer; Phys Thrpy.

BYOUS, ERIC W; Mira Mesa HS; San Diego, CA; (2); Spanish Clb; Ftbl; Wt Lftg; U CA; Phy.

BYRD, ABENA; Lincoln Prep; San Diego, CA; (4); 23/247; Church Yth Grp; Cmnty Wkr; Debate Tm; FCA; FTA; GAA; Letterman Clb; Library Aide; Model UN; Varsity Clb; Psych.

BYRD, DANA; St Marys HS; Stockton, CA; (3); Am Leg Aux Girls St; Church Yth Grp; Pres 4-H; Speech Tm; SADD; Band; Drill Tm; Var Socr; Var Swmmng; High Hon Roll; UOP Recmbinant DNA Smmr Hnrs Pgm 89; Vrsty Water Polo; Acad Achvts Awds Latin & Sci 88 & 89; Sci Research.

BYRD, MAISHA S; Compton HS; Compton, CA; (4); 2/225; Ed Yrbk; VP Jr Cls; Pres Sr Cls; Stat Bsktbl; Sftbl; Var Vllybl; Sec Jr NHS; NHS; Sal; Acad Decthln; Vrsty & Young Blck Schlrs; Spelman Coll; Math.

BYRD, SHANDRICA KHRISTINA; Eisenhower HS; Rialto, CA; (4); Chess Clb; Cmnty Wkr; Capt Varsity Clb; Bsktbl; L Stat Mgr(s); JV Var Vllybl; Hon Roll; NHS; Prfct Atten Awd; Swans Clb Debutante; Soclts Clb Fair Maiden; Clb Vllybl Rvrsd Vllybl Clb 2 Yrs; U CA Riverside; Bio.

BYRD, TIFFINI T; Van Nuys HS; Los Angeles, CA; (4); 43/535; Church Yth Grp; Office Aide; Acpl Chr; Chorus; Stage Crew; Prfct Atten Awd; H E A R T Prgm; Phrmclgy.

BYRNE, BOB E; Castle Park HS; Chula Vista, CA; (2); Band; Jazz Band; Mrchg Band; Pep Band; School Musical; High Hon Roll; Hon Roll; Pres Acad Fit Awd; Won Many Awds Band, Bst Frshmn, Soph Musician, Top Sax; Woodwind Sec Pres; Band Marched Rose Parade 90; UCSD; Comp Engrng.

BYRNS, TOM R; Monte Vista HS; Alamo, CA; (3); 134/352; Church Yth Grp; Ski Clb; Varsity Clb; Bsbl; Ftbl; Trk; Wt Lftg; Wrstlng; Engrng.

BYRON, ELIZABETH M; Villa Park HS; Villa Park, CA; (3); 7/400; Dance Clb; GAA; Hosp Aide; Key Clb; Spanish Clb; SADD; Varsity Clb; Off Frsh Cls; Off Soph Cls; Off Jr Cls; St Qlfr High Jmp Schl Tm.

BYRON, KEITH L; Diamond Bar HS; Diamond Bar, CA; (4); VP Acpl Chr; Treas VP Chorus; School Musical; Swing Chorus; Variety Show; Lit Mag; JV Cheerldng; Hon Roll; De Molay Mstr Cnclr; Peer Cnslng; Acadmc Dcthln; Mt San Antonio Coll; Music.

BYSTRA, JOHN; Mesa Verde HS; Citrus Heights, CA; (4); 6/200; Debate Tm; Drama Clb; Math Tm; Band; Jazz Band; Mrchg Band; Pep Band; School Play; Hon Roll; Ntl Merit SF; Acad Decathalon; U CA Davis; Metallurgist.

BYSTRAK, EDWARD S; Chula Vista HS; Chula Vista, CA; (3); 124/493; Pep Clb; Quiz Bowl; Scholastic Bowl; Ed Phtg Yrbk; Var Crs Cntry; Var Mgr(s); Stat Socr; Var Tennis; Var Trk; Cit Awd; Sports Med.

BYTYCI, LUMNI; Downey HS; Downey, CA; (2); French Clb; JV Sftbl; JV Vllybl; CSF Rep; Interact/Library Clbs; Electronics.

BYUN, CHIYONG; University HS; Los Angeles, CA; (3); Church Yth Grp; Teachers Aide; Temple Yth Grp; Church Choir; Off Jr Cls; Intrml Sftbl; Hon Roll; Prfct Atten Awd; Korean Clb; CSF.

BYUN, DANIEL S; Brea-Olinda HS; Brea, CA; (1); Boy Scts; JV Tennis; Hon Roll; Cmnty Vlntr Pgm; Johns Hopkins U; Pdtrcs.

BYUN, SUSIE; Fountain Valley HS; Fountain Valley, CA; (3); Church Yth Grp; Pep Clb; Acpl Chr; Rep Chorus; Church Choir; School Musical; School Play; Swing Chorus; Cheerldng; Cit Awd; Dance; Arbcs; Crnt Awd; Poly Sci.

CAAGBAY, MYRA O; San Gabriel Acad; W Covina, CA; (4); Pres Church Yth Grp; Band; Chorus; Church Choir; Ed Yrbk; Hist Jr Cls; Hist Sr Cls; Capt Bsktbl; Capt Vllybl; L Ftbl; Loma Linda U Schlrshps Ldrshp & Athltcs; Bnk America Mrt Awd Music.

CABACCANG, ALEXANDER C; Edison HS; Stockton, CA; (3); Latin Clb; VICA; Mgr(s); JV Tennis; Stat Vllybl; Hon Roll; Edison Frgn Lang Dept Latin Excllnc 88-90; CA ST U Sacramento; Cvl Engr.

CABALLA, JENNIFER; El Capitan HS; Lakeside, CA; (4); 15/418; Math Tm; Sec Spanish Clb; Var Trk; High Hon Roll; Hon Roll; El Capitan Acadmc Decthln Tm 89; UCSD; Med.

CABALLERO, CARLOS; Northpark HS; Baldwin Park, CA; (2); Boy Scts; Church Yth Grp; Cmnty Wkr; Math Clb; Teachers Aide; School Play; Yrbk; Cit Awd; Prfct Attndnce Awd; Claremont Coll; Cntrctr.

CABALLERO, DANIEL; John A Rowland HS; Rowland Heights, CA; (4); Pres Spanish Clb; Acpl Chr; Church Choir; Var L Ftbl; Var Capt Socr; Wt Lftg; Hon Roll; Prfct Atten Awd; CS San Bernardino; Med.

CABALLERO, MARC A; Los Altos HS; Hacienda Hts, CA; (2); Bsktbl; Hon Roll; U Of CA Los Angeles.

CABAN, CELESTE S; Mission Viejo HS; Mission Viejo, CA; (2); 219/442; Dance Clb; Sprt Diablos Awd Chrctr, Maturity & Achvts; Word Processor.

CABANILLA, JEANETTE; Brawley Union HS; Brawley, CA; (4); 1/290; Church Yth Grp; Letterman Clb; Sec Math Clb; VP Service Clb; Varsity Clb; Sec Frsh Cls; Sec Jr Cls; Sec Sr Cls; Var Capt Sftbl; Var Capt Vllybl; Cal Poly; Envrnmntl Engnr.

CABASA, MELISSA Y; Golden West HS; Visalia, CA; (2); Dance Clb; Color Guard; Sftbl; Winterguard; Honors Eng & His; Psych.

CABATIC, SHERWIN D; St Ignatius College Prep; San Francisco, CA; (3); 12/244; Art Clb; Intnl Clb; Science Clb; Intrml Bsbl; Intrml Bsktbl; JV Var Trk; Intrml Vllybl.

CABEBE, ELWYN C; Saint Ignatius College Prep; South San Francis, CA; (2); Church Yth Grp; Church Choir; Capt JV Tennis; Hon Roll; Chrstn Life Cmmnty Ldr; UC Berkeley; Pediatrician.

CABELLO, ABEL M; Kingsburg Joint Union HS; Laton, CA; (4); Cmnty Wkr; Teachers Aide; JV Bsbl; Socr; Hon Roll; Mny Schlrshps; Mst Insprtnl Sccr Plyr; Coll Of The Sequoias; Bus Adm.

CABELLON, SUSAN L; University City HS; San Diego, CA; (3); Pres Spanish Clb; SADD; Teachers Aide; Rptr Yrbk; Rep Frsh Cls; Sec Treas Jr NHS; Pres Acad Fit Awd; Green Peace; Pre-Med Physician.

CABERTE, KAREN A; Herbert Hoover HS; Glendale, CA; (3); Cmnty Wkr; Spanish Clb; Rptr Yrbk; Filipino Clb Treas; Jr Statsmn Of Amer; Syracuse Y; Tv Film Prodctn.

CABERTO, KEVIN J; St Francis HS; Glendale, CA; (2); French Clb; JV Bsbl; JV Ftbl; Var Socr; JV Trk; Hon Roll; Pres Acad Fit Awd; CSF; Soccer 2nd Tm All Leag; San Diego; Sci.

CABEZAS, ISIDRO; Pioneer HS; Whittier, CA; (2); Math Clb; Math Tm; Spanish Clb; SADD; Off Soph Cls; Bsbl; Bsktbl; Trk; Wt Lftg; Law.

CABIDA, GARY; East Union HS; Lathrop, CA; (2); Bsktbl; Ftbl; Hon Roll.

CABRAL, CAROLINA; Hamilton Union HS; Hamilton City, CA; (3); Church Yth Grp; Cmnty Wkr; FFA; SADD; Chorus; School Play; Ed Yrbk; Stat Bsbl; JV Var Bsktbl; Var Capt Cheerldng; Acadmc Dcthln; FFA Rgnl Sweetheart; Outstndng Rprtr St Prlmnty Proc; U Of CA Davis; Vet Med.

CABRAL, JENNIFER K; Durham HS; Chico, CA; (3); Debate Tm; FFA; Pep Clb; Ski Clb; Band; Bsktbl; Cheerldng; Golf; Sftbl; FFA Treas 89-90, Sec 90-91; Butte; Flight Attendant.

CABRAL, MARISA V; Balboa HS; San Francisco, CA; (3); Pep Clb; Teachers Aide; Variety Show; Co-Ed Yrbk; Off Soph Cls; Sec Stu Cncl; Var Cheerldng; High Hon Roll; CSF; Psych.

CABRAL, RHODORA; Mission HS; San Francisco, CA; (1); Intnl Clb; ROTC; Chorus; School Musical; School Play; Off Frsh Cls; Vllybl; Cit Awd; Hon Roll; Prfct Atten Awd; Nurse.

CABRAL, ROBERT E; Turlock HS; Turlock, CA; (3); AFS; Treas French Clb; Intnl Clb; Key Clb; Scholastic Bowl; Science Clb; Socr; Rotary Awd; Bio.

CABRAL, TAUNYA M; Highlands HS; Sacramento, CA; (3); SADD; VP Jr Cls; Var JV Powder Puff Ftbl; Var Socr; Var Tennis; Hon Roll; Pres Acad Fit Awd; UC Davis Early Outrch Prog; Schl Rdgntn Awd Geom 88; 4th Plc Voc Ed Day Bus Math 89; CSU Sacramento; Bus.

CABRAL, YOLANDA A; Ganesha HS; Pomona, CA; (4); Ed Nwsp; Cit Awd; Prfct Atten Awd; Vlntr Humane Soc; Vet Med.

CABRALES, MIGUEL A; Chula Vista HS; Chula Vista, CA; (4); 35/505; Chess Clb; Cmnty Wkr; Computer Clb; JA; Math Tm; Pep Clb; Rep Stu Cncl; Var Crs Cntry; JV Socr; Var Tennis; U Of CA San Diego; Politician.

CABREIRA, KENT BENJAMIN; Rio Lindo Adventist Acad; Lodi, CA; (4); Drama Clb; French Clb; Acpl Chr; Chorus; School Play; Capt JV Bsktbl; Var Ftbl; JV Vllybl; Hon Roll; Prfct Atten Awd; Phys Ed Outstndng Awd; Loma Linda U; Psych.

CABRERA, ALVIN D; Alameda HS; Alameda, CA; (2); Computer Clb; Office Aide; Teachers Aide; Golden ST Exam Alg 1; UC Schl; Accntng.

CABRERA, ANNA; Baldwin Park HS; Baldwin Park, CA; (2); Church Yth Grp; Hist Key Clb; Sec Soph Cls; Var Socr; JV Tennis; High Hon Roll; Hon Roll; Library Vol; Honor Soc; 1st Pl Eng Pentathlon; Stanford U; Law.

CABRERA, BENJAMIN; San Bernardino HS; San Bernardino, CA; (2); 1/1000; Treas German Clb; Math Clb; Math Tm; Quiz Bowl; High Hon Roll; Prfct Atten Awd; German Natl Hnr Soc; MESA Outstndng Soph Awd; Challng Bowl Chmpns SBCUSD 90; Physcs.

CABRERA, CARLOS R; Dinuba HS; Dinuba, CA; (3); Church Yth Grp; Office Aide; Band; Chorus; Mrchg Band; Pep Band; School Play; Yrbk; Cheerldng; Mgr(s); Mock Trial 88-91; 1 Of 3 Mem Put Tgthr Jr-Sr Prom 90; Friday Night Live 89-91; UCLA; Bus Mgmt.

CABRERA, EDUARDO; Phillip & Sala Burton HS; San Francisco, CA; (2); Band; Cmptrs.

CABRERA, ERIC; Bishop Ama And Memorial HS; La Puente, CA; (3); Var Hon Roll; NHS; Soc Svc Vlntr Wrk; UC; Mdcn.

CABRERA, HORTENCIA E; Hawthorne HS; Inglewood, CA; (3); Lawyer.

CABRERA, JOSE; Coachella Valley HS; Thermal, CA; (3); Wrstlng; UCLA; Forest Rangr.

CABRERA, JOSE; Pius X HS; Maywood, CA; (3); JV Var Ftbl; Hon Roll; Telecomm.

CABRERA, MARICELA; Sanger HS; Del Rey, CA; (2); Church Yth Grp; Computer Clb; French Clb; FBLA; FHA; Latin Clb; Math Clb; Office Aide; ROTC; Science Clb; PTA Schlrshp Awd.

CABRERA, MARK A; Tulare Western HS; Tulare, CA; (3); Church Yth Grp; Teachers Aide; Chorus; Church Choir; Rep Frsh Cls; Var Capt Golf; High Hon Roll; Spanish NHS; CSF; Tulare Western Accrdtn Team; Stu Needing Asstnc Pgm; Comp Engrng Sci.

CABRERA, MARYHELEN; Sanger HS; Del Rey, CA; (1); Computer Clb; FHA; Office Aide; ROTC; Spanish Clb; Teachers Aide; Bsbl.

CABRERA, ROSA M; Mt Pleasant HS; San Jose, CA; (1); French Clb; Math Clb; Science Clb; SADD; Sftbl; Hon Roll; Pres Acad Fit Awd; Gate Stu; UCLA; Law.

CABRERA, STEPHANIE A; Los Altos HS; Hacienda Hgts, CA; (3); Intnl Clb; Science Clb; Church Choir; Ed Nwsp; Ed Lit Mag; Hon Roll; Prm Spclst Prm Cmmtte; U Of CA San Diego; Jrnlsm.

CABRERA, YVETTE; Dos Pueblos HS; Goleta, CA; (4); 36/320; Pep Clb; Pres Stu Cncl; JV Cheerldng; Var Capt Pom Pon; Hon Roll; NHS; Prfct Atten Awd; Rotary Awd; Math, Engrng, Sci & Achvt Clb Co-Pres; Soroptimist Intl Yth Awd; Occidental Coll; Pre-Med.

CABREROS, MICHELLE R; Desert HS; Lancaster, CA; (2); Math Tm; JV Bsktbl; Var Vllybl; Hon Roll.

CABUAY, JACQUELINE A; Warren HS; Downey, CA; (3); Ed Nwsp; CSF; Booster Bear Awd; Golden St Exams Awd Rcgntn; Optmst Essay Wrtng Cert Rcgntn; Jrnlsm.

CABUNOC, JOYCE; Saddleback HS; Santa Ana, CA; (2); French Clb; Sec Science Clb; Spanish Clb; Rptr Yrbk; JV Trk; JV Vllybl; Prfct Atten Awd; CA Schlrshp Fed; Frgn Lang Awd; Acad Ltr; UCLA; Arch.

CABUNOC, MELODY; Saddleback HS; Santa Ana, CA; (2); Science Clb; SADD; CSF; Grls Lgue.

CABUNTALA, JEANETH M; William Workman HS; West Covina, CA; (3); Intnl Clb; Office Aide; Science Clb; Spanish Clb; Yrbk; Treas Jr Cls; Stat Tennis; Hon Roll; Prfct Atten Awd; Aviation Clb Treas; Loyola Marymount; Bus.

CACAL, CHERYL D; South San Francisco HS; Daly City, CA; (2); French Clb; FBLA; Spanish Clb; Teachers Aide; Rptr Yrbk; JV Sftbl; Hon Roll; Pres Acad Fit Awd; CA Schlrshp Fed; Asian Amer Clb; CA Polytech ST U; Commnctn.

CACANANTA, CARLA L; Rancho Alamitos HS; Garden Grove, CA; (3); Science Clb; Off Frsh Cls; High Hon Roll; CSF; Outstndng Jr Frgn Lang Awd 89-90 Spansh; Peer Cnslng Clb; CSU Fullerton; Accntng.

CACANANTA, OLIVER V; Livermore HS; Livermore, CA; (3); High Hon Roll; Hon Roll; CSF; Acad Achvt Awd; Acad Exllnc Awd; CA ST U; Pharmacy.

CACAO, MELINDA; St Patrick-St Vincent HS; Vallejo, CA; (2); Cmnty Wkr; Church Choir; High Hon Roll; Pres Acad Fit Awd; Awd Acad Achvt Filipino Cmmnty Solano Cnty Inc; CSF; Pep Flag Tm.

CACERES, TERESA A; El Rancho HS; Pico Rivera, CA; (4); 31/530; Stage Crew; Sec Sr Cls; Powder Puff Ftbl; Var Trk; Var Vllybl; High Hon Roll; Cres Hnr Awd; Seal Bearer CSF; Biola U; Nurse.

CACERES, VERONICA; Eagle Rock HS; Glendale, CA; (3); Church Yth Grp; Girl Scts; Spanish Clb; Church Choir; Yrbk; Gym; Vllybl; Pres Acad Fit Awd; UC Davis; Zoology.

CACHO JR, ALFREDO; La Puente HS; La Puente, CA; (2); Comp Repair.

CACHUELA, FRANCES ANN R; Bishop Montgomery HS; Hawthorne, CA; (2); Cmnty Wkr; Key Clb; High Hon Roll; CSF Awd; Algebra I Hnrs Cert Of Awd; UCLA; Engrng.

CACIANTI, PHILLIP J; Calaveras HS; Valley Springs, CA; (3); 12/200; German Clb; Golf; Hon Roll; Advncd CAD; UC Davis; Comp Prgmr.

CADDEL, CINDY L; Cajon HS; San Bernardino, CA; (2); Church Yth Grp; Drama Clb; Girl Scts; School Musical; School Play; Cheerldng; Hon Roll; Theatre.

CADDEL, JEFF; Cajon HS; San Bernadino, CA; (4); 14/358; Church Yth Grp; Cmnty Wkr; JA; Letterman Clb; Scholastic Bowl; Ski Clb; Varsity Clb; Socr; Swmmng; Tennis.

CADE, LATEEFAH I; Mc Clymonds HS; Oakland, CA; (3); #3 In Class; Pep Clb; Chorus; Rptr Nwsp; Rep Frsh Cls; Rep Soph Cls; Rep Jr Cls; Sec Sr Cls; Cheerldng; Tennis; Hon Roll; Spellman; Lawyer.

CADE, SUSAN M; Hemet HS; Hemet, CA; (2); Church Yth Grp; Cmnty Wkr; Debate Tm; SADD; Acpl Chr; Church Choir; VP Frsh Cls; Rep Stu Cncl; JV Bsktbl; Hon Roll; UCLA; Anatomy.

CADENA, JACQUELINE; William Workman HS; Valinda, CA; (2); JV Score Keeper; JV Vllybl; Hon Roll; Prfct Atten Awd; Friend To Friend Clb Treas; Scl Workr.

CADENA, MIGUEL A; St Monica HS; Santa Monica, CA; (3); 7/120; Var Crs Cntry; JV Ftbl; Hon Roll; U Of Sthrn CA; Aeroespc Engrng.

CADENA, RENE N; Santa Ana HS; Santa Ana, CA; (3); FCA; Latin Clb; Letterman Clb; Ftbl; Wt Lftg; Wrstlng; Prfct Atten Awd; USC; Chem.

CADENA, SHEILA R; Redwood HS; Visalia, CA; (3); Church Yth Grp; GAA; Teachers Aide; Church Choir; Yrbk; Score Keeper; Sftbl; Hon Roll; Fresno ST; Phys Thrpst.

CADIGAL, SUSAN; Mount Pleasant HS; San Jose, CA; (4); 58/534; Acpl Chr; Off Frsh Cls; Stu Cncl; Tennis; Trk; NHS; San Jose ST U; Nrsg.

CADILE, CASEY D; Castilleja HS; Los Altos, CA; (3); Math Tm; Treas Frsh Cls; Off Soph Cls; Stu Cncl; JV Var Bsktbl; Var Crs Cntry; Var Trk; High Hon Roll; Wildlife Consrvtn; Physics.

CADION, JOHANNA C; Oak Grove HS; San Jose, CA; (1); Cmnty Wkr; Filipino Yth Orgnztn; Scty Wmn Engrs; Hghr Outrch Ed Prog; Nrsng.

CADIZ, ADRIAN; Baldwin Park HS; Baldwin Park, CA; (3); Band; Mrchg Band; Pep Band; Var Trk; High Hon Roll; Nurse.

CADMUS, JENNIFER E; Arvin HS; Arvin, CA; (1); French Clb; Ski Clb; Chorus; Rep Frsh Cls; Cheerldng; Hon Roll; CSF.

CADOURA, RANIA W; Brea Olinda HS; Brea, CA; (2); UCLA; Psych.

CADWISING, GARY B; Liberty Baptist Schl; San Jose, CA; (4); 2/21; Church Yth Grp; Drama Clb; Office Aide; Church Choir; Nwsp; Ed Yrbk; Pres Frsh Cls; Pres Soph Cls; VP Jr Cls; Rep Stu Cncl; Bank Of Amer Plaque; Santa Clara Cty Yth Hall Of Fame; Concordia Coll; Bio.

CADY, ADAM S; Mira Costa HS; Manhattan Beach, CA; (2); Key Clb; JV Vllybl; High Hon Roll; Hon Roll; Slvr Mdlst US Jr Olympcs Vllybl; CSF; Bus.

CADY, JOANNA; El Toro HS; El Toro, CA; (1); German Clb; Sftbl; High Hon Roll; Natl Tang Soo Do Cngrss Karate Red Belt; FL ST U; Bio.

CADY, MICHELLE M; Ferndale HS; Ferndale, CA; (2); #3 In Class; Church Yth Grp; Cmnty Wkr; SADD; Phtg Yrbk; Bsktbl; Sftbl; Vllybl; Hon Roll; CSF; Hmbldt-Del Norte All Cnty Sftbl Awd; CA Poly Pomona; Acctng.

CAFASSO, DONNA L; Sir Francis Drake HS; San Anselmo, CA; (4); 47/147; Ski Clb; Spanish Clb; School Musical; School Play; Stage Crew; Variety Show; Ed Yrbk; VP Stu Cncl; Bsktbl; Capt Cheerldng; Grad Speaker; Hmcmng Prncss 89; SSTA Drama Cmptn Pantomine Rnnr Up 87; WA ST U; Nrsng.

CAGULADA, KAREN A; Louisville HS; Northridge, CA; (2); Church Yth Grp; GAA; Hosp Aide; Science Clb; Stu Cncl; JV Bsktbl; JV Swmmng; JV Tennis; High Hon Roll; Polynesian Dancing; Piano.

CAHILL, ALEXANDRA; Gompers Secondary Schl; San Diego, CA; (2); Cmnty Wkr; Computer Clb; Key Clb; Model UN; School Play; Mgr(s); JV Trk; Var L Vllybl; High Hon Roll; Hon Roll; S Army Reserv Natl Schlr Athl Awd; CSF Hnr Awd; ASB Rep Elec & Cmmssnr Athltcs Elect; UC Berkeley; Anthrplgy.

CAHILL, MELISSA L; Bakersfield West HS; Bakersfield, CA; (2); Debate Tm; Drama Clb; NFL; Spanish Clb; Speech Tm; SADD; Varsity Clb; Var Tennis; Hon Roll; Interact Club; Cal Poly San Luis Obispo; Ed.

CAHN, BRYCE M; Woodland HS; Woodland, CA; (3); Thesps; Acpl Chr; School Musical; School Play; Rptr School Musical; Ed Yrbk; Stu Cncl; High Hon Roll; Pres Acad Fit Awd; Cmnty Theater; Drama/Lit.

CAHN, MELISSA J; Whittier Christian HS; Whittier, CA; (1); Church Yth Grp; Hosp Aide; Hon Roll; CSF High Honor Scholarship Certificate; Horsebackriding; Guitar; College; Music Agent.

CAI, SAM YUE-YONG; Galileo HS; San Francisco, CA; (2); Off Soph Cls; Bsbl; Bsktbl; Ftbl; Socr; Tennis; Vllybl.

CAIAZZO, WILLIAM; Edison HS; Huntington Beach, CA; (2); Church Yth Grp; Model UN; High Hon Roll; Exclld In Gld St Exam-Algb; Arch.

CAILAO, BRENDA; Moreau HS; Newark, CA; (2); Church Yth Grp; Band; JV Cheerldng; Hon Roll; Bus.

CAIN, ANNE M; Turlock Joint Union HS; Turlock, CA; (2); 92/570; Church Yth Grp; Drama Clb; Girl Scts; Hosp Aide; Office Aide; Science Clb; Teachers Aide; Church Choir; Rptr Nwsp; High Hon Roll; Piano; Modesto JC; Bus.

CAIN, CAROL ANN; Fontana HS; Fontana, CA; (3); Church Yth Grp; Cmnty Wkr; Teachers Aide; High Hon Roll; CA Schlrshp Red; Marine Rsrch.

CAIN, DAVID; Apple Valley Christian HS; Apple Valley, CA; (4); 5/13; Church Yth Grp; Cmnty Wkr; Teachers Aide; Pep Band; Phtg Yrbk; Treas Pres Stu Cncl; Vllybl; High Hon Roll; Hon Roll; Outstndng Achvt Life Sci & Engl Awds 89-90; Excllnc In Hstry Awd 88-90; Biola U; Engl.

CAIN, JENNIFER; Claremont HS; Claremont, CA; (3); Drama Clb; Ski Clb; Spanish Clb; Thesps; Drill Tm; School Musical; School Play; Stage Crew; Yrbk; Hon Roll; Comp Appl Cert; UC Los Angeles; Psych.

CAIN, JESSICA M; Livermore HS; Livermore, CA; (3); Church Yth Grp; Teachers Aide; Band; Chorus; Church Choir; Jazz Band; Mrchg Band; Orch; School Musical; Hon Roll; CA St Hnr Band; Music.

CAIN, MATA E; Victor Valley HS; Victorville, CA; (3); Boy Scts; Church Yth Grp; Temple Yth Grp; Hon Roll; Indstrl Arts Awd; GSE Hnrble Mntn.

CAIN, MICA E; Victorville HS; Victorville, CA; (3); Church Yth Grp; Engrng.

CAIN, MICHAEL A; Tulare Union HS; Tulare, CA; (2); Church Yth Grp; Band; Jazz Band; Sec Frsh Cls; JV Socr; Var Swmmng; Hon Roll; Water Polo JV, Capt; Med.

CAIRO, LORI C; La Habra HS; Whittier, CA; (4); 20/360; Cmnty Wkr; FBLA; Intnl Clb; Letterman Clb; Service Clb; Teachers Aide; Varsity Clb; Treas Pep Clb; Rptr Yrbk; VP Frsh Cls; CSF; Stu Leag; Occptnl Thrpy.

CAITHAMER, JENNIFER L; Orange Lutheran HS; Orange, CA; (2); Stat Score Keeper; Var L Tennis; Orange Cty Acad Decathlon.

CAJERO, RUBEN; Senior HS; Roseville, CA; (2); Aud/Vis; Ftbl; Wt Lftg; Spring Little League Ump; Electronics.

CAJIGAL, CHRISTINA D; El Toro HS; El Toro, CA; (2); 36/557; Church Yth Grp; Drill Tm; Mrchg Band; Cit Awd; High Hon Roll; Jr NHS; High Honors In Golden State Exam For 1st Year Algebra; Im In Csf; I Love Volleyball; English Literature Teacher.

CAJIGAS, GRACE; Montgomery HS; San Diego, CA; (4); 1/410; Hosp Aide; Key Clb; Quiz Bowl; Service Clb; Teachers Aide; Ed Nwsp; Lit Mag; Off Stu Cncl; Cit Awd; High Hon Roll; Jostens Fndtn Recognition Awrd; Bank Of Am Plaque Wnnr-Sci & Math; ASB Distinguished Srvc Awrd; San Diego ST U; Bus Admin.

CAJILES, CHARLENE C; John H Francis Polytechnic HS; Panorama City, CA; (3); Spanish Clb; Pep Band; Hon Roll; Prfct Atten Awd; Nrsng.

CAJIUAT, JUSTIN H; Santa Clara HS; Oxnard, CA; (3); Church Yth Grp; Letterman Clb; Teachers Aide; JV Var Ftbl; Hon Roll; Span Clb; Treas Of Clb; CSUN; Bus Ec.

CALAC, SHALOME L; Forest Lake Christian Schl; Auburn, CA; (2); Church Yth Grp; Spanish Clb; Varsity Clb; Chorus; School Musical; School Play; VP Frsh Cls; VP Soph Cls; Rep Stu Cncl; Bsktbl; Plywrt Cntst Wnr; Pblsh-Wrt Fmly Nwsltr; Fre-Lnc Wrtr.

CALAGUAS, JENNIFER M; Lemoore HS; Lemoore, CA; (3); Cmnty Wkr; Intnl Clb; VP Spanish Clb; Rep Jr Cls; JV Bsktbl; JV Tennis; Hon Roll; Prfct Atten Awd; CSF Clb; Phot Clb Sec; U Of The Pacific; Psych.

CALAGUAS, RAUL A; Notre Dame HS; Riverside, CA; (4); Hon Roll; U Of CA Riverside; Bus.

CALAGUI, ANTONIO A; Sacred Heart Cathedral Prep; Daly City, CA; (1); Cmnty Wkr; Hosp Aide; Science Clb; JV Tennis; Hon Roll; Shotokan Karate Prple Blt; UCLA; Pre Med.

CALAGUI, VENUS; Sacred Heart Cathedral Prep; Daly City, CA; (2); GAA; Spanish Clb; Var Tennis; Hon Roll; Bus.

CALALANG, ETHEL; San Gabriel Acad; Palmdale, CA; (3); Church Yth Grp; Teachers Aide; Chorus; Rep Jr Cls; Intrml Bsktbl; Gym; Intrml Socr; Intrml Sftbl; Intrml Vllybl; NHS; Pacific Union Coll; Nrsng.

CALBES, EMILY L; John Muir HS; Pasadena, CA; (2); Treas FBLA; Library Aide; Ed Lit Mag; Jrnlsm.

CALCANTE, BETH; Newbury Park HS; Newbury Park, CA; (4); Church Yth Grp; GAA; Varsity Clb; Bsktbl; Powder Puff Ftbl; Socr; Sftbl; Tennis; Hon Roll; Prfct Atten Awd; Sftbl Hall Of Fame; CIF Catcher 1st Tm; Northridge; Vet.

CALDERA, JENNIFER A; Hawthorne HS; Lawndale, CA; (2); Church Yth Grp; Cmnty Wkr; Rep Key Clb; Service Clb; Church Choir; Mrchg Band; New Life Clb; Poli Sci.

CALDERA, PAULAMARIE R; Eagle Rock HS; Los Angeles, CA; (3); Cmnty Wkr; Latin Clb; Teachers Aide; Jazz Band; Orch; Mgr(s); Var Sftbl; Cit Awd; Hon Roll; Los Angeles Police Explorer; Comm Kids Tutor; Police Officer.

CALDERON, BEATRIZ; Apple Valley HS; Apple Valley, CA; (3); Hon Roll; Victor Valley Coll; Child Dev.

CALDERON, BENJAMIN A; St Marys HS; Stockton, CA; (2); Science Clb; Band; Jazz Band; Mrchg Band; Pep Band; Stu Cncl; High Hon Roll; Hon Roll; 1st Pl Rgnl Sci Bowl Cmptn Genetics; 4th Pl Nor Cal Sci Bowl Cmptn Genetics; Physics.

CALDERON, CHRISTINA T; Banning HS; Banning, CA; (2); Model UN; Color Guard; Drill Tm; Mrchg Band; JV Sftbl; Acad Ltr; Most Insprtnl JR Var Sftbl Tm; Outstndng Soph Awd Clr Grd; Harvard; Law.

CALDERON, CIELO; Coast Union HS; Cambria, CA; (2); 2/55; AFS; Church Yth Grp; SADD; Pres Frsh Cls; VP Soph Cls; JV Cheerldng; High Hon Roll; CSF; Fshn Dsgn.

CALDERON, ELI; Cantwell HS; Baldwin Park, CA; (4); Spanish Clb; JV Var Bsbl; Var Bsktbl; Hon Roll; UC Riverside; Bus Admin.

CALDERON, GENE A; San Lorenzo HS; Hayward, CA; (2); Church Yth Grp; Scholastic Bowl; Hon Roll; UC Berkleyes Pre-Coll Acad; Minority Ldrshp Grp; UC Berkeley; Engrng.

CALDERON, JENNIFER; Bishop Amat HS; West Covina, CA; (4); 43/400; GAA; Pep Clb; Drill Tm; L Pom Pon; Hon Roll; CSF; Slvr Scrn Clb; Engr.

CALDERON, LAURA; Riverbank HS; Riverbank, CA; (1); Tennis; Engr.

CALDERON, LUIS P; Higland Park HS; Los Angeles, CA; (3); Dance Clb; Library Aide; Jazz Band; Cit Awd; Martial Arts Kung Fu; Weight Training; Glendale Coll; Law.

CALDERON, MARIO A; Brea-Olinda HS; Brea, CA; (2); 41/336; Chess Clb; Church Yth Grp; Band; Jazz Band; Mrchg Band; Pep Band; Crs Cntry; Trk; High Hon Roll; Jr NHS; UC Berkeley; Genetic Engr.

CALDERON, MARTHA; Santa Maria HS; Santa Maria, CA; (2); Church Yth Grp; Spanish Clb; Temple Yth Grp; Amigos Unidos; UCSB; Teacher.

CALDERON, RANDY; Baldwin Park HS; Baldwin Park, CA; (3); High Hon Roll; Prfct Atten Awd; Goldn State Exam Awd Algb & Geom; Acad Achvt Awd; Electrncs.

CALDERON, RAY; Indio HS; Indio, CA; (1); JV Bsktbl; Var Ftbl; Var Trk; Cit Awd; Hon Roll; Pres Acad Fit Awd.

CALDERON, REBECCA; Bishop Anat Memorial HS; Whittier, CA; (3); Office Aide; Var L Crs Cntry; Var L Trk; Hon Roll; CA Schlrshp Fdrtn; Work/Expernc Pgm; Silvr Screen Clb; Loyola Marymount U; Bus.

CALDERON, ROSA E; Pasadena HS; Pasadena, CA; (1); Intrml Swmmng; Law Enfrcmnt.

CALDERON, SERGIO A; Garey HS; Pomona, CA; (3); Am Leg Boys St; Band; Mrchg Band; Most Outstndng Hstry Stu; Hstry Teacher.

CALDERON, TRINA; Burbank HS; Burbank, CA; (2); Church Yth Grp; Dance Clb; Debate Tm; English Clb; Spanish Clb; Speech Tm; Ed Nwsp; Pres Acad Fit Awd; UC Berkley; Jrnlsm.

CALDERON, VIDAL; Venice HS; Inglewood, CA; (3); El Camino Coll.

CALDERON, ZULMA; Pius X HS; Compton, CA; (3); Church Yth Grp; Var Cheerldng; Hon Roll; Bus Admin.

CALDERWOOD, LISA S; Monrovia HS; Monrovia, CA; (3); Church Yth Grp; Treas Drama Clb; Science Clb; Chorus; Capt Flag Corp; JV Sftbl; Hon Roll; Marine Bio.

CALDWELL, CAROL; South Torrance HS; Torrance, CA; (4); Church Yth Grp; Band; Chorus; Church Choir; Color Guard; Flag Corp; Jazz Band; Mrchg Band; Orch; Pep Band; U S CA; Ed.

CALDWELL, DAWN R; Fremont Christian HS; Fremont, CA; (3); Church Yth Grp; French Clb; Pep Clb; Teachers Aide; Chorus; Stat Bsbl; JV Cheerldng; Hon Roll.

CALDWELL, GAYNEL D; Washington Preparotory HS; Los Angeles, CA; (3); Dance Clb; Drama Clb; Teachers Aide; Drill Tm; Variety Show; Cheerldng; Cit Awd; Hon Roll; Prof Dancer.

CALDWELL, HENRY H; Boron HS; Boron, CA; (4); 10/40; Pres English Clb; Letterman Clb; Math Tm; Band; Nwsp; Stu Cncl; Capt Bsbl; Ftbl; Trk; Capt Wrstlng; 2nd Team All Kern Co, All Desert Inyo Leag Ftbl; Sthrn Sectn All Star Bsbl; Bakersfield Coll; Sci.

CALDWELL, JASON D; Los Amigos HS; Santa Ana, CA; (3); 22/301; Boy Scts; Mgr Jr Cls; Pres Sr Cls; JV Ftbl; Hon Roll; NHS; Jr Var Water Polo; Bus Mgmt.

CALDWELL, LISA MARIE; Granada Hills HS; Northridge, CA; (2); Church Yth Grp; Cmnty Wkr; Library Aide; Ski Clb; Yrbk; Sftbl; Cit Awd; Hon Roll; Frontline Fndtn-Wrkng With Homeless; Sun Schl Tchr; Fshn Dsgnr.

CALDWELL, SHARMEL N; Luther Burbank HS; Sacramento, CA; (3); Church Yth Grp; Office Aide; ROTC; Church Choir; Drill Tm; School Play; Gym; Trk; Cit Awd; Hon Roll; Prsnl Apprnce Awd; Seamnshp; Hnr Stu; Prtcptn Awd & Outstndnd Sci Awd; Sac ST U; Brdcstng.

CALER, VINA AILEEN; Wagner HS; APO San Francisc, CA; (2); 78/411; Intnl Clb; Sftbl; Vllybl; Hon Roll; Medal From Senior Softball Team; High Honor Roll Since Elementary; IN U; Medicine.

CALGER, DEIRDRE M; Antelope Valley HS; Lancaster, CA; (3); 9/631; Intnl Clb; Spanish Clb; Teachers Aide; Rep Soph Cls; Rep Jr Cls; High Hon Roll; Masonic Awd; Grls St Fnlst; Intl Order Rainbow For Grls; Dance Tm-Treas.

CALHOON, BROOKE; Calvary Chapel HS; Lake Forest, CA; (2); Aud/Vis; Church Yth Grp; Pres Pep Clb; Ski Clb; Var Cheerldng; Cit Awd; Hon Roll; Pres Acad Fit Awd; Bus.

CALHOUN, CARRIE L; Pioneer HS; San Jose, CA; (3); Church Yth Grp; Cmnty Wkr; Vllybl; Hon Roll; Congressional Yth Ldrshp Cncl; UC Riverside; Orthoppedic.

CALHOUN, DESERIE A; Pioneer HS; San Jose, CA; (2); Cheerldng; Pom Pon; Trk; Hon Roll; NHS; UC Davis; Bus.

CALHOUN, FLORAMARIA; Rosary HS; Fullerton, CA; (4); 24/132; Science Clb; Variety Show; Ed Nwsp; Yrbk; Lit Mag; High Hon Roll; Hon Roll; NHS; CSF; Jrnlsm.

CALHOUN, HEATHER J; Marymount HS; Los Angeles, CA; (3); Dance Clb; Drama Clb; Hosp Aide; SADD; Thesps; Chorus; School Musical; School Play; Stage Crew; Mst Dedctd Choir Awd; Loyola Marymount U; Law.

CALHOUN, JOHN; Colfax HS; Colfax, CA; (4); 10/160; Ski Clb; Var Socr; High Hon Roll; Bank Of Amer Achvt Awd Fld Comp Sci; Colfax HS Comp Sci Stu; Stu Of Mnth; UC Davis; Comp Sci.

CALIBOSO, NOEL D; Channel Islands HS; Oxnard, CA; (4); 4/475; Cmnty Wkr; Science Clb; Teachers Aide; Hon Roll; Prfct Atten Awd; Pres Acad Fit Awd; Defense Attorney For Mock Trial Tm; Cal Poly; Electrical Engr.

CALIC, ALEX; Alameda HS; Alameda, CA; (4); 29/325; Art Clb; French Clb; Var Bsktbl; Var Score Keeper; Intrml Wt Lftg; High Hon Roll; Pres Acad Fit Awd; Schlr Athlt; Acadc A Math, Sci, Frgn Lang & Scl Studies; Athltc Awd; Pepperdine U; Intl Bus.

CALICA, JENNIFER C; Wallenburg Traditional HS; San Francisco, CA; (3); Art Clb; Chess Clb; Cmnty Wkr; Debate Tm; Drama Clb; English Clb; Library Aide; Math Clb; NFL; Office Aide; Sculpting; Riflery; Poetry; MIT; Mech Engrng.

CALIMQUIM, RODNEY; Esperanza HS; Yorba Linda, CA; (4); 58/530; Church Yth Grp; German Clb; Letterman Clb; Varsity Clb; Vllybl; Hon Roll; Top 25; CSF; Asian Clb; UCR; Bus Admin.

CALIN, ANNALORA; Red Bluff Union HS; Red Bluff, CA; (2); 27/443; Church Yth Grp; Rep Frsh Cls; Rep Soph Cls; Stu Cncl; Capt L Cheerldng; Hon Roll; Prfct Atten Awd; HOBY Yth Ldrshp Smnr Ambssdr; Elks Stu Of Mnth Awd; CA Schlrshp Fndtn; Med.

CALIP, JEANETTE B; Dinuba HS; Dinuba, CA; (4); 18/168; Church Yth Grp; VP Drama Clb; Service Clb; Chorus; Church Choir; Color Guard; School Musical; School Play; Hon Roll; CA All-State Hnr Choir; Veterans Of Frgn War Spch Cmptn; Arts Rcgntn & Talent Srch; Juilliard; Music.

CALITRI, MONICA C; Norco SR HS; Corona, CA; (3); Girl Scts; Model UN; Speech Tm; Varsity Clb; Swmmng; Cit Awd; Hon Roll; Rotary Intl Frgn Exchnge Stu Smmr 89; Intl Law.

CALKINS, ERIN E; Hemet HS; Idyllwild, CA; (3); 6/547; Church Yth Grp; Cit Awd; High Hon Roll; Rotary Awd; Daisy Chn Hnr Escrt; Bullpup Hnr Awd 87-88; U Of CA San Diego; Pre-Med.

CALKINS, MATTHEW W; Tamalpais HS; Mill Valley, CA; (4); 7/231; Band; Jazz Band; Orch; High Hon Roll; Ntl Merit SF; Pres/Fndr Dipolomacy Club; Pol Sci.

CALKINS, MELISSA N; Rim Of The World HS; Cedar Glen, CA; (1); Church Yth Grp; Dance Clb; French Clb; Rep Frsh Cls; Hon Roll; Art.

CALKINS, STACI L; Rio Lindo Adventist Acad; Eureka, CA; (3); Church Yth Grp; Cmnty Wkr; Office Aide; Ski Clb; Spanish Clb; Band; Chorus; Orch; Pres Stu Cncl; Intrml Bsktbl; ASB VP 1990-91; Loma Linda U; Medicine.

CALL, BAMBI M; Fred C Beyer HS; Modesto, CA; (1); Pep Clb; SADD; Hon Roll; UCLA; Bus.

CALL, CAROLINE; Saratoga HS; Saratoga, CA; (4); Pres Church Yth Grp; Pep Clb; Church Choir; School Musical; Rep Soph Cls; JV Var Bsktbl; JV Capt Cheerldng; JV Var Diving; Powder Puff Ftbl; Pres Acad Fit Awd; BYU Schlrshp; Jazz Choir; BYU; Pdtrc Psych.

CALLAGHAN, JOHN D; Modoc HS; Alturas, CA; (4); 4-H; JV L Bsktbl; Var L Crs Cntry; JV L Ftbl; Var L Trk; 4-H Awd; Hon Roll; Aviation Club; Eastern OR ST Coll; Vet.

CALLAHAM, DEANNA L; Fall Friver JR SR HS; Mc Arthur, CA; (3); 4-H; Pres FBLA; Off Sr Cls; Var JV Bsktbl; Var JV Vllybl; 4-H Awd; Lassen JC; Phys Ed.

CALLAHAN, AARON P; Sacramento HS; Sacramento, CA; (2); 40/500.

CALLAHAN, CHRISTOPHER R; Fairfield HS; Fairfield, CA; (3); 27/480; ROTC; High Hon Roll; Hon Roll; NHS; Ntl Merit SF; Physcs.

CALLAHAN, CRISTINA R; St Monica HS; Los Angeles, CA; (4); Drama Clb; Science Clb; Ski Clb; Teachers Aide; Thesps; School Musical; School Play; Stage Crew; Swing Chorus; Yrbk; Outstndng Achvt Artstc Desgn Awd; Vrs Schl Role Models; U Of Southern CA; Theatre Arts.

CALLAHAN, DENNIS; Huntington Beach HS; Huntington Bch, CA; (4); 76/457; Varsity Clb; Var Capt Bsktbl; Var Vllybl; Hon Roll; Grad W/Hnrs; Humboldt ST; Environmentl Engr.

CALLAHAN, JEAN M; Cupertino HS; Cupertino, CA; (3); Service Clb; Teachers Aide; Varsity Clb; Swmmng; Girls Water Polo Tm; Cls Actvts; Hstry.

CALLAHAN, JOHN; Paraclete HS; Leona Valley, CA; (4); Church Yth Grp; Treas Key Clb; Letterman Clb; Var L Ftbl; JV Trk; High Hon Roll; Hon Roll; NHS; NEDT Awd; UCLA; Engrng.

CALLAHAN, LISA R; Thomas Downey HS; Modesto, CA; (1); Dance Clb; U Of The Pacific; Educ.

CALLAHAN, SHANNON D; J Eugene Mc Ateer HS; San Francisco, CA; (3); Drama Clb; Acpl Chr; Chorus; School Musical; School Play; Sec Jr Cls; Sec Stu Cncl; JV Sftbl; Stat Vllybl; Hon Roll; Marriot Schlrshp Comptn; Yng Musicians Pgm UC Berkeley; Schl Wrtng Comptn; Musician.

CALLAHAN, TAMMI; Red Bluff HS; Red Bluff, CA; (3); Church Yth Grp; Cmnty Wkr; Dance Clb; Office Aide; Teachers Aide; Yrbk; Sec Frsh Cls; Rep Soph Cls; Rep Stu Cncl; Capt Var Cheerldng; Chrldng Rbbns; Fshn Shw; Sr Prom Bnft 90; Smmr Cnslr; Camp Cnslr; Shasta C; Tchng.

CALLAN, MEGAN E; The Bishops Schl; Solana Beach, CA; (3); Art Clb; Pres Church Yth Grp; Cmnty Wkr; SADD; Thesps; Acpl Chr; Chorus; Church Choir; School Musical; School Play; Horses; Tri-M Music Hnr Soc; Psych.

CALLAN, MELISSA; Barstow HS; Barstow, CA; (2); Hon Roll; Real Estate.

CALLANAN, MELANIE M; South Gate HS; S Gate, CA; (2); Debate Tm; GAA; Quiz Bowl; Scholastic Bowl; Swmmng; Med.

CALLANDER, KAREN A; James Madison HS; San Diego, CA; (2); 1/359; Drama Clb; GAA; NFL; Speech Tm; Cit Awd; High Hon Roll; Pres Acad Fit Awd; Badminton; CSF; UCSD; Envrnmntl Sci.

CALLANDRILLO, ANTHONY M; Riverbank HS; Riverbank, CA; (3); 10/110; Cmnty Wkr; Letterman Clb; Quiz Bowl; Teachers Aide; Varsity Clb; JV Bsbl; JV Var Bsktbl; JV Var Ftbl; JV Var Trk; Hon Roll; Archaeology.

CALLAWAY, CARI; Los Alamitos HS; Los Alamitos, CA; (3); Cmnty Wkr; Capt Drill Tm; High Hon Roll; CSF; Ntl Chrty Lgue; Ped.

CALLAWAY, TAMMIE J; Freedom Christian Schl; North Highlands, CA; (2); Sec Church Yth Grp; Office Aide; Church Choir; School Musical; School Play; Sftbl; Cit Awd; Hon Roll; Chrstn Character Awd; Sacramento ST U; Psych.

CALLE, LUIS ALBERTO; Don Bosco Technical Inst; Fontana, CA; (1); 21/244; Drama Clb; School Play; JV Swmmng; Hon Roll; NEDT Awd; Opt Clb Awd; Pres Acad Fit Awd; Water Polo Player; Materials Sci.

CALLEJO, ROBERT S; Prospect HS; Saratoga, CA; (1); JV Bsbl; JV Ftbl; Hon Roll.

CALLICOTT, JEFF L; Eldorado/Emerson HS; Irvine, CA; (3); Boy Scts; Church Yth Grp; Chorus; Orch; Yrbk; NEDT Awd; Astronomy.

CALLISON, LOGAN C; Fall River HS; Fall River Mlls, CA; (3); Art Clb; Church Yth Grp; Debate Tm; FFA; Hon Roll; UC Santa Barbara; Actor.

CALO, ROSELLE B; Porterville HS; Terra Bella, CA; (3); Pres GAA; Intnl Clb; Science Clb; Band; Mrchg Band; Rep Stu Cncl; Score Keeper; Hon Roll; UCLA; Lib Arts.

CALOCA, IRENE; James A Garfield HS; Los Angeles, CA; (2); Church Yth Grp; Cmnty Wkr; Drama Clb; Thesps; Church Choir; Drill Tm; School Musical; School Play; Stage Crew; Variety Show; Most Insprtnl Prfrmr Trphy; Eastside Boys & Girls Club Vlntr; Chrldng & Drill Team Asst Mgr; Drama.

CALOIA JR, WILLIAM P; John W North HS; Riverside, CA; (2); Boy Scts; Key Clb; Hon Roll; 1st Pl Auto Cad Riverside Cnty; PTA Rflctns Art Contest; Arch.

CALUAG, ARIEL J; Leuzinger HS; Lawndale, CA; (3); Art Clb; Pres Chess Clb; Church Yth Grp; Computer Clb; Key Clb; Off Soph Cls; Var Crs Cntry; Var Trk; Music; Microbio.

CALVERT, JESSICA G; Mt View HS; Los Altos, CA; (2); Church Yth Grp; Dance Clb; Teachers Aide; School Musical; High Hon Roll; NHS; Dancng, Modelng, Camp Cnslr; San Francisco ST; Bus.

CALVERT, MATTHEW H; Bella Vista HS; Citrus Heights, CA; (2); 12/406; Spanish Clb; JV Bsbl; JV Socr; NHS; Spanish NHS; Piano.

CALVILLO, ISAIAS G; Arvin HS; Lamont, CA; (3); Math Clb; VP Jr Cls; Crs Cntry; Trk; Wrstlng; High Hon Roll; Hon Roll; U CA-SANTA Barbara; Law.

CALVILLO, MARIA I; Eisenhower HS; San Bernardino, CA; (2); Church Yth Grp; Computer Clb; Chorus; Tennis; Vllybl; Hmwrk Clb; Ltr K Clb; Piece Ofcr.

CALVIN, JESSICA L; Irvine HS; Irvine, CA; (1); 91/580; Band; Rep Stu Cncl; Sci.

CALVIN, MICHAEL; James Lick HS; San Jose, CA; (4); 16/257; Boy Scts; Church Yth Grp; Cmnty Wkr; Ntl Merit SF; Intnl Clb; Red Cross Aide; Science Clb; Speech Tm; Band; Jazz Band; Eagle Scout; Marine Bio.

CALVIRD, JENNIFER L; Amos Alonzo Stagg HS; Stockton, CA; (2); Drama Clb; Teachers Aide; Hon Roll; Dance Show; Theatrical Cosmotology.

CALVO, JESUS; Modesto HS; Modesto, CA; (3); Math Clb; Math Tm; Office Aide; Band; Hon Roll; NHS; STEP Pgm; PSP Pgm; Math.

CAM, HA TRUONG THI; Costa Mesa HS; Santa Ana, CA; (3); 31/238; Intnl Clb; Bsbl; Bsktbl; Score Keeper; Swmmng; Tennis; Trk; Vllybl; Wt Lftg; High Hon Roll; Orang Coast Coll; Comp.

CAMACHO, ADRIANNE C; La Serna HS; Whittier, CA; (3); 116/393; GAA; Acpl Chr; Chorus; Variety Show; JV Sftbl; JV Swmmng; Var JV Vllybl; Vllybl Clb 3 Yrs; Ed.

CAMACHO, ALBERT M; Don Bosco Techinical Inst; La Puente, CA; (3); Church Yth Grp; Cmnty Wkr.

CAMACHO, ARTHUR; North Park HS; Baldwin Park, CA; (1); Art Clb; Church Yth Grp; Cmnty Wkr; Library Aide; Math Clb; Math Tm; Office Aide; Science Clb; SADD; School Play; Electrncs; Span; ITT Tech; Comp.

CAMACHO, BRETT; Palmdale HS; Agua Dulce, CA; (4); 93/592; Church Yth Grp; Cmnty Wkr; FFA; Speech Tm; Teachers Aide; VICA; Stu Cncl; Wrstlng; Hon Roll; Lion Awd; Bank Of Amer Achvt Awd Fnlst; St FFA Degree, Natl Convntn; CA Poly; Ag Instrctr.

CAMACHO, CENIA Y; Bell Gardens HS; Bell Gardens, CA; (1); Prfct Atten Awd; USC; Lwyr.

CAMACHO, DIANA E; Manual Arts HS; Los Angeles, CA; (3); Drama Clb; Teachers Aide; School Musical; Variety Show; High Hon Roll; Freedms Fndtns Cnfrnc Vly Forge; Cnfrnc W/Tchrs & Schlrs USC; Pre-Law.

CAMACHO JR, GUILLERMO ANDRES; De La Salle HS; Honolulu, HI; (4); Church Yth Grp; Cmnty Wkr; Teachers Aide; Anderrsons Commnctn Schlrshp; Mexican Amer Cultural Assn Schlrshp; Intl Studies Assn Frgn Lng Schlrshp; U Of Honolulu; Cinematgrphy.

CAMACHO, ILAYANA; Warren HS; Bell Gardens, CA; (2); Powder Puff Ftbl; CSF; U Of Southern CA; Jrnlsm.

CAMACHO JR, JOE PAUL; Don Bosco Technical Inst; Los Angeles, CA; (2); 24/212; Var Bsktbl; Hon Roll; NHS; NEDT Awd; Campus Ministry; Gldn Tgr Awd; Engrng.

CAMACHO, JUDEEN C; St Genevieve HS; Mission Hls, CA; (4); Hosp Aide; VP JA; Pep Clb; SADD; Chorus; Drill Tm.

CAMACHO, MARIA A; Paraclete HS; Quartz Hills, CA; (3); Church Yth Grp; Debate Tm; Hosp Aide; SADD; Stage Crew; Capt Socr; Hon Roll; Peer Helpr; Cal Northridge; Physiolgy.

CAMACHO, OSBALDO; Bell HS; Bell, CA; (3); Rep Frsh Cls; JV Bsktbl; UC San Diego; Comp Engr.

CAMACHO, PATRICIA T; John F Kennedy HS; Buena Park, CA; (1); UC Irvine; Bus.

CAMACHO, TREENA R; Antioch HS; Pittsburg, CA; (4); 17/585; FBLA; Office Aide; Pep Clb; Ski Clb; Teachers Aide; Gym; Var Trk; Hon Roll; Pres Acad Fit Awd; Acad Ltrmns Clu; Hnr Guard 89; Homecoming Queen; CA U; Ec.

CAMAQUIN, JAYBOY L; Orosi HS; Orosi, CA; (2); English Clb; FFA; Science Clb; Cit Awd; Hon Roll; Awd Of Merit Outstndng Achvt-Sci & Engl; Kings River CC; Pedtrcn.

CAMARA, JOSEPH R; Turlock HS; Delhi, CA; (2); #43 In Class; FFA; Ftbl; Socr; Wt Lftg; Hon Roll; Yth Sccr Ref/Coach; CA Poly-San Luis Obispo; Sci.

CAMARCE, ANGELINE C; Vallejo SR HS; Vallejo, CA; (4); Teachers Aide; Hon Roll; Filipino Cmnty Orgnztn Awd; Solano CC; Acctng.

CAMARENA, ENRIQUE E; Southwest HS; San Diego, CA; (3); JV Var Bsbl; JV Var Ftbl; Hon Roll; Bus.

CAMARENA, NORMA; Cajon HS; San Bernardino, CA; (3); Hgh GPA.

CAMARENA, YVONNE G; Silver Valley HS; Fort Irwin, CA; (2); Church Yth Grp; GAA; Letterman Clb; Sec Soph Cls; Var JV Bsktbl; Var JV Crs Cntry; Gym; Hon Roll; Law.

CAMARENA, ZORAIDA Z; Central Union HS; El Centro, CA; (3); Bus.

CAMARILLO, SANDY; Tulare Western HS; Tulare, CA; (2); Band; Hon Roll; Hspnc Yth Ldrshp Awds; Migrant Awd GPA; Hnr Engl & Hstry Clsses; Law.

CAMBAY, CHERYL; St Joseph HS; Yorba Linda, CA; (2); 49/196; Church Yth Grp; Drama Clb; Hosp Aide; Spanish Clb; SADD; Variety Show; Var JV Cheerldng; Hon Roll; Yth Peer Cnslng; Peer Cnslr Cert Rcgntn; CSF; U Of CA Irvine; Med.

CAMBERDELLA, CARA; San Marcos HS; Santa Barbara, CA; (4); 11/330; Cmnty Wkr; Hosp Aide; Letterman Clb; Nwsp; Stat Bsktbl; Co-Ed Cheerldng; Var L Sftbl; JV Tennis; High Hon Roll; NHS; Chmpn Eqstrn Rider; USC.

CAMBEROS, SERGIO; Oxnard HS; Oxnard, CA; (3); 27/700; SADD; Hon Roll; Prfct Atten Awd.

CAMBOURIS, ANDY J; Mountain View HS; Los Altos, CA; (3); Teachers Aide; Varsity Clb; JV Var Bsbl; JV Bsktbl; JV Var Ftbl; All League Bsbl; Sports Therapy.

CAMCAM, STEPHEN J; Salinas HS; Salinas, CA; (4); 38/357; Ski Clb; Var Trk; High Hon Roll; Hon Roll; Prfct Atten Awd; Hartnell Coll.

CAMERON, BRYAN THOMAS; Woodrow Wilson HS; Long Beach, CA; (4); Long Beach City Coll; Accntng.

CAMERON, CHAD A; Nevada Union HS; Nevada City, CA; (3); Boy Scts; Library Aide; Var JV Bsbl; Ftbl; Marksmnshp Clb.

CAMERON, IAN T; Napa HS; Napa, CA; (3); Boy Scts; Key Clb; VP Frsh Cls; Var Crs Cntry; JV Swmmng; JV Tennis; Intrml Vllybl; Var Wrstlng; Sierra Clb; Alfred U; Chem Engr.

CAMERON, MELISSA M; Mesa Verde HS; Citrus Heights, CA; (2); 93/257; Spanish Clb; Phtg Rptr Yrbk; Stu Reaching Out; Friday Night Live; Teaching.

CAMILING, ERIC M; Irvine HS; Irvine, CA; (4); AFS; Hosp Aide; Key Clb; Library Aide; Scholastic Bowl; Science Clb; Teachers Aide; Ed Nwsp; Ntl Merit SF; Pres Acad Fit Awd; Acad Decthln Comptn Awds; Pres IHS Chns Clb; Ec Brnz Mdl; Bio.

CAMILO, LYNN R; Mater Dei HS; Costa Mesa, CA; (2); Cmnty Wkr; Drama Clb; Latin Clb; School Musical; School Play; Stage Crew; Hon Roll; Hardest Wrkr Trophy Drama Club Awds; Natl Piano-Playing Audtions; Eng Tchr.

CAMINATA, JEFFREY P; St Marys HS; Stockton, CA; (2); Debate Tm; Model UN; NFL; Speech Tm; Band; Mrchg Band; Pep Band; Stage Crew; Rep Soph Cls; Rep Jr Cls; Stu In Prvntn Alcohol & Drug Awrnss Pgm; Law.

CAMINITI, SANDY L; Redlands HS; Redlands, CA; (3); 58/896; Church Yth Grp; Letterman Clb; Pep Clb; Chorus; Treas Stu Cncl; Cheerldng; JV Var Tennis; Cit Awd; Hon Roll; CA Schlrshp Federation; Civic Aux Of Jr Women Federation Of Amer; Westmont Coll; Math; Bus.

CAMMILLERI, GAIUS S; Arcadia HS; Arcadia, CA; (3); 17/640; Am Leg Boys St; Church Yth Grp; Band; Drm Mjr(t); Mrchg Band; Orch; Pres Frsh Cls; VP Jr Cls; Var JV Bsktbl; High Hon Roll; The Harvard Bk Awd; HOBY Fndtn Stu Ldr; Ivy League; Pol Sci.

CAMOU, ALAIN; John W North HS; Riverside, CA; (4); Church Yth Grp; Varsity Clb; Intrml Bsbl; Intrml JV Bsktbl; Var Capt Ftbl; JV Wt Lftg; French Hon Soc; Hon Roll; Jr NHS; NHS; Hnrb Mntn Grad; Congrssnl Yth Ldrshp Cncl; UC Riverside; Psych.

CAMOZZI, CHRISTINA K; Sir Francis Drake HS; San Anselmo, CA; (2); Ski Clb; JV Bsktbl; JV Powder Puff Ftbl; JV Sftbl; High Hon Roll; Hon Roll; NHS; YMCA Youth And Govt; Students For Social Responsibility; Schl Recognition Golden State Exam Algebra; College; Environmental Sci.

CAMP, BAYLISS; Sacramento HS; Sacramento, CA; (3); 7/386; AFS; Chess Clb; Drama Clb; Ski Clb; School Play; Treas Soph Cls; Pres Jr Cls; CSF; CTY Johns Hopkins; Stu Reachng Out & Friday Nght Live; Drama.

CAMP, KEN A; Canyon Springs HS; Moreno Valley, CA; (3); Band; Mrchg Band; Orch; Pep Band; JV Var Bsktbl; Score Keeper; High Hon Roll; Hon Roll; Prfct Atten Awd; Cngrssnl Schlr CA Rep Natl Yng Ldrs Conf 90; AP Eng & US His 89-90; UCLA; Cmptr Sci.

CAMP, SHANNA; Southport Christian Acad; San Ysidro, CA; (4); Church Yth Grp; Office Aide; Teachers Aide; Hon Roll; Accntng.

CAMP, SHAWN E; Lemoore HS; Lemoore, CA; (3); Pres Church Yth Grp; JV Bsbl; JV Socr; Cit Awd; Hon Roll; Little Lg Umpr; Babe Ruth Umpre.

CAMP, THOMAS L; San Juan HS; Citrus Heights, CA; (4); 37/268; SADD; Teachers Aide; Hon Roll; People To People Frndshp Caravan USSR 90; CSU Sacramento; Comp Sci.

CAMP, TOM; Canyon Springs HS; Moreno Valley, CA; (2); Band; Mrchg Band; Pep Band; JV Bsktbl; High Hon Roll; Hon Roll; Prfct Atten Awd; Pres Acad Fit Awd; Pres Schlr.

CAMPA, DAVID; La Puente HS; La Puente, CA; (3); Bsbl; Bsktbl; Var L Ftbl; Wt Lftg; Hon Roll; Daisey Chain Hnr Guard; CA Geo Fld Study; Pepperdine U; Psych.

CAMPA, FERNANDO A; Tranquillity HS; Firebaugh, CA; (1); School Play; Socr; Trk; Wt Lftg; Cit Awd; Hon Roll; USC; Arch.

CAMPANA, GINAMARIE; St Francis HS; Sacramento, CA; (3); Debate Tm; Latin Clb; Science Clb; SADD; Var Swmmng; Var Trk; Hon Roll; Latin Hnr Soc; Hgh Hnrs Latin Excllnc; Pre-Med.

CAMPANALE, JESSICA L; Atwater HS; Atwater, CA; (2); Cmnty Wkr; French Clb; Hon Roll; Schlstc Art Awds- 2 Gld Mdls, 1 Hnrb Mntn, 1 Natl Awd; Castle Air Force Base Vlntr Of The Yr; Cal Poly; Engr.

CAMPANELLA, ERIC W; Rubidoux HS; Riverside, CA; (4); Art Clb; Chess Clb; French Clb; Yrbk; Float Dsgns; Flm Mkng.

CAMPBELL, BETH A; Moorpark HS; Moorpark, CA; (4); 17/160; Teachers Aide; Band; Drm Mjr(t); Jazz Band; Mrchg Band; Pep Band; High Hon Roll; Hon Roll; Pres Acad Fit Awd; John Phillip Sousa Awd; Best Musician 1988-89; Chldhd Dev.

CAMPBELL, BRETT P; Mt Carmel HS; San Diego, CA; (2); Ski Clb; Socr; Hon Roll.

CAMPBELL, CARMEN Y; Altahoma HS; Alta Loma, CA; (4); Church Yth Grp; Cmnty Wkr; Capt Tennis; Cit Awd; High Hon Roll; Hon Roll; Opt Clb Awd; Pres Acad Fit Awd; Sal; Yth In Govt; Pres Of Ecology Clb; Athltc Acad Awd From The Army; U Of CA Irvine.

CAMPBELL, CATRINA; Dos Palos Joint Union HS; Dos Palos, CA; (2); FFA; Var Tennis; Cngrssnl Yth Ldrshp Cncl; Accntng.

CAMPBELL, CHRIS; Liberty Union HS; Byron, CA; (3); 11/375; Am Leg Boys St; Church Yth Grp; Pres Acpl Chr; Band; Church Choir; Jazz Band; School Musical; Swing Chorus; Socr; High Hon Roll; Northern CA Hnr Choir; CSF & 1st Rnnr Up Boys ST; Bio.

CAMPBELL, CHRIS K; Loyola HS; La Canada Flintri, CA; (2); Boy Scts; German Clb; Letterman Clb; Rptr Nwsp; JV Trk; Outstndng Yth Awd; Ivy Lgue; Law.

CAMPBELL, CHRISTOPHER T; Arcadia HS; Arcadia, CA; (3); 115/646; Boy Scts; FCA; Intrml Bsktbl; Var Crs Cntry; Var Trk; NHS; Principals Recognition Roll; CA Poly Pomona; Arch.

CAMPBELL, COLLEEN M; Mayfield SR HS; La Canada Flintri, CA; (2); AFS; Church Yth Grp; GAA; Hosp Aide; Red Cross Aide; Service Clb; Ski Clb; SADD; JV Capt Bsktbl; Var Trk; Piano Lessons; Med.

CAMPBELL, DARCY L; Templeton HS; Templeton, CA; (2); Bsktbl; Sftbl; Vllybl; Hon Roll; Htl Mgmt.

CAMPBELL, DARIN; Thousand Oaks HS; Thousand Oaks, CA; (3); 19/514; Church Yth Grp; JA; Math Tm; JV Ftbl; JV Socr; Wt Lftg; JV Wrstlng; Hon Roll; Jr NHS; Pres Acad Fit Awd; 7 AP Classes; Several Awrds For Artwork; Never Rcvd Less Than 4 As On A Single Report Card; Pepperdine; Graphic Arts.

CAMPBELL, DIANA L; Independence HS; San Jose, CA; (3); VP French Clb; German Clb; Science Clb; CSF; Vet.

CAMPBELL, EDWARD F; Hemet HS; Hemet, CA; (1); MSJC.

CAMPBELL, ELISABETH R; Antelope Valley HS; Lancaster, CA; (3); 20/631; Am Leg Aux Girls St; Intnl Clb; Math Tm; Sec Spanish Clb; Off Frsh Cls; Off Soph Cls; Off Jr Cls; L Var Swmmng; High Hon Roll; Hon Roll; CSF VP; Jr Honorline 90; CO Coll; Poltcl Sci.

CAMPBELL, GREG C; Temecula Valley HS; Temecula, CA; (3); 72/512; Church Yth Grp; Cmnty Wkr; Letterman Clb; Ski Clb; SADD; Varsity Clb; Rep Frsh Cls; VP Jr Cls; Stu Cncl; Var Ftbl; Rotary Ldrshp Awd; Stu Month; 3 Sport Varsity Ltrmn All League Hnrs; Psych.

CAMPBELL, JAMES J; Bonita Vista HS; Chula Vista, CA; (3); Church Yth Grp; Cmnty Wkr; Letterman Clb; Model UN; Pep Clb; Varsity Clb; Var Ftbl; Var Trk; Wt Lftg; Hon Roll; UCSD; Engrng.

CAMPBELL, JAMES SCOTT; Mira Loma HS; Fair Oaks, CA; (4); 8/257; Chess Clb; VP German Clb; VP Math Clb; Yrbk; JV Var Bsbl; JV Crs Cntry; Var Socr; High Hon Roll; NHS; CA Schlstc Fed; All CUC Leg Sccr Goalie; UC Santa Barbara; Bus.

CAMPBELL, JAMIE L; Pasadena HS; Altadena, CA; (1); Church Yth Grp; French Clb; ROTC; Drill Tm; High Hon Roll; Pres Acad Fit Awd; Engr.

CAMPBELL, JENNIFER L; Vacaville HS; Vacaville, CA; (3); 4-H; Cit Awd; Hon Roll; SPCA Club.

CAMPBELL, JENNY L; Chaparral HS; Santee, CA; (4); Teachers Aide; Rep Stu Cncl; Cit Awd; Outstndng Ctzn Hnr; El Cajon Clb RYLA Drshp Conf; Flght Attendnt.

CAMPBELL, JODI L; Caruthers Union HS; Fresno, CA; (4); 17/70; FCA; FBLA; FHA; GAA; Math Clb; Capt Pep Clb; SADD; Teachers Aide; Varsity Clb; School Play; Bnk Amer Awd Bus.

CAMPBELL, JODI L; Nevada Union HS; Grass Valley, CA; (3); Church Yth Grp; Teachers Aide; Acpl Chr; Chorus; Church Choir; Select Choir Trvld USSR Poland 89; Azusa Pacific U; Music Perfmnc.

CAMPBELL, JOLENE; Yucca Valley HS; Yucca Valley, CA; (2); Church Yth Grp; FCA; Math Clb; JV Cheerldng; Var Sftbl; High Hon Roll; Kiwanis Awd; Taught Gymnstcs Sonlight Acad Gymnstcs; CSF; The University Clb; Air Force Acad; Arntcl Engrng.

CAMPBELL, JONATHAN E; J H Francis Polytechnic HS; N Hollywood, CA; (3); Am Leg Boys St; Pep Clb; Color Guard; JV Capt Bsbl; L Var Ftbl; Hon Roll; Outstndng Frosh; Pro Bsbl Player.

CAMPBELL, KELLY A; Berean Christian HS; Concord, CA; (4); 11/65; Church Yth Grp; Cmnty Wkr; Hosp Aide; Cit Awd; High Hon Roll; Hmcmng Princess; Mst Consistent Stu Writing; Oustndg Physcl Achvt Aerobics; The Masters Coll; Nursing.

CAMPBELL, KEVIN W; San Marin HS; Novato, CA; (4); U Of CA L A.

CAMPBELL, KRISTIE; Mira Loma HS; Carmichael, CA; (3); 33/284; Dance Clb; Teachers Aide; Ed Nwsp; Stu Cncl; JV Var Sftbl; JV Var Vllybl; High Hon Roll; Hon Roll; Mock Trial Attorney; Stu Reaching Out, Friday Night Live; Suprm Crt Jstc; Jrnlsm.

CAMPBELL, LORRAINE; Mission College Prep; Templeton, CA; (3); Church Yth Grp; Cmnty Wkr; VP Sec 4-H; Model UN; Office Aide; Teachers Aide; Chorus; Drill Tm; 4-H Awd; High Hon Roll; Natl Vaulting Tm Chmpn 89; Dance; Pres Yng Republican Cmmtte; Intl Relations.

CAMPBELL, MARK A; Carlsbad HS; Oceanside, CA; (4); Church Yth Grp; Pres Letterman Clb; Ski Clb; SADD; Teachers Aide; Pres Varsity Clb; Band; Drill Tm; Mrchg Band; Pep Band; Peer Cnclr; Certified Scuba Diver; Cmmrcl Airline Pilot.

CAMPBELL, MICHELLE; C K Mc Clatchy HS; Sacramento, CA; (2); 1/538; Key Clb; Off Soph Cls; JV Socr; Hon Roll; Prfct Atten Awd; Acad Excel Awd; Med.

CAMPBELL, MICHELLE L; Antelope Valley HS; Lancaster, CA; (3); Church Yth Grp; Office Aide; Teachers Aide; Chorus; Rep Frsh Cls; Score Keeper; High Hon Roll; Advncd Plcmnt Anatomy; U Of CA San Diego; Marine Bio.

CAMPBELL, PATRICE M; Monte Vista HS; Walnut Creek, CA; (4); Church Yth Grp; Debate Tm; Chorus; VP Frsh Cls; Rep Stu Cncl; Co-Capt Intrml Socr; Var Trk; Hon Roll; Speech Tm; Teachers Aide; Jack & Jill Of Amer Assn; Mexicali Missions Outreach; Publicity Rep; UC San Diego; Econ.

CAMPBELL, RAYCEAN D; Channel Island HS; Oxnard, CA; (1); Church Yth Grp; Var Bsbl; Bsktbl; Ftbl; Hon Roll; Prfct Atten Awd; NC U; Med.

CAMPBELL, SHELENE R; Fortuna Union HS; Fortuna, CA; (3); Hosp Aide; Letterman Clb; Pres Pep Clb; Ski Clb; Teachers Aide; Powder Puff Ftbl; Var Trk; Rally Comm 88-89; Amer Coll Sacremento; Chem.

CAMPBELL, TAMMIE; Argonaut HS; Jackson, CA; (2); VP Pres Church Yth Grp; 4-H; Sec FHA; Key Clb; Band; Tennis; Hon Roll; Church Choir; Mrchg Band; Score Keeper; Natl Phys Fitness Awd; Golden St Exam-Math Wnnr; 2nd Pl Scripture Mastery-Church Seminary Pgm; BYU; Math Ed.

CAMPBELL, TISHA M; Oxnard HS; Oxnard, CA; (3); Art Clb; Church Yth Grp; Cmnty Wkr; Computer Clb; Debate Tm; GAA; JA; Model UN; Spanish Clb; Chorus; Pepperine U; Bus Mgmt.

CAMPBELL, TOBI L; Beaumont HS; Beaumont, CA; (1); Church Yth Grp; Teachers Aide; Flag Corp; Pep Band; Hon Roll; Prfct Atten Awd; Shield Team Capt; Bus.

CAMPBELL, WAYMEN G; Cayon HS; Pasadena, CA; (3); Art Clb; Computer Clb; Dance Clb; Drama Clb; Chorus; Bus.

CAMPBELL-STOELTING, EWAN; Coronado HS; Coronado, CA; (3); Debate Tm; Drama Clb; English Clb; Model UN; Capt Quiz Bowl; Capt Scholastic Bowl; Ski Clb; School Musical; Stage Crew; Rptr Nwsp; Vrsty Water Polo; Round Table Club; Hstry.

CAMPE, ZETH; The Thatcher Schl; Inverness, CA; (4); School Musical; School Play; Nwsp; JV Crs Cntry; Var L Lcrss; Ntl Merit Ltr; U Of Chicago.

CAMPING, KIM; Ontario Christian HS; Riverside, CA; (4); 15/54; Church Yth Grp; Pep Clb; School Musical; Off Soph Cls; Off Jr Cls; Off Sr Cls; Stu Cncl; Cheerldng; Hon Roll; Hmcmng Qn; Mst Frndlst; CA ST San Bernardino; Sociogy.

CAMPLIN, CHRISTINA J; Capistran Valley Christian HS; San Juan Capistra, CA; (2); Church Yth Grp; FCA; Girl Scts; JV Bsbl; JV Trk; Yth Group Cnslr; Church Organ Stu Led Ministries Publcty Dir; Span Teacher.

CAMPOS, ABIGAIL LORRAINE; Alverno HS; Duarte, CA; (4); 3/73; Cmnty Wkr; Hosp Aide; Science Clb; Service Clb; Sec Frsh Cls; Stu Cncl; Bausch & Lomb Sci Awd; Cit Awd; DAR Awd; High Hon Roll; Outstndg Yth Yr LA Cty Comm Yth; Chrstn Svc Awd LA Archdiocese; Bnk Amer Awd Engl; NHS Schlrshp Awd; CSU Fullerton; Spch Path.

CAMPOS, ANGEL H; Ontario HS; Ontario, CA; (3); Varsity Clb; Band; Jazz Band; Mrchg Band; Pep Band; Var Bsbl; Hon Roll; CA-POLY-POMONA.

CAMPOS, CHARLES; Pittsburg HS; Pittsburg, CA; (3); Intrsts Plyng Ftbl; Cadman Awd-Acadc Excllnce; Law.

CAMPOS, DARCY; Lynwood HS; Lynwood, CA; (3); Math Clb; Teachers Aide; Stage Crew; Var Ftbl; Var Wt Lftg; Hon Roll; Jr NHS; NHS; UCLA; Med.

CAMPOS, DELIA M; Delano HS; Delano, CA; (4); Church Yth Grp; Computer Clb; Spanish Clb; Socr; Cit Awd; High Hon Roll; Hon Roll; Prfct Atten Awd; Pres & VP Maya Clb; Bakersfield CA ST U; Commnctn.

CAMPOS, GABRIEL M; Coachella Valley HS; Coachella, CA; (3); MECHA Clb Advsr 90; Accntng.

CAMPOS, GISELLE; Jefferson HS; Daly City, CA; (2); Latin Clb; Red Cross Aide; Science Clb; Stu Cncl; High Hon Roll; Hon Roll; UC Berkeley; Bus.

CAMPOS, IRENE; Pius X HS; Paramount, CA; (4); 22/185; Cmnty Wkr; High Hon Roll; Ntl Merit Ltr; Hispanic Clb; CSU; Intl Relations.

CAMPOS, JENNIFER; Cajon HS; San Bernardino, CA; (3); Church Yth Grp; GAA; Pep Clb; Flag Corp; Off Frsh Cls; Off Soph Cls; Off Jr Cls; Stu Cncl; Var Capt Cheerldng; Choreographed Dances Elem Schl Studs Perform; Practice Jazz Dance & Gymnastics Outside Schl; Court Reporting.

CAMPOS, JOANNE R; Mission San Jose HS; Fremont, CA; (1); 1/500; JA; Band; Mrchg Band; Orch; Pep Band; School Musical; High Hon Roll; Hon Roll; Pres Acad Fit Awd; CSF; CA St Senate Alg Awd; Bus Mgmt.

CAMPOS, KELLY L; Notre Dame HS; Del Rey Oaks, CA; (3); JV Sftbl; Var Trk; Hon Roll; CSF; Young Life; Matheletics Comptn; Aerospace Engrng.

CAMPOS, LUIS E; Southwest HS; San Diego, CA; (4); 7/498; Computer Clb; Drama Clb; JA; Library Aide; SADD; Thesps; School Musical; School Play; Variety Show; Cit Awd; CA Schlrshp Fed; U Of CA San Diego; Comp Sci.

CAMPOS, LUZ M; Ontario HS; Ontario, CA; (3); Art Clb; Dance Clb; Cit Awd; Hon Roll; Prfct Atten Awd.

CAMPOS, LYDIA; San Diego Acad; Chula Vista, CA; (4); 1/41; Church Yth Grp; Pep Clb; SADD; Teachers Aide; Off Frsh Cls; Off Soph Cls; Off Jr Cls; Sec Sr Cls; Cit Awd; High Hon Roll; CSF Clb; Hiking/Camping Clb; US Natl Math Awd; Pacific Union Coll; Elem Ed.

CAMPOS, MARGARET L; Avenal HS; Avenal, CA; (2); Science Clb; Chorus; JV Vllybl; Cit Awd; Voc Ed Olympics; Child Psych.

CAMPOS, MARIA EUGENIA; El Rancho HS; Pico Rivera, CA; (4); Cmnty Wkr; German Clb; Hosp Aide; Science Clb; Teachers Aide; Var JV Swmmng; Adv Plcmnt Bio Clb; Lab Asstn; U Of Southern CA; Biochem.

CAMPOS, MARIA F; Manual Arts HS; Los Angeles, CA; (2); PAL; Partnership Prgm UCLA.

CAMPOS, MARIA Y; Grant Union HS; Sacramento, CA; (3); Church Yth Grp; Pres Spanish Clb; Phtg Yrbk; Cit Awd; High Hon Roll; Pres Acad Fit Awd; Hispanic Stu Assn; Vol Feeding Homeless Around Community; CA ST U Sacramento; Bio.

CAMPOS, RAMIRO; Sonoma Valley HS; Boyes Hot Springs, CA; (4); Cmnty Wkr; VP Spanish Clb; High Hon Roll; Hon Roll; NHS; Prfct Atten Awd; CSF; UC Berkeley; Chem Engrng.

CAMPOS, SUSANA; Bassett HS; La Puente, CA; (2); Dance Clb; Girl Scts; Latin Clb; Phtg Yrbk; Doctorate Tourist Bus.

CAMPOS, TERESA; Downtown HS; Pacifica, CA; (3); Computer Clb; Office Aide; Teachers Aide; Stu Cncl; Hon Roll; Peer Hlpr; Crmnl Law.

CAMPOS, TONI V; San Gorgonio HS; Highland, CA; (3); Office Aide; Rep Stu Cncl; Score Keeper; UNLV; Intl Bus.

CAMPOS, WILLIAM S; Ontario HS; Ontario, CA; (3); 71/543; Spanish Clb; VP Jr Cls; Stu Cncl; Var L Tennis; Hon Roll; Prfct Atten Awd; Dec 88 Stu Mnth; 89 Tnns Sngls MVP.

CAMPROS, TOMIEANNA; Atascadero HS; Gilmer, TX; (4); Am Leg Aux Girls St; French Clb; NFL; Speech Tm; Yrbk; Swmmng; Cit Awd; High Hon Roll; Lion Awd; Pres Acad Fit Awd; Commnctns.

CAMPTON, IRIKA R; Oceana HS; Pacifica, CA; (3); Stu Cncl; Co-Capt Var Cheerldng; Hon Roll; Bus.

CAMPWALA, TASNEEM; Bishop Amat HS; West Covina, CA; (3); English Clb; French Clb; Ed Lit Mag; Stu Cncl; High Hon Roll; NHS; NEDT Awd; Englsh & Bio 1st Hnrs; CSF; Sci.

CAMUSO, ELAINE M; Davis HS; Davis, CA; (3); Key Clb; Pep Clb; Spanish Clb; Teachers Aide; Hon Roll; Pres Acad Fit Awd; CA St U; Jrnlsm.

CAMUTIN, GINA P; Hogan SR HS; Vallejo, CA; (3); Church Yth Grp; Drama Clb; Science Clb; Spanish Clb; Teachers Aide; Church Choir; School Play; Stage Crew; Nwsp; Val.

CANADAY JR, PHILLIP R; Central Union HS; El Centro, CA; (3); Church Yth Grp; Quiz Bowl; Spanish Clb; Band; Jazz Band; Mrchg Band; Pep Band; JV Bsktbl; JV Ftbl; JV Socr; Prncpls List; U Of Dallas; Pharm.

CANADAY, REBECCA A; Armijo HS; Suisun, CA; (1); Ski Clb; Var Tennis; High Hon Roll; Badminton Vrsty; CA Schlrshp Fed; Stu Govt Class; U CA Davis; Biolgcl Sci.

CANADY, DANIEL V; Monterey HS; Seaside, CA; (2); Church Yth Grp; Cmnty Wkr; Drama Clb; School Musical; School Play; JV Bsbl; JV Ftbl; Wt Lftg; Hon Roll; Sprts Med.

CANADY, ELISSA J; Monterey HS; Seaside, CA; (2); Church Yth Grp; Drama Clb; Hosp Aide; School Musical; School Play; Sec Frsh Cls; Rep Soph Cls; High Hon Roll; Peer Ed; CA Schlrshp Fed.

CANADY, FELICIA L; Highlands HS; Sacramento, CA; (2); Church Yth Grp; French Clb; Model UN; Church Choir; Powder Puff Ftbl; Wt Lftg; High Hon Roll; Hon Roll; Pres Acad Fit Awd; Spellman; Med.

CANADY, JOSEPH R; Enterprise HS; Redding, CA; (2); Math Tm; Office Aide; Science Clb; Spanish Clb; JV Bsktbl; Intl Bus.

CANALES, FERNANDO; Paso Robles HS; Paso Robles, CA; (1); Teachers Aide; Off Frsh Cls; Bsktbl; High Hon Roll; Prfct Atten Awd; Stanford.

CANALES, MIRIAM; Tulare Union HS; Tulare, CA; (2); 28/487; Church Yth Grp; Stu Cncl; JV Var Score Keeper; JV Sftbl; JV Capt Vllybl; High Hon Roll; Hon Roll; Crwnd Missionette Hnr Star Chrch; Piano Lssns; USC; Med.

CANAVAN, MEGHAN L; Modesto HS; Modesto, CA; (1); Key Clb; Mrchg Band; Trk; Georgetown; Med Sci.

CANAVESIO, RAYMOND A; Fairfield HS; Fairfield, CA; (3); JV Var Bsbl; JV Var Ftbl; Wt Lftg.

CANCHOLA, JOSE L; Coachella Valley HS; Coachella, CA; (3); FFA; Varsity Clb; Var L Crs Cntry; Var L Trk; Hon Roll; Supvr Golf Crse.

CANCHOLA, ORLANDO E; Antelope Valley HS; Lancaster, CA; (3); 47/631; Am Leg Boys St; VP Letterman Clb; Spanish Clb; Varsity Clb; Off Frsh Cls; Off Soph Cls; Off Jr Cls; L Ftbl; L Trk; High Hon Roll; USC.

CANCIAMILLA, JOSEPHINE G; Pioneer HS; San Jose, CA; (3); 4/265; High Hon Roll; Santa Clara U; Bus Mgmt.

CANCINO, CANDICE; Desert JR/Sr HS; Edwards, CA; (2); Spanish Clb; VP Soph Cls; Var L Tennis; Var L Trk; Prfct Atten Awd; Spc Olympcs Vlntr; UOP; Phrmcy.

CANDELARIA, ALVINA G; San Benito HS; San Juan Bautista, CA; (3); French Clb; Hon Roll; MECHA; Psych.

CANEPA, NIAOMI; Monterey HS; Monterey, CA; (3); Church Yth Grp; JA; Teachers Aide; Var Capt Cheerldng; High Hon Roll; Jr NHS; NHS; Prfct Atten Awd; Ski; BUS Acctnt.

CANEZ, BLANCA O; Brawley Union HS; Brawley, CA; (1); Church Yth Grp; Doctor.

CANFIELD, CHRISTINE; Christian HS; Pine Valley, CA; (3); Pep Clb; Ski Clb; Treas Spanish Clb; VP Frsh Cls; Rep Soph Cls; JV Cheerldng; Var L Sftbl; JV Vllybl; High Hon Roll; NHS.

CANFIELD, DAVE N; El Toro HS; El Toro, CA; (3); 149/480; Boy Scts; Church Yth Grp; Varsity Clb; Church Choir; Bsktbl; Ftbl; Wt Lftg; Hon Roll; Comm.

CANISSO, AMY; Atwater HS; Livingston, CA; (2); Church Yth Grp; FCA; 4-H; Intnl Clb; Sec Frsh Cls; Rep Soph Cls; Var Socr; Var Trk; 4-H Awd; Rotary Awd; Mrktng.

CANJURA JR, ISRAEL; Balboa HS; San Francisco, CA; (2); ROTC; Color Guard; Drill Tm; Tennis; Hon Roll; Stanford; Astronaut.

CANLAS, AIMEE; Oxnard HS; Oxnard, CA; (3); 1/645; Capt Quiz Bowl; Drama Clb; Hosp Aide; NFL; Service Clb; Spanish Clb; Speech Tm; SADD; Teachers Aide; School Musical; Acad Decthln; Point Mugo Sci Chllnge Telmtry Awd.

CANLAS, AMADOR; Oxnard HS; Oxnard, CA; (4); 1/400; English Clb; French Clb; Math Clb; Quiz Bowl; Science Clb; Service Clb; Spanish Clb; Rep Jr Cls; Bausch & Lomb Sci Awd; High Hon Roll; UC Berkeley.

CANLAS, KIM D; Nogales HS; Walnut, CA; (3); Band; Jazz Band; Mrchg Band; Orch; Tennis; High Hon Roll; Pres Acad Fit Awd; Aeronautical Engr.

CANLAS, LEONARD JOE T; San Gabriel Acad; Valinda, CA; (2); Church Yth Grp; Teachers Aide; Chorus; Church Choir; Off Soph Cls; NHS; Spllng Bee 1st Pl 87-88; LLU; Med.

CANNATA, JESS A; Poway HS; Poway, CA; (1); Boy Scts; Church Yth Grp; Stage Crew; Hon Roll; Cal Poly; Philosophy.

CANNELLA, JOHN; Mountain View HS; Mountain View, CA; (3); Band; Jazz Band; Var Golf; Hon Roll; Ntl Merit Schol; Mrchd 100th Trnmnt Roses Parade W/Band & Tour W/The Symphonic Band To HI; Archlgy.

CANNELLA, LISA; Porterville HS; Ducor, CA; (3); Church Yth Grp; 4-H; Hosp Aide; Pep Clb; Service Clb; Varsity Clb; Nwsp; Var Cheerldng; Var Pom Pon; 4-H Awd; Own Radio Pgm; 4h 8 Yrs; Academic Decathlon Tm; Sect Govt Ed Today; Wash DC Congressional Smnr Part; Pepperdine; Telecommunications.

CANNON, ALANYA C; S C P A O'ffarrell HS; San Diego, CA; (1); #3 In Class; Art Clb; Dance Clb; Spanish Clb; Church Choir; School Musical; Cit Awd; High Hon Roll; Hon Roll; Pres Acad Fit Awd; CSF; CJSF; Achvmt Awds Spnsh, Music, Dance; Outstdng Acad Awds Math, Hstry, Engl; Math.

CANNON, ALISHEA L; Woodland HS; Woodland, CA; (3); SADD; Acpl Chr; Intrml Bsktbl; Intrml JV Trk; Cit Awd; Legal Sec.

CANNON, CRYSTAL; Clovis West HS; Fresno, CA; (3); Church Yth Grp; Intnl Clb; Pep Clb; Ski Clb; VP Soph Cls; Var Cheerldng; JV Swmmng; High Hon Roll; Dncng; Chrgrphd Chrsqds; Piano, Violin Plyng; CA Schlrshp Fed; BYU; Psych.

CANNON, DAVID; East Union HS; Manteca, CA; (3); 14/314; Church Yth Grp; Band; Mrchg Band; Orch; Crs Cntry; Trk; Hon Roll; UC Davis; Law.

CANNON, DENISE; Arcadia HS; Arcadia, CA; (1); Dance Clb; Chorus; Drill Tm; Sec Frsh Cls; Stu Cncl; Stat Bsktbl; Hon Roll; Rotary Awd; Arcadia JR All Amer Ftbl Chrldr; Chrldr Coach; Psych.

CANNON, JEFFREY; Mira Mesa HS; Orange Park, FL; (2); 1/860; Capt Aud/Vis; Church Yth Grp; JA; Math Tm; Quiz Bowl; Varsity Clb; Rep Frsh Cls; Bsbl; Crs Cntry; Tennis; USAF; Aeronauticl Engr.

CANNON, LLOYD A; Hoover HS; Fresno, CA; (3); Var Ftbl; Var Trk; Var Wt Lftg; UC Berkely; Elec Engr.

CANNON, MARNEE E; Bonita Vista HS; Bonita, CA; (2); Church Yth Grp; Cmnty Wkr; Office Aide; Chorus; Nwsp; Rep Stu Cncl; Var Cheerldng; Spnsh Lang Awd.

CANNON, MATTHEW W; Mc Kinleyville HS; Mckinleyville, CA; (3); Am Leg Boys St; Boy Scts; SADD; Teachers Aide; Var L Bsbl; Var L Bsktbl; Hon Roll; Orthopedic Surgeon.

CANNON, MIKO L; Washington Preparatory HS; Los Angeles, CA; (2); Church Yth Grp; Drama Clb; FBLA; Girl Scts; Church Choir; Drill Tm; Cheerldng; Sftbl; UCLA; Sci.

CANNON, SAM; Mc Kinleyville HS; Mc Kinleyville, CA; (1); Boy Scts; Church Yth Grp; JV Bsktbl; Pilot.

CANNON, SEAN B; Oakmont HS; Roseville, CA; (2); Boy Scts; Stage Crew; Variety Show; JV Vllybl; BYU; Sci.

CANNON-FULKS, LAURA M; Notre Dame HS; Salinas, CA; (3); Past Pres Jr Cath Dtrs Of Amer Ct; Awded Acad Cert Fr; Comm.

CANO, AMY; North Salinas HS; Salinas, CA; (2); Science Clb; Color Guard; High Hon Roll; Stu Of Mnth For Sci; Med.

CANO, CARLOS; Oxnard HS; Oxnard, CA; (3); 72/460; Art Clb; Future Ldrs Amer; Concerned Stu Org Network; Optometrist.

CANO, DANA; Coast Union HS; Cambria, CA; (2); Church Yth Grp; FHA; GAA; SADD; JV Sftbl; Var Tennis.

CANO, ESMERALDA; Mt Whitney HS; Farmersville, CA; (2); Church Yth Grp; Early Outreach Pgm; VUSD Migrant Pgm; Writing Poetry; UC Santa Cruz; Psychology.

CANO JR, JOSE L; Bishop Amat HS; Baldwin Park, CA; (3); Drama Clb; Vllybl; Wt Lftg; Silver Screen Club; CA ST; Bus.

CANO, LOUIE; Monache HS; Porterville, CA; (4); 10/321; Am Leg Boys St; Church Yth Grp; Teachers Aide; Stu Cncl; JV Tennis; JV Wrstlng; High Hon Roll; Optimetric Techn; UCLA; Bio.

CANO, PATRICIA; Roosevelt HS; Los Angeles, CA; (4); Cmnty Wkr; JA; Key Clb; SADD; Stu Cncl; Trk; Cit Awd; High Hon Roll; Hon Roll; Prfct Atten Awd; Census 90 Awd; MESA Medal, Awd; Ephebian Soc; Occidental Coll; Scl Worker.

CANON, STACEY A; Burbank HS; Burbank, CA; (2); Church Yth Grp; Cmnty Wkr; Letterman Clb; Library Aide; Chorus; Church Choir; School Play; Sec Soph Cls; Var JV Vllybl; High Hon Roll; Amer Lgn Schl Awd; Prncpls Awd Geom; Presdntl Phys Ftng Awd.

CANON, STEVEN J; Burbank HS; Burbank, CA; (2); Church Yth Grp; Cmnty Wkr; Letterman Clb; Band; Jazz Band; JV Bsktbl; JV Trk; High Hon Roll; Pres Acad Fit Awd; Amer Legn Schl Awd; Golden St Acad Exclnc Alg Hnrs, Geom Hgh Hnrs; Pres Phys Fit Awd.

CANONES, ROWENA A; Etiwanda HS; Rancho Cucamonga, CA; (3); Church Yth Grp; Math Clb; Speech Tm; Band; Mrchg Band; Animal Care; Friday Night Live Club; UC Riverside; Medicine.

CANOY, ERIN LABRA; William C Overfelt HS; San Jose, CA; (1); Color Guard; Drill Tm; Mrchg Band; Orch; Cheerldng; High Hon Roll; Hon Roll; Prfct Atten Awd; Pres Acad Fit Awd.

CANOZA, ARLENE C; Notre Dame HS; Corona Hills, CA; (2); 48/155; French Clb; Hosp Aide; Trk; Hon Roll; Law.

CANRINUS, TERESA M; Grossmont HS; El Cajon, CA; (3); Drama Clb; SADD; School Play; Rptr Nwsp; Pres Frsh Cls; Pres Soph Cls; Pres Stu Cncl; Powder Puff Ftbl; JV Capt Tennis; Yng Envrnmntlsts Club; Spng Fshn Show Mstr Ceremonies; Stu Cncl Cmmssnr Pblcty; Brdcst Jrnlsm.

CANTE, ALICIA; Southwest HS; San Diego, CA; (2); Dance Clb; Office Aide; Teachers Aide; Chorus; JV Socr; JV Sftbl; JV Vllybl; Cit Awd; Hon Roll; Prfct Atten Awd; Arch.

CANTELMI, DANIEL S; Tulare HS; Tulare, CA; (2); 51/461; Church Yth Grp; Letterman Clb; Varsity Clb; JV Bsktbl; Var Ftbl; Var Tennis; Hon Roll; CSF; Chrch Yth Choir; Sports Thrpy.

CANTER, TANJA; Bullard HS; Fresno, CA; (3); 41/565; German Clb; Key Clb; Ski Clb; SADD; Var Bsktbl; JV Sftbl; Var Capt Vllybl; All Trnmnt Cntrl Vlybl Trnmnt 89; Bsktbl Coaches Awd 89; Soccer Coach; UCLA; Sports Med.

CANTERBERRY JR, LARRY G; Arvin HS; Bakersfield, CA; (2); Computer Clb; Letterman Clb; Pep Clb; Ski Clb; Varsity Clb; Var Capt Ftbl; Var Capt Golf; Var Wt Lftg; Cit Awd; High Hon Roll; Bakersfield JC; Elec Engr.

CANTERO, SUSANA M; Notre Dame Acad; Los Angeles, CA; (3); Dance Clb; Spanish Clb; Church Choir; Variety Show; VP NHS; Ntl Merit Ltr; Music; Dance; Amnesty Intl; UC Berkeley.

CANTHAL, STEPHAN; El Camino Real HS; West Hills, CA; (3); Drama Clb; Thesps; School Play; Kingsmen Soc Club VP; USC; Arch.

CANTILLO, JOHN P; San Leandro HS; San Leandro, CA; (3); 38/361; Boy Scts; Chess Clb; Church Yth Grp; Dance Clb; Science Clb; Chorus; Church Choir; JV Bsbl; Intrml Tennis; Hon Roll; Brigham Young U; Med.

CANTONG, ARNOLD; Jefferson HS; Daly City, CA; (4); 76/254; Intrml Bsktbl; JV Trk; Hon Roll; Camp Cnslr Outdoor Ed; Gldn St Schlr Schl Rcgntn Awd 87; Scuba Diving, Swimming, Cycling & Hiking; San Jose ST U; Aviation.

CANTORIA, JENNIFER C; Azusa HS; Azusa, CA; (4); 5/233; Pep Clb; SADD; Ed Nwsp; Rep Sr Cls; High Hon Roll; Hon Roll; NHS; CSF Silver Medalist Seal Bearer; Badminton Vrsty Tm; Mock Trial Tm; Prom Cmmtte; Azusa Pacific U; Chem.

CANTORNA, NANCY C; Delano HS; Delano, CA; (3); #12 In Class; FHA; Chorus; High Hon Roll; Hon Roll; Prfct Atten Awd; Untd Filipino Orgnztn Secy; GATE Pgm; Athenian Soc.

CANTRELL, AMBER M; John Glenn HS; Norwalk, CA; (3); Dance Clb; Drama Clb; Spanish Clb; Thesps; School Musical; School Play; Swing Chorus; Variety Show; Hon Roll; UC Davis; Vet.

CANTRELL, DEDRA A; University HS; Irvine, CA; (3); 70/551; JV Bsktbl; JV Swmmng; JV Trk.

CANTRELL, JENNIFER; Bethel Baptist Schl; Garden Grove, CA; (2); Church Yth Grp; Teachers Aide; Church Choir; School Play; Rep Stu Cncl; Capt Cheerldng; Var Vllybl; Hon Roll; Pensacola Christian Coll; Educ.

CANTRELL, KRISTIN MICHELLE; Los Alamitos HS; Los Alamitos, CA; (3); Debate Tm; Drama Clb; NFL; Service Clb; Spanish Clb; SADD; Chorus; School Musical; Rptr Nwsp; Rep Soph Cls; CSF; Westpoint; Law.

CANTRELL, TRACY D; Vanden HS; Indianapolis, IN; (1); 15/250; Church Yth Grp; Computer Clb; Ski Clb; Band; Chorus; Pep Band; Bsbl; Socr; Wrstlng; Mc Donalds Achvt Awds; IN ST; Law Enfrcmnt.

CANTRELLE, JULIE A; Burlingame HS; Belmont, CA; (3); Art Clb; Cmnty Wkr; Drama Clb; Red Cross Aide; Chorus; Stage Crew; Phtg Nwsp; Phtg Yrbk; Hon Roll; CA Explorer Srch, Rescue Unit; Photgrphy; Bowling; CA ST Sacramento; Tchng.

CANTU, BOBBY; Paso Robles HS; Paso Robles, CA; (2); Letterman Clb; Varsity Clb; Var Bsbl; Var Capt Bsktbl; Var Wt Lftg; Cit Awd; Hon Roll; UCSB; Bus.

CANTU, CARMEN M; Firebaugh HS; Mendota, CA; (3); 3/89; Church Yth Grp; FBLA; SADD; Teachers Aide; Rep Stu Cncl; Var Stat Bsbl; JV Tennis; JV Stat Wrstlng; High Hon Roll; Hon Roll; CSF; UCLA; Dentl.

CANTU, CHARLES M; James Logan HS; Union City, CA; (3); Debate Tm; NFL; Speech Tm; Varsity Clb; Ftbl; Wrstlng; Maritial Arts/Kayukenbo 2 Yrs; Lawyer.

CANTU, NICOLE DANIELLA; San Pedro HS; San Pedro, CA; (3); Drama Clb; Office Aide; Pep Clb; Scholastic Bowl; Teachers Aide; Drill Tm; School Musical; School Play; Variety Show; Cheerldng; Grad Speakr 9th Grade; Brnze Awd; U Of HI.

CANU, DINA; Lemoore HS; Lemoore, CA; (2); FHA; Pep Clb; Spanish Clb; Chorus; JV Cheerldng; Interact Clb.

CAO, AN; La Sierra HS; Riverside, CA; (3); Church Yth Grp; Service Clb; VICA; Rep Jr Cls; Vllybl; Cit Awd; Hon Roll; Prfct Atten Awd; Pres Acad Fit Awd; CSF; Cal Poly Pomona.

CAO, BACH-MAI T; Bolsa Grande HS; Garden Grove, CA; (2); 2/359; Office Aide.

CAO, BANG K; Milpitas HS; Milpitas, CA; (4); Letterman Clb; Varsity Clb; Var Tennis; Hon Roll; Prfct Atten Awd; Pres Acad Fit Awd; MVP Tennis; San Jose ST; Bus.

CAO, DUNG; Wilcox HS; Santa Clara, CA; (3); San Jose ST; Engr.

CAO, HA; Casa Grande HS; Petaluma, CA; (2); French Clb; Var Crs Cntry; Var Trk; NHS; Prfct Atten Awd; Goldn St Exm Geom Hgh Hnrs.

CAO, HIEN M; Fresno HS; Fresno, CA; (4); 1/450; French Clb; Key Clb; SADD; Rptr Nwsp; JV Var Bsbl; Tennis; High Hon Roll; Masonic Awd; Val; UCLA; Bio.

CAO, JIA HUAN G; Lowell HS; San Francisco, CA; (2); Band; Volleyball Club; Intl Relations Club; Commercial Art.

CAO, KATIE M; Workman HS; West Covina, CA; (2); Intnl Clb; Science Clb; Schl Schlr; UCLA; Comp Prgmr.

CAO, LAN T; Oakland HS; Oakland, CA; (2); Key Clb; Orch; Cit Awd; Hon Roll; Prfct Atten Awd; CSF Awd; Asian Stu Union; Pediatrician.

CAO, LOI V; Leuzinger HS; Lawndale, CA; (2); Chorus; High Hon Roll; Hon Roll; Chem Engrng.

CAO, NHAN H; San Gabriel HS; San Gabriel, CA; (3); Teachers Aide; Hon Roll.

CAO, QUYNHMAI D; Los Amigos HS; Santa Ana, CA; (2); 14/365; Dance Clb; VP French Clb; German Clb; Key Clb; Pep Clb; Ed Nwsp; Stu Cncl; Var Cheerldng; JV Tennis; Hon Roll; Vietnamese Clb-Sec; Korean Clb; Dnc Team; UCLA; Med.

CAO, ROBERT Q; Bellarmine College Prep; San Jose, CA; (4); Library Aide; Service Clb; Spanish Clb; SADD; Intrml Ftbl; Intrml Sftbl; Var L Trk; Intrml Vllybl; Hon Roll; Principals Letter Of Commendation 86-87; U CA-DAVIS; Econ.

CAO, THANH; Marina HS; Westminster, CA; (4); Math Clb; High Hon Roll; Prfct Atten Awd; Acad Ftnss Awd; Golden Shield Awd Englsh; UC Irvine; Biolgcl Sci.

CAO, THUYEN N; Galileo HS; San Francisco, CA; (4); JA; Red Cross Aide; ROTC; Drill Tm; Lit Mag; Diablo Valley; Educ.

CAO, VALERIE; Mercy HS; San Francisco, CA; (3); Boy Scts; Cmnty Wkr; Girl Scts; Hosp Aide; Math Clb; Red Cross Aide; Service Clb; Teachers Aide; Hon Roll; Prfct Atten Awd; CSF; Health Professions.

CAO, YUE; Buena Park HS; Buena Park, CA; (4); Computer Clb; Key Clb; Math Clb; Quiz Bowl; Church Choir; Jr NHS; CSF; CHS Clubs; U Of CA Berkeley.

CAPANGPANAGAN, MISTY R; College Park HS; Martinez, CA; (1); Church Yth Grp; Teachers Aide; Var Swmmng.

CAPEL, KATHRYN D; Oakmont HS; Roseville, CA; (2); Church Yth Grp; Cmnty Wkr; Drama Clb; Service Clb; SADD; VP Pres Soph Cls; Hon Roll; Pres Acad Fit Awd; Yng Life; Westmont.

CAPELLE, GREGG W; Redlands HS; Redlands, CA; (2); Boy Scts; German Clb; Key Clb; Ski Clb; Band; Hon Roll; Sccr & Bsktbl; Order Arrow Sctn Secty; U Of CA; Bus.

CAPERS, LALITA; Oakland Tech; Oakland, CA; (2); Church Yth Grp; Teachers Aide; Church Choir; Treas Jr Cls; Cheerldng; Hon Roll; Hmcmng Countess; Navy Adopt A Stu Prgm; Want To Be Singer & Cheographer; Lawyer.

CAPILI, JEANNE; Milpitas HS; Milpitas, CA; (3); Dance Clb; Model UN; Spanish Clb; Rep Stu Cncl; JV Tennis; Med.

CAPISTRAN, AZUCENA; George Washington HS; Los Angeles, CA; (4); Church Yth Grp; GAA; Latin Clb; Math Clb; Science Clb; Drill Tm; Trk; High Hon Roll; CSF; MESA; CSU Long Beach; Comp Sci.

CAPISTRANO, CARL E; Don Bosco Techinical Inst; Diamond Bar, CA; (3); Church Yth Grp; Dance Clb; Key Clb; JV Bsktbl; Trk; Vllybl; NHS; Var Water Polo Tm; CA Poly Pomona; Elec Engr.

CAPITOLA, CARYN; Aptos HS; Aptos, CA; (3); 10/303; SADD; Church Choir; School Musical; Ed Nwsp; Rep Soph Cls; Rep Jr Cls; Sec Treas Stu Cncl; Capt Cheerldng; Powder Puff Ftbl; High Hon Roll; JSA; Cabrillo JC; Pblc Rltns.

CAPLAN, DANNY M; Huntington Beach HS; Huntington Bch, CA; (2); Boy Scts; Key Clb; Model UN; Spanish Clb; Temple Yth Grp; High Hon Roll; HRHS Tower Awd; UC Schl; Aerospace Engnrng.

CAPLAN, MARTIN H; The Athenian Schl; Pleasanton, CA; (4); Boy Scts; Cmnty Wkr; Library Aide; School Play; Stage Crew; Ed Nwsp; Phtg Yrbk; Lit Mag; Stu Cncl; Socr; Athenian Greenpeace Orgnztn; Davis CA U; Philosophy.

CAPLE, ROSEMARIE C; Hueneme HS; Port Hueneme, CA; (2); FBLA; Hosp Aide; Chorus; School Play; Rptr Nwsp; Off Frsh Cls; JV Bsktbl; Mgr(s); Score Keeper; JV Socr; Math Tm.

CAPLETTE, MELISSA; Indio HS; Indio, CA; (2); 12/530; Drama Clb; School Play; Var L Cheerldng; Hon Roll; John Hopkins Ctr For Advncmnt Acadmclly Tlntd Yth; Lw.

CAPLIS, CHRISTINE S; Foothill HS; Santa Ana, CA; (3); 56/328; Church Yth Grp; Cmnty Wkr; German Clb; SADD; Chorus; School Musical; Rep Sr Cls; Var Swmmng; Cit Awd; Hon Roll; German Dept Awd; Cncl Church Elem Schl Kids; U CA San Diego; Intl Relations.

CAPOBIANCO, GINA M; Bishop Amat HS; La Verne, CA; (3); JV Stat Bsktbl; Var Mgr(s); Var Score Keeper; Hon Roll; NHS; Crtv Wrtng Clb Pres; Freelance Wrtr.

CAPOBRES, KAREN A; Monterey Bay Acad; San Gabriel, CA; (3); Church Yth Grp; Office Aide; Teachers Aide; Church Choir; Rptr Nwsp; Yrbk; Treas Jr Cls; Stu Cncl; Hon Roll; Jrnlsm.

CAPOCCIAMA, GINA T; Ocean View HS; Huntington Beach, CA; (1); Stat Bsktbl; JV Cheerldng; US Davis; Vet.

CAPOGEANNIS, ARISTOMENIS W; Bellarmine College Prep; Saratoga, CA; (3); 22/308; Church Yth Grp; Pres Hosp Aide; Bowling Coach; Pres Vol Alexin Brothers Hosp; Tae Kwon Do.

CAPORUSSO, NICOLE L; San Leandro HS; San Leandro, CA; (3); 23/361; Teachers Aide; Yrbk; Off Frsh Cls; Off Sr Cls; JV Bsktbl; Var Swmmng; JV Vllybl; Hon Roll; Cmmnty Vlntr Police Dept For DARE Prgm; Bus Mgt.

CAPOZZA, SUSAN M; Saratoga HS; Saratoga, CA; (3); Cmnty Wkr; Debate Tm; Intnl Clb; NFL; Spanish Clb; Off Sr Cls; Swmmng; Hon Roll; Mst Imprvd Debate Awd; Econ.

CAPPETO, CHRISTINE MARIE; Claremont HS; Claremont, CA; (4); 15/385; Cmnty Wkr; French Clb; Teachers Aide; Thesps; Stage Crew; L Crs Cntry; Var L Trk; High Hon Roll; Pres Acad Fit Awd; Amnsty Intl; Bowdoin Coll.

CAPPOCCHI, AARON J; Village Christian HS; Burbank, CA; (3); 17/130; Church Yth Grp; Drama Clb; Mu Alpha Theta; School Play; Amtr Wrtr; Chmpns; Smths Fan Clb; Fn Arts.

CAPRARO, DOMINIQUE T; Troy HS; Yorba Linda, CA; (1); DAR Awd; French Hon Soc; High Hon Roll; Jr NHS; Rotary Awd; Work After Schl Family Bus; Loves Sports; Bus.

CAPSHAW, EMILY R; Hamilton Music Acad; Los Angeles, CA; (2); Drama Clb; Drill Tm; Drama.

CAPSTICK, MARISOL Y; Pinole Valley HS; Pinole, CA; (1); Church Yth Grp; Dance Clb; Pep Clb; Spanish Clb; Church Choir; Rep Frsh Cls; Cheerldng; Gym; Score Keeper; Cit Awd; Stanford; Bus.

CAPUANO, CARA; Marina HS; Huntington Bch, CA; (3); German Clb; Pres Service Clb; Spanish Clb; Capt Flag Corp; Yrbk; Off Stu Cncl; High Hon Roll; Ntl Merit Ltr; Vrsty Badminton; Gldn Shields Awd Nominee; U Of CA; Bio Sci.

CAPUCHINO, ELAINE J; Hanford HS; Hanford, CA; (2); Church Yth Grp; Stanford; Phy.

CAPULE, DENNIS; Saint Ignatius College Prep; Daly City, CA; (4); Cmnty Wkr; Hosp Aide; Wt Lftg; French Hon Soc; Hon Roll; NHS; Prfct Atten Awd; Pres Acad Fit Awd; Chrstn Life Cmnty; Asian Stu Coalition; CA Schlrshp Fed; Med.

CARACAS, SHERRILL; Southwest HS; San Diego, CA; (3); 67/498; Key Clb; Library Aide; Drill Tm; Rptr Nwsp; Yrbk; Rep Soph Cls; Rep Jr Cls; Hon Roll; Pan Asian; Sword & Shield.

CARACOZA, VICTOR; Southwest HS; San Ysidro, CA; (2); Office Aide; Var Bsbl; JV Socr; Wt Lftg; AVIO; AZ U; Engrng.

CARACOZA, XOCHITL; Southwest HS; San Ysidro, CA; (4); Office Aide; Spanish Clb; Cit Awd; Hon Roll; Prfct Atten Awd; San Diego ST U; Educ.

CARADONNA, MICHAEL A; Bellarmine College Prep; Los Altos, CA; (3); 7/300; Service Clb; Rptr Nwsp; Rensselaer Sci/Math Mdlst 90; Spcl Awds Wnnr Santa Clara Cnty Sci/Engrng Fair 90; Stu Athltc Trnr; Med.

CARAHER, TIM J; St Francis HS; Glendale, CA; (2); FCA; Pep Clb; VP Frsh Cls; VP Soph Cls; VP Jr Cls; JV Var Bsbl; Var L Ftbl; Hon Roll; NHS; CSF.

CARANCI, ANTONIA T; St Paul HS; Whittier, CA; (3); Church Yth Grp; Cmnty Wkr; Girl Scts; Hon Roll; NHS; Pres Acad Fit Awd; U Of Southern CA; Pedtrcn.

CARATACHEA, DELIA R; St Francis HS; Mountain View, CA; (2); Vllybl; Acctg.

CARAVALLO, JANEY; Newark Memorial HS; Newark, CA; (3); Drama Clb; FBLA; Letterman Clb; Office Aide; Spanish Clb; Teachers Aide; Varsity Clb; Yrbk; Stu Cncl; Var Mgr Bsktbl; Econ Awd; Pres Phys Fit; Santa Brabara Bus Coll; Acctng.

CARAWAY, JENNIFER M; Madera HS; Madera, CA; (1); JV Bsbl; Var Trk; Intrml Vllybl; UCSD; Med Doc.

CARBAJAL, DE NYSE; San Pasqual Acad; Buena Park, CA; (4); 7/43; Church Yth Grp; Cmnty Wkr; Office Aide; Spanish Clb; Teachers Aide; Band; Ed Yrbk; VP Frsh Cls; Sec Soph Cls; VP Stu Cncl; Girls Clb; CA ST Fullerton; Phys Thrpy.

CARBAJAL, JOSEPH LOUIS; Santiago HS; Garden Grove, CA; (3); JV Bsbl; Var JV Bsktbl; USC; Engrng.

CARBAJAL, KARINA J; Central Union HS; El Centro, CA; (1); Church Yth Grp; GAA; Spanish Clb; Teachers Aide; Chorus; Cit Awd; Hon Roll; Stanford U; Lawyer.

CARBAJAL, LETICIA; Baldwin Park HS; Baldwin Park, CA; (2); Band; Mrchg Band; Pep Band; Bsktbl; Sftbl; Vllybl; Hon Roll; Letterwoman Clb.

CARBAJAL, LIZBETH H; Calexico HS; Calexico, CA; (3); Spanish Clb; Teachers Aide; Srptmst 3 Clb; Spec Olympcs Coach; Spnsh Lit AP Clb; Sales Mgr.

CARBAJAL, MARIO; Poly HS; Riverside, CA; (2); Rptr Nwsp; VP Frsh Cls; Pres Soph Cls; Hon Roll; Brdcst Jrnlsm.

CARBAJAL, PEDRO; Tranquillity HS; Mendota, CA; (3); Teachers Aide; Band; Mrchg Band; Bsbl; Ftbl; Trk; Wt Lftg; Wrstlng; AZ UTI; Diesel Mechnc.

CARBAJO, CHARLES S; Daniel Murphy HS; Los Angeles, CA; (1); Intrml Bsbl; JV Ftbl; Intrml Wt Lftg; Hon Roll; US Air Force Acad; Law Enfrcmt.

CARBIN, CYNTHIA N; Washington HS; Fremont, CA; (3); 26/306; Church Yth Grp; Drill Tm; Var Trk; Med Explrers; Schlrshp Fdrtn-CA; Piano; Med Rsrch.

CARBONE, JANETTE; Warren HS; Downey, CA; (3); French Clb; Office Aide; Pep Clb; JV Var Cheerldng; Gym; Powder Puff Ftbl; Hon Roll; Kiwanis Awd; Pres Acad Fit Awd; Yth Ldrshp Project; Peer Counselor; Argentine Schl At USC; Gymnastics To Compete Natl Cmptn In FL; UCLA; Obstetrician.

CARBONE, NICOLE C; Trabuco Hills HS; Mission Viejo, CA; (2); 21/415; Church Yth Grp; Debate Tm; Spanish Clb; Speech Tm; JV Vllybl; Hon Roll; Kiwanis Awd; Lion Awd; NHS; Cousteau Soc; Earth Clb; Surfrider Fndtn; Spnsh Dstgshd Schlr Awd; Sailing.

CARBONEL, JOSILU; Vivian Webb Schl; Claremont, CA; (3); Art Clb; Church Yth Grp; Cmnty Wkr; Intnl Clb; Latin Clb; Spanish Clb; Phtg Yrbk; Rep Stu Cncl; Var Bsktbl; Swmmng; Scuba Dvng, Wind Srfng, Water Skng & Saig; FL U; Intl Pltcs.

CARBONELL, LEILANI ANN; Nogales HS; Fontana, CA; (4); Dance Clb; VP Science Clb; School Play; Ed Yrbk; Lit Mag; Stu Cncl; Hon Roll; Prfct Atten Awd; Bdmntn Team-JR Vrsty; Natl Young Ldrs Conf; Prom Queens 90; Olympians Clb; UCLA; Pltcl Sci.

CARBRAL, CAROL; Hamilton Union HS; Hamilton City, CA; (3); Church Yth Grp; Cmnty Wkr; FFA; Scholastic Bowl; SADD; Teachers Aide; Chorus; School Play; Ed Yrbk; JV Bsktbl; Director Stu Activities/Rally Commissioner; FFA Regional Sweetheart; FFA Officer 3 Years; U Of CA Davis; Veterinarian.

CARCALLAS, HAZEL; Encinal HS; Alameda, CA; (3); 3/246; Key Clb; ROTC; Church Choir; Orch; Yrbk; Cheerldng; Pom Pon; High Hon Roll; Pres Acad Fit Awd; CA Schlrshp Fdrtn; Filepino Cultrl Dance Troupe; U CA; Bus.

CARCALLAS, HYEIA; Encinal HS; Alameda, CA; (4); 8/210; Pres Key Clb; ROTC; Church Choir; Mrchg Band; Orch; Pres Soph Cls; Cheerldng; Pom Pon; Cit Awd; DAR Awd; Tch Piano Lssns; Cmmnty Wrk, Meals On Wheels; U San Francisco; Nrsng.

CARDARONELLA, LARA N; Redwood HS; Visalia, CA; (2); Church Yth Grp; Socr; Hon Roll; NHS; Biola U.

CARDEN, AMY M; St Josephs HS; Santa Maria, CA; (3); Church Yth Grp; Teachers Aide; Church Choir; Rptr Nwsp; Off Sr Cls; JV Socr; JV Swmmng; St Marys Clg; Engl Teacher.

CARDENAS, CARMEN D; Red Bluff Union HS; Cottonwood, CA; (3); Church Yth Grp; Pres FCA; Teachers Aide; Church Choir; VP Sr Cls; Var Crs Cntry; JV Trk; Hon Roll; Kiwanis Awd; CSF-SEC; Fri Night Live Clb; Mst Imprvd-Track 88; Mst Inspirational-Track 89.

CARDENAS, DANIEL C; River City HS; W Sacramento, CA; (3); Am Leg Boys St; French Clb; SADD; School Play; Treas Stu Cncl; Hon Roll; Mock Trial Tm; Upward Bound; 5 Schlstc Achvts; Law.

CARDENAS, DORA ALICIA; Porterville HS; Terra Bella, CA; (3); French Clb; GAA; Band; Mrchg Band; Var Crs Cntry; JV Score Keeper; JV Sftbl; Var Trk; UC Davis; Elect Engr.

CARDENAS, EDLYNN D.; Valley HS; Sacramento, CA; (2); 33/434; Church Yth Grp; Dance Clb; Rptr Yrbk; Off Jr Cls; JV Var Cheerldng; Hon Roll; Pres Acad Fit Awd; Asilomar; NCD Early Outreach Pgm; CA Schlrshp Fed; UC Davis; Pediatrician.

CARDENAS, HECTOR; Mt View HS; El Monte, CA; (1); Art Clb; Hon Roll; Prfct Atten Awd; Comp Prgrmr.

CARDENAS, JESUS; Tranquillity Union HS; Mendota, CA; (3); Ftbl; Trk; Wt Lftg; Cit Awd; Athltc; Bank Mgr; Fresno ST U; Bank Mgr.

CARDENAS, JUAN CARLOS; Thomas Jefferson HS; Los Angeles, CA; (4); Church Yth Grp; JA; ROTC; JV Crs Cntry; JV Trk; Hon Roll; Schlr Athl Of Yr; CSULA.

CARDENAS, LIZA E; James Lick HS; San Jose, CA; (3); Intnl Clb; Library Aide; Speech Tm; Hon Roll; Portuguese Clb Pres; Bibliophile Soc; Cmnty Marching Band.

CARDENAS, MARITZA; Montebello HS; Los Angeles, CA; (1); Dance Clb; English Clb; Chorus; Tennis; JSA; USC; Bus Adm.

CARDENAS, MILTON C; James Lick HS; San Jose, CA; (1); JV Ftbl; Trk; CSF; Gftd/Tlntd Educ; Portuguese Clb.

CARDENAS, MONIA; Santa Maria HS; Santa Maria, CA; (2); Teachers Aide; Sftbl; Vllybl; Upward Bnd Pgm; Law.

CARDENAS, NANCY J; Anderson HS; Anderson, CA; (3); Debate Tm; Drama Clb; FFA; Office Aide; SADD; Teachers Aide; Acpl Chr; 1st Judging Livestock Shasta Coll; 1st Horse Riding Xmas Parade; FFA Ofcr & Sweetheart.

CARDENAS, PAUL A; Valley View HS; Moreno Valley, CA; (2); ROTC; Stu Cncl; Ftbl; Hon Roll; Sns Amer Rvltn; Gldn St Exm Hnr Awd; Astrntcl Engr.

CARDENAS, PETER A; Leuzinger HS; Hawthorne, CA; (3); French Clb; Teachers Aide; Cit Awd; Hon Roll; Prfct Atten Awd; Acting.

CARDENAS, SAMANTHA; Brea Olinda HS; Fullerton, CA; (1); Sftbl; Vllybl; Jr NHS; Prfct Atten Awd; Natl Chmpn Sftbl Tm 89.

CARDENAS, SUSAN C; San Lorenzo HS; Hayward, CA; (2); Band; Jazz Band; JV Cheerldng; Trk; High Hon Roll; Med.

CARDENAS, VERONICA L; Thomas Downey HS; Ceres, CA; (1); Sftbl; Tennis; Hon Roll; Jazz & Musical Comedy P J School Of Dance; Piano Lessons; Model; Cal Poly; Physical Therapist.

CARDENO, HOSANNA JEAN G; Casa Roble Fundamental HS; Orangevale, CA; (3); 37/390; Orch; Cit Awd; Hon Roll.

CARDIEL, ELAINE L; Roseville HS; Rocklin, CA; (3); 19/411; Drama Clb; French Clb; German Clb; Jazz Band; Pep Band; NHS; CSF; Jnr Music Symphny; Nrthrn Sacrmnto Vly Hnr Choir; Sierra Coll HS Hnr Band; Music.

CARDIN, CHRIS E; Westwood HS; Westwood, CA; (2); Letterman Clb; Teachers Aide; VICA; Bsbl; Bsktbl; Ftbl; Wt Lftg; Hon Roll; Pres Acad Fit Awd; Air Force; Fly.

CARDONA, ANDRE G; Lu Sierra HS; Riverside, CA; (2); Bsbl; Ftbl; Sftbl; Wt Lftg; Baseball.

CARDONA, CAMILLE; Villa Park HS; Orange, CA; (2); Cmnty Wkr; Drama Clb; Key Clb; Office Aide; Spanish Clb; Teachers Aide; JV Crs Cntry; JV Sftbl; JV Trk; Hon Roll; Tchr.

CARDONA, IRENE; Reedley HS; Reedle Y, CA; (4); Pres Church Yth Grp; FBLA; FTA; German Clb; Hosp Aide; Intnl Clb; Key Clb; Science Clb; VP Spanish Clb; SADD; All Amer Hall Of Fame Music; Fresno Pacific Coll; Elem Tchr.

CARDONA, JOHANNA A; Magnolia HS; Costamesa, CA; (1); Trk; French Hon Soc; Frnch Frgn Lang; Lang.

CARDONA, JOSHUA G; Orestimba HS; Newman, CA; (2); Cmnty Wkr; Science Clb; Spanish Clb; JV Bsbl; Capt JV Ftbl; Hon Roll.

CARDONA, NEVIA D; Colton HS; Grand Terrace, CA; (2); Drama Clb; FFA; Library Aide; Office Aide; Chorus; Rep Stu Cncl; Hon Roll; Prfct Atten Awd; Pepperdine U; Psych.

CARDONA, NICKI; Central Union HS; El Centro, CA; (3); Church Yth Grp; Pep Clb; Hon Roll; Tall Flags; ASB Cmmssnr Of Stu Svcs; UCSD; Bus.

CARDONA, PATTY JEAN; Mills HS; Millbrae, CA; (3); Church Yth Grp; Pep Clb; Stage Crew; Cheerldng; Vllybl; Pres Acad Fit Awd; Army Reserve.

CARDONA, SARA L; Bloomington HS; Bloomington, CA; (3); Phtg Yrbk; VP Soph Cls; Var JV Bsktbl; Var L Crs Cntry; JV Var Score Keeper; Var Tennis; Var Trk; High Hon Roll; Hon Roll; Jr NHS; Hnrbl Mntn Var Girls Bsktbl; Graphic Art.

CARDONA, TRACEY E; Beaumont HS; Cherry Valley, CA; (3); Sec Varsity Clb; JV Bsktbl; Var Sftbl; Var Co-Capt Vllybl; Hon Roll; Pres Acad Fit Awd; CA ST Poly Pomona; Adv.

CARDOSA, ANDREA M; Notre Dame HS; Perris, CA; (3); Treas Soph Cls; Rep Jr Cls; Var Capt Bsktbl; Capt Powder Puff Ftbl; JV Sftbl; Var L Vllybl; High Hon Roll; NHS; Med.

CARDOSO, DENNIS A; James Lick HS; San Jose, CA; (3); Letterman Clb; Varsity Clb; Var L Socr; High Hon Roll; Hon Roll; Art Show Awd; San Jose ST U; Bus Admin.

CARDOZA, ANNETTE N; Chino HS; Chino, CA; (2); Science Clb; JV Sftbl; High Hon Roll.

CARDOZA, GILBERT V; Ramona HS; Riverside, CA; (1); 75/298; JV Capt Bsbl; Baseball Coaches Awd; Comp Sci.

CARDOZA, JAMIE L; Turlock HS; Turlock, CA; (3); Church Yth Grp; Office Aide; Teachers Aide; Sftbl; City Smmr League Sftbl; Bus.

CARDOZA, JOHNNY R; Turlock HS; Turlock, CA; (2); 145/700; Rptr Nwsp; JV Ftbl; JV Trk; JV Wt Lftg; Civil Engrng.

CARDOZA, MISTY R; Mt Whitney HS; Tulare, CA; (2); Pep Clb; Hon Roll; Secretary Crafts Club; SAS; Keywanettes; Business.

CARDOZA, PAUL; La Puente HS; La Puente, CA; (1); JV Ftbl; Var Tennis; Var Wt Lftg; Hon Roll; Bus.

CARDWELL, ELIZABETH; Rolling Hills HS; Torrance, CA; (4); 157/300; Computer Clb; 4-H; Girl Scts; Chorus; 4-H Awd; High Hon Roll; Hon Roll; Reserve Champ Equitation LSAC & Champ Pleasure LSAC Horses; Harbor Coll; Nrsng.

CARDWELL, YVONNE; David Starr Jordan HS; Lakewood, CA; (2); Church Yth Grp; Chorus; Drill Tm; Rptr Nwsp; Yrbk; VP Frsh Cls; Cheerldng; Cit Awd; Hon Roll; English Clb; Outstndng Ldrshp Awd; CATP.

CAREDIO, ATHENA M; Los Banos HS; Los Banos, CA; (2); Letterman Clb; Color Guard; JV Bsktbl; Var Trk; Hon Roll; Prfct Atten Awd; Pres Acad Fit Awd; Office Aide; FBLA; Bsktbl All Tourney MIP, Best Ball Handler Awds 1989; Outstndg Phy Ftns Awd; Track Medals; CSU Stanislaus; Oceangrphy.

CARELOCK, JEROME; Aimijo HS; Suisun, CA; (3); FBLA; Var Bsbl; Var Bsktbl; Var Ftbl; Bus Admin.

CAREN, KIMBERLY; Laurel HS; Los Alamitos, CA; (2); Teachers Aide; Cheerldng; Pres Acad Fit Awd; Jrnlsm.

CARESS, KIMBERLY; Rowland HS; Livermore, CA; (2); Pep Clb; Teachers Aide; JV Cheerldng; Var Score Keeper; Hon Roll; BYU; Bus.

CAREY, GINA M; Mercy HS; San Bruno, CA; (2); 21/104; Church Yth Grp; Service Clb; High Hon Roll; NHS; Pres Acad Fit Awd; CSF; Italian Clb-Pres 89-90; Irish Dancer; Stus Aware Of Abused Substances; U Of San Francisco; Ed.

CAREY, JENNIFER DIANE; Shasta HS; Redding, CA; (4); 2/325; Math Tm; Model UN; Science Clb; Rptr Nwsp; Off Soph Cls; Var Co-Capt Cheerldng; Var Crs Cntry; Var Trk; Pres Acad Fit Awd; Sal; Soccer Coach; Shasta Cty Young Woman Of Yr; CSF Life Mem; Stanford U; Hospital Admin.

CAREY, JENNIFER M; Carmel HS; Big Sur, CA; (4); 6/173; Cmnty Wkr; Pres Band; Pres Jazz Band; Orch; Var Capt Fld Hcky; Var Swmmng; DAR Awd; High Hon Roll; Kiwanis Awd; Pres Schlr; CSF, Vp; Wilderness Club; Humboldt ST U; Wildlife Mgmt.

CAREY, KATHLEEN L; Hesperia HS; Hesperia, CA; (3); Drama Clb; FBLA; Hosp Aide; Ski Clb; SADD; Teachers Aide; School Play; Hon Roll; Corp Lwyr.

CAREY, PETER C; San Clemente HS; San Clemente, CA; (1); German Clb; Socr; Avid Sccr Plyr; Local Boys Clb Stu; Coach Boys Sccr; Local Yth Grp Stu; Involved In Feed The Homeless; UCI.

CAREY, ROBERT; Victor Valley HS; Victorville, CA; (2); Boy Scts; French Clb; JV Ftbl; US Air Force Acad; Engrng.

CAREY, SETH; Brethren HS; Long Beach, CA; (1); 1/100; Church Yth Grp; Acpl Chr; School Musical; Bsktbl; High Hon Roll.

CAREY, STEVEN D; San Clemente HS; San Clemente, CA; (1); Teachers Aide; Socr; Avid Sccr Plyr; Coach Sccr; Involved In Feeding The Homeless; UCI.

CAREY, VINCENT M; St Ignatius Preparatory Coll; Pacifica, CA; (2); Church Yth Grp; CSF Ex Brd Yng Rep; Jr Statsmn Amer,Vrsty Crew Rcvd Coachs Awd; Chrstn Surfing Asso.

CARGILL, CHRISTIANE E; Lutheran HS Of Orange County; Santa Ana, CA; (3); 23/94; Church Yth Grp; Chorus; School Musical; Variety Show; JV Cheerldng; Trk; French Hon Soc; Hon Roll; Wntr Chrch Camp Camp Cnslr; Unltd Wrrnty Pianist; Music.

CARGILL, CHRISTINE R; Chino HS; Chino, CA; (3); Girl Scts; Cit Awd; Hon Roll; Comp Sci Silver Spur Awd; Cheffey CC; Psych.

CARHART, CHRISTINE A; Grace Davis HS; Modesto, CA; (2); Var L Socr; Var Trk; Cit Awd; Numerous Sccr Awds & Tms 88-90; Ed.

CARI, ANGELEE D; Casa Roble Fundamental HS; Orangevale, CA; (2); #205 In Class; Church Yth Grp; Girl Scts; Ski Clb; Var Socr; Humboldt; Marine Bio.

CARIAGA, ANGELO S; Nogales HS; La Puente, CA; (3); Lit Mag; Stu Cncl; Bsktbl; Hon Roll; Golden St Exam Awd; Hnr Stu; UCLA; Acctng.

CARIAS, BOBBY; Fairfield HS; Suisun City, CA; (2); Boy Scts; Rptr Nwsp; Rep Frsh Cls; JV Ftbl; JV Trk; JV Wrstlng; Cit Awd; Hon Roll; Prfct Atten Awd; UCLA; Law.

CARIC, MELINDA; Orange Glen HS; Valley Center, CA; (1); Band; Mrchg Band; Hon Roll; Concrt Band; Med.

CARIC, TRACEE M; Garus Memorial HS; Delano, CA; (3); Cmnty Wkr; Drama Clb; Pres Sec 4-H; Letterman Clb; Pep Clb; Science Clb; Band; Var Swmmng; Plyng Piano; Stu Orfnzd For Svc; Peer Cnslng; Psych.

CARIG, MADONNA F; Hemet HS; Hemet, CA; (4); AFS; French Clb; Bsktbl; Intl Clb; Mt San Jacinto Coll; Poly Sci.

CARILLO, RAFAILITA; James A Garfield HS; Los Angeles, CA; (2); Cmnty Wkr; Dance Clb; Science Clb; Prfct Atten Awd; Rotary Awd; Art.

CARINGAL, MARY GAY M; Notre Dame Acad; Los Angeles, CA; (3); Treas Frsh Cls; Sec Soph Cls; Hon Roll; NHS; Prfct Atten Awd; Bus Admin.

CARINI, GIANNA E; Casa Grande HS; Petaluma, CA; (2); Office Aide; Teachers Aide; Vllybl; Hon Roll; Comp, Word Prcssng & Offc Skills Achvt Awds; Most Consistant Awd Bio; Santa Rosa JC; Vet.

CARINO, DEBBI; Hogan SR HS; Vallejo, CA; (3); Treas Sec Drama Clb; 4-H; Pres French Clb; School Play; DAR Awd; Pres Acad Fit Awd; Acad Decathlon; Peer Hlprs; Teens Teachers Projet Commit.

CARINO, MONICA; Mira Mesa HS; San Diego, CA; (2); Chorus; Cit Awd; NHS; Prfct Atten Awd; Santa Barbara U; Bus.

CARISIO, LISA; Mariposa County HS; Mariposa, CA; (3); 2/120; Dance Clb; Pep Clb; Ski Clb; Chorus; Drill Tm; Pres Soph Cls; Pres Jr Cls; Capt Cheerldng; Trk; High Hon Roll; Outstndng Engl Stu Awd; CSF Pres; Commnctns.

CARL, KATHLEEN J; Mt Carmel HS; San Diego, CA; (2); Church Yth Grp; Girl Scts; Crs Cntry; Trk; Cit Awd; Hon Roll; Prfct Atten Awd; Pres Acad Fit Awd; Safe Rides Clb; CSF; Schl Standout Awd.

CARLET, ROMUALDO C; Foothill HS; San Jose, CA; (4); 5/110; Chess Clb; Computer Clb; Library Aide; SADD; Teachers Aide; Varsity Clb; Drm Mjr(t); Nwsp; Pres Frsh Cls; VP Soph Cls; Stu Mnth; Mayors Yth Conf; Dist Press Conf; Aerospace Engr.

CARLETON, MELISSA A; Edison/Camputech HS; Fresno, CA; (1); 55/450; Church Yth Grp; JV Swmmng; JV Vllybl; Env Clb; Edison Soc High Adv; Merit Roll Schlr; U C Coll; Cnslng.

CARLEY, DEBRAH S; Mount Whitney HS; Visalia, CA; (3); Pep Clb; Spanish Clb; Sacramento ST; Child Psych.

CARLEY, JOHN L; Dana Hills HS; Laguna Niguel, CA; (1); Church Yth Grp; Computer Clb; Letterman Clb; Math Clb; Math Tm; Quiz Bowl; Scholastic Bowl; Science Clb; Varsity Clb; Swmmng; 1st Pl Orange Cnty All Around Swmmr; Schlr Athl Awd; Med.

CARLIN, KEVIN P; Bullard HS; Fresno, CA; (2); Church Yth Grp; FCA; Hosp Aide; US Santa Cruz; Marine Bio.

CARLIN, MICHELLE; Capistrano Valley HS; Mission Viejo, CA; (3); Church Yth Grp; Cmnty Wkr; High Hon Roll; Hon Roll; BYU.

CARLIN, MIKE P; Orange Glen HS; Escondido, CA; (3); Lit Mag; Hon Roll; Cnty-Wide Sbjct A Exam Write-Off 90 Outstndng Achvt; Los Angeles Ventura Cnty Shrt Story 2nd Pl; U Southern CA; Medcl.

CARLIN, RICHARD L; Montebello HS; Montebello, CA; (4); 106/560; Letterman Clb; Red Cross Aide; SADD; Band; Mrchg Band; Pep Band; Swmmng; Hon Roll; Prfct Atten Awd; Water Polo Capt 2nd Team All Witmont Leag; CSULA; Avtn.

CARLIS, MARCUS W; Canyon Springs HS; Moreno Valley, CA; (2); Ftbl; JV Trk; JV Wt Lftg; Hon Roll; Accntnt.

CARLISLE, JASON D; Elk Grove HS; Sacramento, CA; (3); 74/609; Ed Nwsp; JV Ftbl; Hon Roll; Glf; Spnsh; Sprts Cllctbls; Accntng.

CARLISLE, JENI; Willits HS; Sonoma, CA; (3); 20/120; School Play; Stage Crew; Variety Show; High Hon Roll; Hon Roll; Pres Schlr; Peer Cnslr; Santa Rosa JC.

CARLISLE, KACI D; Whittier Christian HS; Whittier, CA; (3); Church Yth Grp; Band; Mrchg Band; Pep Band; JV Var Cheerldng; Gym; CA ST Fullerton; Bus.

CARLOCK, JULIE M; Selma HS; Selma, CA; (1); Var L Bsktbl; Var L Swmmng; Var L Vllybl; Hon Roll; Raisin Cnty Aqutcs Swm Team 1982; Sierra Pacific Vllybl Clb; Wrk Part Time Lcl Nwspr; Fresno ST U; Sprts Med.

CARLON IV, LOYAL D; Ramona HS; Ramona, CA; (2); Scholastic Bowl; Ski Clb; Ftbl; Var L Socr.

CARLOS, CARSON A; Southwest HS; San Diego, CA; (3); 19/493; Pres Computer Clb; Drama Clb; Math Clb; Quiz Bowl; ROTC; Science Clb; Chorus; Drill Tm; High Hon Roll; Pres Acad Fit Awd.

CARLOS, DIANA ANGELICA; Saint Michaels HS; Los Angeles, CA; (1); 1/119; Spanish Clb; Hon Roll; Prfct Atten Awd; Hghst GPA Trophy; Achvt Awds; USC; Jrnlsm.

CARLOS, EVELIA; Norte Vista HS; Riverside, CA; (1); Teachers Aide; Cit Awd; Hon Roll; Probation Officer.

CARLOS, GEORGE; Bell Gardens HS; Bell Gardens, CA; (2); Band; Jazz Band; Mrchg Band; Pep Band; Bsbl; UCLA; Law.

CARLOS, JERRYMAIN M; Milpitas HS; Milpitas, CA; (1); JV Wrstlng; Coachs Awd; Principals Schlrshp Awd; UC Berkeley; Phy.

CARLOS, KRISTA K; Polytechnic HS; Riverside, CA; (2); Band; Mrchg Band; Hon Roll; Prfct Atten Awd; Var Badminton; Wind Ensmbl.

CARLOS, MOISES; St Bernard HS; Los Angeles, CA; (3); Church Yth Grp; Cmnty Wkr; Intnl Clb; Latin Clb; Crs Cntry; Ftbl; Knights Columbus Cmnty Svc Awd; Dept Parks/Rec Little Leag Umpire; Law.

CARLOS, NORMA; St Michaels HS; Los Angeles, CA; (4); 1/65; Church Yth Grp; Spanish Clb; Chorus; Stu Cncl; High Hon Roll; Hon Roll; NHS; Prfct Atten Awd; Sci Essy Cont Rcgntn Awds; Hghst GPA; CSF; Med.

CARLSEN, STEPHEN E; Prospect HS; San Jose, CA; (1); Boy Scts; Church Yth Grp; Cmnty Wkr; Math Clb; Science Clb; Crs Cntry; Trk; High Hon Roll; St Schlr; Life Sct; UC Berkeley; Law.

CARLSON, AMY; Village Christian Schls; Shadow Hills, CA; (3); Church Yth Grp; Drama Clb; VP French Clb; Letterman Clb; Co-Capt Drill Tm; School Play; Var Bsktbl; Marine Bio.

CARLSON, AMY L; Mountain View HS; Los Altos, CA; (3); 24/293; Am Leg Aux Girls St; Pres Spanish Clb; Sec Mrchg Band; Orch; Var Swmmng; High Hon Roll; Ntl Merit Ltr; Schl Impvt Cncl; Harvard Bk Awd; Exec Wmn Intl Outstndg Stu; Intl Rel.

CARLSON, APRIL A; Livermore HS; Livermore, CA; (3); Pres Church Yth Grp; Pep Clb; Sec Spanish Clb; Chorus; Church Choir; Ed Nwsp; Rep Stu Cncl; Hon Roll; Co-Head Positive Stu Recgntn Cmmtte; Staff Rcgntn Cmmtte; Edtr; Law.

CARLSON, CANDACE; Woodbridge HS; Irvine, CA; (4); Am Leg Aux Girls St; Church Yth Grp; Cmnty Wkr; Pep Clb; Red Cross Aide; Service Clb; Spanish Clb; Off Frsh Cls; Pres Soph Cls; Pres Jr Cls; Natl Charity Leag; Irvine Yth Vlntr Of Yr 88; Homcmng Qn 89; AZ ST U; Poltcl Sci.

CARLSON, DANA C; Petaluma HS; Petaluma, CA; (3); 39/267; Cmnty Wkr; French Clb; Letterman Clb; SADD; Varsity Clb; Pres Soph Cls; Treas Jr Cls; VP Stu Cncl; Var JV Bsktbl; Var Capt Crs Cntry; CSF; Phys Thrpy.

CARLSON, DANIKA; Edison HS; Huntington Beach, CA; (1); Sec Church Yth Grp; Model UN; Drill Tm; High Hon Roll; Brigham Young U.

CARLSON, DAVID; Mt Whitney HS; Visalia, CA; (2); AFS; Chess Clb; Church Yth Grp; Debate Tm; Key Clb; NFL; SADD; Mrchg Band; Yrbk; JV Socr; Harvard; Med.

CARLSON, DEREK G; Arcata HS; Mc Kinleyville, CA; (3); Church Yth Grp; Math Tm; Scholastic Bowl; Teachers Aide; Var L Bsbl; Var L Bsktbl; High Hon Roll; Top Ten Cls; Gldn ST Hgh Hnrs Gmtry.

CARLSON, JOEL; El Capitan HS; Lakeside, CA; (4); 11/430; JV Trk; Hon Roll; U CA San Diego; Anthrplgy.

CARLSON, JONATHAN M; San Gorgonio HS; Highland, CA; (3); Am Leg Boys St; VP Pres Latin Clb; Letterman Clb; Spanish Clb; Crs Cntry; Trk; Hon Roll; NHS; Spanish NHS; Mock Trl Tm; Cal Poly San Luis Obispo; Arch.

CARLSON, JUSTIN; Arcata HS; Mc Kinleyville, CA; (1); Boy Scts; Church Yth Grp; SADD; Band; Mrchg Band; Pep Band; High Hon Roll; Church Handbell Choir; Sr League Bsbll; Elect Engr.

CARLSON, KAREN L; Colton HS; Grand Terrace, CA; (2); Rptr Yrbk; Var L Vllybl; High Hon Roll; Sportswest Vlybl Clb; UC Berkeley; Optometry.

CARLSON, KIMBERLEY; Los Alamitos HS; Seal Beach, CA; (3); Church Yth Grp; NFL; Speech Tm; Teachers Aide; Orch; JV Crs Cntry; JV Trk; Hon Roll; Prfct Atten Awd.

CARLSON, KRISTIN M; El Capitan HS; Lakeside, CA; (2); #63 In Class; Church Yth Grp; SADD; JV Bsktbl; JV Mgr(s); Hon Roll; Amnesty Intl; UCSD; Phy.

CARLSON, MARK A; Santa Clara HS; Santa Clara, CA; (2); Hon Roll; Elect Engrng.

CARLSON, MICHELLE M; Santa Teresa HS; San Jose, CA; (1); JV Vllybl; Hon Roll; UC Davis; Vet Med.

CARLSON, PAMELA E; Newbury Park HS; Newbury Park, CA; (2); 25/372; SADD; Sec Band; Sec Mrchg Band; Orch; Hon Roll; Ntl Merit Schol; All Sthrn CA Hnr Band; Ventura Cnty Hnr Band; Professional Oboeist.

CARLSON, REBECCA L; James Lick HS; San Jose, CA; (1); Hon Roll; Magnet Prgm; Cmmnction & Ldrshp; UCLA; Film Dir.

CARLSON, RICHARD A; Sierra Vista HS; Baldwin Park, CA; (1); Swmmng; Hon Roll; Marine Bio.

CARLSON, SARAH; Mt Whitney HS; Visalia, CA; (4); 5/373; AFS; Church Yth Grp; FBLA; Treas Math Clb; Band; JV Bsktbl; Var L Swmmng; Cit Awd; Hon Roll; NHS; Keywanettes; CA Schlrshp Fed.

CARLSON, SHARI A; Norte Vista HS; Riverside, CA; (2); 21/445; Church Yth Grp; Drama Clb; Hosp Aide; Pres JA; School Play; Mgr Stage Crew; Swmmng; High Hon Roll; CSF; Golden St Ex Acad Exc Awd Geo.

CARLSON, SHAUN C; Alta Loma HS; Alta Loma, CA; (2); Ski Clb; Varsity Clb; Phtg Yrbk; Tennis; Cit Awd; High Hon Roll; Prfct Atten Awd; Brooks Inst; Photo.

CARLSON, STEPHEN O; Mountain View HS; Los Altos, CA; (4); 1/237; Spanish Clb; Varsity Clb; Var L Swmmng; High Hon Roll; Ntl Merit SF; Wate Polo Var Ltr; Aquatic Club, Coaches Awd, Most Imprvd Sr; Cert Achvt-Frgn Lang Assoc; Soc Stud Awd; Pre-Law.

CARLSON, VIKKI K; Edison HS; Huntington Bch, CA; (4); 9/500; Model UN; Quiz Bowl; Drm Mjr(t); Jazz Band; Mrchg Band; Pep Band; High Hon Roll; Ntl Merit Ltr; Pres Acad Fit Awd; Acad Cmptn; Stu Teacher; Brigham Young U; Commnctns.

CARLSTON, DAVID L; Las Lomas HS; Walnut Creek, CA; (3); Church Yth Grp; Drama Clb; German Clb; School Play; Var Bsbl; Hon Roll; Rose Hallman; Engrng.

CARLTON, MATTHEW A; Rio Americano HS; Carmichael, CA; (3); 10/290; Boy Scts; Pres Math Tm; NFL; Red Cross Aide; Scholastic Bowl; Science Clb; Pres Spanish Clb; Speech Tm; Teachers Aide; Acpl Chr; UC Berkeley; Math.

CARLUCCI, TY R; Dos Palos HS; Dos Palos, CA; (3); FBLA; Band; Mrchg Band; Ftbl; Wrstlng; Aviation.

CARLYLE, RICHARD A; Hueneme HS; Oxnard, CA; (2); Church Yth Grp; Hon Roll; Stud Amer Kempo Karate; Acad Schlrs Awd; Comp Sci.

CARMACK, HEATHER; Hemet HS; Hemet, CA; (4); 22/517; Treas Church Yth Grp; Key Clb; Letterman Clb; Var L Crs Cntry; Var L Trk; Elks Awd; High Hon Roll; Pres CSF; Loma Linda U; Med.

CARMAN, MIKE S; Summerville Union HS; Twain Harte, CA; (2); High Hon Roll; Hon Roll; Prfct Atten Awd; Carpenter.

CARMICHAEL, LISA; Mt Shasta HS; Mt Shasta, CA; (4); Am Leg Aux Girls St; Cmnty Wkr; Drama Clb; Ski Clb; Chorus; School Musical; Stage Crew; Rptr Nwsp; Rptr Yrbk; Pres Frsh Cls; U Of OR; Hstry.

CARMICHAEL, SEAN A; Washington HS; Fremont, CA; (3); JV Bsbl; JV Bsktbl; Var Crs Cntry; JV Socr.

CARMO, NICOLE; Foothill HS; Pleasanton, CA; (3); #9 In Class; Cmnty Wkr; Varsity Clb; JCL; Color Guard; Drill Tm; Capt Flag Corp; Mrchg Band; Capt Trk; High Hon Roll; Golden St Exam Achvt Awd; Track/Color Guard Ltrs; Graphic Design.

CARMONA, ADELA M; University Of San Diego HS; San Diego, CA; (2); Computer Clb; Office Aide; SADD; Fld Hcky; JV Swmmng; Wt Lftg; Pres Acad Fit Awd; San Diego ST U; Speech Thrpy.

CARMONA, ALEJANDRO; Warren HS; Downey, CA; (2); Engrng.

CARMONA, AMY; Foothill HS; Bakersfield, CA; (3); 36/378; Pep Clb; Teachers Aide; JV Capt Cheerldng; Pom Pon; Stock Broker.

CARMONA, ARMANDO J; Montclair HS; Montclair, CA; (3); Plt.

CARMONA, EVANGELINA R; Victor Valley HS; Victorville, CA; (1); Church Yth Grp; Chorus; UCLA; Interior Dsgn.

CARMONA, EVELIA; Mt Whitney HS; Farmersville, CA; (3); Church Yth Grp; Dance Clb; Key Clb.

CARMONA, FRANCIS; Kerman HS; Kerman, CA; (4); 74/123; Church Yth Grp; Cmnty Wkr; German Clb; Spanish Clb; Teachers Aide; Cit Awd; Prfct Atten Awd; Author Of Several Published Poems; Fresno City Coll; Leg Sec.

CARMONA, HECTOR; Hanford Joint Union HS; Hanford, CA; (2); 151/520; Nwsp; Yrbk; JV Bsbl; JV Ftbl; Wt Lftg; Envolved With MESA For 2 Years; Envolved With BSH Club; USC; Physical Therapist.

CARMONA, LUIS E; Arvin HS; Lamont, CA; (3); Computer Clb; JA; Library Aide; Math Clb; Science Clb; Spanish Clb; Teachers Aide; Pep Band; Cit Awd; Hon Roll; U CA Santa Barbara; Chem Engr.

CARNAHAN, MATT; Fairfield HS; Fairfield, CA; (3); Pres Soph Cls; VP Jr Cls; Var Bsbl; Var Ftbl; Wt Lftg; Hon Roll; Prfct Atten Awd; Pres Acad Fit Awd; Powder Puff Ftbl; Wrstlng; Acadmc Ltrmn; Fghtr Pilot.

CARNEY, ADAM M; Hesperia HS; Hesperia, CA; (3); 3/613; Church Yth Grp; Cmnty Wkr; Key Clb; Ski Clb; Varsity Clb; JV Bsbl; Var L Ftbl; JV Golf; Var L Socr; High Hon Roll; Engrng.

CARNEY, JULIE C; San Gabriel HS; San Gabriel, CA; (2); Pep Clb; Service Clb; SADD; Chorus; Drill Tm; Variety Show; Off Jr Cls; Cheerldng; Pom Pon; Swmmng; CA Schlrshp Fdrtn; Chrldng Sqd Capt; Secy Of Recrds & Correspondnc; Georgetown U; Law.

CARNEY, MICHAEL A; Villa Park HS; Orange, CA; (3); French Clb; Key Clb; Ski Clb; Spanish Clb; SADD; Teachers Aide; Yrbk; Off Jr Cls; Off Sr Cls; Bsbl; USC; Lawyer.

CARNEY, PAUL A; Bishop O'dowd HS; Castro Valley, CA; (2); Hon Roll.

CARO, MARIA I; John Burroughs HS; Burbank, CA; (4); Church Yth Grp; Computer Clb; Debate Tm; Drama Clb; Latin Clb; Spanish Clb; Speech Tm; Teachers Aide; Varsity Clb; Band; Valley Coll; Bus.

CAROLINA, JAZMINE; Out Reach Indepent HS; Pomona, CA; (3); Dance Clb; Drama Clb; Model UN; School Play; Nwsp; Yrbk; Bsbl; Bsktbl; Gym; Sftbl; Model.

CARON, JEFF E; Fort Bragg HS; Ft Bragg, CA; (4); Am Leg Boys St; Cmnty Wkr; Drama Clb; Math Tm; SADD; Ed Nwsp; Lit Mag; Pres Frsh Cls; Pres Soph Cls; Pres Jr Cls; Boston U; Aerospc Engrng.

CAROSA, ROSANNA F; Sacred Heart HS; Los Angeles, CA; (3); Cmnty Wkr; Library Aide; 2nd Hnrs Prnclplg Hnr Roll; Guitar; Loyola.

CAROSINO, LISA M; SCPA O'farrell HS; San Diego, CA; (2); Church Yth Grp; Dance Clb; Spanish Clb; SADD; Drill Tm; Hon Roll; UC Irvine; Psych.

CAROSONE, JEFFREY V; Casa Roble Fundamental HS; Citrus Heights, CA; (2); 12/471; AFS; Spanish Clb; Cit Awd; High Hon Roll; NHS; CA Schlrshp Fed; Friday Night Live.

CARPENTER, AMBER D; Poway HS; San Diego, CA; (2); Model UN; NFL; VP Speech Tm; Band; Mrchg Band; Orch; School Musical; Rptr Nwsp; High Hon Roll; Hon Roll; 2nd PTSA.

CARPENTER, APRIL L; Grossmont HS; La Mesa, CA; (3); 79/385; Cmnty Wkr; Hosp Aide; Psych.

CARPENTER, BRANDON M; Edison HS; Fresno, CA; (1); Ski Clb; JV Bsbl; JV Socr; Fresno City Coll; Anstslgy.

CARPENTER, DEBORAH LYNNE; Pleasant Valley HS; Chico, CA; (4); 23/215; Church Yth Grp; Debate Tm; French Clb; SADD; Ed Yrbk; VP Sr Cls; Fld Hcky; Pres Acad Fit Awd; Yth Envrnmntl Advcts Pres; Intract Pres; Amer Lgn Awd; CSUC; Soclgy.

CARPENTER, DENNIS J; Pioneer HS; San Jose, CA; (3); Chico ST U; Comp Science.

CARPENTER, EMILY A; St Joseph Notre Dame HS; Alameda, CA; (3); Cmnty Wkr; Intnl Clb; Model UN; Teachers Aide; Rptr Nwsp; Yrbk; JV Var Cheerldng; High Hon Roll; Hon Roll; Self Determntn Awd; Davis U CA; Psycht.

CARPENTER, JACQUELINE J; Louisville HS; Woodland Hills, CA; (3); 4/65; Drama Clb; FHA; Chorus; School Play; Rptr Nwsp; Bsktbl; NHS; Outstndng Yth Awd San Fernando Vly Repblcn Bus Wmn Rnnr Up; UC Berkley; Law.

CARPENTER, JEFFREY; Liberty Union HS; Brentwood, CA; (1); 2/307; Am Leg Boys St; VP FCA; Letterman Clb; SADD; Varsity Clb; Acpl Chr; Nwsp; Rep Frsh Cls; Pres Soph Cls; Off Jr Cls; Peer Cnslng; USCG Acad.

CARPENTER, KRISTIN K; Aptos HS; Aptos, CA; (1); French Clb; Rep Frsh Cls; Off Soph Cls; Var L Trk; Hon Roll; Pres Acad Fit Awd; CA Schlrshp Fed; Numerous Gymnastics Awds & Hnrs; Cinematology.

CARPENTER, LISA NOEL; Pleasant Valley HS; Chico, CA; (4); 7/215; Church Yth Grp; GAA; SADD; Acpl Chr; Band; Capt Flag Corp; Sec Frsh Cls; Var Crs Cntry; Var Swmmng; JV Trk; CA ST U Chico; Recrtn Admin.

CARPENTER, MICHAEL W; Thomas Downey HS; Modesto, CA; (2); Chess Clb; Computer Clb; Math Clb; Band; Wt Lftg; Comp Tech.

CARPENTER, NATALIE; Fred C Beyer HS; Modesto, CA; (4); 54/548; Art Clb; Science Clb; Variety Show; Yrbk; Cit Awd; Hon Roll; Smi-Fnlst Grls ST Cmp Ryl Hnrb Mntn-Pc Essy Cont; CSF Smifnlst CBYEP; Bckstg Dnc Co; Fn Arts.

CARPENTER, PATRIC S; San Bernardino HS; San Bernardino, CA; (3); 73/373; Letterman Clb; Office Aide; SADD; Varsity Clb; Var Bsbl; Ftbl; JV Tennis; Bus.

CARPENTERO, JENNIFER; Ontario HS; Ontario, CA; (1); Church Yth Grp; Cit Awd; High Hon Roll; Hon Roll; Prfct Atten Awd; St Schlr; Engl Awd; UCLA; Nrsng.

CARPENTIER, ALISON; Centennial HS; Corona, CA; (1); Var Swmmng; High Hon Roll; NHS; Pres Acad Fit Awd; Hnrs On 89 Golden St Exam Algebra; Vrsty Awd Swmmng; U Of CA 89 Acad Tlnt Srch Acad Merit Awd; Bus.

CARPOWICH, MARK D; University City HS; San Diego, CA; (3); Boy Scts; Church Yth Grp; Model UN; Scholastic Bowl; Teachers Aide; Rptr Nwsp; Rep Jr Cls; JV Var Swmmng; JV Var Wrstlng; Hon Roll; Piano; Sports Reporter Local Newspaper; Jrnlsm.

CARR, ADAM T; Pittsburg HS; Pittsburg, CA; (2); Aud/Vis; Boy Scts; Rep Frsh Cls; Hon Roll; Prfct Atten Awd; Europn Trvl Clb; Humbolt ST U CA; Wldlf Mgmt.

CARR, BRIAN A; Ponderosa HS; Placerville, CA; (1); #1 In Class; French Clb; Hon Roll; 2nd Pl Optmst Oratrcl Awd Cameron Park.

CARR, CATHY; Mc Lane HS; Fresno, CA; (2); 19/600; Drama Clb; SADD; School Musical; School Play; Var Cheerldng; Hon Roll; Prfct Atten Awd; Pres Acad Fit Awd; Fresno ST; Tchr.

CARR, DION G; St Francis HS; Sunnyvale, CA; (3); 108/289; JV Bsbl; High Hon Roll; Hon Roll; U San Diego; Engr.

CARR, JEROME D; Saddleback HS; Santa Ana, CA; (2); Dance Clb; Ftbl; Var Score Keeper; JV Trk; BSU; USC; Bus.

CARR, JERON H; Mark Kepple HS; Monterey Park, CA; (1); 3/625; Boy Scts; Treas Drama Clb; Science Clb; Mrchg Band; School Play; L Var Sftbl; High Hon Roll; Cert Apprctn City Hall Volunteer OR Srvc Club; Vrsty Coachs Awd Boys Swmmng; 1st Pl Prsndtl Awd BSA; Physics.

CARR, JOANNA; Lowell HS; San Francisco, CA; (2); Cmnty Wkr; Debate Tm; Speech Tm; Teachers Aide; Lit Mag; Var Rowing Tm; Vlntr; Med.

CARR, JOSHUA E; Mojave HS; Mojave, CA; (1); 1/136; Var Golf; Var Mgr(s); Cit Awd; High Hon Roll; Prfct Atten Awd; Val; Astronautics.

CARR, KRISTINA L; Atwater HS; Atwater, CA; (3); FCA; Pep Clb; Teachers Aide; VP Soph Cls; Off Jr Cls; VP Sr Cls; JV Var Cheerldng; Gym; Hon Roll; Pres Acad Fit Awd; Mst Imprvd Chrldr; AZ ST U; Bus.

CARR, MARTIN D; Armijo HS; Fairfield, CA; (4); 2/376; Off Soph Cls; Pres Jr Cls; Capt Bsktbl; Capt Socr; DAR Awd; High Hon Roll; Ntl Merit Schol; Sal; Amer Acad Achvt; Schlr/Athl Of Yr; UC San Diego.

CARR, WILLIAM R; Poway HS; Poway, CA; (2); Varsity Clb; Band; Drm Mjr(t); Mrchg Band; Var Diving; Hon Roll; Cls Cmmssnr; UCLA; Med.

CARRALES, CATHARINE E; San Diego HS; San Diego, CA; (3); 20/460; Church Yth Grp; Cmnty Wkr; GAA; Treas Intnl Clb; Key Clb; Sec Sr Cls; Var Crs Cntry; Var Socr; Var Swmmng; Rtry Yth Ldrshp; Natl Cncl Tchrs Of Englsh Cntst; Head Cnslr San Diegp Police Dept Sfty Ptrl Camp; Intl Rltns.

CARRANZA, ADELINA; Etiwanda HS; Etiwanda, CA; (4); 70/542; Rep Stu Cncl; Peer Counseling; Honor Band; Cal ST Long Beach; Pol Science.

CARRANZA, BESSY; Theodore Roosevelt HS; Los Angeles, CA; (2); 3/32; Girl Scts; Office Aide; Socr; Cit Awd; Prfct Atten Awd; Cnslrs Hnr Roll; UCSC; Med.

CARRANZA, JUAN C; Baldwin Park HS; Baldwin Park, CA; (1); Boy Scts; Bsktbl; Cit Awd; High Hon Roll; Hon Roll; Prfct Atten Awd; JV Badminton Tm; Comp Prgmr.

CARRANZA, LETICIA; Porterville HS; Porterville, CA; (3); Art Clb; Church Yth Grp; JA; Hon Roll; Sci Awd; Cap Ldrs; Med.

CARRANZA, PATRICIA; Grossmont HS; El Cajon, CA; (4); 29/400; Art Clb; English Clb; Sec French Clb; VP Math Clb; Orch; School Musical; Ed Lit Mag; Jr Cls; Sr Cls; Stu Cncl; UCSD; Med.

CARRASCO, JACQUELINE; Baldwin Park HS; Baldwin Park, CA; (2); Church Yth Grp; Teachers Aide; Orch; High Hon Roll; Hon Roll; Prfct Atten Awd; Upward Bound Acad & Smmr Prog; Heywanetts Club; Pre-Law.

CARRASCO, JOSE L; Rosemead HS; San Gabriel, CA; (3); FCA; Intnl Clb; Thesps; School Play; Variety Show; JV Var Ftbl; JV Trk; Hon Roll; CA Schlstc Fed; Outstndng Achvt Sci; USC.

CARRASCO, MARIA N; Tranquillity Union HS; San Joaquin, CA; (3); SADD; Rptr Nwsp; JV Bsktbl; Socr; JV Tennis; Hon Roll; MECHA Clb; Aeronautics.

CARRAWAY, JENEA; Narbonne HS; Harbor City, CA; (2); Church Yth Grp; Cmnty Wkr; French Clb; Pep Clb; Pep Band; Stage Crew; Rep Frsh Cls; Rep Soph Cls; Cheerldng; Prfct Atten Awd; Howard U; Med.

CARREJO, GABE G; Summerville HS; Tuolumne, CA; (3); 5/140; FCA; Quiz Bowl; Ski Clb; Spanish Clb; Teachers Aide; VP Sr Cls; Treas Stu Cncl; Var Capt Bsbl; Var Capt Bsktbl; Hon Roll; GSE Geom; Asst Var Vllybl Coach; Var Bsktbl; Bus Mgmt.

CARREKER, CEZANNE; Carson HS; Carson, CA; (2); Rptr Yrbk; JV Crs Cntry; Capt Trk; Hon Roll; CA ST Dominguez; Law.

CARRICK, SHERI; Yosemite Union HS; Coarsegold, CA; (3); Ed Yrbk; Hon Roll; CSF; Graphic Desgn.

CARRICO, JEFFREY; San Ramon Valley HS; San Ramon, CA; (3); 125/400; Band; Jazz Band; Mrchg Band; Orch; School Musical; Var Trk; Soc Manufacturing Engr; U Of CA Santa Barbara; Engr.

CARRIERE, ALISON; Willows HS; Glenn, CA; (4); 4/109; Church Yth Grp; Cmnty Wkr; FBLA; Key Clb; Service Clb; Ski Clb; Varsity Clb; Sec Frsh Cls; VP Jr Cls; Stu Cncl; CSF; N St Tnns Champs 89; St Marys; Comms.

CARRIERE, SHELLEY; Willows HS; Glenn, CA; (4); Am Leg Aux Girls St; VP Treas Church Yth Grp; FBLA; Key Clb; Letterman Clb; Ski Clb; Teachers Aide; VP Frsh Cls; Treas Soph Cls; Sec Jr Cls; Santa Clara U.

CARRILLO, ANDREW; Santa Clara HS; Oxnard, CA; (4); 16/176; Stu Cncl; JV Var Ftbl; Var Capt Socr; NHS; CSF; MIT; Math.

CARRILLO, CARLOS; Bell Gardens HS; Bell Gardens, CA; (2); 66/268; Church Yth Grp; Hon Roll; Cal ST Long Beach; Elec Engr.

CARRILLO, CARMEN H; Ocean View HS; Huntington Beach, CA; (3); Girl Scts; Pep Clb; Band; Jazz Band; Mrchg Band; Orch; Pep Band; Rep Frsh Cls; VP Stu Cncl; Score Keeper; Comp Pgmr.

CARRILLO, CARMEN O; Roosevelt HS; Los Angeles, CA; (3); Key Clb; Yrbk; Stu Cncl; Cheerldng; Powder Puff Ftbl; Hon Roll.

CARRILLO, DAPHNIE R; Notre Dame HS; San Jose, CA; (3); 21/90; Drama Clb; Hosp Aide; Intnl Clb; VP Soph Cls; High Hon Roll; NHS; Pres Acad Fit Awd; CSF; Commnctns.

CARRILLO, ILDI FONSO; Brawley Union HS; Brawley, CA; (3); 8/375; Church Yth Grp; Cmnty Wkr; Pres FBLA; Pep Clb; Treas Jr Cls; Stu Cncl; Hon Roll; CLYLC; RYLA; UC Los Angeles; Psych.

CARRILLO, LAURA M; Chaffey HS; Alta Loma, CA; (3); 15/650; Drill Tm; Flag Corp; High Hon Roll; Lulac; CSF; Ivy Chain; Psych.

CARRILLO, MARCOS; Selma HS; Selma, CA; (2); 66/257; Spanish Clb; Varsity Clb; Var Capt Crs Cntry; JV Socr; Var Trk; Hon Roll; Span.

CARRILLO, MARIA LAURA; Brawley Union HS; Brawley, CA; (4); AFS; Church Yth Grp; Cmnty Wkr; Dance Clb; Latin Clb; Letterman Clb; Pep Clb; Spanish Clb; SADD; Band; Outstndng Dancer Awd; UC San Diego; Intl Bus.

CARRILLO, MARITZA; St Joseph HS; Bell Gardens, CA; (3); Cmnty Wkr; Science Clb; Spanish Clb; Hon Roll; St Schlr; UCSJ & Untd Colors Of St Joseph Clb; UCLA; Bus Admin.

CARRILLO, MICHELLE A; Central Union HS; El Centro, CA; (2); Church Yth Grp; Cmnty Wkr; Rep Frsh Cls; Cert Chstn Ldrshp Skills; Chrch Muscl; U Of San Diego; Psych.

CARRILLO, NORMA; Tulare Western HS; Tulare, CA; (3); Dance Clb; Spanish Clb; Capt Color Guard; Pres Sr Cls; Hon Roll; Cls Prncss; Comp Bus.

CARRILLO, RUDY; Coachella Valley HS; Coachella, CA; (2); Church Yth Grp; VICA; Golf; Tennis; Acad Exclince Awd Mech Drawng; Acad Achvt Tnns Awd; Draftng.

CARRILLO, RUTH M; J Eugene Mc Ateer HS; San Francisco, CA; (4); Cmnty Wkr; Latin Clb; Crs Cntry; Trk; Hon Roll; Pres Acad Fit Awd; Engl Acad Achvt; UC Berkeley; Commnctns.

CARRILLO, TINA M; El Toro HS; El Toro, CA; (4); 57/514; Quiz Bowl; Scholastic Bowl; Teachers Aide; Hist Band; Mrchg Band; Swmmng; High Hon Roll; Hon Roll; Grls Lgu VP, Inter Clb Cncl Rep & Histrn; Cnty Acad Dcthln; UC Santa Cruz; Pltcl Sci.

CARRILLO, VANESSA D; Sacred Heart HS; Alhambra, CA; (3); Ski Clb; Stage Crew; Var Bsktbl; Hon Roll; Kiwanis Awd; Art/Tech Awd; Basic Art Awd; Engl Excllnc Awd; Obstetrics.

CARRILLO-JIMENEZ, RODOLFO; Carson HS; San Pedro, CA; (3); Computer Clb; German Clb; Science Clb; Rep Jr Cls; Rep Sr Cls; Rotary Awd; Natl Sci Fndtn; CA Schlrshp Fedrtn Member; Membr Amer Inst Aeronautics & Astrntcs; Aerospc Med.

CARRION, DEBBIE; Winters HS; Winters, CA; (4); AFS; Pres FBLA; Ski Clb; Pres Soph Cls; VP Sr Cls; JV Var Bsktbl; JV Vllybl; Hon Roll; CA Schlrshp Fed Sec, Treas; UCD; Intl Relations.

CARRION, KIM; Fall River JR-SR HS; Cassel, CA; (2); Art Clb; FBLA; Sec Soph Cls; Var L Crs Cntry; JV Trk; JV Vllybl; High Hon Roll; CSF; Yth To Yth Tn Ldr; CASC Dlgte.

CARRIZALES, MELINDA E; Kearny HS; San Diego, CA; (3); French Clb; Letterman Clb; SADD; Chorus; Off Jr Cls; Socr; Tennis; Hon Roll.

CARRIZOSA, KENNETH S; Glendale Adventist Acad; Los Angeles, CA; (4); 12/79; Band; Chorus; School Play; Yrbk; Off Jr Cls; Off Sr Cls; VP Stu Cncl; Hon Roll; Ntl Merit Schol; Bank Of Amer Plq Wnnr; Congrsnl Schl Ntl Yth Ldrs Conf Wash DC 90; Walla Walla Coll; Engr.

CARROLL, AMANDA J; Torrey Pines HS; Solana Beach, CA; (3); 74/457; Church Yth Grp; Hosp Aide; SADD; Nwsp; JV Swmmng; Co-Capt Vllybl; Hon Roll; Hnrs Gldn ST Exam Algbr I; CSF; Schlr Athlt.

CARROLL, BETH M; Mission College Prep; Shell Beach, CA; (2); Key Clb; Ed Yrbk; VP Frsh Cls; Var Capt Bsktbl; Powder Puff Ftbl; Var Capt Vllybl; High Hon Roll; Hon Roll; Frosh Hsty Awd; Math & Engl Awds; MVP Vllbl JV.

CARROLL, BONNIE J; Bonita Vista HS; Bonita, CA; (3); Office Aide; Teachers Aide; Hon Roll; Voice Dem Awd; Hnr Rl; Auto Racing; Southwestern CC; Engl Lit.

CARROLL, CHRISTOPHER P; Paramount HS; Paramount, CA; (3); Church Yth Grp; Cmnty Wkr; Letterman Clb; Red Cross Aide; Varsity Clb; Lit Mag; Var Swmmng; Outstndng Writers Awd; Schl Swmmng Record; Jr Var MVP Water Polo; CSULB; Ed.

CARROLL, JOHN R; Montgomery HS; Santa Rosa, CA; (2); Drama Clb; French Clb; Teachers Aide; School Play; Stage Crew; Phtg Rptr Yrbk; Intrml Bsbl; Intrml Bsktbl; Intrml Ftbl; L Var Golf; Natl Math Test; Lamp Of Knowledge Awd; CSF; AZ ST; Dentistry.

CARROLL, JULIE S; Mission College Prep; Shell Beach, CA; (3); Am Leg Aux Girls St; Treas Key Clb; Teachers Aide; Varsity Clb; Pres Soph Cls; Stu Cncl; Var Capt Bsktbl; Var Vllybl; High Hon Roll; Rotary Awd; Rlgn & Phys Ed Awds 88; Roz Ferrini Mem Awd 88; Stu Ldrshp Awd 90; Bus Mgmnt.

CARROLL, KATHERINE; Palisades HS; Pacific Palisades, CA; (3); Church Yth Grp; Off Soph Cls; Var L Sftbl; Hon Roll; NHS; Working Smmrs Day Camp Cnslr; Bus Adm.

CARROLL, MICHELLE; Santa Paula Union HS; Santa Paula, CA; (4); Church Yth Grp; Letterman Clb; Teachers Aide; Sec Stu Cncl; Var Score Keeper; Var Socr; Var Sftbl; Var Tennis; Hon Roll; Opt Clb Awd; Nrsng.

CARROLL, NICOLE J; Ventura HS; Ventura, CA; (4); Church Yth Grp; Service Clb; Spanish Clb; JV Var Bsktbl; Var Tennis; JV Trk; Gov Hon Prg Awd; High Hon Roll; Hon Roll; All Lg Plyrs Hnrb Mntn Bsktbl; Abilene Chrstn U; Ed.

CARROLL, RYAN; Fred C Beyer HS; Riverbank, CA; (3); Church Yth Grp; Science Clb; High Hon Roll; SADD; Socr; Nwsp; Key Clb; Church Choir; Cit Awd; Hon Roll; Acad Dcthln; CA Poly; Blgcl Sci.

CARROLL, SARAH E; Orange Glen HS; Fallbrook, CA; (3); 1/458; French Clb; FFA; Key Clb; JV Capt Tennis; NHS; HOBY Ldrshp Cnfrnc 89; Vly Forge Ldrshp Cnfrnc 90; Mst Vlbl Plyr Awd Tnns 88-89; Schlr Ath Awd 87-89.

CARROLL, TOM; Hayward HS; Hayward, CA; (1); Church Yth Grp; Band; Jazz Band; Mrchg Band; Pep Band; Pres Frsh Cls; Pres Soph Cls; JV Ftbl; Var Socr; Hon Roll; Music.

CARRON, SHELLEY M; Bonita HS; La Verne, CA; (4); French Clb; Teachers Aide; Chorus; Hon Roll; U Of La Verne; Ed.

CARRON-ROWE, ANDY P; Oak Grove HS; San Jose, CA; (2); Computer Clb; Letterman Clb; Red Cross Aide; Ski Clb; Var L Bsbl; Var L Socr; Hon Roll; Prfct Atten Awd; Bus.

CARROZZO, ERIC L; West HS; Torrance, CA; (1); Aud/Vis; Drama Clb; Teachers Aide; Cit Awd; Yth Cncl Pres; Comp Pgmr.

CARRUTHERS, ANN L; St Joseph HS; Long Beach, CA; (3); Church Yth Grp; Hon Roll; Park Vllybl & Bsktbl Teams; Snow Skiing; Acctg.

CARRUTHERS, JULIE A; Palm Desert HS; Rancho Mirage, CA; (4); 8/319; Church Yth Grp; French Clb; Key Clb; Model UN; SADD; Teachers Aide; School Play; Ed Yrbk; Crs Cntry; Trk; CSF; Sr Rep 89-90 CSF; Interact; U Of CA Santa Cruz; Astrnmy.

CARRUTHERS, TONY S; St Francis HS; Altadena, CA; (2); Cmnty Wkr; Pep Clb; Spanish Clb; Rep Frsh Cls; JV L Bsktbl; Hon Roll; NEDT Awd; Pres Acad Fit Awd; Spanish NHS; Screen Actors Guild; Acad Hall Of Fame; Duke; Med.

CARSEL, JENNIFER R; San Luis Obispo HS; San Luis Obispo, CA; (2); Intnl Clb; Ski Clb; SADD; Hon Roll; Outdoors Clb; UCLA; Law.

CARSON, AUDRA L; Valley Christian HS; Downey, CA; (2); Church Yth Grp; Drill Tm; Rep Jr Cls; Stu Cncl; Bsktbl; JV Var Cheerldng; Camper Ldrshp Trng.

CARSON, CHARISSA J; Grossmont HS; La Mesa, CA; (1); Church Yth Grp; Debate Tm; Math Clb; Spanish Clb; Orch; Cit Awd; Hon Roll; Pres Acad Fit Awd; Piano Player/Hgh Recommendtn; Hrns Math/Wrld Hstry/Engl; UCLA; Poli Sci.

CARSON, DAVID; Arcadia HS; Arcadia, CA; (3); Church Yth Grp; German Clb; JV Swmmng; Wtr Polo; AFA; Pilot.

CARSON, DENISE S; Beaumont HS; Beaumont, CA; (1); Hosp Aide; Math Clb; Science Clb; Band; Mrchg Band; Pep Band; Rep Yrbk; Hon Roll; UCLA; Physician.

CARSON, MICHAEL J; Colfax HS; Meadow Vista, CA; (4); 4-H; FBLA; Teachers Aide; JV Trk; JV Wt Lftg; 4-H Awd; Hon Roll; Woodleaf Cnslr; ROP Creer W/Children; Sierra Coll; Elem Educ.

CARSWELL, ALTON C; Atwater HS; Winton, CA; (2); Spanish Clb; SADD; Band; Mrchg Band; High Hon Roll; Prfct Atten Awd; Falconcrest Awd 6 Times; UCLA; Med.

CARTAGENA, CARMEN M; Lindsay HS; Lindsay, CA; (2); Drama Clb; SADD; Off Frsh Cls; Stat Bsktbl; Stat Swmmng; Hon Roll; Teen Work 90; Tulare Co Atac Force; Peer Cnslr; Laverne U; Bus Admin.

CARTER, ALYSSA B; Lakewood SR HS; Lakewood, CA; (3); Church Yth Grp; German Clb; School Musical; Off Soph Cls; Hon Roll; NHS; Dance Tm Co-Capt/Capt; Woodbury U; Inter Dsgn.

CARTER, ANGELA A; Tennyson HS; Hayward, CA; (3); ROTC; Cit Awd; High Hon Roll; VICA Clb; Bus.

CARTER, APRIL; Exeter Union HS; Farmersville, CA; (1); FFA; Chorus; Stage Crew; Vllybl; Hon Roll; Schl Bd Outstndng Achvmnt Awd Stu Mnth; Stanford; Psychtrst.

CARTER, BLAYNE A; Westlake HS; Westlake Vlg, CA; (2); Drama Clb; SADD; School Play; JV Tennis; High Hon Roll; Hon Roll; Pres Acad Fit Awd; CSF; Interact Clb.

CARTER, BRETT; Napa HS; Napa, CA; (2); 10/400; Swing Chorus; High Hon Roll; Church Yth Grp; Chorus; Socr; Tennis; Swmmng; Key Clb; Ntl Merit Ltr; Cmnty Wkr; Schl Imprvmnt Pgm Cncl; Chm Sr Tea Cmmtte; Bus.

CARTER, BRIAN S; Arcadia HS; Arcadia, CA; (3); 100/650; Pres Church Yth Grp; Cmnty Wkr; Letterman Clb; Var Swmmng; Hon Roll; NHS; Pres Acad Fit Awd; Var Water Polo; Chrch Hndbll Chr; Chem.

CARTER, CARRIE; Bishop Union HS; Bishop, CA; (4); 3/150; Sec AFS; Am Leg Aux Girls St; Church Yth Grp; Pres 4-H; French Clb; Letterman Clb; Pep Clb; Ski Clb; Speech Tm; Church Choir; Qn Of Inyo, Mono & Alpine Cnty Fair 90; U CA Santa Barbara; Educ.

CARTER, CARRIE R; Golden West HS; Visalia, CA; (2); Hon Roll; Academic Letters; English.

CARTER, CHRIS; West Valley Christian Schl; Winnetka, CA; (2); Drama Clb; Band; Drm Mjr(t); Mrchg Band; Davis U; Vet Med.

CARTER, CHRISTOPHER G; Hesperia HS; Hesperia, CA; (2); Church Yth Grp; ROTC; Spanish Clb; Cit Awd; High Hon Roll; Cnslr 6th Grd Eclgy Cmp; CSF; Awd HS 5th Annl Creative Wrtng Celbrtn; Christ College Irvine; Educ Dir.

CARTER, CHRISTY A; St Francis HS; Santa Clara, CA; (4); Church Yth Grp; Intnl Clb; Service Clb; SADD; Band; High Hon Roll; Hon Roll; Radio Clb Music Dir; Envrnmnt Clb; Amnsty Intl; San Francisco ST.

CARTER, CRYSTAL; Pines HS; Santa Rosa, CA; (3); Church Yth Grp; FFA; Teachers Aide; Chorus; JV Vllybl; Hon Roll; FFA Hnrb Mntn; UC Davis; Vet Med.

CARTER, CRYSTAL S; Apple Valley SR HS; Apple Valley, CA; (3); FFA; Hair Stylst.

CARTER, DESMOND; Bellflower HS; Compton, CA; (1); Boy Scts; Church Yth Grp; Band; Church Choir; Mrchg Band; School Musical; Bsktbl; Trk; Cit Awd; Hon Roll; Mst Improved Stu Of Week; UNLV Rebels; Engr.

CARTER, ERIC; Beverly Hills HS; Van Nuys, CA; (4); Debate Tm; NFL; VP Spanish Clb; Speech Tm; Nwsp; Rep Soph Cls; Ntl Merit SF; UC Berkeley.

CARTER, ERIC; Calvary Chapel HS; Santa Ana, CA; (2); Church Yth Grp; JV Bsktbl; JV Vllybl; Skimboarding, Surfing; UCI; Theology.

CARTER, GINN E; Bret Harte Union HS; Murphys, CA; (2); JV Vllybl; Wt Lftg; High Hon Roll; Hon Roll; Campus Clb; Friday Nite Live; Lib Arts.

CARTER, JASON L; Fontana HS; Fontana, CA; (3); Service Clb; Church Yth Grp; School Play; Phtg Yrbk; Cert Scuba Diver; Cal Poly Pomona; Arch.

CARTER, JEFF C; Paradise HS; Paradise, CA; (3); 23/236; Church Yth Grp; Letterman Clb; Rptr Nwsp; Trk; High Hon Roll; Hon Roll; Ski Team; CSF; Chico ST; Bus.

CARTER, JENNIFER L; Big Pine HS; Big Pine, CA; (3); Pres Girl Scts; Ski Clb; Spanish Clb; Crs Cntry; Grgn Lang; Silver Awd; San Diego ST U; Nursing.

CARTER, JUINA R; Skyline HS; Oakland, CA; (4); Sec Boy Scts; Church Yth Grp; Hosp Aide; Office Aide; Teachers Aide; Chorus; Orch; Pres Schlr; Golden Gate Algebra Awd 87; Law Exploxer Post Awd 88; UC Berkeley; Poltcl Sci.

CARTER, JULIE A; Westridge Schl; South Pasadena, CA; (4); Hosp Aide; Sec Service Clb; Spanish Clb; Drill Tm; Rep Soph Cls; VP Stu Cncl; Var Capt Bsktbl; Var Sftbl; Var Capt Tennis; Ntl Merit Ltr; Cum Laude Soc Inductee; Drtmth Clb Bk Awd; LEAD Pgm-Bus U Of MD Smmr Pgm; Bio.

CARTER, KIMBANISHA L; East Union HS; Manteca, CA; (1); Scholastic Bowl; Church Choir; Trk; Wt Lftg; Cit Awd; High Hon Roll; UC Davis; Vet.

CARTER, LAUREL MARIE; Marysville HS; Marysville, CA; (4); 1/194; Church Yth Grp; Debate Tm; Letterman Clb; NFL; School Play; Rep Stu Cncl; JV Bsktbl; Var Mgr(s); Powder Puff Ftbl; Swmmng; Campfire; CA Schlrshp Fed Treas; Natural Hstry Clb Pres; Exchange Clb Stu Of Yr Dist Wnnr; Humboldt ST U; Bio Sci.

CARTER, LEE AARON; Capital Christian HS; Placerville, CA; (3); Church Yth Grp; JV Bsbl; Var Ftbl; Hon Roll; MVP Ftbl; Sierra Coll; Arch.

CARTER, LISA M; Marysville HS; Marysville, CA; (1); 1/225; Church Yth Grp; Band; Drm Mjr(t); Mrchg Band; Pep Band; Swmmng; High Hon Roll; Rotary Awd; Campfire; Natural Hstry Clb.

CARTER, MARINA L; Cerritos HS; Cerritos, CA; (4); Teachers Aide; Jazz Band; Jazz Band Awd; Vrs Mrt Awds; Stu Yr; Fullerton Coll; Music.

CARTER, MEGAN; Archbishop Mitty HS; Santa Clara, CA; (2); 1/230.

CARTER, MICHAEL A; Vacaville HS; Vacaville, CA; (3); Bsktbl; Ftbl; Trk; Cit Awd; Hon Roll; Prfct Atten Awd; Merit Awd; Rec Golden ST Test; Amer Ed Assist Schlrshp; UC-DAVIS; Elec Engr.

CARTER, MIESHA L; King Drew Medical Magnet HS; Carson, CA; (3); Church Yth Grp; Pep Clb; Church Choir; Pep Band; School Play; Nwsp; Trk; Cit Awd; Hon Roll; Cal ST U Irvine; Pediatrics.

CARTER, MIKE R; Rim Of The World HS; Blue Jay, CA; (3); 59/259; L Var Bsbl; L Var Ftbl; Var Wt Lftg; Hon Roll; Golden St Exam For Geometry; Most Otstndng Running Back; Schlr Athlete; Engrng.

CARTER, NICOLE H; San Gorgonio HS; Highland, CA; (4); Church Yth Grp; German Clb; Teachers Aide; Hon Roll; NHS; Dangling Participles; CA ST San Bernardino; Law.

CARTER, OMOBISA M; Oakland HS; Oakland, CA; (2); Girl Scts; Hosp Aide; Cit Awd; Hon Roll.

CARTER, RE ANNE D; Calaveras HS; Glencoe, CA; (2); AFS; Art Clb; Var Letterman Clb; JV Pep Clb; Red Cross Aide; Varsity Clb; Sec Soph Cls; Stu Cncl; JV Cheerldng; JV Pom Pon; Jrnlsm.

CARTER, RICHARD J; East Bakersfield HS; Bakersfield, CA; (4); 8/398; Pres Chess Clb; JA; Pres Key Clb; Pres Math Clb; Co-Ed Math Tm; SADD; Hon Roll; Ntl Merit Ltr; Pres Acad Fit Awd; Natl Bicntnnl Cmptn Lcl & St; Acad Dcthln; CA Poly-San Luis Obispo; Engrg.

CARTER, RICHARD J; Mission Viejo HS; Mission Viejo, CA; (3); German Clb; Math Tm; Natl Beta Clb; NFL; JV Var Swmmng; High Hon Roll; NHS; Water Polo Team Jr Vrsty.

CARTER, RUBY R; Montclair HS; Montclair, CA; (1); Church Yth Grp; Girl Scts; Teachers Aide; Band; Church Choir; Drill Tm; Cit Awd; Hon Roll; Prfct Atten Awd; Cosmotologist.

CARTER, SANDRA; Palo Verde HS; Blythe, CA; (4); 25/157; 4-H; Teachers Aide; School Musical; School Play; Stage Crew; JV Cheerldng; 4-H Awd; Hon Roll; Voice Dem Awd; Grossmont Coll; Nurse.

CARTER, SHANNON C; Prospect HS; San Jose, CA; (1); Sci.

CARTER, STEVE B; Irvine HS; Irvine, CA; (1); Socr.

CARTWRIGHT, VANESSA M; Porterville HS; Porterville, CA; (4); 20/298; Church Yth Grp; Cmnty Wkr; French Clb; Office Aide; JV Capt Bsktbl; Var Capt Trk; Var Capt Vllybl; High Hon Roll; Pres Acad Fit Awd; CSF; Cap Mentoring Pgm; City Trk Team Asst Coach; U CA Fresno; Liberal Stds.

CARUSO, MICHAEL; San Fernando Valley Acad; Agua Dulce, CA; (3); Ski Clb; Varsity Clb; Acpl Chr; Band; Chorus; School Musical; School Play; Ed Yrbk; Off Jr Cls; Capt Var Vllybl; Loma Linda U.

CARUTHERS, BRENT; Palmdale HS; Palmdale, CA; (3); Letterman Clb; Spanish Clb; SADD; Teachers Aide; School Play; Off Jr Cls; Vllybl; High Hon Roll; Hon Roll; San Diego ST; Techncl Engrng.

CARVAJAL, CATHERINE; San Francisco University HS; San Francisco, CA; (4); Var Bsktbl; Var Sftbl; Var Vllybl; Badminton Tm No 1 Singles.

CARVAJAL, GUADALUPE; Nathaniel Narbonne HS; Harbor City, CA; (3); FHA; Key Clb; Hon Roll.

CARVAJAL, SOCORRO; Cajon HS; San Bernardino, CA; (2); Cert Rcgntn Frnch & Wrld Hstry.

CARVALHO, ADRIAN; Casa Grande HS; Petaluma, CA; (3); 66/250; Varsity Clb; JV Bsbl; Var L Ftbl; Hon Roll.

CARVALHO, ANA M; Turlock HS; Turlock, CA; (1); Church Yth Grp; Cmnty Wkr; Dance Clb; Teachers Aide; Chorus; Church Choir; Variety Show; Cit Awd; High Hon Roll; Hon Roll; Vet Med.

CARVALHO, ROBERT; Saint Paul HS; La Habra, CA; (3); Drama Clb; JCL; Band; Chorus; Church Choir; School Musical; Rep Jr Cls; High Hon Roll; NHS; Ntl Merit SF.

CARVER, CANDACE R; Apple Valley HS; Apple Valley, CA; (2); Spanish Clb; Nwsp; Jrnlsm.

CARVER, ERIK; Los Alamitos HS; Los Alamitos, CA; (3); Church Yth Grp; Cmnty Wkr; High Hon Roll; Hon Roll; Eclgy Clb Pres; CSF.

CARVER, HOLLY E; Kern Valley HS; Kernville, CA; (2); VP Sec 4-H; FFA; JV Bsktbl; Var Powder Puff Ftbl; Var L Trk; Hon Roll; Exchng Clb Awd; Med.

CARVER, LISA; Chino HS; Chino, CA; (3); Church Yth Grp; Pep Clb; SADD; Stu Cncl; JV Var Cheerldng; Var Powder Puff Ftbl; JV Swmmng; Cit Awd; High Hon Roll; Hon Roll; Princps Honor Rl; Silver Spur Nom; Stdnts Who Excel Math And Histry.

CARVER, RICHARD P; Del Campo HS; Carmichael, CA; (1); 20/461; Boy Scts; Chess Clb; ROTC; SADD; Band; Color Guard; Drill Tm; Mrchg Band; Hon Roll; Outstndng Fresh Cadet AFJROTC Ca-863; Bronze ROTC Mdl Sons Of Amer Revolution; CA Schlrshp Fed; Annapolis; Aerospace Sci.

CARVER, TERRI; Geyserville HS; Geyserville, CA; (4); 4/20; Am Leg Aux Girls St; Cmnty Wkr; Hosp Aide; SADD; Teachers Aide; Drill Tm; Yrbk; Off Jr Cls; Off Sr Cls; Stu Cncl; Santa Rosa JC; Resource Spclst.

CARY, LAURA; Reedley HS; Reedley, CA; (3); French Clb; FBLA; German Clb; Intnl Clb; Pep Clb; SADD; Yrbk; Cheerldng; Hon Roll; Prfct Atten Awd; Santa Cruz; Animal Sci.

CASALMAN, STEPHANIE C; Fontana HS; Fontana, CA; (3); Pres Pep Clb; Orch; Cheerldng; High Hon Roll; Prfct Atten Awd; CSF; Z Clb; Acad Gld Mdlst; Bus Achvt Awd Comp Sci; UCLA; Pedtrcn.

CASARAY, CHRISTINA; San Lorenzo HS; San Lorenzo, CA; (1); Church Yth Grp; Yrbk; JV Cheerldng; Var Pom Pon; Trk; Comp Oper.

CASAREZ, KRIS V; Glendale HS; Glendale, CA; (4); Drama Clb; Ski Clb; SADD; School Play; Sftbl; Schlrshp LAMADD; Pals Schlrshp; Most Inspirational Player For Softball 90; Grip/Gaffer.

CASAS, GUSTAVO; Garfield HS; Los Angeles, CA; (2); Cit Awd; Prfct Atten Awd; CSF; UC Santa Cruz; Accntnt.

CASAS, LEOBARDO; Fontana HS; Fontana, CA; (2); Wt Lftg.

CASAS, LUIS F; Montgomery HS; San Diego, CA; (2); Var Socr.

CASAS, NORMA; Chula Vista HS; National City, CA; (2); Church Yth Grp; Pep Clb; Teachers Aide; Perfect Attendance; UCSD; Physcn.

CASAS, SERGIO; Blair HS; Pasadena, CA; (1); Pasadena City Coll; Arch.

CASAYSAYAN, RONALD R; Antelope Valley HS; Lancaster, CA; (4); 22/570; Chess Clb; VP Church Yth Grp; Computer Clb; Spanish Clb; Church Choir; Socr; Cit Awd; High Hon Roll; NHS; Pres Acad Fit Awd; Loyola Marymount U; Bus Admin.

CASCERES, BYRON; Bellermine Jefferson HS; Burbank, CA; (1); Var Tennis; Cit Awd; Hon Roll; NHS; Hnrs At Entrnc Bell Jeff; Spcl Rcgntn Exmplry Bhvr Drng Actvts; Acdmc Hnr Awd Rbbns 89, 90; USC; Bus.

CASCIO, ANGELA M; Acad Of Our Lady Of Peace; Bonita, CA; (2); Score Keeper; Hon Roll; Christian Yth Theater & Crew; Piano; CSF; Teacher.

CASE, JEANINE M; Glendora HS; Glendora, CA; (3); Church Yth Grp; Teachers Aide; JV Capt Bsktbl; Hon Roll; Vrsty Badmntn; Hnr Grd; Nurse.

CASE, JEFF N; Ventura HS; Ventura, CA; (3); Church Yth Grp; JV L Ftbl; Wt Lftg; JV L Wrstlng; High Hon Roll; Hon Roll; 2nd Pl Amercnsm Essay Cont; U Of CA San Diego; Med.

CASE, SEAN; Tomales HS; Inverness, CA; (3); Drama Clb; Ski Clb; Jazz Band; Mrchg Band; Pep Band; School Play; Treas Stu Cncl; Ftbl; Wt Lftg; Hon Roll; Engrng.

CASE, STEVEN; Novato HS; Novato, CA; (1); Church Yth Grp; Band; Jazz Band; Mrchg Band; Diving; Swmmng; Hon Roll; Water Polo V.

CASERMAN, KAREN; Hesperia HS; Hesperia, CA; (3); Church Yth Grp; FFA; Stu Cncl; Hon Roll; Deans List Awd; Cert Of Recognition Spnsh; Victory Valley Coll; Dntl Hygn.

CASEY, AMY D; Irvington HS; Fremont, CA; (2); 36/360; Art Clb; Church Yth Grp; French Clb; German Clb; Math Clb; Spanish Clb; Stu Cncl; JV Var Bsktbl; JV Swmmng; JV Vllybl; REACH America; Mst Inspirational Bsktbl, Vllybl, Swmmng; UCLA; Phy.

CASEY, BRANDON A; St Francis HS; San Jose, CA; (1); 95/388; Boy Scts; Service Clb; Hon Roll; Philmont National Boy Scout Ranch Backpacking Trip Participant; Annapolis Naval Acad; Nvl Pilot.

CASEY, LISA; Archbiship Motty HS; Santa Clara, CA; (3); 1/255; Cmnty Wkr; Math Tm; Science Clb; SADD; Rptr Lit Mag; High Hon Roll; NHS; Pres Acad Fit Awd; Clscl Ballet; Envrnmnt Clb; CSF; Psych.

CASH, MATHEW; Golden West HS; Ivanhoe, CA; (4); Band; Jazz Band; Mrchg Band; Pep Band; Var Trk; Section Leader Saxaphones 3 Yrs; UC Davis; Civ Engr.

CASILLAS JR, ESTEBAN; Hilltop HS; Bonita, CA; (3); Church Yth Grp; Pep Clb; SADD; JV Ftbl; Var Golf; Var Trk; Real Est.

CASILLAS, ROBERT A; Hueneme HS; Oxnard, CA; (3); JV Crs Cntry; Capt Var Tennis; JV Trk; High Hon Roll; Math, Engrng, Sci Achvt Club Stu Yr & Pres; Med.

CASILLAS, VIANEY; Downey HS; Downey, CA; (3); JA; Science Clb; SADD; Hon Roll; Prfct Atten Awd; Untd Latino Cncl-Outreach Pgm; U Long Beach ST; Elem Tchr.

CASINO, LEILA G; Holy Family HS; Los Angeles, CA; (3); Phtg Yrbk; Treas Jr Cls; Hist Stu Cncl; JV Var Bsktbl; JV Vllybl; Hon Roll; Prfct Atten Awd; U CA Irvine; Medcl Doctor.

CASMERO, CARLA M; Marina 15871 Springdale HS; Huntington Beach, CA; (2); Church Yth Grp; JA; Spanish Clb; JV Tennis; Hon Roll; AASA; AFS; Dance; U Of CA; Jrnlsm.

CASNATT, ANNE C; Atwater HS; Merced, CA; (3); Church Yth Grp; Cmnty Wkr; SADD; Teachers Aide; Church Choir; Crs Cntry; Score Keeper; Merced Coll; Tchr.

CASPERS, MEGAN; Oroville HS; Oroville, CA; (3); 7/259; GAA; Intnl Clb; Key Clb; SADD; Off Soph Cls; Cheerldng; Capt Powder Puff Ftbl; Var L Socr; Var L Trk; High Hon Roll.

CASS, ERIN D; Novato HS; Novato, CA; (2); Church Yth Grp; French Clb; ROTC; Band; Mrchg Band; Swmmng; Hon Roll; CMEA Band Competition; UC Davis; Law.

CASS, GREG T; Torry Pines HS; Rancho Santa Fe, CA; (3); Boy Scts; Ed Nwsp; Treas Jr Cls; Stu Cncl; Capt Var Ftbl; Var Socr; Var Trk; Pres Wt Lftg; High Hon Roll; Rotary Awd; CA Schlrshp Fed Sealbearer; High Hnrs CA Golden St Exam Algebra, Geom; Ivy League Coll; Bus.

CASSADAY, SUZANNE L; Redwood HS; Visalia, CA; (2); 35/396; Church Yth Grp; Spanish Clb; SADD; Band; Mrchg Band; Pep Band; Ed Nwsp; Score Keeper; High Hon Roll; CSF; Acad Lttr; Elem Ed.

CASSELL, DAMON; Marina HS; Huntington Bch, CA; (4); 141/505; Boy Scts; Cmnty Wkr; Ski Clb; Ftbl; JV Capt Socr; Wt Lftg; Mst Imprfd Stu Awd; OCC; Geology.

CASSEM, JUDITH D; Canyon Springs HS; Moreno Valley, CA; (2); 3/420; Church Yth Grp; English Clb; Hosp Aide; Spanish Clb; Vllybl; High Hon Roll; Prfct Atten Awd; Pres Acad Fit Awd; Gymnstcs; Amer Math Exam; Sci.

CASSIDY, JANET A; John W North HS; Riverside, CA; (2); Band; Mrchg Band; Pep Band; Var Socr; Hon Roll; 1st Team 3rd Pl Sccr 89-90; MVP Sccr Team; Art.

CASSIDY, JASON; South Bay Christian HS; Sunnyvale, CA; (1); Boy Scts; Natl Beta Clb; Stage Crew; Bsbl; Bsktbl; Socr; Sftbl; Cit Awd; NHS; Prfct Atten Awd; Stanford-Berkley.

CASSIDY, ROBERT C; San Pasqual Acad; S Gate, CA; (4); 5/50; Cmnty Wkr; Ski Clb; Treas Soph Cls; Treas Sr Cls; Bsktbl; Gym; Capt Sftbl; Capt Vllybl; High Hon Roll; CA Schlrshp Fdrtn; CA ST U, Long Bch; Med.

CASSITY, DUSTY; Madison HS; San Diego, CA; (2); 98/359; Ski Clb; Variety Show; JV Capt Cheerldng; Gym; Powder Puff Ftbl; Mbr Scnd Rnkd JV Chr Sqd CA; Prttm Mbr Vrsty Chr Sqd; Prtm Mbr Vrsty Chr Sqd San Diego Cnty Chmpns.

CASSMAN, CRYSTAL JOY; Kelseyville HS; Lakeport, CA; (3); 7/100; Boy Scts; Letterman Clb; Office Aide; Pep Clb; Ski Clb; SADD; Varsity Clb; Chorus; Drill Tm; Pres Soph Cls; UC San Diego.

CASTAGNINI, TINA; Las Lomas HS; Walnut Creek, CA; (1); 13/267; Church Yth Grp; French Clb; Band; Nwsp; JV Bsktbl; JV Sftbl; JV Vllybl; High Hon Roll; Hon Roll; Phy.

CASTANEDA, AMBER; Eisenhower HS; Rialto, CA; (2); Dance Clb; Letterman Clb; Acpl Chr; Chorus; Stu Cncl; Cheerldng; Gym; Cit Awd; Hon Roll; Prfct Atten Awd; Math.

CASTANEDA, BRIAN T; Daniel Murphy Catholic HS; Los Angeles, CA; (4); 21/87; Cmnty Wkr; Chorus; Sec Sr Cls; Capt Var Vllybl; Hon Roll; 89-90 Archdiocesan Christian Srvce Awd; Religion Dept Awd; Vlybl Coachs Awd; U Southern CA; Accntng.

CASTANEDA, CARLA P; Ripon HS; Ripon, CA; (3); 2/120; Math Tm; High Hon Roll; Hon Roll; Hnrs Golden St Exam Gem 89; CSF 87-90; Clericl Job Locl Bus; Finance.

CASTANEDA, CATHY; West HS; Bakersfield, CA; (2); Intnl Clb; Spanish Clb; JV Cheerldng; Hon Roll; MESA; Pedtrcs.

CASTANEDA, ELISA; Strathmore Union HS; Strathmore, CA; (4); #2 In Class; Church Yth Grp; FFA; Letterman Clb; Stu Cncl; Bsktbl; Pom Pon; Trk; Vllybl; High Hon Roll; Val; Porterville Coll; Medcl.

CASTANEDA, ELIZABETH; Mountain View HS; El Monte, CA; (2); Cit Awd; High Hon Roll; Hon Roll; FIDM; Fshn Dsgnr.

CASTANEDA, GUADALUPE F; Saint Anthony HS; Carson, CA; (2); Cmnty Wkr; Letterman Clb; Spanish Clb; Var Sftbl; JV Vllybl; Hon Roll; CSF; UCLA; Govt.

CASTANEDA, HOLLY K; Pasadena HS; Altadena, CA; (1); Prfct Atten Awd; Acad Performance & Excllnc; Cal ST; Pediatrics.

CASTANEDA, JASON T; East Bakersfield HS; Bakersfield, CA; (2); Band; Mrchg Band; Pep Band; JV Bsktbl; JV Ftbl; Wt Lftg; Cit Awd; High Hon Roll; Alg Golden St Exam Hnrs; Outstndng Hlth Careers Engl & Bio Stu; UCLA; Law.

CASTANEDA, MARTHA E; Live Oak HS; Live Oak, CA; (3); Drama Clb; FHA; Office Aide; VP Spanish Clb; SADD; Treas Frsh Cls; Pres Soph Cls; Bsktbl; Trk; Hon Roll; Publicity Coord 89-90; Sr Class Yell Ldr 90; Assoc Stu Body Pres 90; Public Rel.

CASTANEDA, MARTHA R; Ygnacio Valley HS; Concord, CA; (3); Church Yth Grp; Cmnty Wkr; Girl Scts; Latin Clb; Varsity Clb; Acpl Chr; Chorus; Church Choir; Color Guard; Mrchg Band; Prncpl Hnr Stu; Mst Val Singer Choir Awd; Air Frc Acad; Sci.

CASTANEDA, REBECCA; Tulare Union HS; Tulare, CA; (4); Hosp Aide; Band; Color Guard; Flag Corp; Mrchg Band; Hon Roll; Prfct Atten Awd; Spanish NHS; Outstndng Bus Stu Dec 89; Hosptl Vlntr; Bus.

CASTANEDA, ROCIO; Mt Diablo HS; Concord, CA; (3); Latin Clb; Spanish Clb; SADD; Sec Jr Cls; Stu Cncl; Mt Diablo Mgr; Sacramento ST U; Bus.

CASTANEDA, SYLVIA; Central Union HS; El Centro, CA; (3); Hon Roll; U Of CA; Elem Ed.

CASTANEDA, YVETTE D; Brawley Union HS; Brawley, CA; (1); Band; Mrchg Band; Cheerldng.

CASTANO, IZTLA R; Chula Vista HS; National City, CA; (2); Girl Scts; Spanish Clb; Band; JSA; Sngng; U IL; Archlgst.

CASTANON, FRANCISCO; Lindsay HS; Lindsay, CA; (3); 5/140; Am Leg Boys St; Spanish Clb; Nwsp; Yrbk; Bausch & Lomb Sci Awd; Hon Roll; Acad Decathalon.

CASTANON, GLORIA; Napa HS; Napa, CA; (1); Church Yth Grp; Key Clb; Yrbk; Off Frsh Cls; Pacific Union Coll; Nurse.

CASTANON, GREYS; John H Francis Polytechnic HS; North Hollywood, CA; (3); Pres VICA; Ed Yrbk; High Hon Roll; Ind Arts Awd; Medallion Awd; LA Vally Coll; Pilotry.

CASTEEL, KRISTY J; Nevada Union HS; Grass Valley, CA; (1); Church Yth Grp; French Clb; Acpl Chr; Chorus; Church Choir; Vcl Prfrmng Music.

CASTEEL, REBECCA; Atwater HS; Winton, CA; (2); SADD; Sclgy.

CASTELBLANCO, CECI; Alameda HS; Alameda, CA; (2); 21/279; Art Clb; School Musical; Off Soph Cls; Stu Cncl; Cheerldng; Hon Roll; Jujitsu; Unity Clb; ESL Class Aide; CO U Boulder.

CASTELLANO, JUANITA B; Golden West HS; Visalia, CA; (2); Latin Clb; Kiwanis Awd; Santa Barbara; Bus.

CASTELLANOS, ALMA; East Union HS; Manteca, CA; (3); 18/315; Church Yth Grp; Letterman Clb; Capt Varsity Clb; Yrbk; VP Jr Cls; Var Capt Vllybl; Cit Awd; High Hon Roll; Hon Roll; Prfct Atten Awd; Cal Poly; Engr.

CASTELLANOS, AMBER; Lakewood SR HS; Lakewood, CA; (4); 20/750; Color Guard; Ed Yrbk; Sec Jr Cls; VP Stu Cncl; Stat Bsbl; Powder Puff Ftbl; NHS; Pres Acad Fit Awd; Spanish NHS; CSF; Acctng.

CASTELLANOS, EVE M; San Joaquin Memorial HS; Sanger, CA; (2); Debate Tm; Spanish Clb; Speech Tm; Nwsp; Hon Roll; Friday Night Live 9th & 10th; Step To College At Fresno State Univ; UC Berkely.

CASTELLANOS, FORTINO; Casa Grande HS; Santa Rosa, CA; (2); Hosp Aide; Ftbl; Socr.

CASTELLANOS, HECTOR S; Leuzinger HS; Lennox, CA; (2); 100/347; Church Yth Grp; Spanish Clb; Intrml Bsbl; Cit Awd; Hon Roll; Prfct Atten Awd; USC; Arch.

CASTELLANOS, MARCELA; Kingsburg HS; Kingsburg, CA; (2); FFA; Hon Roll; Fresno ST; Comp Prgmr.

CASTELLANOS, MARIA A; Leuzinger HS; Lennox, CA; (2); 1/400; Spanish Clb; Band; Mrchg Band; Off Frsh Cls; Cit Awd; Hon Roll; Prfct Atten Awd.

CASTELLANOS, RENE A; Skyline HS; Oakland, CA; (3); Computer Clb; Latin Clb; Intrml Bsbl; Intrml Sftbl; Cit Awd; Hon Roll; Folklore Dancing.

CASTELLANOS, VERONICA E; American HS; Union City, CA; (4); Debate Tm; French Clb; Model UN; Spanish Clb; Hon Roll; Prfct Atten Awd; Meml Schlsp 90; Golden St Exam Hnrs Geom 88; Bank Of America Achvmt Awd Cmptr Stud 90; Bus Acad Fremont; Acctg.

CASTELLANOZ, DANIEL; Tulare Western HS; Tulare, CA; (3); Church Yth Grp; Band; Church Choir; Jazz Band; Mrchg Band; Pep Band; Ftbl; Wrstlng; Hnr Band; Phonix Inst Of Tchnlgy; Drftsmn.

CASTER, LISA K; O'farrell SCPA HS; San Diego, CA; (4); 16/114; Pres Art Clb; Church Yth Grp; Library Aide; Cit Awd; Hon Roll; Pres Acad Fit Awd; Top 5% PSAT Tst; Dept Hnrs For Color & Dsgn; Frlnc Ilstr.

CASTER, PETER; Modesto HS; Modesto, CA; (4); Art Clb; Bus Profs of Am; FBLA; Intnl Clb; Math Clb; Math Tm; Q&S; Scholastic Bowl; Service Clb; Ed Nwsp; Stanford.

CASTERSON, MARCI C; Hanford Jt Union HS; Hanford, CA; (2); 68/521; Church Yth Grp; Cmnty Wkr; 4-H; Teachers Aide; Var L Crs Cntry; Var L Trk; Hon Roll; Chorus; Bsktbl; Gym; Twice Most Dedicated Cross Cntry Rnr; Twice Outstndng Dstnc Rnr Track; 1st Pl Wmns 2 Mi Smky Bear Run; UC Davis; Vet Sci.

CASTGLLANOS, JESUS; Lynwood HS; Lynwood, CA; (4); Key Clb; Intrml JV Ftbl; Intrml Vllybl; Intrml Wt Lftg; Kiki Camarena Case Is Very Important To Me; UCLA; Drug Enforcing Agent.

CASTILLO, A MIREYA; Bishop Amat HS; San Gabriel, CA; (4); 20/395; Ed Yrbk; Hon Roll; NHS; CA Schlrshp Fedrtn; Hstry.

CASTILLO, AILEEN A; Notre Dame HS; San Jose, CA; (3); 19/90; High Hon Roll; CSF; Cbn Ldr-Walden W Cmp; Engrng.

CASTILLO, ALICE H; Los Altos HS; Hacienda Hts, CA; (3); Art Clb; Church Yth Grp; Dance Clb; Pep Clb; Chorus; Church Choir; Drill Tm; Sec Sr Cls; Rep Stu Cncl; JV Cheerldng; Jr Cls Sr Prom Spclst; Bwlng Clb; Prdctn Choir; Arch-Desgn.

CASTILLO, ALMA ROSA; Montgomery HS; Santa Rosa, CA; (3); Teachers Aide; Friday Night Clb; Law.

CASTILLO, AMY A; Mater Dei HS; Santa Ana, CA; (3); Cmnty Wkr; Color Guard; Flag Corp; DAR Awd; Loyola Marymount; Bus.

CASTILLO, ANGELICA; Coachella Valley HS; Thermal, CA; (2); NFL; Speech Tm; Band; Mrchg Band; Orch; Pres Frsh Cls; Pres Soph Cls; Hon Roll; Opt Clb Awd; S CA Drumline Circuit; U Of CA-LOS Angeles; Atty.

CASTILLO, ARACELI; Sacred Heart Of Jesus HS; Los Angeles, CA; (3); 3/98; Rep Jr Cls; Pres Stu Cncl; NHS; Prfct Atten Awd; Natl Span Exm 2nd Pl 88 & 89.

CASTILLO, AURELYN; Jefferson HS; Daly City, CA; (2); Math Tm; Yrbk; Off Soph Cls; Mgr(s); Score Keeper; U Of CA San Diego; Bus Mgmt.

CASTILLO, BRANDON; Elk Grove HS; Park City, UT; (2); 19/700; Boy Scts; Bus Profs of Am; Church Yth Grp; Drama Clb; Letterman Clb; Speech Tm; JV Ftbl; Var Swmmng; High Hon Roll; Jr NHS; CA Schlrshp Fed; Acad Ltr; Stanford; Cmmnctns.

CASTILLO, CESAR R; Castle Park HS; Chula Vista, CA; (1); 30/614; French Clb; SDSU; Zoology.

CASTILLO, CHARLES P; Abraham Lincoln HS; San Jose, CA; (4); 41/256; Spanish Clb; Hon Roll; Acadmc Dcthln Team; Natl Bicentennial Comptn St Fnls; Santa Clara Cnty Yth Expo 1st & 2nd Awds Wrtng; Elizabethtown Coll; Cmmnctns.

CASTILLO, CRISTINE C; Immaculate Conception Acad; San Francisco, CA; (2); Church Yth Grp; French Clb; GAA; Pep Clb; Chorus; Nwsp; Lit Mag; Hon Roll; Cert Achvt Russian Peope Friends Or Foes; Astrophysical Engr.

CASTILLO, FEL; Gilroy HS; Gilroy, CA; (3); 1/450; AFS; JV Crs Cntry; Var Trk; High Hon Roll; Prfct Atten Awd; High Hnrs Golden St Exam Geom, Algebra I&II; Stu Month Schltc Achvt 87-88; CSF Treas, VP; Med.

CASTILLO, FRANK; Montgomery HS; San Diego, CA; (2); Church Yth Grp; Band; Tennis; Cit Awd; High Hon Roll; Masonic Awd; Prfct Atten Awd; UCSD; Civil Engrng.

CASTILLO, ILIANA Y; Workman HS; San Bernardino, CA; (3); 102/268; Church Yth Grp; GAA; Church Choir; Drill Tm; Stage Crew; Powder Puff Ftbl; Score Keeper; Sftbl; Hon Roll; CA ST Fllrtn; Paralgl Stds.

CASTILLO, ISABEL; Santa Monica HS; Santa Monica, CA; (2); Band; Color Guard; Flag Corp; Mrchg Band; Orch; Enjoy Wrtng Poetry; UCLA Prtnrshp Pgm; UCLA; Med.

CASTILLO, JANET; Woodside HS; Redwood City, CA; (2); Cmnty Wkr; Latin Clb; Off Soph Cls; Cit Awd; Hon Roll; Prfct Atten Awd; Real Estate.

CASTILLO, JESSICA A; Sunset HS; Hayward, CA; (3); Var Cheerldng; English Clb; Hon Roll; Acad Achvt Awds; Chabot Coll; Dentstry.

CASTILLO, JESUS M; Abraham Lincoln HS; San Jose, CA; (4); 56/280; Pres Computer Clb; FHA; Rep Stu Cncl; Prfct Atten Awd; Fnlst Bicentenial Comp; San Jose ST U; Comp.

CASTILLO, JOE A; Eagle Rock HS; Los Angeles, CA; (2); Church Yth Grp; Jazz Band; Boy Scts; JV Bsbl; Law.

CASTILLO, JONATHAN C; Grant HS; Sacramento, CA; (3); Church Yth Grp; Drama Clb; Intnl Clb; Science Clb; Spanish Clb; Stu Cncl; CA ST U Sacramento; Radio-TV.

CASTILLO, JOSEPH N; Pasadena HS; Pasadena, CA; (4); 70/329; Cmnty Wkr; Acpl Chr; Band; Jazz Band; Mrchg Band; Orch; Pep Band; School Musical; Variety Show; Hon Roll; John Philip Sousa Awd; Faculty Hnrs Music; Tourn Roses Hnr Band 89-90; Pasadena CC; Music Ed.

CASTILLO, JUAN; Santa Paula Union HS; Santa Paula, CA; (2); 23/400; JV Ftbl; Capt JV Socr; JV Trk; High Hon Roll; Hon Roll; USC; Phy.

CASTILLO, KARLA ELIZABETH; Pasadena HS; Pasadena, CA; (2); Tennis; Hon Roll; CSF Clb Pres; Paralgl.

CASTILLO, KIM M; A A Stagg HS; Stockton, CA; (3); Cmnty Wkr; Dance Clb; Intnl Clb; Service Clb; SADD; Temple Yth Grp; Hon Roll; UC Davis Early Outreach Pgm; Delta JC; Zoology.

CASTILLO, LISA M; Anaheim HS; Anaheim, CA; (3); Teachers Aide; Cheerldng.

CASTILLO, LUZ M; Watsonville HS; Watsonville, CA; (2); 33/545; Pep Clb; JV Cheerldng; Hon Roll; Art.

CASTILLO, MARVIN; Madrane HS; San Rafael, CA; (3); Boy Scts; Off Jr Cls; High Hon Roll; Hon Roll; Joey Ciatti Achvmnt, Cnstnt Achvr Awds; Stu Of Mnth; U Of Honduras.

CASTILLO, PATRICIA M; San Benito HS; Hollister, CA; (3); Church Yth Grp; Trk; San Jose ST; Bus.

CASTILLO, RICARDO H; Chino HS; Chino, CA; (3); Computer Clb; School Play; JV Var Bsbl; Hon Roll; Prfct Atten Awd; Pres Acad Fit Awd; Ca ST U; Comp Prgmng.

CASTILLO, RICHARD R; Pater Noster HS; Los Angeles, CA; (3); #7 In Class; Church Yth Grp; Letterman Clb; Phtg Yrbk; VP Soph Cls; JV Var Bsktbl; Var Capt Vllybl; NHS; Med.

CASTILLO, ROBERT; Orosi HS; Orosi, CA; (3); Boy Scts; Church Yth Grp; Cmnty Wkr; Drama Clb; FFA; Letterman Clb; Spanish Clb; SADD; Varsity Clb; Band; Prom Chm; Frstry Tm; Ldrshp Clss; Columbia; Fire Sci.

CASTILLO, ROBERT A; Chula Vista HS; San Diego, CA; (1); Church Yth Grp; Service Clb; Pres Frsh Cls; JV Ftbl; JV Trk; Asian Fllwshp; CSF; Cal Poly San Luis Obispo; Engr.

CASTILLO, RODEL; Fremont HS; Sunnyvale, CA; (3); Band; Mrchg Band; JV Crs Cntry; Intrml Wt Lftg; JV Wrstlng; Wrkng Part-Time; Pre-Dentistry.

CASTILLO, ROSA A; Thomas Downey HS; Modesto, CA; (3); Cit Awd; Hon Roll; Prfct Atten Awd; Downey Knight Achvt Awd; Modesto JR Coll; Ped Nrs.

CASTILLO, ROSE; Liberty Union HS; Brentwood, CA; (3); French Clb; FHA; Intnl Clb; NFL; Pep Clb; Speech Tm; Var Cheerldng; Hon Roll; CSF; Friday Night Live; UCLA; Med.

CASTILLO, ROXANA E; Pinole Valley HS; Hercules, CA; (2); Hon Roll; Stanford; Pre-Law.

CASTILLO, RUBEN E; Schurr HS; Monterey Park, CA; (3); Boy Scts; Ftbl; Trk; Wt Lftg; Wrstlng; Fire Dept Explores-Capt; County Fire Acad Grad; Fire Fighter Paramedic.

CASTILLO, RUSSELL K; Cordova SR HS; Mather A F B, CA; (3); 89/467; Boy Scts; Church Yth Grp; Band; Mrchg Band; Pep Band; Off Frsh Cls; Trk; High Hon Roll; Ntl Merit SF; Civil Air Patrol.

CASTILLO, SHAROL; Saint Michaels HS; Los Angeles, CA; (4); 4-H; FBLA; Spanish Clb; Church Choir; Off Frsh Cls; 4-H Awd; High Hon Roll; NHS; Stu Mnth; Awd Math Dev Reading; CA ST; Bus Adm.

CASTILLO, SONYA I; Merced High North; Merced, CA; (2); Drama Clb; VP SADD; Acpl Chr; Chorus; Orch; Hon Roll; Peer Cnslng; Musc.

CASTILLO, TONY; Orosi HS; Orosi, CA; (3); Nwsp; Yrbk; Bus Programmer.

CASTILLO, XOCHITL; Santa Paula HS; Santa Paula, CA; (3); SADD; Jazz Band; Mrchg Band; Var Bsktbl; Var Socr; Var Sftbl; Var Vllybl; Cit Awd; Hon Roll; CSF; USC; Bus.

CASTILLON, LETICIA P; Westlake HS; Thousand Oaks, CA; (2); Church Yth Grp; Dance Clb; SADD; Chorus; Cit Awd; Hon Roll; Pres Acad Fit Awd; Int Dsgn.

CASTLE, CHADWICK B; Canyon Springs HS; Moreno Valley, CA; (4); 27/550; Church Yth Grp; Pres FBLA; Key Clb; Ski Clb; Band; Church Choir; Jazz Band; Mrchg Band; Pres Stu Cncl; Trk; 3rd Pl Entrprnship ST FBLA 89 & 2nd Pl 90; Prncpls Awd 90; PA U; Multntnl Finance.

CASTLE, JOHN; Bret Harte Union HS; Douglas Flat, CA; (1); 10/200; FFA; Var Wrstlng; High Hon Roll.

CASTLE, TAMMY; Inland Christian Schl; Rialto, CA; (3); 1/13; Church Yth Grp; Drama Clb; Hosp Aide; Speech Tm; Church Choir; School Musical; School Play; Variety Show; Pres Jr Cls; L Cheerldng; Recorded Record W/ Sngng Grp; Chrstn Character Awds; Loma Linda U; Nrsng.

CASTLE, TRACY A; Mt Carmel HS; San Diego, CA; (4); Art Clb; English Clb; German Clb; Key Clb; Pep Clb; Teachers Aide; Band; School Musical; School Play; Nwsp; Seattle U; Poly Sci.

CASTLEBERRY, ROBERT A; Seaside HS; Fort Ord, CA; (2); Boy Scts; Cmnty Wkr; ROTC; Mgr(s); Upward Bnd Notewrthy Stu Offc Asst; Arch.

CASTLES, KRISTIN D; Woodland HS; Woodland, CA; (2); Church Yth Grp; Cmnty Wkr; FBLA; FFA; Girl Scts; SADD; Band; Church Choir; Jazz Band; Mrchg Band; Handbell Choir; Music Ed.

CASTOR, GERRY; La Puente HS; La Puente, CA; (2); Key Clb; Band; Mrchg Band; Pep Band; Ftbl; Wt Lftg; Cit Awd; Prfct Atten Awd; Cal State Fullerton.

CASTRA, MARIA G; Wasco Union HS; Wasco, CA; (4); 42/180; Powder Puff Ftbl; High Hon Roll; Hon Roll; Migrant Clb VP; Tchrs Now & Tomorrow VP; CA ST Bakersfield; Bus Admin.

CASTRELLON, PATRICIA; San Fernando HS; Pacoima, CA; (3); Band; Mrchg Band; Powder Puff Ftbl; High Hon Roll; Hon Roll; Prfct Atten Awd; Band & Drill Tm Champ 88-90,City Champ,Perfrm Braillo Inst,Elks Clb,City Hall,Stdm,Mayor Of San Fran; UCLA; Bus Comm Advertzmnt.

CASTRILLO, PAULINE DOLORES; Golden West HS; Visalia, CA; (4); Sec FBLA; FHA; Band; Mrchg Band; Pep Band; Hon Roll; Coll Of The Sequoias; Bus.

CASTRILLON, HUMBERTO; Bishop Montgomery HS; Torrance, CA; (4); 5/354; Computer Clb; Key Clb; Hon Roll; Natl Hspnc Schlr Awds Pgm Semifnlst; CA Schlrshp Fdrtn; Mech Engrng.

CASTRO, AARON; Notre Dame HS; San Bernadino, CA; (1); 14/130; Church Yth Grp; Church Choir; Var L Swmmng; High Hon Roll; U Redlands Cmnty Schl Arts Mrt Awd Schlrshp 89-90; Harvard; Doctor.

CASTRO, ADRIAN EDGARDO; Don Bosco Tech Inst; Temple City, CA; (2); 1/211; Boy Scts; Church Yth Grp; JV Var Socr; High Hon Roll; NHS; NEDT Awd; Campus Ministry; JV Soccer Schlr Ath Awd; DBTI Excllnce Tech Rotation Awd; Harvey Mudd Coll; Engrng.

CASTRO, ALEXANDRA; Atascadero HS; Atascadero, CA; (2); Color Guard; Flag Corp; CA Poly U; Bus.

CASTRO, ANA L; Notre Dame Acad; Los Angeles, CA; (3); 29/130; Church Yth Grp; Cmnty Wkr; Science Clb; Spanish Clb; SADD; Cit Awd; Hon Roll; Prfct Atten Awd.

CASTRO, ANAMAIDA M; Central Union HS; Seeley, CA; (2); Church Yth Grp; Hon Roll; Cal Poly; Psych.

CASTRO, ANDREA D; Coachella Valley HS; Coachella, CA; (3); 25/436; Hosp Aide; Varsity Clb; VP Jr Cls; JV Capt Bsktbl; Score Keeper; Var Tennis; Hon Roll; Law.

CASTRO, ARTURO; St Paul HS; South Gate, CA; (3); 15/315; VP Debate Tm; Drama Clb; JCL; Treas Latin Clb; NFL; VP Speech Tm; Chorus; School Musical; School Play; Stage Crew; CA Schlrshp Fdrtn; Latin Natl Hnrs Scty; Natl Frnsc Lg Degree Excllnc; Crmnl Law.

CASTRO, BRENDA R; University HS; Los Angeles, CA; (2); Church Yth Grp; Stu Cncl; Fashion Designer.

CASTRO, CENIA X; International Studies Acad; San Francisco, CA; (3); French Clb; Hosp Aide; Latin Clb; Spanish Clb; Teachers Aide; Capt Sftbl; Hon Roll; Spanish NHS; Sprts Awds; UCB; Doctor.

CASTRO, CRISTINA M; Foothill HS; Bakersfield, CA; (2); Teachers Aide; Mrchg Band; JV Crs Cntry; JV Socr; Var L Tennis; Hon Roll; Mst Imprvd Plyr Tennis Team; Circle F Mrchng Band; Stanford; Comm.

CASTRO, DE ANNA L; Firebaugh HS; Mendota, CA; (3); 17/90; Art Clb; Church Yth Grp; Trk; Hon Roll; Ldrshp; Mecha Club; Law.

CASTRO, DIANA E; Oakdale HS; Oakdale, CA; (2); Crs Cntry; Hon Roll; Acad Awd; Law.

CASTRO, DONNA A; Sacred Heart Of Jesus HS; Los Angeles, CA; (3); School Play; Bausch & Lomb Sci Awd; High Hon Roll; NHS; Math Tutor; Aerosp Engrng.

CASTRO, EINJAR; Bishop Amat Memorial HS; Diamond Bar, CA; (3); Church Yth Grp; Cmnty Wkr; Med.

CASTRO, ELAINE O; Morse HS; San Diego, CA; (3); Yrbk; ASB Assoctd Stu Bdy; Elem Educ.

CASTRO, ELVIRA; Hamilton Acad Of Music; Los Angeles, CA; (2); Cmnty Wkr; Drama Clb; Hosp Aide; Letterman Clb; Chorus; Drill Tm; School Musical; School Play; Variety Show; Bsktbl; NASA Orbiter Tm; Stu Site Cncl Hamilton Acad Of Music; CA Yth Theatre; Bus.

CASTRO, ELZBY; March Mountain HS; Moreno Valley, CA; (3); SADD; Off Jr Cls; Bsktbl; Vllybl; Cit Awd; Hon Roll; Prfct Atten Awd; Stu Of Mnth Feb 90; Bnkng.

CASTRO, ESTELA; California HS; Whittier, CA; (2); JV Vllybl; Rio Hondo; Physician.

CASTRO, ESTHER M; Colton HS; Colton, CA; (1); Bus Profs of Am; Church Yth Grp; GAA; Rep Frsh Cls; JV Fld Hcky; Var Sftbl; JV Vllybl; Hon Roll; Lion Awd; Pres Acad Fit Awd; Future Ldrs Of Amer; Grls League; U Of Redlands; Stngrphr Crt.

CASTRO, EVELYN D; Palmdale HS; Palmdale, CA; (4); Debate Tm; Speech Tm; Rep Frsh Cls; Rep Soph Cls; Rep Jr Cls; Stu Cncl; Crs Cntry; Socr; Hon Roll; Pres Acad Fit Awd; Close Up; Running Club Secy; Antelope Vly Coll; Law.

CASTRO, JOSE F; Southwest HS; San Ysidro, CA; (4); Chess Clb; Hon Roll; San Diego ST U; Chem.

CASTRO, JOSE R; Eisenhower HS; Rialto, CA; (2); CA Poly; Arch.

CASTRO, JOSEPH; Oxnard HS; Oxnard, CA; (4); 24/441; Aud/Vis; English Clb; Key Clb; Library Aide; Library Aide; Science Clb; Rep Frsh Cls; Bsbl; Hon Roll; USC; Bus Admin.

CASTRO, KARRIE A; Santa Paula Union HS; Santa Paula, CA; (3); 42/242; SADD; Var Sftbl; Hon Roll; CA Interschlstc Fed-Southern Section & Acad Tm Hnrb Mntn; U Of CA Santa Barbara; Bus.

CASTRO, LYDIA ICELA; Inglewood HS; Inglewood, CA; (2); French Clb; Latin Clb; JV Vllybl; Cit Awd; Hon Roll; Math Teacher.

CASTRO, MARC N; Horgan SR HS; Vallejo, CA; (3); Am Leg Boys St; VP Drama Clb; Treas Key Clb; Pep Clb; Science Clb; Spanish Clb; SADD; School Musical; Phtg Nwsp; Rep Jr Cls; Pres Hogans Friday Nigh Live Chapter; VP Interact Clb Rotary; Acadmc Decathlon Team; Sports Med.

CASTRO, MARIA; Arvin HS; Lamont, CA; (2); French Clb; Ski Clb; Color Guard; Hon Roll; MESA-MATH/Engrng/Sci/Achvt; MECHA; Math.

CASTRO, MARIA; Presentation HS; San Francisco, CA; (3); Church Yth Grp; Math Clb; Teachers Aide; Phtg Nwsp; Phtg Yrbk; Stu Cncl; Cheerldng; JV Var Crs Cntry; NHS; Prfct Atten Awd; Plyd Piano 11 Yrs; CSF; Athltcs Prog; Bus Admin.

CASTRO, MARIVIC; Bishop Amat Memorial HS; West Covina, CA; (4); 16/407; Dance Clb; Drama Clb; Chorus; Church Choir; Co-Capt Drill Tm; High Hon Roll; Hon Roll; NHS; CSF; CA ST Los Angeles; Nrsng.

CASTRO, MIGUEL; Oakland Technical HS; Oakland, CA; (1); Boy Scts; L Sftbl; Hon Roll; Golden St Exam Algebra Hnrs; Stanford Jr U; Pediatrics.

CASTRO, NANCY; Fontana HS; Fontana, CA; (1); Drama Clb; Library Aide; SADD; Vllybl; Stu Of Month Awd; Stanford U; Inter Decorator.

CASTRO, RENEE L; Tracy HS; Tracy, CA; (3); 109/431; Dance Clb; Girl Scts; Library Aide; Office Aide; Pep Clb; Chorus; Var Cheerldng; JV Vllybl; Hon Roll; Pen Pals; Rdng; Waterskiing; Bus.

CASTRO, RUTH ANN E; El Camino HS; S San Francisco, CA; (3); JV Capt Vllybl; Hon Roll; Alg Awd; Cal Berkeley; Pre-Law.

CASTRO, STEVE R; Hanford Union HS; Hanford, CA; (1); Church Yth Grp; FFA; SADD; Church Choir; Mrchg Band.

CASTRO, VALERIE G; San Gabriel Mission HS; El Monte, CA; (3); Drama Clb; GAA; Hon Roll; JAM; UC San Diego; Cmptrs.

CASTRO, VERONICA IMELDA; Calipatria HS; Calipatria, CA; (2); Yrbk; VP Soph Cls; JV Bsktbl; JV Vllybl; Hon Roll; U CA-SAN Diego; Bus Mgmt.

CASTRO, VICTOR; Mar Vista HS; Imperial Beach, CA; (2); Ftbl; Golf; Wrstlng; Enjoy Pyng Guitar; Love Music; Love Riding Scooters; Enjoy Swim,Run,Ply Rqt Bl & Cycling; Engrng Mech.

CASTRO, VIRGINIA; Sierra Vista HS; Baldwin Park, CA; (1); Church Yth Grp; Speech Tm; School Play; Stage Crew; JV Tennis; Var Trk; High Hon Roll; Opt Clb Awd; Pres Acad Fit Awd; 1st Pl Engl Pnthln; 1st Pl Optmst Oratorical Cntst; UCLA; English.

CASTRO, VIVIAN; St Genevieve Schl; Sepulveda, CA; (3); Computer Clb; Dance Clb; Drama Clb; English Clb; Math Clb; Math Tm; Spanish Clb; Teachers Aide; Thesps; Chorus; Stanford; Nrsng.

CASTRO, WENDY; Savanna HS; Anaheim, CA; (2); JV Var Bsktbl; JV Var Tennis; Var L Trk; High Hon Roll; Athlt Of The Yr; Stanford; Engr.

CASTRO, WILLIAM E; La Sierra HS; Riverside, CA; (2); Varsity Clb; JV Ftbl; Var Tennis; Civil Engrng.

CASTRO, WILLIAM H; Mark Keppel HS; Monterey Park, CA; (3); Math Clb; JV Var Socr; High Hon Roll; Hon Roll; Prfct Atten Awd; GSE Geom Hnrs; Awd Atmtv Excllnc.

CASTRO-BERTERA, CARMELITA M; Pinole Valley HS; Richmond, CA; (1); Church Yth Grp; Cmnty Wkr; School Play; Rep Frsh Cls; JV Vllybl; Hon Roll; Goldn St Exam Acad Excllnce Awd; Phys Thrpst.

CASTROVERDE, CANDICE; Foothill HS; Bakersfield, CA; (3); 11/358; Treas Frsh Cls; Treas Soph Cls; Stu Cncl; Var L Cheerldng; Var Capt Powder Puff Ftbl; L Capt Socr; Capt L Tennis; High Hon Roll; Hon Roll; Gottchalks Hi-Debs; Mck Trl Tm; Mst Imprvd Orch 88; Mst Imprvd Tnns 89; MVP Tnns 90; Mst Outstndng Paint; Bio.

CASUGA, EILEEN P; Armijo HS; Fairfield, CA; (2); AFS; Ski Clb; Drill Tm; Cit Awd; Hon Roll; Jr NHS; NHS; Prfct Atten Awd; Pres Acad Fit Awd; Amsian American Club; Stu Leadership; Med.

CASUPANAN, MARVIN L; Bishop Amat HS; West Covina, CA; (2); Church Yth Grp; Cmnty Wkr; Dance Clb; Ftbl; Trk; Wt Lftg; Wrstlng; Hon Roll; Barkada Dance Club; Bicycle Club; UCLA; Med Dr.

CATALAN, HECTOR; Santiago HS; Garden Grove, CA; (2); 24/497; Letterman Clb; Spanish Clb; SADD; Varsity Clb; Bsktbl; Vllybl; Hon Roll; Law.

CATALDO, JASON; Mesa Verde HS; Citrus Heights, CA; (2); 19/257; Stat Bsbl; Var Ftbl; Score Keeper; Wt Lftg; High Hon Roll; Hon Roll; Pres Acad Fit Awd; Amer Leg Awd.

CATALINE, JANEEN M; Woodcrest Christian HS; Moreno Valley, CA; (3); Chorus; Treas Stu Cncl; Cit Awd; High Hon Roll; NEDT Awd; Education.

CATANESE, STACEY; Beyer HS; Modesto, CA; (4); 10/526; Am Leg Aux Girls St; Church Yth Grp; Pres Sec Drama Clb; Service Clb; SADD; School Play; Rptr Nwsp; Cit Awd; Hon Roll; Spcl Olympcs Coord; Sci & Engl Medal Of Hnr; CSU Fresno; Spch Pthlgy.

CATANZARITE, MICHELLE E; Turlock HS; Turlock, CA; (3); 169/530; Church Yth Grp; Cmnty Wkr; Key Clb; Pep Clb; Teachers Aide; Church Choir; Phtg Yrbk; OR ST; Lbrl Arts.

CATBAGAN, FLORA MAY F; Hawthorne HS; Hawthorne, CA; (2); English Clb; Math Tm; Science Clb; Service Clb; High Hon Roll; Med.

CATE, REGGIE N; Yucaipa HS; Yucaipa, CA; (3); French Clb; Letterman Clb; Bsbl; Wt Lftg; Cit Awd; Hon Roll; Bst Dfns Vrsty Bsbll All Lg Acad Awd; Hozoni Atet Grdtn Ushr; Mth.

CATE, TERRIE J; San Pasqual HS; Escondido, CA; (2); GAA; JA; SADD; VP Frsh Cls; Stu Cncl; Socr; Capt JV Sftbl; Cit Awd; High Hon Roll; NEDT Awd; Algebra Golden St Exam Hnrs; Psych.

CATER, TANESHA; Far West HS; Oakland, CA; (4); 5/25; Cmnty Wkr; Hosp Aide; Nwsp; Yrbk; Tennis; Cit Awd; High Hon Roll; Hon Roll; Stu Body Sec; Vlntr Hlth Ctr; Vlntr Lcl Elem Schl; Bio.

CATES, RYAN D; John Burroughs SR HS; Burbank, CA; (2); Church Yth Grp; Teachers Aide; Ed Nwsp; Phtg Yrbk; Pres Frsh Cls; JV L Bsbl; Bsktbl; L Ftbl; Hon Roll; NHS; Sister City Exchng Stu-To Japan; Cinematogrphy.

CATHCART, NICOLE D; Torrey Pines HS; Rancho Santa Fe, CA; (2); 137/503; Cmnty Wkr; VP SADD; Hon Roll; Chld Psych.

CATILO, LYN D; Vallejo SR HS; Vallejo, CA; (4); Girl Scts; Math Clb; Science Clb; Prfct Atten Awd; Contra Costa Coll; Nrsng.

CATINDIG, LEI ANN R; Bishop Amat Memorial HS; West Covina, CA; (2); French Clb; High Hon Roll; Hon Roll; NHS; CA Schlrshp Fed; Adopt-A-Grandparent; Friday Night Live; UCLA; Nrs.

CATINDIG, MARIA; La Puente HS; La Puente, CA; (4); High Hon Roll; Hon Roll; Ntl Merit SF; Bank Of Amer Achvt Awd Math; 3 Yr Schl Schlr Plaque; 2nd Schl Sci Fair; Greenpeace/Amnsty Intl; USC.

CATLE, MARY GRACE M; St Joseph HS; Downey, CA; (3); Cmnty Wkr; Drama Clb; Library Aide; Spanish Clb; Teachers Aide; School Play; Cit Awd; Hon Roll; Vol Chldrns Preschl & Elderly; Spanish Clb; CA ST U; Medcn.

CATLETT, STEVEN C; Woodbridge HS; Irvine, CA; (4); 6/400; Boy Scts; Treas German Clb; Math Tm.

CATO, AXACAEL; Pasadena HS; Pasadena, CA; (1); Stu Of Mnth; Cal ST U; Aerospc Engr.

CATO, KEVIN; Fairfield HS; Fairfield, CA; (2); Sec Band; Drm Mjr(t); Jazz Band; Mrchg Band; Pep Band; Sec Frsh Cls; Cit Awd; High Hon Roll; Hon Roll; NHS; Bowlng; Long Beach; Music.

CATO, MARK A; Imperial HS; La Crescenta, CA; (2); Chorus; Church Choir; School Musical; Pres Frsh Cls; Intrml Bsktbl; L Trk; Intrml Vllybl; L Wt Lftg; Cit Awd; Hon Roll; UCLA.

CATON, GREG J; Ramona HS; Ramona, CA; (2); Bus Profs of Am; Cmnty Wkr; FBLA; Intrml Bsbl; Intrml Golf; Berkley; Lawyer.

CATON, ROBERT O; Saint Ignatius College Prep; San Francisco, CA; (3); Art Clb; Ski Clb; Band; Jazz Band; Orch; Pep Band; Var L Lcrss; San Francisco ST U; Arch.

CATON, TINA; Rancho Alamitos HS; Garden Grove, CA; (1); Church Yth Grp; Office Aide; Aud/Vis; Chorus; Church Choir; Cypress Coll; Nrsng.

CATON, TONYA; Faith Christian HS; Bangor, CA; (2); 2/25; Church Yth Grp; VP Stu Cncl; Score Keeper; Stat Sftbl; High Hon Roll; CSF; Med.

CATRON, JILL D; Arroyo Grande HS; Arroyo Grande, CA; (1); Var Socr; Var Trk; Hon Roll; Pres Acad Fit Awd; AFS Rcrdng Sec; ASO Soccer; Mentor Pgm.

CATRON, SU; Arlington HS; Riverside, CA; (4); 6/335; Art Clb; Cmnty Wkr; Debate Tm; SADD; Lit Mag; Tennis; Cit Awd; High Hon Roll; Pres Acad Fit Awd; Sal; U Of CA Riverside; Bio.

CATTANACH, SUZANNE; Saint Bonaventure HS; Ventura, CA; (3); Rptr Nwsp; Yrbk; JV Var Bsktbl; Var Trk; JV Var Vllybl.

CATTANI, MARY; Garces Memorial HS; Bakersfield, CA; (1); 1/185; Cmnty Wkr; Service Clb; High Hon Roll; CA Schlrshp Fdrtn; Travel Clb; Outstdng Cls Std Awd; World Hstry Awd; Harvard U; Bus.

CATTRONE, TINA M; College Park HS; Pleasant Hill, CA; (1); Church Yth Grp; Hosp Aide; Spanish Clb; Var Socr; JV Sftbl; High Hon Roll; Hon Roll; CSF; UC Davis; Medicine.

CAUBIN, CRISTIN; Oak Ridge HS; El Dorado Hills, CA; (3); Church Yth Grp; Hosp Aide; Yrbk; Stu Cncl; Hon Roll; CA ST Sacramento; Intl Bus.

CAUDILL, CARRIE S; Irvine HS; Irvine, CA; (2); 2/500; Church Yth Grp; School Play; Var Sftbl; JV Capt Vllybl; Hon Roll; Math Heritage Awd; Hstry Heritage Medallion; Education.

CAUDILL, PAMELA; Palm Desert HS; Palm Desert, CA; (3); Church Yth Grp; Girl Scts; Hosp Aide; Library Aide; Office Aide; Band; Jazz Band; Mrchg Band; Pep Band; Bsktbl; Pepperdine; Psych.

CAUDILL, SHAWN L; Monache HS; Porterville, CA; (2); Church Yth Grp; Prfct Atten Awd; Comp Prgmr.

CAUDLE, KRISTI L; Escondido HS; Escondido, CA; (4); Am Leg Aux Girls St; Church Yth Grp; Dance Clb; Drama Clb; School Musical; Cit Awd; High Hon Roll; Rotary Awd; St Marys Clg; Social Work.

CAUDLE, SCOTT E; Escondido HS; Escondido, CA; (1); Boy Scts; Church Yth Grp; JV Ftbl; JV Socr; JV Trk; Cit Awd; High Hon Roll; Pres Acad Fit Awd.

CAUDLE, THOMAS C; La Sierra SR HS; Riverside, CA; (1); Drama Clb; School Play; Stage Crew; Ftbl; Hon Roll; Pres Acad Fit Awd.

CAUDWELL, JESSICA; St Francis HS; Sacramento, CA; (3); Church Yth Grp; Cmnty Wkr; SADD; Variety Show; Var Capt Cheerldng; Sccr Plyr & Rfree; Tutor Bio & Span; Jr Curatar; Cheers At Spec Olympcs; UC Davis.

CAUFIELD, KELLY; John F Kennedy HS; Fremont, CA; (2); Pep Clb; SADD; Var Cheerldng; Var Pom Pon; Hon Roll; Prfct Atten Awd; Pres Acad Fit Awd; Golden St Exam, Alg I Hnrs; UC Santa Cruz; Bio.

CAUFIELD, KRISTIN; Valley Christian HS; Pleasanton, CA; (3); French Clb; Thesps; Ed Nwsp; Ed Yrbk; Hist Jr Cls; Var Bsktbl; Hon Roll; NHS; CA Hnrs Soc.

CAULFIELD, MIKE K; Bishop O'dowd HS; Berkeley, CA; (2); Boy Scts; Church Yth Grp; Drama Clb; Science Clb; Ski Clb; Band; Tennis; Hon Roll.

CAULFIELD, MONIQUE A; Helix HS; El Cajon, CA; (2); 77/450; Church Yth Grp; English Clb; GAA; Science Clb; Diving; Socr; Sftbl; Wt Lftg; High Hon Roll; Hon Roll; 2nd Pl Awd Dsgn Airplane Aero Spc Museum; Shwng Yth Art Had Picture Shppd Egypt Show; UC Berkley; Med.

CAULKINS, TRYSSA; Summerville HS; Tuolumne, CA; (2); Drama Clb; Ski Clb; Band; Hon Roll; Lawyer.

CAUNAN, MARIA ERMA MIA B; Bishop Amat Mem HS; W Covina, CA; (3); Church Yth Grp; Cmnty Wkr; Treas Dance Clb; Office Aide; Teachers Aide; High Hon Roll; Hon Roll; NHS; Pres Acad Fit Awd; CA Schlrshp Fed; Cert, Trophies Piano & Voice; UCLA; Actrl Sci.

CAUNTAY, KRISHNA L; Notre Dame HS; Salinas, CA; (2); 3/83; Cmnty Wkr; 4-H; JV Bsbl; JV Trk; JV Vllybl; 4-H Awd; High Hon Roll; Lion Awd; Dancing; Fshn Dsgng; Reading; Painting; Photo; Psych.

CAUSEY III, EMMIT M; Fontana HS; Fontana, CA; (2); Swmmng; Water Polo Tm; Photo; Annapolis; Navy Fighter Pilot.

CAUTON, KENDALL OMAR E; Richmond HS; San Pablo, CA; (2); Office Aide; Spanish Clb; Teachers Aide; Varsity Clb; Var Bsktbl; Stat Score Keeper; Hon Roll.

CAVAGNUOLO, KELLY M; Hayward HS; Hayward, CA; (2); 34/300; Hon Roll; Poetry Pblshed Lit Mag; Ct Rprtr Trng Ctr SF; Ct Rprtr.

CAVALHO, MIKE; Modesto HS; Modesto, CA; (2); Boy Scts; Bsktbl; Mech Engr.

CAVALIERE, LISA; Tamalpais HS; Mill Valley, CA; (4); 30/231; Ski Clb; Treas Spanish Clb; Rep Stu Cncl; JV Bsktbl; JV Var Sftbl; High Hon Roll; Hon Roll; Amigos De Las Americas Volntr Prgm SA Countries; U Of MA Amherst; Bus.

CAVALLI, ANDREA; Calaveras HS; Mokelumne Hill, CA; (3); Church Yth Grp; Cmnty Wkr; 4-H; Crs Cntry; Trk; Vllybl; Cit Awd; 4-H Awd; Hon Roll; Prfct Atten Awd; Aviation Grnd Schl; Wood Working; Cmmrcl Pilot.

CAVALLINI, CASSANDRA; Carlmont HS; San Carlos, CA; (3); 16/326; Church Yth Grp; 4-H; Girl Scts; Flag Corp; Ed Yrbk; Capt Swmmng; High Hon Roll; Masonic Awd; Pres Acad Fit Awd; Jobs Dghtrs Hnrd Qn; Camp Cnslr; Demolay Swthrt; Santa Cruz U; Marine Bio.

CAVANAGH, KRISTA; Thomas Downey HS; Modesto, CA; (3); French Clb; SADD; Band; Mrchg Band; Crs Cntry; Trk; NHS; Eng.

CAVANAUGH, BRIANA E; Buena Park HS; La Palma, CA; (1); 83/438; Chess Clb; Drama Clb; Stage Crew; L Var Swmmng; High Hon Roll; CSF; Irish Steppe Dancer; UCLA; Perf Art.

CAVANAUGH, NATALIE M; West Covina HS; W Covina, CA; (3); FBLA; GAA; Letterman Clb; SADD; Teachers Aide; Varsity Clb; Stu Cncl; Ftbl; Var Capt Socr; Bus Profs of Am; Teaching.

CAVAZOS, JOANN; Hueneme HS; Oxnard, CA; (1); Play Bsktbl, Listeng To Musc, Dancng; Bus Week; Mgr Fash Store.

CAVAZOS, LUCINDA; Lemoore Union HS; Lemoore, CA; (3); Art Clb; JV Bsktbl; Hon Roll; Prfct Atten Awd; JC; Fshn Mrchndsng.

CAVAZOS, PABLO; Mc Farland HS; Mc Farland, CA; (3); Art Clb; Band; Bsktbl; Crs Cntry; Trk; Wrstlng; AZ ST; Bus.

CAVENEY, CHRIS M; Santa Teresa HS; San Jose, CA; (2); French Clb; Science Clb; Socr; Close Up; Life Grd; UC Santa Barbara; Engrng.

CAVERO, HAIDEE C; Amos Alonzo Stagg HS; Stockton, CA; (1); High Hon Roll; Prfct Atten Awd.

CAVES, JODY; Corona HS; Corona, CA; (2); Church Yth Grp; Church Choir; Mst Imprvd Awd; Hnr Clses; Poetry; CA ST; Chiropractor.

CAVESTANY, LEE B; St Ignatius College Prep; S San Francisco, CA; (3); 76/244; Art Clb; Cmnty Wkr; Varsity Clb; School Play; Var L Ftbl; JV Trk; Hon Roll; CSF; Santa Clara U; Bus.

CAVOLA, STEPHEN; Clovis HS; Fresno, CA; (3); German Clb; Latin Clb; Math Clb; Science Clb; SADD; Hon Roll; CSF; Golden St Exam Hgh Hnrs Alg, Hnrs Geom; Hstry Day County Cmptn; Qlfr Cngrssnl Schlr; Math.

CAWARING, RACHELE S; Alhambra HS; Martinez, CA; (2); 3/214; Math Tm; Band; Jazz Band; Mrchg Band; Var L Tennis; High Hon Roll; GSE Schlr; Yth Cmmtte; Bus Law.

CAWSTON, HEATHER; Valley Christian HS; San Jose, CA; (3); Church Yth Grp; French Clb; Office Aide; Chorus; Church Choir; Rptr Nwsp; Stat Bsbl; Powder Puff Ftbl; Hon Roll; Fashion Desgnr.

CAYABO, LORENCE S; Orosi HS; Orosi, CA; (3); Latin Clb; SADD; Rptr Nwsp; Ed Yrbk; Rep Stu Cncl; JV Bsktbl; Hon Roll; HI-Y Cmnty Srvc Club; City Coll Of San Francisco.

CAYANAN, IRENE G; Lowell HS; San Francisco, CA; (3); Church Yth Grp; Drama Clb; ROTC; Speech Tm; Ntl Frnscs Leag; U C Davis; Med.

CAYLOR, COREENA O; Rio Lindo Acad; Healdsburg, CA; (3); Spanish Clb; Acpl Chr; Band; Chorus; Orch; Variety Show; Pres Stu Cncl; High Hon Roll; Prfct Atten Awd; Pacific Union Coll; Opthalmlgy.

CAYOSA, EDENGRACE; Van Nuys HS; Los Angeles, CA; (4); 81/535; Sec Church Yth Grp; Capt Drill Tm; Mrchg Band; Cit Awd; Hon Roll; Ntl Merit Ltr; Prfct Atten Awd; Pres Acad Fit Awd; Army Rotc Schlrhsp; UCLA; Engr.

CAYOSA, GRACE; Van Nuys HS; Los Angeles, CA; (4); 81/535; Capt Drill Tm; Mrchg Band; Ed Yrbk; NHS; Prfct Atten Awd; Phys Engrng.

CAYTON, DONNA L; Marysville HS; Marysville, CA; (3); Church Yth Grp; Key Clb; Service Clb; Spanish Clb; SADD; Teachers Aide; Band; Mrchg Band; Sec Yrbk; High Hon Roll; Jr Red Crss; CSF; Sonoma ST; Bus Mgmt.

CAYWOOD, JO ANNA; Western Christian HS; Azusa, CA; (3); Church Yth Grp; Pres Cmnty Wkr; FCA; Pep Clb; Pres Service Clb; Teachers Aide; Chorus; Rep Jr Cls; Stu Cncl; Var JV Cheerldng; UCLA; Bus Admin.

CAZALE, MICHAEL; Lincoln HS; Stockton, CA; (3); 180/550; Office Aide; Hon Roll; Bus.

CAZARES, ANGELICA; Indio HS; Indio, CA; (1); Dance Clb; U Of Sana Barbara; Doctor.

CAZARES, JOSE; San Diego HS; Coronado, CA; (2); French Clb; Intrml Crs Cntry; JV Ftbl; Cit Awd; French Hon Soc; High Hon Roll; Pres Acad Fit Awd; Pres Schlr; Tutor; Arch.

CAZARES, RICK J; Selma HS; Selma, CA; (3); 21/221; Band; Mrchg Band; Pep Band; Variety Show; Var Bsbl; Var Bsktbl; Var Ftbl; Wt Lftg; High Hon Roll; Hon Roll; Fresno ST U; Police Sci.

CAZAREZ, CENEN; Coachella Valley HS; Thermal, CA; (3); Socr; High Hon Roll; Hon Roll; Mecha Club; Perfect Attndnc Awd; Alg Awd; Math Teacher.

CAZORLA, MARINA; C K Mc Clatchy SR HS; Sacramento, CA; (4); 33/443; Church Yth Grp; Library Aide; Sec Spanish Clb; Yrbk; Rep Frsh Cls; VP Soph Cls; Intrml Tennis; Hon Roll; Ntl Merit SF; CA Schlrshp Fed; Stu Acad Intl Studies; UC Davis; Intl Rltns.

CDE BACA, TRICIA; Pioneer Baptist HS; Norwalk, CA; (2); 1/13; Church Yth Grp; Cmnty Wkr; Drama Clb; Pep Clb; Teachers Aide; School Play; Var Bsktbl; Var Mgr(s); Var Vllybl; Cit Awd; Pensacola Christian Coll.

CEA, ELIZABETH; La Sierra Acad; Riverside, CA; (2); Church Yth Grp; Cmnty Wkr; FCA; Spanish Clb; Varsity Clb; Band; Chorus; Church Choir; School Musical; Cit Awd; UCLA; Med.

CEBALLOS, BRENDA P; Glendale HS; Glendale, CA; (2); VP Church Yth Grp; Service Clb; Acpl Chr; Chorus; Church Choir; School Musical; School Play; Music & Dance Actvts; Psych.

CEBALLOS, JEANNETTE Y; Mira Mesa HS; San Diego, CA; (2); Church Yth Grp; Cmnty Wkr; Hon Roll; Ambssdrs To Asia Cmptn; Jrnlsm.

CEBALLOS, LAURA; William Workman HS; Valinda, CA; (1); Legal Attrny.

CEBE, CHARLES K; Clairemont HS; San Diego, CA; (3); 2/235; Boy Scts; Science Clb; Orch; Tennis; High Hon Roll.

CEBE, LAURA P; Clairemont HS; San Diego, CA; (1); 6/260; Var JV Cheerldng; JV Swmmng; High Hon Roll; Hon Roll.

CECCHETTINI, AMY D; El Dorado HS; Placerville, CA; (3); 20/387; Science Clb; Service Clb; Teachers Aide; Var Tennis; Var Trk; High Hon Roll; Prfct Atten Awd; CSF.

CECCHINI, JEANNINE; Liberty Union HS; Oakley, CA; (4); 27/350; Cmnty Wkr; Dance Clb; Debate Tm; Math Tm; Pep Clb; Red Cross Aide; Ski Clb; SADD; Teachers Aide; Varsity Clb; Ntl Dance Team Champshp Orlando FL 89; Sut Mnth 87-90; Mock Trl; 145 Cmmsnr For Blood Dr; UC Sys; Engrng.

CECIC-KARUZIC, MARKO; Santa Rosa HS; Santa Rosa, CA; (4); Church Yth Grp; Cmnty Wkr; French Clb; Speech Tm; SADD; Acpl Chr; Var L Ftbl; Ntl Merit Ltr; Hon Roll; Safe Rides Orgnztn; USC; Pre Med.

CECIL, JODI; North HS; Bakersfield, CA; (4); 12/350; Church Yth Grp; 4-H; French Clb; FFA; Sec Soph Cls; 4-H Awd; Hon Roll; NHS; Pres Acad Fit Awd; Dance Extramrl; Vet Med.

CECIL, TARA; Savanna HS; Anaheim, CA; (2); Church Yth Grp; Church Choir; JV Var Swmmng; Waterpolo Team.

CEDANO, JAIME; Bell Gardens HS; Bell Gardens, CA; (4); 54/529; Art Clb; Ed Yrbk; Score Keeper; Hon Roll; Prfct Atten Awd; Welders America Clb VP; AZ; Grphc Comp Dsgn.

CEDENO, ROBERT A; Amdrew Hill HS; San Jose, CA; (3); Church Yth Grp; Spanish Clb; Varsity Clb; Socr; Migranl Ed Clb VP 89-90; UC Davis; Med.

CEDILLO, AUBREE; Whitney HS; Cerritos, CA; (3); Pres Drama Clb; Key Clb; Spanish Clb; Thesps; Band; Drm Mjr(t); Orch; School Musical; High Hon Roll; NHS; Orange Cty HS Of Arts; CSF; Los Angeles Cty Yth Symphony Orch Cncl Hnr Orch; UCLA; Perfrmnce Cmmnctns.

CEDILLOS, ERIKA; Schurr HS; Moreno Valley, CA; (4); 43/580; French Clb; Spanish Clb; SADD; Rptr Nwsp; Rep Jr Cls; Rep Sr Cls; Rep Stu Cncl; High Hon Roll; Pres Acad Fit Awd; Grls Leag; Basic Clb; CSF; UCLA; Bus Ecnmcs.

CEDILLOS, KARINA; Schurr HS; Moreno Valley, CA; (4); 65/580; Spanish Clb; SADD; Rptr Nwsp; Off Jr Cls; Off Sr Cls; Hon Roll; B A S I Clb; Prom Commtte; UC Riverside; Biomed.

CEFALONI, ANDRAYA; San Lorenzo Valley HS; Santa Cruz, CA; (4); Church Yth Grp; Debate Tm; French Clb; Key Clb; Library Aide; Pep Clb; Speech Tm; Teachers Aide; Chorus; Color Guard; Hnrd Queen Jobs Daughters; Dominican Coll; Art Hstry.

CEIGERKANSKY, LARA L; East Bakersfield HS; Bakersfield, CA; (4); 21/429; 4-H; Intnl Clb; Key Clb; Var Socr; Trk; 4-H Awd; High Hon Roll; Golden St Exam Honors 87-88; Keywanettes; CSU Bakersfield; Engr.

CEJA, MARTHA; Palo Verde HS; Blythe, CA; (2); Drama Clb; Pep Clb; Spanish Clb; Flag Corp; VP Soph Cls; Crs Cntry; Hon Roll; S-Clb; Treas Pep Clb; Awd Outstndng Sportmshp Cross Cntry.

CEJA, SOCORRO; Coachella Valley HS; Mecca, CA; (2); Spanish Clb; Hon Roll; Bnk Of Amer Awd Frgn Lang; MECHA Clb; Dance.

CELANI, JIM V; Antelope Valley HS; Lancaster, CA; (2); 15/810; JA; Var Swmmng; High Hon Roll; Air Force Acad; Comp.

CELAYA, MARK A; Pater Noster HS; Los Angeles, CA; (3); 1/50; Varsity Clb; Rep Frsh Cls; VP Jr Cls; Pres Stu Cncl; JV Bsktbl; Var Ftbl; JV Trk; Hon Roll; NHS; NEDT Awd; Mariposa Pgm Achvt Awd; CSF; Lead Bus Pgm.

CELESTIAL, JEANNIE J; Dr James J Hogan HS; Vallejo, CA; (2); French Clb; SADD; Teachers Aide; Flag Corp; Sec Treas Stu Cncl; Cheerldng; Pom Pon; Stat Wrstlng; Hon Roll; Pres Schlr; Golden St Exam Algebra I Hnrs & Geom High Honors; Engrng.

CELESTIN, MORGIANA; Far West HS; Oakland, CA; (2); 2/11; Math Clb; Office Aide; Teachers Aide; Pres Soph Cls; Cit Awd; High Hon Roll; Poetry; CA ST Hayward; Comp Sci.

CELESTINE, SAMUEL R; Fellowship Schl; Ridgecrest, CA; (2); Capt Quiz Bowl; School Play; Var Bsktbl; Var Ftbl; Var Score Keeper; Stat Vllybl; Hon Roll; 2nd Pl Natls Male Duet.

CELIK, AYTEK ESEN; Claremont HS; Claremont, CA; (4); 2/384; Debate Tm; Drama Clb; Intnl Clb; VP Math Clb; Math Tm; Pres Science Clb; VP Spanish Clb; Speech Tm; SADD; Thesps; Acadmc Dcthln Pres 1st Pl Intrvw; Wmn Engnrs Awd; Yale U; Sci.

CELIO, JENNIFER; Rosary HS; La Mirada, CA; (4); 13/140; Science Clb; Hon Roll; NHS; Campus Ministry Ldrshp; Commrcl Illustrator.

CELIO, SHERRY; Center HS; North Highlands, CA; (4); Church Yth Grp; Office Aide; Teachers Aide; Ed Yrbk; Pom Pon; Score Keeper; Jr Clss Hmcmng Princess; Sr Ball Queen; Sierra Coll; Graphic Arts.

CELIS, MARICHELLE C; Bishop O'dowd HS; Pinole, CA; (3); Hosp Aide; Teachers Aide; High Hon Roll; Hon Roll; CSF; Pre-Med.

CELLA, JENNIFER M; Whittier Christian HS; Diamond Bar, CA; (3); Church Yth Grp; Speech Tm; Drill Tm; Var JV Cheerldng; Powder Puff Ftbl; High Hon Roll; NHS; Ca Schlrshp Fndtn.

CEMAN, CANYON A; Mira Costa HS; Manhattan Beach, CA; (4); 1/376; Key Clb; Math Clb; Quiz Bowl; Scholastic Bowl; Spanish Clb; Varsity Clb; Bsktbl; Vllybl; High Hon Roll; Ntl Merit SF; Scholar Athlete 4 Yrs.

CENIDOZA, THERESA B; Mountain View HS; Milpitas, CA; (3); 27/319; Dance Clb; Intnl Clb; Pres Band; VP Soph Cls; Stu Cncl; Var Cheerldng; High Hon Roll; Fnlst I Have A Dream Essy Cntst; SIP; FYO Secy, VP; Schl Svc Awd 87-88; Stu Mnth 89; Eng.

CENTENO, DANA; Paraclete HS; Littlerock, CA; (2); Church Yth Grp; Pres 4-H; Treas SADD; Pres Chorus; 4-H Awd; Hon Roll; Interact Clb; Chld Psych.

CENTENO, JOHN; Amos Alonzo Stagg HS; Stockton, CA; (1); Red Cross Aide; Teachers Aide; Hon Roll.

CENTURINO, SCOTT D; Casa Roble Fundamental HS; Orangevale, CA; (4); 1/400; German Clb; Math Tm; Science Clb; Hist Service Clb; Elks Awd; NHS; Ntl Merit SF; Mck Trl; Acad Dcthln; Sci Olympd; MA Inst Of Tech; Aerontcl Engr.

CEPEDA, LINDA; Dinuba HS; Dinuba, CA; (3); Hon Roll; Sec Treas Jr Cls; Sec Treas Sr Cls; Stu Cncl; Acad Awds; Mecha Clb; Fresno ST.

CERDA, ALEJANDRA DE LA; Fremont HS; Sunnyvale, CA; (1); Teachers Aide; Rep Stu Cncl; High Hon Roll; La Raya Unida Coll Prgm; Tech.

CERDA, LAURA M; Santa Paula Union HS; Santa Paula, CA; (3); Am Leg Aux Girls St; Cmnty Wkr; Band; Mrchg Band; Pep Band; Nwsp; Pres Jr Cls; Bsktbl; Crs Cntry; Trk; CA Poly; Social Sci.

CERDA, ROBERT P; Sierra Vista HS; Baldwin Park, CA; (3); Letterman Clb; JV Var Ftbl; JV Var Trk; Law.

CERDA, SALVADOR; Garey HS; Pomona, CA; (3); Key Clb; Varsity Clb; Var Bsbl; High Hon Roll; Hon Roll; Prfct Atten Awd; Arch.

CERDA, VELINDA; Montebello HS; Pico Rivera, CA; (2); Church Yth Grp; Chorus; Trk; Psych.

CERDEIRO, FLAVIA M; Edison HS; Huntington Bch, CA; (4); Dance Clb; Bus.

CEREGATTI, SUSAN J; Torrence HS; Torrance, CA; (4); Treas Computer Clb; French Clb; JA; Office Aide; Pep Clb; Chorus; Co-Capt Color Guard; School Musical; Hon Roll; Natl Awd For Music Arion Awd 1989; City Wide Awd For Industrial Arts; Plaque Winner For Industrial Art; Accounting/Vocal Arts.

CEREGHINO, SUSAN E; Sequoia HS; San Carlos, CA; (2); Girl Scts; Pep Clb; SADD; Teachers Aide; Drill Tm; Off Soph Cls; Cheerldng; Socr; Sftbl; Swmmng; Peer Resource Proj, Cnslng, Tutor; UCLA; Lawyr.

CERF, KIMBERLY; Harbor HS; Boulder Creek, CA; (1); Drama Clb; Girl Scts; School Musical; Rep Soph Cls; GS Gld Ldrshp Awd; Dsgnd & Facilitate Anti Drug & Suicide Wrkshps For Teens; Ecological Bus Consultant.

CERIO, DANIEL; Brethren JR/Sr HS; Downey, CA; (2); Var Bsktbl; JV Ftbl; High Hon Roll; CSF.

CERMAK, ANDREA L; Oakmont HS; Roseville, CA; (4); 26/397; German Clb; GAA; Hosp Aide; SADD; Varsity Clb; Band; Mrchg Band; Pep Band; Rptr Nwsp; Stat Socr; Acad Mrt Awd; Edwin S Schellhous Memrl Schlrshp; Thelma Zerbe Memrl Schlrshp Frm Soroptomist; CSUS; Nrsng.

CERNA, LEON D; Hesperia HS; Hesperia, CA; (2); Church Yth Grp; Spanish Clb; Varsity Clb; Jazz Band; Mrchg Band; JV Bsktbl; Var L Ftbl; Var L Golf; Cit Awd; High Hon Roll; University Clb; Stanford; Law.

CERNA, STEVE C; Rancho Cotate HS; Rohnert Park, CA; (2); German Clb; Var Bsbl; JV Socr; High Hon Roll; Stanford U; Med.

CERNEANT, SHELLEY D; San Clemente HS; San Clemente, CA; (2); Spanish Clb; Intrml Bsktbl.

CERON, AKILES A; San Marcos HS; Santa Barbara, CA; (3); 71/380; Pres Church Yth Grp; German Clb; Red Cross Aide; Church Choir; Var Ftbl; Var Trk; Var Wt Lftg; Hon Roll; 1st Pl UCSB Lang Olympiad; German Amer Prtnrshp Pgm; Lang.

CERON, DANIEL; Calexico HS; Calexico, CA; (2); Church Yth Grp; Math Tm; Chorus; Hon Roll; UCSD; Comp Engrng.

CERROBLANCO JR, ARMANDO; Parlier HS; Parlier, CA; (2); Drama Clb; Science Clb; School Play; High Hon Roll; Math Awds Algebra II; Comp Sci Awd Bio; Performing Arts Awd; Math.

CERTONIO, JERRY; Quartz Hill HS; Lancaster, CA; (4); 6/541; Math Tm; Quiz Bowl; Spanish Clb; High Hon Roll; NHS; Sal; NASA SHARP Pgm 89; CSF 86-90; GATE 86-89; UCLA; Comp Sci.

CERVANTES, ADRIAN; Calexico HS; Calexico, CA; (2); Church Yth Grp; JV Bsbl; Bsktbl; JV Crs Cntry; JV Score Keeper; Hon Roll; Golden St Exm Awd.

CERVANTES, ARMANDO; Bishop Montgomery HS; Harbor City, CA; (3); 22/465; Computer Clb; French Clb; FBLA; Letterman Clb; Bsbl; Bsktbl; Ftbl; Socr; Cit Awd; Hon Roll; Vrsty Bsbl Team MVP, All-League; Stanford U; Bus.

CERVANTES, CLARISA; South San Francisco HS; S San Francisco, CA; (2); Church Yth Grp; French Clb; FBLA; Spanish Clb; Hon Roll; Pres Acad Fit Awd; Business.

CERVANTES, CLAUDIA; Garfield HS; Los Angeles, CA; (3); Cmnty Wkr; ROTC; Color Guard; Drill Tm; Prfct Atten Awd; Walk Amer; KLOS; Feed Homeless; Fulerton; Psych.

CERVANTES, DAVEY A; Lynwood HS; Lynwood, CA; (2); ROTC; SADD; Teachers Aide; JV Bsbl; JV Bsktbl; UC Irvine; Psych.

CERVANTES, DIANA; Magnolia HS; Anaheim, CA; (2); Var Bsktbl; Var Sftbl; JV Vllybl; Arch.

CERVANTES, DIANA B; Channel Islands HS; Oxnard, CA; (3); Drama Clb; Latin Clb; Spanish Clb; Speech Tm; Band; Chorus; Church Choir; Jazz Band; Mrchg Band; School Musical; Outstndng Stu Bilingual Pgm; Outstndng Achvt Coll Prep; Speaker Of Wk Future Ldrs Of Amer Camp; Harvard; Law.

CERVANTES, ELIZABETH; Helix HS; Lemon Grove, CA; (3); 37/487; Stu Cncl; Church Yth Grp; Hon Roll; CSF; Top 10 Pct; Ran For Jr Class Treas; Bsktbl; U Of CA San Diego; Med.

CERVANTES, JAYNE M; Lindsay HS; Lindsay, CA; (3); Church Yth Grp; FHA; Spanish Clb; Teachers Aide; JV Tennis; Cit Awd; Hon Roll; Friday Night Live; Acad Awd; Outstndng Achvmnt Awd; Cal Poly; Chld Psych.

CERVANTES, JERRY; Porterville HS; Porterville, CA; (3); FBLA; Science Clb; Mrchg Band; Yrbk; Fresno ST; Naval Aviation.

CERVANTES, JULIE; Banning HS; Wilmington, CA; (4); Cmnty Wkr; VP Math Clb; VP Science Clb; Cit Awd; Pres Acad Fit Awd; Mecha Hispanic Clb; Peer Tutor; Loyola Marymount; Engrng.

CERVANTES, LILIANA; Los Altos HS; Hacienda Hts, CA; (3); 78/376; Church Yth Grp; Cmnty Wkr; Chorus; Church Choir; Rep Stu Cncl; Hon Roll; Bus Admin.

CERVANTES, MARIA; Helix HS; Lemon Grove, CA; (2); 237/487; Church Yth Grp; JV Bsktbl; Bsktbl Awd; Avid Awd; Bsktbl; Cmptr Prgmr.

CERVANTES, MARIA D; Lindsay HS; Lindsay, CA; (3); Art Clb; Sec Church Yth Grp; Spanish Clb; Church Choir; Sec Sr Cls; Cit Awd; Hon Roll; Prfct Atten Awd; Mecha Clb Secy; Snta Brbra.

CERVANTES, MARISOL; Roosevelt HS; Los Angeles, CA; (3); Hon Roll; Psych.

CERVANTES, MARTIN A; Loma Linda Acad; Redlands, CA; (3); Ski Clb; JV Crs Cntry; Snow Skiing, Snwbrdng; Water Skiing; Backpckng; Law.

CERVANTES, MELANIE M; Fontana HS; Fontana, CA; (3); 55/1147; Church Yth Grp; Service Clb; Ski Clb; Pres Frsh Cls; Pres Soph Cls; Pres Jr Cls; Stu Cncl; JV Bsktbl; Var Crs Cntry; Var Sftbl; CA Schlrshp Fndtn; Zontz Clb Pres 90-91; Frgn Lang.

CERVANTES, MIGUEL; Whittier HS; Whittier, CA; (1); 33/475; Intrml Bsbl; Intrml Capt Ftbl; Cit Awd; Hon Roll; Aviations.

CERVANTES, TYRA; West Hills HS; Santee, CA; (2); 57/260; Drill Tm; Capt JV Cheerldng; Hon Roll; Gldn St Exam High Hnrs; UCSD; Zoology.

CERVANTES, VERONICA; Garfield HS; Los Angeles, CA; (2); Church Yth Grp; Girl Scts; Teachers Aide; Acpl Chr; Church Choir; Yrbk; Stu Cncl; Powder Puff Ftbl; Sftbl; Swmmng; Upward Bound Pgm; Psych.

CERVANTEZ, ROSEMARY; Buena HS; Ventura, CA; (2); Church Yth Grp; Socr; Vllybl; Prfct Atten Awd; Pres Acad Fit Awd.

CERVELLI BOPP, LISA M; Kerman HS; Kerman, CA; (4); 12/120; Letterman Clb; Office Aide; SADD; Teachers Aide; Yrbk; JV Var Bsktbl; Var L Vllybl; Hon Roll; Pres Acad Fit Awd; CSF; Fresno City.

CERVINKA, PETER J; Davis SR HS; Davis, CA; (4); Chess Clb; Computer Clb; French Clb; FFA; Key Clb; Science Clb; Spanish Clb; Chorus; Rep Sr Cls; Rep Stu Cncl; U Of CA Davis; Forestry.

CESENA, FRANCINE Y; Will C Crawford HS; San Diego, CA; (2); Church Yth Grp; Dance Clb; GAA; Girl Scts; Spanish Clb; SADD; Mrchg Band; Stu Cncl; JV Var Sftbl; Alg Goldn St Exam Awd; AZ ST U; Acctnt.

CESENA, LETTY; Woodland HS; Woodland, CA; (3); Hon Roll; Prfct Atten Awd; Mbr Early Outreach Program; Natl Hnr Society Mbr; Sacramento ST; Business.

CESENA, YESENIA Y; St Joseph HS; Hawaiian Gardens, CA; (3); 21/200; Church Yth Grp; Drama Clb; Spanish Clb; SADD; High Hon Roll; Hon Roll; NEDT Awd.

CESPEDES, RAFAEL I; Sunset HS; Hayward, CA; (2); 4/237; High Hon Roll; Hon Roll; Gldn St Exam Hnrs; Scl Sci & Math Achvt; Scl Sci.

CESTA, ANTHONY D; Bellarmine Jefferson HS; Burbank, CA; (3); 8/150; Debate Tm; NFL; Speech Tm; Capt Bsbl; Capt Ftbl; Capt Socr; NHS; CSF.

CEVALLOS, CARLOS A; Saddleback HS; Santa Ana, CA; (3); Service Clb; Var Bsbl; Cit Awd; Hon Roll; Prfct Atten Awd; Bst Dfns Awd Vrsty Bsbl 90; All Legue Team Bsbl 90; 4 Yrs Rcrtn Bsktbl Coach Cmnty; Pro Bsbl Plyr.

CEZAR, CARINA; Garden Grove HS; Garden Grove, CA; (4); 7/332; Cmnty Wkr; English Clb; French Clb; Hosp Aide; Teachers Aide; Elks Awd; High Hon Roll; Hon Roll; NHS; Girls Leag Brd Mem; Friends Agnst Driving Drunk; UC Irvine; Bio Sci.

CHA, CHIA NENG; Rio Linda SR HS; Sacramento, CA; (3); Math Tm; Science Clb; Vllybl; Cit Awd; Hon Roll; SE Asian Devlpmnt Club; UC Davis; Doc.

CHA, EDDIE C; Sunny Hills HS; Fullerton, CA; (3); 72/340; Cmnty Wkr; Intnl Clb; Key Clb; Pres Model UN; Rptr Nwsp; Stu Cncl; JV L Crs Cntry; High Hon Roll; Stu Senate; Schl Site Cncl; CA Schlrshp Fed; Intl Rltns.

CHA, HEEMIN MONICA; Saddleback HS; Santa Ana, CA; (3); Church Yth Grp; Cmnty Wkr; Drama Clb; French Clb; FBLA; Science Clb; School Play; Vllybl; CSF; Var Badmntn; CIF; Pre-Law.

CHA, KIA; Edison HS; Fresno, CA; (1); FTA; JV Sftbl; Tennis; High Hon Roll; CSF Club; Southeast Asian Club; GSE Hnrs Awd Algebra I; Physician.

CHA, LENG; Fresno HS; Fresno, CA; (3); 30/500; Boy Scts; Pres Church Yth Grp; French Clb; FBLA; Pres Intnl Clb; Model UN; Var Tennis; Cit Awd; French Hon Soc; Pres Acad Fit Awd; Leag Mst Imprvd Tnns Plyr 89-90; Medcl.

CHA, MAIXIM; Hiram W Johnson HS; Sacramento, CA; (2); 8/618; Church Yth Grp; FHA; Library Aide; Church Choir.

CHA, MAY YEE; Fresno HS; Pinedale, CA; (3); Office Aide; Pep Clb; Teachers Aide; Chorus; JV Cheerldng; Prfct Atten Awd; Asian Clb Actvts Dir; Mrt Awds-Acad; Tchrs Tmrrw FBLA; Fresno ST U; Elem Schl Tchr.

CHA, PANGNGEA; Los Amigos HS; Santa Ana, CA; (2); French Clb; Spanish Clb; Rptr Nwsp; Trk; Hon Roll.

CHA, PETER W; Narbonne HS; Carson, CA; (2); Church Yth Grp; Vllybl; High Hon Roll; Hon Roll; Chrch Yth Dept VP; UCI; Engrng.

CHA, SEONGJIN; Bonita Vista HS; Bonita, CA; (3); 1/530; Cit Awd; High Hon Roll; Hon Roll; Jr NHS; Tnns Clb; Pre-Med.

CHA, SOO-JIN; Bonita Vista SR HS; Bonita, CA; (4); 9/532; Mu Alpha Theta; Cit Awd; Hon Roll; Prfct Atten Awd; CSF; Acadmc Ltr Awd; Math Hnr Soc; Bio.

CHA, XIA; Roosevelt HS; Fresno, CA; (4); Science Clb; School Musical; Socr; Tennis; Vllybl; Wrstlng; Hon Roll; UC San Diego; Biochem Engr.

CHABOT, SHAWN; Gilroy HS; Gilroy, CA; (1); 40/500; Boy Scts; 4-H; Ftbl; Trk; Wt Lftg; Hon Roll; Schlr Athl Ftbll; U Of GA; Law Enf.

CHABOT, STACY; Righetti HS; Santa Maria, CA; (3); French Clb; Band; Mrchg Band; Pep Band; Cit Awd; High Hon Roll; GATE Frnch; Acad Decthln Tm; Stanford U; Social Sci.

CHACE, ANDY; Coronado HS; Coronado, CA; (3); 35/150; Boy Scts; Letterman Clb; Phtg Yrbk; JV Bsbl; Var Crs Cntry; Var Diving; NHS; UC; Bus Law.

CHACKO, JULIE A; Novato HS; Novato, CA; (4); 1/241; Key Clb; Spanish Clb; JV Var Bsktbl; Capt Powder Puff Ftbl; Var L Tennis; Var Trk; Hon Roll; Pres Acad Fit Awd; Val; Unocal Fndtn Schlrshp; Most Outstndng Hnr Stu; CSF; U Of CA San Diego; Pre Med.

CHACON, ADELA YANET; Fremont HS; Sunnyvale, CA; (2); Church Yth Grp; Latin Clb; De Anza Coll; Arch.

CHACON, CHRISTOPHER; Glendale HS; Glendale, CA; (2); JV Capt Bsbl; Cit Awd; High Hon Roll; Hon Roll; Foods Vctnl Awd; Hmrm Rep; Yth & Govt Yth Grp; U Of Southern CA; Med.

CHACON, CINDY V; Nogales HS; W Covina, CA; (2); Science Clb; Hon Roll; Prfct Atten Awd; CSF; Ed.

CHACON, MARIO E; Los Angeles HS; Los Angeles, CA; (4); Science Clb; Hon Roll; Prfct Atten Awd; SMC; Med.

CHACON, RACHEL; Alisal HS; Salinas, CA; (4); Office Aide; Teachers Aide; Score Keeper; Trk; Wt Lftg; Cit Awd; Hon Roll; Pres Acad Fit Awd; VP Alcohol Drug Abuse Prvntn Team; CA Grant A Schlrshp; Alisal Schl Dist Cert Of Outstndng Achvt; UC Santa Barbara; Admin Jstc.

CHACON, TINA L; Hemet HS; Hemet, CA; (2); Hon Roll.

CHADDERTON, RODNEY O; Hamilton HS Academy Of Music; Los Angeles, CA; (3); Band; Mrchg Band; CA ST Northridge; Aeronautics.

CHADDOCK, DEBORAH; Calaveras HS; Linden, CA; (2); Pres Treas 4-H; Treas FFA; JV Capt Bsktbl; JV Capt Vllybl; 4-H Awd; High Hon Roll; Secy CA Jr Simmental Assn; Treas Mokelume Mounties Mounted Drill Tm; CA Simmental Queen; UC Davis; Equine Speclst.

CHADICK, JENNIFER; Palmdale HS; Palmdale, CA; (3); Drill Tm; Powder Puff Ftbl; Brooks Coll; Sci.

CHADWICK III, JW U; Bloomington HS; Bloomington, CA; (4); Boy Scts; Drama Clb; Library Aide; Teachers Aide; Trk; Wt Lftg; Hon Roll.

CHADWICK, JENNIFER; Ernest Righetti HS; Santa Maria, CA; (3); FHA; Drill Tm; Jr Stsmn Amer; Cal Oly; Arch.

CHADWICK, MYKE; Palmdale HS; Palmdale, CA; (4); Key Clb; Pep Clb; Ski Clb; SADD; Yrbk; Var Co-Capt Cheerldng; Powder Puff Ftbl; Hon Roll; Parent-Tchr-Stu; CSF; Hmcmng Prncss; Real Estate.

CHADWICK, RETHA; Rincon Valley Christian HS; Santa Rosa, CA; (3); Church Yth Grp; Band; Chorus; Church Choir; Mrchg Band; School Play; Variety Show; Stu Cncl; Cit Awd; High Hon Roll; Salavation Army Volunteer; Western Baptist Coll; Pharmacy.

CHAFFIN, JULIE M; Tranquillity Union HS; Cantua Creek, CA; (3); Computer Clb; Letterman Clb; Library Aide; Flag Corp; Stat Ftbl; Var Vllybl; Hon Roll; 4-H; French Clb; Office Aide; Word Prcssng & Advncd Bus Skills Certs; Bus Hnr Soc; Fresno City; Medcl Asstnt Admin.

CHAFFIN, SAMANTHA L; Saddleback HS; Santa Ana, CA; (1); Cheerldng; CSF; Mock Trial; Marine Bio.

CHAGOLLA, LYDIA A; Bret Harte HS; Avery, CA; (2); Hon Roll; Vocational Olympics 3rd Pl Graphics; Bret Hart Block Lttr For Schlstc Achvt; Harvard; Criminal Law.

CHAGOLLAN, SAMANTHA L; Edison HS; Huntington Beach, CA; (3); 29/425; Model UN; Acpl Chr; Madrigal Ensmbl; Jr Class Cncl; Yng Conservatory Players; UCLA; Lib Arts.

CHAHMELIKIAN, SHAGHIG; Ferrahian HS; Van Nuys, CA; (2); School Play; Var Bsktbl; Var Vllybl; Armenian Yth Fed; Amer Hstry Awd; Homentmn Athltc; Grphc Art.

CHAHUA, GEORGE; Hungtinton Park HS; Los Angeles, CA; (3); Boy Scts; Teachers Aide; Gym; Swmmng; AP Span Cls; Real Estate.

CHAI, CHUCKRA; Leigh HS; San Jose, CA; (3); 1/300; Am Leg Boys St; Chess Clb; Debate Tm; Treas Pres Key Clb; Math Clb; Math Tm; NFL; VP Treas Spanish Clb; Sec Treas Jr Cls; Hon Roll.

CHAI, JERRY C; St Francis HS; Alhambra, CA; (2); Math Clb; Math Tm; Ed Yrbk; High Hon Roll; Hon Roll; NHS; Pres Acad Fit Awd; Asian-Amer Club; CSF.

CHAI, JULIE S; Santa Teresa HS; San Jose, CA; (3); Church Yth Grp; Drama Clb; Model UN; Q&S; Spanish Clb; SADD; Ed Nwsp; Rep Frsh Cls; Rep Soph Cls; Rep Jr Cls; UCSD; Med.

CHAI, SU YON; Milpitas HS; Milpitas, CA; (1); Pres Church Yth Grp; Church Choir; Sec Frsh Cls; Stat Score Keeper; Hon Roll; Prfct Atten Awd; Write Church Nwspr; UC Berkely; Jrnlsm.

CHAIDEZ, ADRIAN; Burroughs HS; Burbank, CA; (3); Teachers Aide; Chorus; Orch; Stu Cncl; Socr; Wt Lftg; Hon Roll; Prfct Atten Awd; Mst Imprvd Stu; UC Davis; Vet.

CHAING, CHY; Downey HS; Downey, CA; (3); Church Yth Grp; FBLA; Intnl Clb; Office Aide; Science Clb; Service Clb; High Hon Roll; Lion Awd; Prfct Atten Awd; Pres Acad Fit Awd.

CHAIREZ, ELIAS S; Brawley Union HS; Brawley, CA; (3); 10/300; Church Yth Grp; Teachers Aide; Church Choir; Stu Cncl; Bsktbl; Var Tennis; Elks Awd; Hon Roll; Cmnty Scer Coach; Cal Poly; Math.

CHAIVORAPOL, CHITTRA; Westminster HS; Midway City, CA; (3); Hosp Aide; Key Clb; Spanish Clb; Off Jr Cls; Fld Hcky; High Hon Roll; CSF; Advncd Plcmnt Clb; U CA; Pre-Med.

CHAKRABARTI, INDIRA; Arcadia HS; Arcadia, CA; (3); 66/700; VP Red Cross Aide; Teachers Aide; Band; Mrchg Band; Orch; Ed Yrbk; Bsktbl; Sftbl; JV Stat Swmmng; Vllybl; Amnsty Intl Clb Pres; UC San Diego; Engl Lit.

CHAKRAPANI, RAMESH; Whitney HS; Cerritos, CA; (1); Latin Clb; Science Clb; Balavihar; Mridangum; Bus.

CHALFANT, KATHY A; Fremont HS; Sunnyvale, CA; (4); 65/357; Church Yth Grp; Chorus; Fld Hcky; Tennis; Hon Roll; Berkeley; Real Estate Law.

CHALIAN, HOORI; Burbank HS; Burbank, CA; (2); Dance Clb; Girl Scts; Hosp Aide; Spanish Clb; Drill Tm; Rep Frsh Cls; Treas Yth Organ; Z Club; Arch.

CHALMERS, AMANDA; Don Antonio Lugo HS; Chino, CA; (3); Drama Clb; Hosp Aide; Teachers Aide; Thesps; School Play; Stage Crew; Phtg Yrbk; Chptr Vp & St Gld Mdl Wnnr HOSA Extmprns Spkng; Pr Cnclr; Algbr Tutr; UCLA; Nrsng.

CHALMERS, CHRISTY T; Sutter HS; Yuba City, CA; (4); Drama Clb; Intnl Clb; Letterman Clb; Teachers Aide; School Play; Stage Crew; Variety Show; Ed Nwsp; Ed Yrbk; Var L Bsktbl; CSF Life; CSU Chico; Cmmnctns.

CHALMERS, LAURA J; Casa Grande HS; Petaluma, CA; (2); 64/295; Cmnty Wkr; Dance Clb; Hosp Aide; SADD; Drill Tm; Crs Cntry; Vllybl; Hon Roll; CPR Cls; Sonoma ST; Vet Sci.

CHAMBERLAIN, ASENATH; Pioneer HS; San Jose, CA; (1); Cmnty Wkr; JV Bsktbl; JV Var Sftbl; Var Tennis; High Hon Roll; CSF; Stanford; Law.

CHAMBERLAIN, DAMON V; Casa Roble Fundamental HS; Orangevale, CA; (4); 155/325; Boy Scts; German Clb; JV Var Crs Cntry; JV Var Trk; Vrs Mdls & Trphs Trck/Crs Cntry; 3rd Pl CA St Trck Mt 1600; Nrthrn CA Hall Fame Trck; Ricks Coll; Educ.

CHAMBERLAIN, DANA; Riverdale HS; Laton, CA; (3); Church Yth Grp; Pres FFA; Ski Clb; SADD; Band; Pres Sr Cls; Tennis; High Hon Roll; Dance Clb; GAA; CSF VP 89-90; Acad Decathln 89-91; Fresno ST; Ag Bus.

CHAMBERLAIN, JACKIE M; Victory Christian Schl; Carmichael, CA; (2); Church Yth Grp; Pep Clb; Cheerldng; Gym; Hon Roll; Psych.

CHAMBERLIN III, ROBERT V; Woodland HS; Woodland, CA; (4); Drama Clb; French Clb; High Hon Roll; Hon Roll; Jr NHS; Pres Acad Fit Awd; Congrssnl Yth Ldrshp Awd Schlr 90; CSF; Amer JC; Bus Econ.

CHAMBERS, BRENDA; Yosemite HS; Oakhurst, CA; (4); 9/175; Church Yth Grp; French Clb; JV Tennis; High Hon Roll; Exch Stdnt Denmark 88-89; Jobs Dghts Past Hnrd Qun; Secy Teen Ctr; Intl Rel.

CHAMBERS, CYNTHIA D; Edison HS; Stockton, CA; (1); Orch; JV Bsktbl; UC Davis; Vet.

CHAMBERS, HAYWOOD B; Victorvalley HS; Victorville, CA; (3); Letterman Clb; Varsity Clb; Chorus; Church Choir; Stage Crew; Variety Show; VP Soph Cls; VP Jr Cls; Pres Sr Cls; Rep Stu Cncl; NAACP Jr Brnch, Pres; Pres Sr Cls; San Andres Wrtlng 1st Pl Wnnr 3 Yrs; San Diego ST U; Pilot.

CHAMBERS, HEATHER A; Diamond Bar HS; Chino Hills, CA; (4); Church Yth Grp; Office Aide; Off Sr Cls; Stu Cncl; Stat Bsktbl; Hon Roll; Pres Acad Fit Awd; San Diego ST Coll; Jrnlsm.

CHAMBERS, RANDY S; Carson HS; Carson, CA; (3); Chess Clb; Computer Clb; Band; Jazz Band; Sec Stu Cncl; JV Crs Cntry; JV Trk; Cit Awd; High Hon Roll; Prfct Atten Awd; Cmrcl Pilot.

CHAMBERS, REBECCA; Corona HS; Corona, CA; (4); Church Yth Grp; Drama Clb; GAA; Teachers Aide; School Play; Cheerldng; Hon Roll; Ldrshp Cmp; Kndrgrtn Tchr.

CHAMBERS, SARA A; Mt Whitney HS; Visalia, CA; (1); Church Yth Grp; FFA; Chorus; Church Choir; Color Guard; Swmmng; UNLV; Bus.

CHAMBERS, SARAH; Central Valley HS; Redding, CA; (4); 1/180; AFS; Cmnty Wkr; Pres Soph Cls; Pres Jr Cls; Pres Stu Cncl; Var Cheerldng; Var Tennis; Var Trk; DAR Awd; High Hon Roll; UCLA; Bio.

CHAMBERS, STACEY; Apple Valley Christian HS; Apple Valley, CA; (3); 1/18; Church Yth Grp; Teachers Aide; Chorus; Var L Bsktbl; Var L Sftbl; Stat Vllybl; High Hon Roll; Spec Olympics Coach; Awana Yth Pgm Ldr; Bus Mgmt.

CHAMBERS, TANISHA; Washington HS; Los Angeles, CA; (2).

CHAMBERS, VICKY L; Arlington HS; Riverside, CA; (3); 4/460; Church Yth Grp; FBLA; Library Aide; Spanish Clb; Church Choir; Stu Cncl; Intrml Powder Puff Ftbl; Hon Roll; NHS; Yth To Yth/Fri Night Live; Top 10-AZ St Math Cntst; Black Stu Union-Treas; Accntng.

CHAMBLEE, DONALD THOMAS; Clayton Valley HS; Concord, CA; (2); Ftbl; Wt Lftg; Hon Roll; Krte; Mtrcyclng; Wldng; Diablo Vlly Coll.

CHAMBLEE, JEFFREY; Calvary Baptist Christian HS; Fairfield, CA; (2); 1/5; Church Yth Grp; Var L Bsktbl; Var L Socr; Var L Sftbl; High Hon Roll; Schl Sci Fair 2nd Pl; AACS NC Comp Sci Fair Ust Bio Sci; AACS NC Comp Humerous Interpretation 3rd; Duke U; Law.

CHAMBLEE, RICHARD D; Calvary Baptist Christian Schl; Fairfield, CA; (3); 1/7; Church Yth Grp; Debate Tm; Church Choir; Co-Ed Yrbk; Pres Jr Cls; Pres Sr Cls; JV Var Bsktbl; Var L Socr; L Var Sftbl; Cit Awd; AACS 1st Pl Sci Fair Regnl Div; AACS 1st Pl Expository Essay Cont St Div; Pensacola Chrstn Coll; Missions.

CHAMBLISS, STEVE; Fountain Valley HS; Fountain Valley, CA; (2); VP JA.

CHAMMAS, AUDREY J; University HS; Irvine, CA; (3); 90/530; JV Socr; Var Swmmng; JV Tennis; French Hon Soc; Hon Roll; Girls Lg; UCLA; Med.

CHAMMAS, GUY; St Margarets Schl; Capistrano Beach, CA; (4); 1/25; Science Clb; Rptr Nwsp; Treas Stu Cncl; Var Crs Cntry; Var Capt Socr; Var Tennis; High Hon Roll; Val; Envrmntl Action Clb; Ecology Clb; Bio.

CHAMORRO, GISETTE M; Pioneer HS; San Jose, CA; (3); Church Yth Grp; Cmnty Wkr; JA; Math Clb; Spanish Clb; Varsity Clb; Off Frsh Cls; Off Soph Cls; Off Jr Cls; Off Sr Cls; Young Women Of Yr, Schlrshp Pgm 91; CSF 3 Yrs; Natl Hnr Soc 2 Yrs; Peer Tutor; Numerous Awds/Hnrs Achvt.

CHAMPLIN, JOHN C; George Washington HS; San Francisco, CA; (3); Boy Scts; Drama Clb; Intnl Clb; NFL; Ski Clb; Speech Tm; School Play; Rep Frsh Cls; Rep Soph Cls; JV Trk; Crew; Demolay.

CHAN, ALAN K; Etiwanda HS; Fontana, CA; (2); 1/30; Hon Roll; Pres Acad Fit Awd; Phrmcy.

CHAN, ALAN K; Skyline HS; Oakland, CA; (2); German Clb; Capt Vllybl; Hon Roll; GSE Hnrs Alg & Geom; Arch.

CHAN, ALBERT; Petaluma HS; Petaluma, CA; (4); 1/278; French Clb; Science Clb; Varsity Clb; Rep Frsh Cls; Treas Jr Cls; Treas Stu Cncl; High Hon Roll; Hon Roll; NHS; Ntl Merit Ltr.

CHAN, ALICE; Abraham Lincoln HS; San Francisco, CA; (2); Yrbk; Hon Roll; Soph Club; Lincs Soc; Grphc Arts.

CHAN, ALLAN L; Fountain Valley HS; Fountain Valley, CA; (2); Science Clb; Spanish Clb; High Hon Roll; Hon Roll; UC Davis; Pre Med.

CHAN, AMY; Lincoln HS; Stockton, CA; (4); 30/650; Church Yth Grp; Debate Tm; FBLA; VP Key Clb; Math Clb; Mu Alpha Theta; NFL; Sec Science Clb; Spanish Clb; Speech Tm; CA Schlrshp Fed; SALSA Stu Advancng Lang Spanish Assoc VP; Asian Clb VP Sec; USC Cal Poly; Arch.

CHAN, AMY; Lowell HS; San Francisco, CA; (3); SADD; Vlntr At St Marys Hsptl & Schl Offc; Archtctr & Engnrng Clb; Red Crss Clb; Sls Prsn At Kermese; Busi.

CHAN, ANDREA K; Saint Josephs Notre Dame HS; Oakland, CA; (3); Church Yth Grp; Intnl Clb; Office Aide; Hon Roll; NHS; Prfct Atten Awd; Social Justice Committee; Cal Poly; Pre-Law.

CHAN, ANDREW K; Fairfield HS; Fairfield, CA; (1); 9/31; Solano Coll; Comp Prgmr.

CHAN, ANITA; West HS; Bakersfield, CA; (1); Church Yth Grp; Hon Roll.

CHAN, ANITA M; San Gabriel HS; Alhambra, CA; (1); Chess Clb; French Clb; Math Clb; Band; High Hon Roll; Hon Roll; CSF; Med.

CHAN, ANITA N; John A Rowland HS; Rowland Hts, CA; (4); 84/600; Science Clb; Treas Spanish Clb; JV Tennis; High Hon Roll; Hon Roll; Prfct Atten Awd; Pres Acad Fit Awd; CSF; Acad Decthln Team; Interact Clb; UC Riverside; Bus Admin.

CHAN, BENJAMIN E; St Ignatius College Prep; Hercules, CA; (2); Science Clb; Hon Roll; Crew; Viking Sccr; CSF; Chinese; Russian; Kung Fu; Cornell; Doctor.

CHAN, BEVERLY P; San Gabriel HS; San Gabriel, CA; (2); Service Clb; Sec Spanish Clb; Pres Jr Cls; Stat Mgr(s); Capt Var Tennis; High Hon Roll; Jr NHS; Courtesy Cmmtee; CSF; AP Hstry, Geometry, Algebra; Coachs Awd Var Tennis.

CHAN, BILLY H; Flintridge Prep; San Marino, CA; (3); Computer Clb; JCL; Latin Clb; Math Clb; Science Clb; Orch; Pep Band; School Musical; Variety Show; Ed Yrbk; VP Flatridge Chaptr Of Stus For Exploration & Dev Of Sp; Latin Hnr Soc; Cal Tech; Biochem.

CHAN, BRIAN; Phillip & Sala Burton Academic HS; San Francisco, CA; (2); Church Yth Grp; Computer Clb; Treas Math Clb; Science Clb; Church Choir; Orch; Treas Frsh Cls; Treas Soph Cls; Hon Roll; Astronomy.

CHAN, BRYAN H; Lowell HS; San Francisco, CA; (2); Service Clb; Band; Mrchg Band; Orch; Pep Band; JV Trk; Jr Statesmn Amer; Recgntn Gldn St Alg Exm; Elec Engrng.

CHAN, CALONA; Notre Dame HS; Redwood City, CA; (2); Sec French Clb; Library Aide; Model UN; Teachers Aide; School Musical; JV Socr; JV Vllybl; Hon Roll; NHS; Go Clb; Chinese Lang; Bus.

CHAN, CANDACE; Skyline HS; Oakland, CA; (2); Key Clb; SADD; Band; Orch; Sftbl; Tennis; Vllybl; Hon Roll; CSF.

CHAN, CARRIE; South Pasadena HS; South Pasadena, CA; (2); Cmnty Wkr; Dance Clb; GAA; Scholastic Bowl; Service Clb; Ski Clb; SADD; Drill Tm; Pres Soph Cls; Mgr(s); Child Pysch.

CHAN, CHRISTOPHER; South Hills HS; Covina, CA; (4); 12/250; Debate Tm; Model UN; Quiz Bowl; Science Clb; Thesps; Varsity Clb; School Musical; School Play; Nwsp; Off Sr Cls; Vrsty Tennis Capt; Pres JR Statesmen Of Amer Chptr; VP Saracens; USC; Intl Bus.

CHAN, CHRISTOPHER V; St Ignatius College Prep; Hercules, CA; (4); 2/288; Sec Chess Clb; Hosp Aide; Pres Science Clb; Ed Nwsp; Bausch & Lomb Sci Awd; High Hon Roll; Natl Mrt Fnlst; Rcyclng Clb; Sci Fiction & Fantasy Clb; UC Berkeley.

CHAN, CICI; Encinal HS; Alameda, CA; (3); 17/233; Key Clb; Teachers Aide; Chorus; High Hon Roll; Var Bdmntn; Gldn ST Exm Alg Hnrs & Hgh Hnrs Geom.

CHAN, CLINT C; Bishop O'dowd HS; Oakland, CA; (2); Church Yth Grp; Orch; Engrng.

CHAN, CONNIE M; George Washington HS; San Francisco, CA; (2); High Hon Roll; Hon Roll; Ntl Merit Schol; Prncpl Cabinet; Chinese Amer Club; Gen Svc Soc; UC Davis; Bus.

CHAN, CURTIS W; Marina HS; Huntington Beach, CA; (2); Pres JA; Key Clb; Math Clb; Math Tm; Spanish Clb; Off Soph Cls; Bsktbl; Socr; JV Tennis; Hon Roll.

CHAN, CYNTHIA Y; Sacred Heart Prep; Foster City, CA; (4); 19/58; VP Cmnty Wkr; Model UN; Ski Clb; SADD; School Play; Ed Yrbk; Lit Mag; Hon Roll; NHS; Rensselaer Polytechnic; Arch.

CHAN, DAVID C; Alameda HS; Alameda, CA; (3); Church Yth Grp; Cmnty Wkr; Hosp Aide; Office Aide; Red Cross Aide; Science Clb; Spanish Clb; Chorus; Church Choir; Lit Mag; CSF; Asian Club; Korean Club Pblcty Ofcr; U CA Berkeley; Civil Engrng.

CHAN, DENISE; Petaluma HS; Petaluma, CA; (3); 1/260; Cmnty Wkr; Debate Tm; French Clb; Intnl Clb; Service Clb; Speech Tm; Pres Frsh Cls; JV Cheerldng; Bausch & Lomb Sci Awd; High Hon Roll; Stanford U.

CHAN, DEREK K; Servite HS; Whittier, CA; (2); 21/154; Debate Tm; Speech Tm; Hon Roll; NHS; NEDT Awd; CSF Dir; People To People Yth Sci Sxchnge Soviet Union.

CHAN, EILEEN; Thomas Edison HS; Stockton, CA; (2); Church Yth Grp; Cmnty Wkr; Hosp Aide; JV Swmmng; Hon Roll; NHS; Conflct Mgmt; Jobs Dghtrs; CSU Coll; Med.

CHAN, ELBERT; Hayward HS; Hayward, CA; (2); Teachers Aide; Cit Awd; Hon Roll; Prfct Atten Awd; Sci.

CHAN, EMILY W; Abraham Lincoln HS; San Francisco, CA; (2); Acpl Chr; Fencing; CSF; Gldn St Exam; Pharmacist.

CHAN, ERIC; Oakland HS; Castro Valley, CA; (3); German Clb; Key Clb; Math Clb; Math Tm; Science Clb; Hon Roll; Natl Math League Awd; UC Davis; Civil Engrng.

CHAN, ESSIE; Oakland HS; Oakland, CA; (3); Computer Clb; Science Clb; SADD; JV L Vllybl; Keywanettes Historian; Badminton; Engrng.

CHAN, FLORENE; Skyline HS; Oakland, CA; (4); Library Aide; Cit Awd; Hon Roll; Prfct Atten Awd.

CHAN, GALVIN; Lowell HS; San Francisco, CA; (2); Cmnty Wkr; Computer Clb; JV Bsbl; JV Bsktbl; Hon Roll; U Of CA; Compzd Sprts Med.

CHAN, HELEN O; Artesia HS; Norwalk, CA; (3); Science Clb; Spanish Clb; Hon Roll; Chinese Club; CA ST Poly; Bus.

CHAN, HOWARD; Wallenburg Traditional HS; San Francisco, CA; (4); 10/160; Boy Scts; French Clb; Sec Intnl Clb; Red Cross Aide; Science Clb; Teachers Aide; Yrbk; Sec Stu Cncl; High Hon Roll; Hon Roll; IM Fencing Tm; PG&E Exploring Prgm; U Of Pacific; Mgt Eng.

CHAN, HUAN LIN; Schurr HS; Monterey Park, CA; (3); Chess Clb; Computer Clb; VP French Clb; Math Clb; Math Tm; Scholastic Bowl; Hon Roll; Prfct Atten Awd; Tchng Tomrrw Cert Outstndng Achvt Instrnl Cmptn; Gldn St Exm Acad Excllnce Awd 87-88; CSF; UCLA; Med.

CHAN, HUAN-LIN; Schurr HS; Monterey Park, CA; (3); Chess Clb; Computer Clb; VP French Clb; Math Clb; Hon Roll; Prfct Atten Awd; CSF; Golden St Exam Acad Excllnc Awd; Touching Tomorrow Instructional Computing Awd; UCLA; Med.

CHAN, HUAN-OAI; Schurr HS; Monterey Park, CA; (2); Computer Clb; Library Aide; Math Clb; SADD; Hon Roll; CSF; UC Berkeley; Arch.

CHAN, JAYSTON S; South San Francisco HS; S San Francisco, CA; (3); 1/275; Am Leg Boys St; Computer Clb; Treas FBLA; VP Math Clb; VP Stu Cncl; Capt Crs Cntry; Trk; Bausch & Lomb Sci Awd; High Hon Roll; Ntl Merit SF; St Hstry Day 90; Amer HS Math Exam Sch Wnnr 90; Qlfd Amer Invtnl Math Exam; CSF; Engrng.

CHAN, JENNIFER; Charter Oak HS; Covina, CA; (3); Sec Treas Church Yth Grp; Mgr Nwsp; Stat Ftbl; Var L Socr; Hon Roll; NHS.

CHAN, JENNIFER; Menlo Schl; Menlo Park, CA; (4); 4/107; Cmnty Wkr; Hosp Aide; Var Sftbl; Var Vllybl; High Hon Roll; Ntl Merit Ltr; Rotary Awd; 90 Bank Of America Achvt Awd-Math; 90 Bank Of America Achvt Awd-Art; Chamber Music-Clarinet Piano; Dartmouth Coll; Biochemistry.

CHAN, JENNIFER; Oakland Technical HS; Oakland, CA; (4); Math Clb; Bsbl; Bsktbl; Sftbl; Swmmng; Vllybl; Cit Awd; High Hon Roll; Hon Roll; San Francisco ST U; Bus Admin.

CHAN, JEREMY J; Burlingame HS; San Francisco, CA; (3); Treas Church Yth Grp; French Clb; Math Clb; Band; Jazz Band; Mrchg Band; JV Var Tennis; Hon Roll; CSF 87-89; Congrssnl Schlr.

CHAN, JOSEPH L; San Gabriel HS; San Gabriel, CA; (3); Church Yth Grp; Cmnty Wkr; Key Clb; Letterman Clb; Spanish Clb; Varsity Clb; Intrml Bsktbl; JV Var Tennis; Hon Roll; Chrch/Fllwshp Grp.

CHAN, JOSETTE M; St Joseph HS; Long Beach, CA; (3); Debate Tm; Ski Clb; Stage Crew; Nwsp; Hon Roll; Pres Jr Cls; Rep Stu Cncl; Parsons Schl-Design; Grphic Dsn.

CHAN, JUSTINA K; Eagle Rock HS; Los Angeles, CA; (2); Teachers Aide; High Hon Roll; Hon Roll; Prfct Atten Awd; Bank Proof Saturday Cls; Chinese Clb; Awd Asian Pacific Heritage Wk; U S CA; :Bus Prfssnl.

CHAN, KEAN-MING; Skyline HS; Oakland, CA; (2); Sec Computer Clb; Key Clb; Math Clb; Val; Engl/Sci Trophies; Engrng.

CHAN, KENNETH; Bonita Vista HS; Bonita, CA; (4); 6/532; Tennis; FCA; NHS; UCLA; Med.

CHAN, KEVIN; West Covina HS; W Covina, CA; (4); Art Clb; Chess Clb; Debate Tm; German Clb; Science Clb; Hon Roll; NHS; JV, V MVP Bdmntn Tm 88 & 89; Grmn Natl Hnr Soc; San Gabriel Vly Chnese Cltrl Assn Yth Grp VP 88-90; UC Riverside; Bio-Med.

CHAN, KIT; Mark Keppel HS; Rosemead, CA; (1); Debate Tm; Math Clb; High Hon Roll; Hon Roll; CSF; Octagon Clb; U Of CA; Bus Admin.

CHAN, LAILANI C; Edison HS; Stockton, CA; (3); JV Tennis; High Hon Roll; Hon Roll; NHS; Sac ST; Astronaut.

CHAN, LAWRENCE G; Bellarmine Coll Prep; Milpitas, CA; (3); 50/300; Pres Church Yth Grp; Service Clb; Ed Nwsp; Intrml Capt Ftbl; Intrml Capt Sftbl; Intrml Capt Vllybl; JV Wrstlng; Pres Acad Fit Awd; 20 Hrs Wk Public Rltns Ofcr For Cnty; Campus Ministry Ldrshp Cncl; Created Paint War Games Club/Pres.

CHAN, LINA; Lowell HS; San Francisco, CA; (3); Red Cross Aide; Science Clb; Teachers Aide; High Hon Roll; Mandarin Speech Cont Wnnr 3rd Pl; Drug & Health Essay Cont Hnrb Mntn; Bio Club; U CA Berkeley; Optmtry.

CHAN, LISA; Schurr HS; Rosemead, CA; (4); Cmnty Wkr; Key Clb; Q&S; Flag Corp; Ed Nwsp; High Hon Roll; NHS; Pres Acad Fit Awd; CSF Treas; Yale Bk Awd; UCLA.

CHAN, LISA A; Los Altos HS; Los Altos, CA; (4); 24/318; VP Treas Service Clb; Sec SADD; Phtg Yrbk; Var Swmmng; High Hon Roll; Ntl Merit SF; Pres Acad Fit Awd; Outstndng Cert Natl Latin Exam; Vrsty Ltr Badmntn; UCLA; Ec.

CHAN, LISA W; Skyline HS; Oakland, CA; (3); Key Clb; Math Tm; SADD; Band; Orch; Pep Band; School Musical; Treas Jr Cls; Pres Stu Cncl; High Hon Roll; Smith Bk Awd; Bus/Law.

CHAN, MABEL; Abraham Lincoln HS; San Francisco, CA; (1); Church Yth Grp; School Musical; School Play; Ed Nwsp; Yrbk; Lit Mag; Rep Frsh Cls; Hon Roll; Jr NHS; Pres Acad Fit Awd; Bus.

CHAN, MARY BONITA M; Hillsdale HS; San Mateo, CA; (3); Math Clb; Math Tm; Science Clb; Soc Of Wmn Engrs Cert Of Merit 90; Math Tm Cmptn Cert Of Merit 87-0; Outstndng Stu Awd; Uc Berkeley; Biochem.

CHAN, MARY J; Mission HS; San Francisco, CA; (3); Teachers Aide; Rep Soph Cls; Var Vllybl; Hon Roll; CSF Hnr Soc; UC Berkeley; Accntnt.

CHAN, MARY M; Oakland HS; Oakland, CA; (1); German Clb; Nwsp; Trk; Hon Roll; Badminton Team; CJSF; Shclrsp Awd.

CHAN, MICHAEL H; Arcadia HS; Temple City, CA; (3); 106/643; Ftbl; Hon Roll; Korean Clb; Algling Clb; Excllnct Atten Awd; UC; Airline Pilot.

CHAN, MING Y; Oakland Technical HS; Oakland, CA; (2); Math Tm; Cit Awd; Hon Roll; Val; Bridge Clb; Historical Trivia; Yth Empowerment Advocates; Arch.

CHAN, MONICA; Edison HS; Stockton, CA; (2); Hon Roll; Engrng.

CHAN, NORMAN; Lowell HS; San Francisco, CA; (4); 41/626; Teachers Aide; High Hon Roll; Hon Roll; Jr NHS; Ntl Merit SF; Pres Acad Fit Awd; UC Berkeley; Phy Sci.

CHAN, PAMELA; Abraham Lincoln HS; San Francisco, CA; (2); French Clb; Latin Clb; High Hon Roll; CSF; Medicine.

CHAN, PATRICIA; West Covina HS; W Covina, CA; (4); 9/479; Art Clb; Science Clb; Spanish Clb; High Hon Roll; Acad Awd; Var Badminton Wd; Most Promising Frshmn Awd; U CA Riverside; Dsgn.

CHAN, PATTY; Davis SR HS; Davis, CA; (4); 37/370; AFS; German Clb; Key Clb; Yrbk; Treas Soph Cls; Treas Jr Cls; Treas Sr Cls; Var Crs Cntry; Co-Capt JV Vllybl; DAR Awd; Chinese Amer Elaine Shen Awd; Bnk Of Amer Engl Cert Wnnr; Human Relations Cover Dsgn Wnnr; U CA Santa Barbara; Pre-Bus.

CHAN, PEGGY; Diamond Bar HS; Walnut, CA; (2); German Clb; Key Clb; Rptr Nwsp; JV Tennis; Hon Roll; CSF.

CHAN, PERRY; Tennyson HS; Hayward, CA; (4); 5/250; Computer Clb; Debate Tm; Variety Show; Ed Nwsp; Prfct Atten Awd; Pres Acad Fit Awd; Bank Of Am-Achvt Awd For Eng As A 2nd Lang; CA Alumni Assn Berkeley Scholarship; Honor At Graduation; UC Berkeley; Civil Engrng.

CHAN, PRISCILLA C; Los Altos HS; Hacienda Hgts, CA; (4); Church Yth Grp; Intnl Clb; Model UN; Sec Band; Sec Mrchg Band; Pres Acad Fit Awd; Band Mst Imprvd Wind Ensmble 88 & 89; UC San Diego.

CHAN, QUENTIN; Edison HS; Stockton, CA; (1); Math Clb; NFL; Speech Tm; High Hon Roll; NHS; CSF; U CA Berkeley; Med.

CHAN, RUFINA; Lowell HS; San Francisco, CA; (2); Red Cross Aide; Orch; Cmptr Prgmr.

CHAN, SAMUEL; George Washington HS; San Francisco, CA; (2); Church Yth Grp; Key Clb; Red Cross Aide; Service Clb; Spanish Clb; Teachers Aide; Band; Rep Soph Cls; Ftbl; High Hon Roll; U CA-DAVIS; Bus.

CHAN, STACIE; Mills HS; Millbrae, CA; (3); 15/295; Church Yth Grp; Debate Tm; Intnl Clb; Band; Church Choir; Jazz Band; Orch; Rptr Nwsp; Lit Mag; Rep Stu Cncl; Pres Of Interact Club JR Division Of Rotary; Play Oboe In CA Youth Symphony; Stu At SF Consv Of Mus; U; International Economics.

CHAN, STANLEY G; Lowell HS; San Francisco, CA; (3); Q&S; Scholastic Bowl; Science Clb; Service Clb; Varsity Clb; JV Var Tennis; High Hon Roll; NHS; Csf; Goldn St Exam High Hnrs Alg & Geom; All-City Tnns Vrsty Doubles Fnlst; UCLA; Bus Mgmt.

CHAN, STEFANIE M; Skyline HS; Oakland, CA; (3); Cmnty Wkr; Hosp Aide; Key Clb; Treas Frsh Cls; High Hon Roll; Hon Roll; CSF; Yth Endng & Envrnmntl Clb; Easter Seals Vlntr.

CHAN, STELLA K; Santa Teresa HS; San Jose, CA; (3); Hosp Aide; Math Clb; Spanish Clb; School Musical; Var Vllybl; Hospital Vlntr; San Jose ST U; Nurse.

CHAN, STELLA M; Skyline HS; Oakland, CA; (3); Pres Key Clb; Math Clb; Math Tm; Office Aide; Red Cross Aide; Sec Service Clb; Art Clb; Lit Mag; Off Frsh Cls; Sec Jr Cls; Marcus A Footer Ed Inst Achvmnt Awd; U Of Ca Berkeley.

CHAN, STEVEN C; John Swett HS; Rodeo, CA; (2); 3/120; FBLA; Science Clb; Ed Nwsp; Rep Jr Cls; Rep Stu Cncl; JV Capt Bsktbl; Var L Tennis; Hon Roll; CSF Treas; Amercn Chem Soc Awd; CA Math Leag Awd.

CHAN, TIMOTHY; University HS; Irvine, CA; (3); 2/568; Pres Chess Clb; Pres Math Clb; NFL; Pres Science Clb; Var Speech Tm; Lit Mag; Var Tennis; Sci Rsrch Oncogene Lba UCI, Pblsh Paper 91; Jr Sci/Hmnts Sypmsm Fllwshp Sthrn CA Acad Sci; Med.

CHAN, TONY; Piedmont HS; Piedmont, CA; (3); Crs Cntry; Trk; NCS Schltc Athl; East Shore Athltc Leag Chmpn 89; Athl Of Month; Med.

CHAN, VICTON; Inglewood HS; Inglewood, CA; (2); Chess Clb; FBLA; Ed Nwsp; JV Crs Cntry; Intrml Trk; Cit Awd; High Hon Roll; Hon Roll; Ntl Merit Ltr; Prfct Atten Awd; 1st Astronaut Engr Bld 1st Ever Spcshp Go Far Away & Discvr Planets; UCLA; Astrontcl Engr.

CHAN, VINSON K; William Howard Taft HS; Reseda, CA; (2); Chess Clb; Computer Clb; Service Clb; High Hon Roll; Prfct Atten Awd; Goldn St Exam High Hnrs Alg & Geom; Math.

CHAN, VIVIAN; George Washington HS; San Francisco, CA; (3); Cmnty Wkr; Red Cross Aide; Service Clb; High Hon Roll; Hon Roll; BASIS; San Francisco ST U; Bus.

CHAN, WAI YEE; Irvine HS; Irvine, CA; (3); 77/512; Hosp Aide; Band; Jazz Band; Mrchg Band; School Musical; Hon Roll; Hlth Occptn Stus Of Amer; Med.

CHAN, WILLIAM; Colton HS; Loma Linda, CA; (3); Computer Clb; Hosp Aide; Key Clb; Letterman Clb; VP Science Clb; Varsity Clb; Var Tennis; Cit Awd; High Hon Roll; Hon Roll; Pre-Medicine.

CHAN, YVONNE; George Washington HS; San Francisco, CA; (2); Cmnty Wkr; High Hon Roll; Photogrphy Clb; San Francisco ST; Art.

CHANANA, VANI K; Hillsdale HS; San Mateo, CA; (3); ESL Aide For 2 Yrs; CSM.

CHANAWATR, BRYAN; Brea-Olinda HS; Brea, CA; (3); 6/400; Key Clb; Nwsp; Var Capt Socr; Var Capt Tennis; Hon Roll; Jr NHS; Safe Rides.

CHANCE, JENNA C; Carpinteria HS; Carpinteria, CA; (3); Computer Clb; Tennis; Trk; Hon Roll; Comp Aided Drftng.

CHANCE, MICHAEL A; San Clemente HS; San Clemente, CA; (1); Var Bsbl; Capt Ftbl; Psyclgy.

CHANCHEA, BORITH; Roosevelt HS; Fresno, CA; (4); 33/621; Library Aide; Teachers Aide; Hon Roll; Prfct Atten Awd; Hnr In Golden St Exam Geom; CSU; Civil Engr.

CHAND, ANDREW A; Luther Burbank HS; Sacramento, CA; (3); FFA; Socr; Cit Awd; Engrng.

CHAND, REETA; Woodrow Wilson HS; San Francisco, CA; (3); JA; Office Aide; Teachers Aide; Sec Jr Cls; Bsbl; Bsktbl; Ftbl; Swmmng; Tennis; Hon Roll; Law.

CHAND, SIDDHARTHA A; Herbert Hoover HS; Fresno, CA; (3); Debate Tm; NFL; Speech Tm; School Play; Ed Nwsp; Tennis; ST Fnlst Frnscs; Law.

CHANDLER, CYNTHIA A; Coast Union HS; Cambria, CA; (4); Church Yth Grp; Drama Clb; German Clb; Spanish Clb; Teachers Aide; Chorus; Church Choir; High Hon Roll; Hon Roll; Sierra JC; Early Chldhd Ed.

CHANDLER, ERIC C; Victor Valley HS; Victorville, CA; (2); JV Ftbl; Var Wt Lftg; Var Wrstlng; Accntnt.

CHANDLER, IVY; Nogales HS; Walnut, CA; (3); 35/542; Church Yth Grp; VP Spanish Clb; Var Swmmng; High Hon Roll; Hon Roll; Aquatic Clb Secy; Peer Helpers; Azusa Pacific U; Counseling.

CHANDLER, JODY; Fall River HS; Fall River Mills, CA; (3); FFA; Letterman Clb; Ski Clb; SADD; Stu Cncl; Var Cheerldng; Hon Roll; Shasta Coll; Ag.

CHANDLER, KALA; Piedmont HS; Piedmont, CA; (3); Church Yth Grp; SADD; Rptr Nwsp; Rep Jr Cls; Rep Sr Cls; Rep Stu Cncl; Var L Bsktbl; Var L Crs Cntry; Var L Sftbl; Campfire Cnslr; Med.

CHANDLER, KAMI; Lassen Union HS; Susanville, CA; (4); 48/230; Church Yth Grp; Cmnty Wkr; Letterman Clb; Office Aide; Pep Clb; Teachers Aide; Variety Show; Rep Frsh Cls; Rep Soph Cls; Bsbl; 2nd Rnnr-Up Elks Teenager Of Yr; Rotary Yth Exch To Sweden; Vol Adopt A Grand Parent; Real Estate.

CHANDLER, LAURA L; San Gorgonio HS; San Bernardino, CA; (3); Cmnty Wkr; Key Clb; Office Aide; Ski Clb; SADD; Teachers Aide; Pres Jr Cls; Rep Stu Cncl; Capt Powder Puff Ftbl; Cit Awd; UCI; Bus.

CHANDLER, SCOTT S; Fullerton Union HS; Fullerton, CA; (4); Letterman Clb; Office Aide; Varsity Clb; Var L Socr; Var L Swmmng; Water Polo Var Ltr; Rancho Satiago Coll; Pol Sci.

CHANDLER, TODD; Damien HS; Ontario, CA; (3); 31/181; Cmnty Wkr; Rep Jr Cls; JV Bsbl; Capt Bsktbl; Var Ftbl; DAR Awd; Hon Roll; Comm Svc Yth Soccer Prog.

CHANDLER, TRAMPIS D; Clovis HS; Clovis, CA; (2); Wrstlng; UC Davis; Vet.

CHANDLER, TRINETTE RENEE; San Diego HS; San Diego, CA; (4); 60/380; Spanish Clb; Hist Stu Cncl; Hon Roll; Pres Of Black Stu Union; Natl Phi Delta Kappa Schlrshp Wnnr; Carnegie Mellon U; Elec Engr.

CHANDNANI, RAJESH K; Gretchen Whitney HS; Cerritos, CA; (3); FBLA; VP JA; Pres Key Clb; Lbrn Band; Ed Nwsp; Dnfth Awd; High Hon Roll; Principals Advisory Brd Chrprsn; CSF VP; Law.

CHANDRA, ASHWINI; Williams HS; Williams, CA; (1); Hon Roll; Acad Tlnt Srch; UC Davis; Law.

CHANDRA, GITA; River City HS; W Sacramento, CA; (3); Ski Clb; Spanish Clb; SADD; Teachers Aide; Off Frsh Cls; Bsktbl; Vllybl; Cit Awd; Hon Roll; Prfct Atten Awd; Peer Grp; Stanford; Bus.

CHANDRA, ROSIE; Modesto HS; Modesto, CA; (3); Model UN; Office Aide; Teachers Aide; Tennis; Stanislaus ST U; Reg Nrs.

CHANEY, EPHRIAM JEROME; Hogan SR HS; Vallejo, CA; (4); 4-H; Chorus; Church Choir; Acad Excllnc Awd; Mem Sickle Cell Anemia Fndtn; Sacramento ST Coll; Arch Engr.

CHANEY, HEIDI M; Rio Lindo Acad; Ukiah, CA; (4); Art Clb; Church Yth Grp; FCA; French Clb; Ski Clb; Teachers Aide; Acpl Chr; Band; Chorus; Church Choir; Pacific Union Coll; Phys Thrpy.

CHANEY, JENNIFER A; Merced HS; Merced, CA; (3); 4-H; French Clb; Color Guard; Drill Tm; Ed Lit Mag; Elks Awd; 4-H Awd; Hon Roll; Lion Awd; Mid Valley Saddle Club Jr Grp Pres.

CHANEY, JUSTIN; Ambassador Baptist HS; Mira Loma, CA; (1); 3/30; Varsity Clb; Var L Bsbl; Var L Bsktbl; Var L Ftbl; Hon Roll.

CHANEY, KIRK; Arroyo Grande HS; Arroyo Grande, CA; (2); JV Var Ftbl; JV Trk; Surfing; Riding Motorcycles; Work Grocers; Cuesta Coll; Gen Contr.

CHANEY, MICHAEL J; San Luis Obispo HS; San Luis Obispo, CA; (1); Crs Cntry; Trk; Hon Roll.

CHANEY, NATHANIA L; Sir Francis Drake HS; San Anselmo, CA; (4); 1/140; School Play; Stage Crew; Rep Soph Cls; JV Vllybl; Bausch & Lomb Sci Awd; High Hon Roll; St Schlr; Val; Hon Roll; Amnesty Intl; Freedom Writer; Natl Mrt Fnlst; Regents Schlr; UC Davis; Chem.

CHANEY, RHONDA L; Red Bluff Union HS; Red Bluff, CA; (3); 4-H; Girl Scts; Library Aide; ROTC; SADD; Band; Hon Roll; Bowling; U Of San Diego; Library.

CHANEY, SYLVIA YOLANDA; Saddleback HS; Santa Ana, CA; (3); Cmnty Wkr; Pep Clb; SADD; Stu Cncl; JV Var Bsktbl; Var L Cheerldng; JV Pom Pon; Var L Trk; Black Stu Union; Performed All Around The World At The O C Arts Ctr; Spelman Coll; Bus.

CHANG, ALAN; Montery Bay Acad; Camarillo, CA; (4); 7/115; Church Yth Grp; Cmnty Wkr; English Clb; Math Clb; Science Clb; Ski Clb; Spanish Clb; Chorus; Church Choir; VP Frsh Cls; UC Berkeley; Intl Bus Law.

CHANG, ALEX; San Gabriel HS; Alhambra, CA; (1); Key Clb; JV Swmmng; U Of CA Irvine; Surgeon.

CHANG, ALEXANDER; Glen A Wilson HS; Hacienda Hts, CA; (3); 30/500; Church Yth Grp; Varsity Clb; Band; Church Choir; Jazz Band; Mrchg Band; Orch; Hon Roll; Prfct Atten Awd; Badminton Tm; Cal St LA Saturday Conservatory Of Music; Tennis Clb; Cal ST Northridge; Bus.

CHANG, ALICE; Gunn HS; Palo Alto, CA; (3); Cmnty Wkr; Debate Tm; French Clb; JA; Office Aide; Speech Tm; Rptr Nwsp; JV Var Cheerldng; Gym; Pom Pon; Pres Jr Stsmn Amer Clb; Mock Trial Team; Barnard Coll; Pol Sci.

CHANG, ALING L; University HS; Irvine, CA; (4); Spanish NHS; Pediatrics.

CHANG, ALLEN C; De Anza HS; Richmond, CA; (3); Science Clb; Ski Clb; Treas Jr Cls; Treas Sr Cls; JV Var Ftbl; Var Tennis; High Hon Roll; Hon Roll; UC Berkeley; Engrng.

CHANG, ANN S; Sunny Hills HS; Fullerton, CA; (2); 154/464; VP Church Yth Grp; Var Swmmng; Hon Roll; Arch.

CHANG, ANNE C; George Washington HS; San Francisco, CA; (3); Math Clb; Science Clb; High Hon Roll; Hon Roll; Math, Algebra & Chem Achvt Certs; Accntnt.

CHANG, ANNIE; University HS; Irvine, CA; (1); French Clb; Key Clb; Orch; School Musical; Hon Roll; Orange Cnty Acad Decthln 4th Pl; Laureate Awd Engl; Math AP Calcls; Math.

CHANG, APHONE; Arlington HS; Riverside, CA; (4); 13/350; Treas Rptr FBLA; Scholastic Bowl; JV Bsktbl; Pres Acad Fit Awd; CSF Life Mbr; Zonta Career Clb; JV Badminton; U Of CA Riverside; Bus Admn.

CHANG, ARTHUR; Saratoga HS; Saratoga, CA; (3); 13/228; Teachers Aide; Crs Cntry; Trk; Wt Lftg; CSF; U CA Santa Barbara Schlr Day; Robotech.

CHANG, AUGUSTINE; San Ramon Valley HS; San Ramon, CA; (4); 43/403; Computer Clb; Drama Clb; FBLA; Intnl Clb; Key Clb; Pep Clb; Band; Chorus; Mrchg Band; Orch; CA Schlrshp Fed; Biochem.

CHANG, BENJAMIN W; Miramonte HS; Moraga, CA; (4); Chess Clb; Debate Tm; Drama Clb; French Clb; NFL; Science Clb; Rep Frsh Cls; Rep Stu Cncl; Intrml Socr; VP L Trk; Crss Cntry Skiing Team; Peer Tutor; Photo Clb; U CA Berkeley; Econ.

CHANG, BETTY Y; Abraham Lincoln HS; San Francisco, CA; (4); 14/444; Cmnty Wkr; Office Aide; Teachers Aide; High Hon Roll; Acad Of Finance; Bnk Amer Achvt Awd Appld Arts; CSF Pres; UC Berkeley; Elec Engrng.

CHANG, BRIAN P; Brea-Olinda HS; Brea, CA; (1); Church Yth Grp; Band; Church Choir; Mrchg Band; Pep Band; Bsktbl; Ftbl; Trk; High Hon Roll; Hon Roll; Chinese Lang Schl; Piano Guild Awd; Music Tchr Assoc Awd; Cert Of Merit; Pthlgst.

CHANG, BRUCE; Whitney HS; Cerritos, CA; (2); Drama Clb; Key Clb; Math Tm; Model UN; Orch; Hon Roll; Pres Acad Fit Awd; CA Jr Schlrhsp Fed; Astronomy Clb; Scrapbook Artist Clss Prtcptn 89-90; Bio.

CHANG, CAROL S; Woodbridge HS; Irvine, CA; (4); JA; SADD; Chorus; Trk; Hon Roll; NHS; Awrd Englsh & Sci Sntnl Awrd; U Of CA; Psych.

CHANG, CHAE-SIK; Seaside HS; Marina, CA; (3); 10/200; Spanish Clb; Teachers Aide; Socr; High Hon Roll; NHS; Golden ST Geometry Exam High Hnr 89; Outstndng Acad Excllnc In Schl Awd 88-90; UC Davis; Bus.

CHANG, CHARLIE; Diamond Bar HS; Walnut, CA; (2); #2 In Class; Chess Clb; German Clb; Intnl Clb; Key Clb; Science Clb; Rptr Nwsp; Lit Mag; Intrml Bsktbl; Intrml Tennis; Proofcheck Reader For Elem Schl; CA Tech; Engrng.

CHANG, CHING-WEN; Culver City HS; Culver City, CA; (1); Cit Awd; Hon Roll.

CHANG, CHRISTINA; Cornelia Connelly HS; Hacienda Hghts, CA; (3); Cmnty Wkr; German Clb; GAA; Hosp Aide; Intnl Clb; Model UN; Science Clb; Mgr Yrbk; Tennis; Trk; Natl Ldrshp & Service Awd; Natl Jr Tnns Leag Chmpnshp Trnmnt 3rd Pl; Cls Play Bst T Shirt Awd; Med.

CHANG, CHRISTINA A; Lowell HS; San Francisco, CA; (3); Church Yth Grp; Office Aide; Teachers Aide; High Hon Roll; Ntl Merit Ltr; Gldn St Exam Alg Hnrs Awd 88; Gldn St Exam Geom Hnrs Awd 89; Piano; UC Davis.

CHANG, CHRISTINE; Newbury Park HS; Newbury Park, CA; (3); 3/347; Church Yth Grp; Hosp Aide; Pres Spanish Clb; VP SADD; Co-Capt Color Guard; Treas Frsh Cls; Treas Jr Cls; Treas Sr Cls; JV Tennis; High Hon Roll; Med.

CHANG, CHUN; San Leandro HS; San Leandro, CA; (3); 13/399; Computer Clb; Key Clb; Math Clb; Math Tm; Cit Awd; Prfct Atten Awd; Golden St Exam 1st Yr Alg Hgh Hnrs; Outstndng Smmr Schl Stu; Interact Clb; Stu Art Rcgntn 89; UC Berkeley; Chemcl Engrng.

CHANG, CLARK C; La Canada HS; La Canada, CA; (3); Pres Chess Clb; Treas Key Clb; Math Clb; Math Tm; Mu Alpha Theta; Science Clb; Orch; JV Capt Tennis; NHS; Violin S CA; ST Hnr Orchestra:Cmptrs; Engr.

CHANG, CLEMENT; University HS; Los Angeles, CA; (3); Chess Clb; High Hon Roll; Hon Roll; NHS; Ntl Merit Ltr; Pres Schlr.

CHANG, CLIFTON; El Toro HS; El Toro, CA; (2); 14/557; Church Yth Grp; German Clb; Key Clb; JV Socr; Swmmng; High Hon Roll; Hon Roll; Top 20; Wtr Polo; Chrmn Meals On Wheels For Key Clb; Bus.

CHANG, DANIELLE D; Henry M Gunn HS; Los Altos, CA; (4); French Clb; Nwsp; Off Sr Cls; French Studies Sorbonne U Smmr 89; Social Psych Columbia U Smmr 88; Jrnlsm Oxford U Smmr 87; Barnard Coll; Jrnlsm.

CHANG, DAVID; Hiram Johnson HS; Sacramento, CA; (2); 12/182; Hon Roll; CA ST U; Accntng.

CHANG, DAVID H; Arcadia HS; Arcadia, CA; (3); Art Clb; Service Clb; Orch; Tennis; Hon Roll; NHS; Prfct Atten Awd; VP & Treas, Korean Clb; CSF; Arch.

CHANG, DAVIE T; Whitney HS; Lakewood, CA; (3); Drama Clb; Key Clb; Var Crs Cntry; Var Trk; Var Wt Lftg; High Hon Roll; Cycling; Repair Automobiles; CA ST Polytech Inst; Engrng.

CHANG, DEANNA; Wallenberg HS; San Francisco, CA; (1); Church Yth Grp; Var Tennis; High Hon Roll; Hon Roll; Occidental; Marine Bio.

CHANG, DONNA; George Washington HS; San Francisco, CA; (4); Chess Clb; Hon Roll; Acad Of Art Coll Mrt Awd; 90 Poster Cont-Mst Colorful Wnnr; U CA-BERKELEY; Art.

CHANG, DORRIE E; Birmingham HS; Reseda, CA; (3); FBLA; Hosp Aide; Key Clb; Math Tm; Service Clb; SADD; Yrbk; Off Frsh Cls; Hist Soph Cls; Off Jr Cls; Rensselaer Medal For Math & Sci; CSF; Earth Rights Club Treas, Recycling Cmmtte; Stanford; Physician.

CHANG, DRIA; Fresno HS; Fresno, CA; (4); 3/24; Nwsp; Yrbk; Vllybl; Hon Roll; SE Asian Club Pres 89; All City Vlybl Tm Made City All-Star Game; MVP Var Vlybl & Tm Capt; Fresno ST U; Hlth Sci.

CHANG, EDWARD; Whitney HS; Cerritos, CA; (1); 5/155; Intrml Bsktbl; Var Trk; High Hon Roll; Hon Roll; Golden St Exam Hgh Hnrs; Korean & Chinese Clb; Coachs Awd In Bsktbl; Engrng.

CHANG, EMILY N; Las Lomas HS; Walnut Creek, CA; (1); 1/249; JCL; JV Sftbl; High Hon Roll; Underclassman Awd For Eng; Contra Costa Chinese Schl; Private Piano Lessons; Eng.

CHANG, ERIC; John A Rowland HS; Rowland Hgts, CA; (4); German Clb; Science Clb; JV Var Ftbl; JV Var Trk; High Hon Roll; Pres Acad Fit Awd; Pres Schlr; CSF; Interact Clb; U CA-LOS Angeles; Elec Engr.

CHANG, FRANCIS; Monta Vista HS; Cupertino, CA; (3); Church Yth Grp; Cmnty Wkr; Debate Tm; Hosp Aide; JA; Math Clb; Math Tm; NFL; Science Clb; Speech Tm; Med.

CHANG, FRANK H; Artesia HS; Artesia, CA; (3); 9/400; Intnl Clb; Science Clb; Spanish Clb; High Hon Roll; UCLA; Comp Sci.

CHANG, FREDDY F; Diamond Bar HS; Diamond Bar, CA; (3); 36/535; Intnl Clb; Library Aide; Scholastic Bowl; Science Clb; Tennis; Hon Roll; Prfct Atten Awd.

CHANG, GILBERT K; South San Francisco HS; South San Francis, CA; (3); 20/200; Computer Clb; Math Clb; Spanish Clb; Teachers Aide; Bsktbl; Score Keeper; High Hon Roll; Prfct Atten Awd; CSF Clb; Badminton; Asian Amer Clb; Comp Engr.

CHANG, GRACE Y; Edison HS; Huntington Beach, CA; (1); Model UN; JV Swmmng; Prfct Atten Awd; Violin; Piano; U CA Irvine; Phy.

CHANG, HEEYEON; Narbonne Math/Science Magnet HS; San Pedro, CA; (2); Church Yth Grp; Debate Tm; Hosp Aide; Service Clb; JV Tennis; Hon Roll; Prfct Atten Awd; Acad Decathlon; Keywanette Clb; LAUSD Natl Womens Hstry Mnth 90 Essay Cont 2nd Pl; Bus.

CHANG, HENRY; John Marshall HS; Los Angeles, CA; (3); Chess Clb; Drama Clb; Red Cross Aide; Service Clb; Capt Mrchg Band; School Play; Nwsp; Yrbk; Off Frsh Cls; Stu Cncl; DARE Pgm Speaker; Bus.

CHANG, HOWARD Y; University HS; Irvine, CA; (4); 4/500; Capt Debate Tm; Capt Math Tm; NFL; Science Clb; Intrml Trk; High Hon Roll; Lion Awd; Ntl Merit SF; Sal; Spanish NHS; USA Today All USA HS Acad Team 2nd Team; Amer Jr Acad Sci; Harvard; Med.

CHANG, I-LI; College Park HS; Pleasant Hill, CA; (3); French Clb; Intnl Clb; Secy Asian Clb; U Of San Francisco; Bus.

CHANG, IRENE C; Narbonne HS; Harbor City, CA; (4); Girl Scts; JA; Key Clb; Office Aide; Pep Clb; Service Clb; Teachers Aide; Band; Hon Roll; Lion Awd; Lions Clb/Hrbr City Voc Awd; R B Haley Mem Schlrshp Awd; S Bay Hrbr Ind/Educ Cncl Awd; Bk Of Amer Achvt; San Diego ST U; Bus.

CHANG, JAE D; Chaminade College Prep; West Hills, CA; (3); Pres Church Yth Grp; Band; Mrchg Band; Lit Mag; Rep Stu Cncl; JV Ftbl; Var Swmmng; Hon Roll; NHS; Vlntr Tech Hosptl Phrmcy; Arch.

CHANG, JANET; Mills HS; San Bruno, CA; (3); Church Yth Grp; Intnl Clb; Band; Church Choir; Pep Band; Mgr Swmmng; High Hon Roll; Hon Roll; Earth Clb; Interact; Pre Med.

CHANG, JASON; Warren HS; Downey, CA; (3); Art Clb; Church Yth Grp; Mu Alpha Theta; Spanish Clb; Church Choir; Var Vllybl; Hon Roll; St Schlr; Won 4th Place In School Art Show; U CA In Los Angeles; Sci.

CHANG, JASON M; Sonora HS; La Habra, CA; (4); 11/305; Boy Scts; Computer Clb; Intnl Clb; Sec Math Clb; Math Tm; Science Clb; Spanish Clb; Var Tennis; Hon Roll; NHS; UCLA; Elect Engrng.

CHANG, JEFF W; Whitney HS; Cerritos, CA; (1); Church Yth Grp; Nwsp; NHS; CA JR Schlrshp Fndtn; Med.

CHANG, JENNIFER; Santa Monica HS; Santa Monica, CA; (4); Church Yth Grp; Math Clb; Math Tm; Pep Clb; Teachers Aide; Band; Drill Tm; Mrchg Band; Ed Yrbk; Off Frsh Cls; USC.

CHANG, JENNIFER Y; Piedmont HS; Piedmont, CA; (3); 1/125; Pres Debate Tm; French Clb; Model UN; NFL; Science Clb; Pres Speech Tm; Orch; Nwsp; High Hon Roll; Hon Roll; Yng Peoples Symp Orch, Berkeley, 1st Violinist; CSF Pres; Alpha Clan Hnr Soc Treas.

CHANG, JEREMY Y; George Washington HS; San Francisco, CA; (3); Computer Clb; Math Clb; Science Clb; Service Clb; Teachers Aide; High Hon Roll; UC; Chem.

CHANG, JESSICA Y; Sonora HS; Fullerton, CA; (2); 1/313; Art Clb; Pres Chess Clb; FBLA; Rep GAA; Math Clb; Spanish Clb; Drill Tm; Hon Roll; Var Crs Cntry; JV Socr; Mst Insprtnl Vrsty Bdmntn Tm; 5th Pl Lit Orange Cnty Acad Dcthln; Emrgng Ldr Pgm CA ST U Fullerton; UC Berkeley; Sci.

CHANG, JIMMY T; Cupertino HS; Cupertino, CA; (2); FBLA; Spanish Clb; Rptr Nwsp; Lit Mag; UCLA; Med.

CHANG, JOAN- YING; Valencia HS; Placentia, CA; (2); Church Yth Grp; Cmnty Wkr; Science Clb; School Play; Nwsp; Trk; GATE Pgm; Miss Teen Orange Cnty 90; UC Berkeley.

CHANG, JOANNE K; Glendale Adventist Acad; Pasadena, CA; (4); 1/80; Hosp Aide; Office Aide; Teachers Aide; Band; Chorus; Yrbk; Sec Stu Cncl; High Hon Roll; VP NHS; Prfct Atten Awd; Pacific Union Coll; Phy.

CHANG, JOHN C; Glen A Wilson HS; Diamond Bar, CA; (4); Church Yth Grp; Computer Clb; German Clb; Hosp Aide; Science Clb; Speech Tm; Gym; High Hon Roll; Hon Roll; Pres Acad Fit Awd; 1st Pl Glen A Wilson Art Show; 1st Pl Spch Cntst For Sccs; Art Wrk Pblshd In Dist Ltry Mag; UCLA; Pre-Med.

CHANG, JOHN F; Fontana HS; Fontana, CA; (3); Math Tm; Band; Mrchg Band; Tennis; Trk; Hon Roll; Pres Acad Fit Awd; Sci, Math & Hstry Stu Of Ry; 1st Pl Math Fld Day; 1st Pl Natl Math Leag; Acadmc Dcthln; J P Sousa Awd; U Of CA Irvine; Engrng.

CHANG, JOHN I; Irvine HS; Irvine, CA; (2); Orch; Hon Roll; Bus.

CHANG, JOHN WOI; John F Kennedy HS; Buena Park, CA; (3); Computer Clb; Key Clb; High Hon Roll; Hon Roll; NEDT Awd; Pres Acad Fit Awd; CSF Top 25 Awd Golden St Exam; Cal Tech; Engrng.

CHANG, JOYCE; Saratoga HS; Saratoga, CA; (1); Cmnty Wkr; Debate Tm; Drama Clb; NFL; Service Clb; Speech Tm; Chorus; Stage Crew; High Hon Roll; Pres Acad Fit Awd; Bus.

CHANG, JUDY P; Raoul Wallenberg Traditional HS; San Francisco, CA; (1); Hon Roll; Berkeley; Writer.

CHANG, JULIE T; Mission HS; San Francisco, CA; (4); 2/275; Boy Scts; Cmnty Wkr; Ed Nwsp; Pres Soph Cls; Treas Stu Cncl; Ntl Merit Ltr; Fencing; Part Time Job; U Of Calif; Biochemistry.

CHANG, JULLIE J; Richard Gahr HS; Cerritos, CA; (3); French Clb; Teachers Aide; Off Sr Cls; JV Var Tennis; Hon Roll; MVP Tnns; Century 2000 Scl Sci Club; Tnns Club 89-90 Dir Of Pblcty, 90-91 Dir Of Act; Int Dsgn.

CHANG, KAI; Culver City HS; Culver City, CA; (3); French Clb; Off Soph Cls; JV Tennis.

CHANG, KAREN; Abraham Lincoln HS; San Francisco, CA; (1); Church Yth Grp; FCA; Acpl Chr; Church Choir; Hon Roll; Harvard U; Med.

CHANG, KAREN H; Irvine HS; Irvine, CA; (2); 121/605; Key Clb; Pep Clb; SADD; Drill Tm; Pep Band; JV Cheerldng; Schlrshp South Coast Chinese Cltrl Assn; Med.

CHANG, KARINNA M; El Camino HS; Daly City, CA; (3); Church Yth Grp; Thesps; School Musical; San Francisco ST; Accntng.

CHANG, KHAI; Redwood HS; Visalia, CA; (3); Church Yth Grp; Cmnty Wkr; Teachers Aide; Church Choir; Cit Awd; Hon Roll; Med.

CHANG, LI-WEI; Oak Park HS; Agoura Hills, CA; (1); Key Clb; Treas Pep Band; JV Socr; Hon Roll; Prfct Atten Awd; Peer Cnslng; CSF; UCLA; Bus.

CHANG, LINDA L; De Anza HS; El Sobrante, CA; (3); Church Yth Grp; Office Aide; Science Clb; Variety Show; Rep Stu Cncl; Var Tennis; Hon Roll; 2nd Pl MSF Bay Area Sci Fair; Schl Bio Olympid; Psych.

CHANG, MARCELLA; Sherman Oaks CES; Sun Valley, CA; (4); 1/97; Cmnty Wkr; Dance Clb; Debate Tm; Treas French Clb; NFL; Service Clb; Spanish Clb; Speech Tm; Ed Nwsp; Stu Cncl; Peer Coll Cnslr; Hmcmng Pep Rally & Dance Chrprsn; Bank Of Amer Achvt Awd Liberal Arts; CA U Northridge; Accntnt.

CHANG, MARGARET; Alhambra HS; Alhambra, CA; (4); German Clb; Treas Amnsty Intl 89-90; Na Alii; Tutor To Peers; Delta Epsilon Phi Awd; Phrmcy.

CHANG, MASON; Monta Vista HS; Cupertino, CA; (4); 29/378; Church Yth Grp; Math Clb; Church Choir; Var Trk; NHS; Pres Acad Fit Awd; Hnrbl Mntn Math Contest Santa Clara U; Tutor Several Math Subjects; Camp Cnslr; U CA Davis; Aerosp Eng.

CHANG, MATT A; Lincoln HS; Stockton, CA; (3); 170/590; Aud/Vis; Cmnty Wkr; Letterman Clb; Varsity Clb; Bsktbl; Trk; Hon Roll.

CHANG, MAY; Oak Park HS; Agoura Hills, CA; (1); Key Clb; JV Socr; JV Sftbl; JV Vllybl; High Hon Roll; Peer Cnslng; Key Clb Sec; Piano; JV Sccr Mst Imprvd Plyr; JV Sftbl MVP.

CHANG, MELODY; Thomas Downey HS; Modesto, CA; (3); 1/547; Church Yth Grp; French Clb; Key Clb; Math Tm; NFL; VP Science Clb; Service Clb; Off Jr Cls; Cit Awd; Hon Roll; Amer Chemcl Soc Chem Awd; Sci Olympiad Tm 89-90; Qualfd Hnrs On Golden St Exam Geom; CA Schlrshp Fed; UCLA; Comp Sci.

CHANG, MYRA; Aragon HS; San Mateo, CA; (4); Church Yth Grp; JA; Gym; Tennis; Trk; Asian/Amrcn Clb Scrtry; Bdmntn; Vrsty & Jv Ltrs; Bus.

CHANG, NADINE; Woodbridge HS; Irvine, CA; (3); 18/425; Church Yth Grp; French Clb; Hosp Aide; Service Clb; Drill Tm; High Hon Roll; Hon Roll; St Schlr.

CHANG, NOLAN; Brea Olinda HS; Brea, CA; (1); French Clb; Intnl Clb; Band; Mrchg Band; Pep Band; School Musical; Tennis; High Hon Roll; Hon Roll; Jr NHS; UCI; Med.

CHANG, PAI-LING; Torrey Pines HS; San Diego, CA; (4); Cmnty Wkr; VP French Clb; Hosp Aide; JCL; Chorus; School Play; Ntl Merit SF; BMTA Cmptn Wnnr 89; SLT Music Clb Awd 87; Natl Frnch Exm Awds 86-89; Natl Lat Tst Awds 88-89; Med.

CHANG, PETER; Arcadia HS; Arcadia, CA; (3); JA; Band; Mrchg Band; Bsbl; Ftbl; Hon Roll; USC; Bus.

CHANG, PETER; Ukiah HS; Ukiah, CA; (1); 7/532; Chess Clb; Math Tm; Orch; High Hon Roll; Pres Acad Fit Awd; Var Crs Cntry; JV Trk; JV Wrstlng; Symphony Orch; Stanford U.

CHANG, PETER E; University HS; Irvine, CA; (3); Spanish Clb; Lit Mag; Intrml Crs Cntry; JV Trk; Wt Lftg; Spanish NHS; Lameate Awd Excllnce Intro To Pascal; Prtcptn 9th Grd Acad Decathlon Tm; Law.

CHANG, REBECCA; Sunny Hills HS; Fullerton, CA; (3); 17/410; Church Yth Grp; Cmnty Wkr; Debate Tm; Hosp Aide; Intnl Clb; Spanish Clb; JV Tennis; High Hon Roll; Rotary Awd; Travld Greece Theory Knowldge Pgm; Intl Baccalaureate Pgm; UCLA; Economics.

CHANG, RICHARD C; Schurr HS; Covina, CA; (3); Bus Profs of Am; Treas Chess Clb; Teachers Aide; High Hon Roll; Hon Roll; Prfct Atten Awd; CA Schltc Fed; Golden St Exam High Hnrs; UCLA; Med.

CHANG, RICHARD T; San Rafael HS; San Rafael, CA; (3); Hon Roll; Cnty Sci Fair 2nd Pl; ATDP Smmr Berkeley Pgm; Golden St Exam Geom Hnr.

CHANG, RICKY; St Lawrence Acad; San Jose, CA; (4); 2/25; Chess Clb; Computer Clb; Math Clb; Teachers Aide; Pres Sr Cls; High Hon Roll; NHS; JR Statesman; Comp Sci.

CHANG, ROBIA S; Sir Francis Drake HS; Fairfax, CA; (2); Teachers Aide; Band; Pep Band; Var Capt Cheerldng; Hon Roll; Honor Crew; Calif Scholarship Federation.

CHANG, ROSY; Mira Mesa HS; San Diego, CA; (2); French Clb; Science Clb; Cit Awd; Hon Roll; NHS; Wrld Rlf Club; U Of CA; Studio Engr.

CHANG, RUBY; Gretchen Whitney HS; Lakewood, CA; (4); Art Clb; FBLA; Mrchg Band; Nwsp; JV Swmmng; High Hon Roll; Pres Acad Fit Awd; Poetry Clb Treas; CSF Sealbearer; Jr Hnr Guard; U Of Sthrn CA; Phrmcy.

CHANG, RYAN Y; American HS; Fremont, CA; (2); 16/385; Intnl Clb; Quiz Bowl; Bsktbl; Tennis; High Hon Roll; Hon Roll; Stanford; Crim Law.

CHANG, SANDY H; Lowell HS; San Francisco, CA; (3); Art Clb; Chess Clb; English Clb; Hosp Aide; Office Aide; Pep Clb; Science Clb; Teachers Aide; Orch; Badminton Team; Chinese Club; Kermesse & Winterfair.

CHANG, SANDY M; Whitney HS; Cerritos, CA; (1); Service Clb; JV Tennis; Hon Roll; Medcl Clb; Stu For The Ethical Trtmnt Of Animals.

CHANG, SHARON C; Narbonne HS; Harbor City, CA; (3); Girl Scts; JA; Key Clb; Service Clb; Teachers Aide; Prfct Atten Awd; CSF; Bus.

CHANG, SHOUA; Edison HS; Fresno, CA; (2); French Clb; Hon Roll; UC Santa Cruz; Tchng.

CHANG, SHU CHING; Rubidoux HS; Riverside, CA; (4); French Clb; Science Clb; Teachers Aide; Chorus; Color Guard; Bsktbl; GATE Clb; CSF; Stu Of Wk Math & Bio & Deans List; Cal Poly Pomona; Math.

CHANG, SHUNAN; Milpitas HS; Milpitas, CA; (3); JV Wrstlng; Hon Roll; Chinese Clb; Astrnmny Clb; Surgeon.

CHANG, SIMON C; Lowell HS; San Francisco, CA; (3); Boy Scts; Office Aide; Red Cross Aide; Orch; Shield & Scroll; CA Schlrshp Fed; Vllybl Clb; UC Berkeley.

CHANG, SOPHIA W; Abraham Lincoln HS; San Francisco, CA; (3); Cmnty Wkr; Chorus; Hon Roll; Acad Of Finance; Close-Up Pgm; Mandarin Clb Treas; Chico Ag Exchng Pgm; Golden St Math Exam Hnr Awds; UCLA; Bus Admin.

CHANG, STELLA; San Fernando HS; Granada Hills, CA; (3); Am Leg Aux Girls St; Debate Tm; Science Clb; Yrbk; Lit Mag; Stu Cncl; Var Tennis; High Hon Roll; Hon Roll; NHS; CSF.

CHANG, STEPHEN J; Whitney HS; Cerritos, CA; (2); Intnl Clb; JA; Key Clb; Band; Mrchg Band; Nwsp; Yrbk; Var Trk; Cit Awd; Pres Acad Fit Awd; Won ABC Dist Art Cntsts; UCLA; Arch.

CHANG, STEVE; Alameda HS; Alameda, CA; (3); 14/287; Church Yth Grp; Teachers Aide; Church Choir; Rep Jr Cls; JV Ftbl; Var Trk; High Hon Roll; Hon Roll; CSF; Acad Excllnc Awd Geo; UC Berkeley; Engnrng.

CHANG, STEVE H; John Burroughs HS; Burbank, CA; (2); VP Church Yth Grp; JA; Teachers Aide; Band; Chorus; Church Choir; Orch; Off Frsh Cls; Stu Cncl; JV Bsbl; Amer Legn Awd; Awana Clb Ldr; JR High Fclty Memrl Awd.

CHANG, STEVEN H; Servite HS; Fullerton, CA; (2); Aud/Vis; VP Computer Clb; Debate Tm; NEDT High Achvt Awd; Black Belt Taw Kwon Do; Stu Exchng To Russia; Arch Dsgn.

CHANG, SUN JOO; John F Kennedy HS; Granada Hills, CA; (3); Church Yth Grp; Key Clb; Math Clb; Hon Roll; UCLA; Bus.

CHANG, SUNG W; Wilcox HS; Santa Clara, CA; (2); French Clb; Ftbl; Hon Roll; San Jose ST; Bus Mgmnt.

CHANG, TERESA J; San Dieguito HS; La Costa, CA; (2); Stage Crew; Rptr Nwsp; Hon Roll; Law.

CHANG, TERRY Y; Irvine HS; Irvine, CA; (3); Cmnty Wkr; Intnl Clb; Key Clb; Band; Bus.

CHANG, THOR; Mc Lane HS; Fresno, CA; (4); English Clb; French Clb; FTA; Science Clb; School Play; Yrbk; Bsktbl; Vllybl; Prfct Atten Awd; CSUF; Elec Engrng.

CHANG, TONY L; Torrey Pines HS; San Diego, CA; (2); Church Yth Grp; FCA; Varsity Clb; Band; JV Bsbl; JV Bsktbl; JV Wt Lftg; Hon Roll; Ntl Merit Ltr; Pres Acad Fit Awd; Diegueno Jr HS Ath Of Yr 88-89; San Dieguito HS Bsbl MVP; Stanford; Bus.

CHANG, VICTOR; Irvine HS; Irvine, CA; (4); 2/550; Chess Clb; Quiz Bowl; Scholastic Bowl; Science Clb; Acclrtd HS Schlr U CA Irvine; Outstndng Stu Bio; Mem US Acad Decathlon Tm For Sch; Wnnr Heritage Awd; Harvard; Lawyr.

CHANG, VICTOR; Los Altos HS; Hacienda Hts, CA; (2); 98/398; Band; Mrchg Band; Bsktbl; Vllybl; Hon Roll; Prfct Atten Awd; U CA-IRVINE; Comp Sys Analysis.

CHANG, WAYNE W; Villa Park HS; Anaheim, CA; (3); VP Computer Clb; French Clb; Key Clb; Science Clb; Yrbk; Rep Soph Cls; High Hon Roll; NHS; CA Schlrshp Fed Pres; Jr Stsmn Of Amer Treas; UCLA; Engrng.

CHANG, WILLIAM; Mark Keppel HS; Monterey Park, CA; (3); JV Bsktbl; Var Tennis; Hon Roll; 2nd Pl & Hnrbl Mntn Awds-Woodwrkg Projcts LA Cty Fair 88 & 89; JR Cncl & Prom Cmmttes; Engrng.

CHANG, WILLIAM M; Irvine HS; Irvine, CA; (3); Hosp Aide; Key Clb; JV Ftbl; Var Trk; High Hon Roll; Hon Roll; USC; Biomed.

CHANG, WINLOR L; Los Amigos HS; Fountain Valley, CA; (2); 5/365; Church Yth Grp; Spanish Clb; Band; Mrchg Band; JV Bsbl; JV Bsktbl; High Hon Roll; Hon Roll; Jr NHS.

CHANG LO, LOUIS; George Washington HS; San Francisco, CA; (3); Intnl Clb; Math Clb; Math Tm; Spanish Clb; School Play; Off Jr Cls; Bsbl; Bsktbl; Spanish NHS; Badminton; San Francisco ST; Bus.

CHANI, RACHEL R; Rim Of The World HS; Running Springs, CA; (3); 25/274; Church Yth Grp; Debate Tm; Chorus; French Hon Soc; Hon Roll; CA ST San Ernardino; Educ.

CHANNELL, HIRAM J; Don Antonio Lugo HS; Chino, CA; (2); JV Bsktbl; Score Keeper; Cit Awd; Arch Drafing; Delta Sigma Theta Teen Lift; Golden Conquest Awd; Cal Poly Pomona U; Bio-Chem.

CHANSIRIK, SUVIT; Millikan HS; Long Beach, CA; (3); JA; LBCC; Elec Engr.

CHANTHILACK, SUPHAPHORN; Amos Avonzo Stagg HS; Stockton, CA; (2); Yrbk; UC Davis; Pediatrics.

CHAO, ANDREW; Whitney HS; Cerritos, CA; (3); Latin Clb; Letterman Clb; Math Tm; Varsity Clb; Band; Mrchg Band; Nwsp; Crs Cntry; Trk; High Hon Roll; Law.

CHAO, EDWARD; Bishop Amat HS; Azusa, CA; (4); 12/395; Speech Tm; Thesps; Rep Stu Cncl; High Hon Roll; NHS; Ntl Merit Ltr; CSF 88 & 89; Engl Dept Awd-2nd Pl 87-88; Slvr Screen Clb; Life Sci.

CHAO, JIM Y; South HS; Bakersfield, CA; (3); Pres Chess Clb; French Clb; Treas Intnl Clb; Key Clb; Intrml Tennis; High Hon Roll; Hon Roll; 1st Pl S CA HS Chess Chmpnshps; Astrophysics.

CHAO, KOUNG C; Rosemead HS; Rosemead, CA; (3); Computer Clb; Key Clb; Math Clb; Bsktbl; Prfct Atten Awd; Engr.

CHAO, LILY; Glen A Wilson HS; Hacienda Hgts, CA; (3); German Clb; Sec Service Clb; Chorus; High Hon Roll; Hon Roll; Prfct Atten Awd; Pres Acad Fit Awd; Gldn St High Hnrs Geom & Alg; UCLA; Biochem.

CHAO, SEANG S; Mark Keppel HS; Monterey Park, CA; (3); FBLA; JA; Key Clb; Service Clb; School Musical; Cit Awd; High Hon Roll; Ntl Merit Schol; Prfct Atten Awd; Acctng.

CHAO, SOPHIA; John Swett HS; Hercules, CA; (2); Science Clb; Band; Mrchg Band; School Play; Lit Mag; Rep Frsh Cls; Rep Soph Cls; Rep Stu Cncl; Cheerldng; Swmmng; Assmbly Campbells Yth Cmmtte; UC Berkeley; Pediatrician.

CHAO, SUK YUEN; Independence HS; San Jose, CA; (3); Science Clb; Jazz Band; Chinese Clb; UC Davis; Bus.

CHAO, TOMMY S; Gahr HS; Cerritos, CA; (3); 4/500; Cmnty Wkr; Math Tm; Teachers Aide; JV Trk; Hon Roll; Pres Acad Fit Awd; Chinese Clb Pres; U CA Berkeley; Envrnmntl Dsgn.

CHAPA, ELISA I; Pioneer HS; San Jose, CA; (3); 29/333; Cmnty Wkr; Hosp Aide; Yrbk; Off Soph Cls; Off Jr Cls; Var Trk; NHS; Interact Club VP & Lt Gov; Young Life; CSF; Intl Bus.

CHAPA, JOHNNY M; Lindsay HS; Lindsay, CA; (2); Drama Clb; Spanish Clb; Bsktbl; Ftbl; Trk.

CHAPARRO, ANGIE A; Santa Clara HS; Oxnard, CA; (2); 8/180; Church Yth Grp; Cmnty Wkr; Varsity Clb; Var Capt Bsktbl; Var L Vllybl; High Hon Roll; Hon Roll; NHS; Prfct Atten Awd; Pres Acad Fit Awd; HOBY Schl Rep; CSF; Future Ldrs Of Amer; UC Berkeley; Educ.

CHAPARRO, SANDRA C; Bishop Amat Memorial HS; La Puente, CA; (2); Office Aide; Spanish Clb; Color Guard; Cit Awd; Hon Roll; NHS; Prfct Atten Awd; Psych.

CHAPARRO, STEVEN A; Chino HS; Chino, CA; (2); Treas VP Church Yth Grp; Model UN; Band; Church Choir; Mrchg Band; Pres Frsh Cls; Rep Soph Cls; JV Bsbl; JV Bsktbl; JV Ftbl; Stu Ldrshp; Peer Resistance Trng; Stu Who Excells; Prin Awd; CA Poly Pomona; Elec Engrng.

CHAPARYAN, GOHAR; John Muir HS; Pasadena, CA; (3); FBLA; Office Aide; Service Clb; Teachers Aide; JV Vllybl; Armenian Clb; Mustang Readers; Schl Site Cncl; Stu Ldrshp Conf; Recvd Parsons Recgntn Awd; U Of La Verne; Comp Sci.

CHAPEY, DEVA; San Dieguito HS; Encinitas, CA; (2); Nwsp; Yrbk; Hon Roll; Pres Acad Fit Awd; GSE 1st Yr Alg Hnrs; Photo.

CHAPLIN, JASON; San Dieguito HS; Annandale, VA; (3); 279/570; Church Yth Grp; Cmnty Wkr; Science Clb; Church Choir; JV Var Ftbl; Var Swmmng; Intrml Wt Lftg; Bus.

CHAPMAN, BRIDGET A; Hiram Johnson HS; Sacramento, CA; (1); Rep Church Yth Grp; Friday Night Live; REACT Vlntr; Teacher.

CHAPMAN, ERICA; Orland Joint Union HS; Orland, CA; (1); 9/160; Church Yth Grp; JV Bsktbl; Cheerldng; High Hon Roll; Chrch Yth Grp Secy; Bus.

CHAPMAN, ISAAC A; Alhambra HS; Martinez, CA; (3); 13/213; Boy Scts; Math Clb; Math Tm; Science Clb; Nwsp; Lit Mag; JV Bsktbl; Var Socr; Hon Roll; Ntl Merit Ltr; UC Berkeley; Physicist.

CHAPMAN, LANA; Fairfield HS; Fairfield, CA; (1); Drama Clb; English Clb; FFA; Math Clb; Teachers Aide; Bsktbl; Actress.

CHAPMAN, PATRICIA A; Downey HS; Downey, CA; (3); Key Clb; School Play; Var Swmmng; Hon Roll; UCSB; Bus.

CHAPMAN, ROBERT; Edison HS; Huntington Bch, CA; (2); Boy Scts; German Clb; Key Clb; Capt Math Tm; Teachers Aide; Acad Decathlon Co Capt Soph Tm; JV Kiwanis Bowl; Amer Chem Soc Outstndng Stu; Astrophysics.

CHAPMAN, ROBERT D; Katella HS; Anaheim, CA; (1); JV Diving; JV Ftbl; JV Wt Lftg; JV Wrstlng; Fullerton; Dsgnr.

CHAPMAN, SABRINA; Northgate HS; Walnut Creek, CA; (3); Church Yth Grp; Cmnty Wkr; Dance Clb; Spanish Clb; Teachers Aide; Band; Drill Tm; L Cheerldng; Miss Suprsnstnl Fresno USA Camp 89; Ltr Girl Co-Capt 89; Dance Prod 90; Sacramento ST U; Comm.

CHAPMAN, SCOTT E; San Marcos HS; San Marcos, CA; (3); Key Clb; Letterman Clb; Library Aide; Pep Clb; Varsity Clb; Stu Cncl; Cheerldng; Ftbl; Swmmng; Wt Lftg.

CHAPMAN, SHANNA H; Los Alamitos HS; Cypress, CA; (1); Church Yth Grp; Drama Clb; French Clb; Teachers Aide; Jazz Band; Crs Cntry; Gym; Trk; Cypress JC; Educ.

CHAPPELL, MODENA L; Sweetwater HS; National City, CA; (4); JA; SADD; Teachers Aide; Mgr(s); Var Swmmng; Mgr Tennis; Cit Awd; Hon Roll; Prfct Atten Awd; Outstndng Achvmnt Schlrshp; Cert Achvmnt Bsc Alg; San Diego ST; Math.

CHAPPELL, STEPHEN J; Bella Vista HS; Orangevale, CA; (2); 128/406; Spanish Clb; Civil Air Patrl; Sr Major Bsbl; Embry-Riddle Aeronautical U.

CHAPPELL, TODD; Lincoln HS; Stockton, CA; (3); Church Yth Grp; Letterman Clb; Varsity Clb; High Hon Roll; Var Swmmng; Var Water Polo; Tiger Aquatics U Of Pacific, Swmtm 10 Yrs; Carrying Part Time Job Baskin Robbins; CISV; UC; Engr.

CHAPPLE, JOANNA L; Ernest Righetti HS; Santa Maria, CA; (3); Art Clb; Church Yth Grp; Chorus; Hon Roll; Stu Deans List.

CHAPTON, DAWN D; Temecula Valley HS; Temecula, CA; (2); Office Aide; Ski Clb; Teachers Aide; NBL BMX Racing-Wrld Cup; ABA BMX Racing-CA Gold Cup Wnnr; Fishng Derby-1st; Horse Show-Grand Chmpn; U CA-REDLANDS; Horse Trainer.

CHARETTE, CHANTAL M; Los Alamitos HS; Los Alamitos, CA; (1); Church Yth Grp; Cmnty Wkr; Church Choir; Color Guard; JV Bsktbl; JV Crs Cntry; JV Trk; UCLA; Sci.

CHAREZ, MARGARET M; Le Grand Union HS; Planada, CA; (3); Drama Clb; Spanish Clb; School Play; Treas Jr Cls; Cheerldng; Hon Roll; Acad Decathalon; Rotary Ldrshp Camp Royal; CA Bus Week 90; Guidance Cnslng.

CHARKINS, KEVIN; Bloomington Christian HS; Wrightwood, CA; (3); 1/13; Church Yth Grp; Rep Frsh Cls; Rep Soph Cls; VP Stu Cncl; Var Bsbl; JV Var Ftbl; Mgr(s); Wt Lftg; Var Capt Wrstlng; Hon Roll; Lbrl Arts.

CHARLEBOIS, RENEE L; Poway HS; Ramona, CA; (1); Church Yth Grp; Stat Bsktbl; JV Crs Cntry; JV Trk; Pres Acad Fit Awd; U CA; Psych.

CHARLES, AIGA; Alverno HS; Pasadena, CA; (1); 10/90; Service Clb; Rep Frsh Cls; Var Bsktbl; Hon Roll; Alg Awd.

CHARLES, NATALIE; Rio Linda HS; Elverta, CA; (4); 7/260; Church Yth Grp; Dance Clb; Debate Tm; Drama Clb; Speech Tm; Church Choir; School Play; Pres Stu Cncl; Cheerldng; High Hon Roll; Jr Prom Qn 89; Friday Night Live; Close-Up Pgm; Sacramento ST U; Commnctns.

CHARLESWORTH, TERI A; Granada HS; Livermore, CA; (4); French Clb; Chorus; Church Choir; Orch; School Musical; Variety Show; Socr; Mst Vlble Choir Mem Awd; Grad Early; Schlrshp CA Baptist Coll; CA Baptist Coll; Music.

CHARLSON, LESLIE E; Berkeley HS; Berkeley, CA; (3); Cmnty Wkr; French Clb; Key Clb; Library Aide; Hon Roll; Pres Acad Fit Awd; JV Crs Cntry; Var L Gym.

CHARLTON, KELLIE; Cajon SR HS; San Bernardino, CA; (1); Church Yth Grp; Cmnty Wkr; Hosp Aide; Cit Awd; Var Socr; JV Sftbl; Natl Charity League; USC; Law.

CHARLTON, MARJORIE; Palos Verdes HS; Palos Vrds Pen, CA; (4); Chess Clb; Church Yth Grp; Cmnty Wkr; Pres Service Clb; Rotary Awd; Training & Showing Horses; Ms Jr Amer Pag Semi Fnlst; Marquette U; Med.

CHARTARIFSKY, ILANA; Torrey Pines HS; Solana Beach, CA; (3); 231/422; Office Aide; Swmmng; Hon Roll; Psych.

CHASE, MICHELLE M; Pacifica HS; Cypress, CA; (3); Church Yth Grp; Cmnty Wkr; Drama Clb; Library Aide; SADD; Rep Frsh Cls; Rep Soph Cls; Var Powder Puff Ftbl; Law.

CHASE, STEVAN D; Escondido HS; Escondido, CA; (1); Church Yth Grp; Cmnty Wkr; Teachers Aide; Church Choir; Phtg Yrbk; Rep Frsh Cls; JV Tennis; Hon Roll; Escondido HS Jr Vrsty Tnns Awd; Ldrshp, Sprtmnshp & Athlete Ablty.

CHASENGNOU, XAY; River City HS; West Sacramento, CA; (3); Teachers Aide; Ftbl; Socr; Tennis; Vllybl; Wt Lftg; Police.

CHASTAIN, BERNARD A; Eureka SR HS; Eureka, CA; (3); Pres Band; Jazz Band; Mrchg Band; Orch; Pep Band; Socr; Hon Roll; Ldrshp Conf NM; Humboldt ST U; Fisheries.

CHATFIELD, MARGARET; Mc Kinleyville HS; Mc Kinleyville, CA; (3); Treas Key Clb; Jazz Band; Rep Frsh Cls; Rep Soph Cls; Sec Stu Cncl; Var Capt Tennis; High Hon Roll; Prfct Atten Awd; Northern CA Hnr Band; CA Schlrshp Fed VP.

CHATLOS, TINA M; Ramona HS; Riverside, CA; (2); Mgr(s); Trk; Cit Awd; Hon Roll; Pres Acad Fit Awd; Avid; C-Clb; Lawyer.

CHATMAN, COURTENAY; San Juan HS; Citrus Heights, CA; (1); 2/300; Chorus; Rep Frsh Cls; Bsktbl; Capt Cheerldng; Trk; High Hon Roll; Prfct Atten Awd; Pres Acad Fit Awd; Black Stu Union Club; Spelman; Arch Engr.

CHATMAN, KIMBERLYN M; Mayfield SR Schl; Altadena, CA; (2); AFS; Church Yth Grp; GAA; Ski Clb; Chorus; High Hon Roll; Piano; UCLA; Bus.

CHATTERJEE, SANDEEP; Serra HS; Foster City, CA; (3); 4/197; Boy Scts; Cmnty Wkr; Math Tm; Teachers Aide; Color Guard; Rptr Lit Mag; JV Trk; High Hon Roll; Ntl Merit Ltr; Pres Acad Fit Awd; Eagle Scout BSA 88; Acad Awds Math, Foreign Lang, Sci; CSF; UC Berkeley; Elec Engr.

CHATTON, CRYSTAL D; Orange Glen HS; Escondido, CA; (3); Church Yth Grp; Sec VP FFA; Hon Roll; FFA Awd Project Compltn; Outstndng FFA Meb 1989; Di Kalb Awd 1990; Top Horse Judge FFA 1990; Cal Poly San Louis Obispo; Vet.

CHAU, AN; Hoover HS; San Diego, CA; (3); Key Clb; Math Clb; Math Tm; Model UN; NFL; Cit Awd; High Hon Roll; Hon Roll; Jr NHS; NHS; Acad Achvt In Math; Golden St Exam Hgh Hnrs Geom, Alg; SDSU; Bus.

CHAU, BINH THIEN; Hoover HS; San Diego, CA; (1); Math Clb; Acad Clb; Engrng.

CHAU, CUONG T; San Rafael HS; Novato, CA; (4); 39/219; Intnl Clb; Hon Roll; CA ST U Hayward; Bus Admin.

CHAU, HAI K; William C Overfelt HS; San Jose, CA; (1); Science Clb; High Hon Roll; Hon Roll; CSF; Stanford; Aerospc Engrng.

CHAU, HELEN T; Leuzinger HS; Lawndale, CA; (2); 12/800; French Clb; Sec Soph Cls; Stu Cncl; Var Crs Cntry; JV Trk; Prfct Atten Awd; Med.

CHAU, KHOEUNG T; Los Amigos HS; Santa Ana, CA; (2); 65/475; Key Clb; Spanish Clb; JV Vllybl; Hon Roll; Korean Club; Chinese Club; UCI; Arch Engrng.

CHAU, LAN S; San Diego HS; San Diego, CA; (3); Key Clb; Math Clb; Science Clb; Batminton Tm; Project Stop; CA Schlrshp Fed; Med.

CHAU, LINDA; Abraham Lincoln HS; San Francisco, CA; (2); Hon Roll; Chinese Club; Badminton Team; San Francisco ST U; Bus Admin.

CHAU, MINH T; Abraham Lincoln HS; San Jose, CA; (4); JV Wrstlng; Pres Acad Fit Awd; US Air Force Math & Sci Awd; Bank Of Amer Achvt Awd Comp; NASA Orbiter Naming Prgm 88; Santa Clara U; Comp Sci.

CHAU, MOUN Y; Montclair HS; Montclair, CA; (3); 3/267; Cmnty Wkr; Rptr Nwsp; High Hon Roll; Natl Latin I Exam Gold Medal; Natl Latin II Exam Silver Medal.

CHAU, PHOEUNG YAN; Downtown Business Magnet HS; Los Angeles, CA; (4); 3/170; French Clb; FBLA; Treas Key Clb; Yrbk; Hist Jr Cls; Sec Sr Cls; Hon Roll; NHS; Bus Profs of Am; Chess Clb.

CHAU, QUAN JENNY; Mark Keppel HS; Monterey Park, CA; (3); Sec Key Clb; Sec Mu Alpha Theta; Rptr Yrbk; JV Swmmng; Cit Awd; Prfct Atten Awd; Bus Mgmt.

CHAU, SAN-PHAY; King Drew Medical Magnet HS; Los Angeles, CA; (3); Library Aide; Math Clb; Science Clb; Intrml Vllybl; Hon Roll; JETS Awd; Prfct Atten Awd; R M Pyles Boys Camp Staff; UC Berkeley; Biomed Engrng.

CHAU, THAO T; Bolsa Grande HS; Westminster, CA; (2); 50/332; Chess Clb; Tennis; Hon Roll; CSU Pomona; Math.

CHAU, THO N; Lowell HS; San Francisco, CA; (3); German Clb; Intrml Vllybl; Cltrl & Educl Exch Prgm; Dance Prfmnc; Day Care Ctr Vlntr; Psych.

CHAU, TUAN Q; Hoover HS; San Diego, CA; (3); 1/400; French Clb; Intnl Clb; Key Clb; Math Clb; Math Tm; NFL; Office Aide; L Var Tennis; High Hon Roll; NHS; Prjct Step Ldrshp Clb; CA Tech Berkeley; Civil Engr.

CHAU, VAN H; Bolsa Grande HS; Garden Grove, CA; (3); Cit Awd; Hon Roll; Prfct Atten Awd; Vietnamese & Chinese Clb; CSF Mem; Fshn Merch.

CHAU, VAN T; George Washington HS; San Francisco, CA; (2); Hon Roll; US Davis; Bus.

CHAUDHRY, FAISAL; Kennedy HS; La Palma, CA; (2); AFS; CA ST Long Beach; Bus.

CHAUDHRY, SHAKIL; Woodland HS; Woodland, CA; (3); Cmnty Wkr; VP FBLA; Capt Library Aide; SADD; Ed Nwsp; Ed Yrbk; Rep Jr Cls; Hon Roll; Prfct Atten Awd; Rep Frsh Cls; Pre-Med.

CHAUDOIR, CHRISTOPHER J; Bellarmine College Prep; Hillsborough, CA; (3); 46/315; Cmnty Wkr; Capt Debate Tm; NFL; Speech Tm; VP SADD; Ed Nwsp; Ed Yrbk; Rep Frsh Cls; Var Crs Cntry; Jr Statesmn Of Am-Fndr; Scl Involvmnt Corps; Prncpls Commndntn Lttr; UCLA; Bus.

CHAUDRY, SAMAN; Pinole Valley HS; Hercules, CA; (1); Dance Clb; Drama Clb; French Clb; Pres Soph Cls; Rep Stu Cncl; JV Sftbl; Var Trk; Vllybl; French Hon Soc; 4-H Awd; Cultrl Fairs; Arts & Wine Fstvls; U Of CA Berkeley; Genetcs.

CHAV, HEY; Artesia HS; Lakewood, CA; (3); Intnl Clb; Science Clb; Drill Tm; PAL Clb; Comp Pgmr.

CHAVAN, SHELDON; James Lick HS; San Jose, CA; (2); Band; Jazz Band; Mrchg Band; Orch; Pep Band; School Musical; Ftbl; Hon Roll; Pres Acad Fit Awd; Jzz Sxphnst; Stanford; Law.

CHAVARIN, ADRIANA; Chula Vista HS; Chula Vista, CA; (3); 30/493; Pep Clb; SADD; Drill Tm; Cit Awd; Prfct Atten Awd; Pres Acad Fit Awd; Peer Cnlsng VP, Comssnr Fndrsrs; San Diego Cnty Coll Ready Wrt Off; CSF; People To People Stu Ambssdr; U Of San Diego; Elem Educ.

CHAVARIN, NORA; Sacred Heart Of Jesus HS; Los Angeles, CA; (3); GAA; Letterman Clb; Treas Soph Cls; Var Sftbl; Capt Var Trk; Hon Roll; Natl & Advncd Plcmnt Spanish Exams; Cal ST Long Beach; Intrior Dsg.

CHAVARRIA, FATIMA; Lakewood HS; Lakewood, CA; (4); 104/657; Aud/Vis; GAA; Letterman Clb; Varsity Clb; Rep Soph Cls; Rep Jr Cls; Pres Sr Cls; Pres Stu Cncl; Capt Powder Puff Ftbl; Stat Socr; CA ST U Long Beach.

CHAVARRIA, MARSHA; Bishop Amat Memorial HS; Baldwin Park, CA; (4); 26/400; Drama Clb; Pep Clb; Spanish Clb; Drill Tm; School Play; Stage Crew; VP Capt Cheerldng; Hon Roll; NHS; CSF; Poltcl Sci.

CHAVARRIA, MICHAEL J; Amos Alonzo Stagg HS; Stockton, CA; (3); Key Clb; Enrolled Med Pgm Schl.

CHAVES, SIMONE M; Mayfield SR HS; Bradbury, CA; (2); Varsity Clb; DAR Awd; Hon Roll; Equestrian Var Co-Capt Tm; USC; Med.

CHAVES, SONYA Y; Ramona HS; Ramona, CA; (3); Amnsty Intl; Engl Stu Of Month; Interior Dsgn.

CHAVEZ, ALBA; Gahr HS; Artesia, CA; (4); 5/500; Office Aide; Teachers Aide; School Play; High Hon Roll; Sthrn CA Educ Grant Wnnr; Excptnl Schlr Rnnr Up 90; Bank Of Amer Awd Wnnr, Indstrl Arts; Cerritos Coll; CPA.

CHAVEZ, AMANDA L; Mountain View HS; El Monte, CA; (1); Am Leg Aux Girls St; GAA; Pep Clb; SADD; Flag Corp; Mrchg Band; Yrbk; Off Jr Cls; Off Sr Cls; Stu Cncl; Girl Athletic Phys Ftnss Awd; USC; Lawyer.

CHAVEZ, ANA M; Downey HS; Downey, CA; (3); Cit Awd; Hon Roll; Acctng.

CHAVEZ, ANGELICA M; Gonzales Union HS Dist; Gonzalez, CA; (2); Library Aide; SADD; Pep Band; High Hon Roll; Hon Roll; Prfct Atten Awd; CSF; Ed.

CHAVEZ, ANNIE; Porterville HS; Porterville, CA; (1); Church Yth Grp; 4-H; Drill Tm; Cheerldng; Swmmng; Vllybl; Hon Roll; Interior Dsgn.

CHAVEZ, ANTHONY ROBERT; Bellarmine College Prep; Los Gatos, CA; (1); Boy Scts; Cmnty Wkr; Debate Tm; Service Clb; Intrml Bsktbl; Intrml Ftbl; Intrml Sftbl; JV Trk; Piano 8 Yrs; Campbell Moreland Pony Colt Bsbl Lg; Intrgeneratnl Proj Vlntr.

CHAVEZ, ARMANDO D; Arvin HS; Lamont, CA; (2); Boy Scts; Teachers Aide; Band; Jazz Band; Mrchg Band; Pep Band; Score Keeper; Wrstlng; Cit Awd; High Hon Roll; Writing Awd; UCSB; Music.

CHAVEZ, AYDEE; Linden HS; Linden, CA; (1); 5/141; High Hon Roll; Hon Roll; Sacramento ST U; Engrng.

CHAVEZ, BLAS F; Richard Gahr HS; Artesia, CA; (2); Cmnty Wkr; Computer Clb; French Clb; Math Tm; Spanish Clb; Teachers Aide; Wt Lftg.

CHAVEZ, BRIAN E.; Estancia HS; Costa Mesa, CA; (3); 2/300; VP French Clb; Band; Drm Mjr(t); Jazz Band; Mrchg Band; Orch; Pep Band; School Musical; Bausch & Lomb Sci Awd; High Hon Roll; Outstndng Math Achvmnt Awd; Outstndng Music Awd 3 Yrs; Partcpnt In Schl Acad Decathlon & Kiwanis Bowl; Biomedical Science Medicine.

CHAVEZ, CANDELARIA V; Saint Anthony HS; Long Beach, CA; (3); Hon Roll; Accounting Or Nursing.

CHAVEZ, CARMELITA M; Vista HS; Vista, CA; (3); 9/425; Am Leg Aux Girls St; Key Clb; Pep Clb; Teachers Aide; Flag Corp; Stu Cncl; High Hon Roll; Acad Tm; CSF; Intl Rltns.

CHAVEZ, DAVID E; Bonita Vista HS; Bonita, CA; (3); 4/556; Church Yth Grp; Key Clb; Pep Clb; Off Frsh Cls; Off Sr Cls; JV Trk; Hon Roll; Outstndng Stu Engl, Span, US Hstry.

CHAVEZ, EDUARDO; Sierra Vista HS; Baldwin Park, CA; (1); Boy Scts; Teachers Aide; Off Frsh Cls; Bsbl; Ftbl; Cit Awd; High Hon Roll; Hon Roll; Stu Of Month; UCLA; Teacher.

CHAVEZ, ERASMO C; Queen Of Angels Seminary; Venice, CA; (4); Art Clb; Aud/Vis; Church Yth Grp; Library Aide; Science Clb; School Play; Ed Yrbk; VP Jr Cls; JV Ftbl; Intrml Socr; Sci Prjct & Drawings/Dsgns Awds; Cal ST Long Beach; Ind Dsgn.

CHAVEZ, EZEQUIEL; Gahr HS; Artesia, CA; (3); Crs Cntry; Wrstlng; Cycling; Cerritos CC; Arch.

CHAVEZ, JENNIE; Coachella Valley HS; Coachella, CA; (3); Church Yth Grp; Cmnty Wkr; Math Clb; Varsity Clb; Tennis; Hon Roll; Sportmns Clb.

CHAVEZ, JOSEPH J; Don Bosco Technical Inst; Pico Rivera, CA; (3); Honorary Awds In Electronics Tech & English; Varsity Water Polo; Electrical Engineering.

CHAVEZ, JUAN C; Lemoore HS; Stratford, CA; (3); Rep Jr Cls; Bsbl; Trk; Hon Roll; Fresno ST.

CHAVEZ, JUDY L; Monte Vista HS; Spring Valley, CA; (1); Chorus; Mgr Bsktbl; Harvard; Med.

CHAVEZ, JUDY S; Redlands HS; Redlands, CA; (3); Church Yth Grp; Cmnty Wkr; Drama Clb; Spanish Clb; CA ST; Engrng.

CHAVEZ, KAREN; Pioneer HS; Whittier, CA; (2); Drill Tm; JV Swmmng; Var Tennis; High Hon Roll; Math Engrng Sci Assn; Expanded Hrzns Secy; Omega; Phy.

CHAVEZ, LAURIE M; Saint Joseph HS; Garden Grove, CA; (2); Church Yth Grp; Cmnty Wkr; GAA; Var Socr; High Hon Roll; St Schlr; Travlng Sccr Tm; Garden Grove Sccr Clb; UCI; Pre-Med.

CHAVEZ, LUIS M; Woodrow Wilson HS; Long Beach, CA; (2); Pres Science Clb; Orch; Stage Crew; Off Frsh Cls; Stu Cncl; Bsbl; Vllybl; Hon Roll; NHS; Opt Clb Awd; Jr Optimist Clb Awd; Schlrshp Soc; Loyala; Aerospace Engr.

CHAVEZ, LUZ J; Bell Gardens HS; Bell Gardens, CA; (2); Spanish Clb; Teachers Aide; Drill Tm; High Hon Roll; Cal Poly Pomona; Lbrl Arts.

CHAVEZ, MAGGIE; Roosevelt HS; Los Angeles, CA; (3); Cmnty Wkr; Dance Clb; Rep Cheerldng; Pom Pon; Pep Squad; ELAC; Probation Officer.

CHAVEZ, MARGARET L; Montebello HS; Pico Rivera, CA; (1); Church Yth Grp; FCA; Varsity Clb; Chrch Excllnce Awd; Comp Oprtr/Prgmr.

CHAVEZ, MARIANNE; St Paul HS; Pico Rivera, CA; (3); Am Leg Aux Girls St; Church Yth Grp; Rptr Nwsp; Pres Sr Cls; Var Bsktbl; Var Crs Cntry; Var Trk; Hon Roll; NHS; Dance Clb; Athlte Yr 89-90; Whittier Coll; Broadcaster.

CHAVEZ, MARISA V; Samuel F B Morse HS; San Diego, CA; (2); Treas Intnl Clb; Model UN; Mrchg Band; Pres Frsh Cls; Cit Awd; Jr NHS; Prfct Atten Awd; Letterettes Banner Tm; CSF; San Diego ST U; Nurse.

CHAVEZ, MARISELA; Woodrow Wilson HS; Los Angeles, CA; (4); 39/500; Drama Clb; Ed Nwsp; Yrbk; Hon Roll; Pres Acad Fit Awd; Occidental Coll Upward Bnd.

CHAVEZ, MARISOL; Roosevelt HS; Los Angeles, CA; (2); Church Yth Grp; Cmnty Wkr; Dance Clb; School Musical; School Play; Bsbl; Bsktbl; Cit Awd; Hon Roll; Alateens Secy & Treas; Comp.

CHAVEZ, MELISSA D; South San Francisco HS; South San Francis, CA; (2); Cmnty Wkr; FBLA; Hosp Aide; Spanish Clb; JV Bsktbl; JV Var Sftbl; JV Tennis; High Hon Roll; CSF; Stu Of Month Engl Hnrs; Tennis Clb; San Francisco ST U; OR Nurse.

CHAVEZ, MERLINDA D; South San Francisco HS; South San Francis, CA; (2); Cmnty Wkr; FBLA; Hosp Aide; Spanish Clb; Band; JV Bsktbl; Var JV Sftbl; JV Tennis; High Hon Roll; Bio Stu Of Yr; CSF; Creative Productn/Outstndng Achvt-Engl 2 H; San Francisco ST U; Nrsng.

CHAVEZ, MICHAEL F; St John Bosco HS; La Mirada, CA; (1); Jr NHS.

CHAVEZ, MICHAEL S; Santa Teresa HS; San Jose, CA; (3); Church Yth Grp; Letterman Clb; Ski Clb; Var Diving; Intrml Swmmng; Cit Awd; Intrml Trk; Intrml Vllybl; Law.

CHAVEZ, MONICA I; Don Antonio Lugo HS; Chino, CA; (3); 19/770; Dance Clb; French Clb; Math Tm; Variety Show; Cit Awd; High Hon Roll; Hon Roll; Fshn Inst Of Dsgn; Fshn Merch.

CHAVEZ, NORMA F; Exeter Union HS; Clovis, CA; (4); 22/165; Am Leg Aux Girls St; Church Yth Grp; Letterman Clb; Pep Clb; Band; Chorus; Mrchg Band; Stu Cncl; Var JV Cheerldng; JV Sftbl; Farmersville Schl Dist Schlrshp; CSU Hispanics Schlrshp; CSU Fresno; Lbrl Stds.

CHAVEZ, OSCAR A; Shafter HS; Shafter, CA; (3); 16/204; Rptr FFA; German Clb; Pep Clb; Var Bsbl; Var Ftbl; JV Socr; Hon Roll; UCLA; Medicine-Doctor.

CHAVEZ, PATRICIA V; Colton HS; Colton, CA; (3); Var Crs Cntry; Trk; Hon Roll.

CHAVEZ, ROBERT; Cantwell HS; Los Angeles, CA; (3); 2/55; Letterman Clb; Spanish Clb; Rptr Nwsp; Crs Cntry; Trk; Hon Roll; Sec NHS; CSF; Crss Cntry Mst Vlbl Rnnr Awd; Prfct Atten; UCLA; Chem.

CHAVEZ, SOCORRO; Baldwin Park HS; Baldwin Park, CA; (1); Science Clb; Socr; Trk; Lawyer.

CHAVEZ, VERONICA; Pius X HS; Lynwood, CA; (2); High Hon Roll; Hon Roll; Prfct Atten Awd; Pblcty Chrprsn & Rep-Christian Action Mvmnt; Folklorico; Stanford; Elec.

CHAVEZ, VICTOR A; Garfield HS; Los Angeles, CA; (2); Teachers Aide; Varsity Clb; Bsbl; Bsktbl; Ftbl; Sftbl; Trk; Cit Awd; Hon Roll; Prfct Atten Awd; USC Med-Cor Prog; CA Schlrshp Fed; Med.

CHAVIRA, ALEJANDRO; Garfield HS; Los Angeles, CA; (2).

CHAVIRA, ALEX; Back Bay HS; Newport Beach, CA; (2); Comp Sci.

CHAVIRA, BLAS C; Bonita HS; La Verne, CA; (2); Nwsp; Yrbk; Hon Roll; CA Poly; Bus.

CHAVIRA, DAVID S; Our Lady Queen Of Angels Seminary; Azusa, CA; (4); 10/23; School Play; Yrbk; VP Sr Cls; Stu Cncl; Intrml Swmmng; Intrml Trk; CA ST Fullerton; Theatre Arts.

CHAVIRA, MIKE; Huntington Beach HS; Huntington Beach, CA; (3); Varsity Clb; Var L Bsbl; Var L Ftbl; Ca Schlrshp Fed Clb; Tower Awrds; Ap Eur History; Geom; Pre-Calculus; Bus.

CHAVIRA, NICOLE; Cajon HS; San Bernardino, CA; (1); Key Clb; SADD; Sec Score Keeper; JV Tennis; Bus.

CHAVIRA, REBECCA A; San Dimas HS; San Dimas, CA; (3); Church Yth Grp; GAA; Socr; Trk; High Hon Roll; Hon Roll; CA Schlrshp Pgm; Crmnl Justice.

CHAVIS, DIMITRI A; Durham HS; Chico, CA; (3); Church Yth Grp; Cmnty Wkr; FFA; Var Bsktbl; JV Crs Cntry; JV Trk; Hon Roll; Math Stu Yr; Engrng.

CHAYA, ERI; Gardena HS; Gardena, CA; (3); Intnl Clb; Treas Frsh Cls; PTA Schlrshp-Otis Parsons Art Inst; Satrdy Hgh-Art Ctr Pasdna; Grphc Arts.

CHAYRA, DINA LOUISE; Dos Pueblos HS; Santa Barbara, CA; (3); 35/350; Cmnty Wkr; Hosp Aide; Pep Clb; Science Clb; Ski Clb; Varsity Clb; Stu Cncl; Var Cheerldng; Var Tennis; NHS; Ped.

CHE, DIEU-THUY C; Santa Ana HS; Santa Ana, CA; (4); 4/400; Art Clb; Cmnty Wkr; Computer Clb; French Clb; Girl Scts; Hosp Aide; JA; Key Clb; Math Clb; Spanish Clb; Vietnamese Clb VP; Avco Excel Awd; Close Up; UC Irvine; Chem.

CHE, HUY; Oakland HS; Oakland, CA; (3); French Clb; German Clb; Key Clb; Treas Math Clb; Math Tm; Var Tennis.

CHE, STEPHEN; Temple City HS; Temple City, CA; (2); Boy Scts; Church Yth Grp; Key Clb; JV L Trk; High Hon Roll; Hon Roll; Spec Interest Astronomy; Invlvd Astronomy Clubs; 3rd Pl AZ Sci/Engr Fair; Physics.

CHE, TRANG; Valley HS; Santa Ana, CA; (4); 4/300; Office Aide; Temple Yth Grp; Orch; Cit Awd; DAR Awd; High Hon Roll; Prfct Atten Awd; Pres Acad Fit Awd; CSF Outstndng Achvt Awd; Golden St Schlr; Outstndng Acad Achvt Awd; Cal-Poly U; Finance.

CHE, WILLIAM; Abraham Lincoln HS; San Francisco, CA; (2); Yrbk; Cal Poly; Mech Engr.

CHEA, CHITA; Edison HS; Fresno, CA; (2); Computer Clb; VP Pres FBLA; Hon Roll; SE Asian/Amer Clb; CSF; VITA; CPA.

CHEA, FELIX; Millikan JR HS; Los Angeles, CA; (1); Computer Clb; Intnl Clb; Yrbk; Off Frsh Cls; Hon Roll; CJSF; Engrng.

CHEA, NGON I; Gardena HS; Gardena, CA; (3); Trk; Wt Lftg; Asian Yth Grp; CSF; Harvard; Bus Admin.

CHEA, SAMETH; Modesto HS; Modesto, CA; (2); Math Clb; STANISLAUS U; Nrs.

CHEA, WILLIE L; George Washington HS; San Francisco, CA; (2); High Hon Roll; Hon Roll; U Of CA; Comp Sci.

CHEADLE, SARAH; Mack HS; Trinidad, CA; (1); Teachers Aide; Hon Roll.

CHEAH, BRANDON; Granada Hills HS; Granada Hills, CA; (3).

CHEAM, DADA; Garden Grove HS; Garden Grove, CA; (1); 15/100; Intrml Bsktbl; JV Trk; Hon Roll; Jr NHS; Prfct Atten Awd; Pres Acad Fit Awd; UCLA.

CHEAR, VISNA K; Palm Springs HS; Palm Springs, CA; (3); Art Clb; Sal; Hnrb Mntn Cngrssnl Art Cmptn 89; Vlntr Wrk Mrl Artst; My Amer Art Cont; UC Davis; Med.

CHEATWOOD, LANCE; King City Joint Union HS; King City, CA; (3); Computer Clb; Intnl Clb; Chorus; JV Var Bsbl; Var Bsktbl; Intrml Diving; Intrml Golf; Intrml Swmmng; Hon Roll; Phy Ed.

CHEATWOOD, MARY; Palo Verde HS; Blythe, CA; (4); 11/153; Drama Clb; Pep Clb; Service Clb; Nwsp; Cheerldng; High Hon Roll; Hon Roll; NHS; Pres Acad Fit Awd; U Of CA.

CHEAV, KOUNTHEA T; Eisenhower HS; San Bernardino, CA; (3); Sftbl; Tennis; Vllybl; Hon Roll; Asian Club; Cert Of Awd For Outstndng Typing Achvt; Typing.

CHEBOWSKI, SUZY A; Victor Valley HS; Victorville, CA; (3); 12/750; Pres Church Yth Grp; Cmnty Wkr; Girl Scts; Key Clb; Letterman Clb; Office Aide; Yrbk; Hon Roll; CSF Treas; Schl Hm Ecnmncs Awd; CA ST San Bernardino; Elem Ed.

CHECCO, JESSICA L; Villa Park HS; Orange, CA; (2); Drama Clb; French Clb; Key Clb; School Musical; Off Jr Cls; Var Socr; Hon Roll; NHS; 1st Team Soccer All League; Athl Schlr Awd; U CA Santa Cruz; Intl Relation.

CHECKETTS, NATHAN P; Newark Memorial HS; Newark, CA; (3); 4/396; Boy Scts; Church Yth Grp; Service Clb; SADD; Teachers Aide; Church Choir; JV Var Ftbl; Wt Lftg; JV Var Wrstlng; Bausch & Lomb Sci Awd; NASA Space Seed Prjct; Sci Cmp Cnslr; Gldn St Xms Hi Hnrs; Brigham Young; Intl Rltns.

CHECO, KELLY M; Antelope Valley HS; Lancaster, CA; (2); 42/708; FFA; Hosp Aide; Office Aide; Pep Clb; High Hon Roll; CSF; Sccr Clb; The Debs; Stu Wk.

CHEE, ANGELA; Mayfair HS; Cerritos, CA; (3); 6/200; Am Leg Aux Girls St; Pres Ski Clb; SADD; Pres Jr Cls; High Hon Roll; Opt Clb Awd; Miss CA Natl Teen Ager; Miss NTA 3rd Rnnr Up; Peer Cnslg; Hnr Guard; Prm Comm; CSF; Cmmnctns.

CHEE, MICHAEL W; Lowell HS; San Francisco, CA; (3); Treas Boy Scts; Chess Clb; Math Tm; Q&S; Science Clb; Rptr Nwsp; Ntl Merit Ltr; Golden St Exam Algebra, Geom High Hnrs; Med Explorers Post 496 Treas; Pre-Med.

CHEE, MICHELLE; Phillip & Sala Burton HS; San Francisco, CA; (2); Math Clb; Ski Clb; Mdcl Explr Pst 496; Piano-6 Yrs; UC Davis; Fshn Dsgnr.

CHEE, ROBERT S; Glen A Wilson HS; Hacienda Hgts, CA; (2); Key Clb; JV Bsktbl; JV Trk; High Hon Roll; Hon Roll; Asian-Amer Clb; Tnns Clb.

CHEE, SUEYING M; Del Campo HS; Carmichael, CA; (3); 17/446; French Clb; NHS; CSF; Wood Wrkmnshp Awd.

CHEEK, LAURA M; Clovis HS; Fresno, CA; (1); Church Yth Grp; Cmnty Wkr; Drama Clb; School Musical; School Play; Stage Crew; High Hon Roll; Hon Roll; Vlntr Fresno Zoo Rain Frst; Eclgy Clb; Peace Corps.

CHEEK, MARNEY LEIGH; Sunny Hills HS; Fullerton, CA; (4); 4/410; Cmnty Wkr; Hosp Aide; Treas Spanish Clb; Nwsp; Var Socr; High Hon Roll; Masonic Awd; Pres NHS; Ntl Merit SF; Rotary Awd; Jr Statesmen Amer Mayor Region; Natl Charity Leag; Acad Decathlon Team Capt; 3rd Overall Indvl Comptn; Attorney.

CHEEKS JR, MARVIN G; Paso Robles HS; San Miguel, CA; (2); Boy Scts; Church Yth Grp; JV Trk; Crtfd Wldr.

CHEESEMAN, TED; Athenian HS; Saratoga, CA; (3); Science Clb; Service Clb; School Play; Nwsp; Socr; Avud Rock/Ice Climber; Kodak Photo Awd; Lilia Servence Bio Sci Awd; CVMA Sci Fair Awds; Fld Trps E Afr; Prescott Coll; Bio.

CHEHADE, SALLY A; Roseville HS; Sacramento, CA; (2); French Clb; Hon Roll.

CHELEBIAN, ARMINE; Armenian Mesrobian Schl; Montebello, CA; (3); Church Yth Grp; Pep Clb; Nwsp; Lit Mag; Socr; Sftbl; Art.

CHELETTE, JEFF; Ramona HS; Riverside, CA; (3); 106/403; Church Yth Grp; Teachers Aide; Acpl Chr; Chorus; Church Choir; UC Berkeley; Law.

CHELINE, NINA R; Don Antonio Lugo HS; Chino, CA; (3); Teachers Aide; Cit Awd; Long Beach ST; Adv.

CHEM, SYLORS; Woodrow Wilson HS; Long Beach, CA; (2); Hon Roll; Prfct Atten Awd; CSF; Congrssnl Schlr; UCLA; Medcl.

CHEN, ALAN; Mission Viejo HS; Laguna Hills, CA; (3); Library Aide; Ntl Merit SF; Acad Decathalan; Knowledge Mstr; Engrng.

CHEN, ALAN T; John F Kennedy HS; La Palma, CA; (3); Cmnty Wkr; Computer Clb; FBLA; Key Clb; JV Tennis; High Hon Roll; Pres Acad Fit Awd.

CHEN, ALICE; Highlands HS; Sacramento, CA; (2); 1/330; Scholastic Bowl; JV Crs Cntry; Var Tennis; Var Trk; High Hon Roll; Prfct Atten Awd; Ecology Clb; CA St Schlrshp Fdrtn; Columbia Coll; Sci.

CHEN, ALICE; San Jacinto HS; San Jacinto, CA; (2); Church Yth Grp; Letterman Clb; Spanish Clb; Stat Bsbl; Stat Ftbl; Var Golf; JV Sftbl; JV Var Vllybl; Hon Roll; Prfct Atten Awd; Numerous UCR Pgms; Mock Trial; Prom Cmmtte; Bus.

CHEN, ALICE Y; Diamond Bar HS; Walnut, CA; (3); Church Yth Grp; French Clb; Intnl Clb; Key Clb; SADD; Hon Roll; CSF.

CHEN, ALLISON XIAN; Phillip & Sala Burton HS; San Francisco, CA; (3); Computer Clb; German Clb; Spanish Clb; Band; Orch; Hon Roll; Prfct Atten Awd; Exclnnc-1st Yr Spnsh Hnr; Cert Acadc Achvt-Engl 4; U Of CA Davis; Med.

CHEN, ANDREW; Diamond Bard HS; Diamond Bar, CA; (3); 1/498; Hosp Aide; Key Clb; Math Tm; Service Clb; Ed Lit Mag; Tennis; Hon Roll; Badminton JV; Jr Statesmen Of Amer Treas; Bio.

CHEN, ANDREW T; San Luis Obispo SR HS; San Luis Obispo, CA; (2); 12/319; Chess Clb; Church Yth Grp; Orch; JV Crs Cntry; JV Socr; Var Trk; High Hon Roll.

CHEN, ANGELA C; San Gabriel HS; Rosemead, CA; (2); Sec French Clb; Bsktbl; Var Cheerldng; Hon Roll; Acad Dcthln Club; Schl Rcgntn In Golden St Exam; Cert Of Achvt In Typewriting 50 WPM; Finish U; Bus.

CHEN, ANNE; Capistrano Valley HS; Laguna Niguel, CA; (3); Church Yth Grp; German Clb; Hosp Aide; Office Aide; Band; Church Choir; Nwsp; Hon Roll; All Str Orange Cnty HS Hnrlst Awd; CSF Frshmn Rep, Gld Ltr Cmssnr; Pblshd High Life Sec LA Tms Nwsp; Westmont Coll; Liberal Stds.

CHEN, ANNIE T; Alhambra HS; Alhambra, CA; (3); Model UN; Service Clb; Co-Capt Color Guard; CSF; Stu Lglstr; Stu For Bttr Constitution; UCLA; Bio.

CHEN, ANNIE T; University HS; Irvine, CA; (2); #3 In Class; Library Aide; Math Tm; Office Aide; Orch; JV Bsktbl; High Hon Roll.

CHEN, AUDREY M; St Joseph HS; Cerritos, CA; (3); Am Leg Aux Girls St; Pres VP Debate Tm; GAA; Hosp Aide; Variety Show; Treas Frsh Cls; Pres Soph Cls; Pres Stu Cncl; Powder Puff Ftbl; JV Var Tennis; HOBY Ldrshp Awd; Southern CA Yth Citizenship Smnr; Phy.

CHEN, BETSY; Los Alamitos HS; Seal Beach, CA; (3); Cmnty Wkr; French Clb; FBLA; Math Tm; Model UN; Science Clb; Spanish Clb; Speech Tm; JV Tennis; Hon Roll; Piano; UCLA; Envir Sci.

CHEN, BILLY; Fountain Valley HS; Fountain Valley, CA; (2); JA; Science Clb; High Hon Roll; Hon Roll; CSF; Chns Clb; Bdmntn; UCLA; Med.

CHEN, BRIAN Y; Edison HS; Huntington Beach, CA; (3); 18/425; Debate Tm; JA; Key Clb; Model UN; Quiz Bowl; Ski Clb; Spanish Clb; SADD; Rep Jr Cls; Var L Socr; Plympc Dvlpmnt Pgm CA St Tm Sccr; Orange Cty Acdmc Dcthln; CA Schlstc Fed Offcr & Seal Bearer.

CHEN, BRYAN K; Albany HS; Albany, CA; (2); 1/190; Spanish Clb; Band; Jazz Band; Mrchg Band; VP Soph Cls; Var Crs Cntry; Intrml Sftbl; Intrml Vllybl; Hon Roll; Chem Clb.

CHEN, CALVIN C; St Ignatius College Prep; San Francisco, CA; (2); Rep French Clb; Wt Lftg; Hon Roll; Martial Arts; CA Schlrshp Fed Exec Brd; Chrstn Life Cmnty; Stanford U; Bus.

CHEN, CAROL Y; Cerritos HS; Artesia, CA; (4); 22/544; Art Clb; Computer Clb; French Clb; JCL; Math Clb; Science Clb; Chorus; Hon Roll; Pres Acad Fit Awd; Stu Sentor SR; Math Awd; Treas For Chinese Clutural Clb; U CA San Diego; Biochem.

CHEN, CAROLINE J; Westlake Schl; Los Angeles, CA; (4); Cmnty Wkr; French Clb; Hosp Aide; Math Tm; Model UN; JV Swmmng; Intrml Tennis; NHS; Ntl Merit SF; Intnl Clb; Johns Hopkins U Talent Search; Stanford U; Biochem.

CHEN, CATHERINE; Torrance HS; Torrance, CA; (3); JCL; Latin Clb; Pep Clb; Pres Service Clb; Treas SADD; Drill Tm; Yrbk; Hist Sec Frsh Cls; Treas Soph Cls; Hist Jr Cls; CA Schlrshp Fed Pres; Acad Decathalon Tm Mem 90-91; Exchng Stu Kashiwa Japan 90.

CHEN, CHIA-HUNG; Etiwanda HS; Rancho Cucamonga, CA; (2); VICA; Cit Awd; Prfct Atten Awd; Adventure Clb; Harvard; Comp Sci.

CHEN, CHRISTINE H; University HS; Irvine, CA; (3); 24/551; Sec Dance Clb; French Clb; NFL; Science Clb; Service Clb; Speech Tm; Mgr Stage Crew; French Hon Soc; Hon Roll; CA Schlrshp Fed; Physics.

CHEN, CHUN LING; Oakland HS; Oakland, CA; (4); Church Yth Grp; Off Frsh Cls; Vllybl; Chinese Clb; University Coll; Bus.

CHEN, CINDY I; Irvine HS; Irvine, CA; (4); 1/550; AFS; Off Church Yth Grp; French Clb; Sec Key Clb; Math Tm; Orch; Ed Yrbk; Hon Roll; JETS Awd; Ntl Merit SF; Chem Team.

CHEN, DANIEL E; Leland HS; San Jose, CA; (4); 67/393; VP Church Yth Grp; French Clb; Science Clb; Church Choir; Intrml Bsktbl; Ntl Merit SF; Med.

CHEN, DAVID; Fountain Valley HS; Fountain Valley, CA; (1); Church Yth Grp; FCA; Math Clb; Math Tm; Teachers Aide; Acpl Chr; Church Choir; High Hon Roll; Hon Roll; UCI; Math.

CHEN, DAVID C; Cerritos HS; Cerritos, CA; (2); Math Clb; Hon Roll; UCLA; Bus.

CHEN, DAVID T; John F Kennedy HS; La Palma, CA; (2); Computer Clb; FBLA; Key Clb; Chorus; Var Score Keeper; Var Swmmng; Hon Roll; Pres Acad Fit Awd; Waterpolo-Vrsty; Stanford; Bus.

CHEN, DIH-YIH; Whitney HS; Cerritos, CA; (2); 42/168; Church Yth Grp; VP JA; Key Clb; Band; Mrchg Band; JV Swmmng; Pres Acad Fit Awd; CSF; Med.

CHEN, DYE-ZONE A; Mountain View HS; Mountain View, CA; (3); 1/319; Orch; High Hon Roll; Ntl Merit Ltr; Pres Acad Fit Awd; Interact Clb; JV Badmntn; Mtn Biking; Physics.

CHEN, ECHUNG; Luther Burbank HS; Sacramento, CA; (4); 74/300; Math Clb; ROTC; Teachers Aide; Drill Tm; Phtg Yrbk; JV Tennis; Sons American Revolution; UC Davis; Dsgn.

CHEN, ELLEN Y; San Gabriel HS; Rosemead, CA; (3); Church Yth Grp; Dance Clb; Key Clb; Spanish Clb; JV Swmmng; Hon Roll; Mock Trial; Acad Decathlon; Engl.

CHEN, EMILY PEI-YI; San Gabriel HS; San Gabriel, CA; (3); Church Yth Grp; Cmnty Wkr; Acpl Chr; Hon Roll; Peer Cnslng Pgm; Acad Decathlon Clb; UCLA; Pre-Med.

CHEN, ERIC; Cabrillo HS; Lompoc, CA; (3); 1/210; Church Yth Grp; Cmnty Wkr; FBLA; German Clb; Letterman Clb; Math Tm; SADD; Ed Yrbk; VP Soph Cls; VP Jr Cls.

CHEN, GINA Y; Downey HS; Downey, CA; (3); Am Leg Aux Girls St; French Clb; Sec Intnl Clb; Math Clb; Sec Science Clb; Var Tennis; High Hon Roll; Keywanettes Club CA, NV & HI Cnvtn Chrmn 90-91, Treas 89-90; CSF; Harvard Smmr Schl 90; Law.

CHEN, GRACE; Earl Warren HS; Downey, CA; (4); 8/415; Pres Intnl Clb; Pres Science Clb; Sec Service Clb; SADD; Treas Sr Cls; Ntl Merit Ltr; Rotary Awd; Stu Of Mnth & Yr 89; Natl Sci Olympiad Tm 1st Pl 89 & 90; Music Tchrs Assn CA Hnrs Fstvl 87 & 88; UC Berkeley; Biochem.

CHEN, GRACE; Kennedy HS; La Palma, CA; (1); Church Yth Grp; Cmnty Wkr; JV Swmmng; JV Tennis; UCLA; Bus.

CHEN, GRACE; Ocean View HS; Huntington Bch, CA; (2); Church Yth Grp; FBLA; Key Clb; Model UN; Pep Clb; Pres Jr Cls; Cheerldng; Powder Puff Ftbl; Trk; Gov Hon Prg Awd; CSF; Athltc Schlr Awd; Stanford; Law.

CHEN, GRACE H; Casa Grande HS; Petaluma, CA; (3); Church Yth Grp; Cmnty Wkr; Computer Clb; French Clb; FBLA; Church Choir; Var Trk; High Hon Roll; Badminton; UC Berkeley; Acctng.

CHEN, GRACE W; De Anza HS; Richmond, CA; (3); Math Clb; Science Clb; Band; Mrchg Band; Sftbl; Vllybl; Friday Ngt Live 4 Yrs; Interior Des.

CHEN, HSIAO FAN; Abraham Lincoln HS; San Francisco, CA; (3); Art Clb; Cmnty Wkr; Dance Clb; Yrbk; Tennis.

CHEN, HUBERT D; Bishop O Dowd HS; San Leandro, CA; (3); Church Yth Grp; Crs Cntry; Trk; Ntl Merit Ltr.

CHEN, HUI YA HELEN; San Gabriel HS; Alhambra, CA; (4); 2/737; AFS; Debate Tm; FBLA; Pres German Clb; NFL; Pres Science Clb; SADD; Teachers Aide; Crs Cntry; Elks Awd; Red Cross Yth Group First Aid Offcr; U CA Berkeley.

CHEN, HUI-LIN J; La Reina HS; Thousand Oaks, CA; (2); Dance Clb; Drama Clb; Stage Crew; Variety Show; Rptr Yrbk; High Hon Roll; CJSF; UCLA.

CHEN, INGRID P; Glen A Wilson HS; Hacienda Hgts, CA; (2); Church Yth Grp; German Clb; Hon Roll; Ping Pong Champ; Tutor Elem Schl Kids.

CHEN, JAMES F; Irvine HS; Irvine, CA; (2); 2/583; Church Yth Grp; Key Clb; Orch; JV Tennis; High Hon Roll; CSF; Chinese Clb; UC Berkley; Med.

CHEN, JAMES L; Lowell HS; San Francisco, CA; (2); Chess Clb; Hosp Aide; JV Tennis; High Hon Roll; Math Tutor; CA Schlrshp Fed.

CHEN, JANE; Fountain Valley HS; Fountain Valley, CA; (3); JA; Red Cross Aide; Science Clb; High Hon Roll; Hon Roll; CSF; UCLA; Med.

CHEN, JEN T; University HS; Irvine, CA; (3); French Clb; Hosp Aide; Key Clb; Math Clb; Science Clb; Nwsp; Bsktbl; JV Tennis; French Hon Soc; High Hon Roll; CSF; Golden St Ex Awd Geo; UPHSS U Prog For HS Schlrs.

CHEN, JENNIFER; San Rafael HS; San Rafael, CA; (3); 4/273; Chess Clb; Debate Tm; Key Clb; Science Clb; SADD; Teachers Aide; Stage Crew; High Hon Roll; Hon Roll; Pres Acad Fit Awd; Saferides-Explrer Boy Scout Post; C-Lern-Schl Rfrm Pgm Stu Rep; Pianst; Med.

CHEN, JENNY J; University City HS; San Diego, CA; (3); 1/350; Math Tm; Model UN; SADD; Var L Tennis; High Hon Roll; Prfct Atten Awd; Pres Acad Fit Awd; La Jolla Music Fstvl Cmptn 1st Pl; Golden St Exam Hgh Hnr; Math Tm Cmptn At UCSD 3rd Pl; U CA Berkeley; Arch.

CHEN, JIALI; Oakland HS; Oakland, CA; (2); Math Clb; Math Tm; Spanish Clb; Teachers Aide; UC Berkeley; Bus Mgmt.

CHEN, JIM; Santa Monica HS; Santa Monica, CA; (4); Cit Awd; High Hon Roll; Hon Roll; Honorary Schltc Awd; Outstndng Scl Stds Stu Of Yr; UC Los Angeles; Med.

CHEN, JIONG; San Gabriel HS; San Gabriel, CA; (3); Chess Clb; Church Yth Grp; Math Clb; Math Tm; Science Clb; Hon Roll; Sci.

CHEN, JOANNE; Diamond Bar HS; Walnut, CA; (2); Church Yth Grp; French Clb; Key Clb; CSF; '92 Cmmtte.

CHEN, JOANNE; San Luis Obispo HS; San Luis Obispo, CA; (2); 52/319; Church Yth Grp; Band; Mrchg Band; Yrbk; Hon Roll; Prfct Atten Awd; AAUW:Theater.

CHEN, JOE; George Washington HS; San Francisco, CA; (2); Rep Stu Cncl; Var Bsbl; JV Bsktbl; Hon Roll; Pres Acad Fit Awd; Acctng.

CHEN, JOSEPH; John F Kennedy HS; La Palma, CA; (2); FBLA; Key Clb; Chorus; JV Swmmng; High Hon Roll; Pres Acad Fit Awd; Water Polo; CSF.

CHEN, JOSEPH; Lowell HS; San Francisco, CA; (3); Cmnty Wkr; Drama Clb; Hosp Aide; Latin Clb; Office Aide; Teachers Aide; Varsity Clb; School Play; Crs Cntry; Trk; Georgetown U; Intl Rel.

CHEN, JOYCE; Ocean View HS; Huntington Bch, CA; (4); 10/435; Church Yth Grp; Cmnty Wkr; FBLA; Model UN; Office Aide; Spanish Clb; Variety Show; Var JV Cheerldng; High Hon Roll; Ntl Merit SF; CSF Sec; Soc Women Engrs Cert Mrt & Yrs Excllnc Sci & Math; Claremont Mc Kenna Coll; Engrng.

CHEN, KATHERINE J; John F Kennedy HS; La Palma, CA; (3); Church Yth Grp; Key Clb; Chorus; Church Choir; Msc Tcher Asst 87-88; Sthrn Cal JR Bach Fstv Rgnl Awd 87-89; UCLA; Music.

CHEN, KATHY; Glen A Wilson HS; Hacienda Hts, CA; (2); Art Clb; Church Yth Grp; Band; Mrchg Band; Orch; High Hon Roll; Hon Roll.

CHEN, KENNETH; Sunny Hills HS; Buena Park, CA; (2); 26/402; Pres Chess Clb; Pres Computer Clb; French Clb; Model UN; Quiz Bowl; Science Clb; High Hon Roll; Ntl Merit SF; Pres Acad Fit Awd; Acadmc Dec Cnty 1st Pl 90; Bus Admin.

CHEN, KEVIN; West HS; Torrance, CA; (1); UC Berkeley.

CHEN, LARRY; Baldwin HS; Baldwin Park, CA; (3); Math Tm; High Hon Roll; Prfct Atten Awd; Comp Sci.

CHEN, LESLIE; Carlmont HS; Redwood City, CA; (3); Band; Chorus; Pres Acad Fit Awd; Piano/Art Stu; Cmmrcl Art-Dsgn.

CHEN, LILIA; Flintridge Preparatory Schl; Arcadia, CA; (1); Pep Clb; Capt Cheerldng; High Hon Roll; Stanford; Bus.

CHEN, LILY; Montclair HS; Montclair, CA; (4); 6/400; Rptr Nwsp; JV Tennis; JV Trk; Enrnmntl/Hiking Clb; GATE; CSF; U CA Riverside.

CHEN, LINDA Y; Downey HS; Downey, CA; (4); 1/425; Pres Treas French Clb; VP Math Clb; Pres VP Science Clb; Pres Sec Service Clb; Stu Cncl; Var Capt Bsktbl; Var Capt Tennis; Bausch & Lomb Sci Awd; Val; Powder Puff Ftbl; Westinghouse Sci Tlnt Srch; Hnrs Grp Bk Amer; Sci & Math Awd CSF; UC Berkeley; Engr.

CHEN, LISA; Piedmont Hills HS; San Jose, CA; (4); 16/372; Math Tm; Office Aide; Orch; Hon Roll; CSF; UCLA; Bio.

CHEN, LISA F; J E Mc Ateer HS; San Francisco, CA; (3); Teachers Aide; High Hon Roll; Chinese Clb.

CHEN, LYDIA X L; Mission HS; San Francisco, CA; (4); Cmnty Wkr; Girl Scts; Library Aide; Service Clb; Teachers Aide; Vllybl; Hon Roll; CSF Scrtry; UC Davis; Lndscp Arch.

CHEN, MARGARET; Rosary HS; Fullerton, CA; (2); 1/148; Acpl Chr; Chorus; Rptr Nwsp; JV Vllybl; High Hon Roll; Val; Cncrt Pnst 10 Yrs; Schlr Athlt Awd; Med.

CHEN, MARIAN T; Foothill HS; Orange, CA; (2); Church Yth Grp; Sec Key Clb; Orch; JV Tennis; High Hon Roll; NEDT Awd; Orange Cty Yth Symphony Orch Mem; CSF.

CHEN, MARISA K; Santa Barbara HS; Santa Barbara, CA; (3); Science Clb; Phtg Yrbk; Rep Stu Cncl; Capt JV Bsktbl; Var JV Tennis.

CHEN, MEGAN H; Bishop O'dowd HS; Oakland, CA; (3); Var L Swmmng.

CHEN, MEILI; Oakland HS; Oakland, CA; (3); Teachers Aide; Fresh Wind Clb; UC Berkeley; Accntng.

CHEN, MIAO LI; Sacramento HS; Sacramento, CA; (2); 23/505; CSF Clb; UCD Clb; Asian & Chinese Clb; UC Davis; Phrmcst.

CHEN, MICHAEL; Schurr HS; Monterey Park, CA; (3); Chess Clb; Cmnty Wkr; Key Clb; Math Clb; Math Tm; SADD; JV Tennis; High Hon Roll; NHS; Prfct Atten Awd; Bus Club Pres; Amnesty Intl; Citizen Bee Alt Fnlst.

CHEN, MICHAEL G; Whitney HS; Cerritos, CA; (2); 1/168; JA; Band; Mrchg Band; JV Socr; JV Trk.

CHEN, MILES; Bishop Amat Memorial HS; Walnut, CA; (3); Socr; NHS; Art Graphic Desgn; Engrng.

CHEN, NANCY; Mark Keppel HS; San Gabriel, CA; (2); Church Yth Grp; Key Clb; Service Clb; Varsity Clb; Var Tennis; Pres Acad Fit Awd; UCLA.

CHEN, NANCY E; Upland HS; Upland, CA; (2); 1/760; Math Clb; Ski Clb; Orch; JV Swmmng; JV Tennis; High Hon Roll; Hon Roll; Mock Trial-Bst Defense Attrny Awd; JSA Attndnce Yale U; Piano Awds-Bach Fstvl Fnlst; Lawyer.

CHEN, NELLIE E; George Washington HS; San Francisco, CA; (3); Church Yth Grp; Chorus; Church Choir; Hon Roll; CSF; Conservatory Music; Mandarin Spch Cntst; Pharmacy.

CHEN, NICK Z; Mission HS; San Francisco, CA; (4); Boy Scts; Library Aide; Red Cross Aide; Treas Science Clb; Acpl Chr; JV Bsbl; U CA-DAVIS.

CHEN, NINA N; J E Mc Ateer HS; San Francisco, CA; (3); Library Aide; Office Aide; Rep Jr Cls; Intrml Hon Roll; San Francisco U.

CHEN, NOLA; Marymount HS; Los Angeles, CA; (3); Art Clb; Cmnty Wkr; High Hon Roll; Ntl Merit Ltr; Schl Concert; Bk Clb; Stu Support; Med.

CHEN, OSCAR; Highlands HS; Sacramento, CA; (3); 2/250; Debate Tm; Quiz Bowl; Var Swmmng; High Hon Roll; CSF; Schlr Lttr; Elec Engrnt.

CHEN, PAUL; Nogales HS; W Covina, CA; (2); #747 In Class; Computer Clb; Science Clb; Hon Roll; Prfct Atten Awd; Friend To Friend; CSF; Peer Helpers; Caltech; Phys Sci.

CHEN, PETER JIAN-PAN; Phillip & Sala Burton HS; San Francisco, CA; (3); Computer Clb; Math Clb; High Hon Roll; Outstndng Stu Ldrshp Awd; UC Davis; Comp Sci.

CHEN, PHILIP C; Chadwick Schl; Palos Vrds Pen, CA; (4); Variety Show; Nwsp; Var Capt Tennis; Hon Roll; Ntl Merit Schol; Spanish NHS; Cum Laude Soc; All Amer Schlr 89; Comp Awd 88; Stanford U; Mech Engrng.

CHEN, RAYMOND; George Washington HS; San Francisco, CA; (3); Church Yth Grp; Computer Clb; Math Clb; Science Clb; High Hon Roll; U CA Brkly; Engrng.

CHEN, RAYMOND Y; Whitney HS; Cerritos, CA; (2); Sec Church Yth Grp; Key Clb; Letterman Clb; Varsity Clb; Church Choir; Nwsp; Rptr Yrbk; Var L Crs Cntry; Var L Trk; Fndr HS Cycling Club; Cornell.

CHEN, ROBERT J; Arcadia HS; Arcadia, CA; (2); 27/670; FBLA; Math Clb; Science Clb; Service Clb; Var Bsktbl; High Hon Roll; NHS; Prfct Atten Awd; UCLA; Med.

CHEN, ROBIN C; Los Altos HS; Hacienda Hts, CA; (3); Teachers Aide; Golden St Geom, Alge I Hnr; Prncpls Hnr Roll; Engr.

CHEN, ROSE ANNA; University HS; Newport Beach, CA; (4); French Clb; Intnl Clb; Key Clb; Pres Science Clb; Ski Clb; Southern CA Jr Acad Of Sci 87-89; Girls Leag Cmmtte 88-89; CSU; Bio.

CHEN, SANDY T; Fremont HS; Sunnyvale, CA; (2); Debate Tm; French Clb; NFL; Service Clb; Speech Tm; Teachers Aide; CA Schlrshp Fdrtn; Badminton; Prtcptd With Toronto Royal Schl Exams Piano Vly With 1st Cls Hnrs.

CHEN, SHELLEY W; C K Mc Clatchy SR HS; Sacramento, CA; (3); 94/418; French Clb; Math Clb; Spanish Clb; SADD; Phtg Yrbk; Cit Awd; Prfct Atten Awd; Tnns Club; CSUS; Bus.

CHEN, SHIRLEY; San Mateo HS; Hillsborough, CA; (4); Teachers Aide; JV Tennis; Graphic Dsgn.

CHEN, STEPHANIE C; Pacifica HS; Garden Grove, CA; (3); 13/274; Spanish Clb; SADD; High Hon Roll; Hon Roll; Var Badminton; CSF; Piano Level V; Acctng.

CHEN, STEPHEN; Cupertino HS; Santa Clara, CA; (3); 1/256; FBLA; Math Clb; Math Tm; Red Cross Aide; Science Clb; Var Tennis; High Hon Roll; Hon Roll; NHS; Spanish NHS; Sci Olympiad; Indstrl Engrng.

CHEN, STEPHEN J; Miraleste HS; Rancho Palos Vrds, CA; (4); 13/173; Pres Math Clb; Model UN; Sec Spanish Clb; Pres Band; Chorus; Drm Mjr(t); Jazz Band; Mrchg Band; School Musical; School Play; Derrell Harline Mem Music Awd; Schlr Pgm.

CHEN, TED C; Capuchino HS; Millbrae, CA; (1); Letterman Clb; JV Var Bsbl; JV Bsktbl; Hon Roll; Prfct Atten Awd; Pres Acad Fit Awd; Sports.

CHEN, TEMPE K; Lowell HS; San Francisco, CA; (1); Church Yth Grp; Office Aide; Chorus; Church Choir; School Musical; GSE Hnrs Plcmnt; UCB; Sci.

CHEN, TERANCE; Servite HS; Anaheim, CA; (3); 16/149; Debate Tm; Var Tennis.

CHEN, TERESA H; Fremont Christian HS; Fremont, CA; (1); Socr; High Hon Roll; MA Inst; Arch.

CHEN, TIM CHIH-SHENG; South San Francisco HS; S San Francisco, CA; (3); Pres VP Church Yth Grp; Computer Clb; Math Clb; Church Choir; Stu Cncl; Capt Bsktbl; JV Var Trk; CSF Awds Blcok Ltr & Star; Outstanding Achvt Span; Golden St Exm Hgh Hnrs Alg I & Geom; UCLA; Physics.

CHEN, TIMOTHY M; San Rafael HS; San Rafael, CA; (2); 1/256; High Hnrs Golden St Exam; CSFAP Calculus.

CHEN, TONY; Lowell HS; San Francisco, CA; (2); Church Yth Grp; FCA; Orch; JV Bsktbl; Hon Roll; UC Berkley; Elect Engr.

CHEN, TRILIA; Lowell HS; San Francisco, CA; (2); Drama Clb; Band; Gldn St Exm Hgh Hnrs Alg; CSF; Backpacking Club.

CHEN, VIVIEN WENIVEN; Eagle Rock HS; Arcadia, CA; (4); Chess Clb; Science Clb; High Hon Roll; Hon Roll; JETS Awd; Irvine CA U; Cvl Engrng.

CHEN, WEI-TAO; Phillip & Sala Burton Acad HS; San Francisco, CA; (2); Computer Clb; School Musical; High Hon Roll; UC; Comp.

CHEN, WEI-YU; Arcakia HS; Temple City, CA; (4); 18/635; Church Yth Grp; Pres Sec French Clb; FBLA; Sec Red Cross Aide; Service Clb; Teachers Aide; Pres Orch; High Hon Roll; Hon Roll; NHS; CSF; Natl Bicntnnl Cmptn 1st Pl Dist, 3rd Pl St; CJSF Hnr Awd; Acad Excel Geo W/ Hnrs; Musician Of Mth; UC Berkeley; Biochem.

CHEN, WEN-I; Mark Keppel HS; San Gabriel, CA; (4); Teachers Aide; Sec Acpl Chr; Sec Chorus; Clbs Chinese, Bowling, Friendship; Outstndng Chorus; Aztec Concert Choir 88-90; CA ST Of L A; Bus.

CHEN, WENPIN; Gahr HS; Cerritos, CA; (3); Chinese Club; :CPA.

CHEN, WINNIE K; Carlsbad HS; Carlsbad, CA; (3); 18/370; Hosp Aide; Pres Key Clb; Ed Nwsp; Off Soph Cls; Stu Cncl; Cheerldng; Var L Trk; Hon Roll; Pres Acad Fit Awd; 2 Yr Natl Jr Olympian Trk & Field.

CHEN, XIN; Redlands HS; Loma Linda, CA; (4); Cit Awd; Dist Schlr Awd 88-89; Schlr Awd Engl & Math; Comp Pgrmng; San Diego CA U; Comp Sci.

CHEN, XIN LI; Edison HS; Stockton, CA; (2); Hon Roll; UC Davis; Engr.

CHEN, YA-CHIN; Oxnard HS; Oxnard, CA; (3); 7/480; Art Clb; Debate Tm; Intnl Clb; Math Clb; Service Clb; Spanish Clb; SADD; Rep Frsh Cls; VP Soph Cls; Prfct Atten Awd; CA Scholastic Federation Secretary; Bio/ Chemistry.

CHEN, YAO-NING; Galileo HS; San Francisco, CA; (4); Bus.

CHENEY, GREG J; Portola JR SR HS; Portola, CA; (1); 2/65; Boy Scts; Church Yth Grp; Band; Swing Chorus; Pres Soph Cls; JV Bsbl; JV Bsktbl; JV Ftbl; Hon Roll; Yth/Yth Clb.

CHENEY, JUNE C; Clayton Valley HS; Concord, CA; (2); Church Yth Grp; Band; Mrchg Band; Orch; School Musical; Rep Frsh Cls; High Hon Roll; Prfct Atten Awd; Pres Acad Fit Awd; Young Peoples Symph Orch; Boy Area Wind Wymph; CSF; Pro Flutist.

CHENG, AMY; Abraham Lincoln HS; San Francisco, CA; (2); Library Aide; Orch; UC, Berkeley.

CHENG, CALVIN Z; Lowell HS; San Francisco, CA; (3); VP Debate Tm; VP NFL; VP Speech Tm; Ed Nwsp; Intrml Vllybl; Ntl Merit Ltr; Fncng Tm; Mem Of CA Schlrshp Fdrtn & Cowell Shld & Scroll Hnr Scty; Wnnr UCLA Almni Ass Bk Awrd; Political Sci.

CHENG, CINDY S; Arcadia HS; Arcadia, CA; (2); FBLA; Math Clb; Math Tm; Science Clb; Service Clb; Band; Drill Tm; Mrchg Band; Orch; Pep Band; Bio Clb Ofcr Of Cmmnctns; Octagon Clb; CJSF Gld Seal Grad; Gldn St Exam Schl Rcgntn; Med.

CHENG, DAWN; Highlands HS; North Highlands, CA; (2); 2/300; Art Clb; French Clb; Socr; Tennis; Cit Awd; High Hon Roll; Prfct Atten Awd; U CA Davis; Art.

CHENG, DENNIS; Fountain Valley HS; Fountain Valley, CA; (3); Church Yth Grp; JCL; Latin Clb; Science Clb; JV Swmmng; High Hon Roll; Hon Roll; Piano 10 Yrs; Triathlon; Bus.

CHENG, ERIC K; George Washington HS; San Francisco, CA; (3); Cmnty Wkr; VP Computer Clb; German Clb; Key Clb; Math Clb; Off Red Cross Aide; Science Clb; Service Clb; High Hon Roll; Cert Of Achvt; San Francisco PTA Reflections Hnrb Mntn 90; Golden Gate Exam Of Geom High Hnrs; Bio.

CHENG, ERIC T; Piedmont Hills HS; Fremont, CA; (1); Church Yth Grp; Lit Mag; High Hon Roll; Taiwanese Chinese Schl; Piano Awds; Stanford; Med.

CHENG, FONG-PO; Mark Keppel HS; Monterey Park, CA; (3); Latin Clb; Mu Alpha Theta; Hist Spanish Clb; Chorus; JV Vllybl; Hon Roll; Prfct Atten Awd; NCCJ Yth Ldrshp Cert 89-90; Resrc Yth Ldr 89; CSF; Gldn St Exam Alg.

CHENG, GARY T; Brea Olinda HS; Brea, CA; (2); 3/344; Treas Intnl Clb; Yrbk; Sec Bsktbl; JV Ftbl; Gov Hon Prg Awd; High Hon Roll; Jr NHS; Prfct Atten Awd; Ftbl Lineman Of Yr; Geom Golden St Exam High Hnrs; Stanford.

CHENG, GENE; Santa Monica HS; Santa Monica, CA; (3); Ski Clb; Bsktbl; Trk; CA Schlrshp Fed.

CHENG, HELENA; Lowell HS; San Francisco, CA; (3); French Clb; Red Cross Aide; Scholastic Bowl; SADD; Teachers Aide; Band; Rep Jr Cls; JV Vllybl; High Hon Roll; NHS; Pharmacist/Accountant.

CHENG, HUN S; Mark Keppel HS; El Monte, CA; (2); 35/500; Debate Tm; Math Clb; JV Vllybl; Hon Roll; High Hnr Roll; JCSF; Prfct Atten Awd; UC Riverside; Med.

CHENG, IRENE C; Mills HS; Burlingame, CA; (2); Aud/Vis; Sec Chess Clb; Church Yth Grp; Debate Tm; Hosp Aide; Math Tm; Hist Service Clb; Orch; Pres Lit Mag; Mgr(s).

CHENG, JEFFREY J; Miraleste HS; Rancho Palos Verd, CA; (4); German Clb; Key Clb; Model UN; Band; Jazz Band; Mrchg Band; Hon Roll; JV Capt Tennis; Outstndng Muscn Awd; Reed Coll; Bus.

CHENG, KAREN M; Ramona Convent HS; Montebello, CA; (3); Art Clb; Church Yth Grp; Cmnty Wkr; GAA; Model UN; Chorus; Treas Stu Cncl; Mgr(s); Score Keeper; Var Co-Capt Tennis; Engl Medallion Awd Wnnr; Philomathean Hnr Soc; CSF; 1st Prz Short Story Cont 88-89; U CA; Jrnlsm.

CHENG, LARRY; Bellarmine College Prep; San Jose, CA; (4); 6/305; Cmnty Wkr; Debate Tm; Hosp Aide; NFL; Speech Tm; Teachers Aide; Rptr Nwsp; Ed Yrbk; Pres Acad Fit Awd; Rotary Awd; Member Of Social Involvement Core Group And Planning; Social Community Service Award; U Of Calif; Business Economics.

CHENG, LARRY W; La Jolla Country Day Schl; Encinitas, CA; (2); Cmnty Wkr; Sec Treas Jr Cls; Var Capt Bsktbl; Var Ftbl; Var Trk; High Hon Roll; Hon Roll; Bsktbl Most Imprvd; Trk Most Vlbl Fld Athl; 1st Athl To Qlfy From LJCD For Vaquero Trk Chmpnshps; Bus.

CHENG, LEON; Lowell HS; San Francisco, CA; (3); Church Yth Grp; Hosp Aide; Latin Clb; Red Cross Aide; Science Clb; Teachers Aide; High Hon Roll; Medical Explorers Post 496; Med Club; UC Berkeley; Biochem.

CHENG, LILY; Galileo HS; San Francisco, CA; (3); Bus Profs of Am; Computer Clb; FBLA; Math Clb; Ski Clb; Band; School Musical; Vllybl; NEDT Awd; UC Berkeley; Bus.

CHENG, LINKER K; Sunset HS; Hayward, CA; (3); Hon Roll; Outstndng Acad Achvt Golden St Exm Geom W/Hnrs 89; Comp Sci.

CHENG, LOREN; Sunny Hills HS; Fullerton, CA; (3); 7/430; Boy Scts; Cmnty Wkr; Pres Sec Computer Clb; Debate Tm; Sec Spanish Clb; Stu Cncl; Var Trk; High Hon Roll; NHS; Ntl Merit SF; Engrng Tech Soc Treas 89-90; Engrng Tech Soc Pres 90-91; BS Ldrshps Corps; Patrol Ldrs 3 Terms; Life Rk; Med.

CHENG, LUISA WAI WAI; Woodrow Wilson HS; San Francisco, CA; (3); Art Clb; Drama Clb; Science Clb; Vllybl; Hon Roll; CSF; Chinese Stu Clb; Hnr Soc; Biochem.

CHENG, MAY; San Marin HS; San Rafael, CA; (4); 10/242; French Clb; Teachers Aide; Swmmng; Pres Acad Fit Awd; CSF; Blood Dr Cmmtte; Gldn St Exm Geom Hgh Hnr; UC Berkeley; Comp Sci.

CHENG, MICHAEL C; Oakland HS; Oakland, CA; (2); French Clb; Key Clb; Math Clb; Math Tm; Sftbl; Cit Awd; Hon Roll; Prfct Atten Awd; Marcus Foster Awd; CSF; UC Berkeley; Arch.

CHENG, MONA; Southwestern Acad; San Marino, CA; (2); Letterman Clb; Varsity Clb; School Play; Ed Yrbk; Stu Cncl; Capt Bsktbl; Mgr(s); Score Keeper; Capt Vllybl; Rotary Awd; Vlybl CIF Mst Vlble Plyr; Marine Bio.

CHENG, MONA; Southwestern Acad; Temple City, CA; (2); Letterman Clb; Varsity Clb; Yrbk; Rep Stu Cncl; Stat Mgr(s); Var Vllybl; Hon Roll; CA Intrschlstc Fed Acad Vlybl Tm Hnr; CIF Vly Leag 1st Tm Hnrs Vlyvl; UCLA; Chem.

CHENG, NANCY Y; Berkely HS; Berkeley, CA; (4); Intnl Clb; Teachers Aide; Church Choir; Hon Roll; Dulci Jubilo Inc Merit Awd Berkeley Smmr Schl Wrtng Crs 89; Acadmc Awd 90; Contra Costa JC; Comp Sci.

CHENG, PAMELA; Homestead HS; Sunnyvale, CA; (1); Bsktbl; French Hon Soc; Jr NHS; NHS; Pres Acad Fit Awd; Environmental Club Secy; Cosmetology.

CHENG, PEGGY; San Rafael HS; Danville, CA; (3); Art Clb; Church Yth Grp; PEACE.

CHENG, PETER C; Rosemead HS; Rosemead, CA; (2); Treas Church Yth Grp; JV Tennis; Prncpls Hnr Roll; Golden St Schlr 89; Schl Rcgntn Geom; CSF Ftrst Clb New Encounter; Engrng.

CHENG, ROBERT H; Villa Park HS; Orange, CA; (3); Key Clb; Math Tm; Science Clb; Hon Roll; NHS; St Schlr; AHSME Schl Wnr.

CHENG, SANDRA T; San Marino HS; San Gabriel, CA; (3); 40/260; Art Clb; Cmnty Wkr; Dance Clb; Math Clb; NFL; Office Aide; Red Cross Aide; Treas Pres Service Clb; Trk.

CHENG, SHIRLEY; George Washington HS; San Francisco, CA; (3); Cmnty Wkr; Dance Clb; Band; Hon Roll; Eagles Svc Soc; CSF; Chinese Am Clb.

CHENG, STEVE K Y; John F Kennedy HS; Buena Park, CA; (2); Art Clb; Church Yth Grp; Computer Clb; Science Clb; Hon Roll; JV Badminton; Athletic Sprts Awd; Med.

CHENG, TIFFANY; San Gabriel HS; Alhambra, CA; (4); 1/28; Church Yth Grp; Cmnty Wkr; Intnl Clb; SADD; Church Choir; High Hon Roll; Hon Roll; Prfct Atten Awd; UCLA.

CHENG, TINA W; Los Altos HS; Palos Verdes Est, CA; (2); Art Clb; Intnl Clb; Key Clb; JV Swmmng; High Hon Roll; Hon Roll; Pres Acad Fit Awd; Dist Wnnr Natl Piano Aud; Hgh Rtd Pre Clcls Sop; Indvdl Mth Pgm.

CHENG, TONY; El Dorado HS; Placentia, CA; (4); 10/350; Computer Clb; Intnl Clb; High Hon Roll; Pres Acad Fit Awd; Mock Trial; Acadmc Dcthln; Natl Merit Cmmndtn; CSF; U Of CA Berkeley; Arch.

CHENG, TSAI-CHU; Nogales HS; Walnut, CA; (3); 11/800; Pres Computer Clb; Intnl Clb; Science Clb; Yrbk; Var Trk; High Hon Roll; CSF.

CHENG, VIVIAN; Southwestern Acad; South Pasadena, CA; (3); Varsity Clb; Yrbk; Var Vllybl; Gld Awd-Hghst Achvts; MIP Vrsty Vllybl 89; UCLA.

CHENG, WILLIAM; San Gabriel HS; San Gabriel, CA; (3); Girls Bsktbl Tm Mgr; USC; Engrng.

CHENG, WILSON HSI CHIN; George Washington HS; San Francisco, CA; (3); Intnl Clb; Science Clb; Vllybl; Stanford; Elec Engr.

CHENNAULT, TAMMY K; Hemet HS; Hemet, CA; (4); 88/518; German Clb; Treas Letterman Clb; Treas Pep Clb; Ed Yrbk; Var L Trk; Mt San Jacinto; Hstry.

CHERKIS, YEFIM; George Washington HS; San Francisco, CA; (3); Var Tennis; Close-Up Pgm.

CHERNISKY, CHRISTIE L; Fairfield HS; Fairfield, CA; (1); Color Guard; Flag Corp; Mrchg Band; High Hon Roll; Hon Roll; Ntl Merit Ltr; Med.

CHERPIN, WENDY M; Fontana HS; Fontana, CA; (4); 79/800; Aud/Vis; Science Clb; Band; Mrchg Band; School Musical; School Play; Hon Roll; Daisy Chain; Z Clb; Badmntn Vrsty; San Diego ST U; Astrnmy.

CHERRY, ALLISON D; Bella Vista HS; Fair Oaks, CA; (2); 32/406; Drama Clb; Spanish Clb; School Musical; School Play; Global Impact; Law.

CHERRY, ERIN R; Turlock HS; Turlock, CA; (2); 4-H; Hon Roll; CA ST; Pedtrcn.

CHERRY, JASON W; North HS; Bakersfield, CA; (3); 1/368; Am Leg Boys St; Church Yth Grp; FCA; VP Hosp Aide; Letterman Clb; Acpl Chr; School Musical; Var Ftbl; High Hon Roll; Treas NHS; CSF; CA St Hnr Choir; Earthwatch Stu Expedition Awd; Med.

CHERRY, LAWAN; Fairfax HS; Los Angeles, CA; (2); Varsity Clb; Stage Crew; Yrbk; Stu Cncl; JV Bsktbl; JV Ftbl; Loyola ST U; Obstetrcs.

CHERRY, NYESHA M; Morningside HS; Los Angeles, CA; (3); Church Yth Grp; Drama Clb; Church Choir; MESA; Peer Cnslr; Church Debutante Essay Awd Wnnr 88; CA ST U-Northrdg; Law.

CHERUNG, NARO; David Starr Jordan HS; Long Beach, CA; (4); Math Clb; Math Tm; Science Clb; Teachers Aide; Vllybl; High Hon Roll; Ntl Merit Ltr; Pres Acad Fit Awd; Outstndng Awd In Amer Chemcl Soc 2 Yrs; Acad Ltr; UC Riverside; Engrng.

CHESKATY, JULIE; Francis W Parker HS; Santee, CA; (2); Cmnty Wkr; GAA; Letterman Clb; Spanish Clb; SADD; Varsity Clb; Yrbk; Var Bsktbl; Powder Puff Ftbl; Var Sftbl; Vllybll 2nd Tm All League Div III; Smr Lge Basktbl; Phys Thrpy.

CHESNUTT, MELISSA J; Newark Memorial HS; Newark, CA; (2); 61/545; Church Yth Grp; Hon Roll; NHS; Dance Clss; Wrkng Swmmng Aide.

CHETBUNDIT, JARUWAN; James Monroe HS; Sepulveda, CA; (2); Library Aide; Teachers Aide; Cit Awd; Pres Acad Fit Awd; CSF Clb; CA U Of Northridge; Comp Pgmr.

CHEUNG, ALVIN F H; South Pasadena HS; S Pasadena, CA; (2); Computer Clb; Latin Clb; Math Clb; Science Clb; Golden St Exam Alg High Hnr Awd, Geom Hnr Awd; UC Berkeley; Comp Engrng.

CHEUNG, ALVIN K; St Ignatius College Prep; San Francisco, CA; (3); Church Yth Grp; Cmnty Wkr; Phtg Nwsp; Phtg Yrbk; JV Trk; JV Vllybl; Hon Roll; CSF; Pre Med.

CHEUNG, BILLY K; Lincoln HS; San Francisco, CA; (2); Ski Clb; JV Tennis; Cmpgn CA; Cmptrs.

CHEUNG, CHRISTOPHER M; Aragon HS; San Mateo, CA; (3); Church Yth Grp; Crs Cntry; Ftbl; JV Trk; High Hon Roll; UC Davis; Mech Engrng.

CHEUNG, CRISTINA K; Mercy HS; San Francisco, CA; (3); Intnl Clb; Math Clb; Spanish Clb; School Musical; School Play; Hon Roll; Enjoy Dancing Class; Engrg.

CHEUNG, EDDY TIMLAND; Palos Verdes HS; Rancho Palos Vrds, CA; (3); 35/343; Cmnty Wkr; Model UN; Service Clb; Spanish Clb; SADD; Trk; High Hon Roll; Hon Roll; NHS; Pres Acad Fit Awd; Goldn St Exam Geom High Hnrs; Cert Prtcptn Annl Peninsula HS Juried Art Show; Brown; Med.

CHEUNG, ETHAN; Lowell HS; San Francisco, CA; (2); Latin Clb; Library Aide; Science Clb; Harvard; Medic.

CHEUNG, GLORIA H; Walnut HS; Walnut, CA; (4); 26/380; Church Yth Grp; Dance Clb; Key Clb; Pres Chorus; School Musical; Ed Lit Mag; Stu Cncl; High Hon Roll; CSF; Vocal Music Hall Of Fame; Vocal Prfmnc.

CHEUNG, HELEN; Piedmont HS; Piedmont, CA; (4); German Clb; Science Clb; Spanish Clb; SADD; Teachers Aide; Outstndng Bus Educ Awd 90; CA ST U-Hayward; Nrsng.

CHEUNG, HUMPHREY; Redlands SR HS; Redlands, CA; (2); Chess Clb; Pres Computer Clb; JA; Quiz Bowl; Teachers Aide; Cit Awd; Hon Roll; Opt Clb Awd; Prfct Atten Awd; Pres Acad Fit Awd; Mrtl Arts; Hlpd Bld IBM PC In 9th Grd; Harvard; Bus.

CHEUNG, IGNATIUS; Mills HS; Millbrae, CA; (4); 18/280; Math Tm; Teachers Aide; High Hon Roll; Pres Acad Fit Awd; U CA Berkeley; Molecular Bio.

CHEUNG, JASON Y; Galileo HS; San Francisco, CA; (3); Chess Clb; Computer Clb; Math Clb; Band; JV Bsktbl; Var Socr; JV Swmmng; High Hon Roll; Prfct Atten Awd; CA Schlrshp Fedrtn; U Of CA; Comp Sci.

CHEUNG, KAIDICK; E K Mc Clatchy HS; Sacramento, CA; (3); French Clb; Hon Roll; Ntl Merit SF; Pres Acad Fit Awd; Golden St Exam Hnrs; Gtr Sac Vo-Ed Fair 2nd; Aerospace Engrng.

CHEUNG, LAI SEI; Schurr HS; San Gabriel, CA; (3); 13/500; Hosp Aide; Key Clb; Math Clb; Spanish Clb; Mgr Nwsp; Bsktbl; Var L Trk; Hon Roll; Prfct Atten Awd; Athtc Awd; Eclgy Club; Bsktbll Schlr Athlt Awd; Duke U; Bio.

CHEUNG, MIA; Alameda HS; Oakland, CA; (2); English Clb; Chorus; School Musical; UC Berkeley; Designer.

CHEUNG, OLIVER K; Los Angeles Baptist HS; Sepulveda, CA; (3); 15/103; Sec Church Yth Grp; Church Choir; School Play; Var Mgr(s); Var Vllybl; High Hon Roll; Hon Roll; 2 Time Sch Ping-Pong Chmp; UC Davis; Cmptr Prgrmng.

CHEUNG, PHILIP; Bonita HS; La Verne, CA; (2); Debate Tm; SADD; Band; Jazz Band; JV Tennis; High Hon Roll; Jr NHS; Church Yth Grp; French Clb; Mrchg Band; Claremont Yng Musicns Orch; Acad Olympd Tm; Pres/Fndr Dbt Clb.

CHEUNG, RAYMOND C; Los Altos HS; Hacienda Hgts, CA; (4); Library Aide; Varsity Clb; Acpl Chr; Var Vllybl; Natl Jr Olympc Vlybl Chmpnshps 3rd Pl 88; UCLA.

CHEUNG, RONNY; Mount Pleasant HS; San Jose, CA; (2); CSF; Natl Block Awds; UCLA; Arch.

CHEUNG, ROSELYN V; University HS; Irvine, CA; (3); 91/521; French Clb; Hosp Aide; Band; Mrchg Band; Treas Sr Cls; Var L Swmmng; French Hon Soc; Cert Of Mrt Piano Adv Lvl Hnrs Priv; Pres Msc Clb; Sylophone Perf Priv; Psych.

CHEUNG, SUSAN; San Gabriel HS; Alhambra, CA; (2); French Clb; Red Cross Aide; Spanish Clb; Flag Corp; Hon Roll; Pres Acad Fit Awd; Knights & Ladies; E Clb; CSF.

CHEUNG, TIMMY; Alameda HS; Alameda, CA; (2); 15/287; Hon Roll.

CHEUNG, VIVIEN; Chinese Christian Schls; Oakland, CA; (1); 1/11; Sec Church Yth Grp; Hon Roll.

CHEUNG, WILSON; George Miller Schurr HS; Monterey Park, CA; (2); Computer Clb; Ed Nwsp; Hon Roll.

CHEUY, LIN L; Mc Clatchy HS; Sacramento, CA; (1).

CHEVEZ, VICTOR M; Hawthorne HS; Hawthorne, CA; (2); JV Bsbl; Var Ftbl; JV Wrstlng; UCLA; Arch.

CHEVOYA, ANDREA; Yosemite HS; Oakhurst, CA; (4); Church Yth Grp; Service Clb; Chorus; Rep Frsh Cls; Rep Stu Cncl; Var Sftbl; Stat Wrstlng; High Hon Roll; Pre Med.

CHEW, GEOFFREY T; University City HS; San Diego, CA; (3); 131/373; Cmnty Wkr; SADD; L Golf; Ntl Merit SF; Mem CSF; Outstndng Achvmnt Awd; Hnr Roll U HS; U Of CA San Diego; Astrophyscs.

CHEW, LISA M; North HS; Oildale, CA; (3); Church Yth Grp; Cmnty Wkr; Rptr Yrbk; High Hon Roll; Top Acad Awd Cert Of Comptn Fashn Merh 89-90; Lyles Coll Bty 90-91; Biola Christian Coll; Elem Teac.

CHEW, MICHAEL F; Abraham Lincoln HS; San Francisco, CA; (2); Church Yth Grp; Math.

CHEW, MICHELLE; Chinese Christian Schls; Castro Valley, CA; (1); Treas Church Yth Grp; Office Aide; Orch; Intrml Vllybl; Hon Roll.

CHEW, RYAN T; Santa Teresa HS; San Jose, CA; (3); 48/500; Science Clb; Spanish Clb; Intrml Bsktbl; Intrml Socr; Intrml Vllybl; Hon Roll; CA Schlrshp Fed; US Acad Decathlon; UC Davis.

CHEW, TAMARA; San Ramon Valley HS; San Ramon, CA; (3); 126/420; Chrmn Church Yth Grp; Teachers Aide; Band; Mrchg Band; Orch; School Musical; Hon Roll; Nrsng.

CHEW, TIM S; Mission College Preparatory HS; San Luis Obispo, CA; (3); Stage Crew; JV Bsktbl; Var Ftbl; Var Golf; Var Score Keeper; Intrml Vllybl; Var High Hon Roll; Var Hon Roll; Engr.

CHEY, ELIZABETH; John Glenn HS; Norwalk, CA; (2); Key Clb; Ed Nwsp; Off Frsh Cls; Off Soph Cls; Pres Jr Cls; Stu Cncl; JV Vllybl; High Hon Roll; Variety Show; HOBY Ambassador; Stu Of Others Sec; Press-Telegram Minority Seminar; Northwestern; Jrnlsm.

CHEY, MICHELE; Rosary HS; Fullerton, CA; (4); 7/135; Church Yth Grp; Cmnty Wkr; Speech Tm; Teachers Aide; Varsity Clb; Off Jr Cls; Stu Cncl; JV Capt Bsktbl; Trk; Cit Awd; Campus Mnstry Retreat Team; CA U San Diego.

CHHAI, PISETH; Lakewood HS; Long Beach, CA; (3); Ftbl; Trk; Wrstlng; Hon Roll; UC Santa Barbara.

CHHAY, LARA; George Washington HS; San Francisco, CA; (2); High Hon Roll; CSF; Vollybl Clb; 2nd Pl Mandarin Spch Cntst; Lawyer.

CHHAY, PISEY; Edison HS; Stockton, CA; (2); Church Yth Grp; French Clb; Math Clb; Math Tm; Science Clb; Var Socr; Var Swmmng; French Hon Soc; Gov Hon Prg Awd; High Hon Roll; Alpine Club; Explr Boy Scts; CA Poly SLO; Envrnmntl Engr.

CHHEM, CHANRAV A; Roosevelt HS; Fresno, CA; (3); Nrsng.

CHHEN, CHUNG K; Baldwin Park HS; Baldwin Park, CA; (4); Boy Scts; Church Yth Grp; Cmnty Wkr; Computer Clb; FBLA; Math Clb; Hon Roll; Prfct Atten Awd; ROP; CSU Pomona; Bus.

CHHENG, DANIELLE; Downey HS; Downey, CA; (3); French Clb; Intnl Clb; Science Clb; Service Clb; Varsity Clb; Tennis; USC; Intl Bus.

CHHENG, PHARA; Pittsburg HS; Pittsburg, CA; (1); JV Bsktbl.

CHHOR, JENNIFER K; Lincoln HS; Los Angeles, CA; (1); Teachers Aide; Off Frsh Cls; Stu Cncl.

CHHOR, MUY CHOU; Whitney HS; Lakewood, CA; (2); 32/168; Art Clb; Cmnty Wkr; Dance Clb; Drama Clb; Sec VP JA; Rep Key Clb; Spanish Clb; Mrchg Band; Hon Roll; Working With Blind People; Bicycling & Cooking; Bus.

CHHORN, SAMBATH; A A Stagg HS; Stockton, CA; (2); Socr; High Hon Roll; Hon Roll; X-Ray Tech.

CHHOUEN, DARA; Hoover HS; San Diego, CA; (3); French Clb; Intnl Clb; Cit Awd; Hon Roll; NHS; Prfct Atten Awd; Cert Mrt.

CHHUN, AMTHON; Saddleback HS; Santa Ana, CA; (4); 52/540; Church Yth Grp; Spanish Clb; Intrml Trk; High Hon Roll; NHS; Ntl Merit Ltr; Vietnms Clb; UCI; Biolgcl Sci.

CHHUN, CHANDARA; Amos Alonzo Stagg HS; Stockton, CA; (1); Teachers Aide; High Hon Roll; Sec Of Cambodian Club; Child Abuse Prvntn Cncl; UC Davis; Sec.

CHI, HOWARD H; Artesia HS; Artesia, CA; (2); Church Yth Grp; Science Clb; Chorus; Church Choir; Chinese Clb; Cal Tech; Physics.

CHI, LISA; Stagg HS; Stockton, CA; (3); Treas Frsh Cls; High Hon Roll; Hon Roll; CSF; Sgft Arms Stu Take Action Not Drugs.

CHI, ONEIDA; Abraham Lincoln HS; San Francisco, CA; (3); Ski Clb; Sftbl; Lincs Clb; Clss Of 1991; U CA Santa Barbara.

CHI, SHARON; San Gabriel HS; S San Gabriel, CA; (4); 113/737; Art Clb; French Clb; FBLA; Office Aide; Spanish Clb; SADD; Teachers Aide; Varsity Clb; Rep Stu Cncl; Intrml Bsktbl; U CA Riverside; Bus.

CHI, WAN C; Ramona Convent Secondary Schl; Montebello, CA; (3); GAA; Model UN; Var L Trk; Bausch & Lomb Sci Awd; NHS; NEDT Awd.

CHI LIK, ERIC POON; Los Altos HS; Hacienda Hts, CA; (3); Church Yth Grp; Cmnty Wkr; Computer Clb; Red Cross Aide; Band; Chorus; School Musical; Swmmng; Tennis; Prfct Atten Awd; Tnns Coachs Awd, Los Altos Prncpl Hnr Rll 90; Cngrssnl Schlr Rep CA Natl Yng Ldrs Cnfrnc.

CHIA, BENNY; Monte Vista HS; Danville, CA; (3); Computer Clb; Intnl Clb; Math Clb; Model UN; Pep Clb; Prfct Atten Awd; Engl Awd; UC Davis; Dsgn.

CHIA, DAN; Ukiah HS; Ukiah, CA; (4); 7/450; Am Leg Boys St; Church Yth Grp; Orch; Crs Cntry; Socr; Tennis; Pres Acad Fit Awd; U CA-DAVIS; Environmntl Engr.

CHIA, DAVID S; Pacifica HS; Cypress, CA; (3); 4/274; Computer Clb; Pres Math Clb; Math Tm; Quiz Bowl; Scholastic Bowl; Hon Roll; Ntl Merit Ltr; US Acad Decathlon Tm Mem; CSF; Math Awd; U Of CA Irvine; Cmptr Sci.

CHIA, DENNIS J; Glen A Wilson HS; Hacienda Heights, CA; (4); 5/370; Hosp Aide; VP Treas Intnl Clb; VP Key Clb; Service Clb; Var JV Bsktbl; High Hon Roll; Ntl Merit SF; Med.

CHIA, JENNY L; Pacifica HS; Cypress, CA; (1); Hon Roll; SCF Stu; Schlr Of Qtr; Math Medallion & Wrld Hist Hnrs Medallion; Acctg.

CHIA, JESSICA; Palo Alto HS; Palo Alto, CA; (2); Church Yth Grp; Debate Tm; Intnl Clb; Key Clb; NFL; Rptr Nwsp; Sci Dept Awds.

CHIANCHITLERT, VICTOR; Mark Keppel HS; Monterey Park, CA; (2); Office Aide; Off Soph Cls; Off Jr Cls; Mgr(s); Vllybl; High Hon Roll; Hon Roll; Carpenter.

CHIANG, CARL C; San Rafael HS; San Rafael, CA; (4); Cmnty Wkr; German Clb; Intnl Clb; Key Clb; Library Aide; Orch; Var L Crs Cntry; Var L Trk; Hon Roll; Pres Acad Fit Awd; CSF; Robert Selmi Awd; U Of San Francisco; Bio Chem.

CHIANG, CATHY C; Mills HS; Millbrae, CA; (3); 4/290; Am Leg Aux Girls St; Sec Church Yth Grp; Debate Tm; Intnl Clb; Church Choir; School Play; Rep Frsh Cls; Treas Soph Cls; Var Crs Cntry; JV Tennis; San Mateo Cnty Fair Voice Cmptn 3rd Pl; CTA Cert Of Merit Piano Hnrs Rctl; Treas Rotarys Interact Clb; Bus Adm.

CHIANG, CHRIS KUO CHUAN; Arroyo Grande HS; Grover City, CA; (4); Chess Clb; Pres Acad Fit Awd; Astropho & Astronomy; U Of CA Berkeley; Molclr Bio.

CHIANG, CRAIG C; Santa Teresa HS; San Jose, CA; (3); Chess Clb; Debate Tm; FBLA; German Clb; Sec Model UN; Science Clb; Stu Cncl; Var Tennis; NHS; CSF; Awd Excllnc Natl HS Mdl Untd Ntn; UC Berkeley; Poli Sci.

CHIANG, JEANNE; Del Campo HS; Fair Oaks, CA; (3); 71/449; SADD; Band; Drill Tm; Mrchg Band; Var Tennis; NHS; CSF; UC Davis; Commnctns.

CHIANG, JEFFREY C; Milpitas HS; Milpitas, CA; (2); 112/536; Boy Scts; French Clb; Red Cross Aide; Trk; Hon Roll; Astronomy Clb; Chinese Clb; Sci.

CHIANG, JU-HUEI; Schurr HS; Montebello, CA; (4); 11/590; Hosp Aide; Intnl Clb; Teachers Aide; JV Tennis; High Hon Roll; Ntl Merit Ltr; Prfct Atten Awd; Pres Acad Fit Awd; CSF; Rockwell Intl; Chinese Clb; UC Los Angeles; Bio.

CHIANG, LYNDA; Venice High Magnet Schl; Los Angeles, CA; (2); Cmnty Wkr; Intnl Clb; Var Tennis; Prfct Atten Awd; CSF; GATE.

CHIANG, MIN-TE ERIC; Davis SR HS; Davis, CA; (3); Teachers Aide; Intemural Table Tennis.

CHIANG, NANCY A; Palos Verdes HS; Rncho Palos Vrdes, CA; (4); Hosp Aide; Service Clb; SADD; JV Trk; Cit Awd; French Hon Soc; High Hon Roll; NHS; Ntl Merit Ltr; 1st Pl PTSA Cont Visual Arts 90; 1st Pl Cmnty Pstr Cont 88, 90; 3rd Pl Lcl Pstr Cont 89; CSF; U CA Los Angeles; Arch.

CHIANG, SUSAN N; Venice High Magnet Schl; Los Angeles, CA; (2); Cmnty Wkr; Intnl Clb; JV Tennis; Prfct Atten Awd; St Schlr; CA Fed Schlrshp; Chatelaines; USC; Comp.

CHIANG, TONY C; Cerritos HS; Cerritos, CA; (2); Tennis; Jap NHS; Bus.

CHIANG, WARREN; Villa Park HS; Villa Park, CA; (3); Orch; Var Tennis; High Hon Roll; Hon Roll; NHS; UCLA; Comp Sci.

CHIANGTONG, VITAVAS; Mayfair HS; Bellflower, CA; (1); 1/30; English Clb; JA; Key Clb; SADD; Bsktbl; Crs Cntry; Cit Awd; High Hon Roll; Prfct Atten Awd; Asian Clb; Literary Clb; Engrng.

CHIARA, STACEY; Oak Grove HS; San Jose, CA; (3); 30/658; Church Yth Grp; Dance Clb; French Clb; Hosp Aide; Key Clb; Ski Clb; Rptr Nwsp; Sec Frsh Cls; JV Capt Sftbl; High Hon Roll; UC Davis; Nrsng.

CHIARAMONTE, COREY P; Paso Robles HS; Paso Robles, CA; (1); Church Yth Grp; Band; Color Guard; Mrchg Band; Pep Band; Variety Show; JV Socr; JV Trk; Hon Roll; CA CAP; Air Frc Acad; Pilot.

CHIATE, CARLEE M; Santa Monica HS; Malibu, CA; (2); Ski Clb; Equestrian Clb; Ed.

CHICCONI, JENNIFER; Sierra Joint Union HS; Madera, CA; (2); Church Yth Grp; Cmnty Wkr; Dance Clb; JA; SADD; Church Choir; Diving; Swmmng; Trk; Hon Roll; Dancing 8 Yrs, Conventions CA; ST U; Med.

CHICHKANOFF, GREGORY E; Adrian Wilcox HS; Santa Clara, CA; (2); 57/400; Boy Scts; JA; Golden St Exam-Alg I Hnrs; Physicist.

CHIEM, GIALE T; Walkenberg Traditional HS; San Francisco, CA; (1); Vllybl; Hon Roll; Ped.

CHIEM, HOANG; Mark Keppel HS; San Gabriel, CA; (3); 26/208; Sec FBLA; Math Clb; Mu Alpha Theta; Teachers Aide; Cit Awd; High Hon Roll; Hon Roll; Prfct Atten Awd; CA Schlrshp Fdrtn; Octagon Clb Secy; Bus Admin.

CHIEM, MINH I; Mc Clatchy HS; Sacramento, CA; (2); 30/127; Cit Awd; Prfct Atten Awd; Harvard; Doctor.

CHIEM, NU A; Mark Keppel HS; San Gabriel, CA; (1); FBLA; Math Clb; Mu Alpha Theta; Cit Awd; High Hon Roll; Hon Roll; Pres Schlr; CA Schlrshp Fdrtn; Engrng.

CHIEN, DEBBIE W; Alhambra HS; Alhambra, CA; (3); Pres FBLA; Math Clb; Red Cross Aide; Science Clb; Service Clb; Mgr Yrbk; Off Jr Cls; Cit Awd; San Gabriel Vly Indstrl Cncl Medallion Plaque Wnnr; Golden St Exam Algebra Hnr; Ivy League; Bus Admin.

CHIEN, JENNIFER C; La Quinta HS; Westminster, CA; (3); 1/333; Key Clb; VP Science Clb; JV Tennis; Elks Awd; NHS; Ntl Merit Ltr; NEDT Awd; Rotary Awd; Ethnic Rltns Cncl; Scty Of Women Engrs Mrt Awd; Psych.

CHIEN, JULIE C; Lowell HS; San Francisco, CA; (4); 18/658; Cmnty Wkr; Drama Clb; Teachers Aide; Orch; Intrml Gym; Intrml Tennis; Ntl Merit SF; Chinese Clb Pres; Shield Hnr Soc; Cls 90 Rgstry Rep.

CHIEN, LINDA; University HS; Irvine, CA; (2); 5/520; Library Aide; Color Guard; Yrbk; High Hon Roll; Laureate Awds-Math, Engl, Socl Sci; Gldn St Math Exam-Hgh Hnrs Alg I & Geom; CSF.

CHIEN, RUTH S; Whittier Christian HS; La Habra, CA; (2); Church Yth Grp; Chorus; Church Choir; Color Guard; CA Schlrshp Fed.

CHIEN, SHELLEY; Culver City HS; Culver City, CA; (3); Service Clb; Phrmcy.

CHIEN, TERESA K; Mark Keppel HS; Monterey Park, CA; (1); Math Clb; Mu Alpha Theta; Hon Roll; CA Schlrshp Fed Mem; Stanford; Psych.

CHIEN, WAYNE W F; Esperanza HS; Yorba Linda, CA; (2); Key Clb; Model UN; Quiz Bowl; Spanish Clb; Yrbk; Var Tennis; VP Chinese Clb; Mst Vlbl Acad Dcthln Team; Elec Engrng.

CHIEN, WEI-KONG P; El Toro HS; El Toro, CA; (3); JV Socr; Med.

CHIEN, YVONNE; Mills HS; Millbrae, CA; (3); Church Yth Grp; Treas Sec Intnl Clb; Var Tennis; Prncpls Awd Outstndng Schlstc Achvt; People To People Exch Prgm To Soviet Union; GATE; Corp Law.

CHIGWIDA, TONGAI; Pasadena HS; Pasadena, CA; (2); JV Ftbl; JV Trk; Hon Roll; CSF; Congrsnl Schlr.

CHIH, PAUL TSUNG-YU; Eitwanda HS; West Orange, NJ; (3); Boy Scts; Comp Prgmr.

CHIH, YIA-FANG; Arcadia HS; Temple City, CA; (4); Church Yth Grp; Computer Clb; Library Aide; Math Clb; Science Clb; Spanish Clb; Church Choir; Hon Roll; JETS Awd; NHS; Sunday Schl Teacher; UCLA; Law.

CHIKA, ANGELA; Grossmont HS; El Cajon, CA; (3); 60/429; FBLA; High Hon Roll; Hon Roll; Spanish NHS; UCSD; Med.

CHILCOT, MEREDITH; Calabasas HS; Calabasas, CA; (2); Drama Clb; Pep Clb; Ski Clb; Spanish Clb; SADD; Thesps; Yrbk; JV Var Cheerldng; Score Keeper; JV Sftbl; Happy, I Care & Spirit Clbs; Commnty Gulf Celebrity Trnmt; Chrldr Awd 90; U CA; Child Psycht.

CHILCOT, NICOLE; Calabasas HS; Calabasas Park, CA; (4); SADD; Stage Crew; Cheerldng; Swmmng; UC Davis; Human Devlpmnt.

CHILD, BRENDA L; San Gorgonio HS; Highland, CA; (3); Pres Church Yth Grp; German Clb; Church Choir; Hon Roll; Highland 1st Ward Volleyball Team; U C Riverside.

CHILD, DANIEL; Wm S Hart HS; Valencia, CA; (4); 42/420; Boy Scts; Math Clb; Math Tm; Mu Alpha Theta; Teachers Aide; Stat Intrml Bsktbl; JV Crs Cntry; Intrml Ftbl; Intrml Socr; JV Trk; Eagle Sct; CSF; Boys St Fnlst; U CA Santa Barbara; Engrng.

CHILD, MICHAEL; Hart HS; Valencia, CA; (2); Boy Scts; Math Clb; Band; Mrchg Band; Pep Band; School Musical; Hon Roll; Eagle Sct; CSF; Hnr Band.

CHILDENS, JASON W; Live Oak HS; Morgan Hill, CA; (3); 31/636; VP German Clb; Ski Clb; Teachers Aide; Band; Jazz Band; L Swmmng; Hon Roll; Pres Acad Fit Awd; V Swmmng; Starter V Water Polo; MVP Swmmng; UCLA; Pre-Med.

CHILDERS, CORRI; Lincoln HS; Stockton, CA; (4); 62/536; Hosp Aide; Sec Service Clb; SADD; Var Powder Puff Ftbl; Hon Roll.

CHILDERS, DERNEEKA S; Cajon HS; San Bernardino, CA; (1); Church Yth Grp; Cmnty Wkr; Spanish Clb; Church Choir; Co-Ed Lit Mag; Just-A TAD; Pepperdine U; Comp Sci.

CHILDERS, KACI L; Atwater HS; Atwater, CA; (1); FFA; Rptr Nwsp; Rep Frsh Cls; Swmmng; FFA ST Chmpn Novice Prlmntry; FFA Horse Jdgng/Bst Infrmd Grnhnd Tm; Cal Poly; Ag.

CHILDERS, MAKESHIA R; St Michaels HS; Los Angeles, CA; (3); GAA; Hosp Aide; Office Aide; Teachers Aide; Church Choir; School Play; Variety Show; Ed Nwsp; Yrbk; Stu Cncl; MVP Var Vllybl; Outstndng Yth Of Yr Awd 90; USC; Poltcl Sci.

CHILDRESS, LIZ; St Michaels HS; Los Angeles, CA; (4); FBLA; Hosp Aide; School Play; Stage Crew; Variety Show; Phtg Rptr Yrbk; Sec Sr Cls; Cheerldng; Hon Roll; NHS; Young Black Schlr Cert Achvt; Natl Hnr Roll; CSU Fullerton; Nrsng.

CHILDS, DAVID; Abraham Lincoln HS; Stockton, CA; (4); 104/513; Spanish Clb; Orch; L Var Swmmng; Cntrl Vly Yth Symp-1st Violin; CA St Hnrs Orch-1st Violin; Concert Mstr-Lncln HS Hnrs Orch; U Of Pacific; Symp Orch.

CHILDS, RONALD N; Burroughs HS; Ridgecrest, CA; (3); 4-H; FBLA; Band; Mrchg Band; School Play; 4-H Awd; Hon Roll; Elec Eng.

CHILES, KATRINA C; Washington Preparatory HS; Los Angeles, CA; (3); Cmnty Wkr; ROTC; Service Clb; Chorus; JV Swmmng; Masonic Awd; El Cameo; Psych.

CHILSON, THERESA M; Fairfield HS; Fairfield, CA; (2); Church Yth Grp; Drama Clb; School Musical; Variety Show; Cit Awd; Church Gift Shop & Library; GATE; Schl Cnslr.

CHILTON, JAREMI D; Argaunot HS; Pine Grove, CA; (3); Boy Scts; Church Yth Grp; FBLA; Var Ftbl; JV Socr; Var Trk; Var Wt Lftg; Elks Awd; High Hon Roll; Hon Roll; BYU; Engrng Math.

CHIM, KEVIN; Lowell HS; San Francisco, CA; (2); Science Clb; Orch; Sci.

CHIM, MUYKUNG; Hoover HS; San Diego, CA; (3); French Clb; Intnl Clb; Math Clb; Cit Awd; High Hon Roll; NHS; Prfct Atten Awd; Top Mark Clb; Outstndng Ctzn Clb; SDSU; Bus Admin.

CHIM, MUYLENG; Hoover HS; San Diego, CA; (1); Cit Awd; High Hon Roll; NHS; Prfct Atten Awd; Top Of The Mark Club; Outstndng Ctzn Club.

CHIM, NICHOLAS; Piedmont HS; Piedmont, CA; (3); French Clb; Yrbk; Off Frsh Cls; Stu Cncl; Crs Cntry; Trk; Hon Roll; Art/Photo; 1st Pl In Logo Cntst Oakland Yth Orch; 2nd Pl Selix Frmlwr T-Shirt Dsgn.

CHIMA, PURMINDER K; Sutter Union HS; Yuba City, CA; (3); Hon Roll; Biochem.

CHIMIENTI, TAUNA; Reedley HS; Orange Cove, CA; (4); 126/332; Am Leg Aux Girls St; Church Yth Grp; FCA; Pres French Clb; FBLA; Teachers Aide; Chorus; Drill Tm; School Play; Stat Bsktbl; Christ Coll Irvine; Eng Prof.

CHIN, ADRIAN; Glen A Wilson HS; Hacienda Heights, CA; (2); Computer Clb; Science Clb; Band; Mrchg Band; JV Swmmng; High Hon Roll; Prfct Atten Awd; Water Polo; JR Stsmn Of Amer; Dist Hstry Day Wnnr; Harvard U; Bus.

CHIN, ANGELA YUE; Phillip & Sala Burton Academic HS; San Francisco, CA; (3); Math Clb; Ski Clb; Chorus; Rptr Nwsp; 4-H Awd; High Hon Roll; Hon Roll; JETS; UC Berkeley; Biochem.

CHIN, BRYAN N; Ocean View HS; Westminster, CA; (1).

CHIN, CONNIE; San Diego HS; San Diego, CA; (3); #1 In Class; Science Clb; Nwsp; Yrbk; Sec Soph Cls; High Hon Roll; Treas NHS; Ntl Merit Ltr; Opt Clb Awd; Standford Book Awd; Pre-Med.

CHIN, EDITH E; Chula Vista HS; Chula Vista, CA; (4); Gym; MECHA Club; Southwestern Coll; Bus Admin.

CHIN, EUDORA N; Lowell HS; San Francisco, CA; (4); Cmnty Wkr; French Clb; Rep Service Clb; Speech Tm; Rep Stu Cncl; Swmmng; NHS; Ntl Merit SF; Prt Tm Job.

CHIN, FEODOR B; Lowell HS; San Francisco, CA; (2); Cmnty Wkr; NFL; Orch; Nwsp; Pres Frsh Cls; Rep Soph Cls; VP Stu Cncl; Var Swmmng; Vrsty Fncng; Registry Pres; Schl Radio Anncr.

CHIN, GEORGE; Bellarmine Coll Prep; San Jose, CA; (3); 134/340; Cmnty Wkr; Stage Crew; Var Diving; Ntl Merit SF; UC Riverside; Med.

CHIN, IRENE C; Alameda HS; Alameda, CA; (2); 21/275; Church Yth Grp; Treas Spanish Clb; Asian Clb Treas; William K Holt Sci Schlrshp; CA Schlrshp Fdrtn; U Of CA Berkeley; Comp Sci.

CHIN, IRENE M; James Logan HS; Hayward, CA; (3); Computer Clb; Office Aide; Teachers Aide; Cit Awd; Hon Roll; Prfct Atten Awd; Asian Clb; Acctng.

CHIN, JANINE L; Lowell HS; San Francisco, CA; (3); NFL; Service Clb; Speech Tm; Speech Tm; Teachers Aide; Shield & L Honor Society Pres; Vice President Medical Explorer Post 496; CA Schlrshp Fed Member; Pediatrician.

CHIN, JENEFER L; Francis Polytechnic HS; North Hollywood, CA; (3); Church Yth Grp; Hosp Aide; Office Aide; Science Clb; Service Clb; Sec Sr Cls; Stu Cncl; High Hon Roll; Hon Roll; CSF; Acad Club; Mrktng.

CHIN, JENNIFER A; Alameda HS; Alameda, CA; (2); 1/290; Pres Frsh Cls; Pres Soph Cls.

CHIN, JENNIFER T; Irvine HS; Irvine, CA; (2); Key Clb; Off Soph Cls.

CHIN, JOE H; Lowell HS; San Francisco, CA; (3); Chess Clb; Science Clb; Service Clb; Teachers Aide; Hon Roll; CSF; Bio Club.

CHIN, LAWRENCE D; George Washington HS; San Francisco, CA; (2); Computer Clb; Service Clb; Band; Jazz Band; High Hon Roll; Explorers Post; U CA-BERKELEY; Mech Engr.

CHIN, LILY; Oakland HS; Oakland, CA; (2); French Clb; School Musical; U Of CA Burkeley; Bus.

CHIN, MARILYN L; Abraham Lincoln HS; San Francisco, CA; (3); Teachers Aide; Cit Awd; High Hon Roll; Prfct Atten Awd; CA Schlrshp Fed; Japanese Club; ST Coll; Bus.

CHIN, MARK; Whitney HS; Cerritos, CA; (2); JA; Treas Jr Cls; Var Trk; Hon Roll; Prfct Atten Awd; Pres Acad Fit Awd; CA Schlrshp Fed; High Hnrs For Gldn St Geo Exam; UCLA; Med.

CHIN, MILDRED J; San Gabriel HS; Rosemead, CA; (2); Church Yth Grp; Dance Clb; Debate Tm; Girl Scts; Key Clb; NFL; Pep Clb; Church Choir; Variety Show; Pres Acad Fit Awd; Play Piano; Collect Stamps; Interct Clb; UC Santa Barbara; Intr Dsgn.

CHIN, RHONDA; Schurr HS; Montebello, CA; (2); Hon Roll; Chinese Intl Club; CSF.

CHIN, SABRINA F; John F Kennedy HS; Buena Park, CA; (3); Computer Clb; FBLA; Key Clb; JV Tennis; Badminton Mst Improved; Golden St Exam Rcgntn Alg I & Hnrs Geom; Yellow Blt Kung Fu.

CHIN, SANDY; Lowell HS; San Francisco, CA; (2); Cmnty Wkr; Hosp Aide; Office Aide; Band; CSF; Golden ST Exam 1st Yr Algbr High Nrs.

CHIN, SHARON K; Hayward HS; Hayward, CA; (1); Church Yth Grp; Band; Flag Corp; Office Aide; Spanish Clb; Score Keeper; Vllybl; Hon Roll; Piano & Flute; Stanford; Med Sci.

CHIN, SHAUN S; Santa Teresa HS; San Jose, CA; (3); #12 In Class; Intnl Clb; Model UN; Lit Mag; Var Tennis; High Hon Roll; Hon Roll; Phy.

CHIN, SHAUNA Y; Schurr HS; Montebello, CA; (3); Teachers Aide; Hon Roll; Chinese Intl Clb; CSF.

CHIN, VICTOR M; San Gabriel HS; Rosemead, CA; (3); FBLA; Key Clb; Varsity Clb; Var Capt Tennis; Hon Roll; Outstandng Achvt Merit Awd Arch Drftng; Gldn St Exam Awd Geom; Outstndng Achvt Merit Awd Mech Drftng; U Of S CA; Arch.

CHIN-CHEN, YA; Oxnard HS; Oxnard, CA; (3); #7 In Class; Art Clb; Debate Tm; Math Clb; Spanish Clb; SADD; Rep Frsh Cls; VP Soph Cls; Cit Awd; Prfct Atten Awd; CSF; Inter Act; Asian/Amercn Clb; Bio Chem.

CHING, ALVIN Y; Artesia HS; Lakewood, CA; (4); 2/317; VP Science Clb; VP Service Clb; Rep Jr Cls; Treas Stu Cncl; JV Var Bsbl; Elks Awd; High Hon Roll; Ntl Merit Ltr; Sal; CA Schlrshp Fed 100%; Conestoga Awd Wnnr Math & Sci; Bnk Of Amer Plaque Wnnr Math & Sci; UCLA; Elec Engrng.

CHING, ANGELICA; George Moller Schurr HS; Monterey Park, CA; (1); Hon Roll; Prfct Atten Awd; 1st Pl 9th Annual Cinco De Mayo Essay Cont; Schlrshp By U Southern CA; Phrmcy.

CHING, DANIEL; San Leandro HS; San Leandro, CA; (3); 39/361; Computer Clb; Rep Soph Cls; JV Tennis; High Hon Roll; Hon Roll; Prfct Atten Awd; Pres Acad Fit Awd; Natl Yng Ldrs Conf Rep; Nova Vista Symphony Violin Solo 89; 1st Pl Instrumntl Pacific Musicical Soc; Music Performance.

CHING, KARL H; Lowell HS; San Francisco, CA; (2); Cmnty Wkr; German Clb; Var Swmmng; Hon Roll; Doctor.

CHING, LEO; Pinole Valley HS; Hercules, CA; (2); Debate Tm; NFL; Science Clb; Speech Tm; Thesps; JV Var Crs Cntry; JV Var Tennis; JV Trk; Var Wt Lftg; Hon Roll; Fireman.

CHING, WENDY; Los Altos HS; Hacienda Hts, CA; (1); 30/330; Hon Roll; Pres Acad Fit Awd; UCLA; Chem Engr.

CHINN, ALLISON H; Arcata HS; Arcata, CA; (4); 1/170; AFS; Drama Clb; French Clb; Band; Chorus; Jazz Band; School Musical; Variety Show; Ed Lit Mag; Cit Awd; Reed Coll.

CHINN, JENNIFER L; Novato HS; Novato, CA; (1); Girl Scts; Hon Roll; UC Santa Barbara; Bus Econ.

CHINN, LESLIE L; Fontana HS; Fontana, CA; (2); Ski Clb; Rep Frsh Cls; Rep Soph Cls; Sftbl; Intl Explorers; U IL; Bus Admin.

CHINN, LILY; Huntington Beach HS; Huntington Bch, CA; (4); 3/497; Key Clb; Math Clb; Model UN; Teachers Aide; Varsity Clb; Yrbk; Rep Frsh Cls; Stat Fld Hcky; JV Var Vllybl; Hon Roll; 2nd Pl UNA-USA Natl Essay Cont; Principals Awd; Hnrb Mntn Jack In Box Essay Cont 90; U CA Berkeley; Bus.

CHINN, MARISA L; Lowell HS; San Francisco, CA; (2); Hosp Aide; CSF; UCLA; Urbn Plnng.

CHINNIAH, BALARAJ T; John Marshall Fndmntl; Pasadena, CA; (4); 10/145; Aud/Vis; Chess Clb; Cmnty Wkr; JA; Key Clb; Church Choir; Var JV Crs Cntry; JV Tennis; Var JV Trk; Cit Awd; Honor Roll; Kiwanis Award; Natl Honor Society; Perfect Attendance Award; Presidential Acad Fitnss Award; Swarthmore Coll; Electrical Eng.

CHINNOCK, GAYLE L; Monterey Bay Acad; Redlands, CA; (1); Church Yth Grp; Office Aide; Ski Clb; Band; Pres Frsh Cls; Intrml Powder Puff Ftbl; Intrml Vllybl; High Hon Roll; Prfct Atten Awd; Pres Acad Fit Awd.

CHINNOCK, JULIE A; Monterey Bay Acad; Camino, CA; (4); Library Aide; Band; Chorus; School Musical; Ed Yrbk; Intrml Socr; Intrml Sftbl; Intrml Vllybl; High Hon Roll; Prfct Atten Awd; Bank Amer Awd Hstry; Oceanaires; Mrt Schlrshp; Pacific Union Coll; Elem Educ.

CHIO JR, ARTURO B; Walnut HS; Walnut, CA; (2); Key Clb; Church Choir; Mgr Yrbk; Crs Cntry; Trk; Hon Roll; Photo; UCLA; Biochem.

CHIONG, EMILY C; Eagle Rock HS; Los Angeles, CA; (2); JV Swmmng; Hon Roll; Pres Acad Fit Awd; Acad Decathlon; Piano; Law.

CHIOSSI, DENA A; Healdsburg HS; Healdsburg, CA; (4); 24/221; Cmnty Wkr; 4-H; Key Clb; Office Aide; Off Jr Cls; JV Bsktbl; Var Trk; Cit Awd; High Hon Roll; Hon Roll; Typing, Bsktbl, Trck Awds 1986-89; Schlr Athltc 1988-89; Fair Bd, Rotary, Doyle Schlrshps; Santa Rosa JC; Nrsng.

CHIOU, TERRY T; Artesia HS; Cerritos, CA; (3); Science Clb; JV Vllybl; Harvard Bk Prz; Bible Study; UCLA; Sci Rsrch.

CHIPPAS, NICOLE A; El Dorado HS; Placentia, CA; (2); 1/360; French Clb; Chorus; Hon Roll; NHS.

CHIQUETTE, JENNIFER R; Los Altos HS; Hacienda Hts, CA; (3); Science Clb; Var JV Pom Pon; Powder Puff Ftbl; Hon Roll; Pres Acad Fit Awd; UCLA; Med.

CHIQUITO, JULISSA M; Victor Valley HS; Victorville, CA; (3); Dance Clb; French Clb; Science Clb; Chorus; School Musical; Swing Chorus; Variety Show; Hon Roll; Environment; Frgn Affairs; World Cultures; Engl.

CHIRIANO, JASON; Damien HS; Pomona, CA; (2); 33/268; Church Yth Grp; Speech Tm; Ftbl; Swmmng; Trk; High Hon Roll; Bowling Clb; U CA San Diego; Bus.

CHIRRICK, SHERRY L; Hilmar HS; Hilmar, CA; (3); Church Yth Grp; 4-H; Hosp Aide; Band; Flag Corp; Rptr Nwsp; High Hon Roll; Hon Roll; CSF; 90 Merced Cnty Acad Decthln & Wn Schlrshp; Wn 1st Pl Catgry Rymed Poetry Wrtng Fstvl; Zoology.

CHIS, CAMELIA; Beyer HS; Modesto, CA; (4); 50/520; Church Yth Grp; Cmnty Wkr; FBLA; Pep Clb; Science Clb; Spanish Clb; Church Choir; JV Tennis; Hon Roll; Bus Admin.

CHISHOLM, JESSICA A; Hemet HS; Hemet, CA; (3); Sec Church Yth Grp; Pedtrcn.

CHISM, JUDY L; Casa Grande HS; Petaluma, CA; (3); 19/298; Church Yth Grp; Girl Scts; Varsity Clb; Swmmng; High Hon Roll; NHS; Prfct Atten Awd; Tchng.

CHISUM, DUSTIN T; North HS; Bakersfield, CA; (3); Crs Cntry; Trk; Hon Roll; Pres Acad Fit Awd; Wtr Skng; Off Rd Drvng; Cnsrvtn Prjcts; Arch.

CHITAPHAN, SASIPEN; Baldwin Park HS; Baldwin Park, CA; (2); Band; Mrchg Band; Hon Roll; Inter Dsgn.

CHITILIAN, SARINE; Herbert Hoover HS; Glendale, CA; (3); Drama Clb; Key Clb; Spanish Clb; Cit Awd; Law.

CHIU, ANITA K; Rosemead HS; Temple City, CA; (2); Cmnty Wkr; Computer Clb; FBLA; Service Clb; Spanish Clb; JV Tennis; High Hon Roll; Prfct Atten Awd; CSF; Stu Mnth Frgn Lang Jan 89, & Sci Feb 90; 1st Pl Grp Jrcts Hstry Day; 1T Pl NML Alb II; Bus.

CHIU, ANNE; Sunny Hills HS; Fullerton, CA; (3); 37/430; Art Clb; Computer Clb; Science Clb; Spanish Clb; Acpl Chr; High Hon Roll; Chinese Painting; UCLA; Pre Law.

CHIU, ANNIE; Arcadia HS; Arcadia, CA; (2); Drill Tm; Yrbk; Var Cheerldng; Tennis; Cit Awd; Pres Acad Fit Awd; UCLA; Bus.

CHIU, ANNIE S; Edison HS; Huntington Beach, CA; (4); 1/511; English Clb; Treas French Clb; Hosp Aide; Sec Intnl Clb; JA; Model UN; French Hon Soc; Ntl Merit SF; Keywanettes Treas & Pres; Peer Assist Leag; Med.

CHIU, CHARLIE NAN-CHAO; Saint Ignatius College Prep; San Francisco, CA; (3); 12/244; Science Clb; Teachers Aide; Chorus; Tennis; Trk; Hon Roll; YMCA Vlntr; Recycling Club; CSF.

CHIU, CLIFFORD; Montebello HS; Montebello, CA; (1); 7/500; Key Clb; Quiz Bowl; Ski Clb; SADD; School Play; Yrbk; Stu Cncl; Var Tennis; High Hon Roll; UCLA; Doctor.

CHIU, DAVID FU-MAN; Westmoor HS; So San Francisc, CA; (4); 2/367; Chess Clb; Church Yth Grp; Computer Clb; Math Clb; Varsity Clb; JV Bsktbl; Var Tennis; High Hon Roll; Jr NHS; Masonic Awd; Bank Of Amer Cert; Tandy Technlgy Schlr Awd; CA Schlrshp Fdrtn; U Of CA Berkeley; Mech Engrng.

CHIU, DENNY TYH CHING; Don Lugo HS; Chino, CA; (4); Church Yth Grp; Key Clb; Science Clb; Teachers Aide; JV Bsbl; JV Trk; Hon Roll; NHS; Golden St Exam Hnrs; Golden Conquest Awd; UCLA; Med.

CHIU, ELI; Alameda HS; Concord, CA; (4); French Clb; Science Clb; Debate Tm Constitutional Bicntnl Cmptn; Piano; U CA Berkeley; Bus Adm.

CHIU, ERIC; Buena Park HS; Buena Park, CA; (4); French Clb; Intnl Clb; Math Clb; Teachers Aide; Varsity Clb; High Hon Roll; Hon Roll; Prfct Atten Awd; Asian Clb; Vrsty Bdnmtn Clb Capt, MVP; CSF Life Mem; U Of CA Irvine; Bio.

CHIU, HENRY; Mount Whitney HS; Visalia, CA; (2); Art Clb; Computer Clb; FBLA; Key Clb; Math Clb; Math Tm; Science Clb; Orch; Cit Awd; DAR Awd; 3-D Materials; PSAT 95%; Stanford; Comp Sci.

CHIU, HENRY; Sunny Hills HS; Fullerton, CA; (2); Boy Scts; Computer Clb; FBLA; High Hon Roll; Prfct Atten Awd; Comic Bk Clb Treas; Harvard; Bus Mgmt.

CHIU, JENNIFER F; Miramonte HS; Moraga, CA; (4); 7/278; Hosp Aide; Model UN; Spanish Clb; Treas Stu Cncl; High Hon Roll; Piano-Cert Merit, Brnch & Convtn Hnrs, Panel Hnrs; Harvard Bk; Pblcty Ofcr Soviet Clb.

CHIU, JILLIAN J; Yucaipa HS; Yucaipa, CA; (3); Drama Clb; VP Key Clb; Pep Clb; Spanish Clb; Color Guard; Var Trk; Hon Roll; Prfct Atten Awd; Pres Acad Fit Awd; Amer Lgn Marmolejo Aux Awd; Hozoni Atvt Jr Usher Female; Optometry.

CHIU, LAURA W; San Leandro HS; San Leandro, CA; (3); 53/361; Cmnty Wkr; Key Clb; Teachers Aide; Stage Crew; Yrbk; Stat Bsbl; Stat Bsktbl; JV Vllybl; High Hon Roll; NHS.

CHIU, LAWRENCE; Palm Springs HS; Cathedral City, CA; (2); Hon Roll; Kiwanis Awd; Prfct Atten Awd; Silver Sands Awd; UCLA; Physics.

CHIU, LING W; Savanna HS; Buena Park, CA; (2); Intnl Clb; Chorus; Jazz Band; Bsktbl; Trk; UCLA.

CHIU, MARCIA; Diamond Bar HS; Walnut, CA; (2); Church Yth Grp; Intnl Clb; Science Clb; Prfct Atten Awd; Schl Recog CA Golden St Exam Math; Deans Math Hnr List; Vlybl; Bsktbl; Law.

CHIU, MARGARET; Abraham Lincoln HS; San Francisco, CA; (1); Yrbk; Sec Frsh Cls; Sec Soph Cls; Frshmn Clb; Lincolns Soc.

CHIU, MELVIN W; St Patrick-St Vincent HS; Vallejo, CA; (1); High Hon Roll; Piano; UC Berkeley; Natural Sci.

CHIU, MICHAEL J; Pioneer HS; San Jose, CA; (1); Spanish Clb; JV Tennis; CA Schltc Fed; UC Berkeley; Engrng.

CHIU, NIA; Casa Grande HS; Petaluma, CA; (4); 17/262; Church Yth Grp; Treas French Clb; Church Choir; JV Cheerldng; Hon Roll; NHS; Prfct Atten Awd; Pres Acad Fit Awd; U Of CA Irvine; Psych.

CHIU, PAO Y; Whitney HS; Cerritos, CA; (3); Cmnty Wkr; Hosp Aide; Key Clb; Var Trk; High Hon Roll; Ntl Merit Ltr; CSF; Violin Recitals; Med.

CHIU, PE YUEH; Oakland Technical HS; Oakland, CA; (3); Chess Clb; Science Clb; Var Tennis; Hon Roll; Prfct Atten Awd.

CHIU, PEGGY; Pinole Valley HS; Hercules, CA; (2); Spanish Clb; High Hon Roll; Hon Roll; CA Schlrshp Fed; Tennis League.

CHIU, PHILLIP; George Washington HS; San Francisco, CA; (1); JV Bsbl; High Hon Roll; Hon Roll; Med.

CHIU, ROBERT J; Polytechnic Schl; San Marino, CA; (4); Chess Clb; Math Clb; Science Clb; Spanish Clb; Orch; School Musical; JV Tennis; Hon Roll; Ntl Merit Ltr; ARTS 3rd Level Awd In Music.

CHIU, STANLEY S; Sunny Hills HS; Fullerton, CA; (3); 47/430; Chess Clb; Computer Clb; Science Clb; Spanish Clb; School Musical; High Hon Roll; Goldn St Exams-Alg I Hnrs/Geomtry High Hhnrs; Continentl Math League-Dstnctn; Natl Span Exams-Dstnctn; Comp Sci.

CHIU, SYLVIA; Fountain Valley HS; Fountain Valley, CA; (3); Church Yth Grp; Cmnty Wkr; JA; Red Cross Aide; Science Clb; Spanish Clb; JV Fld Hcky; High Hon Roll; Jr NHS; Piano; JV Badminton.

CHIU, TARA L; Los Angeles Baptist HS; Northridge, CA; (3); Church Yth Grp; Cmnty Wkr; Pep Clb; Service Clb; Teachers Aide; Drill Tm; Lit Mag; JV Var Trk; Hon Roll; CSF; Interior Dsgn.

CHIU, VI K; U S Grant HS; Monterey Park, CA; (4); 1/650; High Hon Roll; Hon Roll; Ntl Merit SF; Pres Acad Fit Awd; CA Acad Dcthln; Engrng Clb; Hrvrd Prz Bk Amer Chmcl Scty-Outstndng Achvt In Sthrn CA; UCLA; Biochem.

CHIU, WAI-NGAN; San Gabriel HS; Alhambra, CA; (2); French Clb; Spanish Clb; SADD; Teachers Aide; Chorus; High Hon Roll; Red Cross Yth Vol.

CHIU, WAI-SUM; San Gabriel HS; Alhambra, CA; (1); French Clb; FBLA; Tennis; Hon Roll; Mock Trial.

CHIU, WEI-MIN; Bonita Vista HS; Chula Vista, CA; (4); Church Yth Grp; Intnl Clb; Key Clb; Science Clb; Lit Mag; Cit Awd; High Hon Roll; Hon Roll; Prfct Atten Awd; Bank Of Amer Sci Awd; Tandy Tech Awd; Intrl Baccalaureate Diploma Candidacy; CA Schlrshp Fed Life Memb; U Of CA-SAN Diego; Appld Math.

CHIW, AZUCENA; Calexico HS; Calexico, CA; (2); Church Yth Grp; Church Choir.

CHIZEWSKI, MICHAEL W; Gompers HS; San Diego, CA; (2); 36/145; Boy Scts; Chess Clb; Science Clb; Comp.

CHMIEL, SCOTT R; El Cajon Valley HS; El Cajon, CA; (4); 2/379; Boy Scts; Church Yth Grp; Cmnty Wkr; Library Aide; Sec Science Clb; Band; Mrchg Band; Orch; Pep Band; Stu Cncl; Aero Enge.

CHNG, DENISE; Oxnard HS; Oxnard, CA; (1); 1/818; Intnl Clb; Letterman Clb; Score Keeper; Cit Awd; High Hon Roll; Hon Roll; CSF; Early Acad Outreach; Acad Awd; U CA Santa Barbara; Elec Engr.

CHO, BETTY M; Pinole Valley HS; Hercules, CA; (2); Church Yth Grp; Debate Tm; French Clb; NFL; Speech Tm; SADD; Teachers Aide; Acpl Chr; School Musical; Rptr Nwsp; Algebra I Hnrs & Golden ST Exam Awd; Columbia U; Law.

CHO, CAMILLA K; Bishop Amat Memorial HS; West Covina, CA; (1); Church Yth Grp; High Hon Roll; Prfct Atten Awd; Piano; UCLA.

CHO, CHONG U; Anaheim HS; Anaheim, CA; (3); Cmnty Wkr; Computer Clb; Key Clb; Sec Stu Cncl; Intrml Mgr Ftbl; Var Trk; Var Wt Lftg; Hon Roll; Prfct Atten Awd; Engrng.

CHO, CHU J; Bolsa Grande HS; Anaheim, CA; (3); #338 In Class; Spanish Clb; Band; Mrchg Band; Orch; Pep Band; Swmmng; Hon Roll; USC; Phrmst.

CHO, DAVID; John F Kennedy HS; Buena Park, CA; (1); Church Yth Grp; Key Clb; US Table Tnns Assn; Engrng.

CHO, DAVID H; Whitney HS; Cerritos, CA; (2); Debate Tm; Model UN; Service Clb; Band; Mrchg Band; Var Tennis; High Hon Roll; Hon Roll; Prfct Atten Awd; Pres Acad Fit Awd; CJSF Club; Scrpbk Photogrpr; Comm Fndrsng.

CHO, GRACE; Magnolia HS; Anaheim, CA; (2); Church Yth Grp; Mrchg Band; Orch; Pep Band; JV Capt Swmmng; JV Tennis; High Hon Roll; Natl Hnr Soc Clb; GATE Clb; Standford; Aerospace Engr.

CHO, INES M; Whittier Christian HS; Hacienda Hts, CA; (4); 30/168; VP Church Yth Grp; VP French Clb; Hosp Aide; Band; Mrchg Band; Yrbk; Var Tennis.

CHO, JONGCHUL; La Quinta HS; Westminster, CA; (2); VP Chess Clb; Church Yth Grp; Key Clb; Red Cross Aide; Rep Orch; Tennis; High Hon Roll; Hon Roll; NHS; Rotary Awd; GATE; Dist Hnr Orch 88-90; Med.

CHO, JOOBEE; Calabasas HS; Calabasas, CA; (2); Church Yth Grp; Dance Clb; Debate Tm; French Clb; Hosp Aide; Pep Clb; Church Choir; Drill Tm; Orch; School Musical; Berkley; Commnctns.

CHO, JULIE J; Notre Dame HS; Morgan Hill, CA; (2); 2/76; Church Yth Grp; Science Clb; SADD; Chorus; Sec Stu Cncl; Vllybl; High Hon Roll; Hon Roll; NHS; Prfct Atten Awd; CSF; UCLA; Cardiology.

CHO, KATHRYN; Vivian Webb Schl; Montebello, CA; (4); Church Yth Grp; Cmnty Wkr; Latin Clb; Library Aide; Ski Clb; Chorus; Church Choir; School Musical; School Play; Variety Show; Womns Hstry Jo Hartley Endwd Prz Wnnr; Charles E Weisbrod Awd Clssc Langs & Hstry; Pol Sci.

CHO, KEVIN; Cerritos HS; Cerritos, CA; (2); Math Clb; Chinese Club Act Ofcr; UC; Comp Engr.

CHO, MARK P; San Pedro HS; San Pedro, CA; (3); Bsbl; Cit Awd; Hon Roll; Prfct Atten Awd; U Of Riverside; Bus.

CHO, MICHAEL; John F Kennedy HS; Los Angeles, CA; (3); Cmnty Wkr; English Clb; Key Clb; Orch; Cit Awd; Hon Roll; Prfct Atten Awd; Wrtr Japanese Animation Mgzn Animekko; Mem Library Book Club & CSF; Writing.

CHO, NAOMI; Banning HS; Banning, CA; (3); 7/208; Church Yth Grp; Intnl Clb; Model UN; Band; Jazz Band; Mrchg Band; School Musical; Sec Jr Cls; Pres Sr Cls; Swmmng.

CHO, PAUL Y; John H Francis Polytechnic HS; Sun Valley, CA; (2); Hon Roll; Gldn St Exam Geom High Hnrs; Outstndng Achvt Math; Excllnc Frgn Lang Spnsh; Outstndng Stu Awd; Engrng.

CHO, PETER S; Chula Vista HS; Chula Vista, CA; (3); Am Leg Boys St; Office Aide; Ftbl; Trk; Wt Lftg; Cit Awd; High Hon Roll; Hon Roll; Prfct Atten Awd; CSF; Schlrshp Awd; Stanford; Elec Engr.

CHO, RICHARD S; Servite HS; Buena Park, CA; (2); 10/143; Church Yth Grp; Cmnty Wkr; Drama Clb; Hosp Aide; Service Clb; Stage Crew; Yrbk; Lit Mag; Crs Cntry; Hon Roll; Jr Statemen Amer; Safe Rides; CSF; Phrmcy Aide; Amnesty Intl; Pre-Med.

CHO, SALLIE H; Carlsbad HS; Carlsbad, CA; (1); Church Yth Grp; Science Clb; Service Clb; SADD; Crs Cntry; Trk; Cit Awd; Hon Roll; Hstry & Interact Clb; CSF; UCSD; Bus.

CHO, SANG-CHRIS; Sunny Hills HS; Fullerton, CA; (3); 90/432; Church Yth Grp; French Clb; Intnl Clb; Key Clb; Letterman Clb; Model UN; Ski Clb; Varsity Clb; Var Socr; Var Trk; Gldn St Exam Geo Hnr; Socl Sci.

CHO, SEAN; Sunny Hill HS; Irvine, CA; (2); Intrml Crs Cntry; Intrml Trk; La Crosse Athltc Awd Track And Fld 89; Heritage Awds; Cert Of Merit Yth Of Mnth 86; Stu Of Month 88; Fash Dsgnr.

CHO, STEVE; Bellflower HS; Bellflower, CA; (3); 13/300; Boy Scts; Church Yth Grp; Cmnty Wkr; Key Clb; Math Clb; Mu Alpha Theta; Varsity Clb; Church Choir; Var L Crs Cntry; Var L Tennis; CSF; Fencing Let Capt; Professor.

CHO, STEVE; Norco HS; Lorona, CA; (3); 35/400; Wt Lftg; Wrstlng; Hon Roll; UCLA; Med.

CHO, SUSIE; Bolsa Grande HS; Garden Grove, CA; (3); 59/200; Church Yth Grp; Pep Clb; Spanish Clb; Stu Cncl; JV Bsktbl; Var Cheerldng; JV Score Keeper; Var Socr; Var Trk; Hon Roll; Girls Leag; UCLA; Law.

CHO, TONY; Whitney HS; Cerritos, CA; (2); Model UN; JR High Vlybl Tm; High Hnrs Golden ST Exam; UCLA; Law.

CHO, YUN-JUNG; Concord HS; Concord, CA; (3); Church Yth Grp; Model UN; ROTC; SADD; Teachers Aide; Drill Tm; Hon Roll; UCLA; Bus.

CHOATE, ABIGAIL K; Piedmont HS; Piedmont, CA; (3); Dance Clb; Drama Clb; Thesps; Varsity Clb; Yrbk; Rep Stu Cncl; Pom Pon; Trk; Hon Roll; Pres Acad Fit Awd; Intl Sch Bangkok Thailand.

CHOATE, CATHERINE A; Redlands HS; Redlands, CA; (2); Church Yth Grp; Cmnty Wkr; Dance Clb; Ski Clb; School Play; Stage Crew; Swmmng; Great Y Circus; Dance; Law.

CHOATE, SHARON ANNETTE; Lodi HS; Stockton, CA; (4); 95/400; Socr; FBLA; Spanish Clb; Teachers Aide; Acpl Chr; Chorus; Church Choir; Variety Show; Hon Roll; U San Francisco; Psych.

CHOBDEE, JAY; Glen A Wilson HS; Hacienda Heights, CA; (2); Church Yth Grp; Hosp Aide; Key Clb; Science Clb; Band; Mrchg Band; Intrml Socr; Intrml Trk; Cit Awd; High Hon Roll; Dist Hist Day Wnnr; Co Hist Day Fnlst; Alg & Geo Hnrs Gldn St Exam; Med.

CHODOS, LEON S; Salinas HS; Salinas, CA; (2); Church Yth Grp; Band; Jazz Band; Mrchg Band; Orch; Pep Band; School Musical; Prfct Atten Awd; Eastman Schl Of Music; Music.

CHODOS, MARC; Palisades HS; Los Angeles, CA; (3); Debate Tm; Math Clb; Teachers Aide; Var L Crs Cntry; Var L Trk; Bausch & Lomb Sci Awd; High Hon Roll; NHS; Pres Acad Fit Awd; Rand Corp Awd For Frgn Plcy Paper US Soviet Rltns; Med.

CHOE, CHARLES H; Flintridge Preparatory Schl; Glendale, CA; (3); JCL; Pres Latin Clb; Mgr(s); Var Tennis; Hon Roll; Jr NHS; 1st Runner-Up Hnr Stu Of Yr 88; 2nd Runner-Up 89; John W Neupauer Latin Awd.

CHOE, CHONG U; Bella Vista HS; Orangevale, CA; (3); 7/400; VP Church Yth Grp; French Clb; VP FBLA; German Clb; Science Clb; Rptr Nwsp; Pres French Hon Soc; NHS; Mock Trial; Friday Night Live Sec; Pre-Law.

CHOE, GRACE S; Mountain View HS; Mountain View, CA; (4); JA; Service Clb; Orch; Ed Yrbk; VP Frsh Cls; Pres Jr Cls; High Hon Roll; Hon Roll; Peer Cnslng; Hmcmng Chrprsn; Stu Mnth; UC Davis.

CHOE, HENRY; Earnest Righetti HS; Santa Maria, CA; (2); JV Crs Cntry; JV Trk; Cit Awd; Hon Roll; Arch.

CHOE, JENNY; Miraleste HS; Ranchos Palos Ver, CA; (3); 47/137; Church Yth Grp; Cmnty Wkr; Math Clb; Math Tm; SADD; Teachers Aide; Chorus; Church Choir; Orch; Cit Awd; UC Irvine.

CHOE, JOON; Simi Valley HS; Simi Valley, CA; (4); Church Choir; Mrchg Band; Orch; NHS; UC Irvine; Comp Sci.

CHOE, JULIE; Whittier HS; Whittier, CA; (4); 2/435; Hosp Aide; Math Tm; Model UN; Teachers Aide; Color Guard; Lit Mag; Var Tennis; Elks Awd; High Hon Roll; Sal; CSF; Srptmst Yth Ctznshp Awd; MESA; UCLA; Bio.

CHOHAN, PARDEEP S; Caruthers Union HS; Caruthers, CA; (3); Pres Sec FBLA; Church Yth Grp; Computer Clb; Letterman Clb; Math Clb; Office Aide; Spanish Clb; Speech Tm; SADD; Teachers Aide; HS Stu Of Yr; Strtr On Vrsty Ftbl Tm; Mem Sci Olympiad Tm; Mock Trial Tm; UCLA; Med Sci.

CHOI, ALVIN; William Workman HS; La Puente, CA; (2); Art Clb; Church Yth Grp; Intnl Clb; SADD; Swmmng; High Hon Roll; Prfct Atten Awd; Badminton Tm 89-90; 3rd Southern CA Tae Kwon Do Champnshp Brnz Mdl; Elliott-Pope Prep Sch; Comp Sci.

CHOI, ANGELA H; Rim Of The World HS; Crestline, CA; (2); VP Art Clb; Treas French Clb; Church Choir; Sec Soph Cls; Stat Bsktbl; French Hon Soc; High Hon Roll; Lk Arrowhead Hnrs Arts Assn; SAC Secy; JSA; Pasadena Art Ctr; Grphc Dsgn.

CHOI, ANTHONY K; Warren HS; Downey, CA; (4); 14/385; Pres Computer Clb; FBLA; Key Clb; Math Tm; Kiwanis Awd; Pres Acad Fit Awd; Chinese Club; JR Stsmn Amer; CSF; UCLA; Comp Sci.

CHOI, BRIAN B; California HS; Whittier, CA; (2); Art Clb; SADD; Mgr(s); Vllybl; Cit Awd; Hon Roll; Advtsng.

CHOI, CATHERINE; Alta Loma HS; Alta Loma, CA; (3); 31/582; VP Church Yth Grp; Hosp Aide; Spanish Clb; Color Guard; Rptr Ed Nwsp; High Hon Roll; Prfct Atten Awd; CSF; Goldn St Exam Geom 88; UCLA.

CHOI, CHARLIE; Heritage HS; Fullerton, CA; (4); 1/13; Science Clb; Ski Clb; Pres Sr Cls; Capt Var Bsbl; Var Bsktbl; Var Ftbl; Hon Roll; Val; Arch.

CHOI, CHRISTINE M; Carlmont HS; Redwood City, CA; (3); Intnl Clb; Key Clb; Math Clb; School Play; Nwsp; Yrbk; Hon Roll; Mth Awd Outstndng Achvmnt; Hstrn CSF; Acad Dcthln.

CHOI, DAVID; El Camino HS; West Hills, CA; (3); Service Clb; Var Tennis; Tennis Schlr Athl; USC; Bus.

CHOI, EDWARD; John F Kennedy HS; Corona, CA; (4); Church Yth Grp; Treas Key Clb; Hon Roll; CA Schlrshp Fed; Gldn St Awd Geometry Hnrs; Cal Poly Pomona; Arch.

CHOI, ERIC; Narbonne HS; Torrance, CA; (3); Key Clb; Math Clb; Hon Roll; Prfct Atten Awd; Pres Acad Fit Awd; Engr.

CHOI, ESTHER; South Hills HS; Covina, CA; (4); 45/257; VP Sec Church Yth Grp; Drama Clb; School Musical; Variety Show; JV Var Cheerldng; Var Trk; High Hon Roll; Hon Roll; NHS; Pres Acad Fit Awd; U Of CA Los Angeles; Piano.

CHOI, ESTHER H; Montebello HS; Montebello, CA; (1); Church Yth Grp; Acpl Chr; Church Choir; Variety Show; Bsktbl; Mgr(s); Score Keeper; Trk; High Hon Roll; Hon Roll; CSF; UC Berekely; Med.

CHOI, GIL; Fountain Valley HS; Fountain Valley, CA; (2); Church Yth Grp; Computer Clb; Bsktbl; JV Tennis; UC Irvine; Med.

CHOI, GRACE Y; Santa Teresa HS; San Jose, CA; (1); Church Yth Grp; Drama Clb; Church Choir; Cheerldng; Hon Roll; UCLA; Design.

CHOI, HEE J; Glendale HS; Glendale, CA; (3); Church Yth Grp; Drama Clb; ROTC; Spanish Clb; Acpl Chr; CA Schlrshp Fed; Med.

CHOI, HELEN O; Granada Hills HS; Northridge, CA; (2); Church Yth Grp; Teachers Aide; Pres Frsh Cls; Stu Cncl; High Hon Roll; Hon Roll; Jrnlsm.

CHOI, HERMAN C; Temple City HS; Arcadia, CA; (3); Bus Profs of Am; Computer Clb; FBLA; Key Clb; Math Clb; Math Tm; Mu Alpha Theta; Science Clb; SADD; Var Tnns; Var Trk; Acad Dcthln; CA Schlrshp Fed; Jr Statesman Assmbly; UC San Diego; Med.

CHOI, HYON CHONG; Alhambra HS; Martinez, CA; (3); 11/208; Math Clb; Science Clb; Teachers Aide; Hon Roll; Tutor For Englsh Class; Peer Supprtr; Acad Decthln; Psych.

CHOI, IVAN K; Lowell HS; San Francisco, CA; (4); 10/626; Cmnty Wkr; JA; Teachers Aide; JV Socr; Bausch & Lomb Sci Awd; NHS; Ntl Merit SF; Econ Essy Cont Wnnr; 1st Pl Sci Chllg; MIT; Elec Engrg.

CHOI, IVAN P; South Pasadena HS; S Pasadena, CA; (3); Cmnty Wkr; Pres Key Clb; Latin Clb; Ed Nwsp; Treas Frsh Cls; VP Soph Cls; Var Crs Cntry; JV Socr; JV Trk; Var Vllybl; Yth In Govt; CA Assn Of Stu Cncls; Boston U; Psych.

CHOI, JAE H; Anaheim HS; Anaheim, CA; (4); NHS; Prfct Atten Awd; Astronomy; Friendship Club; Cal Poly Pomona; Chem Engrg.

CHOI, JAI H; Bishop Montgomery HS; Harbor City, CA; (2); Church Yth Grp; JV Ftbl; Wt Lftg; Hon Roll; Weight Lift-A-Thon 90; UCLA; Arch.

CHOI, JAMES H; Monterey HS; Marina, CA; (3); Church Yth Grp; Varsity Clb; Band; Jazz Band; Mrchg Band; Orch; Var Wrstlng; High Hon Roll; Hon Roll; UC Davis; Engrng.

CHOI, JANE; Herbert Hoover HS; Glendale, CA; (3); Church Yth Grp; Cmnty Wkr; Hosp Aide; Key Clb; Med.

CHOI, JEFFERSON; El Dorado HS; Placentia, CA; (3); 50/320; Church Yth Grp; Cmnty Wkr; Intnl Clb; VP Soph Cls; Stu Cncl; JV Vllybl; Var Wrstlng; High Hon Roll; Hon Roll; Physics & Ecology Clubs; CSF; Med.

CHOI, JIM H; Rowland HS; Walnut, CA; (3); Stage Crew; Cit Awd; Hon Roll; Cal Poly; Engr.

CHOI, JIYUN; Los Angeles HS; Los Angeles, CA; (3); Church Yth Grp; French Clb; Hon Roll; UCLA; Dentist.

CHOI, JOANNE Y; Canyon HS; Anaheim, CA; (2); French Clb; GAA; JV Bsktbl; CA Schlrshp Fed Clb; Top 50 Soph & Fresh 89-90; Asian Clb; U Of CA Irvine; Comp Sci.

CHOI, JUNGHEE; Santa Fe HS; Norwalk, CA; (4); Art Clb; Church Yth Grp; FBLA; Service Clb; Jazz Band; Crs Cntry; Tennis; Trk; Hon Roll; Golden St Exam For Alg I & Geom; Cal Poly; Grphc Dsgn.

CHOI, KATHY S; John Marshall Fund HS; Pasadena, CA; (3); Church Yth Grp; Dance Clb; Key Clb; Pep Clb; Red Cross Aide; Science Clb; Church Choir; Flag Corp; Orch; Yrbk; Pratt; Fshn Dsgn.

CHOI, KEVIN; Western HS; Anaheim, CA; (4); Boy Scts; Chess Clb; Church Yth Grp; Cmnty Wkr; Computer Clb; Math Clb; Socr; Swmmng; Jr NHS; NHS; 1st Drftng Yth Expo Orange Co; 2nd Drftng II Voc Olympics; Intl Bus.

CHOI, MIERIENA; Armijo HS; Fairfield, CA; (1); AFS; Band; Rep Mrchg Band; Orch; Pep Band; Off Frsh Cls; High Hon Roll; Asian Amer Clb; CA Schlrshp Fed.

CHOI, MIKE; Glendale Adventist Acad; Los Angeles, CA; (1); 14/70; Church Yth Grp; Teachers Aide; Chorus; Orch; Hon Roll; Sports Bsbl, Bsktbl, Bllybl, Surfing, Hockey, Swimming; Music Violin, Guitar, Drums; Art; Commercial Arts.

CHOI, MINA; Los Angeles Ctr For Enriched Studies; Los Angeles, CA; (3); Church Yth Grp; Cmnty Wkr; Office Aide; Spanish Clb; Orch; Gym; Ldrshp; Yng Asian Schlrs; CA Schlrshp Fed; Knights & Ladies; Corp Law.

CHOI, MINDY H; Brea Olinda HS; Brea, CA; (3); Art Clb; Church Yth Grp; Sftbl; Vllybl; High Hon Roll; Hon Roll; Yrbk; UCI; Psych.

CHOI, NAOMI; Capistrano Valley HS; Laguana Miguel, CA; (3); Church Yth Grp; Teachers Aide; JV Gym; Cit Awd; Acad Achvt Awd; Jr Hnr Escort; Hstrcl Soc Clb; UCSB; Ed.

CHOI, SAM S; San Pasqual HS; San Diego, CA; (2); Scholastic Bowl; Hon Roll; Engr.

CHOI, SAM YOUNG; Righetti HS; Santa Maria, CA; (1); Church Yth Grp; Band; Mrchg Band; Rep Stu Cncl; Socr; Vllybl; CA Schlrshp Fed; US Mltry Acad; Engr.

CHOI, SAMUEL W; Mark Keppel HS; Monterey Park, CA; (3); Key Clb; Math Clb; Mu Alpha Theta; Science Clb; Hnrs Golden St Exam Alg & Geom; Jan Ying Benevolent Assn Schlrshp; Comp Sci.

CHOI, SANDY; Westlake Schl; Beverly Hills, CA; (3); Cmnty Wkr; Sec Debate Tm; Drama Clb; Model UN; Sec NFL; Pep Clb; Service Clb; Speech Tm; SADD; Thesps; Eastern Asian Stds Club Pres & Co-Founder; Westlake Orgnztn For Women; Intl Relations.

CHOI, SERENA M; John A Rowland HS; Rowland Hts, CA; (4); Church Yth Grp; Treas French Clb; Pep Clb; Science Clb; Service Clb; Rptr Phtg Yrbk; Cheerldng; French Hon Soc; High Hon Roll; Hon Roll; UC-IRVINE.

CHOI, STEVE; Dorsey HS; Los Angeles, CA; (2); Ftbl; Wt Lftg; Hon Roll; Ftbl; Fire Fghtr.

CHOI, SUN HA; Chatsworth HS; Chatsworth, CA; (2); Church Yth Grp; FCA; Spanish Clb; Off Soph Cls; JV Ftbl; Hon Roll; Prfct Atten Awd; Bio.

CHOI, SUNG; Herbert Hoover HS; Fresno, CA; (2); Swmmng; Tennis; High Hon Roll; Hon Roll; Water Polo; Princpls Awd; Mock Trial; UCLA; Engrg.

CHOI, SUNG H; Hullard HS; Pinedale, CA; (2); Math Clb; Mech Engrng.

CHOI, SUNG HUI; Culver City HS; Culver City, CA; (2); Church Yth Grp; Dance Clb; Variety Show; Nwsp; Yrbk; Cit Awd; High Hon Roll; Golden St Exam High Hnr Alg I, High Hnr Geom; Chem.

CHOI, VICTORIA; El Cerrito HS; El Cerrito, CA; (4); 41/350; DECA; Office Aide; Science Clb; Teachers Aide; Band; Jazz Band; Orch; School Play; Lit Mag; High Hon Roll; Stu Conservation Assn; U CA Santa Barbara; Fine Arts.

CHOI, YEE W; Ramona Convent HS; El Monte, CA; (3); 5/100; Art Clb; Church Yth Grp; Model UN; Church Choir; Rptr Nwsp; VP Frsh Cls; Treas Jr Cls; NHS; CSF; GPA Awd; Med.

CHOI, YOUNG; Bellflower HS; Bellflower, CA; (2); 1/384; Score Keeper; Intnl Clb; Spanish Clb; Drill Tm; U Yale; Physcn.

CHON, CINDY H; Glen A Wilson HS; Hacienda Hgts, CA; (4); Cmnty Wkr; Hosp Aide; Key Clb; Ski Clb; Drill Tm; Var Cheerldng; High Hon Roll; Hon Roll; Prfct Atten Awd; Pres Schlr; Piano; Bst Dancr Drll Tm; Goldn St Exm Hgh Hnrs Alg I & Geom; UC Santa Barbara; Bus.

CHON, HAMILTON; North Hollywood HS; Studio City, CA; (3); Am Leg Boys St; Pres Ski Clb; Spanish Clb; Varsity Clb; Orch; School Musical; Off Frsh Cls; Var Ftbl; Wt Lftg; Congrsnl Schlr Natl Young Ldrs WA DC Conf.

CHON, PHILIP B; Crescenta Valley HS; La Crescenta, CA; (4); 31/390; VP Church Yth Grp; German Clb; Hosp Aide; Key Clb; Math Clb; Mu Alpha Theta; Band; Jazz Band; Mrchg Band; JV L Bsktbl; Ca Schlrshp Fed-Sealbearer; CA U San Diego; Bio.

CHONG, ALBERT; Sunny Hills HS; Fullerton, CA; (2); 1/450; French Clb; Intnl Clb; JV Bsktbl; JV Tennis; NHS; Prfct Atten Awd; Rotary Awd; Medicine.

CHONG, ANA; Chula Vista HS; Chula Vista, CA; (3); 3/493; Computer Clb; Pep Clb; SADD; Rptr Nwsp; Prfct Atten Awd; Pres Acad Fit Awd; GSE Acad Excllnc & Outstndng Achvmnt Awds; CSF; Peer Cntct.

CHONG, DAVID G; Clovis HS; Clovis, CA; (3); Band; Jazz Band; Mrchg Band; Pep Band; Hon Roll; CA ST U Fresno; Music.

CHONG, EUNCHU C; Warren HS; Downey, CA; (2); Art Clb; Scholastic Bowl; Service Clb; Spanish Clb; Var Trk; Korean Club; Peer Cnslng; Bible Club; UC Berkeley; Bus Law.

CHONG, FATCHHIV; Mira Mesa HS; San Diego, CA; (2); 1/797; Math Tm; Band; Mrchg Band; Off Soph Cls; Cit Awd; High Hon Roll; Pres Acad Fit Awd; CA Schsltc Fed; Teens Hlpng Other Teens; Med.

CHONG, FATTHOV; Mira Mesa HS; San Diego, CA; (3); 32/777; Teachers Aide; JV Trk; Hon Roll; Prfct Atten Awd; Pres Acad Fit Awd; CA Schlrshp Fed; Engrng.

CHONG, IN-SOO; Gardena HS; Gardena, CA; (2); Sec Treas Church Yth Grp; Service Clb; JV Tennis; Oscar Awd; HS Tsck Force; UC Berkeley; Medcl.

CHONG, JINYI; Helix HS; San Diego, CA; (2); 28/449; Sec Treas Drama Clb; French Clb; Intnl Clb; School Play; Stage Crew; JV Tennis; Trk; Hon Roll; JSA; Stanford; Law.

CHONG, MEE-RA; Downey HS; Downey, CA; (2); Church Yth Grp; Church Yth Grp; Treas Key Clb; Math Clb; Pres Science Clb; SADD; Band; Mrchg Band; High Hon Roll; Pres Acad Fit Awd; Obstetrcs.

CHONG, MICHAEL; Sonora HS; La Habra, CA; (2); 15/305; Art Clb; Church Yth Grp; Science Clb; Spanish Clb; VP Soph Cls; JV Ftbl; JV Tennis; High Hon Roll; HOBY Ambssdr; UCLA; Med.

CHONG, SU K; Oxnard HS; Oxnard, CA; (3); Church Yth Grp; Variety Show; Hon Roll; Art.

CHONG, SYLVIA; Granada Hills HS; Granada Hills, CA; (3); VP Debate Tm; NFL; Pres Speech Tm; Jazz Band; Orch; School Play; Lit Mag; High Hon Roll; Ntl Merit Ltr; Pres Acad Fit Awd; Writer.

CHONG, YON H; Polytechnic HS; Riverside, CA; (1); 31/555; Key Clb; Chorus; High Hon Roll; Hon Roll; Prfct Atten Awd; CSF; UC Berkeley; Intl Relations.

CHOO, ALLAN; Los Altos HS; Hacienda Hts, CA; (2); Boy Scts; Var Vllybl; Sccr; Cal-Poly; Elec Engr.

CHOO, JINA; Rosary HS; Fullerton, CA; (2); French Clb; Hosp Aide; Pep Clb; Science Clb; Ski Clb; Speech Tm; High Hon Roll; Hon Roll; JSA; CSF; Stu Recogntn Awd; UCLA; Med.

CHOOBOON, CHARTSAK; Saint Anthony HS; Long Beach, CA; (3); French Clb; High Hon Roll; Hon Roll; NHS; CA Scholarship Federation; Electrial Engineering.

CHOPPING, MONICA E; Mt Carmel HS; San Diego, CA; (2); Band; Mrchg Band; U S Space Acad Huntsville AL 2 Cert Awds; Aerospace Engrng.

CHOPRA, AMIT; Whitney HS; Cerritos, CA; (3); Pres FBLA; Hosp Aide; JA; Sec Key Clb; Rptr Nwsp; Rep Stu Cncl; Var Crs Cntry; Var Trk; Hon Roll; NHS; Genetics Rsrch Asst Beckman Rsrch Inst City Of Hope; Scsf Outstndng Svc Awd; Volunteer Lib & Park; Med.

CHOPRA, ANAND; American HS; Fremont, CA; (4); 28/360; Cmnty Wkr; Model UN; Scholastic Bowl; Science Clb; SADD; Stu Cncl; Tennis; Wt Lftg; High Hon Roll; Hon Roll; U CA Davis; Med.

CHOPRA, SHAGUN; Berkeley HS; Berkeley, CA; (4); Computer Clb; Pres French Clb; Science Clb; Rptr Yrbk; Ed Lit Mag; Gov Hon Prg Awd; High Hon Roll; Hon Roll; CSF Pres; Z Club; Fencing Club; Model Congress Pres; Asian Stu VP; Photo Club Pres; MIT Awd; UC Berkeley; Med.

CHORN, MITH; A.a. Stagg HS; Stockton, CA; (1); Aud/Vis; Bsktbl; High Hon Roll; Pres Acad Fit Awd; Math Awd; Comp Tech.

CHOU, ANITA; Dana Hills HS; Laguna Beach, CA; (1); Teachers Aide; Hon Roll; GSE Algebra High Honor; Dolphin Of The Month; Reading Achvment Awd; UCB; CPA.

CHOU, BRIAN; Mission Bay HS; San Diego, CA; (3); Key Clb; VP Jr Cls; Var Tennis; Cit Awd; High Hon Roll; Rotary Awd; Scripps Clnc Rsrch Inst Intrn 90; Intrn Natl Marine Fisheries Svc 88-89; UCLA; Sci.

CHOU, CAROL; Abraham Lincoln HS; San Francisco, CA; (3); Chorus; Swmmng; Hon Roll; Fshn Dsgnr.

CHOU, CHING; Lowell HS; San Francisco, CA; (3); Q&S; Red Cross Aide; Sec Science Clb; Teachers Aide; High Hon Roll; Ntl Merit SF; CA Invtnl Chemathon 90 1st Pl Trphy; Harvard Bk Awd 90; CSF; Harvard; Med.

CHOU, EVA; Los Albos HS; Hacienda Hts, CA; (1); 1/384; Church Yth Grp; Cmnty Wkr; Band; Church Choir; Mrchg Band; Hon Roll; Kywntts; CSF; Optmtry.

CHOU, JACK; Ontario HS; Ontario, CA; (1); JV Crs Cntry; JV Trk; Cycling; Cal Poly; Auto Desgnr.

CHOU, JAY; Taft Union HS; Taft, CA; (4); 3/202; AFS; Church Yth Grp; Computer Clb; French Clb; Speech Tm; SADD; Rptr Nwsp; Trk; High Hon Roll; Hon Roll; Acad Decathlon Tm 89-90; Mock Trial Tm 88-89; CSF 87-90; UC Berkeley; Nutrition.

CHOU, JEFF; Mills HS; Burlingame, CA; (2); Math Tm; Var JV Tennis; CSF; Intl Bus.

CHOU, JOY J; University HS; Irvine, CA; (3); Off Church Yth Grp; Intnl Clb; Teachers Aide; Chorus; Church Choir; Hon Roll; 1st Pl Chinese Harp Cont; Comp Sci.

CHOU, JUDY Y; Sonora HS; Fullerton, CA; (2); 16/313; Art Clb; Chess Clb; FBLA; GAA; Math Clb; Spanish Clb; Drill Tm; Tennis; High Hon Roll; Cal St Fullerton Emrgn Ldrs Pgm; Cypress Coll Chinese New Yr Mstr Of Crmny; UC Berkeley; Sci.

CHOU, LILY; Los Alamitos HS; Seal Beach, CA; (3); Church Yth Grp; Treas French Clb; Math Clb; Q&S; Science Clb; Ski Clb; Ed Yrbk; High Hon Roll; Intrct Clb Cmnty Svc Exec Brd; Cert Merit Piano.

CHOU, LILY A; Bonita Vista HS; Chula Vista, CA; (2); 1/600; Art Clb; Rptr Nwsp; Sec Rptr Yrbk; Lit Mag; Cit Awd; High Hon Roll; Prfct Atten Awd; Prin Adv Comm; Rcgntn Of Excl In Span; Peer Tutoring; U Of CA Santa Cruz; Psych.

CHOU, LINDA; Lincoln HS; Stockton, CA; (3); 1/600; Cmnty Wkr; Sec Treas Mu Alpha Theta; SADD; Orch; Lit Mag; Var Tennis; High Hon Roll; Pres Acad Fit Awd; Yng Schlrs Pgm-Natl Sci Fndtn At UC Davis 89; Stanislaus Mthmtcs Cmptn-Algbr II 1st Pl 89; UC Berkeley; Med.

CHOU, LUANN; Arcadia HS; Arcadia, CA; (4); Drama Clb; Pep Clb; Teachers Aide; Orch; Sec Stu Cncl; Var Cheerldng; Spec Olympcs Vlntr; Long Beach ST; Bus.

CHOU, ROY H; Sunny Hills HS; Fullerton, CA; (3); Chess Clb; Cmnty Wkr; Sec Computer Clb; VP JA; Math Tm; Spanish Clb; Band; Mrchg Band; Pep Band; Variety Show; Badmntn Tm-Var 89-90; Music Instrmntlst Mag Merit Awd 87-88; CA Inst Of Tech; Elec Engrng.

CHOU, RUBY; Sunny Hills HS; Fullerton, CA; (4); Church Yth Grp; Computer Clb; Letterman Clb; Library Aide; Science Clb; Spanish Clb; Teachers Aide; Mrchg Band; School Musical; High Hon Roll; Outstndng Athltc Awd-Vrsty Badminton 89-90; CA Jazz Fstvl-5th Pl Trophy Intermediate 88-89; Boston U; Med.

CHOU, RUTH C; Mira Costa HS; Redondo Beach, CA; (3); Key Clb; Science Clb; Yrbk; Cit Awd; Hon Roll; S-Clb; Medcl.

CHOUDHARY, MONOJ; Gahr HS; Norwalk, CA; (1); French Clb; Intnl Clb; School Play; Pres Acad Fit Awd; Blue Award; Gold Award; Gahr; Political Science.

CHOUDHARY, TANUJA; Whitney HS; Norwalk, CA; (3); Drama Clb; Key Clb; Spanish Clb; High Hon Roll; Hon Roll; CSF; Med.

CHOUGH, HELEN; Fred C Beyer HS; Modesto, CA; (3); Ski Clb; Spanish Clb; SADD; Teachers Aide; Intrml Swmmng; Cit Awd; Hon Roll; Prfct Atten Awd; Fri Nght Lv Clb; Smifnlst Hugh O'brien Ldrshp Smnr; Tnwrk Ldrshp Conf 88; Sci.

CHOUGH, JENNIFER; Troy HS; Anaheim, CA; (2); Church Yth Grp; Drama Clb; Key Clb; Church Choir; School Play; Rptr Nwsp; JV Bsktbl; Capt Var Vllybl; NHS; Rotary Awd; Brnz Mdl Karate; Badminton Tm Var; U Of CA Irvine; Pre-Med.

CHOUINARD, JOEL; Valley Christian HS; Hollister, CA; (3); Church Yth Grp; Cmnty Wkr; Red Cross Aide; Spanish Clb; Band; Drm Mjr(t); Mrchg Band; Orch; Pep Band; School Musical; Lifeguarding; Archery & Hunting; Le Tourneau; Flght Career.

CHOW, ALAN S; Lowell HS; San Francisco, CA; (2); Red Cross Aide; Jr Statesmen Of Amer; Amnesty Intl.

CHOW, ALAN W; George Washington HS; San Francisco, CA; (1); U Of CA-BERKELEY; Arch.

CHOW, ANNA L; Woodbridge HS; Irvine, CA; (4); Church Yth Grp; Sec Pres JCL; Sec Pres Latin Clb; SADD; Teachers Aide; High Hon Roll; Sec Jr NHS; Sec NHS; Pres Acad Fit Awd; Piano Teacher; Swmmng & Vllybl; Sentinel Awdes Sci & Latin, Latin Hon Soc; U Of CA; Kinesiology.

CHOW, DAVID; Mark Keppel HS; Monterey Park, CA; (1); Math Clb; Science Clb; Bsktbl; Tnns; Comp; Arch.

CHOW, ELIE; Lincoln HS; Stockton, CA; (3); 36/592; Latin Clb; Mu Alpha Theta; SADD; Hon Roll; CA Schltc Fed; Bus.

CHOW, GARY K; Tokay HS; Stockton, CA; (4); JV Trk; Hon Roll.

CHOW, JAMES; San Gabriel HS; Rosemead, CA; (1); French Clb; Hon Roll; UCLA; Pediatrics.

CHOW, JANICE; John F Kennedy HS; Sacramento, CA; (3); 16/616; AFS; Sec Church Yth Grp; Cmnty Wkr; Hosp Aide; SADD; Teachers Aide; Orch; School Musical; Rep Frsh Cls; Rep Soph Cls; Chmbr Orch Clb Pres; CSF; Med.

CHOW, JINNY M; John A Rowland HS; Rowland Heights, CA; (2); 1/300; Church Yth Grp; Cmnty Wkr; Math Clb; Science Clb; Spanish Clb; Acpl Chr; High Hon Roll; Prfct Atten Awd.

CHOW, JONATHAN; Palo Alto SR HS; Palo Alto, CA; (4); 1/300; Hosp Aide; Ed Nwsp; Rep Soph Cls; VP Sec Stu Cncl; Var Trk; Vllybl; Wt Lftg; Ntl Merit SF; JV Crs Cntry; Asian Cultrl Exchng Pres; Multicultrl Cmmttee Agnst Racism; Med.

CHOW, JOSEPH; Palo Alto SR HS; Palo Alto, CA; (2); Church Yth Grp; Intnl Clb; Key Clb; Service Clb; Teachers Aide; Ed Nwsp; Rep Frsh Cls; Off Soph Cls; Var Swmmng; JV Tennis; VP CA Schlrshp Fed; Pres Asian Cltrl Exch; Site Cncl Rep; Jr Vrsty Water Polo; Vlntr Stanford Hosp.

CHOW, KENNY K; Westmoor HS; Daly City, CA; (4); 1/370; Chess Clb; Cmnty Wkr; Math Clb; Rep Sr Cls; JV Crs Cntry; Var Tennis; High Hon Roll; NHS; Pres Acad Fit Awd; Val; Tandy Tech Schlr Awd; Bank Of America Cert Winner Math; CA Body Of Scottish Rite Awd; U CA Berkeley; Mech Engr.

CHOW, KRISTY; Hawthorne HS; Lennox, CA; (2); Hon Roll; Cnsrvtn Scintst.

CHOW, MABEL M; Westmoor HS; Daly City, CA; (3); GAA; Service Clb; JV Tennis; Hon Roll; CA Schlrshp Fed; Coll Entrance Club; Bus.

CHOW, MING-FAWN; Edison HS; Huntington Beach, CA; (1); Church Yth Grp; Model UN; Lit Mag; Chinese Club; CA Schlrshp Fed; Peer Asst League; MUN Awds; Comp.

CHOW, MIRIAM; Schurr HS; Montebello, CA; (4); Spanish Clb; SADD; Teachers Aide; Rptr Nwsp; JV Tennis; Prfct Atten Awd; Jr Var MVP Tnns 88-89; Prfct Atten 4 Yrs; CA Schlrshp Fed; CA ST Los Angeles; Sociology.

CHOW, PAMELA L; Lowell HS; San Francisco, CA; (2); Office Aide; Red Cross Aide; SADD; St Schlr.

CHOW, PATRICIA; Villa Park HS; Villa Park, CA; (2); French Clb; German Clb; Intnl Clb; Key Clb; Latin Clb; Science Clb; Spanish Clb; Rptr Nwsp; Rptr Yrbk; Rptr Lit Mag; Mock Trl; Acadc Decathl; St Sci Olympiad.

CHOW, REGINA; Schurr HS; Montebello, CA; (1); SADD; Band; Chorus; Mrchg Band; Nwsp; Hon Roll; Prfct Atten Awd; Pres Acad Fit Awd; Pianist; UCI; Pedtrcn.

CHOW, ROLAND W; Westmoor HS; Daly City, CA; (3); 4/30; Church Yth Grp; Math Clb; Church Choir; Hnrs Golden St Geo Exam; STRIVE; JV/Vrsty Bdmttn; Sci.

CHOW, SCOTT; Lincoln HS; Stockton, CA; (3); 11/592; French Clb; FBLA; Key Clb; Math Clb; Mu Alpha Theta; JV Crs Cntry; JV Trk; High Hon Roll; Pres Acad Fit Awd; Pltcl Clb; Interact Clb; Law.

CHOW, SOPHIA; Lowell HS; San Francisco, CA; (3); Hosp Aide; Office Aide; Red Cross Aide; Pre Med Club; Pre Med.

CHOW, VICTOR; Schurr HS; West Covina, CA; (4); 420/500; Math Tm; Var Tennis; Gldn St Exam-Geom Hnrs; Mt San Antine Coll; Cvl Engrng.

CHOW, VINCENT Y; Balboa HS; San Francisco, CA; (3); 2/25; Art Clb; Hon Roll; Chinese Clb; CSF; Golden St Exam Hnrs Geom 89; UC Berkeley.

CHOW, WAI L; Schurr HS; Monterey Park, CA; (1); Boy Scts; Math Clb; Hon Roll; CSF; Bio Chem.

CHOW, WINNIE; Lynbrook HS; San Jose, CA; (3); 17/270; Treas Church Yth Grp; Debate Tm; Key Clb; NFL; Service Clb; Spanish Clb; Speech Tm; Chorus; Church Choir; High Hon Roll; Badmntn Vrsty & JR Vrsty; UCLA; Ec.

CHOW, YOLANDA L; Abraham Lincoln HS; San Francisco, CA; (2); Hon Roll.

CHOWNING, TRICIA D; Cornelia Connelly HS; Whittier, CA; (1); Cmnty Wkr; Drama Clb; School Play; High Hon Roll; JR Stsmn Of Amer-Secy Treas; Stanford Smmr Schl-Amer Govt & Spch; Hgh Hnrs Golden St Exam Alg; Law.

CHOY, JULIANA; South San Francisco HS; Pacifica, CA; (3); 10/350; French Clb; Math Clb; Math Tm; Ed Nwsp; Pres Stu Cncl; JV Var Tennis; Hon Roll; NHS; HOBY Ldrshp Awd; Girls ST; Xerox Awd-Humanities, Soc Sci; UCSD; Bus.

CHOY, NANCY C; Mark Keppel HS; Monterey Park, CA; (3); FBLA; CA ST U Of LA; Ecs.

CHRESTENSEN, KURT; Edison HS; Huntington Beach, CA; (2); Trk.

CHRICHTON, KIMBERLY; Eureka HS; Eureka, CA; (4); 2/300; Am Leg Aux Girls St; Ski Clb; Teachers Aide; Orch; School Play; Rep Soph Cls; Sec Stu Cncl; Tennis; High Hon Roll; Sal; CA Schlstc Fed Life Mbr; U Of CA Davis; Intl Relations.

CHRISMAN, SHERRI R; Capistrano Valley HS; Mission Viejo, CA; (4); Drama Clb; Pep Clb; Science Clb; SADD; Yrbk; Gym; Tennis; Trk; Bst Spprtng Actrss 89; Radford U; Pltcl Sci.

CHRIST, COURTNEY; Thomas Downey HS; Blythe, CA; (1); French Clb; Band; Mrchg Band; Pep Band; Stage Crew; Hon Roll; Cmnty Wkr.

CHRIST, MICHAEL J; Rio Mesa HS; Camarillo, CA; (3); 123/400; Chess Clb; JV Capt Vllybl; Boy Of Yr; UCSD; Marine Bio.

CHRISTEN, ANTHONY T; St Ignatius College Prep; San Francisco, CA; (3); 31/244; Service Clb; Ski Clb; Rptr Nwsp; Sec Stu Cncl; Var Crs Cntry; Var Ftbl; Var Lcrss; Hon Roll; Ltrgy Grp; Rlly Cmmttee; DR.

CHRISTENSEN, CAINE P; Kingsbury HS; Kingsburg, CA; (3); Chess Clb; Dance Clb; Math Clb; Mu Alpha Theta; Science Clb; Spanish Clb; Var Socr; Var Tennis; Hon Roll; 1st Tm All Leag Sccr; Acad Block K; Pre-Med.

CHRISTENSEN, CAREY L; Foothill Farms SR HS; Sacramento, CA; (2); Jazz Band; Orch; High Hon Roll; Hon Roll; All St Hnr Orch; Music.

CHRISTENSEN, CHAD; Poway HS; Poway, CA; (3); 15/761; Boy Scts; Church Yth Grp; Scholastic Bowl; Band; Jazz Band; Mrchg Band; Orch; Hon Roll; NHS; Intract Clb; Egl Sct; Brigham Young U; Sci.

CHRISTENSEN, CHRISTY; Anaheim HS; Anaheim, CA; (3); Teachers Aide; Hon Roll; UCI; Law.

CHRISTENSEN, CHRISTY J; Temecula Valley HS; Temecula, CA; (2); Church Yth Grp; Cmnty Wkr; DECA; Drill Tm.

CHRISTENSEN, ERIC G; Simi Valley HS; Simi Valley, CA; (2); Boy Scts; Band; Jazz Band; Mrchg Band; Orch; Pep Band; Jr NHS; Water Polo; Drumline; UT ST; Crime Sci.

CHRISTENSEN, ERIC J; Etiwanda HS; Alta Loma, CA; (2); Art Clb; Boy Scts; Church Yth Grp; Cmnty Wkr; Varsity Clb; Ftbl; Wt Lftg; Hon Roll; Yngst To Show Wrk Invtnl Art Show; Pres Chrch Yth Grp, Capt Of Soccer Team; Lnmn Capt Ftbll; San Francisco Schl/Arts; Art.

CHRISTENSEN, ERIC W; Washington HS; Fremont, CA; (3); Var L Bsktbl; Intrml Vllybl; Ntl Merit Ltr; Golden ST Exam Hgh Hnrs Alg 87, Geom 88.

CHRISTENSEN, HEATHER; Clovis HS; Clovis, CA; (1); Church Yth Grp; Dance Clb; Drama Clb; NFL; Speech Tm; School Musical; School Play; Hon Roll; Dance Clas; Lawyer.

CHRISTENSEN, HEIDI G; Canoga Park HS; Canoga Park, CA; (2); Water Skiing, Snow Skiing; Fly Plane, Play Sftbl, Vllybl, Badmittn; Pilot.

CHRISTENSEN, INGRID E; Argonaut HS; Jackson, CA; (2); 1/102; Treas Rep FHA; Key Clb; Science Clb; Band; Mrchg Band; Stat Bsktbl; Stat Sftbl; High Hon Roll; Treas Soph Cls; Coord For Sch Chaptr Of CA; Sci Olympd Team; Biochem.

CHRISTENSEN, JASON; Victory Valley HS; Victorville, CA; (2); Wrstlng; Air Force Acad; Mltry.

CHRISTENSEN, JOSH; Southwestern Acad; Ridgecrest, CA; (2); Church Yth Grp; Var Bsbl; Var Bsktbl; Var Crs Cntry; Capt Socr; Trk; Athltc Awds Crs Cntry CIF 1st Tm All League - 2 Sccr Most Insprtnl; U Of MI; Orthpdc Surgeon.

CHRISTENSEN, JULIE; John Swett HS; Rodeo, CA; (2); Church Yth Grp; Drama Clb; Math Tm; Science Clb; SADD; Band; Church Choir; Mrchg Band; School Play; Rep Nwsp; Azusa Pacific Mexico Outreach 89 & 90; UCLA; Adv.

CHRISTENSEN, KELLI J; Don Lugo HS; Chino, CA; (2); Pres Church Yth Grp; Cmnty Wkr; Hosp Aide; Yrbk; Nursing.

CHRISTENSEN, LEAH M; Poway HS; Poway, CA; (2); Church Yth Grp; Letterman Clb; Varsity Clb; Chorus; Rep Soph Cls; Var Diving; Hon Roll; Pres Acad Fit Awd; CA Schlrshp Fed; Water Polo; Brigham Young U; Physics.

CHRISTENSEN, MARK S; Trabuco Hills HS; Mission Viejo, CA; (2); 4/330; Cmnty Wkr; Spanish Clb; Var Capt Golf; High Hon Roll; NHS; Outstndng Achvt Hnrs Geom, Engl Hnrs & Spanish III.

CHRISTENSEN, MICHELLE; Poway HS; Poway, CA; (3); Varsity Clb; Var Gym; Var Socr; Hon Roll; Prfct Atten Awd; Letterman Clb; Achiever Of Mnth Consumer & Family Stds; Elem Ed.

CHRISTENSEN, STACEY; Marina HS; Huntington Bch, CA; (4); Church Yth Grp; Dance Clb; Office Aide; Pep Clb; Varsity Clb; Drill Tm; Pep Band; Cheerldng; Gym; Pom Pon; ARMY; Aviation.

CHRISTENSEN, STACEY; San Marin HS; Novato, CA; (3); Church Yth Grp; Teachers Aide; Chorus; School Musical; Friday Night Live Publcty Chrprsn; U OR; Hstry.

CHRISTENSEN, STEPHANIE; St Lawrence Acad; Santa Clara, CA; (3); 1/34; Math Clb; Chorus; Yrbk; VP Frsh Cls; Pres Soph Cls; Var Socr; JV Sftbl; High Hon Roll; Jr NHS; NHS; Stdnt Bdy Treas 89-90; Rsrch Mdl Fld.

CHRISTENSEN, STEVE; Rancho Cotate HS; Rohnert Park, CA; (4); 37/200; Boy Scts; JA; Teachers Aide; Variety Show; Off Soph Cls; Var L Bsbl; JV Stat Bsktbl; Var Capt Ftbl; Stat Score Keeper; Intrml Sftbl; Santa Barbara City Coll; Acctng.

CHRISTENSEN, TRACEY L; Poway HS; Poway, CA; (3); Office Aide; Varsity Clb; Diving; Var Capt Socr; High Hon Roll; Hon Roll; Mst Vlble Team Plyr Sccr-Awd 89-90; Cert Of Merit-Lit 1 & 2 & Amer Lit II; Cert Of Merit-Alg 1 & 2; Elem Ed.

CHRISTENSEN, TRISHA L; Woodland HS; Woodland, CA; (2); Church Yth Grp; FFA; Intnl Clb; SADD; Ed Nwsp; Phtg Yrbk; Treas Frsh Cls; Stu Cncl; JV Bsktbl; JV Crs Cntry; Wldrnss Clb; Cert Of Mrt Hghst Stndng Future Farmer; Chptr Schlrshp & Ldrshp FFA; Arch.

CHRISTENSON, AMY; Riverdale HS; Caruthers, CA; (3); 2/70; Am Leg Aux Girls St; Church Yth Grp; FFA; Pres GAA; Treas Letterman Clb; Office Aide; Pep Clb; VP Science Clb; Treas Ski Clb; Ed Yrbk; Outstndng Stu Span & Engl Awd; Bus Admin.

CHRISTENSON, RYAN A; Apple Valley HS; Apple Valley, CA; (2); Var Bsbl; Var Bsktbl; Hon Roll; CPA.

CHRISTENSON, TINA A; South City HS; South San Francis, CA; (3); Rep Jr Cls; Swmmng; Italian Clb; San Francisco ST U; Teacher.

CHRISTHERNA, ERIKA; James Monroe HS; Los Angeles, CA; (4); Science Clb; Rptr Nwsp; Rep Soph Cls; Rep Stu Cncl; Var Trk; Knights & Ladies; CA Schlrshp Fed; Ecological Soc Clb Chief Of Commtte; LACC.

CHRISTIAN, ALIZA L; North Hills Christian Schl; Vallejo, CA; (2); Aud/Vis; Girl Scts; Office Aide; Church Choir; Drill Tm; Sci Awds.

CHRISTIAN, CHARITY A; San Pasqual HS; Bard, CA; (2); 5/30; FFA; Pep Clb; SADD; Teachers Aide; Band; Mrchg Band; Pep Band; School Musical; Yrbk; Cheerldng; AZ Western Coll; Law.

CHRISTIAN, MARY E; Manteca HS; Manteca, CA; (1); 82/457; SADD; Chorus; Hon Roll; Keywanettes Pres; Mst Imprvd Choir Awd; Notre Dame Coll; Dance.

CHRISTIAN, MICHAEL; Francis W Parker HS; San Diego, CA; (3); 1/60; Cmnty Wkr; Math Tm; School Musical; School Play; Var JV Ftbl; Var Trk; High Hon Roll; Hon Roll; Ntl Merit SF; Val; Yth Volntrs Assn; Saferide Drvr; Vrsty Sailng Tm; U Of CA Los Angeles; Engrng.

CHRISTIAN, SHAMVONE M; San Lorenzo HS; Oakland, CA; (2); Cheerldng; Trk; Peer Cnslr; Cert Of Merit-Attitd; Chld Psycht.

CHRISTIAN, SHAWN T; Mt Empire Unified HS; Descanso, CA; (3); Church Yth Grp; 4-H; German Clb; Letterman Clb; JV Var Bsbl; JV Var Ftbl; Var Wt Lftg; Hon Roll; Pres Acad Fit Awd; Bsktbl.

CHRISTIAN-LUTHY, BRENDA; Bloomington Christian HS; Rialto, CA; (2); 1/30; Church Yth Grp; Cmnty Wkr; Ed Nwsp; Sec Stu Cncl; Cheerldng; High Hon Roll; Pres Acad Fit Awd; Eckerd Coll FL; Marine Bio.

CHRISTIANSEN, AMY J; Ygnacio Valley HS; Walnut Creek, CA; (1); Sec Treas Frsh Cls; Hon Roll; Lion Awd; Woodman Of The World Scty; CA ST Schl; Teacher.

CHRISTIANSEN, BENT V; Corona HS; Corona, CA; (2); JV Bsktbl; High Hon Roll; Pres Acad Fit Awd; Arch.

CHRISTIANSEN, ERIKA LYNNE; Turlock HS; Turlock, CA; (4); AFS; Art Clb; Cmnty Wkr; French Clb; Office Aide; Scholastic Bowl; SADD; Yrbk; High Hon Roll; Hon Roll; Amnsty Intl; D J At CSUS Radio Station; Greenpeace; San Diego ST U; Brdcst Jrnlst.

CHRISTIANSEN, TERESA L; Ferndale Union HS; Ferndale, CA; (3); FFA; Pep Clb; Ski Clb; Yrbk; Sec Frsh Cls; Sec Soph Cls; Sec Jr Cls; JV Var Bsktbl; Var Sftbl; JV Var Vllybl; Santa Rosa JC; Bus.

CHRISTIANSON, BRENT C; San Pedro HS; Rancho Palos Verd, CA; (3); Cmnty Wkr; Teachers Aide; JV Var Vllybl; Hon Roll; Vet Med.

CHRISTIANSON, KIRK L; Canyon Country HS; Canyon Country, CA; (4); Boy Scts; Church Yth Grp; Teachers Aide; Varsity Clb; NHS; BYU; Real Estate.

CHRISTIANSON, MATTHEW D; Yucaipa HS; Yucaipa, CA; (2); Church Yth Grp; Bsbl; Bsktbl; Yucaipa Vly Lttl League All Stars; San Bernardino ST; Bus.

CHRISTIDES, GEORGE H; Warren HS; Downey, CA; (2); Church Yth Grp; Mrchg Band; Orch; Pres Acad Fit Awd; CSF; Surgeon.

CHRISTIDIS, EVIE; Norwalk HS; Norwalk, CA; (4); 12/292; Sec Service Clb; Sec SADD; Church Choir; Ed Nwsp; Yrbk; Stu Cncl; Cheerldng; Powder Puff Ftbl; Cit Awd; High Hon Roll; Presbytrn Inter Cmnty Hsptl Schlrshp; La Mirada Axlry Hsp Schlrshp; Prncpls Awd 90; CA ST Long Beach; Pre-Med.

CHRISTINA, TONY; Fortuna Union HS; Carlotta, CA; (3); SADD; High Hon Roll; CSF; Acad Exclnce Awd-Golden St; Natl Cncl Of Teachers Of Math; Us Natl Math Awd; Schlstc All-Amer Awd; Cal Poly; Engrng.

CHRISTOFER, CHRIS; Temecula Valley HS; Murrieta, CA; (2); JV Bsktbl; High Hon Roll; Hon Roll; Prfct Atten Awd; Arch.

CHRISTOPH, FRANK A; Harvard Schl; Los Angeles, CA; (4); Hon Roll; Ntl Merit SF; Var Fencing.

CHRISTOPHER, ALLYN D; Rosemead HS; San Gabriel, CA; (1); Church Yth Grp; Cmnty Wkr; Kiwanis Awd; UC Irvine; Vet Sci.

CHRISTOPHERSON, DARYL D; Vallejo SR HS; Vallejo, CA; (4); Am Leg Boys St; Church Yth Grp; Letterman Clb; Office Aide; JV Var Bsbl; High Hon Roll; Hon Roll; Prfct Atten Awd; San Francisco ST U; Bus.

CHRUMA, KATERINA P; Mesa Verde HS; Citrus Heights, CA; (1); 1/279; English Clb; Band; High Hon Roll; Hon Roll; Kiwanis Awd; Prfct Atten Awd; Sci.

CHU, AGNES; Kelseyville HS; Kelseyville, CA; (4); 2/79; Sec SADD; Phtg Rptr Yrbk; Treas Jr Cls; Sec Sr Cls; Var Tennis; Var Trk; High Hon Roll; Pres Acad Fit Awd; Sal; U CA Irvine.

CHU, ALICE K; Eagle Rock JR/Sr HS; Monterey Park, CA; (3); Acpl Chr; Band; Drill Tm; Ed Nwsp; Off Frsh Cls; JV Stat Bsktbl; Var L Trk; Hon Roll; Ntl Merit Ltr; Pres Acad Fit Awd; True Eagle Awd; JV Bsktbl MVP; Biopsych.

CHU, ANNA; Schurr HS; Los Angeles, CA; (3); Church Yth Grp; Hosp Aide; Intnl Clb; Service Clb; SADD; Teachers Aide; Hon Roll; Ntl Merit Ltr; Grls League; The Gees Assoc Schlrshp; Cngrssnl Schlr Rep CA; U S CA; Pharm.

CHU, CAMILLE; Mountain View HS; Los Altos, CA; (3); VP Frsh Cls; JV Socr; High Hon Roll; Intrct; CSF.

CHU, CARRIE; Abraham Lincoln HS; San Francisco, CA; (3); Teachers Aide; Chorus; San Francisco ST Coll; Teacher.

CHU, CHECK G; Lowell HS; San Francisco, CA; (3); Am Leg Boys St; Chess Clb; Science Clb; Teachers Aide; Crs Cntry; Shield & Scroll Hon Soc; Vllybl Club.

CHU, CHRISTIAN A; Fountain Valley HS; Fountain Valley, CA; (1); French Clb; High Hon Roll; PTSA Stu Awd; U Of CA; Med.

CHU, DAVE; Taft Union HS; Taft, CA; (4); 8/190; Pres VP AFS; Aud/Vis; Debate Tm; Chrmn Treas Drama Clb; Pres Off French Clb; Treas Key Clb; Teachers Aide; Ed Yrbk; Tennis; High Hon Roll; Outstndng SR; Choir; Friday Nght Life; UCI; Pltcl Sci.

CHU, DAVID; Aragon HS; San Mateo, CA; (4); 17/353; Treas Am Leg Boys St; JA; Letterman Clb; Yrbk; Rep Stu Cncl; Var Bsbl; Var Crs Cntry; Elks Awd; High Hon Roll; Kiwanis Awd; Lgsltv Intrn Cncl Mayors; CA Schlrshp Fed 100 Prcnt Membership; Slvr Sword For Schl Svc Awd; Georgetown U; Bus Admin.

CHU, DAVIS; George Washington HS; San Francisco, CA; (1); Hon Roll.

CHU, DEANNA L; J Eugene Mc Ateer/Schl Of The Arts; San Francisco, CA; (2); Debate Tm; Ski Clb; Band; Church Choir; Jazz Band; Orch; School Musical; Off Frsh Cls; Mgr(s); Var Trk; CA Schlrshp Fed; Schl Of Arts San Francisco; UC Berkly Sch Optmtry; Optmtry.

CHU, DONNY; Encinal HS; Alameda, CA; (4); 15/229; ROTC; High Hon Roll; Hon Roll; Golden St Exam Awd Excllnc Geom; CSF Stu; ROTC Cadet Qtr Excllnc ROTC.

CHU, ERIC M; Abraham Lincoln HS; San Francisco, CA; (2); Church Yth Grp; FCA; Church Choir; JV Bsbl; Cit Awd; Chrch Musical; Chrch Sftbl Team; UC Berkeley; Bus.

CHU, ERWIN; George Washington HS; San Francisco, CA; (2); Church Yth Grp; FCA; Church Choir; JV Trk; High Hon Roll; Hon Roll; Chinese Amer Clb; Rifle Mrksmnshp Explorer Pgm; CA Schlrshp Fed; San Francisco ST U; Bus.

CHU, FRANCIS C; John A Rowland HS; Rowland Heights, CA; (3); Math Clb; Math Tm; Tennis; Bausch & Lomb Sci Awd; High Hon Roll; NHS; Prfct Atten Awd; Hgh Hnrs SCAMPI; Cert Mrt CA Math Leag; Awd Excllnce Natl Sci Olympd; Math.

CHU, HELEN M; Skyline HS; Oakland, CA; (2); Key Clb; Score Keeper; Sftbl; Vllybl; Cit Awd; Hon Roll; UCLA.

CHU, HENRY H; Whitney HS; Cerritos, CA; (3); Church Yth Grp; Intnl Clb; Key Clb; Church Choir; Orch; JV Bsktbl; Var Trk; Intrml Vllybl.

CHU, JONATHAN; Lowell HS; San Francisco, CA; (3); Chess Clb; Cmnty Wkr; German Clb; Science Clb; Service Clb; Rptr Nwsp; Rep Frsh Cls; Rep Soph Cls; Rep Jr Cls; Intrml Bsktbl; CSF; Spcl Educ Tutor; Comp Lab Asst; UC, Davis; Med.

CHU, JOSEPHINE; Los Altos HS; Hacienda Hgts, CA; (3); Teachers Aide; Color Guard; Flag Corp; JV Swmmng; JV Tennis; Hon Roll; UCI; Bus.

CHU, KEVIN; Marina HS; Huntington Bch, CA; (2); JCL; Latin Clb; Ski Clb; Swmmng; Jr NHS; Water Polo.

CHU, KIMBERLY J; American HS; Fremont, CA; (4); 19/323; Cmnty Wkr; Sec Drama Clb; Hist French Clb; German Clb; Sec Model UN; Quiz Bowl; Scholastic Bowl; Service Clb; Spanish Clb; SADD; Bank Amer Fine Arts Plaq; CSF; Amer HS Beautification; UC Irvine; Scl Ecology.

CHU, LUN-CHUN; San Gabriel HS; San Gabriel, CA; (3); Math Tm; Hon Roll; Chapt I Acad Achvt; Sci Dept Awd; UCLA; Elec Engrng.

CHU, MAILIN L; Mission San Jose HS; Fremont, CA; (1); Ski Clb; JV Tennis; Peer Cnslng; Reach For Options; CSF.

CHU, MICHAEL; San Marine HS; Pasadena, CA; (4); 50/250; JCL; Math Clb; Var Trk; JV Vllybl; Hon Roll; UCLA; Engineering.

CHU, MING SHIR; George Washington HS; San Francisco, CA; (2); Sec Intnl Clb; Sec Service Clb; JV Swmmng; High Hon Roll; Hon Roll; NHS; Art Cont Awd 89; Annual Swimming Cmptn-Two Bronze Mdls 90; U CA Berkeley; Math.

CHU, NANCY C; Arcadia HS; Arcadia, CA; (3); 15/639; Treas French Clb; Rep FBLA; Hosp Aide; Sec Math Clb; Treas Science Clb; Sec Orch; NHS; Prfct Atten Awd; Prncpl Cellist Schl Orch; Padadena Yng Musician Orch; CSF; Gldn St Exam Geom Hgh Hnrs; KIOWAS; UC Berkeley; Phrmcy.

CHU, RAYMOND; Washington HS; San Francisco, CA; (3); Boy Scts; Church Yth Grp; FCA; SADD; Teachers Aide; Church Choir; Bsktbl; Swmmng; Hon Roll; San Francisco ST U; Bus.

CHU, ROBERT S; Berkeley HS; El Cerrito, CA; (3); Church Yth Grp; Golden St Exam-Geom Hgh Hnrs; CSF; Vrsty Badminton.

CHU, SELINA L; San Gabriel HS; Rosemead, CA; (1); French Clb; Intrml Tennis; Cit Awd; Hon Roll; Pres Acad Fit Awd.

CHU, WING; George Washington HS; San Francisco, CA; (4); 184/600; Math Clb; Teachers Aide; High Hon Roll; Hon Roll; San Francisco ST; Acctng.

CHUA, EMILY R; Immaculate Heart HS; Los Angeles, CA; (3); Church Yth Grp; Cmnty Wkr; GAA; Chorus; Church Choir; JV Vllybl; Nrsng.

CHUA, JERGEN ANN; St Genevieve HS; Sepulveda, CA; (3); Church Choir; Nwsp; Var Socr; Mgr Sftbl; Hon Roll; Mock Trial; CSF; Med.

CHUA, MELINDA M; Will C Wood HS; Vacaville, CA; (2); Church Yth Grp; Science Clb; Chorus; Church Choir; Drill Tm; School Musical; High Hon Roll; VP Sec Jr NHS; Prfct Atten Awd; Vacaville Tlntd Teen Cntst & Fiesta Days Tlnt Show Wnnr; Natl Jr Hnr Chior; Stu For Peace Treas; Music.

CHUA, PANYA; Royal HS; Simi Valley, CA; (4); 7/500; Boy Scts; French Clb; Math Tm; Science Clb; Stu Cncl; Intrml Bsktbl; Var Socr; Cit Awd; High Hon Roll; Hon Roll; Religious Affltn; Mudy Thai Kickboxing Acad; UCLA; Mech Eng.

CHUA, QUEENA L; Los Angeles Baptist HS; North Hollywood, CA; (3); 1/100; Pres Church Yth Grp; Drama Clb; Drill Tm; School Play; Stat JV Trk; Hon Roll; Opt Clb Awd; CSF; Comp Sci.

CHUAN, HELEN; San Rafael HS; San Rafael, CA; (3); German Clb; Key Clb; Spanish Clb; Band; Chorus; Pep Band; Vllybl; U CA-SANTA Cruz; Marine Bio.

CHUANG, ABRAHAM W; Irvine HS; Irvine, CA; (2); 96/400; Church Yth Grp; Key Clb; Var L Swmmng; Cit Awd; Hon Roll; Jr NHS; Pres Acad Fit Awd; Water Polo Tm; Stanford; Arch.

CHUANG, DEANA K; Gretchen Whitney HS; Cerritos, CA; (4); Pres FBLA; Key Clb; Ed Nwsp; Ed Yrbk; JV Tennis; High Hon Roll; NHS; Ntl Merit SF; Prncpls Advsry Brd; Msc Tchrs Assoc Of CA Cert Merit Achvmnt Piano.

CHUANG, HELEN D; Granada Hills HS; Northridge, CA; (4); 6/596; Hosp Aide; Service Clb; SADD; Rptr Nwsp; Yrbk; Capt L Crs Cntry; L Co-Capt Trk; High Hon Roll; Kiwanis Awd; Pr Coll Cnslr; U Of CA Berkely.

CHUARTA, RICKY I; Alhambra HS; Alhambra, CA; (3); Church Yth Grp; Spanish Clb; Swmmng; Pres Acad Fit Awd; Hi-Y-Club Le Fraternite; Piano, Trumpet & Synthesizer; Bus.

CHUATECO, CHARLES C; Don Bosco Technical Inst; Montebello, CA; (2); JV Trk; JV Vllybl; Astan Impressions DJ; Don Bosco Tech.

CHUCK, LAURA; Lowell HS; San Francisco, CA; (3); Cmnty Wkr; Red Cross Aide; Science Clb; Service Clb; SADD; Nwsp; High Hon Roll; Hon Roll; Prfct Atten Awd; Acad Awd; Jrnlsm Awd; Cmnty Vlntr; Pre-Med.

CHUCK, ORLENA K; Lowell HS; San Francisco, CA; (3); Treas Church Yth Grp; Science Clb; Church Choir; Piano Lessons 12 Yrs.

CHUE, YE PAO; Oroville HS; Oroville, CA; (2); Church Yth Grp; Nwsp; Hon Roll; Prfct Atten Awd; Mechnc.

CHUH, ERICH A; Serra HS; San Mateo, CA; (3); Boy Scts; High Hon Roll; Hon Roll; Bowling Clb; Trivia Clb; Engrng.

CHUI, WILLIAM H; Clovis HS; Clovis, CA; (3); 1/512; Cmnty Wkr; Computer Clb; Debate Tm; Treas Math Clb; Math Tm; NFL; Science Clb; Speech Tm; JV Tennis; High Hon Roll; Acad Dcthln; JETS Tm; His Day 3rd Pl Fresno Cty; Aerosp Eng.

CHUN, DAVID J; Warren HS; Walnut, CA; (4); 4/375; Rep Am Leg Boys St; Pres Church Yth Grp; VP FBLA; Math Clb; Math Tm; Science Clb; Ski Clb; JV Bsktbl; Elks Awd; Gov Hon Prg Awd; Amherst Coll; Med.

CHUN, EDWARD M; Skyline HS; Oakland, CA; (3); Key Clb; Science Clb; Yrbk; Stu Cncl; JV Var Crs Cntry; Var Trk; Hon Roll; Prfct Atten Awd; Skyline Keywanettes; Bret Harte Schl 7-11 Mgr; EARO; Elec Engrng.

CHUN, HELEN; Dinuba HS; Dinuba, CA; (4); Hosp Aide; Service Clb; Hon Roll; Prfct Atten Awd; Rotary Awd; Band Dir Awd; U CA Santa Barbara; Bio.

CHUN, KYOUNG JIN; Mt Carmel HS; San Diego, CA; (3); Computer Clb; Rptr Nwsp; JV Tennis; Cit Awd; Hon Roll; Prfct Atten Awd; Engr.

CHUN, RYAN J; South San Francisco HS; South San Francis, CA; (3); Math Clb; Tennis; Jr NHS; Prfct Atten Awd; Pres Acad Fit Awd; St Fnls Natl Hstry Day Media Grp Div; UC Davis; Med.

CHUN, SHANA; Westlake Schl; Pacific Palisds, CA; (2); Cmnty Wkr; Drama Clb; Varsity Clb; Orch; JV Var Socr; Var Sftbl; Piano Guild; Mrt Cert-S Yth Music Fstvl; Psych.

CHUN, SUNG YONG; North Salinas HS; Salinas, CA; (2); Spanish Clb; Nwsp; Trk; Cit Awd; High Hon Roll; NHS; Berkley U; Bus.

CHUN, YOUNG J; Torrance HS; Torrance, CA; (2); 23/440; Church Yth Grp; French Clb; Intnl Clb; Teachers Aide; Band; Church Choir; Mrchg Band; Pep Band; Cit Awd; Chrch Librarian; Origental Mssn Chrch Choir; Engrng.

CHUNBOMRUNG, NARISA R; Culver City HS; Culver City, CA; (3); Church Yth Grp; Dance Clb; School Musical; Rep Soph Cls; Rep Jr Cls; Var Mgr Bsbl; Mgr(s); Hon Roll; CSF; Math.

CHUNG, AMELIA NGA-MEI; Alhambra HS; Alhambra, CA; (3); Intnl Clb; Golden St Exam Acadmc Excll Awd; CSF; UCLA; Envrnmntl Sci.

CHUNG, CHANG; Western HS; Stanton, CA; (4); Pres Church Yth Grp; French Clb; Jr NHS; NHS; Pacific Tae Kwondo Champ 3rd Pl Blkblt Div 87; Yth Expo 1st & 2nd Pl Drftng 87; UCI; Biochem.

CHUNG, CHRISTINA A; Whitney HS; Cerritos, CA; (1); VP Church Yth Grp; Pep Clb; Church Choir; Off Frsh Cls; JV Cheerldng; High Hon Roll; Hon Roll; Educ.

CHUNG, CHU EUN; Canyan Spring HS; Moreno Valley, CA; (2); 4-H Awd; Gov Hon Prg Awd; High Hon Roll; Cert Awd History Cls; Prncpls Hnr Rl; Outstndng Achvt, Outstndng Stu Alg; UCR; Doctor.

CHUNG, DANIEL YONG; Burbank HS; Los Angeles, CA; (4); Var Pres Acad Fit Awd; Acad Decathlon Tm & Club; Korean Club; Golden St Exam High Hnr; UCLA; Comp Software Dsgn.

CHUNG, DAVID; Albany HS; Albany, CA; (1); Hon Roll; Comp Engrng.

CHUNG, DONNY; Alameda HS; Alameda, CA; (1); CSF; U C Berkeley; Engr.

CHUNG, EDWARD C; Servite HS; Laguna Nigael, CA; (3); School Musical; School Play; Acad Dcthln; JSA LDC; Tri-Scl Safe Rides The Stand; Loyola Marymout U; Pltcl Sci.

CHUNG, ERIC; Cerritos HS; Cerritos, CA; (2); 1/565; Church Yth Grp; Cmnty Wkr; Math Clb; Science Clb; JV Tennis; High Hon Roll; Gldn St Exam Awd For Geom; Berkleley CA U; Bio.

CHUNG, EUN JIN; Gahr HS; Artesia, CA; (1); Church Yth Grp; Girl Scts; Chorus; Church Choir; Orch; Cit Awd; Hon Roll; UCLA.

CHUNG, EVANGELINE P; Chino HS; Ontario, CA; (3); Treas Art Clb; Sec Church Yth Grp; Pep Clb; Ski Clb; Var Trk; JV Vllybl; High Hon Roll; Asian Club; CSF; Arch.

CHUNG, FRANCES; Tustin HS; Tustin, CA; (2); Church Yth Grp; Science Clb; Var Cheerldng; High Hon Roll; Hon Roll; CSF; Korean Club; Top 25 Awd; UC Irvine; Tchr.

CHUNG, FRANK WEI-WEN; Fremont Christian HS; Fremont, CA; (2); Art Clb; Chess Clb; Math Clb; Science Clb; JV Vllybl; Table Tennis; Calligraphy; Origami; Stanford; Technology.

CHUNG, GRACE; West Covina HS; West Covina, CA; (1); Science Clb; JV Tennis; Hon Roll; CA Schlrshp Fed; Friday Night Live; Visage Club; CAL Poly; Fshn Dsgn.

CHUNG, HANH; C K Mc Clatchy HS; Sacramento, CA; (4); 70/337; Bus Accntng.

CHUNG, HANNAH L; University/San Joaquin HS; Irvine, CA; (3); Church Yth Grp; FCA; JCL; Latin Clb; Cit Awd; JV Trk; JV Vllybl; Stu Of Month; 110 Percent Vllybl Awd; U S CA; Bus Admin.

CHUNG, HEIDI A; Estancia HS; Costa Mesa, CA; (3); 2/315; Debate Tm; French Clb; Treas Key Clb; NFL; Pres Speech Tm; Chorus; JV Tennis; High Hon Roll; Masonic Awd; Mock Trial Attrny.

CHUNG, HO K; Mountain View HS; El Monte, CA; (4); 2/371; Computer Clb; High Hon Roll; Prfct Atten Awd; Sal; CSF; Bnk America Sci/Math Achvt & Schl Dist Brd Trustees Awds; Pacific Horizon Clb; UC Los Angeles; Arch.

CHUNG, JACKIE; Arcadia HS; Arcadia, CA; (4); 2/641; Hosp Aide; Red Cross Aide; Science Clb; Service Clb; JV Tennis; Hon Roll; JETS Awd; NHS; Pres Acad Fit Awd; Sal; Natl Bicentennial Constitution Cmptn-3rd Pl St; Amer Acad Achvt Awd; Stu Ldr Of Yr; MIT; Med.

CHUNG, JAMES W; John F Kennedy HS; La Palma, CA; (4); Pres Church Yth Grp; Chrmn Computer Clb; Pres Varsity Clb; Chorus; Rep Jr Cls; VP Sr Cls; JV Var Ftbl; JV Tennis; NHS; Pres Acad Fit Awd; Gldn St Exam Hnrs Geom; Mr Shamrock Most Preferred Soph; Frshmn Ftbl Lg Champs; UC Berkeley; Bio-Chem.

CHUNG, JANE; La Serna HS; Whittier, CA; (1); 1/480; SADD; Orch; JV Tennis; Cit Awd; High Hon Roll; Teachers Aide.

CHUNG, JANET; Lowell HS; San Francisco, CA; (2); Chess Clb; Office Aide; Science Clb; Orch; High Hon Roll; Pres Acad Fit Awd; Chinese Clb Treas 89-90; Chinese Spch Cntst 2nd Pl; Registry Rep; MA Inst Of Tech; Comp.

CHUNG, JASON C; Irvine HS; Irvine, CA; (1); 2/580; Chess Clb; Math Tm; Acadmc Dcthln Team.

CHUNG, JENNIFER K; Abraham Lincoln HS; San Francisco, CA; (3); Art Clb; Church Yth Grp; Cmnty Wkr; FCA; Service Clb; Church Choir; Yrbk; Lincolns Acad Achvmnt; 1st Pl Sci Project; Day-Camp Cunslr; San Francisco ST U; Occptl Thr.

CHUNG, JI YOON; Prospect HS; Campbell, CA; (4); 1/185; VP Church Yth Grp; Cmnty Wkr; Key Clb; Math Clb; Science Clb; Spanish Clb; Church Choir; JV Var Tennis; Pres Acad Fit Awd; Stu Spc & Bio Rsrchr Prog NASA; 1st Clcls Dist Math Cntst; UC Berkeley; Engr.

CHUNG, JI-HEI JULIANNE; Schurr HS; Rowland Hts, CA; (4); 1/580; Key Clb; NFL; Treas Speech Tm; Bausch & Lomb Sci Awd; NHS; Opt Clb Awd; Pres Acad Fit Awd; Sal; Tandy Schlr Awd; CSF; Grad Spkr; MIT; Mech Engrng.

CHUNG, JOHN; Bishop Montgomery HS; Torrance, CA; (3); Art Clb; VP Church Yth Grp; Computer Clb; JA; Ski Clb; JV Capt Bsktbl; Hon Roll; Ntl Merit SF; Bsktbl Most Hustle & Coaches MVP; Bus.

CHUNG, JULIE; Marina HS; Huntington Bch, CA; (4); 24/484; Pres Church Yth Grp; Cmnty Wkr; JCL; Key Clb; Sec Latin Clb; Color Guard; Ed Nwsp; Lit Mag; Sec Frsh Cls; Off Jr Cls; Stud Mnth; Publshd Poet; Intl Rltns.

CHUNG, JUNE; John F Kennedy HS; La Palma, CA; (2); VP Church Yth Grp; Key Clb; Mrchg Band; Orch; Rptr Yrbk; High Hon Roll; Hon Roll; Pres Acad Fit Awd; CSF; Brown; Law.

CHUNG, KIM T; Oakland HS; Oakland, CA; (3); Library Aide; Spanish Clb; Teachers Aide; Cit Awd; Hon Roll; Keywanette Clb; Freshwind Clb; Invest-In-Amer Cert Of Merit; UC-BERKELEY; Comp Sci.

CHUNG, KRISTEN Y; Irvine HS; Irvine, CA; (2); Church Yth Grp; Cit Awd; Jr Vol W Med Ctr; CSF; UCLA; Med.

CHUNG, KYUNG W; Arcadia HS; Arcadia, CA; (2); 39/605; Art Clb; Church Yth Grp; Debate Tm; Library Aide; Chorus; Church Choir; Orch; Hon Roll; NHS; Pres Acad Fit Awd; Korean-Amer Assoc Awd 1st Pl Spch; Hnr Grl Awd; Phys Ftns Awd; UCLA; Law.

CHUNG, LIKSEE; Aragon HS; San Mateo, CA; (2); Church Yth Grp; Hon Roll.

CHUNG, LINH M; Los Angeles HS; Los Angeles, CA; (4); Office Aide; Teachers Aide; Swmmng; Vllybl; Wt Lftg; Hon Roll; Chnese Clb; Schlstc Hnr; L A Trade Tech.

CHUNG, LISA E; Bonita Vista HS; Chula Vista, CA; (2); 1/600; Hosp Aide; Intnl Clb; Cit Awd; Hon Roll; UCSD; Med.

CHUNG, LOAN; Carlsbad HS; Vista, CA; (2); 28/462; Key Clb; Crs Cntry; Pres Acad Fit Awd; CSF.

CHUNG, MELISSA; Trabuco Hills HS; Rancho Santa Ma, CA; (4); Key Clb; Spanish Clb; Mgr Nwsp; JV Tennis; Hon Roll; NHS; CSF; UCI; Law Accntnt.

CHUNG, MIA; Torrey Pines HS; Rancho Santa Fe, CA; (4); 4/448; Debate Tm; Intnl Clb; NFL; Speech Tm; Ed Nwsp; Ed Lit Mag; Var Fld Hcky; JV Swmmng; High Hon Roll; Ntl Merit SF; Acad Tm-N County Acad Lg; Smith Bk Awd 89; Outstndng Span Stu 88.

CHUNG, NGHIA; International Studies Acad; San Francisco, CA; (3); Dance Clb; Teachers Aide; Stage Crew; Variety Show; High Hon Roll; Hon Roll; San Francisco ST U; Comp Sci.

CHUNG, ROWENA; Chinese Christian Schls; Oakland, CA; (4); Chrmn Church Yth Grp; Church Choir; Drm Mjr(t); Mrchg Band; Intrml Vllybl; High Hon Roll; Hon Roll; Annl Sci Exhbtn 1st Pl, 2nd Pl; Guild Natl Piano Audtns Local Wnnr, St Wnnr; Spch Cntst 2nd Pl; Mktg.

CHUNG, SE CHAN; Don Antonio Lugo HS; Chino, CA; (4); 1/510; Church Yth Grp; Spanish Clb; Bsktbl; Var Tennis; High Hon Roll; NHS; Prfct Atten Awd; Sal; Korean Schl; UCLA; Ecnmcs.

CHUNG, SEHEE; Don Antonio Lugo HS; Chino, CA; (2); Church Yth Grp; Church Choir; Var Tennis; Hon Roll; Pres Acad Fit Awd; Gldn Conquest Awd; Vrstn Tnns; Hnr Stu Awd; UCLA; Bus Mgmt.

CHUNG, SEONYEE S; Granada Hills HS; Arleta, CA; (2); Church Yth Grp; Debate Tm; SADD; JV Bsktbl; Jr Statesmn Amer; UCLA; Med.

CHUNG, SEUNG WON; Faith Baptist HS; Woodland Hills, CA; (2); Church Yth Grp; Cmnty Wkr; Debate Tm; Hosp Aide; Speech Tm; Band; Chorus; Church Choir; Color Guard; Mrchg Band; PLASTIC Surgery.

CHUNG, SEUNG WOO; Sunset HS; Hayward, CA; (2); #280 In Class; Comp Sci.

CHUNG, SIN HO; Gahr HS; Norwalk, CA; (3); Var High Hon Roll; Var Hon Roll; Var Prfct Atten Awd; Blue Awd Chem; UCLA; Engrng.

CHUNG, SUSANA C; Oakland HS; Oakland, CA; (2); French Clb; Spanish Clb; Badminton; UC Berkeley; Engr.

CHUNG, SUSIE; Chinese Christian Schls; Oakland, CA; (4); 4/9; Church Yth Grp; Pres GAA; Hosp Aide; Speech Tm; Church Choir; Mrchg Band; Intrml Sftbl; Intrml Vllybl; Hon Roll; Pres Acad Fit Awd; Amer Coll Of Musicians; Amateur Athl Union Of US; UC Berkeley; Law.

CHUNG, THANH M; W C Overfelt HS; San Jose, CA; (4); Vietnamese Clb; San Jose ST U; Bio.

CHUNG, TINA H; John A Rowland HS; Walnut, CA; (2); Science Clb; Drill Tm; High Hon Roll; Hon Roll; Intrct Clb; CA Schlrshp Fed; UC Berkeley; Tchng.

CHUNG, UYN JOO; Cypress HS; Stanton, CA; (2); Sec Church Yth Grp; Intnl Clb; Key Clb; Cheerldng; Piano/Violin; UCLA; Lang.

CHUNG, VAN T; Los Angeles HS; Los Angeles, CA; (4); Tennis; Vllybl; Wt Lftg; Hon Roll; Chinese Clb; Achve CA Schlrshp Fdrtn; Los Angeles Trade-Tech.

CHUNG, WILLIAM; Abraham Lincoln HS; San Francisco, CA; (3); Church Yth Grp; VP Cmnty Wkr; Key Clb; Science Clb; Hon Roll; Prfct Atten Awd; Yth Ed Prgm Drug Ed; CA Schlrshp Fed; UC Davis.

CHUNG, YUEN; Sierra Vista HS; Baldwin Park, CA; (2); Debate Tm; Pres French Clb; Math Clb; Science Clb; Treas Speech Tm; Rep Stu Cncl; JV Tennis; High Hon Roll; Opt Clb Awd; Awd Of Excllnc Rgnl Sci Olympiad Trnmnt; CA Polytechnic U Pomona Access To Hghr Ed Achvt Awd.

CHUNN, CASSANDRA D; Trona HS; Trona, CA; (2); Debate Tm; Speech Tm; Jazz Band; Pep Band; JV Bsktbl; JV Vllybl; Hon Roll; Voice Dem Awd; Kndrgrtn Teacher.

CHUONG, MAI; Hiram Johnson West Campus HS; Sacramento, CA; (2); 34/182; ROTC; NHS; Schlstic Excellnce Awd; Leadershp Medallion; Volunteer Teachers Aide Summer Schl; Berkeley; Archaeology.

CHURCH, ANNE; Sherman E Burroughs HS; Ridgecrest, CA; (4); 8/300; Math Clb; Band; Drm Mjr(t); Jazz Band; Mrchg Band; Orch; School Musical; Rep Stu Cncl; High Hon Roll; Ntl Merit Ltr; Bk Of Amer Fine Arts Plaque Wnnr; Mentor Stu Naval Weapons Ctr; UC Santa Cruz.

CHURCH, BRENNON A; Mira Mesa HS; San Diego, CA; (2); Aud/Vis; Letterman Clb; Pep Clb; Band; Jazz Band; Mrchg Band; Orch; Pep Band; Cit Awd; Video Update; Worchester Poly Tech; Med.

CHURCH, JENNY; Westwood HS; Westwood, CA; (4); 1/25; Spanish Clb; Sec Band; Sec Frsh Cls; Sec Soph Cls; Sec Treas Stu Cncl; Var Capt Bsktbl; Var L Trk; Var Capt Vllybl; Elks Awd; Ntl Merit Ltr.

CHURCH, MICHELLE L; Jurupa Valley HS; Pedley, CA; (2); 1/550; Pres Spanish Clb; JV L Bsktbl; Capt L Sftbl; High Hon Roll; Invlvd W/CSF; UCLA; Tchr/Sftbl Coach.

CHURCH, TIERNIE E; West HS; Bakersfield, CA; (4); Church Yth Grp; Library Aide; Science Clb; Ski Clb; Color Guard; Socr; Hon Roll; Jr NHS; NHS; Pres Acad Fit Awd; Westmont Coll; Bus.

CHURCHLAND, ANNE KATHRYN; Torrey Pines HS; Solana Beach, CA; (2); Drama Clb; Letterman Clb; Red Cross Aide; Thesps; School Musical; School Play; Stage Crew; Variety Show; Hon Roll; Philsphy.

CHURCHMAN, TRISA L; Roseville HS; Rocklin, CA; (3); 104/411; Pres Church Yth Grp; German Clb; Key Clb; Science Clb; Stu Cncl; Tennis; Hon Roll; Golden State Exam; Received High Honors; Principals Advisory Comm; School Dance Prdctn In City Theater; U ST U; Elementary Education.

CHURCHWELL, GARY; Bethel Christian HS; Lancaster, CA; (2); 1/32; Drama Clb; Chorus; Var JV Ftbl; Cit Awd; High Hon Roll; UC Riverside; Med.

CHURCHWELL JR, GARY; Bethel Christian HS; Lancaster, CA; (2); 1/28; Var Bsbl; Var Ftbl; Cit Awd; High Hon Roll; UC Riverside; Med.

CHURCHWELL, KEVIN; Bethel Christian HS; Lancaster, CA; (1); 3/30; Church Yth Grp; Var Bsktbl; JV Ftbl; Trk; Hon Roll; USC; Astrnmy.

CHURMA, LORRIE L; Washington HS; Fremont, CA; (2) Church Yth Grp; Cmnty Wkr; Pep Clb; Var Socr; JV Sftbl; JV Vllybl; Hon Roll; Lttrd Vrsty In Soccr; Elem Ed.

CHWEE, LILA L; Lowell HS; San Francisco, CA; (3); Intnl Clb; SADD; Teachers Aide; Chorus; Amnesty Intl; U Of CA Santa Barbara; Advrtsg.

CHWEH, CRYSTAL; Los Alamitos HS; Seal Beach, CA; (3); Church Yth Grp; NFL; Speech Tm; Church Choir; Hon Roll; Ecology Club; Gldn St Exams-Geom Hnrs; CSF.

CHXINN, ALLISON H; Arcata HS; Arcata, CA; (4); 1/165; AFS; Drama Clb; French Clb; Acpl Chr; Band; Chorus; Jazz Band; Mrchg Band; Orch; School Musical; Art-Wtrclr, Drwng, Sclptng, Shasta Concerto Cont Wnr; Cmnty Musical Theater; Nor Cal Hnr Band; Reed Coll; Liberal.

CHYN, DING-LY; Abraham Lincoln HS; San Francisco, CA; (4); 5/420; High Hon Roll; Hon Roll; Math Dept Outtndng Achvt Awd; Gldn St Alg Exm Hgh Hnr, Geomtry Exm Hnr; Engr Wk Outstndng Stu Awd; UC Berkeley; Engr.

CHYUN, GRACE S; Irvine HS; Irvine, CA; (2); Flag Corp; Orch.

CIABATTARI, TERESA; St Vincent HS; Petaluma, CA; (3); 2/63; Cmnty Wkr; Pres French Clb; Girl Scts; NFL; Speech Tm; School Play; Yrbk; Sec Treas Soph Cls; Rep Stu Cncl; Stat Bsktbl; Friday Night Live Pres; Chld Psych.

CIANCIULLI, LUCIANNA M; Notre Dame HS; Riverside, CA; (1); 4/189; SADD; High Hon Roll; Stu Cncl Treas 90-91; Religious Ed; UCLA; Psych.

CIARAMITARO, SYLVIA L; La Habra HS; La Habra, CA; (4); 22/344; Chorus; Hon Roll; Prfct Atten Awd; Top 100 Stu; Mrt Of Outstnd Achvt In Engl, Hlth, & AP US Hist; The US Intl U; Intl Rltns.

CICALO, ERIN J; University Of San Diego HS; San Diego, CA; (2); Cmnty Wkr; SADD; Swmmng; JV Var Tennis; Coordntd Recycl Pgm; Sanctn Lvl Tnns Plyr-Trvlng Tm; U Of CA Davis; Envrnmntl Law.

CICCANTI, MIA; Redlands HS; Redlands, CA; (2); Church Yth Grp; Cmnty Wkr; Ski Clb; Chorus; Orch; VP Frsh Cls; JV Vllybl; Cit Awd; Hon Roll; March Of Dimes, Walk Amer; Evangelist Healing Team; Speak In Front Of Groups Of People; Pepperdine U; Bus.

CICCARELLI, JOE; Christian Brothers HS; Sacramento, CA; (2); French Clb; Tennis; High Hon Roll; CSF; Cal Poly; Arch.

CIELO, ALMA L; Turlock HS; Turlock, CA; (3); 9/550; Pres AFS; Key Clb; Letterman Clb; Pres Treas Orch; Var L Crs Cntry; JV Swmmng; JV Trk; CSF Secy; Stanislaus Symphny; Camp Royal For Girls; U CA Berkeley; Bio.

CIERLEY, BRYAN L; La Habra HS; La Habra, CA; (3); 17/331; Am Leg Boys St; Pep Clb; Chrmn Jr Cls; Var Ftbl; Var Socr; Hon Roll; NHS; Top 100 Wnnr; CA Schlrshp Assoc; U CA Irvine.

CIESLIKOWSKI, JULIE; Palm Desert HS; Rancho Mirage, CA; (3); Key Clb; Hon Roll; CA Schlrshp Fdrtn; Acad Ltr; Lawyer.

CIGLIANO, STEPHANIE; Mary Star Of The Sea HS; San Pedro, CA; (4); 1/45; Cmnty Wkr; GAA; VP Math Clb; Capt Pep Clb; Teachers Aide; Capt Flag Corp; Ed Yrbk; Hon Roll; NHS; CA ST U Dominguez Hills.

CILMI, KRISTINA; Redlands HS; Redlands, CA; (2); 3/992; Church Yth Grp; JV Co-Capt Cheerldng; Cit Awd; High Hon Roll; 3 Dept Awds Frgn Lang, Engl & PE; Chrldng Advsrs Awd; Jrnlsm.

CIMA, BROCK C; San Pasqual HS; Escondido, CA; (2); Church Yth Grp; JV Bsktbl; JV Golf; Prfct Atten Awd; Communications Sports Broadcst.

CIMINO, MICHAEL A; Mayfair HS; Lakewood, CA; (1); Band; Mrchg Band; Pep Band; Aerospace Engrng.

CINCOTTA, CHRISTOPHER J; Hesperia HS; Hesperia, CA; (2); Cmnty Wkr; ROTC; SADD; Color Guard; JV Intrml Bsktbl; Hon Roll; Top Gun Awd Smstr ROTC; Cadet Mnth Awd; Air Force.

CINENSE, SICILY A; Sherman E Burroughs HS; Ridgecrest, CA; (3); Pep Clb; Spanish Clb; SADD; Teachers Aide; Phtg Yrbk; Lit Mag; Trk; Hon Roll; U Of Santa Barbara; Psych.

CIRCO, DOMINIC; Skyline HS; Oakland, CA; (2); L Lcrss; Hon Roll; Vrsty Ltr Lacrosse; Vrsty Skiing; Hnr Roll; U Of CA San Diego.

CIRIDON, JENNIFER W; Bishop Armat Memorial HS; West Covina, CA; (3); Cmnty Wkr; Drama Clb; Teachers Aide; Variety Show; Trk; High Hon Roll; NHS; CSF; U C Irvine; Med.

CIRIDON, JESSICA W; Bishop Amat Memorial HS; West Covina, CA; (1); Drama Clb; Variety Show; Trk; Hon Roll; Prfct Atten Awd; Pres Acad Fit Awd; Cmnty Wkr; USC; Bus.

CISLER, GEOFF; Mission San Jose HS; Fremont, CA; (1); Boy Scts; Math Tm; JV Trk; High Hon Roll; Algebra Golden St Exam High Hnrs; Math.

CISNEROS, ARTEMIO; Atwater HS; Atwater, CA; (3); Socr; Hon Roll; Merced Coll; Automobile Mech.

CISNEROS, BLAS A; Delano HS; Delano, CA; (3); Teachers Aide; Cit Awd; Hon Roll; Prfct Atten Awd; Law.

CISNEROS, CESAR A; Corcoran HS; Corcoran, CA; (3); Cmnty Wkr; Letterman Clb; Math Clb; Varsity Clb; Bsbl; Bsktbl; Crs Cntry; Ftbl; Socr; Trk; UC System; Bus Mgt.

CISNEROS, CLARISSA C; Central Union HS; El Centro, CA; (3); 75/687; Drama Clb; Office Aide; Teachers Aide; School Play; Rptr Phtg Yrbk; VP Jr Cls; JV Var Cheerldng; JV Var Pom Pon; JV Var Tennis; Hon Roll; Modeling, Traveling; Acctng.

CISNEROS, DAVID H; St Paul HS; Norwalk, CA; (3); 32/285; JV Bsbl; Wt Lftg; Hon Roll; NHS; March For Hunger; Justice Bakery; Bus Mrktng.

CISNEROS, IRMA M; Point Loma HS; San Diego, CA; (3); 80/431; French Clb; German Clb; Intnl Clb; Cit Awd; French Hon Soc; Prfct Atten Awd; Ldrshp Grp 89-90; Frgn Affairs.

CISNEROS, LUPE; River City HS; W Sacramento, CA; (1); 3/30; Mrchg Band; Bsbl; Ftbl; Hon Roll; Law.

CISNEROS, STEPHANIE; Valencia HS; Yorba Linda, CA; (2); Pres Soph Cls; Rep Stu Cncl; JV Cheerldng; JV Pom Pon; High Hon Roll; Pres Acad Fit Awd; CA Schlrshp Fed; Distinguished Schlr; USC; Psych.

CISNEROS, TORY C; St Francis HS; Alhambra, CA; (2); Chess Clb; Church Yth Grp; Ski Clb; L Ftbl; L Trk; Wt Lftg; Hon Roll; CSF; UCLA; Bus Admin.

CISNEROZ, AMY; Napa HS; Tulsa, OK; (4); Office Aide; Teachers Aide; Varsity Clb; Bsktbl; Powder Puff Ftbl; Hon Roll; NSU; TV Brdcstng.

CIVITELLO, JADE; Cardinal Newman HS; Santa Rosa, CA; (1); Cmnty Wkr; Rptr Nwsp; Intrml Bsbl; Intrml Bsktbl; High Hon Roll; Pres Schlr; John Hopkins; Bsbll.

CLAASSEN, F KEVIN; Sanger HS; Sanger, CA; (2); Church Yth Grp; FCA; Science Clb; Ski Clb; Var Golf; JV Socr; Hon Roll; Goshen Coll; Sci.

CLAASSEN, RYAN L; Sanger HS; Sanger, CA; (4); 1/350; Golf; High Hon Roll; Pres Acad Fit Awd; Val; CSF; Goshen Coll; Bio.

CLABAUGH, JENNIFER E; El Toro HS; El Toro, CA; (1); JV Socr; JV Sftbl; JV Capt Vllybl; Hon Roll; Excllnc Awds-Earth Sci.

CLABAUGH, SHELLEY S; Pomona HS; Pomona, CA; (3); Church Yth Grp; Girl Scts; Teachers Aide; Band; Church Choir; Mrchg Band; Cit Awd; Hon Roll; Word Processor Secy.

CLACK, CRISTIN M; Carmel HS; Carmel, CA; (2); Church Yth Grp; Pres Frsh Cls; Pres Soph Cls; Fld Hcky; Capt Swmmng; High Hon Roll; NHS; Prfct Atten Awd; Top 100 GPA Awd 2 Yrs; HOBY Fdtn Smnr Sthrn CA; Military Ordr Of Wrld Wars Ldrshp Conf; Med.

CLAIR, HEATHER; Barstow HS; Barstow, CA; (1); AFS; Church Yth Grp; Science Clb; Band; Drill Tm; Yrbk; Cheerldng; JV Mgr(s); JV Stat Sftbl; High Hon Roll; Image Modeling Face Finders Studio 89; Models For Amer Short Story; Air Force Acad; Engrng.

CLAIR, JASON A; Tustin HS; Tustin, CA; (2); Boy Scts; Church Yth Grp; Drama Clb; FCA; School Play; Stage Crew; Ftbl; Wt Lftg; Wrstlng; Hon Roll; SADD; CA ST Fullerton; Perfrmng Art.

CLAMPITT, RYAN M; La Quinta HS; Fountain Valley, CA; (1); Boy Scts; Computer Clb; Debate Tm; Drama Clb; ROTC; Ski Clb; Band; Jazz Band; Nwsp; Yrbk; Air Force; Bus.

CLANCI, VINCE J; Casa Roble HS; Citrus Heights, CA; (2); 4/465; Church Yth Grp; Letterman Clb; Spanish Clb; JV Ftbl; Var L Wrstlng; High Hon Roll; NHS; Conflict Mgmt; UC Davis; Med.

CLANCY, JENNIFER E; Antelope Valley HS; Lancaster, CA; (2); Church Yth Grp; Hosp Aide; Service Clb; Cit Awd; Hon Roll; Law.

CLANIN, KEVIN J; Liberty Union HS; Oakley, CA; (1); SADD; Stage Crew; Phtg Yrbk; Var Tennis; Hon Roll; Friday Night Live.

CLANOR, BELINDA; Mira Mesa HS; San Diego, CA; (2); Church Yth Grp; Spanish Clb; Drill Tm; Nwsp; Var Trk; Hon Roll; Golden St Exam Schl Recognition; Engrng.

CLANTON, RYAN D; Monclair HS; Cucamonga, CA; (3); Bsbl; Capt L Ftbl; L Trk; Wt Lftg; Hon Roll; Prfct Atten Awd; Pres Acad Fit Awd; FL ST; Ftbll Coach.

CLAPA, EMANUEL; John Glenn HS; Norwalk, CA; (4); Art Clb; Church Choir; Var Socr; Hon Roll; Cerritos Coll; Bio.

CLAPHAM, BRETT M; Junipero Serra HS; San Diego, CA; (3); VP Science Clb; Varsity Clb; Var L Swmmng; Pres Acad Fit Awd; UC Santa Cruz; Envrnmntl Plng.

CLAPP, DAVID G; Los Gatos HS; Los Gatos, CA; (3); Boy Scts; Varsity Clb; Ftbl; Socr; Tennis; Trk; Wt Lftg; Lion Awd; Cal Poly; Engnrng.

CLAPP, SANDRA D; Oakdale Joint Union HS; Waterford, CA; (1); Spanish Clb; JCL; AFS; High Hon Roll; USAF Acad; Marine Bio.

CLAPSADL, CHERYL A; Coronado HS; Coronado, CA; (4); VP Art Clb; VP Drama Clb; Sec Service Clb; SADD; Teachers Aide; Varsity Clb; School Musical; Rep Frsh Cls; Var Socr; Sftbl; Northern AZ U; Psych.

CLARDY, MELISSA L; Etiwanda HS; Alta Loma, CA; (2); JA; JV Bsktbl; JV Swmmng; High Hon Roll; CSF; U Of CA; Bio.

CLARIN, EDSEL A; Don Bosco Technical Inst; West Covina, CA; (4); 19/49; Yrbk; Stat Trk; High Hon Roll; NHS; Ntl Merit Ltr; Awd For Excel, Theology 2nd Pl; Campus Ministry Grp; Cal Poly Pomna; Comp Tech.

CLARK, ALISON D; Etiwanda HS; Cucamonga, CA; (2); Drama Clb; FHA; SADD; Color Guard; High Hon Roll; Arts.

CLARK, AMY; Lodi HS; Acampo, CA; (1); Intrml Cheerldng; High Hon Roll; Santa Barbara ST Coll; Law.

CLARK, AMY J; Tracy Joint Union HS; Tracy, CA; (2); 1/500; Church Yth Grp; Teachers Aide; Church Choir; Variety Show; JV Crs Cntry; High Hon Roll; Hon Roll; CSF; Pres Chrch Yth Grp; Jr Miss Contestant; GSE Hnrs Alg; Brigham Young U; Ed.

CLARK, ANDREA C; Hillsdale HS; San Mateo, CA; (3); Church Yth Grp; 4-H; Office Aide; Service Clb; Varsity Clb; Var Vllybl; High Hon Roll; Math Awd Trig & Math Analysis; Svc Commission Squad Ldr; CO U Boulder; Bus Admin.

CLARK, ANDREW N; Saratoga HS; Saratoga, CA; (3); 26/234; Debate Tm; NFL; Speech Tm; Chorus; Var L Crs Cntry; Var L Trk; JV Wrstlng; Hon Roll; Pres Acad Fit Awd; 90 MIT Ldrshp Awd; Writers Clb; U S Military Acad West Point.

CLARK, BECKY; Ribet Acad; Rosemead, CA; (4); 1/27; Church Yth Grp; Pres Spanish Clb; Teachers Aide; Pres Soph Cls; Rep Sr Cls; Rep Stu Cncl; Capt Var Bsktbl; Var Sftbl; Var Vllybl; High Hon Roll; Accrdttn Cmmtte; Rookie Yr,Mst Imprvd Bsebl,Sftbl,Vllyl; Spnsh,Math,Engl,Sci,PE Awds Mst Outstnd Stu; U Of La Verne;Engrng.

CLARK, BRADLEY C; Hemet HS; Hemet, CA; (2); 27/520; Church Yth Grp; Var Bsbl; Bsktbl; Var Ftbl; Wt Lftg; Sunday Schl Teacher.

CLARK, CHRIS; St Marys College HS; El Cerrito, CA; (2); 3/30; Church Yth Grp; JV Ftbl; JV Trk; High Hon Roll; CSF; Sports Med.

CLARK, CHRISTEN G; Village Christian HS; La Crescenta, CA; (3); Stat Trk; Art; Skiing; Pasadena City Coll; Art.

CLARK, CHRISTOPHER A; Arroyo Grande HS; Arroyo Grande, CA; (3); Boy Scts; Church Yth Grp; Key Clb; Teachers Aide; Phtg Nwsp; Ed Yrbk; VP Jr Cls; Mgr(s); JV Tennis; Hon Roll; UNLV; Bus.

CLARK, DARIN H; Bonita Vista HS; Bonita, CA; (2); Model UN; Acpl Chr; Chorus; Treas Jr Cls; JV Var Ftbl; Var Capt Socr; JV Vllybl; Prfct Atten Awd; Music Machine 2 Yrs.

CLARK, DAVID A; Bakersfield HS; Bakersfield, CA; (3); 62/718; Debate Tm; JA; Key Clb; NFL; Science Clb; Speech Tm; JV Crs Cntry; JV Trk; Hon Roll; Opt Clb Awd; Congressional Yth Ldrshp Cncl; Sccr; Poet; Mech Engrng.

CLARK, DONALD A; Fremont HS; Sunnyvale, CA; (3); Aud/Vis; Boy Scts; Computer Clb; JCL; Latin Clb; Teachers Aide; School Play; Rep Frsh Cls; Rep Soph Cls; JV Sftbl; Assembly Cmmtte Pres; Sci-Fi Club.

CLARK, ELIZABETH; Monte Vista HS; Walnut Creek, CA; (1); Girl Scts; Chorus; Yrbk; Var Swmmng; Friday Nght Live; Pblshd Poems; Won Awd-Bst Lit Stu; Mc Gill U Canada; Phys Thrpy.

CLARK, ELIZABETH A; Sanger HS; Sanger, CA; (2); 1/375; Sec Model UN; Off ROTC; Science Clb; Color Guard; Cit Awd; High Hon Roll; Masonic Awd; NEDT Awd; CSF; US Naval Acad; Lawyer.

CLARK, HALLIE K; Apple Valley HS; Apple Valley, CA; (3); 60/300; Key Clb; Chorus; Swing Chorus; Var Crs Cntry; High Hon Roll; Hon Roll; Piano; Church Vlntr; Bio Sci.

CLARK, JARED; Vacaville HS; Vacaville, CA; (2); Hon Roll.

CLARK, JASON; El Toro HS; El Toro, CA; (2); Chess Clb; Hosp Aide; Intnl Clb; Scholastic Bowl; Socr; Vllybl; High Hon Roll; Hon Roll; Prfct Atten Awd; Pres Acad Fit Awd; Grand Prz Sci Fair Awd; Ucla; Med.

CLARK, JENNIFER; The Bishops Schl; Del Mar, CA; (3); Rep AFS; Cmnty Wkr; Model UN; Spanish Clb; Varsity Clb; Sec Treas Jr Cls; Var Socr; Var Capt Tennis; Coach Indr Soccer At Boys/Grls Clb; Soccer 2nd Tm CIF Goalkeeper; Rice; Intl Bus.

CLARK, JENNIFER G; Westridge School For Girls; San Marino, CA; (4); Model UN; Chorus; Ed Nwsp; Lit Mag; Nuclear Awarenss Grp; Jrnlst Pasadena Star News; Ntl Cncl Tchrs Engl Achvt Awd; Jrnlsm.

CLARK, JENNIFER L; Royal HS; Simi Valley, CA; (3); Prfct Atten Awd; Otis Parson; Fshn Dsgn.

CLARK, JENNIFER M; Ramona HS; Riverside, CA; (3); 40/420; Dance Clb; Letterman Clb; Pep Clb; Varsity Clb; Flag Corp; Variety Show; L Var Cheerldng; L Var Swmmng; Hon Roll; Gymstcs; Public Spkng; Psych.

CLARK, JEREMY J; Sonora HS; Sonora, CA; (4); 116/390; Debate Tm; Letterman Clb; Ski Clb; Varsity Clb; Var Bsbl; Var Capt Ftbl; Wt Lftg; Fresno ST U; Law.

CLARK, JESSE A; Fresno Adventist Acad; Fresno, CA; (2); 3/30; Church Yth Grp; FCA; Teachers Aide; Band; Chorus; VP Frsh Cls; Pres Stu Cncl; Var Intrml Bsktbl; Var Capt Ftbl; Hon Roll; Walla Walla Coll; Brdcst.

CLARK, JESSICA L; Seoul American HS; APO San Fran, CA; (3); Church Yth Grp; Quiz Bowl; Science Clb; SADD; Band; Mrchg Band; Rptr Nwsp; Hon Roll; NHS; All-Amer Schlr, Geomtry & Intl Frgn Lng Awd Grmn USAA; Harding U; Hstry.

CLARK, JOANNE; Highland HS; Bakersfield, CA; (4); FBLA; Library Aide; Office Aide; SADD; Teachers Aide; Band; Orch; Trk; Bus Ed, Comp, Law, Legal Courses; Career CC; Shorthand Rptr.

CLARK, JOSHUA; Casa Roble HS; Citrus Heights, CA; (3); 16/317; Computer Clb; Spanish Clb; Ed Nwsp; Cit Awd; Pres Acad Fit Awd; Claremont-Mc Kenna Coll; Engrng.

CLARK, JUSTIN T; Rancho Alamitos HS; Garden Grove, CA; (1); Church Yth Grp; Band; Jazz Band; Mrchg Band; Rep Stu Cncl; Bsktbl; Trk; Vllybl; Hon Roll; Long Beach ST; Bus.

CLARK, KAREN; Boron HS; Boron, CA; (4); 1/36; Church Yth Grp; Math Tm; VP Sr Cls; Var Cheerldng; DAR Awd; Hon Roll; NHS; Pres Acad Fit Awd; Val; Treas Frsh Cls; CSF; Ricks Coll; Dntl Hygn.

CLARK, KATHLEEN E; San Gorgonio HS; Highland, CA; (3); German Clb; Pep Clb; Adv Curr Expl Soc, ACES; Amer Mensa LTD; Envrnmntl Act, Green Soc; Engl.

CLARK, KIM; Highland HS; Bakersfield, CA; (3); Pres FHA; Teachers Aide; Hon Roll; Innr Clb Cncl; Athltc Trnr; Bakersfield JC; Kndrgrtn Tchr.

CLARK, KIRSTEN; Cope JR HS; Redlands, CA; (1); Pep Clb; Ski Clb; Nwsp; Cheerldng; Pom Pon; Hon Roll; Opt Clb Awd; Prfct Atten Awd; Pres Acad Fit Awd; Bst Chrldng Sqd; Ldrshp; Eagle Ldr; UC Davis; Vet.

CLARK, KRISTI L; Hiram Johnson HS; Sacramento, CA; (4); 6/86; Cmnty Wkr; Band; School Musical; Hon Roll; Culture Clb; Stu Store Mgr; Sacramento City JC; Advrtsng.

CLARK, LATRICE YUETTE; George Washington Prep; Los Angeles, CA; (2); Drill Tm; Tennis; Cit Awd; Hon Roll; Bus.

CLARK, LISA; Levzinger HS; Lawndale, CA; (2); Pres Frsh Cls; Stu Cncl; JV Socr; JV Sftbl; Hon Roll; CSF; UCLA; Med.

CLARK, LUCILLE R; Mater Dei HS; Orange, CA; (3); Church Yth Grp; Cmnty Wkr; French Clb; Pep Clb; Variety Show; JV Var Cheerldng; Gym; JV Trk; Stat Wrstlng; Hon Roll; Dnc Fr Pope LA Clsm; All Mater Dei Chrldrs; Dsnylnd Pep Sqd Pigskin Clssc; Ed.

CLARK, LUCY J; Rio Americano HS; Sacramento, CA; (3); Cmnty Wkr; French Clb; Intnl Clb; Model UN; Science Clb; Teachers Aide; Acpl Chr; Intl Rainbow, Wrthy Advsr; Envrnmntl Planning.

CLARK, LYNAE; Monte Vista HS; Spring Valley, CA; (2); 15/310; Church Yth Grp; Dance Clb; VP French Clb; Pep Clb; Rep Jr Cls; Stu Cncl; JV Cheerldng; JV Sftbl; Jr NHS; Pres Acad Fit Awd; Brdcst Jrnlsm.

CLARK, MARIN; Simi Valley HS; Simi Valley, CA; (3); 1/664; Speech Tm; SADD; Var Capt Cheerldng; Var Swmmng; High Hon Roll; NHS; Pres Acad Fit Awd; Rotary Awd; Golden St Achvt Alg & Geom; Oxford U.

CLARK, MARK A; Antioch SR HS; Antioch, CA; (2); Ski Clb; Teachers Aide; JV Crs Cntry; JV Trk; Comp Sci.

CLARK, MARYANN; Vanden HS; Vacaville, CA; (4); 5/140; Church Yth Grp; Speech Tm; Teachers Aide; Drill Tm; Rptr Nwsp; Var L Crs Cntry; Var Sftbl; Var Capt Trk; High Hon Roll; Pres Acad Fit Awd; U Of Miami.

CLARK, MATTHEW C; Ramona HS; Ramona, CA; (3); 148/300; Art Clb; Church Yth Grp; Acpl Chr; Chorus; Church Choir; Swing Chorus; Hon Roll; Music Educ.

CLARK, MICHELLE D; Los Amigos HS; Santa Ana, CA; (3); 39/294; Chorus; Flag Corp; Mrchg Band; Tennis; Hon Roll; Jr NHS; Lion Awd; Ntl Merit Ltr; Keywntts PR Dir; OCAD Slvr Mdl Lit.

CLARK, MICHELLE E; California HS; San Ramon, CA; (3); 70/380; Church Yth Grp; Letterman Clb; Teachers Aide; JV Crs Cntry; Var L Trk; High Hon Roll; Outstndng Bio Stu; Sci Stu Of Mnth; Vlntr Wrk Chldrns Hm Society; Diablo Valley CC; Chld Dvlpmnt.

CLARK, MISTI F; Arvin HS; Lamont, CA; (2); Church Yth Grp; GAA; Letterman Clb; Ski Clb; SADD; Teachers Aide; Varsity Clb; Off Jr Cls; Var Capt Sftbl; Var Vllybl; UC Santa Barbara; Criminal Law.

CLARK, NATALIE A; Salinas HS; Salinas, CA; (2); Art Clb; Cmnty Wkr; Drama Clb; Spanish Clb; Hon Roll; VP Stu For Better Earth; Art Hstry.

CLARK, NICOLE C; Del Oro HS; Loomis, CA; (3); 6/266; Hon Roll; CA Schlrshp Fdr; Cum Laude Frgn Lang Awd German; Golden ST Exam Geo.

CLARK, REBECCA; Ribet Acad; Rosemead, CA; (4); 1/29; Church Yth Grp; Math Clb; Nwsp; Pres Soph Cls; Rep Sr Cls; Rep Stu Cncl; Var Capt Bsktbl; Var Sftbl; Var Vllybl; High Hon Roll; Accrdtn Cmmttee-Rep; U Of La Verne; Comp Sci.

CLARK, RICHARD C; Ventura HS; Ventura, CA; (3); Chess Clb; Church Yth Grp; Letterman Clb; Varsity Clb; JV Bsbl; JV Bsktbl; JV Var Ftbl; Intrml Wt Lftg; Sports Wrtr.

CLARK, ROBERT; El Cameno Real HS; Chatsworth, CA; (4); Chess Clb; German Clb; JA; Scholastic Bowl; Orch; Lit Mag; JETS Awd; Pres Renaisance Clb; CA ST U San Jose; Aero Engnr.

CLARK, ROGER A; Redwood Christian HS; Castro Valley, CA; (2); Aud/Vis; Church Yth Grp; Spanish Clb; Speech Tm; Chorus; Church Choir; School Play; Stage Crew; Prfct Atten Awd; Lead Tenor Choir; Sang Solos HS & Chrch Choirs; Azusa Pacific U; Music.

CLARK, RONA M; St Bernard HS; Los Angeles, CA; (3); GAA; Thesps; Chorus; School Musical; Var Trk; U La Verne; Psych.

CLARK, RUBY; Mt Eden HS; Hayward, CA; (3); 19/279; Computer Clb; Cheerldng; Hon Roll; CSF; U Of CA Santa Barbara; Psych.

CLARK, RUTH; Woodcrest Christian HS; Highland, CA; (2); Church Yth Grp; FCA; GAA; Teachers Aide; JV Bsktbl; Var Score Keeper; JV Vllybl; Cit Awd; Hon Roll; NHS; San Diego ST U; Travel Agnt.

CLARK, SHANNON L; Casa Robles HS; Orangevale, CA; (2); Hon Roll; JC; Social Work.

CLARK, SHAUNA D; Tulare Union HS; Tulare, CA; (2); Model UN; ROTC; SADD; Bsktbl; Swmmng; Vllybl; Wt Lftg; UCLA; Lawyer.

CLARK, SHAWN K; Mesa Verde HS; Citrus Heights, CA; (2); 23/193; Boy Scts; Church Yth Grp; Band; Pep Band; Bsktbl; Crs Cntry; Trk; Hon Roll; Prfct Atten Awd; Eagle Sct Order Of Arrow; BYU; Arch.

CLARK, SHELLEY A; El Toro HS; El Toro, CA; (3); Church Yth Grp; Chorus; Church Choir; Color Guard; Drill Tm; Flag Corp; Stage Crew; Variety Show; Hon Roll; Worshp Church Team & Cmmty Svc Church Nursery; Church Sound System; Azusa Pacific; Vocal.

CLARK, STACEY L; Ukiah HS; Redwood Valley, CA; (3); Ed Phtg Nwsp; Rep Stu Cncl; Stat Bsbl; Stat Ftbl; Hmcmng; Chico ST U; Comm.

CLARK, STACY; Foothill HS; Sacramento, CA; (3); Church Yth Grp; Science Clb; Church Choir; Capt Cheerldng; Capt Pom Pon; Powder Puff Ftbl; Hon Roll; CSF; Psych.

CLARK, STEPHANIE; Bloomington Christian Schl; Rialto, CA; (1); Rep Frsh Cls; Stu Cncl; JV Cheerldng; Mgr(s); Score Keeper; Var Vllybl; Hon Roll; Dbl A Stu; CA ST Fullerton; Bus Admin.

CLARK, SUZANNE E; Savanna HS; Buena Park, CA; (2); GAA; Intnl Clb; Service Clb; Chorus; Var Gym; Vllybl.

CLARK, TAMMY; Lincoln HS; Stockton, CA; (4); 149/500; Treas Church Yth Grp; Cmnty Wkr; English Clb; French Clb; Intnl Clb; Office Aide; Treas SADD; Church Choir; Stage Crew; Hon Roll; B-Z Stu; U Of CA; Engl.

CLARK, TARYN; Lowell HS; San Francisco, CA; (2); VP Sec Church Yth Grp; Cmnty Wkr; Church Choir; Variety Show; Yrbk; Stu Cncl; JV Cheerldng; VP Of Registry; Brdcstng.

CLARK, THERESA; Fellowship Schl; Ridgecrest, CA; (4); Church Yth Grp; Yrbk; Bsktbl; Score Keeper; Trk; Vllybl; Cit Awd; Hon Roll; ACE St Cnvntn.

CLARK, WENDY L; San Bernardino HS; San Bernardino, CA; (3); Church Yth Grp; Cmnty Wkr; Letterman Clb; Church Choir; Hon Roll; Area Chmbr Of Cmmr Awd-Cld Devlpmnt; CSF; Point Loma Nazrne Coll; Accntng.

CLARKE, ANGELA; La Canada HS; La Canada-Flint, CA; (3); 6/287; Church Yth Grp; Key Clb; Math Clb; Mu Alpha Theta; Office Aide; Teachers Aide; Chorus; Church Choir; High Hon Roll; NHS; Outstndng Musician Concert Choir; Rcvd Honors Algebra/Geom Golden St Exam; CSF; Brigham Young U; Elem Sch Teach.

CLARKE, JEFF S; Arroyo Grande HS; Nipomo, CA; (2); 123/600; Hon Roll; Cal Poly; Arch.

CLARKE, MARY B; Grossmont HS; El Cajon, CA; (3); 120/385; Cmnty Wkr; Office Aide; Pep Clb; Speech Tm; Teachers Aide; Varsity Clb; Rep Sr Cls; Rep Stu Cncl; Var Swmmng; Pres Acad Fit Awd; Swmmng For Priv Swim Team 6 Yrs Plcd 8 Ntl Jr Olympics; Elem Sch Teacher.

CLARKE, PAMELA S; Las Lomas HS; Walnut Creek, CA; (4); 50/250; Cmnty Wkr; Drama Clb; French Clb; Girl Scts; Intnl Clb; Teachers Aide; Stage Crew; Hon Roll; Poetry Pblshd Amer Poetry Assn Anthlgy 89; Lcl Peer Cnslng, Spprt Grps; Humboldt ST U; Psych.

CLARKE, RACHEL P; Eagle Rock HS; Los Angeles, CA; (3); Thesps; School Play; Swmmng; Wt Lftg; Intrstd Wrtng & Wrkng Smtms Pblshd; Trvld Thrgh China & S Amer; Humboltd U; Psychlgy.

CLARKE, RANJIT K; Bishop Montgomery HS; Gardena, CA; (4); JV Bsktbl; Var L Crs Cntry; Var L Trk; Hon Roll; Deans Hnr Roll 87-89; CSF Sealbearer 87-90; USC; Mechanical Engrng.

CLARKE, SHANNON; Rancho Buena Vista HS; Vista, CA; (3); Rep Church Yth Grp; Debate Tm; Ed Nwsp; Ed Lit Mag; JV Var Socr; Hon Roll; French Clb; Key Clb; Pep Clb; Spanish Clb; CSF; Amnesty Intl; Art Schl; Earth Day/Global Awareness Publicity Commtte Pres; Jrnlsm.

CLARKE, SONYA R; Aliso HS; Northridge, CA; (2); High Hon Roll; Hon Roll; CSUN.

CLARKE, TERRA; Arroyo HS; San Leandro, CA; (3); SADD; Variety Show; Lit Mag; L Var Sftbl; Cit Awd; High Hon Roll; Prfct Atten Awd; St Schlr; Golden St Exam Hnrs Math 88 & 89; North Coast Sctnl CSA 89 & 90; U CA Berkeley; Sports.

CLARKSON, JAY R; John F Kennedy HS; Sacramento, CA; (3); Spanish Clb; Speech Tm; Band; Color Guard; Mrchg Band; Orch; Pep Band; Stat Bsktbl; Var Crs Cntry; Var Vllybl; Russian/Intrptr.

CLARKSON, ROBIN L; Chaffey HS; Ontario, CA; (1); Church Yth Grp; Cmnty Wkr; Dance Clb; Hosp Aide; Key Clb; High Hon Roll; CSF; Pediatrics.

CLAROS, FLORENCE YAO; Fremont HS; Sunnyvale, CA; (2); 1/421; Debate Tm; NFL; Service Clb; Speech Tm; L Var Bsktbl; JV Sftbl; JV Tennis; Art Acad & Speech Red & White Awds 90; All Leag Hnrs Sftbl.

CLAROS, GERLIE O; Abraham Lincoln HS; San Francisco, CA; (3); Var Bsktbl; Var Sftbl; Var Vllybl; Hon Roll.

CLAROS, OSWALD; St John Bosco HS; Downey, CA; (2); Boy Scts; Ftbl; Trk; Vllybl; Wt Lftg; Wrstlng; Hon Roll; Outdoorsmn Clb; UC Santa Barbara; Medcl Doctr.

CLARY, JOLENE M; Calaveras HS; San Andreas, CA; (2); 45/360; FFA; Hon Roll; FFA Prjct Comptn Gold Awds Rgnl Lvl; U Of CA Davis; Vet Sci.

CLARY, NIKKI; Antioch HS; Antioch, CA; (3); Spanish Clb; SADD; Acpl Chr; Band; Chorus; Church Choir; Flag Corp; Mrchg Band; DAR Awd; Pres Acad Fit Awd; Sacramento ST; Srgcl Nrsng.

CLASON, CHRISTIE L; John Marshall Fund HS; Pasadena, CA; (3); AFS; Church Yth Grp; Dance Clb; Drama Clb; Key Clb; Pep Clb; Church Choir; Var L Cheerldng; Var L Socr; Var L Trk; Leag Champ In Trck; FAS Summr Trp To Czechoslovakia; Flute Instr; UCI; Pulbi Rltns.

CLAUSELL, SHERRY S; Pasadena HS; Pasadena, CA; (2); Hon Roll; Black Stu Union; Job Asst Sec Disposal Co; Law.

CLAUSEN, KIMBERLY E; Upland HS; Upland, CA; (2); Rptr Phtg Yrbk; JV Capt Sftbl; Sftbl MVP Awd Svrl Tms; Pediatrics.

CLAVE, MICHELLE L; Etiwanda HS; Alta Loma, CA; (2); 9/782; Dance Clb; JA; Spanish Clb; Speech Tm; Lit Mag; Treas Frsh Cls; High Hon Roll; Voice Dem Awd; CSF; GATE Hnrs Cls; Law.

CLAWSON, ALYSHIA F; Pasadena HS; Sierra Madre, CA; (3); Pres Debate Tm; Science Clb; Spanish Clb; Pres Speech Tm; Ed Lit Mag; Pres Frsh Cls; Pres Soph Cls; Hon Roll; Ntl Merit Schol; Opt Clb Awd; LA Stu Coalition; Amnesty Intl; Brotherhood/Sisterhd USA.

CLAWSON, BRIAN C; Victorvalley HS; Victorville, CA; (2); FBLA; JV Wrstlng; Bus.

CLAWSON, MICHELLE L; Mira Mesa HS; San Diego, CA; (2); Cmnty Wkr; Hosp Aide; Library Aide; Science Clb; Band; Mrchg Band; Orch; Pep Band; Comm Pilot; Pilot/Aviation.

CLAXTON, SAUNDRA; Beyer HS; Modesto, CA; (2); NFL; Pep Clb; Speech Tm; Stat Score Keeper; Hon Roll; S-Clb; Fri Nght Live; CSF; U C Riverside; Psych.

CLAY, ADAM B; Skyline HS; Oakland, CA; (3); Thesps; School Musical; School Play; Stage Crew; Nwsp; Acad Art Coll Smmr Art Exprnce Schlrshp; Commercl Art.

CLAY, BRIAN J; Santana HS; Santee, CA; (3); 1/290; Am Leg Boys St; Debate Tm; Letterman Clb; Model UN; Quiz Bowl; Speech Tm; Off Jr Cls; Off Sr Cls; JV Bsktbl; High Hon Roll; Jr Honor Guard; Chem.

CLAY, ERIKA M; Troy HS; Yorba Linda, CA; (2); 39/300; Key Clb; Treas Spanish Clb; Rptr Nwsp; Var L Crs Cntry; Var L Socr; Var L Trk; High Hon Roll; Hon Roll; Rotary Awd; Stu Of Mnth-Intgrtd Sci & Tech 90; Delta Sigma Theta Cmmnty Svc/Schlrshp Fndrsr; Spcl Recognition Plq; Harvard; OB.

CLAY, SHAWN P; Selma HS; Selma, CA; (1); Church Yth Grp; Cmnty Wkr; Debate Tm; Drama Clb; Service Clb; Ski Clb; Spanish Clb; Speech Tm; SADD; School Play; Schools Early Bird Mock Trial Team; Commissioner Of Activities For 90-91 School Year; Roteraty Interac; Law School.

CLAY, TISHA M; Pomona HS; Pomona, CA; (1); Church Yth Grp; Hosp Aide; Stanford; Accntng.

CLAYBORN, RALINDA; St Anthony HS; Long Beach, CA; (2); Drill Tm; Ntl Merit Schol; Merit Schlrshp; Drill Tm Ldrshp & Ctznshp Awd; Co-Capt Drill Tm; Own My Own Bus.

CLAYBURG, NANCY L; Atascadero HS; Atascadero, CA; (1); Church Yth Grp; Hon Roll; Rec Soccer League.

CLAYPOOLE, KENNY; River City HS; West Sacramento, CA; (1); JV Bsbl; JV Bsktbl; Mst Inspiratnl-Bsktbl; Forestry.

CLAYTON, CHELSEA D; Rim Of The World HS; Crestline, CA; (3); Drama Clb; French Clb; Thesps; School Play; Stage Crew; Variety Show; JV Tennis; Gldn St Exams Algebra & Amer Hist; Art Hist.

CLAYTON, CHRISTOPHER W; Bonita Vista HS; Chula Vista, CA; (2); Boy Scts; SADD; JV Crs Cntry; DAR Awd; Pres Acad Fit Awd; U Of CA.

CLAYTON, HOLLY A; Foothill HS; Santa Ana, CA; (4); 14/325; Cmnty Wkr; Key Clb; Red Cross Aide; Teachers Aide; High Hon Roll; Ntl Merit SF; CA Schlrshp Fdrtn Seal Bearer; Assisteen; La Campanas Deb; UN Of S CA; Bus.

CLAYTON, JESSICA T; Burroughs HS; Ridgecrest, CA; (3); Office Aide; Pep Clb; Teachers Aide; Stat Bsktbl; Cheerldng; Powder Puff Ftbl; High Hon Roll; Hon Roll; Delta Kappa Gamma Awd; Stu Ot The Month; CJSF; Law.

CLAYTON, LA TISHA; Downey HS; Downey, CA; (2); Church Yth Grp; FBLA; GAA; Hosp Aide; Office Aide; Teachers Aide; Rptr Yrbk; JV L Bsktbl; JV Score Keeper; Schlstc All Amer Awd; UC Berkeley; Law.

CLAYTON, MICHELLE M; Corona HS; Corona, CA; (2); Church Yth Grp; Computer Clb; Drama Clb; GAA; Girl Scts; Spanish Clb; JV Bsktbl; JV Trk; Cit Awd; Hon Roll; Lawyer.

CLAYTON, SARAH; Fairfield HS; Fairfield, CA; (1); Church Yth Grp; Off Frsh Cls; Stu Cncl; Sftbl; Hon Roll.

CLAYTOR, SHANE; Bethel Christian HS; Lancaster, CA; (2); Aud/Vis; Church Yth Grp; JV Bsbl; JV Bsktbl; JV Ftbl; Hon Roll; Masters Coll.

CLEARY, LISA A; Casa Grande HS; Petaluma, CA; (3); German Clb; Teachers Aide; Var Cit Awd; Hon Roll; NHS; Frgn Lang Awd; Law Enfrcmnt.

CLEARY, NICOLE D; Sanger HS; Fresno, CA; (2); Church Yth Grp; French Clb; Model UN; Chorus; Rptr Nwsp; High Hon Roll; Armenian Club; CSF; U San Diego; Child Psych.

CLEM, CHRIS D; Foothill HS; Santa Ana, CA; (2); Boy Scts; Church Yth Grp; German Clb; JV Ftbl; Wt Lftg; Hon Roll; Tulane U; Med.

CLEMENS, KERI LYNN; Bether Christian HS; Lancaster, CA; (2); Church Yth Grp; Drama Clb; Chorus; Church Choir; Bsbl; JV Var Cheerldng; Trk; High Hon Roll; Pres Acad Fit Awd; Au Coll; Vtrnrn.

CLEMENT, MELANIE C; Enterprise HS; Redding, CA; (3); French Clb; Cosmetology; Fashion Dsgn.

CLEMENTE, AIDE; Alisal HS; Salinas, CA; (3); French Clb; High Hon Roll; Hon Roll; Prfct Atten Awd; Soph Schlrshp Awd Top 10 Stu; Educ.

CLEMENTE, ERIK JOHN Q; John Marshall HS; Los Angeles, CA; (3); Church Yth Grp; Drama Clb; French Clb; Key Clb; Chorus; Stage Crew; Rep Stu Cncl; Var L Socr; Var L Tennis; Duke; Med.

CLEMENTE, MARY; Archbishop Mitty HS; San Jose, CA; (3); 10/255; Art Clb; Hosp Aide; Math Tm; SADD; Chorus; Var Cheerldng; JV Fld Hcky; High Hon Roll; NHS; Amnesty Intl; U CA San Diego; Bus.

CLEMENTIN, MONICA A; Skyline HS; Oakland, CA; (2); Cmnty Wkr; Computer Clb; Dance Clb; Teachers Aide; High Hon Roll; Hon Roll; Peer Counselor.

CLEMENTS, ALISHA I; Weed HS; Weed, CA; (4); 11/42; GAA; Pep Clb; Ski Clb; Teachers Aide; Chorus; Bsktbl; Cheerldng; Sftbl; Trk; Vllybl; Coll Siskiyous; Teacher.

CLEMENZA, NOVA MARIA; Eureka HS; Eureka, CA; (1); High Hon Roll; Pres Acad Fit Awd; CSF; Stu Sprts Athltc Trnr; Cal Poly San Luis Obispo; Arch.

CLEMENZA, SEAN M; Eureka SR HS; Eureka, CA; (4); 2/305; Variety Show; Var L Ftbl; Powder Puff Ftbl; Var JV Trk; Wt Lftg; Var JV Wrstlng; High Hon Roll; Golden St Exam Perfect Score Geom; CSF Pres & Life Mem 90; U CA Davis Regents Schlr; U CA Davis; Chem Eng.

CLEMMER, MITZI M; Faith Christian HS; Yuba City, CA; (2); Church Yth Grp; Band; Mrchg Band; High Hon Roll; Hon Roll; Var Bsktbl; Var Sftbl; Let Acad; Coaches Awd Bsktbl; Stu Of Mnth; Air Force Acad.

CLEMO, STEPHANIE; Nevada Union HS; Grass Valley, CA; (2); 1/500; Church Yth Grp; Rptr 4-H; School Play; Ed Sec Soph Cls; Rep Stu Cncl; Stat Bsktbl; Capt Cheerldng; Var Trk; High Hon Roll; Prfct Atten Awd; CSF; Princpls Schlr Awd 89 & 90; Gldn St Exam-Hnrs 1st Yr Alg; U Of CA Los Angeles; Law.

CLEMO, TARRA D; Oakmont HS; Roseville, CA; (1); Drama Clb; Spanish Clb; Variety Show; Bsktbl; Var Swmmng; Stat Vllybl; Hon Roll; Stanford.

CLEVELAND, AMY K; University City HS; San Diego, CA; (3); 49/373; Church Yth Grp; Model UN; Office Aide; SADD; Var JV Bsktbl; JV Sftbl; Var Vllybl; Hon Roll; CSF; Bsktbl MVP & Mst Insprtnl Plyr; Vlybl Mst Imprvd; Ldrshp Grp; Law.

CLEVELAND, KRISTIN M; Tracy HS; Tracy, CA; (1); 51/565; Church Yth Grp; Drama Clb; School Musical; Gym; Hon Roll; U Of SC; Ped.

CLEVELAND, NATHAN L; Enterprise HS; Redding, CA; (3); Math Clb; Acpl Chr; Band; Drm Mjr(t); Mrchg Band; Orch; Pep Band; School Musical; Swing Chorus; Variety Show; Youth To Youth Stus Committed To Drug Free Life; Model & Choreogrphy For Alpine Outfitter Ski Wear; Engrng.

CLEVELAND, TISHNA; George Washington Prep HS; Los Angeles, CA; (3); Am Leg Aux Girls St; Cmnty Wkr; Teachers Aide; Cheerldng; Trk; Cit Awd; Hon Roll; Law.

CLEVERLEY, MARIA M; Beyer HS; Modesto, CA; (1); Dance Clb; Variety Show; Hon Roll; Jrnlsm.

CLIBORN, ELAINE M; Carson HS; Carson, CA; (2); Treas German Clb; Capt Drill Tm; Var Cheerldng; Var Gym; Cit Awd; Hon Roll; CSF; Acad Dcthln.

CLICK, CARMEN S; Fontana HS; Fontana, CA; (3); Drama Clb; Acpl Chr; Color Guard; Mgr(s); Hon Roll; Achvmnt Awd 2 Slvr Mdls; Z Clb JR Rep; Campus Life Ssctry Of Actvts; CA ST San Bernardino; Bus.

CLIFFORD, KATHRYN M; Fremont HS; Garland, TX; (4); Pres Church Yth Grp; Dance Clb; Drama Clb; SADD; Drill Tm; Ed Yrbk; Rep Jr Cls; Elks Awd; High Hon Roll; NHS; Engl Awd; NCTE Cntstnt; Cross Age Sci Tchng; Brigham Young U; Bio.

CLIFFORD, KATIE; Paradise Adventist Acad; Oroville, CA; (4); Church Yth Grp; Cmnty Wkr; Ski Clb; Teachers Aide; Chorus; School Musical; School Play; Yrbk; Cit Awd; Hon Roll; Pacific Union Coll; Psych.

CLIFFORD, LARRY; Palo Verde Valley HS; Blythe, CA; (3); Letterman Clb; School Musical; Variety Show; VP Jr Cls; VP Stu Cncl; JV Var Ftbl; High Hon Roll; Hon Roll; NHS; Rotary Awd; Yth Congress; Rotry Yth Ldrshp Awd; Congressional Yth Ldrshp Cncl; Bus Mgmt.

CLIFFORD, MARK B; Palo Verde Valley HS; Blythe, CA; (2); Rep Stu Cncl; JV Var Bsktbl; JV Var Ftbl; JV Golf; Intrml Wt Lftg; Hon Roll; Cngrssnl Yth Ldrshp Cncl.

CLIFFORD III, ROLAND O; Twenty Nine Palms HS; Twenty Nine Pal, CA; (4); Art Clb; Drama Clb; Nwsp; Yrbk; Lit Mag; Var L Crs Cntry; Var Ftbl; 89 Congrssnl Art Cmptn Hnrb Mntn Awd; Commercial Art.

CLIFTON, CINDY L; Tulare Western HS; Tulare, CA; (4); 7/226; Church Yth Grp; 4-H; Office Aide; Hon Roll; Span Awd; Sci Awd; Math Awd; CA ST Bakersfield; Bus.

CLIFTON, HEATHER; Poway HS; Poway, CA; (3); Church Yth Grp; Ski Clb; SADD; Off Jr Cls; JV Swmmng; Hon Roll; UC Santa Barbara.

CLIFTON, MONIQUE N; Montclair HS; Montclair, CA; (1); Church Yth Grp; Key Clb; Church Choir; JV Socr; Stat Sftbl; USC; Interior Dsgn.

CLIMENSON, ERNIE T; Helix HS; San Diego, CA; (3); 44/460; Math Tm; Tennis; Hon Roll; Gldn St Exam Alg High Hnrs, Geom Hnrs; USC D; Aeronautics.

CLINE, BRANDI; El Dorado HS; Placerville, CA; (4); Church Yth Grp; Band; Drm Mjr(t); Mrchg Band; Pres Acad Fit Awd; Outstndng Band Stu 86 & 88; John Phillip Sousa Awd 89-90; Nrthrn CA Hnr Band 87-90; Stu Achvt Awd Span; U Of CA Santa Cruz.

CLINE, SHEILA; Reedley HS; Reedley, CA; (4); French Clb; FFA; FTA; German Clb; Intnl Clb; Service Clb; Band; Jazz Band; Mrchg Band; Pep Band; Camp Royal; Golden St Exam Geom Hnrs; CA Schlrshp Fed; Lewis & Clark Coll; Intl Affrs.

CLINKENBEARD, LANENA; Norte Vista HS; Riverside, CA; (2); Dance Clb; FFA; FHA; Hon Roll; Prfct Atten Awd; Child Dvlpmnt.

CLINSCALES, TRACY; Rialto JR HS; Rialto, CA; (1); Church Yth Grp; Girl Scts; Teachers Aide; Ed Nwsp; Bsbl; Cheerldng; Gym; Socr; Sftbl; Trk; Stanford U; Bus Mgmt.

CLINTON, DWAYNE A; Mater Dei HS; Garden Grove, CA; (1); Boy Scts; Hon Roll; Pres Acad Fit Awd.

CLINTON, REBECCA M; Aptos HS; Watsonville, CA; (1); Pres 4-H; Band; Jazz Band; Orch; Pep Band; 4-H Awd; Hon Roll; Yth Sympn-Princpl Flute; Jr Ldr-Rabbits & Arts/Crafts-4 H; Harvard; Marine Bio.

CLINTON, STEPHEN W; Fillmore HS; Tulare, CA; (3); Church Yth Grp; Treas Debate Tm; Drama Clb; FCA; FFA; JA; Letterman Clb; Bsbl; Ftbl; Wrstlng; Hnr Rl Sports; Bsbl.

CLIPPAND, JAMIE M; Redondo HS; Redondo Beach, CA; (4); 28/435; L Capt Crs Cntry; L Capt Trk; Hon Roll; Kiwanis Awd; Pres Acad Fit Awd; Rotary Awd; Pr Cnslng; Long Beach ST; Educ.

CLOE, ALAN D; Ukiah HS; Ukiah, CA; (3); 5/310; Yrbk; Hon Roll; Prfct Atten Awd; Congrssnl Schlr; Stanford; Aerospace.

CLONINGER, BEN; Beaumont HS; Cherry Valley, CA; (3); 31/200; Var Tennis; Hon Roll; Prfct Atten Awd; Pre-Med.

CLONINGER, JAMES E; Monterey Bay Acad; Parachute, CO; (1); Church Yth Grp; FCA; 4-H; Intrml Bsktbl; Intrml Ftbl; Intrml Vllybl; Hon Roll; Pres Acad Fit Awd; Arch Engrng.

CLONINGER, ROBERT; John F Kennedy HS; Sacramento, CA; (3); 10/515; Church Yth Grp; Ski Clb; SADD; Rptr Yrbk; VP Rep Frsh Cls; Pres Rep Soph Cls; Rep Jr Cls; Rep Stu Cncl; Var JV Socr; Var JV Trk; Pre-Med.

CLOSE, DAVID M; Oak Ridge HS; El Dorado Hills, CA; (3); 2/261; Church Yth Grp; NFL; Thesps; School Play; Lit Mag; JV Socr; High Hon Roll; NHS; Pres Acad Fit Awd; Rotary Awd; Piano Pfrmnc & Cmpstn; Psych.

CLOSE, RYAN P; North Tahoe HS; Tahoe City, CA; (1); 14/105; Band; JV Bsbl; JV Ftbl; Hon Roll; Engr.

CLOSSEY, LUKE S; Carlsbad HS; Carlsbad, CA; (1); Capt Scholastic Bowl; Science Clb; JV Tennis; CA Schlrshp Fed; Math.

CLOSSMAN, CHANDRA D; Valley View HS; Moreno Valley, CA; (1); Drama Clb; Stage Crew; JV Socr; Var Trk; Hon Roll; CIF 880; Mst Outstndng Offnsv Sccr Plyr; Hse & Snte; UCLA; Math.

CLOTHIER, MARCI; Christian HS; Spring Valley, CA; (4); 13/99; Rep Church Yth Grp; Drama Clb; Girl Scts; Sec Science Clb; Church Choir; Var L Cheerldng; Cit Awd; NHS; Rotry Yth Ldrshp Awd; CSF Seal Bearer; Chrmn Accredtn Cmmtte; U Of CA San Diego; Psych.

CLOUD, DANA M; Turlock HS; Turlock, CA; (4); 36/520; AFS; Key Clb; NFL; Speech Tm; Capt Cheerldng; JV Mgr(s); High Hon Roll; Girls Leag; Interact; Medic Alert Vlntr; CSU; Elem Tchr.

CLOUGH, LISA; Aquinas HS; San Bernardino, CA; (2); Cmnty Wkr; Hosp Aide; Teachers Aide; Pvt Instgtns.

CLOUGH, MARK L; Arvin HS; Arvin, CA; (1); Yrbk; Ftbl; Wt Lftg; Hon Roll; English Honors; Photography.

CLOUSER, NATALIE J; Irvine HS; Irvine, CA; (3); 86/550; Band; Jazz Band; Mrchg Band; Orch; Pep Band; School Musical; Hon Roll; IA ST U; Spcl Educ.

CLOUTIER, MICHELE; South Tahoe HS; S Lake Tahoe, CA; (3); 1/300; Key Clb; Varsity Clb; Yrbk; Yrbk; Treas Soph Cls; Stu Cncl; Bsktbl; Vllybl; High Hon Roll; Hon Roll; Jr Statemn Amer; CA Schlrshp Fdrtn; Hnrbl Mntn Zone & St Bsktbl; Hnrbl Mntn Vllybl; Bus.

CLOUTIER, PAUL; Orange Glen HS; Escondido, CA; (1); 40/600; Stage Crew; Ftbl; Wt Lftg; Wrstlng; Hon Roll; Pres Acad Fit Awd; Beach Vlybl; 2nd Golden St Exam Alg; 1st USC Alg Exam; U CA Santa Barbara; Arch.

CLOWARD, RIKI A; Richard Gahr HS; Norwalk, CA; (3); Church Yth Grp; Var Pep Clb; Spanish Clb; Off Sr Cls; Cheerldng; Var Socr; Swmmng; High Hon Roll; Prfct Atten Awd; Blue & Gold Awds; USC; Sprts Med.

CLOYD, GRACE D; Foothill HS; Pleasanton, CA; (4); 100/332; Sec SADD; Capt Color Guard; Capt Flag Corp; Mrchg Band; Gldn St Exam-Geom Schl Rcgntn Hnrs; Intr Dsgn.

CLOYS, ADAM; Bloomington Christian HS; Bloomington, CA; (2); Church Yth Grp; Drama Clb; Teachers Aide; Variety Show; Rep Soph Cls; Stat Bsktbl; L Ftbl; Mgr(s); L Stat Wrstlng; High Hon Roll; U Of S CA; Sprts Med.

CLUCK, SHAUNA; Lassen HS; Janesville, CA; (4); 10/200; Intnl Clb; Ski Clb; Spanish Clb; VP Frsh Cls; Rep Stu Cncl; JV Gym; Powder Puff Ftbl; JV Swmmng; Elks Awd; High Hon Roll; Exchng Stu Spain.

CLUCK, TINA; Christian Center HS; Rio Vista, CA; (3); Church Yth Grp; Letterman Clb; Chorus; Church Choir; Ed Yrbk; JV Cheerldng; Capt Sftbl; Capt Vllybl; Hcmng Princess; Ctznshp Awd; Bethany Bible Coll; Psych.

CLUFF, ADAM A; California HS; Whittier, CA; (2); Church Yth Grp; Var Bsbl; Bsktbl; MVP Frshmn Bsbl; Coaches Awd Frshmn Bsktbl; Brigham Young U; Law.

CLUFF, LYNEEN; Woodland HS; Esparto, CA; (2); Church Yth Grp; SADD; Church Choir; High Hon Roll; Hon Roll; Ballet & Folk Dance Private Study; BYU; Engl.

CLYMENS JR, THOMAS EDWARD; Liberty Union HS; Oakley, CA; (1); JV Ftbl; JV Trk; Wt Lftg; Hon Roll; E Diablo Yth Sccr League; Bsbl; Dntst.

CLYMO, DAN; El Camino HS; Sacramento, CA; (3); JV Bsbl; UC Santa Cruz; Hstry.

CNOI, RUTH; Troy HS; Fullerton, CA; (4); 13/310; Rep Church Yth Grp; NFL; Church Choir; Drill Tm; Mgr Nwsp; Var Cheerldng; High Hon Roll; Masonic Awd; Sec NHS; Troy Tech Program; My Youth Group Went To Mexico During Spring Break & Summer To Build Buildings; CA ST U; Bus Admin Accntnt.

CO, AILEEN L; Lowell HS; San Francisco, CA; (2); SADD; Bdmntn Tm JV; Wntrfr Decrtn Cmmtte; Red Crss Clb; CSF; Vlntr Offc Wrkr; Gldn St Exam Hgh Hnrs; Block L; UC Davis.

CO, CHARLES QUY P; Levzinger HS; Lennox, CA; (4); Math Clb; Science Clb; Cit Awd; High Hon Roll; Hon Roll; Prfct Atten Awd; Pres Acad Fit Awd; Vietnamese Club; California Sealbearer Federation; Cal State U Long Beach; Pre Bus.

CO, CLAUDINE; Edison HS; Huntington Beach, CA; (3); Church Yth Grp; Intnl Clb; Model UN; Sec Quiz Bowl; Spanish Clb; SADD; Rep Soph Cls; Rep Jr Cls; Pres Stu Cncl; Hon Roll; Scriputre Instr/Catechist; Distngshed Schlr; English.

CO, EVANGELINE T; Abraham Lincoln HS; San Francisco, CA; (3); Intnl Clb; Scholastic Bowl; Nrsng.

CO, GERALDINE C; Dana Hills HS; Laguna Niguel, CA; (3); Cmnty Wkr; High Hon Roll; Hon Roll; Prfct Atten Awd; Stu Agnst A Vnshng Envrnmnt; CSF; Saddleback Coll; Dntstry.

CO, NA MY; Don Antonio Lugo HS; Chino, CA; (4); 28/689; Cmnty Wkr; FBLA; Library Aide; Math Clb; Science Clb; Varsity Clb; Yrbk; Tennis; Cit Awd; Hon Roll; FIDM; Fshn Dsgnr.

CO, SEAN ALBERT; El Camino Fundamental HS; Carmichael, CA; (3); 112/366; Boy Scts; Church Yth Grp; Key Clb; SADD; Crs Cntry; US Cycling Fed Bicyle Racer.

COADY, DANIEL J; Servite HS; Fullerton, CA; (3); Red Cross Aide; Pres Jr Cls; Rep Stu Cncl; Bsktbl; Trk; Hon Roll; NEDT Awd; Bus.

COATE, HEATHER R; Encina HS; Sacramento, CA; (3); 15/212; SADD; Lit Mag; Vllybl; High Hon Roll; Hon Roll; Most Improved Player Vllybl; Stu Of Mnth Visual Arts; Worked At Local Jr HS As Math Tutor; San Diego ST U; Chem.

COATS, ALBERT W; Grant HS; Sacramento, CA; (3); Spanish Clb; High Hon Roll; Sac ST; Education.

COATS JR, RICHARD C; Apple Valley SR HS; Apple Valley, CA; (3); Cmnty Wkr; Letterman Clb; Teachers Aide; Varsity Clb; Var Bsbl; Var Ftbl; Cit Awd; All San Andreas Leag Vrsty Ptchr; Lwst ERA; Vrsty Ftbl; Ed.

COATS, TAMMIE; Sutter Union HS; Sutter, CA; (3); 9/87; Church Yth Grp; Cmnty Wkr; Pres FBLA; Sec FFA; Intnl Clb; Teachers Aide; School Play; Stage Crew; Variety Show; Ed Phtg Nwsp; CSF, Treas; Yuba Coll.

COBAR, CLAUDIA A; Alverno HS; Temple City, CA; (3); Science Clb; Rptr Mgr Nwsp; Var JV Swmmng; Swmmng MVP & Mst Dedctd Plyr; Campus LIFE; Engrng.

COBAR, FAITH T; James Hogan SR HS; Vallejo, CA; (3); Church Yth Grp; Spanish Clb; Speech Tm; SADD; Teachers Aide; Drill Tm; Hon Roll; Jr NHS; Pres Acad Fit Awd; CSF; Badminton V; Acad Achvt Awd; San Francisco ST Coll; Nrsng.

COBB, ANDREA; Oakdale HS; Oakdale, CA; (2); Dance Clb; Chorus; Cit Awd; High Hon Roll; Hon Roll; Pres Schlr; Army; Electrnc Engr.

COBB, CARISA; Arlington HS; Riverside, CA; (4); 24/336; Church Yth Grp; Cmnty Wkr; Letterman Clb; Pep Clb; Teachers Aide; Church Choir; Lit Mag; Stu Cncl; Var Cheerldng; High Hon Roll; CSF; Bnk America Scl Stds Mrt Awd; CA Baptist Coll; Behvrl Sci.

COBB, ERIN J; Fresno HS; Fresno, CA; (2); Var L Swmmng; High Hon Roll; Hon Roll; Prfct Atten Awd; Most Imprvd Swmmr; Prncpls Awd Acadmc Excllnc; Vrsty Water Polo Coaches Awd; Acadmc Achvt Awd Art 89-90; U Of CA San Diego; Marine Bio.

COBB, JULIE I; Flintridge Prep; La Canada Flintri, CA; (3); Church Yth Grp; JCL; Latin Clb; Church Choir; Yrbk; Off Sr Cls; Socr; Tennis; High Hon Roll; NHS.

COBB, MAISHA J; American HS; Fremont, CA; (4); 26/326; Cmnty Wkr; Office Aide; Spanish Clb; Speech Tm; SADD; Teachers Aide; Rep Jr Cls; Off Stu Cncl; High Hon Roll; Hon Roll; Top 6 Pct Blck Stdt Takg PSAT 88; Blck Stdt Union Clb; CA Schlstc Fed; Psych.

COBB, MICHELLE; Notre Dame HS; San Jose, CA; (2); Service Clb; Stage Crew; High Hon Roll; Hon Roll; Spcl Olympics Vlntr.

COBB, MISTI C; Redlands HS; Redlands, CA; (3); Cheerldng; Pres Acad Fit Awd; Ldrshp Class; Cal U; Psych.

COBB, TAWNYA J; Turlock HS; Turlock, CA; (2); FFA; Hon Roll; CA-POLY; Horse Chiropractor.

COBB, THOMAS C; Fresno Christian HS; Madera, CA; (3); Chorus; Yrbk; Lit Mag; VP Frsh Cls; Treas Sr Cls; Var Ftbl; High Hon Roll; Rotary Awd; CSF; Choir Ensmbl; Genetics.

COBB, TRACY M; San Bernardino HS; San Bernardino, CA; (3); VP Church Yth Grp; Hon Roll; Church Choir; Outstndng Achvt; Perf Attend; Cal ST; Bus Admin.

COBBETT, CHRISTIE L; Bishop Union HS; Bishop, CA; (3); High Hon Roll; Hon Roll; NHS; Natl HS Rodeo Assn; CA Polytech U; Bus.

COBBLEY, CLYDE L; Quincy JR/Sr HS; Quincy, CA; (1); Boy Scts; Ftbl; Golf; Pro Golfer.

COBBS, TRAVIS L; Live Oak HS; San Jose, CA; (3); 12/530; Church Yth Grp; Band; Mrchg Band; Orch; Pep Band; Hon Roll; Comp Aided Dsgn.

COBIAN, CAROLINA; Baldwin Park HS; Baldwin Park, CA; (3); FBLA; Sec Letterman Clb; Spanish Clb; Sec Soph Cls; Off Jr Cls; Var Bsktbl; Var Trk; Hon Roll; HOBY 89; Ambsdr Baldwin Park HS Central CA; Engrng.

COBIAN, IVAN; Cantwell HS; N Whitter, CA; (1); JV Bsbl; Hon Roll; Med.

COBILLAS, JENNIFER; Notre Dame HS; San Jose, CA; (2); Church Yth Grp; Cmnty Wkr; JV Bsktbl; JV Vllybl; High Hon Roll; 89 San Jose Mayors Yth Conf Rep; MIT; Engrng.

COBLE, GEMMY LYNN; Mt Whitney HS; Goshen, CA; (4); French Clb; Key Clb; Teachers Aide; JV Bsktbl; JV Crs Cntry; Stat Score Keeper; Var Capt Trk; W Yosemite Leag Discus Chmpn; UCLA; Pedtrcs.

COBOS, PATRICIA; Sunset HS; Hayward, CA; (3); 42/198; Church Yth Grp; Drama Clb; Teachers Aide; Hon Roll; Ecology Clb; Bus Exec.

COBOS, SAUNDRA C; Santa Clara HS; Oxnard, CA; (3); 2/175; Varsity Clb; Sec Frsh Cls; Rep Soph Cls; Off Jr Cls; Stu Cncl; Var Capt Bsktbl; High Hon Roll; NHS; Genl Excllnc Awd; Natl Fed Of Music Clbs-Natl Hnr Awd; Future Ldrs Of Am; Stanford; Med.

COBOS, SINDY; Chino HS; Ontario, CA; (3); Church Yth Grp; Science Clb; SADD; Band; Church Choir; Mrchg Band; Pep Band; Sftbl; Var Tennis; Futr Ldrs Of Amer; U Of CA Riverside; Orthdntst.

COBURN, AMY MICHELLE; Bellarmine-Jefferson HS; Burbank, CA; (2); 1/150; Cmnty Wkr; Debate Tm; 4-H; Math Clb; Science Clb; Spanish Clb; Speech Tm; High Hon Roll; NHS; Equestrian Tm; CSF; Voluntr Dr Shaws Vet Clinic; Vet.

COBURN II, BARRY C; De La Salle HS; Concord, CA; (3); Ski Clb; Teachers Aide; Stage Crew; Phtg Yrbk; Var Bsbl; Hon Roll; Med.

COBURN, KATHRYN G; Bullard HS; Fresno, CA; (2); Church Yth Grp; Debate Tm; FCA; Intnl Clb; French Clb; SADD; Color Guard; Flag Corp; Rotary Awd; Hi-Deb For Gottschalks.

COBURN, TESSA P; Merced HS North; Merced, CA; (2); FBLA; Spanish Clb; Hon Roll; Wildlife Preservation; Yale U; Linguistics.

COCHRAN, DANIEL; Rio Lindo Adventist Acad; Angwin, CA; (3); Band; Pacific Union Coll; Bus Admin.

COCHRAN, JENNIFER L; Turlock HS; Turlock, CA; (4); Church Yth Grp; Teachers Aide; Acpl Chr; Chorus; Color Guard; Flag Corp; Modesto JC; Dental Hygiene.

COCHRAN, TIFFANY J; Alexander Hamilton HS; Los Angeles, CA; (2); Church Yth Grp; Cmnty Wkr; Computer Clb; Drama Clb; Office Aide; Science Clb; Service Clb; Teachers Aide; Church Choir; School Play; Top Teen Sof Amer Cert Of Outstndng Svc; Myrs Cmndtn For Drug Abs Prvntn On Yth Rcgntn Day; Hwrd U; Brdcst Jrnlst.

COCHRANE, APRILLE; Blackford HS; San Jose, CA; (3); 66/238; Var JV Bsktbl; Var JV Trk; Cal Berkeley; Psych.

COCHRANE, KEVIN V; Amador Valley HS; Pleasanton, CA; (4); 7/413; Church Yth Grp; Var L Crs Cntry; Var Mgr(s); Var L Trk; Hon Roll; Lion Awd; Ntl Merit SF; Rotary Awd; CSF VP; Stanford; Econ.

COCHRANE, RACHEL K; Sunny Hills HS; Fullerton, CA; (3); 116/420; Cmnty Wkr; JA; Spanish Clb; SADD; Acpl Chr; Ed Nwsp; Hon Roll; Acad Achvt Awd Life Sci; 13th Pl Southern CA Jrnlsm Ed Assn Write-Off Cmptn; Jrnlsm.

COCKERHAM, CRAIG A; Irvington HS; Fremont, CA; (2); Church Yth Grp; JV Crs Cntry; Var Socr; High Hon Roll; Hon Roll; CA Schlrshp Fed; Schl Athl Sccr 89; Stu Month; Air Force Acad; Pilot.

COCKEY, JEFFREY W E; Del Campo HS; Fair Oaks, CA; (2); 54/468; SADD; Socr; Hon Roll; Stanford; Bus Law.

COCKRELL, ROBIN; Walnut HS; Walnut, CA; (3); 35/420; Key Clb; Pep Clb; Ski Clb; SADD; VP Frsh Cls; Stu Cncl; JV Var Cheerldng; Var Trk; Intrml JV Vllybl; High Hon Roll; Honor Guard; Class Cabinet; Cal Poly; Math.

COCKRUM, JOSHUA R; Victor Valley HS; Victorville, CA; (3); 42/416; Church Yth Grp; Band; Drm Mjr(t); Jazz Band; Mrchg Band; Pep Band; Hon Roll; Mck Trl Tm; Pres CSF 90-91; Physics.

COCO, RACHEL; Foothill SR HS; Sacramento, CA; (1); Church Yth Grp; Girl Scts; Quiz Bowl; Sec Spanish Clb; SADD; Band; Bsbl; Bsktbl; Tennis; Cit Awd; Princeton; Psych.

COCOBA, ANTHONY L; Samuel F B Morse HS; San Diego, CA; (3); VP Chess Clb; Math Clb; Science Clb; High Hon Roll; Hon Roll; Sci Olympcs; Elec Engr.

CODDINGTON, ABBY; Mc Kinleyville HS; Mc Kinleyville, CA; (2); Church Yth Grp; FBLA; Prfct Atten Awd; U Of CA; Bus.

CODDINGTON, LARA; Mendocino HS; Caspar, CA; (3); French Clb; Bsktbl; Socr; High Hon Roll; Prfct Atten Awd; Span III, Math III Awds; Mst Exmplry Stu Upward Bound; Humboldt.

CODEMO, CHRISTINA M; Notre Dame HS; San Mateo, CA; (4); Library Aide; Treas Science Clb; School Play; Ed Yrbk; Hon Roll; NHS; Pres Acad Fit Awd; Jr Statesmn Amer Clb; CSF Awd Clb; Vol Tutoring Math & Engl; U San Francisco; Bio.

CODERRE, MICHELLE; Rosary HS; Anaheim, CA; (3); Cmnty Wkr; Hosp Aide; Pep Clb; Science Clb; Spanish Clb; Vllybl; High Hon Roll; CSF; Safe Rides; Schlr Athlt Awd; U CA Irvine; Comp Sci.

CODY, CAROLYN E; Mills HS; Millbrae, CA; (3); Church Yth Grp; Teachers Aide; Var Capt Cheerldng; Var Trk; Irish Dancing Champ.

CODY, LEVI; Trinity HS; Weaverville, CA; (3); Boy Scts; Cmnty Wkr; VP FFA; JV Var Ftbl; Var Wrstlng; Hon Roll; Pres Acad Fit Awd; UC Davis; Ag Finance.

COE, CHRISTINE; Portola JR-SR HS; Portola, CA; (2); Church Yth Grp; Drama Clb; Teachers Aide; Swing Chorus; Var Capt Bsktbl; JV Gym; Var Sftbl; JV Swmmng; Var Capt Vllybl; High Hon Roll; Jrnlsm.

COE, CORIE A; Del Oro HS; Loomis, CA; (2); 1/225; Church Yth Grp; Var Capt Cheerldng; Ftbl; Var L Swmmng; High Hon Roll; Lion Awd; CSF; Cum Laude Awd; Bio.

COEL, ANNE J; Lower Lake HS; Lower Lake, CA; (3); Chorus; Hon Roll; JV Trk; Outstanding Student Organization; U Of CA Davis.

COELHO, JULIE; Orestimba HS; Newman, CA; (1); Spanish Clb; Hon Roll; CSF; Nurse.

COELHO, STACY; Turlock HS; Turlock, CA; (1); Church Yth Grp; Cheerldng; Modesto JC; Math.

COEN, SHANNON S; Santa Cruz HS; Santa Cruz, CA; (3); Art Clb; Ski Clb; Spanish Clb; Nwsp; Yrbk; Lit Mag; Hon Roll; Ntl Merit SF; Bicycle Racing; Comp; Ind Dsgn.

COFFEE, MICHELLE; Redlands HS; Redlands, CA; (3); Church Yth Grp; Key Clb; Teachers Aide; Church Choir; Hon Roll; Pres Acad Fit Awd; Nursing.

COFFEEN, JENNIFER A; Encina HS; Sacramento, CA; (3); 38/210; SADD; Yrbk; Rep Stu Cncl; Var Cheerldng; Hon Roll.

COFFENBERRY, SHARI A; San Ramon Valley HS; San Ramon, CA; (2); Involved In Dance Dept But Not In The Dance Club; Diablo Valley Coll; Teaching.

COFFEY, JASON A; Serrano HS; Wrightwood, CA; (2); Ftbl; Wt Lftg; Hon Roll; JV Mst Imprvd Ftbl; Serrano Athltc Boosters Clb Awd.

COFFEY, JASON C; Rancho Cotate HS; Rohnert Park, CA; (2); Drama Clb; School Musical; School Play; Hon Roll; Coll Oregon St; Theater Arts.

COFFIN, MELISSA; Palm Springs HS; Palm Springs, CA; (4); 4/500; Sec Debate Tm; Treas French Clb; Sec Service Clb; JV L Crs Cntry; Var Powder Puff Ftbl; Cit Awd; High Hon Roll; Lion Awd; Pres Acad Fit Awd; CSF; Us Acad Deca; Scripps Womens Coll; Intl Rel.

COFFMAN, AMY K; Liberty Christian HS; Huntington Beach, CA; (2); Church Yth Grp; Cmnty Wkr; Chorus; School Musical; Rep Frsh Cls; Treas Soph Cls; Stu Cncl; Var Bsktbl; Var Sftbl; Var Vllybl; Hmcmng Prncss; Mighty In Spirit Awd; Biola; Jrnlsm.

COFFMAN, BRENDA M; San Dieguito Union HS; Olivenhain, CA; (3); Teachers Aide; Var Bsktbl; JV Sftbl; Ambssdr Hugh O'brian Yth Fndtn Sthrn CA Ldrshp Smnr 89; Schl Rcgntn Algbr CA St Exm 88; U Of CA San Diego; Sci.

COFFMAN, CYNTHIA M; Louisville HS; Chatsworth, CA; (3); Art Clb; FHA; SADD; Lit Mag; Hon Roll; Ntl Merit Ltr; Japanese Study; Bio.

COFFMAN, EZEKIAL J; Sweetwater HS; National City, CA; (3); 121/429; Band; JV Capt Ftbl; Var Capt Swmmng; JV Trk; JV Capt Vllybl; Pres Acad Fit Awd.

COFFMAN, JAY; Los Alamitos HS; Seal Beach, CA; (4); Am Leg Boys St; Boy Scts; Church Yth Grp; VP FBLA; NFL; Service Clb; Sec VP Speech Tm; Treas Band; Chorus; School Musical; Stu Of Mnth; PTSA Person Of The Wk; ASB Cmmssnr Of Stu & Cmmnty Svcs; U Of CA; Schl Tchr.

COFFMAN, JEFFREY A; Oxnard HS; Oxnard, CA; (3); French Clb; Temple Yth Grp; Hon Roll; Temple Yth Grp; U Of CA Santa Barbara; Antrplg.

COFIELD, KIMBERLY D; Victor Valley HS; Victorville, CA; (2); French Clb; Key Clb; ITT Tech Inst; Robotics Engr.

COFONI, MARIKA A; Torrey Pines HS; Solana Beach, CA; (4); Church Yth Grp; Swmmng; Asst Swim Coach; U Of CT; Elem Ed.

COGAN, CHRISTIAN M; Bishop O Dowd HS; Oakland, CA; (2); Thesps; School Musical; School Play; Hon Roll; Wrtr.

COGAN, DANIEL S; Glen A Wilson HS; Hacienda Hts, CA; (2); Band; Mrchg Band; JV Wrstlng; VP Gmrs Gld & Brdg Clb; UC Irvine; Elec Engr.

COGAN, ERIN M; Ygnacio Valley HS; Pleasant Hill, CA; (1); Church Yth Grp; Teachers Aide; Var L Socr; Hon Roll; Girls St Sccr Team 89.

COGSWELL, BRIAN J; Santa Barbara HS; Santa Barbara, CA; (4); 39/470; Church Yth Grp; Math Tm; Teachers Aide; Var JV Bsbl; Hon Roll; NHS; Ntl Merit SF; Stanford; Ec.

COGSWELL, KEVIN L; Santa Barbara HS; Santa Barbara, CA; (2); German Clb; JV Bsbl; Cit Awd; Prfct Atten Awd; GAPP Exch Stu In Germany; AZ ST; Prof Athlete.

COHEN, AMY B; La Quinta HS; Westminster, CA; (1); Drama Clb; GAA; Girl Scts; Key Clb; Intrml Sftbl; Cit Awd; Hon Roll; Pres Acad Fit Awd; Soc Worker.

COHEN, DAMIAN G; Carlmont HS; Belmont, CA; (2); Rep Frsh Cls; Rep Soph Cls; JV Bsbl; JV Socr; Hon Roll; Golden St Exam Cert Mrt Alg I & Geom; Amnsty Intl; Cal Berkeley; Poltcl Sci.

COHEN JR, DAVID L; Fremont Christian HS; Hayward, CA; (3); Church Yth Grp; Office Aide; Ski Clb; School Play; Hon Roll; Cert Of Awd Adv Bio; CA ST U; Bio.

COHEN, DIANA JOY; University City HS; San Diego, CA; (4); Dance Clb; Red Cross Aide; Science Clb; SADD; Temple Yth Grp; Nwsp; JV Bsktbl; Elks Awd; High Hon Roll; Hon Roll; CSF Treas; Berkeley Alumni Schlrshp; Bnai Brith Youth Org; BERKELEY; Chem Engr.

COHEN, JEFF B; William Howard Taft HS; Woodland Hills, CA; (2); Temple Yth Grp; Pres Soph Cls; Bsbl; L Capt Ftbl; JV L Trk; Var Wt Lftg; Hon Roll; Prfssnl Actor TV & Movies; Prdctn Asst.

COHEN, JEREMY A; Dos Pueblos HS; Goleta, CA; (3); NHS; Torah Stdy; Backpacking.

COHEN, KIMBERLEY A; Van Nuys HS; Panorama City, CA; (4); 165/592; Cmnty Wkr; Math Tm; Quiz Bowl; Rep Frsh Cls; Rep Soph Cls; Rep Jr Cls; Rep Sr Cls; Var Powder Puff Ftbl; Var Score Keeper; JV Sftbl; Stu Vlntr GLAZA; Vet Asst; CO ST U; Vet Med.

COHEN, LEE M; Canyon HS; Canyon Country, CA; (4); 4/430; Am Leg Boys St; Drama Clb; Letterman Clb; Spanish Clb; Teachers Aide; Capt Varsity Clb; Var Capt Crs Cntry; Var Capt Trk; High Hon Roll; Hon Roll; CSF Sealbearer; Schlr Athlete 90; Am Assn Of Tchrs-Span & Portuguese Mdls; Occidental Coll; Bio.

COHEN, MABELLE; La Center For Enriched Studies; Los Angeles, CA; (4); Cmnty Wkr; Hosp Aide; Intnl Clb; Office Aide; Science Clb; Service Clb; Teachers Aide; Temple Yth Grp; Orch; Nwsp; Stu Govt Chairperson And Founder Intl Race Rels Comm; Acadmc Dec; Volunteer Tutor Teacher Asst; Brandeis U; Med.

COHEN, MICHAEL; Marina HS; Huntington Bch, CA; (4); AFS; Debate Tm; JA; Teachers Aide.

COHEN, NATALYA; Washington HS; San Diego, CA; (3); 7/306; Computer Clb; Debate Tm; Drama Clb; English Clb; Science Clb; Chorus; School Musical; School Play; Var Vllybl; JV Badminton; Comp Sci.

COHENNO, DOROTHY; Needles HS; Needles, CA; (4); 5/56; Office Aide; Teachers Aide; Mrchg Band; Cit Awd; High Hon Roll; Lion Awd; Rep Frsh Cls; Rep Jr Cls; VP Sr Cls; Stat Bsbl; San Diego ST U.

COHN, ALLYSON; Miraleste HS; Rancho Palos Verd, CA; (4); French Clb; Hosp Aide; Service Clb; Yrbk; Capt JV Tennis; French Hon Soc; Hon Roll; NHS; Pres Acad Fit Awd; Principals Advisory Cncl; ASB Publicity; Asst; UCLA; Bus.

COHN, BRIAN; Silver Creek HS; San Jose, CA; (4); French Clb; Key Clb; Letterman Clb; NFL; Pep Clb; Quiz Bowl; Service Clb; Speech Tm; Teachers Aide; School Musical; ASB Pres; Interact Clb VP; Jnr Cls Treas; UC Berkeley; Bus Admin.

COHN, JENNIFER E; Miraleste HS; Rancho Palos Vrds, CA; (4); 1/200; Hosp Aide; Drill Tm; Var Cheerldng; JV Tennis; High Hon Roll; NHS; Pres Acad Fit Awd; Spanish NHS; Val; Assisteens Golden Angel Awd; Prin Advisory Cncl; 2nd Pl Herbert/Albright Essay Cont; UC Berkeley; Civil Engrng.

COIBION JR, ROBERT A; El Molino HS; Sebastopol, CA; (2); Church Yth Grp; Hon Roll; Campus Life; Arch.

COJULUN, KATHERINE; Birmingham HS; Van Nuys, CA; (3); Aud/Vis; Church Yth Grp; Cmnty Wkr; Dance Clb; Drama Clb; FHA; Girl Scts; JA; Spanish Clb; Drill Tm; UCLA; Phy.

COKE, MATTHEW J; Nordhoff HS; Ojai, CA; (4); Chess Clb; Church Yth Grp; JA; Letterman Clb; Math Clb; Quiz Bowl; Varsity Clb; Var JV Bsbl; Var JV Ftbl; Wt Lftg.

COKELEY, KIRSTEN; Acalanes HS; Lafayette, CA; (1); Church Yth Grp; Drama Clb; Powder Puff Ftbl.

COKER, BONNIE LEIGH; Torrey Pines HS; San Diego, CA; (2); Jazz Band; Mrchg Band; Band Secy, Sctn Ldr, Rep, Pblcty Chrmn; Velvet Knghts Drm Corp; Grl Scts; Cncrt Band; CSF; Bach-Rock Clb; Music.

COKER, JASON W; Yuba City HS; Yuba City, CA; (3); Church Yth Grp; FCA; Church Choir; Stu Cncl; JV Wrstlng; Hon Roll; Tns Fr Lf; NW Coll; Tchr.

COKKINOS, FAITH H; St Joseph HS; Downey, CA; (2); 16/196; Church Yth Grp; Drama Clb; Hon Roll; CSF; Cal ST U Long Beach; Bio.

COLBERT, ADA V; Gladstone HS; Azusa, CA; (3); 65/330; Teachers Aide; Varsity Clb; Stu Cncl; Var Bsktbl; Var Vllybl; Hon Roll; Montview Lg Vrsty Bsktbl 89-90; Comm.

COLBERT, JASON C; San Luis Obispo HS; San Luis Obispo, CA; (2); Intrml Mgr Bsbl; JV Socr; JV Tennis; Hon Roll; UCLA; Law.

COLBERT, LAURA; Marina HS; Huntington Bch, CA; (4); 84/505; Drama Clb; Ski Clb; Spanish Clb; Treas Sr Cls; Stat Score Keeper; JV Tennis; JR Statewsmenb Amer; U San Diego; Lawyer.

COLBERT, MICHELE; Marina HS; Huntington Bch, CA; (2); Rep Debate Tm; Model UN; Pep Clb; Spanish Clb; Treas Frsh Cls; Treas Soph Cls; Stat Score Keeper; JV Tennis; High Hon Roll; Hon Roll; Athls Agnst Substnc Abuse; Arch.

COLBURN, MELISSA; Ponderosa HS; Shingle Springs, CA; (4); 25/289; Church Yth Grp; Cmnty Wkr; Spanish Clb; Teachers Aide; Church Choir; Stat Bsktbl; Cheerldng; Hon Roll; Block P Schlrshp; CSF; Humbolt ST Coll; Bio.

COLBY, MICHAEL A; Argonaut HS; Jackson, CA; (2); Church Yth Grp; JV Bsktbl; Law.

COLBY, RONNIE J; Fall River HS; Fall River Mills, CA; (2); Church Yth Grp; 4-H; FFA; JV Ftbl; JV Var Wt Lftg; 4-H Awd; Hon Roll; Pres Acad Fit Awd; Play Golf; Ski; Spcl Intrsts Hntng Fshng Drvng; Extc Cars & Music; UC Davis; Bus Mngmnt.

COLBY, TIFFANY D; Napa HS; Napa, CA; (3); High Hon Roll; Hon Roll; Univ CA Davis Cmmty Schlrshp Sci Prgm; Contra Costa Cty AIDS Task Frc; Life Sci.

COLDSNOW, ADELE E; Orestimba HS; Newman, CA; (3); Library Aide; Office Aide; SADD; Teachers Aide; VP Stu Cncl; JV Var Bsktbl; JV Var Powder Puff Ftbl; JV Var Sftbl; Hon Roll; Rtry Yth Ldrshp Cmp; Real Est.

COLE, BECKY A; Lutheran HS; Orange, CA; (2); Cmnty Wkr; Var Bsktbl; Var Trk; Child Psych.

COLE, CANDICE M; Desert HS; Edwards, CA; (2); Band; Mrchg Band; Pep Band; School Musical; Hon Roll; Prfct Atten Awd; Medallion For Outstanding Section Leader; CA ST Northridge; Law.

COLE, CARRIE L; Skyline HS; Oakland, CA; (3); 3/550; SADD; Band; Mrchg Band; Pep Band; Variety Show; Rep Soph Cls; Stat Bsktbl; Intrml Cheerldng; JV Trk; High Hon Roll; CSF; Outstndng Jr Girl Sci & Math Glnd St Wmn Engrng; Princeton Awd; Phys Thrpy.

COLE, CHENETTE; South Bay Lutheran HS; Los Angeles, CA; (4); 3/17; Am Leg Aux Girls St; Church Choir; Rptr Yrbk; Rep Jr Cls; Pres Sr Cls; Pres Stu Cncl; Var Sftbl; Var Vllybl; Hon Roll; NCCJ Yth Ldr; Syracuse U; Law.

COLE, CHRIS L; Durham HS; Oroville, CA; (2); Letterman Clb; Ski Clb; Yrbk; Crs Cntry; Trk; Wrstlng; Hon Roll; UC Santa Barbara; Disc Jockey.

COLE, CHRIS L; Mt Whitney HS; Visalia, CA; (1); Pep Clb; Chorus; School Musical; Rep Frsh Cls; Bsbl; Ftbl; JV Socr; Hon Roll; Pres Acad Fit Awd; Stanford; Psych.

COLE, CRYSTAL; Capital Christian Schl; Sacramento, CA; (3); 10/70; Church Yth Grp; Office Aide; Ski Clb; Teachers Aide; Rptr Nwsp; Yrbk; VP Frsh Cls; VP Soph Cls; VP Jr Cls; Var Cheerldng; Bob L Erickson Schlrshp; Pepperdine; Psych.

COLE, CYNTHIA; Los Alamitos HS; Los Alamitos, CA; (3); Church Yth Grp; Science Clb; Service Clb; Spanish Clb; Band; Mrchg Band; Hon Roll; S-Clb; CSF.

COLE, DAVID M; El Camino Real HS; Woodland Hills, CA; (2); Aud/Vis; Math Clb; SADD; Nwsp; CAMERATA; Classical Arts Clb; U Of CO Boulder; Marine Bio.

COLE, DEREK P; Elk Grove HS; Rancho Murieta, CA; (2); 70/550; SADD; Rep Stu Cncl; JV Ftbl; Hon Roll; CSF; Acadmc Ltr; Physics.

COLE, DREAMA D; St Joesph Notre Dame HS; Oakland, CA; (3); JA; JV Bsktbl; Hon Roll; NHS; UC Davis; Bus Admin.

COLE, ERICH F; San Marcos HS; San Marcos, CA; (3); Boy Scts; Key Clb; Ftbl; Ftbl Photo 3 Yrs; Bus.

COLE, FAUNIA A; Tehachapi HS; Keene, CA; (3); Drama Clb; FHA; School Play; Phtg Yrbk; Sec Sr Cls; Powder Puff Ftbl; JV Sftbl; JV Var Vllybl; Wt Lftg; Hon Roll; Yng Wmn Yr Wn Fitnss; Dance Cmmtts; MVP Sftbl; Mst Insprtnl Vllybl; Pacific; Commnctns.

COLE, JENNIFER L; Vintage HS; American Canyon, CA; (2); Computer Clb; German Clb; Girl Scts; Church Choir; School Play; High Hon Roll; NAPA Coll; Psychtry.

COLE, JONATHAN O; Pomona HS; Pomona, CA; (4); Art Clb; Teachers Aide; Chorus; Wt Lftg; Cit Awd; Hon Roll; Act-So Pntng 1st Pl; Blk Engrng Camp 89; Mega Acadc & Prtcptn Awd; CAL Poly; Arch.

COLE, KELLY A; Coronado HS; Coronado, CA; (3); 1/170; Art Clb; Church Yth Grp; Cmnty Wkr; VP French Clb; Key Clb; Letterman Clb; Service Clb; Ed Yrbk; Off Yrbk; Sec Soph Cls; Rotry Yth Ldrshp Awd; Dartmouth U Bk Awd; CA Schlstc Fed; Georgetown; Hstry.

COLE, LARRY G; Chowchilla Union HS; Chowchilla, CA; (4); Church Yth Grp; Church Choir; Hon Roll; Warrior Hnr Roll; Dsgnr Cover For Soph Poetry Book; Art Awd Dsgnr & Ad Cont; Navy; Evnglst.

COLE, LORIE A; Palm Springs HS; Cathedral City, CA; (3); Church Yth Grp; Cmnty Wkr; Debate Tm; Var Stat Vllybl; Hon Roll; Prfct Atten Awd; Wilde Woode Gifted Chldrns Prgrm; Untd Meth Yth Mission Prjct; Advrtsng.

COLE, LUCY A; Eagle Rock JR/Sr HS; Los Angeles, CA; (2); Church Yth Grp; Girl Scts; Key Clb; Chorus; School Play; Hon Roll; Pres Acad Fit Awd; Closeup Gvrnmnt Awrnss; Smmr Exchng Stu To W Germany; Liberal Arts Coll; Humnts.

COLE, MARK; Alta Loma HS; Garland, TX; (4); JETS Awd; Automotive.

COLE, MEREDITH M; Thousand Oaks HS; Newbury Park, CA; (4); Band; Jazz Band; Mrchg Band; Orch; UCLA; Bio.

COLE, PAUL W; Eagle Rock JR/Sr HS; Los Angeles, CA; (2); Boy Scts; Church Yth Grp; Library Aide; Church Choir; Crs Cntry; Trk; Hon Roll; Prfct Atten Awd; Star Trek Clb; Brigham Young U; Acctng.

COLE, ROCHELLE L; Rim Of The World HS; Cedar Glen, CA; (1); German Clb; Band; Drm Mjr(t); Mrchg Band; Orch; Off Frsh Cls; Off Soph Cls; Var Cit Awd; Hon Roll; Pres Acad Fit Awd; Marine Zoology.

COLE, RODERICK J; Chino HS; Chino, CA; (3); Am Leg Boys St; Var L Bsktbl; L Trk; Hon Roll; UCLA Partnrshp Pgm; Slctd Outstndng Mth Stu 89-90; USC; Broadcasting.

COLE, SAMONE L; George Washington Prep HS; Los Angeles, CA; (2); Var Cheerldng; Var Trk; Hon Roll; Marthonians Clb; CA St Champnshp Trk.

COLE, SUZANNE D; Arrowhead Christian Acad; San Bernardino, CA; (3); 1/14; Church Yth Grp; Scholastic Bowl; Chorus; Treas Frsh Cls; Var Bsktbl; Var Sftbl; Cit Awd; High Hon Roll; NHS; Pres Acad Fit Awd; Wilderness Clb; Bus.

COLE, TRACEY K; Beyer HS; Modesto, CA; (4); 286/506; Church Yth Grp; Teachers Aide; Band; Church Choir; Mrchg Band; Hon Roll; Patriot Awd/Bus 89; MJC; Chrstn Cnslr.

COLEGROVE, JENNIFER N; Oakdale HS; Oakdale, CA; (3); 35/300; Ed Yrbk; Powder Puff Ftbl; Hon Roll; Brooks Insti Of Photo; Photo.

COLEMAN, ANGIE; Monta Vista HS; Cupertino, CA; (4); 8/400; VP JA; Acpl Chr; Church Choir; Treas Frsh Cls; JV Capt Cheerldng; Var Pom Pon; Hon Roll; NHS; Ntl Merit Ltr; Pres Acad Fit Awd; CSF; Bnk America Achvt Awd Wnnr; UC Santa Barbara; Econ.

COLEMAN, BLAKE C; Bishop O'dowd HS; Oakland, CA; (3); 100/250; Intrml Vllybl; Hon Roll; Ntl Merit SF; Private Pilot Flght Instrctn; Aerntcl Engrng.

COLEMAN, CALVIN A; Carlsbad HS; Carlsbad, CA; (3); Office Aide; Teachers Aide; Bsktbl; Ftbl; Trk; Hon Roll; Pr Cnslng; Hmn Reltns Cmmtte; Sports Med.

COLEMAN, CHINHAYI; Saint Marys Acad; Los Angeles, CA; (4); 1/84; Hosp Aide; Model UN; Pres Frsh Cls; Hon Roll; NHS; Spanish NHS; Yng Blck Schlrs; Trng Smll Chldrn; Lawyer.

COLEMAN, DAVID; Gateway Christian Acad; San Bernadino, CA; (1); 3/12; Boy Scts; Church Yth Grp; Church Choir; Color Guard; School Play; Yrbk; Rep Stu Cncl; Bsktbl; Cit Awd; Hon Roll; Hrsbck Rdng & Skiing; 2nd Clss Scout; Vet.

COLEMAN, JEREMY M; East Bakersfield HS; Bakersfield, CA; (1); Math Tm; Chorus; JV Bsktbl; Capt Sftbl; Cit Awd; Hon Roll; Prfct Atten Awd; CA ST U-Fullerton; Bsbl.

COLEMAN, JOAN M; Eisenhower HS; Rialto, CA; (3); Key Clb; Office Aide; Pep Clb; Sec Science Clb; Service Clb; Speech Tm; Stu Cncl; Mgr(s); JV Socr; JV Sftbl; Munic Airport Yth Cmmssnr; Amer Legn Cert Schl Awd; Cngrssnl Yth Ldrshp Cncl; Pres Acad Achvt Awd; CA ST San Bernardino; Brdcstr.

COLEMAN, JON C; Elk Grove HS; Sacramento, CA; (4); 36/588; Photo Lcl Art Exhbt; Wtng Music Lcl Rck Band; Musicn.

COLEMAN, KATHLEEN E; Bishop Amat Memorial HS; West Covina, CA; (3); Cmnty Wkr; Teachers Aide; Drill Tm; Powder Puff Ftbl; Score Keeper; JV Trk; Wrstlng; High Hon Roll; Vlntr Cnslr Rec Camp Mntlly Retarded; Loyola Marymount; HS Tchr.

COLEMAN, KEISHA; Inglewood HS; Inglewood, CA; (2); Church Yth Grp; Cmnty Wkr; Office Aide; Red Cross Aide; ROTC; Band; Mrchg Band; JV Sftbl; Hon Roll; Aids Prjct Los Angeles Vlntr Food Bank; Simons Rock Of Bard Coll; Med.

COLEMAN, KIMBERLEIGH M; Palmdale HS; Palmdale, CA; (4); 17/586; French Clb; Mgr Bsktbl; Hon Roll; Pres Acad Fit Awd; Dickinson Coll; Art His.

COLEMAN, KIRSTEN L; Orange Glen HS; Escondido, CA; (1); 110/647; Hon Roll; AZ ST; Arch.

COLEMAN, KISHER M; Vallejo SR HS; Vallejo, CA; (3); Office Aide; Pep Clb; SADD; Stu Cncl; Var Cheerldng; Var L Trk; Var Vllybl; Hon Roll.

COLEMAN, LA TREASE M; Artesia HS; Long Beach, CA; (3); GAA; Band; JV Var Bsktbl; JV Sftbl; Hon Roll; Yng, Black & Gftd Awd; Cmpus Life Clb; PAL Club; Aero Engr.

COLEMAN, LATASHA J; Lakewood SR HS; Lakewood, CA; (4); Church Yth Grp; German Clb; Key Clb; Office Aide; Orch; Kiwanis Awd; NHS; Pres Acad Fit Awd; CSF; Long Beach City Coll.

COLEMAN, LISA M; El Toro HS; El Toro, CA; (3); Church Yth Grp; Cmnty Wkr; Scholastic Bowl; Teachers Aide; Chorus; Capt Drill Tm; High Hon Roll; Opt Clb Awd; Orange Cty Acdmc Dcthln; Med.

COLEMAN, MATTHEW J; Desert HS; California City, CA; (4); 13/81; FBLA; Band; Rep Soph Cls; Rep Stu Cncl; Var Capt Ftbl; Var Trk; Hon Roll; CA Moch Trail Tm 89-90; Otstndng Black Stu Of Antelope Valley Black Heritage Cncl; Otstndng Band Awds; FL A&M U; Bus Admin.

COLEMAN, MELISSA; Rosary HS; Placentia, CA; (3); Spanish Clb; Sftbl; Tennis; High Hon Roll; Hon Roll; NHS; CSF; Safe Rides; USD; Bus.

COLEMAN, NICOLE M; Merced HS; Merced, CA; (3); FBLA; Hon Roll; Prfct Atten Awd; CSF; Bus Admin.

COLEMAN, SARAH K; Claremont HS; Claremont, CA; (1); Dance Clb; Pep Clb; Drill Tm; Socr; Swmmng; High Hon Roll; Hon Roll; Girls Lge; Engl.

COLEMAN, STEPHANIE; Gateway Christian Acad; San Bernardino, CA; (3); 1/4; Church Yth Grp; Office Aide; Teachers Aide; Church Choir; School Play; Nwsp; Yrbk; Pres Rep Stu Cncl; Cit Awd; High Hon Roll; Bible Qzzng; Cal Poly; Cvl Engr.

COLEMAN, STEPHEN R; East Bakersfield HS; Bakersfield, CA; (3); 52/441; Pres Drama Clb; VP German Clb; Key Clb; Thesps; Chorus; School Musical; School Play; Cit Awd; Hon Roll; Prfct Atten Awd; CA ST U Fullerton; Educ.

COLEMAN, TAMARA L; John F Kennedy HS; Sacramento, CA; (3); Treas Church Yth Grp; JA; Church Choir; Var Cheerldng; Var Powder Puff Ftbl; Var Sftbl; Hon Roll; Asst Sunda Schl Teacher; Cert Hnr Schltcs; Psych.

COLEMAN, TAMECA S; Galileo HS; San Francisco, CA; (1); Drama Clb; ROTC; Band; School Play; Hon Roll; Spellman Coll; Law.

COLEMAN, TERESA L; Palmdale HS; Palmdale, CA; (4); 55/510; Drama Clb; Spanish Clb; Teachers Aide; Thesps; School Play; Stage Crew; Off Jr Cls; Off Sr Cls; Swmmng; Pres Acad Fit Awd; CA Scholastic Federation-Life Member; GPA Over 3.17 Since Soph Yr; 19 Units Coll Credit During HS; CSU Nrthrdge; Theatre Arts Tch.

COLEMAN, TIFFINI S; Brethren HS; Carson, CA; (3); Church Yth Grp; Girl Scts; Pep Clb; Teachers Aide; Church Choir; Off Frsh Cls; Stu Cncl; L Trk; Hon Roll; Prfct Atten Awd; U CA Santa Barbara; Crmnl Just.

COLEMAN, YVONNE G; Sonora HS; Sonora, CA; (4); Am Leg Aux Girls St; Church Yth Grp; Teachers Aide; Varsity Clb; JV Var Bsktbl; Stat Ftbl; Score Keeper; JV Var Sftbl; JV Var Vllybl; Stat Wt Lftg; Johnson & Wales U; Hotel/Rest.

COLEMAN-SCOTT, JENE D; Palmdale HS; Palmdale, CA; (3); Church Yth Grp; Girl Scts; Office Aide; Teachers Aide; Church Choir; Drill Tm; JV Bsktbl; Cheerldng; Hon Roll; Prfct Atten Awd; CSU Nrthrdg Upward Bound Pgm; Fisk U; Bus Admin.

COLETTO, REGINA J; Gilroy HS; Gilroy, CA; (4); 77/511; Cmnty Wkr; GAA; JV VP Cheerldng; VP JV Score Keeper; JV Sftbl; Hon Roll; Sftbl Lttl Leag All Stars; Schlr Athlt Awd; Fresno ST U; Psych.

COLEY, ERIN M; Rancho Buena Vista HS; Vista, CA; (4); 22/403; Office Aide; Pres SADD; Chorus; Ed Lit Mag; Rep Frsh Cls; Mgr L Swmmng; High Hon Roll; Hon Roll; Jr NHS; San Francisco ST U; Psych.

COLEY, JASON S; Modesto HS; Modesto, CA; (3); AFS; FBLA; Ski Clb; Bsktbl; Var Golf; Cit Awd; Hon Roll; GAP Prgm Germany Smmr 90; Bus.

COLGAN, KERI; Ramona HS; Riverside, CA; (2); 33/490; Church Yth Grp; Latin Clb; Pep Clb; Off Soph Cls; JV Cheerldng; Trk; Hon Roll; NHS; Friday Night Live; UCR; Elem Ed.

COLGAN, MATTHEW R; Bishop O'dowd HS; Alameda, CA; (2); Drama Clb; Band; School Musical; School Play; Lcrss; Hon Roll; Drama Smmr Wrkshp; Work Luckys Bagger; Skim Brdng; Drama.

COLGATE, ERIN; Dos Pueblos HS; Goleta, CA; (2); 66/313; Church Yth Grp; Cmnty Wkr; Debate Tm; Drama Clb; Letterman Clb; SADD; Varsity Clb; Stage Crew; Variety Show; Var Diving; Usherettes; Marine Bio Club; Fri Night Live; UC Santa Cruz; Acctng.

COLIN, LAURA; James Monroe HS; Panorama, CA; (1); French Clb; Drill Tm; CSUN; Music Engr.

COLLACO, HEATHER A; Skyline HS; Oakland, CA; (3); Church Yth Grp; Computer Clb; Hosp Aide; Key Clb; Rptr Nwsp; Yrbk; Crs Cntry; Cit Awd; Hon Roll; Badmntn; Optometry.

COLLARD, MELANIE D; Twentynine Palms HS; Twentynine Plms, CA; (2); 13/225; Treas AFS; Science Clb; SADD; Stu Cncl; Hon Roll; CSF; Friday Night Live.

COLLAZO, AMELIA; Ramona HS; Ramona, CA; (2); Treas Latin Clb; Socr; CSF; Migrnt Educ Upward Boud Smmr Pgm; Stu Mnth Awds; UC Berkeley; Law.

COLLAZO, GUSTAVO; Pius X HS; South Gate, CA; (4); 7/183; Math Clb; VP Mu Alpha Theta; Science Clb; Spanish Clb; Pres Sr Cls; Bausch & Lomb Sci Awd; High Hon Roll; NHS; Ntl Hispnc Schlrshp Semi-Fnlst; CSF; USC; Comptr Sci.

COLLAZO, JAVIER E; Pius X HS; South Gate, CA; (3); Chess Clb; Letterman Clb; Bsktbl; JV Var Crs Cntry; JV Var Trk; Speech Cont Wnnr; U Southern CA; Law.

COLLAZO, SILVIA; Ramona HS; Ramona, CA; (2); Cmnty Wkr; Pres Latin Clb; Spanish Clb; Migrant Ed; Stu Of Mnth Engl I & II, Alg & Alg IB; UCLA; Phy.

COLLER, BETH; Oceana HS; Pacifica, CA; (4); Library Aide; Teachers Aide; Co-Ed Nwsp; Rep Soph Cls; Rep Jr Cls; Stu Cncl; Cheerldng; Hon Roll.

COLLERSON, EMMA L; Santa Cruz HS; Santa Cruz, CA; (2); Sec French Clb; Band; U CA; Vet.

COLLEY, OCEAN; North HS; Bakersfield, CA; (2); Speech Tm; Teachers Aide; Color Guard; Flag Corp; Cit Awd; Hon Roll; Bio.

COLLEYJR., CLYDE B; Sacramento HS; Sacramento, CA; (4); Art Clb; Aud/Vis; Cmnty Wkr; Drama Clb; Library Aide; School Play; Lit Mag; Cit Awd; Lion Awd; Pres Acad Fit Awd; Commnctns.

COLLIER, JANA M; Bellarmine-Jefferson HS; Los Angeles, CA; (4); 20/110; Church Yth Grp; GAA; Math Clb; Science Clb; Sec Treas Soph Cls; Sec Treas Jr Cls; Sec Sr Cls; Var Bsktbl; Var Tennis; Hon Roll; Michael Maggiaro Scholarship; CA ST U; Business Computers.

COLLIER, JO LENE; Monte Vista HS; Spring Valley, CA; (4); Dance Clb; Office Aide; Pep Clb; Teachers Aide; Drill Tm; Rptr Nwsp; Stat Wrstlng; Hon Roll; Ntl Merit Ltr; Hd Mat Maid; Mat Maid Yr; Dnc Tm Stu Yr; Stephens Coll.

COLLIER, KEVIN M; Bellarmine-Jefferson HS; Los Angeles, CA; (2); Church Yth Grp; Math Clb; Science Clb; Spanish Clb; JV Bsktbl; Var Tennis; High Hon Roll; NHS; Math.

COLLIER, MELISSA; Sacred Heart Of Jesus HS; La Mirada, CA; (4); 1/121; GAA; Pres Letterman Clb; Pres Soph Cls; Pres Sr Cls; Trk; Var Capt Vllybl; Bausch & Lomb Sci Awd; Dnfth Awd; Lion Awd; NHS; Princeton U; Intrntl Rltns.

COLLIER, MICHELLE J; Eagle Rock HS; Los Angeles, CA; (3); Service Clb; Drill Tm; Rptr Nwsp; Yrbk; Pasadena; Ed.

COLLIGAN, TRACIE; California HS; San Ramon, CA; (3); Service Clb; Band; Mrchg Band; JV Crs Cntry; Var JV Sftbl; Hon Roll; Music Awd; Capt JV Sftbl Team; Athl Of Mnth; All Leag Sftbl Team Hnrbl Mntn.

COLLIGNON, KAREN; Palmdale HS; Palmdale, CA; (4); 50/500; FFA; Drill Tm; Capt Off Flag Corp; Rptr Nwsp; Elks Awd; NHS; Pres Acad Fit Awd; Rotary Awd; Keywanettes Sec; Falcon Guide; Engl.

COLLIGNON, KATHERINE D; Bishop O'dowd HS; Berkeley, CA; (3); Church Yth Grp; Cmnty Wkr; Ski Clb; Acpl Chr; Chorus; Nwsp; High Hon Roll; Ntl Merit Ltr; Amnesty Intl; Jr Statesmen Am; San Francisco Girls Chorus Ensemble.

COLLINS, ADAM S; Montclair HS; Montclair, CA; (2); Teachers Aide; L JV Socr; Hon Roll; JV Soccer Team MVP; UN Las Vegas.

COLLINS, ALISA; El Camino Real HS; Woodland Hills, CA; (2); Cmnty Wkr; Rep Frsh Cls; Rep Soph Cls; Stu Cncl; JV Tennis; CSF; UC Irvine; Psych.

COLLINS, CAREN A; Calvary Chapel HS; Garden Grove, CA; (2); Stu Cncl; Var Sftbl; Hon Roll; Sftbl Most Imprvd Player; Elem Schl Teacher.

COLLINS, CHADWICK; Oak Park HS; Agoura Hills, CA; (1); JV Ftbl; JV Trk; Pr Cnslng; Rep ASB Ldrshp.

COLLINS, CHRISTINE; Western HS; Anaheim, CA; (1); GAA; Pep Clb; SADD; Off Frsh Cls; Bsktbl; Cheerldng; Var Score Keeper; Glrs Lgue; SOS; Stanford; Bus.

COLLINS, CHRISTINE L; Pasadena HS; Pasadena, CA; (3); AFS; Church Yth Grp; French Clb; Hosp Aide; SADD; Acpl Chr; School Musical; Variety Show; Var L Swmmng; Hon Roll; CSF; Frng Lang Spk Off; Dance; Librl Arts.

COLLINS, CORY R; Hamilton HS; Los Angeles, CA; (2); Debate Tm; Teachers Aide; Off Frsh Cls; JV Ftbl; JV Golf; Var Wt Lftg; High Hon Roll; Hon Roll; NHS; JSA; AZ ST U; Pro Golfer.

COLLINS, DEMAYNE; Lowell HS; San Francisco, CA; (3); Cmnty Wkr; Computer Clb; FBLA; JA; Math Tm; Science Clb; Orch; Swing Chorus; JV Var Bsktbl; JV Var Ftbl; San Diego ST; Bus/Marktng/Acct.

COLLINS JR, EDWARD J; San Francisco University HS; San Francisco, CA; (4); Church Yth Grp; Cmnty Wkr; Drama Clb; Intnl Clb; Spanish Clb; Acpl Chr; Chorus; School Musical; School Play; JV Crs Cntry; Ntl Achvmnt Schlrshp Prog Outstndng Ngro Stu; Harvard U; Intl Bus Rltns.

COLLINS, ESTHER; Saddleback HS; Santa Ana, CA; (1); French Clb; Yrbk; Cit Awd; DAR Awd; Pres Acad Fit Awd; UCLA; Jrnlsm.

COLLINS, GINGER N; Los Alamitos HS; Los Alamitos, CA; (3); Teachers Aide; Varsity Clb; Var Gym; Ecology Club; S CA Gymnastic Champ; GYMNASTICS MVP 90; Gymnast Of Yr 89.

COLLINS, JENNIFER; Norco HS; Corona, CA; (3); French Clb; Model UN; Office Aide; Service Clb; School Play; Rep Jr Cls; Off Sr Cls; JV Var Cheerldng; Powder Puff Ftbl; Captain JV Cheerleading; Member CA Scholastic Federation As Sophomore; San Diego ST U; Liberal Arts.

COLLINS, JENNIFER A; Leffingwell HS; Norwalk, CA; (3); Church Yth Grp; Drama Clb; Cheerldng; Vllybl; High Hon Roll; Hon Roll; Physical Therapist.

COLLINS, JENNIFER I; Lodi HS; Lodi, CA; (3); French Clb; Library Aide; Acpl Chr; Hon Roll; Psych.

COLLINS, JENNIFER L; Pinole Valley HS; Pinole, CA; (1); Band; Jazz Band; Orch; Gym; Vllybl; Stanford; Marine Bio.

COLLINS, JIMMY; Trinity HS; Trinity Center, CA; (2); Ski Clb; Var JV Ftbl; L JV Trk; L Var Wrstlng; Cal Poly.

COLLINS, JULIANNE M; Coarondelet HS; Clayton, CA; (3); Church Yth Grp; Cmnty Wkr; Drama Clb; Model UN; Rep VP Ski Clb; Rep Frsh Cls; Stu Cncl; Var Cheerldng; Powder Puff Ftbl; High Hon Roll; Outstndng Teenager Awd; CSF; Friday Night Live Promoting Sober Parites & Against Drunk Drvng; Psych.

COLLINS, KAREN M; Poway HS; Poway, CA; (4); 8/714; Letterman Clb; Math Clb; Model UN; Mu Alpha Theta; Ski Clb; SADD; Teachers Aide; Powder Puff Ftbl; Var Capt Socr; Sftbl; 2nd Tm All Leag Socr; UC Davis; Bus.

COLLINS, KATHLEEN; Paraclete HS; Leona Valley, CA; (3); Church Yth Grp; Drama Clb; Key Clb; Pep Clb; SADD; Var Cheerldng; High Hon Roll; Hon Roll; NHS; Z Clb Histrn; Peer Tutor; CSF.

COLLINS, KELLEY L; Woodcrest Christian HS; Riverside, CA; (3); Hosp Aide; Teachers Aide; Var Sftbl; Var Vllybl; Med.

COLLINS, KENDRA E; A A Stagg HS; Stockton, CA; (1); Church Yth Grp; Cmnty Wkr; Dance Clb; Drama Clb; Intnl Clb; JA; SADD; Thesps; Varsity Clb; Church Choir; Spec Olympic Vol; Asst Sign Lang Cls; Berkeley U; Pediatric.

COLLINS, KIM J; Trabuco Hills HS; El Toro, CA; (4); 1/350; Church Yth Grp; Spanish Clb; Ed Nwsp; JV Vllybl; DAR Awd; Elks Awd; Kiwanis Awd; NHS; Pres Acad Fit Awd; Val; Pepperdine U.

COLLINS, LATOYA; Kennedy HS; L V T, CA; (3); Office Aide; Teachers Aide; Drill Tm; Yrbk; Cheerldng; Powder Puff Ftbl; Martin Luther King Clb; Ldrshp; Drill Team Girl Of Yr; Schl Pres; Chld Psych.

COLLINS, LOREINA; Atwater HS; Winton, CA; (4); 1/391; Church Yth Grp; Teachers Aide; Bausch & Lomb Sci Awd; Kiwanis Awd; Ntl Merit Ltr; Pres Acad Fit Awd; Val; Science Clb; Ed Yrbk; High Hon Roll; CSF Lftm; Gld Cord; U Of Rochester; Engrng.

COLLINS, MELISSA L; Red Bluff HS; Red Bluff, CA; (1); Key Clb; SADD; Hon Roll.

COLLINS, MICHELE; Torrey Pines HS; Del Mar, CA; (1); SADD; Wt Lftg; UC Davis; Vet.

COLLINS, REBECCA E; Dixon HS; Dixon, CA; (3); 4-H; French Clb; FFA; Hosp Aide; Intnl Clb; UC Davis; Biological Sciences.

COLLINS, SARAH; Las Plumas HS; Oroville, CA; (1); Pres Church Yth Grp; FHA; VP Frsh Cls; Pres Soph Cls; Stu Cncl; Var JV Score Keeper; Hon Roll; Social Wrkr.

COLLINS, SPENCER A; Saddleback HS; Santa Ana, CA; (1); VP French Clb; MESA Clb; Orange Cty Acad Dcthln Hnrbl Mntn Essy; U CA Davis; Zlgy.

COLLINS, TRACY M; Oakland Technical HS; Oakland, CA; (4); 9/220; Church Yth Grp; Var Capt Swmmng; Hon Roll; NHS; Pres Schlr; Statesmen Assn; Histrcl Trivia; U Of San Francisco; Intl Bus.

COLLUM, CYNTHIA E; Redwood HS; Visalia, CA; (4); Church Yth Grp; French Clb; FBLA; Church Choir; Swmmng; Hon Roll; Pres Acad Fit Awd; CSF; Acad Decthln Tm; Clg Of Sequoia; Accntnt.

COLMENARES, BLANCA R; Liberty Union HS; Oakley, CA; (2); 51/381; Church Yth Grp; Office Aide; Bus.

COLMENARES, CARLOS; Rio Mesa HS; Oxnard, CA; (3); Stu Of Mnth; Perfect Attndnce For JR Yr; Elec.

COLNIC, ANN; Warren HS; Downey, CA; (4); 19/400; French Clb; Science Clb; Service Clb; Pres Sr Cls; Capt Cheerldng; Capt Pom Pon; L Trk; Cit Awd; High Hon Roll; Hon Roll; Bellflower Prfrmng Arts Soloist; Pres Children And The Amer Rvltn; CA Golden ST Geo Awd; U Of Oregoon; Dance Thrpst.

COLOMA, EILEEN ALABANZA; Northgate HS; Walnut Creek, CA; (4); Cmnty Wkr; Hosp Aide; Band; Flag Corp; Mrchg Band; Nwsp; Crs Cntry; Trk; Hon Roll; Churhc Lector-Yth Ministry; Diablo & Rossmoor Schlrshps; Holocaust Educator; Sunday Mass Facilitator; U CA San Diego.

COLOMA, MARIA LANIE M; Robert A Millikan HS; Long Beach, CA; (2); English Clb; Girl Scts; Math Clb; Science Clb; Pres Frsh Cls; VP Stu Cncl; Prfct Atten Awd; Val; Badminton V; Bst Prctcl Arts; 3rd Pl Moore Leag Badminton Trnmt; UCLA; Arch.

COLOMBI, TRACY L; Clear Lake HS; Lakeport, CA; (3); 4/80; JV Bsktbl; Hon Roll; Hosp Vlntr; Mendocino Coll Mdrn Dnc, Sprng Dnc Fstvl; Cert Achvt Mrn Sci; DR.

COLOMEDA, SOFIA T; Cordova HS; Rancho Cordova, CA; (3); Cmnty Wkr; Drama Clb; German Clb; Key Clb; SADD; Teachers Aide; Acpl Chr; Church Choir; School Musical; School Play; Bus Ed Awd Kybrdng I; Friday Night Live; UCLA; Mass Commnctns.

COLON, DAVID; Mountain View Acad; Milpitas, CA; (4); Drama Clb; Spanish Clb; Varsity Clb; Band; Yrbk; Phtg Frsh Cls; Phtg Jr Cls; Phtg Sr Cls; Bsktbl; Ftbl; San Jose ST U; Phy Thrpst.

COLON, ELIZABETH; Yerba Buena HS; San Jose, CA; (2); Sftbl; Hon Roll; MESA Club; Capitalist Club Secy; Pediatrician.

COLON, ELSBETH; Yerba Buena HS; San Jose, CA; (2); Sftbl; Hon Roll; MESA Club; Capitalist Club Secy; Pediatrician.

COLON, JAMES N; Edison SR HS; Stockton, CA; (2); Church Yth Grp; Cmnty Wkr; Hon Roll; Congressional Yth Ldrshp Cncl; Bsktbl; Marine Bio.

COLON, PRISCILLA; Seaside HS; Ft Belvoir, VA; (4); Office Aide; Spanish Clb; Teachers Aide; Tutor Spnsh; VA ST U; Accntng.

COLON, VANESSA M; St Bernard HS; Inglewood, CA; (3); Cit Awd; Hon Roll; Poetry Writer; CA Schlrshp Fed Club; Latino Club; UCLA; Jrnlsm.

COLSON, ANETTE; El Dorado HS; Placerville, CA; (4); Church Yth Grp; Office Aide; Speech Tm; Teachers Aide; Flag Corp; Stat Bsktbl; Stat Trk; Hon Roll; NHS; Pres Acad Fit Awd; Secy JR Stsmn Amer; Pepperdine U; Bus Admin.

COLSON, TANGELA T; Cordova SR HS; Rancho Cordova, CA; (2); Church Yth Grp; Dance Clb; Drama Clb; Model UN; Pep Clb; SADD; Teachers Aide; Drill Tm; School Play; Stage Crew; Qlfr Natl Trk/Field In Relay, Long Jump; UC Davis; Psych.

COLSTON, DAMONE G; Inglewood HS; Inglewood, CA; (2); Drama Clb; Ftbl; Trk; Hon Roll; Trk Fnls & Coaches Awd; Stanford; Elec Engre.

COLT, JAMES D; Garces Memorial HS; Bakersfield, CA; (3); 2/250; Key Clb; Math Tm; Lit Mag; High Hon Roll; Early Accept USC 90; U Southern CA; Pol Sci.

COLTHIRST, ANTHONY D; Saddle Back HS; Santa Ana, CA; (3); Chorus; Stu Cncl; Var Ftbl; Var Trk; Cit Awd; Southern CA U; Eng.

COLTON, MONICA T; Highlands HS; North Highlands, CA; (3); Hon Roll; Sacramento ST; Phy.

COLVILLE, TRENT J; Poway HS; Poway, CA; (3); Cmnty Wkr; Hon Roll; CSF; Bus.

COLVIN, HEATHER L; Brea Olinda HS; Brea, CA; (2); GAA; Varsity Clb; Chorus; JV Capt Sftbl; Var Socr; Var Vllybl; Stat Wrstlng; Hon Roll; Jr NHS; Prfct Atten Awd; Brea Soccer Assn; Law Enforcement.

COLVIN, ROBERT P; Crescenta Valley HS; Glendale, CA; (4); Mu Alpha Theta; ROTC; Spanish Clb; Color Guard; Amrcn Lgn Schlstc Excclnce Awd; CA ST U Northridge; Comp Sci.

COLYN, NIRA; Lassen Union HS; Susanville, CA; (4); 11/160; Letterman Clb; Rptr Nwsp; Ed Yrbk; Rep Stu Cncl; Crs Cntry; Trk; High Hon Roll; NHS; Pres Acad Fit Awd; CA Schlstc Fed 100% Awd Wnnr; St Johns Coll; Lit.

COMAN, TRINA Y; Rim Of The World HS; Blue Jay, CA; (3); Church Yth Grp; Pres Frsh Cls; Rep Stu Cncl; Var Sftbl; JV Vllybl; MVP Awd Jr JV Vllybl; CA ST Fullerton; Law.

COMBS, AMY E; Hoover HS; Fresno, CA; (2); 64/685; JV Sftbl; Hon Roll; Fresno ST; Spcl Ed Tchr.

COMBS, JOEY ALLEN; Oakdale HS; Oakdale, CA; (3); Ski Clb; Teachers Aide; Varsity Clb; School Musical; School Play; JV Var Bsbl; Var Wt Lftg; Var Wrstlng; Law.

COMBS, LORRAINE N; La Mirada HS; Whittier, CA; (2); Debate Tm; Hosp Aide; NFL; Speech Tm; Stage Crew; Trk; High Hon Roll; Yale U; Crmnl Law.

COMBS, MISTY; Hesperia HS; Hesperia, CA; (2); Pep Clb; Cheerldng; Hon Roll; Court Reporter.

COMBS, SARAH J; Fresno Christian HS; Fresno, CA; (2); Church Yth Grp; Chorus; Rptr Nwsp; High Hon Roll; Yth Grp Msc Ldrshp; Englsh.

COMBS, SHANDRIKA R; Skyline HS; Oakland, CA; (3); Cmnty Wkr; Drama Clb; Teachers Aide; Thesps; School Musical; School Play; Stage Crew; Variety Show; Hon Roll; St Schlr; Yth Ending Hunger; Med.

COMEE, STEPHANY; Rosary HS; Yorba Linda, CA; (3); Church Yth Grp; Science Clb; School Play; Sftbl; Hon Roll; NHS; Mock Trial; Retreat Tm; UC Santa Barbara; Marine Bio.

COMFORT, JEFF D; Hughson Union HS; Hughson, CA; (4); Lit Mag; Var Ftbl; Swmmng; Var Trk; Hon Roll; Super Stu Awd; Nmrs Art Awds; CSU Stanislaus; Phys Thrpy.

COMISSO, CHRISTY T; Mayfield SR HS; Arcadia, CA; (3); AFS; Church Yth Grp; Hosp Aide; SADD; Chorus; Ed Nwsp; Intrml Tennis; Intrml Trk; Hon Roll; NHS; Accntng.

COMPAGNON, ANDRES; William Hart HS; Newhall, CA; (2); Cop.

COMPANI, ERICIA; Ygnacio Valley HS; Pittsburg, CA; (3); Pep Clb; Teachers Aide; Bsktbl; Trk; Cit Awd; Hon Roll; BSU Clb; Commrcl Art.

COMPANION, JOHN; Seaside HS; Fort Ord, CA; (3); Art Clb; ROTC; Bsktbl; Vllybl; Hon Roll; Leeward Coll; Art.

COMPTON, HEATHER JEANNINE; Perris HS; Nuevo, CA; (4); Pres SADD; Teachers Aide; Pres Stu Cncl; Var Capt Socr; Cit Awd; Hon Roll; Brd Of Trustees Stu Rep; Stu Comm WASC Chairprsn; Cal ST U Fresno; Physcl Thrpy.

COMPTON, MARCELINA L; Roosevelt HS; Fresno, CA; (2); Church Yth Grp; Band; Chorus; Color Guard; Flag Corp; Mrchg Band; JV Crs Cntry; JV Trk; Hon Roll; RIF; Fresno City; Educ.

COMPTON, MINDY L; Oak Ridge HS; Sacramento, CA; (3); Cmnty Wkr; Intnl Clb; Math Clb; Math Tm; Service Clb; School Play; Ed Nwsp; Rptr Yrbk; Off Frsh Cls; Pres Soph Cls; CSF Mem Coord & Svc Awd; Sierra Club; Greenpeace Mem; Intern CA ST Lands Commission; Kenpo Karate Stu; U CA; Phys Sci.

COMPTON, SONNY J; Central Valley HS; Round Mountain, CA; (3); 11/273; Am Leg Boys St; Var L Wrstlng; Hon Roll; Cert Scuba Diver; Cardin Vasular Srgy.

COMPTON, SUSAN; Ventura HS; Ventura, CA; (3); 36/431; Am Leg Aux Girls St; Church Yth Grp; Drama Clb; Pep Clb; SADD; Thesps; School Play; Var Cheerldng; High Hon Roll; Hon Roll; Ventura Coll; Law.

COMPUESTO, MARIA; Samuel F B Morse HS; San Diego, CA; (4); French Clb; Office Aide; Capt Flag Corp; French Hon Soc; Hon Roll; Jr NHS; NHS; Ldrshp Awd; San Diego Cnty Essy, Write-Off Outstndng Achvt; San Diego ST U; Ed Psych.

CONCEPCION, AL; Lemoore HS; Lemoore, CA; (2); Art Clb; Dance Clb; JV Ftbl; JV Trk; Hon Roll; Cal Poly; Engrng.

CONCEPCION, DENNIS C; Los Angeles HS; Los Angeles, CA; (3); Rep Jr Cls; JV Tennis.

CONCEPCION, LALAINE; Lakewood HS; Long Beach, CA; (3); Drama Clb; Red Cross Aide; Science Clb; Spanish Clb; School Musical; School Play; Stage Crew; Cit Awd; Hon Roll; Lion Awd; Soph Senate; Psych.

CONCEPCION, LAWRENCE; Bellarmine Jefferson HS; Glendale, CA; (1); Church Yth Grp; Cmnty Wkr; JV Bsbl; Var Socr; Prfct Atten Awd; UCLA; Arch.

CONCEPCION, MARICEL C; Saint Genevieve HS; Van Nuys, CA; (3); French Clb; Nwsp; Yrbk; Hon Roll; Unity Clb; UCLA; Nrsng.

CONDE, ANDRE G; Orange Glen HS; Escondido, CA; (3); 23/458; Rep Jr Cls; Rep Stu Cncl; JV Socr; Cit Awd; High Hon Roll; Hon Roll; NHS; Prfct Atten Awd; CSF; Associated Stu Body; Bradley U; Physiology.

CONDE, JOY; Fresno Adventist Acad; Clovis, CA; (4); 2/30; Cmnty Wkr; FCA; Band; Chorus; Sec Soph Cls; Treas Jr Cls; Treas Sr Cls; Bsktbl; Gym; Treas NHS; Pacific Union Coll; Pre-Med.

CONDIT, CAREN M; El Camino Fundamental HS; Carmichael, CA; (3); Church Yth Grp; Cmnty Wkr; Latin Clb; Teachers Aide; Church Choir; Variety Show; Cit Awd; High Hon Roll; Hon Roll; NHS; Writing Awd; Ldr In Natl Yth Cnfrnce; Coll; Tchng Accntnt.

CONE, MARIAH B; San Gabriel HS; San Gabriel, CA; (2); AFS; Debate Tm; Key Clb; NFL; SADD; Rep Jr Cls; JV Crs Cntry; Var Swmmng; Hon Roll; Opt Clb Awd; USC; Philosphy.

CONERLY, MARTINA; Luther Burbank SR HS; Sacramento, CA; (3); Rep Church Yth Grp; Rep Dance Clb; Rep Drama Clb; Rep FHA; Rep FTA; Rep Pep Clb; Rep ROTC; Rep Drill Tm; Rep School Play; Sec Rep Jr Cls; Grambling U.

CONG, KHOANH H; Alhambra HS; Alhambra, CA; (3); Computer Clb; UCLA; Banking.

CONG, LIZ Q; George Washington HS; San Francisco, CA; (2); French Clb; German Clb; Chorus; Hon Roll; Psych.

CONG-TANG, NHAT-THUY T; Berkeley HS; Berkeley, CA; (3); 3/30; #1 Mixed Dbl In Badminton Tm; UC Davis; Pharmacy.

CONGER, CARRIE ANN; Fairfield HS; Rustburg, VA; (1); Church Yth Grp; Girl Scts; Flag Corp; CJSF; Tall Flags Squad; San Diego ST; Marine Bio.

CONINX, MARIANNE E; El Camino Real HS; Westhills, CA; (2); Teachers Aide; Mgr(s); Score Keeper; L Trk; U NE-LAS Vegas; Engr.

CONKLE, MARC; Madera HS; Madera, CA; (3); 16/540; Boy Scts; Science Clb; Rep Soph Cls; JV Tennis; Hon Roll; Pres Schlr; Rotary Awd; Camp Royal Ldrshp Smmr Camp 90; Flying-Soloed 90; CSF; Tutor; USAF Acad; Airline Pilot.

CONKLIN, KYLE D; Antelope Valley HS; Lancaster, CA; (3); 78/798; Church Yth Grp; Teachers Aide; Cit Awd; Hon Roll; CA Schlrshp Fed; Harvard; Acctng.

CONLEY, ADAM J; Notre Dame HS; Colton, CA; (1); Church Yth Grp; JA; Varsity Clb; JV Bsktbl; JV Ftbl; Var L Swmmng; Var Wt Lftg; High Hon Roll; Hon Roll; Jr NHS.

CONLEY, CHRIS J; Coalinga Union HS; Coalinga, CA; (2); FFA; Band; Var Tennis; Hon Roll.

CONLEY, COLLEEN M; Fontana HS; Fontana, CA; (2); Band; Mrchg Band; Hon Roll; Legstve Cncl; Indian Culture Clb; Foods/Nutrition Clb; Accntnt.

CONLEY, JEFF; Middletown HS; Middletown, CA; (4); 13/64; Pres FFA; JV Var Bsbl; JV Var Bsktbl; JV Ftbl; Elks Awd; Hon Roll; Rotary Awd; Outstndng Sr Agri Awd; Chico ST U; Agri.

CONLEY, KELLI Q; Louisville HS; Westlake Vlg, CA; (1); Art Clb; Dance Clb; Drama Clb; GAA; Hosp Aide; Science Clb; Ski Clb; Pres Soph Cls; JV Capt Sftbl; Natl Charity Leag Cmmnty Svc Awd.

CONLEY, RENEE; Reedley HS; Reedley, CA; (4); 58/352; Church Yth Grp; FCA; French Clb; FBLA; German Clb; Pep Clb; Varsity Clb; Treas Sr Cls; JV Var Cheerldng; JV Var Tennis; Frnch Clb VP; Entre Novs Sectry; Law.

CONLEY, SHERELLE N; Encinal HS; Alameda, CA; (3); FBLA; Key Clb; Bsktbl; San Francisco ST; Law.

CONLEY, TAMMY J; La Sierra HS; Riverside, CA; (2); Church Yth Grp; FBLA; Chorus; JV Bsktbl; Var Crs Cntry; Var Capt Trk; JV Vllybl; Friday Night Live; Show Choir Clb Sec; San Diego ST U; Law.

CONLEY, TANISHA M; Fontana HS; Fontana, CA; (3); Drama Clb; Hon Roll; Drama Awd; CA Poly; Teach.

CONN, ANDREA L; Colfax HS; Colfax, CA; (2); 36/197; 4-H; Red Cross Aide; Chorus; Flag Corp; Swmmng; Wt Lftg; Schl Rcgntn Gldn St Exam Alg; ID Unit For Band; U NE Reno; Med.

CONN, JEFF E; Narbonne HS; Rancho Palos Ver, CA; (2); Church Yth Grp; School Play; Stage Crew; Phtg Nwsp; Phtg Yrbk; JV L Tennis; Trk; Wt Lftg; Cit Awd; Hon Roll; Envrnmnt Clb; 1st Pl Photojrnlsm Awd, Rgnl JEA Cntst; Supr Photo Jrnlsm Awds Natl JEA Cntst; Brooks Inst Of Photo; Photo.

CONN, NANCY M; Del Norte HS; Crescent City, CA; (3); Band; Flag Corp; Jazz Band; Pep Band; School Play; Bsktbl; Cheerldng; Vllybl; Butte Coll; Intr Dsgn.

CONNAUGHTON, ERIK; Cajon HS; Sn Bernardino, CA; (4); 7/359; Elks Awd; NHS; CSF Treas; Intl Rltns.

CONNEAU, JANEEN D; Sonora HS; Sonora, CA; (3); 4-H; FFA; Nwsp; 4-H Awd; Star Grnhnd FFA; Horse Shws & Schl Rodeo; CA St Hrsmns Assoc; San Louis Obispo Poly; Hrs Ind.

CONNELL, CHRISTINE M; John Burroughs HS; Burbank, CA; (3); French Clb; Letterman Clb; Library Aide; Pres Service Clb; Teachers Aide; Stage Crew; Pres Stu Cncl; JV L Bsktbl; Var L Trk; Hon Roll; Cmp Fire Eqstrn Grp; YABA.

CONNELL, DIANE L; Eisenhower HS; San Bernardino, CA; (2); Cmnty Wkr; Office Aide; Teachers Aide; Rptr Nwsp; Ltr K Clb; C Clb; Dentistry.

CONNELL, GREGORY A; Homestead HS; Sunnyvale, CA; (1); JV Bsbl; Var Socr; UCSD; Accntnt.

CONNELLY, ROBBIN A; Pomona HS; Pomona, CA; (1); Hon Roll; Citizenship In Art I; Mt Sac Coll; Sec.

CONNELLY, SANDRA M; Imperial HS; Pasadena, CA; (2); Church Yth Grp; Chorus; Intrml Bsktbl; Var Sftbl; Intrml Vllybl; Hon Roll; Vllybll & Chrldng Chrch Youth Prog; Ambassador Coll; Fash.

CONNELLY, STACI A; Santa Clara HS; San Jose, CA; (3); Church Yth Grp; Capt Chess Clb; Var L Swmmng; Pres Acad Fit Awd; Outstndng Spnsh Achvt Awd 89-90; Santa Clara U; Law.

CONNER, BRAD J; Vaca HS; Vacaville, CA; (2); JV Socr; JV Wrstlng; Cit Awd; High Hon Roll; Hon Roll; Prfct Atten Awd.

CONNER, BRIAN J; Bear River HS; Auburn, CA; (2); Band; Jazz Band; Pep Band; JV Capt Socr; High Hon Roll; Hnrs Rnkng Gldn ST Exam Geom; 3rd Pl ST Lvl Odyssey Mind Comp.

CONNER, DENENEA L; Covina HS; West Covina, CA; (2); French Clb; Reading & Exercise; Accntng/Bkkpng.

CONNER, ITONYA C; Fremont HS; Oakland, CA; (4); Pres Church Yth Grp; Dance Clb; Mgr Yrbk; Pres Soph Cls; Pres Jr Cls; Pres Sr Cls; Cheerldng; Var Capt Sftbl; Mst Outstndng Ldrshp Awd; Hayward ST; Bus Admin.

CONNER, KIM; Lodi Acad; Lodi, CA; (2); 1/32; Church Yth Grp; Office Aide; Ski Clb; Band; Bsbl; Bsktbl; Var Ftbl; Capt Gym; Score Keeper; Vllybl; Natl Ftnss Awd; Band Musician Yr; San Diego ST U; Grphc Dsgn.

CONNER, MATTHEW J; Redwood Christian HS; Castro Valley, CA; (3); Am Leg Boys St; Church Yth Grp; Band; Jazz Band; Pres Soph Cls; Sec Jr Cls; Var Bsbl; Var Bsktbl; Var Socr; High Hon Roll; CSF; Chrstn Svc Brigade; U CA Berkely; Engrng.

CONNER, MICHELLE LYNN; South HS; Bakersfield, CA; (4); 59/397; High Hon Roll; Hon Roll; Prfct Atten Awd; CSU Bakersfield; Comp Sci.

CONNICK, CHRISTY R; St Patricks-St Vincents HS; Vallejo, CA; (1); Girl Scts; Hosp Aide; Crs Cntry; Hon Roll; Med.

CONNOLLY, CLAYTON; Rim Of The World HS; Lake Arrowhead, CA; (1); Church Yth Grp; English Clb; Ftbl; Socr; Wt Lftg; High Hon Roll; Hon Roll; UC Irvine; Orthpdc.

CONNOLLY, TERESA M; Trinity HS; Weaverville, CA; (3); Church Yth Grp; Cmnty Wkr; 4-H; FFA; Ski Clb; Sftbl; Var Vllybl; Cit Awd; High Hon Roll; Hon Roll; U Of Davis CA; Psych.

CONNON, PAUL; Capistrano Valley Christian HS; Mission Viejo, CA; (3); Var L Bsbl; Var L Socr; Hon Roll.

CONNOR, TRACY E; La Reina HS; Westlake Village, CA; (2); 1/90; Drama Clb; Hosp Aide; Sec Chorus; Mgr Stage Crew; Rep Nwsp; Ed Yrbk; Sec Treas Soph Cls; NHS; Mock Trl Comptn Defense Lawyer; Vet Med.

CONRAD, DUSTIN S; Chino HS; Chino, CA; (3); FCA; JV Var Ftbl.

CONRAD, JEFFREY; Saint Joseph HS; Santa Maria, CA; (3); Cmnty Wkr; Library Aide; Office Aide; Quiz Bowl; Teachers Aide; Rep Stu Cncl; High Hon Roll; Hon Roll; Var Bsktbl; Var Socr; 3rd Prize-CDA Lit Cont; Stanford; Law.

CONRAD, LAURA; San Marcos HS; Santa Barbara, CA; (4); Drama Clb; School Musical; Hon Roll; Pres Acad Fit Awd; St Schlr; CA Arts Schlr; U CA Irvine; Dance.

CONRAD JR, MICHAEL B; Corona SR HS; Corona, CA; (3); Pres Stu Cncl; Var L Wrstlng; U CA.

CONRAD, MICHAEL D; Lodi HS; Stockton, CA; (3); 72/518; Var Ftbl; Var Trk; Wt Lftg; Hon Roll; Prfct Atten Awd.

CONRAD, MICHELE N; San Gorgonio HS; San Bernardino, CA; (3); Cmnty Wkr; Hosp Aide; Latin Clb; Science Clb; School Musical; School Play; Stage Crew; Rep Frsh Cls; High Hon Roll; NHS; Cert Of Merit In Piano; Ca Schlrshp Fdrtn Slbrer; Spnsh Prnctn Cntst Awded; Irvine CA U; Elec Engrng.

CONRAD, MONICA; Los Banos HS; Los Banos, CA; (2); Math Clb; Science Clb; High Hon Roll; Peer Cnslng; Psych.

CONRADSON, KATIE N; Lutheran HS; Santa Ana, CA; (3); 2/100; Church Yth Grp; Hosp Aide; Quiz Bowl; Scholastic Bowl; Speech Tm; Teachers Aide; Stu Cncl; High Hon Roll; Lion Awd; NHS; Values In Action Awd; Am Legn Auxiliary Girls ST; U CA Irvine; Pre Med.

CONROW, RHONDA K; North HS; Bakersfield, CA; (4); VP Bus Profs of Am; Cmnty Wkr; Office Aide; Teachers Aide; Intrml Powder Puff Ftbl; Hon Roll; Bus Club Schlrshp; Bakersfield Coll; Nrsng.

CONSHAFTER, JANA L; Bakersfield HS; Bakersfield, CA; (2); Church Yth Grp; ROTC; Color Guard; Drill Tm; Rep Stu Cncl; Hon Roll; Cadet 1st Lt Operation Off 3rd In Command; ROTC; Bus.

CONSOLACION, THEODORA B; Lowell HS; San Francisco, CA; (2); SADD; Vlybl Clb; CSF; Bus.

CONSTANZA, PATRICIA; Alexander Hamilton HS; Los Angeles, CA; (3); Drill Tm; Variety Show; L Pom Pon; Hon Roll; UCLA; Arch.

CONSUNJI, TRISHA F; Anaheim HS; Anaheim, CA; (3); Quiz Bowl; Spanish Clb; Teachers Aide; Variety Show; NY U; Writer.

CONTE, LISA J; Huntington Beach HS; Huntington Beach, CA; (1); Red Cross Aide; Sec Soph Cls; Var Socr; JV Trk; Vllybl; Hon Roll; HS Al Reboin Frshmn Awd Prtcptn 3 Sprts; Bus.

CONTI, GINA; St Francis HS; Roseville, CA; (1); SADD; Church Choir; JV L Bsktbl; Var L Swmmng; High Hon Roll; Prfct Atten Awd; CSF; Awd Excl Theology & Math; U WA; Bus.

CONTINELLI, AARON M; Mountain Empire HS; Pine Valley, CA; (2); VP Jr Cls; Var Bsbl; JV Ftbl; Hon Roll; Pres Acad Fit Awd; Aeronautical Engr.

CONTINO, ASHLEY C; Alverno HS; Sierra Madre, CA; (2); Church Yth Grp; Chorus; Church Choir; School Musical; Stage Crew; Rep Soph Cls; NHS; USC; Theatres.

CONTINO, DAWN K; Castle Park HS; Chula Vista, CA; (4); Church Yth Grp; Letterman Clb; Service Clb; SADD; Rep Stu Cncl; Stat Bsktbl; Var Crs Cntry; JV Socr; Var Trk; High Hon Roll; Law Enfrcmnt.

CONTREARAS, RICHARD; Bellarmine College Prep; San Jose, CA; (4); 35/306; Speech Tm; Ed Nwsp; Intrml Bsktbl; Intrml Stat Ftbl; Intrml Sftbl; Intrml Vllybl; JV Wrstlng; Engrng.

CONTRERAS, ANGIE; Palm Springs HS; Desert Hot Spring, CA; (3); Drill Tm; Mrchg Band; Prfct Atten Awd; Awd Hnr; Northern AZ U; Astronomy.

CONTRERAS, CATALINA; San Gabriel Mission HS; Los Angeles, CA; (3); 3/127; Church Yth Grp; French Clb; GAA; VP Jr Cls; VP Stu Cncl; VP Bsktbl; JV Crs Cntry; DAR Awd; NHS; Prfct Atten Awd; HOBY Award; UCLA; Pharmacy.

CONTRERAS, CHRISTINA M; Bonita Vista HS; Bonita, CA; (2); Church Yth Grp; Cmnty Wkr; Dance Clb; Office Aide; Chorus; Variety Show; Trk; Cit Awd; Prfct Atten Awd; Pres Acad Fit Awd; UCLA; Pblc Rltns.

CONTRERAS, DANNY; Etiwanda HS; Atla Loma, CA; (3); Wt Lftg; Var Wrstlng; Hon Roll; ITT; Elect.

CONTRERAS, DESIREE I; San Bernardino HS; San Bernardino, CA; (2); Aud/Vis; English Clb; Cit Awd; Dnfth Awd; Prfct Atten Awd; Crafton Hills Coll; Cosmtlgy.

CONTRERAS, EDUARDO G; Yucaipa HS; Yucaipa, CA; (3); Spanish Clb; Prfct Atten Awd; Frstry.

CONTRERAS, FELIX; Selma HS; Selma, CA; (2); 24/250; Cmnty Wkr; Teachers Aide; Crs Cntry; Socr; Hon Roll; Prfct Atten Awd; Vly Rgnl Oprtnty Pgm A Stu; Goals Yth Pgm; Fresno ST U; Pilot.

CONTRERAS, FLAVIOLA; Turlock HS; Turlock, CA; (3); Office Aide; Mgr Nwsp; Cit Awd; Hon Roll; Prfct Atten Awd; ICONS; Teacher.

CONTRERAS, GABRIELA; Grace Davis HS; Modesto, CA; (2); Drama Clb; Latin Clb.

CONTRERAS, ISABEL; San Bernardino HS; San Bernardino, CA; (2); #64 In Class; Sftbl; Vllybl; Outstndg Athl Of Yr 89-90; CA ST San Bernardino.

CONTRERAS, JEAN M; East Bakersfield HS; Bakersfield, CA; (2); School Play; Hon Roll; MESA; GATE Pgm; Adv Drama; Law.

CONTRERAS, JESSICA LISSETTE; South San Francisco HS; San Francisco, CA; (4); Church Yth Grp; GAA; Latin Clb; Teachers Aide; Temple Yth Grp; Score Keeper; Var Swmmng; Cit Awd; Outstndng Acad Achvt Awd; San Francisco ST; Psych.

CONTRERAS, JILL R; East Union HS; Manteca, CA; (2); 22/400; Cmnty Wkr; Drama Clb; Letterman Clb; Speech Tm; Stage Crew; VP Soph Cls; Stu Cncl; JV Capt Cheerldng; Var Pom Pon; Hon Roll; Keywannettes VP; CSF; Sacramento ST; Law.

CONTRERAS, JOSE J; Woodrow Wilson HS; Los Angeles, CA; (3); Orch; JV Bsktbl; Score Keeper; JV Vllybl; MESA; Acad Dcthln Team; Civil Engrng.

CONTRERAS, JOSEFA; Grant Union HS; Sacramento, CA; (2); Office Aide; High Hon Roll; Hon Roll; Amer Allnce Achvmnt Awrd; Hnr Block Cert; Catherine Wallace Mem Schlshp; U Davis; Dental Asstnt.

CONTRERAS, JUAN J; Tranquillity Union HS; Tranquillity, CA; (3); Var Tennis; High Hon Roll; MCCHA Clb.

CONTRERAS, LOUIE-MARC; Monterey Bay Acad; Vallejo, CA; (4); 1/120; Band; Chorus; Yrbk; Pres Stu Cncl; Intrml Bsktbl; Intrml Ftbl; Cit Awd; Prfct Atten Awd; Med.

CONTRERAS, MARCI Y; Bonita Vista HS; Chula Vista, CA; (2); Church Yth Grp; Hosp Aide; Band; JV Cheerldng; JV Pom Pon; Pres Acad Fit Awd; Ucla; Pediatrician.

CONTRERAS, MARIA E; Our Lady Loretto-Bishop Conaty HS; Los Angeles, CA; (3); Art Clb; Church Yth Grp; FBLA; Hon Roll; Hnrb Mntn; Med.

CONTRERAS, MARIO A; Wasco Union HS; Wasco, CA; (2); Hon Roll; Pres Acad Fit Awd; Engrng.

CONTRERAS, MELISSA R; Los Banos HS; Los Banos, CA; (1); Off Soph Cls; Stu Cncl; Bsktbl; Sftbl; Hon Roll.

CONTRERAS, MIKE D; Lindsay HS; Lindsay, CA; (1); Rep Soph Cls; JV Bsktbl; JV Ftbl; Hon Roll; UCLA; Bus.

CONTRERAS, NANCY M; Woodland HS; Woodland, CA; (3); Ski Clb; Rep Frsh Cls; Off Sr Cls; Stu Cncl; JV Var Bsktbl; Var Powder Puff Ftbl; Intrml JV Vllybl; Hon Roll; Excllnce Lang Arts; Stu Wk; Stu Mnth; Imprvd Acad Prfrmnce; Accntnt.

CONTRERAS, PAUL ROMAN; Fontana HS; Fontana, CA; (2); Cmnty Wkr; Varsity Clb; Ftbl; Hon Roll; Principals Hnr Roll; USC; Jrnlsm.

CONTRERAS, REBECCA A; San Lvis HS; Los Banos, CA; (3); Girl Scts; Office Aide; Teachers Aide; Band; School Play; Hon Roll; Prfct Atten Awd.

CONTRERAS, ROSA M; Bishop Amat HS; La Verne, CA; (3); Var Vllybl; NHS; CSF; 2nd Team Angeles Leag-Vrsty Vllybl 88 & 89; 88 Coaches Awd/89 MVP-VLLYBL; Vet Med.

CONTRERAS, SONIA E; Le Grand Union HS; Le Grand, CA; (3); Drama Clb; Teachers Aide; Stage Crew; Rgnl Occuptnl Pgm.

CONTRERAS, SYLVIA; King City Joint Union HS; Greenfield, CA; (2); Church Yth Grp; Drama Clb; Stage Crew; Sftbl; Hon Roll; Intl Ordr Rainbow Grls; Cmrcl Clb; Interact; U Of CA; OB/Gyn.

CONTRERAS, SYLVIA A; Pasadena HS; Pasadena, CA; (3); L JV Sftbl; JV Vllybl; Intr Decorator.

CONTRERAS, TANYA M; Hilltop HS; San Diego, CA; (2); JV Bsktbl; Var Fld Hcky; Var Sftbl; Field/ I Made 1st All Metro And 2nd All-CIF.

CONTRERAS, VERONICA; Golden West HS; Visalia, CA; (2); Church Yth Grp; FHA; JV Bsktbl; JV Crs Cntry; JV Swmmng; Var L Trk; Hon Roll; CSF; Rally Club; UC Santa Barbara; Bus Law.

CONTRERAS, VERONICA E; Mt Pleasant HS; San Jose, CA; (3); Church Yth Grp; School Play; Var Crs Cntry; Var Trk; High Hon Roll; Hon Roll; NHS; CSF Treas; MESA; Supt Stu Advsry Cmmtte.

CONTRERAS, VICTORIA I; Mount Pleasant HS; San Jose, CA; (3); 34/477; Church Yth Grp; Rep Stu Cncl; Var Crs Cntry; Var Trk; Hon Roll; NHS; MESA; Assoc Stu Bdy Cmmssnr Rlls; CSF.

CONTRERAS, WILLIAM D; Merced HS North; Merced, CA; (2); Office Aide; Bsbl; Wt Lftg; Wrstlng; Hon Roll; Fresno ST U; Meatcutter.

CONTREVAS, ELIZABETH; Clairemont HS; San Diego, CA; (4); 50/200; Church Yth Grp; French Clb; Spanish Clb; Yrbk; Bsktbl; Crs Cntry; Trk; Spanish NHS; San Diego ST U; Sci Hlth.

CONVERSE, HEATHER L; Ponderosa HS; Diamond Springs, CA; (3); 16/268; Chess Clb; Sec Church Yth Grp; Debate Tm; Spanish Clb; Speech Tm; Rep Frsh Cls; Var Swmmng; Var Tennis; Hon Roll; Jr NHS; Naval Acad; Poltcl Sci.

CONVERSE, JESSE; Springs Of Living Water Acad; Chico, CA; (1); Church Yth Grp; Chorus; Off Frsh Cls; Stu Cncl; Bsktbl.

CONWAY, KERRY; San Dieguito HS; Carlsbad, CA; (1); Church Yth Grp; Dance Clb; Library Aide; Office Aide; Teachers Aide; Drill Tm; JV Sftbl; Hon Roll; Theatre.

CONWELL, CHAD; Wm S Hart HS; Valencia, CA; (4); 6/500; Boy Scts; English Clb; French Clb; Intnl Clb; Mu Alpha Theta; Scholastic Bowl; Science Clb; Ski Clb; Band; Jazz Band; UC Berkeley; Poltcl Sci.

COOGAN, AMBER R; Coast Union HS; Cambria, CA; (4); Pres AFS; Church Yth Grp; Spanish Clb; SADD; Var Bsktbl; JV Sftbl; Cit Awd; Hon Roll; Bst Art Stu Awd; Pub Awd; Photo Cert; FIDM; Fash Des.

COOK, ABRAHAM D; Bellermine-Jefferson HS; Sun Valley, CA; (1); Letterman Clb; Varsity Clb; Nwsp; Pres Soph Cls; JV L Ftbl; JV L Trk; High Hon Roll; Pres Acad Fit Awd; Writer.

COOK III, ALONZO; Westmoor HS; Daly City, CA; (2); Art Clb; Cmnty Wkr; Hon Roll; CSF; Math Tutorng Clb; WISHBONE; Graphic Arts.

COOK, AMY N; Branham HS; San Jose, CA; (1); Art Clb; Church Yth Grp; Yrbk; Var Bsktbl; Var Sftbl; Var Vllybl; Hon Roll; Prfct Atten Awd; Acpl Chr; School Musical; Design & Ad Cont Hnr Awd; Lib Arts.

COOK, ANDREW J; Fred C Beyer HS; Modesto, CA; (3); German Clb; JCL; Key Clb; Quiz Bowl; Scholastic Bowl; SADD; Socr; Swmmng; Trk; Gldn ST Math Exm; Acad Dcthln Mdlst; Lang.

COOK, BRANDI E.; St Bernard HS; Eureka, CA; (3); Church Yth Grp; Cmnty Wkr; Service Clb; Teachers Aide; Rptr Yrbk; JV Var Cheerldng; JV Trk; JV Vllybl; Hon Roll; Jr/Sr Prm Dcrtng Cmmtte; Sr Clss Sec & Treas 90-91; Coll Of Redwoods; Elem Sch Tchr.

COOK, CARMEN; Adolfo Camarillo HS; Camarillo, CA; (4); VP Church Yth Grp; French Clb; Drill Tm; Yrbk; Score Keeper; IN U Bloomington; Sports Med.

COOK, CASSANDRA L; Irvine HS; Irvine, CA; (2); AFS; Heritage Awd Wnnr-Math/Sci/Engl; Child Psych.

COOK, CHEVONNA; Miracle Baptist Christian Schl; Moreno Valley, CA; (1); 2/23; Ed Nwsp; Sec Frsh Cls; Pres Stu Cncl; Capt Cheerldng; Swmmng; Vllybl; Lawyer.

COOK, CHLOE Y; Hesperia Christian HS; Hesperia, CA; (3); 1/35; Church Yth Grp; Scholastic Bowl; Teachers Aide; Band; Var Bsktbl; Var Crs Cntry; Var Trk; High Hon Roll; CSF VP.

COOK, DARLA R; Arvin HS; Bakersfield, CA; (3); 31/276; VICA; Rptr Nwsp; Cit Awd; High Hon Roll; Library Sci.

COOK, ELIZABETH; San Dimas HS; San Dimas, CA; (3); Spanish Clb; SADD; Tennis; Cit Awd; Hon Roll; Ntl Merit SF; Pres Acad Fit Awd; UC Riverside; Crmnl Law.

COOK, ELIZABETH A; College Park HS; Martinez, CA; (2); Art Clb; Drama Clb; German Clb; Teachers Aide; JV Var Swmmng.

COOK, JAMES C; Mission Viejo HS; Mission Viejo, CA; (4); 14/475; Teachers Aide; Var Bsktbl; JV Golf; Capt Socr; Var Capt Tennis; High Hon Roll; NHS; Ntl Merit Ltr; Pres Acad Fit Awd; CSF; U CA Berkeley; Bus.

COOK, JAMIE G; East Nicolaus HS; Rio Oso, CA; (3); Friday Night Live; Sierra Coll; Jrnlsm.

COOK, JANETTE; Tulare Union HS; Tulare, CA; (3); Art Clb; Hon Roll; Csmtlgy; Music Guitar; Art Drawng; UCLA; Comm.

COOK, JANINA; Carson HS; Carson, CA; (3); FTA; Drill Tm; Hon Roll; Prfct Atten Awd; Cls Speaker; Nrsng.

COOK, JEFFERY W; Central Catholic HS; Modesto, CA; (3); Letterman Clb; Yrbk; Var Bsbl; Var JV Bsktbl; Var JV Ftbl; Wt Lftg; Hon Roll; Prfct Atten Awd; Tm MVP Ftbl & Bsktbl; All City Tm Bsktbl; U Of CA Berkeley.

COOK, JEFFRY W; Lompoc HS; Ventura, CA; (4); 2/280; Bus Profs of Am; Cmnty Wkr; Treas DECA; Pres FBLA; Scholastic Bowl; Hon Roll; NHS; Sal; 3rd Pl Fnlst In Bank Of Amer Achvt Awd; CSF; Englsh Achvt Awd 90; San Diego ST U; Accnttng.

COOK, JENNIFER D; Westminster HS; Westminster, CA; (1); Church Yth Grp; Teachers Aide; Bsktbl; Score Keeper; Trk; Nrs.

COOK, JESSICA L; Oakmont HS; Roseville, CA; (3); Drama Clb; German Clb; Variety Show; JV Bsktbl; Var Trk; JV Vllybl; Hon Roll; NHS; US Space Acad Rght Stuff Engrng Awd; Young Astrnts Pgm Guest Spkr; Astronautics-Astronaut.

COOK, MELAINE M; Hoover HS; Fresno, CA; (2); Church Yth Grp; Color Guard; JV Gym; Interior Dsgn.

COOK, MELODY JOY; South Fork HS; Miranda, CA; (3); Nwsp; Intrml Vllybl; My Own Column In Schl Nwspaper; Humboldt ST U; Jrnlsm.

COOK, MICHAEL W; Covina HS; Pocatello, ID; (4); Boy Scts; Church Yth Grp; FFA; Teachers Aide; Cit Awd; Elks Awd; Hon Roll; Pres Acad Fit Awd; Bsbl Fan Clb; Eagle Scout; ID ST U; US Postal Inspctr.

COOK, MICHELLE M; Serrano HS; Wrightwood, CA; (1); Church Yth Grp; FBLA; Varsity Clb; Var L Band; Var L Mrchg Band; Var L Orch; JV L Vllybl; High Hon Roll; Hon Roll; Pres Acad Fit Awd; 3rd Pl Outstndng FBLA Stu.

COOK, PHILIP A; Newprt Harbor HS; Costa Mesa, CA; (3); 17/350; Am Leg Boys St; JCL; Latin Clb; Var L Golf; Hon Roll; Pres Acad Fit Awd; Architecture.

COOK, REBECCA A; Rio Lindo Adventist Acad; Springville, UT; (2); Church Yth Grp; Office Aide; Chorus; Church Choir; Hon Roll; Nrsg.

COOK, TARA; Whittier HS; Whittier, CA; (4); Church Yth Grp; Pep Clb; Teachers Aide; Hon Roll; Dnc Clb Sec; Outstndng Ctzn & Achvt Merit Awds; Prncpls Lst; Rio Hondo Coll; Nrsng.

COOK, TIFFANEY; Lompoc HS; Ventura, CA; (2); Church Yth Grp; Cmnty Wkr; FBLA; FFA; Letterman Clb; SADD; Bsktbl; Mgr(s); Score Keeper; Swmmng; CSF; Floral Team; Art Show; San Diego ST; Hrtcltr.

COOK, TONY; Tulare Western HS; Grover City, CA; (4); ROTC; Teachers Aide; Hon Roll; Bnk Of Amer Achvt Awd Applied Arts; Acad Awd In Indus Arts; Cert Outstndng Achvt Indus Arts; Bus.

COOK, TYSON M; Gardena HS; Gardena, CA; (4); Sprt Ed Nwsp; Var Ftbl; Cit Awd; Video Prod Class; El Camino CC; Elec Tech.

COOKE, CHARMIAN D; El Toro HS; El Toro, CA; (3); 70/480; Church Yth Grp; Rptr Nwsp; Trk; High Hon Roll; Hon Roll; Pro-Life Clinic Vlntr; CSF; Girls League; TV Brdcstng.

COOKE, MARY; Sonoma Valley HS; Sonoma, CA; (3); Speech Tm; Powder Puff Ftbl; Trk; Interact Clb; Engrng.

COOKE, SEAN; Dublin HS; Dublin, CA; (4); 3/150; Church Yth Grp; Speech Tm; Teachers Aide; Varsity Clb; VP Stu Cncl; Var Ftbl; Var Socr; Var Swmmng; Var Tennis; Var Vllybl; UC San Diego; Pediatrics.

COOKE, STACEY; Folsom HS; Folsom, CA; (4); Church Yth Grp; GAA; Pep Clb; Ski Clb; Church Choir; Yrbk; Stu Cncl; Cheerldng; Socr; Trk; The Masters Coll; Orthodontist.

COOKE, STEFANIE M; Lowell HS; San Francisco, CA; (2); Church Yth Grp; Cmnty Wkr; JA; SADD; Var Gym; Var Trk; Adventure Alliance Clb; Scl Worker.

COOKINHAM, CHAD G; Castle Park HS; Chula Vista, CA; (3); 48/422; GATE-GFTD & Tlntd Educ; CSF-CA Schlrshp Fdrtn; UCLA; Comp Prgmr.

COOKSEY, MARTINE M; Irvine HS; Irvine, CA; (2); 3/600; Crs Cntry; Trk; Hon Roll; Humanities.

COOKSON, DONALD EARL CLEGG; Etiwanda HS; Reedville, VA; (4); Spanish Clb; Var Bsbl; Cit Awd; High Hon Roll; Hon Roll; Prfct Atten Awd; Spanish Stu Of Yr; VA Union U.

COOKSON, DUANE W C; Etwanda HS; Reedville, VA; (4); 110/485; Math Clb; Spanish Clb; Var L Bsbl; Intrml Bsktbl; Intrml Fld Hcky; Intrml Ftbl; Var Intrml Golf; Hon Roll; Prfct Atten Awd; Old Dominion U; Accntng.

COOLEY, EVIE J; Ponderosa HS; Placerville, CA; (1); 4-H; Girl Scts; Teachers Aide; Band; Mrchg Band; Orch; Pep Band; JV Swmmng; Intrml Vllybl; Hon Roll; System Analyst.

COOLEY, JENNIFER L; Fontana HS; Fontana, CA; (2); Phtg Nwsp; Phtg Yrbk; WA ST; Law.

COOLEY, MARY; St Genevieve HS; Panorama City, CA; (3); Art Clb; Computer Clb; French Clb; Chorus; Socr; High Hon Roll; Unity Clb; Mck Trl; CSF; Arch.

COOLIDGE, BRIAN C; Glendora HS; Glendora, CA; (3); Key Clb; Pres Math Clb; Pres Math Tm; Ski Clb; SADD; JV Trk; High Hon Roll; Hon Roll; Ntl Merit SF; Badminton; CA Schlrshp Fed; MIT; Engrng.

COOLIDGE, ELIZABETH C; Bonita Vista HS; Chula Vista, CA; (3); Cit Awd; High Hon Roll; Hon Roll; S CA Jr Bach Fstvl 89, Wnnr 90; USSR Cert Of Mrt 87-88; Astronomy.

COOLIDGE, PIPER L; Hiram Johnson HS; Sacramento, CA; (3); Church Yth Grp; Drama Clb; Key Clb; Spanish Clb; Teachers Aide; Stage Crew; Nwsp; Yrbk; VP Frsh Cls; Off Jr Cls; Saferides; Photog Stu; STAND; Sac City; Engl.

COOMBS, RENE; Quincy JR-SR HS; Quincy, CA; (4); 4/87; Pres FBLA; Model UN; Spanish Clb; Chorus; Rptr Yrbk; Sftbl; Hon Roll; Masonic Awd; NHS; Pres Acad Fit Awd; Gldn St Grom Exam Hgh Hnrs; #1 Typst In CA; Bus Awd; CSU Chico; Accntng.

COON, BROOKE R; Hanford HS; Hanford, CA; (2); Dance Clb; FBLA; FFA; Teachers Aide; Co-Capt Drill Tm; Trk; High Hon Roll; Hon Roll; Jr NHS; Hnrs Math & Engl; UC Santa Barbara; Psych.

COONEY, BRIAN G; Gompers Secondary HS; San Diego, CA; (2); 50/145; Band; School Musical; Variety Show; Ftbl; Math-Comp Basic Achvt Awd; Engrng.

COONEY, DENNIS M; Napa HS; Napa, CA; (2); 31/438; Boy Scts; Cmnty Wkr; 4-H; Model UN; Teachers Aide; Band; Chorus; School Musical; School Play; Var Bsbl; Vlntr Cnslr Lght Hse Of The Blind & Elem Stu Wk Camps; U Of MI; Cnslng.

COONEY, MEGAN; Sonoma Valley HS; Sonoma, CA; (4); Art Clb; Rptr Nwsp; Var Crs Cntry; Intrml Swmmng; JV Trk; High Hon Roll; Hon Roll; Chico ST U; Teacher.

COONS, LESLIE M; Junipero Serra HS; Poway, CA; (3); 35/391; Church Yth Grp; Cmnty Wkr; French Clb; Hosp Aide; Letterman Clb; Office Aide; Pep Clb; Teachers Aide; Varsity Clb; Acpl Chr; Smmr Candy Sales Ftbl Fnd Rsr; MESA; Sales Clerk; U Of Southern CA; Bio.

COONS, SYLVESTER L; Benicia HS; Benicia, CA; (3); Boy Scts; Band; Mrchg Band; School Musical; JV Var Crs Cntry; JV Var Trk; Hon Roll; Arch.

COOP, COURTNEY; Rio Americano HS; Sacramento, CA; (3); 63/290; Church Yth Grp; Cmnty Wkr; Dance Clb; Chorus; Drill Tm; Var Vllybl; High Hon Roll; Hon Roll; Pres Acad Fit Awd; Cmnty Srvce Prfrmng Grp; BYU; Commnctns.

COOPER, AARON; George Washington Preparatory HS; Los Angeles, CA; (2); 3/800; Church Yth Grp; Band; High Hon Roll; Benjamin E Mays Achvt Awd; Coca Cola Awd; Amer Lgn Awd; MESA Clb; Acad/Schlrshp All Sbjcts Awd; CSF; USC; Pre-Med.

COOPER, ADRIENNE M; Skyline HS; Oakland, CA; (2); Church Yth Grp; Cmnty Wkr; ROTC; Teachers Aide; Church Choir; Spelman; Ed.

COOPER, ANGELA N; Mt Carmel HS; San Diego, CA; (2); Hist Frsh Cls; Off Soph Cls; Stu Cncl; Var Bsktbl; Var Crs Cntry; Var Trk; Prfct Atten Awd; 4th Pl St Crss Cnty & Trk; 7th Pl St Bsktbl; U CA; Sprts Med.

COOPER, BRIDGETTE D; Boron HS; Boron, CA; (2); Cmnty Wkr; Library Aide; Teachers Aide; Stage Crew; Stu Cncl; Sftbl; AZ ST U; Acctng.

COOPER, CAMILLE L; Saint Francis HS; Mountain View, CA; (3); 85/300; Nwsp; Var JV Trk; Hon Roll; Interact Clb; CA U; Pre Law.

COOPER, CHRISTOPHER J; Clovis West HS; Fresno, CA; (3); Top Soccer Player Invited To Attend Claremont; Claremont; Engrng.

COOPER, CHRISTOPHER M; Workman HS; La Puente, CA; (3); German Clb; Band; Chorus; School Musical; School Play; De Vry; Robotical Engrng.

COOPER, DANAMAYE C; Crescenta Valley HS; La Crescenta, CA; (4); 12/381; Sec French Clb; Intnl Clb; Pres Key Clb; Mu Alpha Theta; Treas Service Clb; Teachers Aide; Drill Tm; Rptr Nwsp; Cheerldng; French Hon Soc; Golden St Alg Ex Exc Awd Cert; Perf Atten Cert; CSF; UCLA; Pre-Med.

COOPER, DANEIDA L; Grossmont HS; La Mesa, CA; (1); Church Yth Grp; GAA; JV Bsktbl; Var Trk; Intrml Vllybl; Wt Lftg; Girls League; Athletic Awd Track; 1st Shot Put.

COOPER, FLOYD; Hiram W Johnson HS; Sacramento, CA; (3); 80/368; Computer Clb; Math Clb; Math Tm; Ed Nwsp; Yrbk; JV Var Bsbl; Bsktbl; Hon Roll; NHS; Prfct Atten Awd; Sac City Coll; Engrng.

COOPER, HEATHER; Ygnacio Valley HS; Martinez, CA; (2); Church Yth Grp; Dance Clb; Drama Clb; Girl Scts; Office Aide; Spanish Clb; School Musical; School Play; Variety Show; NCA Natl Chmpn Clayton Vly All Strs Chrldng/Pom Pon Sqd 89-90; NCA Natls, Rgnls & Cola Chmp; UC Santa Barbara; Marine Bio.

COOPER, HODARI TOUSSAINT; Eden Christian Acad; Oakland, CA; (2); Church Yth Grp; Cmnty Wkr; Computer Clb; Debate Tm; Math Clb; Teachers Aide; Temple Yth Grp; VP Frsh Cls; Pres Soph Cls; VP Jr Cls; Alameda Coll Comp Sci Cls; Bus Law.

COOPER, JANET L; Ventura HS; Ventura, CA; (3); Girl Scts; Pep Clb; Stu Cncl; Var Capt Cheerldng; Hon Roll; San Diego ST; Elem Teacher.

COOPER, JESSICA L; Mesa Verde HS; Citrus Heights, CA; (2); 1/257; High Hon Roll; Frgn Lang Hnr; Wrtng Excllnc Awd; Top GPA Schltc, Acad Awds; Ministry.

COOPER, KAREN R; Cupertino HS; San Jose, CA; (3); 1/300; Church Yth Grp; Cmnty Wkr; Treas Key Clb; Pep Clb; Treas Service Clb; Band; Treas Frsh Cls; Rep Jr Cls; Rep Stu Cncl; JV Diving; Gold Awds Art; Schlr Athl Sccr, Swmmng & Gymnstcs; Team Ldr Sccr; Berkeley; Arch.

COOPER, KATHERINE J; John F Kennedy HS; Granada Hills, CA; (3); Teachers Aide; Child Care; UC-SANTA Barbara; Deaf Chldrn.

COOPER, KIMBERLEE K; Sonora Union HS; Sonora, CA; (3); FFA; Intnl Clb; Teachers Aide; School Musical; Rptr Yrbk; Hon Roll; Ag Econ.

COOPER, KIMBERLY J; San Jacinto HS; Cathedral City, CA; (3); Drama Clb; French Clb; Girl Scts; SADD; Vllybl; Cit Awd; Lion Awd; MCAAD; Art.

COOPER, KIMBERLY J; Skyline HS; Oakland, CA; (2); Dance Clb; Variety Show; Var Cheerldng; Cit Awd; Hon Roll; Pres Schlr; Pblc Spkr; Miss Teen CA Pgnt; Dance Co Nuba Dance Thtre; Pblc Spkng.

COOPER, LAURA; Live Oak HS; Morgan Hill, CA; (3); Church Yth Grp; Dance Clb; SADD; Church Choir; Color Guard; School Musical; Rptr Nwsp; Swmmng; Hon Roll; Dr Martin Luther Coll; Teacher.

COOPER, LAVENDER; Pasadena HS; Pasadena, CA; (3); Dance Clb; JA; Math Clb; Science Clb; Cit Awd; High Hon Roll; Hon Roll; Prfct Atten Awd; MESA Club; UCLA; Medicine Pediatrician.

COOPER, MICHELE M; La Reina HS; Thousand Oaks, CA; (3); 34/68; Church Yth Grp; Drama Clb; SADD; Church Choir; Variety Show; Yrbk; Lit Mag; Cit Awd; Hon Roll; Prfct Atten Awd; Mock Trail Cmptns-Atty-89 County Chmpns; Acad Decathln Team; Campus Ministry; Philosophy.

COOPER, MIKAEL KWAME W; Eisenhower HS; San Bernardino, CA; (3); Church Yth Grp; Dance Clb; FCA; Varsity Clb; Band; Church Choir; School Musical; Variety Show; Bsbl; JV Var Ftbl; Miami U; Engr.

COOPER, PRISCILLA V; Castlemont HS; Oakland, CA; (2); Hon Roll.

COOPER, SHERYL A; Pioneer HS; San Jose, CA; (1); Cmnty Wkr; JV Bsktbl; Var Sftbl; Hon Roll; Interact Clb; CSF; Peer Tutor.

COOPER, STACY L; Southwest HS; San Diego, CA; (3); Church Yth Grp; Cmnty Wkr; SADD; Teachers Aide; Cit Awd; High Hon Roll; Pres Acad Fit Awd; Soccer Buddies; San Diego ST U; Elem Ed.

COOPER, STEPHANIE E; Montgomery HS; Santa Rosa, CA; (3); Office Aide; Hon Roll; SRJC; Bus Law.

COOPER, TIMOTHY R; Bonita Vista HS; Bonita, CA; (2); Stage Crew; Yrbk; Civil Art Patrol; Us Naval Acad; Aviation.

COOPER, TOSHA L; John F Kennedy HS; Sacramento, CA; (1); 162/564; Band; School Musical; Nurse.

COOPERSMITH, MARC; Tustin HS; Tustin, CA; (2); Var Chess Clb; Sec Latin Clb; Sec Science Clb; Acad Tm Capt; Top 25; Soc Studies Dept Awd; Cal ST Fullerton; Intl Rltns.

COOPMAN, SCOTT W; Thomas Downey HS; Modesto, CA; (3); Var L Bsktbl; Var L Ftbl; Cit Awd; Prfct Atten Awd; CSF; Outstndng Ctzn; UCLA; Pediatrics.

COPE, KELLEY; Hilmar HS; Hilmar, CA; (3); AFS; Church Yth Grp; Drama Clb; 4-H; FFA; Letterman Clb; Ski Clb; SADD; Teachers Aide; School Play; Fresno ST.

COPE, KEVIN S; Novato HS; Novato, CA; (3); Cmnty Wkr; JA; Spanish Clb; Teachers Aide; Nwsp; Off Jr Cls; Off Sr Cls; Rep Stu Cncl; Intrml Bsktbl; Var Swmmng; Water Polo; Comp Sci.

COPE, KRISTI H; Polytechnic HS; Riverside, CA; (2); Church Yth Grp; Church Choir; Hon Roll; Prfct Atten Awd; Pres Acad Fit Awd; Chrch Missions Orgnztn; Walk-A-Thons Juvnl Diabetes; Europe Trip.

COPE, MICHELLE; St Lawrence Acad; Santa Clara, CA; (3); 3/28; Girl Scts; Rptr Nwsp; Yrbk; Treas Sr Cls; Var Socr; Var Vllybl; Hon Roll; Jr NHS; NHS; Supv Grt Amer Amsmnt Pk; Amnsty Intntl; Engl.

COPELAND, BENJAMIN A; Edison Computech HS; Fresno, CA; (1); Hon Roll; U MI; Med.

COPELAND, BOBBY L; Redlands HS; Redlands, CA; (2); Chess Clb; Church Yth Grp; Cmnty Wkr; JV L Socr; L Var Trk; Wt Lftg; Church Yth Group VP; Presdntl Acad Ftnss Awd; Golden St Exam; Acad Excllnc Awd; High Acad Hnr Awds.

COPELAND, DAVID A; Nevada Union HS; Grass Valley, CA; (2); 12/535; Boy Scts; Rep Stu Cncl; Hon Roll; Fri Night Live VP; FNL Outstndng Yth Awd Cmmty Svc; Gldn St Exam Hgh Hnrs Alg; Physics.

COPELAND, DAVID L; San Gabriel HS; San Gabriel, CA; (3); Crs Cntry; Trk.

COPELAND, STENA G; Moreno Valley HS; Moreno Valley, CA; (3); French Clb; Teachers Aide; High Hon Roll; Hon Roll; Prfct Atten Awd; Cal ST San Bernardino; Medcl.

COPELAND, STEPHANIE; Lincoln HS; Stockton, CA; (4); 49/513; Church Yth Grp; Office Aide; Lit Mag; High Hon Roll; Hon Roll; Masonic Awd; CSF; Delta CC; Spcl Ed.

COPENBARGER, ERIN A; Irvine HS; Irvine, CA; (3); 44/512; Hon Roll; Amnesty Intl; Stu For Soc Rspnsblty; Close-Up; Intl Rltns.

COPENHAVER, DAVID; Cardinal Newman HS; Santa Rosa, CA; (1); Computer Clb; Spanish Clb; Bsktbl; Hon Roll; Med.

COPES, STEPHANIE A; University City HS; San Diego, CA; (3); Spanish Clb; SADD; Orch; Yrbk; Jr NHS; Pres Acad Fit Awd; Schltc All Amer; CA Schlrshp Fed; Culture Clb; Sci.

COPPA, GENE A; Los Altos HS; Hacienda Hts, CA; (3); Letterman Clb; Varsity Clb; Acpl Chr; Chorus; Mrchg Band; Var L Socr; JV Swmmng; Hon Roll; Pres Acad Fit Awd; Math Golden St Awd; UCLA.

COPPENGER, ANGIE; Yuraipa HS; Yucaipa, CA; (3); Church Yth Grp; French Clb; Letterman Clb; JV Var Cheerldng; Var Socr; Vllybl; Hon Roll; Pres Acad Fit Awd; Hnrs Grp; Ed.

COPPIN, SAERA E; Bear River HS; Auburn, CA; (2); 27/220; Acpl Chr; Chorus; Cit Awd; High Hon Roll; Hon Roll; Opt Clb Awd; Rotary Awd; UC Santa Cruz; Liberal Arts.

COPPINGER, MATTHEW J; Edison HS; Fresno, CA; (3); 74/240; Church Yth Grp; Stu Cncl; Var Crs Cntry; Var Socr; Var Trk; Hon Roll; Lttrd Vrsty Soccer As Frosh & Won NYL Chmpnshp; Vrsty Trk Tm Invtatnl Cmptitns; Envrnmntl Stud.

COPPLE, BILL; Carson HS; Terrance, CA; (2); Boy Scts; Church Yth Grp; Ftbl; Prfct Atten Awd; Eagle Sct; Outstndng Stu Trphy; Hstry Outstndng Achvt Trphy; US Air Frc Acad; Aviator.

COPPOLA, LIANA; Mater Dei HS; Los Alamitos, CA; (1); JV Var Crs Cntry; Trk; Concours Natl De Francais Cert; Hnrs In Frnch,Algebra Geom & Bio; Italian Speaking; Med.

COPREN, KIRSTEN ANNE; Loyalton HS; Sattley, CA; (4); 1/31; Rptr FBLA; Rep Stu Cncl; Var JV Bsktbl; Var JV Trk; Var JV Vllybl; High Hon Roll; Val; Ski Clb; Spanish Clb; School Play; All Leag Vllybl, Bkstlbl & Track; Natl Schlr/Athl Awd; CSF Pres; UC Berkeley; Entomology.

CORBAN, DANIEL W; Fountain Valley HS; Fountain Valley, CA; (2); Church Yth Grp; FCA; Letterman Clb; Church Choir; Intrml Crs Cntry; Var Socr; Intrml Vllybl; Hon Roll; Biola U; Theology.

CORBETT, MARK D; Los Banos HS; Los Banos, CA; (2); Boy Scts; Church Yth Grp; Library Aide; Band; Cit Awd; Hon Roll; UCSD; Missnry.

CORBETT, MICHELE L; Tulare Union HS; Tulare, CA; (3); Church Yth Grp; Drama Clb; 4-H; French Clb; FFA; JA; High Hon Roll; CA Schltc Fed Club.

CORBETT, STEPHANIE; Ocean View HS; Huntington Bch, CA; (3); 16/400; Cmnty Wkr; Debate Tm; Model UN; Scholastic Bowl; Capt JV Cheerldng; JV Var Mgr(s); Var Powder Puff Ftbl; High Hon Roll; Gldn Hwk Awd For Biological Sci; Stu Accreditation Cncl; Sci.

CORBIN, ERICA S; St Micheals HS; Los Angeles, CA; (2); GAA; Vllybl; Cal ST Long Beach.

CORBIN, REGINA L; Huntington Beach HS; Huntington Bch, CA; (3); Church Yth Grp; SADD; Varsity Clb; Var Socr; Var Sftbl; Var Trk; JV Vllybl; Jr Lifeguards; Sccr MVP 88-89; 1st Pl Shotput & Discuss Vrsty Trk 90; Scndry Ed.

CORBO, JULIE; La Jolla Country Day Schl; La Jolla, CA; (4); Acpl Chr; School Musical; Stage Crew; Var Capt Bsktbl; Var Sftbl; Var Capt Vllybl; High Hon Roll; Hon Roll; Music Dept Awd; Hagey Grls Sprts Awd; UCSD.

CORDANI, STEPHEN C; Whittier Christian HS; Whittier, CA; (2); Church Yth Grp; Weight Liftng; Elect Engr.

CORDANO, DAWN M; Paradise HS; Magalia, CA; (3); Church Yth Grp; Girl Scts; NFL; Pep Clb; Teachers Aide; Rptr Nwsp; Jobs Daughters; Dist Forensic Leag Trophy 4th Pl Semi-Fnlst; Butte Coll; Teacher.

CORDEIRO, BENJAMIN; John Marshall HS; Pasadena, CA; (3); Boy Scts; Church Yth Grp; Teachers Aide; Church Choir; JV Bsbl; JV Var Bsktbl; JV Var Crs Cntry; JV Trk; High Hon Roll; Hon Roll; Comp Repair.

CORDELL, TIM M; Sacred Heart Cathedral HS; Pacifica, CA; (1); Boy Scts; Hon Roll; Coll Of San Mateo; Nrsng.

CORDERO, ISAAC; Chula Vista HS; Chula Vista, CA; (2); AFS; Bus Profs of Am; Cmnty Wkr; Computer Clb; English Clb; FFA; Hosp Aide; Library Aide; Office Aide; Red Cross Aide; Arch.

CORDERO, MELISSA G; Vista HS; Vista, CA; (4); 46/377; Aud/Vis; Church Yth Grp; Debate Tm; Pres Drama Clb; Spanish Clb; School Musical; Stage Crew; Stu Cncl; JV Var Vllybl; High Hon Roll; Tele Commnctns.

CORDES, CHUCK M; Ponderosa HS; Diamond Springs, CA; (4); Church Yth Grp; 4-H; Letterman Clb; Varsity Clb; Socr; 4-H Awd; Hon Roll; Jr NHS; Mst Val Plyr Var Sccr; Amer River Coll; Bus.

CORDES, FRANCIS A; Ponderosa HS; Diamon Springs, CA; (4); Church Yth Grp; 4-H; Letterman Clb; Varsity Clb; Phtg Yrbk; Socr; 4-H Awd; Jr NHS; Opt Clb Awd; Jostens Photography Awd; James P Morton Schlrshp Awd; Tracy Memrl Schlrshp; Al Collins Graphic Dsgn Schl.

CORDIA, JOY; Saddleback HS; Santa Ana, CA; (2); Hosp Aide; Piano; Spcl Intst Music; Tchr.

CORDIAK, SHELLY LYN; West Covina HS; W Covina, CA; (4); Church Yth Grp; Debate Tm; Varsity Clb; Rptr Nwsp; Trk; Gov Hon Prg Awd; High Hon Roll; Hon Roll; St Schlr; Miss Catlina Island 1990; Miss San Gabriel Valley Tn 1989; Eng.

CORDOBA, ROLANDO A; Capuchino HS; San Bruno, CA; (1).

CORDOVA, AMBER M; Etiwanda HS; Alta Loma, CA; (2); Art Clb; FHA; Latin Clb; Ski Clb; SADD; Hon Roll; Art.

CORDOVA, ANTHONY T; Erma Duncan Polytechnical HS; Fresno, CA; (1); FFA; Jrnlsm.

CORDOVA, MARIA G; Polythechnic HS; Long Beach, CA; (3); Art Clb; Cmnty Wkr; Debate Tm; Drama Clb; Hosp Aide; Library Aide; Spanish Clb; Speech Tm; Teachers Aide; School Musical; Poly PACE; Schlrshp Clb; Prncpls Awdee; UC Berkeley; Law.

CORDOVA, MARIA L; Hawthorne HS; Hawthorne, CA; (1); Teachers Aide; Swmmng; A P Span Stu; Police Offcr.

CORDOVA, MARTHA C; Pasadena HS; Pasadena, CA; (3); Spanish Clb; Drill Tm; Flag Corp; Stage Crew; Off Frsh Cls; Off Soph Cls; Prfct Atten Awd; Pangentry Corp For Athltc Actvts; UCLA; Publc Rltns.

CORDOVA, ROBERTO; Shafter HS; Shafter, CA; (3); Art Clb; Teachers Aide; Var Crs Cntry; Var Trk; High Hon Roll; Hon Roll; MESA Club; UC Davis Engrng Smmr Rsdncy Pgm; Peer Cnslr.

CORDOVA, ROMULO A; Central Union HS; El Centro, CA; (2); Chess Clb; Church Yth Grp; Corp Law.

CORDOVA, SANDRA L; Clovis West HS; Pinedale, CA; (3); Cmnty Wkr; Fresno City Coll; Computers.

CORDOVA, SARA; Strathmore HS; Lindsay, CA; (2); Drama Clb; Letterman Clb; Office Aide; SADD; School Play; Rep Soph Cls; JV Bsktbl; Var Cheerldng; Var Sftbl; Hon Roll; Big Brother/Big Sister; Criminology.

CORDOVA, VALERIE A; Abraham Lincoln SR HS; San Jose, CA; (3); Red Cross Aide; Band; Mrchg Band; JV Sftbl; Hon Roll; St Schlr; Math/Engrng/Sci Achvts-Sec/Mst Imprvd Awd; Engrng Summer Residency Pgm; Med.

CORDOVA, VERA L; Clovis HS; Fresno, CA; (4); Office Aide; Teachers Aide; Band; Jazz Band; Mrchg Band; Pep Band; Hon Roll; Best Attitude Band Awd; UC Davis; Psych.

CORDOVA, VERONICA E; Mountain Empire HS; Campo, CA; (3); Rep German Clb; Office Aide; Spanish Clb; SADD; Varsity Clb; Var Bsktbl; Var Sftbl; Var Vllybl; Hon Roll; Sec Jr Cls.

CORDS, JACKIE A; Fullerton Union HS; Fullerton, CA; (1); 76/486; Cmnty Wkr; Drama Clb; Thesps; Chorus; School Musical; School Play; Stage Crew; Tennis; Hon Roll; USC; Bus.

CORDUA, JENNIFER; Lindsay HS; Lindsay, CA; (3); 1/140; Am Leg Aux Girls St; Key Clb; Ed Yrbk; Sec Frsh Cls; Sec Soph Cls; Sec Jr Cls; Treas Stu Cncl; Var Cheerldng; Swmmng; Vllybl; HOBY Conf; Presdntl Clssrm; Bus Law.

CORDURA, ALDO E; Etiwanda HS; Rancho Cucamonga, CA; (3); Var Bsktbl; Hon Roll; NHS; Prfct Atten Awd.

CORENSON, AMANDA L; Oak Park HS; Agoura Hills, CA; (3); 24/90; Debate Tm; GAA; NFL; Office Aide; Pep Clb; Speech Tm; Teachers Aide; Stu Cncl; JV Capt Bsktbl; Bradley U; Spcl Ed.

COREY, VALERIE M; Ripon HS; Ripon, CA; (1); Church Yth Grp; 4-H; 4-H Awd; UC Davis; Lwyr.

CORFMAN, DESIREE M; Central Union HS; El Centro, CA; (2); Hon Roll; Jobs Dghtrs.

CORK, DANIEL L; Borrego Springs HS; Borrego Springs, CA; (4); 1/26; Church Yth Grp; Office Aide; Orch; Ed Nwsp; Sec Jr Cls; Pres Stu Cncl; Stat Bsbl; Stat Bsktbl; Stat Ftbl; Stat Sftbl; Princpls Outstndng Stu Awd; Statistics.

CORK, SEAN T; Redlands HS; Highland, CA; (4); 1st Pl Wnnr Writing Celebration 88; DARE Pgm; UC Santa Cruz; Engl.

CORK, STEPHANIE M; Borrego Springs HS; Borrego Springs, CA; (3); 6/25; Church Yth Grp; Key Clb; Library Aide; Chorus; Variety Show; Pres Jr Cls; Mgr Stu Cncl; Stat Bsktbl; Stat Sftbl; Tchng.

CORKS, ARTESHA L; Antelop Valley HS; Lancaster, CA; (3); Church Yth Grp; Cmnty Wkr; JA; Pep Clb; Service Clb; Spanish Clb; Teachers Aide; Church Choir; Stu Cncl; Cit Awd; UNLV; Psych.

CORLEY, SHAWN; Mt Whitney HS; Visalia, CA; (4); Church Yth Grp; Cmnty Wkr; Debate Tm; Sec Treas FFA; Teachers Aide; JV Wrstlng; Hon Roll; Tulare Co Jr Fair Bd; Farm Bureau Intern/Yng Frmr & Rancher; Rgnl FFA Rptr/Merit Awd Cow Palace; CA ST U Fresno; Ag Educ.

CORMACK, ANNA; St Margarets HS; Newport Beach, CA; (3); Intnl Clb; Var Fld Hcky; Var Sftbl; Var Swmmng; Hon Roll; Cultrl Arts Clb; Melbourne U; Arch.

CORMACK, SALLY M; St Margarets Schl; Newport Beach, CA; (3); Debate Tm; Pres Intnl Clb; Chorus; Orch; Var Fld Hcky; Var Gym; Var Tennis; High Hon Roll; Law.

CORMAN, TANYA J; Newark Memorial HS; Newark, CA; (3); 1/355; Rep SADD; Treas Stu Cncl; Capt Crs Cntry; Var Trk; High Hon Roll; Ntl Merit SF; Pres Acad Fit Awd; CSF; Goldn St Exam Hnrs Geom; Interact Clb; Sociology.

CORMANY, ASHLEY LYNN; Mount Carmel HS; Aledo, TX; (4); 82/741; Nwsp; VP Stu Cncl; Kiwanis Awd; Hmn Rltns Cmmtte; CASC; UCLA.

CORMIER, MARGAUX A; Edison HS; Fresno, CA; (1); Cmnty Wkr; Acad Achvt Awd; CA ST Hayward; Erly Chldhd Dv.

CORMIER, PATRICK B; Pasadena HS; Pasadena, CA; (1); Church Yth Grp; French Clb; Socr; Swmmng.

CORNEJO, LAURA V; Montebello HS; Montebello, CA; (2); Church Yth Grp; Chorus; JV Capt Cheerldng; Swmmng; UCLA; Med.

CORNELISON, RUSSELL A; Clovis HS; Clovis, CA; (2); Boy Scts; VP Treas 4-H; Band; Color Guard; Mrchg Band; Pep Band; JV Wrstlng; 4-H Awd; Hon Roll; Annapolis; Navy Fighter Pilot.

CORNELISSEN, CHRISTOPHER B; Carmel HS; Carmel, CA; (3); 11/147; Boy Scts; Treas Hosp Aide; Model UN; Teachers Aide; Band; School Play; Crs Cntry; High Hon Roll; Hon Roll; Eagle Sct; Hnr Band.

CORNELIUS, AZURA H; San Andreas HS; San Bernardino, CA; (4); Cmnty Wkr; Drama Clb; VICA; Variety Show; JV Bsktbl; JV Swmmng; Yng Blck Schlrs; Sociology.

CORNELIUS, EVELYN L; Novato HS; Novato, CA; (3); Band; Mrchg Band; Hon Roll; Reg Nurse.

CORNELIUS, STACY N; Saint Joseph HS; Long Beach, CA; (3); Cmnty Wkr; Debate Tm; GAA; Hosp Aide; Pep Clb; Spanish Clb; Rep Jr Cls; Rep Stu Cncl; JV Var Cheerldng; Var Powder Puff Ftbl; CSF; Peer Cnslng Prog; Hnrs & Advncd Plcmnt Cls; Phy Thrpy.

CORNELIUSON, SUSAN K; Bullard HS; Fresno, CA; (2); #1 In Class; German Clb; Band; Color Guard; Mrchg Band; Var Swmmng; High Hon Roll; U CA; Med.

CORNELL, CHRISTINE K; Village HS; Pleasanton, CA; (3); Hon Roll; Acctnt.

CORNELL, MEREDITH C; Clovis West HS; Fresno, CA; (2); FCA; Intnl Clb; Letterman Clb; SADD; Varsity Clb; Var Bsktbl; Socr; Var Sftbl; Var Vllybl; Bsktbl Rkie Yr 89; Sftbl Coach Awd, MIP 89 & 90; Bsktbl Lk Tahoe Trnmt Al-Str Tm.

CORNER, LETITIA M; Cabrillo HS; Lompoc, CA; (3); Hosp Aide; JA; Sftbl; Hon Roll; March Of Dimes Walk; Acctng.

CORNET, JOHN H; Berkeley HS; Berkeley, CA; (3); Boy Scts; Lit Mag; JV Crs Cntry; Mgr(s); Score Keeper; Hon Roll; BSA Eagle Scout; Schl So Athltc Arts Badminton Tm Capt, Mgr & Scrkpr.

CORNETT, BEN L; Villa Park HS; Villa Park, CA; (2); Church Yth Grp; VP German Clb; Key Clb; JV Ftbl; Var Golf; Cit Awd; High Hon Roll; Hon Roll; NHS; Ger Camp 90; Irvine Companys Envrnmntl Conf 90; Sci Olympd 88; UCLA; Med.

CORNETT, KENDRA M; Kingsburg Joint Union HS; Kingsburg, CA; (2); Church Yth Grp; Cmnty Wkr; Letterman Clb; Cheerldng; High Hon Roll; Jr Engrg Tech Soc Club; Odyssey Of Mind; St Fnlst Miss Teenage America Contest; Ecologist.

CORNILS, KEVIN P; Vintage HS; Napa, CA; (3); 1/380; Am Leg Boys St; Boy Scts; Church Yth Grp; Pres Key Clb; Chorus; Stu Cncl; JV Var Socr; JV Var Tennis; VP NHS; Bus.

CORNISH, ALLISON R; St Francis HS; Redwood City, CA; (2); 233/356; Church Yth Grp; Spanish Clb; SADD; Yrbk; Socr; Hon Roll; Miss Teen CA Pgnt; Foothill:Dnsst.

CORNISH, CATHERINE E; Bret Harte Union HS; Murphys, CA; (2); Dance Clb; Girl Scts; Key Clb; Pep Clb; Band; Mrchg Band; Off Frsh Cls; Off Jr Cls; Cheerldng; Hon Roll; Gldn St Math Awd Geom Hnrs; Unvrsl Dance Team Invtn To Tour Europe; UC Santa Barbara; Dance.

CORNISH, LISA A; Grossmont HS; La Mesa, CA; (2); 1/489; Church Yth Grp; FBLA; Math Tm; Var Gym; High Hon Roll; Pres Acad Fit Awd.

CORNMAN, TE ATA L; Mesa Verde HS; Citrus Heights, CA; (2); 22/257; Church Yth Grp; Dance Clb; FTA; Teachers Aide; Variety Show; Sftbl; High Hon Roll; Hon Roll; NHS; Pres Acad Fit Awd.

CORNWELL, ANDREW M; Nevada Union HS; Nevada City, CA; (1); Acpl Chr; Chorus; Ed Lit Mag; Crs Cntry; Vocal Music.

COROLLO, SHELLY; El Cerrito HS; El Cerrito, CA; (2); Church Yth Grp; SADD; Off Soph Cls; Hon Roll; Prfct Atten Awd; Sci.

CORONA, CARLOS JUAN; Calexico HS; Calexico, CA; (1); JV Ftbl; JV Trk; JV Wt Lftg; JV Wrstlng; Hon Roll; DEA Agent.

CORONA, GINA; Anaheim HS; Anaheim, CA; (4); Debate Tm; Latin Clb; Spanish Clb; Teachers Aide; Nwsp; Yrbk; Sftbl; Cypress CC; Jrnlsm.

CORONA, HUGO C; Aptos HS; Freedom, CA; (1); #83 In Class; JV Socr; UCLA; Sprts Med.

CORONA, KATHY; Fontana HS; Fontana, CA; (2); Bsktbl; Crs Cntry; Trk; Vllybl; Comp Sci.

CORONA, MARTHA P; Channel Islands HS; Oxnard, CA; (4); 18/489; Sec Dance Clb; Pres French Clb; Library Aide; Hon Roll; Pres Acad Fit Awd; MESA Treas; CSF; UC Berkeley; Bus Admin.

CORONA, OCTAVIO; Mater Dei HS; Santa Ana, CA; (2); Band; Mrchg Band; Pep Band; Socr; Hon Roll; CSF; Law.

CORONA, ROSA E; Herbert Hoover HS; Glendale, CA; (2); Church Yth Grp; French Clb; Hon Roll; TV Jrnlsm.

CORONA, ROY R; Eisenhower HS; Rialto, CA; (4); 6/663; SADD; Teachers Aide; Var Capt Tennis; Cit Awd; High Hon Roll; Hon Roll; NHS; Ntl Merit Ltr; Pres Acad Fit Awd; Golden St Exam Geom Hnrs; Outstndng In Frnch I, II & Accntng; Claremont Mc Kenna Coll; Accntg.

CORONADO, CYNTHIA; Brawley Union HS; Brawley, CA; (1); Pep Clb; JV Capt Cheerldng; High Hon Roll; Acad Ltr; CPR Card.

CORONADO, JUAN F; Brawley Union HS; Brawley, CA; (1); Comp Pgmr.

CORONADO, LUCIA A; River City HS; W Sacramento, CA; (2); Church Yth Grp; SADD; Rptr Yrbk; JV Var Bsktbl; Hon Roll; Club MESA.

CORONADO, MARIA DE L PILAR G; Mercy HS; San Bruno, CA; (4); 6/104; French Clb; Chorus; Church Choir; Hon Roll; Pres Acad Fit Awd; Pres Schlr; CA Schlrshp Fed; Hnrs Entrnc Stu; Coll Of Notre Dame; Eng.

CORONADO, SERGIO R; Hoover HS; Burbank, CA; (3); Church Yth Grp; Var Swmmng; Cit Awd; Hon Roll; Prfct Atten Awd; Vrsty Team Waterpolo; CA ST Los Angeles; Bus.

CORONADO, TRICIA ANN; Don Antonio Lugo HS; Chino, CA; (2); 22/750; Drama Clb; Ski Clb; Spanish Clb; Cheerldng; Pom Pon; Score Keeper; Trk; High Hon Roll; Hon Roll; CSF; Pep Commissioner; UCLA; Bus Law.

CORONADO, YVETTE; Yerba Buena HS; San Jose, CA; (2); Hon Roll; Pre Engrng Magnet Pgm; MESA; JETS; GATE; Strategic Plnng Cmmtte; Stanford; Microbio.

CORPUZ, EDWARD MARC; Independence HS; San Jose, CA; (2); Band; Jazz Band; Mrchg Band; Pep Band; School Musical; Intrml Vllybl; Univ Coll Opportunities; SEEDS.

CORR, COLIN C; Novato HS; Novato, CA; (2); Latin Clb; Lit Mag; JV Ftbl; JV Capt Lcrss; Hon Roll; Pres Acad Fit Awd; Cmmrcl Art.

CORR, ERIKA L; Roseville HS; Roseville, CA; (2); Hosp Aide; Pep Clb; Drill Tm; Jazz Band; Mrchg Band; Var Trk; Child/Adlscnt Psych.

CORRAL JR, ADAUTO D; Bell Gardens HS; Commerce, CA; (4); Church Yth Grp; Drama Clb; FCA; Letterman Clb; Stage Crew; Var Ftbl; Var Trk; Hon Roll; Prfct Atten Awd; New Life Clb; San Diego ST U; Comp Sci.

CORRAL, ERIKA; Erika Corral HS; El Centro, CA; (1); Hon Roll; UCLA; Bus.

CORRAL, MARTIN; St John Bosco HS; Norwalk, CA; (4); 23/250; French Clb; Pres Key Clb; Office Aide; SADD; Band; Hon Roll; NHS; Ntl Merit SF; U Of Southern CA; Psych.

CORRAL, PALMA A; Santa Maria HS; Santa Maria, CA; (2); 90/600; Drama Clb; Chorus; School Musical; School Play; Stage Crew; Hon Roll; Lit, Music, Art; Lit.

CORRAL, ROGELIO; St Bernard HS; Inglewood, CA; (3); Cmnty Wkr; Latin Clb; JV Var Bsbl; Cit Awd; Acctng.

CORRALES, ERIC J; Indio HS; Indio, CA; (4); 41/348; Cmnty Wkr; Teachers Aide; Cit Awd; Hon Roll; Chrch Knights Columbus Awd; Bsbl; Bsktbl; Collct Bsbl & Sports Cards; CA ST Fullerton; Sports Brdcs.

CORRALES, LAURA L; Washington Prep HS; Los Angeles, CA; (3); Latin Clb; ROTC; Band; Color Guard; Orch; Hon Roll; Writer.

CORREA, CHRISTY S; John F Kennedy HS; Sacramento, CA; (4); 242/388; Church Yth Grp; Debate Tm; Hosp Aide; Intnl Clb; Key Clb; Red Cross Aide; Spanish Clb; SADD; Cheerldng; Hon Roll; Cngrssnl Schlr; MVP Sftbl 88; Chrstn Mssns; AZ Pacific U; Med.

CORREA, EDITH; Workman HS; Valinda, CA; (2); Var Swmmng; Accepted SIOP In Cal Poly Pomona Coll; Coll; Drafting Arch.

CORREA, JESSE; Monache HS; Porterville, CA; (3); Art Clb; Chess Clb; Debate Tm; FCA; 4-H; Letterman Clb; SADD; Teachers Aide; Varsity Clb; Var L Bsbl; Humboldt ST; Wildlife.

CORREA, KARINA A; Pasadena HS; Pasadena, CA; (2); Church Yth Grp; ROTC; Drill Tm; NJROTC Natl Sojourners; USC; Comp Pgmng.

CORREA, ROCIO T; Saunas HS; Salinas, CA; (4); 9/350; Sec Church Yth Grp; English Clb; VP French Clb; Sec Treas GAA; Key Clb; Teachers Aide; Church Choir; JV Bsktbl; JV Sftbl; Cit Awd; Bank Amer Awd Frnch Deprtmnt; Co-Chmps JV Bsktbl; UC Berkeley; Law/Bus.

CORREA, SABINA; Princeton JR SR HS; Butte City, CA; (3); 3/17; Yrbk; Rep Frsh Cls; Treas Stu Cncl; Var Bsktbl; Cheerldng; Stat Ftbl; Var Sftbl; Var Vllybl; Hon Roll; Pres Schlr; CSF Secy; Stu Of Qtr; Blck P; Grls ST Alt; Chicano Ltno Yth Ldrshp Conf 89, Peer Cnslr 90.

CORREIA, KIMBERLY; Patterson HS; Patterson, CA; (2); AFS; Pep Clb; Ski Clb; Spanish Clb; SADD; Cheerldng; Hon Roll; UC Santa Barbara; TV Brdcstng.

CORRODI, JOHN T; Santa Monica HS; Malibu, CA; (2); Am Leg Boys St; Bus Profs of Am; FCA; SADD; Variety Show; Yrbk; Gym; Swmmng; Hon Roll; Bus.

CORSELLO, JASON N; Live Oak HS; San Jose, CA; (3); 27/639; Debate Tm; Pep Clb; Phtg Yrbk; Stu Cncl; Var Golf; Hon Roll; Jr Golf Assn; Med.

CORSETTI, JASON C; Giahz HS; Cerritos, CA; (3); 22/220; Spanish Clb; Teachers Aide; Intrml JV Bsbl; High Hon Roll; Hon Roll; CSU Fullerton; Bus.

CORSO, SEAN; Canyon Springs HS; Moreno Valley, CA; (2); Teachers Aide; Cit Awd; High Hon Roll; Hon Roll; UC Berkeley; Corp Mgmt.

CORTES, ARACELI; San Gabriel HS; Montebello, CA; (3); Drama Clb; VP French Clb; FBLA; Rep Jr Cls; French Hon Soc; High Hon Roll; Hon Roll; NHS; Medallion Awd Frnch; Peer Cnslr; Pitzer; Psych.

CORTES, BERHA; Notre Dame Acad; Culver City, CA; (4); Church Yth Grp; Intnl Clb; Flag Corp; Yrbk; Rep Frsh Cls; Cheerldng; NHS; CA Schlrshp Fdrtn; Harvard Book Prize; Natl Hispanic Schlrshp Awd Pgm Semi-Fnlst; Law.

CORTES, CARLOS A; Rio Mesa HS; Oxnard, CA; (3); Chess Clb; Letterman Clb; Varsity Clb; Var Tennis; Cit Awd; High Hon Roll; Hon Roll; CSF; Aerosp Engr.

CORTES, ELIZABETH; Antioch SR HS; Antioch, CA; (4); Chorus; Hl Loa Coll; Pre-Law.

CORTES, JOSE; Pioneer HS; Whittier, CA; (4); Boy Scts; Drama Clb; Office Aide; Red Cross Aide; Teachers Aide; Stage Crew; JV Bsktbl; JV Crs Cntry; Var Swmmng; JV Wt Lftg; Engrng.

CORTES, JOSE S; Notre Dame HS; Corona, CA; (1); 3/200; SADD; Capt Bsbl; Capt Ftbl; Wt Lftg; Wrstlng; High Hon Roll; Pres Acad Fit Awd; Stanford U; Prfssnl Sports.

CORTES, KAREN; Southwest HS; San Diego, CA; (4); 46/483; Pep Clb; Pres SADD; Rep Stu Cncl; Var Cheerldng; High Hon Roll; ASB Cmssnr Pep; CSF; Extrrdnry Effrt Awd; ASB Wrker Yr Awd; Scl Sci Stu Mnth; Sci.

CORTES, LIZETTE M; La Habra HS; La Habra, CA; (4); Drama Clb; Intnl Clb; Key Clb; Quiz Bowl; Science Clb; Spanish Clb; Research Prjct Spnsrd By Sthrn CA Jr Acad Of Sci; Sci Olympiad; CS Long Beach; Microbiology.

CORTES, MARIBEL; Winters HS; Winters, CA; (2); SADD; Teachers Aide; Stage Crew; JV Bsktbl; JV Vllybl; Hon Roll.

CORTES, MELISSA L; Baptist Christian HS; Hemet, CA; (3); Ed Yrbk; Pres Sr Cls; Var Capt Bsktbl; Var Sftbl; Hon Roll; MVP Sftbl; All Chrstn Leag Sftbl; All Chrstn Leag Bsktbl Hnrbl Mntn; Fshn Mrchndsng.

CORTES, MONICA S; King City Joint Union HS; Greenfield, CA; (3); Pres Art Clb; Debate Tm; Sec Drama Clb; Scholastic Bowl; Pres Speech Tm; Band; Jazz Band; Mrchg Band; School Play; Var L Crs Cntry; Lions Clb Spch Cntst Clb Fnlst 89; Lions Clb Wnr 90; Engl.

CORTES, ROBERT B; Rio Mesa HS; Oxnard, CA; (1); 1/493; JV Tennis; Cit Awd; High Hon Roll; Hon Roll; CSF; Arch.

CORTES, ROGELIO C; Baldwin Park HS; Baldwin Park, CA; (2); High Hon Roll; Hon Roll; Prfct Atten Awd; Arch.

CORTES, ZENIA; La Sierra Acad; Riverside, CA; (2); Church Yth Grp; Teachers Aide; Varsity Clb; Orch; Var L Bsktbl; Var L Vllybl; High Hon Roll; Hon Roll; NHS; Superior Achvt Cert-Comp Applictns; Outstndng Achvt-Alg I 88; Hghst Span Grad 88-90.

CORTESE, ANDREA V; Pioneer HS; San Jose, CA; (1); Cmnty Wkr; Amnesty Intl; Skiing; Jazz Dncng; UC Davis; Dr.

CORTEZ, ADRIANA; Santa Paula Union HS; Santa Paula, CA; (2); Migrant Pgm Club; North Ridge; Psych.

CORTEZ, ANGELICA; Notre Dame Acad; Los Angeles, CA; (3); Spanish Clb; Hon Roll; Social Jstc Clb; Cal Poly Pomona; Vet Med.

CORTEZ, CANDY; Selma HS; Selma, CA; (3); 21/212; Chorus; Bsktbl; Sftbl; Vllybl; Hon Roll; Cngrssnl Yth Schlr; Teach Eng.

CORTEZ, CARLOS B; Mc Farland HS; Mc Farland, CA; (3); Church Yth Grp; VICA; Band; Mrchg Band; Wt Lftg; JV Wrstlng; Hon Roll; Prfct Atten Awd; Alt Boys St-Top Stu; Cal Poly; Arch.

CORTEZ, CHRISTINA D; Mt Whitney HS; Visalia, CA; (4); FFA; Spanish Clb; SADD; Band; Mrchg Band; Pep Band; Rptr Nwsp; Hon Roll; NHS; CSF; Acad, Music & Jrnlsm Ltrs; Culturl Exchnge Stu Spain Smmr 89; UC Davis; Pre-Med.

CORTEZ, CLAUDIA; San Jacinto HS; San Jacinto, CA; (3); Church Yth Grp; High Hon Roll; French Clb; Pres FBLA; Office Aide; Drill Tm; Prfct Atten Awd; Cal ST San Bernardino; Bus.

CORTEZ, CRISTINA; Lynwood HS; Lynwood, CA; (1).

CORTEZ, DEBBIE ANN; Winters HS; Winters, CA; (4); Sec AFS; Church Yth Grp; Pres FBLA; Office Aide; Pep Clb; Teachers Aide; Mgr Yrbk; Hon Roll; CSF Gold Sealbearer; Accntng.

CORTEZ, EDUARDO L; Baldwin Park HS; Baldwin Park, CA; (2); JV Capt Bsktbl; Capt Ftbl; Cit Awd; Acctng.

CORTEZ, ELVA; Banning HS; Wilmington, CA; (2); Church Yth Grp; French Clb; Drill Tm; Jazz Band; School Play; VP Soph Cls; Rep Stu Cncl; Cit Awd; High Hon Roll; Hon Roll; Soroptimist Awd; CJSF Pres; ASB Pres, Sec; UC Santa Barbara; Law.

CORTEZ, EVA; Wasco Union HS; Wasco, CA; (2); FHA; Sftbl; Cal ST.

CORTEZ, IGNACIO; High Lands HS; Sacramento, CA; (3); Socr; Wt Lftg; Prfct Atten Awd; Spcl Olympcs; Wood Shp; Sacramento ST U; Carpenter.

CORTEZ, JAMES V; St Anthony HS; Long Beach, CA; (3); 3/130; Cmnty Wkr; Teachers Aide; School Musical; Nwsp; VP Sr Cls; JV Crs Cntry; Var JV Trk; High Hon Roll; NHS; CSF; St Anthony Mrt Schlrshp; Schl Campus Minstry Grp; Bus.

CORTEZ, JUAN A; Baldwin Park HS; Baldwin Park, CA; (3); Spanish Clb; Socr; High Hon Roll; Hon Roll; Comp Engr.

CORTEZ, JULIZA A; Santa Maria HS; Santa Maria, CA; (3); Church Yth Grp; Cmnty Wkr; Pres FHA; Spanish Clb; Stu Cncl; Capt Powder Puff Ftbl; JV Var Vllybl; Coll Campus Explrs Sec; Var Vllybl MVP; Seattle Pacific U; Bus Mgt.

CORTEZ, KIMBERLY N; Norte Vista HS; Riverside, CA; (3); 38/336; Dance Clb; FBLA; Office Aide; Pep Clb; Science Clb; SADD; Varsity Clb; Off Nwsp; Off Yrbk; Stat Swmmng; Hnr Court; PAL Peer Cnslng; Psych.

CORTEZ, LINDA C; Montebello HS; Los Angeles, CA; (3); SADD; Teachers Aide; Sec Acpl Chr; Chorus; Var Cheerldng; JV Powder Puff Ftbl; Cit Awd; Hon Roll; Modern Dance; Hawaiian Dance; Mst Inspirational & Mst Dedicated Chrldr 89-90; CA ST.

CORTEZ, MANDY E; William S Hart HS; Valencia, CA; (2); Drill Tm; Stu Cncl; Vet.

CORTEZ, MARTHA E; East Bakersfield HS; Bakersfield, CA; (2); German Clb; Teachers Aide; Hon Roll; Bkrsfld Coll; Med.

CORTEZ, ROSALINDA; Tulare Western HS; Tulare, CA; (2); Band; Color Guard; Rep Frsh Cls; Pres Soph Cls; Var Socr; JV Sftbl; Hon Roll; Engl & Frshmn Stds Awds; Participation Awd.

CORTEZ, SONIA M; Huntington Beach HS; Huntington Bch, CA; (3); French Clb; Key Clb; Office Aide; Spanish Clb; Cit Awd; High Hon Roll; Hon Roll; U CA Irvine; Frgn Lang.

CORTEZ, VERONICA; Baldwin Park HS; Baldwin Park, CA; (1); SADD; Band; Mrchg Band; Off Frsh Cls; Tennis; Hon Roll; Prfct Atten Awd; CPA.

CORTEZ, VERONICA; Huntington Park HS; Huntington Park, CA; (1); French Clb; Tall Flags 4 Parades; Ucla; Word Processor.

CORTEZ, VICTORIA A; Orestimba HS; Modesto, CA; (2); SADD; Hon Roll; Cmptrs.

CORTINAS, JAIME; Cantwell HS; Los Angeles, CA; (1); Bsbl; Var Bsktbl; Tgk & Fld; US Air Force.

CORTOPASSI, VALERIE A; John F Kennedy HS; Sacramento, CA; (3); Stu Cncl; JV Var Cheerldng; High Hon Roll; CSF; Nordstrom Brass Plum Fshn Brd; Stanford.

CORVI, MICHELE; Notre Dame HS; San Bruno, CA; (1); Church Yth Grp; Debate Tm; GAA; Red Cross Aide; Bsktbl; Var Sftbl; JV Swmmng; Hon Roll; Swm Instrctr; Spirit Awd; Athltc Awd Swmmng, Sftbl; Attorney At Law.

CORVO, YVETTE M; Woodland HS; Woodland, CA; (4); 22/409; 4-H; Treas Pres Band; Church Choir; Mrchg Band; School Musical; Stage Crew; Nwsp; Hon Roll; Jr NHS; Prfct Atten Awd; CSF; Outstndng Achvt In Geom Awd.

CORWIN, ERICA; Mira Costa HS; Manhattan Beach, CA; (2); Church Yth Grp; Key Clb; Church Choir; Drill Tm; Hon Roll; Pres Acad Fit Awd; UCLA; Tchng.

CORY, JULIANA S; Los Angeles Baptist HS; Tarzana, CA; (3); 7/101; French Clb; Office Aide; Service Clb; Chorus; Var Crs Cntry; Var Trk; Hon Roll; Ntl Merit Ltr; Opt Clb Awd; Big Sister Pgm Schl; CA Schlrshp Fed Mem; Awded For Straight A; Psych.

CORYELLE, STEPHEN E; Independence HS; San Jose, CA; (3); German Clb; Intrml Ftbl; Intrml Socr; Intrml Sftbl; Intrml Vllybl; Civil Air Patrl Billy Mitchell Awd; Aerospace Sci.

CORZO, WILLIAM; Pater Noster HS; Los Angeles, CA; (2); Bsktbl; Ftbl; Trk; High Hon Roll; USC; Engr.

COSGRIFF, COREY K; Granada Hills HS; Northridge, CA; (3); Church Yth Grp; Stage Crew; Wt Lftg; High Hon Roll; Hon Roll; UCLA; Acctnt.

COSGROVE, MICHELLE R; Grace M Davis HS; Modesto, CA; (4); 46/485; Pep Clb; Band; Cit Awd; High Hon Roll; Hon Roll; NHS; Teachers Aide Data Processing Class; Wwahs 88-89; Modesto JR; Marine Biology.

COSICO, MARC; Bishop Amat HS; West Covina, CA; (2); Intrml JV Bsktbl; Intrml Trk.

COSMOT, JOSEPH; Ygnacio Valley HS; Walnut Creek, CA; (3); Boy Scts; Church Yth Grp; Computer Clb; Intrml Bsbl; JV Socr; Intrml Swmmng; Intrml Wt Lftg; Accntnt.

COSTA, AARON; Western Christian HS; Upland, CA; (3); Church Yth Grp; Ski Clb; Teachers Aide; Rptr Nwsp; VP Stu Cncl; Intrml Ftbl; Hon Roll; Ethics Cls Most Insprtnl 1989-90; Bus.

COSTA, AMY-MARIE V; Tulare Union HS; Tulare, CA; (4); 2/385; Ed Nwsp; High Hon Roll; Val; Portuguese Clb; Outstndng Achvmnt Cert Hnrs Engl, Sci & Scl Stud; CA Schlrshp Fed 90; COS; Lw.

COSTA, ANNABEL A; Los Banos HS; Los Banos, CA; (2); Church Yth Grp; Drama Clb; Intnl Clb; Acpl Chr; Church Choir; Stage Crew; Rep Soph Cls; Score Keeper; Hon Roll; PR SRO; Child Psych.

COSTA, ANNABELA M; Tulare Union HS; Tulare, CA; (3); 77/401; Off Bus Profs of Am; Church Yth Grp; Rep Frsh Cls; Rep Soph Cls; Rep Jr Cls; Hon Roll; Prfct Atten Awd; Portuguese Club, Vp, Pres; Ldrshp; ASB, Active Stu Body, Prom Cmmtte; Hi-Deb Modeling Group; COS; Bus Adm.

COSTA, CHAD A; Hanford HS; Hanford, CA; (3); Church Yth Grp; Cmnty Wkr; Church Choir; Stage Crew; Bsbl; Ftbl; Wt Lftg; Cit Awd; 1st Pl Ca Preaching Cntst; 1st Pl Weight Lifting Cntst; So CA Coll; Yth Pastor.

COSTA, DAMIAN; Christian Brothers HS; Elk Grove, CA; (3); Church Yth Grp; Computer Clb; German Clb; SADD; School Play; Pres Soph Cls; Intrml Bsktbl; Intrml Ftbl; High Hon Roll; Drama Clb; CA Schlrshp Fdrtn; Purdue U; Engrng.

COSTA, JASON D; Modesto Christian HS; Modesto, CA; (3); Church Yth Grp; VP Sr Cls; Var Bsbl; Var Ftbl; Var Wt Lftg; Hon Roll; Arch.

COSTA, JOSEPH C; San Bernardino HS; San Bernardino, CA; (3); Chess Clb; ROTC; Crs Cntry; Trk; Hon Roll; Prfct Atten Awd; Cal ST Long Bch.

COSTA, LESTER D; Tulare Union HS; Tulare, CA; (4); 57/368; Church Yth Grp; Drama Clb; Ed Nwsp; Rep Jr Cls; Rep Sr Cls; JV Crs Cntry; Var Ftbl; Var Capt Trk; Var Capt Wrstlng; NHS; Portugese Clb Pres & VP; San Diego ST U; Bio.

COSTA, MARY AILEEN V; Carson HS; Carson, CA; (4); 7/500; Church Yth Grp; Science Clb; Service Clb; Ed Yrbk; Treas Jr Cls; Tennis; Vllybl; Cit Awd; High Hon Roll; Pres Acad Fit Awd; Filipino Clb, Pres, VP & Sectry; Natl Schlr/Athlte Awd US Army Reserve; Las Madrinas; Interact; CA ST U; Elec Engrng.

COSTA, MICHAEL; Independence HS; San Jose, CA; (4); 19/850; Church Yth Grp; Science Clb; Stage Crew; Intrml Socr; Intrml Sftbl; Hon Roll; NHS; Prtgs Clb-Pres & VP; Mck Trl Clb Sec-Treas; Natl Sci Olympd 88; Physcs Dstnctn Awd 89; U Of CA Berkeley; Engrng.

COSTA, SHELLY; Hanford Joint Union HS; Hanford, CA; (1); FHA; Intnl Clb; Office Aide; JV Swmmng; Dancing, Bike Riding, Water Skiing.

COSTA, SOPHIA H; Turlock HS; Turlock, CA; (1); Acpl Chr; Chorus; Swing Chorus; Airline Attendant.

COSTA, STEPHANIE D; Tracy Joint Union HS; Tracy, CA; (4); 21/359; Ed Yrbk; Rptr Lit Mag; Stat Ftbl; Stat Swmmng; Var L Vllybl; JV Var Wt Lftg; High Hon Roll; Hon Roll; Friends Spec Olympcs; Bank Amer Achvt; San Joaquin Delta Coll; Educ.

COSTA, STEVE; Bear River HS; Grass Valley, CA; (2); Boy Scts; Church Yth Grp; Drama Clb; Service Clb; School Play; Bsktbl; Golf; High Hon Roll; Odessy Of The Mind World Finalist; Selected For Hugh Obrien Youth Ldrshp Awd; Brigham Young U; Design & Adver.

COSTALES, PRECIOUS; Alameda HS; Alameda, CA; (4); Science Clb; Ed Yrbk; Hist Soph Cls; Rep Jr Cls; Hon Roll; Pres Acad Fit Awd; Natl Airmotive Schlrshp Recpnt; Asian Club Schlrshp Recipient; CLODS Member; Boston U; Jrnlsm.

COSTANTINO, MARY; San Marcos HS; Escondido, CA; (2); Drama Clb; Band; Drm Mjr(t); Mrchg Band; JV Tennis; DAR Awd; High Hon Roll; Hon Roll; Poets Soc & Sci Fctn Clbs; Slvr & Gldn Poet Awds; Outstndng Soph Awd Mrchng Band; CA Poly San Luis Obisbo; Vet.

COSTANZA, LISA; Antioch HS; Antioch, CA; (2); Key Clb; Letterman Clb; Pep Clb; VP Jr Cls; Cheerldng; Pom Pon; Swmmng; Hon Roll; Swmmng Lssns Instrctr; Coach Antioch Yth Ftbl Chrldrs; Aerobics, Wghtlftng Excrsc Pgm; U Of CA San Diego; Psych.

COSTAUZA, LORI A; Antioch SR HS; Antioch, CA; (2); 123/748; Teachers Aide; Hon Roll; East Clb; CSF; :Marine Biolgst.

COSTELLO, BRANDON M; Prospect HS; San Jose, CA; (1); JV Ftbl; JV Socr; JV Tennis; Math.

COSTELLO, CHAD; Don Lugo HS; Chino, CA; (3); Ftbl; Gov Hon Prg Awd; High Hon Roll; Hon Roll; Frnch Clb; Geom St Awd; Engrng.

COSTELLO, DENIS; Leuzinger HS; Hawthorne, CA; (2); JA; Off Soph Cls; Stu Cncl; JV Var Bsbl; Ftbl; Hon Roll; Stu Cncl Cmmssnr Of Athltcs; UCLA; Med.

COSTELLO, JASON M; Montclair HS; Rancho Cucamonga, CA; (1); Science Clb; JV Tennis; High Hon Roll; GATE & Envrnmntl Clbs; Envrnmntl Sci.

COSTELLO, JOHN P; Pescadero HS; Pescadero, CA; (3); Boy Scts; JA; Band; School Play; Ed Yrbk; Pres Frsh Cls; Pres Soph Cls; Pres Jr Cls; Pres Sr Cls; Sec Stu Cncl; UC Berkely; Accntng.

COSTELLO, JULIE M; Montgomery HS; Santa Rosa, CA; (3); Sec Pres Key Clb; Spanish Clb; Mrchg Band; Var Socr; JV Var Sftbl; Trk; Hon Roll; Math.

COSTELLO, KIMBERLY; Linoln HS; Stockton, CA; (3); Rptr Nwsp; Hon Roll; Hrbl Recog-GSE Exam; Yth Rec Referee; Gftd/Hrs Clsses.

COSTIGLIOLO, BRIAN; Linden HS; Linden, CA; (1); Church Yth Grp; Ski Clb; JV Bsbl; JV Bsktbl; JV Ftbl; Hon Roll; Cal Poly San Luis Obispo; Arch.

COSTIN, JAKE; Yosemite HS; Coarsegold, CA; (3); Ski Clb; JV Bsktbl; JV Ftbl; JV Mgr(s); Var Tennis; Hon Roll; Mock Trial Team; Ivy League Coll; Law.

COTA, BRANDON B; Rubidoux HS; Riverside, CA; (2); 7/364; Church Yth Grp; FBLA; Spanish Clb; Var Ftbl; Var Golf; Cit Awd; Mecha Club; USC; Bus Mgmt.

COTA, CORINNA M; Atwater HS; Atwater, CA; (4); FCA; Red Cross Aide; Science Clb; SADD; Varsity Clb; Powder Puff Ftbl; Socr; Sftbl; Hon Roll; Prfct Atten Awd; Scr Schlrshp; Best Ofnsv Plyr Soccer; Best Def Sftbl; Merced Coll; Art.

COTA, CYNTHIA; Bonita Vista HS; Chula Vista, CA; (2); Church Yth Grp; Chorus; UCSD.

COTA, JENNIFER; La Reina HS; Camarillo, CA; (3); GAA; Letterman Clb; Office Aide; Service Clb; Varsity Clb; Rep Jr Cls; Var Crs Cntry; Var Socr; Cit Awd; St Schlr; Span Natl Hnr Soc; Awd Excllnce Visual Arts; Nwsp & Yrbk Staff.

COTA, JOSE L; Bonita Vista HS; National City, CA; (4); Southwestern Coll; Math.

COTA, LAURIE L; Canyon HS; Canyon Country, CA; (4); Drama Clb; Teachers Aide; Nwsp; Pres Soph Cls; Trk; USC; Libl Art.

COTA, LORETTA M; Coachella Valley HS; Coachella, CA; (3); 135/400; Art Clb; Church Yth Grp; Varsity Clb; Phtg Yrbk; Sec Jr Cls; Sec Stu Cncl; JV Bsktbl; Var Tennis; JV Vllybl; CA ST Fullerton; Communictns.

COTA, REBECCA M; Calexico HS; Calexico, CA; (2); Art Clb; Library Aide; Office Aide; Spanish Clb; SADD; Teachers Aide; Phtg Yrbk; Hon Roll; 3 Comp Awds; Spnsh Tchr.

COTE, ELISE C.; Poway HS; Poway, CA; (2); Church Yth Grp; Cmnty Wkr; Dance Clb; Model UN; Pep Clb; Ski Clb; JV Cheerldng; JV Pom Pon; Hon Roll; CA Jr Schlrshp Fed.

COTE, JENNIFER; Bonita Vista HS; Bonita, CA; (3); Intnl Clb; Pep Clb; Var Crs Cntry; Var Trk; Cit Awd; Hon Roll; Vlntr Of Mnth; Dynamic Dvd Awd; San Diego Zoo Schl; U Of CA-DAVIS; Vet.

COTE, PATRICIA ANN; Cabrillo HS; VAFB, CA; (3); ROTC; Hon Roll; Vet.

COTERO, ADALBERTO; Blair HS; Pasadena, CA; (1); Socr; Hon Roll; Med.

COTEY, DAWN E; Yosemite HS; Ahwahnee, CA; (3); FFA; High Hon Roll; Hon Roll; US Law & Jstc Mock Trl; Vlntr For Mntn Crisis Ctr; Fresno ST U; Crmnl Law.

COTEY, DIANA; Yosemite HS; Ahwahnee, CA; (1); Hon Roll; Mtn Crisis Ctr Vlntr; Fresno City Coll; Scl Wrk.

COTO, AMANDA; Leuzinger HS; Lawndale, CA; (3); Cmnty Wkr; Dance Clb; Debate Tm; Drama Clb; Pep Clb; Science Clb; Drill Tm; Hist Frsh Cls; Sec Soph Cls; Rep Jr Cls; Acad Decathlon; Advanced Dance; Latinos Del Tiempo Nuevo; Sociology.

COTRONEO, STEVE J; California HS; Whittier, CA; (4); Cmnty Wkr; Teachers Aide; Cit Awd; Spring Art Show; Spcl Efcts Demstrtn Art Cls; TV.

COTTENGIN, KAMA C; North HS; Bakersfield, CA; (3); #33 In Class; Drama Clb; Chorus; Hon Roll; Bakersfld Coll Solo Fstvl Wnnr; Prfrmng Arts.

COTTER, SARAH C; Sacramento Adventist Acad; Citrus Heights, CA; (3); 1/40; Church Yth Grp; Cmnty Wkr; Debate Tm; Ski Clb; Band; JV Bsktbl; JV Tennis; Var Trk; Var Vllybl; High Hon Roll; Elec Engrng.

COTTER, TIFFANI; Sierra Jt Un HS; Madera, CA; (4); 5/165; Art Clb; Cmnty Wkr; Pres 4-H; Model UN; Pep Clb; Ski Clb; Spanish Clb; SADD; Varsity Clb; Pres Stu Cncl; Amer Lgn Top Grl, Brd Trusts Top Fml Stu Awd; Hi-Deb Schl Rep & Secy; U Of CA San Diego; Pre-Med.

COTTINGHAM, MELISSA; Capo Valley Christian Schl; San Juan Capistra, CA; (2); Church Yth Grp; Cmnty Wkr; Var Socr; JV Sftbl; JV Vllybl; High Hon Roll; Hon Roll; Pres Acad Fit Awd; Girl Scts; Speech Tm; UCSB; Neo-Natal Nrsng.

COTTINGIM, BRANDI; Hesperia Christian HS; Apple Valley, CA; (1); 1/40; Quiz Bowl; Band; JV Cheerldng; Var Sftbl; High Hon Roll; Achvd Grtst Goal Accptng Jesus As Prsnl Lork & Savior; Biola; Engrng.

COTTON, DAVID D; El Cerrito HS; El Cerrito, CA; (2); Hon Roll; CA Schlrshp Fdrtn; ECHS Awd; Jr Olympc Archry Devlpmnt Pgm.

COTTON, JULIANN A; West Covina HS; West Covina, CA; (1); Church Yth Grp; Drama Clb; Hosp Aide; Pep Clb; Red Cross Aide; School Musical; School Play; Ed Phtg Yrbk; Rptr Lit Mag; Rep Stu Cncl; UCLA; Pltcl Sci.

COTTON, STEVE; El Modena HS; Orange, CA; (2); 1/500; French Clb; Science Clb; Tennis; Cit Awd; High Hon Roll; NHS; Ntl Merit Ltr; Sci.

COTTRELL, DEEANA S; Hemet HS; Hemet, CA; (3); 16/475; Church Yth Grp; Rptr Nwsp; High Hon Roll; Hon Roll; Daisy Chain Hnr Escort Grad Ceremony 90; Brigham Young U; Elem Educ.

COTTRELL, ELIZABETH A; Hesperia HS; Hesperia, CA; (2); Church Yth Grp; Band; Mrchg Band; Hon Roll; CSF; U Of CA; Music.

COUCH, JEROME K; Del Campo HS; Carmichael, CA; (3); 60/446; Spanish Clb; Band; Mrchg Band; Pep Band; Var Crs Cntry; Var Trk; Ntl Merit SF; Acad Decath Tm; Fri Night Live; UC Davis; Envrnmntl Engr.

COUCH, SONYA R; Skyline HS; Oakland, CA; (3); Girl Scts; Band; Chorus; Mrchg Band; School Musical; School Play; Pres Frsh Cls; Rep Stu Cncl; Var Capt Bsktbl; Var Cheerldng.

COUGHLIN, CLAIRE E; Willits HS; Willits, CA; (3); AFS; Cmnty Wkr; Drama Clb; Spanish Clb; Teachers Aide; School Musical; Var Cheerldng; High Hon Roll; Hon Roll; Stu Lion; Willits Frontier Lioness Clb 87-90; Bus.

COUGHLIN, TRACI R; Pinole Valley HS; San Pablo, CA; (1); Church Yth Grp; Drama Clb; Teachers Aide; Stage Crew; Gym; Hon Roll; UC Davis; Chld Psych.

COULSTON, ERIN L; Carondelet HS; Clayton, CA; (3); 14/162; Church Yth Grp; Ski Clb; Yrbk; Rep Frsh Cls; Var JV Crs Cntry; Var JV Swmmng; JV Trk; High Hon Roll; NHS; Spanish NHS; Yth Educator; Peer Cnslr.

COULTAS, STEPHANIE M; Imperial HS; Sunland, CA; (2); Church Yth Grp; Chorus; Variety Show; Cheerldng; Socr; Vet.

COULTER, ANDREA R; Exeter Union HS; Exeter, CA; (4); FBLA; High Hon Roll; Hon Roll; Coll Of The Sequoias; Bus Adm.

COULTER, JULIE; Mar Vista HS; San Diego, CA; (3); Pep Clb; ROTC; SADD; Teachers Aide; Color Guard; Stu Cncl; Hon Roll.

COULTER, MARK W; Mills HS; Millbrae, CA; (3); Office Aide; Service Clb; Teachers Aide; Hon Roll; South CA; Bus.

COULTER, RACHELLE; San Benito HS; Hollister, CA; (2); Drama Clb; SADD; School Play; Stage Crew; Golf; Hon Roll; All Hnr Clses; Gldn St Math Awd Alg; Sci.

COULTER, ROBERT J; Hanford Joint Union HS; Hanford, CA; (2); Drama Clb; Intnl Clb; Acpl Chr; School Play; Var Swmmng; Hon Roll; Spanish Clb; Peer Cnslr 89-90; Frgn Exch Stu Sweden 90-91; US Naval Acad; Ariline Pilot.

COULTER, SHANNON R; Tulare Union HS; Tulare, CA; (4); JV Var Crs Cntry; JV Var Trk; Coll Of Sequoias; Comp Mechncs.

COUNTS, MELISSA J; Bakersfield HS; Bakersfield, CA; (2); 4-H; FHA; SADD; Band; Mrchg Band; Orch; Cit Awd; Hon Roll; NHS; Cert Of Awd Spcl Achvt Civics; Cert Of Recog Outstndg Perf Music; U CA ST Bakersfield; Sclgy.

COURET, LISA N; Edison-Computech HS; Fresno, CA; (1); French Clb; Math Clb; Science Clb; Ski Clb; JV Bsktbl; JV Sftbl; JV Vllybl; Hon Roll; ESHA.

COURON, AARON C; Chino HS; Chino, CA; (3); Letterman Clb; Band; Mrchg Band; High Hon Roll; Prfct Atten Awd; Distngshd Schlr Pgm; UCLA.

COURSEY, GEORGANNA L; India HS; Indio, CA; (1); Color Guard; UCLA; Actng.

COURTEAU, DEVIN C; Marin Catholic HS; Novato, CA; (4); 7/200; Hon Roll; NHS; Ntl Merit SF; CSF; Deans Lst; U Of CA-BERKELEY; Bus Admin.

COURTER, WHITNEY W; Placer HS; Auburn, CA; (2); Church Yth Grp; Ski Clb; Spanish Clb; Trk; Vllybl; Hon Roll; Cross Cntry Skiing Vrsty Mst Vlbl Girl; Eng.

COURTNEY, JEREMIAH S; American HS; Fremont, CA; (3); 73/310; ROTC; Teachers Aide; Hon Roll; ROP Stu Mth; Elec.

COURTRIGHT, JOSHUA; Victor Valley Christian HS; Victorville, CA; (4); 8/23; Boy Scts; Hosp Aide; Teachers Aide; School Play; JV Bsktbl; Hon Roll; Rotary Awd; San Diego ST U; Bus Admin.

COURTRIGHT, KATHLEEN D; Carondelet HS; Walnut Creek, CA; (3); Hosp Aide; Nwsp; Rep Frsh Cls; Rep Soph Cls; Rep Jr Cls; VP Sr Cls; Rep Stu Cncl; French Hon Soc; Hon Roll; NHS; Fri Night Live.

COURTRIGHT, MICHELLE L; Ernest Righetti HS; Santa Maria, CA; (2); 1/400; French Clb; Teachers Aide; JV Capt Sftbl; Var Tennis; High Hon Roll; Stanford; Phys Thrpy.

COURY, BEKKI M; Mater Dei HS; Santa Ana, CA; (3); Cmnty Wkr; French Clb; Hosp Aide; Ski Clb; Swmmng.

COUSINS, JENNIFER M; Tustin HS; Tustin, CA; (1); Church Yth Grp; Cmnty Wkr; Pep Clb; Drill Tm; Var Cheerldng; Cit Awd; Hon Roll; Orange Cty Acad Decthln; CA Schlrshp Fedrtn; Golden St Exm Alg Hnrs; Stanford U; Child Psych.

COUSINS, PETER M; Hughson HS; Ceres, CA; (4); 1/125; 4-H; FFA; Math Clb; Science Clb; Ed Nwsp; L Socr; L Trk; Cit Awd; DAR Awd; 4-H Awd; Editor Indep Schl Nwspaper; Head Dlgte CA Dlgtn To 89 Model Assmbly; 90 Delegate Natl 4-H Conf; Stanford U; Bio.

COUVRETTE, REBECCA L; Helix HS; La Mesa, CA; (4); 6/367; AFS; Am Leg Aux Girls St; Church Yth Grp; Cmnty Wkr; Girl Scts; Hosp Aide; Stat Yrbk; Kiwanis Awd; UC San Diego; Sociology.

COUZENS, KIMBERLY; Bishop Amat Memorial HS; West Covina, CA; (3); Treas SADD; Hon Roll; Pres Acad Fit Awd; Mt Sac; Educ.

COVARRUBIAS, ALEX; Nogales HS; La Puente, CA; (2); Teachers Aide; Rep Frsh Cls; JV Ftbl; Var Trk; Hon Roll.

COVARRUBIAS, ALMA; Imperial HS; San Diego, CA; (4); 10/80; Pep Clb; Spanish Clb; SADD; Teachers Aide; Yrbk; Sec Jr Cls; Sec Stu Cncl; Sftbl; Hon Roll; Pres Acad Fit Awd; CSF; Fri Night Live; San Diego ST U; Nrsng.

COVARRUBIAS, ANA B; Santana HS; Santee, CA; (3); 5/290; Sec Church Yth Grp; Intnl Clb; Church Choir; Var L Bsktbl; Hon Roll; Hnrs Golden St Exam Geom.

COVARRUBIAS, ANGEL; Williams HS; Williams, CA; (3); FFA; Spanish Clb; Nwsp; Bsktbl; Ftbl; Hon Roll; Med.

COVARRUBIAS, CLAUDIA; Alisal HS; Salinas, CA; (2); Diving; Cit Awd; Hon Roll; Biligual Gate Club; Teacher.

COVARRUBIAS, KRISTINA M; Santa Teresa HS; San Jose, CA; (4); 9/450; Pres Church Yth Grp; Q&S; Science Clb; Spanish Clb; Pres SADD; Church Choir; Ed Yrbk; Var Jr Cls; Pres Stu Cncl; Var Socr; Acad Decathlon Stu Coach; Church Mission Trips; Dist 2 Youth Citizen Of Yr; UC Davis.

COVARRUBIAS, MINERVA B; Santa Clara HS; Oxnard, CA; (4); 4/168; Cmnty Wkr; Pres Computer Clb; GAA; Hosp Aide; Pep Clb; Var Score Keeper; Var L Vllybl; High Hon Roll; Pres NHS; Pres Acad Fit Awd.

COVARRUBIAS, PABLO R; San Diego HS; San Diego, CA; (3); Treas Frsh Cls; NHS; Golden St Exam-Geom Hnrs Awd; Outstndng Ctznshp Trophy; CSF 90; Engrng.

COVE, SEAN D; Bakersfield HS; Bakersfield, CA; (3); 135/713; Church Yth Grp; Var L Tennis; High Hon Roll; Hon Roll; Prfct Atten Awd; Stu Store Supvsr; Bakersfield Coll; Bus.

COVELL, CHRISTMAS N; Leland HS; San Jose, CA; (4); 112/415; Intnl Clb; JA; Spanish Clb; Gym; Trk; Hon Roll; San Jose ST U; Aerospc Engrng.

COVELL, KRISTIN S; Carmel HS; Carmel Valley, CA; (2); Church Yth Grp; High Hon Roll; Hon Roll; CSF; Phys Thrpy.

COVENEY, CHRISTY J; Lincoln HS; Lodi, CA; (4); 179/513; Hon Roll; U CA Sacramento; Elem Schl Tch.

COVERDALE, REBECCA E; Victor Valley HS; George Afb, CA; (3); Sec Church Yth Grp; Drama Clb; Church Choir; Sec Swing Chorus; Hon Roll; Spec Educ.

COVERSTONE, AMY; Herlong HS; Herlong, CA; (1); 1/40; Church Yth Grp; SADD; Yrbk; Fine Arts Clb; Law.

COVERT, CHARISSE M; Cordova SR HS; Rancho Cordova, CA; (3); Science Clb; Pres Acad Fit Awd; Camp Horsemanship Assn; Sacramento ST; Dentist.

COVERT, JARED C; Atwater HS; Atwater, CA; (3); FFA; Merced JC; Ag Bus.

COVERT, KRISTIN A; Torrey Pines HS; Del Mar, CA; (4); 95/500; Art Clb; Church Yth Grp; Hon Roll; Hnrs Smnrs; Regnl Ice Skating Cmptn; Excllnc In Art Awd; U CA Santa Cruz; Genetics.

COVERT, RACHAEL; Rim Of The World HS; Crestline, CA; (4); 59/206; Church Yth Grp; Pep Clb; Band; Mrchg Band; Pep Band; JV Cheerldng; Hon Roll; Prfct Atten Awd; Sr All-Amer Hall Of Fame Band Hnrs; Grace Bible Coll; Early Chldhd.

COVEY, RON; Vintage HS; Napa, CA; (2).

COVEY, THERESA B; Garces Memorial HS; Bakersfield, CA; (4); Varsity Clb; Var L Bsktbl; Var L Sftbl; Var L Trk; Hon Roll; CA Schlrshp Fndtn; USC; Fshn Merch.

COVINGTON, JENNIFER L; Fall River Joint Union Schl; Fall River Mills, CA; (2); Art Clb; Church Yth Grp; Cmnty Wkr; ROTC; Teachers Aide; Hon Roll; Campbell Bobby Sox Sfbl; Outstndng Achvt Wrtng Awd 89; 1st Pl Pen & Ink, 3rd Pl Sculpture Vo Ed Fair; San Jose ST U; Interior Dsgn.

COVINGTON, MIKE C; Lindsay HS; Lindsay, CA; (2); Church Yth Grp; Letterman Clb; Varsity Clb; JV Var Bsbl; JV Capt Bsktbl; JV Ftbl; Pres Acad Fit Awd; CA All-Star Baseball Team To Play In Sweden; Cal-Hi Sports For Pitching & Hitting In Baseball.

COVINGTON, SHERI K; Clovis West HS; Fresno, CA; (2); Church Yth Grp; FCA; FBLA; Ski Clb; VP Soph Cls; Stu Cncl; Cheerldng; Swmmng; Vllybl; High Hon Roll; UC San Diego; Math.

COWAN, CASSANDRA L; Mojave HS; California City, CA; (3); 9/100; Church Yth Grp; Girl Scts; Spanish Clb; Band; Mrchg Band; Pep Band; Var Mgr(s); Var Powder Puff Ftbl; Var Score Keeper; Var Sftbl; Bus.

COWART, CHARLES; Casa Grande HS; Rohnert Park, CA; (2); 5/300; Treas Chess Clb; Church Yth Grp; Computer Clb; French Clb; Intnl Clb; High Hon Roll; NHS; County Math Leapfrog Wnnr; Schl Spelling Bee Fnlst; Sunday Schl Teacher; Onom; UC Berkeley; Writing.

COWDERY, KERI; Covina HS; West Covina, CA; (1); 9/350; Treas Frsh Cls; Treas Soph Cls; Bsktbl; JV L Swmmng; L Var Tennis; Hon Roll; Mst Vlble Swmmr; Bus.

COWELL, AARON J; Yucaipa HS; Yucaipa, CA; (2); 24/441; Cmnty Wkr; Key Clb; Spanish Clb; High Hon Roll; Hon Roll; Prfct Atten Awd; Acad Ltr Recipient; AZ ST; Ed Admin.

COWELL, JENNIFER L; Livermore HS; Livermore, CA; (2); Church Yth Grp; Cmnty Wkr; FBLA; Mrchg Band; Ed Phtg Yrbk; JV Swmmng; Hon Roll; Prfct Atten Awd; Pres Acad Fit Awd; Friday Night Live; UC San Francisco; Med.

COWELL, STACY E; Quincy JR/Sr HS; Quincy, CA; (3); Library Aide; Chorus; Pres Frsh Cls; Pres Soph Cls; Pres Jr Cls; Rep Sr Cls; JV Var Bsktbl; Var Cheerldng; Var Sftbl; JV Var Vllybl; Medcl.

COWIESON, WILLIAM J; Riverside Polytechnic HS; Riverside, CA; (4); Math Tm; ROTC; DAR Awd; High Hon Roll; Ntl Merit SF; Prfct Atten Awd; Columbia U NYC; Cvl Engrng.

COWLES, SHILO; Brethren HS; Long Beach, CA; (1); Church Yth Grp; Girl Scts; Band; Jazz Band; Mrchg Band; Pep Band; Sftbl; Capt Vllybl; GSA Silver Awd.

COWLEY, CHRISTINE; El Toro HS; Mission Viejo, CA; (4); Key Clb; Rep Stu Cncl; Hon Roll; Frnscs Tm VP, Scrtry & Fnd Rsng Chm; Vrsty Debater Cngrss Orgnl Ortry; CA Poly Pomona; Urban Plnng.

COWLEY, JESSICA; Thousand Oaks HS; Thousand Oaks, CA; (2); 55/560; Speech Tm; SADD; Color Guard; Hon Roll; NHS; Mbr Of Cty Of Thousand Oaks Youth Commison; TOHS Ambassador; Vet Med.

COWLING, KEITH D; Chula Vista HS; Chula Vista, CA; (1); Intnl Clb; U CA-SANTA Cruz; Advrtsng.

COX, AARON J; La Habra HS; Whittier, CA; (2); German Clb; Swmmng; High Hon Roll; Hon Roll; Pres Acad Fit Awd; Water Polo; U Of HI; Arch.

COX, AUBREY; Brawley Union HS; Calipatria, CA; (3); 2/346; AFS; Am Leg Aux Girls St; Math Clb; Math Tm; Office Aide; Science Clb; SADD; Thesps; Intrml JV Cheerldng; Var L Crs Cntry; CSF; Acad Decathlon; UCLA; Bio Sci.

COX, CHRISTINA A; Oakmont HS; Roseville, CA; (3); 70/450; Drama Clb; SADD; School Play; Variety Show; JV Cheerldng; Hon Roll; UC Davis; Business.

COX, CHRISTINE; South HS; Bakersfield, CA; (4); 7/350; Church Yth Grp; Sec FTA; Teachers Aide; Bus Profs of Am; Stu Cncl; JV Var Sftbl; JV Var Vllybl; High Hon Roll; NHS; CA Schlrshp Fed; Pepperdine U; Elem Schl Tchr.

COX, CHRISTINE R; Hoover HS; Fresno, CA; (1); Church Yth Grp; Cmnty Wkr; Hosp Aide; Score Keeper; Socr; High Hon Roll; Hgh Hnrs Alg Gldn St Exam; U Of CA Los Angeles; Med.

COX, CHRISTOPHER A; Culver City HS; Culver City, CA; (3); Boy Scts; Jazz Band; Orch; School Musical; Capt Var Swmmng; Elks Awd; Hon Roll; Pres Acad Fit Awd; Boys St 90; Vrsty Water Polo Capt; Golden St Math Awd Geom; Astro Physics.

COX, CHRISTOPHER C; Tulare Union HS; Tulare, CA; (3); Church Yth Grp; FFA; Var Bsktbl; Hon Roll; San Diego ST; CPA.

COX, DIANA; Simi Valley HS; Simi Valley, CA; (2); Gov Hon Prg Awd; Thesps; School Musical; Variety Show; Cmnty Theatre; Acting.

COX, ELIZABETH LYNN; Hoover HS; Fresno, CA; (4); 1/350; Church Yth Grp; Cmnty Wkr; French Clb; Pep Clb; SADD; Ed Nwsp; Cheerldng; Pom Pon; Cit Awd; High Hon Roll; UCLA; Dance.

COX, ERIC R; Atwater HS; Atwater, CA; (2); Red Cross Aide; Science Clb; Spanish Clb; Color Guard; Nwsp; Phtg Yrbk; Intrml Bsktbl; Var L Crs Cntry; JV L Tennis; Intrml Wrstlng; Cvl Air Patrol/Cadet Color Grd Commander; Natl Sci Olympiad Awd; Presdntl Physcl Ftnss Awd; AF Acad; Physics.

COX, HARPER; Laguna Beach HS; Laguna Beach, CA; (1); Art Clb; French Clb; Pep Clb; Ski Clb; Drill Tm; Cheerldng; Pom Pon; NY; Art.

COX, HEATHER L; Cornelia Connelly HS; Anaheim, CA; (1); Church Yth Grp; Lbrn Chorus; School Play; High Hon Roll; Jr Statesmn Of Amer; Chrstn Actn VP; U Of San Diego; Tchr.

COX, JACK E; Antelope Valley HS; Lancaster, CA; (3); Ski Clb; VP Frsh Cls; VP Soph Cls; JV Var Bsbl; JV Ftbl; High Hon Roll; Hon Roll; CSF; Chiropractor.

COX, JASON M; Foothill HS; Sacramento, CA; (2); Church Yth Grp; German Clb; Bsbl; Cit Awd; Hon Roll; Atty.

COX, JEFFERSON S; Flintridge Preparatory Schl; Pasadena, CA; (3); AFS; Church Yth Grp; Debate Tm; Key Clb; Latin Clb; School Play; Var Tennis; Bausch & Lomb Sci Awd; DAR Awd; High Hon Roll; Cif Acdmc Tm Tennis Hnrbl Ment; Ntl Jr Clsscl Legue; Ntl Latin Ex; His.

COX, JENNY; Golden West HS; Visalia, CA; (2); Church Yth Grp; Chorus; Church Choir; Color Guard; Flag Corp; School Musical; School Play; Variety Show; Hon Roll; CA Ambssdrs Music Singer 90; Music Ltr; COS; Music.

COX, JESSE P; San Luis Obispo HS; Avila Beach, CA; (1); Hon Roll; Pres Acad Fit Awd; Air Force; Pilot.

COX, JOSEPH; Sonoma Valley HS; Sonoma, CA; (3); 48/200; AFS; Cmnty Wkr; Intnl Clb; Model UN; Yrbk; Ed Lit Mag; High Hon Roll; Hon Roll; Photo; Comp; MIT; Law.

COX, JUSTIN T; Bullard HS; Fresno, CA; (4); 10/437; Cmnty Wkr; Debate Tm; Drama Clb; Intnl Clb; Spanish Clb; SADD; School Play; Pres Schlr; Bullard Schlrshp Awd Govt, Hstry, Economics.

COX, KEISHA MARIA; Central Union HS; Elcentro, CA; (3); FHA; Girl Scts; JA; Spanish Clb; SADD; Thesps; Chorus; School Play; Vllybl; High Hon Roll; Bus Mgmt.

COX, KIMBERLY; Westwood HS; Westwood, CA; (4); 3/23; Am Leg Aux Girls St; Pres FBLA; Pres VP Band; Drm Mjr(t); VP Jr Cls; Pres Stu Cncl; Var L Bsktbl; Capt Sftbl; Elks Awd; High Hon Roll; King Orange Bowl Parade; OSU; Forensic Sci.

COX, LORI J; Simi Valley HS; Simi Valley, CA; (3); San Diego Coll.

COX, MARY A; Las Lomas HS; Walnut Creek, CA; (2); Rptr Nwsp; Var Sftbl; CA Schlrhp Fed; Friday Night Live; Bus.

COX, MELISSA L; Montgomery HS; Santa Rosa, CA; (2); French Clb; Pep Clb; Ed Yrbk; JV Bsktbl; Cheerldng; Var Socr; Var Sftbl; Vllybl; High Hon Roll; Jr NHS.

COX, MICHAEL W; Ramona HS; Riverside, CA; (3); 12/406; Intrml Ftbl; L Var Swmmng; High Hon Roll; Pres Acad Fit Awd; Water Polo Ltr, Awds; 1st P Riverisde Cty Ind Ed Expo 89; Lab Rsrch.

COX, MICHELE; Highland HS; Bakersfield, CA; (2); Church Yth Grp; Dance Clb; Debate Tm; Key Clb; NFL; Orch; Off Frsh Cls; Crs Cntry; Swmmng; Trk; USC; Engrng.

COX, R; Lemoore Union HS; Lemoore, CA; (2); Rptr Bus Profs of Am; Church Yth Grp; Drama Clb; Rptr FBLA; Chorus; Church Choir; Hon Roll; USNSCC 3 Years; Company Commander; Leading Petty Officer; CA Maritime Acad; Bus Admin.

COX, SHARIFA; Los Alamitos HS; Long Beach, CA; (3); Dance Clb; GAA; JA; Letterman Clb; Pep Clb; Spanish Clb; Teachers Aide; Varsity Clb; School Play; Variety Show; UCLA; Med.

COX, TRISHA L; Paramount HS; Paramount, CA; (2); #6 In Class; Letterman Clb; Pep Clb; Service Clb; Pres Frsh Cls; Cheerldng; Sftbl; Cit Awd; High Hon Roll; CA Schltc Fed; Coaches Awd Vrsty Sftbl; Mvp Vrsty Sftbl; Mst Outstndng JR Vrsty Chrldr; UCLA.

COXWELL, BETH; Amador HS; Pleasanton, CA; (4); 114/402; Church Yth Grp; Cmnty Wkr; Drama Clb; Teachers Aide; Var Trk; Hon Roll; Chrstn Cncl; Miss Amer Coed Pageant; Soccer League; U CA Santa Barbara; Law.

COY, MICHELLE M; Bourroughs HS; Ridgecrest, CA; (2); Am Leg Aux Girls St; Art Clb; Church Yth Grp; Cmnty Wkr; Drama Clb; GAA; Girl Scts; Intnl Clb; Key Clb; Pep Clb; Law.

COYAZO, DENISE; Colton HS; Colton, CA; (3); Church Yth Grp; Cmnty Wkr; SADD; Teachers Aide; Band; Mrchg Band; Pep Band; Rep Stu Cncl; Var Cheerldng; Var Pom Pon; Future Leaders Of Amer; San Diego ST; Psych.

COYLE, RYAN; Madera HS; Madera, CA; (4); Am Leg Aux Girls St; Teachers Aide; Bsbl; Var Vllybl; Hon Roll; Interact; Deptmntl Awd Alg II; Vllybl Assn; Fresno ST; Bus Admin.

COYNE, A HEATHER; Woodside HS; Redwood City, CA; (4); 4/280; Cmnty Wkr; French Clb; Hosp Aide; Intnl Clb; Flag Corp; Mrchg Band; High Hon Roll; Ntl Merit SF; Piano; Statsmn Am; Save Earth Clb; Bryn Mawr; Intl Rel.

COYNE, CATHLEEN M; St Patrick-St Vincent HS; Vallejo, CA; (1); Cmnty Wkr; Pep Clb; Treas Frsh Cls; Bsktbl; Cheerldng; Sftbl; Hon Roll; Miss Natl Tngr-Nrthrn CA Rgnl Pgnt.

COYT, MARIA GUADALUPE; Alisal HS; Salinas, CA; (1); Art Clb; Dance Clb; Girl Scts; Hosp Aide; Swing Chorus; Cheerldng; Swmmng; Tennis; Hon Roll; Ntl Merit Schol.

COZ, KELLY A; Oxnard HS; Oxnard, CA; (3); Hosp Aide; Off Jr Cls; Stu Cncl; Tennis; High Hon Roll; Hon Roll; UCSB; Psych.

COZBY, MARCIA; Bakersfield HS; Bakersfield, CA; (2); Dance Clb; Chorus; Hon Roll; CSF.

COZENS, SHANNON W; George Washington HS; San Francisco, CA; (4); Church Yth Grp; Ski Clb; Bsktbl; Tennis; Hon Roll; Northern AZ U.

CRABBE, PHILIP; The College Preparatory Schl; Oakland, CA; (4); Cmnty Wkr; Chorus; Jazz Band; Orch; School Musical; Var Bsktbl; Var Crs Cntry; Var Socr; Var Vllybl; Ntl Merit Ltr; Natl Hspnc Schlr Semifnlst; U Of CA Los Angeles; Bus.

CRACKNELL, KATHLEEN; Carlmont HS; Belmont, CA; (2); Church Yth Grp; Cmnty Wkr; Teachers Aide; School Play; Diving; Tennis; Extra Japanese Lang Stdy; Photo; Bond U; Mrn Bio.

CRADDOCK, JEREMY M; Summerville HS; Tuolumne, CA; (3); FFA; ROTC; Ski Clb; Color Guard; JV Bsktbl; JV Socr; Stat Sftbl; JV Var Trk; High Hon Roll; Hon Roll; Cert-First Aid; Cert-CPR; Hembolt ST; CDF.

CRADDOCK, SUMMER; Fairfield HS; Fairfield, CA; (2); Stat Wrstlng; Law.

CRAFTON, STEPHEN; Garces Memorial HS; Bakersfield, CA; (2); Boy Scts; Cmnty Wkr; Drama Clb; JA; Key Clb; Letterman Clb; Ski Clb; Orch; School Play; Stage Crew; Golf Tm Coachs Awd; Stanford; Law.

CRAIG, DAVID; Cajon HS; San Bernardino, CA; (3); AFS; Church Yth Grp; Key Clb; Quiz Bowl; Crs Cntry; Tennis; Trk; Hon Roll; NHS; Rtry Life Schlrshp; Statesmen America Treas; CSF.

CRAIG, DEBORAH; Sanleandro HS; Castro Valley, CA; (3); Off Jr Cls; French Hon Soc; High Hon Roll; Christian Life Coll; Rgstrd Nrs.

CRAIG III, FLOYD; San Diego HS; San Diego, CA; (3); 154/420; Aud/Vis; Church Yth Grp; FCA; Office Aide; Var Capt Bsktbl; Sftbl; Cit Awd; Prfct Atten Awd; Moorehouse Coll; Pathology.

CRAIG, JENNIFER; Sonora HS; Sonora, CA; (2); 1/336; Church Yth Grp; Science Clb; Band; Mrchg Band; JV Sftbl; JV Tennis; High Hon Roll; CSF; Close-Up; BYU; Fashion Design.

CRAIG, JULIA J; Thomas Downey HS; Modesto, CA; (3); Hosp Aide; Band; Church Choir; Jazz Band; Mrchg Band; Pep Band; Hon Roll; CSF; Intr Dsgn.

CRAIG, KIMBERLY A; Chula Vista HS; Chula Vista, CA; (2); Debate Tm; GAA; Girl Scts; Pep Clb; Quiz Bowl; Var Socr; Cit Awd.

CRAIG, KIMBERLY J; Arlington HS; Riverside, CA; (3); Church Yth Grp; Teachers Aide; Chorus; Church Choir; JV Sftbl; Var Trk; Stu Of Month Drivers Ed; Vocal Music Dept Cert Of Recognition; Music.

CRAIG, LAURA G; Ferndale Union HS; Ferndale, CA; (2); Church Yth Grp; Drama Clb; English Clb; Spanish Clb; Chorus; Tennis; Chico; Trvl Agnt.

CRAIG, MICHELE E; Marymount HS; Studio City, CA; (2); Cmnty Wkr; School Play; JV Crs Cntry; Var Trk; High Hon Roll; Lee Strasberg Theatre Inst Drama Stu; Natl Charity Leag Ticktocker; Jr Tnns Leag; Yale; Entrtnmnt Law.

CRAIL, JEFF L; La Serna HS; Whittier, CA; (3); 12/393; Var Bsktbl; Var Ftbl; Var Vllybl; Hon Roll; Prfct Atten Awd; Top 100 Stu; Prncpls Lst; UCLA; Bus.

CRAIN, DEBBIE L; Taft Union HS; Taft, CA; (3); 12/200; Church Yth Grp; Acpl Chr; Chorus; Church Choir; Rptr Nwsp; High Hon Roll; Hon Roll; Chrstn Ministries.

CRAIN, JEFF S; Central Catholic HS; Modesto, CA; (3); Church Yth Grp; Math Tm; Scholastic Bowl; Spanish Clb; VP Soph Cls; JV Var Swmmng; High Hon Roll; Ntl Merit Ltr; Gld & Slvr Mdls-Sci Olympd; Sigma Xi Rsrch Soc; Mst Val Swmmr 89-90; Med.

CRAM, HEATHER C; Western HS; Cypress, CA; (2); Church Yth Grp; GAA; JA; Pep Clb; Varsity Clb; Sec Soph Cls; Stu Cncl; Var Socr; Var Trk; Cit Awd; Soph Homcmng Princess; Bus.

CRAMER, CINDY; Oakhill HS; Chatsworth, CA; (4); Drama Clb; Ski Clb; Teachers Aide; School Play; Ed Yrbk; VP Stu Cncl; Cheerldng; Hon Roll; NHS; Pres Acad Fit Awd.

CRAMER, DENNIS E; Notre Dame HS; Norco, CA; (3); 3/140; Varsity Clb; Treas Jr Cls; Pres Stu Cncl; Var Bsbl; Var Ftbl; Var Socr; High Hon Roll; Med.

CRAMER, JEFFREY R; Trabuco Hills HS; Mission Viejo, CA; (2); 9/415; Church Yth Grp; Math Tm; JV Ftbl; JV Socr; JV Vllybl; Hon Roll; NHS; CSF.

CRAMER, JILL E; Arroyo Grande HS; Arroyo Grande, CA; (1); 1/580; Church Yth Grp; FCA; Variety Show; JV Cheerldng; JV Vllybl; High Hon Roll; Acad Excllnc Awd; CA Schlstc Fed.

CRAMER, KEVIN; San Bernardino HS; San Bernardino, CA; (3); 13/350; Boy Scts; Key Clb; Spanish Clb; Ftbl; Var Tennis; NHS; Hon Roll; MESA 88-90; Cal Poly; Laser/Physics.

CRAMER, NICHOLAS K; Mission College Prep; San Luis Obispo, CA; (2); Boy Scts; Var Socr; Hon Roll; Eagle Sct; Los Ninos Walkathon 90; Sci Awd; CA Poly SLO; Elec Engrng.

CRAMER, REBECCA J; Polytechnic HS; Riverside, CA; (2); Church Yth Grp; Cmnty Wkr; Drama Clb; GAA; Letterman Clb; Model UN; SADD; Teachers Aide; JV Bsktbl; Score Keeper; Sports Therapy.

CRANDALL, HUNTER JUSTIN; Delano HS; Delano, CA; (4); 2/350; Pres Letterman Clb; Yrbk; Swmmng; Wt Lftg; Pres NHS; Pres Acad Fit Awd; VP Stu Cncl; Mock Trial; Acad Decathlon; Friday Night Live; West Point; Engrng.

CRANDALL, JAMES B; Live Oak HS; Gridley, CA; (4); Drama Clb; FTA; School Play; Rptr Nwsp; Stu Cncl; Hon Roll; Yuba Coll; Tchr.

CRANDALL, TARA A; Redlands HS; Redlands, CA; (2); U Of CA Riverside; Psych.

CRANE, ADAM; Canyon HS; Canyon Country, CA; (2); JV Bsktbl; Schlr Athlt Awd Bsktbl.

CRANE, CYNTHIA D; New Port Harbor HS; Newport Beach, CA; (4); Church Yth Grp; Cmnty Wkr; Ski Clb; Sec Treas Spanish Clb; Pres Frsh Cls; Var Swmmng; Intrml Tennis; Hon Roll; Pres Acad Fit Awd; J V Badminton; Sr Hmcmng Prncss; San Diego U.

CRANE, JENNY K; North Tahoe HS; Carnelian Bay, CA; (3); 5/64; SADD; Band; Jazz Band; Powder Puff Ftbl; Hon Roll; Opt Clb Awd; Pres Acad Fit Awd; CSF Treas & Secy; Acad Clb; Big Brother/Big Sister Pgm; Music.

CRANE, JORDAN; Gardena HS; Gardena, CA; (3); Aud/Vis; Drama Clb; French Clb; School Play; Variety Show; Prfct Atten Awd; Stnd-Up Comedy Act; UCLA; Elec Engrg.

CRANE, JUSTIN D; Chaminade College Prep; Woodland Hills, CA; (2); JV Socr; Hon Roll.

CRANE, LAURA L; Bonita Vista HS; Bonita, CA; (2); Church Yth Grp; SADD; Church Choir; Variety Show; Var L Socr; Var L Trk; High Hon Roll; Hon Roll; Church Bsktbl & Vlybl; Sunday Schl Pres Mai Maid Cncl; PYU; Ocean Grph.

CRANE, SARAH S; University City HS; San Diego, CA; (3); Pres AFS; Math Tm; Scholastic Bowl; Science Clb; High Hon Roll; Gldn Sst Math Awd; AFS Exchng Stu Australia 1990; Yng Art Awd; Anmtn.

CRANE, TAMRA L; Castro Valley HS; Castro Valley, CA; (3); Church Yth Grp; Drama Clb; German Clb; Acpl Chr; Band; Chorus; Church Choir; Orch; School Musical; Variety Show; CA ST Hnr Choir Mem Soph Yr; Dept Awds Fine Arts, Engl, Home Ec; BYU; Engl.

CRANE, WILLIAM M; North Tahoe HS; Carnelian Bay, CA; (3); 1/70; Rep Cmnty Wkr; Pep Clb; SADD; Band; Jazz Band; Pep Band; Crs Cntry; Trk; High Hon Roll; Hon Roll; NTPUD Rep; Golden St Exam Awds; Naval Acad; Pilot.

CRANFILL, CHER A; San Gorgonio HS; San Bernardino, CA; (4); Pres Chorus; Stat Wrstlng; Hon Roll; Show Choir-Dance; Interior Design.

CRANFORD, JOHN; Strathmore Union HS; Lindsay, CA; (2); 3/90; Boy Scts; Chess Clb; JV Ftbl; JV Tennis; High Hon Roll; Scicon Cnslr; Berkley; Police Psych.

CRANMER, JASON J; Bonita HS; La Verne, CA; (1); French Clb; Cit Awd; Hon Roll; Avid Bwler; Brdcstng.

CRASS, CAROLINE LEEANN; Kingsburg Joint Union HS; Kingsburg, CA; (1); Church Yth Grp; SADD; Rptr Nwsp; JV Swmmng; High Hon Roll; Hon Roll; Acad Block K.

CRAVALHO, SADIE; Oakdale HS; Oakdale, CA; (2); Cheerldng; Sftbl; Hon Roll; Pharm.

CRAVEN, TRAVIS; Santa Monica HS; Santa Monica, CA; (2); Church Yth Grp; JV Bsbl; Capt Bsktbl; JV Capt Ftbl; Var Trk; Var Wt Lftg; Hon Roll; Most Insprtnl JV Ftbl; U Of Miami; Phys Thrpy.

CRAWFORD, ANNE L; Rio Americano HS; Carmichael, CA; (4); 1/259; Art Clb; Cmnty Wkr; Math Tm; Nwsp; Ed Nwsp; Lit Mag; NHS; Ntl Merit Schol; Pres Acad Fit Awd; Val; UCLA Alumni Schlrshp; Robert C Byrd Schlrshp; UCLA; Theatre Set Dsgn.

CRAWFORD, BRADLEY D; Woodland HS; Woodland, CA; (3); 1/500; Church Yth Grp; Teachers Aide; Rep Frsh Cls; Off Sr Cls; Stu Cncl; Var Capt Bsktbl; Ftbl; Var Socr; High Hon Roll; Jr NHS; CSF; U Of CA; Civil Engr.

CRAWFORD, BRIAN D; Foothill HS; Sacramento, CA; (3); Letterman Clb; Varsity Clb; Var L Bsbl; JV Bsktbl; Intrml Ftbl; Var L Socr; MVP Socr; Offnsve Plyr Yr Bsbl; Schl Recgntn GSE Math; Hnrs GSE Math Exm Geom; Sports Thrpy.

CRAWFORD, CASEY; Castilleja HS; Saratoga, CA; (3); Art Clb; Cmnty Wkr; Math Tm; Speech Tm; Variety Show; Rep Soph Cls; Off Jr Cls; Stu Cncl; Socr; High Hon Roll; Amnsty Intrntl; Greenpeace; Jnr Statsmn Amer; Math.

CRAWFORD, CHRISTOPHER BRETT; Capistrano Valley HS; San Clemente, CA; (3); Church Yth Grp; Cmnty Wkr; Drama Clb; FCA; Science Clb; School Play; JV L Swmmng; Prfct Atten Awd; Water Polo JV Ltr; Srfng Exile Surf Tm Mem San Clemente; USC; Radio & TV.

CRAWFORD, DANIELLE; Los Gatos HS; Los Gatos, CA; (4); 175/374; Girl Scts; Library Aide; Office Aide; Band; Mrchg Band; School Musical; School Play; Stage Crew; Score Keeper; Drg Fre Fshn Shw; San Jose ST U; Bus.

CRAWFORD, DEBBY M; Etiwanda HS; Alta Loma, CA; (2); Church Yth Grp; Office Aide; Red Cross Aide; Cit Awd; Hon Roll; Pres Acad Fit Awd; Poet, Wrtr Wrk Been Pblshd; P/T Vol Chldrns Day Care Ctr; Int Desgn.

CRAWFORD, DINA K; Livermore HS; Livermore, CA; (1); 41/454; FFA; Band; Mrchg Band; High Hon Roll; Bus.

CRAWFORD, JACQUELYN M; Carpinteria HS; Carpinteria, CA; (2); #3 In Class; Church Yth Grp; Cmnty Wkr; Drama Clb; Letterman Clb; NFL; Pep Clb; Varsity Clb; School Play; Rptr Nwsp; Cheerldng; Ivy Leag Schl; Comm.

CRAWFORD, JARED N; Livermore HS; Livermore, CA; (3); #30 In Class; Art Clb; FBLA; Spanish Clb; Varsity Clb; Orch; Var Swmmng; High Hon Roll; Hon Roll; Pres Acad Fit Awd; Phys Achvt Awd; Acad Achvt Awd; Rookie Yr Awd Swmmng; Bio.

CRAWFORD, JEANIE; Happy Camp HS; Seiad Valley, CA; (4); 2/21; Am Leg Aux Girls St; FBLA; Teachers Aide; Chorus; Variety Show; VP Frsh Cls; Pres Soph Cls; Pres Jr Cls; Pres Sr Cls; Pres Stu Cncl; Certfd 1st Responder/CPR/1st Aide; Acad Decathln; Stu Of Yr 90; Heald Bus Coll; Hosp Admin.

CRAWFORD, JONATHAN E; St Bernard HS; Los Angeles, CA; (3); Boy Scts; Chess Clb; Hon Roll; Rep Frsh Cls; Asian Clb; Cycling Clb; Tigers Bskbl Leag; U CA.

CRAWFORD, KELLY L; Marina HS; Huntington Beach, CA; (2); Rep Drama Clb; Spanish Clb; Rep Thesps; School Musical; School Play; JV Cheerldng; Var Pom Pon; High Hon Roll; Pep Clb; Service Clb; Natl Charity Leag VP; Golden Shield Awd Cert Wnnr; Huntington Harbour Philharmonic Jrs.

CRAWFORD, KENNETH SCOTT; Thomas Downey HS; Modesto, CA; (4); 100/420; Boy Scts; Church Yth Grp; Sec FCA; Letterman Clb; Pep Clb; Ski Clb; SADD; Capt Varsity Clb; Rep Sr Cls; JV Bsbl; Knights Achvt Awd; MV Trk Athl; CCC Hnrb Mntn Ftbl; Modesto Jr; Bus Admin.

CRAWFORD, KIMBERLY M; Downey HS; Downey, CA; (2); Church Yth Grp; Cit Awd; Pres Acad Fit Awd; Jbs Dghtrs/Hnrd Qn; Pacific Christian Coll; Teach.

CRAWFORD, MARK A; Paradise HS; Paradise, CA; (1); Church Yth Grp; Trk; Hon Roll; Golden St Exam Alg Hnrs; CA ST U Chico; Bus Mgmt.

CRAWFORD, ROGER; Magnolia HS; Anaheim, CA; (4); 10/300; Am Leg Boys St; Cmnty Wkr; Stu Cncl; Var L Crs Cntry; Var L Socr; Var L Trk; High Hon Roll; NHS; Pres Acad Fit Awd; Calif Scholastic Federation; U Of Cal; Electrical Engineer.

CRAWFORD, SCOTT; Magnolia HS; Anaheim, CA; (4); 14/300; Am Leg Boys St; Phtg Yrbk; Stu Cncl; Var L Ftbl; Var L Socr; Var L Trk; High Hon Roll; NHS; Prfct Atten Awd; Cal Scholastic Federation; U Of Cal; Biochemistry.

CRAWFORD, SHELLEY MARIE; Hesperia HS; Hesperia, CA; (4); FBLA; Science Clb; Ski Clb; Spanish Clb; SADD; JV Sftbl; Cit Awd; High Hon Roll; Hon Roll; NHS; Prncpls Hnr List; Deans List; CA ST San Bernardino; Pol Sci.

CRAWLEY, BRANDEE; Alta Loma HS; Alta Loma, CA; (1); Church Yth Grp; Dance Clb; Drama Clb; GAA; Variety Show; Bsktbl; Sftbl; BSU Club; Performing Arts.

CREAGER, STEVEN M; Montgomery HS; Santa Rosa, CA; (4); Spanish Clb; High Hon Roll; Engrng.

CREAMER, SANDRA; Lynbrook HS; San Jose, CA; (4); 10/300; Pres JA; Chorus; JV Bsktbl; Var JV Swmmng; Pres NHS; Ntl Merit Ltr; Pres Acad Fit Awd; Pres 88-89 Santa Clara Cnty Achvrs Assoc; VP 89-90 Span Hnr Soc; Wnne PG&E Schlrshp; Alumni Schlrshp; UC Berkley; Bus.

CREART, DONNA L; Bear River HS; Grass Valley, CA; (2); 41/210; Drama Clb; SADD; School Play; Yrbk; Off Soph Cls; Bsktbl; Sftbl; Cit Awd; Hon Roll; Sac ST; Psych.

CREDO, ALLAN V; Sierra Vista HS; Baldwin Park, CA; (3); Art Clb; Intrml Bsktbl; Graphic Arts.

CREECH, BRENDA L; East Union HS; Manteca, CA; (3); Church Yth Grp; French Clb; Library Aide; Pep Clb; Teachers Aide; School Play; Stage Crew; Variety Show; 2nd Pl Spch Comptn Rotary Clb; CSU Stanislaus; Ed.

CREECH, KRISTA M; Vallejo SR HS; Vallejo, CA; (3); Church Yth Grp; Office Aide; Teachers Aide; Acpl Chr; Church Choir; Acad Ltr.

CREEK, CATHI J; University City HS; San Diego, CA; (4); Church Yth Grp; Model UN; JV Bsktbl; JV Trk; JV Vllybl; Hon Roll; Prfct Atten Awd; Pres Acad Fit Awd; Supr Acad Achvmnt Awds; 2nd Pl In San Diego Sci & Engr Fr; U CA Irvine; Bus.

CREEL, WAYNE A; San Dimas HS; San Dimas, CA; (4); Pres Church Yth Grp; VICA; Ed Yrbk; VP Soph Cls; JV Diving; JV Vllybl; Var Wt Lftg; Hon Roll; Order Merit Schlrshp; Stu Gov; Cal Poly Tech; Arch.

CREESE, CHIANE; Fred C Beyer HS; Riverbank, CA; (4); Spanish Clb; SADD; Teachers Aide; Acpl Chr; Chorus; Swing Chorus; Trk; Cit Awd; Hon Roll; Modesto JC; Psych.

CREIGHTON, ALYSSA M; Kern Valley HS; Weldon, CA; (2); 4-H; Var L Bsktbl; Var L Tennis; Var L Trk; High Hon Roll; Church Yth Grp; Cmnty Wkr; Drama Clb; FBLA; Letterman Clb; CSF; Exchng Club Stu Yr; GSE Alg 1 Hghst Hnr; Mock Trl; HOBY Fnlst; Sci Fair MVP; Geom Wnnr Sal Bursey; Math.

CREIGHTON, BOBBY A; Irvine HS; Irvine, CA; (4); Chess Clb; Church Yth Grp; Ski Clb; JV Bsbl; Capt Var Socr; Capt JV Vllybl; Hon Roll; Jr NHS; Natl Yng Ldrs Conf; Rep Irvine Hgh Interview Lcl Nwspaprs; Rep Irvine Hgh Cncl Mtng; Pepperdine; Bus.

CREIGHTON, SANDY; Kern Valley HS; Weldon, CA; (4); 4/128; Am Leg Aux Girls St; Church Yth Grp; Pres Drama Clb; Rptr FFA; School Play; Var Capt Bsktbl; Sftbl; Var Capt Tennis; Elks Awd; Pres Acad Fit Awd; HOBY; Pres Classrm; U CA Davis; Intl Ag.

CRELENCIA, JASON PETER A; Garey HS; Pomona, CA; (3); MESA; Erly Outreach Pgm; CA ST Fullerton; Grphc Arts.

CRELLIN, CHAD; North HS; Bakersfield, CA; (2); Church Yth Grp; French Clb; Key Clb; Wrstlng; Hon Roll.

CRELLIN, SCOTT; Bonita Vista HS; Bonita, CA; (1); Church Yth Grp; Model UN; Intrml Bsktbl; Cit Awd.

CREMASCOLI, DUSTIN W; Southwest HS; San Diego, CA; (1); 4/335; Speech Tm; Var Crs Cntry; Var Vllybl; Cit Awd; Hon Roll; Green Peace Assn; Natl Audobon Soc; CA Schlstc Fed; Zoology.

CREMEANS, CORINNE; Hemet HS; Hemet, CA; (3); Church Yth Grp; Dance Clb; Pep Clb; Varsity Clb; Cheerldng; Pom Pon; Powder Puff Ftbl; Socr; Voice Dem Awd; Outstndng Hstry Stu Awd; Christian Clb Mem & Histrn; Vlntr Wk Mexico; Westmont; Bible.

CREMER, ANGELA L; East Bakersfield HS; Bakersfield, CA; (2); Girl Scts; JA; Treas Band; Treas Mrchg Band; Pep Band; Tennis; Hon Roll; Video Yrbk Staff; CSF; Rgmnt Of The Light Yth Band; Med.

CREMER, SHANNON; Quartz Hill HS; Lancaster, CA; (2); JV Cheerldng; CSF; Z-Clb; Brdcstng Jrnlsm.

CRENSHAW, MICHELE; Lemoore HS; Kettleman City, CA; (3); Church Yth Grp; Treas Computer Clb; SADD; Trk; High Hon Roll; Hon Roll; Vlntr Elem Schl; West Hills CC; Dentistry.

CRESPO, HERMINIA; King City HS; Greenfield, CA; (3); Church Yth Grp; Teachers Aide; Stage Crew; Yrbk; Sftbl; Hon Roll; Maya Clb; Cmrcl Clb; Riverside Coll; Bus.

CRESTEJO, VERONICA P; Don Antonio Lugo HS; Chino, CA; (2); Church Yth Grp; Cmnty Wkr; Hon Roll; CA Schlrshp Fed; U Southern CA; Lawyer.

CRETE, JESSICA; Calvary Chapel HS; Santa Ana, CA; (1); Church Yth Grp; Teachers Aide; Ed Nwsp; Yrbk; Var Sftbl; JV Vllybl.

CRETS, STEPHANIE L; Woodland HS; Woodland, CA; (3); Ski Clb; Teachers Aide; Socr; Cmnty Wkr; Capt L Vllybl; Capt Capt Bsktbl; Gym; Score Keeper; Trk; Hon Roll; U CA D; Speech Thrpst.

CREVISTON, STACY L; Gretchen A Whitney HS; Cerritos, CA; (3); Art Clb; Drama Clb; JA; Key Clb; Spanish Clb; Nwsp; Yrbk; High Hon Roll; Math Tutor; Engrng.

CREW, DARIN W; Rio Vista HS; Rio Vista, CA; (4); 3/55; Pres AFS; French Clb; Q&S; Quiz Bowl; Pres Science Clb; SADD; Teachers Aide; Ed Nwsp; Ed Yrbk; Rep Soph Cls; Bank Amer Outstndng Swmmr; Bank Amer Cert Scl Stds; AFS Switzerland; CA Poly; Engrng.

CREWS, CRISTA; O'farrell SCPA; San Diego, CA; (2); Church Yth Grp; School Musical; Hon Roll; Piano; Voice; San Diego Jr Theatre & Chrstn Yth Theatre; San Diego ST U; Brdcst Journls.

CREWS, JENNIFER L; Nevada Union HS; Grass Valley, CA; (3); 63/280; Intnl Clb; Acpl Chr; Chorus; Amnsty Intl; Srptmst Intl Awd; Dance.

CREWS, KRISTIN R; St Bonaventure HS; Ventura, CA; (3); 4/117; Church Yth Grp; Variety Show; Nwsp; Hist Soph Cls; High Hon Roll; NHS; CSF; Piano Bach Fstvls; Nutcracker Perf.

CRIAZZO, BREE A; Templeton HS; Templeton, CA; (1); Computer Clb; Dance Clb; Ed Yrbk; Bsktbl; Cheerldng; Pom Pon; Powder Puff Ftbl; Sftbl; Vllybl; San Diego ST U; Comp Engrng.

CRICHTON, KIMBERLY; Eureka HS; Eureka, CA; (4); 2/300; Am Leg Aux Girls St; Ski Clb; Teachers Aide; Orch; School Play; Rep Soph Cls; Sec Stu Cncl; Tennis; High Hon Roll; Sal; CA Schlstc Fed-Life Mbr; U Of CA; Intl Relations.

CRIM, CATHY G; El Dorado HS; Placerville, CA; (3); 1/376; Ski Clb; VP Frsh Cls; Rep Soph Cls; Stu Cncl; Var Tennis; High Hon Roll; NHS; Ntl Merit SF; Pres Acad Fit Awd; Pres Schlr; Kirkwood Ski Tm 2 Yrs; Jr Statesmn Amer Grad 90 Stanford Smmr Schl; Jr Olympcs Skiing 4th Pl 90; Sports Med.

CRIM, KOREY; Palo Verde HS; Blythe, CA; (4); 19/120; Key Clb; Office Aide; SADD; Nwsp; Score Keeper; High Hon Roll; NHS; Prfct Atten Awd; Pres Acad Fit Awd; CA Jnr Schlrsp Fed; Ca Schlrshp Fed.

CRINER, KIM; Rim Of The World HS; Lake Arrowhead, CA; (2); 81/352; Sftbl; Vllybl; Hon Roll; 4V Norco Vllybl Trnmnt MVP 89; 2nd Tm All Leag Vrsty Sftbl 2nd Base 90; UC Irvine; Sports Med.

CRISLER, S MICHAEL; Prospect HS; Santa Clara, CA; (4); Band; School Musical; School Play; Stage Crew; Phtg Nwsp; Santa Clara Vanguard; Acad Decathlon; San Francisco ST U; Music Ed.

CRISOLOGO, RESTIE C; Edison HS; Stockton, CA; (1); Ed Lit Mag; Intrml Bsktbl; Hon Roll.

CRISOSTOMO, AIMEE F; Saint Joseph HS; Lakewood, CA; (3); Church Yth Grp; Cmnty Wkr; Debate Tm; Drama Clb; Key Clb; Science Clb; Spanish Clb; Sec SADD; Flag Corp; High Hon Roll; CSF; Aerospace Engrng.

CRISP, MELISSA; Valley HS; Santa Ana, CA; (1); Girl Scts; Nwsp; Yrbk; Hon Roll; NHS; Stu Advsry Cncl On Drug Abuse.

CRISS, PRESTON W; Los Altos HS; Hacienda Hgts, CA; (3); Letterman Clb; Var L Swmmng; Wt Lftg; Hon Roll; Vrsty Waterpolo; Jr Statesman Officer; Explorers; Golden St Schlr; UCSD.

CRISTOBAL, ETHAN S; Monterey HS; Seaside, CA; (3); High Hon Roll; Close-Up; Monterey Penninsula Fencing Club; Comp Sci.

CRISWELL, BRIAN R; Santa Cruz HS; Santa Cruz, CA; (4); Church Yth Grp; Cmnty Wkr; Ski Clb; Spanish Clb; Ftbl; Vllybl; Cabrillo Coll; Bus.

CRITCHFIELD, SAMUEL E; John F Kennedy HS; Granada Hills, CA; (3); Ftbl; Golf; Math.

CRITCHFIELD, STACEY ANN; Bundy Canyon Christian HS; Canyon Lake, CA; (2); 1/15; Church Yth Grp; Office Aide; Teachers Aide; Yrbk; Off Frsh Cls; Stu Cncl; Var L Bsktbl; Var L Sftbl; Var L Vllybl; Cit Awd; Stu Of Month-Acad; Stu Ambssdr To USSR 90; 1st Team All Leag Bsktbl 89-90; Harvard U; Poly Sci.

CRITTENDEN, STEPHANIE; Westmont HS; Campbell, CA; (3); 13/250; French Clb; Key Clb; NFL; Pep Clb; Speech Tm; School Play; Lit Mag; Cheerldng; Powder Puff Ftbl; Swmmng; Song Grl 89-90; UC Santa Cruz; Lbrl Arts.

CRIVELLI, KEVIN J; Turlock HS; Turlock, CA; (4); 63/540; Church Yth Grp; Letterman Clb; SADD; Teachers Aide; Varsity Clb; Var L Bsbl; Var L Bsktbl; High Hon Roll; CSF; 1st Team All-Leag Bsbl; Acad All-Leag Ath; CA ST U Stanislaus; Lib Studs.

CRIVELLO, GINA M; San Jacinto HS; San Jacinto, CA; (4); 3/124; Cmnty Wkr; Capt Quiz Bowl; Pres Spanish Clb; School Play; Nwsp; VP Jr Cls; Pres Stu Cncl; DAR Awd; Prfct Atten Awd; Pom Pon; Clss Histrn Rank 3; Teens Agnst Drgs Pres; Mock Trial 3 Yrs; CSUSB; Cultrl Anthrplgst.

CRNICH, KRISTI; Eureka HS; Eureka, CA; (1); French Clb; Ski Clb; Hon Roll; Var Sftbl; Law.

CROAN, STEPHANIE; Fremont Christian HS; Fremont, CA; (1); Church Yth Grp; GAA; Teachers Aide; Varsity Clb; School Musical; Yrbk; JV Bsktbl; Intrml Capt Sftbl; Var Capt Vllybl; Vlybl Assn; UCLA; Engl.

CROCKER, AMANDA D; Santa Monica HS; Santa Monica, CA; (3); Church Yth Grp; Pres Drama Clb; Sec French Clb; School Musical; School Play; Stage Crew; Hon Roll; House Of Rep; Numerous Drama Clb Awds; Congressional Yth Ldrshp Cncl Natl Yng Ldrs Conf; Commnctns.

CROCKER, MICHAEL P; Irvington HS; Fremont, CA; (2); 15/350; Church Yth Grp; Dance Clb; Letterman Clb; Acpl Chr; Stu Cncl; Bsktbl; Crs Cntry; Golf; High Hon Roll; Hon Roll; US House Of Rep Page; Voices Of Future; TX A&M; Hstry.

CROCKETT, BRIAN R; Rosemead HS; Rosemead, CA; (2); Boy Scts; Key Clb.

CROCKETT, CARMEN; Garey HS; Pomona, CA; (2); Church Yth Grp; Co-Capt Cheerldng; Gym; MESA; Medicine,Pediatrics.

CROCKETT, SHANNINE S; Ganesha HS; Pomona, CA; (2); Cit Awd; Law.

CROCKETT, SHERYL; Bonita Vista HS; Chula Vista, CA; (3); Cmnty Wkr; Hosp Aide; Teachers Aide; JV Swmmng; Cit Awd; Hon Roll; SAC Peer Tutor; Standard Acadmc Ftnss Awd; Southwestern La Jolla; Elem Tch.

CROCKETT, STEPHANIE; Liberty Christian HS; Red Bluff, CA; (3); Church Yth Grp; Pep Clb; Chorus; Stat Bsktbl; Cheerldng; Biola U; Bus Advrtsng.

CROFF, DANNY L; Pittsburg HS; Pittsburg, CA; (2); Chico ST; Engrng.

CROFT, JENNIFER L; Ramona HS; Ramona, CA; (2); Key Clb; Cit Awd; Prfct Atten Awd; US Pony Club; Peer Counseling; San Diego ST U; Hotel Mgmt.

CROFT, LORIN M; Fontana HS; Fontana, CA; (3); Pep Clb; L Drill Tm; JV Bsktbl; Var L Cheerldng; Var L Pom Pon; Var L Trk; High Hon Roll; Hon Roll; Z Clb; Prncpls Hnr Roll; U CA San Diego; Chem.

CROFTON, WENDY J; Sanger HS; Sanger, CA; (2); Drama Clb; German Clb; Girl Scts; Intnl Clb; Color Guard; Hnrb Mntn Creative Writing; Med.

CROLL, SHANNON M; Academy Of Our Lady Of Peace; Spring Valley, CA; (3); Church Yth Grp; GAA; Math Tm; Ski Clb; Var L Socr; High Hon Roll; NHS; NEDT Awd; Opt Clb Awd; Spanish NHS; San Diegos Yng Woman Of Yr; Union-Tribune Schlr Athl Awd; Mc Carty Schlrshp; Bio.

CROMER, BOBBIE S; North Salinas HS; Salinas, CA; (3); Church Yth Grp; Band; Jazz Band; Mrchg Band; Pep Band; Cit Awd; High Hon Roll; Hon Roll; Top One Hundred Students Award; AR ST; Business Adminstration.

CROMPTON, REBECCA; Redwood HS; Visalia, CA; (4); Spanish Clb; Chorus; JV Bsktbl; Var Trk; Hon Roll; NHS; Acad Ltr; CSF; Fresno Pacific; Accntnt.

CROMWELL, MADELYNE C; Montgomery HS; Santa Rosa, CA; (2); Church Yth Grp; Spanish Clb; Treas Jr Cls; JV Sftbl; High Hon Roll; Hon Roll; Jr NHS; Opt Clb Awd; Pres Acad Fit Awd; Cal Poly; Elec Engrng.

CRONICAN, ERIN; Orange Glen HS; Escondido, CA; (1); 63/947; Drama Clb; Acpl Chr; School Play; Stage Crew; Score Keeper; Var Tennis; High Hon Roll; Hon Roll; Wings Youtheatre Company; Lcl Tennis Trnmnts/1st Pl Var Div; Theatr Arts.

CRONIN, JOHN C; Cabrillo HS; Vafb, CA; (2); Church Yth Grp; Band.

CRONIN, JOHN W; John Marshall Fundamental HS; Pasadena, CA; (3); Church Yth Grp; Treas Science Clb; Cit Awd; Hon Roll; NHS; Bus.

CRONIN, THOMAS D; St Joseph Notre Dame HS; Alameda, CA; (3); Science Clb; Var L Crs Cntry; Var L Socr; Var L Trk; High Hon Roll; NHS; Ntl Merit SF; St Schlr; Engrng.

CRONKHITE, ERENDIRA; Venice HS; Culver City, CA; (2); Treas Service Clb; Teachers Aide; Orch; Co-Ed Nwsp; Co-Ed Yrbk; Pres Stu Cncl; Var Bsktbl; Var Trk; Var Vllybl; Cit Awd; Math.

CRONKITE, KARISMA A; O'farrel Schl Of Performing Arts; Spokane, WA; (2); 1/187; Art Clb; Church Yth Grp; Dance Clb; Drama Clb; Hon Roll; Schslte Achvmt; Art Exploratn Distnctn Awd; Education Ctr Art Shw; Wrld Hstry Awd; CAG Art Disply; Harvard U; Med.

CROOK, PATRICIA; Clovis HS; Fresno, CA; (3); Church Yth Grp; Dance Clb; Debate Tm; Spanish Clb; Speech Tm; SADD; Chorus; Hon Roll; Handbell Choir; Cmmrcl Airline Pilot.

CROPPER, DOREA M R; Oakland Technical HS; Oakland, CA; (3); Dance Clb; SADD; School Musical; School Play; High Hon Roll; Performing Arts.

CROPPER, KIM; Miramonte HS; Moraga, CA; (4); 69/285; School Musical; Pres Sr Cls; Cheerldng; Pom Pon; Tennis; High Hon Roll; Cls Prncss; Prncpls Awd; Concord Pavilion Musical Theatre Schlrshp; Dept Choral Awd; Brigham Young U; Music Dance.

CROPPER, NICOLE; Fairfax HS; Los Angeles, CA; (2); Dance Clb; Drama Clb; French Clb; Math Clb; Teachers Aide; School Musical; Variety Show; Variety Show; Cit Awd; High Hon Roll; Best Stu Career Planning Cls; UC Northridge; Acting.

CROSBY, JASON M; Ukiah JR Acad; Willits, CA; (2); Church Yth Grp; Cmnty Wkr; Teachers Aide; Chorus; Color Guard; Drill Tm; Nwsp; Swmmng; Pathfinder Of Yr; Cnslr In Trng; Lrt Recgntn Mendocino Coll ASB 89-90; Rio Lindo Acad; Art.

CROSBY, KARI LYNN; Fresno Christian HS; Fresno, CA; (4); Letterman Clb; Teachers Aide; Band; Chorus; Mrchg Band; Lit Mag; High Hon Roll; Hon Roll; Ntl Merit Ltr; Pres Acad Fit Awd; Mozart Choir Schl; Chrch Hndbl Choir; Biola; Ped.

CROSBY, KELLY A; Antelope Valley HS; Lancaster, CA; (3); Church Yth Grp; Treas Frsh Cls; Rep Soph Cls; Rep Jr Cls; Capt Var Swmmng; Hon Roll; Kiwanis Awd; NHS; Prom Crt; Swmmng; UCSD; Intl Rltns.

CROSBY, ROBERT S; Ukiah JR Acad; Willits, CA; (2); Church Yth Grp; Cmnty Wkr; Teachers Aide; Chorus; Swmmng; Cnslr Trng Pathfinder Clb, Pathfinder Of Yr; Mssnry Work NM; Rio Lindo Acad; Engl.

CROSBY, SCOTT; Santa Ana Valley HS; Santa Ana, CA; (4); 3/340; Key Clb; Rep Sr Cls; Capt Var Bsbl; High Hon Roll; Ntl Merit Ltr; Stanford U; Engrng.

CROSBY, VINCENT A; Sunset HS; Hayward, CA; (4); 11/25; High Hon Roll.

CROSIER, MICHAEL C; Fairfield HS; Fairfield, CA; (4); Hon Roll.

CROSNO, GALA; San Leandro HS; San Leandro, CA; (2); Cmnty Wkr; Drama Clb; School Play; Variety Show; Bsktbl; Cheerldng; Sftbl; 1st Vrty Show 89; Outstndnt Awd Drama 88-89; AZ ST; TV Brdcstng.

CROSS, DEANNA L; Roseville HS; Roseville, CA; (3); 85/420; German Clb; Spanish Clb; Sec Jr Cls; JV Sftbl; JV Var Swmmng; Stat Vllybl; Hon Roll; Stu Govt; Walk Amer; Graphic Arts.

CROSS, DOROTHY V; Norte Vista HS; Riverside, CA; (2); SADD; Varsity Clb; VP Frsh Cls; VP Soph Cls; Off Jr Cls; Stu Cncl; JV Var Bsktbl; Var Trk; Var Capt Vllybl; Hon Roll; Pedtrcn.

CROSS, HANNAH L; Serrano HS; Wrightwood, CA; (3); Model UN; Drm Mjr(t); Jazz Band; Mrchg Band; Pep Band; Yrbk; JV Sftbl; High Hon Roll; Schlstc All Amer; Jr Hnr Grd; UC Irvine; Psych.

CROSS, KARIN; Hesperia HS; Hesperia, CA; (3); 20/600; Church Yth Grp; Cmnty Wkr; Key Clb; Acpl Chr; Chorus; Church Choir; Flag Corp; Orch; Stu Cncl; Cheerldng; Math.

CROSS, KATHLEEN S; North Monterey County HS; Salinas, CA; (2); Church Yth Grp; SADD; High Hon Roll; Hon Roll; Pres Acad Fit Awd; Sec Soph Cls; Sec Jr Cls; JV Var Cheerldng; Var Socr; JV Sftbl.

CROSS JR, TERRY K; Roosevelt HS; Fresno, CA; (3); VP SADD; Hon Roll; Eart Sci Awd; Bus.

CROSS, ZACHARY; Lincoln Prep HS; San Diego, CA; (3); FCA; Varsity Clb; Lit Mag; JV Bsktbl; Var Ftbl; JV Trk; Hon Roll; Ellis H Casson Awd 87-89; San Diego Union Tribune All Acad Tm; Girard Found Awd For Acad Excllnc; Morehouse; Chem-Engr.

CROSSON, LIZ K; Lincoln HS; Stockton, CA; (1); Orch; Socr; Swmmng; High Hon Roll.

CROSSWY, TONYA E; Western HS; Tipton, CA; (3); JA; Teachers Aide; Hon Roll; Child Care & Dev; Fresno ST; Child Care.

CROTEAU, LOUISE C; San Dieguito HS; La Costa, CA; (2); Church Yth Grp; Church Choir; Drill Tm; Score Keeper; Socr; Sftbl; Vllybl; U CA San Diego; Law.

CROTSLEY, KEVIN M; Calaveras HS; Valley Springs, CA; (3); Pres FBLA; Teachers Aide; Rptr Nwsp; Phtg Yrbk; Off Sr Cls; Stu Cncl; Ftbl; Tennis; Cit Awd; High Hon Roll; Co Estblshd Earth Awarenee Grp; Lifeguard Cnslr; Tchrs Aide Sport Game Coordntr Sunshine Preschl; U Of CA Santa Barbara; Bus.

CROTTY, MOLLY A; Kolbe Academy; Napa, CA; (2); Art Clb; Debate Tm; Drama Clb; Latin Clb; Chorus; Church Choir; School Musical; School Play; Stage Crew; Sec Frsh Cls; Voice Of Democracy Speech Cont; Natl U Of Ireland; Art.

CROUCH, KIMBERLY KAREN; Royal HS; Simi Valley, CA; (4); Var Capt Swmmng; Hon Roll; Jr NHS; NHS; Pres Acad Fit Awd; UC Santa Barabara.

CROUCH, TYLER L; Tustin HS; Tustin, CA; (3); 106/446; Latin Clb; Band; Mrchg Band; High Hon Roll; Hon Roll; Tech Educ Awd; CSF; Band Ltr; U CA Irvine; Designing Engr.

CROUGH, BROOK L; Mt Shasta HS; Weed, CA; (2); Debate Tm; Speech Tm; Inst Of Chldrns Lit Gftd Yng Wrtrs; Writer.

CROUSE, KIM E; Norco HS; Norco, CA; (2); Church Yth Grp; Girl Scts; Scholastic Bowl; Spanish Clb; Chorus; JV Socr; Hon Roll; Pres Acad Fit Awd.

CROUSE, SHELLY; Cordova SR HS; Rancho Cordova, CA; (4); 12/469; Sec JA; Model UN; Orch; Rptr Yrbk; Rep Soph Cls; Rep Jr Cls; Rep Sr Cls; JV Bsktbl; JV Trk; High Hon Roll; Intl Yth Studied-Frgn Exchange; CA Schlrshp Fdrtn-Treas; Berkeley CA U; Pltcl Sci.

CROW, DARBY A; Monte Vista HS; Spring Valley, CA; (3); 10/396; Yrbk; L Var Swmmng; Hon Roll; Golden St Exam High Hnrs Geom.

CROW, DORIS R; Tulare Western HS; Tulare, CA; (3); Drm Mjr(t); Flag Corp; Hon Roll; Baton Twirling Wrld, Natl & Valley Chmpnshps; Fresno ST U.

CROW, HEATHER D; Rio Mesa HS; Oxnard, CA; (1); Varsity Clb; Var Sftbl; Hon Roll; UNLV.

CROW, JENNIFER K; El Camino Real HS; West Hills, CA; (2); Sec Boy Scts; Pres Girl Scts; High Hon Roll; CSF; Equestrian Club; Earth Reunion Club; Teacher.

CROW, MISSI; Madera HS; Madera, CA; (4); 13/480; Church Yth Grp; Ski Clb; Speech Tm; Off Soph Cls; Sec Stu Cncl; Powder Puff Ftbl; Tennis; Lion Awd; Prfct Atten Awd; Pres Acad Fit Awd; Lions Clb Spch Wnnr 90; Fresno ST; Psych.

CROWDER, ELICE M; Brea Olinda HS; Brea, CA; (3); French Clb; SADD; Varsity Clb; Yrbk; Var L Socr; Var L Tennis; Hon Roll.

CROWDER, JARED M; Don Lugo HS; Chino Hills, CA; (2); Boy Scts; Church Yth Grp; Spanish Clb; Church Choir; Bsktbl; Ftbl; Wt Lftg; Hon Roll; Eagle Scout Awd; BYU; Optomologist.

CROWE, DINA A; Apple Valley HS; Apple Valley, CA; (3); Church Yth Grp; Pres English Clb; Teachers Aide; Chorus; Church Choir; Swing Chorus; Rptr Nwsp; Var Powder Puff Ftbl; Stat Trk; High Hon Roll; Chrgrphrs Chc Bst Dncr; Shwchr Awd; 1st Plc San Bernardino Ctys Wrtng Clbrtn; MVP Pwdrpf Ftbl; Cal Poly San Luis; Eng Tchr.

CROWELL, DAWN F; El Cajon Valley HS; El Cajon, CA; (3); 14/393; GAA; Letterman Clb; Ski Clb; Varsity Clb; Crs Cntry; Socr; Trk; Med.

CROWELL, JENNIFER M; Granite Hills HS; Alpine, CA; (3); English Clb; Chorus; Swing Chorus; Variety Show; Ed Nwsp; Gym; Cit Awd; High Hon Roll; Hon Roll; San Diego ST U; Jrnlsm.

CROWLEY, MONE T; Valley HS; Sacramento, CA; (4); Cmnty Wkr; FTA; Math Tm; Teachers Aide; Variety Show; Treas Stu Cncl; Var Capt Bsktbl; Capt Ftbl; JV Trk; Elks Awd; Blck Stu Union Treas; Ath Cnsl Rep Bsktbl; Finance Cmmtte Elk Grove Uni-Fied Schl Dist; Teacher.

CROWLEY, TERRI D; Corona HS; Corona, CA; (3); 35/402; Boy Scts; Library Aide; Band; Drm Mjr(t); Jazz Band; Mrchg Band; Orch; Pep Band; Variety Show; Rep Stu Cncl; SCSBOA; All Sthrn Hnr Band; Tourn Of Roses Hnr Band; John Phillip Sousa Hnr Band; Music.

CROWN, HEATHER; John F Kennedy HS; Granada Hills, CA; (4); Dance Clb; SADD; Drill Tm; Var Cheerldng; Var Pom Pon; Hon Roll; Pres Acad Fit Awd; CA ST U Northridge; Astrnmy.

CROWN, SARAH R; Reseda HS; Tarzana, CA; (1); Temple Yth Grp; Babysitting; Reading; Swimming; UCLA; Psych.

CROWNOVER, BERNADETTEE; Paradise HS; Paradise, CA; (1); 2/318; Art Clb; Church Yth Grp; Cmnty Wkr; German Clb; GAA; Hosp Aide; Pep Clb; SADD; Band; Chorus; Swim Aide Paradises Paul Bryan Aquatic Pk Rec & Pks Dept; Schlrshp CSU; UCLA; Ob-Gyn.

CROY, SUSIE; Marysville HS; Marysville, CA; (2); Church Yth Grp; Girl Scts; Library Aide; Treas Pep Clb; Teachers Aide; Color Guard; Capt Flag Corp; School Play; Rptr Nwsp; Rep Stu Cncl; Yuba JC; Bio.

CRUDAINGTON, DAREN; Terra Linda HS; San Rafael, CA; (3); Ski Clb; Swmmng; Tennis; Hon Roll; Schlrshp Soc; Bus.

CRUDEN, BRETT; Poway HS; Poway, CA; (3); 20/761; Treas Pres Computer Clb; FBLA; Treas Pres Math Clb; Scholastic Bowl; Science Clb; JV Var Swmmng; High Hon Roll; NHS; German Clb; Math Tm; CSF; Intrct Clb; Math.

CRUIKSHANK, DAVID E; Crescenta Valley HS; Glendale, CA; (4); 5/380; Church Yth Grp; Drama Clb; Key Clb; Mu Alpha Theta; Spanish Clb; School Play; Yrbk; Ed Lit Mag; NHS; Ntl Merit Ltr; CSF Sealbearer & Secy; UCLA Almumni Schlrshp; Amer Lgn Schlrshp; UCLA; Aerospace Engrng.

CRUISE, DAVID TODD; Nevada Union HS; Grass Valley, CA; (4); 41/477; Church Yth Grp; Debate Tm; French Clb; Math Tm; Scholastic Bowl; Teachers Aide; Crs Cntry; High Hon Roll; NHS; Ntl Merit SF; People To People Stu Ambssdrs Russia 90; CA ST U Sacramento; Engrng.

CRUM, JODY; Fall River HS; Mc Arthur, CA; (4); 6/60; FFA; Varsity Clb; Yrbk; Treas Sr Cls; Var JV Bsktbl; Var Cheerldng; Var Sftbl; High Hon Roll; Hon Roll; CSF; U Of CA Davis; Soclgy.

CRUM, JOE M; Beyer HS; Modesto, CA; (3); VP AFS; Spanish Clb; Speech Tm; Teachers Aide; Var Bsbl; Var Bsktbl; Intrml Tennis; Intrml Wt Lftg; Hon Roll; Conf Bsktbl Champs; Cal Poly SLO; Bus Mgmt.

CRUM, MELINDA; Los Altos HS; Hacienda Hts, CA; (3); 135/376; Band; Color Guard; Mrchg Band; Var L Bsktbl; Var L Vllybl; Hon Roll; Prfct Atten Awd; Jr Hnr Guard; Cmnty Vlntr Vet Hosp; Flag Carrier 100th Trnmt Roses Parade; Bus.

CRUMB, DEREK G; Gompers Secondary HS; San Diego, CA; (2); 41/145; Band; JV Vllybl; Hon Roll; Sci Olympiad; Embry-Riddle; Aerontcl Sci.

CRUMB, DEVIN JEFFREY; Don Bosco Technical Inst; Pasadena, CA; (2); Aud/Vis; Boy Scts; Stage Crew; PADI-AOW Suba Diver; CA Poly-San Luis Obispo; Elect.

CRUMMEY, VIKTORIA G; Armijo HS; Fairfield, CA; (3); AFS; Church Yth Grp; Dance Clb; German Clb; Ski Clb; Swmmng; Hon Roll; Pre-Law.

CRUMP, BROOKE; Esperanza HS; Yorba Linda, CA; (2); Cmnty Wkr; Drama Clb; French Clb; Pep Clb; Var Bsktbl; Var L Trk; High Hon Roll; Hon Roll; World Hstry Excllnc Awd; Girls Leag; 4th Rnk Orange Cnty Hgh Jumper Jr Var; UCLA; Med.

CRUMP, RODNEY; William M Taft HS; New York, NY; (1); Drama Clb; Scholastic Bowl; Nwsp; Lit Mag; VP Frsh Cls; Rep Soph Cls; Rep Stu Cncl; Ntl Merit SF; Natl Champ Acad Decathlon Tm; Telluride Schlr; Columbia U.

CRUMPTON, DAVID M; El Camino HS; Oceanside, CA; (4); French Clb; Teachers Aide; Bsktbl; Hon Roll; OABSE Awd; Blck Stu Acadmc Awd; Acadmc Leag; Hnrs Grad; Palomar Coll; Engrng.

CRUMRINE, DANA; Gilroy HS; Gilroy, CA; (4); 114/500; Church Yth Grp; Cmnty Wkr; Dance Clb; 4-H; FBLA; FFA; Red Cross Aide; Speech Tm; Teachers Aide; 4-H Awd; San Jose ST; Educ.

CRUNKLETON, KATHERINE; Foothill HS; Santa Ana, CA; (4); Pres Church Yth Grp; English Clb; French Clb; Pep Clb; Red Cross Aide; Flag Corp; High Hon Roll; CSF Sealbearer; Early Morning Seminar Grad; Young Womens Pgm Medallion Of Completion; Ricks Coll; Comp Analyst.

CRUTCHER, BRYNDYN; Luther Burbank Acad/Math Sci & Enginrng; Sacramento, CA; (2); Church Yth Grp; Cmnty Wkr; Letterman Clb; Varsity Clb; Var Bsbl; JV Ftbl; Capt Var Vllybl; Cit Awd; Hon Roll; Prfct Atten Awd; Pepperdine U; Educ.

CRUTCHER, LAURA I; Ukiah HS; Ukiah, CA; (3); GAA; Rptr Nwsp; JV Bsktbl; Capt Sftbl; Var Tennis; Hon Roll; Mst Insprtnl Tnns & Bsktbl; MVP Sftbl; UC Santa Barbara; Law.

CRUTCHER, LESLIE; Fremont Christian HS; Fremont, CA; (2); Ski Clb; Pres Frsh Cls; Socr; Vllybl; Hon Roll; UC; Bus.

CRUTCHER, LONA C; Credence HS; Susanville, CA; (3); Elks Awd; Prfct Atten Awd; 2nd Rnnr Up Elks Stu Yr; Comp.

CRUTCHFIELD, TENESHA L; Montclair HS; Ontario, CA; (2); Acpl Chr; Band; Chorus; Jazz Band; School Musical; Attorney.

CRUZ, ALFONSO B; Coachella Valley HS; Coachella, CA; (3); 40/240; Varsity Clb; Var Ftbl; Hon Roll; St Marys; Engr.

CRUZ, ANNA MARIE; Live Oak HS; Morgan Hill, CA; (3); 18/580; French Clb; FBLA; Key Clb; Band; Mrchg Band; Co-Ed Lit Mag; Stu Cncl; Cit Awd; High Hon Roll; Lion Awd; Bdmntn; CA Schlrshp Fed Scrtry; UC Davis; Bio Med Engrng.

CRUZ, ARISTOTLE H; James Logan HS; Union City, CA; (3); Church Yth Grp; Computer Clb; Hon Roll; Cadd Drftng; Badminton; UC-BERKELEY; Aeron Engrng.

CRUZ, CARLA N; James Logan HS; Union City, CA; (3); Church Yth Grp; French Clb; Intnl Clb; Ed Yrbk; High Hon Roll; Hon Roll; Pres Acad Fit Awd; Partnrshp Prgm UC Berkeley 87-90; Pre-Coll Acad-UC Berkeley 88-90; Church Chldrns Choir Orgnst; UC Santa Barbara; Mass Cmmnctn.

CRUZ, DARRYL D; Rancho Alamitos HS; Garden Grove, CA; (3); 22/264; Yrbk; Treas Jr Cls; Bsktbl; Var Ftbl; Var Wt Lftg; Hon Roll; NEDT Awd; Pres Schlr.

CRUZ, DEBBIE; Chino HS; Ontario, CA; (3); FHA; Spanish Clb; Hon Roll; Real Estate.

CRUZ, DOLORES; Hilltop HS; Chula Vista, CA; (4); 7/439; Intnl Clb; Office Aide; Teachers Aide; Chorus; Variety Show; Cit Awd; Hon Roll; Pres Acad Fit Awd; San Diego ST U; Bus Admin.

CRUZ, EMILE IRVING; Simi Valley HS; Simi Valley, CA; (4); 5/730; Spanish Clb; Jazz Band; Orch; Var L Bsbl; JV Ftbl; Intrml Socr; Var Capt Wrstlng; Elks Awd; High Hon Roll; Jr NHS; CA Fdrtn Of Schlrs Life Tm Stu; Rocketdyne Div Of Rockwell Intl Partners In Engrng Excllnc Schlrshp; U CA San Diego; Engrng.

CRUZ, ERIC M; San Gorgonio HS; Highland, CA; (3); JV Crs Cntry; Cit Awd; Hon Roll; Prfct Atten Awd; Schlrs Awd; Poly Sci.

CRUZ, GLORIA; Paramount HS; Paramount, CA; (3); Sec FHA; Prfct Atten Awd; Coll Clb; UC Irvine.

CRUZ, GREGORY; Mission HS; San Francisco, CA; (1); JV Bsbl; Hon Roll.

CRUZ, HENRY; St Genevieve HS; N Hollywood, CA; (4); JV Vllybl; Hon Roll; Prfct Atten Awd; CA ST U; Bus Admin.

CRUZ, JAQUELINE; S Tahoe HS; S Lake Tahoe, CA; (3).

CRUZ, JENNIFER D; El Dorado HS; Yorba Linda, CA; (3); Church Yth Grp; Dance Clb; Intnl Clb; Church Choir; High Hon Roll; Hon Roll; NHS; Eclgy Clb; Msnry; CA Baptist Coll; Scndry Ed.

CRUZ, JOHANN M; Sacred Heart Cathedral HS; San Francisco, CA; (1); Var Tennis; Med.

CRUZ, KAREN V; Mayfair HS; Lakewood, CA; (3); Dance Clb; Pep Clb; Mrchg Band; High Hon Roll; Hon Roll; Spanish NHS; Modelng John Robert Powers; Dept Awd For Bus; UC Irvine; Pedtrcn.

CRUZ, LAURA A; John Glenn HS; Norwalk, CA; (3); Sec Treas Drama Clb; Spanish Clb; Thesps; School Play; Cit Awd; Hon Roll; Theater.

CRUZ III, LOUIS R; Escondido HS; Escondido, CA; (3); Am Leg Boys St; Yrbk; Bsbl; JV Ftbl; Hon Roll; Econ.

CRUZ, LYNN MAE T; Notre Dame HS; San Jose, CA; (3); 10/90; Hosp Aide; Intrml Bsktbl; Var Socr; Capt Var Tennis; Var Trk; Intrml Vllybl; High Hon Roll; NHS; Scl Involvement Corps; CSF; Vrsty Letter Block & 2nd Tm All Leag Sccr; UCLA; Pediatrics.

CRUZ, MARIA A; Mater Dei HS; Orange, CA; (3); Cmnty Wkr; Hosp Aide; High Hon Roll; Hon Roll; NHS; Pre-Med.

CRUZ, MARIA C; Thomas Edison HS; Stockton, CA; (2); Church Yth Grp; Dance Clb; JV Var Score Keeper; High Hon Roll; Hon Roll; Gftd & Tlntd Educ Club; Military.

CRUZ, MARISA D; Fontana HS; Fontana, CA; (2); 64/1110; Treas Debate Tm; Treas Speech Tm; Band; Mrchg Band; VP Frsh Cls; Hon Roll.

CRUZ, MIREA; Mesa Verde HS; Citrus Heights, CA; (2); 11/300; Church Yth Grp; Dance Clb; Band; Chorus; Church Choir; Variety Show; High Hon Roll; Hon Roll; Rep Of Frshmn Visit Other Schl; Mini/Cultural Olympic; Piano Accmpnst Evry Actvty That Includes Piano; Stanford; Brain Surgeon.

CRUZ, NATHAN W; Montecito HS; Collegedale, TN; (4); Church Yth Grp; Spanish Clb; Off Soph Cls; Intrml Bsbl; Intrml Bsktbl; Intrml Ftbl; Intrml Socr; Intrml Sftbl; Capt Vllybl; Intrml Wt Lftg.

CRUZ JR, OCTAVIO G; Livingston HS; Delhi, CA; (3); Chess Clb; SADD; Band; Mrchg Band; Var Bsbl; High Hon Roll; Hon Roll; CSF; Mrchng Band 1st Pl; Fresno ST; Dntst.

CRUZ, PALOMA A; Eagle Rock HS; Los Angeles, CA; (3); Pres Thesps; School Musical; School Play; Variety Show; Pres Frsh Cls; VP Jr Cls; Rep Sr Cls; Stu Cncl; Var Trk; JV Vllybl; Poetry/Creatve Wrtng; Author.

CRUZ, PAUL M; Central Union HS; El Centro, CA; (2); Tennis; Desert Vly Leag For Boys; Mst Imprvd 2nd Yr Boys Tnns Team.

CRUZ, RANDY C; Pittsburg HS; Pittsburg, CA; (2); Pres Rep Soph Cls; Stu Cncl; JV Tennis; High Hon Roll; Prfct Atten Awd; Gldn St Exam Hgh Hnrs Geom/Alg; US Naval Acad; Aerosp Engrng.

CRUZ II, REYMUNDO R; Fontana HS; Fontana, CA; (3); Church Yth Grp; Cmnty Wkr; Teachers Aide; Phtg Nwsp; Phtg Yrbk; Bsktbl; Crs Cntry; Prfct Atten Awd; Mech Engrng.

CRUZ, ROBERT; Fillmore HS; Fillmore, CA; (1); Cit Awd; Hon Roll; Prfct Atten Awd; Electrnc Tech.

CRUZ, ROBYN M; Bishop Amat Memorial HS; Hacienda Hts, CA; (2); Church Yth Grp; Var Capt Crs Cntry; JV Socr; Var Trk; Photography, Slvr Scrn Club; USC; Photogrphy.

CRUZ, ROCHELLE J; James Logan HS; Hayward, CA; (3); SADD; Band; Mrchg Band; Pep Band; Elctd Stu Dir Of James Logan Band 1989-90; Elctd SR Mgr For Band 1990-91; Med.

CRUZ, RODEL L E; James Logan HS; Union City, CA; (3); FTA; Teachers Aide; JV Swmmng; Cit Awd; Hon Roll; UC Berkeley; Journalism.

CRUZ, VERONICA; Burbank HS; Burbank, CA; (3); Math Tm; Office Aide; Science Clb; Cit Awd; JETS Awd; Prfct Atten Awd; Pres Acad Fit Awd; CSF; Natl Cncl Tchrs Engl Wrtng Cmptn Rep 90; Engl Spkng Union Shakespeare Cmtpn 90; Acctng.

CRUZ, ZORAYA; Baldwin Park HS; Baldwin Park, CA; (2); Church Yth Grp; Dance Clb; Pep Clb; Lit Mag; L Capt Cheerldng; JETS Awd; Var Songleading; Psych.

CRYDER, MICHELLE M; Salinas HS; Salinas, CA; (2); Church Yth Grp; Drama Clb; Library Aide; Office Aide; Teachers Aide; Thesps; Church Choir; Stage Crew; High Hon Roll; Hon Roll; Award Spanish 3-4; Salinas Gold Cd High Acad Achvmnt; Sacramento St U; Journalism.

CRYSTAL, TORRES; San Jose High Acad; San Jose, CA; (2); Drill Tm; Cheerldng; Sftbl; San Jose ST; Acctnt.

CSEPELY, EDITH; Saint Francis HS; Sunnyvale, CA; (2); Girl Scts; Intnl Clb; Math Clb; Science Clb; Service Clb; SADD; Church Choir; Color Guard; High Hon Roll; Hon Roll; CSF; Bio.

CSINSI, GINA L; Gahr HS; Norwalk, CA; (2); Church Yth Grp; Hon Roll; Vet.

CUADRA, ISABEL; Selma HS; Selma, CA; (2); Church Yth Grp; Cmnty Wkr; French Clb; Hosp Aide; Variety Show; Bsktbl; Trk; High Hon Roll; Hon Roll; Part Time Job Doing Ofc Work; USC; Chld Psych.

CUAMATZI, AIDA; Sierra Vista HS; Baldwin Park, CA; (3); Church Yth Grp; Girl Scts; Stu Cncl; Cit Awd; Hon Roll; Ntl Merit Ltr; Prfct Atten Awd; U Of Calpoly; Engrng.

CUBE, ANTHONY; Rowland HS; Rowland Heights, CA; (2); French Clb; Trk; Dance Group.

CUBILLAS, ALVARO; Herbert Hoover HS; Glendale, CA; (4); 23/524; Church Yth Grp; Dance Clb; Debate Tm; VP FCA; Hosp Aide; Pres Letterman Clb; Rep Soph Cls; Rep Jr Cls; Var L Ftbl; Var L Trk; UCLA Almns Assoc Awd; CSF Slbrer; Natl Hspnc Schlr Awd; Loyola Marymount U; History.

CUCH, MARVELLA M; Sherman Indian HS; Fort Duchesne, UT; (3); Drama Clb; Office Aide; Drill Tm; VP Stu Cncl; Cheerldng; JV Mgr(s); High Hon Roll; NHS; Cmnty Wkr; Mr Miss Ute Tribe 90-91; Outreach Pgm; U Of CA Irvine; Law.

CUDIAMAT, ARDENE J; Nagales HS; Walnut, CA; (2); Bsktbl; Sftbl; JV Tennis; Hon Roll; Pres Acad Fit Awd; Acad Achvt Excllnc Engl; Arch.

CUE, JACKIE; Westlake HS; Thousand Oaks, CA; (3); 130/450; SADD; VP Jr Cls; Rep Stu Cncl; Var Capt Mgr(s); Hon Roll; Westlake Ambassador; Jr Hmcmng Prncss; Rep ASG Asso Stu Gov; JSA & Interact Govtmnt; Bus.

CUELLAR, DANIEL; Hoover HS; Fresno, CA; (2); Spanish Clb; JV Socr; Var Trk; High Hon Roll; Hon Roll; MESA.

CUELLAR, ELSIE; Schurr HS; Los Angeles, CA; (3); Office Aide; Band; Jazz Band; Mrchg Band; Pep Band; Hon Roll; Prfct Atten Awd; Tres Band; Hotel & Rest Admin.

CUELLAR, STACEY M; Arvin HS; Bakersfield, CA; (3); Pres Computer Clb; Math Clb; SADD; Teachers Aide; Band; Mrchg Band; Sftbl; Hon Roll; Outstndng Band Awd; Mesa Stu; Outstndng Engl Awd; CA ST U-Bakersfield; Music.

CUENCA, MARITZA I; St Joseph HS; Anaheim, CA; (3); Church Yth Grp; Treas French Clb; SADD; High Hon Roll; Hon Roll; Psych.

CUENCA-ORTIZ, ELEIDA; Central Union HS; El Centro, CA; (2); Church Yth Grp; English Clb; German Clb; L Flag Corp; Mrchg Band; Hon Roll; Stanford; Med.

CUESTA, MILO B; Chaffey HS; Upland, CA; (4); Teachers Aide; High Hon Roll; Bckwrds King; Wrtng Celebrtn Cty Wnnr; Gldn St Exam Hghst Score; U CA Davis; Envrnmntl Plcy.

CUEVA, ANGELICA; Baldwin Park HS; Baldwin Park, CA; (2); Science Clb; High Hon Roll; Hon Roll; Prfct Atten Awd; Psychtrst.

CUEVA, CAROLINA; Sweetwater HS; National City, CA; (2); Art Clb; Dance Clb; Drama Clb; Office Aide; Spanish Clb; Teachers Aide; School Play; Stage Crew; Variety Show; Rptr Nwsp; Modeling Club.

CUEVA, CHRIS R; Mater Dei HS; Irvine, CA; (3); Boy Scts; Cmnty Wkr; French Clb; Band; Jazz Band; Mrchg Band; Pep Band; NHS; Outstndng Vlntr Svc Ed Prgm 88; Carnation Vlntr Rcgntn; CA Poly San Luis Obisbo; Arch.

CUEVA, CLAUDIA; Academy Of Our Lady Of Peace; San Diego, CA; (2); Cmnty Wkr; Office Aide; Spanish Clb; Teachers Aide; San Diego ST U; Law.

CUEVA, JUAN; Hawthorne HS; Inglewood, CA; (1); Church Yth Grp; Hon Roll; Loyola Marymount U.

CUEVA, LUGDY; Bishop Amat HS; Valinda, CA; (3); VP Latin Clb; Cit Awd; Hon Roll; FTA; Pres Acad Fit Awd; Fri Ngt Live Clb, CSF Clb & Slvr Scrn Clb; Spec Olympcs; Happy Tms Prog Schlrshp; Arch.

CUEVA, SERGIO; Artesia HS; Hawaiian Gardens, CA; (1); JV Jr Cls; JV Socr; Cit Awd; Hon Roll; Prfct Atten Awd; Pres Acad Fit Awd; Surf Club; CA Jr Schlrshp Fed; CSULB; Bus.

CUEVAS, ANA M; San Benito HS; Hollister, CA; (3); 27/370; Key Clb; Santa Cruz U; Cnslr.

CUEVAS, ANGELICA M; Montgomery HS; San Ysidro, CA; (2); Off Soph Cls; Tonalamatl; Letterettes; Waterpolo; Southwestern Coll; Bus Adm.

CUEVAS, CATHERINE D; Mar Vista HS; Imperial Beach, CA; (2); #4 In Class; High Hon Roll; Hon Roll; Prfct Atten Awd; Hall Of Chmpns-Frgn Lang; Outstndng French Stu Awd; Acctng.

CUEVAS, ERIC R; Orestimba HS; Patterson, CA; (4); Spanish Clb; VICA; School Musical; School Play; Ftbl; Trk; Hon Roll; 6 Art Awds Drwng; Engr.

CUEVAS, GABRIELLA N; St Joseph HS; Cerritos, CA; (3); Church Yth Grp; Drama Clb; SADD; Teachers Aide; Phtg Yrbk; Hon Roll; Photo Awd; Photo.

CUEVAS, GEORGE N; Twentynine Palms HS; Twentynine Palms, CA; (3); Letterman Clb; Science Clb; VP Sr Cls; Rep Stu Cncl; JV Var Crs Cntry; Var Swmmng; JV Var Trk; Wt Lftg; Hon Roll; Prfct Atten Awd; Accntng.

CUEVAS, LEE C; Sanger HS; Sanger, CA; (2); Drama Clb; Model UN; Speech Tm; Flag Corp; Stage Crew; JV Socr; U Of CA Santa Cruz; Bus.

CUEVAS, LUCIA M; Coachella Valley HS; Coachella, CA; (2); FBLA; Drill Tm; Hon Roll; Prfct Atten Awd; Bus.

CUEVAS, MARCO A; Central Union HS; El Centro, CA; (2); 229/430; Color Guard; Ftbl; Wt Lftg; Wrstlng; Cit Awd; Prfct Atten Awd; Imprl Cnty Shrff Explrs; Central Union HS; DEA.

CUEVAS, MIREYA; John H Francis Polytechnic HS; Sun Valley, CA; (4); Dance Clb; French Clb; L Drill Tm; Ed Yrbk; Powder Puff Ftbl; Cit Awd; High Hon Roll; Hon Roll; Prfct Atten Awd; Los Angeles Valley Coll; Law.

CUEVAS, SUZIE; Livingston HS; Livingston, CA; (1); French Clb; Girl Scts; Sec Frsh Cls; JV Bsktbl; JV Score Keeper; Hon Roll; Frnch & Spnsh Clb Europe Trip.

CUEVO, CHRISTOPHER D; Pasadena HS; Pasadena, CA; (2); Comp Sci.

CUFFLIN, KARYN J; La Serna HS; Whittier, CA; (2); 47/450; Church Yth Grp; Tennis; Hon Roll; Bus.

CUIZON, MELIZZA C; University City HS; San Diego, CA; (3); 88/373; Spanish Clb; SADD; Ed Yrbk; Lit Mag; Off Soph Cls; Off Jr Cls; Hon Roll; NHS; Culture Club; Reprographics; U CA San Diego; Bus.

CUKINGNAN, MARIETTA D; Miraleste HS; Rolling Hills, CA; (3); 8/149; Church Yth Grp; Hosp Aide; Spanish Clb; Chorus; Powder Puff Ftbl; Swmmng; High Hon Roll; Hon Roll; Spanish NHS; Alturist Clb; UCLA; Pediatrician.

CULBERSON, CHRISTY; Pioneer HS; San Jose, CA; (4); 109/308; Sec FFA; FHA; Earthday Clb; Cptn Mascots; Envrnmntal Studies.

CULBERTSON, KELLY A; Techachapi HS; Barrow, AK; (3); Stage Crew; Rptr Nwsp; Yrbk; Sec Frsh Cls; Sec Soph Cls; Var Bsktbl; Var Crs Cntry; High Hon Roll; Hon Roll; NHS; U Of S CA; Vet Sci.

CULBERTSON, MAYA; O'farrell SCPA HS; San Diego, CA; (2); 1/187; Dance Clb; School Musical; School Play; Stage Crew; Cit Awd; High Hon Roll; Hon Roll; Dnc CA Ballet Co; UC Berkely; Math.

CULLEN, KRISTEN H; Louisville HS; Northridge, CA; (3); VP Pres FHA; GAA; Treas Sec Service Clb; Crs Cntry; Trk; NHS; Ntl Merit Ltr.

CULLEN, MICHELLE R; Tehachapi HS; Tehachapi, CA; (3); Church Yth Grp; Computer Clb; FHA; Band; Chorus; School Musical; Swmmng; High Hon Roll; Hon Roll; Lion Awd; Band Awd; Choral Awd; S CA Coll; Tchr.

CULLEN, RODNEY; Coast Joint Union HS; Cambria, CA; (4); 5/70; AFS; Church Yth Grp; FBLA; FFA; Red Cross Aide; SADD; Ed Yrbk; Capt L Ftbl; Var L Socr; Var Trk; CA Schltc Fndtn Seal Bearer/Life Time Mem; Amer Drug Free Powerlifting Assn; Ftbl All ST Bike Schlr; Cal Poly San Luis Obispo; Bus.

CULLISON, JAMES; Saint Francis HS; Sunnyvale, CA; (4); 17/324; Debate Tm; NFL; Speech Tm; School Play; Nwsp; JV Tennis; High Hon Roll; NHS; Ntl Merit Ltr; Natl Cncl Tchrs Engl Wrtng Achvt Awd; Pol Sci.

CULLUM, BRIAN P; Mission Viejo HS; Mission Viejo, CA; (2); 78/425; Cmnty Wkr; Spanish Clb; Band; Mrchg Band; Pep Band; Rep Stu Cncl; Crs Cntry; JV Socr; Wt Lftg; Hon Roll; Drftng Clb; Crss Cntry Awd; CSF; CA Poli Sanlo; Grphc Art.

CULLUM, CATIE; Edison HS; Huntington Beach, CA; (2); Church Yth Grp; Dance Clb; Lit Mag; Ballet Stu; Picked To Preform Swan Lake Green Fstvl; UCLA; Dance.

CULLUM, DAVID C; Mission HS; Mission Viejo, CA; (2); 52/425; Cmnty Wkr; Spanish Clb; Band; Mrchg Band; Pep Band; Rep Stu Cncl; Crs Cntry; JV Socr; Wt Lftg; Hon Roll; CSF; Crss Cntry Awds; U Of CO; Bus.

CULMONE, MICHEAL J; Burroughs HS; Ridgecrest, CA; (2); Aud/Vis; Drama Clb; FBLA; Thesps; School Musical; School Play; Stage Crew; Variety Show; Cit Awd; Hon Roll; Adv.

CULP, DEBORAH; Glen A Wilson HS; Hacienda Heights, CA; (4); 70/370; Church Yth Grp; Teachers Aide; Chorus; Co-Capt Flag Corp; Hon Roll; Pres Acad Fit Awd; Biola U.

CULPEPPER, ALEXANDRIA S; Pasadena HS; Pasadena, CA; (3); Church Yth Grp; Pep Clb; Church Choir; Yrbk; Capt Cheerldng; Vllybl; Blck Stu Union; Yng Blck Schlr; Spelman U; Neonatology Doc.

CULPEPPER, ELIZABETH L; Palo Alto SR HS; Palo Alto, CA; (4); Church Yth Grp; Orch; Ed Nwsp; L Swmmng; NHS; Ntl Merit SF; Locl Newspr Intrshp; Sunday Schl Tchr; Engl.

CULVERSON, AMY M; Stagg HS; Stockton, CA; (2); Drama Clb; Band; Engl Teacher.

CUMMINGS, CAMILLE; Los Gatos HS; Los Gatos, CA; (3); 17/341; Pep Clb; Chorus; Variety Show; JV Var Cheerldng; High Hon Roll; Hon Roll; Pres Schlr; Geom Golden St Exam Hnrs; Excllnc In Frgn Lang, Spanish & Chrldng; U CA Santa Barbara; Law.

CUMMINGS, CATHERINE M; Live Oak HS; Morgan Hill, CA; (4); Girl Scts; Teachers Aide; Ftbl; Wrstlng; Hon Roll; Prfct Atten Awd; CSF; Yth Sci Inst Vlntr; CSU Fullerton; Phys Thrpy.

CUMMINGS, DAWN M; Garces Memorial HS; Bakersfield, CA; (3); 31/150; Cmnty Wkr; Hosp Aide; Key Clb; Science Clb; Service Clb; High Hon Roll; Hon Roll; Campus Ministry Tm; Peer Cnslg; CSF; Med.

CUMMINGS, DUWANDA J; Castlemont HS; Oakland, CA; (2); Dance Clb; Hosp Aide; Church Choir; Cit Awd; Hon Roll; Fshn Mdlng; San Francisco ST; Bio.

CUMMINGS, GINA; Pacific Union College Prep; Angwin, CA; (4); 2/25; Church Yth Grp; Cmnty Wkr; Office Aide; Spanish Clb; Band; Chorus; Ed Nwsp; VP Stu Cncl; Swmmng; Ntl Merit SF; Coll Orch 4 Yrs; Violin Tchr F/Chldrn 4 Yrs; Semeon C Williams Awd Strng Prfrmnc; Loma Linda U; OB/Gyn.

CUMMINGS III, GORDON B; Thomas Downey HS; Modesto, CA; (3); Spanish Clb; Teachers Aide; JV Bsbl; 2nd Pl St Drug Essay Cont; Asst Coach Elks Clb Bsbl; Babe Ruth Bsbl Ump; Boise ST; Phys Ed.

CUMMINGS, MARK J; Rio Mesa HS; Camarillo, CA; (4); Cmnty Wkr; Math Tm; Quiz Bowl; Teachers Aide; JV Crs Cntry; JV Golf; JV Socr; High Hon Roll; Hon Roll; NHS; Hmbldt ST; Corp Law.

CUMMINGS, MARSHELL D; L B David Starr Jordan HS; Long Beach, CA; (4); JA; SADD; Teachers Aide; Varsity Clb; Rep Sr Cls; JV Var Bsktbl; Hon Roll; Yng Black Schlrs; CSU Dominguez Hls; Bus.

CUMMINGS, PAUL A; Apple Valley HS; Apple Valley, CA; (2); Church Yth Grp; Key Clb; Band; Chorus; Drm Mjr(t); Mrchg Band; Swing Chorus; High Hon Roll; Hon Roll; 2nd Chair Trumpet Cnty Hnr Band; Stanford; Anthropology.

CUMMINGS, VALERIE A; San Luis SR HS; San Luis Obispo, CA; (2); Church Yth Grp; Key Clb; JV Swmmng; Pres Acad Fit Awd; Sports; CA Polytech U; Med.

CUMMINS, JANET E; Antelope Valley HS; Lancaster, CA; (4); Church Yth Grp; Cmnty Wkr; German Clb; Science Clb; JV Var Tennis; Cit Awd; High Hon Roll; Pres Acad Fit Awd; JR Hnr Line; CA Schlrshp Fed Seal Bearer Or Life; High Hnrs On Natl German Test; Antelope Valley CC; Ameri Hsty.

CUMMINS, JENNIFER L; Louisville HS; Northridge, CA; (3); Church Yth Grp; GAA; Varsity Clb; Chorus; School Musical; School Play; Socr; Vllybl; Hon Roll; Walt Disneys Doers & Drmrs Hnry Awd; Chem, Rlgn I, Bus, Amer Exprnc, Englsh & Hstry Awds; Santa Clara; Vslly Imprd Tchr.

CUMMINS, JODIE; Antelope Valley HS; Lancaster, CA; (4); 1/500; Cmnty Wkr; German Clb; Science Clb; Teachers Aide; JV Var Tennis; Hnr Line 89; CSF; Commndtn Bus Ed; Antelope Valley CC.

CUMMINS, JOSHUA W; Lodi HS; Lodi, CA; (3); Church Yth Grp; FCA; JA; Key Clb; Letterman Clb; Ski Clb; Varsity Clb; Bsbl; Capt Bsktbl; Ftbl; 2nd Pl Shaklee Smart Start Cont Shaklee & Jr Achvt; Spcl Olympcs Vlntr; Pepperdine; Bus Mgmt.

CUMMINS, MARCY D; North HS; Oildale, CA; (2); French Clb; ROTC; Teachers Aide; Vllybl; Hon Roll; CSF; GATE Clb; JROTC Drill Team.

CUNANAN, CATHERINE J; Diamond Bar HS; Chino, CA; (4); Art Clb; Church Yth Grp; Dance Clb; Debate Tm; Science Clb; Teachers Aide; Chorus; Yrbk; JV Var Vllybl; Bst In Comp Sci; Excllnc In Art Awd; Mst Inspirational Vllybl; CA Polytech U; Comp Info Systm.

CUNANAN, HELAINE; St Joseph HS; Cypress, CA; (2); 20/196; Church Yth Grp; GAA; Hosp Aide; Pep Clb; Spanish Clb; SADD; Drill Tm; Nwsp; High Hon Roll; CSF; Algebra I Awd; UCI; Law.

CUNDIFF, KARINA E; Karina Cundiff HS; Hemet, CA; (2); Church Yth Grp; Drama Clb; Intnl Clb; Key Clb; Service Clb; Spanish Clb; Temple Yth Grp; Thesps; School Play; Stage Crew; Lawyer.

CUNG, XUAN-NGA; Santa Teresa HS; San Jose, CA; (3); SADD; Temple Yth Grp; Varsity Clb; Rep Stu Cncl; Var Tennis; Intrml Vllybl; Hon Roll; St Schlr; Vietamese Clb Treas; U CA Davis; Phrmctcl Chem.

CUNHA, PAUL D; Santa Clara HS; Santa Clara, CA; (1); Church Yth Grp; Cmnty Wkr; Teachers Aide; Rptr Nwsp; Phtg Yrbk; JV Capt Bsbl; Wt Lftg; JV Wrstlng; Lion Awd; Wnnr Chmpnshp Santa Clara Lions; SCU; Grphc Art.

CUNHA, SUZANNE; Petaluma HS; Penngrove, CA; (3); Church Yth Grp; Intnl Clb; Spanish Clb; Var Cheerldng; Hon Roll; Fash Desgn.

CUNNIFFE, CHRISTINE A; Garces Memorial HS; Bakersfield, CA; (3); 29/115; Am Leg Aux Girls St; Hosp Aide; Chorus; Mrchg Band; Orch; Pep Band; High Hon Roll; Hnr Band; Acad Decathln 6th Pl Ec; Mem CSF; Med.

CUNNINGHAM, CODY J; Ramona HS; Ramona, CA; (2); Var Bsktbl; Var Vllybl; Hnrs Gldn St Exm; Bsktbl Tm Rep 32 Schl Slvr St Trnmnt; Top 4% Math CTBS, Top 5% Rdng Natn Wide; Engr.

CUNNINGHAM, JASON S; Norte Vista HS; Riverside, CA; (2); 82/444; FFA; Trk; Hon Roll; Part-Time Job; Law.

CUNNINGHAM, JOHN M; Mission San Jose HS; Fremont, CA; (4); 60/350; Teachers Aide; Hon Roll; Pres Acad Fit Awd; Gail Meyers Schlrshp Spcl Avcht Awd; Bk Am Awd; CA ST-HAYWARD; Accntg.

CUNNINGHAM, ROBERT A; Turlock HS; Turlock, CA; (3); 13/600; Church Yth Grp; NFL; Speech Tm; Teachers Aide; Church Choir; Orch; Ntl Merit Ltr; CA Schlrshp Fed; Interact Clb; Golden St Exam Geom Awd; Ministry.

CUNNINGS, BONNER; Yosemite Union HS; Oakhurst, CA; (3); Church Yth Grp; Drama Clb; School Play; Ftbl; Trk; Wt Lftg; Cit Awd; High Hon Roll; Pres Acad Fit Awd; 2nd Deg Blck Belt Tae Kwondo; 1st ST 4th Ntn JR Olympcs Trpl Jump; Bio.

CUPP, CHRISTOPHER L; Lemoore Union HS; Lemoore, CA; (4); French Clb; JV Var Tennis; Hon Roll; Acadmc Dcthln Team; Humanities Club; Tnns Club; CA ST U Fresno; Archeology.

CUPP, CORBY R; Lemoore Union HS; Lemoore, CA; (2); Cmmrcl Artst.

CURATOLO, MELINA; Grossmont HS; El Cajon, CA; (2); 113/431; SADD; Acadmc Excllnc Awd Gldn St Exam; U Of CA Berkeley; Comp Sci.

CURB, ADINA M; Sonora HS; Brea, CA; (3); Pep Clb; Ski Clb; VP Frsh Cls; Rep Soph Cls; Pres Sr Cls; Capt Cheerldng; Powder Puff Ftbl; Var Socr; Var Tennis; Cit Awd; UCSB; Educ.

CURD, MELANIE; Downey HS; Downey, CA; (2); Church Yth Grp; CA Schlrshp Fed; Bus Mgmt.

CURD, STEVEN; Saugus HS; Santa Clarita, CA; (4); Var L Ftbl; Intrml Wrstlng; Ntl Merit SF; USC; Marketing.

CURI, MIGUEL F; Azusa HS; Azusa, CA; (3); Church Yth Grp; JV Trk; Hon Roll.

CURIEL, ALMA I; Fillmore HS; Fillmore, CA; (4); 3/170; Art Clb; Spanish Clb; Teachers Aide; Cit Awd; Hon Roll; Prfct Atten Awd; Rotary Awd; Bank Of Amer Levy Schlrshp; Jimenez Schlrshp; Tandy Corp Schlrshp; CSU Northridge; Bus Admin.

CURIEL, ARTURO; Napa HS; Napa, CA; (2); Ftbl; Trk; Bus Mgnt.

CURIEL, JULIAN A; Lindsay HS; Lindsay, CA; (2); FFA; Hon Roll.

CURIEL, MARTIN E; Central Union HS; Seeley, CA; (2); Church Yth Grp; French Clb; Rep Soph Cls; JV Bsktbl; JV Crs Cntry; JV Trk; Hon Roll; JETS Awd; Prfct Atten Awd; Val; Auto Dsgnr.

CURIEL, VERONICA F; Bell HS; Huntington Park, CA; (3); Church Yth Grp; Computer Clb; Dance Clb; Drama Clb; Office Aide; Service Clb; Teachers Aide; School Play; Off Soph Cls; Off Jr Cls; Stu Week Plnng Cmmtt; Career Day At Dominguez Hills.

CURIOCA, PATTY; Chula Vista HS; Chula Vista, CA; (1); 77/605; Office Aide; Pep Clb; Teachers Aide; Band; Mrchg Band; Var Crs Cntry; Var Trk; Cit Awd; Pres Acad Fit Awd; Church Yth Grp; Mecha Club Pres; X-Cntry VMP; Sccr Roudies Club; AVID; UCLA; Law.

CURL, HEATHER M; College Park HS; Concord, CA; (3); Girl Scts; SADD; Teachers Aide; Band; Jazz Band; Mrchg Band; Pep Band; Lit Mag; Band Cncl; Stu Of Mnth; UCSB; Law.

CURL, SONYA M; Norco SR HS; Norco, CA; (2); 33/404; Model UN; Pep Clb; Chorus; School Play; Stage Crew; Intrml Bsktbl; Intrml Sftbl; High Hon Roll; Hon Roll; Pres Acad Fit Awd; Bus Mgmt.

CURLESS, JAY R; Eagle Rock HS; Los Angeles, CA; (3); Boy Scts; Stage Crew; Golf; Tennis.

CURLEY, BRANDON K; Antelope Valley HS; Lancaster, CA; (3); 14/631; Church Yth Grp; German Clb; Cit Awd; High Hon Roll; Masonic Awd; Ntl Merit Ltr; Pres Acad Fit Awd; CSF; Biola U; Physics.

CURNOW, DIANE; West Valley Christian Church Schl; Chatsworth, CA; (3); Chess Clb; Speech Tm; Teachers Aide; Church Choir; Hon Roll; Walked 20 Miles For Life.

CURRAN, CHANTELLE V; San Gorgonio HS; Highland, CA; (3); Treas AFS; Church Yth Grp; German Clb; Tennis; Pres Acad Fit Awd; Rptr Yrbk; CSF; Interact/Rotary Clb; Badminton; Nrsg.

CURRAN, JOHN J; Mater Dei HS; Santa Ana, CA; (3); Church Yth Grp; Cmnty Wkr; Debate Tm; Hosp Aide; Spanish Clb; VP Sr Cls; Stu Cncl; Var Socr; JV Trk; High Hon Roll; GOP CA Headquarters Volunteer; Spcl Olympics Volunteer; Stanford; Bus.

CURRIE, CHRISTINE P; Etiwanda HS; Alta Loma, CA; (2); Church Yth Grp; French Clb; Intnl Clb; Marine Bio.

CURRIE, MELANIE M; Del Norte HS; Crescent City, CA; (2); VP Soph Cls; Dntl Asstnt.

CURRIER, KIMBERLY; Walnut HS; Walnut, CA; (2); German Clb; Teachers Aide; Flag Corp; High Hon Roll; Hon Roll; Deans List; Ger Hnr Soc; Mt San Antonio Coll; Elng Prof.

CURRY, CHRIS R; Irving HS; Irvine, CA; (2); Church Yth Grp; JV Bsbl; JV Ftbl; JV Wt Lftg; Hon Roll; Pres Acad Fit Awd; Little Leag, Sr Leag All Stars Ctchr; Photo Jrnlsm.

CURRY JR, CHRIS W; North Valley Christian HS; Redding, CA; (4); 2/10; Church Yth Grp; Nwsp; Yrbk; Treas Stu Cncl; Var JV Bsktbl; High Hon Roll; Hon Roll; Sal; Art; Writing; Photo; CA Polytech ST U; Biomdcl Eng.

CURRY, DWIGHT E; Morningside HS; Inglewood, CA; (2); Var Bsktbl; Var Trk; Cit Awd; Hon Roll; Prfct Atten Awd; UCLA; Prfssnl Sports.

CURRY, JACQUELINE; Sacred Heart Cathedral Prep; San Francisco, CA; (4); 70/200; Letterman Clb; Band; Off Sr Cls; JV Bsktbl; Var Cheerldng; Var Swmmng; Var Tennis; Swmmng MVP; CSU Long Beach; Bio.

CURRY, JUSTIN; Paraclete HS; Lancaster, CA; (3); Key Clb; Letterman Clb; Bsbl; Bsktbl; Hon Roll; Bus.

CURRY, KIMBERLY D; Argonaut HS; Ione, CA; (2); AFS; Church Yth Grp; FBLA; Spanish Clb; JV Cheerldng; High Hon Roll; U Of CA; Genetics.

CURRY, MICHELE A; Brea Olinda HS; Placentia, CA; (2); GAA; Band; Pep Band; Ed Lit Mag; Stat Swmmng; High Hon Roll; Hon Roll; Gntc Engr.

CURRY, MICHELLE; La Sierra HS; Riverside, CA; (3); Math Clb; SADD; Band; Mrchg Band; JV Capt Sftbl; High Hon Roll; Hon Roll; CA Schlrshp Fed; John Phillip Sousa Hnr Band; Band Cncl.

CURRY JR, RICHARD; La Sierra HS; Riverside, CA; (1); Var Socr; Var Trk; High Hon Roll; CA Schlrshp Fed; Clb Sccr.

CURTEANU, CARMEN S; Bolsa Grande HS; Garden Grove, CA; (3); 40/54; Church Yth Grp; Drama Clb; German Clb; Church Choir; Orch; School Play; Hon Roll; CSF 2 Yrs; Goldenwest; Retail Clthng Merch.

CURTIN, TRACY; Ramona HS; Riverside, CA; (3); 68/403; French Clb; Letterman Clb; Pep Clb; Teachers Aide; Co-Ed Nwsp; Stu Cncl; Var Cheerldng; French Hon Soc; Intl Comm.

CURTIS, BRANDON L; Foothill SR HS; Sacramento, CA; (1); Chess Clb; Science Clb; Hon Roll; Sci Olympiad; Astronaut.

CURTIS, CORIE; Banning HS; Banning, CA; (3); Computer Clb; Dance Clb; Drama Clb; Pep Clb; Speech Tm; VICA; Cheerldng; Pom Pon; Powder Puff Ftbl; Cit Awd; Stu Of Mnth; Tac Grl; Howard U; Chld Dev.

CURTIS, DUSTIN R; San Clemente HS; San Juan Capistra, CA; (2); Church Yth Grp; Cmnty Wkr; Spanish Clb; Teachers Aide; JV Socr; JV Capt Vllybl; Hon Roll; MVP Vlly Bl Frshmn & JV Tms; UCSB; Bus.

CURTIS, JASON DANIEL; St Augustine HS; San Diego, CA; (4); Boy Scts; Church Yth Grp; School Play; Rptr Nwsp; Pres Sr Cls; Var L Ftbl; Var L Tennis; Var L Vllybl; Elks Awd; Santa Clara U; Poltcl Sci.

CURTIS, JOHN; Palm Springs Christian HS; Desert Hot Sprgs, CA; (3); Varsity Clb; Church Choir; School Play; Variety Show; VP Stu Cncl; Var Bsbl; Var Bsktbl; Var Ftbl; Var Trk; Wt Lftg; UCLA; Sci.

CURTIS, LINDA; Mt Carmel HS; San Diego, CA; (3); Church Yth Grp; French Clb; German Clb; Nwsp; Sec Stu Cncl; Sftbl; Jr NHS; San Luis Obispo; Intl Rel.

CURTIS, MICHELE M; Pioneer HS; Whittier, CA; (4); #49 In Class; Office Aide; Ski Clb; Teachers Aide; Drill Tm; Stage Crew; Photo; Teacher.

CURTIS, MONIQUE R; Ramona HS; Ramona, CA; (2); GAA; Letterman Clb; Off Frsh Cls; VP Soph Cls; Pres Jr Cls; Var Socr; Var Trk; JV Vllybl; Art.

CURTIS, NICOLE L; Ramona HS; Ramona, CA; (2); Church Yth Grp; GAA; Varsity Clb; Treas Jr Cls; Var Socr; Var Trk; JV Vllybl; Pres Acad Fit Awd; Bus.

CURTIS, RHEA V; Novato HS; Novato, CA; (2); School Play; Stage Crew; Elem Tchr.

CURTNER, DINA L; Modesto HS; Modesto, CA; (2); Cmnty Wkr; SADD; Teachers Aide; Color Guard; Gym; Swmmng; Psych.

CURTO, TOBY; Newport Christian HS; Irvine, CA; (1); 2/20; Church Yth Grp; School Play; Rptr Yrbk; Rep Frsh Cls; Var Bsktbl; Var Vllybl; High Hon Roll; Stanford; Law.

CURTONI, ANN M; Central Catholic HS; Oakdale, CA; (3); Rep Church Yth Grp; GAA; Ski Clb; Varsity Clb; Capt Var Bsktbl; JV Powder Puff Ftbl; JV Sftbl; VP Var Trk; Var Capt Vllybl; Hon Roll; Bsktbl Prncss, MVP 89-90; Art.

CURZ, JOSE R; Mater Dei HS; Santa Ana, CA; (3); Church Yth Grp; Cmnty Wkr; ROTC; SADD; Off Frsh Cls; Stu Cncl; Ftbl; Hon Roll; NHS; USC; Bus.

CUSACK, LISA M; Mission Viejo HS; Mission Viejo, CA; (1); 93/360; Orch; School Musical.

CUSEY, ERIN; Mother Lode Christian HS; Sonora, CA; (2); 2/20; Church Yth Grp; Chorus; Pres Frsh Cls; Stu Cncl; JV Sftbl; JV Vllybl; Hon Roll; Frshmn Hmcmng Prncss; Ldrshp Team With Chrch.

CUSEY, JOHN; Mother Lode Christian Schl; Sonora, CA; (4); 2/20; Am Leg Boys St; Church Yth Grp; Band; Drm Mjr(t); Pres Jr Cls; Pres Stu Cncl; Var L Bsbl; Var L Bsktbl; Var Capt Socr; Hon Roll; Pol Sci.

CUSHMAN, BONNY; Tomales HS; Pt Reyes Station, CA; (3); Church Yth Grp; Drama Clb; Ski Clb; Spanish Clb; SADD; School Play; Trk; High Hon Roll; Hon Roll; St Schlr; Art Awd; Coaches Awd; Engl & Hstr Awds; Yale; Med.

CUSHMAN, CARRIE A; San Andreas HS; San Bernardino, CA; (3); Letterman Clb; Sec Jr Cls; Sec Stu Cncl; Vllybl; High Hon Roll; Hon Roll; Century Club; Yth To Yth Cert; Psych.

CUSHMAN, JOSH; Palo Verde HS; Blythe, CA; (3); Teachers Aide; Band; Jazz Band; Mrchg Band; Orch; Pep Band; Hon Roll; John Phillip Sousa Awd; NAU; Vet.

CUSHMAN, LEAH C; Berkeley HS; Oakland, CA; (3); Temple Yth Grp; Stage Crew; Yrbk; Hon Roll; Ntl Merit Ltr; St Schlr; Study Abroad 89 Israel, 90 Oxford; Camp Jr Cnslr; CA Coll Of Arts & Crafts Smmr Stu; Design.

CUSHMAN, TRACIE; Hughson Union HS; Hughson, CA; (4); Pres Church Yth Grp; 4-H; GAA; Sec Intnl Clb; Var Pep Clb; Var Scholastic Bowl; Speech Tm; SADD; Varsity Clb; School Play; Acad Decathlon; Fri Night Live Clb; Modesto JC; Accntng.

CUSTER, JENNIFER; St Joseph HS; Long Beach, CA; (2); Church Yth Grp; Dance Clb; GAA; Ski Clb; Drill Tm; Pres Frsh Cls; Var Cheerldng; Hon Roll; YMCA Yth & Govt Senator; Nathin Cummings Yth Ambssdr Awd; UC Berkeley; Law.

CUSUMANO, CHRISTY A; Clovis West HS; Fresno, CA; (3); FCA; 4-H; Scholastic Bowl; Spanish Clb; Church Choir; Stage Crew; JV Swmmng; Hon Roll; Fresno ST U; Bus Mgmt.

CUTHILL, ANGELA M; Bret Harte HS; Arnold, CA; (2); Church Yth Grp; Drama Clb; Service Clb; School Musical; School Play; Rptr Nwsp; Friday Night Live Officer; Bible Quizzing; Mission Trip; Point Loma Nazarene Coll; Actng.

CUTLER, AMY R; Clayton Valley HS; Walnut Creek, CA; (3); 1/445; Cmnty Wkr; SADD; Temple Yth Grp; Chorus; Orch; Stat Bsktbl; High Hon Roll; CSF; Outstndng Musician; Music Prfmnc.

CUTLER, REBECCA A; Hoover HS; Fresno, CA; (3); 1/500; Church Yth Grp; Spanish Clb; Varsity Clb; Bsktbl; Crs Cntry; Socr; Sftbl; Trk; High Hon Roll; Pres Acad Fit Awd; Jr Achvr; Patriot Awd; CSF.

CUTRIGHT, DAVID; Trabuco Hills HS; Yucca Valley, CA; (1); 70/350; Hon Roll; Bl Rbbn Yth Expo Art Shw Orange Cnty; SR Mjr Bsbl; Rdng Mtrcycls; Archtctr.

CUTTING, JONATHAN E; San Ramon Valley HS; Danville, CA; (1); Boy Scts; Church Yth Grp; Crs Cntry; Trk; High Hon Roll; Acad Decathlon Tm 90-91; Outstndng Frshmn Sci Stu Awd.

CUTTON, TRACIE B; Victor Valley SR HS; Victorville, CA; (2); Church Yth Grp; Christanity; Oral Roberts U; Sci.

CUVIELLO, DAWN E; James Lick HS; San Jose, CA; (2); San Jose ST; Vet.

CUVIELLO, JANETTE E; James Lick HS; San Jose, CA; (2); Cmnty Wkr; Pep Clb; JV Capt Cheerldng; Stat Swmmng; Hon Roll; Leadership Club; UCLA; Dramatic Arts.

CUYLER, CORINNE; Miraleste HS; Rolling Hills Est, CA; (3); Church Yth Grp; Cmnty Wkr; Dance Clb; Pres Key Clb; Pep Clb; Service Clb; SADD; Varsity Clb; Variety Show; Var Capt Cheerldng; Miss Teen Magzn Smi-Fnlst Spr Model Srch; PA Profssnl Schl Of Ballet; Joffrey Profssnl Schl Of Ballet; NY U; Dance.

CYPHER, JENNIFER A; William Workman HS; Valinda, CA; (2); Drama Clb; Intnl Clb; Cal Poly Pomona; Psych.

CYPRESS, ALICIA F; Irvine HS; Irvine, CA; (2); 100/552; Key Clb; Temple Yth Grp; Rptr Nwsp; Lit Mag; High Hon Roll; Hon Roll; CSF; EAF; Jrnlsm.

CZERWINSKI, HEATHER A; Pasadena HS; Sierra Madre, CA; (2); Church Yth Grp; Var Crs Cntry; Var Trk; Psychology.

CZOSEK, VIRGINIA C; Presentation HS; San Jose, CA; (4); 3/134; Church Yth Grp; Cmnty Wkr; Drama Clb; Math Clb; Service Clb; Spanish Clb; SADD; High Hon Roll; NHS; Ntl Merit SF; Libl Arts Plaq; CSF; Sci Plaq; Math Cert; Outstndng Acadmc Achvt Awd GPA; Natl Merit Finlst; Santa Clara U; Hstry.

D ABLAING, LAURIE M; Chula Vista HS; Chula Vista, CA; (3); Drama Clb; Color Guard; School Play; Yrbk; Prfct Atten Awd; SPEAK Stu Peace Eqlty Anml Rghts & Knwldg; Fine Arts.

D AMELIO, KRISTI; Charter Oak HS; Covina, CA; (3); Church Yth Grp; Stage Crew; Rptr Nwsp; Var Capt Pom Pon; Trk; High Hon Roll; Hon Roll; NHS; Pres Acad Fit Awd; Accntng.

D ANDREA, JENNIFER L; Irvine HS; Irvine, CA; (2); Church Yth Grp; GAA; Hosp Aide; Sec Ski Clb; Rep Stu Cncl; JV Capt Tennis; Hon Roll; Pres Acad Fit Awd; Law.

D ANELLA, CARMELLA; Cornelia Connelly HS; Anaheim, CA; (2); Drama Clb; Speech Tm; School Play; Trk; Hon Roll; Bst Actrss Awd Frsh Soph Cls Plys; Hnrs Entrnc Exam Mater Dei HS; UC Berkley; Psych.

D ANGELO, JASON MARK; Poway HS; Poway, CA; (4); 7/714; Kiwanis Awd; NHS; Engl.

D ANGELO, MICHELLE S; Poway HS; Poway, CA; (2); VP Drama Clb; VP Thesps; Chorus; School Musical; School Play; Stage Crew; Swing Chorus; High Hon Roll; Safe Rides; Friday Nght Live; Prfrmng Arts.

D ANIELLO, EMILY S; Pinole Valley HS; Pinole, CA; (2); Debate Tm; Ski Clb; Phtg Yrbk; Off Soph Cls; Sec Jr Cls; JV Capt Bsktbl; Var Diving; JV Var Swmmng; JV Var Vllybl; Hon Roll; CIF Schlr Athl; Marine Bio.

D ANNA, ALEXANDER M; Bellarmine College Prep; San Jose, CA; (3); 5/289; Cmnty Wkr; Letterman Clb; Varsity Clb; Var L Bsktbl; High Hon Roll; Hon Roll; Intrml Ftbl; Intrml Sftbl; Intrml Vllybl; Vrsty Bsktbl Coachs Awd; Princpls Lttr; Boston Coll Bk Awd; Law.

D ARCY, PATRICK D; Bellarmine College Prep; San Jose, CA; (3); 100/300; Aud/Vis; SADD; Paintball Tm Capt; CAP; Airline Pilot.

D AURIA II, JOHN C; North Monterey County HS; Salinas, CA; (2); 3/360; Church Yth Grp; French Clb; Ski Clb; SADD; Jazz Band; Off Soph Cls; Ftbl; Trk; Wt Lftg; Cit Awd; Publshd Poems Poetry Anthlgy Of Amer; Hnrs Awd Hlth, Frnch, Engl & Wrld Cultres; USAF Acad; Pilot.

D AURORA, STEVEN L; Woodland HS; Woodland, CA; (3); Band; Jazz Band; Mrchg Band; Pep Band; Var Trk; Comp Sci.

D ORNELLAS, LISA M; Moorpark HS; Moorpark, CA; (3); FBLA; Co-Capt Color Guard.

DA COSTA, KIMBERLY; Don Antonio Lugo HS; Chino, CA; (1); Church Yth Grp; Cmnty Wkr; Drama Clb; Stage Crew; High Hon Roll; Stu Wk Awd; CSF.

DA MOUDE, JEFFREY H; San Pasqual HS; Escondido, CA; (2); Church Yth Grp; FFA; JV Intrml Bsbl; Intrml Socr; Hon Roll.

DA PRA, STEPHANIE L; St Joseph HS; Bellflower, CA; (2); Debate Tm; JV Bsktbl; Hon Roll; Med.

DA ROSA, MARLINE E; Watsonville HS; Watsonville, CA; (2); #72 In Class; Church Yth Grp; Library Aide; Math Tm; Office Aide; Pep Clb; Church Choir; Hon Roll; Prfct Atten Awd; Sec Frsh Cls; CSF; Jnr CSF; UC Santa Barbara; Bio.

DAAMEN, JENNIFER; Valley Christian HS; Byron, CA; (4); 3/26; Church Yth Grp; Sec Frsh Cls; Treas Soph Cls; Pres Sr Cls; Cheerldng; High Hon Roll; NHS; Rotary Awd; Stu Pilot; Swm Tm; Embry Riddle Aeronautical U.

DABKOSKA, WANDA; Lowell HS; San Francisco, CA; (2); Cmnty Wkr; JV Trk; Hon Roll; Ntl Merit Ltr; Blk Stu Union; Japanese Clb.

DABLO, CHERYL; Loma Linda Acad; San Bernardino, CA; (4); Rptr Yrbk; Sec Soph Cls; Off Jr Cls; VP Sr Cls; NHS; Pres Acad Fit Awd; Pres Schlr; Cmnty Wkr; Drama Clb; Floor Hockey Team-Capt; Bank Of Am Achvt Awd; Loma Linda U Riverside; Engl.

DABNEY, LUCAS E; Sunny Hills HS; La Mirada, CA; (2); Bus Profs of Am; Church Yth Grp; French Clb; FBLA; Quiz Bowl; Band; Jazz Band; Mrchg Band; Pep Band; Stage Crew; JC Cptn Water Polo; Annapolis; Sci.

DABNEY, MELISSA A; Turlock HS; Turlock, CA; (3); Church Yth Grp; Cmnty Wkr; Hosp Aide; Rep Soph Cls; Crs Cntry; Trk; Hon Roll; Bus.

DACHTLER, AMIE C; Oak Ridge HS; El Dorado Hills, CA; (1); 1/300; Girl Scts; Red Cross Aide; SADD; Var Swmmng; Stat Tennis; High Hon Roll; Stu Awd; CA Schlrshp Fdrtn; Stu In Engl, Geom & Comp Applctn; Aero Engrng.

DACIO III, JOSE C; De La Salle HS; Vallejo, CA; (4); 27/208; Church Yth Grp; Drama Clb; Hosp Aide; Orch; School Musical; Ed Yrbk; Rep Soph Cls; JV Crs Cntry; Var Trk; Hon Roll; Campus Mnstry; Cal Poly; Aero Engnrng.

DACZKOWSKI, LISA; Rosary HS; Fullerton, CA; (2); Debate Tm; French Clb; Variety Show; Var L Socr; JV Vllybl; High Hon Roll; Jr NHS; Prfrmng Arts Grp-Pvt Dnc Studio-Inclding Cmptns.

DADABHOY, FARHANA; Culver City HS; Culver, CA; (4); Off Frsh Cls; Off Soph Cls; Off Jr Cls; Off Sr Cls; Mgr(s); Hon Roll; Dept Of Sci Stu Of Month Awd; Syracuse U; Educ.

DADDORIO, DOMINIQUE A; Orange Glen HS; Valley Center, CA; (4); Teachers Aide; Powder Puff Ftbl; Swmmng; UCLA; Psycht.

DAETWILER, JAROD J; Rim Of The World HS; Cedar Glen, CA; (3); 54/2100; Art Clb; Socr; Cit Awd; Hon Roll; Prfct Atten Awd; Arrowhead Arts Assn; Commercial Art.

DAFTARY, NIKHIL; St Marys HS; Stockton, CA; (2); Boy Scts; Church Yth Grp; Debate Tm; Model UN; Var Crs Cntry; High Hon Roll; Pres Acad Fit Awd; Intl Bus.

DAGARAG, MIRASOL; Cypress HS; Cypress, CA; (3); Church Yth Grp; Intnl Clb; Science Clb; Teachers Aide; Chorus; Stage Crew; Hon Roll; Interact Clb; Yng Schlr Prm; CSF; Cert Awd Phys Educ & Choir; Tutor Vlntr; Organ Rectl 87 & 88; CSULB; Nurse.

DAGDAGAN, EDGARDO; SCPA HS; San Diego, CA; (2); 76/151; Band; Orch; Hon Roll; Prfct Atten Awd; Dist In Instr Music; Elec.

DAGERT, CHANTELLE D; Los Alamitos HS; Los Alamitos, CA; (3); Cmnty Wkr; French Clb; Chorus; Peace Child; Assisteens; Intl Relations.

DAGHLARIAN, NATALIE; Holy Martyrs Ferrahian HS; Granada Hills, CA; (4); Art Clb; Cmnty Wkr; Quiz Bowl; Teachers Aide; Chorus; Church Choir; Pres Sr Cls; Rep Stu Cncl; JV Bsktbl; Woodbury U; Arch.

DAGNINO, ALIX; Palo Verde HS; Blythe, CA; (2); JV Bsbl; JV Cheerldng; High Hon Roll; Hon Roll; NHS; Child Psych.

DAGSAAN, CINDY L; Carson HS; Carson, CA; (2); Church Yth Grp; Dance Clb; Service Clb; Color Guard; Drill Tm; Orch; Off Frsh Cls; Stu Cncl; Swmmng; Cit Awd; Miss Teen BASCA 90 Wnnr; Filipino Folkdance Grp; UCLA; Doctor.

DAGUMAN, BRAINARD R; Edison HS; Stockton, CA; (3); Boy Scts; Science Clb; Teachers Aide; Band; Yrbk; Vllybl; Wt Lftg; Hon Roll; Spansh Hnr Cert; Elec Engrng.

DAHAN, OMRI; Redwood HS; Larkspur, CA; (3); SADD; Varsity Clb; Stu Cncl; Capt L Golf; Cit Awd; High Hon Roll; Hon Roll; Cmnty Wkr; Service Clb; Teachers Aide; Mt Tamalpais Bus Ldrshp Awd; Peer Cnslng Prgm Ldr; Br Stu & Faciliatator Redwood Impact.

DAHDUL, WASILA A; Richard Gahr HS; Cerritos, CA; (2); Hon Roll; Bio.

DAHL, DANIELLE E; Canyon HS; Santa Clarita, CA; (4); 33/520; FBLA; Teachers Aide; Cit Awd; Pres Acad Fit Awd; Rotary Awd; CA Schlrshp Fdr; UCLA; Frgn Lang.

DAHL, RYAN C; Sacramento HS; Sacramento, CA; (2); 104/500; Church Yth Grp; Ski Clb; Teachers Aide; Var Crs Cntry; Var Trk; Phys Ther.

DAHL, VANESSA E; Downey HS; Modesto, CA; (2); Cmnty Wkr; 4-H; Girl Scts; Orch; Variety Show; Cal-Western Applsa High Pt Awd; Cechetti Cncl Grade II Bllt Awd; CIT GS Cncl; UC Davis; Vet Med.

DAHLBERG, JOHN D; Mission Viejo HS; Mission Viejo, CA; (4); Office Aide; L Var Ftbl; Trk; Cit Awd; Kiwanis Awd; Gold & Silver Medals Sweepstaks OC Fair 89; U Redlands; Bus.

DAHLEN, JENNIFER M; Valley HS; Santa Ana, CA; (3); Am Leg Aux Girls St; Church Yth Grp; Cmnty Wkr; Variety Show; Ed Yrbk; Score Keeper; Swmmng; Hon Roll; Swmmng Mst Miles Awd 2 Yrs; Girls St Alt; Bus Admin.

DAHLGREN, KRISTEN LAINE; Arcadia HS; Arcadia, CA; (3); 215/639; Church Yth Grp; Girl Scts; Teachers Aide; JV L Swmmng; Hon Roll; Pres Acad Fit Awd; Camping,Hiking,Snowskiing,Waterskiing,Swimming,Rock Climbing; Stu Ldrshp Team; Trips Mexico Spread Chr; Pt Loma Nazarene Coll; Bus Mgmt.

DAHLIN, ERIN A; Vista HS; Vista, CA; (3); 22/422; Church Yth Grp; Treas Key Clb; Ski Clb; Flag Corp; Variety Show; Rep Frsh Cls; Rep Soph Cls; Hon Roll; Cmmnctns.

DAHLKE, CHAD R; Dana Hills HS; Laguna Niguel, CA; (1); Intrml Bsbl; Intrml Ftbl; Intrml Wt Lftg; Hon Roll; Pres Acad Fit Awd; U Of CA Irvine; Antmy/Physlgy.

DAHLQUIST, RUTH M; Kingsburg HS; Kingsburg, CA; (1); Church Yth Grp; Math Clb; Math Tm; Mu Alpha Theta; Band; Jazz Band; Mrchg Band; Pep Band; High Hon Roll; Rotary Awd; Fresno-Madera Cnty Hnr Band; Fresno St U Solo Music Fest Excllnt Ratng Piano; Sci.

DAHMAN, JONATHAN; San Joaquin Memorial HS; Madera, CA; (2); Church Yth Grp; Hon Roll; Bsbl; Markmnshp; US Naval Acad Annapolis; Engr.

DAHOMA, PALMINA; St Genevieve HS; Sylmar, CA; (2); English Stud Awd.

DAIGLE, JAMES M; Foothill HS; Bakersfield, CA; (1); High Hon Roll; Prfct Atten Awd.

DAIGLE, TAMI JAINE; Montclair HS; Chino, CA; (4); 119/400; Ed Yrbk; Stu Cncl; Capt Var Cheerldng; Prom Crt; Sweethearts Crt; Creative & Spirit Awds In Yrbk; Law.

DAIL, JENNY; Concord HS; Concord, CA; (1); Church Yth Grp; Ski Clb; SADD; JV Cheerldng; JV Pom Pon; Hon Roll; Sci & Math.

DAIL, SUNDERPAL S; Selma HS; Selma, CA; (4); 8/192; Intnl Clb; Cit Awd; High Hon Roll; Prfct Atten Awd; CSF; Gldn St Exam Alg Hnrs; Bnk Amer Awd For Achvt In Applied Arts; CSU Fresno; Pre Med.

DAILEY, CATHERINE A; Monterey HS; Monterey, CA; (1); Girl Scts; Thesps; Flag Corp; JV Fld Hcky; JV Trk; High Hon Roll; Physician.

DAILEY, SEAN M; Cloverdale HS; Cloverdale, CA; (2); 1/67; Letterman Clb; Pres Frsh Cls; Rep Soph Cls; JV Bsbl; JV Bsktbl; JV Ftbl; Stanford U; Political Science.

DAILLAK, STEVE J; Morro Bay HS; Morro Bay, CA; (3); Var Trk; Hon Roll; Peer Cnslng; Cnslng.

DAILO, JENNIFER; St Joseph HS; La Mirada, CA; (2); GAA; Hosp Aide; Variety Show; Rptr Yrbk; JV Cheerldng; Hon Roll; Pres Acad Fit Awd; UC Berkeley; Med Sci.

DAILY, TAMMIE C; Argonaut HS; Ione, CA; (2); GAA; Varsity Clb; Capt Drill Tm; Capt Flag Corp; Sftbl; High Hon Roll; Masonic Awd; Letterman Clb; Spanish Clb; Bsktbl; Peer Cnslr; Crisis Htln; Job Dghtrs; Fmly Lwyr.

DAINES, SHERRI R; Richmond HS; San Pablo, CA; (1); Band; Jazz Band; Mrchg Band; Writer.

DAIRE, JASIRI S; Bishop Amat HS; Compton, CA; (3); Letterman Clb; School Play; Bsktbl; Trk; Hon Roll; Cal ST Northridge.

DAKIS, GEORGETTE D; Notre Dame HS; San Mateo, CA; (2); Church Yth Grp; Cmnty Wkr; Dance Clb; Debate Tm; Teachers Aide; School Play; Rptr Nwsp; Pres Frsh Cls; Hon Roll; NEDT Awd; CSF; Yth Cptn Walk-A-Thon Hnr; Tutr Samartn House; AHEPA Mdl Schlstc Excllnce; Swmmng Instr; 2 Cert Spr; Med.

DAKIS, PAMFILIA; Lowell HS; San Francisco, CA; (2); Church Yth Grp; French Clb; SADD; Church Choir; Cit Awd; Hon Roll; Hellenic Club; Greek Dancing Group; Church Sr Girls Bsktbl Team; UC Berkeley.

DAL PONTE, DENISE B; Immaculate Heart HS; Los Angeles, CA; (3); GAA; Hist Frsh Cls; Stu Cncl; Var JV Bsktbl; Var Crs Cntry; Var Sftbl; Hon Roll; MVP Bsktbl; Hstry Awd 90; Phy Ther.

DAL PORTO, ALBERT B; Linden HS; Linden, CA; (4); FFA; Letterman Clb; SADD; Teachers Aide; Varsity Clb; Pres Jr Cls; JV Var Bsbl; Capt Var Bsktbl; JV Ftbl; Hon Roll; Bk Of Amer Excllnce Ag Awd; Dekalb-Pfitzer Outstndng Sr Awd; CA Poly; Crop Sci.

DALAL, ANJANA D; Stephen W Kearney HS; San Diego, CA; (2); 1/378; Dance Clb; Debate Tm; Intnl Clb; Office Aide; Quiz Bowl; Spanish Clb; Speech Tm; Teachers Aide; Temple Yth Grp; School Musical; Gldn St Exam Hnrs Awd; Acad Leag; Indian Yth Assn; Syracuse U; Brdcst Jrnlsm.

DALAL, MARK F; Canyon HS; Canyon Country, CA; (4); French Clb; Teachers Aide; Var Tennis; High Hon Roll; NHS; Pres Acad Fit Awd; Pres Schlr; Rtry Clb; Loyola Marymount U; Biochem.

DALE, KERRY L; California HS; San Ramon, CA; (3); Cmnty Wkr; Teachers Aide; Varsity Clb; Var Crs Cntry; Var Trk; Hon Roll; Stu Of Mnth.

DALE, SUZANNE M; Ocean View HS; Westminster, CA; (1); Church Yth Grp; Model UN; Score Keeper; Stat Swmmng; Var L Tennis; Hon Roll; Orange Cnty Tnns Assn Lawrence Cup Tm; Anthropologist.

DALESSANDRO, JOANNA L; Chula Vista HS; San Diego, CA; (3); 100/535; Intnl Clb; Pep Clb; Stu Cncl; Var Diving; Var Swmmng; Rotary Awd; ASB Co-Cmssnr Finance & Pep; UN Las Vegas; Acctng.

DALEY, JACQUELYN JOAN; El Dorado HS; Placerville, CA; (3); 4/365; Am Leg Aux Girls St; Cmnty Wkr; Pres 4-H; Sec Service Clb; Rep Stu Cncl; JV Crs Cntry; Var L Trk; 4-H Awd; High Hon Roll; NHS; CSF Scrtry & Treas; Stanford U; Pre-Med.

DALEY, LIZABETH T; San Clemente HS; San Clemente, CA; (4); Church Yth Grp; 4-H; Office Aide; Acpl Chr; JV Var Socr; JV Trk; PS I Care Clb; Loud Crowd Clb; SOS Clb; MI ST U; Art.

DALI, JONATHAN P; Kern Valley HS; Lake Isabella, CA; (1); Boy Scts; Church Yth Grp; Spanish Clb; BYU; Animal Sci.

DALIDA, ALEX; Redwood HS; Visalia, CA; (3); 28/290; FBLA; German Clb; Key Clb; Math Clb; Math Tm; Var Tennis; High Hon Roll; Prfct Atten Awd; Bus Admin.

DALISAY, IVAN; Bishop Amat HS; Diamond Bar, CA; (4); 40/400; Band; Mrchg Band; Pep Band; Hon Roll; Altar Boys; CSF Schlrshp Fed; 2nd Hnrs Fine Arts & Indstrl Arts; Engrng.

DALITZ, MICHELE R; North Salinas HS; Salinas, CA; (3); Church Yth Grp; Drama Clb; Chorus; School Play; Yrbk; Rep Stu Cncl; Cheerldng; Swmmng; Vllybl; High Hon Roll; Gldn St Exam Algebra Natl Rcgntn; Gldn St Exam Geo Hnrs; U Of CO; Med.

DALIVA, LELIA B; Edison HS; Stockton, CA; (3); Office Aide; Treas Jr Cls; Treas Sr Cls; Rep Stu Cncl; JV Trk; French Hon Soc; Hon Roll; Hnrs & Natl Hnrs Fr Cont; Hnrs Golden St Exam Algebra; Ldrshp; Bus.

DALLAS, DEANN C; Mission Viejo HS; Laguna Hills, CA; (1); Drama Clb; Thesps; Trk; Vllybl; Fashion Mrchndsng.

DALLAS, ERIC G; Redwood HS; Larkspur, CA; (3); Church Yth Grp; Cmnty Wkr; Intnl Clb; Pres Letterman Clb; L Capt Tennis; Hon Roll; NHS; Vol Wrk San Fran Earthquake; Asian Stu Assn; Cornell; Hotel/Rest Mgt.

DALLEN, THOMAS D; West Torrance HS; Torrance, CA; (3); Church Yth Grp; Cmnty Wkr; JA; Letterman Clb; Office Aide; SADD; Varsity Clb; Chorus; School Musical; Rptr Nwsp; Athl Awds Ftbl All Leag, All Area, Bsbl All Leag, Tm Amer; Bus.

DALLING, ANTONIETTE D; Apple Valley HS; Apple Valley, CA; (1); GAA; Spanish Clb; Sftbl; Vllybl; Hon Roll; USC.

DALLOSTA, ANGELA M; Indio HS; Indio, CA; (2); Law.

DALONZO, CHRISTINE; Lincoln HS; Stockton, CA; (3); Cmnty Wkr; Hosp Aide; SADD; Var JV Swmmng; High Hon Roll; Hon Roll; Pres Acad Fit Awd; All-Amer Swmmng 8th Pl Jr Natl Mt; Yr Rnd Swmmng; Psych.

DALSIMER, GAYLEEN P; Rim Of The World HS; Crestline, CA; (4); Church Yth Grp; Drama Clb; Color Guard; Hon Roll; Ruthless Trths; Chrsnt Bible Study; Stu Venture, Chrstn Grp.

DALTON, ASHLEY G; Grace M Davis HS; Modesto, CA; (3); Amer Assn Of U Women; Dentistry.

DALTON, JENNIFER A; Glendale HS; Glendale, CA; (2); Church Yth Grp; Chorus; Church Choir; Off Jr Cls; Capt Bsktbl; Var Sftbl; Var Vllybl.

DALTON, JEREMIAH A; Gateway Community Schl; Oxnard, CA; (4); Aud/Vis; Cmnty Wkr; Office Aide; Yrbk; Hon Roll.

DALTON, MANDY; Granada Hills HS; Northridge, CA; (3); 1/800; Pres Church Yth Grp; Pres Debate Tm; Pres Soph Cls; Pres Jr Cls; Sec Stu Cncl; Var Cheerldng; Kiwanis Awd; Ntl Merit Ltr; Pres Acad Fit Awd; Val; Brigham Young U.

DALTON, PAUL G; Santa Clara HS; Port Hueneme, CA; (3); Church Yth Grp; Letterman Clb; Office Aide; Off Frsh Cls; Var Golf; High Hon Roll; Hon Roll; MVP Vrsty Golf; Pepperdine; Bus Admin.

DALTON, ZACK J; Piedmont HS; Piedmont, CA; (2); Aud/Vis; English Clb; JA; Spanish Clb; Varsity Clb; Yrbk; JV Var Bsbl; JV Bsktbl; Hon Roll; Bus.

DALURAYA, ROBERT A; Irvine HS; Irvine, CA; (2); French Clb; Ftbl; Hon Roll.

DALVA, SHAYNE; Concord HS; Pacific Palisades, CA; (1); Drama Clb; Speech Tm; Temple Yth Grp; Thesps; Chorus; School Play; Eng Lit; History; Creative Wrtng; Drama; UCLA; Engl.

DALY, ALAN B; Irvington HS; Fremont, CA; (3); Crmnlgy.

DALY, KEVIN A; Valhalla HS; El Cajon, CA; (1); Cmnty Wkr; Key Clb; Letterman Clb; Band; Jazz Band; Mrchg Band; Intrml Bsktbl; JV Ftbl; Intrml Cmnty Wkr; Hon Roll; UC Berkeley; Pre Med.

DALY, KRESTA N; Analy HS; Sebastopol, CA; (3); 20/236; Debate Tm; Spanish Clb; Speech Tm; SADD; Nwsp; Lit Mag; Rep Stu Cncl; USSR Trip Schlrshp; Acadmc Ltr; Best Debator Awd Jr Statemen Of Amer; Pltcl Sci.

DALY, NATASHA; Huntington Beach HS; Huntington Beach, CA; (3); Drill Tm; Var Score Keeper; Stat Vllybl; Hon Roll; Part Time Job; Psych.

DAM, KRISTINA; Rim Of The World HS; Blue Jay, CA; (2); 18/352; Letterman Clb; Spanish Clb; Off Soph Cls; Stat Bsktbl; Crs Cntry; Trk; Prfct Atten Awd; Acad Lttr; Lake Arrowhead Arts Auxilliary; UCLA; Med.

DAM, LOAN K; Luther Burbank SR HS; Sacramento, CA; (2); 22/509; French Clb; Cit Awd; Hon Roll; U CA; Comp Sci Engr.

DAM, THANG T; Diamond Bar HS; Diamond Bar, CA; (3); 120/500; Debate Tm; Hosp Aide; Intnl Clb; Library Aide; Treas Spanish Clb; SADD; Phtg Nwsp; Intrml Swmmng; Intrml Tennis; Cit Awd; USC; Pre Med.

DAM, THAO P; George Washington HS; San Francisco, CA; (1); Hon Roll; Nrsng.

DAM, TIEN; Diamond Bar HS; Diamond Bar, CA; (4); 20/455; VP Sec French Clb; Hosp Aide; Intnl Clb; Science Clb; Nwsp; Pres Jr Cls; Stu Cncl; Var Tennis; Hon Roll; Pres Acad Fit Awd; UC Riverside; Biomed Sci.

DAMAS, SHERRY L; Hilmar Unified HS; Hilmar, CA; (4); FFA; SADD; Sec Frsh Cls; Sec Soph Cls; JV Sftbl; Vllybl; Girls Bloch Clb; Spirit Clb; Bus.

DAMASEN, DEANNA; Hogan HS; Vallejo, CA; (2); Cmnty Wkr; Spanish Clb; SADD; Drill Tm; Cheerldng; Var Tennis; Uc Davis; Med.

DAMATO, VALERIE A; Calvary Chapel HS; Santa Ana, CA; (4); Church Yth Grp; Office Aide; Teachers Aide; Church Choir; Vllybl; Hmcmng Prncss; MVP; Yth Cncl Exec Chrch Yth Grp; Rancho Santiago Coll; Intr Dsgn.

DAMIAN, LETICIA; Indio HS; Indio, CA; (2); French Clb; Band; Church Choir; Mrchg Band; Hon Roll; Real Estate.

DAMM, CHRISTOPHER R; Coast Union HS; Cambria, CA; (3); AFS; Cmnty Wkr; 4-H; French Clb; Science Clb; JV Bsktbl; Var L Tennis; 4-H Awd; Hon Roll; Pres Acad Fit Awd; Cngrssnl Schlr; His Day St Awd; Sci Fair Winner; His.

DAMM, EMILY A; Redwood HS; Visalia, CA; (3); Church Yth Grp; Cmnty Wkr; German Clb; Girl Scts; Teachers Aide; Band; Chorus; Color Guard; School Musical; Off Frsh Cls; Berkeley; Orthodntst.

DAMMANN, SARAH M; Westlake Schl; Los Angeles, CA; (2); Church Yth Grp; VP French Clb; Library Aide; Thesps; Pres Acpl Chr; Chorus; Pres Church Choir; Orch; School Musical; School Play; Natl Charity Leag; Pro Acting; Flute; Med.

DAMON, AMETHYST C; California HS; San Ramon, CA; (4); Cmnty Wkr; Teachers Aide; Rep Frsh Cls; Rep Soph Cls; Var Powder Puff Ftbl; Hon Roll; Bi-Centennial Civics, St Fnls; CA ST U; Nrsng.

DAMON, JULIE E; Santa Teresa HS; San Jose, CA; (1); Art; Read; Art.

DAMPIER, JUSTIN M; Lone Pine HS; Lone Pine, CA; (1); Drama Clb; Library Aide; Ski Clb; SADD; Teachers Aide; School Play; JV Ftbl; Prfct Atten Awd; Boy Scts; Mock Trial; Air Force Acad; Pilot.

DAMRON, DAVID M; Glendora HS; Glendora, CA; (4); 11/375; Computer Clb; Math Clb; SADD; Treas Stu Cncl; JV Var Socr; High Hon Roll; Hon Roll; Pres Acad Fit Awd; Grad Hnr Guard 89; CSF Lifetime; Distngshd Schl Banquet Usher 89; Eductnl Grant 90; N AZ U; Acctng.

DANA, CARMEL; Loretto HS; North Highlands, CA; (3); 5/60; Church Yth Grp; Intnl Clb; Teachers Aide; Varsity Clb; Vllybl; High Hon Roll; Hon Roll; Prfct Atten Awd; Med.

DANA, NEIL; San Ramon Valley HS; Danville, CA; (3); 100/410; Key Clb; Band; JV Crs Cntry; JV Socr; Var Trk; Bus.

DANAO, JEAN; Dublin HS; Dublin, CA; (2); 1/224; FBLA; Hon Roll; CSF; High Hnrs GSE Alg.

DANCOURT, JENNY Y; Etiwanda HS; Rancho Cuccamonga, CA; (2); JA; Acpl Chr; Chorus; Hon Roll; Psychology.

DANCY, TIARA B; Millikan HS; Long Beach, CA; (3); Church Yth Grp; Teachers Aide; Chorus; Church Choir; School Musical; Cit Awd; San Diego ST; Paralegal.

DANE, BETH R; Edison HS; Stockton, CA; (4); Church Yth Grp; Hosp Aide; Intnl Clb; SADD; Teachers Aide; Stu Cncl; Stat Bsktbl; Score Keeper; U Of San Deigo; CPA.

DANE, SUBE T; Montgomery HS; Santa Rosa, CA; (4); Cmnty Wkr; GAA; Pep Clb; Spanish Clb; Teachers Aide; Drill Tm; Sec Frsh Cls; High Hon Roll; Jr NHS; Pres Schlr; Stu Of Yr; John R Foulger Awd; UC Santa Barbara; Psych.

DANEKE, TONYA; Palmdale HS; San Bernardino, CA; (4); 68/510; Chess Clb; Office Aide; Science Clb; Treas Service Clb; Teachers Aide; Band; Mrchg Band; Pep Band; Treas Jr Cls; Treas Stu Cncl; Yth Of Mnth-June 90; Acad Excllnc Cert-Sch Dist & Cert Bus Ed Excllnc; San Bernardino; Fnanc.

DANG, ALISON; Arvin HS; Arvin, CA; (3); Computer Clb; Drama Clb; Math Clb; Ski Clb; SADD; Child Psych.

DANG, AMY K; Hoover HS; Fresno, CA; (3); Art Clb; Cmnty Wkr; Girl Scts; Hosp Aide; Library Aide; Chorus; Stage Crew; JV Gym; JV Socr; JV Sftbl; Law.

DANG, ANH B; Saddleback HS; Santa Ana, CA; (2); Sec French Clb; Hist Science Clb; Ed Yrbk; Hon Roll; Vlntr Wrk; Pdtrcn.

DANG, ANHTHU T; El Toro HS; Laguna Hills, CA; (2); 10/557; Drill Tm; High Hon Roll; Opthalmolgy.

DANG, BANG PHI; Saddleback HS; Santa Ana, CA; (4); 2/520; Chess Clb; English Clb; French Clb; Math Clb; Math Tm; Mu Alpha Theta; Science Clb; Band; Golden St Awds; Acad Achvt Awds; Outstndg Achvt Awds; CSF Seal Bearer; Acad Dcthln Hon Ment Awds; CA Inst Tech; Comp Sci.

DANG, CHIN V; Monterey HS; Seaside, CA; (3); Teachers Aide; Hon Roll; Santa Cruz U; Teacher.

DANG, DIEM T; Dos Pueblos HS; Goleta, CA; (2); 1/300; Intnl Clb; Math Clb; Tennis; High Hon Roll; Hon Roll; Jr NHS; NHS; Prfct Atten Awd; Pres Acad Fit Awd; Pre-Med.

DANG, HUNG VAN; Oxnard HS; Oxnard, CA; (3); 44/479; Computer Clb; Var Wrstlng; Hon Roll; Hnrs Goldn St Exm 1st Yr Alg; CA Poly; Aerospace Engrng.

DANG, KIEULY; Santa Clara HS; Santa Clara, CA; (2); French Clb; Orch; Pedtrcn.

DANG, KRYSTINE C; Savanna HS; Anaheim, CA; (4); 11/285; Key Clb; Pep Clb; Red Cross Aide; Science Clb; Service Clb; Band; Mrchg Band; Stu Cncl; High Hon Roll; NHS; Outstndng Jr Performance Awd-Band; Girls Leag-Pres; U Of CA-IRVINE; Bio.

DANG, LINH V; Seaside HS; Marina, CA; (4); 2/258; AFS; Cmnty Wkr; FBLA; Spanish Clb; Var Tennis; High Hon Roll; NHS; Prfct Atten Awd; Sal; Spanish NHS; Cal Poly San Luis Obispo; Engr.

DANG, MINH T; Garfield HS Magnet; Los Angeles, CA; (2); Ed Nwsp; Prfct Atten Awd.

DANG, MINH T; Harbor HS; Santa Cruz, CA; (4); 11/275; Debate Tm; VP JA; VP Key Clb; Varsity Clb; Pres Chorus; VP Stu Cncl; Socr; High Hon Roll; Pres Schlr; Rotary Awd; CA Poly ST U; Pre-Med.

DANG, NGAN N; Elk Grove HS; Sacramento, CA; (4); Church Yth Grp; Library Aide; Hon Roll; CA ST U Sacramneto; Elec Engr.

DANG, NGUYEN T; Berkeley HS; Oakland, CA; (3); Church Yth Grp; Tennis; High Hon Roll; Val; BAYC; Oklnd Mayors Exc Tennis Yth Prgm; CAL; Arch.

DANG, PHONG XUAN; Bolsa Grande HS; Westminister, CA; (4); Chess Clb; Socr; High Hon Roll; Golden W Coll; Comp Prgmg.

DANG, PHUNG K; Lowell HS; San Francisco, CA; (3); Red Cross Aide; Chinese & Vllybll Clubs; Acctng.

DANG, SUSAN H; Encinal HS; Alameda, CA; (2); Art Clb; Dance Clb; Key Clb; Stage Crew; Swmmng; Vllybl; Prfct Atten Awd; Pom Pon Squad; Schl Musical; Fash.

DANG, SUSIE T; Westminster HS; Westminster, CA; (2); Spanish Clb; Chorus; Leo Awd Westminster HS.

DANG, THAO N; James Madison HS; San Diego, CA; (4); 1/347; Church Yth Grp; Office Aide; Teachers Aide; Yrbk; Powder Puff Ftbl; Var Capt Vllybl; Dnfth Awd; High Hon Roll; Hon Roll; Prfct Atten Awd; Vietnamese & Am Parents & Tchrs Assoc Awd For Schlstcs; Tres CA Schlstc Fed; Sec Delta Club; UCLA.

DANG, TON; Saddleback HS; Santa Ana, CA; (1); Chess Clb; French Clb; Quiz Bowl; Tennis; Prfct Atten Awd; Bus.

DANG, TRAN B; Colton HS; Colton, CA; (2); FBLA; Q&S; Co-Ed Nwsp; Treas Frsh Cls; Fld Hcky; NHS; Harvard U; Pharm.

DANG, TRUNG; El Toro HS; Laguna Hills, CA; (3); 13/500; French Clb; Key Clb; Trk; High Hon Roll; Pres Acad Fit Awd; Orange Cnty Acad Dcthln; CSF; El Toro HS Cmmndble Chrgr; Med.

DANG, TUAN TRAN; Saddleback HS; Santa Ana, CA; (1); Cmnty Wkr; Computer Clb; French Clb; Pep Clb; Science Clb; Tennis; Cit Awd; High Hon Roll; NHS; 1st Dist, 1st Orange Cnty Sci Fair; UCI; Phy.

DANG, TUNG M; Mira Mesa HS; San Diego, CA; (1); French Clb; Intnl Clb; Cit Awd; French Hon Soc; Pres Acad Fit Awd; CA Jr Schlrshp Fed & CA Schltc Fed; Bio Clb & Wildcat Clb Adv; Tae Kwon Do; CA St Polytech U; Arch.

DANG, TY B; Clairemont HS; San Diego, CA; (3); Letterman Clb; Science Clb; Ski Clb; Rep Stu Cncl; Trk; High Hon Roll; California Scholarship Federation; U Of CA San Diego; Chemistry.

DANG, VAN; San Gabriel HS; West Covina, CA; (3); French Clb; Sec Science Clb; Var Capt Vllybl; Cit Awd; High Hon Roll; Hon Roll; Keywants Serv Clb; Girls Leag; CSF; UC San Diego; Pre Med.

DANG, VIVIAN-HANG D; George Washington HS; San Francisco, CA; (2); Hon Roll; CSF; David Cultural Exchng Pgm; San Francisco ST U; Pharmacy.

DANG, XUAN C; Fremont HS; Sunnyvale, CA; (4); 36/389; Math Tm; NHS; Geo Golden St Exam Honors; San Jose ST U; Comp Engrng.

DANGELO, PABLO; San Gabriel HS; San Gabriel, CA; (2); Spanish Clb; Bsbl; Socr; Cit Awd; Hon Roll; Peer Cnslng; Frng Lang Comptn Spnsh Brnz Mdl; Cal ST LA; Sociology.

DANGOTT, ERIC; Edison HS; Huntington Beach, CA; (3); Aud/Vis; Key Clb; Math Tm; Capt Quiz Bowl; Ed Lit Mag; Cit Awd; Kiwanis Awd; HOBY Yth Fndtn 89; Yth Ambssdr Svt Union; Capt & Awd Wnnr Orng Co Acad Decath; Comms.

DANGVU, THUY; Los Amigos HS; Santa Ana, CA; (3); 5/312; Library Aide; Orch; Cit Awd; High Hon Roll; Hon Roll; Prfct Atten Awd; Med.

DANIEL, AARON R; Livermore HS; Livermore, CA; (1); Boy Scts; Church Yth Grp; Library Aide; Band; Mrchg Band; High Hon Roll.

DANIEL, GABRIEL C; Santa Barbara HS; Santa Barbara, CA; (3); Church Yth Grp; ROTC; Color Guard; Drill Tm; Off Frsh Cls; Socr; Vllybl; Wrstlng; Prfct Atten Awd; CAP Cvl Air Patrl USAF Aux Mitchell Awd; Ragfheon Flyng Clb FAA Prvt Pilot; US Air Frc Acad; Aerontcl Engr.

DANIEL, GREGORY D; Enterprise HS; Redding, CA; (4); Bus Profs of Am; Model UN; Yrbk; Stu Cncl; Hon Roll; CA ST U Chico; Poltcl Sci.

DANIEL, HEIDI M; Ukiah HS; Ukiah, CA; (2); 48/409; Hosp Aide; Teachers Aide; Hon Roll; Outstndng Achvt Bus Math; Mendocino CC; Spcl Educ.

DANIEL, KIM M; Fairfield HS; Fairfield, CA; (1); Church Yth Grp; Teachers Aide; Wrtng Fiction & Love Stories; Howard U; Poltcl Sci.

DANIEL, LITA N; Yucaipa HS; Yucaipa, CA; (2); 32/424; Art Clb; Spanish Clb; Swing Chorus; JV Crs Cntry; JV Sftbl; High Hon Roll; Hon Roll; Prfct Atten Awd; Pres Acad Fit Awd.

DANIEL, LUCY; Borrego Springs HS; Borrego Springs, CA; (3); Art Clb; Key Clb; Office Aide; SADD; Pres Frsh Cls; Pres Soph Cls; Sec Treas Stu Cncl; Bsbl; JV Var Bsktbl; L Sftbl; HOBY Yth Fndtn; Most Outstndng Stus Awd; Pol Sci.

DANIEL, MARTINEZ; Calexico HS; Calexico, CA; (1); FBLA; JV Wrstlng; Bus.

DANIEL, PAUL C; Orange Glen HS; Escondido, CA; (3); 1/500; Boy Scts; Church Yth Grp; Swmmng; Hon Roll; NHS; Ntl Merit Ltr; Water Polo; 3rd Pl Shrt Crse; CA Schlstc Fed; Assctd Stu Body Commssnr Stu Rights Relations; Coll.

DANIELE, TERESA P; Moorpark HS; Moorpark, CA; (3); Computer Clb; Teachers Aide; Frshmn Soph JR Clb Clbs; Health Office Aid; Pediatrician.

DANIELS, ALEXANDRA M; Oak Ridge HS; Mather A F B, CA; (2); 30/277; Church Yth Grp; FCA; SADD; Sec Frsh Cls; JV Var Bsktbl; Var Swmmng; JV Tennis; JV Vllybl; Hon Roll; Jr NHS; Environmentalist Club; U CA Sch; Comm.

DANIELS, ALICIA A; Rio Americano HS; Carmichael, CA; (3); 31/290; Church Yth Grp; Service Clb; SADD; JV Capt Bsktbl; High Hon Roll; Hon Roll; Acadmc Ltr; CSF; Jr Statemen Of Amer; Cal Poly San Luis Obispo; Arch.

DANIELS, CHRISTINE A; Chino HS; Chino, CA; (2); Drama Clb; GAA; Pep Clb; Var Sftbl; High Hon Roll; Hon Roll.

DANIELS, HESTER C; Capistrano Valley Christian Schls; San Juan Capistra, CA; (2); Church Yth Grp; Letterman Clb; Varsity Clb; Var Bsktbl; Vllybl; Pt Loma Nazarene Coll; Educ.

DANIELS, JESSICA N; Inglewood HS; Inglewood, CA; (3); Church Yth Grp; JA; Teachers Aide; Church Choir; Hon Roll; San Diego ST U; Chld Dev.

DANIELS, KELLEY; Loretto HS; Citrus Heights, CA; (1); JV Vllybl; High Hon Roll; Hon Roll.

DANIELS, KIMBERLY; Mt Carmel HS; San Diego, CA; (2); Church Yth Grp; Flag Corp; Sntr 89 Elctrl Cnvntn; Bus.

DANIELS, KIMBERLY A; Arcadia HS; Arcadia, CA; (2); 192/695; Church Yth Grp; Drama Clb; Ski Clb; Color Guard; Drill Tm; School Play; Pres Acad Fit Awd; LA Cnty HS For Arts 90-91; UCLA; Actng.

DANIELS, LAURA; Glen A Wilson HS; Hacienda Heights, CA; (3); 99/433; Library Aide; Chorus; Church Choir; Sec Drill Tm; Swing Chorus; Hon Roll; 2nd Lt Drill Tm; US Natl Chmps Med Dance & Lg Mltry Tm; CO Coll; Neo Natal Nrsng.

DANIELS, LORI B; Torrey Pines HS; Del Mar, CA; (3); 1/460; Pres Math Tm; Var Capt Quiz Bowl; Spanish Clb; Speech Tm; SADD; Lit Mag; Var Bsktbl; High Hon Roll; Hon Roll; Rotary Awd; Harvard Bk Awd; Soccer Recreational City Tm 12 Yrs; Rensselaer Polytech Awd Sci & Math.

DANIELS, MARILEE; Kings Christian HS; Hanford, CA; (2); 2/17; Church Yth Grp; Acpl Chr; Chorus; Rep Frsh Cls; Stu Cncl; Var Bsktbl; Var Vllybl; Cit Awd; Hon Roll; CSF; Med.

DANIELS, MORGAN A; Servite HS; Irvine, CA; (2); JV Socr; JV Tennis; NHS; CSF; Co-MVP JV Tnns Tm; Duke Coll.

DANIELS, RONALD L; Paso Robles HS; Paso Robles, CA; (3); Var JV Ftbl; JV Trk; Wt Lftg; JV Wrstlng; High Hon Roll; Hon Roll; Ntl Merit Ltr; Engr.

DANIELS, TRACY R; Rim Of The World HS; Lake Arrowhead, CA; (1); 1/435; Teachers Aide; JV Socr; Var Vllybl; Cit Awd; High Hon Roll; Hon Roll; Prfct Atten Awd; Med.

DANIELSON, BILL E; Torrey Pines HS; Solana Beach, CA; (2); 12/515; Ed Nwsp; JV Crs Cntry; Ftbl; JV Trk; Hon Roll; Opt Clb Awd; Pres Acad Fit Awd; JEA Jrnlsm Cont Awd; CA Schlrshp Fed; Engl.

DANIELSON, ELIZABETH K; San Rafael HS; San Rafael, CA; (1); Drama Clb; Band; Orch; Pep Band; School Musical; School Play; Cheerldng; Hon Roll; CA Schlrshp Fed; UC Berkeley; Law.

DANIELSON, JAMES R; Los Alamitos HS; Seal Beach, CA; (3); Computer Clb; Math Clb; Model UN; Science Clb; Spanish Clb; Physics.

DANIELSON, KAREN; San Ramon Valley HS; Danville, CA; (4); VP Art Clb; Church Yth Grp; Pep Clb; Chorus; Church Choir; Stage Crew; JV Var Cheerldng; CSSSA 89; Achvd Hnrs CA St Exmnr Geo Test; BYU; Visual Arts.

DANIELSON, KRISTIN E; Grossmont HS; Spring Valley, CA; (1); Dance Clb; Hosp Aide; Powder Puff Ftbl; Socr; JV Sftbl; Vllybl; Hon Roll; Prfct Atten Awd; Pres Acad Fit Awd; UC Irvine; Pilot.

DANIELSON, STEVE; Hesperia HS; Hesperia, CA; (2); Teachers Aide; High Hon Roll; Hon Roll; Science.

DANIMURA, KEKENTIA K; Luther Burbank HS; Sacramento, CA; (2); 61/389; Spanish Clb; Rptr Yrbk; Sec Soph Cls; Sec Jr Cls; Score Keeper; Var Vllybl; Cit Awd; Hon Roll; Prfct Atten Awd; MA U; Chld Psych.

DANKA, KURTIS P; North HS; Bakersfield, CA; (2); Teachers Aide; Bsktbl; Trk; High Hon Roll; Kiwanis Awd; CSF; Elect Engr.

DANKER, MARINA M; Eureka HS; Eureka, CA; (1); Hon Roll; Stanford; Engr.

DANKO, HARGITA; Mission San Jose HS; Fremont, CA; (2); Oblone JC; Marine Bio.

DANKS, CINDY L; Rubidoux HS; Riverside, CA; (4); 33/578; Teachers Aide; Chorus; Color Guard; Drill Tm; Rep Flag Corp; Mrchg Band; Rep Soph Cls; Hon Roll; CA ST U; Elem Educ.

DANLAG, DARREL M; Glendale HS; Glendale, CA; (2); Var Crs Cntry; Var Trk; OR ST; Archtctr.

DANNER, ERIKA L; San Luis Obispo HS; San Luis Obispo, CA; (4); Church Yth Grp; Band; Pep Band; Var L Bsktbl; Var L Crs Cntry; Var L Trk; Coaches Awd Crss Cntry; Mst Dedicated Trk Plyr; Cuesta Coll.

DANON, RAELENE C; Lincoln HS; San Jose, CA; (3); 42/356; Pres French Clb; Hosp Aide; Capt Color Guard; Mgr Socr; Var JV Vllybl; Hon Roll; Art Spcl Prjct; Poetry Anthlgy; U Of CO Boulder.

DANRIDGE, MONIQUE M; Lowell HS; San Francisco, CA; (3); Cmnty Wkr; Latin Clb; ROTC; Drill Tm; Orch; Prfct Atten Awd; Blck Stu Union, Pre-Med Clb Treas; MESA VP; Howard U; Pre-Med.

DANSA, ANDY J; Modesto HS; Modesto, CA; (2); Latin Clb; Math Clb; Spanish Clb; Bsbl; Bsktbl; Ftbl; Swmmng; Wt Lftg; Wrstlng; High Hon Roll; Pilot.

DANSBY, ANGELICA Y; Seaside HS; Seaside, CA; (2); Church Yth Grp; Church Choir; Score Keeper; Sftbl; Vllybl; Hon Roll; Bus Law.

DANSBY, SARA; Bolsa Grande HS; Westminster, CA; (2); Chorus; School Musical; Socr; Sftbl; USC; Music.

DANSIE, CHRISTOPHER; James Lick HS; San Jose, CA; (2); Boy Scts; Band; Jazz Band; Mrchg Band; JV Bsktbl; Band Hnrs From Amer Musical Fndtn; BYU; Oral Srgn.

DANZEISEN, AMY; San Juan HS; Citrus Hgts, CA; (3); 32/330; Church Yth Grp; Flag Corp; Mrchg Band; Hon Roll; Psych.

DANZIGER, KATHRYN E; S C P A HS; San Diego, CA; (1); 1/250; Dance Clb; French Clb; Hon Roll; Figr Sktg; Jrnlsm.

DAO, DANNY T; Mountain View HS; Mountain View, CA; (3); 87/400; French Clb; JV Ftbl; Wt Lftg; Hon Roll; Jr NHS; NHS; Engrng Explorer Sct; UC Davis; Pre-Law.

DAO, DUONG; Lincoln HS; Stockton, CA; (3); 94/592; Aud/Vis; Math Clb; Mu Alpha Theta; Science Clb; SADD; Crs Cntry; Cit Awd; Hon Roll; Crtfct Hon Wrld Hist Cultr & Geogrph; Crtfct Hon Japanese; Crtfct Awd Schl Recgntn Golden St Exam; UC Davis; Bus.

DAO, HIEU C; Glendale HS; Glendale, CA; (2); Cmnty Wkr; JV Bsktbl; Var Vllybl; Cal Tech; Aero Eng.

DAO, KEVIN PHUONG; Los Amigos HS; Santa Ana, CA; (2); Variety Show; JV Capt Tennis; High Hon Roll; Hon Roll; Ping Pong; Shooting & Hntng; UCLA; Bus Admin.

DAO, KIMBERLY; Westminster HS; Westminster, CA; (3); Church Yth Grp; French Clb; Hosp Aide; Key Clb; Latin Clb; ROTC; Service Clb; Spanish Clb; Varsity Clb; Off Jr Cls; UC Davis; Med/Pediatrics.

DAO, LE D; Oak Graove HS; San Jose, CA; (2); Cmnty Wkr; Computer Clb; French Clb; Key Clb; Math Clb; Math Tm; SADD; Variety Show; Yrbk; JV Vllybl; Tech & Soc Essay Cntst Hnrbl Mntn; Math Hnr Schlrshp Soc; UC Santa Barbara; Psycht.

DAO, LYNIEL S; Lowell HS; San Francisco, CA; (3); Office Aide; Gldn St Gmtry Hnrs Awd; UC Berkeley; Engrng.

DAO, PHUONG; Santiago HS; Santa Ana, CA; (1); JV Swmmng; Cit Awd; Schls Stars Clb; Phrmcy.

DAO, TERI N; Mira Mesa HS; San Diego, CA; (4); 52/749; Intnl Clb; Flag Corp; Hon Roll; Pres Acad Fit Awd; AVID Pgm; ROP; UCSD; Arch.

DAO, THANH; Taft Union HS; Tupman, CA; (3); 7/200; Var Capt Crs Cntry; Var Capt Tennis; High Hon Roll; Prfct Atten Awd; Mst Insprtnl Rnnr Crss Cntry; Schlr Athl Of Week.

DAO, THERESA H; Gahr HS; Cerritos, CA; (3); FBLA; Hon Roll; CSF; Home Clb; Blue Ang Gold Awd; CA ST Long Beach; Bus.

DAO, THI N; Bolsa Grande HS; Garden Grove, CA; (1); Hon Roll.

DAO, VAN; Leuzinger HS; Hawthorne, CA; (3); Science Clb; Sec Stu Cncl; Score Keeper; Var Socr; JV Trk; Capt Var Vllybl; Interact Clb; Cal Poly Pomona; Civil Engrng.

DAO, WENDY UYEN; Trabuco Hills HS; El Toro, CA; (2); Church Yth Grp; French Clb; JV Vllybl; UCLA; Bus Law.

DAOS, FAUSTO; John F Kennedy HS; Sacramento, CA; (2); 70/525; Band; Mrchg Band; Pep Band; Var Swmmng; Pres Acad Fit Awd; Marine Bio.

DAOUST III, W CHARLES H; East Nicholas HS; Elverta, CA; (2); Cmnty Wkr; Var Bsbl; Var Ftbl; Var Swmmng; Cit Awd; Hon Roll; Prfct Atten Awd; UC Davis; Animal Bio.

DAPPOLLONIO, KIM; Roseville HS; Rocklin, CA; (4); Church Yth Grp; Dance Clb; Girl Scts; SADD; Teachers Aide; School Musical; Nwsp; Bsktbl; Swmmng; Vllybl; Mst Outstndng Worker; Mst Productive Stu Awd; Sierra Coll; Nursing.

DARANCIANG, LISA R; Chula Vista HS; San Diego, CA; (3); 15/535; Hosp Aide; Math Tm; Pep Clb; SADD; Teachers Aide; Band; Mrchg Band; Orch; JV Bsktbl; JV Sftbl; Maria Clara De Pilipinas; Offcr In Chrge Ladies Of Elegnc; SW Fstvl Supr Awd Duet Xylophone; Engrng.

DARAVONG, KETMANY; Savanna HS; Anaheim, CA; (3); Intnl Clb; Coll; Comp.

DARDEN, DESIREE A; Corona Del Mar HS; Newport Beach, CA; (4); 56/320; Cmnty Wkr; Key Clb; Spanish Clb; Teachers Aide; Band; Orch; Stage Crew; Lit Mag; Crs Cntry; Swmmng; Goldn St Exam Acad Excllnvce Awd Geom; PAL; UC San Diego; Pre-Med.

DARDEN, TED D; Imperial HS; Arcadia, CA; (2); Church Yth Grp; Dance Clb; Chorus; Trk; Wt Lftg; Wrstlng; Cit Awd; High Hon Roll; Cert Scuba Diver LA Cnty; Med.

DARE, LISA; San Mateo HS; Foster City, CA; (3); Church Yth Grp; Math Clb; Math Tm; Model UN; Spanish Clb; Band; Church Choir; Mrchg Band; Pep Band; JV Gym; Goldn ST Exam Geom; Currclm & Policy Comm; Amer Musicl Fndtn 2 Yrs; Asian Clb Pres.

DARIMONT, AMY M; Corona HS; Corona, CA; (2); 65/473; Church Yth Grp; Cmnty Wkr; GAA; Girl Scts; Teachers Aide; JV Bsktbl; JV Score Keeper; JV Sftbl; JV Vllybl; Hon Roll; Math.

DARJI, PRAKASH; Western HS; Anaheim, CA; (4); Debate Tm; Drama Clb; NFL; Service Clb; Speech Tm; Rep Sr Cls; High Hon Roll; Chess Clb; Computer Clb; Pep Clb; CA Schlrshp Fed; Geo Gldn St Exam Hnrs; Ldrshp Acad 88; Engrng.

DARLING, JENNIFER; Chico SR HS; Chico, CA; (4); Church Yth Grp; JA; Key Clb; Letterman Clb; Cheerldng; Crs Cntry; Diving; Downhill Ski Team; Bus Stu Qtr; U Of CA Santa Cruz.

DARLING, KAREN M; Colfax HS; Weimar, CA; (3); 6/156; Church Yth Grp; VP Pep Clb; VP Science Clb; Rep Service Clb; Rep SADD; Ed Yrbk; Sec Sr Cls; Stat Bsktbl; Capt Powder Puff Ftbl; Capt Var Sftbl; Alpha Omega Hnr Soc; UCSD; Radiology.

DARLING, KARLA; Casa Grande HS; Petaluma, CA; (3); Dance Clb; German Clb; Office Aide; Band; Color Guard; Drill Tm; Flag Corp; Mrchg Band; Hon Roll; Most Imprvd Gauchoette Awd; Ped.

DARLING, MICHELE; San Ramon HS; Danville, CA; (2); 8/400; Teachers Aide; Ed Nwsp; High Hon Roll; High Ofcr Jobs Daughters; UCLA; Bus Admn.

DARLINGTON, JASON K; Serrano HS; Phelan, CA; (2); FFA; JV Var Trk; Hon Roll; Pres Acad Fit Awd; MVP Trck & Fld 2 Yrs; JV 110 M Hghg Hrdle Schl Rcrd; Dentistry.

DARLINGTON, MATT P; Paradise HS; Paradise, CA; (3); 25/300; Var Am Leg Boys St; Var Cmnty Wkr; Key Clb; Varsity Clb; Acpl Chr; Band; Chorus; Jazz Band; Mrchg Band; Pres Soph Cls; Doctor.

DARPINO, JAMES T; Channel Islands HS; Oxnard, CA; (2); Boy Scts; Crs Cntry; Trk; High Hon Roll; Hon Roll; Church Yth Grp; Cmnty Wkr; Drama Clb; HS Lttrmn-Crss Cntry & Track; Athltc Schlr; Dist Hnr Roll Stu; Math Tutor-Coll Stu Basic Alg; UCSB; Arch.

DARR, TERRIE L; Thomas Dewey HS; Modesto, CA; (3); Church Yth Grp; Key Clb; Spanish Clb; Church Choir; School Play; Stage Crew; Var Socr; JV Swmmng; High Hon Roll; Hon Roll; CSF; MVP Soccer; Rcvd Awd 4.0 GPA; Psych.

DARROW, DEE DEE; Madera HS; Madera, CA; (2); Drama Clb; School Play; Cheerldng; Tennis; Hon Roll; Prfct Atten Awd; Pop Warner Chrldr Grp Coach; Schl Mascot 90-91; U Santa Barbara; Child Psych.

DARROW, JASON; Calvary Chapel HS; Santa Ana, CA; (2); Hon Roll; Bus.

DARVILLE, CHRIS J; Oroville HS; Oroville, CA; (1); Letterman Clb; Intrml JV Ftbl; Intrml JV Trk; High Hon Roll; Prfct Atten Awd; U MI.

DARWAZEH, KISMET W; Novato HS; Novato, CA; (1); French Clb; Band; Mrchg Band; Pep Band; Lit Mag; Hon Roll; CSF Schl Chptr Frosh Rep; CA Music Edctrs Assn Solo/Nsmbl Fest Superior Rtg; Stanford; Ped.

DASALLA, MYLINN L; Polytechnic HS; Sun Valley, CA; (3); Dance Clb; French Clb; Chorus; Church Choir; Stage Crew; Rep Jr Cls; Hon Roll; CJSF; Dana Production; Acctnt.

DASHTIZAD, BABAK A; Canoga Park HS; Woodland Hills, CA; (2); French Clb; Band; Mrchg Band; Pep Band; USC; Arch.

DASKAROLIS, PETER T; Skyline HS; Oakland, CA; (3); Church Yth Grp; Cmnty Wkr; Chorus; Rep Frsh Cls; High Hon Roll; Pres Acad Fit Awd; Jr Statsmn America Treas 90-91; Tn Schl Prsntr Lssns Of Holocaust; Tn Crm Prvntn Cnfrnc Schlrshp 87; U Of CA; Hstry.

DASS, ASHANI D; Hayward HS; Hayward, CA; (1); FBLA; Spanish Clb; Law.

DASWANI, ADARSH; Marina HS; Huntington Beach, CA; (1); Band; Mrchg Band; High Hon Roll; Distgshd Schlr Pgm; Stanford; Fin.

DATE, AMIT S; Canyon HS; Canyon Country, CA; (1); 1/600; Quiz Bowl; JV Tennis; High Hon Roll; Hon Roll; CSF.

DATTA, SHRIMATI; San Luis Obispo HS; San Luis Obispo, CA; (2); 19/319; Hosp Aide; Intnl Clb; Key Clb; SADD; JV Tennis; Hon Roll; Violinist San Luis Obispo Cnty Sympny; Space Shuttle Prjct Launched 91; CA Schlrshp Fed; Sci Fld.

DATTARAY, ANNA; Artesia HS; Lakewood, CA; (2); Intnl Clb; JA; ROTC; Science Clb; Spanish Clb; Intrml Swmmng; Intrml Tennis; Cit Awd; Hon Roll; Ntl Merit Ltr; Stanford; Law.

DATTOMA, LUCIA L; St Genevieve HS; Sylmar, CA; (3); Rptr Nwsp; Ed Yrbk; Rep Soph Cls; Sec Stu Cncl; Allen Robbins Awd 88; Yng Mens Inst Essay Comptn Cert Of Achvt 90; Ed.

DATTOMA, PALMINA; St Genevieve HS; Sylmar, CA; (2); Cosmtlgy.

DATUIN, MARY GRACE P; Phillip & Sala Burton Academic HS; San Francisco, CA; (3); Church Yth Grp; Cmnty Wkr; Teachers Aide; Chorus; Church Choir; School Musical; Hon Roll; Acad Achvtmnt Cert 88-90; St Kevins Church Artechist; San Francisco ST; Speech Thpst.

DATWYLER, SAUL A; Calaveras HS; Valley Springs, CA; (2); 7/200; VICA; JV Bsbl; JV Ftbl; High Hon Roll; CA Polytech ST U; Arch.

DATWYLER, SHANNON L; Del Campo HS; Citrus Heights, CA; (3); 99/446; German Clb; Lbrn Band; Jazz Band; Mrchg Band; Pep Band; Var L Swmmng; JV Water Polo; Treas Friday Night Live; Med.

DAU, BRIAN T; St John Bosco HS; Los Alamitos, CA; (2); Church Yth Grp; Debate Tm; Speech Tm; Rptr Nwsp; Ed Yrbk; JV Socr; High Hon Roll; Hon Roll; NHS; Jr Statesman Govt Wkshp Washington DC; Poly Sci.

DAU, DAN J; Fairfield HS; Suisun City, CA; (2); Drama Clb; School Musical; School Play; Stage Crew; Variety Show; High Hon Roll; Hon Roll; NHS; Marine Bio.

DAU, SASHA R; Santa Fe Christian HS; New Rochelle, NY; (4); Church Yth Grp; Dance Clb; Drama Clb; Ski Clb; Teachers Aide; School Musical; School Play; Lit Mag; Off Sr Cls; Powder Puff Ftbl; San Francisco ST U; Bus.

DAU, THERESA T; Long Beach Polytechnic HS; Long Beach, CA; (3); Math Clb; Math Tm; Ed Nwsp; Ed Yrbk; JV L Tennis; DAR Awd; Hon Roll; Lion Awd; NHS; Pres Acad Fit Awd; Hnrble Mntn Long Beach Centnnl Poster Cont; Outstndng Muralist SYETP Mural; Mst Imprvd GPA Awd; CA Poly San Luis Obispo; Arch.

DAUB, TRACY R; Wm S Hart HS; Santa Clarita, CA; (2); JV Socr; JV Trk; CSF.

DAUGHERTY, C ZANE; Valley Christian HS; San Jose, CA; (4); 2/70; Church Yth Grp; Cmnty Wkr; School Play; Capt Ftbl; Trk; Wt Lftg; Cit Awd; Hon Roll; Prfct Atten Awd; CSF; Hmcmng Prince.

DAUN, STACEY E; Oak Ridge HS; El Dorado Hills, CA; (1); Art Clb; Church Yth Grp; Cmnty Wkr; JV Socr; Hon Roll; Mst Vlby Dfnsv Plyr; People To People Yth Ambssdr USSR; Sierra Svc Prjct.

DAUOD, LEYTH; Woodbridge HS; Irvine, CA; (3); Pres JA; Office Aide; Teachers Aide; Ftbl; Vllybl; Wt Lftg; Spcl Rcgntn Sprts; Ocngrphy.

DAUZ, JOCELYN A; Sweetwater Union HS; National City, CA; (3); 39/429; Church Yth Grp; Sec English Clb; Science Clb; Flag Corp; Variety Show; Cit Awd; High Hon Roll; Prfct Atten Awd; COPAO Faire; Filipino-Amer Yth Advocates Chaplain; Med.

DAVALIAN, GEVORK; John Marshall HS; Pasadena, CA; (3); Church Yth Grp; Cmnty Wkr; Cit Awd; Hon Roll; Chrch Bsktbl; UCLA; Electronics.

DAVALIAN, MARI; John Marshall Fundamental HS; Pasadena, CA; (1); Church Yth Grp; Science Clb; Hon Roll; Satrdy Tchr Armenian Ctr; Family Cnslr.

DAVALOS, CHRISTINE A; Los Altos HS; Hacienda Hts, CA; (2); Church Yth Grp; Band; Drill Tm; Mrchg Band; Swmmng; Hon Roll; Swmng Outstndng Achvt; Pedtrcn.

DAVE, GIATRI; Los Alamitos HS; Los Alamitos, CA; (4); Drama Clb; Hosp Aide; Model UN; Chorus; School Play; Yrbk; Cheerldng; Hon Roll; CA Schltc Fed; Miss Amer Coed Semifnlst; Jr Hnr Guard; U Of CA Irvine; Pre-Med.

DAVE, TIKA F; Fontana HS; Fontana, CA; (2); Hon Roll; Prfct Atten Awd; Black Stu Union; Stu Mnth; Schl Essay Cntst Wnnr; Bus.

DAVELAAR, KERRI; Valley Christian HS; Paramount, CA; (2); Church Yth Grp; Cmnty Wkr; 4-H; Teachers Aide; Church Choir; Drill Tm; Stat Bsktbl; HOBY Fndtn Ldrshp Awd; Elem Educ.

DAVENPORT, ALLISON; Gustine HS; Gustine, CA; (4); 1/55; Am Leg Aux Girls St; Drama Clb; Model UN; Treas Frsh Cls; Pres Soph Cls; Sec Stu Cncl; Tennis; Val; Acadmc Decathalon Medlst Schlrshp Wnnr; Peer Cnslng; St Marys Coll CA; Tchng.

DAVENPORT, BRANDON; Atascadero HS; Atascadero, CA; (4); Church Yth Grp; Var L Ftbl; L Swmmng; Hon Roll; Prfct Atten Awd; Cuesta Coll; Bus.

DAVENPORT, ERIC J; Clovis HS; Fresno, CA; (2); Var Swmmng; Certfd Lifegrd; HS Hikng Clb.

DAVENPORT, MARY A; W C Overfelt HS; Lovettsville, VA; (2); Var Swmmng; Hon Roll; St Schlr; Stanford; Med.

DAVES, DOROTHY A; North HS; Oildale, CA; (2); Hon Roll; Bus.

DAVID, ALFREDO; Los Angeles HS; Los Angeles, CA; (4); Aud/Vis; Cmnty Wkr; Intnl Clb; Office Aide; Spanish Clb; Rptr Nwsp; High Hon Roll; Hon Roll; Prncpls Awd; Peer Cnslr; 3rd Pl Pepsi Schlrshp Cntst CA; Chicago Yth Ldrshp Cnfrnc-Malibu 90; West Los Angeles Coll; Trvl.

DAVID, BRIAN T; Thousand Oaks HS; Thousand Oaks, CA; (3); 46/538; Church Yth Grp; Math Clb; Math Tm; Science Clb; Spanish Clb; Band; Mrchg Band; Orch; Pep Band; Hon Roll; Band Cncl Rep; Stu Sntr; Mck Trl; Med.

DAVID, EDEL P; Sierra Vista HS; Baldwin Park, CA; (1); Church Yth Grp; Rptr Nwsp; Phtg Yrbk; Vllybl; High Hon Roll; Prfct Atten Awd; Pres Acad Fit Awd; Berkeley; Law.

DAVID, GIA N; Bonita Vista HS; Chula Vista, CA; (1); Church Yth Grp; Off Soph Cls; Cit Awd; Hon Roll.

DAVID, LIZA J; Victor Valley HS; Victorville, CA; (3); 2/416; Hosp Aide; Key Clb; Pep Clb; Sec Spanish Clb; Band; Mrchg Band; Ed Nwsp; Off Sr Cls; Stu Cncl; Sports Jrnlsm.

DAVID, SIENNA R; Arroyo Grande HS; Arroyo Grande, CA; (1); Church Yth Grp; Variety Show; JV Cheerldng.

DAVID, VIVIAN; Fred C Beyer HS; Ceres, CA; (4); 45/506; Debate Tm; NFL; Speech Tm; Teachers Aide; Cit Awd; Hon Roll; Lion Awd; NHS; CSF; Explrs Clb; UC Santa Barbara; Pre-Law.

DAVID, YIM M; Lowell HS; San Francisco, CA; (2); Cmnty Wkr; Rep Frsh Cls; Crs Cntry; Trk; 2dn Pl All City 6n Meter Hurdles; CA Polytechnic; Engr.

DAVIDBADAL, KEVIN; Monroe HS; Northridge, CA; (1); Band; Jazz Band; Mrchg Band; Pep Band; School Musical; Hon Roll; Prfct Atten Awd; Music.

DAVIDIAN, YOLANDA M; La Canada HS; La Canada-Flint, CA; (4); 20/250; Girl Scts; Teachers Aide; Var Bsktbl; Powder Puff Ftbl; Var Trk; Var JV Vllybl; Pres Acad Fit Awd; Val; CSF; US Marine Corps US Army Res Schlr/Ath Awd; CIF Southern Section Stu; Los Angeles; Pre Med.

DAVIDOVICH, STEPHANIE J; Norco SR HS; Norco, CA; (2); Church Yth Grp; FFA; FFA Floral Culture Cert; Bus.

DAVIDSON, CANDI L; Fort Bragg HS; Fort Bragg, CA; (2); Pres Church Yth Grp; Cmnty Wkr; SADD; Chorus; Church Choir; Stat Socr; Hon Roll; Peer Cnslng; Piano Cmptn Awds & Hnrs; Chamber Sngrs; CMEA Music Fstvl; Intntl Piano Guild 7 Yrs; Western Bapt Bible Coll; Psych.

DAVIDSON, DANIELLE; St Michaels HS; Los Angeles, CA; (3); 1/40; Drama Clb; Pres GAA; Teachers Aide; School Play; Stage Crew; Rptr Nwsp; Ed Yrbk; Rep Stu Cncl; Var Bsktbl; Var Trk; Ctzn Bee Comp Xerox Schlrshp Humanities; Acad Decathelon; Athlete Of Yr; Highest GPA 3 Yrs; UCLA; Pre-Med.

DAVIDSON, JAMES W; Flintridge Prep Schl; Pasadena, CA; (3); AFS; Treas Soph Cls; Treas Jr Cls; Var Crs Cntry; JV Capt Socr; Var Trk; NHS; Ntl Merit SF; Writng.

DAVIDSON, JAYSON A; Del Campo HS; Fair Oaks, CA; (3); 9/580; Am Leg Boys St; Church Yth Grp; Debate Tm; Letterman Clb; Speech Tm; Rep Jr Cls; Socr; Swmmng; Trk; Wrstlng; 1st Pl Optimist Clb Oratorical Speech & Frgn War Vets Speech Conts; Semi Fnlst Law Day Debates; Stanford; Bus.

DAVIDSON, JENNIFER L; Del Campo HS; Fair Oaks, CA; (1); Church Yth Grp; Girl Scts; ROTC; Band; Color Guard; Drill Tm; USAFA; Pilot.

DAVIDSON, JILL; Del Campo HS; Carmichael, CA; (4); 47/430; French Clb; Speech Tm; Church Choir; Variety Show; Rep Sr Cls; Stu Cncl; Var JV Bsktbl; Var JV Swmmng; High Hon Roll; Hon Roll; CSF; Ricks; Child Psych.

DAVIDSON, JOYCE; Palisades HS; Los Angeles, CA; (3); Cmnty Wkr; Girl Scts; Teachers Aide; Off Soph Cls; Off Jr Cls; JV Stat Sftbl; High Hon Roll; Hon Roll; Pres Acad Fit Awd; Town Cryer Of Year; U CA San Diego; Psych.

DAVIDSON, MELANIE; Faith Christian HS; Gridley, CA; (4); Am Leg Aux Girls St; Treas Church Yth Grp; Drama Clb; English Clb; Library Aide; Teachers Aide; Church Choir; School Play; Var Vllybl; High Hon Roll; Mexico Outrch; Bus.

DAVIDSON, NIKKI L; Washington HS; Fremont, CA; (3); Drama Clb; Ski Clb; Cheerldng; Var Pom Pon; Powder Puff Ftbl; Close-Up.

DAVIDSON, RYAN A; South HS; Bakersfield, CA; (3); 60/450; JA; Library Aide; Teachers Aide; Crs Cntry; Ftbl; Socr; Trk; Hon Roll; Pres Acad Fit Awd; Phys Ftnss Cls; Mobil Oil Excllnc Club; Cal ST U; Bus.

DAVIDSON, SEAN J; Western Christian HS; San Dimas, CA; (3); 6/95; Church Yth Grp; Cmnty Wkr; Letterman Clb; Church Choir; Pres Frsh Cls; Pres Soph Cls; Pres Jr Cls; Var L Bsbl; Var L Ftbl; Intrml Golf; CA Schlrshp Fed; Pre Law.

DAVIDSON, SUZANN; Foothill HS; Sacramento, CA; (2); Church Yth Grp; Science Clb; Spanish Clb; SADD; Powder Puff Ftbl; Swmmng; Hon Roll; Friday Night Live; U Of Santa Barbara; Psych.

DAVIES, GREG M; Bellarmine College Prep; Los Gatos, CA; (1); Cmnty Wkr; Service Clb; JV Swmmng; Hon Roll; Medcl.

DAVIES, HEATHER; Los Angeles Baptist HS; Sepulveda, CA; (4); 16/90; Church Yth Grp; English Clb; French Clb; Chorus; Off Sr Cls; JV Sftbl; High Hon Roll; Hon Roll; NHS; Young Republicans Club; Brigham Young U; Atty.

DAVIES, JESSICA L; Bonita Vista HS; Bonita, CA; (3); 2/559; AFS; Varsity Clb; Ed Nwsp; Rep Jr Cls; Stu Cncl; JV Swmmng; Var Tennis; Hon Roll; Anthropology.

DAVIES, JONATHAN L; Clovis West HS; Clovis, CA; (3); Office Aide; Ski Clb; Swmmng; Vrsty Water Polo Tm; JR Olymp Tm; City Clg Orch; CSF & GATE Clbs; CA Young Amb Of Music Trip; Bio.

DAVIES, JULIE M; Chula Vista HS; Lemon Grove, CA; (3); 51/535; Hosp Aide; Variety Show; Var Cheerldng; Outstndng Achvt Awd For Cnty Wide Subject A Writeoff 90; CA Schlrshp Fed; UCLA; Geophysics.

DAVIES, KATHLEEN; Los Angeles Baptist HS; Sepulveda, CA; (3); 32/100; Church Yth Grp; French Clb; Office Aide; Pep Clb; Sec Treas Jr Cls; Off Sr Cls; Stat Bsktbl; Score Keeper; Hon Roll; BYU; Elem Ed.

DAVIES, MICHAEL; Liberty Union HS; Oakley, CA; (4); 1/304; Am Leg Boys St; FCA; Letterman Clb; Office Aide; SADD; Teachers Aide; Varsity Clb; Rptr Nwsp; VP Soph Cls; VP Jr Cls; Hmcmng Cmmttr Chrprsn; Club Cncl Chrmn; Schlr Ath Yr Brentwood News; Us Nvl Acad; Engrng.

DAVIES, MIRIAM A; Davis SR HS; Woodland, CA; (4); Pep Clb; Teachers Aide; Chorus; School Musical; Sec Stu Cncl; Capt JV Cheerldng; Var Capt Pom Pon; Var Swmmng; Jr NHS; JV Bsktbl; CSF; CA ST U Fresno; Phys Thrpy.

DAVIES, SASHA; San Rafael HS; San Rafael, CA; (3); 9/230; Cmnty Wkr; Pres Frsh Cls; Rep Soph Cls; Stu Cncl; JV Bsktbl; Var Socr; Var Swmmng; Var Tennis; Hon Roll; Yth Commission; HOBY Yth Fndtn; Close-Up.

DAVILA, ARLEEN C; Terra Nova HS; Pacifica, CA; (2); 14/30; Cmnty Wkr; Debate Tm; Teachers Aide; Rptr Nwsp; Rep Stu Cncl; Score Keeper; JV Swmmng; Hon Roll; Jr Statesmen Amer; UC; Natl Rptr.

DAVILA, DAVID A; Brea-Olinda HS; Brea, CA; (3); 12/295; Boy Scts; Hosp Aide; Pres Treas Key Clb; L Var Socr; Var Trk; High Hon Roll; NHS; Pres Acad Fit Awd; Clinic Soccer Head Coach Of Kickin Kangaroos 88; Pediatrician.

DAVILA, FELICIA; Bishop Amat HS; N Whittier, CA; (3); Hon Roll; NHS; Spanish NHS; CSF; Loyola Mrymnt; Med.

DAVILA, FRANCISCA; Sutter HS; Robbins, CA; (2); FHA; Science Clb; Spanish Clb; Nwsp; Var Cheerldng; Hon Roll; UCLA; Pre-Law.

DAVILA, SARA; Fred C Beyer HS; Modesto, CA; (3); Church Yth Grp; Debate Tm; Hosp Aide; NFL; Pep Clb; SADD; Yrbk; Cit Awd; Hon Roll; Head Delg Asilomar Ldrshp Conf; Steerng Cmmtte Beyer Green Party; Philsophy Clb.

DAVIS, ABEBI SAFIYA; Lynwood Adventist Acad; Los Angeles, CA; (3); 2/25; Church Yth Grp; Drama Clb; School Play; Pres Soph Cls; Var Sftbl; High Hon Roll; Deprtmntl Awd Career Educ; Chrch Yth Usher; Cert Athltc Achvt; Oakwood Adventst Coll; Bus Mgmt.

DAVIS, ABIGAIL H; Novato HS; Novato, CA; (4); 29/241; Am Leg Aux Girls St; Church Yth Grp; Drama Clb; SADD; Church Choir; School Play; Stu Cncl; Stat Bsktbl; Cheerldng; Pres Acad Fit Awd; Biola U; Cmmnctns.

DAVIS, ALICIA; Vintage HS; Napa, CA; (4); Dance Clb; Band; Chorus; Mrchg Band; Pep Band; School Play; Music Achvt Awd; Head Majorette; Dance.

DAVIS, ALISON J; Central Union HS; Imperial, CA; (1); Church Yth Grp; Speech Tm; Flag Corp; Hon Roll.

DAVIS, AMY; Hogan SR HS; Vallejo, CA; (3); French Clb; Teachers Aide; Stu Cncl; Crs Cntry; Trk; Hon Roll; Yth Ecology Clb Founder; Teaching.

DAVIS, AMY D; Modesto HS; Modesto, CA; (1); Dance Clb; Drama Clb; Stage Crew; Hon Roll; Dance Productions; Dancing.

DAVIS, AMY MICHELE; Dana Hills HS; Laguna Niguel, CA; (4); Church Yth Grp; Key Clb; Var L Swmmng; Kiwanis Awd; Hmcmng Crt 89-90; Wntr Frml Queen 89-90; U Of CA-IRVINE; Poli Sci.

DAVIS, ANDREA K; Pinole Valley HS; Pinole, CA; (1); Church Yth Grp; Drama Clb; Spanish Clb; Variety Show; JV Sftbl; High Hon Roll; Hon Roll.

DAVIS, ANDREW M; Poway HS; Poway, CA; (1); Boy Scts; Church Yth Grp; Band; Mrchg Band; School Musical; JV Bsktbl; JV Vllybl; Hon Roll; Ordr Of Arrow BSA; All S CA Hnr Band; AAU Bsktbl Pcfc SW 15 Under Div Champ; Stanford; Lawyer.

DAVIS, ANGELA; Willows HS; Willows, CA; (2); Key Clb; Sec Frsh Cls; Sec Soph Cls; Stat Score Keeper; JV Vllybl; Hon Roll; Chico ST U; Math.

DAVIS, ANGELIA D; Andrew Hill HS; San Jose, CA; (3); Drama Clb; Hosp Aide; Teachers Aide; Chorus; School Play; Sftbl; Vllybl; Peer Counselor; San Jose ST U; Law Enfrcmnt.

DAVIS, ANGELIQUE M; Mount Diablo HS; Pittsburg, CA; (1); French Clb; FBLA; Hon Roll; Bus.

DAVIS, ANTHONI; Saddleback HS; Santa Ana, CA; (2); French Clb; FBLA; Letterman Clb; Pres Frsh Cls; JV Capt Bsktbl; JV Capt Ftbl; Var Capt Trk; Hon Roll; Blk Stu Union; CA ST Fullerton; Cmnctns.

DAVIS, ANTHONY W; Rio Mesa HS; Oxnard, CA; (3); Art Clb; Boy Scts; Church Yth Grp; Church Choir; Ftbl; Trk; Wt Lftg; High Hon Roll; Hon Roll; Aid To Drafting, Taught On Comp; Cal ST Bakersfield; Cvl Engr.

DAVIS, APRIL C; Antelope Valley HS; Lancaster, CA; (2); 144/804; Church Yth Grp; Hosp Aide; Band; Mrchg Band; Pep Band; Hon Roll; Peer Helping; Stu Of Wk; Engl Ed.

DAVIS, BETSY E; Sutter Union HS; Meridian, CA; (2); Church Yth Grp; Cmnty Wkr; FBLA; FFA; GAA; Pep Clb; SADD; Teachers Aide; Varsity Clb; Var Cheerldng; Friday Nite Live; CA ST U Chico; Hotel Mgmt.

DAVIS, BREE E; Palisades HS; Los Angeles, CA; (2); Church Yth Grp; Cmnty Wkr; Office Aide; Pep Clb; Red Cross Aide; VP Soph Cls; Rep Stu Cncl; Stat Ftbl; Var Trk; Top Teens America Area VI Correspndng Sec, Treas, Histrn; NAACP; UNCF; Spelman Coll; Child Devlpmnt.

DAVIS, BRETT J; Mission Viego HS; Mission Viejo, CA; (4); Boy Scts; Teachers Aide; VICA; Phtg Ed Nwsp; Cit Awd; Elks Awd; Photo Jrnlst.

DAVIS, BRIAN D; Placer HS; Auburn, CA; (2); Key Clb; JV Bsbl; Psych.

DAVIS, BROOKS I; Ramona HS; Riverside, CA; (3); 14/410; French Clb; Band; Jazz Band; Mrchg Band; Orch; Pep Band; School Musical; JV Var Crs Cntry; High Hon Roll; Pres Acad Fit Awd; Remote Cntrl Car Racing; Dntstry.

DAVIS, CARMEN; St Joseph Notre Dame HS; Alameda, CA; (3); 4/120; Church Yth Grp; Science Clb; Ski Clb; Spanish Clb; Teachers Aide; School Play; Rptr Nwsp; Phtg Yrbk; Sec Soph Cls; Off Jr Cls; SF HOBY Sem N CA; Pres Alameda Law Post; Earthquake Relief Vol; Lang.

DAVIS, CATHLIN M; San Leandro HS; San Leandro, CA; (2); 5/233; VP Church Yth Grp; Dance Clb; JA; Teachers Aide; Chorus; Swing Chorus; Hon Roll; Jr NHS; Pres Acad Fit Awd; Futrstc Fans Of Sci Fi Assocs Fndr & Pres; Engl Tchr.

DAVIS, CELESTE A; George Washington HS; San Francisco, CA; (3); Cmnty Wkr; JA; Letterman Clb; Ski Clb; Teachers Aide; Mgr Varsity Clb; Stage Crew; Stat Ftbl; Stat Wrstlng; High Hon Roll; Youth Court; Enterprise Apprenticeship Program; Junior Statesmen Of America; U Of California.

DAVIS, CHAD; East Union HS; French Camp, CA; (4); 6/264; VP Science Clb; Var Bsbl; JV Bsktbl; Var Ftbl; Block E U Clb; U Of CA Santa Barbara; Marine.

DAVIS, CHAD E; Victor Valley HS; Victorville, CA; (4); French Clb; Key Clb; Letterman Clb; Pres Spanish Clb; Mgr VP Tennis; Trk; High Hon Roll; Loma Linda U; Dntstry.

DAVIS, CHRISTOPHER C; San Bernardino HS; San Bernardino, CA; (2); Boy Scts; Church Yth Grp; Key Clb; NFL; Spanish Clb; Tennis; Hon Roll; Acadmc Dcthln; Pilot.

DAVIS, CHYRON; Brethren HS; Long Beach, CA; (3); 5/55; Church Yth Grp; Math Tm; Science Clb; Pres Jr Cls; Sec Stu Cncl; Vllybl; Cit Awd; Pres Acad Fit Awd; Comp Natl NFSTL Piano Adjdctn 2 Yrs; Med.

DAVIS, CINDY; Palm Desert HS; Thousand Palms, CA; (4); 24/230; 4-H; Girl Scts; Library Aide; Yrbk; High Hon Roll; Grl Sct Menorah Awd; Film/TV Prodctn.

DAVIS, CLARA L; Bonita Vista HS; Bonita, CA; (3); 1/578; Girl Scts; Model UN; Pep Clb; Quiz Bowl; Scholastic Bowl; Pres Science Clb; Ed Nwsp; Ed Yrbk; Rep Stu Cncl; Cit Awd; Outstndng Stu Soc Stds Dept 88; CA Gldn St Geo Exm Hnrs 88; Bio Hnrs Acad Awd 89; Hnrs Eng Acad Awd 89; U Of CA SD; Bio.

DAVIS, CLINTON R; Oak Park HS; Agoura Hills, CA; (1); JV Socr; Hon Roll; Pres Acad Fit Awd; Ayso Soccer; UCLA; Mathmtcs.

DAVIS, CYNTHIA; San Gorgonio HS; Highland, CA; (4); Church Yth Grp; Ski Clb; Varsity Clb; Acpl Chr; Chorus; Powder Puff Ftbl; Socr; Sftbl; Vllybl; Hon Roll; Hmcmng Qn; Alive Clb; Ctznshp Awd; Gorodn Coll; Med.

DAVIS, DANIELLE N; Alverno HS; Altadena, CA; (2); 34/70; Church Yth Grp; Girl Scts; Hosp Aide; Advncd Placemnt Bio; UCLA; Psycht.

DAVIS, DANNY J; Valley HS; Sacramento, CA; (3); Church Yth Grp; FBLA; Office Aide; Rptr Yrbk; Bsbl; JV Var Ftbl; JV Trk; JV Var Wt Lftg; Sacramento ST; Sprts Thrpy.

DAVIS, DARREN G; Nevada Union HS; Nevada City, CA; (3); 24/525; Intnl Clb; SADD; Ed Nwsp; Rep Frsh Cls; Off Jr Cls; Var L Golf; Score Keeper; High Hon Roll; Pres Acad Fit Awd; Prncpls Advsry Brd Cmmssnr; Cmmtte To Slct Interum Prncpl; Gldn St Exam Geom Hnrs; Geo Washington U; Brdcst Jrnlsm.

DAVIS, DAWN D; North HS; Bakersfield, CA; (3); 26/348; Dance Clb; Spanish Clb; Pres Acad Fit Awd; Spanish NHS; Golden Empire Arabian Horse Soc; Model A Ford Clb Of Am; Country At Heart Dnc Team; CA ST U; Engr.

DAVIS, DEAN F; Granada HS; Livermore, CA; (4); Varsity Clb; Bsbl; L Var Crs Cntry; Ftbl; L Var Trk; Var Capt Wrstlng; Project Alert Teen Leader; Ohio State & Wrestle.

DAVIS, DEBI N; Oak Ridge HS; Cameron Park, CA; (3); 19/262; Am Leg Aux Girls St; Cmnty Wkr; Debate Tm; NFL; Science Clb; Speech Tm; Ed Lit Mag; High Hon Roll; NHS; Opt Clb Awd; Fndng Pres Envrnmntlst Clb; Prof Dancer; UC Irvine; Envrnmntl Consrvtn.

DAVIS, DEBRA L; Castle Park HS; Chula Vista, CA; (4); 35/328; French Clb; Teachers Aide; JV Var Bsktbl; JV Var Sftbl; JV Var Vllybl; San Diego ST; Intl Bus.

DAVIS, DONALD D; Thomas Downey HS; Modesto, CA; (4); Letterman Clb; Chorus; Modesto JC.

DAVIS, DORIS; Argonaut HS; Sacramento, CA; (4); 3/33; Church Yth Grp; Cmnty Wkr; Drama Clb; English Clb; 4-H; FBLA; FHA; Math Clb; ROTC; School Play; Memphis ST Coll; Drama.

DAVIS, ERICA M; Mount Pleasant HS; San Jose, CA; (1); Dance Clb; Gym; Trk; Link Inc Awd; Howard; Bus.

DAVIS, GARY A; Livermore HS; Livermore, CA; (3); 40/470; ROTC; SADD; Varsity Clb; Var Ftbl; Var Capt Socr; High Hon Roll; Hon Roll; Rotary Awd; 3.5 Grd Avg; Plyd St Slct Sccr Tms; Sprts Med.

DAVIS, GAVIN L; Atwater HS; Atwater, CA; (2); JV Socr; JV Swmmng; Hon Roll; Prfct Atten Awd; De Molay Master Cnslr; CA Poly; Landscape Dsgn.

DAVIS, GEORGE E; Carson HS; Victorville, CA; (2); Church Yth Grp; FTA; Band; Chorus; Church Choir; Mrchg Band; High Hon Roll; UC Berkeley; Psych.

DAVIS, GLEN M; Sutter Union HS; Yuba City, CA; (3); Pres 4-H; FBLA; Intnl Clb; Letterman Clb; Spanish Clb; Rptr Nwsp; Yrbk; JV Var Trk; JV Var Wrstlng; 4-H Awd; Deomolay; Soccer City Lge; Yuba Coll; Ntl Rsrcs.

DAVIS, GLENN E; Montclair HS; Ontario, CA; (1); Church Yth Grp; Computer Clb; Intrml L Bsbl; Capt L Bsktbl; Hon Roll; NHS.

DAVIS III, GLENN R; Moreno Valley HS; Moreno Valley, CA; (3); French Clb; ROTC; Flag Corp; L Var Golf; Hon Roll; Law Enfrcmnt.

DAVIS, GWEN R; Riverdale HS; Riverdale, CA; (3); Drama Clb; VP FTA; Pep Clb; SADD; Chorus; Phtg Yrbk; Hon Roll; Academic Achievement Award; Fresno City College; Drama.

DAVIS, HEATHER A; Valhalla HS; Jamul, CA; (3); 94/408; Drama Clb; Ski Clb; SADD; Attnd Cmmty Coll During HS Assoc Deg; Embry-Riddle; Arntcl Engrng.

DAVIS, HEATHER D; Watsonville HS; Watsonville, CA; (3); 5/500; Am Leg Aux Girls St; Debate Tm; 4-H; Model UN; Pep Clb; Ski Clb; JV Var Bsktbl; Var Capt Swmmng; 4-H Awd; Hon Roll; Fmly Thrpy.

DAVIS, HEATHER E; Whitney HS; Cerritos, CA; (3); JA; VP Key Clb; Rptr Nwsp; Var L Trk; High Hon Roll; NHS; Opt Clb Awd; Pres Acad Fit Awd; Yng Gftd & Black Schlr; Mcdonalds Black Hist Maker Of 90; Harvard U; Pol Sci.

DAVIS, HEIDI A; Alameda HS; Alameda, CA; (3); 14/276; Key Clb; Teachers Aide; Acpl Chr; Rep Stu Cncl; JV Bsktbl; JV Vllybl; Hon Roll; CSF.

DAVIS, HILLERY; Ukiah HS; Ukiah, CA; (2); Band; School Musical; Cheerldng; Powder Puff Ftbl; Pres Acad Fit Awd; Red Cross Certified 1st Aid & CPR; UC Davis; Interior Dsgn.

DAVIS, JAMES; Elk Grove HS; Elk Grove, CA; (2); Art Clb; Boy Scts; Debate Tm; French Clb; Model UN; Scholastic Bowl; Jr Statesman Of Amer; Acad Talent Search; CA St Exposition Jr Exh Art Awd; Acad Olym Gld & Bronze Medl.

DAVIS, JAMES A; Galt HS; Galt, CA; (4); Boy Scts; Intnl Clb; Letterman Clb; Ed Yrbk; Var L Ftbl; Var L Golf; High Hon Roll; Pres Acad Fit Awd; Cal ST Chico; Vet Med.

DAVIS, JAMIE; Ontario HS; Ontario, CA; (2); Letterman Clb; Varsity Clb; JV Socr; JV Sftbl; Var Tennis; Hon Roll; Prfct Atten Awd; UC Riverside; Law.

DAVIS, JASON W; Apple Valley HS; Apple Valley, CA; (1); Boy Scts; Key Clb; Ski Clb; JV Trk; Hon Roll; Eagle Scout.

DAVIS, JENNIFER; Fairfield HS; Fairfield, CA; (4); French Clb; Key Clb; Rptr Nwsp; Off Jr Cls; Rep Sr Cls; Rep Stu Cncl; JV Cheerldng; Var Capt Pom Pon; Powder Puff Ftbl; French Hon Soc; Sacramento ST U; Pol Sci.

DAVIS, JENNIFER; Newport Christian HS; Fountain Vly, CA; (3); Am Leg Aux Girls St; Debate Tm; Pep Clb; Pres Ski Clb; Rep Soph Cls; Pres Stu Cncl; Stat Bsbl; Var Capt Cheerldng; High Hon Roll; Hon Roll; US Chrldr Achvt Awd; Scuba Dive Cert; UCLA; Lib Arts.

DAVIS, JENNIFER; Paramount HS; Bellflower, CA; (2); Cit Awd; Hon Roll; Bus.

DAVIS, JENNIFER D; River City HS; W Sacramento, CA; (1); Spanish Clb; Capt Gym; Cit Awd; Hon Roll; UC Davis; Typing.

DAVIS, JENNIFER E; Redwood HS; Visalia, CA; (1); FFA; Nwsp; Socr; Swmmng; Hon Roll; UC Davis; Vet Med.

DAVIS, JENNIFER L; Rubidoux HS; Riverside, CA; (4); AFS; Spanish Clb; Prfct Atten Awd; Bus.

DAVIS, JESS; Eureka HS; Eureka, CA; (3); Ski Clb; Bsktbl; Tennis; High Hon Roll; U CA; Envrnmntl Bio.

DAVIS, JESSICA G; Tulare Western HS; Tulare, CA; (3); Treas Bus Profs of Am; Church Yth Grp; Intnl Clb; NFL; Office Aide; Speech Tm; Band; Swmmng; Hon Roll; Brigham Young U; Mrktng.

DAVIS, JOHNNIE MAE; Mission HS; San Francisco, CA; (1); Computer Clb; Teachers Aide; Hon Roll; San Francisco City Coll; Comp.

DAVIS, JOSHUA A; Clovis HS; Clovis, CA; (1); Drama Clb; Spanish Clb; School Musical; School Play; Socr; Hon Roll; Prfct Atten Awd; Pres Acad Fit Awd; Chiropractics.

DAVIS, JULIE; Lee Ware HS; Buena Park, CA; (4); Church Yth Grp; Office Aide; Teachers Aide; Church Choir; JV Stat Bsktbl; JV Stat Ftbl; JV Var Vllybl; Hon Roll; Recrtnl Thrpst.

DAVIS, JUSTIN M; Apple Valley HS; Apple Valley, CA; (1); Key Clb; Hon Roll; Stanford U.

DAVIS, KARALEE A; Norco HS; Norco, CA; (1); Church Yth Grp; Cmnty Wkr; Hosp Aide; Service Clb; Church Choir; Variety Show; Bsktbl; Vllybl; Schl Choir; Girls Leag Frosh Rep; BYU.

DAVIS, KASSANDRA L; Yosemite HS; Raymond, CA; (2); Church Yth Grp; French Clb; Church Choir; Hon Roll; Santa Barbara U; Bus.

DAVIS, KENNETH A; John Swett HS; Rodeo, CA; (2); Church Yth Grp; Science Clb; Band; Jazz Band; Mrchg Band; Pres Frsh Cls; VP Soph Cls; Rep Stu Cncl; JV Bsbl; JV Capt Bsktbl; CA Schlrshp Assoc; Prsdntl Physcl Ftns Awd; Friday Night Live; Doctor.

DAVIS, KENNETH R; Washington HS; Fremont, CA; (3); 56/306; Boy Scts; Pres Church Yth Grp; Ski Clb; SADD; Teachers Aide; Rptr Yrbk; VP Frsh Cls; Off Soph Cls; Pres Jr Cls; Pres Stu Cncl; Brigham Young U; Bus.

DAVIS, KIMBERLY; Fairfield HS; Fairfield, CA; (2); Mrchg Band; Rep Frsh Cls; VP Soph Cls; JV Co-Capt Cheerldng; JV Sftbl.

DAVIS, KIMBERLY A; Pinole Valley HS; Pinole, CA; (3); Computer Clb; Rptr Nwsp; Hon Roll; Pres Acad Fit Awd; CA Congressional Schlr; Diablo Valley Coll; Ed.

DAVIS, KIMBERLY D; St Bernard HS; Inglewood, CA; (3); Ed Yrbk; Lit Mag; Treas Soph Cls; Treas Sr Cls; JV Trk; Cit Awd; Smmr Stdy Abroad Pgm Schlrshp Wnnr; Howard U; Brdcstng.

DAVIS, KRISTIN M; Hogan SR HS; Vallejo, CA; (1); Church Yth Grp; Debate Tm; Key Clb; Office Aide; Teachers Aide; Sftbl; Vllybl; Hon Roll.

DAVIS, LA SHAYE; Washington Prep; Los Angeles, CA; (4); Church Yth Grp; Cmnty Wkr; Drama Clb; Office Aide; Pep Clb; Service Clb; Chorus; Church Choir; Hon Roll; Knght & Lds; Emprsses; Miss Model Miss Egsostn Pgnt 89; CA ST U Long Beach; Law.

DAVIS, LATRICE; Pasadena HS; Pasadena, CA; (3); Church Yth Grp; Computer Clb; Debate Tm; Drama Clb; Office Aide; ROTC; Teachers Aide; Acpl Chr; Chorus; Church Choir; Lawyer.

DAVIS, LAURA J; Huntington Beach HS; Huntington Beach, CA; (2); Church Yth Grp; Dance Clb; Key Clb; Model UN; Swing Chorus; Jr NHS; Treas-Jr Bd Of Dir-Orange Cnty Chldrns Theatre; Vclst/Actress Orange Cnty Chldrns Theatre; Music.

DAVIS, LYNDA KAY; Turlock HS; Turlock, CA; (2); High Hon Roll; Clsrm Achvt Awds; UCLA.

DAVIS, LYNN; Bonita Vista HS; Chula Vista, CA; (2); Church Yth Grp; Chorus; Church Choir; Rep Stu Cncl; JV Cheerldng; JV Vllybl; Cit Awd; High Hon Roll; Mdl Clb; Stu Mtn 11-88; Mst Imprvd Cert Frnch; CSF; Cert Hgh Scrng Gldn St Math Exm 89; Solo/Ensmble Fst; Music.

DAVIS, MARCEL L; Southbay Christian HS; San Jose, CA; (4); 8/24; Cmnty Wkr; 4-H; Letterman Clb; Natl Beta Clb; Spanish Clb; Varsity Clb; VP Jr Cls; Rep Sr Cls; Rep Stu Cncl; Var Bsbl; Santa Clara U; Mech.

DAVIS, MARIKA D; J Eugene Mc Ateer HS; San Francisco, CA; (3); Acpl Chr; Chorus; School Musical; Hon Roll; USA/Ussr Exchng Prgm; Russian Tea Clb; CA Schlrshp Fed Clb; Mc Ateer Coll Society Club; Art.

DAVIS, MARVIN M; Fontana HS; Fontana, CA; (3); Church Yth Grp; Hon Roll; Achvmnt Awd; Mngmnt.

DAVIS, MATHEW; Etiwanda HS; Alta Loma, CA; (2); Scholastic Bowl; Science Clb; Spanish Clb; Var Socr; JV Tennis; Hon Roll; Olympc Dvlpmnt Pgm Soccer; CA Explrs Pro Soccer Dvlpmnt Pgm; IN U; Bus.

DAVIS, MATT F L; Capistrano Valley HS; Coto De Caza, CA; (3); Boy Scts; Church Yth Grp; German Clb; Pres Sec Band; Church Choir; Sec Jazz Band; Capt Mrchg Band; Orch; Pep Band; Louis Armstrong Jazz Awd; R G Canning Otstndng Yth Awd; Capistrane Valley HS Bst Musician 88-90.

DAVIS, MATTHEW; Faith Christian HS; Marysville, CA; (3); 1/20; Church Yth Grp; JV Capt Bsktbl; L Socr; High Hon Roll; Hon Roll; Prfct Atten Awd; CSF 87-90; Writers & Elec Clb; CA ST U; Acctng.

DAVIS, MATTHEW; Yosemite Union HS; Coarsegold, CA; (2); 23/195; Boy Scts; Church Yth Grp; French Clb; Ski Clb; VP VICA; Band; Jazz Band; JV Socr; JV Tennis; High Hon Roll; Poet; Cnslr; Christian Heritage Coll; Psych.

DAVIS, MELISSA M; Rim Of The World HS; Crestline, CA; (1); 1/435; Art Clb; Church Yth Grp; English Clb; French Clb; Teachers Aide; High Hon Roll; Prfct Atten Awd; Bus.

DAVIS, MELISSA R; Downey HS; Vernon, CA; (2); Service Clb; Chorus; Hon Roll; CA Schlrshp Fed; American Coll Applied Arts.

DAVIS, MICHAEL L; San Marcos HS; Santa Barbara, CA; (2); Church Yth Grp; Rep Stu Cncl; JV Socr; JV Swmmng; Hon Roll; Pres Acad Fit Awd.

DAVIS, MICHAEL N; Ramona HS; Ramona, CA; (2); Church Yth Grp; Letterman Clb; Varsity Clb; Bsbl; Bsktbl; Ftbl; Elec Engr.

DAVIS, MICHAEL W; Mar Vista HS; San Diego, CA; (1); 2/530; Teachers Aide; High Hon Roll; Hon Roll; Prfct Atten Awd; UCLA; Phys Sci.

DAVIS, MICHAEL W; Twentynine Palms HS; Twentynine Palms, CA; (1); Boy Scts; Rep Frsh Cls; Rep Stu Cncl; JV Ftbl.

DAVIS, MICHELE A; Palisades HS; Calistoga, CA; (4); Pres SADD; Teachers Aide; VP Sr Cls; JV Vllybl; Cit Awd; Hon Roll; Prfct Atten Awd; Peer Hlpr/W Cert; Awd Cmpltng Pgm At UC Davis Bio; Santa Rosa JR Coll.

DAVIS, MICHELLE J; Willow Glen HS; San Jose, CA; (2); Rptr Nwsp; Ed Yrbk; Hon Roll; Wtrss; Crt Rprtr.

DAVIS, MICHELLE L; Armijo HS; Fairfield, CA; (1); AFS; Band; Off Frsh Cls; High Hon Roll; CA Schlrshp Fed; U Of CA Davis; Ped.

DAVIS, MICHELLE M; Willow Park HS; Lucerne Valley, CA; (3); Computer Clb; Drama Clb; Library Aide; Office Aide; SADD; Teachers Aide; Nwsp; Yrbk; Comp Prcssng.

DAVIS, MONA; Fremont HS; Oakland, CA; (3); #26 In Class; Girl Scts; ROTC; Band; Drill Tm; Cheerldng; Ftbl; Sftbl; Trk; Cit Awd; High Hon Roll; Howard U; Obstetrcn.

DAVIS, MONICA; Los Angeles Baptist HS; Van Nuys, CA; (3); 9/100; Church Yth Grp; Cmnty Wkr; French Clb; GAA; Service Clb; Chorus; Off Frsh Cls; Jr Cls; Stu Cncl; Var Capt Sftbl; Tnns Clb; Sci Awd; Bst Dfns, 1st Tm Al-Leag Vllybl; 2nd Tm Al-Leag Sftbl; Athlt Wk Awd; Piano; UCI; Pre-Med.

DAVIS, MUJAJI S; Fontana HS; Bloomington, CA; (3); Hon Roll.

DAVIS, MYKELL D; Skyline HS; Oakland, CA; (2); Church Yth Grp; Cmnty Wkr; Office Aide; Drill Tm; Ed Nwsp; Off Frsh Cls; Rep Stu Cncl; Var Bsktbl; Hon Roll; Sktchng; Wrkng With Cmptrs; Drftng Dsgnr.

DAVIS, NICHOLLE; Los Alamitos HS; Huntington Bch, CA; (3); Varsity Clb; Capt L Swmmng; Hon Roll; St Schlr; Amnsty Intl; Santa Barbara U; Real Estate.

DAVIS, NICOLE; Paramount HS; Paramount, CA; (3); 77/439; Cit Awd; Hon Roll; Ebony Essnc Clb; Long Bch ST Coll; Dntl Asst.

DAVIS, NIKKI L; Fowler HS; Fowler, CA; (3); FCA; FFA; SADD; Band; Chorus; Stu Cncl; Var Bsktbl; Var Cheerldng; Var Sftbl; Var Vllybl; Fresno Pacific Coll; Knslgy.

DAVIS, PAUL; Poway HS; Poway, CA; (3); 61/763; Boy Scts; Church Yth Grp; Scholastic Bowl; Thesps; Band; Jazz Band; Mrchg Band; High Hon Roll; Hon Roll; NHS; CSF; Aerspc Engr.

DAVIS, RAMELL; Vallejo SR HS; Vallejo, CA; (3); Hon Roll; Jr NHS; NHS; Ntl Merit Ltr; Success Acadmc Achvt Awd; Pre Med.

DAVIS, REBECCA; Anacapa HS; Goleta, CA; (3); Church Yth Grp; Cmnty Wkr; Girl Scts; Office Aide; SADD; Teachers Aide; Band; Chorus; School Play; Stage Crew; Cnclr 6th Grd Cmp; Vlntr Awd; Outstndng Achvt Awd Geom; Clark U; Law.

DAVIS, REBECCA J; Mesa Verde HS; Citrus Heights, CA; (2); English Clb; Sec French Clb; Rptr Nwsp; JV Mgr(s); Var Score Keeper; Intrml Wt Lftg; Hon Roll; Cert Scuba Diver; Bus.

DAVIS, REBECCA S; Clear Lake HS; Lakeport, CA; (3); 1/85; Teachers Aide; Band; Sec Soph Cls; Sec Sr Cls; JV Bsktbl; Var Sftbl; JV Var Vllybl; CA Schlstc Fed; US Army Jr Sci & Hum Symposium At UN Reno 90; UC Berkeley.

DAVIS II, ROBERT J; Golden West HS; Visalia, CA; (2); German Clb; Intnl Clb; High Hon Roll; Hon Roll; St Schlr; Acad Ltr; Independent Order Of Forester; Med.

DAVIS, ROBYN; Calvary Chapel HS; Irvine, CA; (3); 1/39; Church Yth Grp; Cmnty Wkr; Dance Clb; Spanish Clb; Teachers Aide; Acpl Chr; Chorus; Hon Roll; Mexico Ministry; Feeding The Poor Ministry; Irvine Valley Coll; Frgn Lang.

DAVIS, ROSLYN; Dominguez HS; Compton, CA; (2); Math Clb; Math Tm; Science Clb; Varsity Clb; Cit Awd; High Hon Roll; Hon Roll; Prfct Atten Awd; MESA Outstndng Stu Awd; Respirtry Thrpy.

DAVIS, SARAH R; North Salinas HS; Salinas, CA; (4); Boy Scts; Ed Yrbk; High Hon Roll; Hon Roll; Explorers; Hartnell Coll; Comp.

DAVIS, SCOTT E; Mc Kinleyville HS; Trinidad, CA; (2); Scholastic Bowl; Rep Speech Tm; SADD; Rep Stu Cncl; JV Bsktbl; Var Socr; Var Trk; CA Schlrshp Fed Pres Sch Club; Won Humboldt Cty Sci Fair 90.

DAVIS, SHANNON L; Orange Glen HS; Escondido, CA; (3); Church Yth Grp; Cmnty Wkr; Drama Clb; SADD; Capt Flag Corp; Mrchg Band; Rptr Nwsp; Rptr Yrbk; High Hon Roll; Hon Roll; Brdcst Jrnlsm.

DAVIS, SHANNON R; Mission Viejo HS; El Toro, CA; (3); 39/434; Key Clb; Band; Jazz Band; Mrchg Band; Orch; Pep Band; School Musical; High Hon Roll; Hon Roll; Ntl Merit Ltr; Gldn St Hgh Hnrs Geomtry Awd; U Of CA Irvine Wind Ensmbl 2 Yrs Advncd Hrmny & Cmpstn Stdy; U Of Chicago; Arts.

DAVIS, SHERRILL J; Montclair HS; Montclair, CA; (2); Church Yth Grp; Drama Clb; Thesps; School Play; JV Var Swmmng; Water Polo; Golden St Exam 1st Yr Alg With Hnrs; GATE Clb.

DAVIS, SHILA J; Modesto HS; Modesto, CA; (1); Camp Cnslr; Stanislaus U.

DAVIS, SONIA; Sherman Oaks Center Enriched Studies; Los Angeles, CA; (4); French Clb; Spanish Clb; Speech Tm; Teachers Aide; Rep Frsh Cls; Cit Awd; Hon Roll; Acad Decthln Tm; CA Schlrshp Fed; Natl Frnsc League; CA ST Santa Barbara.

DAVIS, STACY E; East Bakersfield HS; Bakersfield, CA; (2); Chorus; Mrchg Band; Sec Soph Cls; Capt JV Cheerldng; JV Socr; Hon Roll; CSF; Solo Majorette; CA Ambassadors Of Music European Tour 90; Acad Ltr.

DAVIS, STEPHANIE; Montgomery HS; Santa Rosa, CA; (2); French Clb; Pep Clb; Trk; Jr NHS; Pres Acad Fit Awd; Badmntn Vrsty.

DAVIS, STEPHANIE; West Hills HS; Santee, CA; (3); 77/233; Cmnty Wkr; Office Aide; Capt Var Cheerldng; Gym; Edtrs Choice Poetry 90; Fundraisers Amer Hrt Assoc, Spcl Olympics; Phys Educ.

DAVIS, STEPHEN J; Bret Harte HS; Angels Camp, CA; (2); JV Var Bsktbl; JV Var Crs Cntry; JV Var Trk; Hon Roll.

DAVIS, TAMARA; Bishop O Dowd HS; San Leandro, CA; (4); Treas Boy Scts; Cmnty Wkr; Math Clb; Math Tm; Trk; High Hon Roll; Pres Acad Fit Awd; Natl Hispanic Schlr Awds Smifnlst; Mrt Schlrshp U Of CA San Diego; CSF Lfe Mbr; U Of CA San Diego; Bio.

DAVIS, TARRA S; Buena Park HS; Buena Park, CA; (3); Church Yth Grp; Pep Clb; Teachers Aide; JV Var Mgr(s); JV Var Score Keeper; Var Trk; High Hon Roll; Hon Roll; CSF; Bus.

DAVIS, THOMAS I; Helix HS; Lemon Grove, CA; (4); 21/365; Science Clb; Teachers Aide; Ed Lit Mag; Otstndng Eng Stu; Bst Lit Smbssn 90 Lit Mag; CA Schlrshp Fdr Life Mbr Achvmnt; U Of CA San Diego; Marine Bio.

DAVIS, TIFFANY C; Woodrow Wilson HS; Long Beach, CA; (3); Cmnty Wkr; Dance Clb; Key Clb; Pep Clb; SADD; Drill Tm; Variety Show; Ed Nwsp; Cheerldng; Powder Puff Ftbl; Prncpls Advrsry Cncl; Peer Cncl; Bus Admin.

DAVIS, TIFFANY G; Roseville HS; Roseville, CA; (2); 16/445; Church Yth Grp; Spanish Clb; Church Choir; Rptr Nwsp; Friday Night Live; Hi Hnrs Gldn St Exam-Alg; Acad Slvr Mdl & Merit Awd; Byu; Actg.

DAVIS, TONI D; Foothills HS; Sacramento, CA; (1); Chorus; School Musical; Hon Roll; Prfct Atten Awd; Stanford; Pre-Med.

DAVIS, TRACY; Los Alamitos HS; Seal Beach, CA; (3); Service Clb; Stu Cncl; Var Co-Capt Cheerldng; High Hon Roll; NHS; Golden ST Exams & High Hnrs Geomtry & Algbr Hnrs; Outstndng Englsh Stu & Wrld Cultures Stu; Astrnt.

DAVIS, TRAVIS H; Banning HS; Carson, CA; (3); Ski Clb; Varsity Clb; School Play; Pres Frsh Cls; Off Soph Cls; Off Jr Cls; Capt Var Ftbl; Var Trk; Wt Lftg; Cit Awd; USC; Bus Mgmt.

DAVIS, VICTORIA L; Torrey Pines HS; Encinitas, CA; (3); Key Clb; SADD; Var Fld Hcky; Var Swmmng; Cit Awd; High Hon Roll; Hon Roll; NHS; Pres Acad Fit Awd; Outstndng Achvt & Swmmng Coachs Awds; PA ST; Pre-Med.

DAVIS, WENDY; Casa Grande HS; Petaluma, CA; (1); French Clb; Girl Scts; Var Trk; Hon Roll; IA ST U; Vet.

DAVIS-MARSH, ERIKA J; Mar Vista HS; Imp Beach, CA; (3); 1/434; Am Leg Aux Girls St; Pep Clb; Variety Show; VP Soph Cls; L Var Swmmng; Var Tennis; Hon Roll; Voice Dem Awd; Acad Superbowl; Vrsty Water Polo Ltr; Aeronautical Engrng.

DAVISON, ASHER; Santa Monica HS; Santa Monica, CA; (4); 1/700; Debate Tm; French Clb; Pres Math Tm; Band; Mrchg Band; Orch; School Musical; High Hon Roll; Kiwanis Awd; Ntl Merit SF; Kiwanis Awd 1st Pl Instrumntl Solo Comptn; 117 AHSME 88; Yth And Govt 89-90.

DAVISON, BETSY; Ferndale HS; Ferndale, CA; (2); Church Yth Grp; JV Bsktbl; JV Sftbl; Beautician.

DAVISON II, DEAN; Golden West HS; Visalia, CA; (4); 28/400; Debate Tm; Math Clb; Math Tm; Pep Clb; Science Clb; Rep Stu Cncl; Var Socr; JV Wrstlng; High Hon Roll; Hon Roll; Sci Olympiad Medal Wnnr; SCICON Cnslr For 6th Grade Stus; Engr Apprentice For US Army; GA Tech; Electrical Engrng.

DAVISON JR, JOHN C; North HS; Bakersfield, CA; (4); Pres Drama Clb; JA; Teachers Aide; School Play; Mgr Stage Crew; Best In Drama Awd; Camp Keep Yth Cnslr; Cal Poly; Arch.

DAVISON, KELLY K; El Cajon Valley HS; El Cajon, CA; (3); 49/458; Dance Clb; Teachers Aide; Variety Show; Treas Frsh Cls; Gym; Socr; Swmmng; Vllybl; Hon Roll; Achvt Awd; Young Life; Marine Bio.

DAVISON, RUTH E; Victor Valley Union HS; Victorville, CA; (3); Church Yth Grp; Cmnty Wkr; Computer Clb; Spanish Clb; Vllybl; Hon Roll; Chrch Yth Activities; Computers.

DAVISON, VERONICA; Cordova SR HS; Rancho Cordova, CA; (4); 24/443; French Clb; Ed Yrbk; Ed Lit Mag; High Hon Roll; Pres Acad Fit Awd; Natrl Hlprs-Peer Cnslng Grp; UC Davis; Cmmnctns.

DAVISSON, MELANIE M; Poway HS; Poway, CA; (3); Church Yth Grp; 4-H; Speech Tm; Varsity Clb; Band; Orch; Var Trk; 4-H Awd; Hon Roll; Judo; Pre-Law.

DAVY, JENETTE L; Trabuco Hills HS; Trabuco Canyon, CA; (2); Church Yth Grp; FBLA; Spanish Clb; Sftbl; Pres Acad Fit Awd; UC Irvine; Medcl.

DAVY, MATTHEW; Irvine HS; Irvine, CA; (1); Church Yth Grp; Ski Clb; Off Frsh Cls; Ftbl; Wt Lftg; Wrstlng; CSF; UCSD; Oceanlgy.

DAW, BRAD E; Torrey Pines HS; San Diego, CA; (2); JV Golf; Alg Golden St Exam Hnrs 89; Bus.

DAWES, CHARLES C; Dana Hills HS; Laguna Niguel, CA; (3); Church Yth Grp; Key Clb; Ski Clb; Varsity Clb; Stu Cncl; Var L Ftbl; Var L Golf; Opt Clb Awd; Chrch Altar Boy; Ftbl Mst Imprvd, MVP 88, 89; USD; Mnfctrs Rep.

DAWES, KEVIN D; Artesia HS; Lakewood, CA; (4); 103/312; Boy Scts; Church Yth Grp; JA; Trk; Wrstlng; High Hon Roll; Hon Roll; UC San Diego; Engrng.

DAWSON, AMY R; Sacramento Adventist Acad; Fair Oaks, CA; (2); Church Yth Grp; Off Frsh Cls; Sec Soph Cls.

DAWSON, ANDRE L; Hanford Union HS; Hanford, CA; (2); VP Frsh Cls; VP Soph Cls; Stu Cncl; JV Bsbl; JV Ftbl; JV Socr; JV Wrstlng; Hon Roll; Santa Barbara; Poltcl Sci.

DAWSON, CHAD K; Atascadero HS; Atascadero, CA; (3); JV Bsbl; JV Bsktbl; JV Var Trk; Winners Circle Awds Span & Bus; CA Polytech ST U; Bus.

DAWSON, CYNDI L; Rio Vista HS; Rio Vista, CA; (3); AFS; Ed FHA; Science Clb; SADD; Rep Soph Cls; VP Sr Cls; JV Var Bsktbl; Var Sftbl; Var Trk; JV Var Vllybl; Olympc Fstvl Cyclng 89 & 90; Mrn Bio.

DAWSON, ERIC; Chaffey HS; Ontario, CA; (2); Bus.

DAWSON, FREDRICK E; Paramount HS; Paramount, CA; (3); 58/320; FCA; Letterman Clb; JV Bsbl; Var Ftbl; JV Wrstlng; Hon Roll; Prfct Atten Awd.

DAWSON, GRANT; Palo Alto HS; Palo Alto, CA; (2); Teachers Aide; Ed Nwsp; Hon Roll; Schl Writing Awds 1st & 3rd Pl; Bus.

DAWSON, IAN J; Arcata HS; Mc Kinleyville, CA; (1); SADD; JV Bsktbl; JV Crs Cntry; Hon Roll; Top 10 Frshmn Clss.

DAWSON, JESSICA; Chico SR HS; Chico, CA; (2); Church Yth Grp; Pep Clb; Band; Chorus; Mrchg Band; JV Cheerldng; Hon Roll; Vet Med.

DAWSON, KELLY; Redlands SR HS; Redlands, CA; (4); Debate Tm; Drama Clb; NFL; Speech Tm; Band; School Musical; Yrbk; Bsktbl; Capt JV Socr; High Hon Roll; UC Irvine.

DAWSON, MATT A; Tustin HS; Santa Ana, CA; (2); Boy Scts; Cit Awd; Surf Clb & Team; Chef.

DAWSON, MICHAEL A; Magnolia HS; Stanton, CA; (3); Band; Orch; Pep Band; Swmmng; UCLA; Art.

DAWSON, SARAH E; Hoover HS; Fresno, CA; (1); Church Yth Grp; Hosp Aide; L Var Crs Cntry; JV Socr; L Var Trk; Pres Acad Fit Awd; US Air Frc Acad; Astronaut.

DAWSON, SHANE R; Porterville HS; Springville, CA; (3); Teachers Aide; Band; Jazz Band; Mrchg Band; Pep Band; Var Trk; Music Awd; Porterville Coll; Music.

DAWSON, TAMU E; Skyline HS; Oakland, CA; (2); Office Aide; Hon Roll; Schl Recgntn Golden St Exams Alg; Neighborhood Schlr; Top Scores CTBS Testing; Spelman Coll; Frgn Lang.

DAY, ASHLEY E; Carlmont HS; San Carlos, CA; (3); Off Soph Cls; Off Jr Cls; Interact Club; Psych.

DAY, CARA M; Delta HS; Courtland, CA; (3); Am Leg Aux Girls St; Church Yth Grp; FHA; Varsity Clb; Chorus; Var L Bsktbl; JV L Sftbl; Var L Trk; Var L Vllybl; High Hon Roll; Close-Up Pgm Washington DC; Acad Decathalon; All League Selection Track; Mineral Law.

DAY, CHRISTINA MARIE; Westminster HS; Westminster, CA; (4); Church Yth Grp; Key Clb; Band; Mrchg Band; Orch; Pep Band; Var Fld Hcky; Orange Coast; Fshn Dsgnr.

DAY, COURTNEY; Leuzinger HS; Lawndale, CA; (3); Church Yth Grp; Cmnty Wkr; Dance Clb; Teachers Aide; Church Choir; Certified Yth Hlth Educator; CA Inst Of Arts; Music.

DAY, HOLLIS W; Nevada Union HS; Penn Valley, CA; (3); Library Aide; Teachers Aide; Camp Cnslr; Snowbrdng; Sacramento ST; Tchr.

DAY, JEFF; Placer HS; Auburn, CA; (3); 57/312; Boy Scts; Ski Clb; Spanish Clb; Teachers Aide; Trk; High Hon Roll; Hon Roll; Pltcl Sci.

DAY, JERRY; Dinuba HS; Dinuba, CA; (3); Rep Chorus; Mrchg Band; Var L Golf; Hole In One Sea Pines Golf Crs 89; Fresno ST U; Ed.

DAY, JULIE A; Sonora HS; La Habra, CA; (3); Treas Pres Church Yth Grp; Debate Tm; French Clb; Ed Lit Mag; Pres Soph Cls; Hon Roll; Ntl Merit Ltr; JV Var Swmmng; Discovery Clb Actvty Mgr.

DAY, MONICA; Thousand Oaks HS; Thousand Oaks, CA; (2); Hon Roll; Lifegrd PE Ldrshp; Soclgy.

DAY, REGINA M; Robert A Millikan HS; Long Beach, CA; (4); Church Yth Grp; Dance Clb; FBLA; SADD; Teachers Aide; Cit Awd; Electrncs; Pr Cnslng; Vlntr Cnslng; Long Beach City Coll; Electrncs.

DAY, TIFFANY; Kern Valley HS; Weldon, CA; (2); Church Yth Grp; 4-H; FFA; Pep Clb; Spanish Clb; SADD; Church Choir; JV Cheerldng; Var Powder Puff Ftbl; Var Tennis; UC Northridge; Phys Thrpy.

DAY, WILLIAM F; John F Kennedy HS; Buena Park, CA; (2); Boy Scts; JV Ftbl; JV Trk; JV Wrstlng; Prfct Atten Awd; Math.

DAYA, ALY S; Kennedy HS; Granada Hills, CA; (3); Art Clb; Computer Clb; French Clb; Ed Lit Mag; JV Bsbl; Var Bsktbl; Var Trk; Pblctns Annl Art Awd; CSUN; Comp Engrng.

DAYAO, DOROTHY; St Patrick-St Vincent HS; Vallejo, CA; (3); Debate Tm; Chorus; Lit Mag; Treas Jr Cls; High Hon Roll; Hon Roll; CSF; Prom Cmmtte; Teachers Aide; Stanford U; Math.

DAYCO, CATHERINE; Berean Christian HS; Concord, CA; (4); Church Yth Grp; School Musical; Pres Frsh Cls; Pres Sr Cls; Stu Cncl; Var L Socr; Var L Vllybl; High Hon Roll; Stu Body VP; Schlr Athlt Awd 89-90; Chrstn Stu Ldrshp; Biola U; Bus Admin.

DAYLA, NILAM; Culver City HS; Culver City, CA; (3).

DAYLEG, RAY-FRANCIS Z; James Logan HS; Union City, CA; (3); Rptr Nwsp; JV Ftbl; Powder Puff Ftbl; Var Tennis; Hon Roll.

DAYTON, SHANIKO; Woodland HS; Woodland, CA; (2); Church Yth Grp; Cmnty Wkr; SADD; Sftbl; Trk; Cit Awd; Chrch Attendnce Awd; U Of OR; Lawyer.

DAZA, JUDY A; Bellarmine-Jefferson HS; Burbank, CA; (4); 7/120; Hosp Aide; Math Clb; Science Clb; Teachers Aide; Rep Frsh Cls; Capt VP Bsktbl; JV Capt Crs Cntry; Var Capt Sftbl; Trk; High Hon Roll; Bnk America Schlr/Achvt Lbrl Arts; Magna Cum Laude; M&ms Schlr/Athl Awd; Army Schlr/Athl; UC Irvine; Bio Sci.

DAZA, KARINA K; Lowell HS; San Francisco, CA; (2); Church Yth Grp; Stage Crew; CSF; Art; Photo; UC Berkeley.

DE ALBA, CARLOS; Castle Park HS; Chula Vista, CA; (3); 5/422; Latin Clb; Cit Awd; Acdmc Achvrs; VP MECHA Clb.

DE AMICIS, TRACY A; Lowell HS; San Francisco, CA; (2); Church Yth Grp; NFL; JV Socr; Italian Club; CSF; Exch Stu To Italy.

DE ANDA, CHRISTINE; Covina HS; West Covina, CA; (4); 15/266; Am Leg Aux Girls St; Model UN; Office Aide; Service Clb; Teachers Aide; Off Frsh Cls; Off Soph Cls; Off Jr Cls; Pres Stu Cncl; High Hon Roll; CSF Pres; U Of La Verne; Elem Tchr.

DE ANDA, YOLANDA; Sacred Heart Of Jesus HS; Los Angeles, CA; (3); GAA; School Play; Yrbk; Hon Roll; Treas NHS; Awd 5th Pl 90 Natl Span Exm; Lawyer.

DE ANDREA, LIV X; Aptos HS; Aptos, CA; (1); #1 In Class; Debate Tm; Pres French Clb; SADD; Pres Acad Fit Awd; Jr Statesman Of Amer; CA Schl Culinary Arts; Chef.

DE ARCE, ANA H; Lowell HS; San Francisco, CA; (2); Jr Statesman Ass; Ballet; Psycht.

DE ARCOS, EVIE S; Nevada Union HS; Grass Valley, CA; (3); 18/535; Church Yth Grp; Varsity Clb; Chorus; Mgr Bsktbl; Mgr(s); Co-Capt Var Vllybl; High Hon Roll; Hon Roll; Math.

DE ASIS, JANE C; Santa Teresa HS; San Jose, CA; (3); French Clb; Spanish Clb; Crs Cntry; Trk; UC Davis; Elec Engr.

DE AVILA, JOHN S; Tulare Union HS; Tulare, CA; (1); FFA; Hon Roll; LUS; Ag.

DE AVILA, LUCI M; Tulare Joint Union HS; Tulare, CA; (2); Church Yth Grp; Hon Roll; Prfct Atten Awd; SES Soc Espirto Santo; CA Schlstc Fed; Fresno ST U; Tchr.

DE AVILA, SHANNON; El Toro HS; El Toro, CA; (2); Church Yth Grp; Cmnty Wkr; GAA; Var Socr; JV Vllybl; Hon Roll; U Santa Barbara; Dsgnr.

DE BAETS, STACIE N; Selma HS; Selma, CA; (3); Church Yth Grp; Band; Mrchg Band; Pep Band; Stat Bsktbl; L Var Sftbl; Engl Ed.

DE BERNARDI, AMBER; Mesa Verde HS; Citrus Heights, CA; (2); Amer River Clg; Photogrphy.

DE BOER, MONICA; Modesto HS; Modesto, CA; (4); 9/460; Church Yth Grp; Dance Clb; Drama Clb; Teachers Aide; Church Choir; Stat Ftbl; Hon Roll; CA Schlrshp Fed; Visit Art Galleries; Comp Tutor; CA ST U Stanislaus; Corp Law.

DE BORD, LEORE C; Winters HS; Winters, CA; (2); Pep Clb; SADD; Band; Drill Tm; Cheerldng; Hon Roll; Model.

DE BORO, KRISTIN L; Morro Bay SR HS; Morro Bay, CA; (3); 20/220; JCL; Latin Clb; Office Aide; Pep Clb; JV Diving; Powder Puff Ftbl; Var L Swmmng; Hon Roll; Pres Acad Fit Awd; Phys Therapy.

DE BORTOLI, KRISTEN; Mc Cloud HS; Mc Cloud, CA; (4); 2/30; Am Leg Aux Girls St; FBLA; FHA; Teachers Aide; Capt Varsity Clb; Band; Pep Band; Pres Frsh Cls; Pres Jr Cls; Rep Stu Cncl; MVP Evrgrn Leag Bsktbl; All Leag Vllybl; Coll Of Siskiyous; Elem Educ.

DE BOURG, HANNA; Calvary Chapel HS; Santa Ana, CA; (2); Nwsp; JV Tennis; JV Trk; Hon Roll; Pres Acad Fit Awd.

DE CAMP, INGE K; Rincon Valley Christian HS; Santa Rosa, CA; (3); Church Yth Grp; Spanish Clb; Chorus; Cit Awd; Ensmbl; Bus.

DE CARO, MICHAEL; Terra Nova HS; Pacifica, CA; (4); Church Yth Grp; Computer Clb; VP French Clb; Letterman Clb; Varsity Clb; Pres Frsh Cls; VP Stu Cncl; Ftbl; Swmmng; Wrstlng; Civil Air Ptrl; Semi-Fnlst AROTC, AFROTC, NROTC; Biochem.

DE CASAS JR, ARMANDO; Garey HS; Pomona, CA; (3); Var Bsbl; JV Bsktbl; UNLV; Sports Medicine.

DE CASAS, MONICA; Rosary HS; Placentia, CA; (3); Church Yth Grp; Cmnty Wkr; Spanish Clb; Variety Show; Hon Roll; NEDT Awd; St Schlr; Vllybl; Safe Rides; US Acad Decathlon Tm & 2nd Pl In Essay; Med.

DE CONTRERAS, DANIELLE C; Roosevelt HS; Fresno, CA; (3); Spanish Clb; Band; Mrchg Band; School Musical; School Play; Yrbk; Var Sftbl; Var Vllybl; Hon Roll; Pres Acad Fit Awd; Work Grocers; Camp Cnslr; Math Achvmt Plaques & Cert; U CA Santa Barbara; Child Psyc.

DE CORSE, RICHARD A; San Pasqual HS; Winterhaven, CA; (3); Am Leg Boys St; 4-H; FFA; Letterman Clb; Spanish Clb; SADD; Var L Bsbl; Var L Ftbl; 4-H Awd; High Hon Roll; AZ Western Coll; Engrng.

DE CRISTOFARO, STEVEN M; Rio Vista HS; Rio Vista, CA; (3); FHA; Letterman Clb; SADD; Nwsp; Yrbk; VP Soph Cls; Sec Stu Cncl; JV Var Bsbl; JV Var Ftbl; Var L Trk; Bus.

DE DARIO, DOLORES E; Alverno HS; San Gabriel, CA; (3); 16/67; Church Yth Grp; Teachers Aide; Chorus; Church Choir; School Musical; Yrbk; Pres Frsh Cls; Treas Soph Cls; VP Jr Cls; Stu Cncl; 13th Strhn CA Annl Yth Ctznshp Smnr; 1-2-1 Clb; CSF; Chld Devlpmnt.

DE FELICE, TIA M; Redlands HS; Redlands, CA; (4); 40/864; Church Yth Grp; FCA; Pres Pep Clb; Spanish Clb; Pres Chorus; Drill Tm; School Play; Powder Puff Ftbl; Hon Roll; San Diego ST U; Bus.

DE FERRARI, CHAD C; Thomas Downey HS; Modesto, CA; (3); Aud/Vis; Chess Clb; Church Yth Grp; Debate Tm; Key Clb; NFL; Speech Tm; SADD; Variety Show; Phtg Yrbk; Thomas Downey Knight Achvt Awd; St Qlfyng Congress & Debate Awd; UC Davis; Broadcasting.

DE FONTENELLE, SHERRY; South East Lutheran HS; Huntington Park, CA; (4); 4/13; Pep Clb; Teachers Aide; Cit Awd; High Hon Roll; Hon Roll; Pres Acad Fit Awd; Stu Of Yr Ojeda Piano Studio 87; Frgn Lang Awd 88; ELAC; Law.

DE GARMO, R AARON; Palo Verde HS; Blythe, CA; (2); Boy Scts; Drama Clb; JV Var Ftbl; High Hon Roll; Hon Roll; NHS; CSF; Intrct Clb; UCLA; Med.

DE GARMO, RICHARD A; Palo Verde HS; San Jacinto, CA; (2); 1/300; Boy Scts; Drama Clb; Var Ftbl; JV Trk; Wt Lftg; High Hon Roll; NHS; CA Schlrshp Fed; Interact Clb; UCLA; Med.

DE GOVIA, MARIO J; North Hollywood HS; Los Angeles, CA; (4); Boy Scts; Capt Debate Tm; Speech Tm; Band; Jazz Band; Mrchg Band; Ed Lit Mag; Intrml Bsktbl; Hon Roll; Ntl Merit SF; Young Schlr; UCLA Alumni Awd 89; Berkeley; Corp Lawyr.

DE GRAFFENREID, KELLY; Ontario HS; Ontario, CA; (3); Pep Clb; Ski Clb; Spanish Clb; Teachers Aide; Cheerldng; High Hon Roll; Hon Roll; Mst Spirited 88-89 Pep Squad; Nrsng.

DE GRAFFENREID, MICHAEL R; Bellarmine College Prep; San Jose, CA; (3); Church Yth Grp; Letterman Clb; Varsity Clb; Var L Wrstlng; Ntl Merit SF; Pres Acad Fit Awd; Played Acousti/Elec Guitar; 1st Pl Wrstlg Lg; Cal Poly; Biochem.

DE GROOT, SARAH; Perris HS; Sun City, CA; (2); 12/697; Church Yth Grp; Cmnty Wkr; Debate Tm; Drama Clb; Sec Chorus; Letterman Clb; Spanish Clb; SADD; Varsity Clb; School Play; Mock Trial Team Law; Interact Club Pres; Rotarian Yth Ldrshp Awd; Schlr Athl; ASB Club Cncl; Acadmc Ltrs; Bio.

DE GROOTE, CHRISTEN M; A A Stagg HS; Stockton, CA; (1); JV Vllybl; Var Pres Acad Fit Awd; U C Davis; Microbio.

DE GROOTE, DAWN; Amos Alonzo Stagg HS; Stockton, CA; (2); Hon Roll; Prfct Atten Awd; Musical Theater; HOSA Assn; MIT; Microbio.

DE GUIA, ALMA MARIE; Chaminade College Prep; Mission Hills, CA; (3); Art Clb; Church Yth Grp; Dance Clb; Drama Clb; Thesps; School Musical; School Play; Variety Show; Yrbk; Var Cheerldng; Won Title Ms CA Coed Hostess 89 & Currntly Ms Mission Hills 90.

DE GUIA, CAROLYN U; Artesia HS; Hawaiian Gardens, CA; (2); Intnl Clb; Science Clb; Spanish Clb; School Play; Rep Soph Cls; Sec Jr Cls; Stu Cncl; JV Tennis; Hon Roll; Nrsng.

DE GUZMAN, ARTURO D; Garey HS; Pomona, CA; (2); VP Stu Cncl; NHS; UC Berkeley; Mech Engrng.

DE GUZMAN, CARLOTA L; Westmoor HS; Daly City, CA; (2); Spanish Clb; CA Schlrshp Fndtn; Newcomers Clb; Piano; San Francisco ST U; Music.

DE GUZMAN, CAROLYN U; Bellarmine-Jefferson HS; North Hollywood, CA; (2); Teachers Aide; School Musical; Variety Show; Var Capt Pom Pon; Cit Awd; High Hon Roll; NHS; CA Schlrshp Fed; UCLA; Dnstry.

DE GUZMAN, LEIZEL; Channel Island HS; Oxnard, CA; (4); Church Yth Grp; Teachers Aide; Drill Tm; Cit Awd; Prfct Atten Awd; Acad Achvt Awd; Acctng.

DE GUZMAN, MYLENE T; So San Francisco HS; S San Francisco, CA; (2); Cmnty Wkr; Drama Clb; French Clb; FBLA; Math Clb; Spanish Clb; Off Frsh Cls; Off Soph Cls; JV Swmmng; High Hon Roll; CSF; Stu Mnth Awd Sci; Outstndng Engl Stu 89-90; Jrnlsm.

DE GUZMAN, RAYNEIL C; Servite HS; Cerritos, CA; (2); Boy Scts; Socr; JR Statemen Of Amer; UCLA; Bus.

DE GUZMAN, RYAN; Christian Brothers HS; Sacramento, CA; (2); 2/142; Science Clb; Spanish Clb; SADD; Sec Soph Cls; JV Tennis; High Hon Roll; NHS; SRO-STUS Rchng Out-Drg Awrnss Tchng Elem Schls; CSF-CA Schlrshp Fdrtn.

DE HAVEN, AUDREY; Chester JR/Sr HS; Chester, CA; (3); 4/45; Am Leg Aux Girls St; Art Clb; Cmnty Wkr; Letterman Clb; ROTC; Spanish Clb; Teachers Aide; Varsity Clb; VP Soph Cls; Pres Jr Cls; All Leag Vllybl & Bsktbl; Schlr Athl 3 Yrs; CSF; HOBY; Sports Med.

DE HAVEN, NICOLE E; Boron HS; Boron, CA; (3); 3/60; Math Tm; Pres Frsh Cls; VP Jr Cls; JV Capt Bsktbl; Var Capt Cheerldng; Sftbl; Var Capt Vllybl; NHS; Commssnr Of Publicity; ASB Pres; Acad Decathlon; Bus Admin.

DE HOFF, SCOTT L; Las Plumas HS; Palermo, CA; (2); Letterman Clb; Var Bsbl; JV Bsktbl; JV Ftbl; Var Wt Lftg; Bus.

DE HOYOS, ISRAEL E; King City HS; King City, CA; (3); Church Yth Grp; Band; Jazz Band; Mrchg Band; High Hon Roll; Hon Roll; Bus.

DE IULIIS, JENNIFER A; Moorpark HS; Moorpark, CA; (2); 114/250; JV Bsktbl; JV Co-Capt Cheerldng; Hon Roll; Poetry Finalist Watermark Press 90; English/Art/Modeling.

DE JESUS, JOSE N; Irvine HS; Irvine, CA; (2); Intrml Bsbl; High Hon Roll; CSF; USC; Engrng.

DE JESUS, SANDRA; Poway HS; Poway, CA; (4); Intnl Clb; VP Science Clb; Teachers Aide; Band; Cit Awd; High Hon Roll; Hon Roll; Jr NHS; NHS; Dncng; Bike Rdng; 4.0 Awd; Hstry Tchr.

DE JONG, CARLA; Central Valley Chrstn; Porterville, CA; (4); Church Yth Grp; Spanish Clb; Church Choir; Stage Crew; Sec Soph Cls; Var Vllybl; Hon Roll; Opt Clb Awd; Otstndng Typist; Coaches Awd Vllybl; Calvin Coll.

DE JONG, HEIDI; Escondido HS; Escondido, CA; (3); Church Yth Grp; Hosp Aide; Key Clb; Science Clb; Capt Vllybl; High Hon Roll; Hon Roll; Gldn St Math Awd Hghst Hnrs; CSF; Coll Rdy Wrtrs Prjct Outstnch Achvt Schlrshp Awd; Corp Law.

DE JONG, RICK A; College Park HS; Pleasant Hill, CA; (4); 43/311; AFS; French Clb; JA; Model UN; Band; Jazz Band; Mrchg Band; St Marys Coll.

DE JONGE, MELANIE S; Tracy HS; Tracy, CA; (2); Church Yth Grp; French Clb; Chorus; High Hon Roll; Nvlst.

DE LA CALZADA, MARIPAZ; Bishop Amat Memorial HS; La Puente, CA; (3); Cmnty Wkr; French Clb; Chorus; School Musical; Hon Roll; Vol At Cath Worker Kitchen E LA; Cert Apprctn DHCC Devlpmntlly Disabled; Silver Screen Club; Agri.

DE LA CERDA, ANDREA K; Whittier HS; Whittier, CA; (4); Letterman Clb; Teachers Aide; Varsity Clb; Stu Cncl; Var Socr; Var JV Swmmng; Hon Roll; NHS; Indstry Ed Cncl Medlln Awd Wnnr-Wrk Exprnc; Swm Clb VP; Na Alii Svc Y-Clb; RIANNS Svc Clb VP; USC; Bus.

DE LA CERDA, EUGENE; San Jose High Acad; San Jose, CA; (3); 14/207; Boy Scts; JV Var Bsktbl; Hon Roll; Prfct Atten Awd; CSF; Navy; Engr.

DE LA CERRA, MANUEL; Chaminade Coll Prep; Canoga Park, CA; (4); 9/250; Key Clb; Spanish Clb; Band; Yrbk; Rep Frsh Cls; JV Bsbl; JV Bsktbl; JV Ftbl; High Hon Roll; Hon Roll; Embry-Riddle Arntl U; Avncs.

DE LA CRUZ, ALISON M; Carson HS; Carson, CA; (2); Computer Clb; Drama Clb; Service Clb; Teachers Aide; Band; Mrchg Band; Nwsp; Treas Stu Cncl; Mgr(s); Sftbl.

DE LA CRUZ, DENISE D; Bishop Amat HS; Rosemead, CA; (3); Dance Clb; Cit Awd; Hon Roll; Sftbl; Chrstn Service For Parish; Silver Screen & Fshn Outlook Clbs; Bus.

DE LA CRUZ, SONIA ISABEL; Central Union HS; El Centro, CA; (2); Treas Spanish Clb; JV Bsktbl; Var Trk; JV Vllybl; Hon Roll; Frdy Nght Live Clb Scrtry; Cnlsr.

DE LA CRUZ, VERONICA; Venice HS; Los Angeles, CA; (4); 22/450; Cmnty Wkr; Debate Tm; Hosp Aide; Orch; School Musical; Treas Sr Cls; Rep Stu Cncl; Var L Sftbl; Hon Roll; Opt Clb Awd; S CA Rep Chicano/Latino Ldrshp St Conf; Fulfllmnt Fund Schlr; Yth Opprtnts Fndtn Schlr; Stanford U; Scl Sci.

DE LA FUENTE, JOE A; Saddleback HS; Santa Ana, CA; (3); Letterman Clb; Varsity Clb; Ftbl; Trk; Wt Lftg; Wrstlng; Fresno ST; Bus.

DE LA FUENTE, NICOLE N; Hoover HS; Glendale, CA; (2); Church Yth Grp; Dance Clb; Letterman Clb; Pep Clb; Variety Show; JV Cheerldng; Gym; USC; Dance.

DE LA FUENTE, RANDOLPH G; Loyola HS; Rosemead, CA; (2); Art Clb; Chess Clb; Cmnty Wkr; Computer Clb; Debate Tm; Drama Clb; French Clb; Hosp Aide; Latin Clb; Scholastic Bowl; Reconstructive Surgery.

DE LA JARA, INGRID; Fairfield HS; Fairfield, CA; (2); Art Clb; Drama Clb; School Musical; School Play; Stage Crew; Variety Show; Hon Roll; CSSSA Arts Schlr 90; Illustration.

DE LA MAZA, HELEN M; University HS; Irvine, CA; (3); 59/551; Pres English Clb; Girl Scts; NFL; Capt Speech Tm; Church Choir; JV Crs Cntry; JV Trk; High Hon Roll; Spanish NHS; Volunteer Arbor Animal Hosp; Counselor Camp Joe Scherman; Laureate Award Medallion Spanish 89-90; Veterinarian.

DE LA O, JESSE; St Genevieve HS; Panorama City, CA; (3); French Clb; Letterman Clb; Pep Clb; Spanish Clb; SADD; VP Stu Cncl; Var Capt Bsktbl; Var Crs Cntry; Var Ftbl; Var Capt Vllybl; Pepperdine U; Bus Admin.

DE LA PAZ, CECILIA; San Gabriel HS; Montebello, CA; (3); Am Leg Aux Girls St; Church Yth Grp; Cmnty Wkr; Hosp Aide; Key Clb; SADD; Church Choir; Ed Nwsp; High Hon Roll; Hon Roll; Bst Jr Jrnlst; Treas Courtesy Cmmtte; Srch & Rescue Squad; U Of Santa Barbara; Jrnlsm.

DE LA RIVA, JOSE J; Saddleback HS; Santa Ana, CA; (3); JV Bsbl; Var Wrstlng; MESA; Entrance Hnrs; Arch Engr.

DE LA ROSA, MARISSA; Gardena HS; Gardena, CA; (3); Am Leg Aux Girls St; Pres Sec Service Clb; Spanish Clb; Rep Soph Cls; Stu Cncl; UCLA Bk Awd; CSF Pres & Sgt-At-Arms; MESA; Attrny.

DE LA ROSA, MARY G; James Logan HS; Union City, CA; (3); 62/972; Church Yth Grp; Teachers Aide; Band; Mrchg Band; Pep Band; School Musical; Hon Roll; Pre-Coll Acad U CA-BERKELEY 89/90; Stu Senator 90; Bst Rookie Band Awd; U CA-BERKELEY; Bio.

DE LA TERRA, MARTHA M; Pittsburg HS; Pittsburg, CA; (1); Prfct Atten Awd; Acdmc Excllnc; Ctzn Day Awd; Doc.

DE LA TORRE, ANGELICA; Ramona Convent HS; Los Angeles, CA; (3); Art Clb; Cmnty Wkr; GAA; Latin Clb; Woodbury U; Bus Adm.

DE LA TORRE, COLUMBA; Albany HS; Emeryville, CA; (4); AFS; Church Yth Grp; Cmnty Wkr; Service Clb; Spanish Clb; Sftbl; Hon Roll; Pres Acad Fit Awd; Goldn St Exam High Hnrs Alg; UC Berkeley.

DE LA TORRE, EDUARDO XAVIER; Pinole Valley HS; Hercules, CA; (3); Boy Scts; Crs Cntry; Trk; Hon Roll.

DE LA TORRE, MARIA C; Buena HS; Ventura, CA; (2); Cit Awd; Hon Roll; Prfct Atten Awd; CSF; Interact Club; Writer.

DE LA TORRE, MARTHA C; Ontario HS; Ontario, CA; (3); Hon Roll; Prfct Atten Awd; Work.

DE LA TORRE, ROLANDO; John F Kennedy HS; Buena Park, CA; (3); 22/450; Am Leg Boys St; Church Yth Grp; Letterman Clb; Teachers Aide; Varsity Clb; Acpl Chr; Swing Chorus; Treas Soph Cls; Stu Cncl; Ftbl; Disneylands Dreamers/Doers Hnrb Mntn; Bus/Econ.

DE LA VEGA, AGNES F; Mount Eden HS; Hayward, CA; (3); 27/270; Hosp Aide; Rptr Yrbk; Hist Sr Cls; JV Tennis; High Hon Roll; Csf; Goldn St Exam Geom Hnr 89; Coll Clb Treas; Partnrshp Pgm UC Berkeley; UC Berkeley; Pre-Med.

DE LANEY, CARLA E; Highlands HS; N Highlands, CA; (4); Art Clb; Sprt Ed Rptr Nwsp; Sftbl; Vllybl; High Hon Roll; Prfct Atten Awd; Pres Acad Fit Awd; Pres Schlr; Law Team; Schlr Lttr; Bus Admin.

DE LANGE, VINCENT P; Pittsburg HS; Pittsburg, CA; (4); 1/303; Church Yth Grp; Debate Tm; FBLA; Pres Key Clb; Pres Mu Alpha Theta; Pres Science Clb; SADD; Bsktbl; Var Capt Tennis; Bausch & Lomb Sci Awd; Rotary Yth Ldrshp Camp Rep; 2nd Pl HS Sci Fair Cntst; Yth Edctrs Pgm; Stanford U; Engrng.

DE LAO, JESSE; Palo Verde HS; Blythe, CA; (2); JV Bsbl; Var Crs Cntry; Var Trk; Var Wrstlng; Bus Adm.

DE LAO, JESSE; St Genevieve HS; Panorama City, CA; (3); French Clb; Letterman Clb; Pep Clb; Red Cross Aide; Spanish Clb; SADD; Var Bsktbl; JV Crs Cntry; Var Ftbl; Var Vllybl; Pepperdine U; Bus Admin.

DE LARA, VICKY; Beaumont HS; Beaumont, CA; (4); 22/140; Office Aide; Band; Mrchg Band; Pep Band; Stat Bsktbl; Var L Crs Cntry; Var L Trk; JV Vllybl; Hon Roll; Prfct Atten Awd; Jr Hnr Escort; Crss Cntry & Trk Coaches Awd; Crafton Hills Coll; Comp Sci.

DE LAURA, PAULA R; Capistrano Valley HS; Mission Viejo, CA; (3); Church Yth Grp; FCA; GAA; Varsity Clb; Rep Sr Cls; Stu Cncl; Cheerldng; Score Keeper; Vllybl; Water & Snow Skng; Long Beach ST U; Nrs.

DE LEON, ELLEN; John A Rowland HS; Walnut, CA; (2); Church Yth Grp; Cmnty Wkr; Science Clb; Varsity Clb; Tennis; Trk; Cit Awd; Gov Hon Prg Awd; High Hon Roll; Hon Roll; UC Berkeley; Accntng.

DE LEON, HEIDI F; John A Rowland HS; Walnut, CA; (4); French Clb; Science Clb; Powder Puff Ftbl; Vllybl; High Hon Roll; Hon Roll; Treas Creative Writing Club; CA ST Northridge; Pre-Bus.

DE LEON, IRIS M; Montebello HS; Montebello, CA; (3); Dance Clb; SADD; Teachers Aide; VP Acpl Chr; Chorus; Var Capt Cheerldng; Var Score Keeper; Most Vlbl Showcheer Chrldng 89-90; Choreogrphy Of Yr 88-89; Real Est Agent.

DE LEON, JAVIER L; Clayton Valley HS; Clayton, CA; (2); Red Cross Aide; Pres Frsh Cls; Off Soph Cls; Stu Cncl; JV Socr; Hon Roll; Pres Acad Fit Awd; Pres Schlr; SITE Cncl; U Of CA Berkeley; Med.

DE LEON, JOHN P; Sanger HS; Sanger, CA; (2); Intrml Var Bsbl; Intrml Bsktbl; JV Socr; USC; Bus.

DE LEON JR, JORGE; Mater Dei HS; Santa Ana, CA; (4); 75/526; Church Yth Grp; Cmnty Wkr; Hosp Aide; Spanish Clb; Score Keeper; JV Vllybl; Hon Roll; NHS; Pres Acad Fit Awd; CSF; Yth Opprtnts Fndtn Excptnl Schlr Awd; Schl Campus Mnstry; UC Irvine; Medcl.

DE LEON, JORGE A; Bellarmine College Prep; San Jose, CA; (3); 57/300; Cmnty Wkr; SADD; Trk.

DE LEON, KATINA M; O'farrell SCPA; San Diego, CA; (3); Dance Clb; Letterman Clb; Varsity Clb; Ed Yrbk; Treas Soph Cls; Var Cheerldng; Cit Awd; High Hon Roll; Ntl Merit Ltr; Prfct Atten Awd; CSF & CJSF; All Am HS Stu Awd; San Diego Jazz Co; Oxford; Lit.

DE LEON, LORRAINE R; St Jospeh HS; Norwalk, CA; (3); 10/180; Hosp Aide; Office Aide; SADD; Yrbk; High Hon Roll; Hon Roll; Prfct Atten Awd; CSF; UC; Pharm.

DE LEON, MARIA LUCIA; Woodland HS; Woodland, CA; (2); 1/750; Cmnty Wkr; Pres VP FBLA; Key Clb; Spanish Clb; Phtg Nwsp; Phtg Yrbk; Off Frsh Cls; Stu Cncl; Mgr(s); Var Tennis; HOBY Fndtn Ambssdr.

DE LEON, MELISA LISA; St Francis HS; Mountain View, CA; (1); 137/400; Pep Clb; SADD; Band; Mrchg Band; Mrchg Band; Pep Band; School Musical; JV Cheerldng; JV Gym; High Hon Roll; Stanford; Psych.

DE LEON, MICHAEL B; Valley HS; Elk Grove, CA; (2); SADD; Var Tennis; Hon Roll; San Francisco ST; Comp Sci.

DE LEON, OLIVIA; Porterville HS; Porterville, CA; (4); GAA; Latin Clb; Spanish Clb; SADD; Geolgy Clb; Hnrs Awd-Tp 10 Pct Cls; Acad Ltr, Emblm, 2 Hnrs Awds Engl; Art Awd-Strght A; Porterville Coll; Lgl Asst.

DE LEON, SAMUEL; Pinole Valley HS; Hercules, CA; (1); Elec Engr.

DE LEON, TATE; Rim Of The World HS; Blue Jay, CA; (2); 32/354; Art Clb; Chess Clb; Computer Clb; GAA; Letterman Clb; Ski Clb; Varsity Clb; Bsktbl; Golf; Socr; CA Schlstc Fed; Radiologist.

DE LEON, WENDY C; Bell Gardens HS; Bell Gardens, CA; (3); French Clb; Spanish Clb; Prfct Atten Awd; CSF; Sch Rcgntn CA Golden St Exm Alg; Spanish Challenge Exm; CA ST Long Beach; Accntng.

DE LLANOS, ESTELA; Notre Dame Acad; Santa Monica, CA; (3); 2/110; Church Yth Grp; Cmnty Wkr; Debate Tm; NFL; Office Aide; Quiz Bowl; Sec Spanish Clb; Speech Tm; Chorus; School Musical; Campus Mnstry Pres; Music Clb Adv Rep.

DE LOACH, KIMBERLY N; Hillsdale HS; Foster City, CA; (3); Cmnty Wkr; Chorus; Hon Roll; CA Gldn St Alg Awd; 2nd Yr Frnch Awd; CSF Clb; Coll Of San Mateo; Psych.

DE LOS REYES, CHARISMA V; Samuel F B Morse HS; San Diego, CA; (2); Church Yth Grp; FTA; Intnl Clb; Chorus; Church Choir; School Play; Rep Stu Cncl; JV Capt Cheerldng; Hon Roll; Prfct Atten Awd; San Diego All-Str Chrldng Sqd; UC Santa Cruz; Edctnl Psych.

DE LOS REYES, JENNIFER F; Nogales HS; Walnut, CA; (3); 21/628; JV Bsktbl; High Hon Roll; Prfct Atten Awd; CSF; Acad Achvt Awd Eng; Schlr/Athl.

DE LOS REYES, MARITES P; Eagle Rock JR/Sr HS; Los Angeles, CA; (1); Key Clb; Var Tennis; Hon Roll.

DE LOS SANTOS, ROMER A; North Hollywood HS; North Hollywood, CA; (3); Spanish Clb; Teachers Aide; Chorus; Hon Roll; UCLA; Acctng.

DE LOS SANTOS, ROMMEL; Lower Lake HS; Clearlake, CA; (4); 4/120; Am Leg Boys St; Church Yth Grp; Pres Stu Cncl; Capt Tennis; Elks Awd; Hon Roll; Pres Acad Fit Awd; Gldn St Exam; Acad Excllnc Awd Geom Hnrs; Cert Of Recgntn CA Acad Dcthln 1989; CA Polytech U; Mechncl Engrng.

DE LOS SANTOS, YOLANDA; Ramona HS; Ramona, CA; (3); Computer Clb; Pep Clb; Spanish Clb; Socr; Sftbl; UCSD; Comp Sci.

DE LOZA, KITZIA K; La Puente HS; La Puente, CA; (3); #2 In Class; Service Clb; Pres Band; Pres Mrchg Band; Off Jr Cls; Off Sr Cls; Var L Tennis; Hon Roll; Prfct Atten Awd; JV Badminton Team; Earth Rehab; Amnesty Intl; UC Irvine; Psychology Spanish.

DE LUCA, NICCOLO S; Bishop O Dowd HS; Oakland, CA; (2); Spanish Clb; Mrchg Band; Pep Band; Rep Soph Cls; Rep Stu Cncl; JV Lcrss.

DE LUCE, JA NEAN; Hemet HS; Hemet, CA; (4); Cmnty Wkr; Office Aide; Pep Clb; Teachers Aide; Drill Tm; Var Mgr(s); Trk; Peer Cnslng; Cross Aid Tutor; Mt San Jacinto; Chld Dev.

DE LUCIA, CARLO; Canyon HS; Anaheim, CA; (1); Church Yth Grp; Cmnty Wkr; Key Clb; Stage Crew; Rep Frsh Cls; Pres Soph Cls; Bsbl; Ftbl; High Hon Roll; Hon Roll; Med.

DE LUNA, ERICK; Saint Anthony HS; Long Beach, CA; (2); Var Ftbl; Hon Roll; Math; Chrstn Srvc; Bus Admin/Acctng; UCLA; CPA.

DE LUNA, MELANIE H; University HS; Irvine, CA; (2); 41/508; Cmnty Wkr; Dance Clb; Office Aide; Ski Clb; Hon Roll.

DE MARIA, ROBERT A; Bassett HS; La Puente, CA; (3); Capt Cheerldng; Aerntcs.

DE MARTINI, CHRISTA; Ramona HS; Ramona, CA; (2); 26/345; Art Clb; Dance Clb; French Clb; Library Aide; Pep Clb; Scholastic Bowl; Drill Tm; GSE Acad Excellencew Award In Geometry; Student Of Month Honors World Civilizatn; Stdnt Month Draftng; U Of Calif; Architecture.

DE MARTINI, STEVEN D; Nevada Union HS; Nevada City, CA; (3); 46/500; Chess Clb; Cmnty Wkr; Chorus; JV Bsbl; JV Bsktbl; Boys St; BYU.

DE MERS, CARRYE L; Willow Glen HS; San Jose, CA; (3); 23/480; Drama Clb; Girl Scts; Q&S; SADD; School Play; Lit Mag; Hon Roll; Ed Nwsp; Amnesty Intl; Photo Clb; Engl Lit.

DE MEY, BROCK L; San Pasqual HS; Escondido, CA; (3); Office Aide; Pres Ski Clb; Pres Frsh Cls; Rep Soph Cls; Var Ftbl; Powder Puff Ftbl; Wt Lftg; Pres Acad Fit Awd; Rotary Awd; NAU; Bus.

DE MEYER, MARIA N; Durham HS; Durham, CA; (3); Teachers Aide; Rptr Yrbk; Sec Frsh Cls; Rep Soph Cls; JV Bsktbl; Chico ST U; Psych.

DE MONNER, STACY MICHELLE; Carondelet HS; Pittsburg, CA; (4); 33/185; Church Yth Grp; Cmnty Wkr; Dance Clb; Hosp Aide; Co-Capt Flag Corp; Rep Stu Cncl; High Hon Roll; NHS; Spanish NHS; Voice Dem Awd; Friday Night Live; Opus De Chrstn Crls Soc/Svc Cmnty Wrk Clb; Prjct 2nd Chance; Campus Ministry; CSU Sacramento; Spch Pthlgy.

DE MONTE, JENNIFER M; Brea-Olinda HS; Brea, CA; (1); Dance Clb; School Play; Jr NHS; Pres Acad Fit Awd; CSF; Med.

DE MUTH, JEFF M; Tulare HS; Tulare, CA; (2); Church Yth Grp; Band; Jazz Band; Mrchg Band; JV Socr; Var L Swmmng; High Hon Roll; Prfct Atten Awd; Vrsty Waterpolo; CSF; Golden St Exam Geom High Hnrs; Engrng.

DE NEEFE, STEVE J; La Mirada HS; La Mirada, CA; (2); Church Yth Grp; Debate Tm; Math Clb; Math Tm; NFL; Speech Tm; JV Var Crs Cntry; JV Trk; High Hon Roll; Project Independence; Spec Olympics; Elec Engr.

DE OCAMPO, THELMA R; Channel Islands HS; Oxnard, CA; (3); 95/573; Science Clb; Band; Mrchg Band; Sec Frsh Cls; Sec Soph Cls; Sec Stu Cncl; Var Tennis; Hon Roll; Student Athlete Scholar Award; U C San Diego; Computer Science.

DE PAUL, ERIC L; Orange Glen HS; Escondido, CA; (3); Drama Clb; Pep Clb; Thesps; School Musical; School Play; Rptr Nwsp; Wt Lftg; NHS; Peer Cnslr; Black Belt-Karate; Indstrl Psych.

DE PAULA, CONNIE F; Pioneer HS; Whittier, CA; (4); 7/303; French Clb; Key Clb; Ed Nwsp; Off Sr Cls; Capt Tennis; Hon Roll; Kiwanis Awd; US Army Reserve Natl Schlr Athlt Awd; Outstndng Engl Stu Of Yr 88-89; Bank Of Amer Achvtmnt Engl Awd; CA U Los Angeles; Bus.

DE PAULO, AUDNEY L; Trabuco Hills HS; El Toro, CA; (2); Letterman Clb; Spanish Clb; Ed Yrbk; Var JV Bsbl; Var Ftbl; Var Wt Lftg; Delphi Acad Coaching; Jrnlsm.

DE PREE, JOHN; Mt Shasta HS; Mt Shasta, CA; (2); 1/100; Ski Clb; High Hon Roll; CSF Siskiyou Cnty BMC Champ 88; Engrng.

DE PUCCI, ANNE M; Analy HS; Sebastopol, CA; (3); 66/234; French Clb; FFA; Hon Roll; Psych.

DE RAMIREZ, BRENDA VERONICA T; San Juan HS; Citrus Heights, CA; (3); Church Yth Grp; GAA; Teachers Aide; Varsity Clb; Band; School Musical; Var Bsktbl; Var Score Keeper; Var Socr; 1st Yr Band Awd; Principals Hnr List; Pediatric Nrsng.

DE RIJKE, ELLEN A; Cupertino HS; Cupertino, CA; (2); German Clb; Orch; Socr; Vllybl.

DE ROBERTIS, ALEX; Palisades HS; Pacific Palisades, CA; (3); Chess Clb; Hon Roll; Lion Awd; Pres Acad Fit Awd; Fluent Engl, Spnsh; Knowledge Of German, Frnch Lang; Med.

DE ROCO, ERIN; Oroville HS; Oroville, CA; (3); Office Aide; Ski Clb; Pres Frsh Cls; JV Var Bsktbl; Var Powder Puff Ftbl; Var L Tennis; JV Var Trk; JV L Vllybl; Hon Roll; Girls Block O; Student Of The Month In Vocational Arts; All League In Track & Field; CA ST U; Registered Nurse.

DE ROSA, MARISSA; Bishop Amat HS; San Dimas, CA; (3); Girl Scts; Pep Clb; Drill Tm; Variety Show; Stu Cncl; JV Var Cheerldng; Cit Awd; Hon Roll; NHS; San Diego U; Adv.

DE ROSA, TAMMY A; St Joseph HS; Santa Maria, CA; (3); 21/125; Cmnty Wkr; GAA; Hosp Aide; Key Clb; Letterman Clb; Spanish Clb; SADD; Varsity Clb; Band; Swmmng; Premed.

DE ROSE, ALLISON M; Santa Fe Christian HS; Rancho Santa Fe, CA; (3); 5/30; Cmnty Wkr; Hosp Aide; Key Clb; Chorus; Ed Yrbk; Var Tennis; JV Vllybl; Cit Awd; Gov Hon Prg Awd; High Hon Roll; Amer Govt Smnr/Cong Packard; USD; Dist Attnry.

DE RUSSY, SARA; Hillsdale HS; San Mateo, CA; (4); 47/296; Church Yth Grp; VP Frsh Cls; Pres Soph Cls; Pres Jr Cls; Pres Sr Cls; JV Var Tennis; Dnfth Awd; Hon Roll; HOBY Fndtn Awd; San Mateo Yth Advsry Cncl; Elem Ed.

DE RUYTER, EMMA L; Bonita Vista HS; Bonita, CA; (1); 26/535; Church Yth Grp; Girl Scts; Ed Nwsp; Ed Yrbk; JV Socr; 2nd Annual Macintosh Apple Writing Cont Hnrb Mntn 4th Pl; Nwsp In Ed Stu Writing Cont Hnrb Mntn 90; Philosophy.

DE SALLES, MARISA A; Valley HS; Sacramento, CA; (3); 15/650; Am Leg Aux Girls St; Pres FTA; Service Clb; SADD; Rep Sr Cls; High Hon Roll; Ntl Merit Ltr; Cmnty Wkr; Computer Clb; Teachers Aide; CSF; Black Stu Union Pres; JR Asilomar Delgtn; Comp.

DE SANTE, KIMBERLEY; North Salinas HS; Salinas, CA; (2); Church Yth Grp; Band; Color Guard; Flag Corp; Mrchg Band; Pep Band; High Hon Roll; Hon Roll; Rotary Awd; Dentistry.

DE SANTIS, DEANNA L; Carondelet HS; Walnut Creek, CA; (3); Church Yth Grp; Sec French Clb; Hosp Aide; Ski Clb; Rep Sr Cls; Sec French Hon Soc; Hon Roll; NHS; Nursing.

DE SANTOS, MICHELE; Hesperia HS; Apple Valley, CA; (4); 8/460; French Clb; FHA; Pep Clb; Teachers Aide; Rep Jr Cls; Rep Sr Cls; Tennis; High Hon Roll; Hon Roll; Univ Clb; CSF; CA ST San Bernardino; Psych.

DE SANTOS, TANYA R; Marymount HS; Los Angeles, CA; (2); FBLA; Hosp Aide; Speech Tm; SADD; Yrbk; Lit Mag; VP Frsh Cls; Pres Soph Cls; Art Clb; Cmnty Wkr; Schl Ambssdr HOBY Ldrshp St Confrnc; Stu Cncl Rep CA Assn Of Stu Cncls Rgn 14-16; Teen Tutors Alg; Stanford; Intl Bus.

DE SARRO, ANGELA; Don Antonio Lugo HS; Chino, CA; (2); Chorus; School Musical; Socr; CA ST Fullerton; Bus.

DE SENA, JENNIFER A; Fountain Valley HS; Fountain Valley, CA; (3); Teachers Aide; Band; Mrchg Band; Pep Band; High Hon Roll; Hon Roll; Hstry Coronet Awd; South Coast Coll; Court Reprtng.

DE SHIELDS, AMY; La Reina HS; Thousand Oaks, CA; (2); Drama Clb; GAA; SADD; Varsity Clb; School Musical; School Play; Stage Crew; Var Cheerldng; Gym; Hon Roll; Mst Sprtd Vrsty Chrldr Awd; Coach Jr High Chrldng Sqd; Peer Cnslng; Psych.

DE SILVA, NICHOLE L; Rancho Cotate HS; Rohnert Park, CA; (3); Ed Nwsp; Hon Roll; Gateway Rdng Cncls Yng Wrtrs Awd; Outstndng Wrtr Awd; Outstndng Achvt Spnsh II Awd; CSF.

DE SIMONE, FRANK M; Leuzinger HS; Hawthorne, CA; (2); Key Clb; JV Trk; Hon Roll; Rotary Awd; Yth & Govt; CSF; Trvl Club; U Of Southern CA; Comp Engr.

DE SISTO, HEATHER; The Acadamy Of Our Lady Of Peace; San Diego, CA; (1); Cmnty Wkr; Speech Tm; School Play; Hon Roll; Drama Theatre; Schlrshp Old Globe Theatre; CSF.

DE SOTO, SHELLEY K F; Clovis West HS; Fresno, CA; (3); Drama Clb; Intnl Clb; Spanish Clb; Stage Crew; Co-Ed Lit Mag; Treas Frsh Cls; Treas Stu Cncl; JV Gym; Var Tennis; High Hon Roll; Med.

DE SOUSA, BARBARA M P; Washington HS; Fremont, CA; (3); 24/306; Yrbk; Powder Puff Ftbl; Hon Roll; Peer Cnslng; U OfCA Hayward; Bus.

DE SOUSA, JOANA T; Turlock HS; Turlock, CA; (4); 68/520; Sec AFS; Art Clb; Church Yth Grp; Drama Clb; French Clb; FBLA; Key Clb; Science Clb; Speech Tm; JV Swmmng; Frgn Exc Stu Brazil; US Intl U; Intl Rel.

DE SOUSA-DIAS, CATHERINE; Palo Verde HS; Blythe, CA; (3); Pres Church Yth Grp; Pres 4-H; Band; Sec Chorus; Church Choir; Drm Mjr(t); Mrchg Band; Cit Awd; 4-H Awd; Hon Roll; John Philip Sousa Awd; Phys Thrpy.

DE SUES, MICHELLE C; Workman HS; La Puente, CA; (2); Chorus; L Swing Chorus; Var L Swmmng; Mst Outstndng Soph-Choir; Biola Coll; Chld Devlpmnt.

DE SUES, MINDY E; William Workman HS; La Puente, CA; (3); German Clb; L Chorus; Hon Roll; Mst Spirited Choir, Pins, Bars; Mt San Antonio JC; Hort.

DE SURRA, DESIREE; Tomales HS; Catati, CA; (3); Letterman Clb; Spanish Clb; VP Soph Cls; Sec Jr Cls; VP Stu Cncl; Stat Bsktbl; Cheerldng; Var Sftbl; Var Vllybl; High Hon Roll; UCLA; Psych.

DE VAUL, PAUL L; Atwater HS; Atwater, CA; (2); Var Trk; Hon Roll; Bus.

DE VAULT, MICHELLE L; Davis HS; Davis, CA; (3); 34/405; Rptr Nwsp; Powder Puff Ftbl; Var L Tennis; Pres Acad Fit Awd; CSF; Ltr Badmntn Tn; Hi-Deb Pgm; Bus.

DE VEAS, WILLSON J; Hamilton Union HS; Orland, CA; (3); Church Yth Grp; SADD; Band; VP Jr Cls; Hon Roll; Lion Awd; Ntl Merit SF; Spelling Bee Chmpn; Vocational Ed Cmptn 90-1st Pl-Word Prcssng; 89 Praise Festvl-Art/Music Awds; Biola U; Cmmnctns.

DE VENECIA, MARK L; Serra HS; San Mateo, CA; (4); 2/200; VP Debate Tm; Rptr Nwsp; Mgr Yrbk; VP Jr Cls; Sec Treas Sr Cls; Var Swmmng; Pres Acad Fit Awd; Rotary Awd; Amnesty Intl Pres; Northwestern U.

DE VERA, ARLENE N; Holy Family HS; Los Angeles, CA; (3); Phtg Yrbk; Scl Action Clb; Pre-Med.

DE VERA, ARNEL P; Roseville HS; Roseville, CA; (3); Hon Roll; Roseville HS Principals Advisory Cmmite JR Class Rep; Fri Night Live; Sanjose ST U; Architectual.

DE VERA, CHERYL; Bonita Vista HS; Bonita, CA; (4); 58/521; Teachers Aide; Treas Sr Cls; Acctg.

DE VERA, JOHANNA; Loma Linda Acad; Loma Linda, CA; (2); Church Yth Grp; Varsity Clb; Band; Sec Frsh Cls; VP Soph Cls; Var Bsktbl; Var Ftbl; Gym; Var Sftbl; Var Vllybl; Sprtswoman Of Year 89-90; Med.

DE VERA, JON N; University HS; Lake Forest, CA; (2); Chess Clb; Drama Clb; Intnl Clb; Key Clb; Rep Jr Cls; JV Trk.

DE VERE JR, JOHN J; Canyon Springs HS; Moreno Valley, CA; (3); Boy Scts; Church Yth Grp; Chorus; Church Choir; Swmmng; Wrstlng; Teens Agnst Drugs; Law.

DE VILBISS, CHRISTINA L; Enterprise HS; Redding, CA; (4); 57/459; Computer Clb; FBLA; Letterman Clb; Varsity Clb; Var L Bsktbl; Stat Swmmng; Var L Trk; Elks Awd; Hon Roll; Pres Acad Fit Awd; AFROTC Full Rd Schlrshp; MVP Fld Evnts Track; Stu Of Month Cmptr Sci; Cmptr Engnrng.

DE VILLE, DE ETTE; Rio Lindo Adventist Acad; Mansfield, TX; (4); 6/96; French Clb; Ski Clb; Band; Orch; Stage Crew; Variety Show; Nwsp; Ed Yrbk; VP Jr Cls; Off Sr Cls; U TX Arlington; Art.

DE VINE, THERESA M; Independence HS; San Jose, CA; (3); Cmnty Wkr; German Clb; Hosp Aide; Flag Corp; Swmmng; Yng Astronauts Pgm Pres; Air Force Acad; Aeronautics.

DE VITA, GINA M; Antelope Valley HS; Lancaster, CA; (3); 44/632; Church Yth Grp; Pres Drama Clb; Pres Pep Clb; Spanish Clb; Rptr Yrbk; Hon Roll; Pres Acad Fit Awd; Girls St; Aifs Schrlshp; Debonnaires; Criminal Law.

DE VITO, DAVID A; Mission Viego HS; Mission Viejo, CA; (4); 10/424; Model UN; JV Wrstlng; Stat Elks Awd; Hon Roll; NHS; Pres Acad Fit Awd; Duke U; Ecnmcs.

DE VITO, JENNIFER Y; Notre Dame HS; Riverside, CA; (1); 14/165; High Hon Roll; U Of CA Riverside.

DE VON, KELLY; Ontario HS; Ontario, CA; (3); GAA; Teachers Aide; Color Guard; Var JV Bsktbl; Prfct Atten Awd.

DE VRIES, FRANCESCA; Carlmont HS; San Carlos, CA; (4); Cmnty Wkr; Drama Clb; Chorus; Trk; Wt Lftg; Pres Acad Fit Awd; Peer Rsrc Prjct; Ldrshp, Poetry, Sngng, Ballet, Actng, Bkng & Wrtng Awds; Phtgrphy & Rdng Bgrphs; Acad Of Arts; Prfrmng Arts.

DE VRIES, MATTHEW S; Rim Of The World HS; Blue Jay, CA; (2); Church Yth Grp; Ski Clb; Church Choir; JV Bsktbl; Hon Roll; Piano Lssns 5 Yrs; Schl Rcgntn Gldn ST Exam Geom; Ecnmcs.

DE VRIES, NEAL D; Rim Of The World HS; Blue Jay, CA; (1); 1/450; Church Yth Grp; Church Choir; Capt Bsktbl; Hon Roll; NHS; Piano.

DE WAAL, JOHAN; Santa Ana Valley HS; Santa Ana, CA; (1); 16/1159; Hosp Aide; Key Clb; Quiz Bowl; Scholastic Bowl; Hon Roll; Jr NHS; Dcthln Team; Mesa UCI Prtnrshp Pgm; JV Badminton; Engrng.

DE WALD, KIM; Kerman HS; Fresno, CA; (3); 10/132; Church Yth Grp; Math Tm; School Play; Ed Yrbk; Score Keeper; High Hon Roll; Acadmc K; Fresno ST; Bus.

DE WEESE, BRIAN; Winters Joint Union HS; Winters, CA; (3); FFA; Letterman Clb; Teachers Aide; JV Ftbl; JV Trk; High Hon Roll; Hon Roll; Fire Cadet; CSF.

DE WITT, NATALEIGH; Bear River HS; Grass Valley, CA; (3); 19/250; SADD; Acpl Chr; Chorus; School Musical; VP Frsh Cls; VP Soph Cls; Pres Jr Cls; Rep Stu Cncl; JV Var Bsktbl; Cit Awd; MVP Bsktbl; Hnr Chr 88; Englsh Hrns 88-89stu Rep Jop Intrvw Cmmtte; UOP; Music.

DE YOUNG, ANDREA; Arrowhead Christian Acad; Redlands, CA; (3); Letterman Clb; Math Clb; Office Aide; Varsity Clb; VP Jr Cls; Var L Bsktbl; Var L Sftbl; Var L Vllybl; High Hon Roll; NHS; Dort Coll; Elem Ed.

DE YOUNG, CHRISTINE E; Village Christian Schls; Sunland, CA; (3); Church Yth Grp; Drama Clb; Office Aide; Spanish Clb; Band; Mrchg Band; Pep Band; JV Sftbl; Doing Social Community Work In Mexico & Mississippi; I Love To Around And Work With People; UCLA; Psychology.

DE YOUNG, DONNA R; Village Christian HS; Sunland, CA; (2); Score Keeper; Sftbl; Trk; Hon Roll; Reg Nurse.

DE YOUNG, LESLIE; Modesto HS; Modesto, CA; (2); Drama Clb; Office Aide; Ski Clb; SADD; Band; Color Guard; Yrbk; Stu Cncl; Var Intrml Powder Puff Ftbl; Var JV Sftbl; Stanford; Child Psych.

DE YOUNG, SHERYL; Village Christian HS; Sunland, CA; (3); 20/123; Church Yth Grp; Drama Clb; Spanish Clb; Band; Drm Mjr(t); Jazz Band; Stage Crew; Yrbk; Var Crs Cntry; Var Trk; CSF; Track; Music Performance Education.

DE YOUNG, STEVE; Arrowhead Christian Acad; Redlands, CA; (1); Chess Clb; Church Yth Grp; Math Clb; Scholastic Bowl; Teachers Aide; Pres Frsh Cls; Rep Stu Cncl; Var L Vllybl; High Hon Roll; Sal; John Hopkins Univ Ctr For Advancement Acad Talented Yth CA ST Awd 1988; Le Tourneau Univ; Engrng.

DEA, CANDACE F; Alhambra HS; Monterey Park, CA; (3); Debate Tm; Model UN; NFL; Rptr Nwsp; Las Moras Svc Clb VP; CSF; 7th Pl Trphy In Debate; Phys Thrpy.

DEA, MELVIN K; San Marino HS; San Marino, CA; (4); 17/265; Art Clb; Intnl Clb; JCL; Latin Clb; Math Clb; Math Tm; Model UN; Science Clb; Nwsp; Yrbk; Pres Amnesty Intl, Math Clb; VP Sci Clb; 3rd Pl Sr Biochem Div Los Angeles Cnty Sci Fr.

DEACON, BRADI M; Poway HS; Chandler, AZ; (4); Debate Tm; Teachers Aide; Band; Color Guard; Young Playwrights; Amnesty Intl; N AZ U; Ed.

DEAL, DANIEL; Lincoln HS; Stockton, CA; (3); Science Clb; High Hon Roll; Magna Cum Laude Ntl Ltn Exm; Cum Laude Ntl Ltn Exm; Cmptr Prog.

DEAL, JAMES E; St Ignatious HS; San Francisco, CA; (2); Pres Drama Clb; Pep Clb; Red Cross Aide; Thesps; School Musical; School Play; Ed Nwsp; Vllybl; High Hon Roll; Play Guitar & Piano; Band Crew; UCSB; Actor.

DEAL, TIMOTHY R; Gilroy HS; Gilroy, CA; (1); Boy Scts; Church Yth Grp; FTA; Diving; Swmmng; Wrstlng; Hon Roll; MVP Diving; SJSU; Teaching.

DEAMUS, STEFANIE E; Canyon HS; Monrovia, CA; (4); Teachers Aide; Church Choir; School Play; Nwsp; Yrbk; Stu Cncl; Vllybl; Several Awds For Stu Of Wk; Pasadena City Coll; Bus.

DEAN, ALEX; Inglewood HS; Los Angeles, CA; (4); Church Yth Grp; ROTC; UCLA; Engr.

DEAN, ANDREA T; Mission Viejo HS; Laguna Beach, CA; (2); 116/442; Var L Trk; JV Vllybl; Prfsl Trk.

DEAN, APRIL D; Imperial Schls; Pasadena, CA; (2); 5/30; Church Yth Grp; FBLA; Speech Tm; Teachers Aide; Chorus; Church Choir; Swing Chorus; Capt Cheerldng; Gym; Score Keeper; Yth Cncl; Cert Excllnce Vllybl & Chrldng; FL ST U; Bus.

DEAN, BARBARA; Mc Lane HS; Fresno, CA; (4); 7/437; Church Yth Grp; Model UN; Band; Mrchg Band; High Hon Roll; NHS; Pres Acad Fit Awd; Played Bagpipes; Stu Employment Achvt Awd; UC Santa Barbara.

DEAN, BRIAN D; Don Antonio Lugo HS; Chino, CA; (2); Ski Clb; JV Wrstlng; Hon Roll; Golden St Exam Recognition; Drftng Pgm; CA Poly; Arch.

DEAN, CURTIS W; Fontana HS; Fontana, CA; (2); Var L Swmmng; Hon Roll; Comp Tech.

DEAN, ELIZABETH; Mt Whitney HS; Visalia, CA; (4); Church Yth Grp; DECA; Spanish Clb; SADD; Band; Chorus; Church Choir; Mrchg Band; School Play; Var Swmmng; DECA-N CA Dist Pres 89-90/St VP 89-90; Ricks Coll; Intl Bus.

DEAN, FRANK; Palm Springs HS; Palm Springs, CA; (3); Comp Pgmng.

DEAN, GEOFFREY A; Clovis HS; Clovis, CA; (2); Church Yth Grp; FCA; SADD; Band; Jazz Band; Mrchg Band; Orch; Pep Band; JV Bsbl; High Hon Roll; Acad Block C; Fresno ST U; Music.

DEAN, HEATHER; Caruthers Union HS; Caruthers, CA; (3); FBLA; German Clb; Math Clb; Pep Clb; SADD; Teachers Aide; Varsity Clb; Sec Frsh Cls; Pres Soph Cls; Pres Jr Cls; Coachs Var Tnns Awd; MIP Var Vlybl; Outstndng Stu Jr 89-90.

DEAN, JASBEEN; Alexander Hamilton HS; Los Angeles, CA; (2); Nrsng.

DEAN, JENNIFER; Kingsburg HS; Kingsburg, CA; (2); Speech Tm; School Play; Stage Crew; Crs Cntry; Score Keeper; Trk; Hon Roll; Tchr.

DEAN, KRISTAL D; Paradise HS; Paradise, CA; (1); Church Yth Grp; Chorus; Church Choir; Hon Roll; Drama Clb; Red Crss Aid; Medcl.

DEAN, LA TOYIA S; Canyon Springs HS; Moreno Valley, CA; (3); Drama Clb; Teachers Aide; Color Guard; School Play; Nwsp; Stu Cncl; Trk; Hon Roll; Ntl Merit Ltr; Prfct Atten Awd; FL ST U; Comp Tech.

DEAN, RENEE; Ponderosa HS; Diamond Springs, CA; (1); Church Yth Grp; FFA; Chld Care.

DEAN, ROBERT J; St Vincent HS; Sebastopol, CA; (3); Boy Scts; Church Yth Grp; Letterman Clb; Var Bsbl; Var Ftbl; Intrml Sftbl; Intrml Vllybl; Hon Roll; Prfct Atten Awd; Sr Leag Bsbl All Star 87 88 89; Schlr Athl; Golden St Math Awd; Engrng.

DEAN, TESHOMBE R; East Bakersfield HS; Bakersfield, CA; (2); Ftbl; Hon Roll; BSU; MESA; Engrg.

DEANER, JODI M; Clovis HS; Clovis, CA; (1); Church Yth Grp; High Hon Roll; Hon Roll; Sparthanian Of Mnth 88; Apprctn Awd 88-89; Marine Bio.

DEANER, SHANNON M; Liberty Christian HS; Cottonwood, CA; (4); 1/25; Church Yth Grp; Pep Clb; Ed Yrbk; Sec Frsh Cls; Pres Jr Cls; VP Stu Cncl; Val; HS Tour Choir; Faith Baptist Bible; Secy.

DEARBORN, KARITH; Napa HS; Napa, CA; (3); Church Yth Grp; Cmnty Wkr; JA; Key Clb; Model UN; Office Aide; Pep Clb; SADD; Teachers Aide; Stage Crew; U Pacific; Intl Relations.

DEARING, BETHANEY; Encinal HS; Alameda, CA; (4); 5/209; Church Yth Grp; Treas Key Clb; Natl Beta Clb; Nwsp; Var Crs Cntry; Var Fld Hcky; Var Swmmng; High Hon Roll; Prfct Atten Awd; Santa Clara U; Engl.

DEARMIN, MICHELLE R; Tracy Joint Union HS; Tracy, CA; (3); Church Yth Grp; SADD; Chorus; Sftbl; Trk; Biola U; Nrsng.

DEAS, JANELLE; Rincon Valley Christian HS; Cotati, CA; (4); 2/15; Art Clb; Church Yth Grp; Drill Tm; School Play; Yrbk; Pres Stu Cncl; L Vllybl; Cit Awd; High Hon Roll; Sal; CSF; Pensacola Christian Coll.

DEAS, LAURA R; Vacaville HS; Vacaville, CA; (3); Church Yth Grp; Key Clb; Band; Treas Frsh Cls; Rep Soph Cls; Rep Jr Cls; Tennis; High Hon Roll; Jr NHS.

DEASE, KATHRYN; Academy Of Our Lady Of Peace; San Diego, CA; (2); Church Yth Grp; Cmnty Wkr; GAA; Hosp Aide; SADD; School Musical; School Play; Just So No Clb; U OR; Telecommnctns.

DEASON, SOPHIE; Rubidoux HS; Riverside, CA; (4); 38/572; French Clb; FFA; Letterman Clb; Teachers Aide; Varsity Clb; Pres Jr Cls; Rep Sr Cls; Stu Cncl; Socr; Capt Swmmng; Jr Rodeo Assn; San Diego ST; Animal Training.

DEAVERS, PAUL S; Poway HS; Vista, CA; (2); Boy Scts; Stu Cncl; JV Ftbl; JV Wrstlng; Hon Roll; ASB Cmmssnr Publicty; ROTC; Officer.

DEBANO, SARAH M; Mesa Verde HS; Citrus Heights, CA; (2); English Clb; Hon Roll; Prfct Atten Awd; Fshn Dsgn.

DEBOER, SHELLY M; Atwater HS; Atwater, CA; (3); Law.

DECHAIRO, BRYAN; Orange Glen HS; Valley Center, CA; (3); 10/458; Key Clb; Math Tm; Spanish Clb; Hon Roll; Sec NHS; CSF; Culture Club; Phys Educ Adhvt Awd; Med Doc.

DECKER, ANGELA L; Arcata HS; Arcata, CA; (4); Church Yth Grp; French Clb; SADD; Teachers Aide; School Musical; School Play; Sec Jr Cls; Sec Stu Cncl; JV Crs Cntry; Cit Awd; Stus Exhibiting Common Sense Clb-Co Moderator; Psych.

DECKER, LAURIE L; Lakewood HS; Lakewood, CA; (4); Church Yth Grp; Cmnty Wkr; Dance Clb; Drama Clb; Q&S; Service Clb; Church Choir; Drill Tm; School Play; Ed Nwsp; Outstandng Spch & Drama Stu; Insight Awd Psych; CA ST U Long Beach.

DECKER, MICHAEL R; Whittier Christian HS; Cypress, CA; (4); 1/180; Church Yth Grp; Science Clb; Chorus; JV Bsbl; JV Bsktbl; Var Tennis; Val; Investment Club; Applied Law Club; USC; Bio.

DECKER, RACHEL M; San Jose HS Acad; San Jose, CA; (2); Drama Clb; French Clb; Hosp Aide; Temple Yth Grp; School Play; Swmmng; Hon Roll; Rep Soph Cls; Badminton Team.

DEDIOS, BEGONA C; Glendale HS; Glendale, CA; (3); Drama Clb; Kung Fu Class; French; Pathology.

DEEDS, VALERIE; Edison HS; Huntington Bch, CA; (4); Color It Orange Art; Acadmc Booster Art; 6 Art Awds Sr Yr; Long Beach ST; Bus.

DEEGAN, ELIZABETH G; Irvine HS; Irvine, CA; (3); Dance Clb; Drama Clb; Pres French Clb; Key Clb; Ski Clb; Teachers Aide; Co-Capt Flag Corp; Rep Stu Cncl; Capt Awds 88; CSU Fullerton; Mrktng.

DEELEY, WENDY A; Edison HS; Huntington Bch, CA; (4); Church Yth Grp; Key Clb; Stat Trk.

DEENEY, JEFF H; Carlmont HS; Belmont, CA; (3); Var Tennis; Math Awd.

DEERING, BRINDA C; Norte Vista SR HS; Riverside, CA; (2); 31/435; Letterman Clb; Teachers Aide; Varsity Clb; Band; Mrchg Band; Pep Band; Var Stat Sftbl; Var Swmmng; Cit Awd; High Hon Roll; Peer Counseling Grp; Stu Task Force Pgm 88-89; Psych.

DEERMAN, JOSH M; Kearny HS; San Diego, CA; (2); 29/378; Scholastic Bowl; Band; Cit Awd; Hon Roll; Pres SAVE Clb Stu Agnst Violnc-Drugs; Attnd Yth-Yth Western St Conf Claremont CA 88; Cal Poly; Arch.

DEFFNER, ELISABETH M; Villa Park HS; Orange, CA; (3); Drama Clb; Sec German Clb; Intnl Clb; Spanish Clb; Lit Mag; Hon Roll; NHS; CSF Mem; Creative Wrtg.

DEFFNER, PETER R; San Leandro HS; San Leandro, CA; (3); 82/399; Church Yth Grp; Computer Clb; Church Choir; Orch; Var Bsbl; Var Bsktbl; Hon Roll; Pres Acad Fit Awd.

DEFILIPPI, GIULIANA V; Louisville HS; Canoga Park, CA; (4); Treas Art Clb; GAA; Science Clb; Stage Crew; Yrbk; Var Cheerldng; Var Capt Swmmng; Bank Amer Frgn Lang; Harvard Lang Cmptn Cert Excllnce & Suprty; Span V AP Cls Awd; Swmng Coachs Awd; Pierce Coll; Pre-Med.

DEFUENTES, KIRSTIE L; Nevada Union HS; North San Juan, CA; (3); Aud/Vis; Model UN; Color Guard; Ed Nwsp; Ed Yrbk; JV Sftbl; Cit Awd; Hon Roll; NV Union HS Mnth Video Mag Edtr; NV Union HS Video Yrbk Edtr; Hnrb Mntn Video Cont; Chico ST; Telecomms.

DEGAITAS, PARASKEVOULA T; Carlsbad HS; Carlsbad, CA; (3); 122/370; Assoc Mem Success Connection.

DEGNAN, SETH D; Grace M Davis HS; Modesto, CA; (2); Church Yth Grp; Band; Chorus; Church Choir; Stage Crew; Bsbl; Bsktbl; Socr; Sftbl; Vllybl; Touring Church Drama & Choir; U CA Stanislaus; Archtct.

DEGORICIJA, VEDRAN; Cupertino HS; Cupertino, CA; (2); Spanish Clb; JV Swmmng; CSF; Cal Tech; Elec Engr.

DEHAENE, ANN M; Lindsay HS; Lindsay, CA; (2); Church Yth Grp; VP Drama Clb; Sec Key Clb; School Musical; School Play; Stage Crew; Treas Frsh Cls; High Hon Roll; St Schlr; Engl Awd; Life Sci.

DEHART, ROBERT; Liberty Union HS; Brentwood, CA; (3); 20/400; Chess Clb; Latin Clb; Band; Jazz Band; Mrchg Band; Pep Band; JV Bsbl; Var L Ftbl; JV Trk; Hnrs Gldn ST Exam-1st Yr Alg & Geom; NCS/Jack In The Box Schlr Athlt Awd; Schl Athlt-Ftbl; Airforce Adac; Helicptr Pilot.

DEHAVEN, LISA J; Oak Ridge HS; El Dorado Hills, CA; (3); Church Yth Grp; FCA; FBLA; Science Clb; Spanish Clb; SADD; Chorus; Off Frsh Cls; Hon Roll; Jr NHS; CA ST U; Bus Admin.

DEHGHAN, HEDIEH; Oakmont HS; Rocklin, CA; (3); Science Clb; Ski Clb; Spanish Clb; SADD; Rptr Nwsp; Tennis; High Hon Roll; Hon Roll; VP Amnesty Intl; Davis U; Med.

DEHLINGER, ROBBIE J; Pittsburg HS; Pittsburg, CA; (2); Band; Church Choir; Jazz Band; Mrchg Band; Pep Band; School Play; Cmnty Theater; Pres Performing Arts Clb; Cnty Hstry Day Awd 90; Music.

DEHQANZADA, YAHYA A; Woodland HS; Woodland, CA; (3); French Clb; Trk; Cit Awd; Hon Roll; Prfct Atten Awd; Wrld Hstry, Geom & Typng Awds; UC Berkeley; Law.

DEHRLEIN, PATTI A; Yucca Valley HS; Yucca Valley, CA; (3); Teachers Aide; Yrbk; Score Keeper; Hon Roll; Loyola Marymount.

DEICAS-BERCOVICI, ARIELA; La Jolla HS; La Jolla, CA; (2); French Clb; SADD; Temple Yth Grp; Acpl Chr; Chorus; School Musical; Variety Show; Hon Roll; Law.

DEININGER, SCOTT; Coalinga HS; Coalinga, CA; (3); Boy Scts; Church Yth Grp; VP Debate Tm; Drama Clb; FCA; School Play; Stage Crew; Rptr Nwsp; Var Bsktbl; JV Ftbl; Resdntl Hnrs Pgm; USC; Engl.

DEIRO, KIMBERLI D; Bret Harte Union HS; Murphys, CA; (2); Church Yth Grp; Cmnty Wkr; Hon Roll; Teen Psych.

DEIWERT, SARAH E; Southbay Christian HS; Menlo Park, CA; (3); Church Yth Grp; French Clb; Teachers Aide; Stage Crew; Var Bsktbl; Var Vllybl; AYSO Sccr; Fashion Desgn.

DEKENS, PETRA S; Huntington Beach HS; Huntington Beach, CA; (2); French Clb; Swmmng; Pres Schl Clb Hb Teen; Zoology.

DEL BONTA, ERIN S; Bishop O'dowd HS; Oakland, CA; (2); Church Yth Grp; Hosp Aide; Chorus; School Musical; School Play; Score Keeper; Swmmng; Cit Awd; Hon Roll; Sci Hnrs Bio; Oakland Youth Chorus; CA U San Diego; Marine Bio.

DEL CARLO, ANNA L; El Sereno HS; Carmichael, CA; (3); Teachers Aide; Hon Roll; Prfct Atten Awd; Athlc Clb; Fshn Mrchndsng.

DEL CHIARO, BERNADETTE; Somoma Valley HS; Sonoma, CA; (4); 20/269; Art Clb; Cmnty Wkr; Service Clb; JV Capt Bsktbl; Var Powder Puff Ftbl; JV Sftbl; High Hon Roll; Jr Statesmen Amer; CSF Life; UC Berkeley; Earth Sci.

DEL FIERRO, KIMBERLY N; Hogan SR HS; Vallejo, CA; (2); Science Clb; Spanish Clb; SADD; Drill Tm; Rptr Nwsp; Var L Cheerldng; Var L Pom Pon; Hon Roll; Acad Achvt Awd, Block Ltr; CA Schlrshp Fed; Honor Soc; UC Berkeley.

DEL FIERRO, MAIA N; Hogan SR HS; Vallejo, CA; (3); Science Clb; Spanish Clb; Drill Tm; Rptr Nwsp; Var L Cheerldng; Var L Pom Pon; Hon Roll; CA Schlrshp Fed; Hnr Soc; Acad Achvt Awd, Ltr; UC Berkeley; Life Sci.

DEL FONZO, STEPHANIE; Mater Dei HS; La Palma, CA; (1); Church Yth Grp; Drill Tm; High Hon Roll; Med.

DEL PORTO, AMY SARAH; Lincoln HS; Stockton, CA; (3); Church Yth Grp; Drama Clb; Thesps; Acpl Chr; Chorus; School Musical; School Play; Variety Show; Hon Roll; Music Ltr; Chamber Ensmbl.

DEL REAL, ADRIANA; Calipatria HS; Calipatria, CA; (2); FBLA; Spanish Clb; High Hon Roll; Hon Roll; Prfct Atten Awd; Spnsh Clb Secy; Law.

DEL REAL, M GUADALUPE; Gladstone HS; Azusa, CA; (3); 188/267; High Hon Roll; Hon Roll; Mt San Antonio Coll; Trvl Agnt.

DEL ROSARIO, ANTOINETTE G; Hogan SR HS; Vallejo, CA; (3); Treas Drama Clb; Science Clb; Spanish Clb; SADD; Teachers Aide; School Musical; School Play; Mgr Yrbk; Bausch & Lomb Sci Awd; Hon Roll; CA Schlrshp Fed-Treas; Var Badminton; Prfrmng Arts Clb; UC Berkeley; Bus Admin.

DEL ROSARIO, ARLENE P; John Swett HS; Rodeo, CA; (2); Church Yth Grp; SADD; Band; Drm Mjr(t); Mrchg Band; VP Frsh Cls; Off Soph Cls; Sec Jr Cls; Pom Pon; Hon Roll; U Of Los Angeles; Bus.

DEL ROSARIO, JANELLE I; Canyon Springs HS; Moreno Valley, CA; (1); Hon Roll; Private Gymnstcs KIPS- Cmptd At Natls Past 5 Yrs.

DEL ROSARIO, MARSHA V; Arlington HS; Riverside, CA; (2); Aud/Vis; Teachers Aide; Dnfth Awd; Hon Roll; Jr NHS; Vlntr Wrk Hsptl; Mhrlka Clb; Math Awd; UCR; Phrmcy.

DEL ROSARIO, PAT; William Workman HS; Valinda, CA; (4); 3/200; Am Leg Aux Girls St; Pres Sec Intnl Clb; Science Clb; Ski Clb; Nwsp; Treas Stu Cncl; Tennis; DAR Awd; High Hon Roll; Pres Schlr; Vrsty Badmntn-Capt/Leag Chmpns/2nd Pl Doubles; Lobo Of Yr 90; Engl Bank Of Am Awd; CA ST U-Fullerton; Hotel Mgmt.

DEL ROSARIO, RICKY J; Monterey HS; Seaside, CA; (2); Ed Nwsp; Intrml Bsktbl; JV Var Ftbl; Var Tennis; High Hon Roll; Fellowship Of Christian Athl Camp Schlrshp; Dentistry.

DEL TORO, EDUARDO; Downey HS; Downey, CA; (3).

DELA CRUZ, AURORA MICHELLE; Hayward HS; Hayward, CA; (2); Pres Sec Church Yth Grp; Church Choir; Var Bsktbl; Var Vllybl; U NC; Elem Teacher.

DELA CRUZ, FELISA; Skyline HS; Oakland, CA; (2); German Clb; ROTC; Drill Tm; U San Francisco; CPA.

DELA CRUZ, HEIDEE A; St Genevieve HS; Sepulveda, CA; (2); Spanish Clb.

DELA CRUZ, KRISTINE ANN; Don Antonio Lugo HS; Chino Hills, CA; (2); Cmnty Wkr; Hosp Aide; Acpl Chr; Chorus; School Play; Variety Show; JV Swmmng; High Hon Roll; Hon Roll; CAL ST; Engr.

DELA CRUZ, RONNIE O; Westmoor HS; Daly City, CA; (2); Bsktbl; Crs Cntry; Wrstlng; Hon Roll; Env Issues; UC Berkeley; Ped.

DELA LLANA, HENRY S; Sierra Vista HS; Baldwin Park, CA; (2); Math Clb; Science Clb; Speech Tm; Var Tennis; High Hon Roll; Opt Clb Awd; JV Water Polo; Engrng.

DELA PAZ, KRISTINE; American HS; Fremont, CA; (3); Math Clb; Science Clb; Treas Frsh Cls; Hon Roll; Filipino Stu Union; Asian Clb; Interact; Med.

DELA RIVA, SARA G; Del Campo HS; Fair Oaks, CA; (3); 109/446; Art Clb; Church Yth Grp; Cmnty Wkr; FBLA; Intnl Clb; Spanish Clb; Teachers Aide; JV Swmmng; Chldrns Rspte Cntr Vlntr; Rnwy Htln CA Vlntr; U SAN Francisco; Psych.

DELA ROSA, CARLOS; Patterson HS; Patterson, CA; (3); AFS; Art Clb; Church Yth Grp; FHA; Ski Clb; SADD; Chorus; Ed Yrbk; Treas Soph Cls; VP Stu Cncl; Mens Hnr Soc; Child Psych.

DELA ROSA, FELIZ G; Bellarmine Jefferson HS; Glendale, CA; (2); Spanish Clb; High Hon Roll; Piano; Reading Books; CSF; Entrprnrshp.

DELACRUZ, GERARDO C; North Hollywood HS; Reseda, CA; (4); French Clb; Teachers Aide; Varsity Clb; Vllybl; Wt Lftg; Cit Awd; High Hon Roll; Prfct Atten Awd; UCLA; Elec Engr.

DELAGO, DAVID J; Antioch HS; Antioch, CA; (2); Hon Roll; Pres Acad Fit Awd; Pacific Coast Champ 89; Cntrl Pacific Champ 90; Natl Chmpnshps 4th Pl 90; Ind Engr.

DELANEY, LAURA CATHRINE; Trona HS; Trona, CA; (3); 2/34; JV Var Bsktbl; Var Crs Cntry; Var Trk; JV Var Vllybl; NHS; Dance Tm.

DELAO, FREDDY A; La Puente HS; La Puente, CA; (2); JA; Teachers Aide; Yrbk; Var Tennis; Cit Awd; High Hon Roll; Prfct Atten Awd; Pres Acad Fit Awd; Pres Schlr; CSF; Engr.

DELAREA, MICHELE A; Mission HS; San Gabriel, CA; (2); 13/147; Church Yth Grp; Drama Clb; Math Clb; Pep Clb; Science Clb; Hon Roll; Prfct Atten Awd; CA Schlrshp Fed; Comp Prgmmng.

DELATORRE, ALVA ILEANA; Hamilton Union HS; Hamilton City, CA; (3); Spanish Clb; SADD; Hon Roll; Outstndng Achvt-Phys Ed/Art Hstry; CA U.

DELBERT, GINI R; Cajon HS; San Bernardino, CA; (2); 38/503; AFS; Debate Tm; Hosp Aide; SADD; Ed Nwsp; Lit Mag; Hon Roll; NHS; CSF; Mock Trl Outstndg Pretrial Prosecuting Atty; Acadc Decath; Jrnlst.

DELCOMA, JULIE; Yucca Valley HS; Yucca Valley, CA; (4); Pep Clb; Teachers Aide; Varsity Clb; Nwsp; Pres Jr Cls; Bsbl; Bsktbl; Cheerldng; Gym; Pom Pon; University Clb; Medcl Asstnt.

DELE CRUZ, TERESA; Delta HS; Clarksburg, CA; (3); SADD; Hon Roll.

DELEHOY, JULIE; Delano HS; Delano, CA; (4); 5/300; Rptr FBLA; Letterman Clb; Teachers Aide; Var Mgr(s); JV Vllybl; Hon Roll; NHS; Opt Clb Awd; Pres Acad Fit Awd; Math, Engrng, Sci Achv; Prlmntrn, Scrtry, Schlrshp Wnnr; Bank Of Amer Plaque Wnnr Lbrl Arts; Fresno ST U; Lbrl Studies.

DELEO, KIM; Dana Hills HS; Laguna Niguel, CA; (4); Church Yth Grp; French Clb; Spanish Clb; SADD; Teachers Aide; Capt Drill Tm; Rep Stu Cncl; VP Capt Cheerldng; Pres Acad Fit Awd; Davis U; Psych.

DELEON, ALEX G; Selma HS; Selma, CA; (4); 32/193; Letterman Clb; SADD; Band; Jazz Band; Mrchg Band; Pep Band; Cheerldng; Tennis; Vllybl; UC Davis; Medcl.

DELEON, MANUEL A; Central Union HS; El Centro, CA; (3); Aud/Vis.

DELESKI, LIZA J; Yucca Valley HS; Yucca Valley, CA; (3); 1/150; Cit Awd; High Hon Roll; Pres Schlr; Rotary Awd; Congrssnl Yth Ldrshp Cncl Wash DC; ABWA Schlrshp; UC Santa Cruz; Law.

DELFIN, LISA; Bishop Amat Memorial HS; West Covina, CA; (3); Church Yth Grp; Drill Tm; Pres Frsh Cls; Stu Cncl; JV Var Cheerldng; Hon Roll; NHS; Brnz Medal Congrssnl Awd; USC; Phys Therapy.

DELFIN, MARIA; Encinal HS; Alameda, CA; (4); Ed Nwsp; VP Sec Frsh Cls; Sec Soph Cls; Sec Jr Cls; Pres Sr Cls; Rep Stu Cncl; JV Crs Cntry; Bnk Of Amer Awd Commnctns; William K Holt Sci Schlrshp; UC Berkeley; Mass Commnctns.

DELGADILLO, CAMIE; East Bakersfield HS; Bakersfield, CA; (2); Church Yth Grp; Teachers Aide; Hon Roll; Natl Ms Teen Contestnt; Phys Thrpy.

DELGADILLO, JULIO E; Garfield HS; Los Angeles, CA; (2); Science Clb; Trk; Prfct Atten Awd; Advanced Placement & Hnrs Cls; Awd From UCLA Mariposa Pgm Acad Achvt; Yale U; Med.

DELGADILLO, LISA; Tracy Joint Union HS; Tracy, CA; (2); 19/525; Letterman Clb; Pep Clb; Ski Clb; SADD; Acpl Chr; Jazz Band; Cheerldng; High Hon Roll; Jr Miss Olympics Cmptn 90; Bus.

DELGADILLO, STEED L; Ontario HS; Ontario, CA; (3); Var Bsbl; Hon Roll; Prfct Atten Awd; Phys Educ Achvt Awd.

DELGADO, ALMA L; Oakland HS; Oakland, CA; (2); Church Yth Grp; FHA; Band; Cit Awd; Hon Roll; Fashion Designer.

DELGADO, ANTONIO T; Carlsbad HS; Oceanside, CA; (1); Aud/Vis; Scholastic Bowl; School Play; Stage Crew; Ftbl; Wrstlng; Pop Warner Outstndng Schlr Athl; Aeronautics.

DELGADO, APRIL R; Etiwanda HS; Alta Loma, CA; (2); Hist FBLA; Band; Mrchg Band; Hon Roll; Pres Acad Fit Awd; Cal Poly Pomona U; Marketing.

DELGADO, BRYAN A; John Burroughs HS; Burbank, CA; (4); Teachers Aide; L Bsktbl; JV L Crs Cntry; JV L Trk; Hon Roll; CJSF; U Redlands; Bus.

DELGADO, DIANE F; Huntington Beach HS; Huntington Beach, CA; (2); Tower Awd For Bio; Orange Coast Coll; Comp.

DELGADO, ELIZABETH; Alain Le Roy Locke HS; Los Angeles, CA; (3); Off ROTC; Stu Cncl; CO ST Doming Hl; Spch Thrpst.

DELGADO, JENNIFER E; Aragon HS; San Mateo, CA; (2); Pep Clb; SADD; Chorus; Stage Crew; Off Soph Cls; Off Jr Cls; JV Cheerldng; Var Pom Pon; Big Brths/Big Sistrs; Svc Comssnr; San Francisco ST; Marine Vet.

DELGADO, JESSICA M; Yucca Valley HS; Landers, CA; (1); Library Aide; Altrnt Chrldr; Rchrds Bty Coll; Cosmotology.

DELGADO, JOSE J; Roosevelt HS; Los Angeles, CA; (3); Debate Tm; Key Clb; Ed Nwsp; Hon Roll; Prfct Atten Awd; MA Inst Of Tech; Elec Engr.

DELGADO, JULIE A; Chaffey HS; Ontario, CA; (3); Pep Clb; Spanish Clb; Band; Jazz Band; Mrchg Band; Pep Band; Var Crs Cntry; Var L Trk; High Hon Roll; Hon Roll; Music; CA ST Los Angeles; Music.

DELGADO, LISA; Apple Valley HS; Apple Valley, CA; (3); Dance Clb; Drama Clb; Model UN; Pep Clb; Off Frsh Cls; Off Soph Cls; Off Jr Cls; Cheerldng.

DELGADO, MARIA G; Hamilton HS Academy Of Music; Los Angeles, CA; (3); Office Aide; Teachers Aide; Band; Mrchg Band; Cit Awd; High Hon Roll; Hon Roll; Prfct Atten Awd.

DELGADO, MICHAEL A; Etiwanda HS; Etiwanda, CA; (2); Boy Scts; Computer Clb; French Clb; Math Clb; Band; Cit Awd; Prfct Atten Awd.

DELGADO, MONICA; Lakewood HS; Long Beach, CA; (2); English Clb; SADD; Yrbk; Vllybl; Cit Awd; Navy; Lawyer.

DELGADO, OSCAR; Morningside HS; Inglewood, CA; (2); Boy Scts; Spanish Clb; Hon Roll; Northrop U; Electro-Mchncl Engr.

DELGADO, SANDY; San Gabriel Mission HS; San Gabriel, CA; (3); Art Clb; FBLA; Spanish Clb; Co-Ed Yrbk; Cit Awd; High Hon Roll; NHS; 2nd Pl LA Essay Cont MADD 90; 1st Pl Jr Vlntr USC Womens Hosp; Spnsh Clb Sec; Loyola Marymount U; Phy.

DELGADO, SERGIO; Southwest HS; San Ysidro, CA; (2); Cit Awd; Scholar Awd; Comp Tech.

DELGHANI, TINA; Granada Hills HS; Northridge, CA; (2); Drama Clb; Stu To Stu; UCLA; Law.

DELGRECO, TONY A; San Luis Obispo HS; San Luis Obispo, CA; (1); 58/380; JV Socr; Cal Poly; Poli Sci.

DELIN, CHRISTOPHER ALAN; Daniel Murphy Catholic HS; N Hollywood, CA; (4); CA ST U Northridge.

DELIRA, STEVE F; Bishop Amat HS; Rowland Hts, CA; (3); Boy Scts; VP Band; Mrchg Band; Pep Band; Rptr Yrbk; NHS; Eagle Scout; 2nd Hnrs Music; UC San Diego; Pathology.

DELISLE, ANNETTE F; Live Oak HS; Morgan Hill, CA; (3); Church Yth Grp; Cmnty Wkr; FCA; FBLA; GAA; Pep Clb; SADD; Var L Socr; Var L Sftbl; Hon Roll; Westmont; Bus.

DELISLE, FRANK DENNIS; Live Oak HS; Morgan Hill, CA; (4); Church Yth Grp; Cmnty Wkr; VP Pep Clb; VP Stu Cncl; JV Bsbl; Var L Socr; Cit Awd; Elks Awd; Hon Roll; San Jose ST U; Bus.

DELL, PETER A; San Marcos HS; Santa Barbara, CA; (3); 8/400; Key Clb; Drm Mjr(t); Jazz Band; Pep Band; Ntl Merit Ltr; UCLA; Motn Pictr Drctr.

DELLA RIPA, MICHELE; St Genieviève HS; Loomis, CA; (4); Pep Clb; Chorus; Pres Jr Cls; Rep Sr Cls; Var Capt Cheerldng; Hon Roll; Hmcmng Prncss; Prom Cmmtte; Liturgy & Unity Clbs; Sacramento ST; Engl.

DELLACAMERA, ANGELA M; Mission Viejo HS; Mission Viejo, CA; (3); 70/444; Church Yth Grp; Capt Color Guard; Capt Flag Corp; Pres Acad Fit Awd; Outstndng Tall Flag Awd; Bst New Membr Color Guard Awd; Piano 6 Yrs; Safe Rides; Loyola Marymount U; Elem Educ.

DELLACAMERA, TERESA A; Mission Viejo HS; Mission Viejo, CA; (1); Pres Color Guard; Flag Corp; Hon Roll; Pres Acad Fit Awd; CA Schlrshp Fed; Piano; Bst New Color Guard Awd; Loyola Marymount U.

DELLAHA, ELIZABETH S; Balboa HS; San Francisco, CA; (2); ROTC; Color Guard; Orch; Sec Frsh Cls; High Hon Roll; Hon Roll; CSF; 100 Bucs Svc Soc; ROTC Drum Corps; Marine Bio.

DELLAMAGGIORE, GINA; Lincoln HS; Stockton, CA; (1); 48/660; Latin Clb; Variety Show; Cheerldng; Hon Roll; Studio I Prfssnl Model; Teach Begnning Tap; Pepperdine; Bus Admin.

DELLEPERE, AMY; Tomales HS; Badega Bay, CA; (4); FFA; Band; Jazz Band; Pep Band; Off Sr Cls; Stu Cncl; Bsktbl; Sftbl; High Hon Roll; Lion Awd; ST Farmer; Fresno ST; Agri Ed.

DELLERA, JENNIFER G; Loyalton HS; Loyalton, CA; (3); Am Leg Aux Girls St; 4-H; FBLA; Letterman Clb; Spanish Clb; Rep Nwsp; Treas Frsh Cls; Sec Soph Cls; Sec Jr Cls; Sec Stu Cncl; Stu Trnr; Hmcmng Prncs; CSU; Sports Med.

DELONG, JULIE; Alhambra HS; Martinez, CA; (2); Dance Clb; Cheerldng; Sftbl; Hon Roll.

DELONG, LAURA; Mountain View HS; Los Altos Hills, CA; (3); Church Yth Grp; Cmnty Wkr; Dance Clb; Rep Soph Cls; JV Var Cheerldng; JV Diving; Var Gym; Var Pom Pon; JV Powder Puff Ftbl; Hon Roll; 7th Cntrl Coast Gymnstcs Sctnl; Stanford Dvng Tm; Law.

DELOS ANGELES, RODNEY F; Milpitas HS; Milpitas, CA; (2); Hon Roll; Bsktbl; Rdng Bks; Engrng.

DELOUISE, BETH A; Vintage HS; Napa, CA; (2); Church Yth Grp; JV Vllybl; Hnr Soc.

DELP, BRANDON C; Berkeley HS; Berkeley, CA; (3); Treas Band; Orch; Var Capt Ftbl; Hon Roll; NHS; Med.

DELUNA, JUANITA C; Napa HS; Napa, CA; (1); Church Yth Grp; Hon Roll.

DELY, SHANAGH; Benicia HS; Benicia, CA; (3); 10/250; Am Leg Aux Girls St; FBLA; Key Clb; Service Clb; SADD; Var Bsktbl; Powder Puff Ftbl; Var Trk; Var Vllybl; High Hon Roll.

DEMAI, SCOTT; Berkeley HS; Albany, CA; (3); Church Yth Grp; French Clb; Ski Clb; Teachers Aide; Var Swmmng; Jr Olympcs; Ntl Yth Conf; UCLA; Sprts Psych.

DEMAN, ANDREW F; Valley HS; Sacramento, CA; (3); Drama Clb; FFA; Office Aide; Red Cross Aide; Service Clb; Spanish Clb; SADD; Thesps; School Play; Hon Roll; Pre Trl Prsctr Mock Trl 4th Cty; Acad Deca; Sac ST; Crmnl Just.

DEMARCHI, DEBORAH M; Mission Viejo HS; Mission Viejo, CA; (2); Church Yth Grp; Pep Clb; SADD; Score Keeper; Var L Socr; JV Trk; Intrml Vllybl; Pres Acad Fit Awd; Var Sccr Coachs Awd; All Lge Hnrbl Mntn 89; Grls Lge Plnnd Schl Actvts; Olmpc Dev Prog Wmns Sccr; Arch.

DEMARCHI, VERA; Temelula Valley HS; Temecula, CA; (4); 15/379; NFL; Speech Tm; Yrbk; High Hon Roll; Hon Roll; Azusa Pacific U; Bio.

DEMAREE, EDITH E; Fremont HS; Sunnyvale, CA; (4); Intnl Clb; Teachers Aide; High Hon Roll; Hon Roll; NHS; Prfct Atten Awd; Econ Stu Of Yr-90; De Anza Coll; Jrnlsm.

DEMAREST, KRISTIN R; Galt HS; Herald, CA; (3); Church Yth Grp; Church Choir; Sacramento ST U; Doctor.

DEMAREST, MARK S; Galt HS; Herald, CA; (2); Church Yth Grp; Church Choir; High Hon Roll; Engl Awd; Frgn Lang Awd German; Phys Ed Awd; Sacramento ST U; Bio.

DEMAREST, TANYA DARLENE; El Dorado HS; Placerville, CA; (3); Church Yth Grp; Cmnty Wkr; Math Tm; Treas Service Clb; SADD; Teachers Aide; High Hon Roll; Hon Roll; CSF; Literacy Action Cncl Tutor; UC Davis; Pediatrics.

DEMBO, CRYSTAL D; Moreno Valley HS; Moreno Vly, CA; (3); Chorus.

DEMBOWSKI, KEIRA; Skyline HS; Oakland, CA; (3); Cmnty Wkr; Debate Tm; Key Clb; Varsity Clb; Yrbk; Off Soph Cls; Off Sr Cls; Rep Stu Cncl; L Var Swmmng.

DEMELLO, JOANNIE A; Santa Clara HS; Santa Clara, CA; (2); Drama Clb; French Clb; Girl Scts; JA; Service Clb; Chorus; School Musical; School Play; Yrbk; Sec Treas Jr Cls; Wildrnss Adventrs Clb; Ballet; Jazz; Acrobts; CA Schlrshp Fed; Drama.

DEMERS, JEFFERY M; Valley View HS; Moreno Valley, CA; (1); Hon Roll; Voice Dem Awd; Interact Clb; Doctor.

DEMERS, WENDY; El Cajon Valley HS; El Cajon, CA; (3); 39/400; JV Socr; JV Sftbl; Var Vllybl; Hon Roll; UCLA; Arspc Engrng.

DEMESA, EDWARD; Vallejo SR HS; Vallejo, CA; (2); JV Ftbl; JV Trk; UCLA; Comp Sci.

DEMETER, ALINA; Los Alamitos HS; Los Alamitos, CA; (4); Cmnty Wkr; FBLA; German Clb; Intnl Clb; Model UN; NFL; Q&S; Ski Clb; Spanish Clb; Speech Tm; USC; Film.

DEMIANEW, MONICA L; Atwater HS; Atwater, CA; (3); Church Yth Grp; French Clb; Church Choir; Hon Roll; Natl & CA Rodeo Assn & Pac Coast Cttng Hrs Assn; Interact Club; Hrs Trng & Rdng; Intl Rels.

DEMINK, DAVE L; Bear River HS; Grass Valley, CA; (2); Church Yth Grp; FFA; Bsbl; Ftbl; Trk; Wt Lftg; Hon Roll; Pres Acad Fit Awd; Aerosp Engrng.

DEMIRDJIAN, RENEE D; Carlsbad HS; Carlsbad, CA; (1); Science Clb; Var L Bsktbl; Var L Sftbl; Hon Roll; Pres Acad Fit Awd; Mar Biol.

DEMIROVIC, ALMA; Dublin HS; Dublin, CA; (4); 5/150; FBLA; Teachers Aide; Var Tennis; Hon Roll; Occidental Coll; Med.

DEMONTEVERDE, GAIL MARIE G; Pasadena HS; Pasadena, CA; (3); Church Yth Grp; Cmnty Wkr; Q&S; Spanish Clb; Teachers Aide; Acpl Chr; Church Choir; Ed Yrbk; Stat Crs Cntry; Mgr(s); CSF; V, JV Badminton Team; Psych.

DEMPSEY, JACOB O; Grace M Davis HS; Modesto, CA; (2); French Clb; Ski Clb; Thesps; Rep Soph Cls; JV Var Swmmng; Pursuit Of Exclnc Awd; USC; Acct Exec.

DEMPSEY, KELLY; South Tahoe HS; South Lake Tahoe, CA; (2); Cmnty Wkr; Drama Clb; Speech Tm; Thesps; School Play; Hon Roll; 1st/2nd Pl Schl Dist Sci Fair; Gymnstcs-GAD Gym; Jr Statesmn Of Am; Cornell; Real Est Lawyer.

DEMPSEY, MARISSA J; Wm S Hart HS; Newhall, CA; (3); Drama Clb; FBLA; Drill Tm; School Play; Safe Rides.

DEMPSEY, SEAN T; Bishop Amat Memorial HS; Covina, CA; (3); Varsity Clb; Ftbl; Var Socr; Var Vllybl; ST Cup Champs Sccr 89; Vrsty Sccr; All Angelus Leg 1st Team Sccr 89-90.

DENEEN, BEN; Edison HS; Stockton, CA; (1); Boy Scts; Lit Mag; JV Bsktbl; Capt JV Ftbl; High Hon Roll; Pres Acad Fit Awd; CA-BERKELEY; Genetic Engr.

DENETTE, KEITH; Oxnard Union HS; Port Hueneme, CA; (4); Capt Chess Clb; ROTC; Rep VICA; Capt Crs Cntry; Hon Roll; Dving; Swmmng; Trck; Santa Barbara Cty Coll; Mre Bio.

DENG, RANDY; Woodrow Wilson HS; San Francisco, CA; (1); Teachers Aide; Hon Roll; Bus.

DENG, THOMAS; Dr James Hogan SR HS; Vallejo, CA; (4); 1/400; Pres Chess Clb; Pres English Clb; VP Math Clb; Service Clb; Spanish Clb; SADD; VP Band; VP Mrchg Band; Ed Nwsp; L Var Crs Cntry; Acad Decthln Tm Capt; CA Schlrshp Fdrtn Pres; Nuclear Engrng.

DENIS, KELLY; Turlock HS; Turlock, CA; (2); 206/655; Treas Pres FBLA; Letterman Clb; Pep Clb; Bsktbl; Capt Cheerldng; Mgr(s); FBLA St Sectn Offcr & Rcrdng Secy; Stanislaus ST; Bus Admin.

DENISON, ANDY E; Antioch HS; Antioch, CA; (2); 58/738; Boy Scts; Church Yth Grp; Hon Roll; BYU; Math.

DENISON, JUSTIN J; Lemoore Union HS; Laton, CA; (3); Church Yth Grp; Cmnty Wkr; Letterman Clb; Teachers Aide; Stage Crew; Trk; De Molay; Schl Disc Jcky; Lawyer.

DENIZ, ANGELA NICOLE; Madera HS; Madera, CA; (3); Pres Church Yth Grp; Hosp Aide; Service Clb; Band; Off Frsh Cls; Treas Soph Cls; Stu Cncl; Var Cheerldng; High Hon Roll; Hon Roll; Miss Teen Of America Schlsp & Recog Pgnt 90; Top 10 Jr Class; Var Song Qlfr USA Natl Cmptn; U Santa Clara; Chiropractor.

DENIZ, KELLI; Livingston HS; Delhi, CA; (4); French Clb; FHA; Teachers Aide; Hon Roll.

DENKERS, CHRIS W; Etiwanda HS; Rancho Cucamonga, CA; (4); Church Yth Grp; Letterman Clb; Spanish Clb; Teachers Aide; Intrml Bsktbl; Var Tennis; Hon Roll; Brigham Yng U; Med.

DENKINS, JAMMI N; Hilltop HS; San Diego, CA; (2); Bus Profs of Am; Church Yth Grp; Drama Clb; Speech Tm; SADD; Pres Church Choir; School Play; Var Bsktbl; Var Vllybl; Hon Roll; NANB & PW; Blck Stu Union; Splmn Coll; Fdrl Prsctr.

DENNEY, CHRIS J; Torrance HS; Torrance, CA; (2); Wt Lftg; JV Wrstlng; Cit Awd; Wrstlng Camp Schlrshp SCWA; Gldn St Agl Exm Wth Hnrs; Sci.

DENNEY, NATHAN D; Red Bluff HS; Red Bluff, CA; (2); Church Yth Grp; Cmnty Wkr; FFA; Hon Roll; Firefighting Course; Chico Coll; Engrng.

DENNEY, PATRICIA M; Alhambra HS; Alhambra, CA; (3); GAA; Girl Scts; Letterman Clb; Office Aide; Varsity Clb; Stat Swmmng; JV Var Vllybl; Cit Awd; Hon Roll; Prfct Atten Awd; CSF; Tri Hi Y Club Le Aikanes Sgt At Arms; USC; Med Doc.

DENNI, MICHALE J; Lindsay HS; Lindsay, CA; (2); Church Yth Grp; Ski Clb; Yrbk; Rep Jr Cls; JV Var Bsktbl; Var Sftbl; JV Var Vllybl; Natrl Hlprs; Sequoias.

DENNIE, VERONICA L; John F Kennedy HS; Sacramento, CA; (2); 122/525; Church Choir; Hon Roll; Hmcmng Prncss; Achvt Awd From Parents Of Blck Stu Achvt; Bus.

DENNIS, KRISTIE; Calvary Chapel HS; Huntington Beach, CA; (3); Church Yth Grp; Drama Clb; Teachers Aide; Chorus; School Play; Pres Soph Cls; Var Bsktbl; Var Sftbl; Var Vllybl; High Hon Roll; Tchg Sundy Schl; Vrsty Vlybl Coachs Awd; Biola U; Educ.

DENNIS, LEAH A; King City HS; King City, CA; (3); 2/275; Treas 4-H; Girl Scts; Sec Treas Speech Tm; Pres Band; Orch; Treas Stu Cncl; Var JV Crs Cntry; High Hon Roll; Lion Awd; Rotary Awd.

DENNIS, PHILLIP S; Santa Barbara HS; Santa Barbara, CA; (3); Scholastic Bowl; School Play; Stage Crew; Nwsp; JV Bsbl; JV Lcrss; JV Socr; JV Tennis; Intrml Vllybl; Hon Roll; CO U Boulder; Frfghtr.

DENNIS, RALPH R; Castro Valley HS; Castro Valley, CA; (4); 7/338; Art Clb; School Musical; School Play; Ed Lit Mag; Sec Sr Cls; Hon Roll; Ntl Merit SF; Amnsty Intl Schl Clb; Nclr Physics.

DENNIS, RITA F; San Fernando Magnet HS; Pacoima, CA; (3); Church Yth Grp; Science Clb; Band; School Play; Stu Cncl; Cit Awd; Hon Roll; Mecha; Peer Cnslr; Southern CA Coll; Psycht.

DENNIS, ROBERT M; La Quinta HS; Westminster, CA; (3); Hon Roll; Bch Vllybl; PSYCH.

DENNISH, ANDREW S; Torrey Pines HS; Rancho Santa Fe, CA; (2); 109/503; Church Yth Grp; Rptr Nwsp; Intrml Trk; Elks Awd; Scuba Diving; Piano; Jrnlsm.

DENNISON III, JAMES TORRENCE; Orange Glen HS; Escondido, CA; (4); Yrbk; JV Trk; Elks Awd; NHS; Pres Acad Fit Awd; CA Schlrshp Fed CSF Life; Racquetbl; Engl.

DENNISON, KRISTIN A; Orange Glen HS; Escondido, CA; (3); 10/460; VP French Clb; Teachers Aide; JV Vllybl; High Hon Roll; NHS; Culture Club VP; Active Extra-Curricular Music Prgms; CSF; Show Choir; Engl.

DENNO, JOHN P; Atwater HS; Atwater, CA; (3); Church Yth Grp; FCA; SADD; Variety Show; Rep Frsh Cls; Off Soph Cls; VP Jr Cls; Stu Cncl; JV Var Bsbl; Mgr Bsktbl; Mst Insprtnl Jr Var Ftbl; CA Assn Stu Cncl; Wrtng Poetry; Fresno ST; Prsnl Ftnss Cnsltnt.

DENNY, NICHOLAS J; Fountain Valley HS; Fountain Valley, CA; (1); Hon Roll.

DENNY, VINCE L; East Union HS; Manteca, CA; (1); Intrml Bsbl; High Hon Roll; Hon Roll; Prfct Atten Awd; Stanford; Doctor.

DENNY, WILLIAM A; Mission Viejo HS; Mission Viejo, CA; (3); Boy Scts; Model UN; Pres Sr Cls; JV Var Bsbl; Bsktbl; Ftbl; Wt Lftg; Hon Roll; NHS; Saferides; Drafting Club; Alt Action.

DENONCOURT, JENNIFER IRENE; Amador Valley HS; Pleasanton, CA; (4); 70/402; Teachers Aide; Mgr Nwsp; Ed Yrbk; Rep Stu Cncl; JV Var Sftbl; Var Capt Tennis; Cert Of Recog Outstndg Achvt Chldcare; NCS Schl Athl Awd 3.83 GPA; Cert Achvt Study Of Constitution; Chico ST; Lbrl Arts.

DENSLEY, JESSICA; Point Loma HS; San Diego, CA; (2); 137/482; Letterman Clb; JV Crs Cntry; JV Trk; Cit Awd; Hon Roll; Prfct Atten Awd; Pres Acad Fit Awd; UCSD; Pre-Med.

DENSON, JOANNA; Immanuel Christian Schl; Ridgecrest, CA; (2); Church Yth Grp; Drill Tm; Var Bsktbl; Var Sftbl; Var Trk; JV Vllybl; Hon Roll; Med.

DENSON, TRENEKIA D; Etiwanda HS; Rancho Cucamonga, CA; (2); Church Yth Grp; Church Choir; Trk; Hon Roll; Congressnal Schlr; Spelman Coll; Psychlgy.

DENTON, AMY M; Sunny Hills HS; Fullerton, CA; (3); 45/437; Latin Clb; Red Cross Aide; Varsity Clb; Mgr VP Swmmng; High Hon Roll; ASB; Girls Athletic Comissioner; Latin Club Sec; Science Medical.

DENTON, JARROD M; Redwood Acad; Santa Rosa, CA; (2); Church Yth Grp; FCA; Quiz Bowl; Ski Clb; Cit Awd; Hon Roll; Prfct Atten Awd; Pres Acad Fit Awd; VP Frsh Cls; Off Soph Cls; OR ST; Arch.

DENVER, COLLEEN; Leland HS; San Jose, CA; (4); 60/372; JA; Key Clb; Spanish Clb; Co-Capt Cheerldng; Hon Roll; Pres Acad Fit Awd; CSF; Sr Women; Gldn St Awds Alg & Geom; UC Santa Barbara; Accntng.

DEOCALES, MICHAEL R; St Genevieve HS; North Hollywood, CA; (3); Boy Scts; Church Yth Grp; French Clb; Letterman Clb; Pep Clb; SADD; Rptr Nwsp; Phtg Yrbk; Var Bsktbl; JV Crs Cntry; Coll Of Dentistry NJ.

DEPEDRO, KAREN; Aptos HS; Aptos, CA; (3); French Clb; Key Clb; Chorus; Cheerldng; Fashion.

DEPEW, TINA M; El Camino HS; Westwood, MA; (3); 10/340; French Clb; SADD; Lit Mag; Capt Var Crs Cntry; Capt Var Trk; Hon Roll; Crss Cntry All CIF Top 10 San Diego Cnty; Blade Ctznshp Awd Schlr Athl; CSF; CA Coll; Educ.

DEPINA, VIVIAN M; Sunset HS; Hayward, CA; (3); Chorus; JV Sftbl; CA ST Hayward; Bus.

DEPPEN, DANIEL M; Etna Union HS; Etna, CA; (3); Bsktbl; Ftbl; Hon Roll; Hiking; Radio Instillation; De Vry Inst Of Tech; Elec Engr.

DER, HENRY; Grant Union HS; Sacramento, CA; (3); Science Clb; Jazz Band; Mrchg Band; Hon Roll; Prfct Atten Awd; CA ST U Sacramento; Elect Eng.

DER, RICHARD C; Schurr HS; Montebello, CA; (4); 37/590; Math Clb; Math Tm; Hon Roll; Prfct Atten Awd; Pres Acad Fit Awd; CA Schlrshp Fed Lf Mem; Ctzn Bee; U CA Los Angeles; Bio.

DER SARKISSIAN, CAROL; Village Christian HS; North Hollywood, CA; (4); 8/119; Hosp Aide; Math Clb; Mu Alpha Theta; Spanish Clb; Drill Tm; Yrbk; Powder Puff Ftbl; USC; Bio.

DER-GRIGORIAN, TALIN; La Canada HS; La Canada Flintri, CA; (3); Girl Scts; Red Cross Aide; Nwsp; Bsktbl; Rotary Awd; BIA Model Cont 1st Pl Awd; Most Val Stu Architectur Clss Awd; Alg & Geo Golden Test Exams Awded; Sthrn CA Inst Of Architector.

DERBISH, ALLYSON L; Etiwanda HS; Alta Loma, CA; (1); Art Clb; Church Yth Grp; Drama Clb; Ski Clb; Bus.

DERBY, HEATHER; Rosary HS; Garden Grove, CA; (4); 61/135; French Clb; Library Aide; Pep Clb; Ed Yrbk; Cheerldng; Hon Roll; NHS; Bank Of America Art Award; Rosary High School Medal For Yearbook; Red & Gold Fashion Captain; Fashion Inst Design; Fashion De.

DERBY, LISA; Valley Christian HS; San Jose, CA; (3); 1/55; Dance Clb; Band; Mrchg Band; Sec Soph Cls; Var Cheerldng; Var Pom Pon; Var Trk; JV Vllybl; High Hon Roll; Poltcl Sci.

DERBY, SHERI; Highlands HS; N Highlands, CA; (3); Band; Drm Mjr(t); Mrchg Band; High Hon Roll; Hon Roll; Jerry Lee; Cosmetology.

DERBY, SUSAN D; Woodcrest Christain Schl; Perris, CA; (1); Church Yth Grp; 4-H; 4-H Awd; High Hon Roll; Piano Stu; Psych.

DERECHO, ABIGAIL T; Narbonne HS; Lomita, CA; (4); 4/457; French Clb; Key Clb; Speech Tm; Teachers Aide; Drill Tm; School Play; Nwsp; Cheerldng; High Hon Roll; Kiwanis Awd; Honored Achvtmnt In Wrtng Ntl Cncl Tchrs Englsh; English.

DERICKSON, LAUREL A; Sonoma Valley HS; Glen Ellen, CA; (4); Pres 4-H; Pres FFA; Intnl Clb; 4-H Awd; Hon Roll; Kiwanis Awd; Ag Sci Stu Of The Yr 87; Natl Yth Ldrshp Awd; Ag Awds; Sana Rosa; Animal Bhrvl Psych.

DERKUM, MICHELLE; El Segundo HS; El Segundo, CA; (3); Spanish Clb; Drill Tm; Bsktbl; Trk; Hon Roll; Acad Decthln; Air Force; Engr.

DEROSA, ROSEANN; Mission Viejo HS; Mission Viejo, CA; (2); Key Clb; Model UN; Rep Jr Cls; Stat Bsktbl; JV Crs Cntry; JV Trk; UCLA; Bus.

DERR, MARIAH; Carmel HS; Carmel Valley, CA; (4); 5/168; Dance Clb; Drama Clb; Teachers Aide; Band; School Play; Capt Var Swmmng; High Hon Roll; Kiwanis Awd; Reserve Chmpn In Hrseback Rdng,Wstrn; Now Ride Engl; Loyola U; Flm Prdctns Actng.

DERRICK, KIM; Pioneer Baptist HS; La Miranda, CA; (2); 2/11; Bus.

DERRYBERRY, TRICIA; Kingsburg HS; Kingsburg, CA; (3); Church Yth Grp; Drama Clb; Science Clb; Speech Tm; Teachers Aide; Church Choir; School Play; Stage Crew; Lit Mag; Tennis; Poetry Pblctns, Jets Team; Odyssy Of Mind, Sci Olympd; Sci Sympsm; UC Davis; Bio.

DERSAKISSIAN, CAROL; Village Christian HS; N Hollywood, CA; (4); 8/119; Hosp Aide; Math Clb; Mu Alpha Theta; Spanish Clb; Drill Tm; Yrbk; NHS; Jobs Daughters; USC; Bio Sci.

DES MARETS, CHRISTIAN N; Azusa HS; Azusa, CA; (3); 5/275; French Clb; Letterman Clb; Quiz Bowl; Var Capt Bsbl; Var Capt Bsktbl; Hon Roll; NHS; Pres Acad Fit Awd; Loyola Marymount U; Sociology.

DESAI, ANISH B; Whitney HS; Cerritos, CA; (2); 1/168; Math Tm; Band; Ed Nwsp; Cit Awd; Hon Roll.

DESAI, DIPTI; South Tahoe HS; S Lake Tahoe, CA; (4); Hon Roll; CSF; UC Davis; Phrmcy.

DESAI, KALPANA; Arcadia HS; Arcadia, CA; (3); AFS; French Clb; Rptr Nwsp; Phtg Yrbk; JV Bsktbl; JV Tennis; Prfct Atten Awd; Pres Acad Fit Awd; Peace Clb; Writers Bloc; Bio.

DESAI, SANDEEP; South Tahoe HS; S Lake Tahoe, CA; (3); JA; JV Tennis; High Hon Roll; Hon Roll; Prfct Atten Awd; Pres Acad Fit Awd; Specl ROP Course VTV; UC Davis; Med.

DESAI, SEEMA; South Tahoe HS; S Lake Tahoe, CA; (3); #1 In Class; JA; Cit Awd; High Hon Roll; Hon Roll; Prfct Atten Awd; Pres Acad Fit Awd; UC Davis; Med.

DESAI, SHEFALI; Burbank HS; Burbank, CA; (3); Science Clb; Drill Tm; Rep Stu Cncl; JV Cheerldng; Mgr Sftbl; Mgr Swmmng; Cit Awd; Hon Roll; Pres Acad Fit Awd; CSF; Zonta Clb; Bus.

DESAI, TEJAS; Saddleback HS; Santa Ana, CA; (4); 57/517; FBLA; Spanish Clb; Vllybl; Hon Roll; Jr NHS; CA Schlrshp Fed; Karate Clb; Comp Sci.

DESHA, EMMALENA KAHEALANI; Presentation HS; Pacifica, CA; (4); 3/97; Church Yth Grp; Cmnty Wkr; Letterman Clb; Teachers Aide; Co-Ed Yrbk; Var Vllybl; High Hon Roll; Pres NHS; NEDT Awd; Pres Acad Fit Awd; CSF; Engl Hnr Medal; Bnk America Cert Lab Sci; UC Santa Barbara; Law.

DESHMUKH, SUNITA S; Canyon HS; Anaheim Hills, CA; (4); Cmnty Wkr; Pres Math Clb; Math Tm; Mu Alpha Theta; Quiz Bowl; Scholastic Bowl; Service Clb; Nwsp; High Hon Roll; Masonic Awd; Grls Leag Treas; CSF.

DESHPANDE, ANNISSA; Fountain Valley HS; Fountain Valley, CA; (3); German Clb; Red Cross Aide; Band; Mrchg Band; Pep Band; Rep Stu Cncl; JV Fld Hcky; Hon Roll; CSF; Eng.

DESLAURIER, ANN; Granite Hills HS; El Cajon, CA; (2); Drama Clb; Acpl Chr; Chorus; Rep Frsh Cls; JV Cheerldng; Sftbl; Trk; Cit Awd; Amer Girl Leag Sftbl; UCSD; Law.

DESPIRITO, EVERETT; San Diego Acad; National City, CA; (4); Church Yth Grp; Cmnty Wkr; Computer Clb; Teachers Aide; Chorus; Mrchg Band; School Play; Rptr Nwsp; Rptr Yrbk; Off Jr Cls; La Sierra U; Elem Ed.

DESTEFANI, ROBERT L; Serra HS; San Carlos, CA; (2); JV Tennis; 4-H Awd; 8 Man Var Crew; Trivia Clb; Bio.

DETJEN, EMILY; Hanford Union HS; Hanford, CA; (1); Church Yth Grp; Band; Mrchg Band; School Musical; Variety Show; Swmmng; Fresno ST; Pediatrics Nrs.

DETRICK, DENISE M; El Camino Fundamental HS; Carmichael, CA; (3); 186/376; German Clb; Girl Scts; Pep Clb; Cheerldng; Tennis; Wt Lftg; U Of San Diego; Bus.

DETTNER, KATHRYN; Lowell HS; San Francisco, CA; (2); Drama Clb; Office Aide; Pres Acad Fit Awd; Shrt Stry Clb; Sci.

DETWEILER, SHANNON L; The Bishops Schl; Del Mar, CA; (3); Model UN; Spanish Clb; Vllybl; High Hon Roll; Hon Roll; Natl Charity League.

DEUEL, BETHANNE A; Antelope Valley HS; Lancaster, CA; (4); Math Tm; Spanish Clb; Off Frsh Cls; Pres Stu Cncl; Powder Puff Ftbl; Var Trk; High Hon Roll; Pres Acad Fit Awd; Voice Dem Awd; Peer Hlpr; CA Schlrshp Fed Lf Mem; Yth Govt Cnclwmn; U CA Davis; Pre-Med.

DEUEL, SUSAN K; Live Oak HS; Live Oak, CA; (3); 1/90; Drama Clb; Spanish Clb; Band; Chorus; School Play; Nwsp; Bsktbl; Trk; Bausch & Lomb Sci Awd; High Hon Roll; Sutter Cnty Juvenile Just Cmmssn; CSF; Cmmnctns.

DEUKMEDJIAN, TARA C; La Reina HS; Camarillo, CA; (2); 5/100; GAA; Hosp Aide; Letterman Clb; Service Clb; Rptr Phtg Nwsp; Sec Frsh Cls; Var L Bsktbl; JV Vllybl; Cit Awd; French Hon Soc; WINGS; AGBU; Play Bsktbl, Vllybl, Trk & Swmmng For This Orgnztn; UC San Diego; Med.

DEUTSCH, CRAIG E; Rio Americano HS; Sacramento, CA; (3); 28/300; Church Yth Grp; Cmnty Wkr; Debate Tm; Key Clb; Spanish Clb; Teachers Aide; Band; Swmmng; High Hon Roll; Pres Acad Fit Awd; Stanford; Bus.

DEUTSCH, ERICA; North Hollywood HS; Los Angeles, CA; (3); French Clb; Treas Service Clb; Yrbk; VP Frsh Cls; Pres Jr Cls; Hist Stu Cncl; Cheerldng; Valley Safe Rides; Acad Decathlon Tm.

DEUTSCH, FRANCES; Southern Ca Christian HS; Diamond Bar, CA; (2); 1/50; Bus Profs of Am; Church Yth Grp; German Clb; JV Vllybl; Hon Roll.

DEVEAU, ANDREA M; Oak Ridge HS; Cameron Park, CA; (1); Art Clb; Ski Clb; Varsity Clb; VP Frsh Cls; Var Socr; Var Tennis; High Hon Roll; Hon Roll; Pres Acad Fit Awd; Stu Ldrshp; CSF.

DEVEAU JR, DAVID M; North HS; Bakersfield, CA; (3); 70/368; Church Yth Grp; FCA; Letterman Clb; Chorus; JV Var Ftbl; Var Socr; Intrml Trk; Wt Lftg; Elks Awd; Hon Roll; Chrch Muscl; Clb Sccr; Bus.

DEVELTER, ERIN R; Oroville HS; Oroville, CA; (2); 1/215; Church Yth Grp; Girl Scts; Church Choir; Capt Bsktbl; JV Trk; JV Vllybl; High Hon Roll; Hon Roll; Envrnmntl Club Co-Ldr; Girls Block O Sprts Club; Phys Thrpy.

DEVENISH, NICOLLE; Miramonte HS; Orinda, CA; (4); Intnl Clb; NFL; Spanish Clb; Speech Tm; Rep Jr Cls; Sec Sr Cls; Stu Cncl; Swmmng; NHS; U C Berkeley.

DEVERA, APRIL R; Roseville HS; Roseville, CA; (2); 45/458; Hon Roll; California Scholarship Federation; Friday Night Live; U Of CA; Medical.

DEVERA, EILEEN; Alisal HS; Salinas, CA; (3); English Clb; Teachers Aide; School Play; Stage Crew; Var Cheerldng; Var Tennis; Var Trk; Hon Roll.

DEVEREUX, KIMBERLY E; Atwater HS; Winton, CA; (3); Am Leg Aux Girls St; FCA; French Clb; Pres Girl Scts; Treas JA; JV Bsktbl; JV Var Swmmng; Var Tennis; High Hon Roll; CCC Al Acad Leag Tnns, Swmng; Falcon Crest Awds-Tp Stu Frnch, Chem; Frnch I Awd-Hghst GPA; USAFA; Math.

DEVERT, KRISTI A; Casa Grande HS; Petaluma, CA; (3); GAA; Intnl Clb; Letterman Clb; Ski Clb; SADD; Varsity Clb; Rptr Nwsp; VP Frsh Cls; Stu Cncl; Var Bsktbl; Athltc Cmmssnr; Natl Sccr Tm 89-90; Cmnctns.

DEVIN, EVA MARIE; Novato HS; Novato, CA; (3); Church Yth Grp; Pres Frsh Cls; Pres Soph Cls; Stu Cncl; Bsktbl; Mgr(s); Score Keeper; Vllybl; Cit Awd; Hon Roll; Horse Back Rider; Young People Vlntr; Bus.

DEVINE, CHRISTOPHER A; Moore Bay HS; Los Osos, CA; (4); 35/245; Church Yth Grp; Spanish Clb; Teachers Aide; Varsity Clb; Rep Jr Cls; Rep Sr Cls; Var Capt Bsbl; Var Capt Socr; Elks Awd; Hon Roll; Inds Art Stu Of Yr 90; Los Padres Athltc Leag Soccer/Bsbl 90; Cuesta Coll; Psych.

DEVINE, SARA V; Madera HS; Madera, CA; (3); Computer Clb; 4-H; FBLA; GAA; Pep Clb; SADD; Teachers Aide; Drill Tm; Stage Crew; Off Soph Cls; Mascot; Prelaw.

DEVLIN, SHELBY L; Monterey HS; Monterey, CA; (2); Church Yth Grp; Chorus; JV Crs Cntry; Sccr; Elem Educ.

DEVORE, AMBER L; Mt Shasta HS; Mount Shasta, CA; (2); Chorus; High Hon Roll; Hon Roll; Horses; Writer.

DEWAR, SCOTT L; Eisenhower HS; Rialto, CA; (3); Boy Scts; Church Yth Grp; Intrml Ftbl; Var L Trk; Hon Roll; Comp Sci.

DEWEESE, CHRISTOPHER N; Edison HS; Stockton, CA; (2); Rep Soph Cls; VP Jr Cls; JV Bsktbl; JV Ftbl; Stat Sftbl; Hon Roll; Pres Acad Fit Awd; Child Abuse Cncl; Med.

DEWEESE, EDUARDO; Moreno Valley HS; Moreno Vly, CA; (4); Computer Clb; Spanish Clb; Teachers Aide; JV Wt Lftg; Comp Sci.

DEWEY, DAVID J; Manteca HS; Manteca, CA; (2); SADD; Bsbl; Tennis; Hon Roll; CSF; Acad Decathlon Team.

DEWEY, ROBERT J; Riverdale HS; Riverdale, CA; (3); Am Leg Boys St; Pres FFA; Letterman Clb; Ski Clb; Chrmn SADD; Stage Crew; JV Bsktbl; Var Capt Ftbl; L Var Trk; Cit Awd; Acadmeic Decathalon; Fresno ST; Physcial Therapy.

DEWEY, TOMMY J; Brookside Christian HS; Stockton, CA; (3); L Var Bsbl; L Var Bsktbl; L Var Socr; Hon Roll; Mst Imprvd Plyr Bsktbl; Bsbl Coachs Awd; Military.

DEWLEN, CRISTI; Albany HS; Roswell, GA; (4); Church Yth Grp; Cmnty Wkr; French Clb; SADD; Chorus; Orch; Pres Frsh Cls; Rep Jr Cls; Rep Stu Cncl; Capt Cheerldng; Chrch Cls Pres; Brigham Young U.

DEWOODY, CRYSTAL; Chino HS; Chino, CA; (3); Drama Clb; Office Aide; Pep Clb; Ski Clb; Teachers Aide; Thesps; School Play; Cheerldng; JV Cheerldng; JV Vllybl; UCLA; Pediatrician.

DEXHEIMER, SEAN P; Fountain Valley HS; Fountain Valley, CA; (2); Treas Ski Clb; Bowlng Clb Pres; CO ST; Rest/Hotel Mgmt.

DEXTER, KEN; Oxnard HS; Oxnard, CA; (3); 15/645; Art Clb; Computer Clb; Teachers Aide; Rptr Nwsp; Rep Stu Cncl; High Hon Roll; Hon Roll; Pres Acad Fit Awd; Sci Fair 1st Pl 87-88; Ventura Cnty Sci Fair 1st Pl 87 & 89 3rd Pl 88; UCLA; Film.

DEYCH, GREGORY; Fair Fax HS; Los Angeles, CA; (3); Cmnty Wkr; School Play; Rep Soph Cls; Var Ntl Merit Ltr; UC Berkeley.

DEYNATA, ROSENDO; Southwest HS; San Diego, CA; (2); Art Clb; Drama Clb; Intnl Clb; Office Aide; Science Clb; Teachers Aide; Bsktbl; Vllybl; Cit Awd; Hon Roll; Comps; Comm Coll; Arch.

DEYO, SUZANNE M; Pleasant Valley HS; Chico, CA; (4); 8/215; Church Yth Grp; Drama Clb; GAA; Pep Clb; Spanish Clb; SADD; Varsity Clb; School Play; Rep Soph Cls; Rep Sr Cls; Advsry Cncl Pres; Stu Mnth; Super Achvt Chem; UC Davis; Food Biochem.

DHA, ONKAR S; James Logan HS; Union City, CA; (3); 77/835; Art Clb; FBLA; JA; Math Clb; Science Clb; Treas Frsh Cls; Rep Soph Cls; Rep Stu Cncl; Tennis; Cit Awd; U CA Berkeley; Pre-Med.

DHADDA, INDERPAL S; Roseville HS; Rocklin, CA; (3); L Socr; Intmrls; Ply Sccr For Leag Team; UC Davis; Aero Engrng.

DHALIWAL, MANJIT S; Caruthers HS; Fresno, CA; (3); 2/160; Computer Clb; FBLA; Intnl Clb; Letterman Clb; Math Clb; Math Tm; Office Aide; Spanish Clb; SADD; Teachers Aide; CA Schlrshp Fed 3 Yrs; Yng Republicans Of Amer; Stanford; Comp Engrng.

DHAMI, HARPREET K; James Logan HS; Union City, CA; (3); Art Clb; Hosp Aide; Bsbl; Bsktbl; Golf; Tennis; Trk; Stanford U; Med.

DHAR, ARUNIMA; Corona Del Mar HS; Corona Del Mar, CA; (3); French Clb; Teachers Aide; Chorus; NHS; Frnch Clb Pres 88-89; CSF; UCLA.

DHATCHAYANGKUL, CYNTHIA; Crescenta Valley HS; La Crescenta, CA; (3); Pres Sec Church Yth Grp; Intnl Clb; Math Clb; Mu Alpha Theta; Chorus; Church Choir; Crs Cntry; Swmmng; Trk; NHS; CSF; Golden State Exam High Hnrs.

DHESI, RAVINDER S; Tranquillity Union HS; San Joaquin, CA; (3); 1/200; FBLA; Teachers Aide; High Hon Roll; Hon Roll; Stu Of Yr; U Of Los Angeles; Comp Engrng.

DHILLON, AMARJIT; Edison HS; Fresno, CA; (1); Intrml Socr; Fresno ST U; Elec Engr.

DHILLON, ASHA; La Reina HS; Agoura Hills, CA; (2); 1/92; Cmnty Wkr; GAA; SADD; Rptr Nwsp; Rptr Yrbk; Rptr Lit Mag; Pres Frsh Cls; Pres Soph Cls; Off Jr Cls; Off Sr Cls; HOBY Sem Rep; Co Champ Mock Trial Team, 9th St; Oxford England U; Law.

DHILLON, DALVINDER S; De Anza HS; Richmond, CA; (3); Cmnty Wkr; French Clb; Pres Math Clb; Math Tm; Science Clb; High Hon Roll; Aud/Vis; Chess Clb; Rchmnd Unfd Sch Dist Spllng Chmpn 89-90; CA St HS Spllng Bee Fnlst 88; Contra Costa Cnty Sci Fair 89; UC Berkeley; Astrophysics.

DHILLON, MANBIR S; Warren HS; Downey, CA; (1); Computer Clb; Engrng.

DHIRI, PRIYA; Diamond Bar HS; Diamond Bar, CA; (2); Key Clb; Science Clb; Spanish Clb; SADD; Off Soph Cls; Tennis; Hon Roll; Member Of And Indian Youth Association; On The Badminton Team; UCLA; Medicine.

DI CAMIMATE, ASCANIO L; Loyola HS; Los Angeles, CA; (2); Debate Tm; Swmmng; Trk; Hon Roll; Frnch Natl Cong 3rd & 5th 89 & 90; Firearns Enthsts Soc Clb; Christian Life Cmmnty Clb; Law.

DI COCCO, PATRICK G; Victor Valley HS; Victorville, CA; (3); Intrml Fld Hcky; High Hon Roll; Hon Roll; OR ST Coll; Bus.

DI DONATO, MANOLO; Liberty Union HS; Belmont, CA; (3); FFA; Library Aide; Teachers Aide; Off Jr Cls; Socr; Wt Lftg; Prfct Atten Awd; Stu Mnth FFA; Navy; NASA Engr.

DI GEROLAMO, CHRISTA L; Newbury Park HS; Newbury Park, CA; (3); 110/360; JV Socr; JV Var Sftbl; Hon Roll; N AZ U; Interior Dsgn.

DI GIACOMO, LISA V; La Jolla Country Day Schl; San Diego, CA; (4); Pres AFS; Cmnty Wkr; French Clb; Spanish Clb; Speech Tm; Capt Var Cheerldng; Gym; Sftbl; Hon Roll; Rotary Awd; San Diego ST U; Comm.

DI GIORGIO, VIRGINIA; Holy Family HS; Los Angeles, CA; (2); Chorus; Var Trk; Hon Roll; Prfct Atten Awd; Crt Rprtr.

DI GRANDE, LUIGI; Sacred Heart Cathedral HS; San Francisco, CA; (2); Boy Scts; Computer Clb; Stage Crew; Hon Roll; Annapolis Nvl Acad; Pilot.

DI LAURA, DANIELLE; La Canada HS; Bradbury, CA; (4); Drama Clb; JA; Key Clb; Service Clb; Teachers Aide; Var Tennis; Pres Acad Fit Awd; Chorus; Art Ctr Coll Dsgn Pasadena CA; CA ST U Fullerton; Commnctns.

DI LEO, GIA G; St Joseph HS; La Palma, CA; (2); 9/196; Debate Tm; Ski Clb; SADD; Cit Awd; High Hon Roll; Snow Skiing; UC Irvine; Law.

DI LORENZO, TONY M; Banning HS; Banning, CA; (3); Boy Scts; Chess Clb; Church Yth Grp; Cmnty Wkr; Model UN; Spanish Clb; Teachers Aide; Pres Soph Cls; Pres Jr Cls; Pres Stu Cncl; UC Davis; Envrnmntl Engr.

DI MAIO, HEATHER K; Ramona HS; Ramona, CA; (2); 10/345; Cit Awd; Hon Roll; NHS; Prfct Atten Awd; UC Davis; Vet Med.

DI MARION, BRAD; Woodrow Wilson HS; Long Beach, CA; (2); JV Bsbl; Hon Roll; Pres Acad Fit Awd; Jr Var Water Polo; CO U; Bus.

DI MUNDO, GAVIN K; Atascadero HS; Atascadero, CA; (2); Boy Scts; Band; Mrchg Band; Orch; Pep Band; School Musical; Rep Stu Cncl; Stat Bsktbl; Hon Roll; CSF Treas; Chem Engrng.

DI PAOLO, JOANA; Cypress HS; Cypress, CA; (2); Church Yth Grp; Girl Scts; Chorus; Church Choir; Color Guard; Drm Mjr(t); Hon Roll; NHS; Calamity Cloggers; Dancer.

DI PIETRO, ANDREA M; Ramona HS; Ramona, CA; (2); Var Socr; JV Vllybl; Marine Bio.

DI PIETRO, VINCENT M; Bellarmine College Prep; San Ramon, CA; (3); Cmnty Wkr; School Play; Crs Cntry; Ntl Merit Ltr; Service Clb.

DI PIETRO, VIRGINIA L; Mojave HS; California City, CA; (2); Church Yth Grp; Drama Clb; FHA; Girl Scts; Office Aide; Spanish Clb; School Musical; School Play; Variety Show; Hon Roll.

DI PROFIO, KELLY M; Westminster HS; Westminster, CA; (3); Drill Tm; Acad Booster Club Ltr; Annual Royal Banquet.

DI RAFFAELE, DIANA; El Capitan HS; Lakeside, CA; (4); 13/418; FBLA; GAA; Spanish Clb; Varsity Clb; Rep Stu Cncl; Var Swmmng; Var Tennis; Hon Roll; U Of CA Santa Barbara; Med.

DI RE, MICHELLE C; St Joseph HS; Cerritos, CA; (2); 1/200; Church Yth Grp; GAA; Hosp Aide; Science Clb; Service Clb; SADD; JV Bsktbl; Capt JV Sftbl; JV Vllybl; High Hon Roll; HOBY Awd Wnnr; Med.

DI VERGILIO, ADAM W; San Luis Obispo HS; San Luis Obispo, CA; (2); 1/319; Sec German Clb; Intnl Clb; Stage Crew; VP L Crs Cntry; VP L Trk; High Hon Roll; CA Schlrshp Fed; Trk Div Fnls; U Of OR Eugene; Physics.

DIAAB, MARYAM; Lakewood SR HS; Long Beach, CA; (1); Church Yth Grp; Girl Scts; Church Choir; Stage Crew; Rep Frsh Cls; Var Crs Cntry; JV Trk; Silver Awd; CA Schlrshp Fed; Yng Black Schlrs Clb; U Of CA; Drama.

DIAMOND, QWINTRICE M; Bonita Vista HS; San Diego, CA; (3); Church Yth Grp; Debate Tm; GAA; Office Aide; Pep Clb; Speech Tm; Teachers Aide; Chorus; Church Choir; Stu Intern US Congrssmn Jim Bates; Delg Ldrsh Excllnc Camp; VP Yng Amer SS Cls; Law.

DIAMONTOPOUIOS, TIA; Torrey Pines HS; Del Mar, CA; (1); Violin 4 Yrs; Karate; Pepperdine; Jrnlsm.

DIANAND, JENNIFER; Fairfield HS; Fairfield, CA; (2); VP Church Yth Grp; Debate Tm; VP Math Clb; Math Tm; VP Science Clb; Chorus; Church Choir; Rep Frsh Cls; Intrml Tennis; Cit Awd; JSA; CSF; Santa Clara U; Bus.

DIANATY, ALI R; Eagle Rock JR/Sr HS; Los Angeles, CA; (2); Off Jr Cls; Tennis; Pres Acad Fit Awd; CA Jr Schlrshp Fed; CA Poly Pomona; Engrng.

DIANCE, VERONICA H; Antelope Valley HS; Lancaster, CA; (3); 121/631; Computer Clb; Bsktbl; Sftbl; Vllybl; High Hon Roll; Hon Roll; Prfct Atten Awd; Spanish NHS; Child Care Asst; UCLA; Teacher.

DIAS, ANTONIO P; Homestead HS; Sunnyvale, CA; (3); 1/383; French Clb; FBLA; Service Clb; Ed Nwsp; French Hon Soc; NHS; CSF; 3rd Bus Engl FBLA Conf; Distnctn In Math & Comp Sci; Comp Sci.

DIAS, DIANE; North HS; Bakersfield, CA; (2); Chorus; School Play; Cheerldng; Crs Cntry; Mgr(s); Score Keeper; Trk; Vllybl; Cit Awd; High Hon Roll; Aerobics, Swmmng, Tnns; Berkeley; Law.

DIAS, DINA S; Hilmar HS; Hilmar, CA; (3); Treas FFA; Var Trk; Hon Roll; Bus.

DIAS, EDDIE M; Riverbank HS; Modesto, CA; (4); Office Aide; Teachers Aide; JV Var Bsbl; JV Var Bsktbl; JV Var Ftbl; JV Var Powder Puff Ftbl; Cit Awd; Hon Roll; Outstndng SR Athlete; Bank Am Acchvt Awd; Voc Achvt Bldg Contr Awd; Modesto JR Coll; Drftng.

DIAS, LINDA; Chico SR HS; Chico, CA; (3); 20/354; Church Yth Grp; Spanish Clb; SADD; Chorus; Ed Nwsp; Ed Yrbk; Pres Stu Cncl; Bsktbl; JV Var Cheerldng; Cit Awd; Am Legn Cert Of Schl Awd; Principals Awd; ANPA Schlst Jrnlst Awd; Red/Gold Svc Awd; Mst Valuable Pep Sq; Bus Mgmt.

DIAZ, ADELINA; El Toro HS; El Toro, CA; (4); FTA; Pep Clb; SADD; Teachers Aide; Pres Chorus; School Musical; Stage Crew; Swing Chorus; High Hon Roll; Hon Roll; CA Schlrshp Fed; Vocal Music Librarian; Gldn St Exam; Math Ed.

DIAZ, AMELIA; Liberty Union HS; Antioch, CA; (2); Hon Roll; Prfct Atten Awd; Mdcn.

DIAZ, ANTHONY F; Pasadena HS; Pasadena, CA; (2); Church Yth Grp; VP JA; Stage Crew; Intrml Mgr Trk; High Hon Roll; Hon Roll; CSF; MESA Outstndng Stu & Rep; Comp Engrng.

DIAZ, ARTURO; Fontana HS; Fontana, CA; (2); Boy Scts; Cit Awd; Hon Roll; Schl Slvr Mdl; Span Spkr; Russian Stu; UCLA; Psych.

DIAZ, BERNADETTE; Kingsburg HS; Traver, CA; (1); FFA; Accntng; UCLA; Law.

DIAZ, BEVERLY; Twentynine Palms HS; Gaithersburg, MD; (3); 9/180; Hosp Aide; Red Cross Aide; Teachers Aide; Band; Chorus; Pom Pon; Swmmng; Tennis; Vllybl; Hon Roll; Vllybl MVP; Sprtmnshp Awd; All League, Hnrb Mntn De Anza League; Jrnlsm.

DIAZ, BRICEIDA; St Genevieve HS; North Hollywood, CA; (3); French Clb; Red Cross Aide; Socr; Hon Roll; Stu Cncl Cmps Cmmssnr; Cmpgn Mgr Cnvntn; CSUN Northridgee; Pre-Law.

DIAZ, CAREY C; Palm Springs HS; Cathedral City, CA; (3); Church Yth Grp; French Clb; Var Swmmng; Hon Roll; Pianist; Chrch Nrsry Wrkr; Chld Psych.

DIAZ, CARLOS; Serra HS; San Mateo, CA; (2); Boy Scts; Pres Frsh Cls; VP Soph Cls; Sec Jr Cls; High Hon Roll; Hon Roll; Santa Clara U; Ped.

DIAZ, CARLOS M; Chowchilla Union HS; Chowchilla, CA; (4); Pres Church Yth Grp; FBLA; Library Aide; Rep Stu Cncl; Var Trk; Hon Roll; Part-Time Job; Chrstn Heritage Coll; Lawyer.

DIAZ, CAROLINE I; Wilcox HS; Santa Clara, CA; (1); Chess Clb; Drama Clb; French Clb; German Clb; JA; Latin Clb; Library Aide; Math Clb; Office Aide; Spanish Clb; Mission Coll; Nrs.

DIAZ, CATHERINE R; Bishop Amat Memorial HS; Rowland Hts, CA; (4); 82/392; Drama Clb; Sec Math Clb; School Musical; Rptr Yrbk; Rep Sr Cls; High Hon Roll; NHS; Friday Night Live; Barkado Clb Sec 88-90; Christian Srvce Vlntr; UC Irvine; Psychobio.

DIAZ, CINDY A; Redlands SR HS; Redlands, CA; (3); Church Yth Grp; Ski Clb; Band; Capt Flag Corp; Off Frsh Cls; Rep Soph Cls; Rep Jr Cls; Rep Sr Cls; Vllybl; Cmnty Wkr; U Of CA Riverside; Ed.

DIAZ, DEBORAH; Garey HS; Pomona, CA; (2); Church Yth Grp; 4-H; Spanish Clb; Church Choir; Pediatric.

DIAZ, ELIDIA; Carlmont HS; Belmont, CA; (3); Church Yth Grp; Spanish Clb; Math Hnr; Achvt In All Subjects; San Jose ST U; Engr.

DIAZ, ESTELA; Liberty Union HS; Brentwood, CA; (1); 1/444; Chorus; Sec Soph Cls; Co-Capt Cheerldng; High Hon Roll; Lw.

DIAZ, ESTHER; Oxnard HS; Oxnard, CA; (3); Teachers Aide; Oxnard Coll.

DIAZ, EVA MARIA; Castle Park HS; Chula Vista, CA; (3); 36/473; Cmnty Wkr; SADD; Cit Awd; Hon Roll; Masonic Awd; Awd Pssng Coll Wrtng Tst; Eng Essy Natl U; Law.

DIAZ, FERNANDO C; Edison HS; Stockton, CA; (3); Art Clb; Spanish Clb; Nwsp; Socr; Wrstlng; Hon Roll; Delta Coll; Comp Engr.

DIAZ, FERNIE L; Oakdale HS; Oakdale, CA; (2); Trk; UCLA; Engrng.

DIAZ, FRED J; King City HS; King City, CA; (2); Drama Clb; Quiz Bowl; Teachers Aide; School Play; Hon Roll; Pharmacy.

DIAZ, GABBY; Saddleback HS; Santa Ana, CA; (1); AFS; Art Clb; Bus Profs of Am; Computer Clb; Dance Clb; Drama Clb; GAA; JA; Math Tm; Orch; Harvard; Law.

DIAZ, GABRIELA V; Los Altos HS; Hacienda Hts, CA; (3); Science Clb; Drill Tm; Hon Roll; Santa Barbar U; Psych.

DIAZ, GERARDO; St Monicas HS; Santa Monica, CA; (3); Bus.

DIAZ, JAIME; Burbank SR HS; Burbank, CA; (4); 78/429; Var Socr; Var Trk; CA Poly Pomona; Aerospc Engr.

DIAZ, JANNELL F; La Sierra Acad; Corona, CA; (2); Spanish Clb; Teachers Aide; Band; VP Frsh Cls; Treas Soph Cls; Bsktbl; Ice Hcky; Score Keeper; Sftbl; Vllybl; Cmpltn Persnlty & Mdlng Schl J W Rawlings; CS St Fnlst Tn Pgnt; LLU; Med.

DIAZ, JOSE L; Galt HS; Thornton, CA; (4); Spanish Clb; Teachers Aide; Varsity Clb; Capt Socr; Hon Roll; MVP Soccer, Player Of Yr 89-90; Delta Coll; Law Enfrcmnt.

DIAZ, JOSE L; La Serna/Montclair HS; Montclair, CA; (3); Hon Roll; Boys Clb; Stu Of Mnth; Outstndng Phys Ed Stu; Medal Excllnce Sci.

DIAZ, LEONARD B; Bellermine-Jefferson HS; Los Angeles, CA; (1); Boy Scts; VP Soph Cls; JV Bsktbl; JV Crs Cntry; JV Trk; High Hon Roll; Bosy & Girls Clb; UCLA; Archlgst.

DIAZ, LIGIA L; Sherman Oaks CES; Van Nuys, CA; (3); Teachers Aide; Drill Tm; JV Pom Pon; Fulfillment Fund Schlrshp; Schl Ser Knights; CSUN; Bus.

DIAZ, LILLIANA A; Corcoran HS; Corcoran, CA; (4); 3/110; Am Leg Aux Girls St; Church Yth Grp; FBLA; Sec Science Clb; Sec Varsity Clb; Sec Treas Stu Cncl; Stat Bsktbl; Var Crs Cntry; Var Trk; Cit Awd; Boswell Schlrshp; U Of Redlands Schlrshp; Bicultural Awd; U Of Redlands; Engl Spnsh Lwyr.

DIAZ, LOURDES A; Anaheim HS; Anaheim, CA; (3); Dance Clb; School Musical; JV Sftbl; MAES Clb; CA ST-FULLERTON; Engrng.

DIAZ, LUPE; Indio HS; Indio, CA; (1); Color Guard; Cit Awd; Hon Roll; Prfct Atten Awd; Real Estate.

DIAZ, MARIA D; Sweetwater HS; National City, CA; (3); Hon Roll; Math Cmptr Sci.

DIAZ, MARIA G; Watsonville HS; Watsonville, CA; (2); Teachers Aide; Hon Roll; CA Schlrshp Fed.

DIAZ, MARSHA; Etiwanda HS; Fontana, CA; (2); Vllybl; High Hon Roll; Hon Roll; CA ST Fullerton; Phy.

DIAZ, MARY; Lincoln HS; Lincoln, CA; (2); 25/186; Church Yth Grp; Spanish Clb; Rep Frsh Cls; Gov Hon Prg Awd; Intl Stud Assn Schlrshp.

DIAZ, MATTHEW; Gompers Secondary Sch; San Diego, CA; (2); 57/672; Chess Clb; Math Clb; Science Clb; Spanish Clb; Rep Frsh Cls; Hon Roll; NHS; Stanford; Engrng.

DIAZ, MAURO; Pater Noster HS; Los Angeles, CA; (3); 4/45; Drama Clb; Chorus; Stage Crew; Pres Frsh Cls; Pres Sr Cls; Hon Roll; NHS; Yrbk; Chrstn Svc; Hstry Awds; U S CA; Accntng.

DIAZ, MIGUEL A; Mount Pleasant HS; San Jose, CA; (2); Latin Clb; High Hon Roll; Hon Roll; Prfct Atten Awd; Pres Acad Fit Awd; Spnsh III Spcl Awd Excllnc 89-90; San Jose ST U; Engr.

DIAZ, MILADIS E; Santa Ana HS; Santa Ana, CA; (2); Art Clb; Latin Clb; Crs Cntry; NHS; UC Irvine; Pediatrician.

DIAZ, MIRNA; South Gate HS; S Gate, CA; (3); JV Sftbl; Hon Roll; Prfct Atten Awd; Med.

DIAZ, NANCY; Mt Pleasant HS; San Jose, CA; (4); JA; Spanish Clb; Nwsp; Off Sr Cls; Hon Roll; NHS; Chicano Yth Ldrshp Cnfrnc In Sacramento; Life Membrshp CSF; Hrnr Roll; San Jose ST; Pre Med.

DIAZ, NATHANIEL P; Don Bosco Technical Inst; Pico Rivera, CA; (3); Art Clb; Chess Clb; Drama Clb; School Play; Yrbk; Hon Roll; NHS; NEDT Awd; Pres Acad Fit Awd; Gldn Tiger All Arnd Achvt Awd; Costume Dsgn Romeo Juliet Play 89; Bosco Tech Ltrmn Soc Patch Dsgn 88; Don Bosco Tech Inst; Grphc Dsgn.

DIAZ, NICOLAS M; Garfield HS; Los Angeles, CA; (2); Hon Roll; Prfct Atten Awd; Gldn St Exam Geom; Cmptr Prgrmmng.

DIAZ, OSCAR; South Gate HS; South Gate, CA; (4); 14/612; Math Clb; Math Tm; Nwsp; High Hon Roll; Hon Roll; NHS; Pres Acad Fit Awd; 90 Uth Opprtnties Fndtn Excptnl Schlr; 90 HS Math Dept Awd; 89 HS Sci Dept Awd; U Notre Dame; Physics.

DIAZ, PAM; Lincoln Prep HS; San Diego, CA; (1); 20/173; JV Sftbl; JV Vllybl; Hon Roll; San Diego ST U; Acctnt.

DIAZ, PATRICIA; Gonzales Union HS; Soledad, CA; (4); 2/169; Am Leg Aux Girls St; Church Yth Grp; Spanish Clb; VP SADD; School Play; High Hon Roll; Sal; CSF VP; Interact Club; UC Davis; Bio.

DIAZ, RAFAEL A; Dublin HS; Dublin, CA; (3); Socr; Trk; Vllybl; Hon Roll; Cert Accmplshmnt; Cert Hnr; Med.

DIAZ, RALPH; Capuchino HS; San Bruno, CA; (2); Church Yth Grp; Letterman Clb; SADD; Stu Cncl; Var Capt Bsbl; JV Bsktbl; Engr.

DIAZ, RALPH R; Woodlake Union HS; Woodlake, CA; (2); FFA; JV Capt Bsbl; JV Capt Ftbl; Var Wrstlng; Hon Roll; Frshmn Ftbl Capt Awd JV Ftbl Best Defnsv Plyr Awd; Back Awd.

DIAZ, RAY; Bishop Amat HS; Baldwin Park, CA; (2); Intrml Crs Cntry; NEDT Awd; Cal Tech; Engrng.

DIAZ, RICARDO; Bellarmine Jefferson HS; Burbank, CA; (1); Spanish Clb; Color Guard; JV Bsbl; JV Bsktbl; High Hon Roll; Stu Of Month; All Star Little Leag Bsbl; UCLA; Med.

DIAZ, ROBERT MICHAEL; Palm Desert HS; Palm Desert, CA; (4); Boy Scts; Church Yth Grp; Cmnty Wkr; Teachers Aide; Bsbl; Ftbl; Hon Roll; Geom Cert Hnr; Jr Golf Assn; YMCA Yth Ctr Vlntr; Cal Poly San Luis Obispo; Engr.

DIAZ, RODERICK; Bishop Amat Memorial HS; Pomona, CA; (3); Cmnty Wkr; Math Clb; High Hon Roll; NHS; NEDT Awd; CSF; Spec Olympcs Vlntr; Acdmc Decthln.

DIAZ, RONNIE; Liberty Union HS; Oakley, CA; (3); Debate Tm; NFL; Treas Speech Tm; Teachers Aide; School Play; Stage Crew; Rptr Nwsp; Var Tennis; High Hon Roll; Voice Dem Awd.

DIAZ, ROSSYBELL; Seaside HS; Ft Knox, KY; (2); Drama Clb; Red Cross Aide; Thesps; School Musical; School Play; Sec Frsh Cls; VP Soph Cls; Var Crs Cntry; Var Tennis; JV Var Trk; Jrnlsm.

DIAZ, SANDRA L; Arroyo HS; El Monte, CA; (4); 103/423; Key Clb; SADD; Acpl Chr; Chorus; Vllybl; Hon Roll; Kiwanis Awd; CA Schltc Fed; Cal Poly Pomona; Accntng.

DIAZ, SERGIO E; Venice HS; Los Angeles, CA; (2); Cmnty Wkr; Letterman Clb; Library Aide; Math Clb; Office Aide; Stage Crew; Yrbk; VP Frsh Cls; Treas Jr Cls; Rep Stu Cncl; Mst Outstndng Argonaut/Argnaut With Hghst Svc Hrs Awds; Cmmnctns.

DIAZ, SOCORRO; Paramount HS; South Gate, CA; (2); 72/666; Band; Cit Awd; Prfct Atten Awd; Bus.

DIAZ, STEVE; San Fernando HS; Pacoima, CA; (3); Boy Scts; Church Yth Grp; Var Capt Ftbl; JV Trk; Var Capt Wt Lftg; Cit Awd; Hon Roll; All Leag Tm Ftbl 88 & 89; Boy Scy Yr Awd 86; Royal Rangr Lt Cmmnr Outpost 209; Comp Info Systms.

DIAZ, SYLVIA; La Puente HS; La Puente, CA; (3); Hon Roll; Accntng.

DIAZ, VICTOR; King City Joint Union HS; King City, CA; (2); FFA; Band; Mrchg Band; JV Bsktbl; JV Ftbl; JV Trk; JV Wt Lftg; U Of Tech Inst; Auto.

DIAZ, VICTORIA A; Colton HS; Colton, CA; (1); Rep Frsh Cls; JV Bsktbl; JV Sftbl; Marine Bio.

DIAZ, YESSENIA; Baldwin Park HS; Baldwin Park, CA; (3); Church Yth Grp; Math Clb; Science Clb; Yrbk; Rep Jr Cls; Cit Awd; High Hon Roll; NHS; Prfct Atten Awd; UCLA; Psych.

DIAZ, YVETTE; Livermore HS; Livermore, CA; (1); Cheerldng; Hon Roll; Choreographer.

DIAZ DE LEON, JUANITA; Bishop Montgomery HS; Torrance, CA; (2); High Hon Roll; Ca Schlrshp Fed; Cert Of Awd 88-89 Sch Yr Alg & Morality; Cert Of Wad 89-90 Geo & Frnch.

DIAZ DE LEON, NANCY; Bishop Amat HS; Diamond Bar, CA; (3); Church Yth Grp; Hosp Aide; Varsity Clb; Var Tennis; Hon Roll; CA Schlrshp Fed; Lanternman ST Hosp Vlntr; Work Experience Pgm; Loyola Marymount U.

DIBB, HEATHER; Concord HS; Concord, CA; (3); 39/280; Pep Clb; SADD; Teachers Aide; Flag Corp; Stu Cncl; L Cheerldng; Pom Pon; Hon Roll; Harvard; Criminal Law.

DIBBLEE, HARRISON F; Huntington Beach HS; Huntington Beach, CA; (1); Boy Scts; Intrml Ftbl; Intrml Trk; USC; Bus.

DICE, CHRISTY K; Oakdale HS; Oakdale, CA; (3); Hosp Aide; Teachers Aide; JV Powder Puff Ftbl; CNA Hosp; Obstrcn.

DICELY, CHRISTOPHER M; Benicia HS; Benicia, CA; (4); Chess Clb; Computer Clb; Debate Tm; French Clb; Pres FBLA; Math Tm; NFL; JV Ftbl; Ntl Merit SF; Adcmc Decthln; Comp Sci.

DICHOSA, ARNOLD E; Pater Noster HS; Los Angeles, CA; (3); 6/30; Dance Clb; Drama Clb; Yrbk; VP Stu Cncl; Stat Ftbl; Var Capt Vllybl; Hon Roll; NHS; CA ST; Engr.

DICK, TODD M; Ramona HS; Ramona, CA; (3); Letterman Clb; Var Bsbl; Var Bsktbl; Var Ftbl; Var Wt Lftg; High Hon Roll; Hon Roll; Pres Acad Fit Awd.

DICKARD, CRYSTAL I; Nevada Union HS; Camptonville, CA; (2); 1/500; Intnl Clb; Chorus; High Hon Roll; Piano; Ballet; CA Schlrshp Fed; Med.

DICKENS, DAVID; Exeter HS; Exeter, CA; (4); Am Leg Boys St; Pres Chess Clb; Church Yth Grp; Pres Drama Clb; Pres FBLA; Acpl Chr; Pres Chorus; School Musical; School Play; Stage Crew; Schlstc Achvt Math Awd; Bk Amer Comp Sci Awd; Acad Dcthln Awds, Mdls; Sci Olympd Awd Wnr; Pepperdine U; Music.

DICKENSHEETS, ANDREA; Hoopa Valley HS; Willow Creek, CA; (3); 2/50; Key Clb; Pep Clb; SADD; Ed Nwsp; Rptr Yrbk; Sec Sr Cls; Var Capt Cheerldng; Var L Sftbl; Var L Trk; Wt Lftg; Poetry Awds; Schlr Athlt Awd; Humboldt ST U; Bus Admin.

DICKER, DAVID J; Poway HS; San Diego, CA; (4); 71/668; FBLA; Key Clb; Spanish Clb; Var Ftbl; High Hon Roll; Ntl Merit Ltr; Pres Acad Fit Awd; UW Madison; Commnctns.

DICKERMAN, LEXA M; Del Campo HS; Fair Oaks, CA; (2); 16/465; French Clb; Hosp Aide; Ed Nwsp; Var Crs Cntry; Var Trk; Hon Roll; NHS; Stu Rchng Out Pres-In-Trng; CSF; CA U; Bio.

DICKERSON, CHAD E; Escalon HS; Escalon, CA; (3); 25/150; Capt Quiz Bowl; Band; Treas Sr Cls; L Var Bsbl; L Capt Bsktbl; L JV Ftbl; L Capt Socr; Cit Awd; Hon Roll; Prfct Atten Awd; Band Awd Acad Excllnce; Schlr/Athlte Awds; MVP Awd Bsktbl 2 Yrs; Tm Cptn Awd Bsktbl; Stanislaus ST; Accntng.

DICKERSON, CHRISHONE N; George Washington Prep HS; Los Angeles, CA; (2); GAA; JA; Math Clb; VP Jr Cls; Rep Stu Cncl; JV Bsktbl; JV Gym; Cit Awd; High Hon Roll; Hon Roll; Cls Jr Princess 89; Most Intelligent 89; 2nd Pl Acad Achvt Awd 89; UCLA; Bus.

DICKERSON, DALE W; Fontana HS; Bloomington, CA; (2); Rep Frsh Cls; JV Bsbl; Var Ftbl; Bus Accntng.

DICKERSON, JOEL; Orange Glen HS; Escondido, CA; (1); German Clb; Math Tm; Quiz Bowl; Scholastic Bowl; Socr; Tennis; High Hon Roll; Hon Roll; Econ.

DICKERSON, LAURA; Fred C Beyer HS; Modesto, CA; (4); 5/506; German Clb; Service Clb; Var Capt Crs Cntry; Var Trk; Cit Awd; High Hon Roll; Hon Roll; CSF; Comp Sci Engrng.

DICKEY, ANGELA M; Fontana HS; Fontana, CA; (2); Hon Roll; Educ.

DICKEY, KANDACE; Oak Ridge HS; El Dorado Hills, CA; (4); 51/235; Church Yth Grp; Cmnty Wkr; SADD; Church Choir; Variety Show; Stu Cncl; JV Var Cheerldng; Mgr Trk; High Hon Roll; Hon Roll; Friday Night Live; Dance; CA ST U; Optometry.

DICKEY, MICHELLE; Imperial HS; Lu Verne, IA; (4); 8/81; Am Leg Aux Girls St; 4-H; FFA; Treas SADD; Nwsp; Pres Sr Cls; Elks Awd; Hon Roll; Lion Awd; Fri Nigh Live-Treas; CSF-SEC; KS ST U; Animal Sci.

DICKEY, WILLIAM G; Santana HS; Santee, CA; (2); 34/379; JV Ftbl; Var Wt Lftg; High Hon Roll; Hon Roll; Golden State Exam Algebra High Hnrs; USD; Real Estate.

DICKIE, KATHLEEN E; Eisenhower HS; Rialto, CA; (3); Aud/Vis; Office Aide; Teachers Aide; Hon Roll.

DICKINSON, CHRISTINE L; Valhalla HS; Jamul, CA; (4); 175/412; Church Yth Grp; Cmnty Wkr; Drama Clb; French Clb; Intnl Clb; Thesps; School Play; Amnsty Intl Clb; Frnch Clb Ofcr JR Yr; Creatv Wrtg.

DICKINSON, ELIZABETH A; San Bernardino HS; San Bernardino, CA; (3); 53/540; Hon Roll; Rotary Awd; Phoenix Hnr Club; Interact Club; Rotary Life Club; Comm.

DICKINSON, ROBERT L; San Bernardino HS; San Bernardino, CA; (4); Band; Mrchg Band; Ed Yrbk; High Hon Roll; NHS; Pres Acad Fit Awd; Rotary Awd; Acadc Dcthln; Odyssy Mind; UC Berkeley.

DICKINSON, TIM; Palo Alto HS; Palo Alto, CA; (2); Drama Clb; Key Clb; Spanish Clb; Thesps; School Play; Nwsp; Rep Frsh Cls; Rep Soph Cls; Rep Stu Cncl; JV Trk; Engl Awd.

DICKMAN, JASON; Poway HS; Poway, CA; (3); 17/600; Boy Scts; Church Yth Grp; High Hon Roll; Hon Roll; NHS; Bsktbl; Brigham Yng U; Bus Mgmt.

DICKMAN III, RALPH E; Poway HS; Poway, CA; (4); 140/720; Boy Scts; Church Yth Grp; Chorus; Church Choir; Hon Roll; Prfct Atten Awd; CSF; Eagle Sct; Brigham Young U; Dntstry.

DICKOVER, MICHELE A; Thousand Oaks HS; Thousand Oaks, CA; (3); 51/542; Girl Scts; Band; Mrchg Band; DAR Awd; High Hon Roll; Hon Roll; Prfct Atten Awd; Turn Around Awd; Comp Sci.

DICKSON, CLINT J; Live Oak HS; Morgan Hill, CA; (3); Spanish Clb; Rep Soph Cls; Var Tennis; JV Trk; Hon Roll; Lion Awd; Ntl Merit Ltr; Pres Acad Fit Awd; St & Natl Off Rd Cyclng Race Intrmdt Div; Essay Hnrb Mntn; CA Poly San Luis Obispo; Arspc.

DICKSON, CRYSTA L; Redlands HS; Highland, CA; (2); Pres Ski Clb; Ed Nwsp; Yrbk; CSU San Bernardino; Dntl Hygst.

DICKSON, JENNIFER L; Credence HS; Susanville, CA; (3); Hosp Aide; Office Aide; Teachers Aide; Ed Nwsp; Yrbk.

DICKSON, MARY; Corona HS; Corona, CA; (2); Sec Church Yth Grp; Ski Clb; Chorus; Church Choir; Cit Awd; Acad Ltr; U Of CA San Francisco; Bus.

DICKSON, NICOLE D; Canyon Springs HS; Moreno Valley, CA; (4); Art Clb; Church Yth Grp; Letterman Clb; Varsity Clb; Rep Frsh Cls; Rep Soph Cls; Rep Jr Cls; Rep Sr Cls; Rep Stu Cncl; JV Bsktbl; Most Imprvd Bsktbl; CSF; Cyn Spgs 1st Girls Frshmn Bsktbl Team; Riverside City Coll; Bus Admin.

DICTOS, ALEX S; Washington Union HS; Fresno, CA; (4); 13/180; CSF; Fresno ST; Indstrl Engrng.

DIDEHVARSADR, FARID; Pasadena HS; Alhambra, CA; (2); Chess Clb; German Clb; Teachers Aide; JV Var Socr; JV Var Tennis; Table Tennis Clb; CSF; Physcn.

DIDEHVARSADR, MOJDEH; Pasadena HS; Alhambra, CA; (3); Chess Clb; German Clb; Teachers Aide; Varsity Clb; Tennis; Var Badminton; CSF; Table Tennis Club; Ucla; Med.

DIDEK, KELLY; Poway HS; Poway, CA; (3); Drama Clb; VP Pres SADD; Stage Crew; JV Sftbl; Stat Wrstlng; High Hon Roll; Hon Roll; NHS; Amnsty Intntl.

DIDOT, CELESTE D; Nevada Union HS; Grass Valley, CA; (3); Church Yth Grp; Drama Clb; Teachers Aide; Thesps; Chorus; School Musical; School Play; Variety Show; JV Sftbl; JV Vllybl; San Diego ST; Psych.

DIEC, THANH H; Milpitas HS; Milpitas, CA; (4); Debate Tm; JA; Scholastic Bowl; Band; Mrchg Band; Orch; Pep Band; School Musical; Stu Cncl; Hon Roll; Cert Of Awd Acadmc Excllnc Physcs, APUS Hstry; Acadmc Ltr; CSF; Santa Clara U; Bus Adm.

DIEGO, LISA A; Monache HS; Poplar, CA; (3); Letterman Clb; Teachers Aide; Band; Mrchg Band; Pep Band; JV Sftbl; JV Var Vllybl; High Hon Roll; Hon Roll; Prfct Atten Awd; Acadc Achvts For Lang Arts; Fresno ST; Chld Psych.

DIEGO, SALVADOR; University HS; South Gate, CA; (3); Intrml Bsktbl; Hon Roll.

DIEHL, ELIZABETH J; Hueneme HS; Port Hueneme, CA; (3); 2/375; Church Yth Grp; Dance Clb; Office Aide; Teachers Aide; VP Soph Cls; Treas Jr Cls; Stu Cncl; Swmmng; High Hon Roll; CSF; Acad Excllnc Awd Math & Phys Educ; UCSB.

DIEHM, TANYA M; Weed HS; Weed, CA; (4); 1/42; Am Leg Aux Girls St; Church Yth Grp; Sec Key Clb; Letterman Clb; Office Aide; Ski Clb; Speech Tm; Band; Pres Soph Cls; Pres Stu Cncl; Vlntr Rescue Sqd & Fire Dept; Hgh Hnrs Gldn St Exm Geom; Acad Decthln; U Of CA Davis; Med.

DIEMER, BRIAN; Valley Christian HS; Dublin, CA; (4); 3/25; Color Guard; Var L Bsktbl; Var L Socr; Cit Awd; DAR Awd; High Hon Roll; NHS; Aud/Vis; Church Yth Grp; CA EMT; Cngrsnl USAF Acad; Cvl Air Ptrl Cdt Of Yr; Prncpls Ldrshp Awd; USAF Acad; Engr.

DIEMERT, AMY J; Laguna Hills HS; Laguna Hills, CA; (2); 83/352; Church Yth Grp; Yrbk; Hon Roll; Ed.

DIEMOZ, LISA G; Napa HS; Napa, CA; (4); #1 In Class; Key Clb; Letterman Clb; SADD; Chorus; Church Choir; Pres Frsh Cls; Var Bsktbl; Var Capt Crs Cntry; Var Powder Puff Ftbl; Var Capt Socr; UCLA; Rsrch Scntst.

DIEP, ANDY T; Alhambra HS; Alhambra, CA; (2); Band; Bsktbl; Badminton; Bus.

DIEP, BETSY-BINH; San Gabriel HS; Rosemead, CA; (3); Cmnty Wkr; German Clb; Math Tm; Q&S; Science Clb; Service Clb; SADD; Nwsp; Ed Lit Mag; Cit Awd; Hstry Profssr.

DIEP, DAVID; Alhambra HS; Alhambra, CA; (3); Office Aide; Science Clb; Intrml Bsktbl; Spnsh Hnr Soc, Scl Clb, Jr Fndrsrs & Jr Cncl; Pre-Med.

DIEP, DU T; Thomas Downey HS; Modesto, CA; (3); German Clb; Hosp Aide; SADD; Teachers Aide; Cit Awd; High Hon Roll; CA Schlrshp Fed; CA Davis U; Bus.

DIEP, JACKIE P; Edison HS; Huntington Beach, CA; (3); German Clb; Model UN; Science Clb; Spanish Clb; Speech Tm; SADD; Ed Lit Mag; JV Trk; Pres Acad Fit Awd; International Relations.

DIEP, JOE; Rosemead HS; Rosemead, CA; (3); Am Leg Boys St; FCA; FBLA; Key Clb; Math Clb; Office Aide; Teachers Aide; Varsity Clb; Var Capt Bsktbl; Var L Trk; CSF VP.

DIEP, KIM BINH; Fountain Valley HS; Huntington Bch, CA; (3); French Clb; Science Clb; Hon Roll; Prfct Atten Awd; CSF; Outstndng Athltc Achvt Awd; JV Badmntn; Medcl.

DIEP, LINDA; San Gabriel HS; San Gabriel, CA; (2); Cmnty Wkr; Spanish Clb; SADD; Acpl Chr; Chorus; School Musical; JV Swmmng; Hon Roll; Interact Club; Cert Achvt Music; Interested In Music, Singing & Brdwy Musicals; Bus.

DIEP, LY H; San Gabriel HS; Rosemead, CA; (3); FBLA; Teachers Aide; Yrbk; Hon Roll; Vietnms Club; Cngrssnl Schlr; Cal Poly Pomona; Bus Mngmnt.

DIEP, LYNN; Galileo HS; San Francisco, CA; (2); Church Yth Grp; Hon Roll; Soph Pep Clb; Cls Svc Apprectn Awd; Fshn Mrchndsng.

DIEP, MAU; Mark Keppel HS; Monterey Park, CA; (3); French Clb; FBLA; Pres Key Clb; Math Clb; Mu Alpha Theta; Intrml JV Bsktbl; High Hon Roll; Prfct Atten Awd; Intrml Tennis; CSF Golden St Exam Awd Surrealist Wrtngs; Cal Tech; Electrnc Engr.

DIEP, TAI; San Gabriel HS; Rosemead, CA; (3); Key Clb; JV Var Bsktbl; JV Crs Cntry; Hon Roll; CSF; Cal Pomona Polytech; Arch.

DIEP, TAM; Modesto HS; Modesto, CA; (2); Intnl Clb; Math Clb; Spanish Clb; Cit Awd; High Hon Roll; CSF; UOP Stockton; Pharm.

DIEP, TERESA HIEU; Phillip And Sala Burton HS; San Francisco, CA; (2); High Hon Roll; Japanese Clb; Rdg Bks; Med.

DIEP, THANH X; Glendale HS; Glendale, CA; (3); Acpl Chr; Chorus; UC Irving; Phrmcy.

DIEP, THI N; Mark Keppel HS; Monterey Park, CA; (3); Debate Tm; FBLA; Math Clb; Math Tm; Mu Alpha Theta; Pres Sec NFL; High Hon Roll; Lion Awd; Opt Clb Awd; Octagon Svc Club VP; Bus.

DIEP, THI T; Thomas Downey HS; Modesto, CA; (1); Science Clb; Chorus; Cit Awd; Hon Roll; Prfct Atten Awd; CSF; Tchr.

DIEP, THU L; Chaffey HS; Ontario, CA; (2); High Hon Roll; CA Schlrshp Fndtn; HEF Awd Algebra Computer Literacy; Fashion Designer.

DIEP, TRINH; Saddle-Back HS; Santa Ana, CA; (4); Prfct Atten Awd; Rgnl Occptn Pgm Schlrsyp; Acadmc Awd; Fullerton U; Bus Admin.

DIEP, VI V; Will C Crawford HS; San Diego, CA; (1); Hon Roll; Pres Schlr; Friends Library; Harvard; Law.

DIEPERSLOOT, ELISABETH A; Redwood HS; Visalia, CA; (4); Church Yth Grp; Key Clb; Math Clb; Math Tm; Pep Clb; Quiz Bowl; Science Clb; Service Clb; Spanish Clb; Speech Tm; CSF Seal Bearor; UCSD; Urban Geography.

DIETEL, MICHAEL A; Capistrano Valley Christian HS; Dana Point, CA; (2); Var Ftbl; Var Socr.

DIETS, CANDI M; Norte Vista HS; Fowleton, IN; (2); Computer Clb; FBLA; GAA; JA; ROTC; Spanish Clb; Color Guard; Drill Tm; Flag Corp; Mrchg Band; Aeronautics.

DIETTERLE, DEBORAH; Rosary HS; Fullerton, CA; (3); Church Yth Grp; Dance Clb; Hosp Aide; Variety Show; JV Swmmng; High Hon Roll; NHS; Mock Trl; Law.

DIETZ, LILI K; Durham HS; Durham, CA; (1); FHA; Hon Roll; Acctng.

DIEZSI, LIAM DONALD; Burney JR SR HS; Burney, CA; (2); Church Yth Grp; Acpl Chr; Band; Church Choir; School Musical; Var Cheerldng; Socr; Var Trk; Var Wrstlng; Hon Roll; Entertainer.

DIFFENBAUGH, NOAH; Mount Madonna Schl; Watsonville, CA; (2); Cmnty Wkr; Drama Clb; Ski Clb; School Musical; School Play; Yrbk; Treas Frsh Cls; VP Soph Cls; Bsktbl; Vllybl; Math Tutor; Stanford; Med.

DIFUNTORUM, ANDREA; St Patrick - St Vincent HS; Fairfield, CA; (3); 42/144; Church Yth Grp; Cmnty Wkr; Pep Clb; SADD; Rep Sr Cls; Stu Cncl; Var Bsktbl; Var Cheerldng; High Hon Roll; Hon Roll; CA ST U; Marketing Rtl Mngr.

DIFUNTORUM, SHERRY L; Las Lomas HS; Walnut Creek, CA; (3); Art Clb; Church Yth Grp; Dance Clb; Intnl Clb; Model UN; Art.

DIGGS, KRISTIN A; Woodland HS; Woodland, CA; (3); Rep English Clb; Treas French Clb; Key Clb; Ski Clb; SADD; Teachers Aide; School Musical; Pres Soph Cls; Pres Jr Cls; Rep Sr Cls; Neurology.

DIGIULIO, DENA; Savanna HS; Buena Park, CA; (3); Color Guard; Fullerton JC; Cosmtlgst.

DIGNAN, CASEY MICHAEL; St Michaels Prep; Costa Mesa, CA; (3); School Play; Stage Crew; Yrbk; Var Bsktbl; Hon Roll; Jr NHS; NHS; Maint Supvr Stu Govt; Acad Decath.

DIGREGORIO, ELAINA M; Notre Dame Acad; Culver City, CA; (3); Church Yth Grp; GAA; Girl Scts; Treas Chorus; Church Choir; School Musical; Variety Show; Ed Yrbk; Capt Socr; Hon Roll; Campus Ministry Pres; Educ.

DIJKSTRA, HELEN B; Bakersfield HS; Bakersfield, CA; (2); Church Yth Grp; German Clb; Key Clb; Band; Drm Mjr(t); Mrchg Band; Pep Band; Intrml Bsktbl; Var Trk; Intrml Vllybl.

DIKOUSMAN, JOHNEE J; Beyer HS; Modesto, CA; (1); High Hon Roll; Hon Roll; Elec Engr.

DIKRANIAN, ARMEN H; Armenian Mesrobian HS; Montebello, CA; (3); 1/40; Boy Scts; Church Yth Grp; Quiz Bowl; Rptr Nwsp; Treas Stu Cncl; Var Socr; Var Trk; High Hon Roll; Pres Acad Fit Awd; USC; Phy.

DILBECK, JASON K; Durham HS; Durham, CA; (3); Drama Clb; Letterman Clb; Red Cross Aide; ROTC; SADD; Teachers Aide; Thesps; Varsity Clb; Color Guard; Chorus; Stu Body City Cncl Rep; Peer Support Grp; Hstry.

DILBECK, MICHELLE; Mount Dia Blo HS; Pittsburg, CA; (1); French Clb; JV Bsktbl; Hon Roll; GATE; Talented Education; Med Schl Brain Surgeon.

DILENA, STEPHANIE; Tomales HS; Pt Reyes Station, CA; (2); Church Yth Grp; Cmnty Wkr; 4-H; Ski Clb; Off Soph Cls; Cheerldng; Score Keeper; Vllybl; Cit Awd; 4-H Awd; Eng Awd-Outstndng Frshmn-Wrtng; Bst Dfns Awd-Vllybl; Spnsh Awd; St Marys U; Tchr.

DILGER, ERIC W; Antelope Valley HS; Lancaster, CA; (3); 169/587; Computer Clb; German Clb; Intnl Clb; Band; Drill Tm; Drm Mjr(t); Jazz Band; Mrchg Band; Orch; Pep Band; Concert Band; Classical Music; Russian Imperilism; Denver U; Music Ed.

DILLARD, ANDREA N; Pius X HS; Long Beach, CA; (3); GAA; Pep Clb; Hon Roll; JV Var Bsktbl; JV Trk; Gospel Choir; Coaches Awd Bsktbl & Trk; Math Ed.

DILLARD, REO TERAO; Bridgemont HS; San Francisco, CA; (3); Letterman Clb; Var Crs Cntry; Var Trk; Wt Lftg; Hon Roll; Prncpls Awd Acad Mst Imprvd 89-90; Engrng.

DILLARD, TAMIE M; Montclair HS; Rialto, CA; (3); 2/33; Drama Clb; JA; Red Cross Aide; Thesps; Varsity Clb; School Play; Stage Crew; JV Crs Cntry; Var Score Keeper; Trk; Intl Order Of The Rainbow For Girls; Stu Of The Mnth.

DILLAVOU, JASON; Chico SR HS; Chico, CA; (3); 25/364; Church Yth Grp; Letterman Clb; Ski Clb; Teachers Aide; Varsity Clb; Ftbl; Trk; Hon Roll; Pres Acad Fit Awd; Engrng.

DILLENBURG, HEATHER; Fred C Beyer HS; Modesto, CA; (4); 56/520; Off Cmnty Wkr; Treas Drama Clb; FBLA; Capt Hosp Aide; Red Cross Aide; Service Clb; Ski Clb; Spanish Clb; Teachers Aide; Varsity Clb; Natl Ldrshp & Svc Awd; Law Explorers Clb; Vlnteer At Dist Attrnys Ofc; Cal Poly; Pre-Law.

DILLEY, KERITH; Sonoma Valley HS; Sonoma, CA; (4); 8/269; Debate Tm; NFL; School Musical; School Play; Ed Nwsp; Var Powder Puff Ftbl; High Hon Roll; CSF; Acad Decathlon Team 2 Yrs; UCLA; Bus.

DILLMAN, AMIE L; Pacifica HS; Cypress, CA; (3); 7/273; Quiz Bowl; Spanish Clb; Band; Jazz Band; Mrchg Band; Socr; Vllybl; Hon Roll; CSF Fund Raiser Coord; Notre Dame U; Chld Dvlpmnt Psyc.

DILLON, ARIANA; Abraham Lincoln HS; San Francisco, CA; (2); Cmnty Wkr; Intnl Clb; Spanish Clb; Teachers Aide; Acpl Chr; Chorus; High Hon Roll; Hon Roll; Sngng Rnbws Yth Ensmbl; Creative Wrtng Wrk Publshd; 19th Cntry Cltrl Evnts Lvng Hist Centre; San Francisco ST U; Elem Ed.

DILLON, CHRISTOPHER; Grace Christian HS; Atascadero, CA; (4); #1 In Class; Church Yth Grp; Cmnty Wkr; Drama Clb; Variety Show; Cit Awd; High Hon Roll; Kiwanis Awd; Prfct Atten Awd; Val; 1st 2nd & 3rd Pl Mndy Clb Music Schlrshp Cmptn; Guest Solist With San Luis Obispo Cnty Symphy Orch; Eastman Schl Of Music; Pianist.

DILLON, CODI; Mt Shasta HS; Mt Shasta, CA; (4); 3/76; Church Yth Grp; Chorus; School Musical; Swing Chorus; Sec Frsh Cls; Rotary Awd; VP Sr Cls; U CA Santa Cruz; Bus.

DILLON, ERIC W; La Habra HS; La Habra, CA; (3); Band; Socr; Trk; Hon Roll; Surf.

DILLON, MARYANN M; San Gorgonio HS; San Bernardino, CA; (4); FBLA; Mayors Crime Task Force; Valley Coll; Mrktng.

DILLON, MICHELE; Thomas Downey HS; Modesto, CA; (1); Dance Clb; Science Clb; Cheerldng; Hon Roll; Fresno ST U; Phys Thrpst.

DILLON, SARAH; Faith Christian HS; Yuba City, CA; (2); Church Yth Grp; GAA; Spanish Clb; Varsity Clb; Church Choir; Drill Tm; Rep Soph Cls; Cheerldng; Var Pom Pon; Var Sftbl; Azusa Pacific Coll.

DIMA, RODICA A; Del Campo HS; Sacramento, CA; (2); French Clb; Hosp Aide; SADD; Variety Show; Cit Awd; Prfct Atten Awd; UC Davis; Dentist.

DIMACALI, DEXTER C; Samuel F B Morse HS; San Diego, CA; (3); Office Aide; Science Clb; Hon Roll; Prfct Atten Awd; Pres Acad Fit Awd; CA Schlrshp Fed; Orthodontics.

DIMACULANGAN, RAMONITO S; Glendora HS; Costa Mesa, CA; (4); Church Yth Grp; Cmnty Wkr; VP Computer Clb; JA; Key Clb; VP Math Clb; Spanish Clb; Pres SADD; Orch; Var Tennis; Fri Night Live Rep 87-88, Mtg Coord 88-89; Pres 89-90; Mayors Task Force Agnst Drug & Alcohol Abuse 90; U Of CA Irvine; Elec Engrng.

DIMALANTA, ERIC V; Nogales HS; Walnut, CA; (2); 27/747; Science Clb; Stu Cncl; High Hon Roll; Hon Roll; Vrsty Fencing Tm; Golden St Exam Geom Schl Recognition; CSF.

DIMAPILIS, ALBERT"STRINGFELLOW"; Baldwin Park HS; Baldwin Park, CA; (4); Aud/Vis; Drama Clb; Science Clb; Teachers Aide; Band; Chorus; School Play; Stage Crew; Lit Mag; Stu Cncl; Best Comedic Perf '90 Drama Dept; Cloak,Daggers & Macgyvers Soc 88-90; Olympic Sum Camp Cnslr; CA ST U; Mus,Arts,Journalism.

DIMAPORO, ANNA CHARINA O; Polytechnic HS; N Hollywood, CA; (2); Dance Clb; Library Aide; Tennis; Hon Roll; Jr NHS; Ntl Merit Ltr; CSUN; RN.

DIMARANAN, MARY S; Glendale HS; Glendale, CA; (3); 72/670; Office Aide; Capt Drill Tm; Ed Nwsp; Capt Pom Pon; Hon Roll; Jr NHS; NHS; California Scholarship Federation; Filipino Club; Medical Explorer Program; Dentristry Nursing.

DIMICK, MAVRI; Laguna Hills HS; Laguna Hills, CA; (3); Church Yth Grp; Pep Clb; SADD; Yrbk; Rep Frsh Cls; JV Var Cheerldng; Swmmng; Trk; Cit Awd; Hon Roll; Art; BYU; Cmnctns.

DIMINO, DONNA; California HS; San Ramon, CA; (3); Cmnty Wkr; Hosp Aide; Intnl Clb; Q&S; Co-Capt Cheerldng; Capt Pom Pon; JV Capt Sftbl; Var Vllybl; Treas NHS; Pres Rotary Awd; UCSD; Pre Med.

DIMOCK, JEANETTE E; Acalanes HS; Lafayette, CA; (1); Dance Clb; Drama Clb; Hon Roll; Pres Acad Fit Awd; Nationally Ranked Rhythmic Gymnast; Ballet; Jazz Dance.

DIMOND, JODI C; Carlsbad HS; Carlsbad, CA; (1); Church Yth Grp; GAA; Pep Clb; SADD; Capt Socr; Capt Sftbl; Cit Awd; High Hon Roll; Pres Acad Fit Awd.

DINA, PETER T; Calvary Baptist HS; La Verne, CA; (3); Church Yth Grp; Teachers Aide; L Bsbl; Trk; L Vllybl; Hon Roll; Civil Air Patrol; Vllybl Mst Insprtnl; Marine Aviation.

DINAN, JENNIFER; Cupertino HS; Cupertino, CA; (4); Teachers Aide; Drill Tm; JV Co-Capt Cheerldng; Powder Puff Ftbl; Socr; Tennis; De Anza Clg; Fnnce.

DINELLI, CATHERINE; Antioch SR HS; Antioch, CA; (3); 4-H; Chorus; Var Socr; 4-H Awd; Hon Roll; Amer Jr Qrtr Hrs Assn; Pacific Cst Qrtr Hrs Assn; CA Amateur Qrtr Hrs Exhbtrs Assn; Tchng.

DINES, VIKI J; Rio Linda SR HS; Rio Linda, CA; (3); ROTC; Teachers Aide; Band; Color Guard; Drill Tm; Hon Roll; UCLA; Pilot.

DINGEE, JOSH B; Gompers Seconday; San Diego, CA; (3); 1/84; Stage Crew; Variety Show; Lit Mag; Cit Awd; High Hon Roll; Hon Roll; Pres Acad Fit Awd; San Diegans For A More Peaceful World Cert; Yale U Book Award; Musician/Songwriter; Engineering Civil.

DINGMAN, JULIE; Barstow HS; Barstow, CA; (2); Flag Corp; Score Keeper; High Hon Roll; Hon Roll; UNLV.

DINGMAN, TRACY M; Las Plumas HS; Oroville, CA; (2); 7/272; Church Yth Grp; High Hon Roll; Hon Roll; Bus.

DINH, DIEP T; La Quinta HS; Westminster, CA; (4); 33/338; French Clb; Pres Intnl Clb; Latin Clb; Math Clb; Science Clb; Vllybl; NHS; Badminton; CSF Bearer; UCI; Bio Sci.

DINH, DUNG; San Lorenzo HS; San Leandro, CA; (2); Asian Woman Grp.

DINH, HOANG V; Granada Hills HS; Northridge, CA; (2); Computer Clb; Science Clb; Teachers Aide; Bsbl; Bsktbl; Ftbl; Swmmng; JV Tennis; Trk; Vllybl; Frgn Lang Awd Span; 4 Consctv Prncpls Hnr Lists; Silver Seal Awd Tech Arts; U Of CA; Elec Engr.

DINH, JENNY; Saddleback HS; Santa Ana, CA; (2); Cmnty Wkr; French Clb; JV Tennis; High Hon Roll; Pres Acad Fit Awd; Karate Clb; Outside Piano Prfrmnce; Orange Cnty Acad Dcthln; U Of CA Irvine; Chiropractic.

DINH, KIEU H; Bolsa Grande HS; Garden Grove, CA; (2); 2/377; Spanish Clb; Var L Crs Cntry; Var L Trk; Hon Roll; CSF; Vietnamese Clb; UCLA; Bus.

DINH, LONG; Santa Teresa HS; San Jose, CA; (2); Chess Clb; Debate Tm; Drama Clb; French Clb; German Clb; JA; Spanish Clb; Varsity Clb; Variety Show; Yrbk; Vietnamese Club; Stanford.

DINH, MARK L; Turlock HS; Turlock, CA; (2); 1/400; Science Clb; Speech Tm; VP VICA; Var Tennis; Var Vllybl; Pres Acad Fit Awd; Vo Indstrl Clubs Of Amer Rgnl & St Comptn Gold Mdls; Cty Math Comptn Silver Mdl; Sci Olymiad Comptn; UC Berkeley; Biochem.

DINH, NGOC V; Bolsa Grande HS; Garden Grove, CA; (2); Teachers Aide; Lit Mag; Crs Cntry; Sftbl; Vllybl; Cit Awd; Hon Roll; Carpenter; Drftg; Carpenter.

DINH, NGUYEN N; Saddleback HS; Santa Ana, CA; (1); Hosp Aide; Cit Awd; Prfct Atten Awd; Pres Acad Fit Awd; CSF; Vietnamese Clb; UCI; Med.

DINH, NHU; Mission Viejo HS; Mission Viejo, CA; (3); Church Yth Grp; Intnl Clb; Key Clb; Pep Clb; Spanish Clb; SADD; Hon Roll; NHS; Bio-Graphics; Jr Statesmn Of Amer; Grls Leag; Stanford; Bio.

DINH, QUOC ANN; Poway HS; Poway, CA; (4); Hosp Aide; Key Clb; Service Clb; Nwsp; Var Crs Cntry; High Hon Roll; Kiwanis Awd; NHS; Pres Acad Fit Awd; Volunteer Tutors Pres; UCSD; Teaching.

DINH, QUYEN; Saddleback HS; Santa Ana, CA; (3); Cmnty Wkr; French Clb; Scholastic Bowl; SADD; Variety Show; JV Tennis; Hon Roll; Pres Acad Fit Awd; Badminton; Karata Club; Outside Piano Prfmncs; U CA Irvine; Chiropractor.

DINH, QUYEN T; Hoover HS; San Diego, CA; (4); 16/298; French Clb; Cit Awd; French Hon Soc; Hon Roll; NHS; Ntl Merit SF; Natl Libr Poetry Semifnlst Poem Cntst; UCSD; Dentist.

DINH, THANG Q; Bellflower HS; Bellflower, CA; (3); 7/276; Sec Computer Clb; FBLA; Letterman Clb; Rep Mu Alpha Theta; Nwsp; Var L Crs Cntry; Var L Socr; Var L Trk; Cit Awd; High Hon Roll; CAUSA; Gldn St Exm Geomtry High Hnrs; CSF; UC Berkeley; Elec Engr.

DINH, THANH; La Quinta HS; Westminster, CA; (2); 2/354; Sec Chess Clb; French Clb; German Clb; Key Clb; Latin Clb; Letterman Clb; Library Aide; Math Clb; Pep Clb; Science Clb; CSF Jr Secy; Vietnamese Clug; UCI; Bio.

DINH, THANH T; Saddleback HS; Santa Ana, CA; (3); Chess Clb; Mu Alpha Theta; Science Clb; Spanish Clb; Tennis; Vllybl; 2 Acadmc Ltrs; High Hnr Golden St Exam; UCI; Pharmcst.

DINH, THAO M; Sunset HS; Hayward, CA; (3); 1/240; Capt Var Tennis; High Hon Roll; Hon Roll; Ecology Club; Badminton; Law.

DINH, THIEN PHUONG; Rancho Buena Vista HS; Oceanside, CA; (4); 3/467; Chess Clb; Math Clb; Math Tm; Quiz Bowl; Scholastic Bowl; Off Soph Cls; High Hon Roll; Pres Acad Fit Awd; CSF; Sci Olympiad; Intl Baccalaureate Pgm; UC San Diego; Genetics.

DINH, TRANG; Baldwin Park HS; Baldwin Park, CA; (1); Math Clb; Science Clb; JV Tennis; Pres Acad Fit Awd.

DINH, TRINH; Baldwin Park HS; Baldwin Park, CA; (4); 7/397; Spanish Clb; Tennis; High Hon Roll; NHS; Prfct Atten Awd; Pres Acad Fit Awd; CSF; Schlstc All-Amer.

DINH, XUAN T; Poway HS; Poway, CA; (2); 1/800; Quiz Bowl; Spanish Clb; JV Tennis; High Hon Roll; Duke U; Med.

DINH, YEN N; Andrew Hill HS; San Jose, CA; (3); San Jose ST U; Accntnt.

DINIS, FRANCISCO M; Thomas Downey HS; Modesto, CA; (3); Teachers Aide; Hon Roll; Modesto JC; US Hstry.

DINNEEN, KATIE; St Rose Acad; San Francisco, CA; (4); 23/91; GAA; Model UN; Teachers Aide; Lit Mag; Hon Roll; NHS; Pres Acad Fit Awd; Amnesty Intl Pres; JR Stsmn Of Amer; Close-Up Pgm DC; U CA Santa Cruz; Engl.

DINO, LEAH S; Hogan SR HS; Vallejo, CA; (3); Spanish Clb; Band; Mrchg Band; Pep Band; Yrbk; High Hon Roll; CSF.

DINO, MARIANNE; Bishop Amat Memorial HS; West Covina, CA; (4); 59/400; Hosp Aide; Speech Tm; Rep Frsh Cls; Hon Roll; NHS; St Schlr; 1st Stu Exchng Rep Fukuoka JP; Piano Stu; Amnsty Amer Clb; Brown; Commnctns.

DINOLFI, GINA; Edison HS; Huntington Beach, CA; (2); Drama Clb; Pep Clb; Ski Clb; School Musical; School Play; Stage Crew; Variety Show; Cheerldng; Gym; AZ ST U; Engrng.

DINSE, JENNIFER L; Oakmont HS; Roseville, CA; (3); Church Yth Grp; Service Clb; Ed Nwsp; Rep Stu Cncl; Var Sftbl; High Hon Roll; FNL Pblcty Pstn Hld; CA Schlstc Fdr VP; Eng.

DINSMORE, DANIEL A; Antelope Valley HS; Lancaster, CA; (3); Sec Letterman Clb; Spanish Clb; SADD; Varsity Clb; Off Frsh Cls; Off Soph Cls; Off Jr Cls; Off Sr Cls; Mgr Stu Cncl; JV Var Ftbl; Stus Agnst Gng Actvty; AVHS Ftbl Bstrs Stu Plyrs; Antlp Vlly Spec Olmpcs Eqstrn Prog; OH U; Sprts Mgmt.

DIONISIO, ARISTOTLE R; Lowell HS; San Francisco, CA; (2); Church Yth Grp; ROTC; Teachers Aide; Chorus; Color Guard; Drill Tm; Hon Roll; NEDT Awd; Pres Acad Fit Awd; U Of CA; Med.

DIONNE, ERIN M; Laguna Hills HS; Laguna Hills, CA; (1); 23/326; French Clb; SADD; Band; Mrchg Band; French Hon Soc; High Hon Roll; CSF; Orange Cty Alliance Francaise Cont 2nd Pl Frnch II; Dartmouth U; Jrnlsm.

DIONNE, MONICA; St Genevieve HS; Panorama City, CA; (2); Church Yth Grp; Sftbl; High Hon Roll; Prfrm At Piano Mscl Rctls Mnthly; Awds & Cert For Prfmrng At Rgnl Fstvls; CSU Nrthrdg; Intr Dsgn.

DIORIO, JAMES; Trabuco Hills HS; Balboa Isl, CA; (2); Boy Scts; Chess Clb; Scholastic Bowl; Ed Yrbk; Intrml Wrstlng; YMCA; 3rd Pl Overal In Orange Cnty Acadc Dclthln; USC; Med.

DIOSDADO, DENISE; Baldwin Park HS; Baldwin Park, CA; (2); Church Yth Grp; Science Clb; High Hon Roll; Hon Roll; Acad Achvt Awd; Comp Prgmr.

DIPPO, KELLI; Argonaut HS; Jackson, CA; (4); Church Yth Grp; Cmnty Wkr; French Clb; FHA; Key Clb; Library Aide; Office Aide; Teachers Aide; Mrchg Band; Pep Band; Ntl Lib Poetry, Acad Excl Awds; CA Hwy Ptrl 11-99 Fnd Schlrshp; Sonoma ST U; Psych.

DIRIGE, LEILANI A; Alta Loma HS; Rancho Cucamong, CA; (3); Dance Clb; School Play; Treas Frsh Cls; Treas Soph Cls; Hon Roll; Intnl Order Jobs Daughters Post Honored Queen; Wrtr Of Yr 1987-88; Legion Of Mary 1987-88, Div Pres; UCLA; Nrsng.

DIRKES, ANDREW; Educational Dynamics Inc; Poway, CA; (3); Church Yth Grp; Debate Tm; French Clb; Pres VP Key Clb; Capt Quiz Bowl; Capt Scholastic Bowl; School Play; Ed Nwsp; Pres VP Stu Cncl; Intrml Bsktbl; UC Fullerton; Poltcl Sci.

DIRKS, JELENA M; Grossmont HS; La Mesa, CA; (2); 1/431; Church Yth Grp; German Clb; Intnl Clb; Acpl Chr; Orch; High Hon Roll; Hon Roll; San Diego Yth Symphony Oboe; Music.

DIRKS, JENNIFER M; El Dorado HS; Fullerton, CA; (1); Church Yth Grp; Drama Clb; Intnl Clb; Band; Mrchg Band; High Hon Roll; Chrch Ldrshp; CSF.

DIRKS, JEREMY J; Gilroy HS; Gilroy, CA; (1); Boy Scts; Church Yth Grp; Cmnty Wkr; Red Cross Aide; Capt Bsktbl; JV Ftbl.

DISCENZA, KENNETH J; Grossmont HS; El Cajon, CA; (2); 11/400; VP Key Clb; SADD; Stu Cncl; Var Socr; Var Tennis; Hon Roll; Pres Acad Fit Awd; CA Schlstc Fed.

DISHMON, COREY; Mt Pleasant HS; San Jose, CA; (3); 2/400; VP French Clb; Ed Nwsp; Treas Jr Cls; VP Sr Cls; JV Sftbl; High Hon Roll; Hon Roll; NHS; Secy CSF; Psych.

DISILVESTRO, ANGELINE M; Temecula Valley HS; Temecula, CA; (2); 30/420; Church Yth Grp; Cmnty Wkr; Color Guard; Drill Tm; Brooks Coll; Inter Dsgn.

DISO, JONATHAN L; Bonita Vista HS; Chula Vista, CA; (2); 125/500; Spanish Clb; Cit Awd; Hon Roll; Prfct Atten Awd; Asian Cultrl Clb; Bowling; Hnrs GSE.

DISTEFANO, CATHERINE; Schurr HS; Montebello, CA; (4); 150/580; Girl Scts; Teachers Aide; VP Varsity Clb; Off Jr Cls; Var L Sftbl; L Vllybl; All League Hnrb Mntn Sftbl 86-87, 89-90; Vlybl MVP 87; Sftbl Most Insprtnl 88; Rio Hondo Coll; Phys Ed.

DITH, NEARYROAT; Hoover SR HS; San Diego, CA; (3); 64/365; Church Yth Grp; French Clb; Teachers Aide; Church Choir; Sftbl; Cit Awd; Prfct Atten Awd; Chrch-Ldr Yth Grp & Speech Yng Wmn Grp; Socl Wrkr.

DITLEVSEN, DAVID F; San Ramon Valley HS; Danville, CA; (2); Hon Roll; Math.

DITMAR, SHAUN D; Rim Of The World HS; Lake Arrowhead, CA; (2); 43/352; Intrml Golf; Hon Roll; Novice Mens Natl Comptr Figure Sktng 90; UNLV; Figure Skating Coach.

DITTMAR, SANDRA J; Ygnacio Valley HS; Walnut Creek, CA; (3); Church Yth Grp; German Clb; Band; Mrchg Band; Orch.

DITTNER, ERIKA; Mission Viejo HS; Mission Viejo, CA; (4); 38/454; Church Yth Grp; Drama Clb; Thesps; Chorus; School Musical; School Play; Cheerldng; Hon Roll; NHS; CSF; Girls League; Prfrmng Arts.

DITTY, ANGELA; St Genevieve HS; Panorama City, CA; (3); Sec French Clb; Pep Clb; Teachers Aide; Rptr Nwsp; Rptr Yrbk; Var Chess Clb; Hon Roll; NEDT Awd; Educ.

DITULLIO, NICOLE M; Westlake HS; Thousand Oaks, CA; (2); Service Clb; SADD; Hon Roll; Pinao Cert Of Merit Awds; Golf; Hnrbl Mntn Dist Sci Fair; Mrktng.

DIVA, CLAIRE F; Grant Union HS; Sacramento, CA; (3); French Clb; Girl Scts; Science Clb; Band; Jazz Band; Mrchg Band; Orch; Pep Band; Vllybl; Prfct Atten Awd; Arts Acad For Creative Excl Best Instrumental; Recog Outstndng Music Achvmt Marching Band; Sacramento ST U; Law.

DIVA, MANUEL L; Richard Gahr HS; Norwalk, CA; (3); Pres Intnl Clb; VP JA; Office Aide; Chorus; Ed Nwsp; Hon Roll; Blue/Gold Awd Frnch; UCI; Chem Engr.

DIVINAGRACIA, JOEL; Artesia HS; Cerritos, CA; (3); Church Yth Grp; Hon Roll; Filipino Club; CSF; Artesia Pioneer Pride Awd; Cal ST Poly Pomona; Engr.

DIVINO, DIANE M; Dana Hills HS; Laguna Niguel, CA; (1); JV Var Socr; Trk; MVP JV Sccr Awd 90; Schlr Athlt Awd JV Sccr Hghst GPA; Mst Vlbl Shtpt & Dscs Plyr Trk Awd; Bus Admin.

DIVITA, DAVID SCOTT; Marin Catholic HS; Novato, CA; (4); 3/200; Cmnty Wkr; Drama Clb; French Clb; Intnl Clb; Pep Clb; Speech Tm; Thesps; School Musical; School Play; Variety Show; Bank Am Plaque Achvt Liberal Arts; Columbia; Comparative Lit.

DIWA, NEPHTHYS G; Channel Islands HS; Oxnard, CA; (3); Cmnty Wkr; Sec Drill Tm; Off Stu Cncl; Capt Bsktbl; Powder Puff Ftbl; High Hon Roll; Hon Roll; Prfct Atten Awd; CA Schlrshp Fed; Dist Hnr Rll; Acdmc Awrdclthng 1 & 2; UCLA.

DIXON, ALICIA M; Folsom HS; Folsom, CA; (3); 13/187; Intnl Clb; Model UN; Treas Frsh Cls; Treas Soph Cls; Hon Roll; NHS; Friday Night Live Treas; CSF Mem; Fashn Merch.

DIXON, APRIL L; St Marys Acad; Inglewood, CA; (2); Church Yth Grp; Church Choir; Hon Roll; Wrld Cvlztn Hnrbl Mntn; Outstndng Ctznshp Awd; Spelman Coll; Ped.

DIXON, DESIREE A; San Clemente HS; San Clemente, CA; (3); Drama Clb; Ski Clb; Chorus; Variety Show; Elks Awd; Loyola Mary Mount; Law.

DIXON, EMILY; Lowell HS; San Francisco, CA; (2); Drama Clb; School Play; Phtg Nwsp; Acting Study; Greek Clb; Italian Clb; Stu Exch Prgm Italy; Yale.

DIXON, HEATHER M; Chaffey HS; Ontario, CA; (1); Key Clb; Outstndng Achvt, French; Mst Imprvd, Hist; USC; Atty.

DIXON, JASON R; Shafter HS; Shafter, CA; (3); 20/207; Church Yth Grp; Drama Clb; German Clb; Church Choir; Var Ftbl; Var Wt Lftg; Hon Roll; Sheriffs Dept Explr; Aerospc Engrng.

DIXON, JENNY L; Mira Mesa HS; San Diego, CA; (4); 1/839; Am Leg Aux Girls St; Ed Yrbk; Elks Awd; High Hon Roll; Hon Roll; NHS; Pres Acad Fit Awd; Val; UCI.

DIXON, JEREMY S; Taft Union HS; Taft, CA; (3); 20/150; Band; Mrchg Band; Golf; Hon Roll; Mst Imprvd Stu Band 88-89; Friday Night Live; Taft JC.

DIXON, KIRSTEN L; San Dimas HS; San Dimas, CA; (4); Drama Clb; Intnl Clb; Pep Clb; Swmmng; Tennis; Trk; Keywanettes Club; Cal Poly; Computer Info Systems.

DIXON, MARINA; Rancho Buena Vista HS; Vista, CA; (2); 28/530; UCSD; Bus.

DIXON, RANDI M; Sierra Joint Union HS; Shaver Lake, CA; (2); Drama Clb; Pep Clb; Ski Clb; SADD; Ed Yrbk; Var Cheerldng; JV Swmmng; JV Trk; US Space Acad Lvl I & II; US Air Force Acad; Aeronautics.

DIXON, SHANNON Y; Temecula Valley HS; Temecula, CA; (3); Fld Hcky; Trk; Vllybl; Cit Awd; Hon Roll; Bus.

DIXON, SHUNTELL; Washington Prep HS; Los Angeles, CA; (3); Drill Tm; Trk; Hon Roll; Howard U; Bus.

DIXON, SUZANNE M; Sunset HS; Hayward, CA; (3); Church Yth Grp; School Play; Variety Show; JV Bsktbl; Stat Var Trk; Hon Roll; CA ST U; Bus Tech.

DIZIER, VENEITA; San Lorenzo HS; San Lorenzo, CA; (4); Ski Clb; Nwsp; JV Var Bsktbl; JV Var Pom Pon; Var Socr; Capt Trk; Adventure Clb; Treas Minority Ldrshp Grp; CA ST Hayward; Liberal Arts.

DIZON, DINNA; Gonzales Union HS; Soledad, CA; (1); Drill Tm; Hon Roll.

DIZON, ELIZABETH P; De Lano HS; Delano, CA; (3); Hon Roll; Prfct Atten Awd; UCLA; Med.

DIZON, EYRENE D; Kearny HS; San Diego, CA; (2); 29/378; Computer Clb; FBLA; JA; Library Aide; Cit Awd; Hon Roll; NHS; Prfct Atten Awd; Psych.

DIZON, JENNA C; San Marino HS; San Gabriel, CA; (3); Cmnty Wkr; FBLA; JCL; Letterman Clb; Red Cross Aide; Pres Service Clb; Var Cheerldng; Var Capt Socr; Var Capt Swmmng; Var Capt Vllybl; VB, Sccr & Swmmng; All Rio Hondo Lg Hnrbl Mntn; 1st Tm Vlybl Hnrbl Mntn; 2 Yrs Sccr.

DIZON, MANUEL M; El Camino HS; Daly City, CA; (3); Band; Ftbl; Wrstlng; Martial Arts; San Francisco ST; Auto Mechncs.

DIZON, MARICHELLE; Westmoor HS; San Francisco, CA; (2); Aud/Vis; Computer Clb; Dance Clb; German Clb; Hosp Aide; Intnl Clb; Office Aide; SADD; Jazz Band; Bsktbl; San Francisco ST; Nrsng.

DIZON, NOEMI M; Branham HS; San Jose, CA; (2); 27/225; Treas Key Clb; SADD; Yrbk; Pres Frsh Cls; Off Soph Cls; Stu Cncl; Var Bsktbl; JV Vllybl; CFS; Myrs Blue Rbn Cmmtte; HI Dncr; UC Berkeley; Opthlmlgy.

DIZON JR, ROMEO Q; Montclair HS; Montclair, CA; (2); 1/24; Boy Scts; SADD; Teachers Aide; Cit Awd; High Hon Roll; NHS; Prfct Atten Awd; Cert Apprctn Bst Story; Apprctn Awd Cls Hlp; Cert Achvt Math; CA Poly; Electrnc.

DJANG, JASON H; Foothill HS; Santa Ana, CA; (2); Church Yth Grp; Cmnty Wkr; Var JV Ftbl; High Hon Roll; Hon Roll; Yng Reps Clb; CSF; Hnrs & Hgh Hnrs Gldn St Exam.

DO, AMIEE; Notre Dame HS; San Jose, CA; (3); Intnl Clb; VP Frsh Cls; Pres Soph Cls; Treas Jr Cls; Hon Roll; NHS; Pres Acad Fit Awd; CA Schlrshp Fed; Commnctn.

DO, ANH D; Bolsa Grande HS; Westminster, CA; (3); Chess Clb; Computer Clb; Spanish Clb; SADD; JV Tennis; JV Trk; JV Vllybl; JV Wt Lftg; Cit Awd; High Hon Roll; CA ST Fullerton; Bus.

DO, ANH Q; University HS; Irvine, CA; (3); Vietnamese Club Treas; Alliance Francais Comp; Stu UCI Pgm Schlrs; CA U Irvine; Bio.

DO, BAO T; Saugus HS; Saugus, CA; (4); 16/427; Art Clb; Cmnty Wkr; Pres Acad Fit Awd; CSF; Acad Ltr Awds; Cal Poly Pomona; Mech Engrng.

DO, BAO TRAM; Gardena HS; Gardena, CA; (3); French Clb; Intnl Clb; Drill Tm; Vllybl; UC Riverside; Ed.

DO, BINH CAO; Huntington Beach HS; Huntington Bch, CA; (3); Spanish Clb; High Hon Roll; Tower Awds Span & Math; UCI; Med.

DO, CAM N; Westmoor HS; Daly City, CA; (3); SADD; Ed Yrbk; VP Soph Cls; Var Stat Bsktbl; Var Stat Ftbl; Var Trk; Pres Acad Fit Awd; Stu Body Advsry Rep 89-90; Amnsty Intl; Bus.

DO, CINDY; Milpitas HS; Milpitas, CA; (2); French Clb; Rep Frsh Cls; Rep Soph Cls; JV Tennis; UC Davis; Med.

DO, CUC X; John A Rowland HS; Rowland Hts, CA; (4); French Clb; Teachers Aide; Rptr Nwsp; High Hon Roll; Kiwanis Awd; Ntl Merit SF; Pres Acad Fit Awd; UCLA; Elem Engr.

DO, DEE; Novato HS; Novato, CA; (3); Church Yth Grp; Sec French Clb; Sec Lit Mag; Hon Roll; Acad Let Acad Torch; CSF; Yth Alive Christian Religious Clb; Med.

DO, DOI T; A A Stagg HS; Stockton, CA; (1); Hon Roll; NHS; Law.

DO, GIAO; Garden Grove HS; Garden Grove, CA; (1); 53/403; Tennis; Prfct Atten Awd; CA Schlrshp Fed; Badminton Player; UCI; Phrmcst.

DO, HA; La Quinta HS; Santa Ana, CA; (3); Hon Roll.

DO, HANH THUY-AI; Mount Miguel HS; Lemon Grove, CA; (4); 9/350; Church Yth Grp; Office Aide; Spanish Clb; Hon Roll; Prfct Atten Awd; Acad Leag; Tandy Tech Schlrs Awd; CSF; CA Outstndng Stu Awd; San Diego ST U; Bus Admin.

DO, HAONG H; Duncan Poly HS; Fresno, CA; (1); Tennis; Bkkpng.

DO, HENRY D; Irvine HS; Irvine, CA; (2); Boy Scts; Chess Clb; Key Clb; Latin Clb; JV Tennis; Coachs Awd JV Tennis; CSF; Stu For Social Rsponsibility/Vietnamese Club; Med.

DO, HIEU T; Westminster HS; Westminster, CA; (3); Chess Clb; Pres Church Yth Grp; Cmnty Wkr; French Clb; SADD; Teachers Aide; Hon Roll; Act Officer Vietnamese Club; Acad Awd 2nd Yr; Med.

DO, HUNG; La Quinta HS; Fountain Valley, CA; (2); Chess Clb; Key Clb; Science Clb; Tennis; Hon Roll; Rotary Awd; CSF; Schlr Of Qtr; Ldrshp Awd Smmr Camp; Med.

DO, JENNIFER Q; Torrey Pines HS; San Diego, CA; (2); French Clb; Yrbk; Cit Awd; High Hon Roll; Hon Roll; San Diego ST U; Bus.

DO, JOHN; Adrian C Wilcox HS; Santa Clara, CA; (4); 1/435; Chess Clb; Pres FTA; JA; Math Tm; Pres Model UN; Spanish Clb; Band; Drm Mjr(t); Mrchg Band; Orch; CSF Treas; Santa Clara Cnty Acad Dcthln Gld Mdl Sci; U CA Rgnts Schlrshp; UC Berkeley; Elec Engr.

DO, KAREN; Southwest HS; Chula Vista, CA; (3); #1 In Class; Pres Key Clb; Math Tm; High Hon Roll; Regstr CSF; Part Tm Coll Stdt; Outstndng Soph Awd; Berkeley; Engrng.

DO, KATHERINE L; Lowell HS; San Francisco, CA; (2); Quiz Bowl; Var Bsktbl; JV Tennis; St Schlr; All City Tnns 3rd Pl Dbls; Golden St Exam High Hnrs Algebra; Biochem.

DO, KHOAN; Roosevelt HS; Fresno, CA; (2); Church Yth Grp; Dance Clb; SADD; Chorus; Cit Awd; Tchrs Tomrrws Clb & Ldrshp; Chines Folk Dance Trp; ESL Clb; SYETP; Fresno City; Teacher.

DO, LAN N; Edison HS; Fresno, CA; (1); 2/250; Drama Clb; French Clb; Science Clb; School Play; Rptr Nwsp; Lit Mag; Stu Cncl; JV Swmmng; JV Vllybl; French Hon Soc; Peer Cnslr; Frnch Stu Of Yr In Fresno; Outstndng Stu Awd; Vietnamese Parents & Tchrs Assn; Harvard; Pltcl Sci.

DO, LUONG D; Silver Creek HS; San Jose, CA; (2); Computer Clb; French Clb; Hist FBLA; Intnl Clb; High Hon Roll; Hon Roll; Top Vietnamese Stu Of Silver Crk Clb; U CA-BERKELEY; Space Sci.

DO, LUONG TRUNG; Sierra Vista HS; Baldwin Park, CA; (1); Chess Clb; AFS; Math Clb; Bsktbl; Var Tennis; High Hon Roll; Pres Acad Fit Awd; Comp; Vllybl; UCLA; Pre-Med.

DO, MAI UYEN; Irvine HS; Irvine, CA; (3); Tennis; Cit Awd; Hon Roll; Bus.

DO, MARTIN; Homestead HS; Cupertino, CA; (1); JV Bsktbl; JV Tennis; Tae-Kwon-Doe Brwn Blt; Stanford; Pdtrcn.

DO, MY-NGA T; Santa Teresa HS; San Jose, CA; (3); Church Yth Grp; Cmnty Wkr; French Clb; Intnl Clb; Mrchg Band; Tennis; High Hon Roll; Hon Roll; NHS; Badmttn; Cnsl Vietnamese Clb; UC Davis; Med.

DO, NANETTE M; Skyline HS; Oakland, CA; (3); Cmnty Wkr; GAA; Key Clb; SADD; Var Socr; Opt Clb Awd; Piano; UC Davis; Orthdntcs.

DO, ORLANTHA; Hanford Union HS; Hanford, CA; (1); Art Clb; Intnl Clb; Acpl Chr; JV Tennis; Hon Roll; Jr NHS; Academic Letter; UCSD; Animation.

DO, PHUC; Los Amigos HS; Fountain Valley, CA; (2); Boy Scts; Church Yth Grp; Intrml Bsktbl; Hon Roll; NHS; Arch.

DO, STEPHANIE; Santa Teresa HS; San Jose, CA; (3); Model UN; CSF; Amnesty Intl Clb; Vietnamese Clb.

DO, TEDDY T; Kennedy HS; La Palma, CA; (4); Chrmn Computer Clb; Sec Debate Tm; FBLA; Key Clb; Quiz Bowl; Sec Speech Tm; Teachers Aide; Hon Roll; Jr NHS; Ldrshp Acad; UCI; Pre-Med.

DO, THU T; San Gabriel HS; Alhambra, CA; (2); Hon Roll; Cosmetology.

DO, TIMMY D; Irvine HS; Irvine, CA; (3); Boy Scts; Chess Clb; Dance Clb; Key Clb; Latin Clb; Spanish Clb; Var JV Tennis; Black Belt Taekwondo Karate; MVP-RACQUET Clb; Amnesty Intl; Tus For Scl Responsblty; Vietnamese Clb; Optometry.

DO, TONY D; Westminster HS; Garden Grove, CA; (1); Boy Scts; French Clb; Bsktbl; Trk; Cit Awd; High Hon Roll; Lion Awd; Prfct Atten Awd; Rotary Awd; UC Irvine.

DO, TRANG T; Milpitas HS; Milpitas, CA; (2); French Clb; JV Tennis; High Hon Roll; NHS; Jr Statesmen Of Amer; Applied Arts.

DO, TUAN; Rosemead HS; Rosemead, CA; (2); Cit Awd; High Hon Roll; Hon Roll; Prfct Atten Awd; CSF; UCLA.

DO, TUAN; Valley HS; Elk Grove, CA; (3); 8/700; Boy Scts; Cmnty Wkr; French Clb; Math Tm; Red Cross Aide; Teachers Aide; Var Tennis; High Hon Roll; Treas Jr NHS; Secy, Treas CA Schlrshp Fed; UC Davis; Cvl Engr.

DO, TUUYEN; Milpitas HS; Milpitas, CA; (2); French Clb; Rep Stu Cncl; Var Tennis; High Hon Roll; NHS; Dist Rep CA Assn Stu Cncl; Treas Jr Statesmen Amer; V Badminton Girls Singles; Santa Clara U; Bus Mrktng.

DO, UYEN D; Los Amigos HS; Santa Ana, CA; (2); Hon Roll; Santa Ana Vietnamese Vlntr Yth Org; Outstndng Achvt Awd Acad Excllnc; UCI; Pre-Med.

DO, VU T; Los Amigos HS; Fountain Valley, CA; (2); 73/406; Varsity Clb; JV Bsbl; Var Wrstlng; Archtctr.

DO, YOUNG MICHAEL H; Fairfax HS; Los Angeles, CA; (3); Hosp Aide; Rep Jr Cls; Hist Stu Cncl; Intrml Bsktbl; Intrml Ftbl; JV Vllybl; High Hon Roll; Pres Acad Fit Awd; KYC Bsktbl Chmpns; Alpha Knights Hnr Club; U CA Los Angeles.

DOAK, KENNY W; Bloomington HS; Bloomington, CA; (3); Cmnty Wkr; Computer Clb; Hon Roll; U CA-R.

DOAN, BAO-THUY T; Arcata HS; Korbel, CA; (3); Math Tm; SADD; Drill Tm; VP Jr Cls; Sec Stu Cncl; Var Cheerldng; Powder Puff Ftbl; Cit Awd; High Hon Roll; Prfct Atten Awd; Top Ten Awd; High Hnrs Golden St Exam For Geo; Med.

DOAN, BAY; Hueneme HS; Oxnard, CA; (3); USCB; Engr.

DOAN, CHAU-THACH; Valley HS; Santa Ana, CA; (1); Cit Awd; High Hon Roll; Prfct Atten Awd; Sal; Partners Club; CSF; Honors At Entrance; Fullerton; Fashion Designer.

DOAN, CHINH H; Arcata HS; Korbel, CA; (1); 1/200; Math Tm; JV Bsktbl; High Hon Roll; Top 10 Frshmn Stu; 1st Pl Redwood Empire Math Trnmnt; Comp Prgmr; Stanford U; Comp Sci.

DOAN, DAO H; Mark Keppel HS; San Gabriel, CA; (4); 34/637; Cit Awd; High Hon Roll; Hon Roll; Prfct Atten Awd; 1st Yr Alg Hnr On Gldn St Exam; Geom Hnrb Mntn On Gldn St Exam; Pasadena Cty Coll; Bkng Occptns.

DOAN, HIEU; Saddleback HS; Santa Ana, CA; (4); 82/520; French Clb; Chorus; Church Choir; Tennis; Wt Lftg; Cit Awd; 4-H Awd; Hon Roll; Prfct Atten Awd; St Schlr; Cal ST Fullerton U; Educ.

DOAN, HIEU N; Abraham Lincoln HS; San Jose, CA; (3); 1/399; Teachers Aide; Tutor Mid Schl Stu Math.

DOAN, KIMMY; Westminster HS; Westminster, CA; (4); 10/403; Church Yth Grp; Cmnty Wkr; French Clb; Girl Scts; JA; Key Clb; Math Clb; Pep Clb; Ski Clb; Church Choir; All-Amer Chrldr Awd; Corp Law.

DOAN, LINH T; La Quinta HS; Westminster, CA; (1); Cit Awd; Hon Roll; UCI; Bus.

DOAN, MELODY MI GIA; Phillip & Sala Burton Academic HS; San Francisco, CA; (2); Hon Roll; San Francisco ST U; Med.

DOAN, PHI; Milpitas HS; Milpitas, CA; (3); NHS; Amnesty Intl; U Of CA Santa Clara; Law.

DOAN, QUAN; Saddleback HS; Santa Ana, CA; (2); #4 In Class; Chess Clb; Math Clb; Chess Clb; Hist Science Clb; Yrbk; Intrml JV Tennis; High Hon Roll; Orng Cty Acad Decathlon; Geom Golden St Exam Hnrs; Sddlbck Math Dept Gold & Bronze Mdl; CSF; Bus.

DOAN, QUYEN; Dana Hills HS; Laguna Beach, CA; (1); Church Yth Grp; Hosp Aide; SADD; Teachers Aide; Chorus; Hon Roll; Dermatlgy.

DOAN, THANH NGOC; Pinole Valley HS; San Pablo, CA; (4); 1/450; AFS; Boy Scts; Computer Clb; French Clb; Math Clb; Science Clb; SADD; Varsity Clb; JV Socr; JV Tennis; Amnesty Intl Club; CSF; UC Berkeley; Chem Engrng.

DOAN, TIN N; Pinole Valley HS; San Pablo, CA; (2); Boy Scts; Computer Clb; French Clb; Math Clb; Science Clb; Spanish Clb; Ed Nwsp; JV Tennis; High Hon Roll; Pres Acad Fit Awd; Comp Sci.

DOAN, TONY; Duarte HS; Duarte, CA; (4); 5/226; Debate Tm; Key Clb; Sec Office Aide; VP Science Clb; Sec Teachers Aide; Var Bsktbl; JV Crs Cntry; Var Tennis; Cit Awd; Hon Roll; Cngrssnl Yth Ldrshp Cncl Awd; Gold Seal Grad Hghst Hnr Awd; Directors Mem Schlrshp Awd; UCR; Elec Engrng.

DOANE, BRIAN P; Palm Springs HS; Palm Springs, CA; (3); VP Jr Cls; Stu Cncl; Var Bsktbl; Prfct Atten Awd; Rotary Awd; Rotary Ldrshp Camp; Engrng.

DOBASHI, BECKY S; Rosemead HS; Rosemead, CA; (4); 2/310; Church Yth Grp; Spanish Clb; Rep Stu Cncl; Var Tennis; Var Trk; Hon Roll; Sal; CSF Gold Seal Bearer; UC Riverside.

DOBBERT, PENELOPE J; Eisenhower HS; Rialto, CA; (3); Church Yth Grp; Cmnty Wkr; French Clb; Girl Scts; Pep Clb; Teachers Aide; Stat Bsktbl; JV Cheerldng; Hon Roll; Prfct Atten Awd; Friday Night Live; Earth Clb; Azurettes; Bus.

DOBBINS, JEFFREY J; Mayfair HS; Cerritos, CA; (2); 47/250; Church Yth Grp; Band; Chorus; Church Choir; Mrchg Band; High Hon Roll; Hon Roll; Masonic Awd; Pres Acad Fit Awd; Med.

DOBBS, DAVID; Village Christian HS; Burbank, CA; (3); 57/123; Church Yth Grp; Band; Jazz Band; Mrchg Band; Yrbk; Var Crs Cntry; Var Trk; Bus.

DOBBS, MICHAEL; Van Nuys HS; Van Nuys, CA; (4); 71/535; Pres Computer Clb; JA; Teachers Aide; Rep Sr Cls; Intrml Bsktbl; Intrml Sftbl; Intrml Trk; Intrml Vllybl; Pres Acad Fit Awd; Atten Awd; U Of CA Santa Barbara; Cmmnctn.

DOBBS-RAY, KRISTY L; Hanford HS; Hanford, CA; (2); Art Clb; Church Yth Grp; FHA; Office Aide; School Musical; School Play; Intrml Cheerldng; JV Swmmng; JV Trk; Cit Awd; Helped In Special Elimpics-Got Awd; Student Of The Month; Like To Work In Offices; Fresno ST; Primary Teaching.

DOBRINEN, NATASHA L; Lowell HS; San Francisco, CA; (2); Band; Chorus; Orch; Pep Band; School Musical; Swmmng; High Hon Roll; MENC-CHEA Solo; Flute 2 Yrs JR Bach Fstvl/Wrkshps Ransome Wilson/J Baker; Swmg Block L Athl Awd.

DOCKENDORF, DIONNE M; Louisville HS; Encino, CA; (3); Chorus; Off Frsh Cls; Treas Jr Cls; JV Cheerldng; JV Sftbl; High Hon Roll.

DOCKERY, CARA; Madera HS; Madera, CA; (2); Drama Clb; VP Frsh Cls; Pres Soph Cls; Cheerldng; High Hon Roll; Interact Clb; Camp Fire Ldr; Child Dvlpmnt.

DOCKSTADER, DUSTIN; Calipatria HS; Calipatria, CA; (3); Pep Clb; SADD; Varsity Clb; Variety Show; Yrbk; VP Jr Cls; JV Bsbl; Var JV Ftbl; Hon Roll; Pres Acad Fit Awd; Rotary Awd; NAU.

DODD, LESLIE; Woodbridge HS; Port Townsend, WA; (3); 42/425; Church Yth Grp; SADD; Phtg Yrbk; JV Bsktbl; JV Tennis; High Hon Roll; Hon Roll; Pres Acad Fit Awd; Mst Imprvd JV Bsktbl Awd; Mst Imprvd Tnns Awd; Advrtsng.

DODD, SABRINA L; Orange HS; Orange, CA; (2); Church Yth Grp; Chorus; Color Guard.

DODDS, BERNADETTE C; Burney JR/Sr HS; Burney, CA; (1); Church Yth Grp; Band; Church Choir; School Musical; Stat Bsktbl; Cit Awd; Hon Roll; Pres Acad Fit Awd; UC Santa Barbara; Bus.

DODGE, MATTHEW E; Fort Bragg HS; Fort Bragg, CA; (3); 16/115; Am Leg Boys St; Boy Scts; Off Jr Cls; Rep Stu Cncl; Var Bsktbl; Var Ftbl; Var Trk; Hon Roll; Prfct Atten Awd; Cert Achvt Algbr II; San Diego ST; Engrng.

DODGE JR, WILLIAM H; Aptos HS; Watsonville, CA; (2); Church Yth Grp; Treas French Clb; Latin Clb; Teachers Aide; Rep Stu Cncl; Hon Roll; Prfct Atten Awd; CA Schlrshp Fed; Harvard; Corp Lawyer.

DODSON, MELANIE L; Montgomery HS; Glen Ellen, CA; (2); Girl Scts; JA; Spanish Clb; Teachers Aide; Hon Roll; Jr NHS.

DODSON, VERONICA A; Hogan SR HS; Vallejo, CA; (3); Cit Awd; Hon Roll; NHS; Prfct Atten Awd; Hogan Gospel Choir; Acctg.

DOELTZ, MICHAEL C; Bellarmine College Prep; Santa Cruz, CA; (1); Chess Clb; Cmnty Wkr; Computer Clb; Latin Clb; Trk.

DOEVE, ROY E; Don Bosco Technical Insti; Cerritos, CA; (3); Var Bsktbl; Hon Roll; NHS; Ind Educ Cncls Medlln Awd Engl; Golden Tiger Awd; Cal ST Long Bch; Comp Sci.

DOEZIE, JENNIE M; Pasadena HS; Sierra Madre, CA; (3); Church Yth Grp; Drama Clb; German Clb; Hosp Aide; Key Clb; Pep Clb; Acpl Chr; Chorus; Church Choir; Flag Corp; CSF; Zonta Club Intl; Art Ctr Coll Of Dsgn Sat High Pgm Schlrshp; Brigham Young U; Art.

DOFFLEMYER, JESSICA L; Redwood HS; Visalia, CA; (3); Church Yth Grp; Cmnty Wkr; Office Aide; Teachers Aide; Tennis; Hon Roll; Acad Ltr GPA Higher Than 3.67; Visited Elem Schls DARE Pgm As Example Stu; Teach Sunday Sch Class; ED.

DOGBE, SENA; John Muir HS; Altadena, CA; (2); JV Bsbl; JV Capt Socr; Prfct Atten Awd; Church Acolyte; Hampton U; Communications.

DOH, GENE S; Chaminade College Prep; Encino, CA; (2); Pres Church Yth Grp; Sec Model UN; Var Golf; High Hon Roll; CFS; Hstry Clb; Asian Amer Clb.

DOHERTY, DENISE R; Providence HS; Glendale, CA; (2); Church Yth Grp; Ski Clb.

DOHERTY, SHANNON D; San Pasqual HS; Escondido, CA; (1); Ski Clb; Dance; Poetry.

DOHERTY, SUMMER L; Atascadero HS; Atascadero, CA; (1); Var Swmmng; High Hon Roll; CSF; Child Psych.

DOHMAN, DAVID W; Southwest HS; San Diego, CA; (2); 1/627; Church Yth Grp; JV Bsbl; Var Tennis; High Hon Roll; Studies Awd; Religion Awd; Sci Fair 1st Pl Schl & 2nd Pl County; Notre Dame; Medical.

DOHRMANN, GEORGE; Lincoln HS; Stockton, CA; (3); 119/601; Cmnty Wkr; Letterman Clb; Math Clb; Mu Alpha Theta; Ski Clb; Varsity Clb; Ed Nwsp; Var L Ftbl; Hon Roll; NHS; Asilomar Clb; Exclinc In Spanish Awd; U Of Notre Dame; Communctns.

DOIG, JENNIFER R; San Dieguito HS; Rancho La Costa, CA; (2); Church Yth Grp; Drama Clb; Science Clb; Cit Awd; Dance; Dance.

DOLAN, ERIC E; Montgomery HS; Santa Rosa, CA; (2); 45/400; Church Yth Grp; Dance Clb; JA; Key Clb; Letterman Clb; Science Clb; Spanish Clb; Varsity Clb; JV Crs Cntry; Var Swmmng; Pres Soph Action Clb.

DOLAN, GEOFFREY W; Bellarmine College Prep; Los Altos, CA; (3); 1/308; Letterman Clb; Math Tm; Var L Crs Cntry; Var Trk; Ntl Merit Ltr; Gen Excllnce Awd; Engrng.

DOLAN, HEATHER; Fullerton Union HS; Fullerton, CA; (1); 23/408; Church Yth Grp; ROTC; Color Guard; Hon Roll; Rotary Awd; Intl Ordr Of Jobs Daghters-JR Prncss; Nrs Ansthtst.

DOLAN, JOE B; Arcadia HS; Arcadia, CA; (3); Ski Clb; SADD; Stage Crew; Var Ftbl; Bus.

DOLAND, KRISTINA D; Saint Francis HS; Mountain View, CA; (4); Church Yth Grp; Drama Clb; French Clb; SADD; School Play; Hon Roll; Linfield Coll; Psych.

DOLCE, KATHY; Atwater HS; Atwater, CA; (1); Am Leg Aux Girls St; FFA; Key Clb; Band; Color Guard; Flag Corp; Mrchg Band; Variety Show; Hon Roll; Fresno ST; Law.

DOLDER, SCOTT; Oakmont HS; Roseville, CA; (2); 1/450; Cmnty Wkr; Letterman Clb; Ski Clb; Var L Trk; Gov Hon Prg Awd; Frsh Homecmng Flt Cmmtte; 7 Entries Schl Art Shw; Socr; UCLA; Advrtsng.

DOLL, BRAD T; Monte Vista HS; Spring Valley, CA; (2); 24/461; Debate Tm; Q&S; Speech Tm; Nwsp; Var Swmmng; Hon Roll; Vrsty Water Polo; Esperaza Coflman Memrl Awd; Most Insprtnl; Cornell U; Comm.

DOLNICK, JEREMY D; El Dorado HS; Placentia, CA; (4); ROTC; Science Clb; Band; Jazz Band; Mrchg Band; Pep Band; High Hon Roll; Hon Roll; Pres Schlr; $100 Eclgy Clb Schlrshp; CSF; UC Santa Barbara; Law.

DOLSON, DARCY R; Woodlake HS; Exeter, CA; (2); Church Yth Grp; FHA; Key Clb; Pep Clb; Science Clb; Ski Clb; Teachers Aide; School Musical; School Play; Var JV Cheerldng; Young Life; Westmont Coll; Sci.

DOLTON, CHERI L; Brea-Olinda HS; Brea, CA; (1); Church Yth Grp; Var L Swmmng; Vllybl.

DOMAEL, ARSENEI P; Leuzinger HS; Inglewood, CA; (1).

DOMBROWSKI, ED A; Irvine HS; Irvine, CA; (2); Church Yth Grp; Military.

DOMECQ, JASON M; Oak Ridge HS; Shingle Springs, CA; (1); Boy Scts; Chorus; JV Wrstlng; Kendo Karate; Chiroprctr.

DOMEN, JIM R; Troy HS; Yorba Linda, CA; (2); 24/323; Church Yth Grp; VP French Clb; Ed Yrbk; Var Wrstlng; High Hon Roll; Rotary Awd; Intern For Congrssmn William E Dannemeyer; :Pal Peer Cnslng; CSF; UCLA; Orthodontist.

DOMENICI JR, ANTHONY L; Hogan SR HS; Vallejo, CA; (3); Cmnty Wkr; Debate Tm; Drama Clb; Key Clb; Letterman Clb; Service Clb; Spanish Clb; SADD; Teachers Aide; Varsity Clb; CSF Pres; Cngrssnl Yth Ldrshp Cncl Washington DC Delg; Aeronautical Engr.

DOMENIGONI, SHANNON; Hemet HS; Hemet, CA; (3); 47/547; Church Yth Grp; Pres 4-H; Teachers Aide; Band; Flag Corp; Powder Puff Ftbl; Var Socr; Var Trk; 4-H Awd; High Hon Roll; Humboldt ST U; Mrn Bio.

DOMICH, KRISTINA J; Grossmont HS; La Mesa, CA; (1); Art Clb; Science Clb; Orch; Princpls Hnr Roll; Marine Bio.

DOMINGCIL, DELILAH E; Orosi HS; Orosi, CA; (3); 8/177; Sec Treas Church Yth Grp; Sec Drama Clb; Rep SADD; Pres Treas Band; Jazz Band; Pres Treas Mrchg Band; Pep Band; School Musical; School Play; Ed Nwsp; Ldrshp Awd; Hnr Band; Ed.

DOMINGO, AILEEN G; St Genevieve HS; Northridge, CA; (3); Cmnty Wkr; French Clb; High Hon Roll; Hon Roll; NHS.

DOMINGO, BERNARDITO C; Don Bosco Tech; Pico Rivera, CA; (3); Church Yth Grp; Intrml JV Bsktbl; Hon Roll; NHS; Electronics; Vllybl; Bus; Elec Engr.

DOMINGO, CRISTINA V; Carondelet HS; Concord, CA; (4); Cmnty Wkr; Drama Clb; Pep Clb; Service Clb; Stage Crew; Variety Show; Rptr Ed Yrbk; Hon Roll; CSF; UC Santa Barbara; Commcntns.

DOMINGO, FERARI; Bishop Amat HS; West Covina, CA; (4); 59/400; Cmnty Wkr; Chorus; Sec Soph Cls; JV Bsktbl; Var Pom Pon; Hon Roll; NHS; CA Schlrshp Fdrtn; Spnsh II Awd; Wrk-Exprnc Pgm Awd-Chrstn Svc Vlntr; UC Riverside; Envrnmntl Engrng.

DOMINGO, JENNIFER R; Victor Valley SR HS; Victorville, CA; (3); Intrml Wt Lftg; Hon Roll; SDSU; Arch.

DOMINGO, JOHN F; Bishop Amat Memorial HS; West Covina, CA; (2); Dance Clb; Teachers Aide; Stage Crew; Trk; CA ST Polytech; Bus.

DOMINGO, LYNN P; Chula Vista HS; San Diego, CA; (3); 26/500; Church Yth Grp; Computer Clb; Pep Clb; Church Choir; Co-Ed Drill Tm; Nwsp; Trk; Vllybl; Cit Awd; Hon Roll; Asst Commissioner Finance Assoc Stu Body; Pan Asian Clb VP; CSF Mem; Sword & Shld Mem; San Diego U; Bus.

DOMINGO, RAQUEL E; Channel Island HS; Oxnard, CA; (2); Bsktbl; Powder Puff Ftbl; Trk; Vllybl; Int Dsgnr.

DOMINGO, REA; George Dewey HS; FPO San Fran, CA; (3); SADD; JV Cheerldng; JV Mgr Trk; Hon Roll; Honorable Mention In Science Fair; Photography Award; Interact Club; UCSD; Medicine.

DOMINGO, RUTHIE C; Aquinas HS; Highland, CA; (4); 3/100; VP Intnl Clb; Key Clb; Pep Clb; Nwsp; Yrbk; Cheerldng; Pom Pon; High Hon Roll; NHS; Pres Acad Fit Awd; Friday Nite Live; Vera Lopez & David Montano Schlrshp; Acad White Ltr/Gold Bars; Bnk Amer Achvt; USC; Bio.

DOMINGUES, KATHERINE A; St Joseph HS; Santa Maria, CA; (2); 25/142; Service Clb; Nwsp; Pom Pon; High Hon Roll; Folk Grp Choir; Perf Arts.

DOMINGUEZ, ANNA MARIE; Tulare Union HS; Pixley, CA; (4); Cmnty Wkr; Teachers Aide; Yrbk; Hon Roll; Tulare Cty Volunteer Firefighter 89; Coll Of Sequoias; Nrsng.

DOMINGUEZ, BERTA; Rio Mesa HS; Camarillo, CA; (2); AFS; Drama Clb; Spanish Clb; SADD; Varsity Clb; School Play; Bsktbl; Trk; Pres Acad Fit Awd; Law.

DOMINGUEZ, CARLOS; Gompers Secondary HS; San Diego, CA; (2); Var Tennis; JV Vllybl; Opt Clb Awd; UCSD; Comp Prgmr.

DOMINGUEZ, CLAUDIA M; San Benito HS; Hollister, CA; (4); Art Clb; Church Yth Grp; FHA; Office Aide; Teachers Aide; Church Choir; Hon Roll; Pacific Union Coll; Erly Chldhd.

DOMINGUEZ, DENISE S; Brawley Union HS; Brawley, CA; (3); AFS; Church Yth Grp; Pep Clb; Peer Cnslng; Pwdr Pff Wrstlng; UCSD; Cnslng.

DOMINGUEZ, GABBY; Sacred Heart HS; Los Angeles, CA; (3); GAA; Spanish Clb; Color Guard; School Musical; Stu Cncl; Cheerldng; Mgr(s); NHS; Natl Span Exm; 2nd Hnrs Rbn; Loyola U; Educ.

DOMINGUEZ, GABRIELA; Southwest HS; San Diego, CA; (2); Teachers Aide; Variety Show; Intrml Socr; Hon Roll; Dntst.

DOMINGUEZ, GLORIA; Pioneer HS; Whittier, CA; (2); Ski Clb; Acpl Chr; Chorus; Drill Tm; School Musical; School Play; Rep Stu Cncl; Cit Awd; Hon Roll; Pres Acad Fit Awd; Accntng.

DOMINGUEZ, HECTOR A; Manual Arts HS; Los Angeles, CA; (3); Boy Scts; Karate 3 Yrs; Arch.

DOMINGUEZ, MARIA A; King City HS; King City, CA; (3); Latin Clb; High Hon Roll; Hon Roll; Girl Scts; Nrsng.

DOMINGUEZ JR, RAMIRO E; Hoover HS; Fresno, CA; (3); #76 In Class; Tennis; Hon Roll; Comp Sci.

DOMINGUEZ, ROBIN; Don Bosco Tech Inst; Pico Rivera, CA; (2); 30/213; JV Bsbl; JV Crs Cntry; NHS; Campus Mnstry; CA Tech; Aerosp Engrng.

DOMINGUEZ, WILLIAM A; James Monroe HS; Panorama City, CA; (2); Teachers Aide; JV Bsbl; Bsktbl; Wt Lftg; Cit Awd; CTBS Rcgntn; UC Davis; Med.

DOMINICK, JUSTIN E; Chaminade College Prep; Northridge, CA; (3); Cmnty Wkr; Debate Tm; Drama Clb; Model UN; Stage Crew; Nwsp; High Hon Roll; Jr NHS; NHS; Pres Acad Fit Awd; Otstndng Achvt Awd Spnsh,Hstry,Chem,Algebra II & British Lit; Pre-Med.

DOMINICK, SAMUEL A; Alta Loma HS; Alta Loma, CA; (1); Boy Scts; Bsbl; Wrstlng; High Hon Roll; Prfct Atten Awd; Chaffey JC; Marine Bio.

DOMINO, BENJAMIN J; Crescenta Valley HS; Montrose, CA; (2); Math Clb; Mu Alpha Theta; Ed Lit Mag; Sec Frsh Cls; Opt Clb Awd; Law Explrs-Boy Scts; CA Jaycees; CSF; Harvard U; Law.

DOMINQUEZ, ADRIANA; El Rancho HS; Pico Rivera, CA; (2); GAA; Tennis; Coed Caper 37th Annual; Lawyer.

DOMINQUEZ, FABIAN; Castle Park HS; Chula Vista, CA; (3); Art Clb; Bsktbl; USCD; Comm.

DOMPE, NICK A; Tracy Joint Union HS; Tracy, CA; (2); 45/500; Church Yth Grp; French Clb; Orch; Interact Clb Spnsrd Rotary Intl; U Of CA Santa Cruz; Marine Bio.

DON, ERICA L; Canyon HS; Anaheim, CA; (4); 2/450; Off Church Yth Grp; French Clb; Math Clb; Service Clb; Chorus; Ed Lit Mag; Off Soph Cls; High Hon Roll; NHS; Ntl Merit SF; Acad Dcthln.

DON, TROY A; Pasadena HS; Pasadena, CA; (2); German Clb; Socr; Tennis; Hon Roll; CSF 90 Sealbearer; U Southern CA; Engrng.

DONAHOE, JOANNE; C K Mc Clatchy HS; Sacramento, CA; (3); Cmnty Wkr; Drama Clb; Sec French Clb; Pres German Clb; NFL; Sec Speech Tm; Var Bsktbl; Var Crs Cntry; Hon Roll; NHS; Outstndng Acvht In German Level 4 & 5; Speech Comptn St Fnlst 4th Pl; Commnctns.

DONAHUE, COREY; Chowchilla Union HS; Chowchilla, CA; (3); 4-H; Letterman Clb; Office Aide; Varsity Clb; Color Guard; Mrchg Band; VP Jr Cls; Cheerldng; Var Tennis; High Hon Roll; UC Santa Cruz; Acctg.

DONAHUE, JAMIE M; Monte Vista HS; Alamo, CA; (2); Aud/Vis; Science Clb; Teachers Aide; Variety Show; Socr; Wt Lftg; Wrstlng; Sci.

DONAHUE, MEGAN; South Torrance HS; Redondo Beach, CA; (3); 15/440; Church Yth Grp; Drama Clb; Orch; School Play; Hon Roll; CSF; Cngrssnl Yth Ldrshp Conf; Hgh Achvt Eng, Soc Sci, Drama.

DONAIRE, SKARLETH S; Los Altos HS; La Puente, CA; (4); Drill Tm; Hon Roll; Pres Acad Fit Awd; Keywannettes Clb; Schl Schlr; CSF; CA ST U Fullerton; Acctng.

DONAIS, MARY ANN P; Grossmont HS; El Cajon, CA; (2); 62/429; Color Guard; Hon Roll; Outstndng Art Achvt Cert; Span Outstndng Achvt; Math Achvt Cert; San Diego ST U; Bus Mgmt.

DONALD, EMILY; Sacramento Waldorf Schl; Fair Oaks, CA; (4); Drama Clb; Teachers Aide; Jazz Band; Orch; School Musical; School Play; Yrbk; Ntl Merit Ltr; NEDT Awd.

DONALDO, HEIDI; Phillip And Sala Burton HS; Vallejo, CA; (3); Church Yth Grp; Math Clb; Chorus; Nrsng.

DONALDSON, AMY; Modesto Adventist Acad; Modesto, CA; (1); Church Yth Grp; Teachers Aide; Band; Hon Roll; Bell Choir; Art.

DONALDSON, BRADLEY K; Patrick Henry HS; San Diego, CA; (2); 42/530; Nwsp; Yrbk; Rep Stu Cncl; Var L Lcrss; Hon Roll; Awd Of Excel Industrial Arts; Bus.

DONALDSON, DANIELLE D; Pomona HS; W Covina, CA; (2); Key Clb; Latin Clb; Chorus; Trk; High Hon Roll; Hon Roll; MESA; Jr Axllry Pst 252 VP 89-90, Pres 90-91; U S CA; Med.

DONALDSON, JENNIFER A; Downey HS; Downey, CA; (3); Church Yth Grp; Drama Clb; Pilot.

DONALDSON, JERRY R; Silver Valley HS; Newberry Spgs, CA; (2).

DONALDSON, LARA L; Monterey HS; Monterey, CA; (3); 3/220; Church Yth Grp; Girl Scts; Hosp Aide; Yrbk; VP Soph Cls; Sec Sr Cls; Var Fld Hcky; Var Swmmng; Var Capt Trk; Treas NHS; CSF VP; Bio.

DONALDSON, ROCHELLE L; Calico HS; Newberry Spgs, CA; (3); Church Yth Grp; Computer Clb; 4-H; SADD; Teachers Aide; Var Powder Puff Ftbl; 4-H Awd; Hon Roll; Prfct Atten Awd; 4-H Fair; Sftbll Tm; Psych.

DONALDSON, STEVE; Chaffey HS; Ontario, CA; (1); Church Yth Grp; Intrml Diving; Hon Roll; Drama; Stu Of Mnth Typing; Navy; Aviation.

DONALDSON-LEWIS, KRYSTINA M; Mesquite HS; China Lake, CA; (3); Church Yth Grp; Drama Clb; Girl Scts; Hosp Aide; Letterman Clb; Ski Clb; SADD; Varsity Clb; Band; Chorus; Anatomy.

DONART, BRANDY M; St Joseph HS; Long Beach, CA; (2); 46/200; Church Yth Grp; Hosp Aide; Science Clb; Ski Clb; JV Bsktbl; Hon Roll; CSF; CA ST U Long Beach; Aero Engr.

DONAT, MONICA Y; Mira Loma HS; Citrus Hts, CA; (1); 1/246; Church Yth Grp; Treas French Clb; Treas Math Clb; Model UN; Science Clb; Band; Mrchg Band; Pep Band; High Hon Roll; CSF; Engr.

DONATH, JEFF R; Woodbridge HS; Irvine, CA; (3); 65/423; Spanish Clb; SADD; Varsity Clb; Var L Trk; High Hon Roll; CSF; Premed.

DONATI, ELI J; Foothill HS; Bakersfield, CA; (3); VP Treas FFA; JA; Cit Awd; St FFA Awd; CA ST U Fresno; Food Sci.

DONELON, NIKOLE M; St Joseph HS; Long Beach, CA; (3); Church Yth Grp; Cmnty Wkr; Debate Tm; Ski Clb; Speech Tm; SADD; Church Choir; JV Trk; JV Vllybl; Hon Roll; Engl Hnrs; Yth & Govt; Loyola Marymount; Child Psych.

DONG, PHUNG T; Mc Clymonds HS; Oakland, CA; (3); Cit Awd; Hon Roll; U CA-BERKELEY; Interior Dsgn.

DONIAN, WARREN L; Lowell HS; San Francisco, CA; (3); Church Yth Grp; Speech Tm; Thesps; Church Choir; School Play; L Var Ftbl; L Var Wrstlng; CSF; 90 CA Chemathon; Advnture Alliance; U CA; Bus Admin.

DONIGUEZ, ANA M; John H Francis Polythechnic HS; Sun Valley, CA; (3); French Clb; Spanish Clb; Teachers Aide; Hon Roll; Drama; Law.

DONIKIAN, AZAD; San Pedro HS; San Pedro, CA; (3); French Clb; Mu Alpha Theta; Quiz Bowl; Scholastic Bowl; Spanish Clb; SADD; Band; JV Socr; Hon Roll; UCLA; Finance.

DONIS, JEFF; Aragon HS; San Mateo, CA; (1); Church Yth Grp; JV Trk.

DONLUCAS, ESTELA; J A Garfield HS; Los Angeles, CA; (4); 40/670; Cmnty Wkr; French Clb; Library Aide; Math Tm; Office Aide; Service Clb; SADD; Teachers Aide; Band; Mrchg Band; CA Schlrshp Fed; Occidental Coll; Educ.

DONNELLAN, MEGAN; Armijo HS; Fairfield, CA; (1); Church Yth Grp; Band; Mrchg Band; Off Frsh Cls; Hon Roll; NHS.

DONNELLY, CECILE A; Academy Of Our Lady Of Peace; Valley Center, CA; (2); Church Yth Grp; Cmnty Wkr; Hosp Aide; Varsity Clb; School Musical; School Play; Stage Crew; Socr; Swmmng; Hon Roll; Stanford; Bus.

DONNELLY, JUSTIN G; El Camino Real HS; West Hills, CA; (2); Drama Clb; School Play; High Hon Roll; Val; CSF; Sci.

DONNELLY, MARCY; Palm Springs HS; Rancho Mirage, CA; (3); Cmnty Wkr; Drama Clb; Chorus; Hon Roll; Jr Miss Palm Sprngs 89; 1st Rnnr Up Miss Palm Sprngs 90; Natl Chrty Leg; U CA Irvine; Marine Bio.

DONNELLY, MICHAEL D; Leuzinger HS; Lawndale, CA; (3); Church Yth Grp; Debate Tm; FCA; Bsbl; Ftbl; Trk; Wt Lftg; Prfct Atten Awd; 3 Yrs Var Ftbl Ltrmn, Capt; Valentine King Of Cls; Law Enfrcmnt.

DONNELLY, MICHELLE A; Fontana HS; Fontana, CA; (3); Church Yth Grp; Cmnty Wkr; Dance Clb; French Clb; Pep Clb; Teachers Aide; Varsity Clb; Acpl Chr; Church Choir; Drill Tm; Chrldng Advsr; Bible Quiz Tm; Elem Educ.

DONOGHUE, MARK; Antelope Valley HS; Lancaster, CA; (3); 203/547; Church Yth Grp; Drama Clb; Teachers Aide; Varsity Clb; Ed Yrbk; Var L Wrstlng; The Masters Coll; Pastor.

DONOHOE, MELINA M; Sacred Heart Prep; Menlo Park, CA; (2); Church Yth Grp; Cmnty Wkr; Drama Clb; Chorus; School Musical; School Play; Stage Crew; Mgr(s); Var Swmmng; Hon Roll; Admissions Clb; Child Psych.

DONOHUE, JEANNINE P; Huntington Beach HS; Huntington Beach, CA; (3); Key Clb; Pep Clb; Spanish Clb; School Play; High Hon Roll; Hon Roll; Jr NHS; SWAT.

DONOHUE, LISA ANNE; Pleasant Valley HS; Chico, CA; (4); 4-H; GAA; Spanish Clb; Drill Tm; Mrchg Band; Rptr Yrbk; Off Frsh Cls; VP Soph Cls; Treas Jr Cls; Var Socr; CSF Pres; Soroptomst Outstndng Sr; Ski Team Vrsty Ltr; UC Santa Barbara; Intl Law.

DONOHUE, RYAN C; Huntington Beach HS; Huntington Beach, CA; (1); Sunset All-League Water Polo; Music.

DONOHUE, THOMAS M; San Clemente HS; San Clemente, CA; (2); Church Yth Grp; Debate Tm; Crs Cntry; JV Tennis; Cit Awd; Hon Roll; Natl Hnr Scty; Wrld Hstry Awd; Cert Cmmndtn Sci From Acad Booster; Club PTSA Sqan Demente HS; U Of San Diego; Cmmrcl Arln.

DONOVAN, BETTY J; Davis SR HS; Davis, CA; (2); Aud/Vis; Church Yth Grp; Girl Scts; Library Aide; Office Aide; SADD; Teachers Aide; Sftbl; Accntng.

DONOVAN, GERALD P; Del Campo HS; Carmichael, CA; (4); 22/450; Spanish Clb; Band; Jazz Band; Mrchg Band; Pep Band; Yrbk; Capt Trk; Hon Roll; Pres Acad Fit Awd; U Of CA Davis; Chem.

DONOVAN, HEATHER L; Village Christian HS; Tujunga, CA; (3); Debate Tm; Drama Clb; French Clb; FBLA; GAA; Office Aide; Pep Clb; Ski Clb; Speech Tm; SADD; Vllybl Jr Olypmcs; Law Stds Clb; UCLA; Poly Sci.

DONOVAN, JOHN; Placer HS; Newcastle, CA; (3); 2/297; English Clb; VICA; Intrml Ftbl; Intrml Wt Lftg; High Hon Roll; Hon Roll; Sierra Coll; Arntcl Engrng.

DONOVAN, KRISTI; Inland Christian HS; Highland, CA; (3); Church Yth Grp; Office Aide; Var L Bsktbl; Var L Sftbl; Var L Vllybl; High Hon Roll; Prfct Atten Awd; Pres Acad Fit Awd.

DONOVAN, NATHAN R; Atascadero HS; Atascadero, CA; (1); Church Yth Grp; FBLA; Var Socr; JV Wt Lftg; Var Hon Roll; UCSB; Law.

DONOVAN, SHANNON K; Our Lady Of Peace HS; San Diego, CA; (1); GAA; Chorus; Variety Show; Madcaps.

DONOVIEL, TROY A; San Leandro HS; San Leandro, CA; (2); 36/400; Cmnty Wkr; Key Clb; Var Socr; High Hon Roll; Bus.

DOOB, JARED A; Irvington HS; Fremont, CA; (4); 3/241; Sec French Clb; VP German Clb; Sec Spanish Clb; Teachers Aide; Yrbk; High Hon Roll; Pres Acad Fit Awd; CSF Hstrn & VP; Bnk Amer Plaq Sci & Math; U Of CA Davis; Law.

DOOLEY, GARY; Hanford HS; Hanford, CA; (3); 14/521; 4-H; FFA; JV Var Bsbl; 4-H Awd; High Hon Roll; JV Bsbl Tm Best Dfnv Plyr; Kings Co 4-H Ctznshp Delegate To WA DC; FFA Cotton Jdgng & Frar Power; Ag.

DOOLEY, JON K; Santa Teresa HS; San Jose, CA; (2); Church Yth Grp; Office Aide; Ski Clb; JV Trk; AZ ST U.

DOOLEY, TARA M; West Hills HS; Santee, CA; (3); 5/233; Cmnty Wkr; Letterman Clb; Varsity Clb; Chorus; Capt JV Cheerldng; Var Trk; Wt Lftg; Cit Awd; High Hon Roll; Hon Roll; Natl Endowment Humanities Yng Schlr Fellowship; Aerospace Engr.

DOOLITTLE, JOE J; Red Bluff HS; Cottonwood, CA; (2); FFA; Ftbl; Wt Lftg; Wrstlng; High Hon Roll; Hon Roll; Kiwanis Awd; Wldng Awd; Welder.

DOOLITTLE, KRISTEN; Garces Memorial HS; Bakersfield, CA; (2); Drama Clb; Pep Clb; Ski Clb; Drill Tm; School Play; Cheerldng; Pom Pon; High Hon Roll; Dance.

DOOLITTLE, MEGAN C; Torrey Pines HS; Del Mar, CA; (2); 44/503; AFS; Var Crs Cntry; JV Socr; Var L Trk; High Hon Roll; Pres Acad Fit Awd; Reprtr Cls Nwsp; Phys Thrpy.

DOOLY, KELLY; Chico HS; Chico, CA; (2); SADD; Drill Tm; School Play; JV Cheerldng; Var Socr; JV Trk; JV Vllybl; High Hon Roll; Hon Roll; Pres Acad Fit Awd.

DOOMAN, BRYAN L; La Canada HS; La Canada Flintri, CA; (3); 30/276; Key Clb; JV Socr; JV Var Trk; NHS.

DOORNEWAARD, MICHAEL E; Grace M Davis HS; Modesto, CA; (3); Cit Awd; Santa Cruz ST U; Astrnmr.

DOOYEMA, KARI; San Dieguito HS; Encinitas, CA; (4); 18/534; Church Yth Grp; Hosp Aide; Office Aide; Chorus; VP L Crs Cntry; JV Sftbl; VP L Tennis; JV Vllybl; DAR Awd; High Hon Roll; Calif Scholarship Federation Seal Bearer; ASB; Wheaton College; English Lit.

DOPF, DAVID J; Beaumont HS; Cherry Valley, CA; (3); 25/200; Letterman Clb; Bsbl; Ftbl; Wt Lftg; Hon Roll; Med.

DOPSON, RICHARD A; Riverside Polytechnic HS; Riverside, CA; (4); 30/400; High Hon Roll; Hon Roll; CA Schlrshp Fed; UC San Diego.

DOR, OKINA; Woodrow Wilson HS; Long Beach, CA; (3); 1/32; Varsity Clb; Var Vllybl; Gov Hon Prg Awd; High Hon Roll; Hon Roll; Princpl Hnr Roll; Prfct Atten; Arch.

DORA, SHAUNA D; Chino HS; Chino, CA; (3); Church Yth Grp; FHA; SADD; Swmmng; Cit Awd; High Hon Roll; Hon Roll; Prfct Atten Awd; Silver Spur Awd Drivers Ed; Voc Olympics; Nordstoms Fshn Brd; Fshn Inst Dsgn/Merch; Fshn.

DORADO, KIMBERLY R; Hamilton HS Academy Of Music; Los Angeles, CA; (4); 113/500; Spanish Clb; Band; Mrchg Band; Orch; School Musical; Pres Acad Fit Awd; All Dist Hnr Orch; Los Angeles Cnty Hnr Orch; USC Schl Of Music; Music.

DORADO, MONICA; Southwest HS; San Diego, CA; (2); 61/673; Art Clb; SADD; VP Soph Cls; Hon Roll; Pres Acad Fit Awd; Intrml Socr; Intrml Vllybl; Assocd Stu Body; MECHA; Mdlng Clb; UC Santa Cruz; Advtg.

DORAN, ALISA D; Montgomery HS; Santa Rosa, CA; (2); Computer Clb; JA; Orch; JV Bsktbl; JV Sftbl; Hon Roll; Pres Acad Fit Awd; City Spon Soccer; Lamp Of Learning Awd For Acad Excl.

DORAN, SHANNON; Saint Francis HS; Santa Rosa, CA; (4); Cmnty Wkr; Drama Clb; JA; Service Clb; SADD; Thesps; School Musical; School Play; Nwsp; High Hon Roll; Santa Clara U; Psych.

DORCUS, DIANA; Los Altos HS; Hacienda Hts, CA; (3); Key Clb; Var Vllybl; Hon Roll; Psych.

DORFMAN, JENNAFER; Pioneer HS; San Jose, CA; (3); 10/325; Math Clb; Q&S; Service Clb; Pres Spanish Clb; Temple Yth Grp; Ed Nwsp; Sec Frsh Cls; Rep Soph Cls; Sec Jr Cls; Sec Stu Cncl; Peer Cnslr; CSF; Parks & Rcrtn Dept Outstndg Yth; Lawyr.

DORION, ROBERT T; Apple Valley HS; Apple Valley, CA; (2); Mrchg Band; High Hon Roll; U Of MD; Aero.

DORMAN, ELIZABETH; Salinas HS; Salinas, CA; (2); Church Yth Grp; Cmnty Wkr; French Clb; Sec Girl Scts; Pep Clb; Band; Jazz Band; Mrchg Band; Pep Band; JV Cheerldng; Music Cncl; Goldn Buddies; U Of CA San Diego; Med.

DORMIRE, JENNIFER M; Healdsburg HS; Healdsburg, CA; (4); 5/221; Church Yth Grp; Cmnty Wkr; Sprt Ed Nwsp; Rep Stu Cncl; JV Var Bsktbl; JV Var Vllybl; AFS; Drama Clb; Model UN; Rep Frsh Cls; Chrstn Yth Group; US Military Acad Prep Schl.

DORNAN, MARYANN; North Monterey County HS; Salinas, CA; (2); Church Yth Grp; Church Choir; JV Bsktbl; Top Clss Span I; Cal Poly; Atty.

DOROTIK, ALEXANDER T; Live Oak HS; San Martin, CA; (3); FBLA; Var Socr; High Hon Roll; Hon Roll; CSF; Badminton; Law.

DORROUGH, DAVID G; Edison HS; Huntington Beach, CA; (4); 26/483; Aud/Vis; English Clb; Science Clb; Teachers Aide; Ntl Merit SF; CA Math League; 3rd Pl Natl Video Cntst; USC Schl Of Cinema; Film.

DORROUGH, JENNIFER; Palm Desert HS; Palm Desert, CA; (3); Band; Var JV Sftbl; Var JV Vllybl; High Hon Roll; Hon Roll; Prfct Atten Awd; UC Berkeley; Psych.

DORROUGH, SUSIE C; Louisville HS; Woodland Hills, CA; (2); Diving; All Amer HS Athlt; 1st Pl Wnnr CIF 2-A Div; Bus Admin.

DORSEY, JOHN; Caroua Del Mav HS; Newport Beach, CA; (3); 11/315; Hosp Aide; Key Clb; Spanish Clb; Speech Tm; Nwsp; Tennis; Med.

DORSEY, KIMBERLY V; George Washington HS; San Francisco, CA; (2); Dance Clb; Hosp Aide; Hon Roll; U CA Berkeley; Hlth Sci.

DORSEY, RULANDA D; Chula Vista HS; Chula Vista, CA; (3); 115/493; Girl Scts; Pep Clb; Drill Tm; Stage Crew; Variety Show; Stu Cncl; Cit Awd; Hon Roll; Pres Acad Fit Awd; Off Sr Cls; Upward Bound Pgm; Yth Frat; Howard U; Chld Psych.

DOSANJH, AVNINDER K; Ceres HS; Hughson, CA; (4); 21/260; French Clb; Hosp Aide; Service Clb; SADD; Phtg Yrbk; Hon Roll; Pres Acad Fit Awd; Stanislaus Occptnl Olympics 4th Pl; Modesto JC; Nrsng.

DOSANJH, HARJIT; Fred C Beyer HS; Modesto, CA; (3); FBLA; Hosp Aide; Intnl Clb; Spanish Clb; SADD; Cit Awd; High Hon Roll; FCA; Prfct Atten Awd; Explorer Post; CA Schlrshp Fed 3 Yrs; UC Davis; Family Med.

DOSS, JUJUAN; Monte Vista HS; Spring Valley, CA; (1); Bsbl; Bsktbl; Ftbl; Socr; Trk; All-Star Bsbll.

DOSS, STEPHANIE; Colton HS; Colton, CA; (3); Pres Church Yth Grp; Dance Clb; Debate Tm; French Clb; FBLA; Model UN; NFL; Ski Clb; Speech Tm; Color Guard; U Southern CA; Law.

DOSSETT, TERESA; Antelope Valley HS; Lancaster, CA; (2); Dance Clb; Teachers Aide; Hon Roll.

DOSSEY, JASON; Serra HS; Daly City, CA; (2); Boy Scts; Letterman Clb; Ski Clb; Varsity Clb; Var Ftbl; Var Trk; MVP Trk; Qlfd Jr Olympcs; UCLA.

DOSTER, REBECCA; Palmdale HS; Littlerock, CA; (2); 35/813; Debate Tm; Rptr FFA; SADD; Chorus; Hon Roll; Lion Awd; Schltc Achvt Awd RBAA; Amer Hrt Assn; Yng Teen Miss CA; UC Davis; Vet.

DOSTER, TAMMY; Palmdale HS; Littlerock, CA; (3); 68/789; Am Leg Aux Girls St; Debate Tm; French Clb; FFA; JA; Speech Tm; Rep Stu Cncl; Cit Awd; High Hon Roll; Kiwanis Awd; FFA-SCHL VP/AV Sect Pres/Sthrn Rgn Rprtr; Parlimentary Procdr Team-Pres/Asst Coach 89-91; Stu Of Yr; U Of MN; Ag Ed.

DOTSON, DENISE LUCIA; South Bay JR Acad; Carson, CA; (2); Computer Clb; Drama Clb; FTA; Chorus; School Musical; Co-Ed Yrbk; Sec Frsh Cls; Pres Stu Cncl; Vllybl; High Hon Roll; Educ.

DOTSON, NANETTE D; Mojave HS; Mojave, CA; (2); Church Yth Grp; English Clb; Spanish Clb; SADD; JV Bsktbl; Var Sftbl; Cit Awd; High Hon Roll; Hon Roll; Pediatrician.

DOTSON, PATRICK D; Valhalla HS; Jamul, CA; (3); Arch; AZ ST U; Archtrl Engrng.

DOTTA, BILL R; Apple Valley HS; Apple Valley, CA; (3); Math Tm; JV Ftbl; JV Trk; Hon Roll; Karate Orange Belt; Psychlgy.

DOTTEN, CHARA; Mother Lode Christian Schl; Sonora, CA; (1); 1/15; Church Yth Grp; Library Aide; Teachers Aide; Chorus; Flag Corp; Stage Crew; Yrbk; High Hon Roll; Chrch Mscl; Pnst/Rctls; Bllt/Rctls; Chrch Dnc Trp; Fresno Pacific; Mdcl Fld.

DOTTER, DENISE; Los Gatos HS; Los Gatos, CA; (2); Cmnty Wkr; Hosp Aide; Intnl Clb; Envrnmnt.

DOTTS, CHERI J; Fontana HS; Fontana, CA; (2); Church Yth Grp; Band; Mrchg Band; Pep Band; JV Bsktbl; JV Socr; JV Vllybl; Hon Roll; Law.

DOTY, SARAH J; Burney HS; Burney, CA; (2); Church Yth Grp; Band; School Musical; Intrml Socr; JV Trk; Hon Roll; Pres Of Teen Ldrs; CA Schlrshp Fed; Moose Clb Congress.

DOUANGPANGA, SYRIPHONE; Turlock HS; Turlock, CA; (2); Art Clb; Church Yth Grp; Key Clb; Color Guard; Trk; Wt Lftg; Photo; Brooks Inst; Bus.

DOUANGSAVANH, SONETHONG; Wish Schl; Riverside, CA; (4); JV Socr; Hon Roll; Prfct Atten Awd.

DOUANGTA, PAE; Edison HS; Stockton, CA; (3); Hon Roll; Vrsty Badminton; U CA Santa Barbara; Fshn Dsgn.

DOUANGVONGSA, AMONLATH; Duncan Poly HS; Fresno, CA; (2); ROTC; Drill Tm; Vllybl; Hon Roll; Prfct Atten Awd; Pres Acad Fit Awd; Elec Careers; Fresno City Coll; Elec.

DOUGAN, BREE; Foothill HS; Pleasanton, CA; (3); Band; Mrchg Band; Var Swmmng; Hon Roll; USS Swm Tm; CSF; Elem Educ.

DOUGHERTY, BILL R; Paradise HS; Paradise, CA; (1); High Hon Roll; Tech Engr.

DOUGHERTY, DAVID S; Clovis HS; Clovis, CA; (3); Ftbl; High Hon Roll; Hon Roll; CSF; Ecology Clb; Natl Hstry Day 5th Pl, St Hstry Day 1st Pl.

DOUGHTERYT, ROBERT; Mt Whitney HS; Visalia, CA; (3); Church Yth Grp; Var Bsbl; Var Bsktbl; Var Ftbl; Hon Roll; Pres Acad Fit Awd; Vllyplyr Yr Ftbl, Underclsmn All St Tm Ftbl; St Rcrd Cmpltn Prctnge; Law.

DOUGLAS, ALISSA C; Francis W Parker HS; San Diego, CA; (2); Math Tm; SADD; School Play; Rptr Nwsp; Rep Stu Cncl; Var Tennis; Hon Roll; Secretary Of Safe Rides; Member Of Girls League Community Service.

DOUGLAS, GREG E; North HS; Bakersfield, CA; (2); Var Ftbl; Var Trk; Var Wt Lftg.

DOUGLAS, HEATHER L; Greenville JR SR HS; Greenville, CA; (3); Am Leg Aux Girls St; Cmnty Wkr; GAA; Hosp Aide; Library Aide; VP Service Clb; Ski Clb; Varsity Clb; Band; School Play; HOBY; Jr Statesmn CA Poltcs Delgt; Var Ski Tm; Intl Rels.

DOUGLAS, HOLLY A; Calaveras HS; Mokelumne Hill, CA; (3); Church Yth Grp; Cmnty Wkr; Pres 4-H; JA; Teachers Aide; Band; Mrchg Band; 4-H Awd; Hon Roll; Prfct Atten Awd; Deaf Camp Cnslr; Respite Provider; Spec Ed Teacher.

DOUGLAS, J BRANDON; Los Amigos HS; Fountain Valley, CA; (3); Boy Scts; Pres Church Yth Grp; VP Band; Jazz Band; Mrchg Band; School Musical; JV Bsktbl; Var Capt Swmmng; Hon Roll; Jr NHS; Var Water Polo Capt All League 1st Tm Goalie; Bart Whitfield Mst Insprtnl Awd; Swim Tm Capt & MVP.

DOUGLAS, MELISA; Ontario HS; Ontario, CA; (1); Church Yth Grp; Chorus; Church Choir; Prfct Atten Awd; Grd Schl Teacher.

DOUGLAS, REBECCA P; Rio Americano HS; Sacramento, CA; (4); 9/269; Church Yth Grp; French Clb; Service Clb; Ski Clb; Cheerldng; JV Var Socr; Hon Roll; Ntl Merit SF; 1st Pl-San Juan Unfd Schl Dist Writers Fair; Suprior-Ntl Hstry Day; Reed Coll; Engrng.

DOUGLAS, SUSAN L; Fontana HS; Fontana, CA; (3); 78/2000; Ski Clb; Drill Tm; Rep Soph Cls; Cit Awd; Hon Roll; Public Relations.

DOUGLASS, CORY R; Beaumont HS; Beaumont, CA; (3); French Clb; Quiz Bowl; Hon Roll; NHS; Real Estate.

DOUGLASS, ELIZABETH S; Mt Miguel HS; Spring Valley, CA; (4); 22/370; Office Aide; Teachers Aide; Phtg Nwsp; Hon Roll; Lemon Grove Rotary Clb Voctnl/Technel Schlrshp; CSF; Mst Outstndng Photogrphy Stu; Grossmont Coll; Film Makr.

DOUGLASS, SHANNON M; Cajon HS; San Bernardino, CA; (3); DECA; Drama Clb; SADD; School Play; Stage Crew; Ed Nwsp; SEA; Hnr Frnch II; UC Davis; Vet.

DOUGLASS, TAMARA M; Tulare Union HS; Pixley, CA; (4); 42/369; Church Yth Grp; Drama Clb; Band; Mrchg Band; Pep Band; Hon Roll; Mock Trial; Liberal Studies.

DOUNGCHAK, FLINT I; University HS; Irvine, CA; (1); Mrchg Band; Orch; School Musical; JV Socr; Cit Awd; Hon Roll; Pres Acad Fit Awd; ST Ice Hockey; Arch.

DOURBETAS, LAINIE A; Kennedy HS; Buena Park, CA; (2); Sec Church Yth Grp; Dance Clb; GAA; Letterman Clb; SADD; Church Choir; School Play; Bsktbl; Crs Cntry; Trk; UCI; Phy.

DOURIAN, BROOKE E; Chaminade College Prep; Northridge, CA; (3); Cmnty Wkr; Drama Clb; Thesps; Drill Tm; School Musical; School Play; Stage Crew; Hon Roll; Pres Acad Fit Awd.

DOUSHY, GILLES; Bonita Vista HS; Bonita, CA; (3); 7/559; Cmnty Wkr; Cit Awd; High Hon Roll; Cert Prtcptn Amer Chmcl Soc; Gldn St Exam Awd-Geom; Gldn St Exam Awd -U S Hstry; UCSD; Med.

DOUTT, KIRSTEN; Avalon HS; Avalon, CA; (4); 1/20; Am Leg Aux Girls St; Pres VP Letterman Clb; VP Spanish Clb; Ed Yrbk; Ed Lit Mag; Pres Frsh Cls; VP Treas Stu Cncl; Var Capt Bsktbl; Socr; Sftbl; CSF Pres, Secy & VP; Claremont Mckenna Coll.

DOUTT, KRISTEN; Avalon HS; Avalon, CA; (4); 1/20; Am Leg Aux Girls St; Pres Treas Letterman Clb; VP Spanish Clb; Ed Yrbk; VP Stu Cncl; Capt Var Bsktbl; Socr; Sftbl; Pres Acad Fit Awd; Val; CSF Pres, Secy & VP; Claremont Mc Kenna Coll.

DOUTY, NATHAN D; Fresno Christian Schl; Fresno, CA; (3); Church Yth Grp; Teachers Aide; Varsity Clb; Rep Jr Cls; Stu Cncl; L Var Ftbl; L Var Golf; Hon Roll; Biking.

DOUZOS, STEPHANIE; San Leandro HS; San Leandro, CA; (4); Hosp Aide; JA; Key Clb; Ski Clb; Score Keeper; Vllybl; High Hon Roll; Hon Roll; Prfct Atten Awd; Pediatric Practitioner.

DOVE, ADAM M; Salinas HS; Salinas, CA; (3); Cmnty Wkr; English Clb; VP Temple Yth Grp; Varsity Clb; Var Capt Swmmng; High Hon Roll; V Water Polo Capt; Natl Hnr Soc; Bus Admn.

DOVICHI, ERIN; Fred C Beyer HS; Modesto, CA; (3); German Clb; Pep Clb; Service Clb; SADD; Cheerldng; Socr; Trk; Vllybl; Hon Roll; Jnr Asilomar.

DOVIDIO, TRACY; Rosary HS; Whittier, CA; (4); 19/135; Pres Cmnty Wkr; Hosp Aide; Library Aide; Ski Clb; Capt School Play; Capt Var Swmmng; Var Trk; Var Capt Vllybl; Hon Roll; Pres NHS; Pressure Free, Drug Awarenss Assoc Fndr, Pres; CSF; Schlr Athlt Vllybl, Swmmng; Finance.

DOVLATIAN, HASMIK; Pasadena HS; Pasadena, CA; (3); Cmnty Wkr; Drama Clb; French Clb; Library Aide; JV Bsktbl; JV Swmmng; Hon Roll; Phi Delta Kappa Camp; Cls Rep CA Schlrshp Fed; Acad Decathalon; Fndr PHS Chptr Greenpeace; Amnsty Intl; UCLA; Engl.

DOW, JEFF D; Casa Grande HS; Petaluma, CA; (4); Church Yth Grp; Phtg Yrbk; Hon Roll; Doyle Schlrshp; Woodworking/Cabinetry Achvt; Santa Rosa JC; Cabinet Making.

DOW, JILL C; Wm S Hart HS; Newhall, CA; (3); 27/480; FBLA; Hosp Aide; Sec SADD; Sec Jr Cls; Var Cheerldng; Mgr(s); Intrml Powder Puff Ftbl; High Hon Roll; Hon Roll; NHS; CSF; Teen Advsry Co Of SCV; Stu Leag.

DOW, KIM S; Nevada Union HS; Nevada City, CA; (2); Rptr Nwsp; High Hon Roll; BMX Rcng Local & Natl No 1; Golden ST Exam GSE Algbr High Hnrs; Jrnlsm.

DOWD, CLIFFORD; South San Francisco HS; South San Francis, CA; (2); Cmnty Wkr; Band; Orch; Pep Band; Nwsp; Sec Amnesty Intl; Big Bro/Big Sister Prog; Wnnr Spllng Bee 89-90; San Diego U; Educ.

DOWD, GINA A; Santa Cruz HS; Santa Cruz, CA; (1); JV Bsktbl; Hon Roll; Vol Young At Art Fstvl 88-89; Girl Scout Vol; Jrnlsm.

DOWDY, ERIC; Argonaut HS; Ione, CA; (2); AFS; French Clb; Bus.

DOWELL, BILL; West HS; Bakersfield, CA; (1); Ftbl; Hon Roll; University; Auto Mechanic.

DOWELL, LANCE V; University HS; Irvine, CA; (2); Cmnty Wkr; JCL; Latin Clb; JV Swmmng; High Hon Roll; Prfct Atten Awd; JV Water Polo; CSF; U Southern CA; Civil Engr.

DOWELL, MARLO R; Moreno Valley HS; Moreno Valley, CA; (4); Key Clb; High Hon Roll; Hon Roll; NHS; Pres Acad Fit Awd; UC Santa Barbara; Envrnmntl.

DOWELL, STACY; Hoover HS; Fresno, CA; (3); Sec Jr Cls; Var Capt Swmmng; Var Vllybl; Young Woman Of The Yr; Sophomore Princess; CSF Member; Coaches Awd Swimming; WWAHS Sophomore Yr; Fresno ST.

DOWLATSHAHI, NOUSHIN; Irvine HS; Irvine, CA; (4); 21/30; Spk Frnch; Intrsts Philosophy, Music & Astrmny; Play Piano; U AZ; Arspc Engrng.

DOWLING, MAE L; Kingsburg HS; Traver, CA; (4); Chess Clb; Church Yth Grp; Cmnty Wkr; FTA; Mu Alpha Theta; Office Aide; SADD; Teachers Aide; Chorus; Rptr Nwsp; Amer Legn Citiznshp Awd; US Army; Teach.

DOWLING, MATTHEW S; Nevada Union HS; Nevada City, CA; (1); 1/589; Office Aide; Chorus; School Musical; Stage Crew; Stanford U; Med.

DOWNER, TODD A; San Clemente HS; San Clemente, CA; (2); Am Leg Boys St; JV Bsbl; Bsktbl; JV Ftbl; Cit Awd; Hon Roll; R G Canning Yth Achvt Awd; BYU; Bus.

DOWNES, LORI A; River City HS; W Sacramento, CA; (4); 5/120; Am Leg Aux Girls St; Chess Clb; Church Yth Grp; French Clb; AFS; Pep Clb; Speech Tm; SADD; Church Choir; VP Frsh Cls; Mac Laughlin Schlrsyp; Frnch Club Schlrshp; CA Luthern U; Mktng.

DOWNEY, ALTHEA; Northview HS; Covina, CA; (4); Art Clb; Letterman Clb; Capt Pep Clb; VP Soph Cls; Rep Stu Cncl; JV Var Cheerldng; Var Trk; High Hon Roll; Hon Roll; Floyd Myrick Awd For Sci; Girls League; Sci Clb; CSU San Bernardino; Ed Hstry.

DOWNEY, BETH; Cajon HS; San Bernardino, CA; (2); Church Yth Grp; Swmmng; High Hon Roll; Strght A Rprt Crd; Harvard:Srgcl Dr.

DOWNEY, JOHN E; College Park HS; Martinez, CA; (3); Church Yth Grp; Letterman Clb; Teachers Aide; Varsity Clb; Socr; Vllybl; Rally Cmmssnr; Pepprdn U; Soc Sci Tchr.

DOWNING, DANYEL EVETTE; Orosi HS; Orosi, CA; (3); Spanish Clb; SADD; Teachers Aide; Chorus; Nwsp; Yrbk; Score Keeper; Hon Roll; Federicos; Beautican.

DOWNING, GARTLEY EARL B; Elk Grove HS; Sacramento, CA; (4); 36/598; Boy Scts; Church Yth Grp; ROTC; Science Clb; Spanish Clb; Church Choir; Rep Frsh Cls; Sec Soph Cls; Bsktbl; Tennis; Elec.

DOWNING, JASON K; Dana Hills HS; Laguna Niguel, CA; (4); Ski Clb; Teachers Aide; Var Bsbl; Var Bsktbl; Hon Roll; Prfct Atten Awd; UCLA; Bus Acctng.

DOWNING, LISA M; San Pasqual HS; Escondido, CA; (2); Church Yth Grp; Cmnty Wkr; Computer Clb; Dance Clb; Scholastic Bowl; Variety Show; Capt Vllybl; High Hon Roll; Jr NHS; Ntl Merit Ltr; Finlst ST MS Natl Tnager Comp Pgnt 1990; CA Schlrshp Fedrtn FR&SOPH Presd Acdmc Achvmnt Awd 1988; SDSU; Obstetrician.

DOWNS, JEFFREY N; Glendale Adventist Acad; Sunland, CA; (1); Church Yth Grp; FCA; Acpl Chr; Color Guard; Drill Tm; Intrml Bsbl; Intrml Bsktbl; Intrml Ftbl; Intrml Golf; Intrml Vllybl; Pacific Union Coll; Psych.

DOWNS, JENNIFER; Los Alamitos HS; Surfside, CA; (3); Church Yth Grp; Var Pep Clb; Spanish Clb; SADD; JV Var Cheerldng; Hon Roll; NHS; Safe-Rides; CSF; Vet Med.

DOWNS, MICHELLE; Holtville HS; Imperial, CA; (3); 36/160; Bus Profs of Am; Church Yth Grp; FBLA; FFA; FHA; Hosp Aide; Library Aide; Office Aide; Teachers Aide; JV Var Bsktbl; Sci Awds; Comp Tech.

DOWNS, STACEY; Western Regional Christian Acad; San Pablo, CA; (1); Church Yth Grp; Teachers Aide; Ed Yrbk; Pres Stu Cncl; High Hon Roll; WRCA; Beautician.

DOYEL, JOSH R; Fairfield HS; Suisun, CA; (1); Swmmng; City Vallejo Outstndng Schltc Achvt Awd; Bus.

DOYLE, ERIN M; O Farrell Schl Of Creative & Perf Art; San Diego, CA; (1); 1/227; Church Yth Grp; Dance Clb; Spanish Clb; Chorus; Hon Roll; Jr NHS; Piano 8 Yrs; San Diego Jr Thtre.

DOYLE, JENNIFER L; Paradise HS; Magalia, CA; (1); Hon Roll.

DOYLE, JENNIFER M; Chino HS; Chino, CA; (2); Science Clb; Ski Clb; Spanish Clb; JV Socr; Sftbl; High Hon Roll; Hon Roll; Gymnastics Outside Schl; Paint & Draw; Photo; Psych.

DOYLE, JOANNE P; Flintridge Preparatory Schl; South Pasadena, CA; (3); AFS; Cmnty Wkr; French Clb; Hosp Aide; Socr; Sftbl; Tennis; Coach Special Olympics Sccr Tm; Bus MBA.

DOYLE, JOHN ANDREW; Paraclete HS; Pearblossom, CA; (3); Hon Roll; Teacher.

DOYLE, KATHLEEN; St Francis HS; Santa Clara, CA; (2); 89/356; SADD; Var Socr; High Hon Roll; Hon Roll; Santa Clara U; Tchng.

DOYLE, MIRANDA S; Live Oak HS; Morgan Hill, CA; (4); 9/543; Cmnty Wkr; FBLA; SADD; Ed Nwsp; Elks Awd; Ntl Merit Ltr; Pres Acad Fit Awd; Amnsty Intrntl VP; YMCA Yth/Govt Delgtn Pres; Ctzns Angst Drug Abuse; Stanford U; Poltcl Sci.

DOYLE, SABRINA M; Mount Shasta HS; Mount Shasta, CA; (2); 5/80; Ski Clb; High Hon Roll; Hon Roll; CSF; Gldn ST Exam Gmtry Hnrs.

DOYLE-MARCEY, JENNIFER E; Bellarmine-Jefferson HS; Glendale, CA; (3); Cmnty Wkr; Math Clb; Science Clb; Spanish Clb; Stage Crew; Rep Frsh Cls; L Var Bsktbl; Capt L Fld Hcky; Intrml Gym; Capt L Lcrss; Loyola Marymount; Psych.

DOZOIS, AIMEE A; John Muir HS; Altadena, CA; (3); Girl Scts; Service Clb; Flag Corp; Yrbk; Lit Mag; Cheerldng; Socr; Hon Roll; Gold Awd-Grl Scts; Bio.

DRAEGER, BENJAMIN R; North Monterey County HS; Castroville, CA; (2).

DRAEGER, MARNIE K; Yucaipa HS; Yucaipa, CA; (2); Church Yth Grp; Drama Clb; Spanish Clb; Mgr Stage Crew; Cngrsnl Schlr Natl Yng Ldrs Conf 90; Cal ST Fullerton; Drma.

DRAEGER, MIKE C; Cupertino HS; Santa Clara, CA; (4); 1/243; Treas German Clb; Math Tm; Jazz Band; High Hon Roll; NHS; Ntl Merit Ltr; Pres Acad Fit Awd; Val; Tae Kwon Do; Eagle Scout; Santa Clara U; Computer Engr.

DRAKE, BRIAN J; American HS; Fremont, CA; (4); 4/350; Boy Scts; Church Yth Grp; French Clb; Model UN; High Hon Roll; Ntl Merit SF; Engnrng.

DRAKE, JENNEA; Sonoma Valley HS; Sonoma, CA; (2); 20/250; JV Swmmng; DAR Awd; JETS Awd; Pres Acad Fit Awd; Santa Rosa JR Coll; Social Wrk.

DRAKE, MARK D; Eisenhower HS; Rialto, CA; (2); 25/800; Letterman Clb; Rep Frsh Cls; Rep Stu Cncl; Var Swmmng; High Hon Roll; Hon Roll; Jr NHS; Kiwanis Awd; NHS; Radio-Controlled Auto Racing 89; Congression Yth Ldrshp Cncl; Exchange Club Yth Month; Medh Engr.

DRAKE, PAUL E; Santa Clara HS; Santa Clara, CA; (3); Church Yth Grp; JV Var Ftbl; Powder Puff Ftbl; JV Socr; Wt Lftg; JV Wrstlng; Hon Roll; Santa Clara U.

DRAP, AMY P; Saugus HS; Saugus, CA; (4); 42/435; Drama Clb; German Clb; Chorus; School Musical; School Play; Stage Crew; Hon Roll; NHS; Yng Stu Actvsts; Film Directing.

DRAPER, CANDISE; Newark Memorial HS; Newark, CA; (3); 66/545; Stat Bsktbl; High Hon Roll; Spirit Week; Law.

DRAPER, TIMOTHY W; Burlingame HS; Burlingame, CA; (3); Boy Scts; Hnr Acad Excllnc Awd 88-89; UC San Diego; Engrng.

DRAWVER, KRISTIN L; East Nicolaus HS; East Nicolaus, CA; (3); 10/50; Teachers Aide; JV Var Bsktbl; JV Cheerldng; Stat Sftbl; JV Var Vllybl; High Hon Roll; Hon Roll.

DRAYER, DENISE; Greenville JR-SR HS; Greenville, CA; (2); Treas FBLA; VP Pres Frsh Cls; VP Pres Stu Cncl; High Hon Roll; Pres Acad Fit Awd; 3rd Bus Math 89; FBLA Sctn Cnfrnc; 3rd Kybrdng 88.

DRECKMANN, CRISTEL J; Hamilton HS; Los Angeles, CA; (2); Bus.

DREDGE, DEBI E; Monte Vista HS; Walnut Creek, CA; (3); Church Yth Grp; Trk; Natl Charity League.

DREDGE, JOANNE; Tulare Union HS; Tulare, CA; (4); Church Yth Grp; Band; Mrchg Band; Pep Band; Swmmng; Ricks JC; Paralegal.

DREHOBL, APRIL V; Del Campo HS; Sacramento, CA; (3); 110/500; Pres Church Yth Grp; Office Aide; Score Keeper; Swmmng; NHS; BYU; Scl Sci.

DREILING, JEFF M; El Toro HS; El Toro, CA; (2); 137/255; Church Yth Grp; Drama Clb; Band; Mrchg Band; School Musical; School Play; Stage Crew; Hon Roll; Sociology.

DRELL, MARIANNA; Van Nuys HS; N Hollywood, CA; (4); Pres Computer Clb; SADD; Drill Tm; Ed Nwsp; Ed Yrbk; Stu Cncl; Hon Roll; Prfct Atten Awd; Pres Acad Fit Awd; CSF Gld Seal Bearer; U Of Judaism; Bus.

DRENE, JESSE D; Huntington Beach HS; Huntington Beach, CA; (1); Teachers Aide; Bsbl; Wt Lftg; Hon Roll; Prfct Atten Awd; Pres Acad Fit Awd; Tower Awds Fnlst; Pepperdine; Law.

DRENNON, JENNIFER; Oakmont HS; Roseville, CA; (4); Pres Treas Church Yth Grp; Drama Clb; Pep Clb; Spanish Clb; SADD; Teachers Aide; Drill Tm; Cheerldng; Hon Roll; Pres Acad Fit Awd; Cal Luth U; Bus.

DRENSER, BRIDGIT E; Costa Mesa HS; Costa Mesa, CA; (3); Cmnty Wkr; French Clb; Pep Clb; Service Clb; Ski Clb; Var L Tennis; Var Trk; Hon Roll; Cltrl Arts Awd 90; Coaches Awd Tnns Tm 89; Mst Imprvd Tnns & Trck; Envrnmntl Actvts; Psych.

DRESE, STACIE L; Bishop O'dowd HS; Oakland, CA; (3); Art Clb; Church Yth Grp; Hosp Aide; Ski Clb; Socr; High Hon Roll; Yth Grp Cncl; Frgn Svc Pgm To Ecuador; All Lg Vrsty Sccr.

DRESHER, WENDY; Central Union HS; El Centro, CA; (4); 23/420; Church Yth Grp; High Hon Roll; Bank Of Amer Bus Cert; Imperial Valley Coll; Accntng.

DRESNER, KAREN M; Redlands HS; Redlands, CA; (2); French Clb; School Play; Bsktbl; Pres Acad Fit Awd; UCSC; Music.

DRESSER, RENEE L; University HS; Irvine, CA; (1); Swmmng; UC Davis; Vet.

DRESSLER, DONALD R; University HS; Irvine, CA; (3); 172/551; Boy Scts; Church Yth Grp; German Clb; Orch; Var Bsktbl; Var Ftbl; Var Trk; Var Wt Lftg; Hon Roll; Hstry Ed.

DRESSLER, DOUG L; Thomas Downey HS; Modesto, CA; (3); Church Yth Grp; Computer Clb; Spanish Clb; Teachers Aide; Law.

DRESSLER, WILLIAM W; University HS; Irvine, CA; (1); Boy Scts; JCL; Latin Clb; Orch; School Play; Intrml Socr; Intrml Vllybl; Hon Roll.

DREW, KARI L; Grossmont HS; El Cajon, CA; (1); Hosp Aide; Ski Clb; Socr; Vllybl; Hon Roll; Pres Acad Fit Awd; UCSB; Teacher.

DREWRY, CHRISTIE D; Alpaugh Unified Schl; Alpaugh, CA; (4); English Clb; Latin Clb; Teachers Aide; Band; Sec Frsh Cls; Cheerldng; Cit Awd; Hon Roll; Ntl Merit Ltr; Prfct Atten Awd; Spirit Cmmtte; Bank Of Amer Achvt Awd; Most Imprvd SR; Sequoias Coll; Bus.

DREWRY, MATT J; Kings Christian HS; Hanford, CA; (4); 2/11; Church Yth Grp; Ski Clb; Chorus; School Play; Yrbk; VP Frsh Cls; Rep Soph Cls; Rep Jr Cls; VP Stu Cncl; JV Var Bsktbl; Sequoias Coll; Crmnl Jstc.

DREYER, JASON R; Los Amigos HS; Santa Ana, CA; (4); Hon Roll; CA Schlrshp Fed Gld Seal Bear; CA Lthrn U; Acctnt.

DRIER, JASON E; Monterey Bay Acad; Madera, CA; (1).

DRIGGS, KIMBERLY L; Beyer HS; Modesto, CA; (3); AFS; Church Yth Grp; Girl Scts; Ski Clb; SADD; Teachers Aide; Acpl Chr; School Musical; Swmmng; Cit Awd; Fri Nght Lv; Music Awds; Helsinki U; Intl Lang.

DRING, LAURA A; Skyline HS; Oakland, CA; (2); Church Yth Grp; Dance Clb; Drama Clb; Letterman Clb; Sec Thesps; Acpl Chr; Chorus; Church Choir; School Musical; School Play; Prfrmng Arts Pblcty Crew Chf; Adv.

DRISCOLL, JENNY; Agoura HS; Westlake Village, CA; (2); 1/469; Cmnty Wkr; Pep Clb; Ski Clb; Spanish Clb; Var Capt Cheerldng; Pom Pon; High Hon Roll; CSF; Eclgy Clb; Natl Charity Leage; Jazz Dancng; Span Awd; Bus.

DRISKELL, KATHERINE; Loara HS; Anaheim, CA; (3); Key Clb; Science Clb; Color Guard; Swmmng; Hon Roll; Jr NHS; CSF; Ntl Sci Fnd S CA Mdrn Physics Inst Smmr Fllwshp Prgm; Marine Bio.

DRIVER, JOEL; Ontario HS; Riverside, CA; (3); Boy Scts; German Clb; Ftbl; Wt Lftg; Prfct Atten Awd.

DRIVER, MYISHA; Pius X HS; West Los Angeles, CA; (3); Church Yth Grp; Pep Clb; Church Choir; Rptr Nwsp; Var Cheerldng; Var Powder Puff Ftbl; Var Trk; High Hon Roll; Hon Roll; NHS; Pan African Heritage Alliance Alt Treas; Howard U; Bus.

DROB, SUZY; William Howard Taft HS; Woodland Hills, CA; (3); Dance Clb; Drama Clb; JA; Speech Tm; Thesps; School Musical; School Play; Variety Show; Capt Cheerldng; Pres Acad Fit Awd; Dnc With Prfssnl Dnc Co; Actng Clss, Wrkshps, Plys, Prfssnl Career; 8 Hnrs Drama Cmptn Awds; UCLA; Thtr.

DROGAN, CHRIS L; Madison HS; San Diego, CA; (2); Church Yth Grp; Latin Clb; Wt Lftg; Navy Sea Cadet Corps; San Diego ST U; Math.

DROLET, BARBARA C; Sweetwater HS; National City, CA; (2); FTA; Scholastic Bowl; Teachers Aide; Stage Crew; Variety Show; Ed Nwsp; Yrbk; Cit Awd; High Hon Roll; Hon Roll; Brdcstng.

DROLL, NASH P; La Sierra HS; Riverside, CA; (1); Ftbl; L Trk; Intrml Wt Lftg; U Of IA; Sports Med.

DROMGOOLE, MICHELLE M; Rubidoux HS; Riverside, CA; (3); ROTC; Teachers Aide; Drill Tm; Rptr Nwsp; Ftbl; Spirit Clb; Sports Med Clb; Stu Trainer; Accntng.

DRON, JEFF M; Lincoln HS; Stockton, CA; (3); JV Bsbl; Var JV Ftbl.

DROWN, RIVERS C; Fort Dick Bible Acad; Crescent City, CA; (2); Pres Church Yth Grp; Band; Intrml Ftbl; Intrml Tennis; Intrml Wt Lftg; Cit Awd; Hon Roll; Chrch Pblc Spkng, Choir; Brigham Young U; Nvy Fghtr Plt.

DROZDENKO, DANIEL; Southbay Christian HS; Sunnyvale, CA; (3); Church Yth Grp; Chorus; Treas Frsh Cls; Treas Soph Cls; Off Stu Cncl; Var L Bsktbl; Var L Socr; Var L Tennis; High Hon Roll; CSF 87-89; Hmcmng Prince; MINISTER.

DROZDOWSKI, JENNIFER; Rosary HS; Whittier, CA; (2); French Clb; Pep Clb; Var Capt Cheerldng; High Hon Roll.

DROZEK, PASCALE N; Lycee Frangais HS; Castro Valley, CA; (3); French Clb; School Play; Nwsp; Phtg Rptr Yrbk; Pres Frsh Cls; Pres Jr Cls; Crs Cntry; Gym; Swmmng; Jrnlst.

DRULLARD, KRISTI; Linden HS; Stockton, CA; (1); 8/140; 4-H; FHA; Pep Clb; Ski Clb; VP Frsh Cls; JV Cheerldng; JV Pom Pon; JV Sftbl; Vllybl; Cit Awd; Phys Thrpst.

DRUMMOND, PAUL C; Grossmont HS; San Diego, CA; (3); 243/589; DECA; Drama Clb; FBLA; Quiz Bowl; School Play; Wt Lftg; Cit Awd; Prfct Atten Awd; Heartland Human Rltns Orgztn; DECA Presentation Tm; Accntg.

DRUMMOND, SCOTT D; Enterprise HS; Redding, CA; (3); 1/400; Am Leg Boys St; Treas Mu Alpha Theta; Sec Stu Cncl; JV Var Bsbl; JV Var Ftbl; DAR Awd; High Hon Roll; Pres Acad Fit Awd; Rotary Awd; CSF; Stanford; Bus.

DRUMMOND, WENDY L; West HS; Bakersfield, CA; (1); Church Yth Grp; Band; Mrchg Band; JV Swmmng; Hon Roll; GATE; CSF.

DRUMRIGHT, KUMANI; Pinole Valley HS; San Pablo, CA; (4); Hon Roll; Black Ldrshp Conf; Law.

DRURY, GITA J; Palo Alto HS; Palo Alto, CA; (2); French Clb; Key Clb; Letterman Clb; Band; Mrchg Band; Crs Cntry; Trk; Hon Roll; Rachel Austin Awd Sci; Jnr Statesmn Amer Clb.

DRURY, KEVIN P; Clovis West HS; Fresno, CA; (3); Cmnty Wkr; Debate Tm; Var Ftbl; Hon Roll; Pres Acad Fit Awd; CAP Ldrshp Awds; Army Rsrvs 90; West Point; Ofcr.

DRYDEN, DAVID; Capital Christian HS; Citrus Heights, CA; (1); Church Yth Grp; Library Aide; JV Bsbl; JV Bsktbl; High Hon Roll; CSF; IN; Bio.

DRYDEN, DEBBIE L; Woodland HS; Woodland, CA; (3); Church Yth Grp; Drill Tm; Yrbk; Hon Roll; Jr NHS; NHS; Pres Acad Fit Awd; U Of CA Davis; Envrnmntl Hlth.

DRYDEN, JENNIFER; Santa Cruz HS; Santa Cruz, CA; (3); Spanish Clb; Band; Capt Color Guard; Mrchg Band; Womens Hnr Soc; Family Law.

DRYE, CHRISTY M; Liberty Union HS; Oakley, CA; (1); Drama Clb; SADD; School Play; JV Cheerldng; Hon Roll; Work Teaching Chldrn How To Swim Smmr Job; Smmr Swim Team Brentwood Dolphins; Royalty Miss Pagant Sys; Marine Bio.

DU, DIEM-PHUONG; Los Angeles Coll Incentive Mag; Huntington Pk, CA; (4); 16/500; Science Clb; Orch; Ed Nwsp; Var Capt Vllybl; High Hon Roll; Hon Roll; Pres Acad Fit Awd; Sal; Interact Club Secy; Peer Cnslr.

DU, KHANH; Trabuco Hills HS; El Toro, CA; (2); Hosp Aide; Treas Jr Cls; Stat Lcrss; Wt Lftg; Var Wrstlng; Hon Roll; Jr NHS; Certified Nrsng Asst Cert; U CA Irvine; Med.

DU, MICHAEL M; Corona SR HS; Corona, CA; (3); JV Var Tennis; Hon Roll; Air Force Acad; Civil Engr.

DU, PHUONG; Santiago HS; Santa Ana, CA; (1); Computer Clb; Spanish Clb; Vietnamese Clb; Physician.

DU, PHUONG B; Alhambra HS; Alhambra, CA; (3); Library Aide; Teachers Aide; Prfct Atten Awd; CA ST U Los Angeles; Nurse.

DU, PHUONG Q; International Studies Acad; San Francisco, CA; (3); French Clb; Yrbk; Hon Roll; Financial Bus Inc Club; CSF; Shanghai Club; Video Club; Med.

DU, SCOTT; Westminster HS; Westminster, CA; (2); Hon Roll.

DU, SON; Westminster HS; Westminster, CA; (3); Temple Yth Grp; Wt Lftg; Hon Roll; Martial Art Dragon Dance Team; Arch.

DU, THANH K; Mission Bay HS; Vista, CA; (2); Varsity Clb; Jazz Band; JV Crs Cntry; JV Trk; Var Wrstlng; Cit Awd; High Hon Roll; Hon Roll; Mech Engrng.

DU, VICKIE S; Mayfield SR Schl; Glendale, CA; (3); Church Yth Grp; Hosp Aide; Library Aide; SADD; Hon Roll.

DU BE, JANE A; Bella Vista HS; Fair Oaks, CA; (4); 7/400; AFS; Drama Clb; French Clb; Science Clb; Service Clb; SADD; Off Sr Cls; French Hon Soc; High Hon Roll; Hon Roll; Schltc Achvt Awds Frgn Lang, Sci, Hstry, Engl, Wrtng; Whitman Coll; Psych.

DU BOIS, DUSTY; Sacramento HS; Sacramento, CA; (2); Office Aide; Teachers Aide; Crs Cntry; Trk; Hon Roll; Kids Helping Kids Vp; Math.

DU BOIS, SHARON; San Gabriel Mission HS; Rosemead, CA; (4); 14/107; Cmnty Wkr; GAA; Girl Scts; Sec Math Clb; Office Aide; Sec Science Clb; Teachers Aide; Hon Roll; NHS; Campus Mnstry LIFE; Justce Action Mission; Pr Cnslr; Whittier Coll; Educ.

DU BOSE, CHRIS S; Troy HS; Yorba Linda, CA; (2); 34/334; High Hon Roll; 5th Pl Orange Cty Stu Voc Olympics; Gldn St Exam Acad Excllnc Awd-Geometry.

DU BOSE, WADE T; Apple Valley HS; Apple Valley, CA; (1); French Clb; Intrml Socr; Hon Roll; Opt Clb Awd; Cal Poly Pomona; Engrng.

DU BREY, TANESHA R; Saint Michaels HS; Lynwood, CA; (3); Church Yth Grp; Cmnty Wkr; Church Choir; Variety Show; Bsktbl; Fld Hcky; Stu Of Mnth; USC; Paralgl.

DU BROVSKAYA, VERONIKA; Lowell US; Santa Monica, CA; (2); Cmnty Wkr; Dance Clb; Drama Clb; Girl Scts; Hosp Aide; Red Cross Aide; Speech Tm; Temple Yth Grp; Gym; Hon Roll; Medcl.

DU CRAY, JAMIE; Elk Grove HS; Wilton, CA; (1); 4-H; Office Aide; Teachers Aide; Nwsp; Amer JR Quartr Horse Wrld Chmpn In Cttng; Acctng.

DU LYON, BENN A; Pater Noster HS; Los Angeles, CA; (1); Church Yth Grp; Cmnty Wkr; Office Aide; Teachers Aide; Chorus; Bus.

DU PLESSIS, SHELLY M; Canyon Springs HS; Moreno Valley, CA; (2); Art Clb; Cmnty Wkr; Dance Clb; Girl Scts; Ski Clb; Teachers Aide; Varsity Clb; Mgr(s); Sftbl; Swmmng; UCLA; Nrsrgn.

DU PONT, AMY K; Lutheran HS; La Habra, CA; (2); Church Yth Grp; Phtg Yrbk; Rep Jr Cls; Var Socr; Var Sftbl; Var Vllybl; Pres Acad Fit Awd; Schlrshp From Lutheran HS; Orange County Yth Expo Art Awd 90; Medical Field.

DU PONT, CARRI J; Ramona HS; Ramona, CA; (2); 31/345; VP Frsh Cls; JV Socr; Cit Awd; Hon Roll; Bus.

DU RETTE, ALLISON; Bonita Vista HS; Chula Vista, CA; (3); Church Yth Grp; Stu Cncl; JV Crs Cntry; Amrcn Cncr Soc Yth Fllwshp Prgm; Chula Vista Cmmssn; Pre-Med.

DU ROSS, GINA; St Joseph HS; Long Beach, CA; (2); Hon Roll; Chrch Actvts; St Joseph; Art.

DU VAL, ANGELA D; East Bakersfield HS; Bakersfield, CA; (2); DECA; Hon Roll; Numerous Actvts; Phy.

DUANN, TOM; La Quinta HS; Fountain Vly, CA; (3); 48/318; Boy Scts; Chess Clb; Cmnty Wkr; Debate Tm; German Clb; Key Clb; Science Clb; JV Tennis; Hon Roll; Ntl Merit Ltr; Red Cross Ldrshp Dev Ctr; Jr Statesmn Summer Schl-Yale U; Bus Admin.

DUARTE, AMY; Williams HS; Williams, CA; (4); 2/32; Sec FFA; Rep Pep Clb; Spanish Clb; SADD; Teachers Aide; Treas Frsh Cls; Treas Soph Cls; Sec Jr Cls; VP Stu Cncl; JV Var Bsktbl; U CA; Phys Educ.

DUARTE, ARGELIA; Brawley Union HS; Brawley, CA; (1); Lwyr.

DUARTE, BERNER H; Morningside HS; Inglewood, CA; (3); Var Capt Socr; Cit Awd; Hon Roll; Prfct Atten Awd; El Camino Coll; Acctng.

DUARTE, CYNTHIA D; Pittsburg HS; Pittsburg, CA; (3); Art Clb; Aud/Vis; Dance Clb; Drama Clb; Teachers Aide; School Play; Off Jr Cls; Hon Roll; Rotary Awd; Habitat For Humanity; Intr Decor.

DUARTE, EDUARDO; Calexico HS; Calexico, CA; (2); Bus Profs of Am; Cmnty Wkr; FBLA; Key Clb; Service Clb; SADD; Pres Soph Cls; Upward Bound; CSF; HOBY; UC Berkeley; Advertising.

DUARTE, GEORGE; Millikan HS; Long Beach, CA; (3); Teachers Aide; Yrbk; Cit Awd; Hon Roll.

DUARTE, IMELDA M; Pinole Valley HS; Hercules, CA; (3); Church Yth Grp; GAA; Spanish Clb; Nwsp; Rep Frsh Cls; Rep Soph Cls; Rep Jr Cls; Rep Stu Cncl; JV Bsktbl; Var Trk; Interact Clb; Marine Bio.

DUARTE, MARISA B; Mayfield SR Schl; Whittier, CA; (3); AFS; Sec Soph Cls; U Of San Diego; Psych.

DUARTE, MELANIE A; Shafter HS; Bakersfield, CA; (3); Art Clb; Key Clb; Office Aide; Pep Clb; Score Keeper; Tennis; Cal ST Bakersfld; Optometry.

DUARTE, NORBERT S; Atwater HS; Winton, CA; (1); FFA; Band; Mrchg Band; CA ST U Stanislaus; Ag.

DUARTE, REBECCA J; Barstow HS; Barstow, CA; (1); Church Yth Grp; Library Aide; Office Aide; Chorus; Cheerldng; Hon Roll; San Diego U; Bus.

DUARTE, SARA; Castle Park HS; Chula Vista, CA; (4); Sec Art Clb; Church Yth Grp; German Clb; Letterman Clb; Teachers Aide; Varsity Clb; Capt Color Guard; Capt Drill Tm; Ed Lit Mag; Rep Soph Cls; Pathfinder Club Cnslr; Athl Schlr Awd; San Diego ST U; Psych.

DUARTE, YVONNE M; Del Campo HS; Carmichael, CA; (2); 86/460; UCSB; Bus.

DUBE, ERIC; El Camino HS; Oceanside, CA; (3); 2/350; VP Soph Cls; VP Jr Cls; VP Stu Cncl; Var Trk; High Hon Roll; RYLA 90; Presdntl Clsrm.

DUBE, ERIK S; 29 Palms HS; Twentynine Plms, CA; (2); 12/280; Letterman Clb; Crs Cntry; Trk; High Hon Roll; Prfct Atten Awd.

DUBEN, ALAN P; Oak Park HS; Agoura Hills, CA; (1); 18/108; JV Ftbl; Var Trk; Peer Cnslng Prog; Med.

DUBLIN, JAMES; Davis SR HS; El Macero, CA; (3); Ski Clb; Rptr Nwsp; Var Golf; Peer Cnslr.

DUBROVSKY, EDWARD J; Saint Ignatius College Prep HS; San Francisco, CA; (3); Cmnty Wkr; Science Clb; Hon Roll; CSF; USF; Bus Fin.

DUBROWSKIJ, TAMMIE; Bell HS; Bell, CA; (3); Church Yth Grp; Cmnty Wkr; Drama Clb; Pep Clb; Science Clb; Service Clb; VP SADD; Capt Drill Tm; School Play; JV Powder Puff Ftbl; Grls League; Interact Clb; Bus.

DUBY, PAULA K; John F Kennedy HS; Cypress, CA; (2); Bus Profs of Am; Cypress Coll; Lwyr.

DUCH, SAVRY; Oakland HS; Oakland, CA; (3); Art Clb; Computer Clb; English Clb; French Clb; German Clb; Key Clb; Math Clb; Science Clb; Spanish Clb; SADD.

DUCHENE, STACIE M; Savanna HS; Buena Park, CA; (3); Church Yth Grp; Dance Clb; Drill Tm; Ed.

DUCHI, CECELI; Enterprise HS; Redding, CA; (3); Mu Alpha Theta; Chorus; Var Crs Cntry; JV Tennis; High Hon Roll; Rotary Awd; Ecology Clb Pres; Natl Energy Educ Ldrshp Conf Staff Mem; Shasta Coll Vlntr Aide; Medcl Doctor.

DUCHOW, DEANNA A; Morse HS; San Diego, CA; (3); Church Yth Grp; Dance Clb; Drama Clb; ROTC; Science Clb; Church Choir; High Hon Roll; Hon Roll; Jr NHS; Drum Corps; CA Schlstc Fdrtn; Humboldt ST U; Park Mgmt.

DUCKSWORTH, SARAH F; Louisville HS; West Hills, CA; (2); Cmnty Wkr; GAA; VP Soph Cls; Rep Stu Cncl; Var Cheerldng; Hon Roll; AZ ST U; Bus Mgmt.

DUCLOS, ERIKA ANN; Argonaut HS; Jackson, CA; (2); Pres French Clb; FBLA; Band; Mrchg Band; Pres Soph Cls; Pres Stu Cncl; High Hon Roll; Hon Roll; JV Bsktbl; Var Sftbl; CSF; Acadmc Excllnc Awd; Natl Phys Ftnss Awd; Med.

DUCREE, JERMAINE; Inglewood HS; Inglewood, CA; (4); Am Leg Boys St; Church Yth Grp; Var Bsktbl; Crs Cntry; Capt Trk; Hon Roll; Natl Hnr Roll; Lafayette Coll; Mech Engrng.

DUCUSIN, KIMBERLY; Redwood HS; Visalia, CA; (1); Church Yth Grp; Drama Clb; French Clb; Science Clb; SADD; Chorus; Church Choir; Color Guard; Drill Tm; Flag Corp; Oral Interpretation Awd; Vocalist Of Yr Awd; 1st Pl Prcssnst & Winterguard Cmptn; Harvard; Scl Sci.

DUDDY, JENNIFER; St Genevieve HS; Arleta, CA; (4); 8/159; Church Yth Grp; JA; Pep Clb; Red Cross Aide; Drill Tm; Var Cheerldng; High Hon Roll; Psych Awd For Acad Excllnc; Teachers Aide; Prom Cmmtte; LMU; Psych.

DUDLEY, ANGELIQUE M; West HS; Bakersfield, CA; (1); Drama Clb; Spanish Clb; Elem Tchr.

DUDLEY, JULIA; Archbishop Mitty HS; San Jose, CA; (4); 34/215; Cmnty Wkr; French Clb; Math Clb; Yrbk; JV Bsktbl; Var L Trk; Var L Vllybl; French Hon Soc; High Hon Roll; Hon Roll; Jack & Jill Of Amer Orgnztn VP & Pres; Hampton U; Mass Commnctns.

DUDLEY, SIDRA V; Alexander Hamilton HS; Los Angeles, CA; (2); Church Yth Grp; Cmnty Wkr; Girl Scts; Teachers Aide; Tennis; UC Berkeley; Law.

DUEBBER, KRISTIN N; Maranatha HS; San Gabriel, CA; (4); Rptr Ed Yrbk; Hon Roll; Psych, Econ & Art Awds; San Diego ST U; Child Psych.

DUELKE, KIM J; Irvine HS; Irvine, CA; (2); Var Cheerldng; Hon Roll.

DUENAS, GERALD J; Carson HS; Carson, CA; (2); Church Yth Grp; Cmnty Wkr; Band; Jazz Band; Mrchg Band; Orch; Cit Awd; USC; Aero Engrng.

DUENAS, OLIVER; Bakersfield HS; Bakersfield, CA; (2); Intrml Ftbl; Intrml Wt Lftg; Intrml Wrstlng; Law Enforcement.

DUENAS, VERONICA R; William C Overfelt HS; San Jose, CA; (2); Intrml Bsktbl; Intrml Sftbl; Mesa Club; UC-BERKELEY; Engrng.

DUENEZ, ANTHONY A; Colton HS; Colton, CA; (2); Rep Stu Cncl; Intrml Var Bsbl; JV Intrml Ftbl; Hon Roll; Prfct Atten Awd; ITT; Electrnc Tech.

DUERKOP, SILKE; Monerey HS; W Germany; (4); AFS; German Clb; Thesps; Bsktbl; Vllybl; High Hon Roll; 3-D Art Outstndng Stu; Creative Wrtng Spcl Recognition; Educational Fndtn Exchange Stu.

DUERKSEN, DEBBIE B; Monterey Bay Acad; Salt Lake City, UT; (3); Drama Clb; German Clb; Library Aide; Teachers Aide; Church Choir; Ed Nwsp; VP Frsh Cls; Hon Roll; Prfct Atten Awd; Decathln Team; Loma Linda U-Riverside.

DUESING, MICHAEL P; Glendora HS; Glendora, CA; (4); Art Clb; German Clb; Band; Mrchg Band; Orch; Pep Band; Golf; Archt.

DUESTERHOFT, REBECCA; Westlake HS; Thousands Oaks, CA; (2); 150/431; Church Yth Grp; Color Guard; Flag Corp; Cit Awd; Hon Roll; Octagon Clb Hstrn.

DUFF, EVELYN; Wagner HS; APO San Francisc, CA; (4); 14/130; Spanish Clb; Sec Varsity Clb; School Play; Yrbk; Pres Stu Cncl; Powder Puff Ftbl; Var Tennis; Hon Roll; Pres NHS; Pres Acad Fit Awd; Pacaf Teen Ldrshp Awd Korea; Schlrshp Lcl Military Wvs Orgnztn; Grant Air Force Aid Soc; U Of Southern CA; Pre-Engrng.

DUFF, JESSICA; Soquel HS; Santa Cruz, CA; (3); 2/347; Band; Drill Tm; Mrchg Band; Pep Band; High Hon Roll; Ntl Merit Ltr; Prfct Atten Awd; Pres Acad Fit Awd; Sal; Cntrl Coast Sec Hnr Orchstra; Phy Thrpy.

DUFFIELD, CARLYLE; Norco HS; Norco, CA; (3); 14/433; Church Yth Grp; Cmnty Wkr; FBLA; Model UN; School Play; High Hon Roll; Voice Dem Awd; Library Aide; Math Clb; Spanish Clb; Acad Dcthln; Mock Trials; Schl Senate; Crmnl Law.

DUFFIELD, MARK; Canyon Springs HS; Moreno Valley, CA; (4); 55/550; FBLA; Office Aide; Teachers Aide; Off Jr Cls; Stu Cncl; High Hon Roll; Pres Acad Fit Awd; Gldn Sst Exmn Algbra U Hghst Hnrs; RCC; Med.

DUFFY, AMY J; Fresno Christian HS; Fresno, CA; (1); Church Yth Grp; Chorus; JV Tennis; High Hon Roll; Ed.

DUFFY, OWEN N; Bishop Montgomery HS; Torrance, CA; (3); Art Clb; Church Yth Grp; SADD; Crs Cntry; JV Trk; JV Var Vllybl; Tutor; Sales Assoc Various Jobs.

DUGADUGA, JOYCE; Loma Linda Acad; Loma Linda, CA; (3); Church Yth Grp; Dance Clb; French Clb; Office Aide; Temple Yth Grp; Chorus; Church Choir; JV Crs Cntry; Gym; JV Swmmng; La Sierra; Arch.

DUGAN, DAVID S; Del Campo HS; Carmichael, CA; (1); 40/461; Lbrn Boy Scts; 4-H; ROTC; Church Choir; Hon Roll; Comp Prgmng; Engrng.

DUGGAN, DALE A; Eisenhower HS; Rialto, CA; (3); Gov Hon Prg Awd; Hon Roll; NHS; Prfct Atten Awd; Financl Admin.

DUGGAN, SEAN P; Montgomery HS; Santa Rosa, CA; (3); JV Var Bsktbl; High Hon Roll; Jr NHS; Gldn St Exam-Geo With Hnrs; Cert Of Merit Frnch 88-89; MIP Bsktbl 89-90; Econ.

DUGOVIC, NANCY; Selma HS; Selma, CA; (3); 14/210; Church Yth Grp; Drama Clb; FCA; Intnl Clb; Letterman Clb; Office Aide; Ski Clb; Varsity Clb; Off Frsh Cls; Stu Cncl; 1st Tm All Leag Vllybl; Palmer Chiropractic.

DUHAMEL, JAMIE; Banning HS; Wilmington, CA; (3); Church Yth Grp; GAA; Teachers Aide; School Play; Nwsp; Yrbk; Rep Frsh Cls; Rep Sr Cls; VP Stu Cncl; Var Bsktbl; Congrssnl Yth Ldrshp Cncl; 1st Tm All Leag Vllybl Bsktbl Sftbl; Femal Athlt Yr 89; Hmcmng Prncss 2 Yrs; Cal Poly San Luis Obispo; Engr.

DUIMSTRA, DUSTIN J; Nogales HS; Walnut, CA; (2); 16/800; JV Bsbl; VP Ftbl; High Hon Roll; Hon Roll; NHS; Pop Warner Ftbl Little Schlrs 86; UCLA; Comp Sci.

DUJAN, PATRICK; Thousand Oaks HS; Thousand Oaks, CA; (3); 120/541; VP Spanish Clb; Teachers Aide; VP Sr Cls; Stu Cncl; JV Var Socr; JV Trk; Rotary Yth Ldrshp Awd 90 Ldrshp Camp; YMCA Yth Govt Pres 90; Psych.

DUK, CHRISTINE H; Los Amigos HS; Fountain Valley, CA; (3); 10/375; Hon Roll; Kwldg Bowl; Sci Olympd; USC; Phrmcy.

DUKAKIS, DAMON; Oak Park HS; Agoura Hills, CA; (2); JV Ftbl; JV Socr; Var Tennis; Regnl Theatre Prods; Syracuse U; Sprts Photo Jrnlst.

DUKE, BOBBY; Yucaipa HS; Yucaipa, CA; (2); Church Yth Grp; Spanish Clb; Acpl Chr; Pres Frsh Cls; Var L Tennis; High Hon Roll; Alive Clb; Actvts Coord; Theology.

DUKE, CHARLES J; Apple Valley HS; Apple Valley, CA; (1); High Hon Roll; US Space Acad Awd; Apple Valley Hnr Stu; CA Tech; Aero Space.

DUKE, DAVID K; Washington HS; Fremont, CA; (2); 1/310; Boy Scts; Church Yth Grp; JV Swmmng; High Hon Roll; Pres Acad Fit Awd; Eagle Scout Applcnt; JV Water Polo; Painting, Sculpting & Drwng; BYU; Airline Pilot.

DUKES, ANN K; Ventura HS; Ventura, CA; (3); 6/431; Sec Service Clb; Lit Mag; Sec Sr Cls; VP Stu Cncl; JV Var Bsktbl; JV Trk; Hon Roll; Ntl Merit Ltr; CSF; Jr Statesmen Of Amer; Yth Ambssdrs Intl, USSR; Engr.

DUKES, JENNIFER A; Paso Robles HS; Paso Robles, CA; (2); 53/317; Rep Soph Cls; Hon Roll.

DUKHOVNY, RICK; Whitney HS; Cerritos, CA; (2); Var Bsktbl; JV Swmmng; Var Trk; Engr.

DULABH, VIMAL; Encina HS; Sacramento, CA; (2); 4/221; Computer Clb; Lit Mag; Var Tennis; JV Wrstlng; High Hon Roll; Opt Clb Awd; Med.

DULAC, BRIAN MICHAEL; Poway HS; Poway, CA; (4); Boy Scts; Church Yth Grp; Cmnty Wkr; JV Var Tennis; High Hon Roll; Hon Roll; NHS; Pres Acad Fit Awd; Eagl Sct; Recog Outstndng Achvt Spnsh; Recog Locl Kiwns Clb Yth Salute; UCLA; Ecnmcs.

DULATRE, CORRINE L; Sweetwater Union HS; National City, CA; (2); Math Tm; SADD; Drill Tm; Ed Nwsp; Ed Yrbk; Intrml Cheerldng; Cit Awd; High Hon Roll; Hon Roll; Opt Clb Awd; Asian Intl Assn; UCLA; Med.

DULIN, RYAN N; San Jacinto HS; San Jacinto, CA; (2); 7/240; French Clb; Letterman Clb; SADD; Varsity Clb; Var Golf; Var Score Keeper; Cit Awd; DAR Awd; French Hon Soc; Hon Roll; Teens Agnst Drgs; Long Beach U; Intnl Bus.

DULISSE, CARRIE; Fred C Beyer HS; Modesto, CA; (3); VP Drama Clb; German Clb; Hosp Aide; School Play; Variety Show; Hon Roll; S Clb; Philosophy Clb.

DULKIN, RYAN S; Clayton Valley HS; Clayton, CA; (3); Boy Scts; Model UN; Temple Yth Grp; JV Ftbl; Chem Commendation; Med.

DULL, KERIN L; Mission Viejo HS; Mission Viejo, CA; (3); Pres Soph Cls; Stu Cncl; Var Sftbl; Var Vllybl; Var Vlybl Most Imprvd; Var Sftbl MVP & 1st Tm All South Coast Lg.

DULLABH, INDIRA; Lowell HS; San Francisco, CA; (3); Office Aide; SADD; Temple Yth Grp; Hon Roll; Schl Rcgntn In Gldn St Exam For Algebra; CSF; Pre-Med Clb; UC Berkeley; Pre-Med.

DULLACK, KATHRYN M; Santa Margarita HS; San Juan Capis, CA; (3); 11/235; Cmnty Wkr; Rep Stu Cncl; Var Capt Bsktbl; Var Capt Crs Cntry; Var Capt Trk; High Hon Roll; NHS; Stat Ftbl; Bonnie Bell Circle Of Excellence; 2nd Team Cross Country; Finalist Cross Country; Semi Final Basketball; Aeronautical Engineering.

DULLACK, STEVEN; St Michaels Prep; San Juan Capistra, CA; (2); Latin Clb; Var Bsktbl; Hon Roll; Jr NHS; CJSF; USNA Anapolis; Pilot.

DULLAS, CATHERINE M; Cajon HS; San Bernardino, CA; (3); Pres AFS; Key Clb; SADD; Stat Swmmng; NHS; Mock Trial Schl Ltr; Earth First; Frnch Schlrshp; Law.

DULNUAN, FRANCIS; Loyola HS; Los Angeles, CA; (2); Ftbl; Trk; Wt Lftg; Hon Roll; Pres Acad Fit Awd; Chmpnshp Ftbl Tm; Leag Chmpn Trk Tm; UCLA; Med.

DULTZ, SHANE; Oak Park HS; Agoura, CA; (4); 3/88; Treas Chess Clb; Teachers Aide; Hist Stu Cncl; Var L Trk; Vllybl; High Hon Roll; Pres Acad Fit Awd; Bank Of America Plaque Awd Sci, Math; CSF Mem; Peer Cnslng; Best In Sch In Physics, Math; U Puget Soung; Physics.

DULY, AMY; Burbank HS; Burbank, CA; (4); 1/425; Church Yth Grp; Drill Tm; Treas Frsh Cls; Pres Sr Cls; Rep Stu Cncl; JV Var Cheerldng; JV Vllybl; High Hon Roll; Opt Clb Awd; Pres Acad Fit Awd; CSF; Princpls Ldrshp Awd; UC Santa Barbara.

DUMAS, JOHN M; Encina Acad; Sacramento, CA; (3); 28/212; US Marines; Aviation.

DUMAS, KIMBERLY A; Arroyo Grande HS; Pismo Beach, CA; (3); Church Yth Grp; FCA; Teachers Aide; Rptr Nwsp; Score Keeper; Var Swmmng; Netwrk For Drg Free Yth; Law Enfrcmnt.

DUMBRIQUE, ANNA LIZA; Leuzinger HS; Hawthorne, CA; (2); VP Chorus; Stu Cncl; JV Crs Cntry; JV Trk; Hon Roll; FIL-AM Clb; Hnr Clsses; UC San Diego; Accntnt.

DUMMER, DAVE W; Village HS; Pleasanton, CA; (3); Cmnty Wkr; 4-H; Ski Clb; Cit Awd; Hon Roll; Skiing Schl Spnsrd; Hstry, Civics, Wrld Area Studies, Psych Acad Awds; Pblc Spkg Drug Awrnss Cmpgn; San Francisco U; Lawyer.

DUMPIT, PAMELA; Del Campo HS; Fair Oaks, CA; (2); 15/460; Rptr FBLA; Var Trk; CA Schlrshp Fed Mem; Ruture Bus Ldrs Am Mem Month; MS Future Bus Ldr 5th Pl Northern Sec; CA U Davis; Dentistry.

DUNAGAN, KATHERINE E; Victor Valley HS; Adelanto, CA; (4); Ski Clb; Color Guard; Vllybl; Hon Roll; CSF Secy, Lf; Cal Poly Pomona.

DUNAWAY, SANDRA D; Galt HS; Galt, CA; (2); Hosp Aide; Stage Crew; Treas Soph Cls; Cit Awd; High Hon Roll; Cert Of Exllnce German II; Bptst Chrch Yth Grp; Med.

DUNBAR, SUZANNE C; Aptos HS; Aptos, CA; (2); GAA; Key Clb; SADD; VP Frsh Cls; Var Bsktbl; Var Crs Cntry; Var Trk; Cit Awd; Hon Roll; Pres Acad Fit Awd; UC Santa Barbara; Ed.

DUNBAR, TARA A; Red Bluff Union HS; Red Bluff, CA; (3); Office Aide; Spanish Clb; SADD; Hon Roll; Karate Trphys; CSF Mem; Chico ST U.

DUNBARR, JAMES J; Vacaville HS; Vacaville, CA; (3); Church Yth Grp; Quiz Bowl; JV Var Socr; JV Var Wrstlng; High Hon Roll; Hon Roll; Dntstry.

DUNCAN, ASHLEY A; Newport Harbor HS; Newport Beach, CA; (2); JV Socr; JV Tennis; Var Trk; Hon Roll; CSF; U CA Davis; Vet Med.

DUNCAN, BONNIE; Red Bluff HS; Cottonwood, CA; (3); Am Leg Aux Girls St; Church Yth Grp; Drama Clb; School Musical; School Play; High Hon Roll; Hon Roll; Ldrshp Grp Church; Rep Friday Night Live Grp Drug & Alcohol Free Teen; Active Campus Bible Study; Art.

DUNCAN, CRISTI; Central Valley Christian HS; Visalia, CA; (2); Church Yth Grp; Pep Clb; Spanish Clb; Chorus; Stat Bsbl; Var Cheerldng; Hon Roll; Bus.

DUNCAN, GARY S; Wm S Hart HS; Valencia, CA; (2); Church Yth Grp; Hon Roll; Goldn St Exam Geom High Hnrs; CSF; CA Coll; Arch.

DUNCAN, JON R; Monte Vista HS; Danville, CA; (2); 45/440; Boy Scts; Church Yth Grp; JV Bsbl; JV Bsktbl; Hon Roll; Eagle Sct Awd; Coaches Awe Bsktbl; Schlr Athl Awd; Berkeley.

DUNCAN, KARA; Davis SR HS; Davis, CA; (2); Cmnty Wkr; Pep Clb; Ski Clb; Teachers Aide; Yrbk; Cheerldng; JV Fld Hcky; Gym; MVP Gymnastics; Mst Sprtd.

DUNCAN, KEN A; Oakdale HS; Oakdale, CA; (3); Drama Clb; Sec Frsh Cls; JV Var Ftbl; JV Socr; Var Trk; JV Var Wt Lftg; Golden St Exam Algebra.

DUNCAN, KIMBERLY; Chowchilla Union HS; Chowchilla, CA; (3); Pep Clb; Band; Sec Frsh Cls; Var JV Cheerldng; JV Tennis; High Hon Roll.

DUNCAN, MELISSA; Western HS; Anaheim, CA; (4); Pep Clb; Teachers Aide; Varsity Clb; Pres Jr Cls; VP Stu Cncl; JV Var Cheerldng; Hon Roll; NHS; Girls Leag; Pepperdine Yth Ctznshp Smnr 89; Cypress Coll; Nutrition.

DUNCAN, MICHAEL A; South San Francisco HS; South San Francis, CA; (2); Computer Clb; Math Clb; Hon Roll.

DUNCAN, MICHELLE D; Santa Teresa HS; San Jose, CA; (2); Cmnty Wkr; Color Guard; Hon Roll; Pres Acad Fit Awd; Police Magnet Pgm; Police Cadet VP; Mayor Yth Conf San Jose; Law.

DUNCAN, NICOLE M; Fairfield HS; Fairfield, CA; (2); Church Yth Grp; French Clb; Spanish Clb; SADD; Band; Chorus; Church Choir; Jazz Band; Mrchg Band; Rep Stu Cncl; Hnr Band; UC Santa Barbara; Psych.

DUNCAN, SHARI R; Elk Grove HS; Sacramento, CA; (4); 53/544; Church Yth Grp; Teachers Aide; Mgr(s); Powder Puff Ftbl; Socr; Hon Roll; Pres Acad Fit Awd; Comp Hntr Humpr Hrsebck Rdng; CA Schlrshp Fed Life Time Mem; Cal Poly; Aero Engr.

DUNCAN, SONYA L; Mount Diablo HS; W Pittsburg, CA; (1); Church Yth Grp; Hon Roll; Stanford; Medcl.

DUNCAN, STACEY; Mount Carmel HS; San Diego, CA; (3); Socr; Trk; Sundevil Standout Awd; Phys Thrpy.

DUNCAN, TARA L; Del Norte HS; Crescent City, CA; (3); Drill Tm; Yrbk; JV Powder Puff Ftbl; Hon Roll; Butte JC; Bus Mgmt.

DUNCANS, KATINA; Eisenhower HS; Colton, CA; (3); Band; Mrchg Band; Orch; School Musical; Var Capt Bsktbl; Sftbl; JV Capt Vllybl; Cit Awd; High Hon Roll; MAD; MVP Var Bsbl; Art Awd; MIP Music Awds; Bsktbl Player Of Yr 89-90; VA ST; Cmmrcl Artst.

DUNDEE, KAREN A; Don Antonio Lugo HS; Chino, CA; (4); 77/598; Cmnty Wkr; Office Aide; Spanish Clb; Cit Awd; High Hon Roll; Hon Roll; Jr NHS; NHS; CSF; Spanish Schlrshp; Acad Ltrs & Medal; Cal Poly Pomona; Bus Admin.

DUNG, PHAN N; Milpitas HS; Milpitas, CA; (1); French Clb; Hon Roll; Sports; Wrtng; Rdng.

DUNGAN, ANGIE L; Escondido HS; Escondido, CA; (1); Band; Mrchg Band; Pep Band; Attended A Seminar On Save The Trails; Attended Schl Brd Meeting To Fight For Rebldgng Schl Theater; SDSU; Journalism/English.

DUNGAN, LYNN; Exeter Union HS; Exeter, CA; (4); 1/179; Am Leg Aux Girls St; Key Clb; Letterman Clb; Rep Frsh Cls; VP Soph Cls; Pres Jr Cls; Pres Stu Cncl; Var Capt Swmmng; JV Vllybl; DAR Awd; Mock Trial Cmptn-St Fnlsts 88/90; Prncpls Ldrshp Awd; Stanford U; Dsgn Engrng.

DUNHAM, CHRISTY; Canyon HS; Conyon Country, CA; (2); 15/450; Pep Clb; JV Cheerldng; Var Trk; Hon Roll; CSF; UCLA; Grphc Art.

DUNHAM, GEORGE E; Colfax HS; Meadow Vista, CA; (3); 19/165; Treas Yrbk; L Bsbl; L Ftbl; Hon Roll; Cal Poly; Cvl Engr.

DUNHAM, MATTHEW; Bakersfield HS; Bakersfield, CA; (4); 88/707; Church Yth Grp; Hon Roll; JETS Awd; Materials Engrng.

DUNKLEY, MAUREEN; John Glenn HS; Norwalk, CA; (2); Church Yth Grp; Dance Clb; Teachers Aide; Church Choir; School Musical; School Play; Cit Awd; Hon Roll; Prfct Atten Awd; Lwyr.

DUNLAP, OLIVER Q; Las Lomas HS; Walnut Creek, CA; (4); French Clb; Model UN; Scholastic Bowl; Varsity Clb; Orch; School Play; Socr; NHS; Ntl Merit Ltr; Aud/Vis; Attended Emanuel Boys Sch London Eng 84-85, 87; Bronze Mdl 3rd Pl Sci Div Acad Decathalon; Berkeley; Archlgy.

DUNLAP, RACHEL E; Marymount HS; West Hollywood, CA; (3); Dance Clb; Hosp Aide; Science Clb; Spanish Clb; SADD; Chorus; Church Choir; Yrbk; Lit Mag; Trk; Co Fndr Schl Envrnmntl Clb; UCLA; Psych.

DUNLAP, TIMOTHY R; Apple Valley HS; Apple Valley, CA; (2); JA; Letterman Clb; Golf; Hon Roll; CSF; UCLA; Bus Admin.

DUNLEAVY, JILL; Rosary HS; Anaheim Hills, CA; (4); 38/135; JV Sftbl; High Hon Roll; Hon Roll; NHS; Mock Trl Tm 89-90; Stu Section Rep 89-90; Part-Time Job; Nordstrom Brass Plum Fashion Brd; St Marys Coll; Bus.

DUNMIRE, MARTHA-ANNE; Ventura HS; Ventura, CA; (3); Drama Clb; Hosp Aide; JCL; Thesps; School Play; Stage Crew; Swmmng; Tennis; Hon Roll; Career Day Co-Chrprsn; Cal ST Northridge; Phys Thrpy.

DUNN, ADAM B; Willow Glen HS; San Jose, CA; (3); 80/580; Science Clb; Var Capt Crs Cntry; JV Tennis; Var L Trk; Hon Roll; NHS; Ntl Merit SF; Hgh Hnrs On Goldn ST Exam Algbra & Geomtry; Regnl Qlfr In Trck; Bus Mgr.

DUNN, AMANDA L; Alta Loma HS; Alta Loma, CA; (2); Church Yth Grp; Cmnty Wkr; English Clb; Hon Roll; Peer Cnslng; Wrestling Stats; Azuza; Law.

DUNN, BRANDON W; Mc Farland HS; Mc Farland, CA; (3); Boy Scts; Church Yth Grp; Letterman Clb; School Play; Nwsp; Yrbk; Pres Sr Cls; Var Bsbl; JV Bsktbl; Var Ftbl; Bus.

DUNN, BRIAN; Oakmont HS; Roseville, CA; (4); 1/400; Church Yth Grp; VP Frsh Cls; Rep Stu Cncl; JV Bsktbl; JV Socr; Var Trk; High Hon Roll; Ntl Merit Ltr; Val; Math Clb; PG & E Schlrshp; NBA Schlrshp; Stanford.

DUNN, CORY J; Apple Valley HS; Apple Valley, CA; (2); 14/900; Key Clb; Chorus; Flag Corp; Orch; Variety Show; CSF; Princpals Hnr Roll; Med.

DUNN, FELIPE J; San Rafael HS; San Rafael, CA; (3); Cmnty Wkr; Latin Clb; Variety Show; JV Bsktbl; Grphc Arts.

DUNN, HEATHER M; Oakdale HS; Oakdale, CA; (3); Hosp Aide; Ski Clb; Teachers Aide; Varsity Clb; Phtg Yrbk; Rep Stu Cncl; Var Capt Swmmng; Trk; Hi-Deb Modeling Pgm Rep 3 Yrs.

DUNN, JENNIFER; Dana Hills HS; Laguna Niguel, CA; (4); Drama Clb; Capt Flag Corp; School Play; Stage Crew; San Diego ST U; Scndry Ed Math.

DUNN, JENNIFER; Mc Farland HS; Delano, CA; (1); Church Yth Grp; Dance Clb; 4-H; Teachers Aide; Cheerldng; Tennis; 4-H Awd; Hon Roll; CA ST Bakersfield; Teacher.

DUNN, JENNIFER M; Oak Park HS; Agoura Hills, CA; (1); 27/90; Church Yth Grp; Bsktbl; Crs Cntry; Trk; High Hon Roll; Hon Roll; Peer Cnslng.

DUNN, JODI K; Tehachapi HS; Tehachapi, CA; (4); 13/149; Am Leg Aux Girls St; Pres Spanish Clb; Band; Jazz Band; Lit Mag; Rptr Sr Cls; Hon Roll; Pres NHS; Co-Founder Of Envrnmntl Club; CSF Sec; Bakersfield; Engl.

DUNN, KIRSTI A; Orange HS; Orange, CA; (3); Letterman Clb; Varsity Clb; Co-Ed Yrbk; Sftbl; Vllybl; Hon Roll; NHS; Psych.

DUNN, LESLIE N; Trona Joint Unified School District; Trona, CA; (2); 11/24; Dance Clb; GAA; Varsity Clb; Drill Tm; Yrbk; VP Frsh Cls; Rep Soph Cls; VP Stu Cncl; Var Capt Bsktbl; Var Trk; Cert Of Recgntn Dance Team; Athl Awd Most Val Jv Vllybl; Athl Awd Most Val Jv Bsktbl.

DUNN, LETTY M; Orange Glen HS; Escondido, CA; (4); 35/450; Rep Key Clb; Spanish Clb; Band; Jazz Band; Mrchg Band; Orch; School Musical; Hon Roll; Treas NHS; Pres Acad Fit Awd; CSF; Band Cncl Mem; UC Santa Barbara; Span.

DUNN, LIZABETH; St Patrick-St Vincent HS; Vallejo, CA; (2); High Hon Roll.

DUNN, MAISHA; Diamond Bar HS; Diamond Bar, CA; (1); Art Clb; Church Yth Grp; SADD; Chorus; Hon Roll; 1st Pl Miss Pre Teen CA 90; Yale; Lwyr.

DUNN, MIKE; Don Antonio Lugo HS; Chino, CA; (3); Am Leg Boys St; Church Yth Grp; Cmnty Wkr; FCA; German Clb; Letterman Clb; Varsity Clb; Var L Ftbl; Var L Trk; Var Wt Lftg; Civil War Re Enactr; Criminlgy.

DUNN, NATALIE A; Mission Viejo HS; Mission Viejo, CA; (3); 72/444; Church Yth Grp; Teachers Aide; Hon Roll; Spirit Of Diablos Awd; Admin Asst.

DUNN, SHELLEY M; Grace Christian HS; San Diego, CA; (4); 2/36; Church Yth Grp; Drama Clb; French Clb; Band; Nwsp; NHS; Horsebackriding; Christ For The Nations; Mission.

DUNN, SHERRI L; Montclair HS; Ontario, CA; (1); Sftbl; Vllybl; Prfct Atten Awd; Inter Dcrtng.

DUNN, SUZY N; Riverside Polytechnic HS; Riverside, CA; (3); Church Yth Grp; Cmnty Wkr; Pep Clb; Church Choir; Hon Roll; Christian Ldrshp Awd; VP Secy Youth Grp At Church; 3rd Yr Puppet Ministry; Pt Loma Naz Clg; Commnctns.

DUNNE, BETH E; George Washington HS; San Francisco, CA; (3); Ski Clb; SADD; School Play; Rep Frsh Cls; Rep Soph Cls; Sec Jr Cls; Sec Sr Cls; Swmmng; High Hon Roll; Hon Roll; Peer Resrc Ctr Tutor; Gldn St Exam Awd; Spnsh Cert Achvt.

DUNNE, GUNDULA H; Academy Of Our Lady Of Peace; San Diego, CA; (1); Art Clb; Cmnty Wkr; 4-H; Hosp Aide; Math Tm; SADD; School Musical; High Hon Roll; NEDT Awd; CA Schlrshp Fed; Amnesty Intl; Friday Night Live; Cornell; Vet.

DUNNE, KETURAH A; Gompers Secondary HS; San Diego, CA; (1); 1/800; Office Aide; Hon Roll; Jr NHS; Opt Clb Awd; Prfct Atten Awd; Missionary.

DUNNICK, ERIC; Hawthorne HS; Hawthorne, CA; (4); 75/600; Am Leg Boys St; Var Ftbl; Swmmng; Wt Lftg; Wrstlng; Hon Roll; Ntl Merit SF; Service Clb; Rep Frsh Cls; Interact Clb-Trustee Of The Board; CA Schlrshp Fdrtn; LA Cnty Jr Lifeguard; US Naval Acad; Ocean Engrng.

DUNSHEE, JENNIFER; Righetti HS; Santa Maria, CA; (4); 52/356; Am Leg Aux Girls St; Ski Clb; SADD; Band; Mrchg Band; Pres Stu Cncl; Var L Bsktbl; JV Sftbl; JV Var Vllybl; Intrml Wt Lftg; Jr Statesmen Amer; Best Prog; YMCA Vol Haunted House; CA Poly; Bus.

DUNSMOOR, KIMBERLY J; Montgomery HS; Santa Rosa, CA; (2); Cmnty Wkr; Science Clb; Spanish Clb; Teachers Aide; Cheerldng; Sftbl; Vllybl; High Hon Roll; Jr NHS; Outstndng 9th Grade Awd; Schlr Athlt Awds Vllybl, Sftbl; Coaches Awd Sftbl; Span Awd; Clb Vllybl.

DUNSMORE, SCOTT; Montgomery HS; San Diego, CA; (3); 114/400; Church Yth Grp; Drama Clb; Spanish Clb; SADD; Thesps; School Play; Stage Crew; Rep Frsh Cls; Rep Soph Cls; Rep Jr Cls; Arspc Engrng.

DUNSTON, TRACY A; Riverbank HS; Riverbank, CA; (3); 6/110; VP SADD; Hon Roll; Prfct Atten Awd; Pres Acad Fit Awd; CSF Mem; Bio.

DUNTSCH, STEPHANIE L; Trinity HS; Lewiston, CA; (2); Ski Clb; Phtg Yrbk; Pres Soph Cls; JV Bsktbl; Var Gym; Var Trk; JV Vllybl; High Hon Roll; Pres Acad Fit Awd; Vllybl Clb; Teacher.

DUNTUGAN, ALBERT G; Saint Genevieve HS; Arleta, CA; (3); Am Leg Boys St; French Clb; Nwsp; Yrbk; JV Capt Vllybl; High Hon Roll; Hon Roll; CSF; Med.

DUNYON, JENNIFER S; Mission Viejo HS; Mission Viejo, CA; (2); Church Yth Grp; Chorus; Church Choir; JV Trk; Jr NHS; BYU; Nrsng.

DUONG, BAO H; Abraham Lincoln HS; San Francisco, CA; (3); Computer Clb; JA; Math Clb; Math Tm; Scholastic Bowl; Science Clb; High Hon Roll; CSF; Vietnamese Outstndng Stu Awd; Vietnamese Clb; UC Berkeley; Chem.

DUONG, BINH H; Crawford SR HS; San Diego, CA; (2); 1/383; French Clb; Math Tm; Tennis; Hon Roll.

DUONG, DONG; Van Nuys HS; Los Angeles, CA; (3); Teachers Aide; Prfct Atten Awd; Knights & Ladies; E Club; Athenians; UC Riverside.

DUONG, HAI H; Wilcox HS; Santa Clara, CA; (1); JV Tennis; Hon Roll; U CA Berkeley; Med.

DUONG, HIEN; Mark Keppel HS; Monterey Park, CA; (3); Math Clb; Science Clb; Cit Awd; Prfct Atten Awd; CSF; Hnrs Awd Alg I Gldn ST Exm.

DUONG, HIEN B; Elsinore HS; Lake Elsinore, CA; (4); 1/456; French Clb; FBLA; Spanish Clb; Trk; Bausch & Lomb Sci Awd; Hon Roll; NHS; Prfct Atten Awd; Irvine Valley Coll; Pre-Med.

DUONG, HONG; Orange HS; Orange, CA; (4); 21/400; Key Clb; Letterman Clb; Math Clb; Mu Alpha Theta; Varsity Clb; Tennis; Vllybl; Hon Roll; NHS; UCLA; Biochem.

DUONG, HUE L; Alexander Hamilton Academy Of Music; Los Angeles, CA; (3); Hosp Aide; Red Cross Aide; Service Clb; Spanish Clb; Chorus; Flag Corp; Jazz Band; Orch; Lit Mag; Rep Stu Cncl; Cardiology.

DUONG, HUNG; Alhambra HS; Alhambra, CA; (3); Chess Clb; VICA; JV Crs Cntry; Gold Medal In Vica Rgnl Cmptn Elect Tech Field; Elect Engr.

DUONG, JAMES SON; Bassett HS; La Puente, CA; (4); FBLA; Intnl Clb; VP Sr Cls; Var Bsktbl; NHS; Badminton JV&V; Outstndng Sr Awds; VP Assoctd Stu Bdy; Cal Poly Pomona U; Phrmcy.

DUONG, JOSEPHINE L; Oakland HS; Oakland, CA; (3); Computer Clb; Key Clb; Orch; Yrbk; Cit Awd; Hon Roll; Lac Hoang Club Treas; UC Davis.

DUONG, KATHY D; La Quinta HS; Santa Ana, CA; (4); 19/319; Teachers Aide; Orch; Cit Awd; Hon Roll; Bnk Of Amer Achvt Awd; CA Schlrshp Fed; Principals Mdlln; CSUF; Acctng.

DUONG, KIM C; Los Amigos HS; Santa Ana, CA; (3); 9/301; Cmnty Wkr; Hosp Aide; Quiz Bowl; Spanish Clb; Cit Awd; Hon Roll; Jr NHS; NHS; Gldn St Exam Rcgntn; UCSB; Bnkng.

DUONG, LAN T; Corona HS; Corona, CA; (3); 10/411; French Clb; Hosp Aide; Math Clb; Science Clb; Tennis; Yth Ldrshp For Actn; Piano; Dntstry.

DUONG, LE Q; Berkeley HS; Berkeley, CA; (3); French Clb; Intnl Clb; Lit Mag; JV Swmmng; Hon Roll; Hnr Soc; Badminton; UC Berkeley; Engrng.

DUONG, LINDA; Skyline HS; Oakland, CA; (2); Red Cross Aide; Drill Tm; Trk; Vllybl; High Hon Roll; Hon Roll; UC Berkeley.

DUONG, LONG; Mission San Jose HS; Fremont, CA; (3); 5/400; Debate Tm; French Clb; Hosp Aide; Letterman Clb; Math Clb; NFL; Science Clb; Ski Clb; Speech Tm; Varsity Clb; N Coast Sectn CA Finals; CA Chemathon; UCLA; Pre-Med.

DUONG, LUAN T; Corona HS; Corona, CA; (2); French Clb; Socr; Tennis; Hon Roll; AYSO.

DUONG, MICHAEL T; Fremont HS; San Jose, CA; (2); Debate Tm; French Clb; JA; Key Clb; NFL; Service Clb; Speech Tm; Rptr Yrbk; JV Crs Cntry; Var Tennis; Schl Recgntn Gldn St Exam Alg.

DUONG, MYXUAN; Dos Pueblos HS; Goleta, CA; (2); 39/270; Intnl Clb; Math Clb; Band; Mrchg Band; School Musical; Tennis; Hon Roll; NHS; CSF; :Inds Engr.

DUONG, NAM; C K Mc Clatchy HS; Sacramento, CA; (2); Math Clb; Math Tm; High Hon Roll; Acdmc Excllnc Awd Goldn ST Exm Hgh Hnrs; UC Davis; Med.

DUONG, NGHIA H; San Gabriel HS; Rosemead, CA; (1); Hon Roll; Med Field.

DUONG, NHAN H; Lowell HS; San Francisco, CA; (3); Tennis; Gov Hon Prg Awd; Hon Roll; Prfct Atten Awd; Vllybl Clb; Vietnamese Clb; Close Up; Tnns Clb; UC Davis.

DUONG, NHI; San Gabriel HS; San Gabriel, CA; (2); Cit Awd; Hon Roll.

DUONG, NHOC; Lurther Burbank HS; Sacramento, CA; (2); Cit Awd; Hon Roll; Prfct Atten Awd.

DUONG, PHAN N; Mark Keppel HS; Alhambra, CA; (1); FBLA; Hon Roll; Prfct Atten Awd; CSF; Arts.

DUONG, PHAT M; Norwalk HS; Norwalk, CA; (2); 5/400; Key Clb; Math Clb; Math Tm; Crs Cntry; Score Keeper; Trk; Hon Roll; Embry-Riddle; Aerntcl Engrng.

DUONG, PHAT V; Woodrow Wilson HS; Long Beach, CA; (3); #1 In Class; Teachers Aide; Nwsp; High Hon Roll; Hon Roll; NHS; Prfct Atten Awd; Pres Acad Fit Awd; Best Algebra Student; Engineering.

DUONG, PHUONG N; Mark Keppel HS; Alhambra, CA; (3); FBLA; Science Clb; Cit Awd; Hon Roll; Prfct Atten Awd; CSF; Friendshp Clb; U CA; Sci.

DUONG, QANH; Oakland HS; Oakland, CA; (2); Girl Scts; Hosp Aide; Comp Clb; Swmmg; CA ST Hayward; Med.

DUONG, QUOC; Richmond HS; San Pablo, CA; (3); Band; VP Stu Cncl; JV Var Ftbl; Var Tennis; High Hon Roll; Hon Roll; Prfct Atten Awd; Rotary Awd; Army Rsrve Ftbl Schlr/Athl Awd; Jack In Box Tnns Schlr/Athl Awd; CA U; Comp Sci.

DUONG, RATHAR; Robert A Millikan HS; Long Beach, CA; (2); Art Clb; Hon Roll; Prfct Atten Awd; Cambodian Stu Assn; Cal Poly; Arch.

DUONG, RICHARD H; West HS; Torrance, CA; (1); JCL; Latin Clb; Bsktbl; Crs Cntry; Trk; Wrstlng; Cit Awd; Pres Acad Fit Awd; Natl Latin Exam; Martial Arts Awd; Trk & Fld Awd; UC Berkeley; Med Doc.

DUONG, TAN; Edison HS; Stockton, CA; (3); Pres Boy Scts; Math Clb; Science Clb; Var Crs Cntry; NHS; Var Badminton; UC Santa Barbara Young Schlr Pgm; CSF & Photo Club; UCSB; Bio.

DUONG, THANH; Luther Burbank HS; Sacramento, CA; (4); 11/244; French Clb; Math Clb; Math Tm; ROTC; Spanish Clb; Speech Tm; Teachers Aide; Hon Roll; UC Berkeley; Civil Engr.

DUONG, TIEN; Tokay HS; Stockton, CA; (2); Elec Engr.

DUONG, TRANG T; Silvercreek HS; San Jose, CA; (2); Hon Roll; San Jose ST U; Pharm.

DUONG, UT T; Ramona HS; Riverside, CA; (2); 51/447; RCC; Acctg.

DUONG, VAN D; Independence HS; San Jose, CA; (4); 200/800; Pres Hosp Aide; Chrmn Intnl Clb; Model UN; Red Cross Aide; Science Clb; Service Clb; Varsity Clb; Pres Frsh Cls; Rep Soph Cls; Rep Jr Cls; Santa Clara Cnty Yth Ambssdr Schlrshp; Wrld Affrs Cncl Schlrshp; Mayors Yth Rcgntn Awd; De Anza Coll; Intl Rltns.

DUPIRE, GERALD E; Argonaut HS; Jackson, CA; (2); AFS; FBLA; Science Clb; Spanish Clb; High Hon Roll; U San Diego; Marine Bio.

DUPLER, DEANNA M; Artesia HS; Cerritos, CA; (3); 33/371; L Color Guard; Drill Tm; Flag Corp; Mrchg Band; Stat Socr; Intrml Swmmng; Cit Awd; High Hon Roll; Hon Roll; Acad Awds; Pet Asstnc League; CSULB; Phys Therapy.

DUPRE, JODIE A; Mt View HS; Los Altos, CA; (2); French Clb; Teachers Aide; Sec Frsh Cls; JV Sftbl; JV Vllybl; Cit Awd; High Hon Roll; Student Of The Month Economics & Health.

DUPREE, AYANNA L; Oakland Technical HS; Oakland, CA; (2); Quiz Bowl; Off Soph Cls; Hon Roll; Howard; Psych.

DUPREY, JEANINE E; Bella Vista HS; Citrus Heights, CA; (2); SADD; Rptr Nwsp; High Hon Roll; Hon Roll; International Order Of The Rainbow For Girls; UC Davis; Pediatrician.

DUPREY, JENNIFER L; Warren HS; Downey, CA; (3); Ski Clb; Bsktbl; Long Beach; Bus.

DUPUY, CHANTELLE E; Victor Valley HS; Victorville, CA; (2); Church Yth Grp; Drama Clb; Girl Scts; SADD; Band; Var Cheerldng; Hon Roll; Grl Sct Slvr Awd; Lsu; Engl.

DUQUE, ALFREDO; Chaffey HS; Ontario, CA; (3); JV Trk; Arch.

DUQUE, JEANNE; Granger JR HS; National City, CA; (1); 2/268; Church Choir; Ed Nwsp; Ed Yrbk; Co-Capt Cheerldng; Vllybl; High Hon Roll; Hon Roll; Associated Stu Body Rep Gen Mgr; Asian Intl Assn Rep Cmmssnr Actvts; Books & Beyond; Harvard; Law.

DUQUETTE, AIMEE; West HS; Bakersfield, CA; (3); 7/444; Dance Clb; Key Clb; SADD; Drill Tm; Cheerldng; Diving; High Hon Roll; Hon Roll; NHS; Active Teens Against Cmnty Crime; U Of CA; Educ.

DURAN, EMILY; Alemany HS; Granada Hills, CA; (1); Church Yth Grp; Pep Clb; Chorus; Drill Tm; Variety Show; Bsktbl; Hon Roll; Prfct Atten Awd; Psych.

DURAN, JANETTE L; Lindsay HS; Lindsay, CA; (1); GAA; Spanish Clb; SADD; Hon Roll; JV Bsktbl; Var Score Keeper; Var Sftbl; Natrl Hlpr; La Vern; Teacher.

DURAN, JOE C; Live Oak HS; Live Oak, CA; (4); 12/50; FFA; SADD; Stu Cncl; Var Bsbl; Var Capt Ftbl; Var Wrstlng; Hon Roll; Pres Acad Fit Awd; ROP Stu Yr; Blck Lo Pres 89-90; Butte Coll; Elec Tchnlgy.

DURAN, MARIA; Point Loma SR HS; San Diego, CA; (2); 206/482; Interact Club; AVID Club; SDSU; Cosmotologist.

DURAN, SALVADOR J; Alisal HS; Salinas, CA; (2); Cmnty Wkr; Drama Clb; FBLA; Science Clb; VP Frsh Cls; Rep Soph Cls; Cit Awd; Jr NHS; Hon Roll; Ldrshp Awd; Japanese Outstndng Achvt; Sci Tchr.

DURAN, TERESA; Mercy HS; S San Francisco, CA; (3); Cmnty Wkr; French Clb; GAA; Spanish Clb; Chorus; JV Vllybl; Hon Roll; NHS; Prfct Atten Awd; Pace Tm 2 Yrs; Hostess Clb; Dir Greeters; UC Davis; Physcn.

DURAN, YVONNE; Morro Bay SR HS; Morro Bay, CA; (3); 6/200; Drama Clb; School Musical; School Play; Stage Crew; High Hon Roll; Hon Roll; CSF; Cal Poly; Drama.

DURAND, MICHELLE M; Amos Alonzo Stagg HS; Stockton, CA; (1); Debate Tm; NFL; Speech Tm; Thesps; School Musical; High Hon Roll; San Joaquin Cnty Zoological Soc; Stanford U; Jrnlsm.

DURAND, ROBERT M; Loyola HS; Los Angeles, CA; (2); Computer Clb; Rptr Nwsp; Rep Jr Cls; Intrml Bsktbl; Var Swmmng; Hon Roll; Jr NHS; Pres Acad Fit Awd; Water Plo MVP 89; CSF; Swim Instr YMCA; UCLA.

DURANI, AFSANA; San Lorenzo HS; San Leandro, CA; (2); Cmnty Wkr; Intnl Clb; Hon Roll; Big Brothers & Sisters; Minority Grp; Fri Nght Live; Psych.

DURANI, AHMAD ZIA; James Logan HS; Fremont, CA; (4); Cmnty Wkr; English Clb; Office Aide; Spanish Clb; Teachers Aide; Nwsp; Socr; Trk; Vllybl; Wt Lftg.

DURANTE, JOHN W; Upland HS; Upland, CA; (2); Church Yth Grp; Skate Brdng Sponsorship; Frontiersman Camping; Graphic Artist.

DURANTE, TERRI R; San Dimas HS; San Dimas, CA; (2); Church Yth Grp; Cmnty Wkr; Dance Clb; GAA; Pep Clb; Drill Tm; JV Cheerldng; Var Socr; Cit Awd; Hon Roll; Camp Couns.

DURAZO, ELIZABETH; Del Oro HS; N Highlands, CA; (3); 89/266; Teachers Aide; Chorus; Sacramento ST U; Bus Mgmt.

DURBIN, MICHELLE M; Santa Teresa HS; San Jose, CA; (3); French Clb; Hosp Aide; SADD; Yrbk; Hon Roll; San Jose ST; Bus.

DURDEN, WILL K; Argonaut HS; Ione, CA; (2); Boy Scts; FHA; Key Clb; Ski Clb; School Play; Wrstlng; Hon Roll; UCSC; Military Pilot.

DURE, EVELYN F; South Bay Luthern HS; Lennox, CA; (3); Church Yth Grp; Office Aide; Church Choir; School Musical; Var Bsktbl; Var Sftbl; Var Trk; Var Capt Vllybl; High Hon Roll; Hon Roll; Bus.

DUREN, BRIAN A; Lynwood HS; Lynwood, CA; (3); Computer Clb; Debate Tm; Math Clb; Teachers Aide; School Play; JV Bsktbl; Var L Ftbl; Var Trk; Wt Lftg; High Hon Roll; Vrsty Ftbl RB & DB, MVP Offnsve Plyr; Bus.

DURFEE, DANIELLE; Ontario HS; Ontario, CA; (3); 38/452; Church Yth Grp; Cmnty Wkr; Pres VP Key Clb; Science Clb; L Drill Tm; JV Socr; Opt Clb Awd; High Hon Roll; Ntl Merit SF; Intrml Wt Lftg; Sci Fair Awd; Voc Bible Schl-Craft Ldr, Storyteller & Dip Ldr; Marahatha Club; Biola U; Missionary.

DURHAM, BENJAMIN C; University HS; Irvine, CA; (2); Boy Scts; JV Bsbl; JV Bsktbl.

DURHAM, MATT; Chaminade College Prep; Northridge, CA; (3); Boy Scts; VP Soph Cls; VP Stu Cncl; Var L Ftbl; Var L Swmmng; Var Wt Lftg; Hon Roll; UC San Diego; Arch.

DURHAM, RICK D; Anally HS; Sebastopol, CA; (2); Stu Store; Atty.

DURHAM, TINA R; Orange HS; Orange, CA; (3); Church Yth Grp; French Clb; Hosp Aide; Acpl Chr; Church Choir; Drill Tm; Var Cheerldng; JV Swmmng; High Hon Roll; NHS; CSF; Chamber Singer; BYU; Music.

DURK, TRISHA A; Glendora HS; Glendora, CA; (3); Stat Ftbl; Stat Trk; Hon Roll; Hnrs Awd.

DURONCELAY, YASHAWNA K; John W North HS; Riverside, CA; (2); 121/510; Drama Clb; School Musical; School Play; Stage Crew.

DURR, ELIANA; Foothill HS; Pleasanton, CA; (2); French Clb; FBLA; Hosp Aide; U CA; Med.

DURR, LEILA I; Tustin HS; Tustin, CA; (2); 7/477; AFS; Girl Scts; Hosp Aide; Key Clb; Letterman Clb; Stu Cncl; Var L Crs Cntry; Var L Trk; High Hon Roll; Pres Acad Fit Awd.

DURRELL, PAUL M; Yosemite HS; Oakhurst, CA; (2); Church Yth Grp; Drama Clb; French Clb; Pres SADD; School Play; Stage Crew; Ed Yrbk; Treas Jr Cls; L Crs Cntry; Hon Roll; Fresno St U Drama Fest-Set Dsgn Super Rtng; YHS Drama Fstvl-Monologues Command Prfrmnc; Cal Poly San Luis Obisp; Jrnlsm.

DURRER, BETTY L; Fontana HS; Fontana, CA; (2); Church Yth Grp; Chorus; Church Choir; Stage Crew; Crs Cntry; Child Psych.

DURST, ERIN R; Stagg HS; Stockton, CA; (1); Church Yth Grp; Cmnty Wkr; Dance Clb; Drama Clb; GAA; Key Clb; Ski Clb; School Play; Stage Crew; Rep Frsh Cls; Harvard; Bus.

DURYEA, SUZANNE; Bella Vista HS; Fair Oaks, CA; (1); Girl Scts; SADD; JV Powder Puff Ftbl; Var Trk; Fri Night Live; San Diego ST; Jrnlsm.

DUSEK, NICOLE DENISE; Southbay Christian HS; San Jose, CA; (2); Church Yth Grp; Band; Chorus; Church Choir; School Musical; Sec Frsh Cls; VP Soph Cls; Cit Awd; NHS; Teach Piano Lessons.

DUSKIS, MICHAEL; Western HS; Cypress, CA; (4); 8/307; Boy Scts; Drama Clb; NFL; Quiz Bowl; Treas Speech Tm; Band; Nwsp; Chrmn Lit Mag; Hon Roll; NHS; Ptry Clb; CA Schlrshp Fdrtn; Gldn St Exmntn Geo With Hnrs; Cmmnctn.

DUSSERT, ALAIN; Magnolia HS; Anaheim, CA; (4); Band; Jazz Band; Mrchg Band; Orch; Pep Band; Rptr Nwsp; Var Ftbl; JV Wrstlng; NHS; Ntl Merit SF; Ride Oper Knotts Berry Frm; Acad Deca; Stanford; Earth Sci.

DUTCHER, DABRINA D; Sherman E Burroughs HS; Ridgecrest, CA; (2); Pres Church Yth Grp; Pres 4-H; Stage Crew; Rptr Nwsp; Lit Mag; Rep Frsh Cls; Rep Soph Cls; 4-H Awd; High Hon Roll; Jr NHS; Naturalst Clb; Cnty Supervsr Vlntr Work; UC Riverside; Chem.

DUTERTE, ESTHER G; Independence HS; San Jose, CA; (3); Art Clb; Library Aide; Pep Clb; Service Clb; Teachers Aide; Bsktbl; Vllybl; Bdmntn; Real Estate.

DUTHLER, KRISTIN LYNN; Contra Costa Christian HS; Walnut Creek, CA; (4); 4/29; Art Clb; Church Yth Grp; Drama Clb; GAA; Letterman Clb; Office Aide; Ski Clb; Spanish Clb; Teachers Aide; Varsity Clb; Calvin Coll; Phys Thrpy.

DUTRA, AARON S; Liberty Union HS; Brentwood, CA; (1); Cmnty Wkr; 4-H; Hon Roll; Vlntr; Golf; UC Berkeley; Mech Engr.

DUTRA, CARLA F; San Jose High Acad; San Jose, CA; (2); Portugues Clb; Tutor; Evergreen Valley Coll; Comp Prng.

DUTRA, CARRIE M; Hanford HS; Hanford, CA; (2); Church Yth Grp; FBLA; JV Sftbl; Acad Ltr Lamp; Fresno ST; Psych.

DUTRA, DIANA S; Don Antonio Lugo HS; Chino, CA; (2); German Clb; Band; Church Choir; Mrchg Band; Orch; School Musical; School Play; Variety Show; Off Soph Cls; Cit Awd; Lang Interpreter.

DUTRA, SHIRLEY A; North Salinas HS; Salinas, CA; (3); Pep Clb; Spanish Clb; Teachers Aide; Ed Yrbk; High Hon Roll; NHS; Rotary Awd; Peer Ldrshp; Advncd Plcmnt Clb Treas; Geom Golden St Exam Acad Excllnc Awd 89; Sonoma ST U; Educ.

DUTTON, DEBBIE A; Colfax HS; Colfax, CA; (2); 18/194; Church Yth Grp; French Clb; Girl Scts; SADD; Varsity Clb; Var Bsktbl; Var Tennis; High Hon Roll; Fri Night Live; Med.

DUTTON, LISA; Simi Valley HS; Simi Valley, CA; (3); 299/735; Church Yth Grp; Drama Clb; Girl Scts; Chorus; Color Guard; School Musical; Cit Awd; Hon Roll; Pres Acad Fit Awd; Moorpark; RN.

DUTTON, MATTHEW ROBERDS; Nevada Union HS; Grass Valley, CA; (4); 4/500; Capt Var Bsktbl; Ftbl; JV Tennis; High Hon Roll; FCA; NHS; Ntl Merit SF; Pres Acad Fit Awd; U CA Davis Chncllrs Schlr; Ed Comm Schlrshp Fndtn Fnlst; U CA Davis; Engrng.

DUTTON, NIKKI S; Mount Carmel HS; San Diego, CA; (3); FFA; Photo; Hira Yth Pgm 3 Yrs; Animals.

DUYAN, DALE ANTHONY; Bon Bosco Tech Inst; West Covina, CA; (2); Church Yth Grp; Cmnty Wkr; Service Clb; Stage Crew; Cit Awd; High Hon Roll; NHS; Prfct Atten Awd; Pres Acad Fit Awd.

DUYAN, DEBORAH A; San Gabriel Mission HS; W Covina, CA; (4); Math Clb; Science Clb; Hon Roll; NHS; Prfct Atten Awd; CSF; Bank Of America Achvmt Awd Sci; Bank Of America Achvmt Awd Sci; Spec Recog Various Subjects; Loyola Marymount U; Poly Sci.

DUYVESTEYN, WIESKE S; Homestead HS; San Jose, CA; (4); Hosp Aide; Model UN; Teachers Aide; Diving; High Hon Roll; NHS; British O-Levls; MIT; Chem Engrng.

DUZAN, JAMI M; Hawthorne HS; Hawthorne, CA; (1); Church Yth Grp; Drama Clb; Church Choir; School Musical; Dominican Republic Trip; New Lite Clb; Pacific Christian Coll; Psych.

DVORAK, DEVERY; Village Christian Schl; Sun Valley, CA; (3); 20/127; English Clb; Math Clb; Mu Alpha Theta; Science Clb; Spanish Clb; Varsity Clb; VP Sr Cls; Rep Stu Cncl; Vllybl; Hon Roll; UC San Diego; Bio.

DVORAK, KATHARINE A; El Camino HS; Carmichael, CA; (3); 27/366; Key Clb; Cit Awd; NHS; Friday Night Live Club Mem; Northwestern; Jrnlsm.

DWIGHT, LINDA M; Redlands HS; Redlands, CA; (2); Drama Clb; School Play; Stage Crew; Socr; U Redlands; Psych.

DY, AILEEN L; Valley HS; Sacramento, CA; (2); #111 In Class; Intnl Clb; Hon Roll; Pres Acad Fit Awd; Presdntl Awd.

DYAL, JAMES E; Tokay HS; Stockton, CA; (2); 8/700; Boy Scts; Church Yth Grp; JV Swmmng; JV Wrstlng; High Hon Roll; Hon Roll; Rotary Awd; Church Choir; Variety Show; Pres Acad Fit Awd; Engrng.

DYAL, SUSAN; Southbay Christian Schl; Mountain View, CA; (2); Church Yth Grp; Chorus; School Musical; Hon Roll; CSF; Engr.

DYER, CHRIS J; C K Mc Clatchy HS; Sacramento, CA; (1); 167/588; ROTC; Socr; U Of NV; Lit.

DYER, CHRISTINA L; Buena HS; Ventura, CA; (3); Office Aide; Teachers Aide; Variety Show; JV Capt Swmmng; JV Vllybl; Hon Roll; Comp Assisted Engr.

DYER, J GREG; San Dieguito HS; Olivenhain, CA; (2); 24/630; Boy Scts; Church Yth Grp; Quiz Bowl; Scholastic Bowl; Rptr Lit Mag; JV Bsktbl; JV Trk; High Hon Roll; CSF; Law.

DYER, JANELLE M; Los Banos HS; Los Banos, CA; (1); Drama Clb; Rep Frsh Cls; JV Swmmng; High Hon Roll; CSF; Psych.

DYER, JOHN S; Terra Nova HS; Pacifica, CA; (2); Church Yth Grp; Pres DECA; Spanish Clb; SADD; Thesps; Mgr Stage Crew; Sec Soph Cls; VP Stu Cncl; HOBY Ldrshp Awd; Stu Store Mgr; Cal Poly; Bus Admin.

DYER, JORJA CHRISTEEN; Enterprise HS; Redding, CA; (3); 101/420; Church Yth Grp; 4-H; French Clb; Teachers Aide; Cit Awd; 4-H Awd; Hon Roll; Humbolt U; Legal Asstnt.

DYER, ROBERT; Santa Monica HS; Malibu, CA; (4); Treas SADD; Teachers Aide; Band; High Hon Roll; Hon Roll; Jr NHS; Rotary Awd; Sealbearer; Ldrshp Awd Cncrt Band 1987; Treas Of SADD; U Of CA Santa Barbara; Stud.

DYER, SHANNON R; Clovis West HS; Fresno, CA; (3); Intnl Clb; Ski Clb; SADD; Score Keeper; U CA Santa Barbara; Bus Admin.

DYER, TOM; Oak Ridge HS; El Dorado Hills, CA; (2); 61/300; Band; JV Bsktbl; Var Tennis; Hon Roll; UC Berkeley.

DYER, TONJA; Skyline HS; Oakland, CA; (3); Church Yth Grp; Drama Clb; ROTC; Band; Drill Tm; Mrchg Band; School Musical; Variety Show; Rep Frsh Cls; Rep Soph Cls; Upwrd Bnd Mills Coll; Law Post; UC Berkeley Partnrshp Pgm; Hampton Inst; Engrng.

DYKSTRA, ANDY; Chino HS; Chino, CA; (4); Church Yth Grp; Tennis; Hon Roll; Pres Schlr; CA Poly Pomona; Acctng.

DYKSTRA, JENNIFER D; Boron JR/Sr HS; Boron, CA; (2); Church Yth Grp; Band; Jazz Band; Mrchg Band; Pep Band; JV Var Sftbl; JV Var Vllybl; Hon Roll.

DYKSTRA, KYLE D; Valley Christian HS; Bellflower, CA; (3); Boy Scts; Church Yth Grp; Ski Clb; Teachers Aide; Acpl Chr; Church Choir; School Musical; Rep Jr Cls; Sec Sr Cls; Stu Cncl; Azusa Pacific.

DYKSTRA, STEVEN A; California HS; Whittier, CA; (3); 92/338; Aud/Vis; Church Yth Grp; Cmnty Wkr; Computer Clb; Q&S; Quiz Bowl; Service Clb; Teachers Aide; Yrbk; Lit Mag; Nuclear Engrng.

DYONIZIAK, IZA S; Chula Vista HS; Chula Vista, CA; (2); 19/605; Church Yth Grp; Drama Clb; Variety Show; Hon Roll; Pres Acad Fit Awd; Physics.

DYRR, JOANNA; Riverside Poly HS; Riverside, CA; (4); 28/385; Am Leg Aux Girls St; Key Clb; Yrbk; Sec Jr Cls; Stu Cncl; Trk; Hon Roll; Pres Acad Fit Awd; CSF; Water Polo Stats; UCR; Bus.

DYRSSEN, NICOLE J; California Lutheran HS; Vista, CA; (3); Church Yth Grp; Drama Clb; Hosp Aide; JA; Office Aide; Chorus; Church Choir; School Play; Variety Show; Lit Mag; Speech Thrpy.

DYRUD, MARTINUS J; Vacaville HS; Rawlins, WY; (4); 5/570; Boy Scts; Computer Clb; Key Clb; Nwsp; Golf; Hon Roll; NHS; Pres Acad Fit Awd; Pres Schlr; Brown U; Ecnmcs.

DYSART, STEVE; Santa Paul HS; Santa Paula, CA; (2); 100/400; Church Yth Grp; Letterman Clb; Ski Clb; Varsity Clb; JV Var Bsbl; Var Crs Cntry; Var Ftbl; JV Var Socr; JV Wrstlng; Surfing, Plyng Drums; CSULA; Music.

DYSE, MICHAEL M; Grossmont HS; El Cajon, CA; (2); 73/429; Hstry.

DYSON, DE ANNA L; San Marcos HS; San Marcos, CA; (3); Church Yth Grp; Cmnty Wkr; Teachers Aide; Band; Chorus; Jazz Band; Mrchg Band; Pep Band; Hon Roll.

DYSON, DIYA; Orange Glen HS; Escondido, CA; (1); Cmnty Wkr; Drama Clb; Library Aide; Office Aide; Teachers Aide; Orch; School Play; Score Keeper; Trk; Hon Roll; Engrng.

DYSON, ERIC L; Chadwick Schl; Los Angeles, CA; (4); Cmnty Wkr; Letterman Clb; Varsity Clb; Var L Bsktbl; Var L Trk; High Hon Roll; Hon Roll; Skydiving; U Of PA; Law.

DYSON, GINA D; Don Antonio Lugo HS; Chino, CA; (2); 15/700; Church Yth Grp; Key Clb; Var Trk; High Hon Roll; CSF 2 Yrs; Hnr Guard Grad & Baccalaureate Ceremonies.

DZEKOV, JEANNE; Palm Springs HS; Palm Springs, CA; (3); Cmnty Wkr; Hosp Aide; Socr; Cit Awd; Hon Roll; VP Amnetsy Intl; Jr Statesment Of Amer; Pltcl Sci.

DZHEREDZHYAN, ASMIK; Hoover HS; Glendale, CA; (2); Dance Clb; Math Tm; Off Frsh Cls; Tennis; UCLA; Phy.

EACOTT, JULIE; Mount Carmel HS; San Diego, CA; (1); Church Yth Grp; Capt JV Cheerldng; Capt Sftbl; Hon Roll; U Santa Barbara; Photgrphy.

EAGAN, JEANNI M; Mayfair HS; Paramount, CA; (4); 7/180; Dance Clb; English Clb; JA; VP Spanish Clb; Teachers Aide; Variety Show; High Hon Roll; CSF; Hlth Stu Yr 88; Pre-Law.

EAGAN, TIMOTHY M; Rio Lindo Acad; Salt Lake City, UT; (3); Church Yth Grp; German Clb; Ski Clb; Band; Mrchg Band; Co-Ed Yrbk; JV Bsktbl; JV Ftbl; JV Sftbl; JV Wt Lftg; Walla Walla Coll; Airline Plt.

EAGLE, MELODIE; La Jolla Country Day Schl; Rancho Santa Fe, CA; (2); French Clb; Key Clb; Chorus; School Musical; School Play; JV Cheerldng; Hon Roll; Theatre Arts.

EAGLE, RYAN; Los Alamitos HS; Los Alamitos, CA; (3); Ftbl; Wt Lftg; Hon Roll; Qualfd Schl Rcgntn Gldn St Exm Geomtry; Cert Hnr Outstndng Achvt Eng; Wght Lftng, Ftbl; USC; Elec Engr.

EAGLESTON, TRACY L; Oakmont HS; Roseville, CA; (3); Service Clb; SADD; Teachers Aide; Varsity Clb; Sec Stu Cncl; Var Sftbl; Var Vllybl; High Hon Roll.

EAGLETON, DEANNA; Williams HS; Williams, CA; (1); GAA; Sec Frsh Cls; JV Bsktbl; Var Sftbl; JV Vllybl; Hon Roll; CA Schlstc Fdn; UC Davis; MD.

EAGLETON, KELLIE; Abraham Lincoln HS; San Francisco, CA; (2); GAA; VP Soph Cls; Var Bsktbl; Var Sftbl; Var Vllybl; Soph Clb; UC Berkeley; Nursing.

EAGLIN, ROBERT; San Gorgonio HS; San Bernardino, CA; (3); Varsity Clb; Bsktbl; Wt Lftg; Hon Roll; BSU Clb; Psych.

EALEY, KIMBERLY; Washington Prepatory HS; Los Angeles, CA; (3); Church Yth Grp; Math Tm; Teachers Aide; Church Choir; Rep Frsh Cls; Stat Swmmng; Hon Roll; Prfct Atten Awd; Math-Sci Magnet Pgm; Amer Talent Search; Yth Usher Board Pres; CA ST Dominguez Hills; Bus.

EANG, SAN K; J F Kennedy HS; Cypress, CA; (3); 1/30; Bsktbl; Won 2nd Plc Yth Expo Orange Cnty Frgrnds; Dfrftng; CA ST Plytechnic U; Archt.

EANS, TASHAWN; Inglewood HS; Inglewood, CA; (4); Stu Cncl; Var Co-Capt Trk; Var Capt Vllybl; High Hon Roll; Black Hstry Club Outstndng African-Amer; Intl Rltns.

EARL, SHERRAL L; Chester HS; Chester, CA; (2); Church Yth Grp; Drama Clb; School Play; Stat Bsktbl; L Vllybl; Hon Roll; Yth To Yth.

EARL, WAYNE B; Sunset HS; Hayward, CA; (2); Boy Scts; Chess Clb; Computer Clb; ROTC; Teachers Aide; UC Berkley; Lwyr.

EARL, ZACHARY S; Village Christian Schls; Glendale, CA; (1); Chess Clb; Church Yth Grp; Spanish Clb; NHS; Chrch Day Camp Cnslr.

EARLS, EVELYN; Porterville HS; Porterville, CA; (1); Drama Clb; Cheerldng; Nrsng.

EARLY, ROBERT; Foothill HS; Pleasanton, CA; (3); 15/250; Church Yth Grp; FBLA; Rptr Nwsp; VP Frsh Cls; Sec Soph Cls; Treas Jr Cls; JV Bsbl; Var Bsktbl; Var Ftbl; Hon Roll.

EARLY, SANDY L; Grossmont HS; La Mesa, CA; (3); 83/385; School Musical; Lit Mag; Stu Cncl; Hon Roll; Teachers Aide; Acpl Chr; Chorus; Chr Dept Rep; Hnrs Ensmbl & Chr; Tchrs Aide Spcl Ed Stdnts; Cmmssnr Sls 88-89; Tallier Art Cnvntn 89-90; Music.

EARNEST, JENNIFER L; Victor Valley HS; Hesperia, CA; (4); 39/335; Pep Clb; Spanish Clb; Hon Roll; CSF; Schlrshp; San Diego ST U; Marktng.

EARNEST, KEITH; Fall River HS; Mc Arthur, CA; (2); Art Clb; Church Yth Grp; 4-H; FFA; Rep Stu Cncl; DAR Awd; 4-H Awd; High Hon Roll; Hon Roll; Pres Acad Fit Awd; Amer JR Herefrd Assoc Ntl Spch Cntst; CCSF.

EASER, KATHERINE L; Gretchen Whitney HS; Cerritos, CA; (3); Cmnty Wkr; Dance Clb; Drama Clb; JA; Key Clb; Variety Show; Prom Cmmttee.

EASLEY, CHRIS R; Dos Palos HS; Dos Palos, CA; (1); AFS; JV Bsktbl; JV Ftbl; High Hon Roll; CSF.

EASLEY, CHRISTINE; Bear River HS; Auburn, CA; (2); Acpl Chr; Band; Chorus; Jazz Band; Pep Band; Cit Awd; Hon Roll; Hnr Bnd; Music.

EASLEY, LA GINA S; Washington HS; Los Angeles, CA; (3); Office Aide; Teachers Aide; Band; JV Bsktbl; JV Sftbl; JV Vllybl; Hon Roll; Prfct Atten Awd; USC Upwrd Band; Howard U; RN.

EASLEY, SASHA T; Barstow HS; Barstow, CA; (2); 4-H; French Clb; Girl Scts; Teachers Aide; Band; Hon Roll; U Of NV; Nrsng.

EASON, JESSE; Inland Christian HS; San Berdo, CA; (2); Church Yth Grp; Bsktbl; Pres Acad Fit Awd; Engr.

EASON, WALTER J; Richard Gahr HS; Cerritos, CA; (2); ROTC; JV Bsktbl; Trk; Jr NHS; Howard U; Bus Admin.

EAST, KAON-JABBAR P; Senior HS; San Jose, CA; (2); Var L Ftbl; Var L Trk; Hon Roll; Tae Kwon Do; Mdlng; Stanford; Med.

EASTBURN, PAUL J; San Rafael HS; San Rafael, CA; (2); Jazz Band; Orch; Pep Band; Cit Awd; Referee Yth Sccr; Smmr Music Wrkshp; Mscl Citations; Music.

EASTCOTT, MERRILL B; Gahr HS; Cerritos, CA; (3); Boy Scts; Teachers Aide; Wt Lftg; High Hon Roll; Pepperline U; Bus Admn.

EASTER, LOIS M; North HS; Bakersfield, CA; (2); Church Yth Grp; German Clb; JA; ROTC; Color Guard; Drill Tm; DAR Awd; Hon Roll; NHS; Pres Acad Fit Awd; CA Schlst Foundation; Academic Decathalon; Gate Club.

EASTER JR, OTIS T; Edison-Computech HS; Fresno, CA; (1); Band; Mrchg Band; Cit Awd; Hon Roll; Prfct Atten Awd; Comp Prgrmng Achvt Awd; MESA Clb; U Of CA Berkley; Comp Prgrmng.

EASTER, TINA VICTORIA; Pittsburg HS; Pittsburg, CA; (3); 5/335; FBLA; Pep Clb; SADD; Teachers Aide; High Hon Roll; Hon Roll; Spllng Bees 3rd & 4th Pl; Natl Issues Forum Discssns; Comp Sci.

EASTER, TROY L; Canyon Springs HS; Moreno Valley, CA; (4); Computer Clb; Office Aide; SADD; Teachers Aide; Stage Crew; Ftbl; Trk; Wt Lftg; Hon Roll; CSU Long Beach.

EASTERDAY, DAVID A; Thomas Downey HS; Modesto, CA; (3); Nwsp; Var L Bsktbl; Cit Awd; High Hon Roll; Prfct Atten Awd; CSF; Aerospace Engr.

EASTHAM, STEWART M; Oroville HS; Oroville, CA; (3); #2 In Class; JV Bsktbl; JV Var Golf; High Hon Roll; Ntl Merit Ltr; Prfct Atten Awd; Top Ten Prcnt; Cert Of Mrt Yth For Undrstndng Intl Exchng; Engrng.

EASTLAND, ANTHONY; San Diego Acad; San Diego, CA; (1); Teachers Aide; Crs Cntry; Trk; Vllybl; Loma Linda U; Arch.

EASTLAND, LAURA ELLEN; Elsinore HS; Lake Elsinore, CA; (2); Color Guard; Color Guard Pin; Psych.

EASTLICK, RICKY R; Mesa Verde HS; Citrus Heights, CA; (2); 70/257; Var JV Bsbl; MVP-JV Bsbl 89; Sports Jrnlsm.

EASTMAN, BEN N; University HS; Irvine, CA; (3); English Clb; JCL; Science Clb; Off Soph Cls; Chrmn Stu Cncl; Capt Var Swmmng; High Hon Roll; Hon Roll; NHS; NCTE Wrtng Cntst; UIF Hon Mntn Water Polo; Stanford; Engl.

EASTMAN, KELLY M; Villa Park HS; Orange, CA; (3); Church Yth Grp; Hon Roll; NHS; Prncpl Hnr Rl; Psych.

EASTMAN, KUMI; Los Angeles Ctr For Enriched Studies; Los Angeles, CA; (3); Teachers Aide; Stu Cncl; Hon Roll; LAPD Explorers; Chem Clb.

EASTON, JEFF R; Irvine HS; Irvine, CA; (2); 90/550; French Clb; Lcrss; Hon Roll; Acad Of Sci And Tech; Passd Coll Profciency Test Intro To Comp Aid Drftg; Irvine Valley Coll; Comp Prgmg.

EASTON, JULIE A; Montgomery HS; Santa Rosa, CA; (3); Church Yth Grp; Office Aide; Bsktbl; Score Keeper; Vllybl; Hon Roll; Dance Cls; Dominican Coll; Pre-Med.

EASTRIDGE, DUANE D; Hemet HS; Hemet, CA; (4); Boy Scts; Church Yth Grp; FFA; Band; Mrchg Band; Orch; Pep Band; Stage Crew; Riverside Cnty Vlntr Firefghtr; Crafton Hills Coll; Paramedic.

EASTRIDGE, SUZANNE B; Saint Francis HS; Santa Clara, CA; (2); 44/356; SADD; JV Bsktbl; JV Vllybl; High Hon Roll; Pres Acad Fit Awd; St Schlr; Envrnmntl Clb; Bio.

EASTWOOD, AMY B; San Ramon Valley HS; Danville, CA; (2); Art Clb; Chess Clb; Church Yth Grp; Cmnty Wkr; FFA; GAA; Intnl Clb; SADD; Ftbl; Golf; Artist.

EATMON, DANA J; Amos Alonzo Stagg HS; Stockton, CA; (3); Church Yth Grp; Pep Clb; SADD; Teachers Aide; Variety Show; Cheerldng; Sftbl; Hon Roll; Conflict Mgmnt; Sacramento ST U; Law.

EATON, ASHLEY; El Camino HS; Sacramento, CA; (3); Drama Clb; French Clb; Thesps; School Musical; School Play; Variety Show; Drama Awds; Dance; Radio; Theater Arts.

EATON, BRANDON J; Antioch SR HS; Antioch, CA; (3); Letterman Clb; JV Ftbl; Wt Lftg; Var L Wrstlng; Hon Roll.

EATON, DEE ANN L; Sierra Joint Union HS; O Neals, CA; (3); Church Yth Grp; Dance Clb; FHA; GAA; Office Aide; Ski Clb; Spanish Clb; SADD; Teachers Aide; Varsity Clb; Jr Princess; Fresno ST; Psych.

EATON, JULIE M; Live Oak HS; Morgan Hill, CA; (3); 36/450; Church Yth Grp; Pep Clb; Ski Clb; Chorus; Church Choir; VP Jr Cls; Rep Stu Cncl; JV Var Swmmng; Var Trk; Hon Roll; Vrsty Mck Trl Tm; St Marys; Teachng.

EATON, JUNE K; Davis SR HS; Woodland, CA; (3); Church Yth Grp; Cmnty Wkr; Office Aide; Ski Clb; Church Choir; CSF; Peer Helpr; Congrssnl Schlr Natl Young Ldr 90; U CA; Bus Admin.

EATON, LA BRUCE; Cajon HS; San Bernardino, CA; (3); Band; Mrchg Band; Pep Band; MI U; Elem Educ.

EATON, STACEY; Don Antonio Lugo HS; Chino Hills, CA; (2); Church Yth Grp; JV Bsktbl; JV Vllybl; Gldn Cnqust Awd Home Ec; Outstndng Achvt Awd Phys Ed; 1st Pl Schl Interior Dsgn Cmptn; Interior Dsgnr.

EAVIS, CARRIE; El Camino Fundamental HS; Sacramento, CA; (3); 5/421; Teachers Aide; Stage Crew; JV Socr; Var Tennis; High Hon Roll; Hon Roll; NHS; Ntl Merit Ltr; Fri Nght Live Clb; Wldrns Clb; Jrnlsm Clb; CSF; Readers Theatre; Awd Excel Schlrshp; Cert Wrting Excel; Stanford; Bus Mgmt.

EBEL, ERIKA J; Lutheran HS; Irvine, CA; (2); Church Yth Grp; Bsktbl; Trk; Vllybl; Christ Coll Irvine; Educ.

EBEL, LISA; Lutheran HS Of Orange County; Irvine, CA; (3); Church Yth Grp; German Clb; Math Clb; Teachers Aide; Sec Stu Cncl; Var Bsktbl; Var Trk; Var Vllybl; Hon Roll; Rotary Awd; Christ Coll Irvine; Medc Mssnry.

EBENSTEIN, DONNA; Northgate HS; Concord, CA; (2); 2/350; Math Clb; High Hon Roll; CSF; Sci.

EBERHARD, ARMIN D; California Lutheran HS; Oceanside, CA; (3); Church Yth Grp; Chorus; Variety Show; Rptr Nwsp; Pres Stu Cncl; L Bsktbl; L Ftbl; High Hon Roll; Hon Roll; Rowing Club; Law.

EBERHARD, ELLEN D; California Lutheran HS; Oceanside, CA; (2); 1/15; Church Yth Grp; Chorus; Variety Show; Pres Frsh Cls; Pres Soph Cls; Var L Bsktbl; Var L Sftbl; Var L Vllybl; High Hon Roll; Hon Roll; Rwng Clb; U Of CA San Diego; Med.

EBERHARD, SALLY C; Portola JR SR HS; Blairsden, CA; (3); SADD; Hon Roll; Miss Teen Of AZ Schlrshp & Rcgntn Pgnt.

EBERHARDT, MATT J; Fontana HS; Fontana, CA; (3); Hon Roll; Pres Acad Fit Awd; Pres Schlr; Comp Sci.

EBERLE, GWENNE; Santa Margarita HS; Mission Viejo, CA; (1); Cmnty Wkr; FCA; Pep Clb; Var Cheerldng; Gym; High Hon Roll; Hon Roll; Religion, Study Skills & Spanish Awds; UCSD; Lawyer.

EBERT, TODD D; Independence HS; Jackson, CA; (4); 1/25; Art Clb; Boy Scts; Church Yth Grp; Drama Clb; French Clb; Office Aide; Chorus; School Play; Stage Crew; Swing Chorus; Speech Clb Wnnr; Friday Night Live; Vlntr; San Juaquin Delta JC; Psych.

EBLE, TROIANNE; Fred C Beyer HS; Modesto, CA; (3); Church Yth Grp; Hosp Aide; SADD; Chorus; Church Choir; School Musical; Hon Roll; Townsend Opera Chorus; CCD Teacher; U CA Santa Cruz; Molecular Bio.

EBMEYER, BROCK A; Apple Valley HS; Apple Valley, CA; (3); Boy Scts; Bus Profs of Am; Church Yth Grp; Spanish Clb; Teachers Aide; Stu Cncl; Var Bsbl; Var Ftbl; JV Golf; Rotary Awd; BYU; Acctng.

EBNER, CHRISTINE; Irvine HS; Irvine, CA; (4); Church Yth Grp; Vllybl; Hon Roll; CSF; Hertiage Awd Excllnc In Socl Sci; U CA Irvine; Psych.

EBNER, DAMON F; Huntington Beach HS; Huntington Beach, CA; (3); French Clb; Speech Tm; Band; Drm Mjr(t); Jazz Band; Mrchg Band; School Musical; Golf; Coll, Prfsnl Jzz Band; Jzz Band Solo Awds Rgnl Cmptns; Berklee Coll Of Music; Music.

EBORALL, ELAINE; Irvington HS; Fremont, CA; (4); Badmiton; S F ST; Mrktng.

EBRAHEMI, FRED; Bellarmine College Prep; Palo Alto, CA; (3); Cmnty Wkr; Drama Clb; NFL; Speech Tm; Temple Yth Grp; School Play; Variety Show; Phtg Nwsp; Pres Sr Cls; JV Ftbl; Philosphy.

EBRAHIM, BEHSHAD; Dana Hills HS; Laguna Beach, CA; (2); Cmnty Wkr; Debate Tm; Drama Clb; Science Clb; Spanish Clb; Bsktbl; Trk; Vllybl; UCI; Sociology.

EBRAHIMI, MARYAM; Palisades HS; Pacific Palisades, CA; (3); Cmnty Wkr; Math Clb; Rep Jr Cls; Rep Stu Cncl; Pres Acad Fit Awd; Elem Schl Tutoring; Smmr Camp Vlntr; Psych.

EBRAHIMOFF, GIZEL; Fred C Beyer HS; Modesto, CA; (4); 6/529; Church Yth Grp; Office Aide; Ski Clb; Teachers Aide; Church Choir; Cit Awd; Hon Roll; CSF; Modesto JC; Accntng.

EBRIGHT, MATTHEW D; Bellarmine College Prep; Los Gatos, CA; (2); Cmnty Wkr; JV Crs Cntry; JV Trk; JV Wrstlng; 3rtd Pl Bellarmine Coll Prep Sci Fair; Prize From Sun Microsystems Santa Clara Cnty Sci Fair; UCLA; Bus.

EBURY, CHRIS; Avenal HS; Avenal, CA; (4); 3/93; Pep Clb; School Play; Pres Soph Cls; Off Jr Cls; Pres Stu Cncl; High Hon Roll; Treas Sec NHS; Ntl Merit SF; JV Var Bsktbl; Mdlst Acad Decathlon & Tm Capt; U Southern CA; Math.

EBY, MARY E; Redlands HS; Loma Linda, CA; (4); 24/844; Church Yth Grp; German Clb; Key Clb; Scholastic Bowl; Science Clb; Teachers Aide; Band; Chorus; Variety Show; Ed Lit Mag; Hist Awd; CSF; Arch.

ECCLES, CHRIS E; Seaside HS; Ft Ord, CA; (2); JV Ftbl; Intrml Wrstlng; KSU; Psycht.

ECCLES, NICOLE T; Independence HS; San Jose, CA; (3); Pep Clb; VP Frsh Cls; Rep Jr Cls; Rep Stu Cncl; Var Capt Cheerldng; Sftbl; Hon Roll; MESA-PRES; Ballet-10 Yrs; UCLA; Med.

ECHAN, CHRISTA; Calvary Chapel HS; Costa Mesa, CA; (4); Church Yth Grp; Chorus; Sec Stu Cncl; Sftbl; Trk; Vllybl; Cit Awd; Child Development; Missions Club; SCC; Elem Educ.

ECHAVEZ, MELODIE A; Novato HS; Novato, CA; (3); Spanish Clb; Band; Mrchg Band; Pep Band; Var Cheerldng; JV Socr.

ECHAVEZ, RITA P; Notre Dame Acad; Burbank, CA; (4); 45/104; French Clb; Speech Tm; Yrbk; High Hon Roll; Amnsty Intl; Cmps Mnstry; Bstn U; Tchr.

ECHEVARRIA, ANTHONY; Roosevelt HS; Los Angeles, CA; (2); Police Acad; Police Ofcr.

ECHEVERRI, NANCI S; Louisville HS; West Hills, CA; (1); Cmnty Wkr; GAA; Hosp Aide; School Play; Treas Soph Cls; JV Capt Sftbl; High Hon Roll; CA Schrlshp Fed; St Mel Church & Schl Cnfrnc; Rlgn Subjct Awd; Pdtrcs.

ECHEVERRIA, JARRETT V; John F Kennedy HS; Los Angeles, CA; (2); Boy Scts; Church Yth Grp; School Play; Stage Crew; Intrml Ftbl; Intrml Trk; Wt Lftg; Schlr Athlete Awd Ftbl & Track; Italian Achvt Awd; U Sthrn CA; Theatre Arts.

ECHEVERRIA, MARIA; Bell Gardens HS; Bell Gardens, CA; (1); Computer Clb; Drill Tm; Sec Frsh Cls; Cit Awd; Comp Analyst.

ECHOLS, JUSTIN A; College Park HS; Martinez, CA; (1); Boy Scts; Church Yth Grp; Varsity Clb; Hon Roll.

ECHOLS, ORVILETTE; Brethren HS; Los Angeles, CA; (4); Am Leg Aux Girls St; Science Clb; Spanish Clb; Teachers Aide; Acpl Chr; Treas Jr Cls; Sec Stu Cncl; Stat Bsktbl; Stat Ftbl; JV Sftbl; Acad Decathln Medal Wnnr; Gold B Pendant; Sonoma ST U; Bus Admin.

ECKENBURG, DALE W; Nevada Union HS; Nevada City, CA; (3); Library Aide; L Ftbl; Var L Tennis; Cit Awd; Hon Roll; Archery St Chmpnshp Wnnr; Lions Club Awd; AZ ST; Math.

ECKER, CAROLYN; Mt Whitney HS; Visalia, CA; (4); Office Aide; Spanish Clb; Band; Mrchg Band; Pep Band; Crs Cntry; Trk; Hon Roll; Pres Acad Fit Awd; CA Poly; Animal Sci.

ECKERSON, NIKKI L; Los Angeles HS; Los Angeles, CA; (3); 2/350; Church Yth Grp; Dance Clb; School Play; Off Jr Cls; Hon Roll; Prfct Atten Awd; Blk Stu Union; Upward Band Accdntl Coll; UC Santa Cruz; Jrnlsm.

ECKERT, DANIELLA L; Coast Union HS; Cambria, CA; (2); FBLA; Ski Clb; Spanish Clb; SADD; VP Frsh Cls; Treas Stu Cncl; Var Bsktbl; Var Tennis; Hon Roll; Pres Acad Fit Awd; Film.

ECKERT, LISA P; Downey HS; Downey, CA; (2); Hosp Aide; Teachers Aide; Keywanettes; CSF; Vlntr Tutor; Elem Ed.

ECKHOFF, TIFFANY S; San Marcos HS; San Marcos, CA; (3); Church Yth Grp; Key Clb; VP Pep Clb; Teachers Aide; Varsity Clb; Drill Tm; Stu Cncl; Crs Cntry; Mgr(s); Sftbl; Stu Ath Trnr Head Trnr; CA Schlstc Fed Treas; UCLB; Accntng.

ECKLAND, KRISTIN L; Bret Harte Union HS; Arnold, CA; (2); Church Yth Grp; FHA; Spanish Clb; Economist.

ECKLES, ANNE; Carlsbad HS; Carlsbad, CA; (1); Science Clb; Chorus; Gym; Tennis; Trk; Cit Awd; Hon Roll; Prfct Atten Awd; CSF; Interact Clb; John Hopkins; Med.

ECKLUND, CHRISTOPHER D; Paradise HS; Paradise, CA; (2); 1/268; Church Yth Grp; JV Capt Bsktbl; JV Capt Ftbl; Var Tennis; Trk; High Hon Roll; Prfct Atten Awd; Pres Acad Fit Awd; Golden St Exam; Alg I Sch Recogntn Geom Hnrs; Bsktbl Coachs Awd; Tennis Most Inspirtional; Arch.

ECLARINAL, CATHERINE F; Manteca HS; Manteca, CA; (1); 11/457; Band; Mrchg Band; Hon Roll; Hnr Awds In Hnrs Engl I & Geom; UC Davis; Crmnl Law.

ECLARINAL, MELANIE F; Manteca HS; Manteca, CA; (2); 7/420; Color Guard; Hon Roll; St Schlr; CSF; Piano Awd Of Xclnc; UC Davis; Nrs.

ECONOMON, STEPHANIE L; Trabuco Hills HS; El Toro, CA; (4); Pep Clb; Spanish Clb; SADD; Teachers Aide; Rptr Nwsp; Hon Roll; Bus & Coll Prep Engl Distngshd Schlr Awd; Sci/Technlgy Fair; Voc Olympics Acctng Cmptn; Saddleback CC; Bus.

ECONOMY, NIKY; John W North HS; Riverside, CA; (2); 24/520; Sec Church Yth Grp; Capt Pep Clb; Varsity Clb; Capt Cheerldng; Var Socr; JV Var Swmmng; High Hon Roll; Pres Acad Fit Awd; UCLA; Civil Engr.

ECONOMY, SIA; John W North HS; Riverside, CA; (1); 14/637; Treas Church Yth Grp; Cheerldng; JV Socr; Hon Roll; NHS; Pres Acad Fit Awd; Greek Schl; Dance; Piano; Loyola Marymount; Law.

EDDIE, DANYA C; Ganesha HS; Pomona, CA; (2); Hon Roll; Math Engrng Sci Achvt.

EDDINGS, ERIK; Fairfield HS; Fairfield, CA; (2); L Ftbl; JV Trk; JV Wrstlng; Cit Awd; Advsr Blck Stu Union; Mst Outstndng Wrstlr Awd 88-89; Attend Solano JC Smmr 90; San Jose ST; Advrtsmnt.

EDDINGS, JOEL N; West HS; Bakersfield, CA; (1); Debate Tm; NFL; Spanish Clb; Hon Roll; CSF.

EDDINS, MICHELLE; Canyon Springs HS; Anaheim, CA; (4); Pres Church Yth Grp; Cmnty Wkr; Hosp Aide; Red Cross Aide; Thesps; School Musical; School Play; Nwsp; Yrbk; Stu Cncl; Yth Ct; Sundy Sch Tchr; San Diego ST U; TV Comm.

EDDY, ANGELA J; Central Catholic HS; Modesto, CA; (3); 12/54; Letterman Clb; Service Clb; SADD; Varsity Clb; Yrbk; Pres Frsh Cls; Pres Soph Cls; Sec Treas Jr Cls; VP Sr Cls; JV Var Bsktbl; Pre-Med.

EDDY, CINDY; Fairfield HS; Fairfield, CA; (1); Church Yth Grp; Temple Yth Grp; Chorus; JV Bsktbl; JV Vllybl; Cit Awd; Vllybl Mst Imprvd Plyr; Isuza Pacific U; Vocal Prfmnc.

EDDY, MATT W; Alta Loma HS; Cucamonga, CA; (2); Hon Roll; CA ST U; Arch.

EDDY, TONY; Delta HS; Lodi, CA; (2); 1/70; Letterman Clb; Varsity Clb; Rep Soph Cls; VP Jr Cls; High Hon Roll; NHS; JV Var Bsbl; JV Var Bsktbl; JV Ftbl; JV Var Wt Lftg; Stanford; Acctng.

EDEJER, NORALYN M; Channel Islands HS; Oxnard, CA; (4); Office Aide; Hon Roll; Prfct Atten Awd; Ventura Coll; Reg Nurse.

EDELMAN, DEBORAH S; Villa Park HS; Villa Park, CA; (2); Debate Tm; French Clb; Key Clb; Latin Clb; Temple Yth Grp; Color Guard; Drill Tm; School Musical; High Hon Roll; NHS; Acad Decathlon; JR Statesmen Of Amer; Law.

EDGAR, ERIC J; Butte Valley HS; Macdoel, CA; (2); JV Bsbl; JV Bsktbl; JV Ftbl.

EDGAR, HAROLD W; Arlington HS; Riverside, CA; (3); 20/440; Var Socr; JV Tennis; 90 USA Select Soccor Tm, U Of CA Irvine For European Tour; Physcn.

EDGAR, STEPHANIE J; Fred C Beyer HS; Modesto, CA; (2); Hon Roll; Stanislaus; Chld Psycht.

EDGE, CHRISTINA; San Dieguito HS; Carlsbad, CA; (1); Church Yth Grp; French Clb; VP Key Clb; JV Bsktbl; Hon Roll; Prfct Atten Awd; Pres Acad Fit Awd; Asst Coach 8th Grd Bsktbl Tm; GSE Hnrs Geom; Engl.

EDGE, NORMA L; Bishop Amat HS; Diamond Bar, CA; (3); Church Yth Grp; School Musical; Var Crs Cntry; JV Tennis; Var Trk; High Hon Roll; NHS; NEDT Awd; Marywood Camp Counselor; Lanterman Dvlpmntl Center Volunteer; USD; Bus.

EDGERTON, ERIN L; Santa Clara HS; Santa Clara, CA; (2); Church Yth Grp; Service Clb; Chorus; Var Socr; JV Vllybl; Socl Sci.

EDGERTON, KAREN E; Los Gatos HS; Los Gatos, CA; (3); 42/364; Girl Scts; Chorus; Var Swmmng; 4-H Awd; Hon Roll; Ntl Merit Ltr; Grl Sct Slvr & Gld Awd; Gldn St Exam Alg & Geo With Hnrs; Engrng.

EDGEWORTH, ERIC T; Moreno Valley HS; 29 Palms, CA; (4); 14/384; German Clb; Math Clb; Math Tm; Teachers Aide; Nwsp; High Hon Roll; Hon Roll; Jr NHS; NHS; Ntl Merit SF; Acad Dcthln; UC Riverside; Physics.

EDMISTEN, DAVID; Fred C Beyer HS; Modesto, CA; (3); Debate Tm; Pres Key Clb; NFL; Speech Tm; JV Bsktbl; L Tennis; Cit Awd; High Hon Roll; Hon Roll; CA Schlrshp Fed Lifetime Mbr; Jr Asilomar Ldrshp Trng; U Of CA; Bus.

EDMISTON, ATHENA L; Tracy Joint Union HS; Tracy, CA; (2); 15/483; Letterman Clb; SADD; Yrbk; Var Gym; High Hon Roll; Hon Roll; Athlte Mnth May 90; Marine Bio.

EDMISTON, JENNIFER; Yosemite HS; Coarsegold, CA; (4); 9/120; Church Yth Grp; Sec 4-H; Office Aide; Teachers Aide; JV Sftbl; Mgr Trk; 4-H Awd; High Hon Roll; Hon Roll; Ltr Acad; Hmcmng Coronation & Flt; Biola U; Nrsng.

EDMOND, MICHELLE M; Oakland HS; Oakland, CA; (2); Dance Clb; Acpl Chr; Band; Chorus; Church Choir; Drill Tm; Variety Show; Off Soph Cls; Stu Cncl; Cheerldng; Brooks Coll; Med.

EDMONDS, CHELSEY; Concord HS; Concord, CA; (1); Drama Clb; Teachers Aide; JV Cheerldng; JV Pom Pon; Chrldg Sqd Cmptn; Drama.

EDMONDS, DARLA M; Barstow HS; Newberry Springs, CA; (3); Church Yth Grp; Teachers Aide; Cit Awd; Prfct Atten Awd; Acad Imprvmnt Awd; Cert Achvt; Achvt 90th Prcntl Cert Hnr; Yellow Jacket Awd; Cosmtlgst.

EDMONDS, DAVID M; Majave HS; Mojave, CA; (2); Church Yth Grp; Letterman Clb; Spanish Clb; Teachers Aide; Yrbk; Sec Treas Jr Cls; Rep Stu Cncl; Capt JV Bsbl; L Bsktbl; L JV Trk; CSF; Ca ST; Med.

EDMONDS, ERICA A; Archbishop Mitty HS; San Jose, CA; (4); Math Tm; School Play; Ed Yrbk; High Hon Roll; NHS; Ntl Merit SF; HS Chptr Of Amnsty Intl Pres & Fndr; Edtr Of Envrnmntl Clb Nwsltr; Cmmnty Svc/Acad CA Schlr Fd Treas; Pltcl Sci.

EDMONDS, KRISTEN D; Orange Glen HS; Escondido, CA; (2); 21/543; Church Yth Grp; Var Capt Cheerldng; Hon Roll; Schlr Athlt Awd.

EDMONDS, ZACH; Bullard HS; Fresno, CA; (1); Ski Clb; Band; Mrchg Band; Pep Band; Tennis; High Hon Roll; U CA Riverside; Med.

EDMONDSON, DAVID M; Leffingwell Christian HS; Norwalk, CA; (3); 2/25; Church Yth Grp; Swmmng; Tennis; Vllybl; Cerritos Coll; Comp Sci.

EDMUNDS, BONNIE J; Fairfield HS; Fairfield, CA; (1); 4-H; Chorus; Cit Awd; Psych.

EDMUNDS, TIM J; Fresno Christian HS; Fresno, CA; (1); Church Yth Grp; Letterman Clb; Bsbl; Bsktbl; Ftbl; Wt Lftg; High Hon Roll; Engrng.

EDMUNDSON, KIRSTEN L; Portola JR SR HS; Blairsden, CA; (3); 2/45; Am Leg Aux Girls St; Letterman Clb; Office Aide; Rep Frsh Cls; Rep Soph Cls; Pres Jr Cls; Var Aud/Vis; Var Sftbl; Capt Var Vllybl; Sal; Notre Dame; Ob/Gyn.

EDMUNDSON, VANGI; Brethren HS; Cerritos, CA; (4); 1/65; Church Yth Grp; French Clb; GAA; JA; Math Clb; Math Tm; Teachers Aide; Varsity Clb; Ed Yrbk; Rep Stu Cncl; Optimst Good Ctzn Awd; Press/Telegrm Acad Achvt Awd, Jrnlsm; Westmont; Commnctns.

EDPUGANTI, RENUKA; Gretchen Whitney HS; Cerritos, CA; (3); Cmnty Wkr; JA; Key Clb; Red Cross Aide; Thesps; Stage Crew; Off Soph Cls; Hon Roll; NHS; Cerritos Yng Woman Yr Schltc Achvt Awd; CA Schlrhsp Fed; Genetic Engrng.

EDRA, BARBRA K; Bonita Vista HS; San Diego, CA; (2); 1/600; French Clb; Intnl Clb; Flag Corp; Ed Yrbk; Jr NHS; NHS; Val; Adoption Essay Cont; Stanford U; Pre-Law.

EDSON, STEVE L; Mills HS; Millbrae, CA; (3); Var Capt Socr; Var Tennis; Bus.

EDSTROM, ANTHONY J; Edison HS; Fountain Valley, CA; (2); Hon Roll; Cert Scuba Diver; CSF.

EDWARD, ATLAS; Grant Union HS; Sacramento, CA; (2); JV Ftbl; JV Trk; Elec Engr.

EDWARDS, AARON; Ontario HS; Ontario, CA; (3); 9/200; Am Leg Boys St; Debate Tm; French Clb; Treas Key Clb; Ski Clb; Sec Frsh Cls; Var Capt Bsbl; Var Capt Socr; High Hon Roll; Hon Roll; Hnr Ushr-Tp 10 Pct Cls 90; MVP Sccr; UCLA; Engrng.

EDWARDS, ALISHA; Chula Vista HS; National City, CA; (2); Church Yth Grp; Dance Clb; Drama Clb; FBLA; GAA; Pep Clb; Teachers Aide; Drill Tm; School Play; Pres Frsh Cls; Blck Stu Union Awd; Howard U; Law.

EDWARDS, ALKO A; Bishop Amat HS; Diamond Bar, CA; (3); Church Yth Grp; Hosp Aide; Spanish Clb; School Musical; School Play; High Hon Roll; NHS; Pres Acad Fit Awd; Asst Sundy Sch Tchr; Silver Scrn Clb; Bus.

EDWARDS, ALLYCE; George Washington HS; Los Angeles, CA; (3); Church Yth Grp; Dance Clb; Math Clb; Pep Clb; Teachers Aide; Church Choir; Variety Show; Hon Roll; Prfct Atten Awd; UC Santa Barbara; Med.

EDWARDS, AMIE; Lincoln HS; Lincoln, CA; (1); 20/167; Pep Clb; SADD; Bsbl; Socr; Swmmng; Gov Hon Prg Awd; Hon Roll; Peer Cnslr; UCLA; Med.

EDWARDS, BECKY; Glen A Wilson HS; Hacienda Hts, CA; (4); 92/350; Church Yth Grp; Pep Clb; Church Choir; Yrbk; JV Var Cheerldng; Var Powder Puff Ftbl; Hon Roll; Pres Acad Fit Awd; Chrldng Comptn Sq; Ltr Chrldng; Biola U; Lib Studies.

EDWARDS, BRAD S; Porterville HS; Porterville, CA; (3); 1/350; Am Leg Boys St; Church Yth Grp; Band; Mrchg Band; Pep Band; L Var Bsktbl; JV Ftbl; High Hon Roll; Schlr Of Week; Rose Parade 89; Carnegie Hall Prfrmnc; Acad Letter; Acad Achvt Awds Reading & Math.

EDWARDS, BRANDON L; Yucca Valley HS; Yucca Valley, CA; (3); FBLA; Math Clb; Spanish Clb; Var Bsbl; Cit Awd; Hon Roll; Prfct Atten Awd; Pres Acad Fit Awd; 90 Natl Young Ldrs Conf-Congrssnl Yth Ldrshp Cncl; University Clb; CSF; U CA-RIVERSIDE; Nuclear Med.

EDWARDS, BRENT T; San Benito HS; Hollister, CA; (3); 15/350; Boy Scts; Church Yth Grp; Letterman Clb; Library Aide; Ski Clb; Teachers Aide; Var Bsktbl; JV Ftbl; Capt Var Golf; NHS; Gldn St Awd Geom; MVP Golf Team; All Leag, All CCS & 8th In Nrthrn CA Golf; Air Force Acad; Bus.

EDWARDS, BRIAN J; La Canada HS; La Canada Flintri, CA; (3); 30/245; Ski Clb; Var Capt Ftbl; Powder Puff Ftbl; Capt Wt Lftg; High Hon Roll; JETS Awd; NHS; UCSB; Bus.

EDWARDS, CAROLYN J; Canyon HS; Canyon Country, CA; (2); GAA; Letterman Clb; JV L Bsktbl; JV L Sftbl; Hon Roll; Jr NHS; CSF; Hnrs Gldn St Exm Geom; Engrng.

EDWARDS, CHANEL M; Lincoln Prep HS; National City, CA; (2); FCA; Girl Scts; Off Soph Cls; Var Bsbl; Var Bsktbl; Var Trk; Cit Awd; Hon Roll; NC ST; Elem Ed.

EDWARDS, CHARLOTTE; Caruthers Union HS; Raisin City, CA; (3); Church Yth Grp; Math Clb; Pep Clb; Varsity Clb; Bsktbl; Cheerldng; Mgr(s); Tennis; Vllybl; High Hon Roll; Point Loma Nazarene; Rtrd Chldn.

EDWARDS, CHRIS K; Calvary Chapel HS; Lakewood, CA; (2); Boy Scts; Church Yth Grp; FCA; Intrml Bsbl; Var Bsktbl; Intrml Ftbl; Intrml Golf; Intrml Sftbl; Intrml Tennis; Cit Awd; Acad Awd Span; U Of WA; Arch.

EDWARDS, CYNTHIA; Cajon HS; San Bernardino, CA; (2); Hosp Aide; Band; Ed Nwsp; Black Ftr Ldrs; Upward Bnd; TOP; U Of Pacific; Phrmcy.

EDWARDS, DOUGLAS M; North HS; Bakersfield, CA; (1); Boy Scts; French Clb; ROTC; School Play; Mgr Stage Crew; JV Ftbl; Hon Roll; Const Crew; CA Poly; Teacher.

EDWARDS, ERIC D; Torrey Pines HS; Rancho Santa Fe, CA; (3); SADD; School Play; Intrml Socr; Hon Roll; Med.

EDWARDS, FELECIA EKISHA; Crenshaw HS; Los Angeles, CA; (2); Cmnty Wkr; Girl Scts; Hosp Aide; Spanish Clb; Teachers Aide; Hon Roll; Prfct Atten Awd; Pediatrics.

EDWARDS, GLENN; Culver City HS; Culver City, CA; (2); Church Yth Grp; Varsity Clb; Jazz Band; Bsktbl; Tennis; Hon Roll; Full Schlrshp Intl Trmpt Gld; Howard U; Pdtrcn.

EDWARDS, HEATHER A; Brea Olinda HS; Brea, CA; (1); 6/396; Hosp Aide; Intnl Clb; Key Clb; High Hon Roll; Jr NHS; Masonic Awd; Pres Acad Fit Awd; Johns Hopkins U Ctr Tlntd Yth; Acad Tutor; Intl Bus.

EDWARDS, JENNIFER; San Jacinto HS; Hemet, CA; (3); 12/200; VP French Clb; Teachers Aide; Nwsp; Yrbk; Hon Roll; U Of CA Santa Barbara; Psych.

EDWARDS, JENNIFER M; Analy HS; Sebastopol, CA; (2); 9/246; Church Yth Grp; JV Tennis; High Hon Roll; CA Schlrshp Fndtn.

EDWARDS, JENNY R; Westwood HS; Westwood, CA; (3); ROTC; Ski Clb; Teachers Aide; Band; Chorus; Mrchg Band; School Play; Nwsp; Yrbk; Sec Soph Cls; Early Chldhd Educ.

EDWARDS, JIM A; Salinas Union HS; Salinas, CA; (1); Boy Scts; Church Yth Grp; Ski Clb; Band.

EDWARDS, JOHN C; Benicia HS; Benicia, CA; (4); 29/300; Church Yth Grp; Treas Computer Clb; Band; Jazz Band; Mrchg Band; High Hon Roll; Hon Roll; Pres Acad Fit Awd; Pres Schlr; Chico ST CA; Engrng.

EDWARDS, KERRY A; Esperanza HS; Yorba Linda, CA; (3); 37/562; Church Yth Grp; Var Bsktbl; JV Socr; Var Trk; High Hon Roll; Hon Roll.

EDWARDS, KRISTI; Canyon HS; Canyon Country, CA; (4); 9/500; Church Yth Grp; Cmnty Wkr; FBLA; Intnl Clb; Lbrn Band; Church Choir; Jazz Band; Mrchg Band; Elks Awd; Hon Roll; Drama Apprctn Soc Pres; CSUN; Tchr.

EDWARDS, LORI L; Westmoor HS; Daly City, CA; (2); Church Yth Grp; GAA; Spanish Clb; Church Choir; Crs Cntry; Trk; Hon Roll; CSF; Math & Sci Tutoring; Hnrs Alg.

EDWARDS, LOUISA; Monte Vista HS; Danville, CA; (2); Intnl Clb; Chorus; Drill Tm; Hon Roll; Dance; Greenpeace; UC-SANTA Barbara; Mar Bio.

EDWARDS, MICHAEL J; San Gor Gonio HS; Highland, CA; (3); Wrstlng; High Hon Roll; Hon Roll; Jr NHS; Civil Engrng.

EDWARDS, MICHELLE D; James Logan HS; Union City, CA; (3); Art Clb; Office Aide; Ski Clb; SADD; Teachers Aide; Stu Cncl; Powder Puff Ftbl; High Hon Roll; Union City Police Explrs Srgnt; Stu Of Mnth; Photo Achvtmnt Awd 90; Cal ST U Hayward; Crmnl Law.

EDWARDS, NATALIE; Eisenhower HS; Rialto, CA; (3); Cheerldng; Hon Roll; UC Riverside; Engl.

EDWARDS, NATHAN K; Point Loma HS; San Diego, CA; (2); JV Crs Cntry; JV Trk; High Hon Roll; Pres Acad Fit Awd; Point Loma HS Unofficial Campus Psychlgst; UCSD; Exprmntl Psych.

EDWARDS, SHARENE S; Apple Valley HS; Apple Valley, CA; (3); 58/650; Church Yth Grp; Sec French Clb; Key Clb; Pep Clb; Teachers Aide; Co-Capt Cheerldng; Stat Powder Puff Ftbl; Stat Socr; High Hon Roll; Hon Roll; Chrch Lector; TX A & M; Genetics.

EDWARDS, TIFFANY N; Valley View HS; Moreno Valley, CA; (2); Var Stat Bsktbl; Hon Roll; Stanford; Teaching.

EDWARDS, WILLIAM; Fred C Beyer HS; Modesto, CA; (4); 43/500; Boy Scts; JV Var Socr; Cit Awd; High Hon Roll; Hon Roll; Modesto JR Coll; Engrng.

EELLS, ELEANOR R; Atascadero HS; Atascadero, CA; (2); Church Yth Grp; Debate Tm; Pres 4-H; Math Tm; SADD; School Play; Var Tennis; Stat Trk; 4-H Awd; High Hon Roll; CSF 88-90; Mst Imprvd Plyr JV Tnns 88; Coaches Awd Vrsty Tnns 89; Bus Mgmt.

EELLS, LU ANNE; Palm Springs Christian HS; Desert Hot Spgs, CA; (1); Church Yth Grp; Drama Clb; SADD; Off Frsh Cls; Bsktbl; Sftbl; Trk; Vllybl; Hon Roll.

EFFERTZ, MASON A; Orange Lutheran HS; Costa Mesa, CA; (2); Boy Scts; Church Yth Grp; SADD; Bsbl; Bsktbl; Pres Acad Fit Awd.

EFIRD, JOHN G; Bullard HS; Fresno, CA; (2); Cmnty Wkr; Debate Tm; French Clb; Key Clb; NFL; Rep Soph Cls; Rep Jr Cls; Rep Stu Cncl; JV Socr; JV Vllybl; Jr Olympic Vllybl; GSE Acad Excllnc Awd; UC Campus Schl; Econ.

EFRON, NEAL J; Granada Hills HS; Northridge, CA; (2); Intnl Clb; Crs Cntry; Trk; Pres Schlr; Sccr; Dance; UCSD.

EGAN, JOSEPH J; Grossmont HS; El Cajon, CA; (1); Debate Tm; Key Clb; NFL; Speech Tm; Hon Roll; Lion Awd; Bus.

EGAN, JUSTINA L; Chino HS; Chino, CA; (2); Church Yth Grp; Cmnty Wkr; Dance Clb; Stu Cncl; Golden ST Exam Awd Alg I; Fashn Merch.

EGBALIC, EUGERINO C; Balboa HS; San Francisco, CA; (2); Spanish Clb; Prfct Atten Awd; San Francisco ST U; Arch.

EGER, ANNAMARIE R; Fontana HS; Fontana, CA; (2); 42/1189; Church Yth Grp; Scholastic Bowl; Teachers Aide; Intrml Bsktbl; Intrml JV Sftbl; Cit Awd; High Hon Roll; Hon Roll; CA Interschltc Schlrshp Fdrtn; City Leag Sftbl; Cal ST; Math Tchr.

EGGEHORN, BENJAMIN; Pasadena HS; Pasadena, CA; (2); Church Yth Grp; Band; Mrchg Band; Orch; Hon Roll; Music/Electrical Technician.

EGGEMAN, REBECCA D; Montclair HS; Ontario, CA; (3); 14/400; Hosp Aide; Rptr Nwsp; High Hon Roll; Peer Cnslng; Stu Of Mnth; Commnctns.

EGGENBERGER, JENNIFER; Rincon Valley Christian HS; Santa Rosa, CA; (2); Church Yth Grp; Band; Chorus; Mrchg Band; Var L Bsktbl; Var L Vllybl; Cit Awd; Hon Roll; Pre-Med.

EGGER, BRUCE; South West HS; San Diego, CA; (2); 1/400; Boy Scts; SADD; Hon Roll; Masonic Awd; Acad Leag; CSF.

EGGER, DANIEL; Mother Lode Christian HS; Soulsbyville, CA; (4); 1/18; Church Yth Grp; FCA; Yrbk; Pres Frsh Cls; Pres Soph Cls; Pres Jr Cls; Pres Sr Cls; Rep Stu Cncl; Var Bsbl; Var VP Bsktbl; Modesto JC; Civil Engr.

EGGER, SERENITY K; Summerville HS; Tuolumne, CA; (3); Church Yth Grp; Quiz Bowl; Teachers Aide; Acpl Chr; Chorus; Church Choir; JV Bsktbl; JV Cheerldng; Score Keeper; JV Vllybl; Close Up Pgm; Jazz Cmptn 2nd Pl Music Fest 90; Hnr Cls 90-91; Music.

EGGER, TRACY K; Summerville Union HS; Soulsbyville, CA; (3); 1/140; French Clb; Letterman Clb; Quiz Bowl; Varsity Clb; Chorus; School Musical; Variety Show; Pres Frsh Cls; Pres Soph Cls; Pres Stu Cncl; High Hnrs Goldn St Exam Geom; Sci.

EGGERS, JASON; Gilroy HS; Gilroy, CA; (1); 53/450; Church Yth Grp; Temple Yth Grp; High Hon Roll; Hon Roll; Pres Acad Fit Awd; BYU; Arch.

EGGERS, LAURA; La Quinta HS; Westminster, CA; (1); JV Sftbl; Hon Roll; Thrtrcl Make-Up Artst.

EGGL, JONNA D; Newport Harbor HS; Santa Ana, CA; (3); Pep Clb; Capt Flag Corp; Swmmng; Intl Ordr Of Jbs Daghtrs Hnr Queen; Pharm.

EGGLEY, MATT M; Canyon Springs HS; Moreno Valley, CA; (2); Church Yth Grp; French Clb; Natl Beta Clb; Science Clb; Band; Church Choir; JV Ftbl; JV Var Socr; Intrml Wt Lftg; High Hon Roll.

EGHBALI, REYHANEH; William Howard Taft HS; Tarzana, CA; (2); Pres German Clb; Chorus; School Play; JV Tennis; Trk; Pres Acad Fit Awd; CSF; Grmn Amer Schl Assn Vlntr Asst Tchr; Excllnc Grmn Stdy Awd; Pediatrician.

EGU, OBILOH E; Abraham Lincoln HS; Daly City, CA; (4); Drama Clb; French Clb; Science Clb; Church Choir; School Play; Stage Crew; Variety Show; Off Frsh Cls; Crs Cntry; Socr; Frosh Acad Schlsp; Recog Awd; U CA Berkeley; Med.

EGUEZ, MAURICIO Z; Gahr HS; Cerritos, CA; (1); Var Swmmng; Water Polo Tm; Rookie Yr; UC Irvine; Engrng.

EHLERS, DIANE L; Bullard HS; Fresno, CA; (4); 43/455; Key Clb; High Hon Roll; CA Schlrshp Fed Mem Life; UC Santa Barbara; Bus.

EHLERS, JON E; John F Kennedy HS; Sacramento, CA; (3); Ed Yrbk; Rep Frsh Cls; Rep Soph Cls; Rep Jr Cls; Off Sr Cls; Stu Cncl; JV Var Ftbl; Powder Puff Ftbl; JV Socr; Var Trk.

EHLERS, LORI A; Lincoln HS; Stockton, CA; (4); 63/513; Church Yth Grp; Cmnty Wkr; Ski Clb; Spanish Clb; Ed Yrbk; JV Var Swmmng; Hon Roll; Rotary Awd; Asilomar Ldrshp Conf; Assiteens P Res; St Marys Coll; Med.

EHLKE, MATT J; Monta Vista HS; Spring Valley, CA; (2); 56/422; Church Yth Grp; Letterman Clb; JV Capt Bsktbl; Ftbl; Prncpls Hnr Roll.

EHNES, BRIAN E; Grant HS; Sacramento, CA; (2); Cmnty Wkr; SADD; Teachers Aide; Ftbl; Wrstlng; Hon Roll; Med.

EHORN, NANCY; Willows HS; Willows, CA; (4); 12/107; Cmnty Wkr; Pres Girl Scts; SADD; Nwsp; Hon Roll; Girl Scout Silver Ldrshp Awd 89; Butte; Sports Med.

EHORN, TANYA N; Red Bluff Union HS; Red Bluff, CA; (3); 7/350; Church Yth Grp; Math Clb; Math Tm; Mu Alpha Theta; Office Aide; Spanish Clb; SADD; Bsktbl; Sftbl; High Hon Roll; CSF Offcr; Astrlgcl Engr.

EHRKE, SAM RYAN; Woodland HS; Woodland, CA; (3); 30/500; Drama Clb; French Clb; School Musical; Jr NHS; Heros Awd; Bus.

EHRLICH, MAUREEN B; Westmont HS; Campbell, CA; (4); Sec Art Clb; Computer Clb; Drama Clb; Math Clb; Spanish Clb; Thesps; Chorus; School Musical; School Play; Stage Crew; Team Jeopardy; Math Comp Awds; UC Davis Rgnts Schlrshp Fnlst; U Of CA Davis.

EHRLINGER, AMANDA S; University City HS; San Diego, CA; (3); 23/373; Dance Clb; Key Clb; Church Choir; Orch; Mgr Swmmng; Hon Roll; Music; Med.

EHSAN, REBECCA; American HS; Fremont, CA; (4); Model UN; Spanish Clb; Sec SADD; Teachers Aide; Co-Ed Nwsp; Ed Yrbk; Stu Cncl; Elks Awd; Hon Roll; NHS; CA ST U; Marktng.

EI-MANG WU, ALICE; Poway HS; Poway, CA; (4); 7/677; VP AFS; Pres FBLA; Treas Mu Alpha Theta; Orch; Nwsp; Var Swmmng; Kiwanis Awd; Ntl Merit Schol; Most Imprvd Grl Swmmr 1987-88; Summr Intrnshp At Caralina Island Marine Insti; U Of CA Berkeley; Engr Mgr.

EICHBERG, CATHERINE J; Louisville HS; Tarzana, CA; (2); Art Clb; Computer Clb; Drama Clb; GAA; Office Aide; Chorus; School Play; Stage Crew; Nwsp; Rep Frsh Cls; Doctor.

EICHENBERG, ROBERT; Sherman E Burroughs HS; Ridgecrest, CA; (4); Am Leg Boys St; Spanish Clb; Varsity Clb; Phtg Ed Nwsp; Rep Stu Cncl; Bsbl; Var L Socr; Pres Radio Clb; Santa Clara U.

EICHLER, ERIKA C; St Francis HS; Sunnyvale, CA; (3); Service Clb; Speech Tm; SADD; Ed Nwsp; Ed Yrbk; Var Swmmng; High Hon Roll; Hon Roll; NHS; Jr Statesman; Jrnlsm.

EICHMAN, TAD J; Colfax HS; Weimar, CA; (3); 11/165; Pres Church Yth Grp; Teachers Aide; JV Bsbl; JV Bsktbl; Cit Awd; Hon Roll; Religious Spprt Grp; CCD HS Tchr; ST Josephs Smnry; Cath Priest.

EICHORN, JOSHUA M; Piedmont HS; Piedmont, CA; (3); Church Yth Grp; Teachers Aide; Acpl Chr; Boy Scts; Church Choir; School Musical; JV Capt Bsktbl; Tri-M VP; Westmont Coll; Minstry.

EICKHOFF, CHRIS D; The Bishops Schl; Escondido, CA; (3); Church Yth Grp; Rep Frsh Cls; Bsbl; Church Yth Grp; Socr; Trk; Wt Lftg; Med.

EID, HEIDI G; Fred C Beyer HS; Modesto, CA; (1); Church Yth Grp; Hon Roll; Yth Stff 1st Bptst Chrch; Bus Admin.

EIDSMOE, JACOB T; Ukiah HS; Ukiah, CA; (3); Letterman Clb; Red Cross Aide; Science Clb; Teachers Aide; Chorus; Rptr Stu Cncl; Var Capt Swmmng; Ukiah HS Swmmng Blnkt 90; Mst Vlbl Swmmr Awd 89; Astrphyst.

EIDSON, MICHELE; Montclair HS; Ontario, CA; (2); Church Yth Grp; GAA; SADD; JV Socr; Var Trk; Hon Roll; Prfct Atten Awd; Azusa Pacific U; Engl.

EIGENHEER, PETER C; John F Kennedy HS; Sacramento, CA; (4); 110/500; Orch; School Musical; Var Crs Cntry; Var Trk; Outstndng Stu Crss Cntry; Plyd 1st Vln.

EILAR, KIMBERLY ANN; Eisenhower HS; Rialto, CA; (4); Church Yth Grp; Cmnty Wkr; French Clb; Girl Scts; Library Aide; Teachers Aide; Church Choir; School Musical; Yrbk; Sec Frsh Cls; Most Creative Sewer/Awd; Most Imprvd Sewer; Most Productive Sewing Stu; Fashion Inst; Fash Dsgnr.

EINESS, TODD; East Union HS; Manteca, CA; (2); 5/214; Band; High Hon Roll; Prfct Atten Awd; Bus.

EING, CAMERON J; Pasadena HS; Sierra Madre, CA; (1); French Clb; Var Swmmng; JV Water Polo; Vrsty Swim Team.

EING, KIRSTEN M; Pasadena HS; Sierra Madre, CA; (3); French Clb; Var Cheerldng; Z Clb Srvc Organztn; Green Peace; Flag Team & Vrsty Cheer.

EINSTEIN, JENNIFER M; Fountain Valley HS; Fountain Valley, CA; (3); Cmnty Wkr; Rep Red Cross Aide; Teachers Aide; Chorus; School Musical; School Play; High Hon Roll; Ntl Merit Ltr; Humanities Approach Culture; TALIT Prgm; CSF.

EISCHEN, TANYA K; Etiwanda HS; Rancho Cucamonga, CA; (3); Office Aide; Hon Roll; GATE.

EISEMAN, JOSHUA; Newport Harbor HS; Costa Mesa, CA; (3); Aud/Vis; Computer Clb; Speech Tm; Thesps; L Band; Drm Mjr(t); Mrchg Band; School Musical; School Play; Stage Crew; San Luis Obispo; Mech Engrng.

EISEMANN, MELANIE A; Downey HS; Downey, CA; (3); Church Yth Grp; School Play; Hon Roll; Acad Excllnc Awd 89; Gldn St Exam 1st Yr Alg Hnrs; Teen Mssn Holland 87; Mssn Amer Stg Crew 90.

EISENBERGER, NAOMI I; Lowell HS; San Francisco, CA; (2); School Musical; Gym; United Synagogue Yth Secy Treas; Israel Culture Club Secy.

EISENBISE, CHRISTINE E; Clovis HS; Clovis, CA; (3); Church Yth Grp; Dance Clb; Drama Clb; French Clb; Speech Tm; Teachers Aide; Church Choir; School Musical; Hon Roll; CSF; Commnctns.

EISENLORD, ALYSON; Simi Valley HS; Simi Valley, CA; (2); Church Yth Grp; Temple Yth Grp; Stu Cncl; JV Cheerldng; Hebrew Schl Aide; Law.

EISER, ANDY; Los Alamitos HS; Seal Beach, CA; (4); Boy Scts; Pres Math Tm; Co-Capt Quiz Bowl; VP Treas Temple Yth Grp; VP Soph Cls; Off Jr Cls; Off Sr Cls; JV Crs Cntry; Ntl Merit Ltr; Med.

EISLEIN, KELEE; Etiwanda HS; Alta Loma, CA; (4); SADD; Hon Roll; Hgh Achvt In Annual Physics Bowl; Awded Ca Meritimes Merit Schlrshp; CA Meritime Acad; Marine Engr.

EISNER, ERIN E; Mater Dei HS; Anaheim, CA; (2); Church Yth Grp; Rptr Nwsp; JV Socr; Var L Trk; Hon Roll; NHS; Athletic Trngn; Coach Yth Soccer Tm; Sports Med.

EITZEN, CHRISTOPHER J; O'farrell SCPA HS; San Diego, CA; (4); Church Yth Grp; Debate Tm; Letterman Clb; Quiz Bowl; Scholastic Bowl; Chorus; Orch; School Musical; High Hon Roll; NHS; Solo Vln; SSSU Sccr; Srfng; Dntstry.

EKHAML, MARK T; University Of San Diego HS; San Diego, CA; (2); Boy Scts; Off Church Yth Grp; Drama Clb; School Musical; School Play; Stage Crew; JV Trk; Opt Clb Awd; Prfct Atten Awd; Altar Boy Chrch; Acting.

EKLUND, JAMIE C; Birmingham HS; Van Nuys, CA; (3); Letterman Clb; Drill Tm; Cheerldng; Hon Roll; Prfct Atten Awd; CSUN; Bus.

EKNOIAN, SAMANTHA; Selma HS; Selma, CA; (1); Drama Clb; High Hon Roll.

EL ALAMI, SAM S; Manteca HS; Manteca, CA; (3); Boy Scts; Church Yth Grp; VP Computer Clb; Var Wt Lftg; BYU; Electromicroscopy.

EL MASSRY, PETER H; St John Bosco HS; Huntington Park, CA; (2); French Clb; Natl Hnr Soc Srgnt At Arms; JR Statesman Of Amer; Yale; Lib Arts.

EL SONBATY, NANCY; Palisades HS; Pacific Palisades, CA; (4); 16/405; Pres Debate Tm; Letterman Clb; NFL; Service Clb; Speech Tm; Chorus; JV Bsktbl; L Var Sftbl; Intrml Tennis; Intrml Vllybl; CSF Pres; UCLA; Bio-Chem.

EL-HAGE, LILLIAN; Livermore HS; Livermore, CA; (4); 4/300; Var Debate Tm; French Clb; Math Clb; Math Tm; NFL; Red Cross Aide; Speech Tm; SADD; Teachers Aide; Nwsp; U Of CA Davis; Bio.

EL-HAYEK, HANI; St John Bosco HS; Lakewood, CA; (3); Computer Clb; Drama Clb; Key Clb; VP Chorus; Church Choir; School Musical; School Play; Stage Crew; Variety Show; Hon Roll; Religion, Comp Sci, Choir, Span Awds; CA ST; Acting.

ELAHI, ALI; San Dieguito HS; Encinitas, CA; (2); #1 In Class; VP German Clb; Math Tm; Scholastic Bowl; Bsktbl; High Hon Roll; Prfct Atten Awd; Pres Acad Fit Awd; CSF; Acad Team Solid Player Awd; U CA San Diego; Med.

ELAHI-KERMANI, ALI; Sandiegoito HS; Carlsbad, CA; (2); #1 In Class; VP German Clb; Math Tm; Scholastic Bowl; Intrml Bsktbl; High Hon Roll; Prfct Atten Awd; Pres Acad Fit Awd; Member Calif Schlrshp Fed; Acad Teams Solid Player Awd; Take Violin Lessons; UCSO; Medicine.

ELANAGAN, WILLEEN; Fremont HS; Oakland, CA; (3); Church Yth Grp; Spanish Clb; Teachers Aide; Chorus; Church Choir; School Musical; Bsktbl; Sftbl; Hon Roll; Jr Prom Clb; UC Davis; Bus.

ELANDER, JENNIFER; Arroyo Grande HS; Arroyo Grande, CA; (1); Church Yth Grp; Dance Clb; FCA; Capt Cheerldng; JV Swmmng; High Hon Roll; Pepperdine; Law.

ELDER, MARCUS; Desert Christian HS; Lancaster, CA; (2); 1/20; Boy Scts; Church Yth Grp; Band; Stage Crew; Rep Stu Cncl; L Var Crs Cntry; High Hon Roll; Intl Dev.

ELDER, SEAN; Manteca HS; Manteca, CA; (3); 60/400; French Clb; Letterman Clb; Varsity Clb; Bsktbl; Wt Lftg; Cit Awd; Hon Roll; Princpals Engl Awd; Law.

ELDER, SHARON A; Bishop Amat HS; El Monte, CA; (2); Church Yth Grp; Cmnty Wkr; Drama Clb; French Clb; Amnasty International Club; East Cst U; Child Psych Or Dipl.

ELDRIDGE, BRENT S; Irvine HS; Irvine, CA; (1); Bsktbl; Vllybl; Hon Roll; Heritage Award For History.

ELDRIDGE, EDWARD J; Valley HS; Sacramento, CA; (2); 70/408; Church Yth Grp; JV Var Bsktbl; Hon Roll; Fullerton ST; Law.

ELDRIDGE, ETHAN C; Montgomery HS; Santa Rosa, CA; (3); Chorus; Jazz Band; Orch; High Hon Roll; NHS; Pres Acad Fit Awd; Sonoma Cty Jr Symphny.

ELDRIDGE, KATHLEEN A; San Pedro HS; San Pedro, CA; (4); 3/522; Teachers Aide; Rep VP Stu Cncl; VP Capt Sftbl; High Hon Roll; Hon Roll; Pres Acad Fit Awd; CSF; CSF Gold Seal Bearer; Scholar Athl Of Yr; UC Santa Barbara.

ELDRIDGE, MICHELLE; Fred C Beyer HS; Modesto, CA; (4); 74/506; Church Yth Grp; Debate Tm; English Clb; Spanish Clb; Teachers Aide; Bsktbl; Gym; Hon Roll; NHS; Pres Acad Fit Awd; Cvl Air Ptrl; Smmr Scntfc Smnr US Air Force Acad; CA Poly Pomona; Aerntcl Engr.

ELEAZAR, DON; Beverly Hills Prep Schl; Westwood, CA; (4); Art Clb; Chess Clb; Computer Clb; Debate Tm; Quiz Bowl; Science Clb; Varsity Clb; Yrbk; Rep VP Stu Cncl; Bsktbl; Loyola Marymount U; Bus Admin.

ELEFANTE, BETSY; Helix HS; La Mesa, CA; (2); 31/472; French Clb; Pep Clb; Quiz Bowl; Stu Cncl; Crs Cntry; Wt Lftg; High Hon Roll; Hon Roll; UCLA; Aerospace Engrng.

ELFORD, KATHLEEN; Oroville HS; Oroville, CA; (4); 10/185; Church Yth Grp; SADD; Chorus; Church Choir; Capt Flag Corp; Mrchg Band; School Musical; Stage Crew; Treas Stu Cncl; Powder Puff Ftbl; Bnk America Plque Awd Appld Arts; Outstndng Musicn Choir; Soroptimst Girl Month Awd; Butte CC; Accntng.

ELIA, ANDREW; Dos Pueblos HS; Santa Barbara, CA; (3); 2/330; Treas Drama Clb; Math Clb; Math Tm; Science Clb; School Play; Variety Show; Var L Crs Cntry; Var L Trk; Mock Trial Team; Improvisation Troupe.

ELIAS, ANTHONY A; Bellarmine College Prep; Milpitas, CA; (4); 1/300; Debate Tm; Math Clb; Math Tm; NFL; Service Clb; Speech Tm; Intrml Trk; High Hon Roll; Hon Roll; Ntl Merit Ltr; CA Schlrshp Fed; Natl Mrt Fnlst; Schlrshp Awd; Chncllr & Regnt Schlrshp Awd; Tandy Corp Top 2 Awd; US Military Acad; Medcl.

ELIAS, DOMINIC; Damien HS; Pomona, CA; (1); Debate Tm; Speech Tm; Ftbl; Golf; Hon Roll; Golf Club; U Southern CA; Med.

ELIAS, ERIKA; Fremont HS; Sunnyvale, CA; (1); Drama Clb; Flag Corp; School Play; Bsktbl; High Hon Roll; Jr NHS; NHS.

ELIAS, KHALID A; Elk Grove HS; Sacramento, CA; (3); 7/650; Art Clb; Computer Clb; Math Clb; Spanish Clb; Wt Lftg; Cit Awd; High Hon Roll; Prfct Atten Awd; CSF Mem 87-90; U CA Davis; Cmptr Eng.

ELIASON, BLAIR E; Bullard HS; Fresno, CA; (2); 45/508; Tennis; CSF; MVP Tnns Team; Mst Imprvd JV Tnns Team.

ELIJAH, MARSHA L; West HS; Bakersfield, CA; (1); Band; Mrchg Band; Law.

ELINSON, HANNAH; Western HS; Anaheim, CA; (3); Debate Tm; Drama Clb; VP French Clb; NFL; Speech Tm; Diving; Trk; High Hon Roll; Opt Clb Awd; Photo Clb; Svc For Chldrns Hosp; Clb SOS; Ntrl Sci.

ELITE, KRISTIANA E; Lowell HS; San Francisco, CA; (2); Latin Clb; Orch; Hon Roll; Lowell Bsbl Team Mgr; UC Santa Barbara; Dsgn.

ELITE, SHANNON M; Clovis HS; Clovis, CA; (2); Pres Church Yth Grp; Hon Roll; Hikng Clb; Fresno ST U; Medcl.

ELIZABETH, PEREZ A; Don Lugo HS; Chino, CA; (2); Pep Clb; Spanish Clb; L Cheerldng; Var Pom Pon; Var L Trk; Cheer Coach Jr All Amer Ftbl; Del ASB Convntn; Law.

ELIZALDE, SYLVINA; Santa Ana HS; Santa Ana, CA; (2); Cmnty Wkr; FTA; Variety Show; High Hon Roll; Math, Engrng, Sci Achvt; Close Up; Math.

ELIZARRARAS, GEORGE A; J W North HS; Riverside, CA; (3); Church Yth Grp; Bsktbl; High Hon Roll; CSF; JR Stsmn Of Amer; Cal Poly Pomona; Engrng.

ELIZARRARAZ, ANTONIO; Mission Bay HS; San Diego, CA; (2); 87/380; French Clb; Spanish Clb; Cit Awd; Hon Roll.

ELIZARRARAZ, CHRISTINE; Lincoln HS; Stockton, CA; (3); 270/538; Dance Clb; Teachers Aide; Variety Show; JV Var Crs Cntry; Var Trk; Hon Roll; USC Coll; Special Educ.

ELIZARRARAZ, DIANA; Calexico HS; Calexico, CA; (1); Computer Clb; GAA; Office Aide; Spanish Clb; Drill Tm; Bsktbl; Gym; Swmmng; Tennis; High Hon Roll; Principal; Cnslr; IBC.

ELIZONDO, FERNANDO V; Kingsburg Joint Union HS; Kingsburg, CA; (2); FFA; Wt Lftg; Wrstlng; Hon Roll; TX A&M; Agri Engr.

ELIZONDO, RODRIGO; Lynwood HS; Lynwood, CA; (4); 24/500; Math Clb; Varsity Clb; Var JV Socr; Hon Roll; Prfct Atten Awd; Top AP Calc I Stu 89-90; Top 10 AP Physics 89-90; U Of Sthrn CA; Elec Engrng.

ELIZONDO, SYLVIA; Arvin HS; Arvin, CA; (3); 6/150; Church Yth Grp; Computer Clb; Debate Tm; Drama Clb; FBLA; Science Clb; Ski Clb; VP Spanish Clb; Speech Tm; SADD; MESA; CSF; Cal ST Bakersfield; Comp Engr.

ELKINS, BEN A; Apple Valley HS; Apple Valley, CA; (3); Church Yth Grp; Office Aide; SADD; Teachers Aide; L Bsktbl; Tom Pyatt Schlrshp Awd Skill & Dedication Bsktbl; Slama-Jama Bsktbl Blue Chip Lg Reebok; UCSB 90; Law.

ELKINS, ERIC D; Hesperia HS; Hesperia, CA; (3); 13/500; Key Clb; Science Clb; JV Bsktbl; CA Schlstc Fed; Unvrsty Clb; Elec Engr.

ELKINS, MICHELE; Highlands HS; Sacramento, CA; (4); Office Aide; Ed Yrbk; Rep Sr Cls; Cit Awd; High Hon Roll; Pres Acad Fit Awd; Sacramento ST U; Liberal Stds.

ELKINS, TINA; Turlock HS; Keyes, CA; (2); Red Cross Aide; JV Sftbl; Intrml Vllybl; Hon Roll; Comp Prgmr.

ELKISCH, ALAN W; John Wesley North HS; Riverside, CA; (3); Computer Clb; Acad Boostr Clb Phys Sci/Earth Awd 89-90; Motion Pictre Directr.

ELLEDGE, KRISANN RENEE; Esperanza HS; Yorba Linda, CA; (1); French Clb; FBLA; SADD; JV Cheerldng; High Hon Roll; Pres Acad Fit Awd; Esperanza Top 25 Awd Of Merit; Acad Achvmt Lttr 89-90; Harvard Med Schl; Pediatrician.

ELLENBERGER, ANDY C; Central Valley HS; Redding, CA; (1); Hon Roll; Just Say No.

ELLERSON, HEIDI L; Ceres HS; Modesto, CA; (4); Art Clb; Dance Clb; French Clb; FBLA; Intnl Clb; Key Clb; Letterman Clb; Pep Clb; SADD; Church Choir; SR Class Pres; Spec Olympics Chm; Hmcmg Queen; Sacramento ST; Intl Rel.

ELLERY, JENNIFER; Piner HS; Santa Rosa, CA; (1); Band; Mrchg Band; JV Cheerldng; U C Davis; Special Educ.

ELLERY, TRACI L; El Toro HS; El Toro, CA; (3); JV Var Bsktbl; JV Sftbl; MVP Sftbl; UC Santa Barbara; Chld Psych.

ELLESTAD, MERRILY A; Bear River HS; Grass Valley, CA; (2); 1/227; Spanish Clb; Cit Awd; Hon Roll; Prfct Atten Awd.

ELLINGS, JESS B; Norco HS; Corona, CA; (2); Arch.

ELLINGSEN, KRISTINA; Lakewood HS; Lkwd, CA; (3); Dance Clb; Drama Clb; JA; Pep Clb; SADD; Thesps; Orch; School Musical; School Play; Rep Stu Cncl; NYU; Phy.

ELLINGTON, CHRISTINA D; St Francis HS; San Jose, CA; (3); 24/288; Stage Crew; Rptr Nwsp; JV Swmmng; High Hon Roll; CSF; Interact Club; Engl.

ELLINGTON, THERESA A; Buena Park HS; Anaheim, CA; (3); 82/375; Am Leg Aux Girls St; Church Yth Grp; Drama Clb; Letterman Clb; Thesps; Church Choir; School Musical; School Play; Stage Crew; Phtg Yrbk; MVP, 1st Team All Leag Sccr; Pblshd Author Short Story Cont; Sci.

ELLIOTT, BRIDGET J; Hilltop HS; Chula Vista, CA; (2); Intnl Clb; SADD; Rptr Nwsp; JV Socr; Cit Awd; Renaissance Clb; Law.

ELLIOTT, DANIEL P; Mira Loma HS; Sacramento, CA; (3); Treas Drama Clb; French Clb; Thesps; Mgr School Play; Stage Crew; Crmnl Justice.

ELLIOTT, DANIELLE L; Louisville HS; Canoga Park, CA; (3); Cmnty Wkr; Drama Clb; FHA; Chorus; School Musical; JV Swmmng; High Hon Roll; NHS; CSF; Peer Cnslng Grp; Law.

ELLIOTT, DAVID; Loyola HS; Hawthorne, CA; (2); Boy Scts; Church Yth Grp; Debate Tm; NFL; Speech Tm; SADD; Variety Show; Rptr Nwsp; Pres Frsh Cls; Pres Soph Cls; Outstndng Stu Yr; Egl Sct Awd; Law Clb; Med Clb.

ELLIOTT, ELIZABETH; Fred C Beyer HS; Modesto, CA; (3); Church Yth Grp; Service Clb; Teachers Aide; Acpl Chr; Chorus; Var Crs Cntry; Var Trk; Hon Roll; Best Crss Cntry Runner 88; Elem Teacher.

ELLIOTT, ELIZABETH A; Santa Clara HS; Oxnard, CA; (2); 40/200; Church Yth Grp; Cmnty Wkr; Pep Clb; Crs Cntry; Hon Roll; NHS; Grad Barbizon Modeling Schl; Author Of Poetry; Dance-Tap, Ballet & Jazz; UC Berkeley; Surg Nrsng.

ELLIOTT, ERICA E; San Bernardino HS; San Bernardino, CA; (3); Office Aide; Teachers Aide; L Var Swmmng; High Hon Roll; Prfct Atten Awd; Hgh Grade Pt Avg Awd; Barbizon Modeling Schl Grad; U CA R; Bus Mgmt.

ELLIOTT, ERIN M; Laguna Hills HS; Laguna Hills, CA; (2); Church Yth Grp; Drama Clb; Model UN; Drill Tm; School Play; Bsktbl; Hon Roll; Global Connctns Clb VP; Creatv Wrtng Clb; Liberal Arts.

ELLIOTT II, JAMES S; Oak Grove HS; San Jose, CA; (4); Cmnty Wkr; Church Choir; Variety Show; Pres Sr Cls; Stu Cncl; Assoc Stu Body Ldrshp Schlrshp; Air Force; Pilot.

ELLIOTT, JAMES W; Pinole Valley HS; San Pablo, CA; (3); Boy Scts; Band; Drm Mjr(t); Jazz Band; School Musical; Var L Crs Cntry; Var L Trk; High Hon Roll; Hon Roll; Eagle Sct; MVA Trck; CSF; U Of CA Berkeley; Chem Engr.

ELLIOTT, JEANINE R; School Of The Arts; San Francisco, CA; (2); 14/400; Church Yth Grp; Teachers Aide; Church Choir; Orch; Stage Crew; Hon Roll.

ELLIOTT, JENNIFER M; Canyon Springs HS; Moreno Valley, CA; (3); Rptr FBLA; Teachers Aide; Stat Bsktbl; Score Keeper; JV Var Sftbl.

ELLIOTT, JOHN; Armijo HS; Fairfield, CA; (1); Spanish Clb; Comp Achvt Awd; Med.

ELLIOTT, KASEY; Walnut HS; Walnut, CA; (2); 68/479; Church Yth Grp; German Clb; Key Clb; Rptr Nwsp; Hon Roll; Crossfire; BYU.

ELLIOTT, KATE E; Berkeley HS; Oakland, CA; (4); 1/600; Church Yth Grp; Cmnty Wkr; Pres French Clb; Hosp Aide; High Hon Roll; Ntl Merit SF; Photogrphy/Photo Clb; Wellesley Bk Awd; CA Schlrshp Federn Pres; Astronomy.

ELLIOTT, LISA ANN; West HS; Bakersfield, CA; (4); 32/392; Ed Yrbk; Stu Cncl; Var Crs Cntry; JV Swmmng; Hon Roll; NHS; Wings For Life Secy VP; Assisteens Rcrdng Secy; USC; Pol Sci.

ELLIOTT, MARGARET S; Clayton Valley HS; Concord, CA; (4); 95/444; Art Clb; Church Yth Grp; Cmnty Wkr; Drama Clb; GAA; High Hon Roll; Hon Roll; Pres Acad Fit Awd; Sr Womens Service Org; Oustndng Sr Vocal Music; Yrh Congressional Ldrshp Conf 90; Fresno ST.

ELLIOTT, MICHAEL R; Irvine HS; Irvine, CA; (3); 30/520; Cmnty Wkr; French Clb; JA; Key Clb; Service Clb; Ed Nwsp; Yrbk; Rep Stu Cncl; JV Capt Socr; High Hon Roll; Club Sccr; AF Acad Smmr Scientific Seminar 90; Wrld Fnlst Odyssey Of Mind Sci Cmptn 90; Engrng.

ELLIOTT, RYAN; Etiwanda HS; Alta Loma, CA; (2); Chess Clb; French Clb; JA; Ski Clb; Hon Roll; Prfct Atten Awd; CSF; Math.

ELLIOTT, TERI L; Eisenhower HS; Colton, CA; (4); FBLA; Spanish Clb; Sec Sr Cls; Hon Roll; Acad Decthln; Blck Stu Union Sectry; San Deigo ST U; Health.

ELLIOTT, TRACIE; Lower Lake HS; Clearlake Park, CA; (2); 11/146; Pres Drama Clb; Pep Clb; Red Cross Aide; School Play; Ed Nwsp; Cheerldng; High Hon Roll; Hon Roll; Prfct Atten Awd; Dramtic Arts.

ELLIOTT, VERONICA; Grant HS; Sacramento, CA; (4); Model UN; Sftbl; Vllybl; High Hon Roll; Hon Roll; Amer River JC; Legal Asst.

ELLIS, AIMEE; Tulare Union HS; Tulare, CA; (1); FFA; Archlgy.

ELLIS, ANGIE; Arrowhead Christian Acad; San Bernardino, CA; (1); Chess Clb; Church Yth Grp; Drama Clb; Math Clb; Pep Clb; Scholastic Bowl; School Musical; School Play; VP Pres Frsh Cls; Rep Stu Cncl; Interior Dsgn.

ELLIS, CHERI L; Hanford HS; Hanford, CA; (1); Church Yth Grp; FHA; Hon Roll; CSF; Gymnstcs; Stanford.

ELLIS, CHIANTA; Polytechnic HS; Long Beach, CA; (1); Church Yth Grp; Hosp Aide; Pep Clb; Teachers Aide; Grace Sorority; Newscstrs.

ELLIS, CHRISTINA M; Ganesha HS; Pomona, CA; (3); French Clb; Cheerldng; Vllybl; Hon Roll.

ELLIS, DONALD R; Atwater HS; Atwater, CA; (2); FFA; Letterman Clb; JV Crs Cntry; JV Ftbl; JV Socr; JV Trk; JV Wt Lftg; Im In Jays Taekwondo Karate; I Have A Part Time Job After Schl; Airforce & College.

ELLIS, ERIK C; Monte Vista HS; Spring Valley, CA; (2); 31/422; Boy Scts; Church Yth Grp; French Clb; Key Clb; Socr; Trk; Hon Roll; UCSD; Orthdntst.

ELLIS, GREGORY A; Loyola HS; San Pedro, CA; (2); Boy Scts; German Clb; NFL; Speech Tm; Trk; Hon Roll; St Schlr; Law.

ELLIS, JENNYFER L; North HS; Bakersfield, CA; (3); 32/456; Pres Sec Church Yth Grp; Spanish Clb; Church Choir; Phtg Yrbk; Sftbl; Hon Roll; Natl Hnr Soc; Spnsh Hnr Soc; Trk Club; Educ.

ELLIS, JESSE; Burbank HS; Burbank, CA; (3); Boy Scts; Church Yth Grp; Pep Clb; Chorus; Var Cheerldng; Var Swmmng; High Hon Roll; Hon Roll; Prfct Atten Awd; Pres Acad Fit Awd; Civil Air Ptrl; Aviation.

ELLIS, JOHN F; Del Campo HS; Carmichael, CA; (2); Ski Clb; Rep Soph Cls; JV Bsbl; JV Bsktbl; JV Socr; Hon Roll; Ref CFO Sccr Clb; BCI Bsktbl Tm; UCLA AZ Stanford; Bus.

ELLIS, KEITH; Fremont HS; Sunnyvale, CA; (1); Boy Scts; School Play; Ed Yrbk; Vol Cty Sunnyvale Pks & Rcrtn Asst; Law.

ELLIS, LATRICE R; Ma Clymonds HS; Oakland, CA; (1); Girl Scts; Ski Clb; Band; Lit Mag; Cit Awd; Hon Roll; Fresno ST; Comp Typist.

ELLIS, LORI B; Fontana HS; Fontana, CA; (3); Chess Clb; Church Yth Grp; Drama Clb; Teachers Aide; Band; Church Choir; Mrchg Band; Stage Crew; Cit Awd; High Hon Roll; Pnthln Acadc Tm; CSF; Girls ST; U Redlands; Engl.

ELLIS, LYDIA; Bethel Christian HS; Monticello, AR; (2); Var Bsktbl; Var Mgr(s); High Hon Roll; Studied Piano For 5 Consecutive Years; Selected To Play At Southern California Music Conv; Branch Hnrs; Lawyer.

ELLIS, MARCIE; San Ramon Valley HS; Danville, CA; (2); Church Yth Grp; Cmnty Wkr; School Play; Bsktbl; Hon Roll; GAA; SADD; Chorus; Stage Crew; Trk; 2 Mst Promsng Drama Stu Awds; Mustang Soccer Clb, USA Soccer Team England 90.

ELLIS, PATRICK; St Joseph Notre Dame HS; Alameda, CA; (4); 17/94; Am Leg Boys St; Boy Scts; Ski Clb; School Play; VP Jr Cls; Var Crs Cntry; Var Socr; NHS; US Mltry Acad; Military Ofcr.

ELLIS, SHAWNIQUE; Livermore HS; Long Beach, CA; (3); Church Yth Grp; Band; Mrchg Band; Cheerldng; Pom Pon; Cit Awd; Hon Roll; Pres Acad Fit Awd; Peer Cnslr; UCLA; Psych.

ELLIS, STACY L; Garces Memorial HS; Bakersfield, CA; (2); Key Clb; SADD; Stage Crew; JV Sftbl; JV Vllybl; High Hon Roll; CSF; Harvard; Law.

ELLIS, SUNNY A; Redwood HS; Visalia, CA; (2); German Clb; Library Aide; Varsity Clb; Band; Rptr Nwsp; JV Bsktbl; Var Swmmng; Hon Roll; Pres Acad Fit Awd; Acad Ltr; History.

ELLIS, TIMOTHY J; Maranatha HS; Los Angeles, CA; (2); 1/117; Church Yth Grp; Service Clb; Band; Mrchg Band; Pep Band; Var Crs Cntry; JV Socr; Var Trk; High Hon Roll; Cross Cntry & Track Var Ltrs; Photo For Yrbk.

ELLISON, ANDREA LYNN; Foothill HS; Santa Ana, CA; (4); 80/320; Red Cross Aide; Teachers Aide; Chorus; School Musical; Cit Awd; DAR Awd; High Hon Roll; Hon Roll; Nominated Girls State; Cal ST; Psych.

ELLISON, ANTHONY D; Hueneme HS; Oxnard, CA; (3); 38/376; Chess Clb; FBLA; Library Aide; Office Aide; Teachers Aide; School Play; JV Bsktbl; Var Ftbl; Mgr(s); Tennis; U Of NV Las Vegas; Engr.

ELLISON, TERRENCE J; Bellarmine College Preparatory HS; San Jose, CA; (3); Cmnty Wkr; Red Cross Aide; Service Clb; Teachers Aide; Ed Nwsp; Intrml Bsktbl; Vllybll; Music Drums; Swmmng; Pre Med.

ELLISON, TERRY J; Bellarmine College Prep; San Jose, CA; (3); 16/296; Red Cross Aide; Service Clb; Teachers Aide; Nwsp; Bsktbl; Ftbl; Sftbl; Trk; Vllybl; Hon Roll; Invest In Amer Cert Of Merit; Loyola Marymount U; Med.

ELLSBERRY, YALAANDA; Bullard HS; Fresno, CA; (2); Church Yth Grp; Band; Chorus; Nwsp; Off Soph Cls; Golf; Socr; Swmmng; Vllybl; Cit Awd; Awd Stu Of Week; Sprtsmnshp Awd; Mscl Awd; Fresno City Coll; Dist Atty.

ELLSWORTH, JEFFERY A; Walnut HS; Walnut, CA; (2); Ski Clb; Swmmng; Hon Roll; Bus.

ELLSWORTH, MARY B; Mt Whitney HS; Visalia, CA; (1); Key Clb; Orch; Diving; Hon Roll; Gymnstcs; Med.

ELMAS, JEREMY; Capital Christian HS; Fair Oaks, CA; (3); VP Chess Clb; Computer Clb; Var L Ftbl; Var Wrstlng; Cit Awd; High Hon Roll; Pres Acad Fit Awd; Engrng.

ELMENDORF, JAMES H; Redlands HS; Redlands, CA; (3); JV Socr; Hon Roll; Greenpeace; Amnsty Intl; Hamphire Coll; Creatve Wrtng.

ELMORE, SHAMRHA L; Ramona HS; Ramona, CA; (2); Dance Clb; Library Aide; Office Aide; Teachers Aide; Rode Horses San Vicente Pony Clb 88-90; Attained Lvl C-1 SVPC; Law.

ELMS, ROBERT L; Ceres HS; Ceres, CA; (4); 21/273; Church Yth Grp; FBLA; Math Tm; Jazz Band; Mrchg Band; Nwsp; Var L Socr; JV Tennis; Var L Trk; High Hon Roll; Stu Of Mnth May; MVP Jr Var Sccr; CA ST U Fresno; Elec Engrng.

ELORDUY, TODD; Christian Brothers HS; Sacramento, CA; (3); SADD; Var Bsbl; Var Ftbl; NHS; Amer Legion Baseball (All-Star Team); Bus Psych.

ELPUSAN, RINA C; Robert A Millikan HS; Long Beach, CA; (4); Sec Art Clb; Church Yth Grp; Cit Awd; High Hon Roll; Pres Acad Fit Awd; Mdl Merit Art; Prin Hnr Role; Cal ST Long Beach; Bio.

ELQUZA, EMAD A; Los Amigos HS; Fountain Valley, CA; (2); JV Bsktbl; Hon Roll; Jr NHS; NHS; Cngrsnl Yth Ldrshp Cncl; U CA Irvine; Med.

ELSAESSER, CARRIE A; Los Amigos HS; Fountain Valley, CA; (3); 95/301; Church Yth Grp; GAA; Letterman Clb; Varsity Clb; Var Bsktbl; JV Vllybl; Hon Roll; Intl Order Jobs Dghtrs Prncss; Long Beach ST; Vet Med.

ELSBERRY, BRANACA M; The Bishops Schl; La Jolla, CA; (4); Var L Sftbl; Var Capt Tennis; Northwestern U.

ELSEIKALI, JOANE K; Pittsburg HS; Pittsburg, CA; (2); Girl Scts; Math Tm; Orch; Vllybl; Wt Lftg; French Hon Soc; High Hon Roll; Hon Roll; Prfct Atten Awd; Pres Acad Fit Awd; Tutor Awd; Library Hlpr Awd; UC Davis; Sci.

ELSER, KEVIN M; Fairfield HS; Fairfield, CA; (3); Art Clb; Chess Clb; Church Yth Grp; Ftbl; Wt Lftg; Wrstlng; UC Davis CA; Spc Sci.

ELSLEY, KATHERINE R; La Reina HS; Thousand Oaks, CA; (3); 16/67; Church Yth Grp; Hosp Aide; Ed Nwsp; Yrbk; Stu Cncl; Cit Awd; Hon Roll; NHS; Opt Clb Awd; Prfct Atten Awd; Campus Ministry; Amnesty Intl; Psych.

ELSMORE, TAMARA J; Hemet HS; Hemet, CA; (3); 84/547; Church Yth Grp; Cmnty Wkr; Library Aide; Office Aide; Teachers Aide; Chorus; Church Choir; Jazz Band; Cit Awd; Hon Roll; Chrch Orgnst; Trinity Of Lndn Xms Piano Stu; Brigham Yng U; Elem Educ.

ELSOKARY, BASEM M; Monterey HS; Monterey, CA; (2); French Clb; Model UN; High Hon Roll; Hgh Hnrs Golden St Exam Alg; Citation Awd United Nations Assn Natl Essay Cont; Stanford U; Math.

ELSON, JOSH C; St Marys HS; Lodi, CA; (2); Church Yth Grp; Varsity Clb; Ftbl; Tennis; Hon Roll; Jr Statesman.

ELSON, MARK T; Lindsay HS; Lindsay, CA; (2); 1/200; Church Yth Grp; SADD; Church Choir; Pres Soph Cls; Var Bsktbl; Tennis; High Hon Roll; Natrl Hlprs.

ELSTER, GRETCHEN LEE; Bear River HS; Grass Valley, CA; (2); Off Church Yth Grp; Church Choir; Rep Stu Cncl; Capt JV Cheerldng; Sftbl; Hon Roll; Cal Poly; Arch.

ELSTON, BRITTNEY N; Bullard HS; Fresno, CA; (1); Spellman; Jrnlsm.

ELTGROTH, SELENE F; Livermore HS; Livermore, CA; (1); 4-H; Band; Mrchg Band; Stat Wrstlng; High Hon Roll; Command Prfrmnce Solo Ensmble.

ELWESS, APRIL R; Modesto Christian HS; Modesto, CA; (3); Church Yth Grp; Treas Sr Cls; Pianist; Stanislaus U; Hstry.

ELWIN, JEANINE A; Alto Loma HS; Alta Loma, CA; (2); Church Yth Grp; Dance Clb; JV Tennis; Environment; Reading; Music; Fashion Display.

ELWOOD, SUSAN; Bonita Vista HS; Chula Vista, CA; (3); NHS; Treas Church Yth Grp; Chorus; Flag Corp; Yrbk; JV Mgr(s); Cit Awd; SADD; Pep Clb; SEA; Diabetes Contrl & Completns Trial; Poltcl Sci.

ELZIE, LEON; Highlands HS; North Highlands, CA; (3); Office Aide; Speech Tm; Teachers Aide; Band; Jazz Band; Mrchg Band; Pep Band; Pres Frsh Cls; Pres Soph Cls; Rep Stu Cncl; Aeronautical Engrng.

ELZIK, MARIA D; Chaminade College Prep; Santa Monica, CA; (4); Church Yth Grp; Drama Clb; Hosp Aide; Chorus; Church Choir; School Musical; Lit Mag; NHS; Opt Clb Awd; Pres Acad Fit Awd; Piano Won Numerous Awds.

EMANA, BRANDON J; Livingston HS; Delhi, CA; (2); JV Capt Bsktbl; High Hon Roll; Hon Roll.

EMANUEL, KEN W; Sonora HS; Sonora, CA; (2); Computer Clb; Spanish Clb; Hon Roll; Aviation Clb; UC Davis; Pilot.

EMANUELE, DANIELLE; Norco HS; Corona, CA; (2); Ed Yrbk; Intrml Bsktbl; Intrml Var Sftbl; Intrml Trk; Intrml JV Vllybl; Hon Roll; Female Athl Of Yr; Csmtlgy.

EMANUELE, NICHOLE M; Norco HS; Corona, CA; (3); 30/399; Hosp Aide; Model UN; Ed Yrbk; Intrml Bsktbl; Intrml Var Sftbl; Intrml Trk; JV Var Vllybl; Hon Roll; Pres Acad Fit Awd; Female Athlt Of The Yr; Pride Awd; Nrsng.

EMBERSON, TERRY; Strathmore Union HS; Strathmore, CA; (3); 5/77; Am Leg Aux Girls St; Chess Clb; German Clb; JA; Ski Clb; Drill Tm; Var Tennis; Cit Awd; High Hon Roll; Odyssey Mind; Engr.

EMBSHOFF, NICOLE; Palm Desert HS; La Quinta, CA; (4); 21/319; Speech Tm; Teachers Aide; Chorus; High Hon Roll; Rotary Awd; Grt Wrkr Achvmnt Pns; San Bernardino; Nrsng.

EMBUDO, LILIOSA V; Delta HS; Walnut Grove, CA; (4); 5/54; Church Yth Grp; Quiz Bowl; ROTC; Science Clb; SADD; Teachers Aide; Chorus; Church Choir; Drill Tm; Sec Frsh Cls; Sacramento City Coll; Computer.

EMERICK, CHRISTY; Ramona HS; Ramona, CA; (4); 1/256; Am Leg Aux Girls St; Church Yth Grp; Key Clb; Office Aide; Scholastic Bowl; Spanish Clb; SADD; Teachers Aide; VP Jr Cls; Sec Stu Cncl; Peer Cnslr; CA Schlstc Fed; Statesman Of Yr Awd; UC San Diego; Psych.

EMERICK, JASON; Ramona HS; Ramona, CA; (3); 98/294; Church Yth Grp; SADD; Var L Ftbl; Var L Trk; Psych.

EMERICK, KYLE C; Carlsbad HS; Carlsbad, CA; (2); Boy Scts; Church Yth Grp; Key Clb; Ski Clb; School Play; Variety Show; Off Frsh Cls; Bsbl; Bsktbl; Ftbl; Royal Rangrs; Law Enfrcmnt.

EMERSON, AIMEE; Los Alamitos HS; Seal Beach, CA; (3); French Clb; Gym; DAR Awd; CSF; U CA Irvine; Medical.

EMERSON, CHRISTINA M; Santa Paula Union HS; Santa Paula, CA; (2); 42/363; Drama Clb; Key Clb; SADD; Teachers Aide; Var JV Swmmng; Hon Roll; Keywannettes; Chld Psych.

EMERSON, MARNI; Grossmont HS; El Cajon, CA; (3); Church Yth Grp; Tennis; Jet Skiing; Babysitting; Wrkd; Grossmont Coll; Intr/Fshn Dsgn.

EMERY, ADAM F; Chaffey HS; Ontario, CA; (3); 101/560; Church Yth Grp; High Hon Roll; Pin Outstndng Accntng Cls; Schl Ltr Acad Achvt; CA Poly; CPA.

EMERY, ALURA; Sonoma Valley HS; Glen Ellen, CA; (3); 18/278; NFL; Ski Clb; Speech Tm; Varsity Clb; Rep Stu Cncl; Var JV Socr; Var Trk; High Hon Roll; Pres Acad Fit Awd; Chess Clb; Interact Clb; CSF; Astro Engrg.

EMERY, CRISTINA T; Clovis HS; Clovis, CA; (3); SADD; JV Bsktbl; Var Sftbl; Opt Clb Awd; Pres Acad Fit Awd; Cls Activities 91; Art Exhbt Awd; Vrsty Sftbl 1st Pl In Our Vly; Fresno ST; Fshn.

EMERY, ERIK W; Irvine HS; Irvine, CA; (3); 70/521; Church Yth Grp; German Clb; Band; Jazz Band; Mrchg Band; Orch; Pep Band; School Musical; Hon Roll; NHS; Mst Outstndng Musician 2 Yrs; Med.

EMERY, JANA J; O'farrell SCPA HS; San Diego, CA; (2); 1/187; Hon Roll; CA Schlrshp Fdrtn; Outstdng Schlrshp Awd; Golden St Math Exam Schl Recgtn.

EMERY, JENNIFER L; Notre Dame HS; Gilroy, CA; (2); Church Yth Grp; Socr; JV Vllybl; Hon Roll; Pres Acad Fit Awd; Acad Schlrshp; UCLA; Bus.

EMERY, PENNY; Moreno Valley HS; Riverside, CA; (2); Band; Mrchg Band; Hon Roll; Principals List; U OK; Bus.

EMERZIAN, SARA J; Homestead HS; Sunnyvale, CA; (3); Service Clb; Sec Spanish Clb; Mgr Frsh Cls; Var Cheerldng; Var JV Tennis; Hon Roll; NHS; US Hstry & Acad Achvt Awds; UCSB.

EMIR, LAILA M; Mountain View HS; Los Altos, CA; (3); Church Yth Grp; Cmnty Wkr; Dance Clb; Swmmng; Hon Roll; Shadowing, Prepare For Med Stud; Med.

EMIS, NICK; Montgomery HS; Santa Rosa, CA; (2); Boy Scts; Pres 4-H; JA; Math Tm; Intrml Bsbl; Intrml Bsktbl; Intrml Socr; 4-H Awd; NHS; Var Badminton; Sccr; Engrng.

EMLET, DIANA M; Clovis West HS; Fresno, CA; (1); Aud/Vis; Dance Clb; FCA; JV Swmmng; Vllybl; High Hon Roll; Hon Roll; Space Camp; CSF; Air Force Acad; Sci Spclst.

EMMEL, DANA; Cloverdale HS; Cloverdale, CA; (3); 8/69; Band; Mrchg Band; Capt Cheerldng; Var Trk; Cit Awd; High Hon Roll; Hon Roll; CSF; Soc Women Engrs Hnr Awd Sci/Math; Nrsng.

EMMERSEN, TRACY L; Kingsburg Joint Union HS; Kingsburg, CA; (1); Girl Scts; Math Clb; Math Tm; Mu Alpha Theta; SADD; Band; Mrchg Band; JV Tennis; High Hon Roll; US Naval Sea Cadet Corps; Med.

EMMONS, BRENT O; Burbank HS; Burbank, CA; (2); Rep Stu Cncl; Var Swmmng; NHS; Pres Acad Fit Awd; Water Polo Capt; Prsdntl Phys Ftns Awd; UCLA; Med.

EMMONS, DANNY C; Mission San Jose HS; Fremont, CA; (1); Church Yth Grp; Elec Engr.

EMMONS, DAVID J; Aptos HS; Aptos, CA; (1); Var Tennis; High Hon Roll; Water Polo; CA Schlrshp Federation.

EMMONS, JOSH M; Eureka HS; Eureka, CA; (3); Ski Clb; Speech Tm; School Play; VP Jr Cls; JV Bsktbl; JV Var Tennis; DAR Awd; High Hon Roll; Hon Roll; Lion Awd; Harvard; Law.

EMOND, CHUCK G; Montgomery HS; Santa Rosa, CA; (2); JA; Key Clb; Spanish Clb; JV Bsbl; High Hon Roll; Hon Roll; Jr NHS; Stanford; Elec Engr.

EMPASIS, MARK; Shandon HS; San Miguel, CA; (3); 1/30; FFA; Nwsp; Phtg Yrbk; Ftbl; Cit Awd; Hon Roll; Acad Decathlon Team; Hnrs Engl; CSF; Stanford; Bus Admin.

EMPEY, STEVEN M; Lemoore Union HS; Lemoore, CA; (3); Ftbl; Doctor.

EMRALINO, JENNIFER VILLADIEGO; Holy Family HS; Los Angeles, CA; (2); Art Clb; Church Yth Grp; Cmnty Wkr; Hosp Aide; Office Aide; Service Clb; Teachers Aide; Chorus; Church Choir; Ed Nwsp; CSF 89; Campus Ministry Tm; Gaels Chronicle Dedictn Plq; Bus Mgmt.

EMRY, MICHELLE; Pleasant Valley SR HS; Chico, CA; (1); Drama Clb; Girl Scts; Office Aide; Pep Clb; Ski Clb; Spanish Clb; Band; Drill Tm; Orch; School Play; Actress.

ENACHE, TEODOR M; Downey HS; Downey, CA; (3); FBLA; Library Aide; Office Aide; Spanish Clb; Teachers Aide; Bsktbl; Ftbl; Tennis; Gldn ST Exam Alb High Hnrs, Geo Hnrs; Bus.

ENAY, JOEYLYN M; Eisenhower HS; Rialto, CA; (2); Teachers Aide; Acpl Chr; Chorus; Mgr(s); Score Keeper; Tennis; Vllybl; Prfct Atten Awd; Fashion.

ENCARNACION, MARIA C; Nogales HS; La Puente, CA; (3); 77/800; Dance Clb; Pep Clb; Yrbk; Lit Mag; Stu Cncl; Cheerldng; Score Keeper; Hon Roll; Gave Blood 90; Helpd Blood Drive 89; Loyola Marymount; Bus Admin.

ENCARNACION, REY O; Channel Islands HS; Oxnard, CA; (1); Church Yth Grp; French Clb; Science Clb; Rep Stu Cncl; Bsktbl; Var Tennis; UCLA; Counselor.

ENCINAS, ARACELY; Sacred Heart HS; Los Angeles, CA; (3); GAA; Letterman Clb; Varsity Clb; Chorus; JV Bsktbl; Var Sftbl; Capt Vllybl; Hon Roll; NHS; Spanish NHS; Stu Alumni Relations Cmmtte Secy; LIFE; UC Northridge; Environmntl Eng.

ENCINAS, RICARDO; Artesia HS; Lakewood, CA; (1); Spanish Clb; Hon Roll; Engrng.

ENCINAS, VICTORIA; Schurr HS; S San Gabriel, CA; (4); 152/580; Spanish Clb; SADD; Lbrn Band; Mrchg Band; Pep Band; Rptr Yrbk; Hon Roll; Ntl Merit Ltr; Jnr Statesmn Amer; UC San Diego; Liberal Arts.

ENCINIAS, JASON L; Monterey HS; Marina, CA; (1); School Play; Var Bsktbl; Var Crs Cntry; Hon Roll; U Of HI.

ENCISO, MAXINE; Baldwin Park HS; Baldwin Park, CA; (2); Cmnty Wkr; Band; Mrchg Band; Hon Roll; GATE Prgrm Sec.

ENCISO, OMAR H; Mission Bay HS; San Diego, CA; (3); French Clb; FHA; FTA; Intnl Clb; Key Clb; Treas Spanish Clb; School Musical; Hon Roll; Stu Wrk Pgm; San Diego ST U; Bus Mgmt.

ENDA, JEANETTE; Southern CA Christian HS; Irvine, CA; (2); Church Yth Grp; Office Aide; Teachers Aide; Spanish Clb; School Play; Treas Soph Cls; Var Stat Bsktbl; JV Cheerldng; Var Stat Ftbl; High Hon Roll; Highest Achvt Drama; Biola.

ENDERLE, BRYAN; Fred C Beyer HS; Modesto, CA; (2); Church Yth Grp; Math Clb; Math Tm; Hon Roll; CA Schlrshp Fed 2 Yrs; Game Clb; Math.

ENDERMANN, NOAH M; Orange Glen HS; Valley Center, CA; (4); 9/497; Church Yth Grp; Band; Mrchg Band; Pep Band; School Musical; High Hon Roll; NHS; Pres Acad Fit Awd; Stu Of Yr Math; U Of CA San Diego; Chem.

ENDICOTT, MARY K; Carondelet HS; Martinez, CA; (3); 7/170; Cmnty Wkr; Drama Clb; Hosp Aide; Intnl Clb; SADD; School Musical; Ed Nwsp; French Hon Soc; High Hon Roll; NHS; Concord Yth Cncl; William K Holt Sci Schlrshp; UC Berkeley; Space Physics.

ENDO, MICHELLE N; Huntington Beach HS; Huntington Beach, CA; (3); Model UN; Spanish Clb; JV Var Bsktbl; CA Schlrshp Fed; Seyo Yth Bsktbl Lg; Phrmclgy.

ENDO, ROGER A; Culver City HS; Culver City, CA; (3); Cmnty Wkr; Orch; Off Frsh Cls; Off Soph Cls; Off Jr Cls; Off Sr Cls; Stu Cncl; High Hon Roll; Stu Leag VP; Chirons VP.

ENDOSO, ANGELO; Damien HS; Glendale, CA; (1); Debate Tm; NFL; Intrml Socr; Hon Roll; Harvard U; Law.

ENDRES, ANDREA M; Quincy HS; Quincy, CA; (4); Hist 4-H; FBLA; Band; School Musical; Var JV Bsktbl; Socr; Var Capt Vllybl; 4-H Awd; Pres Acad Fit Awd; Pres Schlr; Chico ST; Psych.

ENDRES, JENNA; Dublin HS; Pleasanton, CA; (1); 1/200; Church Yth Grp; Var Socr; High Hon Roll; CSF; Astronomy.

ENDRES, NICHOLAS F; Lowell HS; San Francisco, CA; (2); Church Yth Grp; Debate Tm; NFL; Hist Speech Tm; Band; Jazz Band; Orch; Rwng Jr Vrsty; After Schl Job; Trphy Debate; UC San Diego; Physcs.

ENDRINA, MICHELE F; Jefferson HS; Daly City, CA; (2); Science Clb; Hon Roll; Filipino Amer Clb; Stu Ambssdrs Frndshp Caravan USSR 90; New Comers Clb; Stanford U; Comp Engr.

ENERIZ, CELESTE C; Granada Hills HS; San Fernando, CA; (2); Church Yth Grp; Biolgcl Sci.

ENES, JEFF D; St Ignatius College Prep; San Francisco, CA; (2); JV Bsbl; JV Capt Bsktbl; High Hon Roll; 1st Team All Leag Bsbl & Bsktbl; Stanford; Sports Admin.

ENG, CHANTHY; Woodrow Wilson HS; Long Beach, CA; (3); Library Aide; ROTC; Teachers Aide; Color Guard; Drill Tm; Prasth Club Officer; Personal Management.

ENG, CHRISTINA K; Oak Park HS; Agoura Hills, CA; (2); 2/120; Church Yth Grp; Key Clb; JV Bsktbl; Var Tennis; JV Trk; Golden St Exam Geom Hnrs; Peer Cnslng; CSF.

ENG, CHRISTOPHER L; Nogales HS; W Covina, CA; (2); 11/809; Chess Clb; High Hon Roll; CA St U Pomona Achvt Awd Acadmc Achvt & Prms Fut Success 89; US Riverside Outrch Smmr Pgm 89.

ENG, EDWARD P; Serra HS; San Bruno, CA; (3); JV Socr; Hon Roll; Engrng.

ENG, ELLA; John F Kennedy HS; El Cerrito, CA; (4); 1/250; NFL; Sec SADD; Ed Yrbk; Sec Treas Frsh Cls; Sec Treas Soph Cls; Pres Sr Cls; Rep Stu Cncl; Hon Roll; Val; CSF; Asian Stu Union; U CA Berkeley; Pol Sci.

ENG, GEORGE; Mission Bay HS; San Diego, CA; (3); Rep DECA; FBLA; Key Clb; Library Aide; Model UN; Office Aide; Red Cross Aide; Service Clb; Pres SADD; Teachers Aide; Adv Skirball Inst; Interact; Govt In Motion; Law.

ENG, JEAN L; Oakland HS; Oakland, CA; (3); U CA.

ENG, KATHERINE Y; Homestead HS; Sunnyvale, CA; (3); Art Clb; Service Clb; Teachers Aide; Orch; JV Fld Hcky; Badmington Var.

ENG, KELLEE; Mt Pleasant HS; San Jose, CA; (2); Rptr Yrbk; JV Var Cheerldng; High Hon Roll; CSF.

ENG, TONY; Westmoor HS; Daly City, CA; (3); Art Clb; Cmnty Wkr; Debate Tm; Letterman Clb; Model UN; Rptr Nwsp; VP Soph Cls; Rep Jr Cls; Stu Cncl; Crs Cntry; Giftd & Tlnntd Pgm; Navy Outrch Pgm Ofcr; Yth Of Mnth Awd.

ENG HUNG, BRANDI S; Encinal HS; Port Orchard, WA; (4); 62/212; Teachers Aide; High Hon Roll; Cnslng Aide; Comp Accntng.

ENGEL, ERIC C; San Pasqual HS; Escondido, CA; (2); Spanish Clb; Varsity Clb; Bsbl; Var Crs Cntry; JV Socr; Tennis; Var Trk; Vllybl; Wt Lftg; Prfct Atten Awd; Real Estate.

ENGELHARDT, NIKI; Mira Costa HS; Gardena, CA; (4); Pres French Clb; Key Clb; Pep Clb; Pres Frsh Cls; Var Cheerldng; JV Powder Puff Ftbl; Hon Roll; Scholarship From Hermosa Bch Womens Club; Scholarship From Sandacre; UCLA; Lawyer/Teacher.

ENGELMAN, RAIMIE; Monte Vista HS; El Cajon, CA; (2); Church Yth Grp; Drama Clb; French Clb; Teachers Aide; Var Vllybl; Stu Mnth Phys Educ 2 Tms; Hnrbl Mntn All Leag Tm Vllybl; Natl Frnch Tst; Zoology.

ENGLAND, JOSHUA S; Las Lomas HS; Martinez, CA; (3); Church Yth Grp; Cmnty Wkr; Letterman Clb; ROTC; Var L Bsbl; Var L Bsktbl; WA ST; Bus Mgmt.

ENGLAND, ROB; Arcata HS; Blue Lake, CA; (2); Var L Wrstlng; AZ ST; Bus.

ENGLAND, SHENEE N; Alta Loma HS; Rancho Cucamonga, CA; (2); Pep Clb; Var JV Cheerldng; Var JV Pom Pon; Score Keeper; Flag Corp; Sftbl; JV Swmmng; High Hon Roll; Hon Roll; Pres Acad Fit Awd; Hstry Tchr.

ENGLER, DENISE M; Carondelet HS; Martinez, CA; (3); Church Yth Grp; Cmnty Wkr; Drama Clb; VP Sec 4-H; Ski Clb; Chorus; Church Choir; School Play; Powder Puff Ftbl; JV Var Sftbl; Yth Edctr; CA Schlrshp Fdr; Svc Awd; Drama.

ENGLISH, DAN S; Selma HS; Selma, CA; (3); 52/350; SADD; JV Capt Bsbl; JV Capt Bsktbl; JV Capt Ftbl; Hon Roll; Pres Acad Fit Awd; Ftbl MVP, Bsbl Coaches Awd 88-89; Bsktbl CO-MVP, Bsbl MVP 89-90; Sprt Therapy.

ENGLISH, DAWN E; El Cajon Valley HS; El Cajon, CA; (1); Key Clb; BAD; 1st Responder; Jr Southwestern React; Hospital Vlntr; Phy.

ENGLISH, JAMILA; James Lick HS; San Jose, CA; (1); Church Yth Grp; Drama Clb; GAA; Church Choir; Variety Show; Trk; Project Earth Club; Mock Trial; USAF.

ENGLISH, JIM; Archbishop Mitty HS; San Jose, CA; (3); 13/268; Art Clb; JV Ftbl; JV Trk; High Hon Roll; NHS; CA Carvers Guild; Sci.

ENGLISH, JULIE L; El Toro HS; El Toro, CA; (2); Aud/Vis; Church Yth Grp; Band; Mrchg Band; Orch; Pep Band; Yrbk; High Hon Roll; Hon Roll; Phys Ftnss; UC Davis; Medcl.

ENGLISH, SHARON L; Trabuco Hills HS; El Toro, CA; (1); Church Yth Grp; Cmnty Wkr; French Clb; Cit Awd; Hon Roll.

ENGLISH, STEPHANIE; Hesperia Christian Schl; Hesperia, CA; (4); 1/24; Rep Church Yth Grp; Church Choir; School Musical; Ed Nwsp; Yrbk; Rep Frsh Cls; Var JV Vllybl; High Hon Roll; Opt Clb Awd; Smmr Mssn Trp; CSF VP & Scry Treas; The Masters Clg; Lbrl Arts.

ENGLISH, TIARA STARR; Trabuco Hills HS; Mission Viejo, CA; (1); Art Clb; Church Yth Grp; Cmnty Wkr; Dance Clb; FBLA; Math Clb; Church Choir; Cheerldng; Swmmng; HS Stu Ambssdr Pgm; Grad Cert John Robert Pwrs; U Of HI; Model.

ENGLUND, BERGIT A; Antelope Valley HS; Lancaster, CA; (4); 99/488; ROTC; Spanish Clb; SADD; Pres Treas Acpl Chr; Orch; Hon Roll; CAP; Stu Of Wk 3 Times; Good Guys & Gals Schlrshp; Scl Stds Awd; Music Awd; Outstndng Female Sr Singer; Western ST U Coll Of Law.

ENGSTRAND, PAIGE R; Grossmont HS; El Cajon, CA; (1); Hon Roll; Math.

ENGSTROM, BRETT L; Robert A Millikan HS; Long Beach, CA; (3); Drama Clb; School Play; Stage Crew; Variety Show; Swmmng; Hon Roll; Water Polo Team Capt; Auto & Motorcycle Rcng.

ENGUANCHO, ALOHA B; Samuel F B Moorse HS; San Diego, CA; (3); Church Yth Grp; Cmnty Wkr; Computer Clb; Dance Clb; Drama Clb; Girl Scts; Math Clb; Math Tm; ROTC; Teachers Aide; Nrsng.

ENLOW, ANGELA D; Irvington HS; Fremont, CA; (3); 23/283; Drama Clb; Key Clb; JV Bsktbl; Stat Ftbl; Stat Swmmng; Hon Roll; Drama Clb; San Jose ST U; Sci.

ENNIS, ANDREA M; Escalon HS; Escalon, CA; (2); 14/130; Key Clb; JV Bsktbl; Var Sftbl; JV Vllybl; Hon Roll; Trans Valley Lge All Lge 1st Team Bsbl; Mosesto Bee Carrier Schlrshp Cntst; Schlr Athl Awd; Fresno ST U; Phys Therapy.

ENNIS, JASON A; University HS; Irvine, CA; (3); Computer Clb; Hosp Aide; JA; Math Tm; Intrml Mgr Vllybl; Ntl Merit Ltr; Vlntr Museum Docent; Bus Mgmt.

ENNIS, JOHN W; Chula Vista HS; Chula Vista, CA; (2); Ftbl; Trk; Wt Lftg; Sword & Shld Clb; Crmnl Law-Intl Bus Law; UCLA; Bus.

ENNIS, JUSTIN G; Burroughs HS; Ridgecrest, CA; (4); Church Yth Grp; Debate Tm; Drama Clb; FBLA; Treas Latin Clb; Band; Jazz Band; Mrchg Band; School Musical; School Play; Acadmc Dcthln 1st Pl Econ, 3rd Pl Essay; Abilene Chrstn U; Physics.

ENNIS, MICHAEL R; Garces Memorial HS; Bakersfield, CA; (3); Chess Clb; Church Yth Grp; Drama Clb; Treas French Clb; Ski Clb; School Play; JV Crs Cntry; JV Swmmng; Mock Trial; Work; Poly Sci.

ENNIS, MONETTA L; El Cajon Valley HS; El Cajon, CA; (1); Church Yth Grp; GAA; Sec Frsh Cls; Stu Cncl; Cheerldng; Swmmng; Avid Adv Via Indvdl Dertmntn; Harvard; Law.

ENNS, BENJAMEN T; Apple Valley HS; Apple Valley, CA; (1); Ski Clb; High Hon Roll; Hon Roll; Cal Poly; Engrng.

ENOCHS, CRAIG RICHARD; Bellarmine College Prep; San Jose, CA; (4); 40/315; Capt Debate Tm; NFL; Speech Tm; Nwsp; Off Frsh Cls; Off Soph Cls; Off Jr Cls; Off Sr Cls; Ntl Merit SF; Bank Of Amer Social Stud Awd; Blue Belt Tae Kwon Do; U Houston; Psych.

ENOMOTO, ERIN; Half Moon Bay HS; Half Moon Bay, CA; (4); 18/176; Am Leg Aux Girls St; Church Yth Grp; FBLA; Ed Yrbk; Sec Soph Cls; Sec Stu Cncl; Cit Awd; Hon Roll; Fri Night Live Pres & Fndr; St Legislature Intrn; UC Davis; Law.

ENOMOTO, TERI T; Mark Keppel HS; Monterey Park, CA; (3); Cmnty Wkr; French Clb; Q&S; Service Clb; Rptr Nwsp; Capt Tennis; Hon Roll; Prfct Atten Awd; Mission Valley Leag 2nd Pl Tnns & 1st Pl Doubles; Crown & Sceptre Secy; Prexy Cncl Pres; High Schl Educ.

ENOS, JEFF R; San Rafael HS; San Rafael, CA; (2); Key Clb; Ski Clb; JV Capt Bsbl; JV Capt Ftbl; Bus.

ENQUIST, TRACY; Lemoore Union HS; Lemoore, CA; (2); Chrch Yth Grp; Int Dcrtg.

ENRIGHT, KATHY; Oakmont HS; Roseville, CA; (3); Drill Tm; Cit Awd; Hon Roll; Physics Club; San Diego ST U; Teacher.

ENRIGHT, WENDY M; Tokay HS; Lodi, CA; (2); Church Yth Grp; Latin Clb; Model UN; Speech Tm; Color Guard; School Play; Var Diving; High Hon Roll; Pres Acad Fit Awd; Intl Order Of Rainbow For Grls; Ca Schlrshp Fdrtn; San Diego CA U; Marine Zoology.

ENRIQUEZ, ALICE M; John F Kennedy HS; La Palma, CA; (4); Service Clb; Varsity Clb; Intrml Capt Bsktbl; JV Var Cheerldng; JV Var Vllybl; Hon Roll; All Leag Badmntn; Bsktbl JV MVP; Engl Awd; Comp Sci.

ENRIQUEZ, ANGELICA M; Central Union HS; El Centro, CA; (2); Church Yth Grp; Chorus; Church Choir; School Musical; Swing Chorus; Rep Stu Cncl; Dioceasan Yth Cncl; Imperial Vly Yth Cncl; Parish Cncl; U Of San Diego; Psych.

ENRIQUEZ, BILLY D; Rowland HS; Rowland Heights, CA; (2); Church Yth Grp; Model UN; Var Ftbl; Wt Lftg; Wrstlng; Hon Roll; Modeling.

ENRIQUEZ, CHRISTINA; Washington HS; Fremont, CA; (4); Pep Clb; Ski Clb; Ed Yrbk; Rep Soph Cls; Rep Jr Cls; Rep Sr Cls; Rep Stu Cncl; JV Cheerldng; Powder Puff Ftbl; Outdoor Actvts; Santa Clara U; Corp Law.

ENRIQUEZ, CHRISTOPHER B; Pomona Adventist JR Acad; Montclair, CA; (2); 1/13; Church Yth Grp; Teachers Aide; Chorus; Church Choir; Rptr Nwsp; Yrbk; Pres Frsh Cls; Pres Soph Cls; Pres Stu Cncl; High Hon Roll; Gospel Music Sextet; Loma Linda U; Dntstry.

ENRIQUEZ, ERWIN; Livingston HS; Livingston, CA; (4); 1/200; Am Leg Boys St; Treas Frsh Cls; VP Soph Cls; Intrml Bsktbl; Var Capt Tennis; High Hon Roll; Lion Awd; Prfct Atten Awd; Pres Acad Fit Awd; Cngrssnl Svc & Achvmnt Awd Bronze; CSF Lifetime Mem; Lions Club Yth Exch Stu Japan; U Of CA Davis; Biological Sci.

ENRIQUEZ, FORCELINE C; Galileo HS; San Francisco, CA; (2); Church Yth Grp; ROTC; Hon Roll; Prfct Atten Awd; Filipano Clb; SAI Ldrshp; Cadet Of Yr; Stanford U; Mdcl Fld.

ENRIQUEZ, JANINA; Westminster HS; Westminster, CA; (4); Church Yth Grp; French Clb; JA; Key Clb; Red Cross Aide; Service Clb; Spanish Clb; Teachers Aide; Var JV Score Keeper; Var Capt Swmmng; Gonzalo Mendez Schlrshp; Frankie Martinez Schlrshp; Schlr Athl Swmmng Team 88; CSU Fullerton; Law.

ENRIQUEZ, NANCY M; San Pasqual HS; Escondido, CA; (3); Church Yth Grp; Cmnty Wkr; French Clb; GAA; Teachers Aide; Lit Mag; JV Socr; L Var Sftbl; Wt Lftg; Tchng Sunday Schl; Coaching Sccr; Pepperdine U; Sports Med.

ENSEY, CHARLES; Point Loma HS; San Diego, CA; (3); Boy Scts; Key Clb; Spanish Clb; Speech Tm; Varsity Clb; L Var Ftbl; Var Wt Lftg; Bus Admin.

ENSIGN, JOSH P; Elk Grove HS; Elk Grove, CA; (2); 26/600; Church Yth Grp; JV Ftbl; JV Trk; Intrml Wt Lftg; Cit Awd; High Hon Roll; Hon Roll; Pres Acad Fit Awd; GATE; Wrstlng; Sccr; Elem Stu Pres; Crm Law.

ENSLEY, MIKE J; Mater Dei HS; Laguna Niguel, CA; (1); JV Bsktbl; Hon Roll; Jr NHS; NHS.

ENSOR, KARENA; Patten Acad; Oakland, CA; (2); 1/16; Band; Chorus; Orch; Var Bsktbl; Hon Roll; Pres Acad Fit Awd; ACSI Piano Fest Cmmnd Perf; Rgnl Hnr Bnd; Math Lg Cert Of Merit; Music.

ENTENMAN, ALEX; Skyline HS; Oakland, CA; (2); Boy Scts; Computer Clb; Jazz Band; Hon Roll; Jr NHS; CSU San Luis Obispo; Aviation.

ENTZMINGER, JENNIFER H; Santa Barbara HS; Montecito, CA; (4); Church Yth Grp; Cmnty Wkr; Hosp Aide; Teachers Aide; Treas Jr Cls; Rep Stu Cncl; High Hon Roll; Pres Acad Fit Awd; Prncpls Awd 90; Schlrshp; CA Grant; UCSD; Bichem.

ENYART, LACY; San Juan HS; Citrus Heights, CA; (1); 94/296; Cheerldng; Gym; Chld Psych.

ENYEART, SHERRI A; James Logan HS; Fremont, CA; (3); Church Yth Grp; French Clb; Powder Puff Ftbl; Hon Roll; Close Up; Amer Sign Lang Club; Spcl Educ Deaf Chldrn.

ENZ, PETER W; Beaumont HS; Cherry Valley, CA; (1); Boy Scts; JV Bsktbl; JV Trk; Prfct Atten Awd; U Of NV Las Vegas.

ENZLER, MINDA M; Yucaipa HS; Yucaipa, CA; (3); 11/362; Letterman Clb; Spanish Clb; Var Crs Cntry; Var Trk; Hon Roll; NHS; Math & Sci Achvt Awds; Hozoni Atet; U Of Northern CO; Phys Therapy.

EOM, KELLY Y; Warren HS; Downey, CA; (2); Art Clb; Church Yth Grp; Debate Tm; GAA; Hosp Aide; Intnl Clb; Key Clb; Math Tm; Mu Alpha Theta; Service Clb; CSF; Part Of The Science Olympiad Team; Working With The Academic Decathlon Team; Medical Profession.

EPHLIN, CRISTEN; Atwater HS; Atwater, CA; (2); Treas French Clb; SADD; Ed Yrbk; Pres Frsh Cls; Pres Soph Cls; Pres Jr Cls; Hon Roll; CSF-TREAS; Fri Night Live; Stanford U; Bio Engrng.

EPHREM, DANIEL; Hoover HS; San Diego, CA; (3); French Clb; Var JV Bsktbl; JV Crs Cntry; Hon Roll; Received A Club Award For Student Recognition; U Of CA; Architectural.

EPHREM, MEDHANIE; Herbert Hoover HS; San Diego, CA; (1); 38/671; French Clb; JV Bsktbl; JV Ftbl; Portland ST U; Med.

EPLING, HALEE K; Lorreto HS; Roseville, CA; (1); Bsktbl.

EPPERSON, DAVID C; Bullard HS; Fresno, CA; (1); Church Yth Grp; Spanish Clb; JV Swmmng; Odessey Of Mind; CSF; U C Berkeley; Arch Engr.

EPPERSON, JILL; Placer HS; Auburn, CA; (4); Am Leg Aux Girls St; Church Yth Grp; Pres English Clb; French Clb; Yrbk; Sec Soph Cls; Powder Puff Ftbl; Score Keeper; Var Tennis; High Hon Roll; Schlr/Athl Awd; UC Santa Barbara; Brdcst Jrnls.

EPPERSON, REBECCA B; St Vincent HS; Petaluma, CA; (2); French Clb; Church Choir; Peer Counseling; Sci.

EPPS, WARDELL J; San Gorgonio HS; Highland, CA; (3); 28/500; German Clb; Letterman Clb; Var Capt Bsktbl; Hon Roll; ACES VP; Black Stu Union; NC U; FBI.

EPSTEIN, MICHAEL; Rio Vista HS; Rio Vista, CA; (4); AFS; Q&S; Science Clb; Speech Tm; Ed Nwsp; Yrbk; Hon Roll; CA Acad; Mech Engr.

EPSTEIN, TIFFANY L; Elk Grove HS; Elk Grove, CA; (2); Spanish Clb; SADD; Capt Cheerldng; Score Keeper; Hon Roll; Ldrshp; CSF; Law.

ERARD, DAVID O; Yucaipa HS; Calimesa, CA; (2); Boy Scts; Church Yth Grp; Spanish Clb; Varsity Clb; Var Golf; High Hon Roll; Pres Acad Fit Awd; All Leag Golf 90; All Star Summer Swim Leag; Law.

ERB, JOEL P; Sacramento Waldorf HS; Sonora, CA; (3); Debate Tm; Math Tm; Model UN; Jazz Band; Orch; School Musical; Ed Yrbk; Pres Jr Cls; Rep Stu Cncl; Var Bsbl.

ERBA, THOMAS M; Woodland HS; Woodland, CA; (3); Church Yth Grp; Band; Jazz Band; JV Bsbl; Var Bsktbl; JV Ftbl; Var Tennis; High Hon Roll; Hon Roll; Pres Acad Fit Awd; MVP Awd Bsktbl; 1st Pl Awd Sci Fr; Athl Of Yr; Med.

ERBE, MICHELE M; San Leandro HS; San Leandro, CA; (2); 13/399; Cmnty Wkr; Key Clb; Band; Jazz Band; Orch; JV Sftbl; JV Tennis; High Hon Roll; Hon Roll; Kiwanis Awd; Postr Cmmtte Spirit Wk Cmptn; Hnrs Band.

ERBE, NICHOLAS T; Watsonville HS; Watsonville, CA; (4); Am Leg Boys St; Cmnty Wkr; Math Clb; Ski Clb; Teachers Aide; Rep Soph Cls; Rep Jr Cls; Treas Sr Cls; Stu Cncl; JV Ftbl; Santa Clara U; Phys Thrpy.

ERBES, JASON T; Santa Rosa HS; Windsor, CA; (2); Church Yth Grp; Debate Tm; Treas 4-H; VP FFA; VICA; L Crs Cntry; Socr; L Trk; L Wrstlng; Cit Awd; Rodeo; Cal Poly; Ag.

ERDMANN, JAY; Southwest HS; Say Ysidro, CA; (4); 41/498; Teachers Aide; Wt Lftg; Cit Awd; Hon Roll; Prfct Atten Awd; Bilingual Classes Awd; Sthwstrn Coll.

EREDIA, MARIO S; St Genevieve HS; Woodland Hills, CA; (3); Boy Scts; Sec Model UN; Treas Spanish Clb; Ordr Of Arrow, Brthrhd Hnr Lvl; Chf Nws Ltr Edtr; Natl Ordr Of Arrow Conf Chrmn Malibu Ldg 566; CSUN; Bus.

EREZ, SHACHAR; Culver City HS; Culver City, CA; (1); Debate Tm; Vllybl; Hon Roll; AZA; Yth In Govt; UCLA; Law.

ERGANIAN, JOHN K; Taft HS; Woodland Hills, CA; (2); Cmnty Wkr; Var Bsbl; High Hon Roll; Pres Acad Fit Awd; CA Schltc Fed; Soph Class Steering Cmmtte.

ERIC, DUONG T; Mt Diablo HS; Concord, CA; (3); Am Leg Boys St; FBLA; JA; ROTC; Spanish Clb; SADD; Varsity Clb; Off Jr Cls; VP Sr Cls; Socr; Peer Cnslr; USF; Bus.

ERIC, LAN; San Marino HS; San Marino, CA; (3); FBLA; JCL; Math Clb; Red Cross Aide; Science Clb; Varsity Clb; Var Bsktbl; Var Vllybl; Arch-Dsgn Clb Pres; Med.

ERICKSON, ANDREW J; Folsom HS; Folsom, CA; (3); 7/189; VP Intnl Clb; Math Clb; Math Tm; Model UN; Ski Clb; VP Spanish Clb; VP Soph Cls; VP Jr Cls; VP Sr Cls; Var Bsbl; CA Schlstc Fed; CA Poly; Arch.

ERICKSON, BERNICE L; Winters HS; Winters, CA; (2); Church Yth Grp; Girl Scts; Letterman Clb; Pep Clb; Red Cross Aide; Ski Clb; Drill Tm; L Var Cheerldng; Hon Roll; Friday Night Live; Lfgrd; Lawyer.

ERICKSON, BETSY; Fallbrook HS; Fallbrook, CA; (3); Church Yth Grp; Dance Clb; Drama Clb; Spanish Clb; Church Choir; Variety Show; JV Var Cheerldng; High Hon Roll; Prfrmnc Drama Cls; Arch Engrng.

ERICKSON, DANNY W; Woodcrest Christian HS; Corona, CA; (2); Church Yth Grp; Ski Clb; Varsity Clb; JV Bsktbl; Var L Tennis; High Hon Roll; NHS; Rebldng Car.

ERICKSON, DEBBIE; Downey HS; Downey, CA; (1); Cmnty Wkr; Pep Clb; Cheerldng; Hon Roll; CSF.

ERICKSON, JEREMY D; San Ramon Valley HS; Danville, CA; (2); Boy Scts; Church Yth Grp; Cmnty Wkr; French Clb; JV Crs Cntry; JV Trk; High Hon Roll; Prfct Atten Awd; Schlr Athlt Awd 2 Times; Gldn St Math Alg Awd; Prncpls Awd; Brigham Young U.

ERICKSON, JILL A; Shasta HS; Redding, CA; (3); 14/350; Drama Clb; Sec Science Clb; Hon Roll; Bio.

ERICKSON, KALI SINGH; Pasadena HS; Pasadena, CA; (4); Cmnty Wkr; Pres Debate Tm; Service Clb; Pres Speech Tm; Ed Yrbk; Stu Cncl; Swmmng; Tennis; High Hon Roll; Pres Acad Fit Awd; Active In Rdng Is Fndmntl, Southern CA; CSF; Bk Of Amer Engl Awd; Bowdoin Coll; Hstry.

ERICKSON, KINARA I; Arcata HS; Arcata, CA; (2); AFS; Drama Clb; French Clb; Band; Chorus; Jazz Band; Orch; School Play; Variety Show; French Hon Soc; Recyclng Clb; Rainforest Action Clb; Actress.

ERICKSON, KRISTINE M; Enterprise HS; Redding, CA; (3); 35/405; FBLA; Pres FHA; Intnl Clb; Model UN; Teachers Aide; Acpl Chr; Flag Corp; School Play; Mgr Stage Crew; Nwsp; Sci Olympiad; Camp Cnslr, Envrnmntl Camp; Shasta Coll; Intl Rltns.

ERICKSON, MIKE; Woodcrest Christian HS; Corona, CA; (1); Church Yth Grp; Ski Clb; JV Bsktbl; Var Crs Cntry; High Hon Roll; NHS; Rebldng Car.

ERICKSON, NANCY A; Los Angeles Baptist HS; West Hills, CA; (3); Church Yth Grp; 4-H; Yrbk; Stat Crs Cntry; 4-H Awd; Hon Roll; Opt Clb Awd; 3rd Pl Optimist Clb Essay Cont; CSUN; Pre-Pharmacy.

ERICKSON, RICHARD J; Riverside Poly HS; Riverside, CA; (2); JV Bsktbl; Most Insprtnl Awd Bsktbl.

ERICKSON, SHERI A; Ceres HS; Ceres, CA; (4); 7/220; Treas FBLA; Rep Key Clb; Service Clb; Ski Clb; Stu Cncl; Var Capt Cheerldng; Var Swmmng; Hon Roll; Pres Acad Fit Awd; CSF Treas & Schlrshp; Fibreboard Fndtn Schlrshp; Hi Deb Rep; Stanislaus ST; Bus.

ERICKSON, TODD L; John F Kennedy HS; Sacramento, CA; (1); 44/559; Church Yth Grp; Band; Intrml Bsktbl; High Hon Roll; Piano Lvl VI Cert Mrt Music Tchrs Assn; UCLA.

ERICSEN, DENA L; Roseville HS; Roseville, CA; (3); Dance Clb; Band; JV Socr; Var Tennis; Ed.

ERICSON, JEFF G; Foothill HS; Santa Ana, CA; (2); Church Yth Grp; SADD; Church Choir; JV Bsbl; JV Bsktbl; Intrml Ftbl; Elks Awd; Sci.

ERICSON, MARIA I; Morningside HS; Inglewood, CA; (1); Hon Roll; 2nd Pl Fnlst Natl Math Cont.

ERICSSON, MELISSA D; Weed HS; Weed, CA; (4); Letterman Clb; Pep Clb; Band; Pep Band; Pres Frsh Cls; VP Stu Cncl; Stat Ftbl; Sftbl; Capt Vllybl; High Hon Roll; CSF; Cougar Rlly Sqd Pres; Schlr Athlt; GPA 3.5 Achvr; CA ST U; Bus.

ERICSSON, STACEY D; Homestead HS; Sunnyvale, CA; (3); 40/400; Church Yth Grp; Drama Clb; Thesps; Church Choir; School Play; VP Jr Cls; Rep Stu Cncl; Best Actor 89-90; Cmmnty Theatre Muscls.

ERIE, ANDREA D; Capital Christian HS; Rancho Cordova, CA; (3); Art Clb; Church Yth Grp; Teachers Aide; Church Choir; Off Soph Cls; Treas Jr Cls; Stu Cncl; Sftbl; Hon Roll.

ERIKSON, AMY M; Thousand Oaks HS; Thousand Oaks, CA; (3); Church Yth Grp; Rptr Nwsp; Stat Wrstlng; Yth-To-Yth; Westmont Coll; Jrnlsm.

ERIKSSON, JON DERON; William S Hart HS; Valencia, CA; (4); 1/488; Math Clb; Mu Alpha Theta; Science Clb; Crs Cntry; Tennis; High Hon Roll; NHS; Ntl Merit SF; Opt Clb Awd; Val; Hrvrd Prz Bk Awd; CSF; Ansthslgy.

ERLICH, NINA; Culver City HS; Culver City, CA; (2); Teachers Aide; Lit Mag; Sec Frsh Cls; Off Soph Cls; Rep Stu Cncl; High Hon Roll; Hon Roll; Yth & Govt YMCA; Teen Line Vol Svc; YMCA Camp Cnclr; Psych.

ERLINGER, KELLY J; Desert HS; Edwards, CA; (3); Girl Scts; JA; Spanish Clb; Teachers Aide; Tennis; Hon Roll; Bus Awd Word Proc Dip; FL ST Coll; Nrsng.

ERLINGER, MIKE; Damien HS; Claremont, CA; (3); 65/231; Debate Tm; Speech Tm; Varsity Clb; Rptr Nwsp; Var Swmmng; Hon Roll; Walter Polo; Clscl Guitar Trnng.

ERMIGARAT, KORI D; North HS; Bakersfield, CA; (2); Church Yth Grp; English Clb; GAA; Letterman Clb; Spanish Clb; Teachers Aide; Varsity Clb; Stu Cncl; Var Bsktbl; Var Sftbl; Hnr Mntn Var Vllybl; All Lge Pitcher/All Area Infielder Sftbl; Outstndng Athl Awd; Sports Med.

ERMSHAR, ANNETTE LORENE; Village Christian HS; Flintridge, CA; (4); Church Yth Grp; Cmnty Wkr; Drama Clb; English Clb; French Clb; Service Clb; Ski Clb; Speech Tm; Acpl Chr; Chorus; CSF; Frnch Stdy Abroad Smmr 90; Exchnge Stu Tahiti Smmr 88; Pepperdine U; Pre-Law.

ERMSHAR, PHILIP E A; Ukiah JR Acad; Fresno, CA; (1); 4/13; Church Yth Grp; Chorus; School Musical; Yrbk; Intrml Bsbl; Intrml Bsktbl; Intrml Ftbl; Woodcraft; Natl Bsbl & Ftbl; Skiing & Surfing; Pacifc Union Coll.

ERNST, JEFF A; College Park HS; Pleasant Hill, CA; (3); Pres German Clb; Letterman Clb; Varsity Clb; Capt Ftbl; Wrstlng; High Hon Roll; Hon Roll; St Schlr; Yth Ed; Byu.

ERNST, SAM F; Berkeley HS; Berkeley, CA; (3); Latin Clb; Ed Nwsp; Lit Mag; U CA Santa Cruz; Eng.

ERNSTROM, PAULA JANE; Alhambra HS; Martinez, CA; (3); 24/215; Pres Church Yth Grp; Band; Church Choir; Jazz Band; Mrchg Band; Var L Bsktbl; Stat Trk; Hon Roll; Uahona Hnr Soc Tree Hldr; Gldn St Exam Geom Schl Recgntn; Peer Spprt Grp 90-91; Ricks Coll; Music Educ.

EROL, MELTEM; Ygnacio Valley HS; Pleasant Hill, CA; (2); Spanish Clb; SADD; Orch; Ed Nwsp; Rep Stu Cncl; Concord Yth Cncl; Stu Rep USD Drug Free Schls; Editor In Chief & Communications Commissioner 90-91; UC Berkeley; Law.

ERRO, JODY A; Hesperia HS; Hesperia, CA; (4); 42/453; Church Yth Grp; French Clb; Girl Scts; Teachers Aide; Mgr(s); Stat Sftbl; High Hon Roll; Hon Roll; NHS; Outdoor Ed Cnslr; CA ST-SAN Bernardino; Psych.

ERSKINE, KIMBERLY A; Edison HS; Huntington Beach, CA; (2); Model UN; Mem Cal Teen; Past Hnrd Queen Jobs Daugh Bethel; Yth Gov Day; Pol Sci.

ERSOZ, OZAN; Bonita Vista HS; Chula Vista, CA; (3); Library Aide; SADD; Chorus; Var Socr; Var Swmmng; Bus Admin.

ERSPAN, ALLEGRA C; Casa Grande HS; Petaluma, CA; (3); 69/288; French Clb; Hon Roll; Modeling.

ERTEL, JILL; Capital Christian Schl; Orangevale, CA; (4); 1/50; Art Clb; Sec Church Yth Grp; Office Aide; Chorus; School Musical; Sec Sr Cls; Sftbl; Vllybl; High Hon Roll; NHS; CA Schlrshp Fdrtn; Accntnt.

ERVIN, MYESCHA L; Leuzinger HS; Hawthorne, CA; (3); JA; Chorus; Hon Roll; Ebony Natn Clb; Uno Clb Pres; Peer Tutor; Accntnt; Outstndng Turor Awd; SWE Cert Mrt; Med.

ERVIN, NATALIE F; Oak Ridge HS; Shingle Springs, CA; (2); Art Clb; Cmnty Wkr; Dance Clb; High Hon Roll; Fri Night Live; U CA Davis; Vet.

ERVIN, PAMELA; Compton HS; Carson, CA; (2); Church Yth Grp; Cmnty Wkr; Dance Clb; Pep Clb; Spanish Clb; Teachers Aide; Varsity Clb; Cheerldng; Pom Pon; Powder Puff Ftbl; Spelman; Pre Med.

ERVINE, RANDALL J; Clovis HS; Clovis, CA; (2); SADD; Off Frsh Cls; Sec Treas Soph Cls; Off Jr Cls; Hon Roll.

ERWEL, BRYAN K; Antelope Valley HS; Lancaster, CA; (3); 89/646; Church Yth Grp; Drama Clb; JA; Letterman Clb; Office Aide; Spanish Clb; Varsity Clb; Yrbk; JV Ftbl; Var Golf; Bus.

ERWIN, MAT W; Casa Roble HS; Fair Oaks, CA; (3); 81/450; Varsity Clb; JV Var Bsbl; Var Capt Ftbl; Var Wt Lftg; Hon Roll; Pres Acad Fit Awd; V Bsbl All Leag, All Metro Teams.

ERWIN, MATTHEW J; Sunny Hills HS; Buena Park, CA; (2); FBLA; Intnl Clb; Sec Model UN; Rptr Nwsp; JV Crs Cntry; JV Tennis; High Hon Roll; Most Imprvd For Cross Cntry & Tennis; Bus.

ERWIN, ROBERT D; Hemet HS; Hemet, CA; (3); 16/540; Chess Clb; Church Yth Grp; JV Tennis; High Hon Roll; Hon Roll; Hnr Escort Daisy Chain; Engrng.

ESAINKO, KYMRY; Sacramento Waldorf Schl; Sacramento, CA; (3); Math Tm; Jazz Band; Orch; Pres Stu Cncl; CA St U Sacramento BM Prm Piano; Music.

ESAU, DANNY S; Cajon HS; San Bernardino, CA; (3); Var L Ftbl; Var L Trk; US Air Force Acad; Engrng.

ESCAJEDA, INGRID A; Bonita Vista HS; Bonita, CA; (3); 9/517; Key Clb; SADD; Ed Nwsp; Yrbk; JV Socr; Cit Awd; High Hon Roll; Hon Roll; Prfct Atten Awd; Pres Acad Fit Awd; CSF; Golden St Math Awd High Hnrs; Outstndng Acad Achvt; Genetic Engnrng.

ESCALANTE, ROBERTO A; James Logan HS; Union City, CA; (3); 45/845; Computer Clb; Math Clb; Spanish Clb; JV Socr; Hon Roll; Travel Clb; Stanford; Bus Admin.

ESCALONA, KRISTINE; James Logan HS; Union City, CA; (3); Bus Profs of Am; Dance Clb; FBLA; GAA; Spanish Clb; School Play; JV Var Tennis; High Hon Roll; Hon Roll; Mst Imprvd JV Tnns Plyr Awd; Dentistry.

ESCALONA, REBECCA C; William Worhman HS; Valinda, CA; (2); JV Tennis; Badminton Co Capt JV Tm; Bus.

ESCAMILLA, MIRELLA A; Oxnard HS; Oxnard, CA; (3); French Clb; Hon Roll; Admin.

ESCAMILLA, PETRA; Dos Palos HS; South Dos Palos, CA; (2); Modesto JC.

ESCAMILLA, SAUL; Baldwin Park HS; Baldwin Park, CA; (2); Hon Roll; Civil Engr.

ESCAMILLA, WILLIE; Downey High HS; Modesto, CA; (2); Hon Roll; Const.

ESCANEGA, JOLENE; Schurr HS; Monterey Park, CA; (3); Dance Clb; FHA; Key Clb; Varsity Clb; Drill Tm; USC; Teacher.

ESCANUELA, EMILY JANE; Sweetwater Union HS; National City, CA; (2); Library Aide; Yrbk; Off Frsh Cls; Hon Roll; Frsh Treas; Secy Social Sci Cls; Asian Intl Assn; US Intl U; Intl Bus.

ESCANUELA, MARIBEL; Garfield HS; Los Angeles, CA; (4); Church Yth Grp; SADD; Yrbk; Cit Awd; Hon Roll; Pres Acad Fit Awd; Sal; Mult Cultrl Clb; Folklorico Dance Grp; Mt St Marys; Bus.

ESCARENO, MARIA E; Watsonville HS; Watsonville, CA; (2); Church Yth Grp; Library Aide; Office Aide; Hon Roll; PIC; CSF; MESA; UCLA; Engrng.

ESCARZAGA, ANTONIO R; San Gorgonio HS; Highland, CA; (2); Church Yth Grp; Alive Club Treas; Teen Missions Jamaica; Puppeto Jesus Pres; Moody Bible Inst; Thlgy.

ESCHEMAN, SAM J; Marysville HS; Challenge, CA; (1); JV Bsktbl; JV Capt Ftbl; JV Mgr(s); JV Score Keeper; Mgr Sftbl; JV Wt Lftg; Cit Awd; Hon Roll; Prfct Atten Awd; Sprtsmnshp Awd Ftbl; Mst Imprvd Plyr Bsktbl; Hghst GPA Bsktbl; Physl Ed.

ESCOBAR, BRAD; Tulare Union HS; Tulare, CA; (2); 72/461; Letterman Clb; Varsity Clb; JV Var Bsbl; Var L Ftbl; Var JV Socr; Hon Roll; Vet.

ESCOBAR, EVELYN P; Immaculate Conception Acad; San Francisco, CA; (4); 12/55; Drama Clb; GAA; School Play; Mgr Stage Crew; Co-Ed Yrbk; Rep Frsh Cls; Treas Sr Cls; Intrml Bsktbl; Intrml Vllybl; Hon Roll; Block Scty Of ICA; Svc Awd; Bank Of Amer Achvt Awd For Rlgn & Engl; San Fransisco ST U; Radio/Tv.

ESCOBAR, GABRIELA; Bloomington HS; Bloomington, CA; (2); Hon Roll; Prncpls Hnr Rl 88-90; UCLA; Bus.

ESCOBAR, GINA; Calipatria HS; Calipatria, CA; (2); Church Yth Grp; Dance Clb; 4-H; Stage Crew; Yrbk; Crs Cntry; Hon Roll; Fash.

ESCOBAR, IRMA G; St Joseph HS; Anaheim, CA; (2); 72/100; Hon Roll; Prfct Atten Awd; Cal ST U Long Beach; Fshn Dsgn.

ESCOBAR, JOSE J; Orosi HS; Yettem, CA; (2); Math Clb; Nwsp; Yrbk; Bsktbl; Ftbl; Socr; Cert Awd Orosi Bd Ed; UCLA; Arch.

ESCOBAR, JULIO R; Oakland Tech HS; Oakland, CA; (2); High Hon Roll; Hon Roll; Prfct Atten Awd; MESA; Ptnshp Prgm; Span Awd; Univ Conf Fresno; MIT; Aerosp Eng.

ESCOBAR, LETICIA; Orosi HS; Cutler, CA; (4); 3/125; Cmnty Wkr; Computer Clb; Drama Clb; Math Clb; Office Aide; Quiz Bowl; Speech Tm; SADD; School Musical; School Play; Stu Rep Brd; A Clb; Bank Amer Awd Math; Pblsdh Schl Mag; Mck Trl Tm; Wnr Engl Awd Hghst Acvht; CSF; Fresno ST U; Lawyer.

ESCOBAR, LORI; Amador Valley HS; Pleasanton, CA; (2); #1 In Class; Church Yth Grp; French Clb; JV Cheerldng; French Hon Soc; High Hon Roll; CSF.

ESCOBAR, MANUEL J; Bell Gardens HS; Bell Gardens, CA; (2); Church Yth Grp; Teachers Aide; East LA Coll; Comp Prgmr.

ESCOBAR, MELINDA R; John W North HS; Riverside, CA; (3); Office Aide; Rptr Nwsp; Lit Mag; JV Tennis; High Hon Roll; Hon Roll; Intnl Clb; CSF; Inter-Clb Cncl; IJEA Jrnlsm Awd; UC Riverside; Psych.

ESCOBAR, MICAELA; Sacred Heart Of Jesus HS; Brownsville, TX; (3); Library Aide; Scholastic Bowl; Spanish Clb; Teachers Aide; VICA; Chorus; High Hon Roll; Hon Roll; Jr NHS; NHS; Banking & Reconciling Awd; Real Estate Awd; Comptn Awd; Bus.

ESCOBAR, NOEL A; Hayward HS; Hayward, CA; (2); Wt Lftg; Prof Sprts.

ESCOBAR, RAGINA M; Calipatria HS; Calipatria, CA; (2); Church Yth Grp; Dance Clb; 4-H; Math Tm; Temple Yth Grp; Stage Crew; Yrbk; Crs Cntry; Hon Roll; Frdy Nght Live Stus Agnst Drnk Drvng; Chrch Sftbl, Vlybl; Art.

ESCOBAR, STEVE M; Fairfax HS; Los Angeles, CA; (3); Boy Scts; Chess Clb; Rep Jr Cls; JV Ftbl; Honors & High Honors Gldn St Exam In Math; Acctng.

ESCOBAR, TANYA; Arlington HS; Riverside, CA; (2); Church Yth Grp; Teachers Aide; Teachers Aide; JV Socr; Var Swmmng; High Hon Roll; Pres Acad Fit Awd; CSF; Tutor; Hspnc Outstndng Achvt Awd; UC Irvine; Bio.

ESCOBEDO, ELVIA; Baldwin Park HS; Baldwin Park, CA; (1); Stu Cncl.

ESCOBEDO, HECTOR J; Temecula Valley HS; Murrieta, CA; (3); 84/350; Engr.

ESCOBEDO, NATALIE; Silver Creek HS; San Jose, CA; (2); 52/452; Mrchg Band; High Hon Roll; Certfd Pr Cnslr Santa Clara Cnty; Sbstnc Abs Ntwrk Vlntr; Mth Tutr; Mth.

ESCOLA, LAIF J; Ripon HS; Ripon, CA; (4); 15/95; Stu Cncl; JV Bsktbl; Var JV Ftbl; Var Capt Trk; Hon Roll; Pres Acad Fit Awd; Chico ST U; Bus.

ESCOLAR, DAVID P; St Francis HS; Sunnyvale, CA; (3); 43/300; Church Yth Grp; Cmnty Wkr; SADD; JV Socr; High Hon Roll; Hon Roll; Radio Club.

ESCUDERO, RONNIE J; Mira Mesa HS; San Diego, CA; (2); 1/797; Science Clb; Cit Awd; Prfct Atten Awd; Acad Hnr & Top 100 Stu Awds; Prjct Prvnt Clb; Sci.

ESERA, KAISARA LEON; Los Amigos HS; Santa Ana, CA; (2); Band; Drm Mjr(t); Jazz Band; Mrchg Band; Orch; School Musical; Wt Lftg; Dist Hnr Band; Santa Ana Winds Yth Band; Chapman Clg; Arch.

ESGUERRA, JANICE; St Genevieve HS; Van Nuys, CA; (3); #1 In Class; Dance Clb; Drill Tm; High Hon Roll; Singing/Dancing Concerts.

ESGUERRA, JOYCE ANNE S; Saint Francis HS; Mountain View, CA; (4); Art Clb; Intnl Clb; Service Clb; Band; Jazz Band; Mrchg Band; Orch; Pep Band; School Musical; High Hon Roll; Excllnc In Music From St Francis HS 1989-90; William Crawford Svc Awd 1989-90; CMEA Solo Ensmbl; U Of CA Santa Cruz.

ESHLEMAN, BRENDA; Serrano HS; Oak Hills, CA; (2); Cmnty Wkr; FFA; Band; Mrchg Band; JV Hon Roll; CSF; Ag.

ESKENAZI, ERIC M; Los Alamitos HS; Seal Beach, CA; (3); Drama Clb; English Clb; School Play; Stage Crew; Nwsp; Rep Stu Cncl; Prfct Atten Awd; Orange Cty HS Of Arts; Dir Awd Tech Theater; Princeton U Poetry Cont Hnrb Mntn; Princeton U; Engl.

ESKEW, DANA; Brea-Olinda HS; Brea, CA; (4); 20/301; Church Yth Grp; Dance Clb; JA; Library Aide; Office Aide; Pep Clb; Spanish Clb; Color Guard; Flag Corp; Cit Awd; CSF; Acad Bstr Clb; Mst Enth & Supr Awd; Cal ST Fullerton; Educ.

ESKRIDGE, COSINA R; Lakewood SR HS; Long Beach, CA; (3); GAA; Red Cross Aide; Teachers Aide; Var Sftbl; Cit Awd; Hon Roll; Frshmn Schlrshp Pin; Yng Black Schlrs; LSU; Law.

ESKRIDGE, SEAN M; Thousand Oaks HS; Westlake Village, CA; (3); Church Yth Grp; Cmnty Wkr; Letterman Clb; Teachers Aide; Varsity Clb; JV Var Ftbl; JV Var Wt Lftg; JV Var Wrstlng; Hon Roll; Chrch Yth Grp; Ldrshp Tm; Rfree Yth Flg Ftbl Pgm; Shrff Dept.

ESLINGER, HEIDI R; Rio Lindo Acad; Pleasant Hill, CA; (4); 13/96; Spanish Clb; Stu Cncl; Bsktbl; Ftbl; Gym; Capt Sftbl; Vllybl; High Hon Roll; Prfct Atten Awd; Pres Acad Fit Awd; Pacific Union Coll; Aerospc Eng.

ESLINGER, KRISTIN L; Nevada Union HS; Grass Valley, CA; (3); 23/540; Am Leg Aux Girls St; Pres 4-H; Pres FFA; Var Capt Swmmng; 4-H Awd; High Hon Roll; Hon Roll; Pres Acad Fit Awd; San Luis Obispo U; Ag.

ESMAILZADEH, LISA R; Woodcrest Christian HS; Riverside, CA; (3); French Clb; SADD; Acad Of Amer Poets; Wmns Natl Bk Assn; UC Irvine; Bus.

ESPADAS, CHAPIIN; Baldwin Park HS; Baldwin Park, CA; (3); 42/442; Church Yth Grp; Cmnty Wkr; Math Clb; Treas Frsh Cls; Hon Roll; Acad Pentathlon Wnnr Engl, Soc Stud & Sci; Engrng.

ESPANA, MARIA C; San Fernando HS; Pacoima, CA; (2); Hon Roll; CSUN; Social Work.

ESPARZA, ANTOINETTE E; San Gabriel Mission HS; Los Angeles, CA; (2); 16/127; Church Yth Grp; Cmnty Wkr; Hon Roll; NHS; Hlp Tutor Math; Arch.

ESPARZA, FRANCISCO J; Indio HS; Indio, CA; (3); Dance Clb; Latin Clb; Math Tm; Yrbk; Off Sr Cls; Socr; MECHA Clb; Awd Dance Folklorique Mexico; Arch.

ESPARZA, JAVIER; Baldwin Park HS; Baldwin Park, CA; (2); Hon Roll; Prfct Atten Awd; Bus.

ESPARZA, LUIS A; Leuzinger HS; Lawndale, CA; (2); Art Clb; JV Bsbl; JV Ftbl; Cit Awd; Prfct Atten Awd; El Camino JC Ceramic Class; Art.

ESPARZA, MARIA E; Selma HS; Selma, CA; (4); 15/191; Sec Church Yth Grp; Sec Cmnty Wkr; English Clb; Pres FTA; Hosp Aide; SADD; Rptr Nwsp; Stu Cncl; High Hon Roll; Hon Roll; CSF; Mesa Tutor; Bnk Amer Achvt Awd Hstry & Scl Stds; CSU Fresno; Comp Engrng.

ESPARZA, MARK J; Corona SR HS; Corona, CA; (3); Pres Acad Fit Awd; Rotary Awd; Bus.

ESPARZA, PETER; Selma HS; Selma, CA; (1); 15/326; Church Yth Grp; French Clb; High Hon Roll; Hon Roll; Prfct Atten Awd; Pres Acad Fit Awd.

ESPARZA JR, VICENTE; Oakland HS; Oakland, CA; (4); Art Clb; SADD; Stage Crew; Variety Show; JV Crs Cntry; Intrml Swmmng; Intrml Trk; Srf.

ESPE, TONY; Kern Valley HS; Wofford Heights, CA; (1); UCLA; Psych.

ESPEJO, MARIA; Alemany HS; Saugus, CA; (2); Church Yth Grp; Pep Clb; SADD; Band; VP Frsh Cls; Sec Treas Soph Cls; Cheerldng; Score Keeper; High Hon Roll; NHS; Med.

ESPEJO, VALERIE A; Mt Pleasant HS; San Jose, CA; (1); Rep Frsh Cls; JV Cheerldng; High Hon Roll; Supt Hnrs List; UC Los Angeles; Law.

ESPENSON, KIRT D; Etna HS; Greenview, CA; (3); Church Yth Grp; Debate Tm; FFA; Varsity Clb; Band; Chorus; Church Choir; VP Soph Cls; Capt L Ftbl; JV Capt Ice Hcky; FFA St Outdr Rec Prof Wnnr; FFA Proj Cmptn Outstndng Proj; All-League Ftbl; Cal Poly; Rec.

ESPERO, JENNA; Vacaville HS; Vacaville, CA; (3); Pep Clb; Teachers Aide; Cheerldng; Hon Roll; Psych.

ESPINA, ANDREA S; Clayton Valley HS; Clayton, CA; (3); Hum Fstvl Frgn Lang Cmpstn Wnnr; Tutor; Pol Sci.

ESPINAL, MIGUEL V; San Diego & Mission Bay HS; San Diego, CA; (3); French Clb; Intnl Clb; Yrbk; JV Var Ftbl; Var Socr; Wt Lftg; Hon Roll; Kiwanis Awd; DJ; Acting; GSE Recgntn On Tests.

ESPINDOLA, LAURA; Glendale HS; Glendale, CA; (4); 83/695; French Clb; Office Aide; Service Clb; Spanish Clb; Teachers Aide; Cheerldng; NHS; Pres Acad Fit Awd; Acad Excell Awd 89; CSF; CA ST U-Northridge; Trnsltr.

ESPINDULA, RUDY; Redwood HS; Visalia, CA; (2); Intrml Bsktbl; JV Ftbl; Intrml Trk; Engr.

ESPINELI, SHEILA K; Bishop Amat Memorial HS; La Puente, CA; (2); Drama Clb; French Clb; Church Choir; School Musical; School Play; JV Tennis; JV Vllybl; High Hon Roll; NHS; CA Schlrsp Fed; Law.

ESPING, JILL; Rosary HS; La Mirada, CA; (4); Dance Clb; Ski Clb; School Play; Yrbk; Var Cheerldng; JV Swmmng; Hon Roll; NHS; Church Yth Grp; French Clb; Vrsty & JV Ltr; Acadmc Merit Acctng; Schlr Athl Awd; Pressure Free Assn; AZ ST U; Acctng.

ESPINO, ELSA A; Saddleback HS; Santa Ana, CA; (3); Dance Clb; French Clb; Pep Clb; SADD; Chorus; JV Trk; Var JV Vllybl; Acad Ltr 2 Yrs; SD ST; Psych.

ESPINO, JESSICA; Orosi HS; Orosi, CA; (4); 6/121; Church Yth Grp; Letterman Clb; Pep Clb; Service Clb; SADD; VP Band; Mrchg Band; Pep Band; Variety Show; Yrbk; US Army Rsrve Athlete/Schlr, US Navy Advncd Pgms, CA Music Educators Awds 90; Dominican Coll; Math.

ESPINO, VICTORIA M; Dos Palos HS; Dos Palos, CA; (3); VP AFS; Church Yth Grp; Cmnty Wkr; FHA; Pep Clb; VP SADD; Church Choir; Stu Cncl; Var Cheerldng; Stat Mgr(s); ST Rnnr Up Consumer Ed FHA-HERO 89-90; Merit Awd Semi Fnlst RSP; Peer Cnslng; Teacher.

ESPINOLA, KRISTEN M; Ernest Righetti HS; Santa Maria, CA; (4); 71/356; Church Yth Grp; Cmnty Wkr; FFA; Hosp Aide; Teachers Aide; Varsity Clb; Ed Nwsp; Stat Score Keeper; Hon Roll; HS Rodeo Team VP; Allan Hancock Coll; Bus.

ESPINOSA, ANITA; La Puente HS; La Puente, CA; (2); Church Yth Grp; Sec Drama Clb; Drill Tm; Yrbk; VP Soph Cls; Sec Jr Cls; High Hon Roll; Prfct Atten Awd; Sigma; Acad Decathlon; Jrnlsm.

ESPINOSA, ARMANDO; Sweetwater HS; Chula Vista, CA; (2); 147/543; VP Science Clb; Teachers Aide; JV Var Bsbl; Wrstlng; Cit Awd; Awd Of Mrt Schlrshp; Cert Of Achvt; USC; Aerospace Engr.

ESPINOSA, DANIEL G; Don Bosco Technical Inst; Montebello, CA; (3); Boy Scts; Drama Clb; Band; Mrchg Band; School Play; Crs Cntry; Vllybl; Mech Engrng.

ESPINOSA, DAVID; Gardena HS; Gardena, CA; (3); Aud/Vis; Science Clb; Stage Crew; Ed Rptr Nwsp; Yrbk; VP Hist Jr Cls; Stu Cncl; Cit Awd; Hon Roll; Prfct Atten Awd; MESA Pres; Oscar Rcpnt Awd & Ldrshp Awd; Freelance Photo; Fine Arts.

ESPINOSA, GABRIEL; Gladstone HS; Azusa, CA; (3); Church Yth Grp; Ftbl; CA Poly Pomona; Arch.

ESPINOSA, GENE R; Pinole Valley HS; Hercules, CA; (2); Church Yth Grp; Band; Church Choir; Jazz Band; Mrchg Band; School Musical; JV Crs Cntry; JV Trk; High Hon Roll; Hon Roll; UC Berkeley.

ESPINOSA, MA VERONICA; Roosevelt HS; Los Angeles, CA; (2); Girl Scts; Spanish Clb; SADD; Bsbl; Bsktbl; Spanish NHS; ELAC.

ESPINOSA, MARIA C; King City HS; Greenfield, CA; (4); Church Yth Grp; Computer Clb; English Clb; FTA; Latin Clb; Library Aide; Office Aide; Spanish Clb; SADD; Teachers Aide; Cnslng Cmmtte; Cnslr.

ESPINOSA, MARIA T; Baldwin Park HS; Baldwin Park, CA; (2); Hon Roll; USC; Aerontcl Engrng.

ESPINOSA, MELISA; La Canada HS; La Canada-Flint, CA; (4); 50/250; Capt Color Guard; Jazz Band; NHS; U Of Redlands; Engl.

ESPINOSA, RACHEL L; Bishop Amat HS; Diamond Bar, CA; (1); Hon Roll; Bowling League; Cal Poly; Accntng.

ESPINOSA, RICHARD; Cantwell HS; Los Angeles, CA; (4); 9/54; Am Leg Boys St; Letterman Clb; Science Clb; Spanish Clb; Pres Sr Cls; Var L Ftbl; Var L Trk; Hon Roll; NHS; Pres Acad Fit Awd; Gregg Kabat Schlr Athlte Awd; Amer G I Frm Schlrshp; All Sante Fe Leag Ftbl; UC Santa Cruz; Comp Engrng.

ESPINOSA, ROWENA B; Balboa HS; San Francisco, CA; (2); Ed Nwsp; Pres Jr Cls; Cit Awd; Hon Roll; Prfct Atten Awd; Filipino Clb Scrtry; Clss Pblcty Mgr; U CA; Comm.

ESPINOZA, ANTHONY; San Gorgomlo HS; San Bernardino, CA; (2); Advrtsng.

ESPINOZA, AURORA; Le Grand Union HS; Planada, CA; (2); Church Yth Grp; Math Clb; Teachers Aide; Church Choir; Rep Frsh Cls; VP Soph Cls; JV Bsktbl; JV Sftbl; JV Vllybl; JV Wt Lftg; Fresno St; Nurse.

ESPINOZA, CHRISTINA; James A Garfield HS; Los Angeles, CA; (2); Church Yth Grp; Cmnty Wkr; Orch; School Musical; French Hon Soc; High Hon Roll; Hon Roll; Prfct Atten Awd; CSF; Harvard; Med.

ESPINOZA, CINDY A; St Genevieve HS; Reseda, CA; (3); French Clb; Pep Clb; Chorus; Var Socr; Hon Roll; Mck Trl; CSF; Chld Psych.

ESPINOZA, CONNIE LINDA; W Covina Hills 7th Day Adv Schl; Valinda, CA; (2); Chorus; Hon Roll; UCLA; Pediatrics.

ESPINOZA, ELIZABETH C; Channel Islands HS; Oxnard, CA; (2); UCSB; Law.

ESPINOZA, ERIC C; Cantwell HS; Los Angeles, CA; (3); Aud/Vis; Cmnty Wkr; Office Aide; Oper Small Bus Buyng, Sellng & Trdng Collctbls-Bsbl Crds, Comic Bks, Recrds & CD; UCLA; Brdcstng.

ESPINOZA, FRANCISCA; King City HS; Greenfield, CA; (4); FFA; Hon Roll; Locl Schlrshp Greenfld Womens Clb; Schlrshp Hartnell Coll; Grad HS Hon Roll; Salinas CA; Financial Inst Op.

ESPINOZA, HUGO A; Westminster HS; Westminster, CA; (2); JV Bsbl; UCLA.

ESPINOZA, JASMINE P; San Gabriel Mission HS; Los Angeles, CA; (3); Chorus; Gym; Var Swmmng; CSF; Loyola Marymount U; Med.

ESPINOZA, JOHN M; Holtville HS; Holtville, CA; (4); FFA; FHA; Library Aide; Math Tm; Pep Clb; Teachers Aide; Bsktbl; Hon Roll; PIT; Electrncs.

ESPINOZA, LUPE A; Delta HS; Thornton, CA; (4); 14/57; Office Aide; Spanish Clb; Teachers Aide; Crs Cntry; Trk; Prfct Atten Awd; Hospice Schlrshp; Susan Jane Stowall Awd; CA ST U Sacramento; Nrsng.

ESPINOZA, MARISSA G; San Fernando HS; Pacoima, CA; (4); 20/589; Church Yth Grp; Cmnty Wkr; Office Aide; Service Clb; Ed Yrbk; Rep Stu Cncl; Var Bsktbl; High Hon Roll; Pres Acad Fit Awd; Gftd Clb; U La Verne; Sociology.

ESPINOZA, MARTHA; East HS; Bakersfield, CA; (3); Cmnty Wkr; Computer Clb; FFA; FTA; Nwsp; Off Jr Cls; Cit Awd; Spanish NHS; Med.

ESPINOZA, MIA T; Dos Pueblos HS; Goleta, CA; (2); 73/299; Church Yth Grp; Phys Ed Tchr.

ESPINOZA, MONIQUE R; Buena Park HS; Buena Park, CA; (3); 31/375; Letterman Clb; Varsity Clb; Rep Jr Cls; JV Capt Bsktbl; Var L Sftbl; Var L Vllybl; High Hon Roll; Prfct Atten Awd; CSF; Dstngshd Schlr Awd; Stu Of Mnth French III; Bus Admin.

ESPINOZA, RUBICELA; Sacred Heart Of Mary HS; El Monte, CA; (3); Aud/Vis; Library Aide; Spanish Clb; Speech Tm; Stage Crew; Rptr Nwsp; NHS; CSF; Mother Butler Soc; Cum Laude; Library Clb; Bus.

ESPINOZA, SHERI; Helix HS; La Mesa, CA; (3); Hosp Aide; Off Sr Cls; Var Socr; Var Swmmng; Var Vllybl; YMCA Swm Instr/Life Guard; Stu Body Cmmssnr Of Hmn Rltns; Hlth Admin.

ESPINOZA, SUSANA; Pasadenda HS; Pasadena, CA; (3); Art Clb; Chess Clb; Church Yth Grp; Cmnty Wkr; Computer Clb; Dance Clb; Debate Tm; Drama Clb; English Clb; French Clb; California Scholarship Federation; Upward Bound Program; MESA; JV Badminton Team.

ESPINOZA, VANIA; Colton Christian Schl; San Bernardino, CA; (2); Church Yth Grp; Drama Clb; Pep Clb; Chorus; School Musical; School Play; Bsktbl; Cheerldng; Hon Roll; Accntng.

ESPINUEVA, LENI L; Hogan SR HS; Vallejo, CA; (3); Hosp Aide; Key Clb; Spanish Clb; Teachers Aide; High Hon Roll; CSF; Med.

ESPIRIDION, ORTIZ; Morningside HS; Inglewood, CA; (3); French Clb; Latin Clb; Rep Frsh Cls; VP Soph Cls; VP Jr Cls; Rep Stu Cncl; Var Socr; JV Trk; JV Vllybl; Hon Roll; Hmcmng Crt; Pgnt; UCLA; Bus.

ESPIRITU, JONATHAN P; Don Antonio Lugo HS; Chino, CA; (2); German Clb; JV Var Tennis; Cit Awd; High Hon Roll; Hon Roll; Golden Conquest Schl Awd Germn 88-89 89-90; Stu Of Wk Awd 89; Hnr Stu Cert; Brigham Young U; Phys Ther.

ESPIRITU, JOSEPH G; S San Francisco HS; S San Francisco, CA; (4); Drama Clb; Teachers Aide; Swing Chorus; Lit Mag; JV Wt Lftg; Outstndng Achvt Eng 89; Cert Of Cmpltn Reg Occup Prog Hotel Svc Occ 89-90; U Of HI; Hotel Mgt.

ESPIRITU, KATHLEEN; Paramount HS; Paramount, CA; (2); 36/616; SADD; Cit Awd; Hon Roll; Jr NHS; Opt Clb Awd; Prfct Atten Awd; California Scholastic Federation; College Club; Chief Accountant.

ESPRITT, LAILAH; Vivian Webb Schl; Claremont, CA; (4); Latin Clb; Chorus; Rptr Lit Mag; Stu Cncl; Mgr(s); Powder Puff Ftbl; Sftbl; Trk; Hon Roll; Ntl Merit Schol; Stu Cnslr; Dorm Cncl; Partnership Intl Cultural Awareness Org; Columbia U; Econ.

ESQUEDA, LAURA; Arvin HS; Bakersfield, CA; (1); Church Yth Grp; Dance Clb; Latin Clb; Ski Clb; Spanish Clb; Band; Color Guard; Intrml Bsktbl; Intrml Sftbl; Capt Intrml Vllybl; MECHA; CA Schlrshp; MESA; Teaching.

ESQUER, RAMON; Calexico HS; Calexico, CA; (3); Math Tm; Teachers Aide; Advncd Plcmnt Spnsh Lit Club Treas; CA ST Poly U; Elec Engr.

ESQUIBEL, DAVEY; Chaffey HS; Ontario, CA; (1); Church Yth Grp; Hon Roll; Law Enfrcmnt.

ESQUIBEL, LILIANA M; Chaffey HS; Ontario, CA; (3); 134/557; Rptr Nwsp; JV Bsktbl; Powder Puff Ftbl; JV Var Sftbl; Hon Roll; Lylac; Explr For Ontario Police; MECHA; Comp Sci Tech.

ESQUIBEL, PATRICK C; Casa Grande HS; Petaluma, CA; (2); 68/295; Yrbk; Socr; Trk; NHS; CSF; Cycling; Cal-Poly Pomona; Aero Engr.

ESQUIUEL, MARTHA; Pasadena HS; Pasadena, CA; (3); Ski Clb; Teachers Aide; Cit Awd; Hon Roll; Badminton Tm; Photo Clb; CSF; UC Santa Barbara; Crim Just.

ESQUIVEL, ALEJANDRO B; John Marshall HS; Pasadena, CA; (1); Band; Mrchg Band; Cit Awd; Acad Decthln; Won Gldn St Exam Alg Awd; Arch.

ESQUIVEL, JERONIMO JAY; Channe Islands HS; Oxnard, CA; (3); 4-H; Spanish Clb; SADD; Var L Wrstlng; High Hon Roll; Hon Roll; Natl Yng Ldrs Conf Cngrssnl Schlr 90; Geom & Wrk Exprnc Awds 90; Stanford; Optometry.

ESQUIVEL, MARIO E; San Bernardino HS; San Bernardino, CA; (2); 35/600; Hon Roll; Cal Poly; Elec Engr.

ESQUIVEL, RAYMOND J; Bellarmine College Prep; Santa Clara, CA; (3); 58/300; Debate Tm; Letterman Clb; NFL; Speech Tm; Varsity Clb; Intrml Bsktbl; JV Var Ftbl; Christian Life Cmmnty; Retreat Leader; Comp Sci.

ESSEX, TRINA; Mt Diablo HS; Concord, CA; (2); Spanish Clb; SADD; Drill Tm; Bsktbl; Cheerldng; Powder Puff Ftbl; Socr; Trk; Cit Awd; Hon Roll; UC Davis; Child Psych.

ESSIG, JANNINE; Academy Of Our Lady Of Peace; Poway, CA; (2); Church Yth Grp; Dance Clb; School Play; Rep Soph Cls; Hon Roll; Chrch Lectr; Comm.

ESSLINGER, AMY D; St Joseph HS; Lynwood, CA; (3); Church Yth Grp; Cmnty Wkr; Spanish Clb; SADD; Chorus; Church Choir; High Hon Roll; Hon Roll; NHS; St Pres CA Jr Catholic Dghtrs Amer; CSF; Music.

ESTABILLO, GABRIEL P; Righetti HS; Guadalupe, CA; (2); Band; Hon Roll; Band Ltr; Asian Pacific Club; Upward Bound VP; Cal Poly; Arch.

ESTABROOK, MOLLY C; Livermore HS; Livermore, CA; (2); #11 In Class; Church Yth Grp; French Clb; Band; Mrchg Band; School Musical; Phtg Yrbk; Rep Soph Cls; CSF; Sun Schl Tchr; CORE Ldr; U Of CA.

ESTACIO, RHEA L; Southwest HS; San Diego, CA; (1); 16/350; SADD; Teachers Aide; Temple Yth Grp; Stage Crew; JV Bsktbl; JV Vllybl; Cit Awd; Hon Roll; Masonic Awd; Prfct Atten Awd; Jobs Daughters; San Diego ST U; Elem Tchr.

ESTALILLA, BRENDA P; Mc Lane HS; Fresno, CA; (4); 121/450; Acpl Chr; Chorus; Orch; Swing Chorus; Tri-12 & Prjct Alpha Clbs; Fresno City Coll; Pediatrics.

ESTANISLAO, JON RAY; St John Bosco HS; Montebello, CA; (4); 1/199; Key Clb; Q&S; Ed Nwsp; Lit Mag; Treas Jr Cls; Treas Sr Cls; High Hon Roll; NHS; Ntl Merit SF; Val; Asst Sftbl Coach; Acad Decathlon Tm; CSF; Georgetown U; Intl Bus.

ESTANISLAO, LAARNI C; Mark Keppel HS; Monterey Park, CA; (3); Dance Clb; Latin Clb; Hon Roll; Prfct Atten Awd; Paralegal.

ESTANISLAO, SHANE M; St John Bosco HS; Montebello, CA; (2); Church Yth Grp; Debate Tm; Key Clb; Trk; Hon Roll; NHS; Grphc Dsgnr.

ESTANOL, LAVERNE; Montgomery HS; San Diego, CA; (4); Nwsp; Ed Yrbk; Rep Frsh Cls; Var Crs Cntry; JV Socr; JV Vllybl; NHS; Acad All-Am; Natl Ldrshp Mrt Awds; U Of CA-IRVINE; Comp Sci.

ESTANOL, LUCIEN; Montgomery HS; San Diego, CA; (4); 34/406; FBLA; SADD; Ed Yrbk; Crs Cntry; Socr; Vllybl; Hon Roll; NHS; U Of CA Irvine; Biolgcl Sci.

ESTAVILLO, GLORIA F; Bishop Amat HS; West Covina, CA; (3); Church Yth Grp; Ed Yrbk; Rep Jr Cls; Hon Roll; CSF; U Of Pacific; Engl Lit.

ESTEBAN, RODNEY P; Cerritos HS; Cerritos, CA; (2); Art Clb; Aud/Vis; Cmnty Wkr; Debate Tm; Speech Tm; Variety Show; Prfct Atten Awd; VP Japanes Natl Hnr Soc 90-91; Publcty Drctr Japans Natl Soc 89-90; Outstndng Svc Clb Actvts Awd; Arch.

ESTEPHAN, JACK J; West Covina S D A HS; West Covina, CA; (1); Church Yth Grp; Chorus; Ed Nwsp; Yrbk; VP Stu Cncl; Intrml Bsktbl; Intrml Sftbl; Intrml Vllybl; High Hon Roll; Jrnlst.

ESTERS III, LEONARD; Inglewood HS; Inglewood, CA; (2); ROTC; Teachers Aide; Color Guard; Ftbl; Cit Awd; USC.

ESTES, AMY B; Rio Lindo Adventist Acad; Valley Springs, CA; (2); Spanish Clb; Acpl Chr; Band; Chorus; Church Choir; Orch; Variety Show; High Hon Roll; Pacific Union Coll; Vet Med.

ESTES, CARRIE A; Hanford HS; Hanford, CA; (1); Treas Frsh Cls; Treas Soph Cls; Cheerldng; Diving; Swmmng; Wt Lftg; Hon Roll; Interact.

ESTES, FRANKLIN J; Elsinore HS; Wildomar, CA; (2); 30/580; Letterman Clb; ROTC; Treas Frsh Cls; Var Crs Cntry; JV Ftbl; Var Trk; Var Wrstlng; Hnrs Achvt Gldn St Geom Exm; U Of Southern CA; Engrng.

ESTES, JILL; Rosary HS; Anaheim, CA; (2); Church Yth Grp; French Clb; Hon Roll; NEDT Awd; Equestrian; Psych.

ESTES, KRISTY F; Carlsbad HS; Carlsbad, CA; (3); 67/370; FCA; FBLA; FHA; Pep Clb; Varsity Clb; Off Jr Cls; Stat Bsktbl; Cheerldng; Hon Roll; Pres Acad Fit Awd; UCLA; CPA.

ESTES, LEANN M; Mc Kinleyville HS; Mckinleyville, CA; (3); Church Yth Grp; SADD; Teachers Aide; Cit Awd; High Hon Roll; Hon Roll; Prfct Atten Awd; Phys Ed.

ESTES, LINNEA A; Carmel HS; Carmel Valley, CA; (2); Church Yth Grp; Hon Roll; Poem Published; Piano; Child Care; Psych.

ESTES, PAUL; Palm Springs HS; Palm Springs, CA; (3); Aud/Vis; Chess Clb; Computer Clb; Drama Clb; Stage Crew; People/People Yth Sci Exchng-Comp Sci USSR; Mdlst Drama Stage Lghtng/Electrcn PSHS Slvr Sands Awds; CA Inst Of Tech; Electrncs.

ESTES, STEFANIE J; Amador Valley HS; Pleasanton, CA; (4); 15/420; Church Yth Grp; GAA; Office Aide; Ski Clb; SADD; Teachers Aide; School Play; Stage Crew; Ed Yrbk; High Hon Roll; Schlr Awd-Hgh GPA; Outstndng Edtr Awd-Yrbk Sect Edtr; CA ST U-Sacramento; Bus Admin.

ESTEVEZ, ANA L; Baldwin Park HS; Baldwin Park, CA; (4); 85/390; Cmnty Wkr; Drama Clb; Pres Drill Tm; Ed Yrbk; Bsktbl; Trk; Hon Roll; CA Poly Pomona; Psych.

ESTEVEZ, DAVID; St Bernard HS; Hawthorne, CA; (3); Computer Clb; Letterman Clb; Spanish Clb; Varsity Clb; Band; JV Var Bsbl; Intrml Bsktbl; Intrml Ftbl; Intrml Socr; Cit Awd.

ESTEVEZ, JOSE R; El Camino HS; S San Francisco, CA; (3); School Musical; Variety Show; Var Socr; Bus.

ESTEVEZ-BRETON, ANDREA; Hayward HS; Hayward, CA; (1); Band; Mrchg Band; Stanford; Neurologist.

ESTEY, JULIE ELIZABETH; Highlands HS; Sacramento, CA; (1); Cit Awd; Hon Roll; Pres Schlr; U Of CA LA; Law.

ESTIOCO, MARILEE; Pinole Valley HS; Hercules, CA; (2); Church Yth Grp; Cmnty Wkr; Dance Clb; French Clb; SADD; Acpl Chr; Hon Roll; UC Davis.

ESTIVA, JENNIFER U; St Bernard HS; Inglewood, CA; (3); Hosp Aide; Pep Clb; Spanish Clb; Drill Tm; Flag Corp; Cit Awd; Hon Roll; Asian-Pacific Clb; Loyola Marymount; Bus.

ESTIVA, RODELINE C; John F Kennedy HS; Mission Hills, CA; (3); French Clb; Math Clb; Office Aide; Hon Roll; Peer Tutor; CSF; 89 Goldn St Exam-Geom Hgh Hnrs; Chem Engrng.

ESTLINE, EINAT; University City HS; San Diego, CA; (3); Dance Clb; Model UN; Cit Awd; Hon Roll; Golden St Ex Geom Hnrs; Friday Nght Live Drnkng/Drvng; Ldrshp Grp; Berekley; Math.

ESTOPINAN, NOILA; Whittier HS; Whittier, CA; (4); French Clb; Latin Clb; Spanish Clb; Teachers Aide; JV Crs Cntry; JV Trk; Cit Awd; Hon Roll; Prfct Atten Awd; Champ Wnnr; Achvt Mrt; Cardinal Cup; CSU Fullerton; Spansh/Frnch Ed.

ESTRADA, ALICIA; Tranquillity Union HS; Mendota, CA; (2); French Clb; Pep Clb; Cheerldng; Sftbl; Hon Roll; Fresno ST U; Bus Mgt.

ESTRADA, ANA C; Calexico Adventist Mission Acad; Calexico, CA; (3); UC San Diego; Psych.

ESTRADA, ANGELA; Fontana HS; Fontana, CA; (2); Intrct Clb.

ESTRADA, ANN P; San Gabriel HS; San Gabriel, CA; (2); Varsity Clb; JV Var Crs Cntry; Var Trk; Hon Roll; St Fnlst Miss Amer Teen Pageant; Comp Pgm.

ESTRADA JR, APOLO C; George Washington HS; San Francisco, CA; (2); ROTC; Acpl Chr; Church Choir; School Play; Stage Crew; Cit Awd; High Hon Roll; Prfct Atten Awd; UC Davis Ag Exchng Pgm Delg; Engrng.

ESTRADA JR, ARTHUR A; Hesperia HS; Hesperia, CA; (4); 25/427; Key Clb; VP Treas Spanish Clb; Ed Yrbk; Var Crs Cntry; Var Capt Socr; High Hon Roll; Hon Roll; Prfct Atten Awd; Natl Hspncs Schlr; U Of NV Las Vegas; Accntng.

ESTRADA JR, CARLOS; Beaumont HS; Beaumont, CA; (3); 10/180; French Clb; Band; Jazz Band; Mrchg Band; Pep Band; Pres Frsh Cls; JV Crs Cntry; JV Trk; Hon Roll; Stu Of Mnth April; Jnr Hnr Escort; CSF; Stu Ambssdr-Soviet Union.

ESTRADA, CYNTHIA A; Hesperia HS; Hesperia, CA; (4); 9/600; Spanish Clb; Sec Frsh Cls; Sec Soph Cls; Rep Jr Cls; Rep Sr Cls; Rep Stu Cncl; Var Socr; Var Sftbl; High Hon Roll; Hon Roll; Coachs Awd Var Sftbl; Top 5 Pct Cls; CSU Hispanic Stu Schlrshp Wnnr; Cal ST San Bernardino; Tchr.

ESTRADA, CYNTHIA K; James A Garfield HS; Los Angeles, CA; (2); Service Clb; Teachers Aide; Band; Mrchg Band; Orch; Crs Cntry; Trk; Cit Awd; Hon Roll; Prfct Atten Awd; UCLA Partnershp Pgm; Psych.

ESTRADA, DEANA; Living Way Christian Acad; La Puente, CA; (4); 2/6; Church Yth Grp; Teachers Aide; School Play; Ed Nwsp; Sec Stu Cncl; Vllybl; Hon Roll; Dstngshd Chrstn Stu Awd 88-89; Adult CPA & Stndrd First Aid Certs; UCLA; Psych.

ESTRADA, EDNA Y; Calexico Mission Acad; Imperial, CA; (2); Girl Scts; Math Tm; Varsity Clb; School Play; Var Socr; Capt Swmmng; Capt Vllybl; Cit Awd; High Hon Roll; Hon Roll; Congressional Scholar CA Rep; SDSU; Psych.

ESTRADA, HEIDE; Oxnard HS; Oxnard, CA; (3); French Clb; Library Aide; Cit Awd; High Hon Roll; Hon Roll; Prfct Atten Awd; Acad Achvt Awd; Acad Ltr; Northridge; Health.

ESTRADA, LETICIA RENAE; Pinole Valley HS; San Pablo, CA; (4); Church Yth Grp; SADD; Hon Roll; Pres Acad Fit Awd; Dance Prod 3 Yrs; Yth Educator Pgm; CA Schlrshp Fed; UC Berkeley; Bus Mgmt.

ESTRADA, MAYNARD; Fresno Adventist Acad; Madera, CA; (3); 7/20; Church Yth Grp; FCA; Ski Clb; Band; Sec VP Stu Cncl; Bsbl; Bsktbl; Ftbl; Sftbl; Vllybl; CA ST U Fresno; Phys Thrpy.

ESTRADA, OMAR; Servite HS; Buena Park, CA; (3); 13/149; Boy Scts; Nwsp; Hon Roll; CSF; Safe Rides-Tri Schl; Acad Dcthln Tm; Engrng.

ESTRADA, OTHON; Servite HS; Buena Park, CA; (3); 8/149; Cmnty Wkr; Math Tm; Scholastic Bowl; Nwsp; Trk; NHS; NEDT Awd; Safe Rides.

ESTRADA JR, ROBERT; East Bakersfield HS; Bakersfield, CA; (4); Church Yth Grp; SADD; Teachers Aide; VICA; Bakersfield Coll; Engr.

ESTRADA, RODERICK L; Salesian HS; Pinole, CA; (4); 1/35; Ed Yrbk; Sec Treas Frsh Cls; VP Soph Cls; Pres Jr Cls; Pres Stu Cncl; JV Bsktbl; NHS; Val; Church Yth Grp; JV Bsktbl; Robert C Byrd Schlrshp Wnnr; UC Berkeley Almni Assn Schlrshp Wnnr; Ten Team MVP; UC Berkeley; Bio Sci.

ESTRADA, SARAH; St Genevieve HS; Canoga Park, CA; (4); VP SADD; Ed Nwsp; JV Cheerldng; Var Socr; Var Trk; Capt Vllybl; Ntl Merit Ltr; 1st Pl Chaminade Coll Prep Sci Fair; Hnrn Mntn Los Angeles Cnty Sci Fair; Schlrshp Engrng Sumr Inst; Cornell U; Chem Engrng.

ESTRADA, VERONICA; South HS; Bakersfield, CA; (4); 8/397; Intnl Clb; JA; Pres Band; Pres Mrchg Band; Pep Band; Var JV Swmmng; Intrml Vllybl; Cit Awd; Hon Roll; NHS; Mst Outstndng Bandsman & Musician; Bank Amer Awd Music; Hispanic Exclicne Awd CA St Bakersfield; CA ST U Bakersfield; Bus Admn.

ESTRELLA, GALE L; Fontana HS; Fontana, CA; (1); Church Yth Grp; Cmnty Wkr; SADD; Rep Frsh Cls; Intrml Vllybl; Track; Cycling; Auto Mechanics; Yale; Journalism.

ESTRELLA, MIKE E; Don Antonio Lugo HS; Ontario, CA; (4); 24/680; Am Leg Boys St; Teachers Aide; Variety Show; Pres Frsh Cls; Var Bsbl; Var Ftbl; Var Capt Socr; High Hon Roll; NHS; Pres Schlr; Ftbl Schlr/Athlete Of Yr Awds-Natl Hall Of Fame & Citrus Pepsi; St Marys Coll Of CA; Film.

ESTRICK, MICHELE L; Fullerton HS; Fullerton, CA; (1); 8/350; Church Yth Grp; Pep Clb; Drill Tm; JV Socr; High Hon Roll; Rotary Awd; CSF.

ETCHAMENDY, ROSEMARIE; Garces Memorial HS; Bakersfield, CA; (3); Ski Clb; SADD; High Hon Roll; Hon Roll; Bus.

ETCHEVERRY, MARY ANN; Yuba City HS; Live Oak, CA; (2); 39/500; Church Yth Grp; Girl Scts; Ski Clb; JV Var Cheerldng; Var JV Vllybl; High Hon Roll; Pianist; Grp Dance 1st Pl CA St Tlnt Cmptn; Rep Gottschalks Dept Store As Hi-Deb 90; Dance Instr; USAF; Astronaut.

ETCHEVERS, PAUL; Woodside HS; Redwood City, CA; (2); JV Tennis; Mesa Club; Stanford; Med.

ETEMAD, PONTEA; Louisville HS; Woodland Hills, CA; (1); Drama Clb; JV Sftbl; High Hon Roll; Pres Acad Fit Awd; CSF; UCLA; Brain Srgn.

ETHERTON, TRICIA; Fred C Beyer HS; Modesto, CA; (3); Church Yth Grp; Pep Clb; SADD; Teachers Aide; Chorus; Stat Ftbl; Stat Sftbl; Hon Roll; Pres Acad Fit Awd; Boston U; Sales.

ETO, DANELLE S; Morro Bay HS; Los Osos, CA; (3); 3/230; Teachers Aide; Band; Jazz Band; Stat JV Bsktbl; Var JV Vllybl; High Hon Roll; Ntl Merit Ltr; CSF.

EUBANK, ANDY C; San Marcos HS; San Marcos, CA; (3); Church Yth Grp; 4-H; VP Sr Cls; Var Swmmng; Var Wrstlng; Hon Roll; NHS; Surf Club; UCSB; Phys Thrpst.

EUFUSIA, JENNIFER; Half Moon Bay HS; Half Moon Bay, CA; (4); 36/177; Office Aide; Spanish Clb; Stu Cncl; Hon Roll; Millard Fillmore; Span Club Trip Mexico; U CA Riverside; Math.

EUGENIO, CYNTHIA; Sequoia HS; Fontana, CA; (1); Pep Clb; Cheerldng; Vllybl; Hon Roll.

EUN, KATHY J; Buena Park HS; La Palma, CA; (3); French Clb; Key Clb; Letterman Clb; Science Clb; Ski Clb; Teachers Aide; Ed Nwsp; VP Soph Cls; Score Keeper; Var Socr; CSF; OCAD; JSA Dir Pblcty; UCSD; Dntstry.

EUN, SARAH BO; Buena Park HS; La Palma, CA; (4); Key Clb; VP Science Clb; Ski Clb; Teachers Aide; Capt Drill Tm; High Hon Roll; Kiwanis Awd; Orange Cnty Acad Decathlon 4 Yrs; Austen Arnold Schlrshp Wnnr; CA Schlrshp Fed; UC Davis; Pre-Med.

EUREK, JENNIFER; Foothill HS; Pleasanton, CA; (2); Church Yth Grp; SADD; VP Soph Cls; JV Stu Cncl; JV Sftbl; Pom Pon; CSF; Graphic Dsgnr.

EUSTAQUIO, LILIBETH; Flintridge Sacred Heart Acad; Tujunga, CA; (4); French Clb; Service Clb; Chorus; School Musical; Sec Stu Cncl; Stat Mgr(s); NHS; Assn Cthlc Stu Cnsls Grad Awd For Svc; Rlgs Educ Tchr; Living In Faith Experience Campus Mnstry Team; U Of CA Irvine; Bio.

EVANGELISTA, CINDY C; Eagle Rock HS; Los Angeles, CA; (3); Church Yth Grp; Cmnty Wkr; Intnl Clb; Key Clb; Office Aide; Pep Clb; Red Cross Aide; Science Clb; Service Clb; Teachers Aide; Acad All Amer Schlr Pgm; Chldrns Hsptl Vlntr; Jr Yr Drl Tm Top 10; U Of CA; Med.

EVANOFF, ROULA D; Turlock HS; Turlock, CA; (2); Hon Roll; Prfct Atten Awd; Law.

EVANS, AMBER; Lowell HS; San Francisco, CA; (4); 106/626; Drama Clb; Hosp Aide; Rptr Nwsp; Yrbk; Rep Sr Cls; Ntl Merit Ltr; Pres Acad Fit Awd; Library Aide; Stage Crew; Rep Soph Cls; Adventurers Alliance Cochrmn; Stu Advocates Of Global Awrnss; Amnesty Intl; U Of CA Santa Cruz.

EVANS, ANDREA L; Simi Valley HS; Simi Valley, CA; (3); Church Yth Grp; Yrbk; Bsktbl; Powder Puff Ftbl; UCLA.

EVANS, ANNALISSA; Mission San Jose HS; Fremont, CA; (3); Jazz Band; Var Sftbl; JV Capt Vllybl; Hon Roll; Hgh Hnrs Golden St Exam; Piano.

EVANS, BENJAMIN M; Del Campo HS; Carmichael, CA; (2); 18/460; Variety Show; Rep Soph Cls; JV Bsktbl; JV Ftbl; JV Trk; Boys Vlybl Club; Booster Club AAA Awd; 24 Hour Shkspre Marthn Rdng.

EVANS, BOBBY R; Woodcrest Christian HS; Riverside, CA; (2); 5/32; High Hon Roll; Heart Surgeon.

EVANS, BRENNAN; Avalon SR HS; Avalon, CA; (1); Intrml Golf; Var Socr; High Hon Roll.

EVANS, CARLY N; Warren HS; Downey, CA; (1); Pres Sec Church Yth Grp; FHA; Pep Clb; Architect.

EVANS, CAROLE M; Bonita Vista HS; Bonita, CA; (3); 43/559; Church Yth Grp; Model UN; Service Clb; SADD; Teachers Aide; Varsity Clb; Nwsp; Yrbk; Var Fld Hcky; JV Socr; Foreign Exch Stu Italy; All Acad Fld Hockey Awd.

EVANS, CARRIE; Berean Christian HS; Pittsburg, CA; (3); Drama Clb; Church Choir; School Play; VP Frsh Cls; Stat Bsktbl; Var Cheerldng; ACSI Dstngshd Stu; Psych.

EVANS, CRYSTAL ANN; Vacaville HS; Vacaville, CA; (3); Church Yth Grp; High Hon Roll; Hon Roll; Prfct Atten Awd; Peer Cnslng; Foster Yth; Davis; Psych.

EVANS, CRYSTAL L; Fairfield HS; Fairfield, CA; (4); 23/520; Sec Church Yth Grp; Cmnty Wkr; Dance Clb; French Clb; Teachers Aide; JV Var Cheerldng; Var Pom Pon; French Hon Soc; High Hon Roll; NHS; Howard U; Law.

EVANS, DARREN P; Los Amigos HS; Fountain Valley, CA; (2); 5/365; JV Intrml Bsbl; JV Ftbl; High Hon Roll; Hon Roll; Hnrs Golden St Exam 1st Yr Alg, Hgh Hnrs Geom; Stu Of Mnth June 89; Coachs Awd Frosh Bsbl; Arch.

EVANS, DAWNN M; Ramona HS; Ramona, CA; (2); 25/400; Dance Clb; Chorus; School Play; Amnesty Intl Pres; Envrnmntl Club Treas; Animal Rights Grp; Music.

EVANS, DEREK J; Foothill HS; North Highlands, CA; (3); Church Yth Grp; ROTC; Hon Roll; Mech Eng.

EVANS, ERIKA; Perris HS; Perris, CA; (3); Church Yth Grp; Dance Clb; Pep Clb; Church Choir; Trk; High Hon Roll; Hon Roll; Natl Yth Ldrshp Awd Congrssnl Schlr 89-90; Black Stu Union VP; Friday Night Live; Howard U; Psych.

EVANS, GAIL; Washington Preparatory HS; Los Angeles, CA; (3); Church Yth Grp; Math Clb; Co-Capt Pep Clb; Sec Jr Cls; Pres Sr Cls; Pres Stu Cncl; Hon Roll; Pres Empresses; Knights & Ladies; Peace Clb; Yuskegee U; Pre-Med.

EVANS, GINETTE M; Charter Oak HS; Covina, CA; (2); Chorus; Stage Crew; Sftbl; Hon Roll; Prfct Atten Awd; Miss CA Amer Teen Pgnt 90 Fnlst; Accntng.

EVANS, GRAHAM T; Carmel HS; Carmel, CA; (4); Boy Scts; FFA; Varsity Clb; High Hon Roll; Hon Roll; Cal Poly; Anml Sci.

EVANS, HEATHER A; Mount Carmel HS; San Diego, CA; (1); 1/868; Church Yth Grp; Band; Mrchg Band; Hon Roll; BYU; Wrtr.

EVANS, HEATHER S; Village Christian HS; Lake View Terr, CA; (3); 33/123; English Clb; Letterman Clb; Math Clb; Spanish Clb; Rep Stu Cncl; Var Bsktbl; Var Bsbl; Stat Ftbl; Var Sftbl; JV Vllybl; Coaches Awd & 2nd Team All Leag Vrsty Sftbl; Golden Poet Awd 89; Oral Roberts U; Cmmnctns.

EVANS, HOLLY A; Enterprise HS; Redding, CA; (3); 29/427; Church Yth Grp; Dance Clb; Drill Tm; School Play; Stage Crew; Lit Mag; Pom Pon; High Hon Roll; Hon Roll; Pres Acad Fit Awd; Drill Team Co-Capt 90-91; Piano; Art, Lit & Creative Wrtng; U Of CA-DAVIS; Eng.

EVANS, JAMES M; Prospect HS; San Jose, CA; (3); Yrbk; Treas Jr Cls; Treas Sr Cls; Var Capt Socr; Var Tennis; CA Schlstc Fed; Arch.

EVANS, JANET; John F Kennedy HS; La Palma, CA; (4); Bus Profs of Am; Church Yth Grp; Cmnty Wkr; FBLA; Key Clb; Band; Chorus; Mrchg Band; Pep Band; Stu Cncl; Dsnylnd Svc Awd Jdg; Biola U; Bus Adm.

EVANS, JASON M; John Burroughs HS; Burbank, CA; (3); Am Leg Boys St; French Clb; Treas Spanish Clb; High Hon Roll; Rensselaer Polytech Inst Mdlst 89-90; CA Schlrshp Fed; Burbank Amer Red Cross Yth Grp; Engrng.

EVANS, JEAN M; Santa Monica HS; Santa Monica, CA; (1); Dance Clb; Drama Clb; CA Inst Of Arts; Actng.

EVANS, JEANNETTE; Archbishop Mitty HS; San Jose, CA; (2); 1/209; Church Yth Grp; SADD; High Hon Roll; NHS; Engl/Religion Cert Of Excllnc; U CA San Diego; Intr Dsgn.

EVANS, JENNIFER J; Marysville HS; Marysville, CA; (2); 4/232; Church Yth Grp; Var Trk; Cit Awd; High Hon Roll; Frdy Nght Live Clb; Hghst GPA Trck Tm; Rotry Clb; SR HS Rep At Chrch; U CA Davis; Med.

EVANS, JENNIFER L; Lincoln HS; Sheridan, CA; (3); Sec Church Yth Grp; FFA; Church Choir; JV Bsktbl; Hon Roll; CA St Dept Ed & Indstry Ed Cncl CA Exam Awd; Financial Analyst.

EVANS, JON D; Apple Valley HS; Apple Valley, CA; (4); 45/450; Church Yth Grp; Drama Clb; Math Tm; Pep Clb; Spanish Clb; Var L Tennis; High Hon Roll; Hon Roll; CA Sthrn Sctn Plyof Qrtr Fnlst-Tnns; Oro Fndtn Schlrshp; Wrtng Clbrtn Wnr; San Diego ST U; Mktng.

EVANS, JONI E; Gahr HS; Cypress, CA; (1); Church Yth Grp; Dance Clb; Church Choir; Color Guard; Drm Mjr(t); Flag Corp; Mrchg Band; Gym; Cit Awd; Hon Roll; Debutante Princss/Natl Basic Baton Strutt Chmpn/Queen Of Day/DMA Conts 89; Pediatrics.

EVANS, KATHLEEN M; Mountain View HS; Mountain View, CA; (3); 11/293; Am Leg Aux Girls St; French Clb; Girl Scts; Capt Color Guard; Mrchg Band; High Hon Roll; Ntl Merit Ltr; Envrnmntl Clb; Asian Clb.

EVANS, KIMBERLY; Valley HS; Sacramento, CA; (1); Off Frsh Cls; Cheerldng; Var Socr; Stat Wrstlng; Hon Roll; Stanford U; Child Psych.

EVANS, KORI J; Pinole Valley HS; El Sobrante, CA; (1); Library Aide; Rep Stu Cncl; Hon Roll; Qn Of Intl Order Of Jobs Daughters; Tchr.

EVANS, LAKISHA; Pius X HS; Compton, CA; (4); Pep Clb; Chorus; Cheerldng; Hon Roll; NHS; Magna Cum Laude Plaque; NHS/Csf Life Mem; Math/Frgn Lang/Hstry/Sci/Relgn-Silver Certs; Loyola Marymount U; Acctng.

EVANS, LAURA E; Herbert Hoover HS; Fresno, CA; (4); 1/383; Pres French Clb; NFL; Mrchg Band; Lit Mag; Bausch & Lomb Sci Awd; Ntl Merit SF; Val; CA Schlrshp Fed Chptr Pres; Amnestry Intl Chptr Brd Dir; Natl Cncl Tchrs Engl Achvt Awd, Writing; UC Berkeley; Pol Sci.

EVANS, LISA; Justin Siena HS; Napa, CA; (4); 30/135; Am Leg Aux Girls St; Cmnty Wkr; Ski Clb; Stu Cncl; Bsktbl; Socr; Tennis; U Of CO Boulder.

EVANS, LORI; Oak Ridge HS; El Dorado Hills, CA; (4); 21/223; Sec Frsh Cls; VP Soph Cls; Stu Cncl; JV Var Cheerldng; Hon Roll; CA Schlrshp Fed; Hmcmng & Prom Queens Crt; Outstndng Achvt Bio; AZ ST U; Bus.

EVANS, MEGAN E; Homestead HS; Sunnyvale, CA; (1); Church Yth Grp; Cmnty Wkr; Drama Clb; Hosp Aide; Service Clb; SADD; Thesps; Chorus; Church Choir; School Play; U CA; Elem Ed.

EVANS, MELINDA D; Turlock HS; Turlock, CA; (3); Stanislaus; Bus.

EVANS, MELISSA; Oak Ridge HS; El Dorado Hills, CA; (1); Church Yth Grp; Office Aide; Church Choir; Variety Show; Hon Roll; Friday Night Live Clb; BYU; Beautician.

EVANS, MIKE J; Turlock HS; Hughson, CA; (3); 25/600; Church Yth Grp; Letterman Clb; Service Clb; Teachers Aide; Temple Yth Grp; Varsity Clb; Treas Stu Cncl; Var Wrstlng; Cit Awd; High Hon Roll; Hstry.

EVANS, PATRICIA J; Modesto HS; Modesto, CA; (2); JV Bsktbl; Var Sftbl; Hon Roll; Prfct Atten Awd; CA ST U; Marine Bio.

EVANS, PAUL; Reedley HS; Enumclaw, WA; (4); 7/300; Pres Computer Clb; VP German Clb; Math Tm; Sec Ski Clb; Band; Jazz Band; Mrchg Band; Pep Band; Variety Show; JETS Awd; Acad Decathln; Harvey Mudd Coll; Engrng.

EVANS, PAUL R; El Toro HS; El Toro, CA; (3); Band; Chorus; Jazz Band; Treas Mrchg Band; School Musical; High Hon Roll; Hon Roll; Prfrmng Arts Stu Month 90; Outstng Musicianshp Awds Jazz Festvls; GSE Acadmc Excllnc Awd Ge Hons; Berklee Schl Of Music; Music.

EVANS, RHONDA J; Fontana HS; Fontana, CA; (3); Church Yth Grp; Chorus; Var Capt Bsktbl; Hon Roll; Pres Acad Fit Awd; Azusa Pacific U; Phys Thrpy.

EVANS, ROBERT M; Millikan HS; Long Beach, CA; (2); Var Ftbl; Var Trk; Var Wt Lftg; High Hon Roll; Hon Roll; Prfct Atten Awd; UCLA; Med.

EVANS, SARAH A; Santa Teresa HS; San Jose, CA; (2); Church Yth Grp; French Clb; Spanish Clb; Varsity Clb; VP Crs Cntry; Var Socr; Var Trk; Vllybl; KSTS Schl Radio Station; San Diego ST; Comm.

EVANS, SHANNA; Rosary HS; Placentia, CA; (3); Science Clb; Spanish Clb; JETS Awd; NHS; CSF; Psych.

EVANS, SHARON; San Domenico HS; San Rafael, CA; (4); 4/43; VP French Clb; Math Tm; Pres Lbrn Orch; Sec Stu Cncl; Var Swmmng; Elks Awd; High Hon Roll; Pres Sec NHS; Opt Clb Awd; Pres Acad Fit Awd; Princpl Violst San Fran Cymphny Orch; Marin Edctnl Fndtn Stu In Music; Pomona Coll; Music.

EVANS, SHAUG; Avalon HS; Avalon, CA; (2); 1/30; Church Yth Grp; Ed Nwsp; Yrbk; Lit Mag; Var Golf; Var Socr; High Hon Roll; NHS; Ntl Merit Schol; Val; Aeronauticl Engr.

EVANS, SHERI; Carpinteria HS; Carpinteria, CA; (4); French Clb; Pres FHA; VP Science Clb; Ski Clb; Flag Corp; Ed Yrbk; Hon Roll; Vlntr SB Film Fstvl; UCSB; Geo.

EVANS, TAKIYAH M; Fairfield HS; Fairfield, CA; (1); Acpl Chr; Chorus; Church Choir; Tuskeegee Coll; Law.

EVANS, TERRELL; King Drew Medical Magnet HS; Los Angeles, CA; (2); Hosp Aide; Intrml Bsktbl.

EVANS, TRACEE E; Lowell HS; San Francisco, CA; (3); Band; Pres Church Choir; VP JR Nurses; Editor Of Nwspr; Swimmer With San Fran Merionettes & Golen Gate Synchro; Cal Poly; Grahic Design.

EVANS, WENDY A; Coalinga HS; Coalinga, CA; (4); FFA; Office Aide; Teachers Aide; Color Guard; School Play; Rep Nwsp; Wt Lftg; Hon Roll; Taft Coll; Bus.

EVARISTO, MARSHA V; Notre Dame HS; Fremont, CA; (3); 1/90; Church Yth Grp; Cmnty Wkr; Intnl Clb; Teachers Aide; Chorus; Church Choir; School Play; Nwsp; Lit Mag; Hon Roll; California Scholarship Federation; Social Involvement Core; Retreat Programs; Natl Honor Society; Dentistry.

EVARS, LARRY; El Camino HS; S San Francisco, CA; (4); Office Aide; Teachers Aide; Off Sr Cls; Stu Cncl; Golf; Jr NHS; NHS; San Franciso ST; Finance.

EVELAND, KRISTINE; O'farrell HS; San Diego, CA; (4); Ed Nwsp; Video Prdctns Rprtr; Engl.

EVENSON, FREYA; South Fork HS; Redway, CA; (4); 1/60; Art Clb; Math Clb; Math Tm; Quiz Bowl; Scholastic Bowl; Var Capt Crs Cntry; Var L Trk; High Hon Roll; Ntl Merit Ltr; Rotary Awd; CSF Pres Schl Chptr; Globl Issues Forum Clb; Rotry Intl Stu Mnth Engl; Williams Coll MA.

EVENSON, KIMBERLY; Righetti HS; Santa Maria, CA; (2); Church Yth Grp; Church Choir; Var JV Cheerldng; JV Trk; Spelling Bee 5th In Santa Barbara Cnty; Long Beach ST; Psych.

EVEREST, JULIE I; Yreka HS; Horse Creek, CA; (3); #1 In Class; Church Yth Grp; Sec Treas German Clb; Spanish Clb; Church Choir; Sec Jr Cls.

EVEREST, MARY E; Cordova SR HS; Rancho Cordova, CA; (2); Chorus; Ed Yrbk; Sec Frsh Cls; Hon Roll; NHS; Pres Acad Fit Awd; Chamber Ensemble; Outstndng Choir Stu; Outstndng Concert Choir & Chamber Ensemble Stu; Berklee Coll Of Music; Prfrmnce.

EVERETT, BRIGITTE; Arroyo Grande HS; Pismo Beach, CA; (1); 70/589; Church Yth Grp; NFL; Speech Tm; Cheerldng; Hon Roll; Menlo Coll; Comp Sci.

EVERETT, EVELYN; Fresno Christian HS; Fresno, CA; (4); 1/62; Church Yth Grp; Letterman Clb; Teachers Aide; VP Frsh Cls; Pres Soph Cls; VP Jr Cls; Pres Stu Cncl; Cheerldng; High Hon Roll; Val; Fresno Cnty Jr Miss Pgnt 1st Rnnr Up; Twice Nmntd All Amer Chrldr; Rotary Ldrshp Camp Rep; Bus.

EVERETT, KELLY; Santa Paula Union HS; Santa Paula, CA; (2); JV Cheerldng; Var Socr; Var Trk; Hon Roll; CA Schlrshp Fed; 3rd Pl Grls JV Discus Mdl Frontier League & 3rd Pl Grls Var Discus Mdl.

EVERLING, JENNIFER J; Monterey Bay Acad; Vandenberg Afb, CA; (4); 45/112; Chorus; School Musical; Swing Chorus; Pres Stu Cncl; Capt Bsktbl; Capt Vllybl; High Hon Roll; Hon Roll; Oceanaires 2 Yrs; Chrch Soloist 4 Yrs; Pacific Union Coll; Law.

EVERS, BRANDI D; Vacaville HS; Vacaville, CA; (4); Church Yth Grp; Acpl Chr; Chorus; Church Choir; School Musical; Hon Roll; Superior Music Video Teen Tlnt Cmptn; Bionic Stu Mnth; Most Imprvd/Hghst Grade; Lttr Music/Chorus; Intr Dsgn.

EVERS, STACEY L; Bear River HS; Auburn, CA; (2); 1/200; Church Yth Grp; Dance Clb; School Musical; Rep Frsh Cls; JV L Bsktbl; Var L Tennis; JV L Vllybl; Cit Awd; High Hon Roll.

EVERSOLE, MARCIE; Coast Union HS; Cambria, CA; (3); Am Leg Aux Girls St; Church Yth Grp; FBLA; Pres FHA; Pep Clb; Pres Frsh Cls; Treas Stu Cncl; Capt JV Bsktbl; Capt Var Cheerldng; JV Sftbl; Cmmnctns.

EVERSOLE, SUSAN L; Nevada Union HS; Nevada City, CA; (2); 122/535; Chorus.

EVERT, MELISSA M; Selma HS; Selma, CA; (1); VP Church Yth Grp; Q&S; Teachers Aide; Band; Church Choir; Mrchg Band; Pep Band; Rptr Nwsp; High Hon Roll; NHS; Spelling Bee Winner; Nursery Worker; Working With Small Chldrn; Fresno ST U; Eng Lit Teacher.

EVERTS, PAUL; Escondido HS; Escondido, CA; (3); Teachers Aide; Intrml Wrstlng; Army; Sci.

EVES, NICOLE; Antioch HS; Antioch, CA; (4); 98/614; Cmnty Wkr; Drama Clb; Letterman Clb; Pep Clb; Thesps; Chorus; School Musical; Sec Sr Cls; Hon Roll; Mascot; BRIGHAM Young U; Commnctns.

EVIDENTE, PEARL A; Louisville HS; Woodland Hills, CA; (4); 18/95; Art Clb; Drama Clb; Thesps; Chorus; Church Choir; Swing Chorus; Sec Frsh Cls; Pres Stu Cncl; High Hon Roll; Acadmc Awd Amer Hstry; Acadmc Music Awd Royal Co Chorus; Loyola Marymount; Corp Atty.

EVRETT, APRIL L; Exeter Union HS; Exeter, CA; (1); Church Yth Grp; Chorus; Flag Corp; Mrchg Band; Variety Show; Score Keeper; Stat Trk; Work For The City Of Exeter; Howard; Law.

EVULICH, CHRISTIAN A; Kingsburg HS; Kingsburg, CA; (2); Art Clb; Church Yth Grp; Ski Clb; Yrbk; JV Socr; JV Trk; Hon Roll; Vlybl Clb.

EWAYS, JOHN; Cardinal Newman HS; Santa Rosa, CA; (4); 8/74; French Clb; SADD; Band; Drm Mjr(t); JV Socr; Wt Lftg; Cit Awd; High Hon Roll; Hon Roll; NHS; Karate/Kung Fu; 1st Pl Tnlt Cont; 2nd Pl Crss Cntry Meet; Cal Poly ST U; Arch.

EWIN, ARDEN; Francis Parker HS; La Mesa, CA; (3); Church Yth Grp; Hosp Aide; Pres Key Clb; SADD; Chorus; School Musical; School Play; Rptr Nwsp; Var Crs Cntry; JV Trk; Ambssdr Arnold Raphel Awd-Pakistan; Trvld 2 Yrs Pakistan; Outstndng Stu.

EWING, AMBER; Bloomington HS; Bloomington, CA; (2); Church Yth Grp; Dance Clb; Drama Clb; Off Frsh Cls; Off Soph Cls; Cheerldng; Sftbl; Teacher.

EWING, ANNIE; Helix HS; La Mesa, CA; (3); 27/487; Key Clb; Sec Chorus; Swing Chorus; Yrbk; Stu Cncl; Var Capt Cheerldng; High Hon Roll; CA Schlrshp Fdrtn; Psych.

EWING, BRONWYN; Western Christian HS; Rancho Cucamonga, CA; (4); Church Yth Grp; Drama Clb; Hosp Aide; Pep Clb; Church Choir; School Play; High Hon Roll; Hon Roll; Pres Acad Fit Awd; Mime Mnstrs; CA Schlrshp Fed/Watchmn Awd; Crtfd Scuba Diver; Engl.

EWING, CHERYL E; Lincoln HS; Lincoln, CA; (4); 1/141; Am Leg Aux Girls St; Ski Clb; Spanish Clb; SADD; Ed Yrbk; Pres Sr Cls; Sec VP Stu Cncl; Var Capt Bsktbl; JV Vllybl; Val; USC; Bus.

EWING, ERIN L; Aragon HS; San Mateo, CA; (2); Hosp Aide; SADD; Stage Crew; Yrbk; Off Frsh Cls; Rep Stu Cncl; Var JV Swmmng; High Hon Roll; All Leag Swim Team; Badmntn Team; CSF.

EWING, JOYCE BRADLEY; Workman HS; Valinda, CA; (3); Hon Roll; Bus.

EWING, MARY D; Yosemite HS; Oakhurst, CA; (3); Cmnty Wkr; VP Sec Service Clb; SADD; Teachers Aide; Hon Roll; Engrng.

EWING, VANNESSA L; Bullard HS; Fresno, CA; (1); Church Yth Grp; Debate Tm; FCA; German Clb; NFL; Ski Clb; SADD; Gym; High Hon Roll; CSF; Mst Vlble All-Around JV Gymnst; Law.

EXLEY, TIMOTHY J; Dana Hills HS; Dana Point, CA; (2); 4-H; High Hon Roll; Prfct Atten Awd; Karate Purple Belt; 1st Pl Trphy Sparring & Kata Trnmts; U Of CA Irvine; Sci.

EXNER, KATHLENE; Notre Dame HS; Granada Hills, CA; (2); Drama Clb; SADD; Stage Crew; Cheerldng; Swmmng; Hon Roll; YMCA Cnslr.

EXON, HILARY A; Apple Valley SR HS; Apple Valley, CA; (2); Ski Clb; Spanish Clb; Stat Bsbl; Score Keeper; Var Socr; Intrml Sftbl; Intrml Vllybl; High Hon Roll; Hon Roll; Pres Schlr; Engl.

EYERMAN, MARSHALL D; Temecula Valley HS; Temecula, CA; (3); JV Crs Cntry; JV Socr; Hon Roll; Jr Exchnge Clb Mem.

EYRAUD, JENNIFER M; Mary Mount HS; Pacific Palisades, CA; (3); Church Yth Grp; Cmnty Wkr; French Clb; Chorus; Rptr Lit Mag; Var Swmmng; Phys Thrpst.

EYRE, HELEN L F A; Baron HS; Boron, CA; (2); Art Clb; Church Yth Grp; 4-H; Science Clb; Band; JV Bsktbl; Var Tennis; JV Vllybl; Hon Roll; Marine Bio.

EZELL, SUMMER L; Etiwanda HS; Cucamonga, CA; (2); JA; Band; Mrchg Band; Pep Band; Hon Roll; Prfct Atten Awd; Pepperdine; Acctng.

FAAS III, GEORGE EDWARD; Cabrillo HS; Lompoc, CA; (4); 18/220; Church Yth Grp; Key Clb; Ski Clb; Rptr Phtg Yrbk; Rep Frsh Cls; VP Stu Cncl; Var Ftbl; Capt Golf; JV Wrstlng; High Hon Roll; Summit Seeker 1 Of Top 5 Mst Invlvd Stu Sr Clss; Hmcmng King 89-90; Booster Clb Schlshp; U CA San Diego; Molecular Bio.

FABELA, ESPERANZA D; Pomona HS; Pomona, CA; (3); Cit Awd; Hon Roll; Ntl Merit Ltr.

FABER, KARIN; East Bakersfield HS; Bakersfield, CA; (2); French Clb; German Clb; Pres Girl Scts; JA; Band; Mrchg Band; Pep Band; Hon Roll.

FABER, RENEE J; Don Lugo HS; Chino, CA; (3); 18/800; French Clb; Science Clb; Sec Jr Cls; Var Bsktbl; JV Var Tennis; Var Trk; Cit Awd; Ivy Chain; Howard U; Optmtrst.

FABER, SETH; Coast Union HS; Cambria, CA; (3); Pres Spanish Clb; SADD; VP Jr Cls; Hon Roll; Oceanogrphy.

FABIAN, ANGEL; Madera HS; Madera, CA; (3); Dance Clb; FTA; Hosp Aide; Latin Clb; Science Clb; Variety Show; Rptr Lit Mag; VP Jr Cls; Hon Roll; Smmr Inst Ldrshp & Comp Awrnss; Stanford Med Yth Sci Pgm 2 Yrs; Upward Bound; Camp Royal 90; CSF; Med.

FABIAN, SHARON M; Redlands HS; Loma Linda, CA; (2); Spanish Clb; Culture Clb; Nrsng.

FABRO, EMMA C; Paramount HS; Paramount, CA; (3); FTA; Orch; High Hon Roll; Pres Acad Fit Awd; Pres Schlr.

FABRO, PATRICE K; Regina Caeli HS; Gardena, CA; (3); 4/50; GAA; Varsity Clb; Chorus; Sprt Ed Nwsp; Pres Soph Cls; Treas Stu Cncl; Stat Var Bsktbl; Score Keeper; Capt Var Vllybl; Hon Roll; Prncpls Hnr Rll; Stu Cncl Pres & Natl Hnr Scty Treas, & Vrsty Vlybl Cptn 90-91; Loyola Marymount U; Optmtrst.

FACCIANI, JENNIFER; Fresno Christian HS; Fresno, CA; (2); Church Yth Grp; Cmnty Wkr; School Play; Tennis; High Hon Roll; Med.

FACUNDA, CHERRY C; George Washington HS; San Francisco, CA; (2); Girl Scts; Sec Frsh Cls; Vllybl; Hon Roll; Sn Frnsco Smmr Enrchmnt Pgm; Stnfrd U; Med.

FADILLAH, HONEY C; Gladstone HS; Azusa, CA; (4); Church Yth Grp; Chorus; Yrbk; UCLA; Health Sci.

FADILLAH, VIVI; Gladstone HS; Azusa, CA; (3); Church Yth Grp; FBLA; Speech Tm; CA ST U Los Angeles; Acctng.

FADRI, CHARITY; Monterey Bay Acad; Madera, CA; (4); Church Yth Grp; Ski Clb; Band; Chorus; Church Choir; Variety Show; Ed Yrbk; Lit Mag; Sec Treas Sr Cls; Var Bsktbl; 4 Yr Clb Secy; Girls Clb; Pacific Union Coll; Phys Ther.

FAERBER, MONIQUE; Pioneer HS; San Jose, CA; (4); 9/260; Church Yth Grp; Treas Soph Cls; JV Bsktbl; Capt Var Sftbl; Var Vllybl; High Hon Roll; Hon Roll; NHS; Pres Acad Fit Awd; Outstndng Stu In Microcomputers; Ricks Coll.

FAGAN, ALISON L; Arroyo Grande HS; Oceano, CA; (1); 1/590; Sec Church Yth Grp; SADD; JV Capt Socr; High Hon Roll; Tennis; US Davis; Animal Sci.

FAGAN, JENNIFER; Santa Margarita HS; Dana Point, CA; (3); 12/250; Church Yth Grp; Cmnty Wkr; Red Cross Aide; Pres Band; Mrchg Band; Pep Band; Yrbk; Stat Bsktbl; Swmmng; High Hon Roll; CSF; UCLA.

FAGAN, NICOLE M; Terra Nova HS; Pacifica, CA; (2); Public Relations.

FAGGIOLLY, STEVEN P; Woodside HS; Redwood City, CA; (2); Church Yth Grp; Latin Clb; Letterman Clb; Teachers Aide; Varsity Clb; JV Bsbl; Var JV Socr; JV Trk; Intrml Wt Lftg; Kiwanis Awd; Sccr Tm Trp Europe 2nd Tm; Pilot.

FAGINS, DANIELE J; Buena Park HS; La Palma, CA; (4); Church Yth Grp; Cmnty Wkr; Rep GAA; Letterman Clb; Science Clb; Varsity Clb; JV Var Bsktbl; Var Capt Trk; High Hon Roll; Kiwanis Awd; CSF; Black Heritage Clb; CA ST U Fullerton; Tchr.

FAGOT, MARY; Marymount HS; Beverly Hills, CA; (4); 11/85; Bus Profs of Am; Cmnty Wkr; Stu Cncl; Var Capt Socr; JV Swmmng; Intrml Tennis; JV Trk; Ntl Merit SF; Hstry VP; Fn Arts Clb; Pres Clsrm.

FAGUNDES, DAVID; Damien HS; Claremont, CA; (2); 1/269; Debate Tm; NFL; Speech Tm; High Hon Roll; Pres Acad Fit Awd; Stanford; Law.

FAGUNDES, JOHN M; Chaffey HS; Ontario, CA; (2); 2/400; Church Yth Grp; Dance Clb; Band; High Hon Roll; Environmental Engrng.

FAGUNDES, MARK C; Clovis West HS; Fresno, CA; (3); Var Bsbl; Hon Roll; CSF; UCLA; Bus.

FAHEY, JENNIFER; Mount Miguel HS; Spring Valley, CA; (1); Office Aide; SADD; Acpl Chr; Chorus; Sec Stu Cncl; JV Sftbl; Ensemble Lttr; Summer Sftbl Leag Pitcher; Jrnlsm.

FAHIE, VANCE L; Eisenhower HS; Rialto, CA; (2); Church Yth Grp; Church Choir; Phtg Yrbk; Mgr Bsktbl; Mgr(s); Wt Lftg; Var Wrstlng; Hon Roll; Pres Acad Fit Awd; UC Berkeley; Math Prfssr.

FAHIM, JOSEPH W; Los Amigos HS; Fountain Valley, CA; (3); Church Yth Grp; Spanish Clb; Church Choir; Hon Roll; Chrch Deacon, Newsletter Rptr; U Southern CA; Biomedcl Engr.

FAHOUM, OMAR J; Glendale Adventist Acad; La Crescenta, CA; (4); Chorus; Ed Nwsp; Hon Roll; NHS; Ntl Merit Ltr; Martl Arts; UCLA; Aerospace Engrng.

FAHR, MONICA L; Montclair HS; Fontana, CA; (3); Church Yth Grp; Key Clb; Model UN; Teachers Aide; Ed Nwsp; Rep Frsh Cls; Cit Awd; High Hon Roll; Hon Roll; Prfct Atten Awd; CSF; Asst Financial Mgr.

FAHR, MYNOR R; Nogales HS; Chino Hills, CA; (4); Church Yth Grp; Spanish Clb; Varsity Clb; JV Ftbl; Var Swmmng; Var Wt Lftg; Cit Awd; Hon Roll; Summer Camp Counselor; AP Spanish Stu Awd; UC Santa Cruz; Economics.

FAHRINGER, ERICA K; Mt Whitney HS; Visalia, CA; (2); Cmnty Wkr; French Clb; Office Aide; Temple Yth Grp; Hon Roll; County Mock Trials; UCLA; Bus.

FAILOR, SHANI C; Warren HS; Downey, CA; (2); Girl Scts; Library Aide; Sec SADD; School Play; Rptr Nwsp; Socr; Cit Awd; DAR Awd; Hon Roll; Prfct Atten Awd; SADD Sec; Girl Sct Pres; Bible Clb Ldr; Jrnlsm.

FAIR, BOBBY; Johnson HS; Los Angeles, CA; (4); Bus Profs of Am; Computer Clb; FCA; Hosp Aide; Model UN; Science Clb; Ski Clb; Church Choir; Stage Crew; Nwsp; Comp Clb; Electronics.

FAIR, LA TONYA; South Bay Lutheran HS; Inglewood, CA; (3); Church Yth Grp; Rep Jr Cls; VP Stu Cncl; Var Bsbl; Var Bsktbl; Var Vllybl; Hon Roll; Acctnt.

FAIRBANKS, NAYOMI J; Hueneme HS; Port Hueneme, CA; (3); 46/380; Co-Capt Dance Clb; Drama Clb; Sec SADD; Drill Tm; Mrchg Band; School Musical; Variety Show; Hon Roll; Banner/ID Unit Co Capt; Chld Dev.

FAIRBANKS II, STEPHEN R; Moorpark HS; Moorpark, CA; (2); 2/255; Boy Scts; Pres Church Yth Grp; FBLA; Varsity Clb; Band; Jazz Band; Mrchg Band; Nwsp; Crs Cntry; Wrstlng; CSF; Vrsty & Venture Sctng Pgm; Bus.

FAIRBURN, CHRISTOPHER; Mc Lane HS; Fresno, CA; (2); Church Yth Grp; Science Clb; JV Vllybl; JV Wrstlng; Hon Roll; CSF; Vlntr Forst Svc; Wtr Polo.

FAIRCHILD, CATRINA; Montgomery HS; San Diego, CA; (4); Treas FBLA; FTA; Key Clb; SADD; Nwsp; Stu Cncl; Socr; DAR Awd; Pres Acad Fit Awd; CSF; CA Jrnlsm Educ St Write-Offs Excllnc Awd & Super Pl Newswrtng & News Dsgn; U Of CA Irvine; Pltcl Sci.

FAIRFIELD, KATHERINE M; West Covina HS; Valinda, CA; (4); 66/479; Art Clb; Cmnty Wkr; Math Clb; Spanish Clb; SADD; Rep Frsh Cls; Rep Soph Cls; Cngrssnl Yth Ldrshp Cncl Rep; Natl Jr Bowling Champ Cntr Champ 89-90; RN.

FAIRLEY, RAQUEL K; Valley HS; Sacramento, CA; (3); Chorus; Church Choir; Drill Tm; Stu Cncl; Powder Puff Ftbl; Var Socr; Hon Roll; NHS; Prfct Atten Awd; Bus Admn.

FAITH, BRIAN C; Willow Glen Educational Park HS; San Jose, CA; (1); JV Bsbl; JV Bsktbl; JV Crs Cntry; Hon Roll; CSF; UCLA; Arch.

FAITH, CARLA J; Yreka Union HS; Montague, CA; (3); 36/375; Drama Clb; Girl Scts; Treas VICA; Cit Awd; Hon Roll; Engr.

FAITH, STACY M; Atwater HS; Winton, CA; (2); Church Yth Grp; FCA; FHA; Hosp Aide; Trk; Waterpolo; Friday Night Live; Spon Chld Chrstn Chldrns Fund; Humbolt ST; Bio.

FAJARDO, ALEJANDRINA H; Indio HS; Indio, CA; (2); 132/551; Church Yth Grp; French Clb; Office Aide; Teachers Aide; Chorus; Stu Cncl; Cit Awd; High Hon Roll; Hon Roll; Kiwanis Awd; Stu Mnth Phys Ed; Outstndng Atten Awd; Early Outrch Prog; U CA Riverside; Bus Admin.

FAJARDO, ISABEL; Cajon HS; San Bernardino, CA; (2); Chess Clb; Church Yth Grp; Spanish Clb; Cit Awd; NHS; Prfct Atten Awd; CSF; Ntl Hnr Soc; 2nd Pl Chess Tourn; Harvard; Stckbrkr.

FAJARDO, LAURA C; Alisal HS; Salinas, CA; (3); Drama Clb; Thesps; School Play; Stu Cncl; Sftbl; Swmmng; Tennis; Hon Roll; Camp Royal Rotary Awd; Asian Exchng; Amnesty Intl Club Pres; Pltcl Sci.

FAJARDO, ROSANA; Oxnard HS; Oxnard, CA; (3); Hon Roll; MESA Club; Chem Engr.

FAJARDO, THERESA A; Bella Vista HS; Orangevale, CA; (3); 74/420; Sec Spanish Clb; Sec Frsh Cls; Sec Soph Cls; VP Stu Cncl; JV Var Crs Cntry; Var Fld Hcky; Score Keeper; Var Swmmng; Var Trk; CSF; Friday Night Live Clb; Stus Reaching Out; St Marys.

FAKAROS, MARIA A; Skyline HS; Oakland, CA; (2); Church Yth Grp; Thesps; Chorus; Church Choir; School Play; Ed Nwsp; Ed Yrbk; Rep Stu Cncl; Hon Roll; Elem Chldrn Greek Dnc Dir.

FAKES, BRYCE; Brethren JR/Sr HS; Long Beach, CA; (4); Math Tm; School Play; Ftbl; Hon Roll; US Naval Acad; Aerontcl Engr.

FAKOURY, ZEENA; Piedmont HS; Piedmont, CA; (2); CSF; Goldn St Exam Alg Hnrs; Intl Law.

FALASCHI, ANDREA S; Templeton HS; Templeton, CA; (1); FFA; GAA; Quiz Bowl; Cheerldng; Powder Puff Ftbl; Sftbl; Wt Lftg; Hon Roll; Vet.

FALCONI, DUKE D; Pater Noster HS; Los Angeles, CA; (4); 8/54; Letterman Clb; Yrbk; VP Jr Cls; VP Stu Cncl; Var L Crs Cntry; Var L Trk; Elks Awd; Hon Roll; NHS; Prfct Atten Awd; CSF 86-89; Outstndng Achvt In Marriage 89-90; Crss Cntry/Trk Cert; Outstndng Achvt Span I 87-88; Loyola Marymount U; Comp Engrng.

FALCONI, JESUS R; Pater Noster HS; Los Angeles, CA; (1); 1/61; JV Crs Cntry; JV Trk; Hon Roll; NEDT Awd; Prfct Atten Awd; Alg I Hnrs Excptnl Imprvmnt; Crss Cntry & Trk Cert; Bruce Comanda Cls 69 Meml Trphy; Acadmc Achvt Awds; U Of Southern CA; Sci.

FALEAFINE, MARIE; Andrew Hill HS; San Jose, CA; (1); Chorus; Off Frsh Cls; Vllybl; Stanford U.

FALIN, DENISE K; Vintage HS; Vallejo, CA; (2); Cmnty Wkr; Variety Show; High Hon Roll; Hon Roll; Impact Grp; Real Estate.

FALK, ADAM JONATHAN; Fremont HS; Sunnyvale, CA; (4); 18/300; Cmnty Wkr; Var Debate Tm; DECA; Var NFL; Speech Tm; Sec Temple Yth Grp; VP Thesps; Jazz Band; JV Socr; Elks Awd; Brandels U; Biochem.

FALK, JULIE R; Turlock HS; Turlock, CA; (3); 63/630; AFS; Church Yth Grp; VP FBLA; Hosp Aide; Key Clb; Yrbk; Hon Roll; Voice Dem Awd; Water Polo; CA Schlrshp Fed; Girls Leag.

FALK, THAO L; College Park HS; Pleasant Hill, CA; (2); Spanish Clb; JV Sftbl; Co-Capt Vllybl; MVP 89-90 Vllybl Tm; Friday Night Live Clb; DUC; Psych.

FALKENROTH, JOHN C; California HS; San Ramon, CA; (4); 19/408; Band; Mrchg Band; Var L Crs Cntry; Var L Trk; High Hon Roll; Hon Roll; 4-Yr Natl Merit Spec Schlsp Mc Kesson Fnd; Cross Cntry Sr Awd; Chancellors Schlr; U CA Davis; Med.

FALKENSTIEN, SARA N; Banning HS; Banning, CA; (2); Church Yth Grp; Cmnty Wkr; French Clb; Intnl Clb; Model UN; Teachers Aide; Band; Mrchg Band; JV Bsktbl; Stu Supreme Court Justice; House Of Reps; Constitutional Convention Delg; UCSB.

FALKINHAM, IAN; Lincoln HS; Stockton, CA; (4); 54/513; Chess Clb; Computer Clb; Science Clb; Hon Roll; Tulane U; Physics.

FALKNER, TAWNYA; Hogan SR HS; Benicia, CA; (4); 11/389; Am Leg Aux Girls St; Pres Drama Clb; VP English Clb; Sec Key Clb; Pres VP Ski Clb; Spanish Clb; SADD; School Musical; Rep Soph Cls; Police Actvts Sccr Team; Schl Imprvmnt Brd; Diablo Valley Coll; Arch Engr.

FALLAI, ANNEMARIE J; Bella Vista HS; Orangevale, CA; (3); 64/363; Drama Clb; French Clb; Acpl Chr; School Musical; School Play; Stage Crew; Hon Roll; Ntl Merit Ltr; Drama & Music Depts Awd; Frgn Svc.

FALLETTA, BECKY; South Hills HS; Covina, CA; (2); Church Yth Grp; Drama Clb; Girl Scts; Science Clb; Service Clb; Spanish Clb; Capt Flag Corp; JV Swmmng; Miss Rifle Tm; Writer.

FALLIN, TONI D; John Marshall Fundamental HS; Duarte, CA; (3); Church Yth Grp; Hosp Aide; Red Cross Aide; Chorus; Church Choir; Var Bsktbl; Capt Var Sftbl; Var Capt Vllybl; Cit Awd; Pres Acad Fit Awd; Delta Sigma Theta Sorority Appreciation Awd; Med.

FALLON, ARONWRY J; Napa HS; Napa, CA; (3); Whos Who Among Am H S Stu 88-89; JR Coll; Pediatrician.

FALLON, BETH A; Napa HS; Napa, CA; (3); 83/300; Church Yth Grp; Cmnty Wkr; Hosp Aide; Teachers Aide; Band; Chorus; Yrbk; Off Frsh Cls; Hon Roll; Piano For Natl Guild 10 Yrs; Law.

FALLON, BRUCE TIMOTHY; Poway HS; Poway, CA; (4); 156/714; Boy Scts; Church Yth Grp; Teachers Aide; Varsity Clb; JV Socr; Var Trk; Hon Roll; Pres Acad Fit Awd; San Diego Tribune Schlr Athlte 2 Yrs; CA St Trkc & Fld Qlfr; U Of OR; Arch.

FALLON, CHRISTOPHER M; St John Bosco HS; Los Alamitos, CA; (2); 24/250; Rptr Nwsp; JV Socr; JV Trk; High Hon Roll; Hon Roll; NHS; Outdrsman Clb.

FALLON, JESSE A; University City HS; San Diego, CA; (2); 24/418; Model UN; High Hon Roll; Hon Roll; Pres Acad Fit Awd; Golden St Exam Algebra Hnrs, Geom High Honrs; UCSD.

FALLON, M KATHLEEN; Santa Margarita Catholic HS; Laguna Niguel, CA; (3); 15/225; Hosp Aide; Ed Nwsp; Lit Mag; Rep Stu Cncl; Var Capt Cheerldng; Var Capt Pom Pon; Stat Vllybl; High Hon Roll; Off NHS; Natl Charity Leag Pres; Jrnlsm.

FALLON, MATTHEW T; Ygnacio Valley HS; Pleasant Hill, CA; (2); Drama Clb; SADD; Thesps; Dctd Butokukai Mrtl Arts Systm; Accmplshd Mgcn & Cntng Good Stndng Of Scty Amercn Mgcns; Diablo Valley Coll; Pro Illsnst.

FALLON, MEAVE; Mercy HS; Burlingame, CA; (4); 18/104; Church Yth Grp; GAA; Service Clb; Spanish Clb; Var Capt Bsktbl; Var Sftbl; Var Capt Vllybl; High Hon Roll; NHS; Spanish NHS; CSF; Santa Clara U; Bio.

FALLS, CHANDRA C; Las Plumas HS; Oroville, CA; (2); Church Yth Grp; Cmnty Wkr; Drama Clb; Cheerldng; Var Crs Cntry; Var JV Score Keeper; Var Socr; JV Trk; High Hon Roll; Hon Roll; Chico ST; Phys Thrpst.

FALLS, DEBBIE; Oakmont HS; Granite Bay, CA; (3); Pres Church Yth Grp; Cmnty Wkr; Drama Clb; Service Clb; Ski Clb; SADD; Teachers Aide; Church Choir; Variety Show; Sec Soph Cls; BYU; Elem Ed.

FALONI, DUANE D; Healdsburg HS; Geyserville, CA; (4); 17/221; Hon Roll; NHS; Shasta Coll; Horticulture.

FAMAYIWA, RICK S; St Bernard HS; Inglewood, CA; (3); Var Bsktbl; Law/Pro Bsktbl.

FAMBRO, STACY M; John Muir HS; Altadena, CA; (2); Church Yth Grp; Pep Clb; Service Clb; Band; Jazz Band; Mrchg Band; Pep Band; High Hon Roll; Wind Ensemble; Interact Club; CSF; LA Art Inst; Fash Des.

FAN, HENRY; Culver City HS; Culver City, CA; (3); Service Clb; Varsity Clb; Band; Mrchg Band; Rep Frsh Cls; Rep Soph Cls; Rep Jr Cls; JV Bsktbl; JV Vllybl; Hon Roll; Chirons; CSF; Acad Dcthln; UCLA; Eng.

FAN, RYAN ANDREW; Don Bosco Technical Inst; Alhambra, CA; (1); 4/244; Church Yth Grp; Ski Clb; Bsbl; Bsktbl; Hon Roll; Bowlng; Tnns; Dance; Piano; Altar Boy; Comp; Stanford U; Sports Med.

FANCHER, CAROL; North Monterey County HS; Monterrey, CA; (2); Church Yth Grp; Dance Clb; Teachers Aide; Variety Show; High Hon Roll; Sec Jr NHS; Peer Cnslr; Emplyd Rocky Mt Chclt Fctry.

FANG, BLA; Duncan Polytechnical HS; Fresno, CA; (1); Outdoors Adventure Clb; Duncans Athl Clb; Chorus Clb; Pediatrics.

FANG, CONNIE; Capistrano Valley HS; Mission Viejo, CA; (3); Treas Church Yth Grp; German Clb; Math Tm; Pep Clb; Quiz Bowl; Orch; Var Trk; High Hon Roll; Kiwanis Awd; Ntl Merit Ltr; Acad Decathlon; U Of PA; Bus.

FANG, GROVER; La Jolla Country Day Schl; La Jolla, CA; (2); Church Yth Grp; Cmnty Wkr; Key Clb; Model UN; Office Aide; Spanish Clb; JV Bsktbl; Var Tennis; High Hon Roll.

FANG, HELEN; Fountain Valley HS; Fountain Valley, CA; (4); 52/630; French Clb; Hosp Aide; Pep Clb; Drill Tm; Yrbk; Sec Jr Cls; Hon Roll; Distngshd Schlr & Sealbearer; Drill Tm Co-Capt 88-90; UC Santa Barbara; Social Sci.

FANG, JUNE; Irvine HS; Irvine, CA; (3); 1/512; Quiz Bowl; Science Clb; Ed Nwsp; Capt JV Tennis; English Clb; Cnty Acad Decathlon Tm; Cnty Chmpn For Newswriting; Sunrise Exchange Clb Yth Of Mnth April; Engl Lit.

FANG, MEE; Merced HS; Merced, CA; (2); 4-H; FBLA; Spanish Clb; Hon Roll; Decathlon; Japanese Club; Yth Culture Club; Photo Club; UC Davis; Med.

FANG, MICHAEL M; Sacred Heart Cathedral Prep; San Francisco, CA; (2); Church Yth Grp; Science Clb; Church Choir; Wrstlng; Hon Roll; Engr.

FANG, PAO T; Edison HS; Fresno, CA; (1); 2/30; Computer Clb; Science Clb; Cit Awd; High Hon Roll; Hon Roll; Edison; Elecrical/Comp Engr.

FANG, WALLACE; Hoover HS; Glendale, CA; (2); Japanese Clb; GSE Acad Exclnc Awd; Med.

FANIZZI, SARAH D; Aptos HS; Aptos, CA; (1); Church Yth Grp; Ed Yrbk; Var Crs Cntry; JV Socr; High Hon Roll; CSF; Young Life; Sports Med.

FANNING, JENNIFER; Leffingwell Christian HS; La Mirada, CA; (2); Pres Church Yth Grp; Cmnty Wkr; Var Capt Cheerldng; Cit Awd; High Hon Roll; Prfct Atten Awd.

FANSE, ASHISH; Alameda HS; Alameda, CA; (2); 24/250; Boy Scts; Debate Tm; Spanish Clb; Speech Tm; Var L Socr; Var L Tennis; High Hon Roll; Pres Acad Fit Awd; Wm K Holt Schlrshp; UC Brkly; Elec Engr.

FANT, WILLIAM E; Workman HS; Valinda, CA; (2); USC; Arch.

FANTASIA, ANNA MARIA; Colonial Christian Acad; Sacramento, CA; (4); 1/3; Nwsp; Tennis; High Hon Roll; Hon Roll; Pres Acad Fit Awd; Val; Gldn Poet Awd; Bible Eng Physcs Awds; Pres Cngrtltns Bush/Reagan; Hnr O'donnell Clan In Ireland; U Of CA Davis; Aerospace Engr.

FANTAZIA, JOYCE; Orestimba HS; Newman, CA; (4); 2/65; Dance Clb; Office Aide; Pep Clb; SADD; Teachers Aide; Ed Yrbk; Treas Sr Cls; Treas Stu Cncl; Cheerldng; Pom Pon; Jr Ldrshp; CA Schlrshp Fdrtn; Jr Stsman Of Amer; CA St U Stanislaus; Acctng.

FANTON, LISA A; John F Kennedy HS; Buena Park, CA; (3); Treas FBLA; Hon Roll; CA ST Fullerton; Acctnt.

FANTOZZI, ALICIA; Piedmont HS; Piedmont, CA; (4); AFS; VP JA; Spanish Clb; SADD; Band; School Musical; JV Crs Cntry; Var Capt Trk; Hon Roll; NHS; Tech Class Radio Oper; Advancd Open Watr Scuba Divr; Am Top Wnnr Meter Weatherly; U CA Berkeley; Poltcl Sci.

FANUCCHI, STEPHEN; Shafter HS; Shafter, CA; (3); 45/400; Aud/Vis; Boy Scts; Church Yth Grp; Cmnty Wkr; FCA; 4-H; Key Clb; Letterman Clb; Pep Clb; Ski Clb; Bus.

FAORO, KATE; Petaluma HS; Petaluma, CA; (2); Church Yth Grp; French Clb; SADD; Teachers Aide; Var Trk; High Hon Roll; Hon Roll; UCLA; Pediatric Srgn.

FAOUR, ZEINA; Magnolia HS; Anaheim, CA; (3); Computer Clb; Dance Clb; Drama Clb; English Clb; French Clb; Pep Clb; Ski Clb; Teachers Aide; Varsity Clb; Variety Show; Htl Mgr.

FARADAY, MICHELLE F; Palm Springs HS; Palm Springs, CA; (3); 14/500; Church Yth Grp; Cmnty Wkr; Spanish Clb; Acpl Chr; Chorus; School Musical; High Hon Roll; Hon Roll; Prfct Atten Awd; Silver Sands Choral Music Awd; Meth Church Camp Cnslr; Sthrn CA Coll; Chrstn Cnslr.

FARAJ, MONA A; Notre Dame HS; San Jose, CA; (3); 27/91; JV Cheerldng; Var Vllybl; High Hon Roll; Hon Roll; Jr NHS; NHS.

FARAVARDEH, ARMAN; Mira Mesa HS; San Diego, CA; (2); French Clb; Intnl Clb; Key Clb; Math Tm; Science Clb; Yrbk; Hist Stu Cncl; Cit Awd; NHS; Prfct Atten Awd; CSF; Med.

FARBER, DMITRY A; Clairemont HS; San Diego, CA; (2); Sec Model UN; Yrbk; Ed Lit Mag; Hon Roll; Acad Leag Capt Russian Club; Amnesty Intl Seminar Pgm Secy/Treas; Swedish Club Pres; Eugene Lang Coll; Drama.

FARES, DANIEL; Edison/Computech HS; Fresno, CA; (1); Boy Scts; Science Clb; Hon Roll; BYU; Civil Engrng.

FARGHALLI, NAHLA; Edison HS; Huntington Bch, CA; (2); Church Yth Grp; Key Clb; High Hon Roll; Keywanette Awd 89-90; Pediatrician.

FARGO, JENNIFER; Righetti HS; Santa Maria, CA; (2); 3/452; Socr; French Clb; Girl Scts; Chorus; School Musical; School Play; Natl Exchange Clb Milestones Of Freedon Awd; Campus Chrstn Fllwshp Clb; Biola U; Chem.

FARHADIAN, SHERRY; Granada Hills HS; Granada Hills, CA; (4); Ski Clb; SADD; Teachers Aide; Temple Yth Grp; Var JV Cheerldng; High Hon Roll; NHS; Pres Acad Fit Awd; CSUN; Bus Law.

FARHOOMAND, LADAN; San Dieguito HS; San Marcos, CA; (2); 18/296; Var Capt Vllybl; Cit Awd; High Hon Roll; Hon Roll; Prfct Atten Awd; Pres Acad Fit Awd; CA Jr Schlrshp Fed & CA Schlrshp Fed; Gldn St Exam Acad Excllnc Awd & Allnc Francaise Cert Excllnc; Med.

FARIA, CARY T; Bullard HS; Fresno, CA; (2); Drama Clb; SADD; School Play; UC Davis; Pre-Med.

FARIA, TAMARA DIANNE; Los Banos HS; Los Banos, CA; (3); Drama Clb; FFA; Science Clb; Spanish Clb; Band; Mrchg Band; Pep Band; School Play; Stage Crew; Sec Bsktbl; Wrestling; High Honor Roll; Honor Roll; Natl Honor Society; AZ ST U; Environmental Stds.

FARIAS, ALFREDO T; Sweetwater HS; National City, CA; (3); 26/429; Hon Roll; Var Socr; SDSU; Electrncs Engr.

FARIAS, ALICIA T; Sweetwater HS; National City, CA; (3); 18/429; Spanish Clb; Yrbk; Stat Mgr(s); High Hon Roll; Hon Roll; UCSD; Bus.

FARIAS, GABRIELA; Colton HS; Colton, CA; (3); FFA; Model UN; Teachers Aide; Hon Roll; Soc Wrk.

FARIAS, MARISSA; Lindsay HS; Lindsay, CA; (3); Sec Drama Clb; VP French Clb; VP FBLA; FHA; Sec Key Clb; Spanish Clb; Teachers Aide; School Play; Score Keeper; Hon Roll; Fri Night Live; Coll Of Sequoias.

FARIAS, ROBERT M; Modesto HS; Modesto, CA; (3); DECA; Teachers Aide; Ftbl; Ntl Merit Ltr; Art Show; Distrbtv Ed Clbs Amer; Mgr Of Bus.

FARID, DIANA; University HS; Irvine, CA; (2); Spanish Clb; Cit Awd; Hon Roll; Pres Acad Fit Awd; Lauriete Awd; Golden St Alg; Piano; Med.

FARKAS, JOHN J; Sunny Hills HS; Fullerton, CA; (4); 19/410; Church Yth Grp; Latin Clb; Varsity Clb; Rptr Nwsp; Yrbk; Capt L Swmmng; High Hon Roll; NHS; Ntl Merit SF; UCSD; Medcn.

FARKAS, JULIE A; Pacific Shores Private HS; El Toro, CA; (3); German Clb; Phtg Rptr Yrbk; Rep Soph Cls; Sec Jr Cls; Sec Stu Cncl; Bsbl; High Hon Roll; Hon Roll; Dreamers & Doers Awd Frm Walt Disney; Vrs Awds Algebra, Geom, US Hstry, Engl; Fshn Buyer.

FARLEY, JOANNA; Red Bluff HS; Red Bluff, CA; (1); Comp Prgmr.

FARLEY, TIFFANY D; Sonora Union HS; Sonora, CA; (3); School Play; Stage Crew; Csmtlgy Sonora HS ROP; Vlntrd Lcl Rest Home; Cngrssnl Schlr In Natl Yng Ldrs Cnfrnc; Columbia JC; Law.

FARMEN, JOANN; Liberty Union HS; Byron, CA; (2); Church Yth Grp; Drama Clb; FCA; Speech Tm; Acpl Chr; Jazz Band; School Musical; School Play; Rep Stu Cncl; Hon Roll; Friday Nite Live; Stanford; Pilot.

FARMER, BRANDON M; Edison Computech HS; Fresno, CA; (2); Debate Tm; FBLA; NFL; Ski Clb; JV Bsbl; JV Ftbl; JV Socr; Hon Roll.

FARMER, JEREMIAH; San Luis Obispo HS; San Luis Obispo, CA; (3); 1/302; SADD; Rptr Yrbk; Golden Tiger Awd; 1st Pl Fiction Creative Wrtng Cont; Golden Tiger Fnlst Math.

FARMER, MICHAEL F; Clovis West HS; Clovis, CA; (2); Cmnty Wkr; Ski Clb; Spanish Clb; Teachers Aide; JV Var Ftbl; Wt Lftg; UCLA; Bus.

FARMER, MIKE; Taft Union HS; Taft, CA; (3); 7/190; VP Key Clb; Letterman Clb; Yrbk; Var Capt Crs Cntry; Var Trk; High Hon Roll; Prfct Atten Awd; CSF; Psych.

FARMER, TERESA LYNN; El Toro HS; El Toro, CA; (2); Church Yth Grp; 4-H; Red Cross Aide; Socr; Vllybl; Gov Hon Prg Awd; Hon Roll; Ntl Merit Ltr; Pres Acad Fit Awd; Child Psych.

FARMER, VIRGINIA L; San Luis Obispo HS; San Luis Obispo, CA; (1); Church Yth Grp; German Clb; Intnl Clb; Var Swmmng; Hon Roll; Swm Clb; MVP Swmmg; U Of TX; Arch.

FARN, VICTOR; Norte Vista HS; Riverside, CA; (2); Chess Clb; Hosp Aide; Quiz Bowl; ROTC; Science Clb; JV Tennis; High Hon Roll; Hon Roll; Prfct Atten Awd; Army Drl Tm; Qd Ldr; Cadet Mnth; Eng Tutor; Cal Tech; Aero Engr.

FARNER, JAMES C; Montclair HS; Montclair, CA; (1); JV Tennis; Hon Roll; CA Poly Pomona; Archit.

FARNER, KARNA M; Serrano HS; Phelan, CA; (1); 4-H; Bsktbl; High Hon Roll; Pres Acad Fit Awd; VP 4-H; CO ST U; Bus.

FARNSWORTH, CORINA A; Linden HS; Lodi, CA; (2); 41/153; Church Yth Grp; Drama Clb; Chorus; Color Guard; School Musical; School Play; Stage Crew; Hon Roll; Stu Prevntn Rep.

FARNUM, SARA A; St Joseph HS; Long Beach, CA; (2); Church Yth Grp; Girl Scts; School Play; JV Socr; Hon Roll; Miss Amer Teen ST Fnlst; Spcl Rcgntn Work Engl II Hnrs; Invlvmnt Spcl Olympcs; Jrnlsm.

FAROOQUI, ARMEEN; Santa Monica HS; Santa Monica, CA; (1); Peer Cnslr; USC; CPA.

FAROOQUI, SABA; Leuzinger HS; Gardena, CA; (2); Computer Clb; Dance Clb; Drama Clb; Model UN; Teachers Aide; Chorus; Drill Tm; School Musical; Off Soph Cls; Bsktbl; Air Hostess.

FARR, SHARON M; Savanna HS; Anaheim, CA; (3); Cmnty Wkr; Pep Clb; Red Cross Aide; Variety Show; Pres Soph Cls; Rep Stu Cncl; Powder Puff Ftbl; Sftbl; Vllybl; Anaheim Union HS Dist Bd Of Trustees Schl Rep.

FARR, TODD A; Mira Loma I B HS; Sacramento, CA; (3); 7/350; Cmnty Wkr; Debate Tm; JA; Pep Clb; Off Jr Cls; Tennis; High Hon Roll; Rep Frsh Cls; Rep Soph Cls; Stu Cncl; CSF; Natl Hnr Soc; Stanford; Marine Life.

FARRAR, DANIELLE; Nordhoff HS; Ojai, CA; (2) Church Yth Grp; Stu Cncl; Var Bsktbl; Var Cheerldng; Stat Ftbl; Var Socr; Var Tennis; Var Trk; Hon Roll; Acad Ltrs; CSF.

FARRAR, HOLLY J; Montclair HS; Chino, CA; (4); Church Yth Grp; Cmnty Wkr; FBLA; Teachers Aide; Chorus; Church Choir; Hon Roll; Jnr Engl Awd; Bus Awds; Mt San Antonio Coll; Bus Mgmt.

FARRAR, MICHELLE; Mountain Empire HS; Descanso, CA; (4); Pres Treas German Clb; Pep Clb; Off Sr Cls; Cheerldng; Powder Puff Ftbl; NHS; Friday Night Live Pres; Marine Bio.

FARRAR, SHERRY; Calipatria HS; Calipatria, CA; (3); Pep Clb; SADD; Capt JV Cheerldng; Score Keeper; Socr; ROP Comptrzd Acctng Hnrs Grad; Engl Awd; Cmmnctns.

FARRAR, TERESA ELAINE; Calipatria HS; Calipatria, CA; (2); FHA; Office Aide; JV Cheerldng; JV Sftbl; Fri Night Live; MVP Hnrs Sftbl; Law.

FARRELL, AMY K; Rim Of The World HS; Lake Arrowhead, CA; (3); 15/350; Debate Tm; French Clb; GAA; Letterman Clb; Ed Nwsp; Pres Jr Cls; JV Var Tennis; Hon Roll; NHS; San Bernardino Sherffs Stu Advsry Cncl; Homecmng Jr Prncss 89; U Of The Pacific.

FARRELL, ANGELE M; Our Lady Of Peace Acad; San Diego, CA; (3); Church Yth Grp; Cmnty Wkr; Letterman Clb; School Musical; Variety Show; Cheerldng; Business Management.

FARRELL, COREY; Durham HS; Durham, CA; (4); 1/67; Ski Clb; SADD; Varsity Clb; Band; School Play; Rep Frsh Cls; Treas Sr Cls; Var Bsbl; Var JV Bsktbl; Mgr(s); UC Santa Barbara; Law.

FARRELL, DAVID M; Ramona HS; Ramona, CA; (2); Church Yth Grp; Cit Awd; Carpentry.

FARRELL, JOSEPH B; Mission Viejo HS; Mission Viejo, CA; (2); 26/442; Rep Church Yth Grp; Treas German Clb; Chrmn Model UN; Var Intrml Ftbl; Intrml Socr; Intrml Am Leg Aux Girls St; Var Intrml Wt Lftg; Hon Roll; Ply Cello Sddlbck Cmnty Coll-Orch; Wrk-Alpha Beta 90; Georgetown; Law.

FARRELL, JUDITH; Bonita Vista HS; Chula Vista, CA; (4); Church Yth Grp; School Musical; Swing Chorus; DAR Awd; Dancer; CSF Lifetime Membr; Bus.

FARRELL, MEAGHAN E; North Montery County HS; Salinas, CA; (2); Art Clb; Church Yth Grp; Cmnty Wkr; Dance Clb; Drama Clb; Ski Clb; Speech Tm; SADD; School Musical; School Play; Byu; Linguistics.

FARRELL, PATTY K; Vintage HS; Napa, CA; (2); Church Yth Grp; Key Clb; Acpl Chr; Chorus; Stage Crew; Var Cheerldng; Trk; NHS; Pres Acad Fit Awd; Consumer/Homaking Awd; Record Keeping Awd; Coaches Awd In Trk; Moore Park Coll; Marine Bio.

FARRELL, SEAN M; Colfax HS; Colfax, CA; (3); 25/165; Wrestler.

FARRENS, SYLVIA A; Chula Vista HS; Imperial Beach, CA; (2); Church Yth Grp; Drama Clb; Stage Crew; CA Schlrshp Fed.

FARRINGTON, JUSTIN F; Woodland HS; Woodland, CA; (3); 3/300; Am Leg Boys St; Boy Scts; FBLA; SADD; Bsbl; Golf; Wrstlng; High Hon Roll; Hon Roll; Jr NHS; UC Davis; Engrng.

FARRIOR, ENDENNE L; La Sierra Acad; Montclair, CA; (2); Church Yth Grp; French Clb; Teachers Aide; Band; Chorus; Church Choir; Yrbk; VP Soph Cls; Hon Roll; Cal Poly Pomona Smmr Intnsv Orntn Pgm; Oakwood Coll; Bus.

FARRIS, BARBARA A; Prospect HS; San Jose, CA; (1); Church Yth Grp; Prfct Atten Awd; Typing Awds; ACU.

FARRIS, JEFF S; Torrey Pines HS; Rancho Santa Fe, CA; (3); Band; Jazz Band; Intrml JV Socr; High Hon Roll; Hon Roll; Jr NHS; Pres Acad Fit Awd; U Of WA.

FARRIS, SANDY C; Calvary Chapel HS; Westminster, CA; (2); Church Yth Grp; Teachers Aide; Var Capt Sftbl; Var Vllybl; Hon Roll; Creatv Wrtng Awd; 1st Team All Leag Sftbl; Bst Offnsv Plyr Vrsty Sftbl Team; CA ST Fullerton; Engl.

FARTHING, JESSICA; Whittier HS; Hacienda Hghts, CA; (3); Drama Clb; Thesps; Drill Tm; School Play; Stage Crew; Variety Show; JV Var Cheerldng; Cit Awd; High Hon Roll; Hon Roll; Cardinal 50 Top 10 Clss Hnr Bnqt; SAG Screen Actors Guild; Activ Mem NSA; UCLA; Sci.

FARVID, ALI R; Mission Viejo HS; Mission Viejo, CA; (2); 45/439; Boy Scts; Bsktbl; Trk; High Hon Roll; CSF; UCI; Med.

FASANI, RICK A; Del Oro HS; Roseville, CA; (2); 1/270; Church Yth Grp; Cmnty Wkr; 4-H; Ski Clb; JV Capt Bsbl; JV Capt Bsktbl; JV Capt Ftbl; 4-H Awd; High Hon Roll; NHS; Geom Golden St Exam High Hnrs; CSF; Peat Marwick HS Press Awds Fnlst 90; Sci.

FASCIA, MICHELLE D; Redlands HS; Highland, CA; (2); Drama Clb; Hon Roll; Pres Acad Fit Awd; 2nd Pl Frshmn Life Sci; Law.

FASSETT, DEANNA L; Bella Vista HS; Fair Oaks, CA; (4); 20/341; Spanish Clb; Varsity Clb; Stage Crew; Var Crs Cntry; Var Trk; NHS; Spanish NHS; UC San Diego; Media Arts.

FASSO, DOMINIC C; St Joseph Notre Dame HS; Alameda, CA; (3); Church Yth Grp; Cmnty Wkr; Ed Lit Mag; Var Crs Cntry; High Hon Roll; NHS; Soc Justice Cmmtte; CSF; Outdoors Club.

FASTRING, ROGER B; Grossmont HS; El Cajon, CA; (1); Church Yth Grp; Debate Tm; NFL; Speech Tm; Band; Mrchg Band; Orch; Pep Band; High Hon Roll; Opt Clb Awd; UCLA; Atty.

FATA, MARC; Venice Foreign Language Magnet; Venice, CA; (2); Cmnty Wkr; Bsktbl; Opt Clb Awd; Prfct Atten Awd; Church Yth Grp; Computer Clb; French Clb; JA; Letterman Clb; SADD; Cngrssnl Yth Ldrshp Cncl; USC; Med.

FATHKE, CARRIE A; Lemoore Union HS; Lemoore, CA; (2); Band; Mrchg Band; Pep Band; School Play; Variety Show; Swmmng; Hon Roll; NHS; Rotary Awd.

FATLAND, MERRILEE A; Chaparal HS; El Cajon, CA; (2); Church Yth Grp; English Clb; Girl Scts; Library Aide; Office Aide; Teachers Aide; Nwsp; Cit Awd; DAR Awd; HS Writng Cont 1st Pl Poetry; Secrtrl.

FATOURECHI, FARID; Canoga Park HS; Canoga Park, CA; (2); Band; Prfct Atten Awd; CA ST U; Medicine.

FAUBION, MICHELLE; Huntington Beach HS; Huntington Beach, CA; (3); Cmnty Wkr; Red Cross Aide; Science Clb; Rptr Nwsp; Rep Stu Cncl; Stat Ftbl; Score Keeper; Var Socr; JV Trk; Stat Wrstlng; CSF; Tower Awd; Distngshd Oiler Awd; FL Inst Tech; Aeronauticl Engr.

FAUCETTE, LINDSEY B; Arrayo Grande HS; Shell Beach, CA; (2); 1/568; Pres Church Yth Grp; Sec Intnl Clb; Church Choir; Variety Show; High Hon Roll; Hon Roll; Harvard Bus Schl; Acctnt.

FAULCONER, CHRISTIE; Simi Valley HS; Simi Valley, CA; (2); 53/748; Church Yth Grp; Key Clb; SADD; Drill Tm; Hon Roll; Pres Acad Fit Awd; Golden St Exam In Geom High Hnr; Arch.

FAULKNER, JILL; Woodrow Wilson HS; Long Beach, CA; (4); Church Yth Grp; Dance Clb; Service Clb; Pep Band; Variety Show; Gym; Pom Pon; Socr; High Hon Roll; Hon Roll; CA Schlrshp Fed Seal Bearer; Point Loma Nazarene Coll; Nrsng.

FAULKNER, MARK W; Oak Ridge HS; Cameron Park, CA; (2); Art Clb; Boy Scts; Church Yth Grp; Hon Roll; BYU; Teacher.

FAURE, KARINE I; Foothill HS; Santa Ana, CA; (4); 30/322; AFS; Treas French Clb; GAA; SADD; JV Capt Crs Cntry; Tennis; JV Trk; High Hon Roll; CSF Sealbearer/Life Mem; Keywatette-VP/Pres; Span SR Awd; UC-SAN Diego; Intl Bus.

FAURE, MONIQUE; Shasta HS; Redding, CA; (4); 3/450; Model UN; Acpl Chr; School Musical; Var Cheerldng; Stat Ftbl; High Hon Roll; Pres Acad Fit Awd; Rotary Awd; CSF; Mdrgl Choir; UC-BERKELEY; Math.

FAURE BRAC, GABRIEL; Petaluma HS; Petaluma, CA; (4); 22/270; AFS; Debate Tm; Drama Clb; Treas French Clb; Intnl Clb; Quiz Bowl; Speech Tm; SADD; School Play; Stage Crew; Var Bdmntn; Most Insprtnl; Acad Dcthln Tm; Gldn ST Spch Assoc; 1st Pl Drmtc Interp 89; Stanford; Envrnmntl Cnsltnt.

FAURIA, AMY; Fairfield HS; Fairfield, CA; (2); Letterman Clb; Rep Frsh Cls; Rep Soph Cls; JV Capt Bsktbl; Var Trk; JV Capt Vllybl; High Hon Roll.

FAUROAT, NIKKI; Napa HS; Napa, CA; (1); Church Yth Grp; FCA; School Musical; School Play; Stage Crew; Cheerldng; Gym; Score Keeper; Hon Roll; Jr NHS; Schl Counslr.

FAUSETT, KIMBERLY; El Toro HS; El Toro, CA; (2); 40/800; Pres Church Yth Grp; Drama Clb; Pep Clb; Treas Service Clb; School Play; JV Var Cheerldng; High Hon Roll; Keywanettes Treas; Girls Leag; CSF; Brighamm Yng U; Advrts.

FAUSONE, TOM M; Red Bluff Union HS; Red Bluff, CA; (2); Church Yth Grp; FFA; Hon Roll; Rodeo Actvts; Animal Sci.

FAUSS, JOLENE M; Summerville HS; Twain Harte, CA; (1); Art Clb; Church Yth Grp; Cmnty Wkr; Dance Clb; Drama Clb; French Clb; Teachers Aide; Chorus; School Play; Variety Show; Csmtlgy.

FAUST, ERIKA; Orchard Park Schl; Oakdale, CA; (4); Church Yth Grp; Cmnty Wkr; Dance Clb; Office Aide; Orch; School Musical; Stage Crew; Variety Show; Hon Roll; CA All St Hnr Choir 88-90; Natl HS Hnrs Orch To Finland 90; CA Band Dir All St Band 9/; San Jose ST U; Choreogrphy.

FAUST, LIZABETH A; Chaffey HS; Ontario, CA; (1); Church Yth Grp; Drama Clb; Church Choir; School Play; Score Keeper; Stat Trk; High Hon Roll; Comm Theatre; Green Peace; U Of WA; Psych.

FAUSTO, ROSARIO; Oakdale HS; Oakdale, CA; (2); Computer Clb; Dance Clb; Spanish Clb; UCLA; Law Enfrcmnt.

FAUZY, STEVE R; Encina HS; Sacramento, CA; (3); Varsity Clb; Var Crs Cntry; JV Ftbl; Var Wrstlng; Hon Roll; Cal Poly; Acctng.

FAVELA, GABRIELA A; Schurr HS; Montebello, CA; (3); Church Yth Grp; GAA; Pres Frsh Cls; Cmmty Svc Wrk; Mother Butler Assn Hosp; UC Berkeley; Psych.

FAVELA, RAYMOND C; Imperial HS; Imperial, CA; (4); Teachers Aide; Hon Roll; Prfct Atten Awd; Sal; CSF Treas; UC Riverside; Bus Admin.

FAVELA, RUTH; Woodrow Wilson HS; Los Angeles, CA; (3); Stu Of Month Awd.

FAVILA, MARISA; Kerman HS; Kerman, CA; (3); 7/270; Church Yth Grp; Math Tm; VP Spanish Clb; Ed Nwsp; Capt Var Tennis; Hon Roll; JETS Awd; Chicano-Latino Yth Ldrshp; Acad Decathlon 2nd Math, 3rd Essay; Hi-Deb; Lib Arts.

FAVINI, MELISSA M; San Joaquin Memorial HS; Madera, CA; (2); Church Yth Grp; VP 4-H; GAA; Science Clb; Treas Spanish Clb; JV Swmmng; 4-H Awd; Cngrssnl Schlr Intied To Natl Young Ldrs Conf; Madera Cnty 4-H All Star; 2nd Alt St 4-H Arts & Crfts.

FAWCETT, RHEA; Indio HS; Indio, CA; (2); 85/551; Church Yth Grp; Drama Clb; Model UN; Pep Clb; School Play; Variety Show; JV Cheerldng; Hon Roll; Pres Acad Fit Awd; Pre-Med.

FAWKES, CHRISTOPHER J; Paraclete HS; Agua Dulce, CA; (2); Hon Roll; Tstd & Qlfd GATE Prgrm; CA HS Rodeo Assn Chmpn Tm Tpr Dist 8; Bus.

FAWKES, RYAN B; Lower Lake HS; Clearlake, CA; (4); 2/105; Spanish Clb; Crs Cntry; Trk; Wrstlng; Elks Awd; High Hon Roll; Sal; Boys St; Acadmd Dcthln 1st Pl Cnty Comptn Math; Math Sci Achvt Awd; U Of CA Davis; Elec Engrng.

FAWSON, CHRISTY A; Fairfield HS; Fairfield, CA; (2); Art Clb; Church Yth Grp; Crs Cntry; Trk; Cit Awd; Hon Roll; Pres Acad Fit Awd; 2nd Pl Category Figurative Prisma Color Armijo Art Show; 1st Pl Figurative Prisma Color :Ist Art Shw; Brigham Young U; Law.

FAWVER, JESSICA KAREN; Marian Catholic HS; Chula Vista, CA; (4); 4/100; VP Spanish Clb; Pres Frsh Cls; Pres Jr Cls; Var Capt Bsktbl; Var Capt Sftbl; Var Capt Vllybl; Elks Awd; Kiwanis Awd; NHS; Pres Acad Fit Awd; HOBY; Coca Cola Golden Girl Awd; CSF Pres & Sealbearer; U CA San Diego; US Hstry.

FAY, AARON; Eldorado/Emerson HS; Mission Viejo, CA; (1); Church Yth Grp; Orch; School Play; Biogentics.

FAY, CHRISTA; Oakmont HS; Roseville, CA; (1); Dance Clb; 4-H; Drill Tm; Dnfth Awd; Hon Roll; Pres Acad Fit Awd; Drill Team Awd; U CA; Pilot.

FAY, KELLY; San Pasqual HS; Escondido, CA; (4); 1/359; Am Leg Aux Girls St; Church Yth Grp; Intnl Clb; Pres Spanish Clb; Teachers Aide; Rep Soph Cls; Treas Stu Cncl; Capt Var Crs Cntry; Powder Puff Ftbl; L Var Trk; CO Schl Mines Math/Sci Awd; Agnes Smith Coll Outstndng Achvt Awd; San Diego Trib All Ath/Acad Team 89; Pedtrcn.

FAYETTE, CHARLES A; Turlock HS; Turlock, CA; (2); Trk; Aeronautical Engr.

FAZAL, ARIF; Fred C Beyer HS; Modesto, CA; (2); Key Clb; Math Tm; SADD; JV Bsktbl; Cit Awd; High Hon Roll; JETS Awd.

FAZIO, CLAY C; Mater Dei HS; Fountain Valley, CA; (3); Drama Clb; School Play; Stage Crew; Rep Frsh Cls; Rep Soph Cls; Stu Cncl; Hon Roll; UCI; Elec Engr.

FEAVER, ERIKA; Turlock HS; Turlock, CA; (2); Key Clb; JV Cheerldng; Backstage Dance Co; Pro Dancer.

FEBRERO, ELIZA F; Channel Islands HS; Oxnard, CA; (3); Girl Scts; Church Choir; Hon Roll; Cheerldr In Philippines; UCSB; Comp Pgmr.

FECTEAU, LAINA; Saugus HS; Saugus, CA; (2); 30/600; Church Yth Grp; Drama Clb; School Musical; School Play; Nwsp; High Hon Roll; Hon Roll; NHS; Opt Clb Awd; Writers Soc Club; UCLA; Eng.

FEDDERMAN, BRIAN W; Santa Ynez Valley Union HS; Solvang, CA; (3); 20/165; Cmnty Wkr; Library Aide; Pres Sr Cls; Var L Crs Cntry; Var L Trk; Yng Schlrs Smmr Session; US Navl Acad; Hstry.

FEDERICO, MICHAEL T; Royal HS; Simi Valley, CA; (2); Church Yth Grp; Cmnty Wkr; Office Aide; Service Clb; Yrbk; Mgr Bsktbl; Mgr Crs Cntry; Mgr(s); Mgr Tennis; Mgr Trk; Law Enfrcmnt Explr; Law Enfrcmnt.

FEDRICK, CHAD A; Loyola HS; Manhattan Beach, CA; (2); Letterman Clb; JV Var Bsbl; Capt Ftbl; High Hon Roll; Emmett J Malloyschlrshp Ath & Schlrshp.

FEE, KRISTINA D; Vacaville HS; Vacaville, CA; (3); Am Leg Aux Girls St; Church Yth Grp; French Clb; Key Clb; Pep Clb; Quiz Bowl; Drill Tm; Treas Frsh Cls; Treas Soph Cls; Pres Jr Cls.

FEELEY, JENNIFER V; Branham HS; San Jose, CA; (2); Art Clb; Church Yth Grp; Cmnty Wkr; SADD; Church Choir; Orch; JV Diving; Var Swmmng; Var Trk; Hon Roll; Cert Mrt Outstndng Achvt Span 2; Cert Excllnc Freestyle Swim; Service Ministries; UCLA; Phy.

FEELEY, MELISSA M; Paraclete HS; Palmdale, CA; (2); Church Yth Grp; Cmnty Wkr; Drama Clb; Key Clb; School Play; Var Cheerldng; High Hon Roll; CSF; Span Awd I, II; Relign Awd I, II; Theatre Arts.

FEELY, KIMBERLY C; Big Bear HS; Big Bear City, CA; (4); 1/107; Church Yth Grp; Sec French Clb; Band; Stat Sftbl; Stat Vllybl; Pres Acad Fit Awd; Val; Bnk Of Amer-Lbrl Arts Achvt Awd; Acad Decthln; Intract Clb; U Of CA Snta Brbra; Plntry Sci.

FEEMAN, KEVIN L; Narbonne HS; Lomita, CA; (3); Teachers Aide; Hon Roll; Hi Hnrs Golden St Exam Alg 88, Geom 89; Teacher.

FEENEY, SHELLY R; Irvine HS; Irvine, CA; (3); 12/550; French Clb; Teachers Aide; High Hon Roll; Hon Roll; Heritage Awds-Alg II, Cmpstn, Soc Sci, Chem & Frnch 90; Gldn St Exam Alg I 89; Close-Up Fdntns; CA U; Bio.

FEGURGUR, JENNIFER L; Bonita Vista HS; Bonita, CA; (3); Pep Clb; Ed Nwsp; Cit Awd; Hon Roll; Prfct Atten Awd; Santa Cruz CA U; Oceanography.

FEHER, CHRISTINE J; Foothill HS; Santa Ana, CA; (3); Church Yth Grp; Hosp Aide; Chorus; School Musical; JV Swmmng; Hon Roll; Ntl Merit SF; Safe Rides Clb; Jr Statesmen Of Amer Clb; Newlife Clb.

FEHLIMAN, LISA M; Shasta HS; Redding, CA; (3); Drama Clb; GAA; Varsity Clb; Stage Crew; Rep Soph Cls; Rep Jr Cls; JV Var Bsktbl; JV Var Vllybl; Hon Roll; Hosptl Admin.

FEHLMAN, SHAWN; Eisenhower HS; Fayetteville, NC; (3); Boy Scts; Cmnty Wkr; Debate Tm; Letterman Clb; Spanish Clb; Varsity Clb; Rep Jr Cls; Ftbl; Swmmng; Super Quiz; Engl.

FEHOKO, NAU P; Washington Preparatory HS; Los Angeles, CA; (2); Church Yth Grp; GAA; Chorus; Church Choir; Sftbl; Vllybl; High Hon Roll; Prfct Atten Awd; Pre-Law.

FEIGEN, DENISE; Riverside Poly HS; Riverside, CA; (4); Church Yth Grp; Key Clb; Pep Clb; Pres SADD; Teachers Aide; Church Choir; Variety Show; Var Pom Pon; Rvrside Exchnge Clb, 3rd Tlnt Show Wnnr; Dance; Crtfd Peer Cnslr; Psych.

FEILES, LEE M; Wm S Hart HS; Valencia, CA; (4); 11/250; Chess Clb; Teachers Aide; Band; Hon Roll; Pres Acad Fit Awd; Tae Kwon Do 3 Yrs 1st Degree Black Belt; CA Schlrshp Fed Life Membr Sealbearer; Academic Letter; U Of AZ; Civil Engineering.

FEIMAN, CLIFF J; El Camino Real HS; Woodland Hills, CA; (2); Cmnty Wkr; Variety Show; Off Frsh Cls; VP Soph Cls; Stu Cncl; L Bsktbl; Tennis; Hon Roll; Prfct Atten Awd; UCLA; Music.

FEINSTEIN, JEFFREY A; Apple Valley HS; Apple Valley, CA; (3); 24/734; French Clb; Teachers Aide; High Hon Roll; UC Riverside; Pediatrician.

FEIPEL, JENNIFER A; Boron HS; Boron, CA; (4); 7/37; Teachers Aide; Varsity Clb; Rptr Nwsp; Sec Stu Cncl; Var Cheerldng; Hon Roll; CSF; Mock Trial Team; CSU Fresno; Elem Ed.

FEJARANG, PATTI; Elk Grove HS; Sacramento, CA; (4); 4/530; Am Leg Aux Girls St; Church Yth Grp; Dance Clb; Pres Speech Tm; VP Jr Cls; Pres Sr Cls; Cheerldng; Capt Pom Pon; CSF; U CA Davis; Psych.

FELDMAN, DANNY P; Kennedy HS; Granada Hills, CA; (3); Letterman Clb; Office Aide; Treas Frsh Cls; Rep Soph Cls; Rep Jr Cls; Treas Sr Cls; Rep Stu Cncl; Ftbl; Trk; Hon Roll; George K Porter Awd; UCLA; Chld Psych.

FELDMAN, JULIE; North Salinas HS; Salinas, CA; (4); Pres Church Yth Grp; Spanish Clb; Chorus; Church Choir; Swmmng; High Hon Roll; Hon Roll; Pres Acad Fit Awd; Bus Stu Of Mnth; Corp Law.

FELGER, STACEY M; Rio Mesa HS; Camarillo, CA; (3); 26/549; Cmnty Wkr; Dance Clb; Teachers Aide; Church Choir; Ed Nwsp; Hon Roll; NHS; Peer Cnslng; CA Schlrshp Fed Mem; Loyola Marymount; Engl.

FELICIANO, DAVID E; San Pedro HS; San Pedro, CA; (3); Office Aide; Service Clb; Teachers Aide; Rep Frsh Cls; Rep Soph Cls; Rep Jr Cls; Pres Sr Cls; Stu Cncl; Bsbl; Chess Clb; Future Ldrs Of San Pedro; ARCO Jesse Owens Games Natl Chmnshps 87; Habor Occupational Ctr; Plbg.

FELICIANO, DENNIS S; Saint Ignatius College Prep; Daly City, CA; (3); 29/244; Chess Clb; Science Clb; Hon Roll; Bwlng; Bus.

FELICIANO, FRANCIS; Balboa HS; Daly City, CA; (3); Hon Roll; Capt Vrsty Fncng; Pres Filipino Cltrl Clb.

FELIX, CHRISTINA Y; Whittier Christian HS; Hacienda Hghts, CA; (4); 83/168; Office Aide; Chorus; Church Choir; Cmpsng Music F/Piano; Drwng,Sktchng & Pntng; Wrtng Poetry.

FELIX, CRISTINA; Sacred Heart Of Mary HS; Los Angeles, CA; (4); 15/81; Church Yth Grp; Cmnty Wkr; GAA; Teachers Aide; Nwsp; Ed Yrbk; Hon Roll; NHS; Prfct Atten Awd.

FELIX, ERIKA; North Monterey Country HS; Castroville, CA; (2); Church Yth Grp; Latin Clb; Office Aide; High Hon Roll; Prfct Atten Awd; PGA 3.5; Perfect Grades Awds; UCLA; Cmptr.

FELIX, ERIKA D; Adolfo Camarillo HS; Camarillo, CA; (2); 37/508; Drama Clb; French Clb; Speech Tm; School Play; High Hon Roll; NHS; Prfct Atten Awd; CSF; U Of CA Los Angeles; Thtr Arts.

FELIX, JENNIFER C; St Josephs HS; Yorba Linda, CA; (2); SADD; Variety Show; Hon Roll; AFNA; UC Irvine; Obstrcs.

FELIX II, JOE H; Colton HS; Colton, CA; (2); Model UN; Quiz Bowl; Var Ftbl; Var Wt Lftg; JV Var Wrstlng; Gov Hon Prg Awd; Hon Roll; Jr NHS; Lion Awd; Natl Yng Ldrs Conf; Future Ldrs Amer; Ctzn Bee; UC Santa Barbara; Marine Sci.

FELIX, MIGUEL; Central Union HS; El Centro, CA; (3); Ftbl; Trk; Frmn; USC; Mdcl.

FELIX, NATHAN F; Bishop Amat HS; Whittier, CA; (3); Spanish Clb; JV Bsbl; JV Ftbl; Hon Roll; UCLA; Acctg.

FELIX, RACHEL A; Norco HS; Mira Loma, CA; (1); FHA; UCLA.

FELIX, VICKY; Senior HS; Riverbank, CA; (2); Art Clb; Church Yth Grp; Cmnty Wkr; Dance Clb; Latin Clb; Spanish Clb; Church Choir; Yrbk; Off Soph Cls; Powder Puff Ftbl.

FELIX-GRAFF, SAMANTHA B; Fontana HS; Bloomington, CA; (2); FFA; Quiz Bowl; Scholastic Bowl; Chorus; Hon Roll; Animal Rights Organztn; UC Davis; Zoology.

FELIZ, STACY R; Granada Hills HS; Granada Hills, CA; (2); Church Yth Grp; Speech Tm; SADD; Teachers Aide; JV Cheerldng; Hon Roll; Dance; Thtr/Flm Adtns.

FELKEL, COLLEEN L; Robert Bellarmine Jefferson HS; Tujunga, CA; (3); Pres Soph Cls; JV Sftbl; Hon Roll; Jr NHS; NHS; Worked With Glendale Citys Parks & Recreation Pgm After Schl I Was In Charge Of Sprvsng Chldrns Cls; Education.

FELKEY, SANDY D; San Pedro HS; San Pedro, CA; (2); Rep Church Yth Grp; Cmnty Wkr; Service Clb; Speech Tm; Pres Thesps; School Musical; School Play; JV L Swmmng; High Hon Roll; Hon Roll.

FELLER, BRAD D; Santa Clara HS; Santa Clara, CA; (3); Var L Ftbl; Var L Socr; Acctg.

FELLER, DARCY L; Monte Vista HS; Spring Valley, CA; (2); Pep Clb; Drill Tm; Cit Awd; Hon Roll; Performing Arts.

FELLOWES, KAREN; Burlingame HS; Redwood City, CA; (3); Debate Tm; Pres French Clb; Ski Clb; Off Sr Cls; Stu Cncl; Var Tennis; High Hon Roll; Ldrshp Club; CSF; UASB Rep; UC Berkeley; Hotel Mgmt.

FELONEY, ANN M; Chaminade College Prep; Northridge, CA; (3); Chorus; Lit Mag; Pres Sec Stu Cncl; Var Capt Swmmng; High Hon Roll; NHS; LIFE Team; Staying Alive Pres; CSF.

FELS, JENNY LYNN; Gilroy HS; Gilroy, CA; (1); Church Yth Grp; Dance Clb; Speech Tm; School Musical; JV Fld Hcky; JV Socr; Hon Roll; Missionary Wrk.

FELSCH, BARBARA M; Napa HS; Napa, CA; (4); Church Yth Grp; Drama Clb; Key Clb; Thesps; Acpl Chr; Chorus; School Musical; School Play; Hon Roll; Achvt Awd Schlrshp; Napa JC; Acctng.

FELT, VICKI L; Foothill HS; Sacramento, CA; (4); 3/285; Church Yth Grp; Treas Drama Clb; Spanish Clb; Teachers Aide; Church Choir; Orch; School Musical; Variety Show; High Hon Roll; Hon Roll; Mock Trial Def Atty; St Fnlst Chicago Bd Of Trade Commodity Challenge; Bank Of America Awd Soc Sci; Brigham Young U; Elem Ed.

FELT, WENDY; Newport Christian HS; Costa Mesa, CA; (2); Church Yth Grp; Pep Clb; Ski Clb; Teachers Aide; School Play; Rptr Nwsp; Yrbk; JV Cheerldng; Var Sftbl; High Hon Roll; Fashion.

FELT, WILLIAM G; Foothill HS; Sacramento, CA; (1); Boy Scts; Church Yth Grp; Band; Mrchg Band; Pep Band; Swmmng; Hon Roll; Cmptr.

FELTER, JASON C; Vallejo SR HS; Vallejo, CA; (2); Spanish Clb; Off Soph Cls; Bsktbl; Socr; Hon Roll; Hnr Soc; Stanford U; Arch.

FELTON, VERNON DAVID; De La Salle HS; Clayton, CA; (4); 3/211; Stu Cncl; High Hon Roll; NHS; Ntl Merit Schol; Pres Acad Fit Awd; UC Santa Cruz; Envrnmntl Stds.

FEMAL, STACY L; Downey HS; Downey, CA; (3); Cmnty Wkr; Office Aide; Spanish Clb; SADD; Teachers Aide; Band; Mrchg Band; Pep Band; Police Explrs; Law Enfrcmnt.

FEMATH, JAVIER; Sierra Vista HS; Baldwin Park, CA; (1); Bsbl; Bsktbl; Ftbl.

FEMENIA, MARC; Analy HS; Sebastopol, CA; (4); Var Socr; Var Tennis; Engr.

FENDEL, JOE B; Piedmont HS; Piedmont, CA; (3); Chess Clb; Capt Math Tm; Pres Model UN; Teachers Aide; Temple Yth Grp; JV Trk; Vllybl; Ntl Merit Ltr; Rensselaer Polytech Math/Sci Awd; Edgar M Bronfman Yth Fllwshp Israel; U Of PA Bk Awd; Math Professor.

FENDER, AMY L; Apple Valley SR HS; Apple Valley, CA; (1); Pep Clb; SADD; Chorus; Bsktbl; Hon Roll; Prfct Atten Awd; U Of Newport Beach; Tech Engr.

FENDER, CHERYL R; Maranatha HS; Pasadena, CA; (3); Church Yth Grp; JV Crs Cntry; Tall Flags; CSF; AHSME; Bio Sci.

FENDER, CRAIG H; Casa Roble HS; Orangevale, CA; (2); Drama Clb; German Clb; Intnl Clb; SADD; Varsity Clb; School Musical; School Play; Variety Show; Lit Mag; Var Swmmng; Night Courses Amercn River Coll; Goldn Poet 90, Eddie Lou Cole Pblshr; Reed Coll; Psych.

FENDER, MARK; Brethren HS; Lakewood, CA; (2); Aud/Vis; Church Yth Grp; Math Tm; Stage Crew; High Hon Roll; Stu Store Wrkr; Magic Clb; Sun Schl Tchr.

FENG, CHING T; San Gabriel HS; Alhambra, CA; (2); Hon Roll; Acad Decathlon Clb; Commnctns.

FENG, JIM; Mills HS; Millbrae, CA; (2); Chess Clb; Church Yth Grp; Math Clb; Math Tm; Band; Orch; Mgr(s); Tennis; California Scholarship Federation.

FENIQUITO, FRITZIE; South San Francisco HS; Daly City, CA; (4); FBLA; Hosp Aide; Office Aide; Spanish Clb; SADD; Hon Roll; Prfct Atten Awd; Bnk America Awd; Gradtn Hnrs; San Mateo Coll; Comp Sci.

FENLEY, KEVIN D; Escalon HS; Escalon, CA; (2); German Clb; Key Clb; JV L Tennis; JV L Trk; High Hon Roll; Prfct Atten Awd; CA Schlrshp Fed; Ecology Clb; GATE; Knowledge Bowl; Schlr/Athl Awd; UC Santa Cruz; Humanities.

FENN, BRIAN C; Rim HS; Crestline, CA; (2); 19/360; Boy Scts; Church Yth Grp; Drama Clb; Spanish Clb; Rptr Yrbk; JV Bsktbl; JV Ftbl; L Var Golf; Hon Roll; BYU.

FENNELL, JONATHAN A; Village Christian HS; Simi Valley, CA; (3); 14/120; Church Yth Grp; Spanish Clb; VP Soph Cls; Var L Bsbl; JV Bsktbl; Var L Crs Cntry; Var L Socr; Engrng.

FENNELL, NATHANIEL; Redwood HS; Tiburon, CA; (4); Latin Clb; Redwood Sailing Team Capt; CSF; Sacramento City Coll; Mech Engr.

FENSKE, ERIN; Milpitas HS; Newark, CA; (4); Church Yth Grp; Chorus; Church Choir; Rptr Nwsp; Capt Cheerldng; Hon Roll; Pres Acad Fit Awd; CSF; Ohlone JC.

FENSTER, RAM J; Bridgemont HS; Daly City, CA; (2); Phtg Yrbk; Var Bsktbl; Var Capt Crs Cntry; Var Vllybl; High Hon Roll; Hon Roll; Wrtng.

FENTON, NICOLE L; Casa Grande HS; Petaluma, CA; (2); School Play; Mdl Excel Sci; Marine Life Study; Mrn Bio.

FENTON, TZEITEL; Mc Kinleyville HS; Fieldbrook, CA; (3); #10 In Class; 4-H; Acpl Chr; Crs Cntry; High Hon Roll; Jr NHS; NHS; AFS Frgn Exchnge Stu Brazil.

FENYOE, TIMEA M; Sonora Union HS; Columbia, CA; (4); 3/265; Drama Clb; German Clb; Pres Science Clb; Ski Clb; Rptr Nwsp; Bausch & Lomb Sci Awd; High Hon Roll; Pres Acad Fit Awd; Acad Decathlon; Jr Statesman Fndtn; UC Berkeley; Civil Engrng.

FERAN, SEAN W; Apple Valley HS; Apple Valley, CA; (1); JV Ftbl; Hon Roll; Harvard Law Schl; Law.

FERBER, JUSTIN M; Calabasas HS; Hidden Hills, CA; (2); Boy Scts; Ski Clb; Capt JV Socr; JV Sccr MVP, Vrsty Waterpolo 89-90; CSF; Stanford.

FERGASON, STEPHEN H; Poway HS; Poway, CA; (2); 34/830; JV Crs Cntry; JV Tennis; High Hon Roll; Aeron Engrng.

FERGUSON, AMY; Fremont Christian HS; Newark, CA; (1); Church Yth Grp; JV Var Cheerldng; Singing.

FERGUSON, ANN; Monterey HS; Monterey, CA; (2); Hon Roll; Oral Surgeon.

FERGUSON, BILL E; Tustin HS; Tustin, CA; (2); 134/461; Drama Clb; Thesps; School Play; Stage Crew; Intrml Bsbl; Hon Roll; Schlr-Athlt Awd-Bsbl; Drma Dept Awd.

FERGUSON, BRIAN J; Moreau HS; Hayward, CA; (3); Letterman Clb; Var Bsbl; Var Capt Ftbl; High Hon Roll; Union City Pop Warner Ftbl Team Asstnt Coach; Bus.

FERGUSON, CRYSTAL S; North HS; Riverside, CA; (2); Church Yth Grp; Church Choir; Hon Roll; Brigham Young U; Psych.

FERGUSON, DEL M; Daniel Murphy HS; Los Angeles, CA; (3); Cmnty Wkr; Teachers Aide; Rptr Nwsp; Rptr Yrbk; Off Frsh Cls; Stu Cncl; Hon Roll; Cert Of Recog Coca-Cola & KNBC-TV Fnlst Essay Cont; Achvt Awd Outstndg Achvt Soc Sci; CPA.

FERGUSON, ELISA J; Santa Monica HS; Santa Monica, CA; (2); Chorus; Hon Roll; Santa Monica Gems Awd; Wrld Poetry Golden Poet Awd; Stu Of The Month History Clb; U Of CA Los Angeles; Eng.

FERGUSON, JULIE; Santa Teresa HS; San Jose, CA; (4); Pep Clb; Chorus; Rep Stu Cncl; Heald Mrt Schlrshp; Bus Stu Of Wk; Heald Bus Coll; Accntng.

FERGUSON, JULIE; West HS; Bakersfield, CA; (2); Debate Tm; NFL; Speech Tm; JV Cheerldng; Hon Roll; St Vault Chmpn 88; GATE Engl & Bio Classes; CA ST Coll; Arts.

FERGUSON, RICK; Paradise HS; Paradise, CA; (1); Boy Scts; Church Yth Grp; Ski Clb; JV Tennis; Hon Roll; JV Snw Ski Tm; Egl Sct; LDS Smnry; BYU; Med.

FERGUSON, ROD; Bret Harte HS; Murphys, CA; (1); Cmnty Wkr; Bsktbl; Crs Cntry; Friday Night Live; Mst Imrpvd Crss Cntry; Mech Engr.

FERGUSON, RONA L; Thousand Oaks HS; Thousand Oaks, CA; (3); 33/540; Church Yth Grp; Drama Clb; French Clb; School Play; Rep Stu Cncl; Stat Bsktbl; Var JV Diving; High Hon Roll; Hon Roll; Ntl Merit Ltr; City Yth Cmmssn; Hgh Hnrs Golden St Exam-Alg/Geom.

FERGUSON, STEPHANIE A; Riverbank HS; Riverbank, CA; (2); Treas Church Yth Grp; VP Drama Clb; SADD; VP Thesps; Rep Stu Cncl; Var Cheerldng; Powder Puff Ftbl; Hon Roll.

FERGUSON, THERESA; A A Stagg HS; Stockton, CA; (2); JV Cheerldng; JV Sftbl; Hon Roll; Prfct Atten Awd; Stu Ldrshp; Acctnt.

FERIA, CHRISTINA; Hilltop HS; Chula Vista, CA; (3); 155/495; Office Aide; SADD; Church Choir; Drill Tm; Yrbk; JV Cheerldng; Girls Leag Club Secy; Chrch Lector; USD; Acctng.

FERIA, SERGIO; La Canada HS; La Canada Flintri, CA; (4); Sec Chess Clb; Math Clb; Mu Alpha Theta; Science Clb; Chem Engrng.

FERMIL, DEBBIE D; Chula Vista HS; Chula Vista, CA; (3); 115/535; Church Yth Grp; Dance Clb; Pep Clb; School Musical; Sec Frsh Cls; Cheerldng; Mgr(s); Engl Hnrs Clss & Advncd Plcmnt Hist; 1 Yr Amity Lg Social Clb; U Of San Diego; Bus Mgmt.

FERNAMBURG, DEBBIE; Atascadero HS; Santa Margarita, CA; (1); Girl Scts; Drill Tm; Cit Awd; High Hon Roll; Prfct Atten Awd; Home Ec Sclstc Achvt; Hnrs Englsh; Mdlng; Bus.

FERNANDES, DYLAN A; Valley View HS; Moreno Valley, CA; (1); Church Yth Grp; Speech Tm; Bsbl; Vllybl; Hon Roll; Lion Awd; Outstndng Woodwrkng Achvts; Moreno Valley Disposal Essay Hnrb Mntn; Bus.

FERNANDES, PAMELA D; James Lick HS; San Jose, CA; (3); CSF; Badminton; Bus.

FERNANDES, RENATA; Lincoln HS; Stockton, CA; (4); #34 In Class; FBLA; JV Vllybl; JV Var High Hon Roll; U Sao Paulo Brazil; Commnctns.

FERNANDEZ, ALMA A; River City HS; W Sacramento, CA; (2); Hon Roll; Prfct Atten Awd.

FERNANDEZ, ANDREA; Sacred Heart Of Jesus HS; Los Angeles, CA; (2); Church Yth Grp; GAA; Girl Scts; Teachers Aide; Yrbk; Var Crs Cntry; Var Sftbl; Hon Roll; 4th Cabrini Litry Guild Wrtng Cont; Archdiocese Schlrshp; Engrng.

FERNANDEZ, ANDREW; Bishop Montgomery HS; Torrance, CA; (4); 87/390; Varsity Clb; Ftbl; Trk; Wt Lftg; Ntl Merit SF; Deans List; UCLA; Teacher.

FERNANDEZ, ANGELICA R; College Park HS; Danville, CA; (4); Drama Clb; Pep Clb; School Musical; School Play; Pres Jr Cls; Stu Cncl; Var Capt Cheerldng; Var Capt Pom Pon; Hon Roll; Lion Awd; UCA All-Star Chrldr 89; CA ST U Sacramento.

FERNANDEZ, CAREN M; North Monterey Co HS; Watsonville, CA; (2); SADD; JV Capt Bsktbl; JV Var Trk; Hon Roll; Work With Kids; Read Adventure Booksweightlifting; Math.

FERNANDEZ, CECILIA; Santa Maria HS; Santa Maria, CA; (2).

FERNANDEZ, CESAR T; San Diego HS; San Diego, CA; (3); Cmnty Wkr; Var Tennis; U CA San Diego; Arch.

FERNANDEZ, DANIEL; Gahr HS; Riverside, CA; (4); 10/436; French Clb; VP Frsh Cls; Off Soph Cls; VP Pres Stu Cncl; JV Var Trk; Cit Awd; Elks Awd; High Hon Roll; Pres Acad Fit Awd; Mst Outstndng Stu Of Yr; Top Ten; San Diego ST U; Graphic Dsgn.

FERNANDEZ, DAVE P; Fremont HS; Sunnyvale, CA; (2); 45/450; Drama Clb; School Musical; School Play; JV Bsbl; JV Capt Ftbl; JV Socr; JV Trk; Wt Lftg; High Hon Roll; Hon Roll; UCSB; Broadcasting.

FERNANDEZ, DUNIA; James A Garfield HS; Los Angeles, CA; (2); Church Yth Grp; Capt Math Tm; Sec Treas Frsh Cls; Rep Stu Cncl; JV Bsktbl; Mgr(s); High Hon Roll; NHS; Pres Acad Fit Awd; Pres Schlr; Jr Grnd Mrshll LA Chrstms Parade 88; Pres Outstndng Acadmc Achvt Schlrshps 2 Gold Seal & 1 Slvr; Politics.

FERNANDEZ, ELADIO J; Norte Vista HS; Riverside, CA; (2); JV Bsbl; Wt Lftg; Hon Roll; U CA-RIVERSIDE.

FERNANDEZ, ELENA; Valley HS; Sacramento, CA; (4); Am Leg Aux Girls St; Church Yth Grp; Cmnty Wkr; Hosp Aide; Office Aide; Spanish Clb; Speech Tm; SADD; Teachers Aide; Ed Yrbk; Chicano Latin Yth Ldrshp Conf; Maya Clb Pres; CSF; Sacramento ST U; Bus.

FERNANDEZ, ELPIDIO; Watsonville HS; Watsonville, CA; (2); Wt Lftg; Hon Roll.

FERNANDEZ, ESTHER; Sacred Heart Of Jesus HS; Los Angeles, CA; (3); School Play; Hon Roll; NHS; Prfct Atten Awd; Apprctn Cert-Scott Newman Drug Abuse Prevntn Cmmrcl Cont; Awd Cert-Earth Sci Effort.

FERNANDEZ, FATIMA; Independence HS; San Jose, CA; (4); Cmnty Wkr; Teachers Aide; PE Hnrs 87-88; Spanish Hnrs 88-89; Youth Fellowship; Filipino Clb; De Anza Clg; Nrsng.

FERNANDEZ, FAVIOLA; Lynwood HS; Lynwood, CA; (2); Acctng.

FERNANDEZ, FERNANDO; Chula Vista HS; National City, CA; (3); Var Socr; JV Var Vllybl; MECHA Mem 90-91; Hstrn MECHA; UCLA; Elect Engrng.

FERNANDEZ, FRANCISCO; Orosi HS; Cutler, CA; (3); FFA; Math Clb; Teachers Aide; Chorus; Hon Roll; Chem/U S Hstry Awd; Sequoia Acad Sci.

FERNANDEZ, GABRIEL; Mount Diablo HS; Pacheco, CA; (3); 4/200; JA; Band; Jazz Band; Mrchg Band; Bsktbl; Wt Lftg; High Hon Roll; Hon Roll; Computer Engrng.

FERNANDEZ, GINA; Central Union HS; El Centro, CA; (1); FHA; Pep Clb; Chorus; Law.

FERNANDEZ, GRINJE G; Archbishop Riordan HS; San Francisco, CA; (3); 7/144; Church Yth Grp; Intnl Clb; Band; Pep Band; High Hon Roll; Hon Roll; CA Schlrshp Fed 88-90; Med.

FERNANDEZ, JESSE; Banning HS; Wilmington, CA; (4); 53/630; Computer Clb; French Clb; Intnl Clb; Prfct Atten Awd; HS Involvement Pgm; UCLA; Aerospc Engrng.

FERNANDEZ, JOHN C; Bolsa Grande HS; Garden Grove, CA; (3); Intrml Bsbl; JV Ftbl; Var JV Wrstlng; Hon Roll; San Diego ST U; Civil Engr.

FERNANDEZ, JORGE R; Norte Vista HS; Riverside, CA; (3); Art Clb; FFA; Hon Roll; Painter.

FERNANDEZ, KRISTINE F; Mission Viejo HS; El Toro, CA; (2); Computer Clb; Debate Tm; Model UN; Pep Clb; Cheerldng; High Hon Roll; Hon Roll; Stanford; Law.

FERNANDEZ, LETICIA N; St Monicas HS; Culver City, CA; (3); Key Clb; Co-Capt Flag Corp; Rep Frsh Cls; Sec Treas Jr Cls; Rep Sr Cls; NHS; NEDT Awd; Presdntl Clsrm; US Naval Sea Cadet Corps; Acad Decathln Team; Poltcl Sci.

FERNANDEZ, LILIANA G; Rubidoux HS; Riverside, CA; (4); French Clb; Model UN; Pep Clb; Speech Tm; Acpl Chr; Drill Tm; Off Jr Cls; Off Sr Cls; Capt Cheerldng; Intrml Powder Puff Ftbl; CASC, Future Ldrs Of Am, KSR Of Irvine; USC; Intl Rels.

FERNANDEZ, LUZ ELENA F; Woodrow Wilson HS; Los Angeles, CA; (3); Dance Clb; Math Tm; Science Clb; CSF; Stu Of Mnth Awd Soc Stud; Engrng.

FERNANDEZ, MAGALI; Bell HS; Cudahy, CA; (4); Hon Roll; Prfct Atten Awd; Math Cntsts; Differant U Pgms; Long Bch CA ST; Comp Sci.

FERNANDEZ, MARCOS; Abraham Lincoln HS; San Jose, CA; (3); 39/356; Var Socr; San Jose ST U; Mech Engr.

FERNANDEZ, MARIA LOURDES; Fontana HS; Fontana, CA; (2); Debate Tm; Ski Clb; Ed Nwsp; Rep Frsh Cls; Rep Soph Cls; Hon Roll; CSF; Intl Explorers; Tutorng; Jrnlsm.

FERNANDEZ, MARIO G; Sanger HS; Sanger, CA; (2).

FERNANDEZ, MARK J; Bellarmine College Prep; San Jose, CA; (3); Boy Scts; Cmnty Wkr; Red Cross Aide; Retreat Ldr; Bus Admin.

FERNANDEZ, MARY GRACE; Chula Vista HS; San Diego, CA; (3); Church Yth Grp; Cmnty Wkr; Intnl Clb; Temple Yth Grp; Church Choir; School Musical; Prfct Atten Awd; Pres Acad Fit Awd; Hnrb Mntn Music Comp Attndnc Awd; Play Piano, Guitar, Dance, Sing, Acting, Feed Homeless; Bus.

FERNANDEZ, MICHAEL; Notre Dame HS; Van Nuys, CA; (4); Drama Clb; Letterman Clb; Stage Crew; Nwsp; Var L Crs Cntry; JV Socr; Var L Wrstlng; Hon Roll; NEDT Awd; Knights Of Round Table; Rag Prods.

FERNANDEZ, MIGUEL OSCAR; Colusa HS; Colusa, CA; (3); 7/100; Art Clb; French Clb; FBLA; Hon Roll; CSF Secy; Davis; Bus.

FERNANDEZ, NADINA L; El Dorado HS; Placentia, CA; (4); 8/348; Sec Church Yth Grp; Intnl Clb; Thesps; Chorus; School Musical; School Play; VP Sr Cls; High Hon Roll; VP NHS; Ntl Merit SF; Ntl Hispnc Schl Awds Prog; C A Arts Schlr Dance & Two Yrs Ballet; CSF; Stanford U; Soc Sci.

FERNANDEZ, NATALIE MARIE; Notre Dame HS; Moreno Valley, CA; (1); Cit Awd; Hon Roll; Tennis, Bsktbl, Vllybl; Accntnt.

FERNANDEZ, NWANEE; San Gorgonio HS; Highland, CA; (3); 15/460; Sec Key Clb; Color Guard; High Hon Roll; Jr NHS; NHS; Spanish NHS; CSF; Advsry Bd; U Of CA San Diego; Med.

FERNANDEZ, SANDRA O; Hueneme HS; Port Hueneme, CA; (2); Key Clb; Cit Awd; Hon Roll; Acadmc Awds; Phys Educ Awd; Dntstry.

FERNANDEZ, SOFIA; Phineas Banning HS; Wilmington, CA; (4); 6/550; Cmnty Wkr; Ed Nwsp; Pres Jr Cls; VP Sr Cls; Var Cheerldng; JV Vllybl; Hon Roll; Ntl Hspnc Schlr Awds Pgm Schlr 90; WA Wrkshps Cngrssnl Smnr 89; Gerogetown U; Poltcl Sci.

FERNANDEZ, SONIA; Bishop Amat Memorial HS; La Puente, CA; (3); Church Yth Grp; Cmnty Wkr; Service Clb; Spanish Clb; SADD; Church Choir; Ed Yrbk; Cit Awd; Spanish NHS; DECA; Amnesty Intl Club; Cmmnty Svc Awd; Natl Spnsh Exams; San Diego ST U; Spnsh.

FERNANDEZ, STEVEN M; Hesperia HS; Hesperia, CA; (2); French Clb; JV Ftbl; Var Trk; High Hon Roll; Hon Roll; U Of MI; Psych.

FERNANDEZ, SUZANNE; Paraclete HS; Palmdale, CA; (3); Drama Clb; Key Clb; Pep Clb; Service Clb; SADD; School Play; Yrbk; Rep Stu Cncl; Capt Var Cheerldng; Gym; Z Club VP; Loyola Coll; Pre Med.

FERNANDEZ, SYLVIA; Watsonville HS; Watsonville, CA; (3); Computer Clb; English Clb; Spanish Clb; Teachers Aide; Nwsp; Yrbk; Off Frsh Cls; Bsbl; Bsktbl; Ftbl; Cabrillo Coll; Acctng.

FERNANDEZ, VERNON I; Palma HS; Marina, CA; (3); 7/60; Boy Scts; Varsity Clb; VP Sr Cls; Var Ftbl; Trk; Var Wrstlng; Cit Awd; DAR Awd; High Hon Roll; Hon Roll; Rotary Interact Clb Pres; UC Santa Barbara; Bus Mgmt.

FERNANDEZ, VICTOR; Carson HS; Carson, CA; (3); Cmnty Wkr; Drama Clb; Latin Clb; Office Aide; Speech Tm; Teachers Aide; School Play; Treas Frsh Cls; Rep Stu Cncl; Jr NHS; Gftd & Tlntd Pgm.

FERNANDEZ, WALKIRIA; St Joseph HS; Huntington Park, CA; (2); 76/200; Spanish Clb; Hon Roll; Adv Spnsh; USC; Educ.

FERNANDEZ, YOLANDA; Watsonville HS; Watsonville, CA; (2); Cmnty Wkr; Hon Roll; Santa Cruz St Univ Fldtrp; Cabrillo Coll.

FERNANDO II, DAYANTHA M; Whitney HS; Cerritos, CA; (1); Boy Scts; Church Yth Grp; High Hon Roll; CA Jr Schlrshp Fed.

FERNENDEZ, CHERYL; Southwest HS; San Diego, CA; (3); 19/478; Pres Church Yth Grp; Hosp Aide; Pep Clb; ROTC; Rep Frsh Cls; Rep Jr Cls; Cit Awd; Hon Roll; Prfct Atten Awd; Assoc Stu Body Cmmssnr; Gldn Achvt Awd/Schlrshp; Hi Hnr Rl; Med.

FERRA, HECTOR; Senior HS; Santa Clarita, CA; (3); Boy Scts; Chorus; Church Choir; Stage Crew; Swing Chorus.

FERRAN, AILEEN; Culver City HS; Culver City, CA; (1); Cit Awd; High Hon Roll; CA ST U Long Beach; Comp Engr.

FERRARA, MARA; San Gabriel HS; San Gabriel, CA; (4); Church Yth Grp; Cmnty Wkr; French Clb; Latin Clb; Service Clb; Teachers Aide; Varsity Clb; Band; Church Choir; Mrchg Band; Missionary Work Mexico; San Diego ST; MD.

FERRARA, NATALIE; Thomas Downey HS; Modesto, CA; (4); 117/442; Office Aide; Service Clb; Spanish Clb; Teachers Aide; Orch; Cit Awd; Tres Of The Orchestra For 2 Yrs And Organizing Trips Planning Fund Raisers For The Orchestra; Stanislaus St; Engineering.

FERRARI, MELISSA M; Arroyo Grande HS; Nipomo, CA; (2); 134/625; AFS; Church Yth Grp; Dance Clb; JV Tennis; Hon Roll; CA Polytech ST U; Poly Sci.

FERRARI, ROBIN; Archbishop Mitty HS; San Jose, CA; (2); 6/211; SADD; Trk; Vllybl; High Hon Roll; NHS; Snow Ski; Comp Sci.

FERRARO, DANIELLE R; Cornelia Connelly HS; Downey, CA; (1); Cmnty Wkr; Intnl Clb; Library Aide; Service Clb; School Play; Hon Roll; Jr Statesmen Amer; Assistance Leag Downey; Library Clb; Gangs Out Downey Cmnty Svc Grp; Pepperdine; Brdcstng.

FERRASCI, MARGARET T; Notre Dame HS; Salinas, CA; (2); Church Yth Grp; JV Vllybl; Hon Roll.

FERREIRA, AARON S; Granada HS; Livermore, CA; (4); Var Socr; Var Tennis; Prfct Atten Awd; Pres Acad Fit Awd; Cal Poly San Luis Obispo; Comp.

FERREIRA, ALETHEA; Brethren JR/Sr HS; Gardena, CA; (2); French Clb; Varsity Clb; Acpl Chr; School Play; Pres Soph Cls; Var Socr; Wt Lftg; Cit Awd; High Hon Roll; UCLA; Ob Nrs.

FERREIRA, ERIC A; Edison HS; Stockton, CA; (2); Computer Clb; Scholastic Bowl; School Play; Stage Crew; JV Ftbl; JV Trk; JV Wt Lftg; Drawing; Race Car Driver; Delta; Engrng.

FERREIRA, JENNIFER L; Crescenta Valley HS; La Crescenta, CA; (2); Key Clb; Math Clb; Mu Alpha Theta; Spanish Clb; JV Capt Sftbl; JV Vllybl; NHS; Girls Leag; Osteopathetic Surgeon.

FERREIRA, SAMUEL D; Warren HS; Downey, CA; (2); Ski Clb; Intrml Bsbl; Var Capt Crs Cntry; Var Trk; Cit Awd; Hon Roll; Ntl Merit Schol; Pres Acad Fit Awd; Embry Riddle; Law Enfrcmnt.

FERREL, ANNA; Tulare Union HS; Pixley, CA; (3); Church Yth Grp; Cit Awd; High Hon Roll; Hon Roll; Prfct Atten Awd; Fresno ST Coll; Bus Mgmt.

FERREL, HUGO C; Los Angeles HS; Los Angeles, CA; (3); Dance Clb; Science Clb; Spanish Clb; Stu Cncl; Ftbl; Swmmng; Wt Lftg; U CA Berkeley; Physcs.

FERRELL, EDIE A; Rio Mesa HS; Camarillo, CA; (3); 86/373; Church Yth Grp; Hon Roll; Peer Cnslng; Brigham Young U.

FERRELL, KRISTA M; Paso Robles HS; Paso Robles, CA; (4); 69/250; Aud/Vis; Church Yth Grp; Drama Clb; FBLA; SADD; Band; Jazz Band; Mrchg Band; School Play; Stage Crew; Hiking & Envirnmntl Club; Holy Names Coll; Yth Ministry.

FERRER, ALVIN M; University HS; Los Angeles, CA; (4); 11/650; Chess Clb; Library Aide; Math Clb; Math Tm; Office Aide; Teachers Aide; Lit Mag; Rep Stu Cncl; Intrml Bsktbl; High Hon Roll; Acad Decathlon Team; CSF; Most Imprvd Bsktbl Plyr; U CA Riverside; Biomed.

FERRER, ARLENE; Granger JR HS; San Diego, CA; (1); 8/268; Rptr Ed Nwsp; Yrbk; Intrml Vllybl; High Hon Roll; Hon Roll; Prfct Atten Awd; Asst Cmmssnr Stu Actvts Assoctd Stu Bdy; Books & Beyond; Psych.

FERRER, HAZELLE; Hueneme HS; Port Hueneme, CA; (1); Hon Roll; Stanford; Med.

FERRER, JENNIFER L; Yucca Valley HS; Yucca Valley, CA; (1); JV Bsktbl; JV Sftbl; Wt Lftg; Cit Awd; High Hon Roll; Pres Acad Fit Awd; CA Schlrshp Fed; Top Algbr I Stu; CA U.

FERRER, JULIUS D; Casa Grande HS; Petaluma, CA; (2); French Clb; Ftbl; Crpntry.

FERRER, LEAH R; Mt Pleasant HS; San Jose, CA; (2); VP Frsh Cls; High Hon Roll; Hon Roll; Chorus; School Play; CADD Founder & Pres; Youth Recognition Awd 90; CSF Mem; W Assn Of Shls & Coll.

FERRER, LEILANI B; Vallejo SR HS; Vallejo, CA; (3); Church Yth Grp; Office Aide; Spanish Clb; SADD; Teachers Aide; Sec Frsh Cls; JV Var Vllybl; Hon Roll; Comps; Bus.

FERRER, LISA; Bonita Vista HS; Chula Vista, CA; (4); 1/531; Teachers Aide; Pres Stu Cncl; JV Bsktbl; Var JV Sftbl; Var JV Vllybl; Cit Awd; Hon Roll; Assoc Stu Bdyd Cmmsnr Finance; Asian Cltrl Clb; U Of San Diego; Accntng.

FERRER, MARIA T; Bridgemont HS; San Francisco, CA; (3); 1/22; Church Yth Grp; Band; Church Choir; Mrchg Band; School Musical; Vllybl; Cit Awd; High Hon Roll; Hon Roll; MA Inst Of Tech; Engrng.

FERRER, MELISSA; Sacred Heart Of Jesus HS; Los Angeles, CA; (2); GAA; Chorus; Mgr(s); Sftbl; Vllybl; Hon Roll; UC Santa Barbara; Spcl Ed.

FERRERA, LIZBETH F; King City HS; King City, CA; (3); Cmnty Wkr; Office Aide; Service Clb; Teachers Aide; Hon Roll; Peer Cnslr; Fresno ST U; Cnslr.

FERRERIA, DAVID M; Van Nuys HS; Sunland, CA; (4); JA; ROTC; Jazz Band; Mrchg Band; Orch; School Musical; Off Soph Cls; Off Jr Cls; Off Sr Cls; CA Schlrshp Fed; Jr Statsmn Of Amer; Natl Hspnc Schl Semi Fnlst; Gold Sl Bearer; High Hnr Gldn St Exam.

FERRERIRA, NUNO; Liberty Union HS; Oakley, CA; (2); 62/420; FCA; Chorus; JV Crs Cntry; JV Wrstlng; Hon Roll; Prfct Atten Awd; Stanford; Law.

FERRERO, JENNIFER L; Morro Bay HS; Los Osos, CA; (4); 13/245; Office Aide; Teachers Aide; Yrbk; Sec Treas Soph Cls; High Hon Roll; Pres Acad Fit Awd; Pres Classrm; CSF; Yrbk Bus Mgr, Photgrphr, Reprtr, Edtr; U CA Davis; Intl Rels.

FERRETTI, CARI; San Marin HS; Novato, CA; (2); Pep Clb; SADD; Drill Tm; Rptr Phtg Nwsp; Rep Soph Cls; Rep Stu Cncl; JV Var Cheerldng; JV Var Pom Pon; Hon Roll; Sac ST; TV Brdcstng.

FERREYRA, ALBINA; Fairfax HS; Los Angeles, CA; (3); Cmnty Wkr; Girl Scts; Red Cross Aide; Spanish Clb; Teachers Aide; Orch; School Play; Rptr Nwsp; Prfct Atten Awd; Mock Trial Wtnss; Alpha Knghts Grp Of Hghly Intllctl Stu; Feed Hmlss Grp; Soc Sci.

FERRIOT, JULIE L; Bonita Vista HS; Bonita, CA; (3); 30/550; Church Yth Grp; Key Clb; Model UN; Pep Clb; Rptr Nwsp; Off Frsh Cls; Off Sr Cls; Var Fld Hcky; Cit Awd; High Hon Roll; Mst Imrpvd Bio Stu 89; Mst Imprvd Math Analysis Stu 90.

FERRIS, CHRISTOPHER J; Live Oak HS; Morgan Hill, CA; (3); 4/530; VP Chess Clb; High Hon Roll; NHS; Ntl Merit Ltr; Pres Acad Fit Awd; Var Badminton; Chess Trnmnts; Wrote Comp Pgms; Comp Sci.

FERRIS, DAVID L; Covina HS; West Covina, CA; (3); 1/215; Am Leg Boys St; Model UN; Office Aide; Band; Jazz Band; Mrchg Band; Pep Band; Off Band; Off Jr Cls; VP Stu Cncl; CSF Pres; Civil Air Ptrl; U S Air Force Acad; Engrng.

FERRIS II, RUSSELL A; Azusa HS; Azusa, CA; (3); 22/275; Boy Scts; Church Yth Grp; French Clb; Trk; Wrstlng; High Hon Roll; Hon Roll; CSF; Mock Trial Debate Team; Engrng.

FERRIS, TRACEY; Capistrano Valley HS; Mission Viejo, CA; (4); Hosp Aide; Teachers Aide; Hon Roll; Commendation Cert In Amer Lit; Jr Hnr Escort Grad 88-89; U Of CA Irvine; Elem Tchr.

FERRO, AIMEE K; Carmel HS; Carmel, CA; (3); Cmnty Wkr; Treas FFA; Office Aide; Red Cross Aide; Teachers Aide; Var Sftbl; High Hon Roll; Rotary Awd; Outstndng Achvt Awd FFA; Hartnell Coll; Vet Tech.

FERRO, NANCY S; Norco HS; Norco, CA; (4); FBLA; Model UN; Intrml Stat Bsktbl; Stat Ftbl; Intrml Sftbl; High Hon Roll; NHS; Pres Acad Fit Awd; CA ST San Bernardino; Acctg.

FERROL, REBECCA; Los Alamitos HS; Los Alamitos, CA; (4); Sec French Clb; Service Clb; Teachers Aide; Var Diving; 4 Yr CA Schlstc Fdr.

FERRY, ARMELITA C; International Studies Acad; San Francisco, CA; (3); Yrbk; Treas Soph Cls; Treas Jr Cls; Hon Roll.

FERRY, HEATH A; Carlsbad HS; Carlsbad, CA; (2); 83/400; Boy Scts; Band; Jazz Band; Mrchg Band; School Musical; School Play; Hon Roll; Most Imprvd Music Plyr; Fireman.

FERTIG, BRANDY N; Edison HS; Huntington Beach, CA; (3); Teachers Aide; JV Tennis; Orange Coast Coll.

FERTIG, MARTHA; Lodi HS; Stockton, CA; (4); 41/490; Church Yth Grp; Pres 4-H; Pres FHA; FTA; SADD; Acpl Chr; Cit Awd; 4-H Awd; Kiwanis Awd; Ntl 4-H Conf; Badmntn-Vrsty Lttr; Ntl Ldrshp Conf Wash DC; Adlgst.

FESNIAK, MICHAEL A; San Clemente HS; San Juan Capis, CA; (3); 2nd Pl Bio Sci Fair 88; Cert Cmmndtn Acad Booster Club 89; Jr Ref AYSO 87-89; Mem Cath Chrstn Dev Yth; Loyola-Marymount U; Teacher.

FETHKE, KYLE; Canyon HS; Canyon Country, CA; (2); 10/500; Off Jr Cls; Rep Stu Cncl; Var L Ftbl; JV L Socr; Var L Tennis; Hon Roll; Coachs Awds Ftbl; Vrsty Ftbl & Vrsty Tnns CIF Tms 89-90; UC Schl; Envrnmntl Lw.

FETTERS, GREG N; Enterprise HS; Redding, CA; (3); 65/500; Rep Sr Cls; Var Ftbl; Var Trk; Hon Roll; Peer Counslr; Humbolt.

FEUERBORN, SARAH E; Tustin HS; Tustin, CA; (4); 32/377; AFS; German Clb; GAA; Letterman Clb; Co-Ed Yrbk; Swmmng; High Hon Roll; Hon Roll; U Of CA Irvine; Law.

FEWELL, KEVIN ROBERT; Bella Vista HS; Fair Oaks, CA; (4); Church Yth Grp; Drama Clb; Letterman Clb; Spanish Clb; Bsbl; Socr; High Hon Roll; NHS; Pres Schlr; All St Fndtn Schlrshp; Westmont Presdntl Schlrshp; Westmont; Engrng Physics.

FEYGIN II, ARCADY; Monterey HS; Monterey, CA; (4); 16/280; Pres Chess Clb; Intrml Socr; High Hon Roll; NHS; Golden St Exam Acad Achvt Awd 89; Cert Of Achvt For Outstndng Acad Excllnc 90; U CA Berkeley; Bus Admin.

FICANO, CATHERINE N; Miramesa HS; San Diego, CA; (2); Art Clb; Church Yth Grp; Drama Clb; FHA; Spanish Clb; School Play; Variety Show; Yrbk; San Diego ST; Fashn Desgn.

FICKAS, DAVID L; Arcadia HS; Arcadia, CA; (2); Drama Clb; School Musical; School Play; Stu Cncl; Bst Actr In Drama; Yale U; Actor.

FICKE, BONNIE L; Norte Vista HS; Riverside, CA; (1); Dance Clb; Library Aide; Model UN; Teachers Aide; Cit Awd; High Hon Roll; Hon Roll; NEDT Awd; Sec.

FICKEN, KEVEN; Mt Whitney HS; Visalia, CA; (3); Pres Church Yth Grp; Key Clb; Band; Mrchg Band; Pep Band; JV Crs Cntry; Var Mgr(s); JV Trk; High Hon Roll; U Of CO Boulder; Bio.

FICKLE, KIMBERLEY M; Santa Teresa HS; San Jose, CA; (3); French Clb; Ecology Club.

FIDALEO, BRENDA K; Bishops HS; La Jolla, CA; (3); Cmnty Wkr; Girl Scts; Hosp Aide; Spanish Clb; Off Sr Cls; Hon Roll; Spanish NHS.

FIDLER, TIMOTHY M; Tulare Union HS; Tulare, CA; (3); 147/401; Church Yth Grp; Teachers Aide; JV Bsbl; JV Bsktbl; Var JV Ftbl; Prfct Atten Awd; V Ftbl Ironman Awd; JV Bsktbl Coaches Awd.

FIDUCCIA, DAVID M; Costa Mesa HS; Costa Mesa, CA; (3); Boy Scts; Church Yth Grp; Letterman Clb; Office Aide; Intrml JV Bsbl; JV Var Bsktbl; Var Ftbl; Var Golf; Var Wrstlng; Bus.

FIECHTER, JENNIFER L; Poway HS; Poway, CA; (2); High Hon Roll; Hon Roll; Safe Rides; Stanford; Phy.

FIELD, ANTHONY S; Granada Hills HS; Mission Hills, CA; (2); Church Yth Grp; Cmnty Wkr; FCA; Latin Clb; Science Clb; Spanish Clb; SADD; Church Choir; Bsktbl; Vllybl; USC; Sci.

FIELD, CARLENE; San Bernardino HS; San Bernardino, CA; (2); Church Yth Grp; Key Clb; Pep Clb; Acpl Chr; Band; Chorus; Color Guard; Flag Corp; Mrchg Band; School Play; BYU; Theatre.

FIELD, ERICA C; University HS; Irvine, CA; (2); 44/508; Var Bsktbl; Hon Roll; Jrnlsm.

FIELD, HEATHER; A J Heschel Day Schl; Northridge, CA; (1); 1/40; Cmnty Wkr; Teachers Aide; Temple Yth Grp; Sec Frsh Cls; Sftbl; Trk; Vllybl; High Hon Roll; Pres Acad Fit Awd.

FIELD, KAMAILE; Mt Whitney HS; Visalia, CA; (3); AFS; French Clb; Girl Scts; Pep Clb; Band; Stat Bsktbl; Score Keeper; Hon Roll; CSF CA Schlrshp Fdrtn; Vcl Ensmbl; Bus.

FIELD, LAURA M; Alpaugh HS; Alpaugh, CA; (3); Pep Clb; Teachers Aide; Rep Frsh Cls; Hon Roll; Animal Sci.

FIELD, SHANNON S; Rincon Valley Christian Schl; Santa Rosa, CA; (2); Church Yth Grp; Band; Chorus; Mrchg Band; Cit Awd; High Hon Roll; Pres Acad Fit Awd; Med.

FIELDER, ROBYN; Porterville HS; Porterville, CA; (2); Dance Clb; JV Cheerldng; JV Sftbl; Hon Roll; PAA; Cmptr Prgmr.

FIELDING, ROBERT P; Loyola HS; Arcadia, CA; (2); 1/250; Church Yth Grp; Cmnty Wkr; Hosp Aide; Ed Nwsp; Ed Yrbk; French Hon Soc; Hon Roll; Joel & Astrid Rottman Schlrshp; Loyola Poltcl Soc; Chrch Server; Med.

FIELDS, ASHLEY; Capistrano Valley HS; Laguna Niguel, CA; (3); Church Yth Grp; Pep Clb; Teachers Aide; Church Choir; Capt JV Gym; Prfct Atten Awd; Acad Decathlon; UC San Diego; Engl.

FIELDS, AYANNA S; Palmdale HS; Palmdale, CA; (4); 23/592; Office Aide; Teachers Aide; JV Var Swmmng; JV Var Wrstlng; Cal ST Los Angeles; Elem Ed.

FIELDS, BRYANT D; Central HS; El Centro, CA; (1); Chess Clb; Church Yth Grp; Drama Clb; Pep Clb; Off Soph Cls; Stu Cncl; Ftbl; High Hon Roll; Hon Roll; Black Amer Clb; Friday Night Live; USC; Comp Engr.

FIELDS, DARREN; Apple Valley SR HS; Apple Valley, CA; (2); Office Aide; Off Soph Cls; Socr; High Hon Roll; Hon Roll; Vrsty Sccr-Frshmn, Wn Leag Title; MVP Offnse & Awd CIF Vtd Tms Bst Plyr Leag; U Of San Diego; Vet.

FIELDS, RENEE; San Bernardino HS; San Bernardino, CA; (4); 15/345; Spanish Clb; SADD; Stu Cncl; Sftbl; Tennis; High Hon Roll; NHS; UCLA; Pol Sci.

FIELDS, RODERICK SCOTT; St Patrick-St Vincent HS; Vallejo, CA; (4); 6/141; Chorus; Phtg Yrbk; Rep Stu Cncl; Bausch & Lomb Sci Awd; Elks Awd; High Hon Roll; VP NHS; Pres Acad Fit Awd; Sal; Yth Actvts Cmssn Chrmn; Cal Poly San Luis Obispo; Engr.

FIELY, ANDREA; St Joseph HS; Buena Park, CA; (2); 59/200; Drama Clb; Math Tm; Hon Roll; SADD; CA Natl Schlrshp Fed; Sci.

FIEN, BRIAN J; Tulare Union HS; Tulare, CA; (3); 52/390; Hon Roll; Bio.

FIERMAN, DANICA LEE; Tamalpais HS; Greenbrae, CA; (4); 4/231; Drama Clb; French Clb; VP Frsh Cls; Sec Sr Cls; Rep Stu Cncl; High Hon Roll; Pres Acad Fit Awd; Val; School Play; Rep Soph Cls; People To People HS Stu Ambssdr Pgm Eastern Europe; Time Educ Pgm Stu Wrtng & Art Cmptn 2nd Pl Essy; Pomona Coll.

FIERRO, ABRAHAM; El Cajon Valley HS; El Cajon, CA; (3); Church Yth Grp; Speech Tm; Rptr Nwsp; JV Crs Cntry; Hon Roll; Grossmont Coll; Law Enfrcmnt.

FIERRO, CRAIG A; San Joaquin Memorial HS; Selma, CA; (2); Spanish Clb; JV Capt Bsktbl; U Of NV Las Vegas; Sprts Cmntr.

FIERRO, OLIVIA; Whittier HS; Whittier, CA; (2); 25/465; Hosp Aide; Drill Tm; Variety Show; Pres Frsh Cls; Rep Soph Cls; Stu Cncl; JV Capt Cheerldng; High Hon Roll; Hon Roll; Yng Life Grp.

FIERRO, SUSANA; Downey HS; Downey, CA; (2); Church Yth Grp; Cmnty Wkr; Sec Science Clb; Service Clb; Spanish Clb; Teachers Aide; 90 Hnrb Mntn World Poetry; Keywanettes; Cerritos City Coll; Law.

FIERROS, ROSALIA P; Pittsburg HS; Pittsburg, CA; (2); Stu Cncl; Tennis; Cit Awd; High Hon Roll; Hon Roll; Hstry Day Cmptn Awd; Bus.

FIES, ELISABETH; Montgomery HS; Santa Rosa, CA; (3); Cmnty Wkr; Dance Clb; Debate Tm; Drama Clb; Stage Crew; Nwsp; Cheerldng; Cit Awd; Jr NHS; Pres Acad Fit Awd; Meiklejohn Educ Fndtn Cultrl Litrcy; Greenpeace; Peace 21st Contrbutor; Santa Cruz U.

FIESEL, CATHERINE P; Nevada Union HS; Penn Valley, CA; (3); Cit Awd; High Hon Roll; Fri Night Live; Elem Ed.

FIFER, SHANEY M; Fred C Beyer HS; Modesto, CA; (2); Bus Profs of Am; Band; Mrchg Band; Pep Band; Gym; Hon Roll; NAACP Clb; Tutor; Harvard U; Bus.

FIGGERS, NAKIA; Susan Miller Dorsey HS; Los Angeles, CA; (2); Cmnty Wkr; Dance Clb; Drama Clb; Math Tm; Speech Tm; Teachers Aide; Band; Mrchg Band; School Play; Variety Show; Awd Cnclmn Nate Holden Yth Advcy Ldrshp Inst; St Louis Ol Bispo; Arch Dsgn.

FIGOTEN, JEREMY M; Calabasas HS; Woodland Hills, CA; (2); NFL; Speech Tm; Rptr Nwsp; Game Clb Mem; Jr Statesman Amer Mem; I-Care Clb; Jrnlsm.

FIGUEIREDO, JORGE H; Livingston HS; Livingston, CA; (1); Hon Roll; Gen Stu Cncl; Sci.

FIGUEROA, BIANCA; Palo Verde HS; Blythe, CA; (2); Church Yth Grp; Dance Clb; Drama Clb; School Musical; School Play; Cheerldng; Sftbl; Trk; High Hon Roll; Hon Roll; Jazz Dncng & Cmptn Wnnr 87-90; MS Echo 90; UCSP; Med.

FIGUEROA, CLAUDIA; Central Union HS; El Centro, CA; (3); 12/543; Church Yth Grp; Cmnty Wkr; Hon Roll; Admin Law.

FIGUEROA, DIANA M; Lompoc HS; Lompoc, CA; (1); Hon Roll; Vet.

FIGUEROA, GRISELDA; Alisal HS; Salinas, CA; (2).

FIGUEROA, JORGE G; Calexico HS; Calexico, CA; (2); Intnl Clb; Wt Lftg; Hon Roll; Prfct Atten Awd.

FIGUEROA, LORRAINE; Bishop Amat HS; Walnut, CA; (3); Cmnty Wkr; English Clb; French Clb; Drill Tm; School Musical; Elks Awd; Elem Educ.

FIGUEROA, MARIA C; Coachella Valley HS; Thermal, CA; (2); Hon Roll; Cal Poly San Luis Obispo; Bus.

FIGUEROA, MARIA D; Fontana HS; Fontana, CA; (3); 50/1050; Library Aide; Ski Clb; Teachers Aide; Rep Stu Cncl; Hon Roll; Prfct Atten Awd; Pres Acad Fit Awd; 2 Acadmc Gold Mdls; Daisy Chain; CSF; U Of CA San Diego; Pltcl Sci.

FIGUEROA, MIA; George Washington HS; San Francisco, CA; (2); Computer Clb; Gym; Hon Roll; Pres Acad Fit Awd; Psychlgst.

FIGUEROA, MICHAEL A; Don Bosco Technical Inst; West Covina, CA; (3); 8/280; Math Clb; Yrbk; Hon Roll; NHS; NEDT Awd; CA Schlrshp Fed; USC; Bus Admin.

FIGUEROA, OTTO F; Lynwood HS; Lynwood, CA; (3); 42/650; German Clb; Co-Ed Yrbk; JV Crs Cntry; Var Co-Capt Vllybl; Natl Hnr Soc; Engl Natl Mrt Awd Wnnr; UCLA Partnership & PAL; Civil Engr.

FIGUEROA, PATRICIA T; Calexico HS; Calexico, CA; (1); Key Clb; Pep Clb; Band; Pep Band; Off Frsh Cls; Bsktbl; Tennis; Trk; UCSD; Law Enfrcmnt.

FIGUEROA, RAMON; Bishop Amat HS; Walnut, CA; (3); Cmnty Wkr; French Hon Soc; Hon Roll; NEDT Awd; Slvr Screen Club VP; Cal Poly Pomona; Bus.

FIGUEROA, REBECCA; Narbonne HS; Torrance, CA; (4); Cmnty Wkr; Key Clb; Service Clb; Cit Awd; French Hon Soc; High Hon Roll; Hon Roll; Ntl Merit Schol; Chess Clb; Debate Tm; Mxcn Amer Edctrs Awd; Carson Chmbr Of Cmmrc Awd; Kywntts; Ladies Svc Orgnztn; Attnd Ltn Yth Ldrshp Cnfrn; Loyola Mrymount U; Lbrl Arts.

FIGUEROA, RONA; Mercy HS; San Mateo, CA; (4); 20/104; Church Yth Grp; Cmnty Wkr; Intnl Clb; Ski Clb; Band; Chorus; School Musical; Lit Mag; VP Jr Cls; High Hon Roll; Jr Stsmn Of Amer; Amnsty Intl; Lgstlv Intrnshp; Scripps; Wtr.

FIGUEROA, ROSA M; James A Garfield HS; Los Angeles, CA; (3); Church Yth Grp; Office Aide; Red Cross Aide; Band; Yrbk; Stu Cncl; Cheerldng; Hon Roll.

FIGUEROA, SANDRA L; Bassett HS; West Covina, CA; (4); French Clb; Intnl Clb; Ed Nwsp; NHS; Prfct Atten Awd; Peer Cnslng; Stu Intern On Yrbk Staff; Film Hstry & Production; Mt San Antonio Coll; Engl.

FIGUEROA, VERONICA D; Pinole Valley HS; Pinole, CA; (2); Debate Tm; NFL; Spanish Clb; JV Vllybl; Hon Roll; CSF; Interact Clb; Conflict Mgmt Team; Marine Bio.

FIGUEROA, XAVIER A; Edison HS; Fresno, CA; (4); Hosp Aide; Model UN; Ed Lit Mag; Vllybl; Hon Roll; Pepsi-Fresno Unfd Schl Dist Awd; Acad Decath 1st Pl Essay; UC Davis; Med Rcrds.

FIGUR, BRIAN; Serra HS; Burlingame, CA; (2); High Hon Roll; Hon Roll; Trivia Club; Martial Arts; U Of CA Davis; Vet Med.

FIGURACION, ROWENA; James Lick HS; San Jose, CA; (4); 27/257; Intnl Clb; Hon Roll; NHS; Var Badminton; CSF; Asian Club; CA ST U Sacramento; Bus Admin.

FIJMAN, GREG A; Mission San Jose HS; Fremont, CA; (3); 40/420; Church Yth Grp; Varsity Clb; Socr; Hon Roll; Hgh Hnrs Golden St Exam Alg.

FIKES, KRYSTEN M; Notre Dame HS; San Jose, CA; (3); 4-H; Pres Bus Profs of Am; Sec Soph Cls; Sec Jr Cls; Sec Stu Cncl; Hon Roll; Awds Poetry; Co-Fndr Black Stu Union Notre Dame; Pr Cnslng; Rep Mayors Yth Conf; UCLA; Commnctns.

FILAK, KATHARINE E; Coronado HS; Coronado, CA; (4); 2/124; Cmnty Wkr; Drama Clb; French Clb; JA; Key Clb; Pep Clb; Scholastic Bowl; Service Clb; Teachers Aide; Thesps; Soc Of Wmn Engrs; Math & Sci Awd; UC Berkeley; Ind Engrng.

FILATOFF, ANA STACIA; Madera HS; Madera, CA; (4); Teachers Aide; Color Guard; Hon Roll; Intl Frndshp Club; Spirit Club; Fresno ST U; Psych.

FILES, ELLEN; Fountain Valley HS; Fountain Valley, CA; (1); Band; Mrchg Band; Keywanettes; Cost Des.

FILES, STEPHANIE N; Vaca HS; Vacaville, CA; (3); Service Clb; Crt Reprtr.

FILIA, NANCY M; Woodbridge HS; Irvine, CA; (4); 154/360; GAA; Pep Clb; Pom Pon; Sftbl; OCC; Sales.

FILIO, EUGENE A; James J Hogan HS; Vallejo, CA; (2); Teachers Aide; Co-Ed Nwsp; JV Ftbl; Cit Awd; High Hon Roll; Engrng.

FILIPOVIC, ELENA; Redlands HS; Rialto, CA; (4); 49/879; Cmnty Wkr; Hosp Aide; Key Clb; Science Clb; Service Clb; Spanish Clb; Nwsp; Lit Mag; JV Tennis; High Hon Roll; Acadmc Dcthln 1st Pl Lang Lit, 2nd Pl Interview; Fed Svngs Outstndng Stu Yr Awd; 1st Pl Amer Lgn Essay; Cornell U; Engl.

FILIPPELLO, JESSICA; Dos Pueblos HS; Goleta, CA; (3); Church Yth Grp; French Clb; Pep Clb; Drill Tm; Nwsp; Cheerldng; NHS; Pres Acad Fit Awd; Santa Barbara City Coll.

FILLER, ELENA; Fairfax HS; Los Angeles, CA; (3); Cmnty Wkr; Hosp Aide; Library Aide; Red Cross Aide; Rptr Nwsp; Rep Jr Cls; UCLA Bk Awd; Alpha Knights-NCTE Essay Cntst; Prometheans-AP Chem US Hstry & Engl; UCLA; Med.

FILLMER, MICHAEL S; Thomas Downey HS; Modesto, CA; (2); Church Yth Grp; Pres 4-H; Key Clb; Speech Tm; Ftbl; Swmmng; Hon Roll; Boys Wtr Polo Tm; Med.

FILOMIA, MELINA M; Antelope Valley HS; Lancaster, CA; (3); 20/631; Am Leg Aux Girls St; Spanish Clb; Mrchg Band; Ed Nwsp; Ed Yrbk; Ed Lit Mag; High Hon Roll; Vol Cabin Ldr; Z-Club; CSF.

FIMBRES, MARCELA; Palmdale HS; Palmdale, CA; (2); Spanish Clb; Varsity Clb; Sftbl; Vllybl; Math.

FINATTI, TRACI A; Notre Dame HS; Salinas, CA; (3); 12/70; Intnl Clb; VP Science Clb; JV Var Tennis; Cit Awd; High Hon Roll; Rotary Awd; Swmmng & Bkng; Rdng & Comp; Sci.

FINAU, SALESI T; Berkeley HS; Figi; (4); Boy Scts; Var Ftbl; Var Socr; Var Vllybl; Plyd Rugby For Berkeley HS Vice Capt; U S Pacific; Air Force Pilot.

FINCH, BARBARA; Wasco Union HS; Wasco, CA; (2); FFA; FHA; Library Aide; Teachers Aide; Chorus; Chrmn Frsh Cls; Score Keeper; Hon Roll.

FINCH, BRIDGIT R; Eisenhower HS; Rialto, CA; (3); Key Clb; Nwsp; Bsktbl; Mgr(s); High Hon Roll; Hon Roll; NHS; Fri Nght Lv Treas; Bstr Clb; UC Irvine CA; Spcl Invstgtr.

FINCH, STEVE R; Irvine HS; Irvine, CA; (3); Spanish Clb; JV Socr; JV Trk; Pres Acad Fit Awd; Police Sci.

FINCHER, KELLEN; Covington HS; Bush, LA; (3); Band; Mrchg Band; Bsbl; Superior Rating In Several Band Contests; LA ST U; Cmptr Eng.

FINCK, DIANA; Cypress HS; Cypress, CA; (3); Church Yth Grp; Pep Clb; Teachers Aide; Varsity Clb; Rptr Yrbk; Var Capt Cheerldng; Gym; Var L Socr; High Hon Roll; CSF.

FINE, HALLA R; College Park HS; Pleasant Hill, CA; (3); 30/350; Socr; Hon Roll; Yth Edctr; Prin Advsry Cmmttee; Law.

FINGER, JOLI K; O'farrell SCPA HS; San Diego, CA; (4); 2/115; Church Yth Grp; Drama Clb; Office Aide; Spanish Clb; SADD; Sec Chorus; Church Choir; Variety Show; High Hon Roll; Hon Roll; Point Lonra Naz Coll; Music.

FINK, KATHLEEN M; Vacaville HS; Vacaville, CA; (3); Church Yth Grp; French Clb; Key Clb; Service Clb; Variety Show; DAR Awd; High Hon Roll; Hon Roll; SPCA Clb; Intl Bus.

FINK, MELISSA; Westlake HS; Westlake Vlg, CA; (2); 1/500; Dance Clb; Hosp Aide; SADD; Temple Yth Grp; Chorus; Treas Frsh Cls; High Hon Roll; Pres Acad Fit Awd; CSF.

FINK, NAOMI D; Temecula Valley HS; Temecula, CA; (4); Church Yth Grp; Cmnty Wkr; Chorus; Church Choir; Stage Crew; Ed Nwsp; VP Lit Mag; Mgr Bsktbl; Var Trk; Hon Roll; Palomar JC; Ed.

FINKE, MICHELE; Southbay Christian HS; Cupertino, CA; (4); Church Yth Grp; Drama Clb; Pep Clb; Spanish Clb; Thesps; Chorus; Stage Crew; Sec Jr Cls; Var Cheerldng; Hon Roll; Southern CA Coll; Elem Teacher.

FINKELDEI, LAURA D; Notre Dame HS; San Jose, CA; (4); 8/67; Drama Clb; Science Clb; SADD; Church Choir; School Play; Ed Nwsp; Sec Sr Cls; Hon Roll; NHS; Santa Clara Yth Hall Of Fame; Stu Space/Bio Pgm; Bank Of Amer Cert F/Sci; Sonoma ST U; Comm.

FINKENHAGEN, MELISSA A; Los Alamitos HS; Anaheim, CA; (4); Church Yth Grp; Pep Clb; Teachers Aide; Trk; Host Forgn Exch Stu; Art & Sewing Proj; Long Beach City Coll; Intr Dec.

FINKLER, AMANDA; South Tahoe HS; S Lake Tahoe, CA; (3); 1/210; Church Yth Grp; Debate Tm; Key Clb; Pres Frsh Cls; VP Soph Cls; Treas Jr Cls; JV Cheerldng; JV Var Tennis; Var Trk; High Hon Roll; Arch.

FINLAY, JENNIFER; Faith Christian School; Yuba City, CA; (2); 4/20; Var Cheerldng; Intrml Powder Puff Ftbl; Var Sftbl; Var JV Vllybl; Sftbl All-Lg; Sec, Treas, VP Chrch Yth Cncl.

FINLEY, CHRISTOPHER J; Channel Islands HS; Oxnard, CA; (2); Boy Scts; Key Clb; School Musical; JV Socr; San Diego ST; Police Offcr.

FINLEY, DONALD P; Valhalla HS; El Cajon, CA; (1); Church Yth Grp; Math Clb; Var Socr; Harvard; Lwyr.

FINLEY, LA SHAWN R; El Cerrito HS; Richmond, CA; (2); Crs Cntry; Hon Roll; UC Berkeley; Real Estate.

FINN, ALYSSA M; Louisville HS; Woodland Hills, CA; (2); Art Clb; Service Clb; Var Swmmng; Pres Teenettes; Bio Awd; Child Dev Awd; Berkeley; Phy.

FINN, ANDREA L; Dos Pueblos HS; Santa Barbara, CA; (4); 14/319; Debate Tm; Drama Clb; SADD; Acpl Chr; Ed Yrbk; Rep Stu Cncl; Var Swmmng; NHS; Ntl Merit SF; Pres Acad Fit Awd; CA Art Schlr Art Achvt 89; Santa Barbara Rwng Tm; Wellesley Bk Awd Acad Achvt; Brown U; Commercial Art.

FINN, GINA L; Bret Harte HS; Altaville, CA; (2); Dance Clb; Drama Clb; FHA; FTA; GAA; Math Clb; Math Tm; Model UN; Pep Clb; Science Clb; CA ST Chico ST Coll; Math Ed.

FINN, KATHRYN L; South HS; Bakersfield, CA; (4); Debate Tm; Intnl Clb; Pres Treas Key Clb; Teachers Aide; Band; Jazz Band; Pep Band; Sec Jr Cls; Stu Cncl; L Capt Bsktbl; Army Rsrv Natl Schlr Athlt; Pitzer Coll; Pre-Med.

FINNELL, BRENDA CHRISTINE; St Joseph Notre Dame HS; Alameda, CA; (4); 3/94; Church Yth Grp; Cmnty Wkr; Intnl Clb; Teachers Aide; Ed Rptr Nwsp; Ed Yrbk; Bausch & Lomb Sci Awd; High Hon Roll; NHS; Pres Acad Fit Awd; HOBY; Alameda Newspapr Grp Acad All-Star; Bnk America Cert Commnctns; Mills Coll; Engl.

FINNEY, ALISHA R; Francis Polytechnic HS; Covina, CA; (3); Teachers Aide; Mrchg Band; Orch; Hon Roll; Loyola Marymount; Psych.

FINNEY, DEBORAH L; Bakersfield HS; Bakersfield, CA; (2); Church Yth Grp; FHA; Science Clb; Church Choir; Orch; Hon Roll; CSF; Yth Cncl Membr; Educ.

FINNEY, HEATHER B; Temecula Valley HS; Temecula, CA; (2); Church Yth Grp; GAA; Teachers Aide; Rptr Nwsp; Rep Stu Cncl; JV Bsktbl; Stat Vllybl; UCSD; Marine Bio.

FINNEY, HEATHER L; Corona HS; Corona, CA; (2); 32/468; Church Yth Grp; Office Aide; Science Clb; Crs Cntry; Hon Roll; Pres Acad Fit Awd; 3rd Pl Dutchess & 5th Pl Prncss Amer Fed Of N Amer; Church Yth Drama Team; UC Davis; Vet.

FINNEY, HELENE A; Torrey Pines HS; Del Mar, CA; (4); Aud/Vis; Church Yth Grp; Girl Scts; Church Choir; Capt Flag Corp; Jazz Band; Crs Cntry; Goldn St Exam Hnrs Geom & 1st Yr Alg; UC Santa Cruz; Ministr.

FINNEY, MEGAN S; The Bishops Schl; Rancho Santa Fe, CA; (3); Cmnty Wkr; Pres Drama Clb; School Play; Variety Show; Off Soph Cls; Rep Jr Cls; Off Sr Cls; Capt Var Bsktbl; Swmmng; Cit Awd; Most Imprvd Swmmng Awd; Coaches Awd Bsktbl; Actress.

FINNIE, DELIA; Beaumont HS; Cherry Valley, CA; (3); Church Yth Grp; Library Aide; Pep Clb; Pres Jr Cls; JV Stat Vllybl; High Hon Roll; Sec NHS; Rotary Awd; Sci Fair 2 Yr Sweepstakes Wnnr; Med.

FINNIE, SONJA F; Beaumont HS; Cherry Valley, CA; (4); 1/160; Hosp Aide; Rep Jr Cls; VP Sr Cls; Var Cheerldng; DAR Awd; High Hon Roll; Pres NHS; Pres Acad Fit Awd; Val; Sci Fair Sweepstakes Trophy Wnnr 89-90; U Redlands; Bio.

FINNSTROM, ERICKA L; Herbert Hoover HS; Glendale, CA; (4); Church Yth Grp; Cmnty Wkr; GAA; Hosp Aide; JCL; Key Clb; Latin Clb; Letterman Clb; Teachers Aide; Varsity Clb; Donald Ashman Latin Schlr Awd; USC Merit Schlr; USC; Acctng.

FINSTAD, AMY J; Lassen Union HS; Janesville, CA; (4); 19/150; Pres Church Yth Grp; Cmnty Wkr; Teachers Aide; Band; JV Var Sftbl; Hon Roll; NHS; Pres Acad Fit Awd; All Leag Sftbl; CA ST U Chico; Social Work.

FINUCANE, PHILLIP E; Lincoln HS; Stockton, CA; (4); 26/500; Debate Tm; NFL; Speech Tm; Ed Nwsp; Rep Stu Cncl; Golf; High Hon Roll; Ntl Merit SF; Pres Acad Fit Awd; Stu Trstee; Nuclear Engrng.

FIOCCO, NICKI M; Escondido HS; Escondido, CA; (1); Drama Clb; Varsity Clb; School Play; Pres Frsh Cls; Var Bsktbl; Var Socr; Var Trk; Var Vllybl; Hon Roll; UC Santa Barbara; Psych.

FIOLA, ASIR N; Kennedy HS; Santa Ana, CA; (1); Church Yth Grp; Church Yth Grp; Wt Lftg; Pres Acad Fit Awd; GATE; Doctor.

FIORE, RICHARD S; Mission Viejo HS; Mission Viejo, CA; (3); 25/440; Drama Clb; Key Clb; Model UN; SADD; Teachers Aide; Bsbl; Socr; High Hon Roll; Hon Roll; Jr NHS; Perfrmng Arts; Cmnty Svc; Intl Bacalaureate; Berkeley.

FIR, DIANA; Mercy HS; San Bruno, CA; (4); 12/105; Church Yth Grp; Chorus; Church Choir; High Hon Roll; NHS; Italian Clb; Vocal Performance.

FIRESTON, JULIE H; Robert A Millikan HS; Long Beach, CA; (4); Math Clb; Pres Service Clb; Temple Yth Grp; Jazz Band; Ed Yrbk; JV Var Tennis; JV Var Trk; Hon Roll; NHS; Ntl Merit SF; Law.

FIRGENS, MACKENZIE; Coast Union HS; Cambria, CA; (1); AFS; FHA; Pep Clb; SADD; Variety Show; VP Frsh Cls; JV Sec Cheerldng; JV Co-Capt Pom Pon; Cambria Connection Players; Theatrical Arts.

FIRING, KIRSTEN M; Alameda HS; Alameda, CA; (2); Church Yth Grp; Drama Clb; Thesps; Church Choir; School Musical; School Play; Cheerldng; High Hon Roll; Hon Roll; English.

FIRMAN, ROB; Lodi HS; Lodi, CA; (4); Boy Scts; Church Yth Grp; Band; Jazz Band; Mrchg Band; Pep Band; School Musical; Hon Roll; 2 Yrs Cty Hnr Band 86-90; 3 Yrs CMEA Solo Ensmbl 86-90; 1 Yr St Hnr Band 89-90.

FISCHER, BLAKE R; Live Oak HS; San Jose, CA; (3); Chess Clb; French Clb; Band; Jazz Band; Mrchg Band; Orch; Pep Band; School Musical; Intrml Score Keeper; Hon Roll; Badminton Ltr; Drama Ltr; Jazz Band Canadian Tour 88; Marching Band Tour 90; UCLA; Film Stds.

FISCHER, GUSTAVE R; Servite HS; Anaheim, CA; (3); Church Yth Grp; Jr Statesman Of Amer; U Southern CA; Film Arts.

FISCHER, JESSICA J; Mira Mesa HS; San Diego, CA; (2); Cmnty Wkr; Var Socr; Var Trk; Cit Awd; CJSF; CSF; Olympc Dev Pgm Grls Scr; Sprts Med.

FISCHER, JULIE M; Living Way Christian Acad; Pasadena, CA; (4); 1/6; Church Yth Grp; Band; Church Choir; School Musical; School Play; Variety Show; Rptr Nwsp; Ed Yrbk; Stu Cncl; Var Bsktbl; Promise Future Minstry Awd 89-90; ACSI Distngshd HS Stu List 88-90; Fine/Prfrmng Arts.

FISCHER, KEVIN; Poway HS; Poway, CA; (3); Computer Clb; Key Clb; VP Math Clb; Band; Mrchg Band; High Hon Roll; NHS; CSF; Wind Symphny; Comp Sci.

FISCHER, LAURICE; Capital Christian HS; Sacramento, CA; (1); JV Vllybl; Hon Roll; Aerontcs Clb Sec.

FISCHER, LAURIE L; Clovis West HS; Fresno, CA; (4); 9/550; Pres Church Yth Grp; Cmnty Wkr; Debate Tm; Drama Clb; Intnl Clb; NFL; Speech Tm; SADD; Church Choir; School Play; Natl Energy Educ Devlpmnt Pgm; Pr Cnslr; Exchnge Clb Stu Mnth; BYU.

FISCHER, MICHAEL; St John Boslo HS; Cerritos, CA; (3); 14/200; Key Clb; SADD; Varsity Clb; Treas Stu Cncl; JV Bsbl; Var Crs Cntry; Intrml Ftbl; Var Trk; Hon Roll; CSF; U Of CA Berkeley; Engrng.

FISCHER, MICHELLE R; Polytechnic HS; Long Beach, CA; (2); Church Yth Grp; JV Swmmng; Pool, Bowl, Adore Children; Long Beach City Coll; Chld Care.

FISCHER, NICOLE M; Santa Clara HS; Oxnard, CA; (3); Office Aide; Cheerldng; Hon Roll; Amer Teen Semifnlst; Fshn Dsgn.

FISCHER, PAUL A; Piedmont HS; Piedmont, CA; (4); JA; Model UN; Spanish Clb; School Musical; Rptr Nwsp; JV Crs Cntry; Var Ftbl; Var Socr; Var Trk; Ntl Merit Ltr; Trk MVP 89-90; UCLA.

FISCHER, SCOTT J; Burney JR-SR HS; Burney, CA; (2); Pep Clb; Pres Soph Cls; JV Bsktbl; Var Trk; Hon Roll; Prfct Atten Awd; Pres Acad Fit Awd; Stu Acrddtn Cmmt.

FISCHER, STEPHANIE J; Red Bluff HS; Red Bluff, CA; (2); 1/473; Cmnty Wkr; Mu Alpha Theta; SADD; Stage Crew; High Hon Roll; CSF.

FISCHER, URSULA B; Wilson HS; Hacienda Hgts, CA; (2); Church Yth Grp; Cmnty Wkr; German Clb; Hosp Aide; Band; Mrchg Band; Orch; Var Swmmng; Hon Roll; Pres Acad Fit Awd; Intl Bus.

FISCHER, WILLIAM; Clovis West HS; Fresno, CA; (3); Cmnty Wkr; Ski Clb; Spanish Clb; Rep Jr Cls; JV Socr; Var Tennis; Hon Roll; NHS; Spanish NHS; Jrnlsm.

FISCHER, ZACHARY M; Poway HS; Poway, CA; (1); Church Yth Grp; Scholastic Bowl; Mrchg Band; Orch; School Musical; Swmmng; High Hon Roll; U CA; Med.

FISH, ALIANNE T; Agoura HS; Westlake Vlg, CA; (4); 43/438; Pep Clb; Red Cross Aide; VP Soph Cls; Treas Jr Cls; Stu Cncl; JV Cheerldng; Powder Puff Ftbl; Hon Roll; Pres Acad Fit Awd; Parnt Faclty Clb Schlrshp; Rotry Clb Schlrshp; Prom Qn; U Of AZ; Psych.

FISH, CASSANDRA L; Enterprise HS; Palo Cedro, CA; (3); #107 In Class; Drama Clb; San Diego U; Bus Mgmt.

FISH, CHASTINE ARANAS; Armijo HS; Suisun, CA; (2); SADD; School Musical; Trk; High Hon Roll; Hon Roll; NEDT Awd; St Schlr; Asian Amer Club Pres; CSF; UC Davis; Law.

FISH, KIRSTEN; Los Gatos HS; Los Gatos, CA; (1); School Musical; Yth Advsry Cmmsn Mem; YMCA Ldrs Clb & Day Camp Cnslr; Cmnty Agnst Substance Abuse Fshn Show; Harvard; Law.

FISHER, AMY C; Torrey Pines HS; Solana Beach, CA; (2); 1/503; Rptr Nwsp; Var Crs Cntry; JV Socr; Var Trk; CA Schlrshp Fed; Schlr Athl; Stanford; Phy.

FISHER, ANNMARIE; Fontana HS; Fontana, CA; (2); FBLA; Office Aide; Teachers Aide; Variety Show; Rep Stu Cncl; JV Bsktbl; JV Mgr(s); Var Trk; Cit Awd; Gov Hon Prg Awd; Black Stu Union; CSF; Syracuse; Arch.

FISHER, BRETT T; Troy HS; Fullerton, CA; (2); 52/323; Cit Awd; High Hon Roll; Peer Asst Leag; Japanese Clb; Troy Tech Pgm; Comp Sci.

FISHER, CALEB M; Cabrillo HS; Lompoc, CA; (2); Boy Scts; Church Yth Grp; Band; Jazz Band; Hon Roll; BYU; Cmmrcl Pilot.

FISHER, CATHRYN L; River City HS; W Sacramento, CA; (1); Band; Nwsp; Cheerldng; Trk; Jrnlst.

FISHER, CHRISSY; Hogan HS; Vallejo, CA; (2); Church Yth Grp; Key Clb; Office Aide; Ski Clb; Spanish Clb; Drill Tm; Pres Frsh Cls; Rep Jr Cls; Capt Cheerldng; Diving; San Diego ST; Mass Cmmctns.

FISHER, CHRISTOPHER L; Calvary Chapel HS; Lakewood, CA; (2); Church Yth Grp; Var Trk; Hon Roll; Trk Coachs Awd; Biola; Bio.

FISHER, DERRICK G; Grace M Davis HS; Modesto, CA; (2); VICA; Cal Poly; Arch.

FISHER, ELIZABETH V; Grossmont HS; El Cajon, CA; (1); GAA; School Musical; JV Cheerldng; High Hon Roll; Medicine.

FISHER, EVAN LEE; Hughson Union HS; Hughson, CA; (4); French Clb; Math Clb; Band; Co-Capt Bsktbl; Var Golf; Ntl Merit Ltr; Pres Acad Fit Awd; Chess Clb; Church Yth Grp; Intnl Clb; Acad Decthln; Sci Olympd; CSF; CA ST U Stanislaus; Physcs.

FISHER, GREGG D; Paraclete HS; Lancaster, CA; (2); Boy Scts; Church Yth Grp; JA; Letterman Clb; Var Golf; High Hon Roll; NHS.

FISHER, JEAN; Sacramento HS; Sacramento, CA; (4); 30/370; Art Clb; Cmnty Wkr; Drama Clb; Service Clb; SADD; School Play; Cit Awd; High Hon Roll; Bio Ltr; Engl Compstn Ltr; Rep Switzrlnd Sacramento Sesqcntnnl Essy Cont 89; Mills Coll; Govt.

FISHER, JESSICA H; School Of The Arts; San Francisco, CA; (2); Girl Scts; Pep Clb; Chorus; School Musical; Stage Crew; Bsktbl; Cheerldng; Pom Pon; Chiropractic Care.

FISHER, JIM E; Los Altos HS; Los Altos, CA; (4); 1/350; Rptr Nwsp; Rep Frsh Cls; JV Bsbl; Socr; High Hon Roll; Ntl Merit SF; Rotary Awd; Val; Santa Cruz Bk Awd Excllnc Soc Studies; UC Berkeley; Journ.

FISHER, KATHERINE; Rosary HS; Fullerton, CA; (4); Church Yth Grp; Var Bsktbl; Var Swmmng; Hon Roll; Guild Audition 7 Yrs; San Diego U.

FISHER, KEVIN A; Dana Hills HS; Laguna Niguel, CA; (1); Church Yth Grp; Science Clb; Bsbl; Bsktbl; GATE Pgm.

FISHER, LARA E; Immaculate Heart HS; La Canada Flintri, CA; (3); Aud/Vis; Debate Tm; Drama Clb; Varsity Clb; Hon Roll; Natl Chrty Lg; Prtcptd Cls Up Prgrm WA DC; Eng.

FISHER, LEONARD V; Chico SR HS; Chico, CA; (3); Church Yth Grp; Church Choir; L Socr; JV Trk; Hon Roll; Pres Acad Fit Awd; Yth Delg Ro Natl Episcopalian Convention; Sccr; Engrng.

FISHER, LESLIE; Rosary HS; Fullerton, CA; (1); Science Clb; Ski Clb; Off Soph Cls; Var Swmmng; High Hon Roll; Hon Roll; Cert Of Merit Piano; Gld Audtn Piano; U Of San Diego.

FISHER, LISA M; Pine Hills JR Acad; Auburn, CA; (1); Church Yth Grp; Ed Yrbk.

FISHER, NATHAN; Centennial HS; Norco, CA; (1); Bsktbl; Bus Mgmt.

FISHER, REGAN CHRISTIAN; La Mirada HS; Norwalk, CA; (2); Church Yth Grp; Pres 4-H; Church Choir; 4-H Awd; High Hon Roll; Hon Roll; Prfct Atten Awd; Pres Acad Fit Awd; Biola U; Ed.

FISHER, RICHARD J; El Toro HS; El Toro, CA; (3); Chess Clb; Computer Clb; Arch; Arch.

FISHER, TERRI L; 29 Palms HS; Twentynine Palms, CA; (3); Sec Church Yth Grp; FBLA; SADD; Teachers Aide; VP Jr Cls; Rep Stu Cncl; JV Capt Bsktbl; L Var Sftbl; JV Var Vllybl; Hon Roll; Law.

FISHER, TIMOTHY K; Palo Alto HS; Palo Alto, CA; (2); Church Yth Grp; Cmnty Wkr; Letterman Clb; Band; Jazz Band; Mrchg Band; Ed Nwsp; Rep Soph Cls; Rep Jr Cls; Stu Cncl; Rock N Roll Band Leader; Play Svrl Instruments; UCSB; Bus.

FISHER, TRACY M; Miraleste HS; Rolling Hills, CA; (4); Am Leg Aux Girls St; Church Yth Grp; Cmnty Wkr; Spanish Clb; SADD; Teachers Aide; VICA; Stu Cncl; Dr John Clark Mem Schlrshp Awd 88-89; Outstndng Stu Recogntn Pgm; Fshn Inst Of Dsgn/Mrchnds; Dsgn.

FISHER, WENSDA M; David Starr Jordan HS; Long Beach, CA; (3); Church Yth Grp; Psych.

FISHER, YARA; Grossmont HS; El Cajon, CA; (3); 41/385; Cmnty Wkr; Nwsp; Ed Lit Mag; Stu Cncl; Hon Roll; Pres Acad Fit Awd; Spanish NHS; GEPC; Ldr At Earth Fr 1990; Freedoms Fndtn; SFSU; Stud.

FISHLEDER, AARON J; Woodland HS; Woodland, CA; (2); VP Service Clb; Treas Spanish Clb; Hon Roll; Jr NHS; Schl Imprvmnt Cmmtee; Cls Float; UC Davis; Genetics.

FISK, HOLLI A; Troy HS; Fullerton, CA; (1); Church Yth Grp; JCL; High Hon Roll; Hon Roll; Jr NHS; NHS; Rotary Awd; Natl Latin Exam Cum Laude; Troy Tech Engl I Stu Mnth; Jrnlsm.

FISK, KELLIE D; Brea Olinda HS; Fullerton, CA; (3); Church Yth Grp; Cmnty Wkr; Dance Clb; Drama Clb; French Clb; Pep Clb; JV Cheerldng; Intrml Gym; Score Keeper; Cit Awd; Teach Gym To Chldrn; Mdlng Instr & Model; Law.

FISK, LEAH; San Gorgonio HS; Highland, CA; (4); Church Choir; Hon Roll; Spanish NHS; Zonta Clb Sec; U Of CA Riverside; Law.

FISK, STEPHANIE A; Yucca Valley HS; Yucca Valley, CA; (2); Bus Profs of Am; Church Yth Grp; Math Clb; Band; Sec Soph Cls; Treas Stu Cncl; JV Cheerldng; High Hon Roll; Masonic Awd; Pres Acad Fit Awd; Pre-Law Clb; Pomona Coll; Vet.

FISKE, BRENDA; Ukiah JR Acad; Redwood Valley, CA; (2); Church Yth Grp; Cmnty Wkr; Band; Chorus; Church Choir; School Musical; Ed Nwsp; Yrbk; Sec Pres Stu Cncl; Hon Roll; U CA Davis; Vtrnrn.

FISKE, GEORGE; Skyline HS; Irvine, CA; (2); Church Yth Grp; Cmnty Wkr; Debate Tm; Chorus; Nwsp; Ed Lit Mag; Rep Frsh Cls; Rep Soph Cls; Stu Cncl; Lcrss; Speech Cntst Natl Awd & 3rd & 4th Pl Greek Orthdx Archdrcs; Natl Cncl Teachers Of Engl Awd Lit; Eastern Librl Arts.

FISKE, JASON E; Santa Ynez Valley Union HS; Santa Ynez, CA; (4); 2/172; Church Yth Grp; Service Clb; Spanish Clb; Stat Bsktbl; Var Diving; JV Var Ftbl; JV Trk; Intrml Vllybl; Lion Awd; Sal; Yth & Govt; CSF Seal Bearer; Skiing; Loma Linda U; Phys Thrpy.

FITCH, ANN; Ponderosa HS; Placerville, CA; (2); Church Yth Grp; Cmnty Wkr; Dance Clb; Rep Frsh Cls; Stu Cncl; Capt JV Cheerldng; Cit Awd; High Hon Roll; Prfct Atten Awd; Sunday Schl Tchr; Optmst Clb Spch Fnlst; Jazz Dance; Whitworth Presbyt Coll; Cnslr.

FITCH, JENNIE L; Washington HS; Fremont, CA; (3); French Clb; JA; Letterman Clb; Library Aide; Chorus; School Musical; Yrbk; Powder Puff Ftbl; Swmmng; Sci Fair-1st Pl/Grnd Prz-88; Ricks Coll.

FITCH, RYAN; Bakersfield HS; Bakersfield, CA; (2); Church Yth Grp; JA; JV Bsbl; JV Wrstlng; Hon Roll; Math Tutor; GATE Pgm; UC Irvine; Med.

FITZ, DANIELLE N; San Clemente HS; San Juan Capistra, CA; (2); Band; Drill Tm; Sec Mrchg Band; Orch; Pep Band; Pom Pon; Hon Roll; Pres Acad Fit Awd; Wind Ensmbl Symphnc Band; Georgetown; Bus Law.

FITZ MAURICE, JENNIFER C; Villa Park HS; Orange, CA; (3); French Clb; Key Clb; Off Soph Cls; Off Jr Cls; Var Socr; Vllybl; Hon Roll; NHS; Acad Hnrs Patch NEFF; UCI; Med.

FITZGERALD, ANNE E; Cordova SR HS; Rancho Cordova, CA; (3); Cmnty Wkr; Office Aide; Teachers Aide; Intrml Cheerldng; Stat Swmmng; JV Vllybl; Hon Roll; Natural Hlprs; Chico ST; Psych.

FITZGERALD, DAVID M; Bolsa Grande HS; Westminster, CA; (2); Band; Jazz Band; Mrchg Band; Orch; Pep Band; Music.

FITZGERALD, JESSICA; Oxnard HS; Oxnard, CA; (1); 14/818; JV Var Vllybl; Hon Roll; Prfct Atten Awd; Pres Acad Fit Awd; CSF; Mck Trl Clb & Tm; Fabulous Frshmn Hnr Schl Nwspr; Stanford U; Law.

FITZGERALD, MICHELLE J; Vacaville HS; Vacaville, CA; (3); Church Yth Grp; Teachers Aide; Chorus; Hon Roll; Prfct Atten Awd; Solono Coll; Math.

FITZGERALD, MISTY S; Santa Maria HS; Santa Maria, CA; (3); Church Yth Grp; FBLA; Teachers Aide; Chorus; Powder Puff Ftbl; Cit Awd; Hon Roll; Upwrd Bnd Pgm; CSF.

FITZGERALD, PAMELA E; Oakmont HS; Roseville, CA; (3); Band; Color Guard; Mrchg Band; Acadmc Merit Awd 90; Marine Bio.

FITZGIBBON, MEGAN C; Clayton Valley HS; Clayton, CA; (2); SADD; Teachers Aide; Varsity Clb; Var Socr; Pres Acad Fit Awd; Lawrence Hall Sci Biotech Symposium; CSF; Equestrian & Wnnr Amer Qrtr Horse Assn All Around Awds; Sci.

FITZGIBBONS, TERRENCE J; Loyola HS; Pasadena, CA; (2); Church Yth Grp; Bsktbl; Ftbl; Hon Roll; NEDT Awd.

FITZHERBERT, JONATHAN D; Monte Vista HS; Spring Valley, CA; (3); 4-H; Pres Jr Cls; Stu Cncl; JV Ftbl; L Var Wrstlng; MVP Jr Var Ftbl 88; Math.

FITZJERRELL, DENNIS L; Tehachapi HS; Tehachapi, CA; (3); Boy Scts; Letterman Clb; ROTC; Ski Clb; Ftbl; Trk; Wt Lftg; Hon Roll.

FITZLAFF, SHAWN; Bethel Christian HS; Lancaster, CA; (2); 6/28; Church Yth Grp; JV Bsktbl; JV Ftbl; Hon Roll; Prfct Atten Awd; CA ST U Northridge; Comp Anly.

FITZMAURICE, ANDREA; Moore JR HS; Redlands, CA; (1); Church Yth Grp; Pep Clb; Off Frsh Cls; Cheerldng; Cit Awd.

FITZMAURICE, MARCEL V; Cupertino HS; San Jose, CA; (3); JV Bsbl; Ntl Merit SF; Jr Statesmen Of Amer Chief Of Staff; Explainer Exploratorium 90; Amnesty Intl; Wrtng.

FITZPATRICK, BENJAMIN L; Morro Bay HS; Morro Bay, CA; (3); 9/238; Boy Scts; Drama Clb; JCL; Chorus; School Play; Var L Ftbl; High Hon Roll; Ntl Merit Ltr; Zoology.

FITZPATRICK, BONNIE R; Puc Prep; St Helena, CA; (4); 4/24; Church Yth Grp; Chorus; Stu Cncl; High Hon Roll; Prfct Atten Awd; Pacific Union Coll; Nrsng.

FITZPATRICK, BRIGID; Carondelet HS; San Ramon, CA; (3); Church Yth Grp; Cmnty Wkr; Ski Clb; SADD; Rep Frsh Cls; JV Socr; JV Swmmng; Hon Roll; Spanish NHS; CA Schlrshp Fed; Frgn Lang.

FITZPATRICK, CHARLES D; Rio Americano HS; Sacramento, CA; (3); Art Clb; JV Ftbl; UCLA; Bus.

FITZPATRICK, SUSAN M; Loretto HS; Sacramento, CA; (3); Church Yth Grp; Science Clb; Stu Cncl; Var Capt Bsktbl; Var L Crs Cntry; Var Capt Socr; High Hon Roll; Hon Roll; NEDT Awd; Mem Camp Fire Boys & Girls; MVP Soccer, Bsktbl, Most Sprtd Rnnr Cross Cntry; Outstndng Athlete 89-90.

FITZSIMMONS, KIRSTEN A; Paso Robles HS; Los Osos, CA; (2); 1/350; AFS; Church Yth Grp; Dance Clb; Sec Treas Girl Scts; High Hon Roll; CA Polytech ST U; Optometry.

FITZSIMMONS, MICHAEL; Ygnacio Valley HS; Concord, CA; (2); 4/427; Chess Clb; Church Yth Grp; Band; Jazz Band; Mrchg Band; Pep Band; Lit Mag; High Hon Roll; Pres Acad Fit Awd; Mock Trial; Yng Authors Cont Awd; UCLA; Eng.

FITZSIMON, JENNIFER; Temple City HS; Temple City, CA; (2); VP Pep Clb; Pres Jr Cls; JV Bsktbl; Score Keeper; JV Vllybl; High Hon Roll; Lion Awd; Pepperdine; Acctng.

FIZER, KELLY L; Roseville Joint Union HS; Roseville, CA; (3); Pep Clb; Teachers Aide; Wt Lftg; Auto Shop Achvmnt; Bus.

FLACK, JENNIFER R; Don Antonio Lugo HS; Chino, CA; (3); Church Yth Grp; VP French Clb; VP Pres Science Clb; Treas Jr Cls; Powder Puff Ftbl; Var Swmmng; Rotary Awd; Stu Advsry Cncl Pres; Stu Schl Brd; Yng Woman Of Yr; Yth Drug, Alcohol Awrnss Cngrss.

FLADING, JENNIFER L; San Marcos HS; San Marcos, CA; (2); Dance Clb; Treas Soph Cls; Var Vllybl; High Hon Roll; Hon Roll; People To People Ambs; CSF; UC-SANTA Barbara; Travel.

FLAHERTY, JIM C; Nevada Union HS; Grass Valley, CA; (3); 54/551; Boy Scts; Chess Clb; Teachers Aide; Chorus; Capt Golf; High Hon Roll; Prfct Atten Awd; MVP Awd Glf 90; CA All Leag Mdl Golf 90; 1st Pl David Oxley Memrl Jr Golf Trnmnt 90; Cert Scb Divr; UC Santa Barbara; Golf Pro.

FLAHERTY, KEVIN O; Corona Del Mar HS; Corona Del Mar, CA; (4); Aud/Vis; Computer Clb; Nwsp; Yrbk; Photogrphr Of Yr 90; Video Yrbk Editor; Brooks Inst Of Photography.

FLAHERTY, KRISTI L; Calaveras HS; Wallace, CA; (2); Church Yth Grp; Letterman Clb; Yrbk; JV Var Bsktbl; Var Trk; Capt Var Vllybl; High Hon Roll; CA Schlrshp Fdrtn-VP; Fri Night Live-Treas; Schl Rcrd-Mile 800m X Mile Relay; Med Prof.

FLAHERTY, MICHELE; Fairfield HS; Suisun City, CA; (2); Church Yth Grp; Girl Scts; Color Guard; Flag Corp; Mrchg Band; Rep Frsh Cls; JV L Swmmng; Cit Awd; Hon Roll; AF Acad; Math.

FLAHERTY, RACHEL R; Livermore HS; Livermore, CA; (1); Chess Clb; 4-H; Band; Mrchg Band; Sftbl; 4-H Awd; High Hon Roll; Cmmnd Prfrmnc-Ensmbl Grp; Mst Imprvd Sftbl Plyr; Sftbl Team-Hghst GPA.

FLAHERTY, TAMMY; William C Overfelt HS; San Jose, CA; (1); Daycare.

FLAIM, CHRISTOPHER; Beyer HS; Modesto, CA; (2); Key Clb; Math Clb; Math Tm; Science Clb; JV Crs Cntry; JV Trk; Cit Awd; High Hon Roll; Hon Roll; Piano; Comp; Rcqtbl; Engrng.

FLANAGAN, AMY C; Bullard HS; Fresno, CA; (1); Cmnty Wkr; Color Guard; Mrchg Band; Cit Awd; High Hon Roll; Prfct Atten Awd; Alg Gldn St Exam Awd; UC Berkeley.

FLANAGAN, KELLY G; Don Antonio Lugo HS; Chino, CA; (3); CA ST Fullerton.

FLANAGAN, MICHAEL C; Rio Americano HS; Sacramento, CA; (3); 72/290; Office Aide; Varsity Clb; Off Soph Cls; JV Bsbl; JV Var Bsktbl; JV Var Ftbl; JV Var Wt Lftg; High Hon Roll; Hon Roll; All-Amer Bsktbl 88, 89; All-League Bsktbl 89; UC.

FLANAGAN, MOLLY F; Woodrow Wilson HS; Long Beach, CA; (2); Aud/Vis; Church Yth Grp; German Clb; SADD; Teachers Aide; Acpl Chr; Drill Tm; Cheerldng; Cit Awd; NHS; Lost & Found HS Chrch Club; CSF; CA ST Long Beach; Human Rltns.

FLANAGAN, SHANNON; Fred C Beyer HS; Modesto, CA; (3); Math Clb; SADD; Cit Awd; Hon Roll.

FLANAGAN, VICKI; Skyline HS; Oakland, CA; (4); Key Clb; Teachers Aide; Band; Cit Awd; Diablo Valley CC; Bus.

FLANDERS, KETTI D; Simi Valley HS; Simi Valley, CA; (2); Church Yth Grp; Chorus; Ed Nwsp; JV Trk; Jr NHS.

FLANERY, KIMM; Summerville HS; Tuolumne, CA; (3); Quiz Bowl; Spanish Clb; Chorus; Treas Jr Cls; JV Cheerldng; JV Tennis; JV Trk; AFS; Genetic Engrng; Law; Genetic Engrng.

FLANNERY, CHARLIE O; Santa Barbara HS; Santa Barbara, CA; (3); Boy Scts; Rptr Nwsp; Ftbl; Trk; Ftbl Awd, Mst Inspirational Plyr; Jrnlsm Awds, Mst Likely To Become Brdcstr; USC; Elctrncs.

FLARIDA, AMY L; Norco SR HS; Corona, CA; (4); ROTC; SADD; Teachers Aide; Drill Tm; Rptr Nwsp; Rep Stu Cncl; The American U; Lawyer.

FLATE, LISA; Fairfax HS; Los Angeles, CA; (3); French Clb; Co-Capt Cheerldng; Gym; Pres Acad Fit Awd; Mock Trial Team-Attrny; Law.

FLATEN, ERIK B; Santa Monica HS; Santa Monica, CA; (3); Am Leg Boys St; Church Yth Grp; YMCA Yth & Govt.

FLAUGHER, SHERYL L; Castle Park HS; Chula Vista, CA; (1); 15/614; French Clb; Pep Clb; School Play; Variety Show; Cit Awd; High Hon Roll; Hon Roll; Prfct Atten Awd; Harvard; Law.

FLEEGE, AMY J; El Comino Fundamental HS; Carmichael, CA; (3); Church Yth Grp; Cmnty Wkr; Key Clb; Spanish Clb; SADD; Teachers Aide; Chorus; Sec Sr Cls; Var JV Cheerldng; Cit Awd; Mst Outstndnd Chrldr; Yng Repblcns; Arbcs; UNLV; Fshn Mrktng.

FLEEMAN, CASSANDRA L; Mc Farland HS; Delano, CA; (3); Drama Clb; FTA; Letterman Clb; Varsity Clb; School Play; Variety Show; Rptr Lit Mag; Capt Bsktbl; Capt Sftbl; Var Capt Vllybl; Numerous Athltc Awds Sftbl, Bsktbl & Vlybl; Many Hnr Awds Classes; Medal Eng CP Outstndng Achvt 89; CA ST Bakersfield; Tchr.

FLEET, KEVIN A; Sonora HS; La Habra, CA; (3); 14/200; Cmnty Wkr; Ski Clb; Variety Show; Powder Puff Ftbl; Swmmng; Tennis; Cit Awd; High Hon Roll; Co Cptn Water Polo Tm; VP Ski Clb; Life Grd; Swmmng & Tnns Instr; UCSD; Bus.

FLEISHCER, FLAVIA; John F Kennedy HS; Granada Hills, CA; (4); Stage Crew; Ed Lit Mag; Var Bsktbl; Var Socr; Var Sftbl; Var Trk; 3rd Pl CA St Hal Connolly Schlr Athl Awd; Gallaudet; Law.

FLEMATE, DOUGLAS R; Terra Nova HS; Pacifica, CA; (2); JV Var Ftbl; Hon Roll; Skyline Coll; Bus.

FLEMING, AMY M; Mariposa County HS; La Grange, CA; (2); Church Yth Grp; Drama Clb; Ski Clb; Teachers Aide; School Play; Stage Crew; Sec Stu Cncl; JV Bsktbl; Var Golf; Hon Roll; I Am A Shopper, I Love To Shop; I Enjoy Hanging Out With Friends; Harvard Law; Political Science.

FLEMING, BROOK A; Laguna Hills HS; Laguna Hills, CA; (4); Church Yth Grp; Key Clb; Letterman Clb; SADD; Varsity Clb; Off Jr Cls; Var Capt Tennis; High Hon Roll; Hon Roll; Stanford Natl Tnns Camp Cnslr; Baylor U; Law.

FLEMING, DAVID; Edison HS; Fresno, CA; (1); Bsbl; Hon Roll; Heart Srgn.

FLEMING, MELISSA; Springs Of Living Water Acad; Richardson Spgs, CA; (4); Chorus; Church Choir; Treas Soph Cls; Pres Jr Cls; Capt Vllybl; High Hon Roll; Hon Roll; Azus Pacific U; Pre-Law.

FLEMMING, SHANNON P; Mission Viejo HS; Mission Viejo, CA; (3); School Musical; Stat Bsktbl; Var Ftbl; JV Trk; Hon Roll; U Of CA; Psych.

FLENKER, CASSANDRA A; Dana Hills HS; Laguna Hills, CA; (1); Office Aide; French Hon Soc; Hon Roll; Pres Acad Fit Awd; UCI; Advrtsng.

FLESCHNER, VICKY; Fortuna HS; Fortuna, CA; (1); Pep Clb; Rep Frsh Cls; JV Bsktbl; Powder Puff Ftbl; Trk; Hon Roll.

FLESHER, ROBBIE D; Corona SR HS; Corona, CA; (2); 85/473; Church Yth Grp; Science Clb; Yrbk; Hon Roll; Pres Acad Fit Awd; Intr Dsgn.

FLETCHER, ALICIA SHANAY; Harbor HS; Santa Cruz, CA; (4); 3/250; AFS; Service Clb; SADD; Rep Jr Cls; Stu Cncl; Swmmng; High Hon Roll; Ntl Merit Schol; Pres Acad Fit Awd; Peer Helpr; Duke U; Intl Rltns.

FLETCHER, ANDREW W; Davis SR HS; El Macero, CA; (2); Treas Frsh Cls; Treas Stu Cncl; High Hon Roll; Pres Acad Fit Awd; Made Svrl Invstmnts Stock Market; Drw Trains For Plsr Sld Svrl Drwngs; U Of WA Seattle; Bus.

FLETCHER, KATHY A; Del Oro HS; Loomis, CA; (3); 51/266; Church Yth Grp; Drama Clb; Library Aide; Chorus; Church Choir; Var Swmmng; Hon Roll; Campfire; Bible Study; Friday Night Live.

FLETCHER, KAYDEN T; Oak Ridge HS; Cameron Park, CA; (1); Dance Clb; Ski Clb; Tennis; High Hon Roll; Hon Roll; UC Berkeley; Math.

FLETCHER, KELLY; San Lorenzo Valley HS; Scotts Valley, CA; (3); Am Leg Aux Girls St; Church Yth Grp; Debate Tm; Key Clb; Pep Clb; Spanish Clb; Stu Cncl; JV Cheerldng; Pom Pon; Tennis; Pol Sci.

FLETCHER, KENNY E; Serrano HS; Phelan, CA; (3); Church Yth Grp; Chorus; Church Choir; Crs Cntry; Socr; Hon Roll; Serrano Athl Booster Crss Cntry Insprtnl Prfmnc Awd; CA Interschlstc Fdrtn Sthrn Section Qualifier; Special Effects Artist.

FLETCHER, RONI M; Cajon HS; San Bernardino, CA; (1); Ed Lit Mag.

FLETCHER, ROYAL L; Marina HS; Huntington Beach, CA; (3); 180/461; Boy Scts; Church Yth Grp; Church Choir; Ftbl; Wt Lftg; Wrstlng; Hon Roll; Chrch Spnsrd Sprts Vlybl, Bsktbl & Sftbl 2nd In Rgn; Wrk Bike Shop.

FLICKER, JAI G; Sir Francis Drake HS; Woodacre, CA; (2); Math Clb; Varsity Clb; Var Bsktbl; JV Socr; Off Hon Roll; Off Pres Acad Fit Awd; Outstndng Achvment In Mth; Plcd In Schl Wd Mth Comp; UCLA.

FLICKER, KATIE A; San Ramon Valley HS; Danville, CA; (2); Church Yth Grp; Dance Clb; Ski Clb; School Play; Rep Soph Cls; Stat Bsbl; JV Score Keeper; Sftbl; High Hon Roll; Hon Roll; V Ski Tm; Chrldng Coach; San Barbara.

FLINDERS, MATTHEW; James Lick HS; San Jose, CA; (4); 33/280; Cmnty Wkr; Debate Tm; Drama Clb; Intnl Clb; Service Clb; Speech Tm; School Play; Pres Frsh Cls; Treas Stu Cncl; Hon Roll; Co-Chrmn-Styng Alive-Stu Pgm; ASB Commssnr-Publcty; Mock Trial; Hotel Mgt.

FLINT, COLLEEN L; Fountain Valley HS; Fountain Valley, CA; (4); 59/660; Church Yth Grp; Girl Scts; Red Cross Aide; Drill Tm; Rptr Yrbk; Off Sr Cls; Hon Roll; Distinguished Schlr; Girl Sct Gold Awd; Abilene Chrstn U; Grphc Dsgn.

FLINT, FLOYD E; Modesto HS; Modesto, CA; (2); Boy Scts; Church Yth Grp; Letterman Clb; JV Bsbl; JV Ftbl; Var Trk; JV Wt Lftg; Cit Awd; High Hon Roll; Hon Roll; Oral Roberts U; Med.

FLINT, JODEE; Los Alamitos HS; Seal Beach, CA; (4); Model UN; Sec Spanish Clb; Sec Drill Tm; School Play; Hon Roll; NHS; Ntl Merit SF; Bank Of Amer Awd For Foreign Lang; CSF; Notre Dame.

FLOCK, JENNIFER; Lincoln HS; Stockton, CA; (4); 138/536; Pres Latin Clb; 1st Fml Fgr Sktr Frm Stockton To Mk Ntnls; Fgr Sktng Instrctr In Stockton; San Joaquin Delta Coll; Sci.

FLOJO, JONATHAN R; Novato HS; Novato, CA; (2); Chrmn French Clb; Hosp Aide; Chrmn Key Clb; ROTC; Spanish Clb; Ed Nwsp; Lit Mag; High Hon Roll; Jr NHS; Pres Acad Fit Awd; Marin Humane Soc Vlntr; CSF; Renaissance Faire Actor; Bio Chem.

FLORE, KRISTIN M; Mater Dei HS; Santa Ana, CA; (2); Cmnty Wkr; Dance Clb; Drama Clb; Hosp Aide; Drill Tm; High Hon Roll; Piano.

FLORENDO, MARY ANN; San Lorenzo HS; San Leandro, CA; (4); 24/231; Cmnty Wkr; FBLA; Treas Frsh Cls; VP Stu Cncl; Var Capt Cheerldng; Var Capt Pom Pon; Tennis; High Hon Roll; Hon Roll; Northenr CA Outrigger Canoe Assn; Girls Clb Mentorship; Stu Of The Day Awd; UC Riverside; Bus Admin.

FLORES, ABEL; Roosevelt HS; Los Angeles, CA; (2); Boy Scts; Computer Clb; Math Clb; Bsbl; Bsktbl; Sftbl; Prfct Atten Awd; UC-SANTA Cruz; Crmnl Just.

FLORES, ADRIAN CORDOVA Y; Bonita Vista HS; Bonita, CA; (4); 120/540; Church Yth Grp; Teachers Aide; Var Capt Tennis; Cit Awd; Hon Roll; MVP Tennis Vrsty; 10th Tennis CIF S Sctn; Southwestern CC; Intl Bus.

FLORES, ALESTRA J; Alhambra HS; Martinez, CA; (3); Cmnty Wkr; Dance Clb; Hosp Aide; Latin Clb; Pep Clb; Spanish Clb; Cheerldng; Gov Hon Prg Awd; Hon Roll; Stu Actvts Awd Peer Spprt; Yth Educator 90-91; Psych.

FLORES, ALEX; Bonita HS; La Verne, CA; (3); Church Yth Grp; SADD; Hon Roll; Prfct Atten Awd; Cert Merit Fine Arts; Math Awd; Engrng.

FLORES, ALMA C; Lincoln Med/Hlth Prof Magnet HS; Los Angeles, CA; (4); Church Yth Grp; Cmnty Wkr; FCA; GAA; Quiz Bowl; Sec Science Clb; Varsity Clb; Church Choir; School Play; Variety Show; UCLA; Bio.

FLORES, AMY; Emerson JR HS; Davis, CA; (1); Teachers Aide; Cheerldng; Pom Pon; JV Sftbl; Hon Roll; Pediatrician.

FLORES, ANGELICA; Tulare Western HS; Tulare, CA; (3); Spanish Clb; Church Choir; Cert Of Outstndng Achvt.

FLORES, ANTHONY; Calaveras HS; Valley Springs, CA; (2); 59/250; JV Bsbl; JV Bsktbl; Var Score Keeper; Var Tennis; JV Var Wrstlng; Hon Roll; Humbolt ST; Wildlife Bio.

FLORES, AURORA; Montebello HS; Montebello, CA; (2); Dance Clb; SADD; Cheerldng; JV Crs Cntry; JV Trk; Hon Roll; CA ST Long Beach.

FLORES, BERNADETTE; Eisenhower HS; Rialto, CA; (3); Pep Clb; Drill Tm; Yrbk; Cheerldng; Mgr(s); Trk; Psycht.

FLORES, CELESTE B; Selaco HS; Montebello, CA; (3); Girl Scts; Rptr Nwsp; Pres Stu Cncl; Cheerldng; Sctry JR Natl Assc Of Deaf; CA ST U.

FLORES, CELESTE N; Woodlake Union HS; Woodlake, CA; (2); Pep Clb; Hon Roll; Maya Mexican American Youth Assoc; Coll Of The SequoiasNURSE.

FLORES, CYNTHIA J; Lindsay HS; Lindsay, CA; (2); Art Clb; Drama Clb; Drill Tm; Psych.

FLORES, DAISY V; Edison HS; Stockton, CA; (2); FBLA; Service Clb; Hon Roll; Edisons Math/Sci Magnet Pgm; Schl Recgntn In CA Golden St Exam In Geom; Engrng.

FLORES, DANIEL N; Bishop Amat Memorial HS; Azusa, CA; (3); Church Yth Grp; Teachers Aide; Var L Trk; JV Wrstlng; High Hon Roll; NHS; Pres Acad Fit Awd; 1st Pl Natl Span & Portuguese Tchrs Assn In Natl Span Exam; Loyola Marymount U; Bus Admin.

FLORES, DANIELLE E; Lincoln HS; Stockton, CA; (2); 44/568; Hosp Aide; Mu Alpha Theta; SADD; Hon Roll; Golden St Exam Hnrs Algebra, Geom; Safe Rides; Math.

FLORES, DIANA; Bishop Amat HS; La Puente, CA; (3); Drill Tm; Flag Corp; Zoology.

FLORES, DIANA L; San Jacinto HS; San Jacinto, CA; (2); Church Yth Grp; Spanish Clb; Drill Tm; Stat Trk; Hon Roll; Prfct Atten Awd; Flag & Banner; U CA Riverside; Bus.

FLORES, DIANE M; Chino HS; Chino, CA; (3); 91/594; Church Yth Grp; Drama Clb; Teachers Aide; Yrbk; Hon Roll; Princpls Hnr Roll; Corp Lawyer.

FLORES, EDGARD; Leuzinger HS; Hawthorne, CA; (2); Spanish Clb; Arch.

FLORES, EDME; Southbay Christian Schl; Mountain View, CA; (1); Church Yth Grp; Chorus; Church Choir; School Musical; Tchr Of Sun Schl At Chrch; Sng Solos At Chrch; Spk Spnsh Flntly.

FLORES, ELIZABETH; Leuzinger HS; Hawthorne, CA; (2); Spanish Clb; Var Socr; Cit Awd; Pres Acad Fit Awd; Stu Of Mnth Trophy Math, Pre-Algebra Clss; Stu Of Yr Plaque & Trophy Pre-Algebra Clss; Pediatrician.

FLORES, ELIZABETH; Sacred Heart HS; Los Angeles, CA; (3); Church Yth Grp; Cmnty Wkr; Chorus; Church Choir; Natl Spnsh Exam 3 Yrs; CA ST Long Beach; Acctng.

FLORES, ERIKA L; Colton HS; Colton, CA; (4); FBLA; FFA; Letterman Clb; Teachers Aide; Off Jr Cls; Var JV Bsktbl; JV Sftbl; Cit Awd; NHS; Pres Acad Fit Awd; Usher San Bernardino Symphny; U Of San Diego; Elec Engrng.

FLORES, ERMA L; Los Altos HS; Hacienda Hts, CA; (3); Key Clb; Bsktbl; Cheerldng; Hon Roll; Stu Senate; Accntng.

FLORES, ESMER; Alisal HS; Salinas, CA; (1); Powder Puff Ftbl; Hon Roll; U Of Santa Cruz; Intl Bus.

FLORES, ESMERALDA M; Saddle Back HS; Santa Ana, CA; (2); Drama Clb; French Clb; Red Cross Aide; Bsbl; Diving; Sftbl; Vllybl; Wt Lftg; French Hon Soc; Pres Acad Fit Awd; Sectry.

FLORES, FABIOLA; Sweetwater HS; National City, CA; (2); Cit Awd; Ntl Merit Schol; Pres Acad Fit Awd.

FLORES, FRANCINE R; Coachella Valley HS; Coachella, CA; (3); Cathacist; Church Youth Grp; Natural Helper.

FLORES, FRANK D; Coachella Valley HS; Coachella, CA; (2); JV Ftbl; JV Wt Lftg; JV Wrstlng.

FLORES, GABRIEL; Monroe HS; Mission Hills, CA; (3); Library Aide; Office Aide; Teachers Aide; Cit Awd; CSUN Northridge; Educ.

FLORES, GILBERT M; March Mountain HS; Moreno Valley, CA; (4); School Musical; Stage Crew; Variety Show; Yrbk; Bus.

FLORES, GLORIA M; Los Angeles HS; Los Angeles, CA; (3); Var Bsktbl; Var Sftbl; Cit Awd; Hon Roll; Prfct Atten Awd; Mrt Cert; ESL Mst Imprvd; Prin Hnr Roll; Cert Achvmnt; Schlrshp Cert; Schlstc Hnrs Pin; GPA Mdl; CA ST U Northridge; Cmmnctns.

FLORES, GRISELDA; La Serna HS; Whittier, CA; (3); Key Clb; Teachers Aide; Cit Awd; UC Irvine; Psych.

FLORES, GRISELDA E; Lynwood HS; Lynwood, CA; (2); 285/876; Debate Tm; Library Aide; Cit Awd; Prfct Atten Awd; Cal ST Dominquez Hills; Psych.

FLORES, GUADALUPE; Corona HS; Corona, CA; (2); French Clb; Office Aide; Teachers Aide; Sftbl; Vllybl; Hon Roll; UCLA; Bus Admin.

FLORES, HALMAR; Daniel Murphy HS; Los Angeles, CA; (1); Var Crs Cntry; Var Trk; Aviation.

FLORES, HECTOR; John H Frances Polytechnic HS; Sun Valley, CA; (2); Church Yth Grp; Service Clb; Band; Church Choir; Mrchg Band; School Musical; Hon Roll; Outstndng Stu Awd 90; CSU Northridge; Bus.

FLORES, HENRY; Gilroy HS; Gilroy, CA; (1); JV Ftbl; Wt Lftg; Hon Roll; Outstndng Schltc Athl Awd.

FLORES, JAMES J; Edison-Computech HS; Fresno, CA; (2); Band; Mrchg Band; Pep Band; Socr; Vllybl; Cit Awd; Hon Roll; CSF; Fresno Cmmty Hosp Jr Vol; St Louis Coll Of Phrmcy; Phrmst.

FLORES, JASON R; Delano HS; Delano, CA; (2); Letterman Clb; Stu Cncl; Bsbl; Ftbl; Golf; Wt Lftg; Hon Roll; UC-SAN Diego; Crmnl Law.

FLORES, JAVIER; Caruthers HS; Fresno, CA; (1); Dance Clb; Band; Jazz Band; Mrchg Band; Socr; Fresno ST; Dancing.

FLORES, JESSE; Salinas HS; Salinas, CA; (4); 36/340; Key Clb; Spanish Clb; Hon Roll; Pres Acad Fit Awd; Athl Appreciation Club; Cal Poly; Arch.

FLORES, JESSICA; Woodrow Wilson HS; Los Angeles, CA; (3); Church Yth Grp; French Clb; Explorers Club; Cal ST Long Bch; Interior Dsgn.

FLORES, JOSE DAVID; Don Bosco Technical Inst; Alhambra, CA; (2); Church Yth Grp; Off Jr Cls; JV Var Socr; Cit Awd; NHS; Deans List; MIT; Aerospace Engr.

FLORES, JOSE R; Gilroy HS; Gilroy, CA; (1); Band; Mrchg Band; Pep Band; Hon Roll; Spnsh I Cert Of Achvt; Mst Imprvd Band.

FLORES, JOSEPH O; Pater Noster HS; Los Angeles, CA; (1); 1/30; JV Ftbl; High Hon Roll; NEDT Awd; Hnrs Alg & Engl; Bus.

FLORES, JUAN F; La Puente HS; La Puente, CA; (3); Hon Roll; Bus Admin.

FLORES, LETICIA C; Rio Linda HS; Sacramento, CA; (4); 20/350; Church Yth Grp; English Clb; Pep Clb; Teachers Aide; Band; Chorus; Pres Frsh Cls; JV Bsbl; JV Bsktbl; Cit Awd; UC Davis; Psych.

FLORES, LETICIA YOLANDA; Baldwin Park HS; West Covina, CA; (4); Science Clb; Spanish Clb; Lit Mag; High Hon Roll; Prfct Atten Awd; CA Schlrshp Fdrtn Pres; Kywntts Clb Treas; Acadc Achvt Awd.

FLORES, LINDA; Regina Caeli HS; Compton, CA; (1); Latin Clb; Spanish Clb; Hon Roll.

FLORES, LISA; Saddleback HS; Santa Ana, CA; (3); FBLA; SADD; Pres Frsh Cls; Pres Soph Cls; Rep Jr Cls; Gldn St Exam Geom Hnrs 88.

FLORES, LISA R; St Joseph Girls HS; Long Beach, CA; (3); GAA; SADD; Var Capt Socr; Hon Roll; Clb Sccr St Cup Wnnr 90; Sports Med.

FLORES, LUDWING; Leuzinger HS; Inglewood, CA; (3); Art Clb; Var Bsbl; Var Bsktbl; Var Ftbl; Var Socr; Var Wrstlng; Prfct Atten Awd.

FLORES, LUIS; Tulare Western HS; Tulare, CA; (4); Cmnty Wkr; Teachers Aide; Varsity Clb; JV Bsbl; JV Ftbl; Score Keeper; Var Capt Wrstlng; Hon Roll; Free Style Wrstlng; Greco Roman Wrstlng; Coll Of Sequias; Vet.

FLORES, MARIA DEL CARMEN; Baldwin Park HS; Baldwin Park, CA; (3); Pep Clb; SADD; Lit Mag; Treas Stu Cncl; Stat Bsbl; JV Cheerldng; Hon Roll; Pentathlon Team; CSF Club; Law.

FLORES, MARIA F; Adrian Wilcox HS; Santa Clara, CA; (3); Drama Clb; GAA; JA; Latin Clb; Pep Clb; Spanish Clb; Varsity Clb; VICA; Chorus; Stage Crew; Foothill Coll; Dntl Hygne.

FLORES, MARIA R; Bishop Amat HS; Baldwin Park, CA; (2); Spanish Clb; Hon Roll; Prfct Atten Awd; 1st & 3rd Span Natl Exams; 2nd Hnrs Span II Awd.

FLORES, MERCEDES J; Notre Dame Acad; Los Angeles, CA; (3); Service Clb; Spanish Clb; SADD; Cit Awd; Hon Roll; Spnsh Clb Sec; Northridge U.

FLORES, MICHAEL L; Cantwell HS; Commerce, CA; (3); Drama Clb; Phtg Yrbk; Lit Mag; Intrml Bsbl; Stat Bsktbl; Intrml Ftbl; Intrml Sftbl; Var Trk; Wt Lftg; Intrml Wrstlng; Alumni Assn Tuition Grant; Host & Tour Guide To Japanese Stu; CSF; U Of Sthrn CA; Comp Grphs Dsgn.

FLORES, MONIQUE M; Bakersfield Adventist Acad; Bakersfield, CA; (2); Sec Church Yth Grp; Drama Clb; Teachers Aide; Band; Chorus; Sec Stu Cncl; Pres Acad Fit Awd; Cmnty Wkr; Office Aide; Hon Roll; Choral Awd 89-90; AJY Pathfnd Team Cnslr; Gospel Grp Soprano; Med.

FLORES, MONIQUE V; Rio Mesa HS; Little Rock, CA; (1); Band; Mrchg Band; JV Trk; UCLA; Pediatrics.

FLORES, NATHANIEL; Tulare Union HS; Tulare, CA; (2); Band; Jazz Band; Mrchg Band; Var Diving; Hon Roll; Drumline.

FLORES, NORMA; Lompoc HS; Lompoc, CA; (2); JV Bsktbl; Upwrd Bound Pgm; UCLA; Dancer.

FLORES, PEDRO L; Seaside HS; Ft Ord, CA; (3); Dance Clb; ROTC; Color Guard; Drill Tm; JV Ftbl; High Hon Roll; NHS; Pres Acad Fit Awd; Superior Jr Cadet; JROTC Battalion Cmmdr; Air Force Acad; Med.

FLORES, PETER K; San Bernardino HS; San Bernardino, CA; (2); Chess Clb; Church Yth Grp; Computer Clb; German Clb; Pres Math Clb; Quiz Bowl; Scholastic Bowl; Teachers Aide; High Hon Roll; Hon Roll; Grmn, Math Natl Hnr Soc; MESA; Odyssey Of Mnd; Electrnc Engrng.

FLORES, PHILLIP; Cantwell HS; San Gabriel, CA; (2); Rptr Lit Mag; JV Bsbl; High Hon Roll; Hon Roll; CA ST Polytech U; Arch Engnrg.

FLORES, RACHEL; Montebello HS; Montebello, CA; (3); Acpl Chr; Chorus; Hon Roll; Prfct Atten Awd.

FLORES, REBECCA; Elk Grove HS; Elk Grove, CA; (3); Dance Clb; FBLA; Spanish Clb; SADD; Hon Roll; CSF; U Of CA Davis Outrch Pgm; Psych.

FLORES, RENE; Cantwell HS; Los Angeles, CA; (1); Capt Bsktbl; JV Ftbl; Hon Roll; Archtct.

FLORES, RICARDO L; Bassett HS; La Puente, CA; (3); Teachers Aide; Hon Roll; NHS; Cultrl Exchng Clb Treas; Gldn St Exm 1st Yr Alg Hnrs; Upward Bound Stu 88-90; Comp Sci.

FLORES, RICHIE A; Fremont HS; Sunnyvale, CA; (2); Bsbl; Ftbl; MVP Bsbl.

FLORES, ROBERTA; Western HS; Stanton, CA; (4); Church Yth Grp; Treas French Clb; Chorus; Church Choir; Ed Nwsp; Hon Roll; NHS; Schl Rlgs Educ 1st Grd Tchr; Mount St Marys Coll; Nurse.

FLORES, ROBERTO; Oak Grove HS; San Jose, CA; (4); Church Yth Grp; Computer Clb; Math Clb; Math Tm; Var Crs Cntry; Var Socr; I Am Very Involved With Sports; San Jose St U; Aerospace Engr.

FLORES, ROBERTO; Watsonville HS; Watsonville, CA; (3); 10/600; Math Clb; Varsity Clb; Var Capt Bsbl; Var Capt Ftbl; JV Var Wt Lftg; High Hon Roll; Hon Roll; Prfct Atten Awd; MFSA; CSF.

FLORES, ROSALVA; Buena Park HS; Buena Park, CA; (1); Cert Mrt Exclnce Frnch; Psych.

FLORES, ROSIE M; Palo Verde HS; Blythe, CA; (3); Letterman Clb; Teachers Aide; Chorus; Mgr(s); Score Keeper; Mgr Sftbl; Mgr Vllybl; Hon Roll; Trvl Agt.

FLORES, ROSLINA E; Polytechnic HS; N Hollywood, CA; (2); Drill Tm; Ed Yrbk; Off Frsh Cls; UCLA; Bus.

FLORES, RUBEN; Birmingham HS; Van Nuys, CA; (4); 112/515; Teachers Aide; JV Var Bsbl; JV Var Crs Cntry; Hon Roll; UC Berkeley; Poltcl Sci.

FLORES, RUBEN T; Calexico HS; Calexico, CA; (2); UCSD; Dentist.

FLORES, SERGIO L; Corona HS; Corona, CA; (3); Church Yth Grp; Spanish Clb; JV Ftbl; JV Trk; JV Wrstlng; Cit Awd; Karate.

FLORES, SOCORRO; Notre Dame Acad; Los Angeles, CA; (3); Church Yth Grp; Spanish Clb; SADD; Stage Crew; Crs Cntry; Socr; Cit Awd; Hon Roll; Arch.

FLORES, SONIA E; Fontana HS; Fontana, CA; (3); Band; Mrchg Band; Sftbl; Trk; Vllybl; Hon Roll; Cal Poly; Arch.

FLORES, SONIA L; Sanger HS; Sanger, CA; (2); Latin Clb; Nwsp; Fresno ST Coll; Vet.

FLORES, TERESA; Valley HS; Santa Ana, CA; (3); Quiz Bowl; DAR Awd; High Hon Roll; Jr NHS; Pres Acad Fit Awd; MESA Clb; Partners Coll Clb; Capt Dance Tm.

FLORES, TERESA M; Bishop Amat Memorial HS; La Puente, CA; (1); Church Yth Grp; Drill Tm; Vlntr Hpl 90 Rose Parade Flts; US Navy; Med.

FLORES, VERONICA; Mountain Empire JR/Sr HS; Tecate, CA; (3); Art Clb; VP Spanish Clb; SADD; Teachers Aide; Rgnl Ocptnl Pgm Outstndng Stu Awd, Job Srch Unit; Bilingl Tutor Awd; VP Spring Fstvl; San Diego ST U; Intl Law.

FLORES, YILSEN J; Adrian Wilcox HS; Sunnyvale, CA; (2); 116/400; Church Yth Grp; Fld Hcky; De Anza Coll; Scl Wrkr.

FLORES, ZADICK; Pasadena HS; Pasadena, CA; (2); Church Yth Grp; Acpl Chr; Chorus; School Musical; School Play; Variety Show; Hon Roll; Pasadena City Coll; Med.

FLORES ULIBAS, EFRIEM A; Rio Linda SR HS; Sacramento, CA; (3); Crs Cntry; Ftbl; Trk; Art; CSUS; Lbrl Stds.

FLORES-ROSS, KATRINA V; Temple City HS; Temple City, CA; (2); Church Yth Grp; Cit Awd; Hon Roll; Pres Acad Fit Awd; Grls Leag; Dns Lst; Prncpls Lst; UC Berkeley; Bus.

FLOREZ, GLORIA; Redwood HS; Visalia, CA; (3); Church Yth Grp; Band; Mrchg Band; Var Diving; Var Socr; Hon Roll; Phys Thrpy.

FLOREZ, GUADALUPE R; Indio HS; Indio, CA; (3); 9/420; Computer Clb; Drama Clb; FFA; Science Clb; Teachers Aide; Band; Mrchg Band; School Play; Capt Swmmng; Cit Awd; Future Doctors Of Vet Med; CSF; UC Davis; Vet.

FLOREZ, TINA RENEE; Fontana HS; Fontana, CA; (2); #213 In Class; Ski Clb; VP Frsh Cls; Sec Soph Cls; Sec Jr Cls; Stu Cncl; Cheerldng; Mgr(s); Hon Roll; Sftbl; Wrtng Poems; Mt Sac JC; Bus.

FLORIANI, LUCAS; Mater Dei HS; Huntington Beach, CA; (4); SADD; Stu Cncl; Var Swmmng; NHS; Schl Liason With Cnty Drug Awareness Pgm; U CA San Diego.

FLORIN, MEDA A; Clovis HS; Clovis, CA; (2); Hosp Aide; Letterman Clb; Vllybl; High Hon Roll; Hon Roll; Pres Acad Fit Awd; CA Schlstc Fed 2 Yrs; Ped.

FLOSI, CELESTE; Saint Francis HS; Santa Clara, CA; (3); 29/289; Service Clb; SADD; Nwsp; Yrbk; High Hon Roll; NHS; CSF Offcr; Tutrng Clb; Engrng.

FLOURNOY, ROBYN C; Leuzinger HS; Lawndale, CA; (3); Dance Clb; GAA; Pep Clb; Spanish Clb; Var Cheerldng; Var Crs Cntry; Var Capt Trk; Cit Awd; Hon Roll; NHS; UCLA; Law.

FLOYD, AMY A; Fontana HS; Fontana, CA; (2); Key Clb; High Hon Roll; Hon Roll; Pres Acad Fit Awd; Friday Night Live; SADD; CSF; Engl.

FLOYD, CLARK J; Sutter Union HS; Yuba City, CA; (3); 3/78; Am Leg Boys St; Treas Drama Clb; Intnl Clb; Spanish Clb; School Play; Variety Show; Bsktbl; High Hon Roll; Hon Roll; Rotary Awd; Humboldt ST; Bus Adm.

FLOYD, DEREK E; St Patrick-St Vincent HS; Benicia, CA; (2); Letterman Clb; Varsity Clb; Bsktbl; Ftbl; Wt Lftg; Hon Roll.

FLOYD, JACKIE; Santa Maria HS; Santa Maria, CA; (4); Drama Clb; JA; Chorus; Stage Crew; Powder Puff Ftbl; Socr; Hon Roll; Prfct Atten Awd; CSF Clb; Alan Hancock Coll.

FLOYD, KARI; Brawley Union HS; Brawley, CA; (3); Church Yth Grp; Rep SADD; Stage Crew; Stat Ftbl; Hon Roll; VP Soph Cls; Rep Stu Cncl; Ldrshp; Alt Schl Brd Rep; San Diego ST Coll; Psych.

FLOYD, LESLIE; Shasta HS; Redding, CA; (2); Teachers Aide; Variety Show; JV Vllybl; UCSB; Writer.

FLOYD, SHANNON M; Miramonte HS; Moraga, CA; (1); Girl Scts; Hon Roll; Natl Charity Leag Vlntr; Tnns; Houses Frgn Exchng Stu; UCSB; Marine Bio.

FLOYD, TAVARI R; Westlake HS; Westlake Vil, CA; (4); 44/465; Dance Clb; High Hon Roll; Pres Acad Fit Awd; St Schlr; Frshmn, JV & Var Chrldr; Frshmn Hmcmng Princess; Vol Spec Olympics; U AZ; Bus Admin.

FLOYD, TIM D; Nevada Union HS; Grass Valley, CA; (3); 15/460; Church Yth Grp; Band; Pep Band; JV Var Bsbl; Bsktbl; JV Ftbl; Var Socr; Intrml Sftbl; Trk; High Hon Roll; Tchng.

FLUEGGE, GLENN K; Orange Glen HS; Valley Center, CA; (3); 5/458; Church Yth Grp; Spanish Clb; Varsity Clb; Pres Stu Cncl; JV Var Ftbl; Powder Puff Ftbl; Wt Lftg; JV Var Wrstlng; High Hon Roll; Schlr Sthltc Awd Ftbl & Wrstlng; Concordia Coll; Ministry.

FLUITT, STEPHANIE E; Yucaipa HS; Yucaipa, CA; (1); Church Yth Grp; FBLA; Library Aide; Hon Roll; U Redlands.

FLUM, JASON; Chino HS; Ontario, CA; (2); FCA; JV Bsbl; Var L Ftbl; JV Var Wt Lftg; Hon Roll; Water Skiing; Srfng; Whos Who Amng Amer Hgh Schl Stu Hnr; USC; Ftbll Plyr Bus.

FLUMERFELT, LISA; Hawthorne HS; Hawthorne, CA; (2); Library Aide; Yrbk; Cit Awd; Diaconians Svc Clb; APPI; Hnrs Clss Spsnh, Algb, Engl, Bio; Stanford U; Psychlgy.

FLYGARE, GLENN L; Armijo HS; Suisun City, CA; (2); Boy Scts; Church Yth Grp; Varsity Clb; Band; Color Guard; Jazz Band; Mrchg Band; Pep Band; U Of Pacific; Music.

FLYNN, ERICA C; Norco HS; Norco, CA; (3); #18 In Class; Model UN; Sec Spanish Clb; Yrbk; Bsktbl; Powder Puff Ftbl; JV Sftbl; JV Tennis; High Hon Roll; Pres Acad Fit Awd; Hnr Crt; Girls Leag Club; Acadmc Dcthln; Pre Med.

FLYNN, JENNIFER; Garces Memorial HS; Bakersfield, CA; (4); 6/114; Am Leg Aux Girls St; French Clb; Pres JA; Sec Key Clb; Treas Ski Clb; Powder Puff Ftbl; Var L Tennis; High Hon Roll; Mock Trail; Bus.

FLYNN, KRISTY L; Serrano HS; Phelan, CA; (3); 32/248; Church Yth Grp; Drama Clb; Model UN; Stage Crew; Off Stu Cncl; JV Bsktbl; Var Mgr(s); Hon Roll; Spanish NHS; Law.

FLYNN, RAMIE H; Shasta HS; Redding, CA; (2); Chorus; Cheerldng; Powder Puff Ftbl; Sftbl; Vllybl; Hon Roll; Pres Acad Fit Awd.

FLYNN, SARAH R; Montgomery HS; Santa Rosa, CA; (3); Treas FBLA; Hosp Aide; Treas SADD; Chorus; Stu Cncl; Stat Wrstlng; High Hon Roll; Bus Stu Wk; Stu Rep Adv Cmmtte Bus Dept; Prins Awd 9th Grade; Sacramento ST; Bus.

FLYNN, SUSAN; Notre Dame Acad; Inglewood, CA; (3); Science Clb; Spanish Clb; JV Var Bsktbl; Cit Awd; High Hon Roll; NHS; Sunshine Leag 88-89 Hnrb Mntn Bsktbl; Comp Sci.

FLYNN, TIMOTHY H; Glendora HS; Glendora, CA; (3); 72/375; Boy Scts; English Clb; Spanish Clb; Stu Cncl; JV Capt Cheerldng; Var Capt Ftbl; High Hon Roll; Hnr Guard, All CIF 1st Tm Ftbl 1990; Bus Adm.

FOBBER, ANGELA FRANCES; Ygnacio Valley HS; Walnut Creek, CA; (3); Church Yth Grp; Dance Clb; Drama Clb; Teachers Aide; Thesps; Church Choir; School Play; Stage Crew; Bst Actrss In Drama 1 Act Awd; Diablo Vly Coll; Theatre.

FOBBS, DENNEAH; San Joaquin Memorial HS; Clovis, CA; (1); French Clb; Hosp Aide; Service Clb; Ski Clb; Spanish Clb; JV Cheerldng; Powder Puff Ftbl; J R Metropolitan Museum Clb; Yale; Law.

FOBI, TAY A; Don Antonio Lugo HS; Chino, CA; (3); 60/650; Chorus; Pres Stu Cncl; Score Keeper; L Hon Roll; Med.

FOCKAERT, ABE I; Eureka HS; Eureka, CA; (1); Ski Clb; Pres Soph Cls; Bsbl; Bsktbl; Wt Lftg; Hon Roll; AZ ST U; Contractor.

FODOR, ALEXANDER M; St Marys HS; Stockton, CA; (2); Debate Tm; NFL; Speech Tm; Band; Stage Crew; Rep Nwsp; Exchng Stu Belgium; Kayaking; Play Guitar Ska/Reggae Band; Editor.

FOGAL, CHRISTIA; San Lorenzo HS; San Lorenzo, CA; (2); GAA; Ski Clb; SADD; Treas Band; Jazz Band; Bsktbl; Cheerldng; Pom Pon; Hon Roll; San Jose ST U; Sci.

FOGARTY, SHANA D; South San Francisco HS; South San Francis, CA; (2); Hosp Aide; SADD; Color Guard; Pres Acad Fit Awd; U CA San Fran; Med.

FOGEL, JESSICA; Temecula Valley HS; Temecula, CA; (3); 16/246; Pep Clb; Cheerldng; Trk; High Hon Roll; Hon Roll; Schl Mascot; Pep Squad Pres & VP; San Diego ST U; Engr.

FOGEL, MICHAEL J; San Gorgonio HS; Highland, CA; (3); English Clb; Teachers Aide; Band; Jazz Band; Mrchg Band; Law.

FOGL, JOHANNA L; Notre Dame HS; Redwood City, CA; (2); Hosp Aide; Hon Roll; Aquacades Water Ballet; Bus.

FOGLIATTI, DAVID W; De Anza HS; El Sobrante, CA; (3); Ski Clb; Rep Jr Cls; Off Sr Cls; Ftbl; Trk; Wt Lftg; High Hon Roll; Hon Roll; Schlr Athlt; Physcl Therapy.

FOIN, ERIKA M; Davis SR HS; Davis, CA; (4); 70/365; Dance Clb; Key Clb; Library Aide; Band; Chorus; Orch; Lit Mag; Pres Acad Fit Awd; Drama Clb; English Clb; Acad Decthln; Jr Statesman Of Amer; Lewis & Clark Coll.

FOK, REYNA; Abraham Lincoln HS; San Francisco, CA; (4); 27/440; Church Yth Grp; Cmnty Wkr; Service Clb; Sec Jr Cls; VP Stu Cncl; Var Sftbl; Var L Tennis; Hon Roll; UC Davis; Bio.

FOLENDORF, ANGELA C; Analy HS; Sebastopol, CA; (3); 7/273; Church Yth Grp; 4-H; Var Trk; JV Var Vllybl; High Hon Roll; Hon Roll; Cnslr YMCA; USVBA; Educ.

FOLEY, CHRISTOPHER M; Antelope Valley HS; Lancaster, CA; (3); Var Bsbl; Var Golf; Var Socr; JV Wrstlng; CA Poly Sn Luis Obispo; Arch.

FOLEY, CIARAN M; Capistrano Valley HS; Mission Viejo, CA; (4); Computer Clb; FBLA; Band; Drm Mjr(t); Jazz Band; Mrchg Band; Orch; Pep Band; 2nd Pl St-FBLA Comp Cncpts; Marine Corps Musical Excllnc Awd; Bank Of Amer Achvt Awd-Comp; U CA Irvine; Comp Sci.

FOLEY, JESSICA T; Liberty Union HS; Danville, CA; (1); Bsktbl; Sftbl; Hon Roll; N Coast Section, CIF Distngshd Schlstc Team Bsktbl & Sftbl Awd; CA U Berkley; Jrnlsm.

FOLEY, MARK; Benicia HS; Benicia, CA; (2); Boy Scts; Church Yth Grp; Band; Jazz Band; Mrchg Band; School Musical; JV Bsktbl; JV Socr; High Hon Roll; Rotary Awd; BYU; Med.

FOLEY, MATTHEW D; California Lutheran HS; Garden Grove, CA; (1); Church Yth Grp; Chorus; Stu Cncl; JV Capt Bsktbl; High Hon Roll; Prfct Atten Awd; Knowledge Master Open.

FOLEY, THOMAS; Liberty Union HS; Bethel Island, CA; (3); 15/339; Teachers Aide; Stu Cncl; Var JV Ftbl; Wt Lftg; Hon Roll; NHS; U Of The Pacific; Engrng.

FOLKS, CHRISTY S; Coalunga HS; Coalinga, CA; (4); Library Aide; SADD; Teachers Aide; Band; Mrchg Band; Nwsp; Yrbk; Cit Awd; High Hon Roll; Hon Roll; Asst Ed Yrbk 88-89; Ed 89-90; Wrkd Part Time Since Soph Yr; Bank Of Amer Awd In Comm; Bus Awd Also; Cal Poly; Vet Med.

FOLMAR, MICKI; Newport Christian HS; Irvine, CA; (4); 2/13; Scholastic Bowl; Chorus; School Play; Ed Nwsp; Rep Frsh Cls; Rep Sr Cls; Stu Cncl; Var Cheerldng; High Hon Roll; Ntl Merit SF; Theatre.

FOLSOM, BRENT; Foothill HS; Santa Ana, CA; (3); 17/328; Aud/Vis; Church Yth Grp; Cmnty Wkr; Band; Mrchg Band; Pep Band; Hon Roll; NHS; Pres Acad Fit Awd.

FOLSOM, CYNTHIA L; Ramona HS; Ramona, CA; (2); Church Yth Grp; Cmnty Wkr; Dance Clb; Drama Clb; GAA; Acpl Chr; Band; Chorus; Church Choir; School Musical; Fund Raisers; Child Guidance Cnslr.

FOLSOM, SCOTT; Lower Lake HS; Kelseyville, CA; (3); 4/120; Drama Clb; Pep Clb; Band; Jazz Band; VP Orch; Pep Band; School Play; Stage Crew; Ed Nwsp; Stu Cncl; Odyssey Of The Mind Clb Pres & St Wnnrs; Natl Yth Ldrshp Conf Schlr; Hnr Band; UC Davis; Physician.

FOLTZ, NANCY; Vintage HS; Vallejo, CA; (3); Church Yth Grp; Cmnty Wkr; DECA; Teachers Aide; Stage Crew; Capt Cheerldng; Masonic Awd; Worthy Advisor Rainbow Girls; Span.

FOMTAINE, SHAWN M; Bassett HS; Valinda, CA; (2); Temple Yth Grp; High Hon Roll; UCLA; Pediatrcn.

FONBUENA, RICHARD C; Rio Vista HS; Rio Vista, CA; (3); FFA; Varsity Clb; Co-Ed Yrbk; Var L Bsbl; Var L Bsktbl; Var L Ftbl; Var L Trk; JV Var Wt Lftg; Hon Roll; Prfct Atten Awd; Block RV; Pro Athl.

FONCERRADA, LISA E; Bonita Vista HS; Bonita, CA; (1); 12/537; Girl Scts; Model UN; Chorus; Tennis; Cit Awd; High Hon Roll; Pres Acad Fit Awd; Phy.

FONG, ANETT W K; Oakland HS; Oakland, CA; (2); Math Clb; Engr.

FONG, BARRY; Abraham Lincoln HS; San Francisco, CA; (2); San Francisco ST U; Comp.

FONG, CHUEN-MEI; El Dorado HS; Fullerton, CA; (3); 28/317; Hosp Aide; Aud/Vis; Var Bsktbl; High Hon Roll; Schl Rcgntn Golden St Exam 1st Yr Alg; Dstngshd Schlr; CIF Acad Tm Champ; CSF; UC San Diego; Sports Med.

FONG, DEBBIE; Abraham Lincoln HS; San Francisco, CA; (4); Hosp Aide; Office Aide; Service Clb; Teachers Aide; Ed Yrbk; Rep Frsh Cls; Rep Soph Cls; Rep Jr Cls; Rep Sr Cls; Sec Stu Cncl; San Francisco ST U; Acctnt.

FONG, ELAINE A; Calipatria HS; Niland, CA; (4); 4/75; FBLA; FHA; Pep Clb; Spanish Clb; SADD; Teachers Aide; Rep Frsh Cls; Rep Soph Cls; Off Sr Cls; JV Vllybl; CA ST Polytech U Pomona; Buss.

FONG, ELEANOR; Lowell HS; San Francisco, CA; (3); Debate Tm; French Clb; German Clb; Science Clb; Speech Tm; Chorus; School Musical; Swing Chorus; Yrbk; Americanism Essay For Fleet Reserve Assn; UC Davis.

FONG III, ERNEST K S; Tehachapi HS; Tehachapi, CA; (4); 11/148; Boy Scts; Church Yth Grp; Computer Clb; French Clb; Key Clb; Math Tm; Band; Crs Cntry; Trk; High Hon Roll.

FONG, EVA S; John F Kennedy SR HS; Sacramento, CA; (2); Art Clb; Teachers Aide; Hon Roll; Tchr.

FONG, GAIL; Arcadia HS; Arcadia, CA; (2); 200/599; Dance Clb; Drill Tm; Yrbk; Var Trk; Hon Roll; Prfct Atten Awd; Pres Acad Fit Awd; Jnr Statemn Assn; UCLA; Bus.

FONG, GENEVIE; Galileo HS; San Francisco, CA; (1); Teachers Aide; Cit Awd; High Hon Roll; Prfct Atten Awd; Math.

FONG, JACKIE; Liberty Union HS; Brentwood, CA; (2); Church Yth Grp; SADD; High Hon Roll; Hon Roll; Vlntr; UC Davis; Vet Med.

FONG, JOE; Mira Mesa HS; San Diego, CA; (3); Acad Hnr Awd; Herbert Hoover HS Cert Awd; Comp Sci.

FONG, JULIA S; Lowell HS; San Francisco, CA; (3); Church Yth Grp; Cmnty Wkr; Service Clb; Church Choir; Orch; Var L Crs Cntry; Var L Trk; NHS; CSF.

FONG, KIM; Costa Mesa HS; Costa Mesa, CA; (2); 19/280; Spanish Clb; JV Cheerldng; High Hon Roll; Opt Clb Awd; Miss Amer Coed Pgnt; Hmcmng 89; Walk Amer; Med.

FONG, LAWRENCE C; Chaminade College Prep; Chatsworth, CA; (3); Cmnty Wkr; JV Bsktbl; Mech Engr.

FONG, LISA; Bishop Amat HS; San Pimas, CA; (3); Co-Capt Drill Tm; Hon Roll; Blck Schlstc Achvt Clb; 2nd Hnrs Indl Arts; Psych.

FONG, MELINDA M; Lowell HS; San Francisco, CA; (2); Church Yth Grp; Cmnty Wkr; Church Choir; Mgr(s); Vllybl; MVP-VLLYBL 88; Bst Mgr-Vllybl-89.

FONG, MICHAEL T; Whitney HS; Cerritos, CA; (3); Cmnty Wkr; French Clb; JA; Key Clb; Latin Clb; Ed Nwsp; High Hon Roll; NHS; Sal; Jr Hnr Guard; Natl Merit Schlr.

FONG, RAYMOND; La Serna HS; Whittier, CA; (2); 17/450; Latin Clb; Tennis; Cit Awd; High Hon Roll; Hon Roll; NHS; Prfct Atten Awd; SADD; CA Tech; Engrng.

FONG, RAYMOND M; Bishop O'dowd HS; Alameda, CA; (2); JV Crs Cntry; JV Trk; Hon Roll.

FONG, STEPHANIE; John F Kennedy HS; Sacramento, CA; (3); 98/476; Art Clb; Church Yth Grp; French Clb; FBLA; Teachers Aide; School Musical; Intrml Tennis; Intrml JV Vllybl; Prideship; Elections Cmmtte; UCSD; Pre-Med.

FONG, STEVEN G; Acalanes HS; Lafayette, CA; (4); Spanish Clb; SADD; Varsity Clb; Var Crs Cntry; Var Capt Tennis; JV Trk; Hon Roll; Yth Educators; JSA Summer Sch Stanford U; Congressional Yth Ldrshp Cncl; U CA Berkeley; Bus.

FONG, TONY N; C K Mc Clatchy HS; Sacramento, CA; (4); 29/356; Hon Roll; 4.0 GPA; Prfct Atten; Sacramento City Coll; Math.

FONG, WENDY; International Studies Acad; San Francisco, CA; (3); Drama Clb; Thesps; School Play; Hon Roll; Jrnlsm.

FONG, WENDY X; George Washington HS; San Francisco, CA; (3); Cmnty Wkr; Math Clb; Science Clb; Service Clb; Teachers Aide; High Hon Roll; CA Schlrshp Fdrtn; Gldn St Exam-Hgh Hnrs 1st Yr Alg; Gldn St Exam Hnrs Geom.

FONS, TRACEE L; Colfax HS; Colfax, CA; (2); 58/197; Sierra Coll; Bus.

FONSECA, BERTHA M; Bakersfield HS; Bakersfield, CA; (4); Office Aide; Teachers Aide; Off Sr Cls; Lw Enfrcmt Ofcr.

FONSECA, SEVERO; John H Francis Polytechnic HS; Arleta, CA; (3); Latin Clb; Bsbl; JV Bsktbl; Cal Luthern; Lawyer.

FONSECA, SYLVIA; Rio Mesa HS; Oxnard, CA; (2); 93/401; Latin Clb; Score Keeper; Rnssnc Pgm Hnr.

FONTAINE, DEBORAH; Palisades HS; Los Angeles, CA; (3); Dance Clb; JA; SADD; Teachers Aide; Temple Yth Grp; Chorus; Crs Cntry; High Hon Roll; Hon Roll; Rotary Awd; CSF; Palisades Rotary Wrtng Cont 1st Pl Wnnr; Bus Admin.

FONTAINE, FRIEDA; Palisades HS; Los Angeles, CA; (3); JA; Teachers Aide; Temple Yth Grp; Chorus; Crs Cntry; High Hon Roll; Hon Roll; Rotary Awd; CSF; Bus Admin.

FONTAINE, LAURA E; Rio Americano HS; Fair Oaks, CA; (3); Church Yth Grp; Red Cross Aide; SADD; Church Choir; Ed Yrbk; Sec Sr Cls; JV Var Socr; JV Vllybl; Pres Acad Fit Awd; Involved In Galena Street East A Performing Group; Like To Waterski; Windsurf; Snow Ski; Brigham Young U; Interior Dsgn.

FONTANA, ANNE L; Sutter Union HS; Yuba City, CA; (3); 8/79; FBLA; Girl Scts; ROTC; Band; Mrchg Band; Powder Puff Ftbl; Hon Roll; CSF; Girl Sct Gold Awd; Yuba CC; Acctg.

FONTANA, MARIE; Bishop Amat Memorial HS; Glendora, CA; (4); 38/398; Church Yth Grp; GAA; L Capt Socr; L Capt Vllybl; High Hon Roll; Hon Roll; NHS; CSF; Most Ath Cls 90; Rookie Yr; UC-BERKELEY; Math.

FONTES, BRENT M; Alisal HS; Salinas, CA; (3); FBLA; High Hon Roll; Hon Roll; Prfct Atten Awd; Amnsty Intl; Voygrs; Chem.

FONTES, EMILY; Hilmar Sr HS; Hilmar, CA; (1); Church Yth Grp; SADD; VP Frsh Cls; Var Swmmng; Var Trk; High Hon Roll; AFS; GAA; Bsktbl; Cheerldng; Top 12% Schl; Csf Club 90.

FONTES, JULIE; Bullard HS; Central Point, OR; (2); Ski Clb; School Play; High Hon Roll; Hon Roll; Frsno ST; Bus.

FOOTE, JENNIFER L; Bishop Union HS; Bishop, CA; (3); Chorus; Var JV Sftbl; Var Tennis; Hon Roll; Prfct Atten Awd; Engrng.

FOOTE, TANNYA R; Oroville HS; Oroville, CA; (3); Intnl Clb; Band; Flag Corp; Mrchg Band; Pep Band; School Play; Var Socr; Stat Wrstlng; Hon Roll; Grad Cmmtte; Chico ST; Comp Sci.

FORAN, ANNETTE; Norco HS; Norco, CA; (3); Church Yth Grp; Office Aide; Pres Teachers Aide; Church Choir; School Play; Ed Nwsp; Hon Roll; UCLA; Teach Handcppd Chldrn.

FORBES, KYRIE; Santa Cruz HS; Santa Cruz, CA; (2); Hon Roll; Undrgrad Awd Engl; Work Part Time; Achvt In Art Ornttn Awd.

FORBES, SARAH A; Mt Carmel HS; San Diego, CA; (2); Teachers Aide; Hon Roll; ASB Stu Standout Awd 90; Tchr CA Ballet Schl; Apprntce CA Ballet Co.

FORCEY, KATHRYN; Santa Rosa HS; Santa Rosa, CA; (4); 42/520; Spanish Clb; SADD; Teachers Aide; Chorus; School Musical; School Play; High Hon Roll; Hon Roll; Dole Schlrshp; Whittier Coll; Interior Dsgnr.

FORCINA, ANDREW A; Do Antonio Lugo HS; Chino Hills, CA; (2); Letterman Clb; Varsity Clb; JV Ftbl; Var Trk; Cit Awd; High Hon Roll; Hon Roll; Jr NHS; NHS; Gldn Cnqst Span Awd; Lawyer.

FORD, ARETHA T; Inglewood HS; Inglewood, CA; (2); Church Yth Grp; Chorus; Church Choir; Drill Tm; JETS Awd; Santa Barbara; Med.

FORD, BRYAN A; Rio Lindo Adventist Acad; Provo, UT; (3); 2/50; Computer Clb; Off Soph Cls; Comp Engr.

FORD, CHRISTOPHER R; Victor Valley HS; Victorville, CA; (2); Office Aide; Jr NHS; NHS; FBI.

FORD, CORRINE; Los Gatos HS; Los Gatos, CA; (2); Pres Church Yth Grp; Cmnty Wkr; Service Clb; Church Choir; Sec Soph Cls; JV Swmmng; Hon Roll; Ldrshp Clb Project Ld; Brigham Young U; Elem Teacher.

FORD, DEANN M; Santana HS; Lakeside, CA; (4); 26/560; Teachers Aide; Off Frsh Cls; Off Soph Cls; Off Jr Cls; Off Sr Cls; Var Sftbl; Var Tennis; Hon Roll; Pres Schlr; USIU Full Tuition; CSF High Hnrs; British Lit Excllnc; US Intl U.

FORD, DEIDRE D; Covina HS; Covina, CA; (3); Church Yth Grp; Drama Clb; Girl Scts; Letterman Clb; Pep Clb; SADD; Chorus; School Musical; School Play; Rep Sr Cls; Concert Choir; Daisy Chain 90; Fine Arts.

FORD, DONNIE L; Junipero Serra HS; Los Angeles, CA; (3); Cmnty Wkr; Office Aide; Teachers Aide; JV Ftbl; Wt Lftg.

FORD JR, ERIC S; Apple Valley HS; Apple Valley, CA; (4); 63/545; Church Yth Grp; Drama Clb; German Clb; Key Clb; Math Clb; ROTC; Science Clb; Service Clb; Color Guard; School Play; Amer Legion Awd Acad Exc; Cert Merit; U FL.

FORD, JAMES J; Corona HS; Corona, CA; (2); Drama Clb; Stage Crew; Rptr Lit Mag; JV Ftbl; Mck Trl; U NE Las Vegas; Aerntcl Engr.

FORD, JENNY M; El Toro HS; El Toro, CA; (1); Hon Roll; Pres Acad Fit Awd; Sell My Own Earrings; Cashier At An Amusement Pk; UC San Diego; Marin Bio.

FORD JR, JOHN W; Modoc HS; Alturas, CA; (3); Band; Jazz Band; Mrchg Band; Pep Band; School Play; Var L Trk; Hon Roll; Pres Acad Fit Awd; CSF; USC; Film.

FORD, JOSHUA J; Hueneme HS; Oxnard, CA; (4); 1/354; VP Frsh Cls; VP Soph Cls; Stu Cncl; Var L Socr; Var L Trk; Ntl Merit Ltr; Pres Acad Fit Awd; Val; Cmmssnr Of Justice & Ordr; Cmmssnr Of Athl; Peer Cnslr; U CA San Diego; Engrng.

FORD, KIMBERLY T; Chaffey HS; Rialto, CA; (2); Computer Clb; Spanish Clb; Chorus; Church Choir; Howard U; Ob/Gyn.

FORD, MICHAEL J; Bishop Amat HS; West Covina, CA; (4); Varsity Clb; Intrml Bsktbl; JV Ftbl; Var Trk; Cal Poly Pomona; Real Estate.

FORD, NATHAN; Fred C Beyer HS; Modesto, CA; (3); Drama Clb; School Musical; School Play; Stage Crew; Variety Show; Nwsp; Ed Lit Mag; Hon Roll; NHS; John Hopkins CTU Smmr Prog 87; Acadc Dcthln Tm 89-90; USC; Flm Mkng.

FORD, PAUL W; Fairfield HS; Fairfield, CA; (3); Office Aide; Bsbl; Bsktbl; Ftbl; Tennis; Vllybl; Wt Lftg; Cit Awd; Hon Roll; Valuable Back-Ftbl; Bsbl Awd; Sacramento ST Coll.

FORD, SANDRA M; Rio Mesa HS; Camarillo, CA; (3); 21/368; Var Capt Bsktbl; Var Sftbl; Var Capt Vllybl; Hon Roll; Acad Lttr.

FORD, STACY; John F Kennedy HS; Sacramento, CA; (2); Drama Clb; SADD; Thesps; Cheerldng; Vllybl; Marine Bio.

FORD, VENA M; James J Hogan SR HS; Vallejo, CA; (2); Church Yth Grp; Band; Chorus; Church Choir; Mrchg Band; Pep Band; JV Vllybl; Hon Roll; Bsktbl; SADD; Afro-Amer Stu Union; Upwrd Bnd Pgm Davis CA; Cardiology.

FOREMASTER, KIMBERLY D; Burroughs HS; Ridgecrest, CA; (3); Teachers Aide; Hon Roll; Trvl Through SE Asia 87-89; U Of CO CO Sprngs; Law.

FOREST, DEBBIE A; Hiram Johnson West Campus; Sacramento, CA; (2); Science Clb; Hon Roll; Culture Club; Friday Night Live; UCLA; Lawyer.

FORGEY, JASON A; Alta Loma HS; Alta Loma, CA; (2); Art Clb; Church Yth Grp; FTA; Socr; Badmntn; Cmmrcl Art.

FORKNER, NOAH; Ramona HS; Riverside, CA; (3); 108/403; Lit Mag; JV Trk; Prfct Atten Awd; Bus Law.

FORKUM, TARA K; Salinas HS; Salinas, CA; (4); Art Clb; Church Yth Grp; Cmnty Wkr; French Clb; German Clb; Intnl Clb; Letterman Clb; Varsity Clb; Var Swmmng; Hon Roll; AAU/Mars Awd; Monterey Cnty Frgn Lng Achvmnt Awd; Mst Imprvd/Vrsty Swmmr; Peoples U; Frgn Lng.

FORLAND, SHANNON M; Mesa Grande Acad; Cherry Valley, CA; (3); 1/7; Church Yth Grp; Teachers Aide; Varsity Clb; Chorus; Ed Yrbk; VP Soph Cls; VP Jr Cls; Stu Cncl; Var Vllybl; Cit Awd; Stu Of Mnth Sept 88; Stu Rep To Schl Brd; Phy.

FORLEO, CHRISTINA J; Yosemite HS; Oakhurst, CA; (2); Church Yth Grp; French Clb; SADD; Acpl Chr; Chorus; Church Choir; VP Jr Cls; JV Sftbl; Hon Roll; Honor Choir; Maintain Awareness U And I; Piano; Christian Coll; Missionary.

FORMAN, GARY A; El Cajon Valley HS; Santee, CA; (1); FCA; Library Aide; Ftbl; Hon Roll; Bass Fishing; Swmg; Bowling; Completed 1st Aide Course; TX A&M; Law Enfrcmt.

FORMAN, MARY ELIZABETH; St Patricks-St Vincents HS; Vallejo, CA; (3); 2/146; French Clb; Nwsp; Yrbk; Lit Mag; French Hon Soc; High Hon Roll; Statesmen Amer; CSF; Teenwrk; Communications.

FORMANACK, TAMMY L; San Dimas HS; San Dimas, CA; (2); Letterman Clb; Varsity Clb; JV Socr; Var Swmmng; High Hon Roll; JV Water Polo; 3 Rose Awds; Inter Dectr.

FORMET, KELLY B; Whittier Christian HS; Cerritos, CA; (4); German Clb; Library Aide; Teachers Aide; Ftbl; Trk; Wt Lftg; NHS; Stock Club; Fullerton CC; Comp Sci.

FORMIGLE, IAN C; Miramonte HS; Lafayette, CA; (3); JA; JCL; Latin Clb; Diving; Golf; Bowling For Indpndnt Phys Ed Act; Skiing; Ec.

FORMOSA, KATHRYN H; Edison HS; Huntington Beach, CA; (1); Model UN; Var Crs Cntry; Var Trk; French Clb; Pol Sci.

FORMOSO, RODNEY M; St Genevieve HS; North Hollywood, CA; (3); Letterman Clb; Chorus; JV Vllybl; San Diego ST U; Arch.

FORMULAK, CHRIS; Damien HS; Chino, CA; (2); 54/264; Debate Tm; Speech Tm; Hon Roll; Fishing Clb; Comp Prgmng; Penn ST.

FORNACIARI, TONY; Trinity HS; Junction City, CA; (2); FFA; JV Ftbl; Var Wrstlng; Hon Roll; All Leg Shasta Cascade Leg; FFA Grnhnd Dgree & Chptr Frmr Degree; A-AA Schls Wrstlng Champ; Shasta Coll; Tchr.

FORNEY, JO ANN; Glendale Adventist Acad; Pacoima, CA; (2); 5/57; Church Yth Grp; Teachers Aide; Band; Chorus; Church Choir; Drill Tm; Rptr Nwsp; Treas Frsh Cls; VP Soph Cls; Hon Roll; Meherry; Med.

FORNEY, MELANIE J; St Bernard HS; Inglewood, CA; (3); Pep Clb; Chorus; Capt Drill Tm; School Play; VP Stu Cncl; Var Cheerldng; CA Schlrshp Fed; Black Cultural Awarness; UCLA; Psych.

FORNOS, JENNIFER; San Domenico HS; Novato, CA; (4); 1/43; Cmnty Wkr; Pres French Clb; Yrbk; VP Jr Cls; Off Sr Cls; Stu Cncl; JV Swmmng; Var JV Vllybl; High Hon Roll; NHS; Music Piano Solo & Duet Ensemble.

FORONDA, SASHEEN; Granada Hills HS; Granada Hills, CA; (3); Science Clb; Chorus; Drill Tm; Rep Jr Cls; Stu Cncl; JV Var Cheerldng; JV Var Pom Pon; Cit Awd; High Hon Roll; Hon Roll; UCLA; Med.

FOROUDIAN, JIM; South San Francisco HS; San Bruno, CA; (3); Science Clb; Hon Roll; NHS; Prfct Atten Awd; Pres Acad Fit Awd; Pres Schlr; St Schlr; Badminton; San Jose ST; Elec Engr.

FORRAR, MICHELE; C K Mc Clatchy HS; Sacramento, CA; (3); Church Yth Grp; Cmnty Wkr; Dance Clb; French Clb; Intnl Clb; Band; Chorus; Drill Tm; School Musical; Rep Frsh Cls; Pres Friday Night Live; Prfrmr Anti Sbstnc Abuse Mscl Prgm; Prfrmng Ambssdr 88 Wrlds Fair; Comm.

FORREST, ALICE C; Santa Maria HS; Santa Maria, CA; (3); 49/467; Church Yth Grp; Drama Clb; FBLA; School Musical; School Play; JV Crs Cntry; JV Trk; Hon Roll; Campus Career Clb VP; Stmp Clb; Accntng.

FORREST, CARRIE G; Fallbrook HS; Fallbrook, CA; (1); Ski Clb; Hon Roll; Jr NHS; Pres Acad Fit Awd; Piano; Tnns.

FORRESTER, STEPHANIE L; Shasta HS; Redding, CA; (2); Var Cheerldng; Hon Roll; Friday Night Live; Just Say No Clb; Law.

FORRESTER, VERNON WAYNE; Willits HS; Willits, CA; (4); Boy Scts; SADD; Ftbl; Wrstlng; Hon Roll; Completed 23 Coll Units Mendocino CC; Inlstd Navys Delayed Entry Prog; US Navy.

FORSMAN, PETRA; Casa Grande HS; Petaluma, CA; (3); 26/300; French Clb; Lit Mag; High Hon Roll; Hon Roll; NHS; Hnrs Eng, Hnrs Alg II, Visual Arts Survey & Frnch Achvt Awds; Visual Arts Survey Awd Excllnc; UC Santa Cruz; Math.

FORST, ANN E; Skyline HS; Oakland, CA; (2); Off Soph Cls; Treas Stu Cncl; Var L Bsktbl; Var L Trk; Gov Hon Prg Awd; Hon Roll; Pres Acad Fit Awd; Oadland Yth Chorus; Awd Best Schr; CA Music Ed Assoc Hnr Choir; Law.

FORSTER, ANDREW J; Pioneer SR HS; San Jose, CA; (2); Hon Roll; San Jose ST; Aerospace Engr.

FORSTER, HOLLY; Del Oro HS; Auburn, CA; (2); 12/250; Cmnty Wkr; Flag Corp; French Hon Soc; High Hon Roll; Hon Roll; Sec Auburn Bicycling Clb 89-90; CA Inst Of Arts; Comm Art.

FORSTER, JENNIFER L; Pioneer HS; San Jose, CA; (1); Peer Tutoring; San Jose ST.

FORSTER, LANYA; Santa Cruz HS; Santa Cruz, CA; (3); Teachers Aide; Orch; Swmmng; Hon Roll; Envrnmntl Clb; Eng Awd Of Excl & Perfmnce; UCSC; Marine Phtgrphy.

FORSTOT, JONATHAN S; Grossmont HS; El Cajon, CA; (3); 26/392; Var L Socr; High Hon Roll; Hon Roll; CA Schlstc Fed 3 Yrs; San Diego Tribune Achvt Cert All Acad Tm Sccr; Daisy Chain; Law.

FORSYTH, LINETTE J; Tustin HS; Tustin, CA; (4); Teachers Aide; Nw Lf Clb; Gldn ST Exm Rcgntn Alg, Geom; Prncpls Hnr Rl; Irvine Vly CC.

FORSYTHE, CYNTHIA A; Bishop Montgomery HS; Torrance, CA; (2); Girl Scts; Letterman Clb; Service Clb; Rptr Nwsp; Phtg Yrbk; Var Mgr(s); JV Tennis; Var Trk; High Hon Roll; Hon Roll; Hrsbck Riding; Shwng Mdl Horses; UCLA; Med Fld.

FORSYTHE, JILL D; Arroyo Grande HS; Arroyo Grande, CA; (1); Var JV Crs Cntry; JV Trk; Prfct Atten Awd; Pres Acad Fit Awd; UC Santa Cruz; Elem Ed.

FORSYTHE, KYLE L; Palm Springs HS; Morongo Valley, CA; (3); Am Leg Boys St; Chess Clb; VP French Clb; Ski Clb; SADD; VICA; Phtg Yrbk; JV Var Tennis; Vllybl; High Hon Roll; VICA Cmptn Rgnl Gld Mdl, St; Orgnzd Bys Vllybl Tm; UCLA; Engrng.

FORT, MARK T; Twentynine Palms HS; Twentynine Palm, CA; (4); 24/131; FBLA; Scholastic Bowl; Band; Chorus; Mrchg Band; Pep Band; School Musical; Hon Roll; Rotary Awd; CA All-St Hnr Band & San Bernardino Cnty Hnr Band; Music Clb VP; CA ST U Hayward; Music.

FORTENBERRY, LISA N; Capuchino HS; San Bruno, CA; (2); Pres Service Clb; Band; Mrchg Band; Orch; Pep Band; Cheerldng; Trk; High Hon Roll; Hon Roll; Rotary Awd; Pres Of Interact Vlntr Gp; Bus.

FORTENBERRY, YORUBA; 29 Palms HS; Cedar Hill, TX; (2); Debate Tm; Spanish Clb; SADD; Trk; Cit Awd; Hon Roll; Prfct Atten Awd; Crmnl Law.

FORTES, WARREN; Lincoln HS; Stockton, CA; (3); 200/600; French Clb; JV Crs Cntry; JV Trk; Hon Roll; Ntl Merit Schol; Unification Of World Scientist; CA Poly; Arntcl Engrng.

FORTEZ, JERICO J; Valley HS; Sacramento, CA; (2); JV Ftbl; JV Trk; Hon Roll; Notre Dame; Engrng.

FORTHUN, MONICA; Bishop Montgomery HS; Harbor City, CA; (3); Drama Clb; JA; SADD; Chorus; Mrchg Band; School Musical; School Play; Bus.

FORTIN, MARISSA; Gonzales Union HS; Gonzales, CA; (2); Sec FBLA; Science Clb; Pep Band; Cit Awd; Hon Roll; Interact Club; San Jose ST U; Bus.

FORTINO, GINA; Lower Lake HS; Clearlake, CA; (4); 16/123; Church Yth Grp; Library Aide; Office Aide; Red Cross Aide; Speech Tm; SADD; Teachers Aide; Chorus; Church Choir; Off Sr Cls; Stu Lioness; Friday Night Live Sec; CA Schlrshp Fed VP; Santa Rosa JC; Bus Mgmt.

FORTINO, MICHAEL J; El Camino Fundamental HS; Sacramento, CA; (3); Church Yth Grp; Cmnty Wkr; Debate Tm; Socr; High Hon Roll; Hon Roll; NHS; CSF; Jr Statesman Of Amer; UCD Hnrs Pgm, Humanities Inst; Intl Law.

FORTIS II, GILMAR S; Fillmore HS; Fillmore, CA; (2); Church Yth Grp; Hon Roll; NHS; Screenplay Writer.

FORTMEIER, ANDREW R; Orange Lutheran HS; Orange, CA; (2); Church Yth Grp; FCA; Ftbl; Socr; Hon Roll; Play Strategic War Games/Role Playing Games; Build Model Castles & Villages, Draw Cartoons; Dsgn Games.

FORTMEYER, JUSTIN M; North HS; Bakersfield, CA; (4); 10/372; Church Yth Grp; Letterman Clb; Ski Clb; School Play; Pres Soph Cls; VP Stu Cncl; Var L Ftbl; Cit Awd; Hon Roll; NHS; VFW Awd Schlrshp; U Of Southern CA; Civil Engr.

FORTNER, JESSICA; Los Aslamitos HS; Seal Beach, CA; (4); Cmnty Wkr; French Clb; Intnl Clb; Pep Clb; Science Clb; Service Clb; Ski Clb; Chorus; Color Guard; Variety Show; Natl Commnd Stu 90; Miss Supersnstnl Rlf 88-89; Hmcmng Ct; Frgn Rltns.

FORTNER, NICOLE E; Oakdale HS; Oakdale, CA; (3); Church Yth Grp; Dance Clb; Drama Clb; Pep Clb; Science Clb; Teachers Aide; School Play; Stage Crew; Rep Frsh Cls; Rep Soph Cls; 1st Rnnr Up Oakdale Jr Miss; Yth For Christ; Pt Loma Nazarene Coll; Engl Ed.

FORTUNA, LEAH A; Fremont HS; Sunnyvale, CA; (1); Color Guard; School Play; Bsktbl; NHS.

FORTUNE, JESSICA A; San Lorenzo HS; San Leandro, CA; (2); Hon Roll; Minority Club; Cal ST Hayward; Bus Mgmt.

FOSS, ANDREA; Fairfield HS; Fairfield, CA; (2); Church Yth Grp; SADD; Church Choir; Hon Roll; Marine Biology.

FOSTER, ALYSON A; Palo Alto HS; Palo Alto, CA; (4); Cmnty Wkr; Treas Girl Scts; Math Tm; Stage Crew; Ntl Merit Schol; Gold Star Mem Schlrshp; Womens Clb Schlrshp; Chancellors Schlr; UC Berkeley; Biochem.

FOSTER, AMY K; Concord HS; Concord, CA; (3); Library Aide; Model UN; Acpl Chr; Chorus; School Musical; Ntl Merit Ltr; CA Schlrshp Fed; Jrnlsm.

FOSTER, ANGELA; Washington Prep HS; Los Angeles, CA; (3); 1/570; Church Yth Grp; Co-Capt Pep Clb; Teachers Aide; High Hon Roll; Jr NHS; NHS; Pres Acad Fit Awd; Val; Mesa Club:Ucla Prtnrshp; USC; Pre Med.

FOSTER, ANGELA D; Convent Of The Sacred Heart HS; San Francisco, CA; (4); Pep Clb; Chorus; Sec Jr Cls; Treas Sr Cls; Gym; Var Trk; Hon Roll; Jr Stsmn Of Amer; CSF; Yth Adv Cmmttee.

FOSTER, BILLY R; Roosevelt HS; Fresno, CA; (2); Band; Jazz Band; Mrchg Band; Pep Band; Mrt List; 1st Chr Euphonium Fresno-Madera Hnr Band; 1st Chr Ekuphonium Fresnos Finest; Fresno ST U; Music Tchr.

FOSTER, CLAIRE; Los Gatos HS; Los Gatos, CA; (1); Church Yth Grp; Cmnty Wkr; JV Bsktbl; High Hon Roll.

FOSTER, DEONNA; Amos Alanzo Stagg HS; Stockton, CA; (1); Church Yth Grp; Band; Orch; Trk; Hon Roll; Hnrs Cls; UCLA; Psych.

FOSTER, DESIREE; West Conna Hills SDA Schl; West Covina, CA; (2); Teachers Aide; Chorus; Ed Yrbk; Bsktbl; Ftbl; Vllybl; Hon Roll; Harvard Law Schl; Law.

FOSTER, ERICKA; Marina HS; Huntington Beach, CA; (3); Cmnty Wkr; Dance Clb; French Clb; Pep Clb; Off Jr Cls; Jr Presntn Ntl Chrty Leag; Jr Cls Sec.

FOSTER, FARRAH; Van Nuys HS; Los Angeles, CA; (2); Church Yth Grp; 4-H; SADD; Teachers Aide; Chorus; Church Choir; Stage Crew; Capt Var Cheerldng; Cit Awd; High Hon Roll; Horace Mann JC; Phy.

FOSTER, FRANK J; Los Alamitos HS; Seal Beach, CA; (2); Church Yth Grp; Var Bsbl; Hon Roll; Naval Acad; Doctor.

FOSTER, JENNY A; Lassen HS; Susanville, CA; (3); 3/112; Art Clb; Church Yth Grp; Ski Clb; Teachers Aide; School Play; Score Keeper; JV Stat Trk; High Hon Roll; Hon Roll; Art Achvt Awd; CSSSA Pgm Admssn; CSF; Film Prdctn.

FOSTER, JONATHAN D; A A Stagg HS; Stockton, CA; (2); Band; Jazz Band; Mrchg Band; Pep Band; School Musical; School Play; Stage Crew; Hon Roll; Inter/Adv Guitar; Music Tchr.

FOSTER, KARI L; Brawley Union HS; Brawley, CA; (1); 4-H; Sec FFA; Swmmng; JV Tennis; Team Penning; Cal Poly San Luis Obispo; Ag.

FOSTER, KATHLEEN M; St Francis HS; Sunnyvale, CA; (1); Trk; Hon Roll; DAL Trk Fnls 100m Chmpn; Broke JV 400m Relay Record.

FOSTER, KENDRA; Sonoma Valley HS; Sonoma, CA; (2); 2/252; Church Yth Grp; Cmnty Wkr; Dance Clb; Model UN; SADD; Stage Crew; Pres Frsh Cls; Treas Soph Cls; Sftbl; High Hon Roll; CSF & Interact Clbs; Lab Phys Sci & Engl Awds; Envrnmntl Engr.

FOSTER, MARJORIE L; Fairfield HS; Fairfield, CA; (2); Church Choir; Flag Corp; UC Davis; Comp Prgmr.

FOSTER, NICOLE S; Rubidoux HS; Corona, CA; (4); Church Yth Grp; Cmnty Wkr; Teachers Aide; Hon Roll; Work Handicaped; San Deigo ST; Engl.

FOSTER, SHANNON; Encina HS; Sacramento, CA; (3); 25/212; Cheerldng; Sftbl; Stu Of Mnth Bus; UCSD; Marine Bio.

FOSTER, TIM J; Paradise HS; Paradise, CA; (3); Teachers Aide; JV Var Bsktbl; JV Var Ftbl; Hon Roll; Bsktbl MVP; Ftbl Coachs Awd.

FOTINAKES, ANNA; Cypress HS; Cypress, CA; (3); Church Yth Grp; German Clb; Pep Clb; Chorus; Church Choir; Color Guard; Capt Flag Corp; Hon Roll; Pres Acad Fit Awd; CSF; SCAMPI Summer Pgm 90; Physics.

FOUCH, TRACY; Williams HS; Williams, CA; (3); 3/30; Debate Tm; 4-H; FFA; Pep Clb; Scholastic Bowl; Spanish Clb; SADD; Band; Pep Band; VP Frsh Cls; CSF 88-89; Teaching.

FOULK, HEATHER M; Milpitas HS; Milpitas, CA; (4); Pres Church Yth Grp; Pres JA; Church Choir; Co-Capt Var Bsktbl; JV Var Sftbl; Capt Var Vllybl; Pres Acad Fit Awd; Ath Of Yr; Leo B Murphy Awd; Bill Bebout Awd; BYU; Bus Admin.

FOUNTAIN, CRYSTAL L; Cajon HS; San Bernardino, CA; (3); AFS; Church Yth Grp; Cmnty Wkr; Drama Clb; Key Clb; SADD; School Musical; School Play; Peer Cnslng; Awd Apprctn; Duke; Pediatrics.

FOUNTAINE, COLLEEN A; San Pasqual HS; Escondido, CA; (3); Teachers Aide; Color Guard; Flag Corp; Awd Of Stu Of The Semester; Awd Bets Marcher Of The Flag Tm; Awd Most Imprvd Flag; Bus Mgmt.

FOUST, MICHELLE D; Escondido HS; Escondido, CA; (2); 35/451; Church Yth Grp; Key Clb; Pep Clb; JV Bsktbl; Var Crs Cntry; Hon Roll.

FOWLER, ALIA I; Brea-Olinda HS; Brea, CA; (3); Treas VP GAA; Key Clb; Stat Bsktbl; L Trk; JV Capt Vllybl; High Hon Roll; NHS; Sci.

FOWLER, ANGELA T; John Burroughs HS; Burbank, CA; (3); Teachers Aide; Chorus; Variety Show; Stu Cncl; Bsktbl; Swmmng; Cit Awd; High Hon Roll; Pres Acad Fit Awd; Scuba Diving; CSUN; Bus.

FOWLER, MICHELLE L; Fairfield HS; Fairfield, CA; (2); ROTC; Cit Awd; USAF Acad; Pilot.

FOX, BELINDA; Antioch HS; Antioch, CA; (2); Church Yth Grp; German Clb; Pep Clb; Band; Flag Corp; Mrchg Band; Cheerldng; Pom Pon; Trk; High Hon Roll; Brigham Young U; Vet Med.

FOX, BRAD; Christian HS; El Cajon, CA; (4); Church Yth Grp; Ski Clb; Rptr Nwsp; Rep Stu Cncl; Var L Bsktbl; Var L Ftbl; Capt Intrml Socr; Var L Tennis; Intrml Wt Lftg; High Hon Roll; Bus.

FOX, BRIAN G; Long Beach Polytechnic HS; Long Beach, CA; (4); 75/759; Cmnty Wkr; Key Clb; Quiz Bowl; Scholastic Bowl; Rep Jr Cls; Rep Sr Cls; Stu Cncl; NHS; Ntl Merit Ltr; UC San Diego; Corp Law.

FOX, BRIDGET; Pinole Valley HS; Pinole, CA; (1); Church Yth Grp; Cmnty Wkr; Drama Clb; FCA; GAA; SADD; School Play; Stage Crew; Socr; Swmmng; Bay Oaks Select Grls Soccer Club; St Marys College Moraga; Law.

FOX, CASIE; Mc Kinleyville HS; Trinidad, CA; (3); 1/150; Drama Clb; 4-H; French Clb; School Play; Variety Show; Ed Yrbk; Cit Awd; French Hon Soc; Hon Roll; Prfct Atten Awd; CSF; Ca Summer Schl Of Arts.

FOX, CLARISSA; Dana Hills HS; Laguna Niguil, CA; (1); Church Yth Grp; Stu Cncl; Intrml Swmmng; Piano; Santa Barbara; Psych.

FOX, DEBORAH E; La Jolla County Day Schl; La Jolla, CA; (2); Computer Clb; Girl Scts; Spanish Clb; SADD; Stage Crew; Lit Mag; JV Tennis; High Hon Roll; Spanish NHS; Silver Awd.

FOX, DENELLE; Escondido HS; Escondido, CA; (1); Lwyr.

FOX, EDWARD F; Don Lugo HS; Mira Lona, CA; (3); Computer Clb; Math Clb; Sec VP Temple Yth Grp; JV Socr; Hon Roll; Golden Conquest Awd 2 Yrs; Golden St Exam Acad Achvy Awd Hgh Hnrs; Role Playing Clb; USAFA; Comp Prgmmng.

FOX, GREG D; Hesperia Christian HS; Apple Valley, CA; (3); Rptr Nwsp; Rep Soph Cls; Var Ftbl; Art.

FOX, JENNIFER ANN; Mt Whitney HS; Visalia, CA; (2); Church Yth Grp; Cmnty Wkr; Drama Clb; Thesps; Orch; School Play; Rep Stu Cncl; Hon Roll; Mck Trl Tm; Rnbw Grls; Psych.

FOX, JENNIFER L; Edison HS; Huntington Beach, CA; (4); Band; Chorus; Jazz Band; Mrchg Band; Orch; Pep Band; Lit Mag; Golden Key Performing Arts; Hnr Band 89 & 90; STAR Cert; Scndry Ed.

FOX, JO ANNE E; Cordova SR HS; Rancho Cordova, CA; (3); Debate Tm; Model UN; Stat Crs Cntry; Stat Diving; Stat Swmmng; Stat Trk; Octagon Club; Hnr Scty; Sac ST; Kndgrtn Tchr.

FOX, JOHN; Hoover HS; San Diego, CA; (3); Computer Clb; Teachers Aide; Cit Awd; High Hon Roll; Hon Roll; Prfct Atten Awd; Pres Acad Fit Awd.

FOX, JOSEPH R; Cardinal Newman HS; Santa Rosa, CA; (3); 6/86; Cmnty Wkr; Drama Clb; School Musical; Stage Crew; Yrbk; Sec Jr Cls; Var Tennis; High Hon Roll; Sccr Cty League; Clsscl Piano; Cnfrmtn Yth Grp; CCD 3rd Grd Tchr; CSF; Stanford; Engnr.

FOX, JOSHUA; Don Antonio Lugo HS; Chino, CA; (2); German Clb; Gov Hon Prg Awd; Hon Roll; Math.

FOX, KAREN A; O'farrell SCPA HS; San Diego, CA; (2); Hist Church Yth Grp; Cmnty Wkr; Dance Clb; Treas Spanish Clb; School Play; Hon Roll; Pres Acad Fit Awd; CJSF; CSF; Outstdng Art Achvmt Awd.

FOX, KASEY G; Vintage HS; Napa, CA; (2); Intrml Bsktbl; Intrml Vllybl; Hon Roll.

FOX, KATIE; Saratoga HS; Saratoga, CA; (2); Cmnty Wkr; Hosp Aide; Service Clb; Phtg Nwsp; Rep Frsh Cls; Rep Soph Cls; Stu Cncl; Cheerldng; Capt Tennis; Var Trk; Pres Natl Charity Lg; Cmmnctns.

FOX, KERI; El Capitan HS; Lakeside, CA; (4); 10/418; Cmnty Wkr; Hosp Aide; Intnl Clb; Scholastic Bowl; Science Clb; Spanish Clb; Teachers Aide; Treas Jr Cls; Stu Cncl; JV Swmmng; Fnlst Lions Clb Speech Cont; JR Aux Brd Mbr; Schl Improvemnet Pgm Brd Mbr; Med.

FOX, KIMBERLY A; Roseville HS; Roseville, CA; (2); German Clb; Spanish Clb; Stat Bsktbl; Score Keeper; L Var Socr; High Hon Roll; Stu Athltc Trainer; Sports Med.

FOX, KRISTI S; Fred C Beyer HS; Modesto, CA; (3); Cmnty Wkr; FBLA; Girl Scts; Hosp Aide; JA; Pep Clb; Service Clb; SADD; Teachers Aide; Score Keeper; CSU Long Beach; Phys Thrpy.

FOX, LISA SUZANNE; Tustin HS; Tustin, CA; (1); Church Yth Grp; Band; Mrchg Band.

FOX, MARYLOU R; Highlands HS; N Highlands, CA; (2); 1/40; Hon Roll; Prfct Atten Awd; US Air Frc Acad.

FOX, MATTHEW J; Monte Vista HS; Danville, CA; (4); Church Yth Grp; Letterman Clb; Spanish Clb; SADD; Intrml JV Bsbl; Var L Bsktbl; Var JV Ftbl; NHS; Grad Hnr Stu; Most Imprvd Ply Bsktbl 88-89; Benedictine Coll; Bio.

FOX, MAXWELL A; Harvard Schl; Santa Monica, CA; (4); Boy Scts; NFL; Orch; Nwsp; Var Capt Crs Cntry; Var L Trk; Var Wrstlng; Ntl Merit SF; Eagle Scout; Ju-Jitsu.

FOX, MICHELE M; Oak Ridge HS; El Dorado Hills, CA; (1); Church Yth Grp; Bsktbl; Hon Roll; Frsty Ftbl Team Stu Trnr; CSF; Athltc Trnr.

FOX, MONICA M; Sonora HS; Sonora, CA; (2); SADD; Stat Bsbl; JV Bsktbl; JV Var Crs Cntry; High Hon Roll; Hon Roll; Prfct Atten Awd; Pres Acad Fit Awd; Cmptv Swmmg; Stanford.

FOX, SHANON L; Clovis HS; Fresno, CA; (3); Ski Clb; SADD; Sec Stu Cncl; Var Cheerldng; Var Pom Pon; Ldrshp Camp; Human Relations Day Solo Perf; Hmcmng Atten 88; Pep Choregrapher; Camp Royal 90; FSU; Child Psych.

FOX, WENDY; Pleasant Valley HS; Chico, CA; (4); Church Yth Grp; Acpl Chr; Drm Mjr(t); Jazz Band; Mrchg Band; JV L Bsktbl; Var L Trk; Var L Vllybl; Hon Roll; Pres Acad Fit Awd; John Phillip Sousa Band Awd; Bnk Amer Achvt Awd Fine Arts; Trinity Coll; Elem Ed.

FOY, JASON; Fillmore HS; Fillmore, CA; (1); Church Yth Grp; JV Bsbl; Stat Bsktbl; JV Ftbl; Hon Roll; Acad Achvtduringbsbl; Engrng.

FRABL, BRIAN; Edison HS; Huntington Beach, CA; (1); Model UN; JV Swmmng; Hon Roll; Pres Acad Fit Awd; Camp Jr Lifeguard Pgm; Orange Cnty Acad Decathlon; Starting Smll Schl Paper 90-91; Stanford; Bus Mgmt.

FRACISCO, KATIE; Santa Margarita HS; Mission Viejo, CA; (1); 65/341; Girl Scts; Pep Clb; Var Cheerldng; Prfct Atten Awd; Pres Acad Fit Awd; Keywanettes; CSF.

FRACISCO, ROB M; Trabuco Hills HS; Mission Viejo, CA; (2); 35/369; Cmnty Wkr; French Clb; SADD; Socr; Vllybl; Hon Roll; NHS; CSF; Co-Fndr SAFE; U Of CA; Env Sci.

FRAGOSO, JULISA; St Pius X HS; South Gate, CA; (3); Spanish Clb; Pedeatrician.

FRAGUA, AMY D; Sherman Indian HS; Jemez Pueblo, NM; (1); Health.

FRAILEY, BRODY L; Valhalla HS; La Mesa, CA; (3); 7/408; Boy Scts; Debate Tm; Key Clb; Stu Cncl; JV Crs Cntry; Var Ftbl; Socr; JV Trk; High Hon Roll; Rotary Awd; James S Copley Outstndng Ctznshp & Acad Accmplshmnts Awd; Bst Overall Russian 88-90; Jr St Assn; Yale; Law.

FRAILEY, REBECCA; Garces Memorial HS; Bakersfield, CA; (3); Church Yth Grp; Science Clb; Spanish Clb; SADD; Var Bsktbl; JV Sftbl; Var Vllybl; High Hon Roll; Bio Sci.

FRAIRE, MICHELLE R; Paraclete HS; Littlerock, CA; (2); 20/146; Church Yth Grp; Cmnty Wkr; Debate Tm; High Hon Roll; Hon Roll; St Marys Womens Gld Schlrshp; Educ.

FRAKER, JOHN E; Bellarmine College Prep; Saratoga, CA; (3); 65/300; Church Yth Grp; Cmnty Wkr; Debate Tm; Drama Clb; NFL; Speech Tm; Thesps; Rptr Nwsp; JV Diving; Camp Cnslr; Chrch Choir; UCLA; Hstry/Law.

FRAKES, EUGENE P; Rubidoux HS; Riverside, CA; (4); Computer Clb; VP German Clb; Varsity Clb; Var L Swmmng; Prfct Atten Awd; CA ST U; Frgn Lang.

FRAME, JASON M; Clovis HS; Fresno, CA; (3); Church Yth Grp; 4-H; FFA; Church Choir; Hon Roll; Advntrs Mssns Prog; Columbia Chrstn Coll; Yth Mnstr.

FRANCESCHI, NATASHA S; Analy HS; Bodega, CA; (2); 10/250; Drama Clb; French Clb; School Play; Rptr Nwsp; Ed Yrbk; Lit Mag; High Hon Roll; Pres Acad Fit Awd; Prfrmr Peace Child Intl Mscl Soviet Union & E Coast Tours; Piano; Envrnmntl Awrns Clb.

FRANCESCHINI, ANDREW C; Woodbridge HS; Irvine, CA; (3); Ed Nwsp; Intrml JV Crs Cntry; Intrml JV Trk; Hon Roll; U Of San Diego; Bus Admin.

FRANCESCHINI, NICHOLAS; Fairfield HS; Fairfield, CA; (4); Hon Roll; Prfct Atten Awd; Pres Acad Fit Awd; Med.

FRANCHVILLE, GERALD R; Victor Valley HS; Victorville, CA; (1); Boy Scts; Teachers Aide; Intrml Bsbl; Cit Awd; High Hon Roll; Hon Roll; Parade Mag & Daily Press Outstndng Achvts Trip To Italy; Notre Dame; Psych.

FRANCIS II, ALLEN C; Glendale Adventist Acad; Loma Linda, CA; (4); Aud/Vis; Church Yth Grp; FCA; Hosp Aide; Letterman Clb; Teachers Aide; Varsity Clb; Intrml Var Ftbl; High Hon Roll; NHS; Stu Ambssdr To Dffrnt Cntrs; Orgnztn Of Mu Tau Mu; Loma Linda U; Sci.

FRANCIS, ELIZABETH L; Louisville HS; Woodland Hills, CA; (2); Church Yth Grp; Cmnty Wkr; Dance Clb; Drama Clb; 4-H; French Clb; GAA; Hosp Aide; Teachers Aide; School Play; Sci.

FRANCIS, ERIC J; Turlock HS; Turlock, CA; (4); Cmnty Wkr; Drama Clb; German Clb; NFL; Hist Thesps; School Musical; School Play; Stage Crew; UC Berkeley; Hstry.

FRANCIS, KATIE; Sonora HS; Sonora, CA; (2); 23/325; Cmnty Wkr; Drama Clb; Letterman Clb; Pep Clb; Science Clb; Service Clb; Ski Clb; Acpl Chr; Chorus; School Musical; 1st Cnty & 3rd W Cst Reg Fleet Reserve Assn Essay Cont; Interact Foreign Exchange Student To England; U Of CA; Political Science.

FRANCIS, MICHAEL A; Fontana HS; Fontana, CA; (2); High Hon Roll; Hon Roll; Drwng; CA Poly Pomona; Arch.

FRANCIS, MISSY; Chaminade Coll Prep; Northridge, CA; (3); 1/900; Cmnty Wkr; Model UN; Yrbk; Ed Yrbk; Off Sr Cls; Capt Cheerldng; High Hon Roll; Pres Jr NHS; NHS; Ntl Merit Schol; Best Spprtg Actrss Awd; Valley Assisteens Vice Chmn; Hug-A-Bear Proj; CSF; Stanford U; Law.

FRANCIS, RUDY; Sunset HS; Hayward, CA; (2); JV Bsktbl; JV Ftbl; Hon Roll.

FRANCIS, RYAN; Marysville HS; Marysville, CA; (1); Band; Jazz Band; Mrchg Band; Pep Band; Bsbl; Hon Roll.

FRANCIS, SHERRY L; Santa Rosa HS; Santa Rosa, CA; (2); FFA; Sftbl; Lawyer.

FRANCIS, SOPHIA L; Adolf Leuzinger HS; Hawthorne, CA; (2); Church Yth Grp; Rptr Nwsp; JV Bsktbl; JV Var Trk; JV Vllybl; High Hon Roll; Hon Roll; Chrldng Chrch; Numrs Awds Accordion; Engl.

FRANCIS, TAMER; Alameda HS; Alameda, CA; (4); 17/331; Capt Debate Tm; JA; NFL; Pres Speech Tm; Ed Nwsp; JV Bsbl; High Hon Roll; Hon Roll; Lion Awd; Yale U; Philosophy.

FRANCISCO, DANILO; Cathedral HS; Los Angeles, CA; (3); Math Clb; Service Clb; Teachers Aide; JV Var Tennis; Hon Roll; Calligraphy Club; CSF; UCLA; Astrophysics.

FRANCISCO, DARIUS V; Pittsburg HS; Pittsburg, CA; (2); Prfct Atten Awd; Comp Sci.

FRANCISCO, DUANE N; Nogales HS; Walnut, CA; (4); Science Clb; Band; Mrchg Band; Cit Awd; Hon Roll; De Vry Inst; Bus Orgztn.

FRANCISCO, EDITHA; Glendale HS; Arleta, CA; (4); VP Dance Clb; NHS; Outstndng Dancer 90; Cert Apprctn Svc Dance Dept; CA ST U Northridge; Engrng.

FRANCISCO, JOSEPH A; Castle Park HS; Chula Vista, CA; (3); 50/422; Band; Mrchg Band; Pep Band; Pre-Law.

FRANCISCO, LOPEZ L; Baldwin Park HS; Baldwin Park, CA; (2); Church Yth Grp; FBLA; Band; Mrchg Band; Wrstlng; Hon Roll; Hnr Soc Clb; Law.

FRANCO, ADRIANA J; St Monicas HS; Culver City, CA; (3); Church Yth Grp; Cmnty Wkr; Latin Clb; Church Choir; Hon Roll; Nosotros Clb Tres; Wrkd Orthopedics; Church Yth Grp, Coordinator 1 Yr; Bus.

FRANCO, ANN L; Alisal HS; Salinas, CA; (1).

FRANCO, CHERYL R; James Lick HS; San Jose, CA; (3); 25/287; JV Bsbl; JV Vllybl; Hon Roll; Dept Hnrs Consmr Ed 88-89 & Bus 89-90; San Jose ST; Bus.

FRANCO, CLAUDIA M; Santa Monica HS; Santa Monica, CA; (1); UCLA; Lawyer.

FRANCO, GINA; San Fernando HS; Pacoima, CA; (2); Cmnty Wkr; GAA; Pep Clb; Science Clb; Band; Drill Tm; VP Frsh Cls; Trk; Cit Awd; Hon Roll; MESA Math Engrng Sci Achvt; Future Schlrs; Ergan Kalon Hnr Stu; Crmnl Law.

FRANCO, JON; Beyer HS; Modesto, CA; (2); Key Clb; Math Tm; JV Ftbl; Var Socr; JV Trk; Hon Roll; Sports Med.

FRANCO, JOSE J; Morningside HS; Inglewood, CA; (1); High Hon Roll; Stdy Frnch.

FRANCO, LILA; Bellermine Jefferson HS; Burbank, CA; (1); Church Yth Grp; Teachers Aide; Tennis; Cit Awd; Pdtrcn.

FRANCO, MARGARITA; Dos Palos HS; Dos Palos, CA; (3); 4/136; Church Yth Grp; Cmnty Wkr; VP Science Clb; Variety Show; Crs Cntry; Hon Roll; Acadmc Dcthln; CSF; MECHA VP; SADD; Bus Admin.

FRANCO, MARIA A; Fontana HS; Fontana, CA; (2); Drama Clb; Chorus; Stage Crew; Hon Roll; Madrigals/Show Choir; Boston U Amhearst; Poltcl Sci.

FRANCO, MARICELA; Santa Monica HS; Santa Monica, CA; (2); Latin Clb; Prfct Atten Awd; Fshn Dsgnr.

FRANCO, MELISSA C; Holy Family HS; Los Angeles, CA; (2); Art Clb; Church Yth Grp; Library Aide; Stu Cncl; Accntng.

FRANCO, OLGA L; La Sierra HS; Riverside, CA; (1); Prfct Atten Awd; Acctng.

FRANCO, RICHARD; South HS; Bakersfield, CA; (3); 9/469; Cmnty Wkr; Intnl Clb; Key Clb; Var Tennis; MESA Clb; Interact Clb; Medical Clb; Cal Poly SLO; Arch.

FRANCO, TAMARA S; Orange Glen HS; Escondido, CA; (2); 268/543; Church Yth Grp; Law.

FRANCO, VERONICA; Baldwin Park HS; Baldwin Park, CA; (2); Bus Profs of Am; Church Yth Grp; Band; Mrchg Band; Off Soph Cls; Hon Roll; ROP, Bus Skills; Social Wrkr.

FRANCO, VICTOR H; Aptos HS; Aptos, CA; (1); 1/650; Computer Clb; Math Tm; Hon Roll; Prfct Atten Awd; Pres Acad Fit Awd; CA Schlrshp Fed; Stanford; Physicist.

FRANCO, YVETTE; St Genevieve HS; Van Nuys, CA; (3); VP French Clb; Drill Tm; Socr; U Of CA Los Angeles; Psych.

FRANCOIS, TAMARA; St Bernard HS; Los Angeles, CA; (1); Church Yth Grp; French Clb; Band; Phtg Yrbk; Rep Frsh Cls; JV Vllybl; Hon Roll; CSF; Black Cultural Awareness; Amnesty Intl.

FRANDSEN, LORIE A; Lower Lake HS; Clearlake, CA; (4); 15/111; VP Church Yth Grp; Treas FBLA; Service Clb; Pres VP Spanish Clb; Pres Band; Church Choir; Variety Show; Treas Sr Cls; Stu Cncl; Hon Roll; Natl Talent Cont Girls Trio Plaque Awd; Bank Of Amer Plaque Awd; Semper Fidelis Awd; Heald Bus Coll; Bus.

FRANGIEH, TANIA; Northgate HS; Walnut Creek, CA; (3); Dance Clb; French Clb; SADD; Color Guard; Flag Corp; Mrchg Band; Stage Crew; Variety Show; Rep Soph Cls; Rep Sr Cls; Flag Team Capt; Friday Night Live VP; Trk N Coast Chmpnshps; U CA; Phys Thrpy.

FRANK, ANGELINA M; Bakersfield HS; Bakersfield, CA; (2); Church Yth Grp; Psych.

FRANK, BRIAN; Woodland HS; Woodland, CA; (3); JV Var Bsbl; JV Bsktbl; JV Var Crs Cntry; High Hon Roll; Hon Roll; CSF; Golden St Exam Hgh Hnrs.

FRANK, DAWN C; De Anza HS; El Sobrante, CA; (4); 9/270; French Clb; Ed Nwsp; Ed Lit Mag; JV Swmmng; Hon Roll; Ntl Merit Ltr; Pres Acad Fit Awd; Achvt Awd Ntl Cncl Tchrs Engl; 10 Yrs Ballet & Prfrmncs; 8 Yrs Prfrmng Theater Prodctns; Tchr.

FRANK, DEBORAH; Santa Monica HS; Santa Monica, CA; (4); 12/618; Dance Clb; Band; Mrchg Band; Pep Band; School Musical; Lit Mag; Rep Stu Cncl; Swmmng; Cit Awd; High Hon Roll; People To People Stu Ambsdr To USSAR 89; Simon Music Schlrshp; UC San Diego; Microbio.

FRANK, JACQUELINE; Poway HS; San Diego, CA; (3); SADD; School Play; Rep Frsh Cls; Off Jr Cls; Stat Bsktbl; JV Sftbl; JV Capt Vllybl; High Hon Roll; NHS; Pres Acad Fit Awd; Stanford U; Political Sci.

FRANK, LISA M; San Gorgonio HS; San Bernardino, CA; (3); French Clb; Teachers Aide; Aces Clb; Bio Clb; Pre-Med.

FRANK, MIKE; Escondido HS; Escondido, CA; (1); Var L Bsbl; Capt Bsktbl; Capt Ftbl; Hon Roll.

FRANK, SUSAN R; Analy HS; Sebastopol, CA; (4); Art Clb; Pres Drama Clb; Mgr French Clb; Spanish Clb; Thesps; Acpl Chr; School Musical; Mgr Stage Crew; Rptr Nwsp; Yrbk; Yth For Peace Clb Fndr; Linguistics.

FRANK, TIMOTHY W; Berean Christian HS; Pleasant Hill, CA; (3); Aud/Vis; Church Yth Grp; Computer Clb; Service Clb; Teachers Aide; Wt Lftg; High Hon Roll; Hon Roll; CSF; Mst Promising Writer 88-90; Jr Marshal 89-90; Music.

FRANKE, CHRISTOPHER J; Hemet HS; Hemet, CA; (2); Pres Church Yth Grp; Debate Tm; FCA; Treas Key Clb; Math Clb; Math Tm; Service Clb; Spanish Clb; Speech Tm; Band; Amer Lgn Awd; Bullpup Hnr Awd 88-89; Stanford; Corp Lawyer.

FRANKE, SANDY L; Culver City HS; Culver City, CA; (3); Teachers Aide; Stu Cncl; Off Jr Cls; Off Sr Cls; Vllybl; Cit Awd; Hon Roll; Pres Acad Fit Awd; Heal The Bay Club; Stu Lg; Dolphin Trnr.

FRANKLIN, JENNIFER L; Woodside HS; Redwood City, CA; (2); Church Yth Grp; Intnl Clb; Office Aide; Pres Ski Clb; Var Crs Cntry; Var Trk; JV Vllybl; Hon Roll; CSF; Chrch Yth Grp Mission Trip Mexico; Intl Rltns.

FRANKLIN, JOANNA; Encinal HS; Alameda, CA; (3); 1/280; Church Yth Grp; Sec Key Clb; Band; Church Choir; Orch; Ed Nwsp; High Hon Roll.

FRANKLIN, JOEL P; Live Oak HS; Morgan Hill, CA; (3); 54/571; Church Yth Grp; Debate Tm; French Clb; Math Tm; Service Clb; Band; Jazz Band; Mrchg Band; Cit Awd; High Hon Roll; CSF; Friends Outside Summer Cls Asst; Civil Engr.

FRANKLIN, JOHN R; Grossmont HS; El Cajon, CA; (3); 81/392; Church Yth Grp; Chorus; JV Var Crs Cntry; JV Var Trk; Hon Roll; Choir Awd; Hnrs Ensmble; Meteorology.

FRANKLIN, KATIE; Encinal HS; Alameda, CA; (4); 1/223; Church Yth Grp; VP Key Clb; Band; Jazz Band; Mrchg Band; Orch; School Musical; Bausch & Lomb Sci Awd; High Hon Roll; Ntl Merit SF; Natl Merit Fnlst; Natl Cncl Of Tchrs Of Engl Achvt Awd Wrtng; Advancd HS Stdnts Pgm; U Of Pacific.

FRANKLIN, KIMMION M; Dorsey HS; Inglewood, CA; (2); Chorus; Church Choir; Var Trk; Cit Awd; Howard; Kndrgrtn Tchr.

FRANKLIN, STEPHARNIA; Dorsey HS; Los Angeles, CA; (3); UCLA; Cmmnctns.

FRANKLIN, TIFFANY; Nordhoff HS; Ojai, CA; (2); School Play; JV Cheerldng; Hon Roll.

FRANKLIN, WENDY A; San Rafael HS; San Rafael, CA; (3); Church Yth Grp; Hosp Aide; Key Clb; ROTC; Sftbl; Vllybl; Hon Roll; Acad Achvt Medals; San Francisco ST; Med.

FRANKLIN, WILLIAM B; San Gorgonio HS; Highland, CA; (3); Var Church Yth Grp; Var Socr; Hon Roll; Sthrn CA Jr PGA & Desert Jr Golf Assn; Optimist Jr Wrld Golf Trnmt 89; Bit T St Fnls 89.

FRANKS, KAREN J; Orosi HS; Cutler, CA; (2); Church Yth Grp; Drama Clb; Math Clb; Band; Mrchg Band; School Musical; Tennis; Hon Roll; Mock Trial; Hnr Band; Sci.

FRANKS, TAMARA S; Exeter Union HS; Exeter, CA; (1); Church Yth Grp; FHA; Band; Mrchg Band; Sftbl; Vllybl; Hon Roll; Psych.

FRANKS, TRISHA; Whitney HS; Cerritos, CA; (4); Pres Church Yth Grp; Nwsp; Ed Yrbk; Stu Cncl; Elks Awd; High Hon Roll; Sal; 1st Pl Dist Sci Fair; 1st Pl City Essay Cont; BYU Schlrshp; BYU; Zoolgy.

FRANNEA, TARRI; Katella HS; Anaheim, CA; (2); Church Yth Grp; French Clb; Hosp Aide; Key Clb; Spanish Clb; Drill Tm; Socr; Hon Roll; NHS.

FRANTZ, SHANTA G; Albany HS; Albany, CA; (4); Am Leg Aux Girls St; Cmnty Wkr; Hosp Aide; JA; Service Clb; SADD; Pres Jr Cls; VP Sr Cls; Hon Roll; U CA-SC; Poly Sci.

FRASER, KENNETH N; Montclair HS; Montclair, CA; (3); Hist Key Clb; Model UN; Ski Clb; Phtg Rptr Yrbk; Var Capt Crs Cntry; Var Capt Trk; Var Wrstlng; High Hon Roll; Hon Roll; CA Schlrshp Fed 88-90; Soph Engl Awd; Art Awd 89; Crss Cntry MVP 88-89; Jrnlsm Awd; Outstndng Athl 89; UCR; Med.

FRASER, NIKKI R; Mammoth HS; Mammoth Lakes, CA; (4); 8/47; Cmnty Wkr; Ski Clb; Teachers Aide; Phtg Yrbk; Sec Frsh Cls; Sec Sr Cls; JV Var Bsktbl; Var Cheerldng; JV Var Sftbl; JV Var Vllybl; San Diego ST; Sprts Med.

FRASER, ROBBY C; Chico SR HS; Chico, CA; (3); 92/370; Cmnty Wkr; ROTC; SADD; Teachers Aide; Color Guard; Drill Tm; Lit Mag; Hon Roll; Cngrssnl Ldrshp Cncl Awd; Stu Pilot Licnse; Cvl Air Ptrl Billy Mitchell Awd & Cadet Cmmndr; Air Force Acad; Aero Engr.

FRASER, SHANNON L; John F Kennedy HS; Sacramento, CA; (3); 25/476; Debate Tm; Pres French Clb; German Clb; Latin Clb; Ski Clb; Rep Jr Cls; Intrml Socr; Intrml Sftbl; High Hon Roll; Intl Rltns.

FRASER, SIMONE E; Monte Vista HS; Alamo, CA; (2); Church Yth Grp; Cmnty Wkr; Hosp Aide; Var Tennis; Var Trk; Natl Chrty Leag; Yth & Govrnmnt.

FRATELLO, ANTHONY; R A Mullikan HS; Long Beach, CA; (4); 22/726; Computer Clb; Key Clb; Capt Quiz Bowl; Temple Yth Grp; School Play; Rep Soph Cls; Rep Jr Cls; Rep Sr Cls; Var Swmmng; Hon Roll; Top Score Amer Chem, Soc Hnr Tst; Mogen David AZA Frtnty Chptr 2021; Pomona Coll; Physcs.

FRATTS, JASON J; J F Kennedy HS; Buen Park, CA; (3); Church Yth Grp; Letterman Clb; Teachers Aide; Varsity Clb; School Musical; Stage Crew; Var L Swmmng; High Hon Roll; Hon Roll; Pres Acad Fit Awd; Vrsty Ltr Water Polo; Ply Clsscl Guitar; Bus.

FRATUS, ERIKA C; Villa Park HS; Orange, CA; (3); Cmnty Wkr; Flag Corp; High Hon Roll; Color It Orange-Juried Art Exhibit Fnlst; Disneyland Crtvty Rep; Flag Corp-Lt & Capt Solo Prfrmr; Art.

FRAUSTO, BETTY; Exeter Union HS; Visalia, CA; (2); Sftbl; Vllybl; UCLA; Pedtrcn.

FRAUSTO, BRANDI C; Pasadena HS; Pasadena, CA; (3); Band; Jazz Band; Mrchg Band; Orch; Pep Band; School Musical; Drum Line; Chmbr Sngrs; Mst Prmsng Soph Instrmntl Music; USC; Music.

FRAUTSCHI, JENNIFER S; John Muir HS; Altadena, CA; (4); 1/360; FBLA; Service Clb; Teachers Aide; Orch; Ed Nwsp; Ed Yrbk; Pres Frsh Cls; Hon Roll; Ntl Merit Ltr; Pres Schlr; NFAA ARTS 1st Level Awd Wnnr; Seventeen Magazine/General Motors Natl Concerto Cmptn 1st Pl; USC; Music.

FRAYJO, ELIZABETH; Burbank HS; Burbank, CA; (3); Girl Scts; Office Aide; Crs Cntry; Trk; CA Schlrshp Fed; UC Santa Cruz; Law.

FRAZIER, COURTNEY L; Bullard HS; Fresno, CA; (1); Key Clb; SADD; High Hon Roll; NHS; Pres Acad Fit Awd; Jazz/Ballet Dnc; Stanford; Sci.

FRAZIER, CYNTHIA M; Del Oro HS; Newcastle, CA; (2); 19/267; Church Yth Grp; GAA; Teachers Aide; JV Bsktbl; High Hon Roll; Hon Roll; World Of Poetry Natl Contest Hon Ment; Friday Night Live; Ed.

FRAZIER, MICHELLE K; Armijo HS; Fruit Heights, UT; (3); AFS; Hosp Aide; Pep Clb; Teachers Aide; Stu Cncl; Peace Clb; BYU; Elem Ed.

FRAZIER, TAMARA; Lincoln HS; San Diego, CA; (3); Church Yth Grp; Varsity Clb; Nwsp; Yrbk; Trk; Cit Awd; Hon Roll; Prfct Atten Awd; AKA Debutante 90; Spelman Coll; Med.

FRECHETTE, TI TANISHA; Vallejo SR HS; Vallejo, CA; (2); Church Yth Grp; SADD; Teachers Aide; Off Soph Cls; Gym; Sftbl; High Hon Roll; Bus.

FREDERICK, JENNY S; Huntington Beach HS; Huntington Beach, CA; (2); Acpl Chr; Chorus; Variety Show; High Hon Roll; 1st Pl Regnl Piano Cmptn; Alg Hgh Hnrs Awd; Alg, Enlg Tower Awds; Music.

FREDERICK, THOMAS; Atascadero HS; Eureka, CA; (4); Church Yth Grp; Letterman Clb; Teachers Aide; Nwsp; Var Ftbl; High Hon Roll; Brian Russell Awd-Outstndng Athlt, Stu & Friend; Coll Of The Redwoods; Nutrtn.

FREDERICKS, SHEILA; Piner HS; Santa Rosa, CA; (2); Teachers Aide; Chorus; Santa Rosa JC; Bus.

FREDIANI, JENNIFER A; Calistoga HS; Calistoga, CA; (3); 4/38; Am Leg Aux Girls St; Chess Clb; Drama Clb; School Play; Stat Tennis; High Hon Roll; Hon Roll; Statesmn Amer Assmbly Woman; CSF Treas; Pol Sci.

FREDONA, MELISSA; Andrew P Hill HS; San Jose, CA; (4); Cmnty Wkr; Pres Drama Clb; Pres Girl Scts; Treas Science Clb; School Play; Stage Crew; Treas Soph Cls; Var Crs Cntry; Var Stat Ftbl; Var Socr; Myrs Yth Rcgntn Awd; UC Davis; Vet Med.

FREDRICKSON, JENNIFER L; Walnut HS; Walnut, CA; (4); 22/370; Science Clb; Teachers Aide; Stu Cncl; Var Capt Socr; Var Capt Sftbl; Var Capt Vllybl; High Hon Roll; Pres Acad Fit Awd; JR Hnr Guard; Athl Of Yr; CSF; OH ST U; Astronomy.

FREDRICKSON, SCOTT; Dana Hills HS; Laguna Niguel, CA; (3); Latin Clb; Science Clb; SADD; Ed Nwsp; Stu Cncl; JV Crs Cntry; High Hon Roll; Val; Pres Of Sci Fiction Club; Chem Engrng.

FREE, JENNIFER A; Eisenhower HS; Rialto, CA; (3); Science Clb; Teachers Aide; Band; Mrchg Band; Pep Band; Cit Awd; High Hon Roll; Hon Roll; Lion Awd; Stu Of Mnth & Yr Rialto Exchng Club; Mrchng Eagles Uniform Mgr; Cal ST San Bernardino; Bio Tch.

FREEBERG, KIRSTIN L; San Clemente HS; San Clemente, CA; (2); Church Yth Grp; Ski Clb; Chorus; Co-Ed Yrbk; Intrml Bsktbl; Intrml Vllybl; Sam Clement HSSPRTS Med.

FREED, SHANNON T; Henry M Gunn HS; Palo Alto, CA; (1); Church Yth Grp; Girl Scts; Chorus; JV Sftbl; Ski Clb; Temple Yth Grp; UC Santa Barbara; Teacher.

FREEDMAN, DANIEL F; Agoura HS; Agoura Hills, CA; (4); 98/446; Letterman Clb; Pep Clb; Red Cross Aide; Teachers Aide; Varsity Clb; VP Frsh Cls; Stu Cncl; Var JV Bsbl; Var Cheerldng; Hon Roll; All Leag Bsbl; Acad Athltcs Awd; Stu Vocal Ldr; U Of AZ; Poly Sci.

FREELAND, JEFFREY S; La Habra HS; La Habra, CA; (4); #4 In Class; Quiz Bowl; Science Clb; Tennis; Cit Awd; High Hon Roll; Lion Awd; Prfct Atten Awd; Stu Mnth Bus Dept; Top 100 4 Yrs; Hnrs Entrance; Poltcl Sci.

FREELAND, SHELLY A; Bishop Amat Memeorial HS; La Verne, CA; (2); Church Yth Grp; Drama Clb; School Play; High Hon Roll; NHS; Friday Night Live; Eucharistic Mnstr; Actress.

FREEMAN, ABRAHAM M; Carlsbad HS; Arcata, CA; (4); Jazz Band; Ed Nwsp; Trk; Redwoods; Eng.

FREEMAN, ALLISON; Bullard HS; Fresno, CA; (1); Debate Tm; French Clb; Intnl Clb; Key Clb; NFL; SADD; Georgetown U; Frgn Srvce.

FREEMAN, ANDREW P; Bullard HS; Fresno, CA; (1); Spanish Clb; Tennis; High Hon Roll; Hon Roll; OM; Bsbl Card Clb; Aeronautical Engr.

FREEMAN, BONNIE L; Clovis HS; Fresno, CA; (3); SADD; Comp Sci.

FREEMAN, BRET A; Helix HS; Lemon Grove, CA; (2); 88/449; Boy Scts; Drama Clb; Letterman Clb; Varsity Clb; Band; Mrchg Band; Intrml Bsbl; JV Bsktbl; Var JV Ftbl; Var JV Trk; USC; Auavionics, Electronics.

FREEMAN, C STEFAN; Santa Cruz HS; Santa Cruz, CA; (3); Church Yth Grp; Cmnty Wkr; Ski Clb; Teachers Aide; VP Frsh Cls; Treas Sr Cls; JV Ftbl; Var Golf; Var Ice Hcky; JV Var Socr; Hi Tow Toug Mens Hnr Soc; Econ.

FREEMAN, DARRELL L; Fremont HS; Oakland, CA; (2); Computer Clb; ROTC; Bsktbl; Wt Lftg; Cit Awd; Hon Roll; Law.

FREEMAN, EDWIN; Redwood Christian HS; San Leandro, CA; (2); Church Yth Grp; Drama Clb; Spanish Clb; Speech Tm; School Play; Stage Crew; Forgn Lang & Sports; Ed.

FREEMAN, HEATHER M; La Reina HS; Thousand Oaks, CA; (4); 1/81; GAA; SADD; Nwsp; Rep Stu Cncl; Var Capt Bsktbl; JV Sftbl; Var Vllybl; High Hon Roll; Rep NHS; Opt Clb Awd; Mock Trial Tm; Phys.

FREEMAN, JESSICA E; Chula Vista HS; Imperial Beach, CA; (3); Dance Clb; Pep Clb; Varsity Clb; Drill Tm; Var Cheerldng; JV Swmmng; Cit Awd; Hon Roll; Prfct Atten Awd; U CA-SAN Diego; Marine Bio.

FREEMAN, JULIE M; Notre Dame HS; Redwood City, CA; (2); Church Yth Grp; Debate Tm; Rep Nwsp; Swmmng; Bus.

FREEMAN, KALINA; Modesto HS; Modesto, CA; (2); Church Yth Grp; Church Choir; Var Bsktbl; Var Capt Trk; Var Capt Vllybl; High Hon Roll; Hon Roll; Pres Acad Fit Awd; CA Schlrshp Fdrtn; Mst Outstndng Athlt Grls Trk; Al-Acadc Bsktbl, Trk, Vllybl Tm Cntrl CA Conf.

FREEMAN, KATHLEEN E; Bonita Vista HS; Chula Vista, CA; (1); 53/600; Off Frsh Cls; Off Soph Cls; Cit Awd; Recrtnl Soccer Team; Cal Poly Tech; Arch Engrng.

FREEMAN, MICHELLE L; Ocean View HS; Huntington Beach, CA; (1); JV Bsktbl; Cit Awd; Hon Roll; Pres Acad Fit Awd; Exhbtn Clog Dncng Team; Comptv Clog Dncr; Coaches Awd Bsktbl; Tutor Hndcp Stu; LMU; Educ.

FREEMAN, MIKE R; Grossmont HS; El Cajon, CA; (2); 40/300; Computer Clb; Spanish Clb; SADD; Diving; Swmmng; Tennis; Hon Roll; Prfct Atten Awd; Water Polo; UCSD; Comp Sci.

FREEMAN, MILLER; Piedmont HS; Piedmont, CA; (3); French Clb; SADD; Nwsp; JV Var Bsktbl; JV Trk; Hon Roll; CA Schlrshp Fed; Engrng.

FREEMAN, ROBIN; Trinity HS; Weaverville, CA; (3); Drama Clb; FFA; Chorus; Vocal Jazz Ensmble; Shasta Coll; Music.

FREEMAN, SHANNON M; River City SR HS; West Sacramento, CA; (1); JV Vllybl; Photo.

FREEMAN, TRES W; Etiwanda HS; Rancho Cucamonga, CA; (3); Sec French Clb; Hnrs Goldn St Exm Alg & Geom; Vet Med.

FREER, ALLISON C; Maranatha HS; El Monte, CA; (4); Church Yth Grp; Drama Clb; Spanish Clb; Acpl Chr; Church Choir; School Play; Stu Cncl; Var Bsktbl; High Hon Roll; CA Schlrshp Fed; Dstngshd Chrstn HS Stu; Jack Green Svc Awd; U Of CA; Math.

FREER, LISA M; Armijo HS; Suisun City, CA; (2); AFS; Ski Clb; Tennis; Hon Roll; Ldrshp Cls; Pres Rgn 7 Yth Grp; Redwood Morgan Horse Clb Mem; CA U; Psych.

FREERKING, NORA J; Downieville HS; Downieville, CA; (3); Office Aide; Yrbk; Sec Frsh Cls; Pres Jr Cls; Cheerldng; Score Keeper; Hon Roll; Comp Sci Awd; Excl Job Trng Skls; Outstndng Prtcpnt Awd 90; Secy.

FREGOSO, HECTOR; Le Grand HS; Planada, CA; (2); FFA; Socr; Trk.

FREGOSO, OLIVER; Bonita Vista HS; National City, CA; (2); French Clb; Varsity Clb; Var Socr.

FREGOSO, SANDRA L; Clairemont HS; San Diego, CA; (3); VP French Clb; FTA; Church Choir; Hon Roll; Rotary Awd; Rotary Yth Ldrshp Awd; Bsktbl, Swmming; UCSD; Comp Sci.

FREI, CALLI JO B; Etiwanda HS; Alta Loma, CA; (4); Hon Roll; Chrstn Life Fllwshp Clb; Art; Wrtng; U Of CA Riverside; Law.

FREIDHOF, ANNA M; Apple Valley HS; Apple Valley, CA; (3); Church Yth Grp; Cmnty Wkr; Hosp Aide; Lit Mag; High Hon Roll; Hon Roll; Bus.

FREIDIG, NATHAN J; Placer HS; Auburn, CA; (2); Key Clb; Spanish Clb; U CA; Elec Eng.

FREIDMANN-WADDELL, PATRICE; Ernest Righett I HS; Santa Maria, CA; (1); Church Yth Grp; Cit Awd; High Hon Roll; Stu Of Mo April 90; Play Piano; UCSB; Pediatrics.

FREILICH, AMY S; Fullerton HS; Fullerton, CA; (1); #15 In Class; Cmnty Wkr; Drama Clb; Pep Clb; Thesps; Chorus; Drill Tm; School Musical; School Play; Cheerldng; JV Socr; Natl Hnrs Choir.

FREITAS, ANTHONY JOSEPH; South HS; Bakersfield, CA; (3); Aud/Vis; Church Yth Grp; Cmnty Wkr; Computer Clb; Debate Tm; 4-H; Key Clb; Ski Clb; Speech Tm; Sec Jr Cls; Bus.

FREITAS, DEBORAH A; Del Oro HS; Loomis, CA; (2); 42/396; Ski Clb; JV Capt Bsktbl; Var Capt Cheerldng; Hon Roll; System 5 Karate; Bus & Sls.

FREITAS, ELSIE; Archbishop Mitty HS; Santa Clara, CA; (3); Cmnty Wkr; Hosp Aide; Math Tm; Science Clb; JV Var Bsktbl; Var Trk; High Hon Roll; NHS; Pres Acad Fit Awd; Ofcr CSF.

FREITAS, JERRY A; Arcata HS; Arcata, CA; (3); Spanish Clb; SADD; Yrbk; Cit Awd; High Hon Roll; Pres Luso Amer Yth Cncl; Acad Ltr; CSF.

FREITAS, LISA M; Turlock HS; Turlock, CA; (3); Church Yth Grp; Teachers Aide; U Of Pacific; Bus.

FREITAS, MISSII A; Turlock HS; Ceres, CA; (2); Varsity Clb; Socr; Make-Up Artist.

FREITHOFFER, ROBERT J; Victor Valley SR HS; Victorville, CA; (3); Teachers Aide; JV Var Bsbl; Hon Roll; Golf; Bsbl; U Of NV Las Vegas; Bus.

FREMAN, JASON S; Analy HS; Sebastopol, CA; (2); Art Clb; Boy Scts; Drama Clb; Model UN; Red Cross Aide; Science Clb; Band; Mrchg Band; Pep Band; School Musical; UC Berkeley; Chem.

FRENCH, CRYSTAL S; Atascadero HS; Creston, CA; (1); JV Bsktbl; Sftbl; JV Trk; JV Vllybl; Hon Roll; Civil Air Patrol; US Air Force Acad; Pilot.

FRENCH, CYNTHIA; Center HS; Elverta, CA; (3); 2/200; Debate Tm; French Clb; FBLA; Speech Tm; Chorus; VP Stu Cncl; Cheerldng; Powder Puff Ftbl; VP Sftbl; Stat Wt Lftg; Pres Clsrm Young Americans; HOBY Yuth Smnr; Pres Friday Night Live; Corp Atty.

FRENCH, ERIC W; Fillmore HS; Fillmore, CA; (3); Church Yth Grp; Drama Clb; Teachers Aide; Band; Church Choir; Drm Mjr(t); Jazz Band; Mrchg Band; Pep Band; Nwsp; Harding U; Bus Mgmt.

FRENCH III, JOHN C; Bear River HS; Grass Valley, CA; (2); 4-H; Cit Awd; 4-H Awd; Hon Roll; Pres Acad Fit Awd; Aerospace Engr.

FRENCH, LAURA A; Roosevelt School Of The Arts; Fresno, CA; (4); 51/750; Chess Clb; Church Yth Grp; FCA; German Clb; Acpl Chr; Chorus; Church Choir; Cit Awd; Hon Roll; Fresno Pacific Coll; Music.

FRENCH, LEE; Modesto HS; Modesto, CA; (3); Chess Clb; JV Bsbl; JV Var Bsktbl; Capt JV Ftbl; High Hon Roll; Hon Roll; Soph Homecoming King; Mem CA Schlrshp Fed; Chosen Schl Newspaper Work.

FRENCH, NATHAN P; Carlsbad HS; Carlsbad, CA; (1); 35/546; Church Yth Grp; Scholastic Bowl; SADD; School Musical; High Hon Roll.

FRENCH, RACHAEL; Highlands HS; N Highlands, CA; (3); 1/250; French Clb; Ed Nwsp; High Hon Roll; Pres Acad Fit Awd; Acad Dcthln Tm Cptn; Knowlegde Bowl Tm Cptn; Peer Tutor; UC Davis; Vet Med.

FRENCH, RANDY S; Cajon HS; San Bernardino, CA; (1); Boy Scts; Church Yth Grp; Lit Mag; Hon Roll; New Life Club; Animal Trainer.

FRENG, RACHEL; Northview HS; Covina, CA; (4); Library Aide; Science Clb; Treas SADD; Teachers Aide; Church Choir; Flag Corp; Ed Yrbk; Rep Soph Cls; Capt Cheerldng; Grls Leag Sec; Grls Leag Pres; Citrus Coll; Kndgrtn Tchr.

FRENZEL, HOLLY; El Capitan HS; Lakeside, CA; (4); 4/470; Cmnty Wkr; Dance Clb; Drama Clb; English Clb; French Clb; School Musical; School Play; Variety Show; Ed Lit Mag; NHS; Pblshd Poet; Prdcd Plywrght; Awd Wnng Compsr; Musical Theater.

FRESCHAUF, DAWN N; Woodland HS; Woodland, CA; (3); Church Yth Grp; Key Clb; VP Thesps; School Musical; School Play; Variety Show; Sftbl; JV Vllybl; Hon Roll; NHS; Amer Lgn Schl Awd; Health Sci.

FRESCHI, JULIE M; Miramonte HS; Moraga, CA; (3); AFS; Church Yth Grp; GAA; Latin Clb; Spanish Clb; VP L Diving; Hon Roll; US Pony Club; US Diving; Bus.

FRESQUEZ, NEVA-MARIE; Pinole Valley HS; Hercules, CA; (1); Dance Clb; Rep Stu Cncl; Hon Roll; Ballet; Pinole-Hercules Little Leag Sftbl; Journlsm.

FREUDE, KATHRYN A; Fontana HS; Fontana, CA; (2); Hon Roll; Prfct Atten Awd; Pres Acad Fit Awd; Slvr Achvt Awd Mdl; Engl.

FREUND, DEBORAH; University HS; Los Angeles, CA; (3); Math Tm; Teachers Aide; Temple Yth Grp; VP Frsh Cls; Stu Cncl; Hon Roll; Ntl Merit Ltr; Pres Acad Fit Awd; Lit Magazine.

FREY III, CHARLES EDWIN; Warren HS; Downey, CA; (4); Boy Scts; Church Yth Grp; Cmnty Wkr; Mu Alpha Theta; Teachers Aide; Rep Stu Cncl; Vllybl; CSF; PTA Stu Recgntn Awd 4 Yrs; Downey Parks/Rec Hall Fame; Cal Poly San Lui Obispo; Sci.

FREY, JARROD; Poway HS; Poway, CA; (3); 50/696; French Clb; Intrml Tennis; JV Trk; Hon Roll; NHS; Pres Acad Fit Awd; OK Hnr Soc; CSF; Syracuse U.

FREY, JENNIFER A; Fountain Valley HS; Fountain Valley, CA; (3); 251/624; Dance Clb; Cit Awd; High Hon Roll; Hon Roll; Braill Schl For Blind Vlntr; Acctg.

FREYER, AMY M; Etiwanda HS; Alta Loma, CA; (2); JA; Latin Clb; Var Swmmng; Hon Roll; Prfct Atten Awd; Prvt Yr Rnd Swim Clb; Tchng.

FREYER, EDDIE L; College Park HS; Martinez, CA; (4); Boy Scts; Varsity Clb; Crs Cntry; Trk; Cit Awd; Pres Acad Fit Awd; Eagle Sct; CA ST U Sacramento; Cvl Engr.

FRIAS, BARBARA; Bell Gardens HS; Bell Gardens, CA; (2); French Clb; Band; Mrchg Band; Ed Yrbk; Prfct Atten Awd; Psych.

FRIAS, IMELDA I; Westmoor HS; Daly City, CA; (2); Variety Show; Hon Roll; Young Filipino Entertainers Clb; Math.

FRIAS, LORRAINE A; Edison HS; Stockton, CA; (1); Library Aide; Hon Roll; Math/Sci Magnet Pgrm; Merit Awd Smmr Yth Prgm; Comptr Prgrmmr.

FRIAS, MIKE A; Riordan HS; Daly City, CA; (3); Church Yth Grp; Cmnty Wkr; Latin Clb; Letterman Clb; Varsity Clb; Pres Stu Cncl; Var Capt Wrstlng; Hon Roll; Frnch Awd Outstndng Acad Excllnc; CA Schlrshp Fed; Booster Outstndng Athl Awd; Wrstling Awds & Hnrs; Econ.

FRIAS, PAUL D; Sylmar HS; Sylmar, CA; (2); Var Ftbl.

FRIAS, VERONICA M; Gladstone HS; Azusa, CA; (4); Computer Clb; Ventura Coll; Comm.

FRIBERG, TRAVIS; North HS; Bakersfield, CA; (3); Chess Clb; Church Yth Grp; Cmnty Wkr; English Clb; FCA; 4-H; Office Aide; Ski Clb; Spanish Clb; Chorus; CSF; NW Nazarene Coll.

FRICK, KRISTINA A; Mission San Jose HS; Fremont, CA; (1); Var Trk; Photojrnlst.

FRICKA, KEVIN B; Don Lugo HS; Chino Hills, CA; (3); 6/600; Capt Bsktbl; Hon Roll; NHS; Med.

FRIEBUS, CHRIS; Bonita HS; La Verne, CA; (4); AFS; Am Leg Boys St; Church Yth Grp; Teachers Aide; Thesps; School Play; Var Capt Crs Cntry; Var Trk; Var Capt Wrstlng; High Hon Roll; Natl Schlr/Ath Awd; Booster Schlt/Ath Awd; ASB Sec Bys Ath; CSU-FULLERTON; Theatre Art.

FRIED, MELISSA C; Lodi HS; Lodi, CA; (2); Church Yth Grp; German Clb; Chorus; Hon Roll; Orch; Guitar/Keybrd Player; Art Insst Of Seattle; Music.

FRIEDIK, SUSANA I; Sta Monica HS; Santa Monica, CA; (1); JV Bsktbl; Prfct Atten Awd.

FRIEDLANDER, BRIAN L; Lowell HS; San Francisco, CA; (2); Boy Scts; Ski Clb; Temple Yth Grp; Band; Pep Band; Stu Of CSF; High Hnrs In Golden St Math Exam; Comp Sci.

FRIEDMAN, BONNIE A; University HS; Beverly Hills, CA; (2); School Play.

FRIEDMAN, IVON H; Benicia HS; Benicia, CA; (3); SADD; JV L Bsbl; L Bsktbl; Var L Ftbl; Hon Roll; Stu Tutor; HS Mid Schl Role Model Prgm; Bus Admin.

FRIEDMAN, JARED; Taft HS; Woodland Hills, CA; (2); Boy Scts; Socr.

FRIEDMAN, NATHAN N; Palm Desert HS; Palm Desert, CA; (2); French Clb; U Of CA Irvine Tlnt Srch Cert Rcgntn; U Of CA; Math.

FRIEDMAN, ROSS M; Saratoga HS; Saratoga, CA; (3); Cmnty Wkr; English Clb; Var Crs Cntry; JV Ftbl; Var Trk; High Hon Roll; Math Awd Alg II 89; Mck Trl; Math.

FRIEDMAN, SHONA E; Mendocino Community HS; Mendocino, CA; (1); 89-90 Outstndng Sci Stu; Bus.

FRIEDRICH, KLAUS W; Culver City HS; Culver City, CA; (3); German Clb; JA; Ski Clb; SADD; Var Vllybl; Hon Roll; Blue Hnr Rl; Vrsty Ltr Vllybl; Babe Ruth Bsbl; Engrng.

FRIEND, MARK A; Huntington Beach HS; Huntington Beach, CA; (2); French Clb; Key Clb; Model UN; Red Cross Aide; High Hon Roll; Golfing,Reading,Music; UCLA; Pre-Med.

FRIEND, STEPHENIE L; El Camino Real HS; West Hills, CA; (2); Library Aide; Drill Tm; Var Cheerldng; Stat Mgr(s); Swmmng; Cit Awd; Hon Roll; St Schlr; Steering Cmmtte; St CA Indentified Gifted; U Of CA San Diego; Marine Bio.

FRIES, JENNIFER; Denair HS; Denair, CA; (2); 4-H; Teachers Aide; Hon Roll; Anml Husbndry.

FRIES, MATT; Casa Grande HS; Petaluma, CA; (4); 4/280; Am Leg Boys St; Boy Scts; German Clb; Ski Clb; Varsity Clb; Var Crs Cntry; Capt Var Swmmng; Hon Roll; NHS; Ntl Merit SF; Acad Decathalon; Acad Olympiad; Notre Dame; Intl Affairs.

FRIESEN, ANGELA; Bullard HS; Fresno, CA; (1); Chorus; Hon Roll; Dance; UCLA; Phy.

FRIESER, DIRK A; Hoover HS; Fresno, CA; (1); VP German Clb; Ftbl; JV Swmmng; JV Wrstlng; Pres Acad Fit Awd; Pilot.

FRIIS, TONYA J; Lincoln HS; Stockton, CA; (2); 50/568; Church Yth Grp; Tennis; Hon Roll; Golden St Exam Hnrs Alge; Excllnc In Span II Cert; Commrcl Art.

FRILEY, LISA M; Norte Vista HS; Riverside, CA; (3); 46/336; Hosp Aide; Hon Roll; Vlntr Srvce Awd; Notre Dame Coll OH; Bus Admin.

FRILEY, MELINDA; Notre Vista HS; Riverside, CA; (1); Lwyr.

FRILOT, RICHARD; Baldwin Park HS; Baldwin Park, CA; (3); Key Clb; Lit Mag; Rep Jr Cls; Varsity Badminton; Acad Decath.

FRIMMER, TRACEY E; Calabasas HS; Calabasas, CA; (2); Ski Clb; Rep Soph Cls; Var Socr; JV Capt Sftbl; Hon Roll; Pres Acad Fit Awd; Gldn St Alg Exm Schl Rcgntn.

FRINCKE, JANNA; Foothill HS; Pleasanton, CA; (3); 12/296; English Clb; Teachers Aide; Ed Lit Mag; High Hon Roll; Envrnmntl Clb; Humboldt ST U; Wildlife Mgmt.

FRISBEE, KRISTEN L; Vanden HS; Travis Afb, CA; (3); Church Yth Grp; GAA; Science Clb; SADD; Varsity Clb; JV Var Bsktbl; JV Var Sftbl; Hon Roll; Amer Red Crs CA Cert Lfgrd; Drama.

FRISBIE, ROSEMARY; Willows HS; Willows, CA; (3); Art Clb; Church Yth Grp; FBLA; Girl Scts; Teachers Aide; Temple Yth Grp; Church Choir; Cit Awd; Hon Roll; Prfct Atten Awd; Crrctns.

FRITCH, JIMMY; Herlong HS; Herlong, CA; (4); SADD; Teachers Aide; Varsity Clb; Var Bsbl; Bsktbl; Var Capt Ftbl; Var Trk; Wt Lftg; Wrstlng; Hon Roll; Mgr & Ownr Jimbobs Video 87-90; Hmcmng Kng 89-90; Chico; Bus Admin.

FRITCH, LISA A; Mayfair HS; Bellflower, CA; (1); JA; Office Aide; Cit Awd; Hon Roll; Soccer; U HI; Accntng.

FRITCH, LYNDA G; Andrew P Hill HS; San Jose, CA; (1); Church Yth Grp; Chld Psych.

FRITCHLE, MELISSA A; Mtn View HS; Mountain View, CA; (4); VP Drama Clb; Teachers Aide; Thesps; School Play; Stage Crew; Hon Roll; Peer Counseling; U CA Irvine; Lit Prof.

FRITTS, ANDREW K; Rosamond HS; Rosamond, CA; (2); Church Yth Grp; Chorus; Church Choir; Ftbl; Hon Roll; Hghst Adv Achvt Awd; Air Force; Bus.

FRITTS, CRYSTAL L; Vista HS; Oceanside, CA; (2); FFA; Bsktbl; Trk; Pres Acad Fit Awd; Surfing; Highst GPA FFA Clb; Mira Coasta Coll; Med.

FRITZ, ERIC L; Beaumont HS; Cherry Valley, CA; (4); Boy Scts; Church Yth Grp; School Play; Cit Awd; High Hon Roll; Hon Roll; Prfct Atten Awd; JC San Bernardino; Arch Drftsm.

FRITZ, KERRI; Riverdale HS; Riverdale, CA; (2); Church Yth Grp; GAA; VP SADD; Varsity Clb; Church Choir; JV Score Keeper; Var Sftbl; Var Trk; Var Vllybl; High Hon Roll; Cnslr Chrch Yth Camp; Incoming Sec Girls Athltc Assoc, Jr Cls.

FRITZ, KRISTINA L; Nogales HS; W Covina, CA; (3); 38/628; Girl Scts; Sec Varsity Clb; Rptr Yrbk; Var Capt Bsktbl; Var Sftbl; Var Capt Vllybl; High Hon Roll; Prfct Atten Awd; Pres Acad Fit Awd; Sec Stu Cncl; Trvlng Vlybl Clb Sprtswst; Biolgcl Sci.

FRITZSCHE, CHRIS H; Edison HS; Huntington Beach, CA; (2); Church Yth Grp; Letterman Clb; Model UN; Off Soph Cls; L Var Wrstlng; Sister City Assn; Med.

FRIZZELLE, JENNIFER; Agoura HS; Agoura Hills, CA; (4); 35/438; Pep Clb; SADD; Var Tennis; Var Trk; Hon Roll; CSF Member & Gold Seal Bearer At Grad; U Of Southern CA.

FRIZZI, MARK V; Mira Coma HS; Sacramento, CA; (3); 10/284; Letterman Clb; Varsity Clb; Rep Frsh Cls; Rep Soph Cls; Rep Jr Cls; Var Bsbl; Var Bsktbl; Cit Awd; Elks Awd; High Hon Roll.

FROEBERG, JULIE; Canyon HS; Canyon Country, CA; (3); 152/550; French Clb; Pep Clb; Chorus; Cheerldng; Gym; Sftbl; Cit Awd; Hon Roll; Woodbury; Interior Dsgn.

FROEHLICH, DUSTIN; Torrey Pines HS; Solana Beach, CA; (4); Cmnty Wkr; VICA; 2 Local Schlrshps; Dollars For Scholars; 1st Pl Tech Drafting Drawing 90; VICA Conts; CA ST U Long Beach; Art.

FROELICH, CINDY; Lemoore HS; Lemoore, CA; (3); Pep Clb; Spanish Clb; SADD; Cheerldng; Intl Ordr Of Rainbow Girls; Intl Order Jobs Dghtrs; Fresno ST U; Educ.

FROMAN, APRIL; Thomas Downey HS; Modesto, CA; (3); Church Yth Grp; Pep Clb; Spanish Clb; Speech Tm; Chorus; Ftbl; Powder Puff Ftbl; Wt Lftg; Wrstlng; Hon Roll; Thomas Downey Knghts Music Awd 87-88; Stanford ST; Tchr.

FROMBERG, EVE E; Palm Springs HS; Palm Springs, CA; (4); 25/440; Am Leg Aux Girls St; Cmnty Wkr; Debate Tm; Drama Clb; Office Aide; Thesps; School Musical; School Play; Stage Crew; Rep Stu Cncl; Stu Rep Sch Bd; CA Schlrshp Fdr Slbr; Vlntr Hospice Unit; U Of San Diego; Law.

FROMM, CHRIS M; Redlands HS; Mentone, CA; (2); Boy Scts; ROTC; Ski Clb; Teachers Aide; Drill Tm; School Play; Stage Crew; Ftbl; Intrml Wt Lftg; Order Of Arrow; Engr.

FROMM, STEPHEN A; Montgomery HS; Santa Rosa, CA; (3); Church Yth Grp; French Clb; Teachers Aide; Var Crs Cntry; JV Trk; High Hon Roll; Hon Roll; Frgn Lang Cert Of Merit Frnch; Chem Engrng.

FRONCZAK, JOHN C; Livingston HS; Delhi, CA; (2); VP Stu Cncl; JV Ftbl; JV Trk; Var Wrstlng; Hon Roll; Water/Snow Skiing; Teach.

FROST, ALANA M; Pacific Union College Prep; Angwin, CA; (3); Church Yth Grp; Off Soph Cls; Stu Cncl; Gym; Var Sftbl; Prfct Atten Awd; Pacific Union Coll.

FROST, DOUG; Capistrano Valley HS; Mission Viejo, CA; (3); Boy Scts; Church Yth Grp; JV Socr; JV Capt Vllybl; High Hon Roll; UCSD; Bio.

FROST, EMILY; Willows HS; Corbin, KY; (3); Am Leg Aux Girls St; Church Yth Grp; Key Clb; Church Choir; Score Keeper; High Hon Roll; Hon Roll; Psych.

FROST, JENNIFER C; Rio Lindo Adventist Acad; Napa, CA; (3); Art Clb; Church Yth Grp; Drama Clb; FCA; School Play; Ed Nwsp; VP Stu Cncl; 2 Consctve Wrk Exprnce Awds; People/People Frndshp Caravan Stu Ambssdr Russia; Rio Lindo Advntst Acad; Engl.

FROST, JENNIFER M; St Bonaventure HS; Oak View, CA; (3); 10/122; Cmnty Wkr; Ed Nwsp; High Hon Roll; NHS; St Schlr; Part Time Job.

FROST III, KENNETH A; Terra Linda HS; San Rafael, CA; (4); 5/152; Church Yth Grp; French Clb; Science Clb; Band; Mrchg Band; Pep Band; VP Capt Swmmng; Pres Acad Fit Awd; Vrsty Water Polo Let; Harvard Book Awd Wnnr; Marin Athletic Fndtn Stu/Athlete; Brown U; Ortho Surgery.

FROST, RYAN D; Flintridge Preparatory Schl; La Canada-Flint, CA; (4); 11/96; Boy Scts; JCL; Latin Clb; Ed Yrbk; Var Bsktbl; Capt Var Crs Cntry; Var Trk; Capt Var Vllybl; High Hon Roll; 1st Tm All League Vlybl; Brigham Young U; Bus.

FROST, STACEY J; Chico SR HS; Chico, CA; (4); Teachers Aide; School Play; Stage Crew; CSU; Fshn Merch.

FROYD, RENEE; Petterson HS; Patterson, CA; (4); 1/115; Pres AFS; Am Leg Aux Girls St; Cmnty Wkr; SADD; Cit Awd; High Hon Roll; Pres Acad Fit Awd; Val; Acdmc Dcthln Team Mem; Sec Of Girls Ldrshp; Bnk Of Amer Plaque For Math & Sci; UC Davis; Ped.

FRUDDEN, ALICIA D; King City HS; King City, CA; (2); Church Yth Grp; Treas 4-H; Hon Roll; Interact; Commercial Club; Raising Sheep, Babysitting, Ldrshp Class, Piano Lessons, Swmming; Fresno ST; Elem Schl Teacher.

FRUEHAN, SHANA L; Bishop O'dowd HS; El Cerrito, CA; (3); 4/240; Nwsp; French Hon Soc; CA Schlrshp Fdrtn; Soc Of Wmn Engrs; Engl.

FRUHWIRTH, EVELYN; Western HS; Buena Park, CA; (3); Church Yth Grp; Band; Jazz Band; Mrchg Band; Orch; Cit Awd; Hon Roll; NHS; CSF; UCLA; Teacher.

FRY, JEREMY E; Poway HS; Poway, CA; (2); Church Yth Grp; Band; High Hon Roll; UCLA; Dsng Engr.

FRY, MICHAEL A; San Rafael HS; San Rafael, CA; (2); Bsbl; JV Ftbl; Intrml Wt Lftg.

FRY, SHANNON M; Mt Pleasant HS; San Jose, CA; (1); Var Swmmng; Hon Roll; Ca U; Interior Dsgnr.

FRY, THERESA; Lemoore HS; Lemoore, CA; (3); 124/374; Art Clb; Pep Clb; School Play; Var Cheerldng; JV Diving; JV Gym; Masnc Yth Grp; Ms CA Amer Coed Vlntr Svc 89; Fresno ST; Cmmrcl Art.

FRYCKMAN, CINDY L; Folsom HS; Folsom, CA; (3); 2/187; Church Yth Grp; Model UN; JV Var Bsktbl; JV Var Sftbl; Hon Roll; NHS; Friday Night Live Pres 89-90; Sec 88-89; Church Yth Choir; Lawyer.

FRYE, JACI; Tehachapi HS; Tehachapi, CA; (3); 25/190; Church Yth Grp; Drama Clb; Pep Clb; SADD; Teachers Aide; Church Choir; Sec Frsh Cls; Rep Soph Cls; Rep Stu Cncl; Cheerldng; AZ ST U; Brdcstg/Comm.

FRYE, MARY ANNE; Los Gatos HS; Los Gatos, CA; (4); 9/374; Key Clb; Latin Clb; Math Clb; Math Tm; Service Clb; Teachers Aide; Orch; Rep Frsh Cls; Off Soph Cls; Off Sr Cls; Rice U; Engr.

FU, AMY L; Diamond Bar HS; Diamond Bar, CA; (2); Aud/Vis; Key Clb; Science Clb; Service Clb; Spanish Clb; Var Capt Bsktbl; Var Tennis; Cit Awd; Hon Roll; Var Capt Badminton, S CA Jr Team; Pres Phys Ftns AwdfHS Prin Hnr Roll.

FU, CRYSTAL; Pacifica HS; Garden Grove, CA; (4); 2/256; Scholastic Bowl; Pres Spanish Clb; Nwsp; Stu Cncl; Var Capt Crs Cntry; Var Capt Trk; Hon Roll; Ntl Merit SF; Cross Cntry Leag Champ; Leag 1st Team Track; Writer.

FU, DRUCE I; Canyon HS; Canyon Country, CA; (2); Bsktbl; High Hon Roll; Hon Roll; Jr NHS.

FU, IRENE F; Watsonville HS; Watsonville, CA; (3); 1/500; Church Yth Grp; Off Math Clb; Science Clb; Church Choir; Color Guard; High Hon Roll; Hon Roll; Val; Glnd St Exam Geom Hnrs 88; Stu Mnth For Scl Stds & Bus; UC Davis; Vet.

FU, MIMI; Santa Monica HS; Santa Monica, CA; (4); JA; JCL; Latin Clb; SADD; Band; Mrchg Band; Orch; Rptr Nwsp; Landis, Tara & David Simon Schlrshps; Wind Ensemble; CSF; U CA Los Angeles.

FU, STEPHANIE J; Marina HS; Huntington Beach, CA; (3); Spanish Clb; Lit Mag; Hon Roll; Mdlng; Piano.

FUA-STIANILEI, HELEN S; Montclair HS; Ontario, CA; (3); Teachers Aide; Sftbl; Prfct Atten Awd; Sty Of Yr Awrd; Excllnc Geo; CA ST San Bernardino; Bus.

FUENTES, ANA P; St Joseph HS; Montebello, CA; (3); 41/200; JV Var Bsktbl; Var Crs Cntry; Var Sftbl; JV Vllybl; Hon Roll; CSF; Sports Med.

FUENTES, ARTURO; Selma HS; Selma, CA; (2); 43/257; Band; Jazz Band; Mrchg Band; Pep Band; Ftbl; Wt Lftg; Prfct Atten Awd; Student Ambassador; Computers.

FUENTES, BETTY; Carson HS; Carson, CA; (3); Church Yth Grp; Latin Clb; Band; Church Choir; Capt Drill Tm; Mrchg Band; Cit Awd; Hon Roll; Jr NHS; NHS; CSF; Yth Chrch Grp Choir; CA ST Dominguez Hls; Acctng.

FUENTES JR, ISRAEL; La Puente HS; La Puente, CA; (3); Church Yth Grp; Teachers Aide; Chrch Guitar; Drm Plyr; Bus.

FUENTES, JENNIFER; Saddleback HS; Santa Ana, CA; (3); Drill Tm; Jr NHS; Step Clb; Bus.

FUENTES, JULIANN T; Loretto HS; Carmichael, CA; (1); Church Yth Grp; Office Aide; Red Cross Aide; School Musical; Ed Yrbk; Trk; JV Vllybl; Friday Night Live; Stanford; Med.

FUENTES, LOUIS A; Aurora HS; Calexico, CA; (1); Band; Mrchg Band; Pep Band; Rep Stu Cncl; Hon Roll; Pres Acad Fit Awd; Stanford U; Med.

FUENTES, LUPE; Firebaugh HS; Firebaugh, CA; (3); 8/80; Church Yth Grp; Cmnty Wkr; Dance Clb; FHA; SADD; Teachers Aide; Church Choir; High Hon Roll; Hon Roll; FFA; Fresno ST.

FUENTES, MARIA E; Dos Palos HS; South Dos Palos, CA; (2); Teachers Aide; Crs Cntry; Csmtlgy.

FUENTES, PAULA M; Foothill HS; Bakersfield, CA; (3); Church Yth Grp; Library Aide; Drill Tm; Hon Roll; UCSB; Soc Work.

FUENTES, SONIA; John F Kennedy HS; Los Angeles, CA; (3); Wrld Educ Clb; Lawyer.

FUENTES, SUSAN; Bell Gardens HS; Bell Gardens, CA; (3); French Clb; JV Swmmng.

FUENTES, VICENTE R; Carson HS; Carson, CA; (4); Aud/Vis; Latin Clb; School Play; Stage Crew; Socr; CSULB; Intl Bus.

FUENTES, YOLANDA; San Fernando HS; Pacoima, CA; (2); Band; Jazz Band; Mrchg Band; Sec Jr Cls; Sec Stu Cncl; Cit Awd; Hon Roll; NHS; Prfct Atten Awd; Pres Acad Fit Awd; UCLA; Pediatrician.

FUESS, JUDY; Rosary HS; Garden Grove, CA; (3); Science Clb; Hon Roll; NHS; CA Schlrshp Fed; Decathln Tm; Cvl Engrng.

FUGATE, DIONNE; David Starr Jordan HS; Los Angeles, CA; (4); Cmnty Wkr; Intnl Clb; Office Aide; Drill Tm; Off Sr Cls; Cheerldng; Hon Roll.

FUGATE, HEATHER; Mt Carmel HS; San Diego, CA; (2); Varsity Clb; Var Cheerldng; JV Swmmng; Trk; Stu Cncl; Sundevil Awd.

FUGATE, KATHEE; Calvary Chapel HS; Huntington Beach, CA; (4); Church Yth Grp; Cmnty Wkr; Drama Clb; Hosp Aide; Rep Sr Cls; Stu Cncl; Stat Ftbl; Var Mgr(s); JV Var Vllybl; High Hon Roll; HOBY; Westmont Coll; Commnctns.

FUGATTI, CHRISTINE; Miraleste HS; Ranchos Palos Ver, CA; (3); Cmnty Wkr; Hosp Aide; Service Clb; Spanish Clb; Sprt Ed Nwsp; Off Sr Cls; Cheerldng; JV Socr; Var Trk; Hon Roll; Cmnty Srvce Angel Awd; Assisteens; Jrnlsm.

FUGITT, BENJAMIN B; Poway HS; Poway, CA; (2); Spanish Clb; Orch; Lit Mag; North Cty Civic Yth Orch; Billabong String Trio; CSF; Photography Club; Fencing Club; U CA San Diego; Engrng.

FUGITT, CHRISTY N; Fremont Christian HS; Fremont, CA; (2); Church Yth Grp; German Clb; School Play; JV Bsktbl; Var Socr; DAR Awd; Hon Roll.

FUGLEVAND, JENNIFER C; Louisville HS; Woodland Hills, CA; (2); Dance Clb; School Musical; School Play; High Hon Roll; Hon Roll; Prfct Atten Awd; Prfrmng Arts Clb; UCSB; Law.

FUGLSANG, PATRICIA; Richard E Byrd JR HS; Sun Valley, CA; (1); Drama Clb; Chorus; Capt Drill Tm; School Play; VP Stu Cncl; Capt Cheerldng; Capt Pom Pon; Hon Roll; Pres Acad Fit Awd; Amer Lgn Schl Awd.

FUHRIMAN, DAVID O; Santa Maria HS; Santa Maria, CA; (3); 31/467; Boy Scts; Church Yth Grp; Hon Roll; CSF; UCSB; Microbio.

FUJII, KATHY K; Skyline HS; Oakland, CA; (2); Intnl Clb; Key Clb; Treas Frsh Cls; Stat Sftbl; Var Tennis; Cit Awd; Hon Roll; Pres Acad Fit Awd.

FUJIMOTO, JUNE; Burbank HS; Burbank, CA; (3); Office Aide; Red Cross Aide; VP Science Clb; Rep Stu Cncl; JV Sftbl; JV Tennis; Cit Awd; Treas High Hon Roll; Prfct Atten Awd; Pres Acad Fit Awd; Treasurer Of Z Club; Spec Olympics Tri-Valley Volunteer; Voted Most Insprtl JV Tennis; Assembly Comm; Chemical Engineer.

FUJIMOTO, KATE O; Westlake School For Girls; Studio City, CA; (1); French Clb; Hosp Aide; Rptr Nwsp; Vlntr For Eldrly; Law.

FUJINAMI, KATHY M; Gardena HS; Gardena, CA; (4); 19/425; FTA; JA; Yrbk; Pres Acad Fit Awd; Task Force; Drug, Alchl Prevntn Prgm; CSF; Squires Sch And Cmnty Svc Clb; U CA Irvine; Bio.

FUJINO, MELISSA C; Louisville HS; Agoura Hills, CA; (3); Art Clb; Church Yth Grp; FHA; GAA; Church Choir; Rep Stu Cncl; High Hon Roll; ARC Volunteer; CSF.

FUKADA, MAYUMI; Torrance HS; Torrance, CA; (3); 71/414; Off JA; Service Clb; Off Band; Jazz Band; Off Mrchg Band; Pep Band; School Musical; School Play; Ed Phtg Yrbk; Hist Stu Cncl; US Collegiate Wind Band Europe Tour 90; All St CA Hnr Band 90; Intl Chldrns Choirs Peace Tour USSR; Music.

FUKAMI, TAKUYO DAVID; Flintridge Prep; Monrovia, CA; (3); Boy Scts; Chess Clb; Church Yth Grp; Debate Tm; Hosp Aide; JCL; Key Clb; Latin Clb; Math Clb; Ski Clb; Earthquake Preparedness Cmmtte; Lit Film Clb; UCSD; Psych.

FUKSSHIMOV, IRINA; George Washington HS; San Francisco, CA; (2); Computer Clb; Dance Clb; Debate Tm; Drama Clb; Yrbk; Diving; Gym; Hon Roll; Enuigrated From USSR 87; UCLA; Sci.

FUKUDA, TRACY A; San Gabriel HS; San Gabriel, CA; (2); Debate Tm; JA; NFL; Spanish Clb; Speech Tm; Mrchg Band; JV Tennis; Hon Roll; Lion Awd; Opt Clb Awd; San Gabriel Judo Dojo; Jr Judo Natl 2nd Pl; Stanford; Adolescent Psych.

FUKUMOTO, LYNNE M; Mark Keppel HS; Monterey Park, CA; (2); Drama Clb; Math Clb; Bsktbl; Vllybl; Hon Roll; CSF.

FUKUSHIMA, RUSSELL B; John F Kennedy HS; Sacramento, CA; (2); 103/559; Rep Frsh Cls; Intrml Golf; Intrml Wt Lftg; Intrml Wrstlng; Pres Acad Fit Awd; Bus.

FULAY, ADRIAN; La Salle HS; Arcadia, CA; (4); 19/90; Am Leg Boys St; Church Yth Grp; Service Clb; School Play; Yrbk; Sec Treas Sr Cls; Hon Roll; NHS; Los Angeles Chrstn Svc Mdl-Archdiocese; Loyola Mavymount U; Poly Sci.

FULINARA, JENNY A; Sweetwater Union HS; National City, CA; (2); Dance Clb; Drama Clb; Intnl Clb; Teachers Aide; Chorus; Hon Roll; UCSD; RN.

FULLEN, GILDARDO; Huntington Park HS; Los Angeles, CA; (3); Cmnty Wkr; JV Bsbl; Var Ftbl; Var Wt Lftg; Cit Awd; Hon Roll; Pres Awd Acadmc Achvt; Midget Bsbl Team Asst Coach; USC; Astrnmy.

FULLER, ANDREA M; Centennial HS; Corona, CA; (4); 3/130; Drama Clb; Pres SADD; School Musical; Mgr Stage Crew; Var Cheerldng; Cit Awd; DAR Awd; High Hon Roll; Pres Acad Fit Awd; St Schlr; CA Schlrshp Fed; Bank Of Amer Achvt Awd Plaque; Mayors Schlrshp; NY U; Theatre.

FULLER, ASHLEY J; Davis SR HS; Danville, CA; (4); Church Yth Grp; GAA; Pep Clb; Rep Stu Cncl; Powder Puff Ftbl; Sftbl; Var Vllybl; Hon Roll; NHS; U Of CA Los Angeles; Psych.

FULLER, BRETT L; Brawley Union HS; Brawley, CA; (3); 1/450; Am Leg Boys St; Church Yth Grp; Math Tm; VP Stu Cncl; Wrstlng; High Hon Roll; AZ ST U; Engrng.

FULLER, DEBRA M; Irvine HS; Irvine, CA; (3); Band; Jazz Band; Mrchg Band; Orch; School Musical; Intrml Swmmng; Hon Roll; Pres Acad Fit Awd; Clrnt; Soc Sci Heritage Awd; Hgh Hnr Achvt Golden St Exam Algebra; Arch.

FULLER, DORIAN Q; Lowell HS; San Francisco, CA; (3); Boy Scts; Band; Jazz Band; Rptr Nwsp; Crs Cntry; Trk; Hstry.

FULLER, JAVIER; Notre Dame HS; Sherman Oaks, CA; (4); 55/249; Cmnty Wkr; Computer Clb; JA; Pep Clb; ROTC; JV Bsbl; JV Mgr(s); Hon Roll; Ntl Merit SF; Loyola Marymount U; Comp Sci.

FULLER, JENNIFER L; South San Francisco HS; San Bruno, CA; (3); Math Clb; Teachers Aide; Var Tennis; Var Trk; Hon Roll; Pres Acad Fit Awd; MVP Dist Runnr Girls Var Trk 89; St Of Mnth Sci 87; Golden St Exam Awd 1st Yr Algebra 87.

FULLER, KEVIN R; Fresno Christian HS; Fresno, CA; (2); Church Yth Grp; Letterman Clb; Varsity Clb; Pres Soph Cls; Treas Stu Cncl; Var Bsbl; Var Ftbl; Var Socr; Hon Roll; Pres Acad Fit Awd; Law.

FULLER, LAURA K; Thomas Downey HS; Modesto, CA; (2); Dance Clb; Powder Puff Ftbl; Waterpolo; Svrl Awds Dance; Bst Chrgrphr; Knight Achvt Awd; Julliard; Choreography.

FULLER, LEAH M; Leuzinger HS; Hawthorne, CA; (3); 20/500; Girl Scts; Band; Jazz Band; Mrchg Band; School Musical; High Hon Roll; Hon Roll; Pres Acad Fit Awd; Rotary Awd; CSF; Stanford; Pre-Med.

FULLER, ROBERT; Apple Valley SR HS; Apple Valley, CA; (2); Letterman Clb; Crs Cntry; Socr; Trk; Vllybl; San Diego ST U; Arontcl Engrng.

FULLERTON, CARLI G; J Eugene Mc Ateer HS; San Francisco, CA; (3); Church Yth Grp; Cmnty Wkr; Chorus; High Hon Roll; Ivy League Book Awd; Nrsng.

FULLERTON, MOLLY; Paraclete HS; Lancaster, CA; (3); Church Yth Grp; Drama Clb; Hosp Aide; Key Clb; Teachers Aide; School Play; High Hon Roll; Hon Roll; Teaching.

FULMER, JENNIFER; Bishop O'dowd HS; Oakland, CA; (4); Church Yth Grp; Cmnty Wkr; Church Choir; JV Var Bsktbl; Hon Roll; North Park Coll; Nrsng.

FULTER, STACEY A; Crawford HS; San Diego, CA; (4); Computer Clb; Math Clb; Pep Clb; Yrbk; Hnr Sem San Diego; Co-Fndr Cngrs African Am Stu; Cmmnded Natl Schlrshp Comp; Acctnt.

FULTON, JOY L; Sunny Hills HS; Fullerton, CA; (3); 4-H; JCL; Latin Clb; Var L Tennis; 4-H Awd; Silver Mdl Earth Sci & Latin 3; U Redlands.

FULVIO, ALANA M; Sacred Heart Prep; Belmont, CA; (1); Church Yth Grp; Cmnty Wkr; Phtg Rptr Nwsp; VP Frsh Cls; JV L Bsktbl; Var L Sftbl; Var L Trk; JV L Vllybl; 3rd Pl Bst Sport Story San Mateo Times Nwsp Cont; CYSA U-19 Premr Team; U-16 Dist Team Sccr; Santa Clara.

FUMIA, MELISSA A; Los Gatos HS; Los Gatos, CA; (2); Var Socr; Var Trk; Peace & Envrnmntl Issues.

FUNAOKA, LISA M; John F Kennedy HS; La Palma, CA; (2); Sec Soph Cls; Sec Jr Cls; UCLA; Psych.

FUNDERBURK, CINDY; Atwater HS; Atwater, CA; (2); Church Yth Grp; FCA; French Clb; Intnl Clb; Key Clb; SADD; Band; Church Choir; Mrchg Band; Pep Band; CSF Club; Falcon Crest Awds; Stanford; Med.

FUNES, EVELYN Y; Hamilton Music Acad; Bell Gardens, CA; (2); Band; Color Guard; Mrchg Band; UCLA; Elec Engr.

FUNG, ANDREW; St Ignatius College Prep; Pacifica, CA; (3); 7/244; Cmnty Wkr; Orch; Ed Nwsp; Phtg Yrbk; Intrml Ftbl; Intrml Sftbl; Intrml Vllybl; High Hon Roll; Ntl Merit SF; Smmr Times Nwspr Harvard Smmr Schl 90; NCTE Essay Wrtng Cntst.

FUNG, CARRIE C; Westmoor HS; Daly City, CA; (2); GAA; Math Tm; Spanish Clb; JV Crs Cntry; Var Trk; Hon Roll; CSF; GATE; Coll Entrnc Club; Social Wrkr.

FUNG, DEREK P; St Francis HS; Sunnyvale, CA; (2); 5/356; Church Choir; School Musical; School Play; High Hon Roll; Mst Promising Chorus Stu; Outstndg Achvt Math; Medical.

FUNG, HANG; Paramount HS; Bellflower, CA; (2); 3/666; FTA; Letterman Clb; Bsktbl; Tennis; High Hon Roll; Hon Roll; Opt Clb Awd; Prfct Atten Awd; UCI; HS Tchr.

FUNG, JACKIE; Rolling Hills HS; Rolling Hills Est, CA; (3); Church Yth Grp; Dance Clb; Latin Clb; Pep Clb; Spanish Clb; SADD; Drill Tm; Variety Show; Nwsp; Sec Treas Soph Cls; Drl Tm Sgt.

FUNG, JENNY; San Marcos HS; Vista, CA; (3); Pres Key Clb; Mrchg Band; Pres Soph Cls; Treas Stu Cncl; Cheerldng; Var Fld Hcky; JV Socr; Var Trk; Elks Awd; High Hon Roll; CSF VP; Math.

FUNG, JIMMY; Schurr HS; Montebello, CA; (1); Intnl Clb; SADD; Trk; Hon Roll; Prfct Atten Awd; CA Schlrshp Fed; JR Statesman Am; Chinese Clb.

FUNG, JULIE; Hoover HS; Fresno, CA; (3); 24/500; French Clb; Yrbk; JV Bsktbl; Mgr(s); Score Keeper; Var L Tennis; Hon Roll; CSF; Boston U.

FUNG, NANCY; Schurr HS; Montebello, CA; (2); Cmnty Wkr; Hosp Aide; Intnl Clb; Spanish Clb; SADD; Hon Roll; Prfct Atten Awd; Chinese Clb; Interact Clb; CSF; JSA.

FUNG, TRACY Y; John F Kennedy HS; Sacramento, CA; (1); 1/559; Math Clb; Prtcptd Golden St Exam; Friday Night Live Clb; Harvard U; Law.

FUNG, VICTOR WAI-KUEN; Don Bosco Technical Inst; Monterey Park, CA; (1); 10/244; Dance Clb; Quiz Bowl; Teachers Aide; NHS; Pres Acad Fit Awd; Flying Private Aircraft Out Of Whiteman Airport; Have 90 Hrs Logged; Cal Tech; Pilot Comm Airline.

FUNG, WENDY WING YEE; Phillip And Sala Burton HS; San Francisco, CA; (2); Church Yth Grp; Math Clb; Science Clb; High Hon Roll; 5th Chinese Athtlc Tourny Of Bay Area; Chinese Amer Ctzns Alliance Schlrshp; PLUS Educ Schlrshp; Educ.

FUNG, WINNIE; Galileo HS; San Francisco, CA; (2); Pep Clb; Red Cross Aide; Crs Cntry; Trk; Hon Roll; CSF 90; Psych.

FUNK, CHRIS D; Bullard HS; Fresno, CA; (1); Church Yth Grp; Hon Roll; Fresno ST; Accountant.

FUNKE, CAROLYN J; Grossmont HS; El Cajon, CA; (2); 20/420; Church Yth Grp; Hosp Aide; JV Gym; JV Swmmng; Hon Roll; Jazz Dance; Awd Essy Submttd Skirball Inst; UCSD; Chld Psych.

FUNKHOUSER, BECKY S; Ernest Righetti HS; Orcutt, CA; (2); SADD; Stage Crew; Swing Chorus; Stu Cncl; Girl Scts; Var JV Score Keeper; Hon Roll; Gold Awd Girl Sct; Interact Clb; CA Schltc Fed; Med.

FUNSTON, DAVID P; James Lick HS; San Jose, CA; (2); Drama Clb; 4-H; Math Tm; Stage Crew; JV L Bsktbl; JV L Ftbl; Var L Swmmng; 4-H Awd; High Hon Roll; Engrng.

FUNSTON, YORK; Valhalla HS; El Cajon, CA; (2); 45/451; German Clb; Hon Roll; Cinematography.

FUREDI, CYNTHIA M; Huntington Beach HS; Huntington Beach, CA; (3); Dance Clb; Beach Inc Club; Amnesty Intl Club; Loyola Marymount U; Psych.

FURLONG, LYNNE; Foothill HS; Pleasanton, CA; (3); FFA; Teachers Aide; Nwsp; Hon Roll; 2 Awds FFA; Played Tennis Leag City; Natl Yng Ldrs Confrnc Washington DC; Cngrssnl Schlr; UC Santa Barbara; Hotel Mgmt.

FURLONG, WENDY E; Morro Bay HS; Los Osos, CA; (3); JA; Var Capt Bsktbl; Var Sftbl; JV Vllybl; Hon Roll; Photo; Music; Advanced Ceramics; Bus.

FURMAN, SHELLY; Etiwanda HS; Rancho Cucamonga, CA; (2); Cheerldng; Trk.

FURPHY, CINDY M; Liberty Union HS; Brentwood, CA; (1); Church Yth Grp; FCA; Intrml Swmmng; Var Trk; Pres Acad Fit Awd; Prfrmr.

FURROW, SHERI C; Paraclete HS; Palmdale, CA; (2); Church Yth Grp; French Clb; Church Choir; Trk; Hon Roll; Frgn Lang Hnrs; MTA St Cnvntn Ply Piano, Brnch Hnrs Rctl; UCSB; Music.

FURSE, CORY W; Bellarmine College Prep; Sunnyvale, CA; (3); Cmnty Wkr; Letterman Clb; Ski Clb; L Co-Capt Ftbl; 1st String Var Ftbl 90.

FURST, BENJAMIN A; Oak Park HS; Agoura Hills, CA; (1); Boy Scts; Key Clb; Band; Pep Band; Treas Frsh Cls; Treas Soph Cls; Crs Cntry; JV Socr; High Hon Roll; Pres Acad Fit Awd; Eagle Sct 89; CSF; Peer Cnslng.

FURTADO, MARY S; San Jose High Acad; San Jose, CA; (3); Office Aide; Teachers Aide; Hon Roll; Prfct Atten Awd; Portuguese Club.

FURTWANGLER, JASON; El Dorado HS; Camino, CA; (3); 12/365; Church Yth Grp; Drama Clb; Quiz Bowl; Teachers Aide; School Play; JV Crs Cntry; High Hon Roll; Awds In Bio, Geomtry, Englsh & Spnsh; CSF; OR Sci Schl; Health Tchr.

FURUICHI, KRISTIN M; Skyline HS; Oakland, CA; (3); Church Yth Grp; Key Clb; Service Clb; Band; Orch; School Musical; Sec Soph Cls; VP Stu Cncl; Hon Roll; U Sthrn CA; Tele Cmnctns.

FURUMOTO, KARIN S; Gretchen Whitney HS; La Palma, CA; (2); Dance Clb; Key Clb; Special Education.

FURUTA, MICHAEL; Villa Park HS; Anaheim, CA; (2); Key Clb; Spanish Clb; Off Soph Cls; Bsktbl; High Hon Roll; NHS; 4.0 GPA; CSF; Coaches Awd Bsktbll; Wnnr Bronze Sprtn Svc Awd; U Of CA.

FURUTA, SATOKO; Hillsdale HS; San Mateo, CA; (4); 1/296; Am Leg Aux Girls St; Pres Art Clb; Ed Lit Mag; Sec Frsh Cls; VP Soph Cls; Sec Jr Cls; VP Sr Cls; Var L Tennis; Elks Awd; High Hon Roll; Sec & V P CSF; Hmcmng Princess; JSA, Asian Club, Spec Olympics Vol, Badminton; Graphic/Pkgng Dsgn.

FURZE, ERIC; Edison HS; Fresno, CA; (2); Church Yth Grp; Math Clb; Math Tm; Ski Clb; JV Socr; Var Swmmng; Hon Roll; St Schlr; Water Polo; Engrng Tech Soc; Physics.

FUSCO, BRYAN; Chula Vista HS; Chula Vista, CA; (2); 114/605; Church Yth Grp; Band; Mrchg Band; Pep Band; Cit Awd; Pres Acad Fit Awd; MI ST; Med.

FUSHIMI, HARUKA S; Whitney HS; Cerritos, CA; (2); Variety Show; Sec Jr Cls; JV Var Bsktbl; High Hon Roll; Pres Acad Fit Awd; Japanese Schl Stu Pres; SE Yth Orgnztn Bsktbl; CSF; SYMF Wnnr.

FUSILERO, MARIA D; Mira Loma HS; Sacramento, CA; (3); 29/290; Church Yth Grp; Drama Clb; German Clb; Math Clb; Science Clb; School Play; Ed Yrbk; JV Var Sftbl; JV Vllybl; Hon Roll; Mock Trial; Invlvd In IB Prgm; Sac ST; Cmmnctns.

FUTCH, MINDI K; Monte Vista HS; Spring Valley, CA; (3); 26/396; Hosp Aide; Mu Alpha Theta; Pep Clb; SADD; Cit Awd; Hon Roll; Prfct Atten Awd; CSF; Golden St Exam Hnrb Mntn Awd; 1st Pl Cty Mstrs & Qns YABA Chmpnshp Bowling Rnmnt 1989; Law.

FUZZELL, JUSTIN C; Oakdale HS; Oakdale, CA; (3); Church Yth Grp; Spanish Clb; Teachers Aide; Church Choir; Var Crs Cntry; Var Trk; Hon Roll; B Avg Span I V; A Avg Eng; AF Acad; Psych.

FYE, NICOLE L; Yucaipa HS; Yucaipa, CA; (3); 4/352; Am Leg Aux Girls St; Sec Debate Tm; NFL; Spanish Clb; Sec Speech Tm; JV Vllybl; High Hon Roll; NHS; Opt Clb Awd; Rotary Awd; Engl.

FYFE, JENNIFER N; Pinole Valley HS; Pinole, CA; (1); High Hon Roll; Hon Roll; U Of CA Santa Barbara.

FYKES, MIKISHA KONAI; Inglewood HS; Inglewood, CA; (2); Church Yth Grp; Ms Saint; Usher Bd Dept Asst Secy; Church Yth Dept Bd; Cmptrs.

GAAN, JENNIFER L; Sequoia HS; San Carlos, CA; (2); 11/870; Var Bsktbl; CSF; Golden St Exam Hnrbl Mntn; UCSF; Sprts Med.

GABARD, MATTHEW F; Grace M Davis HS; Modesto, CA; (2); Church Yth Grp; JV Swmmng.

GABAYAN, SHERVIN; Palisades HS; Pacific Palisades, CA; (4); Math Tm; Temple Yth Grp; Yrbk; Var Swmmng; NHS; Pres Acad Fit Awd; Mock Trl Tm; Frdms Fndtn Schlrshp; Peer Cnslng; UCLA.

GABBARD, AMY C; Tulare Union HS; Tulare, CA; (3); 75/401; Teachers Aide; Band; Mrchg Band; Hon Roll; Business.

GABBITA, SAM; John F Kennedy HS; La Palma, CA; (4); Cmnty Wkr; Computer Clb; Debate Tm; FBLA; Key Clb; Service Clb; Speech Tm; French Hon Soc; Hon Roll; NHS; UCLA; Law.

GABHART, MARK T; East Nicolaus HS; East Nicolaus, CA; (3); 4/50; Am Leg Boys St; Church Yth Grp; Letterman Clb; Ski Clb; SADD; Band; Pep Band; Treas Stu Cncl; Var Bsbl; Var Bsktbl; Amer River JC; Bus.

GABLER, CARL M; Cupertino HS; Cupertino, CA; (3); 48/300; JV Var Bsbl; Bus.

GABLER, JULIE S; Live Oak HS; Morgan Hill, CA; (4); 7/535; FBLA; Speech Tm; Mrchg Band; Rep Jr Cls; Trk; NHS; Pres Acad Fit Awd; Church Yth Grp; French Clb; Key Clb; Yth In Gvrnmnt; Mock Trl; U Of S CA; Mrktng.

GABOR, JULIETTE; Aragon HS; Foster City, CA; (2); JV Vllybl; Hon Roll; Clsscl Music Cncrts; Bus.

GABOUREL, GAIL; Notre Dame Acad; Los Angeles, CA; (3); Pres Church Yth Grp; Girl Scts; Hosp Aide; Rep Frsh Cls; Rep Sr Cls; JV Bsktbl; Capt Cheerldng; Cit Awd; High Hon Roll; Hon Roll; Phy.

GABRIEL, JOSEPHINE S; Bonita Vista HS; San Diego, CA; (3); Church Yth Grp; Office Aide; Teachers Aide; Band; Chorus; Church Choir; Drm Mjr(t); Flag Corp; Mrchg Band; Off Soph Cls; African Amer Stu Union Club Treas; Singing; Playing Flute & Piano; NYU; Law.

GABRIEL, LAURI A; Rim Of The World HS; Crestline, CA; (2); Church Yth Grp; Cmnty Wkr; FCA; French Clb; Varsity Clb; Nwsp; Rep Stu Cncl; JV Crs Cntry; Var Trk; Wt Lftg; Chrstn Clb; Straight Up; Photo Clb; Chico ST; Scl Work.

GABRIEL, LYDIA; Whittier Christian HS; Walnut, CA; (3); Dance Clb; French Clb; Law.

GABRIEL, MIRANDA J; University HS; Irvine, CA; (3); French Clb; Teachers Aide; Pres Band; Pres Mrchg Band; French Hon Soc; Frnch Allnc; Laureat Awd 88-89.

GABRIEL, TONY; Sonoma Valley HS; Sonoma, CA; (2); Intnl Clb; JV Bsbl; Var JV Bsktbl; Prfct Atten Awd; Pres Acad Fit Awd.

GABRIEL, VAN; El Camino HS; Oceanside, CA; (3); Var Bsbl; Bwlg Clb Pres; SDSU.

GABRIELE, TOM J; El Camino HS; Carmichael, CA; (3); Hosp Aide; Letterman Clb; Math Tm; Varsity Clb; Bsbl; Cit Awd; High Hon Roll; NHS; Karate; Counseling; Berkley; Physics.

GABRIELSON, JACOB A; Berkeley HS; Berkeley, CA; (4); Ntl Merit SF; CSF Hnr Scty; Berkeley High Stie Enrichmnet Prog:Golden ST Exam Hnrs Geom; Comp Sci.

GACAD, THERESE G; St Joseph Notre Dame HS; Alameda, CA; (3); Cmnty Wkr; Band; Church Choir; High Hon Roll; NHS; CSF; Tutor Kndgrtn; Piano Tchr; Elem Ed.

GACASAN, ROZAN L; St Bonaventure HS; Moorpark, CA; (3); 1/117; Nwsp; Yrbk; Lit Mag; VP Soph Cls; Pres Stu Cncl; JV Bsktbl; Powder Puff Ftbl; Var Tennis; High Hon Roll; NHS; USC; Arch.

GACAYAN, CRISTINA F; Delta HS; Walnut Grove, CA; (3); Chorus; Bsktbl; Crs Cntry; Powder Puff Ftbl; Sftbl; Trk; Vllybl; Prfct Atten Awd; Pres Acad Fit Awd; Doctor.

GACUSAN, LEA M; Homestead HS; Sunnyvale, CA; (4); 58/359; Church Yth Grp; French Clb; FBLA; Service Clb; Teachers Aide; Var Fld Hcky; Jr NHS; NHS; Pres Acad Fit Awd; Spanish NHS; Golden ST Math Exam Awds; CSF Treas; Hewlett Packard Schlrshp; UC-DAVIS; Bio Sci.

GADBERRY, JENNIFER L; Silver Valley HS; Newberry Spgs, CA; (2); Teachers Aide; Bsktbl; Cheerldng; Powder Puff Ftbl; Sftbl; Cit Awd; High Hon Roll; Hon Roll; Mck Trl; Fil Ftbl; Acad Ltr; UNLV; FBI.

GADD, JEFF R; Valley Christian HS; Pleasanton, CA; (2); Church Yth Grp; Pep Clb; Spanish Clb; VP Soph Cls; Bsbl; Var Capt Bsktbl; High Hon Roll; NHS; CA Schlrshp Fed; Mst Insprtnl Bsktbl Plyr; U MO Columbia; Coaching.

GADDIE, KIMBERLY A; Eisenhower HS; Rialto, CA; (3); French Clb; Sec VP Key Clb; Office Aide; High Hon Roll; Hon Roll; Bus.

GADDINI, STACIE A; Notre Dame HS; Belmont, CA; (3); Math Clb; Science Clb; Var Socr; Hon Roll; Equstrians Actvts; Vol Specl Olympcs; Civil Engr.

GADDINI, STACY; Notre Dame HS; Belmont, CA; (3); Math Clb; Science Clb; Var Socr; Hon Roll; Vol Spec Olympics; Cal Poly; Civil Engrng.

GADDIS, JULIE D; Bishop Union HS; Bishop, CA; (3); Church Yth Grp; 4-H; FFA; Ed Nwsp; JV Tennis; Hon Roll; Hrsmnshp; CSF; Vet.

GADDIS, TAHISHA J; Pasadena HS; Pasadena, CA; (2); Church Yth Grp; Stat Bsktbl; Hon Roll; Badmintn; BSU; Howard U.

GADE, JEANINE M; Paraclete HS; Lancaster, CA; (2); Drama Clb; JA; Key Clb; Hon Roll.

GADSBY, JASON S; Leland HS; San Jose, CA; (2); Computer Clb; Tennis; Radio Brdcstng DJ Grds 9-10; FBI.

GAE, DONGSHUNG; College Park HS; Pleasant Hill, CA; (3); VP Church Yth Grp; Cmnty Wkr; German Clb; JA; Math Clb; Spanish Clb; Church Choir; Tennis; Cit Awd; High Hon Roll; Gldn ST Mth Exm Hgh Hnr; Engrng.

GAEBE, GEOFFREY P; Contra Costa Chrisitan HS; Martinez, CA; (3); Boy Scts; Drama Clb; Band; Chorus; School Musical; School Play; Yrbk; Pres Soph Cls; Var Bsbl; Var Cheerldng; ACSI Dstngshd Stu; Criminal Law.

GAEDE, KATRINA M; Pasadena HS; Pasadena, CA; (2); Var Cheerldng; Church Yth Grp; Hon Roll; Pres Acad Fit Awd; CA Schlrsp Fed; Point Loma Nazarene Coll.

GAEDE, SHANNON; Del Mar HS; San Jose, CA; (4); German Clb; Key Clb; Teachers Aide; Acpl Chr; Band; VP Chorus; Capt Color Guard; School Musical; NHS; Pres Acad Fit Awd; Lifetime CSF; Humboldt ST U; Lib Studies.

GAEKE, JENNIFER; Helix HS; La Mesa, CA; (1); Cmnty Wkr; Drama Clb; SADD; Thesps; Acpl Chr; Band; Chorus; Color Guard; Drill Tm; Flag Corp; San Diego ST U; Teacher.

GAERTIG, ROB; Lompoc HS; Lompoc, CA; (4); 49/302; Boy Scts; FBLA; FTA; Thesps; Band; Drm Mjr(t); Mrchg Band; Pep Band; School Play; Cit Awd; U CA Santa Barbara; Elem Educ.

GAETA, DEANNA; John A Rowland HS; Walnut, CA; (3); Off Science Clb; Color Guard; Flag Corp; Lit Mag; High Hon Roll; NHS; CA Schlstc Fed; Bio Awd; Sign Lang Cls; U CA Polytech Pomona; Sci.

GAETA, MERCY; St Bernard HS; Los Angeles, CA; (3); Latin Clb; Spanish Clb; Vllybl; Cit Awd; Med.

GAETA, REBECCA E; Albany HS; Albany, CA; (1); Drama Clb; Pep Clb; Spanish Clb; Acpl Chr; Chorus; School Musical; School Play; Variety Show; Cheerldng; Hon Roll; Alg Hnrs Gldn ST Exm; UC Brkly.

GAFFANEY, SHANNON K; Oak Ridge HS; Cameron Park, CA; (2); AFS; SADD; Rep Frsh Cls; JV Vllybl; CSF; Ski Team Ltr; U Of CA Los Angeles; Vet.

GAGE, CARMEN K; Rim Of The World HS; Crestline, CA; (2); Art Clb; Church Yth Grp; Teachers Aide; Bsktbl; Crs Cntry; Trk; Hon Roll; Prfct Atten Awd; Pres Acad Fit Awd; CIF Fnls In Track & Field; Comm Artist.

GAGE, CHRISTINA; Notre Dame HS; Morgan Hill, CA; (3); AFS; Hosp Aide; Science Clb; SADD; Yrbk; Pres Soph Cls; Off Jr Cls; Off Sr Cls; High Hon Roll; NHS; Jr Statesman Of Amer; CSF; Stcey Mead Memrl Awd.

GAGE, LISA; Oakdale HS; Oakdale, CA; (3); Drama Clb; Acpl Chr; Spanish Clb; School Play; JV Powder Puff Ftbl; Var Tennis; Var Trk; High Hon Roll; Hon Roll; Cmmnctns.

GAGE, ROBYN N; Lowell HS; San Francisco, CA; (2); Hosp Aide; JV Badmntn Tm; Pre-Med Clb; Cardiovsclr Surgeon.

GAGE, ROUCHELLE A; Pittsburg HS; Pittsburg, CA; (3); Var Socr; Cit Awd; Hon Roll; Merit List; U CA Davis; Vet.

GAGEN, HOPE E; Eagle Rock HS; Los Angeles, CA; (3); Teachers Aide; Gym; Tennis; Vllybl; Hon Roll; UCLA; Law.

GAGNON, GAYLORD J; Milpitas HS; Milpitas, CA; (1); Rep Teachers Aide; Phtg Nwsp; JV Ftbl; JV Trk; Hon Roll; U CA Prtnrshp Pgm; U Santa Clara; Engrng.

GAHERTY JR, JOHN J; Canyon HS; Canyon Country, CA; (3); Band; Mrchg Band; JV Ftbl; Band Achvt Awd; Gldn Leag Chmpns-Ftbl; Athltc Awd 88 & 89; CA ST U Northridge; Bus Mgmt.

GAIDE, AMANDA; Troy HS; Fullerton, CA; (2); 7/330; Cmnty Wkr; FCA; GAA; Key Clb; Letterman Clb; Varsity Clb; Rptr Yrbk; Co-Capt Bsktbl; L Trk; Vllybl; Sci Adventure Volunteer; Sci Olympiad Tm 3rd Pl S CA Intl Baccalaureate Pgm; UCD; Med.

GAILAR, TODD C; Monte Vista HS; Danville, CA; (2); 100/475; JV Bsktbl; Var Golf; Wt Lftg; High Hon Roll; Pres Acad Fit Awd; Church Yth Group; Sports Broadcasting.

GAILEY, JOHN A; Escondido HS; Escondido, CA; (3); Church Yth Grp; Science Clb; Ski Clb; Hon Roll; Hgh Hnrs Geom Gldn St Exam; Cal Poly; Bus.

GAINES, AYOKA S; Santa Teresa HS; Mesa, AZ; (2); French Clb; BSLL; Black Stu Union; Coll; Law Legal Aide.

GAINES, CHRISTOPHER; Palm Springs Christian HS; Desert Hot Sprngs, CA; (4); Off Sr Cls; Rep Stu Cncl; Bsbl; Bsktbl; Sftbl; Trk; Mini Trk Clb.

GAINES, ERICA L; Ramona HS; Ramona, CA; (2); Key Clb; Tax Atty.

GAINES, HEATHER M; Yucca Valley HS; Yucca Valley, CA; (2); Drama Clb; School Musical; Stage Crew; High Hon Roll; Hon Roll; Oceanography.

GAINES, LA TANYA N; Pinole Valley HS; Hercules, CA; (1); Dance Clb; Spanish Clb; Gym; UC Davis; Vet.

GAINES, LEXTER N; Verbum Dei HS; Los Angeles, CA; (3); 6/70; Boy Scts; Church Yth Grp; JA; Office Aide; Church Choir; Trk; High Hon Roll; Bio Awd 2nd Pl Sci Fr; USC; Law.

GAINES, MARK; Victor Valley Christian HS; Riverside, CA; (4); Church Yth Grp; Drama Clb; Scholastic Bowl; Speech Tm; Teachers Aide; Church Choir; School Play; Pres Soph Cls; Bsbl; Riverside CC; Bus Admin.

GAINS, NATASHA M; Etiwanda HS; Rancho Cucamonga, CA; (2); Church Choir; Bsktbl; Sftbl; Hon Roll; NHS; Fashn Desgng; Wrtng; Inter Decrtng; Corp Law.

GAITAN, DENISE; Los Alamitos HS; Seal Beach, CA; (3); Teachers Aide; Score Keeper; Hon Roll; Cert Hnr Outstndng Achvmnt; UC Santa Barbara; Law.

GAITAN, MARTIN F; Nogales HS; West Covina, CA; (3); 57/768; Drama Clb; FBLA; Latin Clb; Spanish Clb; Mrchg Band; School Play; Phtg Rptr Yrbk; Phtg Rptr Lit Mag; Off Sr Cls; Ftbl; Scrd Hghst Cls CAS Test; Cal Poly Pomona; Real Est.

GAITHER, ANDREA N; Canyon Springs HS; Moreno Valley, CA; (3); Church Yth Grp; Intnl Clb; ROTC; Ski Clb; SADD; Church Choir; Color Guard; Drill Tm; Var Trk; Cit Awd; Ldrshp Awd ROTC; Super Perfmnc ROTC; UCLA; Pre-Med.

GAITHER, CARRIE A; Woodcrest Christian Schl; Riverside, CA; (2); Ski Clb; Chorus; Var Cheerldng; High Hon Roll; Chrstn Ldrshp.

GAJIWALA, PARESH R; Phillip & Sala Burton Acad; San Francisco, CA; (4); Chess Clb; Math Clb; Rep Frsh Cls; Rep Soph Cls; Rep Jr Cls; Rep Stu Cncl; JV Ftbl; Intrml Socr; Intrml Vllybl; Hon Roll; Golden St Exam Awd-Alg 86-87/Geom; Acad Decathln Team; U CA-BERKELEY; Med.

GAJJAR, NUPOOR A; Whitney HS; Cerritos, CA; (3); French Clb; Hosp Aide; Key Clb; Latin Clb; Var Bsbl; Intrml Vllybl; High Hon Roll; Pres Acad Fit Awd; Med.

GAKOVIC, ERIKA Z; Alhambra HS; Martinez, CA; (3); Intnl Clb; High Hon Roll; Hon Roll; Smmr Schl Arts 90; Course Cat & Stu Hndbk 90-91; Illustration.

GALA, ANAND D; St Bernard HS; Culver City, CA; (3); Letterman Clb; Varsity Clb; Var L Ftbl; Hon Roll; CA Schlrshp Fed; Pre-Med.

GALAN, RAY C; Clovis West HS; Clovis, CA; (2); French Clb; Intnl Clb; Ski Clb; Stu Cncl; JV Bsbl; Intrml Bsktbl; JV Ftbl; Intrml Wt Lftg; High Hon Roll; French Clb Pres; CSF; Coach Grls Bsktbl; Red Cross Lfesvng Crse; Annapolis; Airline Pilot.

GALAN, SHELLI E; Clovis West HS; Clovis, CA; (1); Church Yth Grp; Dance Clb; Debate Tm; Hosp Aide; Speech Tm; SADD; Variety Show; JV Gym; JV Socr; Math.

GALANAKIS, MICHAEL A; Warren HS; Downey, CA; (2); FBLA; JV Tennis; Interact Club VP; Demolay; CSF; Pltcl Sci.

GALANG, CLAIRE M; Mayfield SR Schl; North Hollywood, CA; (2); Hon Roll; Med.

GALANG, GLORIA G; Lowell HS; San Francisco, CA; (3); Church Yth Grp; JA; Q&S; Sec Pres Chorus; School Musical; Rep Frsh Cls; Rep Soph Cls; Sec Jr Cls; VP Sr Cls; Pres Acad Fit Awd; Lowell Filipino-Amer Club Mem, VP, Pres; Golden St Exam Hnrs Algebra, Geom; CA Schlrshp Fed Mem; Cal Poly San Luis Obisbo; Arch.

GALANG, JOAN O; John F Kennedy HS; Sacramento, CA; (1); 103/559; Sec Frsh Cls.

GALANG, RACHEL; Berkeley HS; Berkeley, CA; (3); Cmnty Wkr; Computer Clb; Church Choir; Hon Roll; PROBE; CSF Hnr Scty; ASU; ESU; Pacific Islndr Clb; U CA Berkeley; Psych.

GALANGUE, MARECEL; Walnut HS; Walnut, CA; (3); Aud/Vis; Drama Clb; French Clb; FBLA; Key Clb; SADD; Teachers Aide; Chorus; Rptr Nwsp; Cit Awd; Power Clb Envrnmntl Cncrn; Harvard; Supreme Crt Jdg.

GALANTI, JEFF M; Mt Whitney HS; Visalia, CA; (1); Pep Clb; JV Bsbl; JV Ftbl; Wt Lftg; Hon Roll; UC Los Angeles; Sports Med.

GALAPON, ARLENE MERCADO; Arvin HS; Lamont, CA; (4); Office Aide; Ski Clb; SADD; Capt Color Guard; Mrchg Band; Sec Sr Cls; JV Var Score Keeper; JV Tennis; Cit Awd; High Hon Roll; Bernice Braddon Schlrshp; Kern Cnty Comptn Pltcl Philsphy Hrng Constution & Bill Rghts 2nd Pl Team; Bakersfield Coll; Acctng.

GALARZA, ALBERTO B; El Cajon Valley HS; El Cajon, CA; (4); 24/365; Ski Clb; Spanish Clb; Varsity Clb; Capt Var Socr; Wt Lftg; Eductnl Tlnt Rsrch Schlrshp; CA Grant; Fshn Careers Of CA Coll Full Schlrshp; Fashn Careers CA; Fshn Mrchnds.

GALARZA, VERONICA A; Rosemead HS; Rosemead, CA; (2); Treas Church Yth Grp; Ecology Club; New Encounter; Journalism.

GALASSI, NICOLE; Edison HS; Santa Ana, CA; (3); Cmnty Wkr; Girl Scts; Teachers Aide; Chorus; School Play; Lit Mag; USF; Psych.

GALAVIZ, CHRISTINA M; Bullard HS; Fresno, CA; (1); Church Yth Grp; Score Keeper; Big Brothrs/Big Sistrs Clb; CSF; Harvard; Law.

GALAZ, MAIMU L; Trabuco Hills HS; Rancho Santa Ma, CA; (2); Church Yth Grp; Cmnty Wkr; Hosp Aide; Spanish Clb; UCI; Med.

GALAZYN, SHERRY; Orange HS; Orange Villa Pk., CA; (4); 75/400; Debate Tm; Key Clb; Model UN; Ski Clb; Swmmng; UCSC; Marine Bio.

GALBEATH, JASON; Oak Hill HS; Winnetka, CA; (4); 2/18; Cmnty Wkr; Drama Clb; SADD; School Play; Stage Crew; Yrbk; Rep Jr Cls; Rep Sr Cls; Stu Cncl; JV Bsktbl; Model Senate; Stu Of Yr 89-90; Loyola Marymount U; Commnctns.

GALBRAITH, KENNETH; Burbank HS; Los Angeles, CA; (2); Spanish Clb; Orch; Off Soph Cls; Intrml Tennis; High Hon Roll; Pres Acad Fit Awd; Golden St Exam 89 Geom High Hnrs; Aeronautical Engrng.

GALBREATH, CRISTI C; Carlsbad HS; Carlsbad, CA; (2); 35/400; JV Tennis; JV Trk; Hon Roll; Sci.

GALBSHTEIN, YANA; Los Gatos HS; Los Gatos, CA; (2); Los Gatos Rowing Clb; Marilyns Dance Wrkshp; West Coast Inst Of Tae Kwon Do; Art.

GALDONES, CECILIA J; Bellarmine Jefferson HS; Burbank, CA; (2); Stage Crew; Cit Awd; High Hon Roll; Outstndng Achvt Spnsh Awd; Mst Imprv Stu-Sci; CSF; Arts.

GALE, JASON L; James Monroe HS; Sun Valley, CA; (2); Chess Clb; Teachers Aide; Chorus; Bsbl; Bsktbl; Ftbl; Golf; Swmmng; Wt Lftg; Hon Roll; CSUN; Law.

GALE, NATHANAEL R; Grant Joint Union HS; Sacramento, CA; (3); Pres German Clb; Science Clb; Spanish Clb; Hon Roll; Prfct Atten Awd; Fridy Nght Live; U CA Santa Barbara; Marine Bio.

GALE, PATRICK A; Clovis West HS; Fresno, CA; (3); Church Yth Grp; French Clb; Hosp Aide; Key Clb; Civil Air Patrol; Med.

GALE, ROBIN STACEY; Calabasas HS; Woodland Hills, CA; (3); 22/235; Drama Clb; Pep Clb; Temple Yth Grp; Flag Corp; School Musical; Variety Show; JV Capt Cheerldng; Hon Roll; St Schlr; CSF; Golden St Exam Algebra High Hnrs; Chem Advanced Placement Exam; UC Berkeley; Engrng.

GALE, VANJA A; El Camino Real HS; West Hills, CA; (2); Chorus; Swing Chorus; High Hon Roll; Hon Roll; Ecology Club; UCLA.

GALEON, DANOMAR V; Mount Pleasant HS; San Jose, CA; (2); Chess Clb; Hon Roll; San Jose ST U; Comp Prgmr.

GALEOS, HEIDI C; Independence HS; San Jose, CA; (3); Art Clb; Cmnty Wkr; French Clb; Church Choir; VP Tennis; Badminton Vrsty; Santa Clara U; Bus.

GALERA, CHADIE; Hogan SR HS; Vallejo, CA; (2); Church Yth Grp; Cmnty Wkr; ROTC; Spanish Clb; SADD; Color Guard; Drill Tm; Flag Corp; Rptr Nwsp; Phtg Yrbk; FNL; Santa Clara U; Nrsg.

GALES, STEPHANIE; St Bernard Catholic HS; Los Angeles, CA; (4); Church Yth Grp; Ed Yrbk; Rep Frsh Cls; Mgr Bsktbl; Mgr(s); Rep Frsh Cls; Rep Soph Cls; Rep Jr Cls; Rep Sr Cls; Seton Hall; Poli Sci.

GALETTI, TOBIE LEE; Paso Robles HS; Templeton, CA; (1); FFA; Hosp Aide; Var Swmmng; Hon Roll; Kiwanis Awd.

GALFAYAN, NARINA; Canyon Springs HS; Moreno Valley, CA; (3); Gym; High Hon Roll; Hon Roll; Prfct Atten Awd; Riverside CC; Legal Sec.

GALIAS, TERESA B; Notre Dame Acad; Los Angeles, CA; (3); Library Aide; SADD; Chorus; Yrbk; Cheerldng; Ms Pena Francia 2nd Rnnrup 89-90; Bus Admin.

GALINDO, BENJAMIN; San Diego HS; USAF Academy, CO; (4); 39/350; Drama Clb; Scholastic Bowl; Science Clb; School Play; Rep Stu Cncl; Var L Ftbl; Var L Tennis; Pres Acad Fit Awd; Rotary Awd; Congrssnl Page; Yth Advsry Cncl; All City Acad Leag-Vrsty Capt; Bio Chem.

GALINDO, CAROL; Covina HS; Covina, CA; (2); French Clb; Tennis; Badminton; USC; Ped.

GALINDO, DOMINIC J; Chino HS; Ontario, CA; (2); Church Yth Grp; JV Bsbl; Hon Roll; USC; Arch.

GALINDO, GIRLIE; Balboa HS; San Francisco, CA; (2); Hon Roll.

GALINDO, MARIA G; North Hollywood HS; North Hollywood, CA; (2); French Clb; Rep Frsh Cls; Hon Roll; GATE; UCLA Prtnrshp Pgm; CSF; Bus.

GALINDO, NORMA A; James Lick HS; San Jose, CA; (1); Computer Clb; Dance Clb; Math Tm; Spanish Clb; Yrbk; Off Sr Cls; Cheerldng; Swmmng; Tennis; Hon Roll.

GALINDO, TERESA M; El Dorado HS; Pollock Pines, CA; (3); Teachers Aide; Hon Roll; American River CC; Intr Dsgn.

GALION, TIM M; Tustin HS; Tustin, CA; (1); Band; Mrchg Band; Hon Roll; UCLA.

GALITZEN, SASANNA; Orangewood Acad; Garden Grove, CA; (3); Spanish Clb; Varsity Clb; Chorus; Off Soph Cls; Sec Jr Cls; Var Ftbl; Var Sftbl; Cit Awd; High Hon Roll; Natl Piano Playing Auditions 87-88; Walla Walla Coll; Neurosurgery.

GALLAGHER, CHANDRA D; Morse HS; San Diego, CA; (2); 246/764; Church Yth Grp; Library Aide; Pep Clb; Cit Awd; Tuskegee; Med.

GALLAGHER, CHARLES P; Bellarmine College Prep; San Jose, CA; (2); Church Yth Grp; Cmnty Wkr; Debate Tm; Latin Clb; NFL; Speech Tm; Rptr Nwsp; Stu Cncl; Lion Awd; Opt Clb Awd; Mayors Yth Cnfrnc Delg; Schls Irish Clb Co-Fndr; Harvard; Bus.

GALLAGHER, EALAR; Bishop Amat Memorial HS; Temple City, CA; (3); Church Yth Grp; Pres Soph Cls; Bsbl; Var Ftbl; Var Socr; High Hon Roll; Hon Roll; NEDT Awd; CA Schlrshp Fed; Med.

GALLAGHER, ELIZABETH; Palm Desert HS; Bermuda Dunes, CA; (3); Latin Clb; Library Aide; Band; Flag Corp; Mrchg Band; Var Swmmng; Trk; Vllybl; Hon Roll; Pres Acad Fit Awd.

GALLAGHER, MATT; Mater Dei HS; Santa Ana, CA; (1); Boy Scts; Chess Clb; Church Yth Grp; ROTC; Ftbl; Socr; Marines; ROTC; FBI.

GALLAGHER, PATRICK J; St Vincent De Paul HS; Petaluma, CA; (2); 6/60; Speech Tm; Bsbl; Bsktbl; NHS; Prfct Atten Awd; Spch, Hstry, Engl & Thlgy Awds; Med.

GALLAGHER, SHAWN P; Chula Vista HS; San Diego, CA; (3); 79/493; Pep Clb; Pres SADD; Ed Nwsp; JV Var Bsktbl; Var Trk; San Diego Tribunes All Acad Team; Cert Outstndng Achvt Co Subject A Write-Off; Oceanography.

GALLANT, SARA; Lutheran HS; Anaheim, CA; (2); Church Yth Grp; Red Cross Aide; Service Clb; SADD; Rep Soph Cls; Stu Cncl; Mgr Trk; Cit Awd; Hon Roll; Music Guild Awd; Blood Drive Chrmn; Soph Princess; Psych.

GALLARDO, ELIZA RAQUEL; Valley HS; Elk Grove, CA; (2); 7/434; Nwsp; Var Socr; High Hon Roll; CSF; Giftd Tlntd Ed Clb; Acad Exc Awd; U CA-DAVIS; Vet Med.

GALLARDO, JACKIE; Sacred Heart Cathedral HS; Richmond, CA; (4); 40/190; Capt GAA; Letterman Clb; Rptr Ed Yrbk; Rep Soph Cls; Intrml Jr Cls; Capt Var Bsktbl; Var Cheerldng; Var Sftbl; Hon Roll; Vrsty Bsktbl All-Lgue Hnrb Mntn Team Awd; UC Berkeley; Bio Sci.

GALLARDO, MARIA J; Hawthrone HS; Inglewood, CA; (2); Cit Awd; Hon Roll; Prfct Atten Awd; El Camino Coll; Bus.

GALLARDO, MARTHA E; Bonita Vista HS; Bonita, CA; (2); Ed Nwsp; Phtg Yrbk; Cit Awd; Hon Roll; UCB; Teacher.

GALLARDO, RAUL A; Gladstone HS; Azusa, CA; (3); Socr; Comp Spclst.

GALLAWAY, JASON C; Lindsay HS; Lindsay, CA; (3); Letterman Clb; Spanish Clb; Intrml JV Bsktbl; Intrml JV Ftbl; Var Swmmng; Hon Roll; Pres Acad Fit Awd; Bsktbl JV, MVP & Capt; Frstry.

GALLEGO, CANDICE L; Bishop Amat HS; Upland, CA; (3); Letterman Clb; Drill Tm; Fshn Merch.

GALLEGO, MELISSA S; Bullard HS; Fresno, CA; (2); Church Yth Grp; Intnl Clb; School Musical; Stu Cncl; Var Capt Diving; Var Gym; CA Schlrshp Fed; U CA; Bus.

GALLEGO, PATRICIA; Bellarmine-Jefferson HS; Pasadena, CA; (2); Church Yth Grp; Cmnty Wkr; Pres French Clb; Hosp Aide; Rep Soph Cls; JV Bsktbl; Var Crs Cntry; Ftbl; Var Trk; Cit Awd; Fluent Span; Med.

GALLEGOS, ANA; William Workman HS; West Covina, CA; (2); #11 In Class; Church Yth Grp; GAA; Spanish Clb; Bsktbl; Powder Puff Ftbl; Sftbl; Vllybl; Wt Lftg; Hon Roll; Spanish NHS; Mnt Sac; Dntl Asst.

GALLEGOS, CAROLYNE S; Tulare Union HS; Tulare, CA; (2); GAA; Spanish Clb; Band; Mrchg Band; Sftbl; All Star Tournmnt Hl Sftbl; Fresno ST U; Eng Lit.

GALLEGOS, ERIC J; Charter Oak HS; Covina, CA; (2); Letterman Clb; Varsity Clb; Var Tennis; USC.

GALLEGOS, ERIN L; Folsom HS; Folsom, CA; (3); Model UN; Pres Soph Cls; Pres Jr Cls; Stu Cncl; Var JV Socr; Hon Roll; JV Scr MVP; Mstrss Crmns Jr Prm 90; Vrsty Ltr Sccr.

GALLEGOS, JENNIFER J; Etiwanda HS; Alta Loma, CA; (2); Church Yth Grp; Cmnty Wkr; Dance Clb; Var Swmmng; Hon Roll; Assisteens Of Pomona; Gate Pgm; Amer Composers Fstvl Piano; U Of CA; Educ.

GALLEGOS, JESUS; Pater Noster HS; Los Angeles, CA; (1); 15/70; Yrbk; Sec Frsh Cls; Var Bsbl; Capt Bsktbl; JV Ftbl; UCLA; Comp Engr.

GALLEGOS, KIRSTEN H; Lutheran HS; Santa Ana, CA; (3); Cmnty Wkr; Red Cross Aide; Ski Clb; VP Frsh Cls; Rep Jr Cls; Pres Stu Cncl; Var Mgr(s); Var Socr; Var Tennis; Cit Awd; Santa Ana Assisteens VP, Rcrdng Sec; Water, Snow Skiing; Vllybl; Swmmng.

GALLEGOS, LISA R; Sacred Heart Of Jesus HS; Los Angeles, CA; (2); 7/112; Hosp Aide; Rptr Yrbk; VP Soph Cls; High Hon Roll; NHS; Rep Living Informtn Agc Statesmn Fndtn; Geom & Engl II Awds; PETA; Stanford U; Psych.

GALLEGOS, PAMELA L; Bishop Amat Memorial HS; West Covina, CA; (1); Drama Clb; Church Choir; Rep Frsh Cls; High Hon Roll; Hon Roll; Prfct Atten Awd; Barkada Clb; UCLA; Pediatrician.

GALLEGOS, SHANNON K; John F Kennedy HS; Buena Park, CA; (4); Cmnty Wkr; Drama Clb; Letterman Clb; Red Cross Aide; Teachers Aide; Thesps; Chorus; Church Choir; School Musical; School Play; Teach Swmg; Aid Hearing Impaired Chldrn; College Thtr; Cypress Coll; Actress.

GALLEGOS, SHARON M; Bloomington HS; Bloomington, CA; (2); Church Yth Grp; Drama Clb; Hosp Aide; Treas Key Clb; Ski Clb; Color Guard; Pres Frsh Cls; Pres Soph Cls; JV Sftbl; JV Vllybl; Future Ldrs Amer Pr Cnslr & Mnr Assoc Pres; Friday Nite Live; Med.

GALLEGOS, YESENIA; Venice HS; Los Angeles, CA; (4); Hosp Aide; Rptr Yrbk; Pres Acad Fit Awd; Mesa Pres; Riordan Schlr; Earthwarh Expdtn; Loyola Marymount U; Bus.

GALLEHER, LISA ANN; Temecula Valley HS; Temecula, CA; (3); 10/453; Treas Church Yth Grp; Cmnty Wkr; Drama Clb; Key Clb; Church Choir; Co-Capt Flag Corp; Mrchg Band; Hon Roll; CSF; Loma Linda U; Ind.

GALLENO, HUMBERTO; Damien HS; West Covina, CA; (2); 1/300; Church Yth Grp; Debate Tm; NFL; Speech Tm; Chorus; School Musical; Rep Frsh Cls; Rep Soph Cls; Intrml Socr; JV Swmmng; Spnsh Awd; SYMF 4th Pl 89-San Gabriel Vly Music Tchrs Assoc Of CA; Med.

GALLI, STACEY; Carlsbad HS; Carlsbad, CA; (2); Church Yth Grp; FCA; Pep Clb; Chorus; Church Choir; Var Cheerldng; Gym; Trk; Cit Awd; Kiwanis Awd; Play Piano & Ten; BYU; Kndgtn Tchr.

GALLIGHER, ROSS G; Edison HS; Huntington Bch, CA; (3); Cmnty Wkr; Key Clb; JV Wrstlng; Hon Roll; Golden St Acadc Excllnc Awd In Geom With Hnrs 88; Republcn Clb Treas; Key Clb Sec; Chem Engrng.

GALLIMORE, MISSY GLYNN; Fillmore HS; Santa Paula, CA; (3); Cmnty Wkr; FFA; SADD; Socr; High Hon Roll; Hon Roll; FFA Awds; Peer Cnslng; 1st Rnnr Up Miss Teen Fillmore; CSF; CA ST U Northridge; Phy Thrps.

GALLIVAN, JAMES MICHAEL; Hoover HS; San Diego, CA; (4); Art Clb; Debate Tm; English Clb; FBLA; Library Aide; Office Aide; Vllybl; High Hon Roll; Hon Roll; San Diego ST; Cooking.

GALLO, FAVIO A; Don Bosco HS; San Gabriel, CA; (3); Chess Clb; Cmnty Wkr; JV Socr; Cit Awd; Hon Roll; Bike & Tnns Clbs.

GALLON, HOLLY; Will C Wood HS; Vacaville, CA; (1); Church Yth Grp; Chorus; High Hon Roll; Hon Roll; Piano; Swmmng; Notre Dame; Surgeon.

GALLOPS, AMANDA P; North HS; Bakersfield, CA; (3); Library Aide; Bsktbl; Jr NHS; NHS; Ed.

GALLOWAY, CANDACE P; Regina Caell HS; Gardena, CA; (3); Cmnty Wkr; GAA; Letterman Clb; Pep Clb; SADD; Teachers Aide; Rep Soph Cls; VP Stu Cncl; Var Bsktbl; Cit Awd; Gardena City Yth Cmmssnr; Dvlpr & Mgr Gardena Qns Drill Team; Lincoln U; Math.

GALLOWAY, GINA; Bret Harte HS; Altaville, CA; (1); Church Yth Grp; FFA; FHA; GAA; JA; SADD; JV Bsktbl; JV Sftbl; JV Vllybl; Hon Roll; Showmanship 1st Pl; Reserve Grand Champ FFA Beef; FFA Cal Poly St Convention.

GALLOWAY, HEATHER; Tustin HS; Tustin, CA; (1); Church Yth Grp; Rep Frsh Cls; JV Swmmng; Vllybl; Hon Roll.

GALLOWAY, SHANNON M; Mt Shasta HS; Mount Shasta, CA; (2); Dance Clb; Chorus; JV Trk; Hon Roll; Medcl Rsrch.

GALLUZZO, NOLEEN R; Tustin HS; Tustin, CA; (1); Church Yth Grp; Hon Roll; ASB Stu Cncl; Notre Dame; Interior Dsgn.

GALOVICH JR, TOM; Capital Christian Schl; Sacramento, CA; (2); Church Yth Grp; Ski Clb; JV Bsbl; Capt JV Ftbl; Wt Lftg; U Of Southern CA; Arch.

GALVAN, AMELIA V; Rio Mesa HS; Oxnard, CA; (3); 72/369; Hosp Aide; Band; Jazz Band; Mrchg Band; Prfct Atten Awd; Super Spartan Mnth; Band Secy; Ventura Coll; Nrsng.

GALVAN, ANNA J; Mc Farland HS; Mc Farland, CA; (3); Church Yth Grp; Crs Cntry; Cit Awd; High Hon Roll; Hon Roll; Prfct Atten Awd; Help Kids Learn; Bus Mgr.

GALVAN, GINA M; Oakgrove HS; San Jose, CA; (2); SADD; Flag Corp; Hon Roll; Med.

GALVAN, GUADALUPE A; Nogales HS; La Puente, CA; (3); 122/628; Dance Clb; Cit Awd; Hon Roll; Achvmnt & Rcgntn Awds; ROP Bnkng Occptns Cert Of Cmpltn; Amrcn Coll For Appld Art; Bus.

GALVAN, LYDIA; Livingston HS; Livingston, CA; (3); Pres FBLA; SADD; Var Bsktbl; Powder Puff Ftbl; Hon Roll; Fresno ST; Bus.

GALVAN, MARISA; San Bernardino HS; San Bernardino, CA; (2); AFS; Cmnty Wkr; Debate Tm; Key Clb; Model UN; NFL; Quiz Bowl; Scholastic Bowl; Speech Tm; SADD; Black Stu Union; Jr Statesman Of Amer; CSF.

GALVAN, MARY I; Schurr HS; Los Angeles, CA; (1); JV Var Crs Cntry; Var JV Trk; Hon Roll; Crssc Cntry Grls Coaches Awd; Trck JR Vrsty Athlt Of Yr; UCLA; Sci.

GALVAN, NICKI R; Fresno HS; Fresno, CA; (3); 120/500; Church Yth Grp; Chorus; Ntl Merit Ltr; Fresno City Coll; Child Care.

GALVAN, NICOLE F; St Monica HS; Los Angeles, CA; (2); Latin Clb; Spanish Clb; Drill Tm; Off Jr Cls; Hon Roll; Jr Cls Cncl; Home Rm Rep; Drill Tm Mst Imprvd 89, 3 Yrs On Tm; 2nd Hnrs 89; USC; Med.

GALVAN, NOE; Warren HS; Downey, CA; (2); Cmnty Wkr; Spanish Clb; JV Bsbl; JV Ftbl; Coll; Math.

GALVAN, PATRICIA; Garfield HS; Los Angeles, CA; (2); Cmnty Wkr; French Clb; Hosp Aide; Rptr Yrbk; Hon Roll; Home Ec Mrt Awd; USC; Pediatrics.

GALVAN, RACHEL A; Galt HS; Lodi, CA; (3); Church Yth Grp; High Hon Roll; Hon Roll; Acctg I Awds; Delta JC; Acctnt.

GALVAN, RONALD R; Paramount HS; Paramount, CA; (2); 71/660; Rep Orch; JV Bsbl; JV Bsktbl; Cit Awd; Hon Roll; College Club; Arrowbear Music Camp Schlsp; GSE Schl Recog; Berkeley; Bus.

GALVAN, ROSA; San Marcos HS; Santa Barbara, CA; (1); Band; Mrchg Band; Orch; UCSB; Bus.

GALVEZ, ADRIANA; Workman HS; La Puente, CA; (3); Hon Roll; Friend To Friend; Nrsng.

GALVEZ, AGNES C; St Joseph HS; Cerritos, CA; (3); Debate Tm; Hosp Aide; Flag Corp; Stage Crew; Yrbk; Hon Roll; Prfct Atten Awd; CSF; CCD Helper; Secy Keywanette Clb; CSULB; Nrsng.

GALVEZ, AMY; Nogales HS; Rowland Heights, CA; (1); Hon Roll; Dr.

GALVEZ, ANGELA; William Workman HS; La Puente, CA; (2); VP Church Yth Grp; Color Guard; Capt Flag Corp; Mrchg Band; Rep Stu Cncl; Hon Roll; Prfct Atten Awd; Friend To Friend Secy; AP Spnsh Hnrs; Law.

GALVEZ, CONSUELO M; Pasadena HS; Pasadena, CA; (1); Spanish Clb; Hon Roll; Prfct Atten Awd; Lib Club; CSF; Math.

GALVEZ, GRACIE; San Bernardino HS; Sn Bernardino, CA; (4); 76/376; Church Yth Grp; Teachers Aide; Church Choir; Hon Roll; Mecha Club Hstrn; Zonta Club; Sobobans Secy; UC San Bernardino; Liberal Art.

GALVEZ, NANCY; West Covina HS; West Covina, CA; (1); Bus.

GALVEZ, OLIVER A; Independence HS; San Jose, CA; (2); Var Socr; JV Trk; Chicano Latino Stus Recogntn Of Acad Achvt; San Jose ST U; Elect Engrng.

GALVEZ, ROSA M; William Workman HS; Valinda, CA; (3); MTSAC; Nurse.

GALVEZ, ULYSSES R; Norco HS; Norco, CA; (3); Drama Clb; Office Aide; School Musical; School Play; Ftbl; Swmmng; Wrstlng; Hon Roll; Real Est Agent.

GALYEAN, JENNIFER; Novato HS; Santa Rosa, CA; (2); Church Yth Grp; French Clb; SADD; Lit Mag; Hon Roll; Jr NHS; Bus.

GAMA, DIONNA M; Colton HS; Colton, CA; (2); Church Yth Grp; GAA; Letterman Clb; Teachers Aide; Varsity Clb; Rep Stu Cncl; Var Capt Socr; JV Capt Sftbl; JV Vllybl; High Hon Roll; Child Psych.

GAMARGO, SONYA EVELYN; West HS; Bakersfield, CA; (1); Church Yth Grp; Dance Clb; Spanish Clb; Variety Show; Cheerldng; Mgr(s); Score Keeper; Vllybl; Hon Roll; Mexican Folk Dancer; MESA; MECHA Secy; Fashion Dsgn.

GAMAZON, IAN; Montgomery HS; San Diego, CA; (2); Office Aide; Off Soph Cls; Cit Awd; Prfct Atten Awd; Asian Clb; UCLA; Commrcl Art.

GAMBA, JENNIFER L; Chino HS; Ontario, CA; (3); Church Yth Grp; FCA; Chorus; Drill Tm; Acctng.

GAMBARIN, SEMYON; George Washington HS; San Francisco, CA; (3); Art Clb; Chess Clb; Math Clb; School Play; Socr; Swmmng; Tennis; Vllybl; Comp Pgmr.

GAMBEA, GLORIA B; Eagle Rock HS; Los Angeles, CA; (2); Computer Clb; Office Aide; Service Clb; Varsity Clb; Rptr Nwsp; Yrbk; Rep Frsh Cls; Pres Stu Cncl; Var Vllybl; Cit Awd; Jrnlsm.

GAMBEE, MATTHEW S; Aptos HS; Corralitos, CA; (2); Rptr Nwsp; Water Polo; Hockey Leag; CSF; Syracuse; Jrnlsm.

GAMBERG, KRISTINE; Homestead HS; Sunnyvale, CA; (1); Band; Mrchg Band; Pep Band; JV Fld Hcky; Hon Roll; Rainbw For Grls; Aerobics; UCLA; Law.

GAMBETTY, ABBIGAIL; Enterprise HS; Oak Run, CA; (1); Church Yth Grp; Chorus; Trk; Fri Night Live; UCLA; Law.

GAMBINO, GARRETT C; Bonita Vista HS; Bonita, CA; (2); 84/600; Model UN; School Play; Lit Mag; Hon Roll; Top In Eng Class 89-90; Sci, Eng Awd 88-89; Berkeley; Eng Lit.

GAMBLE, CHAD E; Mesa Verde HS; Sacramento, CA; (3); 10/214; French Clb; Math Clb; Math Tm; Spanish Clb; JV Ftbl; Var Tennis; High Hon Roll; Prfct Atten Awd; Pres Acad Fit Awd; Engrg.

GAMBLE, JUSTIN; St Bernard HS; Inglewood, CA; (3); Chess Clb; Computer Clb; Office Aide; Ski Clb; School Play; Var Trk; Cit Awd; English Clb; Pres Acad Fit Awd; CSF; UCLA; Med Rsrch.

GAMBLE, LISA A; El Cerrito HS; Richmond, CA; (3); Dance Clb; Office Aide; Pep Clb; JV Sftbl; Hon Roll; Nrs.

GAMBLE, SEAN R; Torrey Pines HS; San Diego, CA; (2); 10/500; Church Yth Grp; FBLA; VP German Clb; Latin Clb; Math Tm; Ski Clb; High Hon Roll; Intrml Socr; Var Vllybl; Intl Latin Exam Hnrs; Amer Chemcl Soc Rcgntn; Med.

GAMBLE, SUSAN; Providence HS; Glendale, CA; (3); 1/54; Drama Clb; GAA; Chorus; Drill Tm; School Musical; School Play; Stage Crew; JV Var Cheerldng; Mgr(s); Var Sftbl; CSF; Xerox Awd Scl Sci/Humnts; Sea World Photo Cont 1st Pl Wnnr; Psych.

GAMBOA, FABRICIO; Granada Hills HS; Los Angeles, CA; (2); Cmnty Wkr; FBLA; Service Clb; Band; Mrchg Band; Orch; Trk; Prfct Atten Awd; CSUN; Bus.

GAMBOA, IMELDA M; Morningside HS; Inglewood, CA; (1); Computer Clb; French Clb; Latin Clb; Model UN; Office Aide; Ski Clb; Teachers Aide; School Musical; Yrbk; Off Frsh Cls; Southern CA Regnl Occupational Ctr For 5 Months; Ofc Occupation Typing Calculation Filing WPM; Marines Or UCLA; County Work.

GAMBOA, MARIA S; Woodrow Wilson HS; Los Angeles, CA; (3); Church Yth Grp; Cmnty Wkr; French Clb; ROTC; Color Guard; Orch; School Musical; Prfct Atten Awd; Rep Frsh Cls; Teacher.

GAMBOA, MICHELLE D; Independence HS; San Jose, CA; (2); Church Yth Grp; Cmnty Wkr; FBLA; GAA; Church Choir; Pres Frsh Cls; JV Capt Sftbl; Intrml Vllybl; Cit Awd; MVP Sftbl; Sierra Clb Awd Chrch Altr Srvng; San Jose ST; Bus Mgmt.

GAMBOA, NORBERT V; Mira Mesa HS; San Diego, CA; (2); 36/797; 4-H; Nwsp; Cit Awd; 4-H Awd; Prfct Atten Awd; Pres Acad Fit Awd; 4.0 Clb; 4.0 Awd; CSF; UCSD; Biochem.

GAMBON, WILLY G; Channel Islands HS; Oxnard, CA; (3); Letterman Clb; Varsity Clb; Var Ftbl; JV Trk; Wt Lftg; Prfct Atten Awd; Pres Acad Fit Awd; Cal Poly SLO; Arch Engrng.

GAMER, JASON M; Harvard Schl; Beverly Hills, CA; (4); JA; Band; Jazz Band; Orch; Pep Band; School Musical; JV Swmmng; Mgr Vllybl; Music.

GAMEZ, LAURA P; Katella HS; Anaheim, CA; (2); Spanish Clb; JV Bsktbl; Var Crs Cntry; Intrml L Trk; Mst Imprvd Track; Span III Awd; Say Agnst Gngs; UCLA; Electrnc Engr.

GAMEZ, MARCOS; Kingsburg HS; Kingsburg, CA; (2); 2/190; Scholastic Bowl; SADD; Lit Mag; Gov Hon Prg Awd; High Hon Roll; Lion Awd; Prfct Atten Awd; Rotary Awd; Acad Lttr Gold K; CSF; Stanford U; Life Sci.

GAMITIAN, GARY A; Burlingame HS; Hillsborough, CA; (4); Var Sec Church Yth Grp; French Clb; Var Ftbl; Var Socr; Var Swmmng; Hon Roll; Pres Acad Fit Awd; CSF; James Martin Klijian Schlrshp Wnnr 2 Yrs Chrch Awd; Armenia Stu Assn; UC Davis; Sprts Med.

GAMIZ, GABRIELA; Ganesha HS; Pomona, CA; (3); Church Yth Grp; VP French Clb; Math Clb; Stu Cncl; Var Crs Cntry; JV Vllybl; Cit Awd; Hon Roll; Math, Engr, & Sci Achvts; Cvl Engrng.

GAMMON, ANNETTE; Beyer HS; Modesto, CA; (2); Office Aide; Band; Mrchg Band; Swmmng; Tennis; Hon Roll; Jr NHS; Peopl To Peopl Frndshp Caravn To USSR; Cntrl CA Conf All Conf Tm Swmmng; Pre Med.

GAMONING, ELMERSON G; Chula Vista HS; Chula Vista, CA; (2); Cit Awd; Prfct Atten Awd; Pres Acad Fit Awd; Bus.

GAN, JENNIFER; St Genevieve HS; Van Nuys, CA; (2); Hosp Aide; High Hon Roll; Hon Roll; Hnr Awd-Engl; Mdrn/Jazz Dance; Slvr Mdl-Natl Ltn Exam; Bus.

GAN, JESSIE P; Oak Grove HS; San Jose, CA; (2); Church Yth Grp; Cmnty Wkr; Computer Clb; JA; Math Clb; ROTC; SADD; Color Guard; Hon Roll; Amer Vet Of WWII Awd Excllnc; Sons Of Amer Rvltn; Acadmc Achvt Awd; Pediatrics.

GAN, LEE A; Charminade HS; Canoga Park, CA; (2); Cmnty Wkr; Spanish Clb; High Hon Roll; NHS; Spanish NHS; Asian Am Club; UCLA; Bus.

GAN, MARIA A; St Bonaventure HS; Camarillo, CA; (3); Am Leg Aux Girls St; SADD; Rptr Nwsp; Pres Soph Cls; Rep Stu Cncl; JV Sftbl; Hon Roll; NHS; CSF; Jr Statesman Of Amer; Poltcl Sci.

GAN, RAYMOND; Cupertino HS; Cupertino, CA; (4); 8/251; Boy Scts; Sec Debate Tm; VP Rptr FBLA; NFL; Red Cross Aide; Pres Service Clb; Speech Tm; Church Choir; JV Tennis; NHS; Pretrical Motion Attorney Mock Trial; Stanford Medical Yth Sci Pgm; Regents & Alumni Schlrshps; UC Berkeley; Mech Engrng.

GANDARA, BILLIE JO; Delano HS; Tucson, AZ; (2); Church Yth Grp; JV Sftbl; Cit Awd; Hon Roll; Prfct Atten Awd; Supt Honor Roll; ASB Exemplary Stu Awd; Cmptr Prgmr.

GANDARA, GERARDO A; Abraham Lincoln HS; Los Angeles, CA; (3); Band; Var Ftbl; Wt Lftg; Hon Roll; MESA; Pacific Asian Club; CSF; Civil Engr.

GANDARA, LISA MARIE; Delano HS; Delano, CA; (3); Church Yth Grp; Cit Awd; Hon Roll; U Of AZ; Accntnt.

GANDY, DAVID M; Capital Christian HS; Carmichael, CA; (2); Church Yth Grp; Debate Tm; Drama Clb; Ed Nwsp; Pres Frsh Cls; Stat Bsbl; Capt Ftbl; Literature.

GANDY, RAY A; San Gabriel HS; San Gabriel, CA; (2); JV Ftbl; Cert Of Auto Excllnc; Acad Achvt Awd; Cerritos JC; Auto Mchnc.

GANESAN, AMAND; Saugus HS; Valencia, CA; (4); 9/400; Boy Scts; FBLA; Hosp Aide; Band; Jazz Band; Mrchg Band; Pep Band; Rptr Nwsp; JV Tennis; 4-H Awd; Play Mrdngm, Viena; CA Schlstc Fed; UC Berkeley; Physics.

GANGNATH, CAROLYN R; Analy HS; Sebastopol, CA; (2); Art Clb; Cmnty Wkr; French Clb; Rptr Nwsp; Lit Mag; Invlvmnt Lcl Cmnty Ctr; Gftd, Tlntd Educ.

GANGNATH, CHAD; Orange HS; Garden Grove, CA; (3); Church Yth Grp; JV Trk; Var Wrstlng; Cit Awd; Hon Roll; Cal Poly San Luis Obispo; Arch.

GANIBI, EILEEN M; Pasadena HS; Altadena, CA; (3); Q&S; School Musical; Ed Yrbk; Sec Jr Cls; JV Var Cheerldng; JV Var Crs Cntry; Var Trk; Hon Roll; Vrsty Badmntn Team; Friday Night Live VP; Bus.

GANIRON, MAROLIND V; Bellarmine-Jefferson HS; Los Angeles, CA; (2); GAA; Spanish Clb; Church Choir; Drill Tm; Var Cheerldng; Gym; Var Pom Pon; Score Keeper; JV Sftbl; Var Trk; UCLA; Actress.

GANJIANPOUR, MAHYAR; Taft HS; Encino, CA; (3); Northridge U; Bio.

GANNON, MICHAEL; Beaumont HS; Cherry Valley, CA; (2); Church Yth Grp; JV Bsbl; High Hon Roll; 2nd Pl Schl Sci Fair; UCLA; Law.

GANNON, MICHAEL L; Servite HS; La Habra, CA; (2); Intnl Clb; Math Tm; JV Bsbl; JV Bsktbl; JV Ftbl; Hon Roll; Math Achvt Awd.

GANSEN, DENNIS C; San Benito HS; Hollister, CA; (3); 5/370; Am Leg Boys St; Letterman Clb; VICA; Rep Stu Cncl; Var Ftbl; Var Trk; High Hon Roll; NHS; Ntl Merit Ltr; Egl Sct; Aerntcl Engrng.

GANSNEDER, MATT R; Pioneer HS; San Jose, CA; (2); Band; Nwsp; Yrbk; Bsbl; Bsktbl; Tennis; Hon Roll.

GANT, WENDY; Washington HS; Fremont, CA; (2); Drama Clb; Pep Clb; School Play; Rep Frsh Cls; Off Soph Cls; Stu Cncl; Cheerldng; JV Gym; Var Trk; Hon Roll; Cmmnty Theater; Tap Dance; Film Dir.

GANTT, KRISTA J; Oakmont HS; Roseville, CA; (2); Church Yth Grp; Cmnty Wkr; Drama Clb; Ski Clb; Spanish Clb; SADD; Chorus; Church Choir; Stage Crew; Variety Show; Humboldt; Psych.

GANZALEZ, YANIRA; Hathorne HS; Inglewood, CA; (2); Cal ST.

GANZENHUBER, STEPHEN; Mc Lane HS; Fresno, CA; (2); FCA; Ed Nwsp; Var Crs Cntry; JV Tennis; Var Trk; Hon Roll; Vet.

GANZER, STEVEN J; Galt HS; Galt, CA; (2); 26/294; JV Trk; High Hon Roll; Med.

GAO, LAUREN L; Lowell HS; San Francisco, CA; (2); Red Cross Aide; Science Clb; CSF; Elec Engrng.

GAO, LU YING; Phillip & Sala Burton HS; S San Francisco, CA; (4); 3/200; Cmnty Wkr; Pres Math Clb; High Hon Roll; Hon Roll; San Fran-Osaka Sr City Assn Stu Exch; Sec Mandarin Clb; Hrns Awd Golden ST Exam; Bus Admin.

GAONA, DANETTE; Pius X HS; Paramount, CA; (3); Spanish Clb; Hon Roll; NHS; CSF; Congrssnl Schlr Natl Young Ldrs Conf; Biomed Clb; Bus Admin.

GAONA, SANDI M; East Bakersfield HS; Bakersfield, CA; (3); #17 In Class; High Hon Roll; Hon Roll.

GAPPY, JOE J; Grossmont HS; El Cajon, CA; (2); #20 In Class; Church Yth Grp; Teachers Aide.

GAPPY, NEDA M; Grossmont HS; El Cajon, CA; (3); Church Yth Grp; Rptr Nwsp; Ed Yrbk; Off Frsh Cls; Off Soph Cls; Off Jr Cls; JV Var Bsktbl; Powder Puff Ftbl; JV Var Swmmng; Hon Roll; USD Coll; Commnctns.

GAPUD, GENEVIEVE; Bonita Vista HS; Bonita, CA; (1); JV Tennis; Hon Roll; Dermilologist.

GARABEDIAN, AMY L; Clovis HS; Sanger, CA; (2); SADD; Powder Puff Ftbl; Fresno ST; Nrsng.

GARABEDIAN, JAMES J; Westchester HS; Los Angeles, CA; (2); JA; Service Clb; VICA; Stage Crew; Cit Awd; Hon Roll; Prfct Atten Awd; Rotary Awd; Yth Cmnty Svc; UCLA; Mech Engr.

GARAY, MICHELLE; Ocean View HS; Huntington Bch, CA; (3); 217/430; Cmnty Wkr; Ski Clb; Var Powder Puff Ftbl; Var L Socr; Var L Trk; JV Vllybl; Golden West; Bus.

GARAY, PRISCELLA L; Antioch HS; Antioch, CA; (2); Church Yth Grp; Girl Scts; Bsktbl; Score Keeper; VP Socr; Var Sftbl; JV Vllybl; Var Vllybl; Var Wt Lftg; Prfct Atten Awd; Bsktbl MVP 88-89; Vlybl Mst Mprvd 88-89; AAA Sftbl Chmpnshps N Coast Sec 3rd Pl 90; Vr Sftbl Hnbl Mnt; Los Medanos Coll; Sci.

GARAY, VIVIAN; John Burroughs HS; Burbank, CA; (4); 5/366; Red Cross Aide; Service Clb; Sec Treas Spanish Clb; Ed Nwsp; Ed Yrbk; Stu Cncl; Co-Capt Tennis; Cit Awd; High Hon Roll; Opt Clb Awd; Natl Hispanic Schlrshp Fnlst; Amer Legion Awd; CSF VP; Hmcmng Qn 89; U CA Berkeley.

GARBARINO, PETRICE N; Galt HS; Herald, CA; (3); VP FFA; Intnl Clb; Cheerldng; Hon Roll; Acadmc Decath; CSF; Delta JC; Pre-Med.

GARBER, JEREMY D; Fairfield HS; Suisun City, CA; (2); Boy Scts; Church Yth Grp; Band; Mrchg Band; Crs Cntry; Trk.

GARBERO, HAYDEE D; Helix HS; La Jolla, CA; (4); 24/355; Intnl Clb; Science Clb; JV Swmmng; Hon Roll; Prfct Atten Awd; Otstndng Awd Spanish; CA Schlrshp Fdr; U Of CA San Diego; Bio.

GARCES, ANTHONY; St Augustine HS; San Diego, CA; (4); 10/122; Am Leg Boys St; Model UN; NFL; Treas Soph Cls; VP Jr Cls; VP Stu Cncl; Var Trk; Var Wrstlng; NHS; Rotary Awd; Cum Laude; San Diego Union All Acad Team Track; Fnlst Lions Clb Spch Cont; Outstndng Achvt Relgn I&II; U Of Notre Dame; Liberal Arts.

GARCIA, ALBERTO H; Sssn Clemente HS; San Clemente, CA; (3); Spanish Clb; Wt Lftg; Cit Awd; Academic Achievement Awards For American Literature Adv Comp Science Spanish.

GARCIA, ALEX R; Mountain View HS; S El Monte, CA; (3); Cit Awd; High Hon Roll; Hon Roll; Prfct Atten Awd; Hnrbl Mntn Sci Fr Project; Prin Awd Scl Sci; CA Polytech Pomona; Arch.

GARCIA, ALISIA M; Saint Anthony HS; Long Beach, CA; (2); Hon Roll; Med.

GARCIA, ALIW V; Lemoore HS; Lemoore, CA; (4); Church Yth Grp; Nwsp; Hon Roll; Minority Jrnlsm Wrkshp-Fresno ST U; Jrnlsm.

GARCIA, ALLAN J; Servite HS; Cypress, CA; (4); Church Yth Grp; Cmnty Wkr; Ftbl; Var L Socr; Hon Roll; Jr Statesman Of Amer; JV Sccr MVP.

GARCIA, ALONSO; James A Garfield HS; Montebello, CA; (3); Drama Clb; School Musical; School Play; MED-COR; E Los Angeles HS Ext Pgm; UCLA; Anesthslgst.

GARCIA, AMERICA; Coachella Valley HS; Coachella, CA; (3); Cit Awd; Hon Roll; Prfct Atten Awd; Typing II Award; English II Award; Schored 5 On A P Spanish Test.

GARCIA, AMY D; Antioch HS; Antioch, CA; (2); Church Yth Grp; Pep Clb; Teachers Aide; Sec Stu Cncl; Intrml Cheerldng; Hon Roll; Spnsh/Ltno & East Clb; Chrldr Coach; UC Davis; Lang.

GARCIA, ANA D; Gahr HS; Artesia, CA; (2); 53/490; Church Yth Grp; Dance Clb; Powder Puff Ftbl; Hon Roll; Blue & Gold Awd; Psych.

GARCIA, ANA MARIA; Southwest HS; San Ysidro, CA; (4); 9/498; Drama Clb; Office Aide; San Diego ST U; Med.

GARCIA, ANDREA D; Presentation HS; San Jose, CA; (4); 39/134; Art Clb; Dance Clb; Spanish Clb; Chorus; Yrbk; Hon Roll; Pres Acad Fit Awd; Escaramuza Charra Las Adelitas De San Jose; Honors Arts Society; Presentation Ambassador Club; Santa Clara U; Economics.

GARCIA, ANGEL A; Don Bosco Technical Inst; Monterey Park, CA; (3); Church Yth Grp; Gamng,Comic Clb; UCLA; Grphc Comm.

GARCIA, ANGELA; Park Alternative Ctr; Monrovia, CA; (3); Nwsp; Stu Cncl; Cit Awd; Poetry; Womens Aux Awd; Lit.

GARCIA, ANGELICA; Fillmore HS; Fillmore, CA; (2); Church Yth Grp; SADD; Cit Awd; UCSB Partnership Prgm.

GARCIA, ANGELICA; Polytechnic HS; Pacoima, CA; (3); High Hon Roll; Hon Roll; Catherine Coll; Legal Sectry.

GARCIA, ANGELICA; Riverbank HS; Riverbank, CA; (3); 33/110; Church Yth Grp; Spanish Clb; Bst Of Show Art Awd; Sacramento ST U; Bus.

GARCIA, ANGELICA Y; Bonita Vista HS; National City, CA; (3); Dance Clb; Drama Clb; Varsity Clb; Chorus.

GARCIA, ANGELINE; Bishop Amat Memorial HS; Hacienda Heights, CA; (2); Spanish Clb; Natl Spansh Exam 6th Pl 88-89, 9th Pl 89-90; U Southern CA.

GARCIA, ANGIE; Mt Shasta HS; Mt Shasta, CA; (3); Church Yth Grp; Hosp Aide; Teachers Aide; Chorus; Swing Chorus; Var Trk; Hon Roll; All-Leag Track; COS; Psych.

GARCIA, ANNETTE; Norte Vista HS; Riverside, CA; (2); Dance Clb; Pep Clb; Cheerldng; Pom Pon; Cit Awd; Hon Roll; Prfct Atten Awd; Pres Acad Fit Awd; Bus Admin.

GARCIA, ANSELMO; Senior HS; Santa Ana, CA; (2); Hon Roll; UCI Prtnrshp; UCI; Arch.

GARCIA, ANTHONY; South Bay Lutheran HS; Hawthorne, CA; (4); 4/18; Church Yth Grp; Cmnty Wkr; Drama Clb; Capt Quiz Bowl; School Play; Rep Sr Cls; Capt Var Bsbl; JV Bsktbl; Crs Cntry; Ftbl; UC Northridge; Accntng.

GARCIA, ANTONIO A; Oakdale HS; Waterford, CA; (3); Boy Scts; Church Yth Grp; Math Tm; Quiz Bowl; Scholastic Bowl; Band; Mrchg Band; Pep Band; JV Crs Cntry; JV Swmmng; CA ST U; Engr.

GARCIA, ANTONIO P; Lowell HS; San Francisco, CA; (2); Cmnty Wkr; Office Aide; Science Clb; Service Clb; Teachers Aide; JV Trk; Hon Roll; CSF Schlrshp Fed 90; Clss Evnts Vlntr; U Of CA Davis; Law.

GARCIA, ARMANDO C; Watsonville HS; Watsonville, CA; (2); Cmnty Wkr; FFA; Hon Roll; Prfct Atten Awd; Arch.

GARCIA, BELINA; El Camino HS; Valley Center, CA; (3); GAA; Pep Clb; SADD; Var Crs Cntry; JV Socr; Var Trk; Hon Roll; San Diego Tribune Achvt Cert; Outstndng Acad Achvt; Athltc Achvt; Law/Govt.

GARCIA, BENITO; Modesto HS; Modesto, CA; (2); Prfct Atten Awd; San Luis Obispo; Arch.

GARCIA, BLANCA M; Lynwood HS; Lynwood, CA; (4); Drama Clb; Pep Clb; Spanish Clb; Teachers Aide; Thesps; Flag Corp; School Play; Capt Cheerldng; Spanish NHS; Cinco De May Queen 90; Cerritos CC; Bus Mgmt.

GARCIA, BRENDA L; Manual Arts HS; Los Angeles, CA; (2); Drama Clb; Service Clb; Trk; Acad Decathlon; WA U; Bio.

GARCIA, BRIAN S; Bellarmine College Preparatory HS; San Jose, CA; (3); Varsity Clb; Var L Socr; Wt Lftg; Soccer-Olympc Dvlpmnt Prgm; Ucsb.

GARCIA, BRYAN; Roosevelt HS; Fresno, CA; (4); Church Yth Grp; Letterman Clb; Science Clb; Band; Jazz Band; Var Tennis; Green & Gold Clb; UC Davis; Sci.

GARCIA, CAROLINA; Oristimba HS; Newman, CA; (2); Vllybl; Hon Roll; Stanford U; Fshn Dsgn.

GARCIA, CELINE; Bishop Amat Memorial HS; Hacienda Heights, CA; (4); Spanish Clb; Hon Roll; A P Spnsh Lang Test Score 5 89; U Southern CA.

GARCIA, CESAR; Bell Gardens HS; Bell Gardens, CA; (1); Church Yth Grp; FCA; Ftbl; Wt Lftg; Vet.

GARCIA, CHRISTI L; John Muir HS; Altadena, CA; (2); French Clb; Band; Chorus; Jazz Band; Mrchg Band; Orch; School Musical; Hon Roll.

GARCIA, CHRISTINA; San Jose HS Acad; San Jose, CA; (3); 52/207; Dance Clb; Drill Tm; Sec Jr Cls; JV Cheerldng; Hon Roll.

GARCIA, CHRISTINE L; Bishop Amat Memorial HS; Temple City, CA; (2); Color Guard; Drill Tm; NHS; Acad Excl Phys Ed 2nd Hnrs; Friday Night Live Club Secy; Temple City Ltl Lg Sftbl; Awd Merit Span I; Law.

GARCIA, CYNTHIA; Bishop Amat Memorial HS; Covina, CA; (3); Science Clb; Varsity Clb; Var Socr; JV Sftbl; Hon Roll; NHS; CA Schlrshp Fdrtn; UCLA; Psych.

GARCIA, CYNTHIA; Mater Dei HS; Santa Ana, CA; (1); Vlybl; Cmmndtns Span, Sci, Lit & Relgn; Swmmng; UCLA; Arch.

GARCIA, DANIEL P; Palmdale HS; Palmdale, CA; (2); Art.

GARCIA, DANNY; Livingston HS; Livingston, CA; (1); Art Clb; French Clb; JV Bsbl; JV Ftbl; High Hon Roll; Hon Roll; Pres Acad Fit Awd; UCLA; Chem.

GARCIA, DARNYL J; King City HS; King City, CA; (3); Drama Clb; School Play; Stage Crew; Cheerldng; Hon Roll; Bus Admin.

GARCIA, DAVID; Inglewood HS; Inglewood, CA; (3); Hon Roll; UCLA; Accntng.

GARCIA, DAVID L; Archbishop Riordan HS; San Francisco, CA; (3); 24/140; Latin Clb; Spanish Clb; JV Ftbl; Hon Roll; CSF; Engr.

GARCIA, DELIA M; Workman HS; La Puente, CA; (3); Temple Yth Grp; Hon Roll; Arch.

GARCIA, DENISE; Irvine HS; Irvine, CA; (3); AFS; Spanish Clb; JV Socr; Capt Tennis; Soccer Skills Awd; Jrnlst.

GARCIA, DENISE A; Eisenhower HS; Rialto, CA; (3); Cmnty Wkr; Teachers Aide; Band; Mrchg Band; Pep Band; Stat Wrstlng; Hon Roll; Pre-Law.

GARCIA, DESIREE A; Cajon HS; San Bernardino, CA; (3); Church Yth Grp; Cmnty Wkr; Drama Clb; School Musical; School Play; Bsktbl; Swmmng; Theater.

GARCIA, DONNY; Tulare Western HS; Tulare, CA; (1); Band; Mrchg Band; Pep Band; Bsbl; Var Socr; Hon Roll; Qulfd For XXIII Aau JR Olympc Natl Trk Meet TX; Arch.

GARCIA, EDGAR; University HS; Los Angeles, CA; (2); Hon Roll; Cmnty Bsbl.

GARCIA, ELENA G; Monte Vista HS; Alamo, CA; (2); Drama Clb; Teachers Aide; Stage Crew; Art & Music; CA Coll Of Arts/Crafts; Art.

GARCIA, ELENA M; Providence HS; Burbank, CA; (2); Library Aide; Model UN; NFL; Speech Tm; Chorus; Pres Soph Cls; Var L Trk; JV L Vllybl; Hon Roll; NHS; CA Schlrshp Fed; Law.

GARCIA, ELISA; St Paul HS; Santa Fe Springs, CA; (3); 28/300; Var Cheerldng; Hon Roll; NHS; Spanish NHS; March For Hngr; Tchr.

GARCIA, ELIZABETH L; St Genevieve HS; Sepulveda, CA; (2); Church Yth Grp; French Clb; Hosp Aide; Pep Clb; SADD; Chorus; Drill Tm; Stu Cncl; Hon Roll; Hnrb Mntn Piano; UCLA; Doc.

GARCIA, ELSA R; Bishop Montgomery HS; Gardena, CA; (2); Letterman Clb; Spanish Clb; Church Choir; JV Bsktbl; High Hon Roll; Hon Roll; Prfct Atten Awd; Vlybl.

GARCIA, EMMA RUTH ESTILLORE; John Marshall HS; Los Angeles, CA; (4); 91/685; Treas French Clb; Treas Key Clb; Peer Cnclng; U C Riverside; Pre Bus.

GARCIA, ENRIKA G; El Cajon Valley HS; El Cajon, CA; (1); Drftn.

GARCIA JR, ENRIQUE; Indio HS; Indio, CA; (3); 200/500; Spanish Clb; JV Bsktbl; Prfct Atten; UC Irvine; Pre-Med.

GARCIA, ERICA; Calexico HS; Calexico, CA; (2); Spanish Clb; Teachers Aide; Gym; Kelsey-Jenney Coll; Secrtrl.

GARCIA, ERICA J; Bishop Amat HS; La Puente, CA; (3); Cmnty Wkr; Dance Clb; Drama Clb; French Clb; Spanish Clb; School Play; Hon Roll; NEDT Awd; JR Vol Queen Of The Vly Hosp; Vol At Boys Clb; Law.

GARCIA, FERNANDO; Lakewood HS; Long Beach, CA; (2); UCLA; Arch.

GARCIA, FRANCISCA; Washington Prep; Los Angeles, CA; (3); Spanish Clb; Spanish NHS; Cosmetology.

GARCIA, FRANCO X; Watsonville HS; Watsonville, CA; (2); Intrml Ftbl; Hon Roll; Carbillo Coll; Police Offcr.

GARCIA, FRANK; Granada Hills HS; Northridge, CA; (2); Church Yth Grp; FHA; Math Tm; Quiz Bowl; Service Clb; Teachers Aide; Band; JV Bsktbl; High Hon Roll; Hon Roll; UCLA; Law.

GARCIA, FRANK; Montgomery HS; San Diego, CA; (4); 21/400; Am Leg Boys St; Ed Yrbk; Lit Mag; VP Jr Cls; Pres Sr Cls; L Vllybl; NHS; Pres Acad Fit Awd; Lulac Schlrshp; Schl Svc Awd; CSF; UCSD; Comp Sci.

GARCIA, GABRIEL H; Indio HS; Indio, CA; (2); French Clb; Hosp Aide; Rptr Nwsp; Amnesty Intl Club; Jrnlsm Club; Med.

GARCIA, GABRIELA; Bell Gardens HS; Bell Gardens, CA; (2); Church Yth Grp; Crs Cntry; Trk; Sci.

GARCIA, GABRIELA; Colexio HS; Calexico, CA; (1); Church Yth Grp; Temple Yth Grp; Church Choir; San Diego ST U; Paralegal.

GARCIA, GABRIELA; El Modena HS; Orange, CA; (2); Var Bsktbl; Wt Lftg; Hon Roll; Intr Dec.

GARCIA, GABRIELA; Fontana HS; Fontana, CA; (2); Color Guard; Sftbl.

GARCIA, GARY ZALDY C; Channel Islands HS; Oxnard, CA; (2); Science Clb; Hon Roll; Prfct Atten Awd; CSF; Acad Decathlon; CA Inst Of Tech; Sci/Physics.

GARCIA, GERALDINE; Bishop Amat Memorial HS; Hacienda Heights, CA; (3); Church Yth Grp; Drama Clb; JA; Math Tm; Spanish Clb; Church Choir; Capt Bsktbl; Cit Awd; High Hon Roll; NHS; Notre Dame; Med.

GARCIA, GILBERT; Calexico HS; Calexico, CA; (3); Elctrncs.

GARCIA, GINA C; Cuyama Valley HS; New Cuyama, CA; (2); Church Yth Grp; Cmnty Wkr; Mgr Yrbk; Sec Frsh Cls; Stat Bsktbl; Var Sftbl; JV Vllybl; High Hon Roll; Hon Roll; Lion Awd; Cal ST U.

GARCIA, GLADYS; Tranquillity Union HS; San Joaquin, CA; (3); 16/220; FBLA; High Hon Roll; Hon Roll; India Clb Sectry; CSF 3.0 Or Better; Fresno ST; Bus Admin.

GARCIA, GLORIA L; Alhambra HS; Martinez, CA; (3); 28/214; Church Yth Grp; Intnl Clb; Teachers Aide; Church Choir; Hon Roll; UC Prtnrshp Prgm; Amer Assn U Women Cert Of Merit Fr III.

GARCIA, GREGORY G; Garey HS; Pomona, CA; (2); Church Yth Grp; Var Capt Ftbl; MESA-MATH/Engrng/Sci Achvt; CA ST-FULLERTON; Psych.

GARCIA, GRISELDA P; Sacred Heart HS; Los Angeles, CA; (3); 2nd Pl Natl Spnsh Exam; Score Of 5 On Advanced Placement Spnsh Exam; Nrsng.

GARCIA, GUADALUPE; Silver Creek HS; San Jose, CA; (3); Dance Clb; Latin Clb; Teachers Aide; Band; Color Guard; Mrchg Band; School Musical; School Play; Cheerldng; Gym.

GARCIA, HARRIET J; Willow Glen HS; San Jose, CA; (2); SADD; Badminton Tm; CSF; UC Berkeley; Law.

GARCIA, HECTOR M; Riverbank HS; Modesto, CA; (2); Church Yth Grp; Pres Soph Cls; VP Jr Cls; JV Ftbl; JV Trk; Hon Roll; Bio II Hnrs; Life Sci.

GARCIA, HELEN; Whittier Christian HS; Montebello, CA; (3); Church Yth Grp; English Clb; GAA; Sec Frsh Cls; Sec Soph Cls; Stu Cncl; Crs Cntry; Socr; Hon Roll; Mst Vlbl Crss Cntry; Music.

GARCIA, IRENE; East Bakersfield HS; Bakersfield, CA; (4); 89/400; Intnl Clb; Pres Band; Jazz Band; Pres Mrchg Band; Pres Orch; Pep Band; School Musical; Rep Stu Cncl; Var Socr; Var Sftbl; Mst Outstndng Band Mem 89-90; Mst Outstndng Symphny 89-90; MVP Sftbl; CA ST U Fresno; Music Prof.

GARCIA, ISRAEL; Garfield HS; Los Angeles, CA; (2); Cmnty Wkr; Varsity Clb; Ftbl; Wt Lftg; Cit Awd; Hosp Vlntr Wrk; UCLA; Zoology.

GARCIA, ISSAC; Colton HS; Colton, CA; (3); Boy Scts; Cmnty Wkr; FFA; Teachers Aide; Ftbl; Wt Lftg; Wrstlng; Cit Awd; Hon Roll; Prfct Atten Awd; Phys Thrpy.

GARCIA, IVETTE A; Hamilton HS; Los Angeles, CA; (2); French Clb; Drill Tm; Orch; School Musical; Cit Awd; Hon Roll; Knights & Ladies; Dance.

GARCIA, JACOB R; Maranatha HS; Altadena, CA; (2); Drama Clb; Acpl Chr; Chorus; School Play; JV Socr; CSF; Cmmnty Theatre; Spcl Achvt Awds-Physiology/Hnrs Alb 2/Span 2.

GARCIA, JAIME G; San Benito HS; Hollister, CA; (3); Drama Clb; Letterman Clb; School Play; Ftbl; Trk; Wrstlng; CHP Acad; Law Enforcement.

GARCIA, JAIME O; William Workman HS; Valinda, CA; (3); 14/200; Spanish Clb; Varsity Clb; Var Bsktbl; Rotary Awd; Spanish NHS; Fullerton; Business Adm.

GARCIA, JAMES E; Hiram W Johnson HS; Sacramento, CA; (3); 24/116; Boy Scts; SADD; Teachers Aide; Var L Swmmng; Elks Awd; High Hon Roll; Hon Roll; Gldn St Exam 1st Yr Alg Hnrs; Lawyer.

GARCIA, JASON C; North Tahoe HS; Garnecian Bay, CA; (3); Cmnty Wkr; Office Aide; Varsity Clb; Pres Frsh Cls; Pres Soph Cls; Stu Cncl; Var Bsbl; JV Var Bsktbl; Var Capt Ftbl; Var Wt Lftg; UCLA; Bus.

GARCIA, JAVIER; Arvin HS; Lamont, CA; (2); Art Clb; Debate Tm; Drama Clb; Spanish Clb; Speech Tm; SADD; School Play; Lit Mag; Bsktbl; Ftbl; UCSB; Acctnt.

GARCIA, JAVIER; Garfield HS; Los Angeles, CA; (2); Church Yth Grp; Math Clb; Math Tm; Science Clb; JV Tennis; Prfct Atten Awd; Sci.

GARCIA, JAVIER; Schurr HS; Monterey Park, CA; (3); Am Leg Boys St; Hosp Aide; Key Clb; Spanish Clb; SADD; Ed Nwsp; Hon Roll; VP NHS; Prfct Atten Awd; CSF VP; Medicine.

GARCIA, JAZMIN T; Pasadena HS; Pasadena, CA; (1); Band; Mrchg Band; Var Swmmng; Creatv Writing Clb; Mesa; Harvard Law; Lawyer.

GARCIA, JEFF C; Corona SR HS; Corona, CA; (2); Pres Spanish Clb; Var Ftbl; High Hon Roll; Pres Acad Fit Awd; UC San Diego; Pre-Med.

GARCIA, JESSICA; Oxnard HS; Oxnard, CA; (2); 7/204; English Clb; Treas Intnl Clb; Service Clb; School Play; Stage Crew; Rptr Nwsp; Rep Stu Cncl; Cit Awd; High Hon Roll; Prfct Atten Awd; Spelling Bee 1st Pl; CSF; OHS Peer Helpers; Berkeley; Medicine.

GARCIA, JESSICA R; Palmdale HS; Acton, CA; (3); Latin Clb; Science Clb; Spanish Clb; Powder Puff Ftbl; High Hon Roll; CSF; UCLA; CPA.

GARCIA, JOE; Cantwell HS; Los Angeles, CA; (2); Science Clb; Spanish Clb; Teachers Aide; JV Bsbl; JV Crs Cntry; Hon Roll; Cal ST U; Bus.

GARCIA, JOE M; John Burroughs HS; Burbank, CA; (3); 10/30; Boy Scts; Church Yth Grp; Teachers Aide; Cit Awd; BYU; Bus.

GARCIA, JOHANNIE; Palmdale HS; Palmdale, CA; (4); 80/659; Church Yth Grp; French Clb; JA; Science Clb; Speech Tm; Teachers Aide; Off Jr Cls; Off Sr Cls; Stu Cncl; Hon Roll; Stu GovICC RepCSF; UCLA; Med.

GARCIA, JONNALEE; Etiwanda HS; Alta Loma, CA; (3); 52/586; Church Yth Grp; Pep Clb; Var Cheerldng; Chrldng Schlr Awd 89, 90; Prins Hnr Roll; Future Ldrs Of Amer; Brigham Young U; Bus.

GARCIA, JOSE A; Lindsay HS; Lindsay, CA; (2); Art Clb; Teachers Aide; Var Socr; Var Swmmng; Var Trk; High Hon Roll; Hon Roll; Mech Engr.

GARCIA, JOSE R; Calexico Adventist Mission Sch; Oxnard, CA; (3); 8/15; FBLA; FHA; FTA; SADD; Ftbl; Golf; Trk; Wt Lftg; Wrstlng.

GARCIA, JOSE S; Cantwell HS; Pico Rivera, CA; (3); 8/60; Chess Clb; Cmnty Wkr; Computer Clb; NFL; Science Clb; Spanish Clb; Speech Tm; Nwsp; Hon Roll; NHS; CA Schlrshp Fdrtn; ACE Pgm CSULA; CA Inst Of Tech; Engr.

GARCIA, JUAN; Southeast Lutheran HS; South Gate, CA; (3); 1/10; Nwsp; Yrbk; Rep Frsh Cls; Var L Bsktbl; Var Trk; Var Capt Vllybl; Cit Awd; High Hon Roll; Prfct Atten Awd; Grand Canyon U Phoenix AZ; Sci.

GARCIA, JUAN G; Roosevelt HS; Los Angeles, CA; (2); Mrchg Band; Pep Band; JV Bsbl; Hon Roll; Stanford U; Med.

GARCIA, JUAN P; Avalon HS; Avalon, CA; (4); 4/25; Art Clb; Aud/Vis; Computer Clb; Letterman Clb; Pep Clb; Service Clb; Spanish Clb; Varsity Clb; Phtg Yrbk; Rep Jr Cls; Cal Poly Pomona; Mech Engr.

GARCIA, JUANA B; Oceanside HS; Oceanside, CA; (4); Off Frsh Cls; Hon Roll; Tourist.

GARCIA, JUDY E; Lowell HS; San Francisco, CA; (2); Hosp Aide; ROTC; JV Bsktbl; Fil-Am Club; Med.

GARCIA, JUDY R; University HS; Irvine, CA; (3); Chorus; Hon Roll; Prfct Atten Awd; Laurette Awd Engl; Medl In Music; Orange Coast Coll; Bus.

GARCIA, JULIE A; Corona HS; Corona, CA; (2); #7 In Class; GAA; Letterman Clb; Treas Frsh Cls; Powder Puff Ftbl; L Socr; L Sftbl; High Hon Roll; Pres Acad Fit Awd; Amer Lgn Schl Awd; Med.

GARCIA, KARINA; Mt Pleasant HS; San Jose, CA; (3); Latin Clb; Vllybl; Hon Roll; Art; Spring Art Exhbt Hnrb Mntn; Stu Art Fr 4th Pl.

GARCIA, KARLA; Montebello HS; Pico Rivera, CA; (1); SADD; Chorus; JV Vllybl; Cit Awd; Hon Roll; Prfct Atten Awd; Cal ST Long Beach; Law.

GARCIA, KIMBERLY A; Santiago HS; Santa Ana, CA; (2); 67/498; Church Yth Grp; Library Aide; Teachers Aide; Hon Roll; Prfct Atten Awd; Pres Acad Fit Awd; U Of CA Irvine Prtnrshp Pgm; Nrsry Schl Tchr.

GARCIA, LAURA; Sierra Vista HS; Baldwin Park, CA; (4); 6/306; FBLA; Math Clb; Speech Tm; SADD; Pres Soph Cls; VP Jr Cls; Pres Stu Cncl; DAR Awd; High Hon Roll; Opt Clb Awd; Golden St Exam Hgh Hnr Geom; Natl Hspnc Schlrshp Semifnlst; UCLA; Poltcl Sci.

GARCIA, LAURA D; A A Stagg HS; Stockton, CA; (2); School Play; Upward Bound; Early Outreach Pgm; Phy.

GARCIA, LAURA E; San Fernando HS; Pacoima, CA; (3); Band; Hon Roll; NHS; Prncpls Hnr Rl; Claremont; Bio.

GARCIA, LAWRENCE E; Lindsay HS; Lindsay, CA; (1); Boy Scts; Ftbl; Trk; Wt Lftg; Hon Roll; USC.

GARCIA, LETICIA; Oxnard HS; Oxnard, CA; (3); 4-H; Teachers Aide.

GARCIA, LINDA J; Glendale Adventist Acad; Glendale, CA; (3); 1/65; FCA; Rptr Nwsp; Off Frsh Cls; Treas Sr Cls; Pres Stu Cncl; Var Bsktbl; Var Capt Vllybl; High Hon Roll; Harvard Prz Bk; US Army Reserve Natl Schlr/ Athlt Awd 90; Anesh.

GARCIA, LINDA M; West HS; Bakersfield, CA; (2); Spanish Clb; Drill Tm; Hon Roll; Harvard U; Law.

GARCIA, LORENA; Modesto HS; Modesto, CA; (3); Spanish Clb; Teachers Aide; Hon Roll; Prfct Atten Awd; Tchr.

GARCIA, LOURDES C; San Bernardino HS; San Bernardino, CA; (3); Library Aide; SADD; Teachers Aide; Rptr Nwsp; Rptr Yrbk; Sec Jr Cls; NHS; Acad Dcthln; Upward Bound; MESA; Intl Bus.

GARCIA, LUANNE; El Rancho HS; Pico Rivera, CA; (3); German Clb; Math Clb; Science Clb; Hon Roll; Played Piano Through Music Teachers Of Merit Assoc,Involved In VC Partners; CSF; CA ST Long Beach; Marketing.

GARCIA, LUIS R; Calexico HS; Calexico, CA; (1); Bus Profs of Am; U Of Berkley; Comp Engr.

GARCIA, LUPE H; Pius X HS; Long Beach, CA; (4); 1/180; Service Clb; Teachers Aide; Ed Yrbk; Hon Roll; NHS; Rotary Awd; Val; Bnk Amer Awd Math & Sci; CSF; Loyola Marymount U; Liberal Std.

GARCIA, MAGGIE D; Brawley Union HS; Brawley, CA; (3); Imperial Vly Rgnl Occu Pgrm; Fshn Dsgn.

GARCIA, MALISSA A; Merced HS; Merced, CA; (3); High Hon Roll; Hon Roll; Cert Merit Acad Excllnc 87-88; Stu Cmmndtn Eng & Alg 87-88; Cert Of Achvt Retail Sls/Mrchndsng 89-90.

GARCIA, MARA E; San Pedro HS; Wilmington, CA; (2); Church Yth Grp; Dance Clb; Drama Clb; Acadmc All Stars For Schltc Excllnc.

GARCIA, MARIA; King City JR HS; Greenfield, CA; (3); Designer.

GARCIA, MARIA; Williams HS; Williams, CA; (2).

GARCIA, MARIA E; Central Union HS; El Centro, CA; (3); 90/500; Church Yth Grp; Cmnty Wkr; Pep Clb; Hon Roll; Just Say No Club, Frch Cntst Partcptn Aaward; U Of CA San Diego; Intl Bus.

GARCIA, MARIA LOURDES; Woodrow Wilson HS; San Francisco, CA; (4); Church Yth Grp; Dance Clb; Off Latin Clb; Church Choir; Rptr Yrbk; Trk; Vllybl; Hon Roll; Wilson Hnr Scty.

GARCIA, MARIA LUISA; Centennial HS; Corona, CA; (1); French Clb; Entertaining Bus Or Bus Career.

GARCIA, MARIBEL; Calexico HS; Calexico, CA; (3); 20/30; Church Yth Grp; SADD; Imperial Valley Coll; Comp.

GARCIA, MARIBEL; San Pasqual HS; Escondido, CA; (3); 71/353; Cmnty Wkr; French Clb; Library Aide; Chorus; Church Choir; Shift Mgr At Taco Bell Age 16; USD; Accntng.

GARCIA, MARIO; Modesto HS; Salida, CA; (3); Nwsp; Gym; Hon Roll.

GARCIA, MARIO V; Oakland Technical HS; Oakland, CA; (2); Cmnty Wkr; Variety Show; VP Jr Cls; JV Bsktbl; High Hon Roll; Hnr Soc; Close Up Washington DC Excrsn 89; Padeia Pgm; U Of CA Berkeley.

GARCIA, MARISOL; Fontana HS; Fontana, CA; (3); Church Yth Grp; Hon Roll.

GARCIA, MARTHA; Tranquility HS; Mendota, CA; (3); Band; Mrchg Band; Pep Band; Vllybl; Hon Roll.

GARCIA, MARYANN M; Mount Pleasant HS; San Jose, CA; (2); Church Yth Grp; Drama Clb; Girl Scts; Science Clb; Acpl Chr; School Play; Hon Roll; San Jose ST U; Nrs.

GARCIA, MARYBEL; Hemet HS; Hemet, CA; (2); Teachers Aide.

GARCIA, MARYSOL; Mountain View HS; El Monte, CA; (2); Band; Jazz Band; Mrchg Band; Pep Band; Vrsty Badminton; San Diego ST U; Child Psych.

GARCIA, MAX A; Valley HS; Sacramento, CA; (2); Tennis; Hon Roll; CPA.

GARCIA, MAYA S; San Jacinto HS; San Jacinto, CA; (3); 15/200; Pres AFS; Chess Clb; Cmnty Wkr; Drama Clb; VP Sec French Clb; FFA; Letterman Clb; Pep Clb; Teachers Aide; Drill Tm; Mck Trl; Cnsrvtn Clb VP; Prm, Hmcmng Cmmttes; Jrnlsm Wrkshp; Bld Dnr; Hnds Acrss Amer; U Of CA; Photojrnlsm.

GARCIA, MAYRA V; Palmdale HS; Littlerock, CA; (2); Library Aide; Spanish Clb; Cit Awd; Hon Roll.

GARCIA, MELINDA M; Santa Ana HS; Santa Ana, CA; (3); Capt Dance Clb; Pep Clb; Acpl Chr; School Musical; School Play; Stage Crew; Var Capt Pom Pon; UCLA; Prof Dncr.

GARCIA, MELISSA; St Joseph HS; La Palma, CA; (2); Church Yth Grp; Spanish Clb; SADD; Hon Roll; United Colors Of St Josephs; Fashion Clb; UCLA; Bus Admin.

GARCIA, MELISSA J; American HS; Fremont, CA; (3); French Clb; GAA; Spanish Clb; SADD; Sec Soph Cls; VP Sr Cls; JV Capt Bsktbl; JV Var Sftbl; Capt Sftbl; Hon Roll; Swmmng Instr; U CA; Bus.

GARCIA, MICHAEL; John Glenn HS; Norwalk, CA; (2); Band; Mrchg Band; JV Ftbl; Wt Lftg; Cal ST Long Beach; Dr.

GARCIA, MICHAEL A; Garfield Computer Science/Math Magnet; Los Angeles, CA; (2); Debate Tm; Math Clb; Q&S; Science Clb; Spanish Clb; Ed Nwsp; Ed Lit Mag; High Hon Roll; LAUSD All City Mail In Cntst Sprts 3rd Pl 89; Mariposa Prgm Rcgntn; U Notre Dame; Law.

GARCIA, MICHAEL A; San Fernando CIP Magnet HS; Chatsworth, CA; (2); JA; SADD; Var Ftbl; Wt Lftg; High Hon Roll; Cal Poly U; Aerospace Engrng.

GARCIA, MICHAEL H; Plus X HS; Long Beach, CA; (3); Church Yth Grp; High Hon Roll; Mech Drwng; Mech Drwng.

GARCIA III, MICHAEL J; East Union HS; French Camp, CA; (4); #45 In Class; Teachers Aide; Sprt Ed Nwsp; JV Var Bsbl; JV Var Bsktbl; JV Ftbl; Score Keeper; Hon Roll; Comp Sci.

GARCIA, MICHELLE; Antioch SR HS; Antioch, CA; (4); 11/612; Art Clb; Drama Clb; Key Clb; Letterman Clb; Pep Clb; Spanish Clb; Teachers Aide; School Play; Intrml Bsktbl; JV Crs Cntry; Panther Stridors Rnnng Clb; N Coast Schlr Athlt; Bausch & Lomb Hon Sci Awd Prog; 1; UC San Diego; Ecology.

GARCIA, MICHELLE P; Mt Pleasant HS; San Jose, CA; (3); Band; Orch; Pep Band; NHS; Prfct Atten Awd; San Jose St; Comp.

GARCIA, MISTI L; Kerman HS; Kerman, CA; (2); 17/172; Yrbk; JV Sftbl; Hon Roll; Coaches Awd Sftbl; Fresno ST U; Psych.

GARCIA, MONA LISA S; King City HS; Greenfield, CA; (3); 11/250; Church Yth Grp; Chorus; Drill Tm; Yrbk; Sec Sr Cls; High Hon Roll; Hon Roll; Acad Block Awd; Maya Clb; Commercl Clb; San Jose ST U; Bus.

GARCIA, MONICA; Woodside HS; Redwood City, CA; (3); Church Yth Grp; Hosp Aide; Rptr Nwsp; Ed Yrbk; Rep Soph Cls; Rep Jr Cls; Pres Sr Cls; Rep Stu Cncl; Var Vllybl; Cit Awd; Mid-Peninsula Integrtd & Smith Coll Bk Awds; CSF; Clb Vlybl; Mrktng.

GARCIA, MONICA D; Calexico HS; Calexico, CA; (2); FBLA; Intnl Clb; Band; Mrchg Band; Ed Nwsp; Sisters In Soroptomist S Club; Georgetown U; Law.

GARCIA, MONTE; Fred C Beyer HS; Modesto, CA; (4); 29/500; Boy Scts; Pres Church Yth Grp; Math Clb; Science Clb; SADD; Band; Church Choir; Drm Mjr(t); Jazz Band; Mrchg Band; CA All St Hnr Band; Natl Hspnc Schlr Awd Semi-Fnlst; US Naval Acad Summr Smnr; USC; Aerospace Engrng.

GARCIA, NANCY; Senior HS; Los Angeles, CA; (3); Cmnty Wkr; Hosp Aide; Library Aide; Chorus; Variety Show; Yrbk; Stu Cncl; Hon Roll; NHS; 4th Pl Natl Span Exam 89; Service Awd For Hosp Vlntr; Liturgy Clb.

GARCIA, NANCY MARIE; C K Mc Clatchy HS; Sacramento, CA; (4); 79/337; French Clb; Latin Clb; Chorus; Color Guard; School Musical; School Play; Stage Crew; Variety Show; Sec Jr Cls; Rep Sr Cls; Bnk Of Amer Career Awareness Pgm; Mst Imprvd GPA Notice Awd; U Of San Francisco; Fshn Illust.

GARCIA, NANCY V; Culver City HS; Los Angeles, CA; (2); Amateau Radio Clb; Criminal Law.

GARCIA, NORMA; Abraham Lincoln HS; Los Angeles, CA; (4); FBLA; High Hon Roll; Prfct Atten Awd; NALEO Vlntr; Vlntr Aide Chrch; UCLA HS Partnrshp & Mecha Clb; CA ST U Northridge.

GARCIA, NORMA E; Eagle Rock HS; Los Angeles, CA; (2); Cmnty Wkr; Key Clb; JV Bsktbl; Wt Lftg; Hon Roll; Pres Acad Fit Awd; Schlr Athl Awd; CA Jr Schlrshp Fed Hnr Awd; VP CA Schlrshp Fed Clb 90; Psych.

GARCIA, NORMA X; Pius X HS; South Gate, CA; (3); High Hon Roll; Hon Roll; Rcvd Cert Achvt 3.5 Or Hghr GPA; Enjoy Drawing; Work For Sizzler Steak House Over 1 1/2 Yrs; CA ST U Long Bch; Civil Engr.

GARCIA, OLGA; Mt Pleasant HS; San Jose, CA; (3); Latin Clb; Red Cross Aide; Teachers Aide; Varsity Clb; Vllybl; Hon Roll; Tchr Mexican Folklore Grp; MPHH; Foothill Clg; Flight Attndnt.

GARCIA, OLIVIA ERICA; Redwood HS; Visalia, CA; (2); Aud/Vis; Church Yth Grp; Cmnty Wkr; Key Clb; Library Aide; Church Choir; Swing Chorus; Variety Show; Law.

GARCIA, ORLANDO J; Arroyo Grande HS; Nipomo, CA; (2); JV Socr; Santa Barbara Bus Coll; Acctng.

GARCIA, OSCAR; Pasadena HS; Pasadena, CA; (3); Cmnty Wkr; Latin Clb; JV Socr; MESA; LASA; Pasadena City Coll; Med.

GARCIA, PATRICIA; Locke HS; Los Angeles, CA; (3); Computer Clb; French Clb; Cal ST Domingues; Law.

GARCIA, PATRICIA; Sacred Heart Of Mary HS; Los Angeles, CA; (3); Church Yth Grp; Rep GAA; Pep Clb; Spanish Clb; SADD; Var Capt Cheerldng; Spanish NHS; Cum Laude Hnr Soc; Mother Butler Hnr Soc; CA ST Los Angeles; Bus Admin.

GARCIA, PATRICIA H; San Clemente HS; San Clemente, CA; (1); 3/30; Orch; Bsbl; Crs Cntry; Sftbl; Swmmng; Vllybl; Cit Awd; Acad Achvt; UCLA; Air Force Pilot.

GARCIA, PEDRO Q; Sierra Vista HS; Baldwin Park, CA; (3); Band; Mrchg Band; Var L Swmmng; High Hon Roll; Hon Roll; Grad North West Coll Med & Dent Asstnt; Water Polo Team; Ucla; Phys.

GARCIA, PHILL; Abraham Lincoln HS; San Jose, CA; (3); Chess Clb; Church Yth Grp; JV Tennis; Rl Est Invstng; Financl Securities; Music; Financl Broker.

GARCIA, PILAR M; Redwood HS; Visalia, CA; (3); Church Yth Grp; Cmnty Wkr; Band; Mrchg Band; Pep Band; JV Sftbl; Hon Roll; CSF; Acad Ltr, Pin; Chem.

GARCIA, RAUL R; Sonoma Valley HS; Sonoma, CA; (3); French Clb; Letterman Clb; Model UN; Varsity Clb; Band; Mrchg Band; Sec Jr Cls; Var Capt Swmmng; Hon Roll; Educl Exch France; Arch.

GARCIA, REUBEN A; Mojave HS; California City, CA; (2); Computer Clb; Varsity Clb; Bsbl; Ftbl; Wt Lftg; UCLA; Pilot.

GARCIA, REYNA; W C Overfelt HS; San Jose, CA; (2); San Jose ST; Bus.

GARCIA, RHONDA; Christian Center Schl; Oakley, CA; (4); 1/9; Church Yth Grp; School Play; Yrbk; Treas Sr Cls; Rep Stu Cncl; JV Cheerldng; Var Sftbl; Var Vllybl; Hon Roll; Pres Acad Fit Awd; Bethany Bible Coll; Commnctns.

GARCIA, RICHARD; John Muir HS; Pasadena, CA; (2); JV Bsbl; Engr.

GARCIA, RICHARD; Valley HS; Sacramento, CA; (4); 22/462; JV Bsktbl; Hon Roll; UCD Outreach Prgm; Mesa Club; UC Davis; Soclgy.

GARCIA, RICHARD; William Workman HS; Valinda, CA; (3); 2/285; Spanish Clb; Varsity Clb; Ed Nwsp; Off Frsh Cls; Treas Soph Cls; Var L Swmmng; Wt Lftg; Vrsty Waterpolo Let; Gldn St Exam Algbra Hnrs; High Hnrs Geom; Intl Pltcs.

GARCIA, RICHARD E; Los Angeles HS; Los Angeles, CA; (3); Dance Clb; JCL; Latin Clb; Yrbk; Off Jr Cls; Photo.

GARCIA, RICHARD F; Hawthorne HS; Hawthorne, CA; (2); Computer Clb; English Clb; Key Clb; Math Tm; Science Clb; Nwsp; Off Soph Cls; Stu Cncl; Ftbl; Wt Lftg; Comp Engr.

GARCIA, RIZA S; SCPA O'farrell HS; San Diego, CA; (1); 1/283; Dance Clb; Spanish Clb; School Musical; Stage Crew; Sec Frsh Cls; Hon Roll; CSF; Med.

GARCIA, ROBIN D; Colton HS; Colton, CA; (2); Band; Rep Yrbk; Rep Frsh Cls; JV Socr; Hon Roll; U Prep At Early Acad Trng; San Diego ST U; Chld Psych.

GARCIA, ROSA; San Benito HS; Hollister, CA; (2); Spanish Clb; Meche Club; CSF.

GARCIA, ROSA; Wilson SR HS; Long Beach, CA; (3); VP SADD; Sec Soph Cls; Rep Jr Cls; JV Sftbl; Hon Roll; Jr NHS; Wmns Intl Rights Clb; Green Peace; Amnesty Intl; Dentist.

GARCIA, ROSA M; Eisenhower HS; Rialto, CA; (3); Drill Tm; Flag Corp; Swmmng; Trk; Most Valuable Awd Drill Tm & Flags, Swmmng; Athletic Schlr Awd; Psych.

GARCIA, ROSE MARIA; San Fernando HS Magnet; Pacoima, CA; (2); Drama Clb; Church Choir; School Play; Ed Yrbk; Rep Frsh Cls; Cit Awd; Hon Roll; Ldrshp Cls; Bus.

GARCIA, RUBEN; William C Overfelt HS; San Jose, CA; (4); Var Bsktbl; St Schlr; Filipino Amer Club; Research Electrnc & Electrcl Dsgn; De Anza; Elec Engr.

GARCIA, RUDOLPH E; Santa Clara HS; Santa Clara, CA; (4); Service Clb; VP Stu Cncl; Var Crs Cntry; Var Trk; Hon Roll; Pres Acad Fit Awd; Mbr Amnesty Internl; Cty Schl Brd Rep; Homecmng Prince; Santa Clara U; Accnt.

GARCIA JR, RUPERTO; San Lorenzo HS; San Lorenzo, CA; (2); FBLA; Intnl Clb; Treas Soph Cls; Pres Jr Cls; JV Capt Bsbl; JV Bsktbl; JV Ftbl; Hon Roll; Engrng.

GARCIA, RUTHIE M; Hanford Joint Union HS; Hanford, CA; (2); Church Yth Grp; Cmnty Wkr; Office Aide; Rep Soph Cls; Stat Socr; Var Socr; Var Sftbl; JV Vllybl; High Hon Roll; CSF; MESA; Med.

GARCIA, SAL; Nontebello HS; Los Angeles, CA; (1); Boy Scts; Church Yth Grp; Chorus; Bsbl; UCLA; Business Management.

GARCIA, SAMMY D; Palmdale HS; Palmdale, CA; (3); SADD; Teachers Aide; Law.

GARCIA, SAMUEL; Baldwin Park HS; Baldwin Park, CA; (3); Band; Mrchg Band; Pep Band; JV Ftbl; Hon Roll; UCLA; Engrng.

GARCIA, SANDRA L; St Genevieve HS; Panorama City, CA; (3); French Clb; Pep Clb; Teachers Aide; Sprt Ed Nwsp; Yrbk; Hon Roll; Jrnlsm I Awd; CA ST U Northridge; Elem Tchr.

GARCIA, SERGIO H; Coachella Valley HS; Coachella, CA; (2); Varsity Clb; Ftbl; Gym; Wt Lftg; Wrstlng; Hon Roll; Arch.

GARCIA, SHANAMARIE I; William C Overfelt HS; San Jose, CA; (2); GAA; Church Choir; Var Socr; JV Sftbl; Var Trk; Var Vllybl; Social Worker.

GARCIA, SILVIA; Santa Paula Union HS; Santa Paula, CA; (1); 2/360; 4-H; French Clb; JV Bsktbl; Hon Roll; Cmnty Theatre Grp; Pediatrics.

GARCIA, STACEY B; Ontario HS; Ontario, CA; (3); Drama Clb; GAA; Letterman Clb; Varsity Clb; Stu Cncl; Var Capt Bsktbl; Var Sftbl; Prfct Atten Awd; Spcl Olympcs Vlntr; Law.

GARCIA, STEVE L; Salinas HS; Salinas, CA; (1); Church Yth Grp; Ski Clb; High Hon Roll; Hon Roll; UC Santa Barbara; Law.

GARCIA, SYLVIA F; Lompoc HS; Lompoc, CA; (2); Church Yth Grp; FFA; SADD; Chorus; School Musical; Vllybl; Spanish NHS; Phys Thrpst.

GARCIA, TANYA M; Saugus HS; Saugus, CA; (4); Swmmng; Coll Canyons; Bus Admin.

GARCIA, TISHA A; Modesto HS; Salida, CA; (3); Pres VP FHA; Var Vllybl; Hon Roll; 2nd & 3rd Pl Salad Prep Occptnl Olympics; Elem Tchr.

GARCIA JR, TOMAS O; Selaco HS; Norwalk, CA; (3); 1/60; Pres Jr Cls; Rep Stu Cncl; Capt Bsktbl; JV Ftbl; Hon Roll; Mem HS Jr Natl Assn For Deaf Chapter; Los Angeles Cnty Acad Triathlon; Cal ST U Northridge; Psych.

GARCIA, VANNESSA MICHELLE; Notre Dame HS; San Jose, CA; (1); Church Yth Grp; Science Clb; High Hon Roll; Socieyt Women Engrs; Outstndng Achvt Alg I, Rel, Eng & Span Awds; Notre Dame; Aero Engr.

GARCIA, VERONICA; Calexico HS; Calexico, CA; (2); Rep Jr Cls; JV Bsktbl; Var Trk; Var Vllybl; Hon Roll; Medal JV Bsktbl MVP; Grand Champ Read For Fun Comp; Ftbl Soph Princess; Mdls & Certs In Track; UCSD; Elem Tchr.

GARCIA, VERONICA; Carlsbad HS; Carlsbad, CA; (2); Hon Roll; Chruch Choir; Teach CCD; Med.

GARCIA, VERONICA H; Brawley Union HS; Brawley, CA; (2); 6/300; Band; Mrchg Band; Pep Band; Sec Jr Cls; High Hon Roll; Hon Roll; Prfct Atten Awd; Mock Trial; CSF; Band Sec; Top 20; Dance; Law.

GARCIA, VERONICA P; Sweetwater HS; National City, CA; (3); 59/513; Office Aide; Science Clb; Cit Awd.

GARCIA, VICTOR R; Indio HS; Coachella, CA; (1).

GARCIA, VIRGINIA G; John Marshall Fundamental HS; Pasadena, CA; (3); Church Yth Grp; Drama Clb; Sec Key Clb; Ed Nwsp; Stat Bsbl; Capt Cheerldng; Mgr Socr; Hon Roll; NHS; Pres Acad Fit Awd; CA Schlrshp Fed; Assoc Stu Bdy-Pep Comm/Pblcty Comm; Brdcst Jrnlsm.

GARCIA, YOLANDA; Washington HS; Los Angeles, CA; (3); Band; School Play; Variety Show; Tennis; High Hon Roll; Prfct Atten Awd; 2nd Pl Pep Oratorcl Cont; MESA Clb; Stu Alliance; Brooks Coll; Inter Dsgn.

GARCIA, YVONNE; Roosevelt HS; Los Angeles, CA; (2); Church Yth Grp; Intnl Clb; Key Clb; Chorus; Yrbk; Off Soph Cls; Kiwanis Awd; Bus.

GARCIA, ZULLY; St Paul HS; La Mirada, CA; (3); 13/290; VP French Clb; Teachers Aide; Chorus; French Hon Soc; Hon Roll; NHS; CA Schlrshp Fed; Fr Dept Awd; Dntstry.

GARCIA-OVIES, BIANCA; Bonita Vista HS; Bonita, CA; (1); Chorus; Sftbl; Trk; Cit Awd; Hon Roll; Pres Acad Fit Awd; U Of CA Santa Barbara; Mdcl.

GARCIA-PANDAVENES, PABLO; Saint Marys College HS; Oakland, CA; (4); Boy Scts; VP JA; Co-Capt Varsity Clb; VP Frsh Cls; Bsktbl; Var Ftbl; Swmmng; Wrstlng; High Hon Roll; Hon Roll; CA Scholarship Federation; Outstndg Acad Achvt While Involved In Sports; Black Student Union; Claremont Mc Kenna Coll; Premed.

GARCIA-SIRONI, JULIO; Cantwell HS; Los Angeles, CA; (1); Spanish Clb; Socr; Hon Roll; Cal-Poly; Comp Engnrng.

GARD, DAVID; Antioch Christian Tutorial Schl; Pittsburg, CA; (4); 2/3; Boy Scts; Church Yth Grp; Drama Clb; School Play; Variety Show; Pres Soph Cls; Rep Stu Cncl; Var Bsbl; Var Bsktbl; Var Socr; CSF; Bethany Bible Coll; Minstry.

GARD, JASON M; El Cajon Valley HS; El Cajon, CA; (3); Letterman Clb; Office Aide; Varsity Clb; Stu Cncl; Var Bsbl; Var Ftbl; Wt Lftg; Wrstlng; San Diego ST U; Engr.

GARD, MARISA S; Mater Dei HS; Lakewood, CA; (2); Aud/Vis; Church Yth Grp; Ski Clb; Spanish Clb; Teachers Aide; Chorus; School Musical; JV Socr; Trk; High Hon Roll; Natl Mem Music Tchrs 2nd Yr Piano; CSF; Handbells; Medical Field.

GARDEA, HORTENCIA; Woodrow Wilson HS; Los Angeles, CA; (3); Church Yth Grp; Service Clb; Teachers Aide; Chorus; Var Bsktbl; Var Sftbl; Var Trk; Var Vllybl; Ahtl Of Yr; Marines; Police Officer.

GARDEA, RAMONA; Saddleback HS; Santa Ana, CA; (4); 9/520; Cmnty Wkr; English Clb; Capt Quiz Bowl; Service Clb; Orch; Lit Mag; High Hon Roll; Smith Bk Awd 89; Acad Lttr 87-90; Merit Awd Scl Sci 87-89.

GARDELLA, STEPHENIE J; Lodi HS; Lodi, CA; (4); Sec FFA; German Clb; Intnl Clb; SADD; Orch; School Musical; Hon Roll; Alfred Rageth Memrl Schlrshp; Tina Bazett Memrl Schlrshp; CSF Seal Beaarer; CSU Stanislaus; Music.

GARDENHIRE, TROY; Richard Gahr HS; Cerritos, CA; (2); 80/490; Intrml Bsktbl; Chrch Yth Usher Brd; Blue & Gold Medallion Typng & Engl 89; USC; Bus Mgmt.

GARDINER, MONTEREY R; Berkley HS; Berkeley, CA; (4); Computer Clb; German Clb; Stage Crew; Yrbk; UC Davis; Chem Matrls Sci.

GARDNER, ADRIENNE C; Mount Diablo HS; W Pittsburg, CA; (2); Church Yth Grp; Cmnty Wkr; Drill Tm; Cit Awd; Water Envrmnt Clb.

GARDNER, BETH N; Lincoln HS; San Jose, CA; (3); 1/375; Cmnty Wkr; Dance Clb; Drama Clb; Service Clb; Thesps; Drill Tm; School Musical; School Play; Stage Crew; Variety Show; Bio Stu Of Yr 88-89; UC Davis; Phy.

GARDNER, BOB S; Carlmont HS; Belmont, CA; (2); Letterman Clb; Varsity Clb; Off Soph Cls; JV Var Bsbl; JV Crs Cntry; JV Socr; 2nd Tam AAU All Amer Basebl 90; Eng, His Advncd Placemnt; All Peninsula Athl Leag Basebl, Soccer; U Of CA; Bus.

GARDNER, BRANDON C; Vintage HS; American Canyon, CA; (4); Computer Clb; Nwsp; Hon Roll; Prfct Atten Awd; NAPA Coll; Envrnmntl Prdctn.

GARDNER, BREON J; Berean Christian HS; Alamo, CA; (4); Church Yth Grp; Church Choir; Mgr Stage Crew; Socr; Sftbl; Var Capt Vllybl; High Hon Roll; Hon Roll; ASCI Dstngshd Chrstn Stu Ldrshp/Drama; Theater Schlrshp Seattle Pcfc U Mst Prstgs; Vet Awd 4 Yrs; Seattle Pcfc U; Theater.

GARDNER, CARRIE J; Etiwanda HS; Alta Loma, CA; (3); Church Yth Grp; Pep Clb; Ski Clb; SADD; Church Choir; Rep Frsh Cls; Off Jr Cls; Sec Sr Cls; Var Cheerldng; Hon Roll; Church Yth Grp 1st Cnslr; Mem Envrnmntl Club; 3 Yr Church Smnry Gard; Brigham Young U; Accntng.

GARDNER, CASSIE J; Porterville HS; Porterville, CA; (3); 4-H Awd; Hon Roll; Raise Guide Dogs For The Blind; Youth Group Activities In Church Are Important To Me; Marine Biologist.

GARDNER, CHRIS L; Clovis West HS; Clovis, CA; (3); Church Yth Grp; Cmnty Wkr; Ski Clb; High Hon Roll; Pres Acad Fit Awd; Point Loma Nazarene Coll; Engr.

GARDNER, ELANA T; Cabrillo HS; Lompoc, CA; (2); Church Yth Grp; Drama Clb; JA; Key Clb; Sec Soph Cls; Hon Roll; Treas Of Ethnic Stu Assn; U Of CA Santa Barb; CPA.

GARDNER, JEFF A; Servite HS; Villa Park, CA; (3); 34/161; Ski Clb; Spanish Clb; Var Ftbl; Wt Lftg; Hon Roll; CSF; U Of S CA; Bus.

GARDNER, JENESSA M; Trinity HS; Weaverville, CA; (3); Am Leg Aux Girls St; Cmnty Wkr; GAA; Office Aide; Spanish Clb; Varsity Clb; Rep Frsh Cls; Rep Soph Cls; Mgr Stu Cncl; Var Bsktbl; Wofl Gal Bsktbl; SCL Sftbl Hnrb Mntn; Math.

GARDNER, JENNIFER; Huntington Beach HS; Huntington Beach, CA; (1); Key Clb; Chorus; Kiwanis Awd; Awd Spcl After Schl Actvts; Interior Dsgn.

GARDNER, JENNIFER K; San Dieguito HS; Encinitas, CA; (3); 114/570; Church Yth Grp; Library Aide; Hon Roll; Prfct Atten Awd; CA Schlrshp Fed.

GARDNER, KATIE; St Francis HS; Saratoga, CA; (3); Church Yth Grp; English Clb; 4-H; Intnl Clb; Nwsp; Lit Mag; JV Bsktbl; High Hon Roll; SADD; Ecology Clb; Bsktbl Coach; Tutor; U CA Davis.

GARDNER, LESLIE; El Camino HS; Carmichael, CA; (3); Church Yth Grp; Dance Clb; German Clb; SADD; Orch; Cit Awd; Hon Roll; Teacher.

GARDNER, LINDA; Bishop O Dowd HS; Oakland, CA; (3); Cmnty Wkr; Dance Clb; Office Aide; Band; Chorus; Cheerldng; Hon Roll; Mem Black Stu Union; Coll; Bus Mjr.

GARDNER, TERRI L; Cordova SR HS; Rancho Cordova, CA; (3); 23/452; Model UN; Pep Clb; Band; Orch; Off Frsh Cls; Rep Soph Cls; Stu Cncl; JV Var Cheerldng; VP Jr NHS; Ntl Merit SF; Psych.

GARDNER, TONYA R; Irvine HS; Irvine, CA; (2); AFS; Church Yth Grp; French Clb; Office Aide; Band; Mrchg Band; Orch; Stage Crew; Hon Roll.

GARDUNO, ISABEL F; Sweetwater HS; National City, CA; (3); French Clb; Teachers Aide; Drill Tm; Stage Crew; Cit Awd; Hon Roll; UCSD.

GAREY, AMY H; Granada Hills HS; Northridge, CA; (2); Temple Yth Grp; Yrbk; Hon Roll.

GARFIELD, COBY R; Woodbridge HS; Irvine, CA; (3); Teachers Aide; Phtg Yrbk; Hon Roll; Performance Auto Tuner.

GARFIELD, NICOLE S; Capistrano Valley HS; Mission Viejo, CA; (4); Church Yth Grp; Band; Color Guard; Mrchg Band; BYU; Fshn Merch.

GARFIO, EDUARDO C; Calexico HS; Calexico, CA; (2); 19/300; Cmnty Wkr; French Clb; Teachers Aide; Nwsp; French Hon Soc; Hon Roll; Prtnrshp Pgm 89; Uf Of CA Santa Barbara; Lwyr.

GARFIO, HORACIO; Bassett HS; La Puente, CA; (2); Var L Crs Cntry; JV Trk; Hon Roll; NHS; Prfct Atten Awd; Cultural Exch Club.

GARG, SUNEEL K; St Bonaventure HS; Ventura, CA; (3); 1/136; Boy Scts; Pres Scholastic Bowl; Var Tennis; High Hon Roll; NHS; Ntl Merit Ltr; CSF; Interact Clb; Acctng.

GARIBALDI, SALVADOR; Saint Paul HS; Whittier, CA; (3); Church Yth Grp; Hon Roll; NHS; Spanish NHS; Cycling Clb; Stu Clrk; Arch.

GARIBAY, JUAN; Kingsburg Joint Union HS; Kingsburg, CA; (2); Art Clb; Pep Clb; Teachers Aide; Phtg Yrbk; Pres Soph Cls; Pres Jr Cls; Pres Stu Cncl; Mgr Cheerldng; JV Capt Socr; Var Capt Trk; Fresno City; Bus.

GARIBAY, PATTY; Santiago HS; Santa Ana, CA; (2); Dance Clb; Varsity Clb; Chorus; Hon Roll; Assoc Stu Body; Dntl Asst.

GARIBAY, VERONICA; La Puente HS; La Puente, CA; (3); Teachers Aide; Ed Yrbk; Cit Awd; Hon Roll; Prfct Atten Awd; CSF; Readng Clb; UCLA; Bilingual Tchr.

GARING, ROSS M; Poly Technic HS; Riverside, CA; (1); Church Yth Grp; Cmnty Wkr; Var L Crs Cntry; Var L Trk; Hon Roll; Pres Acad Fit Awd; Bus.

GARINGAN, JOEL A; Christian Brothers HS; Sacramento, CA; (3); Computer Clb; Science Clb; Spanish Clb; JV Bsktbl; Hon Roll; CSF; Erly Outrch Pgm; U Of San Francisco; Aerntcs.

GARIS, JACK R; Bishop Amat HS; Covina, CA; (1); Bsbl; Hon Roll; Prfct Atten Awd; Bsbl Leag Champs; Phantisy Clb; USC; Arch.

GARITA, FRANCO I; San Gorgnio HS; Highland, CA; (3); Teachers Aide; VICA; Intrml Bsbl; Intrml Swmmng; Intrml Wt Lftg; Cit Awd; Bus.

GARLAND, DAVID D; River City HS; W Sacramento, CA; (3); Band; Jazz Band; Mrchg Band; School Play; Var L Swmmng; Hon Roll; Prfct Atten Awd; Past Mstr Cnslr Order Of Demolay; W Sacramento Police Cadets; Peace Offcr.

GARLAND, JENNY; Rolling Hills HS; Rancho Palos Verd, CA; (2); Church Yth Grp; Drama Clb; Church Choir; Drill Tm; Stage Crew; Girls Leag Cls Rep; Biola; Commnctns.

GARLAND, LESLEE L; Golden West HS; Visalia, CA; (2); Church Yth Grp; FCA; Letterman Clb; Pep Clb; Spanish Clb; SADD; Rptr Nwsp; Pres Frsh Cls; Bsktbl; Sftbl; CSF; 4.0 GPA; Pepperdine; Elem Tchr.

GARLAND, STEPHANIE L; Cabrillo HS; Vandenberg AFB, CA; (3); 22/266; Church Yth Grp; FCA; Red Cross Aide; Spanish Clb; Mrchg Band; Pep Band; Rep Soph Cls; JV Capt Cheerldng; Hon Roll; Jr NHS; Envrnmntl Law.

GARLEPP, ERIC R; Don Bosco Tech Inst; Pasadena, CA; (4); 1/225; Church Yth Grp; Letterman Clb; Bsbl; Cit Awd; High Hon Roll; NHS; Ntl Merit Schol; Val; UCLA; Elec Engrng.

GARNER, AMANDA J; Mammoth HS; Crowley Lake, CA; (3); 2/56; Drama Clb; Office Aide; Chorus; School Musical; School Play; Stage Crew; Stu Cncl; Var L Crs Cntry; High Hon Roll; NHS; Chldrns Sccr Coach; AYSC Sccr Ref; Schl Site Cncl Mbr 90; Educ.

GARNER, JASON D; Palmdale HS; Aguadulce, CA; (3); 67/644; Boy Scts; Church Yth Grp; Spanish Clb; JV Var Bsbl; High Hon Roll; Hon Roll; CSF; BYU; Radiology.

GARNER, LEANN M; Fontana HS; Fontana, CA; (4); 39/792; Treas Drama Clb; Teachers Aide; Treas Thesps; School Play; Stage Crew; High Hon Roll; Pres Acad Fit Awd; CA Schlrshp Fed Sealbearer; PHQ; Jobs Dghtrs; CA ST San Bernardino; Accntng.

GARNER, MARK S; Lower Lake HS; Clearlake Oaks, CA; (4); 9/105; VP Pres 4-H; Service Clb; Teachers Aide; Varsity Clb; Var L Ftbl; Wt Lftg; L Wrstlng; 4-H Awd; Hon Roll; Lake Co Farm Bureau Schlrshp; Yuba Coll.

GARNER, MELISSA L; Monterey HS; Seaside, CA; (2); Church Yth Grp; Pres Cmnty Wkr; FCA; Hosp Aide; Math Tm; Orch; Pres Frsh Cls; VP Soph Cls; Rep Jr Cls; Stu Cncl; Canadian Exchng Stu; Ambssdr.

GARNER, MISTY M; East Bakersfield HS; Bakersfield, CA; (4); 17/415; SADD; Pres Frsh Cls; Sec Stu Cncl; Var L Socr; Var L Tennis; High Hon Roll; NHS; Pres Schlr; Cmnty Wkr; Teachers Aide; Pres Keywntts; CSF; DARE; Sprts Acadc Awd; Acadc Ltr; Hstry Clb; Sccr Clb; Kern Cnty Rep Frdms Fndtn; CPA.

GARNER, REIGNA C; Fremont HS; Sunnyvale, CA; (1); JV Trk; Kids Day Ldr; Berkeley; Comp Sci.

GARNETT, ANTHONY M; Richard Gahr HS; Cerritos, CA; (1); Cit Awd; Hon Roll; CA Inst Technology; Comp Engr.

GARNETT, CAROL L; Ygnacio Valley HS; Walnut Creek, CA; (2); Dance Clb; Drama Clb; Key Clb; Spanish Clb; Color Guard; School Musical; High Hon Roll; CSF; Teaching.

GAROFALO, KEVIN J; Marina HS; Huntington Bch, CA; (4); Church Yth Grp; Cmnty Wkr; FBLA; JA; Spanish Clb; SADD; Bsbl; Ftbl; Trk; Wt Lftg; St Johns; Theolgy.

GARRELS, SCOTT; Redlands JR Acad; Mohave Valley, AZ; (2); Aud/Vis; Varsity Clb; School Play; Yrbk; VP Frsh Cls; VP Soph Cls; Intrml Bsbl; Var Intrml Bsktbl; Intrml Fld Hcky; Var Intrml Ftbl; Kenny Dutro Awd; Andrews U; Arch.

GARRETSON, APRIL E; Lodi HS; Lodi, CA; (2); Church Yth Grp; Key Clb; Chorus; Hon Roll; Prfct Atten Awd; CSF; Stanislaus ST; Tchr.

GARRETT, AMANDA L; Summerville Union HS; Tuolumne, CA; (3); Quiz Bowl; Ski Clb; Teachers Aide; Acpl Chr; Chorus; Capt Color Guard; Capt Flag Corp; Variety Show; High Hon Roll; Hon Roll; Signlang; Drum Bugle Corps.

GARRETT, AMY S; Buena HS; Ventura, CA; (2); Church Yth Grp; Color Guard; Hon Roll; Prfct Atten Awd; Interact Club Secy; Gldn St Exam Hnrs Geom.

GARRETT, AUTUMN; Palisades HS; Topanga, CA; (3); Chorus; CSF.

GARRETT, CRAIG M; Miramonte HS; Orinda, CA; (2); Var Trk; CA Schltc Fed; Hnrb Mntn Friends Of Orinda Library Lit Cont.

GARRETT, CYNDI M; Yucaipa HS; Yucaipa, CA; (4); 8/300; French Clb; Key Clb; Sec Treas Jr Cls; Sec Treas Sr Cls; Intrml Bsktbl; Hon Roll; Pres Schlr; HOBY Ldrshp Smnr; Tandy Schlrshp Awd; Rotary Clb Achvt Schlrshp; Trvl Ind.

GARRETT, ERNIE D; Redlands HS; Redlands, CA; (3); 300/1000; Var Bsbl; JV Ftbl; Point Loma Nazarene Coll; Acct.

GARRETT, ERNISE; Narbonne Math/Science Magnet; Los Angeles, CA; (4); 122/400; Church Yth Grp; Cmnty Wkr; Key Clb; Office Aide; Teachers Aide; Church Choir; Treas Stu Cncl; Cit Awd; Hon Roll; Kiwanis Awd; Yng Blck Schlrs; Fulfillment Fund Schlr; Richard Hill Schlrshp Fndtn; U Of La Verne; Med.

GARRETT, HOLLY; Escalon HS; Stockton, CA; (3); 10/126; Cmnty Wkr; 4-H; Pep Clb; Scholastic Bowl; Spanish Clb; SADD; Off Frsh Cls; Off Soph Cls; Off Jr Cls; Stu Cncl; YMCA Youth Government; Student In Prevention-San Juqum; UCSB/Sanford; Law.

GARRETT, JENNIFER; Valhalla HS; El Cajon, CA; (4); 53/435; Church Yth Grp; Key Clb; SADD; JV Var Swmmng; Cit Awd; Hon Roll; Natl Soc Of Women Engrs Awd; CSF; Pt Loma Nazarene Coll; Arch.

GARRETT, JOHN A; Flintridge Preparatory HS; San Marino, CA; (3); Cmnty Wkr; Ski Clb; Var Ftbl; Capt Var Socr; Var Trk; Outdr Clb Pres.

GARRETT, LISA M; Hesperia HS; Hesperia, CA; (2); Drama Clb; Hist French Clb; Ski Clb; Writer.

GARRETT, LUCRECE M; Skyline HS; Oakland, CA; (4); 251/542; Treas Spanish Clb; Sec Church Choir; Off Jr Cls; Rep Sr Cls; Rep Stu Cncl; Sec Cheerldng; Hon Roll; Hayward ST U; Pschology.

GARRETT, MEGAN; Casa Grande HS; Petaluma, CA; (2); 10/300; French Clb; Lit Mag; Var L Crs Cntry; Var Tennis; High Hon Roll; NHS; Prfct Atten Awd; Cngrssnl Schlr; Cngrssnl Yth Ldrshp Cncl; NCS/Cif Schlr Ath Awd; CA Schlrshp Fed; U Of CO Boulder; Psych.

GARRETT, NICOLE; John F Kennedy HS; Granada Hills, CA; (3); JA; Math Clb; Ski Clb; JV Cheerldng; Var Diving; Gym; Var Pom Pon; Var Swmmng; Var Trk; Hon Roll; CSF; Stanford U; Actuary.

GARRETT, RACHAEL L; Winters HS; Winters, CA; (3); 1/75; Church Yth Grp; Office Aide; Pep Clb; Chorus; Church Choir; Var L Trk; High Hon Roll; Rotary Intl Dist 516 Camp Royal; Chrch Yyth Grp Mssn Mexico.

GARRETT, RAYMOND P; Pater Noster HS; Los Angeles, CA; (1); Church Yth Grp; Chorus; JV Bsktbl; JV Crs Cntry; JV Ftbl; JV Trk; Imprvmnt Alg I Hnrs; Syracuse U; Engrng.

GARRETT, SOLOMON M; Atascadero HS; Atascadero, CA; (2); 2/230; AFS; FBLA; SADD; JV Golf; Var Socr; Var Swmmng; JV Tennis; French Hon Soc; High Hon Roll; NHS; 1st Pl County Writing Contest/Poetry; AFS Pres 89-90 St Senator 89-90; Golden St Exam Honors 89 Math.

GARREY, SHAYNE M; Santa Ynez HS; Santa Ynez, CA; (3); Math Tm; Teachers Aide; Sec Sr Cls; JV Bsktbl; Elks Awd; Hon Roll; Refree Coach Elsk Bsktbl Leag; Hgh Hnrs Golden St Geom Exm; History.

GARRIOTT, KIM; Laguna Hills HS; Mission Viejo, CA; (4); 14/360; Key Clb; SADD; Ed Yrbk; JV Cheerldng; Var Trk; Pres Acad Fit Awd; High Hon Roll; Hon Roll; Stage Crew; Drama Clb; Pgnt Of Masters; Peer Cnslr; CSF Sealbearer; UC San Diego; Pre Med.

GARRIS, BARBARA J; Livingston HS; Ballico, CA; (3); 2/320; Am Leg Aux Girls St; French Clb; Library Aide; Quiz Bowl; Science Clb; Yrbk; Rep Soph Cls; High Hon Roll; Hon Roll; Ntl Merit SF; Stu Sounding Bd; CSF Sec; Biology.

GARRIS, RAYE P; Fairfox HS; Los Angeles, CA; (2); Pres Church Yth Grp; Drama Clb; Library Aide; Pep Clb; Quiz Bowl; Church Choir; School Play; Christians On Campus 9th Gr; Med.

GARRISI, MATTHEW M; Whittier Christian HS; Whittier, CA; (2); Church Yth Grp.

GARRISON, CLAIR R C; Mojave HS; California City, CA; (3); Teachers Aide; Flag Corp; U CA Davis; Vet Med.

GARRISON, SANDRA LYN; Pinewood HS; Los Altos Hills, CA; (3); Debate Tm; French Clb; Girl Scts; NFL; Speech Tm; School Play; Rptr Nwsp; Ed Yrbk; Rep Sr Cls; Var Bsktbl; Silver Awd; Natl Forensic Leag Double Ruby Awd; Phi Lambda Omega Natl Hnry Frat; Commnctns.

GARRISON, SASHA M; Palmdale HS; Palmdale, CA; (3); 127/644; Var Bsktbl; Var Powder Puff Ftbl; Var Trk; Ed.

GARRISON, TRAVIS B; El Capitan HS; El Cajon, CA; (3); 32/339; Boy Scts; Church Yth Grp; 4-H; Intnl Clb; Pep Clb; SADD; Hon Roll; Yng Schlrs Smmr Sci Inst 89; Bio.

GARRITY, CHRISTY ANN; Pacifica HS; Garden Grv, CA; (3); 43/437; Church Yth Grp; Dance Clb; Sec Soph Cls; Rep Jr Cls; Stu Cncl; Hon Roll; Brooks Coll; Int Desgn.

GARRO, NICOLE M; Torrey Pines HS; Solana Beach, CA; (2); 32/503; JV Fld Hcky; Hon Roll; AA Sccr; Envrnmntl Stds.

GARSAULT, CHRISTIANNE M; Leuzinger HS; Hawthorne, CA; (4); French Clb; Sec Key Clb; Var Crs Cntry; JV Trk; Hon Roll; Prfct Atten Awd; Pres Acad Fit Awd; Peer Tutor; UC Riverside; Bio.

GARSIDE, JENNIFER F; East Bakerfield HS; Bakersfield, CA; (4); 6/412; FCA; Intnl Clb; JV Var Powder Puff Ftbl; Var Socr; Stat Trk; High Hon Roll; Keywanettes Clb; Cal Poly; Economics.

GARST-GARCIA, HEATHER; Central Catholic HS; Turlock, CA; (3); Art Clb; Church Yth Grp; Cmnty Wkr; Office Aide; Pep Clb; Science Clb; Ski Clb; SADD; JV Var Cheerldng; Var Powder Puff Ftbl; Serra Schlrshp; Envrnmntl Stud.

GARTH, ERINN E; Westlake HS; Thousand Oaks, CA; (2); Cit Awd; Hon Roll.

GARVER, SCOTT L; Tulare Western HS; Waukena, CA; (3); Letterman Clb; Var Socr; Hon Roll; Hgh Hnrs CA Gldn ST Exm Alg & Geom; Fresno ST U.

GARVEY, JUSTINE H; Edison HS; Huntington Beach, CA; (4); 22/483; English Clb; French Clb; German Clb; Intnl Clb; Key Clb; Acpl Chr; Chorus; Ntl Merit SF; Acad Dcthln; History.

GARVEY, THOMAS; James Lick HS; San Jose, CA; (4); 50/320; Math Tm; Stu Cncl; Var Ftbl; Swmmng; Var Trk; Wrstlng; San Jose ST U; Engrng.

GARVEY, VICKI K; James Lick HS; San Jose, CA; (3); Drama Clb; Intnl Clb; Chorus; School Play; Sec Treas Frsh Cls; Stu Cncl; Var Cheerldng; Var Swmmng; Hon Roll; Vrsty Badmntn; Most Imsprtnl 1989; Blue Rbbn San Jose Myrs Yth Cnfrnc; U CA Berkeley; Med.

GARVIN, ERIKA D; Brea-Olinda HS; Brea, CA; (2); Church Yth Grp; Dance Clb; Nwsp; High Hon Roll; Acad Ltr Grl; Math Tutor; Sci.

GARWICK, TRAVIS; Cajon HS; San Bernardino, CA; (3); 43/467; Var Crs Cntry; Var Socr; Cit Awd; High Hon Roll; NHS; Prfct Atten Awd; Pre Jr Sts Men Amer; Stamford; Sci.

GARY, KELA; El Camino HS; Oceanside, CA; (3); French Clb; Office Aide; Yrbk; Hon Roll; Stu Of Mont Awd-Bus Ed; Mira Costa JC; Acctng.

GARY, MICHAEL; Atwater HS; Merced, CA; (2); Church Yth Grp; German Clb; Key Clb; Stat Bsktbl; JV Ftbl; Wt Lftg; High Hon Roll; Hon Roll.

GARZA, ANNETTE J; Westminster HS; Westminster, CA; (2); Visual Arts.

GARZA, ANTHONY; Westminster HS; Westminster, CA; (4); 32/400; JA; Hon Roll; NHS; Ntl Merit SF; Spanish NHS; UCLA; Aerospace Engrng.

GARZA, DORA M; Carson HS; Carson, CA; (2); Church Yth Grp; Drama Clb; High Hon Roll; Indian Clb Princess 88; Am Indian Clb; Stephen M White Jr HS 88-89; Drill Team; Latin Dancing; Prof Modl; UCI; Acctg.

GARZA, EDDIE; Monace HS; Porterville, CA; (2); Spanish Clb; SADD; Intrml JV Bsktbl; Var JV Ftbl; Wt Lftg; Prfct Atten Awd.

GARZA, ERNIE T; Delano Joint Union HS; Delano, CA; (3); Art Clb; FFA; FHA; Letterman Clb; Nwsp; Crs Cntry; Mgr(s); Trk; Hon Roll; Prfct Atten Awd; Vrsty Srvc Awd Outstndng Achvts Crss Cntry; Mst Discplnd.

GARZA, EUDOLIO; Chino HS; Rialto, CA; (2); Teachers Aide; Aerospace Engr.

GARZA, MARIBEL A; North Salinas HS; Salinas, CA; (4); Church Yth Grp; Teachers Aide; Acpl Chr; Church Choir; Color Guard; JV Sftbl; JV Vllybl; Cit Awd; Hon Roll; Stu Of Yr Awd; Hartnell Coll; Math.

GARZA, PATTI S; Oakdale HS; Oakdale, CA; (2); Cmnty Wkr; Latin Clb; JV Sftbl; Hlp Hmls; Just Say No; Loyola Marymount; Chld Devlp.

GARZA, PAULA; Elk Grove HS; Elk Grove, CA; (4); Church Yth Grp; Dance Clb; Library Aide; Ski Clb; SADD; Teachers Aide; Color Guard; Drill Tm; School Musical; Bsktbl; USC; Law.

GARZA, RHONDA; Los Molinos HS; Los Molinos, CA; (4); 4/30; Am Leg Aux Girls St; Drama Clb; GAA; Teachers Aide; Varsity Clb; Ed Nwsp; Yrbk; Rep Stu Cncl; Var Cheerldng; Hon Roll; Score Keeper; Butte Coll; Respiratory Thrpy.

GARZA, SUNSHINE A; Strathmore Union HS; St Rathmore, CA; (3); Church Yth Grp; Drama Clb; FHA; School Play; Hon Roll; Wrd Prcssr.

GARZA, TIMOTEO; Central Union HS; El Centro, CA; (2); FCA; Bsbl; Ftbl; High Hon Roll; Hon Roll; Jr NHS; NHS; Pres Acad Fit Awd; TX A&M U; Engr.

GARZA, TINA L; East Bakersfield HS; Bakersfield, CA; (1); Church Yth Grp; Math Clb; Spanish Clb; Band; Mrchg Band; JV Socr; JV Sftbl; Intrml Vllybl; Prfct Atten Awd; MVP-SFTBL; Bakersfield Coll; Acctng.

GARZA, TRACY; Indio HS; Indio, CA; (4); Art Clb; Library Aide; Office Aide; Teachers Aide; Color Guard; Cit Awd; Prfct Atten Awd; Banking & Finance Course; College Of The Desert; Account.

GARZA, VALERIE; Arvin HS; Arvin, CA; (1); Ski Clb; Cheerldng; OK ST U; Rgstrd Nrs.

GASANG, FERDIE M; Mira Mesa HS; San Diego, CA; (2); 111/797; Math Tm; Mrchg Band; Pep Band; School Musical; Rptr Nwsp; Phtg Yrbk; Stu Cncl; High Hon Roll; Prfct Atten Awd; Pres Acad Fit Awd; Prcssn Bell Plyr Wind Ensmbl & Cncrt; Played All City Hnr Band; U CA San Diego; Med.

GASCA, JUAN M; Mark Keppel HS; Rosemead, CA; (3); Church Band; Music.

GASCON, STEPHANIE T; Amos Alonzo Stagg HS; Stockton, CA; (4); Cmnty Wkr; Hon Roll; Sumitomo Bnk Awd; Mary Bixler Stanton Schlrshp; U Of CA Santa Barb; Marine Bio.

GASDICK, LETICIA; Upland HS; Upland, CA; (2); Church Yth Grp; Letterman Clb; Cheerldng; Trk; Cit Awd; Hon Roll; Ldrshp Cls; UC Santa Barbara; Drafting.

GASIOR, TAUS A; Mira Loma HS; Sacramento, CA; (2); JV Var Ftbl; JV Trk; Var Wt Lftg; UC Santa Barbara; Drg Enfrcmnt.

GASPARA, GINA M; West HS; Torrance, CA; (1); Dance Clb; Drama Clb; Law.

GASPARI, DUSTIN; Faith Baptist Schl; Chatsworth, CA; (4); 1/45; Drama Clb; Letterman Clb; Varsity Clb; Stage Crew; JV Ftbl; Var L Trk; Capt L Wrstlng; High Hon Roll; Val; CSF; CSUN; Bus.

GASPARINE, MICHELLE A; Paraclete HS; Palmdale, CA; (2); Church Yth Grp; JA; Crs Cntry; Trk; Cit Awd; Hon Roll; Law.

GASPARUTTI, MAUREEN L; San Clemente HS; San Clemente, CA; (3); Church Yth Grp; Cmnty Wkr; Red Cross Aide; Teachers Aide; Band; Chorus; Mrchg Band; School Play; JV Swmmng; Cit Awd; Ambssdr.

GASPORRA, RAQUEL; Pius X HS; Paramount, CA; (3); VP Church Yth Grp; Drama Clb; GAA; Varsity Clb; VP Sr Cls; Powder Puff Ftbl; Var Sftbl; Var Vllybl; High Hon Roll; Hon Roll.

GASSNER, MICHELLE; San Clemente HS; San Clemente, CA; (2); Girl Scts; Hosp Aide; Spanish Clb; Acpl Chr; Chorus; Cit Awd.

GAST, JOSH; Christian HS; El Cajon, CA; (3); Church Yth Grp; Science Clb; Ed Nwsp; Var Capt Bsbl; Var JV Ftbl; Hon Roll; CSF; U WI Whitewater World Affrs Seminar; Sports.

GASTELUM, ELIZABETH; Immaculate Heart HS; Los Angeles, CA; (3); 2/120; GAA; Math Clb; Spanish Clb; JV Swmmng; Hon Roll; Ntl Merit Ltr; USC; Med.

GASTELUM, YANY E; Woodrow Wilson HS; Long Beach, CA; (3); Drama Clb; Intnl Clb; JA; Science Clb; Spanish Clb; Off Jr Cls; Lion Awd; Prfct Atten Awd; Pres Acad Fit Awd; Natl Hnrs Soc; Acctng.

GATCHALIAN, CECILIA B; Bloomington HS; Bloomington, CA; (3); 10/260; Teachers Aide; Var JV Tennis; High Hon Roll; NHS; Prfct Atten Awd; CSF; Jr Hnr Grd; Loma Linda U; Nurse.

GATCHALIAN, RACHELLE; Bullard HS; Fresno, CA; (2); Church Yth Grp; Cmnty Wkr; Dance Clb; Intnl Clb; Math Clb; Math Tm; SADD; Chorus; Church Choir; Variety Show; City Dance Troop; Run-Way/Print Model; UC; Med.

GATEB JR, ROMEO B; Bishop Amat Memorial HS; La Puente, CA; (3); Cmnty Wkr; Office Aide; Teachers Aide; Var Bsktbl; Var Vllybl; Hon Roll; CSF Awd; Skirball Inst Of Amer Values Hnrbl Mntn; UCLA; Acctg.

GATES, BRADFORD A; Nevada Union HS; Grass Valley, CA; (3); 126/551; Office Aide; Red Cross Aide; Cit Awd; Hon Roll; Law Enforcement Exploring Sgt, Lt, Capt; Explorer Ofcr Assn Chm; Cmmty Svc; CPR Instr; Sacramento ST U; Drug Enf.

GATES, JENNIFER D; El Dorado HS; Placentia, CA; (2); 50/375; Church Yth Grp; Teachers Aide; High Hon Roll; Stu Mthr Pgm; Chld Care Aide; Photo & Edtr Stu Mthr Yr Bk; MS; Math.

GATES, JULIANNE G; Orange Glen HS; Escondido, CA; (3); 75/458; Church Yth Grp; German Clb; Teachers Aide; Trk; Jr NHS; Visual & Prfmng Art Cert Of Hnr; Pasadena CA Art Ctr; Fine Art.

GATES, JULIE C; Savanna HS; Anaheim, CA; (2); Church Yth Grp; FCA; Pep Clb; Science Clb; Rep Soph Cls; Stu Cncl; Socr; Hon Roll; Pres Acad Fit Awd; UCLA; Attnry.

GATES, KRISTI; Edison HS; Huntington Beach, CA; (2); Church Yth Grp; Pep Clb; Var Cheerldng; Pop Warner Cobras Chrldng Sqd Coach.

GATES, RACHEL N; Lodi HS; Lodi, CA; (3); Acpl Chr; Chorus; CMEA Solo/Ensmble Cmmnd Prfrmnce Awds 88-90; All St Hnr Choir 89 & 90; NAU; Music.

GATES, SHARON M; Pasadena HS; Pasadena, CA; (3); Church Yth Grp; French Clb; Church Choir; Nwsp; Hon Roll; Mandarin Tchr.

GATES, SHERYL L; Foothill HS; Santa Ana, CA; (2); 34/335; French Clb; JV Trk; High Hon Roll; Hon Roll; Hnrs Algb I Gldn St Exam; Athl Awd; CA Schlrshp Fed 89-90; Intr Dsgn.

GATES, TIFFANY S; San Gorgonio HS; San Bernardino, CA; (3); Cmnty Wkr; Pep Clb; Rptr Yrbk; Interior Dsgn.

GATES, VIKKI MICHELLE; Bear River HS; Grass Valley, CA; (2); 1/125; Sec Science Clb; Spanish Clb; Speech Tm; Cit Awd; High Hon Roll; Lion Awd; Pres Of Friday Night Live; Mrktng.

GATH, GREGORY M; St Anthony HS; Long Beach, CA; (3); 1/130; Boy Scts; Cmnty Wkr; Letterman Clb; Var L Crs Cntry; Var L Trk; High Hon Roll; NHS; Ntl Merit SF; Prfct Atten Awd.

GATI, DAVID L; Lowell HS; San Francisco, CA; (3); Band; UCLA; Film.

GATLIN, CARRIE F; Etiwanda HS; Etiwanda, CA; (2); 3/782; French Clb; Intnl Clb; Pres JA; Var L Tennis; High Hon Roll; HOBY St Ambssdr; Mst Imprvd Player Var Tnns 90; Schlr Awd Var Tnns 90; Intl Bus.

GATTEN, MARSHALL T; South Tahoe HS; Tahoe Paradise, CA; (4); 23/223; Sec Math Clb; Ski Clb; Band; Awd-Schl Rcgntn Awd-Gldn St Geo Exam; Arch.

GATTO, CARLA F; Berkley HS; Richmond, CA; (4); French Clb; Key Clb; Dance Proj; UC San Diego; Chmst Csmtlgy.

GATTO, MICHAEL A; Loyola HS; Los Angeles, CA; (3); Church Yth Grp; Cmnty Wkr; German Clb; Trk; Hon Roll; NEDT Awd; Loyola Politrl Soc; Germ Book Awd; Exchng Stu Hamburg Germany.

GAUCI, JENNIFER J; Capuchino HS; San Bruno, CA; (3); Capt Color Guard; Mrchg Band; VP Soph Cls; Rep Stu Cncl; Sftbl; UASB Ldrshp Conf; Skyline Coll; Law Enfrcmnt.

GAUDREAU, JASON C; Vacaville HS; Vacaville, CA; (3); French Clb; Var L Tennis; Hon Roll; Jr NHS; NHS; Pres Acad Fit Awd; Bst Dbls Tm Tnns 89; Poetry/Essy Pblsdh Schl Lit Mag; Natl Mrt Cert; Engl.

GAUHAR, AWAIS A; Corona HS; Corona, CA; (2); 24/475; JV Tennis; High Hon Roll; Pres Acad Fit Awd; Med.

GAUL, TOOSDI M; Vintage HS; Napa, CA; (2).

GAULT, MICHELE D; Casa Roble HS; Orangevale, CA; (2); 32/461; German Clb; Var Socr; High Hon Roll; Prfct Atten Awd; Pres Acad Fit Awd; Slvr Renaissance Card; Bus.

GAUNA, GILBERT M; Santa Maria HS; Santa Maria, CA; (3); Vllybl; Upwrd Bnd Pgm; Cnslrs Resltn Team; Goldn St Exam Schl Recgntn; Allan Hancock Coll; Math.

GAUTREAU, SHELLEE; Louisville HS; Westlake Village, CA; (4); Art Clb; Cmnty Wkr; Sec GAA; SADD; Varsity Clb; Stu Cncl; Capt Var Socr; Capt Var Sftbl; Capt Var Tennis; Hon Roll; Acad Awd Span III; Tnns Leag MVP 89-90; Scer Leag 1st Tm; Phys Thrpy.

GAUTREAUX, BRANDON; East HS; Bakersfield, CA; (1); Intnl Clb; Bsktbl.

GAVAGAN, MONICA L; Desert HS; California City, CA; (2); JV Capt Cheerldng; Cit Awd; Hon Roll; Teaching Summer Cheerleading Class For Cal City Recreation Dept; Business Management.

GAVANKAR, SAMEER S; Sunny Hills HS; Fullerton, CA; (3); 16/420; VP Computer Clb; French Clb; Intnl Clb; Pres Key Clb; Tennis; High Hon Roll; NHS; Ntl Merit Ltr; Rotary Awd; 3 Cnsctv Yrs Ten League Champs, Doubles League Champ, Tm CIF Fnlst & Smfnlst; Acad Wrkshp W Point; UCLA; Med.

GAVEL, NICHOLE; Placer HS; Auburn, CA; (4); Church Yth Grp; 4-H; Ski Clb; Church Choir; School Musical; Crs Cntry; Swmmng; Dnfth Awd; 4-H Awd; Acdmc Decthln & Pianist.

GAVETTE, MICHELLE M; South Valley HS; Ukiah, CA; (4); Church Yth Grp; Cmnty Wkr; SADD; Varsity Clb; Orch; Trk; Cit Awd; Prfct Atten Awd; Val; Safe Rides Treas; Stu Of Yr 89-90; Grad Cmmtte; Super Orch Duet; UC Davis; CPA.

GAVIDIA, WENDY Z; Herbert Hoover HS; Glendale, CA; (3); Pep Clb; Spanish Clb; Cheerldng; Cit Awd; Hon Roll; Wllsly Awd; UCLA; Med.

GAVINO, CHRISTOPHER C; Chula Vista HS; San Diego, CA; (1); 1/250; Quiz Bowl; Scholastic Bowl; Service Clb; Rep Frsh Cls; Prfct Atten Awd; Pres Acad Fit Awd; US Nvl Sea Cdt Corp; CSF Treas; Jr Stsmn Amer; MIT; Poli Sci.

GAVINO, WHIGELMY; San Gabriel Mission HS; Rosemead, CA; (2); Church Yth Grp; Teachers Aide; Cit Awd; Hon Roll; Prfct Atten Awd; Receptionist De Burguerios Dntl Ofc; Prolifer Picket Against Abortion; Soc Wrkr.

GAW, REBECCA; Los Alamitos HS; Seal Beach, CA; (4); Cmnty Wkr; Model UN; Red Cross Aide; Ski Clb; JV Swmmng; Hon Roll; Ntl Merit Ltr.

GAWF, LORI M; Valhalla HS; Rancho San Diego, CA; (2); 26/500; Church Yth Grp; Cmnty Wkr; Drama Clb; 4-H; Spanish Clb; Swmmng.

GAY, AUDREY; Torrey Pines HS; San Diego, CA; (2); Church Yth Grp; Cmnty Wkr; Drama Clb; Girl Scts; Hosp Aide; Teachers Aide; Chorus; School Play; Variety Show; Hon Roll; San Dieguito Playhouse Jr Theater; U Of CA; Music.

GAY, CHERYL J; Saint Francis HS; Sunnyvale, CA; (1); 1/390; JV Bsktbl; JV Swmmng; Stanford; Sci.

GAY, LISA M; Montgomery HS; Santa Rosa, CA; (2); Church Yth Grp; Drama Clb; Pep Clb; Spanish Clb; Teachers Aide; Church Choir; Bsktbl; Crs Cntry; Socr; Trk; UC Santa Cruz; Acctng.

GAY, MELINDA E; Grace Davis HS; Modesto, CA; (3); Art Clb; Teachers Aide; Var Swmmng; Vrsty Waterpolo; Marine Bio.

GAY, TAMMY; Liberty Union HS; Oakley, CA; (4); 17/307; FFA; Girl Scts; Rep Soph Cls; Hon Roll; Blue Birds 4 Wheel Dr Clb; Mud Drags Off Road 4 Wheel Dr Racng; RDA.

GAYDON, ERIC N; Tustin HS; Tustin, CA; (3); Boy Scts; Library Aide; Teachers Aide; Ftbl; Modifieds Unltd Car Clb; Orange Coast Coll; Psycht.

GAYLORD, JEREMY M; Live Oak HS; Morgan Hill, CA; (3); 1/600; Rptr FBLA; Ed Nwsp; Soph Cls; Jr Cls; Sr Cls; High Hon Roll; VP NHS; Ntl Merit SF; Vrsty Badminton.

GAYLORD, MICHELLE; Valley Christian HS; San Jose, CA; (3); 10/66; Church Yth Grp; French Clb; Chorus; Vllybl; High Hon Roll; CSF.

GAYNOR, JAKE B; Willits HS; Willits, CA; (3); 10/110; Band; School Musical; School Play; VP Frsh Cls; Sec Sr Cls; Var L Socr; Var Tennis; Var L Wrstlng; High Hon Roll; Hon Roll; Boys St Alt; CIF Schlr Athl; Wrstlng NCS Athl; CA Arts Schlr; 1st Pl Sci Fair; Outstndng Wrstlng Awd; U CA Santa Cruz; Visual Arts.

GAYNOR, JOHN; Damien HS; San Dimas, CA; (4); 5/191; Ed English Clb; Pres German Clb; Letterman Clb; SADD; Varsity Clb; Chorus; School Musical; Nwsp; Rep Jr Cls; Rep Sr Cls; Acdmc Achvt Awds Chrstn Scrptr & Grmn; Backpckg Clb VP & Pres; CSF & Natl Hnrs Socty; Rice U; Hmnts.

GAYTAN, JESUS A; Kerman HS; Kerman, CA; (3); 25/133; Church Yth Grp; Spanish Clb; Chorus; Church Choir; Hon Roll; Hispanics In Soc Male Conf 90; Credit Cert-Mech Drawing I; Pride Awd; Fresno ST U; Arch.

GAZMEN, MICHELLE S; Bellarmine-Jefferson HS; Los Angeles, CA; (4); Art Clb; Cmnty Wkr; School Play; Sec Frsh Cls; Sec Soph Cls; Cheerldng; Trk; High Hon Roll; Hon Roll; San Diego ST U; Graphic Art.

GAZZAR, BRENDA; Barstown HS; Barstow, CA; (3); Treas AFS; JV Cheerldng; JV Score Keeper; High Hon Roll; Hon Roll; CSF; Peer Counselor; 2nd Rnnr Up Southern CA Miss Natl Teenager Pgnt; Nws Bfrdcstr.

GBUR, JOEY S; Oxnard HS; Oxnard, CA; (3); 56/647; Cmnty Wkr; Letterman Clb; Scholastic Bowl; School Play; Variety Show; Off Jr Cls; Chrmn Stu Cncl; Intrml Ftbl; Var Co-Capt Tennis; High Hon Roll; UCLA; Pre Med.

GE BARA, JOE C; Eisenhower HS; Rialto, CA; (2); 3/38; Chorus; Bsbl; Ftbl; San Diego U; Naval Aviator.

GEALOGO, PATRICK; Don Bosco Technical Inst; Los Angeles, CA; (2); Drama Clb; Acpl Chr; Band; Church Choir; Mrchg Band; School Musical; VP Soph Cls; Cit Awd; NHS; Pres Acad Fit Awd; ABC The Home Show Back To Schl Fashn Sgmnt; CA Tech; Engrng.

GEARHART, DOUGLAS G; Cloverdale HS; Cloverdale, CA; (4); 3/70; Band; Jazz Band; Nwsp; Yrbk; Crs Cntry; Tennis; High Hon Roll; Pres Acad Fit Awd; Congrssnl Schlr; All St Band; Physics Exchng Stu; UC Davis; Physics.

GEARHART, JESSE J; Santa Ynez Valley Union HS; Santa Barbara, CA; (3); 9/161; Band; Jazz Band; Mrchg Band; Pep Band; High Hon Roll; Outstndng Muscianshp Awd 88-90; Frosh Soph Music Awd 89; Stu Action Tm; CSF; High Hnrs Gldn St Exam; Cal Poly Sal Luis Obispo; Comp.

GEARHART, SUZANNE J; Cloverdale HS; Cloverdale, CA; (2); 3/57; Church Yth Grp; Letterman Clb; Band; Jazz Band; Mrchg Band; Pep Band; Var Tennis; High Hon Roll; Hon Roll; Mem CSF; UC Davis; HS Teacher.

GEARLDS, JANET D; Lowell HS; San Francisco, CA; (3); Cmnty Wkr; Debate Tm; JA; NFL; Service Clb; Bsktbl; Trk; Amnesty Intl Grp Coordntr; Hunger Prjct & AIDS Walkathon Vlntr.

GEBB, JUSTIN; Bret Harte Union HS; Murphys, CA; (2); Rep Stu Cncl; JV Bsktbl; JV Ftbl; Var Socr; JV Trk; CSF; Schlr Athlete; Acad Block; Bst Show 2 1st Pl Woodwrkng Calaveras Cnty Fr; Tour Guide Mercer Cavern; U Of CA San Diego; Educ.

GEBB, KIRK W; Bret Harte Union HS; Murphys, CA; (4); AFS; VP Pep Clb; Scholastic Bowl; Teachers Aide; Varsity Clb; Stage Crew; Ftbl; JV Score Keeper; Var Socr; JV Trk; Bank Of America Certificate Industrial Arts; Honors Algebra & Geometry Golden St Exams; NM Inst Mining; Metlrgl.

GEBHARDT, BRYAN C; Washington HS; Fremont, CA; (2); 1/370; Computer Clb; Quiz Bowl; Scholastic Bowl; Service Clb; Treas Soph Cls; High Hon Roll; City Sccr; Piano; CSF; Physics.

GECHTER, RONIT C; Grossmont HS; El Cajon, CA; (2); 43/431; Intnl Clb; Temple Yth Grp; Rptr Yrbk; Mgr Diving; Mgr(s); Score Keeper; Mgr Swmmng; Hon Roll; HS Of Jewish Studies; CSF 88-90; Tap & Jazz Dance Cls; Golden St Exam Hnrs Alg; Bio, Chem, Geom Hnrs; UCSD; Teacher.

GECK, MICHAEL D; Crawford HS; San Diego, CA; (3); Pres Latin Clb; Rep Stu Cncl; Var Capt Golf; Hon Roll; Most Imprv Plyr Water Polo; Humbolt; Landscape.

GEDDES, GEORGE C; Valencia HS; Anaheim, CA; (1); Boy Scts; FBLA; German Clb; Science Clb; Band; Mrchg Band; Pep Band; Mst Imprvd In Band 90; SD Schl Of Mines/Tech; Geology.

GEDDES, WILLIAM A; San Pasqual HS; Escondido, CA; (2); JV Bsktbl; JV Ftbl; Var Trk.

GEDRIMAS, ROBERT MURPHY; Le Grand HS; Le Grand, CA; (2); FFA; Pres Acad Fit Awd; U CA; Physics.

GEE, BARRY T; John F Kennedy HS; La Palma, CA; (3).

GEE, CALVIN; Lowell HS; San Francisco, CA; (2); Red Cross Aide; Intrml Bsbl; Intrml Bsktbl; Intrml Ftbl; Intrml Tennis; Jr NHS; Law.

GEE, CHRISTOPHER; Oakland HS; Oakland, CA; (3); German Clb; Key Clb; Math Tm; JV Swmmng.

GEE, DAISY; Luther Burbank HS; Sacramento, CA; (2); 9/435; Stat Bsktbl; Var Swmmng; Cit Awd; High Hon Roll; Hon Roll; Prfct Atten Awd; Pres Acad Fit Awd; Prin Hnr Roll; Polynesian Club; Engrng.

GEE, ELISE C; Nogales HS; Walnut, CA; (3); 50/542; Cmnty Wkr; Intnl Clb; Science Clb; Rptr Nwsp; Pres Frsh Cls; Off Soph Cls; Off Jr Cls; Sec Stu Cncl; Hon Roll; CA Schltc Press Assn Wrkshp Prtcpnt; ASB Awds Ldrshp Most Vlbl & Dedctd; Dir Awd; Jrnlsm.

GEE, JENNY; Lowell HS; San Francisco, CA; (2); Bowling Clb; Vlntr; San Jose ST; Acctng.

GEE, JOANN M; Casa Grande HS; Petaluma, CA; (2); 24/250; Girl Scts; Spanish Clb; Drill Tm; Hon Roll; NHS; Bio.

GEE, KENNETH SCOTT; Casa Grande HS; Petaluma, CA; (4); 24/250; Math Clb; Science Clb; Spanish Clb; Teachers Aide; Hon Roll; NHS; Pres Acad Fit Awd; UC Davis.

GEE, KENRIC P; Wallenberg Traditional HS; San Francisco, CA; (2); Red Cross Aide; Ski Clb; Hon Roll; Optometry.

GEE, KEVIN A; Alameda HS; Alameda, CA; (4); 3/325; Red Cross Aide; Science Clb; Teachers Aide; Band; Mrchg Band; Rptr Nwsp; Yrbk; Vienna Intl Music Fstvl; Bst Musician SR Cls; Co Cncrtmstr Bay Area Wind Symphny; Arch.

GEE, MARY; St Rose Acad; Daly City, CA; (3); Drama Clb; Hosp Aide; Service Clb; Chorus; Mgr Stage Crew; Nwsp; Yrbk; Co-Ed Lit Mag; Cit Awd; Hon Roll; Med Apprntcshp Pgm; Music Tchrs Assoc CA Cert Mrt Exm; CSF.

GEE, RANDY T; Homestead HS; Sunnyvale, CA; (2); Bsbl; Ftbl; Hon Roll; NHS; U Of CA Davis; Psych.

GEE, REBECCA; Bishop Amat HS; Temple City, CA; (1); Church Yth Grp.

GEE, STEFANIE; Oakland Technical HS; Oakland, CA; (2); Hon Roll; Outstndng Achvt In Acad Awd With Lttr; UC Berkeley; Engrng.

GEE, TINA A; Luther Burbank HS; Sacramento, CA; (3); 16/276; Am Leg Aux Girls St; Drama Clb; VP FTA; VP Jr Cls; Var Bsktbl; Var Swmmng; Hon Roll; Cngrsnl Schlr; Sacramento ST U; Cmnctns.

GEE, TONY; Balboa HS; San Francisco, CA; (3); Spanish Clb; Intrml Tennis; Hon Roll; Prfct Atten Awd; Acad Decathlon; JSA Treas; UC Davis; Engrng.

GEE, TREY; Bella Vista HS; Orangevale, CA; (2); French Clb; Ftbl; Hmcmng Cmmtte 2 Yrs; CA ST U; Bus.

GEENA, REGINA NIETO AKA; Lakewood HS; Lakewood, CA; (3); Debate Tm; Church Choir; Drill Tm; Bsktbl; Capt JV Cheerldng; Sftbl; Vllybl; USC; Brdcstng.

GEHLE, DEBORAH A; Whittier Christian HS; Yorba Linda, CA; (4); 12/179; Church Yth Grp; Drama Clb; Pep Clb; School Play; Rptr Nwsp; Var Crs Cntry; Var Socr; Var Trk; Bus Adm.

GEHLKEN, AARON L; Victor Valley Joint Union HS; Victorville, CA; (2); Pres FBLA; Pres Jr Cls; 8th Pl San Bernardino Accntng Cmptn; Victor Valley Teen Ctr Advocates Chrmn; Whittier Coll; Law.

GEHRINGER, TISHA; Arroyo Grande HS; Arroyo Grande, CA; (4); 61/409; Church Yth Grp; GAA; Teachers Aide; Variety Show; Sec Jr Cls; Stu Cncl; Cheerldng; Cit Awd; Hon Roll; NHS; Saddleback Coll; Pre Law.

GEHRTS, KELLY A; Mtn Empire JR-SR HS; Descanso, CA; (3); GAA; Letterman Clb; Pep Clb; Pres Spanish Clb; Teachers Aide; Rep Soph Cls; Treas Jr Cls; Stu Cncl; Intl Studies.

GEIGER, SARAH B; California Lutheran HS; Belmont, CA; (2); 2/16; Church Yth Grp; Acpl Chr; Chorus; Church Choir; Variety Show; Phtg Ed Yrbk; Sec Frsh Cls; Rep Stu Cncl; Var Bsktbl; Var Sftbl; Chopin Music Awd 2 Yrs; Dr Martin Luther Coll.

GEIL, JOLENE S; William S Hart HS; Valencia, CA; (2); Art Clb; Drama Clb; Math Tm; Pep Clb; Science Clb; School Play; Stage Crew; Rptr Nwsp; Cit Awd; Participated In The MIA Foundation In Techachapi; Special Interest In DOC; Berkley; Internist Pathologist.

GEISDORFF, FERNI R; Summerville HS; Tuolumne, CA; (3); Cmnty Wkr; Teachers Aide; Ftbl; Socr; Wrstlng; Wyaki Fncy Dance-Mewuk Trdtnl Dncng; Woodcuttng; Pres Tuolumne Band Mewuk Indns; Humboldt ST Coll; Oprtng Engr.

GEISE, MATTHEW; St Francis HS; Mountain View, CA; (3); 53/289; Band; Jazz Band; Mrchg Band; Orch; Pep Band; School Musical; Outstndng JR Musician In Schl; Engrng Music.

GEISERT, JULIE ANNE; Kearny HS; San Diego, CA; (2); Key Clb; Library Aide; Chorus; Drill Tm; Yrbk; JV Swmmng; Cit Awd; Hon Roll; Job Sea World; Key Club; Spec Interest Photo; Stanford; Law.

GEISINGER, MATTHEW; Grossmont HS; La Mesa, CA; (4); 12/400; Am Leg Boys St; Church Yth Grp; Cmnty Wkr; Math Clb; Spanish Clb; Lit Mag; Rptr Frsh Cls; Var Bsktbl; Var Ftbl; Var Vllybl; CSF; Fed Mart Grant; U Of CA San Diego; Bio.

GEISSLER, HEIDI L; Lemoore HS; Lemoore, CA; (4); Drama Clb; FBLA; FHA; Letterman Clb; Pep Clb; Spanish Clb; Yrbk; JV Bsktbl; Var JV Cheerldng; Var Pom Pon; Hmcmng JR Cls Prncss & SR Qn; Coll Of Sequioas; Elem Tchr.

GELB, BRUCE E; Carlmont HS; Redwood City, CA; (2); German Clb; Ski Clb; Temple Yth Grp; Nwsp; Off Soph Cls; Lcrss; Hon Roll; NHS; CSF; Sci.

GELFAND, JULIE; Buena Park HS; La Palma, CA; (4); Sec French Clb; Science Clb; Sec Jr Cls; VP Sr Cls; Capt Cheerldng; High Hon Roll; Pres Acad Fit Awd; Richard H Spaulding Schlrshp; CSF; UC Irvien; Psych.

GELFF, FAWN C; Whitney HS; Cerritos, CA; (4); Art Clb; Cmnty Wkr; Drama Clb; Spanish Clb; High Hon Roll; Hon Roll; Pres Acad Fit Awd; Greenpeace; UCLA.

GELFUSO, CHRIS; Damien HS; La Verne, CA; (1); Ski Clb; Band; Jazz Band; Wrstlng; High Hon Roll; Fishing Club; UCLA; Med.

GELFUSO, MARK A; Washington HS; Fremont, CA; (2); 30/400; Art Clb; Church Yth Grp; Letterman Clb; Scholastic Bowl; Ski Clb; Varsity Clb; Ed Nwsp; VP Soph Cls; Var Cheerldng; Var Trk; CA Schlstc Fed; Stanford U Stu Govt Wk; Stu Govt Public Rltns Chairperson; U Southern CA; Brdcst Jrnlsm.

GELHAAR, LAURA L; La Canada HS; La Canada-Flint, CA; (4); Drama Clb; Hosp Aide; JA; SADD; Co-Capt Color Guard; School Play; Stage Crew; NHS; Pres Acad Fit Awd; Trnmnt Proses Hnr Band Tall Flg; Outstndng Dancer; Coach Awd; CA ST U Fresno.

GELHAYE, JAMIE; Antioch HS; Antioch, CA; (3); Teachers Aide; JV Swmmng; Hon Roll; Pres Acad Fit Awd; Psych.

GELI, LEA T; Mercy HS; San Bruno, CA; (3); Cmnty Wkr; Drama Clb; Latin Clb; School Musical; School Play; Var Cheerldng; Hon Roll; Intl Ordr Rainbow Girls PWA; Prfrmng Arts.

GELIGA, FERNANDO; Desert HS; Edwards, CA; (2); Ftbl; FL ST U; Elec Engr.

GELLER, SHERRIE L; Willits HS; Willits, CA; (2); Church Yth Grp; 4-H; Diving; Swmmng; Hon Roll; BYU; Optometry.

GEMBALA, MATTHEW I; Analy HS; Sebastopol, CA; (3); 2/237; Church Yth Grp; Math Tm; Band; Church Choir; Drm Mjr(t); Mrchg Band; Orch; Variety Show; Pres Acad Fit Awd; N CA Hnr Band-Frnch Hnr 88-90; CA All-State Hnr Band-Frnch Hnr 88-90; Trnmnt Of Roses Parade 90; Maranatha Bptst Bible; Pastor.

GEMMA, SHANNON L; Apple Valley HS; Apple Valley, CA; (2); Church Yth Grp; Computer Clb; Dance Clb; Ski Clb; Spanish Clb; Yrbk; Crs Cntry; High Hon Roll; Hon Roll; UC San Diego; Psych.

GEMMER, ANDREA; Alhambra HS; Lafayette, CA; (1); Church Yth Grp; Var Socr; High Hon Roll; Pres Acad Fit Awd; NCS Schlr Athl.

GEMMER, JASON C; Alhambra HS; Lafayette, CA; (2); 1/250; Church Yth Grp; Rptr Nwsp; Stu Cncl; JV Capt Bsbl; JV Bsktbl; JV Ftbl; Intrml Socr; Intrml Wt Lftg; High Hon Roll; NCS Schlr Athlt; Contra Costa Times Carrier Mnth; Gldn ST Exam Hnrs Geom.

GENATO, MARIA JASMINE; Bishop Amat Memorial HS; Phillips Ranch, CA; (4); 56/390; Church Yth Grp; Drama Clb; GAA; Drill Tm; School Play; Sec Sr Cls; Stu Cncl; JV Socr; Hon Roll; NHS; Spcl Olympics Vol; Lanteran St Hosp Mntlly Disables Vol; CA ST Long Bch; Nrsng.

GENDEL, JENNIFER K; Taft HS; Canoga Park, CA; (3); Drama Clb; School Play; Stage Crew; Off Frsh Cls; Off Soph Cls; Off Jr Cls; Hon Roll; Manage A Yogurt Store, Penguins; UCLA; TV Brdcster.

GENERALAO, ANDREW; Skyline HS; Oakland, CA; (3); Computer Clb; Teachers Aide; Varsity Clb; Band; Orch; Var Lcrss; Pres Acad Fit Awd; U Of Santa Barbara; Psych.

GENEREUX, KASI; Rancho Cotati HS; Rohnert Park, CA; (3); Pres Church Yth Grp; Service Clb; Spanish Clb; Teachers Aide; Church Choir; JV Cheerldng; High Hon Roll; Hon Roll; NHS; Nurse.

GENESON, SILAS K; St Ignatius College Prep; San Francisco, CA; (3); Chess Clb; Cmnty Wkr; Ski Clb; Yrbk; Socr; Trk; High Hon Roll.

GENG, AMY; Henry M Gunn HS; Palo Alto, CA; (4); 5/275; FBLA; Hosp Aide; Latin Clb; Service Clb; Teachers Aide; Orch; Ed Lit Mag; JV Crs Cntry; Jr NHS; Ntl Merit SF; Med.

GENNER, MONIQUE; Diamond Bar HS; Diamond Bar, CA; (2); French Clb; Var Trk; Hon Roll; Treas Of Psych Clb; SADD; Nomntng Convtn; U WA; Hotl Bus.

GENOVE, ERANO NOBELLO; Balboa HS; San Francisco, CA; (3); JV Var Bsbl; CSF; Schlr Athltc; UCSF; Civil Engr.

GENTILE, APRIL D; Fresno Christian HS; Fresno, CA; (2); Church Yth Grp; Cmnty Wkr; Dance Clb; Pep Clb; Acpl Chr; Chorus; Church Choir; VP Frsh Cls; VP Soph Cls; Cheerldng; Fresno ST U; Physcl Thrpy.

GENTLES, SHARON DELORES; Pius X HS; Lynwood, CA; (3); Church Yth Grp; Cmnty Wkr; Drama Clb; GAA; Sec Girl Scts; Speech Tm; Capt Cheerldng; Cit Awd; Hon Roll; NHS; CA Miss TEEN 90 Hnr; Vlntr Svc Awd; Cmmrcl Actg; Child Psych.

GENTRY, DIANE C; River City HS; W Sacramento, CA; (2); High Hon Roll; French Clb; Stu Cncl; Cheerldng; Acad Ltrs Alg I, French I, Bio, French II; Gldn St Exams Hnrs Alg; Phares Theatre Ballet Co.

GENTRY, ERIC E; Thousand Oaks HS; Thousand Oaks, CA; (3); 54/584; Boy Scts; Church Yth Grp; Cmnty Wkr; JA; SADD; Teachers Aide; Varsity Clb; Ed Yrbk; Ed Lit Mag; Var Ftbl; Jr Most Vlbl Track Athlt; 1st Jr Editor Yrbk.

GENTRY, JENNIFER; Rubidoux HS; Mira Loma, CA; (4); Drama Clb; School Play; Stage Crew; Ed Nwsp; Hon Roll; Hnrs Golden St Exm Geom; CA ST U Northridge; Math.

GENTRY, JENNIFER J; North HS; Bakersfield, CA; (2); Service Clb; Ski Clb; Bsktbl; JV Vllybl; High Hon Roll; Hon Roll; NHS; Spanish NHS; CSF; Kern River Vllybl Clb; Bus.

GENTRY, JENNIFER N; Westlake HS; Westlake Vlg, CA; (2); 50/450; Church Yth Grp; Letterman Clb; SADD; Var Swmmng; Tennis; Hon Roll; Ambssdr; Art Cls Art Ctr Coll; Bus.

GENTRY, KERRY; Anaheim HS; Anaheim, CA; (4); Sec FBLA; German Clb; Pep Clb; Teachers Aide; Rptr Nwsp; Mgr Yrbk; Powder Puff Ftbl; Score Keeper; Sftbl; Tennis; Girls League; CA ST U Long Beach; Bus Admin.

GENTRY, LEGINA K; Antelrope Valley HS; Lancaster, CA; (3); Church Yth Grp; Cmnty Wkr; French Clb; Pep Clb; Spanish Clb; Teachers Aide; Church Choir; School Play; JV Bsktbl; Var Trk; Stu Of Wk; Outstndng Sprinter; Gymnstcs; Langston U; Paralgl.

GENTRY, LISA A; Cabrillo HS; Lompoc, CA; (3); German Clb; CA Poly; Psych.

GENTRY, LORI L; South HS; Bakersfield, CA; (4); 33/330; Church Yth Grp; FCA; VP Key Clb; Science Clb; Speech Tm; Teachers Aide; Stu Cncl; Capt Tennis; Hon Roll; NHS; Stu Bdy Outstndng Svc Awd; Prncpls Awd; Stu Athltc Trnr; CA ST U Bakersfield; Nrsng.

GENUINO, ARLEEN GRACE R; John F Kennedy HS; La Palma, CA; (2); Cmnty Wkr; FBLA; Hosp Aide; Key Clb; Rptr Phtg Yrbk; High Hon Roll; CA Schlrshp Fnd; Kennedy Uundergrad Awd Phys Ed; St Pious Cath Church SRE Pgm; USC; Ped.

GEONETTA, JENNIFER; Temple City HS; Temple City, CA; (3); Dance Clb; Letterman Clb; Pep Clb; Teachers Aide; JV Varsity Clb; Acpl Chr; Chorus; Rep Stu Cncl; JV Var Cheerldng; JV Sftbl; CSF; UCSD; Poltcl Law.

GEOPFARTH, ALEN E; San Dieguito HS; Encinitas, CA; (2); Aviation.

GEORGE, ALAN J; Carlsbad HS; Carlsbad, CA; (3); Ski Clb; Stage Crew; JV Trk; CA St Lifegrd; Aviation.

GEORGE, CHRISTIANE; James Logan HS; Union City, CA; (3); 15/1000; French Clb; FTA; Intnl Clb; Science Clb; Ski Clb; Powder Puff Ftbl; Hon Roll; Davis U; Med.

GEORGE, CHRISTOPHER A; St Anthony HS; Long Beach, CA; (2); JV Bsbl; JV Bsktbl; Var Mgr(s); Hon Roll; Pres Fishing Club; Notre Dame; Comp Sci.

GEORGE, GUILLERMO; Calexico HS; Calexico, CA; (2); School Play; High Hon Roll; Hon Roll; Prfct Atten Awd; CSF.

GEORGE, JENNIFER; Bethel Christian HS; Lancaster, CA; (1); Church Choir; Var Cheerldng; High Hon Roll; CAPS; Pilot.

GEORGE, JENNIFER M; Foothill HS; Santa Ana, CA; (3); Church Yth Grp; Office Aide; Hon Roll; Math Hnrs; ASU; Merch Mrktng.

GEORGE, JULIE; Porterville HS; Porterville, CA; (4); Church Yth Grp; GAA; Teachers Aide; Jazz Band; Mrchg Band; Pep Band; JV Var Cheerldng; Var Capt Tennis; Hon Roll; Intl Order Jobs Dghtrs Hnrs Qn; CA ST U Long Beach; Engrng.

GEORGE, PETER; Paraclete HS; Lancaster, CA; (4); 19/123; Debate Tm; Hosp Aide; JA; Treas Key Clb; Letterman Clb; Quiz Bowl; Treas Service Clb; Church Choir; Var L Golf; French Hon Soc; CSF; Chrstn Svc Awd; Sacristy Clb; Phrmcst.

GEORGE, SHELLIE J; Diamond Bar HS; Diamond Bar, CA; (1); Church Yth Grp; Drama Clb; Chorus; JV Vllybl; Westmont Coll; Lawyer.

GEORGE, STEPHANIE L; Eureka SR HS; Eureka, CA; (3); Service Clb; Ski Clb; Hon Roll; Pres Acad Fit Awd; Prfrmng Redwood Concert Ballet; Humboldt ST U; Dance.

GEORGIANNI, SHELLEY; Warren HS; Downey, CA; (3); Church Yth Grp; JA; Spanish Clb; SADD; Chorus; Church Choir; Rptr Nwsp; Cit Awd; Cerritos Coll; Engl.

GERA, MANOJ; El Rancho HS; Pico Rivera, CA; (2); Computer Clb; Debate Tm; Key Clb; Math Clb; JV Swmmng; JV Tennis; High Hon Roll; Hon Roll; Prfct Atten Awd; CSF; Math Engrng Sci Achvt; U Of CA Prtnrs; U Of CA Irvine; Chem.

GERADS, KAREN; Our Lady Of Victory Hmschl; Freeport, MN; (4); 4-H; Church Choir; John Birch Soc; St Cloud ST U; Health Sci.

GERAGHTY, SHANNON C; El Toro HS; El Toro, CA; (2); 25/565; Church Yth Grp; JV Bsktbl; JV Sftbl; High Hon Roll; Hon Roll; CSF; Keywanettes Club.

GERARDIN, MICHAEL J; Fresno HS; Fresno, CA; (4); 6/430; Cmnty Wkr; Key Clb; SADD; Ed Nwsp; Bsbl; Tennis; High Hon Roll; Senate; CA Schrlshp Fed; NW Fresno Boy Of Mnth; UC Irvine; Jrnlsm.

GERARDO, MARC J; Saint Ignatius College Prep; San Francisco, CA; (4); 1/300; Rep Church Yth Grp; Cmnty Wkr; Debate Tm; Model UN; NFL; Service Clb; Speech Tm; Teachers Aide; Church Choir; Nwsp; U Of PA Book Awd; Natl Cncl Tchrs Engl Writing Awd; Tennis MVP; Law.

GERASIMATOS, DIMITRI; Western Christian HS; Ontario, CA; (4); Model UN; High Hon Roll; NHS; Ntl Merit SF; Stu For The Explortn & Dvlpmnt Of Sci Secy; Acad Decathlon; MENSA; U CA Berkeley.

GERBASI, BOBBI L; Bolsa Grande HS; Garden Grove, CA; (2); 54/377; VP Church Yth Grp; Treas Drama Clb; Sec Thesps; Band; Chorus; Church Choir; Color Guard; Stat Bsktbl; Cheerldng; Hon Roll; Cngrssnl Schlr; CA ST U Fullerton; Music.

GERBER, APRIL; Bellflower HS; Bellflower, CA; (3); 3/241; Church Yth Grp; Key Clb; Spanish Clb; SADD; Drill Tm; Ed Nwsp; VP Frsh Cls; Pres Soph Cls; Cheerldng; High Hon Roll; HOBY Fndtn Awd Wnr; Natl Assn Stu Cncls Schlrshp; US Air Force Acad; Frnsc Med.

GERBER, MICHAEL A; Moreno Valley HS; Moreno Valley, CA; (3); Hon Roll; Art Mrt Achvt Awd.

GERBER, STEFANI; Casa Roble Fundamental HS; Roseville, CA; (2); 1/481; Cmnty Wkr; Ski Clb; Spanish Clb; Drill Tm; High Hon Roll; NHS; Stu Rchng Out; CA Schlrshp Fed; Fri Nght Lv; Cmmnctns.

GERBER, STEPHANIE L; Sonora HS; Brea, CA; (4); 9/279; Spanish Clb; High Hon Roll; Gldn St Exam Alg Hnrs; Stu Mnth Sci; Bus Cmmnctns.

GEREAUX, RONALD E; Silver Valley HS; Yermo, CA; (3); FBLA; FFA; German Clb; Library Aide; Rptr Nwsp; Socr; Wrstlng; Marine Corp.

GERGEN, BRIAN C; Mater Dei HS; Fountain Valley, CA; (3); German Clb; Science Clb; Intrml JV Swmmng; DAR Awd; High Hon Roll; NHS; CA Schlrshp Fed; Water Polo IM, Jr Var, Var; Surfing Clb Sec; U CA San Diego; Engrng.

GERGER, STEPHANIE C; Wm S Hart HS; Valencia, CA; (4); 11/487; Treas French Clb; Mu Alpha Theta; Temple Yth Grp; Nwsp; Hon Roll; NHS; Ntl Merit SF; Opt Clb Awd; ACA Schlrshp Fed; Claremont Mc Kenna; Law.

GERHARDT, LISA M; Watsonville HS; Watsonville, CA; (1); 27/765; 4-H; 4-H Awd; Teens For Teens Stop AIDS Drama Prdctn; Scientist.

GERICH, BRYN K; Livermore HS; Livermore, CA; (3); Hosp Aide; Rep Frsh Cls; Sec Soph Cls; Sec Jr Cls; Rep Stu Cncl; Var L Socr; Capt L Trk; High Hon Roll; Hon Roll; Pres Acad Fit Awd; CA Schlrshp Prgm; Track & Fld MVP; Ambssdr Hugh Obrian Yth Fndtn Ldrshp Org; Med.

GERICK, AMY; Bret Harte HS; Murphys, CA; (1); AFS; Church Yth Grp; Model UN; Ski Clb; Band; School Musical; School Play; JV Tennis; High Hon Roll; CA Schltc Fed; Frgn Affairs.

GERICKE, ANN M; Del Campo HS; Fair Oaks, CA; (2); 29/460; Drill Tm; Fri Nght Live; CA Schlrshp Fdrtn.

GERINGER, KRISTIN; Kerman HS; Kerman, CA; (3); 4/133; Treas Church Yth Grp; Math Tm; Varsity Clb; Band; Mrchg Band; Treas Jr Cls; Pres Sr Cls; Var JV Cheerldng; Var Swmmng; High Hon Roll; Swmmng Awds, Coaches Awd 89; MVP 90; CSU; Bus.

GERINGER, TRICIA; Central HS; Fresno, CA; (3); 9/202; Pep Clb; Ski Clb; Rep Frsh Cls; Sec Sr Cls; Var Cheerldng; JV Score Keeper; Ldrshp Class Mem; Refusal Skills; Comm.

GERJETS, HEATHER; Rio Mesa HS; Camarillo, CA; (3); 12/400; AFS; Varsity Clb; JV Cheerldng; Var Socr; Var Capt Sftbl; High Hon Roll; NHS; MVP Channel Leag Sftbl; Mvp Socr; Acad Ltr; UCSB; Elem Educ.

GERK, JULIE E; Burlingame HS; Burlingame, CA; (3).

GERMAN, PATTY; El Centro HS; El Centro, CA; (3); Bus.

GERMAN, WENDY J; Corona SR HS; Corona, CA; (2); Yrbk; Cit Awd; Hon Roll; Pres Acad Fit Awd; RCC JR Coll; Comp.

GERMANY, VILA SHEREE B; Golden Gate Acad; Oakland, CA; (1); 1/30; Church Yth Grp; Drama Clb; Quiz Bowl; Acpl Chr; Chorus; School Play; Rptr Nwsp; Cheerldng; High Hon Roll; Most Talented 89-90; Most Prdctv Typist 89-90; Oakwood Coll; Atty.

GERMONE, MONIQUE; Analy HS; Sebastopol, CA; (4); Pres Art Clb; Spanish Clb; CA Schlr Arts 89; 1st Stud Art Show 89; Scuptors Apprntc 89; Exchg Stud-Japan 88; Otis Parsons; Fine Arts.

GERMONO, REUBELLE; American HS; Fremont, CA; (2); Church Yth Grp; Band; Mrchg Band; High Hon Roll; Hon Roll; Concert Band; Piano; Swmmng; Outstndng Achvt Hlth 89; UC; Med.

GEROLAGA, MARIA TERESA R; Holy Family HS; Los Angeles, CA; (2); Church Yth Grp; Cmnty Wkr; Drama Clb; GAA; Teachers Aide; Chorus; School Musical; School Play; Sftbl; Trk; Natl Tennis Assn; Art Instrctn Schl; Campus Mnstry; Piano; Film Dir.

GERONIMO, ALEXANDER R; Archbishop Riordan HS; San Francisco, CA; (3); 24/144; Pres Intnl Clb; Intrml Bsbl; Intrml Bsktbl; Hon Roll; Modern Geom & Bio Awds 88-89; CSF 89-90; Bus Admin.

GERONIMO, VERONIKA; Fontana HS; Fontana, CA; (2); Ed Nwsp; Ed Yrbk; Ed Lit Mag; Stu Cncl; Socr; High Hon Roll; Hon Roll; CSF; Magazine Edtr.

GEROVIAN, EDWARD; Bellarmine-Jefferson HS; Sunland, CA; (2); Var Ftbl; Var Trk; Var Wt Lftg; High Hon Roll; UCLA; Bus.

GERRARD, AMANDA; Diamond Bar HS; Diamond Bar, CA; (3); German Clb; Drill Tm; Hon Roll; Ntl Merit Ltr; CSF; Dance Drill Team Ofcr; Princpls Hnr Roll.

GERRINGER, CINDY L; Fresno Christian HS; Fresno, CA; (3); Church Yth Grp; Hosp Aide; Library Aide; JV Tennis; High Hon Roll; Hon Roll; Prfct Atten Awd; Church Clb; Piano; Fresno ST U; Phrmcy.

GERSH, JORDANNA P; Hamilton HS; Los Angeles, CA; (2); Teachers Aide; Temple Yth Grp; Rep Stu Cncl; Wt Lftg; Cit Awd; San Diego U; Bus.

GERSHENOFF, VALERIE A; Live Oak HS; Morgan Hill, CA; (3); Church Yth Grp; Ed Yrbk; Crs Cntry; Diving; Socr; Trk; Biochem.

GERSHENZON, SABINA; George Washington HS; Castro Valley, CA; (3); Speech Tm; Lit Mag; Dance; Body Building; Biology.

GERSHON, RISA; Los Alamitos HS; Seal Beach, CA; (3); Pep Clb; Spanish Clb; VP Temple Yth Grp; Var L Crs Cntry; Var L Trk; Stat Intrml Vllybl; High Hon Roll; Intrct Cmmnty Svcs; Adpt Grndprnt Vlntr; Scfty/Nfty; Eastern U; Bio.

GERSON, MARINA M; Ocean View HS; Huntington Bch, CA; (4); 11/500; Computer Clb; Girl Scts; Key Clb; Math Clb; Spanish Clb; DAR Awd; Hon Roll; Pres Acad Fit Awd; Girl Scouts Gold/Silver Awds; Bicetennial Hnr Guard; Goldenhawk Engl Awd; Stu Of Month; U CA Santa Cruz; Ecology.

GERTEN, ALLEN A; Moreau HS; San Ramon, CA; (3); Cmnty Wkr; Var Wrstlng; High Hon Roll; Hon Roll; World Of Poetry; CSF; St Marys Of CA.

GERTH, ANGELIKA; Whittier Christian HS; La Mirada, CA; (2); 27/189; Church Yth Grp; German Clb; Off Soph Cls; Var Tennis; Med.

GERTMENIAN, DANIEL; Maranatha HS; Pasadena, CA; (4); 5/106; VP Chess Clb; Church Yth Grp; Math Tm; Spanish Clb; Speech Tm; Mgr Bsktbl; Elks Awd; High Hon Roll; Ntl Merit SF; AACL Schlrshp Wnnr; UCLA; Math.

GERTMENIAN, REBECCA; Polytechnic Schl; Pasadena, CA; (4); Cmnty Wkr; Orch; School Musical; School Play; Ed Lit Mag; Pres Soph Cls; Rep Stu Cncl; Hon Roll; Ntl Merit SF; Chmbr Music-Violist; Cum Laud Soc; Hstry.

GERVACIO, SUSAN D; Dixon HS; Dixon, CA; (3); Church Yth Grp; French Clb; Intnl Clb; Band; Mrchg Band; Crs Cntry; Hon Roll; Solano CC; CPA.

GESE, MEGAN; Escondido HS; Escondido, CA; (1); Pep Clb; Interior Dsgnr.

GESSEL, PETER; Benicia HS; Benicia, CA; (2); Boy Scts; Chess Clb; Band; Jazz Band; Mrchg Band; Orch; School Musical; High Hon Roll; Petrlm Engrng.

GESSERT, REBECCA; El Camino Real HS; Woodland Hills, CA; (2); Church Yth Grp; Drama Clb; Thesps; Band; Church Choir; Color Guard; Flag Corp; Mrchg Band; School Musical; School Play; Best Supporting Actress Drama Play; Acad Excllnc Awd With Hnrs; Schlr Athlt Awd; UCLA; Engl.

GESTIEHR, KRISTI D; El Cajon Valley HS; El Cajon, CA; (2); 150/431; Dance Clb; Drama Clb; Office Aide; SADD; School Play; Variety Show; Treas Frsh Cls; JV Sftbl; 2nd Pl Stars Tomorrow Bty Pgnt; Dance Co; UCLA; Dance.

GESUNDHEIT, JOYCE S; Holy Family HS; Los Angeles, CA; (2); Church Yth Grp; Cmnty Wkr; Hosp Aide; Chorus; Church Choir; Var Sftbl; Cert Ed Dev Natl; Soc Action Club; Standford; Jrnlsm.

GETCHEL, AMY; Woodbridge HS; Irvine, CA; (4); 27/362; Drama Clb; Hosp Aide; Pres Pep Clb; Red Cross Aide; Teachers Aide; School Play; Off Jr Cls; Rep Stu Cncl; Var Capt Pom Pon; Hon Roll; Smith Coll; Psych.

GETROST, MELISSA; South Torrance HS; Avon, CO; (3); 38/350; High Hon Roll; Top Sales Assoc Palos Verdes CA; A P Class JR Yr; Fine Arts.

GETSLA, CHRISTOPHER W; Mission Bay HS; San Diego, CA; (3); Church Yth Grp; Hon Roll; Midaevil Fantasy Combat Organization; UCSA UCLA; Cybernetics Robotc.

GETTELMAN, DEBRA L; Westlake School For Girls; Los Angeles, CA; (4); Cmnty Wkr; Letterman Clb; Ed Yrbk; Hist Soph Cls; Stu Cncl; L Var Swmmng; JV Var Tennis; Photography; Teenline; Brown U Book Awd.

GETTYS, TAREY M; Irvine HS; Irvine, CA; (2); Debate Tm; Speech Tm; Ftbl; Wt Lftg; Wrstlng; Hon Roll; Naval Acad; Med.

GEVORKIAN, ARTIN; Hoover HS; Glendale, CA; (2); ROTC; Spanish Clb; Teachers Aide; High Hon Roll; CSF; UCLA; Med.

GEYOGHLIAN, PETER R; Edison-Computech HS; Fresno, CA; (3); 7/300; Boy Scts; Chess Clb; Computer Clb; French Clb; Math Clb; Math Tm; Model UN; Mrchg Band; JV Bsbl; JV Socr; 5 Th In N CA Sci Olympiad Comp Sci Cmptn; Med.

GHADISHAH, ARASH ROSS; Burlingame HS; Burlingame, CA; (1); Cmnty Wkr; Drama Clb; Score Keeper; Hon Roll; Jr Statesman Of Amer Debate Tm; Smmr Cmp Cnslr; U CA; Attorney.

GHAFARI, SARA; Rio Americano HS; Sacramento, CA; (3); Art Clb; French Clb; Rptr Lit Mag; Socr; Tennis; Crtfct Excllnc For Spr Scr In Wrtng Stndrds Of Proficency Tst; CSUS; Sociology.

GHAFFARI, ARSHIA; Santa Monica HS; Santa Monica, CA; (3); Var Tennis; UC San Diego; Dentistry.

GHAFOORI, RAZIA; Magnolia HS; Anaheim, CA; (3); Drama Clb; Teachers Aide; Pres Sr Cls; Vllybl; Cit Awd; Hon Roll; Ldrshp Acad; Psych.

GHAFOUR, IHSAN; Savanna HS; Anaheim, CA; (3); Art Clb; Science Clb; Crs Cntry; Var Swmmng; Trk; Wrstlng; Hon Roll; Jr NHS; Prfct Atten Awd; Pres Acad Fit Awd; U CA; Elect.

GHAHERI, NEDA; Louisville HS; Woodland Hills, CA; (3); Pres Drama Clb; Hosp Aide; School Play; Rptr Nwsp; Pres Frsh Cls; JV Bsktbl; Hon Roll; Harvard Frgn Lang Cmptn Frnch; Natl Enrgy Fndtn; Microbio.

GHAHRAMAN, HELEN; Foothill HS; Pleasanton, CA; (4); Church Yth Grp; Intnl Clb; Service Clb; SADD; Band; Mrchg Band; French Hon Soc; Hon Roll; Pres Acad Fit Awd; Envrnmntl Clb; CSF, Lfetime; Hnrs Rcgntn Golden St Exams Algebra & Geo; UC Berkeley.

GHALBOURJIAN, VICKI; Pasadena HS; Pasadena, CA; (3); Drama Clb; French Clb; Girl Scts; Library Aide; JV Bsktbl; Hon Roll; Greenpeace Clb; Amnsty Clb.

GHANTOUS, KARYNE; William S Hart HS; Valencia, CA; (4); Math Tm; Mu Alpha Theta; Tennis; SADD; Poltcl Sci Clb; Law.

GHASSEMI, TANNAZ; University HS; Irvine, CA; (2); 12/510; GAA; Spanish Clb; Bsktbl; Vllybl; Cit Awd; Hon Roll; U CA; Bio.

GHAVAMI, ASHKAN; William Howard Taft HS; Tarzana, CA; (3); Library Aide; Stage Crew; JV Bsktbl; Var Ftbl; Var Wt Lftg; Indvdl Music Exprmnt; Bxng; Law.

GHAZI, BEGERED; Valley HS; Sacramento, CA; (1); 25/520; Dance Clb; JV Crs Cntry; JV Mgr(s); Var Tennis; Hon Roll; Footworks-Dance Co; CSF; Fri Night Live; Med.

GHAZIKHANIAN, JENIA; Sonoma Valley HS; Sonoma, CA; (3); 5/275; Debate Tm; Speech Tm; School Musical; School Play; Socr; Cit Awd; High Hon Roll; Hon Roll; CA Schlrshp Fed; U Of CA.

GHAZZAGH, LAYLA; Albany HS; El Cerrito, CA; (1); Hosp Aide; Hon Roll; Stanford; Psych.

GHILARDUCCI, MATTHEW; Edison HS; Fresno, CA; (3); Computer Clb; Math Clb; Math Tm; Science Clb; Ski Clb; JV Golf; JV Vllybl; Cit Awd; High Hon Roll; Hon Roll; GSE Award Geometry; Two Industrial Education Awards At Fresno Fair; Engineering.

GHIO, JENNIFER; Santa Cruz HS; Santa Cruz, CA; (4); 1/250; French Clb; Library Aide; Teachers Aide; Lit Mag; High Hon Roll; Pres Acad Fit Awd; Val; 1st Pl Chem-Cty Sci Fair; Zasu Pitts Poetry Awd-HS Stu Magzn; Deptmntl Awds-Sci & Soc Stud; U Of CA Davis; Eng Lit.

GHISOLFO, ROBERT K; Atwater HS; Atwater, CA; (3); Cmnty Wkr; Teachers Aide; JV Bsbl; Hon Roll; Yth Bsbl Umpire & Coach; Volunteer For Atwater/Winton Lions Club; CA ST Stanislaus; Teacher.

GHOBRIAL, NADER M; Huntington Beach HS; Huntington Beach, CA; (3); Church Yth Grp; Ed Nwsp; Bsktbl; Wt Lftg; Hon Roll; CA ST Long Bch; Cvl Engr.

GHODSI, NEWSHA; San Marin HS; Novato, CA; (4); 3/250; Var Capt Bsktbl; Var Capt Vllybl; High Hon Roll; NHS; Pres Acad Fit Awd; Rotary Awd; Sal; Soc Women Engrs Cert Mrt; Vlybl Hnrb Mntn All-League, Coachs Awd; Bsktbl MIP & MVP; UCLA; Chem Engrng.

GHOLDOIAN, MICHELLE T; Marina HS; Huntington Beach, CA; (2); Drama Clb; Spanish Clb; Thesps; School Musical; School Play; Swing Chorus; VP Soph Cls; JV Cheerldng; Hon Roll; Natl Charity Lg; Philhrmnc Jrs; Comm.

GHOSH, INDRANIL N; Alhambra HS; Monterey Park, CA; (2); Var Socr; Spanish NHS; CA Schlrshp Fed.

GHOSHEA, FARIS; Capo Valley Christian Schl; Laguna Beach, CA; (2); 1/45; JV Bsbl; Stanford U; Dr.

GHOSOPH, SVETLANA; Madera HS; Madera, CA; (2).

GHOVANLOU, PARISSA; Canyon HS; Canyon Country, CA; (3); 34/501; Intrml Bsktbl; Score Keeper; Intrml JV Vllybl; Cit Awd; Hon Roll; NHS; Spanish NHS; CA Schlrshp Fed; Bio.

GIACHETTI, GINA P; Burney JR/Sr HS; Burney, CA; (3); Pres Hist 4-H; Teachers Aide; Band; School Musical; Pres Frsh Cls; Mgr Bsktbl; JV Powder Puff Ftbl; JV Vllybl; 4-H Awd; Hon Roll; Ashland Smmr Smnrs JR 90; Midwstrn Music Cmp U Of KS Smmr 88-89; CSF; Cmmnctns.

GIACOMAN, VANESSA Z; South San Francisco HS; South San Francis, CA; (3); Cmnty Wkr; Latin Clb; Model UN; Office Aide; Science Clb; Spanish Clb; School Musical; Off Sr Cls; Bsktbl; Sftbl; Hstry Day-1st Pl Dist/2nd Pl Co/St Fnlst; Sci/Socl Issues Sympsm Berkeley U-3rd Pl; Hghst Ldrshp Score; Stanford; Sci.

GIACOMETTI, EMANUELE F; Newbury HS; Newbury Park, CA; (1); Bsktbl; Diving; Socr; Swmmng; Tennis; Moorpark; Bus.

GIACOMINI, SARAH E; Fortuna HS; Loleta, CA; (1); Church Yth Grp; VP 4-H; 4-H Awd; High Hon Roll; FFAD; U CA Davis; Bus.

GIALAMAS, ANGIE T; Mayfair HS; Cerritos, CA; (3); Church Yth Grp; English Clb; Office Aide; Teachers Aide; Band; Church Choir; Capt Flag Corp; Mrchg Band; Pep Band; Sec Sr Cls; Lng Bch ST; Cnslng.

GIAMBASTIANI, CHRISTY C; San Rafael HS; San Rafael, CA; (3); 19/226; SADD; Flag Corp; Phtg Yrbk; Lit Mag; Cheerldng; Pom Pon; High Hon Roll; Hon Roll; Friday Nite Live.

GIAMMERINARO, JOY; Grossmont HS; El Cajon, CA; (2); Trk; Hon Roll.

GIAMPAOLI, DIANE R; Santa Rosa HS; Santa Rosa, CA; (4); Church Yth Grp; Cmnty Wkr; GAA; Key Clb; Spanish Clb; SADD; Teachers Aide; Yrbk; Socr; Hon Roll; CA ST U; Phys Thrpy.

GIAMPAOLI, JANET L; St Genevieve HS; Reseda, CA; (3); Church Yth Grp; Pep Clb; Chorus; JV Sftbl; Hon Roll; Law.

GIAN, KHANH D; Hawthorne HS; Hawthorne, CA; (3); Cit Awd; Hon Roll; CSF; U Of Irvine; Med.

GIANELLI, BRIAN; St Marys HS; Stockton, CA; (2); Model UN; Ski Clb; JV Socr; JV Tennis; Stus In Prevention; CSF; UCLA.

GIANG, HUY T; Artesia HS; Lakewood, CA; (2); Intnl Clb; Quiz Bowl; Science Clb; Spanish Clb; Rep Frsh Cls; Rep Soph Cls; Var Tennis; High Hon Roll; Prfct Atten Awd; UCI; Acctng.

GIANG, KIM N; Wallenberg HS; San Francisco, CA; (1); Teachers Aide; Orch; Hon Roll; Dental.

GIANG, LINDA; Saddleback HS; Santa Ana, CA; (2); Mu Alpha Theta; Science Clb; Spanish Clb; Speech Tm; Ed Yrbk; Rep Stu Cncl; JV Tennis; JV Trk; Orange Cnty Acadc Decathlon; 3rd Sci Fair; Acadc Lttr; Berkeley; Bus.

GIANG, MAI T; Mark Keppel HS; San Gabriel, CA; (3); Hosp Aide; Mu Alpha Theta; Q&S; VP Service Clb; Ed Nwsp; Yrbk; Stu Cncl; JV Tennis; High Hon Roll; NHS; Proj Harmony; Crown & Sceptic Sr Hnr Soc; Attnded CASC Ldrshp Camp; Pre Med.

GIANG, VAN A; Rosemead HS; Rosemead, CA; (3); Math Clb; Cit Awd; Hon Roll; Badmntn; Sign Lang Clb; CSF; Engrng.

GIANGRASSO, ANNE-MARIE; Chaminade College Prep; West Hills, CA; (3); Art Clb; Cmnty Wkr; Drama Clb; JA; Office Aide; Thesps; School Musical; School Play; Stage Crew; JV Powder Puff Ftbl; Juliet E Rohde Memorial Awd-Drama 90; Peace & Ecology Clb; Broadcst Jrnlsm.

GIANNECCHINI, KASEY; East Union HS; Manteca, CA; (2); 35/400; Pep Clb; Speech Tm; SADD; Teachers Aide; Yrbk; Sftbl; Cit Awd; Hon Roll; Prfct Atten Awd; Real Estate.

GIANNINI, EBOLI T; Villa Park HS; Orange, CA; (4); 25/450; SADD; Chorus; Pres Orch; Off Jr Cls; Off Sr Cls; Rep Stu Cncl; Var Crs Cntry; VP NHS; Pres Acad Fit Awd; Natl Schl Orch Assoc Awd 90; Gld Mdlln For Msc; Leonard Rosie Mem Schlrshp Awd E Msc Fstvl; Peabody Cnsrvtry; Music.

GIANNINI, GINGER A; Dinuba HS; Dinuba, CA; (3); Pres 4-H; Chorus; Cit Awd; 4-H Awd; High Hon Roll; Madrigals; CA Poly-San Luis Obispo; Arch.

GIARDINELLI, LISA M; Bishop Amat HS; La Verne, CA; (2); Church Yth Grp; Drama Clb; School Play; Sftbl; Hon Roll; NEDT Awd; Child Psych.

GIARRITTA, CARRIE; Encina HS; Sacramento, CA; (4); 1/190; Am Leg Aux Girls St; Church Yth Grp; Computer Clb; French Clb; Service Clb; Teachers Aide; Treas Sr Cls; Elks Awd; High Hon Roll; Hon Roll; Acad Deca Medals; U C San Diego; Sports Med.

GIBB, GEOFF; Bakersfield Acad; Bakersfield, CA; (3); Aud/Vis; Church Yth Grp; Office Aide; Ski Clb; Teachers Aide; Band; Stage Crew; Stu Cncl; Intrml Ftbl; Intrml Socr; USCF Bicycle Racer; Mst Outstndng Male Athl 89-90; UC Davis.

GIBBINS, CHRIS; Trabuco Hills HS; Mission Viejo, CA; (3); Spanish Clb; Band; Drm Mjr(t); Jazz Band; Mrchg Band; Pep Band; Hon Roll; NHS; Outstndng Schlr Awds; UCLA; Engrng.

GIBBINS, GAVIN E; Ramona HS; Riverside, CA; (1); 46/582; Socr; Natl PTA Rflctns Pgm 1st Pl.

GIBBONS, ANGELIQUE M; Grace M Davis HS; Modesto, CA; (2); Dance Clb; Drama Clb; Science Clb; SADD; Band; Mrchg Band; Pep Band; Variety Show; Peer Fcltatng; Peer Sbstnc Spprt Grp; Cnty Adlncn T Cnvntn Wrksp Ldr; Cmnty Rsrc Spkr; Modesto JC.

GIBBONS, ASHLEY A; Roseville HS; Rocklin, CA; (3); Pres Church Yth Grp; German Clb; Teachers Aide; Rptr Nwsp; Lit Mag; VP Stu Cncl; Grad Crmny Ldr 90; RN.

GIBBONS, COLLEEN; South San Francisco HS; S. San Francisco, CA; (1); Band; Cheerldng; Hon Roll; Jr NHS; PAL Sftbl.

GIBBONS, KEVIN L; Palo Verde HS; Blythe, CA; (3); Aud/Vis; FFA; Teachers Aide; JV Bsktbl; Var L Ftbl; Wt Lftg; Var Wrstlng; Hon Roll; Pres Acad Fit Awd; Law Enfrcmnt.

GIBBONS, LAUREL; Palm Spring Christian JR SR HS; Desert Hot Spring, CA; (3); French Clb; Teachers Aide; Chorus; Mgr(s); Score Keeper; Cit Awd; Prfct Atten Awd; Val; Pt Loma Nazarine Coll; Bus.

GIBBONS, ROBERT A; Atascadero HS; Atascadero, CA; (1); Math Clb; Var Bsbl; Var Ftbl; OK U; Cmptr Sci.

GIBBS, CHANDRA; St Genevieve HS; Lakeview Terrace, CA; (4); 16/230; Art Clb; Church Yth Grp; Cmnty Wkr; Dance Clb; Hosp Aide; Pep Clb; SADD; Chorus; Drill Tm; Variety Show; Prfrmng Wrkshp Theater, Dance, Ballet, Jazz, Tap, Drama, Voice; Fnlst Mss Sprstnl USA Chrldng; U CA Loa Angeles; Pre Med.

GIBBS, HEATHER S; Bonita HS; La Verne, CA; (2); SADD; Hon Roll; Pres Acad Fit Awd; Stus For Explrtn & Devlpmnt Of Space; Dance; U Of Southern CA; Law.

GIBBS, JE-NEL; St Genevieve HS; Lakeview Terrace, CA; (2); 9/225; Church Yth Grp; Cmnty Wkr; Dance Clb; Drama Clb; Latin Clb; Pep Clb; Drill Tm; Variety Show; High Hon Roll; Prfrmng Wrkshp Theater Dance, Ballet, Jazz, Tap, Drama, Voice, Piano; Mss Sprstnl USAA Chrldng; UC; Physcn.

GIBBS, JENEL; St Genevieve HS; Lake View Terrace, CA; (2); 10/300; Church Yth Grp; Dance Clb; Drama Clb; Latin Clb; Pep Clb; SADD; Varsity Clb; Drill Tm; Variety Show; Cheerldng; Pre Med.

GIBBS, LINDA; John Marshall Fundmntl Scndry HS; Pasadena, CA; (4); 2/150; Church Yth Grp; Key Clb; Office Aide; Service Clb; Teachers Aide; Key Clb; Church Choir; Ed Nwsp; Rep Frsh Cls; Stu Cncl; Stanford U; Hstry.

GIBBS, ROBERT ASHLEY; Don Bosco Technical Inst; Alhambra, CA; (2); Church Yth Grp; Intrml Bsktbl; Cit Awd; High Hon Roll; Hon Roll; NEDT Awd; CA Poly; Aerospace Engrng.

GIBBS, TAMARA J; Ygnacio Valley HS; Concord, CA; (2); FTA; SADD; Stu Cncl; Concord Yth Cncl; Intl Order Of Rainbow For Girls.

GIBERSON, TARA N; Glendora HS; Glendora, CA; (3); Church Yth Grp; Drama Clb; Key Clb; SADD; Teachers Aide; School Play; Lit Mag; Var L Bsktbl; JV Trk; High Hon Roll; Acad Dcthln; Corp Law.

GIBSON, AMBER; Mt Whitney HS; Visalia, CA; (1); Art Clb; Church Yth Grp; Cmnty Wkr; Rep Stu Cncl; Environmental Club; BYU.

GIBSON, ANDRE M; Luther Burbank HS; Sacramento, CA; (3); Church Yth Grp; Pep Clb; Red Cross Aide; ROTC; Church Choir; Drill Tm; Ftbl; Wt Lftg; Mltry Excllnc Awd By Amer Legion; Outstndng Prfrmnc In Bahalion By US Army; West Point.

GIBSON, ANGELIQUE; Fremont HS; San Jose, CA; (1); Church Yth Grp; FCA; GAA; SADD; Band; Mrchg Band; Var Sec Sftbl; JV Vllybl; Cit Awd; AZ ST U.

GIBSON, ANTHONY T; Riverbank HS; Riverbank, CA; (2); JV Var Ftbl; Var Trk; JV Var Wt Lftg; Cit Awd; Hon Roll; Forest Ranger.

GIBSON, CALEB L; Barstow HS; Barstow, CA; (1); Church Yth Grp; Band; Mrchg Band; Ftbl; Wt Lftg; Wrstlng; Hon Roll; Stanford; Mdcl.

GIBSON, CHERI A; Glen A Wilson HS; Hacienda Hts, CA; (3); Church Yth Grp; Band; Mrchg Band; Powder Puff Ftbl; Var Capt Socr; Var L Trk; Var L Vllybl; High Hon Roll; CSF; Olympc Dvlpmnt Prog; S CA ST Soccer Team; Club Soccer; Bus.

GIBSON, CLAIRE; Trabuco Hills HS; Mission Viejo, CA; (1); UCSB.

GIBSON, JACK J; Whitney HS; Cerritos, CA; (3); Boy Scts; Church Yth Grp; Treas Drama Clb; Church Choir; School Musical; School Play; High Hon Roll; Jr Statesman Amer, VP; Eagle Sct; Bst Actor; Ministry.

GIBSON, KATINA; Lompoc SR HS; Lompoc, CA; (1); Church Yth Grp; FFA; SADD; Chorus; Cit Awd; U C Davis:Nrs Vet.

GIBSON, KIM; Los Alamitos HS; Los Alamitos, CA; (3); Cmnty Wkr; Service Clb; Teachers Aide; Chorus; Color Guard; Flag Corp; Pres Frsh Cls; Off Soph Cls; Off Jr Cls; VP Sr Cls; Gldn ST Xm Awds 87-88; Sci Dept Outstndng Stu Awd 88; Eng Outstndng Stu Awd 90; Jr Hnr Guard Grad 90; UC San Diego; Bio Sci.

GIBSON, MANDI; Red Bluff Union HS; Red Bluff, CA; (2); 7/460; Church Yth Grp; Band; Mrchg Band; Orch; Cheerldng; High Hon Roll; CSF; Gldn St Exam Geom Rcgntn; Steering Cmmtte; UC Davis; Bio.

GIBSON, MICHAEL; Palm Desert HS; Palm Desert, CA; (4); 31/321; Am Leg Boys St; Boy Scts; Church Yth Grp; Cmnty Wkr; Debate Tm; German Clb; ROTC; Var Bsktbl; Trk; Hon Roll; West Point Acad; Hstry.

GIBSON, MIKE; Laguna Beach HS; Laguna Beach, CA; (2); Band; Mrchg Band; Cal Poly; Engrng.

GIBSON, PEGGY; Winters HS; Winters, CA; (4); 16/75; Cmnty Wkr; Sec FBLA; Intnl Clb; Teachers Aide; Ed Nwsp; Pres Acad Fit Awd; Bio Rsrch.

GIBSON, RICHARD A; Valencia HS; Placentia, CA; (4); Boy Scts; Church Yth Grp; Teachers Aide; Band; Church Choir; Mrchg Band; Pep Band; Hon Roll; Retail Shop Ownr.

GIBSON, SARA; Lincoln HS; French Camp, CA; (3); 98/592; NFL; Ski Clb; Speech Tm; JV Vllybl; Hon Roll; Bynd War I Glbl Awrnss Clb; Mrn Bio.

GIBSON, SUZANNE K; Livermore HS; Livermore, CA; (4); Dance Clb; Pep Clb; Varsity Clb; Nwsp; Lit Mag; Var JV Socr; Var L Trk; High Hon Roll; Hon Roll; Golden St Exam Alg & Geom Hnrs; Las Positas; Acctng.

GIBSON, VICKI S; Beaumont HS; Beaumont, CA; (3); Church Yth Grp; Cmnty Wkr; French Clb; FHA; Math Clb; Science Clb; Spanish Clb; Color Guard; Mrchg Band; Ntl Merit Ltr; Award For Hghst Avg Indian Stu; Awd Fashion Design & Merchandizing; Hnr Roll; Jr Hnr Guard; Fashion Merchandizing.

GIBSON, YOURIE; La Mirada HS; La Mirada, CA; (3); Church Yth Grp; Cmnty Wkr; Key Clb; Pep Clb; Spanish Clb; Speech Tm; Band; Var L Color Guard; JV Tennis; Var Trk; Peer Cnslr; SOS Sec & VP; Yth To Yth; Sociology.

GIDDENS, IAN; Cathedral HS; Los Angeles, CA; (4); 3/108; Computer Clb; Math Clb; High Hon Roll; Ca Schalrshp Fed; U Of CA Davis; Vet.

GIDDINGS, BRANDY C; Sonora HS; Sonora, CA; (2); 58/336; Girl Scts; SADD; Var Cheerldng; Cit Awd; Intl Ordr Rainbow; Law.

GIDDINGS, NICOLE L; San Diego Acad; Bonita, CA; (3); Church Yth Grp; Ski Clb; Varsity Clb; VP Band; Chorus; Sec Soph Cls; Capt Bsbl; Capt Ftbl; Capt Gym; High Hon Roll; SA Publcty Dir VP 89-90; Gymnst Yr 88-90; MVP Bsbll 88-90; Pacific Union Coll; Phys Thrpy.

GIDO, CYNTHIA T; Hogan SR HS; Vallejo, CA; (4); Dance Clb; DECA; FBLA; Ski Clb; Band; Mrchg Band; Orch; Pep Band; Variety Show; Gym; Diablo Valley Coll; Bus.

GIENG, ROBERT; Skyline HS; Oakland, CA; (3); Hon Roll; CSU; Bus Law.

GIENG, TRAN S; Lowell HS; San Francisco, CA; (2); Red Cross Aide; Science Clb.

GIER, ANTHONY J; Grossmont HS; San Diego, CA; (4); Church Yth Grp; Cmnty Wkr; Intnl Clb; Chorus; School Play; Rep Stu Cncl; San Diego ST U; Bus.

GIESING, TED; Tracy Joint Union HS; Stockton, CA; (4); 6/459; Am Leg Boys St; Pres 4-H; Pres Stu Cncl; JV Diving; JV Swmmng; Cit Awd; 4-H Awd; High Hon Roll; Rotary Awd; Cal Poly San Luis Obispo; Engr.

GIESSNER, KRISTI; Capuchino HS; San Bruno, CA; (1); Church Yth Grp; Cmnty Wkr; GAA; High Hon Roll; AYSO Soccer Coach; U CA-SAN Diego; Law.

GIETZEN, CHERIE; Los Alamitos HS; Orange, CA; (3); French Clb; Chorus; School Musical; Hon Roll; CA Schltc Soc; Orange Cnty HD Arts Mscl Theater; Grls Ensmbl Chrs; Prfrmng Arts.

GIFFITH, LINDA D; Rio Lindo Adventist Acad; Manteca, CA; (3); Church Yth Grp; Cmnty Wkr; Hosp Aide; Library Aide; Ski Clb; Spanish Clb; Church Choir; Variety Show; Bsktbl; Ftbl; Cert Nurses Asst; CPR Cert; Tchr Kndrgrtn Honduras; Pacific Union Coll; RN.

GIFFORD, MELISSA E; North HS; Bakersfield, CA; (3); French Clb; ROTC; Acpl Chr; Swing Chorus; Variety Show; Hon Roll; U CA Los Angeles.

GIFFORD, PETER B; Sacred Heart Preparatory HS; Palo Alto, CA; (2); Boy Scts; Lit Mag; Sec Treas Soph Cls; Crs Cntry; Socr; High Hon Roll; Hon Roll; NHS; Rotary Awd; Dscpln Cmmttee; Env Club; Skmbrdng & Lacrosse; Med.

GIFFORD, SHII; Liberty Union HS; Oakley, CA; (3); 52/405; FCA; Letterman Clb; Varsity Clb; Var Sftbl; Var Vllybl; Frgn Lang Stud Month-Spnsh; UC Davis; Vet Med.

GIGANTE, TINA M; College Park HS; Pleasant Hill, CA; (3); Church Yth Grp; Drama Clb; Service Clb; Spanish Clb; School Musical; Hon Roll; Youth Edctr; Rep Ot Teen To Teen Hotline; Pres Friday Night Live; St Marys Clg; Psych.

GIGLI, CRAIG A; Carlmont HS; Redwood City, CA; (4); Band; Bsbl; Ftbl; Wt Lftg; Hon Roll; San Mateo; Music.

GIL, CHRISTINA M; Santa Barbara HS; Santa Barbara, CA; (3); Jazz Dance; Cosmetology; Cosmetology.

GIL, CHRISTOPHER M; Clovis West HS; Fresno, CA; (3); Letterman Clb; Ski Clb; Spanish Clb; Rep Stu Cncl; Ftbl; Vllybl; Ldrshp Camp; Bass Clb; CAP Summr Schl Teacher Aide.

GIL, DAVID; Irvine HS; Irvine, CA; (3); 25/520; AFS; Boy Scts; Debate Tm; Ski Clb; Stu Cncl; Intrml JV Ftbl; Intrml JV Vllybl; Intrml Wrstlng; Hon Roll; UCLA; Bus.

GIL, FRITZEL H; Sweetwater Union HS; National City, CA; (3); Hon Roll; Asian Intl Assoc; San Diego ST U; Reg Nurse.

GIL, GEORGE H; Turlock HS; Turlock, CA; (3); 115/700; Church Yth Grp; Cmnty Wkr; Varsity Clb; Var Intrml Bsbl; JV Bsktbl; Intrml Ftbl; Hon Roll; Rotary Awd; Stu Of Month; OR ST U; Forestry.

GIL, LISA M; Bishop Amat HS; West Covina, CA; (3); JV Var Bsktbl; Powder Puff Ftbl; Score Keeper; Var Sftbl; Hon Roll; NHS.

GIL-OSORIO, DIANA I; Santa Cruz HS; Santa Cruz, CA; (3); 1/400; Church Yth Grp; Cmnty Wkr; Drama Clb; Spanish Clb; Hist Thesps; Chorus; School Musical; School Play; Stage Crew; High Hon Roll; Russian Club; Intl Rltns.

GILBERT, APRIL V; Hesperia HS; Hesperia, CA; (2); Church Yth Grp; Bsktbl; Hon Roll; Modeling.

GILBERT, BESSIE E; Del Oro HS; Loomis, CA; (3); 27/266; Church Yth Grp; Chorus; Church Choir; Bsktbl; Socr; Vllybl; High Hon Roll; Hon Roll; Cum Laude Awd; Athl Awd; Sierra Coll; Teacher.

GILBERT, BRIAN A; Moreno Valley HS; Moreno Valley, CA; (3); Model UN; ROTC; Color Guard; Drill Tm; Intrml Bsbl; Intrml Ftbl; Var Wrstlng; Prfct Atten Awd; Pop Warner Stu Coach.

GILBERT, BUFFY; Corcoran HS; Corcoran, CA; (4); 3/130; Pep Clb; Ski Clb; Band; Pep Band; Sec Frsh Cls; Stu Cncl; JV Cheerldng; JV Pom Pon; JV Vllybl; High Hon Roll; Child Psych.

GILBERT, HEIDI; John N North HS; Riverside, CA; (2); 194/510; Swing Chorus; Tennis; Hon Roll; Tnns Awd; Choir Awds; Acappella Choir; Chroprctr.

GILBERT, JENNIFER D; El Camino Real HS; West Hills, CA; (2); Pep Clb; Ski Clb; Teachers Aide; Rep Frsh Cls; Rep Soph Cls; Var Tennis; L Trk; Hon Roll; UCLA; Psych.

GILBERT, JENNIFER G; El Camino Real HS; West Hills, CA; (2); Thesps; High Hon Roll; Hon Roll; CSF; Eclgy Clb; 4th Pl Drama Cmptn; UCLA.

GILBERT, JENNIFER J; Trabuco Hills HS; El Toro, CA; (3); 79/350; Pres Church Yth Grp; School Musical; Stu Cncl; JV Var Bsktbl; JV Var Cheerldng; Intrml Lcrss; Intrml Socr; JV Trk; Intrml Vllybl; Hon Roll; BYU Provo; Elem Ed.

GILBERT, KEVIN C; University HS; Irvine, CA; (3); French Clb; Math Clb; Math Tm; Quiz Bowl; Science Clb; Acad Decathlon.

GILBERT, LISA A; Aptos HS; Aptos, CA; (1); 1/396; Service Clb; Orch; Var Tennis; High Hon Roll; Hon Roll; Prfct Atten Awd; Clarinet Sect Ldr Yth Symphny; Actv Interact Clb.

GILBERT, MARGARET; Santa Paula Union HS; Santa Paula, CA; (4); 20/190; Church Yth Grp; Drama Clb; French Clb; Science Clb; Teachers Aide; Drill Tm; Hon Roll; CA Schlrshp Fed; Wrk Crls Jr; Flmd Wrstlng Tm; Ventura Coll; Robotics.

GILBERT, MICHAEL W; Mount Whitney HS; Visalia, CA; (2); Boy Scts; Sec VICA; Swmmng; Water Polo.

GILBERT, MICHELE L; Tehachapi HS; Tehachapi, CA; (3); Church Yth Grp; French Clb; FHA; Library Aide; Sec Stu Cncl; Powder Puff Ftbl; Cit Awd; Hon Roll; NHS; Pres Acad Fit Awd; CA ST Fullerton.

GILBERT, REBECCA; Davis SR HS; Davis, CA; (4); Band; Mrchg Band; Pep Band; Lit Mag; Sec Frsh Cls; Stu Cncl; JV Socr; Hon Roll; PEACE Club; Crcker Art Museum CCAC Hnrs Drwng Wrkshp; Wrk Exprnc Stu Mnth 89; Humboldt; Art Grphcs.

GILBERT, SHIRIN C; Beacon Christian HS; Foster City, CA; (2); Church Yth Grp; Chorus; Rep Frsh Cls; Sec Pres Stu Cncl; Var Co-Capt Cheerldng; Sftbl; Hon Roll; Daniel Awd Courage To Stand Alone; Cert Of Excllnc Bible; Alg II; Bio.

GILBERT, STEPHANIE F; Modesto HS; Modesto, CA; (3); Church Yth Grp; Dance Clb; Office Aide; Pep Clb; Sec Spanish Clb; Ski Clb; Band; Color Guard; Drill Tm; Mrchg Band; Panther Awds; Outstndng Color Guard Awd; Outstndng Marching Awd; Vet.

GILBERT, STEPHANIE L; San Marcos HS; San Marcos, CA; (3); Cit Awd; Hon Roll; San Diego ST U; Sci.

GILBERT, SUSAN E; Saratoga HS; Saratoga, CA; (1); Drama Clb; Chorus; School Musical; Vllybl; High Hon Roll; Hon Roll; NHS; Law.

GILBERT, TARA; Bret Harte HS; Angels Camp, CA; (2); Drama Clb; Spanish Clb; Band; Chorus; School Musical; School Play; Vllybl; Hon Roll; Friday Night Live Clb; Chorus Lip Awd; U CA Berkeley; Law.

GILBERTSON, JUDY MIYUKI; Pilgrim HS; Los Angeles, CA; (2); Church Yth Grp; Teachers Aide; Chorus; Rep Nwsp; VP Soph Cls; JV Bsktbl; JV Var Vllybl; Cit Awd; Jr NHS; NHS; Japanese Taiko Drums, Zenshuji Zendeko; USC; Bus.

GILCHRIST, BRIAN E; El Cajon Valley HS; El Cajon, CA; (4); 89/297; Letterman Clb; Spanish Clb; Ftbl; Vllybl; Wt Lftg; Hon Roll; Grossmont Coll; Engrng.

GILCHRIST, HEATHER A; Irvine HS; Irvine, CA; (3); Cmnty Wkr; Teachers Aide; Mrchg Band; Var Crs Cntry; Var Socr; Var Trk; Hon Roll; NHS; Heritage Awd/Spanish; Athlete Schlor; Coaches Awd; Var Track Frshm Yr; Mem Schl 1st Aide/Medical Team; UC System; Medical Field.

GILDARD, SIANA-LEA V; Hesperia HS; Hesperia, CA; (2); 32/768; Hist FBLA; Office Aide; Spanish Clb; Var Capt Tennis; Schl Cnty Wrtng Clebration 1st Pl Shrt Stry Poetry; Recgntn Schl Brd Trustees; CA Lthrn U; Lthrn Minister.

GILES, ANGELA M; Mt Diablo HS; W Pittsburg, CA; (2); #1 In Class; French Clb; Rep Frsh Cls; Rep Stu Cncl; Hon Roll; Margaret S Macradie Memrl Schlrshp; Frshmn Undergrad Awd; Exec Bus.

GILES, LARRY T; Temecula Valley HS; Murrieta, CA; (2); Letterman Clb; Varsity Clb; Var JV Ftbl; Var JV Trk; Var Wrstlng; U MI; Phys Thrpy.

GILES, MICHELLE E; Westlake HS; Westlake Vlg, CA; (2); Drama Clb; Hosp Aide; Thesps; School Play; Socr; High Hon Roll; Jrnslm.

GILFILLEN, TRICIA L; Hilltop HS; Chula Vista, CA; (2); Church Yth Grp; SADD; Band; Church Choir; Mrchg Band; Pep Band; Cit Awd; Hon Roll; Outstndng Mscn; CA Schlrshp Fed; UCSD; Pdtrcn.

GILHAM, MICHAEL D; Castle Park HS; Chula Vista, CA; (2); Drama Clb; School Play; Stage Crew; Cit Awd; Prfct Atten Awd; Intrml Bsbl; Intrml Bsktbl; Intrml Ftbl; Intrml Socr; Intrml Sftbl; U S Marine Corp; Sec Forces.

GILHAUSEN, JENNIFER J; Villa Park HS; Orange, CA; (3); Cmnty Wkr; Latin Clb; Lit Mag; CSF; AWS; Art Dsgn.

GILL, BOBBY S; California HS; San Ramon, CA; (4); 380/414; Crs Cntry; Trk; Wt Lftg; UC Davis; Bus.

GILL, GURPREET S; Rio Linda HS; Sacramento, CA; (2); Chess Clb; Quiz Bowl; Science Clb; Temple Yth Grp; High Hon Roll; Aeronautics Clb Scrtry; Kwldge Bowl Awd; Math Dept Awd; UC, Davis; MD.

GILL, INDU; San Pasqual HS; Escondido, CA; (3); Chorus; CA Gldn St Exam Geo & Alg.

GILL, JENNIFER M; Mayfair HS; Lakewood, CA; (3); Church Yth Grp; JA; Letterman Clb; Ski Clb; SADD; Teachers Aide; Varsity Clb; Yrbk; JV Bsktbl; Powder Puff Ftbl; LBCC; Sociology.

GILL, JEREMIAH D; University City HS; Spring Valley, CA; (4); Model UN; Science Clb; Variety Show; Rep Jr Cls; Var L Ftbl; Capt Pom Pon; Powder Puff Ftbl; Var Capt Trk; Hon Roll; Ntl Merit Ltr; Young Life; Black Stu Union Orgnzr; U Of CA Los Angeles; Psych.

GILL, KEISHA M; Dorsey HS; Los Angeles, CA; (2); SADD; Teachers Aide; Chorus; Cheerldng; Diving; Powder Puff Ftbl; Sftbl; Swmmng; Tennis; Trk; Morehouse Coll; FBI.

GILL, LEENA; Simi HS; Simi Valley, CA; (2); Nwsp; Bsktbl; Score Keeper; Trk; Cit Awd; Sprts Edtr Nwsp; Santa Barbara; Bus Mgmt.

GILL, MICHELLE; San Mateo HS; Foster City, CA; (4); 1/330; Debate Tm; Temple Yth Grp; Varsity Clb; Tennis; High Hon Roll; Hon Roll; Mc Conville Awd Spnsh; Trig, Math Anlys Awds; MVP Bdmntn Twc; Tandy Schlr; UCLA; Poli Sci.

GILL, SARAH; Rio Mesa HS; Camarillo, CA; (4); 14/386; Sec VP Drama Clb; School Musical; School Play; Treas Frsh Cls; Sec Sr Cls; Trk; NHS; Opt Clb Awd; Pres Acad Fit Awd; U Of CA Santa Cruz Rgnst Schlrshp; HS Elmont W Michaelson Schlrshp; Camp Cnslr & Israeli Dnc Tchr; U Of CA Santa Cruz; Soclgy.

GILL, SHELLY K; Santa Teresa HS; San Jose, CA; (3); French Clb; Hon Roll.

GILL, TISHA M; American Christian Acad; Cottonwood, CA; (4); 2/11; Drama Clb; Treas 4-H; School Play; VP Sr Cls; Var L Vllybl; 4-H Awd; Sal; CA St Hrsemns Assn-Queen Regn 18 & Wstrn Grl Chmpn; Vllybl MVP 90; Shasta Coll; Dntstry.

GILLELAND, RYAN D; Bullard HS; Fresno, CA; (1); Ski Clb; Swmmng; Vllybl; Hon Roll; Surfrider Fndtn Protect The Ocean; Marine Bio.

GILLEN, ADRIENNE S; Novato HS; Novato, CA; (3); Church Yth Grp; Key Clb; Spanish Clb; Band; School Musical; Lit Mag; Capt Crs Cntry; Var Swmmng; Hon Roll.

GILLESPIE, BARBARA A; Canyon Springs HS; Moreno Valley, CA; (3); Bsktbl; Var L Sftbl; Var L Vllybl; High Hon Roll; Psych.

GILLESPIE, CHRISTINA I; Marymount HS; Los Angeles, CA; (3); Cmnty Wkr; Dance Clb; SADD; Nwsp; Yrbk; Lit Mag; High Hon Roll; St Schlr; Environmental Action Club Founder; Yale Bk Awd; Renselear Polytech Inst Awd For Math & Sci.

GILLESPIE, GRETCHEN; Ponderosa HS; Diamond Springs, CA; (3); 43/316; Am Leg Aux Girls St; Scholastic Bowl; Ski Clb; SADD; Stu Cncl; Trk; Rotary Awd; MVP Ski Team V; All Leag; St Rep; Acad Decathlon Team; Western ST Coll CO; Educ.

GILLETT, LOWELLE K; Etna HS; Callahan, CA; (3); Church Yth Grp; Cmnty Wkr; Chorus; Phtg Nwsp; Capt Bsktbl; JV Socr; Capt Sftbl; JV Trk; JV Vllybl.

GILLETTE, MONICA G; Saint Monica Catholic HS; Los Angeles, CA; (3); Church Yth Grp; French Clb; Sec Treas Key Clb; Pep Clb; VP NHS; CS Schlrshp Fed; Dance Ballet 14 Hrs A Wk; Comm.

GILLETTE, WENDY L; Louisville HS; Calabasas, CA; (3); Pres Church Yth Grp; Cmnty Wkr; Model UN; Acpl Chr; Chorus; Church Choir; School Musical; High Hon Roll; NHS; St Schlr.

GILLEY, CANDACE; Durham HS; Eureka, CA; (4); Art Clb; Church Yth Grp; Key Clb; SADD; Varsity Clb; Band; School Musical; JV Sftbl; Coll Of Redwoods; Engrng.

GILLEY, DANIEL B; Redlands HS; Redlands, CA; (2); 17/1100; CSF; Dept Awd Alge II; Bsbl, Tennis.

GILLIAM, KAREN E; Santana HS; Santee, CA; (4); 89/564; Drama Clb; Sec Intnl Clb; Teachers Aide; Off Jr Cls; Off Sr Cls; Photo Clb; N AZ U; Vet.

GILLIAM, STACEY LYNN; Arroyo Grande HS; Arroyo Grande, CA; (2); 54/239; Church Yth Grp; Cmnty Wkr; FCA; French Clb; GAA; Girl Scts; Varsity Clb; Nwsp; Var Bsbl; Var Bsktbl; Cal Poly; Phys Ed.

GILLIAM, WADE; Wade Gilliam HS; Westminster, CA; (2); 12/31; Church Yth Grp; VP Frsh Cls; Var L Bsbl; JV Bsktbl; Var L Ftbl; Wt Lftg; Hon Roll; All Leag 1st Team Bsbl 1st Base; U Of CA Irvine; Engr.

GILLIAMS, GLENYCE S; El Cerrito HS; Richmond, CA; (2); Church Yth Grp; Debate Tm; Girl Scts; Rep Soph Cls; High Hon Roll; Spanish NHS; Stu Ambssdr Soviet Union Smmr 90; Finance Cmmtee Trnee; U Of CA Berkeley Prtnrshp Prgrm; Yale; Obstrcn.

GILLIAN, LARA T; Armenian Mesrobian HS; Los Angeles, CA; (2); Drama Clb; Library Aide; Quiz Bowl; Teachers Aide; High Hon Roll; Hon Roll; Loyola; Pharmacy.

GILLIATT, DOREA M; Summerville Union HS; Mi-Wuk Village, CA; (3); 1/100; Church Yth Grp; Hosp Aide; Scholastic Bowl; Spanish Clb; Flag Corp; High Hon Roll; Rotary Awd; CSF; Bus Admin.

GILLIES, MICHELLE; Ygnacio Valley HS; Concord, CA; (4); 24/360; Am Leg Aux Girls St; Cmnty Wkr; Debate Tm; GAA; SADD; Teachers Aide; Varsity Clb; Ed Nwsp; Capt Vllybl; Cit Awd; Ecology Clb Fndr & Pres; U Of CA Santa Barbara; Soc Sci.

GILLILAND, AUDREY; Junipero Serra HS; San Diego, CA; (1); Pep Clb; Cheerldng; Cit Awd; High Hon Roll; Prfct Atten Awd.

GILLILAND, ELIZABETH A; Castilleja Schl; Menlo Park, CA; (3); JCL; Math Tm; Treas Frsh Cls; Treas Soph Cls; Var Swmmng; 4-H Awd; Hugh O'brien Yth Ldrshp Smnr 1989; Pres Clsstm 1990; Vrsty Watrpolo; Amnsty Ntl; Slavis Stud.

GILLIS, BRYN A; Dana Hills HS; Laguna Niguel, CA; (3); Stu Cncl; Var L Vllybl; Mssn Vly Vllybl Clb; Wrtng.

GILLIS, RAINIE; Desert Christian HS; Lancaster, CA; (2); Ed Yrbk; Intrml Tennis; High Hon Roll; The Masters Coll; Educ.

GILLISON, DWAYNE E; Bassett HS; La Puente, CA; (3); English Clb; Teachers Aide; Off Jr Cls; Bsbl; Crs Cntry; Ftbl; Trk; Vllybl; Wt Lftg; Wrstlng; ELP/Gate; Acctng.

GILLISPIE, ANIKA; St Bonaventure HS; Camarillo, CA; (2); Church Yth Grp; JV Var Cheerldng; JV Var Socr; Teacher.

GILLOT, ANNIQUE G; Bonita Vista HS; Bonita, CA; (1); Chorus; School Play; JV Swmmng; DAR Awd; 4-H Awd; Hon Roll; Pres Acad Fit Awd.

GILLOT, JANINE S; Bonita Vista HS; Bonita, CA; (2); 1/600; Chorus; JV Swmmng; Cit Awd; High Hon Roll; Hon Roll; Masonic Awd; Ntl Merit Ltr; Natl City Swim Clb; Golden St Exam Geom Hgh Hnrs; US Swmmng; UC Davis; Zoology.

GILLUM, KRISTINA M; Newport Harbor HS; Newport Beach, CA; (2); Chorus; Crs Cntry; Trk; UCI; Math.

GILMAN, MICHAEL; Seaside HS; Henderson, TX; (3); 70/210; Art Clb; Debate Tm; Math Tm; Pep Clb; ROTC; SADD; Color Guard; Drill Tm; Flag Corp; Stage Crew; Marion Military Inst; Mil Sci.

GILMAN, TAMI; Poway HS; San Diego, CA; (3); GAA; Varsity Clb; Stat Socr; Var L Sftbl; JV Vllybl; Hon Roll; NHS; Pres Acad Fit Awd; U CA; Psych.

GILMER, RASHAWN; Mt Eden HS; Hayward, CA; (4); 2/269; Math Clb; Office Aide; Teachers Aide; Var L Bsktbl; Var L Crs Cntry; Powder Puff Ftbl; Var Capt Trk; Hon Roll; Ntl Hispanic Schlrshp Awd Semi-Fnlst; Ntl Naval Officers Assn Schlrshp Wnnr.

GILMORE, ERICLEE R; Fresno Christian HS; Fresno, CA; (2); Church Yth Grp; Sec Frsh Cls; JV Capt Bsktbl; JV Capt Ftbl; JV Var Trk; High Hon Roll; Fresno ST U; Math.

GILMORE, JAMES A; Inglewood HS; Inglewood, CA; (2); Aud/Vis; Band; Nwsp; Off Soph Cls; Hon Roll; Med Doc.

GILMORE, MICHELLE; Mountain Empire HS; Pine Valley, CA; (2); Church Yth Grp; Pep Clb; Spanish Clb; Var Cheerldng; Var Score Keeper; Hon Roll; Hrn Soc Club; Csmtlgy.

GILMORE, TAMARA; Francis Polytechnic HS; Pacoima, CA; (3); Church Yth Grp; Dance Clb; Drama Clb; GAA; Pep Clb; Church Choir; School Play; Var Trk; Hon Roll; Rotary Awd; Trck Awds; Amer Lgn Axlry Girls ST; Natl Baptist Cong; UNLV; Pltcl Sci.

GILPIN, JENNIFER L; Rio Vista HS; Rio Vista, CA; (3); Art Clb; Aud/Vis; Office Aide; Teachers Aide; Hon Roll; Friday Night Live; Modelng.

GILPIN, LISA R; Lindsay HS; Lindsay, CA; (3); FHA; Teachers Aide; Score Keeper; Tennis; Hon Roll; Crt Reprtr.

GIM, BEEIN; Walnut HS; Walnut, CA; (2); French Clb; Key Clb; Letterman Clb; Drill Tm; Sprt Ed Nwsp; Off Soph Cls; Var L Crs Cntry; Var L Trk; High Hon Roll; GATE Clb; CSF; POWER Clb; Comm/Jrnlsm.

GIM, JASON Y; St Anthony HS; Lakewood, CA; (3); Church Yth Grp; Cmnty Wkr; Letterman Clb; Varsity Clb; Ftbl; Powder Puff Ftbl; Trk; Wt Lftg; Cit Awd; High Hon Roll; UC Irvine; Bio.

GIM, TONY; Pilgrim Schl; Los Angeles, CA; (3); Model UN; Stage Crew; Yrbk; Var Bsbl; JV Var Bsktbl; Var Ftbl; Wt Lftg; Cit Awd; Hon Roll; NHS; Berkeley; Law.

GIMENEZ, VERONICA; Marina HS; Huntington Bch, CA; (4); Church Yth Grp; Office Aide; Spanish Clb; Lit Mag; Hon Roll; Gldn Shld Awds Engl,Spnsh; NCETS Acht Wrtng Fnlst; Disneyland Crtv Wrtng Cont; Golden West; Child Psych.

GIN, LISA; Phillip & Sala Burton Academic HS; San Francisco, CA; (2); French Clb; Math Clb; School Musical; 4-H Awd; High Hon Roll; Jr NHS; Comp Sci.

GIN, TIMMY W; Oakland HS; Oakland, CA; (4); 14/400; Key Clb; Math Clb; Math Tm; Nwsp; Ed Yrbk; Hon Roll; Ntl Merit Ltr; UCLA; Aerospace Engrng.

GINES, CORALISSA; John F Kennedy HS; Granada Hills, CA; (3); Church Yth Grp; Dance Clb; Drama Clb; Pep Clb; Thesps; School Musical; School Play; Stage Crew; Variety Show; Cheerldng; San Diego ST; Dnc.

GINES, NIKKI; St Patrick-St Vincent HS; Vallejo, CA; (4); 45/153; Office Aide; Chorus; Sec Frsh Cls; Pres Soph Cls; VP Jr Cls; Var L Crs Cntry; Capt Pom Pon; Var L Trk; Stat Sftbl; Hon Roll; UC Santa Cruz; Econ.

GINGERY, GRANT A; Alameda HS; Alameda, CA; (1); 150/279; Boy Scts; Church Yth Grp; JV Bsktbl; JV Ftbl; Swmmng; Wt Lftg; Bus.

GINGRAS, MONICA; Junipero Serra HS; San Diego, CA; (3); 16/391; Church Yth Grp; Var L Swmmng; Cit Awd; High Hon Roll; Hon Roll; Kiwanis Awd; Comptv Swimmer; CSF.

GINGRICH, JOEL G; Claremont HS; Claremont, CA; (3); 51/500; Church Yth Grp; German Clb; Church Choir; JV Ftbl; Var Tennis; Hon Roll; Ntl Merit Ltr; Pres Acad Fit Awd; Pegasus Acdmc Tlnt Srch; Choir Piano Accmpnst; Music.

GINN, ANTHONY P; Albany HS; Albany, CA; (1); Rptr Nwsp; Hon Roll; USS Swim Team; Piano 10 Yrs; UC Berkeley; Teacher.

GINN, ERIC R; Agoura HS; Moorpark, CA; (4); Latin Clb; Hon Roll; NHS; UC Davis.

GINN, LUCAS L; Hemet HS; Hemet, CA; (3); 2/539; Cmnty Wkr; Pres French Clb; NFL; Science Clb; Speech Tm; Cit Awd; High Hon Roll; Masonic Awd; Won Blue Ribbon Bhvrl Sci Div Inland Sci Fair 90; 3rd Pl Riverside Ounty Hist Day 89; Sovet Area Studies.

GINNATY, MARCUS J; Edison HS; Huntington Beach, CA; (2); Intrml Bsbl; Intrml Bsktbl; Intrml Crs Cntry; Intrml Ftbl; Intrml JV Socr; Intrml Sftbl; Intrml Tennis; USC.

GINO, CAROLYN D; Clovis HS; Clovis, CA; (3); NFL; Speech Tm; Teachers Aide; Hon Roll; Pres Acad Fit Awd; Crtfd Peer Cnslr; GATE; Fresno ST U; Psych.

GINSBERG, KRISTA; Palos Verdes HS; Palos Verdes Est, CA; (4); Cmnty Wkr; Hosp Aide; Service Clb; Drill Tm; Off Sr Cls; Cheerldng; Pres Acad Fit Awd; U Of CO Boulder; Bus.

GINSBURG, LORI R; Mira Mesa HS; San Diego, CA; (2); Drama Clb; School Musical; Variety Show; Rep Frsh Cls; Treas Soph Cls; Rep Stu Cncl; JV Trk; NHS; Pres Acad Fit Awd.

GINSBURG, ROCHELLE MARIE; Los Alamitos HS; Seal Beach, CA; (3); Drama Clb; Spanish Clb; Teachers Aide; Temple Yth Grp; School Musical; School Play; Stage Crew; Hon Roll; CSF.

GINTER, NATASHA; Monterey Bay Acad; Ahwahnee, CA; (4); Ski Clb; Teachers Aide; Band; Orch; School Musical; School Play; Prfct Atten Awd; Pacific Union Coll; Pre-Med.

GINTER, REBECCA A; Simi Valley HS; Simi Valley, CA; (3); 68/664; Cmnty Wkr; Letterman Clb; Spanish Clb; Var Crs Cntry; Var Trk; JV Vllybl; CJSF.

GINTZ, JANA M; Fremont Christian HS; Fremont, CA; (1); Church Yth Grp; Sec Frsh Cls; JV Bsktbl; JV Var Vllybl; High Hon Roll; Hon Roll; CSF; ACSI Sppechmeet 2nd Pl Readers Theater; Sports Awd & Team Player; JV Vlybl Mst Insprtn JV Bskt; His.

GIORDANO, GUIDO; Loyola HS; Glendale, CA; (4); 20/270; Chess Clb; Church Yth Grp; Teachers Aide; Rptr Nwsp; Yrbk; Intrml Bsktbl; Var Socr; Intrml Vllybl; High Hon Roll; Hon Roll; Slct U-16 Sccr Tm CA All-Strs Rep USA Europn Cups; Clsscl Pianist Music Fstvls; Cum Laude Scty; Biochem.

GIORDANO, PHILIP D; Helix HS; La Mesa, CA; (2); 14/472; Church Yth Grp; School Play; Capt JV Bsktbl; Capt JV Ftbl; High Hon Roll; Pres Acad Fit Awd; JV Ftbl Dfnsv Bk Yr; CSF; Prof Athltcs.

GIORGI, CHRIS B; Red Bluff HS; Red Bluff, CA; (3); 84/450; Boy Scts; FFA; Lit Mag; Bsbl; Ftbl; Hon Roll; Pres Acad Fit Awd; Bus Owner.

GIOVACCHINI, ERIN S; Livermore HS; Livermore, CA; (2); Church Yth Grp; FBLA; Band; Church Choir; Rep Frsh Cls; Pres Soph Cls; Pres Jr Cls; Var Swmmng; JV Vllybl; Hon Roll; U Of Pacific; Pediatric Nurse.

GIOVAN, MICHAEL P; Montgomery HS; Santa Rosa, CA; (2); Key Clb; Spanish Clb; Var Golf; High Hon Roll; Jr NHS; Pres Acad Fit Awd; Prncpls Awd, Lamp Of Knowledge 88-89; Math.

GIP, KIU A; Hoover HS; Fresno, CA; (2); #42 In Class; Fresno ST.

GIPSON, DENISE ELIZABETH; Lindhurst HS; Linda, CA; (2); English Clb; Library Aide; Math Tm; ROTC; Science Clb; SADD; Cit Awd; Hon Roll; Jr NHS; Pres Acad Fit Awd; Berkeley; Sci.

GIRALDO, FABIAN; La Puente HS; La Puente, CA; (2); Church Yth Grp; Science Clb; School Play; Yrbk; Treas VP Frsh Cls; Treas Soph Cls; Treas Jr Cls; Var Swmmng; High Hon Roll; Acad Decathlon; Friend To Friend; Stanford U; Bus.

GIRARD, JOSEPH; Serra HS; San Carlos, CA; (3); 4/187; Church Yth Grp; Cmnty Wkr; Computer Clb; Key Clb; Math Clb; Math Tm; Office Aide; Science Clb; Ski Clb; Teachers Aide; Rensselaer Mdl Math & Sci; Harvard Engl Awd; CSF; US Naval Acad; Military Pilot.

GIRARD JR, MICHAEL P; Oakmont HS; Roseville, CA; (2); JV Bsbl; Ftbl; Hon Roll; CABA All-Trnmt Team MVP; AAU All-Amer Team; Miami; Finance.

GIRARD, REBECCA M; Notre Dame Acad; Venice, CA; (3); 1/112; Drama Clb; Pres Chorus; School Musical; Ed Lit Mag; Crs Cntry; Swmmng; Jr NHS; NHS; LA City Lifeguard; Cmpus Mnstry Love; Marine Bio.

GIRARDI, LAURA B; South San Francisco HS; South San Francis, CA; (3); Cmnty Wkr; Hosp Aide; Italian Clb Trea 1989-90; Latinos Unidos Clb 1989-90; Concrnd Stu Clb 1988-89; Bus.

GIRERD, ANDRE RENE; Palo Alto HS; Palo Alto, CA; (2); Boy Scts; Church Yth Grp; Cmnty Wkr; French Clb; Intnl Clb; Teachers Aide; Rptr Nwsp; JV L Swmmng; JV L Wrstlng; BSA Engrng Explorer Post; CSF; AYSO Soccr; MIT; Aerosp Engr.

GIRGIS, ELIZABETH; Providence HS; Burbank, CA; (3); Pep Clb; Rep Frsh Cls; Sec Soph Cls; Stat Cheerldng; High Hon Roll; Hon Roll; NHS; Cngrssnl Yth Ldrshp Cncl; HOPE Clb; Law.

GIRGIS, MILAD T; Saint Monica HS; Los Angeles, CA; (3); Pres Church Yth Grp; JV Bsktbl; High Hon Roll; NHS; Engrng.

GIRGIS, REMON; John Glenn HS; Norwalk, CA; (2); Off Soph Cls; Ftbl; Wt Lftg; Hon Roll; Doctor.

GIRGUIS, MARK; Bishop Amat HS; West Covina, CA; (3); Church Yth Grp; Letterman Clb; Math Clb; Varsity Clb; Var Crs Cntry; Var Trk; High Hon Roll; NHS; CA Schlrshp Fdrtn; UCLA; Bio Med Engrng.

GIRL, PRIYA D; Miramonte HS; Orinda, CA; (1); NFL; Speech Tm; Hon Roll; Indian Dncng.

GIROD, ERIC A; Serra HS; Foster City, CA; (3); Boy Scts; Church Yth Grp; Cmnty Wkr; Office Aide; Ski Clb; JV Socr; VP Trk; Hon Roll; Pres Schlr; Acad Awds Rcvd Math & French; CSF; Violin Stu; Engr.

GIROD, REBECCA S; Notre Dame HS; Foster City, CA; (2); Cmnty Wkr; Dance Clb; French Clb; Office Aide; SADD; Var Socr; Var Trk; Hon Roll; Piano; Acad Awd Alg 90; Jr Statesman Amer; CSF; Cultural Awrnss Clb; Elem Educ.

GIRON, RODERICK R; Bishop Amat HS; Walnut, CA; (2); Hon Roll; Aerosp Engrg.

GIRON, ROMEO; Bellarmine-Jefferson HS; North Hollywood, CA; (2); French Clb; JV Bsbl; High Hon Roll; Hon Roll; San Diego ST U; Marine Bio.

GISH, ANDREA; Modesto HS; Modesto, CA; (4); 4/450; Church Yth Grp; Spanish Clb; Teachers Aide; Acpl Chr; Cit Awd; Hon Roll; Ntl Merit SF; Yth Grp Camp Commtte 90; Stanislaus Cnty Annual Spllng Bee 89; Gate Clb; Bus Mgmt.

GISLER, MELISSA; Brea-Olinda HS; Brea, CA; (4); 27/307; Mgr GAA; JA; Cheerldng; Capt Gym; High Hon Roll; Ntl Merit Ltr; Pres Acad Fit Awd; CSF; Dstngshd Schlr; Wldct Key; UCSB.

GITLIN, MICHAEL; Saratoga HS; Saratoga, CA; (4); Capt Debate Tm; NFL; Speech Tm; Temple Yth Grp; Band; Mrchg Band; Hon Roll; Ntl Merit Ltr.

GIVARGIS, ASHUR P; Armijo HS; Fairfield, CA; (3); Church Yth Grp; Drama Clb; French Clb; Office Aide; Thesps; Chorus; School Play; Mgr Stage Crew; Bsbl; Tennis; Acad Achvt Awd; Dvrc Law.

GIVENS, JENNIFER; Atwater HS; Atwater, CA; (2); Church Yth Grp; Girl Scts; Speech Tm; Band; Mrchg Band; Pep Band; Hon Roll; Teen Rep Pastrl Cncl; CA Schlrshp Fed CSF; MECCA Makng Electvs Cnt Career Achvt.

GIZIOTIS, GEORGE J; Damien HS; Upland, CA; (4); 11/191; Cmnty Wkr; Letterman Clb; Lit Mag; SADD; Off Frsh Cls; Off Soph Cls; Off Jr Cls; Pres Sr Cls; Var Capt Swmmng; High Hon Roll; CSF; Spk Greek Engl Spnsh; Med.

GIZZI, KAREN L; Casa Grande HS; Petaluma, CA; (3); 41/288; Church Yth Grp; Letterman Clb; Varsity Clb; School Musical; School Play; Stage Crew; Variety Show; JV Powder Puff Ftbl; Var Trk; Hon Roll; Bus.

GJERSWALD, JOY; Victor Valley HS; Bagdad, AZ; (1); Girl Scts; Chorus; Cit Awd; High Hon Roll; Hon Roll; Best Fresh Class Health; Trophie For Being Most Helpful Choir; Socl Wrkr.

GLADDEN, JACQUELINE M; Notre Dame HS; San Jose, CA; (2); Church Yth Grp; Off Soph Cls; Stu Cncl; Hon Roll; NHS; NEDT Awd; Pres Acad Fit Awd; Chorus, Relgn, Robot Awds; Cnty Fair Rbbns, Trophs; Jr Statesmn Amer; CA Schlrshp Soc; Tri-M Music Hnrs; Acctng.

GLADNEY, ALANNA; Yosemite HS; Oakhurst, CA; (2); Art Clb; Treas FBLA; Bus.

GLAFKIDES, DIMITRI T; Bishop O'dowd HS; Oakland, CA; (3); Church Yth Grp; Dance Clb; Var JV Ftbl; Hon Roll; Hnrbl Mntn ESAL Ftbl; Bsktbl Chrch Leag.

GLAISTER, WENDY; Fred C Beyer HS; Modesto, CA; (3); Church Yth Grp; Debate Tm; NFL; Spanish Clb; Speech Tm; Cit Awd; Hon Roll; Voice Dem Awd; WCTU Outstndng Spkr Awd; Teen Rpblcns; Natl Spch & Debate 90; Intl Law.

GLANG, THANH V; Silver Creek HS; San Jose, CA; (4); 95/415; De Anza Coll; Comp Sci.

GLANVILLE, RYAN; Mt Whitney HS; Visalia, CA; (2); Church Yth Grp; Teachers Aide; Var Bsktbl; Hon Roll; MVP Bsktbl 2 Yrs.

GLASCOCK, CHER M; San Bernardino HS; San Bernardino, CA; (4); Church Yth Grp; Key Clb; Teachers Aide; High Hon Roll; Hon Roll; Prfct Atten Awd; Quincy Brown Memrl Schlrshp 90; Bnk Of Amer Achvt Awd In Bus 90; San Bernardino Vly Coll; Acctng.

GLASCOE, DEREK R; Huntington Beach HS; Huntington Beach, CA; (2); Church Yth Grp; Var L Bsbl; High Hon Roll; Hon Roll; Pres Acad Fit Awd; Biola U.

GLASGOW, JASON A; Venice HS; Los Angeles, CA; (1); Church Yth Grp; Cmnty Wkr; Latin Clb; Orch; High Hon Roll; U For Yng Amers; Harvard U; Crdlgst.

GLASGOW, MUTALIB; Eagle Rock HS; Los Angeles, CA; (4); 53/350; Chess Clb; Var L Ftbl; Var L Trk; Hon Roll; Pres Acad Fit Awd; Occidental Coll; Engrng.

GLASPY, KEVIN B; Covina HS; Covina, CA; (3); Var Ftbl; Var Trk; Comp Sci.

GLASS, AMEE; Bethel Christian HS; Lancaster, CA; (3); Church Yth Grp; Teachers Aide; Chorus; Church Choir; Variety Show; Bsktbl; Capt Cheerldng; High Hon Roll; The Masters Coll; Ed.

GLASS, EMILY; Canyon Springs HS; Moreno Valley, CA; (2); Ski Clb; Chorus; High Hon Roll; San Diego ST; Chld Psych.

GLASS, JENNIFER L; Thousand Oaks HS; Newbury Park, CA; (2); Hon Roll; NHS; Moorpark Coll; Bio.

GLASS, KIMBERLY M; College Park HS; Pleasant Hill, CA; (3); Church Yth Grp; Cmnty Wkr; Model UN; Spanish Clb; Church Choir; High Hon Roll; Hon Roll; Fri Nght Live VP; Gldn St Exam Alg I High Hnrs; Fleet Resrv Wrtng Awds 1st Pl Dist, 3rd Pl Rgn; Pepperdine U; Cmmnctns.

GLASSER, JUDD L; Nevada Union HS; Penn Valley, CA; (4); 10/473; Letterman Clb; Math Clb; Math Tm; Science Clb; Teachers Aide; Varsity Clb; Rep Stu Cncl; Bsktbl; Swmmng; Bausch & Lomb Sci Awd; US Swmng Clb Tm; Red Cross; Lifeguard/Wtr Sfty Instr; USAF Rcrtg Svc Math/Sci Awd; U Of CA San Diego; Biophysics.

GLAVIN, DANNY P; San Luis Obispo HS; San Luis Obispo, CA; (2); 3/300; JV Bsbl; JV Bsktbl; JV Wt Lftg; Var L Wrstlng; High Hon Roll; CSF; Gldn Tiger Awd Phys Sci; U Of San Diego.

GLAZE, AYANNA; Folsom HS; Folsom, CA; (3); FBLA; FHA; JA; Library Aide; Chorus; Yrbk; Cit Awd; Hon Roll; Black Stu Union; Bus Mgmt.

GLAZZARD, THERESA M; Theresa Glazzard HS; Burney, CA; (1); Pep Clb; Powder Puff Ftbl; Vllybl; Hon Roll; Artist.

GLEASON, ERIN; Sunny Hills HS; Fullerton, CA; (2); 143/464; Church Yth Grp; Cmnty Wkr; Drama Clb; French Clb; Pep Clb; Ski Clb; SADD; Rep Stu Cncl; JV Var Cheerldng; JV Socr; Natl Charity Leag.

GLEASON, JOSHUA; Hesperia Christian HS; Phelan, CA; (1); Church Yth Grp; 4-H; Bsktbl; Crs Cntry; 4-H Awd; Masters Coll.

GLEASON, KATHY; Alemany HS; Mission Hills, CA; (2); SADD; Swmmng.

GLEASON, MICHELE J; Whittier Christian HS; Yorba Linda, CA; (2); Church Yth Grp; Sec Frsh Cls; Sec Soph Cls; Crs Cntry; Trk; Vllybl; CSF; Astronaut.

GLEASON, STEPHANIE M; Holy Family HS; Glendale, CA; (3); Church Yth Grp; Cmnty Wkr; Debate Tm; GAA; Model UN; Service Clb; Varsity Clb; Acpl Chr; Church Choir; Sec Frsh Cls; Chrch Lctr, Choir; Sprts Med.

GLEAVES, TYRELL D; Westmoor HS; Daly City, CA; (3); Ftbl; High Hon Roll; Hon Roll; UC Berkeley; Auditing.

GLEED, JASON W; East Bakersfield HS; Bakersfield, CA; (4); 28/398; Debate Tm; Drama Clb; English Clb; Letterman Clb; Math Clb; NFL; Speech Tm; Teachers Aide; Varsity Clb; School Play; Bicntnnl Cmptn 1st Pl St; Physcs Club; Adv.

GLEIM, WILLIAM; Central HS; Fresno, CA; (4); 8/150; Letterman Clb; Jazz Band; Var JV Ftbl; Var Socr; High Hon Roll; NHS; S CA U; Elec Engr.

GLEITSMAN, CALEB; Aptos HS; Corralitos, CA; (1); 59/389; JV Bsbl; Hon Roll; GATE Engl & World Cultures; Acting.

GLEMBA, FONDA C; Rubidoux HS; Riverside, CA; (4); AFS; Hosp Aide; Spanish Clb; Off Jr Cls; Off Sr Cls; Stat Bsktbl; Stat Ftbl; High Hon Roll; CSF; Zoology.

GLENN, JAMISON; Foothill HS; Pleasanton, CA; (3); 9/296; Swmmng; Hon Roll; Hstrn CA Schlstc Fndtn; Lawyer.

GLENN, KIMIKO; Cajon HS; San Bernardino, CA; (4); Aud/Vis; Church Yth Grp; Drama Clb; 4-H; French Clb; SADD; Teachers Aide; School Musical; School Play; Cit Awd; CA ST U; Bus Mngmtn.

GLENN, KYLIE JANELLE; Immacuiate Heart HS; Los Angeles, CA; (3); Church Yth Grp; Sec Hist Drama Clb; GAA; Pep Clb; Service Clb; Stage Crew; Variety Show; Rep Frsh Cls; Rep Jr Cls; Mgr(s); Amnsty Intl; Jr Mannequin Assisteens; U Of Southern CA; Commnctns.

GLENN, LATASHIA M; Washington HS; Los Angeles, CA; (2); Church Yth Grp; Pep Clb; Speech Tm; Church Choir; Drill Tm; Yrbk; Stu Cncl; Trk; JETS Awd; TOP; Comp Sci.

GLENN, MICHELLE L; Bishop O'dowd HS; Oakland, CA; (2); Hosp Aide; Ski Clb; Stage Crew; Intrml Cheerldng; Var Swmmng; Stat Tennis; Var Vllybl; Hon Roll; Blck Stu Union; Gospel Choir; Spelman; Physics.

GLENN, SCOTT EUGENE; El Dorado HS; Camino, CA; (4); Boy Scts; Church Yth Grp; NFL; School Play; Ed Yrbk; Pres Sr Cls; Capt Vllybl; Cit Awd; DAR Awd; Elks Awd; Page US Hs Of Rep; Smmr Camp Staff Boy Sct Camp 4 Yrs; Brigham Yng U; Poltcl Sci.

GLENNEN, NICOLE F; Skyline HS; Oakland, CA; (2); Church Yth Grp; Cmnty Wkr; Dance Clb; Drama Clb; SADD; Band; Score Keeper; Swmmng; Tennis; High Hon Roll; San Diego ST; Prfrmng Arts.

GLICK, AARON M; San Marcos HS; San Marcos, CA; (2); Boy Scts; Key Clb; Spanish Clb; JV Ftbl; JV Capt Golf; JV Socr; Hon Roll; Prfct Atten Awd; Yth Comm; AZ ST U; Oceanogrphy.

GLIDDEN, JULIE K; Edison HS; Huntington Bch, CA; (2); Church Yth Grp; Model UN; SADD; Rep Frsh Cls; Rep Soph Cls; JV Swmmng; High Hon Roll; Opt Clb Awd; Engl Acad Achvt Awd; Mst Valuable Soph; Yth In Ldrshp Conf; Cmmnctns.

GLIEBE, CHRISTINE E; Homestead HS; Sunnyvale, CA; (3); Church Yth Grp; Teachers Aide; Published Homesteads Grad Program 89 & 90; Typesetter & Aide Homesteads Computer Tech; Wrangler At Sea; JR Coll; Computer Operations.

GLINES, MELINDA E; Moreau HS; Hayward, CA; (4); 6/300; Church Yth Grp; Cmnty Wkr; Drama Clb; Math Clb; Chorus; School Musical; School Play; High Hon Roll; NHS; Ntl Merit SF; Theatre, Musical & Straight Theatre; Theatre.

GLOCKNER, WHITNEY; Sacred Heart Prep; Woodside, CA; (2); Cmnty Wkr; Model UN; Ski Clb; Chorus; Yrbk; High Hon Roll; Crew; Choir Ensemble; Horseback Riding.

GLORIA, KATHERINE; Fred C Beyer HS; Modesto, CA; (3); Church Choir; Jazz Band; Mrchg Band; Pep Band; Cit Awd; Hon Roll; Prfct Atten Awd; Wind Ensemble, Majorette, Friday Night Live; Psycht.

GLORIA, MARILYN N; Stagg HS; Stockton, CA; (4); SADD; Bsktbl; Powder Puff Ftbl; Sftbl; Cit Awd; Air Force; Nrsng.

GLOVER, CHARLIE; Castlemont HS; Oakland, CA; (4); 3/200; Math Clb; Math Tm; Quiz Bowl; Scholastic Bowl; Yrbk; High Hon Roll; Hon Roll; Kiwanis Awd; NHS; Prfct Atten Awd; UC San Diego; Mech Engrng.

GLOVER, DANNY M; Rincon Valley Christian HS; Santa Rosa, CA; (2); Band; Mrchg Band; Pep Band; Cit Awd; Bio.

GLOVER, DONNY R; Orange Glen HS; Escondido, CA; (1); 127/644; German Clb; Hon Roll.

GLOVER, JYL; Napa HS; Napa, CA; (3); 45/400; Key Clb; Pep Clb; Varsity Clb; Rep Stu Cncl; Var Bsktbl; Var Vllybl; Hon Roll; Pres Acad Fit Awd; People To People Yth Sci Exchnge Russia; Marine Bio.

GLOVER, NORLICE D; Gomper Sci/Comp Magnet HS; San Diego, CA; (1); 48/267; Church Choir; Hon Roll; Pedtrcn.

GLOWACKI, MARIE; Rolling Hills HS; Rolling Hills Est, CA; (2); Church Yth Grp; French Clb; GAA; JV Crs Cntry; JV Trk; Newspaper Stf; Glrs League; Ped Med.

GLUBKA, CHRISTOPHER J; Fontana HS; Fontana, CA; (3); 47/1012; Am Leg Boys St; Math Tm; Ski Clb; Var L Ftbl; Wt Lftg; High Hon Roll; Pres Acad Fit Awd; UC San Diego; Aerntcl Engrng.

GLUCK, MASON T; Irvine HS; Irvine, CA; (2); Wt Lftg; Hon Roll; PTA Awd Grd Imprvmnt; CO U; Engr.

GLUECK, JESSE J; De La Salle HS; Walnut Creek, CA; (3); 100/230; Aud/Vis; Church Yth Grp; Intrml Bsktbl; UC San Luis Obispo; Bus.

GLYNN, ALLYSON K; Bonita Vista HS; Bonita, CA; (1); Church Yth Grp; Ed Nwsp; Ed Yrbk; Var Cheerldng; JV Swmmng; Hon Roll; Competitive Gymnstcs Team.

GLYNN, MICHAEL R; Portola JR-SR HS; Portola, CA; (2); Boy Scts; Letterman Clb; Spanish Clb; Varsity Clb; Band; Mrchg Band; Mgr Yrbk; VP Soph Cls; Var L Bsbl; JV L Ftbl; Altar Boy Cath Church; GPA; West Point; Bio.

GLYNN, SEAN P; Granada Hills HS; Northridge, CA; (3); Church Yth Grp; Ed Yrbk; Var Vllybl; CA Lutheran U.

GO, EDDY J; Homestead HS; Sunnyvale, CA; (1); Spanish Clb; Socr; High Hon Roll; CSF; Badminton; UC Berkeley; Engr.

GO, NOEL L; St Anthony HS; Long Beach, CA; (2); Cmnty Wkr; Cit Awd; Hon Roll; Prfct Atten Awd; CSF; Standford U; Med.

GO, VINCENT A; Sequoia HS; Redwood City, CA; (3); Orch; San Fran Cnsrvtry Music; Music.

GOARE, CHRISTA E; Folsom HS; Folsom, CA; (3); Church Yth Grp; Girl Scts; Teachers Aide; Band; Cheerldng; Stat Wrstlng; Hon Roll; Dancing Tennis; Twirl Baton; CA ST; Acctng.

GOATLEY, MICHELLE; Bear River HS; Grass Valley, CA; (4); Cmnty Wkr; Hosp Aide; Letterman Clb; Office Aide; SADD; Teachers Aide; Chorus; Swmmng; High Hon Roll; Sonoma ST U; Psych.

GOBBI, MARY; Tomales HS; Petaluma, CA; (3); FFA; Letterman Clb; Spanish Clb; Ed Nwsp; Rep Soph Cls; JV Cheerldng; JV Var Vllybl; High Hon Roll; Hon Roll; Empire Bus Clg; Court Reporting.

GOBER, KATIE J; Escondido HS; Escondido, CA; (1); Church Yth Grp; Hon Roll; Stu Of Mnth; USD; Poli Sci.

GOCHOEL, LENNA; South Fork HS; Garberville, CA; (4); 6/60; Cmnty Wkr; DECA; Pep Clb; Acpl Chr; School Play; Cheerldng; Crs Cntry; Powder Puff Ftbl; Wt Lftg; Peer Cnslr; CPR & First Aid Certs; Life Guard.

GOCHOEL, YVONNE LENNA; South Fork HS; Garberville, CA; (4); 6/56; Pep Clb; Acpl Chr; School Play; Cheerldng; Crs Cntry; Powder Puff Ftbl; Wt Lftg; Hon Roll; Kiwanis Awd; Pr Cnslr; CSF; Photo; U Of Santa Cruz.

GODBERSON, SAMANTHA L; Mt Whitney HS; Visalia, CA; (3); FBLA; GAA; Hon Roll; Tulare Cnty Sheriff Explr; Campus Life; Fresno ST; Bus Mgmt.

GODDARD, AJ J; Del Notre HS; Crescent City, CA; (1); Library Aide; Quiz Bowl; Teachers Aide; JV Bsbl; JV Bsktbl; Intrml Golf; Stat Score Keeper; Hon Roll; U NE Las Vegas; Commnctns.

GODEZANO, GLEN MARK M; Archbishop Riordan HS; San Francisco, CA; (3); Intnl Clb; Band; Trk; Bausch & Lomb Sci Awd; High Hon Roll; Hon Roll; Pacific Rim Club; Crusader Bro; U Of CA Davis; Civil Engr.

GODFREY, CHARLES; Brethren HS; Cypress, CA; (3); 3/56; Math Tm; Crs Cntry; Var L Socr; High Hon Roll; Hon Roll; Voice Dem Awd; Engrng.

GODFREY, JENNIFER; Casa Roble Fundamental HS; Mt Olive, AL; (2); Treas Sec German Clb; Ski Clb; Stage Crew; Rep Soph Cls; JV Var Swmmng; Cit Awd; High Hon Roll; Hon Roll; NHS; Friday Night Live; Stu Reaching Out; UCLA; Psych.

GODINA, RAMIRO T; El Camino HS; San Luis Rey, CA; (3); 13/364; High Hon Roll; Prfct Atten Awd; CSF; El Camino Sci Awd; Chem.

GODINEZ, ANNA L; Santa Barbara HS; Santa Barbara, CA; (3); Band; Mrchg Band; Pep Band; JV Var Sftbl; Hon Roll; Psych.

GODINEZ, ERIC; Hueneme HS; Oxnard, CA; (1); Boy Scts; Church Yth Grp; JA; Var L Swmmng; Hon Roll; Prfct Atten Awd; UA Tucson; Law.

GODINEZ, ISABEL; Porterville HS; Porterville, CA; (3); Church Yth Grp; Library Aide; Drill Tm; Mrchg Band; Hon Roll; Porterville Coll; CPA.

GODINEZ, JEANETTE; Los Amigos HS; Santa Ana, CA; (3); 8/365; French Clb; Spanish Clb; High Hon Roll; Hon Roll; ROP Nrs Asstnc Cls Awd Of Merit For Compltn; Acadmc Achvt Cert Awd.

GODINEZ, LUCILA A; St Genevieve HS; Arleta, CA; (3); Church Yth Grp; Cmnty Wkr; Drama Clb; Spanish Clb; Speech Tm; SADD; Thesps; School Musical; School Play; Stage Crew; Law.

GODINEZ, MIKE A; San Bernardino HS; San Bernardino, CA; (3); Church Yth Grp; Cmnty Wkr; Off Frsh Cls; Stu Cncl; Trk; DARE Pgm; Law Enfrcmnt.

GODKNECHT, CHERYL L; Lutheran HS; Fullerton, CA; (2); Church Yth Grp; Church Choir; Chrch Musical; Arch.

GODOY, ADRIAN H; Duarte HS; Duarte, CA; (3); Church Yth Grp; Cmnty Wkr; Rptr Nwsp; Lit Mag; Socr; Prfct Atten Awd; Hnr Awd Alge, Comp Applctns; Stu Of Month; Best Article Comp Newsltr; UCLA; Comp Prgmg.

GODOY, CARLOS; Damien HS; Rancho Cucamonga, CA; (2); 23/269; Boy Scts; Spanish Clb; Swmmng; High Hon Roll; NHS; Fishing Clb; MESA-HARVEY Mudd Coll; John-Hopkins; Doctor.

GODOY, ERNIE U; Modesto Adventist Acad; Modesto, CA; (4); 2/20; Church Yth Grp; Pres Soph Cls; Hon Roll; Sal; Bus Mgmt.

GOEBEL, JENNIFER K; Academy Of Our Lady Of Peace; San Diego, CA; (4); 14/128; Church Yth Grp; Cmnty Wkr; Hosp Aide; School Musical; Ed Yrbk; Rep Frsh Cls; Pres Soph Cls; Stu Cncl; Var Capt Tennis; High Hon Roll; Xerox Awd Hmnts/Socl Sci; Bak Ofamer Awd In Englsh; Princpls Awd For Ldrshp; Santa Clara U; Englsh.

GOEBEL, KERI M; Garden Grove HS; Anaheim, CA; (1); Hon Roll.

GOEBEL, LYNN; Novato HS; Novato, CA; (4); 1/257; Girl Scts; Hosp Aide; Key Clb; SADD; Band; Stage Crew; Hon Roll; Pres Acad Fit Awd; Val; CSF Pres, VP & Treas; U Of CA Santa Barbara; Sci.

GOEBEL, MARGARET T; Academy Of Our Lady Of Peace; San Diego, CA; (4); 25/128; Church Yth Grp; Cmnty Wkr; School Musical; School Play; Yrbk; VP Frsh Cls; Rep Soph Cls; Rep Jr Cls; Stu Cncl; Var Tennis; Santa Clara U; Teacher.

GOEDE, SANDRA C; Miraleste HS; Rancho Palos Verd, CA; (3); 32/114; Church Yth Grp; German Clb; Girl Scts; Model UN; SADD; High Hon Roll; Jr NHS; Peer Cnslr; U CA San Diego; Psych.

GOEHRING, HEATHER; Canoga Park HS; Canoga Park, CA; (4); Church Yth Grp; Key Clb; SADD; Drill Tm; Hon Roll; Pres Acad Fit Awd; Pierce JC; Bus.

GOEHRING, NICOLE A; Lodi HS; Woodbridge, CA; (3); 7/530; Church Yth Grp; Cmnty Wkr; Pres Key Clb; NFL; Chorus; Stu Cncl; Var Tennis; High Hon Roll; Lion Awd; MTAC Fstvl Cert; Hnr Stu Rectl 89; Cntry Oaks Reqt Clb; Intl Bus.

GOEMANS, CHRIS G; West HS; Bakersfield, CA; (1); Debate Tm; FCA; NFL; Hon Roll; San Diego ST.

GOENS JR, LARRY G; Bakersfield HS; Bakersfield, CA; (2); Church Yth Grp; FCA; JV L Swmmng; JV L Wrstlng; High Hon Roll; William E More Jr Memrl Awd Sci Fair; JV Leag Chmpn Swimmer 500 Yr Freestyle; Schlstc Achvt Awd Sprts; Architectural Engr.

GOERGENS, SCOTT; Granite Hills HS; El Cajon, CA; (4); 90/450; Church Yth Grp; Stu Cncl; Var Capt Bsktbl; Hon Roll; Semi-Fnlst Natl Hspnc Schlrshp; Bus Admin.

GOESSLING, RYAN R; Folsom HS; Folsom, CA; (3); Model UN; Spanish Clb; Teachers Aide; High Hon Roll; Spanish.

GOETZ, BRYAN J; Irvine HS; Irvine, CA; (1); Cmnty Wkr; Wt Lftg; Wrstlng; Hrtg Awd Diligence In Engl 90; U Of CA; Ocngrphy.

GOETZ, CANDY A; La Sierra HS; Riverside, CA; (3); FBLA; SADD; Teachers Aide; Chorus.

GOETZ, KELLY M; Saint Francis HS; Los Altos Hills, CA; (2); 3/350; Dance Clb; French Clb; Hosp Aide; Chrmn SADD; Teachers Aide; Nwsp; Yrbk; JV Vllybl; High Hon Roll; CSF; John Hopkins Schlr.

GOETZE, LAURA R; St Francis HS; Sunnyvale, CA; (3); 108/289; Church Yth Grp; Cmnty Wkr; Math Clb; Pep Clb; Science Clb; Service Clb; SADD; Var Bsktbl; JV Trk; High Hon Roll; Reading Tutor; FBI.

GOFF, JENNIFER J; Lowell HS; San Francisco, CA; (2); Dance Clb; German Clb; Variety Show; Var JV Socr; Hon Roll; Irish Club; Sccr Club; UC Santa Barbara; Corp Law.

GOFF, KEVIN L; South Fork HS; Garberville, CA; (3); Church Yth Grp; Teachers Aide; Varsity Clb; VICA; Band; Bsktbl; Ftbl; Tennis; High Hon Roll; Hon Roll; Engl Bus Awds.

GOFF, SCOTT D; Mt Miguel HS; Spring Valley, CA; (4); 10/350; Church Yth Grp; Cmnty Wkr; JA; ROTC; Science Clb; Spanish Clb; Drill Tm; Stu Cncl; Capt Var Ftbl; Var Vllybl; Yell Leading; San Luis Obispo; Design Engrng.

GOFF, TANYA E; Washington Prep; Los Angeles, CA; (3); Church Yth Grp; Math Clb; Off Jr Cls; Sec Stu Cncl; Cit Awd; High Hon Roll; Hon Roll; CSF; Pre-Med.

GOFF, TESSA N; Cornelia Connelly HS; Costa Mesa, CA; (1); School Play; Stage Crew; Bsktbl; High Hon Roll; Hon Roll; Jr Statesmen Of Amer; Piano; Cnty Sci & Engrng Fr Jr Engrng 3rd Pl; Landscape Arch.

GOFFE, JAMES; Lemoore HS; Lemoore, CA; (2); Church Yth Grp; Cmnty Wkr; Teachers Aide; Band; Jazz Band; Mrchg Band; Pep Band; Trk; Wrstlng; Hon Roll; Phys Thrpy.

GOFORTH, GRETA M; San Dieguito HS; Encinitas, CA; (2); Hon Roll; Prfct Atten Awd; CSF; U Of CA San Diego; Math.

GOIS JR, RAUL L; Oakdale HS; Oakdale, CA; (3); 9/200; Ski Clb; Teachers Aide; Cit Awd; High Hon Roll; Hon Roll; Track Clb Ldr; Golden St Exam Awd; Hgh GPA Awd; Stanislaus ST; Law Enfrcmnt.

GOITIA III, MANUEL BOAIN; Don Bosco Technical Inst; San Gabriel, CA; (1); 30/240; JV Vllybl; NEDT Awd; Bosco Tech; Arch.

GOITIA, NICHELE M; San Gabriel Mission HS; San Gabriel, CA; (2); Drama Clb; GAA; Pep Clb; Hon Roll; UCLA; Med.

GOJIT, ARVIN; Northview HS; Covina, CA; (1); Intrml Bsktbl; JV Trk; Cal Poly U; Arch.

GOLANT, AIMEE B; University HS; Los Angeles, CA; (3); Letterman Clb; Off Sr Cls; Stu Cncl; Sftbl; Spent 2 Mnths In Israel 89.

GOLBEK, BRENDA S; Kingsburg HS; Dinuba, CA; (3); Church Yth Grp; Teachers Aide; Band; Mrchg Band; Pep Band; School Musical; Police Explorer; Kings River CC; Law Enfrcmnt.

GOLD, KEVIN; Heschel Day Schl; Granada Hills, CA; (1); Temple Yth Grp; Var Bsbl; Capt Bsktbl; Var Ftbl; Pres Acad Fit Awd.

GOLD, MATEA; Mc Clatchy HS; Sacramento, CA; (2); 1/800; Temple Yth Grp; Chorus; High Hon Roll; Barcelonia Spain Study Abroad; CSF; Journlsm.

GOLD, TIMOTHY B; Ramona HS; Ramona, CA; (2); 1/345; Boy Scts; Band; Mrchg Band; Pep Band; Acad Leag Jr Var; BYU; Elec Engrng.

GOLDAN, JESHUAH G; Eureka HS; Eureka, CA; (3); Boy Scts; Drama Clb; JA; Ski Clb; School Play; Rptr Nwsp; Var Tennis; Hon Roll; Hnrs Engl.

GOLDBERG, BRIAN D; Long Beach Polytechnic HS; Long Beach, CA; (4); Cmnty Wkr; Debate Tm; Key Clb; NFL; SADD; Treas Sr Cls; Crs Cntry; Trk; Hon Roll; Pres Locl Chptr Mogen Daird B'rai Britz Yth Orgnztn; Outstndng Stu Hebrew HS; U Of Tudaism Lee Coll; Poli Sci.

GOLDBERG, JENI N; Chaminade College Prep; Chatsworth, CA; (2); Art Clb; Cmnty Wkr; Red Cross Aide; Spanish Clb; Varsity Clb; Chorus; Var Swmmng; Hon Roll; Pres Acad Fit Awd; Los Angeles Cty 2nd & CA 2nd St Sci Fair; Los Angeles Cty 3rd Pl Sci Fair; Sports Psych.

GOLDBERG, MARTIN H; San Fernando HS; Sylmar, CA; (3); Boy Scts; Drama Clb; Office Aide; Pep Clb; School Play; Nwsp; Off Jr Cls; Var Cheerldng; Var Tennis; Hon Roll.

GOLDBOONN, CANDIE M; Armijo HS; Suisun, CA; (2); ROTC; Var Bsktbl; Var Sftbl; Sprts.

GOLDEN, ALIS M; Fairfield HS; Fairfield, CA; (4); FHA; Chorus; Cit Awd; French Hon Soc; Hon Roll; Bank Amer Achvt Awd Home Ec; Home Ec Stu Yr; Acad Ltr; Home Ec.

GOLDEN, DEAN B; Santa Clara HS; Santa Clara, CA; (4); 96/409; Aud/Vis; Pres Church Yth Grp; Cmnty Wkr; Library Aide; Office Aide; Teachers Aide; Band; Chorus; Church Choir; Mrchg Band; Santa Clara Police Cadet 3 Yrs; Pt Loma Nazarene Coll; Rlgn.

GOLDEN, JOHN A; Loyola HS; Arcadia, CA; (2); Pres Acad Fit Awd; Ed Nwsp; Ed Lit Mag; High Hon Roll; Natl Latin Exam Maxima Cum Laude Cert Hrbl Mntn; Natl Forensic Leag Deg Merit; Acadmc Dcthln Team; Physics.

GOLDEN, JOHN S; Clear Lake HS; Lakeport, CA; (3); Am Leg Boys St; Computer Clb; Drama Clb; Jazz Band; Pep Band; School Musical; School Play; Tennis; High Hon Roll; Pres Acad Fit Awd; Acad Decathlon; 1st Pl Yamaha Keyboard Fstvl; Lake Cnty Symphony Orc Cellist.

GOLDEN, LYNN M; Hoover HS; Fresno, CA; (3); 42/550; Church Yth Grp; Girl Scts; VP Science Clb; Treas SADD; Chorus; JV Diving; Var Gym; Ntl Merit Ltr; Asst Athl Trnr; Acad Decathlon; Sci Olympiad; Math.

GOLDEN, ROBERT J; Los Altos HS; Hacienda Hts, CA; (3); Boy Scts; JV Bsktbl; Hon Roll; Prfct Atten Awd; Elec Engrng.

GOLDFIELD, DAN; Tomales HS; Inverness, CA; (4); 4/42; Ed Yrbk; Ed Lit Mag; Rep Frsh Cls; Rep Soph Cls; Rep VP Jr Cls; Stu Cncl; Var Bsktbl; Vlntr Wrk Handcppd; Congressnl Yth Schlr; Top 25 HS Stu Engrng Wrkshp; Cnty Cmmnty Svc Awd; MIT; Engrng.

GOLDGORIN, JACQUELINE L; John F Kennedy HS; La Palma, CA; (3); Pres Debate Tm; Drama Clb; FBLA; Pres Speech Tm; Teachers Aide; Temple Yth Grp; Chorus; School Musical; JV Swmmng; USAF Acad Smmr Scntfc Smnr; Mst Dedctd Awd Swmmng.

GOLDING, TONYA; Hughson Union HS; Hickman, CA; (4); 3/120; Church Yth Grp; Pres VP 4-H; GAA; Library Aide; Math Tm; Ski Clb; SADD; Varsity Clb; Band; Mrchg Band; Camp Royal; Irans Vly Seague Schlr Athlete; Sci Olympiad; Sonoma ST U; Med.

GOLDITCH, JASON D; Aptos HS; Watsonville, CA; (2); Band; Var Ftbl; Wt Lftg; Hon Roll; USC; Engl.

GOLDMAN, AMY; Monterey HS; Monterey, CA; (2); Drama Clb; Var Cheerldng; Hon Roll; UC Santa Barbara; Psych.

GOLDMAN, BETH; Serra HS; San Diego, CA; (4); Model UN; Pep Clb; Capt Drill Tm; Hon Roll; UCSD; Math.

GOLDMAN, DAVID; Bonita Vista JR HS; Bonita, CA; (1); Cmnty Wkr; Letterman Clb; Model UN; Orch; Variety Show; Pres Frsh Cls; VP Soph Cls; Rep Stu Cncl; Var Tennis; Cit Awd; Violin; Inter Bacclrte Pgm; Doctor.

GOLDMAN, JACOB D; Monterey HS; Monterey, CA; (4); 3/280; Band; Jazz Band; Mrchg Band; Orch; JV Bsktbl; Var Swmmng; High Hon Roll; NHS; Rotary Awd; Sal; CXA All St Band; CSF; UCLA.

GOLDMAN, JESSICA B; Miramonte HS; Orinda, CA; (2); 1/200; Debate Tm; NFL; Speech Tm; Temple Yth Grp; Hon Roll; Sports Med.

GOLDSBERRY, ELIZABETH A; C K Mc Clatchy HS; Sacramento, CA; (3); 56/390; French Clb; Ed Yrbk; Pres Frsh Cls; Sec Treas Jr Cls; Var Socr; High Hon Roll; Hon Roll; Mock Trial; Jr Statesmn Amer; CSF.

GOLDSMITH, AREN; Santa Barbara HS; Santa Barbara, CA; (2); Model UN; VP Frsh Cls; Var Tennis; High Hon Roll; JSA; Chrstn Surfing Assn; Yale; Bus.

GOLDSMITH, DENA M; Canyon HS; Anaheim, CA; (1); Church Yth Grp; Drill Tm; Cit Awd.

GOLDSMITH, JENNIE; Chaminade College Prep; Simi Valley, CA; (4); Cmnty Wkr; Key Clb; Red Cross Aide; Service Clb; Hon Roll; Life Team 89; Teens For Teens; American U; Intl Pltcs.

GOLDSMITH, MIKE; De La Salle HS; Walnut Creek, CA; (4); 40/200; Teachers Aide; Bsbl; Ftbl; Trk; Wt Lftg; Hon Roll; Chrstn Invlvmnt; Comm Svcs; Cuesta Coll; Const Mgt.

GOLDSMITH, SHARON S; Savanna HS; Buena Park, CA; (2); Church Yth Grp; Debate Tm; Pep Clb; Science Clb; Treas Soph Cls; Score Keeper; JV Vllybl; Water Skiing, Surfng, Jet Skiing, Reading; Law.

GOLDSTEIN, JENNIFER S; Granada Hills HS; Northridge, CA; (3); Dance Clb; SADD; School Musical; Sec Frsh Cls; Stu Cncl; Pres Acad Fit Awd; Ernest Lawrence Awd; CSUN; Ed.

GOLDSTEIN, LANYA; Providence HS; Burbank, CA; (2); Library Aide; Chorus; Pres Jr Cls; JV Sftbl; JV Vllybl; Outdoors Clb; Bus.

GOLDSTEIN, LUSANA; Mt Miguel HS; San Diego, CA; (4); Am Leg Aux Girls St; Debate Tm; Office Aide; Spanish Clb; Treas Frsh Cls; VP Soph Cls; Pres Jr Cls; Var L Bsktbl; L Crs Cntry; JV Var Vllybl; ISSL Awd; Cal Grant Wnnr; 89 Young Speakrs Awd Lions Clb; San Diego ST U; Sign/Spnsh Lan.

GOLDSTEIN, NECOL M; Fairfield HS; Fairfield, CA; (2); Dance Clb; Drama Clb; French Clb; Drill Tm; School Play; Rep Jr Cls; Cit Awd; High Hon Roll; Hon Roll; NHS; Skiing; Swmmng; Ballet; UC Davis.

GOLDWASSER, BARUCH; Bonita Vista HS; Chula Vista, CA; (4); 20/532; Chess Clb; French Clb; Intnl Clb; Key Clb; Spanish Clb; Temple Yth Grp; Ed Yrbk; Intrml Bsbl; Intrml Bsktbl; JV Ftbl; Semi-Fnlst Natl Hspnc Schlr Awds; Amer Chem Soc; Intl Bcclrt Stu; Harvard; Econ.

GOLETZ, BOWEN P; Mater Dei HS; Irvine, CA; (3); Boy Scts; Cmnty Wkr; Computer Clb; German Clb; Science Clb; Spanish Clb; Band; Mrchg Band; Ed Yrbk; Hon Roll; Cert Achvt-Sci US Marine Corps; Purdue; Engr.

GOLEZ, EDWIN; Serra HS; San Bruno, CA; (2); Church Yth Grp; Cmnty Wkr; Varsity Clb; JV Ftbl; JV Socr; Hon Roll; Columbian Squires VP; CA Poly-San Luis Obispo; Arch.

GOLINO JR, RICHARD A; Armijo HS; Fairfield, CA; (4); 45/385; AFS; ROTC; Var Crs Cntry; High Hon Roll; Asist A Grad Schlrshp; Hgh Hnrs Gldn St Exm; Solano Acad Decthln 90; CA ST U; Bus Admin.

GOLINSKI, CHRISTA A; Mira Loma HS; Citrus Heights, CA; (3); 143/284; Spanish Clb; SADD; Pres Acad Fit Awd; Stanford; Cmmrcl Art.

GOLLATZ, MELISSA; Pacifica HS; Los Alamitos, CA; (3); Church Yth Grp; Hosp Aide; Science Clb; SADD; Vllybl; Hon Roll; Vactnl Bible Schl Child Care, Tchrs Aide & Church Deacon; Vlybl, Soccer, Roller Sktng & Stbl; Police Offcr.

GOLTZ, SCOTT; Del Campo HS; Citrus Heights, CA; (2); Boy Scts; JV Bsbl; Hon Roll.

GOLUBCHIK, NATASHA; Santa Monica HS; Santa Monica, CA; (2); Art Clb; Dance Clb; Ski Clb; Drill Tm; Cit Awd; UCLA; Advrtsmnt.

GOMER, NATHAN D; Marysville HS; Marysville, CA; (4); Debate Tm; NFL; Office Aide; Q&S; SADD; Ed Yrbk; Hon Roll; Creative Writing.

GOMES, AUSTIN R; Lynwood HS; Miami, FL; (3); 1/671; Computer Clb; Math Clb; Band; Mrchg Band; Hon Roll; U Of Miami; Comp Sci.

GOMES, NATHAN D; Bret Harte HS; Murphys, CA; (2); FFA; Ski Clb; Hon Roll; Bear Valley Race Team Skiing; 3rd Plc Vctnl Olympcs; Cmmnty Spnsrd Sccr Tm; Archt Drwng.

GOMES, PHELICIA; Central Catholic HS; Manteca, CA; (3); 6/55; Treas French Clb; Math Tm; Scholastic Bowl; Stu Cncl; Cheerldng; Powder Puff Ftbl; Socr; Sftbl; High Hon Roll; NHS; CA Poly Sn Luis Obispo; Acctng.

GOMES, PHILIP M; Bishop O'dowd HS; San Leandro, CA; (2); 40/250; Jazz Band; Pep Band; Ed Nwsp; Hon Roll.

GOMES-WONG, SUZANNE K; Edison HS; Fresno, CA; (1); Hosp Aide; JCL; Hon Roll; Black Belt Schto Kan Karate; Vol Hlth Club; CSF; Sports Med.

GOMEZ, ADAM A; Tulare Western HS; Tulare, CA; (2); Boy Scts; Mrchg Band; Elec Engr.

GOMEZ, ADRIANA; Dos Palos HS; Dos Palos, CA; (3); Trk; Hon Roll; Prfct Atten Awd; St Schlr; Mecha; San Jose; Legal Sec.

GOMEZ, AIMEE K; Alexander Hamilton Academy Of Music; Torrance, CA; (2); Office Aide; Teachers Aide; Orch; School Musical; High Hon Roll; Hon Roll; Prfct Atten Awd; String Ensemble-Violin; Bowling Jr Scratch Doubles; Achvt Awd & Nevians; UCLA; Law.

GOMEZ, ALAN M; Baldwin Park HS; Baldwin Park, CA; (3); Var Bsbl; Var Capt Bsktbl; Var Ftbl; Hon Roll; Hnrbl Mntn Defensive Back; Psych.

GOMEZ, ALICIA C; Garces Memorial HS; Bakersfield, CA; (4); 50/115; Church Yth Grp; Drama Clb; Science Clb; SADD; Sec Chorus; School Musical; School Play; Stage Crew; CA ST U Bakersfield.

GOMEZ, ALONZO; Pioneer HS; Whittier, CA; (4); 2/300; Office Aide; Var Bsktbl; Hon Roll; Jr Hnr Grd; Grad Hnrs; CA ST Fullerton; Bus.

GOMEZ, AMIEE; Chaffey HS; Upland, CA; (2); Dance Clb; Teachers Aide; JV Score Keeper; JV Score Keeper; High Hon Roll.

GOMEZ, ANTONIO; Hanford Union HS; Hanford, CA; (3); 8/473; Church Yth Grp; Treas FBLA; FHA; Pres Treas Math Clb; Treas Stu Cncl; JV Socr; JV Tennis; High Hon Roll; MESA St Cmptn-2nd Pl Math Team & 2nd Pl Oildrrck 89; FBLA Mst Actv Awd 88; U Of CA Berkeley; Engrng.

GOMEZ, APPLE; Sweetwater HS; National City, CA; (3); Drama Clb; GAA; Pep Clb; Science Clb; Teachers Aide; Varsity Clb; Stage Crew; Ed Nwsp; Stu Cncl; JV Var Bsktbl; SDSU; Physcl Ed Tchr.

GOMEZ, BERNADETTE; Chaffey HS; Cucamonga, CA; (4); 4/560; Hist VP Key Clb; Pep Clb; SADD; Yrbk; High Hon Roll; Ntl Merit SF; Peer Cnslng VP; CA Schlrshp Fed Seal Bearer; Ivy Chain; Acad Dcthln.

GOMEZ, BLANCA; Riverdale Union HS; Burrel, CA; (2); 1/140; 4-H; Pep Clb; Science Clb; Band; JV Co-Capt Bsktbl; 4-H Awd; High Hon Roll; CSF; MECHA; GATE Prog; Cal Poly; Arch.

GOMEZ, CAROL; San Benito HS; Hollister, CA; (1); 11/450; Church Yth Grp; High Hon Roll; Hon Roll; U Of CA Santa Barbara.

GOMEZ, CHRISTINA; Paraclete HS; Lancaster, CA; (3); Drama Clb; Key Clb; School Play; Sec Pep Band; VP Soph Cls; Pres Jr Cls; Var Sftbl; Hon Roll; Rtry Yth Ldrshp Awd; Intract Clb Secy; Cmnctns.

GOMEZ, CHRISTOPHER A; Sonora HS; La Habra, CA; (2); Boy Scts; High Hon Roll; Pres Acad Fit Awd; BSA 885, Scout Of Yr 89; Acad Dcthln Ornge Cty; 3rd Pl Ornge Cty Fair Comp Cmptn; Physics.

GOMEZ, CLAUDIA; Theodore Roosevelt HS; Los Angeles, CA; (2); ROTC; Rptr Nwsp; Lmplghtr Hnr Soc; Coll Core Curriculum Prgrm; Advncd US Hstry; Tchng.

GOMEZ, CLAUDIA L; Los Altos HS; Hacienda Hgts, CA; (3); Church Yth Grp; Cmnty Wkr; 4-H; Teachers Aide; Temple Yth Grp; Church Choir; Socr; Trk; Hon Roll; Prfct Atten Awd; Acad Stu Of Mnth; Var Coaches Awd; Bus.

GOMEZ, CRYSTLE; John F Kennedy HS; Buena Park, CA; (3); SMART Cmmtte; Law.

GOMEZ, DALIA; Santa Monica HS; Santa Monica, CA; (2); Mecha Clb; Baya UCLA; Bus.

GOMEZ, DALIA; William C Overfelt HS; San Jose, CA; (2); Church Yth Grp; Math Tm; Teachers Aide; Chorus; High Hon Roll; Alg 1 Hgh Hnrs Acadmc Excllnc Awd; Cert Merit Bio; Chrch Yth Grp Secy; Early Outreach Pgm; MESA Club; Heald Bus Coll; Acctng.

GOMEZ, DANIEL R; Arvin HS; Lamont, CA; (1); Bsbl; Bsktbl; Military.

GOMEZ, DAVID A; Channel Island HS; Oxnard, CA; (3); Church Yth Grp; Dance Clb; JV Socr; New Horizontal Club; Peer Helper Prog; Doctor.

GOMEZ, DIANA; William S Hart HS; Santa Clarita, CA; (4); 52/458; Church Yth Grp; Teachers Aide; Chorus; Stage Crew; Hon Roll; Prfct Atten Awd; Diane Garner Memrl Schlrshp Rcpnt; Coll Of Canyons; Span Tchr.

GOMEZ, DOLORES; San Benito HS; Hollister, CA; (3); 27/380; Church Yth Grp; Dance Clb; GAA; Band; Church Choir; Color Guard; Mrchg Band; Pep Band; JV Var Crs Cntry; Mgr(s); Amnesty Intl; Leag Latin Amer Yth Cncl.

GOMEZ, ELAINE M; Colton HS; Colton, CA; (2); Rep Stu Cncl; Var Fld Hcky; Hon Roll; Futre Ldrs America; Futre Ldrs America Minor Assn; Child Psych.

GOMEZ, ELVIRA; Tracy Joint Union HS; Stockton, CA; (2); 26/483; Key Clb; High Hon Roll; Hon Roll; CSF; Interact Clb; Leo Clb; Bio.

GOMEZ, EMILIANO J; Rosamond HS; Rosamond, CA; (2); Off Frsh Cls; Bsbl; Cit Awd; Hon Roll; Cal ST; Policeman.

GOMEZ, GABRIELLA C; Herbert Hoover HS; Glendale, CA; (3); Am Leg Aux Girls St; Church Yth Grp; Dance Clb; JCL; Pres Latin Clb; Pep Clb; Drill Tm; Ed Yrbk; Pres Jr Cls; Pres Stu Cncl; Youth & Govt; Pepperdine Univ Outstndng Participant Awd; Pre Law; Political Sci.

GOMEZ, GINA; Gunderson HS; San Jose, CA; (2); Cross Age Pr Cnclr; Soc Women Engrs; Mck Trl; Standford; Law.

GOMEZ, GISELA; Tustin HS; Tustin, CA; (1); High Hon Roll; Hon Roll; Gymnstcs; Vllybl; UCSD; Chld Psych.

GOMEZ, HECTOR H; San Diego HS; San Diego, CA; (3); Boy Scts; Library Aide; Office Aide; Trk; Wrstlng; San Diego ST U; Bus.

GOMEZ, INNA; Montgomery HS; Chula Vista, CA; (2); Var Socr; JV Sftbl.

GOMEZ, IRENE; Chino HS; Chino, CA; (3); Library Aide; Teachers Aide; Cit Awd; Hon Roll.

GOMEZ, JACQUELINE BRIDGET; Ontario HS; Ontario, CA; (4); Church Yth Grp; Dance Clb; Key Clb; Temple Yth Grp; Acpl Chr; Chorus; Church Choir; Gym; High Hon Roll; Hon Roll; GSE Alg Rec; Bell HS Harbor Coll; Smr Intership Pgm UCR.

GOMEZ, JENNIFER; Northview HS; Covina, CA; (3); Church Yth Grp; Pep Clb; Spanish Clb; SADD; Teachers Aide; Varsity Clb; Drill Tm; Yrbk; Rep Sr Cls; Var Cheerldng; CSF; Jobs Daughtrs; Poly Net Pgm; UCLA; Lawyer.

GOMEZ, JESSICA; Hawthorne HS; Inglewood, CA; (2); Dance Clb; Teachers Aide; Chorus; Spec Ed Tchr.

GOMEZ, JESSICA; Redlands HS; E Highlands, CA; (2); Ed Yrbk; Vllybl; Friday Night Live Club; Bus.

GOMEZ, JESSICA R; Beaumont HS; Cherry Valley, CA; (1); Drama Clb; Stat Bsktbl; JV Sftbl; Stat Vllybl; Hon Roll; CSF.

GOMEZ, JESUS F; Oroville HS; Oroville, CA; (1); Boy Scts; Church Yth Grp; Letterman Clb; Temple Yth Grp; Intrml Bsktbl; Var Golf; Cit Awd; Hon Roll; Pres Acad Fit Awd; Comm Yth Theatre; BYU; Bus.

GOMEZ JR, JOHN R; East Union HS; French Camp, CA; (2); 39/411; Band; Mrchg Band; Elec Engr.

GOMEZ, JOSE B; Saddleback HS; Santa Ana, CA; (3).

GOMEZ, JOSE C; Bell Gardens HS; Bell Gardens, CA; (4); Drama Clb; Ftbl; Wt Lftg; Hon Roll; Prfct Atten Awd; Industl Drwg; Woodbury U; Arch.

GOMEZ, JOSE G; Delta HS; Sacramento, CA; (2); JV Var Bsbl; Var JV Ftbl; JV Var Wt Lftg; Hon Roll; CA ST U Sacramento; Engr.

GOMEZ, JOSE R; Kingsburg HS; Kingsburg, CA; (3); Latin Clb; Office Aide; Speech Tm; Teachers Aide; Wt Lftg; Hon Roll; Prfct Atten Awd; Spanish NHS; Lawyer.

GOMEZ, JOY D; Santa Clora HS; Camarillo, CA; (4); Office Aide; Sec Treas Science Clb; Teachers Aide; Varsity Clb; Off Stu Cncl; JV Var Vllybl; Cit Awd; High Hon Roll; Hon Roll; NHS; U Of CA; Biochemistry Biology.

GOMEZ, JUAN G; Cajon HS; San Bernardino, CA; (2); Art Clb; Dance Clb; Latin Clb; Spanish Clb; Stage Crew; Variety Show; Yrbk; Off Soph Cls; Stu Cncl; Socr; UCSB; Teach.

GOMEZ, KENNY W; Wasco Union HS; Wasco, CA; (2); Band; Jazz Band; Mrchg Band; Pep Band; JV Bsbl; JV Ftbl; Var Tennis; High Hon Roll; NHS; Kern Cnty HS Hnr Band; CSUB; Tchr.

GOMEZ, LAURA I; Chaffey HS; Guasti, CA; (1); Dance Clb; French Clb; JV Socr; UCLA; Med.

GOMEZ, LORENA; Paramount HS; Compton, CA; (4); 89/400; VP Sec Church Yth Grp; Treas FBLA; VP Key Clb; Latin Clb; Letterman Clb; Church Choir; JV Tennis; Cit Awd; Prfct Atten Awd; Rotary Awd; Mem Of Corsaires Sorority Svc Club; Most Organized Awd; CA ST U Fullerton; Corp Atty.

GOMEZ, LOUIE E; Mcfarland HS; Mc Farland, CA; (3); Church Yth Grp; VICA; Phtg Yrbk; Hon Roll; San Luis Obispo; Arch.

GOMEZ, LUCIA C; Montebello HS; Montebello, CA; (2); Drama Clb; SADD; Acpl Chr; School Musical; JV Swmmng; Cit Awd; Hon Roll; Choirs; CA ST Los Angeles; Psych.

GOMEZ, LUPITA G; Dos Palos HS; Dos Palos, CA; (3); 4-H; Math Clb; Science Clb; Spanish Clb; SADD; Rptr Nwsp; Phtg Yrbk; Hon Roll; San Jose Coll; Interior Dsgn.

GOMEZ, MAGDA O; Sacred Heart Of Jesus HS; Los Angeles, CA; (2); 3/112; Cmnty Wkr; GAA; Letterman Clb; Varsity Clb; Sec Soph Cls; Var Bsktbl; Var Trk; JV Capt Vllybl; Cit Awd; High Hon Roll; Most Inspirational Bsktbl; Coaches Awd Vlybl; Most Inspirational Track; Stanford; Law.

GOMEZ, MARCIA; Montgomery HS; San Ysidro, CA; (4); Latin Clb; Office Aide; Spanish Clb; Teachers Aide; MECHA.

GOMEZ, MARIA; Dos Palos HS; Dos Palos, CA; (2); Library Aide; Sftbl; Hon Roll; CSF; Mecha-Mexican Chicanos Assn; Merced Coll; Cmptrs.

GOMEZ, MARICRUZ; Caruthers HS; Fresno, CA; (2); Computer Clb; 4-H; Teachers Aide; Gym; Swmmng; Fresno City Coll; Secy.

GOMEZ, MARLA T; Christian Brothers HS; Sacramento, CA; (3); Chorus; Drill Tm; School Play; Treas Soph Cls; Score Keeper; High Hon Roll; NHS; Sac St Early Outrch Pgm Schlrshps; Gen Excllnc HS Schlrshps; Engrng Pgm; UC San Diego; Arch Engr.

GOMEZ, MARTIN E; St Michaels College Prep HS; San Clemente, CA; (1); Art Clb; Pres Service Clb; School Play; Yrbk; Jr NHS; Roomldr In Charge Of Dormatory Room; Acadmc Tutor Natl Hon Soc; Mathmtcs.

GOMEZ, MAURICIO; California HS; Santa Fe Springs, CA; (3); German Clb; Office Aide; Ski Clb; SADD; Teachers Aide; Band; Swmmng; Police Explorer Scout Los Angeles Police Dept; Congress Mem Govt; Green Belt Kung-Fu San Soo; Ucla; Aero.

GOMEZ, MICHAEL; Skyline HS; Oakland, CA; (2); Art Clb; Math Clb; Bsbl; Ftbl; Wt Lftg.

GOMEZ, MICHELE A; Pittsburg HS; Pittsburg, CA; (2); Pep Clb; JV Sftbl; Hon Roll; Psycht.

GOMEZ, MILTON; San Antonio HS; Gardena, CA; (1); Boy Scts; Dance Clb; English Clb; Math Clb; Science Clb; Service Clb; SADD; Teachers Aide; Socr; Wt Lftg; Biolgst.

GOMEZ, NATASHA E; Los Altos HS; Hacienda Hgts, CA; (3); 53/376; Church Yth Grp; Office Aide; Band; Mrchg Band; Hon Roll; Prfct Atten Awd; Pres Acad Fit Awd; Jr Hnr Guard 90; Prncpls Hnr Roll 87-90; Gldn St Exam Schl Rcgntn 87-88; Cal Poly San Luis Obispo; Engr.

GOMEZ, PATTY; Rio Mesa HS; Oxnard, CA; (1); FBLA; Pep Clb; SADD; Pep Band; Cheerldng; Hon Roll; Chrldng Coach 5th Grdrs; Hnr Clses.

GOMEZ, REBECCA; Fontana HS; Fontana, CA; (3); Am Leg Aux Girls St; Church Yth Grp; Office Aide; JV Sftbl; JV Swmmng; Var JV Vllybl; Cit Awd; Hon Roll; Prfct Atten Awd; Daisy Chain.

GOMEZ, RICARDO A; Castle Park HS; Chula Vista, CA; (3); MECHA Clb; CSF; Military Acad.

GOMEZ, ROWENA A; Westmoor HS; Daly City, CA; (3); 1/420; Cmnty Wkr; Pres German Clb; Model UN; Service Clb; Teachers Aide; High Hon Roll; Prfct Atten Awd; CSF; GATE; Tchr St Augustine Rlgs Ed Pgm; Psych.

GOMEZ, SANDRA; Baldwin Park HS; Baldwin Park, CA; (1); Church Yth Grp; Science Clb; Cit Awd; Hon Roll; Pres Acad Fit Awd; Yng Schlrs Inst Marine Bio; Marine Bio.

GOMEZ, SERGIO; Lincoln HS; Los Angeles, CA; (2); Drama Clb; French Clb; Key Clb; Rptr Nwsp; Sec Soph Cls; JV Capt Bsbl; JV Capt Ftbl; Hon Roll; Opt Clb Awd; Prfct Atten Awd; All-City Ftbl; Brdcstng.

GOMEZ, SHELLY A; Coachella Valley HS; Mecca, CA; (2); Math Clb; Hon Roll; Piano Lssns.

GOMEZ, SIMONA M; Rio Mesa HS; Camarillo, CA; (3); Church Yth Grp; Girl Scts; JV Swmmng; Prfct Atten Awd; Wrk Dvlpmntly Dsbld & Handcppd; Psych.

GOMEZ, STEVE A; Pittsburg HS; Pittsburg, CA; (2); JV Capt Bsbl; Ftbl; CA ST U-Fresno; Bus Admin.

GOMEZ, SUZETTE; Calexico HS; Calexico, CA; (2); Dance Clb; Drill Tm; Hon Roll; UCSD; CPA.

GOMEZ, TOMAS L; Sunset HS; Hayward, CA; (3); 3/283; Am Leg Boys St; Science Clb; Teachers Aide; Bausch & Lomb Sci Awd; Cls Mascot; San Jose ST; Bus.

GOMEZ, VERONICA M; South San Francisco HS; South San Francis, CA; (2); Church Yth Grp; German Clb; Key Clb; Latin Clb; Teachers Aide; Hon Roll; Yth Of Yr 89 & 90; Keystone Ldrshp Club Secy 89-90; Stanford U; Law.

GOMEZ, YVETTE E; International Studies Acad; San Francisco, CA; (2); Var Sftbl; Isa Acts Philanthropy Clb; Cert Of Awd Excll Bio & Outstndng Prfrmnc Phys Ed; USAF.

GOMMEL, KENNETH S; Vista HS; Oceanside, CA; (3); 20/422; German Clb; VP Jr Cls; Rep Stu Cncl; Var Capt Ftbl; Var Trk; Hon Roll; German Natl Hnr Soc; Xtra News Radio Acad All Amer Ftbl Tm 89; Long Beach; Physcl Thrpy.

GONDA, ELIZABETH M; St Joseph HS; Lakewood, CA; (3); 90/180; Church Yth Grp; Cmnty Wkr; Spanish Clb; Hon Roll; Prfct Atten Awd.

GONG, BILL S; Pasadena HS; Pasadena, CA; (3); Debate Tm; L Socr; L Tennis; Pres Asian Amer Clb; Ping Pong Clb; Awd From Rensselaer Polytechnic Inst; UC Berkeley; Law.

GONG, CHRISTINE G; Sanger HS; Sanger, CA; (2); 1/375; Sec Model UN; ROTC; Science Clb; JV Tennis; Cit Awd; High Hon Roll; Hon Roll; NEDT Awd; CSF; Congrssnl Yth Ldrshp Conf; Georgetown; Bus.

GONG, JENNY CHUN; Phillip Burton HS; San Francisco, CA; (2); Church Yth Grp; Computer Clb; Math Clb; Band; Orch; High Hon Roll; Hon Roll; Comp; Mth.

GONG, MICHAEL CHRISTOPHER; Wasco Union HS; Wasco, CA; (4); 1/160; Cmnty Wkr; Debate Tm; Sec Math Clb; Pres Service Clb; Ed Yrbk; Pres Frsh Cls; VP Soph Cls; Bsktbl; Golf; Tennis; CSF Schlrshp Fnlst; Bnk America Sci/Math Plque Wnnr; CS Polytechnic ST U SLO.

GONG, NANCY; Lowell HS; San Francisco, CA; (2); French Clb; Red Cross Aide; Stage Crew; Rptr Nwsp; Stu Cncl; U CA Of Davis; Sci.

GONG, ROSE; Wasco Union HS; Wasco, CA; (2); 1/235; Drama Clb; Math Clb; VP Frsh Cls; Pres Soph Cls; Treas Jr Cls; High Hon Roll; Hon Roll; Prfct Atten Awd; Hugh O'brian Fndtn; Hoby Rep; Bus.

GONG, VICTOR; Wasco Union HS; Wasco, CA; (1); Cmnty Wkr; Intnl Clb; VP Frsh Cls; Rep Stu Cncl; Intrml Bsktbl; JV Golf; Cit Awd; High Hon Roll; Prfct Atten Awd; CSF.

GONGAWARE, JULIE LYN; Redlands HS; Redlands, CA; (2); Kimberly Jrs; Wind Ensmbl.

GONI, RICK A; Downey HS; Downey, CA; (2); Bsktbl; High Hon Roll; CSF; Hnrs Awd Golden St Exam 1st Yr Alg; U Of ND; Flight Mgt.

GONSALEZ, DIOGUELINA; Oxnard HS; Oxnard, CA; (1); Church Choir; Stu Cncl; Hon Roll; Future Ldrs Of Amer; Educ.

GONSALVES, ANTHONY J; Turlock HS; Turlock, CA; (2); 79/400; FFA; Rptr Yrbk; JV Bsbl; JV Ftbl; Spirit Club; Fresno ST; History.

GONSALVES, MERCY M; Loretto HS; Sacramento, CA; (2); Church Yth Grp; Drama Clb; Intnl Clb; Math Clb; Science Clb; SADD; Chorus; Drill Tm; Lit Mag; Hon Roll; Cert Of Mrt Piano; UC Davis.

GONSALVES, MIKE A; Grant Joint Union HS; Sacramento, CA; (2); Ftbl; Wt Lftg; Hon Roll; Hnr Block Schlrshp; Outstndng Perfmnc & Achvt In Bio; #1 Clb; Law.

GONSALVES, NICOLE L; Oakmont HS; Citrus Heights, CA; (3); Drama Clb; Teachers Aide; Band; Variety Show; Score Keeper; Hon Roll; Geom Golden St Exam; 2 Frgn Exch Progs, W/Switzerland & France; Teacher.

GONSALVES, ROBYN M; Pittsburg HS; Pittsburg, CA; (3); 154/350; FBLA; Lion Awd; Jbs Dghtrs Bethel, Jr & Sr Custdn, Outer Grd, Librn, Treas, Guide, Jr & Sr Prncss & Hnr Qn; LMC JC; Day Care Bus.

GONZAGA, ALEJANDRO; Foothill HS; Bakersfield, CA; (4); 1/370; Church Yth Grp; Cmnty Wkr; Key Clb; Math Clb; Math Tm; Scholastic Bowl; Spanish Clb; Teachers Aide; Rptr Nwsp; VP Sr Cls; Pres Math, Engnrng, Sci Achvmnt; CA Schlrshp Fed; Harvard Smr Schl; Golden Poet Awd; Stanford U; Archt.

GONZALAZ, LILIANA; Mater Dei HS; Santa Ana, CA; (3); Cmnty Wkr; Teachers Aide; Stat Mgr(s); Hon Roll; UCI; Bus Accntng.

GONZALEA, BRIAN; Glen A Wilson HS; Hacienda Hts, CA; (4); 65/300; Band; Jazz Band; Mrchg Band; Hon Roll; Natl Hspnc Schlrshp Assoc; Hgh Hnrs Golden St Geom Exam; Engrng.

GONZALES, AMBER L; San Pasqual HS; Escondido, CA; (2); Church Yth Grp; Pres Frsh Cls; Var Bsktbl; Var Tennis; Var Trk; CIF Doubles Ten Championships; UCLA; Psych.

GONZALES, ANGELA; Atwater HS; Winton, CA; (2); Church Yth Grp; Cmnty Wkr; 4-H; GAA; Library Aide; SADD; Bsktbl; Sftbl; Vllybl; 4-H Awd; Coach T Ball; Merced CC; Marriage Cnslr.

GONZALES, ANNA M; Lemoore HS; Lemoore, CA; (4); 24/292; Art Clb; Church Yth Grp; Intnl Clb; Spanish Clb; JV Bsktbl; Var Capt Sftbl; Santa Clara U; Mechanical Engr.

GONZALES, ARNEL C; Franklin HS; Vallejo, CA; (1); 1/260; Chorus; Cit Awd; Hon Roll; Jr NHS; Prfct Atten Awd; SUCCESS Pgm; UNLV; Elect Engr.

GONZALES, CLEE L; Mar Vista HS; Imperial Beach, CA; (2); Art Clb; Letterman Clb; Office Aide; SADD; Band; Stage Crew; Nwsp; Yrbk; Off Soph Cls; Bsktbl; Marine Bio.

GONZALES, DAVID R; Summerville Union HS; Mi-Wuk Village, CA; (4); 18/120; Church Yth Grp; Quiz Bowl; Ski Clb; Spanish Clb; SADD; Teachers Aide; Treas Frsh Cls; Treas Soph Cls; VP Jr Cls; Rep Sr Cls; Sacramento ST U; Bio.

GONZALES, DEANNA; Rio Mesa HS; Oxnard, CA; (2); 81/300; Church Yth Grp; Drama Clb; Pep Clb; Yrbk; JV Cheerldng; Stat Score Keeper; JV Trk; Cit Awd; Hon Roll; CSF; Arch.

GONZALES, EMILY; Bishop Amat HS; El Monte, CA; (3); GAA; Drill Tm; Sec Frsh Cls; Sec Soph Cls; Sec Jr Cls; Stu Cncl; JV Vllybl; Hon Roll; NHS; Spanish NHS; Awd Hm Ec; CSF; Vlybl Awd; Jrnlsm.

GONZALES, FRANK R; Bloomington HS; Bloomington, CA; (2); German Clb; Hon Roll; Mock Trials; Acad Cmptn Cls; U Of CA Berkley; Elec Engrng.

GONZALES, GERALD G; James Lick HS; San Jose, CA; (1); Math Tm; JV Bsktbl; Suprintndnts Honr Roll; Mock Trl.

GONZALES, HENRY; San Jose High Acad; San Jose, CA; (2); Hon Roll.

GONZALES, IRIS; Franklin JR HS; Vallejo, CA; (1); #28 In Class; High Hon Roll; Jr NHS; Pediatrician.

GONZALES, ISRAEL; Santa Clara HS; Oxnard, CA; (2); 22/210; Church Yth Grp; Debate Tm; Drama Clb; NFL; Speech Tm; School Play; High Hon Roll; NHS; Actv Tradtnl Japanese Karate Do; UCLA; Bio.

GONZALES, IVY; Franklin JR HS; Vallejo, CA; (1); #48 In Class; Teachers Aide; Cit Awd; High Hon Roll; Jr NHS; Doc.

GONZALES, JAMES D; West Campus Hiram Johnson HS; Sacramento, CA; (2); Rptr Nwsp; Ftbl; Cit Awd; Prfct Atten Awd; Mesa Clb; Comp Data Prcssg Smmr Schl.

GONZALES, JOSE B; North Salinas HS; Salinas, CA; (3); Intrml Ftbl; Var Trk; Elks Awd; High Hon Roll; Rotary Awd; MVP JV Trck; Engrng.

GONZALES, JOSE M; Coalinga HS; Huron, CA; (1); DECA; FBLA; FTA; Teachers Aide; VICA; Nwsp; Var Bsbl; Var Ftbl.

GONZALES, JOSEPH R; James Monroe HS; Panorama City, CA; (1); Boy Scts; Office Aide; Band; School Play; Pres Soph Cls; Rep Stu Cncl; JV Vllybl; Cit Awd; Pres Acad Fit Awd; MVP JV Vlybl; UCLA; Srgn.

GONZALES, KRISTA L; Grossmont HS; El Cajon, CA; (2); Church Yth Grp; SADD; San Diego ST U; Jrnlsm.

GONZALES, LEILANI R; Montgomery HS; San Diego, CA; (2); Teachers Aide; Rep Frsh Cls; Mgr(s); Socr; Tennis; Stat Vllybl; Cit Awd; Hon Roll; Prfct Atten Awd; Top Engl Stu; San Diego ST U; Engl Tchr.

GONZALES, LILYANA; Carlsbad HS; Carlsbad, CA; (3); 38/370; Debate Tm; Drama Clb; Speech Tm; Thesps; Chorus; School Musical; School Play; Capt Cheerldng; Vllybl; High Hon Roll; Advrtsng.

GONZALES, MADONNALISA T; St Joseph HS; Lakewood, CA; (2); 12/273; Cmnty Wkr; Drama Clb; Hosp Aide; Science Clb; Spanish Clb; SADD; Chorus; Hon Roll; Yth Ending Hunger; U CA Irvine; Elec Eng.

GONZALES, MANUEL; Cantwell HS; Los Angeles, CA; (4); Am Leg Boys St; Letterman Clb; Pep Clb; Science Clb; Varsity Clb; School Musical; School Play; Rep Stu Cncl; Var Capt Bsktbl; Gov Hon Prg Awd; Santa Fe Leg MVP,Rio Hondo Vlly MVP, Schl MVP Bsktbl 89-90; Montebello Nwsp Plyr Yr; CIF 1st Tm; CA ST U Los Angeles.

GONZALES, MARIE TRINIDAD M; Jefferson HS; Daly City, CA; (2); Church Yth Grp; Science Clb; Atoms Family 89-90; UCSC; Poli Sci.

GONZALES, MARRINA R; Eisenhower HS; Rialto, CA; (3); GAA; Math Tm; Pep Clb; Cheerldng; Socr; Sftbl; Prfct Atten Awd; Dancer At Dance Studio; U Of CA Riverside; Bus.

GONZALES, MELISSA A; Notre Dame HS; Gilroy, CA; (3); Cmnty Wkr; Intnl Clb; Service Clb; SADD; Stage Crew; Rep Soph Cls; Off Jr Cls; VP Sr Cls; Hon Roll; Ed.

GONZALES, MICHAEL; Hogan SR HS; Vallejo, CA; (4); 4/385; Key Clb; Math Clb; Service Clb; VP Spanish Clb; Var Tennis; High Hon Roll; Pres Acad Fit Awd; Sal; U CA-DAVIS; Aernutcl Engr.

GONZALES, MICHAEL C; Seaside HS; Seaside, CA; (2); AFS; Spanish Clb.

GONZALES, MICHAEL J; Andrew Hill HS; San Jose, CA; (2); Church Yth Grp; Bsbl; Bsktbl; Bsbl MVP; Outstndng Ath; Sprts Med.

GONZALES, MICHAEL L; Thousand Oaks HS; Thousand Oaks, CA; (3); 63/541; SADD; JV Var Bsktbl; JV Var Ftbl; Yth To Yth; Pre-Med.

GONZALES, MICHELLE; East Bakersfield HS; Bakersfield, CA; (4); 4/445; Intnl Clb; Latin Clb; Math Clb; Q&S; Science Clb; Treas Spanish Clb; SADD; Rptr Nwsp; Treas Frsh Cls; Rep Stu Cncl; Qn-Cinco De Mayo Parade; Gottschalk's Hi-Deb; CA Poly San Luis Obispo; Math.

GONZALES, MIRNA E; Brea-Olinda HS; Brea, CA; (3); 38/290; Office Aide; Teachers Aide; Cit Awd; High Hon Roll; Hon Roll; Cal ST Fullerton; RN.

GONZALES, MONIQUE M; Gonzales Union HS; Gonzales, CA; (3); 9/200; Church Yth Grp; JV Bsktbl; Hon Roll; NHS.

GONZALES, NATALIE; Oxnard HS; Oxnard, CA; (2); 17/850; Hon Roll; Pres Acad Fit Awd; UCSB; Phsych.

GONZALES, NERRESSA C; Grace M Davis HS; Modesto, CA; (4); Church Yth Grp; Drama Clb; Speech Tm; Chorus; Phtg Yrbk; Rep Frsh Cls; VP Soph Cls; Cheerldng; Elks Awd; Hon Roll; Stanford; Med.

GONZALES, NICOLE R; Oxnard HS; Oxnard, CA; (3); Office Aide; Teachers Aide; Prfct Atten Awd; San Diego ST U; Poltcl Sci.

GONZALES, NORMAN A; Coachella Valley HS; Coachella, CA; (3); Am Leg Boys St; Debate Tm; Math Clb; Model UN; NFL; Speech Tm; Varsity Clb; Drm Mjr(t); Jazz Band; Mrchg Band; Poltcl Sci.

GONZALES, PATRICIA J; Orosi HS; Cutler, CA; (2); FFA; SADD; Hon Roll; Coll Of Sequoias; Educ.

GONZALES, RAMONA M; Bullard HS; Fresno, CA; (1); Church Yth Grp; Mrchg Band; Prfct Atten Awd; Fresno ST; Med.

GONZALES, RAY A; Fontana HS; Fontana, CA; (3); Boy Scts; Yrbk; Hon Roll; Ran A Marathon; UC Santa Barbara; Ec.

GONZALES, ROY D; Carson HS; Carson, CA; (3); Computer Clb; French Clb; Office Aide; Teachers Aide; Yrbk; JV Crs Cntry; UC Riverside; Aero.

GONZALES, SAMUEL R; San Benito HS; Hollister, CA; (4); AFS; Band; Mrchg Band; Pep Band; High Hon Roll; Hon Roll; Lion Awd; Pres Acad Fit Awd; Sci Exchange Stu To Soviet Union Smmr 89; San Francisco Giants Hnr Marching Band 87; U Of CO Boulder; Sports Med.

GONZALES, SHANNA N; Clouis HS; Fresno, CA; (3); Church Yth Grp; Dance Clb; FBLA; Hosp Aide; Library Aide; Office Aide; Pep Clb; Ski Clb; Spanish Clb; SADD; Rep For Miss Teen Pagent In CA 2 Yrs In Row; Fresno ST; Nrsng.

GONZALES, TANYA; Foothill HS; Bakersfield, CA; (4); 24/250; Am Leg Aux Girls St; Debate Tm; Drama Clb; NFL; Speech Tm; SADD; Acpl Chr; Chorus; School Musical; Hon Roll; Talent Show FHS & Two Yrs Wnnr; Reach For Stars Bakersfld Talent Show & Cruiseship Tlnt Show SS HI; HI U; Profsnl Singer.

GONZALES, VICTOR M; Sierra Vista HS; Baldwin Park, CA; (1); Hon Roll; Prfct Atten Awd; Elec Engr.

GONZALES, YOLANDA; Exeter Union HS; Farmersville, CA; (4); Computer Clb; English Clb; FFA; FHA; Math Tm; Spanish Clb; Teachers Aide; School Play; Trk; Vllybl; Yty Employment Pgm Achvt; Szusa Unified Schl Dist Cert Of Achvt; COS; RN.

GONZALES-TOVAR, MARCELA G; Bisho O Dowd HS; Oakland, CA; (2); Hon Roll; Cinco De Mayo Grp; Span Achvt Awd; Geo Achvt Awd; Law.

GONZALEZ, ADRIAN M; Chaminade College Prep; Simi Valley, CA; (3); Church Yth Grp; Cmnty Wkr; Off Library Aide; Service Clb; Spanish Clb; Speech Tm; Varsity Clb; Chorus; School Musical; Var Crs Cntry; Greenpeace; Amnesty Intl; Teens For Teens; Cornell U; Wrtng.

GONZALEZ, ALBERT; Colton HS; Colton, CA; (2); JV Bsbl; JV Trk; Var Wrstlng; Prfct Atten Awd; Ftbl, Bsbl & Bsktbl Rectnl Pks City Leag; U Of Southern CA; Law Enfrcmnt.

GONZALEZ, ALBERT; Leuzinger HS; Gardena, CA; (3); Prfct Atten Awd.

GONZALEZ, ALBERTO N; Leuzinger HS; Lawndale, CA; (3); Am Leg Boys St; Key Clb; Treas Pres Soph Cls; Pres VP Jr Cls; VP Stu Cncl; JV Capt Bsbl; JV Var Ftbl; Hon Roll; YMCA Yth Of Yr Awd 90, Model Legislature/Court CA, Commssn Chm Yth Sec Of St; Poltcl Sci.

GONZALEZ, ALEJANDRA M; Montebello HS; Montebello, CA; (3); Cmnty Wkr; Girl Scts; Sec VICA; Acpl Chr; Chorus; Cit Awd; Hon Roll; Prfct Atten Awd; UC San Diego; Ed.

GONZALEZ, ALEX; Laton HS; Laton, CA; (2); Church Yth Grp; Var Bsbl; Var Bsktbl; JV Ftbl; Hon Roll; UCLA.

GONZALEZ, ALFONSO E; Southwest HS; San Ysidro, CA; (4); 40/480; JA; Key Clb; Latin Clb; Office Aide; Spanish Clb; Teachers Aide; Cit Awd; NHS; Prfct Atten Awd; Upwrd Bnd; CSF; CLY Ldrshp Cnfrnc Stu; Vlnt Tm At Rstrnt; U Of Miami; Intl Bus.

GONZALEZ, ALFREDO; Villa Park HS; Orange, CA; (2); Boy Scts; Church Yth Grp; FBLA; Stage Crew; JV Ftbl; Intrml Wt Lftg; JV Wrstlng; Hon Roll; Scuba Sfty; USSD; Chrprctr.

GONZALEZ, AMY; Fresno HS; Fresno, CA; (1); Chorus; Crs Cntry; Trk; Photo; Art.

GONZALEZ, ANA; Southwest HS; San Diego, CA; (3); Church Yth Grp; Teachers Aide; Hon Roll; Prfct Atten Awd; USCD; Child Psych.

GONZALEZ, ANDREA; Pasadena HS; Pasadena, CA; (1); High Hon Roll; Hon Roll; MECHA VP; Pasadena Schlrshp Cmmtte; Psych.

GONZALEZ, ANDRES E; Elk Grove HS; Elk Grove, CA; (2); 1/550; Church Yth Grp; Latin Clb; Math Clb; Math Tm; Science Clb; Chorus; Church Choir; Variety Show; Rep Frsh Cls; Rep Soph Cls; CA All St Hon Choir; Toastmasters Intl Spch Clb; MESA.

GONZALEZ, ANGIE; California HS; Whittier, CA; (2); 1/31; Bsktbl; Socr; Tennis; Vllybl; Cit Awd; Hon Roll; Prfct Atten Awd.

GONZALEZ, ANNETTE; Bishopamat Memorial HS; El Monte, CA; (3); Church Yth Grp; French Clb; Red Cross Aide; Spanish Clb; Teachers Aide; Hon Roll; NHS; CSF; Slvr Scrn Clb; Sec Fri Nght Live; USC; Physician.

GONZALEZ, ANTHONY; Roosevelt HS; Los Angeles, CA; (2); Art Clb; Aud/Vis; Computer Clb; Drama Clb; Math Clb; Pep Band; Rptr Nwsp; VP Stu Cncl; Cit Awd; Prfct Atten Awd; Art Prdctn & Grde Achvt Awds; Lincoln Medical Magnet; Med.

GONZALEZ, ARACELI; Morningside HS; Inglewood, CA; (2); Latin Clb; Off Jr Cls; Sftbl; Hon Roll; Inglewood Tech Inst Pgm; Sthrn CA Rgnl Occptnl Ctr.

GONZALEZ, ARMANDO; Pasadena HS; Pasadena, CA; (2); Church Yth Grp; Library Aide; Math Clb; Ftbl; Mth Engr Sci Achvt; CSF; Pasadena City Coll.

GONZALEZ, ATHENA A; Garces Memorial HS; Bakersfield, CA; (3); Church Yth Grp; Cmnty Wkr; Dance Clb; Drama Clb; Pres Service Clb; Teachers Aide; School Play; Stage Crew; Rep Frsh Cls; Rep Soph Cls; Kern Kiwanis JR Miss/Young Woman Of The Year Contestant; Loyola Marymount; Political Sci.

GONZALEZ, BELINDA; Fontana HS; Fontana, CA; (3); FBLA; Teachers Aide; Band; Mrchg Band; Orch; Pep Band; Mgr(s); Score Keeper; Socr; Sftbl; Bus Mgmt.

GONZALEZ, BETTY; Richard Gahr HS; Artesia, CA; (2); 38/490; Blue/Gold Awds For Frnch & Math; USC; Bus.

GONZALEZ, BLANCA R; Saddleback HS; Santa Ana, CA; (3); Church Yth Grp; Computer Clb; Office Aide; Bsktbl; Cit Awd; Hon Roll; Cal ST Fullerton; Comp Spclst.

GONZALEZ, CARMEN; Firebaugh HS; Firebaugh, CA; (4); 3/80; Am Leg Aux Girls St; FTA; Pep Band; Ed Nwsp; Pres Soph Cls; Pres Sr Cls; Co-Capt Bsktbl; Vllybl; Pres Acad Fit Awd; Acad Dcthln Team; CA ST U Fresno; Math.

GONZALEZ, CELIA; Chula Vista HS; San Ysidro, CA; (3); Church Yth Grp; Dance Clb; Girl Scts; Church Choir; Cit Awd; Prfct Atten Awd; Pres Acad Fit Awd; CSF Stu; U CA-SAN Diego; Psych.

GONZALEZ, CESAR; Sanger HS; Sanger, CA; (2); Model UN; ROTC; Drill Tm; Intrml Crs Cntry; JV Capt Socr; Hon Roll; Prfct Atten Awd; Pres Acad Fit Awd; VP MESA; CA Schlrshp Fed; Stanford; Mech Engng.

GONZALEZ, CESAR G; Nogales HS; La Puente, CA; (3); 77/568; High Hon Roll; Hon Roll; Prfct Atten Awd; Mech Engrg.

GONZALEZ, CHRISTINA L; Adelante HS; Roseville, CA; (4); Computer Clb; Office Aide; Teachers Aide; Nwsp; Sftbl; Stu Cncl; Sierra Coll; Engrng.

GONZALEZ, CHRISTINA M; Casa Grande HS; Petaluma, CA; (2); 76/295; Drama Clb; French Clb; Stage Crew; Variety Show; Hon Roll; Jr NHS; NHS; Achvt Awd; Hnrs Eng; U Of San Francisco; Law.

GONZALEZ, CHRISTINA M; San Gabriel Mission HS; Montebello, CA; (3); #2 In Class; GAA; Flag Corp; Bausch & Lomb Sci Awd; High Hon Roll; NHS; Bosco Tech Tall Falg Corp Capt; Medallion Awd Wnnr Math; CSF; Med.

GONZALEZ, CINDI M; James Lick HS; San Jose, CA; (3); Church Yth Grp; Cmnty Wkr; Intnl Clb; Spanish Clb; Teachers Aide; Rptr Rep Nwsp; Var Bsktbl; Hon Roll; UCLA; Jrnlsm.

GONZALEZ, CINDY E; Los Amigos HS; Fountain Valley, CA; (2); Dance Clb; French Clb; Swmmng; Vllybl; Hon Roll; Bus.

GONZALEZ, CLAUDIA; San Pedro HS; San Pedro, CA; (3); Computer Clb; Dance Clb; Office Aide; Off Jr Cls; Cit Awd; Prfct Atten Awd; Commodors Svc Clb; Bus.

GONZALEZ, CLAUDIA; William Workman HS; La Puente, CA; (3); Math Tm; Jazz Band; Mrchg Band; Orch; Hon Roll; Spanish NHS; 3rd Pl Natl Spnsh Exam; Schlrshp For Saturday Music Cls.

GONZALEZ, CRISTINA; Valley HS; Sacramento, CA; (2); 19/434; Church Yth Grp; SADD; JV Var Mgr(s); Var Socr; Wt Lftg; High Hon Roll; Hon Roll; Acad Olympics Hnrs Level; CA Schlrshp Fed:Gifted & Talented Ed; Sacramento ST U; Admin Justice.

GONZALEZ, CYNTHIA S; San Benito HS; Hollister, CA; (3); Art Clb; Church Yth Grp; Math Clb; Science Clb; Church Choir; JV Bsktbl; Var Mgr(s); Hon Roll; Piano Lssns; Mrne Bio.

GONZALEZ, DANIEL; Nogales HS; Walnut, CA; (2); 100/989; Rep Soph Cls; JV Ftbl; JV Wrstlng; Hon Roll; Prfct Atten Awd; Acting; College; Stock Broker.

GONZALEZ, DANIEL F; Cantwell HS; Los Angeles, CA; (3); Cmnty Wkr; Dance Clb; Nwsp; Yrbk; Sec Jr Cls; Stu Cncl; Socr; Hon Roll; Poster Club; Med.

GONZALEZ, DELIANA M; Nogales HS; W Covina, CA; (3); 14/544; Teachers Aide; High Hon Roll; Outstndng Performance IPS & Alg I; MT SAC; Courtroom Reporter.

GONZALEZ, DIANA C; John Burroughs HS; Burbank, CA; (3); JA; Natl Beta Clb; Spanish Clb; Rep Nwsp; Cit Awd; Hon Roll; Prfct Atten Awd; Outstndng Schlrshp; Frgn Lang Awd; Cert Mrt; CSUN; Engr.

GONZALEZ, DIANA M; Fairfield HS; Fairfield, CA; (2); Church Yth Grp; Dance Clb; Drama Clb; ROTC; Spanish Clb; Band; Church Choir; Color Guard; Drill Tm; Mrchg Band; Law.

GONZALEZ, DOLORES; Montebello HS; Montebello, CA; (3); Mrchg Band; Yrbk; Fashion Dsgn.

GONZALEZ, EDDIE; Mc Farland HS; Mc Farland, CA; (4); 20/100; Boy Scts; FFA; Letterman Clb; Bsbl; Mgr(s); Tennis; Wrstlng; Cit Awd; Hon Roll; FFA Ofcr; Star Greenhand & Star Chap Farmer Degrees; Medallion Wnnr Ag; Ag.

GONZALEZ, EDGAR F; Canoga Park HS; Los Angeles, CA; (2); Spanish Clb; Socr; Prfct Atten Awd; Comp Prog.

GONZALEZ, EDUARDO L; Coalinga HS; Huron, CA; (2); 2/175; AFS; Church Yth Grp; FCA; FTA; Math Tm; Band; Mrchg Band; Pep Band; Ed Nwsp; Ed Yrbk; Berkeley U; Arch.

GONZALEZ, EILEEN MICHELLE; Serrano HS; Phelan, CA; (3); Church Yth Grp; French Clb; English; Law.

GONZALEZ, ELAINE; Chestnut Avenue Baptist Acad; Fresno, CA; (1); Drama Clb; Teachers Aide; Chorus; School Musical; School Play; Hghst Grd In Hstry & Engl Cls; Plyd A Part Fresnos Chldrns Plyhse; Stu Of Wk Computech Mid Schl; Cal St U Of Fresno; Attrny.

GONZALEZ, ELEAZAR; Franklin HS; Stockton, CA; (2); Church Yth Grp; Bsbl; Hon Roll; Prfct Atten Awd; Delta Coll; Bus.

GONZALEZ, ELISA; Huntington Beach HS; Huntington Beach, CA; (3); Dance Clb; Orange Coast Coll; Pre-Med.

GONZALEZ, ELIZABETH; Palo Verde HS; Blythe, CA; (2); Spanish Clb; Flag Corp; Hon Roll; NHS; Fut Ldrs Of Amer 88; Tchrs Aide Catechism; U Of San Bernardino; Cnslr.

GONZALEZ, ELIZABETH; Wasco Union HS; Yuma, AZ; (3); Pres Frsh Cls; Powder Puff Ftbl; Hon Roll; Degree Of Schlstc Proficiency; Art Cert; Specl Tiger Of Month; AZ Western Coll; Court Reportr.

GONZALEZ, ELOY; Orosi HS; Cutler, CA; (3); Cmnty Wkr; SADD; Bsbl; Ftbl; Wt Lftg; Cit Awd; High Hon Roll; Hon Roll; Fresno Bee Plyr Wk; All League Plyr Yr; Fresno ST Coll; Bus.

GONZALEZ, ENRIQUE; Berkeley HS; San Pablo, CA; (4); Spanish Clb; Phtg Yrbk; Lit Mag; Hon Roll; Kiwanis Awd; UCO/Mesa Math & Sci Tutor Pgm; La Raza Latinos Unidos Clb; UC Berkeley; Elec Engrng.

GONZALEZ, ERIBERTO A; Montebello HS; Montebello, CA; (2); Socr; Vllybl; Spanish NHS; Engr.

GONZALEZ, ERICA; Orosi HS; Cutler, CA; (3); FHA; Pep Clb; Spanish Clb; SADD; Chorus; Stu Cncl; Cheerldng; Powder Puff Ftbl; Hon Roll; Ldrshp Cls; Pres FHA; JSA; Fresno ST; Bus.

GONZALEZ, ERIKA; Paramount HS; Paramount, CA; (2); Church Yth Grp; Drama Clb; Hosp Aide; Key Clb; Speech Tm; SADD; Pres Frsh Cls; VP Soph Cls; Pres Stu Cncl; Opt Clb Awd.

GONZALEZ, ERIKA J; Loretto-Conaty HS; Los Angeles, CA; (3); 6/106; FBLA; Office Aide; Yrbk; Hon Roll; NHS; Natl Hnr Soc Sec/Treas; Bus Admin.

GONZALEZ, ERNIE; Bell Gardens HS; Commerce, CA; (2); Chess Clb; Church Yth Grp; Bsbl; Tennis; Prfct Atten Awd; U Of San Diego; Bus Admin.

GONZALEZ, EZEQUIEL; Orosi HS; Cutler, CA; (3); Bsbl; Ftbl; Hon Roll; High 4 Clb; Kings River CC; Law Enfrcmnt.

GONZALEZ, FEDALIS A; Monterey HS; Seaside, CA; (2); Drama Clb; Stage Crew; Hon Roll; Fresno ST; Child Care.

GONZALEZ, FERNANDO; Pittsburg HS; Pittsburg, CA; (1); Engr.

GONZALEZ, GABRIEL; La Quinta HS; Westminster, CA; (3); Boy Scts; Letterman Clb; Science Clb; Varsity Clb; Var L Crs Cntry; Var L Trk; Crss Cntry MVP 89-90; Comp Pgmng.

GONZALEZ, GABRIELA V; Central Union HS; El Centro, CA; (4); High Hon Roll; Cls Stu Month; UCSD; Translator.

GONZALEZ, GEORGE A; Burbank HS; Burbank, CA; (2); Teachers Aide; JV Capt Bsbl; JV Capt Ftbl; Hnrs Engl; Hnrs World Cultures; Elec Engrg.

GONZALEZ, GLADYS; Chino HS; Ontario, CA; (3); Sec Pep Clb; Capt Bsbl; JV Capt Bsktbl; Cit Awd; Hon Roll; Prfct Atten Awd; 2nd Pl Typng CUSD Stu Voctnl Skills Cmptn; 3rd Pl Yth Expo Stu Voctnl Olympcs Typng; Med.

GONZALEZ, GLORIA; Santa Ana Valley HS; Santa Ana, CA; (3); Cmnty Wkr; Drama Clb; Pep Clb; Chorus; School Musical; Variety Show; Cheerldng; Sftbl; Tennis; Hon Roll; Cal ST; Psych.

GONZALEZ, GLORIA S; Venice HS; Los Angeles, CA; (2); Orch; Chatelaines Hist; MESA; Bus Educ.

GONZALEZ, GREGORIO; Ramona HS; Ramona, CA; (3); Church Yth Grp; Cmnty Wkr; JA; School Musical; Rptr Nwsp; JV Socr; Masonic Awd; BECA Fndtn & Hispanos Unidos Essay Cntst Wnnr; Musician.

GONZALEZ, GUADALUPE; Baldwin Park HS; Baldwin Park, CA; (1); Band; Mrchg Band; Cit Awd; Hon Roll; UCLA; Law.

GONZALEZ, HENRY H; Fontana HS; Fontana, CA; (3); Intrml Bsbl; High Hon Roll; Pres Acad Fit Awd; CSF; EOP; Law.

GONZALEZ, IMELDA; Gonzales HS; Soledad, CA; (2); Treas Soph Cls; High Hon Roll; Hon Roll; CSF; UC Davis; Surgeon.

GONZALEZ, INES; Mercy HS; S San Francisco, CA; (4); 2/103; Church Yth Grp; Service Clb; Ed Yrbk; Trk; High Hon Roll; Kiwanis Awd; Rotary Awd; CA Assmbly 19th Dist Yth Advsry Comm; JR Statesmn Of Amer, Smmr Schl, Rgnl Nwspr Edtr & Campus Mnst; Engr.

GONZALEZ, INEZ ANDREA; Downey HS; Downey, CA; (2); Church Yth Grp; Teachers Aide; Stage Crew; Variety Show; Lcl & Rgnl Dists Tlnt Cmptns Ballet; Bellflower Prfrmng Arts For 3 Yrs; U Of CA Irvine; Dance.

GONZALEZ, IRENE; California HS; Whittier, CA; (3); Office Aide; Pep Clb; SADD; Capt Tennis; 1st Pl Photo Cntst; UCLA; Crmnl Law.

GONZALEZ, ISAAC I; Edison HS; Fresno, CA; (2); Cmnty Wkr; Cit Awd; Joe Casarez Schlrshp Awd 89-90; Teacher.

GONZALEZ, JAIME; El Capitan HS; Lakeside, CA; (2); Band; Jazz Band; Mrchg Band; Prfct Atten Awd; San Diego ST U; Elec Engr.

GONZALEZ, JANET; Fontana HS; Fontana, CA; (4); 150/800; Principials Hnr Roll; UC Long Beach; Marine Biology.

GONZALEZ, JEFFREY; Don Bosco Technical Inst; Los Angeles, CA; (3); JV Bsbl; JV Score Keeper; Hon Roll; Jr NHS; NHS; Cal Poly Pomona; Elctrncs Engr.

GONZALEZ, JESSE; St Bonaventure HS; Santa Paula, CA; (3); Church Yth Grp; Pres Jr Cls; Var JV Ftbl; Biology.

GONZALEZ JR, JESUS; Sierra Vista HS; Baldwin Park, CA; (1); High Hon Roll; UCLA; Pedtrcn.

GONZALEZ, JONATHAN P; Mater Dei HS; Santa Ana, CA; (1); ROTC; Drill Tm; Gldn St Math Awd.

GONZALEZ, JOSE; John Glenn HS; Norwalk, CA; (2); Art Clb; Computer Clb; Library Aide; Teachers Aide; Off Soph Cls; Ftbl; Wt Lftg; Cit Awd; High Hon Roll; Spanish NHS.

GONZALEZ, JOSE L; Marshall Fundamental HS; Pasadena, CA; (1); Spanish Clb; JV Bsbl; Marshall Fundamental; Arch.

GONZALEZ, JOSE L; Orosi HS; Orosi, CA; (3); Teachers Aide; Hon Roll; Sicon Cnslr; COS; Electrncs.

GONZALEZ, JOSE L; Perris HS Lake Continua; Perris, CA; (4); Socr; Hon Roll; Natl Ed Cntr; Photo.

GONZALEZ, JULIAN; Orosi HS; Orosi, CA; (3); 4/180; Drama Clb; Math Clb; Office Aide; Spanish Clb; SADD; School Play; Variety Show; High Hon Roll; SR Clss Treas 90-91; Yrbk Stf 90-91.

GONZALEZ, KATRINA; Whitney HS; Cerritos, CA; (3); Rep Cmnty Wkr; Sec FBLA; Key Clb; Color Guard; Drill Tm; Rptr Nwsp; High Hon Roll; Hon Roll.

GONZALEZ, KRISTA M; Bella Vista HS; Fair Oaks, CA; (2); SADD; Trk; Intl Mdlng & Tlnt Assn Awds; Jr Model Of Yr 2nd Rnnrup; Sci.

GONZALEZ, LAURA; Samuel F M Morse HS; San Diego, CA; (4); Library Aide; Math Tm; ROTC; Drill Tm; Navy.

GONZALEZ, LAYLA ESTELA; San Fernando HS; San Fernando, CA; (4); 6/2500; Am Leg Aux Girls St; Service Clb; Var Tennis; DAR Awd; Hon Roll; NHS; Ntl Merit SF; Pres Acad Fit Awd; Harvard Bk Prz; CSU Northridge; Pediatrics.

GONZALEZ, LETICIA; Sierra Vista HS; Baldwin Park, CA; (3); French Clb; Hon Roll; Friday Night Live 88-89; Mt San Antonio Coll; Bus.

GONZALEZ, LIDIA; Imperial HS; Imperial, CA; (4); VP AFS; Spanish Clb; SADD; Sprt Ed Nwsp; Phtg Yrbk; Treas Jr Cls; VP Stu Cncl; L Bsktbl; L Sftbl; L Vllybl; CSF; Mock Trial; US Army Res Schlr/Athl Awd; Elec Engrng.

GONZALEZ, LIZ V; Pius X HS; S Gate, CA; (4); Band; Powder Puff Ftbl; Bio Med Club; CA ST Los Angeles; Hlth.

GONZALEZ, LORENA; Exeter Union HS; Farmersville, CA; (1); 10/309; JV Sftbl; High Hon Roll; Hon Roll; UCLA; Law.

GONZALEZ, LORETTA M; Sweetwater Union HS; National City, CA; (2); 97/600; Model UN; Office Aide; Treas Frsh Cls; Bsktbl; Cit Awd; Hon Roll; Pres Acad Fit Awd; Marketing/Management.

GONZALEZ, LOURDES V; Arcadia HS; Arcadia, CA; (3); Teachers Aide; Prncpls Recgntn Hnr Rl; Atten Hnr Rl; Advrtsng.

GONZALEZ, LUCY; Bishop Amat Memorial HS; Valinda, CA; (3); Church Yth Grp; Hosp Aide; Teachers Aide; Chorus; Church Choir; School Musical; Rptr Nwsp; Hon Roll; NHS; Theme Song For Yth Day 90; Voices That Challng; Christn Svc Awd; Cert Of Apprctn Am Nrsng Home Assoc; Civl Rights Law.

GONZALEZ, LUPE; Riverdale HS; Caruthers, CA; (3); Trk; Vllybl; High Hon Roll; Hon Roll; Acad Achvt Awd Art Apprctn; Fresno ST U; Teacher.

GONZALEZ, LYDIA M; Bishop Amat HS; La Puente, CA; (3); Church Yth Grp; Spanish Clb; Teachers Aide; Hon Roll; Christian Sci Clss; Psych.

GONZALEZ, MANUEL; Hueneme HS; Oxnard, CA; (2); Yrbk; Off Sr Cls; Bnkng.

GONZALEZ, MANUEL; Righetti HS; Santa Maria, CA; (1); Church Yth Grp; 4-H; FFA; Teachers Aide; Hon Roll; CA Polytech ST U; Ag Bus Mgmt.

GONZALEZ, MARCELLO A; Blair HS; Pasadena, CA; (2); ROTC; Drill Tm; Wt Lftg; Cit Awd; Hon Roll; Pres Acad Fit Awd; Med.

GONZALEZ, MARCOS M; C K Mc Ciatchy HS; Sacramento, CA; (2); 100/442; ROTC; Teachers Aide; JV Bsbl; Var Ftbl; JV Mgr(s); MVP Bsbl; Ftbl Bst Lnmn Awd; Depaul U; Doctor.

GONZALEZ, MARCUS; Mc Farland HS; Mc Farland, CA; (4); FFA; Varsity Clb; Band; Jazz Band; Mrchg Band; Pep Band; Bsbl; Trk; Wrstlng.

GONZALEZ, MARGARITA; Dana Hills HS; Dana Point, CA; (3); French Clb; Chorus; JV Crs Cntry; Cit Awd; High Hon Roll; Hon Roll; Medical Recptnst Cert ROP; UCLA; Med.

GONZALEZ, MARGARITA; El Rancho HS; Pico Rivera, CA; (1); Cmnty Wkr; Science Clb; High Hon Roll; Hon Roll; Math Engrng Sci Achvt Secy; CSF; U CA Partnership; USC; Sci.

GONZALEZ, MARGARITA; Woodland HS; Knights Landing, CA; (3); Sec Church Yth Grp; 4-H; Church Choir; MESA; EAOP; UC Davis; Spanish Ed.

GONZALEZ, MARIA A; Palo Verde HS; Blythe, CA; (2); Church Yth Grp; FFA; Spanish Clb; SADD; Church Choir; Flag Corp; Crs Cntry; Cit Awd; Hon Roll; Church Yth-Treas; Future Leaders Of Amer; Cal ST-SAN Bernardino; Lawyer.

GONZALEZ, MARIA L; Pasadena HS; Pasadena, CA; (3); Spanish Clb; Sftbl; Tennis; Bus.

GONZALEZ, MARIA OSORIO; Bassett HS; La Puente, CA; (2); Nwsp; Yrbk; Lit Mag; Off Jr Cls; Bsbl; Bsktbl; Golf; Gym; Swmmng; Tennis; Flight Atten.

GONZALEZ, MARIA R; John Burroughs HS; Burbank, CA; (4); Church Yth Grp; Computer Clb; Teachers Aide; Chorus; Church Choir; Off Sr Cls; Accntng.

GONZALEZ, MARIBEL; Pittsburg HS; Pittsburg, CA; (1); Latin Clb; GPA 3.12; Merit List; Bi-Lingual Stu Span & Engl; Stanford; Psych.

GONZALEZ, MARICELA; Bishop Amat HS; West Covina, CA; (4); 17/390; Pep Clb; Cheerldng; Pom Pon; Wt Lftg; High Hon Roll; Hon Roll; NHS; French I First Honors; Top 10% Of Cls; CSF; Lolyola Marymount; Dentistry.

GONZALEZ, MARIO; Napa HS; Napa, CA; (4); AFS; Cmnty Wkr; French Clb; Key Clb; Latin Clb; Spanish Clb; Nwsp; Cit Awd; High Hon Roll; Hon Roll; Treas Amer Frgn Srvc Clb; San-Jose ST U; Comp Sci.

GONZALEZ, MARISOL; Canyon HS; Canyon Country, CA; (3); Dance Clb; Girl Scts; JV Bsbl; JV Swmmng; Art Class Got Put Into Art Instruction School; CA Arts; Cartoonist.

GONZALEZ, MARTHA P; Chula Vista HS; Chula Vista, CA; (3); Spanish Clb; Swmmng; Trk; Fshn Dsgnr.

GONZALEZ, MELISA; Yosemite HS; Coarsegold, CA; (2); Church Yth Grp; French Clb; Cit Awd; Pr Cnslng; Piano; Lang.

GONZALEZ, MELISSA I; Etiwanda HS; Alta Loma, CA; (3); 6/606; Church Yth Grp; Spanish Clb; Church Choir; Lit Mag; JV Var Tennis; Hon Roll; Educ.

GONZALEZ, MICHELE; San Gorgonio HS; San Bernardino, CA; (3); Hist FBLA; Office Aide; Spanish Clb; CSU San Bernardino; Nrsg.

GONZALEZ, MIKE; Orosi HS; Orosi, CA; (2); FFA; Latin Clb; Spanish Clb; Church Choir; Stage Crew; Nwsp; Off Frsh Cls; Off Soph Cls; Off Jr Cls; Bsbl; Ldrshp Awd; Fresno ST; Law Enfrcmt.

GONZALEZ, MIRIAM; Palo Verde HS; Blythe, CA; (3); Church Yth Grp; Pep Clb; Spanish Clb; School Musical; Yrbk; Sec Jr Cls; Sftbl; High Hon Roll; NHS; Pres Acad Fit Awd; CSF; Stanford U; Med.

GONZALEZ, MONICA; Coachella Valley HS; Coachella, CA; (3); Pep Clb; Varsity Clb; Rep Soph Cls; Var Bsktbl; Intrml Var Cheerldng; Var Gym; Var Trk; JV Vllybl; Cal ST Fullerton; Comm.

GONZALEZ, MONICA M; West Valley Christian Schl; Canoga Park, CA; (3); Church Yth Grp; Church Choir; School Musical; School Play; Yrbk; Hon Roll; Spiritual Ldrshp Award; Youth Fellowship Worker; English Awards; Day Care Worker; Speech Awards; Masters Coll; Liberal Arts.

GONZALEZ, NANCY E; Palm Springs HS; Palm Springs, CA; (3); Am Leg Aux Girls St; High Hon Roll; Hon Roll; Rotary Awd; Maya Clb Pres; CSF; Natl French Exam; Teaching.

GONZALEZ, OLIVIA S; Brawley Union HS; Brawley, CA; (4); 20/290; Church Yth Grp; Letterman Clb; Pep Clb; Spanish Clb; SADD; Varsity Clb; L Var Crs Cntry; Powder Puff Ftbl; L Var Trk; Prfct Atten Awd; San Diego ST U; Liberal Arts.

GONZALEZ, OSCAR; James Logan HS; Union City, CA; (3); Hon Roll; Prfct Atten Awd; Partnership Prgm; Arch.

GONZALEZ, PATRICIA; Carson HS; Carson, CA; (2); Latin Clb; Spanish Clb; Hon Roll; Bus.

GONZALEZ, PEDRO A; Irvine HS; Irvine, CA; (2); Lcrss; Cit Awd; Pres Acad Fit Awd; Elec Engrng.

GONZALEZ, RAQUEL; St Francis HS; San Jose, CA; (2); 151/358; SADD; High Hon Roll; Hon Roll; Santa Clara U; Law.

GONZALEZ, REIMEN; Paso Robles HS; Paso Robles, CA; (2); Elks Awd; High Hon Roll; Hon Roll; Mst Imprvd Stu Awd; Air Force; CHP.

GONZALEZ, ROCIO J; Indio HS; Indio, CA; (1); Church Yth Grp; Drill Tm; School Musical; Sftbl; Comp Tech.

GONZALEZ, ROLANDO; Orosi HS; Orosi, CA; (3).

GONZALEZ, ROSA; Riverdale HS; Caruthers, CA; (3); VICA; Trk; Vllybl; High Hon Roll; Hon Roll; Prfct Atten Awd; Vrs Mdls Trck; Accntnt.

GONZALEZ, ROSA M; Paramount HS; South Gate, CA; (3); Teachers Aide; Band; Hon Roll; ROP Crtfd Flrst.

GONZALEZ, ROSALIA; Gary HS; Pomona, CA; (2); Art Clb.

GONZALEZ, ROSAURA; Roosevelt HS; Modesto, CA; (3); L ROTC; Rptr Nwsp; Cit Awd; DAR Awd; Hon Roll; ROTC Drill Tm; CCC; Asst Physcn.

GONZALEZ, RUBEN; Strathmore Union HS; Strathmore, CA; (2); #10 In Class; Latin Clb; Intrml Bsktbl; High Hon Roll; San Luis Obispo; Math.

GONZALEZ, RUBEN A; Gladstone HS; Azusa, CA; (3); Var JV Crs Cntry; JV Trk; Wt Lftg; Prfct Atten Awd.

GONZALEZ, RUDY; Bell Gardens HS; Bell Gardens, CA; (1); FCA; Bsbl; Bsktbl; Ftbl; Wt Lftg; Wrstlng; Pres Acad Fit Awd.

GONZALEZ, SALLY; Elsinore HS; Lake Elsinore, CA; (4); FFA; Letterman Clb; SADD; Teachers Aide; Rep Stu Cncl; Hon Roll; Outstndng Stu-Flrl Dsgn; Top 100-Yng Wrtrs Essy Cont; Stu Of Mnth-Jan; Elem Tchr.

GONZALEZ, SALVADOR; Sanger HS; Sanger, CA; (2); #4 In Class; Debate Tm; Model UN; ROTC; Spanish Clb; Speech Tm; Chorus; Drill Tm; Hon Roll; Prfct Atten Awd; Rotary Awd; Forensics; CSF; Bus.

GONZALEZ, SANDRA; North Salinas HS; Salinas, CA; (4); 29/360; French Clb; Band; Mrchg Band; Swmmng; Hon Roll; NHS; Prfct Atten Awd; Dept Key Awd In Bus; Boise ST U; Bus.

GONZALEZ, SANDRA; San Gabriel HS; Rosemead, CA; (2); Service Clb; JV Sftbl; Cit Awd; Plc Dept Explr; YMCA Kahana Kai.

GONZALEZ, SANDRA N; Le Grand Union HS; Le Grand, CA; (3); Drama Clb; French Clb; Spanish Clb; Teachers Aide; School Musical; School Play; Hon Roll.

GONZALEZ, SONIA; Orestimba HS; Crowslanding, CA; (3); Hosp Aide; Pep Clb; SADD; Color Guard; Flag Corp; Sec Soph Cls; Sec Jr Cls; Hon Roll; Jr Ldrshp; Reg Nurse.

GONZALEZ, SUSANA; Orosi HS; Orosi, CA; (2); Church Yth Grp; Drama Clb; Spanish Clb; Chorus; School Musical; Sec Soph Cls; High Hon Roll; Hon Roll; Mock Trial; CA Schlrshp Fed; Bus.

GONZALEZ, SYLVIA M; La Puente HS; La Puente, CA; (4); Band; Mrchg Band; Orch; Pep Band; Pres Stu Cncl; Hon Roll; Music Dept Awd; Uniform Mgr; Greenpeace; Sigma Club Honoree; Bandsman Awd 89-90; CA ST U Long Beach; Radio.

GONZALEZ, TANYA; Etiwanda HS; Alta Loma, CA; (3); 6/606; Church Yth Grp; Treas Spanish Clb; Ed Lit Mag; Treas Jr Cls; High Hon Roll; Award Defense Atty; San Bernadino Stud Advisory Council; College; Intl Rel Pre Law.

GONZALEZ, TERESA R; Centennial HS; Corona, CA; (4); 22/164; Ed Yrbk; Off Sr Cls; Hon Roll; Cal Poly Pomona; Arch.

GONZALEZ, TITO F; Capuchino HS; Millbrae, CA; (3); Treas Church Yth Grp; Drama Clb; Church Choir; JV Var Bsbl; Bst Actor; Welding Tech.

GONZALEZ, VERONICA I; Palo Verde HS; Blythe, CA; (3); FFA; Hon Roll; Cosmtlgy.

GONZALEZ, VICTOR; Valley View HS; Moreno Valley, CA; (2); Ed Nwsp; Ed Lit Mag; Med.

GONZALEZ, VICTORIA; Sierra Vista HS; Baldwin Park, CA; (2); Chess Clb; Debate Tm; Drama Clb; Library Aide; Pep Clb; Science Clb; Speech Tm; Teachers Aide; Band; Chorus.

GONZALEZ, VIOLETA; Academy Of Our Lady Of Peace; San Diego, CA; (1); Spanish Clb; Church Choir; Sec Frsh Cls; Cheerldng; VP Sftbl; UCSD; Obstetrician.

GONZALEZ, WILLIAM; Wasco HS; Wasco, CA; (2); School Play; Wt Lftg; Hon Roll; JV Bsbl; JV Ftbl; Berkley U; Med.

GONZALEZ, YASMIN TANYA P; Notre Dame HS; Salinas, CA; (2); Cmnty Wkr; Hosp Aide; Science Clb; Tennis; Hon Roll; NHS; CSF; Stanford; Phy.

GONZALEZ M, MA FERNANDA; Adacemy Of Our Lady Of Peace; Coronado, CA; (2); French Clb; Swmmng; Piano.

GOOCH, KELLIE LYNN; Eureka HS; Eureka, CA; (2); Church Yth Grp; Cmnty Wkr; Spanish Clb; SADD; Band; Mrchg Band; Pep Band; School Musical; Hon Roll; ST Champshps Bowling; SDSU; Ed.

GOOD, MARY M; Shasta HS; Bella Vista, CA; (4); Pres Drama Clb; Thesps; School Play; Rptr Nwsp; Rptr Yrbk; Hon Roll; Eclgy Clb; Shasta Coll; Theater.

GOOD, SCOTT M; Bellarmine-Jefferson HS; Burbank, CA; (1); High Hon Roll; Martl Arts; Notre Dame; Commrcl Arch.

GOOD, SHANNON; West Hills HS; Santee, CA; (2); 3/277; Church Yth Grp; Drill Tm; Stat Bsbl; Stat Bsktbl; Stat Trk; Hon Roll; Stu Of Mnth; Miss Drill Down; Stanford; Engrng.

GOOD, STEPHANIE A; Vacaville HS; Vacaville, CA; (4); 6/560; Church Yth Grp; Computer Clb; Natl Beta Clb; Science Clb; Var Capt Bsktbl; Var JV Crs Cntry; JV Var Bausch & Lomb Sci Awd; JV Vllybl; High Hon Roll; Pres Acad Fit Awd; Kiwanis Schlrshp; Tandy Technlgy Schlrs; Consumnes River; Astrophysics.

GOODALE, KERRY LEE; Poway HS; San Diego, CA; (2); Church Yth Grp; Girl Scts; Pep Clb; Ski Clb; Cheerldng; Pom Pon; Cit Awd; Hon Roll; Medcl.

GOODALE, NATALIE J; Southern Calif Christian HS; Anaheim Hills, CA; (2); Church Yth Grp; Church Choir; Hon Roll; NHS; Pacific Coast Bible Bapt Coll.

GOODE, CHRIS; Mount Carmel HS; San Diego, CA; (2); Var Bsktbl; Hon Roll; Pro Bsktbl Plyr.

GOODELL, RAEGAN E; Brea-Olinda HS; Brea, CA; (2); Cmnty Wkr; GAA; Var Gym; Hon Roll; U Of CA Irvine; Hlth.

GOODEN, DUANE L; Damien HS; Pomona, CA; (2); 58/268; JV Trk; Hon Roll; Blk Stu Union; Math.

GOODFRIEND, LEWIS G; Lindsay HS; Lindsay, CA; (1); 10/200; Boy Scts; Church Yth Grp; Math Tm; School Musical; Hon Roll; Reading; BYU; Psych.

GOODHUE, JADE; Arlington HS; Riverside, CA; (2); Church Yth Grp; Hosp Aide; ROTC; Chorus; Drill Tm; Schlrshp Idyllwild Inst Fiesta Inc; Grls JROTC Amercnsm & Ldrshp Pgm; Oral Roberts U; Engl.

GOODKIN, ERIKA D; Oak Meadow HS; Los Angeles, CA; (2); Latin Clb; Chorus; Pres Frsh Cls; High Hon Roll; Val; Actrss; Secy Yng Black Schlrs 89-90; Lead Part Musical-Peace Chld Rep Theatr; USC; Psycht.

GOODMAN, AARON JAMES; Henry M Gunn HS; Palo Alto, CA; (2); Math Clb; Capt Var Diving; Hon Roll; Bridge Clb; Mock Trial Clb-VP; Med.

GOODMAN, AMIE L; Thomas Downey HS; Modesto, CA; (2); Key Clb; NFL; Speech Tm; JV Golf; Var Tennis; CA Schlsp Fed.

GOODMAN, CINDY; Golden West HS; Visalia, CA; (4); 42/321; Pres Church Yth Grp; Cmnty Wkr; Science Clb; Spanish Clb; Teachers Aide; Rptr Nwsp; Lit Mag; CSF; Envrnmntlst Clb; Acad Decthln; Fresno Pacific Coll; English.

GOODMAN, HEATHER L; C K Mc Clatchy HS; Sacramento, CA; (2); 29/442; Cmnty Wkr; French Clb; SADD; Hon Roll.

GOODMAN, JED I; University HS; Los Angeles, CA; (3); Teachers Aide; Stage Crew; Ftbl; UCLA; Flm.

GOODMAN, MELISSA M; Live Oak HS; Live Oak, CA; (3); VP Chess Clb; Church Yth Grp; FHA; Office Aide; Pres Spanish Clb; Church Choir; Sec Jr Cls; Rep Stu Cncl; Hon Roll; Prfct Atten Awd; Acad Exclnc Letter; Acad Decathlon Tm; BYU.

GOODMAN, RACHEL B; Moorpark HS; Moorpark, CA; (2); 13/265; School Play; Var Trk; Stu Mnth April; Trk Ltr; UCLA; Engl Ed.

GOODMAN, RICK A; Oak Ridge HS; El Dorado Hills, CA; (3); 15/275; VP Chess Clb; Church Yth Grp; Debate Tm; FBLA; Intnl Clb; NFL; Speech Tm; School Play; JV Socr; High Hon Roll; Jnr Of Yr 90; U Of WA; Mtn Pctr Dir.

GOODMAN, ROBYN T; Westlake School For Girls; Santa Monica, CA; (2); Drama Clb; French Clb; Thesps; Sec Soph Cls; Rep Jr Cls; Tennis; Yng Prfssnls Co Santa Monica Playhouse; Yale U; Writer.

GOODMANSON, JASON C; Lone Pine HS; Lone Pine, CA; (1); Drama Clb; Service Clb; School Play; Stage Crew; High Hon Roll; Hon Roll; Inyo Cnty Spcl Schltc Awd; Chmbdr Commrce Vlntr; Writr.

GOODRICH, ERIKA; Chataqua HS; Big Bear Lake, CA; (2); Dance Clb.

GOODRICH, JENNY L; Analy HS; Sebastopol, CA; (2); 56/256; Church Yth Grp; FFA; GAA; Yrbk; Var Trk; Sonoma ST; Bus.

GOODRICH, REFELINA M; Seaside HS; Ft Ord, CA; (2); Office Aide; Teachers Aide; Chorus; Hon Roll; Prfct Atten Awd; VA Tech; Accntnt.

GOODRICH, RENEE; Oakland Technical HS; Oakland, CA; (2); Church Choir; Hon Roll; Golden St Exam Acad Awd With Hnrs; Photo; U CA Berkley; Engrng.

GOODRODE, DANIELLE R; Pioneer HS; San Jose, CA; (1); Cmnty Wkr; Rptr Nwsp; JV Tennis; Bllt & Jzz; UOP; Advc Clmnst.

GOODSELL, PATRICK W; Don Antonio Lugo HS; Chino, CA; (4); Chess Clb; Church Yth Grp; Cmnty Wkr; Teachers Aide; High Hon Roll; NHS; Golden Conquest Awd Achvt Comp Sci; IL Inst Tech; Comp Sci.

GOODSELL, REBECCA A; San Dieguito Union HS; Cardiff By The Se, CA; (2); GAA; Office Aide; Socr; Cit Awd; Hon Roll; Pres Acad Fit Awd; CA Schltc Fed; Inventor.

GOODWILL, DANA; St Michaels HS; Torrance, CA; (1); Church Yth Grp; Pep Clb; Church Choir; Variety Show; Rptr Nwsp; Sec Frsh Cls; JV Bsktbl; Var Cheerldng; Hon Roll; Opt Clb Awd; Engl & Religion Awds; UCLA; Comp Exec.

GOODWIN, ANTOINETTE D; Ontario HS; Pomona, CA; (3); Church Yth Grp; French Clb; Girl Scts; Key Clb; Science Clb; SADD; Chorus; Church Choir; School Musical; Variety Show; Outstndng 1st Soprano Treble Choir; Bio, Eng Consistent Effort & Achvmnt Awd; U Southern CA; Bio.

GOODWIN, CRAIG L; Clairemont HS; San Diego, CA; (2); 19/254; Church Yth Grp; Model UN; Office Aide; Var L Bsbl; JV Var Ftbl; Hon Roll; All Harbor League Tm Bsbl; San Diego Jr Golf Assn; ASU; Bus.

GOODWIN, J KEVIN; Hoover HS; Fresno, CA; (3); Bsktbl; Var Lttrd As Team Mgr; Flmd Gmes, Team Stat Istician; CA ST U Fresno; Tchng.

GOODWIN, SHEILA L; Ponderosa HS; Diamond Springs, CA; (1); Cmnty Wkr; 4-H; Acpl Chr; Chorus; School Musical; Variety Show; GATE; OR ST U; Med.

GOODWIN, TAMMY A; Santa Ynez Valley Union HS; Solvang, CA; (3); 4-H; VP FFA; FFA Achvmnt Awd; Natl FFA Fndtn Horse; CA Poly; Horse Trnr.

GOODWIN, TERESA M; Mar Vista HS; San Diego, CA; (1); Dance Clb; Quiz Bowl; Scholastic Bowl; Tennis; Trk; Cit Awd; Hon Roll; UCSD; Srgn.

GOOLD, SHERI L; La Canada HS; La Canada Flintri, CA; (3); Pres Church Yth Grp; Teachers Aide; Church Choir; Chrch Cls; Brigham Young U; Comp.

GOOLSBY, CATHERINE M; Buena Park HS; Buena Park, CA; (3); Q&S; Science Clb; Teachers Aide; Varsity Clb; Ed Nwsp; Sec Stu Cncl; Mgr Bsktbl; Mgr(s); Cit Awd; High Hon Roll; Entrance Hnrs; Girls St Finalist; Jrnlsm Advrs Awd.

GOOSZEN, TAMMY M; Cajon HS; San Bernardino, CA; (3); AFS; VP Sec Church Yth Grp; Girl Scts; SADD; School Musical; School Play; Stage Crew; NHS; VP San Gorgonio GS Cncl Plnng Brd; Spcl Educ.

GOPALAN, NISHA; Mission Viejo HS; Mission Viejo, CA; (2); Key Clb; SADD; Mrchg Band; Hon Roll; CA Schlrshp Fed; Psych.

GOPEZ, JONATHAN; George Washington HS; San Francisco, CA; (2); Chess Clb; Computer Clb; Math Clb; Science Clb; JV Var Crs Cntry; JV Var Trk; USAF; Elect.

GORAYA, NEELU K; Fontana HS; Fontana, CA; (2); School Musical; School Play; Hon Roll; Madrigals; Campus Life; Psych.

GORAYA, SIARA N; West HS; Bakersfield, CA; (1); FBLA; Key Clb; Yrbk; Socr; Cit Awd; Hon Roll; Bus.

GORBEA, ANA LUCY; Roosevelt HS; Los Angeles, CA; (2); Drill Tm; Orch; VP Frsh Cls; Prfct Atten Awd; Health Clb; Cncl Clb; Law.

GORDON, CARYN; San Diego HS; San Diego, CA; (2); 22/611; Cmnty Wkr; Intnl Clb; Key Clb; Library Aide; Model UN; Rptr Nwsp; Honorary Reporter.

GORDON, DEBORAH E; Torrey Pines HS; Solana Beach, CA; (2); Drama Clb; Thesps; School Play; High Hon Roll.

GORDON, HILARY G; West HS; Bakersfield, CA; (1); Church Yth Grp; Ski Clb; Ed Yrbk; Swmmng; High Hon Roll; Hon Roll; OBGYN.

GORDON, JASON E; South Bay Lutheran HS; Los Angeles, CA; (3); Chorus; Sec Stu Cncl; Var Crs Cntry; Prfct Atten Awd; Vlntr Work; UH Manoa; Travel Indstry Mgmt.

GORDON, JENNIFER C; Del Mar HS; Campbell, CA; (4); Key Clb; Science Clb; Acpl Chr; Sec Band; Pres Chorus; School Musical; School Play; Yrbk; Ntl Merit Ltr; Pres Acad Fit Awd; Calif All State Hnr Choir; Lander; Music Tchr.

GORDON, JENNIFER M; Fremont Christian HS; Fremont, CA; (2); Church Yth Grp; Teachers Aide; Treas Frsh Cls; JV Bsktbl; Var Tennis; Hon Roll; Mexico Mssns Trp-Chrch; Nrs.

GORDON, JOHN W; Lemoore HS; Lemoore, CA; (3); 2/323; School Play; Rotary Awd; CA Schlrshp Fed; Top FFA 2 Yrs; FFA Chapt Pres, Sctnl Pres, Rgnl VP; Stanford; Law.

GORDON, KAREN M; Bishop Amat HS; West Covina, CA; (3); Chrmn Cmnty Wkr; Service Clb; Ed Yrbk; Lit Mag; Powder Puff Ftbl; Swmmng; NHS; Pres Acad Fit Awd; HS Stu Ambssdr; Congrssnl Schlr; Law.

GORDON, KATHERINE EMILIE; Atascadero HS; Atascadero, CA; (3); Church Yth Grp; Scholastic Bowl; Band; Drm Mjr(t); Pep Band; School Musical; Hon Roll; CSF; Camp Fire Boys & Girls; Big Sister; Mech Engrng.

GORDON, KATHRYN R; Monte Vista HS; Spring Valley, CA; (3); 47/300; Art Clb; SADD; Hon Roll; 1st & 3rd Pl Schl Art Cont; Hlpd Form Planet Awrnss Clb; Dungeons & Dragons; Artist.

GORDON, LILA D; La Habra HS; Whittier, CA; (2); Drama Clb; FBLA; Pep Clb; Rptr Nwsp; Cit Awd; Hon Roll; Top 100 Mem; Tennis; Stu Mnth Awds Hlth & Lang Arts Depts; Sci.

GORDON, LUKE; Oroville HS; Oroville, CA; (4); 41/184; Letterman Clb; JV Var Ftbl; JV Var Wrstlng; Hon Roll; Comp Engrng.

GORDON, MATTHEW S; Woodland HS; Woodland, CA; (3); Bsktbl; Ftbl; Tennis; Trk; Hon Roll; Jr NHS; CSF; Bus.

GORDON, MICHAEL D; Redlands HS; Mentone, CA; (2); Church Yth Grp; Key Clb; Thesps; Band; JV Bsbl; High Hon Roll; Overseas Politics; Intl Stds.

GORDON, MICHELLE R; Castle Park HS; Chula Vista, CA; (3); 170/385; Church Yth Grp; Cmnty Wkr; Pep Clb; San Diego ST U; Accntng.

GORDON, NEIL J; Clayton Valley HS; Concord, CA; (3); JV Wrstlng; Sci, Gen Phys Sci Cmmndtn; CA Poly; Arch.

GORDON, NMARAISHA G; Castlemont HS; Oakland, CA; (4); FBLA; GAA; Hosp Aide; Red Cross Aide; Stu Cncl; Sftbl; Trk; Hon Roll; Jr NHS; NHS; VP Admin Kaiser Med Explr Pgm; Mentor-Dr Sue Abbles-Kaiser Hosp; Won T&T Schlrshp; CSUH; RN.

GORDON, REGINA M; Paraclete HS; Lancaster, CA; (2); JA; Hon Roll; Art, Music.

GORDON, RICK A; Antelope Valley HS; Lancaster, CA; (3); Boy Scts; Church Yth Grp; Yrbk; Hon Roll; Rogue CC; Frst Rngr.

GORDON, SHEENA M; Bishop O'dowd HS; Oakland, CA; (2); Cmnty Wkr; High Hon Roll; Hon Roll; Cert Of Mrt; Tennis; Semifnlst Poetry Cont; Med.

GORDON, TAMRA; Silver Valley HS; Newberry Spgs, CA; (2); Church Yth Grp; Cmnty Wkr; Letterman Clb; Drill Tm; JV L Bsktbl; Stat Ftbl; JV Var Score Keeper; Var Sftbl; Cit Awd; Hon Roll; Save Our Earth Clb Pres; 1st Pl Rnnr-Up Miss Newberry Spgs 89; Engl Awd; Obstetrics.

GORDON, TERRI L; Oakdale HS; Oakdale, CA; (3); Hosp Aide; Letterman Clb; Spanish Clb; SADD; Teachers Aide; Powder Puff Ftbl; Sftbl; Cit Awd; Teacher.

GORDON, TORY J; San Juan HS; Citrus Heights, CA; (4); 60/280; SADD; Teachers Aide; Var Capt Ftbl; Wt Lftg; Var L Wrstlng; Cit Awd; Elks Awd; High Hon Roll; Prfct Atten Awd; All-Cal Lnbckr Hnrb Mntn; Prin Acad Achvt List; St Marys Coll Moroga; Sprts Med.

GORE, DEBORAH L; John F Kennedy HS; Sacramento, CA; (1); 82/559; 2nd Pl Sacramento City Unifd Schl Dist 90 Real Women Creatve Wrtng Cmptn; CSU Sacramento; Law.

GORE, ERIN S; Skyline HS; Oakland, CA; (3); Key Clb; Speech Tm; Band; Orch; Pep Band; Off Frsh Cls; Rep Soph Cls; Rep Jr Cls; Off Sr Cls; L Swmmng.

GORE, RACQUEL M; Moreno Valley HS; Riverside, CA; (3); Var Trk; High Hon Roll; VA ST; Nrsng.

GORE, TRACY; Herlong HS; Doyle, CA; (2); FBLA; Ed Nwsp; JV Bsktbl; High Hon Roll; Hon Roll; NHS; Bus Awd; Wrtng Awd; Engrng.

GORECKI, RUSSELL JOHN; Moorpark HS; Moorpark, CA; (2); 1/286; Boy Scts; Key Clb; High Hon Roll; Egl Sct; AF Acad; Astro Engrg.

GORFAIN, DANIEL J; Temecula Valley HS; Temecula, CA; (3); Letterman Clb; Varsity Clb; Orch; JV Ftbl; Var Tennis; Var Trk; Cit Awd; Hon Roll; Kiwanis Awd; Pres Acad Fit Awd; UCSD; Oceanographer.

GORHAM, CHAD S; Lindsay HS; Lindsay, CA; (1); Church Yth Grp; Key Clb; Swmmng.

GORHAM, LORRIE A; Saugus HS; Valencia, CA; (4); 34/400; Hon Roll; NHS; CSF; Elem Ed.

GORMAN, GREGORY; Warren HS; Downey, CA; (3); 6/456; Debate Tm; FBLA; VP JA; Service Clb; Pres Ski Clb; Swmmng; Tennis; High Hon Roll; Pres Acad Fit Awd; Water Polo Tm Cptn.

GORMAN, STEPHANIE; Clovis West HS; Fresno, CA; (2); Drama Clb; French Clb; Intnl Clb; Pep Clb; Var Mgr(s); Var Score Keeper; U Of CA San Diego; Crprt Law.

GORMAN, TASHA J; Abraham Lincoln HS; San Jose, CA; (3); Cmnty Wkr; Computer Clb; FFA; Girl Scts; Office Aide; Teachers Aide; Off Jr Cls; Bsktbl; Swmmng; Photo Clb; San Jose City; Law.

GORMAN, TIM; Sonora HS; Fullerton, CA; (2); Art Clb; 4-H; Ski Clb; Teachers Aide; Bsbl; Var Diving; Var Ftbl; Socr; Swmmng; Trk; Advrtsng.

GORMLEY, MELINDA B; Woodrow Wilson HS; Long Beach, CA; (2); Church Yth Grp; Cmnty Wkr; Dance Clb; Key Clb; Pep Clb; Quiz Bowl; Teachers Aide; Drill Tm; JV Cheerldng; Var Swmmng; Med.

GORNIK, DEANNA R; Thomas Downey HS; Modesto, CA; (2); Church Yth Grp; Cmnty Wkr; Hosp Aide; JV Vllybl; Hon Roll; Jrnlsm.

GOROSPE, CARMELA V; Diamond Bar HS; Diamond Bar, CA; (4); Bus Profs of Am; Dance Clb; DECA; FBLA; Letterman Clb; SADD; Teachers Aide; Varsity Clb; Var Bsktbl; Hon Roll; Deans List-Math/Engl; CSF; CA ST U.

GOROSTIETA, ROBERTO J; Daniel Murphy HS; Los Angeles, CA; (2); Boy Scts; Quiz Bowl; Yrbk; Bsbl; Socr; Hon Roll; CSF; Law.

GOROV, JULIE; Santa Monica HS; Santa Monica, CA; (4); 50/700; Dance Clb; Pep Clb; Teachers Aide; Temple Yth Grp; Band; Drill Tm; Stu Cncl; Var Cheerldng; Hon Roll; Opt Clb Awd; CA Schlrshp Assn; Scripps Coll.

GORSI, ARAFAT; Livingston HS; Livingston, CA; (1); FFA; Bsbl; Bsktbl; Crs Cntry; Tennis; Trk; Davis Schl Of Med; Med.

GORSKY, JENNIFER M; Redwood HS; Visalia, CA; (1); Orch; Socr; High Hon Roll; Hon Roll; Jr NHS; Rally Club; Music.

GORSUCH, JEFF A; Huntington Beach HS; Huntington Beach, CA; (1); Model UN; Var L Diving; JV Swmmng; Jr Var Waper Polo.

GORSUCH, WENDI; Esperanza HS; Yorba Linda, CA; (2); 59/571; Color Guard; Rep Stu Cncl; High Hon Roll; Stu Mnt Oct 88; CSF; All Amercn Perfrmnce Flg Tm; U Of Pacific.

GORSZWICK, ERICK J; Carlsbad HS; Carlsbad, CA; (1); 275/400; Boy Scts; Science Clb; Rotary Awd; Interact, Hist & Env Clubs; U Of CA-SAN Diego; Educ.

GORTHY, MANDI J; California HS; San Ramon, CA; (3); Chorus; Var Crs Cntry; Var Trk; Hon Roll; Pres Acad Fit Awd; Mrn Bio.

GORTON, DANIELLE J; San Gabriel HS; San Gabriel, CA; (2); Sec AFS; Church Yth Grp; Debate Tm; Sec Girl Scts; Acpl Chr; Capt Flag Corp; School Musical; Hon Roll; Jr NHS; Pres Acad Fit Awd; Amor Amici YMCA Tri-Hi-Y; Acordian Lssns 6 Yrs; Drama Lssns 5 Yrs; Drama.

GORZKOWSKI, MARGARET A; University HS; Irvine, CA; (3); Church Yth Grp; JV Capt Bsktbl; Politicl Sci.

GOSAL, GURJIT S; Live Oak HS; Live Oak, CA; (3); Var JV Bsktbl; Cit Awd; High Hon Roll; Chico U; Physician.

GOSLING, ANN M; Loretto HS; Carmichael, CA; (3); 10/62; Chorus; School Musical; School Play; Ed Nwsp; Ed Yrbk; Rep Frsh Cls; VP Soph Cls; Rep Jr Cls; VP Stu Cncl; High Hon Roll; Fri Night Live.

GOSS, HEATHER R; Redlands HS; Redlands, CA; (2); Church Yth Grp; GAA; JA; Letterman Clb; Varsity Clb; Drm Mjr(t); Mrchg Band; Socr; Sftbl; Vllybl.

GOSS, MATTHEW D; Burroughs HS; Ridgecrest, CA; (3); Spanish Clb; Teachers Aide; Wrk China Lake Naval Wpns & Ctr In Tech Mentor Pgm; U C Davis; Elec Engr.

GOSSAGE, KARI D; Redlands HS; Redlands, CA; (2); Chorus; Sftbl; JV Vllybl; Pres Acad Fit Awd; Jr Achvrs; WA ST U; Phrmcy.

GOSSE, BONNIE L; Rio Americano HS; Sacramento, CA; (4); 1/269; Church Yth Grp; Cmnty Wkr; Debate Tm; French Clb; Service Clb; SADD; Varsity Clb; Sec Jr Cls; Var L Tennis; High Hon Roll; Stu Rchng Out Spkng Agnst Drugs/Alchl Abuse; Chld Abuse Cncl Sacramento; CA Poly San Luis Obisbo; Arch.

GOSSEN, LEEANN ROSEMARY; Vanden HS; Vacaville, CA; (4); 6/139; Spanish Clb; Sec Sr Cls; Var Cheerldng; Stat Ftbl; JV Socr; VP Capt Trk; High Hon Roll; Pres Acad Fit Awd; Engrng Smmr Resdncy Prgm U Of CA Davis 88; Army Schlr/Athlt Awd 90; UCLA; Arospc Engrng.

GOSSETT, ADAM; North Hollywood HS; N Hollywood, CA; (4); Acpl Chr; Chorus; Swing Chorus; Crs Cntry; Ftbl; Trk; Valley Coll; Hstry Prfssr.

GOSSETTE, PHILLIP; John Marshall Fundamental HS; Pasadena, CA; (3); Cmnty Wkr; Red Cross Aide; Spanish Clb; Rptr Nwsp; Phtg Yrbk; VP Frsh Cls; Var L Bsbl; Var Capt Fld Hcky; Var L Trk; JV Var Wt Lftg; CA Schlrshp Fdrtn; Advncd Plcmnt; Vrsty Ftbl Mst Insprtnl Awd; UC Berkeley; Chld Pscychlgy.

GOTHARD, JENNIFER A; Vacaville HS; Vacaville, CA; (4); 10/530; Cmnty Wkr; Sec SADD; Ed Nwsp; Cit Awd; High Hon Roll; Ntl Merit Ltr; Pres Acad Fit Awd; Tandy Tech Schlr; Congrssnl Schlr; 1st Spllng Bee; U Of CA Davis; Anthropology.

GOTLIBOWSKI, TINA; Pacific Palisades HS; Santa Monica, CA; (3); Church Yth Grp; Diving; Swmmng; Prfct Atten Awd; Pres Acad Fit Awd; St Schlr; Band Distngshd Schlr; Cal Tech; Profssnl Plt.

GOTT, CHRIS; Bear River HS; Grass Valley, CA; (3); 25/200; Aud/Vis; Church Yth Grp; Debate Tm; Science Clb; Treas Spanish Clb; SADD; Church Choir; School Musical; School Play; Stage Crew; Biola U; Law.

GOTT, CLINT; Mission College Prep; San Luis Obispo, CA; (4); 2/35; Var Capt Bsktbl; Elks Awd; Ntl Merit Ltr; Sal; CIF Div I Southern Sectn Chmpn Bsktbl Tm; UCSB.

GOTT, RIKKI J; Yucaipa HS; Yucaipa, CA; (3); Church Yth Grp; Cmnty Wkr; FHA; Hosp Aide; Spanish Clb; Teachers Aide; Chorus; Church Choir; Vllybl; Nurse.

GOTT, RYAN M; Coronado HS; Coronado, CA; (4); Church Yth Grp; Drama Clb; Ski Clb; Thesps; Mrchg Band; School Musical; Stage Crew; Hon Roll; NHS; Schl Svc Awd; CA Lutheran U; Bus Admin.

GOTT, STEFANIE M; Independence HS; San Jose, CA; (3); Cmnty Wkr; VP JA; Service Clb; Teachers Aide; VP Frsh Cls; Off Soph Cls; Stu Cncl; Var L Swmmng; Hon Roll; Achvt-Schl Rcgntn Gldn St Exam Algebra I; Pepperdine U; Finance.

GOTTLIEB, TINA; Arlington HS; Riverside, CA; (4); 21/360; Church Yth Grp; Cmnty Wkr; Teachers Aide; Sftbl; Vllybl; Ntl Merit Schol; Pres Acad Fit Awd; Riverside CC; Chrprtc.

GOTTSCHALK, HILARY J; Culver City HS; Culver City, CA; (3); Church Yth Grp; French Clb; Spanish Clb; Off Frsh Cls; Off Soph Cls; Off Jr Cls; JV Vllybl; Cit Awd; High Hon Roll; Pres Acad Fit Awd; Hrsbck Rdng; CA Schlrshp Fed; Interact Clb; Envrnmntl Sci.

GOUBRAN, GEORGE E; Diamond Bar HS; Diamond Bar, CA; (1); Drama Clb; Intrml Bsktbl; JV Socr; JV Tennis; Hon Roll; Certfd Peer Cnslr; Cal Davis; Law.

GOUDE, NICOLE; Apple Valley SR HS; Apple Valley, CA; (2); Cmnty Wkr; French Clb; Office Aide; Ski Clb; SADD; School Play; Treas Soph Cls; Stu Cncl; Gym; Var Score Keeper; Outstndng Achvt Clss Offcr; ASB; U HI; Bus Admin.

GOUGEON, JENNIFER E; Atascadero HS; Creston, CA; (1); Hon Roll.

GOUGH, ERIN M; Hart HS; Valencia, CA; (3); 44/480; Dance Clb; Drama Clb; French Clb; Pres Chorus; School Musical; School Play; Swing Chorus; Variety Show; Nwsp; Stat Bsktbl; Commnctns.

GOUGH, MELISA M; Palm Springs HS; Cathedral City, CA; (3); Church Yth Grp; Drama Clb; Chorus; School Play; Sec Frsh Cls; Pres Soph Cls; JV Cheerldng; JV Var Score Keeper; Wt Lftg; Hon Roll; Engl.

GOUGISHA, TAMICA; Pittsburg HS; Pittsburg, CA; (3); 58/335; Pep Clb; Ski Clb; Chorus; School Play; Cheerldng; Capt Var Pom Pon; Swmmng; Hon Roll; Dance Clb; Drama Clb; MESA Clb; Debutante For Alpha Kappa Alpha Sorority 90; Spellman Coll; Bus Admin.

GOULART, RAQUEL M; Mt Whitney HS; Visalia, CA; (3); Church Yth Grp; Cmnty Wkr; DECA; 4-H; FBLA; FFA; SADD; Teachers Aide; Sec Soph Cls; Rep Stu Cncl; Walt Disney Strive For Exclnc Awd; Fresno ST; Bus Admin.

GOULARTE, MARLENE L; Pinole Valley HS; Hercules, CA; (2); Band; Color Guard; Hon Roll; CSF; UC Berkeley; Psych.

GOULD, JENNIFER; Coast Joint Union HS; Northpole, AK; (2); FHA; Pep Clb; SADD; Cheerldng; Gym; Pom Pon; Sftbl; Pres Acad Fit Awd; AK ST Coll; Psych.

GOULD, KEVIN A; River City HS; W Sacramento, CA; (1); SADD; JV Capt Bsktbl; JV Crs Cntry; High Hon Roll; Pres Acad Fit Awd; Presdntl Acad Ftns Awd; Hnr Role; Outstndng Achvt Engl; UNLV; Lawyer.

GOULD, LO ANNA; Foothill Farms SR HS; Sacramento, CA; (2); JV Sftbl; High Hon Roll; Hon Roll; Omaha Woodmen Ins Bst Girl Camper Awd; Animal Hlth Tech.

GOULD, ROBYN; Taft HS; Tarzana, CA; (3); Cmnty Wkr; Service Clb; SADD; Chrmn Temple Yth Grp; Drill Tm; Off Jr Cls; Capt Var Cheerldng; Hon Roll; Spanish Clb; Rep Frsh Cls; Rep LAUSD Ldrshp Cnfrnce; Mbr CA Hnrs Soc; Treas SASA; Psych Political Sci.

GOULD, SHANNON; Oakmont HS; Roseville, CA; (2); Church Yth Grp; Drama Clb; Ski Clb; Drill Tm; Trk; Hon Roll; Pilot.

GOULD, STACEY L; Skyline HS; Oakland, CA; (3); Varsity Clb; Chorus; Nwsp; Yrbk; Lit Mag; Stu Cncl; Swmmng; Hon Roll; Envrnmntl Clb.

GOULDING, SHAY; Redwood HS; Visalia, CA; (3); 12/300; Am Leg Aux Girls St; Pres Church Yth Grp; FBLA; German Clb; GAA; Sec Key Clb; Letterman Clb; Pep Clb; Spanish Clb; SADD; Camp Royal Deleg Rotary Ldrshp Camp; Rotary Smmr Exchng Stu; CSF; Wrld Champ Amer Paint Horse Assn; Intl Bus.

GOULDY, JARED K; North Monterey County HS; Castroville, CA; (4); 1/300; Am Leg Boys St; Mgr Dance Clb; Phtg Yrbk; Stu Cncl; High Hon Roll; Treas NHS; Val; CA Schlrshp Fed; James E Black Top Schlrshp Wnnr; U Of CA Riverside; Bus Admnstr.

GOULET, NICHOLAS; Rosamond HS; Mojave, CA; (2); Band; Mrchg Band; Pep Band; JV Bsbl; Hon Roll; Drum Line; Drm Sctn Ldr; Music.

GOURLEY, ANN; Foothill HS; Healdsburg, CA; (2); Var L Trk; High Hon Roll; NEDT Awd; USCB; Psych.

GOUSSEV, DAVID P; Lowell HS; San Francisco, CA; (2); Aud/Vis; Chess Clb; JA; Library Aide; Science Clb; Service Clb; Intrml Bsktbl; High Hon Roll; Prfct Atten Awd; Bus.

GOUTSOS, STACEY; Granada Hills HS; Granada Hills, CA; (3); Library Aide; Office Aide; Drill Tm; Mrchg Band; Swmmng; High Hon Roll; NHS; Val; WISE Women In Sci & Engr Prog; Hghlnd Dancer Captn; Comp Sci.

GOUVAIA, BECKY; Livermore HS; Livermore, CA; (4); Dance Clb; Drama Clb; Office Aide; Pep Clb; Varsity Clb; Ed Nwsp; Rptr Lit Mag; JV Capt Cheerldng; Var Capt Pom Pon; JV Powder Puff Ftbl; NCA All Amer Song Grl 88-89; Nca Natl Champs Song Grls Squad 4th Pl; Sacramento St U; Crmnl Law.

GOVE, KERI L; Westminster HS; Westminster, CA; (4); Church Yth Grp; Cmnty Wkr; Hosp Aide; Office Aide; Spanish Clb; Pres Frsh Cls; Stu Cncl; Cheerldng; Jr NHS; Pres Acad Fit Awd; CA ST Fullerton; Nrsng.

GOVE, KRISTEN D; Woodbridge HS; Irvine, CA; (3); 153/425; Girl Scts; Teachers Aide; Varsity Clb; Phtg Yrbk; Var Sftbl; Vllybl; Bus.

GOVEA, EDUARDO; Chino HS; Chino, CA; (3); Band; Jazz Band; Mrchg Band; Orch; Pep Band; School Musical; Badminton; Yth Band Orgnztn; Rep Band Cncl; Band Dir.

GOVER, STEPHEN B; North HS; Bakersfield, CA; (2); Art Clb; Church Yth Grp; Letterman Clb; Office Aide; Spanish Clb; Teachers Aide; L Capt Ftbl; Cit Awd; Hon Roll; Pres Acad Fit Awd; Helping In Probation Office Talking To Children About Drugs & Alcohol; Play Sports; College; Football; Airline Pilot.

GOVIND, ADRIAN S; Leuzinger HS; Inglewood, CA; (3); Computer Clb; Teachers Aide; Cit Awd; Hon Roll; Prfct Atten Awd; USC; Comp.

GOVINDARAJAN, RAMYA L; Cornelia Connelly HS; Anaheim, CA; (3); Cmnty Wkr; Pres German Clb; Hosp Aide; VP Intnl Clb; Model UN; Speech Tm; VP Stu Cncl; High Hon Roll; NHS; Var L Tennis; Boston Coll; Med.

GOWDY, MATTHEW C; Campolindo HS; Lafayette, CA; (4); Boy Scts; Church Yth Grp; Teachers Aide; Acpl Chr; Chorus; Hon Roll; Ntl Merit Ltr; School Musical; Variety Show; Yth Edctr; UC Davis.

GOWDY, REBECCA M; Lincoln HS; Stockton, CA; (4); 98/513; Drama Clb; Thesps; School Musical; School Play; Stage Crew; Variety Show; Intl Thespian Soc Schlrshp; Fashion Inst; Fashion Desgn.

GOWER, DAYSTAR; Montgomery HS; Santa Rosa, CA; (3); Church Yth Grp; French Clb; Science Clb; Chorus; Math.

GOYNE, SCOTT D; Petaluma HS; Petaluma, CA; (3); FFA; FFA Tm 1st St Ag Mechncs Recd St Gold Embhn Awd; Cal Poly; Electrncs.

GOZAR, ELIZA V; St Joseph HS; Pico Rivera, CA; (2); 5/196; French Clb; Hosp Aide; Science Clb; SADD; Var Drill Tm; Hon Roll; NEDT Awd; Yrbk 90-91; Piano; Dance Tm; CSF 88-90; Law.

GOZDECK, REBEKAH L; San Bernardino HS; San Bernardino, CA; (2); Church Yth Grp; Hosp Aide; School Play; Hon Roll; Kids Agnst Crime, Sectry; Hotline Vlntr.

GRABBE, LYNN M; Imperial HS; Altadena, CA; (3); 1/23; Church Yth Grp; Speech Tm; Chorus; School Musical; School Play; Cit Awd; High Hon Roll; Ntl Merit Schol; Speech Clb Sec, VP; Georgetown U; Poltcl Sci.

GRABEEL, EVERETT L; Ernest Righetti HS; Orcutt, CA; (2); Intrml Bsbl; Intrml Wt Lftg; Hon Roll; Wrtng; CA Poly ST U; Real Estate.

GRABER, ANDREA J; Placer HS; Auburn, CA; (2); 4-H; JV Trk; Photojrnlsm.

GRABIEC, AMBER M; Victory Christian Schl; Citrus Heights, CA; (3); Church Yth Grp; Pep Clb; Chorus; Sec Jr Cls; Var Bsktbl; Var Capt Cheerldng; Cit Awd; Var Sftbl; Class Princess; American River.

GRABLE, JEFFREY V; Mission Viejo HS; Mission Viejo, CA; (3); 66/445; Church Yth Grp; Key Clb; SADD; Band; Church Choir; Jazz Band; Mrchg Band; Pep Band; Hon Roll.

GRABLE, SUZANNE M; Montgomery HS; Santa Rosa, CA; (4); FBLA; Opertn Gettng It Togethr Big Sister; Santa Rosa JC; Arch Draftng.

GRABOWSKI, JESSICA; Woodrow Wilson HS; Signal Hill, CA; (3); Church Yth Grp; Girl Scts; Pep Clb; Quiz Bowl; Teachers Aide; Color Guard; Drill Tm; Flag Corp; UCLA; Pedatrcs.

GRACE, BARBARA A; Montgomery HS; Santa Rosa, CA; (2); Church Yth Grp; Vllybl; Cit Awd; Hon Roll; Biola U; Teacher.

GRACE, JENNIFER; Christian Life Schl; Novato, CA; (1); Church Yth Grp; High Hon Roll; Horseback Riding Show Group.

GRACE, LAURA J; North Salinas HS; Salinas, CA; (3); Pres Church Yth Grp; Dance Clb; Spanish Clb; Teachers Aide; JV Bsktbl; Var Cheerldng; JV Var Swmmng; Hon Roll; Advncd Plcmnt Pgm; Piano; BYU.

GRACE, OWEN R; Laguna Hills HS; Laguna Hills, CA; (1); 17/350; French Clb; Math Clb; Band; Mrchg Band; Trk.

GRACE, SONIA; Alverno HS; San Dimas, CA; (4); Church Yth Grp; Science Clb; Service Clb; Ed Lit Mag; Sec Jr Cls; Socr; High Hon Roll; Hon Roll; NHS; Actvs Cmmssn; La Verne U.

GRACE, TRYCHEL L; El Camino HS; Oceanside, CA; (2); Church Yth Grp; SADD; Band; Church Choir; Drill Tm; Mrchg Band; Pep Band; JV Sftbl; Hon Roll; Chld Psych.

GRACE, WANDA; Christian Life HS; Novato, CA; (1); Church Yth Grp; Band; Church Choir; High Hon Roll.

GRACIA, NADINE; San Marin HS; Novato, CA; (3); #1 In Class; French Clb; Hosp Aide; Band; Pep Band; Var JV Bsktbl; Var Capt Trk; High Hon Roll; NHS; Pres Acad Fit Awd; NCS Schlr/Athlete Track, Bsktbl; Outstndng Stu Sci, Math; Soc Of Women Engrs; Med.

GRACIA, RICARDO J; Casa Grande HS; Petaluma, CA; (2); 52/295; Cmnty Wkr; USC; Crmnl Law.

GRACIA, SANYA HAIDE; Palo Verde Valley HS; Blythe, CA; (2); Key Clb; Am Leg Boys St; Spanish Clb; Band; Flag Corp; Nwsp; Pres Frsh Cls; Stu Cncl; Hon Roll; Creative Writing; Helping Friends Work Out Their Problems Or Just Talking; Working At Mcdonalds In Bly; College; Counselling Children.

GRACZYK, CHRISTINE K; International Studies Acad; San Francisco, CA; (2); Drama Clb; French Clb; SADD; School Play; Rptr Nwsp; Yrbk; French Hon Soc; High Hon Roll; Hon Roll; UC Berkeley; Med.

GRADEN, ANNENA; James Logan HS; Union City, CA; (3); Chorus; Variety Show; BPP Scl Grp; Stanford; Bus.

GRADEN, REBLE L; Victor Valley HS; G A F B, CA; (3); 45/240; Church Yth Grp; Yrbk; JV Sftbl; JV Vllybl; Cit Awd; Hon Roll; Pres Acad Fit Awd; Sports Med.

GRADY, MATT E; Maria Catholic HS; Novato, CA; (4); Var Crs Cntry; Var Trk; Var Wrstlng; Hon Roll; Ntl Merit SF; West Point Military Acad; Milit.

GRAFE, MICHAEL W; Montgomery HS; Santa Rosa, CA; (3); 1/450; Am Leg Boys St; Boy Scts; Letterman Clb; Science Clb; Service Clb; Treas Spanish Clb; Rptr Nwsp; Pres Frsh Cls; Rep Stu Cncl; Var L Crs Cntry; CSF; Exchnge Stu Japan & USSR; Jnr Peoples Clb Pres; Aerospace Med.

GRAFF, ERIN; Patrick Henry HS; San Diego, CA; (4); VP Cmnty Wkr; Yrbk; Off Frsh Cls; Stu Cncl; JV Var Cheerldng; Hon Roll; Jr NHS; Ntl Merit Ltr; Pres Schlr; Coord Cncl VP; CSF Hrn Soc VP & Pres; Amnsty Intl; Grad Cmmtte Co-Chr; JR-SR Prm Cmmtte; Cmp Cnslr; Stanford U; Psych.

GRAFIUS, AMANDA J; Oakdale HS; Oakdale, CA; (3); AFS; 4-H; FFA; Band; Mrchg Band; Pep Band; 4-H Awd; Stanislaus ST U Of CA; Art.

GRAGIRENA, TRINETTE; Garces HS; Bakersfield, CA; (2); 4-H; Key Clb; JV Vllybl; 4-H Awd; High Hon Roll; CSF.

GRAHAM, ARACELI; St Lucys Priory HS; Glendora, CA; (4); 2/111; Church Yth Grp; Drama Clb; Science Clb; Spanish Clb; School Play; Pres Frsh Cls; VP Soph Cls; Treas Jr Cls; Pres Sr Cls; High Hon Roll; Sthrn CA Edison Schlrshp; LA Cnty Outstndng Yth Awd; Marcia Gouin Schlrshp; Coord Cncl Yth Svc Awd; Rice U; Coll Engl Prfssr.

GRAHAM, CHRISTINA; Alisal HS; Salinas, CA; (3); Am Leg Aux Girls St; Pres English Clb; Math Tm; Office Aide; Variety Show; Var Capt Cheerldng; Intrml Pom Pon; Monterey Cnty Acad Decathlon Hnrs Speech Gold Mdl.

GRAHAM, CORDELL; Trabuco Hills HS; El Toro, CA; (1); Church Yth Grp; SADD; Intrml Bsktbl; Intrml Ftbl; JV Socr; 3rd St All Str Sccr Clb Tm; San Diego St; Archtct.

GRAHAM, FRANK; Franklin JR HS; Vallejo, CA; (3); 1/30; French Clb; Teachers Aide; Ftbl; Wt Lftg; Cit Awd; Hon Roll; Ftbl MVP.

GRAHAM, HILLARY; Ventura HS; Ventura, CA; (4); 32/410; Hosp Aide; Sec Spanish Clb; Teachers Aide; Capt Flag Corp; High Hon Roll; Prfct Atten Awd; Pres Acad Fit Awd; Golden State Exam Honors In Algebra & Geometry; Seal Bearer For CA Scholastic Fed; Mem Of Acad Dcthln; UCLA; Biology.

GRAHAM, JOSH R; North HS; Woody, CA; (3); 65/400; Pres Church Yth Grp; Pres FFA; Teachers Aide; JV Ftbl; Hon Roll; CHSRA St Fnls 90; FFA Regl/Sectl/Chptr Beef Prfcny Awds; West Hills JC; Ag Bus.

GRAHAM, JUSTIS A; El Cajon Valley HS; Santee, CA; (1); JV Bsbl; JV Ftbl; JV Socr; West Point.

GRAHAM, KELLY A; Ceres HS; Modesto, CA; (3); Drama Clb; Teachers Aide; School Play; High Hon Roll; Hon Roll; Pres Acad Fit Awd; Slvr Mdl Sac ST Lenaer Drama Cmptn; Prfsnl Model Cmpltn Cert; GSE Awd; Acad Decthln Mem; UCLA; Perfrmng Arts.

GRAHAM, KIMBERLY; Wheatland HS; Beale Afb, CA; (4); 11/100; Sec Church Yth Grp; French Clb; Rptr FBLA; Chorus; Ed Nwsp; Sec Sr Cls; JV Var Tennis; Latinos & Boosters Clb Schlrshps; Jrnlsm.

GRAHAM, LANCEN D; Trinity HS; Big Bar, CA; (1); Var Bsbl; JV Bsktbl; Hon Roll; Arch.

GRAHAM, LESLIE D; San Clemente HS; San Clemente, CA; (1); Cmnty Wkr; German Clb; Office Aide; Flag Corp; Hon Roll; UCI; Medcl.

GRAHAM, LISA R; Brawley Union HS; Westmoreland, CA; (2); 19/358; Church Yth Grp; Sec 4-H; Intnl Clb; Math Tm; SADD; Rep Frsh Cls; Rep Soph Cls; JV Sftbl; JV Vllybl; Dnfth Awd; CSF; Mock Trial Team; Vlybl Co MVP; Crmnl Jstce.

GRAHAM, NATALIE; Bishop Montgomery HS; Rolling Hills Est, CA; (1); GAA; Letterman Clb; SADD; Var Bsktbl; Score Keeper; JV Trk; JV Vllybl; Cit Awd; Hon Roll; Pres Acad Fit Awd; All Leag Bsktbl; Psycht.

GRAHAM, NATASHA I; University HS; Los Angeles, CA; (3); Cmnty Wkr; Debate Tm; Temple Yth Grp; Rptr Nwsp; Rep Frsh Cls; VP Sr Cls; JV Var Bsktbl; JV Var Vllybl; Hon Roll; Basic & TV Prdctn Cert Awd; Intl Mktng.

GRAHAM, NOEL L; Central Union HS; El Centro, CA; (2); Aud/Vis; Church Yth Grp; Pep Clb; SADD; Cit Awd; Hon Roll; Pres Acad Fit Awd; Friday Night Live Treas; Cyclst Clb; Upwrd Bnd Stu; UCLA; Wrtr.

GRAHAM, REBEKAH; King City Union HS; King City, CA; (3); Pres Church Yth Grp; 4-H; Band; Trk; Hon Roll; Peer Counselor; Ricks Coll; Child Dvlpmnt.

GRAHAM, RENEE; Berean Christian HS; Concord, CA; (2); 8/59; Church Yth Grp; Drama Clb; School Musical; School Play; JV Cheerldng; Powder Puff Ftbl; Cit Awd; High Hon Roll; Drama.

GRAHAM, RICHELLE; Grover Cleveland Hmnts Magnet HS; Sepulveda, CA; (4); 6/150; Church Yth Grp; Pres Girl Scts; Phtg Nwsp; VP Frsh Cls; Pres Jr Cls; Pres Sr Cls; Var Swmmng; Hon Roll; Pres Acad Fit Awd; UCLA; Commnctns.

GRAHAM, RODRIGO; Calaveras HS; Valley Springs, CA; (3); Church Yth Grp; SADD; Wrstlng; Hon Roll; CA Poly; Arch.

GRAHAM, RUSSELL ALAN; Elk Grove HS; Elk Grove, CA; (4); 39/482; Boy Scts; VP Church Yth Grp; Speech Tm; SADD; Teachers Aide; Variety Show; Rep Sr Cls; High Hon Roll; Hon Roll; Pres Acad Fit Awd; USAF Acad Honor; Outstanding Sr; Rally Comm Publicity Dir; CSF Life Mem; Santa Clara U; Cmptr Eng.

GRAHAM, SAMANTHA; Hiram Johnson HS; Sacramento, CA; (2); 75/573; Math Engrng Sci Achvts; Blck Stu Union; UC Davis Early Outrch Pgm; UCLA; Arch.

GRAHAM, SARAH N; Arcata HS; Arcata, CA; (2); Drama Clb; Stage Crew; Rptr Nwsp; Hon Roll; Piano 10 Yrs; Wrttn Prgms Kaypro, Mac In Tosh, Commodore; Wrttn Prgm Apprsl Bus Dlng Cmplctd Formulas; Humboldt ST; Sci.

GRAHAM, TAMMY L; Mission Viejo HS; Mission Viejo, CA; (3); 17/441; Cmnty Wkr; Debate Tm; GAA; Key Clb; Letterman Clb; Model UN; Spanish Clb; Teachers Aide; Varsity Clb; Rptr Yrbk; Safe Rides; Yth Agnst Hunger; Psych.

GRAHAM, TRACI; Lemoore Union HS; Hanford, CA; (2); French Clb; Sftbl; Hon Roll; JV Sftbl Capt Awd; CSF; Claremont Mc Kenna; Psych.

GRAHAM-WELLS, IDONA A ADAMS; Dunsmuir HS; Dunsmuir, CA; (2); Church Yth Grp; Pep Clb; Ski Clb; Bsktbl; Cheerldng; Pom Pon; Trk; Vllybl; Hon Roll; NHS; Sngldr; Susanville JR Coll; Flght Atnd.

GRAJEDA, MARIA DEL CARMEN; La Mirada HS; La Mirada, CA; (4); 71/340; Intnl Clb; Key Clb; Office Aide; Spanish Clb; Hist Band; Mrchg Band; Ed Yrbk; Hon Roll; Prfct Atten Awd; Off Frsh Cls; Pr Cnslng Cert; Yth Govt; Cochise Coll; Elem Educ.

GRAMATKY, SHERI; Village Christian HS; Glendale, CA; (4); Drama Clb; Spanish Clb; Drill Tm; Rep Stu Cncl; Var Cheerldng; Var Trk; Church Yth Grp; Missions Club; CSF; Biola U; Psych.

GRAMCKO, KIMBERLY A; Big Pine HS; Bishop, CA; (4); VP Frsh Cls; VP Soph Cls; Sec Rep Sr Cls; Var Bsktbl; Var Crs Cntry; Var Sftbl; Cit Awd; Hon Roll; Grls St Alt; Frosh Prncss; Prom Queen; Engr.

GRAMLICH, BRAD R; Irvine HS; Irvine, CA; (3); Church Yth Grp; Teachers Aide; Yrbk; Capt Bsktbl; Goldn St Exam Schl Hnrs; Bus.

GRAMMATKE, JEFF M; Lodi HS; Lodi, CA; (3); 49/616; Boy Scts; German Clb; Hon Roll; Prfct Atten Awd; Aerospc Engrng.

GRANA, JOLYNNE E; Downey HS; Downey, CA; (3); Church Yth Grp; Key Clb; VP Band; Church Choir; Drm Mjr(t); Jazz Band; Swing Chorus; Rep Jr Cls; VP Stu Cncl; Hon Roll.

GRANADO, JENNIFER A; Los Angeles Baptist HS; Sylmar, CA; (4); Church Yth Grp; Ski Clb; Chorus; Church Choir; Stat Bsbl; Stat Bsktbl; Var Co-Capt Cheerldng; Sftbl; Vllybl; Hon Roll; Coll Canyons JC.

GRANADO, MICHELLE M; Moreno Valley HS; Moreno Valley, CA; (3); Church Yth Grp; Drama Clb; Stage Crew; Bsktbl; Sftbl; NHS; Acad Awds; Sports Awds; Var Ltr; CSF Merit Awd; Rep CA In Cngrssnl Yth Ldrshp Cncl 90; Premed.

GRANADO, ZYLNA M; Arroyo HS; San Leandro, CA; (4); Drama Clb; SADD; Cit Awd; High Hon Roll; Hon Roll; Prfct Atten Awd; Pres Acad Fit Awd; CA ST U-Long Bch; Nrsng.

GRANADOS, RHODA L; Alisal HS; Salinas, CA; (1); Hon Roll; Prfct Atten Awd; JV Bsktbl; CSF; Gftd/Tlntd Ed; Presdntl Phys Ftnss Awd; Stanford; Cmmnctns.

GRANADOS, SANDRA E; Birmingham HS; Los Angeles, CA; (2); Dance Clb; Latin Clb; Spanish Clb; Drill Tm; Vllybl.

GRANADOS, STEVEN A; El Camino Fundamental HS; Citrus Heights, CA; (3); Var Ftbl; JV Socr; JV Swmmng; 1st Rnnr Up Yamaha Natl Electrnc Key Brd Fstvl 84; 1st Pl Sci Fair; Stanford.

GRANATOWSKI, LYNN; University Of San Diego HS; Escondido, CA; (2); Church Yth Grp; Cmnty Wkr; Intnl Clb; Service Clb; Ski Clb; Chorus; Bsktbl; Hon Roll; Opt Clb Awd; CSF; Ambssdr USDHS Corps Team; Piano & Horsbckrdng; U GA; Bus Advrtsng.

GRANDE, GARY E; Bellarmine College Prep; San Jose, CA; (3); Cmnty Wkr; Var Bsktbl; Acctng.

GRANDE, MARCO; San Pedro HS; Los Angeles, CA; (3); Band; Mrchg Band; Off Jr Cls; Stu Cncl; Crs Cntry; Cit Awd; Prfct Atten Awd; Good Grades Awd; Comp Prgmmng.

GRANDOS, DAVID; Royal HS; Simi Valley, CA; (4); 21/600; Letterman Clb; Quiz Bowl; Ftbl; Trk; Hon Roll; NHS; Ntl Merit SF; CA Tech; Comp Engrng.

GRANDOV, JENNIFER; Burlingame HS; Burlingame, CA; (3); Rep Stu Cncl; Hon Roll; UCSB; Physical Thrpy.

GRANDY, JEANETTE D; Edison HS; Huntington Beach, CA; (3); 236/425; Drill Tm; Socr; CSULB; Arch.

GRANDY, KEILANI; Saint Michaels HS; Los Angeles, CA; (1); Church Yth Grp; Church Choir; High Hon Roll; Span, Eng, Phys Ed/Health Awds; Obs/Ped.

GRANGER, HANNAH V; Pasadena HS; Sierra Madre, CA; (3); Church Yth Grp; French Clb; Pep Clb; Acpl Chr; Church Choir; Orch; Var Cheerldng; DAR Awd; Hon Roll.

GRANT, BRETT; St Ignatius HS; San Francisco, CA; (3); VP Church Yth Grp; Debate Tm; Speech Tm; JV Ftbl; JV Trk; High Hon Roll; Hon Roll; CSF; Statesmen Of Amer Dir Publicity; Jack & Jill Inc Pres; UCLA; Physician.

GRANT, DAV-YELL K; El Cerrito HS; Richmond, CA; (4); 35/362; Pres Church Yth Grp; Debate Tm; Speech Tm; Acpl Chr; Flag Corp; School Musical; Var Cheerldng; JV Swmmng; Prnctn Awd Acad Excllnc; Lwyr.

GRANT, JENNA M; The Bishops Schl; La Jolla, CA; (3); Drama Clb; Service Clb; Spanish Clb; Speech Tm; Thesps; Varsity Clb; School Play; Variety Show; Var Fld Hcky; Var Socr.

GRANT III, JOHN E; Bakersfield HS; Bakersfield, CA; (3); NFL; Ed Nwsp; Off Soph Cls; Off Jr Cls; Off Sr Cls; Var L Ftbl; Var L Trk; Hon Roll; Ford Dimension; Stu Wrld Consrvtn, Offcr.

GRANT, JUSTINE T; Eagle Rock HS; Los Angeles, CA; (2); Church Yth Grp; Rep Frsh Cls; Off Stu Cncl; Hon Roll; Rotary Awd; Genisis Environmental Club; Golden State Algebra Test Honor; PSAT Recognition; UCLA; Business & Art.

GRANT, LORI L; Monte Vista HS; Danville, CA; (2); Church Yth Grp; Chorus; JV Bsktbl; Var Crs Cntry; Var Trk; High Hon Roll; 5th Leag Crss Cntry; Athl Of Week Crss Cntry; 1st Mt San Antonio Crss Cntry Invtnl; Super Sprt Bsktbl.

GRANT, PETER; Damien HS; Glendora, CA; (3); 71/217; Cmnty Wkr; Debate Tm; NFL; Speech Tm; Teachers Aide; Swmmng; Hon Roll; Pltcl Sci.

GRANT, ROBIN; Vallejo SR HS; Vallejo, CA; (3); Pres Church Yth Grp; Cmnty Wkr; Dance Clb; Drama Clb; SADD; Teachers Aide; Church Choir; Rptr Nwsp; Lit Mag; VP Sr Cls; Stu Rep NC BSU VP; UC USD Tanner Project Stu; Frmr Dlgt & Teen Grp Pres Grtr Vllj Jck & Jill; Spolman Coll; Pol Sci.

GRANT, ROBYN A; Hamilton Acad Of Music; Van Nuys, CA; (2); Girl Scts; Office Aide; Teachers Aide; Band; Mrchg Band; Awds In Percussion Ensmbl Hamiltons Drum Line; St Identified Highly Gftd; Pierce JC; Interior Dsgn.

GRANT, RYAN M; Thomas Downey HS; Modesto, CA; (4); 1/400; Church Yth Grp; Treas German Clb; NFL; Science Clb; Ed Nwsp; L Crs Cntry; L Trk; High Hon Roll; Ntl Merit SF; Val; Acad Dcthln Tm Top Indiv Rgn 89; Mck Trl Tm; CSF Stu; U Of CA Berkely; Ec.

GRANT-WARD, SHANNON; Notre Dame HS; Studio City, CA; (4); 3/249; Cmnty Wkr; Ski Clb; SADD; Pom Pon; High Hon Roll; St Schlr; U CA-SANTA Barbara.

GRANTHAM, JENNIFER E; Poly HS; Riverside, CA; (2); Church Yth Grp; Aud/Vis; GAA; SADD; Stat Bsktbl; Var L Sftbl; JV Vllybl; Hon Roll; Girls Leag Club Treas; UNLV; Bus.

GRANTHAM, KARI L; John F Kennedy HS; El Cerrito, CA; (4); 3/237; Pres German Clb; NFL; SADD; Thesps; School Musical; School Play; Ed Nwsp; Ed Lit Mag; Stu Cncl; NHS; 3rd Pl Dist Wide Splng Bee; Won 2 Gld Mdls Acad Dcthln; Lesher Cmnctns Outstndng Jrnlst Awd; UC Davis; Pltcl Sci.

GRAPA, JULIO J; Bellarmine College Prep; Saratoga, CA; (4); 89/306; Cmnty Wkr; Debate Tm; Speech Tm; Ed Nwsp; Rep Frsh Cls; Rep Soph Cls; Rep Stu Cncl; Var JV Bsktbl; Intrml Ftbl; Intrml Socr; UC Santa Barbara; Chemcl Engr.

GRAPILON, BRIAN; Southwest HS; San Diego, CA; (3); 25/498; Aud/Vis; Key Clb; Quiz Bowl; Band; Treas Frsh Cls; Clss Cmmtte; Annapolis Acad MD; Grphc Art.

GRAS, SUSANNE; West Covina HS; West Covina, CA; (1); Church Yth Grp; GAA; Science Clb; Var Bsktbl; JV Sftbl; JV Vllybl; Friday Night Live; U Southern CA; Phys Thrpst.

GRASER, CRISTA C; St Joseph HS; Long Beach, CA; (3); Church Yth Grp; French Clb; Girl Scts; SADD; Hon Roll; Optometrst.

GRASH, TIFFANY; Elsinore HS; Canyon Lake, CA; (3); Teachers Aide; Hon Roll; Mt St Marys; Accntng.

GRASHIN, PAL; Berkeley HS; Kensington, CA; (3); Cmnty Wkr; Science Clb; Varsity Clb; Orch; School Musical; Var Crs Cntry; High Hon Roll; Hon Roll; NHS; Letterman Clb; Crew; Water Polo; Cello; Weslyan.

GRASSE, CAROLYN; Saddleback HS; Santa Ana, CA; (4); 75/500; Cmnty Wkr; JA; Office Aide; SADD; Variety Show; Rptr Yrbk; JV Cheerldng; L Var Socr; Pres Schlr; Natl Yth Ldrshp Conf; Presdntl Point Of Light Svc Awd; Stu Company/Econ Pres; Law.

GRASSHOFF, JENNIFER L; Torrey Pines HS; San Diego, CA; (3); 33/457; Aud/Vis; Church Yth Grp; Math Tm; VP Service Clb; Co-Capt Drill Tm; Cheerldng; National Merit Commended Scholar; California Scolarship Federation; Science-Biology.

GRASSI, MELANIE A; Napa HS; Napa, CA; (3); Art Clb; Drama Clb; Chorus; Church Choir; Hon Roll; Rens Poem Awds; Napa JC; Nursing.

GRASSO, JAIME L; Clovis West HS; Fresno, CA; (3); Ski Clb; Chorus; Drill Tm; Swing Chorus; Off Frsh Cls; Off Soph Cls; Var Bsktbl; Var Cheerldng; Var Trk; Hon Roll.

GRAUER, NICOLE; Orange Glen HS; Escondido, CA; (4); 21/435; Church Yth Grp; Math Clb; Spanish Clb; JV Var Tennis; Cit Awd; Hon Roll; NHS; Pres Acad Fit Awd; CA Schlstc Fed; Cnslrs Schlrshp; U Of San Diego; Marine Bio.

GRAUPMANN, LISA M; Highland HS; Bakersfield, CA; (4); 28/291; Church Yth Grp; Drama Clb; Hosp Aide; Key Clb; Math Clb; Pep Clb; Sec Spanish Clb; SADD; Teachers Aide; Acpl Chr; CSF Gold Sear Bearer Grad; WATCH Schlrshp; Facity Artst Srs CA St U Chico; CA ST U Chico; Nurse.

GRAUPMANN, STACY A; Highland HS; Bakersfield, CA; (4); 19/291; Church Yth Grp; VP JA; Key Clb; Math Clb; Pep Clb; Spanish Clb; SADD; Orch; Variety Show; Rep Frsh Cls; Amercn Hrt Assoc Schlrshp; Bakersfield Coll Presdnts Schlrshp; Area Rep Freedms Fndtn Yth Ldrshp Smnr; Bakerfield CC; Nurse.

GRAVADOR, RHODA; Lowell HS; San Francisco, CA; (2); Chorus; Church Choir; School Musical; School Play; Theatre.

GRAVANCE, ROCHELLE M; Laton HS; Laton, CA; (4); 3/50; Pres Sr Cls; FFA; Pres GAA; SADD; Teachers Aide; Color Guard; Pres Frsh Cls; Pres Jr Cls; Stu Cncl; Var Capt Bsktbl; Lib Arts Achvt Awwd; Outstndng Sr Ath; Outstndng Sr Excptl Achvt Awd; Ath Ltrs; Cty MVP; FFA Schlrshp; CA Poly Sn Ls Obsp; Dairy Sci.

GRAVELINE II, EDWIN G; Fresno HS; Fresno, CA; (3); 49/600; Boy Scts; Church Yth Grp; Debate Tm; NFL; Ski Clb; Intrml Bsbl; Intrml Ftbl; VP Golf; High Hon Roll; Mem Teens In Action Youth Commtte; CA Schlrshp Fed; Eagle Scout BSA; Broadcast Journalism.

GRAVELL, DINA; Western HS; Anaheim, CA; (1); Church Yth Grp; Treas Frsh Cls; JV Cheerldng; Var Socr; Girls Leag Clb; Amer Lgn Awd For Ldrshp; Wrestlerettes Clb; Western ST U; Tax Attny.

GRAVELL, LISA; Western HS; Anaheim, CA; (3); #10 In Class; Pep Clb; Varsity Clb; Chorus; Yrbk; VP Capt Socr; VP Capt Trk; Hon Roll; NHS; Grls Lg VP.

GRAVES, ANDREA; Paraclete HS; Palmdale, CA; (4); 17/125; Debate Tm; Drama Clb; Key Clb; Teachers Aide; High Hon Roll; Hon Roll; NHS; Mgr Ftbl Tm; 20th Cngrssnl Dist Hrngs; Assoc Stu Bdy Pblcty Chrprsn; Antelope Valley Coll; Intrprtr.

GRAVES, CARRIE M; Kingsburg Joint Union HS; Kingsburg, CA; (3); Church Yth Grp; SADD; Chorus; Rep Frsh Cls; JV Stat Bsktbl; Trk; JV Vllybl; Hon Roll; Jazz Choir; Azusa Pacific U; Chld Psych.

GRAVES, DAVID R; Kingsburg HS; Kingsburg, CA; (1); Band; Jazz Band; Mrchg Band; JV L Bsbl; JV L Bsktbl; JV L Ftbl; Hon Roll; U CA Los Angeles; Med.

GRAVES, HEATHER L; Poway HS; Poway, CA; (4); Model UN; Band; Mrchg Band; Orch; Pep Band; High Hon Roll; NHS; Pres Acad Fit Awd; Natl Mrt Cmmndtn; Gldn St Exm Hgh Hnrs Alg; Kiwanis Recgntn Outstndng Stu; UC Davis; Vet Med.

GRAVES, JOLIE; Chico SR HS; Chico, CA; (2); Church Yth Grp; Q&S; JV Cheerldng; Crs Cntry; Fld Hcky; Var Socr; Trk; Hon Roll.

GRAVES, KAREN L; Sunset HS; Hayward, CA; (4); 4/186; Art Clb; Key Clb; Math Clb; Red Cross Aide; Teachers Aide; Stu Cncl; Var Bsktbl; High Hon Roll; CSF; Coca-Cola Schlr Athlt; Bank Of Amer Achvt Awd Histry; Chabot Coll.

GRAVES, KAREN R; Bonita Vista HS; Bonita, CA; (3); 5/550; Chorus; Swing Chorus; Ntl Merit SF; Stu In IB Brgm & Acad Dcthln; Tutor; Accmpny Vcl Mscns; Math.

GRAVES, MIYONA; Escondido HS; Escondido, CA; (3); Drama Clb; VP Sec Key Clb; Letterman Clb; School Play; Phtg Yrbk; Stu Cncl; Powder Puff Ftbl; JV Var Swmmng; Hon Roll; Water Polo JV-MST Imprvd; Dramatic Arts.

GRAVES, RONALD; Edison-Computech HS; Fresno, CA; (1); Church Yth Grp; Office Aide; Teachers Aide; Church Choir; Cit Awd; Med.

GRAVES, SCOTT L; Rio Lindo Acad; Ukiah, CA; (3); Church Yth Grp; Cmnty Wkr; FCA; JA; Ski Clb; Spanish Clb; Teachers Aide; Band; Pres Soph Cls; Rep Jr Cls.

GRAVES, SEAN E; Montclair HS; Pomona, CA; (4); FBLA; Teachers Aide; Hon Roll; NHS; Prfct Atten Awd; Sn Antonio Coll-Walnut; Jrnlsm.

GRAVES, TAMARA C; Atwater HS; Atwater, CA; (1); Var Bsktbl; Trk; JV Vllybl; Georgetown; Rdlgy.

GRAVES, TAMMY A; Bret Harte Union HS; Copperopolis, CA; (2); FFA.

GRAVES, TRACY; Dublin HS; Dublin, CA; (2); 5/224; French Clb; FBLA; Band; Color Guard; Flag Corp; Mrchg Band; Stu Cncl; High Hon Roll; Hon Roll; Pres Acad Fit Awd; High Hnrs GSE Alg Geom; Recogntn Of Excllnc In Schlrshp; UCLA; Physics.

GRAVETT, ERIKA Y; San Pedro HS; San Pedro, CA; (4); 53/539; Ed Nwsp; Pres Jr Cls; Pres Sr Cls; Lion Awd; Pres Acad Fit Awd; St Schlr; CA Yth-Govt Video Nws Pgm Prdcr; Ephebian Soc; Pirate Ldrshp Awd; Howard U; Brdcst Jrnlsm.

GRAVLEE, ALAN C; El Camino Fundamental HS; Sacramento, CA; (3); 54/366; Spanish Clb; VICA; Hon Roll; Jr Statsmn Amer; Moot Ct Tm; Cinematgrphy.

GRAY, AMY; Carmel HS; Carmel, CA; (2); 14/149; Teachers Aide; JV Fld Hcky; JV Sftbl; JV Vllybl; High Hon Roll; Hon Roll; Prfct Atten Awd; Rotary Awd; Algebra Golden St Exam.

GRAY, ANNE; Las Lomas HS; Lafayette, CA; (4); 20/260; Cmnty Wkr; Drama Clb; Girl Scts; SADD; Chorus; School Musical; Phtg Nwsp; Elks Awd; High Hon Roll; Hon Roll; St Schlr; Cmmnty Vol 5 Yrs Wldlf Museum; Delta Kappa Gamma Schlrshp; Spcl Intst Irish Dncng, Drwng & Bckpckng; UC Davis; Bio.

GRAY, BELINDA M; Lassen HS; Susanville, CA; (3); 26/200; Ski Clb; Teachers Aide; School Play; Ed Nwsp; Treas Soph Cls; JV Var Fld Hcky; JV Trk; Hon Roll; Awd Mst Imprve Vrsty Fld Hcky; Photo; Aerbcs; Ferrum Coll; Commnctns.

GRAY, CHAD; Bonita Vista HS; Bonita, CA; (2); Key Clb; Office Aide; Rptr Nwsp; Off Jr Cls; Cit Awd; Hon Roll; Writer.

GRAY, DEBBIE; Pacifica HS; Garden Grove, CA; (2); 103/298; Church Yth Grp; Hosp Aide; Sftbl; Psych.

GRAY, DENNIS; Luther Burbank Acad Math Sci & Engrng; Sacramento, CA; (3); 1/276; Boy Scts; Math Clb; Math Tm; Band; Mrchg Band; Orch; Bausch & Lomb Sci Awd; High Hon Roll; Hon Roll; Rotary Awd; Pcfc Cst Entmlgcl Soc; Lpdptrst Soc; Acad Dcthln Hnr Div; Entmlgy.

GRAY, DINAH G; Montebello HS; Los Angeles, CA; (2); Dance Clb; Ski Clb; SADD; Chorus; School Play; Cit Awd; Hon Roll; Ballet; Culture Vultures; Dance.

GRAY, EUN-JOO; Burroughs HS; Ridgecrest, CA; (3); 9/415; Mgr Stage Crew; Rptr Nwsp; Co-Ed Lit Mag; High Hon Roll; Opt Clb Awd; Tech Mntr Stu.

GRAY, HERMES; Redlands HS; Redlands, CA; (2); Hon Roll; 1st Pl St Comptn Drafting; Awd For Hnrs In Math; Arch.

GRAY, JENNIFER A; Central Union HS; El Centro, CA; (2); Church Yth Grp; Cmnty Wkr; Speech Tm; High Hon Roll; CA ST U; Lawyer.

GRAY, JULIET; Chadwick HS; Los Angeles, CA; (4); Hosp Aide; Chorus; School Musical; JV Var Cheerldng; Var Sftbl; Ntl Merit Ltr; Vlntrng In A Day-Care Ctr; Santa Barbara U.

GRAY, KRISTINE A; Castle Park HS; Chula Vista, CA; (1); 15/614; Drama Clb; French Clb; Speech Tm; School Play; Stage Crew; Prfct Atten Awd; Educ.

GRAY, LA TONYA M; George Washington Preparatory HS; Los Angeles, CA; (3); Model UN; Pep Clb; JV Bsktbl; Var Trk; JV Vllybl; Empress Club; Grambling U; Bus Mgmt.

GRAY, LESLIE A; Lodi HS; Lodi, CA; (1); English Clb; Girl Scts; Chorus; Elks Awd; High Hon Roll; Hon Roll; Rvrbt Rscls Dixielnd Jazz Band; Lodi Chldrns Chorus.

GRAY, LISA; Liberty Christian HS; Fountain Valley, CA; (3); Church Yth Grp; FCA; GAA; Teachers Aide; Varsity Clb; Chorus; School Musical; Var Bsktbl; Var Capt Sftbl; Var Vllybl; Phy Ther.

GRAY, MISTY S; Warren HS; Downey, CA; (2); Church Yth Grp; Dance Clb; Pep Clb; Chorus; Cheerldng; Cal ST Fullerton; Tchng.

GRAY, RACHEL; Valley HS; Sacramento, CA; (2); 59/431; SADD; Sprt Ed Nwsp; JV Sftbl; Hon Roll; Piano; Stanford; Marine Bio.

GRAY, RANDY; Santa Monica HS; Santa Monica, CA; (4); 157/604; Church Yth Grp; Varsity Clb; Rep Jr Cls; Off Sr Cls; Swmmng; Vllybl; Opt Clb Awd; Vrstyu Water Polo Tm Capt, All Bay League Mst Vlbl Plyr; Cal Poly, San Luis Ob; Anml Sci.

GRAY, SHAWNA L; Channel Islands HS; Oxnard, CA; (3); Church Yth Grp; Cmnty Wkr; Drama Clb; Teachers Aide; Church Choir; School Play; Hon Roll; Law.

GRAY, SHELLY; Ontario HS; Ontario, CA; (2); Church Yth Grp; Dance Clb; German Clb; GAA; JV Bsktbl; JV Swmmng; JV Vllybl; Cit Awd; Dixie Coll; Coaching.

GRAY, ZAILA; University HS; Santa Ana, CA; (2); Dance Clb; School Musical; School Play; Variety Show; Rep Soph Cls; Cit Awd; BSU Social Chrmn; Choreogrphy; Bus Mgmt.

GRAYBILL, LYNETTE M; Dos Pueblos HS; Goleta, CA; (3); Church Yth Grp; Cmnty Wkr; Office Aide; Teachers Aide; JV Bsktbl; JV Sftbl; UCSB; Psych.

GRAYDON, AMY C; Rosemead HS; Rosemead, CA; (2); Hon Roll; CSF; Ecology Clb.

GRAYS, CHERE A; Wasco Union HS; Wasco, CA; (3); Var Cheerldng; Stat Trk; Hon Roll; NHS; CSF; Black U; Engrng.

GRAYSON, CHARLES C; Abraham Lincoln HS; San Francisco, CA; (3); ROTC; Teachers Aide; Band; Color Guard; Drill Tm; School Musical; Stage Crew; Variety Show; Prfct Atten Awd; 2nd Lieut 90; Hghst Rnkng,Positnd Cadet; Stanford U; Nrsng.

GRAZIAN, COURTNEY; Aptos HS; La Selva Beach, CA; (2); 58/396; JV Bsktbl; Var Trk; CA Poly; Arch Engrng.

GREATOREX, JEFF; Liberty Union HS; Oakley, CA; (2); Boy Scts; High Hon Roll; CA Schlrshp Soc; Rcng Stu Mercury Clss Yacht Assoc; Mdl Boat Bldg & Dsgn; Erly HS Engrance 1 Yr; Berkeley; Med Doctor.

GREAVES, CAREN L; Helix HS; La Mesa, CA; (4); 13/367; Church Yth Grp; Cmnty Wkr; FTA; Hosp Aide; Sec Intnl Clb; Key Clb; Science Clb; Chorus; Church Choir; Ed Lit Mag; BYU; Scndry Ed.

GREAVES, CHERI D; Helix HS; La Mesa, CA; (2); 73/449; Pres Church Yth Grp; French Clb; Var Tennis; Kiwanis Awd; Prfct Atten Awd; Brigham Young U.

GREBBIEN, JENNIFER; Christian HS; El Cajon, CA; (3); Church Yth Grp; Drama Clb; Key Clb; SADD; School Play; Stage Crew; Ed Yrbk; JV Sftbl; Stat Vllybl; Hon Roll; Cal Poly Pomona; Engrng.

GRECIA, ELINORE M; South San Francisco HS; South San Francis, CA; (3); Pres Spanish Clb; Sec Sr Cls; Hist Stu Cncl; JV Vllybl; Asian Amer & Stu Soc Sci Clbs; Hnrb Mntn Chinese Hist Soc; Outstnand Achvt In Span; San Francisco ST U; Elem Educ.

GRECIA, RAQUEL M; South San Francisco HS; South San Francis, CA; (2); Cmnty Wkr; Math Clb; Spanish Clb; Math Clb & Span Clb Mst Cndy Sold Awd.

GRECO, LETICIA M; Etiwanda HS; Alta Loma, CA; (2); Sec Church Yth Grp; Office Aide; Rptr Yrbk; Hon Roll; BYU; Cosmtlgst.

GREELEY, DIANE E; Rio Mesa HS; Camarillo, CA; (4); Church Yth Grp; Drama Clb; Hosp Aide; Key Clb; Stage Crew; Off Jr Cls; Cit Awd; Hon Roll; Kiwanis Awd; Pres Acad Fit Awd; Jrnlsm.

GREELEY, VERONIQUE S; San Diego HS; San Diego, CA; (3); Treas French Clb; Science Clb; Rep Jr Cls; JV Vllybl; French Hon Soc; Hon Roll; Rotary Awd; Intl Bacealaurate Dip; Treas Intl Friendshp Clb; CSF; Vet.

GREEN, ABBY A; Northgate HS; Walnut Creek, CA; (4); 56/279; Cmnty Wkr; Model UN; Teachers Aide; Temple Yth Grp; Band; Mrchg Band; Sec Treas Frsh Cls; Off Soph Cls; Sec Treas Sr Cls; Socr; Yuth Ed; CSF; Acad Ltr; U C Davis.

GREEN, AIMEE L; Lowell HS; San Francisco, CA; (3); Church Yth Grp; Cmnty Wkr; Sec Service Clb; Cit Awd; Minority Outreach Pgm; Phy.

GREEN, AKIBA; Grace M Davis HS; Modesto, CA; (1); VP FFA; Hosp Aide; SADD; Orch; JV Trk; Hon Roll; King-Kennedy Brd Of Dirctrs Yth Pgm; Phy.

GREEN, AMY; Sierra Vista HS; Baldwin Park, CA; (1); #20 In Class; Pep Clb; Intrml Cheerldng; Hon Roll; HARVARD; Med.

GREEN, ANGELA M; Santa Barbara HS; Santa Barbara, CA; (1); Pres Church Yth Grp; Chorus; Church Choir; JV Tennis; Pianist; Pvt Vcl Stdy; Pvt Tnns Coaching.

GREEN, ANTONIO; Carlsbad HS; Oceanside, CA; (4); Drama Clb; Letterman Clb; Var Ftbl; Var Socr; JV Tennis; Var Vllybl; Hon Roll; Membr Success Connection; U Of CA Sd; Microbiology.

GREEN, BLAINE I; Arcata HS; Arcata, CA; (3); Boy Scts; Church Yth Grp; French Clb; Scholastic Bowl; Sec Service Clb; Lit Mag; Tennis; French Hon Soc; High Hon Roll; Ntl Merit Ltr; Eagle Scout; USC; Soc Sci.

GREEN, BRETT M; Leuzinger HS; Hawthorne, CA; (4); Sec Ed Yrbk; Hon Roll; Pres Acad Fit Awd; HS Hnr Entrnc; CSF; Hl Fm-Quietst; El Camino JC; Phys Thrpst.

GREEN, CHANTAL S; Borrego Springs HS; Borrego Springs, CA; (2); 1/35; Cmnty Wkr; Key Clb; Pres SADD; Pres Soph Cls; JV Cheerldng; Cit Awd; High Hon Roll; Prfct Atten Awd; Vet.

GREEN, DANIELLE J; Woodcrest Christian HS; Riverside, CA; (2); Church Yth Grp; Pep Clb; Church Choir; Var L Cheerldng; High Hon Roll; NHS.

GREEN, DARCIE C; Santa Margarita HS; Mission Viejo, CA; (3); Church Yth Grp; Drama Clb; English Clb; Letterman Clb; Library Aide; Spanish Clb; Thesps; Acpl Chr; Chorus; Church Choir; Private Piano & Diction; Voice Lessns Dr Maurice Allard; Chapman Coll; Opera.

GREEN, DEBBIE L; Fontana HS; Fontana, CA; (2); Art Clb; Dance Clb; Girl Scts; Drill Tm; School Play; Sec Soph Cls; Stu Cncl; Sftbl; Swmmng; Cit Awd; Lawyer.

GREEN, ELLIS L; Moorpark HS; Moorpark, CA; (2); Cmnty Wkr; Var Capt Bsktbl; JV Var Ftbl; Score Keeper; Wt Lftg; Hon Roll; Prfct Atten Awd; U Of AR; Bus Finance.

GREEN, GEORGETTE M; Manual Arts HS; Los Angeles, CA; (3); ROTC; Color Guard; Hon Roll; Prfct Atten Awd; Trphy Outstndng Achvt Engl; UCLA; Accntnt.

GREEN, GREGORY A W; Hayward HS; Hayward, CA; (2); Chess Clb; SADD; Acpl Chr; Bsbl; Crs Cntry; Ftbl; High Hon Roll; Hon Roll; NHS; UIL Choir Lvl I Solo 89; USAF Acad; Law Enfrcmnt.

GREEN, ILONA S; Mendocino Community Schl; Albion, CA; (2); Girl Scts; School Play; Hon Roll; Outstndng Photo Awd; Mdl Stu Awd; UCSC; Chld Psych.

GREEN, JANEL; Center HS; North Highlands, CA; (1); Band; Church Choir; JV Cheerldng; Hon Roll; Spellman; Aerospc Engrng.

GREEN, JASON A; Apple Valley HS; George AFB, CA; (1); Church Yth Grp; French Clb; JV Bsbl; Bsktbl; Ftbl; High Hon Roll; Deans List.

GREEN, JENNIFER; San Benito HS; Hollister, CA; (2); 180/379; Drama Clb; Pep Clb; School Musical; School Play; JV Var Cheerldng; Prom Commte; Modeling.

GREEN, JENNIFER C; Dana Hills HS; Dana Point, CA; (1); Church Yth Grp; Cmnty Wkr; Science Clb; Church Choir; Off Soph Cls; JV Sftbl; JV Sftbl Awd; Commnctns.

GREEN, JENNIFER L; Newport Christian HS; Santa Ana, CA; (3); Teachers Aide; Rptr Nwsp; Var Bsktbl; High Hon Roll; PALS; Vllybl Clb 90; USC; Commnctns.

GREEN, JONATHAN; South Tahoe HS; Stateline, NV; (3); VP Jr Cls; Var Wrstlng; High Hon Roll; SJA Clb; CSF Clb; USAF Acad; Engrng.

GREEN, JUSTIN; Pinole Valley HS; Pinole, CA; (1); Prfct Atten Awd; Pinole-Hercules Little Leag Sr Major Div Bsbl Tm 90.

GREEN, KIMBERLY M; Casa Roble Fundamental HS; Orangevale, CA; (3); 112/370; Treas AFS; SADD; Close-Up Fndtn; Photo Club; CA ST U Sacramento; Law.

GREEN, LEAH; San Pasqual HS; Escondido, CA; (3); Church Yth Grp; Dance Clb; FCA; Girl Scts; Temple Yth Grp; Drill Tm; VP Soph Cls; JV Crs Cntry; JV Wt Lftg; Cit Awd; UC Santa Barbara; Biochem.

GREEN, MARTA J; North Hollywood HS; Studio City, CA; (3); Key Clb; Letterman Clb; Mu Alpha Theta; Office Aide; Science Clb; Chorus; JV Capt Cheerldng; Hon Roll; Jr NHS; NHS; Explorers Post 108.

GREEN, MELANIE L; Central Union HS; El Centro, CA; (2); AFS; Debate Tm; German Clb; NFL; Speech Tm; High Hon Roll; Hon Roll; Ntl Merit Ltr; Mock Trial; U CA Berkeley; Law.

GREEN, MELISSA L; Don Lugo HS; Chino, CA; (3); Art Clb; Church Yth Grp; Dance Clb; Drama Clb; FCA; Girl Scts; Office Aide; Band; Chorus; Church Choir; Cnslr.

GREEN, MICHAEL L; California HS; Walnut Creek, CA; (4); 100/450; Debate Tm; Pres French Clb; Intnl Clb; JV Trk; French Hon Soc; Hon Roll; Goldn St Geom Exm Hnrs; UC Davis; Elec Engr.

GREEN, PAULA M; Arlington HS; Riverside, CA; (2); Church Yth Grp; Drama Clb; ROTC; Drill Tm; School Play; Var Bsktbl; Var Crs Cntry; JV Trk; Hon Roll; Pilot.

GREEN, PETER C; Don Lugo HS; Chino, CA; (2); 104/800; Church Yth Grp; Cmnty Wkr; German Clb; Hon Roll; Chino Natl SR League Bsbl; Golden St Exam Algebra & Geom Hnrs; Pepperdine U; Engrng.

GREEN, PHAEDRA M; Imperial HS; Imperial, CA; (3); FFA; Varsity Clb; Pres Stu Cncl; Mgr Bsktbl; Var JV Sftbl; JV Vllybl; Hon Roll; Outstndng Engl Achvt; Vlybl Coachs Awd; Hampton Inst; Acctng.

GREEN, REBECCA J; Anderson Union HS; Anderson, CA; (4); German Clb; Bsktbl; Hon Roll; Shasta JC; Comp/German.

GREEN, REBECCA L; Norco SR HS; Norco, CA; (2); Art Clb; Church Yth Grp; Dance Clb; Chorus; Yrbk; Off Soph Cls; Gym; Swmmng; Cit Awd; Ntl Merit Ltr; UCLA; Acctng.

GREEN, SANAE J; Castle Park HS; Chula Vista, CA; (4); 32/400; Pep Clb; Spanish Clb; Co-Capt Varsity Clb; Ed Nwsp; Rep Frsh Cls; Rep Soph Cls; Treas Sr Cls; Rep Stu Cncl; Co-Capt Cheerldng; Sftbl; Interact Clb; Senator; Lbrl Arts Educ.

GREEN, SARAH M; Berean Chr HS; Concord, CA; (3); 1/72; Church Yth Grp; Intnl Clb; Chorus; School Musical; High Hon Roll; Ntl Merit Ltr; CSF Secy; Frgn Lang.

GREEN, SAUNDRALIN; Stagg HS; Stockton, CA; (3); Speech Tm; Acpl Chr; Church Choir; Variety Show; Cit Awd; Standard Engl Proficiency Pgm 9 Yrs; NAACP Natl Act-So Cont 90; Gramblin ST U; Commnctns.

GREEN, SEAN L; Bret Harte HS; Angels Camp, CA; (2); Drama Clb; Pep Clb; Band; School Musical; School Play; Treas Stu Cncl; Awd Pin Band; Friday Night Live; CA ST U; Jrnlsm.

GREEN, SHAWN; Tustin HS; Tustin, CA; (3); 1/250; Key Clb; Letterman Clb; Bsbl; Bsktbl; Cit Awd; High Hon Roll; NHS; All Seaview League 1st Tm Bsbl 89; Schlr Athlete Bsktbl 87; Bus.

GREEN, SKYE M; Pasadena HS; Sierra Madre, CA; (2); GAA; Pep Clb; Flag Corp; Treas Frsh Cls; JV Bsktbl; Var Cheerldng; Var Capt Crs Cntry; Var Trk; Hon Roll; Ballt Le Petit Dance Studio; Piano Fern Rogers; CSF VP.

GREEN, STACY A; Downtown Business Magnet HS; Los Angeles, CA; (2); Art Clb; Chess Clb; Office Aide; Sign Lang Cls Co-Instrctr; Acad Of Finance; Pntng Cls Bgnng Instrctr; Comp Pgmng.

GREEN, STAN D; Davis SR HS; Davis, CA; (4); Art Clb; Yrbk; JV Bsbl; Intrml JV Bsktbl; Hon Roll; Prfct Atten Awd; Pres Acad Fit Awd; Best In USA Awd For Cover Of Yrbk; Outstndng Art Stu Awd; Congrssnl Art Cmptn 90; UCD; Commrcl Art.

GREEN, STEPHANIE R; Alexander Hamilton HS; Los Angeles, CA; (3); Spanish Clb; Stage Crew; Stat Ftbl; Trk; Hon Roll; Acad Excl; 2 Yrs Lttrmn Track; Nevian; UCLA; Med Field.

GREEN, SUSAN; Rio Linda HS; Sacramento, CA; (3); Hosp Aide; Office Aide; ROTC; Teachers Aide; Sftbl; Hon Roll; JR Coll; Surgical Nrs.

GREEN, SUZANNE M; Upper Lake Union HS; Witter Springs, CA; (4); 1/57; Pres Art Clb; Church Yth Grp; Sec Science Clb; Sec Spanish Clb; Nwsp; Sec Treas Jr Cls; Sec Sr Cls; L Var Bsktbl; L Capt Trk; L Var Vllybl; Cmptd St Trck Chmpnshps 89; Mendocino Coll; Health.

GREEN, TAMMY M; Bullard HS; Fresno, CA; (3); Letterman Clb; Ski Clb; School Play; Lit Mag; Socr; TEAMS USA Intl Sccr Team; Marine Bio.

GREENAWAY, DIOR Y; So Bay JR Acad; Los Angeles, CA; (1); 2/20; Art Clb; Church Yth Grp; Computer Clb; Drama Clb; Chorus; Socr; Vllybl; Hon Roll; Sal.

GREENBERG, ERIC W; Mater Dei HS; Fountain Valley, CA; (2); Var Swmmng; JV Water Polo; Columbia U; Ed.

GREENBERG, JASON ERIC; Glendale HS; Glendale, CA; (2); Var Bsbl; Hon Roll; NHS; Pres Acad Fit Awd; U Of CA Santa Barbara.

GREENBERG, JASON P; Flintridge Preparatory Schl; Los Angeles, CA; (3); Ski Clb; Spanish Clb; Temple Yth Grp; Band; JV Socr; Var Swmmng; Hon Roll; Waterpolo; Law.

GREENBERG, JEREMY; San Ramon Valley HS; San Ramon, CA; (2); Temple Yth Grp; JV Ftbl; Var Wt Lftg; JV Wrstlng; Hon Roll; Prfct Atten Awd; Spanish NHS; Guitar; Sports Nutrition; UCLA; Bus.

GREENBERG, KERI J; Live Oak HS; Morgan Hill, CA; (4); 56/480; French Clb; Band; Mrchg Band; Pep Band; Ed Nwsp; French Hon Soc; High Hon Roll; Hon Roll; Ambian Horse Assn; CA All-St Hnr Band 87-90; County Hnr Band 89/90; CA Poly Sn Luis Obispo; Jrnlsm.

GREENBERG, ROBYN A; Leuzinger HS; Hawthorne, CA; (2); School Play; Stage Crew; Rptr Nwsp; JV Bsktbl; Score Keeper; JV Trk; Prfct Atten Awd; Princeton; Med.

GREENBERG, WENDY M; Live Oak HS; Morgan Hill, CA; (3); Art Clb; Debate Tm; French Clb; FBLA; Teachers Aide; Band; Yrbk; Intrml Bsktbl; Sftbl; High Hon Roll; Nordstrom Fashion Bd Rep; U Of CA; Mrktng.

GREENDALE, LYNELL; Justin-Siena HS; Napa, CA; (3); Cmnty Wkr; Key Clb; Office Aide; Pep Clb; Chorus; School Musical; Var Cheerldng; High Hon Roll; Hon Roll; UC Riverside; Bus Admin.

GREENE, ADRIANA M; Gladstone HS; Azusa, CA; (3); Aud/Vis; SADD; Rep Frsh Cls; Chrmn Stu Cncl; Gym; Swmmng; Hon Roll; Pres Acad Fit Awd; Racial Harmony Schl Camp 88; Defense Atty.

GREENE, ALLISON; Tustin HS; Tustin, CA; (4); 40/400; English Clb; JA; Hist Key Clb; VP Thesps; School Play; Stage Crew; Lit Mag; Rep Stu Cncl; Stat Wrstlng; High Hon Roll; Bst Actress Slf Produced Acad Awds 89; Top 25 Pres Hnr Roll; 2 Awds For Cmmnty Svc At Boys Clb; UC Berkeley.

GREENE, ANDY P; San Luis Obispo HS; San Luis Obispo, CA; (1); 1/300; Math Tm; JV Tennis; High Hon Roll; Music; 3rd Pl Math Cont 89.

GREENE, ARMMOND; Morningside HS; Inglewood, CA; (1); Drama Clb; Band; Mrchg Band; Stage Crew; Var JV Tennis; High Hon Roll; UCLA; Doctor.

GREENE, BENJAMIN; Tustin HS; Tustin, CA; (2); VP Latin Clb; Varsity Clb; Swmmng; High Hon Roll; Hon Roll; Water Polo; U Of CA; Med.

GREENE, DOLLY K; Louiseville HS; Woodland Hills, CA; (1); Pres Girl Scts; Ski Clb; Chorus; School Musical; School Play; Swmmng; Hon Roll; Awd Prtl Schlrshp; Harvard; Bus.

GREENE, ERICA D; Turlock HS; Hughson, CA; (2); 78/618; Letterman Clb; Var L Crs Cntry; Var Capt Trk; MVP Crss Cntry 2 Yrs; Miss Teen Amer; 28th Pl Crss Cntry St Chmpnshps.

GREENE, JANICE; Bolytechnic HS; Riverside, CA; (3); Church Yth Grp; Drama Clb; Chorus; Church Choir; Dance Clb; SADD; Stage Crew; Pres Jr Cls; Howard U; Law.

GREENE, JASON C; Carpinteria HS; Carpinteria, CA; (2); 26/161; Band; Hon Roll; Surfing, Body Boarding; U CA Snta Brbra; Robotics Engr.

GREENE, JASON T; Turlock HS; Hughson, CA; (3); 27/700; Letterman Clb; Var Crs Cntry; Ftbl; Var Trk; Physics.

GREENE, JESSICA J; Armijo HS; Fairfield, CA; (2); Drama Clb; Science Clb; SADD; Band; Color Guard; Mrchg Band; School Play; Hon Roll; Most Imprvd Actr 1988-89; Chef.

GREENE, JOEL; Don Lugo HS; Chino, CA; (2); Mgr Dance Clb; Varsity Clb; School Play; Stage Crew; Variety Show; Cit Awd; High Hon Roll; Hon Roll; JV Ftbl; Var Mgr(s); Presdntl Schlr; Comp Clb; Elect Engr.

GREENE, KARI M; Bakersfield HS; Bakersfield, CA; (3); 16/750; Var Swmmng; Chld Dev.

GREENE, KRISTI; Hogan SR HS; Vallejo, CA; (2); Spanish Clb; SADD; Varsity Clb; Drill Tm; Yrbk; Var L Swmmng; Hon Roll; Athltc Of Wk; Mst Vlbl Swmmr 89 & 90; Stanford; Chld Psych.

GREENE, LYNDA C; Hemet HS; Hemet, CA; (1); 221/517; Church Yth Grp; Library Aide; Teachers Aide; Rptr Nwsp; Stat Bsktbl; Powder Puff Ftbl; JV Sftbl; JV Tennis; Mission Bay Career Ctr; Travel.

GREENE III, MERLE; Hamilton HS; Los Angeles, CA; (3); Library Aide; Office Aide; Teachers Aide; Stage Crew; Bsktbl; Crs Cntry; Trk; Cit Awd; High Hon Roll; Hon Roll; USC; Attrny.

GREENE, NATALIA; Agouora HS; Agoura Hills, CA; (3); 57/484; Chess Clb; FBLA; Key Clb; Pep Clb; VP Soph Cls; Pres Jr Cls; Stu Cncl; JV Trk; Wrstlng; Hon Roll; HOBY; Law.

GREENE, NATASHA A; Edison/Computech HS; Fresno, CA; (2); Church Yth Grp; GAA; Teachers Aide; Church Choir; Var Bsktbl; Var Trk; Cit Awd; Gov Hon Prg Awd; High Hon Roll; Hon Roll; Presdntl Acad Ftns Awd; Mst Vlbl Trk Fld Awd; MVP Awd Grls Bsktbl Camp 89; Harvard U; Doctor.

GREENE, NEVIN R; Rio Americano HS; Carmichael, CA; (3); Ski Clb.

GREENE, XAVIER L; St Bernards HS; Los Angeles, CA; (3); Church Yth Grp; Cmnty Wkr; SADD; Chorus; Jazz Band; Mrchg Band; School Musical; Howard U; Commnctns.

GREENFIELD, PAULETTE N; Arrowhead Christian Acad; Redlands, CA; (3); 3/14; Church Yth Grp; Math Clb; Teachers Aide; Band; L Var Bsktbl; L Var Sftbl; High Hon Roll; NHS; Sal; Prin Awd For Srv; Var Bsktbl All Leag, Mst Inspirational Player.

GREENHALGH, ROB; Bellarmine College Prep; Sunnyvale, CA; (3); 18/300; Church Yth Grp; Cmnty Wkr; Debate Tm; NFL; Service Clb; Speech Tm; SADD; Rptr Nwsp; Off Jr Cls; Rotary Clb Schlrshp Wnnr; Gen Exc Awd; U PA-WHARTON; Intl Finance.

GREENHOUSE, KARA K; Mt Pleasant HS; San Jose, CA; (3); Girl Scts; SADD; Var JV Bsktbl; Var Trk; Hon Roll; YBA; Med.

GREENING, JESSICA M; Troy HS; Fullerton, CA; (2); 32/334; Drama Clb; French Clb; School Play; JV Sftbl; Stat Swmmng; JV Vllybl; High Hon Roll; Jr NHS; NHS; Pres Acad Fit Awd; Clb Vllybl; CA Poly Pomona; Vet.

GREENING, JONATHAN; Long Beach Polytechnic HS; Long Beach, CA; (4); Orch; Var Capt Crs Cntry; JV L Trk; NHS; Ntl Merit SF; Sailing Rep Ed So CA US JR Slng Chmpnshps; Genetics.

GREENLAND, RONNIE J; Rubidoux HS; Riverside, CA; (4); School Play; Stage Crew; Variety Show; JV Ftbl; Ecology Clb-Sec; Envrnmntl Clb-Sec; Surf Clb; Riverside City Coll; Advrtsng.

GREENLEE, ANNE E; San Dieguito HS; Olivenhain, CA; (2); 30/650; Church Yth Grp; JV Swmmng; Hon Roll; Prfct Atten Awd; Pres Acad Fit Awd; Sci Awd; Natl Phys Ftns Awd; Golden St Exam Alg Hnrs; Piano 7 Yrs; CA Schlrshp Fed; Cal Poly San Luis Obispo; Arch.

GREENLEE, CHRIS S; Don Antonio Lugo HS; Chino, CA; (2); Church Yth Grp; Teachers Aide; JV Ftbl; Var Trk; Wt Lftg; Hon Roll; USC; Chiropractor.

GREENLEE, SHANNON; California HS; Whittier, CA; (4); 5/361; Am Leg Aux Girls St; Drama Clb; Hosp Aide; Thesps; Chorus; School Musical; School Play; Stage Crew; High Hon Roll; Pres Acad Fit Awd; Bank Amer Fine Arts 2nd Pl Wnnr; Exchng Clb Ctzn Awd St Fnlst; Life CSF; UCS; Nurse.

GREENLY, LISA; California HS; Whittier, CA; (3); 10/450; Cmnty Wkr; Drama Clb; Service Clb; Mrchg Band; Orch; High Hon Roll; Church Yth Grp; French Clb; Ski Clb; Acad Decthln Top Scorer 3 Yrs; CSF; Whittier Union All Dist Hnr Band 2 Yrs; Arch.

GREENMAN, POPPY C; Castilleja HS; Cupertino, CA; (3); Cmnty Wkr; JCL; Key Clb; Service Clb; Spanish Clb; School Musical; Lit Mag; Pres Frsh Cls; Sec Stu Cncl; JV Socr; Medcl Explorers Rep; Med.

GREENSPAN, ALISON SHERYL; Saratoga HS; Saratoga, CA; (1); 6/290; Cmnty Wkr; Debate Tm; NFL; Q&S; Service Clb; Speech Tm; Temple Yth Grp; Nwsp; High Hon Roll; Ntl Merit Ltr; Literary Magazine Editor; U PA; Law.

GREENWALD, BENJAMIN E; Buena HS; Ventura, CA; (1); Quiz Bowl; Scholastic Bowl; Cit Awd; Hon Roll; St Schlr; Humanities Clb; Berkeley; Astrophysics.

GREENWOOD, ERIC S; Acalanes HS; Lafayette, CA; (3); Letterman Clb; Red Cross Aide; Ski Clb; Spanish Clb; Varsity Clb; JV Bsbl; JV Bsktbl; JV Capt Socr; JV Swmmng; Teams USA Nrthrn CA European Tour Sccr.

GREENWOOD, JACKIE; Fred C Beyer HS; Modesto, CA; (4); Cmnty Wkr; SADD; Teachers Aide; Gym; High Hon Roll; Hon Roll; Aim For A Awd Engl; Miss TEEN CA Cert Achvt; Stanislaus; Bus Adm.

GREENWOOD, MONICA E; Notre Dame Acad; Los Angeles, CA; (4); Church Yth Grp; Cmnty Wkr; SADD; Chorus; Church Choir; Variety Show; Rep Stu Cncl; Cit Awd; Hon Roll; NHS; Queens Cncl Pres; Sarah Lawrence Coll; Music Pfmc.

GREENWOOD, PATRICE; Immaculate Heart HS; Los Angeles, CA; (3); English Clb; Math Clb; Model UN; Spanish Clb; Sec Jr Cls; Stu Cncl; Var Cheerldng; Var Trk; Hon Roll; Spanish NHS; Riordan Pgm; S CA Yth Ctznshp Smnr; CA Schlrshp Fdrtn; Bus.

GREENWOOD, STEVEN J; El Cajon Valley HS; El Cajon, CA; (2); 179/500; Boy Scts; Avid; CA Inst Of Tech; Math.

GREER, DIANA; John Muir HS; Pasadena, CA; (4); Church Yth Grp; Drama Clb; FBLA; Speech Tm; Rptr Nwsp; Stu Cncl; Off Jr Cls; JV Bsktbl; JV Cheerldng; Hon Roll; Cmmty & Hosp Volunteer; Ldrshp Conf For Better Yth Ed & Sch Imprvmt; Spellman; Pblc Defender.

GREER, LORI; Templeton HS; Templeton, CA; (3); 6/73; Cmnty Wkr; Hosp Aide; Office Aide; Teachers Aide; Stat Bsktbl; Hon Roll; Spcl Olympcs Athlt-Whlchr Evnts; Spcl Olympcs Mst Insprtnl Athlt; Sci Fair 1st Pl; Cuesta Coll; Offc Wrkr.

GREER, MICHELLE; Canyon Springs HS; Moreno Valley, CA; (1); Teachers Aide; Flag Corp; Mrchg Band; Hon Roll; Pediatrics.

GREGERSEN, BRENDA; Dos Pueblos HS; Goleta, CA; (2); 39/299; Church Yth Grp; VP L Socr; JV Sftbl; JV VP Vllybl; Jr NHS; NHS; Pres Acad Fit Awd; Santa Barbara Yth Vllybl Assn; Sports Med.

GREGG, ELIZABETH A; Immaculate Heart HS; Los Angeles, CA; (3); 6/112; Church Yth Grp; Cmnty Wkr; Drama Clb; Spanish Clb; High Hon Roll; NEDT Awd; Spanish NHS; CSF; Hnrs Engl Awd; Engl.

GREGG, SHAUNA M; Arroyo Grande HS; Arroyo Grande, CA; (3); Church Yth Grp; Cmnty Wkr; SADD; Teachers Aide; Variety Show; Phtg Yrbk; JV Var Swmmng; Hon Roll; Photo.

GREGOIRE, MARINA M; Willow Glen HS; San Jose, CA; (1); Church Yth Grp; JV Bsktbl; Var Trk; Inter Decorator.

GREGOR, SCOTT M; Chaminade HS; Chatsworth, CA; (2); JV Bsbl; Var L Ftbl; JV Wrstlng; High Hon Roll; Hon Roll; Pre-Med.

GREGORIANS, ANI; Flintridge Preparatroy Schl; Glendale, CA; (3); Art Clb; Drama Clb; French Clb; Chorus; School Musical; Stage Crew; Yrbk; Hon Roll; Set Desgnr & Painter; Prom Cmmtte; LA Scene; Arch.

GREGORINI, HEIDI; Cabrillo HS; Vandenberg AFB, CA; (3); Church Yth Grp; French Clb; Intnl Clb; Office Aide; Pep Clb; SADD; Teachers Aide; Rep Stu Cncl; Stat Diving; Mgr(s); CA Miss TEEN Gnt; Natl Cngrssnl Yth Ldrshp Cncl; CA Luthern; Psych.

GREGORY, ALPHONSO; Fairfax HS; Los Angeles, CA; (2); Dance Clb; Class Achvt Awd; UCLA; Aviator.

GREGORY, ERIC; Piner HS; Santa Rosa, CA; (2); Boy Scts; Church Yth Grp; Debate Tm; FFA; Stage Crew; Rep Soph Cls; Rep Stu Cncl; JV Capt Bsktbl; JV Capt Ftbl; Trk; County Fair-Prz Wnnr Pig/2nd Pl Showman; Stu Of Wk; Bst Defnsv Player-JV Bsktbl; Geolg.

GREGORY, JEAN C; Luther Burbank HS; Sacramento, CA; (2); 1/435; Church Yth Grp; Cmnty Wkr; Church Choir; Var Swmmng; Cit Awd; High Hon Roll; Hon Roll; Toastmasters Intl Yth Ldrshp Pgm Awd; Rcgntn Outstndng GPA Early Acad Outrch Pgmcer; Spellman Coll; Engl.

GREGORY, MARK A; Wm S Hart HS; Newhall, CA; (2); Science Clb; Sci/Hlth; UCLA; Bio.

GREGORY, ROSE M; Sherman E Burroughs HS; Inyokern, CA; (3); 10/415; FHA; Science Clb; Spanish Clb; SADD; Teachers Aide; Rep Jr Cls; Rep Stu Cncl; Cit Awd; High Hon Roll; Jr NHS; Prjct Seed Stu Lcl Mojave Brnch Amer Chem Soc 90; 1st Pl Kern Cnty Sci Fair-Botany 90; Knwldg Mstr Opn; UCSD; Ocngrphy.

GREGORYAN, ARMOND; Flintridge Prep Schl; Glendale, CA; (3); Boy Scts; Drama Clb; French Clb; Key Clb; Letterman Clb; Varsity Clb; Stat Bsktbl; JV Var Swmmng; Cit Awd; French Hon Soc; Play Water Polo Schl; Body Boarding; Disc Jockey; Bus.

GREITL, APRIL L; Mayfair HS; Lakewood, CA; (3); Key Clb; Ski Clb; Rptr Nwsp; VP Soph Cls; VP Jr Cls; Stu Cncl; Cheerldng; Capt Pom Pon; High Hon Roll; Kiwanis Awd; Acad Decthln Tm; CSF; Span Stu Yr 88-89; CA ST Long Beach; Teach.

GREMMELL, KRISTEN; Los Gatos HS; Los Gatos, CA; (2); Boy Scts; Church Yth Grp; Debate Tm; Girl Scts; Letterman Clb; Ski Clb; Speech Tm; Varsity Clb; Church Choir; Var Swmmng; Inner City/Out Of Country Missions; CA Poly; Dental.

GRENFELL, RICHELLE; Redwood HS; Visalia, CA; (4); Latin Clb; Chorus; Church Choir; School Musical; Stage Crew; Yrbk; JV Vllybl; Hon Roll; Fshn Des; Adv Drama Prod; Prom Cmmttee; CSF; St Marys Coll; Fshn Merch.

GRENFELL, TRISHA; Redwood HS; Visalia, CA; (3); FBLA; Teachers Aide; Chorus; Var L Bsktbl; L Var Trk; L Capt Vllybl; Hon Roll; Acad Achvt Lttr; CSF; Nutrition Cmmtte SNAC; Sequoias Coll; Pre-Med.

GRENIER, CHRISTINE; Fairfield HS; Fairfield, CA; (3); Art Clb; German Clb; Key Clb; Service Clb; Rep Frsh Cls; Rep Jr Cls; JV Var Crs Cntry; JV Trk; Hon Roll; NHS; Davis; Bio.

GRENLICH, ERIKA D; Antelope Valley HS; Lancaster, CA; (3); Art Clb; Church Yth Grp; Hon Roll; Kathleen White Esp Memrl Fund Schlrshp; Commrcl Art.

GRENS, SUETTA; West HS; Bakersfield, CA; (3); Chorus; Color Guard; Co-Capt Flag Corp; Hon Roll; RN.

GRESCHKE, TINA; Granada HS; Livermore, CA; (3); Art Clb; JV Cheerldng; High Hon Roll; Hon Roll; Rcgnzng Adlscnt Pblms; Natl Chrldr Assn Chmpnshps; Miss Teen Of Amer Pgnt; Cmmrcl Art.

GRESHAM, BRIAN D; Merced HS; Merced, CA; (3); Church Yth Grp; German Clb; Key Clb; Ftbl; Var Capt Socr; Hon Roll; Pres Acad Fit Awd.

GREWAL, AMRIT; Beyer HS; Modesto, CA; (3); Chess Clb; FBLA; SADD; Cit Awd; Hon Roll; Prfct Atten Awd.

GREWAL, HARDEEP S; John F Kennedy HS; Sacramento, CA; (2); 161/525; Chess Clb; JV Trk; Sci.

GREWAL, JIWAN J; Pasadena HS; Pasadena, CA; (4); Art Clb; Chess Clb; Cmnty Wkr; Computer Clb; Dance Clb; Debate Tm; Drama Clb; English Clb; Hosp Aide; Intnl Clb; CA ST Northridge; Pre-Med.

GREWAL, KIRANDEEP K; Encinal HS; Alameda, CA; (3); 25/222; Hosp Aide; Key Clb; Treas Soph Cls; Capt Crs Cntry; Var Socr; Var Trk; High Hon Roll; Cross Country All League 88-89; PCA At UC Berkeley 89; ATDP At UC Berkeley 90; Sports Medicine.

GREWAL, PATTY; El Cerrito HS; Richmond, CA; (2); Cmnty Wkr; Hosp Aide; Hon Roll; CSF; Yth Edctr; UCLA.

GREWALL, MANNY S; West HS; Torrance, CA; (1); Cit Awd; UCLA; Orthpdst.

GREY, GEORGIA; Santa Barbara HS; Santa Barbara, CA; (4); Art Clb; Dance Clb; English Clb; Teachers Aide; Stage Crew; Cheerldng; Sftbl; Hon Roll; Santa Barbara City Coll; Theatr.

GREY, PAMELA D; Trabuco Hills HS; Rancho Santa Mari, CA; (2); 98/415; Church Yth Grp; Spanish Clb; Band; Jazz Band; Mrchg Band; Orch; Bsktbl; Hon Roll; NHS; CSF; Delphi; Brigham Young U; Child Dev.

GRIARTE, LYNDON S; Baldwin Park HS; Baldwin Park, CA; (3); Church Yth Grp; Off Sr Cls; Tennis; Wrstlng; Cit Awd; Hon Roll; Stu Outreach; Biola U; Teacher.

GRICE, J ALICIA; Torrance HS; Carson, CA; (4); 1/400; VP Debate Tm; Service Clb; Ed Nwsp; Rep Frsh Cls; Rep Stu Cncl; JV Trk; Elks Awd; Hon Roll; Pres Acad Fit Awd; Val; Teen Advocate- South Bay Free Clinic; UC Santa Cruz.

GRIDER, KIMBERLY; Fred C Beyer HS; Modesto, CA; (4); 51/506; Church Yth Grp; Teachers Aide; Stat Bsktbl; Mgr(s); Stat Vllybl; Cit Awd; High Hon Roll; Hon Roll; CSF; Golden ST Exam Algbr High Hnrs; Friday Nght Lve; Elem Ed.

GRIDER, MARK; Chaffey HS; Ontario, CA; (3); Pres Treas German Clb; Lit Mag; High Hon Roll; Ecology.

GRIDER, NIKIA N; Bullard HS; Fresno, CA; (1); Girl Scts; Var Trk; UCLA; Law Enfrcmnt.

GRIDER, REBECCA A; Archbishop Mitty HS; Morgan Hill, CA; (3); Cmnty Wkr; Hosp Aide; Math Tm; SADD; French Hon Soc; High Hon Roll; Hon Roll; NHS; CSF; Amnesty Intl; Cnslr-Crippled Chldrns Soc; UC Davis; Med.

GRIDLEY, LAURA DAWN; Claremont HS; Pomona, CA; (4); Am Leg Aux Girls St; SADD; Rep Jr Cls; Sec Treas Sr Cls; Stu Cncl; Var Swmmng; High Hon Roll; Pres Acad Fit Awd; CIF Athl Achvt Awds; Hmcmng Princess 89-90; CSF; Golden St Exam Awds; Principals Hnr Roll; UC Davis; Law.

GRIEB, BRIAN K; Arroyo Grande HS; Grover City, CA; (1); Hon Roll; Amnesty Intl; Optmtry.

GRIEWANK, NICK R; Rancho Cotati HS; Rohnert Park, CA; (4); JV Var Bsbl; JV Var Bsktbl; JV Ftbl; Hon Roll; Coaches Awd Var Bsktbl; Santa Rosa JC; Bus Mgmt.

GRIFFEN, THOMAS A; Marina HS; Huntington Bch, CA; (4); Boy Scts; Church Yth Grp; Cmnty Wkr; Letterman Clb; Teachers Aide; Bsktbl; Crs Cntry; Ftbl; Socr; Trk; Engl Tutor; Schlr Athlt; Wrld Of Poetry Gldn Poets Awd; US Army; Hgh Schl Tchr.

GRIFFIN, CHAD M; Folsom HS; Folsom, CA; (3); 5/189; Model UN; Ski Clb; JV Var Bsbl; JV Var Ftbl; High Hon Roll; Albertson Athl Wk; Stdnt Wk; 2nd Tm All Leag Ftbl; Engrng.

GRIFFIN, DULSA D; Pioneer HS; San Jose, CA; (1); Church Yth Grp; JV Var Swmmng; Mosesto JC; Interior Dsgn.

GRIFFIN, ELIZABETH A; Oak Park HS; Agoura Hills, CA; (2); 12/106; Church Yth Grp; Key Clb; Pres Frsh Cls; JV L Cheerldng; JV Trk; Hon Roll; Pres Acad Fit Awd; Peer Cnslng; CSF; Hmcmng Prin; Natl Guild Auditions Piano Teachers; UCSB; Bus.

GRIFFIN, HARVEY T; Morningside HS; Inglewood, CA; (2); Math Tm; Hon Roll; 1st Pl Natl Math League; Huntington Park HS Math Fair Hnrb Mntn; Applied Tech.

GRIFFIN, JEREMY; Loyalton HS; Loyalton, CA; (2); 1/35; Church Yth Grp; FFA; Red Cross Aide; Ski Clb; Spanish Clb; SADD; Treas Soph Cls; Rep Stu Cncl; Var Bsbl; JV Capt Bsktbl; Cert Lifeguard; Piano; UCLA; Marine Bio.

GRIFFIN, JIMELL D; Leuzinger HS; Hawthorne, CA; (3); Church Yth Grp; Cmnty Wkr; Intnl Clb; Office Aide; Teachers Aide; Crss Cntry & Trk & Fld Jr Vrsty; John Jay Coll; Crmnl Jstc.

GRIFFIN, JOIE N; Las Plumas HS; Oroville, CA; (2); 4-H; Hosp Aide; Drill Tm; Flag Corp; JV Bsktbl; Score Keeper; 4-H Awd; Hon Roll; Prfct Atten Awd; Dentistry.

GRIFFIN, KIRK A; Fairfield HS; Fairfield, CA; (2); Drama Clb; School Play; Socr; Wrstlng; Hon Roll.

GRIFFIN, KRIS M; Morro Bay HS; Morro Bay, CA; (4); Church Yth Grp; Letterman Clb; Teachers Aide; L Bsbl; Capt Bsktbl; Mgr Ftbl; Hon Roll; Athlt Of Yr; Prep Athlt Wk By Nwsppr; All Leag Bsktbl Cntr; All Cnty Cntr San Luis Obisco Cnty Leag; Cal Poly; Bus Mgmt.

GRIFFIN, LAURETTA J; Norte Vista HS; La Sierra Hts, CA; (1); #50 In Class; Cit Awd; High Hon Roll; Hon Roll; Pres Acad Fit Awd; Law.

GRIFFIN, MELINDA; Avalon HS; Avalon, CA; (1); Pres Frsh Cls; Rep Stu Cncl; Var Cheerldng; Princeton; Law.

GRIFFIN, MITCH T; Loyalton HS; Calpine, CA; (3); Church Yth Grp; Cmnty Wkr; Drama Clb; 4-H; FFA; Ski Clb; Spanish Clb; SADD; School Play; Stage Crew; Rotary Clb Outstndng Stu Awd; CSU; Law Enfrcmnt.

GRIFFIN, SOFIA; Costa Mesa HS; Santa Ana, CA; (4); 25/238; Church Yth Grp; Cmnty Wkr; Drama Clb; Hosp Aide; Thesps; School Play; Stage Crew; Var Cheerldng; Hon Roll; E I Moore Awd; UCI; Bio.

GRIFFIN, STEPHANIE A; Mar Vista HS; Coronado, CA; (2); Off Frsh Cls; Hon Roll; CA Schlrshp Fed; Touring Childrens Show; San Diego ST U; T V Brdcstng.

GRIFFIN, SUZIE; Christian Center Schl; Antioch, CA; (2); Church Yth Grp; Hosp Aide; Pep Clb; Varsity Clb; Yrbk; Sec Frsh Cls; Capt Co-Capt Cheerldng; High Hon Roll; Hon Roll; Yth Choir; Yth Drama; Pepperdine U; Advertising.

GRIFFIN, TIGE R; Coast Union HS; Cayucos, CA; (2); Church Yth Grp; Cmnty Wkr; FCA; Ski Clb; Var L Bsbl; Var L Bsktbl; Trk; Hon Roll; Pres Acad Fit Awd; Hmcmng Kng; 2nd Pl JV Surf Cont; MVP Sprg Bsktbl Cmp; Hghst Bat Avg, Mst RBI, 1st Tm All Leag Bsbl; Oceanography.

GRIFFIN, TRICIA A; Don Antonio Lugo HS; Chino, CA; (2); Church Yth Grp; Band; Drm Mjr(t); Mrchg Band; Pep Band; School Play; Stage Crew; Prfrmng Arts.

GRIFFING, JOHN P; Corona SR HS; Corona, CA; (2); Computer Clb; Science Clb; Lit Mag; Bsktbl; Wt Lftg; Kiwanis Awd; Pres Acad Fit Awd; Gldn St Schlr; Coronas Hrtg Comm His Awd; His Day; Sci.

GRIFFIS, KEVIN L; Washington HS; Los Angeles, CA; (3); Church Yth Grp; FCA; Letterman Clb; Capt Bsktbl; 3rd Best Grd CA; Telecomm.

GRIFFIS, TRICIA J; Trabuco Hills HS; Rancho Santa Mari, CA; (2); San Diego ST U; Engl.

GRIFFITH, AUDREY M; Whitney HS; Bellflower, CA; (3); Church Yth Grp; Drama Clb; Pep Clb; Thesps; Chorus; School Play; Pres Frsh Cls; Pres Stu Cncl; JV Cheerldng; Powder Puff Ftbl; Wrk Disneyland; CSULB; Bus.

GRIFFITH, CHRISTINE; Ferndale Union HS; Ferndale, CA; (3); Drama Clb; Girl Scts; Pres VP Pep Clb; Ski Clb; SADD; Teachers Aide; School Play; Yrbk; Pres Frsh Cls; Rep Jr Cls; Prom Chairman; Head Chairman Prom 90-91; Drama.

GRIFFITH, JENNIFER; Oakdale HS; Oakdale, CA; (4); #2 In Class; Letterman Clb; Yrbk; Sec Sr Cls; Bsktbl; Socr; Swmmng; Tennis; Sal; Soroptamist Yth Ctzn Yr; Life Mem CA Schltc Fed; UC Santa Barbara.

GRIFFITH, RYAN L; Servite HS; Garden Grove, CA; (2); Debate Tm; JV Ftbl; Wt Lftg.

GRIFFITH, STELLA L; Del Oro HS; Loomis, CA; (4); SADD; Chorus; Cert Cmpltn Anml-Vet Careers; Vet.

GRIFFITH, STEPHANIE; Hemet HS; Hemet, CA; (4); French Clb; FBLA; Band; Mrchg Band; Swmmng; Tennis; High Hon Roll; NHS; Pres Schlr; LDS Bus Coll; Acctng.

GRIFFITHS, DES; Woodbridge HS; Irvine, CA; (3); Boy Scts; Cmnty Wkr; Model UN; Off Service Clb; Off SADD; Teachers Aide; Jr NHS; Pres Acad Fit Awd; UCSD; Bus Mrktng.

GRIFFITHS, KYNDRA M; Nevada Union HS; Penn Valley, CA; (3); 37/551; Var L Swmmng; High Hon Roll; Hon Roll; Girls ST; Arch.

GRIFFITHS, PHILIP A; Cupertino HS; Cupertino, CA; (3); Var Bsbl; Skiing; San Jose ST; Advrtsng.

GRIGGS, KAREN N; Monterey HS; Seaside, CA; (3); Art Clb; Church Yth Grp; German Clb; Office Aide; Church Choir; School Musical; School Play; Cheerldng; Diving; Socr; CSF; Monterey Hist Of Art Assn.

GRIGSBY, JJ A; Willows HS; Artois, CA; (2); 9/91; Key Clb; Library Aide; SADD; Cit Awd; Hon Roll.

GRIK, KRISTINE F; Notre Dame Acad; Manhattan Beach, CA; (3); SADD; Church Choir; Pres Soph Cls; Sec Stu Cncl; JV Vllybl; Hon Roll; Church Yth Grp; Cmnty Wkr; Gov Hon Prg Awd; Walk-A-Thons; Mexico Orgnztns; Wrkng Frdm Prsnrs Of Conscious Wrldwide; Psych.

GRILLI, JESSICA; San Ramon Valley HS; San Ramon, CA; (2); Law.

GRIM, MONICA J; Redlands JR Acad; Redlands, CA; (2); Church Yth Grp; Varsity Clb; Yrbk; JV Vllybl; High Hon Roll; Pres Acad Fit Awd.

GRIMALDO, SAMMY R; Canyon HS; Canyon Country, CA; (2); Church Yth Grp; Ftbl; UCLA.

GRIMES, JENNIFER L; El Cajon Valley HS; El Cajon, CA; (2); 46/496; Cmnty Wkr; JV Mgr(s); High Hon Roll; Hon Roll; Art Hstry.

GRIMES, JOHN D; Escondido HS; Escondido, CA; (3); Cmnty Wkr; Band; Mrchg Band; Pep Band; Yrbk; Pro Musician; Arch; San Diego ST U; Arch.

GRIMES, KEITH; Herlong HS; Doyle, CA; (2); FFA; Letterman Clb; Varsity Clb; Ed Nwsp; Stat Bsktbl; Var JV Ftbl; Hon Roll; Ftbl-Mst Imprvd Plyr Awd; Ftbl Vsty Al-Leag-Hnrb Mntn; Harvard; Lwyre.

GRIMES, SHAWN M; Willits HS; Willits, CA; (3); Church Yth Grp; Girl Scts; Nwsp; High Hon Roll; Hon Roll; Prfct Atten Awd.

GRIMSLEY, ASHLEY L; Clovis HS; Clovis, CA; (3); Church Yth Grp; FBLA; Hosp Aide; SADD; Off Jr Cls; Off Sr Cls; L Cheerldng; L Var Pom Pon; L JV Tennis; Rotary Awd; Dep & Cheer Chrgrpher; Miss Teen CA Pgnt 90; Jr Hmcmng Attndnt; Fresno ST; Elem Tchr.

GRINDAL, MATTHEW; Cleveland Humanities HS; North Hollywood, CA; (4); 69/470; Chess Clb; Church Yth Grp; Cmnty Wkr; Office Aide; Service Clb; Speech Tm; SADD; Rep Soph Cls; Off Jr Cls; Rep Sr Cls; Chldrn Of The Amer Rvltn; Pres Of Fray Fermin Lasuen Soc; CA ST Hstrn 89; CA ST U; Sociology.

GRINDSTAFF, ROBERT L; GAHR HS; Artesia, CA; (2); 1/500; Church Yth Grp; Spanish Clb; School Play; High Hon Roll; Hon Roll; Blue/Gold Awds-Alg II/Trig/Bio/Span II-HGHST Achvt.

GRINNELL, MARTA; Escandido HS; Escondido, CA; (3); Red Cross Aide; Science Clb; History Club; California Desert Coalition; San Marcos U; Bus Management.

GRIPP, HEATHER M; Culver City HS; Culver City, CA; (2); JV Socr; Sftbl.

GRISHAM, TRACY; Shasta HS; Shasta, CA; (1); Church Yth Grp; Drama Clb; French Clb; Chorus; Church Choir; School Play; Stage Crew; Variety Show; Hon Roll.

GRISSETTE, KAREN E; Pittsburg HS; Pittsburg, CA; (2); 7/304; Pep Clb; Ski Clb; Flag Corp; Jazz Band; JV Cheerldng; Swmmng; High Hon Roll; Hon Roll; Hnrs Core Cls.

GRISSOM, BRENTON E; East Bakersfield HS; Bakersfield, CA; (3); Boy Scts; Church Yth Grp; Band; Chorus; Mrchg Band; Stage Crew; Intrml Vllybl; Golden Empire Suns Yth Band; Bakersfield Coll.

GRISSOM, KIMBERLY C; Diamond Bar HS; Diamond Bar, CA; (4); Chorus; High Hon Roll; Hon Roll.

GRISSOM, LISA S; Grossmont HS; El Cajon, CA; (3); Church Yth Grp; Teachers Aide; Chorus; Church Choir; School Musical; L JV Bsktbl; L Var Swmmng; Cit Awd; Prfct Atten Awd; Hlp Tch Sndy Schl & Handcppd Stu; Music.

GRISWOLD, MELINDA; Mother Lode Christian HS; Sonora, CA; (4); 1/18; Church Yth Grp; Teachers Aide; Band; Chorus; Mrchg Band; Pep Band; Rep Stu Cncl; Var Bsktbl; JV Cheerldng; Var Sftbl; Ed Coaching.

GRISWOLD, MINDY; Mother Lode Christian HS; Sonora, CA; (4); 1/17; Church Yth Grp; Band; Chorus; Mrchg Band; Bus Profs of Am; Rep Sr Cls; Rep Stu Cncl; JV Var Bsktbl; JV Cheerldng; Var Sftbl; Columbia JC; Elem Educ.

GROAT, LAWRENCE J; Rancho Cotate SR HS; Rohnert Park, CA; (3); French Clb; Letterman Clb; Varsity Clb; Intrml Mgr Bsbl; JV Var Trk; Hon Roll; Acad Athl 89; SRJC; Med.

GROBAN, JOSHUA; Torrey Pines HS; Del Mar, CA; (3); Debate Tm; Speech Tm; School Play; Pres Frsh Cls; Rep Soph Cls; High Hon Roll; Pres Acad Fit Awd; Yth Ending Hunger Treas; Sccr Tm; Law.

GROENE, JOHN A; North County Christian Schl; Atascadero, CA; (2); Chess Clb; Church Yth Grp; Math Tm; Band; Hon Roll; Var Bsbl; JV Bsktbl; Yth Symphny; San Luis Obispo; Atascadero Cmmnty Band; Music Composition.

GROH, JOHN P; Tracy HS; Tracy, CA; (3); 57/401; Church Yth Grp; French Clb; SADD; Wrstlng; Hon Roll; Golden St Exam Schl Rcgntn Algbra & Geom; UC Davis; Vet Med.

GRONEK, SCOTT A; San Gorgonio HS; Highland, CA; (3); 1/430; Am Leg Boys St; Church Yth Grp; Pres French Clb; Letterman Clb; Scholastic Bowl; Science Clb; Pres Service Clb; VP Stu Cncl; Var L Tennis; High Hon Roll; Mck Trl Outstndng Prfrmnc Dfns Attrny 89-90; CSF; ACES.

GRONSKY, KRISTIN; El Cerrito HS; El Cerrito, CA; (3); Church Yth Grp; French Clb; Service Clb; JV Sftbl; High Hon Roll.

GROSE, ZOLTAN; John F Kennedy HS; Richmond, CA; (4); 6/250; Debate Tm; German Clb; NFL; Pres Science Clb; Speech Tm; Teachers Aide; Off Soph Cls; Hon Roll; Bnk Am Plaque Wnnr 90 Math & Sci; Chemathon Trphy Wnnr; U Of Santa Cruz; Molecular Bio.

GROSEL, HENRY G; Jesuit College Prep; Concord, CA; (3); Cmnty Wkr; Drama Clb; French Clb; Math Clb; Spanish Clb; School Play; Hon Roll; Cluf F Fndr; Dscssn Grp Rlvnt Situations; Lang.

GROSS, ALMORA; Marin Acad; Woodacre, CA; (4); Library Aide; Quiz Bowl; School Play; Ed Lit Mag; Rep Soph Cls; Var Bsktbl; High Hon Roll; Ntl Merit Ltr; Pres Schlr; Reed Coll; Lit.

GROSS, DEANNA; Vacaville HS; Vacaville, CA; (4); 12/562; Sec French Clb; SADD; Jazz Band; Mrchg Band; Sec Stu Cncl; Powder Puff Ftbl; Tennis; High Hon Roll; Hon Roll; NHS; UC Davis; Phy.

GROSS, GWENDA L; San Gorgonio HS; Highland, CA; (3); Am Leg Aux Girls St; Treas Jr Cls; Powder Puff Ftbl; JV Swmmng; High Hon Roll; NHS; Spanish NHS; Mock Trial-Atty; CA Schlstc Fed; Advncd Curriculum Explrtn Soc; UCR; Law.

GROSS, JESSICA W; Carlmont HS; Belmont, CA; (3); Office Aide; Teachers Aide; Yrbk; Cheerldng; Hon Roll; Cngrsnl Schlr; Ntl Yng Ldrs Cnfrnce Wshngtn DC; U CA Brkly; Law.

GROSS, MEREDY E; Trabuco Hills HS; Mission Viejo, CA; (1); Church Yth Grp; Yrbk; JV Socr; JV Trk; Vllybl.

GROSS, STEPHANIE; Sherman Oaks Ctr For Enriched Studies; Van Nuys, CA; (3); Cmnty Wkr; Computer Clb; Dance Clb; Debate Tm; English Clb; Office Aide; Pep Clb; Spanish Clb; Speech Tm; SADD; Ped.

GROSSI, SARA E; Casa Grande HS; Petaluma, CA; (4); Drama Clb; Teachers Aide; Powder Puff Ftbl; Hon Roll; Wildlife Bio Awd; Drama Awd; Empire Coll; Travel/Tourism.

GROSSMAN, ADAM D; University HS; Los Angeles, CA; (2); Ftbl; Vllybl; Hon Roll; Synagogue Yth Grp.

GROSSMAN, JAMIE; Westlake HS; Westlake Village, CA; (2); SADD; Temple Yth Grp; Pres Soph Cls; Capt Cheerldng; Hon Roll.

GROSSMAN, JESSICA; Helix HS; La Mesa, CA; (2); 45/472; French Clb; Pres Model UN; SADD; Ed Nwsp; Hon Roll; Crss-Age Tchng Frgn Stu; Psych.

GROSSMAN, TODD C; Kennedy HS; Buena Park, CA; (3); JV Ftbl; JV Wrstlng; Cit Awd; Hon Roll; Prfct Atten Awd; CSU Long Beach; Bus.

GROSSMANN, JASON S; Hoover HS; Fresno, CA; (2); German Clb; Teachers Aide; USC; Law Enfrcmnt.

GROSSWEILER, CHERIE L; East Bakersfield HS; Bakersfield, CA; (2); Rptr Nwsp; Bsktbl; Hon Roll; Greenpeace Effort; CA U; Law.

GROSZ, DENNIS; Millikan HS; Long Beach, CA; (4); 1/620; Rep Art Clb; Key Clb; Math Clb; Math Tm; Quiz Bowl; School Musical; Variety Show; Pres Soph Cls; Pres Jr Cls; Pres Stu Cncl; Hall Fame Awd; Golden Ram Awd Hghst Achvt Athltcs/Acad; MVP Awd Vrsty Swmmng; U Of CA Berkeley.

GROTH, LUCINDA L; Schl Of The Arts; San Francisco, CA; (3); Drama Clb; French Clb; Amnesty Intl Pres; Schl Of The Arts Major Visual Arts Ceramics; Cngrssnl Schlr; Natl Yng Ldrs Conf 90; Ceramics.

GROVE, ELIZABETH; Amador Valley HS; Pleasanton, CA; (2); French Clb; Sec Jr Cls; Cheerldng; French Hon Soc; High Hon Roll; Hon Roll; Cnslr Outdr Ed Pgm; Spkr DARE Pgm.

GROVE, JASON G; Kern Valley HS; Lake Isabella, CA; (1); Pep Clb; JV Bsbl; JV Ftbl; JV Wt Lftg; Hon Roll.

GROVE, NANCY L; Pioneer HS; San Jose, CA; (2); Key Clb; CSF; Peer Tutor; Jobs Dghtrs; Interior Dsgn.

GROVE, STEPHEN; Pioneer HS; San Jose, CA; (4); Boy Scts; Key Clb; Yrbk; Sec Sr Cls; Var Swmmng; Hon Roll; Unesco Design Awd Natl Wnnr 89; CSU Long Beach; Graphic Dsgn.

GROVER, KARA; Wilcox HS; Alviso, CA; (1); Drama Clb; Chorus; Drill Tm; Stage Crew; Hon Roll; Prfct Atten Awd; Wtrskiing; Chld Physcn.

GROVER, KENDRA L; Bret Harte HS; Murphys, CA; (2); Church Yth Grp; Ski Clb; Bsktbl; JV Capt Sftbl; JV Capt Vllybl; High Hon Roll; Hon Roll; CSF; Advanced Ensembles Piano; Interact Treas.

GROVER-NEIMAN, MELISSA; South Fork HS; Miranda, CA; (3); 12/75; SADD; Band; Pep Band; JV Var Bsktbl; JV Crs Cntry; High Hon Roll; Rotary Awd; CSF.

GROVES, ANGIE Z; Gompers HS; San Diego, CA; (2); Church Yth Grp; Office Aide; Color Guard; Drill Tm; Hon Roll; Comp Engr.

GROVES, BRANDY; Cajun HS; Colton, CA; (2); Church Yth Grp; SADD; Ed Lit Mag; High Hon Roll; NHS; CA Schlrshp Fed; LAW.

GROVES, CHRISTOPHER E; Villa Park HS; Orange, CA; (3); VP French Clb; SADD; Chorus; Orch; School Musical; Hon Roll; NHS; Frnch.

GROW, KATHARINE N; El Camino Fundamental HS; Citrus Heights, CA; (3); 74/476; Church Yth Grp; German Clb; Church Choir; Swmmng; Hon Roll; Pres Of German Clb; Friday Night Live; CA ST U; Engrng.

GROWCOCK, JENNIFER L; El Toro HS; El Toro, CA; (3); 105/500; Church Yth Grp; SADD; Teachers Aide; Intrml Bsktbl; Intrml Swmmng; Intrml Tennis; Intrml Vllybl; High Hon Roll; Hon Roll; 1st, 2nd Pl Awds From Orange Cnty Yth Expo; 6th Pl, 8th Pl Awd From Orange Cnty Stu Voc Olympics; Arch.

GROWDEN, MATT E; Providence HS; Burbank, CA; (2); Chess Clb; Drama Clb; Letterman Clb; School Musical; School Play; Crs Cntry; High Hon Roll; St Schlr; Sci.

GRUBB, RYAN; Trinity HS; Tempe, AZ; (2); 4-H; Var Bsbl; Hon Roll; All Star Bslb Tm; AF Acad; Pilot.

GRUBBS, EUNICE; Galileo HS; San Francisco, CA; (2); Dance Clb; Pep Clb; School Play; AF Acad; Nrsng.

GRUBEN, BRET R; Winters HS; Winters, CA; (2); Church Yth Grp; Cmnty Wkr; Letterman Clb; SADD; Teachers Aide; Intrml JV Bsktbl; Intrml JV Ftbl; High Hon Roll; Hon Roll; FNL; CSF; City Winters Firefghtng Cadet; Fire Sci.

GRUBER, KRISTI; Edison HS; Huntington Beach, CA; (4); Church Yth Grp; Drill Tm; Off Jr Cls; Prfct Atten Awd; Drill Team Spirit Ldr/Capt 88-90; OCC; Advrtsng Exec.

GRUEN, JONATHAN D; Bishop O'dowd HS; Oakland, CA; (2); Cmnty Wkr; Letterman Clb; Ski Clb; Ftbl; Lcrss; Yth In Transition Cnslr.

GRUENIG, HEATHER; Oakdale HS; Oakdale, CA; (4); 5/220; Letterman Clb; Nwsp; VP Jr Cls; Rep Stu Cncl; Var Bsktbl; High Hon Roll; Pres Acad Fit Awd; HS Rodeo Assn-Pres Dist 5; Peer Facilitating; Modesto JC.

GRUETZBACH, CHRISTINE M; Redwood Christian HS; Castro Valley, CA; (3); Drama Clb; Speech Tm; Teachers Aide; Chorus; Orch; School Musical; School Play; Var Bsktbl; Var Tennis; High Hon Roll; Oakland Yth Orch Violnst; Redwood Chpl Cmnty Chrch Orch; 19th Intl Yth-Music Fstvl Vienna Austria; Music Prfrmnc.

GRULICH, ALAN B; El Cajon Valley HS; El Cajon, CA; (2); 7/500; Q&S; Teachers Aide; Ed Nwsp; Cit Awd; High Hon Roll; Hon Roll; Jrnlsm Tech Camp; Comm.

GRUMBACH, DANA LATICE; N Hollywood Zoo Magnet HS; Los Angeles, CA; (4); Sec Church Yth Grp; Cmnty Wkr; FFA; Teachers Aide; Church Choir; Rep Sr Cls; Stat Score Keeper; JV Var Swmmng; JV Vllybl; Prfct Atten Awd; L A Cnty Sheriffs Expl Prgm & Cert Grad Sherman Block; 2nd Prncss Debutant 88; Black Identity Club; Cal ST U Northridge; Chld Dev.

GRUMM, ROBERT B; North Tahoe HS; Tahoe City, CA; (3); 6/60; Am Leg Boys St; Church Yth Grp; Drama Clb; Pres SADD; School Musical; VP Jr Cls; Bsktbl; Ftbl; Trk; Hon Roll; Elec Engrng.

GRUNBERG, RACHEL; Oceana HS; Pacifica, CA; (4); 10/120; Am Leg Aux Girls St; Drama Clb; Red Cross Aide; School Play; Rep Soph Cls; Var Cheerldng; Stat Swmmng; Hon Roll; Pres Acad Fit Awd; Math Bank Of Amer Awd; Drama Dept Awd; Dist Stu Of Month; San Francisco ST U; Ed.

GRUNDEL, CARMEN; Del Campo HS; Carmichael, CA; (4); 34/450; Rep Soph Cls; Stu Cncl; Var L Swmmng; High Hon Roll; Hon Roll; NHS; Pres Acad Fit Awd; CSF; Stu Reaching Out Sec; Achvt Awd Photography; Sonoma ST U; Teacher.

GRUNDELL, KAREN A; Newark Memorial HS; Newark, CA; (2); 141/650; Pres Church Yth Grp; Service Clb; SADD; Chorus; Church Choir; 6th Grade Sci Camp Cnslr; Brigham Young U; Chld Psych.

GRUNDMANN, KEVIN; Serra HS; Foster City, CA; (2); Var Ftbl; Var Socr; Var Trk; Wt Lftg; Hon Roll.

GRUNDSTROM, ROBERT J; Foothill HS; Santa Ana, CA; (3); 24/328; Key Clb; Spanish Clb; Var JV Bsbl; High Hon Roll; Hon Roll; Hgh Hnrs Gldn St Math Tsts Geom & Alg; U Of CA; Engrng.

GRUNDT, MELINDA M; Wasco Union HS; Wasco, CA; (2); Sec Soph Cls; Var L Tennis; High Hon Roll; CSF; Wasco Cmnty Schlrshp Cert.

GRUNDVIG, DONNA J; Bear River HS; Auburn, CA; (2); Pres Sec 4-H; Acpl Chr; Band; Chorus; 4-H Awd; MT ST; Law.

GRUNDY, ALVIS E; Concord HS; Delaware, CA; (2); Bsktbl; Cit Awd; Bsktbl Plyr.

GRUSH, J ANDREW; St Francis HS; Sierra Madre, CA; (2); Church Yth Grp; French Clb; Ski Clb; Band; Church Choir; Var Socr; Wt Lftg; Yth Mnstrs Awd 89-90; Guitar; Piano; Kybrd; UC Santa Cruz.

GRUTSIS, JORDANA; Arrowhead Christian Acad; Yucaipa, CA; (4); 4/17; Scholastic Bowl; VP Frsh Cls; Treas Jr Cls; Stu Cncl; Capt Cheerldng; Crs Cntry; Cit Awd; High Hon Roll; NHS; Pres Acad Fit Awd; Medicine.

GRUTSIS, SOPHIA; Arrowhead Christian Acad; Yucaipa, CA; (3); Pep Clb; Scholastic Bowl; Ed Nwsp; Sec Jr Cls; L Cheerldng; Crs Cntry; Cit Awd; High Hon Roll; NHS; Pediatrician.

GU, LING; Oakland HS; Oakland, CA; (3); Sec French Clb; JA; Sec Key Clb; Math Clb; Hist Jr Cls; High Hon Roll; Prfct Atten Awd; Imtrl Badmntn; UC Berkeley Upward Bound Pgm; UC Berkeley; Bus.

GU, YOLANDA Y; Gompers Secondary HS; San Diego, CA; (2); 1/178; Computer Clb; Library Aide; Science Clb; Spanish Clb; Teachers Aide; Sec Jr Cls; Rep Stu Cncl; JV Vllybl; High Hon Roll; NHS; N Cnty Chinese Schl, San Diego Brnch; Piano; Med Fld.

GUADAGNINI, ANGELA; Yosemite HS; Coarsegold, CA; (4); 4/150; Church Yth Grp; French Clb; Math Clb; Math Tm; Varsity Clb; VP VICA; Var Crs Cntry; Var Tennis; High Hon Roll; Cvl Engr.

GUADAGNINI, CHRISTINE; Yosemite HS; Coarsegold, CA; (2); 1/150; Sec FBLA; Service Clb; Var Crs Cntry; Var Trk; High Hon Roll.

GUADAGNO, CELESTE; Cornelia Connelly HS; Whittier, CA; (3); Church Yth Grp; Cmnty Wkr; Intnl Clb; School Play; Yrbk; High Hon Roll; Hon Roll; NHS; Assisteens Auxlry Asstnc League Whittier; Jr Stsmn Of Amer; Outstndng Assisteen Prvsnl Scrpbk Coord; Pre-Med.

GUAN, PAULA; Skyline HS; Oakland, CA; (2); 11/30; Key Clb; Vllybl; Cmptr.

GUAN, SHU HUA; Millikan JR HS; Los Angeles, CA; (1); GAA; Bsktbl; Sftbl; Vllybl; Hon Roll; Prfct Atten Awd; Vanguard/Medallions Clbs; Acctng.

GUARAGLIA, CELESTE E; Ursuline HS; Santa Rosa, CA; (4); 13/98; Cmnty Wkr; French Clb; JV Socr; JV Var Sftbl; High Hon Roll; Hon Roll; Jr NHS; NHS; Opt Clb Awd; Pres Acad Fit Awd; Extnded Lrng Pgm; CSF; Yng Mns Inst Awd; UC Santa Barbara; Bio.

GUARASCIO, DANIELLE D; San Clemente HS; San Clemente, CA; (1); German Clb; Varsity Clb; Socr; Var Mgr Swmmng; Hon Roll; Pres Acad Fit Awd; Stud Of Month 4 Times,Sci Math; Lifeguard & Ocean Swimming,Racing; Physical Therapy.

GUARD, DARREN C; Mater Dei HS; Santa Ana, CA; (3); Boy Scts; JCL; Latin Clb; Pep Clb; Off Sr Cls; Cheerldng; Ftbl; Trk; Eagle Scout.

GUARDADO, LORENA; Woodrow Wilson HS; San Francisco, CA; (4); Boy Scts; Office Aide; ROTC; Color Guard; Yrbk; Treas Jr Cls; Sftbl; Law Enforcement Cadet; San Francisco ST U; Police.

GUARDADO, MIRNA E; King-Drew Med Mag HS; Los Angeles, CA; (3); Spanish Clb; Vllybl; High Hon Roll; Hon Roll; Prfct Atten Awd; Med-Cor Pgm; Acad Achvt Awd; Med.

GUARDARRAMA, JOSEPH A; Whitney HS; Cerritos, CA; (1); Drama Clb; Key Clb; Mock Trail Comptn; Skier; Psych.

GUARNIERI, LAUREN J; Bishop O Dowd HS; Alameda, CA; (3); 50/250; Ski Clb; SADD; Rptr Nwsp; Ed Yrbk; Rep Frsh Cls; Var Swmmng; Off High Hon Roll; Off Pres Acad Fit Awd; All Am Vrsty Swmmr; Denison U; Bus Mngmnt.

GUBERMAN, JOY; Venice HS; Fairfield, CA; (3); Cmnty Wkr; Debate Tm; Ski Clb; Nwsp; Stat Ftbl; Outstndng Achvt Engl Dept.

GUBLER, ALISON; Trabuco Hills HS; Mission Viejo, CA; (2); Key Clb; School Play; Swmmng; Own Small Cleaning Bus; U CA Irvine; Psych.

GUDANI, MARIA L; Eagle Rock HS; Los Angeles, CA; (2); Church Yth Grp; Key Clb; Office Aide; SADD; Yrbk; Off Jr Cls; JV Vllybl; Cit Awd; Hon Roll; Pres Acad Fit Awd; UC Berkeley; Bus.

GUDELJ, TINO M; Carlmont HS; San Carlos, CA; (2); 11/300; Chess Clb; Computer Clb; Intnl Clb; Math Clb; JV Socr; Var Tennis; Hon Roll.

GUDINO, JOB Z; Pater Noster HS; Los Angeles, CA; (2); Art Clb; Chess Clb; Church Yth Grp; Letterman Clb; Var Crs Cntry; JV Trk; Rotary Awd; U Of Southern CA; Arch Engrng.

GUDINO, LAURA; Our Lady Loretto-Bishop Conaty HS; Los Angeles, CA; (3); French Clb; FBLA; Ed Nwsp; Yrbk; Stu Cncl; Hon Roll; NHS; Modeling; Acting; UCLA; Bus Admin.

GUDMUNDSSON, JOHANNA I; Mountain View HS; Mountain View, CA; (3); 16/319; French Clb; German Clb; Flag Corp; Mrchg Band; Var Co-Capt Cheerldng; Swmmng; High Hon Roll; Intl Rel.

GUDRITZ, TRACI; Monrovia HS; Newark, CA; (3); Church Yth Grp; Office Aide; Science Clb; Spanish Clb; Chorus; Church Choir; Flag Corp; Var Swmmng; High Hon Roll; Hon Roll; Photographer.

GUENTERT, JOSUA P; St Ignatius College Prep; San Francisco, CA; (3); Speech Tm; Community Svc Work; Creighton U; Pre-Med.

GUERENA, CITLALLI; Montgomery HS; San Diego, CA; (2); Cit Awd; Hon Roll; Ntl Merit Schol; Southwestern Coll; Engrng.

GUERRA, ABEL J; Montebello HS; Pico Rivera, CA; (1); Church Yth Grp; FCA; SADD; Chorus; JV Crs Cntry; JV Trk; Hon Roll; CSF; GSC; Hmcmng Hlpr; Elem Ed.

GUERRA, ANNA M; Hawthorne HS; Hawthorne, CA; (2); Band; Mrchg Band; Yrbk; Loyola Mary Mount; Reporter.

GUERRA, ESPERANZA D; Mesa Verde HS; Sacramento, CA; (1); 46/279; Church Yth Grp; Cmnty Wkr; Bsktbl; Vllybl; Knights Columbus CA Free Throw Chmpn 90; Optomolgst.

GUERRA, GONZALO; Etiwanda HS; Rancho Cucamonga, CA; (4); 6/525; Art Clb; Dance Clb; French Clb; JA; Key Clb; Science Clb; Ski Clb; Chorus; Tennis; Cit Awd; Gldn St Schlr Alg I & Geom; CSF Lifetime Goldseal Bearer; Ancient Ord Of The Falcon; Art Exhibit.

GUERRA, HECTOR; Kingsburg HS; Kingsburg, CA; (3); US Naval Acad; Pol Sci.

GUERRA, JEFF V; Norte Vista HS; Riverside, CA; (3); Art Clb; Band; Wt Lftg.

GUERRA, KAREN M; Lakewood SR HS; Long Beach, CA; (3); Church Yth Grp; Cmnty Wkr; Dance Clb; Debate Tm; Library Aide; Office Aide; Teachers Aide; Drill Tm; Off Soph Cls; Off Jr Cls; Mock Trial Tm Awd Outstndng Stu Yth/The Law; Law.

GUERRA, MARLO T; Modesto HS; Modesto, CA; (3); Yrbk; Hon Roll; Green Clb; Acctng.

GUERRA, MEGAN; San Benito HS; Hollister, CA; (1); Pep Clb; Temple Yth Grp; Cheerldng; Elks Awd; Hon Roll; Core Tm; Tacsc Ldrshp Pgm.

GUERRA, PATRICIA; Dixon HS; Davis, CA; (4); 57/159; Church Yth Grp; Cmnty Wkr; Latin Clb; Teachers Aide; Church Choir; Outstndng Ftnss Awd; Schlrshp Migrant Ctr Boces NY; CA ST U Sacramento; Scl Wrk.

GUERRA, RANDY L; Palma HS; Hollister, CA; (3); Church Yth Grp; Cmnty Wkr; Spanish Clb; Rptr Yrbk; JV Bsbl; Var Golf; JV Score Keeper; Hon Roll; Core Tm; St Marys Coll Of CA; Mrktng.

GUERRA, RAQUEL; Encina HS; Sacramento, CA; (3); 56/211; Church Yth Grp; Intnl Clb; Spanish Clb; Hon Roll; Brdcstng Publication Anchor.

GUERRA, VICTORIA R; Central Union HS; El Centro, CA; (3); Pep Clb; SADD; Varsity Clb; Band; Mrchg Band; Pep Band; U Coll Of San Diego; Pre-Med.

GUERRERA, DANIEL A; St Patrick St Vincent HS; Suisun, CA; (1); Hon Roll; UC Davis; Archt.

GUERRERO, AMY; Fremont Christian HS; Fremont, CA; (2); Church Yth Grp; Drama Clb; Chorus; Variety Show; Var Socr; Ensmbl Lvng Wtr; Azusa Pacific; Vocal Music.

GUERRERO, ARLENE R; Chula Vista HS; San Diego, CA; (3); Aud/Vis; Library Aide; Stage Crew; Lit Mag; Peer Cntct-Peer Cnslng; Jnr Statesmn Of Amer; Assocd Stu Body; Engl Tchr.

GUERRERO, CYNTHIA P; Carson HS; Carson, CA; (3); Hon Roll; Ntl Merit Schol; CSF.

GUERRERO, DIANA; Le Grand HS; Planada, CA; (2); JV Bsktbl; Var Sftbl; Med.

GUERRERO, EMILIO; Inglewood HS; Inglewood, CA; (2); Latin Clb; Chorus; Hon Roll.

GUERRERO, GARRY L; Senior HS; Salinas, CA; (2); Band; Mrchg Band; Cit Awd; Hon Roll; Prfct Atten Awd.

GUERRERO, GILBERT M; Gilroy HS; Gilroy, CA; (1); 12/511; Math Clb; Science Clb; Bsktbl; Hon Roll; Hewlet-Packard Achvt Through MESA Awd; Physics, Philosophy; Golden St Exam Schl Rcgntn; PHD Physics.

GUERRERO, GLADYS S; Samuel F B Morse HS; San Diego, CA; (2); Pep Clb; Cit Awd; Hon Roll; CSF; Homework Consistncy Awd; UCSD; Bus.

GUERRERO, HUGO; Montclair HS; Ontario, CA; (1); 2/38.

GUERRERO, JACK; Bell HS; Cudahy, CA; (3); 8/650; Debate Tm; Math Clb; Speech Tm; Mrchg Band; Ed Nwsp; Pres Stu Cncl; High Hon Roll; NHS; Jr Statsmn Amer; Poltcl Sci.

GUERRERO, JAVIER; East Union HS; Lathrop, CA; (1); 1/430; Bsktbl; Ftbl; Trk; UCLA; Med.

GUERRERO, JENNIFER C; Chino HS; Chino, CA; (2); Drama Clb; Science Clb; Thesps; School Musical; School Play; Var Swmmng; High Hon Roll; Pres Acad Fit Awd; UCLA; Med Orthpdcs.

GUERRERO, KEVIN M; Shasta HS; Redding, CA; (4); Pres Church Yth Grp; Speech Tm; Band; Pep Band; School Musical; Stu Cncl; JV L Bsbl; JV Var Ftbl; CA Schlrshp Fdr Life Mem; Navy ROTC Schlrshp; U Of CA San Diego; Chmstry.

GUERRERO, LIBRADO; Lincoln HS; Stockton, CA; (3); 39/592; Boy Scts; Math Clb; Mu Alpha Theta; Science Clb; Spanish Clb; JV Wrstlng; High Hon Roll; Engnr.

GUERRERO, MARIO M; Garden Grove HS; Garden Grove, CA; (1); Church Yth Grp; School Play; Nwsp; JV Ftbl; Bus.

GUERRERO, MICHELLE A; Carson HS; Carson, CA; (2); Var Bsktbl; Bsktbl OGDL Olymps Girls Devel Lg; Vrsty Bsktbl Smmr Lg 2 Yrs; Comp LA Games Bsktbl 89.

GUERRERO, NIDIA K; Bassett HS; La Puente, CA; (1); Hon Roll; Trvlng; Cosmetologist.

GUERRERO, RAMONA S; Lompoc SR HS; Lompoc, CA; (3); Boy Scts; FBLA; SADD; Teachers Aide; Band; Chorus; Mrchg Band; Pep Band; School Musical; Rptr Nwsp; Lompoc Vly Amer G I Forum Cert Merit; Upward Bound Offcr 89-90; Band Ltr; United Way Poster Dsgnr; Art.

GUERRERO, REBECCA; Tulare Western HS; Tulare, CA; (4); 9/230; Am Leg Aux Girls St; Church Yth Grp; Office Aide; Teachers Aide; Color Guard; Pres Frsh Cls; VP Soph Cls; Sftbl; Tennis; DAR Awd; CSF Pres 2 Yrs; Assocd Stu Bdy Elctn Co-Chrprsn; Soroptmst Clb Girl Of Month; Coll Of The Sequoius; Educ.

GUERRERO, RENE L; River City HS; W Sacramento, CA; (1); JA; Hon Roll; Outstndng Wdwrkr.

GUERRERO, RICARDO E; Sweetwater HS; National City, CA; (2); Boy Scts; Cmnty Wkr; Science Clb; Band; Mrchg Band; JV Socr; JV Wt Lftg; Hon Roll; Hnr Awd Eng Clss; Engnrng.

GUERRERO, ROSELLA E; Sacramento HS; Sacramento, CA; (2); 35/400; Church Yth Grp; GAA; Math Clb; SADD; Var Bsktbl; Stat Ftbl; Var Socr; Cit Awd; High Hon Roll; Pres Acad Fit Awd; NVP Navy Bay Classic Tourn Sccr; Scshl Athl Trainer; Astronaut.

GUERRERO, TIMOTHY M; Galt HS; Herald, CA; (2); 6/243; Boy Scts; Cmnty Wkr; Drama Clb; Spanish Clb; SADD; Thesps; School Musical; School Play; Stage Crew; Yrbk; Acad Thspn, Bst Tech Drama; Coaches Choice Trk; Cornell U; Envrnmntl Engrng.

GUERRERO, VERONICA C; Delano HS; Delano, CA; (3); Cit Awd; Hon Roll.

GUERRIERO, RYAN E; Temecula Valley HS; Temecula, CA; (2); Cmnty Wkr; Letterman Clb; Varsity Clb; Var L Ftbl; Wt Lftg; Var L Wrstlng; Hon Roll; UCLA; Eng.

GUERRINI, STEVEN B; Santa Rosa HS; Santa Rosa, CA; (3); 91/518; Art Clb; Boy Scts; French Clb; JA; Letterman Clb; Band; Jazz Band; School Musical; Var L Bsktbl; Var L Crs Cntry; Natl Champ Steeplechase; Sports Med.

GUERTIN, STEPHEN D; Clovis HS; Clovis, CA; (2); SADD; JV Socr; Intrml Tennis; JV Trk; Intrml Wt Lftg; Sccr Coach & Ref; Fresno ST U; Bus Mgmt.

GUEST, JARRETT VICTOR; Inglewood HS; Los Angeles, CA; (2); JV Ftbl; Engrng.

GUEST, LAUREN A; Folsom HS; Folsom, CA; (3); Church Yth Grp; Model UN; Church Choir; Yrbk; Socr; Var L Trk; Hon Roll; Acad Decathln Team; Future Problem Solving Team-St Fnlst; Chico ST; Intl Stds.

GUEST, PAUL; Edison/Computech HS; Fresno, CA; (2); Church Yth Grp; SADD; Cheerldng; JV Swmmng; Sci Olympiad Rgnls 1st Comp Comp ST Fnls 88, 2nd Metric Est 89, 3rd Comp Pgm 89; Schl Mascot; Air Force; Comp Sci.

GUETZ, AMY E; Crawford HS; San Diego, CA; (2); Church Yth Grp; French Clb; Hosp Aide; Key Clb; Pep Clb; Hon Roll; CA Schlrshp Fed; CA Poly San Luis Obispo; Arch.

GUEVARA, ALICIA A; Bishop Montgomery HS; Redondo Beach, CA; (2); Ski Clb; SADD; Chorus; Church Choir; Drill Tm; Var Co-Capt Cheerldng; Gym; Swmmng; Wt Lftg; Cit Awd; Med.

GUEVARA, CLAUDIA G; Wasco Unin HS; Wasco, CA; (3); FHA; Office Aide; Teachers Aide; Stage Crew; Cit Awd; Hon Roll; Prfct Atten Awd; B C Coll; Lang.

GUEVARA, JUAN CARLOS; Montclair HS; Ontario, CA; (3); Latin Clb; Var Ftbl; Capt Var Trk; Intrml Wt Lftg; Indstrl Engrng.

GUEVARA, JUDY; Montclair HS; Ontario, CA; (2); 7/560; Cmnty Wkr; SADD; Stat Socr; Var Capt Trk; JV Capt Vllybl; Cit Awd; French Hon Soc; High Hon Roll; GATE Stu; Acadc Engl Awd; UCSD; Chld Psych.

GUEVARA, LISETTE; San Gabriel Mission HS; El Monte, CA; (3); 18/134; Treas French Clb; Hon Roll; CSF; Cert Of Mrt Natl De Francais & Skrbll Essy Cntst; Blue Mem In Mnd Gmes; Hstry.

GUEVARA, NORMA; Mc Lane HS; Fresno, CA; (4); #9 In Class; Teachers Aide; Temple Yth Grp; Cit Awd; High Hon Roll; Hon Roll; Bk Of Amer Cert; The Joseph Y De Young Plq; CSF; Pre-Med.

GUEVARA, PONCHO; Homestead HS; Sunnyvale, CA; (4); Church Yth Grp; Cmnty Wkr; Debate Tm; FBLA; Pep Clb; Spanish Clb; Teachers Aide; Rep Stu Cncl; NHS; Spanish NHS; MECHA Founder/Pres; Commnty Activist; Peer Counseling; UCSD; Bio Engrng.

GUEVARA, SANDRA; Mc Lane HS; Fresno, CA; (3); 3/400; Church Yth Grp; SADD; Hon Roll; Explorers Nature Clb; MESA Clb; Prjct Alpha Clb.

GUEVARA, STARLETT M; Norte Vista HS; Riverside, CA; (2); 59/445; Variety Show; Hon Roll; Law.

GUEVARRA, MICHAEL C; Saint Joseph Notre Dame HS; Alameda, CA; (3); Cmnty Wkr; Hon Roll; Jr NHS; NHS; Prfct Atten Awd; St Schlr; Bsktbl; Engr.

GUEVARRA, SARAH S; Westmoor HS; Vallejo, CA; (3); Yrbk; Hon Roll; Nrsng.

GUFFEY, CLARISSA P; Corona SR HS; Corona, CA; (4); 13/422; Church Yth Grp; Chorus; Stu Cncl; High Hon Roll; Pres Acad Fit Awd; Interact Clb; Ca Scholastic Fed; Cal Poly S L Obispo; Sci.

GUFFEY, MICHELLE L; Sanger HS; Sanger, CA; (2); Acpl Chr; Chorus; Church Choir; Hon Roll; NHS; Prfct Atten Awd; Ply Piano Choir Schl & Chrch; Super & Excclnt Solo CA Music Educ Assoc Solo Fstvl; CSF; Fresno Pacific Coll; Teacher.

GUFFEY, PARIS A; Grossmont HS; Beaverton, OR; (1); Band; Jazz Band; Mrchg Band; Orch; Pep Band; High Hon Roll; Hon Roll; NHS; Prfct Atten Awd; Julliard; Sci.

GUGEL, DAVID R; Mission Viejo HS; Mission Viejo, CA; (3); 10/440; Church Yth Grp; Cmnty Wkr; Key Clb; Spanish Clb; Teachers Aide; JV Bsbl; Var Ftbl; High Hon Roll; CA Schltc Fed; Sports Med.

GUGEL, JONATHAN M; Mission Viejo HS; Mission Viejo, CA; (3); Church Yth Grp; Cmnty Wkr; Spanish Clb; Var JV Bsbl; JV Bsktbl; JV Ftbl; Hon Roll; CSF; UCLA; Pre-Law.

GUHA, ARPITA MONI; Central Union HS; El Centro, CA; (2); Math Tm; Med Schl; Ped.

GUIDI, CHRISTOHER S; Lincoln HS; Stockton, CA; (2); 150/800; French Clb; Bsbl; Bsktbl; Score Keeper; Trk; Pres Acad Fit Awd; UC Berkly; Bus.

GUIDI, CHRISTOPHER J; Grace Davis HS; Modesto, CA; (3); Letterman Clb; Office Aide; Red Cross Aide; Ski Clb; Teachers Aide; Varsity Clb; VICA; Var Trk; Vrsty Water Polo 2 Yrs; Aviation.

GUIEB, JANEL B; James Logan HS; Union City, CA; (3); Powder Puff Ftbl; JV Tennis; RN.

GUIEB, TESSIE M; St Patrick-St Vincent HS; Vallejo, CA; (3); 16/146; VP Chess Clb; Sec Spanish Clb; Aud/Vis; Chorus; Rptr Nwsp; Sec Stu Cncl; High Hon Roll; CSF; Campus Mnstry; UC Berkley; Pre Med.

GUIFFRA, JERRY J; Chana HS; Auburn, CA; (2); Computer Clb; English Clb; FFA; Math Clb; Math Tm; Science Clb; SADD; Teachers Aide; School Play; Stage Crew; Humbolt U; Comp.

GUILD, MARCUS A; San Clemente HS; San Clemente, CA; (2); French Clb; Band; Bsktbl; Trk; Law Enfrcmnt.

GUILFOYLE, MOLLY A; Enterprise HS; Redding, CA; (3); Cmnty Wkr; Teachers Aide; JV L Bsktbl; Var L Trk; Var L Vllybl; Hon Roll; Pres Acad Fit Awd; Schlrshp Fdrtn; Stu Of Quarter & Month; Psych.

GUILLEN, PATRICIA L; Santa Ana HS; Santa Ana, CA; (2); Computer Clb; Speech Tm; Teachers Aide; Chorus; School Play; Sch Teacher.

GUILLERMO, JOYCE; Rancho Buena Vista HS; Vista, CA; (3); 109/465; Office Aide; Teachers Aide; Varsity Clb; Chorus; Drill Tm; Prfct Atten Awd; CJSF; Tech Inst; Bus.

GUILLORY, KRISTINE; Oxnard HS; Hillsboro, OR; (3); Band; Mrchg Band; Hon Roll; 100th Rosebowl Parade Band Marcher; Outstndng Private Lesson Stu Mdl 88; Outstndngband Asst Sect Ldr; Music.

GUIN, ERIN E; Hesperia HS; Hesperia, CA; (3); Pres Church Yth Grp; VP FFA; Teachers Aide; JV Vllybl; Stat Wrstlng; High Hon Roll; Hon Roll; Nazarene Yth Intl Zone Rep; Bible Quiz Tm; Vllybl All Star Tm; Point Loma Nazarene Coll; Bus.

GUIRGUIS, LILA A; Alverno HS; Pasadena, CA; (3); Church Yth Grp; Hosp Aide; Science Clb; Rep Soph Cls; Off Jr Cls; Bsktbl; Diving; Swmmng; Tennis; CSF; Swim Tm Mgr; Prom Cmmtte; UCSD; Marine Bio.

GUJRAL, BIKRAMJEET; Duarte HS; Duarte, CA; (3); Art Clb; Computer Clb; Science Clb; Temple Yth Grp; Nwsp; Bsktbl; Tennis; Spec Awd Bst Graphcs/Art Comp; Awd Schlstc Hnrs Physcs & Alg 2; Awd Future Scientsts Fr 90; UCLA; Elec Engrng.

GUJRAL, RANI K; Savanna HS; Anaheim, CA; (3); Drama Clb; Key Clb; Pep Clb; Science Clb; Service Clb; Teachers Aide; Stage Crew; Rep Soph Cls; Rep Jr Cls; Hon Roll; Outstndng Chem Stu; 1st Pl FABE Typwrtg Contest; Astrnmy.

GULDEN, MELISSA S; Shasta HS; Redding, CA; (3); Church Yth Grp; Drama Clb; Hosp Aide; Thesps; Church Choir; Flag Corp; School Play; Variety Show; Rep Stu Cncl; Hon Roll; U Southern CA; Theatre.

GULENO, MARK E; Loyola HS; Los Angeles, CA; (2); Boy Scts; Church Yth Grp; Computer Clb; Nwsp; High Hon Roll; Egl Sct; UCLA; Comp.

GULLA, VANESSA D; Carmel HS; Carmel, CA; (2); VP AFS; Church Yth Grp; JV Bsktbl; JV Sftbl; JV Tennis; High Hon Roll; CSF; SMART-STUS Making A Right Tomorrow-Evironmntl Clb; U S Space Acad-AL.

GULLEY, SHANAE J; Fremont HS; Oakland, CA; (2); School Musical; Cheerldng; Hon Roll; UNLV.

GULLIFORD JR, ROBERT J; Livermore HS; Livermore, CA; (3); Boy Scts; Pres Church Yth Grp; French Clb; Pres Ski Clb; Band; Jazz Band; Mrchg Band; Nwsp; High Hon Roll; NHS; U Of CA Davis.

GULLIKSEN, MICHELLE A; Franklin HS; Stockton, CA; (4); Office Aide; Teachers Aide; High Hon Roll; Hon Roll; Prfct Atten Awd.

GULLIVER, SHANNON E; San Luis Obispo SR HS; San Luis Obispo, CA; (2); Church Yth Grp; Stu Cncl Stu Yth Opport United SLO Branch; Guitar & Genrl Music; Cal Poly; Eng.

GULSTON, VANIA; North Hollywood High Zoo Magnt Ctr; Los Angeles, CA; (4); Dance Clb; Key Clb; Spanish Clb; Ed Nwsp; Ed Lit Mag; Rep Frsh Cls; JV Crs Cntry; Hon Roll; Ntl Merit Schol; Prncpls Hnr Rl; Jrnlsm Achvt Awd; Engl Achvt Awd; Intl Studs.

GUMAYAGAY, MARK E; Golden West HS; Ivanhoe, CA; (2); Church Yth Grp; French Clb; JV Bsktbl; Hon Roll; CSF; U Of CA Berkeley; Accntng.

GUMBLE, JASN E; Coleville HS; Bridgeport, CA; (3); Band; Nwsp; Yrbk; Ntl Merit SF.

GUMM, JOHN E; Edison-Computech HS; Fresno, CA; (4); 17/216; Pres Church Yth Grp; Capt Debate Tm; Sec Model UN; NFL; Capt Speech Tm; Ed Lit Mag; JV Vllybl; Elks Awd; Hon Roll; Jr NHS; Qlfd CA St Spch Chpmnshps; Qlfd Natl Chmpnshp Spch Trnmnt NFL; Awd Scl Sci Dept Schlr Awd; Pepperdine U; Bus Admin.

GUMMER, JACQUELINE; Coachella Valley HS; Indio, CA; (3); Church Yth Grp; Cmnty Wkr; Girl Scts; Hosp Aide; Varsity Clb; Band; Jazz Band; Mrchg Band; Orch; Pep Band; Pst Hnrd Queen Jobs Dghtrs; U Of CA; Med.

GUMMOW, JOHN P; Serrano HS; Phelan, CA; (3); Boy Scts; Church Yth Grp; Church Choir; JV Bsbl; JV Var Ftbl; Wt Lftg; JV Wrstlng; Hon Roll.

GUMPERT, CHRISTINA M; Village Christian HS; Sun Valley, CA; (3); Spanish Clb; Varsity Clb; JV Bsktbl; Var Sftbl; Var Vllybl; UVLA; Law.

GUMPERT, TARA D; Tracy Joint Union HS; Tracy, CA; (2); 50/483; Church Yth Grp; Drama Clb; German Clb; Hosp Aide; SADD; Chorus; School Musical; School Play; Swmmng; Hon Roll; Water Polo Team; Delta Coll; Psych.

GUNDELL, LISA; Santa Ynez HS; Los Olivos, CA; (3); Drama Clb; FHA; Spanish Clb; Teachers Aide; JV Var Cheerldng; Trk; Hon Roll; UCSB; Bus.

GUNDERSON, GENEVIEVE S; Berkeley HS; Berkeley, CA; (3); Hosp Aide; Latin Clb; Var Swmmng; Hon Roll; Paper On Natl Latin Exam; High Hnrs Golden St Geom Exam, Hnrs GSE Alge.

GUNDLACH, HEIDI; Fortuna Union HS; Scotia, CA; (1); Drama Clb; Variety Show; Camerada Singers; Harvard U; Psych.

GUNHUS, JEFFREY A; Corona HS; Corona, CA; (3); Am Leg Boys St; Church Yth Grp; Var Bsbl; JV Bsktbl; Ftbl; Powder Puff Ftbl; Wt Lftg; High Hon Roll; Opt Clb Awd; Pres Acad Fit Awd; Schlr Athlete Awd; Coaches Awd; Bus.

GUNN, CASEY; Mt Carmel HS; Fairfax Station, VA; (2); Scholastic Bowl; Rptr Nwsp; Sec Soph Cls; JV Tennis; CSF; Mst Insprtnl Awd 89 Acad Tm; U Of WA; Educ.

GUNN, JEFF M; Escodido HS; Escondido, CA; (3); FFA; Yrbk; Hon Roll; Schlrshp Awd FFA 3.5 GPA; Palaomar Coll; Photo.

GUNNERSON, KRISTIN; Edison HS; Huntington Beach, CA; (4); 3/483; Church Yth Grp; Cmnty Wkr; Treas Dance Clb; VP Spanish Clb; Drill Tm; Rep Stu Cncl; JV Var Trk; High Hon Roll; Spanish NHS; Yth Of Mth; Math.

GUNST, CHRISTOPHER L; Mater Dei HS; Huntington Beach, CA; (1); Church Yth Grp; Hon Roll; Spec Olympics Vlntr.

GUNTER, KISHA L; John F Kennedy HS; Richmond, CA; (4); 15/230; French Clb; Math Clb; Ski Clb; Teachers Aide; Mrchg Band; Orch; Off Frsh Cls; Off Soph Cls; Sftbl; Hon Roll; Bus Admin.

GUNTER, LISA A; Will C Wood HS; Vacaville, CA; (1); Church Yth Grp; Flag Corp; Rptr Phtg Yrbk; Hon Roll; Stanford; Bus.

GUO, MARY Z; International Studies HS; San Francisco, CA; (2); Hon Roll; Prfct Atten Awd; Accntng.

GUO, RENEE M; Galileo HS; San Francisco, CA; (2); Hon Roll; Berkeley U.

GUPTA, ALOK K; University HS; Irvine, CA; (3); Boy Scts; Capt Debate Tm; VP FBLA; NFL; Speech Tm; Orch; Hon Roll; Spanish NHS; Acad Decath; CA Schlrshp Fed; Dartmouth Coll; Lbrl Arts.

GUPTA, ANJULA; Los Alamitos HS; Los Alamitos, CA; (4); Cmnty Wkr; Hosp Aide; Pep Clb; Service Clb; Spanish Clb; Stu Cncl; High Hon Roll; Hon Roll; NHS; Amnesty Intl; Med.

GUPTA, JAY M; Marina HS; Huntington Beach, CA; (2); Boy Scts; Math Clb; Math Tm; Band; Rep Frsh Cls; High Hon Roll; St Schlr; MIT; Elec Engrng.

GUPTA, NAV N; Don Antonio Lugo HS; Fontana, CA; (3); Cit Awd; High Hon Roll; NHS; Prfct Atten Awd; CA Poly Pomona; Civil Engrng.

GUPTA, NEERAJ; Hayward HS; Hayward, CA; (4); 1/243; Scholastic Bowl; Mrchg Band; Ed Nwsp; Pres Soph Cls; VP Stu Cncl; Stat Bsktbl; Socr; High Hon Roll; Ntl Merit SF; Val; Badmntn Var Capt, Let & All Lgu; CSF; Sci Fairs 1st Pl HS & 1st & 2nd Pl Bay Area; Comp Sci.

GUPTA, NEHA; Sunny Hills HS; Fullerton, CA; (1); Key Clb; Math Tm; Spanish Clb; Intrml Swmmng; Rotary Awd; Jr Statesmen Of Amer; Stu Offrng Support.

GUPTA, POOJA; Bolsa Grande HS; Garden Grove, CA; (3); Computer Clb; Hosp Aide; Math Clb; Science Clb; Speech Tm; Teachers Aide; JV Socr; JV Swmmng; JV Tennis; Cit Awd; Yth Ldrshp For Action; Vol Work Library; Badminton JV; 3rd Sci & Engrng Fair; Ed.

GUPTA, POOJA; Etiwanda HS; Rancho Cucamonga, CA; (3); 7/782; Treas Chess Clb; JA; Key Clb; Spanish Clb; Cit Awd; High Hon Roll; Prfct Atten Awd; CSF VP; Jr Vrsty Bdmntn Team No 1 Girls Dbls; Outstndng Drvrs Educ Stu Awd; Stanford U; Med.

GUPTA, ROHIT; Corona HS; Corona, CA; (2); 5/473; Cmnty Wkr; Hosp Aide; Library Aide; Bsktbl; JV Tennis; Pres Acad Fit Awd; Val; CA Jr Schlrshp Fed; CA Schlrshp Fed; UCI; Med.

GUPTA, SHALU; Moorpark HS; Moorpark, CA; (2); 1/257; Church Yth Grp; Cmnty Wkr; GAA; JV Bsktbl; High Hon Roll; Indian Classical Dance Perf & Awds; Make Food For Needy In LA; CSF; Boutique Model; UCLA; Med.

GUPTA, SHIRISH; Corona HS; Corona, CA; (3); 2/400; Am Leg Boys St; Treas FBLA; Hosp Aide; Service Clb; Stu Cncl; JV Tennis; High Hon Roll; Pres Acad Fit Awd; CSF Pres; Hstry Day St Fnlst; Mock Trial; Law.

GUPTA, SUNIL K; Hogan SR HS; Vallejo, CA; (3); 1/325; Am Leg Boys St; Pres Drama Clb; VP French Clb; Key Clb; School Musical; School Play; Sec Stu Cncl; Var Crs Cntry; Var Tennis; Xerox Awd, Humanities/Soc Sci.

GUPTA, VANDANA; Casa Roble Fundamental HS; Folsom, CA; (2); AFS; Sec Intnl Clb; Letterman Clb; Math Tm; Ed Nwsp; Var Tennis; Cit Awd; French Hon Soc; High Hon Roll; NHS; Mock Trial Tm 1st Pl Sacramento Cnty Chmpns; Optimist Oratorical Cont 1st Pl; Law.

GUPTA, VIKRAM; San Clemente HS; San Clemente, CA; (2); Cmnty Wkr; Treas FBLA; Science Clb; Service Clb; Spanish Clb; Band; Mrchg Band; Pep Band; High Hon Roll; Hon Roll; Bus Law Comptn-1st Pl FBLA S CA & 5th In St; Schl Stu Of Yr Bus-Cert; Harvard; Law.

GUPTILL, HAYLEY; Eisenhower HS; Rialto, CA; (3); Teachers Aide; Stu Cncl; Cheerldng; Var Socr; JV Sftbl; Var Trk; French Hon Soc; High Hon Roll; NHS; Athltc Schlr Awd; Azurettes; Booster Club Awd; Bus.

GUPTILL, SCOTT; San Diego Acad; Singapore; (1); Church Yth Grp; Teachers Aide; Band; Chorus; Phtg Yrbk; Off Frsh Cls; Hon Roll; Far Eastern Acad Singapore.

GURA, DANIEL J; Santa Monica HS; Santa Monica, CA; (1); JV Bsktbl; High Hon Roll; Pres Schlr; St Schlr; Duke; Cmmnctns.

GURKE, JEFF; Atascadero HS; Atascadero, CA; (1); Cit Awd; UC Berkeley; Vet.

GURKSY, MARK; Liberty Union HS; Brentwood, CA; (4); 5/307; FCA; Letterman Clb; Pep Clb; Scholastic Bowl; Ski Clb; SADD; Varsity Clb; Stage Crew; Ed Nwsp; Treas Soph Cls; Commissioner Of Publicity/Clbs; Friday Night Live Treas; U CA Davis; Intl Relations.

GURLEY, FREDETIYA; Silver Valley HS; Barstow, CA; (3); Computer Clb; German Clb; SADD; Varsity Clb; Chorus; Variety Show; JV Var Bsktbl; JV Vllybl; Hon Roll; Comp.

GURROLA, ADRIANA; Sweetwater HS; National City, CA; (2); 10/30; Southwestern Coll; Sci Commnctn.

GURROLA, ROBERT; Bell Gardens HS; Bell Gardens, CA; (2); Intrml Crs Cntry; Intrml Trk; CA ST; Med.

GURTCHEFF, SHAWN E; Casa Roble Fundamental HS; Orangevale, CA; (2); 5/461; French Clb; Drill Tm; Treas Soph Cls; Var Cheerldng; Stat Score Keeper; Var Swmmng; Gov Hon Prg Awd; High Hon Roll; NHS; Pres Acad Fit Awd; Fri Night Live; Tech Engrng.

GURULE, NICKIE; Hilltop HS; Chula Vista, CA; (3); 53/495; NFL; Pep Clb; SADD; Band; Cheerldng; Socr; Trk; Church Yth Grp; Speech Tm; Mrchg Band; Girls Leag; UCLA; Teaching.

GUSHUE, TERI MARIE; Alta Loma HS; Cucamonga, CA; (2); Church Yth Grp; GAA; Chorus; Bsktbl; Score Keeper; Wt Lftg; Cit Awd; Dance; Outstndng Splng Awds; Princpls Awd; Pediatric.

GUSKAY, HEATHER; Vanden HS; Vacaville, CA; (4); Girl Scts; Hosp Aide; Office Aide; Cheerldng; Powder Puff Ftbl; Sacramento ST; Para-Legal.

GUSMAN, ANDREAS; Garden Grove HS; Garden Grove, CA; (4); 22/350; Cmnty Wkr; Intnl Clb; Latin Clb; Scholastic Bowl; Science Clb; Var Crs Cntry; Var L Tennis; Hon Roll; NHS; Natl Hspnc Schlrs Semi-Fnlst; CSF; Invtntl Acad Workshop; UC Davis; Ag Engrng.

GUSMAN, DOLORES R; California Lutheran HS; North Hollywood, CA; (1); Treas Church Yth Grp; Church Choir; Variety Show; Rptr Nwsp; Off Frsh Cls; JV Bsktbl; Var L Sftbl; Var Vllybl; Hon Roll; Prfct Atten Awd; USC; Law.

GUSMAN, RON J; California Lutheran HS; North Hollywood, CA; (3); Pres Church Yth Grp; Chorus; Church Choir; Stage Crew; Variety Show; Var Bsbl; JV Bsktbl; Var Ftbl; Mgr(s); Score Keeper; Citizenship Trophy; USC; Med.

GUSS, AISHA N; Alta Loma HS; Alta Loma, CA; (2); Church Yth Grp; Dance Clb; Letterman Clb; Teachers Aide; Variety Show; JV Capt Bsktbl; L Trk; Hon Roll; Pres Acad Fit Awd; Peer Cnslng; Black Stu Union Clb Sec; San Diego ST; Bus Law.

GUSS, AUDREY M; Santa Monica HS; Santa Monica, CA; (2); JV Sftbl; Green Repblc Clb; Jrnlsm.

GUST, INGER L; L A Lutheran HS; Van Nuys, CA; (3); Church Yth Grp; Var Vllybl; Hon Roll; NHS; Bus.

GUST, NIKKA L; L A Lutheran HS; Van Nuys, CA; (4); Art Clb; Church Yth Grp; Teachers Aide; Pres Jr Cls; Stu Cncl; Cit Awd; Hon Roll; NHS.

GUSTAFSON, MARK A; Los Angeles Baptist HS; Northridge, CA; (3); Boy Scts; Church Yth Grp; Teachers Aide; Treas Stu Cncl; JV Var Socr; Var Vllybl; High Hon Roll; Hon Roll; Order Of Arrow Chptr Treas, Lodge Treas; Jr Statesmn.

GUSTAFSON, MATTHEU; Cajon HS; San Bernardino, CA; (3); 20/463; Cmnty Wkr; L Band; Jazz Band; Mrchg Band; Pep Band; High Hon Roll; Acad Lttr Acad Excllnc Awd Algebra I Stu Govt Day 89; U S Air Force Acad; Engrng.

GUSTAFSON, PAIGE; Tamalpais HS; Mill Valley, CA; (3); French Clb; Rptr Nwsp; Ed Yrbk; Var Capt Cheerldng; JV Sftbl; JV Tennis; High Hon Roll; JETS Awd; Bio.

GUSTAFSON, TRISTAN; Christian Center HS; Antioch, CA; (2); Church Yth Grp; Chorus; Church Choir; Yrbk; Off Jr Cls; High Hon Roll; Music; Bethany Coll; Music.

GUSTASON, LINDA K; Colton HS; Grand Terrace, CA; (2); High Hon Roll; NHS; Bus.

GUSTASON, PAUL; Colton HS; Colton, CA; (3); Boy Scts; Cmnty Wkr; Debate Tm; Aud/Vis; Photogrphy.

GUSTAVSON, KRISTEN; Gilroy HS; Gilroy, CA; (3); Church Yth Grp; Debate Tm; Drama Clb; Speech Tm; SADD; Acpl Chr; Chorus; Church Choir; Color Guard; School Musical; CA All St Choir.

GUTHARY, REBECCA; Downey HS; Downey, CA; (2); Church Yth Grp; Girl Scts; SADD; Chorus; Church Choir; Kewanettes; Obstrcn.

GUTHRIE, HEATHER D; Mt Carmel HS; San Diego, CA; (2); Church Yth Grp; Cmnty Wkr; Sec Soph Cls; Off Jr Cls; JV Diving; Hon Roll; Prfct Atten Awd; Most Dedicated Diver; CSF; Bus.

GUTHRIE, JAN L; Del Campo HS; Carmichael, CA; (4); Cmnty Wkr; French Clb; FBLA; Ski Clb; Teachers Aide; Chorus; Drill Tm; Stage Crew; Stu Reaching Out Treas; CSU Sacramento; Crmnl Just Adm.

GUTHRIE, JENNIFER; Poway HS; Poway, CA; (2); 44/798; Band; Jazz Band; Mrchg Band; Orch; Pep Band; Diving; Gym; Trk; High Hon Roll.

GUTHRIE, PENELOPE; Poway HS; Poway, CA; (4); 45/668; SADD; Band; Mrchg Band; Orch; High Hon Roll; NHS; VP Emerald Brigade Band; Slvr Rank Awd; UCLA; Med.

GUTIERREZ, ALLAN V; Point Loma HS; San Diego, CA; (3); 104/431; Boy Scts; Cmnty Wkr; Dance Clb; English Clb; JA; Letterman Clb; Q&S; Teachers Aide; Varsity Clb; School Musical; Brnze Mdl Intl Karate 88; USD; Med.

GUTIERREZ, AMBER; Chino HS; Chino, CA; (2); Varsity Clb; Var Socr; Var Sftbl; Hon Roll; Silver Spur Nominee For Physical Education; College; Law.

GUTIERREZ, ANA; Bassett HS; Valinda, CA; (2); Church Yth Grp; Intnl Clb; Band; VP Jr Cls; JV Vllybl; NHS; Bus.

GUTIERREZ, ANA I; Eisenhower HS; Rialto, CA; (4); 110/655; Sec DECA; French Clb; Office Aide; Spanish Clb; High Hon Roll; Hon Roll; California Scholarship Federation; U Of Calif Riverside; Bus Admin.

GUTIERREZ, ANA L; Channel Islands HS; Oxnard, CA; (3); 12/773; Stat Bsktbl; JV Crs Cntry; Var Mgr(s); Var Score Keeper; JV Trk; High Hon Roll; Hon Roll; Masonic Awd; Pres Acad Fit Awd; Academic Letter; Honors In Golden State Exam For Algebra; Honors In Golden State Exam For Geometry; Electrical Engineering.

GUTIERREZ, APRIL M; Gladstone HS; Covina, CA; (3); Teachers Aide; Sec Sr Cls; Stat Swmmng; Var JV Tennis; Hon Roll; CSF.

GUTIERREZ, CAMILLA T; Etiwanda HS; Fontana, CA; (2); Band; Mrchg Band; FIDM Modeling Club; UCLA; Med.

GUTIERREZ, CARLOS; Golden West HS; Visalia, CA; (1); Band; Jazz Band; Mrchg Band; Pep Band; Awd Excllnc Phys Educ; UC Davis; Phy.

GUTIERREZ, CAROLINE; Norwalk HS; Norwalk, CA; (3); English Clb; JA; Math Clb; Service Clb; Acpl Chr; Chorus; Powder Puff Ftbl; Hon Roll; Prfct Atten Awd; Trphy Sch Choir; CA Schlrshp Fed; CA ST U Long Beach; Comp Sci.

GUTIERREZ, CLAUDIA; St Genevieve HS; Arleta, CA; (2); French Clb; Pep Clb; Drill Tm; Pres Frsh Cls; Rep Soph Cls; JV Capt Cheerldng; Score Keeper; JV Sftbl; High Hon Roll; Liturgy Clb; UC Davis; Vet.

GUTIERREZ, CRISTINA A; Lemoore Union HS; Lemoore, CA; (2); Band; Yrbk; Capt Var Swmmng; Pres Jr NHS; Natl Jr Bwlng Cngrs Caribbean Champ 89; Natl Jr Bwlng Chmpnshps Fnlst 89; Fmale 18/Undr Athlt Of Yr 89; U Of CA Davis; Med.

GUTIERREZ, DANIEL W; Canyon Springs HS; Moreno Valley, CA; (3); 45/636; Church Yth Grp; Band; Mrchg Band; Rep Yrbk; Golf; High Hon Roll; Hon Roll; Jr NHS; NHS; Opt Clb Awd; Close-Up; Local Sci Fair 1st Pl Chem; UC Riverside; Engl.

GUTIERREZ, DAVID G; C K Mc Clatchy HS; Sacramento, CA; (3); 102/390; Spanish Clb; Band; Mrchg Band; Orch; JV Bsbl; Var Ftbl; Hon Roll; Math/Engr/Sci Assn-Mst Outstndng Jr; Humanities Intl Stds Pgm; Fri Night Live; Jr Ag Rsrch Apprntc Pgm; U CA-DAVIS; Biochem.

GUTIERREZ, DIANA; Mission HS; Alhambra, CA; (2); Hon Roll; Wrk Expr Prgm; JAM Club; UCLA; Bus Mgmt.

GUTIERREZ, DIANA; St Monicas HS; Los Angeles, CA; (3); Key Clb; Latin Clb; High Hon Roll; NHS; Treas CA Schlrshp Fed; Mem Asian Pacific Club; Accntng.

GUTIERREZ, DIANA L; Sacred Heart Of Jesus HS; Los Angeles, CA; (3); 2/100; Cmnty Wkr; Library Aide; Math Tm; Quiz Bowl; Spanish Clb; Ed Yrbk; Treas Jr Cls; High Hon Roll; VP NHS; Prfct Atten Awd; CA Schlrshp Fed VP; Med.

GUTIERREZ, EDDIE J; Bishop Amat HS; Baldwin Park, CA; (3); Spanish Clb; JV Var Bsktbl; High Hon Roll; Hon Roll; Bus Admin.

GUTIERREZ, EDGAR A; Apple Valley HS; Apple Valley, CA; (2); Spanish Clb; Yrbk; Socr; Vllybl; Cit Awd; Hon Roll; Spanish NHS; Airplane Pilot.

GUTIERREZ, EDUARDO; Carson HS; Carson, CA; (3); Band; Orch; Plumbng.

GUTIERREZ, EMIGUIO; Sierra Vista HS; Baldwin Park, CA; (2); Bsbl; Ftbl; JV Wrstlng; Arch.

GUTIERREZ, ENRIQUE L; Hueneme HS; Oxnard, CA; (3); Art Clb; Computer Clb; English Clb; FHA; Math Clb; Science Clb; Hon Roll.

GUTIERREZ, ESMERALDA D; Brawley Union HS; Westmorland, CA; (3); Cmnty Wkr; FHA; Teachers Aide; Elks Awd; Rotary Awd; Imperial Vly Clg; Psych.

GUTIERREZ, EVELYN E; Notre Dame HS; Rialto, CA; (3); Church Yth Grp; FBLA; GAA; JA; Rialto Police Explr; AZ ST U; Law.

GUTIERREZ, FRANCISCO J; La Mirada HS; Whittier, CA; (4); 8/335; 4-H; FBLA; Key Clb; Math Clb; NFL; Speech Tm; Treas Sr Cls; Trk; High Hon Roll; Prfct Atten Awd; Yth In Govt Cnclmn; CSF; U Of CA Irvine; Civil Engrng.

GUTIERREZ, GRACIE A; Brawley Union HS; Brawley, CA; (1); Band; Mrchg Band; Pep Band; Hon Roll; Music.

GUTIERREZ, GUADALUPE; Bell Gardens HS; Bell Gardens, CA; (1); Yrbk; Tennis; UCLA; Tchr.

GUTIERREZ, HECTOR E; Don Bosco Technical Inst; San Gabriel, CA; (2); Capt JV Socr; NEDT Awd; Campus Minstry Core Tm 89-90; Deans List 89-90; Schlr Athl Awd; Gldn Tiger Awd; 2nd Pl Ldrshp; UCLA; Pedtrcn.

GUTIERREZ, HILDA; James Monroe HS; Pacoima, CA; (4); French Clb; Chorus; Church Choir; Var Capt Tennis; Hon Roll; Pres Acad Fit Awd; CSF; Los Angeles City Silver Sealbearer; Torch & Gold Sealbearer At Grad; UCLA; Law.

GUTIERREZ, HUGO E; Fowler HS; Fowler, CA; (3); 9/90; Church Yth Grp; Drama Clb; Science Clb; Off Soph Cls; Bsbl; Crs Cntry; Socr; Prfct Atten Awd; Golden St Exam Acad Excllnce Awd; Geometry Honors; Outstndng Accomp Excllnce Arch; Fresno ST U; Aeronautical Eng.

GUTIERREZ, IRENE M; Moreau HS; Fremont, CA; (3); Church Yth Grp; Cmnty Wkr; Powder Puff Ftbl; Var Capt Socr; JV Sftbl; Var Trk; Hon Roll; Trvlng City Sccr Tm Won St Cup; Sccr Trnmts; Bus.

GUTIERREZ, ISAIAS M; Delano HS; Earlimart, CA; (4); 13/355; VP Computer Clb; Math Clb; Science Clb; Pres Stu Cncl; Wt Lftg; Hon Roll; Masonic Awd; NHS; Pres Acad Fit Awd; U Of CA San Diego; Comp Engrng.

GUTIERREZ, JENNIFER; Righetti HS; Santa Maria, CA; (1); 1/507; Church Yth Grp; Hosp Aide; SADD; School Play; Stu Cncl; Var Tennis; Cit Awd; High Hon Roll; Teacher.

GUTIERREZ, JESSIE; Paramount HS; Bellflower, CA; (3); 119/402; Cmnty Wkr; Math Clb; Drill Tm; Bsktbl; Sftbl; Cit Awd; Hon Roll; GATE; Lawyr.

GUTIERREZ, JOHN A; El Rancho HS; Pico Rivera, CA; (2); JV Ftbl; JV Wt Lftg; Hon Roll; JETS Awd; Vet.

GUTIERREZ, JOSE J; Edison HS; Fresno, CA; (1); JV Bsbl; Intrml Bsktbl; Intrml Ftbl; Cit Awd; High Hon Roll; Hon Roll; Chrch Invlvmnt Scrptr Rdr; Sprts Babe Ruth, All Strs; Comp Bus Admn.

GUTIERREZ, JOSE J; Porterville HS; Porterville, CA; (3); Church Yth Grp; English Clb; Hosp Aide; Math Clb; Science Clb; Spanish Clb; Cit Awd; Hon Roll; Fresno ST U; Engrng.

GUTIERREZ, JOSE R; Sierra Vista HS; Baldwin Park, CA; (1); 10/450; Co-Ed Yrbk; Ftbl; Wt Lftg; Hon Roll; Gftd & Tlntd Ed Stu; Ucla; Med.

GUTIERREZ, JUDITH; Garfield HS; Los Angeles, CA; (2); Church Yth Grp; Computer Clb; Off Soph Cls; Magnet Pgm; Math.

GUTIERREZ, KAREN; Sacred Heart Cathedral HS; San Francisco, CA; (1); Church Yth Grp; GAA; Chorus; Church Choir; Off Frsh Cls; Bsktbl; Score Keeper; Sftbl; Vllybl; Hon Roll; MVP Vllybl; Cls Spirit Cmmssnr; Stanford U; Obstetrics.

GUTIERREZ, LAURA; Rio Mesa HS; Oxnard, CA; (3).

GUTIERREZ, LISA; Mercy HS; San Bruno, CA; (4); Church Yth Grp; GAA; Intnl Clb; Variety Show; Sec Treas Soph Cls; Sec Stu Cncl; Vllybl; High Hon Roll; Spanish NHS; CSF; UC Santa Barbara.

GUTIERREZ, LISA G; Gonzales HS; Soledad, CA; (2); Capt Drill Tm; MA Inst Of Tech; Indstrl Tech.

GUTIERREZ, LORETTA; Hanford HS; Hanford, CA; (4); 42/410; Church Yth Grp; Rep Drama Clb; FFA; Thesps; School Play; Stage Crew; Rep Jr Cls; Rep Sr Cls; High Hon Roll; Lion Awd; GPA Excllnc; Wntr Ct Prncss; CA Polytech; Chem.

GUTIERREZ, LUIS A; La Habra HS; La Habra, CA; (4); 12/334; Boy Scts; Science Clb; High Hon Roll; Hon Roll; Top 100 Stu Awd; CSF; Stu Mnth Eco; CA ST Polytech U; Elec Engr.

GUTIERREZ, M; Burlingame HS; Hillsborough, CA; (1); Church Yth Grp; Drama Clb; Band; Mrchg Band; Pep Band; Bsbl; Ftbl; Socr; U CA Santa Barbara; Atty.

GUTIERREZ, MARCELA; Roosevelt HS; Los Angeles, CA; (3); Hon Roll.

GUTIERREZ, MARCO A; Richmond HS; San Pablo, CA; (2); Bsbl Cards, Comic Books; Bus.

GUTIERREZ, MARIA D; Baldwin Park HS; Baldwin Park, CA; (2); Science Clb; Spanish Clb; Hon Roll; Cmmnctns.

GUTIERREZ, MARIA P; Granada Hills HS; Los Angeles, CA; (2); Letterman Clb; Spanish Clb; Stu Cncl; Cit Awd; High Hon Roll; Hon Roll; Opt Clb Awd; USC; Law.

GUTIERREZ, MARTHA E; St Genevieve HS; Panorama City, CA; (4); Hosp Aide; Pep Clb; Science Clb; SADD; Drill Tm; Flag Corp; NEDT Awd; Smmr Camp Cnslr; Miss Teen Pgnt Cntstnt; CA ST U Northridge; Med.

GUTIERREZ, MARY; Independence HS; San Jose, CA; (4); 21/825; Church Yth Grp; Cmnty Wkr; Teachers Aide; Rep Jr Cls; Rep Sr Cls; Hon Roll; CSF; Hacer/Mc Donalds Schlrshp; UC Santa Cruz; Psych.

GUTIERREZ, MATTHEW A; Whitney HS; Cerritos, CA; (1); Hon Roll; Bus.

GUTIERREZ, MELISSA M; Chino HS; Ontario, CA; (2); Church Yth Grp; Ski Clb; Stu Cncl; JV Capt Socr; High Hon Roll; Silver Spur Awd In Bio; Jrnlst.

GUTIERREZ, MELISSA MARIE; Dinuba HS; Dinuba, CA; (3); Church Yth Grp; Cmnty Wkr; High Hon Roll; Hon Roll; Prfct Atten Awd; Awds-Phys Sci, Cnsmr Ec, Engl B, U S Hstry, Meal Mgt 90; Don Estes Cosmotology; Csmtlgy.

GUTIERREZ, MICAELA V; Santa Teresa HS; San Jose, CA; (3); 8/480; Service Clb; Speech Tm; Jazz Band; Stu Cncl; NHS; Rotary Awd; Voice Dem Awd; Church Yth Grp; Cmnty Wkr; French Clb; CSF Secy; US Acad Dcthln Cmptn Hnrs Lvl; Phlsphy Clb Pres; Stanford U; Pre-Law.

GUTIERREZ, MIRELLA; Pasadena HS; Pasadena, CA; (1); MECHA & LASA Clb For Hispanics; Hlpng The Hmlss Clb-Fndrsr; Sec.

GUTIERREZ, MONICA; Bullard HS; Fresno, CA; (2); Key Clb; Bullard; Telecommnctns.

GUTIERREZ, NOEMI; Alisal HS; Salinas, CA; (3); Church Yth Grp; Treas French Clb; Hist Stu Cncl; High Hon Roll; Hon Roll; Schl Cnflct Resolution Tm ; CSF; Advncd Plcmnt Clb; Big Buddy Pgm; GATE Educ Clb; Oral Roberts U; Elem Educ.

GUTIERREZ, PATRICIA A; Milpitas HS; Milpitas, CA; (1); Hon Roll; Math/Engrng/Sci/Achvt-MESA.

GUTIERREZ, ROSA A; Baldwin Park HS; Baldwin Park, CA; (2); Var Swmmng; Intrml Mgr Vllybl; Hon Roll.

GUTIERREZ, RUBY; Workman HS; West Covina, CA; (2); Chorus; Comp.

GUTIERREZ, SAL; Casa Grande HS; Petaluma, CA; (1); 84/295; AZ U; Engr.

GUTIERREZ, SERGIO HENRY; Phillip & Sala Burton Academic HS; San Francisco, CA; (3); Computer Clb; English Clb; Science Clb; Lit Mag; Cit Awd; High Hon Roll; Hon Roll; Rotary Awd; Bus Camp; Acad Fncng; AP US His Exmntn; UC Berkeley; Physics.

GUTIERREZ, STACY L; Los Alamitos HS; Los Alamitos, CA; (3); Pep Clb; Chorus; School Musical; Cheerldng; Pom Pon; Hon Roll; Orange Cnty HS Of Arts Dance Dept; Won Miss Los Alamitos Bty Pgnt; Med.

GUTIERREZ, SUSAN L; Dinuba HS; Dinuba, CA; (3); 8/183; Chorus; Hon Roll; Keywanettes; Bus.

GUTIERREZ, SYLVIA M; Carpinteria HS; Carpinteria, CA; (3); Office Aide; Teachers Aide; Drill Tm; Flag Corp; Cit Awd; Hon Roll; Masonic Awd; Engl; Frnch; Sci; Home Ec; Stu Of Mo; Westmont Coll; Bus.

GUTIERREZ, TERRI; Mater Dei HS; Santa Ana, CA; (2); JV Trk; Pres Schlr; 2nd Hnrs, Hnrs & High Hnrs Awds.

GUTIERREZ, TRISHA A; Vacaville HS; Vacaville, CA; (3); Band; Mrchg Band; Var Cheerldng; Powder Puff Ftbl; Hon Roll; Jr NHS; Sftbl; Chrldng Sqd Coach; U Of Southern CA; Bus.

GUTIERREZ, VERONICA; Westminster HS; Westminster, CA; (2); Model UN; Teachers Aide; Cit Awd.

GUTING, TRISH; Sacramento Country Day Schl; Sacramento, CA; (1); Dance Clb; Rptr Yrbk; Var Bsktbl; Var Vllybl; Hon Roll; Merit Schlrshp.

GUTMAN, BRIAN R; Rim Of The World HS; Blue Jay, CA; (2); Ftbl; Wt Lftg; Prfct Atten Awd; Crafton JC; Fire Sci.

GUTNIK, VADIM; University HS; Irvine, CA; (4); 1/500; Pres Chess Clb; Math Tm; Office Aide; Pres Science Clb; JV Trk; JV Wrstlng; Hon Roll; Ntl Merit SF; Sal; Acdmc Decthln; Engrng.

GUTRIDGE, GINO; Christian Center HS; Antioch, CA; (4); 2/9; Church Yth Grp; Drama Clb; Letterman Clb; Pep Clb; SADD; Varsity Clb; Band; Church Choir; School Play; Variety Show; Mmission Grnfld 87; Mexico 88-90; CIF Cntrl Cst Sctn Acad/Athltc Achvmnt Awd; Chrcy Yth Cncl Mem; Bethany Bible Coll; Pstrl.

GUTSCH, MARLEA; Mt Whitney HS; Visalia, CA; (1); FFA; Pep Clb; Orch; Sec Soph Cls; Var Cheerldng; High Hon Roll; St Schlr; Tulare Cty Farm Bureau Intern Pgm; FFA Smart Kid Awd; Stanford; Med.

GUTTSCHUSS, HEIDI A; Rio Linda Acad; Placerville, CA; (3); Co-Capt Church Yth Grp; Ski Clb; Band; Chorus; Church Choir; School Musical; School Play; Variety Show; Off Jr Cls; Pacific Union Coll; Spec Ed.

GUTTY, EDWIN J; Pittsburg HS; Pittsburg, CA; (3); Computer Clb; FBLA; Teachers Aide; Cit Awd.

GUY, CHRISTA; Sonora HS; La Habra, CA; (4); Church Yth Grp; Library Aide; Spanish Clb; Teachers Aide; Lit Mag; Swmmng; Hon Roll; Pres Acad Fit Awd; CA ST U Fullerton; Early Chld.

GUY, CHRISTINE M; St Genevieve HS; Arleta, CA; (2); Church Yth Grp; Drama Clb; JV Bsbl; Hon Roll; Fndtn For Schlstc Advncmnt; U San Diego; Acctng.

GUY, DUSTIN C; Saint Bernard HS; Eureka, CA; (2); JV Var Crs Cntry; JV Trk; High Hon Roll; Pres Acad Fit Awd; Outstndng Achvt Awd-Bio & Math Hero Algb II; Schlr Athl Awd; CA Schlrshp Fed; Accntng.

GUY, NICOLLE M; Del Campo HS; Fair Oaks, CA; (3); 23/446; Rptr Nwsp; Ed VP Lit Mag; Friday Night Live 89; CSF 88-90; Stu For Soc Responsibility 89; Grad Usher 90; CA U; Graphic Dsgn.

GUYER, BENJI S; Glendale HS; Glendale, CA; (2); Boy Scts; Church Yth Grp; Drama Clb; Letterman Clb; Ski Clb; School Play; Var L Swmmng; Hon Roll; Vrsty Wtr Polo; City Spnsrd Ice Hcky; Athlt Wk Swm 89-90.

GUYER, TRAVIS D; Turlock HS; Turlock, CA; (2); 81/800; Bsbl; Ftbl; Wt Lftg; JV Wrstlng; Hon Roll.

GUYTON, BENJAMIN L; Elk Grove HS; Elk Grove, CA; (2); 50/531; Debate Tm; Math Clb; Math Tm; Model UN; Band; Mrchg Band; Pep Band; Hon Roll; NHS; JR Statesmn Of Amer; John Hopkins U Rgnl Awd For Math; Acad Excllnc Awd Golden ST Exam.

GUZ, GABRIELLE; Desert Christian HS; Lancaster, CA; (2); 3/20; Church Yth Grp; Crs Cntry; Cit Awd; High Hon Roll; Hon Roll; Awanas Clb LIT; US Air Frc Acad; Astronaut.

GUZMAN, AARON N; Lemoore HS; Lemoore, CA; (2); Church Yth Grp; Var Bsbl; JV Bsktbl; JV Ftbl; Contntl Amature Bsbl Assn; Sting Slct Sccr Tm; Toronto Blue Jays; UCLA; Bus Admin.

GUZMAN, ANA M; North Hollywood HS; North Hollywood, CA; (3); Orch; Ed Nwsp; High Hon Roll; Pres Schlr; Law.

GUZMAN, ANDRE E; Redland HS; Mentone, CA; (2); Cmnty Wkr; Teachers Aide; School Play; JV Bsbl; JV Bsktbl; Ftbl; Trk; Wt Lftg; USC; Elec Engr.

GUZMAN, ANDREA M; Calvary Baptist HS; Fairfield, CA; (3); Church Yth Grp; Pep Clb; Church Choir; Bsktbl; Var Stat Cheerldng; Sftbl; Trk; Var Co-Capt Vllybl; Hon Roll; Prfct Atten Awd; Tri-St Music Comptn-Piano/Vcl; Grphc Dsgn.

GUZMAN, ANGELICA M; Bonita Vista HS; Chula Vista, CA; (3); Cmnty Wkr; Pep Clb; Cit Awd; High Hon Roll; Hon Roll; CSF; U Southern CA; Pre-Med.

GUZMAN, CECILIA M; Ramona HS; Ramona, CA; (3); 10/280; FBLA; JV Sftbl; JV Vllybl; Cit Awd; Hon Roll; Amnesty Intl; U Of Sthrn CA; Bus Admin.

GUZMAN, CYNTHIA; Bloomington HS; Bloomington, CA; (4); 7/189; Sec Key Clb; Office Aide; Pep Clb; Spanish Clb; Mgr(s); High Hon Roll; VP NHS; Friday Night Live; Riverside CC; Comm.

GUZMAN, DAVID; Alemany HS; Mission Hills, CA; (2); Ftbl; Coll Of The Canyons; Plc Ofcr.

GUZMAN, DAVID; Del Campo HS; Fair Oaks, CA; (4); 10/450; Math Tm; Office Aide; School Play; Rptr Yrbk; NHS; Mesa Earthwatch Explrtn Awd; Natl Hispanic Schlr Awd Semi Fnlst; Stanford U; Elec Engrng.

GUZMAN, ELIUTH L; Firebaugh HS; Firebaugh, CA; (4); Pep Clb; Rep Soph Cls; Sec Jr Cls; Rep Sr Cls; Rep Stu Cncl; Cheerldng; Pom Pon; Engl Hnrs Cls; Engl Awd; Fresno ST; Liberal Studies.

GUZMAN, ELIZA; St Genevieve HS; San Fernando, CA; (3); Pep Clb; SADD; Off Jr Cls; Bsbl; Var Cheerldng; Score Keeper; Loyola Marymount U.

GUZMAN, FRANCISCO J; Le Grand HS; Le Grand, CA; (4); Drama Clb; Spanish Clb; Teachers Aide; Stage Crew; Ftbl; Drwng; Merced Coll; Law Enfrcmnt.

GUZMAN, FRANCISCO J; St Paul HS; Norwalk, CA; (3); 1/300; Sec Debate Tm; French Clb; NFL; Sec Speech Tm; Ed Nwsp; Rep Sr Cls; French Hon Soc; High Hon Roll; NHS; Ntl Merit Ltr; CA Spch Tourn St Semifinalist; Engl.

GUZMAN, IRMA KATHY; Dixon HS; Dixon, CA; (2); Intnl Clb; Color Guard; Vllybl; Hon Roll; U Of CA Davis; Chld Psych.

GUZMAN, ISELA; Alemany HS; Sylmar, CA; (2); UCLA.

GUZMAN, JEANNE A; St Joseph HS; La Mirada, CA; (2); 11/196; Church Yth Grp; Cmnty Wkr; Drama Clb; Key Clb; Science Clb; Spanish Clb; SADD; High Hon Roll; Hon Roll; Prfct Atten Awd; CSF; UC Irvine; Med.

GUZMAN, JENNA RUTH S; Polythecnic HS; N Hollywood, CA; (2); Spanish Clb; Orch; Hon Roll; Prfct Atten Awd; CSF; CJSF; CSUN; Acctng.

GUZMAN, JESUS; St Genevieve HS; San Fernando, CA; (4); 5/159; Pep Clb; Spanish Clb; JV Vllybl; Hon Roll; Prfct Atten Awd; U CA San Diego; Bus.

GUZMAN, LORENA A; Schurr HS; Montebello, CA; (2); Varsity Clb; Var Crs Cntry; Var Trk; Hon Roll; Comp Pgmr.

GUZMAN, MARIA M; East Bakersfield HS; Bakersfield, CA; (2); Church Yth Grp; JA; Latin Clb; Teachers Aide; Hon Roll; Santa Barbara; Pediatric.

GUZMAN, MARISELA; Our Lady Of Loretto Bishop C; Los Angeles, CA; (3); Cmnty Wkr; French Clb; Intnl Clb; Spanish Clb; High Hon Roll; Hon Roll; Prfct Atten Awd; Bus Grls Assn; Princpls Schlrshp Awd; UCLA; Bus Admin.

GUZMAN, MARTIN; Salinas HS; Salinas, CA; (3); Phy.

GUZMAN, MARY LINDA; Santa Barbara HS; Santa Barbara, CA; (4); 75/475; Hosp Aide; Band; Var Capt Cheerldng; Var Sftbl; Cit Awd; High Hon Roll; Hon Roll; NHS; Opt Clb Awd; Pres Acad Fit Awd; Tony Gilbert-Athlete-Citizenship Award; UCLA; Psychology.

GUZMAN, MICHAEL V; St Bernard HS; El Segundo, CA; (3); Church Yth Grp; Var Crs Cntry; Law Enforcement.

GUZMAN, MONICA L; Chino HS; Chino, CA; (2); Spanish Clb; Score Keeper; JV Vllybl; Cit Awd; High Hon Roll; Hon Roll; Prfct Atten Awd; Pres Schlr; Acad Booster Clb Awd; Acad Excllnt Awd; Bus.

GUZMAN, PRISCILLA M; Duncan Polytechnical HS; Fresno, CA; (2); Teachers Aide; Cit Awd; Fri Night Live; Air Trffc Cntrllr.

GUZMAN, RITA; Winters HS; Winters, CA; (3); Ski Clb; SADD; Chorus; Sftbl; Vllybl; Hon Roll; Intr Decoratng.

GUZMAN, SARAH; Central Union HS; El Centro, CA; (1); Church Yth Grp; French Clb; Opt Clb Awd; Psycht.

GUZMAN, VILMA G; Glendale HS; Glendale, CA; (4); 145/690; Church Yth Grp; Teachers Aide; Chorus; Church Choir; Prfct Atten Awd; Nrs Wlth Fare; Coord Evangelism Chrch Yth Group; Discipleship Teacher Jr Kids; Med Asst Dip; Glendale Coll; Nrs.

GUZMON, ISAAC C; Dublin HS; Dublin, CA; (3); Chess Clb; Dance Clb; FBLA; Library Aide; Teachers Aide; School Musical; UCLA; Hstry Teacher.

GUZZETTA, GINA; USD HS; Spring Valley, CA; (4); 83/298; Variety Show; JV Bsktbl; JV Var Cheerldng; Pres Acad Fit Awd; Sons Italy Acad Schlrshp; Santa Clara U; Civil Engrng.

GWINNUP, CHRISTINE; Amos Alonzo Stagg HS; Stockton, CA; (3); Church Yth Grp; Key Clb; Pep Clb; Variety Show; Pres Soph Cls; Cheerldng; Var Socr; JV Var Sftbl; JV Vllybl; High Hon Roll; All Leag 1st Sccr Most Vlbl Awd; Coaches Awd V Sftbl; Coachs Awd Jv Sftbl; Med.

GWINNUP, MISTI; Amos Alonzo Stagg HS; Stockton, CA; (2); Pep Clb; Speech Tm; Variety Show; Sec Frsh Cls; Cheerldng; Var Socr; Var JV Sftbl; JV Vllybl; Stat Wrstlng; High Hon Roll; Jobs Dghtrs; Hnrb Mntn All Leag Sccr 89-90; Law.

GWYNNE, KENDRA C; Novato HS; Novato, CA; (1); School Musical; School Play; Hon Roll; Jobs Dghtrs; Marine Bio.

GYORGY, ALINA; Glendale HS; Glendale, CA; (4); Pres Acad Fit Awd; CSF; Distngshd Grad Impact Pgm; Cert Spcl Achvt Frnch Lang; Glendale Coll; Med.

HA, ANN; San Lorenzo HS; Hayward, CA; (4); 16/200; Church Yth Grp; Hon Roll; Pres Acad Fit Awd; CSF; Asian Clb; CA ST Hayward; Bus.

HA, ANN S; John F Kennedy HS; La Palma, CA; (3); Church Yth Grp; FBLA; Capt Color Guard; Hon Roll; Cal Tech; Graphic Dsgnr.

HA, BINH; Baldwin Park HS; Baldwin Park, CA; (1).

HA, BINH L; Lowell HS; San Francisco, CA; (3); Office Aide; Teachers Aide; School Musical; Stage Crew; Schl Spirit Rally; Winterfaire 89; Chinese & Vllybl Clubs; UC Davis; Tchng.

HA, CHI KIM; Skyline HS; Oakland, CA; (4); 9/580; Sec Church Yth Grp; Treas German Clb; Intnl Clb; Key Clb; Math Clb; Service Clb; High Hon Roll; Hon Roll; NHS; Golden St Exam Algebra, Geom Hnrs; CA Schlrshp Fed Mem; 2 Schlrshp Awd Acad Achvt 87, 88; UC Davis; Hlth Sci.

HA, HANG T; Rancho Alamitos HS; Garden Grove, CA; (3); #11 In Class; Intnl Clb; Science Clb; Teachers Aide; Var High Hon Roll; Var Hon Roll; Engl & Spnsh Valedictorian; UC Irvine; Bus.

HA, KIM Q; Rosemead HS; San Gabriel, CA; (3); FBLA; Intnl Clb; Prfct Atten Awd; Pres Acad Fit Awd; Futurist Clb; Dentist.

HA, QUAN L; Troy HS; Fullerton, CA; (2); 19/329; JV Ftbl; JV Trk; Cit Awd; High Hon Roll; Rotary Awd; GA Tech; Engr.

HA, QUY T; Independence HS; San Jose, CA; (3).

HA, SIMON Y; Rowland HS; Rowland Hts, CA; (2); Church Yth Grp; Science Clb; SADD; Rep Soph Cls; JV Ftbl; Wt Lftg; High Hon Roll; Hon Roll; GSE Schl Rcgntn; Eng.

HA, THANH; Oakland Technical HS; Oakland, CA; (2); Model UN; Rptr Nwsp; High Hon Roll; Oakland Est Bay Symphny.

HA, THOAI V; Orange HS; Orange, CA; (3); French Clb; Key Clb; Chorus; Rep Frsh Cls; VP Soph Cls; Sec Jr Cls; Var Swmmng; High Hon Roll; Hon Roll; NHS; CSF; Natl Yth Ldrs Cngrssnl Schlr Rep.

HA, THUAN Q; Pacifica HS; Garden Grv, CA; (3); Church Yth Grp; Computer Clb; Debate Tm; Spanish Clb; Teachers Aide; Temple Yth Grp; Treas Sr Cls; JV Bsktbl; L Var Trk; JV Vllybl; UCI; Bio.

HAAKONSON, CHRISTINE M; Red Bluff Union HS; Red Bluff, CA; (2); Band; Mrchg Band; Pep Band; School Musical; JV Swmmng; Prfct Atten Awd; Mst Outstndng Frosh Muscn; Hnr Band; Muscn.

HAAN, ERIC B; Burroughs HS; Ridgecrest, CA; (3); Church Yth Grp; Ski Clb; Varsity Clb; Var Socr; Var Trk; Bio.

HAAR, CHARLA D; Delano HS; Delano, CA; (3); Band; Mrchg Band; Pep Band; Hon Roll; Cert Laubach Lit Actn Tutor.

HAARS, KERI; Sequoia HS; San Carlos, CA; (4); Church Yth Grp; VP Debate Tm; Teachers Aide; Ed Yrbk; Stu Cncl; Socr; Trk; Jr Statesmens Logistics; Unsung Hero Schlsp; San Jose ST U; Psych.

HAAS, BRETT D; Bellarmine College Prep; Ben Lomond, CA; (3); 30/300; Cmnty Wkr; Service Clb; Stat Bsbl; Intrml Bsktbl; Intrml Ftbl; YMCA Camp Sci Cnlsr; Forgn Exchng Stu In Mexico; Aerospc Engr.

HAAS, CHRISTY R; Selma HS; Selma, CA; (4); 2/191; FCA; SADD; School Play; Yrbk; Treas Stu Cncl; Var JV Vllybl; Bausch & Lomb Sci Awd; Sal; Drama Clb; Office Aide; Bears Head Awd; Bank Am Math/Sci Plaque Wnnr; Yng Life Wild Life Ldr; Claremont Mc Kenna Clg; Govmnt.

HAAS, HEATHER; Marina HS; Huntington Bch, CA; (1); JCL; Latin Clb; Stat Swmmng; Psych.

HAAS, JAMES G; Lindsay HS; Lindsay, CA; (2); 4-H; JV Bsbl; Bsktbl; Ftbl; Cmnty Wkr; 4-H Awd; Hon Roll; Kiwanis Awd; Frsno ST; Acctg.

HAAS, JENNIFER M; Forest Lake Christian Schl; Grass Valley, CA; (2); 4-H; GAA; Letterman Clb; Teachers Aide; Varsity Clb; Chorus; Var L Bsktbl; Var Capt Cheerldng; Var L Sftbl; Var L Trk; Sacramento ST; Crmnl Justc.

HAAS, JULIE ANN; Neward Memorial HS; Newark, CA; (3); 51/355; Girl Scts; Spanish Clb; SADD; Co-Ed Yrbk; Var JV Crs Cntry; Var Capt Swmmng; Hon Roll; Interact Club Mem, Pres 90-91; Bus Finance.

HAAS, KATHERINE B; Grossmont HS; El Cajon, CA; (1); Sec Church Yth Grp; Ski Clb; AYSO Sccr; LDS Vlybl; LDS Bsktbl; BYU; Pdtrcn.

HAAS, SAMANTHA A; Apple Valley HS; Apple Valley, CA; (3); FFA; Band; Mrchg Band; US Pony Clb; Nrsng.

HAAS, STEPHANIE L; San Gorgonio HS; Highland, CA; (3); English Clb; GAA; JA; Pres Q&S; Varsity Clb; Ed Yrbk; Rep Frsh Cls; Cheerldng; Var Swmmng; Cit Awd; Amer Lgn Awd Ctzn Of Yr; Sherriffs Dept War On Crime Cmmssn Outstndg Ctzn; Jr Miss Amer Fnlst; UCSD; Law Enfrcmnt.

HAASE, TIMOTHY R; Sierra Vista HS; Baldwin Park, CA; (1); Chess Clb; Cmnty Wkr; Math Clb; Science Clb; Band; Mrchg Band; Ftbl; Score Keeper; Friday Nite Live; CA ST Fullerton; Music Drctr.

HABAL, ANTHONY; Hueneme HS; Port Hueneme, CA; (4); Debate Tm; Band; Drm Mjr(t); Jazz Band; Mrchg Band; High Hon Roll; Hon Roll; UCLA; Music.

HABER, MICHAEL G; Morro Bay HS; Los Osos, CA; (3); 2/220; Math Tm; Teachers Aide; JV Bsktbl; JV Var Tennis; Intrml Trk; High Hon Roll; Hon Roll; Coaches Awd Tennis; Cal Poly; Engrng.

HABERBERGER, CAITLIN; Piedmont HS; Piedmont, CA; (4); Cmnty Wkr; SADD; Acpl Chr; Orch; Var Cheerldng; Pres Acad Fit Awd; St Schlr; Crew; CT Coll.

HABERMAN, TERESA; San Leandro HS; San Leandro, CA; (2); Church Yth Grp; Drama Clb; Intnl Clb; Pep Clb; Quiz Bowl; Ski Clb; Var Cheerldng; Hon Roll; UCLA; Acting.

HABIB, TONY; Glendale HS; Glendale, CA; (2); Alg Golden St Exam Hnrs; Mock Trial; CA-POLY Romona; Arch.

HABIBI, MARJAN MIA; Dana Hills HS; Laguna Niguel, CA; (4); Art Clb; Computer Clb; FHA; Math Clb; Ski Clb; Teachers Aide; Nwsp; Off Sr Cls; Tennis; NEDT Awd.

HACHA, VERONICA; Bishop Amat HS; La Puente, CA; (3); Spanish Clb; Color Guard; Var L Sftbl; Work Exprnc Prog; U San Diego; Psych.

HACK, JOHN; Turlock HS; Turlock, CA; (2); 19/650; VP Rptr FFA; German Clb; Hon Roll; Pres Acad Fit Awd; Rotary Awd; ST FFA Cnvntn; Roy Baptista Memrl Schlrshp; Wells Fargo Achvmnt Awd; Fresno ST; Ag.

HACKENBERGER, LISBETH A; Louisville HS; Canoga Park, CA; (4); 1/90; Art Clb; Hosp Aide; Scholastic Bowl; Service Clb; School Musical; School Play; Stage Crew; Rptr Nwsp; High Hon Roll; Hon Roll; Prom Commtte San Franando Vlly Otstndng Yth Awd; CA Schlrshp Fed; Tandy Tech Schlr; Robert C Byrd Hnrs; UC Berkeley; Med.

HACKETHAL, VERONICA; Vivian Webb Schl; Rialto, CA; (4); 1/45; Orch; Trk; Vllybl; Hon Roll; Pres Acad Fit Awd; Rotary Awd; Val; Natl HS Hnr Orch; All St HS Hnr Orch; Dorm Cnslr; Harvard U; Cmmnctns.

HACKETT, PATRICK A; Southwestern Acad; Bradbury, CA; (3); Var Mgr(s); JV Vllybl; Hon Roll; Rotary Awd; Rotary Yth Ldrshp Awd; CA Poly Pomona; Phrmcy.

HACKETT, TIFFANY; Los Gatos HS; Los Gatos, CA; (4); 37/390; Spanish Clb; Variety Show; Intrml Powder Puff Ftbl; JV Var Swmmng; Var Trk; High Hon Roll; Hon Roll; Ntl Hspnc Schlr Awd; Yth Advsry Cmmsn; Exchng Stu Spain 89.

HACKIM, JULIE; Argonaut HS; Ione, CA; (3); Church Yth Grp; Letterman Clb; Band; Mrchg Band; Yrbk; Pres Frsh Cls; Pres Jr Cls; Stu Cncl; Cheerldng; Hon Roll; GSE Schlrshp High Hnr Algebra & Geometry; Site Cncl Cmmtte; Sn Dgo ST U; Bio.

HACKLER, JENNA M; Fairfield HS; Suisun City, CA; (2); Drama Clb; Letterman Clb; Red Cross Aide; JV Socr; Var Trk; Hon Roll; NHS; Sci.

HADA, LEA M; Dana Hills HS; Laguna Niguel, CA; (2); Socr; MVP Awd Sccr Tm; Schlr Athlte Awd Mntng 4.0 Avg Thru Sccr Seasn; Stu Mnth Awd Bio; UCLA.

HADAEGH, PANTEA; Palm Springs HS; Desert Hot Spring, CA; (2); Debate Tm; French Clb; Hosp Aide; Office Aide; High Hon Roll; Hon Roll; Prfct Atten Awd; Outside Schl Tnns Cls; Plaque Wnnr For Frnch Silver Sands Awd; Advncd Math Fnlst Slvr Sands Awd; CA Inst Of Tech; Arspc Engrng.

HADAYA, BASSEL; Paraclete HS; Lancaster, CA; (4); 1/128; Church Yth Grp; Debate Tm; Hosp Aide; Key Clb; Quiz Bowl; Rep Stu Cncl; High Hon Roll; NHS; NEDT Awd; Yth Mnth Sept; CSF Pres; Med.

HADDAD, CHRISTIAN EDWARD; Poway HS; Poway, CA; (3); 16/761; Church Yth Grp; VP German Clb; Ed Lit Mag; JV Ftbl; JV Trk; High Hon Roll; Jr NHS; NHS; CSF; Germ Ntl Hon Soc; Civil Air Patrol Aux; Military Acad; Aero Engr.

HADDAD, LILLY D; Canyon HS; Canyon Country, CA; (4); Cmnty Wkr; Debate Tm; Drama Clb; FBLA; Spanish Clb; Ed Nwsp; Var JV Tennis; High Hon Roll; NHS; Spanish NHS; CSF Schlrshp; CA Poly; Bus Admin.

HADDAD, MORAN; Sherman Oaks CES; Canoga Park, CA; (3); Chess Clb; Teachers Aide; L Sftbl; L Tennis; Hon Roll; High Hnrs Alg I & Geom Golden St Exm; All Leag Tennis Tm; Math.

HADDAD, SALIMAH H; Chino HS; Chino Hills, CA; (3); Hist FHA; VP Hosp Aide; Spanish Clb; High Hon Roll; Hon Roll; Prfct Atten Awd; JV Badmnton; 90 Hrs Cmnty Svc; CSF; U CA Riverside; Genetics.

HADDOX, ERIC; Vacaville HS; Vacaville, CA; (3); Church Yth Grp; Teachers Aide; Church Choir; Nwsp; Rep Frsh Cls; Mbr Philosophy Clb; Solano Coll; Mstrs Of Divinity.

HADJES, DIANA; Fellowship Schl; Ridgecrest, CA; (3); 1/2; 4-H; Yrbk; Bsktbl; Trk; Vllybl; High Hon Roll; Pny Clb; Eqstrn; Bus.

HAEFELE, MARK J; River City HS; W Sacramento, CA; (4); 4/150; Church Yth Grp; Pres JA; Score Keeper; Tennis; Stat Vllybl; Hon Roll; Acad Dcthln MVP 89; Mem Undefeated Bad Boy Club Vlybl Div 89; CSF Lifetime Mem; Aspiring Poet; U CA Davis; Zool.

HAEHN, MEREDETH; Fountain Valley HS; Fountain Valley, CA; (2); Spanish Clb; Flag Corp; JV Crs Cntry; JV Trk; High Hon Roll; San Diego ST U; Gntc Cnslr.

HAEMMERLE, HEATHER; Inland Christian Schl; Rialto, CA; (1); 1/17; Church Yth Grp; Church Choir; School Play; Var Sftbl; Var L Vllybl; High Hon Roll; Cedarville Coll.

HAFALIA, APRIL J A; Lowell HS; San Francisco, CA; (3); Dance Clb; Varsity Clb; Variety Show; Var Gym; Vlntr Cchng Elem Kid Sprts; Karate; Berkley; OB/Gyn.

HAFALIA, MICHAEL E; Sacred Heart Cathedral HS; Daly City, CA; (1); Church Yth Grp; Cmnty Wkr; Red Cross Aide; Capt Bsktbl; Hon Roll; Tae Kwon Do; Volunteer Coach; Prof Bsktbl Player.

HAFAR, BERT H; Happy Camp HS; Seiad Valley, CA; (4); 1/29; Cmnty Wkr; School Musical; Phtg Yrbk; Var Bsktbl; Var Crs Cntry; Var Trk; Cit Awd; High Hon Roll; Lion Awd; Prfct Atten Awd; Humboldt ST U; Biolgcl Sci.

HAFLE, MICHELLE R; Yosemite HS; Coarsegold, CA; (2); Church Yth Grp; Pep Clb; Rptr Nwsp; Pres Jr Cls; Cheerldng; Hon Roll; Santa Barbara U; Engl Profsr.

HAFNER, AMANDA M; Oakmont HS; Roseville, CA; (1); Dance Clb; Letterman Clb; Cheerldng; JV Capt Swmmng; Hon Roll; Friday Nite Live Club; Tennis; Voted Most Insprtnl For JV Swm Tm.

HAGADORN, WARREN L; Troy HS; Fullerton, CA; (2); Outstndng Achvt In Life Sci Cert Of Mrt; Teach.

HAGAN, KELLY L; Villa Park HS; Villa Park, CA; (2); Church Yth Grp; Key Clb; Rep Frsh Cls; Sec Soph Cls; Var Capt Socr; Var Trk; High Hon Roll; NHS; HOBY Ambssdr; Grls Clb Scr Team; Mssnry Wrk Mexico.

HAGAN, KENNETH A; Aptos HS; Watsonville, CA; (4); 62/260; Teachers Aide; JV Bsbl; Hon Roll; CSF; Outside Wrk Experne Pgm Awd; Prfency Cert Awd Acctng; San Jose ST U; Comp Acctng.

HAGAN, ZETHERINE F; John Glenn HS; Norwalk, CA; (2); Letterman Clb; Pres Soph Cls; L Bsktbl; L Trk; High Hon Roll; 1st Team Suburban All League; 2nd Team All CTF; Press Tlgrm Plyr Of Wk; USC; Pdtrcn.

HAGANS, DONNA L; Taft Union HS; Taft, CA; (3); 40/180; Pres Sec Key Clb; SADD; Varsity Clb; JV Var Bsktbl; Var Capt Crs Cntry; Var Swmmng; Var Capt Trk; High Hon Roll; Hon Roll; Soroptimist Intl Girl Of Achvt Awd; CA Coll System; Engl.

HAGE, MARY ELLEN; Gridley HS; Oroville, CA; (4); 6/107; Cmnty Wkr; 4-H; Spanish Clb; Teachers Aide; Variety Show; Hon Roll; NHS; Ntl Merit SF; Pres Acad Fit Awd; Fridy Nght Live Class Offcr Rep; U Of OR.

HAGEDORN, KIM M; El Dorado HS; Placentia, CA; (3); 46/317; Science Clb; Band; Mrchg Band; Cheerldng; High Hon Roll; NHS; CSF; Cal Poly Pomona; Accntng.

HAGEMAN, CATHERINE J; San Benito HS; Hollister, CA; (1); 19/465; Cmnty Wkr; Pep Clb; Ski Clb; JV Cheerldng; JV Tennis; High Hon Roll; Kiwanis Awd; CA Schlrshp Pgm; Prfct Attndnc 89-90; Med Sci.

HAGEMAN, REBECCA; Mojave HS; Mojave, CA; (2); 12/129; High Hon Roll; Hon Roll; CSF; Btcn.

HAGEMANN, KYLE W; Montgomery HS; Santa Rosa, CA; (3); Band; Mrchg Band; Orch; Pep Band; Hon Roll; Vet.

HAGEN, AMBER DAWN; Madison HS; San Diego, CA; (4); 24/368; Church Yth Grp; Drill Tm; Rep Stu Cncl; L Crs Cntry; L Trk; High Hon Roll; Prfct Atten Awd; Bio.

HAGEN, ERIC; Yosemite HS; Oakhurst, CA; (3); Church Yth Grp; Key Clb; Math Clb; Science Clb; Service Clb; SADD; Band; Jazz Band; Rptr Nwsp; JV Trk; Gldn St Schlr; PRIDE; Publc Reltns Ofcr & Altrnt Actvts Directr Campus Anti-Drug Clb; CA Schlrshp Fed; Music Tchr.

HAGEN, G DEAN; San Joaquin HS; Clovis, CA; (2); Key Clb; Spanish Clb; JV Bsbl; Var Wrstlng; 90-91 Key Clb-Lt Gov.

HAGEN, JAMES R; Marina HS; Huntington Beach, CA; (2); Church Yth Grp; JA; Latin Clb; Letterman Clb; Var Swmmng; Hon Roll; Piano; Chrch Actvts; Water Polo Tm; U CA; Sci.

HAGEN, MICHELE L; Clovis HS; Clovis, CA; (2); Church Yth Grp; SADD; Chorus; Fresno ST; Teacher.

HAGEN, PATRICK B; Burbank SR HS; Burbank, CA; (2); Boy Scts; Spanish Clb; Var L Crs Cntry; Var L Trk; High Hon Roll; Hon Roll; Pres Acad Fit Awd; Hghst Scr CAP Tst; Outstndng Stu Wk; AFA; Pilot.

HAGENBAUGH, BARBARA; Montgomery HS; Santa Rosa, CA; (3); 1/400; Cmnty Wkr; Drama Clb; Hosp Aide; Pep Clb; Pres Spanish Clb; Speech Tm; School Play; Ed Yrbk; Rep Frsh Cls; Capt Cheerldng; Work; Stu Rep Sch Site Cncl; Kids Day Steering Comm P R; Journ.

HAGER, DEBBIE L; Aptos HS; Watsonville, CA; (1); 58/396; 4-H; Service Clb; 4-H Awd; Hon Roll; UC Davis; Vet.

HAGER, KIMBERLY; Hoover HS; Fresno, CA; (2); Pep Clb; School Musical; Cheerldng; Tennis; Photo Clb; UCLA; Drma.

HAGER, SARAH E; Victor Valley HS; Victorville, CA; (4); 28/313; Church Yth Grp; Pres French Clb; Pep Clb; Ski Clb; Teachers Aide; Stat Pres Wrstlng; High Hon Roll; Hon Roll; CSF; Boston U; Psych.

HAGERTY, ALISA; Beyer HS; Modesto, CA; (3); Church Yth Grp; Debate Tm; NFL; Pep Clb; Speech Tm; Hon Roll; English.

HAGGARD, JESSICA M; Shasta HS; Redding, CA; (2); Church Yth Grp; Dance Clb; 4-H; Pep Clb; Drill Tm; School Play; JV Cheerldng; 4-H Awd; Hon Roll; IMACF Karate Chmpshp; Jazz Dncg; Shasta JC; RID Dsgntn.

HAGGENMILLER, TODD; Thousand Oaks HS; Thousand Oaks, CA; (3); 63/541; Church Yth Grp; U CA-SANTA Barbara; Engrng.

HAGINS, JASON D; San Benito HS; Hollister, CA; (3); 20/400; Scholastic Bowl; Co-Ed Nwsp; Treas Frsh Cls; JV Bsktbl; Intrml Ftbl; Journ.

HAGINS, JEDD A; Hilmar HS; Turlock, CA; (2); FFA; Hon Roll; Star Chptr Farmr 90; Outstndng Ag Mechnc 89; Cal Poly; Dsgn Engr.

HAGLE, CORA L; Turlock HS; Ceres, CA; (3); Church Yth Grp; FFA; Teachers Aide; Chorus; Church Choir; Wt Lftg; Hon Roll; Prfct Atten Awd; Awd Passing Smnry; Pres Yng Womens Chrch Org; Modesto JC; Social Worker.

HAGLE, DORA R; Turlock HS; Ceres, CA; (3); Church Yth Grp; FFA; Teachers Aide; Chorus; Church Choir; Wt Lftg; Hon Roll; Prfct Atten Awd; Awd Passng Semnry; Outstndng Ornamntl Hortcltre Exhbtn; Modesto JC.

HAGOOD, JENNIFER; Bakersfield HS; Bakersfield, CA; (4); Church Yth Grp; JA; Service Clb; SADD; Teachers Aide; Chorus; Variety Show; Powder Puff Ftbl; Hon Roll; CSF Gold Sealbearer; Humboldt ST U; Audiology.

HAGOPIAN, VICKY; Pasadena HS; Pasadena, CA; (3); Church Yth Grp; Nrsng.

HAHN, AARON; Sonoma Valley HS; Sonoma, CA; (2); 1/250; Cmnty Wkr; FBLA; Model UN; Varsity Clb; Var Tennis; Cit Awd; St Schlr; Golden St Exam 89; Geo With Honors; Med.

HAHN, CHRISTINA H; Whitney HS; Cerritos, CA; (2); Church Yth Grp; Cmnty Wkr; French Clb; FBLA; Hosp Aide; JA; Key Clb; Rep Nwsp.

HAHN, CINDY L; Hanford Union HS; Hanford, CA; (1); Art Clb; Cmnty Wkr; FBLA; Library Aide; High Hon Roll; Jr NHS; CA Schlrshp Fed; CA Poly San Luis Obispo; Engrn.

HAHN, DANNY I; Redlands HS; Redlands, CA; (3); Boy Scts; Debate Tm; FBLA; Key Clb; NFL; Service Clb; Speech Tm; School Play; Stage Crew; JV Swmmng; JV Water Polo; UC Berkeley; Pre-Law.

HAHN, JONG H; Bolsa Grande HS; Garden Grove, CA; (2); 2/377; Chess Clb; Church Yth Grp; French Clb; Latin Clb; Math Clb; Science Clb; Spanish Clb; Var Tennis; Hon Roll; Garden Grove Tennis Dbls League Final Wnnr; Bolsa Grande HS Sngles Table Tennis Trnmnt Wnnr; U Of CA Los Angeles.

HAHN, KAI-UWE; San Clemente HS; San Juan Capistra, CA; (1); Church Yth Grp; German Clb; Tennis; Wrstlng; Cit Awd; Bio.

HAHN, KYRA J; St Bernard HS; Los Angeles, CA; (3); Church Yth Grp; Cmnty Wkr; Chorus; Mgr(s); Score Keeper; Stat Vllybl; Mass Tele Commnctns.

HAHN, SHELLEY L; Lutheran HS Of San Diego; Lemon Grove, CA; (3); 7/21; Church Yth Grp; VP German Clb; Key Clb; Science Clb; Chorus; School Play; Var Bsktbl; Var Sftbl; JV Vllybl; Hon Roll; Equine Sci.

HAHNER, CELESTE; Christian Life HS; Rio Dell, CA; (2); Rep Church Yth Grp; Spanish Clb; Teachers Aide; Yrbk; Pres Soph Cls; Rep Stu Cncl; Hon Roll; Piano 88-90 Prvt Lssns; Bethany Bible Coll; Msc.

HAI, MUI; Lincoln HS; Los Angeles, CA; (4); Computer Clb; English Clb; Bsktbl.

HAID, TASHSA B; Orange Glen HS; Escondido, CA; (3); Hon Roll; NHS; Gldn Poet Awds 88-89; Slvr Poet Awd 90; Writer.

HAIDARY, AHMAD F; El Cajon Valley HS; El Cajon, CA; (3); 2/400; Chess Clb; Intnl Clb; Science Clb; Ed Yrbk; Ed Lit Mag; High Hon Roll; Lion Awd; Sal; Humn Rltns Clb VP & Pres; CSF Pres; Multi Cltrl Clb Treas; U Of CA San Diego; Doctor.

HAIDARY, FAZILA; El Cajon Valley HS; El Cajon, CA; (4); 6/350; English Clb; Ed Lit Mag; Elks Awd; Hon Roll; Hmn Rltns Clb Pres; CSF; Mltcltrl Clb Secy; UCSD; Mdcn.

HAIGHT, DESIREE R; Yreka Union HS; Montague, CA; (3); 8/127; Dance Clb; Pres 4-H; Scholastic Bowl; Spanish Clb; Band; Mrchg Band; Pep Band; Intrml Powder Puff Ftbl; Var Capt Trk; 4-H Awd; Chef.

HAIGHT, KEVIN L; Willow Glen Educational Park HS; San Jose, CA; (2); #1 In Class; Hon Roll; Sci.

HAIGHT, MICHAEL; Maranatha Christian Academy HS; Irvine, CA; (1); Var L Swmmng; Stanford; Law.

HAIGLER, AMANDA D; Redwood Christian HS; Livermore, CA; (3); Church Yth Grp; Drama Clb; Teachers Aide; Varsity Clb; Chorus; Church Choir; School Play; Var Cheerldng; Stat Vllybl; Hon Roll; Point Loma; Phys Thrpy.

HAIGLER, ROBERT B; Mission San Jose HS; Fremont, CA; (1); Boy Scts; Chess Clb; Treas Frsh Cls; JV Swmmng; CSF; Hgh Hnrs-Geom Gldn St Exam; HS Ldrshp Cncl; Engrng.

HAIK, HURSH; Calvary Christian Acad; El Sobrante, CA; (2); 1/15; Church Yth Grp; Teachers Aide; School Play; Nwsp; Yrbk; High Hon Roll; Hon Roll; Stanford; Doctor.

HAILEY, LYTERES A; Barstown HS; Barstow, CA; (3); Church Yth Grp; Cmnty Wkr; Computer Clb; Dance Clb; Office Aide; Teachers Aide; Chorus; Church Choir; Drill Tm; School Play; Amer Educ Asst Cncl; Miss Teen Pgnt 6th Ms Photogenic; Bus Educ 3 Cert Awds; CSU Long Beach; Bus Comp.

HAIM, TOM P; San Rafael HS; San Rafael, CA; (3); 18/226; Spanish Clb; Band; Jazz Band; Pep Band; Bsktbl; Tennis; Hon Roll; CSF; Law.

HAIMAN, CHRIS A; Chico SR HS; Chico, CA; (4); 10/360; Am Leg Boys St; Letterman Clb; Spanish Clb; Varsity Clb; Band; Jazz Band; Pres Jr Cls; Pres Stu Cncl; JV Bsktbl; JV Var Ftbl; U C Berkeley; Genetics.

HAINES, AARON C; George Washington HS; San Francisco, CA; (3); Art Clb; Off Boy Scts; Church Yth Grp; Cmnty Wkr; English Clb; FBLA; Service Clb; JV Wrstlng; Hon Roll.

HAINES, THOMAS; Santa Teresa HS; San Jose, CA; (2); Var Diving; UC Santa Cruz; Bus.

HAIR, JENNIFER; Royal HS; Simi Valley, CA; (3); Church Yth Grp; Cmnty Wkr; SADD; Chorus; Church Choir; Music; Elem Ed.

HAIRGROVE, DEEANN; Mission College Prep; San Luis Obispo, CA; (3); Cmnty Wkr; French Clb; Teachers Aide; Ed Yrbk; Rep Stu Cncl; Hon Roll; Hmcmng Prncss; UCSD; Liberal Arts.

HAIRSTON, TOMIKA R; Paramount HS; Downey, CA; (3); Teachers Aide; Acpl Chr; Chorus; Church Choir; School Musical; School Play; Music Trphys; Cert In Music; AL ST; Prfrmng Arts.

HAIRSTON, VERONICA A; Grace M Davis HS; Modesto, CA; (3); Dntl Asst.

HAISUPA, APICHAI; Hiram Johnson HS; Sacramento, CA; (3); School Play; Rep Soph Cls; Var Bsbl; Var Socr; JV Wrstlng; Hon Roll; NHS; Pres Acad Fit Awd; Gldn St Exam Hnr Cert Geom; U Of CA Davis; Pre Med.

HAJEK, KRISTINA K; Jereann Bowman HS; Saugus, CA; (4); 3/150; Drama Clb; 4-H; Ed Yrbk; Stu Cncl; High Hon Roll; Hon Roll; Outstndng Eng & Yrbk Stu Awd At Grad; Acctpd Fashn Inst Dsgn & Mrchndsg 88; FIDM; Inter Dsgnr.

HAJJ, MARY J; Covina HS; Covina, CA; (2); Cmnty Wkr; French Clb; Hosp Aide; Library Aide; Chorus; Yrbk; Crs Cntry; Cit Awd; Alcyonians Grls Clb; Yth Vlntr Awd; Washington U; Med.

HAKALA, MARJA L; Miramonte HS; Orinda, CA; (3); Sec AFS; Latin Clb; Spanish Clb; Orch; JV Bsktbl; Var Crs Cntry; DAR Awd; Hon Roll; U Of California; Business Mgnt.

HAKIMI, FREDDY F; Foot Hill HS; Laguna Hills, CA; (3); Art Clb; Service Clb; Trk; Wrstlng.

HALBACH, KENDRA D; Clovis West HS; Fresno, CA; (3); Church Yth Grp; Cmnty Wkr; Intnl Clb; Pres Key Clb; Ski Clb; SADD; Varsity Clb; JV Crs Cntry; Var Swmmng; Var Tennis; Big Sisters Fersno; Arch.

HALCON, MARIA S; Alisal HS; Salinas, CA; (2); FBLA; Cheerldng; Powder Puff Ftbl; Score Keeper; Sftbl; ADAPT; UC Santa Barbara; Acctnt.

HALCON, MONICA; North Salinas HS; Salinas, CA; (3); Hosp Aide; Pep Clb; Science Clb; SADD; Yrbk; Var Trk; Cit Awd; High Hon Roll; Hon Roll; Hgh Hnrs Golden ST Exam Algebra; Engnrng.

HALDERMAN, KRISTA M; Modoc HS; Alturas, CA; (2); School Play; JV Crs Cntry; Var Trk; High Hon Roll; CSF; Engl.

HALE, DESIREE M; Notre Dame HS; San Jose, CA; (3); Dance Clb; JV Cheerldng; High Hon Roll; Hon Roll; Law.

HALE, ELIZABETH; Magnolia HS; Anaheim, CA; (3); Color Guard; Yrbk; Cypress Coll; Nrsng.

HALE, JENNIFER N; St Josephs Notre Dame HS; Alameda, CA; (3); Cmnty Wkr; French Clb; Intnl Clb; Varsity Clb; Sftbl; Tennis; High Hon Roll; Hon Roll; Jr NHS; NHS; Outdoors Club; Bud Branch To Support Chldrns Hospital; Equestrian Club; UC Davis; Animal Trainer.

HALE, JOHN D; University City HS; San Diego, CA; (3); Church Yth Grp; Teachers Aide; School Play; Stage Crew; Var Wrstlng; High Hon Roll; Hon Roll; Music Clb Co-Pres; Aeronautical Engrng.

HALE, MELINDA C; Fairfield HS; Suisun City, CA; (2); Girl Scts; Library Aide; Teachers Aide; Bsktbl; Tennis; Vllybl; Hon Roll; Prfct Atten Awd; UCLA; Law.

HALE, SANYIKA B; Junipero Serra HS; Compton, CA; (2); Church Choir; Ed Yrbk; Var Trk.

HALE, TAFFIE; Lower Lake HS; Clearlake, CA; (4); Office Aide; Sec Pep Clb; Cheerldng; Score Keeper; Cit Awd; High Hon Roll; Hon Roll; Rotary Awd; St Schlr; Friday Night Live VP; Outstndng Stu Orgnztn; Soc Wmn Engrns Hghst Hnrs; CSU Sacramento; Psych.

HALE, TANYA M; Mar Vista HS; Imperial Beach, CA; (1); 40/615; Chess Clb; Cmnty Wkr; Library Aide; Cit Awd; Hon Roll; UCSD; Med.

HALES, KRISTEN A; Brea-Olinda HS; Brea, CA; (2); 70/350; Key Clb; Pres Frsh Cls; Pres Soph Cls; Sec Stu Cncl; Socr; Rotary Awd; HOBY Ambassador; Sister City Del To Hanno Japan; Dance; Azusa Pacific U; Teacher.

HALEY, ANDREW; Mt Whitney HS; Visalia, CA; (2); Bus Profs of Am; Church Yth Grp; Acpl Chr; Church Choir; Hon Roll; Engrng.

HALEY, COURTNEY; Fairfax HS; Los Angeles, CA; (2); Computer Clb; Teachers Aide; Church Choir; Intrml Bsbl; Intrml Ftbl; Intrml Swmmng; UCLA; Bus.

HALEY, CYNTHIA D; Galt HS; Galt, CA; (3); 27/167; GAA; Letterman Clb; SADD; JV Var Bsktbl; JV Var Sftbl; Var L Vllybl; Hon Roll; Prfct Atten Awd; Vlybl MVP; Sftbl GEL All Lg 3 Yr Ltrmn; Bsktbl Hnrb Mntn; Nrsng.

HALEY, ERIC B; Huntington Beach HS; Huntington, CA; (3); Church Yth Grp; Var Socr; High Hon Roll; Cngrssnl Yth Ldrshp Cncl; GMI Engrng Inst; Auto Engrng.

HALEY, KELLY KATHLEEN; Arroyo Grande HS; Shell Beach, CA; (4); 37/479; Church Yth Grp; Key Clb; Acpl Chr; High Hon Roll; Prfct Atten Awd; Pres Acad Fit Awd; Stu Yr Awd Engl, Spnsh & Hstry 87; Spcl Olympcs Vlntr; Cal Poly San Luis Obispo; Elem.

HALEY, LORRIE E; Burney JR/Sr HS; Burney, CA; (2); 1/75; Church Yth Grp; Cmnty Wkr; Ski Clb; Yrbk; Lit Mag; Treas Frsh Cls; VP Soph Cls; Rep Stu Cncl; JV Bsktbl; JV Powder Puff Ftbl; CSF; Biola U; Sci.

HALILI, BRIAN J; Channel Islands HS; Oxnard, CA; (3); Art Clb; Church Yth Grp; JA; Off Jr Cls; Off Sr Cls; JV Var Tennis; Cit Awd; Hon Roll; Prfct Atten Awd; Pres Acad Fit Awd; Asian-Amer Clb; Arch Engrng.

HALL, ALLISON S; Monte Vista HS; Danville, CA; (3); 128/356; Church Yth Grp; German Clb; Girl Scts; Teachers Aide; Powder Puff Ftbl; Score Keeper; BYU; Fshn Dsgn.

HALL, AMY L; Shasta HS; Redding, CA; (2); Sec Church Yth Grp; Orch; Socr; Sftbl; Swmmng; Vllybl; Hon Roll; Shasta Yth Symphony; Redding Yth Soccer Lge; Brigham Young U; Music.

HALL, ANGELA L; Washington HS; Los Angeles, CA; (3); Pres Church Yth Grp; FCA; Hosp Aide; Math Clb; Chorus; Church Choir; School Musical; Variety Show; Rep Soph Cls; Off Sr Cls; Acad Awd; CSF; Singer Of Yr Awd; PBSC Oratorical Awd; UCLA; Pre-Med.

HALL, ANN-MARIE K; Branham HS; San Jose, CA; (1); Church Yth Grp; Hosp Aide; Chorus; Church Choir; Flag Corp; JV Cheerldng; Hon Roll; Psych.

HALL, ANSELM P; Loyola HS; Glendale, CA; (1); Chess Clb; Computer Clb; Med.

HALL, BRANDON A; Ontario HS; Ontario, CA; (3); German Clb; Key Clb; Teachers Aide; JV Bsktbl; Crs Cntry; JV Var Tennis; High Hon Roll; Hon Roll; Jr Statesmn Amer Treas; Maranatha Clb; Bus.

HALL, BRANDON W; Delano HS; Delano, CA; (2); Church Yth Grp; JV Bsktbl; JV Ftbl; Wt Lftg; Hon Roll; Prfct Atten Awd; Outstndng Referee, JV MVP Awd, Frosh & JV EYL Chmpns Bsktbl; Explorer Scouts; Teen To Teen; Humboldt ST U; Forestry.

HALL, CHRISTINA L; El Cajon Valley HS; El Cajon, CA; (3); 53/370; Cmnty Wkr; Hon Roll; Prfct Atten Awd; Dead Poets Society; Peer Listener; San Diego ST U; Education.

HALL, CHRISTINA R; Encinal HS; Alameda, CA; (1); Dance Clb; Score Keeper; Sftbl; Vllybl; Hon Roll; Bus.

HALL, CHRISTINA S; Pomona HS; Pomona, CA; (2); Church Yth Grp; Drama Clb; French Clb; Girl Scts; Science Clb; School Play; Sec Jr Cls; Var Trk; JV Vllybl; Hon Roll; UCLA; Pdtrc Srgn.

HALL, CHRISTINE A; Galt HS; Galt, CA; (2); Library Aide; SADD; Teachers Aide; Hon Roll; Law.

HALL, CHRISTINE R; Mc Lane HS; Fresno, CA; (3); Church Yth Grp; Cmnty Wkr; Girl Scts; Hosp Aide; Library Aide; Chorus; Church Choir; Flag Corp; Powder Puff Ftbl; Swmmng; UC Davis; Vet.

HALL, CHRISTOPHER G; Westminster HS; Westminster, CA; (3); Boy Scts; Debate Tm; JCL; Key Clb; Latin Clb; Vllybl; Hon Roll; UCSD; Phys Thrpy.

HALL, DEBRA L; Paramount HS; South Gate, CA; (2); 22/500; Science Clb; SADD; Sftbl; High Hon Roll; Hon Roll; CSF; Coll Clb; UC Irvine; X-Ray Tech.

HALL, DENISE; Coalinga HS; Coalinga, CA; (2); Church Yth Grp; GAA; Letterman Clb; Pep Clb; Church Choir; Color Guard; Variety Show; Bsktbl; Cheerldng; Pom Pon; Edtrs Choice Awd 90 Natl Libry Poetry; 2nd Pl Sci Fr; Star Mnth Art & Lab Bio 90; Sci.

HALL, ELIZABETH G; Newbury Park Adventist Acad; Thousand Oaks, CA; (2); Church Yth Grp; Equestrian; Sprts Ldrshp; Tch Swmmng Tofluentspan Chldrn; Moorpark JC; Jrnlsm.

HALL, GINA; John North HS; Riverside, CA; (3); Hist Drama Clb; Treas German Clb; Model UN; Chorus; Hist Mrchg Band; Orch; Treas Rep Stu Cncl; High Hon Roll; Hnrd Qn Bethel 257 Jbs Dghtrs; UC.

HALL, GREGORY J; Antelope Valley HS; Lancaster, CA; (2); 1/820; Computer Clb; Math Tm; JV Crs Cntry; JV Socr; JV Tennis; High Hon Roll; CA Schlrshp Fed; U Of CA; Bus.

HALL, HENNY A; Fairfield HS; Fairfield, CA; (2); JV Ftbl; JV Trk; Archlgy.

HALL, HUGH D; Sacred Heart Cathedral Prep HS; San Francisco, CA; (2); Rep Soph Cls; Stu Cncl; Capt JV Bsbl; Bsktbl; Capt JV Ftbl; High Hon Roll; Hon Roll; Athletic Awds MVP Ftbl; MVP WCAL Ftbl; Cet For Schltc Achvt Athletic Seasons; Stanford; Ftbll.

HALL, JAMES D; Mount Miguel HS; Spring Valley, CA; (4); 22/389; Co-Ed Yrbk; Off Sr Cls; Swmmng; Capt Water Polo Team; Boys Sportsmanship Awd; Mesa Coll.

HALL, JASON D; Rim Of The World HS; Blue Jay, CA; (3); Ski Clb; Spanish Clb; Varsity Clb; Band; Stu Cncl; Var Ftbl; Var Wrstlng; Hon Roll; CIF-IA Champ Wrestling S Sect; Expert Rock Climber; Pre-Law.

HALL, JASON W; Victor Valley HS; Victorville, CA; (3); 49/424; CA ST Polytech; Aeroscp Engr.

HALL, JEFFREY ALAN; Edison HS; Huntington Beach, CA; (4); Band; Jazz Band; Mrchg Band; Pep Band; Hon Roll; Star Advncd Cert-Perfrmng Arts; Velvet Knights Drum/Bugle Core-Horn Line; U Of CA-IRVINE; Comp Sci.

HALL, JENNIFER; Crescenta Valley HS; Glendale, CA; (2); Mu Alpha Theta; Ed Lit Mag; Var Trk; Opt Clb Awd; CSF; Gldn St Exam Hnrs-Geom; Psych.

HALL, JENNIFER; Santana HS; Lakeside, CA; (1); Model UN; Bsktbl; Cross Ctry; Track; Bus.

HALL, JENNIFER D; Vintage HS; Napa, CA; (4); 22/318; Church Yth Grp; Church Choir; School Musical; Phtg Nwsp; Powder Puff Ftbl; Cit Awd; NHS; St Schlr; Peer Spprt Excllnc Cert; Am Assn Of U Women Schlrshp; Masters Coll; Psych.

HALL, JENNIFER S; San Dimas HS; San Dimas, CA; (3); GAA; Hosp Aide; Sec SADD; Yrbk; Sec Jr Cls; Sec Stu Cncl; JV Sftbl; JV Tennis; High Hon Roll; CA Schlrshp Fed; Smith Coll; Mdcn.

HALL, JOANNE E; Palmdale HS; Little Rock, CA; (3); 100/650; Church Yth Grp; SADD; Chorus; School Play; Hon Roll; Achievers Club; Prfrmng Arts Drama.

HALL II, JOHN E; Rowland HS; Rowland Heights, CA; (2); JV Bsbl; JV Ftbl; JV Wt Lftg; Jr Leag Wrld Series Champ Tm 87; Animtn Prgm Advncd Stu; Weight Liftng Fitbl, Bsbl; Pro Bsbl.

HALL, JOSEPH R; Merced HS; Merced, CA; (2); JV Bsbl; Cit Awd; High Hon Roll; Hon Roll; Fresno ST U; Mech Engrng.

HALL, JOSHUA; Mc Kinleyville HS; Fieldbrook, CA; (3); Cmnty Wkr; Band; Mrchg Band; JV Bsktbl; Cit Awd; Hon Roll; Prfct Atten Awd; Cnslr Week Long Envrnmntl Camp; Attnd Phi Delta Kappa Smmr Inst Prspctv Tchrs; Humboldt ST U; Educ.

HALL JR, KENNY D; L A Baptist HS; Canoga Park, CA; (3); Church Yth Grp; Hon Roll; Contributor To Lit Mag; Hold 99 Pct In US Hist Clss Awd; Meterologist.

HALL, KIMBERLIE L; Montgomery HS; Santa Rosa, CA; (3); FBLA; JA; Science Clb; Sftbl; Swmmng; Hon Roll.

HALL, KRISTINA M; Bella Vista HS; Orangevale, CA; (2); 40/410; Church Yth Grp; Office Aide; Spanish Clb; Band; Rep Soph Cls; High Hon Roll; NHS; Engl, Span, Bus Awds; Schl Spllng Be Chmpn; BYU.

HALL, LAYLA R; Mc Kinleyville HS; Trinidad, CA; (3); 1/150; AFS; Drama Clb; School Play; High Hon Roll; Photo; Drama Awd; Drama Troupe Scl Message Theater Grp; UC Davis; Med.

HALL, LECHELL L; Washington HS; Los Angeles, CA; (3); Church Yth Grp; Church Choir; Hon Roll; Vocal Ensmbl; Pre-Med.

HALL, MEGAN P; El Toro HS; El Toro, CA; (2); 40/557; German Clb; Hosp Aide; Rptr Nwsp; Var Swmmng; High Hon Roll; Hon Roll; Pres Acad Fit Awd; UCSD; Pre Med.

HALL, MERCY L; Fairfield HS; Fairfield, CA; (3); Boy Scts; German Clb; Off Jr Cls; Hon Roll; NHS; Yth Grp Actvts.

HALL, MICHAEL E; Bishop Montgomery HS; Torrance, CA; (3); 88/375; Church Yth Grp; Cmnty Wkr; Ski Clb; Rep Frsh Cls; Rep Soph Cls; Rep Jr Cls; Off Sr Cls; Capt L Bsbl; Var L Ftbl; Var L Trk; Norwalk CA Cardinals Mickey Mantle Natl Chmp-2nd Pl Jr Olympc Chmp.

HALL, MOLLY KATHERINE; Miramonte HS; Orinda, CA; (4); AFS; Cmnty Wkr; French Clb; Sec Intnl Clb; Model UN; Office Aide; Speech Tm; SADD; Pres Jr Cls; Stu Cncl; AAUW Outstndng Stu Awd; Stu Dist Schl Brd; Sch Dist Jnt Comm & Co-Fndr Dist Actvts Comm; Russian Clb; Middlebury VT; Intl Rltns.

HALL, N COLIN; Dana Hills HS; Laguna Niguel, CA; (1); Drama Clb; FCA; Stage Crew; Hon Roll; Pres Acad Fit Awd; Surf Team; UCLA.

HALL, NICHOLAS H; Saint Monica HS; Los Angeles, CA; (2); High Hon Roll; Hon Roll; Ply Drms; Berkeley.

HALL, NICOLE L; John A Rowland HS; Rowland Hts, CA; (2); Pres Church Yth Grp; Pep Clb; Acpl Chr; Cheerldng; Hon Roll; Mt Sac; Pre-Schl Teacher.

HALL, REBECCA; St Patrick - St Vincent HS; Benicia, CA; (2); Rep French Clb; SADD; Teachers Aide; Lit Mag; High Hon Roll; Hon Roll; Frnch Clb Pres 90-91; Tchr.

HALL, REBECCA A; Tustin HS; Tustin, CA; (1); Church Yth Grp; Dance Clb; Pep Clb; Drill Tm; Arch.

HALL, REED; Sonora HS; La Habra, CA; (2); 1/500; Art Clb; Boy Scts; Tennis; Hon Roll; NHS; Pres Acad Fit Awd; JV Water Polo; Gldn St Schlr Hi Hnrs Geomtry; Amer Chem Soc Outstndng Chem Stu Awd; Arch.

HALL, ROSE; Los Angeles Baptist HS; Canoga Park, CA; (3); Church Yth Grp; Teachers Aide; Chorus; School Play; Lit Mag; Hon Roll; Desgn Logo Schl Annl Fshn Show; Svrl Drwng Annl Art Show; Psych.

HALL, SHERRI; Monte Vista Christian Schl; Corralitos, CA; (4); 12/100; Church Yth Grp; Cmnty Wkr; Hosp Aide; Var Capt Sftbl; Var L Tennis; Stat Vllybl; High Hon Roll; CSF; Monterey Peninsula Coll; Nrsng.

HALL, STACY; St Bouaventure HS; Ventura, CA; (1); Church Yth Grp; JV Cheerldng; High Hon Roll; Stanford; Lawyer.

HALL, STEVE D; Monterey HS; Monterey, CA; (3); 75/350; Computer Clb; Band; Jazz Band; Mrchg Band; Orch; Pep Band; JV Crs Cntry; Capt Var Wrstlng; Hon Roll; GSE Hnrs Alg & Geom; Army Resrve MOS Intllgnce Anlyst; Comp Sci.

HALL, STEVEN M; West Campus Hiram Johnson HS; Sacramento, CA; (2); 89/192; Hon Roll; Construction.

HALL, TANAIIA PHELAN; Pittsburg HS; Pittsburg, CA; (2); 75/435; GAA; Varsity Clb; Var Trk; Cit Awd; Hon Roll; Nwsp; Yrbk; Lit Mag; Off Frsh Cls; Off Soph Cls; 1st Pl Hstry Day Cmptn; Hnrs Core Pgm; Stanford; Animal Handler.

HALL, TIM; Savanna HS; Buena Park, CA; (2); High Hon Roll; Hon Roll; Engrng.

HALL, TIMOTHY M; Huntington Beach HS; Huntington Beach, CA; (3); Church Yth Grp; ROTC; Teachers Aide; Chorus; Church Choir; Hon Roll; Jr NHS; Prfct Atten Awd; Tower Awd Physics; Natl Congrssnl Schlr; Theology.

HALL, TRISHA; Palmdale HS; Aqua Dulce, CA; (2); 20/870; Church Yth Grp; Cmnty Wkr; 4-H; FFA; Drill Tm; Flag Corp; Cit Awd; High Hon Roll; Hon Roll; Pres Schlr; Rotary Club Stu Mnth; CSF; Psych Club; US Constitution Awd; Psych.

HALLAM, MELISSA A; Woodcrest Christian Schl; Perris, CA; (1); Church Yth Grp; High Hon Roll; NHS; Mgmt.

HALLBACK, ALLYSON S; Miramonte HS; Orinda, CA; (1); Drama Clb; Var Trk; Jazz Dance Class; Ice Skating; Sewing Classes; Fashion Designer.

HALLBERG, KRISTINA; Big Valley HS; Bieber, CA; (1); 5/32; Church Yth Grp; 4-H; JV Bsktbl; JV Var Cheerldng; JV Trk; Hon Roll; Law.

HALLER, DAVID; Atascadero HS; Atascadero, CA; (1); Chess Clb; Church Yth Grp; Letterman Clb; Band; Mrchg Band; Socr; Swmmng; Tennis; CA Schlrshp Fed; CA Poly San Luis Obispo; Engrn.

HALLIDAY, HEATHER; Oakmont HS; Roseville, CA; (3); 78/398; Drama Clb; Service Clb; Var JV Bsktbl; Var Crs Cntry; Trk; JV Vllybl; Cit Awd; Hon Roll; Pres Acad Fit Awd; Physics Club; Humboldt; Home Ec.

HALLIS, JOHN; Fred C Beyer HS; Modesto, CA; (4); 98/506; Church Yth Grp; SADD; Cit Awd; Hon Roll; Prfct Atten Awd; Patroot Awd Mathmtcs; Bus.

HALLMANN, MICHELLE; Ramona HS; Ramona, CA; (3); Spanish Clb; Off Jr Cls; Rep Stu Cncl; Var Cheerldng; Var Sftbl; Hon Roll; Pres Acad Fit Awd; Ambssdrs Club; CSF; Nrsng.

HALLMARK, OLIVIA G; El Cerrito HS; Richmond, CA; (4); 25/360; Acpl Chr; Band; Chorus; Jazz Band; Mrchg Band; Orch; Pep Band; School Musical; School Play; Yrbk; UC Davis; Med.

HALLOCK, ERIN E; Mount Diablo HS; Pittsburg, CA; (1); Model UN; Spanish Clb; SADD; Polic Acad; Police Offcr.

HALLOCK, JESSICA L; Atascadero HS; Atascadero, CA; (2); 17/323; VP Frsh Cls; Pres Soph Cls; JV Sftbl; Hon Roll; Ldrshp Class; ASB VP 90-91.

HALLOCK, KELLY L; Washington HS; Fremont, CA; (3); 28/320; Church Yth Grp; Dance Clb; Cit Awd; Hon Roll; 2nd Pl CAML Cntst 2 Yrs Algebra II, Trigonometry Then Pre-Calculus; CSF; Yth Alive Club, Sec, Pres; The Masters Coll; Youth Work.

HALLOWS, ANNESSA S; Fairfield HS; Suisun City, CA; (2); Pres Church Yth Grp; GAA; Church Choir; JV Var Crs Cntry; Stat Trk; Hon Roll; Pres Jr NHS; Pres Acad Fit Awd; Sacramento ST U; Chld Dev.

HALLUM, TOM W; San Dimas HS; San Dimas, CA; (2); Boy Scts; Church Yth Grp; JV Crs Cntry; JV Trk; Hon Roll; Prfct Atten Awd; Recd Roses Awd; CA ST Fullerton; Fire Sci.

HALM, BRANDON M; Coronado HS; Coronado, CA; (3); 11/256; Spanish Clb; Teachers Aide; Varsity Clb; Var Tennis; High Hon Roll; Hon Roll; Jr NHS; NHS; San Diego Tribunes All Acadmc 1st Tm; Violin 8 Yrs; Pres San Diego Jr Tnns Cncl; Intl Bus.

HALOG, DEBBIE F; Thomas Edison HS; Stockton, CA; (1); Dance Clb; Drama Clb; Rep Frsh Cls; Hon Roll; Pres Acad Fit Awd; Spanish NHS.

HALPERN, ARIEL K; San Rafael HS; San Rafael, CA; (1); Cmnty Wkr; French Clb; SADD; Var Swmmng; CA Schlrshp Fed; Cmnty Theater.

HALPERN, LISA; La Canada HS; La Canada Flintri, CA; (3); 7/250; Mu Alpha Theta; Ed Yrbk; VP Frsh Cls; Treas Soph Cls; Sec Jr Cls; Treas Sr Cls; Var Crs Cntry; Var Socr; Var Trk; NHS; Site Cncl; PTSA 4th VP.

HALPERN, RANA D; Bishop O'dowd HS; Berkeley, CA; (2); Cmnty Wkr; Varsity Clb; Socr; Sftbl; High Hon Roll; Hon Roll; NEDT Awd; NCS/Jack In Box Schlr Athlte; Georgetown; Pol Sci.

HALSTEAD, CARMEN L; Mesa Verde HS; Citrus Heights, CA; (4); 13/175; Drama Clb; Spanish Clb; Teachers Aide; School Play; Stage Crew; Variety Show; JV Bsktbl; Hon Roll; Acad Decathln Vrsty Team; San Juan Drama Festvl; Sacramento ST U; Theatre Arts.

HALTER, KRISTIN M; Redlands HS; Redlands, CA; (4); 30/900; Church Yth Grp; Pres French Clb; Key Clb; Mrchg Band; Pep Band; School Musical; Cit Awd; Hon Roll; NHS; Pres Acad Fit Awd; UC Irvine; Social Ecology.

HALTERLEIN, JUSTIN; Palm Desert HS; Palm Desert, CA; (2); Intnl Clb; Tennis; High Hon Roll; GSE Hnrs Algb/Geom; Supr Piano Plyr.

HALTERMAN, MELINDA L; Rowland HS; Rowland Heights, CA; (1); Acpl Chr; School Musical; School Play; Nwsp; Gym; Trk; Hon Roll; Stu Of Yr Music; Otstndng Chorus; Cal Poly; Doctor.

HALVA, AARON; Lincoln HS; Stockton, CA; (4); 60/500; Drama Clb; Acpl Chr; VP Chorus; School Musical; School Play; JV Bsktbl; High Hon Roll; Hon Roll; Rck Bnd Plyr Wrld Hngr, Chrty Dncs; Wrtn Melodrmas; Prfrmd Orgnl 1-Act Ply L A Thspn St Shw; Actng.

HAM, ANNE MARY M; St Joseph HS; Huntington Park, CA; (4); Off Church Yth Grp; Cmnty Wkr; VP Treas SADD; High Hon Roll; Hon Roll; Parish Cncl Recrdng Sec; Cal ST U Long Beach.

HAM, SUSY; Skyline HS; Oakland, CA; (2); Key Clb; Library Aide; Orch; Hon Roll; Prfct Atten Awd; UC Berkeley; Law.

HAMADA, PEYRI; San Pasqual HS; Escondido, CA; (2); 10/352; Var L Cheerldng; San Pasqual Stu Trainer; Med.

HAMAGUCHI, KARYN M; Mira Mesa HS; San Diego, CA; (2); 36/795; Dance Clb; Teachers Aide; Drill Tm; Orch; Variety Show; Cit Awd; High Hon Roll; 1988/89 Wangenheim JH Otstndg Mscn Yr; 1988/89 P Warnr Dl Tm 1st Lt; 1990/91 MM HS Dr Tm LT; Ballet; Dietician Dance.

HAMAKER, JUSTIN N; Nevada Union HS; Nevada City, CA; (3); SADD; Cmnty Wkr; Hon Roll; Friday Night Live Pres; Sacrament ST U CA; Elec Engr.

HAMAM, DAWN M; Mater Dei HS; Westminster, CA; (3); Church Yth Grp; Chorus; School Musical; JV Crs Cntry; High Hon Roll; NHS; UC Santa Barbara; Crmnl Law.

HAMAMOTO, DAVID M; Del Campo HS; Fair Oaks, CA; (3); 117/500; Church Yth Grp; FBLA; SADD; Band; Trk; Prfct Atten Awd; CSUS.

HAMANN, MARK E; Canyon Springs HS; Moreno Valley, CA; (2); Teachers Aide; Temple Yth Grp; Varsity Clb; Var Bsbl; Ftbl; Wt Lftg; Wrstlng; Hon Roll; MVP JV Ftbl & Frshmn Coaches Awd Var Wrstln; CIF 2-A Qlfr Var Wrstlng; AZ ST U; Mrktng.

HAMAOUI, KAMIL G; Loyola HS; Woodland Hills, CA; (2); Boy Scts; Letterman Clb; Orch; Variety Show; JV Swmmng; High Hon Roll; Pres Acad Fit Awd; IM Water Polo; Music.

HAMBLEN, DENISE; Lincoln HS; Lincoln, CA; (3); 4-H; Pep Clb; Teachers Aide; Var Trk; JV Vllybl; 4-H Awd; Hon Roll; Sierra Coll; Fash Merch.

HAMBLETON, JODI; El Camino Real HS; Woodland Hills, CA; (3); Math Clb; Service Clb; Drill Tm; Off Frsh Cls; Off Soph Cls; Off Jr Cls; High Hon Roll; Hon Roll; CSF; JR Stsmn Of Amer; Hgh Hnrs Geom Golden St Exam; Engrng.

HAMBY, AIMEE; Mojave HS; California City, CA; (1); Church Yth Grp; Drama Clb; Spanish Clb; Thesps; Flag Corp; School Play; Stage Crew; JV Cheerldng; Hon Roll; Ldrshp Conf; Lit.

HAMBY, COREY J; Modoc HS; Alturas, CA; (3); 5/75; Church Yth Grp; Letterman Clb; Pep Clb; Ski Clb; Varsity Clb; Band; Jazz Band; Mrchg Band; Pep Band; School Musical; Advncd Bio, Alg, Eng Awds; Med.

HAMBY, JOSHUA; Woodland HS; Woodland, CA; (4); 47/420; FBLA; Spanish Clb; Var Bsktbl; JV Crs Cntry; JV Ftbl; JV Var Tennis; JV Trk; Hon Roll; U Of CA Santa Cruz; Comp Engr.

HAMDANI, SYEDA Z; Sacramento HS; Sacramento, CA; (2); 16/500; German Clb; Science Clb; High Hon Roll; NHS; CA Schlrshp Fed; UCD; Acad Excllnc Awd Gldn ST Exam; 1st Yr Alg Hnrs; Jrnlsm.

HAMED, ALI; College Park HS; Pleasant Hill, CA; (1); Art Clb; Computer Clb; Varsity Clb; Bsbl; High Hon Roll; Hon Roll; Comp/Bsbl.

HAMELIN, NICOLE; Marina HS; Huntington Beach, CA; (3); Church Yth Grp; Cmnty Wkr; Office Aide; Chorus; Color Guard; Flag Corp; Hon Roll; Flag Team Prfrmnce Awd; Music.

HAMER, DAVID E; Rio Americano HS; Carmichael, CA; (3); 9/290; Key Clb; Spanish Clb; Temple Yth Grp; Band; Jazz Band; Pep Band; JV Bsbl; JV Bsktbl; Capt Var Socr; Var Trk; Bus.

HAMER, JAKE; The Bishops Schl; La Jolla, CA; (3); Cmnty Wkr; Letterman Clb; SADD; Varsity Clb; Bsbl; Ftbl; Wt Lftg; Hon Roll; Stanford; Med.

HAMID, KYLE A; Canyon HS; Canyon Country, CA; (3); Bsktbl.

HAMID, OMID; Santa Monica HS; Santa Monica, CA; (3); Am Leg Boys St; FBLA; High Hon Roll; U Of CA Los Angeles.

HAMILL, JULIAN M; Bellarmine College Prep; Fremont, CA; (1); Church Yth Grp; Wt Lftg; Wrstlng; Cmmnty Svc Wrk; Psych.

HAMILTON, ALYCIA A; Vintage HS; Vallejo, CA; (2); 98/445; Church Yth Grp; Band; Church Choir; Color Guard; Flag Corp; NAPA JC; Registered Nurse.

HAMILTON, ANGELA; Maxwell HS; Maxwell, CA; (2); 4-H; FFA; Speech Tm; Yrbk; Bsktbl; Sftbl; Vllybl; Cit Awd; Hon Roll; Prfct Atten Awd.

HAMILTON, BARBARA; Cajon HS; San Bbernardino, CA; (2); AFS; Key Clb; Vllybl; NHS; Jobs Dghtrs; Sndy Schl Tchr; CSF.

HAMILTON, BRENNA E; Del Campo HS; Carmichael, CA; (3); French Clb; Hon Roll; Natl Youth Ldrshp Cncl; Advrtsng Internship; Young Republicans Activist; London Sch Of Econ; Intl Econ.

HAMILTON, CARIN A; Oakdale HS; Oakdale, CA; (1); AFS; Church Yth Grp; Debate Tm; Math Tm; Speech Tm; Intrml Tennis; High Hon Roll; Acad Lttrmn; Stanislaus Cnty Math Cmptn; Law.

HAMILTON, CHARLES; Azusa HS; Azusa, CA; (3); Letterman Clb; Varsity Clb; Var Bsbl; Var Ftbl.

HAMILTON, CHRISTOPHER; Bishop Amat HS; West Covina, CA; (3); Aud/Vis; Hon Roll; Prfct Atten Awd; CSF; UCAL; Dir.

HAMILTON, DENNIS D; Bakersfield HS; Bakersfield, CA; (3); 149/718; Boy Scts; Science Clb; Ed Lit Mag; JV Swmmng; Hon Roll; Soc For Creatv Anachronism; Leather Craftng; War Gaming; Engl.

HAMILTON, ETHAN; Hesperia Christian HS; Hesperia, CA; (1); 2/42; Church Yth Grp; Quiz Bowl; Scholastic Bowl; Band; Rep Frsh Cls; Stu Cncl; JV Bsktbl; Var Crs Cntry; High Hon Roll; CA Schlrshp Fed; The Masters Coll; Tchr.

HAMILTON, FELIX S; University HS; Irvine, CA; (3); VP Chess Clb; Debate Tm; Math Clb; Math Tm; NFL; Quiz Bowl; Scholastic Bowl; Pres Science Clb; JV Trk; JV Wrstlng; Scntfc Rsrch; Publications; Various Sci Cmptns; Physical Sci.

HAMILTON, GRACE H; El Cajon Valley HS; El Cajon, CA; (2); 27/390; Church Yth Grp; Office Aide; Rptr Yrbk; Socr; Sftbl; Trk; Vllybl; Hon Roll; Lions Clb, Leos; Yng Life; HS Teacher.

HAMILTON, JASON A; Downey HS; Downey, CA; (2); Math Clb; Rep Soph Cls; Intrml Ftbl; JV Trk; Var Wrstlng; Arch.

HAMILTON, JOSHUA G; Los Gatos HS; Los Gatos, CA; (3); 26/370; Cmnty Wkr; Key Clb; Ed Nwsp; High Hon Roll; Hon Roll; Ntl Merit Ltr; Var L Ftbl; Var L Socr; Var L Trk; Peer Cnslng; Cornell; Law.

HAMILTON, JULIE E; Victor Valley HS; Victorville, CA; (3); Computer Clb; 4-H; ROTC; Spanish Clb; Chorus; Hon Roll; Swmmng; Vllybl; Marine Bio; U Of Loyola; Med.

HAMILTON, KAREN LYNN; Presentation HS; Daly City, CA; (4); 19/101; Cmnty Wkr; Hosp Aide; Library Aide; Service Clb; School Play; Mgr Stage Crew; Off Frsh Cls; Off Soph Cls; Hon Roll; Secy Black Stu Union; Chrstn Fllwshp; U CA Davis; Sci.

HAMILTON, KIMBERLY A; Grace M Davis HS; Modesto, CA; (2); Cmnty Wkr; Girl Scts; Band; Color Guard; Drill Tm; Mrchg Band; Pep Band; JV Var Cheerldng; Var JV Diving; Ftbl; Fresno ST U; Phrmcy.

HAMILTON, KRISTIE; Kerman HS; Kerman, CA; (2); 12/150; Church Yth Grp; FCA; FTA; SADD; Bsktbl; Sftbl; High Hon Roll; Hon Roll; Bike Riding; Teach Chldrn Church; Fresno ST; Chld Dev.

HAMILTON, LESLIE; University City HS; San Diego, CA; (4); VP JA; Office Aide; SADD; Treas Soph Cls; Treas Jr Cls; Rep Sr Cls; Stu Cncl; Var Cheerldng; Cit Awd; Hon Roll; U San Francisco; Psych.

HAMILTON, LISA M; El Camino HS; Oceanside, CA; (4); 74/338; Yrbk; Lit Mag; Var Socr; Hon Roll; Peer Asst; Aviation.

HAMILTON, MANDI; John Swett HS; Rodeo, CA; (2); French Clb; Science Clb; Spanish Clb; Church Choir; School Play; Law.

HAMILTON, MARK D; Southwestern Acad; Pasadena, CA; (2); Aud/Vis; Boy Scts; Church Yth Grp; Cmnty Wkr; Stage Crew; Phtg Yrbk; Rep Stu Cncl; Var Bsbl; Var Crs Cntry; Socr; Sci.

HAMILTON, MARLON K; Long Beach Jordan HS; Los Angeles, CA; (3); Bsbl; Bsktbl; Ftbl; UNLV; Med.

HAMILTON, MARY C; Oakdale HS; Waterford, CA; (2); Hon Roll; Pharmacy Tech.

HAMILTON, MATTHEW; Golden West HS; Visalia, CA; (4); 1/320; Church Yth Grp; VP Math Clb; Teachers Aide; Acpl Chr; Chorus; Church Choir; Pres Sr Cls; Var L Tennis; Elks Awd; Hon Roll; CSF; Mission Cnstrctn Prjct Mex; Bank Amer Plaq Wnnr Liberal Arts; Westmont Coll; Engrng.

HAMILTON, MIKE T; Calaveras HS; San Andreas, CA; (3); Church Yth Grp; Cmnty Wkr; 4-H; Band; Socr; Swmmng; 4-H Awd; Modesto JC; Engrng.

HAMILTON, MINA I; Encina HS; Sacramento, CA; (3); 1/275; Church Yth Grp; Debate Tm; French Clb; Speech Tm; Teachers Aide; Ed Lit Mag; VP Soph Cls; Stu Cncl; Var Vllybl; Hon Roll; Mock Trial; Acad Dcthln; UCLA; Law.

HAMILTON, NALO; Moreno Valley HS; Perris, CA; (3); German Clb; Varsity Clb; Church Choir; Drill Tm; Rptr Yrbk; Stat Bsktbl; Capt Trk; Capt Vllybl; High Hon Roll; Hon Roll; Black Stu Union Sgt At Arms; Stu Against Drugs; Oakwood Coll; OB/Gyn.

HAMILTON, NATHAN P; California HS; Whittier, CA; (3); Treas Drama Clb; Treas Thesps; School Musical; School Play; Stage Crew; Swing Chorus; Variety Show; Dance; Fullerton JC; Entertainment.

HAMILTON, PAUL O; San Benito Union HS; Hollister, CA; (1); #90 In Class; Ski Clb; Intrml Bsktbl; JV Tennis; Intrml Wt Lftg; Band; Princeton; Lawyr.

HAMILTON, SEAN L; Will C Crawford HS; San Diego, CA; (2); 26/402; Church Yth Grp; Band; Hon Roll; Guitar; Music.

HAMILTON, SHAUNA L; San Bernardino HS; San Bernardino, CA; (3); Teachers Aide; Chorus; Stat Trk; Hon Roll; 2 Choir Trphy, Ltr; SAL Champ Track Ltr; CA ST San Bernardino; Engrng.

HAMILTON, SHAWN E; Skyline HS; Oakland, CA; (2); Computer Clb; Science Clb; Jazz Band; CSF; Sunday Schl Tchr; Sci.

HAMILTON, SHAWN M; Sherman E Burroughs HS; Ridgecrest, CA; (3); Am Leg Boys St; Ski Clb; Spanish Clb; Ed Nwsp; Var Boy Scts; Var L Socr; Church Yth Grp; Varsity Clb; Cit Awd; CA Schlrshp Fed Hgh Hnr Rl; Prin Awd; UC Davis; Engrng.

HAMILTON, VICTORIA L; Carlmont HS; Belmont, CA; (2); Computer Clb; Girl Scts; JA; VP Math Clb; Civil Air Patrol; Engrng Clb Treas; Sci.

HAMILTON, WENDY; Willits HS; Willits, CA; (1); Hist AFS; Chorus; High Hon Roll; Hon Roll; Pres Acad Fit Awd; Law.

HAMLIN, CLAUDIA A; Saint Monica HS; Santa Monica, CA; (4); Hosp Aide; Hon Roll; CA ST U Northridge; Phy.

HAMLIN, JERRY W; Troy HS; Yorba Linda, CA; (2); Church Yth Grp; JV Socr; JV Tennis; High Hon Roll; Hon Roll; NHS; Intl Baccalaureate Awd Rec Geom; Hnrs At Entrance; Comp Engr.

HAMM, ANTHONY M; St Anthony HS; Long Beach, CA; (3); Letterman Clb; Varsity Clb; JV Var Crs Cntry; JV Var Socr; JV Var Trk; Hon Roll; L B CA ST Coll; Accntng.

HAMM, JASON C; Foothill HS; Santa Ana, CA; (2); 2/320; Science Clb; Spanish Clb; Temple Yth Grp; JV Swmmng; High Hon Roll; Pres Acad Fit Awd; Acad Decathlon; JV Water Polo; Young Democrats Of Amer; UC Berkeley; Particle Physics.

HAMMACK, LISA A; Chino HS; Chino, CA; (3); Powder Puff Ftbl; Tennis; Hon Roll; Silver Spur Engl Awd Wnnr; Ed.

HAMMANN, JEFFERSON G; George Washington HS; Presidio, CA; (3); 65/690; Boy Scts; ROTC; Teachers Aide; Var L Crs Cntry; Var L Wrstlng; Hon Roll; NHS; Wrstlng 2nd Pl All City San Francisco; Coaches Awd 90; Vrsty Lttr; Trvled Abroad; PA ST; Poly Sci.

HAMMAR, REBECCA R; Dos Pueblos HS; Goleta, CA; (2); #20 In Class; Church Yth Grp; Church Choir; Var Socr; NHS; Teach Preschl At Chrch; UCSB; Marine Bio.

HAMMEL, JENNIFER L; Loretto HS; Sacramento, CA; (2); Drama Clb; SADD; School Play; Stage Crew; Var Tennis; Hon Roll; FNL; Peer Ministry; Hnrb Mntn & Publshng In World Of Poetrys Poetry Cont; Nrsng.

HAMMEL, TASHIA L; Poway HS; Poway, CA; (3); Church Yth Grp; FCA; Math Tm; Ed Nwsp; Sec Frsh Cls; Sec Soph Cls; Var Crs Cntry; Trk; High Hon Roll; NHS; ST Qualifier 3200 & 1600 88-89; SICA Riverto River Cross Cntry Mem 88; Bio Awd 87-88.

HAMMER, HEATHER M; Mater Dei HS; Fountain Valley, CA; (2); Church Yth Grp; Cmnty Wkr; Spanish Clb; CSF.

HAMMER, SHAUN M; Grace M Davis HS; Modesto, CA; (4); 9/425; Church Yth Grp; Debate Tm; Speech Tm; Teachers Aide; JV Fld Hcky; Pres Acad Fit Awd; Bank Am Cert Excllnc Frng Lang Spanish; 1st Pl Congress Debate; Advncd Plcmnt Bio Test Score 4; Point Lama Nazarene Coll; Biomd.

HAMMOND, BRIAN; St John Bosco HS; Garden Grove, CA; (2); 16/200; Church Yth Grp; Key Clb; Sftbl; Hon Roll; NHS; Engl Acad Awd.

HAMMOND, HILLARY; Las Lomas HS; Concord, CA; (4); Drama Clb; Library Aide; Chorus; Stage Crew; Rep Stu Cncl; Vlntr At Runaway Shelter; U Of Portland; Modern Langs.

HAMMOND, VANESSA; Mountain Empire HS; Descanso, CA; (2); Pep Clb; Spanish Clb; Rptr Nwsp; Lit Mag; NHS; JV Ntl Merit Ltr; Friday Night Live; Zoology.

HAMMOND, WILLIAM S; Rancho Alamitos HS; Santa Fe, NM; (2); Chess Clb; Top Stu In Bio Sphmr Class; CA Poly San Luis; Comp.

HAMMONS, BRIAN D; Los Gatos HS; Los Gatos, CA; (2); 1/333; Vllybl; High Hon Roll; Pres Acad Fit Awd; Jr Olympics-Vllybl.

HAMNER, MALISSA M; Serrano HS; Phelan, CA; (1); FBLA; Yrbk; Sec Frsh Cls; Stat Sftbl; Vllybl; High Hon Roll; CA Yth Tennis Fdrtn; FBLA Cmnty Blood Drive; Aeronautics.

HAMPTON, CHRIS A; Yucaipa HS; Yucaipa, CA; (2); Church Yth Grp; Spanish Clb; Teachers Aide; Ftbl; Wt Lftg; Hon Roll; Pres Acad Fit Awd; Cycling; San Diego ST U.

HAMPTON, CHRISTINA; Valley HS; Sacramento, CA; (4); 12/446; JA; Office Aide; SADD; High Hon Roll; Hon Roll; Duplication Aide; Capital Ed Consrtium; Natl Ed Ctr; Jrnlsm.

HAMPTON, DAVID W; Edison-Computech HS; Fresno, CA; (1); Debate Tm; JV Bsbl; JV Socr; Intl Ordr Of Demolay; Gldn St Exmntn Alg Hnrs.

HAMPTON, JALYN M; Skyline HS; Oakland, CA; (3); Church Yth Grp; Cmnty Wkr; Debate Tm; FCA; SADD; Varsity Clb; Chorus; School Musical; Yrbk; L Swmmng; Rural Outreach; Jr Statesmn Amer; UC Davis; Med.

HAMPTON, JANELL M; Skyline HS; Oakland, CA; (2); Church Yth Grp; Cmnty Wkr; Debate Tm; FCA; Science Clb; SADD; Teachers Aide; Yrbk; Var L Sftbl; JV Vllybl; Amnesty Intl; Jr Statemn Amer; Piano; UC Davis.

HAMPTON, LEAH D; Red Bluff Union HS; Red Bluff, CA; (2); SADD; Swmmng; Tennis; Vllybl; Wt Lftg; Shasta Clg.

HAMPTON, ROBERT W; Saint Ignatius College Prep; Tiburon, CA; (3); 72/210; Church Yth Grp; Drama Clb; School Musical; Stage Crew; Psych.

HAMSON, NORMAN R; Torrey Pines HS; Solana Beach, CA; (1); Boy Scts; Church Yth Grp; Bsktbl; Hon Roll; Attorney.

HAN, BEIBEIANNIE; Abraham Lincoln HS; San Francisco, CA; (2); Bus Profs of Am; Ed Lit Mag; High Hon Roll; Hon Roll; Mandarin Clb; Chico Exchnge Pgm; UC Berkeley; Doctor.

HAN, BERNICE H; Schurr HS; Montebello, CA; (1); Key Clb; Pep Clb; Color Guard; Flag Corp; JV L Crs Cntry; JV Trk; Hon Roll; CSF; Sci.

HAN, BO YOUNG; Rowland HS; Rowland Heights, CA; (2); Church Yth Grp; Hosp Aide; Spanish Clb; Church Choir; Rptr Nwsp; JV Tennis; High Hon Roll; Hon Roll.

HAN, CHRISTINE S; Mira Mesa HS; San Diego, CA; (4); 1/800; Cmnty Wkr; Pres Service Clb; Rep Soph Cls; Sec Jr Cls; Rep Sr Cls; Intrml Tennis; NHS; Pres Acad Fit Awd; Val; CA Schlrshp Fed; Stanford U; Med.

HAN, DAPHNE; Mark Keppel HS; Monterey Park, CA; (3); Dance Clb; Library Aide; Office Aide; Teachers Aide; Powder Puff Ftbl; Wt Lftg; Pres Acad Fit Awd; Berkeley U; Bus.

HAN, DENNIS Y; Kennedy HS; Buena Park, CA; (1); Church Yth Grp; Cmnty Wkr; FCA; Key Clb; JV Bsktbl; Cit Awd; Hon Roll; Pres Acad Fit Awd; Lorani Clb; Cmnty Vllybl Team; Cmnty Golf; Engrng.

HAN, EDWARD J; Loyola HS; Alhambra, CA; (2); 1/250; Debate Tm; NFL; Lit Mag; Var Ftbl; Hon Roll; 1st Pl Cinco De Mayo Cntst; Loyola Schlrshp Bst Wrtr.

HAN, HOLLY; Alhambra HS; Monterey Park, CA; (4); 1/690; Church Yth Grp; Computer Clb; Pres English Clb; Math Clb; Model UN; Science Clb; Ed Lit Mag; Rep Stu Cncl; Bausch & Lomb Sci Awd; Val; Westinghouse Top 300 Hnrs Grp; Jnr Sci/Hmnts Stu Fllw; Edison-Mc Graw Schlrshp Pgm; Med.

HAN, HYUNAH; Aragon HS; San Mateo, CA; (3); Varsity Clb; Tennis; Hon Roll; Badminton; UC Davis; Phrmcst.

HAN, JANET K; Rio Mesa HS; Camarillo, CA; (4); 1/374; AFS; Cmnty Wkr; Sec Drama Clb; Hosp Aide; School Play; Sec Stu Cncl; Ntl Merit Ltr; Opt Clb Awd; Pres Acad Fit Awd; Val; UCSD; Bio.

HAN, JENNIFER J; Sonora HS; La Habra, CA; (3); 6/300; Art Clb; Cmnty Wkr; French Clb; FBLA; Math Clb; Science Clb; Ski Clb; Teachers Aide; French Hon Soc; High Hon Roll; CSF; UCLA; Ophthalmologist.

HAN, JIWON; Bolsa Grande HS; Garden Grove, CA; (4); 12/330; Pres German Clb; Math Clb; Science Clb; Sec Jr Cls; Treas Sr Cls; Sec Stu Cncl; Var JV Tennis; Hon Roll; Lead Worshop Walk By Faith Chrch Pastor Howard Yim; SEALBEARER; Orange Cnty Stu Advsry Cncl Agnst Drg; U CA Irvine.

HAN, JOHN; Ripon HS; Escalon, CA; (4); 9/96; Debate Tm; SADD; Varsity Clb; Var Bsbl; Var Ftbl; Var Wrstlng; Gov Hon Prg Awd; High Hon Roll; NHS; Pres Acad Fit Awd; Cal Poly; Econ.

HAN, JOHNEY; Marina HS; Westminster, CA; (4); 11/505; Church Yth Grp; JCL; Key Clb; Latin Clb; Math Clb; Trk; High Hon Roll; Hon Roll; NHS; Pres Acad Fit Awd; Tae Kwon Do Black Belt; Acad Decath; U CA Berkeley; Mech Engrng.

HAN, JONATHAN C; Savanna HS; Anaheim, CA; (4); 5/286; Pres Church Yth Grp; Hosp Aide; Pres JA; Pres Service Clb; Mrchg Band; Ed Nwsp; Rep Stu Cncl; Capt JV Tennis; Ntl Merit Ltr; Pres Acad Fit Awd; U MI Ann Arbor; Elect Engr.

HAN, JULIE J; Granada Hills HS; Northridge, CA; (3); Church Yth Grp; JV Bsktbl; Var JV Cheerldng; JV Trk; JSA.

HAN, KARYN MAI T; Alhambra HS; Alhambra, CA; (2); Office Aide; Cheerldng; La Chandelle Tri-Hi-Y; San Deigo ST U.

HAN, KATHERINE K; Nogales HS; W Covina, CA; (2); Science Clb; VP Jr Cls; High Hon Roll; Hon Roll; Prfct Atten Awd; CSF; Stanford; Phy.

HAN, KILBY J; Eagle Rock HS; Los Angeles, CA; (2); Art Clb; Library Aide; Bsktbl; Hon Roll; Prfct Atten Awd; E Club; Cal ST Los Angeles; Arch.

HAN, KIMBERLEY H; Carondelet HS; Concord, CA; (4); Cmnty Wkr; Ski Clb; Spanish Clb; Chorus; School Musical; School Play; High Hon Roll; Ntl Merit SF; Yth Edctr Pgm; AP Spnsh IV Awd-Acad Excllnc; AHSSP; Stanford U; Psych.

HAN, MEE-JA; Cerritos HS; Cerritos, CA; (1); Church Yth Grp; Cmnty Wkr; Intnl Clb; Math Clb; Math Tm; Service Clb; Band; High Hon Roll; U Of CA Berkeley; Acctng.

HAN, MEI MEI; Lowell HS; San Francisco, CA; (2); Drama Clb; Ski Clb; Rep Stu Cncl; French Hon Soc; Hon Roll; Pacific Rowng Clb Coachs Awd 90; Corp Law.

HAN, NYDIA; St Bonaventure HS; Santa Paula, CA; (3); Church Yth Grp; Hosp Aide; Sec Service Clb; Variety Show; Ed Yrbk; Sec Frsh Cls; Sec Jr Cls; Treas Sr Cls; Var Cheerldng; NHS; Bach Clscl Rmntc Cntmpry Fstvl Wnr; Cert Mrt Pnl; Ventura Cnty Sci Fr 3rd Pl; Miss CA Natl Teen Fnlst; Cmnctns.

HAN, SALLY; Palisades HS; Los Angeles, CA; (4); 1/450; VP Sec Church Yth Grp; Library Aide; Ed Yrbk; Off Jr Cls; Off Sr Cls; Bausch & Lomb Sci Awd; Prfct Atten Awd; Pres Acad Fit Awd; Cert Of Mrt Soc Wmn Engrs; Rensselaer Polytech Inst Mdl.

HAN, SIMON S; Whitney HS; Cerritos, CA; (3); Cmnty Wkr; Pres JA; Hist Key Clb; Rep Model UN; Mgr Nwsp; Rep Jr Cls; Var Socr; Var Capt Tennis; High Hon Roll; Var Bsbl; U Of CA Berkeley; Bus Fin.

HAN, SUE J; King-Drew Medical Magnet HS; Los Angeles, CA; (3); Chess Clb; Church Yth Grp; Math Clb; Church Choir; Hon Roll; Prfct Atten Awd; UCSD; Bio.

HAN, SUE Y; Antelope Valley HS; Lancaster, CA; (3); 19/654; Church Yth Grp; German Clb; Office Aide; Church Choir; Hosp Aide; Service Clb; Spanish Clb; Rep Soph Cls; Off Jr Cls; Stu Cncl; Zonta Club; UCLA; Tchr.

HAN, SUNG H; Santa Clara HS; Santa Clara, CA; (2); Church Yth Grp; Service Clb; Chorus; Church Choir; JV Socr; JV Tennis; JV Trk; High Hon Roll; Hon Roll; Pres Acad Fit Awd; Pediatrics.

HAN, SUSAN H; Gardena HS; Gardena, CA; (4); Church Yth Grp; Cmnty Wkr; FTA; Intnl Clb; Teachers Aide; Varsity Clb; School Play; Variety Show; Ed Yrbk; Tennis; Cal ST Fullerton; Teach.

HAN, TRACY; Marina HS; Westminster, CA; (2); Church Yth Grp; German Clb; Key Clb; Color Guard; Flag Corp; Mrchg Band; High Hon Roll; Peer Asstnc Ldrshp; Family Cnslr.

HAN, UNG; Fountain Valley HS; Fountain Valley, CA; (2); Chess Clb; Church Yth Grp; Tennis; Korean Clb; UC Berkeley.

HAN, YEONG-CHIA; Piedmont HS; Piedmont, CA; (4); Debate Tm; German Clb; Intnl Clb; Model UN; NFL; Pep Clb; Quiz Bowl; Speech Tm; SADD; Band; Modern Music Masters; Gld Awd Music; Natl Forensic League Hnrs Awd; Astrophysics.

HANAFIN, JOSHUA R; Redlands SR HS; Redlands, CA; (2); Band; Mrchg Band; Hon Roll; Jr NHS; NHS; Pres Acad Fit Awd; Outstndng Schlrshp & Ctznshp Awd Sci & Phys Educ 89-90; 1st Degr Black Balt Shodan; US Judo Assn; West Point; Infrantry Offcr.

HANAMAIKAI, JENNIFER L; Savanna HS; Anaheim, CA; (2); Pep Clb; Trk; Vllybl; UCLA; Med.

HANANIA, MITRI; Westmoor HS; Daly City, CA; (4); Hon Roll; Pres Acad Fit Awd; South San Francisco Price Clb; San Francisco ST U; Atty.

HANBERRY, JAMES C; Santa Maria HS; Santa Maria, CA; (2); JV Wrstlng; Cit Awd; Prfct Atten Awd; Air Force Acad; Air Force Piolt.

HANCE, LORI; Notre Dame HS; San Mateo, CA; (2); Church Yth Grp; Cmnty Wkr; Variety Show; Var JV Bsktbl; JV Cheerldng; JV Pom Pon; Socr; Hon Roll; NEDT Awd; San Francisco ST U; Bus.

HANCHETT, MELISSA L; Live Oak HS; San Martin, CA; (3); Art Clb; Church Yth Grp; Debate Tm; 4-H; Teachers Aide; Nwsp; Cit Awd; 4-H Awd; Hon Roll; Pres Acad Fit Awd; Dressage Rdng; Grphc Art.

HANCOCK, AMY; Fairfield HS; Fairfield, CA; (4); Church Yth Grp; Dance Clb; Drama Clb; Teachers Aide; Rep Frsh Cls; Ricks Coll; Dietien.

HANCOCK, CARRIE; Pioneer Baptist HS; Norwalk, CA; (3); 1/10; Church Yth Grp; Cmnty Wkr; Pep Clb; Teachers Aide; School Play; Yrbk; Sec Stu Cncl; Var Cheerldng; Var Sftbl; High Hon Roll; Hghst GPA 88-89; Hmcmng Prncss 87 & 89; Stdy Sgn Lang Cerritos Coll; StanfordSPCH Pthlgy.

HANCOCK, CHERYL L; Irvine HS; Irvine, CA; (1); Key Clb; Pep Clb; Hon Roll; Vol Lcl Hosp.

HANCOCK, HEATHER; Santa Paula HS; Santa Paula, CA; (2); Church Yth Grp; Cmnty Wkr; Pres Key Clb; SADD; Stat Bsktbl; Hon Roll; Pres Acad Fit Awd; Miss Congeniality Miss Teen Santa Paula Pgnt.

HANCOCK, J MATT; Armijo HS; Fairfield, CA; (1); Boy Scts; Church Yth Grp; JV Bsktbl; Var Diving; JV Socr; Var Swmmng; High Hon Roll; Schl Dcthln 4th Pl; BYU; Med.

HANCOCK, JAMES R; Apple Valley HS; Apple Valley, CA; (1).

HANCOCK, LUKAS; Ukiah HS; Calpella, CA; (2); 185/554; U ST CA; Medcl Doctor.

HANCOCK, TIFFANY; Orange Glen HS; Esconddido, CA; (3); French Clb; Pres FFA; Teachers Aide; Pres Acad Fit Awd; FFA Str Chpt Fmr Outstndg Proj 90; 1st Pl Indv FFA Lghthrs Jdg Cal-Poly Pomona 90; G Fleeup Mem Awd; Cal Poly San Luis Obispo; Vet.

HANCORNE, HOPE I; Rio Lindo Adventist Acad; Trinidad, CA; (4); French Clb; Library Aide; Variety Show; Gym; Vllybl; Pacific Union Coll; Accntng.

HAND, ANGELA; Lassen Union HS; Milford, CA; (3); 11/214; Cmnty Wkr; SADD; Drill Tm; Hon Roll; CSF.

HAND, CHRISTOPHER B; Baldwin Park HS; Baldwin Pk, CA; (1); Church Yth Grp; English Clb; FBLA; Science Clb; SADD; Rep Frsh Cls; Stat Bsktbl; JV Ftbl; JV Trk; Wt Lftg; Sftbl Baldwin Pk; 3.8 GPA; UNLV; Teacher.

HAND, HEATHER L; Oak Ridge HS; Shingle Springs, CA; (3); Sec Debate Tm; NFL; Sec Speech Tm; SADD; Lit Mag; Cit Awd; High Hon Roll; Hon Roll; Friday Night Live; CSF; Sacramento ST Coll; Psych.

HAND, KEVIN; Hawthorne HS; Hawthorne, CA; (3); Church Yth Grp; Drama Clb; Office Aide; SADD; Teachers Aide; Church Choir; Var Bsbl; Hon Roll; CA ST LA; Pblc Rltns.

HAND, SHAWN L; Clovis HS; Clovis, CA; (2); Socr.

HANDAL, JENNIFER; Acalanes HS; Lafayette, CA; (4); Am Leg Aux Girls St; Dance Clb; Model UN; Spanish Clb; Speech Tm; VP Jr Cls; Stu Cncl; Intrml Trk; Masonic Awd; Mock Trial; Amnesty Intl; Yth Edctr; Duke U; Pol Sci.

HANDEL, JASON W; Buena Park HS; Buena Park, CA; (3); Letterman Clb; Varsity Clb; Bsbl; Socr; Wrstlng; Sports Med.

HANDLER, GABRIELLE B; El Camino Real HS; Woodland Hills, CA; (2); Intnl Clb; NFL; VP Service Clb; VP Speech Tm; Sec Soph Cls; L Trk; Hon Roll; HOBY Ldrshp Smnr; St Natl Forensic Leag Trnmt; UCLA; Law.

HANDORF, KIERSTEN; Lemoore HS; Lemoore, CA; (3); Dance Clb; Drama Clb; Pep Clb; Flag Corp; School Play; Variety Show; VP Frsh Cls; Cheerldng; NHS; Psychlgst.

HANDS, AFRICA SHERI; John F Kennedy HS; Richmond, CA; (2); Spanish Clb; Hon Roll; Awds For Excl Chm & Geom; Teen Incntv Prgm; Yth In Transition; Prtnrshp; Pre Coll Acad 90; Psych.

HANDY, NICOLA J; Moreno Valley HS; Moreno Valley, CA; (3); Drama Clb; ROTC; Color Guard; Drill Tm; Var L Swmmng; Var L Trk; JROTC Civic Svc Awd; JRTOC Longevity & Fidelity Awd; JROTC Sharp Shooter Awd; U Of CA Los Angeles; Drama.

HANELT, SCOTT A; Del Campo HS; Fair Oaks, CA; (3); 62/446; Teachers Aide; Rep Sr Cls; JV Bsbl; Ftbl; Intrml Wt Lftg; Hon Roll; Hmcmng & Prom Cmmttes; UCSB; Sports Med.

HANEY, LENISE V; Edison HS; Stockton, CA; (3); Church Yth Grp; 4-H; Sec FTA; Girl Scts; Teachers Aide; Yrbk; Rep Stu Cncl; Bsktbl; Vllybl; Hon Roll; U Of Paficic Upward Bound Pgm; Georgetown U; Educ.

HANFLAND, MATTHEW L; Arlington HS; Riverside, CA; (3); Church Yth Grp; Letterman Clb; Varsity Clb; Acpl Chr; School Musical; Swing Chorus; Var Crs Cntry; Var Trk; Hon Roll; Jr NHS; U Of CA Riverside; Dentistry.

HANFT, NICHOLE; Livermore HS; Livermore, CA; (4); 26/372; Church Yth Grp; Pep Clb; Acpl Chr; School Play; Stage Crew; Ed Nwsp; Rptr Lit Mag; Rep Jr Cls; Rep Sr Cls; Chrmn Stu Cncl; Edtr Laburinth-Artistic & Lit Sctn Schl Nwspr; CSF; Berkeley; Art.

HANG, BUU; Saddleback HS; Santa Ana, CA; (1); FBLA; JV Bsktbl; Cit Awd; CA Polytechnic; Drftsmn.

HANG, NGUYEN T; University HS; Irvine, CA; (2); Var Ftbl; Intrml Wrstlng; UCI; Combat Pilot.

HANG, QUOC DUY; Santiago HS; Garden Grove, CA; (2); 1/498; Art Clb; Boy Scts; Cmnty Wkr; Computer Clb; Dance Clb; Debate Tm; French Clb; Hosp Aide; Intnl Clb; Latin Clb; UCR; Pre-Med.

HANG, VINCENT; Abraham Lincoln HS; San Francisco, CA; (4); Library Aide; CA Schlrshp Fed Life Stu; Yth Educator Pgm; San Francisco ST U; Engrng.

HANG, VO; Saddleback HS; Santa Ana, CA; (4); French Clb; Red Cross Aide; Spanish Clb; Tennis; Trk; Cit Awd; Gov Hon Prg Awd; Prfct Atten Awd; Var Lttr-Tennis; Vietnamese Clb & Chinese Clb; UCI Prtnr; CA ST Poly Pomona; ETE.

HANGARTNER, LINDA; Encinal HS; Alameda, CA; (3); Sec Drama Clb; Girl Scts; Mrchg Band; School Musical; Var JV Cheerldng; JV Socr; Var L Swmmng; Hon Roll; St Schlr; Church Yth Grp; Encnls F/Cngssnl Page In WA DC; PTA Rflctns Pgrm 1st Pl; HS Entry Advncd Dist; GATE 80; UCLA; Drama.

HANGO, CHRISTINE M; La Habra HS; La Habra, CA; (2); 1/388; Church Yth Grp; Girl Scts; Band; Jazz Band; Mrchg Band; Pep Band; Film Club; Top Brass.

HANH, LE H; Seaside HS; Marina, CA; (3); AFS; FBLA; Hosp Aide; Temple Yth Grp; Prfct Atten Awd; FBLA Corresponding Secy Of Month; Bus.

HANIF, AMJAD S; Clovis HS; Clovis, CA; (3); Rep Debate Tm; Treas FBLA; Math Tm; Rep NFL; Science Clb; Off Frsh Cls; Off Soph Cls; Rotary Awd; Jr Sci & Humanities Symposium Fnlst; CA St Sci Fr 4th Pl; Civil Engrng.

HANKINSON, CHAD; Saugus HS; Saugus, CA; (4); 23/660; Church Yth Grp; Teachers Aide; Varsity Clb; Pres Soph Cls; Pres Jr Cls; Pres VP Stu Cncl; Var Capt Bsbl; Var Capt Bsktbl; Cit Awd; Masters Coll; Bus.

HANKS, AMBER; Folsom HS; Leesburg,, VA; (1); Off Frsh Cls; Stu Cncl; JV Cheerldng; Hon Roll; Prfct Atten Awd; SRO.

HANKS, STACI; Woodcrest Christian Schl; Riverside, CA; (1); Church Yth Grp; Church Choir; JV Bsktbl; Stat Sftbl; JV Vllybl; High Hon Roll; Piano; Apt Ministries; Chrstn Ldrshp Awd.

HANLE, CARI; Burbank HS; Burbank, CA; (2); Cmnty Wkr; French Clb; Rptr Nwsp; Skiing Tennis & Swmmg; NY U; Med.

HANLEY, DESIREE RENEE; Summerville HS; Twain Harte, CA; (3); French Clb; Pep Clb; Quiz Bowl; Teachers Aide; Nwsp; Yrbk; Lit Mag; JV Capt Cheerldng; Phys Thrpy.

HANLEY, MICHELLE; Etiwanda HS; Alta Loma, CA; (4); 38/500; Pep Clb; School Play; Cheerldng; Tennis; Hon Roll; CSEA Schlrshp Wnnr; 89 Miss CA Cont; CA Poly Pomona; Educ.

HANLEY, TERRI R; Healdsburg SR HS; Benicia, CA; (4); 3/300; Sec AFS; Rep Am Leg Aux Girls St; Art Clb; Pres Boy Scts; Chess Clb; VP Debate Tm; Sec Intnl Clb; Model UN; Q&S; Ski Clb; Karate; Japanese HS Student Exchange Program; BSA Explorers Of America; UC Berkeley; Political Econ.

HANLON, GAIL E; Poway HS; San Diego, CA; (3); Church Yth Grp; Flag Corp; Cal ST Long Beach; Educ.

HANN, BREE; Edison HS; Huntington Bch, CA; (1); Key Clb; Teachers Aide; OCAD Capt; Acad Cmptn Sec; 2(d Pl Spch & 3rd Pl Lit OCAD Awds; Eng.

HANN, LISA M; Gompers Secondary HS; San Diego, CA; (2); 1/145; Church Yth Grp; Model UN; High Hon Roll; NHS.

HANN, SHAUNA N; Mission Viejo HS; Laguna Hills, CA; (1); 128/455; Model UN; Color Guard; Rptr Nwsp; Most Imprvd Awd Color Guard; Dele Awd Sanger MUN Conf; Bus.

HANNA, CHRISTINE N; Redwood HS; Visalia, CA; (4); Rptr Nwsp; Hon Roll; CA ST Long Beach; Jrnlsm.

HANNA, JANINE RENEE; W Covina Hills Adventist Schl; San Dimas, CA; (1); 1/15; Church Yth Grp; Teachers Aide; Ed Yrbk; Stu Cncl; High Hon Roll.

HANNA, JESSICKA E; North Salinas HS; Salinas, CA; (1); Am Leg Aux Girls St; Cmnty Wkr; Drama Clb; Key Clb; SADD; Band; Mrchg Band; Pep Band; School Play; JV Bsktbl; Teach.

HANNA, REBECCA L; Rio Americano HS; Sacramento, CA; (3); Art Clb; Church Yth Grp; Cmnty Wkr; German Clb; NFL; Science Clb; SADD; Church Choir; School Play; Var L Trk; U Of Brtsh Columbia Dendrolgy.

HANNA, SYLVIA; St Monicas HS; Los Angeles, CA; (3); Church Yth Grp; Cmnty Wkr; Pres Sr Cls; JV Vllybl; Hon Roll; CSF; Part-Time Job; U Of CA Los Angeles; Law.

HANNA, WAFA J; El Cajon Valley HS; El Cajon, CA; (4); 10/308; Church Yth Grp; Dance Clb; GAA; Intnl Clb; Letterman Clb; Varsity Clb; Variety Show; Var Capt Crs Cntry; JV Gym; Var Capt Trk; CIF X-Cntry, Trck, CA Intrschlstc Fed; St Qlfr X-Cntry 89-90; Mesa CC Of San Diego; Lnqstcs.

HANNA, WISSAM; San Pasqual HS; Escondido, CA; (3); 114/353; Wt Lftg; JV Wrstlng; Hon Roll; Jr NHS; U CA-SANTA Barbara; Engrng.

HANNAH, Y LONDA M; Washington Prep HS; Compton, CA; (2); ROTC; Band; Church Choir; Cit Awd; Hon Roll; Jr NHS; Acad Achvt Awd; Pediatrcs.

HANNER, JENNIFER; Roosevelt HS; Fresno, CA; (1); Dance Clb; Hosp Aide; Acpl Chr; Chorus; Hon Roll; Ldrshp Roosevelt Live; Piano; Med.

HANNESSON, KATIE M; Davis SR HS; Davis, CA; (2); Church Yth Grp; Spanish Clb; School Play; Off Frsh Cls; JV Vllybl.

HANNIE, LA PORSCHA J; St Michael HS; Los Angeles, CA; (3); Pres Church Yth Grp; Hosp Aide; Library Aide; Spanish Clb; Stage Crew; Variety Show; Hon Roll; Jarvis Christian Coll; Sociolgy.

HANNIE, LAPORSCHA J; St Michaels HS; Los Angeles, CA; (3); Pres Church Yth Grp; Dance Clb; Hosp Aide; Office Aide; Spanish Clb; Stage Crew; Variety Show; Hon Roll; Jarvis Christian Coll; Soclgy.

HANNIGAN, AMBER F; Villa Park HS; Orange, CA; (2); Drama Clb; Key Clb; Spanish Clb; Teachers Aide; Stage Crew; Drama.

HANNON, KATHLEEN; Granada HS; Livermore, CA; (4); 1/330; Church Yth Grp; Sec Science Clb; Pres Science Clb; Spanish Clb; Ed Lit Mag; Var Socr; Var Capt Trk; Var Vllybl; High Hon Roll; Ntl Merit SF; All League & All Section Vllybl; ST Meet Track Comp 330 Low Hurdles, Triple Jump; Envrmntl Engr.

HANNON, PEGGY; Lincoln HS; Stockton, CA; (3); 63/600; Chorus; Lit Mag; High Hon Roll; CSF; Hnrs Geom; Psych.

HANRAHAN, SHELLY A; St Paul HS; La Habra, CA; (3); Cmnty Wkr; Var Socr; Var JV Sftbl; High Hon Roll; NHS; CSF; U CA Davis; Vet.

HANSBROW, BRIAN J; College Park HS; Martinez, CA; (3); Band; Jazz Band; Mrchg Band; Pep Band; Race BMX.

HANSCHE, CHRIS M; Saint Joseph HS; Santa Maria, CA; (3); JA; Science Clb; SADD; Wrk 30 Hrs Wk; Study Music & Ply Guitar.

HANSCOM, KENNY; North HS; Bakersfield, CA; (1); Church Yth Grp; Band; Mrchg Band; Pep Band; JV Socr; Hon Roll; Bio-Chem.

HANSCOME, JENNIFER; Woodbridge HS; Irvine, CA; (2); Drama Clb; Chorus; Drill Tm; Variety Show; Girls League; U CA; Fshn Merch.

HANSEL, JUSTIN; Cardinal Newman HS; Santa Rosa, CA; (2); Service Clb; Spanish Clb; JV Socr; Var Tennis; High Hon Roll; Pres Acad Fit Awd; Santa Clara U.

HANSEN, ANGELA; Mountain Empire HS; Alpine, CA; (3); Drama Clb; Pres VP 4-H; Letterman Clb; Spanish Clb; Teachers Aide; Varsity Clb; Church Choir; VP Soph Cls; VP Pres Stu Cncl; Hon Roll; Rotry Yth Ldrshp Awd; Cls Qn; Tribune Awd; USD; Envrnmntl Engr.

HANSEN, BRIAN E; Lodi HS; Lodi, CA; (2); Teachers Aide; Band; Mrchg Band; Lit Mag; JV Bsktbl; Var Vllybl; Hon Roll; CA Poly; Chem Engr.

HANSEN, BRIAN L; Fresno HS; Fresno, CA; (2); Debate Tm; NFL; Speech Tm; Prfct Atten Awd; Intrml Bsbl; JV Tennis; Frnsics Trnmnt Awd-St; Law.

HANSEN, BRIDGET; St Joseph HS; Santa Maria, CA; (3); Church Yth Grp; GAA; NFL; Science Clb; SADD; Teachers Aide; Rep Nwsp; JV Sftbl; JSA Treasurer & Director Of Innovations; Pre Medicine.

HANSEN, CARRIE F; Bullard HS; Fresno, CA; (1); Art Clb; Cit Awd; Hon Roll; Horseshow Jumping; CSF; Parsons Schl Design; Grphc Dsgn.

HANSEN, CRAIG; Fresno Adventist Acad; Chowchilla, CA; (2); Church Yth Grp; FCA; Ski Clb; Phtg Yrbk; Var Ftbl; Var Sftbl; Aviation.

HANSEN, CYNTHIA; Nevada Union HS; Grass Valley, CA; (4); 10/477; 4-H; Math Tm; Band; Jazz Band; Mrchg Band; School Musical; Stage Crew; Var Capt Crs Cntry; Trk; Elks Awd; Nordic Ski Team Capt; SAFE Envrnmntl Club; CSF; U Of Puget Sound; Music.

HANSEN, DARLEEN; Monta Vista HS; Cupertino, CA; (2); Pres Church Yth Grp; Chorus; Church Choir; Variety Show; Cheerldng; Score Keeper; Swmmng; Trk; Vllybl; Hon Roll; Mst Imprvd Plq Sccr; Cal Poly; Animal Husbndry.

HANSEN, EMILY E; La Reina HS; Camarillo, CA; (2); 1/92; Church Yth Grp; NFL; Hist Speech Tm; Rptr Nwsp; Rep Soph Cls; Rep Jr Cls; Cit Awd; High Hon Roll; NHS; Spanish NHS; CSF; Med.

HANSEN, ERICKA; Capital Christian HS; Fair Oaks, CA; (3); Church Yth Grp; Var Bsktbl; Var Trk; Var Vllybl; High Hon Roll; Aeronautics Club; CSF; Stu Pilot; US Air Force Acad; Aeronaut.

HANSEN, HEATHER; Arlington HS; Riverside, CA; (2); Pep Clb; Hist Soph Cls; Co-Capt Cheerldng; Hon Roll; St Schlr; HOBY Schlr; Yth Grp-Chrch; CSF; Intl Rltns.

HANSEN, HEATHER; Benicia HS; Benicia, CA; (1); Church Yth Grp; Pep Clb; Band; Church Choir; Mrchg Band; Pep Band; Jr NHS.

HANSEN, IANA HOY; La Jolla HS; La Jolla, CA; (4); 114/345; Aud/Vis; Cmnty Wkr; Dance Clb; Drama Clb; Key Clb; Service Clb; Spanish Clb; Thesps; School Musical; School Play; Video Prod-Biweekly Cmps News, Sprts, Var Shw La Jolla Hghlts; Yr Long Emplymnt Athl Shoe Store; NYU; Film Directing.

HANSEN, JEFFREY; Fred C Beyer HS; Modesto, CA; (3); Church Yth Grp; German Clb; Math Clb; Math Tm; Church Choir; Cit Awd; Hon Roll; Robotics & Film Clbs.

HANSEN, JENNIFER M; Santa Barbara HS; Santa Barbara, CA; (3); 63/472; Drama Clb; Pep Clb; Varsity Clb; Chorus; Cheerldng; Pom Pon; Socr; U Of CA; Interior Design.

HANSEN, JENNIFER MICHELLE; Newport Harbor HS; Newport Beach, CA; (4); 35/335; AFS; French Clb; Band; Pep Band; Var L Vllybl; Pres Acad Fit Awd; Socl Sci Clb Secy & Treas; CSF; U Of CA Los Angeles; Hstry.

HANSEN, KARA L; Ceres HS; Ceres, CA; (3); Church Yth Grp; FBLA; Key Clb; Model UN; Stu Cncl; High Hon Roll; Hon Roll; Pres Acad Fit Awd; French Clb; Pep Clb; 5th Pl Future Prob Slvng Team Intl Bowl 88; Acad Decthln Team 90; Valparaiso U; Law.

HANSEN, KARYN; Fresno HS; Fresno, CA; (4); Church Yth Grp; Pep Clb; SADD; Rep Stu Cncl; JV Var Bsktbl; High Hon Roll; Brigham Yng U; Elem Ed.

HANSEN, KATHLEEN M; Cornerstone Christian HS; Camarillo, CA; (1); Church Yth Grp; Cmnty Wkr; Service Clb; Spanish Clb; Var Bsktbl; Var Sftbl; Var Vllybl.

HANSEN, KIRSTEN; Palo Verde HS; Blythe, CA; (3); #3 In Class; Drama Clb; Sec Key Clb; Service Clb; Variety Show; Rptr Nwsp; Rptr Yrbk; Sec Soph Cls; Treas NHS; Mock Trial 10th & 11th; CA Schlrshp Fed Treas; San Diego ST; Ed.

HANSEN, KRIS A; Oak Ridge HS; Rescue, CA; (2); 28/277; Vllybl.

HANSEN, KRISTIN T; West Shores HS; Desert Shores, CA; (4); 1/17; Key Clb; Ed Nwsp; Yrbk; Pres Frsh Cls; Pres Soph Cls; Rep Jr Cls; Sec Stu Cncl; Var Capt Bsktbl; Var Capt Cheerldng; Var Score Keeper; Coll Of The Desert; Nursng.

HANSEN, LISA M; Golden West HS; Visalia, CA; (2); Church Yth Grp; German Clb; Intnl Clb; Science Clb; Sec Band; Mrchg Band; Pep Band; Ed Nwsp; Capt Sftbl; High Hon Roll; Commnctns.

HANSEN, MICHELE L; Ponderosa HS; Placerville, CA; (4); French Clb; Ski Clb; Acpl Chr; Stat Bsbl; JV Tennis; Hon Roll.

HANSEN, MONICA L; Cordova HS; Rancho Cordova, CA; (3); Cmnty Wkr; Hosp Aide; Model UN; Teachers Aide; Acpl Chr; Yrbk; Var Capt Swmmng; JV Var Vllybl; Cit Awd; High Hon Roll; Camp Fire Inc Awandah Awd; Vlybl MVP Awd; CA ST U Of Sacramento; Acctng.

HANSEN, ROBYNN K; Casa Robles HS; Orangevale, CA; (3); Pep Clb; Spanish Clb; Teachers Aide; Drill Tm; Cheerldng; Pom Pon; Score Keeper; Vllybl; Hon Roll; Sac ST; Bus.

HANSEN, SEAN; Granada Hills HS; Granada Hills, CA; (3); Cmnty Wkr; VP FBLA; Ski Clb; Yrbk; VP Frsh Cls; JV Lcrss; JV Wrstlng; Hon Roll; Snowboarder Of Wrld Rnkd 17th; Envrnmntl Hygienst.

HANSEN, SHELLIE L; River City HS; W Sacramento, CA; (3); SADD; Hon Roll; Pres Acad Fit Awd; Sacramento ST U; Acctng.

HANSEN, STACEY; Poway HS; Poway, CA; (1); Church Yth Grp; Band; Church Choir; Mrchg Band; Pep Band; School Musical; School Play; Stage Crew; Variety Show; Bus Mgmt.

HANSEN, TRAVIS; San Bernardino HS; San Bernardino, CA; (3); 14/500; Boy Scts; Church Yth Grp; Computer Clb; FFA; Crs Cntry; Ftbl; Trk; High Hon Roll; Pres Acad Fit Awd; USC.

HANSEN, VANESSA; Capital Christian HS; Fair Oaks, CA; (1); Church Yth Grp; Treas Frsh Cls; Var Bsktbl; JV Vllybl; High Hon Roll; Aeronautics Clb; CSF; Psych.

HANSJELIANA, VICTOR; GAHR HS; Artesia, CA; (2); 5/500; Boy Scts; 4-H; French Clb; JA; JV Swmmng; 4-H Awd; High Hon Roll; Hon Roll; Blue & Gld Awds Math & Engl; Waterpolo Tm; USA Water Polo; UCLA; Mech Engrng.

HANSJI, AARTI S; Cornelia Connelly HS; Anaheim, CA; (4); Cmnty Wkr; Stage Crew; Variety Show; Yrbk; Lit Mag; Off Sr Cls; Tennis; Hon Roll; NHS; Indian Classcl Dancing; Indian Folk Dancing Cmptns-1st/2nd Pl; U Of S CA; Bus.

HANSON, ADAM S; Atwater HS; Atwater, CA; (3); Boy Scts; Church Yth Grp; Church Choir; Var JV Socr; High Hon Roll; Hon Roll; Prfct Atten Awd; Certs A P Bio & Calculus; Var Socr; BYU.

HANSON, ALISON G; The Branson Schl; Ross, CA; (4); Cmnty Wkr; Dance Clb; Drama Clb; Key Clb; School Play; Variety Show; Stu Cncl; Vllybl; Dance Shows; Hnrb Mntn Drama Awd; Acting.

HANSON, AMY A; Tulare Union HS; Pixley, CA; (3); 3/401; Band; Mrchg Band; Var Tennis; High Hon Roll; CA Schlstc Fed; Bio.

HANSON, ANDREA L; Santa Paula Union HS; Santa Paula, CA; (1); 16/360; SADD; JV Cheerldng; Hon Roll; UNLV; Bus.

HANSON, COLE; Palm Desert HS; Palm Desert, CA; (3); JV Bsktbl; Var Golf; CSF.

HANSON JR, DAVID C; St Genevieve HS; Canoga Park, CA; (3); Hon Roll; Mdl Rcktry; Mdlng Civilian & Military Aircrft; Rdng Sci Fctn; Air Trffc Cntrllng.

HANSON, DENISE A; Mira Mesa HS; San Diego, CA; (4); Var Swmmng; JV Tennis; Pres Acad Fit Awd; Top 100 Stu 90; Schl Site Cncl; UC Santa Barbara.

HANSON, ERIC A; Elk Grove HS; Elk Grove, CA; (3); Letterman Clb; Science Clb; SADD; Var Bsbl; JV Ftbl; Mgr Var Mgr(s); Prfct Atten Awd; St Schlr; Acad Achvt Awd; Airline Pilot.

HANSON, JOANNE E; Beaumont HS; Beaumont, CA; (2); Church Yth Grp; Dance Clb; French Clb; Stat Bsktbl; L Mgr(s); Score Keeper; Cit Awd; High Hon Roll; Hon Roll; Stat Ftbl; Azusa Pacific; Child Psych.

HANSON, JOSEPH D; Apple Valley Christian HS; Apple Valley, CA; (3); Church Yth Grp; Teachers Aide; Varsity Clb; Band; Pep Band; Var Bsbl; Var Bsktbl; Var Vllybl; Hon Roll; Azusa Pacific.

HANSON, KELLY D; Tulare Union HS; Pixley, CA; (2); Rep Soph Cls; Rep Stu Cncl; JV Bsktbl; Var Tennis; High Hon Roll; Hon Roll; CA Schlstc Fed; Jrnlsm.

HANSON, LYNN; Moreno Valley HS; Riverside, CA; (2); Teachers Aide; Chorus; Mgr(s); High Hon Roll; Hon Roll; Gldn St Exms Alg; Actrss.

HANSON, MATT J; North County Christian Schl; Atascadero, CA; (2); Aud/Vis; Chess Clb; Church Yth Grp; FCA; Letterman Clb; Math Clb; Math Tm; Band; Chorus; Pep Band; Harbard; Music.

HANSON, MEGAN M; Alta Loma HS; Rancho Cucamonga, CA; (3); #55 In Class; Var Crs Cntry; Var Trk; High Hon Roll; Prfct Atten Awd; MIP X-Cntry & Trck Trphy; Peer Cnslng Awd; Acad Ltr; CSULB; Tchr.

HANSON, MINDI JAE; Apple Valley HS; Apple Valley, CA; (2); 13/742; Hon Roll; CSF; Loma Linda U; Obstetrician.

HANSON, MOLLY M; Temecula Valley HS; Temecula, CA; (4); Church Yth Grp; DECA; SADD; Teachers Aide; High Hon Roll; EARTH Clb-Pres; Bst Attitude; Saddleback; Psych.

HANSON, NATHAN R; Valley Christian HS; Bellflower, CA; (2); Church Yth Grp; JV Socr; High Hon Roll; NHS; Prfct Atten Awd; Amer Freestyle Assn Cont Bike Tricks Mem AFA; Awd Most Yrs Svc Bethany Luth Church; UCLA Stanford; Civil Engr.

HANSON, NICOLE C; Bridgemont HS; San Francisco, CA; (3); Church Yth Grp; Church Choir; Var Cheerldng; High Hon Roll; Hon Roll; Soc Women Engrs High Hnr Math, Sci Awd; San Francisco City Wd Poetry Fstvl Fnlst; Engl Awd.

HANSON, SETH L; Atwater HS; Atwater, CA; (2); Boy Scts; Church Yth Grp; SADD; JV Socr; JV Tennis; High Hon Roll; Pres Acad Fit Awd; Brigham Young U; Dntstry.

HANSON, TODD W; Rio Americano HS; Carmichael, CA; (3); Church Yth Grp; Church Choir; Var L Ftbl; Var JV Trk; Var JV Wt Lftg; Capt L Wrstlng; Art; Top 10 N CA Track; U CA Santa Barbara; Psych.

HANSSEN, JODY L; El Cajon Valley HS; El Cajon, CA; (1); German Clb; Drill Tm; Lit Mag; Rep Frsh Cls; Mgr(s); JV Swmmng; Hon Roll; Teacher.

HANTAKAS, MARY ANN; San Joaquin Memorial HS; Fresno, CA; (4); 11/112; Church Yth Grp; Drama Clb; French Clb; GAA; Science Clb; Hon Roll; Pres Acad Fit Awd; CSF; Bk Amer Achvt Awd-Rlgs Stdy; Cum Laud Grad; U Of CA Davis; Bio Sci.

HANUMAN, SHASHI; Pacifica HS; Cypress, CA; (3); 2/274; French Clb; JV Bsktbl; Vllybl; High Hon Roll; Ntl Merit SF; UC Berkeley; Psycht.

HANZEL, KELLEE S; Dublin HS; Dublin, CA; (3); 56/160; Dance Clb; FBLA; Office Aide; Service Clb; Teachers Aide; Hon Roll; Stu Cncl; Var JV Sftbl; Trk; Stat Wrstlng.

HAO, DAVID H; Saint Monica HS; Culver City, CA; (3); #1 In Class; Pres Chess Clb; Debate Tm; Key Clb; Ski Clb; Trk; Hon Roll; VP Pres NHS; CSF; Cert Mrt Piano; Acad Dcthln; UCLA; Comp Sci.

HAOZOUS, EMILY A; Arcata HS; Arcata, CA; (3); Drama Clb; Jazz Band; Mrchg Band; Orch; School Musical; School Play; Stage Crew; Lit Mag; Socr; Hon Roll; Rainforest Clb; Recycling Clb; Music.

HAR, UN HUI; Saratoga HS; Saratoga, CA; (3); Sec Church Yth Grp; JA; Ed Nwsp; Pres Frsh Cls; Stu Cncl; Co-Capt Var Vllybl; High Hon Roll; Harvard Book Awd; CSF.

HARADA, DONNA P; Simi Valley HS; Simi Valley, CA; (3); 50/665; Spanish Clb; Hon Roll; Jr NHS; Spanish NHS; Psych.

HARADON, JASON; Fountain Valley HS; Fountain Valley, CA; (1); Cit Awd; Hon Roll; Criminal Justice/Police Offcr.

HARALDSEN, LORI J; San Marcos HS; San Marcos, CA; (3); Church Yth Grp; Drama Clb; Teachers Aide; Church Choir; Stat Trk; High Hon Roll; Hon Roll; Outstndng Bus Ed Stu; Golden St Exam-St Hnrs; Yth Advsry Cmmttee-Yth Grp; S CA Coll-Costa Mesa; Bus Adm.

HARALSON, JUSTIN T; La Sierra HS; Riverside, CA; (3); Pres Acad Fit Awd; Congressional Yth Ldrshp Cncl; Golden St Exam Hgh Hnrs Achvt; Stanford U; Art.

HARB, LINDA; Mater Dei HS; Anaheim, CA; (2); Church Yth Grp; Speech Tm; Stat Ftbl; UCLA; Brdcstng.

HARBAUGH, DOUG P; Pasadena HS; Pasadena, CA; (4); Church Yth Grp; Debate Tm; Varsity Clb; Stu Cncl; JV Bsbl; Var Socr; High Hon Roll; Pres Acad Fit Awd; R G Canning Yth Awd; AYSO Referee; AF Acad; Pilot.

HARBER, JENNIFER L; Garden Grove HS; Garden Grove, CA; (3); Cmnty Wkr; French Clb; Intnl Clb; Science Clb; SADD; Chorus; High Hon Roll; Kiwanis Awd; NHS; Prfct Atten Awd; Keywanettes, Sec, VP & Pres; CSF; NHS 3 Yrs; Cmnty Svc 89-90 Mst Dedctd Keywanette Awd.

HARBISON, ANNE M; Bishop Montgomery HS; Rolling Hills Est, CA; (2); Church Yth Grp; Pres 4-H; Letterman Clb; Rptr Nwsp; Rep Stu Cncl; JV Trk; 4-H Awd; NHS; 4-H Loa Angels Cnty All Star 90-91; Camp Cnslr; Ed.

HARBISON, ROXANNE E; Hueneme HS; Port Hueneme, CA; (2); 136/503; Drama Clb; Color Guard; Drill Tm; Flag Corp; Prfct Atten Awd; Cmmnty Sftbl; U Of CA Santa Barb; Psych.

HARBISON, SHAWNEE; Avalon HS; Avalon, CA; (3); Church Yth Grp; Letterman Clb; Sec Jr Cls; Stu Cncl; Cheerldng; Sftbl; High Hon Roll; Engr.

HARBOUR, JENNIFER M; Rim Of The World HS; Cedar Glen, CA; (4); Drama Clb; Pep Clb; Color Guard; Flag Corp; Hon Roll; Clark Coll; Chld Dvlpmnt.

HARBOYAN, LORY G; Armenian Mesrobian HS; Montebello, CA; (2); 1/32; Quiz Bowl; Rptr Nwsp; Rptr Lit Mag; Pres Frsh Cls; Hon Roll; UCLA; Amer Lang & Lit.

HARCOS, KYLE A; University City HS; La Jolla, CA; (3); JV Bsbl; Var L Bsktbl; Var L Ftbl; Var L Socr; Var L Vllybl; Hon Roll; CSF; Cum Laude Ntl Latin Exam; U Of CA; Math.

HARCOS, MOLLY A; St Francis HS; Sacramento, CA; (3); Cmnty Wkr; Intnl Clb; Latin Clb; Acpl Chr; JV Bsktbl; Capt Cheerldng; JV Var Socr; Var Capt Tennis; High Hon Roll; CSF VP; Latin Hnr Soc Latin Excllnc Awd; Sacramento Metropolitan Leag Singles Tnns Champn.

HARDEN, REBECCA; Roseville HS; Roseville, CA; (3); 79/411; Church Yth Grp; Cmnty Wkr; Drama Clb; French Clb; Pep Clb; SADD; School Play; Stage Crew; Tennis; Hon Roll; CA ST U Sacto; Bus Major.

HARDENBROOK, DYLAN; Providence HS; Tujunga, CA; (2); Boy Scts; Chess Clb; Crs Cntry; CSUN; Med.

HARDESTY, JASON M; Hesperia HS; Hesperia, CA; (2); 1/768; Cmnty Wkr; FBLA; SADD; Sprt Ed Yrbk; Trk; High Hon Roll; Hon Roll; CA Poly; Jrnlsm.

HARDEY, JACOB ROGER; Placer HS; Newcastle, CA; (2); 24/352; French Clb; Key Clb; Letterman Clb; Ski Clb; Varsity Clb; Crs Cntry; Trk; Vllybl; French Hon Soc; High Hon Roll; Bio.

HARDIMAN, ANGELA; University City HS; San Diego, CA; (3); Am Leg Aux Girls St; Drama Clb; Model UN; SADD; School Play; Stage Crew; Yrbk; Rep Jr Cls; Mgr(s); Powder Puff Ftbl; Galaxy Award; Citizenship Award; Outstanding Achievement Award.

HARDIN, HEATHER M; Lower Lake HS; Clearlake, CA; (1); Church Yth Grp; Chorus; Church Choir; Hon Roll; Friday Night Live; Piano; CA Baptist Coll; Cnslr.

HARDIN, JOHN A; Summerville HS; Tuolumne, CA; (3); Math Clb; Treas Spanish Clb; Stage Crew; Wt Lftg; L Wrstlng; Cit Awd; Hon Roll; NHS; 1st In Voc Olyumpcs Accntng; CA Bus Wk 90; CA ST Fullerton; Accntng.

HARDIN, PATRICIA M; Inglewood HS; Inglewood, CA; (2); Dance Clb; Hon Roll; GATE; UC Berkeley; Phy.

HARDING, AARON R; Selma HS; Kingsburg, CA; (2); Boy Scts; Pep Clb; Hon Roll; Frosh Engl I Outstndng Awd; Engrng.

HARDING, ANGELA L; University HS; Irvine, CA; (1); Orch; School Musical; JV Socr; Scl Sci & Math Laureate Awd; Stanford; Film.

HARDING, MICHELLE LOUISE; Bear River HS; Grass Valley, CA; (2); JV Tennis; JV Vllybl; High Hon Roll; Pres Acad Fit Awd; UCLA; Med.

HARDING, SCOTT R; Greenville JR-SR HS; Greenville, CA; (3); 3/45; Treas Am Leg Boys St; Drama Clb; Service Clb; Band; Jazz Band; VP Frsh Cls; VP Sr Cls; Var L Bsbl; Var L Ftbl; JV Trk; Dynamics Engrng.

HARDING, SITA R; Santa Cruz HS; Santa Cruz, CA; (2); Cmnty Wkr; Drama Clb; Teachers Aide; Thesps; Chorus; School Play; Variety Show; Global Yth Exch 90-91; Peace Child UN Peace Day; Envrnmntl Clb; Theatre.

HARDMAN, CHANEY J; Poway HS; San Diego, CA; (2); Girl Scts; Orch; Nwsp; JV Crs Cntry; Var L Trk; San Diego Cnty Deputy Shrf Explorer; Law Enfrcmnt.

HARDMAN, ELIZABETH L; Davis SR HS; Davis, CA; (4); Art Clb; French Clb; Key Clb; Ed Lit Mag; Prfct Atten Awd; Pres Acad Fit Awd; Pres Schlr; Davis Rotry Clb Schlrshp; Badminton Tm Var Ltrmn; VP CA Schlrshp Fed; Reed Coll; Professor.

HARDMAN, JOE; San Ramon Valley HS; Danville, CA; (2); Cmnty Wkr; Drama Clb; Band; Mrchg Band; Pep Band; Hon Roll; Stu Ambsdr New Stu; JR Vol Local Hosp; U CO; Pedtrcn.

HARDWICK, HEATHER C; Saint Francis HS; Los Altos, CA; (1); 1/396; Art Clb; Church Yth Grp; JV Bsktbl; High Hon Roll; Dance; Stanford; Math.

HARDWICK, MELISSA; Arlington HS; Riverside, CA; (3); Church Yth Grp; Drill Tm; Variety Show; JV Var Cheerldng; Var L Pom Pon; Hon Roll; CA St Natl Dance Champ; Regnl & Natl Showstopper Dance Champ; Exchng Clb Tlnt Show Wnnr; Long Beach ST; Bus.

HARDY, AMANDA L; American HS; Fremont, CA; (4); 4/310; Cmnty Wkr; Hist French Clb; Office Aide; Service Clb; SADD; Teachers Aide; Var Socr; Stat Wrstlng; High Hon Roll; Hon Roll; Bank Of Amer Plaque Wnnr; City Sccr Coach; UCLA.

HARDY, ANDREA L; Sierra Joint Union HS; Madera, CA; (2); Church Yth Grp; Ski Clb; High Hon Roll; Hon Roll; Mem CA Schlrshp Fed; Mem Natl Hnr Soc; Bus Mngmnt.

HARDY, ANDREA S; Skyline HS; Oakland, CA; (3); Aud/Vis; Church Yth Grp; Debate Tm; Drama Clb; Letterman Clb; Library Aide; Office Aide; Speech Tm; Teachers Aide; Thesps; Intl Order Of Jobs Daughters Hnr Qn; Golden St Exam Algebra Awd; CA Order Jobs Daughters 1st Pl Solo; UC Santa Cruz; Psych.

HARDY, DANIEL B; Bellarmine College Prep; San Jose, CA; (3); 18/320; Debate Tm; Band; Jazz Band; Pep Band; School Musical; Ntl Merit SF; UC Berkeley; Elec Engrng.

HARDY, GRAY ALLEN; Quartz Hill HS; Palmdale, CA; (3); 85/722; Key Clb; Letterman Clb; Teachers Aide; Var JV Ftbl; JV Var Wrstlng; Hon Roll; Schlr Athlete-Ftbl & Wrestling; Antelope Vly Coll.

HARDY, MELISSA; Saint Genevieve HS; Saugus, CA; (4); 5/150; Cmnty Wkr; Teachers Aide; Drill Tm; Nwsp; Yrbk; High Hon Roll; Hon Roll; NHS; Opt Clb Awd; Congrssnl Yth Ldrshp Cncl; Loyola; Pre Bus.

HARDY, RENEE L; Colfax HS; Meadow Vista, CA; (2); 7/197; Church Yth Grp; High Hon Roll; Hon Roll; Alpha Omega; Sierra CC; Chld Psych.

HARDY, RYAN; Mother Lode Christian HS; Sonora, CA; (2); Ski Clb; Band; Chorus; JV Bsbl; JV Bsktbl; 1st Pl Boys Div Dodge Ridge Invtnl Ski Race 89; Most Insprtnl Plyr Awd JV Bsktbl 90; Pacific Union Coll; Sports.

HARDY, SHANNON F; Patrick Henry HS; San Diego, CA; (3); Church Yth Grp; Hosp Aide; Model UN; Office Aide; Service Clb; Teachers Aide; L JV Vllybl; Cit Awd; DAR Awd; High Hon Roll; Interact Svc Clb; CSF; Piano; UCSD; Math.

HARDY, WESLEY M; Monte Vista HS; Spring Valley, CA; (3); 78/373; Church Yth Grp; VICA; Bsbl; Ftbl; Tennis; High Hon Roll; Grossmont Coll; Math.

HARFORD, RACHEL J; Fremont HS; Sunnyvale, CA; (2); Service Clb; School Musical; School Play; Off Trk; Red & White Awrds In Ceramics & German; Awrd Best 3d-Dstrct Art Shwcs; Track-Frshmn Yr 89.

HARGER II, BRADLEY L; California HS; Oakland, CA; (3); Computer Clb; Office Aide; Ski Clb; Chorus; Intrml Wt Lftg; Var Wrstlng; High Hon Roll; Hon Roll; Pres Schlr; Stu Of Mnth; Stu Cnsrvtn Assn Vlntr 89; Robotics.

HARGRAVE, MORGAN S; Etiwanda HS; Alta Loma, CA; (3); 18/850; Key Clb; SADD; Jazz Band; Capt Socr; Wt Lftg; Var Wrstlng; NHS; Schlr Athlete Awd; Co Hnr Band 89; U CA-SANTA Barbara; Sci.

HARGROVE, AMY M; Homestead HS; Sunnyvale, CA; (2); JV Capt Fld Hcky; Var Capt Socr.

HARGROVE, BARBARA G; Estancia HS; Costa Mesa, CA; (4); 11/334; Am Leg Aux Girls St; Girl Scts; Mrchg Band; School Musical; DAR Awd; Hon Roll; Ntl Merit SF; JR Statsmn Amer; Stanford; Gentic Engrng.

HARICE, LATRICIA; St Michaels HS; Los Angeles, CA; (1); Church Yth Grp; Service Clb; Church Choir; School Play; Trk; Hon Roll; Good Samaratin Club; Chld Dvlpmnt.

HARIG, RICK; East Union HS; Manteca, CA; (3); 96/354; Cmnty Wkr; Office Aide; SADD; Teachers Aide; Swmmng; Wt Lftg; Youth To Youth Drg Free Conf; Peer Cnslng; Hmn Rltns Day; STAND; Coach.

HARISH, SAMEER; Mission San Jose HS; Fremont, CA; (1); Science Clb; JV Swmmng; Law Explorer Post; Law.

HARKAVY, JOHN A; Miramonte HS; Orinda, CA; (4); 3/275; Chess Clb; Spanish Clb; Rep Frsh Cls; JV Wrstlng; Ntl Merit SF; CSF; Busboy 10 Hrs A Wk; Interests Aircraft, Automobiles; Exec Auto Corp.

HARKEN, COURTNEY; Grossmont HS; El Cajon, CA; (4); 8/454; Church Yth Grp; SADD; Teachers Aide; JV Tennis; Elks Awd; CSF; Daisy Chain Outstndng JR Help At Graduatn; Church Deacon; CA U Irvine; Tchng.

HARKENRIDER, JESSICA L; Mira Costa HS; Manhattan Beach, CA; (2); Drama Clb; Key Clb; Pep Clb; Scholastic Bowl; Science Clb; Drill Tm; Rep Frsh Cls; Rep Soph Cls; Var Cheerldng; Cit Awd; Loyola Marymount; Psych.

HARKER, RUTH A; Katella HS; Anaheim, CA; (4); Key Clb; Spanish Clb; JV Capt Bsktbl; Powder Puff Ftbl; JV Tennis; Cit Awd; High Hon Roll; Prfct Atten Awd; Pres Acad Fit Awd; Pres Schlr; 4-A CIF Champs & St Fnlsts 89; CA ST U Fullerton; Bus.

HARKER, SERESE; Garces Memorial HS; Bakersfield, CA; (1); Cmnty Wkr; Service Clb; Rep Frsh Cls; JV Sftbl; Intrml Vllybl; High Hon Roll; PBFT Club; Mst Insprtnl Sftbll; Notre Dame; Comms.

HARKEY, JENNIFER; Yucaipa HS; Yucaipa, CA; (3); Letterman Clb; Pep Clb; Spanish Clb; Varsity Clb; Cheerldng; Crs Cntry; Pom Pon; Powder Puff Ftbl; Socr; Sftbl; Crafton Hills; Brdcstng.

HARLAN, HEATHER CATHERINE; Las Lomas HS; Walnut Creek, CA; (4); Hosp Aide; Intnl Clb; SADD; Acpl Chr; Band; Pep Band; School Musical; School Play; Stage Crew; Ed Yrbk; PTA Reflections Contest Awd In Lit 89-90; Sftbl Coach Awd 89-90; Most Vlbl Stafm Mem Yrbk 90; CA Coll Arts & Crafts.

HARLAN, WENDY; San Juan HS; Citrus Heights, CA; (2); JV Cheerldng; Hon Roll; Sacramento ST U; Elec Engrng.

HARLESS, ELIZABETH K; Torrey Pines HS; Del Mar, CA; (3); 88/1500; Church Yth Grp; Girl Scts; Ed Yrbk; Sec Soph Cls; Stat Bsktbl; Hon Roll; Pres Acad Fit Awd; Recycling Block Ldr; Activists Clb; Yth Ending Hunger Clb; UCSB; Commnctns.

HARLICK, DIANA L; Mills HS; Burlingame, CA; (2); Church Yth Grp; Cmnty Wkr; English Clb; French Clb; Hosp Aide; Orch; Var L Crs Cntry; JV Swmmng; Var L Trk; High Hon Roll; CSF; Goldn St Schlr 88-89; Princpals Awd 88-89, 89-90; Film.

HARM, BILLY; Santa Rosa HS; Santa Rosa, CA; (4); 47/530; Church Yth Grp; Spanish Clb; Varsity Clb; L Var Socr; High Hon Roll; Pres Acad Fit Awd; Pres Schlr; CSF; Doyle Schlrshp; Santa Rosa JC.

HARMAN, LIZ; Benicia HS; Benicia, CA; (3); Key Clb; Var Crs Cntry; Var Trk; Hon Roll; Key Clb Sec 90-91; Yrbk Staff 90-91; Santa Cruz; Pblc Rltns.

HARMANING, DAWN; Capital Christian HS; Citrus Heights, CA; (2); Church Yth Grp; Cmnty Wkr; FCA; Library Aide; Office Aide; Pep Clb; Ski Clb; Teachers Aide; School Musical; School Play; CSF; Outstndng Alg Stu Awd; Crtfd Amateur Sftbl Assoc Umpire; UCLA; Engrng.

HARMER, JENNIFER; Shafter HS; Bakesfield, CA; (3); 8/210; Am Leg Aux Girls St; Key Clb; Letterman Clb; Pep Clb; SADD; Yrbk; JV Var Cheerldng; Var Socr; JV Vllybl; Pres & VP Friday Night Live; Phys Thrpy.

HARMISON, JENNIFER M; Mountain Empire JR/Sr HS; Campo, CA; (3); Cmnty Wkr; Girl Scts; Letterman Clb; Pres Spanish Clb; Rep Soph Cls; Rep Jr Cls; Var Sftbl; Var Vllybl; High Hon Roll; Pres Acad Fit Awd; CIF Hnrbl Mntn Sftbl Leagu 90; Natl Yng Ldrs Cnfrnc 90; Sprts Med.

HARMON, DAVID W; Redwood HS; Visalia, CA; (4); Chess Clb; JV Bsktbl; Hon Roll; Lion Awd; CSF; Spcl Olympcs Coach; Sequoias Coll; Mech Engr.

HARMON, GINA; Cajon HS; San Bernardino, CA; (2); Church Yth Grp; Teachers Aide; Cit Awd; UCLA; Tchr.

HARMON, JEFFREY A; East Union HS; Manteca, CA; (1); 2/400; Boy Scts; Key Clb; Bsbl; Bsktbl; Ftbl; Hon Roll; Prfct Atten Awd.

HARMON, JULIE M; Edison HS; Huntington Beach, CA; (3); Pres Church Yth Grp; Rep Key Clb; Natl Beta Clb; Band; Drm Mjr(t); Rptr Nwsp; Rep Stu Cncl; French Hon Soc; Pres Acad Fit Awd; Odyssey Of Mind World Finals Competitr; Diocese Of Lttle Rock Yth Srvc Awd; Engl Tchr.

HARMON, MICHAEL T; Thomas Downey HS; Modesto, CA; (4); Church Yth Grp; Teachers Aide; Church Choir; Trk; Cit Awd; God Squad Club 86-90; Chrcn Ensmbl Group; Cnslng Other In Prblms They Have; Bethany Bible Coll; Psych.

HARMON, STEVE; East Union HS; Manteca, CA; (4); 1/300; Am Leg Boys St; Boy Scts; Treas Pres Key Clb; VP Science Clb; Treas Frsh Cls; JV Var Bsbl; JV Var Bsktbl; JV Ftbl; NHS; Prfct Atten Awd; Stanford U; Poltcl Sci.

HARN, SUZIE; Alhambra HS; Alhambra, CA; (4); 64/690; Church Yth Grp; FBLA; Letterman Clb; Model UN; Teachers Aide; Pres Soph Cls; Co-Capt Cheerldng; Pom Pon; Swmmng; Hon Roll; Irvine U; Bio.

HARNDEN, RICHARD D; Red Bluff HS; Red Bluff, CA; (3); Church Yth Grp; Cmnty Wkr; Key Clb; Letterman Clb; SADD; Stu Cncl; Ftbl; Wt Lftg; Wrstlng; Hon Roll; Class III Stu Pilot Cert; Aerontcl Engrng.

HARNED, MELINDA A; De Anza HS; El Sobrante, CA; (3); Girl Scts; Office Aide; Ski Clb; Teachers Aide; Yrbk; Treas Frsh Cls; Var Bsktbl; Var Capt Swmmng; Hon Roll; Vrsty Waterpolo; MVP Smmng 88-90; N Coast Schlr Athl 89; Embry Riddle Aeronaut U.

HARNISH, ERIC A; Village Christian HS; Van Nuys, CA; (4); Church Yth Grp; English Clb; Spanish Clb; School Play; Rptr Nwsp; VP Sr Cls; Var JV Ftbl; Var JV Socr; Hon Roll; U Of Southern CA.

HARNS, JOEL; Templeton HS; Templeton, CA; (2); Drama Clb; 4-H; Pep Clb; Varsity Clb; Variety Show; Var Bsbl; Var Socr; Wt Lftg; Stat 4-H Awd; Hon Roll; Bus.

HARNTHA, JUTHYMAS; Westlake Schl For Girls; Los Angeles, CA; (3); Cmnty Wkr; Debate Tm; French Clb; JA; Math Tm; Model UN; NFL; Speech Tm; Yrbk; Ed Lit Mag; Current Events Clb; Law.

HARO, ARACELI; Sierra Vista HS; Baldwin Park, CA; (4); 11/267; Science Clb; Speech Tm; Teachers Aide; School Musical; School Play; Vllybl; High Hon Roll; Opt Clb Awd; Pres Acad Fit Awd; US Acad Decathlon Team; CSF; Pomona Coll; Physics.

HARO, DAVID C; John Muir HS; Pasadena, CA; (2); French Clb; FBLA.

HARO, LILIANA; Notre Dame Academy Girls; Culver City, CA; (2); Church Yth Grp; Cmnty Wkr; 4-H; French Clb; Spanish Clb; SADD; Teachers Aide; Cit Awd; Hon Roll; Prfct Atten Awd; UCLA.

HARO, MARIA I; Santa Ana HS; Santa Ana, CA; (2); French Clb; Yrbk; Hon Roll; UCI; Doctor.

HARO JR, ROBERT; Sierra Vista HS; Baldwin Park, CA; (1); Chess Clb; Computer Clb; Science Clb; High Hon Roll; Pres Acad Fit Awd; Guadalupan Soc; CA Inst Of Tech; Nuclear Physc.

HAROLD, MELINDA A; San Dieguito HS; Carlsbad, CA; (2); Church Yth Grp; Pep Clb; School Play; Stage Crew; JV Cheerldng; Var L Trk; Hon Roll; Prfct Atten Awd; U Santa Barbara; Teacher.

HAROUTIAN, ALLISON; Bullard HS; Fresno, CA; (1); Key Clb; SADD; Var Cheerldng; UCSB; Arch.

HARPER, ANEDRA C; Chino HS; Chino, CA; (2); Cmnty Wkr; Letterman Clb; Science Clb; Ski Clb; SADD; Varsity Clb; Band; Jazz Band; Mrchg Band; Pep Band; Law.

HARPER, ANGELA L; Atascadero HS; Atascadero, CA; (4); AFS; Church Yth Grp; Ed Yrbk; Powder Puff Ftbl; Stat Swmmng; Stat Wrstlng; Acad Decathalon Tm; Bob Jones U; Intl Lawyer.

HARPER, ANGELA S; Ponderosa HS; Pollock Pines, CA; (1); Hon Roll; Friday Night Live; Bus.

HARPER, JAKE D; Red Bluff Union HS; Cottonwood, CA; (2); Mu Alpha Theta; Spanish Clb; JV Bsbl; JV Ftbl; Intrml Wt Lftg; JV Wrstlng; Hon Roll.

HARPER, JILL L; Bellarmine-Jefferson HS; Glendale, CA; (2); Orch; Golf; Acting.

HARPER, KENNETH; Armijo HS; Suisun, CA; (4); 28/401; Chess Clb; Church Yth Grp; Math Clb; VICA; Cit Awd; High Hon Roll; Cngrssn Schlr St VA; Hghst Hnrs Goldn St Exm Geom; GA Tech; Nuclear Engrng.

HARPER JR, LENVERT; Leuzinger HS; Hawthorne, CA; (3); Hosp Aide; Red Cross Aide; Hon Roll; Prfct Atten Awd; APPI Pgm; SCROC; U Of CT; Air Force Helo Pilot.

HARPER, MONICA; Tulare Western HS; Tulare, CA; (3); Church Yth Grp; Teachers Aide; Varsity Clb; Off Jr Cls; Socr; Sftbl; Air Force Military Schl; Psych.

HARPER, NICOLE D; East Bakersfield HS; Bakersfield, CA; (2); Drama Clb; Intnl Clb; Chorus; School Musical; School Play; Var Tennis; High Hon Roll; Treas Soph Cls; CA Schlstc Fed; 1 Mnth Germany US Tennis Tm Intl Exchng.

HARPER, SHANELL; St Michaels HS; Los Angeles, CA; (2); 4/50; Church Yth Grp; Church Choir; Trk; Hon Roll; UNLV; Social Psych.

HARR, MICHA N; Clovis HS; Clovis, CA; (1); House Of Reps; Fresno ST U CA; Math.

HARRADINE, BRIAN R; Mt Diablo HS; Concord, CA; (4); 32/221; Drama Clb; Letterman Clb; Pres Model UN; Pres Spanish Clb; Teachers Aide; Drm Mjr(t); School Play; Nwsp; Ed Lit Mag; Stu Cncl; Top 50 Stu Cls 90; U Of CA Davis; Engl.

HARRAL, ALEAH D; Red Bluff Union HS; Los Molinos, CA; (1); FFA; Key Clb; Rep Frsh Cls; Cheerldng; Swmmng; Hon Roll; Piano; Optmtrst.

HARRELL, JERMAINE L; Seaside HS; Marina, CA; (3); Teachers Aide; Chorus; JV Bsktbl; JV Ftbl; JV Trk.

HARRELL, MICHAEL A; Tulare Union HS; Tulare, CA; (3); 62/381; Church Yth Grp; JA; Ed Yrbk; Rep Soph Cls; VP Jr Cls; Hon Roll; Ldrshp Cls; Stu Actvty Dir ASB Cncl 90-91; Cmnctns.

HARRELL, MIKE; Le Moore Union HS; Lemoore, CA; (3); Boy Scts; FBLA; Band; Mrchg Band; Pep Band; Tennis; Hon Roll; Peer Hlprs.

HARRELL, PATASHA E; Eisenhower HS; Rialto, CA; (3); FCA; FBLA; Office Aide; Service Clb; Variety Show; Rep Sr Cls; Chrmn Stu Cncl; Var Capt Cheerldng; Rotary Awd; Blck Stu Union; San Diego ST U; Bus Admin.

HARRELL, ROBIN L; Atwater HS; Atwater, CA; (1); JV Swmmng; High Hon Roll; Schl Sponsrd Athltc Acts; Friday Night Live; UC San Diego; Marine Bio.

HARRELSON, GLENDA; West Covina HS; West Covina, CA; (3); French Clb; Pep Clb; Ski Clb; SADD; Band; Church Choir; Mrchg Band; Pep Band; Rep Soph Cls; Var Pom Pon; UCSB; Librl Arts.

HARRIGAN, DAVID PATRICK; Don Bosco Technical Inst; Hacienda Hghts, CA; (1); 16/244; Boy Scts; Chess Clb; Church Yth Grp; Hon Roll; NEDT Awd; Altar Srvr; Math.

HARRIGAN, NANCY; Highlands HS; Roseville, CA; (4); Library Aide; Off Office Aide; Spanish Clb; Off Lbrn Teachers Aide; Acpl Chr; Sec Sr Cls; Hon Roll; Prfct Atten Awd; Bob Jones U; Elem Schl Teacher.

HARRIMAN, CHRISTINA M; Alverno HS; San Gabriel, CA; (3); Service Clb; Off Frsh Cls; Off Soph Cls; Off Jr Cls; Hon Roll; CSF; Activities Dept; Adv Plcmnt Soc Stud; UCLA; Lawyr.

HARRINGTON, AMY M; Manteca HS; Manteca, CA; (4); 17/336; Drama Clb; Pres 4-H; German Clb; Ski Clb; Thesps; School Play; VP Soph Cls; JV Sftbl; JV Vllybl; High Hon Roll; CSF; Humboldt ST U; Marine Bio.

HARRINGTON, BRIAN R; Bonita HS; La Verne, CA; (2); Boy Scts; Pres Church Yth Grp; French Clb; Crs Cntry; Trk; Hon Roll; Hstry Club; Brigham Young U; Arch Drafter.

HARRINGTON, DAVID W; North HS; Bakersfield, CA; (3); Church Yth Grp; FCA; FFA; Church Choir; Intrml JV Ftbl; Hon Roll; NHS; Supt Of Schls; Principals Southern Hnrs Awd; Cal Poly San Luis Obispo; Arch.

HARRINGTON, JENNIFER M; Louisville HS; Northridge, CA; (2); Church Yth Grp; GAA; Science Clb; Ski Clb; Stat Bsktbl; JV Var Score Keeper; JV Var Sftbl; Intrml JV Vllybl; Htl Mgmt.

HARRINGTON, KRISTA; Eisenhower HS; Rialto, CA; (3); Church Yth Grp; Model UN; Service Clb; Ski Clb; Stu Cncl; Capt Var Cheerldng; Bausch & Lomb Sci Awd; High Hon Roll; Hon Roll; Jr NHS; CSF; Sobobans; Yth Alv; Grphc Dsgn.

HARRINGTON, MICHAEL D; North HS; Bakersfield, CA; (3); 18/382; Am Leg Boys St; Boy Scts; Church Yth Grp; Ski Clb; VP Spanish Clb; Var Socr; Wt Lftg; Gov Hon Prg Awd; High Hon Roll; NHS; Explr Post 76 Canine Trng & Care; Vet.

HARRINGTON, ROBERT J; Bishop O'dowd HS; Alameda, CA; (2); Ski Clb; Var L Bsktbl; High Hon Roll; Ltl Leag Bsbl Umprng; Sccr Rfree; Acad Cngrss/Cnvntn; Schlr Athlt Awd; Yth Sccr Coach; Bio.

HARRINGTON, SHAWN; Rowland HS; Rowland Heights, CA; (3); Church Yth Grp; Band; Jazz Band; Mrchg Band; Pep Band; Hon Roll; Drum Corps; Wrtr Of Yr Engl Cls; Top Tlntd Hnr Band Of CA; Azusa Pacific U; CPA.

HARRINGTON, TAMARA L; Woodcrest Christian Schl; Riverside, CA; (2); Church Yth Grp; Pep Clb; Ski Clb; Score Keeper; Baylor; Int Design.

HARRINGTON, TRACY A; Arcadia HS; Arcadia, CA; (3); Drama Clb; Spanish Clb; Thesps; Band; Mrchg Band; Orch; School Musical; School Play; Hon Roll; NHS; Bus.

HARRION, KARMA V; Rio Mesa HS; Camarillo, CA; (3); 24/145; Church Yth Grp; Varsity Clb; Var L Bsktbl; Var Capt Crs Cntry; JV Var Trk; Hon Roll; NHS; Prfct Atten Awd; Notre Dame; Ornithlgst; Vet.

HARRIS, ADRIENNE DANIELLE; San Pedro HS; High Point, NC; (3); Pep Clb; Sec Science Clb; Color Guard; Rptr Nwsp; Yrbk; Rep Jr Cls; Powder Puff Ftbl; Trk; Hon Roll; Prfct Atten Awd; Abilene Chrstn U; Ag.

HARRIS, ALBERT H; Thomas Downey HS; Modesto, CA; (4); Phoenix Inst Tech; Electrncs.

HARRIS, AMY B; Trabuco Hills HS; El Toro, CA; (4); 9/330; Boy Scts; Pres French Clb; Pres SADD; Teachers Aide; Ed Lit Mag; Cit Awd; High Hon Roll; Sec NHS; Pres Acad Fit Awd; Bank Of Amer Plaque Winner Liberal Arts; Kiwanis Outstanding Student English; CA Schlrshp Fed Winner; U Of San Francisco; English Lit.

HARRIS, AMY L; Atascadero HS; Atascadero, CA; (2); Band; Mrchg Band; Pep Band; Var Socr; Hon Roll.

HARRIS, AMY M; Nathaniel Narronne HS; Lomita, CA; (2); Letterman Clb; Varsity Clb; Rptr Nwsp; Ed Yrbk; Treas Frsh Cls; Var Sftbl; Close Up Prgm; Linguist.

HARRIS, ANDREE J; Santa Teresa HS; San Jose, CA; (2); Church Yth Grp; Science Clb; Ski Clb; Spanish Clb; Crs Cntry; Trk; Cheerldng; Morning Announcmnt Clb; CSF; MVP-TRACK; Math Engrng Sci Assn; Valentine Queen; Golden St Exam-Geom Hnrs; Obstetrics.

HARRIS, ANTHONY T; Kennedy HS; Richmond, CA; (3); Drill Tm.

HARRIS, BETH; Modesto HS; Modesto, CA; (4); 24/500; Church Yth Grp; Cmnty Wkr; Hosp Aide; Teachers Aide; School Play; Rep Soph Cls; Cheerldng; Cit Awd; High Hon Roll; Lion Awd; Madrigals; State; Psych.

HARRIS, BRIAN A; Mesa Verde HS; Citrus Heights, CA; (2); French Clb; JV Bsbl; JV Bsktbl; JV Var Ftbl; Wt Lftg; Cit Awd; Hon Roll; JV Ftbl MVP.

HARRIS, BRIAN J; Edison HS; Huntington Beach, CA; (2); Church Yth Grp; Intrml Ftbl; JV Swmmng; Emerg Med Technqs Orange Coast Coll; U Of CA Irvine; Med.

HARRIS, BRIAN K; Ukiah JR Acad; Willits, CA; (1); Church Yth Grp; Band; Chorus; Drill Tm; Rptr Nwsp; VP Stu Cncl; Capt Bsktbl; Capt Ftbl; Intrml Sftbl; Intrml Vllybl; Comp; Tnns, Golf, Aerobic Training; Ukiah JR Acad; Arch.

HARRIS JR, BURT R; Fairfax HS; Los Angeles, CA; (2); Var Bsktbl; Pres Acad Fit Awd; Math.

HARRIS, CARRIE A; Bonita HS; La Verne, CA; (1); Spanish Clb; Band; Mrchg Band; Orch; Pep Band; School Musical; Variety Show; Cit Awd; High Hon Roll; Hon Roll; Lawyer.

HARRIS, CHRISTINA L; North HS; Bakersfield, CA; (3); Teachers Aide; Hon Roll; Cal ST; Elem Tchr.

HARRIS, CHRISTOPHER PAUL; Clovis West HS; Fresno, CA; (3); 104/525; Quiz Bowl; Band; Jazz Band; Mrchg Band; Orch; Pep Band; School Musical; Co-Ed Lit Mag; Hon Roll; CSF; GATE Stu; Work Part Time Mc Donalds Rest, Employee Of Mnth Oct 89; CA ST U; Music Ed.

HARRIS, DARNELL L; Mission College Prep; San Luis Obispo, CA; (3); Pres Church Yth Grp; Varsity Clb; VP Sr Cls; Var Bsbl; Capt L Ftbl; Intrml Sftbl; Var L Trk; Intrml Vllybl; Hon Roll; Pres Acad Fit Awd; UC Santa Cruz Hstry Awd; Mission Coll Prep Relgn Awd; Cptn 89 Mission Coll Prep Boys CIF Bsktbl Chmp; Bus.

HARRIS, DARREN M; Los Altos HS; Hacienda Hts, CA; (4); 25/400; Letterman Clb; Science Clb; Var Capt Bsbl; Var Ftbl; High Hon Roll; Prfct Atten Awd; Pres Acad Fit Awd; Life Mem CA Schlrshp Fed; 4 Yr Schlr; Bank Of America Achvt In Frgn Lang Awd; U Of CA-IRVINE.

HARRIS, DEBORAH R; Imperial HS; Pasadena, CA; (4); Church Yth Grp; Chorus; Variety Show; Sec Stu Cncl; Var Stat Bsktbl; Mgr(s); Capt Var Sftbl; Var Vllybl; Speech Club Secretary 88-89; Sylvia D Van Derenter Scholarship Award; Ambassador Coll; Home Economics.

HARRIS, DJUANA J; San Gorgonio HS; Highland, CA; (3); Church Yth Grp; Cmnty Wkr; English Clb; Girl Scts; Teachers Aide; Church Choir; Drill Tm; Stu Cncl; Bsktbl; Score Keeper; Swans Debutant; Black Stu Union; Pre-Med.

HARRIS, GIDGET L; El Cerrito HS; Richmond, CA; (1); Cmnty Wkr; English Clb; FTA; Library Aide; Office Aide; Spanish Clb; SADD; Teachers Aide; Chorus; School Play; Hayward ST U; Nrsng.

HARRIS, HANSI Y; Capital Christian HS; W Sacramento, CA; (2); Church Yth Grp; SADD; Teachers Aide; Band; Church Choir; Jazz Band; Mrchg Band; Pep Band; Var Cheerldng; Var Tennis; Sacramento Dixieland Jubilee; MESA; CA Schlrshp Fed; Bethany Bible; Music.

HARRIS, HEATHER; Westwood HS; Westwood, CA; (1); 1/30; Library Aide; Mrchg Band; JV Bsktbl; High Hon Roll; Rotary Awd; Vllybl & Bsktbl Ststcn; MBA.

HARRIS, HILLARY L; Villia Park HS; Orange, CA; (1); Church Yth Grp; Cmnty Wkr; Sftbl; Vllybl; Hon Roll; Prfct Atten Awd; Pres Acad Fit Awd; Yth Stu Body; USC.

HARRIS, JACQUELINE M; Los Altos HS; Hacienda Hts, CA; (1); Church Yth Grp; Band; Jazz Band; Mrchg Band; Orch; Hon Roll; Outstndng Soloist Awd Jazz; All Southern CA Jr HS Jazz Band, Hnr Orch; Music.

HARRIS, JASON A; University HS; Irvine, CA; (3); 100/550; AFS; Spanish Clb; Temple Yth Grp; JV Trk; Var Wrstlng; Hon Roll; NHS; Spanish NHS.

HARRIS, JASON J; Galt Joint Union HS; Galt, CA; (4); Church Yth Grp; FHA; Teachers Aide; Church Choir; Rptr Yrbk; Ftbl; L Trk; Wt Lftg; Hon Roll; U Of Pacific; Physcl Thrpy.

HARRIS, JASON M; Rio Americano HS; Sacramento, CA; (3); 40/290; Boy Scts; French Clb; JCL; Key Clb; Latin Clb; Science Clb; School Play; Chrmn Stu Cncl; Wrstlng; High Hon Roll; Gold Mdl Natl Latin Exam; Golden Poet; Stanford; Lit.

HARRIS, JASON R; Villa Park HS; Orange, CA; (2); Boy Scts; Church Yth Grp; Key Clb; Band; Church Choir; Jazz Band; Mrchg Band; Pep Band; High Hon Roll; NHS; Water Polo JV; Eagle Sct; Med.

HARRIS, JENNIFER J; West HS; Bakersfield, CA; (3); Church Yth Grp; VP Chorus; Bsktbl; Hon Roll; Talents For Christ-Voice 89; Masters Coll; Elem Ed.

HARRIS, JENNIFER K; O'farrell Schl/Creative & Perf Arts; San Diego, CA; (1); Quiz Bowl; Stage Crew; Hon Roll; Photo; Film Making; UCLA; Film Making.

HARRIS, JENNIFER LEE; Antioch SR HS; Antioch, CA; (4); Church Yth Grp; Cmnty Wkr; Office Aide; Teachers Aide; Acpl Chr; Chorus; Church Choir; School Musical; Swing Chorus; High Hon Roll; Outstndng Vocal Stu 90; Azusa Pacific Univ Performing Schlrshp; Azusa Pacific U; Ed.

HARRIS, JENNIFER M; Desert Christian Schl; Lancaster, CA; (2); 5/22; Church Yth Grp; FCA; Teachers Aide; Band; Variety Show; Rptr Nwsp; Phtg Yrbk; Rptr Lit Mag; Rep Frsh Cls; Rep Stu Cncl.

HARRIS, JENNIFER M; Poway HS; San Diego, CA; (3); SADD; Capt Color Guard; High Hon Roll; Hon Roll; CSF; Phys Thrpy.

HARRIS, JEROME L; Palmdale HS; Palmdale, CA; (2); #27 In Class; Band; Jazz Band; Mrchg Band; Var Swmmng; Cit Awd; Hon Roll; CA Schlstc Fed; ROTC.

HARRIS, JILL C; Hanford HS; Hanford, CA; (1); Teachers Aide; JV Vllybl; High Hon Roll; Pepperdine; Lawyer.

HARRIS, JILL R; Paradise HS; Magalia, CA; (3); Church Yth Grp; Pep Clb; Chorus; Drill Tm; School Musical; Rep Sr Cls; Var Capt Cheerldng; Capt Var Pom Pon; Powder Puff Ftbl; Var JV Trk; CSUC; Phys Ed Tchr.

HARRIS, JING JING; Monteray Bay Acad; Lafayette, CA; (3); Art Clb; Dance Clb; Drama Clb; Hosp Aide; Intnl Clb; Math Clb; Science Clb; Speech Tm; Teachers Aide; Acpl Chr; 12 Poems Publshd Jr Text Bks PR China; Outstndng Achvt Awd PR China; Pres Med Sci Clb; Pres Bio Clb; UC Davis; Bio.

HARRIS, JIVITA M; Huntington Beach HS; Huntington Bch, CA; (3); VP Band; Jazz Band; Mrchg Band; Pep Band; School Musical; Hon Roll; Coll; Fashion Design.

HARRIS, JODIE A; Selma HS; Selma, CA; (1); Church Yth Grp; JV Bsktbl; Var Tennis; High Hon Roll; Pres Acad Fit Awd; Chapman Coll; Pharmcy.

HARRIS, JOSH; Hamilton HS Academy Of Music; Los Angeles, CA; (3); Mrchg Band; Orch; School Musical; Variety Show; Bsbl; Hon Roll; Golden St Exam Acad Excllnc Awd; UCSB; Bsbl.

HARRIS, JULI; Dinuba HS; Dinuba, CA; (1); Pep Clb; JV Cheerldng; DAR Awd; Hon Roll; Fresno ST; Teaching.

HARRIS, KAMISHA R; Mayfield SR Schl; Altadena, CA; (2); Church Yth Grp; GAA; Letterman Clb; Library Aide; Red Cross Aide; JV Bsktbl; Var Trk; Hon Roll; CA Schlrshp Fed; Med; Pediatrician.

HARRIS, KAREN D M; Tehachapi HS; Tehachapi, CA; (3); Church Yth Grp; Rptr FHA; Pres SADD; Varsity Clb; Pres Jr Cls; Rep Sr Cls; Var Sftbl; Var Tennis; High Hon Roll; NHS; I Dare You Awd; FHA Aoutstndng Chptr Mem Awd; KY ST U; Sociology.

HARRIS, KATHERINE; Truett Christian HS; Long Beach, CA; (4); Church Yth Grp; Teachers Aide; Church Choir; Rptr Yrbk; Pres Stu Cncl; Cheerldng; Vllybl; Hon Roll; Val; Hyles Anderson Coll; Elem Educ.

HARRIS, KEITH; Downtown Business Magnet HS; Los Angeles, CA; (2); Bus.

HARRIS, KENDRA L; Ventura HS; Santa Paula, CA; (3); 1/451; JA; Pep Clb; SADD; Varsity Clb; Rep Frsh Cls; Rep Soph Cls; Rep Jr Cls; Tennis; High Hon Roll; Hon Roll; Jr Republican; Southern CA Ranked Jr Tennis Player; Economics.

HARRIS, LACONIA E; El Camino HS; St Louis, MO; (4); 29/338; Church Yth Grp; Cmnty Wkr; French Clb; SADD; Teachers Aide; French Hon Soc; Hon Roll; NHS; Pres Schlr; U Of Southern CA; Ecnmcs.

HARRIS, LEAH I; Poway HS; San Diego, CA; (1); 1/802; Quiz Bowl; Scholastic Bowl; Temple Yth Grp; Nwsp; High Hon Roll; Mem Mensa; Johns Hopkins; Med.

HARRIS, MARVIN L; Warren HS; Downey, CA; (1); Bsbl; Bsktbl; Ftbl.

HARRIS, MICHAEL; La Serna HS; Whittier, CA; (3); 22/400; Boy Scts; SADD; Rep Frsh Cls; Rep Soph Cls; Treas Jr Cls; Var L Crs Cntry; Var L Trk; Hon Roll; Pres NHS; Actvt Chrpsn Stu Body; Sci.

HARRIS, MICHAEL C; 29 Palms HS; Twentynine Palms, CA; (3); Boy Scts; Church Yth Grp; Hon Roll; Prfct Atten Awd; Morehouse Coll.

HARRIS, MICHAEL J; Chadwick Schl; Manhattan Beach, CA; (4); Cmnty Wkr; Letterman Clb; Var Bsbl; Hon Roll; Outstndng Negro Stdnt Commdtn; Serra Intl Awd; Northwestern U; Biomed Engrng.

HARRIS, MICHAEL P; Antelope Valley HS; Lancaster, CA; (3); 7/630; Church Yth Grp; Cmnty Wkr; Math Tm; Spanish Clb; Cit Awd; High Hon Roll; Prfct Atten Awd; Design & Engrng Clb Pres & Treas; CA Schlrhsp Fed; Peer Tutor-Higher Math; Architect.

HARRIS, MICHAEL W; Benicia HS; Benicia, CA; (3); Cmnty Wkr; Letterman Clb; Library Aide; SADD; Var Capt Boy Scts; L Ftbl; High Hon Roll; Hon Roll; NHS; Pres Acad Fit Awd; U NC; Med.

HARRIS, MICHELE W; Novato HS; Novato, CA; (2); Sec Church Yth Grp; French Clb; Variety Show; Sec Jr Cls; JV Cheerldng; JV Swmmng; UC Berkley.

HARRIS, PAULA O; Arlington HS; Riverside, CA; (2); Pep Clb; Chorus; School Musical; High Hon Roll; Outstndng Achvt Awd; CSF; Amer Coll; Inter Dectr.

HARRIS, RASHIDA M; Sacred Heart Prep; Stanford, CA; (3); 23/30; Sec Drama Clb; FCA; JA; Drill Tm; Ed Yrbk; Stu Cncl; Cheerldng; Crs Cntry; Trk; JETS Awd; Campus Minstry Club; Art Hstry.

HARRIS, REBECCA; Lincoln HS; Stockton, CA; (3); 9/584; Sec Key Clb; Mu Alpha Theta; NFL; Speech Tm; VP SADD; Ed Lit Mag; High Hon Roll; Assistns Philathrpc Chrprsn; Std Takng Actn Not Drgs Pres; Stds In Prevntn Cnty Rep.

HARRIS, RICK; Brawley Union HS; Brawley, CA; (1); Drama Clb; 4-H; Stage Crew; Off Frsh Cls; Ftbl; Wt Lftg; Hon Roll; Ldrshp.

HARRIS, SAM; Sunny Hills HS; Fullerton, CA; (2); 43/464; FBLA; Off Soph Cls; Crs Cntry; JV Ftbl; Trk; Rotary Interact Clb; SOS Clb; CSF.

HARRIS, SHANNON E; Trabuco Hills HS; Mission Viejo, CA; (2); 76/415; Key Clb; Spanish Clb; SADD; Hon Roll; CSF; Safe Rides; Aerospace.

HARRIS, SHAWN; Thousand Oaks HS; Thousand Oaks, CA; (4); 21/540; VP German Clb; Math Tm; VP Mu Alpha Theta; Science Clb; School Play; Nwsp; Lit Mag; Hon Roll; Amer Lgn Boys St; Berkeley; Chem Engrng.

HARRIS, SHAWNA C; West HS; Bakersfield, CA; (2); Church Yth Grp; Cmnty Wkr; Letterman Clb; Ed Yrbk; Rep Frsh Cls; Bsktbl; Diving; Vllybl; Hon Roll; Wngs For Life Clb-Amer Cncr Soc; Asstngs League; Phys Thrpy.

HARRIS, TAMARA L; Lynwood HS; Lynwood, CA; (3); Church Yth Grp; Church Choir; JV Cheerldng; Capt Cheerldng; Stu Of Mnth-Jan 89-90; U Of NV Las Vegas; Comp.

HARRIS, TAMMY A; Ocean View HS; Costa Mesa, CA; (4); 103/414; Church Yth Grp; Cmnty Wkr; Debate Tm; Speech Tm; Teachers Aide; Band; Church Choir; Jazz Band; Mrchg Band; Pep Band; Band Ltr; Christ Coll Irvine; Pre-Law.

HARRIS, TANISHA A; Bridgemont HS; San Francisco, CA; (2); Girl Scts; Teachers Aide; Pres Frsh Cls; Rep Soph Cls; Rep Jr Cls; Stu Cncl; Vllybl; Hon Roll; Med.

HARRIS, TEANNE L; Norwalk HS; Green Bay, WI; (2); Church Yth Grp; Stage Crew; High Hon Roll; Hon Roll; Acctng.

HARRIS, TOM G; Ventura HS; Ventura, CA; (3); 5/500; Cmnty Wkr; Letterman Clb; JV Bsktbl; Var Swmmng; High Hon Roll; Hon Roll; Prfct Atten Awd; Pres Acad Fit Awd; Vrsty Water Polo; Lfgrd Cmnty Svc.

HARRIS, TRACEY N; Grant HS; Sacramento, CA; (1); Cmnty Wkr; Computer Clb; Dance Clb; Drama Clb; Radio & TV Prodctn; Modelng; Radio/TV.

HARRIS, TRACI L; Southern California Christian HS; Anaheim, CA; (3); Church Yth Grp; Office Aide; Chorus; Church Choir; Drill Tm; Hon Roll; Yth Cnslng.

HARRIS, TRINA T; William C Overfelt HS; San Jose, CA; (2); Church Yth Grp; Band; Church Choir; Mrchg Band; Pep Band; Crs Cntry; Stanford; Surgn.

HARRIS, VANESSA; Pittsburgh HS; Pittsburg, CA; (3); Acpl Chr; Band; Chorus; Mrchg Band; Trk; Vllybl; Humboldt U; Psych.

HARRIS, VERENA D; Hueneme HS; Port Hueneme, CA; (2); JV Bsktbl; Intrml Tennis; Hon Roll; Phrmctcls.

HARRIS, VERONICA E; Pittsburg HS; Pittsburg, CA; (3); Church Yth Grp; Drama Clb; FBLA; Pep Clb; SADD; Chorus; School Play; Tennis; Hon Roll; Bus.

HARRIS, WILLIAM C; Redlands SR HS; Redlands, CA; (3); Cmnty Wkr; Letterman Clb; Teachers Aide; Varsity Clb; Var L Bsktbl; Bus Admin.

HARRISON, BRET J; Village Christian HS; Van Nuys, CA; (2); Church Yth Grp; Yrbk; Ftbl; Trk; USC; Sci.

HARRISON, CHARLENE; Skyline HS; San Lorenzo, CA; (2); GAA; Socr; Hon Roll; Girls Athltc Assn Sccr; Chabot JC; Neurosrgn.

HARRISON, CHRISTOPHER; Capital Christian HS; Sacramento, CA; (2); Pres Church Yth Grp; Church Choir; JV Bsbl; JV Var Bsktbl; JV Ftbl; High Hon Roll; Pres Acad Fit Awd; Stanford U; Bus Ecnmcs.

HARRISON, DARA T; John F Kennedy HS; Sacramento, CA; (3); 48/422; Debate Tm; NFL; Spanish Clb; Speech Tm; Stu Cncl; Hon Roll; MESA; Mech Engrng.

HARRISON, DAWN; Atwater HS; Atwater, CA; (3); Church Yth Grp; Cmnty Wkr; Church Choir; Hon Roll; Interact Clb; Natl Frat Stu Musicians; NYI Cncl Mem; U Of Santa Cruz; Marine Bio.

HARRISON, DEANIE L; Oxnard HS; Oxnard, CA; (3); French Clb; Oxnard Coll.

HARRISON, HARVEY TERRELL; Chino HS; Ontario, CA; (1); Band; Jazz Band; Mrchg Band; Pep Band; JV Ftbl; Silver Spur Awd; Pediatrician.

HARRISON, HATTIE P; St Bernard HS; Hawthorne, CA; (3); Letterman Clb; Pep Clb; Ski Clb; Varsity Clb; Var Crs Cntry; Var Socr; Var Trk; UNLV; Hstry.

HARRISON, HEIDI; Hiram Johnson West Campus HS; Sacramento, CA; (3); 2/120; Pres Church Yth Grp; Cmnty Wkr; Church Choir; Orch; High Hon Roll; Hon Roll; NHS; Play Piano & Violin; Play Sccr & Vllybl; BYU; Hstry Teacher.

HARRISON, JANET L; Riverside Christian HS; Riverside, CA; (1); 2/13; Art Clb; Church Yth Grp; Drama Clb; School Play; Rep Frsh Cls; Rep Stu Cncl; Davidson; Vet Med.

HARRISON, JENNIFER D; Diamond Bar HS; Diamond Bar, CA; (3); Art Clb; Spanish Clb; Capt Color Guard; Variety Show; Archtctrl Design.

HARRISON, JOEL B; Ganesha HS; Diamond Bar, CA; (4); 14/250; Boy Scts; Letterman Clb; Teachers Aide; Band; Hon Roll; Bank Of Amer Achvt Awd Hstry; US Army.

HARRISON, JOSEPH; Antioch HS; Antioch, CA; (3); Teachers Aide; JV Ftbl; Cert Of Apprctn US Air Force; Cert Of Apprctn Matrl Storg P Dist Brnch; San Jose ST; Airline Pilot.

HARRISON, JUSTIN; Trabuco Hills HS; Mission Viejo, CA; (2); Cmnty Wkr; Quiz Bowl; Red Cross Aide; Spanish Clb; Var Golf; High Hon Roll; Hon Roll; Jr NHS; Kiwanis Awd; NHS; CSF.

HARRISON, JUSTINE; Fallbrook Union HS; Fallbrook, CA; (2); 23/572; Church Yth Grp; French Clb; Key Clb; Acpl Chr; Church Choir; Pres Soph Cls; Rep Stu Cncl; JV Var Cheerldng; Var Trk; High Hon Roll; Cotillion Tchr; Prfrmnce Dance Grp; CAR; Westmont; Intl Bus.

HARRISON, KAREN B; Delta HS; West Sacramento, CA; (1); Church Yth Grp; Library Aide; SADD; Band; JV Vllybl; Sci.

HARRISON, KELLY M; Alto Loma HS; Upland, CA; (2); Drama Clb; 4-H; GAA; Ski Clb; School Play; Stage Crew; Gym; Socr; Cit Awd; 4-H Awd; USC; Acting.

HARRISON, NATALIE R; Yucca Valley HS; Morongo Valley, CA; (4); Math Clb; Hon Roll; University Clb; U Redlands; Corp Law.

HARRISON, RICHARD C; Central Catholic HS; Modesto, CA; (3); Cmnty Wkr; Service Clb; Ski Clb; Golf; Socr.

HARRISON, RONECE; Western Christian HS; W Covina, CA; (3); Bus Profs of Am; Ski Clb; High Hon Roll; Sal; Dntstry.

HARRISON, RUSSELL S; Warren HS; Downey, CA; (2); Church Yth Grp; Cmnty Wkr; Debate Tm; SADD; VP Stu Cncl; Crs Cntry; Trk; High Hon Roll; Pres Acad Fit Awd; PTA Awd; CSF; Trk Capt; Biola U; Psych.

HARRISON, SEAONA; Bret Harte HS; Avery, CA; (1); Church Yth Grp; Cmnty Wkr; GAA; Letterman Clb; Ski Clb; Crs Cntry; Trk; Schlr Athlt; Crs Cntry Mst Imprvd; 1st Pl ST Rgnls Crs Cntry.

HARRISON, THERESA R; Analy HS; Sebastopol, CA; (4); Chorus; Sftbl; Wt Lftg; Empire Coll; Legal Sec.

HARRISON, TIFFANY; Lincoln HS; Lincoln, CA; (1); Hon Roll; Pres, 1st Cnslr, Sec Church Yth Group; Helpd Span Club; UC Davis; Anmls.

HARRISON, VICKI; Carmel HS; Carmel, CA; (4); 24/150; Am Leg Aux Girls St; Hosp Aide; VP Key Clb; Sec Stu Cncl; Var Bsktbl; Var Trk; Var Capt Vllybl; High Hon Roll; Pres Acad Fit Awd; Rotary Awd; Yng Life; Peer Cnslng; UC San Diego.

HARRSCH, RHETTA F; Castle Park HS; Chula Vista, CA; (2); 34/473; Co-Capt Color Guard; Flag Corp; UC Santa Cruz; Bus.

HARRSCH, TARA L; Castle Park HS; Chula Vista, CA; (3); Letterman Clb; Speech Tm; SADD; Off Drill Tm; Rep Frsh Cls; Rep Soph Cls; Rep Jr Cls; Tennis; Pres Acad Fit Awd; Girls Lg; Law.

HARRY, ELIORA N; O'farrell SCPA; San Diego, CA; (2); Church Yth Grp; Dance Clb; Math Clb; Spanish Clb; Band; Orch; Pres Soph Cls; Cit Awd; Hon Roll; Plays-West Side Story & Gypsy; Plays-Band & Orch; Jackson ST U; Med.

HARRYMAN, CATHERINE A; Aptos HS; Watsonville, CA; (1); 1/396; Hon Roll; Prfct Atten Awd; Interact Clb; CSF; U CA; Wrtng.

HART, BENJAMIN C; Poway HS; Poway, CA; (4); 60/680; Pres Sec Model UN; Mu Alpha Theta; SADD; High Hon Roll; Hon Roll; NHS; Ntl Merit SF; Pres Acad Fit Awd; UC San Diego; Physics.

HART, CECELIA M; Winters HS; Winters, CA; (2); Church Yth Grp; Drama Clb; Pres Pep Clb; SADD; Chorus; Church Choir; School Play; Stage Crew; Cheerldng; Sly Pk Resdnt Outdr Schl Pgm Cabin Ldr; Yth Day Cmmtte; Yth Day City Attrny; Brigham Young U HI; Corp Atrny.

HART, JUSTIN A; San Diego HS; San Diego, CA; (3); 71/550; Yrbk; Co-Ed Lit Mag; Var Swmmng; Cit Awd; Hon Roll; Prfct Atten Awd; Rotary Awd; Engl.

HART, LIANE J; Oak Park HS; Agoura, CA; (2); 13/119; German Clb; JA; Library Aide; Stat Crs Cntry; Stat Trk; Vllybl; Hon Roll.

HART, MELISSA A; John Glenn HS; Norwalk, CA; (4); 25/290; VP Pres Drama Clb; Office Aide; Teachers Aide; Thesps; School Play; Stage Crew; High Hon Roll; Bst Actress Awd 87-88; Intl Thespian Soc; Elem Tchrs Aide; UCLA; Spcl Ed.

HART, MIKE P; Lindsay HS; Lindsay, CA; (1); Church Yth Grp; FCA; French Clb; Letterman Clb; Band; Mrchg Band; Pep Band; Ftbl; Wt Lftg; Hon Roll; USC; Radiology.

HART, RONNIE B; Ukiah HS; Redwood Valley, CA; (2); 175/554; Church Yth Grp; Var Diving; Var Wrstlng; Comptd 24 Hr Relay; Bus.

HART, THOMAS C; Concord HS; Concord, CA; (3); SADD; Teachers Aide; JV Var Trk; Geom Stu Of Yr 1990; Math Achvt Awd; DVC; Cmptrs.

HART, WAYNE T; Casa Roble HS; Orangevale, CA; (3); 20/390; Boy Scts; Church Yth Grp; German Clb; Pep Clb; Science Clb; Teachers Aide; Hon Roll; NHS; Prfct Atten Awd; CA Schlrshp Fed; BYU; Elctrncs.

HART-JACKSON, CARRIE E; Southwestern Acad; Whittier, CA; (3); 1/30; Church Yth Grp; Debate Tm; GAA; Letterman Clb; Math Clb; Math Tm; Sec Model UN; Pep Clb; Sec Speech Tm; SADD; Ansty Intl; Coustean Svty; Green People; Humboldt ST U; Envrnmntl Engr.

HARTHRONG, ELIZABETH; Hesperia HS; Hesperia, CA; (2); Teachers Aide; Acpl Chr; Band; School Musical; High Hon Roll; Honor Society; Worship Club; Teachers Aide In Summer School; College; Ecology.

HARTLEY, ELISABETH N; Poly HS; Riverside, CA; (1); Cmnty Wkr; Dance Clb; French Clb; FBLA; Key Clb; Pep Clb; SADD; Drill Tm; School Play; Swing Chorus; Blck Stu Union.

HARTLEY, JASON A; Trona HS; Ridgecrest, CA; (3); Pep Clb; Crs Cntry; Trk; High Hon Roll; Fantasy Gaming Assn-Dungeons/Dragons.

HARTLEY, KAREN; Yuba City HS; Yuba City, CA; (4); Church Yth Grp; Treas 4-H; Pres FFA; Spanish Clb; SADD; Score Keeper; Trk; 4-H Awd; High Hon Roll; Pres Acad Fit Awd; Bk Of Amer Cert Ag; Farm Bureau Schlrshp; Pacific Egg & Poultry Assn Schlrshp; Yuba Clg; Ag Ed.

HARTLEY, L KEITH; Hanford Union HS; Hanford, CA; (3); 28/478; VP Church Yth Grp; Math Tm; Spanish Clb; Pres Frsh Cls; Pres Soph Cls; Pres Jr Cls; Stu Cncl; Hon Roll; Jr NHS; Pres Acad Fit Awd; US Naval Acad; Pre-Med.

HARTLEY, SCOTT; Dublin HS; Dublin, CA; (1); 1/200; Math Clb; Math Tm; Band; Jazz Band; Mrchg Band; Pep Band; School Musical; Variety Show; High Hon Roll; Prfct Atten Awd; Fine Art.

HARTLINE, JEFF; East Bakersfield HS; Bakersfield, CA; (2); Aud/Vis; Letterman Clb; Thesps; Stage Crew; Yrbk; Ftbl; Tennis; Wrstlng; Hon Roll; Stereo Tech.

HARTMAN, ALICIA M; Trinity HS; Trinity Center, CA; (3); Var Bsktbl; Capt Var Sftbl; Var Vllybl; Hon Roll; Trinity Christian Fllwshp; Bus.

HARTMAN, DANIEL S; Eureka HS; Eureka, CA; (2); Boy Scts; Treas Key Clb; Ski Clb; Intrml JV Bsktbl; Hon Roll; Hgh Hnrs Gldn ST Exam Alg; CA Poly SLO; Cvl Engrng.

HARTMAN, GREGORY; Torrey Pines HS; San Diego, CA; (3); Church Yth Grp; Pep Clb; JV Var Ftbl; Var Capt Lcrss; Pres Acad Fit Awd; U CA-SANTA Barbara; Poly Sci.

HARTMAN, JENNIFER; Cabrillo HS; Lompoc, CA; (4); 31/220; Church Yth Grp; SADD; Acpl Chr; Chorus; School Musical; Cheerldng; Mgr(s); Swmmng; Elks Awd; High Hon Roll; CA Baptist Coll; Behvrl Sci.

HARTMAN, JENNIFER R; Fontana HS; Fontana, CA; (2); Church Yth Grp; Acpl Chr; Church Choir; School Musical; High Hon Roll; Ntl Merit Ltr; Pres Acad Fit Awd; CSF; Dixie Coll; Music Ed.

HARTMAN, JUSTIN E; Lone Pine HS; Olancha, CA; (2); 8/30; Drama Clb; Spanish Clb; School Play; JV Bsktbl; Hon Roll; Peer Cnslr.

HARTMAN, SANDRA M; Irvine HS; Irvine, CA; (4); 31/580; Church Yth Grp; French Clb; FTA; Pep Clb; Red Cross Aide; Treas Frsh Cls; JV Var Cheerldng; JV Trk; High Hon Roll; Pres Acad Fit Awd; U Of CA Irvine; Bio.

HARTMAN, SHAWNI EDEN; Capistrano Valley Chistian HS; San Juan Capistra, CA; (2); Church Yth Grp; Cmnty Wkr; Dance Clb; FCA; Pep Clb; Service Clb; Varsity Clb; School Musical; Stu Cncl; Var Capt Cheerldng; Mst Insprtnl Awds JV & Var Cheer; Coaches Awd; Bus.

HARTMAN, TERRI L; Irvine HS; Irvine, CA; (4); 21/580; Church Yth Grp; Pres Drama Clb; French Clb; FTA; Pep Clb; Red Cross Aide; Sec Frsh Cls; JV Var Cheerldng; High Hon Roll; Pres Acad Fit Awd; Mc Donnell Douglas Corp Schlsp Awd; U CA Irvine; Poly Sci.

HARTMAN, WENDI; Ernest Righetti HS; Los Alamos, CA; (4); 5/356; Pres 4-H; FBLA; Sec FFA; Office Aide; Teachers Aide; Drill Tm; Flag Corp; 4-H Awd; High Hon Roll; Prfct Atten Awd; Allan Hancock Coll; Dntl Asst.

HARTMANN, STEPHANIE L; Mills HS; Millbrae, CA; (3); Church Yth Grp; 4-H; Var L Bsktbl; Intrml Socr; Var L Trk; Intrml Vllybl; High Hon Roll; Hon Roll; NHS.

HARTNETT, GABRIELLE A; Woodside HS; Redwood City, CA; (2); Var Sftbl; Var Vllybl; V Vllybl.

HARTNETT, KATHLEEN; San Ramon Valley HS; Danville, CA; (4); 11/402; Church Yth Grp; VP Key Clb; Treas SADD; Orch; Stu Cncl; Var Capt Swmmng; High Hon Roll; Sec NHS; CSF Pres; HOBY Ldrshp Sem; Fine Arts Cncl.

HARTNETT, SUZANNE M; Pacifica HS; Garden Grove, CA; (3); 51/280; Boy Scts; Church Yth Grp; Dance Clb; 4-H; Speech Tm; Treas Ski Clb; Treas Jr Cls; JV Var Swmmng; Hon Roll; CSF; Engrng.

HARTRANFT, WENDY; Rosary HS; Orange, CA; (4); 34/140; Science Clb; Spanish Clb; Hon Roll; NHS; CA ST Fullerton; Art.

HARTSELL, JONATHON CRAIG; Woodlake Union HS; Woodlake, CA; (4); 5/135; Cmnty Wkr; Debate Tm; Letterman Clb; Math Tm; Varsity Clb; Var Capt Bsbl; Var Capt Ftbl; Var Capt Wrstlng; Hon Roll; Pres Acad Fit Awd; CSUF Rodman Schlr; Bnk Amer Sci Awd; 1S Marine Corps Schrl-Athl; CSUF; Comp Engrng.

HARTSFIELD, SHERILYN RENEE; Norco HS; Corona, CA; (4); 92/405; Church Yth Grp; Cmnty Wkr; FBLA; Hon Roll; CSF; Girls League; CA ST-SAN Bernadino; Ed.

HARTUNG, MISTY; Cypress HS; Los Alamitos, CA; (2); Pep Clb; Teachers Aide; Varsity Clb; Cheerldng; Socr; Trk; Vllybl; Hon Roll; NHS; Pres Acad Fit Awd; USC Stanford.

HARTWELL, BENJAMIN P; Kern Valley HS; Lake Isabella, CA; (1); Church Yth Grp; Church Yth Grp; Spanish Clb; Bsktbl; Trk; Friday Night Live; Cnty Firefightr.

HARTWELL, JESSICA K; Narbonne HS; Harbor City, CA; (4); Teachers Aide; Yrbk; Lit Mag; Cit Awd; High Hon Roll; Hon Roll; Ntl Merit SF; Pres Acad Fit Awd; Acad Decathlon; Pres Schl Site Cncl; Engl Ed.

HARTWELL, MISTY M; Golden West HS; Visalia, CA; (2); Band; Bowling; Waves Swm Tm; Estes Beauty Schl; Cosmtlgst.

HARTWICH, DARREN M; Adolfo Camarillo HS; Camarillo, CA; (2); 33/506; Boy Scts; Key Clb; Yrbk; High Hon Roll; Hnrs Gldn St Exm 1st Yr Alg; CSF; GATE Mem 2yrs; Bio.

HARTWIG, ADRIANA D; Atascadero HS; Atascadero, CA; (2); Band; Mrchg Band; Pep Band; Hon Roll; CBDA CA St Hnr Band; San Luis Obispo Sr Cnty Hnr Band; Music.

HARTWIG, JENNIFER A; Woodland HS; Woodland, CA; (3); Key Clb; Stu Cncl; Var JV Bsktbl; Var JV Vllybl; Gov Hon Prg Awd; Pres Acad Fit Awd; Mst Imprvd Bsktbl & Vlybl; Cal Poly; Indstrl Engrng.

HARUTUNIANS, MICHAEL; Glendale HS; Glendale, CA; (2); Computer Clb; English Clb; Math Clb; Red Cross Aide; Science Clb; Spanish Clb; SADD; Bsktbl; Tennis; Prfct Atten Awd; UCLA; Psych.

HARVEY, AMBER J; La Serna HS; Whittier, CA; (3); Church Yth Grp; Chorus; Cheerldng; Hotel Mgmt.

HARVEY, EDDIE L; East Bakersfield HS; Bakersfield, CA; (4); 92/441; Church Yth Grp; Teachers Aide; Var L Bsktbl; Var Capt Ftbl; Var L Trk; Wt Lftg; Cit Awd; Hon Roll; Pres Acad Fit Awd; Music; Alpha Kappa Alpha & Kappa Omega Omega Chapt Awd; Bakersfield City Coll; Cnslr.

HARVEY, JANETTA L; Antelope Valley HS; Lancaster, CA; (3); 176/547; Pep Clb; Teachers Aide; Black Stu Union; Antelope Valley Coll; Bus Mgt.

HARVEY, KAREN; Paraclete HS; Lancaster, CA; (3); 14/113; Drama Clb; Key Clb; SADD; Varsity Clb; Co-Capt Crs Cntry; Socr; Trk; High Hon Roll; Hon Roll; NHS; CSF Scry; Znta Clb VP; Ltr Wmn Clb; Bio Sci.

HARVEY, LAKISHA D; Bishop Amat Memorial HS; La Puente, CA; (1); Church Yth Grp; Dance Clb; Drama Clb; Varsity Clb; Church Choir; Var Trk; Hon Roll; Stu Snt.

HARVEY, LATOYA F; Alexander Hamilton HS; Los Angeles, CA; (2); Teachers Aide; Prfct Atten Awd; Bus Admin.

HARVEY, LEIGH; Oroville HS; Oroville, CA; (4); 4-H; SADD; Powder Puff Ftbl; High Hon Roll; Pres Acad Fit Awd; Acad O; Lmp Knwldg; Butte JC; Physcl Thrpst.

HARVEY, MELISSA DANIS; Santa Clara HS; Port Hueneme, CA; (2); Speech Tm; JV Swmmng; Hon Roll; NHS; Opt Clb Awd; Airline Attndnt.

HARVEY, MIKE T; Woodside HS; Redwood City, CA; (2); 11/502; Teachers Aide; Jazz Band; Crs Cntry; Tennis; Pres Acad Fit Awd; Gldn St Exam For Alg; Dstngshd Schlrs.

HARVEY, PAUL WILLIAM; Saint Marys HS; Stockton, CA; (2); 1/200; Debate Tm; JA; Model UN; NFL; Science Clb; Service Clb; Speech Tm; Teachers Aide; Var Wrstlng; Gov Hon Prg Awd; Outstndg Stu Debate Team; 4.0 GPA Acad Awd; Pol Sci.

HARVEY, ROBERT M; Oak Ridge HS; Cameron Park, CA; (1); 1/280; Boy Scts; Chess Clb; Math Tm; Teachers Aide; Trk; Vllybl; Cit Awd; High Hon Roll; Pres Acad Fit Awd; CSF; Aerospc Engr.

HARVEY, ROBIN L; Gilbert East HS; Anaheim, CA; (3); Aud/Vis; Drama Clb; Pep Clb; SADD; Acpl Chr; Chorus; Color Guard; Flag Corp; Variety Show; Nwsp; Fullerton JC; Marine Photgrphy.

HARVEY, ROBYN; Reedley HS; Reedley, CA; (3); Drama Clb; German Clb; Chorus; School Musical; School Play; Rep Frsh Cls; Rep Soph Cls; L Cheerldng; Golf; Powder Puff Ftbl; Bst Actrs Awd 89.

HARVEY, SARAH E; Notre Dame HS; San Jose, CA; (3); 13/90; Church Yth Grp; Sec VP SADD; Rptr Nwsp; Phtg Ed Yrbk; High Hon Roll; Scrctrl Jb Chrch Rctry; Chrch Yth Grp Vlntr; San Jose ST U; Cmmnctns.

HARVEY, SCOTT G; Antelope Valley HS; Lancaster, CA; (2); 37/804; 4-H; JA; Math Tm; Var L Tennis; 4-H Awd; High Hon Roll; Hon Roll; Golden St Math Exam High Hnrs; Photo Clb; UCLA; Elctrnc Engr.

HARVEY, STACY E; Armijo HS; Suisun, CA; (1); AFS; Art Clb; Church Yth Grp; Ski Clb; Off Frsh Cls; High Hon Roll; Jr NHS; HS Supr Achvt Awd Excllnc Outstndng Stu Awd; U S CA; Ped.

HARVEY, WILLIAM W; Manteca HS; Manteca, CA; (3); 75/358; Teachers Aide; Real Estate.

HARVISON, GRACE; Barstow HS; Barstow, CA; (4); Church Yth Grp; Teachers Aide; Powder Puff Ftbl; High Hon Roll; Rifle Team; CSF; Astra; Barstow CC; Comp.

HARWARD, DANIEL; Bonita Vista HS; National City, CA; (2); 125/500; Church Yth Grp; Model UN; JV Bsbl; Capt JV Bsktbl; Cit Awd; High Hon Roll; Hon Roll; Prfct Atten Awd; Mst Imprvd Stu; Humboldt ST U; World Hstry.

HARWOOD, SUZANNE; Livermore HS; Livermore, CA; (3); Church Yth Grp; Cmnty Wkr; JV Bsktbl; High Hon Roll; Hon Roll; CSF; CA St Senate Recgntn Hnr Outstndng Acad Prfrmnce 89 GSE; Stu Actvty Cmmtte; BYU.

HARZOG, MICHAEL E; San Rafael HS; San Rafael, CA; (3); 11/226; Jazz Band; Pep Band; Rptr Yrbk; Var Socr; Var Tennis; Var Wrstlng; High Hon Roll; Hon Roll; NHS; Outstndng Vlntr Srvce Marin Cnty Awd; Schlr Athl Wrstlng & Tnns; Cngrssnl Yth Ldrshp Cncl.

HASAN, HUSNI; North HS; Riverside, CA; (2); 25/526; Teachers Aide; JV Ftbl; Wt Lftg; High Hon Roll; Hon Roll; Schlr Athl Ftbl Team; Podiatrist.

HASAN, MICHELLE; Corona Del Mar HS; Newport Beach, CA; (3); 30/250; Church Yth Grp; Science Clb; Rptr Nwsp; Phtg Yrbk; High Hon Roll; CSF; Brooks Inst Of Photo; Photo.

HASAN, QURATUL A; Diamond Bar HS; Diamond Bar, CA; (1); Chorus; Hon Roll; UCLA; Med.

HASAN, SYED M; Artesia HS; Lakewood, CA; (3); 1/300; Intnl Clb; ROTC; Science Clb; Spanish Clb; Lit Mag; Off Frsh Cls; Bsbl; Capt Fld Hcky; Socr; Trk; Hnr Guard; Hgh Hnrs Alg Exam; UCLA; Phy.

HASEGAWA, JAMES T; Lowell HS; San Francisco, CA; (3); ROTC; Flag Corp; Ntl Merit Ltr; Prfct Atten Awd; Vrsty Rifle Tm & Pistol Tm; Drill Platoon; Engrng.

HASEGAWA, TAMI T; North Torrance HS; Torrance, CA; (4); 43/431; Church Yth Grp; Cmnty Wkr; Intnl Clb; Service Clb; SADD; Teachers Aide; Sftbl; Hon Roll; JA; Republic Bak Ctznshp Awd; CSF Histrn; Peer Counselor; Loyola Marymount U; Liberal Stu.

HASH, JESSICA L; El Camino Fundamental HS; Sacramento, CA; (3); Girl Scts; Acpl Chr; Chorus; JV Swmmng; Photojrnlsm.

HASHA, AMY; Lassen Union HS; Susanville, CA; (4); 1/160; Art Clb; Letterman Clb; Ski Clb; Band; Treas Stu Cncl; VP Fld Hcky; Trk; NHS; Pres Acad Fit Awd; Val.

HASHMY, ASRA; Rosary HS; Fullerton, CA; (3); French Clb; Hosp Aide; Rptr Nwsp; VP Frsh Cls; Hon Roll; LA Times High Life Sctn Schl Rep; Med.

HASKELL, KEVIN; Serra HS; San Mateo, CA; (2); Church Yth Grp; Cmnty Wkr; Teachers Aide; Tennis; Wrstlng; Hon Roll; UC Davis; Pediatrics.

HASKELL, KIM S; Woodside HS; Portola Valley, CA; (2); 36/420; Rep Frsh Cls; Rep Soph Cls; Var Socr; Var Tennis; Var Trk; High Hon Roll; Hon Roll; Pres Acad Fit Awd; Girl Athl Of Yr.

HASKILL, RHONDA J; R A Millikan HS; Long Beach, CA; (4); Church Yth Grp; Cmnty Wkr; Dance Clb; Hosp Aide; Office Aide; Teachers Aide; Chorus; Church Choir; Socr; Sftbl; Dist Medallion; Gold Tassel; Medal Of Merit; LBCC; Secy.

HASKINS, NEIL G; Apple Valley Christian HS; Apple Valley, CA; (3); Church Yth Grp; Var Bsbl; Capt Bsktbl; Var Vllybl; Stu Of Yr Bible; Stu Of Yr His; Engrng.

HASKOVEC, ALEXANDRA; Torrey Pines HS; Solana Beach, CA; (3); 25/427; Art Clb; Service Clb; Phtg Yrbk; Lit Mag; Treas Soph Cls; JV Gym; JV Swmmng; Hon Roll; Ntl Merit SF; Rotary Awd; Envrnmntl Awareness Club; CA Schltc Fed.

HASLER, DAVID G; Kingsburg HS; Kingsburg, CA; (3); Art Clb; Chess Clb; Computer Clb; Socr; Tennis; Hon Roll; Acadmc Ltr Awd; U Of Zurich.

HASLETON, PERRY J; Hiram W Johnson HS; Sacramento, CA; (3); 21/116; Boy Scts; Church Yth Grp; Church Choir; Color Guard; Hon Roll; Eagle Sct With Bronze Palm; BYU; Bus Admin.

HASLETT, GINA M; Modoc HS; Alturas, CA; (2); 10/60; FBLA; Office Aide; SADD; Band; Mrchg Band; Pep Band; School Musical; Nwsp; Powder Puff Ftbl; High Hon Roll; Received All Svc Bars Rainbow Girls; CA Rainbow Girls Worthy Advisor; Shasta CC; Bus Mgt.

HASS, CHERYL L; St Francis HS; Sacramento, CA; (4); 23/145; Debate Tm; Speech Tm; Teachers Aide; Hon Roll; Prfct Atten Awd; 90 CA St Mock Trial Cmptn; Young Mens Inst Essay Cmptn-Achvt Cert; CA ST U-Sacramento; Psych.

HASSAKOURSIAN, YVETTE; Ribet Acad; La Canada, CA; (2); 1/18; Girl Scts; Rep Stu Cncl; Var Bsktbl; Var Sftbl; Var Vllybl; Hon Roll; Prfct Atten Awd; Ribet Acad.

HASSAN, SHAMINA K; Andrew Hill HS; San Jose, CA; (3); French Clb; Yrbk; Prfct Atten Awd; Class Spellout; Bus.

HASSE, REBEKAH; John F Kennedy HS; Granada Hills, CA; (3); Key Clb; Teachers Aide; Rep Stu Cncl; JV Cheerldng; Phys Therapy.

HASSELBACH, MATTHEW W; Manteca HS; Manteca, CA; (2); 12/437; Aud/Vis; French Clb; FBLA; Math Clb; JV Ftbl; High Hon Roll; Prfct Atten Awd; Business.

HASSERD, KATIE; Archbishop Mitty HS; San Jose, CA; (3); 12/250; Church Yth Grp; Cmnty Wkr; Off Soph Cls; Treas Jr Cls; JV Socr; Var Trk; High Hon Roll; Hon Roll; NHS; Outstndg Acad Awds & MVP Sccr.

HASSIM, JAMEELA; Woodrow Wilson HS; Long Beach, CA; (3); Hosp Aide; Intnl Clb; Math Clb; Office Aide; Science Clb; Spanish Clb; Hon Roll; Prfct Atten Awd; Envrnmntl Awrnss Clb; Making Jewelry; Asst Wddng Photo; CA ST U Long Bch; Sci.

HASSOLD, ANETTE M; Novato HS; Novato, CA; (1); Temple Yth Grp; Band; Mrchg Band; Pep Band; Stage Crew; TV Prdctns; Actin; Pediatrician TV Prdctn Acting.

HASSOUN, HAKIM T; Gompers HS; San Diego, CA; (3); 57/163; Church Yth Grp; 4-H; Band; Chorus; Church Choir; Drm Mjr(t); Jazz Band; Variety Show; Wt Lftg; Cit Awd; Rgnl Yth Pgm Awd; San Diego ST U; Elec Engrng.

HASSOUN, JIBRIL S; Gompers HS; San Diego, CA; (2); Hon Roll; Amer Tae Kwondao Assoc 1st Degree Black Belt; Mira Mesa Swim Tm; Marine Sci.

HASTIE, SHIONA; Rancho Bernardo HS; San Diego, CA; (2); Mrchg Band; USC; Pilot.

HASTINGS, LAURA A; Redondo Union HS; Redondo Beach, CA; (4); 21/416; Cmnty Wkr; Drama Clb; French Clb; Math Clb; Quiz Bowl; Science Clb; Service Clb; Rep Stu Cncl; Hon Roll; Pres Acad Fit Awd; Synchronized Swimming; Assisteens Angel Awd; CSF Life Membership; UCLA; Bio.

HASTINGS, MICHELLE L; Carpinteria HS; Carpinteria, CA; (3); 12/145; Cmnty Wkr; French Clb; Office Aide; Trk; Vllybl; Hon Roll; St Schlr; CA Schlrshp Fed; Dep Awds Frnch, Hstry; UCLA; Med.

HASTON, NATHAN H; Carlsbad HS; Carlsbad, CA; (1); English Clb; Quiz Bowl; Scholastic Bowl; Band; Jazz Band; Mrchg Band; Pep Band; Stat Score Keeper; Cit Awd; High Hon Roll.

HASTY, AIMEE; Carson HS; Carson, CA; (3); Art Clb.

HATAMI, DYLAN N; Hogan SR HS; Vallejo, CA; (3); Chess Clb; Spanish Clb; Teachers Aide; Bausch & Lomb Sci Awd; High Hon Roll.

HATAYE, JASON M; Pinole Valley HS; Hercules, CA; (3); French Clb; Intnl Clb; Science Clb; Ski Clb; JV Crs Cntry; Hon Roll; Explorers; Amnesty Intl; Cal Poly; Engrng.

HATCH, AARON Y; St Margaret Scotland Episcopal Schl; Laguna Beach, CA; (3); Drama Clb; Chorus; Church Choir; School Musical; School Play; Stage Crew; Variety Show; Nwsp; Yrbk; Treas Jr Cls; Hnr Rll; Ftlghtrs; Spcl Hstry Awd; Amer Ldrshp Stdy Grp 89; Clsscl Piano.

HATCH, AMY B; Mc Kinleyville HS; Arcata, CA; (2); Church Yth Grp; Cmnty Wkr; Debate Tm; Pres Sec Girl Scts; Key Clb; NFL; Ed Nwsp; Hon Roll; Prfct Atten Awd; Gldn St Exam Alg Awd; Natl Logic/Reasoning Test; Vol Work Easter Seals Camp; Stanford; Humanities.

HATCH, KRISTIN; Righetti HS; Santa Maria, CA; (2); Church Yth Grp; FFA; Teachers Aide; Rptr Nwsp; Hon Roll; Allan Hancock Coll; Bus.

HATCH, MONICA L; Turlock HS; Turlock, CA; (2); 4-H; FFA; GAA; Office Aide; SADD; Teachers Aide; Rptr Nwsp; 4-H Awd; Hon Roll; U CA Stanislaus; Phys Thrpy.

HATCHER, SUZANNE M; Thomas Downey HS; Modesto, CA; (1); VP Sec Church Yth Grp; SADD; Teachers Aide; Acpl Chr; Band; Chorus; Church Choir; Sec Mrchg Band; Pep Band; Hon Roll; Full Symphonic Orch; U Of CA; Bio Sci.

HATCHETT, ALICIA K; Crenshaw HS; Los Angeles, CA; (1); Cmnty Wkr; Gym; Cit Awd; Hon Roll; NHS; Ldrshp Cls; Jrnlsm.

HATFIELD, CHRISTINE E; Hilltop HS; Chula Vista, CA; (3); Office Aide; Teachers Aide; Thesps; Chorus; School Play; Variety Show; JV Bsktbl; JV Fld Hcky; Var Trk; CA Schlrshp Fed; Hnrs & Schl Rcgntn Gldn St Exm; Bio.

HATFIELD, CRISTI; Troy HS; Fullerton, CA; (4); Church Yth Grp; Teachers Aide; Fullerton Coll; Bus.

HATFIELD, JACK R; Paraclete HS; Lancaster, CA; (2); Key Clb; Letterman Clb; Quiz Bowl; SADD; Treas Soph Cls; JV Var Ftbl; Sec Mgr(s); JV Var Socr; High Hon Roll; Hon Roll; CSF; Law.

HATFIELD, JENNIFER L; Woodcrest Christ HS; Riverside, CA; (3); Church Yth Grp; Cmnty Wkr; Office Aide; Red Cross Aide; Bsktbl; Cheerldng; Crs Cntry; Sftbl; Vllybl; Pblshd Poem Natl Library Poetry; Social Sci.

HATFIELD, MEREDITH C; Bullard HS; Fresno, CA; (1); SADD; Drill Tm; Flag Corp; Cheerldng; Prfct Atten Awd; Fresno ST U; Psycht.

HATFIELD, PENELOPE; De Anza HS; Richmond, CA; (4); 46/280; Church Yth Grp; French Clb; Sec Acpl Chr; Yrbk; Rep Stu Cncl; Co-Capt Pom Pon; Capt Socr; Vllybl; Hon Roll; Pres Acad Fit Awd; MVP Sccr; Mst Imprvd Vllybl; CA Grant A Schlrshp; Chief Justice Of Stu Crt; CA ST U Chico; Frgn Lang.

HATFIELD, STEVEN D; Vacaville HS; Vacaville, CA; (3); Hon Roll; Martial Arts; U Of CA; Physcs.

HATLER, CASSANDRA L; Duncan Poly Tech; Fresno, CA; (1); Duncan Athltc Club; Friday Nite Live; Child Psych.

HATTA, ERI; George Washington HS; San Francisco, CA; (3); Math Clb; Science Clb; School Musical; High Hon Roll; Hon Roll; Recod For Excl Sci Awd Wellesley Coll; Cert Participation Camp Enterprise; Intramural Bowling.

HATTAR, JAMES A; San Gorgonio HS; Highland, CA; (3); Cit Awd; Doc.

HATTI, VIKRAM M; Pasadena HS; Pasadena, CA; (2); Chess Clb; JA; Var Swmmng; High Hon Roll; Hon Roll; CA Schlrshp Fed; UCLA; Med.

HATTON, HOLLIE; Seaside HS; Marina, CA; (3); Girl Scts; Red Cross Aide; ROTC; Teachers Aide; Acpl Chr; Band; Drill Tm; Var Swmmng; Wt Lftg; High Hon Roll; Pony Clb; UC Davis; Animal Sci.

HATTON, KELLY J; Taft Union HS; Taft, CA; (3); 28/200; AFS; Aud/Vis; Debate Tm; Key Clb; Pep Clb; SADD; Band; Color Guard; Flag Corp; Jazz Band; Mock Trl; Rly Cmmssn; Friday Nght Live; Bus.

HATTON, M RYAN; Roseville HS; Roseville, CA; (1); Boy Scts; JV Var Bsktbl; Var L Crs Cntry; L Var Trk; High Hon Roll; Pres Acad Fit Awd; Boy Sct Hnr Awd; Loyola Marymont Coll; Math.

HATZKE, CHRIS; Fairfield HS; Fairfield, CA; (1); FHA; JV Bsktbl; JV Ftbl; Hon Roll; Pro Golfer.

HAUB, SARA A; Beyer HS; Modesto, CA; (3); Office Aide; Pep Clb; Teachers Aide; Stat Bsbl; Cheerldng; Score Keeper; Hon Roll.

HAUBRUGE, CHERIDA M; Mojave HS; Mojave, CA; (1); Bsktbl; Vllybl; Hon Roll.

HAUCK, THOMAS L; Torrey Pines HS; Del Mar, CA; (2); 85/503; Boy Scts; SADD; Intrml Bsbl; JV Ftbl; Intrml Socr; JV Wrstlng; Hon Roll; JETS Awd; Guitarist & Singer Local Band; Stanford; Engrng.

HAUG, JON; North Bay Orinda Schl; El Cerrito, CA; (2); Hon Roll; Comp Blltn Brd Sys Co-Sys Oper; Comp Pgmng.

HAUGE, BRYAN E; Paraclete HS; Acton, CA; (2); Socr; Hon Roll; Accntng.

HAUGE, DEWEY J; Woodside HS; Redwood City, CA; (2); Dance Clb; Letterman Clb; Ski Clb; Varsity Clb; JV Bsbl; JV Bsktbl; JV Ftbl.

HAUGE, JASON; Savanna HS; Anaheim, CA; (3); JA; Lbrn Teachers Aide; Rep Soph Cls; Bus.

HAUGE, MATTHEW R; Maranatha HS; Sierra Madre, CA; (2); Church Yth Grp; Drama Clb; Spanish Clb; School Play; Stage Crew; Rep Soph Cls; JV Var Bsbl; JV Ftbl; JV Var Socr; Wt Lftg.

HAUGH, MARK DEWON; Apple Valley HS; Apple Valley, CA; (3); 55/728; French Clb; Key Clb; Ftbl; High Hon Roll; Hon Roll; Wrtng Clb VP; Congrssnl Yth Ldrshp Cncl; Archtr Voctnl Cert; Law.

HAUGHEY, JOHN C; Vista HS; Vista, CA; (2); 11/500; Church Yth Grp; Stu Cncl; L Var Swmmng; High Hon Roll; Acad Achvt Awd; ASB Soph Of Yr; Swmmng CIF Fnlst; JV Waterpolo; Engrng.

HAUK, MATT; Los Alamitos HS; Los Alamitos, CA; (2); Church Yth Grp; FCA; Letterman Clb; Varsity Clb; Church Choir; L Var Ftbl; L Var Trk; Pres Acad Fit Awd; Weight Lifting Awd 2 Yrs; Aero Engr.

HAUKAAS, JEFFREY WILLIAM; Acalanes HS; Lafayette, CA; (3); Church Yth Grp; Drama Clb; School Play; Off Soph Cls; VP Jr Cls; Pres Sr Cls; Var Swmmng; Hon Roll; Rotary Awd; Var Water Polo; Yng Life, Ldrshp; Bus.

HAUMEA, HEATHER N; Dos Palos HS; Dos Palos, CA; (2); FCA; Chorus; Var Bsktbl; Var Sftbl; Var Capt Vllybl; Hon Roll; West Handbl Tm 89 Olympc Fstvl.

HAUMSCHILT, GREGORY D; Galt HS; Galt, CA; (2); Boy Scts; Church Yth Grp; JV Bsbl; Hon Roll; Comp Prgmng.

HAUN, MARK A; Sacramento Adventist Acad; Sacramento, CA; (3); 3/40; Church Yth Grp; Spanish Clb; Band; Hon Roll; NHS; Ntl Merit Ltr; Outstndng Achvt Awd; Pacific Union Coll; Elect Engr.

HAUPTMAN, ESTHER A; Clovis West HS; Fresno, CA; (3); Model UN; Pep Clb; Temple Yth Grp; Orch; Hon Roll; Sing; Stu Tchr Rlgs Schl; UCSB; Law.

HAURY, ERIC P; Torrey Pines HS; Del Mar, CA; (3); 84/475; Aud/Vis; Model UN; Scholastic Bowl; Hon Roll; Ntl Merit Ltr; Author Shrt Strs & Fantasy Novel; Writer.

HAUS, SHARON; Berean Christian HS; Concord, CA; (1); Church Yth Grp; Chorus; School Musical; Stat Bsbl; Var Cheerldng; Score Keeper; Wt Lftg; Southern CA Coll.

HAUSE, CRAIG A; Cypress HS; Cypress, CA; (3); 78/350; Boy Scts; Ftbl; Golf; Tennis; Wt Lftg; Hon Roll; Aerospc Engr.

HAUSERMAN, BRIAN; Idyllwild Schl Of Music And The Arts; Harlingen, TX; (4); 2/95; Speech Tm; School Musical; School Play; Rptr Nwsp; Rep Stu Cncl; Cit Awd; Ntl Merit Schol; Opt Clb Awd; Rotary Awd; Sal; Austin ISD Trustees Schlrshp Awd; CA Schlrshp Federation Seal Bearer; Idyllwild Schlrshp; U Of Cincinnati; Musical Thtre.

HAUSSLER, SALLY; El Camino Fundamental HS; Carmichael, CA; (3); Church Yth Grp; Spanish Clb; Teachers Aide; Church Choir; Swmmng; Friday Night Live; Azuza Pacific; Nrsng.

HAUT, JENNIFER; Lodi HS; Lodi, CA; (4); 18/399; Pres Church Yth Grp; German Clb; Hosp Aide; Sec Treas Science Clb; Pres Band; Church Choir; Jazz Band; Pres Mrchg Band; Pep Band; Cit Awd; Chemathon W/Hnry Mntn; Sci Olympoiad & 3rd Pl Bio Ctgry; Life Mem CA Schlrshp Fed; CA ST U; Bio.

HAUT, SANDRA L; Neveda Union HS; Nevada City, CA; (3); Color Guard.

HAUVER, DAVID K; John Burroughs HS; Burbank, CA; (2); Engr.

HAVEN, BRIAN; Golden West HS; Visalia, CA; (3); 25/300; Band; Mrchg Band; Orch; Pep Band; Hon Roll; Bus.

HAVEN, JANET; Los Alamitos HS; Seal Beach, CA; (3); Cmnty Wkr; Debate Tm; French Clb; Speech Tm; Teachers Aide; Hon Roll; NHS; Russn Cltr.

HAVENER, KATHERINE; Dublin HS; Dublin, CA; (4); 11/174; Drama Clb; French Clb; Service Clb; SADD; Thesps; Chorus; Church Choir; School Musical; School Play; Sec Stu Cncl; CSF VP; Mst Likely To Succeed Awd; Bank Of Amer Outstndng Achvt; MV Stu Schlrshp; Invest In Amer Awd; Bennington Coll; Child Dvlpmnt.

HAVENS, AARON M; Hemet HS; Hemet, CA; (2); 113/729; Band; Jazz Band; Mrchg Band; JV Bsbl; Var L Crs Cntry; Var L Wrstlng; Pres Acad Fit Awd; Hnrs Golden St Exam; USNA; Engr.

HAVENS, JACQUELINE; Mojave HS; Hesperia, CA; (4); School Play.

HAVERLOCK, SCOTT J; Barstow HS; Barstow, CA; (4); 16/250; AFS; Church Yth Grp; Dance Clb; Drama Clb; School Play; Variety Show; Pres Soph Cls; Off Jr Cls; Pres Sr Cls; Var Tennis; CA Youth & Govt,Model Legislature Court; CA Schlrshp Fed; Barston CC; Comm Sports Brcstr.

HAVILAND, BRIAN D; North Monterey County HS; Salinas, CA; (2); 2/400; AFS; Boy Scts; Pres Church Yth Grp; 4-H; VP Ski Clb; SADD; JV Crs Cntry; JV Ftbl; JV Trk; 4-H Awd.

HAVLICEK, LANI K; Morro Bay HS; San Luis Obispo, CA; (4); 8/175; Church Yth Grp; English Clb; Intnl Clb; Band; Mrchg Band; Pep Band; School Play; Ed Yrbk; Intrml Powder Puff Ftbl; Var Socr; Acad Decathalon Tm; CA Schlrshp Fed; Reed Coll; Envrnmntl.

HAWAYEK, JIMMY F; Artesia HS; Lakewood, CA; (3); Var Bsktbl; Var Ftbl; Var Wt Lftg; Hon Roll.

HAWES, NATHAN L; Etiwanda HS; Alta Loma, CA; (2); Church Yth Grp; JV Bsbl; JV Crs Cntry; JV Socr; JV Trk; High Hon Roll; Hon Roll; Pepperdine; Pro Bsbl.

HAWK, KELLY L; Redlands HS; Redlands, CA; (2); Hosp Aide; Office Aide; Pep Clb; Teachers Aide; CA Poly; Bus.

HAWK, MICHELLE L; North HS; Bakersfield, CA; (3); Drama Clb; Business Club; Accntng.

HAWKES, THOMAS N; Fairfield HS; Fairfield, CA; (1); Prfct Atten Awd.

HAWKINS, CHRISTAN LEIGH; Colton HS; Colton, CA; (2); Church Yth Grp; JV Var Bsktbl; MVP Girls Bsktbl 2 Yrs; Schlstc Achvt Awd Hnr Rl For 3 Sports In 1 Yr; Riverside CC; Sports Med.

HAWKINS, DENISE L; Oak Ridge HS; Rescue, CA; (3); 11/280; Church Yth Grp; Cmnty Wkr; 4-H; Intnl Clb; Math Tm; SADD; 4-H Awd; High Hon Roll; Hon Roll; NHS; U Of The Pacific; Pharmacy.

HAWKINS, ELISA; Tracy Joint Union HS; Tracy, CA; (4); 81/355; Cmnty Wkr; Teachers Aide; Lit Mag; Capt Stu Cncl; High Hon Roll; Hon Roll; Stu Leag Rep; Ctrfd CPR & Frst Aid; Sacramento ST; Pre-Med.

HAWKINS, HOLLY M; San Marcos HS; San Marcos, CA; (3); 24/450; French Clb; Band; Mrchg Band; VP Soph Cls; Sec Jr Cls; Treas Stu Cncl; High Hon Roll; Rotary Awd; St Schlr; Music.

HAWKINS, JACQUELYN M; Leuzinger HS; Hawthorne, CA; (3); Teachers Aide; Band; Cit Awd; High Hon Roll; Hon Roll; Pres Acad Fit Awd; Ebony Nation Clb; UCLA; Pre Med.

HAWKINS, JAMES R; Lemoore HS; Lemoore, CA; (3); Var Bsktbl; Var Trk; Hon Roll; CSF; Cal Poly; Sci.

HAWKINS, JENNIFER A; North HS; Bakersfield, CA; (2); Church Yth Grp; FFA; Spanish Clb; Band; Mrchg Band; Pep Band; Score Keeper; Hon Roll; BYU.

HAWKINS, JENNIFER T; Rancho Cotate HS; Rohnert Park, CA; (4); 36/270; Church Yth Grp; Cmnty Wkr; Treas Spanish Clb; Treas Sr Cls; Cheerldng; JV Tennis; Hon Roll; NHS; Rotary Awd; CSF; Safe Rides; Stu Mnth; Sonoma ST U.

HAWKINS, JULIE R; Kingsburg HS; Kingsburg, CA; (1); Cmnty Wkr; 4-H; FFA; SADD; School Play; Stage Crew; 4-H Awd; Hon Roll; Grnhnd Offcr Scrtry; FFA Horse Prfcncy; FFA Horse Jdgng Team, Bst Infrmd Team Grnhnd; CA Poly SLO; Amnl Hsbntry.

HAWKINS, RYAN L; Nevada Union HS; Nevada City, CA; (3); Chorus; Ski Clb; Speech Tm; Intrml Bsktbl; Var Socr; Intrml Wt Lftg; JV Wrstlng; Hon Roll; Law.

HAWKINS, SCOTT A; Thousand Oaks HS; Thousand Oaks, CA; (3); 52/538; Math Tm; Ed Yrbk; JV Crs Cntry; JV Tennis; JV Trk; JV Var Wrstlng; High Hon Roll; Acad All-Amer 88; Goldn St Exam Geom Hnrs 88.

HAWKINS, SHELLEY D; Skyline HS; Oakland, CA; (3); Church Yth Grp; Teachers Aide; Acpl Chr; Jazz Band; Orch; Swing Chorus; Rep Stu Cncl; Vllybl; Hon Roll; Dance Clb; MESA; UC San Diego; Medicine.

HAWKINS, STUART J; Mountain View HS; Mountain View, CA; (2); 1/25; Boy Scts; Computer Clb; French Clb; JA; Math Tm; High Hon Roll; Cert Scuba Diver; Skiing Mdl; Windsurfer & Sailer; Stanford; Fin.

HAWKINS, TAMMI R; Covina HS; Covina, CA; (3); Off Soph Cls; Hon Roll; Prfct Atten Awd; Bus.

HAWKINS, THOMAS; Carmel HS; Carmel Valley, CA; (4); 2/175; Am Leg Boys St; Church Yth Grp; Cmnty Wkr; Debate Tm; French Clb; Math Tm; Quiz Bowl; Scholastic Bowl; Teachers Aide; Band; Water Polo Var 3 Yrs, MVP, Tm Co-Capt; Delg USSR Stu/Teacher Peace Exchange; Stanford; Sci.

HAWKINS, VICKY L; Colton HS; Colton, CA; (4); Church Yth Grp; Office Aide; Varsity Clb; Var Tennis; Hon Roll; Acad Exc; Dentl Assist.

HAWKINS, WADE N; O'farrell SCPA HS; San Diego, CA; (4); Church Yth Grp; Drama Clb; English Clb; Letterman Clb; Teachers Aide; School Musical; School Play; Stage Crew; Variety Show; Prfct Atten Awd; Asst Dir; Jr Theater Schlrshp Awd; K-Arts Video Prod; Film Dir.

HAWKINSON, CHARIS A; Traruco Hills HS; Mission Viejo, CA; (1); German Clb; GAA; Girl Scts; Vllybl; U Of WA; Med.

HAWORTH, MICHELLE; San Benito HS; Hollister, CA; (3); FBLA; GAA; Letterman Clb; Ski Clb; Varsity Clb; Mgr Yrbk; Sftbl; Vllybl; Wt Lftg; Cit Awd; CHSRA 3rd In St Of CA In Pole Bending 88-89; 4th Barrel Racing; Fresno ST; Sports Med.

HAWORTH, ROB; Oakmont HS; Roseville, CA; (1); UC Davis; Arch.

HAWORTH, SAMANTHA; Upper Lake HS; Nice, CA; (3); 1/35; Am Leg Aux Girls St; Science Clb; Spanish Clb; Phtg Rptr Nwsp; Phtg Rptr Yrbk; Pres Frsh Cls; Pres Soph Cls; Pres Jr Cls; Pres Stu Cncl; Var Capt Cheerldng; Tnwrk 90; Scndry Tchr.

HAWORTH, TAMI DIANE; Norbonne HS; Carson, CA; (4); Church Yth Grp; Girl Scts; Office Aide; Teachers Aide; Chorus; Drill Tm; Cheerldng; Hon Roll; Professional Modeling.

HAWS, ANNIE; San Marcos HS; Santa Barbara, CA; (2); Key Clb; Ski Clb; SADD; Teachers Aide; Treas Stu Cncl; Swmmng; Vllybl; Hon Roll; No 1 Clb; Acad Awd; BYU; Teacher.

HAWTHORNE, AARON A; Huntington Beach HS; Huntington Beach, CA; (2); Cmnty Wkr; JV Bsktbl; Ftbl; Hon Roll; Tower Awd.

HAWTHORNE, RACHEL A; Ventura HS; Ventura, CA; (1); 21/511; Church Yth Grp; Church Choir; Variety Show; High Hon Roll; Prfct Atten Awd; City Bsktbl Leag.

HAY, ADAM J; Nevada Union HS; Grass Valley, CA; (1); Acpl Chr; Chorus; JV Swmmng; Hon Roll; Water Polo.

HAY, JONATHAN P; Bellarmine College Prep; San Jose, CA; (3); 62/300; Quiz Bowl; Ski Clb; JV Diving; Cmmnty Svc Tutrng Chldrn; CA U; Sci.

HAY, LENORA T; Mount Diablo HS; Pittsburg, CA; (2); Church Yth Grp; French Clb; Teachers Aide; Variety Show; Rep Frsh Cls; Rep Soph Cls; JV Bsktbl; Stat Ftbl; Powder Puff Ftbl; Var Trk; Fri Night Live; Safe Rides; CSF; Boston U.

HAY, SEAKNGOR; Fremont HS; Oakland, CA; (3); FCA; Math Tm; Temple Yth Grp; Church Choir; Hon Roll; Merrite Coll; Nrsng.

HAYASHI, RICHARD D; Bishop O'dowd HS; Alameda, CA; (2); Cmnty Wkr; Dance Clb; Off Soph Cls; Stu Cncl; JV Trk; High Hon Roll; Engrng.

HAYASHIDA, MICHAEL K; Gardena HS; Gardena, CA; (4); 12/460; Intnl Clb; Pres Latin Clb; ROTC; School Play; Intrml Bsktbl; Wt Lftg; Cit Awd; Opt Clb Awd; Pres Acad Fit Awd; Bank Of Amer Acad Excllnc Awd; UCLA; Microbio.

HAYDEN, JENNIFER; Culver City HS; Poway, CA; (2); JV Var Cheerldng; JV Sftbl; JV Tennis; High Hon Roll; Hon Roll; Golden St Exam Awd Geom; Yth And Govt; Sci.

HAYDEN, LAURA B; Redlands HS; Redlands, CA; (4); 13/821; Church Yth Grp; Ski Clb; Bsktbl; Sftbl; Trk; Vllybl; Cit Awd; High Hon Roll; Pres Schlr; CSF; BYU; Med.

HAYDEN, LISA A; Red Bluff Union HS; Red Bluff, CA; (2); 1/350; Key Clb; Mu Alpha Theta; Stage Crew; High Hon Roll; Kiwanis Awd; NHS; Friday Night Live; Intl Bus.

HAYDEN, MICHAEL L; Hawthorne HS; Hawthorne, CA; (1); Band; Jazz Band; Mrchg Band; Orch; Rep Stu Cncl; Hon Roll; Rookie Of The Year; Scholarship For Marching Band; Engineering.

HAYDU, JENNIFER; Chaminade College Prep; West Hills, CA; (3); Art Clb; School Musical; Variety Show; Powder Puff Ftbl; Vllybl; High Hon Roll; Hon Roll; Peace Club; Cnsvrtn & Envrnmntl Club; UC Santa Cruz; Art.

HAYES, COLLEEN E; Apple Valley Christian Schl; Victorville, CA; (3); Church Yth Grp; Drama Clb; FCA; Pep Clb; Red Cross Aide; School Play; Var Bsktbl; Var Cheerldng; Var Vllybl; DAR Awd; NAA Lvl I Crtfd Archery Instrctr; Red Crss Crtfd Lifeguard; Athl Of Yr; Wright ST U; Nrsng.

HAYES, DAN J; Livermore HS; Livermore, CA; (3); 1/458; Ski Clb; Var Bsbl; JV Socr; High Hon Roll.

HAYES, DANIEL P; Canyon HS; Newhall, CA; (3); 88/501; Church Yth Grp; ROTC; Intrml Bsktbl; Cit Awd; ROTC Flight Cmmander C/Cptn Rank; Point Loma Nazarene Coll; Educ.

HAYES, DAVID; Southwest HS; San Diego, CA; (2); Math Tm; Science Clb; JV Vllybl; Cit Awd; US Air Frc Pilot.

HAYES, DENELLE R; Galileo HS; San Francisco, CA; (4); Church Yth Grp; Treas JA; SADD; Teachers Aide; Variety Show; Var Bsktbl; Score Keeper; Var Sftbl; Hon Roll; BSU Club; Aids Education Team; Street Law Certificate Tri Univ Of San Francisco School Of Law; San Francisco ST U; Bus Admins.

HAYES, GINA L; Faith Christian HS; Marysville, CA; (3); Letterman Clb; Teachers Aide; Varsity Clb; JV Var Cheerldng; JV Var Powder Puff Ftbl; Score Keeper; Vllybl; Cit Awd; Hon Roll; Yuba Coll; Bus.

HAYES, JASON M; Carlsbad HS; Carlsbad, CA; (1); Key Clb; JV Tennis; Hon Roll; Athltc Booster Clb; Stu Athl Of Month; AAHPERD Htl Ftnss Awd; Acctng.

HAYES, JEREMY S; Oakmont HS; Roseville, CA; (2); Mem HS Global Impact Club; UC Santa Barbra; Arch.

HAYES, JOHN W; Carmel HS; Carmel Valley, CA; (3); Boy Scts; Church Yth Grp; Computer Clb; Drama Clb; 4-H; FFA; Intnl Clb; Model UN; SADD; Teachers Aide; Cal Poly Sn Luis Obispo; Engrng.

HAYES, KATHY L; Victor Valley HS; Victorville, CA; (3); 16/450; Key Clb; NFL; Phtg Nwsp; Hon Roll; Jr NHS.

HAYES, KRISTEL; Millikan HS; Long Beach, CA; (4); Dance Clb; VP Sec Key Clb; Pep Clb; Service Clb; Acpl Chr; School Musical; Variety Show; Rep Soph Cls; Rep Jr Cls; Rep Sr Cls; Rotry Yng Sngr Yr; Englsh Mdl Mrt Fnlst; Bank Of Amer Plaque Wnnr Music; UCLA; Musical Theatre.

HAYES, LAUREL A; St Joseph HS; Santa Maria, CA; (3); Church Yth Grp; Pep Clb; Spanish Clb; Yrbk; Var Pom Pon; JV Trk; Hon Roll; Yng Wmn Yr; Outstndng Acad Achvt Cert; Hnrs All Subjcts Cert; Psych.

HAYES, LYDIA M; Moorpark HS; Moorpark, CA; (3); FBLA; Teachers Aide; JV Vllybl; Hon Roll; Olympc Sports Fstvl 89 & Jr Natls 90 Bicycling Comptns; Roller Speed Sktng Natl Comptns 80-89; CA ST U Northridge; Athlt Trn.

HAYES, MARITESS S; San Lorenzo HS; San Lorenzo, CA; (2); Church Yth Grp; Band; Orch; Rep Frsh Cls; Var Trk; JV Vllybl; High Hon Roll; San Francisco Symphny Yth Orch; Oakland Yth Orch; Biomedcl Engr.

HAYES, MELISSA I; Ofarrell SCPA HS; San Diego, CA; (4); Dance Clb; Variety Show; Sec Frsh Cls; Cit Awd; High Hon Roll; Hon Roll; Pres Acad Fit Awd; UC Santa Barbara; Comp Sci.

HAYES, MICHAEL; St Patricks-St Vincents HS; Vallejo, CA; (4); 7/148; Am Leg Boys St; Sec Cmnty Wkr; Science Clb; Service Clb; Teachers Aide; Chorus; Rptr Nwsp; Ed Lit Mag; High Hon Roll; Parnts Clb Cumltv Achvt Awd; Benicia Histrcl Soc; Amercn Hstry.

HAYES, MISTY; Strathmore HS; Strathmore, CA; (2); Art Clb; SADD; Drill Tm; Rptr Yrbk; Cit Awd; High Hon Roll; Hon Roll; Engl Awd; Wrld Hstry Awd; UCLA; Theatre.

HAYES, MISTY S; Edison HS; Huntington Beach, CA; (2); Girl Scts; Band; Mrchg Band; Orch; Pep Band; School Musical; Cit Awd; Body Boarding; Scuba Dvng; Air Force Pilot.

HAYES, OKEMA; Stagg HS; Stockton, CA; (1); Dance Clb; Rep Nwsp; Cheerldng; Off Cit Awd; Prfct Atten Awd; Pres Acad Fit Awd; Dance Awd 1st Pl, Gong Shw In AK; Delta Coll; Rprtr.

HAYES, RAYMOND A; East Bakersfield HS; Bakersfield, CA; (2); JV Bsbl; JV Ftbl; Vllybl; Math, Science.

HAYES, SHANNON A; Del Campo HS; Carmichael, CA; (3); 5/449; Spanish Clb; SADD; Var Socr; Var Tennis; High Hon Roll; NHS; St Schlr; All Metro, Leag Soccer Plyr; Athltc Of Wk 1990; Corp Law.

HAYES, SHAWN E; Edison HS; Huntington Beach, CA; (1); Model UN; Var L Swmmng; Water Polo; Tech Engrng.

HAYES, TREVOR L; Tehachapi HS; Tehachapi, CA; (3); Letterman Clb; Office Aide; Rep Soph Cls; JV L Bsktbl; JV Var Ftbl; Powder Puff Ftbl; Var L Tennis; JV L Trk; Wt Lftg; Hon Roll; Advrtsng.

HAYES, WILLIAM M; Crenshaw HS; Los Angeles, CA; (3); Church Yth Grp; Church Choir; Cit Awd; Hon Roll; Prfct Atten Awd; Cmptr Math.

HAYHURST, TONI D; Sanger HS; Sanger, CA; (3); Church Yth Grp; Cmnty Wkr; Dance Clb; Red Cross Aide; ROTC; Ski Clb; Teachers Aide; Peer Cnslng; Athltc Trng; Fresno ST U; RN.

HAYMAN, SCOTT E; Paraclete HS; Littlerock, CA; (2); Boy Scts; High Hon Roll; Hon Roll; Brown Belt Karate, Asst Instr; Self Defense Classes For Women; Engr.

HAYNES, JASON M; Orange Lutheran HS; Anaheim, CA; (3); 3/100; Church Yth Grp; Chorus; Church Choir; Pres Soph Cls; Var Crs Cntry; Var Socr; Var Trk; Hon Roll; Psych.

HAYNES, JOHN M; Sherman E Burroughs HS; Ridgecrest, CA; (3); Rep Church Yth Grp; FBLA; Pres JCL; Pres Latin Clb; Yrbk; Rep Stu Cncl; JV Golf; JV Socr; Var Trk; Acad Dcthln 3rd Plc Mdl Sci, 2nd Pl Music; Gldn ST Exm Hnrs Alg & Geom; Judge Bike Ct Ridgecrest; USAFA; Poli Sci.

HAYNES, MICHELLE; Livermore HS; Livermore, CA; (1); Girl Scts; Hosp Aide; Latin Clb; Spanish Clb; Capt Cheerldng; High Hon Roll; Hon Roll; Natl Classical League Natl Latin Exam Cum Laude; UCSF; Health.

HAYNES, NICOLE; Bishop Montgomery HS; Torrance, CA; (2); Service Clb; Ski Clb; Pres Frsh Cls; Pres Soph Cls; Pres Jr Cls; Var Socr; Var Trk; Hon Roll; MVP Trk 88-89 & Sccr 88-90; TAC Natl Chmpn Long Jump 90; Stu Of Semester 88-89; UCLA; Sports Med.

HAYNES, RYAN K; Garden Grove HS; Garden Grove, CA; (3); 2/300; Chess Clb; French Clb; Pres Intnl Clb; VP Service Clb; Chorus; Ed Yrbk; Ed Lit Mag; High Hon Roll; Masonic Awd; NHS; Brown Bk Awd Engl; Xerox Social Sci/Hmnts Awd; 1st Pl Schlwide Poetry Cntst.

HAYNES, TAMMY J; Cordova HS; Rancho Cordova, CA; (2); Church Yth Grp; Teachers Aide; Cheerldng; Trk; Vllybl; Hon Roll; Awesome Lancer Awd.

HAYNES, TRAVIS M; Lutheran HS Of Orange County; Anaheim, CA; (2); 3/95; Church Yth Grp; Church Choir; School Musical; Var L Crs Cntry; Var L Socr; Var L Trk; Chrstn Band.

HAYNIE, RONALD J; Ramona HS; Ramona, CA; (3); 15/294; FBLA; Spanish Clb; Pres Acad Fit Awd; CSF; UCSD; Math.

HAYNOSKI, ANNA M; St Genevieve HS; Granada Hills, CA; (3); Drama Clb; Letterman Clb; Pep Clb; Thesps; School Musical; School Play; Rep Soph Cls; VP Jr Cls; Stu Cncl; Var Bsktbl; UCLA; Accntnt.

HAYS, JANET K; Tulare Wester HS; Tulare, CA; (3); JA; Science Clb; Spanish Clb; School Play; Ed Yrbk; Off Stu Cncl; High Hon Roll; Hon Roll; Ntl Merit Ltr; Academic Decathlon Honors Team; Environmental Chemistry.

HAYS, MELISSA L; Hemet HS; Hemet, CA; (4); 28/487; Church Yth Grp; Speech Tm; Ed Nwsp; Stu Cncl; JV Sftbl; JV Tennis; Hon Roll; Masonic Awd; James W Gill Jr Jrnlsm Awd; CA Schltc Fed; Sonoma ST U; Engl.

HAYSLIP, THOMAS; Southwest HS; San Diego, CA; (4); 34/498; Var Ftbl; JV Trk; Cit Awd; Hon Roll; Prfct Atten Awd; Raider Of Week For Hstry; San Diego ST U; Bio.

HAYTAYAN, STEPAN A; Holy Martyrs Armenian HS; Van Nuys, CA; (3); JV Capt Bsktbl; Intrml Vllybl; US Naval Sea Cadet Corps.

HAYWARD, CYNTHIA A; Victor Valley SR HS; Adelanto, CA; (3); Church Yth Grp; Dance Clb; French Clb; Office Aide; Hon Roll; Coll Classes Engl IA & Elem Alg; Mesa ST Coll; Spec Ed Teacher.

HAYWARD, JARED L; Dana Hills HS; Monarch Beach, CA; (2); JV Tennis; JV Vllybl; High Hon Roll; Rotary Awd; CSF; UCSD; Law.

HAYWOOD, CHERIE L; John F Kennedy HS; Granada Hills, CA; (2); Cit Awd; Hon Roll; Jr CSF Treas; Jrnlsm.

HAYWOOD, MAISHA; Skyline HS; Oakland, CA; (2); Spanish Clb; Ed Nwsp; VP Frsh Cls; Rep Stu Cncl; JV Bsktbl; Cit Awd; Hon Roll; Prfct Atten Awd; Chess Clb; Debate Tm; Acad Awd; Jrnlsm Clb Pres; Martin Luther King Jr Ldrshp Awd; Mass Commnctns.

HAZARI, NIRAJ; San Lorenzo HS; Hayward, CA; (2); Intnl Clb; Spanish Clb; Teachers Aide; JV Capt Bsbl; JV Bsktbl; Wt Lftg; High Hon Roll; Prfct Atten Awd; CSF; Asian Clb; Bsbl Crd Clb; Stanford U; Engrng.

HE, JULIE Z; George Washington HS; San Francisco, CA; (3); Math Clb; Red Cross Aide; Science Clb; Service Clb; Swmmng; Tennis; High Hon Roll; CSF; Gifted/Talntd Educ Pgm; Acad Exclnce Awd High Hnrs Gem & Alg; Cert Achvts Vars Clses; Cyclng.

HE, TING MEI; George Washington HS; San Francisco, CA; (2); JV Swmmng; High Hon Roll; Hon Roll; CSF Mem; Univ Of CA Berkeley; Med.

HEAD, LAURA L; Grossmont HS; El Cajon, CA; (2); Church Yth Grp; GAA; Key Clb; Letterman Clb; Office Aide; Pep Clb; Spanish Clb; SADD; Varsity Clb; Stu Cncl; Builders Clb; Santa Barbara ST; Acctng.

HEAL, KIM; Golden Sierra HS; Georgetown, CA; (3); 20/90; Letterman Clb; Spanish Clb; Teachers Aide; Varsity Clb; Chorus; Church Choir; Powder Puff Ftbl; Sftbl; Vllybl; Wt Lftg; Heald Bus Coll; Secy.

HEAL, KORY G; Bonita HS; La Verne, CA; (1); Bus Profs of Am; SADD; JV Socr; High Hon Roll.

HEALD, PATRICIA L; Ontario HS; Ontario, CA; (4); Pep Clb; Spanish Clb; Chorus; School Musical; Var Capt Cheerldng; Swmmng; High Hon Roll; Hon Roll; Prfct Atten Awd; Ivy Chain; CSF; CA St U San Bernardino.

HEALD, TANYA J; Merced HS North; Merced, CA; (4); 23/675; Church Yth Grp; Drama Clb; Spanish Clb; Band; Church Choir; Mrchg Band; Sec Orch; School Musical; High Hon Roll; Hon Roll; CSF Life; Golden St Exam Geom Hnrs; Cert In Bus; Merced Coll; Bi-Ling.

HEALY, LYNNE; Hawthorne HS; Hawthorne, CA; (4); 30/484; Art Clb; VP Church Yth Grp; Cmnty Wkr; Service Clb; Ski Clb; Co-Capt Drill Tm; VP Soph Cls; Var Co-Capt Cheerldng; Hon Roll; GATE Outstndng Achvta Awd; Miss Supersensational Drill Team 88; UC Santa Barbara; Studio Art.

HEALY, SEAN M; Weed HS; Weed, CA; (3); 3/45; Am Leg Boys St; Letterman Clb; Ski Clb; Phtg Yrbk; Pres Jr Cls; Pres Stu Cncl; Var Ftbl; Var Trk; Hon Roll; St Schlr; Chem Hnr Stu; Acad Decathlon Team; UC Davis; Engrng.

HEAP, BRIAN D; Kearny HS; San Diego, CA; (2); Rptr Nwsp; Yrbk; Stu Cncl; Cit Awd; Hon Roll; Jr NHS; Opt Clb Awd; Fri Nght Live Clb L; Sprts Brdcstr/Trnlst.

HEAP, KELLY A; Immaculate Heart HS; La Crescenta, CA; (3); 40/135; Pres Treas Girl Scts; Hosp Aide; Science Clb; Chorus; Drill Tm; Stage Crew; JV Crs Cntry; Hon Roll; GSA Gld, Slvr & Marion Awds; Cardiolgst.

HEARD, ARI-BEN; Mac Ateer HS; San Francisco, CA; (3); School Musical; School Play; Stage Crew; Rep Soph Cls; Hon Roll; Visl Art; Vodeo Tapng Plys; San Francisco U; Acctg.

HEARD, JAMETTE L; Sunny Hills HS; Buena Park, CA; (2); 40/464; Church Yth Grp; Intnl Clb; Model UN; Spanish Clb; JV Bsktbl; Stat Vllybl; Schl Amnesty Intl Club Treas; 2nd & 4th Pl Overall Orange Cnty Acad Decthln; Yale; Law.

HEARD, KRISTI; Upland HS; Upland, CA; (3); Church Yth Grp; Dance Clb; Pep Clb; Chorus; Drill Tm; Cheerldng; Pom Pon; Powder Puff Ftbl; Swmmng; High Hon Roll; CSF; Child Psych.

HEARNE, KIMBERLY; Modesto Christian HS; Modesto, CA; (3); 2/40; Church Yth Grp; Cmnty Wkr; Teachers Aide; Acpl Chr; Chorus; Church Choir; Off Jr Cls; Var L Bsktbl; JV Powder Puff Ftbl; Var L Socr; Modesto Yuth Cmmsn; Trinity Western Canada; Bio.

HEARNE, QUINDOLYN D; North HS; Riverside, CA; (2); Sec Frsh Cls; Rep Stu Cncl; JV Sftbl; Cit Awd; Prfct Atten Awd; Black Stu Union; Outreach Partnership Pgm; Grambling; Psych.

HEARNE, WILLIAM; Hesperia HS; Hesperia, CA; (3); Computer Clb; Spanish Clb; Hon Roll; Prfct Atten Awd; University Club Historian.

HEARRON, MELISSA D; Lindsay HS; Lindsay, CA; (1); Church Yth Grp; SADD; Wt Lftg; Hon Roll; CA Poly Sn Luis Obispo; Arch.

HEASLEY, ANDREA; Cajon HS; San Bernardino, CA; (3); 38/480; Sec AFS; Drama Clb; Key Clb; Teachers Aide; School Musical; School Play; Stage Crew; Ed Lit Mag; High Hon Roll; Hon Roll; Peer Cnslr; CSF; Ed.

HEATH, CLAIRE A; Westlake Schl; Los Angeles, CA; (2); French Clb; SADD; School Play; Mgr Stage Crew; Lit Mag; Rep Stu Cncl; Cheerldng; Intrml Wt Lftg; High Hon Roll; Hon Roll; Dance Concert; Cmmnty Svc Hunger Coalition; Hnrs Concours Natl De Francais; Bus.

HEATH, ROBERT S; Bellarmine Jefferson HS; Los Angeles, CA; (3); 11/110; Yrbk; VP Jr Cls; Stu Cncl; Capt Crs Cntry; Var Trk; Hon Roll; NHS; HOBY; Long Beach ST U; Creatve Wrtng.

HEATH, TRINA L; Channel Islands HS; Oxnard, CA; (4); 13/480; Sec Church Yth Grp; Debate Tm; Drama Clb; Science Clb; Church Choir; High Hon Roll; Hon Roll; Ntl Merit SF; Pres Acad Fit Awd; Acad Decathlon; Young Womanhood Medalion; Summiteer Program; Humboldt ST U; Zoology.

HEATHCOE, GEORGE P; Edison HS; Fresno, CA; (2); JV Ftbl; Hon Roll; Gldn St Schlr; CA Schlrshp Fed; Comp.

HEATHERLY, RYAN; Mt Whitney HS; Visalia, CA; (3); Hon Roll; Fresno ST.

HEAVIN, KRISTIE L; Westminster HS; Westminster, CA; (1); Church Yth Grp; Var JV Swmmng; Hon Roll; NHS; Long Beach ST; Educ.

HEBER, MEGAN; Eureka HS; Eureka, CA; (4); 36/300; Debate Tm; FCA; FFA; Quiz Bowl; SADD; Mrchg Band; Orch; JV Bsktbl; L Cheerldng; Pom Pon; USC; Math.

HEBER, RYAN; Taft Union HS; Taft, CA; (3); 10/250; Boy Scts; VP Stu Cncl; Ftbl; Wt Lftg; Business.

HEBERARD, MAGALI; Lycee Laperouse HS; Los Altos, CA; (3); 2/20; Latin Clb; School Play; Rptr Yrbk; U Of CA.

HEBERLY, JENNIE M; Arcata HS; Blue Lake, CA; (3); 5/200; Church Yth Grp; FCA; GAA; Scholastic Bowl; SADD; Powder Puff Ftbl; Sftbl; Tennis; Hon Roll; CA Poly-Pamona; Indstrl Engr.

HEBERT, DIANE; Lincoln HS; Stockton, CA; (4); Art Clb; Dance Clb; Pep Clb; Spanish Clb; Variety Show; Yrbk; Cheerldng; Pom Pon; Trk; Hon Roll; Violin Instr; Gldn ST Exam Hgh Hnrs; Black Stu Union; UCLA; Bus Admin.

HEBERT, DUANE A; West Torrance HS; Gardena, CA; (3); Church Yth Grp; Chorus; School Play; SCAHA Ice Hockey; Choir Club; Military.

HEBERT, NICOLE L; Mar Vista HS; San Diego, CA; (4); 60/285; Teachers Aide; Chorus; Church Choir; Mgr Socr; HS Faculty Schlrshp; Macintosh Write Stuff Awd; Black Stu Union Sec; CSU San Bernardino; Bus Admin.

HEBRARD JR, CHARLES L; Calaveras HS; San Andreas, CA; (3); 14/180; Church Yth Grp; Var Bsbl; JV Bsktbl; Var Socr; Var Swmmng; JV Trk; Intrml Vllybl; Hon Roll; AFS; German Clb; JR Fair Bd; Friday Night Live; CSF; CA Poly SLO; Arch.

HECHANOVA, CARLA PIA F; Liberty Union HS; Brentwood, CA; (3); Var Vllybl; Mst Imprvd Plyr Vllybl 89-90; Pres Block L 90-91; CSU Hayward; Nrsng.

HECHT, JOANNE; Rosary HS; La Mirada, CA; (3); Science Clb; Varsity Clb; Var Sftbl; High Hon Roll; NHS; CSF; Bus.

HECHT, KIM M; El Toro HS; El Toro, CA; (3); Boy Scts; Dance Clb; Key Clb; Pres Temple Yth Grp; Chorus; High Hon Roll; Hon Roll; CSULB; Phys Thrpy.

HECHT, SHANDI; El Toro HS; El Toro, CA; (4); Hon Roll; Pres Acad Fit Awd; Scl Sci Excllnc Awd; U CA San Diego; Marine Bio.

HECK, SUSIE M; Monte Vista HS; Spring Valley, CA; (3); 65/480; Dance Clb; French Clb; Pep Clb; U San Diego; Bus.

HECKARD, TERESA J; Lee Vining HS; June Lake, CA; (3); Church Yth Grp; School Play; Sec Frsh Cls; VP Soph Cls; Pres Jr Cls; Var Sftbl; Var Vllybl; Philidelphia Schl Of Arts; Art.

HECKMAN, KEVIN S; Troy HS; La Mirada, CA; (2); Church Yth Grp; Computer Clb; FBLA; Spanish Clb; Hon Roll; International Baccalaureate; War Games; Role Playing Games; Cal Poly San Luis Obispo.

HECKMANN, MATTHEW; Est Bakersfield HS; Bakersfield, CA; (2); German Clb; Band; Mrchg Band; Pep Band; Hon Roll; Naval Acad.

HECKSCHER, MAX M; San Rafael HS; San Rafael, CA; (2); Var Swmmng; Hon Roll; Var Water Polo Tm Capt; CA Jr Schlsp Fed; CSF.

HECOX, KAREN; South Hills HS; West Covina, CA; (4); 6/270; Am Leg Aux Girls St; Church Yth Grp; Cmnty Wkr; Intnl Clb; Service Clb; Teachers Aide; Varsity Clb; Variety Show; VP Frsh Cls; Rep Soph Cls; Ath Schlrshp To UCLA; CA Schlr Fed; Acad Ath Schlrshp; UCLA; Physcl Thrpy.

HEDAYI, RUDY SONER; Redlands HS; Redlands, CA; (4); 28/830; Model UN; Teachers Aide; Cit Awd; High Hon Roll; Prfct Atten Awd; CA Schlrshp Fed; UC Riverside; Bio.

HEDBERG, ETHAN A; Bullard HS; Fresno, CA; (1); 95/400; Church Yth Grp; Drama Clb; FCA; German Clb; SADD; Teachers Aide; Band; Orch; Pep Band; Sprt Ed Yrbk; Yng Life/Campus Life; Outstndng Stu Zoology 89, Soclgy 90; Chrch Drama Tm; Biola U; Psych.

HEDDERSON, MONIQUE M; Albany HS; Albany, CA; (2); Girl Scts; Hosp Aide; Science Clb; Spanish Clb; High Hon Roll.

HEDENBERG, ERIC J; Fountain Valley HS; Fountain Valley, CA; (2); JV Trk; Civil Air Patrol; Commsn; Embry Riddle; Military Pilot.

HEDGPETH, BONNIE; Mt Carmel HS; San Diego, CA; (4); Church Yth Grp; Service Clb; Pres Acpl Chr; Band; Chorus; Church Choir; Kiwanis Awd; CA ST U Northridge; Music.

HEDGPETH, KELLI; Folsom HS; Folsom, CA; (3); Am Leg Aux Girls St; Church Yth Grp; Girl Scts; Library Aide; Model UN; Spanish Clb; Trk; Cit Awd; Hon Roll; Rotary Awd; Future Prblm Slvng; Amer Auxilary Legion Essay Cont Awd; U OH Miami; Medcl.

HEDRICK, CHAD A; Mesa Verde HS; Citrus Heights, CA; (2); 56/257; Rep Jr Cls; JV Bsbl; JV Bsktbl; JV Ftbl; Sacremento ST; Law.

HEDRICK, KRISTI; Louisville HS; Northridge, CA; (2); GAA; Pres Soph Cls; JV Swmmng; JV Vllybl; Hon Roll; Art Clb; Church Yth Grp; Dance Clb; Science Clb; Ski Clb; Writing Published; HOBY Smnr; Frgn Lang/-2nd Pl; CSF; UCLA; Law.

HEEKE, SHANNAN; Northview HS; Covina, CA; (3); 1/250; Am Leg Aux Girls St; Spanish Clb; SADD; Capt Flag Corp; High Hon Roll; CA Schlrshp Fdrtn; Accntng.

HEEKIN, KARIE L; El Toro HS; El Toro, CA; (3); 485/560; Drama Clb; Thesps; School Play; Stage Crew; Hon Roll; Crop; Vet Asst; U Of CA Humbolt; Zoology.

HEER, RICKY A; North HS; Bakersfield, CA; (2); JA; Wrstlng; CA ST Bakersfield; Comp.

HEEREN, SETH; Cajon HS; San Bernardino, CA; (4); Cmnty Wkr; JA; Off Sr Cls; Stu Cncl; High Hon Roll; NHS; Rotary Awd; Hewlett-Packard Schlrshp; UCSD; Bus.

HEFFINGTON, WENDY; North Salinas HS; Salinas, CA; (4); Church Yth Grp; Cmnty Wkr; French Clb; Teachers Aide; Sec Jr Cls; High Hon Roll; Hon Roll; Pres Acad Fit Awd; Miss Monterey Cnty Schlrshp Pgnt 1st Rnnrup; Montery Cnty Acadmc Dcthln 5 Mdls; CA St Acadmc Dcthln; UCLA.

HEFLIN, KIMBERLY M; Fowler HS; Selma, CA; (3); Drama Clb; Office Aide; Science Clb; Spanish Clb; SADD; Yrbk; Sec Jr Cls; Var Trk; High Hon Roll; CSF; Friday Nite Live; Cmptr Sci.

HEFNER, JASON R; Vacaville HS; O'fallon, IL; (4); #6 In Class; Church Yth Grp; Drama Clb; Band; Church Choir; Jazz Band; Mrchg Band; School Musical; School Play; Lit Mag; JV Socr; Chrstn Camp Cnslr; UC Santa Barbara; Relgn.

HEGDAHL, HEIDI ANN; Oakdale HS; Oakdale, CA; (4); 1/230; Sec Treas Letterman Clb; Math Tm; Pep Clb; Scholastic Bowl; Teachers Aide; Varsity Clb; Ed Nwsp; Stu Cncl; Var Capt Bsktbl; Var Capt Tennis; CSF; U S Army Rsrve Schlr/Athl Awd; ASB Publc Rltns Cmssnr; BYU; Bus Admin.

HEGDE, MANU; Clovis HS; Clovis, CA; (3); Pres Debate Tm; French Clb; Math Clb; Math Tm; Pres NFL; Science Clb; Speech Tm; SADD; Nwsp; Intrml Tennis; CA ST Sci Fair Med & Hlth 2nd Pl 88 & 3rd Pl 90; Natl Frnscs Trnmnt 3r Pl 88-90; Ntl Hstry Day 5th; Law.

HEGEDUS, GREGORY T; John F Kennedy HS; Granada Hills, CA; (3); Pres Treas Key Clb; Ed Nwsp; Yrbk; Lit Mag; Rep Stu Cncl; JV Bsbl; Ftbl; Kiwanis Awd; Ntl Merit Ltr; 1st Pl Jnrlsm Write Off, Sports; Summer Schlrs; Outstndng Sprts Story; Key Clubber Of Yr; Jrnlsm.

HEGENBART, CHRISTINA L; Ukiah HS; Redwood Valley, CA; (2); Frgn Exchnge Clb; Stu Ldrshp Cls; SAFE Rides.

HEGENBART, HEATHER; Armijo HS; Fairfield, CA; (3); GAA; JV Vllybl; Hon Roll; NHS; Solano CC; Acctng.

HEGEWISCH, KATHERINE C; Red Bluff Union HS; Cottonwood, CA; (2); 1/454; French Clb; Key Clb; Letterman Clb; Math Tm; Mu Alpha Theta; JV Bsktbl; Var Vllybl; Kiwanis Awd; CSF; Golden St Exams High Hnrs Alg I & Geom.

HEHLE, ANDY D; Woodcrest Christian Schl; Riverside, CA; (1); Var Tennis; JV Vllybl; Planetary Soc; Electronics Techn Course; Kung-Fu Schl Orange Belt; Elec Engrng.

HEHR, KIMBERLY; Elk Grove HS; Sacramento, CA; (3); Dance Clb; Spanish Clb; Teachers Aide; Chorus; Color Guard; Cheerldng; Swmmng; Hon Roll; Prfct Atten Awd; Long Beach City; X-Ray Tech.

HEI, RONNY; Cerritos HS; Cerritos, CA; (2); Cmnty Wkr; Debate Tm; FBLA; Key Clb; Model UN; Off Frsh Cls; Off Jr Cls; Stu Cncl; Swmmng; Tennis; Rep Japanese Ntl Hnr Soc; USC; Bus.

HEID, MATT J; Skyline HS; Oakland, CA; (2); Bsktbl; Animal Rights Clb; Sci.

HEIDINGER, JOANNE; Galt HS; Acampo, CA; (4); Intnl Clb; SADD; Band; Jazz Band; Mrchg Band; Pep Band; School Musical; Hon Roll; John Philip Sousa Awd; 88-90 Cnty Hnr Band; Delta; Phys Thrpst.

HEIDMILLER, KARENSA; Herbert Hoover HS; San Diego, CA; (4); Church Yth Grp; French Clb; Church Choir; Var Cheerldng; Hon Roll; Hostess Clb; Ballet.

HEIER, ALISON L; Burney JR SR HS; Burney, CA; (1); Church Yth Grp; Pep Clb; Ski Clb; Chorus; School Musical; Pres Frsh Cls; JV Bsktbl; JV Socr; Fresno ST.

HEIKKINEN, TANIA M; Dana Hills HS; Laguna Niguel, CA; (2); Chorus; Orch; 1 Piano, Comp, WA ST Music Teachers Assn; Rating Superior, Piano Comp Intl Annual Comp Test.

HEIL, ALISON; Sonoma Valley HS; Sonoma, CA; (4); 34/250; Church Yth Grp; Drama Clb; FBLA; Intnl Clb; Stage Crew; Nwsp; Hon Roll; Congrssnl Yth Ldrshp Cncl Nominee; Ldrshp Clss; CSF Pblcty Chrmn; U NE Lincoln; Advrtsng.

HEILBRON, VICKI; St Joseph HS; Long Beach, CA; (3); 3/180; Pep Clb; JV Cheerldng; High Hon Roll; Ntl Merit Ltr; Loyola Marymount U; Med.

HEILIG, CHRIS; San Ramon Valley HS; San Ramon, CA; (2); 4-H; Teachers Aide; Band; Drm Mjr(t); Jazz Band; Mrchg Band; Orch; French Hon Soc; High Hon Roll; NHS; Acad Ltr; Ply Bay Area Wind Symphony; U CA Berkeley; Law.

HEILMANN, MARIE; Bella Vista HS; Fair Oaks, CA; (2); 38/406; Church Yth Grp; Cmnty Wkr; Spanish Clb; Rptr Yrbk; Swmmng; NHS; FNL; Acctng.

HEIM, CRISTAN M; Patrick Henry HS; San Diego, CA; (3); 102/532; Church Yth Grp; Varsity Clb; Yrbk; VP Soph Cls; Trk; Vllybl; High Hon Roll; Tripe E Awd; UCSD.

HEIM JR, MICHAEL L; Portola JR SR HS; Portola, CA; (1); Band; Mrchg Band; Swing Chorus; Hon Roll; Yth/Yth; Doctor.

HEIM, MICHAEL P; Troy HS; Yorba Linda, CA; (1); Var JV Tennis; High Hon Roll; Pres Acad Fit Awd; Med.

HEIMANSON, SHELLY; Oakwood Schl; Studio City, CA; (1); Dance Clb; Drama Clb; Office Aide; Temple Yth Grp; Acpl Chr; Chorus; School Musical; School Play; Variety Show; Yrbk; UCLA; Voice.

HEIMBURG, JONATHAN S; El Capitan HS; Lakeside, CA; (2); Science Clb; Hon Roll; Pres Acad Fit Awd; Pres Schlr; Sci Olympiad Pentathln 1st Pl; Acad League; Site Cncl.

HEIMLICH, RACHEL E; Gahr HS; Cerritos, CA; (2); 98/490; French Clb; Mgr(s); Powder Puff Ftbl; Var Socr; JV Sftbl; Hon Roll; Cerritos Coll; Cosmetology.

HEIN, HEATHER J; Brea-Olinda HS; Brea, CA; (1); Ski Clb; Acpl Chr; Sptlght On Yth Awd; Recog Acad Bstr.

HEIN, TROY M; Portola JR-SR HS; Portola, CA; (2); Letterman Clb; Band; Swing Chorus; Variety Show; Var Bsbl; Var Bsktbl; Hon Roll; Pres Acad Fit Awd; Reach Amer Yth To Yth; U AZ; Sports Cmmnctns.

HEINEMAN, RICK I; Culver City HS; Culver City, CA; (3); Am Leg Boys St; Church Yth Grp; Ski Clb; Off Frsh Cls; VP Soph Cls; Off Jr Cls; Off Sr Cls; Stu Cncl; Var Bsbl; Var Ftbl; House Of Rep; Vrsty Ltrmn Clb; Stu League; Sr Cls Hnrs Clb.

HEINEMANN, ERICA L; Atascadero HS; Atascadero, CA; (4); Church Yth Grp; Dance Clb; Teachers Aide; Hon Roll; Cuesta CC; Elem Schl Tchr.

HEINER, JON; Mills HS; Burlingame, CA; (2); Chess Clb; Math Tm; Socr; Trk; JR ST Of Amer; Soviets & US Awarenss Conf.

HEINIG, DAVID W; Fontana HS; Fontana, CA; (3); Teachers Aide; Phtg Yrbk; Intrml Bsbl; Cvl Air Patrol-Cadet Cmmndr; Friday Night Live-Dsgntd Drvr; UC Riverside; Russian.

HEINISCH, ROBERT C; William S Hart HS; Valencia, CA; (3); Pres Chess Clb; FBLA; Model UN; NFL; Acpl Chr; School Musical; Hon Roll; 88 William Holt Sci Schlrshp Rcpnt Lawrence Hall Of Sci; Nominee Boys St; Top Chess Ply Under 21 CA.

HEINKS, MATTHEW D; Mt Whitney HS; Visalia, CA; (1); Church Yth Grp; Key Clb; JV Crs Cntry; JV Ftbl; JV Socr; JV Trk; Cit Awd; Hon Roll; Pres Acad Fit Awd.

HEINRICH, CHRIS M; Santa Teresa HS; San Jose, CA; (2); Boy Scts; Church Yth Grp; Ski Clb; Spanish Clb; Teachers Aide; JV Bsktbl; Var Ftbl; Var Tennis; JV Trk; Var Wt Lftg; Eagle Sct; UCLA; Law.

HEINRICH, GRANT; Carmel HS; Carmel Valley, CA; (3); 20/160; Chess Clb; Cmnty Wkr; Math Tm; Ski Clb; Spanish Clb; Varsity Clb; Var Golf; Var Socr; Wt Lftg; High Hon Roll; Top 100 In Schl; Surfing; UC Santa Barbara; Engr.

HEINRICH, KARA J; Los Altos HS; Hacienda Hts, CA; (3); Church Yth Grp; Band; Color Guard; Mrchg Band; Hon Roll; Prfct Atten Awd; Speech Path.

HEINZ, CRISTINA S; James Logan HS; Union City, CA; (3); Drama Clb; Teachers Aide; School Play; Stage Crew; Hon Roll; Hnrs Golden St Exam Algebra; Sch Rcgntn Golden St Exam Geom.

HEIPLE, TANYA M; Nevada Union HS; Grass Valley, CA; (3); 31/551; Church Yth Grp; Cmnty Wkr; SADD; Teachers Aide; Church Choir; Color Guard; Flag Corp; High Hon Roll; St Schlr; Mission Wrk; Planning Cmmtte Discovery 91; CSF; Ldrshp Conf; Whitworth Coll.

HEISE, ELIZABETH; North Torrance HS; Torrance, CA; (2); 23/406; Church Yth Grp; Girl Scts; Spanish Clb; SADD; Chorus; Church Choir; Color Guard; Cit Awd; Hon Roll; USC; Phy Thrpy.

HEISER, RACHEL; Dunsmuir HS; Dunsmuir, CA; (4); 1/29; Am Leg Aux Girls St; Church Yth Grp; Drama Clb; Office Aide; Pep Clb; Ski Clb; Band; Church Choir; Pep Band; School Play; Bank America Plq & Mntry Mth/Sci; Tiger Awd Wnnr Stu Govt; Simpson Coll; Psych.

HEISEY, DEREK V; Bonita HS; La Verne, CA; (3); Church Yth Grp; French Clb; Model UN; Band; Chorus; Church Choir; Jazz Band; Hon Roll; CA ST-FULLERTON; Music Perf.

HEISSER, STEPHANIE M; Irvine HS; Ir, CA; (2); Drama Clb; SADD; Hon Roll; Zephyrs Clb; Elem Schl Tchr.

HEITMELER, STEVE E; Redlands HS; Redlands, CA; (3); Ski Clb; Varsity Clb; Band; Mrchg Band; Capt Bsbl; JV Socr; Var Tennis; Hon Roll; Pres Acad Fit Awd; TX A&M; Engrng.

HEITZ, ERIC S; North Monterey County HS; Salinas, CA; (2); Stage Crew; Hon Roll; 1st Pl Envrnmntl Stud Monterey Cnty Sci & Engrng Fair; Elkhorn Slough Natl Estuarine Rsrch Resrv Awd; San Jose ST; Math.

HEITZMANN, SARA M; Mariposa HS; Mariposa, CA; (4); 12/120; Cmnty Wkr; 4-H; GAA; Office Aide; Ski Clb; Teachers Aide; Church Choir; School Play; Stu Cncl; High Hon Roll; CSU Chico.

HEKMAN, WILLIAM; Troy HS; Anaheim, CA; (3); 83/315; German Clb; Scholastic Bowl; Band; Drm Mjr(t); Jazz Band; Hon Roll; All S CA Hnr Band 1989, 1990; CA All St Hnr Band 1989; Music.

HELBIG, LESLIE; Santa Cruz HS; Santa Cruz, CA; (3); Teachers Aide; Chorus; Orch; School Play; Jrnlsm.

HELBLING, ANDREA D; Palm Springs HS; Desert Hot Spgs, CA; (4); Church Yth Grp; Acpl Chr; Band; Chorus; Church Choir; Mrchg Band; School Musical; Cit Awd; Hon Roll; Pres Acad Fit Awd; Slvr Sands Awd; Most Outstndng Instrmntl Music 90; Bnk Amer Achvt Awd; Wmns Club Acadmc Schlrshp; Sthrn CA Coll; Crss Cultural.

HELBLING, RYAN D; Palm Springs HS; Desert Hot Spring, CA; (2); Church Yth Grp; Band; Jazz Band; Mrchg Band; Pep Band; School Musical; JV Bsktbl; JV Crs Cntry; Hon Roll; VP Band Bd 90-91; Church Orch; Southern CA Coll; Music.

HELDBERG, ELIZABETH ANN; J Eugene Mc Ateer HS; Pacifica, CA; (4); Debate Tm; Drama Clb; Hosp Aide; Sec Thesps; Chorus; Church Choir; School Musical; School Play; Stage Crew; Gov Hon Prg Awd; Acad Dcthln; Bst Actrss Trphy In Caronsel; Mills Coll; Theatre.

HELFERS, DEAN J; Center HS; N Highlands, CA; (4); Church Yth Grp; Spanish Clb; SADD; Teachers Aide; Capt Bsktbl; Hon Roll; Medicine.

HELFERT, BREANNA F; El Camino Real HS; Woodland Hills, CA; (3); Letterman Clb; Thesps; School Play; Off Frsh Cls; Off Soph Cls; Off Jr Cls; Gov Hon Prg Awd; High Hon Roll; Hon Roll; Ntl Merit SF; Jr Statesmen Of Amer; Amnesty Intl; Yale U; Theatre Arts.

HELGREN, ERIK B; Lowell HS; San Francisco, CA; (2); Boy Scts; Treas German Clb; Var Socr; CSF; Cal Poly ST U San Luis Obispo.

HELGREN, TANIA V; Lowell HS; San Francisco, CA; (3); French Clb; Pres German Clb; Ski Clb; JV Socr.

HELLAND, LENE-MARIE; Hoover HS; Fresno, CA; (1); Orch; Grnd Prz Wnnr Yng Musicians Cmptns; Fresnos Finest Cmptn Wnnr; Cncrt Mstr All St Orch; Juilliard; Violinist.

HELLER, ROBYN D; The Athenian Schl; Vacaville, CA; (3); Art Clb; Drama Clb; Intnl Clb; Rep Soph Cls; JV Bsktbl; JV Diving; Var Swmmng; JV Vllybl; Greenpeace; Cmmnty Against Substance Abuse-Awd; Amnsty Intl; Film.

HELLER, RUTH A; Valencia HS; Anaheim, CA; (2); Var L Crs Cntry; Var L Trk; High Hon Roll; 2-Time Orange League Champion In High Jump; Coll; Mathematics.

HELLERSTEIN, ELIZABETH; Acalanes HS; Lafayette, CA; (4); Off Model UN; Office Aide; Teachers Aide; Acpl Chr; Chorus; School Musical; Ntl Merit SF; Mck Trl Tm; Dist Schl Bd Rep; Co-Fndr Amnsty Intl Clb; Columbia Coll NY.

HELLWIG, DIANE M; Tulare Union HS; Tulare, CA; (2); Church Yth Grp; SADD; Temple Yth Grp; Church Choir; Hon Roll; Pres Acad Fit Awd; Chrch Yth Cncl; Biola U; Child Psych.

HELM, JULIA; Canyon HS; Santa Clarita, CA; (3); 13/501; Art Clb; Pres Church Yth Grp; Letterman Clb; Church Choir; Yrbk; Treas Soph Cls; Off Jr Cls; Off Sr Cls; Sec Stu Cncl; NHS; CSF; Cotillion; Comms.

HELMAN, JENNIFER; Benicia HS; Benicia, CA; (2); SADD; Band; Mrchg Band; Pep Band; Swing Chorus; Yrbk; Cheerldng; Trk; Hon Roll; Music.

HELMICK, CHRIS K; San Clemente HS; San Clemente, CA; (1); Boy Scts; Church Yth Grp; FCA; German Clb; Swmmng; High Hon Roll; Hon Roll; Schl Spnsrd Ath Act Water Polo; Mst Insprtnl Awd Swmmng; 4th Pl Leg Swim Fnls Backstroke 100 Yrds; Stanford; Math.

HELMICK, HEATHER D; San Clemente HS; San Clemente, CA; (4); Church Yth Grp; Ski Clb; Church Choir; JV Tennis; Cit Awd; High Hon Roll; NHS; Frgn Lang & Scl Sci Poseidon Awd; U CA Davis; Intl Relations.

HELMS, HEATHER; Williams HS; Williams, CA; (1); Band; Mrchg Band; JV Bsktbl; JV Vllybl; High Hon Roll; Law.

HELMS, PATTY; Oxnard HS; Oxnard, CA; (2); Church Yth Grp; Hon Roll; UCLA; Law.

HELMUTH, CHRISTINA M; Thousand Oaks HS; Thousand Oaks, CA; (3); Church Yth Grp; Drama Clb; Acpl Chr; Chorus; Church Choir; Drmtcs.

HELMUTH, TRISHA; Nevada Union HS; Nevada City, CA; (3); Teachers Aide; Chorus; Color Guard; Var Trk; Hon Roll; Chico ST; Chldrn.

HELO, VICTORIA; John F Kennedy HS; Granada Hills, CA; (3); Church Yth Grp; Cmnty Wkr; Dance Clb; Library Aide; Office Aide; Teachers Aide; Chorus; Church Choir; Drill Tm; Yrbk; SWAS; CSUN; Interior Desgn.

HELRING, MICHELLE C; Woodbridge HS; Irvine, CA; (3); Church Yth Grp; Var Socr; Var Sftbl; Self-Esteem Clss; Golden West; Cnslng Juveniles.

HELSLEY, SHAWN T; Monroe HS; Sepulveda, CA; (2); Comp Prgrmr.

HELTON, DEREK A; Lutheran HS; Orange, CA; (2); Church Yth Grp; Band; Chorus; Orch; Pep Band; School Musical; Cit Awd; Hon Roll; Prfct Atten Awd; Pres Acad Fit Awd; Cncrt Choir Accmpnst.

HELVEY, BEN; Arrowhead Christian Acad; Redlands, CA; (2); Church Yth Grp; Cmnty Wkr; Ski Clb; School Musical; Ed Yrbk; Pres Frsh Cls; VP Stu Cncl; L Var Bsktbl; Var Capt Vllybl; Cit Awd; Princpals Awd; Poltcl Sci.

HELZER, TIFFANY; Vanden HS; Travis A.f.b., CA; (2); 31/175; Art Clb; Church Yth Grp; Cmnty Wkr; Drama Clb; English Clb; Rep Latin Clb; Letterman Clb; Office Aide; Science Clb; SADD; Ldrshp Class; Beauty Pageant Model; Yth & Teen Ctr Volunteer; U CA Davis; Bus Econ.

HEM, HAY; Lincoln HS; Stockton, CA; (3); 60/543; High Hon Roll; Hon Roll; Prfct Atten Awd; Delta; Doctor.

HEMBD, RON L; Redlands HS; Redlands, CA; (3); Letterman Clb; Band; Mrchg Band; Diving; Ftbl; Var L Wrstlng; High Hon Roll; Pres Acad Fit Awd; Demolay; Scuba Sfty Cert At Level II; Med.

HEMINGWAY, AMY M; St Francis HS; Cupertino, CA; (3); 40/289; Service Clb; Teachers Aide; Ed Nwsp; Ed Yrbk; Gym; High Hon Roll; NHS; SADD.

HEMINGWAY, DEJA M; Loara HS; Anaheim, CA; (4); Pep Clb; Rep Frsh Cls; Rep Soph Cls; Rep Jr Cls; Rep Sr Cls; Var JV Cheerldng; Powder Puff Ftbl; Hon Roll; NHS; Pep Squad; Prncpls Awd; Cypress JC.

HEMINGWWAY, AMY M; St Francis HS; Cupertino, CA; (3); 40/289; Office Aide; Service Clb; SADD; Ed Nwsp; Ed Yrbk; Gym; High Hon Roll; Jr NHS; NHS; Intl Rltns.

HEMMINGS, IAN D; Lutheran HS; Orange, CA; (3); Aud/Vis; Church Yth Grp; Cmnty Wkr; German Clb; Ed Yrbk; JV Crs Cntry; Mgr(s); Socr; Hon Roll; Church Work-Ldrshp/Help; Christ Coll-Irvine; Med.

HEMPEL, NICHOLLE M; Clovis West HS; Fresno, CA; (3); Hosp Aide; Key Clb; Ski Clb; SADD; Orthodontist.

HEMPHILL, DANI L; Apple Valley HS; Apple Valley, CA; (3); Church Yth Grp; Cmnty Wkr; Model UN; Spanish Clb; Teachers Aide; Church Choir; Swing Chorus; High Hon Roll; Hon Roll; Exec Brd, Stdy Chrprsn Conf Cncl Yth Mnstries United Methdst CA Pacific Conf; Seattle-Pacific U; Christian Ed.

HEMPHILL, LESLIE; Palo Verde HS; Blythe, CA; (2); 1/300; Church Yth Grp; FFA; Service Clb; Rep Stu Cncl; Powder Puff Ftbl; High Hon Roll; NHS; Pres Acad Fit Awd; Hgh Hnrs Gldn St Exm; Prncpls Lst 87-90; Jr Amer Lgn Axlry; Accntnt.

HEMPHILL, STEPHANIE R; Montclair HS; Upland, CA; (4); Art Clb; Debate Tm; Drama Clb; GAA; Key Clb; Office Aide; Speech Tm; SADD; Teachers Aide; Varsity Clb; Poet & Music; UCLA; Crmnl Psych.

HEMPLE, STEVEN C; Calvary Chapel HS; Santa Ana, CA; (2); Church Yth Grp; Bsktbl; Ftbl; Tennis; Trk; Hon Roll; UCLA; Phy.

HEMPSTEAD, KEN D; Bellarmine College Prep; Los Gatos, CA; (4); French Clb; Service Clb; Varsity Clb; Var Swmmng; Waterpolo; Cal Polytechnic ST U; Bio Chem.

HEMPY, KEN J; San Clemente HS; San Clemente, CA; (4); Science Clb; Spanish Clb; Intrml Bsktbl; Var L Tennis; Intrml Wrstlng; Cit Awd; High Hon Roll; Prfct Atten Awd; CSF; Acad Achvt Physics & Spansh; Cal Poly Pomona; Mech Engrng.

HENARES, YVETTE P; Etiwanda HS; Alta Loma, CA; (2); Treas Church Yth Grp; Latin Clb; Office Aide; Church Choir; Cit Awd; Pres Acad Fit Awd; CSF; Outstndng Acad Achvmnt; Stu Mdl Cngrss 200th Annvrsry; Psych.

HENDEL, VICTORIA L; Pioneer HS; San Jose, CA; (3); VP Drama Clb; Q&S; School Play; Stage Crew; Variety Show; Ed Yrbk; Sec Soph Cls; High Hon Roll; NHS; Ntl Merit SF; Engl.

HENDERSON, APRIL M; El Dorado HS; Placentia, CA; (3); #12 In Class; Intnl Clb; Socr; Trk; High Hon Roll.

HENDERSON, BECKY K; Valhalla HS; El Cajon, CA; (4); 58/415; Band; Mrchg Band; Pep Band; Cit Awd; Hon Roll; Prfct Atten Awd; Bnk Amer Awd Bus; Distinguished Stu Awd; Hnr Grad; S W MO ST U; Acctng.

HENDERSON, CARI A; Poway HS; Poway, CA; (2); Church Yth Grp; Computer Clb; Dance Clb; French Clb; Band; Mrchg Band; Orch; Pep Band; Cit Awd; French Hon Soc; Art.

HENDERSON, CHRISTINA L; Ukiah HS; Ukiah, CA; (2); Church Yth Grp; Chorus; Church Choir; Hon Roll; Chld Psych.

HENDERSON, DEVIN L; Clairemont HS; San Diego, CA; (2); Am Leg Boys St; Cmnty Wkr; Letterman Clb; Model UN; Spanish Clb; Varsity Clb; Var Bsbl; Var Ftbl; Var Wt Lftg; Cit Awd; Hmcmng Rep; Congrsnl Schlr Rep CA Natl Young Ldrs Conf.

HENDERSON, ERIK R; Monte Vista HS; Walnut Creek, CA; (2); Letterman Clb; Teachers Aide; JV Ftbl; Var L Tennis; Wt Lftg; Hon Roll; Pres Acad Fit Awd; Fri Night Live; Yth & Govt; Asst Coach; UC-DAVIS; Engrng.

HENDERSON JR, ERNEST L; Brethren HS; Lynwood, CA; (3); Teachers Aide; Chrmn Frsh Cls; Stu Cncl; Var Bsbl; Var Bsktbl; Wt Lftg; Hon Roll; CSF; UCLA; Bus Admin.

HENDERSON, GREGG M; San Ramon Valley HS; Danville, CA; (4); 16/400; Church Yth Grp; Drama Clb; Key Clb; School Play; VP Sr Cls; Var L Swmmng; High Hon Roll; JETS Awd; NHS; Photo Clb VP; Duke.

HENDERSON, JENNIFER; Northhills Christian Schl; Vallejo, CA; (2); Church Yth Grp; Cmnty Wkr; German Clb; Quiz Bowl; Chorus; School Musical; Nwsp; Yrbk; Crs Cntry; High Hon Roll; Hgh Engl Awd; Pilot.

HENDERSON, JENNIFER B; Homestead HS; Los Altos, CA; (4); Spanish Clb; Tennis; Hon Roll; Jr NHS; Ntl Merit Ltr; Althenians; El Camino Hosp Vlntr.

HENDERSON, JENNIFER L; Irvine HS; Irvine, CA; (3); Key Clb; Hon Roll.

HENDERSON, JENNIFER M; Madera HS; Madera, CA; (2); Church Yth Grp; Pres Drama Clb; Pres Sec 4-H; School Musical; School Play; Variety Show; 4-H Awd; Hon Roll; Treas Soph Cls; 4-H All Star; Interact Clb; Horizon; Ucla; Law.

HENDERSON, JOHN O; Riverside Christian HS; Pinon Hills, CA; (2); SADD; Varsity Clb; Var Bsktbl; Var Vllybl; Hon Roll; Outstndng Engl Stu Awd; Cal ST; RN.

HENDERSON, KENDRA J; Las Plumas HS; Oroville, CA; (4); 16/200; GAA; Office Aide; Teachers Aide; Band; Chorus; Mrchg Band; Crs Cntry; Trk; Hon Roll; Chico ST U; Phys Ed.

HENDERSON, LA RONCE; Montclair HS; Montclair, CA; (3); 25/422; Drama Clb; Chorus; Variety Show; Nwsp; Yrbk; Treas Jr Cls; Pres Stu Cncl; Ftbl; Trk; Pres Acad Fit Awd; Brdcst Jrnlsm.

HENDERSON, LAURIE D; La Mirada HS; La Mirada, CA; (2); Church Yth Grp; Hosp Aide; Teachers Aide; Co-Capt Flag Corp; Rptr Lit Mag; Off Frsh Cls; Cit Awd; High Hon Roll; Treas Rep NHS; Prfct Atten Awd; CSF & Schlrthon; Outstndng Spanish Stu; Outstndng Algebra II Stu; Whittier Coll; Chld Dvlpmnt.

HENDERSON, LYNN A; Morro Bay HS; Los Osos, CA; (2); Chess Clb; Church Yth Grp; JCL; Varsity Clb; Sec Jr Cls; JV Crs Cntry; Capt Var Socr; JV Trk; Hon Roll; BYU; Sci.

HENDERSON, MICHAEL T; Bishop O'dowd HS; San Leandro, CA; (3); Trk; High Hon Roll; Schlr Athlete Awd; SHARP Prgm; U CA Los Angeles; Aero Engrng.

HENDERSON, MIKAILA; Eagle Rock HS; Los Angeles, CA; (3); Drill Tm; Stu Cncl; JV Var Bsktbl; Hon Roll; Korean, Pilipino Clb Secy; Asst To Sr Cls; UC System; Psych.

HENDERSON, SCOTT; El Toro HS; El Toro, CA; (3); 4/500; Church Yth Grp; Computer Clb; Math Tm; Stage Crew; JV Swmmng; Tennis; High Hon Roll; Ntl Merit Ltr; UCI Prgm For Ust Yr Chem; Gldn ST Awd High Hnrs Geo & 1st Yr Alg; Arspc Engrng.

HENDERSON, SEAN; Yosemite HS; Bass Lake, CA; (2); Church Yth Grp; Ski Clb; JV Bsktbl; JV Ftbl; Var L Tennis; High Hon Roll; Hon Roll; Art Clb; VICA; Honor Roll Acadmc Ltr; Vrsty Tennis Tm 2nd Pl; US Tennis Assoc; Fresno ST U; Arch.

HENDERSON, SHELI; Crenshaw HS; Los Angeles, CA; (4); Pres Church Yth Grp; JA; ROTC; Varsity Clb; Church Choir; Drill Tm; Orch; School Musical; Var Cheerldng; Hon Roll; Brown U; Law.

HENDERSON, SHERYL; Valhalla HS; La Mesa, CA; (4); 10/412; Church Yth Grp; Hosp Aide; Key Clb; SADD; School Play; Ed Nwsp; High Hon Roll; Dstngshd Acad Pgm; Humanities Enrchmnt Pgm; Fed Mart Schlrshp Awd; Wheaton Coll IL; Commnctns.

HENDERSON, STEVE; Ambassador Baptist HS; Rialto, CA; (2); Church Yth Grp; Bsbl; Ftbl; High Hon Roll; Hon Roll; Weight Liftng; Acctnt.

HENDERSON, TAMIYA RENEE; Armijo HS; Suisun City, CA; (4); Var Trk; Var Stat Wrstlng; Blsck Stu Union 86-90; Sacramento ST; Bus Admin.

HENDERSON, TIFFANIE J; Tustin HS; Tustin, CA; (1); Church Yth Grp; Cmnty Wkr; Girl Scts; Band; Mrchg Band; Pep Band; Chld Psych.

HENDLER, SHANNON; La Canada HS; La Canada Flintri, CA; (3); Cmnty Wkr; Debate Tm; GAA; Hosp Aide; Office Aide; Speech Tm; SADD; Teachers Aide; Rptr Yrbk; Rep Frsh Cls; Prom Cmmssnr; Goodwill Tour Tour/Plyng Russia, Sweden & Finland; Adopt-A-Family Pgm; Bus.

HENDLEY, JOEL M; El Dorado HS; Placerville, CA; (4); 1/290; Church Yth Grp; VP Math Clb; Q&S; Pres Science Clb; Speech Tm; Band; Church Choir; Jazz Band; Mrchg Band; Rptr Nwsp; CSF VP; Ski Tm; Harvey Mudd Coll; Comp Engrng.

HENDRICK, HOLLY V; Dos Pueblos HS; Goleta, CA; (3); 58/320; Church Yth Grp; Cmnty Wkr; SADD; Teachers Aide; Nwsp; NHS; Co-Leader HS Chptr Of Saferides; CA Schltc Fed; Psych Club; Elem Ed.

HENDRICKER, JENNIFER L; Huntington Beach HS; Huntington Beach, CA; (3); French Clb; Drill Tm; Swmmng; CSF Actvts Cmmttee; Tower Awd; Red Crss Clb; Bus.

HENDRICKS, BETH A; Escondido HS; Escondido, CA; (1); Drama Clb; French Clb; Office Aide; Pep Clb; School Play; Score Keeper; Mat Maids-Wrstlng; Law.

HENDRICKS, GINGER C; Antelope Valley HS; Lancaster, CA; (3); 30/631; German Clb; Intnl Clb; Rep Soph Cls; Var Swmmng; Stu For Stu; House Of Reps; CSF; U CA.

HENDRICKS, TIM M; Oak Ridge HS; El Dorado Hills, CA; (1); Ski Clb; Hon Roll; Church Yth Grp; UCSD.

HENDRICKSON, BRIAN D; Analy HS; Sebastopol, CA; (4); 2/212; Pres JA; Math Tm; High Hon Roll; Pres Acad Fit Awd; Sal; CSF; Interact; Harvard Awd For Outstndng Acad Achvt; Santa Rosa JC; Bus.

HENDRICKSON, CELESTE I; Central Union HS; El Centro, CA; (3); Church Yth Grp; French Clb; Pep Clb; Teachers Aide; Band; Chorus; Jazz Band; Mrchg Band; Orch; School Musical; US Navy Lge; San Diego ST U; Naval Aviator.

HENDRICKSON, ERIC M; Diamond Bar HS; Diamond Bar, CA; (2); Boy Scts; Church Yth Grp; German Clb; NHS; Chorus; Church Choir; Swing Chorus; Variety Show; High Hon Roll; Hon Roll; Wmmr MTA Compsr Fstvl St Lvl 1st Pl; Natl Guild Cmpsrs St & Natl Lvl 1st Pl Wnnr; Outstndng Band Stu; Prof Musician.

HENDRICKSON, JOHN K; Huntington Beach HS; Huntington Beach, CA; (1); Debate Tm; Model UN; Spanish Clb; Speech Tm; Teachers Aide; JV Crs Cntry; JV Socr; JV Trk; Yth Govt.

HENDRIX, BETHANY; Calvary Chapel HS; Santa Ana, CA; (1); Church Yth Grp; Teachers Aide; High Hon Roll; Primary Teacher.

HENDRIX, CYNTHIA; Santa Paula HS; Santa Paula, CA; (2); 17/370; Church Yth Grp; VP Frsh Cls; Pres Soph Cls; Capt Cheerldng; Var Socr; JV Sftbl; High Hon Roll; Hon Roll; CSF; Brigham Young U; Educ.

HENDRIX, JASON S; Rubidoux HS; Mira Loma, CA; (4); 43/578; FFA; Var Swmmng; Var Wrstlng; High Hon Roll; Hon Roll; Val; Prom Comm; Pol Sci Clb Mck Trial; GATE Clb; UCR; Med.

HENDRIX, JENNIFER; East Union HS; Manteca, CA; (3); 33/315; Debate Tm; Speech Tm; JV Cheerldng; Var Score Keeper; Cit Awd; High Hon Roll; Psych.

HENDRIX, KRISTINA M; Marysville HS; Marysville, CA; (1); Mgr(s); Score Keeper; Vllybl; High Hon Roll; U Incentive Grant Wnnr; CSUC; Child Psych.

HENDRIX, MICHAEL; Bakersfield HS; Bakersfield, CA; (4); 70/686; Church Yth Grp; Math Clb; Acpl Chr; Tennis; High Hon Roll; Hon Roll; NHS; Math, Engrng, Sci Achvt; Blk Studs Pgrss; Cal Poly; Elec Engrng.

HENDRIXSON, MARK; Reedley HS; Orange Cove, CA; (4); Boy Scts; Church Yth Grp; Computer Clb; FCA; German Clb; Varsity Clb; Pres Sr Cls; Intrml Crs Cntry; Var Swmmng; Intrml Wrstlng; Brigham Young U; Med.

HENDRY, BRIAN J; Midway Baptist HS; Chula Vista, CA; (3); 1/15; Church Yth Grp; Church Choir; School Play; Treas Stu Cncl; JV Var Bsbl; Var Bsktbl; JV Var Ftbl; High Hon Roll; Hon Roll; Bus.

HENDRY, HEATHER; Cabrillo HS; Lompoc, CA; (3); Color Guard; Mrchg Band; High Hon Roll; Hon Roll; Freelancers Drum & Bugle Corps; Tall Flag Mjr; Outstnd Soc Svc Awd; Sonoma ST; Envrnmntl Studies.

HENDRYX, TIFFANY; Los Gatos HS; Los Gatos, CA; (2); JV Swmmng; Pres Acad Fit Awd; Los Gatos Crew Team; Prjct Lead.

HENENFENT, JEFF M; Village Christian Schls; Sun Valley, CA; (2); Boy Scts; Chess Clb; Church Yth Grp; Math Clb; Mu Alpha Theta; Spanish Clb; Rep Frsh Cls; Hon Roll; Exchng Stu Japan Smmr 88; Accntng.

HENG, CHHONG; Santa Teresa HS; San Jose, CA; (2); Magnet Bus Pgm; Stanford; Bus.

HENG, MENG; Millikan JR HS; Los Angeles, CA; (2); JA; Teachers Aide; Cit Awd; High Hon Roll; Vanguard Hnr Soc; Golden St Exam Algebra High Hnrs; UCLA; Bus.

HENG, MENG; Oakland Technical HS; Oakland, CA; (2); Yrbk; Vllybl; Hon Roll; Asian Clb; Bus.

HENG, PROS; Modesto HS; Modesto, CA; (3); Cmptr Svcg; Elec Trades; Electronics; Pharm.

HENG, RATHA; San Gabriel HS; Rosemead, CA; (1); Sec Chess Clb; Sec Church Yth Grp; French Clb; Hon Roll; Jr NHS; CSF.

HENGSTEBECK, CHER L; Tehachapi HS; Tehachapi, CA; (3); Church Yth Grp; FFA; FHA; Office Aide; Teachers Aide; Cheerldng; Score Keeper; Sftbl; Trk; Cit Awd; Psych.

HENKEL, REBECCA; Chaffey HS; Ontario, CA; (3); Church Yth Grp; French Clb; Teachers Aide; Ed Yrbk; Mgr(s); Powder Puff Ftbl; Swmmng; Vllybl; Cit Awd; DAR Awd; Jr Ivy Chn Tp 50 Grls Crry Chn Of Ivy Grdtn; Hmts; Acad Lttr 3.5 Grd Avg; EMT Trng.

HENKER, DIANE; Archbishop Mitty HS; San Jose, CA; (3); #1 In Class; Church Yth Grp; Cmnty Wkr; Girl Scts; Intnl Clb; Math Tm; Service Clb; School Play; High Hon Roll; NHS; Opt Clb Awd; Hsitory Professor.

HENMI, LOREN T; Santa Maria HS; Santa Maria, CA; (3); 62/467; Aud/Vis; FBLA; Yrbk; Ftbl; Natl Yng Ldrs Conf, Washington DC; UC Davis; Bio Sci.

HENNAGER, THERESA; Burney JR/Sr HS; Burney, CA; (4); FBLA; FHA; Office Aide; Hon Roll; Stu Ldrshp; Franklin Pierce Coll; Arch.

HENNEMAN, TANYA A; Berkeley HS; Berkeley, CA; (3); Dance Clb; Chorus; School Musical; School Play; Rptr Nwsp; Var Capt Cheerldng; High Hon Roll; Hon Roll; African Student Association; Senate; Psychology/Pre-Med.

HENNEMANN, CHRISTINE E; Mt Whitney HS; Visalia, CA; (4); 10/373; Cmnty Wkr; Key Clb; Math Clb; Math Tm; Science Clb; Service Clb; Spanish Clb; Off Sr Cls; High Hon Roll; Hon Roll; Life Mem CSF; Lt Govnr Keywanetts CAL-NEV-HA Div 3; VP & Treas Jr Statesmn America; Yth In Govt Sgt; U Of CA Davis; Civil Engrng.

HENNESSEY, SEAN; Fred C Beyer HS; Modesto, CA; (4); 1/500; AFS; Am Leg Boys St; Debate Tm; VP FBLA; German Clb; Math Clb; NFL; Speech Tm; Orch; Ntl Merit SF; JR Stsmn Prog; Awd Schlrshp 89-90; Cong Bdtng Prog; Acadc Dcthln Tm 89-90; Tm Cptn; Harvard; Intl Rltns.

HENNESSY, SHEA; Rim Of The World HS; Running Springs, CA; (2); Aud/Vis; Church Yth Grp; Drama Clb; Ski Clb; Spanish Clb; Drill Tm; Hon Roll; UC San Diego; Med.

HENNING, KIMBERLY A; Villa Park HS; Orange, CA; (3); Church Yth Grp; Intnl Clb; Spanish Clb; Color Guard; JV Socr; JV Trk; Lt Plc Explrs; Accntng.

HENNINGER, AIMEE R; Rim Of The World HS; Running Springs, CA; (1); Church Yth Grp; Chorus; Educ.

HENNINGS, AARON M; San Clemente HS; San Clemente, CA; (1); Church Yth Grp; Socr; Cit Awd; Mission Viejo; Clb Sccr Tm Pataedores 75.

HENNIS-KNOEPFEL, CHERRI K; Fairfield HS; Suisun, CA; (3); FFA; Band; Mrchg Band; Hon Roll; Jr NHS; NHS; Slvr Awd CA FFA; Decthlm Tm; Engl Dept Schlstc Awd; Anything Goes Tm Cmptn; Carrier Mtn; Sessions Mdlng; Marine Bio.

HENNY, CHARLENE; Chico SR HS; Chico, CA; (4); Am Leg Aux Girls St; Church Yth Grp; Pres Hosp Aide; Intnl Clb; Spanish Clb; Band; Mrchg Band; Orch; Pep Band; Co-Ed Nwsp; Henry Mayo Newhall Schlrshp; John Phillip Sousa Awd; N CA HS Hnr Band; Westmont Coll; Doctor.

HENRI, DELPHINE N; Lowell HS; San Francisco, CA; (2); Drama Clb; French Clb; Tennis; Badminton Team; Bus.

HENRICKSON, DOLLIE-JEAN; Lincoln HS; Lincoln, CA; (3); 78/150; Art Clb; Vllybl; Hon Roll; Heald Coll; Legal Secy.

HENRIKSEN, MARTIN; Saint Francis HS; Woodside, CA; (2); Letterman Clb; Service Clb; Ski Clb; Varsity Clb; Var Swmmng; Wt Lftg; Vrsty Water Polo.

HENRIQUES, JILL N; Saint Francis HS; San Jose, CA; (1); Pep Clb; SADD; Rep Yrbk; High Hon Roll; San Jose Jrs Vlybl Clb.

HENRY, BRIAN W; Serrano HS; Wrightwood, CA; (2); JV Bsbl; JV Bsktbl; Hon Roll; Boosters Clb Awd Bsktbl; Coach & Rfree Sccr For AYSO; UCLA; Med.

HENRY, CHADEB C; Skyline HS; Oakland, CA; (2); Church Yth Grp; Chorus; Church Choir; JV Bsktbl; Hon Roll; Oakland Yth Chorus; Gospel Choir; Early Chldhd Devlpmnt.

HENRY, CHRISTOPHER M; Antioch HS; Antioch, CA; (3); 5/607; Church Yth Grp; Spanish Clb; Varsity Clb; JV Bsktbl; Var JV Ftbl; Var JV Trk; Wt Lftg; NHS; Pres Acad Fit Awd; Cal Poly San Luis Obispo; Engr.

HENRY, CYNTHIA H; Torrey Pines HS; Del Mar, CA; (4); Treas SADD; Rptr Nwsp; Hon Roll; Ntl Merit Ltr; Acad Decathlon; CA Schlstc Fed Sealbearer; UC Santa Barbara; Psych.

HENRY, KIMBERLY G; Brethren JR/Sr HS; Buena Park, CA; (2); Acpl Chr; Chorus; School Musical; VP Frsh Cls; Cheerldng; Hon Roll; Val; Royal Servants Intl; Reign Ministries Inc; Clscl Soloist Wnnr ACSI Comp; Biola U; Psych.

HENRY, LEEANN; Casa Grande HS; Petaluma, CA; (3); 9/288; School Play; Cit Awd; High Hon Roll; Hon Roll; Jr NHS; NHS; Spec Stu Of Mnth Awd; CA Schlrshp Fed; UC Santa Barbara; Bio.

HENRY, LISA D; Casa Grande HS; Petaluma, CA; (2); 18/295; French Clb; JV Sftbl; Hon Roll; Jr NHS; NHS; Pres Acad Fit Awd; Achvt Awds Comp Allctns & PE; Schlr Athlte; Sonoma ST U; Bus.

HENRY, SUNYANI P; Eisenhower HS; Rialto, CA; (4); Cmnty Wkr; VP Chorus; Church Choir; Bsktbl; Hon Roll; Schlstc Achvt Awd; Cert Of Recognition Black Stu Union 90; Spcl Olympics Coach; Occidental Coll; Poltcl Sci.

HENRY, TAMMY; Hemet HS; Hemet, CA; (2); Church Yth Grp; FFA; SADD; Powder Puff Ftbl; Socr; Jobs Daughters; Photographer.

HENRY, TARA A; Hogan SR HS; Vallejo, CA; (3); Church Yth Grp; Cmnty Wkr; French Clb; Science Clb; Church Choir; Nwsp; Crs Cntry; Trk; Co-Founder Ecology Clb; CSF Clb; Jrnlsm.

HENSCH, CHAD K; San Dieguito HS; Cardiff By The Se, CA; (2); JV Bsbl; Intrml Wrstlng; Hon Roll; Prfct Atten Awd; Hnrs Algebra And Geom Golden ST Exam; Bus.

HENSEL, BRETT J; Torrey Pines HS; Rancho Santa Fe, CA; (2); 24/503; Church Yth Grp; SADD; Var Vllybl; High Hon Roll; Pres Acad Fit Awd; 2nd Tm All Amer Jr Olympcs Vlybl 90; CA Slchltc Fed.

HENSEL, CURT W; Torrey Pines HS; Rancho Santa Fe, CA; (3); 43/400; Church Yth Grp; Ski Clb; SADD; Nwsp; Var Ftbl; Var Capt Vllybl; Elks Awd; High Hon Roll; Pres Acad Fit Awd; Rotary Awd; RYLA Ldrshp Cnvntn.

HENSEL, DANIEL E; Galt HS; Galt, CA; (3); Var Socr; Var Trk; Hon Roll; Outstndng Vrsty Trk Rnnr.

HENSELER, KERI L; Foothill HS; North Highlands, CA; (2); Church Yth Grp; FTA; Spcl Educ.

HENSHAW, CHRISTINA; Moorpark HS; Moorpark, CA; (2); Church Yth Grp; Church Choir; Variety Show; Treas Frsh Cls; JV Cheerldng; High Hon Roll; Hon Roll; TMTA Intl Modeling/Tlnt Assoc Awd; Fshn Print, Cmmrcl Print, TV Commercial; Cmmrcl Print & Fshn Mdl; BYU; Cmmrcl Art.

HENSHAW, MARION; Lodi HS; Lodi, CA; (4); 12/399; Art Clb; Church Yth Grp; Acpl Chr; Swmmng; High Hon Roll; Kiwanis Awd; Opt Clb Awd; Priv Frgn Exchng Brazil 88; CSF Awd; U Of Puget Sound; Psych.

HENSHAW, NATHAN D; Alvord HS; Riverside, CA; (4); Cmnty Wkr; ROTC; Band; Mrchg Band; VP Bsbl; Clean & Sober Tn Ntwrk; Riverside CC; Cnslr.

HENSHAW, PATRICIA C; Esperanza HS; Yorba Linda, CA; (2); 1/475; Cmnty Wkr; Intnl Clb; Rep Stu Cncl; Var Capt Bsktbl; Var Tennis; High Hon Roll; NHS; CSF; Math.

HENSHAW, TANYA A; Calabasas HS; Topanga, CA; (3); GAA; Sch Equstrn Tm; Med.

HENSLEY, CHRISTIE M; San Bernardino HS; San Bernardino, CA; (3); 55/400; German Clb; SADD; JV Sftbl; JV Tennis; Hon Roll; Natl Grmn Hnr Soc Delta Epsilon Phi; MESA; Translator.

HENSLEY, GREG W; Victor Valley HS; Manassas, VA; (4); Boy Scts; Church Yth Grp; Church Choir; Socr; High Hon Roll; Hon Roll; Prfct Atten Awd.

HENSLEY, KASSIE J; Hemet HS; Hemet, CA; (4); Library Aide; Teachers Aide; Phtg Yrbk; Score Keeper; People For The Ethical Trtmnt Of Animals; Mt San Jacinto Coll; Marine Bio.

HENSLEY, MELISSA D; Cupertino HS; Santa Clara, CA; (3); 16/296; NHS; Interact Clb; UCLA; Psych.

HENSLEY, SETH; Butte Valley HS; Dorris, CA; (2); 1/30; Computer Clb; Teachers Aide; Pres Jr Cls; JV Bsktbl; Var Tennis; High Hon Roll; Lion Awd; CA Schlrshp Fed; B S; Engrng.

HENSLEY, SHAWNA; Nevada Union HS; Nevada City, CA; (4); Drama Clb; English Clb; Hosp Aide; Chorus; School Play; Rep Stu Cncl; High Hon Roll; Hon Roll; Psych.

HENSLEY, TISH A; Live Oak HS; Live Oak, CA; (3); 4/90; Church Yth Grp; Sec Frsh Cls; Treas Stu Cncl; JV Trk; JV Var Vllybl; High Hon Roll; Hon Roll; CSF; Acad Excl Club; Church Ofc Vol Work; Yuba Coll; Bus.

HENSLEY, TRINITY M; Turlock HS; Turlock, CA; (4); 44/600; AFS; Art Clb; Cmnty Wkr; FBLA; Science Clb; SADD; Teachers Aide; Life-Time CSF; CSU Stanislaus; Bus.

HENSON, AMY; Roseville HS; Roseville, CA; (2); 30/400; Church Yth Grp; Pep Clb; Spanish Clb; Cheerldng; High Hon Roll; Acad Achvt Cert, Mdl; Tiger Stripes Awd Pep Squad & Optmstc Attitude; Folk Dncng; Mem Friday Night Live; UC Berkeley; Intl Rel.

HENSON, CHRISTINE M; Canyon HS; Canyon Country, CA; (3); Pres Sec Chorus; UCLA; Arch.

HENSON, JASON; Fontana HS; Fontana, CA; (2); Ftbl; Hon Roll; Doc.

HENSON, JENNIFER L; Modoc HS; Alturas, CA; (4); 1/55; Band; School Play; Yrbk; Var L Sftbl; Var L Trk; Elks Awd; Pres Acad Fit Awd; Val; CBDA All-St Hnr Band; CSU Chico; Engl Teacher.

HENSON, JORY A; Branham HS; San Jose, CA; (2); #22 In Class; Church Yth Grp; Key Clb; SADD; Yrbk; Treas Frsh Cls; JV Bsktbl; Var Tennis; Hon Roll; Prfct Atten Awd; Tnns Mst Imprvd Plyr; UC Irvine.

HENSON, KETURAH L; Lone Pine HS; Randsburg, CA; (3); Math Tm; Pep Clb; Teachers Aide; School Play; Stage Crew; Ed Nwsp; Hon Roll; Acadc Ltr; Hstry Awd; CPA.

HENSON, MICHELE K; Ramona HS; Riverside, CA; (1); 94/580; Drama Clb; Chorus; School Musical.

HENSON, PAMELA; West Chester HS; Los Angeles, CA; (2); Var Bsktbl; Advrtsng.

HENSON, QUIN A; J W North HS; Riverside, CA; (1); JV Bsktbl; Intl Baccalaureate Prep Pgm.

HENSON, SUSANNA; Mater Dei HS; Santa Ana, CA; (3); Cmnty Wkr; Dance Clb; Drama Clb; Pep Clb; Ski Clb; Spanish Clb; Drill Tm; Stage Crew; Rep Stu Cncl; L Var Pom Pon; U Of Southern CA; Psych.

HENTGES, SANDY M; Sunny Hills HS; Fullerton, CA; (2); Church Yth Grp; Hosp Aide; Intnl Clb; Key Clb; Vllybl; Hon Roll; Amnsty Intl.

HENWOOD, JENNIFER R; Lindhurst HS; Marysville, CA; (2); Cmnty Wkr; Teachers Aide; High Hon Roll; Hon Roll; Physcl Ed Awd; Publc Spkng Pgm; Med Sctry.

HENZIE, MATTHEW G; Village Christian Schls; Sunland, CA; (3); 17/123; Church Yth Grp; Var Bsbl; Var Bsktbl; JV Ftbl; CSF.

HEO, THOMAS SUK; Birmingham HS; Van Nuys, CA; (4); Cmnty Wkr; Teachers Aide; Band; Drm Mjr(t); Jazz Band; Mrchg Band; Hon Roll; LAUSD All City Marching Band; Boston U; Pre-Med.

HEPPNER, BRENT; South Hills HS; Covina, CA; (2); 18/278; Science Clb; Var Crs Cntry; Var Tennis; JV Trk; High Hon Roll; Pres Acad Fit Awd; Mchncl Engr.

HER, BAI; Clovis HS; Fresno, CA; (4); 17/540; 4-H; VICA; High Hon Roll; Hon Roll; CSF; Bank Of Amer Achvt Awd; Fresno Fair Is Pl Art Exhibition & Indstrl Arts; UW Milwaukee; Mech Engrng.

HER, FONG; Lincoln Prep HS; San Diego, CA; (3); Pres Art Clb; Drama Clb; FTA; Office Aide; ROTC; Color Guard; Socr; High Hon Roll; Hon Roll; Prfct Atten Awd; Math Awd; Goldn ST Exm; Acad Leag; UCSD; Elec Engr.

HER, JULIE YING; Duncan Poly HS; Fresno, CA; (1); Cmnty Wkr; Computer Clb; FBLA; Intnl Clb; Library Aide; Math Clb; Math Tm; Office Aide; ROTC; SADD; Bus.

HER, KA YING; Edison HS; Stockton, CA; (2); French Clb; Hosp Aide; Teachers Aide; Hon Roll; Gftd & Tlntd Ed Prgms; Hmong Club Secy; Elem Tchr.

HER, LEE; Merced HS; Merced, CA; (4); Office Aide; Teachers Aide; Hon Roll; Prfct Atten Awd; Japanese Clb; YCE; UC Davis; Psych.

HER, MAY KER; Hoover HS; San Diego, CA; (2); Cit Awd; High Hon Roll; Hon Roll.

HER, MEE SANDY; Duncan Polytechnical HS; Fresno, CA; (1); Church Yth Grp; Drama Clb; Office Aide; SADD; Church Choir; Hon Roll; Prin Awd; Teachers Awd; Atten Awd; Fresno ST; Acctng.

HER, ONG; Duncan Poly HS; Pinedale, CA; (4); 1/115; Pres Church Yth Grp; Pres Intnl Clb; VICA; Church Choir; Var Vllybl; Cit Awd; High Hon Roll; Kiwanis Awd; Prfct Atten Awd; Val; Acad Decathlon & Voc Olympic Teams; Fresno ST U; Arch.

HER, PAO; Merced HS North; Merced, CA; (3); Yrbk; Hon Roll; Prfct Atten Awd; Stanislaus Turlock; Accntnt.

HER, STEVE; Western HS; Anaheim, CA; (4); 1/324; Am Leg Boys St; Drama Clb; Pep Clb; Speech Tm; Varsity Clb; Var Tennis; Bausch & Lomb Sci Awd; High Hon Roll; NHS; Hon Roll; CA Schlrshp Fdrtn; Pre-Med.

HER, TENG; Lindhurst HS; Marysville, CA; (4); Art Clb; Church Yth Grp; Science Clb; Church Choir; CSU; Acctng.

HER, TOU B; Turlock HS; Turlock, CA; (3); Art Clb; Church Yth Grp; Spanish Clb; Cit Awd; Hon Roll; Sci Prodject Awd; CA Schlrshp Fed Club; San Luis Obispo; Constr Engrng.

HER, XA; Edison HS; Stockton, CA; (2); Hon Roll.

HER, XAO; Bullard HS; Fresno, CA; (3); French Clb; Ftbl; Socr; CA ST U Fresno; Bus.

HER, XIONG P; Edison HS; Stockton, CA; (3); Chess Clb; Church Yth Grp; Computer Clb; French Clb; Math Clb; Science Clb; Church Choir; High Hon Roll; Hon Roll; NHS; Physics Clb; CSU Sacramento; Comp Sci.

HER II, YA; Kearny HS; San Diego, CA; (2); Boy Scts; Library Aide; Math Tm; Model UN; Nwsp; Yrbk; Cit Awd; Hon Roll; Prfct Atten Awd; UCSD; Graphic Dsgn.

HER, YANG HOUA; Edison Computech HS; Pinedale, CA; (3); Chess Clb; Church Yth Grp; German Clb; Model UN; Band; Tennis; Hon Roll; Pepsie Awd; William Saroyan Wrtg Contest Winner; Odyssey Of Mind St Fnls; Bus.

HERALDO, AIMEE J; William C Overfelt HS; San Jose, CA; (2); Church Yth Grp; Var Tennis; NHS; Sci Lab Asst Overfelt HS; Most Val Doubles Awd-Tennis; 5 Yrs Piano Lessons.

HERANA, ANTHONY M; Armijo HS; Fairfield, CA; (1); AFS; Computer Clb; High Hon Roll; Engrng.

HERB, WENDY; Rosary HS; La Habra, CA; (3); Science Clb; Spanish Clb; Varsity Clb; Variety Show; Off Frsh Cls; JV Var Bsktbl; Var Swmmng; Var JV Vllybl; High Hon Roll; NHS; Schlr Athl 3 Yrs; CA Schlrshp Fdrtn 1 Yr; Acad Merit Eng; Athl Yr; MVP Vrsty Vllybl; Phys Thrpy.

HERBERT, AYANA N; Morningside HS; Inglewood, CA; (1); 1/410; Cit Awd; High Hon Roll; Hon Roll; Prfct Atten Awd; Inglewood Show Team; Doctor.

HERBERT, KELLY L; Durham HS; Durham, CA; (3); GAA; SADD; Rptr Yrbk; Sec Soph Cls; JV Trk; Var Vllybl; Hon Roll; Prfct Atten Awd; Chico ST U; Law.

HERBERT, MARVELYN; Morningside HS; Inglewood, CA; (1); Cit Awd; Hon Roll; Indepndnt Drill Team; Obstetrcs.

HERBERT, ROBYN S; San Benito HS; Hollister, CA; (1); Church Choir; Piano; Music.

HERBERT, SHAUNA M; John Muir HS; Pasadena, CA; (3); Church Yth Grp; Church Choir; Trk; Prfct Atten Awd; BSU; Math, Tnns, Singing; Harvard; Law.

HERBERT, TAMURA LA SHAWN; Washington Prepratory HS; Los Angeles, CA; (3); Co-Capt Pep Clb; Chorus; School Play; Var Sftbl; JV Trk; Prfct Atten Awd; U Of CA Irvine; Chem.

HERBERT, TONYA L; Tonya Linn Herbert HS; Phelan, CA; (3); 8/213; Church Yth Grp; Cmnty Wkr; Dance Clb; Drama Clb; FBLA; Model UN; Science Clb; SADD; Teachers Aide; Thesps; Mock Trial Outstndng Dfns Atty Awd; Rotary Yth Ldrshp Awd; Hnr Guard; Pltcl Sci.

HERBERT, VALERIE T; Notre Dame HS; Carmel, CA; (3); 10/90; Church Yth Grp; Cmnty Wkr; Debate Tm; Science Clb; Spanish Clb; SADD; Chorus; Off Jr Cls; Pres Sr Cls; JV Var Sftbl; Respect Life Commsn; Jr Statesmen Of Amer; Amnesty Intl Commsnrs Publicty; UCSC; Art.

HERBST, JANELLE; Ponderosa HS; Placerville, CA; (3); 9/330; French Clb; VP Rep Jr Cls; Pres Sr Cls; JV Var Cheerldng; JV Var Tennis; L Ntl Merit Schol; Opt Clb Awd; Chorus; School Musical; Gov Hon Prg Awd; CSF; GATE & CASC; UC Santa Barbara; Envrnmntl.

HERBST, MATT T; The Bishops Schl; Poway, CA; (3); Cmnty Wkr; Drama Clb; Science Clb; Teachers Aide; School Musical; School Play; Mgr Stage Crew; Yrbk; JV Tennis; Var Vllybl; Advncd Theatrical Prdctn Dir; Bowling Club Pres; UCLA; Film.

HERCEG, MICHAEL R; Venice HS; Venice, CA; (2); Band; Mrchg Band; Pentathlon Cmptn; Decathln Cls; CA Jr Schlrhsp Fund; CA Schlrshp Fund; All Dist Band & Drill Team; UCLA; Chem.

HERD, DEREK J; Red Bluff Union HS; Red Bluff, CA; (2); 90/250; Church Yth Grp; Wt Lftg; High Hon Roll; Hon Roll; Engr.

HERDMAN, DIANA L; Torrance HS; Torrance, CA; (3); Cmnty Wkr; Dance Clb; GAA; Office Aide; Pep Clb; SADD; Variety Show; Var JV Cheerldng; Score Keeper; AFS; Feed, Send Food To Homeless; Chrldng Hnrs, Awds; San Diego ST U; Bus.

HEREDIA, GUSTAVO E; San Rafael HS; San Rafael, CA; (3); Socr; Engrng.

HEREDIA, IRASEMA; Monte Vista HS; Spring Valley, CA; (3); Spanish Clb; SADD; Var Vllybl; CCN Prgm; Los Amigos Club Rep; Ayamaca Coll; Cmptr Sci.

HEREDIA, JOY; Santana HS; Santee, CA; (4); 22/560; Am Leg Aux Girls St; Church Yth Grp; Ed Yrbk; Off Jr Cls; Off Sr Cls; Var Capt Crs Cntry; Var Capt Trk; Cit Awd; Hon Roll; Cal Poly; Hotl Admin.

HEREDIA, RAUL; Montclair HS; Montclair, CA; (3); Wt Lftg; Var Wrstlng; Hon Roll; Bus.

HERH, CHER; Hoover HS; San Diego, CA; (3); Intnl Clb; Pep Clb; Sec Jr Cls; Powder Puff Ftbl; Cit Awd; Hon Roll; NHS; Campus Bk Clb VP; Top Of The Mark Clb; U CA Santa Barbara; Psych.

HERION, BRANDON J; Clovis West HS; Fresno, CA; (1); Ski Clb.

HERKENHOFF, NICOLE R; Dana Hills HS; Laguna Niguel, CA; (3); Church Yth Grp; Church Choir; Mrchg Band; Pep Band; Stu Cncl; Outstndng Sewing Achvt Awd; HS Yth Grp Ldrshp Awd; Fshn Dsgn.

HERMAN, BRIAN A; Delta HS; Clarksburg, CA; (3); FHA; SADD; Teachers Aide; Chorus; Crs Cntry; Trk; High Hon Roll; Hstry.

HERMAN, BURT; San Marcos HS; Santa Barbara, CA; (3); Key Clb; Temple Yth Grp; Band; Drm Mjr(t); Mrchg Band; Orch; Pep Band; School Musical; Variety Show; Yrbk; PSAT Commended; Stanford.

HERMAN, JOHN; San Joaquin Memorial HS; Albuquerque, NM; (2); Math Clb; Ski Clb; Spanish Clb; Varsity Clb; Bsbl; Ftbl; Socr; Wt Lftg; Hon Roll; Cal Poly San Luis Obispo; Arch.

HERMAN, MARK A; Roseville HS; Rocklin, CA; (3); Church Yth Grp; Pres French Clb; Red Cross Aide; Band; Jazz Band; Mrchg Band; Rptr Yrbk; Lit Mag; Ftbl; Var Swmmng; Pblshd Artcls In Literary Mgzne; Sierra Coll; Comm.

HERMANN, DARCY; Escondido HS; Escondido, CA; (2); Church Yth Grp; Debate Tm; Drama Clb; Math Clb; NFL; ROTC; Speech Tm; SADD; Flag Corp; School Play; Cert Of Acad Awd; Cert Of Commendation; U Of CA.

HERMANN, KRISTINA; Fall River HS; Old Station, CA; (1); Rep SADD; JV Bsktbl; JV Socr; JV Trk; Hon Roll; Just Say No; Youth To Youth; UC Santa Cruz; Trvl Agnt.

HERMANSKI, GREG S; Santa Rosa HS; Santa Rosa, CA; (4); 24/494; JA; SADD; Varsity Clb; Band; Drm Mjr(t); Jazz Band; Mrchg Band; School Musical; Var Bsktbl; L Var Golf; Aerospc Engrng.

HERMOGENO, LANI S; St Joseph HS; Cerritos, CA; (2); Church Choir; Drill Tm; Variety Show; Hon Roll; Piano & Organ; Bus.

HERMOSILLO, KAREN J; Magnolia HS; Stanton, CA; (2); Boy Scts; Church Yth Grp; Math Clb; Teachers Aide; Off Frsh Cls; Socr; High Hon Roll; Hon Roll; Brd Dirctrs Untd Chrstn Ashram Smmr Camp.

HERNANDE, JACKIE; Ontario HS; Montclair, CA; (4); German Clb; Key Clb; Science Clb; Varsity Clb; Crs Cntry; Trk; Hon Roll; Prfct Atten Awd; Math Achvt Awd; Engl Achvt; Cal Poly Pomona; Biochem.

HERNANDEZ, AARON M; Garfield HS; Los Angeles, CA; (2); Church Yth Grp; SADD; Ftbl; Sftbl; Trk; Cit Awd; Hon Roll; Prfct Atten Awd; Mariposa Prog Cert Of Excllnc UCLA; Vlntr In Painting A Portion Of Schl Lockers; UCLA; Bus Admin.

HERNANDEZ, ABEL A; Colton HS; Grand Terrace, CA; (2); Law Enfrcmnt.

HERNANDEZ, ADRIAN C; Chaffey HS; Ontario, CA; (2); JV Bsbl; JV Bsktbl; JV Ftbl; JV Socr; Fontana; Lawyer.

HERNANDEZ, ADRIAN M; Ganesha HS; Pomona, CA; (3); JV Ftbl; Hon Roll; UC Riverside; Med.

HERNANDEZ, ADRIENNE R; Roosevelt HS; Fresno, CA; (2); Band; Mrchg Band; Pep Band; Rep Soph Cls; JV Cheerldng; High Hon Roll; Pres Acad Fit Awd; Harvard U; Law.

HERNANDEZ, ALBA; Cajon HS; San Bernardino, CA; (2); Dance Clb; French Clb; Gym; Sftbl; America Statesmen.

HERNANDEZ, ALBERTO; Paramount HS; Paramount, CA; (4); Boy Scts; Letterman Clb; Var Crs Cntry; Var Trk; Var Wrstlng; Cit Awd; Prfct Atten Awd; Law.

HERNANDEZ, ALEJANDRO; Cathedral HS; Los Angeles, CA; (4); 1/106; Cmnty Wkr; Computer Clb; VP Pres Math Clb; Science Clb; Service Clb; Spanish Clb; Mgr Teachers Aide; Ed Yrbk; High Hon Roll; St Augustine Schlrshp; Taught Comp At Holy Cross Middle Schl/Smmr 89; Wrtng As A Hobby; Loyola Marymount; Cvl Engrng.

HERNANDEZ, ALFREDO; Cantwell HS; Montebello, CA; (1); 4/28; Boy Scts; Trk; Cal ST LA; Engr.

HERNANDEZ, ALMA; Woodland HS; Woodland, CA; (3); Intnl Clb; Key Clb; NFL; Spanish Clb; Speech Tm; School Musical; Rep Frsh Cls; Stu Cncl; JV Bsktbl; Var Capt Socr; SPCA Vlntr; UC Santa Barbara; Animal Trnr.

HERNANDEZ, ANA; Rowland HS; Rowland Heights, CA; (2); JV Sftbl.

HERNANDEZ, ANA MARIA; Notre Dame HS; San Jose, CA; (4); 1/70; Intnl Clb; Sec Science Clb; Rptr Nwsp; Lit Mag; Sec Frsh Cls; Var Cheerldng; High Hon Roll; Val; Alliance Frangaise Schlrshp; Bank Of Amer Plaque Wnnr; U CA Berkeley; French/Spanish.

HERNANDEZ, ANGEL; David Starr Jordan HS; Los Angeles, CA; (1); Band; Var Socr; Var Vllybl; Sci.

HERNANDEZ, ANGELICA; Indio HS; Indio, CA; (1); Color Guard.

HERNANDEZ, ANGELICA M; Pasadena HS; Pasadena, CA; (1); Church Yth Grp; Office Aide; Arch.

HERNANDEZ, ANNA M; Buena Vista HS; Chino, CA; (3); Dance Clb; Hosp Aide; Cit Awd; Baldy View Rgnl Occptnl Pgm Nrsng & Medcl Asst; Riverside CC; Nrsng.

HERNANDEZ, ANTONIO P; La Habra HS; La Habra, CA; (4); Church Yth Grp; Cmnty Wkr; Drama Clb; Letterman Clb; Pep Clb; ROTC; Science Clb; Spanish Clb; SADD; Varsity Clb; Honorary Stu In Oral Commnctns; Sgate Crew.

HERNANDEZ, ARCELIO; Robert A Millikan HS; Long Beach, CA; (4); Church Yth Grp; Teachers Aide; Acpl Chr; School Musical; Var L Socr; Hon Roll; Rotary Awd; Frgn Lang Mdl Of Mrt; Chrch Musician; CSULB; Frgn Lang.

HERNANDEZ, ARTHUR J; John Glenn HS; Norwalk, CA; (3); ROTC; Band; JV Ftbl; JV Socr; Var L Trk; Hon Roll; Phy.

HERNANDEZ, ARTURO; Artesia HS; Hawaiian Gardens, CA; (3); 4/30; Cmnty Wkr; JA; Math Tm; Teachers Aide; Band; Mrchg Band; Pep Band; School Musical; Ftbl; Wt Lftg; Bus.

HERNANDEZ, BAUDELIO E; Garfield HS; Los Angeles, CA; (3); JV Bsbl; Prfct Atten Awd; Pro Bsbl.

HERNANDEZ, BELLE Q; Central Union HS; El Centro, CA; (1); Hon Roll; Early Outreach Pgm; Pediatrician.

HERNANDEZ, BEN C; Los Altos HS; La Puente, CA; (3); 141/368; FCA; Letterman Clb; Varsity Clb; Acpl Chr; Chorus; Church Choir; School Musical; Swing Chorus; Variety Show; Bsbl; Sound Eng.

HERNANDEZ, BERNADETTE A; Mtn View HS; El Monte, CA; (1); Pep Clb; Band; Mrchg Band; JV Cheerldng; U Of S CA; Chldrns Socl Wrkr.

HERNANDEZ, BERNARDO; Watsonville HS; Watsonville, CA; (2); JV Ftbl; U Of Miami.

HERNANDEZ, BERTHA A; Venice HS; Los Angeles, CA; (2); Office Aide; Hon Roll; Prfct Atten Awd; MESA.

HERNANDEZ, BLANCA O; San Pasqual HS; Escondido, CA; (2); Church Yth Grp; UCLA; Engrng.

HERNANDEZ, BRENDA; Hemet HS; Hemet, CA; (2); Med.

HERNANDEZ, BRENDA; William Howard Taft HS; San Fernando, CA; (3); Pitzer; Child Psych.

HERNANDEZ, CARLOS; Don Bosco Technical Inst; Montebello, CA; (4); Church Yth Grp; Hon Roll; NHS; Golden Tiger Awd; Cal Poly Pomona; Elec Engr.

HERNANDEZ, CARLOS A; St Francis HS; Altadena, CA; (2); Cmnty Wkr; Pep Clb; Spanish Clb; Pep Band; Yrbk; Crs Cntry; Trk; Hon Roll; Spanish NHS; Piano; CSF Mem; Clef Club Pres; USC; Poly Sci.

HERNANDEZ, CARMEN; Orosi HS; Orosi, CA; (3); Latin Clb; Spanish Clb; Band; Mrchg Band; Pep Band; Hon Roll; CSF; Fresno ST; Bus.

HERNANDEZ, CHRISTY; Lodi HS; Lodi, CA; (2); Band; High Hon Roll; CSF; Early Acad Outreach Pgm; Outstndng Beginning Band Musician Awd; CA ST U-Sacra; Interior Dsgnr.

HERNANDEZ, CLAUDIA; Bell Gardens HS; Bell Gardens, CA; (2); Cmnty Wkr; Red Cross Aide; Rep Stu Cncl; Prfct Atten Awd; Vol Rio Hondo Boys Club; Vol Red Cross Hlth Fairs; Govt.

HERNANDEZ, DAN; Hawthorne HS; Lennox, CA; (3); Church Yth Grp; Band; Drm Mjr(t); Jazz Band; Mrchg Band; Ftbl; Trk; Watts Hlth Fndtn-Teen Advoc; Tchng.

HERNANDEZ, DAN J; Fremont HS; Sunnyvale, CA; (2); 29/421; Debate Tm; NFL; Speech Tm; Band; Mrchg Band; School Musical; JV Tennis; High Hon Roll; Opt Clb Awd; CSF; CA Inst Of Tech; Mech Engr.

HERNANDEZ, DANA; Fillmore HS; Fillmore, CA; (4); Spanish Clb; SADD; Tennis; High Hon Roll; Hon Roll; Prfct Atten Awd; Pres Acad Fit Awd; Rotary Awd; UC Davis; Vet.

HERNANDEZ, DANIEL A; San Benito HS; Hollister, CA; (2); 53/380; FFA; Key Clb; Letterman Clb; Varsity Clb; VP Soph Cls; Ftbl; Wrstlng; High Hon Roll; Hon Roll; AZ ST; Bus.

HERNANDEZ, DANNY; Lindsay HS; Lindsay, CA; (1); Hon Roll; Fresno ST U; Pharmacy.

HERNANDEZ, DAVID S; San Dimas HS; San Dimas, CA; (2); JV Bsbl; JV Ftbl; JV Wrstlng; 4 Rose Awds; Jr Var Most Outstndng Wrstlr 90; Eng.

HERNANDEZ, DIANA C; Encinal HS; Alameda, CA; (3); 9/220; Treas FBLA; Band; Rptr Nwsp; Rep Jr Cls; JV Cheerldng; Var Tennis; High Hon Roll; Debate Tm; ROTC; SADD; Pre Coll Acad UC Berkeley; JROTC Supr Cadet Awd 89; CSF Treas; U Of CA Berkeley; Bus Admin.

HERNANDEZ, DINA; Lincoln HS; Stockton, CA; (2); 196/530; Dance Clb; Ski Clb; Teachers Aide; Cheerldng; Gym; Pom Pon; Swmmng; Hon Roll; Miss Petite Prncss 88; U Of CA Davis; Bus.

HERNANDEZ, ELIAZAR; Palm Desert HS; Palm Desert, CA; (3); Art Clb; Cmnty Wkr; Computer Clb; Drama Clb; Hosp Aide; Latin Clb; Math Tm; Office Aide; Spanish Clb; Teachers Aide; Coll Of The Desert; Doctor.

HERNANDEZ, ELISABETH M; Victor Valley HS; Victorville, CA; (4); Red Cross Aide; Spanish Clb; Lion Awd; Psych.

HERNANDEZ, ELIZABETH; River City SR HS; Woodland, CA; (3); Hon Roll; MESA; MECHA; Sacramento ST Coll; Probtn Ofc.

HERNANDEZ, ELIZABETH; Schurr HS; Los Angeles, CA; (1); Hon Roll; Phclgy.

HERNANDEZ, ELIZABETH L; Roosevelt HS; Fresno, CA; (3); Spanish Clb; Teachers Aide; Band; Gym; Score Keeper; Sftbl; Cit Awd; Hon Roll; Fresno ST U; Chld Psych.

HERNANDEZ, ELVIRA; Roosevelt HS; Los Angeles, CA; (2); Church Yth Grp; VP Frsh Cls; Hon Roll; Mdcl Career Clb; MESA; Fidm; Fshn Dsgnr.

HERNANDEZ, ERNESTO; Salesian HS; Los Angeles, CA; (2); 15/100; Sec Soph Cls; JV Bsbl; Hon Roll; MVP JV Baseball Team 90; Architecture.

HERNANDEZ, ESTELLA; Montgomery HS; San Diego, CA; (3); Office Aide; Teachers Aide; Var Capt Crs Cntry; Score Keeper; Stat Sftbl; Var Trk; Cit Awd; Schlrshp Awd; Ed.

HERNANDEZ, ETHEL; Channel Islands HS; Oxnard, CA; (3); 37/574; Hon Roll; Prfct Atten Awd; CSF; MESA; Law.

HERNANDEZ, EVANGELINA S; Dinuba HS; Dinuba, CA; (3); Am Leg Aux Girls St; Treas FBLA; Pres Frsh Cls; Sec Treas Soph Cls; JV Score Keeper; Cit Awd; Hon Roll; Prfct Atten Awd; CSF; Outstndnd Achvtmnt Awds Spansh, Engl, Hstry & Accntng; CA ST U Fresno; Accntng.

HERNANDEZ, FRANCISCO; Wasco Union HS; Wasco, CA; (2); Red Cross Aide; JV Bsbl; JV Bsktbl; Hon Roll; Chem.

HERNANDEZ, FREDDIE; El Camino HS; Oceanside, CA; (4); VP French Clb; SADD; Teachers Aide; Yrbk; Capt Bsbl; Wt Lftg; High Hon Roll; Ntl Merit SF; Baseball All League; Pepperdine; Bus.

HERNANDEZ, GABRIEL; John A O'connell HS; San Francisco, CA; (2); Crs Cntry; Var Vllybl; Var Wrstlng; Arch.

HERNANDEZ, GABRIEL P; Edison HS; Stockton, CA; (1); Spanish Clb; SADD; Teachers Aide; Elect Engr.

HERNANDEZ, GEORGINA; Point Loma HS; San Diego, CA; (4); 46/402; Church Yth Grp; Sec French Clb; VP Intnl Clb; Church Choir; Cit Awd; French Hon Soc; Hon Roll; Pres Acad Fit Awd; CA Polytechncl ST U; Int Dsgn.

HERNANDEZ, GERARDO; Sweetwater Union HS; San Diego, CA; (3); UCSD; Bio.

HERNANDEZ, GILBERT F; Chaffey HS; Ontario, CA; (3); 39/500; FBLA; Band; Hon Roll; Pres Acad Fit Awd; Lit Club; CA ST U; Accntng.

HERNANDEZ, GILBERT M; Bellarmine College Prep; San Jose, CA; (4); 112/305; Nwsp; Intrml Ftbl; Intrml Sftbl; GI Forum Schlrshp Awd; Cal Poly; Civil Engrng.

HERNANDEZ, GINA E; Norco SR HS; Norco, CA; (2); Band; Chorus; Hon Roll; Girls Lg Soph Rep; Cal ST Fullerton; Sci.

HERNANDEZ, HORTENCIA; Winters HS; Winters, CA; (3); Cmnty Wkr; FFA; SADD; Varsity Clb; Chorus; School Musical; Nwsp; Off Frsh Cls; Off Jr Cls; Stu Cncl; Chrprsn FFA Denver Trip; 1st Alt Cmp Royal Ldrshp Conf; Yth Cncl; UCLA; Psych.

HERNANDEZ, INGRID Y; Bell HS; Maywood, CA; (3); JV Tennis; Math Tchr.

HERNANDEZ, IRAZEMA G; Indio HS; Indio, CA; (3); 62/400; Spanish Clb; Chorus; Comp Prgmr.

HERNANDEZ, IRENE; Mission Viejo HS; Mission Viejo, CA; (3); JV Var Tennis; Intl Rel.

HERNANDEZ, ISABEL; John Glenn HS; Norwalk, CA; (4); Dance Clb; Flag Corp; Mrchg Band; Cerritos Coll.

HERNANDEZ, ISRAEL; Lynwood HS; Lynwood, CA; (1); 5/600; Math Clb; Math Tm; Science Clb; Rep Frsh Cls; Crs Cntry; Trk; MESA; Electronics Engr.

HERNANDEZ, ISRAEL; Santa Maria HS; Santa Maria, CA; (3); 110/600; JA; Teachers Aide; Nwsp; Intrml Mgr Bsktbl; Intrml Mgr Ftbl; Cit Awd; Hon Roll; Ntl Merit Ltr; Cal Poly; Bus.

HERNANDEZ JR, JAIRO; Warren HS; Downey, CA; (3); 40/403; Spanish Clb; Socr; Vllybl; Hon Roll; Social Science Club; 4.0 Board; Engrng & Med.

HERNANDEZ, JAMES; Pomona HS; Pomona, CA; (3); 3/228; French Clb; Band; Orch; Var L Socr; Var L Tennis; High Hon Roll; Hon Roll; Prfct Atten Awd; Schlrshp Erthwtch Expdtn; Smi-Fnlst Natl Hspnc Schlr Awds Pgm 90; Physcs Clb; Acadc Olympd; MESA; CSF; MA Inst Of Tech; Mech Engr.

HERNANDEZ, JEVIN A; Palma HS; Salinas, CA; (4); 20/100; Church Yth Grp; Dance Clb; Drama Clb; School Play; Pres Sr Cls; Ftbl; Var Trk; Dnfth Awd; High Hon Roll; Hon Roll; Bank Of Amer Achvt Awd Art; Hartnell Schlrshp; Crtfct Awd Art Hist Outstng Accmplshmnt & Excllnc; Hartnell Coll; Law.

HERNANDEZ, JOHNNY T; Antelope Valley Union HS; Lancaster, CA; (2); JV Wrstlng; Cal Tech; Arch.

HERNANDEZ, JORGE L; Roosevelt HS; Los Angeles, CA; (3); Church Yth Grp; Computer Clb; FBLA; JA; JCL; Math Tm; Office Aide; Red Cross Aide; Varsity Clb; Bsbl; UCLA; Law.

HERNANDEZ, JOSE L; Bell Gardens HS; Bell Gardens, CA; (2); Dance Clb; French Clb; Prfct Atten Awd; Law.

HERNANDEZ, JUAN; Gahr HS; Artesia, CA; (1); Latin Clb; Score Keeper; Socr; Fireman.

HERNANDEZ, JULIA A; Workman HS; Valinda, CA; (3); Church Yth Grp; Hon Roll; Acctnt.

HERNANDEZ, KAREN M; Foothill HS; Tustin, CA; (3); 72/320; Church Yth Grp; Debate Tm; GAA; Var Bsktbl; Var Socr; Var Sftbl; Var Vllybl; High Hon Roll; NHS; CSF; Principals Hnr Roll; Christians & Jews Conf.

HERNANDEZ, KARINA; Castle Park HS; Chula Vista, CA; (2); 26/473; Dance Clb; Cit Awd; Prfct Atten Awd; Tchr Of Bllt Flk Music In CPMS.

HERNANDEZ, KATHY; Christian Center Schl; Antioch, CA; (3); Church Yth Grp; Letterman Clb; Ed Yrbk; Sec Frsh Cls; Pres Soph Cls; Rep Stu Cncl; Capt Bsktbl; Capt Sftbl; High Hon Roll; Bethany Bible Coll.

HERNANDEZ, LAURA; Sacred Heart Of Jesus HS; Los Angeles, CA; (3); GAA; Ed Lit Mag; JV Vllybl; Hon Roll; Commercial Art.

HERNANDEZ, LAURA I; Bell HS; Cudahy, CA; (4); Cmnty Wkr; French Clb; SADD; Band; Mrchg Band; Orch; School Musical; School Play; JR Statesmn Of Amer; Music.

HERNANDEZ, LEE ANDREA; Ramona HS; Riverside, CA; (2); 1/582; Girl Scts; Library Aide; Math Clb; Office Aide; Teachers Aide; Chorus; School Musical; School Play; Hon Roll; Pres Acad Fit Awd; Awds, Certs; U Of Riverside CA; Bus.

HERNANDEZ, LEONARD A; Hanford Union HS; Hanford, CA; (2); Church Yth Grp; Teachers Aide; Band; Mrchg Band; Hon Roll; Spec Interest Swim Tm; FBLA; CSU Fresno; Bus.

HERNANDEZ, LETICIA; Saugus HS; Saugus, CA; (4); 70/400; Pep Clb; Off Jr Cls; Off Sr Cls; Var Cheerldng; Var Pom Pon; San Diego ST U; Elem Tchr.

HERNANDEZ, LIZETTE; Our Lady Loretto-Bishop Conaty HS; Los Angeles, CA; (3); 1/110; VP Frsh Cls; VP Soph Cls; Pres Jr Cls; Pres Stu Cncl; Var Bsktbl; Var Vllybl; Hon Roll; NHS; Prfct Atten Awd; Pres Acad Fit Awd; Scty Wmn Engrs; Math Awds; Frnch Awd; USC; Engrng.

HERNANDEZ, LORAINE; Dixon HS; Dixon, CA; (2); AFS; Sec Jr Cls; Var Cheerldng; Hon Roll; CSF; Gynclgst.

HERNANDEZ, LORNA A; Lemoore Union HS; Lemoore, CA; (2); Art Clb; Hon Roll; Acad Decathlon; Commrcl Art.

HERNANDEZ, LORRAINE; Abraham Lincoln HS; San Jose, CA; (2); 16/386; JV Tennis; PTSA Star Wnnr Schl Atten; Santa Clara Cnty 2nd Harvest Food Bnk; Math.

HERNANDEZ, LUCY A; San Lorenzo HS; San Leandro, CA; (2); JV Bsktbl; JV Sftbl; Var Vllybl.

HERNANDEZ, LUIS; St John Bosco HS; Maywood, CA; (3); 55/210; Cmnty Wkr; Drama Clb; Treas French Clb; Letterman Clb; Service Clb; SADD; Varsity Clb; Band; Jazz Band; Mrchg Band; CSF; Civil Engrng.

HERNANDEZ, LUIS A; Red Bluff Union HS; Red Bluff, CA; (3); Letterman Clb; Rptr Yrbk; Rep Stu Cncl; Var L Bsbl; Var L Ftbl; Wt Lftg; Hon Roll; Lion Awd; Law.

HERNANDEZ, MAGALY; Savanna HS; Buena Park, CA; (3); Pep Clb; Chorus; Swing Chorus; Off Frsh Cls; Off Soph Cls; Jr Cls; Stat Bsktbl; JV Var Gym; Hon Roll; NHS.

HERNANDEZ, MARCIA M; Hilltop HS; Chula Vista, CA; (2); Intnl Clb; Pep Clb; Teachers Aide; Cit Awd; Hon Roll; Tourism.

HERNANDEZ, MARCOS J; Lindsay HS; Lindsay, CA; (3); Church Yth Grp; JV Bsbl; Intrml JV Ftbl; High Hon Roll; Hon Roll; Acad Awd; CSF.

HERNANDEZ, MARGARITA; Abraham Lincoln HS; San Francisco, CA; (2); Office Aide; Teachers Aide; Tennis; Vllybl; Hon Roll; Prfct Atten Awd.

HERNANDEZ, MARIA D; Nogales HS; La Puente, CA; (2); Cal Poly U Achvt Awd; Ldrshp Confrnce; High Hnr Awd; Prfct Attndnce; Cal ST Fullerton; Int Dsgnr.

HERNANDEZ, MARIA E; Ramona HS; Ramona, CA; (2); Latin Clb; CSF; UCSD; Psych.

HERNANDEZ, MARIA G; Bell Gardens HS; Bell Gardens, CA; (3); Office Aide; Teachers Aide; Hon Roll; Prfct Atten Awd; Schl Rcgntn Algebra Gldn St Exam; Math.

HERNANDEZ, MARIA I; Woodland SR HS; Woodland, CA; (3); Spanish Clb; Cit Awd; Hon Roll; NHS; Horses; Reading; Sacramento ST U; Bus.

HERNANDEZ, MARIANNA; Fontana HS; Fontana, CA; (2); Hon Roll; CSF; Outstndng Electricity Stu 88-90; Cal Poly Pomona; Comp.

HERNANDEZ, MARTA E; John W North HS; Riverside, CA; (2); Girl Scts; Library Aide; Service Clb; Spanish Clb; Band; Bsktbl; Ftbl; Socr; Sftbl; Swmmng; Accntng.

HERNANDEZ, MARTHA ELVA; Southwest HS; San Ysidro, CA; (4); Treas Pep Clb; Pres Acad Fit Awd; MECHA Secy; Modeling Club Secy; Senate Rep; Southwestern Coll; Math Tchr.

HERNANDEZ, MARTIN; Lynwood HS; Lynwood, CA; (3); 21/800; Cmnty Wkr; Letterman Clb; Math Clb; Spanish Clb; Varsity Clb; Ed Yrbk; Capt Bsbl; Crs Cntry; Ftbl; Cit Awd; UC Irvine; Elec Engrng.

HERNANDEZ, MELANIE; Rubidoux HS; Riverside, CA; (2); VP FTA; Letterman Clb; Quiz Bowl; Spanish Clb; SADD; Varsity Clb; Off Soph Cls; Var Powder Puff Ftbl; Var JV Tennis; Cit Awd; Multiple Year Award For Outstanding Achievement; U Of CA; Computers.

HERNANDEZ, MELISSA; Ramona HS; Ramona, CA; (2).

HERNANDEZ, MERLE; Southern Ca Christian HS; La Palma, CA; (2); Church Yth Grp; Drama Clb; French Clb; GAA; Spanish Clb; Chorus; JV Bsktbl; Powder Puff Ftbl; Var Vllybl; Hon Roll; Bsktbl Trophy MVP; Bus.

HERNANDEZ, MICHAEL; Lindsay HS; Lindsay, CA; (3); FFA; Letterman Clb; Spanish Clb; Var Bsbl; Var Ftbl; Var Socr; Hon Roll; Frdy Nght Lv; Frsno ST; Elec Engrg.

HERNANDEZ JR, MICHAEL ANTHONY; Madera HS; Madera, CA; (2); JV Var Diving; JV Ftbl; Gym; Score Keeper; Hon Roll; Diving Schlrshp Awd; CA Schlrshp Fed; Vlntr Wrk, Comp Asst; Comp Engrng.

HERNANDEZ, MICHAEL G; Brea Olinda HS; Brea, CA; (1); Engr.

HERNANDEZ, MICHELLE; Lemoore HS; Lemoore, CA; (3); Powder Puff Ftbl; High Hon Roll; Hon Roll; Pep Clb; VP Spanish Clb; Teachers Aide; JV Cheerldng; CSF 88-90; 3rd Pl Cal Bowl; 2nd Pl Clovis Pep Clssc.

HERNANDEZ, MILAGROS C; Culver City HS; Los Angeles, CA; (3); Church Yth Grp; Dance Clb; VP Pres Spanish Clb; Teachers Aide; Off Frsh Cls; Off Soph Cls; Off Jr Cls; Cit Awd; Hon Roll; NHS; Chirons; Peer Cnslr; Work A Thon; Med.

HERNANDEZ, MIRABELLE; Fillmore HS; Fillmore, CA; (3); JV Bsktbl; Var Sftbl; Ventur Coll; Nrs.

HERNANDEZ, MONICA R; Sanger HS; Sanger, CA; (2); Debate Tm; Spanish Clb; Treas Frsh Cls; Treas Jr Cls; JV Bsktbl; Socr; Var Trk; Opt Clb Awd; Pres Acad Fit Awd; Stu Govt & Jrnlsm; Goldn Poet Awd "peace"; Pblc Sci.

HERNANDEZ, MYRNA; Fremont HS; Oakland, CA; (2); Church Yth Grp; Temple Yth Grp; Church Choir; School Play; Cit Awd; High Hon Roll; Hon Roll; Law.

HERNANDEZ, NARY; Castle Park HS; Chula Vista, CA; (1); French Clb; Drill Tm; Princeton U; Economics.

HERNANDEZ, NATALIE; Manteca HS; Lathrop, CA; (2); Pep Clb; Sftbl; STAND; Fri Night Live; Stanislaus; Chld Social Worker.

HERNANDEZ, NOE; South HS; Bakersfield, CA; (3); Cit Awd; Elks Awd; High Hon Roll; Hon Roll; Prfct Atten Awd; U Of CA-SAN Diego; Math.

HERNANDEZ, NORMA I; San Fernando HS; Pacoima, CA; (2); Office Aide; Teachers Aide; Drill Tm; Hon Roll; Magnet Pgm; UCLA; Bus.

HERNANDEZ, OCTAVIO; Thomas Downey HS; Modesto, CA; (2); FFA; JV Bsktbl; JV Ftbl.

HERNANDEZ, OLGA L; King City HS; King City, CA; (4); Acpl Chr; Hon Roll; Frgn Lang Awd; Hartnell Coll; Psych.

HERNANDEZ, ORLANDO; Fontana HS; Fontana, CA; (3); Spanish Clb; Socr; Hon Roll; Chaffey Coll; Archtct.

HERNANDEZ, PIA; Ramona Convent HS; Alhambra, CA; (3); Church Yth Grp; Cmnty Wkr; Hosp Aide; Model UN; Spanish Clb; Teachers Aide; Chorus; Mgr Jr Cls; Trk; High Hon Roll; CSF; Helped Pblsh Sociological Artcls/Pamphlets; Philomatheon Soc; Health.

HERNANDEZ, RAMIRO; Orosi HS; Orosi, CA; (3); Church Yth Grp; Cmnty Wkr; SADD; Varsity Clb; Var Capt Bsbl; Var Ftbl; Powder Puff Ftbl; Wt Lftg; Hon Roll; Fresno ST; Phys Ed Tchr.

HERNANDEZ, RAMON E; Irvine HS; Irvine, CA; (3); 45/520; Hosp Aide; Latin Clb; Stu Cncl; Trk; Hon Roll; UCLA; Bio.

HERNANDEZ, RAY; Rosemead HS; Rosemead, CA; (2); FCA; Rep Lit Mag; Rep Soph Cls; VP Jr Cls; Rep Stu Cncl; JV Bsktbl; L VP Ftbl; High Hon Roll; Hon Roll; Dfnsv Plyr Yr Ftbl Awd.

HERNANDEZ, RAYNE E; Fontana HS; Bloomington, CA; (3); Teachers Aide; Band; Orch; Hon Roll; Pres Schlr; Prtnrshp Prgm; CA Jnr Schlrshp Fed; Accntng.

HERNANDEZ, RICKY; Will C Wood HS; Vacaville, CA; (2); Hon Roll; Photo.

HERNANDEZ, RICKY M; La Sierra HS; Riverside, CA; (3); Boy Scts; Letterman Clb; Math Tm; Var L Golf; Hon Roll; Prfct Atten Awd; Cal Poly Pomona; Htl Mgmt.

HERNANDEZ, RODRIGO; Independence HS; San Jose, CA; (3); JV Var Ftbl; Bus.

HERNANDEZ, ROXANN; Sunset HS; Hayward, CA; (2); Engr.

HERNANDEZ, RUBEN M; Roosevelt HS; Fresno, CA; (3); Cit Awd; Hon Roll; Prfct Atten Awd; Pres Acad Fit Awd; Elctrncs Engrng.

HERNANDEZ, SAL; Fontana HS; Fontana, CA; (2); JV Bsbl; JV Ftbl; Hon Roll.

HERNANDEZ, SANDRA; Morningside HS; Inglewood, CA; (3); French Clb; Latin Clb; Yrbk; Vllybl; Hon Roll; Miss Frshmn 87-88; Hnrs Cls; ITI Cls; CA ST Long Beach; Comp Prgmr.

HERNANDEZ, SANDRA; Sacred Heart Of Jesus HS; Los Angeles, CA; (3); Church Yth Grp; Cmnty Wkr; GAA; Hosp Aide; Speech Tm; Chorus; School Play; Yrbk; Off Sr Cls; Off Stu Cncl; Untd Nghbrhd Orgzn; Los Ang Cnsrvtn Grp; Ntlnl Bskbl At Seattle WA 87; UCLA; Medi.

HERNANDEZ, SANDRA A; Coachella Valley HS; Thermal, CA; (2); Math Clb; San Luis Obispo; Comp Elec.

HERNANDEZ, SANDRA E; Notre Dame Acad; Los Angeles, CA; (3); Cmnty Wkr; Library Aide; Red Cross Aide; Spanish Clb; Chorus; Cit Awd; Hon Roll; Amicae; Queens Coll; USC; Law.

HERNANDEZ, SANDRA L; Victor Valley HS; Victorville, CA; (2); French Clb; Nrsng.

HERNANDEZ, SARI E; Red Bluff HS; Red Bluff, CA; (1); GAA; Bsktbl; JV Sftbl; Vllybl; Hon Roll; Paralegal.

HERNANDEZ, SEAN MARCIANO; Bishop Amat HS; Hacienda Heights, CA; (2); 475/957; Church Yth Grp; Drama Clb; Band; School Play; Rep Jr Cls; JV Ftbl; Hon Roll; Jr NHS; NHS; Music Cert Of Mrt; Young Musicians Guild; US Naval Acad; Poltcl Sci.

HERNANDEZ, SERGIO; Pittsburg HS; Pittsburg, CA; (1); Teachers Aide; Wt Lftg; High Hon Roll; Prfct Atten Awd; Los Medanos Coll.

HERNANDEZ, SONIA; Gonzales HS; Greenfield, CA; (2); Cmnty Wkr; Office Aide; Crs Cntry; Trk; Cit Awd; Prfct Atten Awd; Orale Clb; Interact Clb; San Jose ST; Bus.

HERNANDEZ, STEPHANIE L; Glendale Adventist Acad; Los Angeles, CA; (1); 5/64; Church Yth Grp; FCA; Teachers Aide; Band; Chorus; Rptr Nwsp; VP Frsh Cls; Var Bsktbl; Var Vllybl; High Hon Roll.

HERNANDEZ, STEVE E; River City HS; W Sacramento, CA; (2); Sprt Ed Nwsp; VP Frsh Cls; JV Bsbl; Next Big Steps Math Lab Project Stu Asst; Astronomy.

HERNANDEZ, TERESA; Theodore Roosevelt HS; Los Angeles, CA; (2); Aud/Vis; GAA; Library Aide; Teachers Aide; Varsity Clb; Stage Crew; Bsktbl; Sftbl; High Hon Roll; Hon Roll; Math, Engl & Prncpls Awd; UCLA; Psych.

HERNANDEZ, TONI; Paso Robles HS; Paso Robles, CA; (1); Art Clb; Cmnty Wkr; JV Swmmng; Cit Awd; High Hon Roll; Cal Poly; Real Estate.

HERNANDEZ, TROYLENA; San Jacinto HS; San Jacinto, CA; (3); 14/250; Am Leg Aux Girls St; Church Yth Grp; Drama Clb; Model UN; Pep Clb; Spanish Clb; Speech Tm; Thesps; School Play; Hon Roll; Wells Coll; Med.

HERNANDEZ, VERONICA; Saddleback HS; Santa Ana, CA; (3); FBLA; Girl Scts; Yrbk; Var Sftbl; Future Ldrs Of Amer Mnrty Assn; Mock Trial; Amer Fast Pitch Assn.

HERNANDEZ, VICKIE; Tracy HS; Tracy, CA; (3); Church Yth Grp; Band; Church Choir; Hon Roll; Fresno ST; Doctor.

HERNANDEZ, VIKY M; Gardena HS; Gardena, CA; (2); Drama Clb; U CA Santa Barbara; Comp Sci.

HERNANDEZ, VIVIAN; Saint Michaels HS; Los Angeles, CA; (1); Spanish Clb; Church Choir; Hon Roll; Flag Girls; Mt St Marys Coll; Newscstr.

HERNANDEZ, XOCHITL C; Mission College Prep; Grover City, CA; (4); Cmnty Wkr; Drama Clb; Office Aide; School Musical; School Play; Stage Crew; Variety Show; Yrbk; Crs Cntry; Powder Puff Ftbl; Cmnty Svc Awd; Cal Poly U San Luis Obispo; Vet.

HERNANDEZ, YARIMA; Hueneme HS; Oxnard, CA; (1); Off Frsh Cls; High Hon Roll; Hon Roll; Future Ldrs Amer; Computation.

HERNANDEZ, YESENIA R; Andrew P Hill HS; San Jose, CA; (3); Church Yth Grp; ROTC; Teachers Aide; Rptr Nwsp; Stu Cncl; Hon Roll; Upward Bound Prog SJSU MESA; Supeintndnts Stu Cmmtt ESL Tutor; Blue Rbbn Cmmtt Jr Spellout; UOP; Physcl Ther.

HERNANDEZ, YOLANDA M; Hesperia HS; Hesperia, CA; (2); 4-H; Band; Chorus; 4-H Awd; Hon Roll; U C I; Nursing.

HERNANDEZ, YOLED J; Indio HS; Indio, CA; (1); Drama Clb; French Clb; Church Choir; Color Guard; School Play; Variety Show; Peer Cnslng Natural Helper; USC; Liberal Studies.

HERNANDEZ, YVETTE; Escondido HS; Escondido, CA; (4); 30/286; Cmnty Wkr; Debate Tm; Hosp Aide; Key Clb; Model UN; SADD; Powder Puff Ftbl; Trk; Vllybl; Cit Awd; CSF; U Of Davis CA; Vet Med.

HERNANDEZ, YVETTE C; San Fernando HS; San Fernando, CA; (2); Church Yth Grp; Cmnty Wkr; Teachers Aide; Cit Awd; Hon Roll; UCLA; Law.

HERNANDEZ, YVONNE; Coachella Valley HS; Coachella, CA; (3); 53/487; Debate Tm; Pep Clb; Spanish Clb; Speech Tm; Varsity Clb; School Play; Off Frsh Cls; Chess Clb; Tennis; Hon Roll.

HERNANDEZ, ZENEDITH; San Benito HS; Hollister, CA; (2); Church Yth Grp; Cmnty Wkr; Dance Clb; Pep Clb; Band; Church Choir; Mrchg Band; Sec Bus Profs of Am; VP Soph Cls; Capt Cheerldng; All Grl Band; UC Santa Barbara; Chld Psych.

HERNANDEZ, ZOE M; Castle Park HS; Chula Vista, CA; (1); Cmnty Wkr; French Clb; Girl Scts; Nwsp; JV Cheerldng; Var Tennis; Cit Awd; Prfct Atten Awd; UC Santa Cruz; Marine Bio.

HERNANDEZ-POL, JOSE M; Leland HS; San Jose, CA; (4); 1/410; Boy Scts; Church Yth Grp; Science Clb; Intrml Fld Hcky; Intrml Vllybl; High Hon Roll; Ntl Merit SF; Pres Acad Fit Awd; San Jose GI Forum Schlrshp Wnnr; Boston Globe Carrier Awd Middlesex News; Harvard U; Med.

HERNANDO, JOY L; Southwest HS; San Diego, CA; (2); Co-Ed Yrbk; Mgr Frsh Cls; Med.

HERNANDO, LYNETTE G; St Lawrence Acad; San Jose, CA; (4); 9/26; Office Aide; Teachers Aide; Treas Soph Cls; Sec Sr Cls; Hon Roll; Treas NHS; Spansh III, IV & V Awds; Bnk America Awd Spansh; San Francisco ST U.

HERNANDO, VIMERALD; St Patricks-St Vincents HS; Vallejo, CA; (4); Aud/Vis; French Clb; Service Clb; Stage Crew; Nwsp; Cit Awd; High Hon Roll; Hon Roll; Pres Acad Fit Awd; U CA-SANTA Barbara; Med.

HERNDON, LATASHA; Burlingame HS; Hillsborough, CA; (4); Church Yth Grp; Cmnty Wkr; Hosp Aide; Chorus; Church Choir; School Musical; School Play; Black Stu Unin Pres; Interact Clb; Schlrshp Parents Assoc SMUHSD; Smmr Brdge Pgm UC Berkeley; UC Berkeley; Bio Sci.

HERNDON, NICOLE L; La Sierra HS; Riverside, CA; (4); Church Yth Grp; Letterman Clb; Spanish Clb; Teachers Aide; Band; Mrchg Band; Hon Roll; Hnrs Grad; Track Qn 88; Riverside CC; Law.

HERNENDEZ, MARIA E; Hawthorne HS; Lennox, CA; (1); Church Yth Grp; Dance Clb; Off Frsh Cls; Vllybl; APPI; Layola Marymount; Fshn Dsgn.

HEROLD, JENNIFER; Marina HS; Huntington Bch, CA; (2); Treas German Clb; Pres Girl Scts; Sec JA; Hon Roll; Peer Assistnc Lgu; UCLA; Theater.

HERON, MOLLY E; Santa Barbara HS; Santa Barbara, CA; (2); Church Yth Grp; Rep Frsh Cls; Rep Soph Cls; Mock Trial; Cal Poly San Luis Obispo; Tchr.

HEROPOULOS, ANGELO C; Bellarmine College Prep; Santa Clara, CA; (3); Church Yth Grp; Computer Clb; Debate Tm; NFL; Pres Service Clb; Speech Tm; Teachers Aide; Cheerldng; Ftbl; Socr; Ltr Cmmndtn Prin Ofc; People To People Stu Ambssdr Prgm; Ltr Of Praise & Thanks Cmps Mnstry Prgm; LMU Anapolis; Pol Sci.

HERR, KAN RONNIE; Clovis West HS; Clovis, CA; (2); Church Yth Grp; Computer Clb; Variety Show; VP Soph Cls; JV Socr; JV Vllybl; Hon Roll; Asian Clb; Phy.

HERRBACH, TAMARA; San Bernardino HS; San Bernardino, CA; (2); 5/585; Speech Tm; Off Soph Cls; Off Cit Awd; Off High Hon Roll; Off JETS Awd; Off Rotary Awd; California Scholarship Federation; Interact Club; GSE Geometry.

HERREN, GINA; Monterey HS; Monterey, CA; (2); Cmnty Wkr; Drama Clb; Thesps; Chorus; School Play; Yrbk; Capt Cheerldng; Trk; Wt Lftg; Hon Roll; UCLA; Perfrmng Arts.

HERRERA, ADAM MARCUS; East Bakersfield HS; Bakersfield, CA; (3); Church Yth Grp; Rep French Clb; Rep German Clb; Band; Mrchg Band; Pep Band; School Musical; School Play; Stage Crew; Music; Natl Guard; SYETP 2 Yrs; CA ST Bakersfield; Sci Ed.

HERRERA, ALEJANDRA; Winters HS; Winters, CA; (3); Am Leg Aux Girls St; Cmnty Wkr; Sec FFA; SADD; Rptr Nwsp; Off Frsh Cls; Treas Soph Cls; Rptr Jr Cls; Rptr Sr Cls; Stu Cncl; FFA Mdls Chapter Farmer, Greenhand; Various Other FFA Positions; UCLA; Psych.

HERRERA, AMELIA D; St Genevieve HS; Sylmar, CA; (3); Church Yth Grp; Cmnty Wkr; Pep Clb; Proyecto Amistad Grp Church Invlvd To Get Teenagers Invlvd Doing Many Actvts Away From Drugs; UCLA; Pre-Law.

HERRERA, ANDREA; Fremont Christian HS; Newark, CA; (3); Church Yth Grp; Intnl Clb; Ski Clb; Varsity Clb; Stat Bsbl; Var Socr; Var Vllybl; Hon Roll; 1st Team All Leag Vllybl; MVP Offns, MVP Defns Vllybl.

HERRERA, ANGEL; Cathedral HS; Los Angeles, CA; (4); JA; Math Clb; Spanish Clb; Yrbk; Sec Treas Sr Cls; JV Var Ftbl; High Hon Roll; Hon Roll; NHS; Bus.

HERRERA, ANNA; Maranatha HS; Montebello, CA; (4); 9/103; Church Yth Grp; Spanish Clb; Chorus; Sec Stu Cncl; JV Sftbl; High Hon Roll; CA Schlrshp Fed Lftm Mbr; Numerous Super Rtngs & Rbbns Comptv Piano Fstvls; Poltcl Sci.

HERRERA, AUGIE J; Eisenhower HS; Rialto, CA; (3); Math Clb; Nwsp; Ftbl; Trk.

HERRERA, CARLOS J; Eagle Rock HS; Los Angeles, CA; (3); Am Leg Boys St; Red Cross Aide; Spanish Clb; SADD; Band; Off Jr Cls; Off Sr Cls; Cheerldng; Trk; Hon Roll; Golden St Exam Geom Hnrs; Stanford; Arch.

HERRERA, CARLOS R; Redwood HS; Bullhead City, AZ; (4); Am Leg Boys St; Q&S; Ed Nwsp; Acad Decathln Team 89/90; Essay Gold Mdl; Odd Fellows Schlrshp 90; CA St U Minority Jrnlsm Wrkshp-Edtr; USC; Cmmnctns.

HERRERA, CARMEN LUCIA; Delta HS; Clarksburg, CA; (2); Latin Clb; Treas Jr Cls; Bus Admin.

HERRERA, CECILIA; Adrian Wilcox HS; Alviso, CA; (3); Church Yth Grp; Latin Clb; ROTC; Bsktbl; Powder Puff Ftbl; Var Sftbl; Var Vllybl; Prfct Atten Awd; Math Prgm MESA; Ldrshp Prgm Stanford; UC Davis; Vet Med.

HERRERA, CESAR R; Ontairo HS; Ontario, CA; (3); Latin Clb; Teachers Aide; Varsity Clb; Var Capt Ftbl; Var Wt Lftg; Prfct Atten Awd.

HERRERA, DEBRA A; Montebello HS; Montebello, CA; (1); NFL; Office Aide; Chorus; Orch; JV Bsktbl; Score Keeper; Cit Awd; Prfct Atten Awd; Law.

HERRERA, FERNANDO; Don Bosco Techinical Inst; Downey, CA; (1); 12/244; Church Yth Grp; Cmnty Wkr; Var Score Keeper; JV Var Vllybl; High Hon Roll; Hon Roll; Val; Assoc Cathlc Stu Cncls; Schlrshp Knghts Columbus; Ctznshp Awd; Pedrtrcn.

HERRERA, GILBERT; Pasadena HS; Pasadena, CA; (2); CSF; MESA; Engrng.

HERRERA, GINA; River City HS; W Sacramento, CA; (3); Cmnty Wkr; Rep Sr Cls; Hon Roll; Pres Acad Fit Awd; Recrtn Aide Parks/Cmmnct Svc W Soc; Psych.

HERRERA, GLORIA ISELA; Southwest HS; San Ysidro, CA; (4); 78/498; Teachers Aide; Capt Vllybl; Vrsty Vlby; Mdlng Clb; San Diego ST; Chld Psych.

HERRERA, IMELDA; Artesia HS; Hawaiian Gardens, CA; (1); Treas Frsh Cls; High Hon Roll; Part Time Job; Ucla; Computer Science.

HERRERA, JENNIFER; Mt Eden HS; Hayward, CA; (4); 46/252; Teachers Aide; Ed Nwsp; Var Tennis; Hayward Local 790 Shop Stwrd; UC Davis; Mech Engrng.

HERRERA, JESSICA C; Brawley Union HS; Brawley, CA; (3); Church Yth Grp; Service Clb; SADD; Flag Corp; JV Tennis; Hon Roll; 1988 Rookie Of The Year Jv Tennis; 1989 Letter Band; Friend To Friend Club; Seattle U; International Bus.

HERRERA, JOHN W; Servite HS; Orange, CA; (3); 13/145; Drama Clb; Letterman Clb; Thesps; School Musical; School Play; Nwsp; Lit Mag; Off Jr Cls; Stu Cncl; Swmmng; Lit.

HERRERA, JULIE ANN; Brawley Union HS; Brawley, CA; (2); Band; Mrchg Band; Treas Soph Cls; Treas Jr Cls; Hon Roll; UCLA; Ped.

HERRERA, LOUIS; Coachella Valley HS; Coachella, CA; (3); Math Clb; Varsity Clb; Var Tennis; Hon Roll; Prfct Atten Awd; UC San Luis Obispo; Engr.

HERRERA, LOURDES; Francis H Polytechnic HS; Pacoima, CA; (2); Library Aide; Office Aide; Drill Tm; Yrbk; Cit Awd; Hon Roll; Future Schlrs Pgm; CJSF; Dancer.

HERRERA, MARIA C; Bell HS; Maywood, CA; (3); Variety Show; Rptr Nwsp; Stu Cncl; Cit Awd; High Hon Roll; Hon Roll; Georgetown; Lawyer.

HERRERA, NORA JEAN M; Richard Gahr HS; Cerritos, CA; (2); Var Trk; High Hon Roll; Hnrs Bio & Chem; Blue & Gold Awd Acad Excllnc In Soph Engl; CSULB; RN.

HERRERA, RAMON; Jordan HS; Los Angeles, CA; (3); Off Frsh Cls; Gov Hon Prg Awd; High Hon Roll; Hon Roll; Prfct Atten Awd; Comp Engr.

HERRERA, SALINA C; Faith Christian HS; Marysville, CA; (3); Church Yth Grp; Teachers Aide; Hon Roll; Distngshd Christian Stu; Art.

HERRERA, SUSIE; Upland HS; Upland, CA; (4); Church Yth Grp; Key Clb; Teachers Aide; Yrbk; JV Cheerldng; Var Pom Pon; FIDM; Marketing.

HERRERA, TAMI; St Anthony HS; Long Beach, CA; (4); Cmnty Wkr; Drill Tm; Stu Cncl; Capt Cheerldng; Powder Puff Ftbl; Hon Roll; CSF; UCLA; Pltcl Sci.

HERRERA, VIVIAN; Kingsburg HS; Kingsburg, CA; (1); Church Yth Grp; Band; Mrchg Band; Cheerldng; Tennis; High Hon Roll; Rotary Top 40 Stu Awd; Stanford U; Med.

HERRIGES, JEAN M; Prospect HS; San Jose, CA; (4); 21/186; Cmnty Wkr; Dance Clb; Key Clb; Spanish Clb; NHS; Ntl Merit SF; Pres Acad Fit Awd; Badmntn Vrsty Ltr; UC Santa Cruz; Spanish.

HERRIN, CARLA L; South Bay Lutheran HS; Inglewood, CA; (2); Var Co-Capt Vllybl; High Hon Roll; Mst Inspirational Plaque Vllybl; Law.

HERRING, STEVEN J; St Michaels College Prep HS; Rancho, CA; (1); School Play; Stage Crew; Hon Roll; Jr NHS.

HERRING, SUSANNE; Fowler HS; Delrey, CA; (2); Church Yth Grp; Drama Clb; FCA; Letterman Clb; Pep Clb; Service Clb; Sec Spanish Clb; Band; Mrchg Band; Var L Bsktbl; Rainbow Girls-Worthy Advsr; Fresno ST; Public Cmmnctns.

HERRINGTON, PATRICK W; Archbishop Mitty HS; San Jose, CA; (3); Cmnty Wkr; JV Socr; Var Tennis; High Hon Roll; NHS; Bus.

HERRMANN, MICHELLE R; Thomas Downey HS; Modesto, CA; (3); Acpl Chr; Chorus; Swing Chorus; Pres Madrigal Chrs Grp; Piano Lssns; Coll Clb; Chld Cnslr.

HERRMANN, PATRICIA D; Templeton HS; Templeton, CA; (3); Cmnty Wkr; Drama Clb; FFA; German Clb; GAA; Letterman Clb; Office Aide; Science Clb; SADD; Bsktbl; Jrnlsm.

HERRMANN, RUTH; Loma Linda Acad; Loma Linda, CA; (4); 31/124; Church Yth Grp; Teachers Aide; Chorus; Drill Tm; Off Sr Cls; Hon Roll; NHS; Pres Schlr; Smmr Schlrs Pgm Andrws U; LLU Mrt Schlrshp Awd; Pcfc Un Coll; Elem Ed.

HERRON, JAMIE F; Canyon Springs HS; Moreno Valley, CA; (2); Library Aide; Ski Clb; VP Frsh Cls; Socr; Hon Roll.

HERRON, JENNIFER R; La Habra HS; Whittier, CA; (4); Treas Church Yth Grp; Aud/Vis; VP German Clb; Pep Clb; Sec Science Clb; School Play; NHS; Pr Cnsltr; Top 100; UC San Diego; Marine Bio.

HERRON, JULIE; Beyer HS; Riverbank, CA; (2); Debate Tm; NFL; Pep Clb; Service Clb; Speech Tm; SADD; JV Capt Cheerldng; Var Socr; Var Trk; JV Vllybl; CSF; U CA Berkeley.

HERRON, NATHANIEL; San Diego HS; San Diego, CA; (3); Chess Clb; Church Yth Grp; Office Aide; Co-Ed Rptr Nwsp; High Hon Roll; Hon Roll; Bodyboard; UCSD.

HERRON II, RONALD FRANKLIN; Palmdale HS; Palmdale, CA; (2); FBLA; JA; Crs Cntry; Cit Awd; Hon Roll; Prfct Atten Awd; Bus.

HERSANT, KRISTIN T; San Dieguito HS; Carlsbad, CA; (2); 30/650; Church Yth Grp; Ed Nwsp; VP Stu Cncl; JV Trk; High Hon Roll; Hon Roll; Prfct Atten Awd; Pres Acad Fit Awd; CJSF Pres; CSF.

HERSCH, MARCIE L; Marina HS; Huntington Beach, CA; (3); Key Clb; Pep Clb; Spanish Clb; Var L Cheerldng; Var L Crs Cntry; Stat Socr; JV L Trk; High Hon Roll; Math.

HERSH, HEATHER E; Bakersfield HS; Bakersfield, CA; (3); 6/718; Sec Key Clb; Ski Clb; Sec Stu Cncl; Powder Puff Ftbl; JV Swmmng; Ntl Merit Ltr; CA Schlrshp Federation Gold Seal; Stanford U Summer Quarter Intro Courses; Humanities.

HERSHEY, DANIEL W; Mission San Jose HS; Fremont, CA; (3); Boy Scts; Letterman Clb; Ski Clb; Temple Yth Grp; VP Band; Mrchg Band; Orch; Var Capt Ftbl; JV Swmmng; JV Trk; Gldn St Exam Alg Hnrs; All City Hnr Band; U Of CA; Pre Med.

HERSKOWITZ, ROBYN G; Thomas Downey HS; Modesto, CA; (2); Cmnty Wkr; Debate Tm; Key Clb; NFL; Speech Tm; Temple Yth Grp; Rep Soph Cls; Crs Cntry; Trk; Hon Roll; 800M Co & City Meet Champ-Track; Jr Class Pres 1990; Law.

HERSTOFF, TAMMY D; Huntington Beach HS; Huntington Bch, CA; (2); Girl Scts; Model UN; Red Cross Aide; Temple Yth Grp; Var Fld Hcky; JV Swmmng; High Hon Roll; Soccer AYSO; CA Schlrshp Fed; Skiing; USCD.

HERTZER, KEITH R; Las Lomas HS; Walnut Creek, CA; (3); 1/275; Model UN; Var Swmmng; Hon Roll; Acad Dcthln 3rd Pl Indvdl Cnty Level; UC Berkeley; Comp Sci.

HERTZFELDT, DAN C; Mission San Jose HS; Fremont, CA; (3); Cmnty Wkr; Math Clb; Science Clb; JV Ftbl; High Hon Roll; NHS; Pianist 8 Yrs; UC Davis; Zoology.

HERVEY, PAUL R; Dana Hills HS; Laguna Beach, CA; (1); Cal Poly; Arch.

HERWICK, SHAWN; St Helena HS; Saint Helena, CA; (2); 1/100; Key Clb; Math Clb; Math Tm; Pep Clb; Ski Clb; SADD; Teachers Aide; Varsity Clb; Acpl Chr; Band; CSF; NEDT 99 Prcnt On All Areas; GSE Schl Recognition; CA ST; Med.

HERZ, KARINA; Downey HS; Downey, CA; (3); Cmnty Wkr; Pres JA; Teachers Aide; Ed Yrbk; Capt Cheerldng; Hon Roll; Normaneers Svc Clb; CA ST Fullerton; Bus.

HERZFELD, TISHA; Manteca HS; Manteca, CA; (4); 86/300; Pep Clb; Teachers Aide; Varsity Clb; Treas Jr Cls; Cheerldng; Capt Var Sftbl; Vllybl; MVP Pitcher Vrsty Sftbl; Booster Club Schlrshp; Stanislaus ST U.

HERZSTEIN, KIMBERLY A; Santa Clara HS; Oxnard, CA; (3); 17/145; Varsity Clb; Bsktbl; Swmmng; High Hon Roll; Hon Roll; NHS; U Southern CA; Accntng.

HESKY-ZAKNICH, KATHERINE S; North Salinas HS; Salinas, CA; (4); 11/380; Drama Clb; Rep Stu Cncl; Stat Bsktbl; JV Swmmng; High Hon Roll; NHS; Pres Acad Fit Awd; Hnrs-Golden St Exam Alg; Top 100 Schlrs Awd Rotary Club; Stu Yr 89-90; Mt St Marys Coll; Scndry Ed.

HESLEP, JENNIFER L; Selma HS; Selma, CA; (3); 5/200; Am Leg Aux Girls St; Church Yth Grp; Intnl Clb; SADD; Band; Mrchg Band; School Play; Nwsp; Pres Sr Cls; JV Powder Puff Ftbl; CA All St Band; Acad Decathlon; Prom Cmmttee; Tulare Symphony; CSF Treas; Float Cmmttee; Tchr.

HESS, AARON H; Elk Grove HS; Elk Grove, CA; (4); 83/575; Trk; Pres Acad Fit Awd; CA ST Fair 2nd Pl Painting 90; U OR Eugene; Law.

HESS, CHRISTIAN A; Davis SR HS; Davis, CA; (3); Spanish Clb; Pres Acad Fit Awd; St Schlr; Congrssnl Schlr; U Of CA; Anthropology.

HESS, EMILY C; Brea-Olinda HS; Brea, CA; (1); Stat Bsbl; Stat Bsktbl; Stat Score Keeper; JV Tennis.

HESS JR, JAMES C; Mater Dei HS; Anaheim, CA; (3); Boy Scts; Church Yth Grp; French Clb; ROTC; Ski Clb; JV Tennis; Hon Roll; People To People Stu Ambssdr Orient Smmr 90; Bus Admin.

HESS, JENNIFER D; Rio Americano HS; Carmichael, CA; (3); 84/290; Capt Drill Tm; School Play; Readers Theatre; Dramatic Arts.

HESSLING, JENNIFER A; Desert HS; Edwards, CA; (2); Var L Tennis; Hon Roll; Jr NHS; Pres Acad Fit Awd; U Of AZ; Bus Admin.

HESSON, JANINE R; Roseville HS; Rocklin, CA; (2); Church Yth Grp; Dance Clb; Office Aide; SADD; Drill Tm; DARE; Sierra Coll.

HESSON, NATANYA; Lompoc HS; Suisun, CA; (2); Yrbk; JV Bsktbl; Var L Trk; JV Vllybl; High Hon Roll; Pres Acad Fit Awd; Pres Schlr; CA Schlrshp Fed; Math.

HESSON, STEPHANIE; Lincoln HS; Stockton, CA; (1); Church Yth Grp; Cheerldng; Pom Pon; Spcl Olympcs Hlpr; Cla Rep 93; U Of Santa Barbara; Chld Psych.

HETHCOAT, SCOTTY A J; Red Bluff Union HS; Red Bluff, CA; (1); FFA; Ftbl; Wt Lftg; Wrstlng; High Hon Roll; Hon Roll; Tm Rpng Hrsbck Rdng; Bsbl Lttl Lg; Engnrng.

HETHCOCK, JULIE; Modesto Christian HS; Modesto, CA; (3); Church Yth Grp; Teachers Aide; Mgr Yrbk; Cit Awd; High Hon Roll; Pres Acad Fit Awd; Intl Frgn Lang Awd Wnnr; Psych.

HETRICK, LE ANN A; Oak Ridge HS; El Dorado Hills, CA; (1); Art Clb; Church Yth Grp; 4-H; Var Swmmng; Hon Roll; Pres Acad Fit Awd; Envrnmntlst Club; 4-H Offcr; Hrs Show Rbbn Wnnr; UC Davis.

HETTINGA, IAN B; Sierra Vista HS; Baldwin Park, CA; (3); French Clb; Letterman Clb; Speech Tm; Varsity Clb; L Var Swmmng; L Var Wrstlng; Hon Roll; Opt Clb Awd; Vrsty Swmmng Mst Insprtnl 90 & Iron Man Of Yr 89; Arch.

HEU, CHANG P; Clovis West HS; Pinedale, CA; (2); JV Ftbl; Var Trk; Hon Roll; UC Berkeley; Aerospace Engrng.

HEU, VANG; Edison HS; Pinedale, CA; (3); Chess Clb; Church Yth Grp; Cmnty Wkr; Math Clb; Model UN; Tennis; High Hon Roll; Southeast Asian Clb; Odyssy Mnd; JETS; Bus Admin.

HEUSNER, PATRICIA; Santa Fe Christian HS; San Diego, CA; (4); 1/45; Church Yth Grp; Capt Var Cheerldng; Powder Puff Ftbl; L Var Trk; High Hon Roll; NHS; Ntl Merit Ltr; Wheaton Coll; Elem Educ.

HEVANSAVATH, SENGSOURISACK N; Edison HS; Stockton, CA; (2); Church Choir; Hon Roll.

HEVEL, DEREK F; Wilcox HS; Sunnyvale, CA; (2); 14/410; Boy Scts; Spanish Clb; Band; Mrchg Band; Yrbk; CSF; Frshmn Class Math Awd; U CA Davis; Engr.

HEVER, GAL; Thousand Oaks HS; Newbury Park, CA; (3); 27/600; Var Bsktbl; High Hon Roll; Hon Roll; Prfct Atten Awd; UCLA Stanford; Medicine Law.

HEVERLY, MELISSA; Valley Christian HS; Pleasanton, CA; (2); Church Yth Grp; French Clb; Pres Soph Cls; Var Capt Bsktbl; Sftbl; Vllybl; High Hon Roll; NHS; Pres Acad Fit Awd; Most Valuable Player In Varsity Volleyball; Varsity Basketball; 1st Tm All League In Varsity Volleybal.

HEVRON, CHRISTINA M; Bella Vista HS; Orangevale, CA; (4); 4/321; Art Clb; French Clb; Science Clb; SADD; French Hon Soc; Hon Roll; NHS; Awd Mdl For Excllnce In P E 89; Awd Cert Numerous Cls 87-90; Physics Day At CA ST U Sacramento; U Of CA Davis; Chemcl Engrng.

HEWETT, ERIC B; Modesto HS; Modesto, CA; (2); Church Yth Grp; Teachers Aide; Band; Jazz Band; Mrchg Band; Pep Band; School Play; JV Crs Cntry; JV Trk; All Am Hall Of Fame Band Hnrs; Play Trumpt Modesto Perf Arts; Musc.

HEWITT, BONNIE A; Marina HS; Huntington Beach, CA; (2); Aud/Vis; GAA; Pep Clb; Service Clb; Spanish Clb; Varsity Clb; Color Guard; Flag Corp; Cit Awd; Hon Roll; Vrsty Bdmntn Ltr; Vrsty Color Guard; Most Improvd Bdmnt; UC; Comm.

HEWITT, BRYAN W; Grossmont HS; El Cajon, CA; (2); 160/465; Boy Scts; Cmnty Wkr; Off Frsh Cls; Off Soph Cls; Stu Cncl; Var Ftbl; Var Trk; Var Wt Lftg; DAR Awd; Pepperdine; Psych.

HEWKO, ERIN G; Dana Hills HS; Dana Point, CA; (3); Varsity Clb; JV Socr; Var Trk; Var Vllybl; Hon Roll.

HEXBERG, NOELLE A; Los Alamitos HS; Los Alamitos, CA; (3); Church Yth Grp; Spanish Clb; Teachers Aide; Rep Frsh Cls; Var Diving; JV Swmmng; JV Tennis; JV Vllybl; Frgn Lang.

HEYDA, MELINDA J; Louisville HS; West Hills, CA; (1); Church Yth Grp; Dance Clb; Variety Show; High Hon Roll; Grad Of John Robert Powers Mdlng Schl; Mdlng.

HEYDON, KATY E; Poway HS; Poway, CA; (3); Church Yth Grp; Pep Clb; SADD; Varsity Clb; Var JV Tennis; Cit Awd; Hon Roll; U San Diego; Engl.

HEYDT, MARGARET A; Albany HS; Albany, CA; (1); Orch; School Play; Treas Yrbk; Hon Roll; Soc For Creatv Anacronism; UC Berkeley; Archaeology.

HEYERMAN, ELIZABETH L; Enterprise HS; Palo Cedro, CA; (3); Band; Jazz Band; Mrchg Band; Pep Band; Lit Mag; Show Choir; Lit Fest Awds; Scripps; Lit.

HEYFRON, MARY; Shasta HS; Redding, CA; (2); 22/425; Band; Drm Mjr(t); Mrchg Band; School Musical; JV Swmmng; High Hon Roll; Anti-Drug Orgnztns; Law.

HEYN, TYSON; Miraleste HS; Palos Verdes, CA; (4); German Clb; Math Clb; Model UN; Service Clb; Ed Yrbk; Hist Stu Cncl; Hon Roll; NHS; Prin Advsry Comm; AATG Book Awd; YMCA Volunteer; Published Cmptr Prgm PCM Magazine.

HEYNIO, AMY; Palm Springs HS; Palm Desert, CA; (3); Church Yth Grp; FCA; GAA; Intnl Clb; Latin Clb; Math Clb; Swmmng; Hon Roll; Pres Acad Fit Awd; Most Imprvd Swmmr; Slvr Sands Awd Sci; Natl Latin Awd; Princeton; Pre-Med.

HIATT, ADRIENNE L; Monterey Bay Acad; Freedom, CA; (3); 29/95; German Clb; U Of Santa Cruz; Marine Bio.

HIATT, ANDREW D; Mission Viejo HS; Mission Viejo, CA; (3); 45/445; Boy Scts; VP Pres Church Yth Grp; Var Crs Cntry; Var L Trk; High Hon Roll; Bus Mgmt.

HIATT, JASON; Cardinal Newman HS; Cloverdale, CA; (3); 8/78; Cmnty Wkr; JA; Spanish Clb; High Hon Roll; Hon Roll; Peer Fcltr Club.

HIATT, REGINA F; Montclair HS; Montclair, CA; (3); Church Yth Grp; FHA; Intnl Clb; Library Aide; SADD; Church Choir; Gftd/Tlntd Ed; Acctng.

HIBBARD, MICHAEL T M; Hogan HS; Vallejo, CA; (2); Office Aide; Science Clb; Band; Church Choir; Drm Mjr(t); Jazz Band; Mrchg Band; Nwsp; High Hon Roll; NHS; Math Tutor; Schltc Achvt Awds; Solano Cty Hnr Band; Harvard; Bus Admin.

HIBBERT, GEOFFREY; Dana Hills HS; Laguna Niguel, CA; (3); Church Yth Grp; Cmnty Wkr; Math Tm; Stage Crew; Rep Jr Cls; Rep Sr Cls; Rep Stu Cncl; Hon Roll; NHS; Ntl Merit Schol; Engrng.

HIBBERT, LIANNE; The Athenian Schl; Oakland, CA; (3); Cmnty Wkr; Girl Scts; Band; Jazz Band; Orch; School Play; Sec Jr Cls; JV Bsktbl; JV Swmmng; Tennis; Minority Awareness Prog; Better Chance Prog; Cngrssnl Yth Ldrshp Cncl.

HIBBITS, BRANDEE MARIE; Lompoc HS; Lompoc, CA; (4); 3/320; Cmnty Wkr; 4-H; Letterman Clb; Band; Stat Bsbl; L Var Socr; JV Var Vllybl; Cit Awd; Elks Awd; High Hon Roll; Life Mem CA Schlrshp Fed; Acad Decthln Team; Bank Of Amer Lbrl Arts Plaque Wnnr; U Redlands.

HIBBS, ROSS MICHAEL; Marin Catholic HS; Fairfax, CA; (4); 12/197; Ed Nwsp; High Hon Roll; NHS; Prfct Atten Awd; Pres Acad Fit Awd; Rotary Awd; CA Acad Decthln; CSF; CA Poly ST U; Comp Sci.

HICKEY, STEPHANIE M; Estancia HS; Costa Mesa, CA; (1); Church Yth Grp; Pep Clb; Crs Cntry; Trk; Pres Acad Fit Awd; BSU; Fash Dsgnr.

HICKINBOTHAM, CHARLES C; Lincoln HS; Stockton, CA; (3); VP Computer Clb; Teachers Aide; Stage Crew; Phtg Nwsp; High Hon Roll; Close-Up VP/Sec; SPEBQSA; Cinematogrphy.

HICKMAN, DAVID C; El Camino Real HS; West Hills, CA; (2); Math Clb; JV L Trk; JV L Wrstlng.

HICKMAN, ERIC R; Merced Union HS; Merced, CA; (3); Library Aide; Office Aide; Rptr Yrbk; Hon Roll; Prfct Atten Awd; Yng Amer Bowling Alliance; Locl Womens Bowling Assn Schlrshp; Muscular Dystrophy Assn Bowl-A-Thons.

HICKOK, MELISSA S; Escondido HS; Escondido, CA; (3); 7/818; Pres Key Clb; Treas Science Clb; High Hon Roll; Jr NHS; NHS; Pres Awd Acad Ftns; 1st Pl Schl Wrtng Contest; Syracuse; Jrnlsm.

HICKOX, MISTY L; Temple Christian HS; Quail Valley, CA; (1); Church Yth Grp; Capt Cheerldng; Var Score Keeper; Var Vllybl; Hon Roll; Mt San Jacinto Coll For Off Campus Classes Credit/No Credit; CA U San Diego; Behavioral Sci.

HICKS, AMANDA Y; Dixon HS; Dixon, CA; (1); Drama Clb; 4-H; Math Clb; Math Tm; Band; Mrchg Band; School Play; Variety Show; Hon Roll; UC Davis; Forestry.

HICKS, ANGELA A; Clovis HS; Clovis, CA; (2); 2/688; Variety Show; Powder Puff Ftbl; High Hon Roll; Acad Block C; CA Schlrshp Fndtn; Math Engrng Sci Achvt; Bus.

HICKS, BETH A; L A Baptist HS; Spokane, WA; (3); Lit Mag; Stat Bsbl; Stat Crs Cntry; JV Trk; High Hon Roll; Hon Roll; NHS; Top Grade Eng Awd; Excl In Math; Surgeon.

HICKS, BETH J; Kingsburg Joint Union HS; Kingsburg, CA; (3); VP FFA; High Hon Roll; Hon Roll; Jr NHS; Pres Acad Fit Awd; Acad Blokc K Awd; Schlrhsp Awd; Med.

HICKS, BIANCA M; El Cerrito HS; Richmond, CA; (3); Drama Clb; Speech Tm; Teachers Aide; Thesps; Flag Corp; Rep Jr Cls; Tennis; Hon Roll; Modeling; Partnership Student; Writer; Howard U; Architecture.

HICKS, CHARLES M; Las Plumas HS; Berry Creek, CA; (1); Church Yth Grp; 4-H; Bsktbl; JV Crs Cntry; JV Trk; High Hon Roll; Hon Roll; Epsilon Pi Tau Cert Of Merit Electrncs; Cert Of Proficiency-Elctrnc Tech; U Of CA; Aerosp Engrng.

HICKS, CHERON R; John Muir HS; Pasadena, CA; (2); Drum Corps; Med.

HICKS, CHRISTINA; Notre Dame HS; Moreno Valley, CA; (1); 76/165; JV Bsktbl; JV Vllybl; Co-MPV For Bsktbl; UCLA; Actress.

HICKS, CORY A; Hoopa Valley HS; Salyer, CA; (3); 16/50; Teachers Aide; Band; JV Bsktbl; Var Golf; JV Trk; USAF; CA Hwy Ptrl.

HICKS, DALLAS; Central Unified HS; Fresno, CA; (1); Computer Clb; Ski Clb; Yrbk; Stu Cncl; Hon Roll.

HICKS, DORINDA; Washington Prepartory HS; Los Angeles, CA; (3); Computer Clb; Dance Clb; English Clb; Math Clb; Math Tm; Service Clb; Spanish Clb; Teachers Aide; Drill Tm; Off Frsh Cls; DARE Pgm Pres; Law.

HICKS, ELISA; Marantha HS; Duarte, CA; (4); 10/101; Church Yth Grp; Cmnty Wkr; Teachers Aide; Co-Capt Flag Corp; High Hon Roll; Hon Roll; Var Capt Pep Flags; CSF; Marriage/Fmly/Chld Cnslr.

HICKS, ELISHA L; Marlborough Schl; Los Angeles, CA; (4); Church Yth Grp; Hosp Aide; SADD; Lit Mag; Cit Awd; High Hon Roll; NHS; Ntl Merit Ltr; Young Black Schlrs; Jack & Jill Amer Treas; Psych.

HICKS, JANEL O; Calvary Christian Schl; Ridgecrest, CA; (4); Pep Clb; Ski Clb; Nwsp; Yrbk; VP Pres Stu Cncl; Var Bsktbl; Var Cheerldng; JV Sftbl; JV Var Vllybl; Hon Roll; Oral Roberts U; Bus Mgmt.

HICKS, JENNIFER R; Arlington HS; Riverside, CA; (2); Sftbl; Law.

HICKS, JOHN D; Elsinore HS; Lake Elsinore, CA; (3); Intnl Clb; Math Tm; Pep Clb; Teachers Aide; Chrmn Stu Cncl; JV Bsktbl; Var Crs Cntry; Var Tennis; Var Trk; NHS; Tchng.

HICKS, JULIE A; Forest Lake Christian Schl; Auburn, CA; (2); Var Cheerldng; Var Sftbl; Cit Awd; Miyagi Gymnstcs Acad Team; Nutrtn.

HICKS, MARY S; Fred C Beyer HS; Modesto, CA; (3); JV Var Sftbl; Hon Roll; U Of San Diego; Marine Bio.

HICKS, SHANNON; Surprise Valley HS; Cedarville, CA; (3); Cmnty Wkr; Sec FBLA; GAA; Office Aide; Speech Tm; Ed Nwsp; Pres Jr Cls; JV Var Vllybl; Lion Awd; Voice Dem Awd; Lssn Coll; Bus Adm.

HICKS, SHARI; Golden Sierra HS; Pilot Hill, CA; (4); 4/88; Ed Yrbk; Treas Sr Cls; Stu Cncl; Var L Bsktbl; Var Powder Puff Ftbl; Hon Roll; CSF; Sonoma ST U; Envrnmntl Studies.

HICKS, STACY LYN; Dan Antonio Lugo HS; Chino Hills, CA; (2); Church Yth Grp; Girl Scts; Science Clb; NHS; CSF.

HICKS, STEPHANIE M; Walnut HS; Walnut, CA; (4); Church Yth Grp; Dance Clb; FBLA; Pep Clb; SADD; JV Capt Cheerldng; Var Capt Pom Pon; Hon Roll; Prfct Atten Awd; CA Poly San Luis Obispo; Engrn.

HICKS, TAMARA L; North HS; Bakersfield, CA; (2); 10/369; FCA; Key Clb; Pres Chorus; Pres Frsh Cls; Stu Cncl; High Hon Roll; Hon Roll; Jr NHS; NHS; Church Yth Grp; Bakersfield JR Miss; Young Woman Of Yr 90; CSF; Azusa Pacific U; Pre-Med.

HICKS, TESSA W; Venice HS; Venice, CA; (1); Cmnty Wkr; Dance Clb; JV Bsktbl; Pres Soph Cls; Peace Club; Earth Day Cmmtte.

HICKSON, HEATHER M; Santa Teresa HS; San Jose, CA; (1); Church Yth Grp; 4-H; German Clb; JA; Ski Clb; SADD; Band; Mrchg Band; Hon Roll; Prfct Atten Awd; Animals.

HIDALGO, CLAUDIA I; Susan Miller Dorsey HS; Los Angeles, CA; (2); Church Yth Grp; Dance Clb; Hosp Aide; Library Aide; Office Aide; Teachers Aide; Hon Roll; Prfct Atten Awd; Santa Barbara U; Child Psych.

HIDALGO, ELIZABETH; Downey HS; Downey, CA; (1); Vllybl; Bus.

HIDALGO, JENNIFER; Oxnard HS; Oxnard, CA; (3); 35/427; Intnl Clb; Stu Cncl; Var L Socr; Cit Awd; Hon Roll; Prfct Atten Awd; Pres Acad Fit Awd; Math, Engrng, Sci & Achvt Clb; Interact Clb; Pepperdine U; Bus.

HIDALGO, LETICIA; Pioneer HS; Whittier, CA; (2); 23/377; Church Yth Grp; Drill Tm; Stu Cncl; Score Keeper; High Hon Roll; Treas ASB 90-91; Rec Sec Grl Lg 90-91; Psych.

HIDALGO, RAYMOND P; Mount Pleasant HS; San Jose, CA; (3); Church Yth Grp; JA; Library Aide; JV Ftbl; Var L Socr; Hon Roll; US Naval Sea Cadets Corp; Santa Clara U; Pre-Med.

HIDALGO, ROBERTO V; Chula Vista HS; Chula Vista, CA; (2); Cmnty Wkr; Math Tm; Office Aide; Teachers Aide; Nwsp; Wt Lftg; Engr.

HIDEY, LAURIE; Ramona HS; Riverside, CA; (4); 97/497; Church Yth Grp; Girl Scts; Swmmng; RCC; Law.

HIEB, MARIANNE; Monterey Bay Acad; Las Vegas, NV; (3); Church Yth Grp; Cmnty Wkr; French Clb; Red Cross Aide; Ski Clb; Chorus; Church Choir; School Musical; Swing Chorus; Hon Roll; Esp Piano Solo Rectls & Quest Vcl Wrk; Acad Decathln 1st Pl Team Santa Cruz Cnty; Med.

HIGASHI, WAYNE E; Andrew Hill HS; San Jose, CA; (3); 40/380; Teachers Aide; Varsity Clb; Phtg Yrbk; Pres Jr Cls; JV Var Ftbl; JV Var Wrstlng; Hon Roll; Pres Acad Fit Awd; ASB Pres; CCS CIF Schltc Achvt Team; Planning Cmmtte Ldrshp Conf; Bio.

HIGBEE, JASON P; Shafter HS; Bakersfield, CA; (3); 4/215; Am Leg Boys St; Church Yth Grp; FCA; Pres Key Clb; Letterman Clb; Pep Clb; Ski Clb; Varsity Clb; Capt Var Bsktbl; Capt Var Ftbl; UCLA; Sprts Med.

HIGDON, NICOLA S; Grossmont HS; La Mesa, CA; (1); Church Yth Grp; Band; Chorus; Orch; Pep Band; High Hon Roll; Musician Of Yr Awd; Oboist Civic Youth Orch; Music.

HIGGINBOTHAM, COLBY G; Lindsay HS; Lindsay, CA; (3); Library Aide; Spanish Clb; Intrml JV Ftbl; Hon Roll; Acad Decathln.

HIGGINBOTHAM, CYNTHIA; Hamilton Union HS; Orland, CA; (3); Drama Clb; 4-H; FFA; Pep Clb; Quiz Bowl; SADD; School Musical; Capt Cheerldng; Hon Roll; Rep Stu Cncl; Singing; Acting; Dancing; University; Voice/Acting.

HIGGINBOTHAM, DEAN; Capistrano Valley HS; Mission Viejo, CA; (4); 21/500; Boy Scts; Church Yth Grp; BYU; Comp Sci.

HIGGINBOTHAM, JAYSON J; Highlands HS; North Highlands, CA; (1); 4/530; Dance Clb; JV Capt Crs Cntry; JV Trk; High Hon Roll; Prfct Atten Awd; Pres Acad Fit Awd; Cit Awd; Stat Swmmng; Presdntl Phys Ftns Awd; MVP Crss Cntry; Aeronautical Engrng.

HIGGINBOTHAM, JENNIFER; Wasco Union HS; Wasco, CA; (2); FFA; Chorus; Rep Frsh Cls; Rep Soph Cls; Tennis; Hon Roll; Exploresr Prog; Jr Farmers; Bakersfield Coll; Sheriffs Dpty.

HIGGINS, ANDREA M; Del Campo HS; Fair Oaks, CA; (3); 30/446; Art Clb; Pep Clb; Rptr Nwsp; Var Cheerldng; NHS; Advncd Drawing Class; CSF; CA Coll Arts & Crafts; Dsgn.

HIGGINS, ANDREW D; Lowell HS; San Francisco, CA; (3); Boy Scts; Jazz Band; Orch; Musician.

HIGGINS, BARBARA H; Grace M Davis HS; Modesto, CA; (2); Church Yth Grp; French Clb; Band; Church Choir; Mrchg Band; Orch; Cit Awd; Church Orchestra; Kindergarten Teacher.

HIGGINS, BECKY; Mother Lode Christian Schl; Twain Harte, CA; (1); 1/15; Church Yth Grp; Drama Clb; Office Aide; Chorus; Church Choir; Rep Frsh Cls; Var Sftbl; JV Vllybl; High Hon Roll.

HIGGINS, BRIDGETTE; Manteca HS; Manteca, CA; (3); French Clb; Key Clb; Band; Hon Roll; REACH Clb; BETA Clb; Med.

HIGGINS, CARMEN R; Castle Park HS; Chula Vista, CA; (4); Church Yth Grp; JA; Teachers Aide; Rptr Nwsp; Prfct Atten Awd; San Diego ST U; Cvl Lwyr.

HIGGINS, CHANDRA; Mt Carmel HS; San Diego, CA; (2); Church Yth Grp; Hosp Aide; Flag Corp; Mrchg Band; Hon Roll; Medcl.

HIGGINS, CHRISTINA; Mother Lode Christian HS; Twain Harte, CA; (3); Church Yth Grp; Drama Clb; Band; Chorus; Mrchg Band; Pep Band; Rep Soph Cls; Var Sftbl; Hon Roll; Nutritionist.

HIGGINS, HOLLY A; Washington HS; Fremont, CA; (3); 4-H; Psych.

HIGGINS, JULIA KAY; Hesperia HS; Hesperia, CA; (3); Church Yth Grp; French Clb; Key Clb; Nwsp; Var Socr; Hon Roll; Univ & Jrnlsm Club; UCLA; Comm.

HIGGINS, MATTHEW K; Hespera HS; Hesperia, CA; (2); Church Yth Grp; ROTC; Spanish Clb; JV Socr; High Hon Roll; Hon Roll; USAFA; Aerntcs.

HIGGINS, PHILL J; Roseville HS; Roseville, CA; (2); 117/512; Spanish Clb; Var Ftbl; Hon Roll; Pres Acad Fit Awd; Soccer; Law.

HIGGINS JR, WILLIAM CLIVE; Bishop Amat HS; La Puente, CA; (3); Letterman Clb; Math Clb; Varsity Clb; Band; Mrchg Band; Pep Band; Var L Crs Cntry; Trk; High Hon Roll; NHS; CSF; Band Ofcr; Elec Engrg.

HIGGINSON, SARAH R; El Camino HS; Oceanside, CA; (1); Drama Clb; Thesps; Hon Roll; Kiwanis Awd; Advertising.

HIGHAM, MELANIE; Mission Viejo HS; Mission Viejo, CA; (1); 32/455; Pres Church Yth Grp; JV Bsktbl; Hon Roll; Intl Baccalaurette; CSF; BYU.

HIGHTOWER, AMY J; Red Bluff Union HS; Red Bluff, CA; (2); French Clb; Hon Roll; Dance; Theater Prdctn Cls; Art Courses; Csmtlgy.

HIGHTOWER, HEATHER M; Casa Roble Fundamental HS; Orangevale, CA; (4); 3/400; Hist French Clb; Church Choir; School Musical; Stu Cncl; Ntl Merit SF; Church Yth Grp; Cmnty Wkr; Drama Clb; Stage Crew; JV Crs Cntry; Acad Decathlon 3rd Co Overal; Sr Hmcmng Princess; Mock Ct Outstndng Spkr; Fri Nite Live-Pub Chair; Pepperdine U; Psych.

HIGHTOWER, JESSE B; Mojave HS; Mojave, CA; (1); VP Frsh Cls; JV Bsbl; Capt Ftbl; Var Wt Lftg; MI U; Phys Ed.

HIGMAN, RYAN D; Warren HS; Downey, CA; (2); Church Yth Grp; Service Clb; Speech Tm; Church Choir; School Musical; School Play; JV Capt Vllybl; Hon Roll; NHS; Rotary Awd; Jnr Statesmn; Pre-Med.

HIGUCHI, KEIKO; San Domenico Schl; Rnch Palos Verdes, CA; (4); Cmnty Wkr; Spanish Clb; Orch; Ed Yrbk; Var Socr; High Hon Roll; Hon Roll; NHS; Opt Clb Awd; Pres Acad Fit Awd; Marin Youth Vol Awd; Fndr Amnsty Intl Chapter Schl; Duo Pianist Soloist Marin Yth Orchstr; UC Berkeley.

HIGUERA, ANDREA; El Toro HS; El Toro, CA; (4); 1/522; Sec VP Key Clb; Ed Yrbk; VP Sr Cls; Co-Capt L Pom Pon; High Hon Roll; Ntl Merit Ltr; Val; Church Yth Grp; VP Frsh Cls; VP Soph Cls; Homcmng Qn; Natl Hispanic Schlr Wnnr; So CA Yth Ctznshp Smnr Outstndng Partcpnt; Stanford U; Intl Relations.

HILARIDES, TERESA L; Tahoe Truckee HS; Truckee, CA; (4); 11/84; Church Yth Grp; Sec Nwsp; Bsktbl; Powder Puff Ftbl; Hon Roll; CSF; Sty Of Mnth, Bus 89; Brigham Young U; Bilingual Educ.

HILARIO, RACHEL; St Francis HS; Mountain View, CA; (1); 66/388; Church Yth Grp; Intnl Clb; SADD; Band; Church Choir; Mrchg Band; Pep Band; JV Trk; Hon Roll; Tae Kwon Do Karate; Stanford U; Med.

HILBERG, KENNETH L; East Union HS; Manteca, CA; (3); Church Yth Grp; Science Clb; Band; Jazz Band; Mrchg Band; Wrstlng; Hon Roll; Drum & Bugle Corps; Music Tchr.

HILBERT, BECKY; Strathmore Union HS; Porterville, CA; (3); 23/77; Church Yth Grp; Office Aide; Chorus; Color Guard; Drill Tm; Variety Show; VP Soph Cls; Var Swmmng; Hon Roll; NHS; Cnslr Chrstn Yth Cmps; Smmr Mssn Trps; Sun Schl Tchr; Own Bus.

HILBURN, PETER Z; Trinity HS; Douglas City, CA; (2); JV Ftbl; JV Trk; Intrml Wt Lftg; Var Wrstlng; Hon Roll; Peer Hlpr; Air Force Acad.

HILDEBRAND, WILLIAM M; Oak Grove HS; San Jose, CA; (4); Cmnty Wkr; Teachers Aide; Oakgrove Pop Warner Ftbl Natl Chmpns 87-88, Northwest Rgnl Chmpns 86-87; Evergreen CC; Law Enfrcmnt.

HILDEBRANDT, MATTHIAS B; Culver City HS; Culver City, CA; (3); Band; Jazz Band; Mrchg Band; Orch; Wt Lftg; High Hon Roll; Golden St Exam Awd Geomtry; Stu Of Mnth; Bus.

HILDEBRANDT, MERIAH J; Nevada Union HS; Nevada City, CA; (3); SADD; Cit Awd; Hon Roll; UC Davis; Med.

HILE, JENNIFER L; Woodbridge HS; Irvine, CA; (2); Sec AFS; Cmnty Wkr; Treas Spanish Clb; Pres Stu Cncl; Var Socr; Cmnty Wkr; Vllybl; Cit Awd; High Hon Roll; Lion Awd; 2nd Tm All Leag Hnrs; Envrnmntl Law.

HILGER, LES G; Bishop O'dowd HS; Alameda, CA; (3); 8/210; Art Clb; Debate Tm; Hosp Aide; Science Clb; Service Clb; Ski Clb; Off Frsh Cls; Off Sr Cls; Stu Cncl; Var Capt Swmmng; Rtry Yth Ldrshp Awd Schlrshp; Amnsty Intl Pres; JSA VP; Cornell; Bio Sci.

HILL, ADAM E; Wm S Hart HS; Valencia, CA; (2); Stage Crew; Var Golf; JV Capt Socr.

HILL, ANDREA J; Apple Valley HS; Apple Valley, CA; (2); Cit Awd; Hon Roll; CA U; Bus.

HILL, ANGELA C; Walnut HS; Walnut, CA; (2); 14/479; Church Yth Grp; Key Clb; Co-Ed Nwsp; Hon Roll; Crossfire Club; Dance Prodctn; Brigham Young U; Nrsng.

HILL, BRIAN D; San Luis Obispo SR HS; San Luis Obispo, CA; (2); 52/319; Boy Scts; Church Yth Grp; Band; JV Swmmng; Hon Roll; JV Water Polo; BSA 50 Miler Awd; BSA SR Ptrl Ldr; UC Berkeley; Aerontl Engrng.

HILL, BRITTON A; Irvine HS; Irvine, CA; (1); 2/650; Dance Clb; Drama Clb; Thesps; High Hon Roll; 3 Heritage Awds; Berkeley; Law.

HILL, CHARLES; Sequoia HS; San Carlos, CA; (2); 62/200; Var Bsbl; Var Ftbl; Hon Roll; Bsbl Smmr Leag; San Diego ST; Bus.

HILL, CHRISTINE A; California HS; San Ramon, CA; (3); Cmnty Wkr; SADD; Teachers Aide; JV Bsktbl; Hon Roll; Prfct Atten Awd; Sports Med.

HILL, CURTIS L; Grossmont HS; El Cajon, CA; (1); JV Bsktbl; JV Ftbl; SDSU; Comp Tech.

HILL, DANA; Thousand Oaks HS; Thousand Oaks, CA; (2); 13/560; Dance Clb; SADD; Color Guard; Flag Corp; High Hon Roll; Hon Roll; Jr NHS; NHS; Thousand Oaks Teen Bd 88-90; USA Natl Grand Champ Cologrd Tm 90; PTA Reflctns Cntst Awd Wrtng Achvt; USC Davis; Vet Med.

HILL, DANA M; Desert HS; Edwards, CA; (2); Band; Mrchg Band; Pep Band.

HILL, DENISE; Mission Bay HS; San Diego, CA; (1); Art Clb; African Stu Union; Morehouse Coll; Engrng.

HILL, ERIN; Laguna Beach HS; Laguna Beach, CA; (2); Pep Clb; Chorus; School Musical; Variety Show; Cheerldng; Sftbl; Hon Roll; Cert Of Mrt Hnr Stu; Super Awd, CA Chrldr Assn Clinic; Music.

HILL, GEORGETTE M; George Washington Preparatory HS; Carson, CA; (3); Dance Clb; Math Clb; Capt Pep Clb; Chorus; School Musical; Variety Show; High Hon Roll; Prfct Atten Awd; St Schlr; Howard U; Med.

HILL, HENRIA J; Mt Diablo HS; Pittsburg, CA; (4); 22/249; VP French Clb; VP FBLA; Model UN; Lit Mag; Cnfct Mgmnt/Peer Cnslng; Pre Coll Acad; UC Berkeley; Bus Admn.

HILL, J BRANDON; Santiago HS; Garden Grove, CA; (2); 44/538; Pres Church Yth Grp; Drama Clb; French Clb; German Clb; Ski Clb; School Play; Variety Show; Off Soph Cls; Rep Stu Cncl; JV Ftbl; BYU; Med.

HILL, JACKLYN M; Hilltop HS; Chula Vista, CA; (3); 12/495; Chorus; Var Bsktbl; Var Sftbl; CSF; Renaissance Clb; USIU; Design.

HILL, JEREMY; Fred C Beyer HS; Modesto, CA; (4); 5/506; Church Yth Grp; Pres Math Clb; Math Tm; Science Clb; Church Choir; Yrbk; Cit Awd; Hon Roll; Sec Pres; Chess Clb; Acad Decthln-Tm Capt; Sci Olympd-Tm Capt; Grmn-Amer Prtnrshp Pgm; Sci.

HILL, JODY; Oxnard HS; Oxnard, CA; (3); Dance Clb; Band; Mrchg Band; Pep Band; High Hon Roll; Hon Roll; UCSB; Trvl Agnt.

HILL JR, JOE D; Strathmore Union HS; Strathmore, CA; (3); Computer Clb; Letterman Clb; Library Aide; Ski Clb; SADD; Teachers Aide; Var Ftbl; Var Wt Lftg; Cit Awd; Hon Roll; Sci & Phys Ed Awds; Comp Pgrmr.

HILL, JOSEPH R; University City HS; San Diego, CA; (3); Aud/Vis; Ski Clb; Teachers Aide; Var L Swmmng; Ntl Merit Ltr; Pres Acad Fit Awd; Ltr-Wtr Polo Capt; U Of CA; Engr.

HILL, KACEY C; Wm S Hart HS; Newhall, CA; (1); Church Yth Grp; JV Crs Cntry; JV Trk; Intrst Environment Greenpeace; PETA; Bus.

HILL, KATHY L; California HS; San Ramon, CA; (4); French Clb; Cit Awd; Hon Roll; NHS; Pres Acad Fit Awd; Acad Achvt Awd 87-88; Cert Accmplshmnt; Cert Commndtn; U Of Denver.

HILL, KIMBERLEE M; Carona SR HS; Corona, CA; (2); 32/473; Church Yth Grp; Hon Roll; Pres Acad Fit Awd; St Schlr; Epscpl Grls Frndly Socty; U Of CA Irvine Pre-Coll; Chmcl Engrng.

HILL, LEON A; St Bernard HS; Los Angeles, CA; (3); U Of CA Berkeley; Pltcl Sci.

HILL, LONTE A; East Bakesfield HS; Bakersfield, CA; (1); Bsktbl; Crs Cntry; Trk; Vllybl; Hon Roll; Odyssy Mind Cert; MESA Cert Math/Sci/Engrng Clb; Lawyer.

HILL, MARIANNE K; Ramona HS; Ramona, CA; (2); Church Yth Grp; Dance Clb; SADD; Flag Corp; Cit Awd; Hon Roll; Kiwanis Awd; Prfct Atten Awd; Amnesty Intl; Psych.

HILL, MELISSA S; Bullard HS; Fresno, CA; (2); FCA; GAA; Letterman Clb; Varsity Clb; JV Capt Bsktbl; Var L Crs Cntry; JV Sftbl; MVP Bsktbl; V Crss Cntry; JV Track; Bio Awd; Vet.

HILL, MICHAEL; Apple Valley SR HS; Apple Valley, CA; (4); JV Var Bsbl; JV Var Ftbl; JV Wrstlng; Hon Roll; Comp Sci.

HILL, NATALIE; Capistrano Valley HS; Mission Viejo, CA; (2); Church Yth Grp; Church Choir; JV Capt Cheerldng; Hon Roll; BYU; Rdtn Thrpst.

HILL, NICOLE; Cope JR HS; Redlands, CA; (1); Dance Clb; Teachers Aide; Variety Show; Cheerldng; Cit Awd; High Hon Roll; NHS; Prfct Atten Awd; Pres Acad Fit Awd; Law.

HILL, NKOLAS A; Oak Grove HS; San Jose, CA; (2); Boy Scts; German Clb; Photography.

HILL, REBECCA M; George Washington HS; San Francisco, CA; (3); Letterman Clb; Ski Clb; Rep Sr Cls; Var L Vllybl; High Hon Roll; Hon Roll; JR Statesmen Of Amer.

HILL, ROBERT W; Porterville HS; Springville, CA; (3); Hon Roll; CAP Mentor; Engrng.

HILL, RYAN C; Homestead HS; Cupertino, CA; (1); German Clb; Jr NHS; Green & White Awd Acad Achvt Bio.

HILL, SHEILA N; Los Banos HS; Los Banos, CA; (2); Capt Swmmng; Var Trk; JV Vllybl; Hon Roll; ST Coll; Phys Thrpst.

HILL, SHERI S; Corning Union HS; Corning, CA; (3); Church Yth Grp; GAA; Intnl Clb; Office Aide; Science Clb; VP Soph Cls; JV Var Bsktbl; JV Var Sftbl; JV Trk; Var Vllybl; Vlybl Fgntng Crdnl; Shasta Coll; Elem Tchr.

HILL, STEPHANIE; Palm Desert HS; Palm Desert, CA; (2); Chess Clb; Cmnty Wkr; Treas Key Clb; Office Aide; Yrbk; High Hon Roll; Kiwanis Awd; U Of CA; Bus.

HILL, STEPHANIE A; Oakmont HS; Roseville, CA; (4); 25/400; Cmnty Wkr; Drama Clb; Spanish Clb; SADD; Teachers Aide; Var Capt Swmmng; Hon Roll; V Cptn Water Polo; CSF; UC Davis; Marine Bio.

HILL, VICKI L; San Dimas HS; San Dimas, CA; (4); 1/230; GAA; SADD; Var Tennis; High Hon Roll; Ntl Merit Ltr; Val; CSF; Order Mrt Schlrshp; Interact; CA Polytechnic U Pomona; Fnce.

HILL, VICTORIA; Clovis HS; Clovis, CA; (2); Church Yth Grp; German Clb; Science Clb; SADD; Band; Mrchg Band; Pep Band; Sign Lang Clb; Fresno ST U; Med.

HILL, WENDY R; Casa Grande HS; Petaluma, CA; (2); 70/280; Sec Drama Clb; French Clb; SADD; Pres Chorus; School Musical; School Play; Hon Roll; Cmmnty Theater Prodctns; Achvt Awd Choir & Drama; Musical Theater.

HILL, WILLIE L; Narbonne HS; Gardena, CA; (4); 1/457; VP Church Yth Grp; Dance Clb; Church Choir; Ed Nwsp; Pres Stu Cncl; Capt Bsktbl; Score Keeper; Trk; Cit Awd; High Hon Roll; Yng Blck Schlrs Shcl Facilitator; VP/Chrmn Chrch Usher & Jr Deacon Brd; Black Hrtge Essay Cont 1st Pl; Engrng.

HILLARD, ERIK; Palma HS; Salinas, CA; (2); Boy Scts; JV Socr; High Hon Roll; Hon Roll; Ca Schlrshp Federation; Outing Clb; Bus Mngmnt.

HILLE, PATRICIA A; Atwater HS; Atwater, CA; (2); Friday Night Live; Hield Bus Coll; Bus.

HILLER, ELAN WAYNE; Hoover HS; San Diego, CA; (3); 21/499; Church Yth Grp; Intnl Clb; Key Clb; JV Var Ftbl; JV Var Wrstlng; Hon Roll; Jr NHS; A P Physcs Clb.

HILLER, KEITH; Corning Union HS; Flournoy, CA; (3); 4-H; Intnl Clb; Spanish Clb; Tennis; Wt Lftg; Wrstlng; Hon Roll.

HILLIARD, MICHAEL D; Lincoln Prep; San Diego, CA; (3); Church Yth Grp; Office Aide; ROTC; Band; Var Bsbl; Var Ftbl; Hon Roll; Central ST; Pltcl Sci.

HILLIARD, SEAN E; Capistrano Valley HS; Mission Viejo, CA; (3); German Clb; Jr Hnr Escorts.

HILLIARD, SHARLENE M; Antioch HS; Antioch, CA; (2); Church Yth Grp; Cmnty Wkr; Girl Scts; Key Clb; Letterman Clb; Varsity Clb; Acpl Chr; Church Choir; Orch; Pep Band; Athl Of Yr; Hnr Orch; CMEA Bay Stcn; Diablo Vly Yth Symphny; Diablo Yth Sccr Leag; East Cty Chrch Orch.

HILLIKER, JOSH M; Ponderosa HS; Placerville, CA; (3); Acpl Chr; Chorus; Church Choir; Ftbl; Golf; Swmmng; Hon Roll; Comm.

HILLMAN, BONNIE A; South HS; Bakersfield, CA; (3); 30/424; VP Drama Clb; JA; Thesps; School Play; Stage Crew; Hon Roll; Pres Acad Fit Awd; Mock Trial; Law.

HILLMAN, ELIZABETH D; Mission San Jose HS; Fremont, CA; (2); 1/428; JV Bsktbl; JV Vllybl; High Hon Roll; Pres Acad Fit Awd; UC Berkeley Acad Tlnt Dvlpmn Pgm 88-90; CSF; Supr Achvt CA Nvtnl Chemathn 90.

HILLMAN, JENNIFER C; Alta Loma HS; Alta Loma, CA; (4); 6/450; Ed Yrbk; Var Crs Cntry; Var Socr; Var Trk; High Hon Roll; Pres Acad Fit Awd; CSF Sealbearer; CIF Reebok Schlr Athl; Rotry Schlrshp; UCLA; Hstry.

HILLMAN, MARCUS B; Buena HS; Ventura, CA; (2); Church Yth Grp; German Clb; VP Jr Cls; Cit Awd; Prfct Atten Awd; Ger Exch Prgm; Sea Explorers; Interact Club VP; Landscape Arch.

HILLMAN, RYAN; Huntington Beach HS; Huntington Beach, CA; (2); Art Clb; Church Yth Grp; Cmnty Wkr; JA; Key Clb; Office Aide; Science Clb; Ski Clb; Spanish Clb; Teachers Aide; JR Life Guard; UC Irvine; Bus.

HILLS, MELISSA; Palm Srpings Christian HS; Desert Hot Sprngs, CA; (1); Church Yth Grp; Cmnty Wkr; Chorus; Church Choir; School Musical; Stu Cncl; Bsktbl; Cheerldng; Trk; Vllybl; Hrsbck Rdng Awds; Pdtrc Nrs.

HILLY, MARY; Torrey Pines HS; San Diego, CA; (3); 252/472; Dance Clb; Debate Tm; GAA; Latin Clb; Library Aide; Math Clb; Pep Clb; Science Clb; Ski Clb; Speech Tm; Pblc Spkng 2nd Pl City Finals; UC Santa Barbara; Lwyr.

HILMEN, KARENA M; Valhalla HS; La Mesa, CA; (3); 53/438; Am Leg Aux Girls St; Cmnty Wkr; Hosp Aide; Key Clb; Pep Clb; Ski Clb; SADD; Stu Cncl; Hon Roll; SPRITES.

HILO, JOHNNY R; Baldwin Park HS; Baldwin Park, CA; (3); FBLA; Letterman Clb; Teachers Aide; Var Capt Bsbl; JV Bsktbl; JV Capt Ftbl; Hon Roll; Prfct Atten Awd; Pres Acad Fit Awd; Bus.

HILSCHER, SHARI L; Canyon HS; Canyon Country, CA; (2); Acpl Chr; Chorus; Mgr(s); L Var Swmmng; Cit Awd; Hon Roll; Choir Ltr; Acad Ltr; Jrnlsm.

HILSINGER II, ROBERT K; Grant Union HS; Sacramento, CA; (3); Quiz Bowl; ROTC; Hon Roll; 1st Pl Indvdl Drill Cadets; 1st Lieut-Cadet Corps; Comp Pgming.

HILT, JUSTIN J; Pinole Valley HS; Hercules, CA; (3); Hon Roll.

HILTON, JANICE M; El Dorado HS; Diamond Springs, CA; (4); 74/294; Q&S; Acpl Chr; Chorus; School Musical; Phtg Nwsp; Ed Yrbk; Hon Roll; Prfct Atten Awd; Bnk Of Amer Achvt Awd Music; El Dorado Union HS Dist Stu Achvt Awd Fine Arts; Edtr Of Yr; Music Ed.

HILTON, KENNETH T; Vacaville HS; Vacaville, CA; (3); Var Bsbl; Var Ftbl; Wt Lftg; Hon Roll; UC Berkeley; Psych.

HILTON, MARY; Pilgrim Christian Schl; Lynwood, CA; (4); Church Yth Grp; Speech Tm; Teachers Aide; Chorus; Church Choir; Vllybl; High Hon Roll; Most 100s Schl Awd 89-90; Rnnrup Spch Cntst; Cerritos CC; Bus.

HILTON, TYSON L; Huntington Beach HS; Huntington Beach, CA; (2); Model UN; Red Cross Aide; Capt Ftbl; Trk; High Hon Roll; Golden ST Geom Exam High Hnrs; OH ST; Intl Affairs.

HILTY, OZMIN DARIO ZARATE; Brawley Union HS; Westmorland, CA; (2); 4-H; French Clb; Math Tm; Bsbl; Tennis; Wrstlng; High Hon Roll; Aerospace Engrng.

HIM, CHANTHA S; Modesto HS; Modesto, CA; (1); FHA; Hosp Aide; Teachers Aide; Orch; 2nd Pl Dist Salad Prep; U CA Pacific; Dr.

HIMELSEIN, WAYNE; Santa Barbara HS; Santa Barbara, CA; (2); 25/600; Cmnty Wkr; Temple Yth Grp; Bsktbl; Ftbl; JV Trk; Wt Lftg; High Hon Roll; Pres Acad Fit Awd; Harvard; Ec.

HIMENES, FRANK; River City HS; W Sacramento, CA; (1); VICA; High Hon Roll; Hon Roll; American River Coll; Elect Engr.

HIMMELBERGER, HEIDI A; The Bishops Schl; San Diego, CA; (4); Var Socr; Hon Roll; Pres Acad Fit Awd; UC Santa Barbara; Bus.

HINCHY, KAREN; Fountain Valley HS; Ft Valley, CA; (4); 26/630; German Clb; Science Clb; Band; Jazz Band; Mrchg Band; High Hon Roll; Hon Roll; Jr NHS; Ntl Merit Ltr; Pres Acad Fit Awd; Distngshd & Natl Sci Fndtn Young Schlrs; Coronet Awd; Stevens Inst Tech; Mech Engrng.

HINCKLEY, JONATHAN L; South Torrance HS; Torrance, CA; (4); Church Yth Grp; Jazz Band; Orch; Hon Roll; Ntl Merit SF; Pepperdine U; Music Teach.

HINCKS, MEKIELE E; Sonoma Valley HS; Glen Ellen, CA; (1); Sftbl; Pilot.

HINDLE, BRONWYN M; Norco HS; Norco, CA; (3); 9/399; Model UN; High Hon Roll; Pres Acad Fit Awd; CSF; Girls Leag; San Bernardino.

HINDLE, SUZANNE M; Norco HS; Norco, CA; (3); 12/399; Church Yth Grp; Model UN; SADD; High Hon Roll; Pres Acad Fit Awd; Sal; Girls League Treas; CSF; U CA Santa Barbara; Teaching.

HINE, JEAN A; Paramount HS; Paramount, CA; (3); Speech Tm; SADD; Band; Jazz Band; Mrchg Band; Pep Band; Law.

HINES, CANDIE; Santa Ana HS; Santa Ana, CA; (3); Computer Clb; Key Clb; Pep Clb; Science Clb; School Musical; Off Sr Cls; JV Var Cheerldng; Tennis; High Hon Roll; Hon Roll; Acad Vrsty Lttr; AZ U; Sprts Med.

HINES, STEVE K; Orange Glen HS; Escondido, CA; (3); Church Yth Grp; Computer Clb; Nwsp; Hon Roll; Comp Prgmr; Bus Owner; Comp Sci.

HINGARH, NILESH H; Saratoga HS; Saratoga, CA; (2); Scholastic Bowl; Chorus; School Musical; JV Bsktbl; JV Crs Cntry; JV Trk; Hon Roll; Med.

HINH, QUI C; San Gabriel HS; Rosemead, CA; (3); Engrng.

HINK, BRIAN D; Irvine HS; Irvine, CA; (2); JV Var Bsktbl; Hon Roll; Arch.

HINKLE, PHILIP C; Redlands SR HS; Redlands, CA; (3); Sisters City Expressions Of Peace Art Cont 3rd Pl; Chepulechi Art Cont 3rd Pl; Outstndng Phy Ftnss Awd; Art.

HINKLEY, FAITH N; Lincoln HS; Stockton, CA; (4); Latin Clb; Science Clb; Acpl Chr; Chorus; Hon Roll; Ntl Merit Schol; Pres Choirs 89-90; St Hnr Choir 90; Stat Wrstlng Tm 3 Yrs; Music.

HINNENBERG, LISA J; Casa Grande HS; Petaluma, CA; (3); 33/288; Church Yth Grp; German Clb; Girl Scts; Church Choir; High Hon Roll; Hon Roll; NHS; CSF; Bus.

HINOJOS, SOFIA; San Gabriel Mission HS; Monterey Park, CA; (4); 12/108; Pep Clb; Chorus; Var Co-Capt Cheerldng; Hon Roll; Prfct Atten Awd; Alg II Hnrs Awd; Cal ST-LOS Angeles; Bus Mgmt.

HINOJOSA, HECTOR; Rio Mesa HS; Oxnard, CA; (3); Aerosp Engr.

HINOJOSA, JORGE A; Cuyama Valley HS; New Cuyama, CA; (3); Church Yth Grp; FFA; Rep Soph Cls; Off Jr Cls; VP Stu Cncl; Bsbl; JV Var Bsktbl; Var Ftbl; Hon Roll; I Dare You Awd; Bus.

HINOJOSA, LIZZIE D; Central Union HS; El Centro, CA; (3); 20/543; Church Yth Grp; Pres 4-H; Sec FFA; Letterman Clb; Teachers Aide; Sec Soph Cls; Rep Stu Cncl; Swmmng; 4-H Awd; Hon Roll; Stu Mth; Crtfd Al-Brd Dog Grmng Cert; Ownr Dog Grmng Shp; Lwyr.

HINOJOSA, MICHAELE L; Castle Park HS; Chula Vista, CA; (3); German Clb; Sec Sr Cls; Stu Cncl; Mgr(s); Socr; Water Polo; Girls Leag; Enviornmntl Sci.

HINRICHS, BRANDY; Costa Mesa HS; Santa Ana, CA; (4); Cmnty Wkr; French Clb; Teachers Aide; Intrml Swmmng; Hon Roll; HS 1st Annual Poetry Cont 4th Pl; Humboldt; Ecology.

HINS, KAREN; Kern Valley HS; Weldon, CA; (2); Pres 4-H; FFA; Sec Pep Clb; Stat Bsbl; Cheerldng; Powder Puff Ftbl; 4-H Awd; Hon Roll; FFA CA Prepared Pblc Spkng ST Champ; Kern Cnty Miss Wool 90; CA ST U; Ag.

HINSBERGER, ERIKA A; C L Mc Lane HS; Fresno, CA; (2); Cmnty Wkr; 4-H; Pep Clb; Teachers Aide; Rep Stu Cncl; Cheerldng; Pom Pon; 4-H Awd; Many Hnrs & Awds In Horse Show Cmptns; Many Gold Mdls In 4-H Actvts; CSUF; Vet.

HINSHAW, ANNIE; Rosemead HS; Rosemead, CA; (3); Church Yth Grp; FCA; GAA; SADD; Church Choir; JV Bsktbl; Var Powder Puff Ftbl; Var Tennis; Tennis Tm MVP.

HINSON, JASON R; Hillsdale HS; Foster City, CA; (3); Church Yth Grp; Debate Tm; Drama Clb; Spanish Clb; Thesps; School Play; Rep Stu Cncl; Mgr(s); Hon Roll; Law Enfrcmnt.

HINSON, RAFAELITA C; Notre Dame HS For Girls; Salinas, CA; (4); Dance Clb; Science Clb; Spanish Clb; Sec SADD; Chorus; School Musical; Rptr Nwsp; Off Sr Cls; Stu Cncl; Hon Roll; Pres Jr Clb; Actv Dir; Prof Model; Bus Admin.

HINTON, NICOLE L; Pacific Palisades HS; Los Angeles, CA; (2); Church Yth Grp; Pep Clb; Teachers Aide; Church Choir; Rep Frsh Cls; Hon Roll; Rep Soph Cls; CAFE; Comp Clss; Blach Data Prcssng Assoc; Scrkpr T-Ball; Comp Systms Engr.

HINTON, SAMUEL P; Fresno Christian HS; Fresno, CA; (2); 1/60; Church Yth Grp; Acpl Chr; Chorus; VP Stu Cncl; Var Tennis; High Hon Roll; Hon Roll; NHS.

HINZ, AMY L; Livermore HS; Livermore, CA; (1); Church Yth Grp; Cmnty Wkr; Band; Prfct Atten Awd; Campfire; Envrnmntl Clb.

HINZ, TRICIA G; Kennedy HS; Buena Park, CA; (3); Drama Clb; FBLA; Quiz Bowl; Capt Flag Corp; School Play; Var L Swmmng; High Hon Roll; Hon Roll; Pres Acad Fit Awd; US Air Force Acad; Aerontcl En.

HION, CHRISTOPHER Y; Whitney HS; Cerritos, CA; (1); Boy Scts; Church Yth Grp; German Clb; Key Clb; Band; Rep Frsh Cls; JV Bsbl; JV Bsktbl; Hon Roll; Stanford; Med Rsrch.

HIOTT, CHERISE Y; South HS; Bakersfield, CA; (3); 14/458; Church Yth Grp; Hon Roll; NHS; Stu Agnst The Violation Of Earth; CSF; Bakersfield Coll; Bus Mgmt.

HIPKISS, JACKIE L; Sonoma Valley HS; Sonoma, CA; (4); Ed Nwsp; Phtg Yrbk; JV Powder Puff Ftbl; Hon Roll; Explr Sct; Acadmc Dcthln; U Of CA Santa Cruz; Illstrtn.

HIPOLITO, VENUS A; Edison HS; Huntington Beach, CA; (1); Key Clb; Model UN; JV Bsktbl; Octagon Clb; SEYO S E Yth Organztn Bsktbl.

HIPPLE, DAVID BEN; Fillmore HS; Fillmore, CA; (1); Cit Awd; Prfct Atten Awd; Soroptmsts 1st Pl Shrt Story; Outstndng Stu Awd; Electrnc Engr.

HIPPS, CATHERINE M; St Francis HS; Davis, CA; (3); Sftbl; Hon Roll; Phys Educ.

HIRABAYASHI, KIMBERLY E; Gardena HS; Gardena, CA; (3); 20/500; Hosp Aide; Intnl Clb; Service Clb; Ed Nwsp; VP Frsh Cls; Stu Cncl; Var Tennis; High Hon Roll; CSF Treas; CIB L A City 3 A Champs Tennis 89-90; VFW Post 1961 Womens Clb Engl Awd; Teach.

HIRAHARA, TIFFANI A; Sacramento Country Day Schl; Cameron Park, CA; (3); Art Clb; Mgr Yrbk; Rep Jr Cls; Rep Stu Cncl; Var Capt Bsktbl; L Socr; L Trk; AA Clb; MVP Bsktbl; Engrng.

HIRAI, ELISA; Cupertino HS; Cupertino, CA; (3); Hosp Aide; Treas Soph Cls; Treas Jr Cls; VP Sr Cls; JV Capt Bsktbl; Powder Puff Ftbl; JV Vllybl; NHS; Interact Clb; Medcl.

HIRAI, FRANCES A; John F Kennedy HS; Sacramento, CA; (3); 1/476; AFS; Orch; School Musical; High Hon Roll; Chmbr Orch Clb.

HIRANUMA, GEMMA; Los Angeles Center For Enrich Studies; Los Angeles, CA; (3); Cmnty Wkr; Dance Clb; School Musical; School Play; Variety Show; Hon Roll; LA Student Coalition; Brotherhood0sisterhood USA Youth Ldrshp Pgm; Environmental Clb & Opera Clb; USC; Psych.

HIRATSUKA, JENNIFER L; San Gorgonio HS; Highland, CA; (3); AFS; 4-H; ROTC; Off Soph Cls; Var Tennis; Pr Cnslng; Svc Awd ROTC; Brd Mem Yth/Yth; Teach.

HIRMENDI, FARIDOON; Inglewood HS; Inglewood, CA; (4); Art Clb; Computer Clb; VP Drama Clb; Hosp Aide; Var Vllybl; Cit Awd; Hon Roll; CA ST U Northridge; Aero Engr.

HIRNING, MONICA J; Yreka HS; Yreka, CA; (3); 8/170; Am Leg Aux Girls St; Pres Church Yth Grp; Spanish Clb; Co-Capt Flag Corp; School Musical; Ed Nwsp; VP Soph Cls; Stat Bsktbl; Powder Puff Ftbl; U CA Davis.

HIROSE, TARA A; Foothill HS; Santa Ana, CA; (3); 9/328; German Clb; Var Swmmng; Cit Awd; High Hon Roll.

HIROSHIMA, GREGORY M; Sacramento Adventist Acad; Sacramento, CA; (2); 9/48; Church Yth Grp; Ski Clb; Teachers Aide; Band; Bsktbl; Ftbl; Intrml Score Keeper; Intrml Sftbl; Tennis; Band Tour Mgr; Pacific Union Coll; Bus.

HIRSCH, JEREMY; Chatsworth HS; Chatsworth, CA; (4); 23/650; Boy Scts; Temple Yth Grp; Band; Mrchg Band; Rep Frsh Cls; Var L Cheerldng; JV L Swmmng; Var Trk; Cit Awd; Hon Roll; Natl Eagle Scout Assn; U CA Los Angeles; Med Rsrch.

HIRSCH, LALO M; Hilltop HS; Chula Vista, CA; (2); Church Yth Grp; Off Soph Cls; Socr; Surfing.

HIRSCH, TERAMI R; Burbank HS; Burbank, CA; (2); Dance Clb; Drama Clb; Girl Scts; Teachers Aide; Vllybl; Jr NHS; Civic Light Opera.

HIRSCHHORN, JESSICA P; Westlake School For Girls; Los Angeles, CA; (2); Cmnty Wkr; French Clb; Schl Dance Co; Amnsty Intrl; Theater Arts.

HIRST, JUSTIN C; Elk Grove HS; Elk Grove, CA; (1); Boy Scts; Church Yth Grp; JV Crs Cntry; JV Trk; Hon Roll; BYU; Acctnt.

HISHMEH, JULIANA; Mercy HS; San Francisco, CA; (2); 3/120; Church Yth Grp; Dance Clb; School Musical; Var Cheerldng; Var Pom Pon; High Hon Roll; Hon Roll; BSU; CSF; Save The Earth Recycle For Eht Ozone Cmmttee; Stanford U; Law.

HISQUIERDO, DAVID; Gompers Secondary Schl; San Diego, CA; (2); JV Crs Cntry; JV Trk; San Diego ST; Engrng.

HITCHCOCK, BRIAN; Chowchilla Union HS; Chowchilla, CA; (3); Boy Scts; Cmnty Wkr; FFA; SADD; JV Capt Wrstlng; Rptr Yrbk; Rep Stu Cncl; JV Bsbl; JV VP Bsktbl; JV Capt Ftbl; Interact Clb 2 Yrs Sec Torary Awds Wnnr; Feather River Coll; Fire Sci.

HITCHCOCK, JAMIE B; Anaheim HS; Anaheim, CA; (3); Drama Clb; Quiz Bowl; Thesps; School Play; Hon Roll; NHS; Ntl Hnr Soc Secy; Philosophy Club; Psych.

HITE, JASON R; John F Kennedy HS; La Palma, CA; (2); Church Yth Grp; Computer Clb; Teachers Aide; Comp.

HITOMI, LORI KIMIKO; Nogales HS; West Covina, CA; (3); 153/600; Cmnty Wkr; Dance Clb; Pep Clb; Teachers Aide; Rep Stu Cncl; Cheerldng; Hon Roll.

HITT, KATHERINE LYNN; Coronado HS; Coronado, CA; (3); Church Yth Grp; Cmnty Wkr; Drama Clb; Office Aide; Chorus; Church Choir; Variety Show; Stat Bsktbl; Var Powder Puff Ftbl; Var Capt Sftbl; Solo/Duet/Trio Singing; Jazz Dance; Pr Cnclr; Psych.

HIXON, JANELLE R; Roosevelt School Of The Arts; Fresno, CA; (3); French Clb; School Play; Hon Roll; Cmnty Theatre & Dance; Envrnmntl Clb; Jr Larks Clb; UC Santa Barbara; Psych.

HIXON, ROBERT; Monrovia HS; Pomona, CA; (4); Service Clb; Teachers Aide; Band; Mrchg Band; Pep Band; Stu Cncl; Swmmng; Water Polo; Mc Donnel Douglas Stu Of Month; Pres Boys Lg.

HIXSON, DIANA A; Apple Valley HS; Apple Vly, CA; (2); FFA; Spanish Clb; Teachers Aide; JV Sftbl; JV Var Tennis; Hon Roll; ROP Floral Dsgn; Berkley; Psych.

HIYAMA, KATSUHIKO; El Toro HS; El Toro, CA; (4); 4-H; German Clb; Intnl Clb; Key Clb; Math Tm; Rep Sr Cls; JV Crs Cntry; Var Swmmng; Var Wrstlng; 4-H Awd; UCLA; Bus.

HIZON, JENNIFER J; Providence HS; Sun Valley, CA; (2); Church Yth Grp; Dance Clb; Hosp Aide; High Hon Roll; Hon Roll; St Schlr; Asian Club Pblc Rltns Offcr; Med.

HJELDEN, ERIK P; Highlands HS; Sacramento, CA; (3); Var Bsbl; High Hon Roll; Hon Roll; UC Davis; Bus Adm.

HJORTEN, TARA; Eisenhower HS; Rialto, CA; (3); Church Yth Grp; Rptr Nwsp; Treas Frsh Cls; JV Bsktbl; Hon Roll; NHS; Amer Lgn Awd; Ricks JC; Inter Dsgn.

HLUBINKA, MICHELLE IVA THOMAS; Fountain Valley HS; Fountain Valley, CA; (4); 1/630; Cmnty Wkr; Key Clb; Pep Clb; VP Science Clb; Service Clb; Co-Ed Yrbk; Stu Cncl; Elks Awd; High Hon Roll; Ntl Merit Ltr; EPA Envrnmntl Clb Co-Fndr & Pres; CSF Sec; Prix D Honneur Hghst Hnr; Yale U.

HO, ADELINE L; Galileo HS; San Francisco, CA; (4); Rep Dance Clb; Pres JA; Sec Spanish Clb; Stu Cncl; Hon Roll; Peer Tutoring Pgm; San Francisco City; Bus Admin.

HO, AKINA M; Mission HS; San Francisco, CA; (3); Art Clb; Cmnty Wkr; Dance Clb; Debate Tm; French Clb; Office Aide; Varsity Clb; Variety Show; Pres Soph Cls; Pres Stu Cncl; Vol Cmmty Club Pres; Army Reserved Athltc Acad Schlsp 89; U CA Berkeley; Bus.

HO, ALLEN K; Mc Ateer HS; San Francisco, CA; (3); Boy Scts; Church Yth Grp; Cmnty Wkr; Computer Clb; Intnl Clb; Hon Roll; Bdmtn Awd; Arch Dsgn Awd; Engr.

HO, AMY; Sunny Hills HS; Fullerton, CA; (2); Debate Tm; Hosp Aide; Intnl Clb; Key Clb; Ski Clb; Spanish Clb; JV Swmmng; Var Trk; High Hon Roll; Hon Roll; Cert Mrt Stdy Piano; Acad Awd; U Of MI Ann Arbor; Med.

HO, AMY F; Chaminade College Prep; Canoga Park, CA; (3); Cmnty Wkr; Letterman Clb; Service Clb; Band; Chorus; Mrchg Band; Pep Band; Nwsp; High Hon Roll; Hon Roll; Asian-Amer Tour China; Asian Amercn Clb; Astrnmy Clb; Pedtrcn.

HO, ANDY W; Santa Teresa HS; San Jose, CA; (2); Chess Clb; Computer Clb; French Clb; JA; Variety Show; Intrml Vllybl; Wrote Comedy Material; Wrote Plays, Short Stories, Short Novels & Poetry; Corp Law.

HO, BRENDA J; John F Kennedy HS; Sacramento, CA; (3); 34/422; Dance Clb; FBLA; FTA; Office Aide; Color Guard; Hon Roll; CSF; U Of CA Davis; Vet Med.

HO, CARMEN K; South San Ffrancisco HS; South San Francis, CA; (3); Church Yth Grp; FBLA; Math Clb; Chorus; Var Tennis; Hnrs Awd Golden Gate Gmtry Exm; GPA Acad Awds; UC Berkely; Arch Engrng.

HO, CHARLENE CUN; Ontario HS; Ontario, CA; (1); Sftbl; Vllybl; CA Poly U.

HO, CHERYL; Los Gatos HS; Los Gatos, CA; (4); 6/375; Hosp Aide; Chorus; Color Guard; Yrbk; Stu Cncl; JV Capt Cheerldng; High Hon Roll; Ntl Merit Ltr; NEDT Awd; Pres Acad Fit Awd; NYU Schlrshp Bus; NY U; Bus Mgmt.

HO, CHUONG; Moorpark HS; Moorpark, CA; (3); 15/275; Var JV Bsbl; Var JV Ftbl; JV Socr; High Hon Roll; Prfct Atten Awd; MVP Bsbl Frshn & Soph; MIP Frshmn & MVP Soph Ftbl; Outstndng Offnse Awd Sccr Sop; Var Ftbl Fookie Yr.

HO, CONNIE; Canyon HS; Anaheim, CA; (2); Computer Clb; Drama Clb; Spanish Clb; Band; Mgr Mrchg Band; Harvard; Lwyr.

HO, DAN T ESTACION; Bellarmine College Prep; San Jose, CA; (3); Cmnty Wkr; NFL; Speech Tm; Teachers Aide; Thesps; School Play; Ntl Merit Ltr; Vocal Performance Cmptn-2 1st Pls; Soc Involvement Corps Core; U CA-BERKELEY; Sports Med.

HO, DANH CHAU; George Washington HS; San Francisco, CA; (2); Socr; High Hon Roll; CSF; Alg High Hnr; Frnch 4 Achvt; Mech Engrng.

HO, DAVID D; South San Francisco HS; S San Francisco, CA; (3); Am Leg Boys St; Math Clb; Science Clb; JV Bsktbl; Mgr(s); JV Tennis; Ntl Merit SF; Geom Stu Yr; Elem Fnctns Stu Yr; Spllng Bee Wnnr; UC Berkeley; Crtv Wrtng.

HO, DAVID T; Whitney HS; Cerritos, CA; (1); Church Yth Grp; Cmnty Wkr; Key Clb; SADD; Church Choir; Nwsp; JV Socr; High Hon Roll; Hon Roll; Pres Acad Fit Awd; UCLA; Bus Mgmt.

HO, DEBORAH; Encinal HS; Alameda, CA; (3); 15/233; Church Yth Grp; Cmnty Wkr; Key Clb; School Musical; Rptr Yrbk; Pres Soph Cls; VP Jr Cls; Var L Cheerldng; Gym; Var L Pom Pon; Vlntr Spcl Olympcs; UCLA; Liberal Arts.

HO, DIANA QUYNH-DAO; Folsom HS; Folsom, CA; (3); 5/240; Church Yth Grp; French Clb; Treas Intnl Clb; Orch; Nwsp; Yrbk; Rep Jr Cls; Treas Sr Cls; Var Tennis; High Hon Roll; Dentistry.

HO, DUNG; Yerba Buena HS; San Jose, CA; (4); Math Clb; Hon Roll; Chinese, Vietnamese Club; San Jose ST U; Bus Mgmt.

HO, DUY; Baldwin Park HS; Baldwin Park, CA; (2); Computer Clb; SADD; Hon Roll; Memb Tri Cmmnty Photo Schl; UCLA; Math.

HO, EAMON W; Menlo-Atherton HS; Atherton, CA; (4); Ntl Merit SF; Anime Clb Pres; Asian Stu Union; Amer Chem Scty Awd Achvt; Engr.

HO, ESTHER E; Whitney HS; Cerritos, CA; (2); Church Yth Grp; JA; Church Choir; Pres Nwsp; Off Soph Cls; JV Bsktbl; Var Trk; High Hon Roll; Hon Roll; All Star AYSO Sccr Leag; Chinese Schl Tchr; Anti-New Kids On The Block Fedrtn.

HO, EVA; Abraham Lincoln HS; San Francisco, CA; (2); Swmmng; Tennis; Vllybl; Music, Arts & Sci Achvts; Alg Hnrs; UC Berkeley; Nrsng.

HO, FLORA K; Arcadia HS; Arcadia, CA; (3); 11/643; AFS; Church Yth Grp; Rep Math Clb; Math Tm; NFL; Red Cross Aide; Science Clb; Service Clb; Speech Tm; Band; Brown U; Bio Chem.

HO, GILBERT C; St Ignatius College Prep; San Francisco, CA; (3); 7/244; Chess Clb; JV Var Trk; CSF.

HO, HA; Garden Grove HS; Garden Grove, CA; (4); 18/352; Math Tm; Speech Tm; Bsbl; Bsktbl; Ftbl; Socr; Tennis; High Hon Roll; Hon Roll; Prncpls Hnr Roll; Orange Coast Coll; Comp Sci.

HO, HELEN; Abraham Lincoln HS; San Francisco, CA; (3); Intnl Clb; ROTC; Teachers Aide; Color Guard; Drill Tm; Orch; Interact Club.

HO, HELEN L; Mark Keppel HS; Monterey Park, CA; (4); FBLA; Key Clb; Service Clb; Teachers Aide; Chorus; Lit Mag; Lit Mag; Intrml Tennis; Cit Awd; High Hon Roll; LEOS Affiliation Lions Club Intl; 1st Pl Rgnls 22nd, 25th & 30th Constitution Cmptn; U Of Southern CA; Entreprenuer.

HO, HUBERT W; Ocean View HS; Westminster, CA; (3); 25/440; Computer Clb; German Clb; Key Clb; Math Clb; High Hon Roll; Hon Roll; Pres Acad Fit Awd; Gldn Hawk Fnlst Frgn Lang; Co-Fndr Asian Club; UCLA; Bioengrng.

HO, JACQUELINE G; George Washington HS; San Francisco, CA; (2); Drill Tm; Wt Lftg; Hon Roll; Gngrbrd Hse 1st Pl.

HO, JAMES J; Los Gatos HS; Los Gatos, CA; (3); Chess Clb; Hon Roll; Drafting Awds; Hnrs In Golden St Exam Geom; Engrng.

HO, JAVIER O; Corona HS; Corona, CA; (2); 7/425; Treas Science Clb; Teachers Aide; Off Stu Cncl; JV Tennis; High Hon Roll; Pres Acad Fit Awd; Hnrs Gldn St Exm Gom CA; Stu CSF; Bus Admin.

HO, JEANIE; International Studies Acad; San Francisco, CA; (3); Yrbk; Sec Soph Cls; High Hon Roll; Hon Roll; CSF; U CA; Intl Law.

HO, JEANNETTE F; St Francis HS; Sacramento, CA; (3); Church Yth Grp; Cmnty Wkr; Drama Clb; Latin Clb; Math Clb; Math Tm; Office Aide; Service Clb; Teachers Aide; Chorus; CSF Treas; Stu Reaching Out Sec; Fri Night Live; Numerous Dsgn Conts & Writings Conts; Acad & Svc Awds; Cmmnctns.

HO, JENNIFER; Bishop O'dowd HS; Oakland, CA; (3); Church Yth Grp; Ski Clb; Chorus; Church Choir; JV Tennis; High Hon Roll; NEDT Awd.

HO, JENNY; Whitney HS; Cerritos, CA; (3); Church Yth Grp; Cmnty Wkr; French Clb; FBLA; JA; Sec Key Clb; Rptr Nwsp; Ed Yrbk; Hon Roll; City Of Cerritos Lbrary Vlntr; Chinese Cultural Dance; JR Guard & Hnr; Harvad; Bus.

HO, JENNY W S; A Lincoln HS; San Francisco, CA; (3); DECA; Science Clb; Service Clb; Yrbk; U Of CA Los Angeles; Bus.

HO, KAYE K; Pinole Valley HS; Hercules, CA; (3); Art Clb; Drama Clb; English Clb; Math Tm; Teachers Aide; Crs Cntry; Trk; High Hon Roll; Bus.

HO, KIN; West Campus HS; Sacramento, CA; (3); 7/116; FBLA; Science Clb; High Hon Roll; Culture Club VP; Sac ST U; Social Wrk.

HO, KITTY; Fremont Christian HS; Fremont, CA; (3); Dance Clb; Drama Clb; Cit Awd; Hon Roll; Prfct Atten Awd; Berkeley U; Bus Adm.

HO, KRISTINA; University HS; Irvine, CA; (3); #3 In Class; Hosp Aide; Sec JCL; Var L Bsktbl; Hon Roll; Laureate Awds Engl Latin.

HO, KRISTINE; Lincoln HS; Los Angeles, CA; (2); Intnl Clb; Teachers Aide; Chorus; Yrbk; Cit Awd; Hon Roll.

HO, KURT; Daniel Murphy HS; Los Angeles, CA; (4); 19/89; Boy Scts; Church Yth Grp; French Clb; Intnl Clb; Letterman Clb; Red Cross Aide; Yrbk; Pres Sr Cls; JV Var Ftbl; Var Capt Vllybl; Police Explr Post 101; Cmpus Mnstry; Chrstn Svc Awd; U Southern CA; Arch.

HO, LAN SY; Davis SR HS; Davis, CA; (4); Chess Clb; French Clb; Vllybl; Parents Awd 88-89; U Of CA Davis; Chem.

HO, LIANA NICOLE; Newbury Park HS; Newbury Park, CA; (1); 1/361; Church Yth Grp; SADD; Band; Jazz Band; Mrchg Band; Hon Roll; Diplmts Clb; Yrbk Clb; Prncpls Athltc Schlr Awd; Ucla; Optmtrst.

HO, LINH; Edison HS; Stockton, CA; (2); Wt Lftg; Dentist.

HO, LUANN S; Lowell HS; San Francisco, CA; (3); Church Yth Grp; Science Clb; SADD; High Hon Roll; Hon Roll; Acad Excel Awd, Gldn St Exam 88 & 89.

HO, MING H; San Gabriel HS; San Gabriel, CA; (2); Chess Clb; Computer Clb; Science Clb; High Hon Roll; Hon Roll; Outstndng Stu Writer Awd; Sys Operator Comp Bulletin Bd Sys; Engrng.

HO, OSMOND; Glen A Wilson HS; Hacienda Hgts, CA; (4); 26/357; Church Yth Grp; Computer Clb; Science Clb; Spanish Clb; Prfct Atten Awd; Pres Acad Fit Awd; CSF; UCLA; Engrng.

HO, PHUONG-DUNG T; James Madison HS; San Diego, CA; (3); Latin Clb; Math Clb; Mu Alpha Theta; Mrchg Band; Pep Band; Tennis; Hon Roll; Office Aide; Prfct Atten Awd; CSF; Concert Band; USC; Pre-Pharmacy.

HO, RONALD L; Oak Grove HS; San Jose, CA; (2); Drama Clb; Acpl Chr; Chorus; Church Choir; School Musical; Swing Chorus; Variety Show; Cnty Hnrs Choir; Eagles Alive Chrstn Clb; Peer Cnslng; U CA Irvine; Psych.

HO, STACY HSIAO; Culver City HS; Culver City, CA; (3); French Clb; Rep Frsh Cls; Rep Soph Cls; Rep Jr Cls; Rep Sr Cls; JV Tennis; JV Trk; High Hon Roll; Hon Roll; Ntl Merit Schol; Alg & Geo -Gldn ST Exam- Schl Rcgntn; UC Santa Barbara; Pediatrician.

HO, STEPHANIE TRAM; Don Antonio Lugo HS; Chino, CA; (4); Treas French Clb; SADD; High Hon Roll; Hon Roll; NHS; Golden Conquest Awd; Gradwith Hnr; U Of CA; Med.

HO, STEVE; Pacifica HS; Stanton, CA; (2); German Clb; JV Bsktbl; Var Ftbl; Var Wt Lftg; Hon Roll; Prfct Atten Awd; Orange Cnty Acad Decthln Tm Mem; CSF Mem; Schlr Of Quarter; Intl Bus.

HO, STEVE HSI-CHI; Alexander Hamilton HS Music Acad; Gardena, CA; (3); Chess Clb; Spanish Clb; Teachers Aide; Orch; Cit Awd; High Hon Roll; Prfct Atten Awd; U CA Berkeley; Elec.

HO, SUSAN; San Gabriel HS; San Gabriel, CA; (3); Intnl Clb; Spanish Clb; Cit Awd; Hon Roll; Prfct Atten Awd; Val; Bus.

HO, TANYA A; Brea-Olinda HS; Brea, CA; (3); 13/292; Hosp Aide; Sec Key Clb; Ed Yrbk; Stu Cncl; JV Socr; High Hon Roll; Grls Leag; UC San Diego; Bus.

HO, TAO T; Crawford HS; San Diego, CA; (3); French Clb; Nwsp; Socr; Hon Roll; Engrng.

HO, TARA K; Abraham Lincoln HS; San Francisco, CA; (1); Church Yth Grp; FCA; Vllybl; Japanese Club Mem; Outstndng Cmmty Svc Awd; Hnrbl Mntn Vlybl; Policewoman.

HO, THAO N; Valley HS; Sacramento, CA; (3); Computer Clb; Library Aide; Math Clb; SADD; Temple Yth Grp; Hon Roll; CSF; Friday Night Live; U CA Davis Outreach; UC Davis; Comp Engr.

HO, THAO P; Kearny HS; San Diego, CA; (2); JA; Model UN; Office Aide; Teachers Aide; Nwsp; Hon Roll; Lion Awd; Pres Acad Fit Awd; Sal; Recgntn Acad Exc; CA Bus Ed Assoc; Bus.

HO, THY; Mira Mesa HS; San Diego, CA; (2); FHA; SADD; Teachers Aide; Vllybl; Cit Awd; Doc.

HO, TRI; Independence HS; San Jose, CA; (1); French Clb; Ftbl; Wt Lftg; Hon Roll; Engr.

HO, TU M; Herbert Hoover HS; Glendale, CA; (2); French Clb; Cit Awd; Hon Roll; CSF; Japanese Club; UC Berkeley.

HO, WARREN W; Corona HS; Corona, CA; (3); 15/402; School Play; Rptr Nwsp; High Hon Roll; Pres Acad Fit Awd; Mock Trial; CSF; Interact Club; Intl Bus.

HO, WAYNE; Santa Teresa HS; San Jose, CA; (1); JA; Spanish Clb; Intrml Vllybl; High Hon Roll; Prfct Atten Awd; CA Schlrshp Fdrtn; Bus.

HO, YING-SUN; George Washington HS; San Francisco, CA; (1); High Hon Roll; Hon Roll; Peer Resource Ctr; Teen Abuse Tm; Evergreen ST Coll.

HO, YUAN-YUAN; Cerritos HS; Cerritos, CA; (3); Math Clb; Spanish Clb; Hon Roll; UC Berkeley; Bus Admn.

HOAC, NHI H; San Gabriel HS; San Gabriel, CA; (3); French Clb; FBLA; Red Cross Aide; Hon Roll; Interact Clb.

HOADLEY, RENEE MICHELLE; Sacramento HS; Sacramento, CA; (4); 6/388; SADD; Mrchg Band; Pep Band; Cit Awd; High Hon Roll; NHS; CSF Hghst Hnr Awd; Natl Hnr Soc Pin; Bnk Of Amer Achvt Awd; Friday Night Live; Music Awds; American River; Math.

HOAGLAND, ERYN; Fred C Beyer HS; Oakdale, CA; (3); Pep Clb; Service Clb; SADD; Ed Yrbk; Rep Soph Cls; Rep Jr Cls; JV Sftbl; JV Vllybl; Hon Roll; Jrnlsn.

HOAGLAND, REGINA R; Monte Vista HS; Spring Valley, CA; (4); 1/437; Pep Clb; Teachers Aide; Yrbk; Stu Cncl; JV Capt Cheerldng; Capt L Crs Cntry; Capt L Trk; DAR Awd; High Hon Roll; Hon Roll; U Notre Dame.

HOANG, ANH; Garey HS; Pomona, CA; (3); 4/400; Sec Treas French Clb; FBLA; Hosp Aide; JA; Pep Clb; Tennis; Trk; Cit Awd; High Hon Roll; NHS; Outstndng Spnsh I & Alg II Awds; Claremont; Bus Mgmt.

HOANG, BAO; Garey HS; Pomona, CA; (1); Art Clb; Boy Scts; School Play; Bsktbl; JV Tennis; Treas Asian Clb; Natl Acad Ftnss Awd; Frgn Exchng Clb.

HOANG, BAO J; Los Amigos HS; Fountain Valley, CA; (2); Boy Scts; Church Yth Grp; French Clb; Math Clb; Math Tm; Spanish Clb; Score Keeper; Socr; Vllybl; High Hon Roll.

HOANG, BINH; Santa Teresa HS; San Jose, CA; (3); Cmnty Wkr; French Clb; JA; Science Clb; Swmmng; Santa Barnara; Elec Engr.

HOANG, BINH; Westlake HS; Westlake Village, CA; (2); JV Capt Ftbl; Var L Wrstlng.

HOANG, BOUNTHEN G; Pomona HS; Pomona, CA; (2); Tennis; Vllybl; Hon Roll; GATE; CA Poly; Accntng.

HOANG, CHI N; Foothill HS; Sacramento, CA; (1); Orch; High Hon Roll; Hon Roll; UCLA; Pharm.

HOANG, DAVID; Modesto HS; Modesto, CA; (4); 4-H; Intnl Clb; Key Clb; Math Clb; JV Swmmng; Intrml Wrstlng; Cit Awd; Hon Roll; Lion Awd; Prfct Atten Awd.

HOANG, DIEC JESSE T; C K Mc Clatchy HS; Sacramento, CA; (1); SADD; UC Davis Early Acad Pgm Smmr Schl; UC Davis; Biology.

HOANG, DINH T; North Hollywood HS; North Hollywood, CA; (3); Sec Church Yth Grp; JA; Spanish Clb; Intrml Bsktbl; Intrml Trk; Cit Awd; High Hon Roll; Prfct Atten Awd; Gldn St Exam High Hnrs Alg II; CSF Pres 91.

HOANG, GENEVA; Western HS; Anaheim, CA; (3); Nwsp; Hon Roll; Asian Club; UC Irvine; Drmtlgy.

HOANG, HAIVAN V; Ocean View HS; Huntington Beach, CA; (1); JV Crs Cntry; CSF; Bus.

HOANG, HOANG NGUYEN; Hoover SR HS; San Diego, CA; (3).

HOANG, HUY; Sacramento HS; Sacramento, CA; (2); 56/550; Church Yth Grp; Key Clb; Ed Nwsp; VP Soph Cls; VP Jr Cls; Tennis; Wt Lftg; High Hon Roll; Yth Emergency Svc Red Cross; Bus.

HOANG, HUY D T; Marina HS; Huntington Beach, CA; (3); Spanish Clb; High Hon Roll; Hon Roll; Intrml Stat Bsktbl; Score Keeper; Bsktbl Team Schlr Athl; Dentstry.

HOANG, HUY T; Santa Monica HS; Santa Monica, CA; (1); Chorus; Prfct Atten Awd; Yng Entrprnrs Society Club; Engrng.

HOANG, KATHY K; Ganesha High; Pomona, CA; (4); French Clb; Math Tm; Capt Tennis; Hon Roll; CA Schltc Fed Sec; Asian Stus Assn Pres; Cal Poly.

HOANG, LIEN A; Oakland HS; Oakland, CA; (3); Cantonese Clubs; Ctznshp; Schlrshp.

HOANG, LINH TRANG N; Santa Ana HS; Santa Ana, CA; (3); Spanish Clb; Hon Roll; Viet Clb; Padres Y Maestros Unidos Awd; Cal ST Fullerton; Comp Prcsr.

HOANG, LIZ H; Bolsa Grande HS; Garden Grove, CA; (1); Chess Clb; Band; Mrchg Band; Pep Band; High Hon Roll; Hon Roll; Long Beach; Eng.

HOANG, LOC V; Saddleback HS; Santa Ana, CA; (3); Chess Clb; Science Clb; Church Choir; Phtg Yrbk; JV Bsktbl; JV Tennis; CSF; Mock Trial; Golden St Exam Hnrs; UC Schl; Comp Sci.

HOANG, LYNNE; Galileo HS; San Francisco, CA; (3); Scholastic Bowl; Church Choir; Cit Awd; Hon Roll; Chinese Bilingual Clb; San Francisco ST; Secretary.

HOANG, NHA; Santa Ana HS; Santa Ana, CA; (2); Computer Clb; Key Clb; Tennis; UCL; Comp Sci.

HOANG, PATRICK TIEU; San Gabriel HS; Rosemead, CA; (1); 7/35; Girl Scts; School Play; Wt Lftg; Cit Awd; Hon Roll; Pres Acad Fit Awd; Chinese Clb; Bk Amer Acad Achvts Awd; USC; Mdcl.

HOANG, PHONG; Chula Vista HS; Chula Vista, CA; (3); French Clb; Teachers Aide; Cit Awd; Hon Roll; NHS; CSF; Peer Contact; CA U Riverside; Engl Teacher.

HOANG, PHUONG; Oakland HS; Oakland, CA; (2); Girl Scts; Office Aide; Chorus.

HOANG, PHUONG T; The Academy Of Our Lady Of Peace; San Diego, CA; (2); Church Yth Grp; Key Clb; School Musical; Pres Soph Cls; Hon Roll; UCSD; Math.

HOANG, QUAN; C K Mc Clatchy SR HS; Sacramento, CA; (2); #1 In Class; Pres Off Church Yth Grp; French Clb; Key Clb; Math Clb; Math Tm; Hon Roll; CSF; Stnfrd; Engrng.

HOANG, QUY; Gahr HS; Cerritos, CA; (2); Art Clb; Cmnty Wkr; English Clb; JA; Math Clb; Science Clb; SADD; Phtg Yrbk; Off Soph Cls; JV Socr; Cert Achvmnt; Chem.

HOANG, REGINA; Saddleback HS; Santa Ana, CA; (1); SADD; Ed Nwsp; High Hon Roll; Hosp Vlntr; Vllybl; Bus.

HOANG, ROBERT A; Rosemead HS; Rosemead, CA; (2); Cmnty Wkr; Computer Clb; Debate Tm; FBLA; Key Clb; Math Clb; Math Tm; Spanish Clb; Var Tennis; High Hon Roll; UCLA; Med.

HOANG, THAI T; Los Amigos HS; Santa Ana, CA; (3); 2/300; Key Clb; Spanish Clb; JV Bsktbl; Wt Lftg; Hon Roll; Lion Awd; Mills House Art Show 1st Pl Black & White.

HOANG, THANH K; Andrew P Hill HS; San Jose, CA; (2); French Clb; Girl Scts; Hosp Aide; Math Clb; Math Tm; Variety Show; JV Tennis; High Hon Roll; Supt Advsry Cmmtte; Ldrshp Pgm; Mayors Yth Conf; UC Davis; Physcn.

HOANG, THANH MAI DUONG; Hoover HS; San Diego, CA; (4); 16/298; Church Yth Grp; VP French Clb; Intnl Clb; Key Clb; Church Choir; School Play; Cit Awd; High Hon Roll; Hon Roll; Bnk Amer Achvmnt Award; CIF Final Badmntn Award; High GPA Award; Pres Pro Step; UCSA Warren Coll.

HOANG, THANH T; Mira Mesa HS; San Diego, CA; (3); Acad Excllnce Awd GSE; Clsrm Stu Mnth Geom Cls; San Diego ST U; Nurse.

HOANG, THIEU; Walnut HS; Walnut, CA; (3); Intnl Clb; Teachers Aide; JV Tennis; Hon Roll; Doctor.

HOANG, THONG Q; Encina HS; Sacramento, CA; (3); Computer Clb; French Clb; Pres Intnl Clb; Var Tennis; CSF; Mock Trial; U CA Davis; Med.

HOANG, THU K; Franklin HS; Stockton, CA; (2); High Hon Roll; Hon Roll; Top 10 Of Soph Cls; UC Davis; Doctor.

HOANG, THUY; Santa Monica HS; Santa Monica, CA; (3); High Hon Roll; Asian Clb.

HOANG, TIEN; Sacramento HS; Sacramento, CA; (4); 1/395; Key Clb; Math Tm; Red Cross Aide; Sec Treas Science Clb; High Hon Roll; NHS; Hosp Vlntr; Brnz Mdl Rgnl Sci Olympiad Cmptn Prdc Tbl Ctgry; Pres & Hstrn CA Schlrshp Fdrtn; Pdtrcn.

HOANG, TON T; Milpitas HS; San Jose, CA; (2); French Clb; CA Schlrshp Fed; Natl Hnrs Soc.

HOANG, TRANG T; Saddleback HS; Santa Ana, CA; (3); FBLA; Science Clb; CA Fed Schlrshp; U Of Irvine Partner; High Hnr In Golden Exam; UC Irvine; Bio.

HOANG, TRANG TAWNI; Mira Mesa HS; San Diego, CA; (2); #1 In Class; Cmnty Wkr; 4-H; GAA; Key Clb; Science Clb; Service Clb; JV Socr; Cit Awd; 4-H Awd; Jr NHS; World Relief Clb; UC Davis; Forestry/Envrnmntl.

HOANG, TRI-DUNG; Luther Burbank HS; Sacramento, CA; (4); 1/244; French Clb; Math Clb; Science Clb; Bausch & Lomb Sci Awd; Hon Roll; Prfct Atten Awd; Val; Newcomers Club; CSF; UC Davis; Life Sci.

HOANG, TUAN Q; Grace M Davis HS; Modesto, CA; (3); 1/500; Am Leg Boys St; NFL; VP Science Clb; Speech Tm; VP VICA; JV Var Trk; High Hon Roll; Pres Acad Fit Awd; Val; Natl Young Ldrs Confrnc; Sci Olympiad Tm; Cal Tech Pasadena; Engrg.

HOANG, YEN; Robert A Millikan JR HS; Los Angeles, CA; (1); GAA; Intnl Clb; Pres Service Clb; Rep Frsh Cls; Trk; Cit Awd; High Hon Roll; Prfct Atten Awd; CSF Pres; Comp-Sci Clb.

HOANG, YEN A; Oakland HS; Oakland, CA; (3); Cantonese Club; Schlrshp; Ctznshp.

HOAR, KATHRYN G; Arcadia HS; Arcadia, CA; (3); Aud/Vis; VP Church Yth Grp; Hosp Aide; Teachers Aide; Band; Mrchg Band; School Play; Trk; City Ltl Lgu Sftbl; Cal ST Northridge; Chld Psych.

HOARD, LAURA; Lincoln HS; Stockton, CA; (4); Church Yth Grp; SADD; Teachers Aide; Hon Roll; Vol Specl Olympcs 88-89; CPR; Tchr.

HOBAN, LAUREL M; Gilroy HS; Gilroy, CA; (3); Cmnty Wkr; FBLA; Red Cross Aide; Nwsp; JV Swmmng; Hon Roll; CSF; Yosemite Clb; Jrnlst.

HOBART, CHRISTINA S; Clayton Valley HS; Concord, CA; (3); SADD; JV Vllybl; Hon Roll; CA Schlstc Fed.

HOBBARD, CRAIG D; Etna HS; Fort Jones, CA; (3); 4-H; FFA; VP Letterman Clb; Var Bsbl; Var Bsktbl; Var Capt Ftbl; Hon Roll; Human Dev.

HOBBS, ADAM J; Marina HS; Huntington Beach, CA; (1); Drama Clb; JCL; Latin Clb; Thesps; Chorus; School Musical; School Play; Stage Crew; Swing Chorus; Variety Show; Show Choir; UCLA; Theater.

HOBBS, ANGELA; Argonaut HS; Jackson, CA; (1); Pres Frsh Cls; Rep Stu Cncl; Intrml Cheerldng; Intrml Pom Pon.

HOBBS, ERIN; Bonita Vista HS; Bonita, CA; (4); 4/535; Service Clb; Thesps; Ed Nwsp; Yrbk; Cit Awd; Hon Roll; Stu Fine Arts Clb; Stu Envrnmntl Awrnss Clb; Certs Merit IB Bio & IB Wrld Cultures 88; Engl.

HOBBS, JESSICA L; Sonora Union HS; Sonora, CA; (2); 24/350; French Clb; Science Clb; Band; Mrchg Band; JV Tennis; Hon Roll; Commercial Art.

HOBBS, KAREN; Liberty Union HS; Brentwood, CA; (4); 7/225; Hon Roll; Los Medanos Coll; Art.

HOBBS, LEANN; Woodbridge HS; Irvine, CA; (4); 157/379; Cmnty Wkr; Ski Clb; Drill Tm; School Musical; Variety Show; Rptr Yrbk; Off Soph Cls; Var JV Chess Clb; Var Capt Pom Pon; Golden St Exam Hnrs Rcgntn Geom; U AZ; Bus Admin.

HOBBS, LISA A; Pacifica HS; Garden Grove, CA; (2); JV Swmmng; Hon Roll; Commercial Art.

HOBBS, STACI R; Tulare Western HS; Tulare, CA; (4); 10/250; Intnl Clb; Science Clb; High Hon Roll; Pres Acad Fit Awd; Soroptmst Grl Of Mnth; CSF; Coll Of Sequoias; Paralgl.

HOBERT, JEFF P; Dana Hills HS; Laguna Beach, CA; (1); Bsktbl.

HOBLIN, JASON R; Emerson Eldorado HS; Yorba Linda, CA; (2); Yrbk; Bsbl; Physics.

HOBSON, KATHERINE E; San Marcos HS; Santa Barbara, CA; (4); 1/303; Key Clb; Drill Tm; Stu Cncl; JV Swmmng; Ntl Merit SF; Mock Trial Atty; Amnesty Intl Pres; Natl Charity Lg/Ticktockers; Law.

HOBSON, MATT; Huntington Beach HS; Huntington Beach, CA; (3); Ftbl; Hon Roll; Pres Acad Fit Awd; Tower Awd Pin Wnnr Math; Plyr Game Awd Ftbl.

HOBSON, MICHAEL H; Monte Vista HS; Spring Valley, CA; (3); 41/454; Boy Scts; Church Yth Grp; Intnl Clb; Math Clb; Bsktbl; Ftbl; High Hon Roll; Eagle Scout; Hnrs Golden St Ex Geo,U S His.

HOBSON, SCOTT D; Adolfo Camarillo HS; Camarillo, CA; (4); German Clb; Key Clb; Science Clb; Socr; High Hon Roll; Sal; CSF; UC Santa Barbara Rgnts Schlrshp; Natl Hnr Rl; U CA Santa Barbara; Chem.

HOBSON, TIFFANY; Vallejo SR HS; Vallejo, CA; (2); Drama Clb; Model UN; Spanish Clb; SADD; School Play; Ed Nwsp; JV Cheerldng; JV Sftbl; JV Vllybl; Cit Awd; Writing Poems & Stories; 1st White Person In Black Stu Union; Foreign Languages.

HOCH, SEAN R; Ontario HS; Ontario, CA; (2); French Clb; JV Bsbl; Hon Roll; Prfct Atten Awd; CA U; Sci.

HOCHER, LILIANA; Lynwood Adventist Acad; Los Angeles, CA; (2); Drama Clb; GAA; Quiz Bowl; Scholastic Bowl; School Play; Yrbk; Treas Frsh Cls; Stu Cncl; Bsktbl; Cheerldng; Cal Poly San Luis Obispo; Arch.

HOCHGURTEL, DANIEL A; Warren HS; Downey, CA; (1); German Clb; JV Ftbl; JV Wt Lftg; USC; Bus.

HOCHKOEPPLER, TULIO J; Carmel HS; Carmel Valley, CA; (3); 31/144; Letterman Clb; Spanish Clb; Varsity Clb; Band; Orch; Treas Jr Cls; Treas Sr Cls; Var Bsbl; Var Bsktbl; Var Capt Ftbl; Htl Mgmt.

HOCKETT, AMY L; La Sierra HS; Riverside, CA; (2); JV Bsktbl; Var Sftbl; JV Vllybl; Cit Awd; Sftbl MVP; U Sthrn CA; Physcn.

HOCKING, DIANE E; Victor Valley HS; Victorville, CA; (3); Church Yth Grp; Drama Clb; French Clb; Ski Clb; SADD; Thesps; School Play; Hon Roll; CA Arts Schlr; U Burbank-Berkeley; Pol Sci.

HOCKLESS, CYNTHIA E; Eisenhower HS; Bloomington, CA; (3); Var Bsktbl; Var Trk; Hon Roll; Lawyer.

HODEL, CHRISTINA A; Beaumont HS; Cherry Valley, CA; (3); 7/200; Var L Swmmng; Var L Vllybl; Hon Roll; NHS; CSF; UC Riverside; Dentstry.

HODEL, GREGORY R; Don Antonio Lugo HS; Chino, CA; (4); 1/651; French Clb; Capt JV Ftbl; L Capt Trk; High Hon Roll; NHS; Ntl Merit Ltr; Val; Natl Mrt Special Schlrshp; Robert C Byrd Hnrs Schlr; Bank Of Amer Achvt Awd; UCLA.

HODGE, BRANDON M; Tulare Union HS; Tulare, CA; (2); 5/400; Math Clb; Math Tm; Stu Cncl; JV Bsbl; JV Socr; Cit Awd; Hon Roll; Prfct Atten Awd; CSF; Hnrs 1st Yr Algbra Gldn St Exm; Acctng.

HODGE, REBECCA; El Toro HS; El Toro, CA; (3); 75/550; Church Yth Grp; Thesps; School Play; L Var Cheerldng; L Var Pom Pon; High Hon Roll; Hstry Day 1st Pl Dist; CA Schlrshp Fed; Engl.

HODGE, SUZANNE M; Chester HS; Chester, CA; (3); 6/47; Church Yth Grp; Teachers Aide; JV Bsktbl; JV Crs Cntry; Stat Score Keeper; Trk; JV Var Vllybl; High Hon Roll; Eqstrn Sprts; CSF Ofcr; Yth To Yth Anti-Drg Pgm; Sprts Med.

HODGE, TERRA; Redwood HS; Tiburon, CA; (2); Art Clb; Church Yth Grp; Dance Clb; Key Clb; Latin Clb; Quiz Bowl; Ski Clb; Bsktbl; Sftbl; Crew.

HODGE-LANE, RONNELL; Fred C Beyer HS; Modesto, CA; (1); Hon Roll; Piano Class Activities; Psychologist.

HODGES, BRANDON; Foothill HS; Pleasanton, CA; (3); Boy Scts; Church Yth Grp; Pres Frsh Cls; Bsktbl; Hon Roll; Jr NHS; NHS; Pres Acad Fit Awd.

HODGES, DOUGLAS J; Woodland HS; Woodland, CA; (3); Pres Key Clb; VICA; JV Intrml Crs Cntry; JV Intrml Trk; Prfct Atten Awd; Heroes Awd; Auto Tech.

HODGES, JASON; Hanford Joint Union HS; Hanford, CA; (3); FCA; FFA; Band; Jazz Band; Mrchg Band; Pep Band; Var Crs Cntry; Var Trk; Hon Roll; TX A&M; Vet Med.

HODGES, JENNIFER L; Foothill HS; Santa Ana, CA; (2); 77/326; Church Yth Grp; Rptr Nwsp; JV Swmmng; High Hon Roll; Hon Roll; Gldn St Exam Hnrs; CIF Swim Rly 3rd Pl; Amateur Prose Clb; Jrnlsm Awds 89-90; Tchr.

HODGES, KRISTIN; Fred C Beyer HS; Modesto, CA; (4); 32/506; Dance Clb; German Clb; Intnl Clb; Service Clb; SADD; Rep Frsh Cls; Var Cheerldng; Cit Awd; 4-H Awd; High Hon Roll; Smi-Fnlst Paigeshp Pgm WA DC; Smi-Fnlst Cmp Royal, Grls ST; Grmn-Amer Prtnrshp Pgm Exchng; Ag Bus.

HODGES, LAURA M; Fairfield HS; Suisun City, CA; (4); Church Yth Grp; FHA; Hosp Aide; Office Aide; Pep Clb; Teachers Aide; Rep Frsh Cls; JV Cheerldng; Var Gym; JV Score Keeper; Solano CC.

HODGES, MARCI L; Clovis West HS; Clovis, CA; (3); Church Yth Grp; FCA; Ski Clb; Church Choir; Treas Sr Cls; Stu Cncl; Powder Puff Ftbl; High Hon Roll; Piano; Fresno ST U; Bus.

HODGES, SUSAN M; Lutheran HS Of San Diego; Lemon Grove, CA; (4); German Clb; Co-Capt Key Clb; Science Clb; Nwsp; Pres Stu Cncl; Dnfth Awd; High Hon Roll; NHS; Pres Acad Fit Awd; Val; Laurels For Leaders; Prin Ldrshp Awd; Tandy Tech Schlrs Outstndng Stu & Acad Top 2% Awds; UCSD; Animanl Physiology.

HODGES, WES; Tokay HS; Lodi, CA; (2); Pres 4-H; L Swmmng; Hon Roll; Pres Acad Fit Awd; Tn Ldr 4-H; Rgnl Rcrdbk Wnnr 4-H; Cert Lifegrd.

HODGIN, SANDRA L; St Francis HS; Saratoga, CA; (1); Church Yth Grp; Cmnty Wkr; Drill Tm; Vllybl; Hon Roll; Law.

HODGKINSON, ROBIN D; El Cajon Valley HS; El Cajon, CA; (3); 25/440; Key Clb; Bsktbl; Mst Imprvd Player Var Bsktbl 90; Pre-Med.

HODNETT, HEATHER L; William S Hart HS; Valencia, CA; (2); Band; Drill Tm; Mrchg Band; School Musical; School Play; Hon Roll; OK ST U; Elem Tchng.

HODO, LINDA; Central Union HS; El Centro, CA; (2); Church Yth Grp; Cmnty Wkr; Computer Clb; Girl Scts; Pep Clb; U Of Virgin Islands; Photo.

HODO, LOUISE A; Central Union HS; El Centro, CA; (2); VP Girl Scts; CA Poly Ponoma; Coroner.

HODSON, RYAN R; Chaffey HS; Ontario, CA; (3); Boy Scts; Office Aide; Teachers Aide; Intrml Bsbl; Var Ftbl; Powder Puff Ftbl; Wt Lftg; Cal ST Fullerton; Commnctns.

HOE, J SCOTT; North Salinas HS; Salinas, CA; (3); JV Var Trk; JV Var Wt Lftg; High Hon Roll; Hon Roll; Rotary Awd; Engrng.

HOEFER, ERICH; Dos Pueblos HS; Goleta, CA; (3); 14/328; Church Yth Grp; Letterman Clb; Math Clb; Science Clb; Thesps; Acpl Chr; Band; Orch; School Play; Rptr Nwsp; Intl Rltns; Travel To USSR Smmr 89; Intl Rltns.

HOEFS, LARA BETH; University HS; Irvine, CA; (2); 48/500; Church Yth Grp; Cmnty Wkr; Dance Clb; JCL; Cit Awd; Hon Roll; Lauredte Awd Math & Dance; Mission Bell Awd; Choreography/Perf Dance Company.

HOEGGER, ERIC; Phillip & Sala Burton Academic HS; San Francisco, CA; (2); VP Science Clb; High Hon Roll; Cert Achvt World Cvlztn & Study Skls; Eng.

HOEGH, REINA M; University HS; Irvine, CA; (3); VP Cmnty Wkr; Hosp Aide; Pep Clb; Service Clb; Ski Clb; Spanish Clb; Teachers Aide; Var Cheerldng; JV Crs Cntry; Var Pom Pon; CSF; Sci & Spnsh Laureatte Awds; Natl Charity League-Ticktockers; Psych.

HOEKENGA, BRITTA; Montgomery HS; Santa Rosa, CA; (3); 1/500; French Clb; JA; Pep Clb; Teachers Aide; Drill Tm; Capt Flag Corp; Ed Yrbk; Cheerldng; Hon Roll; NHS; Outstndng Achvr Awd JR Achvt; 3yr Mem Grap Called Mekklejohn Travel For Liberal Ed; Med.

HOELSCHER, TINA; Mercy HS; San Francisco, CA; (3); Church Yth Grp; Dance Clb; GAA; Rep Stu Cncl; Var Socr.

HOEM, REBECCA A; Washington HS; Fremont, CA; (2); 10/310; Pres Church Yth Grp; Temple Yth Grp; Church Choir; Variety Show; Hgh Hnrs GSE.

HOERNER, MARILYN; Quartz Hill HS; Lancaster, CA; (2); Church Yth Grp; Drama Clb; French Clb; Teachers Aide; Cit Awd; Hon Roll; CSF; UCLA; Pedtrcn.

HOFACKER, LUKE A; Westlake HS; Thousand Oaks, CA; (2); 25/431; JV Crs Cntry; JV Trk; Hon Roll; Civil Air Patrol Rnk Airman 1st Clss; Waiter Wrk 10-15 Hrs Wk; USAF Acad; Pilot.

HOFER, JASON; Whittier Christian HS; Norwalk, CA; (2); Church Yth Grp; Bsbl; High Hon Roll; Hon Roll; Ntl Merit Ltr; CSF; Cal Poly U; Strctrl Engr.

HOFER, JEANETTE; Casa Grande HS; Petaluma, CA; (4); Teachers Aide; Capt Cheerldng; Pom Pon; Score Keeper; Hon Roll; Santa Rosa Beauty Coll Schlrshp; AAL Schlrshp Aid Assn For Lutherans; 2nd Altr Dairy Princess Dist 3; Santa Rosa Beauty; Csmtlgst.

HOFERER, DAVID FRANCIS; Don Bosco Technical Inst; Rowland Heights, CA; (2); Church Yth Grp; Cmnty Wkr; VP Letterman Clb; Varsity Clb; L Capt Crs Cntry; L Var Trk; High Hon Roll; NHS; HOBY Fndtn Stu Ambssdr; Building Indus Assn 2nd Pl Soph-Residential Div; Engrng.

HOFERER, MARK EDWARD; Don Bosco Technical Inst; Rowland Heights, CA; (1); 25/245; Church Yth Grp; Cmnty Wkr; Letterman Clb; Var L Crs Cntry; Var L Trk; High Hon Roll; Prfct Atten Awd; Campus Ministry; Aviator.

HOFF, CHRISTINA L; Galt Joint Union HS; Galt, CA; (2); Pres Drama Clb; Intnl Clb; Spanish Clb; Thesps; School Musical; School Play; Pres Soph Cls; Mgr Stu Cncl; JV Sftbl; Hon Roll; Spnsh Awd; Physcl Ed Awd; Engl Awd; Pltcl Sci.

HOFF, JENNIFER A; St Francis HS; Los Altos, CA; (3); 99/350; Church Yth Grp; Pres Cmnty Wkr; Letterman Clb; Pep Clb; Service Clb; SADD; Rptr Nwsp; Var JV Trk; JV Var Vllybl; High Hon Roll; Rage Clb Capt 90-91; Pep Clb Of St Francis; Rotary Yth Ldrshp Awd Schlrshp; Nordstrom Brss Plum Fshn Bd; UCLA; Sociology.

HOFFA, KELLY S; Livermore HS; Livermore, CA; (2); FHA; Office Aide; Band; Score Keeper; High Hon Roll; Hon Roll; Outstndng Acadmc Prfrmnc Gldn St Alg Exam 89; Acadmc Excllnc Awd.

HOFFER, AMY H; El Toro HS; El Toro, CA; (3); Church Yth Grp; Dance Clb; Drama Clb; Letterman Clb; Thesps; Chorus; Church Choir; Drill Tm; School Musical; School Play; Girls Leag; Keywanettes; Biola U.

HOFFERT, LAURA C; Atascadero HS; Atascadero, CA; (2); Church Yth Grp; Drama Clb; Thesps; JV Swmmng; Hon Roll; Lawyer.

HOFFMAN, AMIE C; Bonita HS; La Verne, CA; (1); Hon Roll.

HOFFMAN, CARLY M; Madera HS; Madera, CA; (2); Church Yth Grp; 4-H; Intnl Clb; Science Clb; SADD; Hon Roll; Kiwanis Awd; Lrn Trvl Cntrs; Pen Pals All Over Canada , Japan, Malaysia; Kiwans Stu Of Month; BYU; Hstry Teacher.

HOFFMAN, CLARISSA D; Sunny Hills HS; Fullerton, CA; (3); 45/400; Cmnty Wkr; Co-Capt Dance Clb; Capt Debate Tm; Pep Clb; Pres Science Clb; SADD; Pres Band; Pres Frsh Cls; Capt Cheerldng; Hon Roll; Peer Leadership; UCLA; Communications.

HOFFMAN, CLINT; Mountain Empire HS; Descanso, CA; (3); Church Yth Grp; Letterman Clb; Spanish Clb; JV Var Bsbl; JV Var Ftbl; Var Socr; Hon Roll; Pres Acad Fit Awd; Cal Poly; Arch.

HOFFMAN, DARON M; Santa Cruz HS; Santa Cruz, CA; (3); Am Leg Boys St; Debate Tm; Drama Clb; Speech Tm; Thesps; Ed Nwsp; High Hon Roll; Hon Roll; Ntl Merit Ltr; Pres Acad Fit Awd; JR Statesman; Elks Club/Club Zone Reg Oratorical Cont Wnnr; Prfssnl Actor In Shakespeare Santa Cruz; Government/Diplomacy.

HOFFMAN, ELISA R; John F Kennedy HS; Granada Hills, CA; (2); Aud/Vis; Church Yth Grp; Key Clb; Cit Awd; High Hon Roll; Hon Roll; Pres Acad Fit Awd; JR Statesmen Of Amer Treas; CA Schlrshp Fdrtn; US Space Acad Lvl II Grad; Sci.

HOFFMAN, JEFFREY R; Holtville HS; Holtville, CA; (3); AFS; VP FFA; NFL; Pep Clb; Speech Tm; Phtg Yrbk; Stu Cncl; JV Ftbl; JV Var Golf; Var Wrstlng; Cmmnctns.

HOFFMAN, JENNIE L; Calvary Chapel HS; Huntington Beach, CA; (2); Teachers Aide; Var L Sftbl; Var L Vllybl; Sftbl-Plaq Best Defsv Player; Vllybl-Plaq Most Impvd; Chld Care.

HOFFMAN, JENNIFER; University City HS; La Jolla, CA; (4); 1/320; Am Leg Aux Girls St; Scholastic Bowl; Chorus; School Musical; School Play; Ed Nwsp; High Hon Roll; NHS; Ntl Merit Schol; UC Bekeley; Physics.

HOFFMAN, JENNIFER L; Fairfield HS; Fairfield, CA; (3); VP Bus Profs of Am; Church Yth Grp; FBLA; Key Clb; Pres Science Clb; School Play; Variety Show; High Hon Roll; NHS; Pres Of Cnsrvtn Clb; 3rd Pl Acadc Decathalon; U Of Davis; Women Studies.

HOFFMAN, LISA D; Taft Union HS; Taft, CA; (3); 3/180; Drama Clb; Yrbk; VP Jr Cls; JV Var Vllybl; High Hon Roll; Ntl Merit Ltr; Southern Methodist U; Jrnlsm.

HOFFMAN, MITZIE; Southwest HS; San Diego, CA; (4); 16/498; VP JA; SADD; Off Frsh Cls; Rep Sr Cls; Stu Cncl; Intrml Vllybl; Cit Awd; Hon Roll; Prfct Atten Awd; CSF; San Diego ST; Bus Mgmt.

HOFFMAN, RENEE J; West HS; Torrance, CA; (1); 93/340; Church Yth Grp; Drama Clb; Band; Mrchg Band; Hon Roll; Am Yth Soccr Assn All Star.

HOFFMAN, RICHARD; Lakewood HS; Lakewood, CA; (4); Boy Scts; Church Yth Grp; Red Cross Aide; Band; Orch; Var JV Ftbl; Var JV Wrstlng; Elks Awd; Lion Awd; Black Belt Karate; BYU.

HOFFMAN, RYAN S; Thousand Oaks HS; Thousand Oaks, CA; (2); 54/554; Cmnty Wkr; Temple Yth Grp; Hon Roll; Prfct Atten Awd; AYSO Soccer; Amer Fld Hcky; Law.

HOFFMAN, WENDY; Clovis West HS; Fresno, CA; (4); 1/575; Cmnty Wkr; Drama Clb; FBLA; Intnl Clb; Math Clb; Math Tm; NFL; Office Aide; Pep Clb; Speech Tm; Fresno State; Business Admin.

HOFFMANN, GARY R; Petaluma HS; Petaluma, CA; (4); Aud/Vis; Debate Tm; Pres Drama Clb; French Clb; Speech Tm; Pres Thesps; Varsity Clb; School Musical; School Play; Stage Crew; Stu Mnth 90; Actor Yr 90; Mst Insprtnl & Imprvd Swm Tm; CA ST U Chico; Broadcstng.

HOFFMANN, LAMAIA L; Sequoia HS; San Carlos, CA; (2); Church Yth Grp; Letterman Clb; Rep Stu Cncl; L Var Crs Cntry; L Var Socr; Var Trk; Los Amigos De Las Americas-Ecuador Smmr 90 Vlntr; Csf; Amnesty Intl; Golden St Exams; Geom W/Hnrs; Bio Sci.

HOFMANN, CHRISTINA; Mercy HS; San Bruno, CA; (3); French Clb; GAA; Service Clb; Crs Cntry; High Hon Roll; JSA; CSF; Envrnmntl Clb.

HOFMANN, DANIELA; Canyon Springs HS; West Germany; (4); German Clb; Intnl Clb; Ski Clb; Varsity Clb; Gym; Socr; Tennis; Hon Roll; Achvts In Tnns; Marine Bio.

HOFMANN, MARK D; Los Gatos HS; Los Gatos, CA; (2); Boy Scts; Key Clb; Bsktbl; Tennis; Hon Roll; Eagle Scout.

HOFMANN, SANDRA; Rowland HS; Rowland Heights, CA; (3); Band; Drm Mjr(t); Mrchg Band; Cit Awd; Hon Roll; Drum Major Awds; Spcl Ed.

HOFMANN, SATOMI E; San Domenico Schl; San Anselmo, CA; (4); 12/43; Drama Clb; Pres German Clb; Mrchg Band; Orch; School Musical; School Play; Stage Crew; Variety Show; High Hon Roll; Treas NHS; San Domenico Virtuoso Prog; CA Arts Schlr Theatre; NSA; Musical Theatre.

HOFMANN, THAD J; St Joseph-Notre Dame HS; Alameda, CA; (3); JV Var Bsbl; JV Var Bsktbl; High Hon Roll; Hon Roll; Lector St Philip Eri Church 3 Yrs; Impire Little League 1 Yr; Las Vegas U; Bus.

HOFSTETTER, JASON B; Ukiah HS; Petaluma, CA; (3); FFA; Letterman Clb; Varsity Clb; JV Var Ftbl; Var L Trk.

HOFT, PETER; Poway HS; Poway, CA; (2); Church Yth Grp; Cmnty Wkr; German Clb; Science Clb; Hon Roll; NHS; Sccr; Raquetbl Tm; Little Leag Asst Mgr; U Of MI; NROTC.

HOGAN, ADRIENNE Y; Bullard HS; Fresno, CA; (2); 112/450; Debate Tm; NFL; UCLA; Mrktng.

HOGAN, JACK; Corona Del Mar HS; Balboa Island, CA; (3); Church Yth Grp; Key Clb; Letterman Clb; Off Jr Cls; Capt L Crs Cntry; Capt L Trk; High Hon Roll; Hon Roll; Pres Acad Fit Awd; Reached CIF Cross Cntry & Track 800 Meters; PTA Reflections Contest 1st Pl Art & 2nd Pl Poetry; Eng.

HOGAN, JENNIFER; East Bakersfield HS; Bakersfield, CA; (4); Church Yth Grp; Intnl Clb; VP SADD; Chorus; School Play; Hon Roll; YMCA Leaders Club; Bakersfield Coll; Pre-Sch Teach.

HOGAN, KEVIN; Carson HS; Carson, CA; (3); Computer Clb; Ftbl; Trk; Wt Lftg; History Acad Awd; Comp Engr.

HOGAN, KRISTI; Highlands HS; N Highlands, CA; (3); Am Leg Aux Girls St; Cmnty Wkr; Drama Clb; Red Cross Aide; School Play; Ed Nwsp; Friday Night Live Pres; Intl Order Of Jobs Daughers; Teenwork Conf 90; U CA Davis; Intl Relations.

HOGAN, MATTHEW; Poway HS; Carlsbad, CA; (2); Church Yth Grp; English Clb; Speech Tm; Chorus; School Play; Variety Show; Off Frsh Cls; Stu Cncl; Speach & Debate; Orgnl Poetry & Prose; Berkeley U; Jrnlsm.

HOGAN, STEPHANIE A; San Luis Obispo HS; San Luis Obispo, CA; (2); 3/300; Church Yth Grp; Hosp Aide; Key Clb; Pep Clb; SADD; JV Cheerldng; High Hon Roll; JV Trk; CSF; U Of CA Santa Cruz; Chld Psych.

HOGAN, STEVE; Lodi HS; Woodbridge, CA; (4); Boy Scts; Church Yth Grp; 4-H; Key Clb; Acpl Chr; Band; Chorus; Church Choir; Mrchg Band; Socr; Stockton Chorale Australian Tour; Music.

HOGARTH, TARIK J; Daniel Murphy HS; Los Angeles, CA; (1); Var Crs Cntry; Var L Trk; High Hon Roll; Tphy MVP Track 89-90; Stanford; Sftwr Engr.

HOGG, ANGELA D; El Toro HS; Fairfax Station, VA; (1); 31/550; Church Yth Grp; JV Crs Cntry; JV Trk; High Hon Roll; Aeronautical Engrng.

HOGGATT, MYCHAL J; Liberty Christian HS; Westminster, CA; (2); Church Yth Grp; Mrchg Band; Pep Band; School Musical; Rptr Nwsp; Pres Frsh Cls; Rep Stu Cncl; Var L Bsbl; Var L Bsktbl; Var L Ftbl; City League Bsktbl; San Diego ST; Writr.

HOGUE, STEVEN J; Chico SR HS; Chico, CA; (3); Intnl Clb; Office Aide; Teachers Aide; VICA; Band; Rptr Nwsp; Var Trk; Cit Awd; Hon Roll; Civil Air Patrol; Criminology.

HOHENBERGE, JULIE A; Thomas Downey HS; Modesto, CA; (1); Science Clb; Service Clb; CSF; Translator.

HOHN, DAVID T; Lincoln HS; Stockton, CA; (3); 23/570; VICA; Stage Crew; Yrbk; Crs Cntry; Trk; High Hon Roll; Hon Roll; Prfct Atten Awd.

HOHN, JOSHUA N; Upper Lake HS; Upper Lake, CA; (4); 3/57; Am Leg Boys St; Quiz Bowl; SADD; Pres Frsh Cls; Pres Soph Cls; Pres Jr Cls; Pres Stu Cncl; JV Var Ftbl; Elks Awd; Pres Acad Fit Awd; Stu Lion 88-90; Lions Clb; Jvnle Justc/Delqncy Prevntn Cmmssn 88-90, Co-Chrmn; 1st Hnrs Div GPA; CA ST U Chico; Poltcl Sci.

HOISINGTON, APRIL A; La Sierra HS; Riverside, CA; (2); Church Yth Grp; Cmnty Wkr; Drama Clb; FFA; SADD; Chorus; Church Choir; School Play; JV Swmmng; Hon Roll.

HOISINGTON, BILL A; Cajon HS; San Bernardino, CA; (3); Church Yth Grp; Letterman Clb; Office Aide; Varsity Clb; Band; Mrchg Band; JV Ftbl; Var Trk; Cit Awd; Pre-Med.

HOJAT-KASHANI, ALI; Trabuca Hills HS; Mission Viejo, CA; (1); Artist.

HOK, ON; Artesia HS; Lakewood, CA; (3); Vllybl; Wrstlng; Hon Roll; Prfct Atten Awd.

HOK, PHANARY; Artesia HS; Lakewood, CA; (2); Intnl Clb; Science Clb; Spanish Clb; Yrbk; Off Soph Cls; Hon Roll; Acad Lttr Outstndng Acad Achvt 90-91; GATE Prgm; CA Schlrshp Fed; UCI; Doctor.

HOK, TOUCH; Belmont HS; Los Angeles, CA; (3); Chorus; Tennis; Hon Roll; St Schlr; VICA Club; Cntrl Amer Club; Upward Bound; CA ST Bakersfield; Bus.

HOKIT, KATRINA; Wasco Union HS; Wasco, CA; (2); Band; Mrchg Band; Pep Band; Powder Puff Ftbl; Sftbl; Hon Roll; Santa Barbara City; Bus.

HOKMABADI, SEPIDEH; Woodside HS; Menlo Park, CA; (3); 5/250; GAA; Intnl Clb; Office Aide; Varsity Clb; Ed Yrbk; Rep Frsh Cls; Rep Soph Cls; Rep Jr Cls; VP Sr Cls; Stu Cncl; Frndshp Awd; Drmrs & Doers Awd; Chem.

HOLANDA, JASON S; Grace Davis HS; Modesto, CA; (2); JV L Bsbl; JV L Bsktbl; L Ftbl; JV L Trk; Invstmnt Bnkr.

HOLAWAY, JULIE; Saint Bonaventure HS; Ventura, CA; (3); 10/122; Service Clb; Var Cheerldng; Hon Roll; NHS; CSF; 3 Supr Rbbns NCA Camp Dance; Buena Ventura Acad Jazz, Tap & Ballet Clss.

HOLBROOK, DEBORAH; Dixon HS; Vacaville, CA; (1); Drama Clb; Pres 4-H; Math Clb; Math Tm; Band; Mrchg Band; School Play; 4-H Awd; High Hon Roll; Hon Roll; Golden St Exam-Alg I Hnrs; Bus Admin.

HOLBROOK, ROXANNE NANETTE; Del Norte HS; Crescent City, CA; (4); 4/180; Drama Clb; VP Pep Clb; JV Bsktbl; JV Var Sftbl; Var Capt Vllybl; Elks Awd; High Hon Roll; Rotary Awd; Sr Grls Athlt Of Yr; Vllybll White Star; Sonoma ST U; Educ.

HOLBUS, ERIN N; St Francis HS; Carmichael, CA; (2); Dance Clb; Debate Tm; Speech Tm; JV Capt Cheerldng; Var Swmmng; Hon Roll; Manikan Manors Chmpnshp Spirit Team; Fri Night Live.

HOLCK, RYAN D; Ballard HS; Fresno, CA; (2); Aud/Vis; Church Yth Grp; Band; Mrchg Band; Stage Crew; Hon Roll; Golden St Exam Hnrs In Geom.

HOLCOMB, MATTHEW R; Lompoc HS; Lompoc, CA; (3); AFS; Church Yth Grp; Pres Band; Chorus; Jazz Band; Pep Band; Hon Roll; Master Of Crmns For HS SR Schlrshp Nght; Exch Stu To Turkey For Smmr Of 90; CA Schlrshp Fed SR Rep; Math.

HOLCOMB, MELODY D; Selma HS; Selma, CA; (2); 7/257; Church Yth Grp; Drama Clb; Q&S; Service Clb; SADD; School Play; Rptr Yrbk; SETA VP; Mountnrng; CSF; BYU; Med.

HOLCOMB, MIKE G; Oakdale HS; Oakdale, CA; (3); Stu Cncl; Tennis; Music.

HOLCOMBE, KAREN M; J F Kennedy HS; La Palma, CA; (3); Church Yth Grp; FBLA; Quiz Bowl; Band; Church Choir; Color Guard; Mrchg Band; Pep Band; Hon Roll; Frshmn & Soph Bnd Awds.

HOLDEN, KARLEE; Los Gatos HS; Monte Sereno, CA; (2); Girl Scts; Rep Soph Cls; Var Socr; Var Trk; Hon Roll; Lion Awd; Leos & Alfs Clubs; Karate; UC-BERKELEY; Psych.

HOLDEN, MARK W; Thomas Downey HS; Modesto, CA; (4); Cit Awd; Prfct Atten Awd; MJC; Ed.

HOLDEN, MELISSA R; Artesia HS; Lakewood, CA; (2); Church Yth Grp; Spanish Clb; Socr; Sftbl; Capt JV Vllybl; High Hon Roll; PAL; CSF; Vlybl Clb; Med.

HOLDEN, ROBERT J; San Luis Obispo SR HS; San Luis Obispo, CA; (1); Church Yth Grp; Science Clb; JV Socr; JV Swmmng; NASA Slctd 2 Prjcts Send Space Shuttle; CA Poly San Luis Obispo.

HOLDEN, TINA L; Sutter Union HS; Sutter, CA; (2); Drama Clb; FFA; Intnl Clb; Letterman Clb; Spanish Clb; Variety Show; Sftbl; Stat Wrstlng; Hon Roll; Arch.

HOLDEN, TONIA; Willows HS; Willows, CA; (2); Church Yth Grp; Cit Awd; Hon Roll; Kiwanis Awd; Friday Night Live Drug & Alcohol Prvntn Clb & CSF; Comp Prgrmmr.

HOLDEN, VICTORIA L; College Park HS; Pleasant Hill, CA; (3); 2/317; Church Yth Grp; Hosp Aide; High Hon Roll; Outstndng Frshmn Sci Stu Plaque; Stu Of The Mnth; Phi Delta Kappas Smr Camp/Inst Prspctv Tchrs 90; Psych.

HOLDER, LISA M; Independence HS; San Jose, CA; (3); Vlntr Big Brothers/Big Sisters Santa Clara Cnty; Play Northside Theatre Co; San Jose St Advc Spec Educ; Psych.

HOLDER, TAMMY; Tracy HS; Tracy, CA; (2); 5/483; Pres Church Yth Grp; Lit Mag; Var Tennis; High Hon Roll; CSF; BYU.

HOLDING, ANNE L; Henry M Gunn HS; Palo Alto, CA; (4); Church Yth Grp; JV Swmmng.

HOLGADO, SHARITA A; Pinole Valley HS; Hercules, CA; (1).

HOLGUIN, DENISE M; Chino HS; Victorville, CA; (3); Drama Clb; Ski Clb; Spanish Clb; Teachers Aide; JV L Bsktbl; JV Powder Puff Ftbl; JV L Vllybl; Hon Roll; NEDT Awd; Pres Acad Fit Awd; Minimum Comptncy Testng Prfct Awd; Mock Trial Team 89 90; Crmnl Law; Ontario Intl Airln Acad; Flght.

HOLGUIN, FREDDY; Nogales HS; La Puente, CA; (3); Teachers Aide; Varsity Clb; Bsbl; Ftbl; Wt Lftg; Wrstlng; High Hon Roll; Hon Roll; Rio Hondo; Law.

HOLGUIN, KRISTIE D; Thomas Downey HS; Modesto, CA; (3); Sec AFS; Key Clb; Latin Clb; Service Clb; SADD; Socr; Sftbl; Hon Roll; Downey Knight Achvmnt Awrd; U C Davis:Child Psych.

HOLLAND, BRANDON K; Hanford HS; Hanford, CA; (1); Acpl Chr; Chorus; Socr; Trk; Wt Lftg; Hon Roll.

HOLLAND, CARRIE A; Tulare Union HS; Tulare, CA; (2); FFA; Hon Roll; Ag Teacher.

HOLLAND, CHARITY T; Encinal HS; Dallas, TX; (3); 64/223; Church Yth Grp; ROTC; Var Socr; Var Swmmng; Var Vllybl; Hon Roll; Water Polo; Racquetball; Most Outstndng Fml Swmr-Swm Season 90; Jobs Daughters; US Navy.

HOLLAND, DAMIAN; Paraclete Ca; Acton, CA; (4); 4/128; Cmnty Wkr; Intrml Bsbl; Intrml Bsktbl; Intrml Fld Hcky; Intrml Ftbl; Intrml Var Socr; Intrml Sftbl; Intrml Swmmng; Intrml Tennis; Intrml Trk; Berkeley; Astro Engrng.

HOLLAND, DIANA; Fontana HS; Fontana, CA; (2); Hon Roll; U Redlands; Intl Rltns.

HOLLAND, GROVER DALE; Palmdale HS; Littlerock, CA; (3); 15/644; Pres French Clb; High Hon Roll; CSF; Gldn ST Exm In Geo; Psych.

HOLLAND, JENNIFER D; Estancia HS; Costa Mesa, CA; (4); Church Yth Grp; Chorus; Fld Hcky; Sftbl; Swmmng; Orange Coast Coll; Rest Mgt.

HOLLAND, JOHN W; Quincy JR/Sr HS; Quincy, CA; (3); Am Leg Boys St; Boy Scts; Cmnty Wkr; Spanish Clb; Band; VP Soph Cls; Pres Stu Cncl; JV Var Bsktbl; JV Var Ftbl; JV Trk; Eagle Sct; Rotary Yth Ldrshp Awd; Marine Bio.

HOLLAND, JOSEPH A; Ygnacio Valley HS; Pleasant Hill, CA; (3); Boy Scts; Ftbl; Trk; Wt Lftg.

HOLLAND, MICHAH D; Paraclete HS; Acton, CA; (3); School Musical; Cit Awd; High Hon Roll; Hon Roll; Jr NHS; Intrml Bsbl; Intrml Bsktbl; Intrml Fld Hcky; Intrml Ftbl; Intrml Socr; Coll Of Art/Dsgn; Cmmrcl Art.

HOLLAND, MIKE W; Bonita Vista HS; Bonita, CA; (4); Church Yth Grp; Intnl Clb; Math Tm; VICA; Numerous Actvts; SDSU; Bus.

HOLLAND, MORGAN; Clovis West HS; Madera, CA; (3); Cmnty Wkr; Hosp Aide; Intnl Clb; Letterman Clb; Varsity Clb; Rptr Nwsp; L Crs Cntry; L Trk; Hon Roll; Drama Clb; Hlth Care.

HOLLAND, STACY R; El Toro HS; El Toro, CA; (2); 82/536; Rep Key Clb; VP Chorus; Intrml JV Fld Hcky; JV Var Sftbl; High Hon Roll; Hon Roll; Jr NHS; NHS; Pres Acad Fit Awd; UCI Hnr Pgm Chem Hnrs; UCSD; Pre Med.

HOLLCROFT, STEPHANIE M; Clovis West HS; Fresno, CA; (2); Church Yth Grp; Drama Clb; Key Clb; NFL; Ski Clb; Stage Crew; High Hon Roll; UC; Entrnmnt Ind.

HOLLENBECK, DIANA R; Marysville HS; Marysville, CA; (2); Lbrn Band; Jazz Band; Mrchg Band; Pep Band; Hon Roll; Northern CA Hnr Band; Instrumentalist Mag Musicianship Awd; SAC ST U; Crmnl Lawyer.

HOLLEY, CHRISTINA; Artesia HS; Lakewood, CA; (1); Church Yth Grp; Pep Clb; Rep Frsh Cls; Cheerldng; Hon Roll; Bus.

HOLLEY, JASON D; Lincoln HS; Stockton, CA; (3); Ski Clb; Variety Show; Var JV Bsbl; JV Var Ftbl; JV Var Wt Lftg; Hon Roll; Varsity Ftbl Hnrb Mntn; Backpacking; Hunting; Waterskiing; Coll; Waste Mngmnt.

HOLLEY, JENNIFER; Tulare Western HS; Tulare, CA; (3); Drama Clb; Hist Service Clb; Variety Show; Cheerldng; Feather River JC; Envrnmtl Sci.

HOLLIDAY, ERICK B; Mater Dei HS; Westminster, CA; (1); 1/604; Bsktbl; Ftbl; Hon Roll; Acad Excllnc Commendation Engl & Span; Engrng.

HOLLIDAY, JAMIE M; Ontario HS; Ontario, CA; (3); Dance Clb; Band; Mrchg Band; Orch; CSF.

HOLLIDAY, KAREN; Mater Dei HS; Westminster, CA; (4); 1/526; Church Yth Grp; Cmnty Wkr; Spanish Clb; Ed Yrbk; Stu Cncl; Trk; High Hon Roll; NHS; CSF; Natl Hspnc Schlrs Awd Pgm Semi-Fnlst; UC Berkeley.

HOLLIE, SHANNYN D; Capuchino HS; San Bruno, CA; (1); Rep Frsh Cls; Rep Stu Cncl; JV Bsktbl; Var Gym; JV Vllybl; City League Sftbl; Water Skiing Tourns; Snow Skiing; Santa Barbara U; Arch.

HOLLINGSHAUS, WADE J; Mission Viejo HS; Mission Viejo, CA; (3); Boy Scts; Church Yth Grp; Cmnty Wkr; Drama Clb; German Clb; Math Tm; Thesps; Sec Band; Church Choir; Jazz Band; Wrtg.

HOLLINGSHEAD, STACY L; Paraclete HS; Lancaster, CA; (3); SADD; Drill Tm; Yrbk; Rep Frsh Cls; Rep Stu Cncl; High Hon Roll; Hon Roll; NHS; CSF; Bus.

HOLLINGSWORTH, LAURA; Coast Union HS; Cambria, CA; (3); AFS; Church Yth Grp; FBLA; Spanish Clb; SADD; VP Sr Cls; Var Capt Bsktbl; Var Sftbl; Var Vllybl; High Hon Roll; Cuesta.

HOLLINS, JASON C; Santana HS; Santee, CA; (3); 2/290; Quiz Bowl; Teachers Aide; JV Bsbl; JV Socr; Var L Tennis; High Hon Roll; Pres Acad Fit Awd; Rotary Awd; Voice Dem Awd; Jr Hnr Guard; Bus Advertising.

HOLLINS, JASON D; Clovis HS; Clovis, CA; (3); 34/635; Church Yth Grp; FCA; Letterman Clb; Science Clb; Rep Jr Cls; Swmmng; High Hon Roll; Hon Roll; Wtr Polo; USAFA; Pilot.

HOLLIS, ANITA; Bolsa Grande HS; Garden Grove, CA; (3); Church Yth Grp; Drama Clb; Speech Tm; Band; Mrchg Band; Yrbk; Off Frsh Cls; Off Soph Cls; Off Jr Cls; Stu Cncl; Jobs Daughters; Yth Ldrshp For Action; Public Relations.

HOLLIS, MICHELLE; Alameda HS; Alameda, CA; (2); 12/276; Pep Clb; School Musical; School Play; Hist Frsh Cls; JV Pom Pon; Cit Awd; High Hon Roll; Prfct Atten Awd; Pres Acad Fit Awd; Outstndng Actress; CSF; Artstc Vllr Sktr Natl Cham In Age Grp; UC-DAVIS; Vet.

HOLLMAN, MICHAEL W; Cordova SR HS; Rancho Cordova, CA; (3); Model UN; Science Clb; Ski Clb; 3rd Pl Greatr Sacramento Voctnl Ed Fair; CSU Sacramento; Engrng.

HOLLOWATY, ERIC C; Trabuco Hills HS; El Toro, CA; (2); 6/420; Chess Clb; Scholastic Bowl; Service Clb; Spanish Clb; Speech Tm; Lit Mag; JV Golf; Var Lcrss; High Hon Roll; NHS; Acad Decathlon Awd Wnnr; HOBY Ambssdr S CA Smnr; JR Statesmen Summer Schl Yale U; Ivy League; Finance.

HOLLOWAY, MARILYNN; St Paul HS; Whittier, CA; (2); 9/300; Spanish Clb; Drill Tm; JV Capt Cheerldng; Pom Pon; Hon Roll; NHS; Spanish NHS; CSF; USC; Med.

HOLLSTEIN, MONIKA L; Irvine HS; Irvine, CA; (1); Drama Clb; German Clb; JV Sftbl; Spirit Clb.

HOLLY, ALLISON; Porterville HS; Porterville, CA; (1); Church Yth Grp; Pep Clb; Band; Cheerldng; Pom Pon; Swmmng; Hon Roll; Cal Poly.

HOLM, CHIRSTOPHER D; Paraclete HS; Lancaster, CA; (2); Key Clb; Var Crs Cntry; JV Socr; Var Trk; Cal Poly Pomona; Engr.

HOLM, STASHA; Washington Union HS; Fresno, CA; (3); 4/175; Am Leg Aux Girls St; Church Yth Grp; Cmnty Wkr; Drama Clb; FCA; French Clb; FBLA; Intnl Clb; Band; Church Choir; Rotary Yth Ldrshp Camp; Close-Up Fndtn Fllwshp To Washington DC; Soclgy.

HOLMAN, BRITA; Orangewood Adventist Acad; La Habra, CA; (3); Church Yth Grp; Drama Clb; Teachers Aide; Chorus; Stage Crew; Ed Yrbk; Off Soph Cls; Sec Pres Stu Cncl; Hon Roll; Handbell Choir; Pres Assoctd Stu Bdy; Spcl Acad Awd Chem; Stu Agnst Drug Use; Loma Linda U; Med.

HOLMAN, DONALD E; Bonita HS; La Verne, CA; (2); Chorus; Hon Roll; Coin Collecting; U CA Berkeley; Cmptrs.

HOLMAN, KIM D; Live Oak HS; Morgan Hill, CA; (2); Dance Clb; Hosp Aide; Library Aide; Chorus; Flag Corp; Hon Roll.

HOLMAN, KIRK H; Fresno Christian HS; Fresno, CA; (2); Church Yth Grp; Cmnty Wkr; Teachers Aide; Church Choir; Orch; Var Bsbl; Var Bsktbl; Var Ftbl; Hon Roll; Thrpst.

HOLMAN, MELANIE S; Rancho Cotati HS; Rohnert Park, CA; (1); Hon Roll; Pres Acad Fit Awd; Duke U; Psych.

HOLMAN, ROCHELLE R; Rio Lindo Adventist Acad; Stockton, CA; (3); Church Yth Grp; Drama Clb; Office Aide; Spanish Clb; Teachers Aide; Chorus; Variety Show; Stu Cncl; Girls Clb Offcr; Psych.

HOLMES, BETH A; Eureka HS; Eureka, CA; (1); Church Yth Grp; Drama Clb; Chorus; Drill Tm; Orch; Hon Roll; Pres Acad Fit Awd; Val; Symphny Humboldt St U; Dance & Music Lssns; Gymnstcs; U Of CA Davis; Music Teacher.

HOLMES, CHASITY A; Arlington HS; Riverside, CA; (3); Church Yth Grp; Dance Clb; Drama Clb; Teachers Aide; Chorus; Church Choir; Ed Nwsp; Stat Ftbl; JV Socr; JV Swmmng; Work Doctors Office; Law.

HOLMES, ERIC C; Mt Whitney HS; Visalia, CA; (1); FFA; Bsktbl; Hon Roll; CSF; Acad Ltr.

HOLMES, ERIKA L; O'farrell SCPA HS; San Diego, CA; (2); Dance Clb; Drama Clb; Spanish Clb; Teachers Aide; Variety Show; Yrbk; Hon Roll; Pres Acad Fit Awd; Coca Cola Fshn & Img Clb; Arts-Dnc & Chrgrphng; Howard U.

HOLMES JR, HOWARD; Liberty Union HS; Bethel Island, CA; (4); 10/225; FCA; Treas Nwsp; Off Sr Cls; Rep Stu Cncl; JV Ftbl; Hon Roll; NHS; Prfct Atten Awd; Fri Nght Live; CSF; Mech Engrng.

HOLMES, IAN E; Mt Whitney HS; Visalia, CA; (1); Boy Scts; Church Yth Grp; Key Clb; VICA; Crs Cntry; Hon Roll; Cal Poly San Luis Obispo; Archt.

HOLMES, JAMES B; Irvington HS; Fremont, CA; (1); Boy Scts; Church Yth Grp; Drama Clb; Band; Mrchg Band; School Musical; School Play; Mgr Stage Crew; Ftbl; JV Trk; Pilot.

HOLMES, JENNA H; John Swett HS; Port Costa, CA; (2); Cmnty Wkr; Science Clb; Band; Mrchg Band; Lit Mag; Stat Score Keeper; Hon Roll; CSF; Assmblymn Robert Campbells Yth Cmmtte; Marine Bio.

HOLMES, JENNIFER MARIE; Ukiah HS; Ukiah, CA; (4); 14/445; SADD; Treas VP Band; Mrchg Band; Pep Band; Treas Jr Cls; Treas Sr Cls; Stu Cncl; Elks Awd; High Hon Roll; Pres Acad Fit Awd; CSF Treas; Chico St Univ; Music.

HOLMES, JOSEPH A; Ganesha HS; Pomona, CA; (2); Chess Clb; Library Aide; Church Choir; Bsktbl; Ftbl; Wt Lftg; High Hon Roll; Law.

HOLMES, JULIE; Downey HS; Downey, CA; (3); Am Leg Aux Girls St; Church Yth Grp; Treas Pres Cmnty Wkr; Sec French Clb; Intnl Clb; Sec Math Clb; Science Clb; Service Clb; Stu Cncl; JV Capt Tennis; Arch.

HOLMES, KAMILAH; San Diego HS; San Diego, CA; (1); Church Yth Grp; Cmnty Wkr; Variety Show; Yrbk; Cheerldng; Advrtsmnt.

HOLMES, KERRY B; Alameda HS; Alameda, CA; (3); 22/276; Library Aide; Hon Roll; CSF; Elem Ed.

HOLMES, KEVIN M; College Park HS; Martinez, CA; (2); JV Bsbl; JV Bsktbl; Hon Roll; Pres Acad Fit Awd; Bsktbl Mst Imprvd Plyr.

HOLMES, MELISSA; Hemet HS; Hemet, CA; (3); Key Clb; Speech Tm; Thesps; Acpl Chr; Stage Crew; Var Crs Cntry; Opt Clb Awd; CSF Treas; Chiropractor.

HOLMES, MICHELLE T; Albany HS; Albany, CA; (3); Service Clb; Stat Bsktbl; Var Sftbl; High Hon Roll; Hon Roll; Ntl Merit Ltr; Gldn St Math Test Awd; U Irvine CA; Comp Sci.

HOLMES, SARAH K; Foothill HS; Santa Ana, CA; (2); Church Yth Grp; JV Crs Cntry; JV Socr; Var Trk; Hon Roll; Yng Rpblcns Club; Dist Atty.

HOLMES, SHELLEY A; Eureka HS; Arcata, CA; (3); Church Yth Grp; FCA; 4-H; SADD; Acpl Chr; Church Choir; Chrch Vllybl Team; Chrch Yth Cncl Membr; Ballet Intrndte; Jazz Dance; Northwest Nazarene Coll; Mktg.

HOLMES, STEPHANIE L; Canyon HS; Anaheim, CA; (4); 17/550; Church Yth Grp; Cmnty Wkr; Drama Clb; Spanish Clb; Jazz Band; Mrchg Band; School Musical; Lit Mag; DAR Awd; NHS; Work Exprnc; CSF; CA ST U Fullerton; Musc Bus.

HOLMES, WALTER L; Temecula Valley HS; Murrieta, CA; (2); Boy Scts; Drama Clb; School Musical; JV Bsktbl; JV Ftbl; Eagle Sct Awd; UCLA; Psych.

HOLROYD, ELEYCE L; Mission Viejo HS; Mission Viejo, CA; (4); Church Yth Grp; French Clb; Library Aide; Pep Clb; SADD; School Play; Var Capt Tennis; Hon Roll; Pres Acad Fit Awd; CSF; MVP, Mst Vlbl Dbls Vrsty Tnns; Grls Leag Clb; Sonoma ST U; Cmnctns.

HOLSOPPLE, RUSSELL D; Sunset HS; Hayward, CA; (4); Rep Jr Cls; VP Sr Cls; Rep Stu Cncl; High Hon Roll; Hon Roll; CA Schlrshp Fed; Chrch Yth Grp; Choir; CA ST U Hayward; Ed.

HOLT, AMY E; Skyline HS; Oakland, CA; (2); Sec Church Yth Grp; Varsity Clb; Church Choir; Orch; Var L Socr; Var L Trk; Hon Roll; St Schlr; UC Davis; Vet Med.

HOLT, CANDICE M; L A Baptist HS; Bell Canyon, CA; (4); 5/90; French Clb; Drill Tm; School Musical; Ed Yrbk; Var Crs Cntry; Var Trk; High Hon Roll; NHS; CSF; Frnch Excllnce Hnrs; Pepperdine U; Bus.

HOLT, DAVID J; Merced HS North; Merced, CA; (2); Ftbl; Wt Lftg; Fresno St; Bus.

HOLT, ERICA; San Diego HS; San Diego, CA; (3); Spanish Clb; Band; Drm Mjr(t); Mgr Nwsp; Ed Yrbk; Tennis; High Hon Roll; NHS; Pres Acad Fit Awd; CSF; Intl Friendship Club; Hstry Club; USC; Bus.

HOLT, GARY M; Fremont HS; Sunnyvale, CA; (3); 20/420; Boy Scts; Church Yth Grp; Debate Tm; FBLA; German Clb; NFL; VP Speech Tm; Varsity Clb; Rep Stu Cncl; Bsktbl; Mem Natl Eagle Sct Assn; Ldr Of Chrch Yth Grp; Assn Stu Body Cabinet Mem; Corp Law.

HOLT, JOSHUA; Palo Verde HS; Blythe, CA; (2); #1 In Class; Boy Scts; Church Yth Grp; Letterman Clb; Var L Bsktbl; JV L Crs Cntry; High Hon Roll; NHS; CSF.

HOLT, ROBERT; Del Oro HS; Loomis, CA; (3); 1/266; Boy Scts; Church Yth Grp; Teachers Aide; JV Capt Ftbl; High Hon Roll; NHS; St Tm Acad Decathlon In CA Won St Chmpnshp Small Schls; U Of AZ; Med.

HOLT, SHAUNA MARIE; Esperanza HS; Anaheim, CA; (3); 75/630; Church Yth Grp; Drama Clb; Pres Chorus; Church Choir; Color Guard; Stage Crew; Variety Show; High Hon Roll; Hon Roll; Yorba Linda Civic Lght Opera Prfrmnc; Esperanzas Choir Pres; CA ST Fullerton; Educ.

HOLT, TRACEY; El Toro HS; El Toro, CA; (3); Church Yth Grp; Varsity Clb; Orch; Nwsp; Yrbk; Swmmng; High Hon Roll; CSF; Orange Cnty Acad Dcthln; Mock Trial; Engl/Jrnlsm.

HOLTON, JAMES; Lincoln HS; Stockton, CA; (3); 1/630; Science Clb; Ski Clb; Band; Jazz Band; Mrchg Band; Orch; Pep Band; High Hon Roll; Ntl Merit Schol; CSF; Oxford; Biochem.

HOLTZ, DAWN; Wheatland Union HS; Beale A. F. B., CA; (3); Sec FBLA; German Clb; Red Cross Aide; SADD; Jazz Band; Mrchg Band; Pep Band; Var Tennis; Hon Roll; Friday Night Live; CYOC; Psych.

HOLTZ, JOHN C; Ukiah HS; Ukiah, CA; (2); 56/554; Pres Church Yth Grp; SADD; Teachers Aide; Bsktbl; Socr; Trk; Hon Roll; UCLA; Pro Athl.

HOLZ, URSULA; San Luis Obispo HS; Los Osos, CA; (2); 80/319; Pres Mgr Church Yth Grp; Chorus; Church Choir; Hon Roll; Study Trip To Europe; United Mthdst Wmn Conf Delg; Med.

HOM, BRYANT; George Washington HS; San Francisco, CA; (2); Boy Scts; High Hon Roll; Hon Roll; Chinese Amer Clb; CA Schlrshp Fed.

HOM, DORIS S; John Muir HS; Pasadena, CA; (4); French Clb; FBLA; Key Clb; Library Aide; Office Aide; Red Cross Aide; Service Clb; SADD; Teachers Aide; Orch; Svc Awd; Dedicated Svc Awd Actvts; Pasadena Unfd Schl Dist Stu Offer Svc Awd; San Diego ST U; Bus Mgmt.

HOM, ERIC S; A Lincoln HS; San Francisco, CA; (2); Boy Scts; Church Yth Grp; Band; Jazz Band; Orch; Pep Band; U Of CA Davis; Arch.

HOM, JEFF; Santa Paula HS; Santa Paula, CA; (1); 9/363; Hon Roll; Swmmng; Rollr Sktng; Berkley; Doctor.

HOM, MEL-LING C; Grossmont HS; Spring Valley, CA; (2); 32/429; Cmnty Wkr; Hosp Aide; Intnl Clb; Pep Clb; Ski Clb; SADD; Sec Soph Cls; Stu Cncl; JV Gym; JV Swmmng; Martial Arts; UCSD; Med.

HOM, NANCY L; Lowell HS; San Francisco, CA; (3); Church Yth Grp; Cmnty Wkr; JA; Latin Clb; Library Aide; Office Aide; Phrmcy.

HOM, NORMAN; Edison HS; Stockton, CA; (4); 6/367; VP Latin Clb; Band; Mrchg Band; Ed Yrbk; Off Soph Cls; Swmmng; Hon Roll; NHS; Pres Acad Fit Awd; CA Schlrshp Fed Life Mem; Water Polo; Homecoming Ct; U CA Davis; Sociology.

HOM, RAYMOND F; Lowell HS; San Francisco, CA; (3); Computer Clb; Science Clb; Engrng.

HOM, SUSAN K; Lowell HS; San Francisco, CA; (3); Science Clb; Teachers Aide; School Musical; Mgr(s); Chinese Clb Pres 2 Yrs; Red Crss & Pre-Med Clbs.

HOM, SUZANNE; Schurr HS; Monterey Park, CA; (4); 8/580; Church Yth Grp; Cmnty Wkr; Key Clb; SADD; Rptr Nwsp; Rep Stu Cncl; Hon Roll; NHS; Prfct Atten Awd; Pres Acad Fit Awd; U Of PA Bk Awd; UC Irvine Admssn Dstnctn; Tandy Tchnlgy Schlrs; Acad Tp 2 Pct 89-90; UCLA; Psych.

HOM, TIMOTHY; George Washington HS; San Francisco, CA; (3); Church Yth Grp; Key Clb; Service Clb; Church Choir; JV Stat Bsbl; High Hon Roll; Hon Roll; Japanese Clb; Golden St Exm Alg 88, Geom 89 Hnrs; Yth Edctr Drg Awrns Pgm; Arch.

HOMAN, BILL; St Francis HS; Sunnyvale, CA; (3); Boy Scts; Bsbl; High Hon Roll; Hon Roll; Jr NHS; Business Administration.

HOMAN, CLARE L; Live Oak HS; Morgan Hill, CA; (3); Pres Computer Clb; French Clb; Hosp Aide; Mrchg Band; Ed Lit Mag; Rep Stu Cncl; JV Var Diving; Hon Roll; Ntl Merit Ltr; Vrsty Bdmntn.

HOMAR, LISA RENEE; Hesperia HS; Hesperia, CA; (2); Off French Clb; Capt Drill Tm; Ed Yrbk; Hon Roll; Journlsm.

HOMER, JANELLE A; Turlock HS; Turlock, CA; (4); AFS; Debate Tm; Key Clb; Letterman Clb; NFL; Service Clb; Speech Tm; Rotary Awd; Slvr Cngrsnl Awd; Camp Royal Dele; Chico ST; Pol Sci.

HOMER, JERRALEE; Carlsbad HS; Carlsbad, CA; (3); Church Yth Grp; Office Aide; Teachers Aide; Art Awds; Ricks Coll; Ecnmcs.

HON, DEBORAH; Capistrano Valley Christian HS; S Laguna, CA; (4); High Hon Roll; Hon Roll; Pres Acad Fit Awd; Ntl Chrty League; CSF Pres; Alpa Gamma Sgma At Sdlbck Coll; Psych.

HON, KIM; Capistrano Valley Christian HS; S Laguna, CA; (2); Church Yth Grp; Girl Scts; Hosp Aide; Socr; Sftbl; Vllybl; High Hon Roll; Pres Acad Fit Awd; Natl Charity League; CA Schlrshp Fed.

HON, LUKE; Temple City HS; Temple City, CA; (3); Math Clb; Math Tm; Bsktbl; Tennis.

HONEA, DANIELLE A; Monte Vista HS; Spring Valley, CA; (2); Church Yth Grp; Hosp Aide; Chrch Handbell Choir.

HONEA, RYAN; Wasco Union HS; Wasco, CA; (2); FFA; Var L Wrstlng; Hon Roll; CA Poly; History.

HONEYCUTT, LEAH; Davis SR HS; Davis, CA; (4); 99/394; Pep Clb; Spanish Clb; Lit Mag; Var Capt Pom Pon; Bnk Of Amer Achvt Awd; Friday Nite Live; Hi-Deb; BECA Schlrshp Wnr; Cal ST U; Bus Admin.

HONEYFIELD, CRAIG R; La Sierra HS; Riverside, CA; (3); Computer Clb; Varsity Clb; Yrbk; Socr; Swmmng; Elec Engr.

HONG, ALBERT K; Abraham Lincoln HS; San Francisco, CA; (3); Golden ST Exam Awds Alg & Geom; Yth Educatorprgm; Jr Club; UC-BERKELEY; Mech Engrng.

HONG, ALICE M; Central Union HS; El Centro, CA; (2); Debate Tm; Speech Tm; Var Cheerldng; High Hon Roll; Hon Roll; Rotary Awd; Mock Trial Future Lawyers Of Amer; UCLA; Politics.

HONG, AMY; Mark Reppel HS; Rowland Hgts, CA; (3); Church Yth Grp; French Clb; Hosp Aide; Key Clb; Mu Alpha Theta; Church Choir; Sec Stu Cncl; High Hon Roll; Ntl Merit SF; LA Co Yng Woman Of Yr 91; People To People Ambssdr To Japan; CA Arts Schlr-Music; HOBY Ambssdr; UCLA; Pre-Med.

HONG, AUSTIN C; Homestead HS; Cupertino, CA; (3); 1/384; Art Clb; Church Yth Grp; Cmnty Wkr; FBLA; Math Clb; Science Clb; Spanish Clb; Teachers Aide; Orch; School Play; El Camino Yth Symphny; Stanford Blood Bank Vlntr; GATE VP; Berkeley; Bus.

HONG, DARY H; Oakland HS; Oakland, CA; (4); Spanish Clb; Ed Yrbk.

HONG, DAVID; George Washington HS; San Francisco, CA; (3); JA; Varsity Clb; Var Bsktbl; Var Crs Cntry; Var Tennis; Var Trk; Hon Roll; Asian Amer Tnns Fndtn 90; All City Tm Tnns 89-90; 14th Annl S Bay Boy Sngls Champ; U San Francisco; Mech Engr.

HONG, DEBORAH; El Modena HS; Orange, CA; (4); 1/345; Church Yth Grp; French Clb; Key Clb; Chorus; Church Choir; Orch; Mgr Yrbk; Cit Awd; DAR Awd; Elks Awd; Supreme Ct Justce; Mck Trl Tm Defnse Lawyr; CSF; Wharton Schl Of Bus; Law.

HONG, DERRICK; Trabuco Hills HS; Mission Viejo, CA; (2); 1/418; Bsktbl; High Hon Roll; Hon Roll; NHS; Opt Clb Awd; Pres Acad Fit Awd; West Point; Med.

HONG, DOUGLAS D; Piedmont HS; Piedmont, CA; (3); VP Treas Church Yth Grp; Var Crs Cntry; Var Trk; Hon Roll; CSF; Summer Sch Korea Univ; Schlr Athlete.

HONG, DUNG; Herbert Hoover HS; San Diego, CA; (2); French Clb; FTA; Cit Awd; Tutor; Recgntn Acad Excllnce 89-90; San Diego; Arch Technlgy.

HONG, EDWARD; La Canada HS; La Canada Flintri, CA; (3); 40/250; Boy Scts; Chess Clb; Math Clb; Mu Alpha Theta; Acpl Chr; VP Chorus; Church Choir; JV Ftbl; Var Socr; NHS; CFS; Golden St Awd Algebra High Hon; Pre-Med.

HONG, ESTHER; Marlborough Schl; Los Angeles, CA; (4); Cmnty Wkr; Hosp Aide; SADD; Acpl Chr; Chorus; Church Choir; Yrbk; Lit Mag; Sec Soph Cls; High Hon Roll; Badminton Var; Cum Laude Society; Dartmouth Book Awd; Bio.

HONG, HAEJI; El Camino Real HS; West Hills, CA; (3); Math Clb; Orch; High Hon Roll; Hon Roll; Prfct Atten Awd; Kingsmn Clb Secty; Hands Acrss Campus; Deads Poets Soc; Teacher.

HONG, HANNAH S; University HS; Los Angeles, CA; (3); Treas Church Yth Grp; Hosp Aide; Rep Jr Cls; High Hon Roll; Hon Roll; Med.

HONG, HELLEN Y; El Camino Real HS; West Hills, CA; (2); Church Yth Grp; Debate Tm; Speech Tm; Score Keeper; Swmmng; Vllybl; High Hon Roll; Hon Roll; Bible Club.

HONG, HENRY; George Washington HS; San Francisco, CA; (2); Key Clb; Service Clb; Varsity Clb; Off Soph Cls; Var Bsktbl; JV Crs Cntry; Var Tennis; Var Trk; Hon Roll; U San Francisco; Comp Prog.

HONG, JAMES; Skyline HS; Oakland, CA; (3); Intnl Clb; VP Math Clb; Capt Math Tm; High Hon Roll; St Schlr; CIT; Elec Engrng.

HONG, JAMES S; John F Kennedy HS; Granada Hills, CA; (4); Church Yth Grp; Intnl Clb; Math Clb; Red Cross Aide; Teachers Aide; Stat Golf; Socr; Sftbl; Vllybl; Pres Acad Fit Awd; Cngrssnl Yng Ldrshp Conf 90; U Of CA Los Angeles; Comp Sci.

HONG, JENNY; Sonora HS; La Habra, CA; (4); Computer Clb; Key Clb; Science Clb; High Hon Roll; Top 100 Awd; CSF Awd; Amnesty Interntl Clb; UC Irving; Doctor.

HONG, JOOHEE; Culver City HS; Culver City, CA; (1); Church Yth Grp; Service Clb; Church Choir; Cit Awd; High Hon Roll; Hon Roll; Stu Mnth Math & Frgn Lang.

HONG, JULIE; Whitney HS; Cerritos, CA; (2); Church Yth Grp; Cmnty Wkr; Church Choir; Var JV Cheerldng; UCLA; Psych.

HONG, MARGARET; George Washington HS; San Francisco, CA; (4); 41/582; GAA; Teachers Aide; Var Capt Tennis; Cit Awd; Hon Roll; NHS; Prfct Atten Awd; Hnr Ellen Rush Tns Schlrshp; John Clark Memrl Schlrshp; Saul Schlr Masters Awd; All Cty Tnns Chmpn; U Of San Francisco; Phys Educ.

HONG, MICHAEL P; Oak Park HS; Agoura Hills, CA; (2); Golden St Exam Hnr In Geom; Photo Exhibition 3rd Pl; Psych.

HONG, PHAT; Hoover HS; San Diego, CA; (1); French Clb; NFL; Hon Roll; Ntl Merit Ltr; MIT; Bus Adm.

HONG, PHOUAY; Saddelback HS; Santa Ana, CA; (1); FBLA; Spanish Clb; Hon Roll; UCI Partnership Clb; STEP Clb; Comp.

HONG, RICHARD B; Sunny Hills HS; Buena Park, CA; (3); 17/430; Treas Chess Clb; Key Clb; Spanish Clb; Yrbk; Crs Cntry; Trk; High Hon Roll; Rensselaer Polytech Inst Awd; UCLA; Med.

HONG, ROBERT; Hawthorne HS; Hawthorne, CA; (4); Math Clb; Math Tm; Band; Mrchg Band; Crs Cntry; Golf; Score Keeper; Pres Acad Fit Awd; U Of CA Riverside; Math.

HONG, SAM S; Andrew Hill HS; San Jose, CA; (1); Church Yth Grp; Cmnty Wkr; Computer Clb; FCA; Intnl Clb; Science Clb; Spanish Clb; Teachers Aide; Chorus; Church Choir; Odyssy Mnd; Dr.

HONG, SAN A; Gardena HS; Gardena, CA; (3); 1/500; Intnl Clb; JA; Service Clb; Spanish Clb; Rptr Nwsp; VP Stu Cncl; Elks Awd; High Hon Roll; Kiwanis Awd; Opt Clb Awd; Chinese Lang Schl & Other Activities.

HONG, SANDY D; Mountain View HS; El Monte, CA; (2); GAA; Science Clb; Band; Mrchg Band; Pep Band; Rptr Nwsp; JV Tennis; High Hon Roll; Badminton Vrsty; Med Fld.

HONG, SANG Y; Herbert Hoover HS; Glendale, CA; (3); Aud/Vis; Church Yth Grp; FCA; JCL; Key Clb; Latin Clb; Letterman Clb; Stage Crew; Yrbk; Vllybl; Natl Latin Exam Magna Cum Laude; Top Svc Awd; Arch.

HONG, SEUNG I; Granada Hills HS; Northridge, CA; (3); Pres Church Yth Grp; Math Tm; JV Bsbl; Intrml Bsktbl; Cit Awd; High Hon Roll; Hon Roll; Prfct Atten Awd; Pres Acad Fit Awd; Coaches Awd Bsbl.

HONG, TAI; Andrew Hill HS; San Jose, CA; (1).

HONG, THUY P; La Quinta HS; Westminster, CA; (3); FBLA; Spanish Clb; SADD; Prfct Atten Awd; CA ST U Fullerton; Doctor.

HONG, VENUS; West HS; Torrance, CA; (1); Church Yth Grp; Cmnty Wkr; JCL; Latin Clb; Service Clb; Band; Drill Tm; Cit Awd; Hon Roll; Pres Acad Fit Awd; Magna Cum Laude Natl Latin Exam JSL & ACL; Cert Of Merit Piano.

HONG, WENDY M; Balboa HS; San Francisco, CA; (3); Math Clb; Hon Roll; Chinese Club.

HONRADO, KIMBERLY-TERESA I; Mercy HS; Daly City, CA; (4); 38/103; Church Yth Grp; GAA; Intnl Clb; Library Aide; Variety Show; Rptr Yrbk; Rep Frsh Cls; Rep Soph Cls; Rep Jr Cls; Capt Cheerldng; CSF.

HONZIK, THERESE M; St Francis HS; Mountain View, CA; (4); Art Clb; Drama Clb; Intnl Clb; School Musical; School Play; Ed Yrbk; High Hon Roll; NHS; Ntl Merit Ltr; Shakespeare Clb-Bd Dir; Voice Hope/Amnsty Intl; U Of CA Santa Barbara; Engl.

HOO, MICHAEL P; Cleveland HS; Canoga Park, CA; (3); VICA; Tennis; Vllybl; Hon Roll; Northrop U; Aeronautical Engr.

HOOD, BECKIE; Orange Glen HS; Escondido, CA; (1); 42/647; Dance Clb; Band; Hon Roll.

HOOD, BRIAN; Woodland HS; Woodland, CA; (2); Ftbl; Wt Lftg; Wrstlng; Hon Roll; Auto Engrng.

HOOD, CHAD C; Royal HS; Simi Valley, CA; (3); 133/600; Church Yth Grp; Swmmng; Tennis; Cit Awd; Hon Roll; Jr NHS; Water Polo Tm Capt; Palmer Chiropractic Coll; DC.

HOOD, GLORIA LYNETTE; Paramount HS; Norwalk, CA; (4); Church Yth Grp; FBLA; Teachers Aide; Am Leg Boys St; Bsbl; Trk; Vllybl; Cit Awd; Southern U; Bus Admin.

HOOD, JENNIFER; Mariposa County HS; Coulterville, CA; (3); Pep Clb; Var JV Cheerldng; Hon Roll; Merced; Marine Bio.

HOOD, JENNIFER A; Homestead HS; Sunnyvale, CA; (1); Church Yth Grp; Drama Clb; SADD; Church Choir; Drill Tm; Treas Frsh Cls; High Hon Roll; Vrs Cmnty Svc Prjcts; Mrt Stu Readrs Pgm Drng Smmr; Med.

HOOD, JENNIFER H; Montgomery HS; Santa Rosa, CA; (3); Pres Church Yth Grp; Cmnty Wkr; Pres FTA; Library Aide; Band; Church Choir; High Hon Roll; Hon Roll; Outstndng Bible Stu; Outstndng Musician; Yth Smmr Pgm Team; Elem Educ.

HOOD, LISA J; Thomas Downey HS; Modesto, CA; (2); Church Yth Grp; Key Clb; NFL; Spanish Clb; Speech Tm; SADD; Band; Mrchg Band; Pep Band; High Hon Roll; UC Santa Cruz; Jrnlst.

HOODA, SHAMSUDDIN N; Santa Monica HS; Santa Monica, CA; (1); Art Clb; Boy Scts; Chess Clb; Computer Clb; Dance Clb; Math Clb; Math Tm; Science Clb; Temple Yth Grp; School Play; Badmittan Club; UCLA; Med.

HOODENPYLE, MATT J; Rim HS; Lake Arrowhead, CA; (1); Church Yth Grp; FCA; Ski Clb; Var JV Ftbl; Wt Lftg; Hon Roll; Prfct Atten Awd; USC; Engr.

HOOGE, HEIDI; Turlock HS; Turlock, CA; (1); Church Yth Grp; Church Choir; Orch; Yrbk; Var Trk; Cit Awd; High Hon Roll; Hon Roll; Pres Acad Fit Awd; Cnslr & Tchr Hrs Cmp; Wn Cole Awd Orchestra; Chrch Pres Yng Wmns Clss; Drll Tm; CA All Cnfrnc Trk Tm; BYU; Phys Thrpy.

HOOGE, MATTHEW D; Ygnacio Valley HS; Walnut Creek, CA; (3); Church Yth Grp; JV Bsktbl; Var Trk; Pre-Vet.

HOOGES, BRANDON M; Foothill HS; Pleasanton, CA; (3); Boy Scts; Church Yth Grp; Hosp Aide; Pres Frsh Cls; VP Sr Cls; Var Bsktbl; Var Golf; Jr NHS; NHS; Pres Acad Fit Awd; BYU; Sports Med.

HOOKER, BERNADETTE; Tulare Union HS; Tulare, CA; (3); Rep Church Yth Grp; French Clb; Office Aide; Church Choir; Var Capt Bsktbl; Score Keeper; Var Capt Trk; Vllybl; Hon Roll; BSU Club VP; CSF; Bus.

HOOKER, JENNIFER E; Loretto HS; Wilton, CA; (4); 10/52; JA; Office Aide; Service Clb; Co-Capt Drill Tm; Rep Soph Cls; Var L Trk; JV Vllybl; High Hon Roll; Ntl Merit Ltr; Pres Acad Fit Awd; Congressional Yth Ldrshp Cncl; CSU Sacramento; Bus Admin.

HOOKER, KIMBERLEE A; Apple Valley HS; Apple Valley, CA; (3); Office Aide; Teachers Aide; Hon Roll; Pres Acad Fit Awd; CA Schltc Fed.

HOOKER, MARGARET; Newport Harbor HS; Newport Beach, CA; (2); Church Yth Grp; Dance Clb; Drama Clb; French Clb; Key Clb; Pep Clb; Ski Clb; Thesps; School Musical; Ed Yrbk; Dance Wnnrs Car Cmptn.

HOOKER, MELISSA L; Roseville HS; Sacramento, CA; (3); Church Yth Grp; Drama Clb; French Clb; Science Clb; SADD; Teachers Aide; Church Choir; School Musical; School Play; Stage Crew; Tiger Stripes Hgh Grd Alg; Mrt Awds; Ed.

HOOKER, MICHELLE D; Paraclete HS; Palmdale, CA; (2); Hon Roll; Spch Thrpst.

HOOKS, ALETA C; Fontana HS; Fontana, CA; (2); UCLA; Law.

HOON, SUZAN J; Willits HS; Willits, CA; (1); Church Yth Grp; Pep Clb; SADD; Teachers Aide; Chorus; Cheerldng; Hon Roll; Jobs Dghtrs; UC Davis; Vet.

HOOPER, STEPHANIE Y; Eisenhower HS; Rialto, CA; (3); Drill Tm; Bsktbl; Cheerldng; Wt Lftg; Hon Roll; Prfct Atten Awd; Yth On March Christ; Outstndng Female Stu Awd; Pre Med.

HOOSE, KAREN L; North HS; Bakersfield, CA; (2); French Clb; Chorus; Cheerldng; Hon Roll; CA Schlrshp Fed; Acctng.

HOOSER, LISA L; Shafter HS; Shafter, CA; (4); 4/200; Church Yth Grp; Drama Clb; Key Clb; Pep Clb; SADD; Drm Mjr(t); Mrchg Band; School Play; Variety Show; Rptr Nwsp; Past Hnrd Qn Intl Ordr Jobs Dghtrs; Bakersfield Coll; Dentstry.

HOOTON, BRENT E; Artesia HS; Lakewood, CA; (4); VP JA; Math Tm; Science Clb; Teachers Aide; Rep Soph Cls; Rep Jr Cls; Rep Sr Cls; Interact Club; Chf Just Stu Crt; U Of La Verne.

HOOVEN, LAURETTA A; Norco SR HS; Norco, CA; (4); 11/475; Cmnty Wkr; Library Aide; Model UN; Office Aide; Teachers Aide; High Hon Roll; Pres Acad Fit Awd; Webster U; Jrnlsm.

HOOVER, ANDREW P; Aptos HS; Watsonville, CA; (1); 4-H; Teachers Aide; Yrbk; Photo.

HOOVER, ANGEL M; Montecito HS; Ramona, CA; (2); 22/61; Teachers Aide; Chorus; Cit Awd; Environmntl Clb; Engl/Math Outstndng Achvts; Math Ed.

HOOVER, ANNA; Escondido Adventist Acad; Temecula, CA; (1); Chorus; Variety Show; Hon Roll; Prfct Atten Awd; Clown Mnstry.

HOOVER, DAVID L; San Gorgonio HS; San Bernardino, CA; (4); 97/500; Art Clb; French Clb; Schlstc Achvt Lttr; Outstndng Vocational Stu Awd; Valley Coll; Comp Pgrmmr.

HOOVER, DENISE; Poway HS; Poway, CA; (3); 3/761; Church Yth Grp; Key Clb; Var JV Swmmng; Capt JV Vllybl; Hon Roll; NHS; Waterpolo-Stats.

HOOVER, JENNIFER; Canyon HS; Canyon Country, CA; (3); Church Yth Grp; Dance Clb; Girl Scts; Chorus; Swing Chorus; Gym; Cit Awd; Girl Sct Slvr Awds; CSUN; Spcl Educ Tchr.

HOOVER, JEREMY J; Capistrano Valley HS; San Juan Capistra, CA; (3); Church Yth Grp; Trk; Wt Lftg; Wrstlng; Amer Cultures; Historical Soc; San Diego ST; Bus.

HOPE, SHAWN M; Antioch HS; Antioch, CA; (2); Ftbl; Cmptr Prog.

HOPE, TY B; Kennedy High; Sacramento, CA; (2); Band; Jazz Band; Mrchg Band; Ftbl; Wrstlng; Blue Devil Drum & Bugle Corps; N TX ST U; Music.

HOPELIAN, DANIELE L; Clovis HS; Clovis, CA; (1); Drama Clb; FCA; Pep Clb; Stage Crew; Cheerldng; JV Var Swmmng; Hon Roll; Swmng Mst Inspirational Awd; UCLA; Law.

HOPKINS, JULIE; San Pasqual HS; Escondido, CA; (4); 18/250; Church Yth Grp; Var Crs Cntry; Var Socr; Var Trk; Pres Acad Fit Awd; Westmont Coll; Psych.

HOPKINS, MARIA E; Ramona HS; Riverside, CA; (1); Church Yth Grp; Cmnty Wkr; Teachers Aide; Church Choir; English Award; RCC.

HOPKINS, ROBIN N; El Toro HS; El Toro, CA; (2); Church Yth Grp; High Hon Roll; Hon Roll; El Toro HS Excllnc Awd; CSF Mem; Psych.

HOPKINS, SHANNON C; Riverbank HS; Riverbank, CA; (3); 5/125; SADD; Yrbk; High Hon Roll; Hon Roll; CSF; Med.

HOPKINS, TODD D; Arlington HS; Riverside, CA; (3); 41/465; Band; Jazz Band; Mrchg Band; Ftbl; Socr; Swmmng; Tennis; Trk; Hon Roll; Med.

HOPKINS, YAVONDA V RENEE; Luther Burbank HS; Sacramento, CA; (3); 85/389; Church Yth Grp; FHA; GAA; Pep Clb; ROTC; Chorus; Drill Tm; Var Bsktbl; JV Sftbl; Var Trk; Commnctns.

HOPPE, ANNE C; San Dieguito HS; Encinitas, CA; (2); 22/615; Church Yth Grp; Hosp Aide; Library Aide; JV Swmmng; High Hon Roll; Pres Acad Fit Awd; CSF; Natl Sci Olympiad Comptn Bio Wnnr; Med.

HOPPE, BENJAMIN D; Oak Ridge HS; Cameron Park, CA; (3); 21/261; Am Leg Boys St; Boy Scts; Pres Church Yth Grp; SADD; Church Choir; School Play; Lit Mag; JV Bsbl; Intrml Bsktbl; Intrml Ftbl; Schl Dist Awd Excl Drm 89; Rcvd Prtl Schlrshp To U Thtr Wrkshp Brigham Young U; Rcvd Actn Awds; Thtr Art.

HOPPER, JEANETTE L; Bonita Vista HS; Chula Vista, CA; (2); Hosp Aide; Library Aide; Model UN; Teachers Aide; Cit Awd; UCSD; Engl Ed.

HOPPER, JESSICA LYNNE; Buena Park HS; Fullerton, CA; (3); 25/375; Am Leg Aux Girls St; Key Clb; Letterman Clb; Science Clb; Treas Soph Cls; Sec Sr Cls; Mgr(s); Var L Swmmng; Cit Awd; High Hon Roll; CSF; Dstngshd Schlr; Stu Coaltn For Greener Earth Clb; UC Davis; Vet.

HOPPER, MATTHEW SCOTT; Bear River HS; Grass Valley, CA; (2); 19/227; Church Yth Grp; Church Choir; School Play; JV Trk; High Hon Roll; Hon Roll; Odyssy Mnd Wrld Fnlst; UC.

HOPPERT, REBECCA A; Tulare Western HS; Tulare, CA; (3); 1/250; Am Leg Aux Girls St; Church Yth Grp; Pres Chorus; School Play; Co-Ed Yrbk; Ntl Merit Ltr; CSF Treas; US Air Force Acad Smmr Sci Smnr; Stu Rep Schl Brd; Bio.

HOPPING, PAUL A; Covina HS; W Covina, CA; (4); Boy Scts; Church Yth Grp; Letterman Clb; Band; Church Choir; Mrchg Band; Swmmng; Hon Roll; Vigil Order Of Arrow; Ealge Plus 4 Palms; Handbell Choir Chrch; Mt San Antonio Coll.

HOPSITER, MIKE S; Canyon Springs HS; Moreno Valley, CA; (3); High Hon Roll; Hon Roll; 1st Pl Riverside Cty Natl Date Fstvl; Festvl Of Arts Moreno Vly; Art Exhbt 90.

HOPSON, MARYANN E; Hayward HS; Hayward, CA; (2); 13/230; German Clb; Stage Crew; Hon Roll; Pres Acad Fit Awd; Badminton Team Vrsty; Liberal Arts.

HORCASITAS JR, ARTHUR A; Bell Gardens HS; Bell Gardens, CA; (3); Church Yth Grp; Ftbl; Wrstlng.

HORDER, CHE; Clovis HS; Clovis, CA; (1); Church Yth Grp; Math Clb; Math Tm; Band; Mrchg Band; JV Wrstlng; High Hon Roll; FMCMEA High Sch Hnr Band; CA Schltc Fed; ; Clairnet Lessons; Freestyle Wrstlng.

HORDER, MICHELLE; Clovis HS; Clovis, CA; (3); Church Yth Grp; Dance Clb; FCA; Letterman Clb; Varsity Clb; Band; Color Guard; Mrchg Band; Var L Tennis; High Hon Roll; Piano Lessons, Dance Recitals; Honor Band; CFS; Ecology Club; Flute Lessons; Long Beach ST; Interior Dsgn.

HORG, JENNIFER A; Clovis HS; Clovis, CA; (3); SADD; Lit Mag; Rep Jr Cls; Wt Lftg; Hon Roll; Mdlng; Apprd On Craft & Ndlewrk Mag Cover; Fresno City Coll; Psych.

HORGAN, LISA M; Esperanza HS; Yorba Linda, CA; (4); 7/480; Intnl Clb; Math Tm; JV Stat Swmmng; High Hon Roll; NHS; Rotary Awd; March Of Dms Tm Ldr; Styng Alive/Peer Spprt; CSF; U Of CA Irvine; Physcl Sci.

HORIO, RICHARD T; L A Baptist HS; Granada Hills, CA; (3); 6/100; Church Yth Grp; French Clb; Stage Crew; Yrbk; JV Bsbl; Cit Awd; High Hon Roll; Opt Clb Awd; CSF; T-Ball Coach; Speak Engl, Japanese, & French; Arthroscopic Srgn.

HORITA, MISA; Lincoln HS; Stockton, CA; (3); Church Yth Grp; Mu Alpha Theta; Spanish Clb; School Musical; Yrbk; Off Jr Cls; JV Cheerldng; Pom Pon; High Hon Roll; CSF; Interact; Asstns.

HORMAN, HEATHER; Laguna Hills HS; Garden Grove, CA; (4); 27/342; Chess Clb; Ski Clb; Band; Chorus; Mrchg Band; Orch; Pep Band; School Musical; Amer Bank Achvt Awd; Natl Schl Choral Awd; Orange Coast Coll; Music.

HORN, ANGIE J; Orange Glen HS; Valley Center, CA; (3); 120/458; Church Yth Grp; Dance Clb; German Clb; Spanish Clb; Rptr Nwsp; JV Var Tennis; NHS; English.

HORN, DANA; Calaveras HS; Rail Road Flat, CA; (1); Teachers Aide; Cheerldng; Pom Pon; Trk; Vllybl; San Diego ST U; Tchr.

HORN, DARCY D.; Acalanes HS; Lafayette, CA; (3); 27/263; Church Yth Grp; Cmnty Wkr; Teachers Aide; Varsity Clb; Var Intrml Cheerldng; JV Crs Cntry; Var Socr; Var Trk; Hon Roll; US Reserve National Scholar/Athlete Award.

HORN, JEFFREY; Los Alamitos HS; Los Alamitos, CA; (4); Boy Scts; English Clb; Library Aide; Science Clb; Spanish Clb; Temple Yth Grp; Hon Roll; St Schlr; Police Explr Scout; CA ST U Long Beach; Vet.

HORN, JENNIFER; Ramona HS; Riverside, CA; (3); 19/400; French Clb; Pep Clb; Teachers Aide; Rptr Nwsp; Sec Jr Cls; Sec Stu Cncl; JV Cheerldng; Var Pom Pon; Var Trk; CSF; UCLA; Med.

HORN, PATRICIA L; Northview HS; Covina, CA; (2); Church Yth Grp; Letterman Clb; Teachers Aide; Yrbk; JV Bsktbl; Var Tennis; Var Trk; Hon Roll; Preschl Tchr; Coll Prof.

HORNADAY, JEFF M; Capistrano Valley HS; Mission Viejo, CA; (3); German Clb; Rep Stu Cncl; Intrml Crs Cntry; Intrml Trk; Hon Roll; Ntl Merit SF; Pres Acad Fit Awd; CSF; Envrnmntlst Clb; Pomona Coll; Intrntl Reltns.

HORNBACK, NATHAN A; Silver Valley HS; Newberry Spgs, CA; (2); JV Bsktbl; Var Crs Cntry; High Hon Roll.

HORNBACK, TODD W; Torrey Pines HS; Del Mar, CA; (4); 78/450; Church Yth Grp; VP Pres Yng Rpblcns Clb; Peer Cnslr Peercnslng Pgm Schl; CA Schlrshp Fed Sealbearer; U CA Davis; Bus Mngmnt Psych.

HORNBECK, MICHELLE; Modoc HS; Canby, CA; (2); Cmnty Wkr; FHA; Band; Chorus; Powder Puff Ftbl; Vllybl; Cit Awd; Hon Roll; Acad Decathlon; WA ST U; Cosmotologist.

HORNBUCKLE, CHRISTINE M; Garces Memorial HS; Bakersfield, CA; (2); Church Yth Grp; JA; Key Clb; Ski Clb; Church Choir; Variety Show; JV Crs Cntry; JV Sftbl; High Hon Roll; Hon Roll.

HORNE, NATHANAEL S; Santa Barbara HS; Santa Barbara, CA; (3); Boy Scts; Church Yth Grp; Cmnty Wkr; Ski Clb; Teachers Aide; Hon Roll.

HORNER, CATHERINE; Piedmont HS; Piedmont, CA; (1); 2/145; SADD; Acpl Chr; School Musical; Nwsp; Treas Soph Cls; Var Swmmng; High Hon Roll; Ntl Merit Ltr; Pres Acad Fit Awd; Sal; Volunteer Tutor; Dartmouth College.

HORNOR, JASON; Fresno Christian HS; Fresno, CA; (1); Church Yth Grp; Var Bsbl; Hon Roll; Civil Air Patrol; Pilot.

HORNSTEIN, JORDONNA; Ygnacio Valley HS; Concord, CA; (3); Teachers Aide; Temple Yth Grp; School Musical; JV Sftbl; Coach Spec Ed Kids; SITUP; Child Psych.

HOROWITZ, JONATHAN S; John F Kennedy HS; Granada Hills, CA; (2); L Bsktbl; L JV Vllybl; Hon Roll; Jr Statesman Amer Clb; Vtd Mst Insprtnl Plyr JV Vllybl Tm; Schlr Athlte Awd JV Vllybl Tm; UCLA; Poltcl Sci.

HOROWITZ, RUTH; Beverly Hills HS; Beverly Hills, CA; (4); School Play; Variety Show; Hon Roll; Ntl Merit Ltr; Charlie Awd Crtv Wrtg; 89 CA Arts Schlr; Engl.

HORPORNSIRI, SASIKAMOL; Los Altos HS; La Puente, CA; (2); 6/365; High Hon Roll; 2nd Yr CSF; Dist Schlr; UC Berkeley; Bus.

HORR, CAINE; Analy HS; Sebastopol, CA; (3); 155/220; Cmnty Wkr; VICA; Band; Var Trk; VICA Applied Electronics-Reg Gold Medal; Aviation Club; Elec Eng.

HORRELL, DAWN L; Edison HS; Fresno, CA; (2); Latin Clb; Ski Clb; Swmmng; Cit Awd; Environmental Club; Berkeley; Psycht.

HORTA, ANNA; Capital Christian HS; Rancho Cordova, CA; (4); Art Clb; Church Yth Grp; Cmnty Wkr; Drama Clb; Chorus; Church Choir; School Musical; Treas Sr Cls; High Hon Roll; Supr Rtng Awd Natl Fine Arts Fstvl; CSF; Cmmnd Prfrmnc Achvt ASCI Music Fstvl 2 Yrs; Azusa Pacific U; Commrcl Music.

HORTA, ELIZABETH A; Etiwanda HS; Rancho Cucamonga, CA; (2); French Clb; FHA; JA; Spanish Clb; SADD; Color Guard; Flag Corp; High Hon Roll; Hon Roll; CSF; Fshn Inst Dsgn & Mer; Fshn Dsgn.

HORTINELA, TRACI; Capistrano Valley HS; Mission Viejo, CA; (4); Church Yth Grp; VP Pres Hosp Aide; Yrbk; Hon Roll; Saddleback Coll.

HORTON, ADAM J; Hanford Union HS; Hanford, CA; (2); 1/521; Church Yth Grp; Pres Frsh Cls; Off Soph Cls; Stu Cncl; JV Bsbl; High Hon Roll; Outstndng Bio Stu 89-90; Soph Male Schlr Athlt Of Yr; Frshmn Bsbl Dfnsv Player Of Yr; CSF; Pepperdine.

HORTON, BRENDA A; Caruthers Union HS; Caruthers, CA; (3); 3/87; Church Yth Grp; Computer Clb; FBLA; Girl Scts; Math Clb; Spanish Clb; JV Bsktbl; Var Sftbl; High Hon Roll; Lion Awd.

HORTON, BRIAN A; Mt Whitney HS; Visalia, CA; (3); Cmnty Wkr; Letterman Clb; SADD; Var Bsbl; JV Capt Ftbl; Var Wt Lftg; Hon Roll; Prfct Atten Awd; Capt JV Ftbl Tm; COS; Tchr.

HORTON, BRIAN J; Del Mar HS; San Jose, CA; (1); Key Clb; JV Crs Cntry; Var Wrstlng; High Hon Roll; NHS.

HORTON, HOLLY M; Orange Glen HS; Escondido, CA; (3); Cmnty Wkr; Office Aide; SADD; Band; Rptr Nwsp; Recieved My GED; Achievement Award For Hot Line Crisis Training; San Diego St U; Clinical Psych.

HORTON, KAREN L; Portoloa JR-SR HS; Portola, CA; (3); 1/48; Church Yth Grp; Ski Clb; High Hon Roll; Pres Acad Fit Awd; Var Soph Cls; Var L Tennis; Yth To Yth.

HORTON, MEGAN; Rim Of The World HS; Cedarpines Park, CA; (3); 20/300; Am Leg Aux Girls St; High Hon Roll; Hon Roll; Lion Awd; NHS; Intrml Tennis; Var Trk; Var Vllybl; People To People Stu Ambssdr; UCR Pgm; UCLA; Lawyer.

HORTON, MELANIE; Clayton Valley HS; Clayton, CA; (2); Pres Church Yth Grp; Church Choir; JV Vllybl; Prfct Atten Awd; Chrch Sftbl, Bsktbl, Vllybl; Chrch Drma; Hmownrs Assn Swm Tm; Brigham Young U.

HORTON, NICKI L; Canyon Springs HS; Moreno Valley, CA; (4); Church Yth Grp; Debate Tm; Pep Clb; Teachers Aide; Church Choir; Rep Frsh Cls; Rep Soph Cls; Stu Cncl; JV Capt Cheerldng; Trk; Bsktbl Homcmng Princess; Homcmng Princess 90; CA ST-NORTHRIDGE; Econ.

HORVATH, ADRIAN L; Downey HS; Downey, CA; (2); Key Clb; Var Tennis; USC; Bus.

HORVATH, HOLLY; Rosary HS; Whittier, CA; (3); VP Cmnty Wkr; Science Clb; Ski Clb; Rep Soph Cls; JV Tennis; High Hon Roll; Jr NHS; Mock Trl; Ntl Charity Leag; Hgh Hnrs Gldn ST Exms Alg I/Geom; Bus.

HORVATH, JOSEPH D; Mission Viejo HS; Mission Viejo, CA; (1); Boy Scts; Model UN; Law.

HORVATH, SHANNON D; Montgomery HS; Santa Rosa, CA; (2); Church Yth Grp; French Clb; High Hon Roll; Jr NHS; Pres Acad Fit Awd; Golden St Exam High Hnrs Alg & Geom; Biola U; Teacher.

HOSAC, TARA; Leigh HS; San Jose, CA; (4); Drama Clb; French Clb; Speech Tm; Yrbk; Lit Mag; Hon Roll; CSF; Med Explr Post; UCSB; Pre Law.

HOSE, AHMED B; Poway HS; Poway, CA; (2); Varsity Clb; JV Var Wrstlng; Law.

HOSEA, STACY D; George Washington Prep HS; Los Angeles, CA; (1); Chorus; Tennis; Cit Awd; Hon Roll; Arch.

HOSFELD, JEFF C; El Toro HS; El Toro, CA; (4); 198/522; Red Cross Aide; Intrml Bsbl; Intrml Ftbl; Intrml Golf; Hon Roll; San Diego ST; CPA.

HOSFIELD, DAVID B; Montgomery HS; San Diego, CA; (2); Cit Awd; Hon Roll; Prfct Atten Awd; Tutor; Arch.

HOSKIN, KIMBERLY J; Redwood Christian HS; San Leandro, CA; (3); Church Yth Grp; Cmnty Wkr; Drama Clb; Teachers Aide; School Musical; Tennis; Hon Roll; Pres Acad Fit Awd; Ed Nwsp; Ed Yrbk; Piano Cert Of Merit St Recgntn; CSF; Acad Hnrs Engl & French Awds; Piano Cert Of Merit Gold Pin & Mdls; CSU Hayward; CPA.

HOSKING, MICHELLE DAWN; Walnut HS; Walnut, CA; (3); Cmnty Wkr; Dance Clb; Key Clb; JV Sec Pep Clb; Off Jr Cls; Stu Cncl; Stat Bsbl; JV Co-Capt Cheerldng; Stat Ftbl; High Hon Roll; CA Poly Pomona; Math Teacher.

HOSKINS, KARI C; Mt Whitney HS; Visalia, CA; (1); FFA; Hosp Aide; Pep Clb; SADD; Orch; JV Diving; Hon Roll; UCLA; Med.

HOSS, NATALIE K; Ramona HS; Ramona, CA; (3); 13/342; Church Yth Grp; Dance Clb; Drama Clb; Key Clb; School Play; Cit Awd; High Hon Roll; Hon Roll; Prfct Atten Awd; San Diego ST U; Dance.

HOSSEINI, AYME F; Mission Bay HS; San Diego, CA; (4); 165/294; DECA; Key Clb; Mgr Nwsp; Var Treas Fld Hcky; Trk; Teen Inst Cmmtte; Interact Clb Chrmn Electns; U Of San Diego; Law.

HOSSUM, REBECCA; Valley Alternative Magnet Schl; Los Angeles, CA; (3); Church Yth Grp; Hosp Aide; Library Aide; Office Aide; Teachers Aide; Church Choir; Bsbl; Bsktbl; Cit Awd; Accomplshmnt Cert-Mayors Yth Dev Ofc/Bus Indstry Schl/Fulfillmnt Fund Schlrs; UCLA; Law.

HOSTETLER, KERI KRISTEN; Rim Of The World HS; Riverside, CA; (4); 10/238; Drama Clb; Sec French Clb; School Play; French Hon Soc; High Hon Roll; Pres Acad Fit Awd; Drama Awds Bst Supporting Actress 88-89, Bst Actress 89-90; Jr Hnry Ivy Chain 89; Theatre Arts.

HOSTETLER, SASKIA E; Torrey Pines HS; Del Mar, CA; (2); Church Yth Grp; Crs Cntry; Socr; Trk; Hon Roll; Piano 8 Yrs; Pastor Comm; Med.

HOSTETTER, GEOFFREY D; Bishop Amat Memorial HS; San Dimas, CA; (2); Cmnty Wkr; Library Aide; Teachers Aide; Bio Sci.

HOTINE, JENNY M; Modesto Christian HS; Salida, CA; (4); Church Yth Grp; Drama Clb; Teachers Aide; Chorus; Church Choir; School Musical; Ed Yrbk; Hon Roll; Ensmble; Head Chpl Cmmtte; Music.

HOU, ANDREW; Lowell HS; San Francisco, CA; (3); Church Yth Grp; Orch; Var Trk; Kung-Fu Intermd Trnng; Piano.

HOU, JIMMY C; Los Altos HS; Hacienda Hts, CA; (1); Art Clb; Key Clb; Math Clb; Bsktbl; Athltc Actvts-Badminton; U Of CA Los Angeles; Mrktng.

HOU, PAXON; Schurr HS; Montebello, CA; (1); Hon Roll; Prfct Atten Awd; USC; Engr.

HOU, PETER; Burbank SR HS; Burbank, CA; (4); Am Leg Boys St; Pres Chess Clb; Science Clb; Speech Tm; Stu Cncl; Crs Cntry; Co-Capt Tennis; Pres Acad Fit Awd; Acad Decathlon 88-89; CSF; Yth & Govt YMCA 88-89; U CA-BERKELEY; Med.

HOU, RAVINA; Katella HS; Anaheim, CA; (4); French Clb; Key Clb; Spanish Clb; High Hon Roll; Hon Roll; Prfct Atten Awd; Pres Acad Fit Awd; Val; CA Schlrshp Fed Gold Seal Bearer; Engl Stu Yr Awd; Entrance Hnrs; CA ST U Fullerton; Acctng.

HOU, RENEE J; Saratoga HS; Saratoga, CA; (1); Church Yth Grp; Chorus; Hon Roll; Chorus Accmpnst.

HOUCHINS, DAWN; Granite Hills HS; El Cajon, CA; (2); 56/517; Chorus; JV Cheerldng; Cit Awd; Hon Roll.

HOUCK, ZACHARIAH H; Colton HS; Grand Terrace, CA; (2); JV Bsbl; JV Var Ftbl; Medcl.

HOUGE, JENNIFER M; Lower Lake HS; Lower Lake, CA; (3); 11/103; Church Yth Grp; FBLA; Pep Clb; Spanish Clb; Stat Bsktbl; Var Sftbl; High Hon Roll; Hon Roll; Friday Night Live; Rainbow Girls.

HOUGH, ELIZABETH C; Bethel Christian HS; Edwards AFB, CA; (1); Var Cheerldng; High Hon Roll; Tchr.

HOUGHTALING, JACK S; San Pasqual HS; Escondido, CA; (2); French Clb; Hon Roll; Stu Tutor-Math & Wrld Cltrs; Palomar CC; Med.

HOUGHTON, CHRISTY; Victor Valley SR HS; Victorville, CA; (3); Peer Counceling; Victor Valley Coll; Child Care.

HOUGHTON, KIM L; Bella Vista HS; Fair Oaks, CA; (3); 22/363; Church Yth Grp; FBLA; Ski Clb; Spanish Clb; SADD; Var JV Bsktbl; Fridy Nght Live; Wrk In Accntng Comp Consulting Office; Accntnt Engrnr.

HOUGHTON, SARAH A; Atascadero HS; Atascadero, CA; (2); Church Yth Grp; Band; Cit Awd; High Hon Roll; Pres Acad Fit Awd; CA Poly; Archeology.

HOUGLAND, SARA; San Diego Schl Crtv & Prfrmng Arts; San Diego, CA; (3); 37/123; Church Yth Grp; Orch; High Hon Roll; U Of CA San Diego; Arch.

HOULDING, SCOTT C; Madera HS; Madera, CA; (3); Church Yth Grp; Cmnty Wkr; Intnl Clb; Treas Service Clb; Treas Rep Soph Cls; Treas Rep Stu Cncl; Ftbl; JV Golf; High Hon Roll; Hon Roll; Schltc Awd; Dept Awd; GSE Hnrs Awd; CSF Rep; Cal Poly; Ag Bus.

HOULE, CHRIS P; Serra HS; San Mateo, CA; (2); Cmnty Wkr; JV Bsbl; JV Bsktbl; High Hon Roll; Hon Roll; St Schlr; HOBY Ldrshp Awd; Schlr-Ath Awd; CSF; Soph Cert Wnr Forgn Lang.

HOULE, ERIK R; San Gorgonio HS; Highland, CA; (3); French Clb; German Clb; Off Jr Cls; Off Sr Cls; Hon Roll; NHS; Pres Russn Clb; Intl Bus.

HOUNG, LI-JUNG T; Cerritos HS; Cerritos, CA; (3); Intnl Clb; Cit Awd; Jr NHS; Church Yth Grp; Cmnty Wkr; Math Clb; Rep Science Clb; Teachers Aide; Thesps; Score Keeper; Japanese Natl Hnr Soc VP, Pres; Vlntr Rcgntn Awd; Pre-Med.

HOURIZADEH, ELLIE; Taft HS; Woodland Hills, CA; (2); VP Sec Spanish Clb; Sec Temple Yth Grp; JV Capt Bsktbl; Cit Awd; High Hon Roll; Pres Acad Fit Awd; CSF; Mock Trl Cpt & Prsctng Attorney; Law.

HOURMEZIAN, STEVE YOUSIF; El Cajon Valley HS; El Cajon, CA; (2); 60/500; Church Yth Grp; VP Spanish Clb; Church Choir; Cit Awd; Hon Roll; Prfct Atten Awd; Top Sci Stu; UCSD; Cardiology.

HOUSE, MAISHA; John Swett HS; Rodeo, CA; (2); Drama Clb; FBLA; SADD; Band; Mrchg Band; Orch; JV L Bsktbl; Var L Pom Pon; Var L Sftbl; JV L Vllybl; CSF; BSU Black Stu Union; Howard U; Bus.

HOUSEN, ERIC A; Valley Christian HS; San Ramon, CA; (3); Church Yth Grp; Spanish Clb; Varsity Clb; Rep Frsh Cls; Rep Soph Cls; Rep Jr Cls; Var Bsbl; Var Bsktbl; Var Socr; Hon Roll; CSF; Sports Med.

HOUSER, GREGORY; Beyer HS; Modesto, CA; (3); German Clb; Key Clb; Yrbk; Off Jr Cls; Stu Cncl; JV Var Socr; High Hon Roll; Hon Roll; CA ST U; Crmnl Justice.

HOUSER, KELLY; Acalanes HS; Lafayette, CA; (2); Office Aide; SADD; Chorus; Rep Stu Cncl; JV Cheerldng; JV Swmmng; Pres Acad Fit Awd; LMSC Traveling Soccer; DFIC Exch; Peer Cnslr.

HOUSH, MELODI M; Atwater HS; Winton, CA; (1); Church Yth Grp; JV Cheerldng; Stat Trk; Hon Roll; Marine Bio.

HOUSTON, CRAIG; Canyon HS; Canyon Country, CA; (4); 20/480; Drama Clb; FBLA; Library Aide; Spanish Clb; School Play; JV Tennis; High Hon Roll; Hon Roll; Pres Schlr; Spanish NHS; Westmont Coll.

HOUSTON, HOLLY M; San Marino HS; Altadena, CA; (3); Dance Clb; Pep Clb; Science Clb; Service Clb; Cheerldng; Natl Chrty Leag; Amnsty Intl; Bus.

HOUSTON, JANICE M; Mc Clatchy HS; Sacramento, CA; (3); Church Yth Grp; Cmnty Wkr; 4-H; Intnl Clb; Pep Clb; SADD; Hon Roll; Smmr Creative Wrtng Hnrs Pgm, UCLA; Kids On Kampus Vlntr; Sacramento Mayoral Cmpgn Wrkr 87; Chld Psych.

HOUSTON, JOHN C; Ventura HS; Ventura, CA; (4); 31/408; Cmnty Wkr; JA; Letterman Clb; SADD; Teachers Aide; Pres Sr Cls; Var Capt Diving; Var Capt Socr; High Hon Roll; So CA Olympic Dev St Sccr Tm 89; CIF Dvng Fnlst 89; UCI; Math.

HOUSTON, MONIQUE C; Vallejo SR HS; Vallejo, CA; (3); 6/500; Model UN; Teachers Aide; Hon Roll; Jr NHS; Schlstc All Amer Awd; Golden St Hnrs Awd Wnnr Geo, Alg I; Acad Ltr; Gntcs.

HOUSTON, MORTISHA Y; Alhambra HS; Martinez, CA; (3); Band; Drill Tm; Flag Corp; Jazz Band; Mrchg Band; Orch; Pep Band; Stat Var Trk; Hon Roll; Archtctr.

HOUSTON, OLGA; El Cajon Valley HS; El Cajon, CA; (2); Church Yth Grp.

HOUTING, KATHIE A; El Camino Fundamental HS; Sacramento, CA; (3); 109/425; Church Yth Grp; Teachers Aide; Church Choir; Chrprsn Yth Grp Cncl Ldrshp Tm; Southern CA Coll; Sociology.

HOUX, NATHAN G; Thomas Downey HS; Modesto, CA; (4); Chess Clb; JV Var Crs Cntry; JV Ftbl; JV Var Trk; High Hon Roll; Pres Acad Fit Awd; Knight Achvt Awd Acad Excl Math 88-89; High Hnrs Golden St Exam Geom; Life Mem CSF; Cal Poly; Landscape Arch.

HOVANNISIAN, DAMON; Edison Computech HS; Fresno, CA; (2); Ski Clb; JV Bsbl; JV Ftbl; Skeet Shtng Rnkd No 1 Sub Jr In Wrld; UCLA; Bus.

HOVARD, BRANDON; Woodrow Wilson HS; Long Beach, CA; (2); Church Yth Grp; Office Aide; SADD; Vllybl; High Hon Roll; Hon Roll; Lion Awd; NHS; Pres Acad Fit Awd; Jnr Vrsty Vlybl MVP; CSF; Super Achvt Spansh; Stamford; Bus.

HOVDE, HEATHER L; Woodcrest Christian HS; Perris, CA; (2); Drama Clb; Key Clb; Teachers Aide; Acpl Chr; Chorus; School Play; Crs Cntry; Cit Awd; High Hon Roll; NHS; Work With Pre-Schl Chldrn Montessort Schl; Chrstn Ldrshp Aed 90; Early Grad.

HOVELSEN, CHAD E; Los Altos HS; Hacienda Hts, CA; (1); Boy Scts; Church Yth Grp; SADD; Band; Chorus; Church Choir; Mrchg Band; Pep Band; Socr; Vllybl; Mst Imprvd Soccer; Princpals Hnr Rll; Perf Atten; Stanford; Metalergical Engr.

HOVENIC, MICHAEL THOMAS; Chula Vista HS; Poway, CA; (2); 20/205; Boy Scts; Speech Tm; Var Golf; Var Socr; Life Badge Boy Scouts; CSF; Jr Statesmn Assn; Dartmouth; Dentist.

HOVEY, DOUGLAS K; Burbank HS; Burbank, CA; (3); Aud/Vis; French Clb; Teachers Aide; Ed Nwsp; Acadmc Dcthln; People To People Stu Ambssdr Pgm; NY U; Film.

HOVEY, JUSTIN D; Novato HS; San Jose, CA; (4); 1/241; Cmnty Wkr; Teachers Aide; Rptr Yrbk; Pres Frsh Cls; Pres Soph Cls; Rep Jr Cls; Rep Sr Cls; Stu Cncl; Var JV Bsbl; High Hon Roll; Ucla; Poltcl Sci.

HOVEY, RUTH; Valhalla HS; El Cajon, CA; (4); 8/412; Church Yth Grp; Hosp Aide; Key Clb; Chorus; Church Choir; Rptr Nwsp; Ed Yrbk; Var Swmmng; DAR Awd; High Hon Roll; Bob Jones U.

HOVINETZ, CARRIE A; John F Kennedy HS; Buena Park, CA; (3); Teachers Aide; Var L Crs Cntry; Var L Trk; Hon Roll; Woodwrkng Awds Orange Cnty Fr; Hnrs Golden St Exm Alg; Woodworking.

HOVLAND, CARTER J; Miraleste HS; Rolling Hills, CA; (3); JV Bsktbl; JV Ftbl; Var Socr; Var Trk; Hon Roll; New Life & Pddl Tnns Clbs; Tchng.

HOVLAND, LISA J; Edison HS; Huntington Beach, CA; (3); Church Yth Grp; Model UN; Band; Church Choir; Jazz Band; Mrchg Band; Pep Band; High Hon Roll; Hon Roll; Aeron Engr.

HOVORE, TOM; Canyon HS; Canyon Country, CA; (3); 5/600; Debate Tm; FBLA; Band; Jazz Band; Mrchg Band; Pep Band; Bsbl; JV L Bsktbl; Var L Tennis; High Hon Roll; Schltc All-Amer; Acad Letterman; Acad Decathlon; USC; Law.

HOW, MATTHEW D; Troy HS; Yorba Linda, CA; (2); High Hon Roll; Stu Of Mnth Engl Oct & Dec; Awd In Span II, Hstry; CA Schlrshp Fed.

HOWARD, AARON L T; Orange HS; Santa Ana, CA; (3); Church Yth Grp; Intrml Bsbl; Intrml Ftbl; High Hon Roll; NHS; Archry; Marksmn; Baritone; UC San Diego; Marine Bio.

HOWARD, ADAM M; Antelope Valley HS; Lancaster, CA; (3); Church Yth Grp; Service Clb; Ski Clb; SADD; Swmmng; Cit Awd; High Hon Roll; Bys STR; Acad Dcthln; FL ST U; Aerospc Engr.

HOWARD, BRAD A; North HS; Oildale, CA; (3); 20/368; Church Yth Grp; SADD; Crs Cntry; High Hon Roll; NHS; Bilingual; Notre Dame; Psych.

HOWARD, BRIDGET K; Merced HS; Merced, CA; (3); Church Yth Grp; Teachers Aide; Stat JV Bsbl; Var Diving; Hon Roll; Graduated With Gold Cord; Coaches Awd Diving; CSU; Phys Thrpy.

HOWARD, CHRISTINE A; Bishop Amat Memorial HS; Glendora, CA; (2); GAA; Var Capt Vllybl; Vllybl Frshmn MVP Awd Cptn Vrsty; Cyclng Clb; Fshn Outlk Clb; Med.

HOWARD, CHRISTOPHER N; Clovis HS; Clovis, CA; (3); Boy Scts; Church Yth Grp; High Hon Roll; Hon Roll; German; Latin; Davis; Vet.

HOWARD, CINDY; Emeryville HS; Berkeley, CA; (1); Office Aide; Cit Awd; High Hon Roll; Hon Roll; Math, Social Studies, Spanish, World History & Health Achvt Tree Awds; Zoologist.

HOWARD, DANIEL L; Bella Vista HS; Fair Oaks, CA; (4); 14/400; Science Clb; Band; Mrchg Band; High Hon Roll; Ntl Merit Schol; St Schlr; Wnnr Amer River Coll Chem Cntst 89; CA Poly; Envrnmntl Engrng.

HOWARD, DEBBIE K; Edison HS; Huntington Beach, CA; (3); GAA; Ski Clb; Var Swmmng; Var Vllybl; Golden Key Medallion; Swmmng Coachs Awd Jr Var, Mst Imprvd Var; Mst Imprvd Vllybl; USC; Poltcl Sci.

HOWARD, EMILY J; Wilcox HS; Santa Clara, CA; (1); #63 In Class; Drama Clb; Library Aide; Spanish Clb; Color Guard; Stage Crew; Psych.

HOWARD, ETHAN J; Woodside Priory Schl; San Jose, CA; (3); 4/20; Cmnty Wkr; Computer Clb; Sprt Ed Nwsp; Stu Cncl; Var Bsbl; Var Socr; Cit Awd; Hon Roll; NHS; Med.

HOWARD, JEFF; Calaveras HS; San Andreas, CA; (2); 3/236; Pres 4-H; Letterman Clb; VICA; Ed Yrbk; JV L Ftbl; JV L Wrstlng; 4-H Awd; High Hon Roll; Hon Roll; CSF; Friday Night Live; Historical Soc Essay Cont Wnnr; UC Berkeley; Engrng.

HOWARD, JOHN; Brethren HS; Long Beach, CA; (3); 1/60; Pres Church Yth Grp; Acpl Chr; Church Choir; School Musical; VP Jr Cls; Var Crs Cntry; Var Tennis; Var Trk; VP Bsbl; Intrml Bsktbl; Ecclesia; US Acad Decthln Hnrs Div Std; US Air Force Acad; Engrng.

HOWARD, KELLY J; Moreau HS; Fremont, CA; (2); Drama Clb; Ski Clb; Var Swmmng; Hon Roll; Gymnst; USC; Bus.

HOWARD, KRISTINA M; Las Lomas HS; Walnut Creek, CA; (3); AFS; French Clb; Pep Clb; Teachers Aide; Band; Hon Roll; Golden ST Rcgntn Awd In Geom 1988; UCSD; Envrmntl Engr.

HOWARD, LISA LYNN; Clovis West HS; Clovis, CA; (4); Intnl Clb; SADD; Var L Cheerldng; Var L Trk; Hon Roll; Pres Acad Fit Awd; Natl Crwdldr Chmpns 90; Coachs Awd-Trck 90; GATE; AZ ST U; Sprts Med.

HOWARD, MICHELLE L; Fontana HS; Fontana, CA; (3); Color Guard; Stat Bsktbl; Hon Roll; Stu Govt Traveled To Washington DC; Bus.

HOWARD, NATALIE A; North HS; Bakersfield, CA; (2); Sftbl; Hon Roll.

HOWARD, PEARL E; Montclair HS; Ontario, CA; (2); Church Yth Grp; Drama Clb; Pres FHA; Church Choir; Stage Crew; Drama.

HOWARD, ROBERT J; Clovis West HS; Fresno, CA; (3); FTA; German Clb; Letterman Clb; Library Aide; Office Aide; SADD; Teachers Aide; Varsity Clb; Rep Jr Cls; Rep Stu Cncl; Golden Poet Awd; Dukakis For Pres Cmpgn 88; Feinstein For Govnr Cmpgn 90; Gary Condit For Cngrss 88; UCLA; Aerospace Engrng.

HOWARD, SAMANTHA; Southwest HS; San Diego, CA; (2); Church Yth Grp; SADD; Chorus; Church Choir; Rep Frsh Cls; Rep Stu Cncl; Cit Awd; High Hon Roll; Prfct Atten Awd; Pres Acad Fit Awd; Awd Outstndng Music Stu; Bell Choir; Princpls Advsry; UCSD; Nrsng.

HOWARD, SCOTISKA L; Montclair HS; Montclair, CA; (2); SADD; Sec Soph Cls; Sec Stu Cncl; Stu Cncl Certs Achvt & Ltrs; La Verne; Law.

HOWARD, SHARON A; North County Christian HS; Paso Robles, CA; (1); Church Yth Grp; 4-H; Speech Tm; Bsktbl; Vllybl; Real Est.

HOWARD, STEPHANIE; Clovis West HS; Fresno, CA; (3); JV Cheerldng; Coach Awd 87-88; Cert Apprctn 89-90; FSU; Bus Law.

HOWARD, STEPHANIE C; Placer HS; Auburn, CA; (2); Church Yth Grp; Cmnty Wkr; Yrbk; JV Vllybl; Hon Roll; Younglife; Frshmn Princess; Mission Trips To Mexico; Bus.

HOWARD, THERESA; North HS; Bakersfield, CA; (2); Teachers Aide; Mgr(s); Score Keeper; Sftbl; Skiing; Bakersfield Coll; Bus.

HOWARDCOHEN, ISA; Lowell HS; San Francisco, CA; (3); Drama Clb; Red Cross Aide; Teachers Aide; Band; Cert Of Hnr Reg Outstndng Cntrbtn; SF Suicide Prevtn; Awd Of Merit/Outstndng Achvmnt; Teachng Asst; UC Santa Cruz.

HOWATT, KIMBERLY; El Capitan HS; El Cajon, CA; (4); 10/406; Am Leg Aux Girls St; Pep Clb; VP Spanish Clb; Off Soph Cls; Sec Stu Cncl; JV Bsktbl; Var Trk; Var Vllybl; Hon Roll; Lion Awd; ASB Publcty Commssnr; U CA-DAVIS; Poly Sci.

HOWDER, CHRISTY M; Colfax HS; Colfax, CA; (4); Pres Church Yth Grp; Drama Clb; VP Rptr FBLA; Science Clb; Pres Service Clb; School Play; Rptr Phtg Yrbk; Stat Ftbl; Capt Var Sftbl; Hon Roll; Natl Yth Ldr Schlr; Sacramento ST; Vsl Hndcp Tchr.

HOWE, DAVID; Palo Verde HS; Blythe, CA; (2); 14/299; Church Yth Grp; Drama Clb; SADD; Hon Roll; NHS; Rotary Awd; U Of CO Denver; Math.

HOWE, FRED S; Cordova HS; Rancho Cordova, CA; (4); German Clb; VP Frsh Cls; JV Bsktbl; JV Crs Cntry; JV Ftbl; JV Swmmng; Capt Trk; Wt Lftg; Boy Scts; Jazz Band; Natural Hlprs Peer Cnslng; Spartan; Aeronautics.

HOWE, MISTY D; Bullard HS; Fresno, CA; (1); Key Clb; Ski Clb; GATE Cls.

HOWE, RACHEL E; Clovis West HS; Fresno, CA; (3); Church Yth Grp; FBLA; Intnl Clb; Church Choir; Sec Sr Cls; Stu Cncl; JV Gym; High Hon Roll; Hon Roll; Teachers Aide; Yng Women Of Yr Schlrshp Pageant 2nd Pl; Jr Cls Homcmng Attendant Princess; Mexicali Stu Ldr 89-90; Biola U; Psych.

HOWE, SARAH E; Clovis West HS; Fresno, CA; (4); Church Yth Grp; Cmnty Wkr; English Clb; FCA; Intnl Clb; Key Clb; NFL; Service Clb; Yrbk; Rep Stu Cncl; Jnr Miss Pgnt 2nd Rnnr Up 89; Hmecmng-Jnr Prncss, Snr Attndnt 89, 90; Comm.

HOWELL, ANGELIQUE; Woodrow Wilson HS; Long Beach, CA; (3); Drama Clb; Math Tm; Teachers Aide; Chorus; Mgr(s); Trk; High Hon Roll; Jr NHS; Lion Awd; Pres Acad Fit Awd; Engrng.

HOWELL, CHRISTY L; Fontana HS; Fontana, CA; (2); Church Yth Grp; Sftbl; Hon Roll; :Med.

HOWELL, GRACE A; Westmoor HS; Daly City, CA; (2); Drama Clb; Stage Crew; Hon Roll; Palestinian Amer Yth Orgnztn.

HOWELL, JENNIFER; Corning Union HS; Corning, CA; (3); GAA; Ski Clb; Drill Tm; Sec Frsh Cls; Treas Soph Cls; Vllybl; High Hon Roll; Hon Roll; CSF.

HOWELL, JENNIFER K; Fontana HS; Fontana, CA; (4); 131/792; FBLA; JA; Band; High Hon Roll; Hon Roll; Stu Mnth; Exchng Club Schlrshp; FBLA Career & Voc Awd; San Bernardino Valley; Secy.

HOWELL, JOSHUA D; Las Lomas HS; Walnut Creek, CA; (2); Tennis; High Hon Roll; Hon Roll; UC Berkeley; Biochem.

HOWELL, KATIE T; North HS; Bakersfield, CA; (3); 1/270; Am Leg Aux Girls St; Sec Church Yth Grp; FCA; Letterman Clb; Spanish Clb; Varsity Clb; VP Jr Cls; VP Socr; JV Capt Vllybl; Hon Roll; Biola U; Elem Ed.

HOWELL, MARY C; Barstow HS; Hinkley, CA; (3); Church Yth Grp; Teachers Aide; Band; Mrchg Band; Pep Band; Hon Roll; Sctn Ldr Marching Band; UNLV; Lawyer.

HOWELL, SCOTT E; Pioneer HS; San Jose, CA; (2); Boy Scts; Church Yth Grp; Cmnty Wkr; Band; Jazz Band; JV Ftbl; JV Trk; Var Wt Lftg; Var JV Wrstlng; Pres Schlr; Cyclng, Bckpckng; US Air Force Acad; Medivac Unt.

HOWELL, SHANE M; Chula Vista HS; Chula Vista, CA; (3); 75/500; Chess Clb; Church Yth Grp; Cmnty Wkr; Pep Clb; Spanish Clb; SADD; JV Var Bsktbl; JV Diving; Var Tennis; Var Capt Vllybl; All Acadmc Tm Bsktbl, Vllybl; Bsktbl 3 Point Shooter Champ; San Diego ST; Geogrphy.

HOWELL, WILLIAM C; Desert HS; Edwards, CA; (3); Pres Sr Cls; Bausch & Lomb Sci Awd; Cit Awd; Hon Roll; Sci.

HOWELLS, MARIA S; San Juan HS; Rancho Cordova, CA; (1); Drama Clb; Chorus; School Play; Stage Crew; Mgr(s); Chico ST; Cnslr.

HOWERTON, AMY D; O'farrell SCPA HS; San Diego, CA; (1); 26/227; Dance Clb; Chorus; Hon Roll; Jr NHS; NHS; Cmpt Rllr Skater; CA Yth Chorale; O Ferrel; Vet Med.

HOWES, BRANDON; Southwest HS; San Diego, CA; (3); 14/493; Am Leg Boys St; Cmnty Wkr; Letterman Clb; SADD; Varsity Clb; Band; Ed Nwsp; Bsbl; Bsktbl; Diving; Freedms Fndtn Yth Ldrshp Conf; Stanford; Brdcst Jnrlsm.

HOWES, SHANNON M; Alameda HS; Alameda, CA; (4); 39/331; Treas Frsh Cls; Var Capt Swmmng; Var Tennis; Hon Roll.

HOWLAND, ALISON M; Sonora HS; Columbia, CA; (3); 50/280; Church Yth Grp; Ski Clb; Phtg Nwsp; Hon Roll; Video Cmnctns Cls-Edtng, Cmra Wrk; Frstry.

HOWLAND, JULIAN N; Atascadero HS; Atascadero, CA; (2); Drama Clb; French Clb; Hon Roll; La Sorbonne.

HOWLAND, WILLIAM BRIAN; Monterey Bay Acad; Kettering, OH; (3); Church Yth Grp; Drama Clb; Church Choir; School Musical; Var Ftbl; School Play; Variety Show; Yrbk; Stu Cncl; Hon Roll; Missions Projects Other Countries Bldg Churches; Andrews U; Psych.

HOWLETT, KATE M; San Clemente HS; San Juan Capis, CA; (2); Cmnty Wkr; Dance Clb; French Clb; Hosp Aide; NFL; Quiz Bowl; Science Clb; Service Clb; Speech Tm; Cit Awd; Johns Hopkins Prog; Harvard U; Plstc Surgn.

HOWSER III, KENNETH JAY; Madera HS; Madera, CA; (2); Boy Scts; Church Yth Grp; Church Choir; JV Trk; Hon Roll; Dept Awds Geom, Art, Phys Ed; BYU.

HOY, HOLLY A; Alverno HS; Sierra Madre, CA; (3); Service Clb; Play Drums; Enjoy Wrtng Poetry & Svrl Were Pblshd; Artwork Is Important; UC Davis; Vet Med.

HOYT, CRYSTAL L; Victor Valley HS; Victorville, CA; (2); 2/605; Church Yth Grp; Key Clb; Pep Clb; Spanish Clb; JV Cheerldng; High Hon Roll; Prfct Atten Awd; Soph Hghst GPA Awd; World His Achvmt Awd; Pepperdine; Ped.

HOYT, KENNY W; Rio Lindo Adventist Acad; Napa, CA; (3); FCA; Ski Clb; Teachers Aide; School Play; Yrbk; Pres Stu Cncl; Intrml Ftbl; Intrml Sftbl; Intrml Vllybl; CA U; Med.

HOYT, MICHAEL; Holtville HS; Holtville, CA; (4); 4/103; 4-H; FBLA; Math Tm; Pep Clb; Yrbk; VP Jr Cls; Var L Bsbl; Var L Bsktbl; Var L Ftbl; High Hon Roll; Acad All Amer; All Valley Lineman Ftbl; Cal Poly Pomona; Engrng.

HOYT, SARAH J; Irvington HS; Fremont, CA; (2); 23/325; Church Yth Grp; Band; Mrchg Band; JV Cheerldng; JV Swmmng; Hon Roll; Summer Swim Clb; Music Lessons; Mrktng.

HRABA, KRISTEN; San Mateo HS; San Mateo, CA; (4); 90/340; Am Leg Aux Girls St; Rptr Nwsp; Rptr Frsh Cls; VP Soph Cls; Off Jr Cls; Stu Cncl; Capt Var Socr; Capt Var Sftbl; Hon Roll; Rotry Stu Of Yr; Jr Statesmen Of Amer; U CO Boulder; Commnctns.

HREN, KATHERINE A; Louisville HS; Westlake Village, CA; (1); Church Yth Grp; Cmnty Wkr; Drama Clb; Ski Clb; Chorus; VP Soph Cls; JV Cheerldng; High Hon Roll.

HRISTOVA, MARTA K; Eugene Mc Ateer HS; San Francisco, CA; (3); Hon Roll; Badminton Clb; Bio.

HRUBY, TIA; Highland HS; Bakersfield, CA; (4); Teachers Aide; High Hon Roll; Hon Roll; UC Santa Cruz.

HRYNKIEWICZ, JOANN M; Saint Bernards HS; Eureka, CA; (2); Drama Clb; FHA; Girl Scts; Hosp Aide; Teachers Aide; Cruise Dir.

HSEI, VANESSA C; Edison HS; Huntington Beach, CA; (3); Church Yth Grp; French Clb; Intnl Clb; Model UN; Church Choir; High Hon Roll; CSF Ofcr; Cal Teen; PALS.

HSIA, RENEE Y; John A Rowland HS; Rowland Heights, CA; (2); Math Clb; Science Clb; Spanish Clb; Acpl Chr; Cit Awd; High Hon Roll; Prfct Atten Awd; Pres Acad Fit Awd; CSF & Intrct Clb; UCLA; Lwyr.

HSIAO, BYRON C; John F Kennedy HS; Anaheim, CA; (2); Church Yth Grp; Computer Clb; Church Choir; Wt Lftg; Berkeley; Bus Law.

HSIAO, ERIC Z; El Cerrito HS; El Cerrito, CA; (4); Teachers Aide; Mgr Yrbk; VP Stu Cncl; JV Var Tennis; Stat Vllybl; Hon Roll; Pres Acad Fit Awd; U Of CA Los Angeles.

HSIAO, GRACE; John F Kennedy HS; La Palma, CA; (3); Church Yth Grp; 1st Pl & Best Of Show La Palma Clbrtn Of Arts 89; UCLA; Econ.

HSIAO, HUIWEN; Sunny Hills HS; Fullerton, CA; (1); Church Yth Grp; Sec Frsh Cls; Cit Awd; DAR Awd; High Hon Roll; Stanford; Med.

HSIAO, JEFFREY; Lowell HS; San Francisco, CA; (2); Art Clb; Cmnty Wkr; Computer Clb; Pep Clb; Science Clb; Service Clb; JV Crs Cntry; Score Keeper; JV Trk; Cit Awd; CSF; Tnns Clb; Princeton; Aerospace Engr.

HSIAO, LEO L; Gladstone HS; Covina, CA; (3); Pres Church Yth Grp; Science Clb; Teachers Aide; Var Capt Tennis; High Hon Roll; Prfct Atten Awd; CSF.

HSIAO, MYRNA; Lowell HS; San Francisco, CA; (3); Cmnty Wkr; English Clb; Pep Clb; Red Cross Aide; Service Clb; SADD; Orch; High Hon Roll; JV Fncng; Amnsty Intl; CSF; Princeton; Hotel Mgmt.

HSIEH, FRANCES L; Lowell HS; San Francisco, CA; (2); Science Clb; Teachers Aide; Band; Pep Band; Russian Club; Shrt Stry Club; CSF.

HSIEH, JEAN; Homestead HS; Los Altos, CA; (1); Orch; 1st Pl Chinese Schl Art Cntst; CSF; Badmntn.

HSIEH, JENNY C; Irvine HS; Irvine, CA; (2); #1 In Class; French Clb; Intnl Clb; Key Clb; Service Clb; NHS; Heritage Awd; Orange Cnty Acad Dcthln 2 Yrs; Law.

HSIEH, KEVIN R; Lowell HS; San Francisco, CA; (2); Chess Clb; Goldn St Exam 1st Yr Alg High Hnrs; Comp Pgmng.

HSIEH, KOU-YING; St Marys HS; Stockton, CA; (2); Science Clb; Speech Tm; Orch; Var Swmmng; High Hon Roll; Biochem.

HSIEH, PATRICK C; Temple City HS; San Gabriel, CA; (3); 22/400; Var Bsktbl; High Hon Roll; Hon Roll; NHS; UCLA; Arch.

HSIEH, RICHARD C; El Toro HS; El Toro, CA; (3); 1/490; Treas Debate Tm; Treas French Clb; Key Clb; Math Tm; Quiz Bowl; Speech Tm; JV Tennis; JV Trk; High Hon Roll; NATO Essay Cont Wnnr 90; Intl Rltns.

HSIEH, SARAH; Ernest Righetti HS; Santa Maria, CA; (4); 4/356; VP Art Clb; Church Yth Grp; Dance Clb; Math Clb; Science Clb; Cit Awd; High Hon Roll; Hon Roll; CSF; Piano; Acad Lttr; U Of CA LA; Bus.

HSIEH, STEPHANIE; Newport Christian HS; Fountain Valley, CA; (3); 1/20; Church Yth Grp; Quiz Bowl; Scholastic Bowl; Speech Tm; Teachers Aide; School Play; Mgr Stage Crew; High Hon Roll.

HSIEH, VANESSA L; Poway HS; Poway, CA; (4); Church Yth Grp; Hosp Aide; Math Clb; Math Tm; VP Mu Alpha Theta; Scholastic Bowl; SADD; Orch; Ed Yrbk; Ed Lit Mag; Ballet & Jazz Dancing; Piano; Tutor; Med.

HSING, KENNETH H; Fountain Valley HS; Fountain Valley, CA; (1); German Clb; Crs Cntry; JV Trk; Hon Roll; Most Improved Player Cross Country Team; UCI; Engineering.

HSIU, EDWARD Y; Monte Visa HS; Walnut Creek, CA; (2); Cmnty Wkr; Computer Clb; Hosp Aide; Hon Roll; Piano; Academic Decathalon; East Bay Taiwanese Youth; UC Los Angeles; Medical.

HSIUNG, DAISY; John A Rowland HS; Rowland Heights, CA; (2); 20/552; Sec Church Yth Grp; Dance Clb; French Clb; Pres Key Clb; Science Clb; Acpl Chr; Church Choir; School Musical; School Play; Stage Crew; Photo Club Vp; UCLA; Bus Adm.

HSU, ANGEL I; Lowell HS; San Francisco, CA; (3); Treas Band; Orch; CSF; Schl Cleaness Soc; Shield & Scroll Hnrs Soc; Red Cross Clb-Pres, VP, Pub Rel; Hgh Hnrs Golden St; Hstry.

HSU, ANNIE Y; Whitney HS; Cerritos, CA; (1); Art Clb; Drama Clb; Color Guard; Swmmng; High Hon Roll; Chinese Clb; Inner Cncl Publicity; CJSF; Piano.

HSU, AURIE Y; St Margarets Of Scotland HS; Laguna Niguel, CA; (2); Art Clb; Chorus; Pep Band; Variety Show; Bsktbl; Socr; Sftbl; Vllybl; Wt Lftg; High Hon Roll; Fnlst Intl Piano Comptn; Prfrmng Arts.

HSU, CAROL J; Irvine HS; Irvine, CA; (2); 2/530; AFS; Band; Mrchg Band; JV Socr; JV Vllybl; High Hon Roll; Pres Acad Fit Awd; Coachs Awd Vllybll & Sccr; Zoo Vlntr; Heritage Awd Chem & Eng; Sec Educ.

HSU, DANIEL S; Poway HS; San Diego, CA; (2); 100/833; VP FBLA; JV Trk; Hon Roll; CSF; Pres Young Dem; VP Financl Consltnst Sherson Leman Hutton.

HSU, DONALD I; John F Kennedy HS; Cypress, CA; (3); Church Yth Grp; JV Bsktbl; Hon Roll; Pres Acad Fit Awd; UCLA.

HSU, GLORIA; University HS; Irvine, CA; (4); 36/488; JCL; Latin Clb; Teachers Aide; L Var Crs Cntry; Var Trk; High Hon Roll; Stu Of Month 90; Cornell U; Nutritional Sci.

HSU, HELEN; Bullard HS; Fresno, CA; (3); 1/500; Church Yth Grp; Debate Tm; Sec VP French Clb; NFL; Lit Mag; Hon Roll; Ntl Merit Ltr; 1440 On SAT; Prfct 800 On Amer Hstry Achvt Test; Mem Of Oddessey Of The Mind Tm Whch Plcd 2nd Reg Fin; UCLA; Financial Planning.

HSU, JEAN W; John Burroughs HS; Burbank, CA; (4); Chorus; Pres Acad Fit Awd; Cal Poly Ponoma; Bio.

HSU, JENNIFER C; Mills HS; Millbrae, CA; (3); Intnl Clb; Spanish Clb; Bus Admin.

HSU, JEROME; Pinole Valley HS; Hercules, CA; (4); 32/450; Church Yth Grp; Cmnty Wkr; Debate Tm; Hosp Aide; NFL; Speech Tm; Var Tennis; High Hon Roll; Hon Roll; Pres Acad Fit Awd; CSF; U Of CA Berkeley; Frnch Lit.

HSU, JOHN H; Sun Mateo HS; Foster City, CA; (3); JV Var Ftbl; JV Var Trk; JV Wrstlng; High Hon Roll; Hon Roll; City Chinese Clb Yth Grp; CA Schlrshp Fdrtn.

HSU, JOHN Y; Whitney JR SR HS; Cerritos, CA; (2); 1/200; Intnl Clb; Ed Nwsp; JV Swmmng; High Hon Roll; CSF; Karate.

HSU, KENNETH K; J F Kennedy HS; La Palma, CA; (3); Cmnty Wkr; Computer Clb; FBLA; Intnl Clb; Key Clb; Math Tm; Speech Tm; Ed Nwsp; JV Var Tennis; High Hon Roll.

HSU, LILY; Sunny Hills HS; Fullerton, CA; (3); Spanish Clb; Orch; Tennis; High Hon Roll; NHS; Jr Engrng Technel Soc Clb VP; IB Clb Pres; Orange Cnty Yth Symphny Orhcestra.

HSU, LINDA L; San Marino HS; San Marino, CA; (4); French Clb; FBLA; Math Clb; Science Clb; Nwsp.

HSU, PHILLIP S; Poway HS; San Diego, CA; (3); Boy Scts; Church Yth Grp; FBLA; Letterman Clb; Library Aide; Varsity Clb; Var Vllybl; Hon Roll; Bus.

HSU, RAY C; Hillsdale HS; Foster City, CA; (3); French Clb; Math Clb; Math Tm; Ed Yrbk; Tennis; Hon Roll; Mech Engrng.

HSU, SAM; Lowell HS; San Francisco, CA; (2); Rep Frsh Cls.

HSU, SHELTON J; Lowell HS; San Francisco, CA; (2); Church Yth Grp; Cmnty Wkr; Golden State Exam High Honors; Basketball; Pacific Union College; Medicine.

HSU, TIM H; Dana Hills HS; Laguna Niguel, CA; (4); French Clb; Red Cross Aide; Church Choir; Stu Cncl; Ntl Merit SF; Englsh Achvt Awd; 1st Pl Music; Panel Hnrs; UC Brkly; Elec Engrg.

HSU, TONY; University HS; Irvine, CA; (1); Computer Clb; Hosp Aide; Orch; Cit Awd; Hon Roll; Pres Acad Fit Awd; Genetic Engrng.

HSU, YVONNE; Esperanza HS; Yorba Linda, CA; (2); 1/571; Intnl Clb; Treas Soph Cls; JV Tennis; High Hon Roll; Treas NHS; CSF; Girls League Treas.

HSUE, DIANA Y; John A Rowland HS; Rowland Heights, CA; (2); Cmnty Wkr; German Clb; Teachers Aide; Hon Roll; Athletics Badminton; CSF; Princ Hnr Rl; UCLA.

HSUEH, LO; Abraham Lincoln HS; San Francisco, CA; (3); U Of CA Berkeley; Med.

HSZIEH, RANDOLPH T; Redlands HS; Loma Linda, CA; (4); 32/800; Boy Scts; JV Socr; Hon Roll; Badminton JV; UC Irvine; Civil Engrng.

HTOY, SALLY L; San Gabriel HS; Rosemead, CA; (2); Var Vllybl; Cit Awd; Hon Roll; Prfct Atten Awd; Pres Acad Fit Awd; CSF; Acad Decathalon; USC; Pharm.

HU, CHARLES; Poway HS; Poway, CA; (4); 3/700; Pres Sec Computer Clb; Debate Tm; Sec FBLA; Hosp Aide; Pres VP Math Clb; Pres Mu Alpha Theta; Capt Quiz Bowl; Capt Scholastic Bowl; Spanish Clb; Ed Nwsp; 3rd Pl Bus Engl; CA St FBLA; 4th Pl Cal Poly St Math Cmptn; Pres CSF; U Of CA Berkeley; Bio.

HU, ESSA H; South Pasadena HS; South Pasadena, CA; (4); 1/280; Math Clb; Math Tm; Treas Orch; Rptr Nwsp; Ed Lit Mag; JV Tennis; Ntl Merit Ltr; Pres Acad Fit Awd; Rotary Awd; Val; Knowledge Bowl Comptn; CSF; Chinese Club Pres; Golden St Geom Exam Honors; Harvard U.

HU, JAMES C; Mountain View HS; Mountain View, CA; (3); Boy Scts; French Clb; Nwsp; High Hon Roll; Ntl Merit Ltr; Amnesty Intl; Interact Clb; Badminton Var.

HU, TIFFANY; Los Altos HS; Hacienda Hgts, CA; (2); Church Yth Grp; Cmnty Wkr; Intnl Clb; Red Cross Aide; Science Clb; Hon Roll; Prfct Atten Awd; JV Stat Bsktbl; Vlntr COER UCLA Frgn Exchng Pgm Smmr 89 & 90; Keywanette Clb Pres 88-90; CA-NV-HI Keywan Dist Secy; UCLA.

HUA, AARON H; Galileo HS; San Francisco, CA; (2); 2/32; Aud/Vis; 4-H; Science Clb; Teachers Aide; School Play; Rptr Nwsp; VP Jr Cls; Swmmng; Wt Lftg; Hon Roll; U CA-BERKELEY; Bus Mgmt.

HUA, ANH; Alhambra HS; Alhambra, CA; (4); Cmnty Wkr; Dance Clb; Hosp Aide; Office Aide; Red Cross Aide; Teachers Aide; Prfct Atten Awd; Teen Clb; Vietnamese Clb; Medcl Clb; CA ST LA; Bio.

HUA, BAN; U S Grant HS; Los Angeles, CA; (4); Hon Roll; Chinese Clb; 1st Pl Bio Cls; Civil Engrng.

HUA, CHAU; Montclair HS; Montclair, CA; (1); Tennis; High Hon Roll; Prfct Atten Awd; Natl Latin Exm; Envrnmntl Clb.

HUA, DAVID DU-VINH; Bassett HS; La Puente, CA; (3); Treas FBLA; Math Clb; Mu Alpha Theta; Rep Sr Cls; High Hon Roll; NHS; Prfct Atten Awd; GSE Hgh Hnrs Alg I Awd; GSE Hgh Hnrs Geom Awd; Hnr Guard; Harvey Mudd Coll; Comp Engrng.

HUA, JACKIE; Skyline HS; Oakland, CA; (2); Intl Clb Pres; Accntng.

HUA, JIMMY T; Mark Keppel HS; Alhambra, CA; (3); 15/255; Cmnty Wkr; FCA; FBLA; Key Clb; Math Clb; Yrbk; Bsktbl; Tennis; High Hon Roll; Jr NHS; Hnr Soc; 3 Yr Vrsty Bsktbl Cptn; Cngrssnl Schlr Rep CA Natl Yng Ldrs Conf DC; UC Berkeley; Bus Admin.

HUA, KEVIN V; Los Amigos HS; Fountain Valley, CA; (2); Science Clb; Spanish Clb; Bsktbl; Var JV Tennis; Hon Roll; FVU Exchng Stu Japan Schlrshp; UCLA; Pediatrics.

HUA, LEIGH; Sacramento HS; Sacramento, CA; (2); 208/500; School Play; CSUS.

HUA, LILY; Arcadia HS; Arcadia, CA; (2); French Clb; Teachers Aide; UCLA.

HUA, PETER; Oakland Technical HS; Oakland, CA; (2); Chess Clb; Teachers Aide; Orch; Var Tennis; Cit Awd; Marcus A Foster Edctnl Achvt & Stu Yr Spnsh Mrt Awds; St Elizabeth Yth Emplymnt Corp; Lang.

HUA, THIEN L; George Washington HS; San Francisco, CA; (3); Key Clb; Bsktbl; Hon Roll; UC Berkeley; Bio.

HUA, TRINH N; San Gabriel HS; San Gabriel, CA; (2); Pep Clb; SADD; Variety Show; Cit Awd; Hon Roll; Lion Awd; Prfct Atten Awd; Interact Clb; CSF; Engl.

HUA, VANESSA; Miramonte HS; Orinda, CA; (1); Debate Tm; Girl Scts; NFL; Band; Lit Mag; JV Cheerldng; Hon Roll; CSF; Orinda Libr Excllnc Writing Cont Short Story Wnnr; Writer.

HUAMAN, RICARDO J; Bishop Amat Memorial HS; Baldwin Park, CA; (3); Church Yth Grp; Drama Clb; School Play; Hon Roll; Natl Scl Stds Olympiad Distnctn Awds-Wrld Hstry/Am Hstry.

HUAN, EDNA M; Walnut HS; Walnut, CA; (3); Spanish Clb; Cit Awd; Hon Roll; UCLA.

HUAN, NGUYEN M; Los Amigos HS; Santa Ana, CA; (2); Hon Roll; NHS; U Of CA Los Angeles; Engr.

HUANDRA, LILIANI; George Washington HS; San Francisco, CA; (2); Computer Clb; Badmnton Team; Comp Sci.

HUANG, ALEX XUE YUAN; Phillip & Sala Burton Acad HS; San Francisco, CA; (3); Boy Scts; Chess Clb; Computer Clb; Library Aide; Math Clb; Nwsp; 4-H Awd; High Hon Roll; Drama Clb; Teachers Aide; Gldn ST Exam Alg; Cert Acad Achvt Bio, Geom, Engl & Pascal.

HUANG, ALICE C; Arcadia HS; Arcadia, CA; (3); 39/639; AFS; Spanish Clb; Teachers Aide; Pricipals Recogntn Roll; CSF; UCLA; Bus Mgmt.

HUANG, ANGELINA; Mission HS; San Francisco, CA; (4); 1/270; Office Aide; Sec Science Clb; Service Clb; Hon Roll; Val; Robert C Byrd Hnrs Schlrshp; Bank Of Amer Achvt Awd Sci; Life Membership CSF; U CA-LOS Angeles; Elec Engrng.

HUANG, ANNE; Earl Warren SR HS; Downey, CA; (3); Art Clb; Church Yth Grp; French Clb; Pres JA; VP Service Clb; SADD; Rep Frsh Cls; Var L Trk; Var L Vllybl; CSF Pres; Bio.

HUANG, ARTHUR Z; West HS; Torrance, CA; (4); 1/428; Cmnty Wkr; Hosp Aide; VP JA; Service Clb; Sec Band; Mrchg Band; Orch; Pep Band; School Musical; Ed Nwsp; Chrch Trmpt Plyr; Estr Sls Wrkr; CSF; Bio Engr.

HUANG, BAO; C K Mc Clatchy HS; Sacramento, CA; (3); 142/390; Church Yth Grp; ROTC; Bsktbl; Sacramento City Coll.

HUANG, BARRY P; Sunny Hills HS; Fullerton, CA; (3); 34/480; Cmnty Wkr; Computer Clb; Science Clb; Spanish Clb; Teachers Aide; Pres Frsh Cls; JV Crs Cntry; Jr Engrng Tech Clb, Bible Clb & Pres In Sci Clb; AP Chem; Chem Engrng.

HUANG, BENSON X; George Washington HS; San Francisco, CA; (3); Engrng.

HUANG, BI ZHEN; Mission HS; San Francisco, CA; (3); Off Jr Cls; Prfct Atten Awd; CSF; LTS; Engrng.

HUANG, CELIA; Leland HS; San Jose, CA; (3); Intnl Clb; UC Berkeley; Ed.

HUANG, CHARLES; Marina HS; Huntington Bch, CA; (4); JA; Teachers Aide; Yrbk; L Var Bsbl; JV Bsktbl; Bus.

HUANG, CHENG SHENG; George Washington HS; San Francisco, CA; (2); Bsktbl; Engrng.

HUANG, DAVID L; Laguna Hills HS; Laguna Hills, CA; (1); 1/380; Boy Scts; French Clb; VP Math Clb; Capt Math Tm; Teachers Aide; Orch; JV Bsktbl; Opt Clb Awd; Pres Acad Fit Awd; Acad Decathlon Capt; Phy.

HUANG, DAVID S; Fountain Valley HS; Fountain Valley, CA; (3); English Clb; Intnl Clb; NFL; Science Clb; Spanish Clb; Speech Tm; Stu Cncl; CSF; Humanities Org & Ethnic Advsry Forum; UCLA; Law.

HUANG, EDWARD; South HS; Bakersfield, CA; (3); FFA; JA; Hon Roll; Prfct Atten Awd; GBS; GSE Geomtry Hnrs; Hnr Art Cunningham Mem Art Gllry; Bus.

HUANG, ELAINE P; Pacifica HS; Garden Grove, CA; (1); Church Yth Grp; Band; Mrchg Band; JV Stat Tennis; Hon Roll; CSF; UCLA; Psych.

HUANG, EVELYN; John F Kennedy HS; La Palma, CA; (2); Church Yth Grp; Hosp Aide; Key Clb; Jazz Band; Mrchg Band; Orch; JV Tennis; Var Trk; High Hon Roll; CSF; Undrgrad Awd Engl Dept; UCLA; Bio.

HUANG, GRACE W; Blair HS; Pasadena, CA; (4); 4/171; Church Yth Grp; Cmnty Wkr; German Clb; Science Clb; Band; Church Choir; High Hon Roll; Pres Acad Fit Awd; CA Scholarship Federation-Certificate Of Life Membership; Bank Of Amer Achievement Award In Science; U Of CA La; Biochemistry.

HUANG, HARRY HERBERT; San Bernardino HS; San Bernardino, CA; (2); Office Aide; Socr; Cit Awd; High Hon Roll; Prfct Atten Awd; CA ST Polytech U; Arch.

HUANG, HELEN; Sacramento HS; Sacramento, CA; (2); 27/500; Science Clb; Hon Roll; Congrssnl Schlr Natl Yng Ldrs Conf; CSF; UC Davis; Comp Engrng.

HUANG, JAMES; Mills HS; Millbrae, CA; (2); JA; Math Tm; Orch; JV Bsbl; High Hon Roll; Hon Roll; Lion Awd; Pres Acad Fit Awd; CSF; Med.

HUANG, JAMES J; San Marino HS; San Marino, CA; (3); FBLA; Hosp Aide; Math Clb; Teachers Aide; JV Vllybl; Cit Awd; NHS; NEDT Awd; Prfct Atten Awd; 88 Golden State Exam Geometry Honors; Certfcate Of Merit; E Club Outstndng Schlrship; Cert Achv Health; Med.

HUANG, JASON; John F Kennedy HS; La Palma, CA; (3); Computer Clb; Key Clb; Teachers Aide; Ed Nwsp; JV Tennis; Hon Roll; Pres Acad Fit Awd; Gse Exam; Acad Exclnc Awd; Hnr Hnrs; Amer Chem Socty Outstdng Chem Std Awd.

HUANG, JERRY; Lynbrook HS; San Jose, CA; (4); 1/300; Chrmn FBLA; JA; Q&S; Stage Crew; Rptr Nwsp; Var L Ftbl; NHS; Ntl Merit SF; Schlr Ath Ftbl 88-89; Engrng.

HUANG, JIENA; Abraham Lincoln HS; San Francisco, CA; (4); English Clb; Library Aide; Teachers Aide; Arch Engrng.

HUANG, JING; Calvin Simmons JR HS; Oakland, CA; (1); JA; Band; School Musical; Vllybl; High Hon Roll; UC Berkeley; Law.

HUANG, KATHERINE; Glen A Wilson HS; Hacienda Heights, CA; (4); Church Yth Grp; Teachers Aide; Drill Tm; Drill Teams Most Outstndng; Medcl Clb Secy/Pres.

HUANG, KHY L; Granada HS; Los Angeles, CA; (2); FBLA; Cit Awd; Hon Roll; CSF; Comp Pgmng.

HUANG, LILLIAN L; George Washington HS; San Francisco, CA; (3); Church Yth Grp; Key Clb; Math Clb; Science Clb; Service Clb; Chorus; Church Choir; Hon Roll; Church Yth Grp Pres; CSF; Finance.

HUANG, LILY J; Vivian Webb HS; Upland, CA; (4); 2/40; Band; Chorus; Orch; School Musical; School Play; Swing Chorus; Bausch & Lomb Sci Awd; Ntl Merit SF.

HUANG, LILY M; San Marino HS; San Marino, CA; (4); Art Clb; Math Clb; Red Cross Aide; Science Clb; Teachers Aide; UCLA.

HUANG, LISA L; Pacifica HS; Garden Grove, CA; (2); 23/298; JV Swmmng; Hon Roll; CA Schrlshp Fed; Water Polo Score Keeper; UCLA; Teaching.

HUANG, MEL M; Westmoor HS; Daly City, CA; (3); 29/360; Debate Tm; Model UN; Spanish Clb; Teachers Aide; Sec Jr Cls; Var Golf; Var Tennis; Hon Roll; MIT; Physics.

HUANG, MICHAEL S; Edison HS; Huntington Beach, CA; (2); Key Clb; Model UN; JV Tennis; Chinese Clb; OCAD; Jr Var Tnns; Biochem.

HUANG, MICHELLE S; Calabasas HS; Calabasas Hills, CA; (3); Church Yth Grp; Debate Tm; Hosp Aide; Intnl Clb; Math Tm; Service Clb; School Musical; Nwsp; Hon Roll.

HUANG, MIKE; Venice HS; Anaheim, CA; (2); Var Computer Clb; Var Vllybl; Var Hon Roll; Homework Clb; High Math Lectures; Art Lssns; UCLA; Theoretcl Physics.

HUANG, MIKE S; Marina HS; Huntington Beach, CA; (3); Math Clb; Math Tm; High Hon Roll; Hon Roll; Var Plyr Bdmntn; UCLA; Bio.

HUANG, MIMI J; Mount Pleasant HS; San Jose, CA; (3); Math Clb; Math Tm; Service Clb; Ed Yrbk; Rep Stu Cncl; Var Capt Cheerldng; NHS; CSF; Yth Recog Awd Wnnr.

HUANG, NANCY S; James Russell Lowell HS; San Francisco, CA; (2); Church Yth Grp; French Clb; Office Aide; SADD; Church Choir; Day Camp Cnslr; Med.

HUANG, QICHANG EVA; Galileo HS; San Francisco, CA; (3); Computer Clb; Math Clb; SADD; Teachers Aide; Swing Chorus; Swmmng; SFSU; Lawyer.

HUANG, QIZHAO; George Washington HS; San Francisco, CA; (1); Hon Roll; UC-BERKELEY; Educ.

HUANG, RITA; John F Kennedy HS; La Palma, CA; (2); FBLA; Key Clb; Science Clb; Band; Jazz Band; Mrchg Band; Rptr Nwsp; High Hon Roll; CSF; Kiwanis Bowl Acad Team; Drum Cmptn; Bio Undergrad Awd; High Hnr Golden St Exam PSAT Score 1490; Lit.

HUANG, SANDRA; Arcadia HS; Arcadia, CA; (3); 250/650; Hosp Aide; Drill Tm; Rptr Yrbk; Var Sftbl; Hon Roll; Prfct Atten Awd.

HUANG, SHAU-WIN AMY; The Athenian Schl; Danville, CA; (3); Art Clb; Cmnty Wkr; Computer Clb; Dance Clb; Debate Tm; Drama Clb; Math Clb; Science Clb; Service Clb; Church Choir; AWE Death Valley Trp; Ldrshp Trng Course; Hotel Mgmt.

HUANG, SHIH-TIEN; Los Alamitos HS; Garden Grove, CA; (3); Church Yth Grp; FCA; Intnl Clb; Service Clb; Off Frsh Cls; Off Soph Cls; Cit Awd; Hon Roll; Prfct Atten Awd.

HUANG, SHOU-YU; Covina HS; West Covina, CA; (4); Computer Clb; Math Clb; SADD; Temple Yth Grp; JV Tennis; Co MVP Tnns 89-90; Bus.

HUANG, STELLA; John A Rowland HS; Rowland Hts, CA; (4); 35/550; Cmnty Wkr; Intnl Clb; Key Clb; Math Clb; Scholastic Bowl; Science Clb; Spanish Clb; Yrbk; High Hon Roll; Hon Roll; CSF Life; U CA Irvine; Bus Mgmt.

HUANG, STEVEN W; University HS; Irvine, CA; (3); 9/540; Hosp Aide; NFL; Quiz Bowl; Spanish Clb; Orch; Off Frsh Cls; Sec Soph Cls; Off Sr Cls; Swmmng; Pres Spanish NHS; S CA Hnr Orch.

HUANG, TERRY K; University HS; Irvine, CA; (4); Chess Clb; Computer Clb; German Clb; Intnl Clb; Math Clb; Science Clb; Teachers Aide; NHS; CSF; Delta Epsilon Phi; UC Berkeley; Doctor.

HUANG, TONY T; Santa Teresa HS; San Jose, CA; (2); JV Bsktbl; JV Tennis; CSF; Dist Supt List; Bus.

HUANG, TRACY C; Mark Keppel HS; S San Gabriel, CA; (3); #29 In Class; FBLA; Key Clb; Mu Alpha Theta; Science Clb; VP Band; Jazz Band; Mrchg Band; Orch; Hon Roll; Prfct Atten Awd; CA Schlrshp Fed; Leo Club; Outstndng Achvt Span; Outstndng Band Stu; UC Berkeley; Arch.

HUANG, WEI Y; Chaffey HS; Ontario, CA; (1); Hon Roll; Prfct Atten Awd.

HUANG, WILLIAM W; University HS; Irvine, CA; (3); Intnl Clb; JCL; Key Clb; Latin Clb; Science Clb; JV Tennis; UCLA; Elctrcl Engr.

HUANG, YANXIAO; Balboa HS; Daly City, CA; (2); U Of Berkeley; Comp.

HUANG, YUTAO; Galileo HS; San Francisco, CA; (4); City Coll San Francisco.

HUAYLLASCO, JOSEPH RAYMOND; Lowell HS; San Francisco, CA; (3); Gldn St Hnrs Geom, Alg & US Hstry; Amer Inst Arch Dsgn Cmptn; Comp Engr.

HUBBARD, ALBERT D; Leffingwell Christian HS; Los Angeles, CA; (3); Church Yth Grp; JV Capt Bsktbl; Var Ftbl; Wt Lftg; Hon Roll; Mst Imprvd Spnsh Stu; All Leag Awd Ftbl; Phys Ed.

HUBBARD, GREGORY A; Marysville HS; Yuba City, CA; (1); JV Bsktbl; JV Tennis; Cit Awd; Lion Awd.

HUBBARD, KENJI; George Washington HS; San Francisco, CA; (4); 20/582; Computer Clb; Math Clb; Science Clb; Service Clb; Teachers Aide; High Hon Roll; Hon Roll; Ntl Merit Ltr; Pres Acad Fit Awd; UC Berkeley; Electrical Engr.

HUBBARD, KRISTEL; La Quinta HS; Westminster, CA; (2); 42/362; JV Bsktbl; Hon Roll; Mck Trl Wtnss; Prncpls Awd 3.5 GPA; Law.

HUBBARD, LESLIE G; Pittsburg HS; Pittsburg, CA; (2); Bsktbl; Score Keeper; Sftbl; Cit Awd; Hon Roll; Italian Clb; Stanford; Pilot.

HUBBARD, LINDA; Fairfield HS; Suisun, CA; (2); Church Yth Grp; Off Soph Cls; Var Crs Cntry; Var Swmmng; Hon Roll; Intr Dsgn.

HUBBARD, RACHEL; Del Norte HS; Crescent City, CA; (2); Treas Debate Tm; Drama Clb; 4-H; NFL; Pep Clb; Treas Speech Tm; Thesps; School Musical; Crs Cntry; 4-H Awd; Most Dedicated Speaker; CA Arts Scholor 90; Miss Cross Country 9-10; Coll; Drama Law.

HUBBARD, REBECCA L; Lone Pine HS; Lone Pine, CA; (1); Church Yth Grp; Drama Clb; Treas Girl Scts; Service Clb; School Play; Pres Frsh Cls; High Hon Roll; Hon Roll; CA Schlrshp Fed; Horses; Sunday Schl Teacher; Point Loma Nazarene Coll.

HUBBEL, TIMOTHY N; Oakdale HS; Oakdale, CA; (3); 11/375; Cmnty Wkr; Bsbl; Ftbl; Powder Puff Ftbl; High Hon Roll; Modesto JC; Dsnr Engr.

HUBBELL, JANETTE; North HS; Bakersfield, CA; (3); 37/400; Cmnty Wkr; Girl Scts; Teachers Aide; Band; Mrchg Band; Pep Band; Hon Roll; Pres Acad Fit Awd; Bakersfield Coll; 1st Grd Tchr.

HUBBELL, LAURIE M; Chester JR SR HS; Chester, CA; (3); French Clb; Ski Clb; Band; Mrchg Band; Hon Roll.

HUBBS, JUSTIN L; Carlsbad HS; Carlsbad, CA; (2); Ski Clb; JV Socr; Var Tennis; Drftsman Of Smstr; Civil Engrng.

HUBEL, HEATHER A; La Habra HS; Whittier, CA; (3); Church Yth Grp; Drama Clb; Girl Scts; Pep Clb; Teachers Aide; Church Choir; Stage Crew; Variety Show; Cit Awd; High Hon Roll; Cerritos Coll; Gen Ed.

HUBER, AMY E; Santa Barbara HS; Santa Barbara, CA; (3); Church Yth Grp; Cmnty Wkr; German Clb; Intnl Clb; SADD; Cngrssnl Awd Cmmnty Svc Natl Charity Leag; Gftd/Tlntd Educ Pgm; Intl Lang Exchng Germany Smmr; Westmont Coll; Religious Stds.

HUBER, BETH; Valley Christian HS; San Jose, CA; (3); Church Yth Grp; Teachers Aide; Band; Drill Tm; School Musical; Crs Cntry; Trk; High Hon Roll; Chem.

HUBER, DENISE H; Tokay HS; Stockton, CA; (4); German Clb; Hosp Aide; Science Clb; High Hon Roll; Hon Roll; Pres Acad Fit Awd; Rotary Awd; CSF; Bnk America Frgn Lang Awd; Photogrphy Clb VP; San Joaquin Delta Coll; Bio.

HUBER, ELIZABETH M; Narbonne HS; Harbor City, CA; (2); French Clb; Service Clb; Teachers Aide; Plyng Tennis, Track & Cross Cntry; USAF Acad; Arntcl Engr.

HUBER, ERIC B; San Marcos HS; San Marcos, CA; (3); Var Swmmng; High Hon Roll.

HUBER, HANS C; Arroyo Grande HS; Shell Beach, CA; (1); Var Swmmng; Sailing; Windsurfing.

HUBER, JACOB M; San Lorenzo Valley HS; Zayante, CA; (2); Art Clb; Chef.

HUBER, JANET; Burbank HS; Burbank, CA; (2); Drama Clb; Pep Clb; Drill Tm; School Musical; School Play; Cheerldng; Vllybl; Hon Roll; Pres Acad Fit Awd; UCSB; Dramatic Arts.

HUBER, LORI-MARIE; Atwater HS; Atwater, CA; (2); FFA; Socr; Tennis; High Hon Roll; Kiwanis Awd; CSF; FFA Schlrshp Awd & Point Awd; Dancr-Backstage Danc Studio-Schlrshp Pgm; Sci.

HUBER, MATT M; Casa Grande HS; Petaluma, CA; (3); 18/290; French Clb; Varsity Clb; Var Bsktbl; High Hon Roll; Hon Roll; Jr NHS; Bus.

HUBER, MELISSA; Santa Barbara HS; Santa Barbara, CA; (2); 3/430; Vllybl; High Hon Roll; Jr Statesmn Amer; Capri 13 Fleet; Princeton U; History.

HUBERT, KEVIN M; Granada HS; Livermore, CA; (3); Teachers Aide; Band; Hon Roll; Real Est.

HUBERTS, JEFFREY; San Marcos HS; Vista, CA; (2); Key Clb; Var Bsbl; Var Ftbl; Var Socr; High Hon Roll; Hon Roll; Pres Acad Fit Awd; MVP Player Soccer; CA Schltc Fed; UCU; Bus.

HUCKEBA, KELLY L; Warren HS; Bell, CA; (2); Church Yth Grp; Teachers Aide; L Tennis; Hon Roll; Accmplshd Pianist; BYU; Ed.

HUCKELL, MARCI E; Los Gatos HS; Los Gatos, CA; (3); 67/333; Church Yth Grp; Teachers Aide; Var Powder Puff Ftbl; Hon Roll; Ed.

HUCKINS, AMY L; Hilltop HS; Kodiak, AK; (3); Intnl Clb; Office Aide; SADD; Teachers Aide; Var Fld Hcky; Var Socr; Var Capt Swmmng; Cit Awd; Pres Acad Fit Awd; Jobs Dghtrs; US Marine Corps Athlt Awd; Phys Thrpy.

HUDDLESTON, APRIL D; Lassen HS; Milford, CA; (4); 2/180; Sec Art Clb; Ski Clb; SADD; Treas Band; Jazz Band; Mrchg Band; Pep Band; Phtg Rptr Nwsp; High Hon Roll; Pres Acad Fit Awd; CSF; CA Art Schlr 89; Art Inst Of Seattle; Photogrphy.

HUDELSON, JOSEPH H; Serra HS; South San Francis, CA; (2); Boy Scts; Drama Clb; Ski Clb; Church Choir; Thesps; Chorus; School Musical; School Play; Intrml Bsbl; JV Crs Cntry; Summer ACT Theatre Classes, Fitness Cls Coll Level; Sing In Band; Santa Clara U; Bus.

HUDKINS, JENNIFER; Lincoln HS; Stockton, CA; (3); 43/592; French Clb; SADD; CSF; Bee Clb; Interact.

HUDOCK, MATTHEW J; Corona HS; Norco, CA; (3); 51/401; Church Yth Grp; Computer Clb; JV Wrstlng; Cit Awd; High Hon Roll; Hon Roll; US Marine Corps Good Conduct Awd & Cert Of Phys Achvt; Var Acad Ltr; US Marine Corps.

HUDSON, DAVID; Newark Memorial HS; Newark, CA; (4); Drama Clb; SADD; Teachers Aide; Varsity Clb; Band; Jazz Band; School Play; Swmmng; Opt Clb Awd; Var Swim Awd; Golden St Exam Cert Alg Hnrs; Stu Of Mnth Awd; Ohlone Coll; Mrktng.

HUDSON, DEANNA M; John F Kennedy HS; Sacramento, CA; (4); 188/427; Church Yth Grp; Debate Tm; Office Aide; Speech Tm; Band; Mrchg Band; Pep Band; High Hon Roll.

HUDSON, DREW S; Valhalla HS; El Cajon, CA; (1); Debate Tm; Ftbl; Vllybl; 3 Wk Schlrshp To Japan 1 Of 300 West Coast; Bst Pronunctn Spnsh Awd; Cmmndtn Cnty Supt Hghst Scr Engl; UCLA.

HUDSON, JA CINTA; Golden Gate Acad; Vallejo, CA; (1); 2/25; Church Yth Grp; Church Choir; VP Frsh Cls; Hon Roll; Kings Daughtrs Schlrshp 89-90; Gldn Gate Acad Alumni Schlrshp 89-90; Vtd Mst Athltc Grl Cls 89-90; Doctor.

HUDSON, JENNIFER; Taft Union HS; Taft, CA; (3); 12/200; Am Leg Aux Girls St; Key Clb; Letterman Clb; Yrbk; Pres Jr Cls; Var Capt Crs Cntry; Var Swmmng; Var Trk; High Hon Roll; UC Davis; Med.

HUDSON, JOSH R; Calvary Chapel HS; Fountain Valley, CA; (2); Church Yth Grp.

HUDSON, LOUIS E; Red Bluff HS; Red Bluff, CA; (3); Aud/Vis; Debate Tm; FFA; Band; Church Choir; Jazz Band; Mrchg Band; Orch; Pep Band; School Musical; Most Imprvd Band; Perf Arts Ldrshp Team; Star Greenhand FFA; USAF; Stage Sound/Tech.

HUDSON, LYNETTE P; Bonita HS; La Verne, CA; (2); Drama Clb; FBLA; Chorus; Color Guard; School Play; JV Bsktbl; High Hon Roll; Hon Roll; Black Stu Union; CA ST Los Angeles; Bus.

HUDSON, ROBERT W; Redlands HS; Redlands, CA; (2); Letterman Clb; Teachers Aide; Stat Bsbl; Stat Bsktbl; Stat Ftbl; Stat Mgr(s); Stat Trk; Wt Lftg; U Of CA Riverside; Elec Engr.

HUDSON, SONYA W; Washington Prep HS; Los Angeles, CA; (3); Bus Profs of Am; Church Yth Grp; Drama Clb; English Clb; GAA; Service Clb; Speech Tm; Stu Cncl; JV Capt Bsktbl; Var Sftbl; Athletic Awds; USC; Bus Law.

HUDSON, THERESA L; Calipatria HS; Calipatria, CA; (4); 8/68; Sec Drama Clb; 4-H; FBLA; Pres VP FFA; SADD; Teachers Aide; Stu Cncl; Hon Roll; Natl Yng Ldrs Conf Schlr; Imperial Valley Coll; Animl Sci.

HUDSON, TYRUS; Petaluma HS; Petaluma, CA; (3); 2/267; Science Clb; JV Var Bsbl; JV Var Socr; High Hon Roll; Hon Roll; JETS Awd; Ntl Merit Ltr; De Molay; MIT; Aerntcl Engrng.

HUENEMEIER, WENDY A; Central Vally Christian HS; Visalia, CA; (3); Church Yth Grp; SADD; Chorus; Church Choir; Cheerldng; Stat Score Keeper; Church Musical; Azusa Pacific Clg; Teach.

HUERECA, VERONICA; Orosi HS; Orosi, CA; (3); Chorus; Cheerldng; Pom Pon; Hon Roll; Outstndng Acad Awd; Invited Wash DC John M Hines; Russia Stu Ambsdr; Fresno ST; Comp.

HUERTA, ADRIANA; Roosevelt HS; Los Angeles, CA; (3); Cmnty Wkr; School Musical; Stu Cncl; Bsktbl; Powder Puff Ftbl; Sftbl; Vllybl; High Hon Roll; Hon Roll; Prfct Atten Awd; Cal ST Poly Pomona; Archtctr.

HUERTA, DEBBIE; Dos Palos HS; Firebaugh, CA; (3); Church Yth Grp; FHA; GAA; Score Keeper; Sftbl; Fresno ST; Tchr.

HUERTA, ELIZABETH; Saddleback HS; Santa Ana, CA; (1); AFNA; Dance; Acting.

HUERTA, EMILIA; Garfield HS; Los Angeles, CA; (3); Dance Clb; Drill Tm; Ed Nwsp; JV Diving; JV Powder Puff Ftbl; JV Swmmng; Hon Roll; Drill Tm Awd; Cert Of Prtcptn-Swmmg; U Southern CA; Doctor.

HUERTA, ESTHER; Coalinga Huron Unified HS; Huron, CA; (2); Chorus; Color Guard; Hon Roll; 1st Girl Outstndng Achvt; 1st Girl Schlr; UCLA; Law.

HUERTA, JOYCE J; Coachella Valley HS; Indio, CA; (3); 6/387; Church Yth Grp; Cmnty Wkr; Pep Clb; Spanish Clb; Chorus; Church Choir; Pres Sr Cls; Gym; Vllybl; Cit Awd; Choose Life Clb; Trvlrs Clb; Claremonte Coll.

HUERTA, LUISA; Lindsay HS; Lindsay, CA; (2); French Clb; Yrbk; Mst Imprvd Sci; Natural Helprs; Friday Night Live.

HUERTA, MARIA L; Castle Park HS; Chula Vista, CA; (1); 7/614; Drama Clb; Acad Achvrs Clb; UCLA; Econ.

HUERTA, MELISSA; Mt Whitney HS; Goshen, CA; (3); Church Yth Grp; Sec Treas FBLA; Office Aide; Spanish Clb; Hon Roll; Mecha Club; FBLA Mem Mnth; COS; Law.

HUERTA, OSVALDO H; Buena Park HS; Fullerton, CA; (4); 22/304; Church Yth Grp; French Clb; Math Clb; Teachers Aide; Var L Bsktbl; Var L Crs Cntry; Var L Trk; High Hon Roll; Kiwanis Awd; Prfct Atten Awd; CSF; Bk Amer Achvt Awd Eng; Outstndng Stu Soc Sci; CA ST U; Bus Adm.

HUERTA, ROSA; Garfield HS; Los Angeles, CA; (2); UCLA; Law.

HUERTA, ROSAISELA; Theodore Roosevelt HS; Los Angeles, CA; (2); Church Yth Grp; Library Aide; Ed Yrbk; Swmmng; UC Santa Barbara; Int Dcrtr.

HUERTA, RUDY; Calvary Baptist HS; La Verne, CA; (4); 4/8; Drama Clb; Hosp Aide; Bsbl; Cit Awd; Hon Roll; Princp Awd; Art Awd; 3rd Pl Annl Essay Awd; Azusa Pac U; Pre Med Educ.

HUERTA, SANDRA; Castle Park HS; Chula Vista, CA; (1); Drama Clb; French Clb; Hon Roll; UCLA; Law.

HUERTA, SHELLEY A; Nogales HS; Rowland Hgts, CA; (3); Teachers Aide; Tennis; Prfct Atten Awd; Photo, Graphics & Jrnlsm; USC; Photo Jrnlst.

HUERTAS, G DENISE; Castle Park HS; Chula Vista, CA; (1); #5 In Class; French Clb; Acad Achvr Awd; UCSD; Psych.

HUETTNER, ADAM P; Apple Valley HS; Apple Valley, CA; (1); Cit Awd; Sheriff Explorers; Comp; Yale; Attorney.

HUEY, BETTY S; Lowell HS; San Francisco, CA; (2); Cmnty Wkr; Stat JV Bsktbl; Mgr(s); Score Keeper; Var Trk; Grls Bsktbl Coach; UC Davis; Lawyer.

HUEY, KRISTINE; Clayton Valley HS; Clayton, CA; (2); Model UN; Bsktbl; Var Trk; Bio Dept Awd 89-90; Mst Imprvd Bsktbl 88-89; Dsgn.

HUEY, MARK C; Poway HS; Poway, CA; (2); Aud/Vis; Boy Scts; Church Yth Grp; Cmnty Wkr; German Clb; Key Clb; Math Clb; Quiz Bowl; Scholastic Bowl; SADD; Water Polo; Assoc Stu Body; Commsnr Clbs; UCLA; Lawyer.

HUEY, MARY; Alhambra HS; Alhambra, CA; (3); Lit Mag; Envrnmntl Clb; Amnesty Action; CSF; Yale Bk Awd; Bio.

HUFF, DAMON; Washington Preparatory HS; Los Angeles, CA; (3); Letterman Clb; Physiology.

HUFF, JENNIFER L; Prospect HS; San Jose, CA; (1); Church Yth Grp; Prfct Atten Awd; Hgh Hnrs Goldn St Exm 1st Yr Alg Stu.

HUFF, JENNY K; Edison Computech HS; Fresno, CA; (1); 1/450; JCL; JV Swmmng; Tennis; High Hon Roll; Odyssy Of Mind Rgnl & St Chmpns, 3rd Wrld Fnlst Team; CSF; Edison Soc For High Adventure; Marine Bio.

HUFF, SARAH M; Fremont HS; Sunnyvale, CA; (2); Pres Drama Clb; Teachers Aide; Pres Thesps; Acpl Chr; Chorus; School Musical; School Play; Stage Crew; Swing Chorus; Variety Show; Prfrmd In Many Plays & Musicals In Schl & Within The Cmmnty; Amer Acad Of Dramtc Arts; Mscl.

HUFF, VICKI LYNN; Apple Valley HS; Lucerne Valley, CA; (4); Church Yth Grp; Drama Clb; French Clb; Key Clb; Treas Chorus; Flag Corp; Crs Cntry; High Hon Roll; Presidentical Academic Fitness Award For Extraordinary Effort; Choir Section Leader; CA ST Fullerton; Fine Arts.

HUFFMAN, AARON J; Etna Union HS; Fort Jones, CA; (3); 18/68; Boy Scts; Letterman Clb; Office Aide; Teachers Aide; Hon Roll; Babe Ruth Bsbl Best Offensive Plyr.

HUFFMAN, ANDREA; Santa Maria HS; Santa Maria, CA; (4); 4/357; Drama Clb; FBLA; School Play; Ed Nwsp; Hon Roll; Ntl Merit SF; CSF; DC Express.

HUFFMAN, DAVID K; Fortuna Union HS; Fortuna, CA; (3); SADD; Phtg Yrbk; Off Jr Cls; Hist Stu Cncl; High Hon Roll; NHS; CSF; UC Davis; Sci.

HUFFMAN, EMILY DIANE; Moorpark HS; Moorpark, CA; (1); Church Yth Grp; JV Cheerldng; High Hon Roll; Class Treas 90.

HUFFMAN, KRISTI M; Clovis West HS; Fresno, CA; (3); Intnl Clb; Key Clb; NFL; Pres Acad Fit Awd; Fresno ST; Tchng.

HUFFMASTER, ANDREW S; Fairfield HS; Suisun City, CA; (2); Church Yth Grp; Band; Mrchg Band; NHS; CSF; U CA-DAVIS; Aeronautcl Engr.

HUFFMASTER, LYDIA; Maxwell HS; Maxwell, CA; (2); 2/25; Debate Tm; FBLA; FFA; Pres Frsh Cls; Rep Stu Cncl; JV Bsktbl; Var Sftbl; JV Vllybl; Hon Roll; MIP Sftbl 89; MIP Vlybl 89; Western Baptist Coll; Elem Ed.

HUFFMASTER, SALLY; Maxwell HS; Maxwell, CA; (3); 3/30; Church Yth Grp; FFA; Scholastic Bowl; SADD; School Play; Capt Var Bsktbl; Var Cheerldng; Var Sftbl; Capt Var Vllybl; 4-H; Pr Cnslng Pres; Whitworth Coll; Nurse.

HUGEN, APRIL L; Foothill HS; Bakersfield, CA; (2); Church Yth Grp; Band; Mrchg Band; Orch; Pep Band; School Musical; Drumline Cmptns; Bakersfield Yth Symphony; Azusa Pacific U; Pro Musician.

HUGGINS, MARCIA; Armijo HS; Panama City, FL; (4); 84/375; Church Yth Grp; Band; Jazz Band; Mrchg Band; Pep Band; Ed Yrbk; Rep Frsh Cls; Vllybl; Achvmnt Music; Hnr Band; St Hnr Band; Mcdonalds Band; Mst Imprvd Music; Miss Tn CA Pgnt; FL ST U; Cmptr Sys Anlyst.

HUGGINS, MARCIA; Armijo HS; Panama City, FL; (4); 84/374; Band; Jazz Band; Mrchg Band; Pep Band; Ed Yrbk; Rep Frsh Cls; Var Vllybl; Hon Roll; Miss CA Teenage Schlrshp Pgnt; Solano Cnty Hnr Band; Hayward St Hnr Band 2 Yrs; Vlntr Spec Olympcs; Gulfcoast CC; Comp.

HUGGINS, MARISA; Hoover HS; San Diego, CA; (2); Church Yth Grp; Cit Awd; San Diego ST U; Chld Devlpmnt.

HUGHES, AARON J; John F Kennedy HS; Cypress, CA; (1); Church Yth Grp; Band; Jazz Band; Mrchg Band; Pep Band.

HUGHES, ALAN; Gahr HS; Cerritos, CA; (2); Office Aide; Spanish Clb; Intrml Trk; Hon Roll; PTSA Cert Achvt; Golden ST Exam 1st Yr Alg; Hnr Soc; UC Irvine; Military.

HUGHES, ALLISON; Loara HS; Anaheim, CA; (2); 1/400; Key Clb; Spanish Clb; Drill Tm; Rep Frsh Cls; Rep Soph Cls; JV Swmmng; High Hon Roll; Model Legsltre/Ct; Poly Sci.

HUGHES, AUTUMN L; Lincoln HS; Sheridan, CA; (1); 18/170; Art Clb; Office Aide; Pep Clb; SADD; Var Trk; High Hon Roll; Hon Roll; Pres Acad Fit Awd.

HUGHES, BRIAN C; Escondido HS; Escondido, CA; (1); Church Yth Grp; Cmnty Wkr; Teachers Aide; L Capt Bsbl; L Bsktbl; Wt Lftg; Cit Awd; Hon Roll; Schlr Athlt Awd.

HUGHES, BRONWYN E; Sacred Heart Prep; Menlo Park, CA; (2); Yrbk; Var Bsktbl; Var Tennis; Var Trk; Amnesty Intl; Interact Clb; Admissions Clb.

HUGHES, BRYAN B; El Dorado HS; Shingle Springs, CA; (3); Chess Clb; Key Clb; Service Clb; Crs Cntry; Socr; Swmmng; High Hon Roll; Hon Roll; Jr NHS; NHS; Dauksavage Awd-Swmmng; Sprtsmnshp Awd-Swmmng; Susan B Anthony Awd, Advncd Plcmnt Hstry.

HUGHES, CINDY C; Colton HS; Colton, CA; (2); Model UN; Sec Frsh Cls; Pres Soph Cls; Cheerldng; Hon Roll; Badmntn; CA ST San Bernardino; Lawyer.

HUGHES, DEBRA M; Poway HS; Poway, CA; (3); Band; Mrchg Band; High Hon Roll; Intrmrl Co-Ed Sftbl; Envrnmntl Awrnss Clb.

HUGHES, ERIC C; San Diego Acad; Imperial Beach, CA; (3); Ski Clb; Band; Chorus; Stu Cncl; Bsktbl; Vllybl; High Hon Roll; NHS; Boy Scts; Church Yth Grp; Hiking & Camping Clb; Mission Clb To Honduras & Mexico; Loma Linda U; Sports Med.

HUGHES, FRANCIE; San Gabriel HS; San Gabriel, CA; (3); Pres Church Yth Grp; French Clb; Drill Tm; JV Cheerldng; Hon Roll; NHS; Stu Congress.

HUGHES, HEATHER K; San Pasqual HS; Escondido, CA; (2); Office Aide; Acpl Chr; Chorus; Church Choir; School Musical; Swing Chorus; Variety Show; St Schlr; Prime Movers Honorary Drctr; UC San Diego; Vet.

HUGHES, HEATHER L; Hemet HS; Hemet, CA; (4); Church Yth Grp; Pep Clb; School Play; Nwsp; Stu Cncl; Var Crs Cntry; Vllybl; Hon Roll; Lion Awd; Ntl Merit SF; UCSD; Biochem.

HUGHES, JAKE; Van Nuys HS; Los Angeles, CA; (4); Aud/Vis; Drama Clb; Teachers Aide; Thesps; School Musical; School Play; Prfct Atten Awd; Garrett Mc Cuga Schlrshp; Dir.

HUGHES, JASON; El Toro HS; El Toro, CA; (2); Church Yth Grp; Jazz Band; Var L Wrstlng; Hon Roll; CAP Cadet & Pilot; USAFA; Pilot.

HUGHES, JASON; Golden West HS; Ivanhoe, CA; (3); Band; Jazz Band; Pep Band; Drum Line; COS.

HUGHES, JEFFREY M; Rio Lindo Adventist Acad; Napa, CA; (4); Pres Acad Fit Awd; Prfct Atten Awd; Hon Roll; Var Vllybl; Var Gym; Var Ftbl; Var Capt Bsktbl; Var Bsbl; Band; Spanish Clb; Scuba Diving Cert; Sportsmanship Awd; Chrstn Scholar Awd; Sacramento ST U; Intl Bus.

HUGHES, JENNIFER; William S Hart HS; Newhall, CA; (4); 9/490; Church Yth Grp; French Clb; Math Clb; Math Tm; Mu Alpha Theta; High Hon Roll; NHS; Ntl Merit Ltr; Piano Awds Recital 89; CSF; The Masters Coll; Math.

HUGHES, KARNA; San Marin HS; Novato, CA; (3); Debate Tm; French Clb; Intnl Clb; Service Clb; SADD; Band; JV Swmmng; Hon Roll; Ntl Merit Ltr; Marin Yth Cmmssn; Human Rghts Wrksbp; Rainforest Awrnss Grp Fndr.

HUGHES, MARCIE C; Trabuco Hills HS; Trabuco Canyon, CA; (1); Cmnty Wkr; Spanish Clb; SADD; Treas Soph Cls; Var L Socr; JV Trk; JV Vllybl; Law.

HUGHES, MARIE L; C K Mc Clatchy HS; Sacramento, CA; (2); 82/442; Color Guard; Mrchg Band; JV Sftbl; U Of CA Davis; Vet Med.

HUGHES, NICOLE R; Sunset HS; Hayward, CA; (2); Church Yth Grp; Variety Show; Bsktbl; Swmmng; Trk; High Hon Roll; Hon Roll; Schlr Athlte Awd; Fnlst Miss Natl Teenager Pgnt; Duanes Dance Studio Ballet & Jazz; UCLA; Optometrist.

HUGHES III, PAUL R; Sierra Vista HS; Baldwin Park, CA; (1); Chess Clb; Church Yth Grp; Science Clb; Var L Swmmng; Hon Roll; Water Polo JV; Us Navy; Telecmmnctns.

HUGHES, ROMI G; Pinole Valley HS; Hercules, CA; (1); Spanish Clb; Chorus; Church Choir; Bsktbl; JV Vllybl; Hon Roll; U CA Berkeley; Law.

HUGHES, RUSSELL; Eugene Mc Ateer HS; San Francisco, CA; (3); School Play; Variety Show; Wt Lftg; Wrstlng.

HUGHES, SHANNON; Elsinore HS; Lake Elsinore, CA; (2); Drill Tm; Flag Corp; Off Jr Cls; USD; Corp Law.

HUGHES, SHANNON L; El Toro HS; El Toro, CA; (3); 50/520; Church Yth Grp; French Clb; Teachers Aide; Sec Sr Cls; JV Trk; Var Vllybl; High Hon Roll; Hon Roll; Pres Acad Fit Awd; AZ ST U; Bus.

HUGHES, STEFANIE; Santa Teresa HS; San Jose, CA; (3); Church Yth Grp; Dance Clb; French Clb; Science Clb; Band; Color Guard; Flag Corp; Mrchg Band; Cheerldng; Vllybl; ASU; Vet.

HUGHES, TANYA; Hilltop HS; Chula Vista, CA; (4); 56/452; Cmnty Wkr; Dance Clb; Drama Clb; Intnl Clb; Pep Clb; Drill Tm; School Play; Variety Show; Mgr Yrbk; Cheerldng; UCSD; Hearing Imprd Thrpst.

HUGHES, TRAVIS J; Canyon Springs HS; Moreno Valley, CA; (3); ROTC; JV Crs Cntry; JV Trk; JV Wrstlng; Hon Roll; NHS; Civil Air Patrol; Cadet Commander; Mitchells/Earhart Awds; CSF; JROTC Daedalian Awd; Sons Of Amer Legn; American U; Poly Sci.

HUGHLEY, PRENEKA E; San Diego SR HS; San Diego, CA; (4); 71/437; Var FTA; Model UN; Teachers Aide; Cit Awd; Jr NHS; NHS; Opt Clb Awd; Civic Review Awd; Deans List; 9th Gr Grad Benediction In Spanish; Math.

HUGLE, DEENA D; Porterville Union HS; Porterville, CA; (3); Band; Mrchg Band; Pep Band; Rep Stu Cncl; JV Var Bsktbl; Intrml JV Sftbl; Intrml JV Vllybl; Hon Roll.

HUGO, VANESSA A; Redlands HS; Highland, CA; (2); Cmnty Wkr; JA; Pep Clb; Spanish Clb; Teachers Aide; Yrbk; Gym; Trk; Cit Awd; High Hon Roll; Gymnstcs Cls IV Champ 88; Friday Night Life; PACT; TX A&M; Bus.

HUH, AGATHA S; Edison HS; Garden Grove, CA; (2); Church Yth Grp; Key Clb; Acpl Chr; Church Choir; Hon Roll; Piano; Music; Art; Auc Schl; Art.

HUH, AMY; Marina HS; Huntington Bch, CA; (3); Am Leg Aux Girls St; Dance Clb; Rep Key Clb; Sec Spanish Clb; Capt Drill Tm; High Hon Roll; Pres Acad Fit Awd; Church Yth Grp; Cmnty Wkr; Pep Clb; Girls State Finalist; Golden State Exam Honors.

HUI, CARLO; Walnut HS; Walnut, CA; (2); Intrml Tennis; CSF; UC Riverside; Elec Engrng.

HUI, CINDY; Westmoor HS; Daly City, CA; (3); VP Cmnty Wkr; Pres Intnl Clb; Letterman Clb; Co-Capt Pep Clb; Sec Science Clb; SADD; Co-Capt Varsity Clb; Sec Rep Soph Cls; Stu Cncl; JV Var Cheerldng; Student Body Commissioner Of Clubs; Georgetown U; International Bus.

HUI, DAVID; Mills HS; Millbrae, CA; (3); Math Tm; Var L Swmmng; High Hon Roll; Hon Roll; Water Polo Var Lttr; MIP Swmmr Var 90; Guitar; Econ.

HUI, ELIZABETH Y; Eureka SR HS; Eureka, CA; (3); 3/400; Drama Clb; Sec Orch; Stage Crew; High Hon Roll.

HUI, ELLIOT E; Maranatha HS; Arcadia, CA; (4); 1/106; Church Yth Grp; Spanish Clb; Ed Nwsp; JV Capt Socr; Var L Trk; Elks Awd; High Hon Roll; Ntl Merit Schol; Val; Vctn Bible Sch Tchr; MA Inst Tech; Physcs.

HUI, EVA; Albany HS; Albany, CA; (4); Church Yth Grp; Service Clb; Sec Treas Sr Cls; Hon Roll; Pres Acad Fit Awd; Golden St Exm High Hnrs Alg & Geom; Chemathon Hrnbl Achvt Trophy; Associated Stu Govt; U Of CA Los Angeles; Bus Ecs.

HUI, JASON K; Garfield High Computer Science Magnet; Los Angeles, CA; (2); Church Yth Grp; Ed Nwsp; Ed Lit Mag; Hon Roll; Prfct Atten Awd; 39th Annual Los Angeles Cnty Sci & Engrng Fair; Christmas Toy Dr; MIT; Elec Engrng.

HUI, KWONG W; Monte Vista HS; Spring Valley, CA; (3); 110/373; JV Var Ftbl; Hon Roll; Pacific Islander Asian Club; San Diego Union Newspr GPA Ftbl Awd; CSF; CA U; Elem Engr.

HUI, LILY L; Lowell HS; San Francisco, CA; (3); Cmnty Wkr; Red Cross Aide; Hon Roll.

HUI, MAY C; Needles HS; Needles, CA; (4); 2/55; Pres FHA; Sec Key Clb; Library Aide; Rptr Nwsp; Rptr Yrbk; VP Soph Cls; VP Jr Cls; Stu Cncl; Var Cheerldng; Powder Puff Ftbl; CSF; Girls St Alt; Bank America Math/Sci Plque Wnnr; UC Santa Barbara; Commnctns.

HUI, MICHAEL; Galileo HS; San Francisco, CA; (4); 48/350; French Clb; JA; Pep Clb; Science Clb; Teachers Aide; Varsity Clb; Stu Cncl; Tennis; Hon Roll; San Jose ST U; Art.

HUI, PEGGY S; James Logan HS; Union City, CA; (3); 1/795; Church Yth Grp; Math Clb; Science Clb; High Hon Roll; Advanced Placement Club; Student Month.

HUI, SUK; Foothill HS; Pleasanton, CA; (4); Los Positas Coll.

HUI, WENDY T; George Washington HS; San Francisco, CA; (3); Office Aide; Chorus; Orch; Stage Crew; Variety Show; Rep Jr Cls; High Hon Roll; Amer Yth Hostel Ecology Clb; UC Berkeley; Sci.

HUIBREGTSE, WENDY K; Redlands HS; Redlands, CA; (2); 30/992; Church Yth Grp; School Musical; Pres Stu Cncl; JV Trk; High Hon Roll; Pres Acad Fit Awd; Sal; Vocal Music Awd; Presdntl Phys Fitness Awd; Dept Stu Awds In Sci, Frgn Lang; Cmmrcl Art.

HUICOCHEA, GERARDO; Salesian HS; Commerce, CA; (2); French Clb; JV Bsbl; JV Ftbl; Cert Outstndng Acad Excllnce Fine Arts 2nd & Engl II 1st Pl.

HUIDOR, MIGUEL; Mount Whitney HS; Goshen, CA; (4); 11/349; Pres Art Clb; French Clb; Spanish Clb; High Hon Roll; Pres Acad Fit Awd; Acad Decathlon Won Cnty Div; Seal Bearer CSF; Stanford; Fine Arts.

HUIDOR, RAFAEL; Huntington Park HS; Huntington Park, CA; (3); Comm.

HUIE, STACY J; Encinal HS; Alameda, CA; (1); Hon Roll; U CA Berkeley.

HUIZAR, LUCAS; Southbay Christian HS; Milpitas, CA; (1); Church Yth Grp; English Clb; Natl Beta Clb; Var Bsktbl; Ftbl; Hon Roll; Stu Of Mnth; Stu Of Yr; Comp Engr.

HUIZAR, MARIA L; Bell Gardens HS; Bell Gardens, CA; (1); Dance Clb; Yrbk; Prfct Atten Awd; Stu Of Month; Coumbia U; Pediatrician.

HUIZAR, MARICELA; Azusa HS; Azusa, CA; (3); 8/275; Drama Clb; Treas French Clb; Rptr Nwsp; JV Vllybl; Hon Roll; NHS.

HUIZAR, VERONICA; Modesto HS; Modesto, CA; (3); Pres Spanish Clb; Cit Awd; High Hon Roll; Hon Roll; Prfct Atten Awd; MJC; Psych.

HUIZENGA, TIFFANY I; Hesperia HS; Hesperia, CA; (4); Church Yth Grp; Cmnty Wkr; French Clb; FBLA; Letterman Clb; Office Aide; Pep Clb; Red Cross Aide; Science Clb; Ski Clb; Long Beach ST; Sprts Med.

HUIZING, HEATHER M; Southern California Christian HS; Orange, CA; (1); Church Yth Grp; Drama Clb; VP 4-H; School Musical; Stage Crew; 4-H Awd; Hon Roll; NHS; U S CA; Bus.

HUL, SOTHEAVY; Channel Island HS; Oxnard, CA; (2); Ed Yrbk; Hon Roll; U Of AZ; Phrmcy.

HULAN, PIERRE; Fremont HS; Sunnyvale, CA; (2); 75/421; Chess Clb; Science Clb; Jr NHS; Gate Clb; CSF; GSE Golden ST Ex Hgh Hons Alg & Geo; UC Davis; Med.

HULBERT, RICHARD C; Redlands HS; Redlands, CA; (2); Ski Clb; Bsbl; Socr; Cit Awd; Hon Roll; Prfct Atten Awd; Pres Schlr; Rec Bsbl Ump; Sccr Team; Audio Tech.

HULBROCK, AMY I; Edison HS; Huntington Bch, CA; (2); German Clb; JV Socr; JV Sftbl; Sccr Bst Dfns Awd; Sftbl Gldn Bat Awd.

HULL, BRETT T; Pescadero HS; Pescadero, CA; (3); 1/20; Teachers Aide; VP Soph Cls; Var Bsbl; Var Bsktbl; Var Socr; High Hon Roll; Pres Acad Fit Awd.

HULME, MARK; Imperial HS; Pasadena, CA; (1); 1/26; Chorus; VP Frsh Cls; High Hon Roll; Snow Skiing; World Travel; Piano/Trumpet Playing; Arch.

HULS, JEFF; Indio HS; Desert Hot Spgs, CA; (2); 30/760; Church Yth Grp; VP German Clb; Band; Jazz Band; Mrchg Band; Pep Band; Acadc Lttr Twice German I & II; Music.

HULSE, RICK; Porterville HS; Porterville, CA; (3); JV Ftbl; Hon Roll; Kiwanis Awd; Fresno ST; CPA.

HULSEBUS, JACOB L; Saint Francis HS; Tujunga, CA; (2); 17/175; Scholastic Bowl; JV Socr; High Hon Roll; Cycling Clb; CA ST-BERKLY.

HULSEY, JENNIFER; La Sierra HS; Riverside, CA; (4); 7/264; Am Leg Aux Girls St; Drama Clb; Pres VP Science Clb; Thesps; Capt Flag Corp; Phtg Nwsp; Swmmng; Ntl Merit SF; CSF, Histrn; Mock Trial Atty; U Southern CA; Drama.

HULSEY, REBECCA R; Golden West HS; Visalia, CA; (1); Church Yth Grp; Band; Prfct Atten Awd.

HULSEY, TINA KEITHANNE; Thomas Downey HS; Modesto, CA; (2); French Clb; Teachers Aide; Color Guard; Wntr Awd.

HULSHOFF, TONI L; Hilltop HS; Chula Vista, CA; (3); 54/400; Church Yth Grp; Girl Scts; Office Aide; Pep Clb; Teachers Aide; Church Choir; Stu Cncl; Stat Bsktbl; Var Mgr(s); Var Score Keeper; CSF; San Diego ST U; Lib Arts.

HULTBERG, BECKI; Carondelet HS; Martinez, CA; (3); Church Yth Grp; Pep Clb; Rep SADD; Church Choir; Variety Show; Pres Stu Cncl; Var Capt Cheerldng; Powder Puff Ftbl; Trk; Cit Awd; Untd Spirit Assn Applcnt; Peer Cnslr; ISC Cncl; Exec Cncl Pres; JV Cheer/Song Coach; CASC; USA; Poltcl Sci.

HUM, KEVIN; Lowell HS; San Francisco, CA; (3); Hon Roll; U CA; Poltcl Sci.

HUMBERSTONE, CHAD K; Mt Carmel HS; San Diego, CA; (3); Boy Scts; Church Yth Grp; High Hon Roll; Hon Roll; Kiwanis Awd; NHS; Pres Acad Fit Awd; Brigham Young U.

HUMBERT, MEGAN J; Santa Ynez Valley Union HS; Buellton, CA; (3); 2/160; Teachers Aide; Band; Mrchg Band; Pep Band; Stat Ftbl; Var L Swmmng; CSF; Excl Math Awd; Areospace Engr.

HUME, GAIL; Marina HS; Huntington Bch, CA; (4); 174/505; Pep Clb; Ski Clb; Teachers Aide; Hon Roll; San Diego ST; Psych.

HUMES, HEATHER; Huntington Beach HS; Huntington Beach, CA; (3); French Clb; Model UN; Red Cross Aide; Capt Drill Tm; Treas Soph Cls; Hon Roll.

HUMMEL, CHELSEA D; Fall River JR SR HS; Fall River Mills, CA; (2); 4-H; Lit Mag; JV Bsktbl; Var Trk; Cit Awd; 4-H Awd; Hon Roll; Prfct Atten Awd; Yth Soccer Lg Cert Referee & Player.

HUMMEL, REBECCA S; Rio Americano HS; Carmichael, CA; (2); Church Yth Grp; French Clb; Service Clb; Hon Roll; Pres Acad Fit Awd; Outstndng Achvt Painting/Drawing Awd.

HUMPAL, BRENT N; Merced HS; Merced, CA; (3); Church Yth Grp; Band; Church Choir; Jazz Band; Mrchg Band; Orch; Hon Roll; Merced Coll; Pilot.

HUMPHREY, CORINDA; Indio HS; Indio, CA; (1); Capt Cheerldng; Gym; Prfct Atten Awd; CSF; Most Imprvd Chrldr; Engl.

HUMPHREY, ELIZABETH; Manteca HS; Manteca, CA; (2); Pep Clb; Teachers Aide; Yrbk; JV L Cheerldng; Var L Trk; High Hon Roll; Hon Roll; Stanley H Kaplan Schlrshp; Natl Cngrssnl Yth Ldrshp Cncl Washington DC; Prncpls Awds; Psych.

HUMPHREY, NATHAN J; Woodcrest Christian Schl; Riverside, CA; (3); Church Yth Grp; Model UN; Scholastic Bowl; Variety Show; Rep Sec Frsh Cls; Sec Soph Cls; Rep Jr Cls; Sec Sr Cls; Sec Stu Cncl; Crs Cntry; UCR-MUN Cmmndtn NATO Iceland 88; UCR-MUN Actvty Awd 88; Schlrs Bowl Actvty Awd 88; CBC Schlrs Awd; Ivy League; Pltcl Sci.

HUMPHREY, SHELLY; Lassen HS; Chico, CA; (2); Church Yth Grp; SADD; CSU Chico.

HUMPHREY, WENDY Y; Rio Linda HS; Sacramento, CA; (3); Church Yth Grp; Hosp Aide; Hon Roll; Crt Rprtng.

HUMPHREYS, AMANDA; Pleasant Valley HS; Chico, CA; (1); Church Yth Grp; 4-H; Girl Scts; Spanish Clb; Nwsp; Bsktbl Chrldr.

HUMPHREYS, MARCELLA M; Corning Union HS; Corning, CA; (2); Church Yth Grp; GAA; Intnl Clb; Science Clb; Band; JV Fld Hcky; Hon Roll; CSF; Sut Of Mnth Engl 90; Band Ldrshp; Stanford; Polctl Sci.

HUMPHREYS, RACHEL; Tehachapi HS; Tehachapi, CA; (4); 18/149; Pres Church Yth Grp; Nwsp; Ed Lit Mag; Treas Stu Cncl; Hon Roll; Sec NHS; Pres Acad Fit Awd; Mock Trial Team; CSF; Schl Site Cncl; Brigham Young U.

HUMPHREYS, SHANE A; Hogan HS; Vallejo, CA; (4); Debate Tm; French Clb; Math Clb; Stu Cncl; Cheerldng; Crs Cntry; Trk; Hon Roll; Pres Acad Fit Awd; Intrct Clb Pres, Treas, & Pres; U Of CA; Pre-Med.

HUMPHRIES, KARA; Downey HS; Downey, CA; (2); Church Yth Grp; Dance Clb; Pep Clb; Cheerldng; Gym; Cit Awd; Hon Roll; USC; Nrsng.

HUMPHRY, CHRISTY D; Arcata HS; Arcata, CA; (3); Church Yth Grp; Drama Clb; Girl Scts; Speech Tm; Band; Orch; Stage Crew; Variety Show; Cit Awd; French Hon Soc.

HUN, SUNARI; Montclair HS; Montclair, CA; (2); Key Clb; Library Aide; Hon Roll; Prfct Atten Awd.

HUNDAL, GURPREET K; Beyer HS; Modesto, CA; (3); Cmnty Wkr; Cit Awd; Hon Roll; Vctnl Ed Acctng I Stu Awd; BSA Acctng Clb; Phy.

HUNDERTMARK, SARAH; Mission Coll Prep; Arroyo Grande, CA; (3); Church Yth Grp; Cmnty Wkr; Debate Tm; Drama Clb; Model UN; Chorus; School Play; Yrbk; Var L Crs Cntry; High Hon Roll; Chorus Outstndg Stu; Piano Stu; Chrctr Awds; Music.

HUNDLEY, CHRISTI; Westminster HS; Westminster, CA; (1); Church Yth Grp; Pep Clb; Church Choir; Off Frsh Cls; Rep Stu Cncl; Cheerldng; Hon Roll; Prfct Atten Awd.

HUNG, BENJAMIN M; El Camino Fundamental HS; Sacramento, CA; (3); Teachers Aide; Diving; JV Swmmng; Vllybl; Wt Lftg; JV Var Wrstlng; Cit Awd; Hon Roll; NHS; Ntl Merit Ltr; Econ.

HUNG, EMILY; Alameda HS; Alameda, CA; (2); 3/275; Var Tennis; Hon Roll; CSF; Piano 8 Yrs.

HUNG, EUGENE Y; Torrey Pines HS; San Diego, CA; (2); VP Chess Clb; Quiz Bowl; Hon Roll.

HUNG, LING; Ramona Convent Secondary HS; Montebello, CA; (3); Cmnty Wkr; VP French Clb; Model UN; Treas Sr Cls; Var L Tennis; Hon Roll; NHS; Ntl Merit Ltr; NEDT Awd; People To People Ambassador Pgm.

HUNG, PAUL P; Glen A Wilson HS; Hacienda Heights, CA; (3); VP German Clb; VP Key Clb; Band; Ed Nwsp; Tennis; High Hon Roll; Sci.

HUNG, PETER W; San Diego HS; San Diego, CA; (3); 3/415; Church Yth Grp; Math Tm; Pres Jr Cls; L Var Tennis; High Hon Roll; Ntl Merit Ltr; Opt Clb Awd; CSF VP; Mck Trl Atty.

HUNG, PHI D; San Gabriel HS; San Gabriel, CA; (2); Debate Tm; JV Stat Vllybl; Hon Roll; High Hnrs 1st Yr Algbr Golden ST Exam 89; CSF.

HUNGA, NICOLE M; Central Union HS; El Centro, CA; (2); Letterman Clb; NFL; Speech Tm; Orch; Hon Roll; Futurists Soc; Interact Clb; Archeology.

HUNGATE, JASON P; Branhan HS; San Jose, CA; (1); JV Bsbl; Air Force Acad; Airline Pilot.

HUNGERHOLT, KRISTIANNE; Wilcox HS; Sunnyvale, CA; (1); Drama Clb; German Clb; School Play; Amnesty Intl; UC Santa Barbara; Lawyer.

HUNN, ANGELA; Liberty HS; Oakley, CA; (1); Debate Tm; NFL; Speech Tm; Acpl Chr; Stage Crew; Variety Show; Brntwd Cmmnty Thtr; Bob Hunn Evnglstc Assn; Chmbr Sngrs; Brdcst.

HUNNICUTT, BETHANEE; Armona Union Acad; Hanford, CA; (3); 1/12; Church Yth Grp; Drama Clb; Hosp Aide; Spanish Clb; Teachers Aide; Acpl Chr; Band; Chorus; Church Choir; School Play; U CA; Ed.

HUNNICUTT, STEVEN B; Carlsbad HS; Carlsbad, CA; (2); 1/350; Church Yth Grp; Math Tm; High Hon Roll; Prfct Atten Awd; Vllybl Club.

HUNSAKER, CHRISTI L; Bakersfield HS; Bakersfield, CA; (2); Rep Church Yth Grp; FCA; JA; Key Clb; SADD; Chorus; Capt Bsktbl; Sftbl; Capt Vllybl; Hon Roll; MVP Vlybl, Bsktbl; Point Loma Nazarene Coll; Ed.

HUNSHERGER, ALLEN R; Ramona HS; Ramona, CA; (3); 30/294; Boy Scts; Church Yth Grp; VP Key Clb; Church Choir; Var JV Ftbl; JV Tennis; High Hon Roll; Hon Roll; Prfct Atten Awd; CSF; Eagle Sct; UC San Diego; Physics.

HUNSINGER, NANCI ELIZABETH; Beue River HS; Grass Valley, CA; (3); 15/182; Am Leg Aux Girls St; VP Spanish Clb; Teachers Aide; Off Frsh Cls; Off Soph Cls; Bsktbl; Powder Puff Ftbl; Swmmng; Cit Awd; Hon Roll; Cls Float Cmmtte; Capt Of V Swim Team; Cal Poly; Poltcl Sci.

HUNT, ANTHONY N; Mt Whitney HS; Visalia, CA; (1); Chess Clb; FFA; Socr; Hon Roll; FFA Best Informed Greenhand, Creed Recitation Wnnrs; Chef.

HUNT, DAVID R; Milpitas HS; Milpitas, CA; (1); ROTC; Drill Tm; Nwsp; Yrbk; Hon Roll; Hnr Guard; Cmnty Svc; Natl Grd Explrs; Civil Air Patrol; UC Berkeley; Med Doc.

HUNT, DIANE M; Nevada Union HS; Grass Valley, CA; (3); GAA; JV Var Bsktbl; Var Bsktbl; Powder Puff Ftbl; Wt Lftg; Hon Roll; Prfct Atten Awd; Bus.

HUNT, DYLAN A; Arcata HS; Arcata, CA; (1); Math Tm; Chorus; Intrml Wt Lftg; CA Hstry Day 2nd Pl Hstrcl Paper; 1st Pl Team, 4th Pl Indvdl Cnty Mathcounts Comptn; Music.

HUNT, HEATHER; Ponderosa HS; Shingle Springs, CA; (1); Pep Clb; Cheerldng; Jr NHS; Prfct Atten Awd.

HUNT, JASON J; Riverbank HS; Riverbank, CA; (3); Teachers Aide; Hon Roll; Regnl Occpntl Pgm Mrt Awd; Outstndng Stu Bldg Constrctn, Arch & Comp; Constrctn.

HUNT, JENNIFER L; Corning Union HS; Corning, CA; (3); Church Yth Grp; GAA; Science Clb; Church Choir; Yrbk; Hon Roll; Mem CSF; Ricks JC; Jrnlsm.

HUNT, JENNIFER LYNN; Calvary Chapel HS; Fountain Valley, CA; (2); Church Yth Grp; Drama Clb; Office Aide; Drm Mjr(t); High Hon Roll; Hon Roll; Law.

HUNT, JILLIAN; Montery Bay Acad; Arroyo Grande, CA; (3); Church Yth Grp; Drama Clb; Office Aide; Teachers Aide; Chorus; Church Choir; School Musical; School Play; Yrbk; Treas Frsh Cls; Acad Achvt Awd; Pacific Union Coll; Pedtrcn.

HUNT, KARYN M; El Cajon Valley HS; El Cajon, CA; (2); Letterman Clb; Var Crs Cntry; Var Socr; JV Trk; Art; Aviation; Weight Trng; Military Pilot.

HUNT, LAURA; Reedley HS; Reedley, CA; (3); 6/310; Computer Clb; French Clb; Intnl Clb; Office Aide; High Hon Roll; Jr Engrng Tech Soc Clb; CA Gldn St Exam Awd Geometry; Engrng.

HUNT, MICHAEL A; Arcata HS; Arcata, CA; (3); Aud/Vis; Debate Tm; French Clb; Letterman Clb; Math Tm; Yrbk; Rep Frsh Cls; Intrml Bsbl; Intrml Bsktbl; JV Ftbl; UC Berkeley.

HUNT, PASHA L; Palmdale HS; Agua Dulce, CA; (2); Church Yth Grp; Hon Roll; String Ensamble Instr Violin; Gldn ST Exam Rcvd Schl Rec Geom; Mission Aviation.

HUNT, RAYMOND M; El Camino Fundamental HS; Carmichael, CA; (3); 69/376; SADD; Var L Crs Cntry; Var L Trk; JV Wrstlng; Cit Awd; Prfct Atten Awd; SB Coll; Engrng.

HUNT, SARAH; Center HS; Elverta, CA; (2); Church Yth Grp; Treas Frsh Cls; Var Crs Cntry; High Hon Roll; CSF; Elem Ed.

HUNT, TERESA M; Bishop O'dowd HS; Oakland, CA; (2); Art Clb; Ski Clb; JV Swmmng; Bio Hkng Clb; Fint Art.

HUNT, TIFFANI E; Castlemont HS; Oakland, CA; (2); Scholastic Bowl; Stage Crew; Hon Roll.

HUNT, TYLER N; Fresno HS; Fresno, CA; (2); 1/635; Ski Clb; Nwsp; Stu Cncl; JV Bsbl; JV Bsktbl; Hon Roll; CSF; Auto Engr.

HUNTER, AMY V; Golden West HS; Visalia, CA; (2); Drama Clb; Thesps; School Musical; School Play; Var Sftbl; JV Capt Vllybl; Hon Roll; CA Inst Arts; Acting.

HUNTER, APRIL M; Diamond Bar HS; Diamond Bar, CA; (4); Debate Tm; Chorus; School Musical; Swing Chorus; Hon Roll; Yng Amercns; Mck Trl Law Tm; Blck Womens Assoc Schlrshp; NY U; Finance.

HUNTER, BARRY JOHN; Southwest HS; San Diego, CA; (3); Church Yth Grp; ROTC; Thesps; Band; Jazz Band; School Musical; School Play; Stage Crew; Music Tech Ensm-Hgh Tech Music Grp; ASB Cmmssnr Of Sound & Svcs; Studio Engr.

HUNTER, DENNIS A; Porterville HS; Porterville, CA; (3); 20/400; Cmnty Wkr; Science Clb; Lit Mag; Bsbl; JV Bsktbl; Var Capt Crs Cntry; Var Capt Trk; Hon Roll; Prfct Atten Awd; Campus VIP; Amer Indian Clb; Southern CA U; Bus.

HUNTER, HEATHER L; Rancho Cotati HS; Rohnert Park, CA; (2); 5/500; Cmnty Wkr; Bsktbl; Sftbl; Hon Roll; Mst Outstndng Defnsv HS Sftbl Plyr 90; All League 1st Team Catcher 89-90; All Redwood Empire 1st Team; Med.

HUNTER, HOLLY C; Immanuel Christian Schl; Ridgecrest, CA; (4); 4/15; Hon Roll; Pres Acad Fit Awd; Bnk America Achvt Awd Art & Math; Art.

HUNTER, INEDRA; Rialto JR HS; San Bernardino, CA; (1); Church Yth Grp; Pep Clb; Church Choir; School Play; Stu Cncl; Cheerldng; Gym; Mgr(s); Trk; Cit Awd; Prjct Up Beat Coll Awarnss Pgm; Math.

HUNTER, JAMES; Hamilton HS; Los Angeles, CA; (3); Cmnty Wkr; Debate Tm; JA; Letterman Clb; Rptr Nwsp; Rep Jr Cls; Bsbl; JV Soph Cls; Hon Roll; Peoples Awrd; Coll; Bus.

HUNTER, JEFF E; Bellarmine College Prep; Sunnyvale, CA; (3); Letterman Clb; Service Clb; Ski Clb; SADD; Drill Tm; Stat Bsbl; Var Cheerldng; Intrml Ftbl; Intrml Vllybl; JV Var Wrstlng; Tiny Tots Asstnc Vlntr; Flag Ftbl Coach 8th Grade; U CA Santa Barbara.

HUNTER, JOANNA L; Will C Wood HS; Vacaville, CA; (2); Church Yth Grp; Sec Band; Capt Color Guard; Jazz Band; Mrchg Band; JV Vllybl; Cit Awd; Hon Roll; UC Berkeley ATDP Pgm 90; Commnctns.

HUNTER, KARA; Strathmore HS; Strathmore, CA; (1); Tennis; High Hon Roll; CA Poly; Chld Psych.

HUNTER, KELLY A; Atwater HS; Atwater, CA; (2); Drama Clb; Rptr FBLA; Mgr Yrbk; High Hon Roll; Work K-Mart; Read Shakespearan Plays & Write; Environmental Issues.

HUNTER, KRISTA; Strathmore Union HS; Strathmore, CA; (3); 4/80; German Clb; SADD; Tennis; High Hon Roll; Scicon Cnslr; Lbrl Arts.

HUNTER, MARNIE; Santiago HS; Santa Ana, CA; (2); 189/498; Sec Model UN; SADD; Drill Tm; School Play; Variety Show; Cheerldng; Trk; Hon Roll; Bro & Sis Unted Treas; GATE; Cmmnctns.

HUNTER, MATTHEW A; Ukiah HS; Ukiah, CA; (3); 68/439; Aud/Vis; Church Yth Grp; Office Aide; School Musical; School Play; Stage Crew; Swmmng; Bio-Tech Sympsm 88-89; Bio, Chem Hnrs 88-89-90; Elec Techn Head Lghtng Techn; Elec Engrng.

HUNTER, MICHAEL A; Sunny Hills HS; Fullerton, CA; (3); Ski Clb; JV Bsbl; Intrml Bsktbl; JV Ftbl; Intrml Vllybl; Wt Lftg; Hon Roll; City & St Yth In Govt; IM Street Hcky; U Of CA.

HUNTER, SEVGI; Galt HS; Galt, CA; (2); High Hon Roll; Forensic Pathlgy.

HUNTER, SICHANA D; Downey HS; Downey, CA; (3); Church Yth Grp; Chorus; Cit Awd; Hon Roll; Schl Recgntn Golden St Exam; Howard U; Law.

HUNTING, JULIE; Bonita Vista HS; Chula Vista, CA; (1); Church Yth Grp; Cmnty Wkr; Socr; Swmmng; Cit Awd; High Hon Roll; Prfct Atten Awd; Mem USTA; Arch.

HUNTING, MELANIE L; Pacifica HS; Garden Grove, CA; (3); 20/260; Church Yth Grp; GAA; Hosp Aide; Letterman Clb; Science Clb; JV Sftbl; JV Vllybl; Hon Roll; CA Schlstc Fed; Honorary Awd In Hstry.

HUNTINGTON, MICHAEL R; Petaluma HS; Penngrove, CA; (3); 17/267; Boy Scts; Band; Jazz Band; Mrchg Band; Swmmng; High Hon Roll; Hon Roll; CA Schlrshp Fdrtn; Accntng.

HUNTLEY, IAN A; Santa Maria HS; Santa Maria, CA; (3); 12/457; FBLA; Varsity Clb; Bsktbl; Var Tennis; Hon Roll; NHS; Pres Schlr; Spanish NHS; CSF; Acad Tm Hnrbl Mntn In Tnns; U CA San Diego; Pre Med.

HUNTSINGER, CAM R; Marina HS; Huntington Beach, CA; (1); JV Swmmng; UC Irvine; Engrng.

HUNTSMAN, JENNY R V; Yosemite Union HS; Coarsegold, CA; (3); 20/174; Church Yth Grp; Stu Cncl; Var L Bsktbl; Var L Crs Cntry; Stat Sftbl; Var L Trk; Hon Roll; Skiing, Hrsbck Riding, Hiking; Adv Lifesaving & CPR; Pianist; Humboldt; Forestry.

HUNTZINGER, REBECCA E; Hayward HS; Hayward, CA; (3); Pres Church Yth Grp; German Clb; Science Clb; Acpl Chr; Church Choir; Off Sr Cls; JV Bsktbl; Var Trk; Var Vllybl; Hon Roll; Choral Aires; Music.

HUNWICK III, BERNARD B; Venice HS; Venice, CA; (2); School Musical; Yrbk; Stu Cncl; JV Swmmng; Mst Inspiratnl; V Swmmng; Berkeley; Physics.

HUPF, CHRISTOPHER P; Saint Anthony HS; Garden Grove, CA; (2); Boy Scts; Church Yth Grp; Teachers Aide; High Hon Roll; NHS; Bilingual Span Awd; BSA Rank Life; Ordr Arrow; Sci.

HUPPERT, LARA L; Bishop O'dowd HS; San Leandro, CA; (3); Church Yth Grp; Cmnty Wkr; Aud/Vis; Chorus; Church Choir; School Musical; School Play; Stage Crew; Rptr Nwsp; High Hon Roll; Acadmc Achvt Awd US Hstry.

HUQ, SADAT ZUNNURAIN; Downey HS; Downey, CA; (3); 1/400; French Clb; Math Clb; Math Tm; Pres Spanish Clb; Crs Cntry; Trk; High Hon Roll; Interact Pres; Boys Alt St Rep; Yng Invrnmntlst Clb Actvts Chrmn; Sci.

HUR, CAROLINE K; West Lake School For Girls; Los Angeles, CA; (2); French Clb; Math Tm; Ski Clb; Varsity Clb; Band; Mrchg Band; Orch; Var Sftbl; JV Vllybl; Hon Roll.

HURD, JASON W; Los Altos HS; Hacienda Hgts, CA; (3); 69/376; Letterman Clb; Teachers Aide; Var Vllybl; Hon Roll; Prfct Atten Awd; Los Angeles Cnty Fire Dept Explorer; Fire Sci.

HURD, JENNIFER M; Del Campo HS; Citrus Heights, CA; (2); 325/380; Church Yth Grp; FBLA; CA ST U; JR HS Teacher.

HURLBURT, CHRISTY A; Poway HS; Poway, CA; (4); 15/728; Cmnty Wkr; Ed Lit Mag; High Hon Roll; Kiwanis Awd; NHS; Peer Cnslng; Fri Nght Live-Eqvlnt To SADD/Safe Rds.

HURLEY, CRAIG; Fountain Valley HS; Fountain Valley, CA; (3); Boy Scts; Church Yth Grp; Cmnty Wkr; Varsity Clb; Ftbl; Trk; Wt Lftg; Eagle Scout; Mst Imprvd Ftbl Player; BYU; Advertisement.

HURLEY, JON-MARK; North Monterey County HS; Salinas, CA; (3); Treas AFS; Church Yth Grp; Dance Clb; Drm Mjr(t); Jazz Band; Cheerldng; High Hon Roll; Hon Roll; Pres Acad Fit Awd; Performer Of Month, Dance Advanced Awd 90; 1st Pl Spring Board Diving Sctnl Champ; Stanford; Med.

HURLEY, JOSHUA; Portola JR SR HS; Portola, CA; (2); Letterman Clb; Spanish Clb; Varsity Clb; Swing Chorus; Sec Frsh Cls; Rep Soph Cls; VP Jr Cls; Bsktbl; Golf; Trk; Yth To Yth & Drug Free Club; Wstrn St Yth To Yth Conf; Spnsh Club Trip Spain & France 91; U Of CA Santa Cruz; Marine Bio.

HURLEY, SHANNON T; Aptos HS; La Selva Beach, CA; (2); 1/396; Church Yth Grp; Cmnty Wkr; Service Clb; Rep Stu Cncl; JV Bsktbl; JV Vllybl; High Hon Roll; Hon Roll.

HURST, JENNY; Dana Hills HS; Laguna Niguel, CA; (1); Church Yth Grp; Key Clb; Fshn Dsgn.

HURST, KENNETH W; Napa HS; Napa, CA; (1); Napa Valley Phys Dev Awd 90; Pro Bsbl.

HURST, MICHELLE D; Dana Hills HS; Laguna Niguel, CA; (2); Cmnty Wkr; GAA; Girl Scts; Letterman Clb; Varsity Clb; Acpl Chr; Chorus; School Musical; JV Crs Cntry; Gym; UCLA; Ped.

HURST, NICOLE J; Bonita HS; La Verne, CA; (1); FBLA; SADD; Law.

HURST, PAUL P; Shasta HS; Redding, CA; (3); 44/427; Bus Profs of Am; Drama Clb; FBLA; Ftbl; Trk; Vllybl; High Hon Roll; UC Davis; Sprts Med.

HURT, HOLLY C; Schl Of Creative & Perfoming Arts; San Diego, CA; (3); 20/151; Church Yth Grp; Dance Clb; Drama Clb; Girl Scts; Office Aide; Teachers Aide; Church Choir; School Musical; School Play; Variety Show; Hnrs Spanish; Hnrs Dance.

HURT, VERA J; Western Christian HS; W Covina, CA; (4); Pep Clb; Mrchg Band; Var Cheerldng; Var Powder Puff Ftbl; High Hon Roll; Hon Roll; Pres Acad Fit Awd; Solo Twirler; All W Rgnl Miss Majorette; USC; Engrng.

HURTAD, ROSARIO; Pasadena HS; Pasadena, CA; (3); Church Yth Grp; Latin Clb; Var Tennis; Hon Roll; CA Poly Pomona; Vet.

HURTADO, GREG; Central Union HS; El Centro, CA; (2); Intrml JV Bsbl; Intrml Ftbl; Hon Roll; Bus.

HURTADO JR, JOSE MIGUEL; Vanden HS; Travis A F B, CA; (2); 1/175; Boy Scts; Church Yth Grp; Stu Cncl; JV Crs Cntry; High Hon Roll; Jr NHS; Prfct Atten Awd; Gldn St Exam Hnrs For Geo; No 1 Stu In Geo, Engl I & II, Bio, Algebra II & Wrld Hist; Stu Of Mnth 89; Air Force Acad; Aerospc Engr.

HURTADO, JOSUE L; Sierra Vista HS; Baldwin Park, CA; (1); Marine Bio.

HURTADO, LAUREN S; Rosamond HS; Edwards, CA; (2); Art Clb; French Clb; Drill Tm; Rep Soph Cls; Stu Cncl; JV Bsktbl; Cit Awd; Hon Roll; Drawing.

HURTADO, LORIE; Ft Bragg SR HS; Fort Bragg, CA; (2); Church Yth Grp; Cmnty Wkr; Dance Clb; Drama Clb; Latin Clb; Spanish Clb; Teachers Aide; Church Choir; Cheerldng; Pom Pon; Helped Organize Flocorik Dances; Sonoma ST U.

HURTADO, MARCO A; Daniel Murphy HS; Los Angeles, CA; (1); Intrml JV Bsktbl; UCLA; Mech Engrng.

HURTADO, MILENA M; Fillmore HS; Fillmore, CA; (2); Cit Awd; Hon Roll; Acadmc Achvt Awd; Outstndng Achvt Awd; Migrant Club; Sys Analyst.

HURTADO, RAMIRO; Lynwood HS; Lynwood, CA; (4); Math Tm; Var Crs Cntry; Var Socr; Lion Awd; Comp Sci.

HURTE, HEATHER S; Oroville HS; Oroville, CA; (1); Church Yth Grp; Cmnty Wkr; Drama Clb; Church Choir; VP Frsh Cls; Var Crs Cntry; Var Trk; Hon Roll; Pacific Chrstn Coll; Acting.

HURTGEN, RICHEY; Oakdale HS; Oakdale, CA; (2); Church Yth Grp; 4-H; FFA; Quiz Bowl; Spanish Clb; Trk; 4-H Awd; Hon Roll; Outstndng FFA Dairy Exhbtr Stanislaus Co Fair & CA T Fair; Exhbtd Suprme Champ Dfairy Female; Modesto JC; Dairy Sci.

HURTT, BRIAN A; Beacon Christian HS; Foster City, CA; (1); 2/14; Church Yth Grp; Chorus; Church Choir; School Play; Stu Cncl; Socr; Hon Roll; Joshua Awd, Outstnd Chrstn Ldrshp.

HURWITZ, GREGG A; Bellarmine College Prep; Saratoga, CA; (3); 1/330; Cmnty Wkr; Letterman Clb; Service Clb; Teachers Aide; Stage Crew; Nwsp; Crs Cntry; Trk; Wrstlng; Cit Awd; Engl.

HUSAIN, IQBAL; Burlingame HS; Concord, CA; (3); French Clb; Hon Roll; CSF Stu; Prncpls Hnr Rll Cert.

HUSAIN, ZEESHAN S; West Torrance HS; Houston, TX; (4); 1/435; Pres Computer Clb; Sec Rep Math Clb; Math Tm; Rep Stu Cncl; JV L Bsktbl; High Hon Roll; NHS; Ntl Merit Ltr; Pres Acad Fit Awd; Val; Harbor/1CLA Collegium; Caltech Smmr Scndry Schl Sci Pgm; Amer Comp Sci Leag 1st Pl; MA Insti Of Tech; Bio.

HUSAR, KRISTA E; Valhalla HS; El Cajon, CA; (2); Dance Clb; VP Hosp Aide; Intnl Clb; SADD; Trk; Cit Awd; Hon Roll; Golden St Exam For Algebra High Hnrs; CSF; UCSD; Corp Bus.

HUSBANDS, TAMARA A; Skyline HS; Oakland, CA; (3); Rptr Nwsp; Rep Stu Cncl; MESA; UC Prtnrshp; Jrnlsm.

HUSEIN, OMAR; Bullard HS; Fresno, CA; (3); 1/600; Boy Scts; Church Yth Grp; Capt Math Tm; Orch; Pres Rep Stu Cncl; Var L Wrstlng; Capt JETS Awd; Pres Acad Fit Awd; Acad Decathln-Capt; Mensa; Med.

HUSSAIN, ARSHIA; Notre Dame HS; San Jose, CA; (3); Church Yth Grp; Cmnty Wkr; Drama Clb; Hosp Aide; School Play; Rep Soph Cls; High Hon Roll; Hon Roll; NHS; Acadmc Achvt Photo; U Of Sthrn CA; Jrnlsm.

HUSSAIN, SAYAID Z; Patterson SR HS; Patterson, CA; (3); VICA; Acctng.

HUSSEIN, NAFEESA; River City HS; W Sacramento, CA; (1); School Play; Stage Crew; Rptr Nwsp; Hon Roll; Peer Pgm Engrng & Comp Sci; BIONIC.

HUSSEY, MELISSA; Dublin HS; Dublin, CA; (3); 4/287; Church Yth Grp; FBLA; Color Guard; Var Cheerldng; Var Crs Cntry; Pom Pon; Score Keeper; Var Trk; High Hon Roll; Hon Roll; CA Schlrshp Fed; Exalt Clb; Stanford; Med.

HUSTON, KELLY E; Westlake HS; Westlake Vlg, CA; (1); Pres Church Yth Grp; Drama Clb; Math Clb; Spanish Clb; SADD; School Play; VP Soph Cls; Var Crs Cntry; JV Trk; Hon Roll; Georgetown; Med.

HUSTON, KERRY; Encina HS; Sacramento, CA; (3); 16/123; Am Leg Aux Girls St; Letterman Clb; Drill Tm; Lit Mag; Off Jr Cls; Hon Roll; Stu Rchng Out Secy; Rotary Club Rcgtn; Rally Cmmssnr; UCSB; Elem Tchr.

HUSTON, NORA; San Gabriel HS; San Gabriel, CA; (2); AFS; Church Yth Grp; Cmnty Wkr; Acpl Chr; Drill Tm; School Play; Score Keeper; JV Var Swmmng; Tri-Hi-Y Clubs Amoramici; Proj Apprctn; Day Care Tchr.

HUSTON, URIAH J; El Camino HS; Oceanside, CA; (4); Art Clb; NFL; Pep Clb; Speech Tm; School Play; Stage Crew; High Hon Roll; Hon Roll; Kiwanis Awd; Pratt Inst; Graphic Artstry.

HUTAK, VICTORIA R; Duarte HS; Monrovia, CA; (2); 3/250; Church Yth Grp; Treas Key Clb; Science Clb; School Play; Yrbk; Phtg Lit Mag; VP Soph Cls; High Hon Roll; Pres Acad Fit Awd; CA Schlrshp Fed VP; Pomona Coll; Bus.

HUTCHCRAFT, JUSTIN; Cajon HS; San Bernardino, CA; (2); Church Yth Grp; French Hon Soc; NHS; CO Coll; Bus Ownr.

HUTCHEON, SCOTT L; Edison HS; Huntington Bch, CA; (2); Var Socr; Intrml Tennis; Coaches Awd Sccr; Club Sccr; Bus.

HUTCHERSON, STEPHANIE S; St Joseph HS; La Palma, CA; (2); Church Yth Grp; Drama Clb; SADD; Drill Tm; Hon Roll; Piano Lessons 11 Yrs; Play Hymn Music Mrng Church Svcs; Hiking, Bicycling, Swmmng, Snow Skiing; Bus.

HUTCHERSON, TAMMI; Nordhoff HS; Oak View, CA; (4); Art Clb; Cmnty Wkr; Spanish Clb; SADD; Band; Drm Mjr(t); Mrchg Band; Orch; Pep Band; School Musical; Cal Poly; Bus.

HUTCHINGS, BRENT I; Oakridge HS; Huntsville, AL; (2); Boy Scts; Church Yth Grp; SADD; Swmmng; Hon Roll; Schlr/Ath Of Yr 85; BYU; Pre-Med.

HUTCHINGS, JENNIFER F; San Ramon Valley HS; Danville, CA; (3); Art Clb; SADD; Hon Roll; Pres Acad Fit Awd; Art.

HUTCHINGS, TRICIA; Yosemite HS; Raymond, CA; (4); Church Yth Grp; Cmnty Wkr; 4-H; FBLA; GAA; Library Aide; Office Aide; Teachers Aide; Varsity Clb; JV Var Bsktbl; Mercad U; Bus Mgmt.

HUTCHINS, TODD A; Orange Glen HS; Escondido, CA; (3); 125/460; German Clb; Hon Roll.

HUTCHINS, WILL C; Delta HS; Courtland, CA; (2); Sec Jr Cls; JV Bsktbl; Capt Ftbl; JV Trk; Ftbl Capt; Pblc Pskng.

HUTCHISON, JOHNNY F; Antelope Valley HS; Lancaster, CA; (4); 69/521; German Clb; Science Clb; Spanish Clb; Rep Frsh Cls; Rep Soph Cls; Rep Jr Cls; Rep Sr Cls; Stu Cncl; High Hon Roll; Hon Roll; Rotary Clb Yth Mnth Awd; CSF; Antelope Valley Coll; Med.

HUTCHISON, STEFANIE A; Vacaville HS; Vacaville, CA; (4); 79/562; Sec Spanish Clb; Teachers Aide; Ed Yrbk; High Hon Roll; Hon Roll; NHS; CA Schlrshp Fed; Solano CC; Bus.

HUTH, HILLARY H; George Washington HS; San Francisco, CA; (3); NFL; Speech Tm; Rep Frsh Cls; Rep Soph Cls; High Hon Roll; Peer Resource Ctr; Amnesty International Grp Coord; Stus Concerned Over Rocist Evnts.

HUTH, THOMAS; East Bakersfield HS; Bakersfield, CA; (4); FCA; French Clb; Intnl Clb; Key Clb; Teachers Aide; Ed Nwsp; Stu Cncl; Var Crs Cntry; Var Socr; Var Trk.

HUTSELL, JULIE; Coast Union HS; Cambria, CA; (3); AFS; French Clb; FHA; SADD; Yrbk; JV Var Cheerldng; JV Var Sftbl; JV Vllybl; High Hon Roll; Commnctns.

HUTSON, JENNIFER S; Glendora HS; Glendora, CA; (4); 22/375; Math Clb; JV Bsktbl; Stat Swmmng; High Hon Roll; Lion Awd; Fri Ngt Live Club; Soc Of Women Engnrs Awd; U Of CA; Bioengnrng.

HUTT, MARK J; Enterprise HS; Redding, CA; (3); 43/427; Pres JA; Math Clb; Mu Alpha Theta; Pep Clb; VP Science Clb; Treas Frsh Cls; Pres Soph Cls; Pres Stu Cncl; Hon Roll; Boy Scts; U Of CA, Snta Barb; Micro Bio.

HUTTINGA, JACELYN J; Redwood Christian HS; Alameda, CA; (4); Treas Church Yth Grp; Teachers Aide; Chorus; Church Choir; VP Soph Cls; Pres Sr Cls; Var L Trk; Var Capt Vllybl; High Hon Roll; Ntl Merit SF; Parttime Job; Calvin Coll; Frgn Svc Offcr.

HUTTO, HEIDI E; Redwood HS; Visalia, CA; (2); Hon Roll; Prfct Atten Awd; COS; Ed.

HUTTO, K C; Mills HS; Millbrae, CA; (4); Band; Pep Band; Stage Crew; JV Var Bsktbl; Hon Roll; Embry-Riddle Aero U; Aero Sci.

HUTTO, TAMMY; Valley HS; Sacramento, CA; (3); 115/580; Church Yth Grp; Dance Clb; Office Aide; Teachers Aide; Cheerldng; Gym; Hon Roll; Prfct Atten Awd; Child Psych.

HUTTON, CHRISTINA; Chaffey HS; Ontario, CA; (4); 8/526; Pres Church Yth Grp; Pres French Clb; High Hon Roll; CSF Pres; Acad Decathlon Team; Natrl Envrmnt S CA Clb; CSU; Art Hstry.

HUTTON, EVANGELINE F; Redwood Christian HS; San Leandro, CA; (2); Church Yth Grp; Band; Var Bsktbl; JV Var Vllybl; High Hon Roll; Hon Roll; Prfct Atten Awd; Pres Acad Fit Awd; CSF; Sports Awd; Bus.

HUTUHINS, DARREN; Branham HS; San Jose, CA; (4); French Clb; Ski Clb; JV Bsktbl; Var Swmmng; High Hon Roll; CSF; Hnr Soc Life; Uc Berkeley; Law.

HUTZLER, ALICIA; Sunny Hills HS; Fullerton, CA; (1); Church Yth Grp; Dance Clb; Drama Clb; Pep Clb; SADD; Ed Yrbk; Capt JV Cheerldng; Cit Awd; High Hon Roll; Hon Roll; U CA Santa Barbara; Marine Bio.

HUY, DUONG; Sierra Vista HS; Baldwin Park, CA; (3); Socr.

HUYNH, ANH T; Mt Pleasant HS; San Jose, CA; (1); Math Clb.

HUYNH, ANH-LUU T; Mater Dei HS; Fountain Valley, CA; (3); Cmnty Wkr; Hosp Aide; Spanish Clb; Chorus; Rptr Yrbk; Stu Cncl; High Hon Roll; Hon Roll; Jr NHS; NHS; U CA; Pre-Med.

HUYNH, BAO-AN; Pacifica HS; Garden Grove, CA; (2); 14/294; Letterman Clb; Varsity Clb; Bsktbl; Crs Cntry; Tennis; Hon Roll; Prfct Atten Awd; CSF; Gse; UCI; Phy.

HUYNH, BINH THUY; Gardena HS; Gardena, CA; (3); French Clb; Library Aide; JV Vllybl; Hon Roll; Val; HS Libr Assn Pres; CA Schlrshp Fed; Optometry.

HUYNH, CALEB A; Galileo HS; San Francisco, CA; (2); Church Yth Grp; Hon Roll; Art.

HUYNH, CHAN; Santiago HS; Garden Grove, CA; (1); 117/509; SADD; Band; Mrchg Band; Pep Band; Tennis; Hon Roll; Marching Band Freshman Of Yr; USC; Arch.

HUYNH, CHAU M; Oakland Technical HS; Oakland, CA; (4); 3/363; JA; Math Clb; Math Tm; High Hon Roll; Hon Roll; Prfct Atten Awd; Math Outstndng Schlrshp; Acad Achvt Span 3; Golde St Schlrs Of Geom 88; UC Berkeley; Comp Sci.

HUYNH, CHUONG Q; San Gabriel HS; Rosemead, CA; (2); Chess Clb; Debate Tm; NFL; Speech Tm; Bsktbl; High Hon Roll; Hon Roll; Prfct Atten Awd; Medcl Sci.

HUYNH, CUONG; Monterey Park HS; Monterey Park, CA; (4); 29/623; Cmnty Wkr; Debate Tm; Math Clb; NFL; Red Cross Aide; Service Clb; Socr; Cit Awd; Hon Roll; Opt Clb Awd; Cmnty Relations Commissioner For Monterey Park City & Volunteer; Aids Speaker For Amer Red Cross; UCLA; Med.

HUYNH, CYNTHIA L; Saddleback HS; Santa Ana, CA; (1); SADD; Variety Show; Pres Soph Cls; DAR Awd; Prfct Atten Awd; CSF Membr; Mock Trail; USC; Arch.

HUYNH, DAO; Bolsa Grande HS; Westminster, CA; (1).

HUYNH, DAO B; J F Kennedy HS; Glendale, CA; (4); Math Clb; Service Clb; Tennis; Wt Lftg; High Hon Roll; Hon Roll; Northridge CSU; Bus Admin.

HUYNH, DAO D; Santa Teresa HS; San Jose, CA; (3).

HUYNH, DAVID T; American HS; Fremont, CA; (3); 29/351; Gov Hon Prg Awd; High Hon Roll; Hon Roll; Prfct Atten Awd; UC Davis; Pre-Med.

HUYNH, DOANH G; Mayfair HS; Norwalk, CA; (4); 4/200; AFS; French Clb; Intnl Clb; High Hon Roll; Prfct Atten Awd; CSF; Math Dept Awd; Stu Mnth; CA ST U Long Bch; Bus.

HUYNH, DUC; Gardena HS; Gardena, CA; (4); #12 In Class; Sec Key Clb; NFL; Service Clb; Speech Tm; Intrml Bsktbl; Var Tennis; Cit Awd; Hon Roll; Pres Acad Fit Awd; Supr Lincoln Douglas Debate; All City Speech Team; Hands Across Amer Essay Awd; UC Irvine; Civil Engr.

HUYNH, DUKE T; Mark Keppel HS; Monterey Park, CA; (4); 3/600; Chess Clb; Cmnty Wkr; JA; Chrmn Math Clb; Math Tm; Chrmn Mu Alpha Theta; Pres Science Clb; Teachers Aide; Band; Mrchg Band; Jr Medalion Awd; Bk Of Amer Plaque Awd; Harvey Mudd Coll; Comp Sci.

HUYNH, DUNG L; Andrew Hill HS; San Jose, CA; (2); Prfct Atten Awd; JV Badminton; CSF.

HUYNH, EDWARD; Bellarmine College Prep; San Jose, CA; (1); Boy Scts; Service Clb; Rptr Nwsp; Rptr Yrbk; Capt Ftbl; Capt Wrstlng; Tutor; SIC.

HUYNH, FREDERIC; South Pasadena HS; S Pasadena, CA; (4); 21/295; French Clb; L Capt Tennis; Hon Roll; Pres Acad Fit Awd; CSF Seal Bearer; MVP 90 Vrsty Tnns; 90 Cngrssnl Yth Ldrshp Clb; CA Poly Pomona.

HUYNH, HA; Will C Crawford HS; San Diego, CA; (1); Math Tm; High Hon Roll; UCSD; Pre-Med.

HUYNH, HOA V; Huntington Beach HS; Huntington Beach, CA; (2); Var L Bsktbl; Capt Trk; High Hon Roll; Prfct Atten Awd; Engrng.

HUYNH, HONG; Ontario HS; Ontario, CA; (3); 17/500; French Clb; Key Clb; Math Clb; Ski Clb; Teachers Aide; Cit Awd; High Hon Roll; Prfct Atten Awd; Voice Dem Awd.

HUYNH, HONG; Seaside HS; Marina, CA; (3); Art Clb; Chess Clb; Computer Clb; Library Aide; Office Aide; Orch; Nwsp; Off Sr Cls; Bsktbl; Ftbl; San Jose UCS; Bus.

HUYNH, HUE C; San Gabriel HS; Rosemead, CA; (2); French Clb; SADD; High Hon Roll; CA Schlstc Fed; Acad Decathlon.

HUYNH, JASON T; San Gabriel HS; Rosemead, CA; (3); Trk; Design Drftng.

HUYNH, JENNIFER; Saddleback HS; Santa Ana, CA; (2); Cmnty Wkr; Pep Clb; Speech Tm; Variety Show; Nwsp; JV Co-Capt Cheerldng; High Hon Roll; Prfct Atten Awd; CSF Reception Crdntr; Girls League; CA ST Fullerton; Nwsbrdcstr.

HUYNH, JENNY; J F Kennedy HS; Glendale, CA; (4); Math Clb; Teachers Aide; Hon Roll; Pres Schlr; Math Hnr Soc; Arts; CSUN; Bus Admin.

HUYNH, JOHN K; Bellarmine College Prep; San Jose, CA; (3); 8/300; Chess Clb; Service Clb; Varsity Clb; JV Var Crs Cntry; Mgr(s); Var L Tennis; JV Trk; Intrml Vllybl; Indpndnt Aging Prgm; 2 Part Time Jobs; Bus.

HUYNH, JOSEPHINE Y; Mt Diablo HS; W Pittsburg, CA; (3); French Clb; VP FBLA; Asian Club Sec; CSF; UC Berkeley; Accntng.

HUYNH, KHOA D; Glendale HS; Glendale, CA; (3); Cmnty Wkr; SADD; Chorus; Ed Nwsp; Phtg Yrbk; NHS; Val; Glendale Yth & Govt; Amer Lgn Awd; Vietnamese Club Pres; UC Santa Cruz; Intl Bus.

HUYNH, KIET A; Hawthorne HS; Hawthorne, CA; (2); 4/1000; JV Vllybl; Hon Roll; UC Berkeley; Engnr.

HUYNH, KIM T; La Quinta HS; Santa Ana, CA; (3); 103/333; Chess Clb; French Clb; Math Clb; Hon Roll; NHS; JV-BADMNTN; CA Schlrshp Fed; CA ST Fullerton; Accntng.

HUYNH, LAP M; Fremont HS; Sunnyvale, CA; (4); 42/389; Art Clb; French Clb; Variety Show; High Hon Roll; Golden St Exam High Hnr Geom; Cngrssnl Yth Ldrshp; West Valley Coll; Arch.

HUYNH, LINH T; Skyline HS; Oakland, CA; (4); French Clb; Key Clb; High Hon Roll; Hon Roll; UCLA; Real Estate.

HUYNH, LOI T; Luther Burbank HS; Sacramento, CA; (3); Dance Clb; French Clb; Bsktbl; Socr; Vllybl; Wt Lftg; Cit Awd; High Hon Roll; Hon Roll.

HUYNH, LONG; Oxnard HS; Oxnard, CA; (2); 39/604; Rep Stu Cncl; Bsktbl; JV Ftbl; Var Tennis; Photo Clb Pres; CSF; UCSB; Engrng.

HUYNH, LONG B; Fremont HS; Sunnyvale, CA; (1); Debate Tm; NFL; Speech Tm; Ntl Merit Schol; Golden St Exam Hgh Hnrs Algebra I.

HUYNH, LUONG T; San Gabriel HS; San Gabriel, CA; (2); Library Aide; Math Tm; Hon Roll; Physics.

HUYNH, MAI N; Mission Bay HS; San Diego, CA; (2); 1/380; French Clb; Cit Awd; High Hon Roll; CSF Clb; UCI; Bus.

HUYNH, MAN T; San Gabriel HS; San Gabriel, CA; (3); German Clb; Hon Roll; Keywanettes; AP Clb.

HUYNH, MARLENE; Galileo HS; San Francisco, CA; (3); Dance Clb; Hon Roll; Amer Red Cross For Elderlies Volunteer; Elem Ed.

HUYNH, MAY L; International Studies Acad; San Francisco, CA; (3); Yrbk; Hon Roll; Fincl Bus Ink Treas; Stu Store; Pr Cnslng; Shaughas Clb Secty; CA ST U; Chld Psych.

HUYNH, MINH N; Independence HS; San Jose, CA; (3); Chess Clb; Math Clb; Math Tm; Science Clb; Intrml Vllybl; High Hon Roll; CSF-LIFE Member; Outstndng Achvt-Chem; Conscientious Effort-Genl Sci; GSE Geom Hnrs; U CA-IRVINE; Comp Engr.

HUYNH, MINH Q; San Gabriel HS; Monterey Park, CA; (2); Tennis; Hon Roll.

HUYNH, MINH T; Alameda HS; Alameda, CA; (1); 34/299; High Hon Roll; Acad Boostrs; Phys Sci.

HUYNH, NGA T; Andrew Hill HS; San Jose, CA; (2); Cmnty Wkr; Hosp Aide; Teachers Aide; VP Jr Cls; Var Bsktbl; Var Vllybl; UCLA; Bus.

HUYNH, NGA T; Luther Burbank HS; Sacramento, CA; (2); Dance Clb; Teachers Aide; Vllybl; Cit Awd; Hon Roll; Newcomers Clb; Schlrshp Awd Frnch Dept; Cert Recgntn; Office.

HUYNH, NGAN N; La Quinta HS; Westminster, CA; (3); 6/333; French Clb; German Clb; Office Aide; Science Clb; High Hon Roll; Hon Roll; CA Bus Ed Assn Awd; Hi Hnrs Gldn St Exaf-Geom; CSF & Cambodian Club; U CA Irvine; Bio.

HUYNH, NGOC KIM; Skyline HS; Oakland, CA; (3); Church Yth Grp; Dance Clb; Intnl Clb; Key Clb; Math Clb; Math Tm; Service Clb; Band; Church Choir; Jazz Band; Stu Of Month Awd; Bus.

HUYNH, NGOC T; Arlington HS; Riverside, CA; (2); Chorus; Stat Trk; Hon Roll; CSF; Spirit Club; Mock Trial; Law.

HUYNH, PHUONG N; Lincoln HS; San Francisco, CA; (1); Bsbl; Bsktbl; Socr; Sftbl; Tennis; Vllybl; Wt Lftg; Vietnamese Stus Awd; Badminton.

HUYNH, PHUONG THI; Herbert Hoover HS; San Diego, CA; (3); Library Aide; High Hon Roll; GPA Awd; U Of CA San Diego; Flght Attnd.

HUYNH, PHUONG V; La Quinta HS; Santa Ana, CA; (1); Hon Roll; UCLA.

HUYNH, QUANG C; Oakland Technical HS; Oakland, CA; (3); Band; Hon Roll; Haywood; Bus.

HUYNH, QUANG D; Loara HS; Anaheim, CA; (4); Computer Clb; Key Clb; Hon Roll; NHS; CSF, JV Badminton 90; Golden St Exam Geom High Hnrs 88; UC Irvine; Comp Sci.

HUYNH, QUOC V; Seaside HS; Marina, CA; (4); Art Clb; Band; Pep Band; School Musical; Swmmng; Med.

HUYNH, SALLY M; Richard Gahr HS; Cerritos, CA; (2); Church Yth Grp; Drama Clb; French Clb; Off Jr Cls; JV Vllybl; Hon Roll; Teen Fellowship Clb; UC Irvine; Psycht.

HUYNH, STACY TIEN T; Abraham Lincoln HS; San Francisco, CA; (2); Hon Roll; Jr Clb; Acting.

HUYNH, STEPHEN M; Mt Diablo HS; W Pittsburg, CA; (2); 1/200; French Clb; Treas FBLA; Asian Clb; CA Schlrshp Fdrtn; Undrgrad Awd; U Of CA Davis; Bio.

HUYNH, TAI; San Gabriel HS; Rosemead, CA; (3); Cit Awd; Hon Roll; Prfct Atten Awd; Proj Appreciation; Invest In Amer; Art Awd; Bus.

HUYNH, TAN C; Lincoln HS; Stockton, CA; (3); 17/529; Mu Alpha Theta; JV Crs Cntry; JV Trk; French Hon Soc; High Hon Roll; CSF; Vrsty Badmntn; UC Berkeley; Medcl.

HUYNH, THANH T; Nevada Union HS; Grass Valley, CA; (4); 19/448; FBLA; Ski Clb; Varsity Clb; Var Ftbl; Var Tennis; JV Trk; Elks Awd; High Hon Roll; Hon Roll; Goldn St Exam Hnrs; Badmntn Vrsty Athltc Ltr, MVP Awd; CSU; Sacramento; Bus Admin.

HUYNH, THU L; Skyline HS; Oakland, CA; (3); Cmnty Wkr; Drama Clb; Key Clb; Service Clb; Thesps; Chorus; School Musical; Stage Crew; Variety Show; Ed Nwsp; Sons Of Amer Revolution Oratorical Cont; Share The Dream Essay Cont Fnlst; UCLA; Jrnlsm.

HUYNH, THU TAM; Ontario HS; Ontario, CA; (2); Math Clb; Hon Roll; Prfct Atten Awd; Pres Asian Club; Medicine.

HUYNH, THUY GIANG; Calvin Simmons HS; Oakland, CA; (1); 1/35; ROTC; Speech Tm; Color Guard; Drill Tm; Off Frsh Cls; Stu Cncl; Vllybl; Cit Awd; High Hon Roll; Hon Roll; Upward Bound Pgm; Oakland Tech; Med.

HUYNH, TI-AN; Pacifica HS; Garden Grove, CA; (1); Var Dance Clb; Hon Roll; Schlr Of Qrtr; CSF; U CA; Psych.

HUYNH, TIEN; Luther Burbank HS; Sacramento, CA; (4); 54/234; Dance Clb; Bsktbl; High Hon Roll; Hon Roll; Cosumner River Coll; Arch.

HUYNH, TOAN N; San Gabriel HS; San Gabriel, CA; (2); Bsktbl; Ftbl; Trk; Hon Roll; Vietnamese Clb; UNLV; Photo.

HUYNH, TRUC; Hoover HS; Fresno, CA; (4); Science Clb; Spanish Clb; SADD; Treas Soph Cls; Var L Tennis; High Hon Roll; Hon Roll; JETS Awd; CSF; City Schl Phys Ftnss Chmpnshp; UC Irvine; Biological Sci.

HUYNH, TRUNG V; Alisal HS; Salinas, CA; (2); High Hon Roll; Electronic.

HUYNH, TUONG; Oakland HS; Oakland, CA; (4); French Clb; Math Clb; Science Clb; SADD; CA ST U San Jose; Elec Engrng.

HUYNH, TUYEN B.; Sonora HS; Sonora, CA; (3); Am Leg Aux Girls St; Hosp Aide; Pep Clb; Science Clb; Spanish Clb; Pres Bus Profs of Am; Off Soph Cls; Pres Jr Cls; Cheerldng; Sftbl; Interact Dist 523 Govr; CSF Pres; UC Davis.

HUYNH, VAN T; Don Antonio Lugo HS; Chino Hills, CA; (2); 6/850; Teachers Aide; Cit Awd; CSF; Keywanettes; UCLA; Pediatrician.

HUYNH, VIET H; Mark Keppel HS; Monterey Park, CA; (3); Church Choir; Swmmng; Tennis; Wt Lftg; Hon Roll; Prfct Atten Awd; UC Irvine; Med.

HUYNH, XINH X; Lowell HS; San Francisco, CA; (2); Chess Clb; Teachers Aide; Orch; Jr NHS.

HUYNH, XUAN; Stagg HS; Stockton, CA; (2); Math Clb; Science Clb; School Musical; Bsktbl; Tennis; Vllybl; Hon Roll.

HUYNH, YUNG J; Downey HS; Downey, CA; (3); French Clb; Key Clb; Math Clb; Science Clb; SADD; Var Co-Capt Swmmng; Hon Roll; Vsty Water Polo.

HUYSER, SHANNON A; Hesperia HS; Hesperia, CA; (2); Drama Clb; Ski Clb; School Play; Drama; Actress.

HWANG, CHIAO; Mojave HS; Mojave, CA; (2); Math Tm; Mgr(s); Hon Roll; Prfct Atten Awd; CSF.

HWANG, CHRISTINA K; San Dieguito HS; Encinitas, CA; (2); Church Yth Grp; French Clb; Church Choir; Orch; JV Tennis; Cit Awd; High Hon Roll; Hon Roll; Prfct Atten Awd; Pres Acad Fit Awd; Amer Chem Soc Cmptn, Math Dept Awd; Golden St Exam Geom High Hnrs; Natl Frnch Cmptn; Cert Of Achvt; CSF.

HWANG, DAVID S; Whitney HS; Cerritos, CA; (3); Sec French Clb; JA; Key Clb; Latin Clb; Band; Mrchg Band; Orch; Nwsp; Score Keeper; Hon Roll; CSF; City Wide Essay Writing Cont 3rd Pl; Natl Frnch Test 10th Pl CA.

HWANG, EDDIE YUNG C; Mark Keppel HS; Monterey Park, CA; (3); UT Austin; Bus Admin.

HWANG, ELLA; Don Antonio Lugo HS; Chino, CA; (2); Prfct Atten Awd; Golden Conquest Awd Frnch; CSF; Bus.

HWANG, HUNTZ H; Cupertino HS; Cupertino, CA; (2); 33/276; FBLA; German Clb; Rptr Nwsp; Rptr Lit Mag; JV Bsktbl; Var Tennis; Cit Awd; Hon Roll; Prfct Atten Awd; Rotary Awd; Interace Club; Comp Engrng.

HWANG, LAURA; Ventura HS; Ventura, CA; (4); 53/410; Bus Profs of Am; Spanish Clb; Yrbk; JV Var Tennis; High Hon Roll; Hon Roll; NHS; MVP Tnns; CA ST U Long Beach; Bus.

HWANG, LIAN C; Mira Mesa HS; San Diego, CA; (3); 32/777; French Clb; FBLA; Library Aide; Model UN; Cit Awd; Hon Roll; Lion Awd; Pres Acad Fit Awd; 3rd Pl Sci & Engrng Fair; SDSU; Acctng.

HWANG, MARIA C; Alverno HS; Arcadia, CA; (3); 7/65; Cmnty Wkr; VP Model UN; Science Clb; Variety Show; Rptr Nwsp; Off Jr Cls; Off Sr Cls; JV Var Mgr(s); Hon Roll; NHS; Stanford; Engl Educ.

HWANG, SALLY I; George Washington HS; San Francisco, CA; (2); Key Clb; ROTC; Color Guard; Drill Tm; Off Frsh Cls; Hon Roll; 1s Pl All City Individual Drill Down 2 Consecutive Yrs; Superior Jr Cadet Decrtn Award 2 Cnsctv Yrs; San Francisco ST U; Mlty Nrs.

HWANG, SUSAN K; Palm Springs HS; Palm Springs, CA; (3); Church Yth Grp; Debate Tm; Chorus; Sec Treas Jr Cls; Sec Treas Sr Cls; Var Cheerldng; Cit Awd; Hon Roll; Prfct Atten Awd; UCSD; Med.

HWANG, SUSIE BIN-SU; Ramona Convent Secondary Schl; Montebello, CA; (3); 1/97; Hosp Aide; Model UN; Ed Lit Mag; Sec Stu Cncl; Var Swmmng; Lion Awd; NHS; Art Clb; GAA; Letterman Clb; Harvard-Radcliffe Summer Pgm In Sci Schlrshp; HOBY Natl Ambssdr; Chem.

HWANG, TIM; John Burroughs HS; Burbank, CA; (2); Church Yth Grp; Band; Mrchg Band; Ed Nwsp; Ed Yrbk; Lit Mag; Off Chess Clb; Hon Roll; UCSB; Engrng.

HWANG, VIVIAN; Mills HS; Millbrae, CA; (4); Teachers Aide; Bank Of Amer Art Awd 90; Viking Acad Achvt Awd 88-90; San Jose ST U; Grphc Dsgn.

HWEE, CINDY; San Gabriel HS; Rosemead, CA; (1); Treas Chess Clb; JV Swmmng; JV Tennis; Hon Roll; Prfct Atten Awd; Courtsy Clb; CSF; UCLA; Med.

HWEE, CINDY L; Abraham Lincoln HS; San Francisco, CA; (2); Library Aide; Teachers Aide; Hon Roll; San Francisco ST U.

HYARE, TAJINDER; Fred C Beyer HS; Modesto, CA; (4); 10/520; French Clb; FBLA; Science Clb; SADD; Teachers Aide; Cit Awd; High Hon Roll; Hon Roll; NHS; Prfct Atten Awd; CA Schlrshp Fed; Patriot Mdl Oh Hnr In Sci; Soroptimist Clb; UCD; Pharmacy.

HYATT, CAROL; Artesia HS; Lakewood, CA; (3); Church Yth Grp; Cmnty Wkr; Dance Clb; Library Aide; Office Aide; Teachers Aide; Color Guard; Hon Roll; Libry Page Cnty L A; History.

HYATT, MELISSA A; Birmingham HS; Encino, CA; (3); Church Yth Grp; Dance Clb; Drama Clb; French Clb; Temple Yth Grp; Stu Cncl; Hon Roll; Opt Clb Awd; CSF.

HYCHONG, STEVE; Long Beach Polytechnic HS; Long Beach, CA; (3); 1/826; Pres Key Clb; Math Tm; Pres Science Clb; Stu Cncl; Var Wrstlng; Lion Awd; Ntl Merit SF; Val; CSF; Natl Hnr Soc VP; 4.0 Club; 700 Club; MIT; Engrng.

HYDE, MARIAH L; Los Alamitos HS; Anaheim, CA; (3); Church Yth Grp; Drama Clb; Thesps; School Musical; School Play; Variety Show; Stu Cncl; High Hon Roll; HOBY Schlrshp; CA U; Lbrl Arts.

HYDE, REBEKAH ANN; Lassen HS; Susanville, CA; (4); 3/166; Band; JV Var Fld Hcky; JV Trk; Bausch & Lomb Sci Awd; Elks Awd; High Hon Roll; Pres Acad Fit Awd; Ski Clb; School Play; Sch Site Cncl Stu Rep; CSF; Tandy Corp Schlr; CA ST U Chico; Bus Admin.

HYDE, TINA C; Bloomington HS; Bloomington, CA; (2); Church Yth Grp; High Hon Roll.

HYDER, MELANIE L; Cajon HS; San Bernardino, CA; (1); 24/873; Ed Lit Mag; High Hon Roll; Recognition For Engl Schlrshp; Interior Dsgn.

HYLAND, JOANNA; Mercy HS; San Francisco, CA; (3); GAA; Pep Clb; Varsity Clb; Drill Tm; Cheerldng; Pom Pon; Hon Roll; Mst Outstndng Chrldr.

HYMAN, DANIEL; Claremont HS; Claremont, CA; (4); 52/382; Church Yth Grp; Pres Computer Clb; Math Clb; Math Tm; JV Golf; Var Wt Lftg; JETS Awd; Ntl Merit Ltr; Harvey Mudd Coll; Robotics Engr.

HYMAN, ROBERT; Madera HS; Madera, CA; (2); 15/900; 4-H; Ski Clb; Phtg Yrbk; Vllybl; High Hon Roll; Hon Roll; Pepperdine; Lawyr.

HYON, IN; Arlington HS; Riverside, CA; (4); 2/330; Cmnty Wkr; Quiz Bowl; High Hon Roll; Lion Awd; Opt Clb Awd; Pres Acad Fit Awd; Rotary Awd; Val; Mck Trl; Harvey Mudd Coll; Engrng.

HYRES, WILLIAM FREDERIK; Enterprise HS; Redding, CA; (4); 20/300; Chess Clb; Church Yth Grp; Dance Clb; Drama Clb; Math Clb; Math Tm; Mu Alpha Theta; Speech Tm; Thesps; Varsity Clb; Rep CA Frnch Bicentennial Rvltn; Native Sons Spch Cntst Wnnr; Wnnr Of Vars Marathons; San Francisco ST U; Antrplgy.

HYSELL, DENA N; Bonita Vista HS; Bonita, CA; (1); Church Yth Grp; Cmnty Wkr; Rptr Nwsp; Ed Yrbk; Stu Cncl; JV Crs Cntry; JV Socr; JV Trk; High Hon Roll; Optimist Speech Awd; Golden ST Exam Algbr High Hnrs; Law.

HYSELL, DEREK N; Bonita Vista HS; Bonita, CA; (3); Am Leg Boys St; Church Yth Grp; Quiz Bowl; Scholastic Bowl; Ed Yrbk; L Var Crs Cntry; JV Wrstlng; High Hon Roll; Ntl Merit SF; Pres Acad Fit Awd; Freedoms Fndtn; Intl Frndshp Cmmssn Sistr Cts Exchng Stu Mexico; Med.

HYSON, CHAD E; Etiwanda HS; Alta Loma, CA; (2); JA; Ski Clb; Teachers Aide; Tennis; Cit Awd; High Hon Roll; Hon Roll; Stanford; Bus.

HYUN, JOHN S; Rosemead HS; Rosemead, CA; (3); Computer Clb; Science Clb; Prfct Atten Awd; CSF; Prncpls Hnr Roll; Cmptr Sci.

HYUN, JOONHO; Homestead HS; Los Altos, CA; (3); Art Clb; Church Yth Grp; French Clb; Math Tm; Service Clb; SADD; Church Choir; JV Crs Cntry; L Var Trk; L Var Wrstlng; Chrch Yth Grp Ldr; Music; U CA; Bio.

IACCINO, CARY T; Saint Genevieve HS; Sepulveda, CA; (3); French Clb; Letterman Clb; Rptr Yrbk; Var Bsbl; Var Capt Ftbl; Var Socr; High Hon Roll; NEDT Awd; Outstndng Achvt Art; Bsbl Schl Athl Awd; Bus.

IANNACONE, ERIC A; Poway HS; San Diego, CA; (3); Var Ftbl; Wrkd Restaurant Bus; U Of San Diego.

IBA, ELIZABETH J; Santa Monica HS; Santa Monica, CA; (2); Church Yth Grp; Dance Clb; Pep Clb; Hon Roll; Stat Bsbl; Var Cheerldng; Score Keeper; Model Stu Awd; Congrsnl Yth Ldrshp Cncl; Spec Ed.

IBACH, ANGELA M; Elk Grove HS; Elk Grove, CA; (2); 98/531; Church Yth Grp; Pep Clb; SADD; Band; Color Guard; Mrchg Band; Pep Band; Hon Roll; Sacramento ST U; Law.

IBANEZ, JEANKAY; Los Altos HS; Hacienda Hgts, CA; (2); GAA; Socr; Trk; Hon Roll; Outstndng Stu; Prncpls Hnr Roll; Drama.

IBANEZ, PATRICIA; Fontana HS; Fontana, CA; (3); Computer Clb; Office Aide; SADD; Teachers Aide; Acpl Chr; Chorus; Church Choir; Drill Tm; Mrchg Band; Bsktbl; Ladies Glee Pres; Slvr Mdls 3.8 GPA 2 Yrs; Cynthias Beauty Acad; Csmtlgst.

IBARRA, ALEJANDRO A; Watsonville HS; Watsonville, CA; (4); 2/283; Church Yth Grp; Cmnty Wkr; Red Cross Aide; Ski Clb; Spanish Clb; Varsity Clb; Var L Ftbl; Var L Trk; Var Wt Lftg; Hon Roll; MESA; Prtnrshp Pgm; Cal Poly San Luis Obispo; Arch.

IBARRA, ANDREW; Clovis HS; Fresno, CA; (3); Ftbl; Fresno ST; Cartoonst.

IBARRA, ANGEL; Ernest Righetti HS; Guadalupe, CA; (1); Boy Scts; Church Yth Grp; Temple Yth Grp; Band; Church Choir; Intrml Bsbl; Var Crs Cntry; JV Trk; Cit Awd; Prfct Atten Awd; Marimba Band Club; ASB Cnvtn; Hancock JC; Zoologist.

IBARRA, DALILA E; Anaheim HS; Anaheim, CA; (3); Church Yth Grp; Drama Clb; School Musical; School Play; Variety Show; Mgr(s); Score Keeper; Socr; Hon Roll; NHS; Walk America 3 Yrs; Obst.

IBARRA, ESTHER; San Gabriel Mission HS; Los Angeles, CA; (3); 19/117; Church Yth Grp; GAA; Pep Clb; Spanish Clb; Teachers Aide; Pres Sr Cls; Vllybl; Hon Roll; NHS; Prfct Atten Awd; Mdlln Awd Wnnr Bus; YMCA Vllybl & Bsktbl; Retreat Ldr; Oral Hygn.

IBARRA, GLENN J; Balboa HS; San Francisco, CA; (3); Var Hon Roll; CSF; Bodybuilding; San Francisco ST U; Accntng.

IBARRA, GRISELDA; Crawford HS; San Diego, CA; (2); Chorus; Math.

IBARRA, HORACIO; Tranquility Union HS; Cantua Creek, CA; (1); JV Bsktbl; JV Ftbl; MECHA Clb; Cmnty Clb CYC; Bus-Stock Broker; Los Angeles U; Bus.

IBARRA, J JUAN; W C Overfelt HS; San Jose, CA; (3); Socr; Swmmng; Comp.

IBARRA, JESSE; Warren HS; Downey, CA; (3); German Clb; Hon Roll; CSF; Gldn St Exam Rec Alg & Hnrs Geomtry; Gldn Bear Awd Cmptrs; USAF ROTC; Engr.

IBARRA, JUAN G; Sequoia HS; Menlo Park, CA; (3); 2/363; Chess Clb; Band; Chorus; Mrchg Band; School Musical; Phtg Nwsp; Rptr Yrbk; Cit Awd; High Hon Roll; Hon Roll; MESA; CSF; Earthwatch Schlrshp; Stanford; Physician.

IBARRA, LORRAINE; Don Antonio Lugo HS; Chino, CA; (3); VP Pep Clb; Q&S; Church Choir; Phtg Nwsp; Ed Yrbk; Off Frsh Cls; Off Soph Cls; Rep Jr Cls; Var Capt Cheerldng; Capt Powder Puff Ftbl; Friday Night Live; CA Schlrshp Fed; ASB; U Of Southern CA; TV Brdcstng.

IBARRA, LUIS A; Castle Park HS; Chula Vista, CA; (3); 50/385; Pres Church Yth Grp; Treas Dance Clb; SADD; Ed Lit Mag; Stu Cncl; JV Socr; Var Swmmng; Civil Air Patrol 2 Yr Svc Hnr; Cadet Of Yr Hnr 88; Model Rocketry Awd; Civil Air Patrol Badge; Scl Sci.

IBARRA, MICHAEL A; Montebello HS; Montebello, CA; (1); Chorus; School Musical; Bsbl; Ftbl; Prfct Atten Awd; USC; Bus.

IBARRA, RACHEL A; Whitcomb HS; Glendora, CA; (2); JV Var Fld Hcky; Hon Roll; Prfct Atten Awd; Teen-Mother Pgm.

IBARRA, VERONICA; Walnut HS; Walnut, CA; (2); Hon Roll; USC; Lwyr.

IBBETSON, PATRICK K; Edison Computech HS; Fresno, CA; (1); JV Water Polo; Pilot.

IBRAHIM, LAILA; Bloomington HS; Bloomington, CA; (1); Church Yth Grp; Spcl Hnrs 2nd Awd Prncpls Hnr Roll; Teacher.

IBRAHIM, SHREEN; East Union HS; Manteca, CA; (2); 19/400; Hon Roll; Prfct Atten Awd; CSF; CPA.

IBRAHIM, YAHYA; Los Alamitos HS; Los Alamitos, CA; (3); Church Yth Grp; Cmnty Wkr; Letterman Clb; Varsity Clb; Socr; Trk; Cit Awd; High Hon Roll; UCLA; Med.

ICAMEN, RAMON J; L A Lutheran HS; Los Angeles, CA; (2); Letterman Clb; Rep Soph Cls; Var L Bsbl; Var L Crs Cntry; UC Davis; Elctrnc Engr.

ICARANGAL, LILY; Fairfield HS; Suisun City, CA; (3); Rep Stu Cncl; Pom Pon; Hon Roll; UCLA; Bus.

ICARDO, ADAM; Garces Memorial HS; Bakersfield, CA; (2); 18/175; Cmnty Wkr; Key Clb; Letterman Clb; Ski Clb; School Play; Treas Frsh Cls; Treas Jr Cls; L Var Socr; JV L Trk; High Hon Roll; HOBY Ldrshp Awd; People Bound For Trvl; Dplmtc Svc.

ICEDO, DANNY; Riverbank HS; Riverbank, CA; (2); Rep Soph Cls; JV Ftbl; Sac ST U; Med.

ICENAGLE, NNNKIM; Northview HS; Covina, CA; (3); Pres Art Clb; Pep Clb; Teachers Aide; Rptr Yrbk; Bsktbl; JV Var Cheerldng; Comm Of Spcl Events ASB; Girls League 2 Yrs; Art.

ICHIHO, BYRON M; C K Mc Clatchy HS; Sacramento, CA; (3); 139/390; Church Yth Grp; Cmnty Wkr; Teachers Aide; L Var Bsktbl; Asian Club.

ICHIYAMA, JODI; Bishop Montgomery HS; Torrance, CA; (3); Office Aide; Pep Clb; Ski Clb; SADD; Drill Tm; Var L Cheerldng; UCLA; Sprts Med.

ICHO, JEANNE A; Orosi HS; Orosi, CA; (3); Socr; Hon Roll; Bus.

IEST, MARIE L; Fresno Christian HS; Madera, CA; (1); Cit Awd; Hon Roll.

IGANO, GALE H; Arroyo HS; San Lorenzo, CA; (3); Dance Clb; Bsktbl; UC Davis; Chem Engrng.

IGARASHI, CARY R; Saddleback HS; Santa Ana, CA; (3); French Clb; High Hon Roll.

IGARTVA, PHYLLIS; Options For Youth HS; Los Angeles, CA; (2); Hon Roll; Law.

IGLESIAS, ALBERTO J; El Camino HS; Sacramento, CA; (3); 68/366; Boy Scts; Chess Clb; Church Yth Grp; Cmnty Wkr; 4-H; Spanish Clb; Teachers Aide; Varsity Clb; JV Socr; Var Swmmng; Early Out Reach Pgm; JASRAP; MESA; Friday Night Live; Wildrnss Clb; Span.

IGLESIAS, ELIZABETH; Notre Dame Academy HS; Culver City, CA; (3); Drama Clb; Girl Scts; Pep Clb; Spanish Clb; Chorus; School Musical; Co-Capt Cheerldng; Cit Awd; Hon Roll; NHS; HOPE Clb; Camous Ministry; Georgetown U; Intl Rltns.

IGLESIAS, TIRSO; Bishop Amat HS; San Gabriel, CA; (3); 105/399; Letterman Clb; Varsity Clb; Ftbl; Hon Roll; NHS; U Of CA Los Angeles; Sprt Thrp.

IGNACIO, ANNA MARIE M; Encinal HS; Alameda, CA; (4); 23/209; FBLA; VP Spanish Clb; Hon Roll; Asian Clb; Badmntn Vrsty; San Diego ST; Dentistry.

IGNACIO, JENNIFER B; South San Francisco HS; South San Francis, CA; (2); High Hon Roll; CSF.

IGNACIO, MELANIE; South San Francisco HS; South San Francis, CA; (2); Cmnty Wkr; FBLA; Spanish Clb; Ed Nwsp; Pres Frsh Cls; Pres Soph Cls; Pres Jr Cls; Var Tennis; HOBY; Jackie Speier Yth Advsry & Dist Stu Advsry Commtte Reps.

IGNACIO, SAMARAH R; Poly HS; Riverside, CA; (2); Church Yth Grp; Socr; Hon Roll; Girls League; Psych.

IGNACIO, SHERMAN C; Hiram Johnson HS; Sacramento, CA; (3); 47/116; Vllybl; Prfct Atten Awd; CA ST U; Cvl Engr.

IGNACIO, VICTOR J; Davis SR HS; Davis, CA; (3); 78/1200; FFA; Var Bsktbl; Var Ftbl; Var Socr; Wt Lftg; High Hon Roll; CSF; Yth Cncl.

IKEDA, KAOLI R; North Saunas HS; Salinas, CA; (3); Intnl Clb; Off Key Clb; Science Clb; Teachers Aide; Rptr Yrbk; Var Tennis; JV Trk; High Hon Roll; Rotary Awd; Lfs Honors Society Clb Vp; Advanced Placement Clb Vp; Physics Clb; Aero; Engnrng.

IKEDA, TAKAKO; Loara HS; Anaheim, CA; (2); JA; Key Clb; JV Cheerldng; Var Tennis; Hon Roll; CSF.

IKNADOSSIAN, HERMINE; Pasadena HS; Pasadena, CA; (2); Church Yth Grp; Drama Clb; School Musical; Vllybl; Hon Roll; CA Schlrshp Fed; Acad Dcthln; Armnn Clb; Pasadena City Coll; Psych.

ILAGAN, ALAN E; Lowell HS; San Francisco, CA; (3); Office Aide; ROTC; Teachers Aide; Color Guard; Hon Roll; Med.

ILALIO, SUSANA E; Paramount HS; Paramount, CA; (1); Church Yth Grp; Computer Clb; Chorus; Church Choir; Cit Awd; Hon Roll; Law.

ILANO, LIEZZA P; Eagle Rock HS; Los Angeles, CA; (2); Drama Clb; Key Clb; Library Aide; Office Aide; Mgr(s); Peer Cnslr; Envrnmntl Awarnss Clb Offcr; UCLA; Bus Admin.

ILICH, MARIA O; Immaculate Heart HS; Los Angeles, CA; (3); Aud/Vis; Church Yth Grp; Drama Clb; School Play; People/People Stu Ambssdr; Tnns.

ILL, BRIAN A; San Gorgonio HS; Highland, CA; (4); Art Clb; Aud/Vis; Church Yth Grp; Library Aide; Cit Awd; Hon Roll; Prfct Atten Awd; San Bernardino Tchrs Assn Hnrs & Cal St U Hispnc Stu Schlrshps; CSU Sa Bernardino; Meteorlgy.

ILNAY, KIMBERLY R; Casa Roble Fundamental HS; Citrus Heights, CA; (2); 2/485; Church Yth Grp; Band; JV Bsktbl; JV Vllybl; Cit Awd; High Hon Roll; NHS; Multiple Involvement Awd; Outstndng Engl Stu; Friday Night Live; Medcl.

ILOG, BIEN B; Grace Davis HS; Modesto, CA; (3); AFS; Church Yth Grp; Dance Clb; French Clb; Pep Clb; SADD; Band; Church Choir; Cheerldng; Pom Pon; Med.

IM, EDWARD; Cypress HS; Cypress, CA; (4); Am Leg Boys St; Debate Tm; Math Tm; NFL; Speech Tm; Band; Church Choir; Orch; Bsktbl; High Hon Roll; Chrch Yth Grp Pres & Genl Secy; All Sthrn CA Hnr Band; Harvard Coll; Physics.

IM, JOSEPH K; Glen A Wilson HS; Hacienda Hts, CA; (2); Treas Computer Clb; Band; Mrchg Band; Bsktbl; Hon Roll; Acad Exclnc Dist Schlr GPA 3.80-4.00; Cert Awd Exclnc Span I; Acad Exclnc Awd Alg With Hnrs.

IM, SOKOAN; John F Kennedy HS; Buena Park, CA; (2); Vllybl; USC; Ed.

IM, SOO; Hawthorne HS; Torrance, CA; (4); 1/500; Am Leg Aux Girls St; Hosp Aide; Pres Service Clb; Ed Yrbk; Kiwanis Awd; Pres Acad Fit Awd; Rotary Awd; Val; CSF Secy; MIT; Arch.

IM, SOO H; West HS; Torrance, CA; (4); 16/400; Church Yth Grp; Cmnty Wkr; FBLA; Hosp Aide; Intnl Clb; Service Clb; Spanish Clb; Teachers Aide; Church Choir; Ed Yrbk; Jrnlsm Cntst 8th Pl; 3rd Pl PTSA Wrtng Cntst; Gld Mdl Essy Spch; Engl Achvmnt Awds; UC Berkeley; Psych.

IMAHATA, JEANNETTE; Orangewood Acad; Anaheim, CA; (1); Teachers Aide; Chorus; School Musical; VP Frsh Cls; Bsbl; Ftbl; Sftbl; Vllybl; Sportsmanship Awd; Girls Clb; Acad Achvt Awd; La Sierra; Phy.

IMAI, ANN R; Rosemead HS; Rosemead, CA; (4); 13/376; Sec Church Yth Grp; Office Aide; Service Clb; JV Crs Cntry; Var Trk; High Hon Roll; Prfct Atten Awd; Pres Acad Fit Awd; Keywanettes Svc Clb; CSF; NYU; Bus.

IMAI, KERI E; Los Amigos HS; Fountain Valley, CA; (3); Church Yth Grp; Pep Clb; Science Clb; L Var Cheerldng; Gym; Vllybl; Hon Roll; Outstndng Gymnst Awd #1 St Chmpn Blance Bm 86; Humntrn Clb.

IMAI, MIKIKO; La Habra HS; Whittier, CA; (2); Church Yth Grp; Cmnty Wkr; Treas FBLA; Sec German Clb; Var Swmmng; Var Tennis; Cit Awd; High Hon Roll; Var Prfct Atten Awd; Stu Leag.

IMAIZUMI, KINYA; Arcadia HS; Arcadia, CA; (2); Boy Scts; Band; Hon Roll; Kyoto U Japan; Literature.

IMANI, SHADI; Ganesha HS; Diamond Bar, CA; (3); 1/265; Church Yth Grp; Cmnty Wkr; Sec Debate Tm; Treas French Clb; Pres Math Clb; Sec Speech Tm; Rep Stu Cncl; Bausch & Lomb Sci Awd; High Hon Roll; Prfct Atten Awd; Aerospace Engrng.

IMATOMI, NOREEN H; Bishop Montgomery HS; Gardena, CA; (3); Church Yth Grp; Key Clb; Band; Church Choir; Var JV Tennis; Hon Roll; 2nd Degree Brown Karate Belt; Jap Lang Cert.

IMBACH, TIMOTHY P; Cloverdale HS; Cloverdale, CA; (2); Church Yth Grp; Band; Mrchg Band; Stat Bsktbl; Cit Awd; Hon Roll; Prfct Atten Awd; Music.

IMES, BRITT PATRICK; Highland HS; Bakersfield, CA; (4); Cmnty Wkr; VP JA; Key Clb; Office Aide; Spanish Clb; Teachers Aide; Variety Show; Rep Frsh Cls; Rep Jr Cls; Intrml Ftbl; Mock Trial Atty & Witness; CSF; U CA Santa Cruz; Crmnl Jstc.

IMMEL, MARK; The Branson Schl; Mill Valley, CA; (4); Pres Chess Clb; Latin Clb; Math Tm; Quiz Bowl; Sec SADD; Chorus; Jazz Band; School Musical; School Play; Stage Crew; Awds Bio, Chem, Algb, Trig, Calc; Natl Latin Exam Gold Medl; Rensselaer Medl; Princeton Bk Awd.

IMMOOS JR, JAMES D; Seaside HS; Fort Ord, CA; (3); JV Var Bsbl; JV Var Ftbl; Hon Roll; Ntrl Hlprs Clb; MVP Bsbl 88-89; U Of TX; Tchng.

IMOTO, ERIC; Garfield HS; Monterey Park, CA; (3); Chess Clb; Church Yth Grp; Library Aide; Trk; JV Vllybl; Prfct Atten Awd; 2nd Deg Black Belt Kendo; Interact Club; CSF; Cal Poly-Pomona; Arch.

IMPERIO, CEALY JANE; Glendale Adventist Acad; Glendale, CA; (3); Church Yth Grp; Science Clb; Church Choir; School Play; Off Frsh Cls; Treas Soph Cls; Swmmng; Vllybl; Pathfinder Clb; Nrsng.

IN, SOTHY; Wilson HS; Long Beach, CA; (3); Pres Intnl Clb; Sec JA; Office Aide; Spanish Clb; Drill Tm; Rep Soph Cls; Rep Jr Cls; High Hon Roll; NHS; Opt Clb Awd; CSF FEC PRASATH Club; Asian Club; An-Nam Club; Home Ec Award; U Of Cal Irvine; General Doctor.

INAWAT, BRYAN JASON A; Glendale HS; Fontana, CA; (3); 44/1200; Art Clb; Boy Scts; Intnl Clb; Math Clb; Science Clb; Acpl Chr; School Play; Rptr Nwsp; Off Sr Cls; Stu Cncl; Elect Robotics.

INBODY, ASHLEY B; Torrey Pines HS; Del Mar, CA; (3); Church Yth Grp; Cmnty Wkr; GAA; Girl Scts; Key Clb; SADD; Teachers Aide; Varsity Clb; Yrbk; Stat Bsbl; Interior Dsgn.

INCE, EDWARD J; Mesa Verde HS; Citrus Heights, CA; (2); SADD; Cit Awd; Hon Roll; Prfct Atten Awd; Taekwondo Club; Friday Night Live.

INDA, SVEN E; Novato HS; Novato, CA; (1); Church Yth Grp; Key Clb; Band; Mrchg Band; Orch; Pep Band; High Hon Roll; CSF Assoc; Top Stu Engl Awd; Karate-6 Gold Medls-Orange Belt 2nd Deg.

INDYK, BEN; Edison HS; Huntington Beach, CA; (1); Boy Scts; Model UN; JV Wrstlng; Engrng.

INDYK, JUSTIN A; Edison HS; Huntington Beach, CA; (3); Boy Scts; JA; Key Clb; Model UN; Quiz Bowl; Spanish Clb; Band; Mrchg Band; Pep Band; High Hon Roll; Eagle Sct; Fluent In Span; Math.

INENO, PHILIP S; Torrance HS; Torrance, CA; (4); Church Yth Grp; Letterman Clb; Varsity Clb; Rep Frsh Cls; JV Tennis; VP Capt Wrstlng; Cit Awd; El Camino Coll; Grphc Dsgn.

ING, DAVID R; Gardena HS; Gardena, CA; (3); Service Clb; Capt Bsktbl; Cit Awd; Bwlg Clb; Japanese Clb; Gardena FOR Bsktbl.

ING, PEOU T; River City SR HS; W Sacramento, CA; (2); Cit Awd; High Hon Roll; Hon Roll; 9th Grade Straight A; Spec Coll Prep Class; Lawyer.

ING, SOMALY; Woodrow Wilson HS; Long Beach, CA; (4); Intnl Clb; Hon Roll; Jr NHS; NHS; CSF; Pres Acadmc Ftnss Awd 90; Chem Awd 89; SMART 89; CA ST U Long Beach; Nrsng.

INGALLS, INGRID L; Pacific HS; San Bernardino, CA; (1); Church Yth Grp; Library Aide; Office Aide; Spanish Clb; Teachers Aide; Cit Awd; Hon Roll; CA ST; Psych.

INGBRETSON, ERIKA L; Trabuco Hills HS; Hansville, WA; (2); 112/406; Band; Color Guard; Mrchg Band; Orch; School Musical; Saddleback Symphny Orch; Evergreen Coll; Music.

INGEL, KIM; Santa Monica HS; Santa Monica, CA; (3); FBLA; Var Capt Socr; Var Sftbl; Berkeley; Lgl.

INGERSOLL, JESSICA M; Colfax HS; Applegate, CA; (3); Ski Clb; Speech Tm; SADD; Bsbl; Bsktbl; Gym; Vllybl; Lion Awd; Ntl Merit Schol; Harvard Law Schl; Lawyer.

INGERSOLL, SHERRIE L; Mc Kinleyville HS; Mckinleyville, CA; (2); Church Yth Grp; French Clb; SADD; Church Choir; Vllybl; High Hon Roll; Coll Of The Redwoods; Day Care.

INGHAM, ALYSON L; Los Altos HS; Hacienda Hts, CA; (2); Church Yth Grp; Church Choir; Swing Chorus; Var L Crs Cntry; Var L Socr; Var L Trk; Hon Roll; Sierra Lge Hnrb Mntn Soccer; All Vly Lthr Lngr Awd Outstnd Frosh Crs Cnty Rnnr 90; Outstnd Sprntr Awd.

INGHAM, DEANNE K; Los Altos HS; Hacienda Hgts, CA; (3); Church Yth Grp; Science Clb; Chorus; Church Choir; Swing Chorus; Variety Show; Var L Socr; Hon Roll; Skirball Inst Essay Cont Hnbr Mntn; CSF; 2nd Tm All Leag Girls Vrsty Sccr.

INGLE JR, HARRIS; Benicia HS; Benicia, CA; (4); 6/243; Am Leg Boys St; Church Yth Grp; VP JA; Ed Yrbk; Rep Frsh Cls; Treas Soph Cls; JV L Trk; High Hon Roll; NHS; Ntl Merit Schol; Acad Decathlon; MMA Exam; U CA Berkeley; Math.

INGLIMA, BETSY; Thomas Downey HS; Modesto, CA; (1); Letterman Clb; Pep Clb; Ski Clb; Cheerldng; Pom Pon; Hon Roll; St Schlr; CSF; Inter-High Rep.

INGLIS, DANYELE A; Fresno HS; Fresno, CA; (3); #26 In Class; Band; Mrchg Band; Pep Band; Hon Roll.

INGRAM, BRENT; Leffingwell Christian HS; Lakewood, CA; (3); Var L Ftbl; Var L Wrstlng; Cit Awd; High Hon Roll; Hon Roll; Arrwhd Leg Champ Wrstlng 89; AAU Rgnl Frstyle Champ; Duke U; Bus.

INGRAM, JENNIFER; Woodrow Wilson HS; Long Beach, CA; (4); 1/800; Key Clb; Service Clb; Pres VP Stu Cncl; Var Cheerldng; Var Co-Capt Socr; Opt Clb Awd; Pres Acad Fit Awd; Val; Hmcmng Queen; DANCE; UC Berkeley.

INGRAM, TONY A; North HS; Glennville, CA; (2); 4-H; FFA; Hon Roll; Law Enfrcmnt.

INGVOLDSEN, KYLE E; Oroville HS; Oroville, CA; (4); 6/189; Letterman Clb; Math Clb; Ski Clb; SADD; Varsity Clb; Var Bsbl; JV Var Bsktbl; JV Var Ftbl; JV Var Golf; Var Tennis; CA ST U Chico; Elec Engrng.

INIBA, KATHERINE; Workman HS; West Covina, CA; (2); School Play; Variety Show; Cit Awd; High Hon Roll; Hon Roll; Prfct Atten Awd; Hnr Soc; Actress.

INIGO, ERIC T; Poway HS; San Diego, CA; (2); Cmnty Wkr; FBLA; Hosp Aide; Hon Roll; Cal Poly San Luis Obispo; Arch.

INIGUEZ, LUCERO; Indio HS; Indio, CA; (2); 164/551; Church Yth Grp; Computer Clb; Dance Clb; Color Guard; Nwsp; UCLA; Dance.

INIGUEZ, MARIA V; Fairfield HS; Fairfield, CA; (2); Band; Mrchg Band; Pep Band; High Hon Roll; Hon Roll; Music Prtcptn Awd 88-90; Outstndng Prfrmnc Flute Trio.

INKS, AMANDA C; Fairfield HS; Fairfield, CA; (3); Band; Mrchg Band; Hon Roll; City Spnsrd Gymnstc Tm; EP2; CO U; Marktng.

INKS, GROVER M; Bret Harte HS; Murphys, CA; (2); Math Clb; Math Tm; Ski Clb; JV Bsktbl; JV Ftbl; Golf; Trk; Hon Roll; Prof Athlt.

INMAN, BRENDA L; Seaside HS; Ft Ord, CA; (3); Church Yth Grp; Band; Drm Mjr(t); Mrchg Band; Orch; Mgr(s); High Hon Roll; Hon Roll; Jr NHS; Prfct Atten Awd; Ntrl Hlprs Peer Cnslr 87-90; Chrch Parish Cncl 89; Biola U; Elem Ed.

INMAN, JOSHUA; Porterville HS; Porterville, CA; (3); JV Ftbl; JV Var Socr; High Hon Roll; Opt Clb Awd; Camp Royal Rotary Ldrshp Camp; Boys St Fnlst; Humboldt; Forestry.

INMAN, SHERRI D; John W North HS; Riverside, CA; (3); Library Aide; Teachers Aide; Yrbk; JV Mgr(s); Hon Roll; Pres Acad Fit Awd; PAWS; Jr Cls Float Cmmtte; Swm Tm Mgr; Child Care.

INMAN, TARA F; Mira Mesa HS; San Diego, CA; (3); Debate Tm; Treas VP French Clb; NFL; Quiz Bowl; Treas Speech Tm; SADD; Orch; High Hon Roll; Lion Awd; Ntl Merit Ltr; Intl Poltcl Sci.

INNES, LAURA M; Thousand Oaks HS; Thousand Oaks, CA; (3); Intnl Clb; Peer Cnslr; Psych.

INONG, MAYWELL LEONES; Edison HS; Stockton, CA; (2); Sec Church Yth Grp; Science Clb; SADD; Church Choir; High Hon Roll; Hon Roll; NHS; Play Piano; Hnrs In Gldn ST Exmntn For Gmtry; Sun Schl Chrch Tchr; Stanford U; Pdtrcn.

INOUE, SUMIE; Montgomery HS; Santa Rosa, CA; (3); 24/430; Church Yth Grp; English Clb; Varsity Clb; Band; Drill Tm; Mrchg Band; Pep Band; Cheerldng; Var Tennis; High Hon Roll; Badminton Team; Fri Night Live; U Of CA Davis; Intl Bus.

INOUYE, KELLEY; John F Kennedy HS; Buena Park, CA; (4); Church Yth Grp; Cmnty Wkr; Computer Clb; FBLA; VP Pres Key Clb; Office Aide; Varsity Clb; JV Var Tennis; High Hon Roll; Pres Advncd Plcmnt Clb; Undrgrad Awd Phy Ed; UCLA; Chem.

INPRASUETH, KHAMSAN; Richmond HS; San Pablo, CA; (3); Church Yth Grp; Cmnty Wkr; GAA; Intnl Clb; Teachers Aide; Thesps; Varsity Clb; Band; Church Choir; Nwsp; Hayward; Nrsng.

INSALACO, JASON M; Loyola HS; Glendale, CA; (2); German Clb; JV Swmmng; Hon Roll; German Achvt Awd; Poltcl Soc; Ivy Leag.

INSCO, MARK W; Analy HS; Sebastopol, CA; (3); 3/250; Church Yth Grp; Band; Mrchg Band; Var Bsbl; High Hon Roll.

INSELMAN, BRIAN M; Seaside HS; Ft Ord, CA; (4); 15/280; Ski Clb; Ed Yrbk; JV Bsbl; Capt L Ftbl; JV Trk; Intrml Wt Lftg; High Hon Roll; Hon Roll; NHS; Islanders Clb; Schlr/Athlete; UC, Davis.

INSOGNA, ALEXANDRA M; Calistoga HS; Calistoga, CA; (2); 3/50; Church Yth Grp; Cmnty Wkr; Pres Sec Girl Scts; Pres Band; School Play; Sec Stu Cncl; Capt Bsktbl; Co-Capt Vllybl; Pres Acad Fit Awd; Jr Stsmn Of Amer Chaptr Pres.

INTERIANO, FELIX R; Sierra Vista HS; Baldwin Park, CA; (3); Var L Socr; Hon Roll; Engr.

INTHAVONG, LADDAVONE; Orestimba HS; Newman, CA; (3); Stanislaus County; Nurse.

INWIYA, ADRIAN H; Turlock HS; Turlock, CA; (2); Church Yth Grp; Library Aide; Office Aide; Teachers Aide; School Play; Cit Awd; Hon Roll; Prfct Atten Awd; U CA Berkeley; Crmnl Atty.

INWOOD, EMILY M; Fort Bragg HS; Fort Bragg, CA; (2); 2/160; Church Yth Grp; Cmnty Wkr; Rptr Nwsp; Rep Frsh Cls; Rep Soph Cls; Rep Jr Cls; Rep Stu Cncl; Stat Bsktbl; Swmmng; Var Tennis; Cty Spelling Bee 88 & 89; Acad Achvt Certs; Literary Essay 1st Pl; Med.

INZER, KENDRA C; R A Millikan HS; San Pedro, CA; (2); Church Yth Grp; Drama Clb; Sftbl; Vllybl; Hon Roll; Jr Mem Cabrillo Beache Ycht Clb; Attnd SHARP; Cast Mem Of The Glory Of Chrstms Crystal Cath Church; Pre Law.

IOANNOU, PHOPHI A; Bonita HS; La Verne, CA; (3); Bus Profs of Am; Church Yth Grp; Dance Clb; French Clb; FBLA; Girl Scts; Office Aide; Hon Roll; Prfct Atten Awd; Irvine U; Obstetrician.

IOBBI, FABIAN; Redlands HS; Redlands, CA; (3); Debate Tm; Spanish Clb; JV Swmmng; Engrng.

IONESCU-ZANETTI, CRISTIAN; Homestead HS; Sunnyvale, CA; (2); Computer Clb; Math Clb; U CA Santa Barbara Physcs Cntst; Physcs.

IONOFF, KATHERINE N; Notre Dame HS; San Mateo, CA; (2); Church Yth Grp; Debate Tm; Chorus; Church Choir; Hon Roll; Tri M Musc Hnrs Society; Mixd Boys, Girls Chr; Russn Schl; Envrnmnt Clb; Engl.

IP, ALLIS W; Burlingame HS; Burlingame, CA; (2); Math Clb; Rep Stu Cncl; Stat Bsktbl; Mgr(s); Score Keeper; JV Tennis; Var Trk; High Hon Roll; CA Explorer Search & Rescue; Gldn St Exam Alg Rcgntn; Stanford Med Sch; Med.

IP, LESTER S; Servite HS; Monterey Park, CA; (2); NEDT Awd; Cert Achvt For Outstndng Acad Excllnc; CSF; JR Statesmen Of Amer; Stanford U; Engrng.

IP, STEPHANIE Y; John Swett HS; Hercules, CA; (2); Science Clb; Band; Mrchg Band; Rep Soph Cls; Rep Jr Cls; Var Cheerldng; Swmmng; Hon Roll; Chrldng Sargnt Arms; Cncrt Band; Art.

IPPOLITI, JULIE; Hillcrest Christian HS; Granada Hills, CA; (1); Church Yth Grp; Ed Yrbk; Pres Stu Cncl; Var Cheerldng; Trk; Var Vllybl; Hon Roll; Val; CSUN; Med.

IPSON, ANDY C; Montclair HS; Montclair, CA; (2); 4/499; JV Ftbl; Var Mgr(s); Var Trk; Var Wt Lftg; High Hon Roll; Hon Roll; Prfct Atten Awd; Golden St Exam Algebra Hnrs 89; Bio, Engl & Spnsh Awds; GATE & Schlrshp Clbs; U CA; Bus.

IRA, JENNIFER; Del Campo HS; Carmichael, CA; (3); Church Yth Grp; Ed Yrbk; Swmmng; Chrch Choir; Intl Jrnlsm.

IRA, JOY L; California HS; San Ramon, CA; (4); Church Yth Grp; Teachers Aide; JV Var Trk; Cmmnty Vlntr; Church Yth Grp Ldr Pres & VP; Diablo Valley Coll; Bus.

IRACI, MARIA C; Academy Of Our Lady Of Peace; San Diego, CA; (1); Church Yth Grp; Key Clb; Variety Show; Hon Roll; Clothing Designer.

IRANI, HOOMAN M; Canoga Park HS; Reseda, CA; (3); Var Vllybl; Var Wrstlng; Ntl Merit Ltr; CA Schlrshp Fed; U CA Santa Barbara.

IRATO, CAPUCINE; Santa Barbara HS; Santa Barbara, CA; (3); 130/472; JV Var Vllybl; Hon Roll; Santa Barbara Yth Vllybl Assoc-Soph & Jr Yr; Channel Coast Vllybl Clb-Frshmn Yr; Phys Thrpy.

IRAVANI, LEILA M; Villa Park HS; Villa Park, CA; (3); French Clb; Key Clb; High Hon Roll; Jr NHS; NHS; Prfct Atten Awd; Pres Acad Fit Awd; Med.

IRBY, TANISHA L; Loretto HS; Citrus Heights, CA; (4); 12/52; Cmnty Wkr; Debate Tm; Pres JA; Drill Tm; VP Stu Cncl; Sftbl; High Hon Roll; Hon Roll; Pres Acad Fit Awd; Griffin & Veary Lee Holmes Family Scholarship; Sonoma St U; Criminal Just.

IRELAND, JENNIFER; Santa Teresa HS; San Jose, CA; (3); French Clb; Girl Scts; Pep Clb; Science Clb; SADD; Yrbk; Socr; Trk; NHS; Early Chldhd Occup Awd Of Excllnc; Acad Decthln Spprt Team; Psych.

IRELAND, JENNIFER M; Cajon HS; San Bernardino, CA; (3); Outstndng Occuptnl Training Stu Awd; Schlstc Awds-Math/Bio/Restaurant Training; Kids Against Crime; Child Care.

IRFAN, NASEER A; Phillip & Sala Burton Academic HS; San Francisco, CA; (3); Dance Clb; Spanish Clb; Hon Roll; San Francisco ST U; Comp Sci.

IRIAS, DORAMANDA; Our Lady Loretto-Bishop Conaty HS; Los Angeles, CA; (4); Cmnty Wkr; Dance Clb; Pres FBLA; Intnl Clb; Office Aide; Chorus; Drill Tm; School Musical; Phtg Yrbk; Cit Awd; Care Unit Clb; Ambssdrs Clb; Campus Ministry; U Of CA-BERKELEY; Bus Admin.

IRIBARREN, CANDY A; Bakersfield HS; Lebec, CA; (2); JV Trk; JV Vllybl; Hon Roll; UCLA; Doctor.

IRION, NICOLE CHRISTINE; Paraclete HS; Lancaster, CA; (4); Church Yth Grp; Cmnty Wkr; Hosp Aide; JA; Quiz Bowl; Hon Roll; Z Club; Mission Club; CSF; Antelope Valley Coll; Fshn Dsgn.

IRISH, DAWN M; Atwater HS; Atwater, CA; (2); Band; Mrchg Band; Pep Band; Hon Roll; Sctn Ldr-Flutes; Bus.

IRIYE, JUDY M; Mayfair HS; Lakewood, CA; (3); 1/215; Treas Key Clb; SADD; Thesps; School Play; Co-Ed Nwsp; Pres Stu Cncl; Var Capt Vllybl; High Hon Roll; Lakewood Youth Hall Of Fame Schlr Athlt 88-90; Outstndng 11th Grd Stu 90; Law.

IRONS, BRANDI S; Ontario HS; Ontario, CA; (3); VP Art Clb; Key Clb; Spanish Clb; Teachers Aide; Band; Jazz Band; Mrchg Band; Cit Awd; Peer Cnslng-Pres; Peer Cnslr Advsr; U CA; Ed.

IRRERA, GAETANO; El Camino HS; Oceanside, CA; (2); Art Clb; ROTC; SADD; Teachers Aide; Color Guard; School Play; Variety Show; Hon Roll; JETS Awd; Martl Arts; Psych; Cal Tech; Comp Engr.

IRUEGAS, MIREYA; Central Union HS; El Centro, CA; (2); Church Yth Grp; Band; Church Choir; Mrchg Band; Pep Band; Cheerldng; Gym; Hon Roll; Help Troubled Teenagers; Like To Have My Own Business; Like To Have A Place For Kids To Come Stay; UCSD; Child Psychology.

IRVIN, BRIAN T; Wilson HS; Long Beach, CA; (2); Ftbl; JV Socr; Hon Roll; NHS; Prin Merit Awd; UCLA; Arch.

IRVIN, KIRA A; Canyon Springs HS; Moreno Valley, CA; (2); Hon Roll; NY U; Performing Arts.

IRVINE, JEFFREY V; Lakewood HS; Lakewood, CA; (3); 100/850; Drama Clb; Acpl Chr; School Musical; Swing Chorus; Stu Cncl; Crs Cntry; Socr; Wrstlng; Hon Roll; NHS; Humboldt; Law.

IRVING, DRUEMEKA; Pius X HS; Compton, CA; (4); Sec Church Yth Grp; Drama Clb; Math Clb; Spanish Clb; Teachers Aide; VP Frsh Cls; Var Sftbl; Hon Roll; NHS; Sci Slvr Cert; LA Cnty Miss Teen Pgnt Cntstnt 90; CSF; U Of CA Irvine; Psych.

IRWIN, JASON S; Upper Lake HS; Nice, CA; (3); Science Clb; Spanish Clb; SADD; Teachers Aide; Band; Var Ftbl; Capt Trk; JV Wrstlng; Pres Acad Fit Awd; Acad Decathlon; U Of CA Sacramento; Pilot.

IRWIN, JENA L; San Diequito HS; Encinitas, CA; (3); Church Yth Grp; Teachers Aide; Lit Mag; Var Diving; JV Gym; JV Swmmng; Jr NHS; Bus.

IRWIN, JOSHUA; Oak Ridge HS; El Dorado Hills, CA; (3); 45/250; Ftbl; Socr; Hon Roll; Ntl Merit Ltr; Assmblymn YMCA Yth In Govt Pgm; Ref Yth Soccer Lg El Dorado Hills; UC Santa Barbara; Pre-Law.

IRWIN, TISHA C; Mater Dei HS; Santa Ana, CA; (2); Church Yth Grp; French Clb; Hosp Aide; Band; High Hon Roll; CSF; Campus Minstry; Pre-Schl Teacher.

ISAAC, DAWN O.; Indio HS; Yuma, AZ; (2); 56/382; Drama Clb; Pep Clb; JV Co-Capt Cheerldng; Var Gym; Stat Trk; CSF; Frshmn & JV Co-Capt Chrldng; UCLA; Acting.

ISAACS, MELISSA J; Mt Whitney HS; Visalia, CA; (1); Church Yth Grp; Cmnty Wkr; FFA; Court Stngrphr.

ISAACS II, MICHAEL E; Downtown Business Magnet HS; Los Angeles, CA; (2); Cmnty Wkr; Dance Clb; FBLA; Var Bsktbl; Cit Awd; Hon Roll; Acad Of Finace; Hampton U; Bus Admin.

ISAACSON, RALPH R; Norte Vista HS; Riverside, CA; (2); 103/445; VP JA; Ftbl; Hon Roll; Engrng.

ISAAK, JASON; Roosevelt HS; Fresno, CA; (4); 20/569; Church Yth Grp; German Clb; Socr; Hon Roll; Pres Schlr; Stu Of Mnth; Pres Schlrshp Awd Wnnr; Most Imprvd Soccr Plyr 87-88; Fresno Pacific Coll; Art.

ISABEL, VERONICA; Madera HS; Madera, CA; (2); Church Yth Grp; Latin Clb; Band; Church Choir; Mrchg Band; Pep Band; Sftbl; High Hon Roll; Hon Roll; Peer Cnslr; Teatro; Hnrs Top 10 1988-89; Gate Pgm; CSF; Med.

ISABELLE, DEBORAH I; John F Kennedy HS; Richmond, CA; (4); 4/230; SADD; Band; VP Frsh Cls; Rep Soph Cls; Sec Treas Jr Cls; VP Sr Cls; Stat Bsktbl; Stat Ftbl; High Hon Roll; Ntl Merit SF; Soc Of Wmns Engr Highest Honors; Lawrence Berkeley Lab DEHS Hon Prog; Yth Ed Peer Drug Cnsllng; U Of CA Davis; Vet Med.

ISADOR, JODI; El Camino Real HS; West Hills, CA; (3); Capt Drill Tm; Off Frsh Cls; Off Soph Cls; Off Jr Cls; Treas Stu Cncl; Hon Roll; UC Riverside; Bus.

ISBELL, AMY C; Mountain Empire JR-SR HS; Boulevard, CA; (3); SADD; Ed Yrbk; Rep Frsh Cls; Rep Soph Cls; Hon Roll; ROP Outstndng Stu Awd Comp Applctns; Grossmont Coll; Comp.

ISBELL, DAMON B; Woodland HS; Woodland, CA; (3); Drama Clb; FCA; Office Aide; SADD; Teachers Aide; Thesps; School Musical; School Play; JV Bsbl; JV Bsktbl; CSF; U S Air Force Academy.

ISBILL, STEPHEN E; North Salinas HS; Salinas, CA; (4); Var JV Bsktbl; Var Ftbl; High Hon Roll; Hon Roll; Prfct Atten Awd; Harthell JC; Mlmn.

ISCAN, HAYRIYE M; James Logan HS; Union City, CA; (4); 34/622; Cmnty Wkr; FTA; Stage Crew; Hon Roll; Pres Acad Fit Awd; Teach Catechism Our Lady Of Rosary; Outstndng Achvt Span Awd; Grad Magna Cum Laude; Cal ST Hayward; Psych.

ISETTI, DEREK D; St Marys HS; Stockton, CA; (2); 1/200; Drama Clb; NFL; Speech Tm; School Musical; Rep Jr Cls; Var Tennis; High Hon Roll; Water Polo-Jv Most Insprtnl; CSF; Boys Senate; Pediatrician.

ISHAM, EVE; Ernest Righetti HS; Santa Maria, CA; (1); Cmnty Wkr; Cit Awd; Hon Roll; CSF; Ambassadors Club Pres; Radio Clb; Stanford U; Doctor.

ISHEIK, ADAM; Los Alamitos HS; Los Alamitos, CA; (4); Bus Profs of Am; Debate Tm; NFL; Speech Tm; Jazz Band; Swmmng; Water Polo; 2nd Tm All Leag Water Polo; Bus Law.

ISHIDA, TIFFANY; Maranatha HS; San Gabriel, CA; (4); 1/105; Church Yth Grp; Pres Spanish Clb; Rep Nwsp; VP Frsh Cls; VP Stu Cncl; Var Capt Vllybl; High Hon Roll; CSF; Bnk Amer Awd.

ISHIGURO, JENNIFER YAYOI; Vivian Webb Schl; Gardena, CA; (3); 1/45; Cmnty Wkr; Debate Tm; Intnl Clb; Thesps; Orch; School Play; Ed Lit Mag; Dance Clb; German Clb; Ed Nwsp; Japanese Clb Pres; Amnsty Intl; Intl Law.

ISHIHARA, KIM K; Rio Americano HS; Carmichael, CA; (3); Latin Clb; Teachers Aide; Var Bsktbl; Score Keeper; JV Vllybl; High Hon Roll; Hon Roll; Pre-Med.

ISHIKAWA, NORIKO H; Edison HS; Huntington Beach, CA; (2); Church Yth Grp; Model UN; Off Soph Cls; Rep Stu Cncl; JV Swmmng; Hon Roll; UCI; Pediatrician.

ISHIKI, KENNETH K; Warren HS; Downey, CA; (2); Boy Scts; Church Yth Grp; FBLA; Cit Awd; High Hon Roll; Prfct Atten Awd; John Hopkins; Anesthslgst.

ISHIMARU, JANICE; Oak Park HS; Agoura Hills, CA; (2); 4/125; Church Yth Grp; Key Clb; Off Soph Cls; JV Crs Cntry; JV Socr; Var L Trk; Advancd Peer Cnslng; CA Schlrshp Fed; Dead Poets Soc.

ISHIOKA, RICK T; Venice HS; Culver City, CA; (2); Stage Crew; Stu Cncl; Bsktbl; Cit Awd; Hon Roll; Prfct Atten Awd.

ISHIZUKA, EIKO; Schurr HS; Rosemead, CA; (1); JV Tennis; High Hon Roll; Hon Roll; Prfct Atten Awd; Forgn Lang.

ISHIZUKA-CAPP, THAI E; Culver City HS; Culver City, CA; (2); Church Yth Grp; Varsity Clb; Off Soph Cls; Swmmng; Hon Roll; Gldn St Exm Geom Hnrs; Vrsty Ltrs 2; Fashn Desgnr.

ISHMAN, FRANK A; Gahr HS; Cerritos, CA; (3); Boy Scts; Church Choir; Off Sr Cls; Var Cheerldng; Diving; Var Ftbl; Socr; Var Vllybl; Wt Lftg; Var Wrstlng; UCI Schlrs In Training; CIF Acad Tm Hnrb Mntn; Blue, Gold Awd Adv Wood 2 Yrs; UCI; Obstetrcn.

ISIDRO, CHRISTOPHER A; Pinole Valley HS; Hercules, CA; (2); Church Yth Grp; JV Crs Cntry; JV Tennis; High Hon Roll; CSF; UC Berkeley; Comp Sci.

ISIP, PAMELA Z; Eagle Rock HS; Los Angeles, CA; (4); Cit Awd; Hon Roll; Schlrshp Awd; Marine Sci Mdl; Silver Sealbearer; Glendale CC; Nrsng.

ISKANDAR, TIFFANY M; Hesperia HS; Hesperia, CA; (3); French Clb; Hon Roll; Psych.

ISKANDARYAN, ARSINE; Herbert Hoover HS; Glendale, CA; (2); Vllybl; Hon Roll; Figure Ice Sktng In Armenia; Art Clb; Glendale CC; Comp Accntnt.

ISKANDER, GREG; John A Rowland HS; Walnut, CA; (3); Hosp Aide; Letterman Clb; Science Clb; Spanish Clb; Speech Tm; Var Bsktbl; JV Tennis; High Hon Roll; Hon Roll; NHS; CA Schlrshp Fed.

ISKANDER, NADINE; St Margarets Schl; Capistrano Beach, CA; (4); 2/23; Art Clb; Cmnty Wkr; JA; Pres Service Clb; Yrbk; Var Bsktbl; Intrml Swmmng; High Hon Roll; Spnsh Awd; Natl Cncl Tchrs Engl Awd In Writing; Painting & Drawing.

ISLAS, BLANCA A; Lynwood HS; Lynwood, CA; (3); Psych.

ISLAS, DANA K; Enterprise HS; Redding, CA; (4); Church Yth Grp; Cmnty Wkr; Red Cross Aide; Spanish Clb; Chorus; Color Guard; Flag Corp; School Musical; Powder Puff Ftbl; Hon Roll; Chico U; Tchng.

ISLAS, JUDITH; San Gabriel Mission High; Baldwin Park, CA; (2); 16/130; Church Yth Grp; Office Aide; Teachers Aide; Prfct Atten Awd; CA Schlrshp Fed; Cal Poly; Arch.

ISLAS, MICHAEL V; Don Bosco Technical Inst; Baldwin Park, CA; (3); Church Yth Grp; Acad Awds; Cal Poly Pomona; Constrctn Engr.

ISLEY, ALICIA; Novato HS; Novato, CA; (2); Spanish Clb; Hammilton LL Book Asst Editor; Santa Rosa JC; Accntng.

ISLEY, JENNIFER K; Sonora HS; La Habra, CA; (4); Treas Drama Clb; GAA; Ski Clb; Phtg Teachers Aide; School Play; Co-Capt Var Socr; Var Trk; NHS; Madrigals; Whittier Coll; Theatre Ed.

ISLEY, KIMBERLY C; Chaffey HS; Ontario, CA; (1); Band; High Hon Roll; Hon Roll.

ISMAILI, NAHEED; Clayton Valley HS; Concord, CA; (2); Rptr FBLA; Intnl Clb; SADD; Color Guard; Jazz Band; Mrchg Band; Var L Trk; CSF; Outstndg Girl Stu; Harvard U; Med.

ISMAILJEE, SALEHAH; Fullerton HS; Fullerton, CA; (1); FFA; Rotary Awd; Hnrs At Entrnc Awd; Stu Mnth Spnsh I & Engl I; CSF; Cal Poly Pomona; Arch Engrng.

ISOM, LARRY H; Trona HS; Trona, CA; (2); 2/50; Boy Scts; Debate Tm; German Clb; Letterman Clb; Math Clb; Math Tm; Teachers Aide; Pres Frsh Cls; JV Bsktbl; Var Ftbl; Egl Scout; U Of CA San Diego; Engnrng.

ISOMURA, ERIKA M; Torrey Pines HS; San Diego, CA; (4); 21/448; French Clb; Library Aide; Scholastic Bowl; Service Clb; Teachers Aide; Yrbk; High Hon Roll; Ntl Merit SF; High Hnrs Golden ST Geom Exam; Vol Local Theater; Engrng.

ISOMURA, STEVE E; Torrey Pires HS; Del Mar, CA; (2); Chess Clb; VICA; Intrml Wrstlng.

ISRAEL, GREGORY S; Tokay HS; Stockton, CA; (2); 1/700; FCA; Off Soph Cls; Var Trk; High Hon Roll; Japanese Club Pres; CSF; U WA; Teaching.

ISRAELSON, KIMBERLY D; Edison HS; Huntington Beach, CA; (2); Band; Mrchg Band; Pep Band; High Hon Roll; Hon Roll; Yng Rpblcns Clb; Vet.

ISSA, NABIL; Hemet HS; Hemet, CA; (3); 23/670; Church Yth Grp; Cmnty Wkr; Debate Tm; Hosp Aide; Sec Key Clb; NFL; Quiz Bowl; Speech Tm; Ed Nwsp; Ed Yrbk; Var Lttrmn-Waterpolo; Spllg Bee Dist Chmpn; 1st Pl Dist Optmst Clb Oratorical Cont; CSF VP; UCSD; Med.

ISSAGHOLIANTCE, PATRICK; Herbert Hoover HS; Glendale, CA; (2); Boy Scts; Spanish Clb; Bsbl; Bsktbl; Ftbl; Socr; Trk; Vllybl; Wt Lftg; Cit Awd; CA ST Plytechnc U; Arch Engr.

ITO, CRAIG; Willow Glen HS; San Jose, CA; (1); Quiz Bowl; JV Socr; JV Tennis; UC Berkely.

ITO, DAVID A; Brea-Olinda HS; Brea, CA; (2); Boy Scts; Letterman Clb; Bsktbl; Var L Trk; High Hon Roll; Hon Roll; Eagle Scout; Law.

ITOH, AKIKO; Cerritos HS; Cerritos, CA; (4); Key Clb; Office Aide; Teachers Aide; Band; Drill Tm; Mrchg Band; Orch; Yrbk; Tennis; High Hon Roll; Japanese Natl Hnr Soc VP; U Of CA Santa Barbara; Econ.

ITOW, JANICE H; Culver City HS; Culver City, CA; (1); Mgr Drill Tm; Rep Frsh Cls; Cit Awd; High Hon Roll; Hon Roll; Pres Acad Fit Awd; Stu Lgu; UCLA; Pedtrcn.

ITRI, JASON N; Edison HS; Huntington Beach, CA; (1); Boy Scts; Model UN; Ftbl; Socr; Trk; Johns Hopkins; Med.

ITURBE, MARIA I; Inglewood HS; Inglewood, CA; (3); French Clb; Temple Yth Grp; Stat Score Keeper; JV Sftbl; JV Vllybl; Hon Roll; Chiropractor.

ITURRINO, URSULA P; Villanova HS; Columbus, GA; (2); 60/114; Drama Clb; French Clb; Flag Corp; Cheerldng; Socr; Vllybl; VIP; Tn Advsr; Santa Barbara U; Bus Admin.

ITURRIRIA, FRANCISCO J; North HS; Bakersfield, CA; (3); 27/350; Church Yth Grp; Spanish Clb; Var Bsbl; Hon Roll; Prfct Atten Awd; Spanish NHS; CSF; Star Awd Wnnr Bsbl; Hstry Day Comptn St Fnls 4th Pl; Cal Poly SLO; Ag Engrng.

IV, JUNE; Lincoln HS; Stockton, CA; (3); 132/592; English Clb; Key Clb; Mu Alpha Theta; Spanish Clb; Lit Mag; Hon Roll; Prfct Atten Awd; Close-Up Clb VP; Pltcl Clb; Badmttn Team; UC Davis; Csmtc Med.

IVAN, SABRINA A; Etiwanda HS; Alta Loma, CA; (2); Rep Church Yth Grp; Cmnty Wkr; Drama Clb; Church Choir; Hon Roll; Chmber Singers Choir; Parish Cncl; San Francisco Consvrtry Music.

IVANOV, SOFIA T; Immaculate Heart HS; Los Angeles, CA; (3); GAA; Pep Clb; Spanish Clb; JV Crs Cntry; Var Socr; Piano; Bio Sci.

IVERSEN, NAOMI; Notre Dame Schl; Chico, CA; (1); Church Yth Grp; Acpl Chr; Church Choir; School Play; Off Frsh Cls; Bsktbl; Cheerldng; High Hon Roll; Yth Grp Core Ldr; UCLA; Psych.

IVERSON, LEISEL E; Piedmont HS; Piedmont, CA; (3); Church Yth Grp; Hosp Aide; Sec Intnl Clb; SADD; Acpl Chr; Church Choir; School Musical; School Play; Sprt Ed Nwsp; JV Vllybl; Piano 11 Yrs; CMEA Singing Excllnc; Gld/Slvr Ad Musical Schl Pgms; St Olaf; Orthopedics.

IVEY, PAIGE E; Armijo HS; Suisun City, CA; (2); Church Yth Grp; Quiz Bowl; Band; Mrchg Band; Pep Band; Lit Mag; Rep Frsh Cls; Rep Stu Cncl; Var Sftbl; Hon Roll; AFS; Aerospace Engrng.

IVEY, PAUL J; Casa Roble Fundamental HS; Orangevale, CA; (2); 9/461; French Clb; JV Bsktbl; US Yth Sccr Assn; Fri Night Live; Hnr Roll For Acadmc Achvt; Merit Awd 90; Engrng.

IVEY, TANZANIA T; Mt Pleasant HS; San Jose, CA; (1); FBLA; Band; Var Crs Cntry; Var Trk; Accntng.

IVIE, JUSTIN P; Delta HS; Sacramento, CA; (3); Am Leg Boys St; SADD; Varsity Clb; Yrbk; Bsbl; Ftbl; Wt Lftg; Hon Roll; Air Force Acad; Aviation.

IVORY, BRIDGETTE; Etiwanda HS; Alta Loma, CA; (3); FBLA; JA; SADD; Med.

IVORY, OWEN L; Sonora HS; La Habra, CA; (4); 8/330; Boy Scts; Computer Clb; Math Clb; Science Clb; Ski Clb; Var L Socr; JV Trk; High Hon Roll; NHS; Pres Acad Fit Awd; Bank Of Amer Sci & Math Plaq Wnnr; Rgnts Schlr UCI; U Of CA Irvine; Mech Engrng.

IVY, CANDICE C; Etiwanda HS; Alta Loma, CA; (2); JA; Hon Roll; Prfct Atten Awd; Pres Acad Fit Awd; UCLA; Bus.

IVY, DANA D; Santa Ynez Valley Union HS; Santa Ynez, CA; (2); Church Yth Grp; Band; Church Choir; Mrchg Band; Pres Acad Fit Awd; Church Handbell Choir; Embry-Riddle; Aeronautical Engr.

IWAHASA, MELANIE M; Edison HS; Huntington Beach, CA; (2); Church Yth Grp; Var Bsktbl; JV Vllybl.

IWAMOTO, HIROKO; Cupertino HS; Cupertino, CA; (4); 11/250; Pres Church Yth Grp; Flag Corp; Jazz Band; Ed Yrbk; Stu Cncl; Pom Pon; NHS; Ntl Merit Ltr; Drama Clb; German Clb; Bnk Of Amer Lbrl Arts Plque; Chrs Pianist; CSF VP; Cornell U; Engl.

IWANAGA, COURTNEY P; Saratoga HS; Saratoga, CA; (1); Church Yth Grp; Girl Scts; Chorus; Treas Soph Cls; Bsktbl; Swmmng; High Hon Roll; Chrmn CASA; Natl Charity Leag Ofcr.

IWAZ, MARY; Village Christian HS; Glendale, CA; (3); Cmnty Wkr; Drama Clb; GAA; Service Clb; Spanish Clb; Bsktbl; Crs Cntry; Mgr(s); Powder Puff Ftbl; Score Keeper; U La Verne; Law.

IYER, RAJIV; Irvine HS; Irvine, CA; (2); 2/548; Art Clb; French Clb; Rep Stu Cncl; High Hon Roll; Hon Roll; Pres Acad Fit Awd; Intnshp Hoag Mem Hosp Heritage Hnr Bio; ; Cs Fed Indian Yth Assn,AMA,NAR Hnrb Mntn Art; Med.

IYER, SHEILA; Rosary HS; Fullerton, CA; (4); Hosp Aide; Pres Speech Tm; Temple Yth Grp; School Play; Rptr Nwsp; Var Trk; High Hon Roll; NHS; Prfct Atten Awd; Mck Trl; Indian Dncng; UCLA; Phy.

IYER, SWARNA M; Sacred Heart Prep HS; Menlo Park, CA; (2); Cit Awd; High Hon Roll; Play Harmonium; Indian Clsscl Sng; Pdtrcn.

IZADSETA, PARASTOO; Corona HS; Corona, CA; (2); GAA; Library Aide; Ski Clb; Band; Pep Band; Vllybl; Cit Awd; High Hon Roll; Ntl Merit Ltr; CSF Clb; 2nd To None Awd; Achvmnt Awd; Acad Awd; Cert Awd; UCI; Bio.

IZQUIERDO, ALICIA D; Providence HS; Burbank, CA; (2); Church Yth Grp; Cmnty Wkr; Library Aide; Teachers Aide; Chorus; School Musical; JV Vllybl; High Hon Roll; Prfct Atten Awd; CSF; UCLA; Med.

IZU, KEVIN; Piedmont Hills HS; San Jose, CA; (4); 24/336; Boy Scts; Math Tm; Rptr Nwsp; Treas Sr Cls; Var Socr; Var Tennis; High Hon Roll; Rotary Awd; CSF; MESA; Brigham Young U; Mech Engr.

JABALERA, KARINA R; California HS; Whittier, CA; (2); 58/503; SADD; Swmmng; Lang.

JACABAN, DAVID A; Fresno Adventist Acad; Orosi, CA; (3); 1/15; Church Yth Grp; Computer Clb; FCA; JA; Teachers Aide; Band; Chorus; Drill Tm; Yrbk; VP Frsh Cls; SDA Pathfinder Club Pathfinder Of Yr Awd; Loma Linda U; Phys Thrpy.

JACINTO, JAY; Calvary Chapel HS; Fountain Valley, CA; (2); Art Clb; Church Yth Grp; Drama Clb; School Play; Yrbk; JV Ftbl; Var Trk; Reading & Writing Poetry; U CA Irvine; Medical.

JACK, TIMOTHY J; Corona HS; Corona, CA; (3); JV Bsbl; Hon Roll; Jr NHS; Prfct Atten Awd; Pres Acad Fit Awd; Sal; USC; Bus.

JACKLE, JULIE M; Huntington Beach HS; Huntington Beach, CA; (3); 11/550; GAA; Key Clb; Math Clb; Math Tm; Model UN; Ski Clb; Spanish Clb; High Hon Roll; Pres Acad Fit Awd; Var Crs Cntry; Piano Cert Of Mrt; USC; Bus.

JACKLETT, JASON; Mariposa County HS; Mariposa, CA; (4); 7/101; Boy Scts; VP Frsh Cls; Pres Soph Cls; Treas Stu Cncl; Var Capt Trk; DAR Awd; NHS; Pres Acad Fit Awd; St Schlr; FL Coll; Elect Engrng.

JACKMAN, CHERILYN; Turlock Christian Schl; Turlock, CA; (2); 2/30; Church Yth Grp; Office Aide; Band; Church Choir; Mrchg Band; Pep Band; School Musical; JV Cheerldng; High Hon Roll; Hon Roll; Wrote & Publsh Shrt Stories, Essys & Poems; Author.

JACKMON, AMIRA A; Roosevelt HS; Fresno, CA; (3); 21/700; Church Yth Grp; Church Choir; Orch; Pres Sr Cls; JV Tennis; MESA Sec; 2nd VP & Pres United Black Stu Of CA Central Rgn.

JACKOVICS, JULIA M; Piedmont HS; Oakland, CA; (2); Girl Scts; JA; SADD; Var Bsktbl; Var Swmmng; Var Vllybl; Hungarian Scts Ldr; U CA; Psych.

JACKS, BRIAN N; Davis SR HS; Woodland, CA; (3); Church Yth Grp; Cmnty Wkr; Spanish Clb; Band; Jazz Band; Mrchg Band; Orch; Pep Band; School Musical; School Play; U Of CA Davis; Civil Engrng.

JACKS, LESA D; Saddleback HS; Santa Ana, CA; (4); Drama Clb; Speech Tm; Variety Show; Var Bsktbl; Var Trk; Var Vllybl; Psych.

JACKS, ROCHELLE; Gustine HS; Newman, CA; (4); 4-H; FBLA; FFA; Model UN; SADD; Band; Flag Corp; JV Vllybl; Ed Nwsp; Ed Yrbk; JR SR Ldrshp; Acadmc Decthln; MO U Columbia; Jrnlsm.

JACKS, SHANNON T; Armijo HS; Suisun City, CA; (2); Church Yth Grp; Girl Scts; ROTC; Color Guard; Drill Tm; Gym; Trk; Hon Roll; Solano Coll; Nurse.

JACKSON, ADRIAN G; Locke HS; Los Angeles, CA; (2); Church Yth Grp; JV Bsktbl; Hon Roll; Prfct Atten Awd; U Of AZ; Engrng.

JACKSON, ALISSA D; River City HS; W Sacramento, CA; (4); 1/150; Am Leg Aux Girls St; Thesps; Jazz Band; School Musical; Swmmng; Elks Awd; Masonic Awd; Rotary Awd; Val; Acad Decthln; U Of CA Santa Cruz; Marine Bio.

JACKSON, AMINA; Hawthorne HS; Lynwood, CA; (4); AFS; Church Choir; JV Trk; HS Invlvmnt Pgm Northrop; Spanish, Engl Hnrs; CA ST Long Bch; Spanish.

JACKSON, ANGELA N; Monterey HS; Seaside, CA; (3); Church Yth Grp; Teachers Aide; Church Choir; Hon Roll; Natrl Helpers; Monterey Peninsula Coll; Medcl.

JACKSON, ANISSA; Porterville HS; Porterville, CA; (3); Church Yth Grp; Science Clb; Teachers Aide; Drill Tm; JV Sftbl; Hon Roll; Prfct Atten Awd; Mexican Amer Club; Porterville Juniorettes Club.

JACKSON, ANTHONY L; East Bakersfield HS; Bakersfield, CA; (3); 43/448; Boy Scts; Math Clb; Office Aide; SADD; Teachers Aide; Varsity Clb; Var Capt Bsktbl; Var Capt Ftbl; Elks Awd; High Hon Roll; U CA Davis; Med.

JACKSON, APRIL; Palm Desert HS; Palm Desert, CA; (2); Church Yth Grp; Hon Roll; Art Piece Pblshd In Cty Clndr; U CA Irvine; Comp Grphcs.

JACKSON, BENITA; Canyon HS; Anaheim, CA; (4); Am Leg Aux Girls St; Hosp Aide; Mu Alpha Theta; VP Service Clb; Cit Awd; High Hon Roll; NHS; Ntl Merit Ltr; AFL-CIO & UC Berkeley Alumni Schlrshps Wnnr; Yth Ldrshp Action; UC Berkeley; Rsrch Sci.

JACKSON, CAMILLE M; Roosevelt HS; Fresno, CA; (2); Spanish Clb; SADD; Socr; Sftbl; Vllybl; Tutor; Psych.

JACKSON, CHARLES B; Palmdale HS; Littlerock, CA; (4); 49/510; Pres Church Yth Grp; Cmnty Wkr; Teachers Aide; Ftbl; Cit Awd; High Hon Roll; Hon Roll; Pres Acad Fit Awd; Yng, Gftd & Black Awd; CSU Northridge; Comp Sci.

JACKSON, CHRISTINE; Temecula Valley HS; Temecula, CA; (3); Church Yth Grp; SADD; Stage Crew; Cit Awd; Hon Roll; HS Acad Schlrshp; Bus.

JACKSON, CINDIE; Diamond Bar HS; Diamond Bar, CA; (3); 101/500; VP Pep Clb; Drill Tm; JV Cheerldng; Hon Roll; Most Dedicated Songleader 89-90; Sci Stu Of Week; CA Schlrhsp Fed; CA ST U Fullerton; Bus.

JACKSON III, DAILEY; Washington Prep HS; Los Angeles, CA; (4); Pres Church Yth Grp; Capt Debate Tm; Drama Clb; Capt Speech Tm; Jazz Band; Orch; Hon Roll; Humboldt ST U; Bus.

JACKSON, DANA R; Clovis West HS; Fresno, CA; (3); Intnl Clb; High Hon Roll; Hon Roll.

JACKSON, DE ANN; Sierra Joint Union HS; Auberry, CA; (4); 32/175; Letterman Clb; Spanish Clb; Speech Tm; SADD; Teachers Aide; Varsity Clb; School Play; Pres Frsh Cls; VP Soph Cls; Treas Jr Cls; GSE Hnrs; Fresno ST U; Sociolgy.

JACKSON, DENISE M; Valley Christian Acad; Santa Maria, CA; (4); Debate Tm; Chorus; School Play; Co-Ed Yrbk; JV Sftbl; High Hon Roll; Lion Awd; JR Statesmen Amer; Long Beach ST U; Jrnlsm.

JACKSON, DUSTIN T; San Pasqual HS; Winterhaven, CA; (2); #5 In Class; Church Yth Grp; Letterman Clb; Office Aide; Band; VP Frsh Cls; VP Soph Cls; Var Bsbl; Var Ftbl; Var Wt Lftg; Var Wrstlng; AZ Western Coll; Dgnstc Techn.

JACKSON, DWAYNE D; Lynwood HS; Lynwood, CA; (2); Church Yth Grp; Model UN; Office Aide; Band; Mrchg Band; Pep Band; Off Frsh Cls; Off Soph Cls; Cit Awd; UCLA; Comp Prog.

JACKSON, DYLAN J; Fremont HS; Sunnyvale, CA; (2); 1/450; Chess Clb; Debate Tm; FBLA; JA; NFL; Speech Tm; Jr NHS; Geom Golden St Exam High Hnrs; Geom & Alg II Teams; Badminton Team; U CA Berkeley; Comp Sci.

JACKSON, ELESHA; Corona HS; Corona, CA; (2); Computer Clb; Girl Scts; Spanish Clb; Church Choir; School Musical; School Play; JV Bsktbl; Var Trk; Cit Awd; Acad Letter & Cert; UCLA; Orthodontist.

JACKSON, EVERETT; Carlmont HS; East Palo Alto, CA; (2); JV Capt Ftbl; Miami U; Pro Ftbl.

JACKSON, GEORGIA M; Marlborough Schl; Los Angeles, CA; (4); Debate Tm; Girl Scts; Library Aide; Math Tm; NFL; Science Clb; Stage Crew; Mgr(s); Hon Roll; Vrsty Bdmntn Tm; Bus.

JACKSON, HEATHER I; Kingsburg HS; Kingsburg, CA; (2); Sec Church Yth Grp; Drama Clb; Letterman Clb; Sec Science Clb; Teachers Aide; Band; Mrchg Band; Pep Band; Stat Bsktbl; Var Trk; Acadmc Block K Acadmc Ltr 89-90; Young Life; Cal Poly San Luis Ob; Engrng.

JACKSON, JAMAL; Washington P HS; Inglewood, CA; (4); 24/600; Yrbk; Hon Roll; Prfct Atten Awd; CSF; Yng Black Schlrs; FL A&M U; Grphc Arts.

JACKSON, JAMIE L; Notre Dame HS; San Jose, CA; (3); Church Yth Grp; Cmnty Wkr; Hosp Aide; SADD; Church Choir; School Musical; Cheerldng; Pom Pon; Hon Roll; Pres/VP Black Stus Union; Sltd Stu Ambasdor Southren Europe 90; Sltd Rep Yth Govt 90; Psych.

JACKSON, JEFFREY S; Corona Del Mar HS; Newport Beach, CA; (4); AFS; FCA; Letterman Clb; Var Capt Bsktbl; Var Capt Ftbl; U WA; Bus.

JACKSON, JENNIFER; Capistrano Valley HS; Mission Viejo, CA; (3); Pep Clb; Drill Tm; JV Cheerldng; JV Tennis; Cit Awd; Miss Bolivia Ayudo Ninos Bolivianos Clb.

JACKSON, JENNIFER; River City HS; West Sacramento, CA; (1); 13/302; Drama Clb; Hosp Aide; Thesps; JV Cheerldng; Cit Awd; Hon Roll; Jobs Daughters Past Honored Qn; CA Schlrshp Fed; Homcmng Royalty; UCD; Neuro Sci.

JACKSON, JENNIFER C; El Camino HS; Oceanside, CA; (3); Church Yth Grp; Speech Tm; Wrk Cshr/Clr Yogurt Store; Coll; Law.

JACKSON, JENNIFER S; Winters Joint Union HS; Winters, CA; (2); Church Yth Grp; Drama Clb; Library Aide; Pep Clb; SADD; Teachers Aide; School Play; Stage Crew; Friday Night Live; Teaching.

JACKSON, JERI K; Etiwanda HS; Etiwanda, CA; (2); Hrsmnshp Trng & Cmptn; Bus.

JACKSON, JILL E; El Toro HS; El Toro, CA; (1); 28/550; Church Yth Grp; Dance Clb; GAA; Socr; Trk; High Hon Roll; Excllnce Awd For Math; Dncng, Skiing & Campng; Photo.

JACKSON, JILL M; Orestimba HS; Newman, CA; (3); Drama Clb; Pep Clb; Chorus; School Play; Var Cheerldng; Var Tennis; Hon Roll; Mst Imprvd Tnns Plyr; Design.

JACKSON, JONATHAN L; Atwater HS; Atwater, CA; (2); Church Yth Grp; FBLA; Hon Roll; Lubbock Christian Coll; Psych.

JACKSON, JONEEN V; Kingsburg HS; Kingsburg, CA; (2); Church Yth Grp; Cmnty Wkr; Drama Clb; Teachers Aide; Band; Mrchg Band; Mgr Nwsp; Sec Soph Cls; Rep Jr Cls; Var Capt Swmmng; Vllybl Clb; Stu Govt Ldrshp; Acad Block K; Young Life; Sequoias; Advrtsng.

JACKSON, JOSHUA A; Kerman HS; Kerman, CA; (2); 7/150; German Clb; Band; Jazz Band; Mrchg Band; JV Ftbl; Wt Lftg; Hon Roll; Acad Lttr Of Achvt; Fishing & Camping; Frst Rngr.

JACKSON, JULIE L; Tulare Union HS; Tulare, CA; (4); 7/360; Pres French Clb; SADD; Church Choir; Stu Cncl; Var Capt Tennis; High Hon Roll; Val; Church Yth Grp; Teachers Aide; Prfct Atten Awd; CSF Treas; Outstndg Stu Awd Math, Sci, Engl & Bus 89-90; Camp ROYAL Ldrshp Camp 89; CA Polytech SLO; Engrng.

JACKSON, KARI; Arcadia HS; Arcadia, CA; (1); Cmnty Wkr; Dance Clb; Hosp Aide; Teachers Aide; Drill Tm; Sftbl; Tennis; Vllybl; Hon Roll; Berkeley; Law.

JACKSON, KEENAN D; Washington Comm Mag HS; Los Angeles, CA; (3); Chess Clb; Dance Clb; Debate Tm; Drama Clb; Science Clb; Speech Tm; School Play; Trk; Hon Roll; Future Entrprsrs Clb; MESA; Knights & Ladies; Yale; Supreme Ct Jdg.

JACKSON, KELLY W; Mira Mesa HS; San Diego, CA; (2); 71/797; Boy Scts; Church Yth Grp; Stu Cncl; Pres Acad Fit Awd.

JACKSON, KIMBERLY LYNNE; Grace M Davis HS; Modesto, CA; (4); AFS; Church Yth Grp; French Clb; Pep Clb; Chorus; Mrchg Band; Lit Mag; Cit Awd; Law Enfrcmnt.

JACKSON, KOURVAHCIA; Fremont HS; Oakland, CA; (2); Girl Scts; Office Aide; SADD; Teachers Aide; Rptr Nwsp; Rptr Stu Cncl; Media Acad; IWE Pr Tutr.

JACKSON, LAWRENCE B; Barstow HS; Barstow, CA; (2); Church Yth Grp; Church Choir; Bsktbl; Ftbl; Hon Roll.

JACKSON, LISA; Hiram Johnson HS; Sacramento, CA; (1); Band; Mrchg Band; Orch; Swmmng; Cit Awd; Hon Roll.

JACKSON, MALINDA J; Immaculate Heart HS; Los Angeles, CA; (4); High Hon Roll; U CA San Diego; Law.

JACKSON, MICAH DARTAGNAN; Hamilton Music Acad; Los Angeles, CA; (2); Church Yth Grp; Computer Clb; Drama Clb; Office Aide; Varsity Clb; Band; School Play; JV Ftbl; UCLA Prtnrshp Prgm; USC NYSP Smmr Athltc Prgm; NAACP Mem & ACTSO Cmptr; Escort Beta Pi Sigma Ball; UCLA; Arch.

JACKSON, MONICA R; Homestead HS; Sunnyvale, CA; (1); Cmnty Wkr; SADD; Envrnmntl Club; Biologist.

JACKSON, NATHAN; Cardinal Newman HS; Rohnert Park, CA; (2); School Musical; Ftbl; Hon Roll.

JACKSON, NICOLE M; Hiram Johnson HS; Sacramento, CA; (3); 13/116; Church Yth Grp; Var Tennis; Hon Roll; NHS; Cultre Clb; Vrsty Tnns Mst Imprvd Plyr; Commnctns.

JACKSON, PAULA A; Yucaipa HS; Yucaipa, CA; (3); Church Yth Grp; Office Aide; Spanish Clb; Flag Corp; Stage Crew; Bus Comp; CA ST U; CPA.

JACKSON, QUOMIEKO S; Oakland Tech HS; Oakland, CA; (2); Cit Awd; Hon Roll; Bus Mgmt.

JACKSON, RACHELLE D; St Patrick-St Vincents HS; Vallejo, CA; (1); Church Yth Grp; Var Bsktbl; Stat Ftbl; Hon Roll; Sprt Clb; Mrrs Brwn; Cnslr.

JACKSON, RAMON S; Eden Christian Acad; Oakland, CA; (4); Church Yth Grp; Cmnty Wkr; Computer Clb; Debate Tm; English Clb; FBLA; Math Clb; Science Clb; Teachers Aide; Temple Yth Grp; Alameda Coll Comp Sci Cls; Coll Of Alameda; Bus Admin.

JACKSON, REBEKAH; San Lorenzo Valley HS; Boulder Creek, CA; (3); 3/219; Dance Clb; French Clb; Temple Yth Grp; Drill Tm; Ed Nwsp; Pres Frsh Cls; Stu Cncl; Cheerldng; Socr; Rotary Awd; Jrnlsm.

JACKSON, ROBERT; St Bernard HS; Los Angeles, CA; (4); 24/300; Debate Tm; Service Clb; Rptr Nwsp; JV Crs Cntry; JV Trk; Var Hon Roll; CSF; US Cstms Explrs; Martial Arts; UCLA; Acctnt.

JACKSON, RUTHIE E; Magnolia HS; Anaheim, CA; (4); Church Yth Grp; VP Intnl Clb; Rptr Nwsp; JV Tennis; High Hon Roll; Hon Roll; NHS; Hosp Vlntr; CSF; CA ST U Long Beach; Int Dsgn.

JACKSON, RYAN; Monterey HS; Salinas, CA; (4); 21/250; Lit Mag; Var Trk; Bausch & Lomb Sci Awd; High Hon Roll; Hon Roll; Acad Decathlon Co-Capt; Knowledge Bowl; Bk Of Amer Cert, Lab Sci; :Ca Poly Tech; Aeronautical Eng.

JACKSON, SABRINA L; T A P E HS; Davis, CA; (3); Church Yth Grp; Girl Scts; Office Aide; Pep Clb; SADD; Bsktbl; Member Of Friday Night Live.

JACKSON, SPRING D; Los Alamitos HS; Los Alamitos, CA; (2); Dance Clb; Color Guard; Drill Tm; Stage Crew; Wt Lftg; Hon Roll; Mdlng; Career Acad Of Bty; Csmtlgy.

JACKSON, STUART K; Manteca HS; Manteca, CA; (2); FBLA; Band; Mrchg Band; Treas Frsh Cls; Ftbl; Trk; Hon Roll; Peer Resource.

JACKSON, SUSIE; Valley Christian HS; San Jose, CA; (4); Church Yth Grp; Office Aide; Nwsp; Var Bsktbl; Var Pom Pon; Cit Awd; High Hon Roll; I D Sqd Vrsty; Biola U; Commnctns.

JACKSON, TAMICA D; Mira Loma HS; N Highlands, CA; (3); 88/284; Band; Color Guard; Flag Corp; Mrchg Band; Pep Band; Stu Cncl; Cheerldng; Hon Roll; LA ST U; Psych.

JACKSON, TATISHA M; Vallejo SR HS; Vallejo, CA; (3); Drama Clb; SADD; Chorus; Church Choir; School Play; Rptr Nwsp; Var Crs Cntry; Var Trk; Hon Roll; Spelman Coll; Crim Law.

JACKSON, TENISHA D; Fremont HS; Oakland, CA; (1); Girl Scts; ROTC; Chorus; Off Soph Cls; Bsktbl; Sftbl; Vllybl; Cit Awd; Hon Roll; Prfct Atten Awd; Howard U; Law.

JACKSON, TINA; Edison HS; Fresno, CA; (3); Am Leg Aux Girls St; Teachers Aide; Crs Cntry; Pres Schlr; Fresno ST U; Bus Admin.

JACKSON, TRACIE A; Bishop Amat HS; Diamond Bar, CA; (3); Pep Clb; Drill Tm; Var JV Cheerldng; Var Capt Pom Pon; Powder Puff Ftbl; Hon Roll; USC.

JACKSON, TUKALA T; Washignton Prep HS; Starkville, MS; (3); Office Aide; Church Choir; School Musical; Sftbl; High Hon Roll; Hon Roll; Pres Acad Fit Awd; Marthonians Club; Mesa; CSF; Bus Admin.

JACOB, ERIN; Rio Lindo Adventist Acad; Martinez, CA; (3); Church Yth Grp; French Clb; Band; Chorus; Orch; Rptr Yrbk; Hon Roll; Pathfndrs; Religious VP; Pacific Union Coll.

JACOB, JEAN D; Turlock HS; Turlock, CA; (4); 2/630; AFS; Art Clb; Cmnty Wkr; German Clb; Hosp Aide; Key Clb; SADD; Teachers Aide; Lbrn Nwsp; VP NHS; Gottschalks Hi Deb Model; Bank Of America Achvt Award In Liberal Arts; Stu Of The Month; Interact Club; UC; Biologiacl Sciences.

JACOB, SARGON; Sonoma Valley HS; Sonoma, CA; (4); 4/277; Boy Scts; Church Yth Grp; Cmnty Wkr; Var Socr; JV Tennis; High Hon Roll; Hon Roll; Gldng St Exam Hnrs; 99 Pct ASVAB Military Tst; Bodybrdng; UC Santa Cruz; Envrnmntl Engrn.

JACOBO, NOEL; Central Union HS; El Centro, CA; (2); JV VP Bsbl; Var JV Bsktbl; Wt Lftg; Arch.

JACOBS, AARON S; Nevada Union HS; Nevada City, CA; (4); 17/435; Drama Clb; Thesps; Chorus; Jazz Band; School Musical; School Play; Stage Crew; Variety Show; High Hon Roll; Jr NHS; 2nd Pl Lenaea Drama Cmptn Duet Actng; Music.

JACOBS, BRANDY M; San Dieguito HS; La Costa, CA; (2); 101/600; Dance Clb; Var Gym; Hon Roll; UC Santa Barbara; Child Psych.

JACOBS, CARI A; California HS; Whittier, CA; (3); Band; Jazz Band; Mrchg Band; Orch; Pep Band; CA ST Fullerton; Teacher.

JACOBS, CARRIE L; Mission Viejo HS; Mission Viejo, CA; (2); Dance Clb; Drama Clb; Thesps; School Musical; School Play; Variety Show; Cheerldng; Hon Roll; Inter Decrtrng.

JACOBS, DAN R; El Toro HS; El Toro, CA; (3); 140/516; JV Bsbl; Var Socr; Hon Roll.

JACOBS, DASHA; Santa Barbara HS; Santa Barbara, CA; (3); Cmnty Wkr; Debate Tm; Hosp Aide; Temple Yth Grp; Church Choir; Hon Roll; Dance; Piano; Brandeis U; Pre-Med.

JACOBS, EMILY S; Arcata HS; Arcata, CA; (3); Art Clb; Drama Clb; Intnl Clb; SADD; Temple Yth Grp; Trk; Prfct Atten Awd; LAW.

JACOBS, EVAN; Palm Springs HS; Palm Springs, CA; (4); Am Leg Boys St; Acpl Chr; Pres Chorus; High Hon Roll; Ntl Merit Ltr; Pres Acad Fit Awd; Acad Dcthln; JR Stsmn Of Amer VP; CSF Pres; U CA San Diego; Engrng.

JACOBS, GLENN; West Covina HS; W Covina, CA; (3); 44/500; Am Leg Boys St; Letterman Clb; Office Aide; Red Cross Aide; Spanish Clb; SADD; Varsity Clb; Pres Jr Cls; Var L Bsbl; Var L Ftbl; Cmptv Soccer Team ST Cup Chmps 89; MVP Soccer; ASB Pres 90-91; Ftbl Coaches Awd 87-88; UCLA; Jrnlst.

JACOBS, HEATHER L; Village Christian HS; La Crescenta, CA; (4); Hosp Aide; Mu Alpha Theta; Office Aide; Teachers Aide; Chorus; Hon Roll; Biola U; Psych.

JACOBS, JACQUELINE M; Porterville HS; Porterville, CA; (3); Art Clb; French Clb; JA; School Musical; School Play; Nwsp; Hon Roll; Bio.

JACOBS, JENIPHER; Oakmont HS; Roseville, CA; (1); Drama Clb; French Clb; Service Clb; SADD; School Play; Crs Cntry; Trk; High Hon Roll; Pres Acad Fit Awd; Global Impact Clb; Med.

JACOBS, JENNIFER; Dana Hills HS; Dana Point, CA; (1); Church Yth Grp; Cmnty Wkr; Stu Cncl; JV Bsktbl; Socr; JV Sftbl; Cit Awd; Hon Roll; Pres Acad Fit Awd; U CA-SANTA Barbara.

JACOBS, JENNIFER K; Santa Margarita Catholic HS; Rnch Snta Margari, CA; (3); 51/227; Drama Clb; Model UN; School Play; Lit Mag; Swmmng; Hon Roll; NHS; Pre Law.

JACOBS, JULIAN K; Pioneer HS; San Jose, CA; (4); Debate Tm; Key Clb; Spanish Clb; Var Capt Bsbl; Capt Var Ftbl; Hon Roll; Mock Trials Best Def Atty; Outstndng Sr Male Athlt; US Army Reserve Schlr Athlt Awd; Physiology.

JACOBS, LARRY; Covina HS; Covina, CA; (4); Letterman Clb; Teachers Aide; Varsity Clb; JV Var Bsktbl; High Hon Roll; Hon Roll; Athl Schlr 88; CA Schltc Fed 86 88 90; Pres Of Bsktbl Clb 89-90; Congrssnl Schlr 89-90; UCLA; Bus.

JACOBS, MELISSA N; Rio Americano HS; Carmichael, CA; (3); Debate Tm; Spanish Clb; Drill Tm; School Musical; Stage Crew; Nwsp; Stu Cncl; Friday Night Live, Co-Pres 2 Yrs; TV Sta Mgr; Brass Plum Fshn Brd; Commnctns.

JACOBS, PATRICIA Y; O'farrell SCPA HS; San Diego, CA; (2); Band; Jazz Band; Mrchg Band; Pep Band; School Musical; High Hon Roll; Hnr Band; Deptmnt Hnrs Spnsh I & II; Outstndng Achvtmnt Instrmntl Music; Drama.

JACOBS, ROYCE; Herlong HS; Herlong, CA; (4); VP Debate Tm; VP Drama Clb; Letterman Clb; JV Bsktbl; Var Cheerldng; JV Var Ftbl; JV Wt Lftg; Var Wrstlng; Acad Olympcs; Spllng Bee; U Of NV; Computers.

JACOBS, SHIRA; Santa Barbara HS; Santa Barbara, CA; (2); 17/500; Cmnty Wkr; Debate Tm; Drama Clb; Hosp Aide; Church Choir; Rep Frsh Cls; Rep Soph Cls; Rep Stu Cncl; JV Bsktbl; High Hon Roll; Piano; Dance; Ecology Clb; Vassar; Botany.

JACOBS, STAN J; Adolfo Camarillo HS; Oxnard, CA; (2); Church Yth Grp; Computer Clb; VP Debate Tm; German Clb; NFL; VP Speech Tm; Nwsp; Rep Frsh Cls; Rep Soph Cls; High Hon Roll; Law.

JACOBS, TEARMESHA; Washington Prep HS; Los Angeles, CA; (4); 14/520; Church Yth Grp; Girl Scts; Pep Clb; Teachers Aide; Tennis; Cit Awd; Hon Roll; Empress Clb; El Camino JC; Nursing.

JACOBS, TINA S; Abraham Lincoln HS; San Francisco, CA; (1); GATE Pgm; City Coll Of Sn Francisco; Educ.

JACOBSEN, AMY; Casa Grande HS; Petaluma, CA; (3); 30/300; Drama Clb; Letterman Clb; Varsity Clb; School Play; Lit Mag; Var Bsktbl; Powder Puff Ftbl; Var Trk; Hon Roll; NHS; Cal Poly; Bio Sci.

JACOBSEN, AMY; Miramonte HS; Lafayette, CA; (3); Cmnty Wkr; NFL; Speech Tm; Teachers Aide; Var Capt Diving; Var L Gym; Cit Awd; Wrstlng; St Schlr; Particpnt UCSB Smmr Jnrs Prgm; UCSB Ambssdr; CA ST Public Spkng Fnlst 89-90; UCSB; Geolgy.

JACOBSEN, DANIELLE; Amador Valley HS; Pleasanton, CA; (2); Church Yth Grp; Color Guard; Mrchg Band; High Hon Roll; Hon Roll; CSF; CA Golden St Exam Awd Gold Seal Geom.

JACOBSEN, DAVID; Mt Whitney HS; Visalia, CA; (4); Boy Scts; French Clb; Spanish Clb; Sequoias Coll; Frgn Lang.

JACOBSEN, IVY; Kingsburg HS; Reedley, CA; (2); Art Clb; Church Yth Grp; Bsktbl; Tennis; Trk; Hon Roll.

JACOBSEN, LISA N; Dana Hills HS; San Juan Capistra, CA; (1); Church Yth Grp; Hon Roll; Pres Acad Fit Awd; GATE.

JACOBSEN, MICHELLE L; Antelope Valley HS; Lancaster, CA; (4); 11/560; Cmnty Wkr; German Clb; Service Clb; Sec Band; Mrchg Band; Pep Band; Cit Awd; High Hon Roll; Pres Schlr; CSF-HNR Soc-Life Stu; San Diego ST U; Publc Acctng.

JACOBSEN, ZERO J; San Rafael HS; San Rafael, CA; (2); Drama Clb; Variety Show; JV Crs Cntry; JV Trk.

JACOBSOHN, JED A; Berkeley HS; Berkeley, CA; (3); Pep Clb; Ski Clb; Teachers Aide; Band; Ed Nwsp; Treas Frsh Cls; Treas Soph Cls; Treas Jr Cls; Stu Cncl; Hon Roll; Freelance Photo United Press Intl; Photo Jrnlsm.

JACOBSON, CORY L; Corona HS; Corona, CA; (4); 32/472; Church Yth Grp; Drama Clb; FCA; FTA; Letterman Clb; Pep Clb; Q&S; Speech Tm; Varsity Clb; Band; Assoc In-N-Out; Long Beach ST U; Psych.

JACOBSON, KELLY L; North HS; Bakersfield, CA; (1); Ski Clb; Varsity Clb; Var L Crs Cntry; Var L Socr; Var L Tennis; Hon Roll; Schlr Awd V Crss Cntry; Water Skiing; Phrmcy.

JACOBSON, KRISTI T; Lassen Union HS; Janesville, CA; (2); Ski Clb; Band; Stage Crew; Elctrnc Tech.

JACOBSON, MONIQUE; Capital Christian Schl; Sacramento, CA; (4); Sec Frsh Cls; Sec Stu Cncl; Var Sftbl; Var Trk; Var Capt Vllybl; High Hon Roll; CA Schlrshp Fed VP & Lftm; CA Poly; Arch.

JACOBSON, REBECCA ANN; Ventura HS; Ventura, CA; (3); Pep Clb; SADD; JV Cheerldng; Var Pom Pon; JV Trk; OR ST; Teacher.

JACOBSON, RONI; Capistrano Valley HS; Mission Viejo, CA; (3); Drama Clb; German Clb; Teachers Aide; Capt Color Guard; Orch; Cit Awd; High Hon Roll.

JACOBSON, SHEILA; Marina HS; Westminster, CA; (4); Art Clb; Church Yth Grp; French Clb; Pep Clb; Church Choir; Hon Roll; Orange Coast Coll; Advrtsng.

JACOBUS, GREGG A; Bishop Montgomery HS; Gardena, CA; (3); Var JV Bsktbl; Sprts Med.

JACQUETTE, JULIENNE I; Carson HS; Carson, CA; (3); Church Yth Grp; Cmnty Wkr; FTA; SADD; Church Choir; Variety Show; Sec Stu Cncl; Cheerldng; Stat Ftbl; Hon Roll; Delta Sigma Theta-Black Heritage Essay-3rd Pl; Debutante-Alpha Kappa Alpha; Paine Coll-Augusta; Corp Law.

JACQUEZ, CHRIS L; Liberty Union HS; Oakley, CA; (3); Boy Scts; Church Yth Grp; Teachers Aide; Ftbl; Yth Dvlpmnt Entrprs Stu & Job Exchng Hl; Ricks Coll ID; Air Ln Pilot.

JACSON, GWENDOLYN; Washington Prep; Los Angeles, CA; (4); Band; Drm Mjr(t); Jazz Band; Mrchg Band; Stu Cncl; Hon Roll; Prfct Atten Awd; Val; Boston U; Bus.

JADDOU, UR M; Chula Vista HS; Chula Vista, CA; (2); 13/558; Debate Tm; Sec Pep Clb; Yrbk; Treas Frsh Cls; Treas Soph Cls; VP Jr Cls; NHS; Stu Accredtn Cmmttee; Schlwide Stu Senate Rep; Stanford; Lawyer.

JADIA, ROSEMARY R; Fountain Valley HS; Fountain Valley, CA; (1); Spanish Clb; School Play; Variety Show; Off Frsh Cls; Stu Cncl; CSF Clb; PTSA Stu Achvt Awd Engl; Harvard; Med.

JAEGER, TERI LYN; Irvine HS; Irvine, CA; (1); Church Yth Grp; French Clb; Tennis; UCSD; Psycht.

JAFFE, TROY R; Campolindo HS; Moraga, CA; (4); Cmnty Wkr; JA; Rptr Nwsp; Crs Cntry; JV Socr; Trk; High Hon Roll; Ntl Merit SF; Exch Stu To West Grmny.

JAFFIN, JAY; San Ramon Valley HS; San Ramon, CA; (3); FBLA; Band; School Musical; Wrstlng; High Hon Roll; NHS; Musician/Schlr Awd; Golden St Exam Geom Awd; Berkeley; Bus.

JAGARD, KERRI L; Simi Valley HS; Simi Valley, CA; (4); 48/789; Dance Clb; Key Clb; Thesps; Pres Acpl Chr; Pres Chorus; Capt Flag Corp; School Musical; School Play; Swing Chorus; Variety Show; BYU; Music.

JAGER, ERICA R; Presentation HS; San Jose, CA; (4); Art Clb; Cmnty Wkr; Office Aide; Service Clb; High Hon Roll; Pres Acad Fit Awd; Pres Schlr; Mount St Marys Coll Future Tchr Schlrshp; Yth Hall Of Fame; Engl Excllnc; Mount St Marys Coll; Engl.

JAGER, MELANIE; Marina HS; Westminster, CA; (2); Church Yth Grp; Spanish Clb; Off Soph Cls; JV Swmmng; High Hon Roll; Jr NHS; Pres Acad Fit Awd; Scholar Athlete Awd; March Of Dimes Club; Peer Assistance Lg; Brigham Young U; Arch.

JAGLA, TOM A; San Rafael HS; San Rafael, CA; (4); Boy Scts; German Clb; Variety Show; Swmmng; Tennis; High Hon Roll; Hon Roll; Pres Acad Fit Awd; Vrsty Wtr Polo; U Of CA Santa Barbara; Bus.

JAHED, NAVID; University HS; Irvine, CA; (3); 1/550; Debate Tm; French Clb; Math Clb; Math Tm; NFL; Quiz Bowl; Science Clb; Bsktbl; French Hon Soc; High Hon Roll; Med.

JAHIEL, ALEXIS; Los Angeles County HS For The Arts; Hollywood, CA; (4); 64/150; Lit Mag; Rep Stu Cncl; Pres Schlr; LA Cultrl Affrs Dept Awd Creatvty Photo & Hnrbl Mntn Fine Art Photo; KC Art Inst Pres Schlrshp; Kansas City Art Inst; Photo.

JAHNS, AMY C; Poway HS; Poway, CA; (2); SADD; Band; Mrchg Band; Pres Acad Fit Awd; Music; Friday Night Live; U CA; Envrnmntl Stds.

JAHR, TOM N; Village Christian HS; Tujunga, CA; (2); Chess Clb; Church Yth Grp; Cmnty Wkr; Spanish Clb; Band; Mrchg Band; Stage Crew; Yrbk; Ftbl; Socr; Video Game Champ; Cartoonst; Poster Dsgnr Aero Systms Grp; CO ST; Cmmrcl Esgn.

JAIME, ARENAS; Huntington Park HS; Huntington Park, CA; (2); Cmnty Wkr; Hosp Aide; Key Clb; Library Aide; Office Aide; Teachers Aide; Off Soph Cls; Off Jr Cls; Stu Cncl; Tennis; Cert For Being Asst Commissioner Of Publcty; Helped Campaign Re-Elect Cunningham For Cnclmn; Law.

JAIME, GINA D; Pius X HS; South Gate, CA; (3); 5/175; Church Yth Grp; Cmnty Wkr; GAA; Chorus; Bsktbl; Crs Cntry; Sftbl; High Hon Roll; Hon Roll; NHS; Pre-Law.

JAIME, MARTA; Glendora HS; Glendora, CA; (4); 70/375; Church Yth Grp; Service Clb; SADD; Yrbk; Stu Cncl; Tennis; Hon Roll; Pres Acad Fit Awd; Ten Coaches JR Var Awd 86, 2nd Tm Var MUP 88; All Lg, 3rd Pl Bsln Lg 89; 1st Tm Lg Acad Schlr Awd; Azusa Pcfc U; Liberal Studies.

JAIME, SANDRA; Bassett HS; La Puente, CA; (4); 4/260; French Clb; Cit Awd; High Hon Roll; Hon Roll; NHS; 4th In Cls; Recognition For Perfmnce In English AP Tests,US Govt AP Tests; Sonoma ST U; Family Law.

JAIMES, BRENT L; Monrovia HS; Glendora, CA; (4); #19 In Class; Drama Clb; Science Clb; Service Clb; Pres Spanish Clb; SADD; School Musical; Pres Acad Fit Awd; CA Schlrshp Fed Chaptr Hstrn; Fthll Jaycees Outstndng Stu Ldr Awd; U Of CA Berkeley; Arch.

JAIMES, MONICA; San Gabriel Mission HS; Los Angeles, CA; (2); GAA; Var L Crs Cntry; Mgr(s); Var L Trk; Hon Roll; US Long Distance Int Sports Exch Team Mem; Stanford; Law.

JAIMES, TRISTA; Pioneer HS; San Jose, CA; (4); FFA; Library Aide; Mgr(s); L Swmmng; Santa Clara Cnty Humane Soc Vlntr; Chld Dvlpmnt.

JAIN, ANAMIKA; Irvine HS; Irvine, CA; (3); 137/512; AFS; Cmnty Wkr; Intnl Clb; Key Clb; JV Diving; JV Swmmng; Hon Roll; Ethnc Advsry Forum; Stdnts For Scl Rspnsblty; Peer Cnslg; Engrng.

JAIN, KAVITA; Canyon HS; Anaheim, CA; (4); 9/450; French Clb; Math Clb; Ed Nwsp; Hon Roll; NHS; Girls Leag Svc Club Offcr; Prfssnl Clsscl Indian Dance Troupe Tour; Mock Trial Lawyer; USC; Corp Law.

JAIN, KAVITA; Live Oak HS; Morgan Hill, CA; (3); 8/500; Treas French Clb; FBLA; Key Clb; Office Aide; Teachers Aide; Ed Yrbk; Hon Roll; Ntl Merit SF; VP CA Schlrshp Fndtn; Psych.

JAIN, MANAV; Irvine HS; Irvine, CA; (3); 65/512; AFS; VP German Clb; VP JA; Stu For Soc Respnsblty; Amer Fld Svc; Hertge Awds; Soc Sci.

JAIN, SHAFALI; Hiram W Johnson HS; Sacramento, CA; (1); 1/787; Cmnty Wkr; Dance Clb; Drama Clb; Intnl Clb; Orch; School Musical; Hon Roll; Sacramento Indian Yth Assn; Indian Dances; Toastmstrs Intl Yth Ldrshp Pgm; Comp Analyst.

JAISWAL, ANJALI; John Burroughs HS; Burbank, CA; (2); Cmnty Wkr; Key Clb; Science Clb; Rep Stu Cncl; Var Fld Hcky; High Hon Roll; Hon Roll; Opt Clb Awd; SHARE-RELATIONS Commssnr; CSF; Close Up-Schl Rep; Jrnlsm.

JAKOBSON, GABRIEL; Abraham Lincoln HS; San Francisco, CA; (4); VP Computer Clb; Rotary Awd; Bnk Amer Achvt Awd; 2nd Pl In Invest In Amer Econ Cntst; UC Davis; Elec Engr.

JAKOBSON, REVITAL; Abraham Lincoln HS; San Francisco, CA; (2); Intrml Bsktbl; Intrml Vllybl; Int Dcrtr.

JAMAICA, LILIA M; Crenshaw HS; Los Angeles, CA; (2); JA; Library Aide; Office Aide; Pep Clb; Science Clb; Service Clb; Teachers Aide; Chorus; School Musical; School Play; Soc Sci.

JAMANILA II, GABRIEL; Sweetwater Union HS; National City, CA; (3); Boy Scts; Church Yth Grp; Band; Pep Band; JV Trk; U Notre Dame.

JAMES, AIMEE R; Mercy HS; San Francisco, CA; (4); Stage Crew; Nwsp; JV Vllybl; Black & White Photography; City Coll Of San Francisco.

JAMES, ANDREA S; Palmdale HS; Palmdale, CA; (2); Hon Roll; Int Dcrtng.

JAMES, CHANTAE; Chino HS; Chino, CA; (1); Church Yth Grp; Cmnty Wkr; Drama Clb; FFA; FHA; Drill Tm; Nwsp; Off Frsh Cls; Off Soph Cls; Bsktbl; Southern; Psych.

JAMES, CHRISTINA L; Villa Park HS; Orange, CA; (2); Hosp Aide; Treas Latin Clb; Red Cross Aide; Rep Soph Cls; Var Crs Cntry; Hon Roll; NHS; Disneyland Creatvty Challng Speech Finalist; PUSH Prev Drug & Alchl; PAL Peer Asst Ldrshp; Notre Dame; Cardiovascula Srgn.

JAMES, DANIEL S N; Orange Glen HS; Escondido, CA; (3); Church Yth Grp; Cmnty Wkr; French Clb; Band; Jazz Band; Mrchg Band; Orch; Pep Band; JV Crs Cntry; Berklee Schl Music; Musician.

JAMES, DNECE W; Yreka HS; Montague, CA; (3); 3/180; Church Yth Grp; Cmnty Wkr; JV Var Cheerldng; JV Var Powder Puff Ftbl; CSF Treas; All-Amer Schltc Awd.

JAMES, ELICIA; Bret Harte HS; Murphys, CA; (2); FFA; Spanish Clb; Var Tennis; JV Vllybl; High Hon Roll; Friday Night Live; IA ST U; Ped.

JAMES, ERIC L; Hemet HS; Hemet, CA; (2); Church Yth Grp; Teachers Aide; Acpl Chr; Church Choir.

JAMES, ERIC L; Pittsburg HS; Pittsburg, CA; (3); 136/344; FBLA; Cit Awd; Hon Roll; Civil Engrng.

JAMES, EVE A; Canyon Springs HS; Moreno Valley, CA; (3); Girl Scts; ROTC; Church Choir; Hon Roll; Prfct Atten Awd; ROTC Drill Team; Was In Few Parades; Air Force; Engr.

JAMES, GARY; Analy HS; Sebastopol, CA; (4); Church Yth Grp; FFA; Christn Mssnry Outreach Mexico; Police Explrer; Outstndng Crftsmn Woodshp Awd 2 Yrs; Doyle Schlrshp Awd; Santa Rosa JC; Carpentry.

JAMES, GREG; Cypress HS; Cypress, CA; (3); Science Clb; Service Clb; Band; Drm Mjr(t); Mrchg Band; Orch; High Hon Roll; Bio.

JAMES, JARED L; Arvin HS; Arvin, CA; (2); Church Yth Grp; Pep Clb; Band; Chorus; Jazz Band; Off Mrchg Band; Pep Band; Bsbl; Hon Roll; Jr NHS; Bakersfield Coll; Music.

JAMES, JENEAN; Sonora HS; Groveland, CA; (4); 83/250; Drama Clb; French Clb; Office Aide; Teachers Aide; Chorus; School Musical; Stu Cncl; Var Cheerldng; Var Pom Pon; D J For Schl Radio Station; Columbia JC; Elem Ed.

JAMES, JENNIFER W; Fontana HS; Fontana, CA; (4); 97/794; Aud/Vis; Drama Clb; Teachers Aide; Thesps; Acpl Chr; Chorus; School Musical; School Play; Stage Crew; Variety Show; Tri-M Music Awd & Tassal; CSF, Silver Medal 88-90; Outstndng Soprano Acappella Choir 89, Girls Chorus; CA ST; Teacher.

JAMES, JODIE A; Nevada Joint Union HS; Grass Valley, CA; (3); Ski Clb; JV Cheerldng; JV Var Tennis; JV Vllybl; Principals Awd For Acad Achvt; Chico ST U; Phys Thrpy.

JAMES, JULIANNE W; Fontana HS; Fontana, CA; (3); Church Yth Grp; Drama Clb; Service Clb; Acpl Chr; Chorus; Church Choir; School Play; Hon Roll; Madrigals; CSF Silv Mdl Awd; CA St San Bernardino; Engl Tch.

JAMES, KATHERINE E; Arlington HS; Riverside, CA; (3); Teachers Aide; Hon Roll; RCC; Socl Woker.

JAMES, LAURA; Victor Valley HS; Victorville, CA; (2); GAA; Teachers Aide; JV Var Sftbl; JV Var Vllybl; Cit Awd; Hon Roll; Cal ST San Bernadino; Teacher.

JAMES, LISA; Western Christian HS; W Covina, CA; (4); Pres Church Yth Grp; Drill Tm; Variety Show; Off Soph Cls; Rep Jr Cls; Off Sr Cls; Off Stu Cncl; JV Var Cheerldng; Hon Roll; Mt Sac; Nursing.

JAMES, MONICA H; Santa Clara HS; Oxnard, CA; (2); Cmnty Wkr; Debate Tm; Hosp Aide; NFL; Speech Tm; Score Keeper; Hon Roll; NHS; Pres Acad Fit Awd; Elem Ed.

JAMES, NICOLE S; Thomas Downey HS; Modesto, CA; (4); Cit Awd; Hon Roll; Modesto JR Coll; Dental Asst.

JAMES, PETER D; Las Lomas; Walnut Creek, CA; (1); Boy Scts; Spanish Clb; Hon Roll; Reflections Wrtng Cont.

JAMES, SCOTT W; Willows HS; Willows, CA; (2); Boy Scts; Church Yth Grp; Key Clb; Letterman Clb; Pep Clb; Church Choir; Color Guard; Var Cheerldng; JV Var Ftbl; Var Wt Lftg; Congrssnl Yth Ldrshp Cncl; Aeronautic Engr.

JAMES, SHANNON M; Rim Of The World HS; Fountain Valley, CA; (2); Cmnty Wkr; GAA; Service Clb; Var Capt Bsktbl; Trk; Hon Roll; Opt Clb Awd; Stanford.

JAMES, TAMARA D; Mtn View Acad; Sunnyvale, CA; (4); 13/28; Church Yth Grp; French Clb; Ski Clb; Spanish Clb; Chorus; Off Jr Cls; Prfct Atten Awd; Poems Published; Golden Poet Awd 2 Yrs; Edtrs Choice Awd; Walla Walla Coll; Socl Work.

JAMES JR, WILLIAM T; 29 Palms HS; 29 Palms, CA; (1); 4/300; Var JV Bsbl; Cit Awd; High Hon Roll; Hon Roll; Prfct Atten Awd; Pres Acad Fit Awd; U Of Miami FL; Accntng.

JAMESON, ERIK STEPHEN; Walnut HS; Walnut, CA; (4); 43/353; Key Clb; Thesps; School Play; Chess Clb; Off Jr Cls; Off Sr Cls; Hon Roll; Pres Acad Fit Awd; LA Cnty U Of AZ Alumni Schlrshp Wnnr/Rep Women Schlrshp Wnnr; U Of AZ; Archeology.

JAMESON, JASON T; Yucca Valley HS; Yucca Valley, CA; (2); Cit Awd; Hon Roll; Masonic Awd; Awds In Art; Biomedcl Engr.

JAMESON, MAISHA J; Oakland Technical HS; Oakland, CA; (2); 1/445; Art Clb; Pep Clb; Office Aide; Teachers Aide; School Musical; Rptr Nwsp; Hon Roll; Natl Yng Ldrs Conf Cngrsnl Schlr; Chldrn Of War; Yth Empwrmnt Advcts; Stanford; Law.

JAMESON, MICHAEL; Cajon HS; San Bernardino, CA; (3); 35/463; Tennis; JV Trk; Wt Lftg; NHS; CSF; Jr Statesmen O Amer; Natl Hnr Soc; Stanford U; Elec Engrng.

JAMGOCHIAN, GINA MARIE; Bullard HS; Fresno, CA; (4); 30/454; Treas Church Yth Grp; Key Clb; Rep Stu Cncl; Var Tennis; NHS; CSF Lf, Bd Dir; Coach Awd-Tnns; Hnr Rl; Gldn ST Exm Geom Awd; UCLA; Bus.

JAMIESON, AARON R; Westminster HS; Westminster, CA; (1); Boy Scts; Altered Universe Club; Archlgy.

JAMIESON, CARRIE; Napa HS; Napa, CA; (1); Band; City Sftbl Tm; Piano; Swmmng.

JAMIESON, KIM S; Canyon HS; Anaheim, CA; (1); GAA; Capt Pep Clb; SADD; Capt Cheerldng; Stat Socr; Capt Vllybl; Hon Roll; Vlybl Bst Offnsv Plyr; UCLA.

JAMIL, RITA; Monte Vista HS; La Mesa, CA; (2); 15/470; French Clb; Key Clb; Swmmng; Hon Roll; Gldn St Exam Alg Hnr Achvt; Natl Frnch Test; USC; Med.

JAMISON, GABRIELLE L; Mission Bay HS; San Diego, CA; (4); Dance Clb; Drama Clb; SADD; Varsity Clb; Band; School Play; Stu Cncl; Fld Hcky; Powder Puff Ftbl; High Hon Roll; UA Fairbanks; Bio.

JAMISON, LAURA M; Ukian HS; Ukiah, CA; (1); 83/625; Church Yth Grp; Chorus; Church Choir; JV Cheerldng; Physical Therapy.

JAMISON, MICHAEL; Roseville HS; Roseville, CA; (4); 30/360; Church Yth Grp; JA; SADD; JV Var Crs Cntry; JV Trk; Hon Roll; Pres Acad Fit Awd; Vet.

JAMISON, MICHELE L; John Muri HS; Altadena, CA; (2); Pep Clb; Bsktbl; Sftbl; Trk; Cit Awd; Boys Clb; Lawyer.

JAMOSMOS, MARITESS; Edison SR HS; Stockton, CA; (3); Boy Scts; Math Clb; NFL; Science Clb; Speech Tm; SADD; Variety Show; Cheerldng; High Hon Roll; Hon Roll; CSF Sec; Mst Outstndng Sci Stu San Joaquin Cnty 89-90; Keywanettes Clb Treas; Stanford U; Engrng.

JANAK, KEVIN; Don Antonio Lugo HS; Chino Hills, CA; (2); Boy Scts; Church Yth Grp; German Clb; Var Trk; High Hon Roll; Gldn Cnqust Awd Engl; 2nd Pl Wrtng Cntst; Mrn Bio.

JANCE, JUNE M; Woodland HS; Woodland, CA; (2); French Clb; Acpl Chr; Band; School Musical; Hon Roll; Intl Ordr Rnbw For Grls Ofcs Faith Hope Pot Of Gold Rptr; Intl Ordr Of Jobs Dghtrs Ofc Treas; Fr Nt Lv; Penn ST; Astronomy.

JANCI, STEPHANIE A; Armijo HS; Fairfield, CA; (2); Color Guard; Hon Roll; Vocal Trng; Piano Lssns; Edtrs Choice Awd Natl Libr Poetry Cont 90; Russian.

JANES, JACQUIE M; Walnut HS; Walnut, CA; (4); Church Yth Grp; Cmnty Wkr; Debate Tm; Drama Clb; Band; Church Choir; Mrchg Band; Pep Band; School Musical; Stage Crew; Snow Skiing; Mount San Antonio; Arch.

JANG, ANNETTE; Hogan SR HS; Vallejo, CA; (2); SADD; Teachers Aide; Hon Roll; Sal; Hnr Soc; Acad Ltr; Harvard; Law.

JANG, ERIN N; Alpha Beacon Christian Schl; San Carlos, CA; (1); Church Yth Grp; Drama Clb; FCA; School Musical; School Play; Yrbk; Var Sftbl; Var Vllybl; Hon Roll; Pres Acad Fit Awd; All Leag Sftbl Awd 90; Teaching.

JANG, GWENDOLYN M; Lowell HS; San Francisco, CA; (3); GSE Alg & Geom W/Hnrs; Bio Chem.

JANG, SOO; Walnut HS; Walnut, CA; (4); 24/360; German Clb; Hosp Aide; Key Clb; Stu Cncl; L Ftbl; L Socr; Tennis; High Hon Roll; Pres Acad Fit Awd; Cls Of 90 Cabinet; CSF; German Hnr Soc; U CA Irvine; Biolgcl Sci.

JANI, NAVIN M; Irvine HS; Irvine, CA; (2); French Clb; Key Clb; Math Tm; Science Clb; Band; Mrchg Band; Hon Roll; Pres Acad Fit Awd; OCAD; Tae Kwon Do; Stanford; Scintst.

JANIK, KEVIN; Palm Desert HS; Palm Desert, CA; (2); Cmnty Wkr; Key Clb; Model UN; Science Clb; Tennis; High Hon Roll; Hon Roll; Pres Acad Fit Awd; Skiing; Reading & Hiking.

JANIS, STEPHEN P; Damien HS; Upland, CA; (3); 62/217; Spanish Clb; Hon Roll; U Of Southern CA; Dentistry.

JANJIK, TALIN; Herbert Hoover HS; Glendale, CA; (3); Dance Clb; German Clb; Girl Scts; Science Clb; UCLA; Bio Chem.

JANKE, RAINA A; John Burroughs HS; Burbank, CA; (3); Dance Clb; Drama Clb; Spanish Clb; Pres Frsh Cls; Rep Stu Cncl; Hon Roll; Pres Acad Fit Awd; Mem Share Clb Hlps Stu Lss Fortunate; Phtgrphy/Advrtsng.

JANKOUZIAN, RITA; Pasadena HS; Pasadena, CA; (2); 2/30; High Hon Roll; CA Schlrshp Fed; 3 Speech Mts 1st Pl; Sci.

JANKOWSKI, BECKY; Woodbridge HS; Irvine, CA; (1); 32/435; Drama Clb; Pep Clb; Drill Tm; Cheerldng; High Hon Roll; Jr NHS; Pres Acad Fit Awd; Law.

JANKOWSKI, BRIAN T; Mater Dei HS; Fountain Valley, CA; (3); Church Yth Grp; Intrml Ftbl; Intrml Golf; Hon Roll; Jrnlsm.

JANKOWSKY, AMY; Poway HS; San Diego, CA; (2); Church Yth Grp; Model UN; Pep Clb; Cheerldng; Hon Roll; Outstndng Delg Model UN; Tchr Rcgntn Awd; Gldn St Exam Awd.

JANKOWSKY, KARA; Poway HS; San Diego, CA; (4); Church Yth Grp; Letterman Clb; Pep Clb; SADD; Varsity Clb; Variety Show; Capt Var Cheerldng; Powder Puff Ftbl; Hon Roll; NHS; U Of AZ; Psych.

JANMOHAMED, MUNIR S; Sacramento Waldorf Schl; Fair Oaks, CA; (3); Boy Scts; Temple Yth Grp; Chorus; Orch; School Play; Stage Crew; Phtg Yrbk; Treas Soph Cls; JV Bsktbl; Score Keeper; UC Irvine; Doctor.

JANN, LING LESLIE; Pleasant Valley HS; Chico, CA; (4); 11/226; Cmnty Wkr; Hosp Aide; Office Aide; School Play; Trk; Vllybl; Gov Hon Prg Awd; Hon Roll; Pres Acad Fit Awd; CA ST U Chico; Bus.

JANNKE, LAUREN S; Loretto HS; Sacramento, CA; (3); Cmnty Wkr; Dance Clb; SADD; School Musical; Variety Show; Treas Jr Cls; Pres Sr Cls; CA Schlrshp Fdrtn; Cmnctns.

JANOSKI, DAVID J; Corona HS; Corona, CA; (2); 25/470; Var Bsbl; Var Bsktbl; Var Ftbl; High Hon Roll; Pres Acad Fit Awd; Gldn St Exam Hnrs Geom; Math.

JANOUSEK, JEANETTE; Royal HS; Simi Valley, CA; (2); 2/300; Church Yth Grp; Pres French Clb; Treas Intnl Clb; Office Aide; Co-Capt Drill Tm; Jr NHS; Pres Acad Fit Awd; CSF; Carnegie Mellon; Sci/Math.

JANSEN, ERIK; Esperanza HS; Anaheim, CA; (4); Var Debate Tm; NFL; Nwsp; High Hon Roll; Hon Roll; Mock Trl Dfnce Capt; Loyola Marymount U; Pol Sci.

JANSSEN, DAVID L; Cabrillo HS; VAFB, CA; (2); Teachers Aide; JV Bsbl; JV Ftbl; Hon Roll; UNLV; Bus.

JANSSEN, MARY; Bishop Montgomery HS; Lawndale, CA; (3); Office Aide; Vllybl; Hon Roll; VASA Order Amer; Hnrb Mntn Sci Fr; San Diego ST U; Advrtsng.

JANTZEN, LISA; James Lick HS; San Jose, CA; (4); 5/257; Sec Pres Church Yth Grp; Cmnty Wkr; Intnl Clb; VP Service Clb; Rptr Nwsp; Rep Stu Cncl; High Hon Roll; NHS; Rotary Awd; Elem Ed.

JANUARY, DARCELL D; Chaffey HS; Ontario, CA; (3); Church Yth Grp; Cmnty Wkr; FCA; Letterman Clb; Library Aide; Red Cross Aide; SADD; Teachers Aide; Church Choir; Bsktbl.

JANUS, JULIE JEAN; Bear River HS; Grass Valley, CA; (3); 1/200; Band; Jazz Band; Capt Var Crs Cntry; Capt VP Trk; High Hon Roll; Ntl Merit Ltr; MVP 4th In State; Member & Officer CA Schlastsic Fedration; CO ST Boulder.

JANZEN, MARK E; Edison HS; Fresno, CA; (1); Church Yth Grp; Golf; Pres Acad Fit Awd; CSF; Envrmntl Clb; Photo.

JAQUEZ, EZEQUIEL J; Rio Mesa HS; Camarillo, CA; (3); Latin Clb; Letterman Clb.

JAQUEZ, PETULA S; Rio Mesa HS; Camarillo, CA; (3); Church Yth Grp; Church Choir; Var Capt Bsktbl; Hon Roll; Psych.

JAQUEZ JR, STEPHEN ANTHONY; Watsonville HS; Watsonville, CA; (2); Church Yth Grp; Band; Jazz Band; Mrchg Band; Police Ofcr.

JARAMILLA, MARGARET; Oxnard HS; Oxnard, CA; (2); 4/604; Church Yth Grp; Pres Frsh Cls; Off Soph Cls; Pres Stu Cncl; Var Trk; JV Vllybl; High Hon Roll; Hon Roll; VP Asian Amer Clb; 3rd Frgn Lang Acad Olympc; Outstndng Gov Awd; J.V-MVP Trck/Fld; JV Vlybl Coachs Awd; CA ST Berkeley; Med.

JARAMILLO, CLAUDIA E; Mira Mesa HS; San Diego, CA; (3); Acpl Chr; Chorus; Cit Awd; Hon Roll; Music.

JARAMILLO, JENNIFER K; University HS; Los Angeles, CA; (3); JCL; Latin Clb; Office Aide; Service Clb; Variety Show; Pres Frsh Cls; Stu Cncl; Var Capt Cheerldng; Var L Gym; Hon Roll; Most Inspirational Gymnast 89-90; Most Ded Gymnst 88-89; Most Invld Sch Activities 87-88; UCLA; Frgn Lang.

JARAMILLO, JUDITH A; Ventura HS; Ventura, CA; (3); 54/431; Church Yth Grp; Hosp Aide; Letterman Clb; Teachers Aide; Varsity Clb; High Hon Roll; Hon Roll; Prfct Atten Awd; Crtfd Cthlc Catechist; Gldn St Exam Geom Hnrs; Rainbow Coalition; Whittier Coll; Law.

JARAMILLO, LUZ A; Bell HS; Maywood, CA; (3); Church Yth Grp; GAA; Teachers Aide; Varsity Clb; Var Bsktbl; CA ST L A; Elem Teacher.

JAREB, SHIRLEY D; La Quinta HS; Fountain Valley, CA; (3); Dance Clb; GAA; VP Pep Clb; Speech Tm; SADD; Teachers Aide; Variety Show; Rep Jr Cls; Var L Socr; JV Tennis; AZ ST; Law Enfrcmnt.

JARED, MISTIE; West HS; Bakersfield, CA; (4); Dance Clb; Var Cheerldng; Var Capt Pom Pon; Hon Roll; Awd Mst Imprvd Advncd Dnce; CA ST U Bakersfield; Psycht.

JARIANGPRASERT, SUTIDA N; Clovis West HS; Fresno, CA; (3); Key Clb; Orch; Hon Roll; Jr Larcs; GATE; CSF.

JARKA, SHARI L; William S Hart HS; Valencia, CA; (2); Church Yth Grp; FBLA; Swmmng; Hon Roll; Pres Acad Fit Awd; CA Schlrshp Fed.

JARO, JOCELYN R; Poway HS; Poway, CA; (1); Rep Stu Cncl; JV Swmmng; High Hon Roll; Grapplettes.

JARRAR, FRED; Newport Christian HS; Costa Mesa, CA; (3); Chess Clb; Ski Clb; Teachers Aide; Stage Crew; Var Bsbl; Var Bsktbl; Var Vllybl; Hon Roll; Bus Engrng.

JARRELL, HOLLY A; La Sierra HS; Riverside, CA; (1); Treas Church Yth Grp; JV Swmmng; High Hon Roll; CSF; Law.

JARRELL JR, NICHOLAS W; Foothill SR HS; Sacramento, CA; (1); Boy Scts; Chess Clb; VICA; Band; Jazz Band; Pep Band; Ftbl; Hon Roll; Jr Indstrl Arts 1st Awd; Drafting.

JARRELL, SHERI; La Habra HS; Whittier, CA; (4); 51/362; Pep Clb; Drill Tm; Stu Cncl; High Hon Roll; Hon Roll; Golden St Exm Hgh Hnrs; CA ST U Fullerton; Advrtsng.

JARRETT, EVA; South Tahoe HS; S. Lake Tahoe, CA; (4); Church Yth Grp; SADD; Teachers Aide; School Play; Ed Yrbk; Var Capt Cheerldng; Hon Roll; U Of NE, Reno.

JASOBSEN, ERIC W; Redlands HS; Loma Linda, CA; (2); 140/1000; SADD; Mrchg Band; Rptr Nwsp; Redlands Safe Rides Elected To Be Co-Pres; Drafting Club; U Of FL.

JASSO, WAKAI; Moorpark HS; Moorpark, CA; (2); Var Bsbl; Var Ftbl; Var Wt Lftg; Cit Awd; Hon Roll; Entertainmnt.

JASTER, BRENT J; Mission San Jose HS; Fremont, CA; (3); 1/420; Science Clb; Pres Ski Clb; Treas Stu Cncl; Var Bsbl; Var Socr; Elks Awd; Stu Cnsrvtn Assn; Beaverhead Natl Forest; Rotary Yth Ldrshp Awd; Ldrshp Camp.

JAUREGUI, ADRIAN; Lindsay HS; Lindsay, CA; (2); Var Bsbl; Var Ftbl; Hon Roll; Frsno ST U.

JAUREGUI, ELISIA; Santa Paula Union HS; Santa Paula, CA; (3); SADD; Band; Yrbk; Stat Bsktbl; Var JV Sftbl; Stat Wrstlng; Hon Roll; CSF; Social Sci.

JAUREGUI, MAURA R; South San Francisco HS; S San Francisco, CA; (2); JV Sftbl; Hon Roll; Cert Of Recognition 89; Stanford U; Attorney.

JAUREGUI, VERONICA P; Warren HS; Downey, CA; (3); Art Clb; Church Yth Grp; Latin Clb; Office Aide; Spanish Clb; Teachers Aide; Var Mgr Bsktbl; Mgr(s); Score Keeper; JV Swmmng; Peer Counclng Certfct; Babysttr YMCA; UCLA; Med.

JAUREGUI, VIVIANA; Downey HS; Downey, CA; (3); Church Yth Grp; Cmnty Wkr; JA; Teachers Aide; Chorus; Swing Chorus; Var Vllybl; Cit Awd; Hon Roll; Ntl Hnr Rll; UCLA; Bus.

JAUSSAUD, CHELSI; Delano HS; Delano, CA; (2); Letterman Clb; Pep Clb; JV Capt Cheerldng; Hon Roll; NHS; 89 Mst Dedicated Chrldr; CSF; Berkeley; Jrnlsm.

JAVADI, SHERVIN; Fremont HS; Sunnyvale, CA; (4); 11/374; High Hon Roll; Hon Roll; NHS; Pres Acad Fit Awd; San Jose ST U; Mechncl Engr.

JAVDANI, JILA M; Las Lomas HS; Danville, CA; (3); Drama Clb; Teachers Aide; Drill Tm; High Hon Roll; Hon Roll; NHS; Intl Stds.

JAVIER, ELMER R; Whitney HS; Lakewood, CA; (1); Bsktbl; Hon Roll; Engr.

JAVIER, GINGER NAZARENO; Granger JR HS; National City, CA; (1); Intnl Clb; Ed Nwsp; Ed Yrbk; Cit Awd; High Hon Roll; Prfct Atten Awd; Naic Assn San Diego Yth Clb; UCSD; Phy.

JAVIER, MATTHEW R; Gardena HS; Gardena, CA; (2); Church Yth Grp; Latin Clb; Cit Awd; El Camino.

JAVILLO, CLARISSA; Bishop Amat HS; West Covina, CA; (2); Cmnty Wkr; French Clb; Off Soph Cls; Hon Roll; NHS; CSF; Fri Night Live; Optmtry.

JAY, ROENA M; Channel Islands HS; Oxnard, CA; (3); Church Yth Grp; Key Clb; Library Aide; Speech Tm; SADD; Church Choir; High Hon Roll; Hon Roll; Opt Clb Awd; Acad Dcthln Tm Mem; CSF; Bio Clb Scrtry; Ed.

JAY, SUSAN M; Notre Dame Acad; Los Angeles, CA; (4); 1/110; VP Pres Girl Scts; Church Yth Grp; Cmnty Wkr; Service Clb; Speech Tm; Off Jr Cls; Crs Cntry; Sftbl; Cit Awd; French Hon Soc; Amicae Scl Just Club; Acadmc Dcthln 5 Medals; Girl Sct Slvr Ldrshp Awd; U Of Notre Dame; Intl Rltns.

JAY, WILLIAM; Lincoln HS; San Francisco, CA; (2); Church Yth Grp.

JAYADEV, RAJ K; Lynbrook HS; San Jose, CA; (1); Church Yth Grp; Debate Tm; NFL; Speech Tm; VP Soph Cls; Var Crs Cntry; JV Tennis; Pres Acad Fit Awd.

JAYASINGHE, AMALI; Whitney HS; Cerritos, CA; (3); Hosp Aide; JA; Mrchg Band; Variety Show; Ed Nwsp; Off Soph Cls; JV Var Swmmng; Hon Roll; Trs Perfrmng Cmptv Dance Co; VP SETA Stu Ethical Treatmnt Anmls; Premed.

JAYME, CHARMAINE; Manor Baptist Christian Schl; San Leandro, CA; (3); Speech Tm; Chorus; School Musical; School Play; Yrbk; Off Jr Cls; Bsktbl; Vllybl; High Hon Roll; Hon Roll; Spellman U; Intr Dsgn.

JAYME, JAY; Manor Baptist Christian HS; San Leandro, CA; (4); Teachers Aide; Acpl Chr; School Musical; School Play; Ed Nwsp; Yrbk; Pres Jr Cls; Var Bsktbl; Score Keeper; High Hon Roll; U C Berkeley; Pol Sci.

JAYME, MICHAEL; Don Bosco Technical Inst; El Monte, CA; (3); JV Vllybl; Pres Acad Fit Awd; Creative Writing.

JAYNES, PAUL B; Grossmont HS; El Cajon, CA; (2); 62/429; Church Yth Grp; Intnl Clb; JV Socr; Hon Roll; Eagle Scout Awd; Ucsd; Arch.

JAZO, DAVID; Castle Park HS; Chula Vista, CA; (2); 5/500; Computer Clb; Quiz Bowl; Scholastic Bowl; SADD; Socr; Hon Roll; Pres Acad Fit Awd; Blngl Spnsh; Chem Engnrng.

JEANSEAU, BRIAN C; El Toro HS; El Toro, CA; (4); Church Yth Grp; High Hon Roll; Hon Roll; Music.

JEANSONNE, LUCY F; O'farreil SCPA HS; San Diego, CA; (1); Band; School Musical; Hon Roll; Acad Leag; Frgn Lang Clb; San Diego Prep Wind Ensemble 4th Clarinet.

JEAVONS, HEATHER S; Willits HS; Willits, CA; (3); 1/120; GAA; Treas Jr Cls; Score Keeper; Var L Vllybl; Bausch & Lomb Sci Awd; High Hon Roll; Ntl Merit SF; Pr Cnslng; Acad Decthln Cls; Jazz Choir; Stanford; Sci.

JEDLINSKY, MAILE M; Ponderosa HS; Placerville, CA; (3); 8/300; Church Yth Grp; Math Tm; Pep Clb; Chorus; Variety Show; Nwsp; Intrml Bsktbl; High Hon Roll; Student Ambassador To The Soviet Union Summer 90; Communication.

JEFFCOAT, JESSICA K; Poway HS; Poway, CA; (2); 43/798; Church Yth Grp; Treas Drama Clb; Scholastic Bowl; SADD; Thesps; Acpl Chr; Chorus; School Musical; High Hon Roll; CSF; Intl Rltns.

JEFFERIES, RACHEL A; Escondido HS; Escondido, CA; (3); Cmnty Wkr; Drama Clb; Science Clb; School Play; Cit Awd; Hon Roll; Bus.

JEFFERIES, TONYA; Red Bluff HS; Red Bluff, CA; (1); Key Clb; Hon Roll; Marine Life; Chico ST; Bus Acctng.

JEFFERIS, WENDY; Antelope Valley HS; Lancaster, CA; (3); Intnl Clb; VP Spanish Clb; SADD; Phtg Yrbk; Rep Soph Cls; Rep Jr Cls; Cheerldng; Swmmng; Tennis; Hon Roll.

JEFFERS, STEPHANIE R; Trabuco Hills HS; El Toro, CA; (4); French Clb; Quiz Bowl; SADD; Teachers Aide; Chorus; High Hon Roll; Kiwanis Awd; Pres NHS; Ntl Merit Schol; Pres Acad Fit Awd; Orange County Acadc Decath 3 Mdl Wnnr; Keywanettes; Inner Clb Cncl; U Of CA Irvine; Intl Rel.

JEFFERSON, JENNIFER D; Serrano HS; Wrightwood, CA; (2); Chorus; Drill Tm; School Play; High Hon Roll; Hon Roll; Spanish NHS; CSF; Pediatrics.

JEFFERSON, KANIKA W; Newark Memorial HS; Newark, CA; (3); 28/545; Church Yth Grp; Hon Roll; Prfct Atten Awd; Psych.

JEFFERSON, KEVIN L; Senior HS; Garden Grove, CA; (1); Debate Tm; Intrml Bsktbl; Intrml Ftbl; Intrml Trk; Hon Roll; Law.

JEFFERSON, LA VONDA; St Michaels HS; Los Angeles, CA; (4); Office Aide; Teachers Aide; Variety Show; Phtg Yrbk; Hon Roll; Cert Outstndng Effrts Power Rdng; Cngrtns Acad Yr; CA ST Long Beach; Crm Jstce.

JEFFERSON, LATONYA R; Valley HS; Sacramento, CA; (3); 35/600; Debate Tm; Science Clb; Speech Tm; Teachers Aide; Hon Roll; Hewlett Packard Awd Outstndng Jr; MESA Club Treas; UCLA; Econ.

JEFFERSON, LAUREN; San Luis Obispo SR HS; San Luis Obispo, CA; (3); English Clb; JCL; Latin Clb; Var L Crs Cntry; Var L Socr; Var L Trk; High Hon Roll; Hon Roll; CSF; Marine Bio.

JEFFERSON, MELISSA J; Encina HS; Sacramento, CA; (4); Church Yth Grp; JA; SADD; Teachers Aide; Church Choir; Rep Jr Cls; Off Sr Cls; JV Socr; Cit Awd; Hon Roll; CSU-SACRAMENTO; Bus Admin.

JEFFERSON, MICHAEL; Carson HS; Carson, CA; (4); 7/550; Church Yth Grp; Phtg Rptr Yrbk; Off Jr Cls; Off Sr Cls; Stu Cncl; L Ftbl; Var L Trk; High Hon Roll; 12th Grd Ldrshp; Black Heritage; Alpha Kappa Alpha Schlr; CSF Yng Blck Schlrs; Angel Cty Links; US Naval Acad; Psychtry.

JEFFERSON, TIFFANI; George Washington Prep HS; Los Angeles, CA; (2); Chess Clb; Hosp Aide; ROTC; Teachers Aide; Bsktbl; Gym; Hon Roll; Doctor.

JEFFRESS, JENNIFER A; College Park HS; Pleasant Hill, CA; (3); Cmnty Wkr; Letterman Clb; Spanish Clb; Teachers Aide; Varsity Clb; Rptr Nwsp; Stu Cncl; JV Cheerldng; Mgr(s); Score Keeper.

JEFFREY, JASON M; Antioch HS; Antioch, CA; (2); Pres Church Yth Grp; Letterman Clb; Capt JV Ftbl; JV L Trk; Wt Lftg; Prfct Atten Awd; Ftbl Ldrshp Awd 88; Most Vlbl Def Lineman 89; NCS Dstngshd Schltc Tm 89; All City Track 89; Sports Med.

JEFFRIES, HEIDI M; Monterey Bay Acad; Chowchilla, CA; (2); Chorus; Church Choir; School Musical; Bsbl; Sftbl; Hon Roll; Prfct Atten Awd; Monterey Bay Acad; Ped.

JEFFS, CORA E; Modesto HS; Modesto, CA; (4); Church Yth Grp; Girl Scts; Library Aide; Church Choir; JV Bsktbl; JV Sftbl; JV Vllybl; Cit Awd; Hon Roll; Memphis ST; Law.

JEH, MAN HUN; George Washington HS; San Francisco, CA; (3); Computer Clb; High Hon Roll; Hon Roll; Physics.

JELETI, JOHN M; Lincoln HS; Northridge, CA; (4); 18/513; Church Yth Grp; FBLA; Mu Alpha Theta; Science Clb; Jazz Band; Pep Band; JV Var Ftbl; JV Wrstlng; Elks Awd; Val; Head Ushper; Mable Barona Wd Hgst Grade Pt Avg; Schrlshp PTSA 89-90; U Pacific; Phrmcy.

JELLINGHAUSEN, STACI; Granada HS; Livermore, CA; (4); 8/306; Church Yth Grp; Service Clb; Church Choir; Orch; School Musical; High Hon Roll; Pres Acad Fit Awd; Acad Schlrshp-BYU; Band Of Am Plaque-Applied Arts 90; Golden St Exam Geom Hnrs 88; BYU; Bus.

JEN, HENRY; Villanova Prep Schl; Monterey Park, CA; (4); 1/42; Boy Scts; School Play; Sec Sr Cls; JV Bsbl; JV Crs Cntry; JV Trk; Var Vllybl; High Hon Roll; Hon Roll; NHS; Hgh Achvt Math/Sci 89-90; Sigma XI Outstndng Sci Stu; RPI; Elec Engrng.

JEN, LAWRENCE; Herbert Hoover HS; Fresno, CA; (4); 1/500; Am Leg Boys St; Bus Profs of Am; Debate Tm; Sec French Clb; VP FBLA; NFL; Pres Ski Clb; Speech Tm; Acpl Chr; Band; Harvard Summer Schl; Fresno Boy Of Yr; Intl Exch Stu China; Stanford U; Intl Relations.

JEN, SARA; Salinas HS; Salinas, CA; (4); 1/350; Church Yth Grp; French Clb; Math Tm; Color Guard; Nwsp; High Hon Roll; Treas NHS; Prfct Atten Awd; Pres Acad Fit Awd; Val; Rensselaer Mdlst; Amer HS Math Exam Schl Wnnr; Rotary Intnls Camp Royal; Pacific Union Coll; Pre Med.

JENG, GRAY; Los Alamitos HS; Seal Beach, CA; (3); French Clb; Speech Tm; Teachers Aide; Trk; Hon Roll; CSF; USC; Bus.

JENG, HOWARD; Independence HS; San Jose, CA; (3); Science Clb; Intrml Wt Lftg; Wrstlng; Hon Roll; Prfct Atten Awd; Wrestling Clb; Cal Poly SLO; Arch.

JENG, PAMELA; Independence HS; San Jose, CA; (3); Cmnty Wkr; Hosp Aide; Intnl Clb; Latin Clb; Science Clb; Service Clb; Spanish Clb; Speech Tm; Hon Roll; Pres Acad Fit Awd; Wrk Homeless Shltrs; U CA Davis; Hstry.

JENG, REBECCA H; Edison HS; Huntington Beach, CA; (3); Off Church Yth Grp; VP Key Clb; Model UN; Band; Jazz Band; Mrchg Band; Pep Band; JV Trk; Spanish NHS; Engrng.

JENKINS, AINAISHA; Atwater HS; Atwater, CA; (3); Church Yth Grp; Teachers Aide; Chorus; Powder Puff Ftbl; Score Keeper; Trk; Hon Roll; AFS; U Of NY; Ed.

JENKINS, ALEXANDER; Westchester HS; Los Angeles, CA; (4); 11/400; Church Yth Grp; Sec Service Clb; Ed Nwsp; Lit Mag; JV Capt Ftbl; Var Vllybl; Sister Schl Exchange Pgm New Zealand; Yth & Govt Mdl Legis; YMCA Sgt At Arms; U CA Los Angeles; Civil Engr.

JENKINS, BRIAN K; Canyon Springs HS; Moreno Valley, CA; (3); Art Clb; Boy Scts; Church Yth Grp; Cmnty Wkr; FBLA; Crs Cntry; Trk; Hon Roll; Hmcmng Prince; Med.

JENKINS, CARRIE; Valencia HS; Placentia, CA; (4); 25/324; Co-Ed Dance Clb; Sec FBLA; Pep Clb; Service Clb; VP Frsh Cls; Pres Soph Cls; VP Pres Stu Cncl; Score Keeper; DAR Awd; High Hon Roll; Mayors Schlhrshp; Chapman Coll; Soclgy.

JENKINS, DANIELLE LA DEAN; Los Angeles Baptist HS; Northridge, CA; (4); 10/90; Church Yth Grp; English Clb; French Clb; Teachers Aide; Chorus; Cit Awd; High Hon Roll; Hon Roll; NHS; CA Schlrshp Fdrtn 87-90; 3rd Pl Awd Frnch Write On 88; Awds At Grad; UCLA; Dr.

JENKINS, EBONE; Westchester HS; Inglewood, CA; (1); Church Yth Grp; Bus Admin.

JENKINS, ELIZABETH; William Howard Taft HS; Woodland Hills, CA; (2); Girl Scts; Hosp Aide; Rep Frsh Cls; Rep Soph Cls; Rep Stu Cncl; Var Sftbl; JV Swmmng; JV Tennis; High Hon Roll; St Schlr; Intl Stds Assn Spnsh Schlrshp; Miss CA Co-Ed 3rd Rnn-Up; Golden St Exam Hnrs Geom; Pediatrics.

JENKINS, GIVONA; Washington HS; Los Angeles, CA; (2); Church Yth Grp; Girl Scts; ROTC; Church Choir; Rptr Lit Mag; Hon Roll; Prfct Atten Awd; UCLA; Comp Tech.

JENKINS, HEATHER M; Upland HS; Upland, CA; (2); Church Yth Grp; Dance Clb; School Musical; Pres Soph Cls; Rep Stu Cncl; JV Socr; Dance Team; Brigham Young U.

JENKINS, JESSICA M; Mtn Empire HS; Descanso, CA; (2); German Clb; GAA; Office Aide; Pep Clb; JV Vllybl; NHS; Perf Arts.

JENKINS, KELLY ANNE; Temecula Valley HS; Murrieta, CA; (1); Cmnty Wkr; GAA; Hosp Aide; Gym; JV Socr; JV Tennis; Var L Trk; Cit Awd; Hon Roll; Prfct Atten Awd; Bst Track Athl Awd; Mst Pnts Scrd Awd Track; Maintained 4.0; UC Davis; Vet Med.

JENKINS, MICHELLE A; Mater Dei HS; Fullerton, CA; (1); Church Yth Grp; Rep Frsh Cls; Crs Cntry; Socr; French Hon Soc; Pres Acad Fit Awd; Harvard; Psych.

JENKINS, NATASHA D; West Covina HS; West Covina, CA; (1); Church Yth Grp; SADD; Chorus; Church Choir; School Musical; Swing Chorus; Yrbk; Lit Mag; Spellman U; Bus Mgmt.

JENKINS, PAM; Sunny Hills HS; Fullerton, CA; (2); Church Yth Grp; Cmnty Wkr; French Clb; Pep Clb; Cheerldng; Socr; Tennis; High Hon Roll; Rotary Awd.

JENKINS, RICHARD H; C K Mc Clatchy HS; Sacramento, CA; (3); 4/400; Math Clb; Band; Jazz Band; Mrchg Band; Pep Band; School Musical; JV Socr; Var Tennis; High Hon Roll; Ntl Merit Ltr.

JENKINS, SALENA R; Mc Clymonds HS; Oakland, CA; (1); Spanish Clb; Off Frsh Cls; JV Crs Cntry; JV Tennis; Cit Awd; High Hon Roll; Hon Roll; Multiculitre Clb; Tuskegee U; Psych.

JENKINS, SCOTT; Linden HS; Linden, CA; (1); Pres Church Yth Grp; Ski Clb; SADD; Var Bsbl; JV Capt Bsktbl; JV Capt Ftbl; Hon Roll; Pres Acad Fit Awd; Little Leag Coach; Sccr Referee; Babe Ruth Bsbl; U Of CA; Math.

JENKINS, STACEY; Gardena HS; Gardena, CA; (2); Dance Clb; Drama Clb; Girl Scts; School Play; JV Sftbl; Hon Roll.

JENKINS, STACIE; Western Christian HS; West Covina, CA; (3); Church Yth Grp; Pep Clb; Acpl Chr; Chorus; Church Choir; Swing Chorus; Off Jr Cls; Capt Cheerldng; High Hon Roll; Hon Roll; Fine Arts Fstvl 1st Pl Soloist 88; Natl Fine Arts Fstvl Excllnt Rtng; Fine Art Fstvl Sprior Rtng 89; Azusa Pacific U; Music.

JENKINSON, DANETTE A; St Bernard HS; Eureka, CA; (2); Church Yth Grp; Cmnty Wkr; Service Clb; Treas Soph Cls; JV Bsktbl; Var Sftbl; JV Vllybl; High Hon Roll; Hon Roll; NHS; All Tournmnt Awd JV Bsktbl 89.

JENKS, AMBER; Quartz Hill HS; Rosamond, CA; (1); Hosp Aide; SADD; Sftbl; Cit Awd; High Hon Roll; Hon Roll; Pres Schlr; Law.

JENNER, AMY C; Burbank HS; Burbank, CA; (2); Teachers Aide; JV Tennis; Hon Roll; Pres Acad Fit Awd; Faclty Schlrshp Awd; Prncpls Awd; CA Jr Schlrshp Fed Hnr Awd; Hnrb Mntn Burbank Cvc Pride All Yth Essy.

JENNINGS, BRIAN E; Moorpark HS; Moorpark, CA; (2); 10/250; Church Yth Grp; Cmnty Wkr; Math Clb; Ski Clb; Teachers Aide; Variety Show; Nwsp; Rep Frsh Cls; Rep Soph Cls; Treas Jr Cls; Coach Awd Bsktbl Tm; Musketeer Pride Awds-Spnsh II, Geom, Alg II, Engl, Hstry; Stu Mth; Duke U; Med.

JENNINGS, CHRISTI; Lincoln HS; Stockton, CA; (2); 74/588; Church Yth Grp; Chorus; Church Choir; Var JV Cheerldng; Crs Cntry; Gym; Trk; High Hon Roll; Hon Roll; CSF; Biola U; Engl.

JENNINGS, CHRISTINE; Miramonte HS; Orinda, CA; (4); 84/266; Church Yth Grp; Cmnty Wkr; Spanish Clb; Speech Tm; Acpl Chr; Church Choir; School Musical; Cheerldng; Crs Cntry; Natl Hnr Roll 89; Miramonte Parnts Clb Art Awd 90; Orinda Jr Womens Clb 2nd Pl Art Awd 90; UC Davis; Advrtsng.

JENNINGS, DARCY LANAI; Corona Del Mar HS; Corona Del Mar, CA; (1); Church Yth Grp; Cmnty Wkr; Dance Clb; Library Aide; Office Aide; Pep Clb; Service Clb; SADD; Teachers Aide; Variety Show; Sm Fnlst Miss Teenage CA Pgnt 90; UCLA; Law.

JENNINGS, JEFF D; Riverbank HS; Riverbank, CA; (3); Var Capt Bsktbl; Tennis; Trk; Wt Lftg; Hon Roll.

JENNINGS, KRISTA A; Santa Ynez HS; Los Olivos, CA; (2); 41/215; Rptr 4-H; Band; Mrchg Band; JV Bsbl; Hon Roll; Southern CA Jr Bach Fstvl Rgnl Piano; Orthodontist.

JENNINGS, KRISTEN M; Clovis HS; Clovis, CA; (1); Church Yth Grp; FCA; Cheerldng; Swmmng; High Hon Roll; Hon Roll; U CA Santa Barbara; Psych.

JENNINGS, MELISSA; Lodi HS; Lodi, CA; (2); Teachers Aide; Band; Drill Tm; Mrchg Band; Stu Cncl; Hon Roll; Prfct Atten Awd; Var Badmntn Ltr; Sci Camp Cnslr; Chrldng; CA Poly; Poltcl Sci.

JENNINGS IV, PAUL R; Redlands HS; Mentone, CA; (4); Boy Scts; Socr; Bus Dept Awd; CA ST U San Bernardino; Bus.

JENNINGS, SETH E; Fairfield HS; Suisun City, CA; (3); Boy Scts; L Var Trk; Arch.

JENNINGS, TAO A; Redlands HS; Mentone, CA; (2); Boy Scts; Cmnty Wkr; Bsbl; Socr; Pres Acad Fit Awd; CSF; Sci Olympcs Team; Bus.

JENSEN, ALISON C; Alverno HS; Arcadia, CA; (2); 1/78; Church Yth Grp; Treas Science Clb; Rep Frsh Cls; Var Bsktbl; JV Var Vllybl; High Hon Roll; NHS; CSF; Sports Med.

JENSEN, ANDREW I; Berean Christian HS; Walnut Creek, CA; (3); 4/65; Church Yth Grp; Letterman Clb; Stu Cncl; JV Bsbl; Var L Bsktbl; High Hon Roll; MVP Frshmn Bsktbl; Coaches Awd/Most Inspirnl Var Bsktbl; Most Outstndg/Physics Pre-Calculus; UC Berkeley; Economics.

JENSEN, BRENDA J; Lindhurst HS; Marysville, CA; (4); Church Yth Grp; Cmnty Wkr; Drama Clb; Thesps; Church Choir; Rep Stu Cncl; Hon Roll; Yuba Coll; Chld Care.

JENSEN, CAMILLE M; Nordhoff HS; Ojai, CA; (4); Teachers Aide; Tennis; Hon Roll.

JENSEN, CHAD E; Rio Linda HS; Sacramento, CA; (2); JV Bsbl; Var Socr; Hon Roll.

JENSEN, CHANTE VIVIAN; Bellflower HS; Bellflower, CA; (3); Church Yth Grp; Debate Tm; Drama Clb; Treas FBLA; Band; Drm Mjr(t); Jazz Band; Mrchg Band; Pep Band; Off Frsh Cls; Comp Prog.

JENSEN, CHRISTOFFER; Brethren JR SR HS; Lynwood, CA; (1); 4/100; Church Yth Grp; Letterman Clb; Crs Cntry; Hon Roll; U Of Southern CA.

JENSEN, CHRISTY A; Alhambra HS; Martinez, CA; (1); Church Yth Grp; Cmnty Wkr; Hon Roll; Beautify Alhambra Campus Cmmtte; Protest Agnst Toxic Burner; Envrmntl Sci.

JENSEN, COLIN R; Novato HS; Novato, CA; (1); Boy Scts; Church Yth Grp; Key Clb; Band; High Hon Roll; Hon Roll; CSF; Karate; BYU.

JENSEN, CORIE A; Francis W Parker HS; San Diego, CA; (3); Service Clb; Treas Spanish Clb; SADD; Pres Soph Cls; Stu Cncl; Var Tennis; Hon Roll; Rowing Jr Cmptve Crew; Hnrs Semnrs San Diego; MADCAPS; Vet.

JENSEN, DAVID ALLEN; Burbank HS; Burbank, CA; (4); 1/429; Boy Scts; Church Yth Grp; Debate Tm; Pres French Clb; Science Clb; Speech Tm; Lit Mag; JV Var Tennis; Ntl Merit Ltr; Pres Acad Fit Awd; Mock Trail; Brigham Young U; Economics.

JENSEN, DRENA S; Analy HS; Sebastopol, CA; (1); Church Yth Grp; Drama Clb; FFA; JA; SADD; Teachers Aide; VICA; Smmr Cnslr Aid CYO Camp Armstrong; Empire Coll; Acctng.

JENSEN, ERIK R; Canyon HS; Saugus, CA; (3); 77/501; Debate Tm; Drama Clb; FBLA; Var Golf; U CA San Diego; Bus Ec.

JENSEN, HEATHER; Trabuco Hills HS; Trabuco Cyn, CA; (2); Church Yth Grp; German Clb; Pep Clb; Acpl Chr; Chorus; Church Choir; Swing Chorus; JV Co-Capt Cheerldng; Sftbl; Swmmng; Skiing, Water Skiing, Babystng, Rsrch Disabld; Brigham Young U; Soclgy.

JENSEN, J DEAN; Mission San Jose HS; Fremont, CA; (3); Boy Scts; Church Yth Grp; Drama Clb; VP Pres Spanish Clb; Chorus; School Musical; School Play; Trk.

JENSEN, KATHLENE M; Helix HS; Lemon Grove, CA; (4); 38/355; Yrbk; Mem Fasion & Self Image Club; Sr Board & Sr Council; CA Schlrshp Fed; UCSD.

JENSEN, KELLY E; Nevada Union HS; Chicago Park, CA; (3); Chess Clb; Drama Clb; School Play; Stage Crew; Swing Chorus; High Hon Roll; FISH.

JENSEN, KIRSTEN K; Arlington HS; Riverside, CA; (2); Church Yth Grp; ROTC; Color Guard; Teachers Aide; 4-H Awd; Hon Roll; Stu Mth; Gldn Appl Awd; Band Awd; Riverside CC; Nrsng.

JENSEN, KRISTIN L; San Marcos HS; San Marcos, CA; (3); SADD; High Hon Roll; Hon Roll; Palomar; Law.

JENSEN, KYLE A; Linden HS; Stockton, CA; (3); 13/148; Church Yth Grp; Letterman Clb; Band; Church Choir; Mrchg Band; Yrbk; Var Bsktbl; Var Socr; Hon Roll; Rotary Club Ldrshp Camp; Sports Med.

JENSEN, LINN M; Sonora HS; La Habra, CA; (3); 32/282; Art Clb; French Clb; Girl Scts; Office Aide; Lit Mag; Powder Puff Ftbl; Var Swmmng; French Hon Soc; Hon Roll; Girls Leag Publicity Chm; JSA Publicity Chairperson; UCSD; Psych.

JENSEN, LOIS A; Upland HS; Upland, CA; (2); Church Yth Grp; Band; Mrchg Band; Orch; Hon Roll; Hnr Band; San Bernardino Cnty Hnr Band; Sousa Hnr Band; Biomed Engr.

JENSEN, MARIANNE R; Mercy HS; San Francisco, CA; (4); Drama Clb; Model UN; Treas Service Clb; Teachers Aide; School Musical; School Play; Stage Crew; Variety Show; Phtg Nwsp; Rep Sr Cls; Bank Amer Achvt Awd Commnctn; Amnsty Intl; Theater Svc, Dir, & Perfrmnce Awds; San Francisco ST U; Psych.

JENSEN, MEGAN L; Foothill HS; Orange, CA; (3); Computer Clb; Office Aide; Spanish Clb; Teachers Aide; Stat Bsbl; JV Tennis; High Hon Roll; Hon Roll; Jr NHS; UCLA; Pre-Med.

JENSEN, MICHAEL P; Armijo HS; Fairfield, CA; (1); Boy Scts; Jazz Band; Orch; Pep Band; JV Bsbl; Hon Roll; Fairfield Leag Sccr; Yth Symphny; Babe Ruth Bsbl; Bus.

JENSEN, MONICA M; Homestead HS; Los Altos, CA; (1); Church Yth Grp; Cmnty Wkr; Dance Clb; JV Socr; Pres Acad Fit Awd; Envrnmntl Club Fndr; UC Santa Barb; Envrnmntl Sci.

JENSEN, NICOLE T; Rancho Cotate HS; Rohnert Park, CA; (3); Am Leg Aux Girls St; Cmnty Wkr; Yrbk; Cheerldng; Score Keeper; Socr; Hon Roll; Crt Rptr.

JENSEN, PATTI; Western HS; Anaheim, CA; (3); Pep Clb; Sec Frsh Cls; Sec Soph Cls; Pres Jr Cls; JV Var Cheerldng; Hon Roll; CA Schlrshp Fed; Grls Leg; U AZ; Optmtry.

JENSEN, PHILIP; Linden HS; Stockton, CA; (2); 1/143; Church Yth Grp; Letterman Clb; Math Tm; Science Clb; Church Choir; Mrchg Band; Pep Band; JV Bsktbl; Var Socr; JV Trk; Engrng.

JENSEN, RENEE; Needles HS; Needles, CA; (4); 1/52; Am Leg Aux Girls St; Key Clb; School Play; Rep Soph Cls; Rep Jr Cls; Rep Sr Cls; DAR Awd; Pres Acad Fit Awd; Val; Voice Dem Awd; UC Santa Barbara.

JENSEN, SUSAN C; Cupertino HS; Cupertino, CA; (3); 36/297; Red Cross Aide; Pres Key Clb; Speech Tm; Band; Drm Mjr(t); Sec Stu Cncl; Var Sftbl; Capt JV Vllybl; Kiwanis Awd; NHS; Altrvettes Pres Girls Svc Club; Yrbk Editor Of Academics; Intra Dist Cncl Rep IDC Rep; 4 Yr Coll; English.

JENSEN, TAMARA A; Miraleste HS; Ranchos Palos Ver, CA; (3); 33/153; Service Clb; Spanish Clb; SADD; Stu Cncl; Score Keeper; Hon Roll; Pres Acad Fit Awd; ETI 3rd Jr Princess; Congrssnl Yth Ldrshp Cncl Schlr; UC; Law.

JENSEN, TRACI L; El Toro HS; El Toro, CA; (1); Letterman Clb; Var L Socr; JV Sftbl; Vllybl; Hon Roll; JETS Awd; Vlybl Offnsv Plyr Of Yr 89; All Lg Goalie Soccer CIF Div 4a Soccer Champnshp Tm 90; Air Force Acad; Aerontcl Engrng.

JENSEN, TRICIA A; San Joaquin Memorial HS; Fresno, CA; (4); 20/123; FFA; GAA; Letterman Clb; Science Clb; Service Clb; Sec Spanish Clb; Speech Tm; Mgr(s); Powder Puff Ftbl; Tennis; Horses; Piano; Friday Night Live Clb; Fresno ST.

JENSEN, WAYNE C; Del Campo HS; Carmichael, CA; (3); Boy Scts; French Clb; Math Clb; Teachers Aide; Varsity Clb; Var Ftbl; JV Wrstlng; Hon Roll; Sacramento ST; Teacher.

JENSON, KRISTINA E; Baker Valley HS; Baker, CA; (2); Art Clb; GAA; Pres Frsh Cls; Bsktbl; High Hon Roll; Prfct Atten Awd; All League 2nd Team Bsktbl Awd; Artist.

JENSSEN, HOLLY D; Rosamond HS; Rosamond, CA; (2); #1 In Class; Math Tm; VP Soph Cls; Stat Bsktbl; JV Vllybl; High Hon Roll; Bus Mgmt.

JENZEN, JENNIFER L; Arroyo Grande HS; Nipomo, CA; (3); Church Yth Grp; Dance Clb; SADD; Treas Sr Cls; Cheerldng; Buddy Hugger In Spcl Olympics 88; Advncd Peer Communicator 89-90; Peer Counselor 89-90; CA Poly Tech U; Ed.

JEONG, KELLY; Los Alamitos HS; Seal Beach, CA; (4); 1/500; Math Clb; Model UN; Quiz Bowl; Science Clb; Service Clb; Rptr Mgr Nwsp; Var Tennis; Hon Roll; Kiwanis Awd; Cert Meril Piano; Med.

JEONG, LISA; John F Kennedy HS; La Palma, CA; (2); Church Yth Grp; Key Clb; Chorus; Church Choir; School Musical; Swmmng; Tennis; Cit Awd; Hon Roll; NHS; CSF; U Of CA Los Angeles; Law.

JEONG, MELISSA G; Abraham Lincoln HS; San Francisco, CA; (2); Boy Scts; Church Yth Grp; GAA; Red Cross Aide; Off Soph Cls; Gym; Trk; High Hon Roll; Pres Acad Fit Awd; Gldn St Exam Hnrs In Algbr; U CA; Sprts Med.

JEONG, YUKYUNG; Lowell HS; San Francisco, CA; (2); SADD; Orch; Hon Roll; BBSO Schl; BBBS San Francisco; Bus.

JEREMIAS, ROSANNA; Lowell HS; San Francisco, CA; (2); Boy Scts; Church Yth Grp; Cmnty Wkr; Drama Clb; Hosp Aide; Red Cross Aide; Spanish Clb; Nwsp; Hon Roll; Prfct Atten Awd; Laraza Day Prtcpnt; Prmdc 1990 SF Day To Brkrs (15 Crtfd CPR BLS & SFA); Artstc Awd Rsrchng; UCSF; Medical Engr.

JEREZ, JENNIFER J; Roseville HS; Rocklin, CA; (4); 83/400; Cmnty Wkr; Drama Clb; French Clb; Hosp Aide; Ed Nwsp; Yrbk; Ed Lit Mag; Hon Roll; Dudley-Vehmeyer Brown Schlrshp; Tiger Stripes; Fri Night Live; San Diego ST U; Telecomms.

JEREZ, JOSE E; Pasadena HS; Pasadena, CA; (1); Church Yth Grp; Church Choir; JV Socr; Cit Awd; High Hon Roll; Pres Acad Fit Awd; Engrng.

JERNEGAN, DALE; Hemet HS; Hemet, CA; (4); Prncpls Advsry Lst; Mt San Jacinto; Bus.

JERNIGAN II, DANNY E; River City HS; W Sacramento, CA; (1); Math Clb; Bsbl; Ftbl; Wrstlng; Cit Awd; Hon Roll; Prfct Atten Awd; All Hnr Clss; Comp Prgmng.

JERVIS, REGAN L; San Marcos HS; Santa Barbara, CA; (3); Cmnty Wkr; Hosp Aide; JA; Pep Clb; Rptr Yrbk; Hon Roll; Conservation Clb; Golden St Exam Geom Schl Recognition; Commnctns.

JESCHKE, RONI L; Antelope Valley HS; Lancaster, CA; (4); Girl Scts; Hosp Aide; Office Aide; Teachers Aide; Drill Tm; Cit Awd; High Hon Roll; Library Aide; Hon Roll; Z Clb; Wrk Exprnc Pgm.

JESION, KEOGH J; Atwater HS; Winton, CA; (3); Hon Roll; Mdl Rlrdng; Auto Mech.

JESKE, STEPHANIE; Tokay HS; Stockton, CA; (1); 2/900; Church Yth Grp; FCA; German Clb; Cheerldng; High Hon Roll; CA Schlrshp Fed; Phy.

JESPERSEN, TISHARA A; El Toro HS; El Toro, CA; (1); Church Yth Grp; Cmnty Wkr; GAA; Ski Clb; School Play; VP Soph Cls; Gym; JV Socr; Tennis; Var L Trk; Girls Leag; Pepperdine; Psych.

JESSEE, KALIN M; Del Campo HS; Citrus Heights, CA; (3); French Clb; SADD; Chorus; UC Davis; Bio Sci.

JESSEN, STEPHANIE; Fred C Beyer HS; Modesto, CA; (4); 19/500; Teachers Aide; Acpl Chr; Pres Chorus; School Musical; Cit Awd; High Hon Roll; Hon Roll; CMEA 2 Command Perfmncs; Intl Order Jobs Dghtrs 88; Life Mbr CSF 87-90; Comp Prgmr.

JESSER, CHARITY; Dana Hills HS; Laguna Beach, CA; (1); Church Yth Grp; Dance Clb; Drama Clb; Thesps; School Musical; School Play; Stage Crew; Variety Show; Writing Poetry; Reading Liturature, Plays, Etc; Theater.

JESSUP, JON C; Bear River HS; Grass Valley, CA; (2); Art Clb; FBLA; Socr; Gov Hon Prg Awd; Hon Roll; Acting.

JESUS, JOSE GONZALEZ; Watsonville HS; Watsonville, CA; (2); San Jose ST.

JETER, KEVIN D; Lompoc HS; Lompoc, CA; (4); 1/400; Church Yth Grp; Cmnty Wkr; Debate Tm; Letterman Clb; Scholastic Bowl; Service Clb; SADD; Varsity Clb; School Play; Variety Show; Acad Dcthln DARE; Pacesetter; Black Stu Clb; Syracuse U; Phys Ed.

JETT, SCOTT; Sanger HS; Sanger, CA; (3); Am Leg Boys St; Art Clb; Church Yth Grp; Cmnty Wkr; FCA; JA; Letterman Clb; ROTC; Ski Clb; Spanish Clb; Natl Young Leaders Conf; ROTC Cadet Of Month; Natl Swimming & Waterpolo Rec; USNA; Pre Med.

JETTE, JONI L; Modesto HS; Modesto, CA; (3); Hon Roll; ROP Word Prcssng Class; Modesto JC; Comp Prgmg.

JEW, CORRINE L; Lowell HS; San Francisco, CA; (3); Church Yth Grp; Cmnty Wkr; Hosp Aide; Office Aide; Red Cross Aide; Teachers Aide; JV Trk; Cit Awd; Hon Roll; Arch & Engrng Clb; Chemathon 90; Sftbl Clb.

JEW, KENNETH; Abraham Lincoln HS; Los Angeles, CA; (4); Cmnty Wkr; FBLA; Teachers Aide; School Play; Cit Awd; Hon Roll; UC Riverside; Arch.

JEW, ROBERT Y; Lowell HS; San Francisco, CA; (3); Science Clb; Tennis; Jr NHS; Pres Acad Fit Awd; CSF; Scroll Hnr Society; Tennis Clb; Engineering.

JEWELL, PATRICIA C; Crawford HS; San Diego, CA; (4); AFS; Hist Service Clb; Drill Tm; Yrbk; JV Cheerldng; Hon Roll; Pres Acad Fit Awd; Spanish NHS; Grad With Acad Dstnctn; San Diego ST U; Intl Bus.

JEWETT, ORVAL A; South Fork HS; Alderpoint, CA; (3); 6/70; Am Leg Boys St; Art Clb; Boy Scts; Teachers Aide; Rptr Yrbk; Sec Sr Cls; High Hon Roll; Hon Roll; Prfct Atten Awd; Humboldt ST U; Hist.

JHAWAR, MONINDER K; Cornelia Connelly Schl; Fullerton, CA; (2); Chorus; School Play; Hon Roll; Pres Acad Fit Awd; Medcl.

JHUNG, DANIEL Y; Whitney HS; Cerritos, CA; (1); Pres Church Yth Grp; Cmnty Wkr; Key Clb; Variety Show; Ed Nwsp; Pres Frsh Cls; Var Socr; JV Tennis; High Hon Roll; Hon Roll; CS Jr Schlstc Fed Pres; Stu Rep Schl Sit Cncl; Marion Huhn Awd; Educ.

JHUNJHUNWALA, UDAY; Whitney HS; Buena Park, CA; (3); Cmnty Wkr; French Clb; JA; Key Clb; Varsity Clb; JV Var Bsbl; JV Bsktbl; High Hon Roll; Ntl Merit SF; Val.

JI, HELEN R; Esperanza HS; Yorba Linda, CA; (2); Church Yth Grp; Intnl Clb; Speech Tm; Variety Show; JV Tennis; High Hon Roll; Sec NHS; Acad Decthln; CSF; Piano; Bach Fest Hnrbl Mntn.

JIANG, JIMMY J; Lowell HS; San Francisco, CA; (2); Science Clb; Crs Cntry; U CA Berkeley; Cmptr Eng.

JIANG, JONATHAN J; Lowell HS; San Francisco, CA; (3); Boy Scts; Church Yth Grp; Library Aide; Science Clb; Crs Cntry; Algebra, Geom Golden St Exam Hi Hnrs; Berkeley; Math.

JIANG, SCOTT YUCHOU; George Washington HS; San Francisco, CA; (3); Swmmng; San Francisco ST.

JIANG-FEN, GUAN; Woodrow Wilson HS; San Francisco, CA; (4); Spanish Clb; Swmmng; Hon Roll; CSF Awd; Hnr Soc; UC Santa Cruz; Envrnmntl Stds.

JIMENEZ, ADRIAN; James A Garfield HS; Los Angeles, CA; (2); Church Yth Grp; Cmnty Wkr; Library Aide; Teachers Aide; Stu Cncl; Vllybl; Cit Awd; Hon Roll; UC Berkeley; Bus.

JIMENEZ, ALMA R; Mountain View HS; El Monte, CA; (3); Cit Awd; Hon Roll; ROP Comp Applications, Word Processing; Rio Hondo CC; Comp.

JIMENEZ JR, ANGEL; Edison HS; Stockton, CA; (3); Am Leg Boys St; Church Yth Grp; Cmnty Wkr; Key Clb; Spanish Clb; SADD; Band; Church Choir; Jazz Band; Mrchg Band; Stu Prevtn; Engrngn Smmr Resdnt Prgm; Friday Nighy Live Cmmtte; Louie Armstrong Jazz Awd; Civil Engrng.

JIMENEZ, ATANACIO; Gardena HS; Los Angeles, CA; (3); French Clb; Teachers Aide; Cal ST; Electrncs.

JIMENEZ, BARBARA; Turlock HS; Turlock, CA; (2); #29 In Class; Letterman Clb; Teachers Aide; Var Socr; Cit Awd; High Hon Roll; Prfct Atten Awd; Pres Acad Fit Awd; Psych.

JIMENEZ, BERTHA; El Rancho HS; Pico Rivera, CA; (4); 8/550; VP Church Yth Grp; Varsity Clb; Var Crs Cntry; Powder Puff Ftbl; Var Trk; High Hon Roll; Awd Bank Of Am Engl; Schlr Athlt Awd; Wrtrs Of Tmmrw Clb; UCLA.

JIMENEZ, BLANCA E; El Cajon Valley HS; Lakeside, CA; (3); Dance Clb; English Clb; Latin Clb; Spanish Clb; Teachers Aide; Mrchg Band; Stage Crew; Sec Jr Cls; Folk Dance Awd; Bilngl Tchr.

JIMENEZ, CAMALA S; Buena Park HS; Buena Park, CA; (3); 9/409; Church Yth Grp; Key Clb; High Hon Roll; Silverado American Girl Softball; Distinguished Scholar Awards; Honors At Entrance; Calif State; Psychologist.

JIMENEZ, CECILIA M; San Benito HS; Hollister, CA; (3); Pres Spanish Clb; Church Choir; Lit Mag; Hon Roll; SILCA 3 Yrs; Psych.

JIMENEZ JR, CESAR; Carlmont HS; San Carlos, CA; (4); French Clb; Prfct Atten Awd; Cert Mrt Outstndng Achvt Alg I; Cert Mrt Outstndng Accmplshmnt Art; Wk Exp Schlrshp Awd/Spllng Cert; San Jose ST U; Advrtsng.

JIMENEZ, DAVID A; Sacred Heart Cathedral HS; Pacifica, CA; (2); 36/220; Varsity Clb; JV Ftbl; Var Wrstlng; High Hon Roll; Hon Roll; Schlr Pgm.

JIMENEZ, DIANA M; Santa Barbara HS; Santa Barbara, CA; (3); MECHA VP 89-90 & Pres 90-91 Chiacano Stu Mvmnt; Fshn Dsgn.

JIMENEZ JR, FELIPE; Eisenhower HS; Rialto, CA; (2); Church Yth Grp; Church Choir; VP Jr NHS; Pres Acad Fit Awd; UCLA; Phy.

JIMENEZ, FRED S; Riverdale Jt Un HS; Riverdale, CA; (3); #12 In Class; Stage Crew; JV L Bsbl; JV Bsktbl; Var JV Ftbl; Hon Roll; CA ST U Fresno; Phys Ed.

JIMENEZ, FREDERIK V; Gahr HS; Cerritos, CA; (2); JA; JV Crs Cntry; Trk; Wt Lftg; Wrstlng; Hon Roll; Blue & Gold Awds; Track Club; UCLA; Mech Engr.

JIMENEZ, GEORGE EDWARD; Cantwell HS; Los Angeles, CA; (4); 8/53; Drama Clb; School Musical; School Play; Yrbk; Sec Soph Cls; Treas Jr Cls; Sec Sr Cls; Crs Cntry; Hon Roll; NHS; Work Experience; U Of CA Berkeley; Film/English.

JIMENEZ, GRACE; Strathmore HS; Strathmore, CA; (3); 10/77; Library Aide; Office Aide; Var Capt Bsktbl; Var Capt Vllybl; CADENA Clb; CADENA Clb Soc Comm Chpsn VP; Spartan Schlstc Sprts Plaque.

JIMENEZ, GUILLERMO; Hawthorne HS; Lennox, CA; (2); Boy Scts; Drama Clb; Cit Awd; Spanish NHS; UCLA; Machinist.

JIMENEZ, IRENE; Bell Gardens HS; Commerce, CA; (2); Drama Clb; School Play; CSF; Ped.

JIMENEZ, ISMAEL; Southwest HS; San Ysidro, CA; (2); School Musical; Prfct Atten Awd; Hghst Achvr Awd Intro Soc Sci; Archt.

JIMENEZ, JANET; Bell Gardens HS; Bell Gardens, CA; (1); Art Clb; Band; Nwsp; Score Keeper; Columbia; Obstetrics.

JIMENEZ, JORGE; Bell Gardens HS; Huntington Park, CA; (3); Teachers Aide; Socr.

JIMENEZ, JUAN G; Schurr HS; Los Angeles, CA; (3); Cmnty Wkr; Band; Mrchg Band; Var Bsbl; JV Crs Cntry; Little Leag Coach Bsbl 88-89; Engrng.

JIMENEZ, KIMBERLY A; Coalinga HS; Coalinga, CA; (2); Sec Soph Cls; Stat Sftbl; JV Tennis; JV Vllybl; Hon Roll.

JIMENEZ, LAURA; Dos Pueblos HS; Goleta, CA; (4); 5/303; Capt L Swmmng; Jr NHS; NHS; Ntl Merit Schol; Math, Engrng & Sci Achvt Pres; Earthwatch Expedition; Sister Cities Exchng Pgm; Pitzer Coll; Lit.

JIMENEZ, LUIS DIEGO; Fontana HS; Fontana, CA; (2); Scholastic Bowl; Rep Stu Cncl; Intrml Socr; High Hon Roll; Hon Roll; Redlands U; Civil Engrng.

JIMENEZ, MARIA DE LOURDES; Santa Barbara HS; Santa Barbara, CA; (4); 63/466; Treas SADD; Var JV Trk; Hon Roll; Friday Night Live; MESA; UC Berkeley; Intl Rltns.

JIMENEZ, MARIA G; Chula Vista HS; Chula Vista, CA; (4); Zlgy.

JIMENEZ, MIRCALA; Central Union HS; El Centro, CA; (4); 72/892; Church Yth Grp; Pep Clb; SADD; Temple Yth Grp; Color Guard; L Flag Corp; Variety Show; Hon Roll; Imperial Vly Coll; Bus Psych.

JIMENEZ, NOEL M; Tranquillity HS; Mendota, CA; (1); Hon Roll; CSF; Fresno; Dr.

JIMENEZ, REBECCA H; Mountain View HS; El Monte, CA; (1); Princpls Hnrs Rll; Creatve Wrtng Clb; Psych.

JIMENEZ, SANDRA G; Abraham Lincoln HS; Los Angeles, CA; (2); Crs Cntry; Hon Roll; UCLA; Engrng.

JIMENEZ, SHIRLEY; Bishop Amat Memorial HS; Rowland Heights, CA; (3); Art Clb; Math Clb; Ed Lit Mag; High Hon Roll; NHS; Actvts Dir Xanadu Crtv Art Clb; CA Schlrshp Fdrtn; Stanford; Dntstry.

JIMENEZ, TERESA; Nathaniel Narbonne HS; Torrance, CA; (4); Hon Roll; CSU Long Beach; Psych.

JIMENEZ, TIM M; Carpinteria HS; Carpinteria, CA; (2); 44/180; Church Yth Grp; Letterman Clb; Varsity Clb; JV Bsktbl; JV Var Ftbl; Var L Trk; Var Wt Lftg; Hon Roll; Best Back Ftbl; Broke Sch Recrds Long, Triple Jump; Medls Track; Med.

JIMENEZ, VILAIPORN A; Fairfield HS; Fairfield, CA; (1); Girl Scts; Spanish Clb; Yrbk; Hon Roll; Jr NHS; Spanish NHS; Harvard; Bus Admin.

JIMISON, PAT N; Pinole Valley HS; Pinole, CA; (2); JV Bsbl; JV Ftbl; Hon Roll; Sacramento ST; Arch.

JIMMERSON, KEISHA L; Woodrow Wilson HS; Long Beach, CA; (3); Intrml Sftbl; Cit Awd; Hon Roll; USC.

JIN, HELEN S; John A Rowland HS; Rowland Heights, CA; (2); 42/602; French Clb; Science Clb; Acpl Chr; Trk; High Hon Roll; CA Schlrshp Federation; UCR; Pre-Med.

JIN, JUSTIN S; Foothill HS; Fountain Valley, CA; (3); Var Debate Tm; Var English Clb; French Clb; JV Ftbl; JV Wrstlng; Hon Roll; Eclgy Clb Fndr; V Pres In Yng Dmcrts; U C Santa Cruz; Pltcl Sci.

JIN, MICHELLE H; San Gorgfonio HS; San Bernardino, CA; (3); 10/431; Church Yth Grp; French Clb; Key Clb; Powder Puff Ftbl; JV Tennis; Cit Awd; NHS; Aces Clb; CSF; UCLA; Pre-Med.

JIN, PAUL; Damien HS; Rialto, CA; (2); Church Yth Grp; Computer Clb; Ski Clb; Off Frsh Cls; Stu Cncl; Hon Roll; Fishing Clb.

JIN, RICHARD Z; Narbonne HS; Carson, CA; (3); Aud/Vis; Church Yth Grp; Debate Tm; Key Clb; Math Clb; Church Choir; Stage Crew; JV Capt Vllybl; Hon Roll; Prfct Atten Awd; AWANA Ldr; Church Praise Team; Med.

JIN, WALTER S; Loyola HS; Los Angeles, CA; (4); 1/261; Chess Clb; Pres Computer Clb; Debate Tm; Pres Capt Math Clb; NFL; Speech Tm; Pep Band; Ed Nwsp; Ed Yrbk; Phtg Lit Mag; Harvard Prz Bk Awd; Bnk America Achvt Awd; Acad Dcthln Team Capt, Gold/Silver Essay Wrtng Medls; Harvard U.

JINDRICH, ANTONIA E; Tamalpais HS; Mill Valley, CA; (2); Dance Clb; Drama Clb; Orch; High Hon Roll; Prfct Atten Awd; Gymnastics; Violin.

JINE, GUY; Foothill HS; Pleasanton, CA; (3); 100/250; FBLA; Ftbl; Hstry.

JIRANEK, JAMES R; San Pasqual HS; Escondido, CA; (3); 53/353; Letterman Clb; Varsity Clb; Intrml Bsktbl; Var Capt Golf; Hon Roll; Pres Acad Fit Awd; Essy Cmptn UCSD, Recvd Recgntn; Hnrs Gldn St Alg & US Hstry Exms; UCSB; Accntng.

JIRAPISANKUL, SARAWOOTH; Los Angeles HS; Los Angeles, CA; (3); Science Clb; Teachers Aide; Prfct Atten Awd; USC; Bus.

JIU, PIERSON W; Bakersfield HS; Bakersfield, CA; (3); 23/718; Church Yth Grp; Debate Tm; Treas Key Clb; NFL; Science Clb; Teachers Aide; JV Ftbl; High Hon Roll; Hon Roll; Comp; Vllybl; Engr.

JO, CHANG B; Gretchen Whitney HS; Cerritos, CA; (4); 1/170; French Clb; Key Clb; Science Clb; Pres Service Clb; Orch; Ed Nwsp; Var Socr; JV Tennis; Cit Awd; Hon Roll; Music Tchrs Assn CA Cert Merit; Sthwstrn Music Fstvl 85-89; CA Schlrshp Fdrtn VP; Poli Sci.

JO, HYO-JUNG J; La Sierra HS; Riverside, CA; (1); FBLA; Spanish Clb; Nwsp; JV Tennis; High Hon Roll; Ntl Merit Ltr; Prfct Atten Awd; Pres Acad Fit Awd; Principals Awd; Bus.

JO, JANET; Katella HS; Anaheim, CA; (3); Am Leg Aux Girls St; Cmnty Wkr; Hosp Aide; VP Pres Key Clb; Pep Clb; Spanish Clb; Drill Tm; VP Soph Cls; Var Tennis; High Hon Roll; Lt Govr Key Clb; OCAD; CSF; Med.

JO, JUDY; Tracy Joint Union HS; Tracy, CA; (2); 22/483; Orch; Vllybl; Hon Roll; Big Brother & Sister Clb; UC Berkely; Bus.

JOAQUIN, VIVIAN; Los Altos HS; Hacienda Hts, CA; (3); Hon Roll; Teacher.

JOB, JESSICA; Biggs HS; Richvale, CA; (3); 6/46; Yrbk; VP Frsh Cls; Stu Cncl; JV Var Cheerldng; JV Var Score Keeper; JV Var Sftbl; JV Var Vllybl; High Hon Roll; Hon Roll; Prfct Atten Awd; FFA Sweetheart Queen 88; Sftbl All League 3rd Bsmn 90; Butle Clg; Bus.

JOBE, WENDI; Williams HS; Williams, CA; (4); 1/30; Pres SADD; Ed Nwsp; Ed Yrbk; Pres Soph Cls; Sec Jr Cls; Sec Sr Cls; Treas Stu Cncl; Capt Var Bsktbl; Var Trk; Capt Var Vllybl; Juvenile Just Dlnqncy Prvntn Cmmssn; Camproyal Rotary Yth Ldrshp Activities; Co MVP Mid Vly Leg Vlybl; U AK Anchorage; Bus Admin.

JOBSON, JENNIFER R; Oak Ridge HS; El Dorado Hills, CA; (2); 14/290; SADD; Socr; Trk; High Hon Roll; CSF.

JOCHIM-PORTER, MICHELLE C; Venice HS; Santa Monica, CA; (2); Church Yth Grp; Thesps; Band; School Play; JV Cheerldng; Gymanstics Fdrtn Team; CSF; UCLA; Engrng.

JOCHUMS, SARA S; Analy HS; Sebastopol, CA; (3); 35/243; Church Yth Grp; Cmnty Wkr; Drama Clb; Pres French Clb; Girl Scts; Intnl Clb; School Musical; Var Cheerldng; High Hon Roll; St Schlr; Girl Sct Gold Awd; Japanese Exchng Stu Ambssdr To Japan; Sci.

JOE, LORAH L; Skyline HS; Oakland, CA; (3); Cmnty Wkr; Dance Clb; 4-H; Hosp Aide; ROTC; Spanish Clb; Drill Tm; Hon Roll; UC Santa Barbara; Psych.

JOFFE, ERIS; Ponderosa HS; Rescue, CA; (1); German Clb; JCL; VP Service Clb; Band; Drill Tm; Mrchg Band; Pep Band; Lit Mag; JV Cheerldng; Tennis; Child Care/Tchr.

JOGOPULOS, DEBRA L; Pittsburg HS; Pittsburg, CA; (4); 7/277; Am Leg Aux Girls St; 4-H; Pep Clb; SADD; L Co-Capt Cheerldng; L Capt Socr; Elks Awd; 4-H Awd; High Hon Roll; Rotary Awd; Delta Yth Sccr Leag; Italian Travel Clb; Diablo Valley Coll; Bus Admin.

JOH, JEANNIE; Sunny Hills HS; Buena Park, CA; (1); Band; Church Choir; Mrchg Band; Orch; NHS; Pres Acad Fit Awd; WA Pre-Coll Test Erly Entrnc Prgm; Yale U; MD.

JOHAL, SARVJEET K; Dinuba Joint HS; Dinuba, CA; (3); FHA; Key Clb; Rptr Yrbk; Tennis; Sci.

JOHAL, SUKVINDER K; Livingston HS; Livingston, CA; (3); FBLA; Girl Scts; Spanish Clb; Teachers Aide; Church Choir; Phtg Rptr Yrbk; Cit Awd; Hon Roll; Prfct Atten Awd; U Stanislaus; Teacher.

JOHANNSEN, ELISE R; Santa Barbara HS; Santa Barbara, CA; (2); Chorus; Drill Tm; School Musical; School Play; Lit Mag; Cmmnty Theatre; Presdntl Phys Ftns Awd; Singer.

JOHANSEN, DAVE A; Roseville HS; Rocklin, CA; (1); JV Bsbl; JV Socr; Hon Roll; Pres Acad Fit Awd; Mst Imprvd Bsbl Awd.

JOHANSSON, PIA K; Redlands SR HS; Redlands, CA; (4); Hon Roll; Nrsg.

JOHN, CINDY ST; Loyalton HS; Calpine, CA; (3); 1/37; Dance Clb; Drama Clb; VP FBLA; Ed Rptr Nwsp; Phtg Ed Yrbk; Pres Sr Cls; JV Var Cheerldng; Stat Ftbl; Var L Sftbl; Var L Vllybl; CSF; Spansh & Pep Clbs; Southern CA.

JOHN, HEATHER; Justin Siena HS; Angwin, CA; (4); Rep Frsh Cls; Pres Rep Soph Cls; Art Awd; Hnr Roll; U CA Davis; Engl.

JOHN, JESSICA; Palo Verde HS; Blythe, CA; (3); 1/288; Church Yth Grp; Drama Clb; Pep Clb; Pres Soph Cls; Sec Stu Cncl; Hon Roll; NHS; Tap Dance; Schltc All Amercn; Piano; BYU.

JOHN, LUKE K; Crescenta Valley HS; Montrose, CA; (3); Capt Debate Tm; Hosp Aide; Math Clb; Ed Lit Mag; High Hon Roll; NHS; Ntl Merit Ltr; Edtr-In-Chief Of Galactic Chronicles; Edtr Schl Prose/Poetry Jrnls; 2nd Sci Fair; VP Sci-Fi Clb; CSF; Harvard U; Med.

JOHN, MELIND J; Menlo Schl; San Carlos, CA; (4); 1/107; Nwsp; Ed Yrbk; Lit Mag; JV Bsbl; JV Var Crs Cntry; Var Mgr(s); Var Score Keeper; JV Var Socr; Var L Trk; High Hon Roll; Yale Book Awd; Menlo Park, CA Rotary Clb Awds Physcs & Econ; Stanford U; Bus.

JOHNS, BECKY; San Lorenzo HS; San Lorenzo, CA; (2); Church Yth Grp; JV Var Bsktbl; JV Capt Cheerldng; Chabot Coll; Elem Tchr.

JOHNS, DALLIN D; Los Altos HS; Hacienda Hts, CA; (3); Boy Scts; Church Yth Grp; Ski Clb; Band; Mrchg Band; Ftbl; Hon Roll; Brigham Young U; Accntng.

JOHNS, DARREN C; San Marcos HS; Santa Barbara, CA; (2); Var Diving; JV Tennis; Pres Acad Fit Awd; Engr.

JOHNS, DEBRA ANN; Alhambra HS; Alhambra, CA; (3); VP Church Yth Grp; Service Clb; Capt Flag Corp; Alhambra Yth Cmssn Sec; BYU; HS Engl Tchr.

JOHNS, DEIDRE; Woodlake HS; Woodlake, CA; (2); Church Yth Grp; Debate Tm; Drama Clb; 4-H; FHA; Key Clb; Pep Clb; Science Clb; Ski Clb; SADD; CSF Sec; Mst Imprvd Vlybl; GATE; Hnrs Classes.

JOHNS, HEATHER; San Lorenzo HS; San Lorenzo, CA; (4); 5/200; Church Yth Grp; Quiz Bowl; Scholastic Bowl; Service Clb; Teachers Aide; Church Choir; Var JV Cheerldng; Var Trk; High Hon Roll; CSF; Coll Club; UC Davis; Biochem.

JOHNS, JASON; Huntington Beach HS; Huntington Beach, CA; (3); Aud/Vis; Lcl Bands; Cmnctns.

JOHNS, JEREMIAH KNUDSON; Oxnard HS; Oxnard, CA; (3); Chess Clb; Drama Clb; English Clb; French Clb; Quiz Bowl; Band; Stu Cncl; Ecology; Astronomy.

JOHNS, JOANNA L; Salinas HS; Salinas, CA; (2); Church Yth Grp; GAA; SADD; Teachers Aide; Pres Frsh Cls; Rep Stu Cncl; JV Sftbl; Var Trk; JV Vllybl; High Hon Roll; CSF; Stu For A Better Earth; Frshmn Cls Hmecmng Princess.

JOHNS, SCOTT R; Live Oak HS; Morgan Hill, CA; (3); 38/530; Sec Pres Chess Clb; Computer Clb; Band; Jazz Band; Mrchg Band; Pep Band; School Musical; Lit Mag; Intrml Socr; Intrml Sftbl; Several Band Awds; Bus.

JOHNS, SUMMER N; Edison HS; Huntington Beach, CA; (3); Girl Scts; Office Aide; Ski Clb; Trk; Homerm Rep; Orange Coast Coll; Acctng.

JOHNSEN, AARON M; Chana HS; Auburn, CA; (4); Sec FFA; Rptr Nwsp; Intrml Socr; Santa Barbara; Econ.

JOHNSEN, LYZA; Paso Robles HS; Paso Robles, CA; (1); Church Yth Grp; Library Aide; Ski Clb; School Play; Ed Yrbk; Rep Stu Cncl; JV Bsktbl; JV Sftbl; Cit Awd; High Hon Roll; Med.

JOHNSON, AARON J; Argonaut HS; Jackson, CA; (2); Band; Mrchg Band; JV Capt Bsktbl; JV Capt Ftbl; High Hon Roll; U Of CA; Davis; Sprts Med.

JOHNSON, AISHA K; Vallejo SR HS; Vallejo, CA; (2); Church Yth Grp; Cmnty Wkr; Church Choir; San Francisco ST; Art.

JOHNSON, ALANYA J; Lompoc HS; Lompoc, CA; (2); Church Yth Grp; Drama Clb; Pep Clb; Teachers Aide; Band; Drill Tm; JV Mgr(s); JV Trk; Blck Stds Club; Med.

JOHNSON, ALEX M; Buena HS; Ventura, CA; (3); Cit Awd; High Hon Roll; Hon Roll; Acctng.

JOHNSON, ALISON L; Stephen Watts Kearny HS; San Diego, CA; (2); Art Clb; Church Yth Grp; Cmnty Wkr; Letterman Clb; Model UN; Pep Clb; Speech Tm; SADD; Teachers Aide; Varsity Clb; Mst Enthusiastic Soph Awds; Friday Night Live Org; Arch.

JOHNSON, ALLAN D; Maranatha HS; Pasadena, CA; (2); Church Yth Grp; Drama Clb; Letterman Clb; Chorus; Church Choir; School Musical; School Play; JV Crs Cntry; JV Socr; Var Trk; CSF; US Navy; Pilot.

JOHNSON, ALLISON M; Analy HS; Sebastopol, CA; (2); French Clb; Teachers Aide; JV Tennis; Rotary Awd; UC Davis; Vet.

JOHNSON, AMANDA J; Oakdale HS; Oakdale, CA; (1); Church Yth Grp; Dance Clb; FHA; SADD; Chorus; Church Choir; Gym; Sftbl; Vllybl; Cit Awd; Choice Awd Drug Abuse; BYU; Psych.

JOHNSON, AMBER; Vivian Webb HS; San Rafael, CA; (3); Church Yth Grp; School Play; Ed Lit Mag; JV Cheerldng; Var Socr; Var Sftbl; Hon Roll; Paleontology.

JOHNSON, AMY; Miramonte HS; Orinda, CA; (1); Latin Clb; Spanish Clb; Speech Tm; High Hon Roll; JV Swmmng; Piano; Cmpng; CA Schlrshp Fed; Hkng; Fshng; U Of CA.

JOHNSON, AMY; West HS; Bakersfield, CA; (4); Pres Dance Clb; Ski Clb; SADD; Teachers Aide; Variety Show; Stu Cncl; Var Cheerldng; Var Pom Pon; Dnc Clb Schlrshp; Sr Outstndng Dncr Mdl; Bakersfield Coll; Arch.

JOHNSON, AMY L; Cordova SR HS; Sacramento, CA; (3); 14/464; Key Clb; Model UN; Stage Crew; Ed Nwsp; JV Var Crs Cntry; High Hon Roll; Ntl Merit Ltr; Octagon Clb; CSF; Jrnlsm.

JOHNSON, AMY L; Dana Hills HS; Laguna Niguel, CA; (3); Ski Clb; Spanish Clb; Bsktbl; Sftbl; Trk; Church Yth Grp; Teachers Aide; JV Gym; Hon Roll; Part Time Job Pharmacy; Saddleback JR Coll; Photo Jrnl.

JOHNSON, AMY L; Edison HS; Stockton, CA; (1); Church Yth Grp; Speech Tm; SADD; Hon Roll; NHS; UC Davis; Engl.

JOHNSON, AMY L; San Gabriel Mission HS; Monterey Park, CA; (3); 6/116; GAA; Pep Clb; School Musical; Yrbk; Hon Roll; NHS; CSF; 2nd Hnrs Acad; LIFE; Teacher.

JOHNSON, ANDREA C; Monterey HS; Monterey, CA; (3); Church Yth Grp; Teachers Aide; Sftbl; High Hon Roll; Hon Roll; Prfct Atten Awd; Pres Acad Fit Awd.

JOHNSON, ANDRIA D; Immaculate Heart HS; Inglewood, CA; (3); Church Yth Grp; Drama Clb; GAA; School Musical; Rep Frsh Cls; Pres Soph Cls; VP Jr Cls; Pres Stu Cncl; Mgr Swmmng; Hon Roll; APBA; Los Angeles Pediatric Soc; Med.

JOHNSON, ANGELA D; Lompoc HS; Lompoc, CA; (2); Art Clb; Band; Chorus; Mrchg Band; High Hon Roll; Anthrplgy.

JOHNSON, ANGELA R; La Sierra HS; Riverside, CA; (1); Hon Roll; UCSD; Marine Bio.

JOHNSON, ANTOINE D; Gardena HS; Gardena, CA; (2); Library Aide; JV Bsbl; Var Bsktbl; JV Ftbl; Hon Roll; Med.

JOHNSON, ARISHA; Castlemont HS; Oakland, CA; (2); Band; Church Choir; Trk; Hon Roll; UCLA; Jrnlsm.

JOHNSON, ARTHUR W; Whittier Christian HS; Fullerton, CA; (2); Church Yth Grp; Teachers Aide; JV Bsbl; JV Bsktbl; High Hon Roll; Hon Roll; Jr PGA Tour Glf; Hgh Hnr CSF; Stanford; Sci.

JOHNSON, BECKY L; Roseville HS; Roseville, CA; (3); 38/431; Am Leg Aux Girls St; Church Yth Grp; Debate Tm; Pres Pep Clb; School Play; Sec Treas Soph Cls; Rep Jr Cls; Capt Var Cheerldng; Var Capt Powder Puff Ftbl; Var Socr.

JOHNSON, BEN; Rosamond HS; Rosamond, CA; (2); Church Yth Grp; Letterman Clb; Cit Awd; Hon Roll; Masonic Awd; Bsktbl Mgr; Bsbl Statistician; Indust Arts.

JOHNSON, BRANDON S; Hemet HS; Hemet, CA; (2); Boy Scts; Band; Bsktbl; Cit Awd; Hon Roll; Prfct Atten Awd; San Diego ST U; Phrmctcl.

JOHNSON, BRENDA S; Fontana HS; Fontana, CA; (3); Debate Tm; Drama Clb; FFA; Chorus; School Play; Hon Roll; Pres Acad Fit Awd; CSF; Vet.

JOHNSON, BRIAN K; Moreno Valley HS; Moreno Vly, CA; (4); Letterman Clb; JV Ftbl; JV Trk; Hon Roll; Co Curricular Schlstc Achvt; Merit Awd; RCC; Bus.

JOHNSON, BRIAN MICHAEL; Folsom HS; Folsom, CA; (3); 1/189; Am Leg Boys St; Boy Scts; Intnl Clb; Math Clb; Model UN; Var L Crs Cntry; Var L Trk; High Hon Roll; NHS; Rotary Awd; Stu Reaching Out; Friday Night Live; CSF; Engrng.

JOHNSON, BRITTANY; Point Loma HS; San Diego, CA; (3); Key Clb; Model UN; L Cheerldng; Hon Roll; Rotary Awd; Interact & MADCAPS Clbs; Saferides Teen Cnslng.

JOHNSON, BROOK C; Chino HS; Chino, CA; (4); 12/519; Var Socr; Cit Awd; Elks Awd; High Hon Roll; Pres Acad Fit Awd; CSF; Eagle Scout; Voc Cert Drafting; BYU; Bio Chem.

JOHNSON JR, BRUCE D; Redwood Christian HS; Castro Valley, CA; (3); Church Yth Grp; Band; Orch; School Musical; Off Sr Cls; Bsbl; Bsktbl; Crs Cntry; Trk; High Hon Roll; Smmr Mnstry Europe 90; Biola.

JOHNSON, CAMILLE S; Claremont HS; Claremont, CA; (4); 41/417; 4-H; Girl Scts; Ed Yrbk; Swmmng; High Hon Roll; Hon Roll; Ntl Merit SF; Pres Acad Fit Awd; JV Wtr Polo 4 Yrs; CSF-CA Schlrshp Fndtn 4 Yrs; Slvr Awd GS-SCTS; Carleton.

JOHNSON, CARLIN; Fred C Beyer HS; Modesto, CA; (3); School Play; Var Sftbl; High Hon Roll; Hon Roll; Vrsty Wtr Polo; Mrn Bio.

JOHNSON, CARMEN; Santa Teresa HS; San Jose, CA; (4); Drama Clb; FCA; French Clb; Model UN; Pres Band; Pres Mrchg Band; School Musical; Stage Crew; Variety Show; Stu Cncl; Mck Trl Tm 89-90; Acad Decthln Tm 88-90; Hnr Bands 87-88; U Of CA Davis; Anthrplgy.

JOHNSON, CATHERINE D; Chico SR HS; Chico, CA; (3); 38/354; Church Yth Grp; Key Clb; Band; School Play; JV Bsktbl; Var JV Sftbl; JV Var Vllybl; Hon Roll; Pres Acad Fit Awd; Acad Decathlon 1st Pl Interview; MVP Sftbl 89; U Pacific; Pharm.

JOHNSON, CATONA T; Monrovia HS; Monrovia, CA; (3); Aud/Vis; Church Choir; Var Bsktbl; JV Swmmng; Hon Roll; Cert Ath Achvt; USM; RN.

JOHNSON, CELESTE M; Salinas Union HS; Salinas, CA; (2); Church Yth Grp; Band; Mrchg Band; French Hon Soc; Foreign Lang Ger & Fr; Trvl East/West Europe 86-89; Stanford; Med.

JOHNSON, CHANEL M; Highlands HS; North Highlands, CA; (1); Chorus; High Hon Roll; Stu Reaching Out.

JOHNSON, CHARLIE; Mt Whitney HS; Visalia, CA; (3); 56/350; Var Diving; Var Swmmng; Water Polo; UCSD.

JOHNSON, CHERIE; Huntington Beach HS; Huntington Bch, CA; (3); Church Yth Grp; Church Choir; Drill Tm; Trk; Hon Roll; Interior Design.

JOHNSON, CHERISE S; Galileo HS; San Francisco, CA; (2); Dance Clb; Pep Clb; Nwsp; Bsktbl; Cheerldng; Ftbl; Score Keeper; Sftbl; High Hon Roll; Hon Roll; LA Tech; Tchr.

JOHNSON, CHRIS R; Apple Valley HS; Apple Valley, CA; (3); Boy Scts; Pres Church Yth Grp; Varsity Clb; Capt L Bsktbl; Capt L Trk; Cit Awd; Hon Roll; Pres Acad Fit Awd; Eagle Scout Awd; All Leag Bsktbl Team Hnrbl Mention; Mst Valuable Track Athlete 90; Arch.

JOHNSON, CHRISTI L; Sherman H Burroughs HS; Ridgecrest, CA; (3); Church Yth Grp; Dance Clb; Drama Clb; Pres French Clb; Treas FBLA; VP SADD; Thesps; Drill Tm; Drill Tm; Rotary Awd; DARE Role Model; Church Yth Choir; Psych.

JOHNSON, CHRISTOPHER I; Westchester HS; Culver City, CA; (2); JV Trk; Cit Awd; High Hon Roll; Hon Roll; NHS; Pres Acad Fit Awd; YLFA Mem; Planetary Soc; Frnds Of Obsrvtry; UC Berkeley; Astrophysicist.

JOHNSON, CHRISTOPHER J; Armijo HS; Fairfield, CA; (2); Key Clb; High Hon Roll; Hon Roll; Arch.

JOHNSON, CHRISTY; Van Nuys HS; Tujunga, CA; (2); Church Yth Grp; Dance Clb; Drama Clb; Girl Scts; Drill Tm; Pep Band; School Musical; School Play; Stage Crew; Intrml Cheerldng; Jr Mill Am St Pagnt 4th Rnnr Up; UCLA; Directing.

JOHNSON, CINDY; Ramona HS; Ramona, CA; (2); 93/336; Church Yth Grp; GAA; Varsity Clb; Bsktbl; Sftbl; Cit Awd; Hon Roll; Brigham Young U.

JOHNSON, DAN; Banning HS; Banning, CA; (3); Nwsp; Hon Roll; Graphic Artist.

JOHNSON, DANA; Bel-Air Preparatory HS; Yorba Linda, CA; (2); Chess Clb; Church Yth Grp; Cmnty Wkr; Debate Tm; Drama Clb; Varsity Clb; Church Choir; School Play; Rptr Nwsp; Rptr Yrbk; Prfct Atten; Stanford; Law.

JOHNSON, DANA L; Victor Valley HS; Victorville, CA; (2); Church Yth Grp; Church Choir; Hon Roll; Fishers Of Men Club-Chrisitan Schl Club; Point Loma Nazerene ; Social Wk.

JOHNSON, DANIEL J; Mount Diablo HS; Concord, CA; (3); #15 In Class; Service Clb; SADD; Hon Roll; CSF; Aerosp Engr.

JOHNSON, DANIEL J; St John Bosco HS; Whittier, CA; (2); Boy Scts; Band; Mrchg Band; Yrbk; Hon Roll.

JOHNSON, DANIELLE A; Will C Crawford HS; San Diego, CA; (2); Hosp Aide; Pep Clb; Nwsp; Stu Cncl; Mgr(s); Coca Cola Modelng Clb; UC Davis; Philosphy.

JOHNSON, DARREN L; Escondido Adventist Acad; San Diego, CA; (3); Church Yth Grp; Ski Clb; Band; Pep Band; Rptr Nwsp; Off Frsh Cls; VP Jr Cls; Var Bsktbl; Intrml Ftbl; Hon Roll; Jrnlsm.

JOHNSON, DAVID H; El Camino HS; Oceanside, CA; (3); Dance Clb; Speech Tm; SADD; Teachers Aide; Chorus; Variety Show; Hon Roll; Opt Clb Awd; US Intl U; Acting.

JOHNSON, DEMOND; O'farrell JCPA HS; San Diego, CA; (1); Band; Orch; Intrml Bsbl; Intrml Ftbl; Music.

JOHNSON, DENA A; Poway HS; Poway, CA; (2); Church Yth Grp; SADD; Teachers Aide; Varsity Clb; Stat Bsbl; Stat Bsktbl; Var L Swmmng; Tutor Elem Schl Studs; CA U; Ed.

JOHNSON, DEREK E; Rubidouk HS; Riverside, CA; (4); 1/600; Teachers Aide; Rep Frsh Cls; Rep Soph Cls; Capt Jr Cls; Pres Sr Cls; Rep Stu Cncl; L Var Tennis; Capt Vllybl; Cit Awd; High Hon Roll; Boys St; Toys For Tots Chrmn; CSF; Stanford; Pol Sci.

JOHNSON, DEUSHA L; East Union HS; French Camp, CA; (1); Church Yth Grp; Teachers Aide; Church Choir; Prfct Atten Awd.

JOHNSON, DINA; Los Alamitos HS; Seal Beach, CA; (3); Church Yth Grp; Cmnty Wkr; French Clb; Model UN; Science Clb; JV Bsktbl; Var Trk; JV Vllybl; Hon Roll; Safe Rides; Brown; Intl Rel.

JOHNSON, DOMONECK D; Washington Preparatory HS; Los Angeles, CA; (2); Computer Clb; Astronomy.

JOHNSON, DUSTIN L; Torrey Pines HS; Del Mar, CA; (3); Church Yth Grp; Cmnty Wkr; Ski Clb; Rep Soph Cls; JV Ftbl; JV Var Vllybl; Christian Ldrshp Cmp 90; Bus.

JOHNSON, ERIK J; Ygnacio Valley HS; Concord, CA; (2); Boy Scts; Church Yth Grp; Chorus; Var L Trk; Earned Acad Ltr GPA; Bay Vly Athletic Lg Jr Vrsty Discus Champ; CA Interschltc Fed Schlr Athlete; Phys Sci.

JOHNSON, ERIK R; Ventura HS; Ventura, CA; (3); 42/432; Boy Scts; JCL; Latin Clb; Band; Drm Mjr(t); Jazz Band; Mrchg Band; Pep Band; School Play; Hon Roll; Ca Poly San Louis.

JOHNSON, ERIKA L; East Union HS; Manteca, CA; (2); SADD; Band; Jazz Band; Mrchg Band; Pep Band; Trk; Hon Roll; CA ST U Stanlislaus; Music.

JOHNSON, ERIN; Nordhoff HS; Ojai, CA; (4); 10/160; Spanish Clb; Pres Sr Cls; Stu Cncl; Capt Var Bsktbl; Var Powder Puff Ftbl; L Var Sftbl; Capt Var Vllybl; Cit Awd; High Hon Roll; NHS; Outstndng Girl Yr; Ranger Yr; Outstndng Female Athltc Yr; CO Coll.

JOHNSON, EVELYN Y; West Covina HS; W Covina, CA; (3); Church Yth Grp; Varsity Clb; Church Choir; Var Bsktbl; JV Sftbl; Var Vllybl; Wt Lftg; Prfct Atten Awd; Jr Act Dir Friday Night Live; Visage Club; U S CA; Acctg.

JOHNSON, GINA MARIE; Los Angeles Baptist HS; Granada Hills, CA; (4); 3/92; Church Yth Grp; French Clb; Teachers Aide; Church Choir; Lit Mag; Var Crs Cntry; Var Trk; French Hon Soc; High Hon Roll; NHS; CSF Gold Sealbearer; Stanford U; Med.

JOHNSON, GLENN A; River City HS; West Sacramento, CA; (4); Chess Clb; Computer Clb; JA; SADD; Bsktbl; Golf; Cit Awd; High Hon Roll; Prfct Atten Awd; Bank Amer Achvt Awd; Vlntr Fire Dept; Law Enfrcmnt.

JOHNSON, GREG W; Santa Teresa HS; San Jose, CA; (3); Church Yth Grp; Computer Clb; Science Clb; Spanish Clb; Band; Mrchg Band; School Musical; Music; Bsbl; San Jose ST U; Physicist.

JOHNSON, GREGORY E; Valhalla HS; El Cajon, CA; (3); 85/408; Church Yth Grp; FTA; Pres Soph Cls; Hon Roll; HOBY; Campus Life; USD; Bus.

JOHNSON, HEATHER D; Arlington HS; Riverside, CA; (2); Art Clb; ROTC; Golden Apple Awd; US Air Force.

JOHNSON, HEATHER E; Galt HS; Galt, CA; (2); 1/239; Church Yth Grp; Church Choir; Drill Tm; Flag Corp; Variety Show; High Hon Roll; Odyssey Of Mind Regnl Champs; Pres Church Yth Grp; Private Violin Lessons; Brigham Young U; Graphic Desgn.

JOHNSON, HEATHER R; Southern Trinity HS; Bridgeville, CA; (2); 1/18; Church Yth Grp; SADD; Teachers Aide; Pres Frsh Cls; Pres Soph Cls; Bsktbl; Trk; Vllybl; Cit Awd; High Hon Roll; Golden St Exam Awd; OH ST U; Bus.

JOHNSON, HEIDI; Mt Whitney HS; Visalia, CA; (4); Sec Spanish Clb; Teachers Aide; Var JV Tennis; Rckt Clb; Med Creers Clb; Gtschlks Hi-Deb; UC San Diego; Med.

JOHNSON, HEIDI S; Huntington Beach HS; Huntington Beach, CA; (2); JV Trk; Tower Awd Athlts; TAN; Orange Coast Coll; Phys Thrpst.

JOHNSON, JANA M; Gompers Secondary Schl; San Diego, CA; (2); 10/140; Scholastic Bowl; Pres Science Clb; Rep Frsh Cls; JV Cheerldng; High Hon Roll; Hon Roll; Jr NHS; NHS; Opt Clb Awd; Pres Acad Fit Awd; Sci Olympd Pres & Team Capt; German/Russian Clb Pres; UC Berkeley; Astronaut.

JOHNSON, JANEEN; Amos Alonzo Stagg HS; Daly City, CA; (4); Dance Clb; Debate Tm; NFL; Spanish Clb; Speech Tm; Rptr Nwsp; Powder Puff Ftbl; Sftbl; Vllybl; Hon Roll; Skyline Coll; Psychology.

JOHNSON, JANELLE M; Escondido HS; Escondido, CA; (3); 1/400; Church Yth Grp; Teachers Aide; High Hon Roll; Ntl Merit SF; CSF; Daisy Chain; Elem Ed.

JOHNSON, JENETTE; El Segundo HS; El Segundo, CA; (3); AFS; VP French Clb; Sec Science Clb; Capt Color Guard; Capt Flag Corp; Capt JV Bsktbl; L Var Sftbl; Intl Order Of Rainbow Girls, Order Of De Molay, Order Of Jobs Daughters; U CA.

JOHNSON, JENNIFER; Carondelet HS; Martinez, CA; (4); Church Yth Grp; Cmnty Wkr; GAA; Pep Clb; Ski Clb; Rep Frsh Cls; Rep Soph Cls; Rep Jr Cls; Stu Cncl; JV Co-Capt Socr; Yth Edctr; Campus Mnstry Rep; Yng Girls Sftbl Team Asst Coach; St Marys U.

JOHNSON, JENNIFER; Clayton Valley HS; Clayton, CA; (2); Church Yth Grp; SADD; Teachers Aide; Cheerldng; Miss Natl Beauty Pagnt-2nd Pl; Miss Natl Tlnt Pagnt-3rd Pl; Medcl Explr; UCLA; Med.

JOHNSON, JENNIFER; Galt HS; Galt, CA; (1); Pep Clb; Stage Crew; Cheerldng; Var Trk; Hon Roll; Pres Acad Fit Awd; Bus.

JOHNSON, JENNIFER; Poway HS; Poway, CA; (3); Church Yth Grp; Cmnty Wkr; Dance Clb; Debate Tm; NFL; Office Aide; Pep Clb; Speech Tm; SADD; Teachers Aide; Hnrs Band; Stu Of Mnth; U CA Berkely; Law.

JOHNSON, JENNIFER L; Grossmont HS; El Cajon, CA; (3); 27/400; Church Yth Grp; Dance Clb; Variety Show; Lit Mag; High Hon Roll; Psych.

JOHNSON, JENNIFER R; Apple Valley SR HS; Apple Valley, CA; (1); FHA; Office Aide; Ski Clb; Teachers Aide; UNLV.

JOHNSON, JENNY; Arroyo Grande HS; Pismo Beach, CA; (2); 50/625; Cmnty Wkr; NFL; Band; Mrchg Band; Pep Band; JV Swmmng; JV Tennis; Hon Roll; CSF; Rainbow Girlsworthy Advsr; Work Mc Donalds; Co Sr Honor Band 1st Chair Flute; Law.

JOHNSON, JEREMIAH P; North HS; Bakersfield, CA; (2); Boy Scts; Church Yth Grp; Cmnty Wkr; Variety Show; Bsktbl; Tennis; Hon Roll; Pres Acad Fit Awd; Brigham Young U; Bus.

JOHNSON, JERRY O; Tokay HS; Stockton, CA; (2); HI; Police.

JOHNSON, JESSICA; Rio Mesa HS; Camarillo, CA; (1); SADD; JV Cheerldng; San Diego St; Marine Zoology.

JOHNSON, JIMMY L; Fairfield HS; Fairfield, CA; (3); Socr; Wt Lftg; Wrstlng; Hon Roll; UC Davis; Phys Ed.

JOHNSON, JOAHNE L; Palisades HS; Los Angeles, CA; (4); Church Yth Grp; Drama Clb; SADD; Pep Band; School Play; Rep Sr Cls; Rep Stu Cncl; Var Cheerldng; High Hon Roll; NHS; CSF; Flfllmnt Fund Schlrs Awd; Yng Blk Schlrs; 1st Chr God Schlrshp Awd; Yng Achvrs Awd; Ple To Ple Pgm; Hampton U; Interntl Bus.

JOHNSON, JOEY; Woodside HS; Redwood City, CA; (2); Swmmng; Cal Berkeley; Engr.

JOHNSON, JOHN E; Palmdale HS; Palmdale, CA; (4); Chess Clb; Debate Tm; Drama Clb; Math Clb; Math Tm; Quiz Bowl; Speech Tm; Teachers Aide; School Play; Stage Crew; Antelope Valley Coll; Math Tchr.

JOHNSON, JOLYN; Oxnard HS; Oxnard, CA; (2); 4/604; Treas Drama Clb; Thesps; Band; School Musical; School Play; Stage Crew; High Hon Roll; CSF; Acad Ltr; Actng.

JOHNSON, JONAH C; Nevada Union HS; Nevada City, CA; (3); Chess Clb; SADD; Var Swmmng; Hon Roll; Water Polo; Piano; U CA Davis; Paramedic.

JOHNSON, JONATHAN D; North Salinas HS; Salinas, CA; (2); Church Yth Grp; Trk; Hon Roll; Prfct Atten Awd; CA Gldn St Exam Alg Hnrs; Engrng.

JOHNSON, JONNETTA ROSE; Porterville HS; Porterville, CA; (3); Church Yth Grp; GAA; SADD; Band; Mrchg Band; Pep Band; Trk; Hon Roll; San Jose ST; Psych.

JOHNSON, JOSHUA M; Atwater HS; Merced, CA; (4); 2/385; Boy Scts; Ski Clb; Yrbk; High Hon Roll; Hon Roll; Pres Acad Fit Awd; CA Schlrshp Fed; CAP; Bnk Of Amer Achvt Awd; San Jose ST U; Math.

JOHNSON, JULIE; Amador Valley HS; Pleasanton, CA; (1); Church Yth Grp; Cheerldng; Trk; Educ.

JOHNSON, JUSTIN M; Clovis West HS; Fresno, CA; (3); 32/600; Var Trk; High Hon Roll; CA Schlrshp Fed; Bus.

JOHNSON, KAIDI M; Ontario HS; Ontario, CA; (2); 56/567; Letterman Clb; VP Spanish Clb; Var Trk; High Hon Roll; Hon Roll; Prfct Atten Awd; Black Stu Union; Engrng.

JOHNSON, KARA L; Antioch HS; Antioch, CA; (2); 19/721; Spanish Clb; Rptr Nwsp; Hon Roll; Pres Acad Fit Awd; CJSF & CSF; Stu Mentor Sci; Golden ST Exam Gemtry Hnrs; Bio.

JOHNSON, KARENLYNN; Hemet HS; Los Angeles, CA; (2); Church Yth Grp; JV Cheerldng; Intrml Ftbl; Intrml Socr; JV Sftbl; Intrml Swmmng; Intrml Vllybl; Cit Awd; Hon Roll; U CA; Poly Sci.

JOHNSON, KARNA L; Alhambra HS; Martinez, CA; (3); Church Yth Grp; 4-H; Pep Clb; Varsity Clb; Ed Nwsp; Yrbk; Rep Soph Cls; VP Soph Cls; Pres Jr Cls; Stu Cncl; Yth Eductr; GSE Schlr Awd; Dstngshd Schltc Team; North Coast Sctn Awd 89-90; U Of CA.

JOHNSON, KATHERINE; Modesto HS; Modesto, CA; (4); Sec AFS; Church Yth Grp; Acpl Chr; Yrbk; Treas Sr Cls; Hon Roll; Prfct Atten Awd; Acad Dcthln Jr Yr; Alt Gld Mdl; Scrtry/Treas Yng Dmcrts; Modesto JC.

JOHNSON, KATHRYN; St Marys HS; Stockton, CA; (2); Hosp Aide; JV Socr; Hon Roll; Jobs Daughters; Psych.

JOHNSON, KATHY; El Camino SR HS; S. San Francisco, CA; (1); Dance Clb; Drama Clb; Variety Show; Cheerldng; Jr NHS; Kiwanis Awd; Jrnlsm.

JOHNSON, KATHY; The Bishops Schl; San Diego, CA; (2); Church Yth Grp; Hosp Aide; Library Aide; Service Clb; Chorus; Lit Mag; Trk; Wt Lftg; Hon Roll; Spanish NHS; Public Libr Pearl Awd.

JOHNSON, KATIE K; Village Christian HS; Sun Valley, CA; (4); 27/119; Drama Clb; English Clb; Mu Alpha Theta; Spanish Clb; Church Choir; Var Trk; U AZ; Sociology.

JOHNSON, KATRIN M; Santa Teresa HS; San Jose, CA; (2); Drama Clb; French Clb; Spanish Clb; SADD; Band; Jazz Band; Mrchg Band; Pep Band; School Musical; Variety Show; CSF; Acadmc Dec; Chem.

JOHNSON, KATRINA N; Skyline HS; Oakland, CA; (3); Dance Clb; Drama Clb; Thesps; Band; Stage Crew; Hon Roll.

JOHNSON, KEITH W; Pinole Valley HS; Hercules, CA; (3); Teachers Aide; JV Bsktbl; JV Ftbl.

JOHNSON, KELLY E; Aptos HS; Watsonville, CA; (1); Cmnty Wkr; German Clb; Girl Scts; JV Swmmng; Interact Clb, Secy; Piano; UCLA; Chld Psych.

JOHNSON, KEVIN M; Skyline HS; Oakland, CA; (3); Hosp Aide; Hon Roll; Rugby Club.

JOHNSON JR, KEVIN R; Fontana HS; Fontana, CA; (4); 4-H; Church Choir; Variety Show; Ftbl; Vllybl; Wt Lftg; 4-H Awd; Consumer Science Department Awd Excellence In Human Dev; Contracting,Musician.

JOHNSON, KHARY; Santa Barbara HS; Santa Barbara, CA; (3); 243/471; Teachers Aide; Bsktbl; Ftbl; Potentiality Award; Outstanding Academic Achievement Award; Certificate Of Recog CA St Senate; U Of Xavier.

JOHNSON, KIM L; Lick-Wilmerding HS; Sedona, AZ; (4); Cmnty Wkr; Teachers Aide; Chorus; Ed Yrbk; Var Swmmng; Ntl Merit SF; U AZ; Mktng.

JOHNSON, KIMBERLY A; The Bishops Schl; Rancho Santa Fe, CA; (3); Model UN; Var L Bsktbl; Var L Trk; Hon Roll; Ntl Merit Ltr; Intl Studies Diplomacy.

JOHNSON, KIMBERLY L; Westminster HS; Westminster, CA; (2); Drama Clb; School Play; Stage Crew; Off Soph Cls; JV Trk; Pace Bnk Amer Essay Cont; Animal Rights Orgnztns; Publc Brdcstng.

JOHNSON, KRISTA M; Buena HS; Ventura, CA; (4); 10/450; L Church Yth Grp; French Clb; SADD; Band; Mrchg Band; Sec Sr Cls; VP Capt Crs Cntry; JV Trk; High Hon Roll; Pres Acad Fit Awd; Acad Lttr Clb Pres; Grl Of 4th Qrtr; U Of CA Berkeley; Bio Pre-Med.

JOHNSON, KRISTI; St Joseph HS; Bellflower, CA; (4); 68/171; Pep Clb; SADD; Acpl Chr; Chorus; Var Capt Cheerldng; Hon Roll; Karate Rgnls 88; USAKF Jr Olympics-Gold Medal & Slvr Medal 88; USAKF Jr Olympic Bronze Mdls 89; Chapman Coll; Physcl Thrpy.

JOHNSON, KRISTINA L; Del Oro HS; Chico, CA; (4); 56/275; Cmnty Wkr; French Clb; GAA; JA; Math Clb; Red Cross Aide; Ski Clb; SADD; Teachers Aide; Sec Jr Cls; Gldn Eagle Of Wk; Aero Engrng.

JOHNSON, KRISTY J; Fountain Valley HS; Fountain Valley, CA; (1); Church Yth Grp; College; Electrical Engineer.

JOHNSON, KURT E; Ventura HS; Ojai, CA; (3); 14/514; Art Clb; Boy Scts; Treas Drama Clb; German Clb; JCL; Latin Clb; Teachers Aide; Thesps; Cit Awd; High Hon Roll; Maxima Cum Laude, Cum Laude Natl Latin Exams; Arch.

JOHNSON, LAKESHA; Washington Prep; Los Angeles, CA; (3); Church Yth Grp; Chorus; Drill Tm; School Play; Cheerldng; Trk; High Hon Roll; Hon Roll; UCLA; Law.

JOHNSON, LARS; Chaminade College Prep; Northridge, CA; (2); Bus Profs of Am; Church Yth Grp; FBLA; Letterman Clb; Varsity Clb; Rptr Nwsp; Ftbl; Trk; Vllybl; Wrstlng; Clb Vllybl Jr Olympcs; Own Mail Ordr Bus; CSUN; Bus.

JOHNSON, LATONIA; Morningside HS; Inglewood, CA; (3); Church Yth Grp; Hon Roll; Pre-Schl Sunday Schl Tchr; Elem Ed.

JOHNSON, LATRICE R; South Bay Lutheran HS; Chattanooga, TN; (2); Var Sftbl; Hon Roll; Prfct Atten Awd; UCLA; Nrsng.

JOHNSON, LAURA L; Highlands HS; North Highlands, CA; (2); Church Yth Grp; ROTC; SADD; JV Mgr(s); Var Socr; Cit Awd; Hon Roll; St Drill Tm 1st Pl; Exhibtn Drill Tm; Air Force Acad.

JOHNSON, LAURIE A; Mira Loma HS; Sacramento, CA; (3); Latin Clb; Chorus; Color Guard; Bus.

JOHNSON, LAURIE R; Winters HS; Winters, CA; (2); Church Yth Grp; Drama Clb; Girl Scts; Band; JV Bsktbl; CSF; Math.

JOHNSON, LAWRENCE JAYMES; Leffingwell Christian HS; Lynwood, CA; (3); 5/56; Rep Frsh Cls; VP Soph Cls; VP Jr Cls; Capt Var Bsbl; JV Bsktbl; Capt Var Ftbl; High Hon Roll; Outstndng Bio Stu; Bsktbl Coach; FL ST U.

JOHNSON, LESLIE R; Ocean View HS; Westminster, CA; (2); Church Yth Grp; Cmnty Wkr; Chorus; Church Choir; School Musical; Variety Show; Teaching Vietnms Girls ESL; HS Pilot Prgm Chrs; SOS, PALS Teen Suppt Grp; Coll Chr Class; CA ST Fullerton; Soclgy.

JOHNSON, LESTER M; Ukiah HS; Ukiah, CA; (2); 87/554; Band; School Play; Variety Show; Hon Roll; Prfct Atten Awd; Odyssey Of The Mind.

JOHNSON, LINDA; Saddleback HS; Santa Ana, CA; (3); Spanish Clb; SADD; Drill Tm; School Play; Ed Nwsp; Rptr Lit Mag; Hmcmng Prncss 87-88; Bus Mgmt.

JOHNSON, LISA A; St Patrick - St Vincent HS; Vallejo, CA; (2); Cmnty Wkr; Hosp Aide; Pep Clb; Science Clb; Sftbl; CSF; Jr Statesmen Amer.

JOHNSON, LORI; Capital Christian HS; Sacramento, CA; (3); 1/59; Chess Clb; Church Yth Grp; Cmnty Wkr; Church Choir; High Hon Roll; CSF; UC Davis; Phrmcy.

JOHNSON, MARGIE M; Saint Anthony HS; Long Beach, CA; (2); Cmnty Wkr; GAA; Teachers Aide; Varsity Clb; Yrbk; Var Crs Cntry; JV Socr; Pres Acad Fit Awd; Campfire; Part-Time Wrk Dental Ofc; U San Diego; Law.

JOHNSON, MARIO M; South HS; Bakersfield, CA; (3); Var Bsktbl; Var Ftbl; Var Trk; Hon Roll.

JOHNSON, MECHELLE D; Vallejo SR HS; Vallejo, CA; (4); Church Yth Grp; GAA; Church Choir; Rptr Yrbk; VP Frsh Cls; Rep Soph Cls; Rep Jr Cls; VP Stu Cncl; JV Bsktbl; Var Vllybl; Chrstn Character Awd; San Francisco ST U; Cmmnctns.

JOHNSON, MEGAN R; Mtn Empire HS; Descanso, CA; (2); GAA; Letterman Clb; Pep Clb; Spanish Clb; SADD; Varsity Clb; Drill Tm; Pres Frsh Cls; VP Soph Cls; Treas Stu Cncl; SAT Scores 910; Marine Bio.

JOHNSON, MELANIE S; San Dieguito HS; Encinitas, CA; (3); Pres Church Yth Grp; Library Aide; Office Aide; Ski Clb; Church Choir; School Musical; Stage Crew; JV Capt Bsktbl; Intrml Sftbl; Cit Awd; Vlntr Yth League Bsktbl Coach; BYU.

JOHNSON, MICAH D; Edison Computech HS; Fresno, CA; (1); Church Yth Grp; Spanish Clb; Intrml Vllybl; Hon Roll; Vly Chldrns Hosp Vlntr; UC Berkeley; Engrng.

JOHNSON, MICHAEL B; Pinole Valley HS; Pinole, CA; (1); JV Swmmng; High Hon Roll; Hon Roll; Water Polo JV; Pilot.

JOHNSON, MICHELE L; Etiwanda HS; Alta Loma, CA; (3); JCL; Pres Latin Clb; JV Tennis; JV Badmntn; CA ST U; Educ.

JOHNSON, MICHELLE A; Gahr HS; Cerritos, CA; (2); Drama Clb; Cal ST U Long Beach; Law.

JOHNSON, MINDY M; La Sierra HS; Riverside, CA; (1); Band; Mrchg Band; Pep Band; Hon Roll; CSF; S Methodist U; Med.

JOHNSON, MYLINDA L; Brea-Olinda HS; Brea, CA; (3); Temple Yth Grp; Chorus; School Musical; High Hon Roll; Masonic Awd; Vet Offc Vlntr; Vet.

JOHNSON, NAOMI J; Redlands HS; Redlands, CA; (2); Pres Acad Fit Awd; Bus.

JOHNSON, NICOLE; Aptos HS; Aptos, CA; (1); JV Swmmng; Interact Club; Frsno ST U.

JOHNSON, NICOLE; Mount Diablo HS; Concord, CA; (4); High Hon Roll; Black Stu Union; San Francisco ST U; Elec Engr.

JOHNSON, NICOLE; Woodrow Wilson HS; Long Beach, CA; (4); 61/728; Cmnty Wkr; Drama Clb; Key Clb; Rep Frsh Cls; Rep Soph Cls; Rep Jr Cls; Rep Sr Cls; Stu Cncl; JV Tennis; Jr NHS; YMCA Inst; U Of CO-BOULDER; Chld Dev.

JOHNSON, NICOLE E; Antioch HS; Antioch, CA; (4); 123/610; Church Yth Grp; Hosp Aide; Jazz Band; Mrchg Band; Var L Bsktbl; Var L Socr; Var Capt Trk; Var L Vllybl; Hon Roll; Black Stu Union Pres; Pre-Law.

JOHNSON, NICOLE L; Fontana HS; Fontana, CA; (2); Color Guard; Drill Tm; Bsktbl; Tennis; Trk; Hon Roll; Prfct Atten Awd; CJSF; Legislative Cncl; BSU; NC U; Law.

JOHNSON, OCTAVIA K; Vacaville HS; Vacaville, CA; (3); GAA; Hosp Aide; Band; Jazz Band; Mrchg Band; Pep Band; Crs Cntry; Sftbl; Trk; Vllybl; Sacramento ST Coll; Med.

JOHNSON, PAUL N; Gompers Secondary HS; San Diego, CA; (2); Chess Clb; Band; Jazz Band; JV Crs Cntry; Prfct Atten Awd; Sci.

JOHNSON, PENNY C; Mission Bay HS; San Diego, CA; (1); 63/413; Church Yth Grp; Cmnty Wkr; Pep Clb; Hon Roll; Sci & Engrng Fair; Interior Dsgn.

JOHNSON, PETER J; Valley View HS; Moreno Valley, CA; (2); Chess Clb; Church Yth Grp; Var L Bsktbl; Var L Crs Cntry; Var L Trk; Hon Roll; Voice Dem Awd; Archery; Acad Decathlon; Interact; Air Force.

JOHNSON, RACHAEL N; Southern Trinity HS; Dinsmore, CA; (4); 4/17; Drama Clb; Teachers Aide; School Play; Stage Crew; Nwsp; Yrbk; Lit Mag; Pres Frsh Cls; VP Soph Cls; Sec Jr Cls; Stu Of Mnth; Pblctn In Various Lcl Papers & Annuals Of Wrtng; Shasta JR Coll; Jrnlsm.

JOHNSON, RACHEL K; Canyon Springs HS; Moreno Valley, CA; (3); 22/637; Pres Church Yth Grp; Cmnty Wkr; Teachers Aide; Stu Cncl; Stat Mgr(s); Var JV Score Keeper; Var Swmmng; JV Var Tennis; High Hon Roll; Hon Roll; Teens Agnst Drugs; Jr Advncd Plcmnt Engl; Advncd Plcmnt U S Hstry; BYU; Psych.

JOHNSON, RACHEL L; Redlands HS; Redlands, CA; (3); Pres 4-H; Pep Clb; Spanish Clb; Stat Bsktbl; JV Cheerldng; 4-H Awd; CA ST U Long Beach; Pharm.

JOHNSON, RANDY W; Sacramento Country Day HS; Sacramento, CA; (1); Bsbl; Bsktbl; Ntl Merit Schol; Jrnlsm.

JOHNSON, RICHARD L J; Apple Valley HS; Apple Valley, CA; (4); Chess Clb; ROTC; JV Crs Cntry; Hon Roll; Jr NHS; Pres Acad Fit Awd; Amer Kenpo Karate; Fire Fghtng Explr; Body Bldng; Cal ST San Diego; Engr.

JOHNSON, ROBERT; Gompers Secondary HS; San Diego, CA; (2); 17/145; Church Yth Grp; Band; Chorus; Co-Capt Drill Tm; Cit Awd; High Hon Roll; Hon Roll; Jr NHS; Prfct Atten Awd; Pres Acad Fit Awd; UCSD; Med.

JOHNSON, ROBERT; La Salle HS; Pasadena, CA; (3); Chess Clb; Church Yth Grp; Orch; Cit Awd; Hon Roll; NHS; Civil Air Patrol; California Scholarship Federation; Pi Alpha Chi Service Society.

JOHNSON, ROBERT; Saddleback HS; Santa Ana, CA; (3); Aud/Vis; Boy Scts; Cmnty Wkr; FBLA; Science Clb; Spanish Clb; SADD; Teachers Aide; Ed Yrbk; Rep Soph Cls; CSF; Peer Cnslng; Bus.

JOHNSON, ROBERT A; Mission Viejo HS; Mission Viejo, CA; (3); 141/360; Church Yth Grp; Saddleback JC; Pro Vllybl.

JOHNSON, RONALD J; Grace M Davis HS; Modesto, CA; (4); 19/433; Church Yth Grp; JV Bsktbl; Var Crs Cntry; Var Trk; Pres Acad Fit Awd; Rotary Awd; Modesto Roadmen Jr Bike Tm; UCLA; Civil Engr.

JOHNSON, RYAN T; Porterville HS; Porterville, CA; (3); Church Yth Grp; Office Aide; Sec Frsh Cls; Var Bsktbl; Var Ftbl; Var Wrstlng; Hon Roll; PE Stu Of Yr; Ftbl Lineman Of Yr; All Leag Ftbl Plyr; CA Berkeley; Sociology.

JOHNSON, SABRINA; Oroville HS; Oroville, CA; (3); Letterman Clb; SADD; Var Crs Cntry; Mgr(s); JV Var Trk; High Hon Roll; Hon Roll; Cross Age Tutor; Teen Advisor; Comp.

JOHNSON, SAMMY; Credence HS; Susanville, CA; (3); Computer Clb; Math Tm; ROTC; Science Clb; Spanish Clb; Band; Jazz Band; Mrchg Band; Orch; Pep Band.

JOHNSON, SAPHRONIA R; Berkeley HS; Berkeley, CA; (3); Treas Church Yth Grp; Pres Science Clb; VP Acpl Chr; VP Chorus; Pres Church Choir; Sec Jr Cls; JV Bsktbl; JV Sftbl; Stat Wrstlng; MESA Gold Mdl Wnnr Alg; Howard U Washington; Phys Thrpy.

JOHNSON, SARAH; Laguna Beach HS; Laguna Beach, CA; (3); Model UN; Color Guard; Rptr Nwsp; Yrbk; Lit Mag; Hon Roll; NHS; Pres Acad Fit Awd; Acad Decathlon; Amnesty Intl Club Treas; Radio Club; Barnard Coll.

JOHNSON, SARAH E; O'farrell SCPA; San Diego, CA; (1); Dance Clb; Girl Scts; Stage Crew; Hon Roll; Sec 8th Grade.

JOHNSON, SCOTT A; Canyon HS; Canyon Country, CA; (2); Hon Roll; Motorcrss Racing; Stu Of Semester.

JOHNSON, SCOTT C; Pinole Valley HS; Hercules, CA; (2); Church Yth Grp; Cmnty Wkr; Computer Clb; JV Bsbl; Var L Socr; High Hon Roll; Selected USA Soccer Team In Europe; Amnesty Intl Club; Stanford; Med.

JOHNSON, SCOTT C; Simi Valley HS; Simi Valley, CA; (4); 13/700; Letterman Clb; Var Capt Crs Cntry; Intrml Socr; Var Capt Trk; Jr NHS; NHS; Pres Acad Fit Awd; St Schlr; UCLA; Physics.

JOHNSON, SHAUN; Linohurst HS; Marysville, CA; (2); Pres Key Clb; Pep Clb; SADD; Chorus; Off Frsh Cls; Off Soph Cls; Off Jr Cls; Stu Cncl; Cheerldng; Trk; Freshman Homecoming Basketball Princess; Sadie Hawkins Dance Queen; Peer Counseling; Whos Who; Chico St U; Business Attorney.

JOHNSON, SHAWNA; San Dimas HS; San Dimas, CA; (2); 4-H; Stat Bsktbl; Var Crs Cntry; Var Score Keeper; Var Trk; 4-H Awd; Hon Roll; UC Davis; Vet Sci.

JOHNSON, SHAWNTELL; Skyline HS; Oakland, CA; (2); Church Yth Grp; Cmnty Wkr; Red Cross Aide; Church Choir; Orch; School Musical; Rep Frsh Cls; JV Cheerldng; Intrml Vllybl; Cit Awd; Cert Of Mrt Recgntn Of Elem Algebra; Awded Cert Top Grl Awd; Outstndng Achvt Awd; Peer Cnslng Schlrshp; Chld Psych.

JOHNSON, SONIA A; San Leandro HS; San Leandro, CA; (2); Church Yth Grp; GAA; Girl Scts; Teachers Aide; Sec Frsh Cls; JV Bsktbl; Score Keeper; Hon Roll; Architect.

JOHNSON, STACEY A; Apple Valley HS; Apple Valley, CA; (1); Pres Church Yth Grp; Varsity Clb; Var L Socr; Var L Trk; Vllybl; Cit Awd; High Hon Roll; Vrsty Soccer Tm, Outstndng Undrclsmn Plyr; Hlth Care.

JOHNSON, STACEY A; San Jacinto HS; Hemet, CA; (3); Am Leg Aux Girls St; French Clb; Hosp Aide; Spanish Clb; Prfct Atten Awd; CA St San Bernardino; Bus.

JOHNSON, STEPHEN E; Gahr HS; Norwalk, CA; (3); Dance Clb; Band; Jazz Band; Mrchg Band; Orch; Pep Band; School Musical; School Play; Variety Show; JV Bsbl; Chem.

JOHNSON, STEPHEN MICHAEL; Robert A Millikan HS; Trabuco Canyon, CA; (4); 58/623; Church Yth Grp; Computer Clb; Letterman Clb; Teachers Aide; Jazz Band; School Musical; Var Swmmng; High Hon Roll; Vrsty Water Polo; The Way Bible Study-Ldr; Biola U; Bus.

JOHNSON, TAHIS M; Eagle Rock HS; Los Angeles, CA; (2); Church Yth Grp; Cmnty Wkr; Pep Clb; Teachers Aide; Drill Tm; JV Cheerldng; JV Pom Pon; JV Wt Lftg; Hon Roll; CA U; Botanist.

JOHNSON, TAMMY; Palm Springs HS; Palm Springs, CA; (3); Pep Clb; Cheerldng; Hon Roll; Jr Statesmen Of Amer; Inter Dsgn.

JOHNSON, TAUESHA D; Lincoln HS; San Diego, CA; (1); French Clb; Cit Awd; Hon Roll; Early Acad Outreach Pgm; Proj I Believe; Comp Sci.

JOHNSON, TERI E; Escondido HS; Escondido, CA; (3); Drama Clb; Key Clb; Science Clb; Ski Clb; School Play; Stage Crew; Rptr Nwsp; Hon Roll; Member CSF; Rotary Four Way Speech Contest; Annual Law Week Oratorical Contestbest Actress Award; Law Schl; Major In English.

JOHNSON, THERESA M; Inglewood HS; Inglewood, CA; (2); JV Trk; Hon Roll; Ladies & Knights Clb; U Of CA Santa Cruz; Cardiology.

JOHNSON, TIMOTHY; San Lorenzo Valley HS; Boulder Creek, CA; (4); 3/200; Church Yth Grp; Treas French Clb; Key Clb; Teachers Aide; Yrbk; Golf; High Hon Roll; Hon Roll; Ntl Merit SF; Sal; Bnk Amer Plaque Awd Lbrl Arts; UCLA Alumni Assn Schlrshp; Roger B Phelps Memrl Schlrshp; UCLA; Commnctns.

JOHNSON, TIMOTHY W; Hoover HS; Fresno, CA; (3); CA ST U Fresno; Comp Sci.

JOHNSON, TINISHA N; Mercy HS; Pacifica, CA; (3); Prfct Atten Awd; Photo Clb; Black Stu Union; UCLA; Bus.

JOHNSON, TODDRICK J; Monte Vista HS; Spring Valley, CA; (3); Boy Scts; Church Yth Grp; Cmnty Wkr; Temple Yth Grp; Varsity Clb; Church Choir; Variety Show; Yrbk; JV Diving; Ftbl; BYU; Dr.

JOHNSON, TROY D; Castle Park HS; Chula Vista, CA; (2); 30/473; Church Yth Grp; Cmnty Wkr; Church Choir; Rep Stu Cncl; Cit Awd; Hon Roll; Prfct Atten Awd; Assocd Stu Bdy-Bus Mgr; CSF; Acad Achvrs; Educ.

JOHNSON, VANESSA D; Lycee Francais Lape Rouse HS; San Francisco, CA; (1); Econ.

JOHNSON, VERA A; Palm Springs HS; Cathedral City, CA; (2); Teachers Aide; Mgr Yrbk; Rep Frsh Cls; Rep Soph Cls; JV Bsktbl; Var Swmmng; JV Vllybl; Silver Sands 89; Black Stu Union Secy 89; High Mntn Sci Awd 88; Law.

JOHNSON, VIDA; La Jolla Country Day Schl; San Diego, CA; (2); Model UN; Hon Roll; NYU; Teacher.

JOHNSON, WENDY J; Modesto Christian HS; Modesto, CA; (3); 10/34; Pep Clb; Teachers Aide; Pres Frsh Cls; Var Bsktbl; High Hon Roll; Hon Roll; CA Schlrshp Fed Mem, Modesto All-City Grls Bsktbl Tm, All-Sthrn League 1st Tm, Mdsto Chrstn Bst Off; Bus.

JOHNSON, WINONA L; James Lick HS; San Jose, CA; (4); Cmnty Wkr; VP Debate Tm; Intnl Clb; SADD; School Play; Stage Crew; Variety Show; Trk; Hon Roll; Mck Trial Atty-Cndctd In Real Supr Ct; Outstndng Achvt For X-Exmntn Awd; Acad Dcthln; Spnsh Hnr; Santa Clara U; Pltcl Sci.

JOHNSON, YVETTE J; Vista HS; Oceanside, CA; (3); Pres Church Yth Grp; Drama Clb; Pep Clb; Chorus; Church Choir; Yrbk; Off Sr Cls; JV Capt Cheerldng; Crs Cntry; Powder Puff Ftbl; Yth Missionary; Peer Cnslng; DECA; San Diego ST.

JOHNSON, ZACHARY T; California HS; San Ramon, CA; (3); Church Yth Grp; Scholastic Bowl; Var L Crs Cntry; JV Ftbl; Var L Socr; Var L Trk; Wt Lftg; Hon Roll; Pres Acad Fit Awd; Engrng.

JOHNSTON, BARBARA A; Mira Mesa HS; San Diego, CA; (2); 1/850; Hosp Aide; Science Clb; Band; Mrchg Band; Pep Band; Pres Acad Fit Awd; CSF; U Of CA San Diego; Med.

JOHNSTON, BRIAN E; Miraleste HS; Ranchos Palos Ver, CA; (3); Church Yth Grp; Pres Key Clb; Letterman Clb; Spanish Clb; SADD; Cit Awd; High Hon Roll; Hon Roll; Pres Acad Fit Awd; Pres Soph Cls; Congrssnl Schlr; Jr Olympcs Vllybll All Amer,MVP League,1st Team CIF,MVP Team; All Leag Water Polo; Bus.

JOHNSTON, CHERIE B; Clearlake HS; Lakeport, CA; (3); Church Yth Grp; Teachers Aide; Hon Roll; Sec Of Seminary Clss; Attndc Awd; Stu Of Friday Night Live.

JOHNSTON, DESTINY M; Trinity HS; Weaverville, CA; (1); Church Yth Grp; GAA; Girl Scts; Chorus; JV Bsktbl; Fld Hcky; Intrml Gym; Var Sftbl; Hon Roll; Local Teen Center.

JOHNSTON, ERIC M; Bret Harte Union HS; Murphys, CA; (2); Hon Roll; 1st Pl Arch Drwng Calavaras Cnty Fair 90; Hstry.

JOHNSTON, JENNIFER S; Herbert Hoover HS; Fresno, CA; (2); 20/2200; Band; Mrchg Band; Pep Band; Hon Roll; Cmmnd Prfrmnc At Solo & Ensmbl; Elem Schl Tchr.

JOHNSTON, JESSE; El Molino HS; Guerneville, CA; (4); Debate Tm; NFL; Speech Tm; SADD; Cit Awd; Gov Hon Prg Awd; Hon Roll; Lion Awd; Pres Acad Fit Awd; Glnd Gate Spch Assn; Gldn St Schlrs Hghst Hnrs Math.

JOHNSTON, JILL; Fairfield HS; Fairfield, CA; (3); Pep Clb; VP Jr Cls; Cheerldng; Pom Pon; Powder Puff Ftbl; High Hon Roll; Hon Roll; Hmcmg Attdt 87.

JOHNSTON, JILL A; Montgomery HS; Santa Rosa, CA; (2); 1/500; Church Yth Grp; French Clb; Pep Clb; Band; Drm Mjr(t); Mrchg Band; Orch; Pep Band; Yrbk; Rep Stu Cncl; Schlr/Athltc Awd; Jr Olympic Vlybl Tm; Hgh Hnrs Golden St Exam Geom; U Of CA; Bus.

JOHNSTON, JODI M; Mayfair HS; Lakewood, CA; (2); Teachers Aide; Band; Jazz Band; Mrchg Band; Pep Band; JV Sftbl; Law.

JOHNSTON, JOY K; Warren HS; Downey, CA; (2); Pres Acad Fit Awd; Gldn ST Exm; Crtv Wrtng Clb; Engl.

JOHNSTON, KIM A; Lodi HS; Lodi, CA; (2); Band; Mrchg Band; Hon Roll; Law.

JOHNSTON, MAURA K; Cornelia Connelly HS; Fountain Valley, CA; (2); Cmnty Wkr; GAA; Intnl Clb; Service Clb; Thesps; Band; Chorus; School Play; Variety Show; Lit Mag; JR Statesmen Of Amer Clb; CSF; JSA/Stnfrd & Georgetwn Smmr Schl Grad; March Of Dimes Ldrshp Cncl; Poltcl Sci.

JOHNSTON, MICHAEL; Southern Calif Christian HS; Laguna Miguel, CA; (3); Church Yth Grp; Spanish Clb; Treas Sr Cls; Hon Roll; Film.

JOHNSTON, REBECCA; Valley Christian HS; Imperial, CA; (4); Church Yth Grp; Teachers Aide; Church Choir; School Play; High Hon Roll; Rptr Nwsp; Ed Yrbk; Pres Frsh Cls; Pres Stu Cncl; Capt Cheerldng; Visl Display; Christian Heritage; Intern Bus.

JOHNSTON, SHAYNE S; Galileo HS; San Francisco, CA; (2); JV Var Ftbl; Hon Roll; Peer Res Grp; MVP Ftbl; U Of MI; Chem.

JOHNSTON, STEFANIE A; Notre Dame HS; Redwood City, CA; (3); Debate Tm; Hosp Aide; Variety Show; Var Bsktbl; Var Sftbl; Hon Roll; Vrsty Sftbl All-Cnty; CO ST; Bus.

JOHNSTON, THOMAS J; Loyola HS; La Crescenta, CA; (1); Debate Tm; Speech Tm; Ed Nwsp; Award For Outstanding NEDT Scores; Award For Outstanding Entrance Exam Scores; Annapolis Naval Acad; Lawyer.

JOHNZE, BRANDI C; Mountain Empire HS; Mount Laguna, CA; (3); Rptr Lit Mag; Hon Roll; Grossmont Coll; Engl.

JOHSON, KENT S; Roseville HS; Roseville, CA; (3); GAA; Phtg Yrbk; Mtn Clmbng; Fly Fishing; Hiking; CSU; Acctng.

JOKELSON, PAUL; Berkeley HS; Berkeley, CA; (3); Science Clb; School Musical; School Play; Nwsp; Ntl Merit Ltr; Hnrs Geom GSE.

JOLIVETTE, ANDREW J; Sacred Heart Cathedral HS; San Francisco, CA; (1); Rep Frsh Cls; JV Ftbl; JV Trk; Hon Roll; Altar Svr, Poetry Wrtr & Singer; 200 & 100 Meters San Francisco; Bus.

JOLLEY, ALICIA; Glen A Wilson HS; Hacienda Heights, CA; (1); Church Yth Grp; Cmnty Wkr; Dance Clb; Library Aide; SADD; Teachers Aide; Band; Church Choir; Drill Tm; Hon Roll; Vrs Dance Awds; BYU; Teacher.

JOLLEY, KELLY A; Hiram Johnson-West Campus HS; Sacramento, CA; (2); 41/182; School Play; Stage Crew; Swing Chorus; JV Socr; Hon Roll; American River Coll; Int Dec.

JOLLIFF, AMY; Modesto HS; Modesto, CA; (2); AFS; Church Yth Grp; FHA; Math Clb; Acpl Chr; Hon Roll; Rlly Clb; Elem Tchr.

JOLLY, GINA; Elk Grove HS; Sacramento, CA; (4); 85/588; Church Yth Grp; Church Choir; Drill Tm; Cheerldng; Pom Pon; Hon Roll; Drill Tm Best Attitude Awd; Elem Educ.

JOLLY, JACK A; Modesto HS; Modesto, CA; (4); Drama Clb; Teachers Aide; School Play; Stage Crew; Tennis; Stnsls Tlmn Mono Mrt Awd Comp Svcg; 1st Pl Fav Movie Str Dnce; 1st Prz Mst Macho Egg Baby; Modesto JC; Sci.

JON, SAEUNG; El Camino Real HS; Los Angeles, CA; (2); Bsktbl; UCLA; Bus.

JONAS, AARON; Santa Paula HS; Santa Paula, CA; (4); Key Clb; Letterman Clb; Quiz Bowl; Science Clb; Varsity Clb; Var Crs Cntry; Var Trk; Cit Awd; High Hon Roll; Hon Roll; U Of CA-LOS Angeles.

JONAS, JENNIFER; Burbank HS; Burbank, CA; (4); 33/429; VP French Clb; Chorus; Stu Cncl; JV Var Bsktbl; Var Cheerldng; JV Var Vllybl; High Hon Roll; CSF; Ford/Angel Schlr Athl; U UT; Pre-Med.

JONDLE, ALAN; Capital Christian HS; Sacramento, CA; (2); 1/70; Chess Clb; Church Yth Grp; Computer Clb; Service Clb; High Hon Roll; Phy Sci Awd; Geom Awd; Comp Sci.

JONES, ALISIA M; Bunche HS; Oakland, CA; (3); Teachers Aide; Chorus; Cit Awd; High Hon Roll; Hon Roll; Prfct Atten Awd; Most Imprvd; Acad Excllnce; Criminal Lawyer.

JONES, ALLEN; Cardinal Newman HS; Cotati, CA; (2); 1/98; Cmnty Wkr; Spanish Clb; SADD; Var Tennis; Wt Lftg; High Hon Roll; Knights Of Newman.

JONES, AMY; San Benito HS; Hollister, CA; (4); 27/252; Cmnty Wkr; Pep Clb; Ski Clb; Band; Mrchg Band; Rep Frsh Cls; Var Cheerldng; Gym; Hon Roll; Church Yth Grp; Grl Mnth Womens Clb; BYU; Elem Educ.

JONES, AMY LEIGH; Greenville JR/Sr HS; Greenville, CA; (2); Hist Service Clb; Band; Mrchg Band; Pep Band; Cheerldng; Tennis; High Hon Roll; Yth To Yth Club; Postv Cntrbtn To Schl Awd; Tnns Awd; Sacramento ST; Engl Tchr.

JONES, ANGELA; Menlo-Atherton HS; Menlo Park, CA; (4); AFS; Church Yth Grp; Intnl Clb; VP Key Clb; Church Choir; Capt Drill Tm; School Musical; Kiwanis Awd; Ntl Merit Ltr; Pres Acad Fit Awd; Bronze Key Awd For Activities, Bk Of Amer Awd For Engl & AATG Awd; Ampex Excel Awd; Dancer; Stanford U; Tchr.

JONES, ANISSA J; John F Kennedy HS; Richmond, CA; (4); 31/250; Church Yth Grp; Elks Awd; Hon Roll; MESA Pgm; Partnership Pgm; U Of CA Davis; Ag Sci.

JONES, APRIL B; Eisenhower HS; Rialto, CA; (3); Library Aide; Bsktbl; Mgr(s); Trk; High Hon Roll; Elec Tech.

JONES, APRIL M; Roseville HS; Rocklin, CA; (2); 103/445; Spanish Clb; Var Trk; Hon Roll; Prfct Atten Awd; Pres Acad Fit Awd; Prncpls Advsry Cmmtte; Jrnlsm.

JONES, AUNDREI; Golden Gate Acad; Alameda, CA; (2); Acpl Chr; Church Choir; Ed Yrbk; Pres Soph Cls; Bsbl; Bsktbl; Swmmng; Tennis; Vllybl; Hon Roll; Stanford; Surgeon.

JONES, BLAINE K; Foothill HS; Santa Ana, CA; (3); Cmnty Wkr; Drama Clb; Letterman Clb; Thesps; Varsity Clb; School Play; Rep Frsh Cls; Rep Soph Cls; Stu Cncl; Var L Bsbl; All Star Team Coach; Drama.

JONES, BRADLEY T; Northview HS; Covina, CA; (2); Church Yth Grp; FCA; Letterman Clb; Varsity Clb; Var Ftbl; Var Trk; Intrml Wt Lftg; Var Wrstlng; Fire Sci.

JONES, BRANCHE R; Encina HS; Sacramento, CA; (4); Church Yth Grp; Cmnty Wkr; Spanish Clb; SADD; Yrbk; Bsbl; Bsktbl; Socr; Hon Roll; UC Davis Outreach Pgm; Conflict Mgmt; U CA Santa Barbara; Poltcl Sci.

JONES, BRIAN; Cardinal Newman HS; Cotati, CA; (3); 15/100; JA; Spanish Clb; Swmmng; Cit Awd; High Hon Roll; Hon Roll.

JONES, BRIAN; Gahr HS; Cerritos, CA; (1); Church Yth Grp; Band; Mrchg Band; Stu Cncl; Trk; Pres Acad Fit Awd; U Of Long Beach; Phys Thrpst.

JONES, CASEY ELLIOT; Inglewood HS; Los Angeles, CA; (4); 17/490; Art Clb; JA; Rptr Yrbk; Rep Stu Cncl; Ftbl; Tennis; Hon Roll; Rotary Awd; Hist Clb Pres; UC, San Diego; Law.

JONES, CATHLEEN M; Canyon HS; Canyon Country, CA; (1); Var L Socr; Sftbl; Vllybl; CA Schlrshp Fddrtn; GSE Hgh Hnrs Geo; CIF All-Leag Sccr.

JONES, CEDRIC; Washington HS; Los Angeles, CA; (2); Aud/Vis; Bus Profs of Am; Computer Clb; FBLA; VICA; Lit Mag; Off Soph Cls; Bsbl; Bsktbl; Hon Roll; USC; Comp Prgmmr.

JONES, CHAD C; Thousand Oaks HS; Thousand Oaks, CA; (2); Boy Scts; Church Yth Grp; Cmnty Wkr; Drama Clb; SADD; Acpl Chr; School Musical; Variety Show; Var Diving; JV Swmmng; BYU; Space Exploration.

JONES, CHERIE; Novato HS; Novato, CA; (2); Cmnty Wkr; Girl Scts; Office Aide; Red Cross Aide; ROTC; Chorus; Drill Tm; Bsbl; Sftbl; Swmmng; IVC Coll; Pilot.

JONES, CHRIS; Sonoma Valley HS; Sonoma, CA; (4); 51/1108; Cmnty Wkr; Debate Tm; Letterman Clb; NFL; Ski Clb; Speech Tm; Varsity Clb; Yrbk; Rep Sr Cls; Var Crs Cntry; Pres Interact Clb; U CO Boulder; Bus Mgmt.

JONES, CORINA M; Valley HS; Sacramento, CA; (2); Aud/Vis; Church Yth Grp; Cmnty Wkr; FTA; SADD; Cit Awd; Hon Roll; Prfct Atten Awd; Friday Night Live; U Of CA; Elem Schl Tchr.

JONES, CRAIG E; Foothill HS; Santa Ana, CA; (3); 25/350; Off Church Yth Grp; Key Clb; Church Choir; Bsktbl; High Hon Roll; CA Schlrshp Fed Mem; Instituted, Dir Church Handbell Choir; UCLA; Engrng.

JONES, CRYSTAL; San Gorgonio HS; San Bernardino, CA; (2); French Clb; Cheerldng; Sftbl; Schlr Awd For 3.5 GPA; Astronomer.

JONES, CYNTHIA M; Granada HS; Livermore, CA; (4); 12/288; Cmnty Wkr; 4-H; Service Clb; Spanish Clb; Lit Mag; 4-H Awd; Ntl Merit Ltr; Pres Acad Fit Awd; Yth Svc Awd; Degl Mdl Assmbly Orgnztn Amercn States 89; U Of CA Davis; Intrntl Reltns.

JONES, DAMISHA A; Hoover HS; Los Angeles, CA; (3); Church Yth Grp; Science Clb; Teachers Aide; Cheerldng; Cit Awd; Hon Roll; Prfct Atten Awd; African Am Stu Union; Pediatrics.

JONES, DANIELLE S; Agoura HS; Agoura Hills, CA; (2); 48/457; Dance Clb; Hon Roll; Cert Comp Fash Merch; Fash Inst Dsgn/Merch; Merch Mkt.

JONES, DAVID S; Woodside HS; Portola Vly, CA; (3); Church Yth Grp; Stu Cncl; JV Var Crs Cntry; JV Var Trk; Millard Fullmore Trivia Hunt.

JONES, DAWNA; North HS; Bakersfield, CA; (4); 8/400; VP Church Yth Grp; Math Tm; Color Guard; Rptr Nwsp; High Hon Roll; Pres Acad Fit Awd; Spanish NHS; CSF Gold Seal; Bnk Of Amer Frgn Lang Awd; Tandy Corp Acad Awd; CA ST U Bakersfield; Educ.

JONES, DEBORAH; Etiwanda HS; Alta Loma, CA; (2); Church Yth Grp; Acpl Chr; Chorus; School Musical; Swmmng; Tennis; Int Dsgn.

JONES, DENEISHA; Mount Pleasant HS; San Jose, CA; (3); Church Yth Grp; Cmnty Wkr; JA; SADD; Stu Cncl; L Var Bsktbl; Var Capt Powder Puff Ftbl; Var Trk; Cit Awd; Syracuse U; Sports Brdcstng.

JONES, DIANA M; Granada HS; Livermore, CA; (4); Church Yth Grp; Hosp Aide; Pep Clb; SADD; Teachers Aide; Cheerldng; Powder Puff Ftbl; High Hon Roll; Hon Roll; Pres Acad Fit Awd; CA St Talent Comptn Grand Chmpn 87; UC Davis.

JONES, DONALD; Herbert Hoover HS; Prescott Valley, AZ; (2); Var Bsbl; Var Mgr(s); Var Score Keeper; Cit Awd; Hon Roll; Prfct Atten Awd; Pres Acad Fit Awd; San Diego ST; Comp.

JONES, DONALD N; Washington Prep HS; Los Angeles, CA; (3); Band; Jazz Band; Mrchg Band; School Musical; Music.

JONES, DOVIE K; San Gorgonio HS; San Bernardino, CA; (3); Church Yth Grp; Dance Clb; Hosp Aide; Church Choir; Gym; Cit Awd; Hon Roll; Loma Linda U; Med Doctor.

JONES, EDWARD C; Corning Union HS; Corning, CA; (4); VICA; Science Clb; Spanish Clb; Band; Jazz Band; Mrchg Band; JV Intrml Ftbl; Intrml Var Wrstlng; Elks Awd; High Hon Roll; Chico ST; Cvl Engr.

JONES, ELIOTT K; Bishop Montgomery HS; Gardena, CA; (3); Office Aide; Var Bsktbl; Var Trk; Hon Roll; U S Blck Cltrl Clb; Comm.

JONES, ELISHA D; Morningside HS; Inglewood, CA; (3); Drama Clb; Var Cheerldng; Hon Roll; Bus.

JONES, ERIC E; Dana Hills HS; Laguna Niguel, CA; (2); Boy Scts; Church Yth Grp; Socr; Tennis; Outstndng Achvt Comp Ed; Bus.

JONES, ERIC E; Riverbank HS; Oakdale, CA; (2); 1/120; SADD; Band; Jazz Band; Pep Band; VP Frsh Cls; Treas Soph Cls; Treas Jr Cls; JV Bsbl; JV Ftbl; JV Trk; ID Coll; CPA.

JONES, ESSENCE N; San Lorenzo HS; San Leandro, CA; (2); Church Yth Grp; GAA; Bsktbl; Cheerldng; Sftbl; Cit Awd; Hon Roll; Prfct Atten Awd; Coll Club; Peer Conflict Mgr; San Jose ST; Frnsc Med.

JONES, EVAN M; Laguna Beach HS; Laguna Beach, CA; (3); Debate Tm; Drama Clb; French Clb; Chorus; School Musical; School Play; Variety Show; Intrml Bsktbl; Intrml Ftbl; Intrml Lcrss; Snowbrdg & Bodybrdg.

JONES, FLIP M; Hanford HS; Hanford, CA; (2); JV Bsbl; Bus.

JONES, HEATHER S; Encina HS; Sacramento, CA; (2); 17/221; Cmnty Wkr; Church Choir; Yrbk; Var Socr; High Hon Roll; Hon Roll; Stu Reachng Out; Envrnmntl Sci.

JONES, JAEGER P; Hemet HS; Hemet, CA; (2); Boy Scts; Church Yth Grp; Key Clb; Red Cross Aide; Spanish Clb; Varsity Clb; Socr; Eagle Sct; Funeral Directr.

JONES, JAMES D; Lynwood HS; Lynwood, CA; (3); Church Yth Grp; Church Choir; Bsktbl; Ftbl; Trk; Prfct Atten Awd; Bus.

JONES, JAMILLE TARAE; Narbonne HS; Torrance, CA; (3); Dance Clb; Office Aide; Pep Clb; Spanish Clb; Band; Drm Mjr(t); Jazz Band; Mrchg Band; Orch; Pep Band; Stu Union Pres; CA Jr Schlsp Fed; Stu Recog Awd; Law.

JONES, JARILYN S; Eisenhower HS; Rialto, CA; (3); Church Yth Grp; Pres Cmnty Wkr; Drama Clb; Speech Tm; Chorus; Pres Church Choir; School Play; JV Capt Bsktbl; Hon Roll; Prfct Atten Awd; Swons Debutante Club; Miss Black San Bernardino; Valley Coll; Newscaster.

JONES, JAY MICHEAL; North HS; Bakersfield, CA; (2); Church Yth Grp; FCA; French Clb; JA; Key Clb; Library Aide; Office Aide; ROTC; Teachers Aide; Band; Law.

JONES, JEANETTE A; Riverside Poly HS; Riverside, CA; (2); Am Leg Aux Girls St; Score Keeper; Hon Roll; Coachs Awd; Outstndng Athltc Awd; Law.

JONES, JEFFREY L; Bonita Vista HS; San Diego, CA; (4); Chess Clb; Science Clb; Ed Yrbk; Ed Lit Mag; Cit Awd; High Hon Roll; Pres Acad Fit Awd; Pres Schlr; Sal; ASB Commissioner; UCSD; Comp Sci.

JONES, JEFFREY W; Arlington HS; Riverside, CA; (2); Church Yth Grp; JV Ftbl; Helicopter Aviator.

JONES, JENNIE; Mc Kinleyville HS; Mc Kinleyville, CA; (2); Church Yth Grp; Spanish Clb; SADD; Yrbk; Capt Bsktbl; Hon Roll; Prfct Atten Awd; MVP Jr Var Bsktbl; Attend Bsktbl Camp.

JONES, JENNIFER; Gilroy HS; Gilroy, CA; (1); 13/500; Church Yth Grp; Drama Clb; Swmmng; Trk; DAR Awd; Pres Acad Fit Awd; CSF; Golden St Exam Alg Hnrs.

JONES, JENNIFER; Sonoma Valley HS; Sonoma, CA; (4); 5/300; Cmnty Wkr; Dance Clb; NFL; Sec Speech Tm; School Musical; Capt Crs Cntry; Swmmng; Trk; High Hon Roll; Voice Dem Awd; Exch Stu Soviet Union; Aviation; HOBY; Intl Rltns.

JONES, JENNIFER; Yosemite HS; Bass Lake, CA; (4); Teachers Aide; Hon Roll; CA Schlstc Fed; Grphc Art.

JONES, JENNIFER A; East Bakersfield HS; Bakersfield, CA; (1); Church Yth Grp; JA; Band; Church Choir; Mrchg Band; JV L Socr; Hon Roll; Mst Insprtnl Plyr JV Sccr.

JONES, JENNIFER A; Tracy Joint Union HS; Tracy, CA; (2); Church Yth Grp; 4-H; French Clb; Key Clb; Bsktbl; Sftbl; Hon Roll; Pres Acad Fit Awd; Asilomar Club; CSF; Chld Psych.

JONES, JENNIFER E; Sacramento Adventist Acad; Fair Oaks, CA; (3); 4/37; FCA; Science Clb; Band; Chorus; Church Choir; Capt Drill Tm; Rep Jr Cls; Stu Cncl; Intrml Var Bsktbl; Hon Roll; Loma Linda U; Obstrcn.

JONES, JENNIFER L; John A Rowland HS; Rowland Hts, CA; (2); Church Yth Grp; Pep Clb; Pep Band; Rep Soph Cls; Co-Capt Cheerldng; Cit Awd; Hon Roll; Cal Poly; Elem Educ.

JONES, JENNIFER L; Monache HS; Porterville, CA; (3); Am Leg Aux Girls St; Art Clb; Church Yth Grp; Cmnty Wkr; Dance Clb; Drama Clb; Pres Pep Clb; Scholastic Bowl; SADD; Teachers Aide; U Of CA Santa Barbara; Poly Sc.

JONES, JENNIFER M; Garces Memorial HS; Bakersfield, CA; (3); French Clb; Rep Ski Clb; SADD; JV Bsktbl; Elks Awd; High Hon Roll; Masonic Awd; Pres Acad Fit Awd; Val; Poltcl Sci.

JONES, JENNIFER T; Saugus HS; Valencia, CA; (4); Stage Crew; Swmmng; Kiwanis Awd; NHS; Pres Acad Fit Awd; Psych.

JONES, JESSICA L; Arroyo Grande HS; Arroyo Grande, CA; (2); Treas AFS; Pres Church Yth Grp; Dance Clb; SADD; Variety Show; JV Trk; Hon Roll; Comp Grphcs.

JONES, JOANNA M; Centennial HS; Corona, CA; (3); Church Yth Grp; Drama Clb; SADD; Varsity Clb; School Play; Stage Crew; Var Cheerldng; High Hon Roll; Pres Acad Fit Awd; Hstry Clb; Psych.

JONES, JOANNE; Eisenhower HS; Rialto, CA; (2); Swmmng; Hon Roll; Riverside CC; Bio.

JONES, JON A; Orange Glen HS; Escondido, CA; (2); Church Yth Grp; German Clb; Quiz Bowl; Temple Yth Grp; Chorus; Church Choir; JV Var Tennis; Masonic Awd; NHS; Debate Tm; CSF; Acad Decathalon; U CA-SAN Diego; Pre Med.

JONES, JONELLE E; Merced HS; Merced, CA; (1); Church Yth Grp; Church Choir; Orch; Hon Roll; Young Life; Mssnry/Tchr.

JONES, KALONDA E; Apple Valley HS; Apple Valley, CA; (1); Office Aide; Spanish Clb; Hon Roll; NAACD; FL A&M; Bus Mgmt.

JONES, KARISSA; Fontana HS; Fontana, CA; (3); VP Frsh Cls; Rep Stu Cncl; Capt Cheerldng; Var Sftbl; JV Vllybl; Cit Awd; High Hon Roll; NHS; Zonta Clb; 4 Acad Mdls; U San Diego; Pltcl Sci.

JONES, KENDRA; Fallbrook Union HS; Fallbrook, CA; (4); 15/392; French Clb; FHA; Girl Scts; Key Clb; SADD; Teachers Aide; Band; Drm Mjr(t); Mrchg Band; Pep Band; CSF; Acad Team; Girl Sct Gold Awd; U CA San Diego; Bus Mgmt.

JONES, KENNETH C; Etiwanda HS; Alta Loma, CA; (2); VP JA; Var L Tennis; High Hon Roll.

JONES, KENNETH E; Seaside HS; Seaside, CA; (3); Cmnty Wkr; Office Aide; Varsity Clb; JV Bsktbl; JV Var Ftbl; Cit Awd; Hon Roll; Monterey Peninsula Coll; Busine.

JONES, KERELI; Los Gatos HS; Los Gatos, CA; (4); 102/374; Church Yth Grp; JA; Acpl Chr; Chorus; Church Choir; Variety Show; Swmmng; Trk; Pres Acad Fit Awd; Rowing Club; Jazz Purr; Cal Poly San Luis Ob; Scl Sci.

JONES, KERREY A; Clovis West HS; Fresno, CA; (4); DECA; FCA; SADD; Treas Varsity Clb; Rep Jr Cls; Rep Sr Cls; Socr; Sftbl; Vllybl; High Hon Roll; Fresno St U Vlybl Trny Athltc Schlr; Block C W Vrsty Clb Schlrshp; CSU Fresno; Commnctns.

JONES, KEVIN R; Torrance HS; Torrance, CA; (2); Phtg Yrbk; Var Vllybl; Hon Roll; Pres Acad Fit Awd; Ski Clb; Bus.

JONES, KIM; Flintridge Sacred Heart Acad; Glendale, CA; (3); Church Yth Grp; Letterman Clb; VP Math Clb; Red Cross Aide; VP Science Clb; Var Swmmng; CSF; Amnsty Intl; Glendal YMCA Gators Swim Team; Sci.

JONES, KIMBERLY A; Westlake HS; Thousand Oaks, CA; (4); 35/440; Sec Drama Clb; Thesps; School Musical; School Play; Mgr Stage Crew; Rptr Yrbk; High Hon Roll; NHS; Pres Acad Fit Awd; CSF Gld Seal Bearer; CA U Snta Brb; Bus.

JONES, KOREY D; Christian Center Acad; Perris, CA; (4); Church Yth Grp; Cmnty Wkr; Office Aide; Teachers Aide; Rep Jr Cls; Pres Sr Cls; Var L Bsbl; Capt L Bsktbl; Var Ftbl; Score Keeper; Bsktbl Leag MVP; All CIF Bsktbl; Azusa Pacific U; Math.

JONES, KORINNA; Wasco Union HS; Wasco, CA; (4); Pep Clb; Teachers Aide; Chorus; Yrbk; Cheerldng; Powder Puff Ftbl; Sftbl; Vllybl; Hon Roll; NHS; Santa Barbara City Coll; Psych.

JONES, KRISTEN D; Mt Miguel HS; Lemon Grove, CA; (4); 10/405; Church Yth Grp; Church Yth Grp; Ed Yrbk; Stu Cncl; JV Var Swmmng; High Hon Roll; Vrsty Bys Wtr Polo-Mngr; Stu Ldr/Lfgrd Pgm; Prncpls Lttr Cmmndtn; U Of San Diego; Psych.

JONES, LATRICE; Downtown Buis Mag HS; Los Angeles, CA; (4); 14/172; VP Frsh Cls; Pres Sr Cls; Rep Stu Cncl; Hon Roll; UC Riverside; Bus Admin.

JONES, LAVEDA D; Crenshaw HS; Los Angeles, CA; (2); Church Yth Grp; ROTC; Science Clb; Band; Church Choir; Cit Awd; High Hon Roll; Hon Roll; Masonic Awd; Athltc Achvmnt Awd; Psych.

JONES, LEANNE MARIE; Capuchino HS; San Bruno, CA; (4); 56/230; Mrchg Band; VP Frsh Cls; VP Soph Cls; Pres Jr Cls; Pres Sr Cls; Var Capt Bsktbl; VP Capt Sftbl; VP Var Vllybl; Cit Awd; DAR Awd; Bank America Achvt Awd Fine Arts; Herff Jones Ldrshp Awd; Mc Caughey Schlrshp/Athltc Awd; Chico ST U; Telecommnctns.

JONES, LIANA A; Torrey Pines HS; San Diego, CA; (2); 21/503; Hosp Aide; Intnl Clb; Yrbk; Hon Roll; Pres Acad Fit Awd; Japanese Coll Course.

JONES, LISA R; North Hills Christian Schl; Vallejo, CA; (2); 2/13; Computer Clb; Drama Clb; Speech Tm; Teachers Aide; Chorus; School Musical; School Play; Stage Crew; Ed Rptr Nwsp; Yrbk; Prncpls Awd; Facecntng.

JONES, MARK C; Valley HS; Sacramento, CA; (4); 1/450; Treas Church Yth Grp; Service Clb; Drm Mjr(t); Jazz Band; Rep Stu Cncl; Rotary Awd; Val; Sec FBLA; Hosp Aide; Spanish Clb; Hmcmng Royalty; Elks Lodge Stu Of Yr; Princeton U; Intl Rel.

JONES, MATT; Modoc HS; Canby, CA; (2); Pres Treas 4-H; FFA; Teachers Aide; Temple Yth Grp; Yrbk; VP Frsh Cls; Treas Soph Cls; Var Wt Lftg; Var Wrstlng; CA St Rookie Str Wrstlng Yr 89; Chmpn Steer Wrstling 90; 2nd Pl Wrstlng League 90; Cal Ply; Ag.

JONES, MATTHEW M; 29 Palms HS; Locust Grove, VA; (2); Letterman Clb; Science Clb; Crs Cntry; Trk; High Hon Roll; Prfct Atten Awd; U ND; Airline Pilot.

JONES, MAURICE; Junipero Serra HS; Los Angeles, CA; (2); Dance Clb; Bsktbl; Trk; USC; Bus Mgmt.

JONES, MEEGAN; Hemet HS; Hemet, CA; (3); 35/530; Pres Church Yth Grp; SADD; Teachers Aide; Varsity Clb; Var Swmmng; Var Trk; JV Var Vllybl; Cit Awd; High Hon Roll; Pres Acad Fit Awd; Eng & Hist Schlstc Awds 89-90; Stu Vlntr Smmr 90; Brigham Young U; Sprts Med.

JONES, MEG; Laguna Beach HS; Laguna Beach, CA; (2); AFS; Drama Clb; French Clb; Chorus; VP Soph Cls; Bsktbl; Swmmng; Hon Roll; NHS; Pres Schlr; Choral Presentation Soloist 90; Swimming Coaches Awd; Bsktbl Most Imprvd Player Awd; Sci.

JONES, MELISSA; Center HS; Elverta, CA; (1); Hon Roll; Wrkd On Float; Fdnrsng Frshmn Cls; Advrtsng.

JONES, MERIN; Hemet HS; Hemet, CA; (3); Church Yth Grp; Cmnty Wkr; Science Clb; Teachers Aide; Church Choir; Cheerldng; Powder Puff Ftbl; JV Socr; Sftbl; Var L Swmmng; Top Dog Awd; BYU; Phy Therapy.

JONES, MICHAEL; Valley Christian HS; San Jose, CA; (3); 1/66; Church Yth Grp; Office Aide; Service Clb; Chorus; Stage Crew; Trk; Cit Awd; High Hon Roll; San Jose PAL Law Enfrcmnt Unit.

JONES, MICHAEL; Yosemite HS; Bass Lake, CA; (2); Church Yth Grp; Ski Clb; Socr; Tennis; Hon Roll.

JONES, MICHAEL T; Madison HS; San Diego, CA; (3); 33/349; Latin Clb; Jazz Band; L Capt Bsbl; JV Cheerldng; L Capt Ftbl; JV Wrstlng; Hon Roll.

JONES, MICHELE L; Redlands HS; Redlands, CA; (3); 99/905; Church Yth Grp; Office Aide; Scholastic Bowl; Band; Flag Corp; Mrchg Band; Ed Yrbk; Ed Lit Mag; JV Swmmng; Hon Roll; UA Tucson; Envrmntlst.

JONES, MICHELLE; Livermore HS; Livermore, CA; (2); 129/393; Pep Clb; Teachers Aide; JV Capt Bsktbl; JV Cheerldng; Score Keeper; Hon Roll; Ldrshp; Bsktbl Best Offensive Awd; Red Cross Crtfd Lifeguard; CA ST Hayward; Sprts Med.

JONES, MICHELLE K; Liberty Union HS; Byron, CA; (4); Chorus; Color Guard; Drill Tm; Los Medanos Coll; Chld Care.

JONES, MISSY L; Dinuba HS; Dinuba, CA; (4); Art Clb; FBLA; FFA; FHA; JA; Science Clb; Spanish Clb; Teachers Aide; VICA; Cit Awd; U CA Integrated Pest Mgmt Intern; Natural Helpers; UC Davis; Plant Protctn.

JONES, NATASHA B; Santa Teresa HS; San Jose, CA; (2); Church Yth Grp; Band; Church Choir; Mrchg Band; Pep Band; Church Regnl Dance Fest; Pres Church Class; Church Choir Accmpnst; Brigham Young U; Music.

JONES, NICOLE; Analy HS; Sebastopol, CA; (2); Intnl Clb; Pep Clb; Cheerldng; Trk; Chrldg Compt Sqd; Sign Lang Tchr.

JONES, NICOLE; Cajon HS; San Bernardino, CA; (2); Cit Awd; Hon Roll; Loma Linda U; Physcl Ther.

JONES, NICOLE; Canyon HS; Santa Clarita, CA; (4); Church Yth Grp; JV Var Bsktbl; Outstndng Photo; BYU; Phys Educ.

JONES, NICOLE; Del Oro HS; Loomis, CA; (3); 37/274; Cmnty Wkr; Service Clb; SADD; Bsktbl; Socr; Sftbl; Trk; Vllybl; Lion Awd; Masonic Awd; Chico ST; Pub Rel.

JONES, NICOLE; Paramount HS; Paramount, CA; (3); Church Yth Grp; Chorus; Church Choir; Drill Tm; Ebony Essence Clubs; Bus.

JONES, NICOLE S; Bishop O'dowd HS; Vallejo, CA; (3); Bus Profs of Am; German Clb; Band; Ed Nwsp; Rep Frsh Cls; Var Vllybl; Opt Clb Awd; Prfct Atten Awd; Photo; U Of MD; Intl Bus.

JONES, NOAH M; Pioneer HS; Rochester, MN; (3); Intrml Bsktbl; Var L Ftbl; Var L Trk; Var Wt Lftg; Asst Coach PAL Yth Ftbl; MVP Fld Trck; Hnrble Mntn All Leag STAL Ftbl; PE Instr.

JONES, PATRICK; West Campus HS; Hanford, CA; (2); Church Yth Grp; Bsktbl; Ftbl; Trk; Wt Lftg; Wrstlng; Hon Roll; UCLA; Med.

JONES, PEYTON R; Marina HS; Huntington Beach, CA; (3); Lit Mag; Ftbl; Wt Lftg; Outstndng Offnsve Plyr Awd Ftbl; Astronmy Clb; Biola U; Hstry.

JONES, PSHYRA; South Bay JR Acad; Carson, CA; (1); Church Yth Grp; Teachers Aide; Church Choir; School Musical; High Hon Roll; Pres Acad Fit Awd; Val; Cls Pres; NAACP Act-So Pgm; Med.

JONES, RADIAH M; Arlington HS; Riverside, CA; (2); ROTC; Pres Frsh Cls; Var Crs Cntry; Var Sftbl; Hon Roll; Jr NHS; Pediatrics.

JONES, RASHIDI; Dorsey HS; Los Angeles, CA; (3); Church Yth Grp; Cmnty Wkr; Ftbl; Trk; Wt Lftg; Hon Roll; Prfct Atten Awd; Engrng.

JONES, REBECCA; Liberty Union HS; Brentwood, CA; (2); Teachers Aide; Hon Roll; CSF; Cal ST Hawyard; Psych.

JONES, RUSSELL C; Tulare Western HS; Tulare, CA; (3); 70/240; 4-H; Letterman Clb; Science Clb; JV Bsbl; JV Ftbl; Hon Roll; Vocational Olympics Champion In County; Racing Modified Midgets; Air Force Acad; Aurontcl Engr.

JONES, RYAN; Taft Union HS; Taft, CA; (4); 5/180; VP AFS; Debate Tm; VP Treas Drama Clb; VP Sec French Clb; Key Clb; Speech Tm; Teachers Aide; Chorus; School Musical; School Play; UC Davis; Attorney.

JONES, RYAN D; Oxnard HS; Oxnard, CA; (3); Hon Roll; Masonic Awd; Gldn St Exam Schl Rcgntn; Comp.

JONES, RYAN M; Irvine HS; Irvine, CA; (1); Ski Clb; Varsity Clb; Bsbl; Ftbl; Wt Lftg; Cptn Frosh Ftbl; Envrnmntl Studies.

JONES, SAM J; San Luis Obispo SR HS; San Luis Obispo, CA; (2); 15/319; Var Crs Cntry; Var Trk; Cal Poly; Aerospace Engrng.

JONES, SCOTT W; Chaminade College Prep; Northridge, CA; (2); JV Ftbl; Var L Golf; High Hon Roll; Hon Roll; Jr NHS; Hstry Clb; Hnrs At Entrance.

JONES, SETH; T C HS; Arcadia, CA; (3); Drama Clb; German Clb; Varsity Clb; Acpl Chr; Off Soph Cls; JV Var Bsktbl; Ftbl; Tennis; Hon Roll; Pres Acad Fit Awd; MNVP Bsktl Trnmnt; U Of A; Dntl.

JONES, SHARMAINE; Pasadena HS; Pasadena, CA; (2); School Play; Pres Frsh Cls; Cit Awd; St Schlr; USC; Fine Arts.

JONES, SHARON; Lincoln HS; Stockton, CA; (1); 9/540; Church Yth Grp; Cmnty Wkr; Sec Mu Alpha Theta; Pres Chorus; Yrbk; Var Crs Cntry; Capt Var Socr; Var Trk; Kiwanis Awd; Val; MVP Defnsve Vrsty Sccr; Sccr Referee; 6 Vrsty Athltc Ltrs Lifetime Lincolnian Clb; CA Polytech St U; Bus Admin.

JONES, SHAUNESSY M; Notre Dame HS; Campbell, CA; (3); Drama Clb; Sec SADD; Chorus; School Play; Rptr Phtg Nwsp; Rep Soph Cls; Rep Jr Cls; High Hon Roll; Hon Roll; NHS; Robert Frost Poetr Awd 3rd Pl; Campus Mnstry Retreat Ldr; Tchng.

JONES, SHAWN M; Miramonte HS; Orinda, CA; (3); Variety Show; Var Bsktbl; JV Diving; Hon Roll; Jack-Jill Amer; Cal Poly; Arch.

JONES, SHAYLISA D; Washington Prep; Los Angeles, CA; (4); 8/500; Church Choir; Drill Tm; Yrbk; VP Frsh Cls; Rep Stu Cncl; Cheerldng; Gym; Pom Pon; High Hon Roll; Hon Roll; U Of Southern CA; Architecture.

JONES, SHELBY R; Atwater HS; Winton, CA; (3); Boy Scts; Church Yth Grp; FCA; Hosp Aide; Red Cross Aide; SADD; JV Var Ftbl; JV Var Mgr(s); JV Socr; JV Var Wt Lftg; Small Engines Awd; Dentistry.

JONES, STACEY L; Pleasant Valley HS; Chico, CA; (4); Church Yth Grp; Cmnty Wkr; GAA; Ski Clb; Spanish Clb; SADD; Ed Yrbk; Rep Sr Cls; JV Vllybl; DAR Awd; Ski Team St Fnlst; UC Davis; Envrnmntl Sci.

JONES, STACEY M; Inglewood HS; Los Angeles, CA; (4); JA; Church Choir; Mesa; Cal-Soap; Black Hstry Clb; CA ST U Los Angeles; Bus Mgmt.

JONES, STEPHANIE; Crystal Springs Uplands HS; San Mateo, CA; (4); Am Leg Aux Girls St; Q&S; Chorus; Stage Crew; Nwsp; Ed Yrbk; VP Jr Cls; VP Stu Cncl; Var Capt Socr; NHS; Oxfam Amer Pres; Bank Of Amer Frnch Awd; Brown U; Intl Reltns.

JONES, STEPHANIE D; Skyline HS; Oakland, CA; (2); Teachers Aide; Hon Roll; Harvard; Law.

JONES, SUZANNE M; Carlmont HS; Belmont, CA; (3); Office Aide; Teachers Aide; Crs Cntry; Mgr(s); Trk; Wt Lftg; Hon Roll; YES; Peer Cnslg; Supvr & Officiate JR HS Grack & Fld Meets; Frosh Transition Prgm; Sports Thrpy.

JONES, SYLVIA R; A A Stagg HS; Stockton, CA; (3); VP Key Clb; NFL; Spanish Clb; Sec Speech Tm; Thesps; Chorus; Stage Crew; Rep Soph Cls; Var Socr; High Hon Roll; Camp Royal Ldrshp.

JONES, TABATHA L; Mt Whitney HS; Visalia, CA; (1); Church Yth Grp; Band; Chorus; Church Choir; Pep Band; Swmmng; Hon Roll; Church Musical; Phrmcst.

JONES, TAMALA M; Cajon HS; San Bernardino, CA; (3); School Musical; Stage Crew; Lit Mag; Rep Soph Cls; Stu Cncl; Stat Bsbl; Intrntnl Bcclrt Prgm; Hnry Mem Of Bd Of Ed; Elctd ASB Pres; Eng & Us His Hnrs Awd; Wrtng Clbrtn; U Of CA; Tchng.

JONES, TAMU F; John Muir HS; Pasadena, CA; (3); 60/250; Hon Roll; Psych.

JONES, THERESA; Edison HS; Stockton, CA; (3); Bus Profs of Am; Church Yth Grp; Cmnty Wkr; FBLA; Acpl Chr; Chorus; Church Choir; School Musical; Rep Soph Cls; Prfct Atten Awd; Peer Ed Training; BSU Clb; Photo Clb; RN.

JONES, TIA T; Gompers HS; San Diego, CA; (2); Church Yth Grp; Girl Scts; Office Aide; Cit Awd; Hon Roll; Prfct Atten Awd; Howard U; Law.

JONES, TICIA; Southbay Christian HS; Sunnyvale, CA; (2); 8/190; Natl Beta Clb; JV Bsktbl; JV Sftbl; JV Vllybl; Cit Awd; Hon Roll; Ntl Merit Ltr; Pres Acad Fit Awd; Athl Of Yr.

JONES, TIFFANY R; Beaumont HS; Beaumont, CA; (3); 1/200; Quiz Bowl; Teachers Aide; Rptr Nwsp; JV Bsktbl; Stat Ftbl; Var Capt Sftbl; Var Vllybl; High Hon Roll; Treas NHS; Pres Acad Fit Awd; Xerox Awd; CSF-SCHL Chaptr Pres; All Leag Sftbl; Jrnlsm.

JONES, TIMOTHY; Village Christian HS; Burbank, CA; (3); 26/123; Boy Scts; Pres Church Yth Grp; Cmnty Wkr; Church Choir; School Musical; Phtg Yrbk; Var Crs Cntry; Var Socr; Var Trk; High Hon Roll; Outstndng Scout Of Yr Awd; US Naval Acad; Aviator.

JONES, TIMOTHY R; Ontario HS; Ontario, CA; (2); Church Yth Grp; Letterman Clb; Spanish Clb; Varsity Clb; Band; Mrchg Band; Pep Band; Var Wrstlng; Police Officer.

JONES, TRACY; Sierra HS; Auberry, CA; (2); Letterman Clb; Pep Clb; SADD; Sec Soph Cls; Cheerldng; Pom Pon; Tennis; NHS.

JONES, TRACY; Wm S Hart HS; Valencia, CA; (4); 92/498; Church Yth Grp; SADD; Var Capt Cheerldng; Gym; Trk; Pres Acad Fit Awd; Working W/ Homeless; Stu League; CSUN; Bus.

JONES, TUNYA R; Edison HS; Clovis, CA; (4); 62/200; Church Yth Grp; SADD; Church Choir; JV Bsktbl; Trk; Hon Roll; VP Of Club Called Preps; Member Of Anaacp; Hnrd At Black Graduate Celebration; Fresno ST U; Comp Sci.

JONES, VALERIE R; Amos Alonzo Stagg HS; Stockton, CA; (3); Sec Key Clb; VP Speech Tm; Thesps; Acpl Chr; Off Soph Cls; Swing Chorus; Var Socr; Var Swmmng; High Hon Roll; CSF Sctry; POET Clb; Libral Arts Coll.

JONES, VINCE M; Nevada Union HS; Nevada City, CA; (3); 79/550; Hon Roll; Outstndng Ctznshp Letter; ROP Cert-Auto Tune-Up; Sierra Coll; Arch.

JONES, WYKING L; St Bernard HS; Inglewood, CA; (3); Church Yth Grp; Cmnty Wkr; Red Cross Aide; Varsity Clb; Var Capt Bsktbl; All CIF Bsktbl; Var Ltrmn; All Leag Bsktbl; Arch.

JONES, YOLANDA J; Highlands HS; North Highlands, CA; (1); SADD; JV Sftbl; Sut Reaching Out; UCD; Law.

JONES-LAING, KARYN; Los Altos HS; Hacienda Hts, CA; (4); Aud/Vis; Teachers Aide; Varsity Clb; Phtg Yrbk; Var Capt Swmmng; Hon Roll; NHS; Photo Club Vp; Bank Of America Indl Arts Awd; Ralph Neighbors Sports Med Schlsp; Orange Coast JC; Sports Med.

JONG, WANDA; Richard Gahr HS; Cerritos, CA; (2); 67/500; Speech Tm; Color Guard; Hon Roll; Hotel Mgmt.

JONKER, JEFFREY D; San Marino HS; San Marino, CA; (4); Church Yth Grp; Drama Clb; FBLA; Letterman Clb; Math Clb; Science Clb; Thesps; School Play; Stage Crew; Variety Show; Cmnty Cnslng Pgm Cert Pr Cnslr; Ftbl Tm Wn St Chmpnshp; Claremount Mc Kenna Coll; Law.

JONO, AUBREY M; Gardena HS; Gardena, CA; (3); Church Yth Grp; Intnl Clb; Yrbk; Admirals Hgh Hnrs Club; Humanities; UCLA; Pre-Law.

JOO, GLORIA; Warren HS; Downey, CA; (3); Pres Church Yth Grp; JA; Mu Alpha Theta; Pep Clb; Science Clb; Church Choir; Treas Frsh Cls; Var Cheerldng; Var Tennis; Cit Awd; Ledy Natl JR Achvt Conf 89; All Around Player Badmntn-Trphy; Cert Acad Excllnc; Pdtrcn.

JOO, SAM; Buena Park HS; Buena Park, CA; (3); Church Yth Grp; French Clb; Hosp Aide; Letterman Clb; Science Clb; VP Sr Cls; Swmmng; Hon Roll; MVP & Mst Insprtnl Wtr Polo; TAG; Pre-Med.

JOO, YONG T; John F Kennedy HS; La Palma, CA; (3); Treas Computer Clb; FBLA; Key Clb; Speech Tm; Kiwanis Bwl Tm; CA Schlrshp Fdrtn; Cls Rep; Gldn ST Exm-Geom Prfct Scr.

JOPSON, CINDY J; East Nicolaus HS; Wheatland, CA; (2); 1/50; Art Clb; Church Yth Grp; GAA; Letterman Clb; Pep Clb; Ski Clb; Variety Show; Rep Soph Cls; Var JV Bsktbl; Stat Ftbl; Intl Order Of Rainbw Girls Past Wrthy Advsr; CSF; US Air Force Acad; Rsrch.

JOPSON, PAMELA; East Nicolaus HS; Wheatland, CA; (4); 8/41; Am Leg Aux Girls St; Church Yth Grp; GAA; Pres Letterman Clb; Office Aide; Pep Clb; Ski Clb; Sec SADD; Capt Varsity Clb; Var Capt Bsktbl; Amer River Coll.

JOQUIN, RONETTE; Herbert Hoover HS; San Diego, CA; (3); Church Yth Grp; French Clb; Girl Scts; Office Aide; Church Choir; Drill Tm; Hon Roll; Comp.

JORDAHL, CHRISTY L; California Lutheran HS; Fountain Valley, CA; (3); Church Yth Grp; L Cheerldng; L Sftbl; High Hon Roll; High Hnrs The Gldn St Exm Alg I; Hs Hnrs The Gldn St Exam Geo.

JORDAN, AMY E; Montgomery HS; Santa Rosa, CA; (2); Church Yth Grp; Dance Clb; GAA; Pep Clb; Spanish Clb; Teachers Aide; Church Choir; Flag Corp; Bsktbl; Crs Cntry; UC Davis; Envrnmntl Attorney.

JORDAN, BECKY; St Francis HS; Portola Valley, CA; (3); Church Yth Grp; Cmnty Wkr; 4-H; Intnl Clb; Letterman Clb; Service Clb; SADD; Varsity Clb; Bsktbl; Sftbl; Intergenerational Pgm; CYSA Soccer; Work With Elderly.

JORDAN, BEN; Piedmont HS; Piedmont, CA; (3); Var Crs Cntry; Var Trk; Athltcs Cngrss USA; CSF.

JORDAN, CHRISTINE R; Tulare Union HS; Tulare, CA; (3); Art Clb; Hon Roll; UCLA; Radio Brdcstng.

JORDAN, CHRISTOPHER; Coast Christian Schl; Los Angeles, CA; (3); 7/20; Letterman Clb; Spanish Clb; Varsity Clb; Yrbk; Capt Var Bsbl; Capt Var Ftbl; Hon Roll; USC; Bus.

JORDAN, DAVID D; Servite HS; Fullerton, CA; (2); Ski Clb; JV Socr; High Hon Roll; CSF; Stanford U; Med.

JORDAN, JASON M; Bellarmine College Prep; San Jose, CA; (2); 1/296; Cmnty Wkr; Stat Debate Tm; NFL; Speech Tm; Teachers Aide; Varsity Clb; Rep Stu Cncl; Intrml Bsktbl; Var Crs Cntry; JV Trk; Outstndng Awd; Top Hnrs Debater/Speaker; Berkeley; Bus Admin.

JORDAN, KELLIE; Los Alamitos HS; Seal Beach, CA; (4); Church Yth Grp; Pep Clb; Service Clb; Sec Color Guard; Capt Flag Corp; Hon Roll; CSF; Saferides; SR Clss Cmmttee; U Of CA; Spch & Hrng Thrpy.

JORDAN, KIMBERLY; Piedmont Hills HS; San Jose, CA; (3); #203 In Class; Drill Tm; Cheerldng; Dental Asst.

JORDAN II, LOUIS J; Ceres HS; Ceres, CA; (4); Church Yth Grp; Spanish Clb; JV Bsbl; Var Ftbl; Crtfct Achvt Golden St Examintn; U Pacific; Pre Med.

JORDAN, LYNEA R; Sanger HS; Sanger, CA; (2); Church Yth Grp; FCA; 4-H; Intnl Clb; Model UN; Ski Clb; Var L Diving; Var L Swmmng; 4-H Awd; Rotary Awd; Whitworth Coll; Intl Rel.

JORDAN, MELANIE; Cajon HS; San Bernardino, CA; (4); Cmnty Wkr; Drama Clb; Service Clb; School Play; High Hon Roll; CSF; U Of CA Santa Barbara; Psych.

JORDAN, MELISSA M; Norco HS; Corona, CA; (3); 21/399; Hosp Aide; Model UN; Office Aide; SADD; Score Keeper; High Hon Roll; Hon Roll; Pres Acad Fit Awd; Girls Leag; CSF; Educ.

JORDAN, MICHELE R; Rubidoux HS; Mira Loma, CA; (4); #4 In Class; Church Yth Grp; Sec FHA; Model UN; Spanish Clb; Church Choir; High Hon Roll; NHS; Mock Trl Treas; Model Cong; Hnrs Geo Golden St Ex; Brigham Young U; Elem Ed.

JORDAN, MIGUEL R; La Canada HS; La Canada-Flint, CA; (4); 4/235; Church Yth Grp; Hist Key Clb; Math Clb; Science Clb; NHS; Ntl Merit Ltr; Bank Of Amer Sci Awd; Sci Dept Best Physis Stu; National Sci Olympiad-Best Physis Score; Caltech; Engineer.

JORDAN, OWENA R; River City HS; W Sacramento, CA; (3); French Clb; Yrbk; MESA; Early Outreach; Upward Bund Stu Advsry Brd Edtr; U Of CA Davis; Cmmrcl Art.

JORDAN, RACHEL; Stagg HS; Stockton, CA; (1); Church Yth Grp; Dance Clb; Drama Clb; 4-H; Girl Scts; Hosp Aide; Math Tm; Red Cross Aide; Teachers Aide; Band; Outstndng Ctzn Of Yr; UC, Davis; Pro Ftbl.

JORDAN, RAY A; Arlington HS; Riverside, CA; (3); Church Yth Grp; Dance Clb; Teachers Aide; Pres Soph Cls; VP Stu Cncl; Ftbl; Hon Roll; Pres Acad Fit Awd; Pres Stu Govt; 1st Rep For Prin Svc Awd; Bus Mgt.

JORDAN, ROBERT; Cupertino HS; Cupertino, CA; (3); 97/300; Var Ftbl; Powder Puff Ftbl; Var Socr; Var Wt Lftg; Rugby Clb Pres & Capt; Pilot.

JORDAN, SARA J; Analy HS; Sebastopol, CA; (2); Art Clb; Church Yth Grp; Cmnty Wkr; 4-H; Science Clb; Ed Yrbk; Lit Mag; Stat Bsktbl; Score Keeper; Trk; N Coast Schlr Athl; San Diego ST; Teacher.

JORDAN, STEPHEN T; Moreno Valley HS; Moreno Valley, CA; (3); 12/520; Boy Scts; Cmnty Wkr; French Clb; Key Clb; Model UN; ROTC; Drill Tm; High Hon Roll; NHS; AFJROTC Distinguistal Cadet; Air Force Acad; Aero Engr.

JORDAN, TERA; Encinal HS; Alameda, CA; (4); 30/224; Drama Clb; Chorus; School Musical; School Play; Stage Crew; Outstndng Frshmn & Soph Drama Clb; Author.

JORDON, JOHN P; Redlands HS; Redlands, CA; (2); Church Yth Grp; Debate Tm; Intrml Bsktbl; Intrml Ftbl; Intrml Wt Lftg; Cit Awd; Rotary Awd; Team Redlands; Coin Clb; Harvard; Intl Law.

JORDON, MICHAEL; Rubidoux HS; Riverside, CA; (4); 7/500; Am Leg Boys St; Stu Cncl; Var Bsbl; Var Capt Ftbl; Var Wrstlng; High Hon Roll; Hon Roll; Opt Clb Awd; Occidental.

JORENBY, PAULA A; Whittier Christian HS; Whittier, CA; (4); Church Yth Grp; Var Crs Cntry; Var Trk; CSF; Phrmcy.

JORGENSEN, ELIZABETH C; Fairfield HS; Fairfield, CA; (2); Art Clb; English Clb; Flag Corp; Yrbk; Bus.

JORGENSEN, KIRK J; Washington Union HS; Gualala, CA; (2); 5/200; FBLA; Letterman Clb; Q&S; Band; Mrchg Band; Orch; Pep Band; School Musical; Stat Bsktbl; JV Ftbl; CSF; St Hnr Band; UC Berkeley; Bus.

JORGENSEN, KURT M; El Dorado HS; Placentia, CA; (3); 28/317; Var Socr; High Hon Roll; CA Schlrshp Fed; St Schlr; Mech Engrng.

JORGENSEN, SVEN E; Montgomery HS; Santa Rosa, CA; (2); Art Clb; Drama Clb; French Clb; Speech Tm; Ed Yrbk; JV Crs Cntry; JV Trk; Pres Acad Fit Awd; Juggling; Biking; Planet Saving.

JORGENSEN, TRENT; Point Arena HS; Gualala, CA; (3); 2/41; Am Leg Boys St; L Q&S; Mrchg Band; VP Jr Cls; Var L Bsktbl; Var L Tennis; High Hon Roll; Hon Roll; Masonic Awd; CSF Lifetime Mem, Vp Of Clb; U CA Berkeley; Path.

JORGENSON, KELLIE L; Mission Viego HS; Mission Viejo, CA; (2); Church Yth Grp; FCA; Girl Scts; Office Aide; Teachers Aide; Crs Cntry; Cit Awd; Hon Roll; Grls Leag; Tnns; Hrsbck Rdng; Trinity Christian Coll; Educ.

JORNADA, CHARI DELLE H; San Gabriel Acad; Covina, CA; (3); Acpl Chr; Band; Rep Frsh Cls; Rep Soph Cls; Stu Cncl; Intrml Capt Vllybl; NHS; Church Yth Grp; Church Choir; Intrml Bsktbl; Christian Yth Bldrs Sec; 3rd Pl Physcs & SGA Sci Fair 88-89; Floor Hcky Cptn 89-90; Loma Linda U; Med.

JORRITSMA, JAMIE; Ontario Christian HS; Chino, CA; (1); 1/67; Church Yth Grp; Band; Chorus; Pep Band; School Musical; JV Cheerldng; Hon Roll; CA Schlrshp Fed; Music.

JORSKI, DAYTEDEE; Fontana HS; Fontana, CA; (2); Band; Chorus; Mrchg Band; High Hon Roll; Hon Roll; Prfct Atten Awd; Band Cncl.

JOSAFAT, JASON M; Chula Vista HS; San Diego, CA; (2); 108/605; Church Yth Grp; Treas Jr Cls; Var Ftbl; JV Capt Vllybl; Wt Lftg; Hon Roll; Concssns Wrkr; Hnr Clses Bio, Engl & AP Eurpean Hstry; UCSD; Engl.

JOSEPH, JENIFER; Greenville JR/Sr HS; Taylorsville, CA; (4); 6/30; Am Leg Aux Girls St; Sec 4-H; Sec Service Clb; Band; Jazz Band; Phtg Yrbk; Tennis; Capt Vllybl; Hon Roll; Rotary Yth Ldrshp Awd; U NE Reno.

JOSEPH, LASHAWN K; Chaffey HS; Ontario, CA; (3); Church Yth Grp; Church Choir; Var Cheerldng; Powder Puff Ftbl; High Hon Roll; NHS; Prfct Atten Awd; UC Riverside; Obstetrician.

JOSEPH, LISA D; Etiwanda HS; Alta Loma, CA; (4); Church Yth Grp; Cmnty Wkr; Latin Clb; Ski Clb; SADD; Teachers Aide; Lit Mag; High Hon Roll; Hon Roll; U Of CA-IRVINE.

JOSEPH, MICHAEL P; Turlock HS; Turlock, CA; (3); AFS; Church Yth Grp; Band; Church Choir; Jazz Band; Mrchg Band; Orch; Pep Band; Chrch Orch; Music.

JOSEPH, SABRINA; Los Alamitos HS; Long Beach, CA; (3); Stage Crew.

JOSEPH, SAJU; Orange Lutheran HS; Anaheim, CA; (2); Art Clb; Church Yth Grp; Computer Clb; FCA; Letterman Clb; Spanish Clb; Varsity Clb; JV Ftbl; Var Tennis; Var Wrstlng; Dctr Of Med.

JOSEPH, SHARON; Fontana HS; Fontana, CA; (4); 90/792; Art Clb; Intnl Clb; Yrbk; Intrml Bsktbl; Silver Acad Mdl; CA ST U San Bernardino; Bus.

JOSEPH, SHARON; Imperial HS; Pasadena, CA; (3); Church Yth Grp; Drill Tm; Flag Corp; Cheerldng; Swmmng; Trk; Vllybl; Hon Roll; Advncd Accntng Awd; Bus Admin.

JOSEPH, SOPHIA A; Lindhurst HS; Marysville, CA; (2); Cmnty Wkr; Drama Clb; VP Key Clb; SADD; School Play; Rptr Nwsp; Ed Yrbk; Off Frsh Cls; Off Soph Cls; JV Vllybl; Peer Cnslr; Friday Night Live; UCLA; Bus.

JOSEPH, STEPHEN A; Loyola HS; Los Angeles, CA; (2); Church Yth Grp; Var Ftbl; NEDT Awd; Chrstn Life Cmmnty; Mnrty Stus Assn; Schlrshp Upon Entrnc To Loyola; Air Force Acad; Plt.

JOSEPH, TIFFANY; Tri-City Christian Schl; Carlsbad, CA; (2); Church Yth Grp; Var Co-Capt Cheerldng; High Hon Roll; NCA Pom Pon Natl Chmpn; 1st Baptist Chruch Core Grp; Wrtr.

JOSIMOV, NATALIJA; Trabuco Hills HS; Trabuco Canyon, CA; (3); Pep Clb; Spanish Clb; SADD; Teachers Aide; Hon Roll; NHS; CA Schlrshp Fed; Distngshd Schlr Awd Socl Sci; Psych.

JOSING, DEANNA H; Canyon HS; Canyon Country, CA; (1); Ed Yrbk; Hon Roll; Med.

JOSTAD, CHEMAINE R; Davis HS; Modesto, CA; (2); Sftbl; Vllybl.

JOSUE, MELANIE L; Milpitas HS; Milpitas, CA; (2); ROTC; Drill Tm; JV Tennis; Schlr Athlte 3.50 GPA Or Hghgr; Med.

JOUAN, JENNIFER A; Chula Vista HS; Chula Vista, CA; (3); Math Clb; Office Aide; Band; Mrchg Band; Pres Orch; Pep Band; A Member Of SPEAK; Performing Arts.

JOUANEH, EVELYN; College Park HS; Pleasant Hill, CA; (1); Library Aide; Office Aide; Teachers Aide; School Play; Stage Crew; Variety Show; Lit Mag; Cit Awd; Worked In Cafeteria For Coll Park; U Co; Psych.

JOVE, LARRY C; Palm Springs HS; Palm Springs, CA; (3); JV Var Bsktbl; JV Tennis; Hon Roll; Lion Awd; CA Boys St; UNLV; Arch.

JOVEN, JENNIFER L; Simi Valley HS; Simi Valley, CA; (3); Library Aide; Office Aide; Teachers Aide; Jr NHS; NHS; UCSB; Nrnsg.

JOVES, JAMES; Montgomery HS; Kenwood, CA; (3); Art Clb; Boy Scts; Church Yth Grp; JA; Spanish Clb; Rptr Yrbk; Sec Stu Cncl; Trk; Wrstlng; High Hon Roll; Acad Achvt In Art; CSF; Engrng.

JOW, JOYCE S; San Gabriel HS; San Gabriel, CA; (3); 6/700; Pres Church Yth Grp; Key Clb; Science Clb; Spanish Clb; SADD; Church Choir; Var L Swmmng; Var L Vllybl; High Hon Roll; Biochem.

JOY, CELIA; East Bakersfield HS; Bakersfield, CA; (3); Church Yth Grp; French Clb; JA; Band; Jazz Band; Mrchg Band; Pep Band; Write Poems; Vactn Bible Schl Tchr.

JOY, STEPHANIE L; Lower Lake HS; Lower Lake, CA; (2); Chorus; Hon Roll; K Teacher.

JOYCE, EDWARD D; Paraclete HS; Acton, CA; (3); Church Yth Grp; Key Clb; Letterman Clb; Bsbl; Ftbl; Hon Roll; Sprts Med.

JOYCE, JEFFREY M; Lincoln HS; Stockton, CA; (3); 119/538; Cmnty Wkr; Teachers Aide; Var Bsbl; Var Ftbl; Hon Roll; All SJAA Leag Ftbl & Bsbl; Envrnmntl Sci.

JOYCE, JOANNA; Coronado HS; Coronado, CA; (3); #8 In Class; Cmnty Wkr; Drama Clb; Office Aide; Service Clb; Teachers Aide; Off Frsh Cls; Pres Sr Cls; Sec Stu Cncl; JV Socr; JV Sftbl; Rotary Yth Ldrshp Awd; CSF; Usherette; ICC; Acad Leag; Campus Life; UCSD; Bus.

JOYCE, JONA S; Victor Valley SR HS; Helendale, CA; (3); Church Yth Grp; VP Pep Clb; SADD; Hon Roll; Teen Thtre; Humbolt ST U; Marine Bio.

JOYCE, MAUREEN E; Hemet HS; Mountain Center, CA; (3); VP Church Yth Grp; Girl Scts; Teachers Aide; Church Choir; Lion Awd; Engl Dept Achvt Awd; Hnrbl Mntn Crtv Wrtg Cont-U CA San Bernardino; Med.

JOYNER, KA SHEIKA D; South Bay JR Acad; Torrance, CA; (1); Church Yth Grp; Computer Clb; Drama Clb; Hon Roll; Pediatrician.

JOYNT, SARAH E; San Benito HS; Hollister, CA; (4); 16/362; AFS; Church Yth Grp; Drama Clb; 4-H; Intnl Clb; Key Clb; Pep Clb; Science Clb; Spanish Clb; Band; Congress-Bundestag Semi-Fnlst; CSF.

JUAN, ETHEL; Vallejo SR HS; Vallejo, CA; (2); Rptr Nwsp; JV Capt Cheerldng; Pom Pon; Hon Roll; NHS; Vrsty Acad Lttr; Pediatric Nrsng.

JUAN, RAMOS; Mission HS; San Francisco, CA; (3); Church Yth Grp; Yrbk; Off Sr Cls.

JUAN, SHELLEY; San Gabriel Acad; W Covina, CA; (4); Teachers Aide; VP Frsh Cls; Rep Soph Cls; Rep Jr Cls; Intrml Bsktbl; Intrml Ftbl; Intrml Gym; Intrml Socr; Intrml Sftbl; Loma Linda U; Bus.

JUANERO, KENNETH; Oxnard HS; Oxnard, CA; (3); 5/450; Cmnty Wkr; High Hon Roll; Hon Roll; Pres Acad Fit Awd; CSF; Alg Golden St Exam, High Hnrs; Geom Golden St Exam Hnrs; Cal Poly San Luis Obisbo; Engr.

JUAREZ, ANABEL R; Workman HS; La Puente, CA; (2); Drama Clb; School Play; Ed Rptr Nwsp; Hon Roll; Elem Schl Teacher.

JUAREZ, ANN M; Schurr HS; Montebello, CA; (3); Spanish Clb; Hon Roll; Bio.

JUAREZ, CELIA P; Central Union HS; El Centro, CA; (4); 5/500; Am Leg Aux Girls St; Girl Scts; Office Aide; Spanish Clb; Teachers Aide; Cit Awd; High Hon Roll; Hon Roll; Pres Acad Fit Awd; U C Berkeley Alumni Schlrshp 4.0 Avg; END Hatch Schlrshp; Soroptimist Citizenshp Awd; WCF Schlrshp; UC Berkeley; Bus Adm.

JUAREZ, ISIDRO; Calexico HS; Calexico, CA; (1); Basbl; Comp.

JUAREZ, JENNIFE A; Los Amigos HS; Orange, CA; (3); Church Yth Grp; Dance Clb; GAA; Bsktbl; Trk; Vllybl; Wt Lftg; Cal ST Fulerston; Law.

JUAREZ, JOSE G; Saniago HS; Santa Ana, CA; (2); UCLA; Dentist.

JUAREZ, JULIAN; Bishop Amat HS; Arcadia, CA; (1); Varsity Clb; Ftbl; Wrstlng; Hon Roll.

JUAREZ, LILIAN V; Crenshaw HS; Los Angeles, CA; (3); Cit Awd; High Hon Roll; Hon Roll; Prin Hnr Rl; Bus.

JUAREZ, LUIS; Garfield HS; Los Angeles, CA; (3); Explorer; UCLA; Law Enfrcmnt.

JUAREZ, MARCUS R; Brawley Union HS; Brawley, CA; (1); 1/382; Math Tm; JV Ftbl; Var Tennis; High Hon Roll; Hon Roll; CSF; Engr.

JUAREZ, MARIA N; Oakdale HS; Waterford, CA; (2); Band; Mrchg Band; Pep Band; Sacramento U; Inter Dsgn.

JUAREZ, MICHAEL D; Encina HS; Sacramento, CA; (4); 96/163; Boy Scts; Church Yth Grp; Teachers Aide; Ftbl; Socr; Vllybl; AIDS Peer Cnslr; Conflict Mgr; E NM U; Law Enfrcmnt.

JUAREZ III, RAUL; Selma HS; Selma, CA; (1); Drama Clb; Ski Clb; JV Bsbl; JV Bsktbl; JV Ftbl; Trk; Cit Awd; Hon Roll; Prfct Atten Awd; Fresno ST; Lawyer.

JUAREZ, RICHARD I; Brawley Union HS; Brawley, CA; (4); 3/290; Am Leg Boys St; Treas Math Clb; Stu Cncl; Var L Ftbl; Var L Tennis; Cit Awd; Elks Awd; High Hon Roll; Hon Roll; Pres Acad Fit Awd; CSF VP; Rotary Interact Clb; UC Los Angeles; Dentstry.

JUAREZ, ROSALIE; Colton HS; Colton, CA; (3); VP DECA; Teachers Aide; JV Fld Hcky; JV Mgr(s); JV Score Keeper; Hon Roll; Regnl Occptnl Prgm; Fshn Merch; Med.

JUAREZ, SHAYLA M; Encina Acad; Sacramento, CA; (3); 11/212; Church Yth Grp; Spanish Clb; SADD; Teachers Aide; Temple Yth Grp; Church Choir; Drill Tm; Stu Cncl; JV Var Bsktbl; Score Keeper; Assgnd Cnflct Mgrs Tm Stu Of Mnth; MVP Awd 89-90 Vllybl Season; All-League Plyr 1st Tm Vllybl 89-90; Archtctr.

JUAREZ, YENNY; Sweetwater Union HS; National City, CA; (1); Church Yth Grp; Church Choir; Off Frsh Cls; Vllybl; Cit Awd; High Hon Roll; Hon Roll; Prfct Atten Awd; U Of CA San Diego; Med.

JUAREZ, YOLANDA M; St Paul HS; La Puente, CA; (3); 87/350; Pep Clb; Drill Tm; Var Pom Pon; Hon Roll; NHS; Med.

JUAREZ-ROMERO, ROSE M; Norwalk HS; Norwalk, CA; (3); Key Clb; Treas Latin Clb; SADD; Teachers Aide; JV Tennis; Hon Roll; MECHA Club 89-90; CSF 88-89; Maranatha Club 89-90; Sorptmst Club 88-89; Interact Club 89-90; San Diego U; Pediatrician.

JUBB, KRISTIN W; Elk Grove HS; Sacramento, CA; (2); Church Yth Grp; Var Powder Puff Ftbl; Consumnes JC; Bus.

JUCAR, JENNIFER; Rowland HS; Rowland Hts, CA; (3); Cmnty Wkr; Pres Pep Clb; Science Clb; Var Cheerldng; Var Trk; High Hon Roll; NHS; Grls League; UC Santa Barbara; Pre Law.

JUDAH, TOM; Tomales HS; Bodega Bay, CA; (2); Ski Clb; VP Rep Frsh Cls; Treas Rep Soph Cls; VP Stu Cncl; JV Bsktbl; Capt JV Ftbl; Hon Roll; Pres Acad Fit Awd.

JUDD, JESSICA; Turlock HS; Turlock, CA; (2); 10/600; AFS; Key Clb; Letterman Clb; Ed Nwsp; Var Swmmng; Var Tennis; Mst Imprvd V Swmmr 90; Achvd 1st Yr Algebra Hnrs On Golden St Exam; U Of CA Berkeley; Liberal Arts.

JUDD, SAVANNA; Morro Bay HS; Los Osos, CA; (4); 2/225; Cmnty Wkr; English Clb; French Clb; Teachers Aide; Yrbk; Ed Lit Mag; Var Tennis; Cit Awd; Elks Awd; High Hon Roll; CSF; 3rd Pl MB Sci Fair 88; Coachs Aws Tnns 89; Reed Coll; Eng Tchr.

JUDD, TRACI D; Mission Bay HS; San Diego, CA; (3); 96/307; Chorus; Variety Show; Var Capt Fld Hcky; Trk; Hon Roll; Teen Insti; UCLA; Bus.

JUDILLA, ROLYN; Cajon HS; San Bernardino, CA; (2); Cmnty Wkr; Key Clb; Ed Lit Mag; High Hon Roll; Hon Roll; Jr NHS; NHS; Pres Acad Fit Awd; Rotary Awd; Oxford; Med.

JUDKINS, SCOTT W; John A Rowland HS; Walnut, CA; (2); Boy Scts; Hon Roll; CA ST Fullerton; Chiropractor.

JUE, IVAN L; Saint Ignatius College Prep; San Francisco, CA; (3); 62/244; Aud/Vis; Boy Scts; Cmnty Wkr; Debate Tm; Hosp Aide; JA; Office Aide; Science Clb; Service Clb; Ed Nwsp; CSF; Medcl Explorers Post 496; UC Davis; Corp Law.

JUE, TIFFANY C; Bishop Montgomery HS; Harbor City, CA; (3); Cmnty Wkr; Hosp Aide; Service Clb; SADD; Hon Roll; Prfct Atten Awd; CSF, Svc Awd & Club Sr Rep; U Of Southern CA; Bus Adm.

JUERGENS, PATRICIA M; University HS; Irvine, CA; (3); Church Yth Grp; High Hon Roll; Hon Roll; Spanish NHS; Sea Scouts Of America; Laureate Award Winner AP Calculus; Warton Schl Business; Business.

JUHA, MAY F; Lowell HS; San Francisco, CA; (3); Dance Clb; Red Cross Aide; SADD; Teachers Aide; Vllybl; Hon Roll; Palestinian Amer Yth Orgnztn; Arabic Music Singing Grp; UC Berkeley; Psych.

JUHL, PIA; Santa Cruz HS; Santa Cruz, CA; (3); Teachers Aide; Lane County CC; Pre-Med.

JUHNKE, SABRINA A; Hanford HS; Hanford, CA; (4); 3/400; Church Yth Grp; FBLA; School Play; Score Keeper; Var L Swmmng; Hon Roll; Pres Acad Fit Awd; Val; CSF; Jbs Dghtrs; Fresno ST; Bus Admin.

JULES, APRIL; Chino HS; Chino, CA; (3); Drama Clb; Teachers Aide; Thesps; School Play; Powder Puff Ftbl; Socr; Prfct Atten Awd; Ebony Excllnc; Fshn Inst Merch & Dsgn; Int Dsn.

JULIAN, CATHERINE D; Independence HS; San Jose, CA; (2); Off Soph Cls; Hon Roll; Photogrphy.

JULIEN, DAN J; Calaveras HS; Mokelumne Hill, CA; (2); Trk; Gov Hon Prg Awd; Hon Roll; Ger; Art; Drftng; Arch Engr.

JUMA, HUSSEIN S; Santa Monica HS; Santa Monica, CA; (3); Church Yth Grp; Cmnty Wkr; FBLA; Intnl Clb; Astronomy Club; Young Entrepreneur Soc; U Of Southern CA; Accntng.

JUMELET, DOUG A; San Juan HS; Roseville, CA; (4); 60/269; Computer Clb; Spanish Clb; Bsbl; Bsktbl; Socr; Elks Awd; Hon Roll; U Of S CA; Pre-Business.

JUMP, DONNA C; Oak Park HS; Agoura Hills, CA; (4); 38/87; Key Clb; Office Aide; Teachers Aide; Rptr Nwsp; Ed Yrbk; JV Socr; Stat Trk; JV Vllybl; Moorpark CC.

JUN, MARCELO; Mark Keppel HS; Monterey Pk, CA; (4); Stage Crew; Var Capt Swmmng; Cit Awd; Hon Roll; Prfct Atten Awd; Chrch Srvnt Ldrshp Grp; CSU Long Beach; Materials Engr.

JUN, WOO JIN; Nogales HS; W Covina, CA; (2); Science Clb; Var Tennis; Hon Roll.

JUNEMANN, MICHAEL; Cardinal Newman HS; Sebastopol, CA; (2); Church Yth Grp; Latin Clb; Hist Soph Cls; Trk; JV Wrstlng; High Hon Roll; NHS; U Of CA; Sci.

JUNG, BOBBY; Crescenta Valley HS; La Crescenta, CA; (2); Church Yth Grp; Key Clb; Letterman Clb; Math Clb; Mu Alpha Theta; Spanish Clb; Yrbk; Swmmng; Kiwanis Awd; Prfct Atten Awd; Water Polo; CSF Treas; Swmmng Leag Chmpns.

JUNG, JENNIFER D; Skyline HS; Oakland, CA; (4); High Hon Roll; Hon Roll; Pres Acad Fit Awd; Envirnmntl Clb; Amnesty Intl.

JUNG, JEREMY A; Savanna HS; Buena Park, CA; (2); Boy Scts; Church Yth Grp; JA; Science Clb; Trk; JV Wrstlng; High Hon Roll; Arch.

JUNG, JOANNE; Cerritos HS; Artesia, CA; (3); Cmnty Wkr; Pres FBLA; JV Swmmng; Hon Roll; Octagon Clb Sr Rep; Pacific Asian Clb Pre.

JUNG, JULIANE K; Westmoor HS; Daly City, CA; (3); French Clb; VP German Clb; GAA; Service Clb; SADD; Rep Jr Cls; Var Tennis; Hon Roll.

JUNG, KENNETH W; Lowell HS; San Francisco, CA; (3); Cmnty Wkr; Library Aide; ROTC; Ed Nwsp; Intrml Sftbl; JV Trk; NEDT Awd; CSF; Elec Engrng.

JUNG, PARKIN; Lowell HS; San Francisco, CA; (3); Teachers Aide; Korean Clb; Gldn St Exam Geo.

JUNG, SEONG; Woodrow Wilson HS; Long Beach, CA; (2); Arch.

JUNG, SEUNG; J F Kennedy HS; La Palma, CA; (3); Church Yth Grp; Chrmn Computer Clb; Key Clb; Speech Tm; Varsity Clb; Var Ftbl; Var L Tennis; Hon Roll; Pres Acad Fit Awd; CSF; Med.

JUNG, WEYLAND; South Pasadena HS; Pasadena, CA; (4); Cmnty Wkr; Spanish Clb; Jazz Band; Pres Orch; School Musical; Mgr(s); Var JV Vllybl; Ntl Merit Schol; Pres Acad Fit Awd; California Scholarship Federation; Volleyball Rottender League First Team; U Of Ca Irvine; Economics.

JUNGBLUTH, BRETT; Galt HS; Galt, CA; (3); JV Bsbl; Golden St Exam In Algebra I; Golden St Exam In Geom & US Hstry; Pol Sci.

JUNOD, ANN; Rio Americano HS; Sacramento, CA; (3); 29/288; Church Yth Grp; Teachers Aide; School Musical; School Play; Stage Crew; Hon Roll; Rdrs Theater Prod; Comm Dept Awd Bronze, Slvr, Gold; Dept Awds Frnch, Bio, Readers Theater; Lib Arts.

JUNTADO, JENNIFER; Wilcox HS; Santa Clara, CA; (3); FTA; VP Service Clb; Ed Lit Mag; Rally Cncl; Law.

JUNTTI, HELEN M; Sacramento HS; Sacramento, CA; (2); 152/500; Church Yth Grp; Drama Clb; Hosp Aide; Red Cross Aide; Church Choir; Soph Cls; Jr Cls; Am Red Cross Yth Svc Pgm-Pres; Elem Ed.

JURACH, MATT G; El Camino Fundamental HS; Sacramento, CA; (3); 40/370; Church Yth Grp; Latin Clb; Office Aide; Band; Church Choir; NHS; On-Campus Bible Study Mem; Photo Stu Of Yr; Math Tutor.

JURADO, JENNIFER N; Tokay HS; Stockton, CA; (2); 7/650; German Clb; Model UN; High Hon Roll; Dance Co; Fresh Orientation Facilitator; Bus.

JURADO, MICHAEL C; Patrick Henry HS; San Diego, CA; (2); Letterman Clb; JV Bsbl; Cit Awd; High Hon Roll; NHS; Pres Acad Fit Awd.

JURADO, TANYA S; Mayfield SR Schl; San Gabriel, CA; (3); 4/43; AFS; GAA; Var Socr; Var Trk; Hon Roll; CSF; Intl Poli Sci.

JURADO, XAVIER O; Don Bosco Technical Inst; San Gabriel, CA; (2); Sci.

JURGENSEN, PAMELA J; Cordova SR HS; Rancho Cordova, CA; (4); 82/467; Church Yth Grp; Teachers Aide; Church Choir; Yrbk; Lit Mag; 2nd Pl Public Schls Wk Essay Cont; CA Schlrshp Fed; Outstndng Achvt Flds Lf Sci/Engl; Fash Dsgn.

JURGENSON, BILLY R; Paradise HS; Paradise, CA; (2); 39/225; Letterman Clb; JV Bsbl; JV Ftbl; Var Socr; Hon Roll; CSF; UCLA; Phys Ed.

JURGENSON, COLBY A; San Ramon Valley HS; Danville, CA; (2); Cmnty Wkr; JV Bsktbl; Var Ftbl; Var Trk; Hndcppd Chllngr Leag Bsbl Buddy.

JUSSEL, AUDRA ANNE; Grace Davis HS; Modesto, CA; (2); German Clb; Hosp Aide; JV Bsktbl; JV Powder Puff Ftbl; JV Sftbl; Var Trk; Hon Roll; MGSL; Saturday Night Live Clb; UCLA; Phys Thrpy.

JUST, WINDY; Redwood HS; Visalia, CA; (3); 16/280; Key Clb; Q&S; SADD; Ed Nwsp; Var Crs Cntry; JV Var Tennis; Hon Roll; Rqt Clb Sec; Mck Trl Tm; Rlly Clb; Peer Cnslr; Pepperdine U; Communications.

JUSTHAM, MICHELLE D; Del Campo HS; Citrus Heights, CA; (2); 37/460; German Clb; CA Schlrshp Fed; Friday Night Live.

JUSTICE, TERRI D; Yreka HS; Yreka, CA; (4); 5/170; Church Yth Grp; Treas FHA; Teachers Aide; Capt Drill Tm; Mrchg Band; Var Trk; High Hon Roll; Pres Acad Fit Awd; Rotary Awd; St Schlr; Natl Yng Ldrshp Cncl; Engrng.

JUSTICE, YVETTE; Thousand Oaks HS; West Lake Village, CA; (3); 90/595; Church Yth Grp; Debate Tm; Drama Clb; French Clb; Math Tm; Model UN; NFL; Speech Tm; SADD; Acpl Chr; Mock Trial; GLADD; CSF.

JUSTIN, JAMES K; Rim Of The World HS; Running Springs, CA; (3); 86/259; Boy Scts; Letterman Clb; Var L Crs Cntry; Var L Trk; Hon Roll; Prfct Atten Awd; Pharoh Of The Flying Buffaloes Intl Ltd Clb Pres; U Of CA Riverside; Physics.

JUSTIN, SHAWNITA L; Rowland HS; Walnut, CA; (2); Church Yth Grp; Dance Clb; GAA; Nwsp; Bsktbl; Cheerldng; Trk; Cit Awd; High Hon Roll; Hon Roll; Media Commnctns.

JUSTINIANI, MARITONI J; Pinole Valley HS; Pinole, CA; (3); Church Yth Grp; Drama Clb; Math Clb; Science Clb; School Play; Treas Frsh Cls; Hon Roll; Sal; SCORE; Med.

JUUL-BORRE, SARAH; Templeton HS; Templeton, CA; (2); 4/80; Church Yth Grp; Orch; Cit Awd; High Hon Roll; Hon Roll; Fllwshp Chrstn Stu Sec.

JUVERA, CHRISTINA E; Modesto HS; Modesto, CA; (1); Church Yth Grp; Band; Church Choir; Mrchg Band; Pep Band; Prfct Atten Awd; Pdtrcn.

JUWONO, JULIA; Whitney HS; Cerritos, CA; (2); 45/168; Key Clb; Nwsp; Var Bsktbl; JV Tennis; Med.

KAAS, ELIZABETH A; Brea-Olinda HS; Brea, CA; (2); Drama Clb; Speech Tm; School Play; Stage Crew; Hon Roll; Lion Awd; Art.

KABISAMA, TAYAMIKA A; Etiwanda HS; Cucamonga, CA; (2); Church Yth Grp; Dance Clb; French Clb; Drill Tm; Hon Roll; Black Stu Union; Berkley; Attorney.

KABOUR, PHIL M; Novato HS; Novato, CA; (4); 1/269; Church Yth Grp; Key Clb; Socr; High Hon Roll; Pres Acad Fit Awd; Val; UC Davis; Envrmntl Sci.

KACHIRISKY, CARMINA; James A Garfield HS; Los Angeles, CA; (3); FTA; ROTC; Orch; Hon Roll; Prfct Atten Awd; Outstndng Mexican-Amer Stds Achvt; UCLA; Elem Ed.

KACKMEISTER, ALAN; Arroyo Grande HS; Arroyo Grande, CA; (4); 9/394; Am Leg Boys St; Church Yth Grp; Band; Jazz Band; Mrchg Band; Sprt Ed Yrbk; Treas Frsh Cls; Var L Crs Cntry; Var L Socr; Var L Trk; Natl Schlr/Athlte Awd 90; St/Natl Histry Day Awd 89; Bank Amer Yth Achvt Awd; U Of CA Berkeley; Physics.

KADA, KATHRYN A; Mountain View HS; Mountain View, CA; (2); High Hon Roll; Prfct Atten Awd; Asian Clb; San Jose ST; Lbrn.

KADAKIA, ANISH K; Whitney HS; Cerritos, CA; (1); Boy Scts; Computer Clb; Model UN; Trk; Cit Awd; High Hon Roll; Hon Roll; Medcl.

KADDEN, JASON B; El Camino HS; West Hills, CA; (3); Cmnty Wkr; Math Clb; SADD; Prfct Atten Awd; Los Angeles Marthn Atten; Asst Coach Woodland Hlls & West Hls Prks & Recrtn Dept; AZ ST U; Arch.

KADISON, JENNIFER L; John H Francis Polytechnic HS; North Hollywood, CA; (3); Drama Clb; French Clb; School Play; Hon Roll; Outstndng Stu Awd; Frnch Cls Cert Mrt; Psych.

KAFATI, JOSEPH O; Encina HS; Sacramento, CA; (3); JV Var Bsktbl; Cit Awd; High Hon Roll; Most Imprvd Plyr Bsktbl; CSUS; Bus.

KAFKA, JULIE; Fullerton Union HS; Fullerton, CA; (4); 16/325; Cmnty Wkr; Dance Clb; Hosp Aide; Pep Clb; Ski Clb; Teachers Aide; Drill Tm; JV Bsktbl; JV Var Cheerldng; Var Pom Pon; Natl Chrty Leag; Sailing, Skiing; UC Santa Barbara.

KAGAY, JANINE R; Covina HS; Covina, CA; (4); Church Yth Grp; Pres Debate Tm; Sec FFA; Speech Tm; SADD; Church Choir; Gym; Vllybl; Hon Roll; Lion Awd; FFA Schlrshp; ST FFA Deg; De Calb Wnr FFA Awd; Vet Med.

KAHKEDJIAN, AIDA; Pasadena HS; Pasadena, CA; (4); Church Yth Grp; Cmnty Wkr; JA; Speech Tm; Debate Tm; Drama Clb; Model UN; Office Aide; Teachers Aide; Church Choir; Photo 3 Yrs; Music; Chrch Actvts; Pasadena City Coll; Crmnl Law.

KAHLER, LYNDSAY R; Orange Lutheran HS; Santa Ana, CA; (2); Church Yth Grp; Scholastic Bowl; Chorus; Church Choir; School Musical; Nwsp; Var Crs Cntry; Var Trk; High Hon Roll; Pres Jr NHS; Outstndng Concert Choir Schlrshp; Audition To Unlimited Warranty; Hlth 3rd Pl 89; Essay Hlth 5th Pl 90; Music.

KAHN, JULIE; Palisades HS; Los Angeles, CA; (4); 12/455; Cmnty Wkr; Ski Clb; Chorus; VP Sr Cls; VP Stu Cncl; Capt Socr; Trk; Cit Awd; Saferides Coordinator; Wrtng Cont 1st Pl Wnnr.

KAHN, KAREN; San Luis Obispo HS; San Luis Obispo, CA; (3); 80/315; Church Yth Grp; Chorus; Church Choir; Stu Cncl; Var Cheerldng; Powder Puff Ftbl; JV Swmmng; Presdntl Clssrm Rep; Camp Fire; Cal Poly; Child Dev.

KAHN, MARLO A; Miramonte HS; Orinda, CA; (4); Cmnty Wkr; Hosp Aide; NFL; Speech Tm; Rep Soph Cls; Rep Jr Cls; Rep Stu Cncl; Tennis; Voice Dem Awd; Stanford U.

KAHN, SHANA; Lynbrook HS; San Jose, CA; (3); 59/284; FBLA; NFL; Pep Clb; Spanish Clb; Speech Tm; Teachers Aide; Rptr Lit Mag; Stu Cncl; Capt Cheerldng; Stat Wrstlng; VP GATE Clb; Schl Site Cncl; Mst Dedctd JV Sprtldr 88-89; Pre-Law.

KAHNG, MAY; Glen A Wilson HS; Hacienda Hts, CA; (2); Art Clb; Key Clb; Band; Mrchg Band; Var Trk; Hon Roll; Prfct Atten Awd; Amerasian Clb; Wind Ensmbl; CA Schlrshp Fed.

KAIDIN, SHERI ALISSA; Sherman Oaks Center For Enrich Studies; Van Nuys, CA; (3); Dance Clb; Pep Clb; Spanish Clb; Co-Capt Cheerldng; Powder Puff Ftbl; High Hon Roll; Hon Roll; CA Schlrshp Fed; Schl Safety Svc; UC Santa Barbara Outstndng Schlr; Brdcst Commnctns.

KAING, HUOT; John Glenn HS; Norwalk, CA; (3); Chess Clb; Var Science Clb; Var Tennis; Sci; Engrng.

KAIO, BARBARA T; Lowell HS; San Francisco, CA; (3); Cmnty Wkr; Chorus; School Musical; Amnesty Intl; Japanese Clb; Cult Film Clb; CCSF; Psych.

KAISER, POLLY E; Amos Alonzo Stagg HS; Stockton, CA; (1); Debate Tm; Speech Tm; Thesps; School Musical; School Play; Socr; Tennis; High Hon Roll; Lndry Svc Ownr; UCLA; Math.

KAISER, VANESSA Y; Mt Whitney HS; Visalia, CA; (4); FBLA; Spanish Clb; Hon Roll; Pres Acad Fit Awd; CA Schlrshp Fed; CSUF Rodman Schlrshp; Schlrshp Ca Assoc Of Educl Office Profssnls; CUSF; Bus Admin.

KAJI, CHRISTOPHER K; Livingston HS; Livingston, CA; (2); Church Yth Grp; Cmnty Wkr; Rep Stu Cncl; JV Var Bsbl; JV Var Ftbl; Mgr(s); Wt Lftg; Var Wrstlng; High Hon Roll; St Schlr; UC; Bus.

KAJIKAWA, GAVIN T; San Gabriel HS; San Gabriel, CA; (2); Boy Scts; Church Yth Grp; VP JA; Rep Frsh Cls; Rep Soph Cls; JV Ftbl; Capt JV Socr; Var Swmmng; Hon Roll; YMCA Hi-Y Clb Sec, Pres; UCLA; Sprts Med.

KAJITANI, ALEX T; Irvine HS; Irvine, CA; (3); 54/512; Cmnty Wkr; Teachers Aide; Stu Cncl; Swmmng; High Hon Roll; 3 Yr Vrsty Lttrmn Water Polo; Yth Of Mnth; CA Schlrshp Fed.

KAKAR, AMIT; Whitney HS; Cerritos, CA; (1); Key Clb; JV Bsktbl; JV Tennis; PA U; Bus.

KAKIGI, SEAN T; El Cerrito HS; Kensington, CA; (2); Band; JV Tennis; High Hon Roll.

KAKIMOTO, CHARLENE V; Marina HS; Huntington Beach, CA; (3); German Clb; Hosp Aide; Varsity Clb; Yrbk; Pres Jr Cls; Stu Cncl; JV Bsktbl; JV Tennis; Var Trk; Hon Roll; Golden Shield Awd, German; Jeweled Trident Awd, Svc Awd; Prom Jr Princess; CA Girls St Fnlst; Med.

KALAGAYAN, NORIE; Calvary Baptist HS; Suisun City, CA; (3); Church Yth Grp; Pep Clb; School Play; Yrbk; Sec Jr Cls; Var Bsktbl; Vllybl; Cit Awd; Hon Roll; Chrstn Character Awd; Pastors Awd; Bob Jones U; Med.

KALCEVICH, KELLY R; Atwater HS; Atwater, CA; (1); Dance Clb; Cheerldng; Trk; Hon Roll; Ntl Merit Ltr; MECCA Prgm; Med.

KALE, DAVID; Imperial HS; Pasadena, CA; (1); Church Yth Grp; Computer Clb; Spanish Clb; Chorus; School Musical; Intrml Bsktbl; Trk; Cit Awd; Hon Roll; Ambassador Coll; Comp.

KALEMBER, STEVE M; Santa Clara HS; Oxnard, CA; (3); Letterman Clb; Varsity Clb; Sec Jr Cls; Crs Cntry; Socr; USC; Bus Admin.

KALFAYAN, MARY S; Ferrahian HS; Van Nuys, CA; (3); Drama Clb; Quiz Bowl; Cheerldng; Trk; Vllybl; Ntl Merit Ltr; AYF; Vol Spec Olympics 89; Med.

KALIFON, MICOLE; Santa Monica HS; Malibu, CA; (3); SADD; Chorus; Hon Roll.

KALINO, HEATHER J; East Union HS; Manteca, CA; (3); Am Leg Aux Girls St; FFA; Letterman Clb; Varsity Clb; JV Capt Vllybl; Cit Awd; Hon Roll; Grls St Alt; Outstndng Angus Exhbtr 90; Natl Jr Angus Assoc Delg; San Luis Obispo CA Poly; Ag.

KALIS, NICOLE L; Clear Lake HS; Lakeport, CA; (3); 3/81; Am Leg Aux Girls St; Office Aide; SADD; Chorus; VP Sr Cls; Stu Cncl; Hon Roll; Germany 87 & 89; U Of CA; Intl Law.

KALISH, ROBIN E; Rio Americano HS; Sacramento, CA; (3); 20/320; Cmnty Wkr; French Clb; Science Clb; Temple Yth Grp; School Play; Stage Crew; Hon Roll; Ntl Merit Ltr; Flute; Psych.

KALKAT, RAVINDER K; Gridley HS; Gridley, CA; (3); 10/120; Pres Church Yth Grp; Cmnty Wkr; Drama Clb; VP French Clb; Office Aide; Speech Tm; SADD; Stage Crew; Variety Show; Sec Sr Cls; CSF; Migrant Educ Stu Yr 90; ASB Elctns Snr Cls Sectry; CA ST U Chico; Comp Sci.

KALLA, JASON S; Don Lugo HS; Chino, CA; (1); Church Yth Grp; Hon Roll; Prfct Atten Awd; Smmr Schlrshp Art Ctr Coll Of Dsgn 90; Art Ctr Coll Of Dsgn; Trnsprtn.

KALLENBERGER, KATHRYN; West HS; Bakersfield, CA; (4); 25/394; Dance Clb; Debate Tm; GAA; Letterman Clb; Pep Clb; Service Clb; Ed Bus Profs of Am; Stu Cncl; Cheerldng; Swmmng; Gldn St Exam Alg; Bnk Amer Achvt Awd Engl; Bakersfield Coll.

KALLENBERGER, LINDA G; St Bernard HS; Los Angeles, CA; (3); SADD; JV Crs Cntry; L JV Trk; L Var Vllybl; High Hon Roll; Hon Roll; VP NHS; NEDT Awd; Camp Fire Yth Org; CSF.

KALMAN, JULIANNE E; Santa Teresa HS; San Jose, CA; (3); 39/467; Spanish Clb; SADD; Varsity Clb; Crs Cntry; Socr; Sftbl; Trk; Bio.

KALMAN, KATRINA; Santa Teresa HS; San Jose, CA; (4); 19/520; Intnl Clb; Pep Clb; Q&S; Science Clb; Ski Clb; Spanish Clb; SADD; Mgr Nwsp; Stu Cncl; Var Capt Cheerldng; Schl Cty Mock Trial Team; UC San Deigo; Poltcl Sci.

KALRA, ANKUR; Mission San Jose HS; Fremont, CA; (1); 2/30; Church Yth Grp; Ski Clb; Intrml Tennis; Cit Awd; Gov Hon Prg Awd; High Hon Roll; Pres Schlr.

KALT, VIRGINIA; Valley HS; Elk Grove, CA; (2); 89/213; Intnl Clb; Spanish Clb; High Hon Roll; Hon Roll; Prfct Atten Awd; Riding & Shwng Horses; CO ST U; Equine Sci.

KALUA, JEANNINE K; P U C Prep; Angwin, CA; (3); Church Yth Grp; Hosp Aide; Spanish Clb; Acpl Chr; Psychlgy.

KAM, SHERRIE I; San Gorgonio HS; Highland, CA; (3); 41/430; Treas Key Clb; Science Clb; High Hon Roll; NHS; Prfct Atten Awd; Pres Spanish NHS; Rotary Life Prgm Pres & VP; UC Irvine; Bus.

KAM, STEVEN; Bellarmine College Prep; Sunnyvale, CA; (1); Debate Tm; Latin Clb; NFL; Jr NHS.

KAM, STEVEN; Lowell HS; San Francisco, CA; (3); Hon Roll; Kiwanis Awd; Pres Acad Fit Awd; GSE Geo Hnrs; UC-DAVIS; Arch.

KAM, YOUNG S; Whitney HS; Norwalk, CA; (1); Pres Church Yth Grp; Debate Tm; Drama Clb; Hist Key Clb; Sec Model UN; Treas Ski Clb; School Play; Variety Show; Phtg Yrbk; Lit Mag; Conf Bst Delg Awd; Swmmng Leag Fnlst; Mock Trial Bst Defense Attorney; Yale; Crmnl Law.

KAMACHI, KEITH M; Etiwanda HS; Alta Loma, CA; (3); Hon Roll; Engrng.

KAMARGA, LISA; Canyon Springs HS; Moreno Valley, CA; (4); Art Clb; Church Yth Grp; Hon Roll; Riverside CC; Graphic Dsgn.

KAMBAK, JENNIFER; Rosary HS; Fullerton, CA; (2); Cmnty Wkr; Hosp Aide; VP Frsh Cls; Rep Soph Cls; Var Socr; Var Swmmng; Var Tennis; High Hon Roll; Athlt Yr; Cty Fullerton Stu Recgntn Awd.

KAMBITSCH, KRIS M; Santa Cruz HS; Santa Cruz, CA; (3); Hon Roll; Cert Excllnc Outstndng Achvt Lang Arts; Won Essay Cont JR Yr; CA U Santa Cruz; Teaching.

KAMEDA, TOSH; Mountain View HS; Mountain View, CA; (3); 16/319; VP Chess Clb; Pres VP Church Yth Grp; Band; Church Choir; Jazz Band; Mrchg Band; School Musical; High Hon Roll; CSF; Brown Blt Judo; 89 & 90 CA St Judo Chmpnshps; 89 US Judo Fed Jr Natnls; Math.

KAMENY, STEVEN C; Lowell HS; San Francisco, CA; (2); Debate Tm; Drama Clb; NFL; Speech Tm; St Schlr; Short Story Clb; Cult Film Clb; U Of CA; Law.

KAMIGAKI, ALISA; Lincoln HS; Stockton, CA; (3); 22/592; Hist Church Yth Grp; Hosp Aide; Mu Alpha Theta; Mgr Ed Yrbk; Var L Tennis; High Hon Roll; CSF; San Joaquin Vly Schlstc Prss Assn; Yrbk Dsgn 1st Pl; Assisteens; Cmmnty Vlntr; Lib Arts.

KAMIN, MARIA L; Louisville HS; Woodland Hills, CA; (1); Church Yth Grp; Chorus; JV Tennis; High Hon Roll.

KAMINSKI, CHAD F; Lincoln HS; Stockton, CA; (3); Office Aide; Teachers Aide; Band; Jazz Band; Mrchg Band; School Musical; Hon Roll; Cngrssnl Yth Ldrshp Cncl; Berklee Schl Of Music; Music.

KAMINSKI, LORI K; California HS; San Ramon, CA; (3); Ski Clb; High Hon Roll; Hon Roll; CA ST Hayward; Nrsng.

KAMISHER, ROBYN H; Birmingham HS; Encino, CA; (2); FBLA; GAA; SADD; Off Frsh Cls; JV Sftbl; JV Tennis; Hon Roll; 1st Pl Jesse Owens Games; 2nd Tm All Stars JV Sftbl; Johns Hopkins U; Genetic Engr.

KAMIYAMA, KENNETH; Seaside HS; Fort Ord, CA; (2); Spanish Clb; Band; Mrchg Band; Orch; Hon Roll; UC Riverside; Pre-Med.

KAMMERER, MIKE; Newport Harbor HS; Fountain Valley, CA; (3); 25/360; Church Yth Grp; German Clb; Teachers Aide; High Hon Roll; CSF; U CA Irvine; MD.

KAMMINGA, NIKKI; Newark Memorial HS; Newark, CA; (3); 24/545; Library Aide; Office Aide; SADD; Teachers Aide; School Play; Stu Cncl; High Hon Roll; Hon Roll; FIDM San Francisco; Fshn Dsgnr.

KAMOSHITA, AILEEN Y; Schurr HS; Montebello, CA; (1); French Clb; Band; Mrchg Band; Rptr Nwsp; High Hon Roll; Hon Roll; Prfct Atten Awd; Music.

KAMPER, DAVID M; Newport Harbor HS; Newport Beach, CA; (3); 3/350; Temple Yth Grp; Sec Sr Cls; Church Yth Grp; E I Moore & USC Bk Awds.

KAMPER, RHONDA; Mountain Empire HS; Campo, CA; (2); 3/110; Treas 4-H; VP German Clb; Letterman Clb; Pres Band; Capt JV Bsktbl; JV L Sftbl; JV L Vllybl; 4-H Awd; Var L High Hon Roll; Photo Club; Ricks JC; Sprts Med.

KAMPERMAN, PRO Q; Santa Clara HS; Santa Clara, CA; (2); Var Ftbl; JV Tennis; Var Wrstlng; High Hon Roll; Hon Roll; NEDT Awd; Prfct Atten Awd; Hgh Hnrs Wnnr Natl Poppy Math Tst.

KAMPF, KIMBERLY L; Yucaipa HS; Yucaipa, CA; (3); Church Yth Grp; Spanish Clb; Nwsp; Var L Tennis; Alive Clb; Drafting; Arch.

KAMRAS, JASON S; Rio Americano HS; Carmichael, CA; (3); 1/290; Spanish Clb; Lit Mag; Treas Frsh Cls; Treas Pres Stu Cncl; Var JV Swmmng; High Hon Roll; Pres Acad Fit Awd; United Synagogue Yth; Stu Reaching Out; Jr Statesmen Of Amer; Pol Sci.

KAN, ANDREW K; San Leandro HS; San Leandro, CA; (3); 12/360; Math Tm; JV Crs Cntry; Var L Socr; JV Tennis; JV Trk; High Hon Roll; Gldn St Exam Alg & Geom High Honors; UC Berkeley; Engrng.

KAN, ANNA S; Lowell HS; San Francisco, CA; (3); Red Cross Aide; Science Clb; SADD; Teachers Aide; Rptr Nwsp; Shield & Scroll Hnr Scty; CA Schlrshp Fdrtn; Brd Of Schl & Cmmnty Srvcs.

KAN, ERIN; Crescenta Valley HS; La Canada, CA; (4); 1/400; Dance Clb; VP French Clb; Pres Mu Alpha Theta; Orch; Ed Nwsp; Ed Lit Mag; Sec Stu Cncl; Cheerldng; NHS; Pres Acad Fit Awd; Stanford U.

KAN, FARAND C; Whitney HS; Cerritos, CA; (3); French Clb; Pres Latin Clb; Band; Off Nwsp; Var Swmmng; High Hon Roll; Ntl Merit Ltr; Chinese Clb VP; CSF.

KAN, HORACE C; Whitney HS; Cerritos, CA; (4); Church Yth Grp; FBLA; Hosp Aide; Var Swmmng; Ntl Merit SF; Pres Acad Fit Awd; UC Berkley.

KAN, SANDY PUI SHAN; Phillip & Sala Burton Academic HS; San Francisco, CA; (4); Cmnty Wkr; High Hon Roll; Sci Fiction Club; Awds Trig; Part-Time Worker; Doctor.

KAN, SOPHIA; San Leandro HS; San Leandro, CA; (4); 33/347; Cmnty Wkr; Hosp Aide; Library Aide; Service Clb; Teachers Aide; Var L Trk; High Hon Roll; CA Schlrshp Fed; CA ST U Hayward; Nrsng.

KANCHIAN, VIVIAN; Herbert Hoover HS; Glendale, CA; (3); Girl Scts; Teachers Aide; Glendale CC.

KANDA, SNEH L; Kennedy HS; La Palma, CA; (2); FBLA; Hosp Aide; Library Aide; Ed Nwsp; Bsktbl; Pres Acad Fit Awd; Cmnty Wkr; Rcvd Plaques For Bst Health & Ftr Stories Schl Nwspr 89-90; Dbls Plyr JV Bdmntn Tm; CSF; Med.

KANDARIAN, GINA Y; Fowler HS; Fowler, CA; (3); 17/100; Church Yth Grp; Drama Clb; FCA; Pep Clb; Spanish Clb; Rptr Nwsp; Sec Frsh Cls; VP Soph Cls; Sec Stu Cncl; Var Cheerldng; CSF; Prm Chrmn; Fresno City Coll; Law.

KANE, BRIAN F; St Bonaventure HS; Thousand Oaks, CA; (3); 1/125; Church Yth Grp; Hosp Aide; Crs Cntry; Cit Awd; Hon Roll; NHS; Ntl Merit SF; Interact Cmmty Svc Clb; Kenpo Karate; Nwsp Carrier; Los Robdes Hosp Vlntr; Loyola Marymount U; Bio.

KANE, ELIZABETH; Bishop O'dowd HS; Alameda, CA; (3); Ski Clb; Ed Yrbk; Chld Psych.

KANE, JAMIE LYNN; Vallejo SR HS; Vallejo, CA; (3); Office Aide; SADD; Ed Nwsp; Pres Frsh Cls; JV Cheerldng; JV Sftbl; Hon Roll; Jr NHS; Tanner Project; Lucy Fuller Memrl Awd; Spelman Coll; Elem Ed.

KANE, JAY L; Montgomery HS; Santa Rosa, CA; (3); French Clb; Orch; High Hon Roll; Hnr Scty Trea; Boys St; Pomona Coll; Math.

KANE, LUKE A; Ukiah HS; Ukiah, CA; (2); Bsbl; JV Tennis; JV Wrstlng; Tennis; UC Berkeley; Frnch.

KANE, SONYA J; Atwater HS; Winton, CA; (1); JV Bsktbl; Var Sftbl; High Hon Roll; CA Schlrshp Fed; Scl Sci.

KANE, TRINA R; Vacaville HS; Vacaville, CA; (3); Drill Tm; School Musical; School Play; Stage Crew; Drama.

KANEMARKI, TRENT J; Sunny Hills HS; Fullerton, CA; (3); 13/475; Boy Scts; Chess Clb; Church Yth Grp; Cmnty Wkr; Treas Pres Frsh Cls; Stu Cncl; Swmmng; Cit Awd; High Hon Roll; Jr NHS; Bronze Awd; Hnrs Englsh; Ldrshp Awd; JR Gold & Silver Awds; Sci.

KANEMOTO, ERIC R; Armijo HS; Fairfield, CA; (2); Church Yth Grp; Socr; High Hon Roll; CA Schlrshp Fed; Comp; Comp Sci.

KANENOBU, SONOKO K; Arcadia HS; Sierra Madre, CA; (3); 169/639; Debate Tm; Drill Tm; JV Trk; JV Vllybl; Hon Roll; Piano.

KANG, ANNE C; San Dieguito HS; Carlsbad, CA; (2); JV Tennis; Elks Awd; High Hon Roll; Hon Roll; Prfct Atten Awd; Pres Acad Fit Awd; CSF; Piano Level 8 Cert Mrt & Bach Fest Wnnr; Phrmcy.

KANG, BETTY; Arcadia HS; Arcadia, CA; (2); Church Yth Grp; Intnl Clb; Math Clb; Office Aide; Teachers Aide; Church Choir; Flag Corp; Vllybl; Hon Roll; A Cad Excllnc Awd Gldn St Exam; MIT; Dsgn.

KANG, BINNAH; Agoura HS; Agoura Hills, CA; (3); Church Yth Grp; Sec FBLA; Pres Key Clb; Latin Clb; SADD; Church Choir; Nwsp; JV Trk; Hon Roll; Comm.

KANG, CHANBOREMEY; Woodrow Wilson HS; Long Beach, CA; (3); 2/32; French Clb; JA; Spanish Clb; NHS; CSF; Far East Cntry Clb; CSULB; Bus.

KANG, DANIEL; Skyline HS; Oakland, CA; (3); 8/650; Cmnty Wkr; Key Clb; Church Choir; Orch; Var Tennis; High Hon Roll; Ntl Merit Ltr; Yth Act Dir Church Day Camp; Pomona Coll; Bus.

KANG, ESTHER; Alisal HS; Salinas, CA; (3); JA; Treas Soph Cls; Var Cheerldng; JV Var Powder Puff Ftbl; Var Tennis; JV Trk; Cit Awd; Gov Hon Prg Awd; High Hon Roll; Hon Roll; CSF; Jostens Top Ten Awd; Hnrs & Advncd Plcmnt Classes; Stanford; Psych.

KANG, ESTHER M; Van Nuys HS; Los Angeles, CA; (4); 47/550; Sec Natl Beta Clb; Orch; Rep Frsh Cls; Treas Jr Cls; Treas Sr Cls; Pres Treas Stu Cncl; Elks Awd; High Hon Roll; Pres Acad Fit Awd; N Hollywood Rtry Outstndng Grad Awd; CA Schlrshp Fed Gold Seal Bearer; U Of Soutehrn CA; Phrmcy.

KANG, FERNANDO C; Warren HS; Downey, CA; (3); Computer Clb; Debate Tm; Key Clb; Science Clb; Mrchg Band; Orch; Pep Band; Cit Awd; High Hon Roll; CSF; Golden Bear Cert; Golden St Exam Acadmc Excllnc Awd; UCLA; Engrng.

KANG, HEERA S; Irvine HS; Irvine, CA; (2); Church Yth Grp; Intnl Clb; Key Clb; Chorus; Church Choir; Drill Tm; JV Trk; Hon Roll; Russia & Europe Mission Chorus; Chrch Yth Grp Ldrshp; Drll Tm; Nurse.

KANG, HELEN; John A Rowland HS; Rowland Heights, CA; (2); #1 In Class; Church Yth Grp; Science Clb; Spanish Clb; Ed Nwsp; JV Vllybl; High Hon Roll; Pres Acad Fit Awd; GSE Geom High Hnrs; Alg I Hgh Hnrs; Maintained 4.0 GPA; CSF; CSF Clb VP; UC Schl; Doctor.

KANG, JAE K; Sunny Hills HS; Fullerton, CA; (3); 1/430; Cmnty Wkr; Key Clb; Pres Spanish Clb; Bausch & Lomb Sci Awd; High Hon Roll; JETS Awd; NHS; Ntl Merit SF; Frnscs Clb Pres; OCAD Capt.

KANG, JANE; Warren HS; Downey, CA; (4); 1/415; Pres VP Church Yth Grp; Treas Key Clb; Sec Treas Service Clb; Treas Spanish Clb; Var Trk; Var Capt Vllybl; Rotary Awd; Bk Amer Achvt Awd Fnlst Sci/Math; Vol Mnth Awd; Sci Olympiad Tm; Biochem.

KANG, JEAN M; Lowell HS; San Francisco, CA; (2); Treas Church Yth Grp; Band; Rep Frsh Cls; Rep Soph Cls; JV Trk; Stdy Law Oxford Trdtn Prog Oxford England 90.

KANG, JEAN Y; Homestead HS; Sunnyvale, CA; (1); Hon Roll; Jr NHS; Cert Hnr; UC Berkeley.

KANG, KIRANDEEP K; Sequoia HS; Redwood City, CA; (3); #1 In Class; Treas Service Clb; Ed Nwsp; Rep Stu Cncl; Bausch & Lomb Sci Awd; Lion Awd.

KANG, MARGARET K; Esperanza HS; Yorba Linda, CA; (2); Church Yth Grp; Cmnty Wkr; Intnl Clb; Teachers Aide; Acpl Chr; JV Trk; High Hon Roll; NHS; Top 25; U CA Davis; Vet Med.

KANG, MARK C; Artesia HS; Cerritos, CA; (2); Rep Intnl Clb; Rep Science Clb; Rep Spanish Clb; Rep Soph Cls; JV Tennis; Hon Roll; Interact Clb; UCLA; Ped.

KANG, MICHAEL M; Mayfair HS; Lakewood, CA; (2); Computer Clb; Math Clb; Science Clb; Orch; JV Bsktbl; JV Crs Cntry; Cit Awd; Hon Roll; Prfct Atten Awd; Pres Acad Fit Awd; U Of CA.

KANG, MOON-KYOO; Artesia HS; Hawaiian Gardens, CA; (2); Church Yth Grp; Intnl Clb; Science Clb; Vllybl; High Hon Roll; CSF; Interact Clb; Korean Clb VP; Engrng.

KANG, MYONG J; Monterey HS; Seaside, CA; (3); Chess Clb; Temple Yth Grp; Stat Socr; Hon Roll; Monterey Peninsula Coll; Phlspy.

KANG, PHILIP W; John F Kennedy HS; La Palma, CA; (3); Chess Clb; Computer Clb; Key Clb; Ed Nwsp; JV Tennis; High Hon Roll; Hon Roll; Pres Acad Fit Awd; Gldn St Exam Hi Hnrs Alg & Geom; Undergraduate Awd Hlth Educ; U CA Berkeley.

KANG, REYNOLD D; Burbank SR HS; Burbank, CA; (3); Intnl Clb; Math Clb; Orch; Bsktbl; Cit Awd; Hon Roll; Pre Med.

KANG, RICHARD C; San Ramon Valley HS; Danville, CA; (3); 60/300; FBLA; Key Clb; Teachers Aide; JV Crs Cntry; Var Socr; Var Trk; JV Vllybl; High Hon Roll; Hon Roll; Acad Decathlon Team; Principals Schlr Athl Awd; UC Irvine; Sports Med.

KANG, SUNGHOON; Hoover HS; Glendale, CA; (3); Pres Church Yth Grp; Intnl Clb; JCL; Latin Clb; ROTC; Teachers Aide; Trk; High Hon Roll; Prfct Atten Awd; CSF; Chem Engrng.

KANG, TYLER; Dana Hills HS; Laguna Niguel, CA; (1); Spanish Clb; Cit Awd; Hon Roll; High Achvt Awd In Math; Bio Achvt Awd; Stanford; Med.

KANG, WENDY; Piedmont HS; Piedmont, CA; (3); French Clb; Intnl Clb; Math Clb; Math Tm; Science Clb; Orch; School Musical; Prfct Atten Awd; San Francisco Symphny Yth Orch; Yng Musicians Pgm; Chiness Clb; Health Applied Sci.

KANGAS, JOHN K; Porterville HS; Springville, CA; (3); 4-H; JV Bsktbl; Capt Var Ftbl; JV Capt Trk; GET Clb Govr Ed Today; Cngrssnl Sem Washington DC; Pltcl Sci.

KANIEL, NATALIE; Cupertino HS; Cupertino, CA; (3); Drill Tm; Ed Nwsp; Co-Ed Yrbk; Stu Cncl; Capt Var Cheerldng; Powder Puff Ftbl; Swmmng; High Hon Roll; NHS; Ntl Merit Ltr.

KANJI, OMAR; Bel-Air Prep; Santa Monica, CA; (2); Aud/Vis; Church Yth Grp; Cmnty Wkr; Drama Clb; Teachers Aide; School Play; Variety Show; Ed Nwsp; Treas Stu Cncl; High Hon Roll; Stu Of Mnty 88-90; Stanford NY U; Ophthalmology.

KANJI, SHARI H; The Bishops Schl; La Jolla, CA; (4); 12/77; AFS; Cmnty Wkr; French Clb; Model UN; SADD; Teachers Aide; Varsity Clb; Golf; Stage Crew; Rptr Nwsp; UC Irvine; Law.

KANN, SIMON; San Pedro HS; San Pedro, CA; (3); 10/625; Math Tm; Rep Frsh Cls; Rep Soph Cls; Rep Jr Cls; Rep Stu Cncl; Bsktbl; Var Crs Cntry; Intrml Ftbl; Var Trk; Cit Awd; Fnslt Los Angeles Cnty Sci Fair; Schl Rep HOBY Ldrshp Seminar; U Of S CA Hnrs Pgm; Civil Engrng.

KANNER, DANIEL F; San Marino HS; San Gabriel, CA; (3); 36/260; FBLA; Letterman Clb; Model UN; Teachers Aide; Var Capt Swmmng; Swmmng-All Amercn, CA St Chmpn 500 Yd Freestyle.

KANO, LENN; Hamilton HS Humanities Magnet; Los Angeles, CA; (3); School Musical; School Play; Stage Crew; Rep Nwsp; Lit Mag; VP Frsh Cls; Math Tutoring VP Geom Club; MA.

KANSA, ERIC C; Livermore HS; Livermore, CA; (4); 10/290; Church Yth Grp; Pres German Clb; Math Clb; Band; High Hon Roll; Hon Roll; Pres Acad Fit Awd; Valqueros Del Mar Scuba Dvng Clb; CSF; UC San Diego.

KANSAL, MALIN; South San Francisco HS; South San Francis, CA; (2); Computer Clb; French Clb; Sec FBLA; Library Aide; Math Clb; JV Tennis; High Hon Roll; CSF Stu; Asian Amer Clb; Concern Stus Clb; U In CA.

KANTATHAVORN, WONDEE; Downey HS; Downey, CA; (3); Aud/Vis; Teachers Aide; Ed Rptr Yrbk; Rep Stu Cncl; JV Powder Puff Ftbl; Brooks Coll; Inter Dsgn.

KANU, ASIKEH S; Loyola HS; Los Angeles, CA; (2); Computer Clb; Yrbk; Trk; Hon Roll; AATF Frnch Natl Cntst 89; Harvard U; Med.

KANZLER, PATRICK M; Foothill HS; Santa Ana, CA; (2); Pres Sec Latin Clb; JV Crs Cntry; JV Trk; JV Wrstlng; High Hon Roll; Hon Roll; Acad Cmptn; Military.

KAO, CAROLINE C; Arcadia HS; Arcadia, CA; (3); 61/639; Science Clb; Band; Mrchg Band; Orch; School Musical; Yrbk; Var Trk; Cit Awd; NHS; Prfct Atten Awd; CJSF; UCLA; Pharmcy.

KAO, JAMES; Palm Desert HS; Palm Desert, CA; (3); Computer Clb; UCLA; Comp.

KAO, JOSEPHINE Y; Pioneer HS; San Jose, CA; (3); Church Yth Grp; VP French Clb; Hist FBLA; VP Math Clb; Church Choir; Var Tennis; NHS; Mock Trl.

KAO, RACHEL N; Palo Alto HS; Palo Alto, CA; (2); Church Yth Grp; Cmnty Wkr; Debate Tm; Sec Key Clb; Speech Tm; School Play; Ed Nwsp; Off Frsh Cls; Off Soph Cls; JV Tennis; Grnd Prz Wnnr Schl Sci Fair; Stanford U; Psychlgy.

KAO, ROBIN; Archbishop Mitty HS; Saratoga, CA; (3); 14/150; Art Clb; Cmnty Wkr; Computer Clb; Math Clb; Math Tm; Teachers Aide; School Musical; NHS; Prncpl Hnr Roll; Play Violin; Batmntn; N Wstrn U; Pre Med.

KAO, SUSAN; Whitney HS; Cerritos, CA; (1); JCL; Key Clb; High Hon Roll; CA Jr Schlrshp Fed; UC Berkeley.

KAO, VIVIAN; Napa HS; Napa, CA; (4); 8/389; Superinteriors Awd; Bd Of Ed Awd; U Of Pacific; Accntng.

KAO, YUH-TING; Temple City HS; Temple City, CA; (4); 23/400; Dance Clb; Debate Tm; Treas French Clb; Key Clb; Drill Tm; Orch; School Musical; Var Cheerldng; VP NHS; CSF; JS Statesman Of Amer; U CA Irvine; Bus.

KAPLAN, CRAIG W; Bellarmine HS; Los Gatos, CA; (4); 5/301; Temple Yth Grp; Yrbk; Intrml Bsktbl; Intrml Ftbl; Intrml Sftbl; Intrml Vllybl; JV Wrstlng; High Hon Roll; Ntl Merit SF; Pres Acad Fit Awd; UCLA.

KAPLAN, IRINA; G Washington HS; San Francisco, CA; (2); Dance Clb; Off Soph Cls; Comp.

KAPLAN, NEAL; Palisades HS; Pacific Palisades, CA; (3); Drama Clb; Math Clb; Math Tm; School Play; JV Crs Cntry; JV Trk; High Hon Roll; Prfct Atten Awd; Pres Acad Fit Awd; St Schlr; Jr Statesmen Amer.

KAPLAN, SETH L; Sacramento HS; Sacramento, CA; (2); 66/500; Bsbl; Bsktbl; Ftbl; Hon Roll; Work Paper Rt Baskin Robbins; Cllctng Bsbll Crds; MVP Tm Cptn Bsktbll; Bus Admn.

KAPOOR, NATASHA; Carondelet HS; Danville, CA; (3); Cmnty Wkr; Ski Clb; Spanish Clb; Rep Frsh Cls; VP Soph Cls; Pres Jr Cls; Pres Sr Cls; Tennis; Hon Roll; Pr Cnslr; Yth Ed; Psych.

KAPOOR, TAIRA; Brea Olinda HS; Brea, CA; (1); Cmnty Wkr; Cit Awd; Hon Roll; Girls Leag Clb; Pedtrcn.

KAPRELIAN, MARAL; Pasadena HS; Pasadena, CA; (3); Church Yth Grp; Girl Scts; Teachers Aide; Cit Awd; Hon Roll; Vllybl Armenian Yth Organ; Trck Armenian Yth Organ; Pasadena City Coll; Acctng.

KARAKAS, ERIN TRACY; Sonora HS; Moreno Valley, CA; (3); French Clb; Science Clb; Drill Tm; JV Sftbl; JV Vllybl; High Hon Roll; Hon Roll; CSF; Golden St Exam Geom Hnrs.

KARAKASHIAN, MARIA; Clovis West HS; Fresno, CA; (2); Church Yth Grp; Teachers Aide; Cit Awd; Prfct Atten Awd.

KARAKOSSIAN, VARTAN; Pasadena HS; Pasadena, CA; (3); ROTC; Off Frsh Cls; Off Soph Cls; Off Jr Cls; Bsktbl; Socr; Tennis; Vllybl; Intr Dsgn & Indstrl Drftng Stu Of Mnth; Engrng.

KARAKOUZIAN, RAFFI; Ferrahian HS; Santa Monica, CA; (2); Boy Scts; Chorus; Yrbk; Bsktbl; Crs Cntry; Score Keeper; Socr; Trk; Hon Roll; Prfct Atten Awd; Cultural Grps; UCLA; Engrng.

KARALUN, MICHAEL C; San Gorgonio HS; Highland, CA; (3); Church Yth Grp; French Clb; Key Clb; Service Clb; JV Tennis; NHS; CSF; Bus Admin.

KARAPETIAN, GINA; Armenian Mesrobian HS; Montebello, CA; (1); Church Yth Grp; GAA; Rep Frsh Cls; Bsktbl; Trk; Vllybl; Lawyer.

KARBASSI, BEHNAM; Fresno Christian HS; Fresno, CA; (1); Tennis; High Hon Roll; Shotokan Karate; Stanford U; Bus Adm.

KARBUM, CHERI S; Los Amigos HS; Santa Ana, CA; (3); 127/310; Red Cross Aide; Teachers Aide; Stage Crew; Sprt Ed Lit Mag; Rep Jr Cls; Stat Bsktbl; JV Vllybl; Hon Roll; Prom Cmmtte; Humanitarian Clb; Medcl.

KARDOS, JASON S; Monte Vista HS; Spring Valley, CA; (2); Boy Scts; Church Yth Grp; Hon Roll; Scuba Diving; Landscpng; Mdrn Art; Ag.

KARELL, MICHELLE; E Righetti HS; Santa Maria, CA; (4); 12/343; Church Yth Grp; Math Clb; Science Clb; Teachers Aide; School Play; Lit Mag; High Hon Roll; Hon Roll; Photo Club Secy; Jr Statesmen Amer; CSF; Allen Hancock; Envrnmntl Engr.

KARETOV, CATHERINE; Monterey HS; Burbank, CA; (3); Var Cheerldng; USC; Engl.

KARIMI, NEDA; Taft HS; Reseda, CA; (3); French Clb; Hosp Aide; Rep Jr Cls; High Hon Roll; Math, Sci, Socl Stud Prvt Tutr; ESL Stu Vlntr Engl, Trig, Alg; Med.

KARIMYAN, ARMEN; Hoover Herbert HS; Glendale, CA; (3); Math Clb; Bsktbl; Wrstlng; Elec Eng.

KARINJA, INGRID M; Hillsdale HS; San Mateo, CA; (4); Hosp Aide; Teachers Aide; Chorus; Mbr Croation Fraternal Union Of America; Hnr Alpha-Delta-Kappa Awd; Sacramento ST U; Bus Admin.

KARJALA, ALEISHA S; Mayfair HS; Bellflower, CA; (2); AFS; VP Drama Clb; English Clb; Sec Key Clb; Pep Clb; SADD; VP Thesps; School Play; Stage Crew; Variety Show; UCLA; Theatre Arts.

KARL, SHERI L; Torrey Pines HS; Solana Beach, CA; (3); 109/457; Spanish Clb; Drill Tm; JV Capt Fld Hcky; JV Gym; JV Pom Pon; JV Socr; Hon Roll; NHS; Certfd USSF Sccr Refree; UCSD; Geophysics.

KARLE, MATTHEW D; Sanger HS; Sanger, CA; (4); FCA; Office Aide; Teachers Aide; JV Var Bsbl; JV Ftbl; Var L Socr; Cit Awd; Hon Roll; Peer Cmmnctn Club & Cls; FCC Life West; Chrprctr.

KARLIE, MARK S; Kingsburg HS; Kingsburg, CA; (1); FFA; Pres Frsh Cls; JV Bsktbl; JV Ftbl; JV Trk; Hon Roll; Top 40 Stus; Var Ftbl; U Of S CA; Ftbl.

KARLINGER, LIBBY; Lowell HS; San Francisco, CA; (3); Church Yth Grp; Debate Tm; Drama Clb; French Clb; NFL; Speech Tm; Thesps; Treas Orch; School Musical; Stage Crew; Shld & Scrll Hnr & Svc Scty; Stu Advcts Global Awrnss; CMPTV Gymnstcs Tm.

KARMAN, PETER E; California HS; Whittier, CA; (4); 1/360; Church Yth Grp; Q&S; Pres Service Clb; Varsity Clb; Church Choir; Nwsp; Var Capt Crs Cntry; Var Socr; Var Capt Trk; Hon Roll; Bethel Coll; Cmmnctns.

KARP, DAVID; Miramonte HS; Orinda, CA; (4); German Clb; Envrnmnt Now Clb; UC Berkeley; Mech Engrng.

KARP, KELLEY E; Patrick Henry HS; San Diego, CA; (2); 79/530; Model UN; Quiz Bowl; Rptr Yrbk; JV Var Cheerldng; L Var Mgr(s); Cit Awd; Hon Roll; Jr NHS; Prfct Atten Awd; Coordntng Cncl Orgnzd Awareness Alternatives To Drgs; Fine Arts.

KARPENKO, LARA P; San Dieguito HS; Encinitas, CA; (2); Debate Tm; Letterman Clb; NFL; Quiz Bowl; Speech Tm; Ed Yrbk; Lit Mag; Hon Roll; Forensics Dgree Distnctn; Law.

KARPONTINIS, EFFIE M; Chino HS; Chino, CA; (4); Spanish Clb; Teachers Aide; Cit Awd; High Hon Roll; CA Schlrshp Fed; Hnrs Grad; Badminton Jr Var; U CA Riverside; Bus.

KARR, MICHELLE C; Gladstone HS; Glendora, CA; (4); Church Yth Grp; Office Aide; Church Choir; CSF CA Schlrshp Fed.

KARSTETTER, REBECCA J; Barstow HS; Barstow, CA; (1); Band; Mrchg Band; Co-Capt Swmmng; Hon Roll; Jr Olympic Swmmr 88-90; Sthrn CA Q Meet 88-90; CA Intrschlstc Swmmng Champs 3rd Pl 90; Child Psych.

KARVELOT, JASON A; Apple Valley HS; Apple Valley, CA; (2); Church Yth Grp; High Hon Roll; Meteorology.

KAS, RITHY; Mc Clymonds HS; Oakland, CA; (3); Computer Clb; ROTC; Merritte Coll.

KASAMA, PATRICK; William Workman HS; La Puente, CA; (3); 57/289; Boy Scts; Temple Yth Grp; Var Tennis; Cit Awd; Hon Roll; Prfct Atten Awd; Hnr Stu Cert; Achvt Cert; U S CA; Bio Sci.

KASAMEYER, AMY F; Livermore HS; Livermore, CA; (3); 11/411; Church Yth Grp; Sec German Clb; Band; Chorus; Mrchg Band; School Musical; Rep Jr Cls; Ntl Merit Ltr; Homcmng Co Chairmn 90; CSF; Bio.

KASDAN, SIMONETTA D; Sir Francis Drake HS; San Anselmo, CA; (2); Drama Clb; Ski Clb; Teachers Aide; School Play; Stage Crew; Yrbk; JV Cheerldng; JV Socr; Pres Acad Fit Awd; Wilderness Clb; UC Santa Barbara; Interior Dsg.

KASEM, RAKSAN T; Amos Alonzo Stagg HS; Stockton, CA; (2); Church Yth Grp; Teachers Aide; Temple Yth Grp; Rep Stu Cncl; High Hon Roll; Hon Roll; Prfct Atten Awd; Stagg Bdmtn Team; Pres HOSA Clb; Media Arts Clb; Delta Coll; Comp Prgmr.

KASENCHAK, KRISTOPHER; Woodside Priory Schl; Woodside, CA; (3); 9/19; Church Yth Grp; Ski Clb; Nwsp; VP Frsh Cls; VP Soph Cls; VP Jr Cls; VP Stu Cncl; JV Bsbl; Var Lcrss; Var Socr.

KASHEVEROFF, FELICIA; East Union HS; Manteca, CA; (4); 1/264; Church Yth Grp; French Clb; Pres Science Clb; Speech Tm; Pres Thesps; School Play; Stage Crew; Cit Awd; High Hon Roll; Val; CA Schlrshp Fdrtn; Schlstc Achvmt Awd; U Of CA; Dramatic Arts.

KASHIWAGI, MINDEE F; Analy HS; Sebastopol, CA; (4); Am Leg Aux Girls St; 4-H; French Clb; JA; Ed Yrbk; Stu Cncl; Var Vllybl; French Hon Soc; High Hon Roll; Rotary Awd; Badminton Var; U Of CA Davis; Bio Sci.

KASHIWAGI, ROSS B; Analy HS; Sebastopol, CA; (4); 1/211; Am Leg Boys St; 4-H; Pres JA; VICA; Stu Cncl; JV Bsbl; JV Bsktbl; Intrml Vllybl; 4-H Awd; High Hon Roll; CA Polytech ST; Mech Engrng.

KASISCHKE, DOUG; Loma Linda Acad; Redlands, CA; (4); Church Yth Grp; Cmnty Wkr; Drama Clb; Ski Clb; Teachers Aide; Acpl Chr; Band; Chorus; Church Choir; Orch; Loma Linda U; Law.

KASMAR, ANNE G; Marlborough Schl; Los Angeles, CA; (4); Ed Nwsp; JV Co-Capt Tennis; DAR Awd; Ntl Merit SF; Music Ensmbl Piano; Natl Chrty Leag Rec Secy.

KASPAR, EDWARD M; Hueneme HS; Oxnard, CA; (3); 10/396; Quiz Bowl; SADD; Ed Nwsp; Ed Yrbk; Rep Stu Cncl; Intrml Bsbl; High Hon Roll; Masonic Awd; Ntl Merit SF; TASP; Target Handgunning; Hon Cir; Deep Springs Coll; Law Enfrcmnt.

KASPER, BRIAN G; Warren HS; Downey, CA; (2); Boy Scts; Debate Tm; FBLA; Elks Awd; Hon Roll; Pres Acad Fit Awd; Cty Downey Kds Day Hl Fm; CSF.

KASRAVI, BARSAM; Ocean View HS; Huntington Beach, CA; (1); Boy Scts; Model UN; Ski Clb; Yrbk; VP Frsh Cls; Bsktbl; JV Tennis; High Hon Roll; Prfct Atten Awd; Pres Acad Fit Awd; Pdtrtn.

KASSABIAN, LEO; Holy Martyrs HS; Encino, CA; (3); Cmnty Wkr; Bsbl; Socr; Cit Awd; High Hon Roll; Hon Roll; Pres Schlr; Sci.

KASSAJIKIAN, SOSSY; Glendale HS; Glendale, CA; (3); Art Clb; Church Yth Grp; Cmnty Wkr; Red Cross Aide; Science Clb; School Musical; Rep Frsh Cls; Rep Soph Cls; Prfct Atten Awd; YWCA As Y-Teen VP; Art Mautner Schlrshp Instrmntl Achvt Awd; Ballet Lssns; UCLA; Lawyer.

KASSARTIAN, CHRISTINA; Viewpoint Schl; Tarzana, CA; (2); Art Clb; Speech Tm; Lit Mag; Vllybl; Wt Lftg; Arch.

KASSEL, THERESA L; Saint Francis HS; San Jose, CA; (1); 38/388; Drama Clb; SADD; School Musical; Stage Crew; High Hon Roll; U CA Berkeley; Frgn Svc.

KASSENS, LISA A; Antelope Valley HS; Lancaster, CA; (4); Pres Church Yth Grp; Drama Clb; Teachers Aide; School Play; Powder Puff Ftbl; Hon Roll; Home Ec Awd; Yng Wmn Rcgntn Chrch; Smnry Chrch Pgm Grad; Ricks Coll; Hstry Tchr.

KASSLER, ELIZABETH R; Immaculate Heart HS; Sherman Oaks, CA; (3); 7/112; Cmnty Wkr; GAA; Var Trk; JV Var Vllybl; High Hon Roll; Vllybl Coachs Awd 88; Mst Insprtnl 87, 89; Amnsty Intl Stu Rep 90-91; Envrnmntl Prsrvtn Rcyclng; Bio.

KASSMANN, CAREY J; O'farrell Scl Of Creatv-Prfrmg Arts; San Diego, CA; (2); 5/155; Dance Clb; SADD; Hon Roll; Pres Acad Fit Awd.

KAST, GINA N; Mount Diablo HS; W Pittsburg, CA; (1); Cheerldng; Hon Roll; UCLA; Psych.

KASTAMA, ALISON A; Skyline HS; Oakland, CA; (3); Drama Clb; JA; Key Clb; Service Clb; Thesps; Orch; School Musical; School Play; Stage Crew; Cit Awd; Stanford; Arch.

KASTEL, JENNIFER L; Mont Clair HS; Fontana, CA; (2); Intrml Bsktbl; Hon Roll; Ski & Key Clbs; USAF; Lawyer.

KASTEN, KRISTA; Bishop Amat HS; Covina, CA; (3); Cmnty Wkr; Drama Clb; Service Clb; Teachers Aide; High Hon Roll; NHS; Yth Grp Brd Mbr Secry; Chinese Cultr Prfrmng Arts Grp; Rlgs Cmmssnr.

KATACIC, ALEXANDRA; San Pedro HS; San Pedro, CA; (4); 25/525; School Musical; Variety Show; High Hon Roll; NHS; Pres Acad Fit Awd; Pres Schlr; Music Teachers Assn HS Music Diploma; CSF Gold Sealbearer; Knight-Knightette Mem Sr Hnr Club; Los Angeles Harbor Coll; Music.

KATAOKA, CHRISTINE L; Kingsburg HS; Kingsburg, CA; (1); 1/200; Rep FTA; Mu Alpha Theta; SADD; Band; Mrchg Band; Pep Band; High Hon Roll; Acad Block K; Span Essay Wnnr; CA Schlrshp Fed.

KATAOKA, DAWN E; Kingsburg Joint Union HS; Kingsburg, CA; (4); 1/170; Church Yth Grp; Debate Tm; Pres VP Mu Alpha Theta; Band; Ed Yrbk; Var Capt Tennis; Var Capt Vllybl; Bausch & Lomb Sci Awd; Val; Rotary Awd; Stanford U.

KATERELOS, ARI; St Genevieve HS; Panorama City, CA; (2); Latin Clb; JV Ftbl; Hon Roll; LA Pblc Libry Sht Stry Cont; UCLA.

KATHER, MATT H; Los Altos HS; Los Altos, CA; (3); Var JV Bsktbl; JV Crs Cntry; JV Socr; High Hon Roll; Hon Roll; Movie Club; Business.

KATKOV, WILLIAM V; Armenian Mesrobian Sch; Montebello, CA; (3); Church Yth Grp; Quiz Bowl; Ed Nwsp; Sprt Ed Yrbk; Sec Stu Cncl; Var Capt Socr; Cit Awd; Hon Roll; UC San Diego; Marine Bio.

KATO, DEREK; La Quinta HS; Westminster, CA; (3); 1/330; Am Leg Boys St; Boy Scts; Pres VP Key Clb; Var JV Bsbl; High Hon Roll; VP NHS; NEDT Awd; Rotary Awd; CSF Pres, VP & Secy; Yth Ldrshp For Action Constitutional Rghts Fndtn.

KATO, ROBIN E; Carlsbad HS; Zephyr Cove, NV; (1); Color Guard; CSF; Hnrs Pgm; Telecmmnctns.

KATSAS, MARIA A; Alhambra HS; Alhambra, CA; (3); Church Yth Grp; 4-H; French Clb; GAA; Hosp Aide; Teachers Aide; Lit Mag; Rep Stu Cncl; JV Capt Vllybl; Stat Wrstlng; Tri-Hi-Y Clb La Chandelle; Ldr NCCJ Brthd/Sistrhd USA; Maids Athena Grk Cltrl Grp; UC Santa Cruz; Psych.

KATSUHIKO, HIYAMA; El Toro HS; El Toro, CA; (4); 4-H; German Clb; Intnl Clb; Key Clb; Math Tm; Rep Sr Cls; JV Crs Cntry; Var Swmmng; Wrstlng; 4-H Awd; UCLA; Bus.

KATZ, JENNIFER B; Redlands SR HS; Redlands, CA; (3); 73/997; Band; Mrchg Band; School Musical; Hon Roll.

KATZ, MIKE S; Elk Grove HS; Elk Grove, CA; (2); Boy Scts; Temple Yth Grp; High Hon Roll; Hon Roll; Hgh Hnrs Golden St Exam Geom; Acad Ltr; UC Berkeley; Bio.

KATZAKIS, MARIA; Grace M Davis HS; Modesto, CA; (2); Church Yth Grp; Dance Clb; French Clb; Cit Awd; Hon Roll; Greek Orthdox Flk Dnc Fstvl; U CA.

KAUFFOLD, SANDI L; Bonita Vista HS; Chula Vista, CA; (3); 9/536; Pres Church Yth Grp; Band; Chorus; Church Choir; Mrchg Band; Pep Band; Nwsp; DAR Awd; High Hon Roll; Hon Roll; Brigham Yng U; Elem Ed.

KAUFMAN, AMY A; Cornelia Connelly HS; Villa Park, CA; (4); French Clb; GAA; Model UN; School Play; Lit Mag; Cheerldng; Hon Roll; Mount Holyoke Coll.

KAUFMAN, ERIC T; University HS; Los Angeles, CA; (3); Cmnty Wkr; Quiz Bowl; Ski Clb; Lit Mag; Rep Frsh Cls; Rep Stu Cncl; Bsktbl; Hon Roll; Yth Ldrshp Action; Commnctns.

KAUFMAN, JO A; Workman HS; West Covina, CA; (2); Hosp Aide; Intnl Clb; Letterman Clb; Spanish Clb; Var Swmmng; Cit Awd; High Hon Roll; Hon Roll; Prfct Atten Awd; Pres Acad Fit Awd; Mutual; Semenary; CSF; Stanford U; Hrt Srgn.

KAUFMAN, KIMBERLEY A; Bullard HS; Fresno, CA; (2); 1/600; Debate Tm; Hist Hosp Aide; Intnl Clb; Key Clb; NFL; Spanish Clb; SADD; Tennis; High Hon Roll; Attorney.

KAUFMAN, KRISTINA; Casa Grande HS; Petaluma, CA; (4); 1/270; Cmnty Wkr; VP Debate Tm; Library Aide; Pres SADD; Ed Lit Mag; Stu Cncl; Stat Bsktbl; Powder Puff Ftbl; High Hon Roll; NHS; Vlntr Camp Cnslr For Chldrn With Cancer; Lcl Newspr Wkly Columnist; Wellesley Coll; Medical Rsrch.

KAUFMAN, MARIZA; Crawford HS; San Diego, CA; (2); Church Yth Grp; Girl Scts; Variety Show; Rptr Nwsp; Yrbk; JV Bsktbl; JV Capt Cheerldng; JV L Vllybl; Cit Awd; Hon Roll; Friday Night Live FNL Club Against Alcohol; ASB Cmmtte.

KAUFMAN, PEGGY EVA; Half Moon Bay HS; El Granada, CA; (4); 15/176; Drama Clb; Pres Sec French Clb; FHA; Rptr Yrbk; Sec Sr Cls; Var Tennis; Var Trk; Hon Roll; 3rd Pl NPL Finals; NPL Trk Girls Chmpn 90, Girls Tnns Chmpns 89; San Diego ST U; Comp Sci.

KAUFMAN, TERRY; Culver City HS; Culver City, CA; (4); 30/330; Cit Awd; High Hon Roll; Hon Roll; Cmmty Schlrshp; Cal ST U Long Beach; Med Dr.

KAUFMAN-JONES, CHRIS J; Fairfax HS; Los Angeles, CA; (2); Varsity Clb; Bsktbl; Wt Lftg; VA Union U; Pro Bsktbl.

KAUFMANN, BARBIE; Glendale HS; Glendale, CA; (2); Drill Tm; School Play; JV Sftbl; JV Swmmng; Drama; Advrtsng.

KAUFMANN, LUSHA M; Trinity HS; Lewiston, CA; (1); Church Yth Grp; FCA; SADD; High Hon Roll; Hon Roll; Communications.

KAUR, AMAN P; Andrew Hill HS; San Jose, CA; (1); Drama Clb; GAA; Math Tm; Var Swmmng; High Hon Roll; Supts Hnr Roll; Kosho Shorei Kenp 3rd Deg Brwn Belt; Med.

KAUR, AMANPRIT; Atwater HS; Atwater, CA; (1); Computer Clb; Key Clb; Spanish Clb; Chorus; Rep Stu Cncl; Mgr(s); Hon Roll; Prfct Atten Awd; Friday Night Live Clb.

KAUR, JASVINDER; Grant HS; Sacramento, CA; (4); Dance Clb; Drama Clb; French Clb; Model UN; Office Aide; Teachers Aide; School Musical; Cit Awd; DAR Awd; CSF; Cngrssnl Yth Ldrshp Cncl; Acctng.

KAUTH, SARAH; Arroyo Grande HS; Grover City, CA; (3); 176/471; Boy Scts; Church Yth Grp; FCA; NFL; Speech Tm; Chorus; Yrbk; VP Frsh Cls; VP Soph Cls; Rep Jr Cls; Rotry Uyth Ldrshp Assn Awd; U Of OR; Ed.

KAUTZMAN, FRANK S; San Gorgonio HS; Highland, CA; (3); 7/900; Debate Tm; NFL; Speech Tm; Var Capt Swmmng; High Hon Roll; Lion Awd; NHS; Rotary Awd; Vrsty Waterpolo.

KAVANAUGH, JOHNNY J; Serrano HS; Wrightwood, CA; (1); JV Bsktbl; JV Ftbl; JV Trk; JV Wt Lftg.

KAVIANI, CRISTINA; Mt Whitney HS; Visalia, CA; (4); 25/400; Pres 4-H; Yrbk; VP Soph Cls; Pres Jr Cls; Treas Stu Cncl; Capt Tennis; Opt Clb Awd; CSF; Prncpls Ldrshp Awd; Jnr Statesmn Amer Fndr/Pres; Rotary Exchng Stu Spain; Intrntl Relations.

KAWABE, AIMEE K; Buena HS; Ventura, CA; (4); High Hon Roll; Pres Acad Fit Awd; CSF Gold Seal Bearer; Acad Ltr; U Of CA Los Angeles; Bio.

KAWAGUCHI, FRANCES T; Mills HS; Burlingame, CA; (4); Band; Orch; Pep Band; Mgr(s); Tennis; Trk; Hd Mgr Boys Tnns; Mst Imprvd, Mst Cntrbtd; Capt Grls Tnns; Natl Orch Awd; Cncrt Mstrs VP, Pres; Intl Chrstn U; Mltpl Lang.

KAWAGUCHI, YUMIKO; Mission Veijo HS; Mission Viejo, CA; (3); Intnl Clb; Key Clb; Chorus; Foreign Langs.

KAWAHATA, JULIE M; John F Kennedy HS; Sacramento, CA; (3); 95/422; Church Yth Grp; Mrchg Band; Hon Roll; Vrsty Band Lttr; UC Davis.

KAWAI, DRENDA M; Fairfield HS; Fairfield, CA; (3); Hosp Aide; Sec Key Clb; SADD; Drill Tm; Yrbk; Rep Stu Cncl; High Hon Roll; Hon Roll; Jr NHS; NHS; UC Davis.

KAWAMURA, DEBORAH J; West HS; Torrance, CA; (4); 1/435; Off Hosp Aide; Treas Science Clb; Drill Tm; Rptr Nwsp; Sec Stu Cncl; JV Debate Tm; Cit Awd; High Hon Roll; NHS; Ntl Merit SF; Social Studies Clb Pres & Sec; Acad Dcthln Tm; Trrnce Cty Yth Cncl Sec; Med.

KAWANO, MASAYO; El Camino Real HS; West Hills, CA; (3); Bus.

KAWASAKI, BRIAN S; St Ignatius HS; San Francisco, CA; (2); Church Yth Grp; Cmnty Wkr; French Clb; Capt Novice Tm; UCLA; Bus.

KAWKA, ELENORA S; Sunny Hills HS; Fullerton, CA; (2); French Clb; Intnl Clb; Pep Clb; Ski Clb; Spanish Clb; VP Temple Yth Grp; Phtg Nwsp; JV Swmmng; High Hon Roll; Acad Ltr; Swmmng Coachs Awd.

KAY, EMILY; Palisades HS; Pacific Palisades, CA; (3); Dance Clb; Drama Clb; Thesps; Acpl Chr; Drill Tm; School Musical; School Play; Variety Show; Sec Frsh Cls; Stu Cncl; Capt Of Palisades Dance Tm; Prncpls Awd Outstndng Schl Svc; Spotlight Awd; Theatre.

KAY, KATHLEEN M; Palos Verdes HS; Rancho Palos Verd, CA; (3); Church Yth Grp; Cmnty Wkr; SADD; Sprt Ed Nwsp; VP Frsh Cls; Stu Cncl; Crs Cntry; Socr; High Hon Roll; Hon Roll; SOFAH.

KAY, RAYMOND S; River City HS; W Sacramento, CA; (3); 9/300; Chess Clb; Drama Clb; SADD; Teachers Aide; Varsity Clb; Acpl Chr; Chorus; School Play; JV Bsktbl; Capt JV Tennis; 7 Yrs Cty Soccer; World Trvlr; Sacramento ST U; Engrg.

KAY, TIM A; Sunny Hills HS; Fullerton, CA; (4); Church Yth Grp; Teachers Aide; JV Crs Cntry; JV Trk; High Hon Roll; Ntl Merit Schol; Cal Poly Pomona.

KAYLOR, BEKKI; Hanford Joint Union HS; Hanford, CA; (1); Drill Tm; Mesa; Erly Acad Outreach Pgm; Mgrnt Ed Pgm; Comp.

KAYLOR, MICHELLE A; El Toro HS; El Toro, CA; (4); Church Yth Grp; Drama Clb; Pep Clb; Teachers Aide; Thesps; School Play; Yrbk; Sec VP Stu Cncl; Cheerldng; High Hon Roll; Pepperdine U; Brdcst Jrnlsm.

KAZANJIAN, JANAE L; Kingsburg HS; Kingsburg, CA; (3); Church Yth Grp; Pep Clb; SADD; Teachers Aide; Rep Frsh Cls; JV Var Cheerldng; Hon Roll; CA ST Polytechnic U; Tchr.

KAZE, JODIE; Amos Alonzo Stagg HS; Stockton, CA; (2); Church Yth Grp; Church Choir; Tennis; Hon Roll; NEDT Awd; Vlntr; Coachs Awd In Tnns; Psych.

KAZEE, KIMBERLY L; Encina HS; Sacramento, CA; (4); 6/163; Computer Clb; SADD; Teachers Aide; Ed Lit Mag; Chorus; Hon Roll; Engl Stu Of Month; Hnr Stu Cert & Medal; Sacramento ST U; Engl.

KAZEM, WAHID S; Independence HS; San Jose, CA; (3); Ed Nwsp; Pres Sr Cls; JV Trk; Hon Roll; US Army Reserve; UC Davis; Envrnmntl Policy Plg.

KAZIKIEWICZ, CHARITY J; Yucca Valley HS; Yucca Valley, CA; (1); Drill Tm; High Hon Roll; Var Hon Roll; Corp Law.

KAZINEC, BRANDI MONTEE; Fairfield HS; Fairfield, CA; (2); Cmnty Wkr; ROTC; Score Keeper; Swmmng; Pres Frsh Cls; Pres Soph Cls; EMT; Paramdc.

KAZLAUSKAS, AMI L; Canyon HS; Anaheim, CA; (1); Church Yth Grp; Sec Spanish Clb; High Hon Roll.

KAZLAUSKAS, KRISTOFER A; Bellarmine College Prep; San Jose, CA; (2); 1/320; Church Yth Grp; Latin Clb; JV Golf; JV Socr; Intrml Sftbl; High Hon Roll; Numerous Achvts CYSA Clb Sccr.

KAZSUK, CHRISTINA M; Desert Christian HS; Palmdale, CA; (2); Hosp Aide; Office Aide; Teachers Aide; Cit Awd; Hon Roll; Nurse.

KE, ALLAN C; Temple City HS; Temple City, CA; (3); 50/400; Intnl Clb; Key Clb; CSF; Golden St Math Hnr; Comp Engrng.

KE, MALCOLM S J; Gretchen Whitney HS; Cerritos, CA; (1); Boy Scts; Church Yth Grp; Sec Treas Varsity Clb; Stu Cncl; Var Capt Bsktbl; JV Var Tennis; NHS; UC Berkeley.

KEAGY, FREDERICK F; San Luis Obispo HS; San Luis Obispo, CA; (2); 9/265; Key Clb; L Var Socr; High Hon Roll; Math.

KEAGY, SCOTT C; Coast Union HS; Cayucos, CA; (3); 1/65; Treas Pres FBLA; Letterman Clb; Math Clb; Math Tm; Var L Ftbl; Bausch & Lomb Sci Awd; High Hon Roll; Ntl Merit SF; Rotary Awd; Sci Ambsdr USSR People To People Youth Sci Excng; 1st Pl Earthday Essay Cntst; 1st Pl Lions Spkng Cnt; Engr.

KEANE, JUSTIN; Torrey Pines HS; San Diego, CA; (1); Chess Clb; Drama Clb; Teachers Aide; Thesps; School Musical; School Play; Stage Crew; Rep Stu Cncl; Intl Thespian Soc; UCLA; Drama.

KEANE, MARCIE; Foothill HS; Pleasanton, CA; (2); Church Yth Grp; Dance Clb; French Clb; Pep Clb; SADD; JV Cheerldng; JV Pom Pon; JV Swmmng; Hon Roll; Peer Cnslr; Psych.

KEANE, MICHELLE; Foothill SR HS; Sacramento, CA; (2); German Clb; Swmmng; Vllybl; High Hon Roll; Hon Roll; UCLA; Cmmnctns.

KEAR, DANIELLE P; Central Union HS; El Centro, CA; (4); 55/472; French Clb; NFL; Pep Clb; Speech Tm; Pres Soph Cls; Treas Jr Cls; JV Sftbl; Var Swmmng; Hon Roll; Lion Awd; Presdntl Phys Ftnss; CA ST San Bernardino; Bus Adm.

KEARN, KATHLEE LOIS; Desert Christian HS; Desert Center, CA; (2); 1/11; Church Yth Grp; Yrbk; Sec Frsh Cls; Sec Treas Stu Cncl; Var Bsktbl; Var Cheerldng; Var Powder Puff Ftbl; Hon Roll; Cmmnctns.

KEARNEY, DOUGLAS E; John Muir HS; Altadena, CA; (2); Church Yth Grp; Cmnty Wkr; German Clb; Church Choir; Hon Roll; Prfct Atten Awd; Ju-Jitsu; Parsons Stu Mnth; SYMC; MESA; Howard U; Egyptlgy.

KEARNEY, TRAVIS R; Rim Of The World HS; Lake Arrowhead, CA; (3); Boy Scts; Church Yth Grp; Capt Debate Tm; Letterman Clb; Quiz Bowl; Ski Clb; VP Jr Cls; Pres Sr Cls; Stu Cncl; Var Socr; Rock Clmbng; Jr Statesman Of Amer; U CA Boulder; Intl Bus.

KEARNS, JONETTE; Escondido HS; Escondido, CA; (3); FHA; Office Aide; Teachers Aide; Powder Puff Ftbl; Cit Awd; Hon Roll; San Diego ST U; Paralegal.

KEARNS, SHEILA V; Poway HS; Poway, CA; (4); 57/728; Letterman Clb; SADD; Varsity Clb; School Play; Var Powder Puff Ftbl; Var Socr; Var Sftbl; High Hon Roll; NHS; Sftbl 2nd Team All League; Schlr Athlt; CSF; Pre-Med.

KEARNY, JENNIFER; Leland HS; San Jose, CA; (2); Church Yth Grp; Var Crs Cntry; Var Trk; UCSB; Gen Ed.

KEASEY, CARL J; Santa Teresa HS; San Jose, CA; (2); Boy Scts; Computer Clb; SADD; Teachers Aide; Pres Acad Fit Awd; Comp Prgmng; De Anza; Bus.

KEATING, BRETT; Cardinal Newman HS; Santa Rosa, CA; (3); 1/100; Letterman Clb; Ski Clb; Hist Frsh Cls; Intrml JV Bsktbl; Var L Crs Cntry; Var L Trk; High Hon Roll; Peer Facilitator Club; Principals List; Cartoonist; Stanford; Math.

KEATING, JENNIFER E; Redondo Union HS; Redondo Beach, CA; (4); 29/400; Church Yth Grp; Key Clb; Office Aide; Teachers Aide; Yrbk; Capt Socr; JV Var Sftbl; JV Vllybl; Cit Awd; Hon Roll; Army Rsrv Schlr Athlt Awd; El Camino; Pltcl Sci.

KEAY, CORINE M; Victory Christian HS; Orangevale, CA; (2); Church Yth Grp; Science Clb; Var Sftbl; Var Vllybl; Hon Roll; MVP Awd; Hnr Roll; All Leag Athltc Awd 90; Comp Sci.

KECHTER, MELANIE R; California HS; San Ramon, CA; (3); Church Yth Grp; Girl Scts; Ski Clb; Sec Pres Spanish Clb; Teachers Aide; Powder Puff Ftbl; Cit Awd; High Hon Roll; Hon Roll; NHS; Acadc Lttr & 3 Lampof Knwldge Pins; Alg I & Geom Outstndng Achvt Awds; CA Schlrshp Fed Membr; Pre-Med.

KECKLEY, BEVERLY; Monache HS; Porterville, CA; (3); 18/360; Art Clb; Church Yth Grp; Thesps; Acpl Chr; Chorus; School Musical; School Play; Stage Crew; High Hon Roll; Prfct Atten Awd; 89-90 Achievement Awards High Test Scores Reading & Language Arts; Golden State Exam; 10 Yrs Sty Dance.

KEDDINGTON, KRISTIN; Poway HS; Poway, CA; (3); 14/761; AFS; FBLA; Intnl Clb; Math Clb; Service Clb; JV Trk; JV Vllybl; High Hon Roll; NHS; CSF; San Diego U CA; Accntng.

KEDINEOGLU, NADIA; Montebello HS; Montebello, CA; (2); Temple Yth Grp; Cit Awd; Hon Roll; Stu Month.

KEDSLIE, NICOLE; Janta Maria HS; Santa Maria, CA; (3); 1/555; Church Yth Grp; Drama Clb; FBLA; School Play; Sec Soph Cls; Sec Jr Cls; Sec Sr Cls; VP Tennis; Hon Roll; VP Spanish NHS; CA Poly San Luis; Cmptr Sci.

KEE, CLAUDINE S; Mercy HS; San Francisco, CA; (4); 8/157; Hosp Aide; Latin Clb; Quiz Bowl; School Musical; Stage Crew; Yrbk; Cit Awd; Hon Roll; Bnk Of Amer Achvt Awd Social Studies; Life Mem CA Schlrshp Fed; JR Statesmn Amer; San Francisco U; Bus Admin.

KEE, KAREN; Sierra Joint Union HS; Tollhouse, CA; (4); 1/175; Church Yth Grp; Letterman Clb; Model UN; Treas SADD; Off Stu Cncl; JV Bsktbl; Var Swmmng; VP NHS; CSF Pres; UC Davis; Ophthalmogy.

KEEFE, SHERRI L; Sonora Union HS; Jamestown, CA; (3); 1/356; Pres Girl Scts; Spanish Clb; Band; Mrchg Band; Rep Sr Cls; L JV Socr; Var L Sftbl; Var L Vllybl; High Hon Roll; Girl Scout Gold Awd; Primary.

KEEFFE, KATHLEEN D; Pinole Valley HS; Hercules, CA; (4); 31/500; Math Tm; Scholastic Bowl; Teachers Aide; Treas Sr Cls; Rep Stu Cncl; Var Mgr(s); Powder Puff Ftbl; Hon Roll; Pres Acad Fit Awd; Rotary Awd; CSF Life; Ldrshp Grp; Diablo Vly Coll; Aerosp Med.

KEEGAN, NATHAN R; Atwater HS; Atwater, CA; (2); 4-H; Var Trk; 4-H Awd; Bus Mgmt.

KEEGAN, STACY E; Montgomery HS; Santa Rosa, CA; (2); Cmnty Wkr; JA; Spanish Clb; High Hon Roll; Jr NHS; Pres Acad Fit Awd; Lamp Of Knowledge Trophy; Gldn St Exam Awds Alg & Geom; CSF; Herpetology.

KEEHN, CHERYL; Anderson Union HS; Anderson, CA; (3); 48/246; 4-H; FFA; Rptr Nwsp; 4-H Awd; Prfct Atten Awd; CA Gldn St FFA Degr Hnr; Amer Jr Qtrhrs Assn; Prjct Comptn Gold Awd; Chico ST U.

KEELBE, SHANE W; Concord HS; Concord, CA; (3); Art Clb; School Play; Stage Crew; Intrml Wrstlng; Hon Roll; Outstanding Achievements In Arts & Crafts; Outstanding Poet; Outstanding Achievement In Physiology; UCLA; Film Making.

KEELEN, ALLAN; Thomas Downey HS; Modesto, CA; (2); FFA; Band; Jazz Band; Mrchg Band; Pep Band; Forest Firefighter.

KEELER, SARAH E; San Benito HS; Hollister, CA; (1); 1/464; Church Yth Grp; GAA; Pep Clb; Church Choir; Treas Frsh Cls; Var Vllybl; High Hon Roll; Frgn Exchng Clb; CSF; BYU; Psych.

KEELEY, ALLISON M; Woodside HS; Redwood City, CA; (3); German Clb; Band; Drm Mjr(t); Jazz Band; Mrchg Band; Vllybl; High Hon Roll; CSF; Frgn Lang.

KEELEY, KAREN I; Roseville HS; Rocklin, CA; (3); 46/411; Computer Clb; Teachers Aide; High Hon Roll; Hon Roll; CSF; Prin Advisory Comm; CA ST U Sacramento; Archlgy.

KEELING, GREGORY L; Redlands HS; Redlands, CA; (3); 39/900; Boy Scts; Church Yth Grp; Mgr(s); JV Wrstlng; High Hon Roll; Hon Roll; Pres Acad Fit Awd; 1st Pl Redlands Bicycle Classic 89; Spring Select Soccr 89; Hgh Hnrs Golden ST Geom Test; Bus.

KEEN, JENNIFER M; Duarte HS; Duarte, CA; (4); 18/220; Pep Clb; Science Clb; Teachers Aide; Flag Corp; Mrchg Band; Ed Nwsp; Stu Cncl; Cheerldng; Powder Puff Ftbl; Score Keeper; Hnrs Wldng & Wood Wrkng; Stu Cncl; Mt San Antonio; Wldlife Mgmt.

KEENAN, AMY; Carlmont HS; San Carlos, CA; (2); French Clb; Cheerldng; Socr; Trk; Hon Roll.

KEENAN, CYNTHIA M; USD HS; Escondido, CA; (4); Var Capt Socr; Var Trk; Var Vllybl; Kiwanis Awd; Pres Acad Fit Awd; 1st Tm Sccr All Leag & All CIF; St Marys Coll CA; Psych.

KEENAN, JENNIFER; Fresno HS; Fresno, CA; (4); 29/430; Church Yth Grp; Drama Clb; Thesps; Varsity Clb; Acpl Chr; Chorus; Church Choir; School Musical; School Play; Variety Show; All St Hnr Choir; Pepsi FUSD Awd; FSU Solo/Ensmble Fstvl; Fresno ST U; Liberal Stds.

KEENAN, MATTHEW; Palo Verde HS; Blythe, CA; (2); Var Golf; Hon Roll.

KEENE, DAVID W; Tehachapi HS; Tehachapi, CA; (2); Church Yth Grp; Math Tm; Rep Model UN; Ed Yrbk; NHS; Civil Engr.

KEENER, JESSICA; Yosemite HS; Coarsegold, CA; (3); Am Leg Aux Girls St; French Clb; Pep Clb; Var Cheerldng; Cit Awd; High Hon Roll; Hon Roll; Lion Awd; Peer Cnslng Cert; SMT Sngr; Davis U; Elem Educ.

KEENER, R M; Pittsburg HS; San Ramon, CA; (3); Church Yth Grp; Math Clb; Swmmng; Vllybl; Racquetball Trnmnts; CA ST Hayward; Engrng.

KEESEE, DAVID A; Mojave HS; California City, CA; (2); ROTC; Bsbl; Wt Lftg; Hon Roll; Dsbld Amer Vetrns Aux Essay Cont 1st Pl "what Amer Means To Me"; Antelope Valley Coll; Air Force.

KEESIS, HEIDI M; James Logan HS; Union City, CA; (4); 18/651; Church Yth Grp; Capt Color Guard; Mrchg Band; Rep Stu Cncl; JV Var Swmmng; High Hon Roll; Hon Roll; Pres Acad Fit Awd; Colorguard Vet Of Yr Awd; Axlry Hall Of Fame Awd; U Of S CA; Sprts Med Doc.

KEETER, DANIELLE; Ventura HS; Ventura, CA; (2); 115/500; Drama Clb; Color Guard; Mrchg Band; Hon Roll; UCSB; Doc.

KEETH, JENI M; Red Bluff Union HS; Red Bluff, CA; (2); French Clb; Teachers Aide; Var Sftbl; High Hon Roll; Hon Roll; Hon Mntn/All Leag & Coachs Awd Vrsty Sftbl; Athltc Of Wk; Bus.

KEETON, LYNDA R; Santa Rosa HS; Santa Rosa, CA; (4); 50/543; FBLA; FFA; Office Aide; Teachers Aide; Band; Drm Mjr(t); Jazz Band; Mrchg Band; Orch; Pep Band; St Hl Indvdl Farm Rcrds/Accntng CA In FFA; Ownd Bus At 16 88; Trvlng Mst Fvrt Hobby; CA Polytechnic U SLO; Bus Adm.

KEFELEGN, ESSEYE; Athenian Schl; Danville, CA; (3); Cmnty Wkr; Computer Clb; Letterman Clb; Office Aide; Varsity Clb; Rep Frsh Cls; Var Bsktbl; Var Capt Socr; Var Vllybl; Wt Lftg; Var Girls Soccer Asst Coach 2 Yrs; Duke U; Poly Sci.

KEFFER, JAMES; Red Bluff Union HS; Red Bluff, CA; (3); 40/340; Varsity Clb; Rep Frsh Cls; Rep Soph Cls; Rep Jr Cls; Intrml Bsktbl; JV Var Ftbl; Powder Puff Ftbl; JV Trk; JV Wrstlng; Hon Roll; Phys Thrpy.

KEFFURY, CHRISTINE D; Atascadero HS; Atascadero, CA; (4); 6/258; Church Yth Grp; FBLA; SADD; Teachers Aide; Powder Puff Ftbl; Swmmng; High Hon Roll; Pres Acad Fit Awd; Sec Frsh Cls; Sec Soph Cls; CA Polytech-Sn Luis Obispo; Ed.

KEFLEZIGHI, FUSSUMBRHAN R; San Diego HS; San Diego, CA; (3); 27/415; Crs Cntry; Socr; Trk; Pres Acad Fit Awd; Engrng.

KEH, MARIA; Abraham Lincoln HS; San Francisco, CA; (3); Dance Clb; Math Clb; Acpl Chr; Chorus; Off Jr Cls; Hon Roll; San Francisco ST U; Accntng.

KEHL, SHELBY; San Clemente HS; San Clemente, CA; (1); JV Sftbl; Cit Awd; Parent Tchr Stu Assn; Acctng.

KEHLET, STEVEN T; Foothill HS; Santa Ana, CA; (2); 2/120; Boy Scts; French Clb; Latin Clb; Science Clb; Var Swmmng; High Hon Roll; Hon Roll; Eagle Scout; Top Schlr Awd; Vrsty Waterpolo; Stanford U; Elect Engr.

KEHOE, KEATHER; Saratoga HS; Saratoga, CA; (4); 14/280; Treas Debate Tm; VP Intnl Clb; NFL; VP Spanish Clb; Treas Speech Tm; Capt Color Guard; Stage Crew; Hon Roll; Ntl Merit Ltr; Pres Acad Fit Awd; Cornell U; Crimnl Lawyer.

KEHOE, KEVIN; Lakewood HS; Lakewood, CA; (3); Church Yth Grp; JA; Var Capt Swmmng; NHS; Prfct Atten Awd; CSF; Pride Clb.

KEHOE, NATALIE; Aptos HS; Watsonville, CA; (3); Church Yth Grp; Debate Tm; Pep Clb; SADD; Color Guard; Mrchg Band; Stu Cncl; JV Var Cheerldng; Pom Pon; Powder Puff Ftbl; Excllnc In Dance & Chrldng; Law.

KEHOE, TRACY R; Live Oak HS; Live Oak, CA; (4); FFA; VP Letterman Clb; SADD; Teachers Aide; Rep Phtg Nwsp; Rep Sr Cls; Rep Stu Cncl; Var Ftbl; Var Tennis; Var Trk; Yuba Coll; Law Enfrcmnt.

KEIG, JENNIFER M; Vintage HS; Napa, CA; (3); 36/320; Church Yth Grp; 4-H; Office Aide; Spanish Clb; SADD; JV Vllybl; Cit Awd; 4-H Awd; Hon Roll; NHS; U Of CA San Diego; Bus Ec.

KEIGHLEY, JOHN W; Sacramento Adventist Acad; Carmichael, CA; (2); Drama Clb; Ski Clb; Band; Chorus; Pres Frsh Cls; Off Soph Cls; Rep Stu Cncl; Intrml Ftbl; Intrml Sftbl; Intrml Trk; Stanford; Bus.

KEIL, MATTHEW J; El Toro HS; El Toro, CA; (3); 199/499; Var L Ftbl; Intrml Socr; Var L Trk; Wt Lftg; UC Irvine; Psych.

KEIL, MONICA L; Enterprise HS; Redding, CA; (3); Mu Alpha Theta; Science Clb; SADD; Teachers Aide; Flag Corp; Powder Puff Ftbl; UC San Diego; Math Prfssr.

KEIRNAN, NOEL; Foothill HS; Pleasanton, CA; (3); Church Yth Grp; Hon Roll; Greenpeace Spnsr; Srfng; Gldn ST Exam; Humboldt; Mrn Eclgy.

KEIRNS, ROBERT M; Fontana HS; Fontana, CA; (2); Var Crs Cntry; JV Trk; High Hon Roll; Acac Awd-Glf Mdl; UNLV; Auto Engrng.

KEISER, JEFF; Del Campo HS; Sacramento, CA; (2); 5/460; Church Yth Grp; JV Bsktbl; JV Ftbl; High Hon Roll; Schlr-Athlete Terra Nova HS 88-89; Golden St Acad Excllnc Awd.

KEISER, STEPHANIE; Valhalla HS; El Cajon, CA; (2); 50/451; German Clb; Key Clb; SADD; Mgr(s); Swmmng; Water Polo Team; Elected Key Club Treasurer For 1990/91; UC Davis; Vet Med.

KEITH, CHAD L; Sweetwater Union HS; National City, CA; (2); Computer Clb; Quiz Bowl; Scholastic Bowl; School Play; Rptr Nwsp; Rptr Yrbk; Cit Awd; Hon Roll; Prfct Atten Awd; UCSD; Bus Mgmt.

KEITH, DONELLA; Gardena HS; Hawthorne, CA; (4); Varsity Clb; Pres Frsh Cls; Pres Sr Cls; Stu Cncl; Cheerldng; Powder Puff Ftbl; Trk; Hon Roll; Pres Acad Fit Awd; Yng Blck Schlr; Oscar Awd; San Diego ST U; Pre Med.

KEITH, JENNIFER; Herlong HS; Herlong, CA; (3); 1/30; Art Clb; Debate Tm; FBLA; Letterman Clb; Varsity Clb; Variety Show; Rep Soph Cls; Cheerldng; Wt Lftg; High Hon Roll; CA Schlrshp Fdrtn, Jr Statesmn Of Amer; Fine Arts Clb, Sci Camp Cnclr & Engl Awd; San Diego ST U; Bus.

KEITH, JEREMY R; Highland HS; N Highlands, CA; (4); Art Clb; Church Yth Grp; FHA; Science Clb; SADD; Band; Pep Band.

KEITH JR, NATHANAEL; Cajon HS; San Bernardino, CA; (3); Var JV Ftbl; Var Wt Lftg; Var Wrstlng; Cit Awd; Econ.

KEITH, PETER J; Montgomery HS; Santa Rosa, CA; (4); 1/430; Scholastic Bowl; Treas Speech Tm; Ed Nwsp; Ed Yrbk; Var L Crs Cntry; Var L Trk; Ntl Merit SF; French Clb; JA; Science Clb; Harvard Bk Awd; JR Statsmn Am; Oper Gttng To Tgthr.

KEITH, RICHARD K; Hesperia Christian HS; Hesperia, CA; (3); 5/30; Church Yth Grp; Capt Scholastic Bowl; Band; Chorus; High Hon Roll; Hon Roll; Var L Bsbl; JV Bsktbl; Var L Crs Cntry; Var L Ftbl; Comp Sci.

KEKAHUNA, RICHARD NOBORU; Servite HS; Garden Grove, CA; (2); Boy Scts; Library Aide; Math Tm; Hon Roll; NHS; NEDT Awd; Amateur Radio; CSF; Jr Statesman Of Amer; Aerospace.

KELCKA, HEATHER D; Capital Christian HS; Citrus Heights, CA; (3); Computer Clb; Office Aide; Speech Tm; Thesps; School Musical; School Play; Stage Crew; Cit Awd; Hon Roll; Theater Arts.

KELEDJIAN, SHOGHIG Z; Holy Martyrs/Ferrahian HS; Van Nuys, CA; (2).

KELIDDARI, FARHAD; Santa Monica HS; Santa Monica, CA; (3); Teachers Aide; Var Bsktbl; Cit Awd; High Hon Roll; Hon Roll; Boys Clb Amer; CSF; UCLA; Med.

KELL, CHRISTINE D; Thomas Downey HS; Modesto, CA; (4); 17/436; Ed Nwsp; Ed Yrbk; Var L Swmmng; Hon Roll; Pres Acad Fit Awd; Vrsty Water Polo Tm, Ltr; UC Davis; Ag Economics.

KELL, JEANETTE M; Chino HS; Chino, CA; (3); Church Yth Grp; Girl Scts; School Play; JV Var Swmmng; Cit Awd; Hon Roll; Spur Mdl; Congressional Schlr; Chaffey JR Coll; Psych.

KELLAMS, KATHERINE A; San Marcos HS; Santa Barbara, CA; (3); 50/380; Acpl Chr; Ed Nwsp; Treas Frsh Cls; JV Var Bsktbl; JV Swmmng; JV Trk; JV Vllybl; Hon Roll; Lcl Prod Opera; Tutored Alg 1-4, Geo & Trig; UCLA; Politics.

KELLAS, KRISTIN N; Alta Loma HS; Montclair, CA; (4); Acpl Chr; Color Guard; Cheerldng; Chamber Singers; Badminton; Jobs Dghtrs; Politics.

KELLEHER, JENNIFER M; Las Lomas HS; Alamo, CA; (4); 15/250; Church Yth Grp; Dance Clb; Drama Clb; School Play; Nwsp; Sec Soph Cls; Off Sr Cls; Stu Cncl; High Hon Roll; UCLA.

KELLER, CARISA A; Del Mar HS; Campbell, CA; (4); 18/250; Library Aide; JV Bsktbl; Var Socr; Var Tennis; Pres Acad Fit Awd; Pres Schlr; CSF; Vrsty Badminton; UC Santa Barbara; Engrng.

KELLER, CHERYL; Herlong HS; Herlong, CA; (4); 5/26; Am Leg Aux Girls St; Cmnty Wkr; FBLA; Office Aide; SADD; Teachers Aide; Lit Mag; Treas Jr Cls; Pres Treas Stu Cncl; Capt Bsktbl; Tn Wrk Rep 88; Safe Ride Co-Ord; Drug, Alcohol Awareness Group; Lassen CC; Bus Admin.

KELLER, DANIEL A; John F Kennedy HS; Sacramento, CA; (2); Art Clb; ROTC; Var Ftbl; Wt Lftg; Hon Roll; Animation; Japanese Animation; Cartooning; Comp; Cartoonist.

KELLER, DAWN M; Bishop Manogue HS; Woodland, CA; (3); GAA; Teachers Aide; Vllybl; Hon Roll; NHS.

KELLER, DUSTIN; Las Plumas HS; Bangor, CA; (1); Math Clb; Nwsp; Off Frsh Cls; Hon Roll; JETS Awd; UC Santa Cruz; Theoretcl Physc.

KELLER, JENNIFER; Rosary HS; Buena Park, CA; (2); Church Yth Grp; Cmnty Wkr; French Clb; NFL; Speech Tm; School Play; Hon Roll; CA ST Fullerton; Cmmnctns.

KELLER, JOHN J; Woodcrest Christian HS; Norco, CA; (1); JV Bsktbl; Norco Bsktbl Leag; Pat Riley Bsktbl Camp 90; RSVP Bsktbl Camp 90.

KELLER, KERI; Alhambra HS; Martinez, CA; (2); 10/200; Church Yth Grp; Dance Clb; 4-H; Pep Clb; Ski Clb; Teachers Aide; Band; Jazz Band; Mrchg Band; Variety Show; Friday Night Live; Chico.

KELLER, LAURA E; Rio American HS; Sacramento, CA; (3); 51/288; Church Yth Grp; Service Clb; Ski Clb; Band; Church Choir; Var L Sftbl; Var Trk; Var Capt Vllybl; High Hon Roll; Pres Acad Fit Awd; Essay Cntst; Photo Cntsts; Local Mdlng Agncy; Bus.

KELLER, LISA; Cajon HS; San Bernardino, CA; (2); Church Yth Grp; Cmnty Wkr; SADD; NHS; Medcl.

KELLER, MICHELLE; Westminster HS; Westminster, CA; (3); Cheerldng; Fld Hcky; Swmmng; Trk; Hon Roll; Chrldng Sqd Rgnl Cmptn Dallas Ntls; Fld Hcky Tm 90 Sunset Lg Chmps; AZ State; Law.

KELLER, REBECCA E; Bullard HS; Fresno, CA; (2); SADD; Teachers Aide; Temple Yth Grp; Prfct Atten Awd; Zoology.

KELLER, STACI N; Folsom HS; Folsom, CA; (3); Pres Church Yth Grp; Cmnty Wkr; Intnl Clb; Model UN; Pep Clb; Teachers Aide; High Hon Roll; Hon Roll.

KELLER, TARA A; Dos Pueblos HS; Santa Barbara, CA; (1); Church Yth Grp; NHS; CA Schlrshp Fedrtn.

KELLER, THOMAS J; Palos Verdes HS; Rancho Palos Verd, CA; (4); Key Clb; Letterman Clb; Office Aide; Ski Clb; Spanish Clb; Teachers Aide; Var Bsbl; Var Intrml Ftbl; Hon Roll; U CO Boulder.

KELLER, VERONICA F; East Bakersfield HS; Bakersfield, CA; (4); 66/400; Teachers Aide; Chorus; Var Socr; Var Trk; Hon Roll; Eisenhower Fndtn Sci Ambssdr; Sci.

KELLEY, AARON J; Hoover HS; Fresno, CA; (1); Church Yth Grp; Stu Cncl; Tennis; JV Vllybl; Golden St Exam Hnrs In Alg; USC; Comp.

KELLEY, DAVID; Highlands HS; Sacramento, CA; (2); 4/200; Boy Scts; Debate Tm; NFL; Speech Tm; Mrchg Band; Rep Soph Cls; Bsktbl; Socr; Swmmng; 1st Pl Wnnr Black Hstry Wk Essay Cont; Natl Forensics Leag St Qualfr; Marching Band Bst Fresh; Brigham Young U; Bus Law.

KELLEY, DAWN M; North HS; Bakersfield, CA; (2); Pep Clb; Spanish Clb; Chorus; JV Var Cheerldng; Pres Acad Fit Awd; Interact Club; N AZ U; Flight Attndt.

KELLEY, DONNA M; Oakmont HS; Roseville, CA; (2); Church Yth Grp; Band; Mrchg Band; Hon Roll; Point Loma Nazarene Coll; Tchr.

KELLEY, ELMO J; John Wesley North HS; Riverside, CA; (4); 36/300; Church Yth Grp; Spanish Clb; Rptr Yrbk; Cit Awd; Hon Roll; Spanish NHS; Acad Excllnc Schlrshp U CA Riverside; Grad With Hnrbl Mntn; HS-U Pgm UCR 89-90; U CA Riverside; Econ.

KELLEY, ERIN; Moorpark HS; Moorpark, CA; (4); 2/206; Church Yth Grp; VP Band; VP Frsh Cls; VP Stu Cncl; Var L Bsktbl; Var Capt Crs Cntry; Var L Trk; High Hon Roll; CA Hnr Soc-Pres & VP; Princeton U.

KELLEY, KATHY S; Santa Ynez HS; Santa Ynez, CA; (3); Debate Tm; Varsity Clb; Var Socr; Var Trk; Var Capt Vllybl; Pres Acad Fit Awd; Outstndng Stu Trck; CIF Vllybl Tm; Outstndng Vllybl All St Tm; Lompoc Hower Show 88-90; Alfa Clb Chmpn; Hstry.

KELLEY, KEVA PAULA; Fairfield HS; Fairfield, CA; (3); Church Yth Grp; Drama Clb; Teachers Aide; School Play; Rptr Nwsp; Bsktbl; Tennis; Cit Awd; Hon Roll; Prfct Atten Awd; U CA Davis.

KELLEY, KRYSTAL L; Canyon Springs HS; Moreno Valley, CA; (3); Chorus; High Hon Roll; U Of CA Riverside; Counselor.

KELLEY, MARK J; Chico HS; Chico, CA; (4); 16/354; Debate Tm; Drama Clb; Speech Tm; Phtg Yrbk; JV Bsktbl; High Hon Roll; Jr NHS; Pres Acad Fit Awd; Val; Video Club; CSU; Bus Admin.

KELLEY, MELISSA B; Valley Christian HS; Bellflower, CA; (2); Church Yth Grp; Letterman Clb; Office Aide; VP Frsh Cls; Pres Soph Cls; Var L Crs Cntry; Mgr Vllybl; Vrsty Crss Cntry 1st Team All Leag; Fig Sktng ISIA 1st Pl 3 Of 4 Comptns; Art.

KELLEY, ROBERT; Mater Dei HS; Tustin, CA; (2); Church Yth Grp; Cmnty Wkr; Off Soph Cls; Bsbl; Socr.

KELLEY, RYAN M; Del Campo HS; Citrus Heights, CA; (4); 14/429; Teachers Aide; Hon Roll; Pres Acad Fit Awd; CSF; Sacramento Prsnl Comp Users Grp; CSU Sacramento; Comp Engrg.

KELLEY, SAMANTA; Bolsa Grande HS; Westminster, CA; (1); Var L Socr; Hon Roll; Pediatrician.

KELLEY, SHANNON A; La Canada HS; La Canada Flintri, CA; (3); 81/250; Church Yth Grp; Cmnty Wkr; Key Clb; Teachers Aide; Acpl Chr; School Musical; Yrbk; VP Jr Cls; Powder Puff Ftbl; Teach Nursry Schl; Ed.

KELLEY, SHANNON G; Woodland HS; Woodland, CA; (3); Church Yth Grp; FFA; Teachers Aide; Yrbk; Sftbl; Hon Roll; Pwdr Puff Sftbl; Slwptch Sftbl; Chrch Yth Grp Vllybl; Animal Care Clinic Vlntr; Tchng.

KELLEY, TIMOTHY M; Bellarmine College Prep; Los Gatos, CA; (3); Red Cross Aide; Yrbk; Ftbl; JV Trk; Ntl Merit Ltr; Pres BPAC; Tae Kwon Doe Stu; CA St U; Philosphy.

KELLIER, SHAUNETTE K; Montclair HS; Pomona, CA; (3); Office Aide; Band; Orch; Trk; Brooks Coll; Fashn Merch.

KELLIHER, CHRISTI A; Valhalla HS; Jamul, CA; (3); 76/408; Church Yth Grp; Dance Clb; Rptr Nwsp; Off Soph Cls; Off Jr Cls; Ftbl; Wrstlng; Kiwanis Awd; U Of CA Riverside.

KELLISON, JOSHUA GENE; Sweetwater HS; National City, CA; (2); Boy Scts; Church Yth Grp; Hosp Aide; Science Clb; Ski Clb; Thesps; Band; Jazz Band; Mrchg Band; School Play; ASB Outside Concessions; Scienct Honor Award; California JR Ranger; English/Teacher.

KELLOGG, JENNIFER C; John F Kennedy HS; Sacramento, CA; (2); 178/525; JV Socr; Hon Roll; JV Most Outstndng Plyr 1989; Piano.

KELLOGG, KATHLEEN; Morro Bay HS; Albuquerque, NM; (4); 33/223; Dance Clb; Drama Clb; Ski Clb; Varsity Clb; Chorus; School Musical; Swing Chorus; Var JV Cheerldng; Powder Puff Ftbl; Hon Roll; Bank Of Amer Achvt Awd-Fine Arts; Sousa Awd Choir; U Of NM; Fine Arts.

KELLOGG, LEANDER D; Moreno Valley HS; Moreno Valley, CA; (3); Boy Scts; Church Yth Grp; ROTC; Color Guard; Drill Tm; Stage Crew; Rep Stu Cncl; High Hon Roll; Hon Roll; Sns Amer Revltn Natl Awd ROTC; 3rd Pl 2nd Annl Wrtng Cmptn; BYU.

KELLOGG, MISHA; Cajon HS; Devore, CA; (2); Cmnty Wkr; GAA; Key Clb; SADD; Lit Mag; Var L Tennis; Cit Awd; Hon Roll; NHS; CSF; U S Tennis Assoc; Bus.

KELLOGG, ROBERT D; St Ignatius HS; San Francisco, CA; (3); Cmnty Wkr; French Clb; Ski Clb; Nwsp; JV Bsbl; JV Bsktbl; JV Ftbl; Liturgy Group; Jr Statesman Of Amer; Spirit Club; Engl.

KELLY, AARON C; Poway HS; Poway, CA; (3); Varsity Clb; Ftbl; Wt Lftg; Wrstlng; Arch.

KELLY, AMY; Morro Bay HS; Los Osos, CA; (3); 54/213; Drama Clb; French Clb; Chorus; Stage Crew; Off Jr Cls; Hon Roll; Dance; U Of CA Davis; Sci.

KELLY, ANNE J; Poway HS; Poway, CA; (4); 99/679; Church Yth Grp; Cmnty Wkr; Library Aide; Teachers Aide; Church Choir; Orch; Hon Roll; CSF; Palomar Coll; Chld Dvlpmt.

KELLY, ANNE L; El Toro HS; Trabuco Canyon, CA; (3); Treas French Clb; Key Clb; Var Cheerldng; High Hon Roll; CSF; Delphi; Bus.

KELLY, BRANDON J; Washington HS; Fremont, CA; (3); 20/350; Varsity Clb; JV Var Ftbl; Powder Puff Ftbl; Intrml Wt Lftg; Hon Roll; Jr NHS; UCLA; Med.

KELLY, CLINTON S; Royal HS; Simi Valley, CA; (3); Boy Scts; Band; Rep Soph Cls; Cit Awd; High Hon Roll; NHS; Ntl Merit SF; Prfct Atten Awd; UCLA; Chem.

KELLY, COLLEEN; Antioch Unified Schls; Antioch, CA; (3); Rep Frsh Cls; Pep Clb; Var Pom Pon; Hon Roll; Diablo Valley Coll; Art Tchr.

KELLY, CRYSTAL M; Santa Maria HS; Santa Maria, CA; (3); Drama Clb; FFA; Key Clb; Teachers Aide; School Play; Hon Roll.

KELLY, DARRIN T; Shasta HS; Redding, CA; (3); Drama Clb; German Clb; Var L Ftbl; Var Trk; Hon Roll; Peer Tutoring; Wrk 25 Hrs Wk Local Restrnt; Plastic Surgeon.

KELLY, EDITH J; George Washington HS; San Francisco, CA; (3); Church Yth Grp; Dance Clb; Key Clb; Pres Service Clb; School Musical; School Play; Treas Frsh Cls; High Hon Roll; Pres Jr Statesmen Amer; Yth Ambssdr Israel & Japan; HS Span Teacher.

KELLY, FERREN L; Raoul Wallenberg HS; San Francisco, CA; (1); 5/180; GAA; Varsity Clb; Pres Frsh Cls; JV Vllybl; High Hon Roll; UCSF; Pediatrics.

KELLY, JENNIFER A; Diamond Bar HS; Diamond Bar, CA; (2); Church Yth Grp; Cmnty Wkr; German Clb; Key Clb; VP SADD; Varsity Clb; Lit Mag; Tennis; Hon Roll; UC San Diego.

KELLY, JOEL; Western Christian HS; Walnut, CA; (3); Church Yth Grp; JV Var Bsbl; JV Ftbl; Hon Roll; Chrch Chr; Eagle Sct BSA; Bus.

KELLY, KARA LYNN; Corona Del Mar HS; Corona Del Mar, CA; (3); 75/310; Aud/Vis; Church Yth Grp; Cmnty Wkr; Dance Clb; Intnl Clb; JCL; Key Clb; Latin Clb; Pep Clb; SADD; Peer Assistnace Leag Pres; Youth To Youth; Psych.

KELLY, KATHERINE; Modesto HS; Modesto, CA; (1); Church Yth Grp; FHA; Orch; Hon Roll.

KELLY, KRISTIN L; Los Gatos HS; Los Gatos, CA; (2); Key Clb; Var Crs Cntry; Var Trk; High Hon Roll; CASA Fshn Show; Vol Blood Drive Key Club; UC; Psych.

KELLY, LAURIE T; St Genevieve HS; Granada Hills, CA; (3); Dance Clb; Pep Clb; Chorus; Drill Tm; Hon Roll; Mst Insprtnl Dance Tm.

KELLY, LISA; San Ramon Valley HS; Danville, CA; (2); Church Yth Grp; Cmnty Wkr; Chorus; Socr; Sftbl; Hon Roll; Inter Dsgn.

KELLY, MARIAN C; Lynbrook HS; San Jose, CA; (4); 56/293; Chorus; Piano; Axso Sccr; U Of CO Boulder.

KELLY, PAMELA; Homestead HS; Sunnyvale, CA; (3); Church Yth Grp; Girl Scts; Hosp Aide; JA; Teachers Aide; CSF; Golden St Exam Alg & Geom Hnrs.

KELLY, PATRICK J; Bellarmine College Prep; Burlingame, CA; (3); 25/300; Cmnty Wkr; VP Letterman Clb; NFL; Service Clb; Ski Clb; Capt Varsity Clb; Rep Stu Cncl; Intrml Bsktbl; Capt L Crs Cntry; Stat Ftbl.

KELLY, ROBERT C; Beaumont HS; Beaumont, CA; (2); Var Bsbl; Var Bsktbl; JV Capt Ftbl; Hon Roll; U Of CA Los Angeles.

KELLY, THERESA M; Modesto HS; Modesto, CA; (3); Church Yth Grp; Prfct Atten Awd; Psych.

KELLY, TIMOTHY; Claremont HS; Claremont, CA; (4); 39/387; Am Leg Boys St; Church Yth Grp; Pres French Clb; Q&S; Ed Nwsp; Var Capt Crs Cntry; Var Capt Trk; High Hon Roll; Pres Acad Fit Awd; CSF-LIFE; Coll Of William & Mary; Econ.

KELSEY, AMANDA; Brea Olinda HS; Brea, CA; (2); Dance Clb; Key Clb; Stage Crew; March Of Dimes Walk Amer; CA ST Fullerton; Chld Care.

KELSEY, JANE M; Aptos HS; Aptos, CA; (1); 1/400; German Clb; School Musical; Var Swmmng; High Hon Roll; Prfct Atten Awd; Pres Acad Fit Awd; Zenith Clb; Intrct Clb Pres, Area Rep For Dist.

KELSO, MICHELLE M; Bishop O'dowd HS; Oakland, CA; (2); Stage Crew; Drama.

KELSO, PREEYA; Morro Bay HS; Los Osos, CA; (4); 144/226; Church Yth Grp; FBLA; Cit Awd; Hon Roll; ROP Cert; Peer Cnslr; Cursta Coll.

KELTON III, BURL; Del Campo HS; Carmichael, CA; (3); 108/450; Church Yth Grp; Cmnty Wkr; Drama Clb; French Clb; Intnl Clb; ROTC; Teachers Aide; Color Guard; School Play; Ed Nwsp.

KELTZ, JOSEPH V; San Diequito HS; Cardff By The Sea, CA; (3); Letterman Clb; Varsity Clb; JV Crs Cntry; Var Lcrss; Wrstlng.

KEMP, CORY; Los Alamitos HS; Los Alamitos, CA; (3); Boy Scts; Church Yth Grp; Band; Chorus; Jazz Band; Mrchg Band; Pep Band; Hon Roll.

KEMP, DOUG; Calvary Chapel HS; Garden Grove, CA; (4); Chess Clb; Church Yth Grp; Yrbk; Cit Awd; Pres Acad Fit Awd; Music Apprctn; Golden West Coll.

KEMP, KELSEY E; James Logan HS; Union City, CA; (3); Cmnty Wkr; Drama Clb; School Musical; School Play; Stage Crew; Hon Roll; Outing Clb Sec; Campfire; Day Camp; U Of OR; Elem Ed.

KEMP, KIM L; Glendale HS; Glendale, CA; (3); Church Yth Grp; Pres Cmnty Wkr; Ski Clb; Color Guard; Drill Tm; Ed Nwsp; Sec Frsh Cls; Off Sr Cls; Bsktbl; Prfct Atten Awd; Natl Chrty Leag, Pres; San Diego ST; Teacher.

KEMP, MICHELLE A; Greenville JR/Sr HS; Greenville, CA; (3); Church Yth Grp; Drama Clb; Girl Scts; Service Clb; Chorus; Variety Show; Sec Jr Cls; Pres Sr Cls; JV Cheerldng; High Hon Roll; Music.

KEMP, RANDALL; Berean Christian HS; Pittsburg, CA; (4); 3/70; Church Yth Grp; Ski Clb; Rep Stu Cncl; Var L Bsbl; Var L Bsktbl; Var L Socr; Var L Trk; High Hon Roll; Pres Acad Fit Awd; UC Davis; Lib-Info Sci.

KEMP, SHERI N; Saugus HS; Saugus, CA; (3); 4/456; Capt Drill Tm; NHS; CSF; CAPR Awd Spnsh I, II, III, & Engl; Nutrition.

KEMPNER, FRANKLIN J; Mount Diablo HS; Concord, CA; (3); 11/350; FBLA; VP Spanish Clb; SADD; Off Jr Cls; Pres Sr Cls; Rotary Awd; Variety Show; VP Soph Cls; Crs Cntry; Tennis; Asian Clb Pres; Clb Latino; CA Schlstc Fed; Jr Undergrad Plaque; UCLA; Intl Financer.

KEMPS, DOMINIC C; Sacred Heart Prep; Atherton, CA; (2); Model UN; Ski Clb; Chorus; JV Socr; Var Tennis; Hon Roll; NHS.

KEMPTON, HEATHER DENISE; Buena HS; APO New York, NY; (4); 68/456; Church Yth Grp; Drama Clb; JA; Color Guard; Lit Mag; Stu Cncl; Ntl Merit Ltr; Pres Acad Fit Awd; CA Schlrshp Fed Gold Seal Bearer; Girls Leag Brd; Vlntr; Intl Bus.

KENDALL, ARIEL; Lowell HS; San Francisco, CA; (2); Pres Church Yth Grp; Teachers Aide; Chorus; Church Choir; School Musical; VP Frsh Cls; Partnrsp Pgm UC Berkeley; Bio.

KENDALL, JASON J; Glendora HS; Glendora, CA; (3); Church Yth Grp; JV Ftbl; Var Capt Socr; Hon Roll; Golden St Acad Excllnce Awd Geom 89.

KENDALL, MICHAEL L; La Sierra HS; Riverside, CA; (3); JV Var Bsbl; JV Ftbl; Hon Roll; Bsbl Lttr-Var; JV Bsbl & Ftbl; Drftng.

KENDALL, SUZIE A; Sequoia HS; San Carlos, CA; (1); 14/455; Socr; Statesman Amer; CSF; Cal Poly; Int Desgn.

KENDALL, TINA M; Rio Vista HS; Rio Vista, CA; (3); Church Yth Grp; FHA; Letterman Clb; Ed Nwsp; Rptr Yrbk; Sec Jr Cls; Var JV Bsktbl; JV Sftbl; Var Tennis; Var Trk; Sftbl MVP; Butte View League Trk Chmpns, All-League & MVP; Butte View League Tnns Chmpns; Solano CC; Phys Ed Tchr.

KENDALL, TROY W; Torrey Pines HS; San Diego, CA; (3); 128/457; Church Yth Grp; Cmnty Wkr; FCA; SADD; Crs Cntry; Diving; Trk; Hon Roll; Golden St Exam-Geom Hnrs; Grand Awd-500 Arts Festvl; Advrtsng.

KENDIG, JAMIE A; La Reina HS; Thousand Oaks, CA; (2); 1/100; Cmnty Wkr; GAA; Letterman Clb; Rep Frsh Cls; VP Soph Cls; VP Jr Cls; Var Crs Cntry; Var Socr; Var Sftbl; French Hon Soc; JR Alma Mater Schlrshp; Svc Cncl Pin; Ctznshp Hnrs.

KENDRICK, ADAM W; Tulare Union HS; Tulare, CA; (3); Teachers Aide; Hon Roll.

KENELY, BREENA JOY; Torrey Pines HS; San Diego, CA; (2); Church Yth Grp; Cmnty Wkr; Dance Clb; Girl Scts; Hosp Aide; Library Aide; Office Aide; Teachers Aide; Variety Show; Rep Soph Cls; UCSB; Psycht.

KENG, ROBERT; Washington HS; Fremont, CA; (4); 75/340; Hnrs Chem 88-89; Hnrs Physcs 89-90; Marine Reserves; Physcs.

KENI, JYOTSNA; Diamond Bar HS; Diamond Bar, CA; (2); French Clb; Intnl Clb; Math Clb; Math Tm; Science Clb; Service Clb; SADD; Cit Awd; DAR Awd; High Hon Roll; Jr Statesmen Of Amer; CA Schltc Fed; JV Badminton; Engrng.

KENLINE, KIMBERLEE J; Corning Union HS; Corning, CA; (4); 9/122; Cmnty Wkr; Trk; Bank Of Amer Achvmnt Awd; All Leag Sub Sctn; Cert Acad Excllnc In Achvmng; Shasta Coll; Art.

KENNARD, KEVETT; South Gate HS; Los Angeles, CA; (2); Church Yth Grp; Dance Clb; Pep Clb; Drill Tm; JV Bsbl; Cit Awd; Gramlen U; Actrss.

KENNEBECK, KRISTEN M; Saint Josepih HS; Seal Beach, CA; (2); Church Yth Grp; Cmnty Wkr; GAA; JV Sftbl; JV Vllybl; Hon Roll; Bus.

KENNEDY, AARON M; Garden Grove HS; Garden Grove, CA; (3); Church Yth Grp; FCA; Teachers Aide; JV Bsbl; Var Socr; Pres English Clb; Hon Roll; Garden Grove Police Xplr; Clb Scr Tm; Goldenwest JC; Law.

KENNEDY, ADAM; Central Union HS; El Centro, CA; (3); 60/550; Church Yth Grp; Cmnty Wkr; Debate Tm; NFL; Speech Tm; Varsity Clb; Band; Mrchg Band; Pep Band; School Musical; Tnns Teacher & Compete In Trnmnts; U Of CA Berkeley; Bus Law.

KENNEDY, ALEX; Dana Hills HS; Lake Forest, CA; (4); 25/575; Church Yth Grp; Drama Clb; German Clb; Science Clb; SADD; Ed Yrbk; Elks Awd; Hon Roll; Pres Acad Fit Awd; Rotary Awd; U Of CA Irvine; Mech Engrng.

KENNEDY, ANDREW; Cajon HS; San Bernardino, CA; (2); Chess Clb; Key Clb; JV Tennis; UCLA.

KENNEDY, ANTHONY J; Pacifica HS; Stanton, CA; (3); 55/260; Church Yth Grp; SADD; Intrml Bsktbl; Var Vllybl; High Hon Roll; Hon Roll; Pres Acad Fit Awd; Engrng.

KENNEDY, AUTUMN A; Rubidoux HS; Mira Loma, CA; (4); 41/550; JV Var Sftbl; Hon Roll; CSF; JR Coll; Comp Prog.

KENNEDY, BLAKE S; Piedmont HS; Piedmont, CA; (4); Boy Scts; Cmnty Wkr; Spanish Clb; SADD; Acpl Chr; Pres Frsh Cls; JV Ftbl; JV Socr; Var Tennis; High Hon Roll; BS Rank Eagle Scout; Order Of Arrow Hnry; CSF; U CA-BERKELEY; Envrmntl Sci.

KENNEDY, CAILIN K; Orland HS; Orland, CA; (4); 8/111; Church Yth Grp; SADD; Stage Crew; Rep Frsh Cls; Rep Sr Cls; Stu Cncl; Stat Bsbl; Capt Cheerldng; Ntl Merit Ltr; CSF Seal Bearer; GATE; Acad Dcthln Tm; Cal Poly; Bus Admin.

KENNEDY, CHRISTINE M; Sierra Vista HS; Baldwin Park, CA; (3); Cmnty Wkr; Key Clb; Pep Clb; Science Clb; Band; Chorus; Off Soph Cls; Off Sr Cls; Var L Crs Cntry; Trk; YMCA Cnslr Asst; Church Camp Cnslr; HS Literary Mgzn Poems Pblshd; Mt San Antonio U; Psych.

KENNEDY, DANIELLE L; Arcadia HS; Arcadia, CA; (3); Church Yth Grp; Dance Clb; Drama Clb; Ski Clb; Thesps; School Play; Variety Show; Rep Soph Cls; Rep Jr Cls; Capt Cheerldng; Chrch Mssn Trip Ensenada Mexico; Westmont Coll; Commnctns.

KENNEDY, DARLA M; Ponderosa HS; El Dorado, CA; (2); Band; Pep Band; Bsktbl; Hon Roll; Chico ST; CPA.

KENNEDY, DEANNA; Lompoc HS; Lompoc, CA; (2); Drama Clb; Hon Roll; Pres Acad Fit Awd; Awd For Outstndng PE Female; Awd Otstndng Stu Life Skills; Humboldt ST U.

KENNEDY, DON R; Carlsbad HS; Carlsbad, CA; (1); Band; Jazz Band; Mrchg Band; School Musical; Bsktbl; High Hon Roll.

KENNEDY, ERIN; Vista HS; Vista, CA; (4); 41/480; Drama Clb; German Clb; Office Aide; Teachers Aide; Chorus; Stu Cncl; Gym; Swmmng; Cit Awd; Hon Roll; Assoc Stus Of German; Gym Club Pres; Bckyrd Swim Vlntr; Adopt A Family; Soup Kitchen; MV Gymnast; U Of AZ; Nrsng.

KENNEDY, JASON A; Robert A Millikan HS; Long Beach, CA; (4); Boy Scts; Church Yth Grp; Chorus; Church Choir; School Musical; School Play; Swing Chorus; Hon Roll; Bus Medal Of Merit; Long Beach City Coll; Bus.

KENNEDY, JOSHUA; Marysville HS; Marysville, CA; (4); 1/200; Am Leg Boys St; Debate Tm; Key Clb; Pres Letterman Clb; NFL; Pep Clb; Science Clb; Ski Clb; Spanish Clb; SADD; Sci & Math Rgn 2nd Pl; CSF; Outstndng Cntrbtn Track; USMA; Cvl Engr.

KENNEDY, JUANITA; Westlake Schl For Girls; Van Nuys, CA; (4); Cmnty Wkr; Debate Tm; Latin Clb; Letterman Clb; Math Tm; NFL; SADD; Temple Yth Grp; Varsity Clb; High Hon Roll; Natl Ltn Soc Exm Fnlst Gld Mdl; Hd Admssns Cmmtte; Hd Wrtng Ctr Tutrs; Amherst Coll.

KENNEDY, KEVIN R; Barston HS; Barstow, CA; (2); Chess Clb; JV VP Ftbl; JV VP Trk; Cit Awd; Hon Roll; Air Force.

KENNEDY II, LUKE M; Red Bluff HS; Gerber, CA; (3); Church Yth Grp; Cmnty Wkr; 4-H; FFA; JA; Teachers Aide; Bsbl; JV Var Crs Cntry; JV Ftbl; Sftbl; Most Outstndng Runner Cross Cntry; FFA Showmanshp Awd; Game Warden.

KENNEDY, LYNN MICHELE; Bear River HS; Grass Valley, CA; (2); Church Yth Grp; Ski Clb; SADD; Band; Rep Stu Cncl; Cit Awd; High Hon Roll; Hon Roll; Pres Acad Fit Awd; UC Davis; Pre-Med.

KENNEDY JR, MICHAEL LINEHAN; Bishop Amat Memorial HS; Covina, CA; (2); Letterman Clb; Var L Golf; Hon Roll; NHS; Pres Acad Fit Awd; Med.

KENNEDY, PAMELA E; Whitney HS; Cerritos, CA; (4); Drama Clb; Girl Scts; Library Aide; Teachers Aide; Thesps; School Play; U Of OR; Ed.

KENNEDY, SCOTT M; Coronado HS; Coronado, CA; (3); 14/136; Office Aide; High Hon Roll; CSF.

KENNEDY, SHELLEY; San Gabriel Acad; Temple City, CA; (2); Church Yth Grp; Teachers Aide; Chorus; Church Choir; Rep Stu Cncl; Bsktbl; Ftbl; Sftbl; NHS; Pathfinders.

KENNEY, CHARLOTTE J; Vacaville HS; Nine Mile Falls, WA; (2); FFA; Teachers Aide; Cit Awd; High Hon Roll; Hon Roll; Tennis With Classes; Track Bsktbl; Spokane Falls; Eng.

KENNEY, CHRISTINE R; California HS; Whittier, CA; (3); 16/365; French Clb; SADD; JV Bsktbl; Stat Crs Cntry; JV Var Trk; Hon Roll.

KENNEY, JULIE K; Redlands HS; Redlands, CA; (4); 16/908; Art Clb; Pres Church Yth Grp; Pep Clb; Science Clb; Cit Awd; High Hon Roll; CSF Sea Bearer; Brigham Young U Trustees Schlrshp; Hnrs Grad LDS Smnry Pgm; Brigham Young U.

KENNIFER, KAREN L; Irvine HS; Irvine, CA; (3); Office Aide; Off Jr Cls; Rep Stu Cncl; Var L Swmmng; Hon Roll; Charity Club; CSF; Schlr/Athltc Awd; U CA Santa Barbara; Bus.

KENNIGNTON, AARON B; Paraclete HS; Lancaster, CA; (3); Computer Clb; Scholastic Bowl; High Hon Roll; Trig Math Awd; Chem Sci Awd; CSF.

KENNING, JODIE L; Sonora HS; Fullerton, CA; (2); Church Yth Grp; French Clb; Pep Clb; Ski Clb; JV Cheerldng; Hon Roll; Var Badminton MVP.

KENNINGS, SEAN L; Tamalpais HS; Mill Valley, CA; (3); Latin Clb; Scholastic Bowl; Var L Ftbl; Var L Lcrss; JV L Trk; High Hon Roll; Arch.

KENNINGTON, AARON; Paraclete HS; Lancaster, CA; (3); Computer Clb; Quiz Bowl; High Hon Roll; CA Schlstc Federal; Arch Engr.

KENNISON, MEGAN V; St Josephs HS; Santa Maria, CA; (3); Rptr Nwsp; Var Sftbl; JV Var Vllybl; High Hon Roll; Hon Roll; Jr NHS; NHS; CA Schlstc Fed; Schlr Ath; Frgn Lang Clb; Bst Offns Sftbl; Excllnc In All Sbjcts Awd; All Leg Sftbl; UCSD.

KENNON, AMBER L; Montebello HS; Montebello, CA; (2); Church Yth Grp; Drama Clb; Girl Scts; Pep Clb; SADD; Chorus; Church Choir; Color Guard; JV Co-Capt Cheerldng; JV Pom Pon; CSLB; Law.

KENNY, J RYAN; Redlands HS; Redlands, CA; (4); Pres Chess Clb; Treas Debate Tm; NFL; Treas Speech Tm; Var L Trk; Pres Acad Fit Awd; USAF Acadm Appt; MENSA; USAF Acad.

KENNY, MECHELLE LYNN; Patrick Henry HS; San Diego, CA; (4); Hosp Aide; Band; Mrchg Band; Ed Nwsp; Sprt Ed Yrbk; Hon Roll; Jr NHS; Patriot Yr 89-90; Herff-Jones Yrbk Awd 90; Past Hnrd Qn Jbs Dghtrs; Boyd Schl; Flight Attendant.

KENNY, SEAN M; Redlands HS; Redlands, CA; (3); Swmmng; Water Polo; UCUSB; Aerospace Engr.

KENNY, SHANNON L; Santa Barbara HS; Montecito, CA; (3); Lit Mag; Stu Cncl; DAR Awd; Hon Roll; Ballet; Creative Wrtng; Theatre.

KENNY, TERRY; Ramona HS; Riverside, CA; (4); Var Socr; JV Tennis; Lawyer.

KENT, JACQUELINE M; Lakewood HS; Lakewood, CA; (4); Treas Art Clb; Drama Clb; Pres FTA; Treas Pres Intnl Clb; Key Clb; Office Aide; Speech Tm; SADD; Teachers Aide; Lit Mag; PTA Mdlln 87; Gold Tassel-Hnrs Grad 90; Dsgnr/Producer HS Hnr Plaque; Long Bch Cty Coll; Cinematgrphy.

KENT, JAMES J; Bishop Montgomery HS; San Pedro, CA; (2); 31/415; Band; Jazz Band; Mrchg Band; Orch; Stage Crew; High Hon Roll; NHS; Prfct Atten Awd; So CA Drumline Circuit 1st Pl; So Cal Band & Orch Assoc 1st Pl 89-90; Embry Riddle; Aeronaut Sci.

KENT, JULIE A; Fresno Christian HS; Fresno, CA; (2); Church Yth Grp; VP Jr Cls; Cit Awd; High Hon Roll; Hon Roll; JV Vllybl; Mostinsprtnl Awd 1989-90 JR Vrsty Vllybl Tm; Fresno City.

KENT, MATTHEW S; Silver Valley HS; Fort Irwin, CA; (2); Var Bsbl; JV Ftbl; Cit Awd; Hon Roll; Pres Acad Fit Awd; Wntr Fstvl Prncs 90; Vrsty Ltr Awd Bsbl; Med.

KENT, MATTHEW W; Lincoln HS; San Francisco, CA; (3); Nwsp; Var Swmmng; Cls Up Prgrm; Jr Statsmn Amer; Wrld Affrs Cncl; CS U San Luis Obispo; Arts.

KENT, RICHARD E; The Bishops Schl; San Diego, CA; (3); 3/88; French Clb; VP Stu Cncl; JV Tennis; French Hon Soc; High Hon Roll; NHS; Ntl Merit SF; Pres Schlr; Acad Leag; Vrsty Water Polo.

KENT, SHALONDA; Portola JR SR HS; Portola, CA; (2); Church Yth Grp; Dance Clb; Ski Clb; Spanish Clb; Band; Mrchg Band; Swing Chorus; Variety Show; JV Bsktbl; Score Keeper; Drug Free Yth To Yth Club; Trck N Sectns CA Chmpnshps; Music Camp Schlrshps; UC Davis; Jrnlsm.

KENT, TARALYN M; Rim Of The World HS; Twin Peaks, CA; (1); Church Yth Grp; 4-H; 4-H Awd; Hon Roll; Vet.

KENYON, AMY; Etiwanda HS; Alta Loma, CA; (1); Church Yth Grp; Cmnty Wkr; Pep Clb; L Cheerldng; Var L Trk; Hon Roll; UCLA; Sci.

KENYON, ELISA; Tulelake HS; Tulelake, CA; (2); 1/40; Church Yth Grp; School Play; Bsktbl; Vllybl; NHS; Treas FBLA; Treas Frsh Cls; Water Skiing; Friday Night Live; CSF; Teach.

KENYON-VOELKER, SHONEE L; Colfax HS; Nevada City, CA; (3); 5/165; Office Aide; Service Clb; Nwsp; High Hon Roll; Hon Roll; Pres Schlr; Peer Tutor; Acad Dcthln; Loyola Marymount U; Bio Sci.

KEO, PENHBORAMEY; Jordan HS; Long Beach, CA; (4); Debate Tm; Tennis; Hon Roll; Pres Acad Fit Awd; PTA & Rotary Schlrshps; Debate Clb; Chem Team; UC Los Angeles; Hstry.

KEO, SOVANKIRY; East Bakersfield HS; Bakersfield, CA; (3).

KEOBOUTH, BOUNMY; California HS; Whittier, CA; (2).

KEODARA, BOUNPHENG; Hoover SR HS; San Diego, CA; (1); 1/538; Var Socr; Jr NHS; Badmntn; Elec Engrng.

KEOMAHAVONG, SITTHACHONE; Kearny HS; San Diego, CA; (3); English Clb; Var Golf; Var Socr; High Hon Roll; Hon Roll; Ntl Merit SF; Prfct Atten Awd; Mesa Coll.

KEOPADABSY, VIENGKHONE; Amos Alonzo Stagg HS; Stockton, CA; (1); JV Socr; Media Art Clb; 2 2 2 Pgm; Comp Prgmr.

KEOVILAY, AHT M; Hueneme HS; Oxnard, CA; (1); Computer Clb; Crs Cntry; Ftbl; Trk; Prfct Atten Awd; Auto.

KEPHART, CHI; Soquel HS; Soquel, CA; (4); 4/300; Am Leg Aux Girls St; Cmnty Wkr; Model UN; Teachers Aide; JV Tennis; High Hon Roll; Prfct Atten Awd; Sal; HS Hnrs Stu; High Hnrs Golden ST Exam Gemtry; CSF & Hnrs Club; Attnd Local CA U SR Yr; UCLA; Intnl Rltns.

KEPUS, KAREN D; Yuba City HS; Yuba City, CA; (4); #3 In Class; Church Yth Grp; Am Leg Boys St; Sec Ski Clb; Rep Stu Cncl; Swmmng; Trk; High Hon Roll; Hon Roll; Pres Acad Fit Awd; Exchange Clb Outstndng Stu Of Qrtr; NOW Outstndng Sr Woman 90; Chico ST U; Bus.

KERBA, ELIZABETH G; Carlmont HS; Redwood City, CA; (2); #24 In Class; Cmnty Wkr; Key Clb; Math Clb; Tennis; CA Schlrshp Fed.

KERCHER, JENNIFER L; Capistrano Valley HS; Mission Viejo, CA; (3); Church Yth Grp; Pres Chorus; School Musical; JV Crs Cntry; Socr; Var Swmmng; Trk; Hon Roll; UC Santa Barbara.

KERCHER, KATHERYN A; Riverdale HS; Riverdale, CA; (2); 10/134; GAA; Pep Clb; Science Clb; SADD; Cheerldng; Sftbl; Vllybl; High Hon Roll; Hon Roll; Law.

KEREPESZKI, JOHN; Tri-City Christian Schl; Oceanside, CA; (2); High Hon Roll.

KERGER, KERILY N; Flintridge Preparatory Schl; San Gabriel, CA; (4); French Clb; Key Clb; Pres Pep Clb; School Musical; Rptr Yrbk; Capt Var Cheerldng; Var Socr; Sec French Hon Soc; Hon Roll; Ntl Merit SF; Engrng.

KERNAHAN, STEPHANIE; Casa Grande HS; Petaluma, CA; (3); 1/288; Cmnty Wkr; German Clb; Service Clb; Ski Clb; Speech Tm; Var L Crs Cntry; Capt Var Swmmng; FTA; French Clb; Math Or Science.

KERNELLU, KIRAN R; Armijo HS; Fairfield, CA; (1); ROTC; Drill Tm; High Hon Roll; US Air Force Acad; Aerontcs.

KERNKAMP, BELINDA L; Huntington Beach HS; Huntington Beach, CA; (2); Var Fld Hcky; Var Swmmng; Towers Awd; MVP Var Swmmng; Marine Bio.

KERNS, DOUGLAS E; Hesperia USD; Hesperia, CA; (3); Church Yth Grp; Var L Ftbl; Var L Trk; Wt Lftg; VFW Essay Cntst.

KERNS, JENNIFER; C K Mc Clatchy HS; Sacramento, CA; (2); 1/538; Cmnty Wkr; French Clb; Math Clb; Math Tm; Ski Clb; Band; Mrchg Band; VP Frsh Cls; Pres Soph Cls; Var Socr; Hstry Day Indvdl Media 1st CA, 4th Nation 88; Piono Cert Merit Pgm 7 Yrs; Music.

KERNS, JOLIE; C K Mc Cluthcy HS; Sacramento, CA; (3); 15/471; AFS; Ski Clb; Ed Yrbk; Sec Treas Frsh Cls; Pres Soph Cls; JV L Bsktbl; JV Cheerldng; Powder Puff Ftbl; Var L Socr; Var L Tennis; Hstry Day-Grp Media-1st Pl St Of CA 87; Chrmn Hmcmng Actvties 89; Mock Trl 89; Piano/Cert Merit Pgm; Art Dsgn.

KERR, JOHN E; College Park HS; Walnut Creek, CA; (3); Church Yth Grp; Cmnty Wkr; Letterman Clb; Math Clb; Ed Nwsp; Rptr Yrbk; Stu Cncl; Bsbl; Bsktbl; Bst Jrnlsm Stu; Appeard ESPN Schltc Sports Amer; Sacramento ST U; Bus Admin.

KERR, KIMBERLY R; Los Altos HS; Hacienda Hgts, CA; (2); Girl Scts; Key Clb; Nwsp; Hon Roll; Friend To Friend Club Scl Actvts Dir; Archaeology.

KERR, MOLLY B; Marin Acad; Fairfax, CA; (4); 4/80; Pres Drama Clb; Math Clb; Office Aide; Teachers Aide; School Musical; School Play; Stage Crew; Variety Show; Yrbk; High Hon Roll; Choreographer For 3 Musicals; Renaissance Faire Actor, ACT Yng Cnsrvtry; Artistic Director.

KERR, TAMARA; Fall River JR-SR HS; Fall River Mills, CA; (4); FBLA; Library Aide; Teachers Aide; School Musical; Ed Yrbk; High Hon Roll; CSF; Fine Arts Guild; Grphc Art.

KERRANE, SHANNON M; Wm S Hart HS; Valencia, CA; (3); 127/400; FBLA; Hosp Aide; Rep Jr Cls; Stu Cncl; Rotary Awd; Peer Cnslng.

KERRICK, CATHERINE; Colton HS; Colton, CA; (2); Church Yth Grp; Hon Roll; Jr NHS; NHS.

KERRIN, KRISTINA M; Casa Roble HS; Orangevale, CA; (2); 14/461; AFS; Spanish Clb; High Hon Roll; Friday Night Live; Renaissance Pgm; UC Davis; Marine Bio.

KERSEY, ANDREW; Serrano HS; Westminster, CA; (2); Church Yth Grp; High Hon Roll; Hon Roll; Golden St Exam Awd Alge.

KERSH, JACKIE; Hamilton HS; Los Angeles, CA; (2); Cmnty Wkr; Socr; Amnesty Intl; Grnpeace; Boston U; Chld Devlpmnt.

KERSHAW, ANGELIQUE; Bidwell JR HS; Chico, CA; (1); Church Yth Grp; French Clb; Pep Clb; Teachers Aide; Orch; JV Cheerldng; JV Crs Cntry; JV Pom Pon; JV Trk; Hon Roll; Bus.

KESHISHIAN, AKOP J; Pasadena HS; Pasadena, CA; (3); Debate Tm; Speech Tm; Teachers Aide; Bsktbl; High Hon Roll; Hon Roll; Cal Poly; Crmnl Lawyer.

KESHISHIAN, DZHAMILA; Pasadena HS; Pasadena, CA; (3); Art Clb; Cmnty Wkr; Debate Tm; Office Aide; Speech Tm; Hon Roll; Cmnty Svc; Vrs Speech Awds; Recite Poetry On TV, Stages; Piano; USC; Law.

KESLER, GREG S; La Sierra HS; Riverside, CA; (2); FBLA; JA; Letterman Clb; Spanish Clb; SADD; School Play; Yrbk; Var Bsbl; Hon Roll; Prfct Atten Awd; ROP Grphcs Tech Training Cert; UCLA; Phys Thrpy.

KESSLER, JESSICA R; Lassen HS; Susanville, CA; (4); Aud/Vis; Church Yth Grp; Cmnty Wkr; FHA; Library Aide; Office Aide; Pep Clb; SADD; Teachers Aide; VICA; Bus.

KESSLER, JUBAL; Marin Catholic HS; Larkspur, CA; (4); 32/190; Art Clb; Boy Scts; Debate Tm; English Clb; French Clb; Math Tm; Quiz Bowl; Ski Clb; Stage Crew; Nwsp; U CA Davis; Bio-Chem.

KESSLER, KIM; Loara HS; Garden Grove, CA; (3); Pep Clb; Ski Clb; Spanish Clb; Off Frsh Cls; Off Soph Cls; Off Jr Cls; Cheerldng; Powder Puff Ftbl; Intr Dsgn.

KESSMAN, GREG M; Tehachapi HS; Tehachapi, CA; (2); Church Yth Grp; Ski Clb; Rep Frsh Cls; Treas Soph Cls; JV L Bsktbl; Var L Golf; High Hon Roll; Hon Roll; NHS; St Schlr.

KESTING, MATT B; Brea-Olinda HS; Brea, CA; (1); Boy Scts; Band; Mrchg Band; Pep Band; Intrml Ftbl; JV Golf; Intrml Socr; JV Trk; Hon Roll.

KESZEK, AUDREY I; Pasadena Alternative Schl; Pasadena, CA; (3); 1/15; Cmnty Wkr; Rptr Nwsp; Sec Soph Cls; Sec Jr Cls; French Hon Soc; High Hon Roll; Pres Acad Fit Awd; YWCA 17th Annl 2nd Cntry Awd Vlntr Work; Cert Of Rcgntn CA Assmblyman Richard Polanco; The Evergreen ST; Fiction Wrtn.

KETCHAM, BRANNON; Sierra HS; Prather, CA; (4); #1 In Class; Cmnty Wkr; Computer Clb; German Clb; Letterman Clb; Math Tm; Model UN; Office Aide; Red Cross Aide; Science Clb; SADD; Gldn St Alg Hnrs & Geom Hi Hnrs; Pomona Coll; Civil Engrng.

KETCHAM, CAROLINE J; Sierra Joint Union HS; Prather, CA; (2); Cmnty Wkr; GAA; Science Clb; SADD; Varsity Clb; Var L Swmmng; JV Capt Vllybl; High Hon Roll; Jr NHS; NHS; Vllybl Clb-Capt; HOBY Yth Fndtn Ambssdr; WASC Accredation Cmmttee Stu Rep; U CA-SAN Diego; Med.

KETCHAM, MICHELLE R; Morse HS; San Diego, CA; (4); 1/600; Church Yth Grp; Computer Clb; Model UN; Scholastic Bowl; Church Choir; School Play; Jr NHS; NHS; Ntl Merit SF; Ldrshp Awd; Campfire Yth VP, Mdln; UCSD; Engrg.

KETHCART, MICHAEL R; Del Campo HS; Carmichael, CA; (2); JV Bsktbl; Hon Roll.

KETNER, CHERYL L; Hoover HS; Fresno, CA; (3); French Clb; Ski Clb; Off Frsh Cls; Off Soph Cls; Off Jr Cls; Stu Cncl; Capt Socr; Pres Acad Fit Awd; Rotary Club Camp Royal; UCSF.

KETSOUVANHASANE, SIRAKHONE; Banning HS; Banning, CA; (3); French Clb; Office Aide; Spanish Clb; Teachers Aide; School Play; Cit Awd; Hon Roll; Prfct Atten Awd; Friday Night Live Clb; Say No To Drugs; JTPA Pgm; UCR; Health.

KEUS, BRIGITTE R; Hawthornce HS; Hawthorne, CA; (3); GAA; Office Aide; Teachers Aide; Socr; High Hon Roll; Ntl Merit Ltr; San Diego ST; Fshn Dsgnr.

KEUSER, KRISTOPHER A; Bellarmine College Prep; San Jose, CA; (3); 49/315; Church Yth Grp; Cmnty Wkr; Letterman Clb; Service Clb; Varsity Clb; Church Choir; Swmmng; Capt Swm Tm; Cmmdtn Ltr; Gd Prfmnce; Prsnl Cntrbtn; Sprts Med.

KEUTE, TANYA; Bethel Christian HS; Quartz Hill, CA; (2); Church Yth Grp; Teachers Aide; Bsktbl; Sftbl; Vllybl; 4-H Awd; Hon Roll; Barrel Rcng.

KEVAN, JILL; Poway HS; Poway, CA; (3); 45/756; Sec Pres Church Yth Grp; SADD; Varsity Clb; Stu Cncl; JV Var Socr; JV Var Trk; High Hon Roll; Church Choir; NHS; Pr Cnslng; WASC Stu Cncl; HOBY; UC Davis; Elem Ed.

KEWISH, CHARLES J; Katella HS; Anaheim, CA; (4); Boy Scts; Pres Church Yth Grp; Key Clb; Pres Temple Yth Grp; Rep Frsh Cls; VP Soph Cls; Off Jr Cls; Treas Stu Cncl; High Hon Roll; Jr NHS; Yth In Govt Day Mayor; Yth Of Awd Fnlst; Brigham Young U.

KEY, JONATHAN C; Woodland HS; Woodland, CA; (2); Teachers Aide; Band; Mrchg Band; Orch; Bsbl; Ftbl; Score Keeper; Wt Lftg; Hon Roll; Sacramento Area Coll; Police Sc.

KEYES, TIMOTHY F; Mt Whitney HS; Visalia, CA; (3); 30/330; Church Yth Grp; Band; Mrchg Band; JV Crs Cntry; Capt Var Trk; Hon Roll; Commerical Pilot.

KEYLIN, EUGENE L; George Washington HS; San Francisco, CA; (4); Chess Clb; Math Clb; Science Clb; Chorus; School Musical; Bsktbl; Socr; Swmmng; Hon Roll; City Coll San Francisco; Math.

KEYS, JACITA J; John Muir HS; Pasadena, CA; (2); Dance Clb; Service Clb; VP Jr Cls; JV Cheerldng; Ped.

KEYS, LASHAWNA; Santa Barbara HS; Santa Barbara, CA; (3); 209/472; Drill Tm; JV Pom Pon; Var Sftbl; Endowmnt Yth Cmmtte Acad Awd; UCLA; Dentist.

KEYSER, COLLEEN; Washington HS; Fremont, CA; (3); 51/354; Var Gym; Var Trk.

KHA, HUNG; San Gabriel HS; San Gabriel, CA; (2); Spanish Clb; VICA; Bsktbl; Wt Lftg; Rio Hondo; Fireman.

KHA, TUE T; Los Pinos HS; Westminster, CA; (2); Hon Roll; Art Achvt & Awd; Cert Of Achvt; Cmptr Cert; Long Beach U; Arch.

KHA, XUONG NHON; Sunny Hills HS; Fullerton, CA; (3); 100/450; U Of Riverside; Ecnmcs.

KHACHATOURIANS, ARMOND G; Herbert Hoover HS; Glendale, CA; (4); Cmnty Wkr; Debate Tm; Key Clb; High Hon Roll; Pres Acad Fit Awd; CSF; Emt-Ia Emer Med Tech; CA ST U Northridge; Med.

KHADDER, NICK S; Homestead HS; Sunnyvale, CA; (3); 1/383; Boy Scts; Church Yth Grp; Debate Tm; NFL; Ed Nwsp; Var JV Crs Cntry; JV Trk; Hon Roll; Pres Acad Fit Awd; CSF; Law.

KHADEM, ALI; Mountain View HS; Los Altos, CA; (1); Chess Clb; Computer Clb; High Hon Roll; Jr NHS; NHS; U CA Berkeley; Sci.

KHAIAPHONE, KOULAH; Hoover HS; San Diego, CA; (1); Church Yth Grp; Cit Awd; Hon Roll; Jr NHS; Prfct Atten Awd; Teacher.

KHALAF, GEORGE A; Dinole Valley HS; Pinole, CA; (1); Church Yth Grp; German Clb; Bsbl; Wt Lftg; High Hon Roll; Hon Roll; Drwng, Wrtng, Brdcstng; Stanford.

KHALAF, MAHA; Santa Clara HS; Santa Clara, CA; (2); Church Yth Grp; Cmnty Wkr; Pres French Clb; Intnl Clb; Pep Clb; Service Clb; Teachers Aide; Varsity Clb; Variety Show; Stu Cncl; San Francisco Ramallah Yth Club; Ldrshp Cls 88-89; Hnrs Engl Classes; Harvard; Law.

KHALAF, TAMARA; Foothill HS; Santa Ana, CA; (2); Aud/Vis; Church Yth Grp; Cmnty Wkr; German Clb; Key Clb; Tennis; Cit Awd; High Hon Roll; Hon Roll; Piano Stu Of The Yr; Co-Chrmn; Assisteens.

KHALAFIAN, YVETTE; Holy Martyrs Ferrahian HS; Woodland Hills, CA; (3); Boy Scts; Church Yth Grp; Cmnty Wkr; Band; Cit Awd; UCLA; Bio.

KHALIGH, ANDREA M; Fontana HS; Fontana, CA; (3); Chorus; Cit Awd; Hon Roll; Prfct Atten Awd; Zonta Club; Cert Of Awd; Cert Of Mrt; Prin Hnr Roll; Fshn Dsgnr.

KHAMAMKAR, NIVEDITA S; Capistrano Valley HS; Mission Viejo, CA; (3); Hosp Aide; JV Bsktbl; JV Crs Cntry; Var L Sftbl; Hon Roll; Ntl Merit Ltr; Gldn T Exam Acadc Excllnce Awd; Rgnl Sci Olympd 4th Pl; Jr Vrsty Sftbl MVP; Irvine CA U; Biological Sci.

KHAMKOON, VIENGPHONE A; Gompers HS; San Diego, CA; (2); French Clb; Key Clb; Treas Frsh Cls; Sec Soph Cls; Swmmng; JV Capt Vllybl; High Hon Roll; Hon Roll; Jr NHS; NHS; Sci Olympd; Nature Clb; Acad Leag; Stamford U.

KHAMOU, SUMMER S; El Cajon Valley HS; El Cajon, CA; (4); 19/297; Teachers Aide; Mgr Yrbk; High Hon Roll; Hon Roll; Prfct Atten Awd; Grossmont Coll; CPA.

KHAMPHANITH, THAVILAY; Bakersfield HS; Bakersfield, CA; (2); Church Yth Grp; FBLA; Math Clb; Spanish Clb; Vllybl; Hon Roll; APAC Cmmtte; CSF; 2nd Pl Earth Poetry Cntst Bakersfield; CCI; Bus Ed.

KHAMPHILATH, BOUAVONE; Modesto HS; Modesto, CA; (4); 2/450; Dance Clb; Intnl Clb; Key Clb; Math Clb; Spanish Clb; Cit Awd; High Hon Roll; Hon Roll; Lion Awd; Prfct Atten Awd; San Jose ST U; Govmt.

KHAMPHOR, THONGKHOUNE; Lincoln HS; San Diego, CA; (2).

KHAMPHOUMY, KHAMFONG T; Grant Union HS; Sacramento, CA; (2); Intnl Clb; Library Aide; Cit Awd; Hon Roll; Prfct Atten Awd; Awd For Excllnc Frnch II; Cert Of Hnr Acctng I; Bank Of Am Awd Engl; Sonoma ST U; Bus Mgmt.

KHAMPOU, CHANTHY; Woodrow Wilson HS; Long Beach, CA; (4); Church Yth Grp; Hosp Aide; JA; SADD; Off Sr Cls; Stu Cncl; Sftbl; Cit Awd; Hon Roll; NHS; Mock Trial Tm; Key Clb; CSULB; Phys Thrpy.

KHAMSAVATH, LOUNNIVONGSA; Banning HS; Banning, CA; (3); Church Yth Grp; French Clb; Church Choir; Ftbl; Socr; Cit Awd; High Hon Roll; NHS; Prfct Atten Awd; Natl Hnr Soc; Hnr Roll; Prfct Atten Awd; Phy.

KHAMSIVONE, PONNIE; Pittsburg HS; Pittsburg, CA; (2); Hon Roll; Prfct Atten Awd; Acad Achvt Awds; Los Medanos Coll; Cosmetology.

KHAMSOMBAT, LAMMONE; Sweetwater HS; National City, CA; (4); Drama Clb; French Clb; FBLA; Library Aide; Science Clb; SADD; Teachers Aide; Rep Frsh Cls; Cit Awd; Hon Roll; San Diego ST U; Bus Admin.

KHAN, ALYA; Del Campo HS; Carmichael, CA; (2); French Clb; Band; Color Guard; Flag Corp; Mrchg Band; Math.

KHAN, MASOOD R; Alhambra HS; Monterey Park, CA; (2); Debate Tm; Key Clb; NFL; Rep Soph Cls; CSF; UCLA; Bio.

KHAN, SHAZIA R; Valley View HS; Moreno Valley, CA; (1); Speech Tm; Hon Roll; Criminal Law.

KHANDERISH, LILLIE; Turlock HS; Turlock, CA; (4); Church Yth Grp; Cmnty Wkr; French Clb; Nwsp; Photogrphy Awds; CA ST U.

KHANNA, JASPREET; Mission San Jose HS; Fremont, CA; (3); Aud/Vis; VP Church Yth Grp; Hosp Aide; VP Temple Yth Grp; Band; Mrchg Band; Stage Crew; High Hon Roll; Bus.

KHAROD, KETAN U; San Pedro HS; Ft Meade, MD; (4); 1/522; Hosp Aide; Service Clb; Nwsp; VP Stu Cncl; Val; Natl Mrt Fnlst; Schl Mascot; Bank Maer Librl Arts Awd; Georgetown U; Govt.

KHARRAZIAN, DATIS; Torrey Pine HS; Del Mar, CA; (3); Boy Scts; Office Aide; Krte 84-90; Berkeley; Psych.

KHARUFEH, MOHAMMAD M; Armijo HS; Suisun, CA; (3); Key Clb; High Hon Roll; Ldrshp; CA Schlstc Fed; U Of Berkely; Bus Admin.

KHARUFEH, NAJIBA J; Armijo HS; Suisun, CA; (2); Ski Clb; Amer Stu Exchng Prgm; Lawyer.

KHASTOO, DESIREE; Irvine HS; Irvine, CA; (1); Dance Clb; Spanish Clb; Schlrshp Dncng; Carthage Coll; Law.

KHATAMI, PEDDY P; Lowell HS; San Francisco, CA; (2); Boy Scts; Teachers Aide; Nwsp; Ftbl; Sftbl; CSF; Russian Clb; Bowling Leag; UC Berkeley; Jrnlsm.

KHATIB, ABEER M; Redlands SR HS; San Bernardino, CA; (4); ROP Offc Procedures; Comp Applctns; Religious Grp; CA ST U San Bernadino; Law.

KHAUV, HAV C; Fontana HS; Fontana, CA; (4); 1/900; Chess Clb; Math Clb; Math Tm; Science Clb; VICA; Bsktbl; High Hon Roll; Pres Acad Fit Awd; 2 Gold Mdls Vica Regnl Cmptn; Stu Of Mnth 2 Yrs Math Dept; UC Irvine; Elec Engr.

KHAYAT, TINA M; Carsbad HS; Carlsbad, CA; (4); Teachers Aide; Chorus; Stage Crew; Drftng Awd 88 & 89; CA Poly; Arch.

KHAYKIN, MIKHAIL; G Washington HS; San Francisco, CA; (3); Var Socr; Var Swmmng; Hobby Clb; Geogrphy Clb; Berkeley U; Doctor.

KHAZAENI, BABAK; El Camino Real HS; West Hills, CA; (4); 1/575; Computer Clb; Math Clb; Trk; High Hon Roll; Pres Acad Fit Awd; Jr Statesman Of Amer; CA Schlrshp Fdrtn; UCLA; Med.

KHAZAENI, SIAMAK; El Camino Real HS; West Hills, CA; (3); Chess Clb; Library Aide; Office Aide; Teachers Aide; Hon Roll; Coll; Arch.

KHEZRI, MONA; Birmingham HS; Encino, CA; (3); 4-H; Ed Nwsp; Cit Awd; High Hon Roll; Hon Roll; CSF; OTSA; Iranian Jewish Cultural Ctr; UCLA; Doctor.

KHIANTHALAT, SAYTHAVY T; Roosevelt Performing Art HS; Fresno, CA; (2); #41 In Class; Cmnty Wkr; FTA; Hosp Aide; Science Clb; SADD; Roosevelt Lives; ESL Club; UC Davis; Pediatrician.

KHIEU, KUMPIRA; Tokay HS; Stockton, CA; (2); 8/694; Intnl Clb; Trk; Hon Roll; Kemera Ed Clb; Cambodian Clb; UOP; Med Doc.

KHIEV, SAVUTH; Bassett HS; La Puente, CA; (3); 5/30; Cit Awd; CA ST U Los Angeles; Word Prc.

KHIM, CHANTHOU; Hoover HS; Fresno, CA; (3); French Clb; Office Aide; Ski Clb; SADD; Orch; School Musical; Off Frsh Cls; Stu Cncl; Golf; Cit Awd; Fresno ST.

KHINE, KHIN; Bishop Amat HS; Diamond Bar, CA; (1); Drama Clb; Hon Roll; Prfct Atten Awd; Amnsty Intl Mem; Med.

KHO, JAY STEVEN YAP; Don Bosco Technical Inst; Rosemead, CA; (2); Computer Clb; Cit Awd; Hon Roll; NHS; Spcl Mrt Awd-Rio Hondo Coll Tech Cmptn; Engrng.

KHO, TUONG C; San Gabriel HS; San Gabriel, CA; (3); French Clb; FBLA; Key Clb; JV Tennis; Hon Roll; Prfct Atten Awd; Indstrl Art Awd; Tennis Awd; Achvt Awd-Rgnl Occuptnl Pgm; U Of Irvine; Pharmacist.

KHOBOYAN, CHOGHIK; Pasadena HS; Pasadena, CA; (2); Church Yth Grp; Stat Score Keeper; Var Tennis; Hon Roll; Vllybl,Bsktbl & Tennis Armenian Ath Assn; CSF; Friday Night Live Clb; Dental Hyg.

KHODAI, NAGHMEH; Downey HS; Irvine, CA; (3); Cmnty Wkr; French Clb; Math Clb; Pep Clb; Science Clb; Service Clb; Teachers Aide; Nwsp; Ed Yrbk; Hon Roll; Normaneers; CSF Freshman Rep; Spllng Bee Chmpn.

KHODAVERDIAN, ALEXI; Glendale HS; Glendale, CA; (3); Swmmng; Tennis; Vllybl; Prfct Atten Awd; Stu Month; Rop Pgm; Glendale CC; Lathe Oprtr.

KHOE, GINO; J F Kennedy HS; La Palma, CA; (1); Ftbl; Wt Lftg; Cit Awd; Hon Roll; Pres Acad Fit Awd; Hnr Band Anaheim Union Sch Dist; Orange Empire Schlr Tm; Genetic Engrng.

KHOLOS, JENNIFER L; Imperial HS; Arcadia, CA; (3); Church Yth Grp; Speech Tm; Varsity Clb; Golf; Flag Corp; Swing Chorus; Yrbk; Var Bsktbl; Capt Cheerldng; Var Sftbl; Charge Of Decrtns & Other Cmmttes For Prom; Spch Clb Offcr; Charge Of Dcrtns For Thnksgvng Dance; Loyola; Lwyr.

KHONA, DIMPLE K; El-Dorado HS; Placentia, CA; (3); 55/317; Intnl Clb; Math Clb; Science Clb; High Hon Roll; Hon Roll; Yng Schlrs Pgm U CA Santa Barbara; Far East Travel; CA ST U Fullerton; Med.

KHONG, CHUNG S; Bellarmine College Prep; San Jose, CA; (1); Church Yth Grp; Latin Clb; Service Clb; Crs Cntry; Trk; Hon Roll; Prfct Atten Awd; Pres Acad Fit Awd; Chrstn Life Cmnty.

KHOONSRIVONG, THONG LAI B; Lincoln HS; Stockton, CA; (3); Ftbl; UC Davis; Stock Broker.

KHOROZIAN, RAFFY; South San Francisco HS; South San Francis, CA; (3); Red Cross Aide; Teachers Aide; Rep Frsh Cls; Italian Clb.

KHOSROWPOUR, IMAN; Irvine HS; Irvine, CA; (3); Chess Clb; Spanish Clb; Orch; School Musical; JV Swmmng; High Hon Roll; Hon Roll; Pacific Symphony Violion Soloist; Music Camp Schlrshps; Julliard; Music Performance.

KHOU, SAN H; Belmont HS; Los Angeles, CA; (4); 26/600; Cmnty Wkr; FTA; Science Clb; Teachers Aide; VICA; Off Jr Cls; Cit Awd; High Hon Roll; Hon Roll; Lion Awd; Stu Mnth; USC; Phrmcst.

KHOUNPASEUTH, BOUNBANG; Redwood HS; Visalia, CA; (2); FBLA; Latin Clb; Teachers Aide; Hon Roll; CSF.

KHOUNVICHITH, KHEKKEO K; Edison HS; Stockton, CA; (2); Science Clb; Hon Roll; Prfct Atten Awd; Spanish NHS; Laotian Club; UC Davis; Doctor.

KHOURI, ISSA A; South San Francisco HS; South San Francis, CA; (2); 1/300; FBLA; Math Clb; Off Frsh Cls; Off Soph Cls; Capt L Bsbl; Capt L Wrstlng; High Hon Roll; Hon Roll; Stu Yr Alg II Hnrs & Chem Hnrs; Stu Mnth Schl, Math Dept & Sci Dept; JV Bsbl Hustle Awd Wnnr; Chem.

KHOURY, ANNA; St Genevieve HS; Van Nuys, CA; (3); Church Yth Grp; Drama Clb; SADD; Thesps; School Play; Hon Roll; Unity Clb Chrstn Outreach Pgm Clb Pres; CA ST U Northridge; Deaf Stds.

KHOURY, RICHARD; Lawrence Acad; San Jose, CA; (4); 1/30; Math Clb; Math Tm; Office Aide; Science Clb; Teachers Aide; Nwsp; Ed Yrbk; Pres Sr Cls; Tennis; Vllybl; Santa Clara U; Chem.

KHU, TAN; Los Amigos HS; Santa Ana, CA; (2); 37/406; High Hon Roll; Hon Roll.

KHUC, TAM T; San Rafael HS; San Rafael, CA; (3); 12/250; Cmnty Wkr; French Clb; German Clb; Intnl Clb; SADD; High Hon Roll; Hon Roll; Ntl Merit Schol; Golden St Exam Mrts; Concours Natl De Francais Cert Of Mrt; Marin Cty Sci Fair Cert Of Achvt 88-89; UC Berkeley; Law.

KHULLAR, VIVEK; El Toro HS; El Toro, CA; (2); Ftbl; JV Trk; Wt Lftg; Presdntl Phys Ftnss Awd; Modeling Agency; U Of CA Irvine; Bus.

KHUU, DUC; Northgate HS; Walnut Creek, CA; (2); Art Clb; Debate Tm; Math Clb; Model UN; Hon Roll; Best Tutor Awd 89; Mt Diablo Hum Fest Essay Contest Awd; Acad Achvmt Awd; Acad Ltr; U CA Berkeley; Med.

KHUU, HEATHER T; San Gabriel HS; San Gabriel, CA; (2); Debate Tm; NFL; Drill Tm; Cit Awd; Hon Roll; Opt Clb Awd; Harvard U; Law.

KIANG, JULIA; Rosary HS; La Palma, CA; (2); Science Clb; High Hon Roll; Hon Roll; U Of CA; Med.

KIANMAHD, SHARONA; Santa Monica HS; Santa Monica, CA; (3); FBLA; SADD; Teachers Aide; Var Cheerldng; JV Trk; Hon Roll; Public Relations Clb-Treas; CSF; UCLA; Engrng.

KIBBY, SHEREE; Woodland HS; Woodland, CA; (4); 12/421; Key Clb; Service Clb; Spanish Clb; Sec Treas SADD; Band; Color Guard; Mrchg Band; Stage Crew; Lit Mag; Hon Roll; Literary Clb; CA Schlrshp Fed; Woodlnd Dance Acad Ballet Dncr; Santa Cruz U; Math Cmptrs.

KICK, KERRY S; Irvine HS; Irvine, CA; (1); Dance Clb; Drama Clb; French Clb; Pep Clb; Teachers Aide; Chorus; JV Cheerldng; Hon Roll; Dance Teacher Jazz & Tap Irvine Dance Acad; UC Irvine; Dance Teacher.

KIEFER, HEIDI; St Paul HS; Whittier, CA; (3); 68/350; Red Cross Aide; Hon Roll; Ftbl Stu Trainer; Med.

KIEHM, CORINA; North Salinas HS; Salinas, CA; (1); Teachers Aide; Off Soph Cls; Crs Cntry; Fld Hcky; Sftbl; Swmmng; Trk; Wt Lftg; Cit Awd; High Hon Roll; Nurse.

KIEHN, MARCIE; Woodland HS; Woodland, CA; (2); Church Yth Grp; Sec 4-H; SADD; Teachers Aide; Band; Church Choir; Capt Color Guard; Mrchg Band; Pep Band; 4-H Awd; Jobs Dghtrs; Pwdr Puff Sftbl; UCD; Law.

KIEHN, TODD; Pinewood HS; Los Altos, CA; (4); 1/43; Capt Debate Tm; NFL; Speech Tm; School Play; Ed Nwsp; JV Bsktbl; French Hon Soc; High Hon Roll; NHS; Ntl Merit SF.

KIELBASA, ADRIANA D; Fontana HS; Fontana, CA; (3); Cmnty Wkr; High Hon Roll; Hon Roll; CSF Mem; Gldn St Geom Exam High Hnrs.

KIEN, WILLIAM; Rowland HS; Rowland Heights, CA; (2); 47/602; Cmnty Wkr; DECA; Science Clb; JV Crs Cntry; Var Trk; Hon Roll; USC; Med.

KIENAST, SUZANN; College Park HS; Martinez, CA; (2); Teachers Aide; Chorus; Drill Tm; Hon Roll; NHS; Engr.

KIENBORTS, JASON W; San Marcos HS; Santa Barbara, CA; (3); JV Bsktbl; Var Ftbl; High Hon Roll; NHS; Pres Acad Fit Awd; NYU; Film.

KIENBORTS, KELLY LEE; San Marcos HS; Santa Barbara, CA; (2); Off Key Clb; Ski Clb; Yrbk; Capt Var Cheerldng; Var Pom Pon; Hon Roll; Bus.

KIERNAN, PATRICK A; Modesto HS; Salida, CA; (4); Art Clb; French Clb; FFA; Ed Yrbk; Var Diving; Intrml Ftbl; Var Swmmng; JV Trk; Xerox Awd Hum Soc Sci; Elec Sys Engrng.

KIESEL, JASON A; San Pasqual HS; Escondido, CA; (2); 1/416; Church Yth Grp; Cmnty Wkr; Sec Jr Cls; JV Bsbl; Ftbl; Hon Roll; CSF; Vrsty Bsbl GPA Awd; CA Inst Of Tech; Engrng.

KIESLER, DANIELLE; Santa Cruz HS; Santa Cruz, CA; (2); Art Clb; Trk; Hon Roll; Lit,Journlsm & Art; Singing & Drama; Journlsm.

KIESTER, TED C; Hart HS; Valencia, CA; (2); JV Capt Bsbl; JV Ftbl; Capt Frosh & Jr Var Bsbl Tm; U S CA; Major Lg Bsbl Player.

KIEU, FREDERICK B; Santa Clara HS; Santa Clara, CA; (2); Orch; Rep Frsh Cls; Prfct Atten Awd; Medicine.

KIHARA, CHRISTOPHER J; Santa Teresa HS; San Jose, CA; (3); Hist Church Yth Grp; Spanish Clb; SADD; Varsity Clb; JV Var Bsbl; JV Var Bsktbl; JV Ftbl; Hon Roll; CSF; Outstndng Stu Athlete 87-88.

KIKUCHI, KRISTEN M; Rim Of The World HS; Running Springs, CA; (2); Spanish Clb; Teachers Aide; JV Socr; Hon Roll; Prfct Atten Awd; CA Schlstc Fed-Hnry; Jr Stsmn Of Amer; Ed.

KILAGHBIAN, TALIN A; Clovis HS; Clovis, CA; (3); Art Clb; Church Yth Grp; Drama Clb; Math Clb; Math Tm; Science Clb; High Hon Roll; Acad Block C; Creighton U; Med.

KILANI, MARWA; Chatsworth HS; Northridge, CA; (3); Church Yth Grp; Science Clb; SADD; Thesps; Varsity Clb; Rep Soph Cls; Var JV Tennis; Var Trk; Hon Roll; UCLA HS Mnrty Rsrch Pgm; LA Cnty Sci Fr 3rd Pl; UCLA; Med.

KILBY, SHAWNA; Ponderosa HS; Shingle Springs, CA; (1); Church Yth Grp; Cmnty Wkr; JV Trk; Cit Awd; Hon Roll; Prfct Atten Awd; Flute/Piccolo Private Tutrs; Model.

KILEDJIAN, ARPI M; Holy Martyrs Armenian HS; Canoga Park, CA; (3); Var Cheerldng; Var Vllybl.

KILEY, SARAH A; Notre Dame Acad; Los Angeles, CA; (4); 25/112; Debate Tm; Speech Tm; Phtg Yrbk; Cit Awd; High Hon Roll; NHS; CSF; UC Santa Barbara; Aquatic.

KILGORE, AMY; San Bernardino HS; San Bernardino, CA; (2); #4 In Class; SADD; High Hon Roll; Elite Gymnast 88-90; Med.

KILGORE, CHRISTIE; San Bernardino HS; San Bernardino, CA; (2); #7 In Class; SADD; High Hon Roll; Water Polo Tm.

KILGORE, DARIN R; Beyer HS; Modesto, CA; (3); Drama Clb; School Play; Stage Crew; Ed Nwsp; JV Bsktbl; Var L Trk; Hon Roll; Prfct Atten Awd.

KILKENNY, KARIN A; San Dieguito HS; Carlsbad, CA; (2); Church Yth Grp; Dance Clb; Hosp Aide; Office Aide; Science Clb; JV Socr; Var Tennis; Amnesty Intl Clb; Georgetown U; Med.

KILKENNY, NICOLE M; Mercy HS; Pacifica, CA; (2); GAA; Chorus; Stage Crew; Rep Soph Cls; Var JV Bsktbl; Var Sftbl; Hon Roll; Entrance Hnrs; Most Insprtnl Sftbl.

KILLEN, KATHERINE A; Cupertino HS; San Jose, CA; (4); 1/230; Church Yth Grp; VP German Clb; Teachers Aide; Flag Corp; Variety Show; Ed Yrbk; NHS; Ntl Merit Schol; Pres Acad Fit Awd; Val; Badminton JV&V; German Hnr Soc Co-Chair; Bnk Amer Math/Sci Plaq Wnnr; U Of CA San Diego; Biophysics.

KILLEY, BRENT A; Huntington Beach HS; Huntington Bch, CA; (4); 42/500; Model UN; Red Cross Aide; Ski Clb; Band; Jazz Band; Mrchg Band; Pep Band; School Musical; Ice Hcky; Lcrss; Whittler Coll; Engr.

KILLIAN, SCOTT A; San Luis Obispo HS; San Luis Obispo, CA; (2); Astrnmy Clb; Amateur Rodeo Clb; CA Polytech ST U; Engrng.

KILLINGSWORTH, COURTNEY M; Skyline HS; Oakland, CA; (2); Dance Clb; Georgetown; Journalism.

KILLINGSWORTH, JEFF O; Tehachapi HS; Tehachapi, CA; (3); Teachers Aide; Varsity Clb; JV Var Bsbl; JV Var Bsktbl; Cit Awd; Hon Roll; NHS; Prfct Atten Awd; Engrng.

KILMURRAY, FELICITY; Galt HS; Galt, CA; (2); Drama Clb; Pep Clb; Speech Tm; Thesps; School Musical; Cheerldng; Hon Roll; Actrss.

KILPATRICK, AUSTON M; Mt Madonna Schl; Watsonville, CA; (4); #1 In Class; Drama Clb; Ski Clb; School Play; Rep Jr Cls; Treas Sr Cls; Bsktbl; JV Ftbl; Var Capt Vllybl; Stanford; Engr.

KILPATRICK, KYLE R; Brea Olinda HS; Brea, CA; (3); Church Yth Grp; Letterman Clb; Var L Swmmng; Hon Roll; Jr NHS; Pres Acad Fit Awd; Water Polo Capt; Vrsty Ltrmn; All Orange Leag 1st Team; MVP Water Polo; U Of CA Irvine; Bus.

KILPATRICK, MANIKA J; Helix HS; La Mesa, CA; (4); 59/355; Church Yth Grp; Drama Clb; French Clb; Band; Mrchg Band; School Play; Variety Show; Lit Mag; Gldn St Exam-Alg; Drama-Mst Imprvd Prfrmr; Purdue U; Bio.

KILPATRICK, SUSAN M; Kearny SR HS; San Diego, CA; (3); 22/322; Debate Tm; Speech Tm; School Play; Rep Jr Cls; JV Sftbl; Acad Leag 89-90; Badmington Var 87-88; San Diego ST; Elec Engrng.

KILPONEN, JAMES D; Sunny Hills HS; Fullerton, CA; (4); 25/425; Am Leg Boys St; VP Jr Cls; Pres Sr Cls; Pres Jr NHS; Masonic Awd; NHS; Ntl Merit SF; Rotary Awd; Off Soph Cls; JV Swmmng; Waterpolo; Chrmn Yth Bus,Gov; Intl Bus.

KILTON, KIM D; Canyon Springs HS; Moreno Valley, CA; (3); Art Clb; Cmnty Wkr; Dance Clb; GAA; Girl Scts; Ski Clb; Spanish Clb; Teachers Aide; VICA; School Play; Vltr Wrk Nrsng Home; Voctnl Sch Grphc Arts; Columbus ST U; Graphic Arts.

KIM, ALVIN U; Sunny Hills HS; Fullerton, CA; (3); Church Yth Grp; Hosp Aide; Hosp Aide; Intnl Clb; Key Clb; Model UN; Spanish Clb; Speech Tm; Varsity Clb; Rep Stu Cncl; V Water Polo; Rcgntn TSWE Achvt; Awds GSE Math, Scl Sci; Berkely; Law.

KIM, ANATASIA S; Whitney HS; Cerritos, CA; (3); Cmnty Wkr; Hosp Aide; JA; Key Clb; Spanish Clb; Pres Mrchg Band; Orch; Ed Nwsp; Var Swmmng; Pres Acad Fit Awd; JR Stsmn Of Amer Pres; Natl Hnr Scty; S CA Hnr Band; Psych.

KIM, ANDREW C; John F Kennedy HS; La Palma, CA; (3); VP Chess Clb; Sec Computer Clb; Chrmn Key Clb; Teachers Aide; Nwsp; JV Tennis; Hon Roll; Pres Acad Fit Awd; CSF; Gldn St Exam Acad Excllnc Awd; UCLA; Law.

KIM, ANGIE; Fontana HS; Bloomington, CA; (3); Church Yth Grp; Cmnty Wkr; Teachers Aide; Color Guard; Ed Nwsp; Phtg Yrbk; Lit Mag; Stat Swmmng; Cit Awd; Hon Roll; City Vlntr, Envrnmnt; Tchr.

KIM, ANGIE M; John F Kennedy HS; Granada Hills, CA; (4); Church Yth Grp; Key Clb; Speech Tm; Rptr Nwsp; Phtg Yrbk; Sec Frsh Cls; Rep Stu Cncl; JV Golf; Hon Roll; Prfct Atten Awd; Korean Clb Pres, Won Amer Legion Schlrshp Awd; CA ST Nrthrdge; Lbrl Stud.

KIM, ANN; Warren HS; Downey, CA; (3); Pres Church Yth Grp; Debate Tm; Hosp Aide; Key Clb; VP SADD; Sec Frsh Cls; Mgr(s); Var Trk; Var Vllybl; Ntl Merit Ltr; Peer Cnslng; AWANA Ldr; Assnt Athltc Trainer; Med.

KIM, ANNE; Burroughs HS; Burbank, CA; (2); Rptr Nwsp; Rptr Yrbk; Lit Mag; CSF.

KIM, ANNE H; Los Altos HS; West Covina, CA; (3); 56/365; Church Yth Grp; Flag Corp; Hon Roll; Schl Schlr; Keywanettes Clb; Rep CA Natl Yng Ldrs Conf 90.

KIM, ANNICE E; Whitney HS; Cerritos, CA; (2); 68/200; Cmnty Wkr; Drama Clb; Hosp Aide; Key Clb; Latin Clb; Band; Chorus; Mrchg Band; Co-Ed Nwsp; JV Swmmng; JR Statesmen Of Amer Secy; Cls Inner Cncl Co-Edtr Nwsltr & Sports Nwsltr Edtr; Prom Cmmtte 88-90; UCLA; Medcl.

KIM, ANNIE W; Tustin HS; Tustin, CA; (4); Church Yth Grp; JA; Math Tm; Lit Mag; Mgr Tennis; High Hon Roll; NEDT Awd; Pres Acad Fit Awd; UC Irvine; Biochem.

KIM, ANTHONY; Sunny Hills HS; Fullerton, CA; (3); 130/425; Church Yth Grp; Intnl Clb; Key Clb; Letterman Clb; Varsity Clb; Var Capt Bsktbl; Var L Ftbl; Var L Golf; Var Wt Lftg; Intrml Wrstlng; Jr Statesman Of Amer; UCLA; Bus.

KIM, BARBARA K; La Mirada HS; La Mirada, CA; (2); French Clb; Rptr Nwsp; Treas Frsh Cls; Var JV Vllybl; High Hon Roll; Hon Roll; Girls League 10th Grd Pblcst, 11th Grd Actvts Dir; Engrng.

KIM, BILL J; Mayfair HS; Bellflower, CA; (1); JA; Key Clb; Mrchg Band; Pep Band; High Hon Roll; Hon Roll; Prfct Atten Awd; GSE, High Acad Achvt, Outstndng Acad Achvt Awd.

KIM, BRIAN; Crescenta Valley HS; La Crescenta, CA; (4); 17/380; Computer Clb; French Clb; Treas Key Clb; Math Clb; Mu Alpha Theta; Science Clb; Treas Spanish Clb; Yrbk; Pres Acad Fit Awd; Med.

KIM, BRIAN; Upland HS; Upland, CA; (2); Chess Clb; FBLA; Math Clb; Math Tm; JV Swmmng; High Hon Roll; Jr NHS; Kiwanis Awd; Prfct Atten Awd; Harvard; Med.

KIM, BRIAN U; Granada Hills HS; Granada Hills, CA; (4); Science Clb; Chorus; High Hon Roll; Pres Acad Fit Awd; UCLA.

KIM, BYONG JOON; Sunny Hills HS; Fullerton, CA; (4); Church Yth Grp; Spanish Clb; Var Capt Trk; High Hon Roll; Rotary Awd; Asst Dir Church Grammar Camp; Pres Church Yth; Rcvd Coachs Awd Trck; Berkeley; Cvl Engrng.

KIM, CALVIN; Sacramento Adventist Acad; Citrus Heights, CA; (2); Church Yth Grp; Drama Clb; Ski Clb; School Play; Intrml Mgr Gym; Hon Roll; Drama Awd; Med.

KIM, CAROL J; Carson HS; Carson, CA; (2); Church Yth Grp; Teachers Aide; Band; CA St Schlrshp Clb; Acad Awd Span & Engl; Ladies/Squires; Bus Admin.

KIM, CAROLINE; Temple City HS; Temple City, CA; (3); #10 In Class; Cmnty Wkr; Dance Clb; Hosp Aide; Key Clb; Pep Clb; Drill Tm; Orch; School Musical; Rep Frsh Cls; Rep Soph Cls; Sci Fr Spec Awd 1st Pl Ovral Wnnr; Jr Hnr Grd; Sr Svc; U Of CA San Diego; Psych.

KIM, CAROLINE C; Flintridge Prep; Pasadena, CA; (3); Church Yth Grp; Hosp Aide; Chorus; School Musical; Sec Soph Cls; Var Tennis; Hon Roll; NHS; Spanish NHS; UCLA.

KIM, CAROLINE S; Hawthorne HS; Hawthorne, CA; (3); Drama Clb; Hosp Aide; Intnl Clb; Service Clb; Chorus; School Musical; School Play; Stage Crew; Variety Show; Stat Var Bsktbl; CSF; Outstndng Achvt; UC Santa Barbara; Psych.

KIM, CAROLINE S; Whitney HS; Cerritos, CA; (2); Treas Pres Church Yth Grp; Key Clb; Band; Church Choir; Mrchg Band; JV Vllybl; Hon Roll; Pres Acad Fit Awd; Piano; Cmnty Service.

KIM, CECILE; Turlock HS; Turlock, CA; (3); 15/500; AFS; Church Yth Grp; Cmnty Wkr; Hosp Aide; Key Clb; Letterman Clb; NFL; Service Clb; Speech Tm; Varsity Clb; V Waterpolo; Neurosurgeon.

KIM, CHANG M; Burbank SR HS; Burbank, CA; (3); Church Yth Grp; Teachers Aide; Orch; Cit Awd; Hon Roll; UC Prep; Med.

KIM, CHARLES; Servite HS; Fullerton, CA; (3); 7/150; VP Church Yth Grp; Cmnty Wkr; Quiz Bowl; Phtg Yrbk; Var Swmmng; Var Tennis; High Hon Roll; NHS; Ntl Merit Ltr; Vrsty Waterpolo.

KIM, CHONG M; La Quinta HS; Fountain Valley, CA; (1); 2/400; Key Clb; Band; Mrchg Band; Pep Band; Intrml Bsktbl; High Hon Roll; Stanford U.

KIM, CHRIS C; Whitney HS; Cerritos, CA; (1); Debate Tm; Key Clb; Model UN; Service Clb; High Hon Roll; CJSF Hnr Awd; UC; Econ.

KIM, CHUNG KUN; Huntington Beach HS; Huntington Bch, CA; (3); Treas Church Yth Grp; Debate Tm; French Clb; Key Clb; Math Tm; Model UN; Red Cross Aide; Speech Tm; Rep Stu Cncl; Golf; OCKFPC Yth Orch; Harvey Mudd Coll; Engrng.

KIM, CI HYE; Seaside HS; Marina, CA; (3); AFS; Debate Tm; Drama Clb; French Clb; FBLA; Ski Clb; Spanish Clb; Speech Tm; School Play; Yrbk; Engr.

KIM, CLARA H; University HS; Irvine, CA; (3); 22/551; Church Yth Grp; Hosp Aide; Pres Spanish Clb; Pres Orch; High Hon Roll; Pres Acad Fit Awd; Spanish NHS; All St Hnr Orch; All Southern CA Hnr Orch; CSF VP.

KIM, CLARA M; Whitney HS; Cerritos, CA; (1); Debate Tm; Drama Clb; Key Clb; Latin Clb; Model UN; Pep Clb; Chorus; Orch; Nwsp; Off Frsh Cls; Orange Cnty HS Of The Arts; Inter Dsgn.

KIM, DAE YUN; Don Bosco Tech Inst; Montebello, CA; (2); 26/251; Church Yth Grp; Computer Clb; Intrml Bsktbl; JV Vllybl; Hon Roll; NHS; Prfct Atten Awd; CA Schlrshp Fed; Math Relay Team 1st Pl; MA Inst Tech; Metallurgist.

KIM, DAE-WON; Downey HS; Downey, CA; (3); Am Leg Boys St; JA; Pres Key Clb; SADD; Pres Frsh Cls; Pres Soph Cls; Pres Jr Cls; Var Ftbl; Var Trk; Hon Roll; PTA Recognition Awd; Accredidation Comm Stu Comm Chariman; Key Clbs Outstdng; U; Law.

KIM, DALLIA H; West HS; Bakersfield, CA; (1); Chorus; Interact; Piano; Hstry.

KIM, DANIEL; Downey HS; Downey, CA; (1); Art Clb; VP Church Yth Grp; Intnl Clb; Key Clb; Science Clb; JV Tennis; Hon Roll; Aerospc Engnrng.

KIM, DANIEL; Flintridge Prep Schl; Glendale, CA; (3); French Clb; VP Jr Cls; Stu Cncl; JV Bsktbl; Golf; Tennis; French Hon Soc; High Hon Roll; NHS; 1st Runner Up Hnr Stu Of Yr 89; Biochem.

KIM, DAVID; Central Union HS; El Centro, CA; (2); Church Yth Grp; Computer Clb; 4-H; Math Tm; Tennis; Bank Of Amer Rwrd Math; UCLA; Engrng.

KIM, DEAN D; George Washington HS; San Francisco, CA; (2); Intrml Bsktbl; Capt Wt Lftg; High Hon Roll; Hon Roll; Korean Club; UCLA; Hotel Mgr.

KIM, DON; Prospect HS; Campbell, CA; (4); 3/200; Pres Church Yth Grp; Pres Cmnty Wkr; Treas Key Clb; Pres Math Clb; NFL; Speech Tm; Treas Soph Cls; JV Var Crs Cntry; Var Trk; Var JV Wrstlng; UC Berkeley; Math.

KIM, DONNA E; Los Angeles HS; Los Angeles, CA; (4); Aud/Vis; Church Yth Grp; Cmnty Wkr; Intnl Clb; JA; ROTC; Science Clb; Teachers Aide; Band; Variety Show; Principals Awd Jrnlsm; Ephebian Soc Mem; CA Schlrshp Fed Mem.

KIM, DOUGLAS D; Las Lomas HS; Lafayette, CA; (2); Ski Clb; JV Bsktbl; JV Socr; JV Swmmng; JV Tennis; Athltc Awd Tnns & Sccr; Achvt Awd Engl; UC Berkeley; Arch.

KIM, EDWARD K; Artesia HS; Hawaiian Gardens, CA; (3); Cmnty Wkr; Intnl Clb; Model UN; Science Clb; Speech Tm; Teachers Aide; Rep Sr Cls; Rotary Awd; Stu Empwrmnt; Vol Wrk ST Sntr 33rd Dist; Eurpn Hist & Clsscl Lit Music; UCLA; Gov.

KIM, ELBERT K; Glendale Adventist Acad; Woodland Hills, CA; (2); 9/56; Teachers Aide; Band; Off Soph Cls; Stu Cncl; Intrml Vllybl; Hon Roll; Orgnzd Bicycle Rcng; Loma Linda U; Med.

KIM, ELLA; Flintridge Preparatory Schl; Los Angeles, CA; (3); Pres Church Yth Grp; Cmnty Wkr; Hosp Aide; Key Clb; Pep Clb; Red Cross Aide; Service Clb; Pres Spanish Clb; Chorus; School Musical; Stanford; Bus.

KIM, ELLEN CHRISTINA; San Rafael HS; San Rafael, CA; (2); Church Yth Grp; Spanish Clb; School Play; Var Trk; Var Vllybl; Hon Roll; Marin County Fair 2nd Pl; Bay Area Sci Fair Behavioral Sci 3rd Pl 90; U C Davis; Pediatrician.

KIM, ERIC; Cajon HS; San Bernardino, CA; (2); Key Clb; Tennis; High Hon Roll; NHS; Rotary Awd; CSF; Intl Baccalaureate Acadmc Prgm; Plyng Bsbl, Ftbl, Bsktbl; Harvard U; Polticl Sci.

KIM, ERNEST T; University HS; Irvine, CA; (3); 9/550; Chess Clb; Church Yth Grp; Debate Tm; Math Clb; Math Tm; NFL; Science Clb; Speech Tm; High Hon Roll; Pres Acad Fit Awd; Sthrn CA Jr Acad Sci Rsrch Dr Ju-An Hong U Of CA Irvine 89-90; Sddlbck Coll Math Comp 1st Pl Tm 89.

KIM, ESTHER; Narbonne HS; Lomita, CA; (3); Church Yth Grp; Service Clb; Teachers Aide; Church Choir; Sec Rep Frsh Cls; JV Capt Vllybl; Cit Awd; High Hon Roll; Prfct Atten Awd; Cal St U Northridge LAUSD Music Schlrshp Cmptn Hnrb Mntn Piano; Schlr/Athl Awd Vlybl; Mrt Awd; Harvard U; Pediatrics.

KIM, ESTHER; Warren HS; Downey, CA; (4); 10/395; Pres Church Yth Grp; FBLA; Key Clb; L Letterman Clb; Spanish Clb; Var JV Tennis; Var Trk; CSF Pres,VP; Les Amies Club Pres; Delta Kappa Gamma Honoree; UC Berkeley; Sociology.

KIM, ESTHER S; El Toro HS; El Toro, CA; (1); Church Yth Grp; French Clb; Intnl Clb; Cit Awd; High Hon Roll; Pres Acad Fit Awd; Synchrnzd Swmmng; Excllnc Awd Math; Bus.

KIM, EUGENE; Rowland HS; Rowland Heights, CA; (2); Var Ftbl; High Hon Roll; Hon Roll; UCLA; Phy.

KIM, EUGENE J; Clovis West HS; Fresno, CA; (3); 1/600; Cmnty Wkr; English Clb; FBLA; Hosp Aide; Intnl Clb; Key Clb; Math Clb; Math Tm; Science Clb; Orch; Med.

KIM, EUN C; Alameda HS; Alameda, CA; (4); Science Clb; Spanish Clb; Church Choir; High Hon Roll; Korean Clb Treas.

KIM, EUN YEONG; Sunny Hills HS; Fullerton, CA; (1); 37/400; Key Clb; Spanish Clb; Treas Frsh Cls; Pres Soph Cls; Var Trk; High Hon Roll; One Of Top Three Eng Stud; Claremont Mc Kenna.

KIM, EUNICE J; Palo Alto HS; Palo Alto, CA; (2); Teachers Aide; Orch; Rptr Nwsp; Rep Frsh Cls; Rep Soph Cls; L Crs Cntry; L Trk; Theatre; Music Piano, Violin & Viloa; Schl Sci & Fren Awds Lawrence Hall Of Sci UV Berkeley 89.

KIM, EVELYN; Fountain Valley HS; Fountain Valley, CA; (3); Art Clb; French Clb; Key Clb; Ed Nwsp; Intrml Swmmng; Hon Roll; NHS; Red Cross Club Rep; Ethnic Advsry Forum; Oriental Brush Pntng Cntst Wnnr.

KIM, FRANCES; Upland HS; Upland, CA; (4); 2/587; Cmnty Wkr; Hosp Aide; Math Clb; Spanish Clb; Rptr Nwsp; Jr NHS; NHS; Prfct Atten Awd; Pres Schlr; Sal; Bank Of America Schlrshp; USAF Acad Math & Sci Awd; CSF; CA Tech; Medical Phy.

KIM, FRANCES S; Fairfax HS; Los Angeles, CA; (3); Ed Lit Mag; Off Soph Cls; Off Jr Cls; Pres Stu Cncl; Stat Vllybl; Teenline Listenr; Acad Dcthln Team; Corp Law.

KIM, FRED U; John A Rowland HS; Rowland Hts, CA; (3); Church Yth Grp; Cmnty Wkr; Science Clb; Spanish Clb; Stu Cncl; Intrml Bsbl; JV Ftbl; Intrml Tennis; JV Var Trk; Wt Lftg; CSF; Interact Clb; Premed.

KIM, GINA C H; George Washington HS; San Francisco, CA; (2); Am Leg Boys St; Drama Clb; Teachers Aide; School Play; Variety Show; Hon Roll; Best Actress Awd; Peer Rsrc Ctr Staff Stu; Bus.

KIM, GLENN; Downey HS; Downey, CA; (3); 5/500; Am Leg Boys St; Church Yth Grp; Debate Tm; French Clb; JA; Key Clb; Letterman Clb; Math Clb; Math Tm; ROTC; Vllybl, All Leag, All St & All Amer; Tnns All Leag & All St; Fllwshp Natl Acad Sci; Stanford; Bus.

KIM, GLORIA; Palmdale HS; Palmdale, CA; (2); 29/813; Chess Clb; Church Yth Grp; Computer Clb; Intnl Clb; JA; Key Clb; Spanish Clb; SADD; Church Choir; School Musical; Top Pts Cmptr, Chem Cls; Jr Cls Secy; UCLA; Pre-Med.

KIM, GLORIA; San Gabriel Acad; Arcadia, CA; (4); 2/38; Church Yth Grp; Hosp Aide; Teachers Aide; Band; Chorus; Church Choir; Treas Sr Cls; Tennis; Vllybl; Badmington; Bio.

KIM, GRACE; Etiwanda HS; Alta Loma, CA; (3); Am Leg Aux Girls St; Church Yth Grp; Cmnty Wkr; Hosp Aide; Key Clb; Scholastic Bowl; Sec Spanish Clb; Church Choir; Ed Yrbk; Ed Lit Mag; Mock Trial Witness & Lawyer; Envrnmntl Club; Psych.

KIM, GRACE E; University HS; Irvine, CA; (1); Church Yth Grp; Key Clb; Spanish Clb; Orch; School Musical; JV Bsktbl; Hon Roll; Jr NHS; MA Inst Of Tech; Math.

KIM, GRACE HYO JUNG; Village Christian HS; Northridge, CA; (3); 6/123; Church Yth Grp; English Clb; Math Clb; Mu Alpha Theta; Spanish Clb; Rep Stu Cncl; Vllybl; CA Schlrshp Fed.

KIM, GRACE J; Diamond Bar HS; Diamond Bar, CA; (2); 1/500; Church Yth Grp; Cmnty Wkr; Key Clb; Science Clb; Spanish Clb; Rptr Nwsp; JV Tennis; Piano; Chrch Yth Grp; Berkeley; Arch.

KIM, GRANT J; Granada Hills HS; Northridge, CA; (2); Church Yth Grp; JV Ftbl; JV Tennis; Hon Roll; CSF; Univ Of CA; Med.

KIM, HACKJIN; Polytecnic HS; Northridge, CA; (3); French Clb; Nwsp; Wt Lftg; Wrstlng; High Hon Roll; Hon Roll; Prfct Atten Awd; UC Davis; Engr.

KIM, HAEJUNG; Pilgrim Schl; Los Angeles, CA; (2); 3/12; Library Aide; Teachers Aide; Chorus; Orch; Mgr Nwsp; Sec Soph Cls; Sftbl; Vllybl; Hon Roll; Jr NHS; Play The Flute; Pre-Med.

KIM, HAN S; Apple Valley SR HS; Lucerne Valley, CA; (3); Wrstlng; High Hon Roll; Hon Roll; CSF; UC San Diego; Corp Acctnt.

KIM, HARRY; Santa Margarita HS; San Clemente, CA; (3); 15/227; Church Yth Grp; Cmnty Wkr; FCA; Var L Socr; JV Tennis; High Hon Roll; Hon Roll; NHS; Pres Acad Fit Awd; Comp Algb II & Trig Awds; UCLA; Engrng.

KIM, HEATHER C; Esperanza HS; Yorba Linda, CA; (2); 41/571; FCA; Intnl Clb; Pep Clb; Spanish Clb; Drill Tm; School Musical; Cit Awd; High Hon Roll; Pres Acad Fit Awd; Spanish NHS; Girls League; UCLA; Ntrtnst.

KIM, HEESUN; Granada Hills HS; Granada Hills, CA; (3); Prfct Atten Awd.

KIM, HELEN J; Lakewood HS; Lakewood, CA; (4); Pres English Clb; Pres Key Clb; School Play; Ed Yrbk; Sec Stu Cncl; Kiwanis Awd; NHS; VP Art Clb; Sec Church Yth Grp; Cmnty Wkr; CSF Sealbearer; Joan Heller Meml Awd; Lancer Awd; Stu Cncl ASB Cabinet; Stu Cnsultnt; UCLA; Dsgn.

KIM, HELEN J; Richard Gahr HS; Cerritos, CA; (3); 1/550; Church Yth Grp; Cmnty Wkr; French Clb; JA; Nwsp; Phtg Yrbk; Hist Sr Cls; JV Var Swmmng; High Hon Roll; Pres Acad Fit Awd.

KIM, HELEN Y; John F Kennedy HS; Granada Hills, CA; (2); Key Clb; Math Clb; Spanish Clb; Rep Frsh Cls; Cit Awd; Hon Roll; Jr NHS; NHS; UC Berkeley; Med.

KIM, HENRY; West Torrance HS; Torrance, CA; (3); 35/405; Church Yth Grp; Office Aide; JA; Drm Mjr(t); Mrchg Band; Orch; Sec Stu Cncl; JV Trk; High Hon Roll; CSF; West Point Acad; Comp Sci.

KIM, HOWARD; Glen A Wilson HS; Hacienda Heights, CA; (2); 14/425; Key Clb; Science Clb; Mrchg Band; Orch; Ed Nwsp; High Hon Roll; NHS; St Schlr; Soph Rep Fine Arts Clb; Sec Bridge Clb; Tennis Clb; Amerasian Clb; CSF; Open Hse Vlntr; Law.

KIM, HUI DO; Warren HS; Downey, CA; (4); Cmnty Wkr; Debate Tm; FBLA; JA; Key Clb; Letterman Clb; Math Tm; Teachers Aide; Socr; High Hon Roll; Korean Clb; UCLA; Biochem.

KIM, HYUN; Pacifica HS; Garden Grove, CA; (1); Spanish Clb; Trk; Hon Roll; CSF; Cal ST Pomona; Engrng.

KIM, HYUN-HELEN; Sunny Hills HS; Fullerton, CA; (3); Drama Clb; German Clb; Teachers Aide; Thesps; School Musical; Lit Mag; JV Tennis; Hon Roll; Prfct Atten Awd; Pres Acad Fit Awd; Martial Arts; Engl.

KIM, IN; University HS; Irvine, CA; (3); 22/500; French Clb; JV Bsktbl; French Hon Soc; High Hon Roll; Ntl Merit SF; Harvard Smmr Schl 1990; Med.

KIM, IN HEE; Whitney HS; Buena Park, CA; (3); Pres Church Yth Grp; Hosp Aide; Key Clb; Capt Color Guard; Hon Roll; NHS; CSF; CJSF; Dntst.

KIM, IN SOOK; Hoover HS; San Diego, CA; (2); Church Yth Grp; Hon Roll; Principals Honor List; UCSD; Math.

KIM, JAE B; Gahr HS; Cerritos, CA; (3); French Clb; Intnl Clb; Service Clb; Spanish Clb; JV Crs Cntry; JV Trk; High Hon Roll; Hon Roll; Med.

KIM, JAMES J; Gahr HS; Norwalk, CA; (1); JV Trk; Hon Roll; Prfct Atten Awd; Pres Acad Fit Awd; Harvard.

KIM, JAMES J; Gretchen Whitney HS; Cerritos, CA; (3); 1/170; French Clb; FBLA; Key Clb; Latin Clb; High Hon Roll; Ntl Merit Ltr.

KIM, JANE C; John F Kennedy HS; Buena Park, CA; (3); Church Choir; High Hon Roll; Hon Roll; JV Badmntn; GSE Geom Hgh Hnr; Psych.

KIM, JANE CHONG W; Kennedy HS; La Palma, CA; (3); Church Yth Grp; Church Choir; Hon Roll; CSF Hnr Clb; Badminton; Psych.

KIM, JANE J; J F Kennedy HS; La Palma, CA; (3); Art Clb; Sec Church Yth Grp; Intnl Clb; Math Clb; Science Clb; Spanish Clb; Temple Yth Grp; Chorus; Church Choir; School Musical; Choraleers; CA ST Long Beach; Bus Admin.

KIM, JANET; Downey HS; Downey, CA; (3); Church Yth Grp; Intnl Clb; Math Clb; Service Clb; JV Tennis; Prfct Atten Awd; Achvd Hnrs For Alg & Ge For Golden St Exam; Rcrdng Secy & VP For Svc Club; CSF; UCI; Tchng.

KIM, JANETTE; Indio HS; Palm Desert, CA; (2); 50/469; Church Yth Grp; Nwsp; Cheerldng; Var Trk; Cit Awd; Hon Roll; Phys Sci & Engl Hnrs; Phrmcst.

KIM, JANETTE; Palos Verdes HS; Rancho Pls Vrd, CA; (1); 1/300; JCL; VP Latin Clb; Model UN; SADD; Orch; Trk; Hon Roll; Natl Latin Exam Gold Medalist.

KIM, JANEY; University HS; Diamond Bar, CA; (3); Church Yth Grp; FCA; Teachers Aide; Jazz Band; Orch; Rep Stu Cncl; JV Vllybl; Hon Roll; Prfct Atten Awd; Acad & Prncpls Hnr Roll; Schlr/Athlt Awd & Ldrshp; E Clb & Sfty Svc; Korean Clb; Pre-Med.

KIM, JASON; Downey SR HS; Bellflower, CA; (4); Art Clb; Church Yth Grp; Intnl Clb; Key Clb; Math Clb; Science Clb; Ski Clb; Vllybl; High Hon Roll; Stu Senate; Hnrs Golden St Exam Geom; UCLA; Bus Admin.

KIM, JEAN; Immaculate Heart HS; Studio City, CA; (3); French Clb; GAA; Hosp Aide; Math Clb; Mu Alpha Theta; Science Clb; Yrbk; Crs Cntry; Hon Roll; Occidental Coll; Ped.

KIM, JEAN; Los Alamitos HS; Seal Beach, CA; (4); Church Yth Grp; Cmnty Wkr; FBLA; Hosp Aide; Model UN; Pep Clb; ROTC; Service Clb; Spanish Clb; Teachers Aide; U Of CA Berkeley; Bio.

KIM, JEAN H; J F Kennedy HS; La Palma, CA; (1); FBLA; Key Clb; JV Swmmng; Hon Roll; Prfct Atten Awd; Pres Acad Fit Awd.

KIM, JEFFREY C; San Rafael HS; San Rafael, CA; (1); Church Yth Grp; Spanish Clb; Varsity Clb; VICA; JV Var Bsbl; Capt JV Bsktbl; JV Var Ftbl; Intrml Golf; Hon Roll; Trumpet; Atuo Clb.

KIM, JENNY; Los Alamitos HS; Los Alamitos, CA; (2); Cmnty Wkr; High Hon Roll; Hon Roll; Prfct Atten Awd; CSF; U Of CA; Med.

KIM, JENNY J; Bolsa Grande HS; Garden Grove, CA; (3); Art Clb; Spanish Clb; Orch; Cit Awd; Hon Roll; Sch Spon Athlete Act JV Badminton; Cal ST Fullerton; Optics.

KIM, JESSE; California HS; Whittier, CA; (3); Math Clb; Yrbk; Bsktbl; Cit Awd; Prfct Atten Awd.

KIM, JESSICA; Cleveland HS; Tarzana, CA; (1); Church Yth Grp; French Clb; Intnl Clb; Color Guard; Off Frsh Cls; Off Soph Cls; Stu Cncl; High Hon Roll.

KIM, JI YOUNG; Arroyo Grande HS; Santa Maria, CA; (4); 1/400; AFS; FBLA; Hosp Aide; Key Clb; Model UN; SADD; JV Tennis; NHS; Pres Acad Fit Awd; Val; UC Berkeley; Bus Mgmt.

KIM, JI-HO; Eagle Rock HS; Los Angeles, CA; (3); Sec Church Yth Grp; Office Aide; Ski Clb; Teachers Aide; Orch; Phtg Yrbk; Off Jr Cls; Var Ftbl; Var L Trk; Cit Awd; Arch.

KIM, JIM; Lowell HS; San Francisco, CA; (2); Church Yth Grp; Cmnty Wkr; Cthlc Yth Orgnztn Tm Capt; Tae Kwon Do Black Belt.

KIM, JIN WOO; Bishop Amat HS; Rowland Heights, CA; (3); Cmnty Wkr; Math Clb; High Hon Roll; NHS; Ntl Merit Ltr; Spcl Olympcs Event Coord; UC Berkeley; Bio.

KIM, JINAH; Walnut HS; Walnut, CA; (4); 26/365; Drama Clb; FBLA; Pres German Clb; Thesps; Chorus; School Musical; School Play; Variety Show; Ed Nwsp; Ed Lit Mag; U Of CA Los Angeles; Engl.

KIM, JOAN; Mountain View HS; Los Altos, CA; (3); Church Yth Grp; Dance Clb; JA; Treas Sr Cls; JV Var Cheerldng; JV Gym; High Hon Roll; Multicultural Advsry Clb; Amnesty Intl; Interact Clb; Bus.

KIM, JOANNE; Los Alamitos HS; Los Alamitos, CA; (4); Church Yth Grp; Cmnty Wkr; Girl Scts; Hosp Aide; Library Aide; Pep Clb; Spanish Clb; Color Guard; Hon Roll; Pres Acad Fit Awd; Hnr Awd Golden St Exams; U Of CA Los Angeles; Pre-Geom.

KIM, JOEL E; University HS; Irvine, CA; (3); VP Church Yth Grp; French Clb; VP Key Clb; Math Tm; Chorus; Church Choir; JV Bsktbl; French Hon Soc; Hon Roll; Hstry.

KIM, JOHN; St Michaels Prep; Orange, CA; (3); Art Clb; Library Aide; School Play; Nwsp; Yrbk; Jr NHS; NHS; CSF.

KIM, JOHN; Whitney HS; Cerritos, CA; (3); Church Yth Grp; Pres Frsh Cls; Bsktbl; Hon Roll; Jr Hnr Awd; Japanese Clb VP.

KIM, JOHN D; Lakewood SR HS; Long Beach, CA; (3); Am Leg Boys St; JA; Cit Awd; High Hon Roll; Kiwanis Awd; NHS; Ntl Merit Schol; Opt Clb Awd; Prfct Atten Awd; Art Clb; U Of CA Irvine; Acctng.

KIM, JOHN J; Glendale Adventist Acad; Chatsworth, CA; (3); Church Yth Grp; Teachers Aide; Chorus; Orch; VP Soph Cls; Treas Jr Cls; VP Sr Cls; JV Capt Vllybl; Hon Roll; NHS; Algebra I Awd; Engl I Awd; Most Imprvd Singer Awd; Med Tech.

KIM, JOHNNY; Sunny Hills HS; Fullerton, CA; (3); French Clb; Intnl Clb; Science Clb; Off Soph Cls; Water Polo, Swmmng; Physics.

KIM, JOSEPH C; Glendale HS; Glendale, CA; (3); #18 In Class; Church Yth Grp; Pep Clb; Varsity Clb; Acpl Chr; Pres Frsh Cls; Off Soph Cls; Var Swmmng; High Hon Roll; NHS; Var Water Polo; Golden Boys St; UCLA; Psych.

KIM, JOSEPH J; Lowell HS; San Francisco, CA; (3); Latin Clb; Q&S; Quiz Bowl; Science Clb; Band; Pep Band; NHS; Cadet Mnth JROTC; Brnz Mdl Natl Jr Olympcs Tae Kwon Do Chmpnshps; Bst Cmptr Trphy 6th Nor CA Rgn Oly; Doctor.

KIM, JOSEPH N; J Eugene Mc Ateer Schl Of The Arts; San Francisco, CA; (3); Church Yth Grp; Teachers Aide; Band; Golf; Mgr(s); Hon Roll; Vrsty Fncng Capt; Chrch Pblctn Edtr; Mnstry.

KIM, JUDONG; Richard Gahr HS; Cerritos, CA; (3); 15/462; 4-H; Spanish Clb; Ed Yrbk; JV Ftbl; High Hon Roll; Bio.

KIM, JULIE; Woodbridge HS; El Toro, CA; (4); 25/360; Church Yth Grp; JCL; High Hon Roll; Jr NHS; Bnk Amer Awd; Yth Grp Sec; CA Schlrshp Fed; CA Poly Sn Luis Obispo; Arch.

KIM, JUNE; Marlborough Schl; Los Angeles, CA; (4); Cmnty Wkr; Service Clb; SADD; Chorus; Lit Mag; Var JV Crs Cntry; High Hon Roll; Ntl Merit Ltr; Prfct Atten Awd; Numerous Awds In Music Cmptns; 1st Pl In Intl Piano Recording Cmptn; Yale U; Econ.

KIM, JUNG; Irvine HS; Irvine, CA; (3); AFS; Key Clb; Intrml Ftbl; Wt Lftg; JV Var Wrstlng; Cit Awd; CA Schlstcs Fed; U Of CA Los Angeles; Intl Bus.

KIM, JUNG SUSAN M; San Gabriel HS; Highland, CA; (4); 40/725; VP JA; JV Var Pep Clb; Spanish Clb; VP SADD; Yrbk; Rep Frsh Cls; Rep Soph Cls; Rep Jr Cls; Rep Sr Cls; Rep Stu Cncl; HOBY Fndtn Smnr; Hmcmng Prncss 89; CSF; UC Irvine.

KIM, KAREN; San Dimas HS; San Dimas, CA; (3); 17/300; Treas Church Yth Grp; Cmnty Wkr; FCA; Mgr Nwsp; Cit Awd; High Hon Roll; Hon Roll; Amer Hertg Clb; Bus.

KIM, KERRY; San Dieguito HS; Carlsbad, CA; (2); Hon Roll; Prfct Atten Awd; Physics Achvt Awd; CSF; Golden St Exam High Hnrs Alg & Geom; Physics.

KIM, KOO YOUNG K; Irvine HS; Irvine, CA; (3); Church Yth Grp; Orch; Hon Roll; Ntl Merit Ltr; Music Awds; Juilliard; Music.

KIM, KWANG H; Lowell HS; San Francisco, CA; (3); Sec Treas Science Clb; Teachers Aide; Rptr Nwsp; Rep Stu Cncl; Capt Sftbl; CPR Coord Med Explorers; Bio.

KIM, KYONG; Bullard HS; Fresno, CA; (3); 57/550; Computer Clb; French Clb; Intnl Clb; Math Clb; Math Tm; Science Clb; JV Tennis; Cit Awd; High Hon Roll; Prfct Atten Awd; CSF; UCLA; Pre-Med.

KIM, KYONG J; John F Kennedy HS; Buena Park, CA; (4); Church Yth Grp; Computer Clb; Varsity Clb; Var Capt Socr; High Hon Roll; Pomona Coll; Bio.

KIM, KYU; Warren HS; Downey, CA; (2); Computer Clb; Key Clb; Spanish Clb; SADD; JV Tennis; Jnr Statsmn Assmbly; Asst Tnns Coach; Sci.

KIM, KYUNG; Kennedy HS; Granada Hills, CA; (4); 1/700; Pres Church Yth Grp; Treas Debate Tm; Drama Clb; Math Clb; Scholastic Bowl; Church Choir; Intrml Bsktbl; High Hon Roll; Pres Acad Fit Awd; Korean Clb Pres; Acad Decathlon; Golden St High Hnrs; UCLA; Med.

KIM, LANA; Oxnard HS; Oxnard, CA; (3); 8/640; Color Guard; Hon Roll; CSF; UC; Pediatrics.

KIM, LAUREN S; Sunny Hills HS; Fullerton, CA; (2); 15/464; Cmnty Wkr; Intnl Clb; Key Clb; Model UN; JV Swmmng; High Hon Roll; Rotary Awd; Bio.

KIM, LINDA J; Gretchen Whitney HS; Norwalk, CA; (3); Hosp Aide; JA; Office Aide; Variety Show; Rptr Nwsp; Hon Roll; CSF/Cjsf; Korean Clb; Clb Kaiblgan.

KIM, LISA G; Sunny Hills HS; Fullerton, CA; (3); VP Church Yth Grp; Intnl Clb; Key Clb; Teachers Aide; School Play; Hon Roll; UCSB; Advrtsng.

KIM, MALAY; River City HS; West Sacremento, CA; (3); 10/215; French Clb; Hon Roll.

KIM, MARK S; Gladstone HS; Azusa, CA; (3); Church Yth Grp; Cmnty Wkr; FBLA; Science Clb; Nwsp; Sprt Ed Yrbk; Stu Cncl; Capt Var Bsktbl; Var Vllybl; Cit Awd; GATE Prgm; CSF; Prsdntl Acad Ftnss Awd; Aeronautical Engrng.

KIM, MARTIN H; Sacramento Adventist Acad; Citrus Heights, CA; (2); Drama Clb; Ski Clb; Gym; Prfct Atten Awd; Harvard; Med Mssnry.

KIM, MAY J; Calabasas HS; Calabasas, CA; (3); Treas VP Church Yth Grp; Intnl Clb; Church Choir; Swmmng; Vllybl; Hon Roll; UCLA; Chem.

KIM, MICHAEL S; Capistrano Valley HS; Mission Viejo, CA; (3); FBLA; Mrchg Band; Orch; Wrstlng; Mrtl Arts-Blck Blt; USC; Bus Admin.

KIM, MICHAEL S; Serrite HS; La Mirada, CA; (2); JV Bsktbl.

KIM, MICHELLE J; Glen A Wilson HS; Hacienda Hgts, CA; (3); Cmnty Wkr; Office Aide; Var Tennis; High Hon Roll; Treas NHS; Amerasian Clb Treas; Open House Parent-Tchr Conf Coordntr; Fine Arts Clb.

KIM, MICHELLE J; Senior HS; San Francisco, CA; (3); Key Clb; Teachers Aide; Acpl Chr; Chorus; Church Choir; Swmmng; High Hon Roll; Hon Roll; Tutoring.

KIM, MICHELLE J; Villa Park HS; Villa Park, CA; (2); French Clb; Hosp Aide; Key Clb; Nwsp; Yrbk; JV Cheerldng; JV Crs Cntry; NHS.

KIM, MILLER S; Montebello HS; Montebello, CA; (1); Chorus; Hon Roll; Engl.

KIM, MIMI; North HS; Torrance, CA; (2); Pep Clb; Rep Soph Cls; JV Cheerldng; Hon Roll; Jr NHS; Julians/Valiants; Japanese Clb; CSF; UC San Diego; Med.

KIM, MINDY; Don Lugo HS; Chino, CA; (2); VP Church Yth Grp; Var Tennis; Hon Roll; Pres Chorus; Pres Of All Chorus Classes; Psych.

KIM, MINSOO MATTHEW; Buena Park HS; Cerritos, CA; (4); #34 In Class; Aud/Vis; Church Yth Grp; Debate Tm; NFL; Science Clb; Speech Tm; Teachers Aide; Church Choir; Ed Nwsp; Var Tennis; Karate; Korean Clb; Peer Tutrng Cnslr; UC Irvine; Soc Sci.

KIM, MOON HEE; Artesia HS; Lakewood, CA; (4); Tennis; High Hon Roll; Conestoga Trphy; Cal ST Long Beach; Psych.

KIM, MOSES M; Lowell HS; San Francisco, CA; (4); 25/626; Church Yth Grp; JA; Math Tm; Chorus; Crs Cntry; Trk; High Hon Roll; Ntl Merit SF; CA Schlrshp Fed; Scrll Hnr Scty; Biochem.

KIM, NANCY INKYUNG; Claremont HS; Claremont, CA; (4); Debate Tm; SADD; Pres Treas Color Guard; Co-Capt Drill Tm; School Musical; Variety Show; Activities Cmmtte; 3rd Rnr-Up Miss Dance, Drill Tm Northern CA, USA Pgnt, HI Invttnl 90; UC Santa Cruz.

KIM, NAUN; James Logan HS; Hayward, CA; (3); 73/900; Art Clb; Red Cross Aide; Church Choir; Off Frsh Cls; Cit Awd; Hon Roll; Korean Church Pianist; CSF; Travel Club; Special Olympics; Publishing.

KIM, NINA; Los Amigos HS; Fountain Valley, CA; (2); Drama Clb; Sec French Clb; Treas German Clb; Key Clb; Thesps; School Musical; School Play; JV Tennis; Hon Roll; Jr NHS; Korean Clb; Intl Thespian Soc; Golden St Exam Geom Hnrs; UCSB.

KIM, ORIANA; Marina HS; Huntington Bch, CA; (4); 2/505; Church Yth Grp; VP JA; VP Key Clb; Pres Frsh Cls; Pres Soph Cls; Pres Jr Cls; JV Tennis; High Hon Roll; Ntl Merit Ltr; Pres Schlr; United Way Yth Ldrshp Pgm Chrmn; Hntngtn Bch Yth Brd Chrmn; Grad Cmmtte Chrmn; U Of CA Berkeley; Bio.

KIM, PAUL; Adrian C Wilcox HS; Santa Clara, CA; (2); Band; Jazz Band; Mrchg Band; School Musical; Hon Roll; Prfct Atten Awd.

KIM, PAUL H; Arcadia HS; Arcadia, CA; (3); Service Clb; Orch; Var Capt Ftbl; High Hon Roll; Hon Roll; Pres Acad Fit Awd; SR Men An Honorary Svc Grp; Ldr Vrsty Ftbl Prgm; NY U.

KIM, PAUL H; Edison HS; Huntington Beach, CA; (3); Church Yth Grp; Key Clb; Spanish Clb; Var Capt Tennis; Hon Roll; Acad Letter; Peer Assitance Leag; Golden St Exams-Geom 88; UCLA; Med.

KIM, PAUL H; Whitney HS; Cerritos, CA; (3); VP French Clb; JA; Key Clb; Latin Clb; Nwsp; Hon Roll; Hstry Day LA 2nd Pl Group; CSF; Physics.

KIM, PAUL K; Grace M Davis HS; Modesto, CA; (2); Debate Tm; French Clb; FBLA; NFL; Speech Tm; Church Choir; Orch; JV Bsbl; JV Trk; Cit Awd; Elctrnc Engrng.

KIM, PETER Y; Bakersfield HS; Bakersfield, CA; (3); 1/714; Chess Clb; Math Clb; Math Tm; Science Clb; Service Clb; Band; Orch; Lit Mag; High Hon Roll; 3rd Pl CA ST Tak Kwondo Chmpnshps; Math Fld Day CA ST U Of Bakersfield; 1st Pl Math Bwl.

KIM, PHARN; Santa Ana HS; Santa Ana, CA; (3); U C Fullerton; Art.

KIM, PHILLIP S; Gretchen Whitney HS; Cerritos, CA; (3); Pres Church Yth Grp; Cmnty Wkr; Drama Clb; Key Clb; Library Aide; Church Choir; Rptr Nwsp; JV Bsbl; Hon Roll; Fndr Guiding Light Clb.

KIM, PHUONG T; Pinole Valley HS; Rodeo, CA; (3); JA; Hon Roll; Prfct Atten Awd; UC Berkeley; Med.

KIM, RATHA R; Ygnacio Valley HS; Concord, CA; (3); Chess Clb; Debate Tm; Math Clb; Sec Quiz Bowl; Science Clb; Speech Tm; SADD; Band; Mrchg Band; VP Frsh Cls; U Of San Francisco; Ed.

KIM, SAE HWAN; Birmingham HS; Los Angeles, CA; (3); Math Clb; Varsity Clb; School Play; Stu Cncl; Var Socr; High Hon Roll; UCLA; Bus.

KIM, SAMUEL L; Lowell HS; San Francisco, CA; (2); Red Cross Aide; California Scholarship Federation; UC Berkeley; Medicine.

KIM, SANDRA; Clovis West HS; Fresno, CA; (4); 1/504; Church Yth Grp; Office Aide; Band; Church Choir; Sec Frsh Cls; Var Tennis; Wt Lftg; Val; Piano; Jazz, Tap Dance; U CA Davis; Biochem.

KIM, SANDRA; Norco HS; Clearwater, FL; (3); Spanish Clb; Teachers Aide; Cit Awd; High Hon Roll; Prfct Atten Awd; Lang Art & Scl Stds Awds; Acad Excllnc; Bus.

KIM, SARA; El Segundo HS; El Segundo, CA; (1); Pep Clb; Spanish Clb; Sec Treas Frsh Cls; Rep Sec Stu Cncl; JV Cheerldng; High Hon Roll; Frshmn Prncss; Dance Cmmtte; Pblcty Cmmtte; Faculty Relations; Miss Coed Fnslt; Commrcl Art.

KIM, SARA S; Herbert Hoover HS; Glendale, CA; (3); Church Yth Grp; Pres Key Clb; Orch; Ed Nwsp; Yrbk; Sec Frsh Cls; Off Sr Cls; Var Cheerldng; Pom Pon; Cit Awd; Mayors Cmmtte Yth Citizen For Future; Korean Amer HS Mrt Schlrshp 90; JSA; UC Irvine; Layout Dsgnr.

KIM, SARAH; Palisades HS; Los Angeles, CA; (3); Art Clb; Church Yth Grp; Cmnty Wkr; VP Scholastic Bowl; Service Clb; Teachers Aide; Orch; VP Frsh Cls; Off Jr Cls; Prfct Atten Awd; Jr Statesmen Of Amer; Palisades Outreach; Smmr Day Camp Tchr.

KIM, SEAN T; Mills HS; Burlingame, CA; (2); Church Yth Grp; Debate Tm; Hosp Aide; Orch; JV L Bsbl; High Hon Roll; Pres Acad Fit Awd; Cello CA Yth Symphny; Chsn Play 37th Annl Jr Bach Festvl; Engr.

KIM, SEONG E; Central Union HS; El Centro, CA; (4); 21/447; Cmnty Wkr; Computer Clb; Dance Clb; Speech Tm; Orch; Vllybl; Spanish NHS; Acad Mdl; Amer Sign Lang Clb Pres; UC Davis; Med.

KIM, SERAN; Monta Vista HS; Cupertino, CA; (2); French Clb; FBLA; Hosp Aide; Service Clb; Yrbk; Pres Stu Cncl; JV Cheerldng; Var Trk; High Hon Roll; NHS; Stanford U.

KIM, SHARON M; Fullerton HS; Fullerton, CA; (3); 2/369; Church Yth Grp; Cmnty Wkr; VP Debate Tm; French Clb; NFL; VP Speech Tm; Co-Capt Drill Tm; High Hon Roll; VP NHS; Rotary Awd; Sci Olympiad; Theory Of Knowledge Smmr Schl; Anthropology.

KIM, SHARON S; Glendale Adventist Acad; Chatsworth, CA; (2); Art Clb; Church Yth Grp; Teachers Aide; Chorus; Orch; Off Frsh Cls; Off Soph Cls; Off Jr Cls; JV Vllybl; Hon Roll; Alg I Awd; Spd Typst Trphy 89; Geom Awd; Mst Imprvd Sngr Awd; Vet.

KIM, SHIRLEY; Hawthorne HS; Hawthorne, CA; (3); AFS; Cmnty Wkr; Dance Clb; Service Clb; Capt Drill Tm; High Hon Roll; Hon Roll; Jr NHS; Pres Acad Fit Awd; CA Schlrshp Fed; Premed.

KIM, SIYEON; Warren HS; Downey, CA; (4); 18/415; FBLA; Key Clb; Letterman Clb; Teachers Aide; Varsity Clb; JV Mgr(s); JV Var Swmmng; Tennis; High Hon Roll; Pres Acad Fit Awd; Music-Piano; Art Drawing & Painting; Tutoring; Teaching.

KIM, SONANG; Oceana HS; Pacifica, CA; (1); Church Yth Grp; Drama Clb; School Play; Stage Crew; Hon Roll; UC Berkley; Plastic Surgn.

KIM, SONIA; Warren HS; Downey, CA; (3); 24/423; FBLA; High Hon Roll; CSF; Interact Rotary Club; UCLA; Bus.

KIM, SOOK; Lynbrook HS; San Jose, CA; (3); Debate Tm; FBLA; Key Clb; NFL; Spanish Clb; Sec Soph Cls; High Hon Roll; NHS; Opt Clb Awd; FBLA St Cmptn Bus Law 3rd Pl.

KIM, SOYON; Redlands HS; Redlands, CA; (3); Art Clb; Church Yth Grp; FBLA; Hosp Aide; Key Clb; Ski Clb; Rep Frsh Cls; Hon Roll; Kiwanis Awd; Prfct Atten Awd; San Bernardino Cnty Wrtng Celebrtn Author Awd Poem; Orgnzd Schl Attndnc March Dimes Walk Am 88.

KIM, STAN S; Orange HS; Orange, CA; (4); 3/450; Pres Church Yth Grp; Drama Clb; Hosp Aide; Mu Alpha Theta; Church Choir; Hon Roll; NHS; Prfct Atten Awd; Gale Pattison Ldrshp Awd; Jnr Vlnr Schlstc Awd; U Of CA Irvine; Bio.

KIM, STEVE; La Vista HS; Fullerton, CA; (3); Boy Scts; Church Yth Grp; FCA; Nwsp; Yrbk; Hon Roll; Prfct Atten Awd; ITT Tech; Comp.

KIM, STEVE; Los Altos HS; Hacienda Hgts, CA; (2); Church Yth Grp; Letterman Clb; Varsity Clb; Wrstlng; Cit Awd; Hon Roll; Prfct Atten Awd; Arch.

KIM, STEVE S; El Toro HS; El Toro, CA; (3); 1/500; VP French Clb; VP Key Clb; Letterman Clb; Math Tm; Quiz Bowl; Bsktbl; JV Var Vllybl; High Hon Roll; Ntl Merit Ltr; Med.

KIM, STEVE S; Santa Clara HS; Camarillo, CA; (3); Am Leg Boys St; French Clb; School Play; Off Frsh Cls; Off Soph Cls; VP Jr Cls; Off Sr Cls; JV Trk; Hon Roll; NHS; Bach Fstvl Rgnl Fnlst Piano; Mount St Marys Ldrshp Conf; UCLA; Civil Engrng.

KIM, SU LINDA A; Alameda HS; Alameda, CA; (3); Church Yth Grp; Treas Frsh Cls; Off Soph Cls; Sec Jr Cls; VP Sr Cls; JV Var Cheerldng; High Hon Roll; Rotary Awd; RYLA Camp Rotary Yth Ldrshp Awd; Top 10% Trophy Wnnr 88-89; UC Berkeley; Poltcl Sci.

KIM, SU YEON; Burbank HS; Burbank, CA; (3); French Clb; Red Cross Aide; Science Clb; High Hon Roll; Hon Roll; Prfct Atten Awd; Pres Acad Fit Awd; High Hnrs Golden St Exam Alg, Geom; Korean Clb.

KIM, SUE; Walnut HS; Walnut, CA; (2); Debate Tm; FBLA; German Clb; Key Clb; Ski Clb; Yrbk; Off Soph Cls; Crs Cntry; Swmmng; High Hon Roll; Med.

KIM, SUE Y; University HS; Irvine, CA; (2); 13/508; French Clb; Hosp Aide; Key Clb; Var L Crs Cntry; JV Trk; French Hon Soc; Hon Roll; Olympc Style Rowing Crew; Envrnmntl Club.

KIM, SUELYN; John A Rowland HS; Rowland Heights, CA; (2); Key Clb; High Hon Roll; Hon Roll; Prfct Atten Awd; UC Berkeley; Cmptr Sci.

KIM, SUN; Coast Christian Schls; Torrance, CA; (1); 3/26; Church Yth Grp; Teachers Aide; Tennis; Stanford.

KIM, SUN; Villa Park HS; Orange, CA; (2); Church Yth Grp; Cmnty Wkr; Hosp Aide; Spanish Clb; Church Choir; Rptr Nwsp; Intrml Bsktbl; JV Swmmng; High Hon Roll; Jr NHS; Asian Clb VP; Mock Trl Wtnss; Acad Dcthln; Writer.

KIM, SUNG E; John F Kennedy HS; Cypress, CA; (3); Chess Clb; Pres Church Yth Grp; Speech Tm; Band; Church Choir; Mrchg Band; JV Var Ftbl; Var Tennis; Hon Roll; 3rd Degree Black Belt Tae Kwon Do; UC San Diego; Med.

KIM, SUNG H; Westminster HS; Westminster, CA; (1); Latin Clb; Intrml Ftbl; JV Wrstlng; Hon Roll.

KIM, SUNG HEE; Arcadia HS; Arcadia, CA; (2); #8 In Class; Art Clb; VP Church Yth Grp; Hosp Aide; Orch; Cheerldng; Hon Roll; NHS; Pres Acad Fit Awd; Korean Club Treas; Stanford; Pediatrician.

KIM, SUNG T; Buena Park HS; Anaheim, CA; (3); 6/400; Art Clb; Church Yth Grp; Math Clb; Science Clb; Church Choir; High Hon Roll; CSF; Stu Of Month Physics, Scl Sci & Trig/Hnr; Korean & Aisan Clbs; Medcl.

KIM, SUNG-YONG; Artesia HS; Lakewood, CA; (1); Church Yth Grp; Golf; High Hon Roll.

KIM, SUNG-YOON; Gahr HS; Cerritos, CA; (1); Church Yth Grp; Intnl Clb; Math Tm; Var Gym; Cit Awd; Hon Roll; Prfct Atten Awd; Pres Acad Fit Awd; UCI; Tchr.

KIM, SUSAN; Bishop Amat HS; Walnut, CA; (4); 14/411; Church Yth Grp; Cmnty Wkr; Red Cross Aide; Co-Capt Color Guard; High Hon Roll; NHS; Silver Screen Clb Sec; UC Berkeley; Lawyer.

KIM, SUSAN B; College Park HS; Martinez, CA; (3); Church Yth Grp; Hosp Aide; SADD; Teachers Aide; Hon Roll; Law.

KIM, SUSAN K; South San Francisco HS; South San Francis, CA; (2); Computer Clb; FBLA; Math Clb; High Hon Roll; CSF; Asian Amer Club; Cert Of Merit Prgm Piano; UCLA; Lawyer.

KIM, TAE H; Bullard HS; Clovis, CA; (4); 1/450; Model UN; Science Clb; Trk; Hon Roll; Kiwanis Awd; Rotary Awd; Val; 49th Westinghouse Natl Sci Tlnt Srch Fnlst; 1st Biochem Intl Sci Fair; Reed Coll; Molecular Bio.

KIM, TAE K; Charter Oak HS; Glendora, CA; (4); Debate Tm; Science Clb; Thesps; School Musical; School Play; High Hon Roll; NHS; Pres Acad Fit Awd; Badminton JV; CA Schlrshp Fed Mem; UC Riverside; Biomed.

KIM, THE SUN; Glendale HS; Glendale, CA; (3); Sec Art Clb; Sec FBLA; Pres Spanish Clb; VP SADD; Drill Tm; Pres Frsh Cls; Pres Soph Cls; Var Cheerldng; JV Capt Tennis; NHS; Psych.

KIM, TO H; Fremont HS; Sunnyvale, CA; (4); Debate Tm; Drama Clb; Library Aide; NFL; JV Socr; JV Tennis; 1st Deg Blck Blt Tae Kwon Do; De Anza JC; Med.

KIM, TODD; Menlo-Atherton HS; Menlo Park, CA; (4); 13/340; Church Yth Grp; Key Clb; Letterman Clb; Math Clb; Band; Church Choir; Jazz Band; Off Soph Cls; Off Jr Cls; Var Bsbl; CSF; Pres; Swarthmore Coll.

KIM, TOKHYUN DAVEY; Fairfax HS; Los Angeles, CA; (4); 45/650; SADD; Stu Cncl; JV Var Bsbl; Intrml Mgr Ftbl; Cit Awd; High Hon Roll; Cngrssnl Yth Schlr; UCLA; Ec.

KIM, TOM; Prospect HS; Campbell, CA; (3); 64/274; Church Yth Grp; Hon Roll; USCF Bcycl Racng.

KIM, TRACY; Bonita Vista HS; Bonita, CA; (2); Church Yth Grp; Flag Corp; Cit Awd; Hon Roll.

KIM, VARY; River City HS; W Sacramento, CA; (1); French Clb; CA Schlrshp Fndtn.

KIM, VICTOR Y; Palma HS; Salinas, CA; (4); 2/90; Phtg Yrbk; NHS; Pres Acad Fit Awd; Sal; Science Clb; Rep Nwsp; High Hon Roll; CSF; Intract; Bk Amer Plaque Wnnr, Lbrl Art; James J Cecilian Mem Schlrshp For Math; Knwldge Bowl; Spch; UC Berkeley; Acctng.

KIM, WILLAIM P; Warren HS; Downey, CA; (2); Sec Church Yth Grp; Computer Clb; Debate Tm; French Clb; Key Clb; Band; Mrchg Band; Pep Band; Prfct Atten Awd; Bus.

KIM, WILLIAM; Granada Hills HS; Northridge, CA; (2); Church Yth Grp; Office Aide; Ski Clb; Dancing; Sports.

KIM, WON I; Tustin HS; Tustin, CA; (2); 5/460; VP Church Yth Grp; Science Clb; Church Choir; JV Bsktbl; Hon Roll; Thlgy.

KIM, WOO YOUNG; Los Angeles HS; Los Angeles, CA; (4); Intnl Clb; Temple Yth Grp; Varsity Clb; Church Choir; Off Jr Cls; Off Sr Cls; Stu Cncl; JV Var Vllybl; Cit Awd; Rcgnzd Hgh Golden St Exam Score; UCL; Fine Arts Industrial.

KIM, WOOJAY; Bishop Amat HS; Diamond Bar, CA; (4); 2/400; Cmnty Wkr; JV Bsktbl; Var Tennis; High Hon Roll; Hon Roll; NHS; Ntl Merit SF; Religious Commissioner; UCLA; Med.

KIM, YE O; Woodbridge HS; Irvine, CA; (4); Church Yth Grp; Cmnty Wkr; German Clb; Intnl Clb; Library Aide; Office Aide; ROTC; SADD; Teachers Aide; Acpl Chr; UCI; Music.

KIM, YOO JIN; Crossroads Schl; Los Angeles, CA; (2); Orch; Music.

KIM, YOO M; Grant HS; North Hollywood, CA; (2); Church Yth Grp; Office Aide; SADD; Teachers Aide; VP Stu Cncl; Hon Roll; Prfct Atten Awd; Service Clb; Cit Awd; CSF; UCLA.

KIM, YOON JONG; Alhambra HS; Alhambra, CA; (3); Church Yth Grp; Service Clb; School Musical; Lanakila YMCA Club Tri-Hi-Y; Optometry.

KIM, YOUNG; Arcadia HS; Arcadia, CA; (2); Boy Scts; Church Yth Grp; Mrchg Band; Orch; Rptr Nwsp; JV Swmmng; Cit Awd; Hon Roll; Prfct Atten Awd; Pres Acad Fit Awd; UC Berkeley; Arch.

KIM, YOUNG; Miramonte HS; Orinda, CA; (1); Debate Tm; NFL; Tennis; Hon Roll.

KIM, YOUNG; Westmoor HS; Daly City, CA; (3); 7/300; Boy Scts; Church Yth Grp; Debate Tm; Intnl Clb; Math Clb; Math Tm; Model UN; Spanish Clb; SADD; Varsity Clb; UCLA; Bio.

KIM, YOUSUN; Culver City HS; Culver City, CA; (3); Cmnty Wkr; Debate Tm; Sec French Clb; Speech Tm; Off Soph Cls; Off Jr Cls; French Hon Soc; Hon Roll; Lion Awd; NHS; Thatcher Schl Smmr Sci Prgm; Bio-Med.

KIM, YUN J; Rowland HS; Rowland Heights, CA; (3); Church Yth Grp; French Clb; FBLA; Hosp Aide; Key Clb; Math Clb; High Hon Roll; Hon Roll; Prfct Atten Awd; Chrch Band.

KIMANH, NGUYEN THI; Edison HS; Stockton, CA; (3); French Clb; Hon Roll; UC Davis; Med.

KIMBALL, BENJAMIN A; Lindsay HS; Lindsay, CA; (1); 4/200; Boy Scts; Church Yth Grp; JV Ftbl; Score Keeper; Elks Awd; Hon Roll; Brigham Young U; Comp Prgmr.

KIMBALL, BEVERLY MONIQUE; John A Rowland HS; Diamond Bar, CA; (4); High Hon Roll; Hon Roll; Science Clb; Stu Yr; Mt San Antonio Coll; Photo.

KIMBALL, DYANA; Burlingame HS; Burlingame, CA; (1); Church Yth Grp; Drama Clb; Church Choir; School Musical; School Play; Off Frsh Cls; Off Soph Cls; JV Bsktbl; Stat Vllybl; Hon Roll; Chrstn Camp Cnslr; Missionary.

KIMBALL, JACOB C; Yucca Valley HS; Morongo Valley, CA; (3); 2/225; Am Leg Boys St; Church Yth Grp; Debate Tm; FBLA; Letterman Clb; Math Clb; NFL; Quiz Bowl; Spanish Clb; SADD; CSF Pres; Sprts Jrnlst.

KIMBERLIN, BRIAN M; Indio HS; Indio, CA; (3); Teachers Aide; Prfct Atten Awd; Ltr Wd Shp; Natl Sci Olympd; Coll Of Desert.

KIMBIRK, ANTHONY JOHN; Colton HS; Colton, CA; (2); Var L Ftbl; JV L Wt Lftg; JV L Wrstlng; Hon Roll; St Schlr; Golden St Algebra Exam Recognition From St Sen Reubin S Ayala; Acad Cmptn; Lifeguard; Aeronautical Engrng.

KIMBROUGH, TAMARA D; La Canada HS; La Canada-Flint, CA; (4); 14/256; Church Yth Grp; Intnl Clb; Key Clb; Ed Yrbk; Sec Sr Cls; Capt Powder Puff Ftbl; Vllybl; High Hon Roll; Kiwanis Awd; NHS; Cmnty & Natl Hnr Soc Schlrshps; Franklin/Marshall Coll; Bus Adm.

KIMELMAN, OLEG; Washington HS; San Francisco, CA; (2); JV Bsktbl; JV Ftbl; JV Trk; High Hon Roll; Hon Roll; Use Comps; San Francisco ST; Comp Pgm.

KIMES, BRANDI; Hesperia HS; Hesperia, CA; (2); Office Aide; Pep Clb; Cmnty Wkr; SADD; Teachers Aide; Orch; Pep Band; Stat Bsktbl; Stat Score Keeper; Camp Cnslr; U CA Riverside; Teacher.

KIMMEL, ALLISON R; Granada Hills HS; Northridge, CA; (2); GAA; Temple Yth Grp; Yrbk; Cheerldng; Socr; Hon Roll; Pres Acad Fit Awd; Med.

KIMMEL, KATHERINE N; Poway HS; San Diego, CA; (2); Key Clb; Pep Clb; SADD; Hon Roll; Pres Acad Fit Awd; Amnesty Intl; Tnns Pgm; Bus.

KIMMEL, MELANIE D; Serrano HS; Phelan, CA; (3); 1/213; Church Yth Grp; Sec French Clb; Quiz Bowl; Ed Yrbk; Stat Bsktbl; JV Var Sftbl; High Hon Roll; Jr NHS; Hnr Guard; Sci Fair Wnnr; Stu Month & Wrtng Celebration; UCR; Elem Educ.

KIMONT, MASON W; Santa Teresa HS; San Jose, CA; (2); Teachers Aide; Jazz Band; School Musical; Variety Show; Ftbl; Wt Lftg; Hon Roll; UCLA; Law.

KIMSEY, STACEY D; S Cal Christian HS; Costa Mesa, CA; (4); 1/60; Church Yth Grp; VP Spanish Clb; Ed Nwsp; Stu Cncl; High Hon Roll; Pres NHS; Ntl Merit SF; Stu Advsry Brd; Whitelines Staff Anti Drug Nwsltr; YMCA Swim Tm; Westmont Coll; Englsh Wrtng.

KIMSON, PATRICIA R; Mt Diablo HS; Pittsburg, CA; (4); 1/204; Am Leg Aux Girls St; French Clb; Hosp Aide; Model UN; VP Jr Cls; Pres Sr Cls; Rep Stu Cncl; Var Tennis; DAR Awd; Val; Undrgrad Awd; Danc Prdctn; UC Davis; Bio Sci.

KIMURA, AMI; Berean Christian HS; Concord, CA; (4); 4/66; Co-Ed Yrbk; High Hon Roll; Hon Roll; Hnr Stu; CA Schltc Fed Pres & Lftm Mem; ACSI Dstngshd Chrstn HS Stu Acad; UC Davis.

KIMURA, ANDY S; San Gabriel HS; San Gabriel, CA; (2); French Clb; Hon Roll; Comp Tle Commnctns.

KIMURA, ROBYN L; Sacramento Adventist Acad; Sacramento, CA; (3); Church Yth Grp; Teachers Aide; Band; Off Jr Cls; Hon Roll; NHS; Prfct Atten Awd; Acad Ltr 89; Chem Awd 90; Bio Awd 89; Phy.

KIMURA, SARINA; Adrian C Wilcox HS; Sunnyvale, CA; (4); Am Leg Aux Girls St; French Clb; Band; Co-Capt Drill Tm; Pres Frsh Cls; Rep Soph Cls; Rep Jr Cls; Stu Cncl; JV Tennis; Hon Roll; UCLA; Psych.

KIN, TONY; Mira Costa HS; Manhattan Beach, CA; (4); Cmnty Wkr; Teachers Aide; JV Bsktbl; Cit Awd; Hon Roll; Pres Acad Fit Awd; The Amer U; Pol Sci.

KINCADE III, ROBERT; Fontana HS; Fontana, CA; (2); Bus Profs of Am; Bsktbl; Bus.

KINCAID, D ANNE; Sonora HS; La Habra, CA; (4); 12/279; Pep Clb; Spanish Clb; Yrbk; High Hon Roll; NHS; Pres Acad Fit Awd; CSF; U CA Santa Barbara Regents Schlr; UC Santa Barbara; Spansh.

KINCAID, MICHAEL C; Mission Viejo HS; Mission Viejo, CA; (1); 7/400; Model UN; Spanish Clb; Crs Cntry; Trk; JR Stsmn Amer; Prin Hnr Roll.

KINCY, DARIAN; Monrovia HS; Monrovia, CA; (3); Dance Clb; Drama Clb; Office Aide; Teachers Aide; Varsity Clb; School Musical; School Play; Rptr Nwsp; Rptr Yrbk; Var Bsktbl; Awd Bus Eng, Jrnlsm Outstndng Wrk; Stu Wk; UCLA; Bus.

KINDER, GRETCHEN M; Thomas Downey HS; Modesto, CA; (1); Church Yth Grp; Drama Clb; Band; Mrchg Band; Stage Crew; JV Swmmng; Var Tennis; High Hon Roll; Mssnry Wrk Mexico; CSF; Social Work.

KINDER, JOHN H; Foothill HS; Santa Ana, CA; (2); JV Bsbl; Otsd Actvts, Motorsprots Pro Am Kart Rcng 88 Road Rcng Chmpn JR Div 89; Dirt Chpn Kart Rcng Assn; Phys Thrpy.

KINDERMANN, AMY; Paso Robles HS; Paso Robles, CA; (1); Church Yth Grp; Intrml Cheerldng; Score Keeper; Law.

KINDLE, DAVID M; Aptos HS; Santa Cruz, CA; (2); Band; Jazz Band; Mrchg Band; Pep Band; Ftbl; High Hon Roll; Prfct Atten Awd; CSF; Law.

KINDRICK, ARMINDA; Highlands HS; North Highlands, CA; (3); Church Yth Grp; Cmnty Wkr; Red Cross Aide; Spanish Clb; Rptr Nwsp; High Hon Roll; Masonic Awd; Post Hnrd Qn; Friday Night Live Sec; Swthrt Sacrmnto Chptr De Molay; Intl Stud.

KINERMON, TERESA; Chula Vista HS; San Diego, CA; (3); 53/535; French Clb; Band; Mrchg Band; Orch; Cit Awd; Mathmtc Engr Sci Achvt Clb; Blck Stu Union,Schlrshp Fedrtn; U WI Madison; Bio-Med Engr.

KINETZ, ERIKA T; Bishop Montgomery HS; Manhattan Beach, CA; (4); 1/354; Letterman Clb; NFL; Ski Clb; Speech Tm; SADD; Drill Tm; VP Co-Capt Cheerldng; High Hon Roll; NHS; Ntl Merit SF; Co-Capt Dnc Tm; Sci & Mth Excllnc; Caer Bonnag Slvr Mdl Tp Acad Prfrmnc; Intl Rltns.

KING, ALLISON; Campbell Hall HS; Sherman Oaks, CA; (3); FCA; Ski Clb; Aud/Vis; Ed Yrbk; Off Frsh Cls; Off Soph Cls; Pres Sr Cls; JV Var Cheerldng; Diving; Gym; Jr Hmcmng Princess; Human Behavior.

KING, ANDRA R; Trabuco Hills HS; El Toro, CA; (1); Art Clb; Church Yth Grp; French Clb; Hon Roll; Art.

KING, ANDREA M; Corona HS; Corona, CA; (2); 148/473; 4-H; Yrbk; Socr; Trk; Math.

KING, BECKIE; Coronado HS; Coronado, CA; (4); Cmnty Wkr; FCA; Service Clb; Yrbk; Capt Bsktbl; Fld Hcky; Var Mgr Sftbl; Hon Roll; NHS; Spanish NHS; CSU Fresno; Marine Sci.

KING, BECKY J; Santa Teresa HS; San Jose, CA; (1); Temple Yth Grp; Piano 7 Yrs; Flute 4 Yrs; UC Santa Barbara.

KING, BECKY L; Sonora HS; Kirkland, WA; (2); 80/336; Dance Clb; Drama Clb; Ski Clb; Spanish Clb; JV Cheerldng; JV Pom Pon; Hon Roll; AFS; Long Beach ST.

KING, CARRIE E; San Bonito HS; Hollister, CA; (2); Art Clb; Church Yth Grp; Cmnty Wkr; Dance Clb; Drama Clb; English Clb; 4-H; GAA; Intnl Clb; Letterman Clb; Stu Congrss; Drama Awd; Ed.

KING, CATHERINE A; Westlake HS; Westlake Village, CA; (2); 1/432; Church Yth Grp; French Clb; Office Aide; JV Tennis; High Hon Roll; CSF.

KING, CHANEL L; Skyline HS; Oakland, CA; (3); Cmnty Wkr; Service Clb; Ski Clb; Rep Frsh Cls; Var Trk; Cit Awd; High Hon Roll; Hon Roll; Pres Acad Fit Awd; Georgetown U; Phy.

KING, CLINT J; Porterville HS; Springville, CA; (3); Cmnty Wkr; Science Clb; School Play; Rptr Nwsp; Jrnlst.

KING, COREY; Cajon HS; Devers, TX; (3); 8/430; Boy Scts; Church Yth Grp; Treas Key Clb; Ed Lit Mag; Rep Frsh Cls; Var L Crs Cntry; JV Trk; High Hon Roll; Natl Yth Ldrshp Cert Merit; Egl Scout; Nuclr Engrng.

KING, DEREK; Vista HS; Vista, CA; (3); FFA.

KING, DIONNE; Colton HS; San Bernardino, CA; (4); 7/329; Key Clb; NFL; Speech Tm; Var L Cheerldng; L Trk; NHS; Pres Acad Fit Awd; Rep Stu Cncl; Jeopardy Teen Trnmt 89-90; U Of CA Irvine; Psycht.

KING, DUSTIN D; Esperanza HS; Yorba Linda, CA; (3); Boy Scts; Ski Clb; Rep Frsh Cls; Bsktbl; Ftbl; Trk; Vllybl; Wt Lftg; Hon Roll; Prfct Atten Awd; Intermural Bsktbl; Stanford; Advertising.

KING, ELAINE Y; University HS; Irvine, CA; (2); 5/500; Hosp Aide; Intnl Clb; Library Aide; Math Clb; Math Tm; Orch; School Musical; French Hon Soc; High Hon Roll; Med Club Secy; CSF; Alg & Geom Of Golden St Exams With Sntrs Rcgntn; Sci Fair Fnlst.

KING, EMILY; Hartford Union HS; Hanford, CA; (1); JV L Tennis; High Hon Roll; Jr NHS; Frgn Exch Clb; CSF.

KING, ERIC W; Central Union HS; El Centro, CA; (4); 12/450; AFS; Computer Clb; Math Tm; Quiz Bowl; VP Science Clb; Spanish Clb; Hon Roll; Pres Acad Fit Awd; CA Acad Decthln; Coin Collctng; TX A&M U; Petroleum Engrng.

KING, ERIN M; Cabrillo HS; Lompoc, CA; (3); Church Yth Grp; Drama Clb; Spanish Clb; Chorus; Church Choir; Yrbk; Sftbl; Vllybl; Engl.

KING, GARY R; Bellarmine College Prep; San Jose, CA; (3); 54/300; Cmnty Wkr; Hosp Aide; Band; Bsbl; Intrml Ftbl; Intrml Sftbl; Accntng.

KING, JAMIE L; Tokay HS; Lodi, CA; (3); Church Yth Grp; FCA; German Clb; Key Clb; Variety Show; Rptr Nwsp; Yrbk; Crs Cntry; Socr; Trk; Sci Ambssdr Soviet Union People/People; Doers/Dreamers Awd; UC San Diego; Marine Bio.

KING, JENNIFER E; San Marcos HS; Santa Barbara, CA; (2); Church Yth Grp; Drama Clb; Band; Chorus; Drill Tm; Mrchg Band; School Musical; Variety Show; Nwsp; Hon Roll; Cmmnctns.

KING, JENNIFER M; St Josephs HS; Downey, CA; (3); 6/180; Cmnty Wkr; Drama Clb; Hon Roll; Art; Play Piano; CSF; Graphic Art.

KING, JEREMY; Bellarmine HS; San Jose, CA; (2); JV Wrstlng.

KING, JONATHAN E; Fontana HS; Fontana, CA; (3); 9/1147; Am Leg Boys St; Aud/Vis; Boy Scts; Church Yth Grp; FBLA; Service Clb; Color Guard; School Play; Rptr Nwsp; Phtg Yrbk; Eagle Sct 4 Palms; Sccr; Pony/Colt Leag Bsbl; CSF; Stanford; Marketing.

KING, KATRINA D; Leuzinger HS; Inglewood, CA; (2); Church Yth Grp; Teachers Aide; Band; Church Choir; Drm Mjr(t); Mrchg Band; School Musical; Hon Roll; U Of S CA; Law.

KING, KEVIN; Victor Valley HS; Eagle River, AK; (2); Spanish Clb; Hon Roll; Hnr Spnsh Cls.

KING, KURSTEN; Los Gatos HS; Los Gatos, CA; (4); Church Yth Grp; Key Clb; Pep Clb; Chorus; Church Choir; Variety Show; JV Var Cheerldng; High Hon Roll; Hon Roll; Cal Poly SLO; Home Ec.

KING, LA MONTE; St Bernard HS; Inglewood, CA; (3); Boy Scts; Cmnty Wkr; Library Aide; Teachers Aide; Stu Cncl; Bsktbl; Trk; Pres Schlr; Flying Lssns; Morehouse; Airline Pilot.

KING, LYNISA B; Mira Mesa HS; San Diego, CA; (2); French Clb; Band; Drm Mjr(t); Jazz Band; Mrchg Band; Pep Band; JV Sftbl; JV Tennis; Cit Awd; Hon Roll; Teens Helping Other Teens; Stu Cncl Band; All City Hnr Band; Harvard U; Lawyer.

KING, MARGIE; Fullerton HS; Fullerton, CA; (2); JV Capt Bsktbl; JV Vllybl; UCI; Med.

KING, MARY CARMEL; University Of San Diego HS; San Diego, CA; (4); 50/298; Cmnty Wkr; Hosp Aide; Model UN; Service Clb; Teachers Aide; Church Choir; Score Keeper; Sftbl; High Hon Roll; Hon Roll; Cmnty Svc Awd; CSF; U Of CA San Diego; Psych.

KING, MATT D; Del Norte HS; Crescent City, CA; (3); Church Yth Grp; Cmnty Wkr; 4-H; FFA; SADD; Band; Mrchg Band; Pep Band; School Musical; Music.

KING, NICOLE O; Living Way Christian Acad; Pasadena, CA; (3); 2/3; Pep Clb; Teachers Aide; Church Choir; Bsktbl; Sftbl; Vllybl; Cit Awd; Hon Roll; Mst Inspiratnl Plyr Plq Bsktbl; Bsktbl Vlybl & Sftbl Cert; Ctznshp Cert; Cmmrcl Art.

KING, PETER J; Analy HS; Sebastopol, CA; (4); 20/220; Aud/Vis; Church Yth Grp; Letterman Clb; Office Aide; Service Clb; Spanish Clb; SADD; Teachers Aide; Varsity Clb; Nwsp; Doyle, Peter Suacehi Athl, Moore-Patterson Acad Schlrshps; Santa Rosa JC; Jrnlsm.

KING, ROBERT; Victor Valley Christian Schl; Victorville, CA; (4); Church Yth Grp; Cmnty Wkr; Scholastic Bowl; Spanish Clb; Speech Tm; School Musical; School Play; Stage Crew; Variety Show; Yrbk; People People Stu Ambssdr; UC Santa Barbara Film Cmmnctn.

KING, RUBY L; Hilmar HS; Stevenson, CA; (3); Church Yth Grp; Hon Roll; ROP; Bus.

KING, SHARI A; Redwood Christian HS; San Leandro, CA; (3); Church Yth Grp; Drama Clb; Office Aide; Chorus; School Play; ACSI Spch Fnlst; Day Care Cnslr; Pepperdine U; Dntstry.

KING, SHAWN F; Edison HS; Huntington Beach, CA; (3); 2nd Team All-League Tnns 2 Yrs; UCLA; Cinematogrphy.

KING, SHERRI M; Tulare Western HS; Tulare, CA; (3); Model UN; ROTC; Teachers Aide; Chorus; Hon Roll; Mck Trl; Acad Awd Art; Art.

KING, STACY; Lincoln HS; Stockton, CA; (3); Church Yth Grp; Office Aide; Teachers Aide; Church Choir; Var Swmmng; Hon Roll; Water Polo Stat Keeper; Pharm.

KING, TERESA J; University City HS; San Diego, CA; (4); Intnl Clb; SADD; Teachers Aide; Rptr Nwsp; Rptr Lit Mag; Cit Awd; High Hon Roll; Hon Roll; Prfct Atten Awd; Jobs Dghtrs Treas & 4th Mssngr; Poems Pblshd Schl Yrbk 88-90; Jbs Dghtrs Schlrshp 89-90; U Of CA San Diego; Economics.

KING, THOMAS H; San Dieguito HS; Cardiff, CA; (3); French Clb; Varsity Clb; Rep Stu Cncl; Var Crs Cntry; Var Trk; Stat Wrstlng; High Hon Roll; NHS; Ntl Merit Ltr.

KING, TOLA V; John Glenn HS; Paramount, CA; (3); Church Yth Grp; Drill Tm; Flag Corp; Cheerldng; Cit Awd; Hon Roll; MESA; Studs For Others; Oral Roberts U; Law.

KING, TRACEY D; South HS; Bakersfield, CA; (3); 69/458; Church Yth Grp; JA; Teachers Aide; Paralegal.

KING, TROY L; Mc Ateer HS; San Francisco, CA; (4); Teachers Aide; Band; Jazz Band; Pep Band; Stage Crew; Wt Lftg; Hon Roll; SAT Prep Hlpr; Math Tutor; Peer Cnslr; U CA Berkeley; Bus Admin.

KING, URSULA D; Lincoln Prep HS; San Diego, CA; (4); 40/216; Debate Tm; FTA; ROTC; Color Guard; High Hon Roll; Hon Roll; U Of CA-IRVINE; Bio.

KING, VERONIQUE S; Abraham Lincoln HS; San Francisco, CA; (2); Cheerldng; Outdoors Clb; Zoo Vlntr.

KING, VINA M; Anderson HS; Anderson, CA; (2); Church Yth Grp; Acpl Chr; Med.

KINGAARD, JACOB J; San Dieguito HS; Encinitas, CA; (2); Church Yth Grp; Cmnty Wkr; Cit Awd; Surfing; Yth Soccer Ch; Photogpy; UCSD; Photojrnlsm.

KINGERY, STANLEY C; Calvary Chapel HS; Irvine, CA; (3); Church Yth Grp; JV Socr; Var Vllybl; Hon Roll; Golden St Exam W/Hnrs; Bus.

KINGSLEY, JENNIFER L; Hueneme HS; Oxnard, CA; (1); Church Yth Grp; 4-H; Girl Scts; Chorus; Bsktbl; 4-H Awd; High Hon Roll; Hon Roll; Channel Isl Photo Soc; Bio.

KINKAID, TAMMY L; Oroville HS; Oroville, CA; (4); Office Aide; SADD; Hon Roll; Bk Am Cert Achvt Bus; Stu Mnth Bus Hm Ec; Butte Coll; Bus.

KINN, ARIANE A; Arcata HS; Trinidad, CA; (3); Phtg Yrbk; French Hon Soc; Hon Roll; CSF; Ltr Acad.

KINN, JEREMY; Hemet HS; Hemet, CA; (3); Church Yth Grp; JV Bsktbl; Var Crs Cntry; Hon Roll; Psych.

KINNARD, SEAN M; Southwestern Acad; San Pedro, CA; (1); Aud/Vis; Teachers Aide; Yrbk; Off Stu Cncl; Hon Roll; Outward Bound.

KINNE, JOY; Banning HS; Banning, CA; (3); Church Yth Grp; Spanish Clb; Rptr Nwsp; Var Bsktbl; Hon Roll; Cosmtlgst.

KINNEY, JOSHUA O; Woodside HS; Redwood City, CA; (2); 99/400; Church Yth Grp; Capt Var Bsbl; Hon Roll; Pop Warner Ftbl Schltc Natl Semi-Fnlst; Commnctns.

KINOSHITA, LISA; Lynbrook HS; San Jose, CA; (3); 55/282; Cmnty Wkr; Hosp Aide; Pep Clb; Service Clb; Spanish Clb; Chorus; Sec Jr Cls; Var JV Cheerldng; CSF; Psych.

KINOSHITA, SHERRI E; Nogales HS; W Covina, CA; (2); Rptr Nwsp; Tennis; High Hon Roll; UCLA.

KINSCHER, ERIK; Capo Valley Christian HS; Sa J Capistrano, CA; (3); Church Yth Grp; Office Aide; Var Socr; Cit Awd; Pres Acad Fit Awd; Black Belt Tae Kwon Do; Mntn Biking; BMX Bkng.

KINSCHER, INGRID Y; Capistrano Valley Christian Schls; San Juan Capistra, CA; (2); Church Yth Grp; Cmnty Wkr; Letterman Clb; Varsity Clb; L Var Socr; Athltc Awd Sccr; Acad Awd; Loma Linda U; Medcl Phy.

KINSELLA, TIMOTHY J; Alhambra HS; Martinez, CA; (2); VICA; JV Ftbl; Hon Roll; Drftng, Arch; Arch.

KINSEY, MATTHEW J; Paradise HS; Magalia, CA; (1); Hon Roll.

KINSMAN, FELICIA T; Edison HS; Stockton, CA; (1); Church Yth Grp; Hon Roll; Spanish Excl Awd; Delta Coll; Law.

KIOUSIS, SPIRO K; Turlock HS; Turlock, CA; (3); Church Yth Grp; Debate Tm; Speech Tm; Varsity Clb; Var Crs Cntry; JV Ftbl; Var Wrstlng; Gov Hon Prg Awd; High Hon Roll; Hon Roll; UCLA; Cmmnctn.

KIPER, CRISTIN L; San Leandro HS; San Leandro, CA; (3); 52/361; Church Yth Grp; Ski Clb; Band; Off Jr Cls; Stat Bsktbl; Stat Ftbl; JV Swmmng; Vlntr Sulphur Crk Wldlife Refuge; Valley Beauty Coll; Cosmtlgst.

KIPNIS, MARINA; Mission San Jose HS; Fremont, CA; (3); Hosp Aide; Science Clb; Swmmng; Hon Roll; Pres Acad Fit Awd; Treas French Clb; Poltcl Sci.

KIPNIS, RACHEL N; Lowell HS; San Francisco, CA; (3); Chorus; School Musical; Music Apprctn Soc Fndr & Pres 89-90; Amnest Intl 89-90; Rgstry Rep 89-90; Vocal Musician.

KIPP, LORI J; Monterey HS; Monterey, CA; (4); 15/270; Church Yth Grp; Cmnty Wkr; German Clb; Teachers Aide; Rptr Nwsp; Var Swmmng; High Hon Roll; NHS; German Natl Hnr Soc VP; Bank Of Amer Awd For Frgn Lang; UC Santa Barbara; Bio Sci.

KIPP, SHARON A; Hillsdale HS; San Mateo, CA; (3); Church Yth Grp; Office Aide; Teachers Aide; Outstndng Stu Awd Spanish I & II, US Hstry & Child Dvlpmnt; Accantng.

KIRBY, KARLA; West Valley Christian Schl; West Hills, CA; (4); 1/7; Church Yth Grp; Band; Chorus; Church Choir; Sec Yrbk; Stu Cncl; Var L Bsktbl; Var L Vllybl; High Hon Roll; Pres Acad Fit Awd; Ozark Chrstn Coll; Bus.

KIRBY, MICHELLE L; King City Joint Union HS; King City, CA; (3); 4/220; Am Leg Aux Girls St; Red Cross Aide; SADD; Band; Jazz Band; Mrchg Band; Pep Band; Bausch & Lomb Sci Awd; High Hon Roll; Sec Frsh Cls; Friday Nite Live Charge Sober Grad; 1st Pl Jr Cls Scheid Writing Cont; Southern CA U; Pre-Med.

KIRBY, MONICA L; Bullard HS; Fresno, CA; (2); #1 In Class; FCA; German Clb; Crs Cntry; Socr; Trk; Pres Acad Fit Awd; Pres Schlr.

KIRBY, SARAH D; Hoover HS; Fresno, CA; (2); Church Yth Grp; Swmmng; Hon Roll; CA ST U Fresno; Psych.

KIRBY, TIFFINY; Channel Islands HS; Oxnard, CA; (4); 111/480; Church Yth Grp; FBLA; Hosp Aide; SADD; Flag Corp; Intrml Vllybl; Hon Roll; Bus.

KIRCH, SHELLEY T; Mount Shasta HS; Mount Shasta, CA; (2); 14/87; Red Cross Aide; Band; Chorus; Pep Band; Pres Soph Cls; Rep Stu Cncl; Stat Bsbl; JV Bsktbl; JV Var Vllybl; Hon Roll; JV Vllybl Best Defense; JV Bsktbl MVP, All Tourney Soph; Var Vllybl All League Hnrs; Stanford; Law.

KIRCHBERGER, JODY; El Camino HS; Carmichael, CA; (3); 66/366; Var JV Swmmng; JV Wt Lftg; Hon Roll; Raquetball; Hnr Roll Algebra I & Geom Awds; UC Schl; Marine Bio.

KIRCHNER, MICHELLE E; Diamond Bar HS; Diamond Bar, CA; (2); Church Yth Grp; French Clb; SADD; Socr; Hon Roll; Public Relations.

KIRIN, BRIAN J; Westminster HS; Westminster, CA; (4); 60/411; Boy Scts; Letterman Clb; Teachers Aide; JV Var Ftbl; High Hon Roll; Hon Roll; Eagle Scout; Goldenwest Coll; Elec Engr.

KIRK, ANTHONY; Carson HS; Carson, CA; (3); Boy Scts; Church Yth Grp; Church Choir; JV Ftbl; Var Socr; Var Sftbl; Var Swmmng; JV Trk; Var Wt Lftg; Achvt Awd Outstndng Stu Hstry Cls; Super Effort Awd 87-88; Presdntl Phys Ftnss Awd; CA ST Long Beach; Comp.

KIRK III, CHARLES E; De Anza HS; El Sobrante, CA; (3); Letterman Clb; Varsity Clb; JV Var Bsbl; Intrml Bsktbl; Intrml Ftbl; Hon Roll; Psych.

KIRK, JASON; Sonoma Valley HS; Sonoma, CA; (2); 9/252; Cmnty Wkr; Model UN; Var Tennis; High Hon Roll; Soccer Lge; Stu Senator For Hmrm; UC Davis; Med.

KIRK, KATHERINE I; Victor Valley HS; Victorville, CA; (3); Spanish Clb; Teachers Aide; Paralegal.

KIRK, KELLEM L; Trinity HS; Burnt Ranch, CA; (1); Boy Scts; High Hon Roll; Hon Roll; Engrng.

KIRK, KELLY; Highlands HS; Rio Linda, CA; (3); FTA; Rptr Yrbk; Sec Frsh Cls; Sec Soph Cls; Sec Jr Cls; Pres Sr Cls; Var Capt Bsktbl; Var Capt Cheerldng; Var JV Sftbl; JV Vllybl; Sacramento ST; Elem Ed.

KIRK, TERRY S; Hillcrest Christian Schl; Simi Valley, CA; (4); 2/6; Boy Scts; Teachers Aide; School Musical; Phtg Ed Yrbk; Rep Soph Cls; Bsbl; High Hon Roll; Debate Tm; People To People HS Ambssdr Northern Europe Smmr 89; U Southern CA; Anthroplgy.

KIRKBRIDE, BRIAN; Yosemite HS; Coarsegold, CA; (2); Church Yth Grp; Library Aide; Band; Jazz Band; Hon Roll; Goldn St Exam Hnrs; Christ Coll; Music.

KIRKEBY, KARL M; Loyola HS; La Canada Flintri, CA; (2); Boy Scts; Cmnty Wkr; JV L Bsktbl; JV L Socr; JV L Tennis; Intrml Vllybl; High Hon Roll; NHS; Spanish NHS; Egle Sct Awd.

KIRKHAM, ROBERT J; Big Bear HS; Big Bear Lake, CA; (4); 15/105; Boy Scts; SADD; Var Ftbl; Intrml Wt Lftg; JV Wrstlng; High Hon Roll; Hon Roll; Pres Acad Fit Awd; Rotary Awd; Interact Clb; Schlr Ath Awd Wrstlng 87-88; Spec Athl Awd Ftbl 88-89; CA ST-SAN Bernardino; Accntnt.

KIRKJAN, GREGORY; Palm Desert HS; Indio, CA; (3); 12/400; Key Clb; Science Clb; High Hon Roll; CSF; UCLA; Sci.

KIRKLAND, ROXANNE; Etiwanda HS; Manteca, CA; (3); Church Yth Grp; Church Choir; JV Capt Bsktbl; JV Trk; Prfct Atten Awd; Wrtng Poetry; Fshn Merch.

KIRKPATRICK, CLIFFORD; Christian HS; Tecate, CA; (3); 8/80; Church Yth Grp; Drama Clb; Library Aide; Teachers Aide; Variety Show; Rptr Nwsp; Var L Bsbl; Var L Ftbl; Var L Socr; Acadmc Olympcs; Civil Air Ptrl; Glider Flying; Pltcl Sci.

KIRKPATRICK, KAREN J; Loyalton HS; Calpine, CA; (3); 4-H; FBLA; Hosp Aide; Ski Clb; SADD; Nwsp; Sec Sr Cls; Var JV Cheerldng; Var JV Pom Pon; Var Sftbl; Child Psych.

KIRKWOOD, KIRSTAN KIER; Villa Park HS; Villa Park, CA; (3); Cmnty Wkr; GAA; Key Clb; Ski Clb; SADD; Teachers Aide; Varsity Clb; JV Var Sftbl; Hon Roll; Bobby Sox & All Stars; Coaches Awd; Chld Psych.

KIRLAND, BRIAN J; Mater Dei HS; Costa Mesa, CA; (2); Cmnty Wkr; German Clb; JV Swmmng; High Hon Roll; NHS; Cptn JV Waterpolo Tm; CSF; UCSD; Engrng.

KIRN, AMY R; Mariposa County HS; Mariposa, CA; (4); 17/101; Church Yth Grp; Ski Clb; Teachers Aide; Chorus; VP Jr Cls; VP Stu Cncl; JV Var Vllybl; Cit Awd; Hon Roll; Pres Acad Fit Awd; Prin Ldrshp Awd; Yosemite Schlrshp; Somona ST; Envrnmntl Planning.

KIRRENE, JOSEPH C; Encina HS; Sacramento, CA; (3); 25/228; Spanish Clb; SADD; Ed Nwsp; Lit Mag; VP Frsh Cls; JV Vllybl; Cit Awd; Hon Roll; Prfct Atten Awd; Aud/Vis; Encinas Fitness Elite; Stu Of Month-Span; Hnr Classes; Santa Clara U; Psych.

KIRRER, JEFF A; Mater Dei HS; Fountain Valley, CA; (3); Church Yth Grp; Varsity Clb; Bsktbl; Ftbl; Golf; Chrch Yth Grp; Peer Mnstry.

KIRSCH, BRIAN B; Casa Grande HS; Petaluma, CA; (2); 43/295; JV Bsbl; Hon Roll; Schlr Athlete Achvng 3.83 While On JV Bsbl; Achvt Awd Algebra I, Phys Ed; U Of NV Las Vegas; Bus Lawyr.

KIRSCHNER, MONICA M; El Camino HS; Oceanside, CA; (3); 14/364; Church Yth Grp; Speech Tm; Church Choir; Sec Sr Cls; JV Bsktbl; Swmmng; Hon Roll; His Club Pres; Earth Club Secy; Amer Govt Seminar; Christ Coll; Soc.

KIRSHEN, MARC P; Mt Carmel HS; San Diego, CA; (3); 141/767; Cmnty Wkr; Q&S; Ed Nwsp; Var Tennis; Sun Devil Stndout Schl & Cmnty; UCLA; Cmmnctn.

KIRSTEN, BRENT H; Mission Bay HS; San Diego, CA; (3); 58/307; Letterman Clb; Var Capt Ftbl; Var Capt Socr; High Hon Roll; Kiwanis Awd; Pres Acad Fit Awd; Off Soph Cls; Off Jr Cls; Var Vllybl; 3 Sport Ltrmn; 1st Team All Leag Rookie Yr Sccr; MVP, 2nd Team All Leag Ftbl; ASB Cmmssnr Athltcs; Physiology.

KIRTLAN, JASON G; Delta HS; Clarksburg, CA; (4); Am Leg Boys St; Church Yth Grp; SADD; Varsity Clb; Pres Sr Cls; Rep Stu Cncl; Var Capt Bsbl; Capt Bsktbl; JV Crs Cntry; Opt Clb Awd; US Army Rsv Natl Schlr/Athltc Awd; Sacramento City.

KISBYE, MAX J; Arroyo Grande HS; Shell Beach, CA; (2); 82/580; Office Aide; Var Bsktbl; Var Ftbl; Trk; Hon Roll; USC; Bus.

KISER, SHANNON G; Clovis HS; Fresno, CA; (4); Cmnty Wkr; Dance Clb; English Clb; FBLA; NFL; Variety Show; Off Sr Cls; Rep Stu Cncl; Var Powder Puff Ftbl; Stat Swmmng; JR SR Prm Chrprsn; Hi-Deb Rep Clovis HS Gottschalks 88-90; Intnlpblctn Fnlst 90; UCLA; Bus Mgmt.

KISNER, CAMMIE; Rio Mesa HS; Camarillo, CA; (1); Aud/Vis; Church Yth Grp; Band; Color Guard; Drill Tm; Flag Corp; Jazz Band; Orch.

KISNER, CARMEN Y; Rio Mesa HS; Camarillo, CA; (3); 36/365; Church Yth Grp; FCA; Letterman Clb; Church Choir; Nwsp; Lit Mag; Mgr(s); Swmmng; Psych.

KISOW, AIMEE; Mater Dei HS; Orange, CA; (4); Church Yth Grp; Var Capt Crs Cntry; Var L Trk; High Hon Roll; NHS; Pres Acad Fit Awd; CSF; Athltic Bd; U San Diego.

KISSANE, CARRIE A; Torrey Pines HS; San Diego, CA; (3); 191/457; Church Yth Grp; SADD; JV Var Cheerldng; Var Gym; Letterman Clb; Pep Clb; Ski Clb; Varsity Clb; Variety Show; Cit Awd; Nrthrn AZ U; Hotel Mgmt.

KISSELBURG, MORGAN W; Adolf Leuzinger HS; Lawndale, CA; (2); Church Yth Grp; Ftbl; Trk.

KISSICK, STEPHANIE; Tri-City Christian Schl; Carlsbad, CA; (2); 1/20; Church Yth Grp; Spanish Clb; Speech Tm; Church Choir; Cheerldng; High Hon Roll; 90 TCCS Sci Fair Grand Prz; 90 Southern CA ACSI Sci Fair Blue Rbbn; Ed.

KISSOON, NATALIA A; James Lick HS; San Jose, CA; (3); Church Yth Grp; Cmnty Wkr; VICA; Math Tm; Speech Tm; Teachers Aide; Church Choir; Variety Show; Rptr Nwsp; Pres VP Frsh Cls; NAACP Outstndng Achvt Awd; Firemans Assn Talent Show Wnnr; Church Easter Play Asst Dir; Hayward U; Bus.

KISZONAS, SANDRA L; Chino HS; Ontario, CA; (3); Church Yth Grp; Teachers Aide; Powder Puff Ftbl; High Hon Roll; Prfct Atten Awd; Sch Recog Golden St Exam Alge; Acctg.

KITAZAWA, YOHEI; University City HS; San Diego, CA; (3); 110/373; JV Var Ftbl; JV Var Trk; JV Var Wrstlng; Cit Awd; Hon Roll; Prfct Atten Awd; Japanese Schl; UC San Diego; Engr.

KITCHELL, DAVID E; Tehachapi HS; Tehachapi, CA; (3); 24/220; Boy Scts; French Clb; SADD; Rep Stu Cncl; Var Crs Cntry; Var Trk; Hon Roll; Friday Nght Live; Rocket Clb Pres; Scintst.

KITCHEN, DOUG L; Hoover HS; Glendale, CA; (2); Boy Scts; Band; Bsbl; Ftbl; Golf; High Hon Roll; Ntl Merit Schol.

KITCHEN, STEPHANIE D; Dublin HS; Dublin, CA; (3); 20/160; Cmnty Wkr; JA; Office Aide; Spanish Clb; Teachers Aide; Color Guard; Drill Tm; Flag Corp; Variety Show; Hon Roll; Semi-Fnlst Star Search 88; Tap, Jazz & Ballet; CA ST U; Scl Sci.

KITSINIAN, SAKO A; Diamond Bar HS; Diamond Bar, CA; (3); French Clb; FBLA; Service Clb; Am Leg Aux Girls St; Stu Cncl; JV Var Trk; Hon Roll; USAF Acad; Aeron Engr.

KITTIDUMRONGKOOL, KEITH; Bellarmine-Jefferson HS; N Hollywood, CA; (3); 25/160; Math Clb; Science Clb; Spanish Clb; Hon Roll; NHS; Pthlgy.

KITTREDGE, NICK; Capistrano Valley HS; San Juan Cpstrano, CA; (3); FCA; Rep Frsh Cls; Rep Soph Cls; Rep Jr Cls; Var Swmmng; Hon Roll; Prfct Atten Awd; SB Commissioner Of Athl/Campus Service; All Amer Consideration For Swimming; Bus Admin.

KITZMAN, SHAWNE T; California HS; Whittier, CA; (3); 9/369; VP English Clb; Pres Ski Clb; Varsity Clb; Var Tennis; Var Trk; Notre Dame; Author.

KIUHAN, MICHEL J; Whitney HS; Cerritos, CA; (3); Boy Scts; Church Yth Grp; Pres French Clb; VP JA; Latin Clb; Spanish Clb; Band; Rep Soph Cls; Swmmng; Hon Roll; Waterpolo Vrsty Cptn; Intl Bus.

KIVETT, AMY C; Bullard HS; Fresno, CA; (1); French Clb; SADD; CSF; Hnr Rl; Stanford; Inter Dsgn.

KIYOI, KEVIN P; Alhambra HS; Martinez, CA; (4); 3/220; Boy Scts; Church Yth Grp; Letterman Clb; Math Clb; Science Clb; Band; Jazz Band; Stu Cncl; Var Crs Cntry; Var Ftbl; Wrstlng Clb Pres; UC Berkeley; Mineral Engrng.

KIYOI, MATTHEW D; Alhambra HS; Martinez, CA; (3); 35/214; Boy Scts; Teachers Aide; Band; Jazz Band; Mrchg Band; Variety Show; Stu Cncl; Crs Cntry; Diving; Wrstlng; St Marys; Nrsng.

KIYOTA, MELODEE Y; George Washington HS; San Francisco, CA; (2); Cmnty Wkr; Teachers Aide; Stu Cncl; Vllybl; High Hon Roll; Hon Roll; Japanese Bsktbl League; Japanese Cmnty Yth Grp Cncl.

KIZIRIAN, YEGHIG; Holy Martyrs Ferrahian HS; Van Nuys, CA; (2); Quiz Bowl; School Play; JV Bsktbl; Trk; Hon Roll; Pres Acad Fit Awd; Excllnc Amer Stds Schlrshp; Bio.

KIZOREK, MICHELE LEAH; Bear River HS; Grass Valley, CA; (4); 7/150; Am Leg Aux Girls St; Letterman Clb; Spanish Clb; SADD; Rep Stu Cncl; Stat Bsbl; Stat Ftbl; Var Capt Vllybl; Cit Awd; High Hon Roll; Ski Team; U CO; Envrmntl Design.

KIZZIAR, KARIN M; Rio Lindo Acad; Hayfork, CA; (4); Ski Clb; Band; Orch; Pres Frsh Cls; Intrml Bsbl; Intrml Bsktbl; Gym; Score Keeper; Intrml Vllybl; Prfct Atten Awd; Pacific Union Coll.

KJERULF, BRIAN; Lincoln HS; Stockton, CA; (4); 1/536; Boy Scts; Ski Clb; Band; Jazz Band; Mrchg Band; Orch; Pep Band; Hon Roll; Val; CSF; CA Inst Of Tech; Physics.

KLASA, JOANNA; Pacific Grove HS; Seaside, CA; (3); Teachers Aide; Chorus; Co-Capt Flag Corp; JV Swmmng; Hon Roll; Surgcl Nrsng.

KLASKY, KAREN A; Granada Hills HS; Northridge, CA; (2); Debate Tm; Hosp Aide; Pres Spanish Clb; Temple Yth Grp; Sec Frsh Cls; Stu Cncl; Cit Awd; High Hon Roll; Hon Roll; Jr NHS; Mock Trial Pros Atty 2nd Pl Semifnls; Stu Govt Planning Act; Most Svc To Schl Awd; UCLA; Med.

KLATT, KARIE J; Norco SR HS; Corona, CA; (2); Art Clb; Rptr Yrbk; JV Bsktbl; Var Trk; Var Vllybl; Hon Roll; Prfct Atten Awd; Pres Acad Fit Awd; Riverside CC; Acctng.

KLATZKER, SOFIA F; Hamilton HS Academy Of Music; North Hollywood, CA; (2); Hon Roll; CA Arts Schlr 90.

KLAUS, KEVIN H; Loyola HS; Culver City, CA; (1); Church Yth Grp; Snr Leag Bsbl.

KLAVER, KAREN; Piedmont Hills HS; San Jose, CA; (4); Am Leg Aux Girls St; Church Yth Grp; Cmnty Wkr; Dance Clb; Key Clb; Model UN; Pep Clb; Red Cross Aide; Service Clb; Spanish Clb; CSF; Amnesty Intl; UC Santa Barbara; Intl Rltns.

KLAWITTER, CHRISTIAN R; Chaminade College Prep; Woodland Hills, CA; (3); Model UN; Ed Lit Mag; Off Jr Cls; L Ftbl; Retreat Ldr Living Faith Exper Life Prgm; CSF; High Sierra Clb; Creative Wrtng.

KLEBANER, ALEX; George Washington HS; San Francisco, CA; (3); Pres Soph Cls; Socr; Wt Lftg; George Washington; Dentist.

KLEBAU, MARYANN K; So Cal Christian HS; Fountain Valley, CA; (3); Church Yth Grp; Office Aide; Chorus; Sec Stu Cncl; Stat Bsbl; Hon Roll.

KLEBE, TERESA; Yuba City HS; Yuba City, CA; (4); 63/470; Pres Art Clb; Church Yth Grp; Intnl Clb; Pep Clb; SADD; Variety Show; Stu Cncl; JV Var Cheerldng; Capt Powder Puff Ftbl; High Hon Roll; Bnk America Art Awd Wnnr; Teachers Dept Hnrs Awd Art; PEACE Clb; American River JC; Art.

KLECKNER, TAMRA; Canyon Springs HS; Riverside, CA; (1); Church Yth Grp; Dance Clb; Drama Clb; Pep Clb; Chorus; Drill Tm; Flag Corp; Mrchg Band; School Play; Stage Crew; Modeling.

KLEIN, BLYTHE S; John F Kennedy HS; Granada Hills, CA; (2); Key Clb; Ed Yrbk; High Hon Roll; Pres Acad Fit Awd; Algebra Hnrs Golden St Exam; CJSF Secy; CSF; Yrbk Awd; Schlrshp Awd; U CA; Pediatrics.

KLEIN, ERIKA B; Capistrano Valley HS; Mission Viejo, CA; (3); GAA; Rptr Nwsp; JV Socr; Trk; Cit Awd; Amer Yth Sccr Orgnztn; Santa Cruz; Jrnlsm.

KLEIN, ERIN A; Bonita HS; La Verne, CA; (1); French Clb; Girl Scts; Nwsp; Yrbk; Score Keeper; Pres Acad Fit Awd; Algebra & Geom Golden St Exam Awd; Stu Agnst Violation Of Earth Clb.

KLEIN, JASON; Poway HS; San Diego, CA; (3); Ski Clb; Temple Yth Grp; JV Var Bsktbl; JV Trk; High Hon Roll; Hon Roll; Jr NHS; NHS; UC Schl; Psych.

KLEIN, JEROD T; Sunny Hills HS; Fullerton, CA; (3); 15/450; AFS; Am Leg Boys St; Sec Church Yth Grp; Model UN; Spanish Clb; Rep Stu Cncl; Var Capt Socr; High Hon Roll; Jr NHS; Ntl Merit SF; Psych.

KLEIN, KEVIN M; Paraclete HS; Lancaster, CA; (2); Key Clb; School Play; Stage Crew; Ed Nwsp; Stu Cncl; JV Ftbl; JV Trk; JV Wt Lftg; Loyola Marymount U; Comedy.

KLEIN, KIMBERLY E; Capistrano Valley HS; Mission Viejo, CA; (3); Church Yth Grp; Dance Clb; Church Choir; Drill Tm; New Life Leader; Drill Tm Awd; Biola U; Elem Ed.

KLEIN, ROBERT; Loara HS; Anaheim, CA; (4); 10/380; Church Yth Grp; Rep Key Clb; Treas Stu Cncl; Var Capt Socr; High Hon Roll; NHS; Pres Acad Fit Awd; Val; Mock Trl Team Captn; Acad Decathlon Team; U Southern CA; Poltcl Sci.

KLEIN, SHERI; Santa Teresa HS; San Jose, CA; (2); Church Yth Grp; Drama Clb; Spanish Clb; JV Crs Cntry; Hon Roll; U Santa Barbara; Tchr.

KLEIN, STEVEN M; Santa Clara HS; Oxnard, CA; (2); Letterman Clb; Stage Crew; Rep Soph Cls; Var Mgr Bsbl; Var Mgr Ftbl; Mgr(s); Var Mgr Socr; Sci.

KLEINEDLER, ANNE M; Bishop Amat HS; Temple City, CA; (3); Church Yth Grp; Church Choir; Var JV Cheerldng; Hon Roll; NHS; CSF; U Of CA Los Angeles; Jrnlsm.

KLEINER, FIANA; Granada Hills HS; Northridge, CA; (3); Thesps; Drill Tm; School Play; Rep Nwsp; Yrbk; Hon Roll; St Fnlst Miss CA Coed Pgnt; SADD.

KLEINER, MARAT; Fairfax HS; Los Angeles, CA; (4); 12/650; Science Clb; Intrml Bsktbl; Intrml Socr; Intrml Tennis; Var Vllybl; High Hon Roll; Tandy Tech Schlrs; CSF; Jewish Stu Union; U Of CA Santa Barbara; Bio.

KLEINGARTNER, JENNIE L; Turlock HS; Turlock, CA; (4); 81/510; Church Yth Grp; Pep Clb; Teachers Aide; Band; CA ST U Stanislaus; Tchr.

KLEINSMITH, BRIAN P; Brea-Olinda HS; Brea, CA; (4); 32/245; Church Yth Grp; Cmnty Wkr; French Clb; L Var Socr; Intrml Tennis; Cit Awd; High Hon Roll; Hon Roll; Prfct Atten Awd; Eng.

KLEIS, RYAN; Los Amigos HS; Fountain Valley, CA; (2); Intrml Bsktbl; Intrml Ftbl; Intrml Trk; Hon Roll; Mst Imprvd Plyr Ftbl & Trk; Long Beach ST; Electroncs.

KLEM, ERICH R; Mission College Prep; San Luis Obispo, CA; (3); Cmnty Wkr; Teachers Aide; Yrbk; Var Socr; High Hon Roll; Hon Roll; Pres Sr Cls; Chem.

KLEMENT, MARTIN C; Calabasas HS; Woodland Hills, CA; (4); 13/315; Boy Scts; Math Tm; Tennis; Hon Roll; Ntl Merit SF; Eagl Sct 89; Engrng.

KLEMENTSSON, LINDA P; Elk Grove HS; Sacramento, CA; (4); Socr; Hon Roll; Exchnge Stu US.

KLEMM, AMY K; Paraclete HS; Lake Hughes, CA; (2); Church Yth Grp; Cmnty Wkr; Drama Clb; Pres JA; School Play; Treas Frsh Cls; Hon Roll; UNLV; Htl-Rsrt Mgmt.

KLEMM, KEVIN A; Foothill HS; Santa Ana, CA; (3); Church Yth Grp; Drama Clb; FCA; Ski Clb; Thesps; Church Choir; School Musical; School Play; Stage Crew; Var Swmmng; Motorcycle Mchns & Racing Tm; Geologist.

KLEMP, CARRI A; Savanna HS; Anaheim, CA; (3); Pep Clb; Teachers Aide; Sec Stu Cncl; Hon Roll; Spanish NHS.

KLEMS, JULIA; Berkeley HS; Berkeley, CA; (3); Church Yth Grp; Chorus; Lit Mag; Sec Frsh Cls; Sec Soph Cls; Hon Roll; Ntl Merit Ltr; Golden St Exam Geom Hgh Hnrs; HS Dance Production.

KLEPADLO, BRIAN G; Mater Dei HS; Placentia, CA; (3); Cmnty Wkr; Letterman Clb; Varsity Clb; Var L Ftbl; Var Wt Lftg; Bus.

KLEVEN, MAUREEN A; Alameda HS; Alameda, CA; (2); 8/275; GAA; Teachers Aide; JV Bsktbl; High Hon Roll; Hon Roll.

KLEVER, KIM; Del Norte County HS; Crescent City, CA; (3); 15/221; 4-H; Yrbk; Cheerldng; Powder Puff Ftbl; High Hon Roll; CA Schlrshp Fndtn; U Of CA Davis; Pub Rel.

KLEVER, KRIS WALTER; Del Norte County HS; Crescent City, CA; (4); 12/250; Boy Scts; School Musical; Yrbk; High Hon Roll; Prfct Atten Awd; Golden ST Awd; Rotary Schlrshp; CSF; Advncmnt Placement US Hstry Exam; U S CA; Fullerton; Micro Reserc.

KLEVESAHL, DAVID; Pioneer HS; San Jose, CA; (3); 55/333; Hon Roll; Gol; Music Play Drums; San Jose ST U; Business.

KLEVESAHL, ERICA A; Pioneer HS; San Jose, CA; (1); 1/375; Cmnty Wkr; Hon Roll; CSF; Horseback Riding 3-Day Evnt; Cal Poly; Vet Sci.

KLIBBE, SAMANTHA L; Ramona HS; Ramona, CA; (2); Cmnty Wkr; JV Socr; Var Tennis; U CA-BERKELEY.

KLIER, JITKA; North Salinas HS; Salinas, CA; (3); AFS; German Clb; Intnl Clb; Band; School Play; Var JV Fld Hcky; Var JV Swmmng; Stat Wrstlng; High Hon Roll; Hon Roll; MS Vlntr; Marine Bio.

KLIEVER, SHAWNA L; Bloomington HS; Bloomington, CA; (2); 47/503; Church Yth Grp; Band; Color Guard; Flag Corp; Mrchg Band; Pep Band; Law Enfrcmnt.

KLIEWER, CYNTHIA S; Clovis HS; Clovis, CA; (3); Church Yth Grp; French Clb; JV Socr; Fresno Pacific; Phys Thrpy.

KLIEWER, MICHAEL D; Bellarmine College Prep; San Jose, CA; (4); Service Clb; JV Crs Cntry; Intrml Ftbl; Intrml Vllybl; KSKJ HS Schlrshp 86-89; KSKJ Coll Schlrshp 90; Cal Poly San Luis Obispo; Cmptr.

KLINE, CHRISTINA M; Monte Vista HS; Spring Valley, CA; (2); Church Yth Grp; Spanish Clb; Mgr(s); Score Keeper; Wt Lftg; Hon Roll; Prncss Cntstnt Mother Goose Parade; UCSD; Tchr.

KLINE, ERIK; Bellarmine College Prep; Saratoga, CA; (4); 1/308; VP Chess Clb; Cmnty Wkr; Hosp Aide; VP Math Clb; Treas Science Clb; Pep Band; JV Var Wrstlng; Ntl Merit Schol; Computer Clb; MIT Ldrshp Awd Sci/Math 89; SHARP Pgm NASA 89 & 90; Fnlst Natl Mrt Schlrshp Fndtn; Black Schlrshp Fn; MA Inst Of Tech; Math.

KLINE, GALEN T; Novato HS; Novato, CA; (3); Band; Jazz Band; Mrchg Band; Orch; Pep Band; Var Trk; Hon Roll; CA ST Hayward; Symphony.

KLINE, LAUREL E; Novato HS; Novato, CA; (3); Drama Clb; French Clb; Key Clb; Latin Clb; Library Aide; Chorus; School Musical; High Hon Roll; Ntl Merit SF; CMEA; Bus.

KLINT, AMIE; Mount Whitney HS; Visalia, CA; (3); Church Yth Grp; Chorus; High Hon Roll; Hon Roll; CSF; 1st Pl Dist-Wd Spnsh Cmptn; Biola U; Psych.

KLINTWORTH, ROBERT C; Paso Robles HS; Paso Robles, CA; (3); 1/320; AFS; Church Yth Grp; Var L Bsbl; Prfct Atten Awd; Lcl History Day Wnnr.

KLOBUCHER, DEREK J; Kadena HS; APO Sn Francisco, CA; (2); 33/355; Boy Scts; Science Clb; Spanish Clb; Band; Mrchg Band; Var Boy Scts; Hon Roll; Jr NHS; Prfct Atten Awd.

KLOCKENTEGER, KELLY; Workman HS; Victorville, CA; (2); Band; Jazz Band; Cit Awd; Prfct Atten Awd; Top 10 Stu Physcl Sci Dept; Outstng Band; Orthodontst.

KLOECKNER, KYLE W; Lodi HS; Lodi, CA; (2); VICA; Capt JV Ftbl; L Trk; High Hon Roll; Prfct Atten Awd; People To People Friendshp Caravan; Stanford U; Engrng.

KLOPPING, WILLIAM E; Apple Valley SR HS; Apple Valley, CA; (1); Church Yth Grp; Aeropsc Engr.

KLOPSON, NAKELLE M; Orestimba HS; Newman, CA; (3); Letterman Clb; Pep Clb; Stat Ftbl; Var Pom Pon; Var Powder Puff Ftbl; Var Sftbl; Var JV Vllybl; Hon Roll; Stanislaus ST; Bus.

KLOSTER, CHRISTINA A; Central HS; Fresno, CA; (2); 4-H; FBLA; FFA; FTA; 4-H Awd; Hon Roll; CSF; Amercn Southdown Shp Brdrs Assn; CA Poly; Ag Teachering.

KLOSTER, MARK S; Las Lomas HS; Walnut Crk, CA; (3); 63/275; Acpl Chr; School Musical; JV Golf; Var Ice Hcky; JV Socr; JV Vllybl; Undrclsmn Awd Achvt 90; Chmbr Cmmrc Career Day 90; CMEA Hnr Choir 87; Engrng.

KLOSTER, MICHAEL; Central Unified HS; Fresno, CA; (4); 4-H; FFA; Intnl Clb; Science Clb; Stu Cncl; Cit Awd; 4-H Awd; Natl Mdl Orgnztn Amer ST 4-H Rep; Cmp Ryl-Rtry Yth & Ldrshp; Natl 4-H Cngrss 88.

KLOTZ, BRENDA V; Mater Dei HS; Santa Ana, CA; (1); Church Yth Grp; Cmnty Wkr; Drill Tm; CPA.

KLOUDA, JULIE A; Rio Americano HS; Sacramento, CA; (3); 29/290; French Clb; Service Clb; Ski Clb; Phtg Nwsp; High Hon Roll; Apprentice Trainer G K Arabian Ctr; Engrng.

KLUMPP, MICHELLE L; Orange Glen HS; Escondido, CA; (3); 39/500; Church Yth Grp; Girl Scts; Spanish Clb; Church Choir; Yrbk; Score Keeper; Sftbl; High Hon Roll; Hon Roll; NHS; CSF Secy; CA Luthern U; Tchng.

KLUNGTVET, MEKA L; Orland HS; Paradise, CA; (4); 10/111; Drama Clb; English Clb; School Play; Sec Frsh Cls; VP Soph Cls; Rep Stu Cncl; High Hon Roll; Pres Acad Fit Awd; Letterman Clb; Pep Clb; GATE Club; CSF; Gldn St Math Exam Hnrs; CA ST U Chico; Tchng.

KLVANA, NICOLE C; William S Hart HS; Newhall, CA; (3); FBLA; VICA; Hon Roll; Pres Acad Fit Awd; CSF; UC San Diego; Intl Relations.

KLYSE, JULIE M; Oak Ridge HS; El Dorado Hills, CA; (3); 23/262; Pres Church Yth Grp; Cmnty Wkr; Stu Cncl; Capt Var Cheerldng; High Hon Roll; Yth & Govt; UC Santa Barbara; Phys Thrpy.

KMELNITSKY, DMITRY; Hamilton High Acad Of Music; Northridge, CA; (3); Variety Show; Tennis; Hon Roll; NHS; Athletic Award.

KMIECEK, MICHELE; Mt Pleasant HS; Naperville, IL; (2); 87/467; Art Clb; Cmnty Wkr; SADD; Teachers Aide; Hon Roll; Cardinals Against Driving Drunk; Civil Air Patrol; WA ST; Spec Ed.

KMINEK, JO A; Bear River HS; Grass Valley, CA; (2); 19/227; 4-H; Cit Awd; 4-H Awd; High Hon Roll; Hon Roll; Humboldt U; Psych.

KNAPP, BILLY J; Colfax HS; Meadow Vista, CA; (3); 18/155; Letterman Clb; L Bsbl; L Bsktbl; L Ftbl; JV Trk; Intrml Vllybl; Intrml Wt Lftg; Engr.

KNAPP, CHRISTINE M; Channel Islands HS; Oxnard, CA; (3); Key Clb; Yrbk; Hon Roll; Banner Precision Squad Capt; Peer Helpers; Law.

KNAPP, KRIS; Fallbrook HS; Fallbrook, CA; (4); 4/400; Boy Scts; Church Yth Grp; Scholastic Bowl; JV Crs Cntry; JV Trk; Bausch & Lomb Sci Awd; Hon Roll; Ntl Merit Ltr; Pres Schlr; UC Berkeley; Physics.

KNAPP, R JASON; El Toro HS; El Toro, CA; (4); Art Clb; Letterman Clb; Stage Crew; JV Bsbl; VP Wrstlng; Hon Roll; MVP Wrstlng 86-87; Coachs Awd Wrstlng 89-90; Dsgn Sr Awd & Baccalaureate Covers; CA ST; Med.

KNAPP, RICKY; Modesto HS; Salida, CA; (1); Boy Scts; Chess Clb; Church Yth Grp; JV Socr; JV Swmmng; Hon Roll; Pres Acad Fit Awd; JV Waterpolo; OR ST U; Oceangrphy.

KNAPP, SHANNON M; Grossmont HS; El Cajon, CA; (2); 1/431; VP Pres German Clb; NFL; Speech Tm; Flag Corp; Lit Mag; Hon Roll; Pres Acad Fit Awd; 2nd Pl & Rnnr Up Optimist Clb Oratoracle Cont; Fnlst LA Times/Cathay Pacific Airline Essay Cont.

KNAPP, TIMOTHY M; West HS; Torrance, CA; (3); Varsity Clb; Ed Lit Mag; Capt Crs Cntry; JV Socr; Var Trk; Cit Awd; Achvt Awd Arts-Crfts; Al-Ocean Crss Cntry 89.

KNAPP, TINA; Woodrow Wilson HS; Long Beach, CA; (4); 58/758; Church Yth Grp; Key Clb; Capt Drill Tm; Var Capt Trk; High Hon Roll; NHS; Pres Acad Fit Awd; Pres French Clb; Bsbl; Bsktbl; Phi Beta Kappa Seal Bearer For CSF; Gold W High Activity Pts; Zygomas; U CA Irvine; Eng.

KNARR, STEPHANY M; San Gorgonio HS; San Bernardino, CA; (3); Church Yth Grp; Cmnty Wkr; Awd High Achvt Geom Goldn St Exam; Acctng.

KNAUS, LYNN M; Irvington HS; Fremont, CA; (1); Church Yth Grp; Cmnty Wkr; Band; Jazz Band; Mrchg Band; Pep Band; School Musical; Rep Stu Cncl; Var Trk; Hon Roll; Bethany Bible Coll; Child Psych.

KNAUSS, JESSICA K; Mc Kinleyville HS; Mckinleyville, CA; (1); Drama Clb; School Play; High Hon Roll; Prfct Atten Awd; Engl.

KNEBEL, JENIFER L; Carlsbad HS; Carlsbad, CA; (3); 57/350; Treas Key Clb; SADD; Varsity Clb; Chorus; Church Choir; Yrbk; Var Capt Crs Cntry; JV Tennis; Var Capt Trk; Pres Acad Fit Awd; CSF.

KNECHT, CARL R; Eisenhower HS; Rialto, CA; (4); 22/655; Chess Clb; VP Key Clb; Library Aide; High Hon Roll; NHS; Pres Acad Fit Awd; Friday Night Live Sec 88-90; Cal Poly Pomona.

KNECHT, GINA L; Chino HS; Chino, CA; (3); Church Yth Grp; Spanish Clb; Band; Church Choir; Drm Mjr(t); Jazz Band; Mrchg Band; Pep Band; School Musical; Stage Crew; Prfrmng Arts Medal; Music.

KNECHT, KATHY; Hogan HS; Vallejo, CA; (2); Church Yth Grp; Key Clb; SADD; Drill Tm; Swmmng; Hon Roll; SDSU; Socl Svcs.

KNEEBONE, CHRIS D; Coachella Valley HS; Coachella, CA; (3); Tennis; Hon Roll; San Diego; Med.

KNEELAND, DANETTE JEAN; Fresno Christian HS; Prather, CA; (3); Art Clb; Church Yth Grp; Drama Clb; GAA; Teachers Aide; Chorus; School Play; Stage Crew; Yrbk; Gym; Hghst Acad Achvt Bible 89-90; Biola U; Art Bus Grphc Dsgn.

KNEELAND JR, PHILLIP; Clovis HS; Fresno, CA; (2); JV Golf; Hon Roll; Cpa.

KNEISEL, ALESHA R; Paraclete HS; Quartz Hill, CA; (2); Church Yth Grp; Drama Clb; School Play; VP Jr Cls; Cheerldng; Powder Puff Ftbl; High Hon Roll; NHS; Rotary Awd; CSF; Drama.

KNEISLY, TIFFANY LYNN; Nogalas HS; La Puente, CA; (2); 54/800; Teachers Aide; JV Vllybl; Cit Awd; High Hon Roll; Hon Roll; Pres Acad Fit Awd.

KNIFFEN, SUSANNA C; Coast Joint Union HS; Cayucos, CA; (2); #2 In Class; AFS; Church Yth Grp; FBLA; JV Sftbl; JV Vllybl; High Hon Roll; NHS; 1st Pl CA Hstry Day Comptn 90; Acad Awd Span, Eng, Sci; Intl Law.

KNIFTON, CARRIE; North County Christian Schl; Paso Robles, CA; (3); 1/6; Church Yth Grp; Math Tm; Teachers Aide; Chorus; School Play; Stu Cncl; Stat Bsktbl; Var Cheerldng; JV Var Vllybl; Hon Roll; Won 1st Pl Lapidary Show; Azuza Pacific U; Ed.

KNIGHT, AARON E; Orange Glen HS; Valley Center, CA; (3); 19/458; Church Yth Grp; Treas Key Clb; Spanish Clb; Acpl Chr; Pres Band; Mrchg Band; Pep Band; JV Trk; NHS; Acad Decathlon.

KNIGHT, DOUG E; Mission Bay HS; San Diego, CA; (4); 4/325; Letterman Clb; Varsity Clb; Var Bsbl; Var Crs Cntry; Var Capt Socr; High Hon Roll; Kiwanis Awd; UCSB; Envrnmntl Engr.

KNIGHT, HAVEN S; Berkeley HS; Berkeley, CA; (2); High Hon Roll; Pres Acad Fit Awd; Jr Var Water Polo; Var Crew; Princeton; Sci.

KNIGHT, JASON; Hogan SR HS; Vallejo, CA; (4); Boy Scts; Key Clb; Ski Clb; Spanish Clb; JV Var Bsbl; JV Var Ftbl; Hon Roll; Prfct Atten Awd.

KNIGHT, JUSTIN J; St Marys HS; Lodi, CA; (2); Church Yth Grp; Model UN; Ed Nwsp; JV Capt Bsbl; JV Capt Socr; High Hon Roll; CSF; USSF Registered Referee; Sccr MVP; Bsbl Mst Imprvd.

KNIGHT, KATHLEEN M; Los Amigos HS; Fountain Valley, CA; (4); 65/300; Church Yth Grp; Teachers Aide; Band; Drill Tm; Capt Flag Corp; Mrchg Band; Swmmng; Outstndng Tall Flag Person Band Schlrshp; Golden West Coll; Accntng.

KNIGHT, LADONA E; Pius X HS; Cerritos, CA; (4); 9/178; Church Yth Grp; Drama Clb; Girl Scts; Church Choir; High Hon Roll; Hon Roll; NHS; Voice Dem Awd; CSF; Grad Magna Cum Laude; Boston U; Lawyer.

KNIGHT, NGUYON; St Michaels Prep; Redondo Beach, CA; (1); Art Clb; Bskbl,Wghtlftng, Spanish Lang.

KNIGHT, NICKI R; Ramona HS; Ramona, CA; (3); 13/450; Dance Clb; Spanish Clb; Varsity Clb; School Play; Rep Stu Cncl; Capt Var Bsktbl; Var Trk; Var Vllybl; High Hon Roll; Pres Acad Fit Awd; BYU; Law.

KNIGHT, NICOLE D; Gardena HS; Gardena, CA; (3); Church Yth Grp; Pep Clb; Sec Church Choir; Mrchg Band; Ed Nwsp; Stat Bsktbl; Score Keeper; Sftbl; UCO; Pres Yth Usher Brd; Grambling ST U; Bus.

KNIGHT, SUZANNE E; Apple Valley SR HS; Apple Valley, CA; (1); Church Yth Grp; Hosp Aide; Letterman Clb; Spanish Clb; Church Choir; Var Bsktbl; Stat Ftbl; Var Trk; Wt Lftg; High Hon Roll; Stanford; Ped.

KNIGHT, TAMMY M; Shasta HS; Redding, CA; (2); AFS; Drama Clb; Hon Roll; Engl.

KNIGHT, TRAVIS J; Ramona HS; Ramona, CA; (2); 1/300; Bsktbl; Vllybl; High Hon Roll; Duke; Med.

KNIGHT, VANESSA M; Arroyo Grande HS; Arroyo Grande, CA; (4); 30/550; Mgr AFS; Am Leg Aux Girls St; Debate Tm; NFL; Speech Tm; Teachers Aide; Var Tennis; Hon Roll; Pres Acad Fit Awd; CA St Chmpn Ortry Frnscs; Hstry Day St Lvl; Clrmnt Mcknna Coll; Intl Rltns.

KNIGHTS, LORI; Saddleback HS; Santa Ana, CA; (3); Office Aide; Pep Clb; Yrbk; Ed Lit Mag; Creatv Wrtng Clb; Engl Clb; Engl.

KNITTLE, MARIE R; Modesto HS; Modesto, CA; (3); Treas FBLA; Teachers Aide; Hon Roll; Modesta JR Coll; Pediatrician.

KNOBLAUCH, MARK A; Clovis HS; Clovis, CA; (3); Dance Clb; Drama Clb; Acpl Chr; Chorus; Church Choir; Orch; School Musical; School Play; Hon Roll; Fresno Madara County Hnr Chair; Wrld Showcase Fstvl Natl Champs; Fresno ST; Vocal Music.

KNODORKOVSKY, KARINA M; Skyline HS; Oakland, CA; (3); Cmnty Wkr; Dance Clb; Key Clb; Varsity Clb; VP Stu Cncl; Socr; Tennis; Hon Roll; Exchng Pgm To USSR 89; Ballet Cnsrvtry 11 Yrs; Piano 11 Yrs; Modeling; Jazz; Law.

KNOEPFLE, KIRSTEN S; Sonora HS; La Haba Hts, CA; (3); 8/292; Scholastic Bowl; Science Clb; Ski Clb; Chrmn Jr Cls; Hon Roll; Pres Acad Fit Awd; JV Bsktbl; Var Powder Puff Ftbl; JV Swmmng; Var Capt Tennis; 3 Yrs Top 100; UCSD; Anthrplgy.

KNOLLENBERG, CLIFFORD F; Kerman HS; Fresno, CA; (2); 4/170; German Clb; Math Tm; Rep Frsh Cls; Stu Cncl; Var Swmmng; Hon Roll; Voice Dem Awd; VP Teachers Of Tomorrow; CSF; VP Interact; Aerospace Engr.

KNOOP, KELLY L; Ponderosa HS; Rescue, CA; (4); 42/278; GAA; SADD; Band; Mrchg Band; Pep Band; Rep Sr Cls; Var L Socr; High Hon Roll; Hon Roll; Tracy & Stella Mem Schlrshp; Friday Night Live; Moorepark; Exotic Animal Trng.

KNOPF, ERIC R; Edison HS; Huntington Beach, CA; (3); Library Aide; Model UN; Ski Clb; Jr NHS; Bicycle Clb; Mun Conf Stanford, Georgetown.

KNOPP, ERIC A; Cupertino HS; Cupertino, CA; (1); FBLA; Fld Hcky; CSF; Cmpltd Alg II 90; Purdue; Crmnl Law.

KNOPP, MICHELLE L; Paradise SR HS; Magalia, CA; (2); 1/268; Teachers Aide; High Hon Roll; Prfct Atten Awd; CA Schlrshp Fed; CA HS Prfcncy Exam; U CA; Scndry Spnsh Tchr.

KNOTT, BRENDA E; Mater Dei HS; Huntington Beach, CA; (1); Church Yth Grp; Pep Clb; Capt Cheerldng; Cit Awd; High Hon Roll; NHS; CA Schlrshp Fed; Piano; Swmmng, Gymnstcs & Day Camp Cnslr; U CA San Diego; Med.

KNOWLDEN, LORI M; El Cajon Valley HS; El Cajon, CA; (2); 95/431; Cmnty Wkr; Drama Clb; Chorus; School Play; Variety Show; Acting.

KNOWLES, CATHERINE H; Channel Islands HS; Oxnard, CA; (3); Girl Scts; Band; Mrchg Band; Pep Band; Sci.

KNOWLES, JENNIFER M; Mt Whitney HS; Visalia, CA; (2); Pep Clb; JV Cheerldng; CSF; Keywanettes; Earth Aid; U CA Santa Barbara.

KNOWLTON, JENNIFER L; Amador Valley HS; Pleasanton, CA; (4); Teachers Aide; Color Guard; Hon Roll; Marine Bio.

KNOX, ANTOINETTE T; Eisenhower HS; Rialto, CA; (2); Varsity Clb; Bsktbl; Swmmng; Trk; High Hon Roll; Peer Cnslr; High GPA; U S CA; Math.

KNOX, DEBORAH L; Corona HS; Corona, CA; (3); Church Yth Grp; Office Aide; SADD; Yrbk; JV Crs Cntry; Var Swmmng; Pres Acad Fit Awd; CO ST.

KNOX, HEATHER L; Shafter HS; Shafter, CA; (4); 10/250; Chess Clb; Pres Hosp Aide; Key Clb; Pep Clb; SADD; School Musical; Var L Socr; Cit Awd; Ntl Merit SF; Pres Acad Fit Awd; Pepperdine U; Pre-Law.

KNOX, INGER; Rim Of The World HS; Blue Jay, CA; (3); 21/259; Art Clb; Church Yth Grp; German Clb; Pep Clb; Chorus; Ed Nwsp; Ed Yrbk; Stat Bsktbl; High Hon Roll; Hon Roll; Acad Lttr Jr Yr; CA St San Bernardino; Wrtng.

KNOX, KEITH W; Vintage HS; Napa, CA; (4); 57/350; FCA; Teachers Aide; Sec Jr Cls; JV Var Socr; Cit Awd; Hon Roll; Bank Of Amer Achvt Awd; Napa Valley Coll; Arch.

KNOX, LEONARD; Ganesha HS; Pomona, CA; (2); Bsbl; Bsktbl.

KNOX, MATTHEW; Earl Warren HS; Downey, CA; (3); 11/460; Am Leg Boys St; Key Clb; Mu Alpha Theta; Teachers Aide; Var L Bsbl; Intrml Bsktbl; High Hon Roll; St Schlr; Glnd St Exam Hgh Hnrs Alg & Geom; Acadmc Ltr Wnnr; Greenpeace; Elec Engr.

KNOX, MONICA; Ukiah HS; Potter Valley, CA; (4); Band; Nor Cal Hnr Band; Law.

KNUDSEN, JENNIFER A; Hanford HS; Hanford, CA; (3); Church Yth Grp; Cmnty Wkr; Dance Clb; Score Keeper; Hon Roll; CSF; San Francisco ST; Psych.

KNUDSEN, JON; Mt Whitney HS; Visalia, CA; (1); Boy Scts; FFA; Acpl Chr; Chorus; Church Choir; Ftbl; Swmmng; Wt Lftg; Hon Roll; Prfct Atten Awd; Bwlng Awds; UCLA; Music.

KNUDSEN, KRISTA L; Hanford Union HS; Hanford, CA; (1); Church Yth Grp; Cmnty Wkr; Drama Clb; FHA; School Musical; School Play; High Hon Roll; Dance Clb; Speech Tm; Jr NHS; Acad & Drama Lttrs; 1st Pl St Cnvntn Ntrtn Div; CSF; Drama.

KNUFF, JENNIFER; Bonita Vista HS; Bonita, CA; (3); Cmnty Wkr; Model UN; Pep Clb; Service Clb; Yrbk; Lit Mag; Cit Awd; Hon Roll; Treasurer Environmental Club; President Interact Club; Political Science.

KNUPFER, JASON L; Woodside HS; Redwood City, CA; (2); Church Yth Grp; Var Bsbl; JV Bsktbl; Hnrb Mntn Vrsty All-League Bsbl Team.

KNUTSON, KERI M; Valhalla HS; El Cajon, CA; (3); 42/408; Var Swmmng; Elem Ed.

KNUTSON, LARS A; Troy HS; Yorba Linda, CA; (2); Bsktbl; Var Tennis; Cit Awd; High Hon Roll; MVP Tennis; CSF; U CA; Astrnmy.

KO, ANDREW PIN-WEI; Glen A Wilson HS; Hacienda Hgts, CA; (2); Computer Clb; German Clb; High Hon Roll; Bridge Clb Pres.

KO, CINDY; Napa HS; Napa, CA; (4); 1/350; Am Leg Aux Girls St; Cmnty Wkr; Key Clb; SADD; Rep Frsh Cls; Rep VP Soph Cls; Rep Sr Cls; Hon Roll; NHS; Pres Acad Fit Awd; Juvenile Justice Delinquency Privention Cmnssn; Top 1% Soc/Napa Vly Yth Cmmssn; Bd Ed Sclr; UC Davis; Elec Engrng.

KO, CLARA; Lowell HS; San Francisco, CA; (2); Cmnty Wkr; Chorus; School Musical; High Hon Roll; Rehrsl Accmpnst Adv Chorus; Red Belt Tae Kwon Do; Chinese Club; Sanford U; Lwyr.

KO, CLAUDINE C; University HS; Irvine, CA; (2); Cmnty Wkr; Intnl Clb; JCL; Latin Clb; Variety Show; Rptr Nwsp; JV Crs Cntry; JV Trk; NHS; Jrnslm.

KO, ELLEN C; San Dimas HS; San Dimas, CA; (3); Co-Ed Yrbk; Hon Roll; Jr Var & Var Badminton; CA Schlrshp Fed; Literary Hnrs Soc.

KO, FANNY C; San Gabriel HS; Alhambra, CA; (3); 23/727; Hon Roll; CSF; Acad Decathlon; Acad Excllnc Awd; UCLA; Law.

KO, HYONG C; Foothill HS; Sacramento, CA; (2); Tennis; Hon Roll; Mech Engr.

KO, JOSEPH; Saint Ingatius College Prep; San Francisco, CA; (2); Cmnty Wkr; French Clb; Trk; Hon Roll; VP Frnch Clb; Psych.

KO, LILLY P; Galileo HS; San Francisco, CA; (2); Pep Clb; Varsity Clb; Band; Sec Soph Cls; VP Jr Cls; Var Vllybl; Hon Roll; Pres Acad Fit Awd; Badmntn Tm; UC Davis; Lawyer.

KO, PHILLIP; Lincoln HS; San Francisco, CA; (1); Cow Poly; Cvl Engr.

KO, RAYMOND; Bullard HS; Fresno, CA; (3); 80/500; Debate Tm; NFL; Ski Clb; Speech Tm; School Play; Var Tennis; High Hnrs Golden ST Exam Geom; Hnrs Golden ST Exam Alg.

KO, ROGER W; Chaminade HS; Northridge, CA; (2); Art Clb; Bsktbl; High Hon Roll; CSF; Hstry Club.

KO, SANG; Highlands HS; Sacramento, CA; (4); Math Clb; Hon Roll; Pres Acad Fit Awd; Physics, Bio, US Hstry, Engl; CA ST U; Civil Engrng.

KO, SOPHIA; Los Altos HS; Hacienda Hgts, CA; (3); 39/376; Cmnty Wkr; Key Clb; Teachers Aide; Church Choir; Hon Roll; Prfct Atten Awd; Jr Hnrs Guard; Sci Fair Grand Prize Wnnr; Badminton Team.

KO, SUNNIA C; Skyline HS; Oakland, CA; (3); 10/600; Cmnty Wkr; Key Clb; Teachers Aide; Band; Orch; Ed Nwsp; Yrbk; VP Frsh Cls; Treas Stu Cncl; Sftbl; Rotary Yth Ldrshp Awd; Golden St Alg & Geomtry Hgh Hnrs Awd; Marcus A Foster Ed Inst Achvmnt Awd; Stanford.

KO, TOMMY; Saddleback HS; Santa Ana, CA; (3); Church Yth Grp; Pep Clb; Science Clb; Ski Clb; Spanish Clb; SADD; Varsity Clb; VP Jr Cls; Var L Swmmng; Hon Roll; Var Water Polo Team; USAP Clb; Music-Top Jr Choir; USC; Accntng.

KO, VICKY Y; Skyline HS; Oakland, CA; (2); Library Aide; Math Clb; Math Tm; ROTC; Teachers Aide; Orch; School Musical; Vllybl; Cit Awd; Hon Roll; ROTC Hnr Guard Platoon; UC Berkeley; Elec Engrng.

KO, VIRGINIA; Lowell HS; San Francisco, CA; (2); CSF Mem; Red Cross Club Mem; Med Explorers Mem; Med.

KO, WENDY; Napa HS; Napa, CA; (1); #1 In Class; Key Clb; SADD; Cit Awd; Hon Roll; 1st Pl Poetry Cont RENS; 2nd Pl Creative Writing Cont RENS; Cert Excllnc GPA; Teacher.

KO, WYNNE S; Lowell HS; San Francisco, CA; (3); Science Clb; Teachers Aide; Orch; Shield Hr Soc; Golden St Exam Algebra & Gmtry; Red Cross Clb Pblc Rltns Ofcr; CA Schsp Fed; Premed Clb; Biological Science/Physician.

KO, YOUNG S; Santa Clara HS; Santa Clara, CA; (3); Pres Church Yth Grp; German Clb; VP JA; Church Choir; JV Socr; JV Trk; Hon Roll; Prfct Atten Awd; Var Badmntn Team; Guitar; Hon Guard; Treas Korean Club; CSF; Psych.

KOBAYASHI, MICHIYO; Warren HS; Downey, CA; (2); Art Clb; Church Yth Grp; Chrmn Temple Yth Grp; JV Capt Vllybl; CA Schltc Fed Awd 89-90; JV Vllybl MIP 88-89; MVP 89-90; Piano 10 Yrs; Flute 3 Yrs; Psych.

KOBERG, MINDY J; Folsom HS; Folsom, CA; (3); GAA; Letterman Clb; Model UN; Pep Clb; SADD; Teachers Aide; Varsity Clb; Off Frsh Cls; Off Soph Cls; Off Jr Cls.

KOBERLEIN, BRANDI; Folsom HS; Folsom, CA; (3); 38/189; Church Yth Grp; Model UN; Sec Pep Clb; Teachers Aide; Church Choir; JV Var Bsktbl; JV Crs Cntry; High Hon Roll; Hon Roll; Futre Prblm Slvng 1st Pl; Frdy Nght Live; Sci.

KOBERSTEIN, GWEN; Antioch HS; Antioch, CA; (4); 115/600; Pres Church Yth Grp; Drama Clb; Letterman Clb; Pep Clb; Band; Color Guard; Flag Corp; Jazz Band; Mrchg Band; Orch; Ricks Coll; Med.

KOBIALKA, SEMYON; University HS; San Francisco, CA; (4); Jazz Band; Orch; School Musical; SF Yth Orch; Karate Awds; 1st Pl Vamos Pacific Musical Soc & Cello Club; Music.

KOBLE, CHRISTOPHER M; Paramount HS; Lakewood, CA; (2); 78/616; Band; Mrchg Band; Pep Band; Hon Roll; VP Computer Clb; Teachers Aide; CA ST U Long Beachs Upwrd Bnd Prgrm Smmr 89; Cmptr Prgrmng; Pepperdine U; Cmptr Prgrmng.

KOBLE, JASON P; Southfork HS; Weott, CA; (3); VICA; JV Var Ftbl; Rotary Awd; Humboldt ST; Carpentry.

KOBZOFF, NICOLETTE N; Downey HS; Downey, CA; (4); Church Yth Grp; Cmnty Wkr; Chrmn Hosp Aide; Service Clb; Rptr Nwsp; Stu Cncl; JV Tennis; Cal ST U; Jrnslm.

KOCH, BECKY; Agoura HS; Westlake Vil, CA; (3); 95/487; Church Yth Grp; Dance Clb; Pep Clb; Teachers Aide; Chorus; Drill Tm; Swing Chorus; Cheerldng; Capt Pom Pon; Hon Roll; Natl Charity Leag-Pres; Bst Dancer-Sounds Of Clss 90-91; TV.

KOCH, DAVID BRIAN; Poway HS; Poway, CA; (3); Church Yth Grp; Varsity Clb; Rep Soph Cls; Rep Sr Cls; Stu Cncl; Wrstlng; Hon Roll; NHS; Schlr-Athlt, Al-Leag Wrstlng 89-90; Al-CIF 89-90; UC Berkeley; Scndry Ed.

KOCH, ELIZABETH A; Grossmont HS; La Mesa, CA; (1); Church Yth Grp; Drama Clb; Service Clb; School Play; Rep Stu Cncl; JV Cheerldng; Hon Roll; UC Santa Barbara; Jrnlsm.

KOCH, JAMES; Lassen HS; Susanville, CA; (2); 34/265; Church Yth Grp; VICA; Score Keeper; Socr; Trk; High Hon Roll; Hon Roll; Sci.

KOCH, MATT J; Gahr HS; Norwalk, CA; (3); Spanish Clb; Socr; Hon Roll; Home Clb; Blue & Gold Awd; UC Riverside; Med.

KOCH, TIMORY; Dana Hills HS; Monarch Beach, CA; (1); Dance Clb; Dance Tm; Advertising.

KOCHAVATR, JOHN T; Ontario HS; Ontario, CA; (3); 3/600; VP Art Clb; Cmnty Wkr; Key Clb; Pres Speech Tm; Pres Jr Cls; Var Tennis; Cit Awd; High Hon Roll; Opt Clb Awd; Rotary Awd; Jr World Golf Prtcpnt; SCPGAJGA; MVP, Most Imprvd & Coaches Tnns Awds; UCLA; Sci.

KOCHERGEN, TRISHA L; Bullard HS; Fresno, CA; (2); Church Yth Grp; FCA; SADD; Powder Puff Ftbl; Trk; Hon Roll; Biola; Med.

KOCHHEISER, BRENDA A; Hoover HS; Fresno, CA; (4); Art.

KOCMICH, LORI; Bullard HS; Fresno, CA; (2); 57/566; Ski Clb; Spanish Clb; SADD; Ed Yrbk; Hon Roll; Sailing; San Diego ST; Bus.

KODANI, RAY; Rio Linda SR HS; Sacramento, CA; (2); Spanish Clb; SADD; Yrbk; Hon Roll; U Of Miami; Radio DJ.

KODIS, NICOLE M; Villa Park HS; Orange, CA; (3); Office Aide; Teachers Aide; High Hon Roll; Hon Roll; Stu Of The Mnth; Fullerton; Advrtsng.

KOEDYKER, KRISTEN; Indio HS; Indio, CA; (4); 60/400; Church Yth Grp; Drama Clb; Chorus; Church Choir; School Play; Pres Jr Cls; Var Cheerldng; Var Powder Puff Ftbl; Var Sftbl; JV Swmmng; ACSI Dstnghsd HS Arts; Phi Delta Kappa Schlrshp; Educ.

KOEHLER, CHRISTINA L; Crescenta Valley HS; Glendale, CA; (2); Cmnty Wkr; Hosp Aide; Intnl Clb; Mu Alpha Theta; Service Clb; Spanish Clb; Chorus; JV Capt Bsktbl; JV Trk; Youth & Govt; Ldrshp Developmnt Pgm; Loyola Marymount; Corporate Law.

KOEHLER, DAWN; Canyon Springs HS; Moreno Valley, CA; (2); French Clb; Yrbk; Var Trk; Spirit Clb; Intr Dsgn.

KOEHN, JENIFER; Eureka HS; Eureka, CA; (2); Church Yth Grp; Ski Clb; SADD; Treas Frsh Cls; Off Soph Cls; Off Jr Cls; JV Capt Cheerldng; Socr; Hon Roll; Active In Bicycling; Helped Eureka Food Bank & Bowled For Kids Sake; Obtained Pen Pal Japan, Spain; St Marys; Elem Ed.

KOEHN, MARK D; Poway HS; Poway, CA; (3); Church Yth Grp; FCA; Acpl Chr; Chorus; Church Choir; Swing Chorus; Trk; JV Vllybl; High Hon Roll; Hon Roll; Trophy Best Sport At Word Of Life Vlybl Tourn.

KOELBEL, KELLY; Leland HS; San Jose, CA; (2); 85/442; Church Yth Grp; GAA; Key Clb; SADD; Pres Soph Cls; Stu Cncl; JV Cheerldng; Var Socr; Hon Roll.

KOENIG, KIMBERLY A; Tamalpais HS; Mill Valley, CA; (4); 10/239; Dance Clb; Drama Clb; Pres French Clb; School Play; High Hon Roll; Hon Roll; Bnk Of Amer Plaque Wnnr Fine Arts; Peer Cnclr; Theatre Teacher; UCLA; Theatre.

KOENIG, SARAH C; Poway HS; Poway, CA; (3); 85/714; Church Yth Grp; Chorus; JV Swmmng; Hon Roll; Kewanettes Clb; CSF; U Of CA; Engl Teach.

KOENS, KELLI ANN; Ernest Righetti HS; Santa Maria, CA; (3); 18/336; Teachers Aide; Stu Cncl; JV Var Cheerldng; JV Var Sftbl; High Hon Roll; Hon Roll; CSF; Bus.

KOEPKE, MICHELLE; Chaffey HS; Ontario, CA; (4); 8/478; Church Yth Grp; Drama Clb; Pep Clb; Science Clb; School Play; Yrbk; High Hon Roll; NHS; Rotary Awd; CA Inst Of The Arts; Art.

KOEPPEN, CATHERINE ELISE; Woodland HS; Esparto, CA; (4); 25/475; Pres Key Clb; Jazz Band; Nwsp; Lit Mag; Hon Roll; NHS; Ntl Merit Ltr; SADD; School Musical; Stage Crew; Intl Order Jobs Dghtrs Prncss; Acadmc Dcthln; CSF; Cornell Coll; Engl.

KOERS, ESTHER H; So Pasadena HS; S Pasadena, CA; (4); 135/293; Church Yth Grp; Cmnty Wkr; Drama Clb; SADD; Teachers Aide; School Play; Var L Mgr(s); Var Powder Puff Ftbl; Var L Swmmng; Homcmng Qn; CA ST LA; Engl.

KOFAHL, ANDRA; Willits HS; Willits, CA; (2); Church Yth Grp; Hosp Aide; SADD; Mrchg Band; Trk; Vllybl; Cit Awd; High Hon Roll; Hon Roll; Pres Acad Fit Awd; Santa Rosa JC; Pediatrics.

KOGER, NICOLE; Lemoore HS; Lemoore, CA; (2); JV Crs Cntry; Var Trk; Hon Roll; Hgh Pnt Achvr Socl Stud; CSF; U CA Irvine; Ad.

KOH, JINA E; Huntington Beach HS; Huntington Bch, CA; (3); Church Yth Grp; French Clb; Model UN; Red Cross Aide; Church Choir; Orch; U CA; Dermatology.

KOH, KAREN L; Arcadia HS; Arcadia, CA; (2); 74/605; Dance Clb; Drill Tm; Flag Corp; Variety Show; Ed Yrbk; Hon Roll; NHS; Pres Acad Fit Awd; Organ Piano Flute & Guitar; CA Jr Schlrshp Fed Hnrs; Korean Clb; Jrs Stsmn Of Amer; Chinese Schl; Med.

KOH, YOUNG; Buena Park HS; Fullerton, CA; (4); Church Yth Grp; Science Clb; Korean Clb.

KOHARA, PAUL; Carlmont HS; Belmont, CA; (4); 12/261; Boy Scts; VP Church Yth Grp; Off Frsh Cls; VP Soph Cls; Bsktbl; Var Tennis; Wt Lftg; Pres Acad Fit Awd; Pres Schlr; CSF; Asian Amer Club; Schl Math Hnrs; UC Berkeley; Civil Engrng.

KOHLER, CHRIS L; Alameda HS; Alameda, CA; (4); 45/325; Art Clb; Spanish Clb; VICA; Hon Roll; Ntl Merit SF; Cal Poly SLO; Grphc Dsgn.

KOHLER, CHRISTOPHER M; Pasadena HS; Sierra Madre, CA; (3); Var L Bsbl; Var L Ftbl; Hon Roll; USC Smr Hnrs Pgm; CSF; Hnrs Grd Geom Gldn St Exm; Stanford; Sports Med.

KOHLER, MATTHEW D; Canyon Springs HS; Riverside, CA; (3); Intnl Clb; Intrml Bsbl; High Hon Roll; Co-Capt NHS; Electrcl Engnrng.

KOHLER, REBECCA; Artesia HS; Lakewood, CA; (1); Church Yth Grp; Intnl Clb; Science Clb; Church Choir; Stu Cncl; JV Tennis; Long Beach U; Nrsg.

KOHLER, SUSANNAH C; Alameda HS; Alameda, CA; (2); 32/275; Jazz Band; JV Vllybl; High Hon Roll; Dixieland Band; Outstndng Soloist Santa Cruz Jazz Fes 89; Microbio.

KOHOUT, MELISSA R; Atascadero HS; Atascadero, CA; (1); Drama Clb; Drill Tm; High Hon Roll; Camp Counselor Speech & Hearng Impaired Kids; Speech Pathlgy.

KOHOUT, MINDY; Corona HS; Corona, CA; (3); 65/430; Church Yth Grp; Girl Scts; Office Aide; Pep Clb; Color Guard; Flag Corp; Gym; Ntl Merit Ltr; Pres Acad Fit Awd.

KOHUT, ANA N; Woodside HS; Redwood City, CA; (4); 32/271; French Clb; Drill Tm; Mrchg Band; Off Sr Cls; Vllybl; Hon Roll; Kiwanis Awd; Opt Clb Awd; Pres Acad Fit Awd; KQED Auction Vlntr; Millard Fillmore Tricia Clb; Ltr Tm Capt; Peer Hlpr; UCLA; Ecnmcs.

KOKAME, HIROSHI J; Drew College Prep; San Francisco, CA; (3); Chess Clb; Chorus; San Francisco ST; Bus Adm.

KOKIATKULKIJ, JINNIE; Bellflower HS; Bellflower, CA; (3); 7/276; Hist Key Clb; Math Clb; Pres Spanish Clb; Var Tennis; High Hon Roll; CSF; Outstndng Stu Awd Spnsh I & Geom; Goldn St Exm Awd Hnrs Geom; UCLA; Bio.

KOKJER, RACHEL K; Oak Ridge HS; Cameron Park, CA; (2); 2/290; Church Yth Grp; Debate Tm; NFL; Church Choir; Acpl Chr; Band; Chorus; Church Choir; Cit Awd; High Hon Roll; Attend 9th Grade Canadian Acad In Kolse Japan; CA St Spch & Debate Champ 90; Extmrns Spkng & Oxford; Intl Rel.

KOKOT, NIELS; Montgomery HS; Santa Rosa, CA; (3); 1/450; French Clb; JA; Rptr Nwsp; Var Bsbl; High Hon Roll; Pres Jr NHS; Sci.

KOKX, TYLER D; Dana Hills HS; Dana Point, CA; (3); Var Ftbl; JV Var Socr; Var Wt Lftg; FL ST; Math.

KOLASA, BRYAN; Los Alamitos HS; Los Alamitos, CA; (2); Science Clb; Spanish Clb; JV Bsbl; Var Ftbl; JV Socr; Hon Roll; CSF; Marine Bio.

KOLB, HEATHER A; Rio Linda SR HS; Elverta, CA; (2); Hon Roll; ROP Pgm; Fshn Dsgn.

KOLDE, HEATHER; Alta Loma HS; Alta Loma, CA; (4); 2/450; Am Leg Aux Girls St; Church Yth Grp; Cmnty Wkr; Girl Scts; Key Clb; Pep Clb; Service Clb; SADD; Church Choir; Stu Cncl; Bsln Leag Outstndng SR; Chffy Trust Schlrshp Awd; UCLA; Law.

KOLENIC, SCOTT R; Rancho Bernardo HS; San Diego, CA; (2); Letterman Clb; Intrml Bsktbl; JV Crs Cntry; Var L Trk; Hon Roll.

KOLKMAN, JOY A; Simi Valley HS; Simi Valley, CA; (3); Church Yth Grp; ROTC; Chorus; Church Choir; Jazz Band; Bsktbl; Trk; Vllybl; Moorpark Coll; Bus.

KOLL, CARLA; San Benito HS; Hollister, CA; (3); Church Yth Grp; Cmnty Wkr; Pep Clb; SADD; Teachers Aide; Varsity Clb; Ed Yrbk; Rep Frsh Cls; Rep Soph Cls; Cheerldng; Rally Clb; Pharmacy.

KOLL, MEGHAN E; Paso Robles HS; Paso Robles, CA; (2); Church Yth Grp; Girl Scts; Swmmng; Tennis; High Hon Roll; Hikng & Envrnmntl Club; Sousson Fndtn Yosemite Vlntr; Syracuse U; Tchng Engl.

KOLLAR, MEGAN A; San Gorgonio HS; Highland, CA; (3); Aud/Vis; Church Yth Grp; Cmnty Wkr; French Clb; Yrbk; Powder Puff Ftbl; JV Socr; JV Swmmng; Var Trk; Hon Roll; Most Imprvd Awd JV Swmmng; Spcl Olympcs Vlntr; Aces Club; Pilot.

KOLLAR, ROBERT; La Serna HS; Whittier, CA; (4); Church Yth Grp; Drama Clb; Cmnty Wkr; Spanish Clb; Thesps; School Play; Rep Jr Cls; Rep Sr Cls; Rep Stu Cncl; JV Crs Cntry; CSF; Lance, Dstngshd Schlr Awds; Fnlst Drma Tchrs Assn Sthrn CA Fll Fstvl; Chsn Cndt Imprvstn Wrkshp; U Of CA Irvine.

KOLLMEYER, STACEY R; Oakdale HS; Waterford, CA; (1); Church Yth Grp; Swmmng; Hon Roll; Cont Miss Waterfrd Cont; CSF Membr; Vrsty Swm Team; Conflict Mgr.

KOLMER, KRISTIN K; Bella Vista HS; Citrus Heights, CA; (2); 79/406; Church Yth Grp; Spanish Clb; JV Crs Cntry; Var Trk; Ped.

KOLOWSKI, PAULETTE L; Pittsburg HS; Pittsburg, CA; (2); JV Bsktbl; Hon Roll; St Schlr; Schl Recog Awd Outstndg Achvt Alg; William A Cadman Memrl Spts Awd; Princeton; Engrng.

KOLSTER, STEVE P; Colfax HS; Auburn, CA; (3); 2/160; Church Yth Grp; SADD; Bsktbl; Ftbl; Tennis; High Hon Roll; Spirit Club; U Of CA Santa Barbara; Acctng.

KOLVA, JULIE P; James Madison HS; San Diego, CA; (4); 51/348; Cmnty Wkr; Band; Mrchg Band; Orch; Pep Band; Hon Roll; CA Schlstc Fdrtn; U Of CA, San Diego; Comp Engr.

KOLZE, SARA; East Union HS; Spanaway, WA; (2); #1 In Class; French Clb; Teachers Aide; Stu Cncl; Cheerldng; Vllybl; Cit Awd; High Hon Roll; Peer Cnslng; Stanford; Bus.

KOMANY, KITIDETH; Pittsburg HS; Pittsburg, CA; (2); 9/424; JA; Var Tennis; Hon Roll; Prfct Atten Awd; Pres Acad Fit Awd; Tnns Rookie Of Yr; All-Amer Acad Achvt Awd; Special Interest In Astronomyh; UC Davis; Biophys.

KOMAROMI, DAN; Sonora HS; Fullerton, CA; (3); Ski Clb; Variety Show; Lit Mag; Powder Puff Ftbl; Hon Roll; Jr NHS; NHS; Published Articles & Pgms In Magazines; Music Perf.

KOMATSUZAKI, AMY; Branham HS; San Jose, CA; (3); 1/259; Pres French Clb; Ed Yrbk; Stu Cncl; Bsktbl; Tennis; Trk; Vllybl; High Hon Roll; Prfct Atten Awd; Bst Shw Tech Drwng; MIT; Aero Engr.

KOMO, MATTHEW J; St Francis HS; Los Altos, CA; (1); Bsktbl; Ftbl; Wt Lftg; Ahtl Of Yr.

KONCHIGERI, RAVI H; University HS; Irvine, CA; (3); 1/551; Pres Debate Tm; Math Tm; NFL; Science Clb; Spanish Clb; Pres Speech Tm; JV Crs Cntry; Var Trk; High Hon Roll; Hon Roll; CA HS Speech Assn St Trnmnt; Orange Cnty Acad Decathlon Individual Awds; Stanford; Med.

KONDEJA, ANNA; Palm Desert HS; Indian Wells, CA; (3); Church Yth Grp; Chorus; Church Choir; Var Gym; Arts.

KONDELIK, CAROLYN; Canyon Springs HS; Phoenix, AZ; (4); Cmnty Wkr; Intnl Clb; Letterman Clb; Ski Clb; Teachers Aide; Varsity Clb; Stu Cncl; Var L Swmmng; High Hon Roll; Hon Roll; U CA Riverside; Med Sci.

KONDO, GRANT T; Sanger HS; Fresno, CA; (3); Pres Church Yth Grp; VP Church Yth Grp; Capt Model UN; Science Clb; Chorus; Stu Cncl; VP Tennis; Rotary Club Camp Royal Ldrshp; Mem CA Schlrshp Fed Rep; Chem.

KONDOR, LIVIA; Alameda HS; Alameda, CA; (3); 1/276; Spanish Clb; Crs Cntry; Swmmng; High Hon Roll; UC Berkeley.

KONDRASHOFF, BRANDY C; Chula Vista HS; Chula Vista, CA; (2); Church Yth Grp; Teachers Aide; Ed Nwsp; Mgr Sftbl; Child Psych.

KONDUS, KRISTINE L; Fontana HS; Fontana, CA; (3); 13/1024; Church Yth Grp; Drama Clb; Stat Swmmng; Var Tennis; High Hon Roll; 3 Acad Gold Mdls; UC San Diego; Med.

KONEGEN, ELIZABETH A; Cupertino HS; Santa Clara, CA; (2); Pres Church Yth Grp; Band; Church Choir; Mrchg Band; Orch; Pep Band; JV Fld Hcky; Wt Lftg; Medicine.

KONG, ANGELA; Abraham Lincoln HS; San Francisco, CA; (1); Orch; Yrbk; Treas Frsh Cls; VP Soph Cls; Lincolns Soc.

KONG, ANNA W; Oakland HS; Oakland, CA; (3); 5/35; Church Yth Grp; Cmnty Wkr; Library Aide; Office Aide; Temple Yth Grp; Nwsp; Yrbk; Lit Mag; Bsbl; Bsktbl; U C Berkeley; Nrsng.

KONG, CHEN S; Modesto HS; Modesto, CA; (3); Rep Intnl Clb; Speech Tm; Pres SADD; Orch; Yrbk; VP Sr Cls; Hon Roll; Stu Curriculum; Mock Trial; Young Democrat Treas; HONEST; Teenwork Staff Cert Of Appreciation; Human Service.

KONG, CHRISTOPHER; George Washington HS; San Francisco, CA; (2); Teachers Aide; JV Bsbl; High Hon Roll; Gldn St Exam-Algb-Hgh Hnrs; UC Berkeley; Ed.

KONG, DORIS M; Abraham Lincoln HS; San Francisco, CA; (2); FCA; Rep Soph Cls; Var Capt Sftbl; Var Vllybl; High Hon Roll; Hon Roll; CSF; Lincs; Outstndng Citznshp; UC Berkeley; Bus.

KONG, FAYE; Franklin HS; Stockton, CA; (4); Cmnty Wkr; Computer Clb; Drama Clb; JA; Office Aide; Red Cross Aide; ROTC; Teachers Aide; Color Guard; Drill Tm; Forever Young Clb; TOPS; CSU Sacramento; Bus.

KONG, GARHENG A; Edison HS; Fresno, CA; (2); 1/480; Chess Clb; Math Clb; Math Tm; Ski Clb; Orch; VP Stu Cncl; Var Vllybl; High Hon Roll; JETS Awd; Pepsi Schlr Awd 90; JETS Tm 1st Pl Northern CA; Odyssey Of Mind 1st Pl CA St, 4th Pl World Comptn.

KONG, GARYUN B; Edison HS; Fresno, CA; (1); 1/400; Cmnty Wkr; Math Clb; Math Tm; Ski Clb; JV Bsktbl; JV Tennis; Vllybl; High Hon Roll; Jr Fresno Metropolitan Museum Clb; CA Goldent St Geom Hnr Awd; Pepsi Schlr Awd 90.

KONG, JACKSON C; Richard Gahr HS; Artesia, CA; (1); Church Yth Grp; Band; Jazz Band; Mrchg Band; Orch; School Musical; Hon Roll; Pres Acad Fit Awd; CSF; Natl Teacher & Parents Achvt Awd; UPS; UCLA; Med.

KONG, JENNY; University HS; Irvine, CA; (1); JCL; Cheerldng; Hon Roll; Natl Latin Hnr Scty; Law.

KONG, KASERIN TAMMIE; Nogales HS; Walnut, CA; (2); 1/800; Science Clb; Off Drill Tm; Mrchg Band; High Hon Roll; Vrsty Modern Dance Team Club; CSF; Hnrs Eng, Hnrs Phys Sci Awds; 20th Century Wrld Hstry Awd; Stanford; Med.

KONG, MEI-MEI; Homestead HS; Sunnyvale, CA; (1); Art Clb; Cmnty Wkr; FBLA; Spanish Clb; Band; Rep Stu Cncl; JV Bsktbl; JV Vllybl; Cit Awd; High Hon Roll; Badmntn Var; Sunnyvale Alumni Schlrshp; GATE Clb; UC Davis; Lwyr.

KONG, PAMELA M; Skyline HS; Oakland, CA; (2); Church Yth Grp; Key Clb; Service Clb; Hon Roll; Pres Acad Fit Awd; CSF; Asian Stu Union; UCLA; Elec Engrng.

KONG, SOPHEA; Modesto HS; Modesto, CA; (4); Vllybl; Modesto JC.

KONG, STEVE V; Homestead HS; Sunnyvale, CA; (1); JV Badminton; MIT; Mech Engr.

KONG, SURENA; Woodrow Wilson HS; Long Beach, CA; (3); German Clb; Intnl Clb; Spanish Clb; Rep Soph Cls; Mgr(s); Intrml Co-Capt Vllybl; Hon Roll; NHS; Prfct Atten Awd; Pres Acad Fit Awd; UC Los Angeles; Medcl.

KONGBOUNMEE, KHAMDY; Luther Burbank HS; Sacramento, CA; (3); Art Clb; ROTC; Speech Tm; Off Jr Cls; Socr; Swmmng; Vllybl; Cit Awd; Hon Roll.

KONGKASEM, CYNTHIA; Holy Family HS; Los Angeles, CA; (3); Hosp Aide; Chorus; Crs Cntry; Trk; Prfct Atten Awd; Humane Soc Of US; Loyola Marymount U; Elem Educ.

KONGKASURIYACHAI, DARIN; Nogales HS; Walnut, CA; (3); 5/653; Key Clb; Service Clb; SADD; Teachers Aide; JV Tennis; High Hon Roll; Hon Roll; Prfct Atten Awd; Pres Acad Fit Awd; Pres Schlr; Gldn St Exam Algebra Hnrs; Svc Stu Of Yr 88; U Of CA Los Angeles; Pre Med.

KONIGSMARK, ERIC; Avalon HS; Avalon, CA; (3); Var Golf; High Hon Roll; Hon Roll; Spanish.

KONING, HEIDI A; Woodcrest Christian HS; Riverside, CA; (2); Church Yth Grp; Sec Church Choir; Var Math Clb; Var Sftbl; Var Vllybl; High Hon Roll; HOBY Ambassador 90; Hand Bell Choir; Tch & Take Painting Classes; Heartsong Ensmbl Choir; Math.

KONING, LYNDA E; Piner HS; Santa Rosa, CA; (2); FFA; Girl Scts; Key Clb; Band; Mrchg Band; Amer Red Cross Yth Emer Svcs; Train Dogs For Blind.

KONING, SHAWNN K; Woodcrest Christian HS; Riverside, CA; (1); Church Yth Grp; Church Choir; Co-Capt JV Bsktbl; Var Sftbl; Capt JV Vllybl; High Hon Roll; Handbell Choir; Asst Sound Tech On Kelsey & Yamaha Mixers For Live Performances; Sound Engrng.

KONISHI, MARIKO; Torrance HS; Torrance, CA; (4); Cmnty Wkr; Intnl Clb; JA; Latin Clb; Spanish Clb; Cit Awd; Hon Roll; Bank Of Am Schlrshp Awd; Yth Vlntr; U Southern CA; Intl Bus.

KONN, LISA M; Esperanza HS; Yorba Linda, CA; (3); 73/562; Church Yth Grp; Treas 4-H; Hosp Aide; Sec Church Choir; Mrchg Band; Stat Swmmng; 4-H Awd; Hon Roll; NHS; CSF.

KONNO, CHERYL M; Milpitas HS; Milpitas, CA; (2); 13/536; ROTC; VP Frsh Cls; VP Soph Cls; Stat Bsktbl; Score Keeper; High Hon Roll; JR Schlrs Of Am; Yng Life; UC Davis.

KONO, STACY; San Ramon Valley HS; San Ramon, CA; (3); 8/420; Art Clb; Pres Church Yth Grp; Hosp Aide; Intnl Clb; Rptr Yrbk; Intrml Trk; Hon Roll; Amnesty Intl VP; Hnr Frnch; Japanese; Reed; Humanities.

KONRAD, NATHAN; San Ramon Valley HS; Danville, CA; (2); Church Yth Grp; FBLA; Biomed Engrng.

KONSHAK, SARAH; Poway HS; Poway, CA; (2); Drama Clb; Model UN; Thesps; School Musical; School Play; Stage Crew; Variety Show; Phtg Nwsp; Hon Roll; Photgrphy; Wtrs Influence; Theatre Guild; Soc Sci.

KONYALIAN, TAMAR; Ribet Acad; Glendale, CA; (1); 1/24; Church Yth Grp; Orch; Bsktbl; Sftbl; Vllybl; Cit Awd; Hon Roll; Harvard; Med.

KONZELMAN, KAREN E; Arcadia HS; Arcadia, CA; (3); Ski Clb; School Play; Intrml Bsktbl; Var Crs Cntry; Stat Mgr(s); JV Var Socr; Var Trk; High Hon Roll; Prfct Atten Awd; Pres Acad Fit Awd; Sccr-CIF/Leag Wnnr 89; CIF Relay Team Quaterfinals 90; Horse Showing; Tom Sawyer Camp Cnslr.

KOO, AMY K; Lowell HS; San Francisco, CA; (3); Office Aide; Band; Rep Soph Cls; Bausch & Lomb Sci Awd; Med Explr Post 496 Secy; CSF; Bowling Leag; Sheild Hnr Soc; Chinese Clb; Bio Clb.

KOO, BRANDT M; Warren HS; Downey, CA; (4); 14/413; Computer Clb; Debate Tm; FBLA; Key Clb; Office Aide; Stat Bsktbl; Ntl Merit SF; Pres Acad Fit Awd; CSF; Ec.

KOO, CHUL H; Downey HS; Downey, CA; (3); Boy Scts; JA; Key Clb; Spanish Clb; SADD; Var JV Trk; Var Wrstlng; UCLA; Arch.

KOO, CLAURIO; Westmoor HS; Daly City, CA; (3); Art Clb; GAA; Spanish Clb; Var Vllybl; Hon Roll; Outstndng Athlete Awd; MVP Badminton.

KOO, EVAN K; Whitney HS; Cerritos, CA; (3); Art Clb; Church Yth Grp; FBLA; Key Clb; Church Choir; Var L Bsktbl; Mgr(s); Hon Roll; Korean Club; SCF; Bus.

KOO, HOWARD; Lowell HS; San Francisco, CA; (2); Cmnty Wkr; Debate Tm; Intnl Clb; Red Cross Aide; Science Clb; Band; Mrchg Band; Orch; JV Trk; High Hon Roll; Hnrd Schlr Of Gldn St Exmntn; Cmmnty Svcs & Othr Act Of Cls Of 92; UCLA; Comp Sci.

KOO, NAAREE; Burbank HS; Burbank, CA; (4); 1/429; Red Cross Aide; Science Clb; Band; Pres Schlr; CSF; Z-Clb; Berkeley.

KOO, RICHARD P; Bellarmine College Prep; San Jose, CA; (3); 15/300; Teachers Aide; Var Swmmng; U CA Davis; Chem.

KOO, THOMAS H; Birmingham HS; Van Nuys, CA; (1); Church Yth Grp; Band; Jazz Band; Mrchg Band; Hon Roll; Golden St Exam Algebra I; Stanford; Med Phys.

KOO, VINCENT; Abraham Lincoln HS; San Francisco, CA; (2); CSF; Chinese Clb; High Hnr Gldn St Exam Geom; San Francisco ST U; Acctnt.

KOO, VIVIAN W; Abraham Lincoln HS; San Francisco, CA; (4); Library Aide; Office Aide; Teachers Aide; Chorus; Church Choir; High Hon Roll; CSF; Bowling Tm; Chinese & Canton Clbs; UC Berkeley; Accntng.

KOOB, JENNY L; Atwater HS; Merced, CA; (1); Debate Tm; FFA; GAA; Teachers Aide; Nwsp; Yrbk; Score Keeper; Sftbl; Wrstlng; High Hon Roll; Atwater Mat Maid; Hnr Roll; Fresno ST; Bus.

KOOIMAN, BRIAN L; Orange Glen HS; Escondido, CA; (3); 35/400; Bsbl; Ftbl; Wt Lftg; Hon Roll; CSA; Schlr Athl Awd.

KOOIMAN, JENNESS ANNE; Tomaves HS; Port Reyes Sta, CA; (3); Art Clb; Ski Clb; Spanish Clb; Treas Sec Frsh Cls; Sec Soph Cls; VP Treas Jr Cls; Stat Score Keeper; High Hon Roll; Hon Roll; Grls St; Vet.

KOOK, SPENCER Y; Warren HS; Downey, CA; (2); Art Clb; Sec Debate Tm; Key Clb; Crs Cntry; Trk; Law.

KOON, SHAWNA M; Palm Springs HS; Palm Springs, CA; (4); Church Yth Grp; Chorus; Hon Roll; Ntl Merit Ltr; Jr Statesmen Amer; CA Schltc Fed; TX Chrstn U; Bus Admin.

KOONCE, NANCY L; Fremont HS; Sunnyvale, CA; (4); 98/385; Spanish Clb; Capt Color Guard; School Play; Yrbk; Rep Stu Cncl; Hon Roll; Sci Camp Cnslr; 1st Pl-Alameda Poetry Cont; De Anza JC; Acctng.

KOONTZ, KERRI A; Los Angeles Baptist HS; Sepulveda, CA; (3); Drama Clb; Letterman Clb; Varsity Clb; School Play; Score Keeper; Var Trk; Var Vllybl; W Coast Sideout Vllybl Clb; Scndry Ed.

KOOPMANN, RAYNA M; Manteca HS; Manteca, CA; (3); 11/400; English Clb; Treas Pep Clb; SADD; Cheerldng; High Hon Roll; NHS; Keywannettes Lt Gvrnr; U Of Pacifc Sci Awd, San Joaquin Cnty; Outstndng Chem Stu; U Fo Santa Barbara; Engrng.

KOOPS, NICOLE R; Atwater HS; Atwater, CA; (2); Computer Clb; Dance Clb; Key Clb; Bsktbl; Swmmng; Vllybl; Cit Awd.

KOPEC, SANDRA; Costa Mesa HS; Costa Mesa, CA; (2); 35/250; Pep Clb; Cheerldng; Pom Pon; Hon Roll; Grphc Art.

KOPER, OLIVIA F; Burbank HS; Burbank, CA; (2); Cmnty Wkr; Hosp Aide; School Play; Stage Crew; Rep Frsh Cls; Bsktbl; Stat Sftbl; Cit Awd; Pres Acad Fit Awd; Hgh Hnrs-Geom Gldn St Exm; Soc Sci Awd; Outstndng Spnsh Stu Awd; CSF; CJSF; Bus.

KOPICKA, JARMILA S; Rubidoux HS; Riverside, CA; (4); 40/575; AFS; Rep Jr Cls; Powder Puff Ftbl; Stat Wrstlng; High Hon Roll; Hon Roll; Badminton MVP; GATE Clb Pltcl Sci Clb; Prm Cmmtte; U Of CA Riverside; Bus Admin.

KOPIKO, KAREN; S F Christian HS; San Francisco, CA; (4); 1/20; School Play; Pres Soph Cls; Pres Jr Cls; Stat Bsktbl; Var L Sftbl; Vllybl; High Hon Roll; Val; Hmcmng Queen 89-90; Natl Chrstn Hnr Soc 86-90; UCLA.

KOPP, ELIZABETH M; Casa Grande HS; Petaluma, CA; (1); Letterman Clb; Varsity Clb; Var Trk; Hon Roll; NHS; Pres Acad Fit Awd; Gymnastics Northern CA Lvl 6 ST Vault; Rcgnzd Outstndng Achvt Bio, Global Studies, Phys Ed 89-90; Sports Med.

KOPP, KIMBERLEIGH N; Serra JR-SR HS; San Diego, CA; (3); 18/391; Drama Clb; French Clb; Capt Drill Tm; Nwsp; Cit Awd; Hon Roll; Peer Tutor; Poetry Awd; Psych.

KOPPEL, AHRIN B; Apple Valley HS; Apple Valley, CA; (1); Pep Clb; Ski Clb; Spanish Clb; VP Frsh Cls; Cheerldng; Gym; High Hon Roll; CSF; Arch.

KORAKAS, ANNA M; Modesto HS; Modesto, CA; (3); AFS; Church Yth Grp; Drama Clb; French Clb; Key Clb; Ski Clb; Color Guard; Flag Corp; Var Gym; Var Trk; Coll; Accounting.

KORDIS, CANDI; Escondido HS; Ephrata, WA; (2); Church Yth Grp; Teachers Aide; Drill Tm; JV Capt Bsktbl; Var Trk; JV Vllybl; Hon Roll; Pres Acad Fit Awd; SAFTYE; Hrsbck Rdng; Law.

KORDOSKY, JENNIFER; Oxnard HS; Oxnard, CA; (2); 8/604; Pep Clb; Yrbk; Var Tennis; High Hon Roll; Prfct Atten Awd; Soc Of Woman Engrs Math Awd; CSF; 1st Pl Typing Cont 88-89; Acad Ltr; U CA Berkeley.

KORFMACHER, KURT A; Redlands SR HS; Redlands, CA; (3); 30/930; Boy Scts; German Clb; Letterman Clb; Library Aide; Band; School Musical; Nwsp; Var L Crs Cntry; JV Trk; High Hon Roll; CSF; All-Sthrn CA & All-San Bernardino Co Hnr Bnds; UC-SANTA Barbara; Bio.

KORING, KELLY MARIE; Bear River HS; Grass Valley, CA; (4); 10/160; Church Yth Grp; Letterman Clb; SADD; Church Choir; Yrbk; Rep Frsh Cls; Rep Soph Cls; Rep Jr Cls; Stat Bsbl; JV Var Bsktbl; Chrmn & Cnslr CASC; CA Pol San Lui Obispo; Grph Ds.

KORKKO, KIMBERLY A; Alta Loma HS; Alta Loma, CA; (3); 65/522; Church Yth Grp; Cmnty Wkr; Dance Clb; FTA; GAA; Pep Clb; Ski Clb; Spanish Clb; Teachers Aide; Varsity Clb; CA Jr Mss Yng Wmn Yr St Fnlst; UC Irvine; Elem Educ.

KORNBLUTH, DAVID A; Trabuco Hills HS; El Toro, CA; (2); Pep Clb; Spanish Clb; SADD; Varsity Clb; JV Swmmng; Hon Roll; Water Polo.

KORNELL, NATHAN H; Santa Barbara HS; Santa Barbara, CA; (2); 33/430; JV Bsktbl; Var Vllybl; High Hon Roll.

KOROCK, NICOLE; Southbay Christian Schl; Sunnyvale, CA; (4); 5/30; Church Yth Grp; Pep Clb; Chorus; Church Choir; School Musical; School Play; Sec Soph Cls; Sec Sr Cls; Var Cheerldng; VP CSF; Yth Cncl Sec.

KOROMAH, ELI; Fontana HS; Fontana, CA; (3); Cmnty Wkr; Chorus; Trk; Hon Roll; Accntng.

KORSMEIER, ALISON; Berean Christian HS; Concord, CA; (1); Church Yth Grp; Sec Frsh Cls; Stu Cncl; JV Cheerldng; Var Sftbl; Hon Roll.

KORTEERAKUL, ISRIYA E; Pasadena HS; Pasadena, CA; (3); Church Yth Grp; English Clb; French Clb; Girl Scts; Acpl Chr; Chorus; Church Choir; Drm Mjr(t); Off Jr Cls; Swmmng; Badminton; Bangkok Chldrn Chorus; UCLA; Arch.

KORTH, TESS; St Joseph Notre Dame HS; Hayward, CA; (4); Cmnty Wkr; French Clb; FHA; Library Aide; Pep Clb; Red Cross Aide; SADD; Teachers Aide; Pres Frsh Cls; Stu Cncl; Red Cross Awd Erthquake 89 Dmg Assmnt; Natl French Cntst; Natl Wmns Pltcl Caucus Awd; Intl Htl Mngmnt.

KORTHAUER, DANA M; Dana Hills HS; Laguna Niguel, CA; (1); Church Yth Grp; Hon Roll; Pres Acad Fit Awd; NW Talent Srch IN SATS; Anestelsgist.

KORTZ, SUSANNE; Dos Pueblos HS; Goleta, CA; (3); 4/338; Church Yth Grp; French Clb; Intnl Clb; Math Clb; Science Clb; High Hon Roll; NHS; 2nd Prz St Art Cont; Arch.

KOSINSKI, KIMBERLY M; Atwater HS; Atwater, CA; (1); FBLA; Key Clb; Boston U; Law.

KOSKELA, YVONNE S; Workman HS; West Covina, CA; (2); Intnl Clb; Science Clb; Mrchg Band; Hon Roll; District Scholar; Tri-M Music Hnr Society; Outstndng Sophomore Band.

KOSKELIN, JENNIFER LEE; College Park HS; Martinez, CA; (4); 25/311; Church Yth Grp; German Clb; JA; Band; Rep Soph Cls; Var Sftbl; Var Tennis; Var Trk; Hon Roll; Pres Acad Fit Awd; Teen Entrtnmnt Corp; Amnsty Intl; Yth Ed Pgm; Santa Clara U.

KOSKI, JODY; Fort Bragg HS; Santa Rosa, CA; (4); #4 In Class; Stage Crew; Yrbk; Var Tennis; High Hon Roll; Hon Roll; CSF; AIFS; Santa Rosa JC; Math.

KOSMALA, JULIE A; Santa Teresa HS; San Jose, CA; (3); Science Clb; Ski Clb; Varsity Clb; Swmmng; KSTS; Swmmng Achvt Awds; UC Santa Barbara; Med.

KOSMATKA, MICHAEL W; Moorpark HS; Moorpark, CA; (2); Art Clb; Math Tm; Cal Poly San Luis Obispo; Arch.

KOSOFSKY, KAREN; Montclair College Prep; Encino, CA; (3); Pep Clb; Ski Clb; Stu Cncl; JV Bsktbl; Capt Var Cheerldng; Var Pom Pon; Var Sftbl; JV Var Vllybl; Hon Roll; NHS.

KOSOL, EVE A; Homestead HS; Los Altos, CA; (1); Color Guard.

KOSONSANONG, VICHAY S; Bassett HS; La Puente, CA; (2); Art Clb; French Clb; FBLA; Bsktbl; Powder Puff Ftbl; Vllybl; Gov Hon Prg Awd; High Hon Roll; Hon Roll; Jr NHS; UCLA; Med.

KOSONSANONG, VILAY; Bassett HS; La Puente, CA; (3); French Clb; FBLA; Intnl Clb; Treas Jr Cls; Gov Hon Prg Awd; Hon Roll; Treas NHS; Hnr Guard Grad 90; Varsit Badmitton; Bus.

KOSS, LESLIE ANN; University Of San Diego HS; Rancho La Costa, CA; (4); Church Yth Grp; Cmnty Wkr; Ed Mgr Yrbk; Lit Mag; JV Swmmng; High Hon Roll; Pres Acad Fit Awd; Congrssnl Schlr Natl Young Ldrs Conf; Comptv Figure Skater; U Of San Diego; US Coast Guard.

KOSTRIKIN, LIZA V; Santa Rosa HS; Santa Rosa, CA; (4); VP Art Clb; Church Yth Grp; Math Tm; Spanish Clb; Orch; School Musical; School Play; Hon Roll; Santa Rosa JC Doyle Occuptnl Ed Awd; CSF Life Mbr; Santa Rosa JC; Accntng.

KOSTUCHEK, TANYA J; San Francisco Christian Schl; San Francisco, CA; (4); Church Yth Grp; Drama Clb; Teachers Aide; Chorus; Church Choir; Rptr Nwsp; Yrbk; Treas Sr Cls; High Hon Roll; Hon Roll; Prncpls List; Merit Roll; Cert Of Merit; San Francisco ST.

KOTAKI, KAORI; Pioneer HS; San Jose, CA; (4); French Clb; VP FBLA; Math Clb; Science Clb; Service Clb; Teachers Aide; High Hon Roll; Hon Roll; NHS; Pres Acad Fit Awd; Peet Tutoring Assoc Orgnzr; Tutoring Schlrshp; CA Schlrshp Fed; Hnr & Svc Clb; Intrct Clb; San Jose ST U; Comp Engr.

KOTECHA, ANAND; South Tahoe HS; S Lake Tahoe, CA; (3); Tennis; High Hon Roll; Hon Roll; CSF; Vkng TV; UCLA; Bus.

KOTELES, JAMES A; Lodi HS; Lodi, CA; (2); Boy Scts; Science Clb; Acpl Chr; Mrchg Band; Pep Band; Hon Roll; VP Culture & Lit Clb; VP Envrnmntl Awrnss Clb; UC Berkeley; Poly Sci.

KOTHMAN, GREGORY P; Big Pine HS; Big Pine, CA; (2); Church Yth Grp; Ski Clb; Var Bsbl; Var Crs Cntry; Cit Awd; Hon Roll; Suprntndnts Spcl Recgntn Outstndng Citizen.

KOTOWSKI, ANDREW F; Bellarmine College Prep; Campbell, CA; (3); Computer Clb; Letterman Clb; Red Cross Aide; Service Clb; SADD; Teachers Aide; Stat Bsktbl; Ntl Merit SF; Law.

KOTTAS, KASIE; Bellflower HS; Bellflower, CA; (4); 8/250; Cmnty Wkr; GAA; Letterman Clb; Office Aide; Scholastic Bowl; Ed Nwsp; Rep Frsh Cls; Sec Soph Cls; Sec Jr Cls; Sec Stu Cncl; Bank Of Amer Outstng HS Stu Engl; Tandy Most Outstng Sci Stu; Bellflower Womans Clb Schlrshp Wnnr; CA ST Long Beach; Social Wrk.

KOTZMAN, WILLIAM K; Loyola HS; Los Angeles, CA; (1); Church Yth Grp; JV Socr; JV Vllybl; Hon Roll; Outstndng Stu In Cls; HS Mrt Schlrshp; Med Sci.

KOUNAS, JASON P; San Gorgonio HS; Highland, CA; (4); Letterman Clb; Spanish Clb; Teachers Aide; Varsity Clb; Var JV Bsbl; Ftbl; Powder Puff Ftbl; Wt Lftg; JV Wrstlng; Hon Roll; Coached Powder Puff Ftbl Tm; Coaches Awd For Bsbl; Phy-Ed.

KOURY, VANESSA M; Notre Dame Acad; Los Angeles, CA; (4); 7/100; Treas Sec Debate Tm; Drama Clb; NFL; Treas Sec Speech Tm; School Play; Stage Crew; Cit Awd; French Hon Soc; High Hon Roll; Hon Roll; ST Stu Congress Qlfr; Sec/Treas Queens Cncl; CSF; JSA Smmr Sch 89 At Georgetown; Georgetown U; Pol Sci.

KOUSSER, RACHEL M; John Muir HS; Altadena, CA; (4); Dance Clb; Pres French Clb; Pres Service Clb; Drill Tm; Flag Corp; Ed Yrbk; Ed Lit Mag; Ntl Merit SF; Acadmc Dcthln Tm; Sci Fair-1st Prz-Bio Sci Div; Lit.

KOUSSER, THAD B; John Muir HS; Altadena, CA; (2); 1/400; Sprt Ed Nwsp; Ed Lit Mag; Var Swmmng; Var Wt Lftg; Interact Clb Bd & Treas; Var Swm Team MVP; Pacific Leag 100 Yd Bckstrk Chmpn; Politician.

KOUYOUMJIAN, VASKIN; La Salle HS; Sierra Madre, CA; (4); 7/80; Chess Clb; Computer Clb; Math Clb; Pep Clb; Science Clb; Service Clb; Band; Chorus; Jazz Band; Pep Band; Alpha Delta Mu Art Soc Pres; Magna Cum Laude; CA Polytech U Pomona.

KOVACH, ELENA M; Santa Clara HS; Santa Clara, CA; (2); Church Yth Grp; JV Tennis; Var Trk; Super Svc Awd; Chmpnshp Cert-Athltc Leag; Span II/Iii Excllnc Merit Awd.

KOVACH, GERDA H; Azusa HS; Azusa, CA; (4); 23/187; Church Yth Grp; Letterman Clb; Office Aide; Teachers Aide; Varsity Clb; Var Sftbl; Hon Roll; NHS; ASCC Schlrshp Citrus Coll; Citrus Azusa Pacific U; Rn.

KOVACH, MATT A; Huntington Beach HS; Huntington Beach, CA; (3); Model UN; Var L Crs Cntry; JV L Trk; High Hon Roll; CSF.

KOVACK, BERNADETTE G; Immaculate Heart HS; Montrose, CA; (2); Church Yth Grp; Chorus; U Of CA Los Angeles; Paralegal.

KOVACS, KATALIN A; Nogales HS; La Puente, CA; (3); 171/542; Teachers Aide; Chorus; Off Jr Cls; Merits Award; Certificat Jobs Course; Teacher Leg Secretary.

KOVACS, TIMOTHY R; Novato HS; Sierra Vista, AZ; (2); Boy Scts; Church Yth Grp; Band; Jazz Band; Mrchg Band; Pep Band; School Musical; JV Ftbl; Hon Roll; Golden St Exam High Hnrs Geom; BYU; Math.

KOVAR, JANA L; Village Christian Schls; Glendale, CA; (3); Mu Alpha Theta; Band; Drm Mjr(t); Jazz Band; Mrchg Band; Pep Band; Bsktbl; Var Sftbl; Var Vllybl; OR ST U; Pre Med.

KOWAL, TENA M; Roosevelt HS; Fresno, CA; (1); Am Leg Aux Girls St; Church Yth Grp; Church Choir; School Play; JV Swmmng; Cit Awd; High Hon Roll; Hon Roll; Ballet Jazz Dance; Awd CSUF Invtnl; Law.

KOWAL, VINCENT C; Workman HS; La Puente, CA; (2); Hon Roll; Art Ctr Coll Of Dsgn; Archt.

KOWALAK, CHRISTIE L; Pioneer HS; San Jose, CA; (3); German Clb; Swmmng; YMCA; U CA Davis; Vet.

KOWARDY, KEVIN J; Oak Ridge HS; Rescue, CA; (1); Music Piano; Drums; Math.

KOYAMA, JASON K; Venice HS; Los Angeles, CA; (2); Boy Scts; Church Yth Grp; Cmnty Wkr; Orch; Hon Roll; Opt Clb Awd; Prfct Atten Awd.

KOZAR, MICHAEL A; Fillmore HS; Fillmore, CA; (4); Letterman Clb; Bsbl; Ftbl; All-Ventura Cnty Bsbl & Ftbl; Woodbury U; Arch.

KOZELCHIK, ZOLISSA A; Pasadena HS; Pasadena, CA; (3); Church Yth Grp; L Acpl Chr; Church Choir; School Musical; Var L Bsktbl; JV Var Sftbl; Var Trk; Hon Roll; Pres Acad Fit Awd; CSF; Med.

KOZIKOWSKI, ERIC M; Indio HS; Indio, CA; (1); FFA; Band; Ftbl; Wt Lftg.

KOZIN, ILYA; Fairfax HS; Van Nuys, CA; (2); Cit Awd; Hon Roll.

KOZLAK, MICHELLE; Woodbridge HS; Irvine, CA; (3); 57/425; Cmnty Wkr; Drama Clb; Key Clb; Service Clb; School Play; Cheerldng; Hon Roll; CSF 89; Most Vlble Pepstr Awd 89-90; Frgn Lang.

KOZONO, DAVID E; Walnut HS; Walnut, CA; (2); 1/475; Debate Tm; French Clb; Key Clb; Service Clb; Off Soph Cls; CSF; GATE; Sci Fictn; Top Score AHSME Tst Schl 90; Doctor.

KOZUCH, TONY J; St Ignatius College Prep; San Francisco, CA; (3); 19/243; Pres Service Clb; Chorus; Jazz Band; Orch; Pep Band; Stu Cncl; JV Crs Cntry; Var JV Golf; JV Tennis; Pep Clb; Intrntl Bus.

KOZUKA, MAYU; Carlmont HS; Belmont, CA; (3); 2/280; Cmnty Wkr; Pres GAA; Office Aide; Rptr Nwsp; VP Sr Cls; JV Tennis; Hon Roll; Vrsty Badmntn.

KRAAI, RYAN E; Rio Mesa HS; Camarillo, CA; (3); Boy Scts; JV Vllybl; Fire Cadet Pgm; Engr.

KRAFFT, ANGELINA M; Andrew Hill HS; San Jose, CA; (1); Bsbl; Bsktbl; Sftbl; Swmmng; Hon Roll; Pres Acad Fit Awd; Advncd Math Prgm; Med Magnet Prgm; Berkeley; Astrnt.

KRAFT, DIANA; Apple Valley HS; Apple Valley, CA; (4); 1/435; French Clb; Pres Key Clb; Spanish Clb; Pres Stu Cncl; Var Cheerldng; Cit Awd; Val; CSF Pres; San Bernardino Cnty Suns All-Cnty Acad Team; Jnr Statesmn America Fndr/Pres; Stanford U; Intl Rltns.

KRAFT, JOY; Agoura HS; Westlake Village, CA; (2); SADD Co-Pres.

KRAFT, KELLY D; Valley Christian Acad; Santa Maria, CA; (4); 7/17; Church Yth Grp; Office Aide; Teachers Aide; School Play; Rptr Nwsp; Rptr Yrbk; Pres Sr Cls; Pres Stu Cncl; Var Capt Bsbl; Var L Bsktbl; Coast Vly All-Conf Team-Ftbl/2nd Team Bsbl; Pensacola Christn; Bus.

KRAFT, KEVIN J; Apple Valley HS; Apple Valley, CA; (1); Key Clb; JV Tennis; Jr Statesmen Of Amer; CSF.

KRAFT, LISA M; Fairfield HS; Fairfield, CA; (2); Church Yth Grp; GAA; JV Crs Cntry; Var Sftbl; Cit Awd; Psych.

KRAGH, KATHY; Rio Mesa HS; Camarillo, CA; (3); Church Yth Grp; Cmnty Wkr; Dance Clb; Drama Clb; 4-H; Intnl Clb; Math Tm; Pep Clb; Service Clb; Teachers Aide; Gymnstcs Coach; Peer Cnslr; Engl Ed.

KRAHNKE, RICHARD; Foothill HS; Pleasanton, CA; (4); 32/321; Church Yth Grp; Intnl Clb; Teachers Aide; Rep Stu Cncl; JV Bsbl; Var JV Ftbl; Ice Hcky; High Hon Roll; Hon Roll; St Schlr; U Of CT; Biochem.

KRAKER, DARREN; Bonita Vista HS; Bonita, CA; (3); High Hon Roll; Hon Roll; Bus.

KRAKLOW, ALAN J; Claremont HS; San Diego, CA; (3); 46/208; Var L Swmmng; Waterpolo MVP & Co-Capt; Mesa Coll; Marine Sci.

KRALEVICH, NICHOLAS N; Kerman HS; Kerman, CA; (2); 1/180; Math Tm; Spanish Clb; Band; Rep Jr Cls; High Hon Roll; JETS Awd; Math Exam Awd; UC Davis; Engr.

KRALJEV, DARREN M; Sacred Heart Prep; San Carlos, CA; (3); Cmnty Wkr; Computer Clb; Var Tennis; High Hon Roll; Hon Roll; NHS; Music Tchrs Assn CA Cert Mrt Achvt Stdy Piano Level 5; MIT; Comp Sci.

KRAMER, BRIAN D; Independence HS; San Jose, CA; (2); Var Socr; Gate Stu; Santa Cura U; Graphic Arts.

KRAMER, BRYAN J; Pioneer HS; San Jose, CA; (1); Boy Scts; Service Clb; Spanish Clb; Temple Yth Grp; Band; Jazz Band; Treas Frsh Cls; Var Tennis; High Hon Roll; CSF; San Jose City Mayors Yth Cncl; Sch Pgm Imprvmnt Cncl; U CA; Law.

KRAMER, DAVID W; Tomales HS; Point Reyes Stati, CA; (3).

KRAMER, LAURA A; Berkeley HS; Berkeley, CA; (3); High Hon Roll; Crew Team; Engl.

KRAMER, LONNIE T; Burroughs HS; Ridgecrest, CA; (3); Church Yth Grp; Debate Tm; JCL; Latin Clb; NFL; Hon Roll; NHS; Pres Acad Fit Awd; MUN; Mock Trl; UNLV; Diplomatic Trnsltr.

KRAMER, STACIA S; Diamond Bar HS; Chino Hills, CA; (4); Fullerton JC; Csmtlgy.

KRAMER, SUZANNE L; Patrick Henry HS; San Diego, CA; (3); Hosp Aide; Model UN; Quiz Bowl; Lit Mag; Jr NHS; Ntl Merit SF; Pres Acad Fit Awd; Drama Prod Cls; WA ST U; Drama.

KRAMLING, ERIC; Fred C Beyer HS; Modesto, CA; (3); Debate Tm; German Clb; Sec Key Clb; NFL; Ski Clb; Speech Tm; Rep Frsh Cls; Var Golf; Hon Roll; Bus.

KRANE, SONJA; Torrey Pines HS; Del Mar, CA; (2); 19/503; French Clb; Hosp Aide; Speech Tm; JV Cheerldng; JV Crs Cntry; Var L Gym; Hon Roll; Math.

KRANTZ, BRANDI R; Woodbridge HS; Irvine, CA; (4); 1/400; English Clb; French Clb; Pep Clb; Science Clb; Pres Temple Yth Grp; Rep Stu Cncl; Var Capt Swmmng; Hon Roll; Pres Jr NHS; Ntl Merit SF; Liberal Arts.

KRANTZ, MYRA K; Calaveras HS; San Andreas, CA; (3); 5/160; Varsity Clb; VICA; JV Var Bsktbl; JV Var Sftbl; JV Var Vllybl; High Hon Roll; Hon Roll; Voctnl Olympics 2nd Pl; Chico ST U; Engr.

KRANZ, KIRSTEN A; Clear Lake HS; Lakeport, CA; (3); Chorus; School Musical; JV Var Cheerldng; High Hon Roll; Pres Acad Fit Awd; Val; CSF; U Of CA; Marine Sci.

KRANZBERG, JENNIFER L; Desert Christian HS; Lancaster, CA; (1); Church Yth Grp; Drama Clb; Chorus; School Play; Crs Cntry; Sftbl; Cit Awd; Hon Roll; Drama Clb Pres; Actng.

KRANZBERG, JOSEPH E; Antelope Valley HS; Lancaster, CA; (2); Church Yth Grp; JV Ftbl; Wt Lftg; Cit Awd; Hon Roll; Missions.

KRANZLER, MYKEAH; Santa Clara HS; Saratoga, CA; (3); Yrbk; Powder Puff Ftbl; Hon Roll; Rotary Awd; Broadcasting.

KRATT, KIMBERLY C; Clovis HS; Clovis, CA; (3); Stage Crew; Sftbl; High Hon Roll; Hon Roll; Fresno ST; Bus.

KRATZ, DOUGLAS L; Burbank HS; Glendale, CA; (3); VP Key Clb; Letterman Clb; Pres Treas Frsh Cls; VP Soph Cls; JV Var Swmmng; High Hon Roll; Pres Acad Fit Awd.

KRATZER, TINA M; San Pasqual HS; Escondido, CA; (2); FFA; Cal Poly San Luis Obispo; Vet.

KRAUDE, DREW; Galt HS; Galt, CA; (3); 33/226; Church Yth Grp; Cmnty Wkr; Teachers Aide; L Var Bsbl; L Capt Bsktbl; L Var Socr; L Var Trk; Hon Roll; Bsktbl Schl Rcrd 19 Pts Gm; Vrsty Bsbl Bat .417 Seasn; Gldn St Exm Geom Recgntn; Law Enfrcmnt.

KRAUS, SCOTT M; Cajon HS; San Bernardino, CA; (3); Quiz Bowl; Rep Frsh Cls; Rep Soph Cls; Var L Bsbl; Var L Crs Cntry; Var L Socr; Cit Awd; Rotary Awd; CA ST U; Exec Advrtsng.

KRAUSE, AARON E; Edison HS; Huntington Beach, CA; (1); Boy Scts; Model UN; Band; Mrchg Band; Hon Roll; USC.

KRAUSE, DONALD E; Chino HS; Chino, CA; (2); 55/658; Church Yth Grp; Bsbl; JV Bsktbl; High Hon Roll; Hon Roll; Pres Acad Fit Awd; Mst Inspiratnl Plyr JV Bsktbl 89-90; Comp Sci.

KRAUSE, DOROTHY L; Gladstone HS; Azusa, CA; (4); 8/250; Church Yth Grp; Band; Jazz Band; Mrchg Band; Pep Band; Bsktbl; Vllybl; High Hon Roll; Hon Roll; NHS; Cngrssnl Yth Ldrshp Cncl Cngrssnl Schlr; Most Imprvd Band Awd 87; Bnk Amer Fine Arts Awd 90; U Of Southern CA; Arch.

KRAUSE, JOSEPH N; Saint Ignatius College Prep; San Francisco, CA; (3); 35/266; Drama Clb; Pep Clb; Service Clb; Thesps; Band; Pep Band; School Play; Nwsp; Var Lcrss; Hon Roll; Plays Guitar, Piano; Crfew Team; Jensen Schlrshp Awd 3 Yrs.

KRAUSE, KAREN S; Bullard HS; Fresno, CA; (1); FCA; Var Gym; Hon Roll; Pres Acad Fit Awd; Gymnastics St Chmpn Lvl 8 90; MVP Clovis Acad Gymnastics 90.

KRAUSE, KARINE; Novato HS; San Rafael, CA; (2); Church Yth Grp; Drama Clb; Teachers Aide; Church Choir; School Play; High Hon Roll; Hon Roll; Pres Acad Fit Awd; CSF; Yth Alive.

KRAUSE, KARL A; Novato HS; San Rafael, CA; (2); Boy Scts; Church Yth Grp; Cmnty Wkr; Drama Clb; ROTC; Spanish Clb; Crs Cntry; Ftbl; Elks Awd; Drama Team At Church; Pilot.

KRAUSE, MOLLY T; San Lorenzo Valley HS; Boulder Creek, CA; (2); Girl Scts; Spanish Clb; Hon Roll; Frdy Nght Lv Clb.

KRAUSE, REBECCA ANN; College Park HS; Pleasant Hill, CA; (3); Church Yth Grp; Letterman Clb; Service Clb; Varsity Clb; Church Choir; Variety Show; Var Co-Capt Bsktbl; Var Trk; High Hon Roll; Hon Roll; Won Schl PTA Cntst; Art Awds; Mst Imprvd JR Yr Trck; Brigham Yng U; Math.

KRAUSS, STEPHEN; San Ramon Valley HS; Danville, CA; (3); Intrml Bsktbl; JV Var Ftbl; Bus.

KRAWEZ, BRIAN A; Dublin HS; Dublin, CA; (3); FBLA; Ed Nwsp; JV Crs Cntry; Var Swmmng; JV Wrstlng; High Hon Roll; Hon Roll; Mck Trl; CSF; Interact; U Of Berkeley; Law.

KREAGER, JEANNE M; Whittier Christian HS; La Habra Heights, CA; (2); 19/185; Church Yth Grp; French Clb; Sec Frsh Cls; JV Tennis; Stat Vllybl; Prfct Atten Awd; St Schlr; Surf Clb & Tm.

KRECHMER, DANIEL P; Palo Alto HS; Palo Alto, CA; (4); Boy Scts; Cmnty Wkr; Drama Clb; Thesps; Chorus; School Musical; School Play; Stage Crew; Lit Mag; Boston U; Drama.

KREIDE, ANITA T; Bishop Montgomery HS; Lawndale, CA; (3); Boy Scts; Hosp Aide; Ski Clb; Bsktbl; Hon Roll; Yth & Govt YWCA; Cert Med Termnplgst; Eng Achvt Dept Awd; UCLA.

KREIDEN, NINA; Monte Vista HS; Walnut Creek, CA; (3); 54/356; Church Yth Grp; SADD; Teachers Aide; High Hon Roll; Hon Roll; Dept Of Englsh Awd; Bus Admin.

KREIDL, KEN; Aragon HS; San Mateo, CA; (4); JA; Sprt Ed Nwsp; VP Jr Cls; Var L Socr; Capt L Tennis; Elks Awd; High Hon Roll; Pres Acad Fit Awd; Water Polo Capt Vrsty Letter; Princeton U; Sports Med.

KREIL, JEFFREY E; Bolsa Grande HS; Garden Grove, CA; (2); Drama Clb; Spanish Clb; Rep Frsh Cls; Rep Soph Cls; JV Bsktbl; Var Swmmng; Hon Roll; Med.

KREITZ JR, RICHARD C; Lutheran HS; Upland, CA; (3); ROTC; Var Bsktbl; Var Capt Ftbl; Var Trk; JV Wrstlng; Hstry.

KRELL, SHERRY L; Encina HS; Sacramento, CA; (3); 1/212; Cmnty Wkr; Treas VP Spanish Clb; SADD; Rptr Nwsp; Ed Lit Mag; Sec Jr Cls; Var L Sftbl; Cit Awd; High Hon Roll; Opt Clb Awd; Aerosp Engr.

KREMENLIEV, MIGUEL; Ygnacio Valley HS; Concord, CA; (3); 3/450; Spanish Clb; Varsity Clb; Var Swmmng; Wt Lftg; Bausch & Lomb Sci Awd; High Hon Roll; Hon Roll; Var Water Polo.

KREMPELY, MICHELLE; Roseville Joint Union HS; Rocklin, CA; (1); Church Yth Grp; Drama Clb; German Clb; Red Cross Aide; JV Vllybl; Cit Awd; Hon Roll; Cvl Air Ptrl AF Axlry; Stu Ambsdr Prgms Frndshp Caravan; AF Acad; Aero Engr.

KRENG, VIRANY M; Ramona Convent Secondary Schl; Monterey Park, CA; (3); Art Clb; Cmnty Wkr; Red Cross Aide; Rptr Nwsp; Treas Soph Cls; High Hon Roll; NHS; Ntl Merit Ltr; CSF; Philomathean Soc; Med.

KRENGEL, KIRSTIN N; Santa Clara HS; Santa Clara, CA; (3); Spanish Clb; Band; Mrchg Band; Powder Puff Ftbl; Var L Swmmng; Hon Roll; All-Amrcn Smmng 87 & 89; Spnsh Mrt Awd 87 & 89.

KRENTZ, ANNAMARIE; Upper Lake HS; Nice, CA; (3); Church Yth Grp; FBLA; Library Aide; Spanish Clb; Teachers Aide; Hon Roll; Prfct Atten Awd; Bus.

KRESGE, KIMBERLY; Hilltop HS; Chula Vista, CA; (4); Church Yth Grp; Cmnty Wkr; Dance Clb; Drama Clb; French Clb; Intnl Clb; Pep Clb; SADD; Variety Show; Var Cheerldng; USIU; Dnc Chorgrph.

KRESTA, CARIE M; Corona SR HS; Corona, CA; (2); 72/450; Church Yth Grp; Drama Clb; Office Aide; Yrbk; Var Mgr(s); Score Keeper; JV Socr; Var Tennis; Hon Roll; Vlntr Los Angeles Zoo; UC Davis; Vet Med.

KRESTA, TAMMY; Redwood HS; Visalia, CA; (3); Church Yth Grp; Cmnty Wkr; Drama Clb; German Clb; Math Clb; Math Tm; Chorus; School Musical; School Play; Ed Nwsp; Wrk Pblshed In Natl Library Of Poetry Bk Of Anthology; Mock Trial; Acad Decathelon; UC Los Angeles; Brdcst Jrnlsm.

KRIEG, JESSICA L; Turlock HS; Turlock, CA; (2); #49 In Class; JV Sftbl; Var Tennis; Block T Clb.

KRIEGER, ROBIN J; Claremont HS; Claremont, CA; (3); Q&S; Stage Crew; Ed Nwsp; JV Crs Cntry; JV Trk; DAR Awd; Hon Roll; Pres Acad Fit Awd; Amnesty Intl; Acad Decathalon.

KRIENS, PAULA; Yucaipa HS; Yucaipa, CA; (1); Spanish Clb; Yrbk; JV Bsktbl; CSF; Comp.

KRINER, HEATHER R; Foothill HS; Pleasanton, CA; (3); 28/290; Math Clb; Service Clb; SADD; Teachers Aide; Band; Mrchg Band; Pep Band; French Hon Soc; Hon Roll; Jr NHS; CSF; Cum GAP Recogntn; Outstndng Phys Ed Achvt; Mrktng.

KRISCHER, BRADLEY D; San Rafael HS; San Rafael, CA; (3); 25/225; Am Leg Boys St; SADD; Temple Yth Grp; JV Ftbl; Var Golf; Var Swmmng; Hon Roll; U CA; Bus Adm.

KRISHNA, ANAND; Sunny Hills HS; La Palma, CA; (3); 41/430; Cmnty Wkr; Debate Tm; Pres Intnl Clb; Temple Yth Grp; Var L Crs Cntry; Var L Trk; High Hon Roll; Jr Statesmen Of Amer; Intl Baccalaureate Pgm; Psych.

KRISHNA, FELIX; Capuchino HS; San Bruno, CA; (2); Church Yth Grp; Letterman Clb; Office Aide; Bsktbl; Ftbl; Mgr(s); Score Keeper; Tennis; Hon Roll; UNLV; Bus Law.

KRISHNAMURTHY, USHA; Whitney HS; Lakewood, CA; (3); FBLA; Hosp Aide; Library Aide; Office Aide; Yrbk; High Hon Roll; Indian Classical Dance & Music; Piano; Psych.

KRISHNAN, DEV A; Pittsburgh HS; Pittsburg, CA; (2); 17/304; Church Yth Grp; SADD; VP Rep Jr Cls; JV Bsbl; JV Bsktbl; JV Tennis; JV Trk; High Hon Roll; Prfct Atten Awd; Italian Travel Clb; Stu Congress Rep; Hnrs Core.

KRISHNAREDDY, SUMANA; Huntington Beach HS; Huntington Beach, CA; (1); Debate Tm; Model UN; Speech Tm; Band; Mrchg Band; Orch; Pep Band; School Musical; Phtg Ed Yrbk.

KRISHNASWAMY, RAHUL S; El Dorado HS; Yorba Linda, CA; (2); 1/340; Boy Scts; Cmnty Wkr; Hosp Aide; Intnl Clb; Treas Science Clb; Temple Yth Grp; JV Bsktbl; High Hon Roll; NHS; Pres Acad Fit Awd; CSF; Mock Trial Pre Trial Atty; HOBY Ambssdr; UCLA; Polticl Sci.

KRISTIANSEN, DENISE A; Victor Valley HS; Victorville, CA; (3); Hosp Aide; ROTC; Hon Roll; Dept Cmmndtn Scl Sci; Cert Apprctn George AFB Family Svcs; Vlntr Month; UNLV; Bus.

KRISTIANSEN, KARSTEN S; Strathmore Union HS; Porterville, CA; (4); 1/70; Debate Tm; Letterman Clb; Speech Tm; SADD; Teachers Aide; Varsity Clb; Socr; Cit Awd; Elks Awd; High Hon Roll; Stanford U; Med.

KRISTOVICH, DINELLE M; South San Francisco HS; South San Francis, CA; (4); Dance Clb; Drama Clb; Treas FBLA; Stage Crew; Acad Awd Achvt 3.0-3.49 GPA; Awd Mst Imprvd Wrtng Prjct Write Pgm; Water Ski; Accntng.

KRITNER, ANN M; Century HS; Santa Ana, CA; (2); Church Yth Grp; Dance Clb; Model UN; Variety Show; Stu Cncl; Bsbl; Trk; Hon Roll; Hnrs Prjcts Awd; Outstndng Stu Advrtsmnt; Davis; Law.

KRITZER, AMY J; Granada Hills HS; Northridge, CA; (3); VP Girl Scts; JA; SADD; Teachers Aide; VP Temple Yth Grp; Drill Tm; Rptr Nwsp; Rep Frsh Cls; High Hon Roll; Hon Roll; Stanford; Comm.

KRITZER, HEATHER L; Poway HS; Poway, CA; (4); 153/689; SADD; Varsity Clb; Ed Nwsp; Off Jr Cls; Rep Sr Cls; Var L Sftbl; Var L Tennis; High Hon Roll; Hon Roll; Area Pnhllnc Schlshp Wnnr; Voted MVP Sftbll Tm; Chsn All League 1st Tm Sftbll; U Of AZ; Pblc Admin.

KRIVITZ, CHRISTIE; El Capitan HS; Lakeside, CA; (4); 16/425; Church Yth Grp; Cmnty Wkr; Key Clb; Letterman Clb; Pres Pep Clb; Sec Service Clb; SADD; Teachers Aide; Varsity Clb; Variety Show; Rgnls & Natls CA St Delg; Amnstry Intrntl Clb; Pepperdien U; Commncnts.

KRIZEK, LAURA LIN; Saugus HS; Saugus, CA; (3); 5/450; Teachers Aide; Hon Roll; CSF; Outstndng Frnch Stu Awd; Stanford; Law.

KRIZO, PHAEDRA; Tulelake HS; Tulelake, CA; (4); Drama Clb; FBLA; Sec Ski Clb; Teachers Aide; School Play; Var JV Bsktbl; JV L Cheerldng; Var Vllybl; High Hon Roll; Fri Night Live; UC Santa Barbara; Actng.

KROEGER, DEREK; Santa Cruz HS; Santa Cruz, CA; (2); 1/275; Band; Mrchg Band; JV Bsktbl; JV Ftbl; JV Socr; Hon Roll; CA Schlrshp Fed; Bus.

KROEKER, CHRISTINE R; Clovis West HS; Fresno, CA; (4); 42/535; Church Yth Grp; FHA; Intnl Clb; Rptr Yrbk; High Hon Roll; Hon Roll; CA Schlrshp Fed; Forensics Tm; Fresno City Coll; Pre-Med.

KROG, KARIN L; Rim Of The World HS; Blue Jay, CA; (2); Church Yth Grp; Dance Clb; Debate Tm; Pep Clb; Teachers Aide; Chorus; Church Choir; Stu Cncl; Capt Cheerldng; Socr; U Of S CA-SANTA Barbara; Psych.

KROGSTAD, KAREN E; James Lick HS; San Jose, CA; (2); Cmnty Wkr; Drama Clb; Red Cross Aide; Stu Cncl; Bsktbl; Sftbl; Vllybl; Hon Roll; Pres Acad Fit Awd; Pedtrcn.

KROGSTAD, KIMBERLY A; James Lick HS; San Jose, CA; (3); Cmnty Wkr; Red Cross Aide; Rptr Nwsp; Off Jr Cls; Off Sr Cls; Stu Cncl; Swmmng; Hon Roll; Rotary Awd.

KROHN, CINDY; Tracy Joint Union HS; Tracy, CA; (4); 350/450; Church Yth Grp; FFA; FHA; Teachers Aide; Church Choir; Flag Corp; Hon Roll; 680 Vlntr Hrs V A Med Ctr; Ladies Axlry Veterans Frgn Wars 1537.

KROLL, KRISTINA K; Etiwanda HS; Alta Loma, CA; (2); Chess Clb; Church Yth Grp; Rep Speech Tm; Band; Mrchg Band; Pep Band; High Hon Roll; Prfct Atten Awd; Animal Rights Clb; Wind Ensmbl; Gifted/Talented Ed St Gates Or Hons; Tchr For The Deaf.

KRONBETTER, JULIE; Bullard HS; Fresno, CA; (3); Am Leg Aux Girls St; Church Yth Grp; Cmnty Wkr; FCA; Hosp Aide; Hist Key Clb; Sec Ski Clb; SADD; Rep Stu Cncl; Capt Cheerldng; Chosen To Attnd Camp Royal; CA Schlrshp Fed; HS Rep For Fresno Unifd Schl Dist Stu Advsry Bd; Santa Clara; Comm.

KROON, AMY B; Escalon HS; Escalon, CA; (2); 18/140; Church Yth Grp; German Clb; Key Clb; JV L Bsktbl; Powder Puff Ftbl; JV L Sftbl; Hon Roll; Prfct Atten Awd; Engrng.

KROON, TOD N; Escalon HS; Escalon, CA; (3); 10/144; Church Yth Grp; Cmnty Wkr; Key Clb; Var Ftbl; Var Trk; Hon Roll; Kiwanis Awd; Azuza Pacific; Sprts Med.

KROPAC, HEATHER L; Mayfield SR HS; Pasadena, CA; (3); Library Aide; SADD; Bsktbl; Hon Roll; NHS; Physcn.

KROPP, JEFF A; Chaminade College Prep; Woodland Hills, CA; (3); Art Clb; JV Ftbl; JV Trk; Wt Lftg; Hon Roll; Pres Acad Fit Awd; Sci Fair; Dancing; Horsebck Rdng.

KROS, SONYA; Monte Vista Christian HS; San Leandro, CA; (4); Church Yth Grp; Chorus; Var Swmmng; Hon Roll; Chabot CC.

KROTIK, JOANNA L; Atwater HS; Winton, CA; (1); FHA; Key Clb; Swmmng; Hon Roll; Merced Coll.

KROVAS, ELIZABETH L; Corona HS; Corona, CA; (2); Church Yth Grp; Debate Tm; Speech Tm; Chorus; Church Choir; Bsktbl; Law.

KRUECKEL, KATHY A; Bella Vista HS; Fair Oaks, CA; (3); 20/363; French Clb; Spanish Clb; Sec Stu Cncl; JV Cheerldng; Var Pom Pon; JV Var Swmmng; JV Var Tennis; Hon Roll; Schlstc Achvt Awd Sci, Soc Sci; U CA; Med.

KRUEGER, CLINT E; Carlmont HS; Belmont, CA; (3); 48/400; Cmnty Wkr; Letterman Clb; Varsity Clb; Band; Jazz Band; Pep Band; Stage Crew; Variety Show; Fld Trp; Ftbl; Socr; CPI San Luis Obispo; Aviation.

KRUEGER, JULIE A; Valhalla HS; El Cajon, CA; (2); 120/445; Church Yth Grp; Cmnty Wkr; German Clb; SADD; JV Bsktbl; L Var Swmmng; UCSD; Med.

KRUG, LEANNE; Newbury Park HS; Newbury Park, CA; (3); 11/347; Color Guard; Rep Stu Cncl; High Hon Roll; Hon Roll; Most Spiritd Awd, Var Ltr Colorgrd; Best Sprtsmnshp Awd Bobby Sox Sftbl; Plyd Sccr; Cal Poly San Luis; Arch.

KRUPA, ROBERT S; Dos Palos Joint Union HS; Dos Palos, CA; (2); Tennis; Hon Roll; RN.

KRUPICKA, DANIEL J; Poway HS; San Diego, CA; (3); Aud/Vis; Cmnty Wkr; Model UN; Quiz Bowl; Science Clb; Lit Mag; Hon Roll; NHS; Hnrs Gldn St Exam-Geom; Military; Physcs.

KRUPPA, CHRISTIANA; Atwater HS; Winton, CA; (2); Church Yth Grp; FCA; Var Bsktbl; JV Sftbl; JV Vllybl; High Hon Roll; Hon Roll; MVP Awd Sftbl, Vllybl; Natl Wnnr Piano Guild Cmptn 5 Yrs; Schlrshp Wnnr Piano Cmptn Merced Womens Clb; UOP.

KRUSE, ADINA M; Montclair HS; Montclair, CA; (2); Church Yth Grp; Band; Mrchg Band; Pep Band; Hon Roll; Prfct Atten Awd; Cert Mrt Prfrmnce; Cert Achvt Band; Chaffey; Accntng.

KRUSE, CHARITY; Junipero Serra HS; San Diego, CA; (3); Cmnty Wkr; Teachers Aide; Ed Nwsp; Cit Awd; Prfct Atten Awd; Comp Sci.

KRUSE, KAREN; Dana Hills HS; Dana Point, CA; (1); Boy Scts; Church Yth Grp; French Clb; Teachers Aide; Cit Awd; Hon Roll; Orange Cnty Marine Inst Vlntr; Stanford U; Ed.

KRUSE, TOBY; Dana Hills HS; S Laguna, CA; (1); Var Ftbl; Var Vllybl; Var Wt Lftg; Hon Roll; Berkley; Architech.

KRUSI, KATIE L; Nevada Union HS; Nevada City, CA; (2); JV Capt Sftbl; Hon Roll; Mst Imprvd Plyr Awd Sftbl 88-89; NV Cnty Grls Sftbl Tm 88-89; PG & E Kite Fstvl 89; Hnr Engl I & II; San Diego ST; Advrtsng.

KRUTIAK, JULIE A; Whitney HS; Cerritos, CA; (2); 1/200; High Hon Roll; MIT; Engr.

KRYSTAL, BARBARA; Ygnacio Valley HS; Concord, CA; (4); Dance Clb; Drama Clb; Pres German Clb; Key Clb; Teachers Aide; School Play; Ed Yrbk; Hist Frsh Cls; Hon Roll; Ecology Club Pres; Gldn Poet Awd; Fncng, Tap/Jazz Dance; U CA Santa Barbara; Intl Rel.

KRYSTALL, ZAN; Arroyo Grande HS; Grover City, CA; (1); Cit Awd; High Hon Roll; Hon Roll; Prfct Atten Awd; Pres Acad Fit Awd; Recog Wrtg Abilities; Sgn Lang, Drawng & Painting; Wrtg.

KRYWE, TOM J; Branham HS; San Jose, CA; (4); Treas Jr Cls; Pres Sr Cls; Stu Cncl; JV Var Bsbl; JV Var Bsktbl; JV Var Ftbl; High Hon Roll; Hon Roll; NHS; Santa Clara U; Acctng.

KSANDER, SKYE; Santa Cruz HS; Santa Cruz, CA; (1); Band; Hon Roll; Mem Santa Cruz Hgh Surf Tm; Brown Belt-Tae Kwon Do; Avid Surfer.

KU, EMERALD M; John A Rowland HS; Rowland Hts, CA; (4); French Clb; Intnl Clb; Key Clb; Science Clb; Teachers Aide; High Hon Roll; Pres Acad Fit Awd; JV-BADMNTN; CSF-ACTVTY Dir; UC Irvine Hnr; Cornell; Htl Mgmnt.

KU, FREDERICK M; John A Rowland HS; Rowland Heights, CA; (2); Church Yth Grp; French Clb; Intnl Clb; Key Clb; Science Clb; Service Clb; High Hon Roll; Prfct Atten Awd; JV Badminton; Hgh Hnrs On GSE In Algebra I 89; UCLA; Bus.

KU, HYANG M; Warren HS; Downey, CA; (3); Art Clb; Sec Church Yth Grp; French Clb; FBLA; Treas Key Clb; Letterman Clb; VP Math Clb; VP Mu Alpha Theta; Science Clb; Varsity Clb; UCLA.

KU, MARY; Lynbrook HS; San Jose, CA; (3); Debate Tm; French Clb; Treas FBLA; VP JA; VP Key Clb; NFL; Var Tennis.

KU, ROBERTSEN; Fremont HS; Sunnyvale, CA; (3); Boy Scts; Pres Chess Clb; Debate Tm; DECA; NFL; Speech Tm; JV Tennis; Engrng.

KUAN, JEFFREY; Torrey Pines HS; Cardiff, CA; (3); Band; Drm Mjr(t); Jazz Band; Mrchg Band; Pep Band; Lit Mag; Hon Roll; Cyclng Clb; UCSD; Arch.

KUAN, WEI; James Lick HS; San Jose, CA; (4); 1/250; Intnl Clb; Math Clb; Math Tm; Teachers Aide; Tennis; High Hon Roll; NHS; Prfct Atten Awd; Pres Acad Fit Awd; Bank Of Amer Achvt Awd Math; Tandy Tech Schlrs; Dsrvng Stu Schlrshp; U CA Davis; Cmptr Sci.

KUANG, STEVE Z; Mc Clatchy HS; Sacramento, CA; (2); 62/450; French Clb; JV Trk; Elec Engnr.

KUANG, SUHUA; Galileo HS; San Francisco, CA; (3); Art Clb; Quiz Bowl; School Musical; Variety Show; Tennis; SFSU; Fshn Dsgn.

KUANG, YANFANG; International Studies Of Acad; San Francisco, CA; (2); High Hon Roll; Japanese Clb; CA Schlrshp Fed; Ed.

KUBACKY, URSULA; Loretto HS; Sacramento, CA; (4); 2/55; Cmnty Wkr; Debate Tm; Math Tm; Red Cross Aide; Science Clb; Chorus; Ed Nwsp; Rep Frsh Cls; Pres Soph Cls; Rep Stu Cncl; Friday Night Live; Wellesley Coll MA; Biochem.

KUBANCIK, ALEXAS M; Skyline HS; Oakland, CA; (2); Thesps; School Musical; School Play; Stage Crew; Variety Show; Thespian Of Yr 89-90; Actng.

KUBANDA, CHRISTINE L; Elsinore HS; Lake Elsinore, CA; (3); Church Yth Grp; Cmnty Wkr; Drama Clb; ROTC; Thesps; School Play; Stage Crew; Var Swmmng; Hon Roll; Lifeguard Cert; ROTC 2nd Lt Schltc Awd; BYU.

KUBEL, BRIAN; Dos Pueblos HS; Goleta, CA; (3); 40/380; Church Yth Grp; ROTC; Color Guard; JV Bsktbl; JV Tennis; NHS; St Schlr; Surf Clb; Rsrv Offcrs Assn Of Amer; Mntn Bkng; Med.

KUBERNICK, SAMUEL; Los Alamitos HS; Seal Beach, CA; (3); Service Clb; Spanish Clb; Rptr Nwsp; Var Swmmng; Lion Awd; Var Water Polo Ltrmn; Class Cmmtte; Commctns.

KUBICEK, BEN S; Mission Bay HS; San Diego, CA; (2); Church Yth Grp; Var Ftbl; Var Vllybl; Cit Awd; High Hon Roll; Cmnty Wkr; Teachers Aide; Tn Yr Awd Piano Gld Natl Piano Plyng Adtns; CA Poly San Luis Obispo; Arch.

KUBICEK, TANIA; Lindsay HS; Lindsay, CA; (3); FBLA; Var L Vllybl; Hon Roll; Bus Mgmt.

KUBLER, MICHAEL D; Central Union HS; Calexico, CA; (2); German Clb; Speech Tm; 4-H Awd; Pres Schlr; Annapolis; Aerospc Engr.

KUBO, AILEEN; Monterey Bay Acad; Japan; (4); Ski Clb; Varsity Clb; Band; Chorus; Orch; Variety Show; Ed Lit Mag; Rptr Jr Cls; Var Vllybl; Prfct Atten Awd; 4 Yr Club; Girls Club; Pacific Union Coll; Advrtsg Dsg.

KUBOTA, TIMO; El Toro HS; El Toro, CA; (2); Socr; Hon Roll; Rotary Awd; 1st Pl Yth Expo Arch Cmptn, 10th Pl Zrch Drwng; Mst Imprvd JV Sccr 90; Arch.

KUBOYAMA, LANCE T; Schurr HS; Montebello, CA; (1); Band; Mrchg Band; Orch; Pep Band; Hon Roll; VP A D Eurpean Hstry Trvl Clb.

KUCKENBAKER, LORI; Riverdale HS; Riverdale, CA; (4); 3/90; Am Leg Aux Girls St; Treas GAA; SADD; Pres Varsity Clb; Pres Soph Cls; Treas Stu Cncl; Var Cheerldng; Capt Var Sftbl; Capt Var Vllybl; CA Polytech San Luis O; Arch.

KUDAMATSU, MINEKO REBECCA; Westmoor HS; Daly City, CA; (3); Art Clb; Debate Tm; 4-H; JA; Spanish Clb; SADD; Drill Tm; Mrchg Band; Pep Band; Off Frsh Cls; Intl Wrld Peace Yth Org Rep; Mrchng Band 1st Prz; UC Berkeley.

KUDER, RYAN A; San Dieguito HS; Encinitas, CA; (2); 30/620; Quiz Bowl; Sec Soph Cls; JV Golf; JV Socr; High Hon Roll; Schl Recgntn CA Math Leag 88-89; Outstndng Span Stu 90; CSF; Harvard; Bus.

KUDLU, PURNIMA; Ygnacio Valley HS; Concord, CA; (2); Hosp Aide; Sec Key Clb; Spanish Clb; JV Capt Vllybl; Comm Plays Musicals; Med.

KUDRNA, JULIE D; Eureka HS; Eureka, CA; (2); Church Yth Grp; Ski Clb; Chorus; Off Frsh Cls; Rep Soph Cls; Bsktbl; Trk; Vllybl; Hon Roll; Pres Acad Fit Awd; Santa Clara U; Psych.

KUE, KA; Thomas Edison HS; Stockton, CA; (2); Church Yth Grp; Cmnty Wkr; Band; Jazz Band; Mrchg Band; School Musical; Nwsp; Stu Cncl; Hon Roll; Cit Awd; Soroptimist S Clb; Care Clb; Heritage Fstvls; UC Davis; Mrktng.

KUEBLER, RACHAEL A; Hayward HS; Castro Valley, CA; (2); 17/237; Spanish Clb; Var Trk; High Honors Awd Golden State Exam Algebra; Medicine.

KUEBLER, SCOTT E; San Dimas HS; San Dimas, CA; (3); Varsity Clb; VICA; Var Bsbl; Hon Roll; WA ST U; Arch.

KUEH, GARY; Etiwanda HS; Alta Loma, CA; (3); 2/630; Key Clb; Pres Speech Tm; NHS; Mck Trl; Acadc Dcthln; JV Bdmntn.

KUEH, JASON; Etiwanda HS; Alta Loma, CA; (3); 3/640; Key Clb; Scholastic Bowl; Ed Lit Mag; NHS; Mock Trial; Pr Trl Atty; Tutoring Algebra II; UC System; Med Rsrch.

KUENZI, KAYNE K; Mar Vista HS; Imperial Beach, CA; (4); 5/285; Church Yth Grp; Pep Clb; School Musical; Stu Cncl; Hon Roll; Southwestern Coll; Librl Arts.

KUEST, JASON; Sacramento Adventist Acad; Folsom, CA; (3); 10/40; Church Yth Grp; Ski Clb; Chorus; Stu Cncl; Bus.

KUEST, WENDY A; El Camino HS; Oceanside, CA; (2); 34/426; Pep Clb; School Play; Hon Roll; Outstndng Sci Cls Stu Mdl; Frnch Cls Pin; Engl.

KUEY, SHANG-CHI KATY; Cerritos HS; Cerritos, CA; (1); Treas JCL; Science Clb; Hon Roll; UNICEF 89; 4th Pl Hot Air Balln Cntst; MA Inst Of Tech; Sci.

KUHFAL, HEIDI; Hogan HS; Vallejo, CA; (2); Cmnty Wkr; Teachers Aide; School Play; Ltr Co-Capt; Band Dir Right Hand Awd; Music.

KUHL, JOANN; Fontana HS; Fontana, CA; (2); Band; Mrchg Band; Pep Band; Sftbl; High Hon Roll; Hon Roll; Prfct Atten Awd; Bus Admin.

KUHLMEIER, VALERIE A; Chaminade College Prep; West Hills, CA; (3); 3/200; Cmnty Wkr; Chorus; Ed Lit Mag; Var L Sftbl; Hon Roll; NHS; Opt Clb Awd; Commnctns.

KUHN, KITTY; Lindhurst HS; Marysville, CA; (3); Pres 4-H; Pep Clb; SADD; School Play; Variety Show; Rep Frsh Cls; Rep Soph Cls; Rep Jr Cls; Rep Stu Cncl; JV Var Cheerldng; Cnty Dress Revue Wnnr 90; Corp Law.

KUHN, KRISTIN; Brawley Union HS; Brawley, CA; (1); Rptr 4-H; Hon Roll; Tnns Lessons; Raise Show Steer; Ride Horses; UCLA; Lawyer.

KUHN, MATT; Valley Christian HS; San Ramon, CA; (4); 4/27; Church Yth Grp; Yrbk; VP Jr Cls; VP Stu Cncl; Socr; Hon Roll; NHS; Rotary Clb Stu Awd; San Jose ST U; Comp Sci.

KUHN, PAULA Y; Montgomery HS; Santa Rosa, CA; (3); Art Clb; Church Yth Grp; Office Aide; Var Vllybl; Cit Awd; Hon Roll; Pres Acad Fit Awd; Study Piano; Stu Of Wk; Berkley; Intl Bus Law.

KUHS, JONATHAN S; Thousand Oaks HS; Thousand Oaks, CA; (2); Var Trk; U CA; Engrng.

KUIPERS, BRIAN W; Don Antonio Lugo HS; Chino, CA; (4); 14/651; Church Yth Grp; High Hon Roll; NHS; Calvin Coll; Acctng.

KUIPERS, RACHEL K; Don Antonio Lugo HS; Chino, CA; (2); JV Socr; Var L Trk; JV Vllybl; Cit Awd; High Hon Roll; Cert Of Recognition; Golden Conquest Awd Cert; Calvin Coll MI.

KUJAK, BRIAN L; Lutheran HS; Yorba Linda, CA; (2); Church Yth Grp; JV Golf; Wt Lftg; JV Wrstlng; CSUF; Indstrl Dsgn.

KUKAS, JEREMY P; Mt Whitney HS; Visalia, CA; (1); FFA; Capt JV Ftbl; JV Trk; Capt JV Wrstlng; AZ ST; Sport Thrpy.

KUKENAS, ALGIS; Cathedral HS; Los Angeles, CA; (4); Math Clb; JV Socr; JV Trk; High Hon Roll; Christian Action Club; CSF; Cal Tech; Elec Engr.

KUKKONEN III, CARL; La Canada HS; La Canada, CA; (3); 16/250; Boy Scts; German Clb; Intnl Clb; Key Clb; Math Clb; Mu Alpha Theta; Band; Drm Mjr(t); Jazz Band; Mrchg Band; Ice Hockey Capt; Breeding/Showing Birds; Amer Assn Of Teachers Of German.

KULA, GENA N; Del Norte HS; Crescent City, CA; (2); Spanish Clb; Hon Roll; Sacramento ST; Psych.

KULAGA, TANYA M; Leuzinger HS; Hawthorne, CA; (1); Church Yth Grp; Key Clb; High Hon Roll; Pres Acad Fit Awd; Psychothrpy.

KULBE, ROBERT; Sierra Joint Union HS; Madera, CA; (2); Church Yth Grp; FFA; SADD; NHS; Pres Acad Fit Awd; JV Trk; FFA Best Informd Tm; Sch Rally Clb; Long Beach ST; Bio.

KULBERTIS, MELANIE; Escondido HS; Escondido, CA; (1); Drama Clb; Pep Clb; Chorus; Flag Corp; Photo.

KULICK, MICHAEL J; Norco SR HS; Norco, CA; (2); 144/460; Cmnty Wkr; Ftbl; Cmmnty Svc Work For Lions Clb; Cmmnty Svc Work SR Ctzns; Bus Admin.

KULIK, KRISTEN L; Valley HS; Sacramento, CA; (2); 15/435; Dance Clb; Var Gym; Intrml Wt Lftg; Hon Roll; Prfct Atten Awd.

KULISCH, STEPHEN; Lincoln HS; Stockton, CA; (3); 230/600; Boy Scts; Church Yth Grp; Band; Mrchg Band; Pep Band; Diving; Ftbl; Socr; Wt Lftg; Cmptv Sccr; Northwestern U; Physcl Thrpy.

KULKARNI, MANOJ A; Mission Viejo HS; Mission Viejo, CA; (2); 1/500; Boy Scts; Key Clb; Model UN; Hon Roll; Acad Dcthln; Jr Stsmn Amer; Stanford; Dr.

KULUKIAN, IDA; Holy Martyrs/Ferrahn Armenian Schl; Granada Hills, CA; (2); Girl Scts; Band; Mrchg Band; School Play; Hon Roll; CSUN; Engl.

KUM, TOM B; Foot Hill HS; Santa Ana, CA; (3); 2nd Pl Engrng Awd; 2nd Pl Skatebrdng; Mech Engrng.

KUMAGAI, BRYCE S; Bellarmine College Prep; San Jose, CA; (1); Boy Scts; Cmnty Wkr; Band; Mrchg Band; Orch; Pep Band; Architect.

KUMAR, MOHINI L; Sequoia HS; East Palo Alto, CA; (3); FBLA; High Hon Roll; Prfct Atten Awd; Val; Acad All-Amer Schlr Prog 87; E Ralo Alto Chamber Of Commerce; Vldctrn; Supers Awd; Stanford U; Med.

KUMAR, NAVEEN N; Ygnacio Valley HS; Martinez, CA; (1); Boy Scts; Math Clb; High Hon Roll; UC Berkeley; Physician.

KUMAR, RACHEL; Mission Viejo HS; Mission Viejo, CA; (1); 6/400; Church Yth Grp; Key Clb; Socr; Trk; High Hon Roll; Yth Ending Hngr Clb; Piano; UCLA; Med.

KUMAR, RONALD R; W C Overfelt HS; San Jose, CA; (1); Computer Clb; Math Clb; Cit Awd; Aerospc Engr.

KUMAR, SHALINI; Beyer HS; Modesto, CA; (3); Drama Clb; Ski Clb; SADD; Teachers Aide; Cit Awd; High Hon Roll; Hon Roll; Prfct Atten Awd; CSF; UOP; Phrmcst.

KUMAR, SUNJAY; Edison HS; Huntington Beach, CA; (1); #8 In Class; Boy Scts; Debate Tm; Drama Clb; FBLA; Model UN; Science Clb; Temple Yth Grp; VICA; Yrbk; Stu Cncl; MUN Awds & Most Prmsng Frshmn; Temple Yth Group; Gftd Chldren Pgm; U CA Irvine; Med.

KUMETAT, DARREN J; Sonora HS; Groveland, CA; (4); Ski Clb; Band; Jazz Band; Mrchg Band; High Hon Roll; Pres Acad Fit Awd; Rotary Awd; UOP; Chem.

KUMLER, JUSTIN M; Modesto HS; Modesto, CA; (2); Church Yth Grp; JV Ftbl; JV Socr; Prfct Atten Awd; Gldn ST Schlr; Arch.

KUMMER, KIMBERLY; West HS; Bakersfield, CA; (1); Girl Scts; JV Bsktbl; JV Sftbl; JV Vllybl; Cit Awd; Hon Roll; Prfct Atten Awd; CA ST Bakersfield; Chldrn.

KUNCZE, KAREN; Vanden HS; Vacaville, CA; (4); 4/139; VP Pres Spanish Clb; SADD; Teachers Aide; Stat Bsktbl; Var Mgr(s); JV Var Tennis; High Hon Roll; NHS; Pres Acad Fit Awd; Tutoring Acad Ltr; Solano CC; Engrng.

KUNCZE, KRISTINE Y; Vanden HS; Vacaville, CA; (1); 38/211; Drill Tm; Var Trk.

KUNG, CALINA; Skyline HS; Oakland, CA; (3); Church Yth Grp; Intnl Clb; Key Clb; Pep Clb; Service Clb; SADD; Color Guard; Drill Tm; Var Cheerldng; Var Pom Pon.

KUNG, GUY; Live Oak HS; Morgan Hill, CA; (3); French Clb; FBLA; Teachers Aide; Intrml Crs Cntry; Intrml Tennis; Cit Awd; Hon Roll; Prfct Atten Awd; Bio.

KUNG, IRENE Y M; Villa Park HS; Orange, CA; (3); Art Clb; Drama Clb; French Clb; Key Clb; Science Clb; Yrbk; JV Swmmng; NHS; Girls St Alt Rep; Aeronaut Engr.

KUNG, JONATHAN A; Las Lomas HS; Walnut Creek, CA; (4); Band; High Hon Roll; Certs & Hnrs Music; All-St Band 90; UC Berkeley; Comp Sci.

KUNG, SUE A; Lowell HS; San Francisco, CA; (3); Cmnty Wkr; Computer Clb; JA; JCL; Q&S; Science Clb; Service Clb; SADD; Teachers Aide; Ed Nwsp; Japantown Bwlng Leag 1st Pl Grls 2 Tms; UC Berkeley; Bio.

KUNG, WAI; Mt Pleasant HS; San Jose, CA; (2); Chess Clb; Math Tm; High Hon Roll; Hon Roll; Ceramic Art Awd.

KUNG, YUNG-SHIN A; Bellarmine College Prep; Santa Clara, CA; (1); Cmnty Wkr; Debate Tm; Latin Clb; NFL; Pres Acad Fit Awd; US Tennis Assn Stu.

KUNG, ZHI ANNIE; Alhambra HS; Alhambra, CA; (4); 1/33; Office Aide; Teachers Aide; Yrbk; Off Sr Cls; Peer Tutor; Pasadena City Coll; Chemcl Engr.

KUNITAKE, BRYAN A; Hawthorne HS; Hawthorne, CA; (2); Service Clb; Teachers Aide; Var L Crs Cntry; JV Trk; JV Wrstlng; Hon Roll.

KUNIYUKI, KEN T; Torrance HS; Torrance, CA; (4); 1/393; Chess Clb; Debate Tm; Pres Science Clb; Service Clb; Nwsp; Cit Awd; Hon Roll; Ntl Merit SF; Acad Decathlon; Citizen Bee Civics Comp, 3rd Pl Ntl, 3rd Pl ST, 1st Pl Rgnl; CSF; Statistics.

KUNKEL, KIM; Hesperia Christian HS; Victorville, CA; (4); Church Yth Grp; Teachers Aide; Church Choir; Pep Band; School Musical; School Play; Var Bsktbl; Var Sftbl; Var Vllybl; Hon Roll; MVP Chrstn Lgue Vllybl; Sr Prncss; Phy Ed.

KUNTZ, KRISTIN M; Hanford HS; Hanford, CA; (2); Church Yth Grp; Office Aide; Treas Frsh Cls; Rep Soph Cls; Var Swmmng; Hon Roll; Interact Clb; CSF; Acctng.

KUNZ, JENNIFER M; Sierra Ft Union HS; Big Creek, CA; (3); Church Yth Grp; FBLA; GAA; Letterman Clb; SADD; Varsity Clb; Treas Jr Cls; Stu Cncl; Var JV Bsktbl; Var Swmmng; HOBY Ambssdr; Div III St Chmpn Vllybl Tm 89; Educ.

KUNZ, REBECCA; Templeton HS; Templeton, CA; (3); Church Yth Grp; Drama Clb; Chorus; Church Choir; School Play; VP Stu Cncl; Var Bsktbl; Powder Puff Ftbl; Var Capt Vllybl; High Hon Roll; Brigham Young U.

KUO, CHRISTINE; Upland HS; Upland, CA; (2); Key Clb; Var JV Vllybl; NHS; Highlander Ed Fndtn Awd; CSF; Cmmrcl Dsgn.

KUO, ELISA L; Lincoln HS; Daly City, CA; (3); Yrbk; Graphic & Fashn Desgn; Drawing, Painting; Bus Mgt; UC Berkeley; Design.

KUO, HELEN; Northgate HS; Walnut Creek, CA; (4); 1/280; Ed Nwsp; JV Bsktbl; Var L Crs Cntry; Var L Trk; Ntl Merit SF; Pres Acad Fit Awd; Pres Schlr; Val; Piano Player; Junior Volunteer At Kaiser Hospital; Yale U.

KUO, KANE E; Whitney HS; Cerritos, CA; (3); 1/179; Church Yth Grp; Orch; Nwsp; Pres Jr Cls; Var Crs Cntry; High Hon Roll; Ntl Merit Ltr; Church Yth Music Ldr, HS Band; Missionary Teams Mexico, AZ; Jr Hnr Guard Capt; Med.

KUO, MAY M; Dana Hills HS; Laguna Beach, CA; (1); French Clb; GAA; SADD; Teachers Aide; JV Tennis; High Hon Roll; Hon Roll; Prfct Atten Awd; Rotary Awd; Tnns Schlr Athl; Frnch Clb Pres; Stu Of Yr In Frnch II, Engl I ACC, Bio; Stanford; Bio.

KUO, SZY-CHI ALICE; John H Francis Polytechnic HS; N Hollywood, CA; (4); French Clb; Math Tm; Science Clb; Spanish Clb; Band; Jazz Band; Nwsp; Cit Awd; High Hon Roll; Hon Roll; Cal Poly Pomona; Cmptr Sci.

KUO, WILBUR Y; El Camino Real HS; West Hill, CA; (3); Debate Tm; Math Clb; NFL; Speech Tm; High Hon Roll; Prfct Atten Awd; Rockwell-LAUSD Comp Sci Compton 1st Pl Schlrshp; Jr Statesman Of Amer; CSF; John Hopkins U; Med.

KUOCH, KOING; Andrew Hill HS; San Jose, CA; (1); Hosp Aide; Math Tm; VP Soph Cls; Tennis; High Hon Roll; Medical Magnet; Odyssey Of The Mind; MIT; Engrng.

KUONEN, VANESSA JORY; Saugus HS; Saugus, CA; (3); 11/460; Am Leg Aux Girls St; Church Yth Grp; Ed Yrbk; Treas Soph Cls; VP Jr Cls; Pres Sr Cls; Stu Cncl; Var L Trk; Hon Roll; Treas NHS; Vet.

KUP, EDDY; Palisades HS; Pacific Palisades, CA; (3); Chess Clb; Math Clb; Math Tm; Chorus; Part Time Job Pharm Tech; CA Tech; Arch.

KUPELIAN, ARPI; Terra Linda HS; Corte Madera, CA; (4); Acpl Chr; Chorus; Jazz Band; Orch; JV Var Crs Cntry; JV Trk; Yrbk Hnr; Marin Living Mag Intrvw; San Francsco Cnsrvty; Pianist.

KUPERMAN, ALEKSANDR; George Washington HS; San Francisco, CA; (3); Chess Clb; Temple Yth Grp; UC Berkeley; Bus Admin.

KUPPERS, LAURIE; Alemany HS; Sepulveda, CA; (4); 5/400; Letterman Clb; Office Aide; Pres Pep Clb; Ski Clb; Varsity Clb; Variety Show; Stu Cncl; Cheerldng; High Hon Roll; Hon Roll; Hmcmng Prncss; Aids Project LA; CSF; Cal Grant A; Burns Grant Loyola Marymount; Bnk Amer Engl Awd; Loyola Marymount U; Bus.

KURAGAMI, CYNTHIA Y; Savanna HS; Buena Park, CA; (3); 1/314; Intnl Clb; Key Clb; Science Clb; Service Clb; Stat Bsktbl; Var L Tennis; Bausch & Lomb Sci Awd; CA Schlstc Fed Treas 90-91; Bus.

KURBAN, MARK R; Providence HS; Burbank, CA; (2); Pres Chess Clb; Debate Tm; NFL; Speech Tm; L Stat Crs Cntry; High Hon Roll; CA Schlrshp Fed; Astrophysics.

KURIHARA, JUNNOSUKE; Saint Francis HS; Saratoga, CA; (2); Boy Scts; Nwsp; JV Tennis; Ntl Piano Plyng Auditions; John Hopkins U; Bio Engr.

KURIHARA, LESLEE; Dinuba HS; Dinuba, CA; (2); Pep Clb; Chorus; Church Choir; Lit Mag; Cheerldng; Pom Pon; Powder Puff Ftbl; Score Keeper; Swmmng; Hon Roll; Princeton; Law.

KURIMAY, DANNY M; Souther Calif Christian HS; Westminster, CA; (3); Church Yth Grp; FCA; Letterman Clb; Teachers Aide; Varsity Clb; Variety Show; Stu Cncl; Ftbl; Wt Lftg; Hon Roll; Bible Study & Praise/Worship Ldr; Biola.

KURISU, GLENN A; Clovis West HS; Fresno, CA; (2); Socr; Tennis; High Hon Roll; UCLA; Engr.

KURITSUBO, KIMBERLY; Yerba Buena HS; San Jose, CA; (2); Girl Scts; Band; School Musical; Cheerldng; Band Executive Council; Peer Counselor; San Jose St; Law.

KURJATKO, ADINA I; Notre Dame HS; Redwood City, CA; (2); 1/100; French Clb; Math Clb; Science Clb; Nwsp; Cheerldng; JV Tennis; Hon Roll; NHS; Cresmont Conservatory Of Music Pianist; CSF; Med.

KURKJIAN, ROBERT J; Los Alamitos HS; Seal Beach, CA; (3); Boy Scts; Debate Tm; Model UN; NFL; Ski Clb; Speech Tm; SADD; Nwsp; Cit Awd; High Hon Roll; Stnfrd; Law.

KURLAWALLA, CHRISTINE SOPHI; Laguna Hills HS; Laguna Hills, CA; (4); 4/356; Key Clb; Math Clb; Hon Roll; Pres Acad Fit Awd; Key Clb Stu Of Mnth; CA Schlrshp Fed Mdln Schlr & Sealbearer; Tandy Tech Schl; Bnk Amer Achvt Awd Math; U Of CA Irvine; Pre-Med.

KURLYAND, VITALY; Cleveland Humanities Magnet HS; Sherman Oaks, CA; (4); Chess Clb; Cmnty Wkr; Debate Tm; French Clb; NFL; Speech Tm; Temple Yth Grp; Tennis; Cit Awd; High Hon Roll; CA Lgsltr Assmbly Cert Rec; Gldn Poet Awd; Wrld Of Poetry; N Shore Anml Lgue Bnfctrs Awd; Lib Svc Awd.

KURNIADI, ALWIN I; Sunset HS; Hayward, CA; (1); 64/188; Boy Scts; Church Yth Grp; Hon Roll; Close-Up; Comp Info Systems.

KUROKI, TAMIKO; Coachella Valley HS; Coachella, CA; (4); 9/315; Office Aide; Pep Clb; Teachers Aide; Band; Drm Mjr(t); Mrchg Band; Cheerldng; Gym; Pom Pon; Hon Roll; Coll Of The Desert; Nrsng.

KUROSAKI, KYLE Y; Mark Keppel HS; Monterey Park, CA; (3); Tennis; JV Wrstlng; Artstc Roller Sktr; Invtd US Olympc Ftvl 90 Cmpte Rlr Skt; Plcd Svl Tms Natl Artst Rlr Skt; USD; Bio.

KURPIEWSKI, STEVEN J; Patrick Henry HS; San Diego, CA; (3); 30/528; Office Aide; Quiz Bowl; Lcrss; Jr NHS; Soccr Comptv Clb Tm; UCSD; Marine Bio.

KURTZ, CHRISTOPHER S; Seaside HS; Fort Ord, CA; (2); Boy Scts; ROTC; Color Guard; US Air Force Acad; Pilot.

KURTZ, JUDAH S; Dana Hills HS; Dana Point, CA; (1); JCL; Latin Clb; Science Clb; Chorus; Orch; School Musical; Stat Tennis; All-Southern CA Hnr Orch; Capistrano Unifd Schl Dist Instrmntl Music Awd; Harvard U; Cardiology.

KURTZ, RODERICK O; Fountain Valley HS; Fountain Valley, CA; (3); Boy Scts; Pres German Clb; Off Frsh Cls; Off Soph Cls; Treas Jr Cls; Stu Cncl; Tennis; High Hon Roll; Jr NHS; Ntl Merit SF; Huntington Bch Jr Lfegrd-Capt; Cngrssnl Schlr-Natl Yng Ldrs Cnfrnc; Mc Donnel Douglas Engrng Explr Pst; Aeronaut Engrng.

KURTZ, STACEY R; North HS; Bakersfield, CA; (3); 33/350; Church Yth Grp; Spanish Clb; Teachers Aide; Hon Roll; Ntl Merit Ltr; Spanish NHS; The Masters Coll; Chld Dvlpmnt.

KURTZMAN, STEPHANIE; Dos Pueblos HS; Goleta, CA; (3); 4/338; Drama Clb; Library Aide; Math Tm; Pep Clb; Science Clb; Temple Yth Grp; School Play; Stage Crew; Variety Show; Rep Stu Cncl; Scl Sci.

KURZ, BRANDEE R; Strathmore Union HS; Strathmore, CA; (3); Letterman Clb; Pep Clb; Ski Clb; Stu Cncl; Var Bsktbl; Powder Puff Ftbl; Var Sftbl; Var Vllybl; Hon Roll; Bobby Sox Sftbl.

KURZ, JILL; Mills HS; Hillsborough, CA; (4); Church Yth Grp; Teachers Aide; Church Choir; Sec Sr Cls; Var Crs Cntry; Var Trk; Hon Roll; Pres Acad Fit Awd; Crss Cntry 2nd Pl Team CA St Meet; San Francisco ST U; RN.

KURZ, JULIE R; Norco HS; Corona, CA; (3); 32/347; Model UN; SADD; Phtg Nwsp; Var Bsktbl; Var Trk; High Hon Roll; All Acad Tm Awd; Long Beach ST; Educ.

KUSANO, KEN; Poway HS; Poway, CA; (3); 58/761; JV Ftbl; JV Wrstlng; Hon Roll; NHS; Minato Gukven Jpns Schl; CSF; Engrng.

KUSANO, SANDRA; Mountain View HS; Mountain View, CA; (3); French Clb; Band; Chorus; Mrchg Band; Orch; Co-Ed Nwsp; Socr; High Hon Roll; CSF; Amnsty Ingl; UCLA; Jrnlsm.

KUSE, EDDIE J; Warren HS; Downey, CA; (2); JV Bsbl; Var Ftbl; Comp Sci.

KUSHNER, MIKE J; Fremont HS; Sunnyvale, CA; (2); Debate Tm; FBLA; JA; NFL; Speech Tm; Hon Roll; NHS; Bowling Schlrshp; Amateur Filmmaker; Sch Envrnmntl Clb.

KUSHNIR, LARISA; Redwood HS; Visalia, CA; (2); GAA; Latin Clb; Varsity Clb; Rptr Nwsp; Var Capt Bsktbl; Var Capt Sftbl; JV Capt Vllybl; Wt Lftg; Hon Roll; Sierra Pacific Vllybl Clb; Bobby Sox All Star 6 Yrs; Sci.

KUSS, SARAH; Garces Memorial HS; Bakersfield, CA; (2); 2/170; Ed Lit Mag; Var Cheerldng; High Hon Roll; CSF; People Bnd For Trvl Clb.

KUSUMA, IMELDA; Homestead HS; Sunnyvale, CA; (1); Hon Roll; Jr NHS; CSF.

KUSUNOKI, NINA; Saint Bernard HS; Playa Del Rey, CA; (3); Cmnty Wkr; French Clb; Pep Clb; Treas Service Clb; Ski Clb; Cit Awd; Cal ST Long Beach; Bus.

KUTCH, KOREEN A.; Costa Mesa HS; Costa Mesa, CA; (4); 91/350; Pep Clb; Stu Cncl; Var Capt Cheerldng; JV Trk; Prncpls Spcl Svc Awd; Orange Coast Coll; Cmmnctns.

KUTSCH, CASSANDRA L; Mission Bay HS; San Diego, CA; (2); 10/380; Church Yth Grp; Chorus; Church Choir; School Musical; Swing Chorus; High Hon Roll; Hon Roll; Outstnd Soph Swing Choir; Acvht Soc Stud Awd 89-90; Stu Of Mnth French V, Algebra & Adv Wrld Hist; U Of CA San Diego; Engl.

KUTTNER, MARC A; Daniel Murphy HS; Los Angeles, CA; (4); 24/89; Church Yth Grp; Letterman Clb; Teachers Aide; Thesps; School Play; Stage Crew; Yrbk; Crs Cntry; Trk; Hon Roll; Radio Cntrlld Modlr; Sacramento City Coll; Pilot.

KUWAHARA, TIFFANY F; Gardena HS; Gardena, CA; (3); Intnl Clb; Service Clb; Ed Frsh Cls; Treas Jr Cls; Stu Cncl; Var Tennis; Cit Awd; Zoology.

KUWANO, JOYCE K; Live Oak HS; Morgan Hill, CA; (3); 5/530; Church Yth Grp; VP Sec French Clb; FBLA; Key Clb; Var Swmmng; High Hon Roll; Jr NHS; Prfct Atten Awd; Church Music Chrprsn; Japanese Schl.

KUYKENDALL, CHRISTINA; Yosemite HS; Coarsegold, CA; (2); Pep Clb; Spanish Clb; Variety Show; Cheerldng; Trk; Cit Awd; High Hon Roll; Hon Roll; Prfct Atten Awd; Pres Acad Fit Awd; Presdntl Phys Ftnss Awd; Chrprctr.

KUYKENDALL, KIMBERLEE A; Bonita Vista HS; Bonita, CA; (2); Nwsp; Co-Ed Yrbk; Cit Awd.

KUYKENDALL, TIMOTHY ANDREW; Idllywild Schl Of Music & The Arts; Laguna Niguel, CA; (4); Band; Mrchg Band; Orch; School Musical; Var Bsktbl; All Southern CA Hnr Band; Spec Proj Wrtng, Arranging & Perfrmng Compact Disc; Water Polo Capt; Prof Muscn.

KUZMA, KEVIN W; Burbank HS; Burbank, CA; (2); French Clb; Orch; School Musical; L JV Socr; Hon Roll; Pres Acad Fit Awd; CSF; Sons Union Vetrns; Frnch Awd.

KUZNETSOV, POLINA; Cupertino HS; Cupertino, CA; (2); 1/350; Teachers Aide; Tennis; High Hon Roll; Interact Club; Golden St Exam Hi Hnrs; Skiing; U CA Santa Cruz; Math.

KWAK, ANGIE; Crescenta Valley HS; La Crescenta, CA; (3); Hosp Aide; Key Clb; Sec Mu Alpha Theta; Spanish Clb; Drill Tm; Co-Ed Yrbk; Pres Frsh Cls; Pres Soph Cls; NHS; Prfct Atten Awd; Mascot; Stu Cngrss Rep; Accredidation Cmmtte; Lawyer.

KWAK, ANNA B; Rosemead HS; San Gabriel, CA; (4); Computer Clb; Sec Debate Tm; Pres Service Clb; Teachers Aide; Church Choir; Mrchg Band; Pep Band; JV Tennis; NHS; Chrch Clb; Cal Poly Pomona; Engrng Tech.

KWAK, CAROLINE; Oceana HS; San Bruno, CA; (4); 1/180; Computer Clb; SADD; Rptr Nwsp; Var Gym; Var Tennis; DAR Awd; Elks Awd; High Hon Roll; NEDT Awd; Pres Acad Fit Awd; U S Army Rsrve Natl Schlr/Athl Mdl Awd; Asian Clb Pres; MA Inst Technology.

KWAK, JASON T; Whitney HS; Cerritos, CA; (3); Art Clb; FBLA; JA; Key Clb; High Hon Roll; Hon Roll; U CA Berkeley.

KWAK, MYUNG-HEE K; Norwalk HS; Norwalk, CA; (2); Church Yth Grp; Key Clb; Band; Pep Band; Stu Cncl; Tennis; Trk; High Hon Roll; Hon Roll; Teachers Aide; CSF; Teens For Teens Clb; U CA; Nrsng.

KWAK, YOUNG; John A Rowland HS; Chino Hills, CA; (2); Church Yth Grp; Math Clb; Science Clb; Spanish Clb; Band; Mrchg Band; Pep Band; High Hon Roll; Prfct Atten Awd; Golden St Exam Algebra I & Geom High Hnrs; Southwestern Yth Music Fstvl 2nd Pl Duet, 3rd Pl Solo.

KWAN, ALVIN; Bridgemont HS; San Francisco, CA; (3); FHA.

KWAN, AMY JIE SHAN; J Eugene Mcateer HS; San Francisco, CA; (3); Boy Scts; Teachers Aide; Hon Roll; Badminton Tm; Cert Scty Women Engrs; Engrng.

KWAN, ANGELA; Ramona Convent Secondary Schl; Rowland Heights, CA; (2); GAA; Model UN; Trk; Grls Athltc Assoc Awd; U CA Irvine; Phy.

KWAN, ANNA; John Marshall HS; Los Angeles, CA; (3); Key Clb; Office Aide; Spanish Clb; JV Var Sftbl; NHS; Prfct Atten Awd; Schlr Athlt Awd 90; Outstndng Schltc Achvt 89-90; Schlrshp Achvt 88; Bus.

KWAN, ANNE; Lowell HS; San Francisco, CA; (4); Church Yth Grp; Cmnty Wkr; GAA; JA; Pep Clb; Variety Show; Ed Yrbk; Var Cheerldng; Var JV Gym; Intrml Vllybl; Outstndng Stu Bus Exec Womens Intl; Mgmt Awd; Hnrs Golden St Ex Alg,Geo; U CA-DAVIS; Intl Rel.

KWAN, BARBARA GARSYN; Brea-Olinda HS; Brea, CA; (4); 21/310; Bus Profs of Am; Computer Clb; Dance Clb; Drama Clb; Hosp Aide; Intnl Clb; Math Clb; Science Clb; Chorus; School Play; Pharmacy.

KWAN, GORDON HY; Lowell HS; San Francisco, CA; (3); Smmr Bslb Leag; UC Davis; Med.

KWAN, HARRY; Saint Ignatius College Prep; San Francisco, CA; (2).

KWAN, HELENA H; George Washington HS; San Francisco, CA; (4); 5/575; Chess Clb; Key Clb; Math Clb; Science Clb; Service Clb; Cit Awd; High Hon Roll; Hon Roll; Ntl Merit Ltr; Architecture.

KWAN, JENNY S; Skyline HS; Oakland, CA; (3); Science Clb; Yrbk; Treas Frsh Cls; JV Bsbl; JV Vllybl; Cit Awd; Hon Roll; CA Schlstc Fed; Bus.

KWAN, JUDY; Lowell HS; San Francisco, CA; (3); Spanish Clb; Teachers Aide; Orch; JV Crs Cntry; Hon Roll; Volunteering.

KWAN, JULIE D; J Eugene Mc Ateer HS; San Francisco, CA; (3); Chinese Club; Social Wrkr.

KWAN, JULIE W; Gardena HS; Gardena, CA; (3); Intnl Clb; JCL; Latin Clb; SADD; Off Frsh Cls; High Hon Roll; Hon Roll.

KWAN, KATRINA M; South San Francisco HS; San Bruno, CA; (2); 1/350; VP Computer Clb; French Clb; FBLA; Math Clb; Science Clb; Ed Nwsp; Stu Cncl; Var Trk; JV Vllybl; High Hon Roll; Hstry Day St Comptr; Chinese Hstrcl Socty Awd; Stanford U; Med.

KWAN, LOCK K; George Washington HS; San Francisco, CA; (2); Teachers Aide; Crs Cntry; Trk; High Hon Roll; Hon Roll; Perestroika New Ave Cmmnctn Art Cntst Best Grphc Awd; Gen Svc Soc; Chinese Amer Club; UC Berkele; Aeronautic Engr.

KWAN, RANDY J; Miramonte HS; Orinda, CA; (1); Debate Tm; NFL; Speech Tm; High Hon Roll; Lion Awd; Pres Acad Fit Awd.

KWAN, ROBERT H; Arroyo HS; Arcadia, CA; (4); Am Leg Boys St; Boy Scts; Church Yth Grp; Letterman Clb; Office Aide; Varsity Clb; Var L Ftbl; Var Capt Trk; Kiwanis Awd; Am Legn Schl Awd 85; Congrssnl Schlr-Congrssnl Yth Ldrshp Cncl 90.

KWAN, ROSA; Santa Paula Union HS; Santa Paula, CA; (2); 1/379; Treas Key Clb; Science Clb; SADD; Var Vllybl; High Hon Roll; Prfct Atten Awd; CSF; Peer Cnslr.

KWAN, SHIRLEY Y; John F Kennedy HS; Sacramento, CA; (2); 44/559; Hon Roll; Adv.

KWASNESKI, ANN M; Montgomery HS; Kenwood, CA; (3); 65/440; French Clb; Ski Clb; Tennis; Hon Roll; Edith Snypp Memrl Awd In Piano; U Of CA Davis; Englsh.

KWAY, CYNTHIA; Mission San Jose HS; Fremont, CA; (4); 7/364; Science Clb; Chorus; Hon Roll; NHS; Pres Acad Fit Awd; Leo Clb; CA Schlrshp Fed; UC Davis; Vet.

KWE, FRANCISCO E; Newark Memorial HS; Newark, CA; (3); Hist DECA; French Clb; Intnl Clb; Teachers Aide; Yrbk; Hon Roll; Commercl Art.

KWOCK, JANET L; Ocean View HS; Huntington Beach, CA; (1); Model UN; U CA Riverside; Chem.

KWOK, CYNTHIA K; George Washington HS; San Francisco, CA; (2); Chorus; Hon Roll; Eagles Svc Soc; Prncpls Cabinet; Bus.

KWOK, ELAINE M; Fremont HS; Sunnyvale, CA; (2); JV Tennis; Hon Roll; Acctng Awd; CPA.

KWOK, JEFFREY C; St Ignatius HS; Pacifica, CA; (3); 7/250; Art Clb; JA; Intrml Bsbl; JV Crs Cntry; Intrml Ftbl; Var Trk; Wt Lftg; High Hon Roll; Hon Roll; UC Berkeley; Engrng.

KWOK, JON S Y; Rosemead HS; Rosemead, CA; (3); Chess Clb; Computer Clb; Intnl Clb; Key Clb; Math Clb; Science Clb; Cit Awd; High Hon Roll; Hon Roll; Indstrl Technlgy Acad Achvt Awd; 90 1st Pl HS Chess Chmpn; Engrng.

KWOK, KATHLEEN E; Abraham Lincoln HS; San Francisco, CA; (2); Teachers Aide; Hon Roll; Jr NHS; Sphmr Clb; CA Schlrshp Fdr; Hgh Hnrs Gldn St Exam Algbra; Phrmclgy.

KWOK, KAY MAY; St Joseph HS; Santa Maria, CA; (1); 1/142; Sec 4-H; Key Clb; Ski Clb; Pres Frsh Cls; JV Capt Cheerldng; Var Trk; 4-H Awd; High Hon Roll; Treas Jr NHS.

KWOK, KERMAN; Madera HS; Madera, CA; (4); 5/450; Pres Church Yth Grp; FBLA; Hosp Aide; Science Clb; Teachers Aide; Church Choir; Elks Awd; High Hon Roll; Pres Acad Fit Awd; Exch Club Boy Of Month 89; Mader Cty Acad Dcthln Tm Mem 88-89; Perf 2 Solo Organ Recitals 87 & 90; U CA Davis; Bio Sci.

KWOK, RAYMOND W; Hogan SR HS; Vallejo, CA; (3); Chess Clb; Hon Roll.

KWOK, SHARON M; Lowell HS; San Francisco, CA; (2); Church Yth Grp; Debate Tm; Drama Clb; Math Clb; Math Tm; Chorus; Church Choir; Orch; School Musical; High Hon Roll; Standford; Med.

KWOK, VALERIE K; Poway HS; San Diego, CA; (2); Hosp Aide; NFL; Speech Tm; Band; Lit Mag; High Hon Roll; Hon Roll; Interact Club; Law.

KWOK, WINNIE; A A Stagg HS; Stockton, CA; (2); NFL; Spanish Clb; Speech Tm; High Hon Roll; Prfct Atten Awd; Var Ltr Badmntn; CSF; HOSA.

KWON, ANGIE; Notre Dame HS; Burbank, CA; (4); 23/249; JA; Latin Clb; Ski Clb; SADD; Band; JV Trk; High Hon Roll; NEDT Awd; Pres Acad Fit Awd; Valley Safe Rides; CSF Pres; Amnesty Intl; UCLA; Optometry.

KWON, ARLENE; Thousand Oaks HS; Thousand Oaks, CA; (3); 50/541; Church Yth Grp; Spanish Clb; Chorus; Lit Mag; Hon Roll; Prfct Atten Awd; Continental Math League.

KWON, BO-KYUNG; Chaffey HS; Upland, CA; (4); 2/526; Am Leg Aux Girls St; Church Yth Grp; French Clb; Hosp Aide; Treas Pep Clb; Yrbk; Powder Puff Ftbl; High Hon Roll; Lion Awd; Sal; 2nd Pl Hnr Lang/Lit Acad Decathlon 89-90; 2nd Pl Wnnr Econ Essay Cont; Chaffey Alumni Schlrshp; UCLA; Pre Med.

KWON, HELEN; Crescenta Valley HS; Montrose, CA; (3); Cmnty Wkr; Hosp Aide; Key Clb; Math Clb; Mu Alpha Theta; Pep Clb; Spanish Clb; Drill Tm; Ed Yrbk; JV Cheerldng; UC Berkeley; Pharmacy.

KWON, HYEJEONG; Antelope Valley HS; Palmdale, CA; (4); Scholastic Bowl; Service Clb; Spanish Clb; Capt Cheerldng; Hon Roll; Pres Acad Fit Awd; CSF Pres; U Of CA; Psych.

KWON, JOHN J; Santa Clara HS; Camarillo, CA; (2); U Of PA Wharton; Bus.

KWON, JOSEPH; Downey HS; Downey, CA; (4); Church Yth Grp; Score Keeper; Var Co-Capt Vllybl; Hon Roll; Prfct Atten Awd; Hgh Hnrs Gldn St Exm Alg & Geo; UCSB; Bus Admin.

KWON, JUNIOR H; Garden Grove HS; Garden Grove, CA; (3); Church Yth Grp; JV Bsktbl; Var L Socr; Hon Roll; Prfct Atten Awd; Korean Clb; Bus Mgmt.

KWON, PATRICIA; Campbell Hall HS; Van Nuys, CA; (3); Church Yth Grp; Dance Clb; Service Clb; Ski Clb; SADD; School Musical; Rptr Nwsp; Var Cheerldng; Var Mgr(s); Var Score Keeper; Law.

KWON, PETER; Whitney HS; Lakewood, CA; (2); JA; JV Bsbl; Bsktbl; Hon Roll; CSF; Golden ST Xm; UC Berkeley.

KWON, RUTH; John A Rowland HS; La Puente, CA; (3); Church Yth Grp; Science Clb; Spanish Clb; High Hon Roll; Hon Roll; Interact Clb; CSF; UCLA; Bus.

KWON, RYAN; Taft HS; Los Angeles, CA; (3); Art Clb; Var Crs Cntry; JV Tennis; Var Trk; JV Vllybl; Prfct Atten Awd; Golden St Exam Hnrs; Dentistry.

KWON, SOO A; Narbonne HS; Harbor City, CA; (3); NFL; Treas Speech Tm; JV Sftbl; JV Tennis; High Hon Roll; Prfct Atten Awd; Pres Acad Fit Awd; Keywanettes Historian; Congrssnl Bronze Awd; CSF VP; John Hopkins U; Pediatrics.

KWON, SOPHIA; San Dieguito HS; Carlsbad, CA; (2); 17/520; Key Clb; Band; JV Tennis; Hon Roll; Prfct Atten Awd; CSF; Acad League; Press Clb; U C San Diego; Biochem.

KWON, SUNNY; Antioch HS; Antioch, CA; (4); 8/599; Am Leg Aux Girls St; Church Yth Grp; Rep Pep Clb; Sec Speech Tm; Orch; Treas Soph Cls; Treas Jr Cls; Pres Stu Cncl; Cheerldng; Hon Roll; UC Santa Barb; Pltcl Sci.

KWON, UK X; Palm Springs HS; Palm Springs, CA; (3); 1/802; Am Leg Boys St; Tennis; Elks Awd; High Hon Roll; Hon Roll; Amnsty Intl; UCSD; Med.

KWONG, ANNA; Skyline HS; Oakland, CA; (4); 25/542; Church Yth Grp; Key Clb; Math Tm; Teachers Aide; Band; Church Choir; Pres Stu Cncl; Vllybl; High Hon Roll; NHS; CA Schlrshp Fed Sealbearer; Marcus A Foster Ed Inst Achvt Awd, Clorox Co Schlrshp; CA ST Haward; Liberal Stu.

KWONG, BEN; Lowell HS; San Francisco, CA; (2).

KWONG, BONNIE; Alhambra HS; Alhambra, CA; (2); Spanish Clb; USC; Bus.

KWONG, BONNIE; Lowell HS; San Francisco, CA; (2); Debate Tm; NFL; Teachers Aide; Rep Frsh Cls; Rep Soph Cls; Hon Roll; CSF; Spirit Week; Color Wars; Big Bro/Big Sis Assn; Kermesse; Forensics; Bus.

KWONG, DONALD; Carpinteria HS; Santa Barbara, CA; (3); Math Tm; Teachers Aide; Yrbk; Var Crs Cntry; JV Socr; Var Trk; Math Awd Elem Fnctns; Sci Awd Physics; Scl Stds Awd US Hstry I; U Of CA Los Angeles; Psych.

KWONG, JESSICA D; Gahr HS; Artesia, CA; (3); Debate Tm; Model UN; Spanish Clb; Speech Tm; Teachers Aide; Rptr Yrbk; Hon Roll; Blue & Gold Awd Engl 88-89; L A Acad Decathlon 3rd Pl Speech & Essay Wrtng 89-90; Engl.

KWONG, JUSTIN Y; Sacramento HS; Sacramento, CA; (2); 1/500; Chess Clb; Computer Clb; JV Crs Cntry; Var Tennis; Hon Roll; CSF; Acadmc Excllnc Awd; JV Crss Cntry Team Trphy Metro Chmps; Princeton; Math.

KWONG, KAREN S; Lowell HS; San Francisco, CA; (2); Church Yth Grp; French Clb; SADD; Chorus; Church Choir; Chinese Club; Dance Class; Golden St Exam High Hnr Algebra/Geom.

KWONG, LINLY; Valley HS; Sacramento, CA; (4); 3/400; Math Clb; Teachers Aide; Mrchg Band; Pep Band; School Musical; JV Var Vllybl; High Hon Roll; Pres Acad Fit Awd; Bank Of Am Achvt Awd Math; GATE Clb Pres; CSF Pres, Life Stu & 100 Pct Stu; U Of CA Davis; Bio Sci.

KWONG, MANDY; Lowell HS; San Francisco, CA; (3); Boy Scts; Cmnty Wkr; Hosp Aide; Q&S; Red Cross Aide; Teachers Aide; CSF; 89-90 Mandarin Speech Cont Hnrb Mntn; Golden St Exam High Hnr Alg & Geom; UC Berkeley; Medcl.

KWONG, MICHAEL; Abraham Lincoln HS; San Francisco, CA; (3); Bus Profs of Am; Teachers Aide; Debate Tm; Hon Roll; Golden ST Schlr Geom; UCLA; Intl Trade.

KWONG, RICHARD; Pilgrim HS; Los Angeles, CA; (2); 1/13; Art Clb; Computer Clb; JV Var Bsktbl; JV Var Ftbl; JV Var Vllybl; Cit Awd; Hon Roll; Jr NHS; NHS; Prfct Atten Awd; Referee HS Vlybl; Cnslr Plgrm Day Camp; Phrmcy.

KWONG, ROBERT; Lowell HS; San Francisco, CA; (3); Chess Clb; Science Clb; Orch; Mandarin Spch Cont; Bay Area Sci Cont; Comp Asst.

KWONG, WEI W; Balboa HS; San Francisco, CA; (3); Hon Roll; Prfct Atten Awd; CSF; Chinese Benvlnt Clb; Jr Statesmn Amer.

KY, DANY; Los Amigos HS; Garden Grove, CA; (3); 45/301; Key Clb; Hon Roll; NHS; Phys Ed Awd 88-89; Keywanette Awd; Bus.

KY, HEIDI; El Cajon Valley HS; El Cajon, CA; (3); 3/370; Rptr Nwsp; Lit Mag; High Hon Roll; Hon Roll; CSF; Multicultural Club.

KY, JANE C; Fremont HS; Sunnyvale, CA; (2); 60/400; Church Yth Grp; Score Keeper; JV Vllybl; Cit Awd; High Hon Roll; Hon Roll; NHS; Bdmntn Vrsty; Med.

KY, VEROCK; Reedley HS; Reedley, CA; (4); 37/330; Debate Tm; French Clb; FBLA; German Clb; Spanish Clb; Teachers Aide; Hon Roll; Kings River CC; Dentist.

KYAW, KHINE; Westmoor HS; Daly City, CA; (1); German Clb; Rep Frsh Cls; Hon Roll; Carl Vinson Clb; GATE; Tennis.

KYE, STELLA; University HS; Irvine, CA; (3); Church Yth Grp; JCL; Key Clb; Latin Clb; Service Clb; Spanish Clb; Cit Awd; Hon Roll; Pr Asstnce Ldrshp Awd Orange Cnty Dept Educ; Acad Excllnce Awd 2 Gldn St Exm & Natl Ltn Exm; Mrch/Dims.

KYLE, CHRIS D; Carlsbad HS; Oceanside, CA; (1); Church Yth Grp; Drama Clb; Thesps; School Play; Hon Roll; Prfct Atten Awd; U Of HI; Marine Bio.

KYLE, WENDY J; El Camino HS; Sacramento, CA; (3); 11/366; School Musical; School Play; JV Var Bsktbl; JV Var Vllybl; Cit Awd; NHS; Prfct Atten Awd; All-League Plyr Vllybl; Most Imprvd Plyr Awd Bsktbl & Vllybl.

KYMES, SHANNON; Desert JR/Sr HS; Edwards, CA; (1); Church Yth Grp; FBLA; SADD; Sec Frsh Cls; Sec Stu Cncl; JV Co-Capt Cheerldng; Var Sftbl; Acad Excllnc; U TX Austin; Accntng.

KYRIACOU, CHRISTOPHER; Lowell HS; San Francisco, CA; (2); Church Yth Grp; Dance Clb; FCA; Teachers Aide; JV Bsktbl; Hon Roll; Pres Acad Fit Awd; Hellenic Club; U Of CA; Lang.

KYRIAKIS, TINA; Mills HS; Millbrae, CA; (3); Drama Clb; Chorus; School Musical; Variety Show; High Hon Roll; Hon Roll; CSF; Schl Stu Store Mgr; Supr Vcl Rtng CA Music Edctrs Assoc; Real Estate Broker.

KYSER, MATTHEW P; Irvine HS; Irvine, CA; (2); 53/500; Church Yth Grp; Cmnty Wkr; Key Clb; Ski Clb; Golf; Socr; Hon Roll; Doctor.

KYSER, MELANIE L; Norco SR HS; Norco, CA; (2); Church Yth Grp; FHA; Girl Scts; Church Choir; Rptr Yrbk; JV Cheerldng; JV Gym; JV Trk; Hon Roll; Prfct Atten Awd; Los Angeles Trade Tech; Dsgnr.

KYU, DON; Washington HS; San Francisco, CA; (1); JV Bsbl; JV Ftbl; Hon Roll; Jr NHS.

L HERAULT, BRANDON; Lemoore HS; Lemoore, CA; (3); FBLA; Treas Spanish Clb; Rptr Nwsp; Var Golf; Var JV Tennis; Hon Roll; Acad Decathalon; UCSB; Bus.

L HEUREUX, STEPHANIE A; Carlsbad HS; Carlsbad, CA; (2); 1/350; Cmnty Wkr; Girl Scts; Key Clb; Scholastic Bowl; SADD; Cheerldng; Hon Roll; Rotary Awd; Rotary Yth Exchng Stu Japan; Cmmr Cty Carlsband Sister Cty Cmmssn; East Asian Stds.

LA, BILL; Oakland HS; Oakland, CA; (2); JV Ftbl; Hon Roll; Actor.

LA, EVELYN HANH T; Schurr HS; Monterey Park, CA; (3); Pep Clb; Teachers Aide; Varsity Clb; Acpl Chr; Band; Mrchg Band; Yrbk; Var JV Cheerldng; Var Capt Pom Pon; Hon Roll; Various Beauty Pageant Prtcpnt; Grls Leag; Head Chrldr/Head Capt Schurr Hgh Prep Squad; U Of CA, Berkeley; Bus.

LA, HELEN; Alhambra HS; Alhambra, CA; (2); Office Aide; Service Clb; Swmmng; Hon Roll; Social Clb; Bus Advrtsmnt.

LA, HONG L; Crawford HS; San Diego, CA; (2); Hon Roll; CSF; Bus Mgmt.

LA, HUE T; Mountain View HS; S El Monte, CA; (2); Hon Roll; CSF Clb; Dr.

LA, HUONG K; Rosemead HS; Rosemead, CA; (2); Cmnty Wkr; GAA; Intnl Clb; Math Clb; Science Clb; Service Clb; Lit Mag; Capt Crs Cntry; Var Trk; High Hon Roll; CSF; Judicial Brd; Friday Night Live; Bus.

LA, JANET; Abraham Lincoln HS; San Francisco, CA; (2); 4-H; Teachers Aide; Chorus; Rep Frsh Cls; Rep Soph Cls; Cit Awd; 4-H Awd; High Hon Roll; Hon Roll; Prfct Atten Awd; San Francisco ST U; Law.

LA, KIM; Granada Hill HS; Los Angeles, CA; (2); Church Yth Grp; Cmnty Wkr; Girl Scts; Hosp Aide; Office Aide; Teachers Aide; Bsbl; Bsktbl; Score Keeper; Vllybl; Chldrn Ctr Vlntr; UCSD; Adv Exec.

LA, LE-KIM; Rosemead HS; Rosemead, CA; (2); Cmnty Wkr; Computer Clb; GAA; Intnl Clb; Math Clb; Science Clb; Hist Service Clb; Lit Mag; Capt Crs Cntry; JV Trk; CSF; Judicial Brd; Friday Night Live; Teach.

LA, MIKE L; La Mirada HS; La Mirada, CA; (2); FBLA; Spanish Clb; Rep Frsh Cls; Rep Soph Cls; Var Tennis; Hon Roll; Prfct Atten Awd; Wrkng & Hlpng People; CSU; Bus Law.

LA, MINH; Baldwin Park HS; Baldwin Park, CA; (1); Church Yth Grp; Intrml Bsktbl; Intrml Trk; Cit Awd; Hon Roll; Prfct Atten Awd; Pres Schlr; Gftd & Tlntd Educ.

LA, NHU; Mark Keppel HS; Monterey Park, CA; (2); DAR Awd; Jr Var Badminton; Peace Org; UC Riverside; Med.

LA, PHUONG; Mark Keppel HS; Monterey Park, CA; (2); Math Clb; SADD; Jr Var Badminton; United For Peace; U Of CA Irvine; Arch.

LA, PHUONG-ANH T; La Quinta HS; Westminster, CA; (3); 12/333; French Clb; Key Clb; Math Clb; Treas SADD; High Hon Roll; Hon Roll; CSF; Schlr Of Qtr; Royal Bnqt Cert Wnnr Phys Ed.

LA, THANH C; Bassett HS; La Puente, CA; (2); FBLA; Cit Awd; Hon Roll; Jr NHS; NHS; UCLA; Bus Mgmt.

LA, VAN H; Tustin HS; Tustin, CA; (3); 71/446; Aud/Vis; Intnl Clb; Key Clb; Science Clb; Intrml Bsktbl; Intrml Fld Hcky; Intrml Ftbl; JV Vllybl; Hon Roll; Pres Acad Fit Awd; Korean,Vietnamese & Ethic Clbs; CSF; Roller Hockey; Body Surf; Chrstn & Jew Breakfast; Vllybl 2nd Pl; CSUF; Dentistry.

LA, VI; Bassett HS; La Puente, CA; (4); 10/277; FBLA; Teachers Aide; Church Yth Grp; High Hon Roll; NHS; Prfct Atten Awd; Vrsty Badminton; Talent Search Pgm Cal St Los Angeles; CSU Polytech Pomona; Intl Bus.

LA BARGE, SCOTT M; Quartz Hill HS; Lancaster, CA; (4); 1/560; Drama Clb; French Clb; Key Clb; Varsity Clb; Band; Jazz Band; Mrchg Band; Pep Band; School Play; Ed Lit Mag; U DE; Philosophy.

LA BEAUD, ANGELLE D; Lowell HS; San Francisco, CA; (2); Office Aide; Band; Italian Clb; Art; Poetry; Music; Med Rsrch.

LA BERGE, KATHY S; El Cajon Valley HS; El Cajon, CA; (3); 33/296; FTA; GAA; Pres Sec Key Clb; Speech Tm; Ed Yrbk; Rep Stu Cncl; Var Fld Hcky; JV Sftbl; Var Tennis; Hon Roll; San Diego ST U; Educ.

LA BUTE, MONTIAGO X; Mt Diablo HS; W Pittsburg, CA; (3); English Clb; JA; Model UN; Variety Show; Ed Nwsp; Lit Mag; JV Tennis; High Hon Roll; Hon Roll; Play Drums; UC Davis CA; Bio Chem.

LA CHAPELLE, KATRINA R; Vallejo SR HS; Vallejo, CA; (2); SADD; Hon Roll; UC Berkeley; Lawyer.

LA CUES, MICHELLE I; Apple Valley HS; Apple Valley, CA; (3); French Clb; Band; Mrchg Band; Hon Roll; CA ST U.

LA FORTE, ANISSA; Orange Glen HS; Escondido, CA; (3); 118/460; JV Capt Bsktbl; Church Yth Grp; Chorus; Church Choir; Hon Roll; NHS; MVP Jr Var Bsktbl 88-89; Ready Writhers Project Cert Outstanding Achvmt 90; Eng.

LA FRANCHI, KIM A; San Rafael HS; San Rafael, CA; (3); 15/284; Key Clb; Spanish Clb; SADD; Ed Nwsp; Stu Cncl; Var Capt Bsktbl; Var Capt Tennis; Var Trk; Hon Roll.

LA LONDE, NIKKI R; Edison HS; Huntington Beach, CA; (2); Church Yth Grp; Cheerldng; Pepperdine; Corp Law.

LA LUZERNE, WENDY NATALIE; Grant HS; Broderick, CA; (1); Band; Jazz Band; Mrchg Band; Pep Band; Stage Crew; Rptr Nwsp; Yrbk; High Hon Roll; Hon Roll; Opt Clb Awd; Stu Reaching Out; Mrchng Band Beginning Piano Excllnc Awd; Opng Act For Blck Film Mkrs Awd 89-90; CSUS; Music Educ.

LA MARK, ALICIA M; Mt Shasta HS; Mount Shasta, CA; (2); JV Powder Puff Ftbl; JV Sftbl; JV Vllybl; Hon Roll; CSF; Vlntrs Fire Prvntn CA Dept Frstry Pgm; Humboldt ST U; Frstry.

LA MARR, YEAPHANA A; Encina HS; Sacramento, CA; (4); Var Capt Sftbl; Hon Roll; Tutor; CSU Chico; Pre-Med.

LA MERE, JEFFREY P; Oak Ridge HS; El Dorado Hills, CA; (3); 8/270; Am Leg Boys St; SADD; Pres Frsh Cls; Rep Soph Cls; Rep Jr Cls; JV Var Bsktbl; JV Capt Ftbl; High Hon Roll; Ntl Merit Ltr; Rotary Awd; CSF.

LA MONT, JENNIFER D; Central Union HS; Oak Harbor, WA; (2); Church Yth Grp; Chorus; Flag Corp; Red Crss Certf Lifeguard 2 Yrs; U Of Western WA; Nrsng.

LA MONTAGNE, ARBON D; Sutter Union HS; Sutter, CA; (3); 1/79; Church Yth Grp; Intnl Clb; High Hon Roll; Hon Roll; Prfct Atten Awd; Bst Shw Vctnl Ed Olympcs Yuba City 1989-90; Gld Mdl Sutter Cnty Acad Dcthln, St 1989-90; 4.0 GPA; CA ST U Chico; Math.

LA MUNYON, ADAM L; Whittier Christian HS; Yorba Linda, CA; (2); Speech Tm; Yrbk; Bsbl; Trk; OK ST; Law Enfrcmnt.

LA MUNYON, RYAN; Liberty HS; Brentwood, CA; (3); Church Yth Grp; Computer Clb; Quiz Bowl; Scholastic Bowl; SADD; VICA; Off Frsh Cls; Rep Stu Cncl; Var Bsbl; JV Bsktbl; Stu Mnth Awd.

LA O, CHRIEZL L; Chula Vista HS; San Diego, CA; (3); 48/535; Computer Clb; Pep Clb; Ed Yrbk; JV Vllybl; Cit Awd; Masonic Awd; Pres Acad Fit Awd; Pan Asian Clb; Dentstry.

LA PLANTE, ISREAL D; Mt Shasta HS; Mount Shasta, CA; (3); AFS; Teachers Aide; School Musical; Stage Crew; Var JV Ftbl; Pres Acad Fit Awd; Pres Schlr; High Hnrs Golden St Exam Geom; Tchr.

LA PLANTE, JEANNE A; Marymount HS; Los Angeles, CA; (3); Pres Drama Clb; Science Clb; Speech Tm; Thesps; Chorus; School Musical; School Play; Stage Crew; Lit Mag; Pres Soph Cls; Cmmnctns.

LA POINT, SHALOM; Mesa Verde HS; Citrus Heights, CA; (3); 23/225; Am Leg Aux Girls St; Cmnty Wkr; Red Cross Aide; Spanish Clb; Sprt Ed Nwsp; Rptr Frsh Cls; Rptr Soph Cls; Rptr Stu Cncl; Var Bsktbl; Var Vllybl; Stud Rchng Out; Mock Trl Witness & Instr; UC Davis; Comm.

LA POINTE, JOSYELLA C; Hamilton Academy Of Music; Los Angeles, CA; (2); Spanish Clb; School Play; VP Soph Cls; Pres Jr Cls; Theatr Arts.

LA QUIRE, JENNETTE; El Capitan HS; El Cajon, CA; (4); 9/460; Pres French Clb; Intnl Clb; Varsity Clb; Var Capt Crs Cntry; Var Trk; High Hon Roll; Tribune Athl/Acad Awd; Arch.

LA RIVA, YVONNE; Phineas Banning HS; Wilmington, CA; (4); 9/551; Church Yth Grp; FTA; Intnl Clb; Teachers Aide; Church Choir; Stu Cncl; Var Capt Swmmng; High Hon Roll; Pres Schlr; Interact Clb; CSF Sealbearer; Ephebian Soc; Educ.

LA ROCQUE, JENNIFER L; Poway HS; San Diego, CA; (4); 32/679; Church Yth Grp; SADD; Rptr Yrbk; Rep Stu Cncl; Powder Puff Ftbl; JV Tennis; High Hon Roll; Hon Roll; Kiwanis Awd; NHS; U Of CA; Med.

LA ROSA, DEVIN D; Modesto HS; Modesto, CA; (3); Ed Nwsp; Var L Bsktbl; JV Trk; Hon Roll; Ntl Merit Ltr; CA Schlrshp Fed; Aerontcl Engrng.

LA ROSA, KATHRYN KELLY; Alhambra HS; Martinez, CA; (4); 7/215; Cmnty Wkr; Math Clb; Teachers Aide; Yrbk; Stu Cncl; Var Capt Diving; Var Socr; High Hon Roll; Kiwanis Awd; Cmp Fire Wo-He-Lo Mdlln 90; Math Engr.

LA RUE, BRENDA; Napa HS; Napa, CA; (4); 20/385; Am Leg Aux Girls St; Church Yth Grp; Key Clb; Math Clb; SADD; Teachers Aide; Mrchg Band; Var Bsktbl; Var Trk; Hon Roll; Samuel Merritt Coll; Med.

LA VALLO, GINA; Vista HS; Vista, CA; (4); 29/400; Am Leg Aux Girls St; Pres Stu Cncl; Var JV Fld Hcky; JV Socr; Cit Awd; Hon Roll; Pres Acad Fit Awd; Rotary Awd; Peer Cnslr; Kelly Rae Olson Melo Awd; Pnthr Yr; U Of CA Santa Barbara; Politic.

LA VALLO, KERRI J; Antioch SR HS; Antioch, CA; (4); 69/605; Spanish Clb; Sec Chorus; Swing Chorus; High Hon Roll; Hon Roll.

LA VELLE, SUZANNE M; Corona HS; Corona, CA; (2); Drama Clb; Letterman Clb; Science Clb; School Play; Rep Frsh Cls; Stu Cncl; Intrml Vllybl; Pres Acad Fit Awd; AZ ST U; Bus.

LA VORICO, GINA M; Woodland HS; Woodland, CA; (3); Drill Tm; Score Keeper; Sftbl; Tennis; Amnsty Intl; CA ST U Sacramento; Bus.

LABABIT, CATHERINE M; Hanford Union HS; Hanford, CA; (2); FBLA; FHA; Tennis; Hon Roll.

LABARBER, STACI L; Edison SR HS; Stockton, CA; (1); Rep Debate Tm; Rep Speech Tm; Rptr Nwsp; Pres Frsh Cls; Pres Soph Cls; Stu Cncl; Hon Roll.

LABAT, EBONY A; Mercy HS; San Francisco, CA; (4); 56/164; Yrbk; Rep Frsh Cls; Rep Soph Cls; Hon Roll; Black Stu Union Treas 2 Yrs; Black Stu Union Choir; San Diego ST U; Bus Adm.

LABATE, DONA T; Dona Labate HS; San Jose, CA; (2); Art Clb; Science Clb; Artwrk Dsplyd Spring Fuire; Dntl Care Wrkng Dntls Offc; U Of San Jose; Nrsng.

LABAYEN, AILEEN; Norte Vista HS; Riverside, CA; (3); Dance Clb; JA; Var Cheerldng; Hon Roll; Bus.

LABIO, MERILOU GALLIGUEZ; Diamond Bar HS; Walnut, CA; (4); Pres Sec Chorus; Variety Show; Intrml Vllybl; Hon Roll; Pres Acad Fit Awd; Madrigal Choir Pres & Secy; Vocal Jazz Choir Pres; Show Choir Pres; CA Poly Pomona; Civil Engrng.

LABIT, JESSICA A; Apple Valley HS; Apple Valley, CA; (2); Rep Church Yth Grp; ROTC; Rep Frsh Cls; Pres Stu Cncl; Score Keeper; Hon Roll; Yth Cnslr; Acting.

LABRADOR, ROWENA S; Whitney HS; Cerritos, CA; (1); Church Yth Grp; Dance Clb; Color Guard; Drill Tm; Flag Corp; Jazz Dance.

LABRECQUE, MICHELLE; Concord HS; Concord, CA; (3); Debate Tm; GAA; Model UN; SADD; Teachers Aide; Chorus; Yrbk; Bsktbl; Hon Roll.

LAC, DEREK T; George Washington HS; San Francisco, CA; (3); Computer Clb; Crs Cntry; High Hon Roll; Hon Roll; Fencing; Cmptr Sci.

LAC, JAMES M; Los Amigos HS; Fountain Valley, CA; (3); French Clb; JV Bsktbl; JV Vllybl.

LAC, TIFFANY; George Washington HS; San Francisco, CA; (4); Intnl Clb; Key Clb; Red Cross Aide; Cit Awd; Hon Roll; Kiwanis Awd; Gen Srvc Soc; Spcl Olympcs; San Francisco ST U; Nrsng.

LAC, VU; Hemet HS; Hemet, CA; (2); Varsity Clb; JV Bsktbl; JV Ftbl; Var Trk; Wt Lftg; Elks Awd; Hon Roll; Jr NHS; MVP Ftbl 2 Yrs.

LACAR, LEN; Samuel F B Morse HS; San Diego, CA; (3); VP Science Clb; Variety Show; Sprt Ed Yrbk; Mgr(s); Co-Capt Vllybl; Hon Roll; NHS; Opt Clb Awd; Prfct Atten Awd; Pres Acad Fit Awd; SDCS Staff Bulleton Super Rtng; Jr Optimists Of Yr; UCLA; Sci.

LACAYO R, MA VERONICA; Hollywood HS; Los Angeles, CA; (4); Spanish Clb; Off Sr Cls; Gym; Cit Awd; Hon Roll; Silver Seal, Engl & Scl Stds Awds; Cal ST Los Angeles; Mech Engr.

LACEY, AIMEE; O'farrell SCPA HS; San Diego, CA; (3); 1/151; Letterman Clb; Spanish Clb; Variety Show; Cit Awd; High Hon Roll.

LACEY, DINA M; Clayton Valley HS; Clayton, CA; (1); Dance Clb; Gym; Cit Awd; Hon Roll; Lion Awd; Pres Acad Fit Awd; Vrsty Lttr Gymnstcs; Stanford U; Physcn.

LACEY, MARIO; San Gorgonio HS; San Bernardino, CA; (3); Am Leg Boys St; Church Yth Grp; Band; Var Crs Cntry; Intrml Ftbl; Var Trk; Cit Awd; Hon Roll; Prfct Atten Awd; UCR; Electronics.

LACEY, MARLON G; San Gorgonio HS; San Bernardino, CA; (3); Church Yth Grp; Off Jr Cls; Crs Cntry; Ftbl; Trk; Hon Roll.

LACEY, TIMOTHY J; Templeton HS; Paso Robles, CA; (3); Church Yth Grp; Cmnty Wkr; FFA; Hosp Aide; Sec Science Clb; Socr; Vllybl; Cit Awd; Hon Roll; Voice Dem Awd; Helicopter Flight Schl; Exchng Stu USSR; Sign Lang Clss; Environmental Engrng.

LACHBERG, MICHAEL T; San Gabriel HS; Rosemead, CA; (3); Chess Clb; Drama Clb; Stage Crew; JV Bsktbl; JV Crs Cntry; Hon Roll; Pres Acad Fit Awd; Acctng.

LACHER, TOM; De La Salle HS; Concord, CA; (3); 9/219; Am Leg Boys St; Sec Treas Spanish Clb; Rep Frsh Cls; Rep Soph Cls; Rep Jr Cls; VP Sr Cls; Rep Stu Cncl; Bsktbl; Crs Cntry; Stat Ftbl; City Of Concord Yth Cncl 90-91; Oakland Diocesan Reach Cong Delg; Campus Ministry; Chem Engrng.

LACHO, CAROLYN A; Independence HS; San Jose, CA; (4); Teachers Aide; Outstndng Achvt ESL & Engl Cls; San Jose ST; Chem Engr.

LACK, CHARLIE W; Kingsburg HS; Kingsburg, CA; (2); Church Yth Grp; JV Ftbl; JV Golf; JV Wrstlng; Hon Roll; CA Maritime Acad; Marine Trans.

LACKEY, CHANTAL A; Westlake Schl; Santa Monica, CA; (2); Church Yth Grp; Cmnty Wkr; Debate Tm; Pres VP French Clb; Thesps; Chorus; School Musical; School Play; Natl Frnch Cont 4th Pl Natlly High Level.

LACOCK, SARAH K; Apple Valley HS; Apple Valley, CA; (2); Church Yth Grp; School Play; Hon Roll; Teachers Aide.

LACONICO, MICHAEL J; Saint Francis HS; Duarte, CA; (2); Chess Clb; Pep Clb; Spanish Clb; Yrbk; Hon Roll; NHS; Spanish NHS; CSF; Fishing Clb; CA Polytechnic; Comp Sci.

LACORTE, ERIN S; Cerritos HS; Cerritos, CA; (1); GAA; Band; Mrchg Band; School Musical; JV Socr; Var Trk; Intrml Wt Lftg; Hon Roll; Cerritos JC; Eng.

LACOVARA, JENNIFER A; Morro Bay HS; Los Osos, CA; (3); 7/215; AFS; Intnl Clb; JCL; School Play; Var Crs Cntry; Var Trk; High Hon Roll; CA Schlrshp Fed Club; Tchng.

LACROIX, GARY; Willows HS; Willows, CA; (3); 1/85; Var JV Bsktbl; Var JV Ftbl; High Hon Roll; Block W Clb Ath; CSF.

LACSAMANA, GENEVIEVE; Granada Hills HS; Northridge, CA; (4); Church Yth Grp; Hosp Aide; Varsity Clb; Chorus; L Cheerldng; Vllybl; Hon Roll; CA ST U Northridge; Psych.

LACSON, CATHERINE C; Dr James J Hogan HS; Vallejo, CA; (3); Art Clb; Drama Clb; Science Clb; Teachers Aide; Chorus; School Play; Rptr Nwsp; Ed Yrbk; High Hon Roll; Hon Roll; CSF; Vrsty Badmntn; Art.

LACSON, MARIA REGINA I; Staint Anthony HS; Long Beach, CA; (3); Ntl Merit Schol; Phy.

LACY, CHRISTINE M; Fontana HS; Fontana, CA; (2); Dentstry.

LACY, LORI LAVELLE; North Monterey County HS; Salinas, CA; (3); Dance Clb; Drama Clb; Girl Scts; SADD; Variety Show; Nwsp; Vllybl; High Hon Roll; Hon Roll; Prfct Atten Awd; Acad Awds; Certs Achvts; Hartnell; Medcl Recrds.

LACY, SAMANTHA R; Irvington HS; Fremont, CA; (3); Key Clb; JV Var Bsktbl; JV Swmmng; JV Var Vllybl; Hon Roll; San Diego ST U; Firefighter.

LADD, ALLAN M; Hemet HS; Hemet, CA; (2); U Of CA Riverside.

LADD, JEFF A; Modesto HS; Modesto, CA; (1); JV Bsktbl; JV Golf; Hon Roll; Acadc All Conf Tm Golf.

LADD, MARY; Benicia HS; Benicia, CA; (3); Church Yth Grp; Cmnty Wkr; JA; Key Clb; Varsity Clb; Color Guard; Ed Nwsp; Rptr Yrbk; JV Var Bsktbl; High Hon Roll; Soph Rep Pres Key Clb; Quake 89 Outreach; Organized Donkey Bsktbl Fndrsr; San Fran ST U; Jrnlsn.

LADEN, TANYA M; Louisville HS; Woodland Hills, CA; (3); Cmnty Wkr; Drama Clb; School Musical; Nwsp; Off Soph Cls; Hon Roll; Awd For Engl II; Philosophy.

LADNER II, JUDITH; Colfax HS; Colfax, CA; (3); Science Clb; Cheerldng; Vllybl; Hon Roll; CA ST U Sacramento; Cvl Engr.

LAFAURIE, JEN I M; Louisville HS; Woodland Hills, CA; (2); Church Yth Grp; Sec Science Clb; Ski Clb; Stage Crew; Trk; Hon Roll; Prfct Atten Awd; CA Schlrshp Fed; Explorer Clb Pres; Hnrbl Mntn La Cnty Sci Fr, Hlth,Physics Soc; Awd Mrt Amer Vacuum.

LAFAURIE, LEAH R; Mt Whitney HS; Visalia, CA; (1); Church Yth Grp; Art Clb; Sftbl; Vllybl; CA Schlrshp Fedrtn; Photgrphy; Acad Ltr; U Of CA.

LAFIGUERA, MARICRIS B; Workman HS; West Covina, CA; (3); 16/81; German Clb; Intnl Clb; Rep Key Clb; VP Science Clb; Ski Clb; Spanish Clb; Ed Rptr Nwsp; Off Jr Cls; Stu Cncl; Mgr(s); Brnz Cngrsnl Awd; CA Schlrshp Fdrtn; U CA Irvine; Bus Adm.

LAFLIN, BONNIE-JILL; Concord HS; Concord, CA; (1); Cmnty Wkr; Model UN; Ski Clb; Cheerldng; Var Trk; Dance Grp Natl Cmptn Wnnr; Trk Spcl Olympic Coach; U Irvine; Prfssnl Dancer.

LAFORGA, ABIGAIL M; St Monica HS; Los Angeles, CA; (3); Cmnty Wkr; Intnl Clb; Pep Clb; Stage Crew; Stu Cncl; Cheerldng; Hon Roll; NHS; U Of CA Santa Cruz; Bio.

LAFRANCHI, SUZANNE J; Notre Dame HS; San Jose, CA; (3); 1/90; Intnl Clb; Chorus; School Musical; School Play; Ed Nwsp; Lit Mag; Pres Jr Cls; Pres Stu Cncl; Swmmng; High Hon Roll; Hnbl Mntn Poetry Cntst; Pblshd Poem/Grt Poems Of Westrn Wrld; 1st & 3rd Pl In Spnsh Poetry Cntst; Psych.

LAGALA, STACEY C; Poway HS; Poway, CA; (4); Cmnty Wkr; Drama Clb; Ski Clb; Rep Stu Cncl; Cheerldng; JV Var Mgr(s); Powder Puff Ftbl; Score Keeper; Stat Wrstlng; Peer Cnslr; Stu Athltc Trnr; U Of AZ; Sports Thrpy.

LAGAMAYO, MARK PHILIP C; Southwest HS; San Diego, CA; (2); Prfct Atten Awd; Hnr Clss Engl; Sci-Aerosp Engrng-Astrnmy-Astrphyscs-Wrld Hist/Culture Awds; UCSD; Aerosp Engrng.

LAGANA, ELISA; Monterey HS; Carmel, CA; (4); Rptr Nwsp; Hon Roll; Italian Club VP & Pres; Menlo Coll; Psych.

LAGATTA, VINCE; Cardinal Newman HS; Santa Rosa, CA; (2); Church Yth Grp; Church Choir; VP Frsh Cls; Pres Soph Cls; JV Bsbl; JV Bsktbl; Var Capt Ftbl; High Hon Roll; Hon Roll; All Around Stu; Pop Warner Coll Schlrshp; Law.

LAGATTUTA, LAUREN; Alverno HS; Arcadia, CA; (3); 17/60; Chorus; Pres Jr Cls; Rep Stu Cncl; Offcl Govt Cabnt Sec Of Commnctns; House Rep; Psych.

LAGE, MIKE P; Fullerton Union HS; Fullerton, CA; (1); 52/432; Bsbl; Ftbl; Hon Roll; Cmmrcl Pilot.

LAGER, JEANNETTE C; Miraleste HS; Rancho Pls Vrds, CA; (3); 15/153; Church Yth Grp; Model UN; Service Clb; Off Sr Cls; Capt Var Cheerldng; JV Socr; High Hon Roll; NHS; Spanish NHS; UCLA; Med.

LAGMAY, PHOEBE C; Carson HS; Carson, CA; (2); Intnl Clb; Drill Tm; Cit Awd; High Hon Roll; Prfct Atten Awd; Pres Acad Fit Awd; Asian Club, CA Jr Schlrshp Fed; Outstndng Achvt Awd CA Schlrshp Fed; Banners Squad.

LAGNEAUX, ANGELA C; Roseville HS; Rocklin, CA; (3); 43/411; Drama Clb; Science Clb; Spanish Clb; School Musical; School Play; Stage Crew; Var Crs Cntry; Var Trk; High Hon Roll; CSF; Davis; Envrnmntl Stds.

LAGO, EDUARDO A; Hogan HS; Vallejo, CA; (3); Chess Clb; VP French Clb; ROTC; JV Ftbl; Wrstlng; Var L Wrstlng; Civil Engr.

LAGOMARSINO, FRANK S; A A Stagg HS; Stockton, CA; (1); Church Yth Grp; Intrml Bsktbl; High Hon Roll; Hon Roll; NHS; Anesthesiology.

LAGOMARSINO, GINA; Rio Americano HS; Carmichael, CA; (3); 1/290; Church Yth Grp; Spanish Clb; Band; Treas Soph Cls; Pres Jr Cls; Pres Sr Cls; Ntl Merit Ltr; Service Clb; Pep Band; Lit Mag; Jr Statesmen Amer Sec & Conference Coord; Ca Schlrshp Fed Pres & Sec; Friday Night Live; Polical Sci.

LAGRIMAS, JUDETH V; Mira Mesa HS; San Diego, CA; (2); Spanish Clb; Band; Jazz Band; Mrchg Band; Pep Band; Cit Awd; Prfct Atten Awd; CSF; U CA; Med.

LAGUNA, ART NAZABAL; Tranquility Union HS; Mendota, CA; (2); Boy Scts; Church Yth Grp; Cit Awd; Hon Roll; Outstndng Stu Awd; Stu Pilot; Motorcros Racing; Fresno ST; Law Enfrcmnt.

LAGUNA, MICHAEL; Bishop Amat HS; Huntclair, CA; (1); Intrml Bsbl; Intrml Bsktbl; Intrml Ftbl; Hon Roll; UCLA; Accntng.

LAH, JOHN J; Troy HS; Yorba Linda, CA; (2); 17/334; Church Yth Grp; Math Clb; Band; Bsktbl; Art Clb; Tennis; High Hon Roll; Hon Roll; Rotary Awd; PAL; UCSD; Pre-Med.

LAHAV, ORI S; William Howard Taft HS; Van Nuys, CA; (2); Cmnty Wkr; Computer Clb; Debate Tm; VP French Clb; Treas Intnl Clb; Ski Clb; Speech Tm; Temple Yth Grp; Ed Nwsp; JV L Trk; Hstry, Lang Art, Sci, Engl Achvmtn Awds.

LAHMANN, MARTIN; Arroyo Grande HS; Arroyo Grande, CA; (4); 93/435; AFS; Church Yth Grp; Stat Bsbl; Var Socr; Architectural Engineering.

LAHMON, JODI L; Armijo HS; Fairfield, CA; (2); Church Yth Grp; JV Cheerldng; Phys Thrpy.

LAI, BENJAMIN Y; Canyon Springs HS; Moreno Valley, CA; (4); FBLA; High Hon Roll; Hon Roll; Art Awds; Arch.

LAI, CHRISTINE; George Washington HS; San Francisco, CA; (2); Hon Roll; Bus Admin.

LAI, EUGENE; San Ramon Valley HS; San Ramon, CA; (4); 36/387; Church Yth Grp; Computer Clb; Math Clb; Teachers Aide; High Hon Roll; Gldn St Exam In Geo Hgh Hnr; San Jose ST U; Comp Sci.

LAI, GENA; Torrey Pines HS; San Diego, CA; (3); 6/457; Key Clb; Acpl Chr; Band; Chorus; Nwsp; Sec Soph Cls; Stu Cncl; JV Crs Cntry; JV Capt Vllybl; Hon Roll; Scripps Clinic Intrnshp Wnnr; Hghst Achvt-Engl/Bio; U CA SB Undergrad Fellowshp/Prz Cmptn-Semifnlst; Neurosci.

LAI, HO Y; Lowell HS; San Francisco, CA; (3); Science Clb; Service Clb; Teachers Aide; Vlntrd Rcrtn Ctr Hndcppd; Vlybl & Tnns Clb; CA Schlrshp Fdrtn; Spcl Ed.

LAI, JAMES C; Montclair HS; Montclair, CA; (2); Wt Lftg; Cit Awd; High Hon Roll; Engr.

LAI, JAMES W; Villa Park HS; Orange, CA; (3); Key Clb; Bsktbl; Cit Awd; High Hon Roll; Hon Roll; NHS; CSF; Bus.

LAI, JENNIFER C; Diamond Bar HS; Diamond Bar, CA; (2); French Clb; Key Clb; Library Aide; Science Clb; Tennis; Hon Roll; Bdmntn; CSF.

LAI, JOHN; Mt Pleasant HS; San Jose, CA; (2); Chess Clb; Tennis; Vietnamese Clb; Asian Clb.

LAI, JUDY Y; Arcadia HS; Arcadia, CA; (3); 31/639; Hist Art Clb; Church Yth Grp; Co-Capt Hosp Aide; Teachers Aide; Church Choir; Color Guard; Drill Tm; Yrbk; Var Trk; Intrml Vllybl; Electric Bass Guitar; Teacher Sunday Schl & Bible Stud; Love Dogs & Kids; Berkeley; Vet Med.

LAI, LINDA; San Ramon Valley HS; San Ramon, CA; (4); 65/387; Church Yth Grp; Intnl Clb; JA; Library Aide; Teachers Aide; Variety Show; Hon Roll; San Jose ST U; Nutrition.

LAI, MING SHYAN; Gahr HS; Artesia, CA; (3); Church Yth Grp; Computer Clb; Hon Roll; Chinese Club; UC Irvine; Engrng.

LAI, QUANG C; Montclair HS; Montclair, CA; (1); Library Aide; Var Bsbl; Ftbl; Wrstlng; High Hon Roll; Hon Roll; Prfct Atten Awd.

LAI, SAMMY C; San Gabriel HS; San Gabriel, CA; (2); Computer Clb; Debate Tm; Key Clb; NFL; Science Clb; Speech Tm; Hon Roll; Opt Clb Awd; JV Tennis; Debate ST Qualyfier Double; Intl Trade Awd; Harvard; Law.

LAI, SON C; Lakewood SR HS; Long Beach, CA; (3); Cmnty Wkr; French Clb; Intnl Clb; Ed Yrbk; Off Jr Cls; Stu Cncl; Cit Awd; Prfct Atten Awd; Pres Acad Fit Awd; CSF; Golden St Ex; Chem Cntst Exmtn; USC; Comp Engr.

LAI, STEVE P; Bakersfield HS; Bakersfield, CA; (2); Boy Scts; Chess Clb; FCA; Teachers Aide; JV Crs Cntry; Intrml Ftbl; JV Trk; JV Wrstlng; Hon Roll; Bio; Devry Inst; Cmptr Prgmng.

LAI, THAI Q; Independence HS; Sunnyvale, CA; (3); Science Clb; Socr; Badminton; Most Improved 1987-88 88-89; Soccer Top Scorer 87-88 88-89; Gmtry Honor 87-88 Golden St Exam; UC Davis.

LAI, TSE; Mountain View HS; El Monte, CA; (1); JV Tennis; Hon Roll; Jr Var Badminton 89-90.

LAI, VAN T; Notre Dame Acad; Los Angeles, CA; (3); Church Yth Grp; Service Clb; SADD; Yrbk; Lit Mag; Pres Frsh Cls; Rep Jr Cls; Hon Roll; APLA; U CA Santa Barbara; Visl Arts.

LAI, WENDY; Mt Whitney HS; Visalia, CA; (2); Art Clb; 1st Pl Tulane Cnty Grand Jury Art Cont; CSF; 3 Times Acad Ltr Awd; UCLA; Art.

LAI, WILLY H; West HS; Torrance, CA; (3); 24/400; Church Yth Grp; Computer Clb; Intnl Clb; JA; Math Clb; Service Clb; Varsity Clb; Var Tennis; High Hon Roll; Prfct Atten Awd; Most Artistic Awd; Most Imprvd Tnns Awd; Asian Cultural Club; U Of CA; Arch.

LAINE, REBECCA; Palm Desert HS; Bermuda Dunes, CA; (2); Treas SADD; School Play; High Hon Roll; Rotary Awd; St Schlr; Mock Trl Tm; Natural Hlprs; Earthquake Rlf Fund; Notre Dame; Lwyr.

LAIRD, BRIAN; Cerritos HS; Cerritos, CA; (4); Hon Roll; Acquring Pilots Lic Federal Avtn Admin; Embry Riddle Aeron U; Aeron Eng.

LAIRD, DIANA; Portola JR SR HS; Clio, CA; (3); Office Aide; ROTC; Ski Clb; Teachers Aide; JV Bsktbl; Var JV Vllybl; High Hon Roll; Hon Roll; Rep Frsh Cls; Treas Soph Cls; Ski Team; Phys Thrpst.

LAIRD, JENIFER S; Alhambra HS; Martinez, CA; (3); 15/205; Am Leg Aux Girls St; Treas 4-H; Pep Clb; Varsity Clb; Phtg Yrbk; Sec Treas Jr Cls; Pres Sr Cls; JV Bsktbl; JV Cheerldng; Var Sftbl; CSF; Rodeo; Adv.

LAIRD, PIPER; St Helena HS; Saint Helena, CA; (4); Pres 4-H; Treas Key Clb; Model UN; Service Clb; Chorus; School Musical; Yrbk; Rep Frsh Cls; VP Soph Cls; Rep Jr Cls; Slctd For Nat Model Assmbly Org Of Am St; Ctznshp Washington Focus; World Focus Del; Nat 4-H; Vol Tv Stn; CSU; Government Intl Relations.

LAJOIE, HEATHER; Willits HS; Willits, CA; (3); GAA; Letterman Clb; SADD; Varsity Clb; Var Golf.

LAKE, HEIDI; Palm Desert HS; Mt Center, CA; (2); Church Yth Grp; Drama Clb; Key Clb; High Hon Roll; Whittier Coll; Tchr.

LAKE, JAMES A; Galt HS; Galt, CA; (3); 26/200; Boy Scts; Letterman Clb; Teachers Aide; Var Bsktbl; JV Ftbl; High Hon Roll; Hon Roll; Pres Acad Fit Awd; Cert Excllnc Hstry; All Leag V Bsktbl; Phys Thrpy.

LAKE, PARKER D; Bishop Amat Memorial HS; Pomona, CA; (3); Drama Clb; Letterman Clb; Varsity Clb; School Play; Ed Nwsp; Lit Mag; Off Sr Cls; L Ftbl; L Trk; Var Wt Lftg; Cmnty Service Awds; One In The Spirit; Spec Olympics Coach; USC; Bus.

LAKE, TANYA; Acad Of Our Lady Of Peace; San Diego, CA; (2); High Hon Roll; Hon Roll; NEDT Awd; Acad Leag Tm; Engrng.

LAKEMAN, RUSSELL E; Milpitas HS; Milpitas, CA; (3); Church Yth Grp; Spanish Clb; Var Ftbl; Wt Lftg; Hon Roll; Vlntrd Veterans Admin Hosp; Cal Poly; Mech Engr.

LAKHANI, BILAL M; Magnolia HS; Anaheim, CA; (1); Office Aide; Cit Awd; Hon Roll; Prfct Atten Awd; Cypress Coll; Arch.

LAKIN, GLEN A; Brea-Olinda HS; Brea, CA; (1); Boy Scts; Church Yth Grp; Intrml Socr; JV Trk; Hon Roll; Prfct Atten Awd; Pres Acad Fit Awd; Rotary Awd; CSF; Eagle Scout; Stu Mnth 89; Cal Poly; Arch.

LAL, MANJU; Upland HS; Upland, CA; (2); Trk; Hon Roll; Pres Acad Fit Awd; Gastorenterology.

LAL, RAVINESH A; Woodrow Wilson HS; San Francisco, CA; (3); School Play; Yrbk; Cit Awd; Hon Roll; Med.

LALA, BIRAJ K; Harbor HS; Scotts Valley, CA; (4); 1/250; Am Leg Boys St; Pres JA; School Musical; School Play; Ed Nwsp; High Hon Roll; Jr NHS; Pres Acad Fit Awd; Rotary Awd; Val; Bnk Amer Plaq Awd Liberal Arts; Bio, Jrnlsm, Scl Stds, Drama & Engl Awds; Omega Nu & Parker Schlrshps; U Of CA Berkeley; Bus.

LALANDE, KAREN N; Lutheran HS; Orange, CA; (2); Church Yth Grp; Pep Clb; Ski Clb; Yrbk; JV L Sftbl; Intrml Vllybl; Juniorettes Pres; Chapman Coll; Art.

LALATA, JACKIE C; North Salinas HS; Salinas, CA; (4); Dance Clb; Office Aide; Science Clb; Teachers Aide; Cit Awd; High Hon Roll; Hon Roll; Prfct Atten; Hartnell Coll; Bus.

LALL, PREM H; Lowell HS; San Francisco, CA; (4); 51/650; Cmnty Wkr; Red Cross Aide; Yrbk; Ntl Merit SF; Pres Pre-Med Club; CSF Rep; Treas Jr Statesmen Amer; UCSF Minority Rsrch Apprenticeship; Stanford; Opthalmology.

LALLANA, KATHRYN; Independence HS; San Jose, CA; (4); Church Yth Grp; GAA; Band; Church Choir; Mrchg Band; School Musical; Sec Jr Cls; VP Sr Cls; NHS; Var Badminton Tm Mst Imprvd Awd; Band Mst Outstndng Woodwind Awd & Sr Awd; Grnd Chmp CA St Tlnt Cmptn; San Jose ST U; Bio Sci.

LALLIER, ALLEN E; Central Union HS; El Centro, CA; (4); Debate Tm; DECA; FFA; Pep Clb; Speech Tm; Band; Jazz Band; Mrchg Band; Orch; Pep Band; Engrng.

LALONGISIP, ELENA; Oceana HS; Daly City, CA; (2); Church Yth Grp; Math Clb; Math Tm; Spanish Clb; Thesps; Church Choir; Yrbk; Treas Frsh Cls; Bsktbl; Vllybl; Filipino Clb; Acctng.

LAM, AGNES; James Lick HS; San Jose, CA; (2); Chorus.

LAM, ALAN S; Sunny Hills HS; Fullerton, CA; (2); 2/440; Church Yth Grp; Cmnty Wkr; Intnl Clb; Orch; Crs Cntry; JV Swmmng; High Hon Roll; VP NHS; Prfct Atten Awd; Rotary Awd; Acad Medals In Mathematics Science And Foreign Language; 3rd Pl In Amer String Tchrs Assoc Comp; Acad; Harvard; Pre Med.

LAM, ALTON F; San Lorenzo HS; San Leandro, CA; (4); 3/214; Scholastic Bowl; Trk; High Hon Roll; Ntl Merit Ltr; Sal; Peer Tutor; CSF Seal Bearer; Asian Clb; UC Berkeley; Mech Engr.

LAM, AN CHI; Abraham Lincoln HS; San Francisco, CA; (2); 4-H; Hosp Aide; Teachers Aide; Yrbk; Hon Roll; CSF Clb; U C Berkeley; Bus.

LAM, ANDERSON; San Gabriel HS; San Gabriel, CA; (3); VICA; Hon Roll; Cal Poly Pomona; Civil Engr.

LAM, ANN; John Marshall Fund Secondary HS; Pasadena, CA; (3); Debate Tm; Library Aide; Science Clb; Service Clb; Tennis; Hon Roll; NHS; Prfct Atten Awd; Pres Acad Fit Awd; CSF; Acad Dcthln Tm; Bus.

LAM, BERNICE M; Lowell HS; San Francisco, CA; (2); Teachers Aide; Stanford; Pediatrics.

LAM, BOBBY; Lincoln HS; Los Angeles, CA; (2); Dance Clb; Math Clb; Yrbk; Bsktbl; Trk; High Hon Roll; Hon Roll; Engr.

LAM, BONNIE C; Pinole Valley HS; Hercules, CA; (1); High Hon Roll.

LAM, BRENDEN M; J E Mc Ateer HS; San Francisco, CA; (3); Computer Clb; ROTC; Spanish Clb; Teachers Aide; Band; Drill Tm; Crs Cntry; Vllybl; Hon Roll; Chnese Clb; UC Davis; Engrg.

LAM, CECILIA; La Mirada HS; La Mirada, CA; (4); Key Clb; High Hon Roll; Hon Roll; Girls Leag Sec; Golden St Exam Hnrs; Outstndng Achvt In Peer Counseling; Long Beach City Coll; Intl Bus.

LAM, CHRISTINA Y; Mark Keppel HS; Monterey Park, CA; (1); Science Clb; JV Swmmng; Hon Roll; Prfct Atten Awd; Coachs Awd Swmmng Jr Var 90; Var Swmmg Ltr Awd; UCLA; Sci.

LAM, CHUNG H; Irvine HS; Irvine, CA; (4); Key Clb; Intnl Clb; Var Capt Tennis; U Of CA Irvine; Bio Sci.

LAM, CHUNG L; Granada HS; Los Angeles, CA; (2); Aircrft Mech.

LAM, CINDA K; Oakland HS; Oakland, CA; (3); Cmnty Wkr; Dance Clb; French Clb; Service Clb; SADD; Teachers Aide; Off Jr Cls; JV Vllybl; Hon Roll; Kiwanis Awd; World Hstry Map Cont 1st Pl Prfrmnce; FIDM; Fshn Dsgn.

LAM, CO; Lincoln HS; Los Angeles, CA; (2); Tennis; Hon Roll; Prfct Atten Awd; Cert Of Achvt; CSF.

LAM, CUONG H; Leuzinger HS; Hawthorne, CA; (3); Computer Clb; French Clb; Library Aide; Math Clb; Science Clb; Trk; Vllybl; Hon Roll; Prfct Atten Awd; Biochem.

LAM, CUONG P; Fremont HS; Sunnyvale, CA; (2); Chess Clb; Vllybl; Collecting Bsbl Cards, Comic Bks, Coins; Rdng Books; Stanford; Doctor.

LAM, CYNDI M; Alameda HS; Alameda, CA; (2); 22/275; Church Yth Grp; Key Clb; Science Clb; Spanish Clb; Hon Roll; Rcrdng Sec Of Asian Clb; CA Schlrshp Fdrtn; UC Berkeley; Engrng.

LAM, DANE T; Mt Diablo HS; Pittsburg, CA; (3); Church Yth Grp; French Clb; FBLA; UC Berkeley; Pediatrics.

LAM, DAVE H; Lowell HS; San Francisco, CA; (2); Church Yth Grp; JA; Teachers Aide; Cit Awd; Pres Acad Fit Awd; Vietnamese Clb VP; UCLA; Envrnmntl Engrng.

LAM, DON; Abraham Lincoln HS; Los Angeles, CA; (2).

LAM, DUNG; Savanna HS; Anaheim, CA; (2); VP Intnl Clb; Key Clb; Service Clb; Var Tennis; Var Trk; CSF Club Mem; Berkeley; Astronomy.

LAM, DUNG N; George Washington HS; San Francisco, CA; (2); Math Clb; Science Clb; Band; Red Crss Clb; Chinese Amer Clb; UCLA; Civil Engr.

LAM, ELISA; Mark Keffel HS; Monterey Park, CA; (2); 74/350; Hosp Aide; Treas Key Clb; Teachers Aide; Nwsp; Hon Roll; Amer/Asians Clb; Hstrn YMCA Awded Club Of Yr 89; Vlntr Hstrcl Museum; Pedtrcs.

LAM, ELVIS; Oakland HS; Oakland, CA; (3); Church Yth Grp; Cmnty Wkr; Pres French Clb; Key Clb; Math Clb; Yrbk; Var Tennis; JV Capt Vllybl; Cit Awd; Gov Hon Prg Awd; Archery Club; Physics & Frnch Awds; UC Berkeley; Civil Engrng.

LAM, ERIC P; John A Rowland HS; Walnut, CA; (2); High Hon Roll; Hon Roll; Intro Elec Hgh Achvt Awd; CA Poly Pomona; Elec.

LAM, FRANK; C K Mc Clatchy HS; Sacramento, CA; (4); 14/443; Cmnty Wkr; Math Clb; Math Tm; Quiz Bowl; Science Clb; Spanish Clb; High Hon Roll; Hon Roll; Prfct Atten Awd; 1st Pl Hnrs In Essay Contests 1st Pl In Greater Sacramentos Voc Fair.

LAM, GARVIN B; San Gabriel HS; San Gabriel, CA; (2); Pres Acad Fit Awd; Engrng.

LAM, HAI; Encina HS; Sacramento, CA; (4); Computer Clb; French Clb; Intnl Clb; Rptr Yrbk; Var Tennis; Hon Roll; CSU Sacramento.

LAM, HANH THI; Rosemead HS; San Gabriel, CA; (3); Dance Clb; Intnl Clb; Office Aide; High Hon Roll; Hon Roll; Pres Acad Fit Awd; Sign Lang; CSF; Prfct Acad Awd Cert; UC Riverside; Bus Mgmt.

LAM, HARRY C; Ygnacio Valley HS; Concord, CA; (2); 1/500; Hosp Aide; Key Clb; Model UN; Band; Trk; Guitar.

LAM, HELEN; Dublin HS; Dublin, CA; (1); 1/229; Drama Clb; Band; Jazz Band; Mrchg Band; Var Swmmng; High Hon Roll; High Hnrs Alg & Geo Golden St Exm; Engrng.

LAM, HOA V; Fresno HS; Fresno, CA; (3); Treas French Clb; FBLA; FTA; GAA; Math Clb; Math Tm; Varsity Clb; Var Capt Tennis; Cit Awd; French Hon Soc; CSF; Asian Amer Clb; Cal Poly; Engrng.

LAM, HUGH; Oakland Technical HS; Oakland, CA; (2); Math Tm; Science Clb; Tennis; JV Wrstlng; Hon Roll; Math & Acad Excllnce Awds; Asian Clb.

LAM, HUNG; Bellflower HS; Bellflower, CA; (3); 2/276; Treas Computer Clb; VP FBLA; Hosp Aide; JA; Library Aide; Mu Alpha Theta; Quiz Bowl; Scholastic Bowl; Ed Nwsp; High Hon Roll; Pre-Med.

LAM, JANE PHAN; Oakland HS; Oakland, CA; (3); German Clb; JA; Key Clb; Ed Mgr Yrbk; Var Bsktbl; Var Vllybl; High Hon Roll; Hon Roll; Hong Kong Chus; Jack London VP; UCLA; Bus Mgmt.

LAM, JANET W; San Gabriel HS; San Gabriel, CA; (3); Service Clb; Spanish Clb; Hon Roll; Pres Acad Fit Awd; Ucla; Dermatology.

LAM, JASON W; Carlmont HS; Redwood City, CA; (2); Math Clb; Tennis; CSF; Arch.

LAM, JIMMY; San Gabriel HS; San Gabriel, CA; (4); French Clb; Office Aide; SADD; Co-Ed Yrbk; Off Sr Cls; Stu Cncl; Var Capt Swmmng; Hon Roll; CSU Long Beach; Bus Admin.

LAM, JONATHAN K; Phillip & Sala Burton Academic HS; San Francisco, CA; (3); Computer Clb; Math Clb; Band; Phtg Ed Yrbk; Stu Cncl; Intrml Sftbl; Cit Awd; Hon Roll; Ntl Merit Schol; Pres Acad Fit Awd; Church Young Adult Clb-Co Organzr; MVP Intramural Sftbl/Vllybl; Golden St Exam-Agl Hnr; Geom Recogntn; U CA-BERKELEY; Comp Sci.

LAM, KIA; Redland SR HS; Highland, CA; (4); 56/836; French Clb; Hon Roll; NHS; Prfct Atten Awd; Asian Clb Pres & VP; CA Schlrshp Fed; Hunger Buster; CA ST San Bvernardino; Accntg.

LAM, KIEN LOI CYNTHIA; Granada Hills HS; Los Angeles, CA; (2); Yrbk; Cit Awd; Hon Roll; UCLA; Csmtlgy.

LAM, KIU D; Lincoln HS; Los Angeles, CA; (2); FBLA; Hon Roll; Yth Cmnty Srv.

LAM, LILI; San Leandro HS; San Leandro, CA; (3); 48/362; Church Yth Grp; Mrchg Band; Hon Roll; Prfct Atten Awd; Octagon Clb; 1st Pl Mandarin Spch Cntst; Attainment Level Chrysler Fund AAU Phys Ftnss Prgm; UC Davis; Bio.

LAM, LOUIS L; Abraham Lincoln HS; San Francisco, CA; (1); CA Schlrshp Federation.

LAM, LUI; Luther Burbank HS; Sacramento, CA; (3); 58/276; Cit Awd; Vietnam Clb.

LAM, MAGGIE XUAN; Mark Keppel HS; Monterey Park, CA; (4); 27/637; FBLA; Math Clb; Mu Alpha Theta; Cit Awd; Hon Roll; Prfct Atten Awd; Pres Acad Fit Awd; 1988 Golden ST Exam Geometry High Hnors; 1987 Golden ST Exam In 1st Yr Algebra Hnors; Call ST LA; Electrl Engng.

LAM, MAI; Baldwin Park HS; Baldwin Park, CA; (1); Math Clb; Science Clb.

LAM, MAI; C K Mc Clatchy HS; Sacramento, CA; (4); Library Aide; Cit Awd; Prfct Atten Awd; ROP; Scrmnto Cty Coll; Bus.

LAM, MAI; Millikan JR HS; Los Angeles, CA; (1); Treas Service Clb; Teachers Aide; Cit Awd; Hon Roll; Ntl Merit Schol; Prfct Atten Awd; Yng Author; Girls Athl Clb; Jazz & Exercise Clb; Med.

LAM, MAN KIN; International Studies Acad; San Francisco, CA; (3); High Hon Roll; Prfct Atten Awd.

LAM, MANDY H; Oakland HS; Oakland, CA; (2); Pres Math Clb; Math Tm; Science Clb; Treas Spanish Clb; High Hon Roll; Hon Roll; Badmntn Tn; UC Berkeley; Engrng.

LAM, MIKE V; Oakland HS; Oakland, CA; (3); German Clb; Key Clb; Car Awd & Car Security Awd Comm; Vllybl; Tennis & Swmmng; UC Davis; Arch.

LAM, MUI H; San Gabriel HS; Rosemead, CA; (4); Cit Awd; High Hon Roll; ROP Intr Dsgn Cert; ROP Ofc Occptns Cert; Bus.

LAM, NAVY J; Tokay HS; Stockton, CA; (2); 28/742; Boy Scts; Latin Clb; Socr; NEDT Awd; Prfct Atten Awd; U Of Pacific; Arch.

LAM, NGA T; Polytechnic HS; Sun Valley, CA; (4); Cit Awd; Hon Roll; Pres Acad Fit Awd; Bank Of Ameri Achvt Awd; Inds Awd Drafting; Medallion Awd Inds Ed; Arch.

LAM, NGAN T; Mark Keppel HS; Rosemead, CA; (3); FBLA; Key Clb; Hon Roll; Prfct Atten Awd; UCLA; Law.

LAM, NGHIEP S; San Rafael HS; San Rafael, CA; (3); Hon Roll; Auto Mech.

LAM, NGUYEN; Wallenberg HS; San Francisco, CA; (2); Intnl Clb; Var Socr; High Hon Roll; Hon Roll; Prfct Atten Awd; Engrng.

LAM, OANH; Independence HS; San Jose, CA; (3); Girl Scts; Math Clb; Math Tm; Teachers Aide; Prfct Atten Awd; E Side Union HS Dist Math Cntst Awd 88.

LAM, PAMELA Y; Arcadia HS; Arcadia, CA; (2); 28/605; Art Clb; JA; Library Aide; Pep Clb; Teachers Aide; Rep Nwsp; High Hon Roll; NHS; Prfct Atten Awd; Pres Acad Fit Awd.

LAM, PEGGY K; Westmoor HS; Daly City, CA; (3); Chorus; Hon Roll; Coll Entrnc Club; Chinese Club; San Francisco ST U; Bus Admin.

LAM, PHUOC; Phillip & Sala Burton A HS; San Francisco, CA; (3); Bsbl; Bsktbl; Ftbl; Socr; Sftbl; Swmmng; Tennis; Trk; Vllybl; Hon Roll; Vietnamese Club Apprctn Club 90; Cert Acadmc Achvt GPA; Cert Acadmc Achvt Advncd Cmpstn; U Of San Francisco; Clerk.

LAM, PHUOC K; Grace Davis HS; Modesto, CA; (3); Treas Key Clb; JV Var Ftbl; JV Socr; JV Var Trk; Colley Club Pres; Peer Facilitator; CSF Treas.

LAM, QUAN T; John Burroughs HS; Burbank, CA; (4); Stu Cncl; Var L Tennis; Hon Roll; Prfct Atten Awd; Pres Acad Fit Awd; SHARE Club; UC Northridge; Pediatrics.

LAM, QUYNH; San Gabriel HS; Rosemead, CA; (4); Cit Awd; Hon Roll.

LAM, RAYMOND; Senior HS; San Francisco, CA; (2); Orch; Crs Cntry; Prfct Atten Awd; Gldn St Exm Rcgntn Alg I.

LAM, ROBERT; George Washington HS; San Francisco, CA; (3); Stanford; Bus.

LAM, SANH T; Lowell HS; San Francisco, CA; (3); Rep Cmnty Wkr; Office Aide; Rep Red Cross Aide; Rep Science Clb; Rep Service Clb; Var Swmmng; High Hon Roll; Foreign Lang Labs Treas; Rep Archtctrel Design.

LAM, SAU LAI; John Marshall HS; Los Angeles, CA; (4); 14/703; Am Leg Aux Girls St; Cmnty Wkr; JCL; Latin Clb; Teachers Aide; Jr NHS; NHS; Prfct Atten Awd; $100 Schlrshp Los Angeles Chinese Wmns Clb; Riordan Schlrs; Citznshp Hnry Soc And CSF; U CA Los Angeles; Finance.

LAM, SENG M; Mark Keppel HS; Rosemead, CA; (1); Math Clb; Prfct Atten Awd; CSF; United For Peace.

LAM, STACY; Workman HS; West Covina, CA; (2); Intnl Clb; Hon Roll; U Of CA ST Fullerton; Bus.

LAM, STANLEY K; Mark Keppel HS; Monterey Park, CA; (3); 3/500; Debate Tm; Rep Key Clb; Math Clb; NFL; Rep Science Clb; Ftbl; High Hon Roll; Opt Clb Awd.

LAM, STEPHEN; Rosemead HS; Rosemead, CA; (2); 2/35; Computer Clb; Key Clb; Math Clb; High Hon Roll; Hon Roll; Sign Lang Clb; Var Badminton Tm; CA Schlrshp Fed; UC Berkeley; Bus.

LAM, SUZANNE; John Marshall Fundamental HS; Pasadena, CA; (4); 1/147; Chess Clb; Key Clb; Pres Math Clb; Pres Science Clb; Rptr Nwsp; Ed Yrbk; Sec Frsh Cls; Bausch & Lomb Sci Awd; NHS; CSF VP; U Rochester; Med.

LAM, TAI D; Millikan HS; Long Beach, CA; (4); 26/726; Key Clb; Am Leg Aux Girls St; Band; Jazz Band; Mrchg Band; Orch; School Musical; Phtg Yrbk; Rep Frsh Cls; Pres Sr Cls; Jr Optimist Speech Cont-3rd Pl; CA ST-LONG Beach; Cmmnctn.

LAM, TAM QUANG; Hoover HS; San Diego, CA; (3); Computer Clb; French Clb; Math Clb; Wrstlng; Cit Awd; High Hon Roll; Hon Roll; Prfct Atten Awd; Comp.

LAM, TAN B; San Gabriel HS; San Gabriel, CA; (4); Off Jr Cls; Tennis; High Hon Roll; Phycht.

LAM, TERESA; George Washington HS; San Francisco, CA; (2).

LAM, THUY; Norte Vista HS; Riverside, CA; (3); French Clb; Treas FBLA; VP Q&S; Treas Science Clb; Ed Yrbk; Lit Mag; Rep Stu Cncl; Stat Swmmng; High Hon Roll; CA Schlrshp Fed VP; Mock Trl; Daisy Chain Hnr Crt; U CA Riverside; Ecnmcs.

LAM, TINH Q; Lincoln HS; Los Angeles, CA; (2); Hon Roll; Gldn St Exam Acadmc Excllnc Awd; CSF; Med.

LAM, TOM P; Sacred Heart Cathedral Prep; Pacifica, CA; (1); Bsbl; Bsktbl; Ftbl; Hon Roll; Bus.

LAM, TRUNG C; Mountain View HS; El Monte, CA; (1); School Musical; Hon Roll; Ntl Merit Ltr; Prfct Atten Awd.

LAM, VAN S; San Rafael HS; San Rafael, CA; (4); Var Trk; Hon Roll; Pres Acad Fit Awd; Robert Royle Awd; Bnk Amer Achvt Awd; UC Davis; Comp Sci.

LAM, WALLACE; Mills HS; Millbrae, CA; (3); Chess Clb; French Clb; Intnl Clb; Math Clb; Math Tm; Science Clb; High Hon Roll; CA Schlrshp Fed Sec; Stanford; Med.

LAM, WINNIE Y; Lowell HS; San Francisco, CA; (2); Office Aide; SADD; CA Schlrshp Fed; Schl Spirit Week; Big Brthr, Sistr Orgnztn; Cls Svc Prjct; Golden St Exam High Hnrs; U Of CA; Medcl.

LAM, YASSI; Willows HS; Willows, CA; (2); Red Cross Aide; Hon Roll; CA U Brkly; Soclgy.

LAMADRID, JOEANN D; George Washington HS; San Francisco, CA; (2); Cmnty Wkr; Service Clb; Rep Frsh Cls; Rep Soph Cls; Hon Roll; Close Up Clb; JV Badmntn; Ed.

LAMAS, FERNANDO D; Baldwin Park HS; Baldwin Park, CA; (1); 350/1993; Rep Frsh Cls; VP Soph Cls; Rep Stu Cncl; JV Swmmng; Hon Roll; Water Polo; UCLA; Doctor.

LAMB, DARLA; Immanuel Christian Schl; Ridgecrest, CA; (4); Church Yth Grp; Cmnty Wkr; Chorus; Church Choir; Sec Sr Cls; Var Cheerldng; Var Sftbl; Var Vllybl; Var Cit Awd; Var High Hon Roll; Coachs Awd Vlybl; Cerro Coso CC; Accntng.

LAMB, JENNIFER M; Alhambra HS; Martinez, CA; (3); Dance Clb; Band; Jazz Band; Mrchg Band; Score Keeper; Socr; Hon Roll; Camp Counselor; Swim Inst; Teachers Aid; UC Santa Barbra; Bus Ec.

LAMB, KATHRYN R; Irvine HS; Irvine, CA; (1); Church Yth Grp; Church Choir; Southwest Ctr-Feed Homeless; Mexico Easter Proj-Build Homes In Tiajuana.

LAMB, KENNETH W; Woodbridge HS; Irvine, CA; (3); Boy Scts; Chess Clb; Church Yth Grp; Pres Drama Clb; VP JA; School Musical; School Play; Variety Show; Intrml Fld Hcky; High Hon Roll; Natl Conf Chrstns & Jews Smnr Schl Rep; Schl Sentinel Awd Math & Scl Sci; Syracuse U; Sprtscstr.

LAMB, SCOTT T; Gahr HS; Artesia, CA; (3); 231/400; Var L Ftbl; Art Ninjutsu; Write Ptry; Police Ofcr.

LAMB, STEPHANIE; San Luis Obispo HS; San Luis Obispo, CA; (2); Hon Roll; Jr NHS; CSF; CA JR Schlrshp.

LAMB, STEVE D; Edison/Computech HS; Fresno, CA; (2); Church Yth Grp; Ski Clb; SADD; Stu Cncl; JV Diving; JV Golf; Cit Awd; High Hon Roll; Hon Roll; CSF; Goldn St Exam High Hnrs; UCSD; Aerospace Engrng.

LAMB, TAMMY L; North HS; Bakersfield, CA; (2); Church Yth Grp; Office Aide; Teachers Aide; Church Choir; High Hon Roll; Hon Roll; NHS; VP Rotary Awd; Spanish NHS; CSF; Wld Life Eclgy Clb Pres; Hstry.

LAMBEL, SHAUNESE M; Fresno HS; Fresno, CA; (1); JCL; Hon Roll; Prfct Atten Awd; Acad Ltr; Math & Engl Dept Awds; Vet.

LAMBERT, ANDREA K; Santa Rosa HS; Santa Rosa, CA; (4); 3/480; Am Leg Aux Girls St; Cmnty Wkr; Dance Clb; Pres Sec Key Clb; Spanish Clb; Chorus; School Musical; Hon Roll; Kiwanis Awd; Rotary Awd; Piano Cert Mrt, Sr Pin; UC San Diego.

LAMBERT, ELLAYNA D; Prospect HS; San Jose, CA; (1); Church Yth Grp; Teachers Aide; Chorus; Church Choir; Bsktbl; San Jose ST; Bus.

LAMBERT, HOLLY K; Troy HS; Yorba Linda, CA; (2); 12/334; Drill Tm; High Hon Roll; Rotary Awd; Peer Cnslr; CSF; Cert Mrt In Fr; Interior Decorator.

LAMBERT, LEKETA DONICE; Oakland Tech HS; Oakland, CA; (3); Pres Sr Cls; Church Yth Grp; Girl Scts; SADD; Teachers Aide; Chorus; Church Choir; Drill Tm; Variety Show; Phtg Yrbk; Legal Asst; KY ST; Law.

LAMBERT, MATTHEW; Antioch HS; Antioch, CA; (4); 1/583; Boy Scts; Mu Alpha Theta; Ski Clb; Rptr Nwsp; Phtg Yrbk; Var Trk; JV Wrstlng; Hon Roll; Val; Acad Dcthln Team; Acad Lttrmn Clb; CA Schlrshp Fed Pres; UC Davis; Arntcl Engrng.

LAMBERT, MISTY; Long Beach Jordan HS; Westminster, CA; (1); Church Yth Grp; Dance Clb; FTA; Teachers Aide; Drill Tm; Cheerldng; Cit Awd; Hon Roll; Church Choir; LBCC; Teacher.

LAMBERTH, JASON; Marina HS; Huntington Beach, CA; (3); Latin Clb; Intrml JV Bsbl; Intrml Wrstlng; Hon Roll; UCLA; Acctg.

LAMBERTI, JOSEPH N; Pioneer HS; San Jose, CA; (2); Treas Frsh Cls; Pres Soph Cls; Swmmng; JV Wt Lftg; High Hon Roll; NHS; CSF; County Sci Fair; U CA-IRVINE; Engr.

LAMBERTON, JILL; Loma Linda Acad; Loma Linda, CA; (3); Church Yth Grp; Teachers Aide; Band; Chorus; Rptr Yrbk; VP Frsh Cls; Stu Cncl; Cit Awd; High Hon Roll; Hon Roll; Stu Of Month 88; Stu Of Yr 88-89; Walla Walla Coll; Engl.

LAMBIE, JAMAICA; Edison HS; Stockton, CA; (1); NFL; Science Clb; Speech Tm; High Hon Roll; Hon Roll; Sci Olympiad Team; Gftd & Tlntd Educ; Acad Tlnt Srch CA St U; U CA Berkeley; Civil Engrng.

LAMBRECHT, ANDREA; Fontana HS; Fontana, CA; (3); Church Yth Grp; Rep Jr Cls; Cit Awd; Legislative Council; Ped.

LAMBSON, HEATHER E; Trinity HS; Junction City, CA; (2); Church Yth Grp; Drama Clb; Pres 4-H; Ski Clb; SADD; Church Choir; Bsktbl; 4-H Awd; High Hon Roll; Tchr.

LAME, DIETRICH D; South Pasadena HS; South Pasadena, CA; (4); Boy Scts; Debate Tm; German Clb; Quiz Bowl; Scholastic Bowl; JV Crs Cntry; Var Capt Trk; JV Wrstlng; Ntl Merit SF; Comp Prgmr; Sci.

LAMEDMAN, LISA A; Canyon HS; Canyon Country, CA; (1); Teachers Aide; U CA Irving; Doctor.

LAMERDIN, KRISTEN D; Casa Roble Fundamental HS; Citrus Heights, CA; (2); 42/461; Church Yth Grp; GAA; Letterman Clb; Spanish Clb; Teachers Aide; Gym; Cit Awd; High Hon Roll; Hon Roll; Acadm Block; Cls 3 St Chmpn Gymnstcs; Phys Thrpy.

LAMEY, KELLY A; Notre Dame HS; Belmont, CA; (2); Art Clb; Cmnty Wkr; FBLA; GAA; Pep Clb; Ski Clb; Sec Treas Frsh Cls; Rep Soph Cls; Rep Jr Cls; Swmmng; Psych.

LAMKE, AURORA X; Dublin HS; Dublin, CA; (4); 20/158; Capt Var Bsktbl; Var Capt Sftbl; Hon Roll.

LAMKE, PANDORA Z; Dublin HS; Dublin, CA; (4); 29/158; GAA; Office Aide; Teachers Aide; Varsity Clb; Socr; Sftbl; Trk; High Hon Roll; Hon Roll; MVP Vrsty Sccr; Animal Sci.

LAMKIN, HEIDI P; Los Amigos HS; Santa Ana, CA; (2); Church Yth Grp; Chorus; School Musical; Variety Show; High Hon Roll; Hon Roll; Keywanettes Banner Squad Awd; Bible Clb.

LAMM, MANUEL J; San Pedro HS; San Pedro, CA; (4); Art Clb; Cmnty Wkr; Debate Tm; NFL; Speech Tm; Natl Frnsc Leag Dgree Dstnctn; Emlio Pucci Schlrshp; Amer Coll Appld Arts; Cmrcl Art.

LAMONS, MICHAEL D; Hogan SR HS; Vallejo, CA; (3); Church Yth Grp; Var JV Bsktbl; JV Trk; Hon Roll; NHS; Play Drums In Chrch; Musical Instruments; Lrng Music.

LAMONT, JOSHUA R; Gompers Secondary HS; San Diego, CA; (2); Math Clb; Math Tm; Capt Quiz Bowl; Sec Science Clb; Spanish Clb; Speech Tm; Teachers Aide; VP Frsh Cls; Pres Soph Cls; VP Stu Cncl; Sci Olympiad Natl Chmpnshp; CA Schltc Fed & HOBY Delg; Congrssnl Distgshd Svc Awd; Pediatrics.

LAMOREAUX, TRICIA M; Central Union HS; El Centro, CA; (1); Church Yth Grp; Letterman Clb; Pep Clb; Orch; Capt Cheerldng; Var Gym; Hon Roll; Teacher.

LAMOS, SHEERIE L; El Rancho Verde HS; Hayward, CA; (3); Church Yth Grp; Teachers Aide; Temple Yth Grp; Rep Frsh Cls; Rep Soph Cls; Rep Jr Cls; JV Bsktbl; Cheerldng; Hon Roll; Coach Grade Schl Bsktbl; Start Pgm Teens Who Have Voices Todays Soc.

LAMOUNTRY, NITSA; Encina HS; Sacramento, CA; (3); 33/212; French Clb; Intnl Clb; Stu Mnth; CSUS; Professor.

LAMPITOC, LUVELYN J; Arroyo Grande HS; Arroyo Grande, CA; (4); 1/400; Hosp Aide; Key Clb; Yrbk; VP Sr Cls; JV Tennis; Elks Awd; High Hon Roll; Pres Acad Fit Awd; Val; Acad Decathlon Hnrs Div; Filipino Yth Club Pres; CSF Lifer; CA Polytechnic ST U; Arch.

LAMPKIN, RAY JANETTE L; Carson HS; Carson, CA; (2); Office Aide; Teachers Aide; Bsktbl; Sftbl; Trk; Hon Roll; Awd For Hlpng At Schl; Acctng.

LAMPMAN, MICHELLE; The Linfield Schl; Temecula, CA; (1); JV Vllybl; Hon Roll; Pres Acad Fit Awd.

LAMPRON, HEATHER; Foothill Farms HS; Sacramento, CA; (1); Church Yth Grp; German Clb; SADD; Powder Puff Ftbl; Swmmng; Vllybl; Jrnlsm.

LAMSONG, SORIKANE; Elsinore Union HS; Lake Elsinore, CA; (3); 89/472; Church Yth Grp; French Clb; FBLA; Science Clb; Trk; LEO Clb; Acad Dcthln; Dr.

LAMUG, ALBERT P; Carson HS; Carson, CA; (4); Math Clb; Science Clb; Service Clb; Stat Ftbl; Hon Roll; Lion Awd; NHS; Envolled Gifted Pgm; Rcvd Bank Am Awd; A Avg SR; UCLA; Elec Engr.

LAN, ANDREW J; Harvard Schl; Los Angeles, CA; (4); Chess Clb; Computer Clb; JA; Math Tm; Model UN; NFL; Orch; School Musical; Yrbk; Stat L Bsktbl; 1st Prz Ntl Olympiada Spkn Russian; 1st San Diego ST U Strng Qrts; Biolgcl Sci.

LAN, MICHELLE C; Whitney HS; Cerritos, CA; (3); 1/170; FBLA; Key Clb; Science Clb; Phtg Yrbk; Swmmng; Hon Roll; Pres Schlr; CSF; Illuminations Pres; Sci.

LANA, CHERYL A; Miramonte HS; Orinda, CA; (2); NFL; Spanish Clb; Speech Tm; Varsity Clb; Rep Frsh Cls; VP Soph Cls; Sec Jr Cls; Socr; Swmmng; Hon Roll; CSF; Stanford; Graphi Dsgn.

LANCASTER, BROOKE; Silver Valley HS; Ft Irwin, CA; (2); 1/147; Church Yth Grp; Cmnty Wkr; Letterman Clb; Treas Soph Cls; Stu Cncl; Var L Crs Cntry; Cit Awd; High Hon Roll; Hon Roll; Pres Acad Fit Awd; Excllnce Engl & Frnch; Bst 1st Yr Rnnr Awd Crs Cntry; U Of FL; Psych.

LANCASTER, JEFF P; Westminster HS; Midway City, CA; (3); Letterman Clb; Spanish Clb; Teachers Aide; Band; Ftbl; Trk; Wt Lftg; Wrstlng; Hon Roll; Orange Coast Coll; Law.

LANCASTER, NICOLLE A; Redwood Christian HS; San Ramon, CA; (3); Church Yth Grp; FCA; Letterman Clb; Teachers Aide; Chorus; Off Frsh Cls; Var Socr; Var Sftbl; Var Vllybl; Sccr Lg 1st Pl Southern Alameda Cnty Trvlng Tm; 1st Tm All League Scc; MVP 2 Yrs Sccr; Chabot JC; Bus Mgmt.

LANCASTER, SHERISE R; Fred C Beyer HS; Modesto, CA; (1); Var L Trk; JV Vllybl; Hon Roll.

LANCE, BRETT M; Chino HS; Chino, CA; (3); Boy Scts; Cmnty Wkr; German Clb; JV Var Ftbl; Var Golf; JV Var Wt Lftg; Cit Awd; Hon Roll; Fishing; Camping; Maintaining Landscape; UC Davis; Landscape Arch.

LAND, ERIC J; Willows HS; Willows, CA; (3); 58/85; Aud/Vis; FFA; Key Clb; ROTC; Speech Tm; School Play; Cheerldng; Crs Cntry; Trk; Mltry Police.

LANDAGAN, EVA REA I; Hilltop HS; Chula Vista, CA; (2); SADD; Teachers Aide; Color Guard; Orch; Prfct Atten Awd; Outstndng Achvt; Cert Achvt Schlrshp & Ctznshp; Cngrsnl Awd Of Merit; UCLA; Nrsng.

LANDAVERDE, AIDA M; Burlingame HS; Burlingame, CA; (3); Teachers Aide; Orch; Yrbk; Pres Soph Cls; Sec Jr Cls; Stu Cncl; Bsktbl; Mgr(s); Sftbl; Tennis; Outdoor Ed Cnslr 90; San Mateo Coll; Scl Work.

LANDAZURI, JAVIER I; Saint Francis HS; Sunnyvale, CA; (1); 159/388; Boy Scts; Hon Roll; Order Of Arrow Lodge Vice Chief; Law.

LANDE, ERIK S; Orange Glen HS; Lancaster, CA; (1); 1/647; L Trk; High Hon Roll; Hon Roll; Acad Leag; Schlr Athltc Awd.

LANDER, LISA; La Habra HS; Fountain Valley, CA; (3); Pep Clb; Var JV Tennis; Congress Jr Yr; Top 100 Three Yrs; Student Of Month Spanish III Foods; UC Irvine; Psych.

LANDEROS, CLAUDIA; Schurr HS; Los Angeles, CA; (2); Drill Tm; Prfct Atten Awd; Hermanos Clb; USC; Fmly Thrpst.

LANDIN, ERIKA A; Vallejo SR HS; Vallejo, CA; (3); Spanish Clb; SADD; Teachers Aide; Band; Mrchg Band; Hon Roll.

LANDIS, ERIN B; East Bakersfield HS; Bakersfield, CA; (1); Church Yth Grp; Intnl Clb; Sec Key Clb; Rep Frsh Cls; Var Tennis; Vllybl; Hon Roll; Pepperdine; Bus.

LANDKROHN, PATTI; Saddleback HS; Santa Ana, CA; (2); Pep Clb; Drill Tm; Sec Treas Frsh Cls; Hon Roll; UCLA; Law.

LANDMESSER, MELISSA J; Etiwanda HS; Fontana, CA; (3); #45 In Class; Teachers Aide; Bsktbl; Tennis; Hnr Guard; Athltc Acadmc Awd; Chaffey; Bus.

LANDON, CAROLYN T; Independence HS; San Jose, CA; (4); Church Yth Grp; Church Choir; School Musical; Intrml Vllybl; Hon Roll; VP Yth Grp; CSF; Sharp Smmr Apprntce Rsrch Pgm Moffet Fld 90; Engrng.

LANDON, HEATHER; Tulare Union HS; Tulare, CA; (3); 7/401; Cmnty Wkr; Drama Clb; SADD; Band; Mrchg Band; Stage Crew; Rep Stu Cncl; High Hon Roll; Hon Roll; Svc Awd 88-90; Mck Trl 88-90; Music Ltr 89; U Of CA Irvine; Bio.

LANDON, JENNIFER M; Granada Hills HS; Northridge, CA; (2); Stat Vllybl; Hon Roll; UCSB; Envrnmntl Rsrch.

LANDON, SERENA L; El Toro HS; El Toro, CA; (3); 57/480; VP Chorus; Drill Tm; Yrbk; Var L Cheerldng; Var L Pom Pon; High Hon Roll; Hon Roll; Outstndng Choral 89-90; Mst Enthusiastic Songleader Awd 89-90; U Santa Cruz; Theater Arts.

LANDRETH, ELLYN A; Trinty HS; Weaverville, CA; (2); AFS; Church Yth Grp; Drama Clb; German Clb; Hosp Aide; SADD; Church Choir; Yrbk; Hon Roll; U CA-DAVIS; Ed.

LANDRETH, EMILY JANE; North Salinas HS; Salinas, CA; (3); AFS; Church Yth Grp; English Clb; French Clb; Scholastic Bowl; Orch; High Hon Roll; Hon Roll; NHS; Ntl Merit Ltr; Stu Mem Of Monterey Bay Symphny; Mem Cmnty Coll Drama Co; Mem Of Acad Dectlhn Tm; U Of CA.

LANDRETH, NELLEKA J; Palmdale HS; Saugus, CA; (3); 120/650; Debate Tm; Pres 4-H; Speech Tm; Rep Nwsp; Powder Puff Ftbl; 4-H Awd; Voice Dem Awd; Resrve Natl Chmpn Paso Fino Horses; West Coast Chmpn 88-90; UCSD; Commnctns.

LANDRY, CHRISTOPHER P; San Dieguito HS; Cardiff By The Se, CA; (3); Aud/Vis; Rptr Nwsp; Var Capt Lcrss; Aviation.

LANDRY, LONECIA L; St Michaels HS; Los Angeles, CA; (3); Variety Show; Pres Jr Cls; VP Stu Cncl; Var Sftbl; Chrldr Capt, All Star Trphy; UNLV.

LANDRY, MELISSA M; Casa Grande HS; Petaluma, CA; (2); 57/295; Church Yth Grp; Hosp Aide; Var Trk; Hon Roll; NHS; Scl Work.

LANDRY, NINA; Santa Clara HS; Santa Clara, CA; (2); JCL; JV Trk; Prfct Atten Awd; Art.

LANDRY, SCOTT E; San Dimas HS; San Dimas, CA; (3); Church Yth Grp; Math Tm; Golf; Alfred Mistern Acad Olympiad Awd 89-90; CSF; Stu Excllnc Roses Awd; Physics.

LANDT, CARYLYN; Academy Of Our Lady Of Peace; San Diego, CA; (1); GAA; Hon Roll; Sons Am Revolution Bronze Ctznshp Mdl; Hnry ST Pres Chldrn Am Rev; San Diego Icettes Prcsn Ice Sktg.

LANDUA, CANDACE E; Bella Vista HS; Fair Oaks, CA; (2); 48/406; Church Yth Grp; Treas German Clb; SADD; Var L Swmmng; Tennis; Kiwanis Awd; Schlstc Achvt Awd Phys Ed; Standards Proficiency Test Cert Of Exclnc.

LANDY, MONTE; El Capiton HS; Lakeside, CA; (4); 29/420; DECA; Key Clb; Science Clb; Service Clb; Spanish Clb; SADD; Teachers Aide; Varsity Clb; Var Stat Vllybl; Cit Awd; Natl DECA Comptn; San Diego ST U; Mktng.

LANE, AMY E; Saint Vincent HS; Petaluma, CA; (3); Cmnty Wkr; French Clb; Letterman Clb; SADD; Varsity Clb; Ed Yrbk; Var Trk; Var Vllybl; NHS; NEDT Awd; CSF.

LANE, ANDREW; Orestimba HS; Newman, CA; (1); Church Yth Grp; Var Bsbl; Hon Roll.

LANE, BARTON F; Los Altas HS; Los Altos, CA; (1); Church Yth Grp; SADD; JV Bsktbl; Var Swmmng; Intrml Vllybl; High Hon Roll; Ntl Merit SF; Pres Acad Fit Awd; Stanford U; Natural Science.

LANE, BROOK R; Boron JR/Sr HS; Boron, CA; (2); Capt JV Cheerldng; Var Sftbl; Accntng.

LANE, ELIZABETH S; Lowell HS; San Francisco, CA; (3); Girl Scts; Q&S; Pres Sec Science Clb; Teachers Aide; Nwsp; Socr; Gov Hon Prg Awd; High Hon Roll; St Schlr; Rensselaer Polytech Inst Awd Math & Sci; CA Arts Schlr; Acad Of Art Awd Of Mrt; UCSF Smmr Intern; Sci.

LANE, FRANK; Oakland HS; Oakland, CA; (3); Boy Scts; Church Yth Grp; Cmnty Wkr; Drama Clb; ROTC; SADD; Teachers Aide; Band; Church Choir; Color Guard; Sonoma ST U; Psych.

LANE, HEATHER D; Woodlake Union HS; Woodlake, CA; (2); Church Yth Grp; Drama Clb; Pep Clb; Science Clb; SADD; Church Choir; Cit Awd; High Hon Roll; Hon Roll; Psych.

LANE, HEATHER L; Bakersfield HS; Bakersfield, CA; (4); 1/729; Church Yth Grp; Math Tm; SADD; Teachers Aide; Orch; Var Swmmng; Hon Roll; Ntl Merit SF; Opt Clb Awd; CA Schlrshp Fed Treas; Chem Engrng.

LANE, JENNIFER D; Analy HS; Santa Rosa, CA; (2); Debate Tm; Pres VP 4-H; French Clb; Service Clb; Orch; School Musical; Nwsp; Co-Ed Lit Mag; Hon Roll; Drama Clb; Jrnlsm.

LANE, JULIE A; Oak Park HS; Agoura, CA; (1); Church Yth Grp; Treas Key Clb; Treas Service Clb; School Musical; VP Frsh Cls; Stat Drill Tm; JV Cheerldng; Pepperdine U; Med.

LANE, LISA D; Homestead HS; San Jose, CA; (1); School Play; Stage Crew; Sec Soph Cls; JV Cheerldng; UC-RIVERSIDE; Brdcstng.

LANE, MELISSA A; Woodlake Union HS; Woodlake, CA; (3); Church Yth Grp; 4-H; FFA; FHA; GAA; Science Clb; Band; Church Choir; Tennis; 4-H Awd.

LANE, MICHAEL J; Monache HS; Porterville, CA; (3); Am Leg Boys St; Science Clb; Teachers Aide; Tennis; High Hon Roll; Lion Awd; Prfct Atten Awd; Voice Dem Awd; Sci Olympiad Tm; Ed.

LANE, MICHAEL L; El Camino HS; Oceanside, CA; (3); Computer Clb; Teachers Aide; Hon Roll; Srvyr.

LANE, MICHELLE V; Huntington Beach HS; Huntington Beach, CA; (2); Model UN; Cit Awd; Pres Acad Fit Awd; Nutrtnst.

LANE, PAM K; Vacaville HS; Vacaville, CA; (3); Pres Church Yth Grp; Pres Hosp Aide; Treas Service Clb; Hon Roll; Jr NHS; Sonoma ST; Pre-Med.

LANE, RASHIEDA T; Inglewood HS; Inglewood, CA; (2); Cmnty Wkr; ROTC; Spanish Clb; Drill Tm; School Play; Intrml Vllybl; Yale; Pre Med.

LANE, SEAN C; Moreno Valley HS; Moreno Vly, CA; (3); Church Yth Grp; Cmnty Wkr; Var Ftbl; Var Wt Lftg; Hon Roll.

LANG, CARRIE E; Eureka SR HS; Eureka, CA; (3); 3/425; VP Pres Drama Clb; Thesps; Sec Orch; School Play; High Hon Roll; CSF Offcr & VP; Keywannettes Clb; Envrnmntl Awareness Clb; CA Arts Schlr Attended CA Art Smmr Schl.

LANG, CATHY; Alta Loma HS; Alta Loma, CA; (2); Score Keeper; French Clb; Hosp Aide; VP Frsh Cls; VP Jr Cls; Swmmng; Trk; Hon Roll; Schl & Fed Govt; Loma Linda U; Psych.

LANG, CHANTRA A; Independence HS; San Jose, CA; (2); Prfct Atten Awd; Cambodian Clb; SEED Pgm; Bus.

LANG, DONALD J; Monta Vista HS; Cupertino, CA; (4); 180/400; Boy Scts; Church Yth Grp; Band; Mrchg Band; Orch; Pep Band; Ntl Merit SF; CA All St Hnr Band; Intl Reltns.

LANG, JEF; Morro Bay HS; Morro Bay, CA; (3); Chess Clb; Drama Clb; JA; Key Clb; Letterman Clb; Thesps; Chorus; Stage Crew; JV L Ftbl; Peer Comm Prgm; Cal Poly; Teach Theatre.

LANG, LINDSAY; Fresno HS; Fresno, CA; (4); 75/500; Drama Clb; FCA; French Clb; German Clb; JCL; Latin Clb; Teachers Aide; Hist Thesps; School Musical; School Play; CSF 90; People To People Stu Ambassador Pgm 88; Intl Stds.

LANG, NOAH D; Irvine HS; Irvine, CA; (2); 10/550; Key Clb; Sprt Ed Nwsp; High Hon Roll; NHS; Staff Reprtr; Heritage Awd Soc Sci.

LANG, VAN B; Fremont HS; Sunnyvale, CA; (3); FBLA; Intnl Clb; Hon Roll; Riverside; Bus.

LANGE, JOAN P; Los Altos HS; Hacienda Hts, CA; (2); 16/398; Intnl Clb; Yrbk; Stat JV Bsktbl; Hon Roll; Prfct Atten Awd; Keywanettes Secy; CSF; Friend To Friend; Arch.

LANGE, KERRY; Redwood HS; Visalia, CA; (3); 46/348; Church Yth Grp; French Clb; Chorus; School Musical; School Play; Rep Stu Cncl; Var JV Socr; JV Swmmng; Hon Roll; Pres Acad Fit Awd; CA Schltc Fed; Chmbr Singers.

LANGE, PAUL A; Southern Calif Christian Schl; Anaheim, CA; (3); Church Yth Grp; Intnl Clb; Office Aide; Treas Stu Cncl; JV Capt Bsktbl; Var Ftbl; High Hon Roll; Hon Roll; Phys Thrpy.

LANGE, RENEE E; Oak Ridge HS; El Dorado Hills, CA; (1); Church Yth Grp; Girl Scts; SADD; Vllybl; High Hon Roll; Optmtrst.

LANGELIER, LUKE J; Santa Clara HS; Oxnard, CA; (2); Church Yth Grp.

LANGELIER, MISTY L; Valley View HS; Moreno Valley, CA; (1); Yrbk; Socr; Swmmng; Tennis; High Hon Roll; Hon Roll; Greenpeace; Humboldt; Marine Bio.

LANGENFELD, STEPHANIE M; Trabuco Hills HS; Mission Viejo, CA; (2); 1/408; Church Yth Grp; VP French Clb; Science Clb; Color Guard; Yrbk; Stage Crew; Rptr Nwsp; High Hon Roll; Kiwanis Awd; Rep NHS; Mock Trl Team Lwyr; Orange Cnty Acadc Dcthln Team.

LANGFORD, CHARLES D; Mountain Empire HS; Boulevard, CA; (3); 1/100; Am Leg Boys St; Band; Stage Crew; Treas Soph Cls; JV Capt Bsktbl; High Hon Roll; NHS; Ntl Merit Ltr; Val; Church Yth Grp; Publictn Stu Handbook; Acad Achvt; USAFA; Aero Engrng.

LANGFORD, JASON L; Arlington HS; Riverside, CA; (3); Ftbl; Hon Roll; UCR.

LANGFUS, JENNIFER E; North Hollywood HS; Toluca Lake, CA; (2); Teachers Aide; Temple Yth Grp; Var Tennis; Hon Roll; U Of PA; Politics Law.

LANGHAM, CHRISTOPHER M; Trona HS; Trona, CA; (4); 18/46; Boy Scts; Sec Church Yth Grp; Intnl Clb; SADD; VICA; Band; Mrchg Band; Eagle Scout; Church Sports-Bsktbl/Vllybl/Sftbl; Yng Mens Grp; Cerro Coso CC; Ed.

LANGHAM, JOHN R; St Genevieve HS; Van Nuys, CA; (3); Boy Scts; Model UN; Office Aide; Crs Cntry; Hon Roll; Egl Sct Awd; Prsh Atr Srvr; Plt.

LANGHAM, KRISTOFER A; University City HS; San Diego, CA; (2); 24/418; Math Tm; Model UN; Hon Roll; Prfct Atten Awd; Pres Acad Fit Awd; CA St Math Awd 89; Hgh Hnrs Golden St Exam Alg & Geom; Sigma Math Leag Gold Mdl & Mst Vlbl Tm Mbr.

LANGHAM, NANCY M; Irvington HS; Fremont, CA; (1); Church Yth Grp; Band; Church Choir; Jazz Band; Mrchg Band; School Musical; Rptr Nwsp; High Hon Roll; Hon Roll; Hnr Band; Mills Coll; Music.

LANGHELD, BRENDA L; Whitney HS; Cerritos, CA; (3); Cmnty Wkr; Debate Tm; JA; Key Clb; Church Choir; Color Guard; Var L Swmmng; High Hon Roll; NHS; Semi Fnlst Cngrss Bundstagg Yth Exchng Prgm; People To People Friendship Caravan 89.

LANGHELD, DEBORAH A; Whitney HS; Cerritos, CA; (3); Cmnty Wkr; Debate Tm; Sec JA; Church Choir; Crs Cntry; Swmmng; High Hon Roll; NHS; Pres Acad Fit Awd; People To People Frndshp Caravan To Soviet Nion 89; CSF & JSA; Fnlst Lions Club Spch Contest; Naval Acad; Aerontcl Engrng.

LANGHORNE-JOHNSON, MONIQUE; Vallejo SR HS; Vallejo, CA; (2); Treas Church Yth Grp; French Clb; Teachers Aide; Treas Church Choir; Drill Tm; JV Bsktbl; JV Cheerldng; Cit Awd; Hon Roll; Prfct Atten Awd; Black Stu Union; Golden St Exam Algebra I Hnrs; Corp Law.

LANGILLE, MARK DAVID; Moreno Valley HS; Moreno Valley, CA; (3); Church Yth Grp; Variety Show; High Hon Roll; Prfct Atten Awd; 1st Pl Geom Dsgn Cont; Talent Show 87, 88, 90; Art Show 87-88; U Of CA Riverside; Engl.

LANGIS, CHRISTAL; Lower Lake HS; Clearlake, CA; (3); Am Leg Aux Girls St; Church Yth Grp; High Hon Roll; Hon Roll; Odyssy Mind Clb; Friday Night Live Clb; UC Santa Cruz; Engls Teacher.

LANGIT, EMANUEL M; Phillip & Sala Burton Academic HS; San Francisco, CA; (4); 54/169; Jazz Band; High Hon Roll; Hon Roll; U Of CA Santa Cruz; Physics.

LANGLEY, BRIAN; Paso Robles HS; Paso Robles, CA; (4); Church Yth Grp; Band; Drm Mjr(t); Jazz Band; Mrchg Band; Pep Band; Stage Crew; JV Ftbl; Var Socr; Intrml Vllybl; John Phillip Souza Awd; 2nd Pl Drum Mjr Pismo Bch; San Diego ST.

LANGLEY, BRIAN D; South HS; Bakersfield, CA; (3); 11/469; Band; Mrchg Band; Pep Band; Var Golf; Socr; High Hon Roll; Hon Roll; NHS; Pres Acad Fit Awd; Arch.

LANGLEY, JASON; Clovis HS; Clovis, CA; (3); Teachers Aide; High Hon Roll; Hon Roll; CSF; Acad Block C; Hkng Clb; Cal Poly; Engr.

LANGLEY, JEFFREY RAY; Antelope Valley HS; Lancaster, CA; (3); Church Yth Grp; JA; Letterman Clb; Office Aide; Rptr Frsh Cls; Treas Soph Cls; Stu Cncl; Var Ftbl; Var Golf; Wt Lftg; Orthdntst.

LANGLEY, SIMON J; Lone Pine HS; Lone Pine, CA; (3); 1/26; Am Leg Boys St; Band; School Play; Variety Show; Rep Frsh Cls; Pres Soph Cls; Pres Jr Cls; VP Stu Cncl; Var Bsbl; Stat Bsktbl; Sking; Guitar, Bass & Drums; Mathletes; UCSB; Music.

LANGLIE, NINA R; Monterey HS; Monterey, CA; (3); AFS; Model UN; Thesps; Chorus; Orch; School Musical; School Play; Rep Stu Cncl; High Hon Roll; Ntl Merit SF; Cngrss Bundestag Schlrshp.

LANGOON, STAR; Ventura HS; Ventura, CA; (3); Church Yth Grp; Hon Roll; Prfct Atten Awd; Ldrshp; Spirit Clb; Girls Lgu; UC Santa Cruz; Bus Mngr.

LANGS, CINNAMON; Irvington HS; Fremont, CA; (2); Dance Clb; GAA; Pres Frsh Cls; Sec Soph Cls; JV Trk; JV Vllybl; Hon Roll; Fremont Hub Model; Fremont Dance; Ohlone Coll.

LANGSTON, BRYAN S; Ygnacio Valley HS; Walnut Creek, CA; (4); Boy Scts; Church Yth Grp; Letterman Clb; Varsity Clb; Band; Church Choir; Variety Show; Crs Cntry; Tennis; Ricks Coll.

LANGSTON, NIKI D; Shafter HS; Bakersfield, CA; (4); Church Yth Grp; Drama Clb; Jazz Band; VP Mrchg Band; Pep Band; School Play; Hon Roll; Extraordinary Stus Am, Music Stu 89; SR Music Awd 90; Bakersfield Coll; Interor Dsgnr.

LANI, JANELLE; Rosary HS; Yorba Linda, CA; (3); Church Yth Grp; Cmnty Wkr; Office Aide; Pep Clb; Science Clb; Spanish Clb; Chorus; School Musical; Stage Crew; Rep Frsh Cls; CSF; Accntng.

LANIER, KERI; Woodland HS; Woodland, CA; (3); French Clb; Treas Key Clb; Yrbk; Intrml Bsktbl; Intrml Co-Capt Vllybl; Intrml Jr NHS; JV Var NHS; Intrml Pres Acad Fit Awd; Var St Schlr; Ray A Kroc Yth Achvt Awd; Amnesty Intl; CA Schlrshp Fed; Art.

LANIER, KRISTY; Redlands HS; Redlands, CA; (2); GAA; Pep Clb; Chorus; Intrml Socr; Cit Awd; DAR Awd; Hon Roll; Pres Acad Fit Awd; Poem Pblshd In Book; AYSO Sccr; Clthng.

LANIER, TIM D; Hilltop HS; Chula Vista, CA; (2); Church Yth Grp; JV Bsbl; JV Ftbl; Wt Lftg; JV Var Wrstlng; Hon Roll.

LANIGAN, KERRY; Palos Verdes HS; Palos Verdes Est, CA; (3); 8/350; Cmnty Wkr; Treas Rep Service Clb; School Musical; Off Jr Cls; Off Sr Cls; Cheerldng; Pres Pom Pon; Trk; High Hon Roll; NHS.

LANIGAN, REBECCA; Fred C Beyer HS; Modesto, CA; (3); L Band; L Mrchg Band; L Pep Band; Cit Awd; Hon Roll; CSF; Stnsls Co Hnr Bnd & Orch.

LANIR, MICHELLE; Dos Pueblos HS; Santa Barbara, CA; (3); 9/338; Teachers Aide; Band; Drill Tm; NHS; Golden St High Geom Hnrs; CSF; Majorette Tm Co-Capt; Mathematics.

LANK, LIZ; Boron HS; Boron, CA; (2); Church Yth Grp; Dance Clb; Letterman Clb; Sec Frsh Cls; Treas Soph Cls; JV Bsktbl; Var Pom Pon; Var Trk; Var JV Vllybl; JV Hon Roll; AV Coll; Accntng.

LANKFORD, LISA C; Mater Dei HS; Orange, CA; (1); Church Yth Grp; Cmnty Wkr; Girl Scts; Hosp Aide; High Hon Roll; Hon Roll; Jr NHS; Asst Teacher SS Chrch; Slvr Awd 2nd Highest Hnr GS; CSF.

LANKFORD, MICHELLE; Paraclete HS; Lancaster, CA; (4); 12/123; Debate Tm; Drama Clb; Hosp Aide; Quiz Bowl; Spanish Clb; Speech Tm; School Play; Sec Jr Cls; Sec Stu Cncl; Cit Awd; Prm Cmmtte; UCI; Law.

LANKSTER, LA DONNE C; Canyon Springs HS; Moreno Valley, CA; (1); Church Yth Grp; Church Choir; High Hon Roll; Blck Stu Union; NAACP Act-So Cmptn; Hampton U; Lawyer.

LANN, DINA S; North Hollywood/Zoo Magnet HS; Canoga Park, CA; (2); Cmnty Wkr; Var Sftbl; Var Vllybl; High Hon Roll; Hon Roll; NHS; Zoo Crew; Camp Cnslr; Ed.

LANNAK, STACEY C; Foothill HS; Sacramento, CA; (4); Church Yth Grp; Sec 4-H; Letterman Clb; Office Aide; Teachers Aide; Varsity Clb; Chorus; Church Choir; Co-Capt Drill Tm; Rep Soph Cls; Symposium On Lvng In The Info Age; Rcvd Outstndng Engl 12-C Awd; Rcvd Schlr Athlete Awd; Sacramento CA ST U; Pltcl Sci.

LANNING, BRENT J; San Ramon Valley HS; Danville, CA; (4); 3/400; Church Yth Grp; Var JV Bsktbl; Var Capt Tennis; DAR Awd; High Hon Roll; Jr NHS; NHS; Pres Acad Fit Awd; UCLA.

LANNING, DREW C; Monterey HS; Monterey, CA; (2); Trk; Archlgy.

LANNING, MORGEN J; Mc Kinleyville HS; Trinidad, CA; (1); Var Socr; Var Wt Lftg; Var Wrstlng; Cit Awd; Hon Roll; Prfct Atten Awd; Amer Legn Cert.

LANO, DESTINEY D; Amos Alonzo Stagg HS; Stockton, CA; (1); Drill Tm; Dlta Yth Ftbl Chrldr; U HI; Cmptr Sci.

LANPHEAR, PATRICIA L; Hesperia HS; Hesperia, CA; (3); Hon Roll; Optmtry.

LANSVILLE, JOHN C; Barstow HS; Barstow, CA; (4); 10/250; AFS; Letterman Clb; Service Clb; Stu Cncl; Var Capt Tennis; High Hon Roll; Jr NHS; Opt Clb Awd; Pres Acad Fit Awd; Bank Of Amer Achvt Awd; MVP Tnns; Stu Of Month; U Redlands; Bus Admin.

LANT, BRIE L; Mesa Verde HS; Citrus Heights, CA; (2); 16/257; Spanish Clb; Var Sftbl; Hon Roll; Stu Reaching Out; Pediatrics.

LANTERMAN, COREY M; John W North HS; Riverside, CA; (3); Teachers Aide; Cerritos JC; Auto Tech.

LANTING, BRIAN C; Mt Whitney HS; Visalia, CA; (1); FFA; JV Socr; Fresno ST U; Hwy Patrol Offcr.

LANTINGA, SAM O; Mesa Verde HS; Citrus Heights, CA; (2); 7/257; Spanish Clb.

LANTSBERGER, RUSTY W; Kern Valley HS; Kernville, CA; (1); FFA; Pres Frsh Cls; Pres Soph Cls; Wt Lftg; Wrstlng; Hon Roll; CA Poly; Ag.

LANTZ, ELISA; Pomona Catholic HS; Upland, CA; (3); 1/100; Cmnty Wkr; GAA; Hosp Aide; Letterman Clb; Pep Clb; Stu Cncl; Capt L Cheerldng; Bausch & Lomb Sci Awd; High Hon Roll; NHS; Stanford; Bio.

LANTZ, MICHELLE M; Mira Mesa HS; San Diego, CA; (3); Drama Clb; RN.

LANUM, CHRISTIE; Atwater HS; Winton, CA; (3); FBLA; FFA; SADD; Color Guard; Mrchg Band; High Hon Roll; Prfct Atten Awd; Winton Sprng Fstbl Qn; Schlstc Achvt FFA Hghst GPA Jr.

LANUZA, EDUARDO J; Mission HS; San Francisco, CA; (3); Latin Clb; Band; Hon Roll; Outstndng Prfrmnc Trphy Bgnng Band; Step To Coll Pgm; San Francisco ST U.

LANZA, JENNIFER; Palmdale HS; Acton, CA; (2); Dance Clb; Debate Tm; Drama Clb; Speech Tm; Teachers Aide; Cheerldng; Sftbl; Cit Awd; Hon Roll; U Of San Diego; Jrnlsm.

LAO, BURT B; Bishop Amat Memorial HS; West Covina, CA; (2); Aud/Vis; Church Yth Grp; Yrbk; Summer Camp Cnslr; Cal Poly Pomona; CPA.

LAO, EASTTINA NGEK; Mayfield SR Schl; Alhambra, CA; (3); 8/18; SADD; School Play; Stage Crew; Lit Mag; Tennis; Bd Of Govr General Alumni Assn Bk Awd; Stanford; Intl Relations.

LAO, MELANIE M; Eagle Rock JR/Sr HS; Los Angeles, CA; (2); Drill Tm; Hon Roll; CJSF; E-Club; U Of S CA.

LAO, MICHELLE M; Eagle Rock HS; Los Angeles, CA; (2); Key Clb; Acpl Chr; Var Tennis; Hon Roll; Forestry.

LAO, THAI B; Artesia HS; Lakewood, CA; (2); Hon Roll; Pres Acad Fit Awd; Archt.

LAO, VINH TAN; Elk Grove HS; Sacramento, CA; (3); 15/500; Var Tennis; Hon Roll; CSF; Acad Ltr Awd; Sci Olympd Tm; Med.

LAPADULA, MARC M; San Dieguito Union HS; La Costa, CA; (2); Stu Cncl; JV Crs Cntry; JV Ftbl; JV Trk; JV Wt Lftg; Pres Acad Fit Awd; Hon Roll; USC; Aviation.

LAPAYESE, YVETTE V; St Joseph HS; Downey, CA; (3); 8/180; Hosp Aide; SADD; Rep Jr Cls; Sec Stu Cncl; Var Powder Puff Ftbl; High Hon Roll; Peer Counselor; Stu Of Yr Awd; CA Schlrshp Fed Treas; Poltcl Sci.

LAPID, ROY P; Lowell HS; San Francisco, CA; (2); JV Var Bsbl; Capt Var Ftbl; Wt Lftg; Hon Roll; Fil-Am Club; Ltl Leag Bsbl Umpire; Stanford U; Med.

LAPIN, JACKSON P; Carlmont HS; Belmont, CA; (2); Var Socr; Var Trk; Hon Roll; Pres Acad Fit Awd; Peninsula Athltc Leag Awds Trck & Pole Vltng; #2 Stu Schl Fitnss 89-90; Belmont Red Rbbn Wk, Jst Sy No; Engrng.

LAPKIN, EMILY N; Palm Springs HS; Palm Springs, CA; (3); Treas Drama Clb; School Musical; School Play; High Hon Roll; CA Schlrshp Fed; Jr Statesmen Of Amer; Amnesty Intl; Natl Charity Leag Treas; Writing.

LAPOINTE, ALYCIA M; South Pasadena HS; South Pasadena, CA; (3); Church Yth Grp; Girl Scts; Spanish Clb; Teachers Aide; Rep Sr Cls; Stu Cncl; Var Bsktbl; Var Capt Trk; Hon Roll; Prfct Atten Awd; Law Clb; African Amer Clb; UCSD; Obgyn.

LAPOINTE, JASON P; Esperanza HS; Anaheim, CA; (2); 47/2000; Bsktbl; Wt Lftg; Cit Awd; Gov Hon Prg Awd; High Hon Roll; Hon Roll; NHS; Pres Acad Fit Awd; High Hnrs Golden St Exam Geom; Embryriddle; Aero Eng.

LAPPIN, DAVID B; St Paul HS; La Habra, CA; (3); 11/313; Boy Scts; JCL; Latin Clb; Var Tennis; High Hon Roll; Hon Roll; NHS; Tnns Tm MVP 90; 3rd Roman Hstry CJCL; Claremont Mc Kenna; Chem Engrng.

LARA, ALEJANDRO; St John Bosco HS; Bell, CA; (2); Computer Clb; Key Clb; Band; Mrchg Band; Orch; Pep Band; Intrml Vllybl; Interested In Working With Special Effects Make Up; Veterinarian.

LARA, ALEXIS M; Skyline HS; Oakland, CA; (2); Rptr Yrbk; Stu Cncl; Vllybl; Cit Awd; Hon Roll; Pres Acad Fit Awd; Law.

LARA, ANA M; Sacred Heart Of Jesus HS; Los Angeles, CA; (3); GAA; School Play; Yrbk; Hon Roll; NHS; Spanish NHS; Religion Awd; NHS Clb; Vlntr Santa Martha Hosp; Bus.

LARA, ANITA; Whitney HS; Riverside, CA; (3); 115/174; Church Yth Grp; Spanish Clb; Var Bsktbl; Var Crs Cntry; Swmmng; Hon Roll; Missionette Tchr 3 Yrs; Humboldt; Envrnmntl Sci.

LARA, ARTURO C; Bell HS; Cudahy, CA; (2); High Hon Roll; MESA.

LARA, BETSABEL; Sierra Vista HS; Baldwin Park, CA; (3); Cmnty Wkr; Hosp Aide; SADD; Band; Color Guard; Flag Corp; Jazz Band; Variety Show; High Hon Roll; Studing CNA; ASB Secy 90-91; RN.

LARA, ENRIQUE G; Mar Vista HS; Imperial Beach, CA; (2); 82/414; Cmnty Wkr; School Musical.

LARA, GERARDO; John F Kennedy HS; Fremont, CA; (4); 9/275; Cmnty Wkr; School Play; Co-Ed Yrbk; Treas Stu Cncl; Var Crs Cntry; Cit Awd; High Hon Roll; Pres Schlr; Rotary Awd; Bld Dr Coord; Stanford U.

LARA, IRENE; Castle Park HS; Chula Vista, CA; (3); 2/450; Drama Clb; Speech Tm; Rptr Nwsp; Ed Lit Mag; Pres Jr Cls; JV Var Socr; Hon Roll; French Clb; School Play; Sec Treas Frsh Cls; CA Schlstc Fed; Snte Stu; Acad Achievers.

LARA, LISANNE; Diamond Bar HS; Diamond Bar, CA; (1); German Clb; Girl Scts; SADD; Chorus; Color Guard; Swing Chorus; Psych.

LARA, LUCILLE M; North Salinas HS; Salinas, CA; (3); Band; Mrchg Band; Orch; Pep Band; High Hon Roll; Hon Roll; Goldn St Exam-Alg 1 Hnrs.

LARA, PETER; Atwater HS; Atwater, CA; (2); Bsbl; Ftbl; Hon Roll; In Top Ten High Scores Acad Bio; Medcl/Doctor.

LARA, SHEILA; La Puente HS; La Puente, CA; (2); Dance Clb; Drill Tm; Stat Ftbl; Hon Roll; Court Rep.

LARA-VEGA, SVETLANA K; Vacaville HS; Vacaville, CA; (3); Church Yth Grp; Intnl Clb; Spanish Clb; SADD; Drill Tm; Rep Soph Cls; Var Powder Puff Ftbl; Cit Awd; Hon Roll; Prfct Atten Awd; S Club; Peer Cnslg; Sacramento ST U; Astronomer.

LARANJO, ISABEL M; Los Banos HS; Los Banos, CA; (3); Cmnty Wkr; FBLA; Science Clb; Spanish Clb; Hon Roll; Interact Club; Fshn Mrchndsng.

LARCHE, GENESEE A; Grace M Davis HS; Modesto, CA; (1); Hist Service Clb; Trk; Cit Awd; MYF; Child Psych.

LARCO, ANITA V; St Joseph HS; La Palma, CA; (2); Cmnty Wkr; French Clb; SADD; Hon Roll; Algebra I Award; Religion I Award; United Colors Of St Joseph Club; UCI; Business/Finance.

LARD, ERIC; Lassen Union HS; Janesville, CA; (3); 33/254; Boy Scts; Church Yth Grp; Ski Clb; Pres Soph Cls; Rep Stu Cncl; Ftbl; Socr; Trk; Elks Awd; Pres Acad Fit Awd; HOBY; Engrng.

LARES, HECTOR; Winters HS; Winters, CA; (4); SADD; Varsity Clb; VP Stu Cncl; Var Capt Ftbl; Trk; Hon Roll; Amigos Unidos, Pres & VP; CA ST U; Sacramento; Intl Rltn.

LARGE, SUZANNE F; Yosemite HS; Oakhurst, CA; (3); Church Yth Grp; FHA; GAA; Pep Clb; Science Clb; SADD; Score Keeper; Tennis; High Hon Roll; Hon Roll; Nrsg.

LARI, FIROUZEH; Tamalpais HS; Mill Valley, CA; (4); 5/239; Pres French Clb; Orch; Rep Stu Cncl; High Hon Roll; NHS; Ntl Merit Ltr; Pres Acad Fit Awd; Val; James B Black Schlrshp $4000; David D Hawkins Math Awd 1st Pl; Bank Of Amer Awd; Cert Phys Sci; Stanford U; Economics.

LARIOS, LORENA; Washington Prep HS Comm Arts; Los Angeles, CA; (2); Office Aide; JV Tennis; Cit Awd; Hon Roll; Prfct Atten Awd; Talnt Srch; Cmmnctns Arts Magnet; UCLA; Jrnlsm.

LARIOS, MARIA G; Garfield HS; Los Angeles, CA; (4); Church Yth Grp; Office Aide; Pep Clb; Teachers Aide; Drill Tm; Rptr Nwsp; Treas Jr Cls; Rep Stu Cncl; Cheerldng; Prfct Atten Awd; UCLA; Bus.

LARIOS, MONICA; Bell Gardens HS; Commerce, CA; (4); 9/510; FTA; Q&S; SADD; Teachers Aide; Ed Nwsp; Stu Cncl; Powder Puff Ftbl; Hon Roll; Prfct Atten Awd; CSF; Santa Clara U; Hstry.

LARIOSA, LARRY; Southwest HS; San Diego, CA; (2); Cmnty Wkr; Intnl Clb; Key Clb; SADD; Band; Variety Show; Hon Roll; Ntl Merit Ltr; Peace Clb; ASB Concessns; Acdmc Leag; U Of San Diego; Law.

LARKIN, BRIAN J; Garces Memorial HS; Bakersfield, CA; (2); Rep Jr Cls; Var L Bsktbl; JV Ftbl; High Hon Roll; CSF; People Bound For Travel Club; Notre Dame; Phys Thrpy.

LARKIN, CHRISTINA; Tracy Joint Union HS; Stockton, CA; (4); 8/453; Pres 4-H; Pres Key Clb; NFL; Speech Tm; Treas Jr Cls; Treas Stu Cncl; Bsktbl; Vllybl; 4-H Awd; NHS; STAND; Delta Coll; Law.

LARKIN, JENNIFER J; Arlington HS; Riverside, CA; (3); Church Yth Grp; Drama Clb; Thesps; Chorus; Church Choir; School Play; Stage Crew; Socr; Hon Roll; Crmnl Lwyr.

LARKIN, PENNIE; Tracy Joint Union HS; Stockton, CA; (3); 4-H; Key Clb; SADD; Var Diving; Var Score Keeper; Var Vllybl; Cit Awd; 4-H Awd; Club Vllybl In Tracy; Peer Cnslng; Statistcn For V Diving; UCSB; Marine Bio.

LARKIN, TODD; Garces Memorial HS; Bakersfield, CA; (3); 1/150; Science Clb; Var Bsktbl; JV Ftbl; JV Socr; High Hon Roll; Top Ranked No 1 Stu; CSF; People Bound Trvl Clb; Aerospace.

LARKIN, VICKI M; Ramona HS; Ramona, CA; (2); Church Yth Grp; Dance Clb; Drama Clb; Thesps; School Musical; Ricks Coll; Musical Theater.

LARKINS, BRENT C; Santa Teresa HS; San Jose, CA; (2); JV Bsktbl; JV Ftbl; Var Socr; JV Wt Lftg; Hon Roll; Prfct Atten Awd.

LARNER, RUSTY J; Morro Bay HS; Morro Bay, CA; (4); 16/210; Speech Tm; High Hon Roll; Hon Roll; Ntl Merit SF; Acad Dcthln; Engrng.

LARON, CONNIE D; Livermore HS; Livermore, CA; (3); Bus Profs of Am; Computer Clb; FCA; FBLA; Intnl Clb; JA; JCL; Office Aide; Spanish Clb; VICA.

LARRABEE, HEATHER N; Poway HS; Poway, CA; (3); Band; Mrchg Band; Humboldt ST U; Chld Psych.

LARRABEE, NICOLE D; Marina HS; Huntington Beach, CA; (3); Ski Clb; Spanish Clb; Drill Tm; Hon Roll; Goldn Shield Awd; U San Diego; Commnctns.

LARRABURE, ANNE-MARIE; Ontario HS; Ontario, CA; (2); Letterman Clb; Var Socr; JV Vllybl; Hon Roll; Tags Of 92; CA Schlrshp Fed,& Clbs Forgn Language Clb.

LARRIEU, PHILIP J; Portola JR-SR HS; Portola, CA; (2); Cmnty Wkr; Letterman Clb; Science Clb; Ski Clb; Teachers Aide; Band; Swing Chorus; Sec Jr Cls; JV Ftbl; JV Trk; MIT.

LARRISON, ANGIE C; Mojave HS; Mojave, CA; (2); Church Yth Grp; Spanish Clb; Drill Tm; Sftbl; Hon Roll; Acctng.

LARRY, WROTEN; Washington HS; Los Angeles, CA; (4); Letterman Clb; Bsktbl; Prfct Atten Awd; UNLV; Elect Engr.

LARSEN, ALI M; Santa Teresa HS; San Jose, CA; (2); Church Yth Grp; French Clb; Church Choir; Swmmng; Brigham Yng U.

LARSEN, CHRIS R; Marysville HS; Marysville, CA; (2); Stat Bsbl; Stat Bsktbl; JV Ftbl; JV Var Score Keeper; Stat Trk; UNLV; Bus.

LARSEN, DAVID P; Tustin HS; Tustin, CA; (3); 19/446; Church Yth Grp; JV Socr; JV Wrstlng; High Hon Roll; NEDT Awd; Top 25 Awd; CSF; Golden St Exmn Hgh Hnrs Geom, Hnrs Alg.

LARSEN, ERIN S; Ramona HS; Ramona, CA; (3); Church Yth Grp; Cmnty Wkr; Treas VP SADD; Teachers Aide; Variety Show; Phtg Nwsp; Stat Var Gym; Cit Awd; High Hon Roll; Hon Roll; Accpt Cngrssnl Yth Ldrshp Cncl 90; Ballet Instr; Photgrphy Tchr.

LARSEN, JOHN A; East Nicolaus HS; Trowbridge, CA; (4); 23/40; Church Yth Grp; Ftbl; Trk; Wt Lftg; Mechanic.

LARSEN, MELISSA; Vista HS; Oceanside, CA; (3); 9/400; Church Yth Grp; French Clb; Science Clb; Teachers Aide; Sec Band; Lbrn Mrchg Band; High Hon Roll; NHS; Pres Acad Fit Awd; Physics.

LARSEN, TIFFANY; Hillsdale HS; Foster City, CA; (3); Church Yth Grp; Pep Clb; Service Clb; Rep Frsh Cls; JV Var Cheerldng; Hon Roll; CSF; Engl Dept Awd; Brigham Young U.

LARSON, BELLA A; University City HS; San Diego, CA; (3); Church Yth Grp; Cmnty Wkr; Hosp Aide; Intnl Clb; Phtg Yrbk; High Hon Roll; Hon Roll; Prfct Atten Awd; Pres Acad Fit Awd; UCSD; Pre-Med.

LARSON, CHRIS W; Valencia HS; Anaheim, CA; (2); Boy Scts; Treas Chess Clb; German Clb; Math Tm; Science Clb; Tennis; U C Irvine; Comp Sci.

LARSON, CHRISTA C; Montclair HS; Montclair, CA; (2); Church Yth Grp; Key Clb; Chorus; Kindergarden Teacher.

LARSON, DANA; Simi Valley HS; Simi Valley, CA; (3); 226/666; Drill Tm; Rptr Nwsp; Sec Stu Cncl; Mgr Tnns; Drll Tm; Grad Spch; Eastern OR ST; Elem Ed.

LARSON, DANIEL D; El Toro HS; El Toro, CA; (3).

LARSON, EDWARD C; Nevada Union HS; Penn Valley, CA; (3); 42/551; Model UN; Teachers Aide; Cit Awd; Hon Roll; Bus.

LARSON, HANS P; Monterey HS; Monterey, CA; (2);*AFS; Church Yth Grp; Cmnty Wkr; FCA; Letterman Clb; Model UN; Teachers Aide; Crs Cntry; JV Ftbl; JV Capt Wrstlng; Mst Outstndng JV Wrstlr 90; Tm Capt JV Wrstlng 90; Slippery Rock; Engl.

LARSON, HEATHER L; Porterville HS; Hot Springs, CA; (3); Teachers Aide; Drill Tm; Hm Ecnmcs Awd; Coll Of Sequoias; Marine Bio.

LARSON, JARED E; Grossmont HS; El Cajon, CA; (3); 58/385; Church Yth Grp; Letterman Clb; JV Var Bsktbl; JV Var Ftbl; Hon Roll; Forestry.

LARSON, JEFF A; Marysville HS; Marysville, CA; (3); Boy Scts; Cmnty Wkr; VP Ski Clb; Band; Jazz Band; Mrchg Band; Pep Band; Cit Awd; Hon Roll; Wt Lftg; Eagle Scout; Pilots License; Vol Fireman; CPR Cert 88 & 89; Woodleaf Cnslr; Flying.

LARSON, JENNIFER N; Bolsa Grande HS; Garden Grove, CA; (2); 36/350; Girl Scts; Service Clb; Spanish Clb; Rep Frsh Cls; Rep Soph Cls; Stu Cncl; Capt Chess Clb; Score Keeper; Hon Roll; NHS; Fisherman Clb; Engl.

LARSON, JULIEANNE M; Rio Lindo Adventist Acad; San Gabriel, CA; (3); Church Yth Grp; Spanish Clb; Variety Show; Off Soph Cls; Stat Bsktbl; Score Keeper; Sftbl; Wt Lftg.

LARSON, KEITH A; Manteca HS; Manteca, CA; (3); 62/358; Varsity Clb; Stu Cncl; JV Var Bsktbl; JV Ftbl; Hon Roll; Fresno ST U; Bus Mgmt.

LARSON, KRISTIN J; Yucca Valley HS; Joshua Tree, CA; (3); Church Yth Grp; Girl Scts; Band; Mrchg Band; Nwsp; Cit Awd; High Hon Roll; Hon Roll; Pres Acad Fit Awd; Vet.

LARSON, MARLA; Winters HS; Winters, CA; (1); Cmnty Wkr; Letterman Clb; SADD; Drill Tm; Sec Frsh Cls; Stat Bsktbl; JV Swmmng; JV Vllybl; High Hon Roll; Hon Roll; Twn Yth Cmmssn; CSF; Fri Nght Live; Phy.

LARSON, MATTHEW J; Elsinore HS; Wildomar, CA; (3); 5/419; Band; Mrchg Band; Pep Band; CSF; Top Engl Awd 3 Yrs; Top Wrld Hist; To Bio.

LARSON, NICOLE L; Hemet HS; Hemet, CA; (2); Var Trk; Short Flag & Banner Sqd; U CA Riverside; Child Psych.

LARSON, PER B; Marshall Fundamental HS; Pasadena, CA; (3); Boy Scts; VP Soph Cls; VP Jr Cls; Pres Stu Cncl; Var Capt Ftbl; Var Capt Socr; JV Var Trk; High Hon Roll; NHS; Ntl Merit Ltr; Chrch Sftbl, Vllybl & Bsktbl; Pasadena Plyr Yr Ftbl; All San Gabriel Vlly Sccr Tm.

LARSON, RANDY S; Villa Park HS; Villa Park, CA; (2); Boy Scts; Key Clb; Letterman Clb; SADD; Varsity Clb; Nwsp; Rep Soph Cls; Var Swmmng; High Hon Roll; Pres Acad Fit Awd; U Of S CA.

LARSON, TINA M; North HS; Bakersfield, CA; (2); Church Yth Grp; Cmnty Wkr; L Dance Clb; French Clb; Teachers Aide; Variety Show; Var Cheerldng; Hon Roll; Full Scholarship To Joffrey Ballet; Studied With San Fran Ballet; Screen Actors Guild; Natl Commercials; Dance; Performing Arts.

LARSON, VIKTORIA J; Novato HS; Novato, CA; (2); 2/225; Sec Church Yth Grp; Sec Key Clb; Speech Tm; Band; Lit Mag; Var Mgr Trk; High Hon Roll; NHS; Wrthy Advsr Intl Ordr Rnbw Grls; U CA; Pltcs.

LASAM, MARY JANE A; Mt Carmel HS; San Diego, CA; (2); Key Clb; Prfct Atten Awd; Pblc Reltns Cmmssnr-Races Untd 89-90; Nrth Cty Acad Leag 88-89; Sundevil Stndouts Awd 89; CSF 88-90; U Of CA Berkeley; Bus Admin.

LASATER, SHANNON G; South HS; Bakersfield, CA; (3); Socr; Tennis; Vllybl; Hon Roll; Clb Sccr; Clb Vllybl.

LASELL, BEKKI; Hiram Johnson West Campus HS; Sacramento, CA; (3); English Clb; Hosp Aide; Office Aide; SADD; Teachers Aide; JV Var Swmmng; Hon Roll; U CA Davis; Sci.

LASIC, ROBERT V; San Gabriel HS; Rosemead, CA; (3); VP Computer Clb; Treas FBLA; Spanish Clb; Church Choir; School Play; Sprt Ed Nwsp; Yrbk; Crs Cntry; High Hon Roll; MASO Historian/Rptr; Med.

LASKA, MICHELLE; Lemoore HS; Hanford, CA; (4); 48/290; Church Yth Grp; Hist FBLA; FHA; Teachers Aide; Band; Mrchg Band; Pep Band; Ed Nwsp; Hon Roll; Acad Decathlon; 1st Pl Schl Spelling Bee; Humanities Clb; CA ST Bakersfield; Jrnlsm.

LASKA, PAUL S; Apple Valley SR HS; Apple Valley, CA; (3); Church Yth Grp; German Clb; Treas Chorus; CA Poly Pomona; Arch.

LASKY, BAIA J; San Diego HS; San Diego, CA; (3); Drama Clb; Intnl Clb; Science Clb; School Play; Tennis; High Hon Roll; NHS; Pres Acad Fit Awd; Piano Cert Merit Brnch Hnrs; Invent Amer 2nd Pl Sch, 3rd Pl Cnty; Clsscl Ballet; Biochem.

LASQUETE, EDWARD S; Mt Pleasant HS; San Jose, CA; (3); Art Clb; Phtg Rptr Yrbk; Var Capt Trk; Hon Roll; NHS; Cal Poly San Luis Obispo; Med.

LASSANSKE, PAULA JEAN; Lodi HS; Lodi, CA; (3); Church Yth Grp; Dance Clb; 4-H; GAA; Girl Scts; Spanish Clb; Acpl Chr; Band; Chorus; Church Choir; Bus.

LASSITER, AUDREY L; Moreno Valley HS; Moreno Valley, CA; (4); 22/383; Church Yth Grp; Cmnty Wkr; Red Cross Aide; Teachers Aide; Ed Nwsp; Rptr Yrbk; Rep Frsh Cls; High Hon Roll; Hon Roll; Pres Acad Fit Awd; Gftd Tlntd Eductnl Pgm; US Ldrshp Mrt Awd; US Achvt Awd; U Southern CA; Brdcst Jrnlsm.

LASTER, ANNETTE; Pasadena HS; Pasadena, CA; (2); Church Yth Grp; Cmnty Wkr; Church Choir; JV Bsktbl; Hon Roll; CSF Fnlst Miss America CO-ED Pgnt 90; Usher Of Yr New Revelation Bapt 1988-89; Pastors Awd 89; Law.

LASTRE, OSVELIO C; Bell HS; Bell, CA; (3); Key Clb; Math Clb; Science Clb; Rep Jr Cls; Capt Swmmng; Hon Roll; Knghts & Ladies Hnrs Socty; AP Spnsh Lang & Lit Tests; CO ST U; Comm.

LASTRELLA, CLIFF; St Patrick-St Vincent HS; Vallejo, CA; (4); 12/152; Letterman Clb; Sec Frsh Cls; Pres Soph Cls; Pres Jr Cls; Pres Sr Cls; Intrml Bsktbl; Var L Wrstlng; CSF; Engr.

LASTRO, JOSE A; Wasco Union HS; Wasco, CA; (3); Spanish Clb; JV Bsbl; Var Crs Cntry; Var Capt Socr; High Hon Roll; Hon Roll; Ntl Merit Ltr; CA Poly Sn Luis Obispo; Engr.

LASUA, ANYAS E H; San Lorenzo HS; San Leandro, CA; (2); JV Bsktbl; Var L Sftbl; Var L Vllybl; Innervisions; Coll Club; Comp Sci.

LATCHIE, LEKESHIA R; Seaside HS; Fort Ord, CA; (2); Church Yth Grp; FBLA; Teachers Aide; Church Choir; Cit Awd; Hon Roll; Prfct Atten Awd; Pediatrics.

LATHAM, JACQUELINE; Canyon Springs HS; Moreno Valley, CA; (2); Service Clb; Church Choir; Var Cheerldng; High Hon Roll; NHS; Church Yth Grp; Dance Clb; FBLA; Pep Clb; Colle Schlrshp Fndtn; Hnrs Awd Golden St Geom Exam; Bio Stu Yr 3rd Pl; 2nd Pl Sci Fair Behvrl Sci; Pre-Med.

LATHIGARA, RAJ P; Live Oak HS; Morgan Hill, CA; (3); 65/550; Debate Tm; SADD; Lit Mag; Tennis; Hon Roll; UC Berkeley.

LATIF, MAHAM; Del Campo HS; Carmichael, CA; (3); 150/446; American River Coll; Acctng.

LATINI, MARK A; Huntington Beach HS; Huntington Beach, CA; (2); Church Yth Grp; Red Cross Aide; Spanish Clb; Socr; Wt Lftg; Hon Roll; Yth Ambssdr To USSR; U CA.

LATOUR, ANGELIQUE; St Anthony HS; Compton, CA; (1); Church Yth Grp; Cmnty Wkr; Hon Roll; Bible Stdys Hnrs Awd; Math, Engr & Sci Achvmnt; Zoology.

LATRIECE, WATKINS S; John Muir HS; Pasadena, CA; (3); Debate Tm; Girl Scts; Flag Corp; Svc Awd Schl Canteen; Stu Aide; Cal ST Fullterton; Nrs.

LATRONICA, BILL C; Merced HS; Snelling, CA; (4); Church Yth Grp; FFA; Intrml Bsktbl; High Hon Roll; Pres Acad Fit Awd; CSF; Pr Cnslng; Bloss Memrl Schlrshp; Bethany Bible Coll; Psych.

LATTA, TRISTAN; Capital Christian HS; Rancho Cordova, CA; (1); Drama Clb; Girl Scts; Ski Clb; Teachers Aide; Thesps; Chorus; Church Choir; School Musical; School Play; Stage Crew; Hmcmng Cmmtte; Ed.

LATTANAPHOM, NOUKOUN; Mc Clymonds HS; Oakland, CA; (1); Cmnty Wkr; GAA; Temple Yth Grp; Pres Frsh Cls; Bsktbl; Vllybl; Cit Awd; Hon Roll; Pres Acad Fit Awd; Yth Cmmssnr Oakland; Wrtr.

LATTIN, ANDREA; Enterprise HS; Redding, CA; (3); 3/427; Am Leg Aux Girls St; Treas Jr Cls; Var JV Cheerldng; Powder Puff Ftbl; JV Var Sftbl; High Hon Roll; Hon Roll; Pres Acad Fit Awd; CSF Lf; Spnsh, Phys Ed Outstndng Stu Awd; Stanford U; Bus Law.

LAU, AILSA H; Woodrow Wilson HS; Los Angeles, CA; (3); Key Clb; Teachers Aide; Band; Hon Roll; CSF Clb; Acad Excel Awd Geo; Achvt Awd Chem; Psycht.

LAU, ALBERT; Woodrow Wilson HS; Los Angeles, CA; (4); 3/553; Key Clb; Math Tm; Ed Yrbk; High Hon Roll; Prfct Atten Awd; Sal; CSF; Gldn St Exam Hgh Hnrs Geom; Peer Tutor; UCLA.

LAU, ALICE; J Eugene Mc Ateer HS; San Francisco, CA; (4); Teachers Aide; High Hon Roll; Hon Roll; Pres Acad Fit Awd; Sch Of Arts-Visual; Merit Awd Smmr Yth Emplymnt Pgm 89; UC Davis; Comp Sci.

LAU, ALICE; Woodbridge HS; Irvine, CA; (3); Computer Clb; Hon Roll; Lgn Of Mary; U Of CA Irvine; Med.

LAU, BENNY H; Arroyo Grande HS; Grover City, CA; (3); Key Clb; JV Bsktbl; Hon Roll; Cal Poly San Luis Obispo; Comp.

LAU, BONNIE; Abraham Lincoln HS; San Francisco, CA; (2); Var Swmmng; CA Schlrshp Fed; Close Up Prog For New Americans; Trip To Washington DC; Boy Scouts Of America; UC Davis; Pharmacy.

LAU, BRIAN C; Terrance HS; Torrance, CA; (3); Teachers Aide; JV Socr; JV Wrstlng; Cit Awd; Gaming Soc; Long Beach; Accntng.

LAU, CARMEN; George Washington HS; San Francisco, CA; (2); French Clb; German Clb; Red Cross Aide; Hon Roll; Japanese Club; CSF; General Service Soc; UC Berkeley; Accntng.

LAU, CASEY KIEN CHUNG; Granada Hills HS; Northridge, CA; (2); Cmnty Wkr; DECA; SADD; Ed Yrbk; Rep Frsh Cls; Pres Stu Cncl; Cit Awd; Pres Acad Fit Awd; Jr Statesmen Amer; Chinese Culture Clb; Dntstry.

LAU, CLAUDIA; John Burroughs HS; Burbank, CA; (4); Cmnty Wkr; Dance Clb; Varsity Clb; Pep Band; Cheerldng; Valley Coll; Intl Bus.

LAU, CONNIE H; George Washington HS; San Francisco, CA; (2); High Hon Roll; Hon Roll; CSF; UC Santa Barbara; Intrior Dsgn.

LAU, CONNIE H; Pasadena HS; Pasadena, CA; (3); Hosp Aide; Math Clb; Speech Tm; Var Tennis; Hon Roll; Pres Tbl Tnns Clb; Zonata Clb; CSF; Phrmcst.

LAU, DAVID S; Alhambra HS; Monterey Park, CA; (2); German Clb; Stat Bsktbl; Mgr(s); Comp Sci.

LAU, DENISE Y; Abraham Lincoln HS; San Francisco, CA; (2); Gym; Chinese Clb; CSF; U CA Los Angeles; Arch.

LAU, DINH X; Cupertino HS; San Jose, CA; (2); FBLA; Hon Roll; Chinese Culture Club; Asian American Club; Med.

LAU, DONNA; C K Mc Clatchy HS; Sacramento, CA; (3); 1/567; Church Yth Grp; Treas Pres French Clb; German Clb; Hosp Aide; Sec Key Clb; VP Math Clb; Science Clb; SADD; JV Var Vllybl; High Hon Roll; Anml Rghts & Envrnmntl Actvst; Boston U.

LAU, DOUG B; North HS; Bakersfield, CA; (4); 4/390; Math Tm; Scholastic Bowl; Pres Science Clb; Teachers Aide; Yrbk; Var Tennis; High Hon Roll; Pres Acad Fit Awd; Pres Schlr; St Schlr; Acad Dcthln; Mock Trial; Natl Young Ldrs Conf; USC; Commrcl Art/Dsgn.

LAU, ERICA; Raal Wallenberg Trad HS; San Francisco, CA; (1); Church Yth Grp; Church Choir; Treas Soph Cls; High Hon Roll; Hon Roll; Jr NHS; Galla Sallame Ldrshp Schlrshp Awd; Hlpng Hnds Clb; Pdtrcn.

LAU, ERNEST; J E Mc Ateer HS; San Francisco, CA; (3); Red Cross Aide; Teachers Aide; Hon Roll; Civil Engrng.

LAU, EVELYN S; San Gabriel HS; Alhambra, CA; (1); Spanish Clb; SADD; Chorus; Drill Tm; Rep Stu Cncl; Hon Roll; CSF.

LAU, FELIX; Mark Keppel HS; Monterey Park, CA; (4); 131/637; Pres FBLA; Sec Key Clb; Sec Math Clb; Science Clb; Yrbk; Stu Cncl; Hon Roll; Leo Club Secy & Prlmntrn; 4th Pl Mr Future Bus Ldr 1990; CSF; U Of CA Irvine; Bus Admin.

LAU, JACOB E; North HS; Bakersfield, CA; (2); 1/475; Computer Clb; Var Math Tm; Var L Tennis; High Hon Roll; VP Wildlife Clb; CFS; GATE Clb; Johns Hopkins U; Med.

LAU, JASON; St Ignatius College Prep; Daly City, CA; (3); 23/244; Cmnty Wkr; Science Clb; Hon Roll; Asian Stu Coalition; Christian Life Cmnty; CSF; Accntng.

LAU, JENNIFER; Chinese Christian Schls; Oakland, CA; (2); Church Yth Grp; Office Aide; Church Choir; Mrchg Band; Intrml Vllybl; High Hon Roll; Hon Roll.

LAU, JOANNA; Abraham Lincoln HS; San Francisco, CA; (2); ROTC; Ed Nwsp; Rep Frsh Cls; Rep Soph Cls; Hon Roll; Prfct Atten Awd; CSF; 89 Goldn St Schlr; MA Inst Tech; Indstrl Engrng.

LAU, JOHN ZE FENG; Phillip & Sala Burton Academic HS; San Francisco, CA; (4); 37/180; Bus Profs of Am; Chess Clb; Cmnty Wkr; Office Aide; Teachers Aide; Yrbk; Intrml Swmmng; Intrml Tennis; Intrml Vllybl; High Hon Roll; Acad Dcthln; Civ Engrng.

LAU, JULIA F; American HS; Fremont, CA; (4); 5/319; Church Yth Grp; Drama Clb; Sec French Clb; German Clb; Spanish Clb; SADD; Variety Show; Yrbk; Var Cheerldng; JV Swmmng; CA SCHLRSHP Fed Cls Rep; U Of CA Los Angeles; Commnctns.

LAU, KELLEY M; Skyline HS; Oakland, CA; (2); Key Clb; Mgr Yrbk; VP Frsh Cls; Var Sftbl; Var Tennis; Vllybl; Ldrshp Cls; Doris Betty Awd; Run Stu Store; Bus Mgmt.

LAU, LUIS A; Livingston HS; Livingston, CA; (1); French Clb; Red Cross Aide; Nwsp; Rep Stu Cncl; Intrml Bsbl; Hon Roll; Prfct Atten Awd; Math Hnrs Golden St Exm Alg I; U Of CA San Diego; Arch Engr.

LAU, MARCIA; Carlmont HS; San Carlos, CA; (2); 29/200; Capt JV Vllybl; High Hon Roll; CSF; Asian Clb Rep; Soph Brd; Davis U; Doctor.

LAU, MIN H; Mission HS; San Francisco, CA; (3); Teachers Aide; Phtg Yrbk; Treas Jr Cls; Treas Sr Cls; Cit Awd; Hon Roll; Prfct Atten Awd; CSF; Learning Through Srvce Hnr; San Francisco ST U; Med.

LAU, ONHING; Delano HS; Delano, CA; (4); Art Clb; Bus Profs of Am; Computer Clb; Key Clb; Bsktbl; Ftbl; Tennis; High Hon Roll; NHS; CIF Tnns Chmpnshps; Hnr Rl; Hnrbl Mntn Al-Area Schlr-Athlt; UC Davis; Bus.

LAU, PARKNING; Skyline HS; Oakland, CA; (2); Cit Awd.

LAU, PATRICIA; Calexico HS; Calexico, CA; (2); Church Yth Grp; Pep Clb; Church Choir.

LAU, ROBERT; Abraham Lincoln HS; San Francisco, CA; (3); Ski Clb; Var Ftbl; Var Trk; UCLA; Bus.

LAU, SALLY; Mission HS; San Francisco, CA; (3); Off Jr Cls; Hon Roll; CSF; Learning Thru Serving; Nrsng.

LAU, SIUFU; Fontana HS; Fontana, CA; (2); Quiz Bowl; Scholastic Bowl; High Hon Roll; Hon Roll; Prfct Atten Awd; Chem.

LAU, SUZANNE S; Eagle Rock HS; Los Angeles, CA; (2); Church Yth Grp; Key Clb; JV Tennis; Hon Roll.

LAU, TERENCE; Bonita HS; La Verne, CA; (2); 5/350; Debate Tm; French Clb; JV Bsktbl; JV Bdmtn; CA Schlrshp Fdr.

LAU, TERRENCE Y; Sacred Heart Cathedral Prep; San Francisco, CA; (1); Bsktbl; JV Ftbl; JV Tennis; JV Wt Lftg; NHS; Pres Acad Fit Awd; 1st Hnrs; WCAL Frosh Champs-Bsktbl 89-90; UCLA; MD.

LAU, TRACY Y; A Lincoln HS; San Francisco, CA; (4); Drama Clb; Varsity Clb; School Play; Stu Cncl; Intrml Bsktbl; Intrml Vllybl; AP Hnr Calculus; Photo Clb; Csf; Chinese Clb; UC Berkeley; Arch.

LAU, WAI YAN; Rio Americano HS; Carmichael, CA; (3); Church Yth Grp; Math Tm; Spanish Clb; Teachers Aide; Acpl Chr; Var L Trk; JV Vllybl; High Hon Roll; Hon Roll; Pres Acad Fit Awd; Bus.

LAUB, CAROLYN; Dos Pueblos HS; Santa Barbara, CA; (3); 4/350; Church Yth Grp; Cmnty Wkr; Drama Clb; French Clb; Intnl Clb; Pres Math Clb; Math Tm; Science Clb; School Play; Stage Crew; Mock Trial Tm; Math Tm Awds.

LAUBY, PAIGE M; El Toro HS; El Toro, CA; (4); Yrbk; L Var Bsktbl; L Var Socr; L Var Sftbl; Pres Acad Fit Awd; CIF Sftbl Plyr Of Yr; LA Times Plyr Of Yr; All CIF & All Leag; Leag & Tm MVP; U NC Chapel Hill; Jrnlsm.

LAUER, BRITTANY R; San Ramon Valley HS; Danville, CA; (4); 10/410; Church Yth Grp; Dance Clb; Drama Clb; Key Clb; SADD; Band; Orch; School Musical; Stu Cncl; Diving; Mst Insprtnl Awd Vrsty Dvng 89; Lead Ballet Prdctn; UCLA; Interntl Law.

LAUER, GRIFFEN; San Ramon Valley HS; Danville, CA; (2); Church Yth Grp; Teachers Aide; Band; Jazz Band; Var Crs Cntry; JV Socr; Var Trk; High Hon Roll; Pres Schlr; UCLA.

LAUGHARN, KEVIN C; University HS; Irvine, CA; (2); Boy Scts; Church Yth Grp; Ski Clb; Swmmng; Vllybl; Surfing Comptns; Landscape Arch.

LAUGHLIN, BARBARA D; North Monterey County HS; Castroville, CA; (2); Aud/Vis; Bus Profs of Am; FHA; SADD; Drill Tm; Cit Awd; Hon Roll.

LAUGHLIN, PATRICIA M; Tehachapi HS; Tehachapi, CA; (3); Church Yth Grp; Drama Clb; 4-H; FFA; Ski Clb; Teachers Aide; 4-H Awd; High Hon Roll; Hon Roll; Coll Of/Sequoias; Prbtn Ofcr.

LAUGHLIN, SHEILAGH; Palm Desert HS; Indian Wells, CA; (2); Church Yth Grp; Cmnty Wkr; Drama Clb; Pep Clb; Bus Profs of Am; Stage Crew; JV Cheerldng; High Hon Roll; Drama Clb Cert Of Apprctn; Bullocks Teen Bd; UCLA; Brdcstng.

LAUGUICO, SUZETTE I; Glendale Adventist Acad; Los Angeles, CA; (2); 10/55; Hosp Aide; Teachers Aide; Acpl Chr; Rptr Nwsp; High Hon Roll; Prfct Atten Awd; Med.

LAUNIUS, KAMI SUREE; Corning Union HS; Corning, CA; (4); 11/170; Dance Clb; Drama Clb; GAA; Intnl Clb; Science Clb; Ski Clb; SADD; Band; Drill Tm; Flag Corp; CSF; Acad Awds; Butte Coll; Hlth.

LAURANILLA, SAMUEL T; Edison HS; Stockton, CA; (1); Intrml Crs Cntry; Intrml Trk; Cit Awd; Hon Roll.

LAUREANO, HECTOR; Palisades HS; Los Angeles, CA; (4); 11/445; Latino Awareness Clb; U Of CA LA; Aerospc Engrng.

LAUREANO, MARYANNE; Fountain Valley High; Fountain Valley, CA; (1); Pres Frsh Cls; Off Soph Cls; College; Corporate Law.

LAUREN, CHRISTIE; Carlmont HS; San Carlos, CA; (4); Teachers Aide; Band; Var Bsktbl; Var Crs Cntry; Cit Awd; Prfct Atten Awd; Outstndng Achvts Math 87-89; Presdntl Acad Ftns Awd 90; Sierra Acad Aeronautics; Aviatn.

LAURENCE, PATRICK M; Saint Francis HS; Pasadena, CA; (2); 9/150; Church Yth Grp; Cmnty Wkr; Ski Clb; Teachers Aide; Rptr Yrbk; JV Ftbl; Var Trk; Var Wt Lftg; NHS; NEDT Awd; CA Schlrshp Fed; Del Rey Leag Triple Jump Chmpn; Western Amer Hstry Collection; Notre Dame.

LAURENCE, TED; Thousand Oaks HS; Thousand Oaks, CA; (3); 1/500; Boy Scts; Church Yth Grp; Art Clb; JV Swmmng; High Hon Roll; CSF; Astronomy; Rock Music Keybrds; CA Tech; Astrophysics.

LAURI, JOCELYN; Fontana HS; Fontana, CA; (2); Band; Mrchg Band; High Hon Roll; San Bernardino All Cnty Hnr Band; Acadmc Gold Medal; Harvard; Bus.

LAURICIO, RICHARD F; Delano HS; Delano, CA; (3); Art Clb; Chess Clb; Church Yth Grp; Computer Clb; French Clb; Key Clb; JV Tennis; JV Trk; JV Wt Lftg; Hon Roll; MESA Club; Robotics.

LAURIE, CHARLES A; El Toro HS; El Toro, CA; (2); Boy Scts; Church Yth Grp; French Clb; Key Clb; Var Tennis; Pres Acad Fit Awd; 1st Pl Orange Cnty Hstry Day Cmptn, 4th Pl St; Engrng.

LAURITZEN, SHAWNETTE; Rubidoux HS; Riverside, CA; (4); Am Leg Aux Girls St; Church Yth Grp; Dance Clb; Office Aide; Pep Clb; Chorus; Rep Frsh Cls; Rep Soph Cls; Sec Rep Stu Cncl; Var Capt Cheerldng; Chrch Yng Wm Mdln & Cert Campcrftr; Stu Gvnrmnt Hnrs; Brigham Young U.

LAUSMAN, ANDREA Y; Branham HS; Canada; (1); French Clb; Stage Crew; Rep Frsh Cls; Swmmng; Trk; Harvard; Obstetrician.

LAUTERBACH, KAREN M; Villanjua Prep; Oxnard, CA; (4); 5/44; Pres Schlr.

LAUTERBACH, RYAN; Bret Harte HS; Avery, CA; (1); Ski Clb; JV Bsktbl; Var Socr; High Hon Roll; Schlr Athlete Awd Pin.

LAUTI, ELIZABETH L; Jefferson HS; San Francisco, CA; (2); Church Yth Grp; FCA; Girl Scts; Chorus; Church Choir; Off Frsh Cls; Score Keeper; Sftbl; Vllybl; Helping Out Others; Working With Comps; Lawyer.

LAUTI, GARY E; Carson HS; Carson, CA; (3); Church Yth Grp; Var Ftbl; Wt Lftg; Naval Acad; Civil Engrng.

LAUTMAN, STEVEN A; Bishop Amat HS; West Covina, CA; (2); Math Clb; NEDT Awd; Prfct Atten Awd; CSF; UCLA; Comp Sci.

LAUTT, ADAM; Desert Christian HS; Palmdale, CA; (2); Aud/Vis; Ed Nwsp; Cit Awd; High Hon Roll; Sal; Val; Aerosp.

LAUZIER, CHRIS J; Edison HS; Mission Viejo, CA; (3); Pres Ski Clb; Phtg Yrbk; Var Ftbl; Var Vllybl; Scuba Diving Instr; Snow Ski Racer; Acting Schl; Civil Air Patrol Sgt & Pilots License; Job-Sprt Chalet; Acting.

LAVAGNINO, THERESA M; Folsom HS; Folsom, CA; (3); 10/170; Model UN; Mrchg Band; Rptr Nwsp; Var Capt Bsktbl; JV Var Sftbl; JV Vllybl; Hon Roll; NHS; FNL; SRO; CSF; Ed.

LAVENDER, KYSHA; Leuzinger HS; Hawthorne, CA; (3); Library Aide; Teachers Aide; School Play; Prfct Atten Awd; Long Beach ST; Acctng.

LAVERDIERE, MICHAEL; St Bernard HS; El Segundo, CA; (2); Art Clb; French Clb; Band; Jazz Band; Mrchg Band; Pep Band; JV Trk; CA Schlrshp Fed; Hmrm Rep; JV Shotput Capt; Mc Gill; Crmnl Law.

LAVEY, THOMAS; Santa Clara HS; Port Hueneme, CA; (3); Sec Sr Cls; Sec Stu Cncl; JV Bsbl; JV Crs Cntry; Var Trk; Hon Roll; NHS; Bus.

LAVEZZOLI, DAVID J; Casa Grande HS; Petaluma, CA; (2); 27/295; Boy Scts; Band; Jazz Band; Mrchg Band; Pep Band; Var Crs Cntry; JV Trk; Var Wrstlng; Hon Roll; NHS; CSF; Olde Adobe Assn; Military.

LAVEZZOLI, THOMAS J; Casa Grande HS; Petaluma, CA; (2); 37/295; Boy Scts; Band; Jazz Band; Mrchg Band; School Musical; Var Tennis; Var Wrstlng; High Hon Roll; Hon Roll; Jr NHS; CSF; Olde Adobe Assoc; Petaluma Area Pilots Assoc; Med.

LAVIN, MARIANNE; Junipero Serra HS; San Diego, CA; (3); 52/391; Chorus; Drill Tm; School Musical; Stage Crew; Variety Show; Yrbk; Powder Puff Ftbl; Hon Roll; Altrnt Pepperdine Yth Smnr; Yrbk Outstndng Cntrbtr; U Of AZ; Psych.

LAVINE, BILLY H; Bonita Vista HS; San Diego, CA; (2); JV Bsbl; JV Ftbl; Forensic Path.

LAVIS, MARTIN R; Andrew Hill HS; San Jose, CA; (3); Math Tm; Comp Sci.

LAVOIE, TODD; Wilson HS; Long Beach, CA; (3); 80/760; Rep Stu Cncl; Hon Roll; DECA; Berkeley; Accntng.

LAVOIE, TONY; Wilson HS; Long Beach, CA; (3); 75/733; DECA; Speech Tm; Hon Roll; Jr NHS; NHS; St Schlr; Press Telegram Stock Mrkt Game; Finance.

LAW, AMY; Victory Christian Schl; Cardiff, CA; (3); 1/12; Church Yth Grp; Pres Key Clb; Church Choir; School Play; Rptr Yrbk; Pres Soph Cls; VP Jr Cls; Var Bsktbl; Var Cheerldng; Intrml Powder Puff Ftbl; Appreatice Local Christian Radio Station CA Schlrshp Fed; Mexican Missions & Camp Cnslr; Radio Broadcaster.

LAW, ANN MARIE; Marina HS; Huntington Beach, CA; (2); High Hon Roll; Crisis Eclgy Clb; Golden Shield Honr.

LAW, EDMOND C; Garfield Computer Sci Magnet HS; Los Angeles, CA; (2); Capt Math Tm; Rptr Nwsp; Hon Roll; Prfct Atten Awd; MIT; Comp Sci.

LAW, HELEN; Baldwin Park HS; Baldwin Park, CA; (4); 2/397; Hosp Aide; Key Clb; Math Clb; DAR Awd; High Hon Roll; NHS; Sal; Rptr Nwsp; VP Sr Cls; Stu Cncl Clb Acctnt; Actvts Cmmsnr Of Stu Cncl; Upward Bnd; U Of PA; Bus Admin.

LAW, JULIE; Central Union HS; El Centro, CA; (1); Church Yth Grp; French Clb; Spanish Clb; Temple Yth Grp; Band; Church Choir; Mrchg Band; Pep Band; School Musical; Var Tennis; Hon Roll; BYU.

LAW, KARIE A; Mission Viejo HS; Mission Viejo, CA; (2); 67/442; Church Yth Grp; Intrml Crs Cntry; JV Socr; JV Trk; Intrml Vllybl; Hon Roll; Prfct Atten Awd; Pres Acad Fit Awd; JV Girls Soccer League Coaches Awd; Spirit Diables Awd; Most Imprvd JV Cross Cntry; UC Davis; Med.

LAW, SUNDAY P; Berkeley HS; Berkeley, CA; (4); Drama Clb; Ski Clb; Teachers Aide; School Play; Stage Crew; Nwsp; Rptr Yrbk; High Hon Roll; Jr NHS; Val; Creating Our Future Yth Env Actn Group; Anthropology.

LAW, TIM Y; Woodrow Wilson HS; San Francisco, CA; (3); FBLA; Science Clb; Yrbk; Swmmng; Hon Roll; Pres Acad Fit Awd; Golden St Exam High Honors; CSF; Honor Soc; Friday Night Live; Drug Free Clb; UCSB; Math.

LAWENDA, STEVEN; El Camino Real HS; West Hills, CA; (2); Cmnty Wkr; High Hon Roll; CA Schlrshp Fdrtn; Jr Statesmen Of Amer; Gldn St Exam-Geom; UC; Bus.

LAWLESS, JOHN A; Fresno HS; Fresno, CA; (3); #25 In Class; JCL; VP Latin Clb; Var Bsbl; Hon Roll.

LAWLESS, SEAN P; Morro Bay HS; Morro Bay, CA; (2); 39/280; Computer Clb; Var Bsbl; Var Crs Cntry; High Hon Roll; Hon Roll; Comp Prgmr.

LAWNICZAK, JON R; San Diego HS; San Diego, CA; (3); 30/415; French Clb; Ski Clb; Rep Frsh Cls; Treas Stu Cncl; JV Var Ftbl; JV Trk; Hon Roll; NHS; U S Air Force Acad; Pilot.

LAWRENCE, BEN J; Oak Ridge HS; El Dorado Hills, CA; (1); 47/295; Church Yth Grp; Bsktbl; JV Socr; Hon Roll; Engrng.

LAWRENCE, BYRON; Schurr HS; Rosemead, CA; (4); Pres Art Clb; Key Clb; Hon Roll; Pres Acad Fit Awd; CA Schlrshp Fed; HS Art Awds; HS Artist Of Yr; Woodbury U; Graphic Design.

LAWRENCE, CHRISTINE; Lincoln HS; Stockton, CA; (3); 47/633; Church Yth Grp; Cmnty Wkr; Mu Alpha Theta; Band; Stage Crew; JV Tennis; High Hon Roll; Hon Roll; Spanish NHS; Camp Fire-Treas; Schl Recgntn-Goldn St Exam-Geo; Landscp Arch.

LAWRENCE, CINNAMON A; Hanford Joint Union HS; Hanford, CA; (1); 4-H; FFA; FHA; Rptr Nwsp; Cheerldng; Swmmng; Chldrn Cnslr.

LAWRENCE, DAVID M; Paraclete HS; Lancaster, CA; (2); Key Clb; JV Var Bsktbl; Cit Awd; High Hon Roll; Hon Roll; Engr.

LAWRENCE, DAWN; Herlong HS; Doyle, CA; (3); Pres Art Clb; FBLA; Sec VP SADD; Nwsp; Treas Frsh Cls; Stat Ftbl; High Hon Roll; NHS; CSF VP; Natl Hnr Rll; JSA; Sacramento ST; Jrnlsm.

LAWRENCE, IAN A; Flintridge Prep; Duarte, CA; (3); AFS; Science Clb; Pres Spanish Clb; Ed Yrbk; Var Swmmng; High Hon Roll; Hon Roll; Jr NHS; NHS; Spanish NHS; Wtr Polo Vrsty; Awd For Excllnc Grmn.

LAWRENCE, JUSTIN P; Galt Joint Union HS; Herald, CA; (3); 15/209; Church Yth Grp; Stat Bsktbl; JV Var Ftbl; Intrml Socr; JV L Trk; Var Wt Lftg; Gov Hon Prg Awd; High Hon Roll; Hon Roll; Prfct Atten Awd; Golden St Exam Geometry Recognition; CA Poly; Elec Engrng.

LAWRENCE, KRISTIINA R; Escondido HS; Escondido, CA; (3); Church Yth Grp; Band; Flag Corp; Mrchg Band; JV L Trk; Cit Awd; Prfct Atten Awd; Best Acad Imprvmnt Awd; Jr Var Mat Maids; Graphic Art.

LAWRENCE, MIKE A; Grace M Davis HS; Modesto, CA; (4); German Clb; Bsbl; Bsktbl; Ftbl; Gldn St Exam Alg & Geom Hnrs; Stanislaus ST U; Phrmcy.

LAWRENCE, SELENA; Edison HS; Stockton, CA; (2); GAA; Acpl Chr; Chorus; School Musical; Var Bsktbl; Var Sftbl; Var Trk; Hon Roll; Pres Acad Fit Awd; Air Force.

LAWRENCE, TINA M; Antelope Valley HS; Lancaster, CA; (3); 109/631; Pres Church Yth Grp; Church Choir; Interior Decorator.

LAWRENCE, TREVOR I; Hamilton Academy Of Music; Studio City, CA; (2); Teachers Aide; Band; Jazz Band; Mrchg Band; Orch; Pep Band; School Musical; School Play; Variety Show; Bsktbl; Musicfest Intl Outstndng Drummer; New Schl Coll Schlrshp; All St Jazz Band; Howard U; Entertainer.

LAWS, JEFF J; Ramona HS; Ramona, CA; (2); 4-H; Bsktbl; Ftbl; JV Socr; JV Trk.

LAWS, SHARAWN; Sunshine HS; San Francisco, CA; (3); Church Yth Grp; ROTC; Teachers Aide; Church Choir; School Play; Cit Awd; Hon Roll; Reg Nrs.

LAWSON, BEN P; Paradise HS; Paradise, CA; (3); Letterman Clb; Jr Cls; L Var Ftbl; L Var Trk; Wt Lftg; Hon Roll; Pres Acad Fit Awd; Mst Vlbl Athl; Var Trk 3 Yrs; Var Ltrmn 2 Sports Freshman Yr; Sports Med.

LAWSON, CRAIG A; California HS; Hayward, CA; (4); Sprt Ed Nwsp; Var Bsbl; Mgr(s); Score Keeper; Hon Roll; Acad Lttr 3rd Smstr; Stu Of Mnth San Ramon Rtry Clb 90; PA Anncr Bys Bsktbl; Diablo Valley Coll; Cmmnctns.

LAWSON II, GARY; Coronado HS; Coronado, CA; (3); 4/115; Church Yth Grp; Intnl Clb; Key Clb; Office Aide; Quiz Bowl; L Bsktbl; L Ftbl; Powder Puff Ftbl; High Hon Roll; NHS; Kiwanis Essy Awd Wnnr; Xerox Hmnts/Scl Stds Awd; Ftbl Schlr Athlt; Georgetown; Bus.

LAWSON, HEIDI J; College Park HS; Pleasant Hill, CA; (1); Blck Stu Union; Early Outreach Pgm; Dancing, Rapping, Wrtng Songs; UC Berkeley; Engl.

LAWSON, LATISIA; St Michaels HS; Los Angeles, CA; (4); Dance Clb; VP Jr Cls; Hon Roll; Yng Blck Schlr; Cal ST Dominiquez; Crmnl Just.

LAWSON, LISA; Abundant Life Christian Acad; Highland, CA; (2); 1/10; Math Clb; Teachers Aide; Yrbk; Stu Cncl; Var Bsktbl; Var Cheerldng; Var Sftbl; Var Vllybl; Hon Roll.

LAWSON, LISA; San Benito HS; Hollister, CA; (3); 3/402; Debate Tm; GAA; Pep Clb; Science Clb; Off Soph Cls; Treas Jr Cls; Tennis; Trk; High Hon Roll; Hon Roll; Bio.

LAWSON, NATHAN J; Atwater HS; Merced, CA; (1); Church Yth Grp; Cmnty Wkr; Kiwanis Awd.

LAWSON, SARAH; Grossmont HS; La Mesa, CA; (3); 187/376; Am Leg Aux Girls St; JCL; Teachers Aide; Varsity Clb; Phtg Lit Mag; JV Socr; Var Swmmng; Ntl Merit Ltr; Pres Acad Fit Awd; Sprites; ASU.

LAWTON II, MARVIN M; Washington Prep; Los Angeles, CA; (3); Church Yth Grp; Math Clb; Teachers Aide; Church Choir; School Play; Off Jr Cls; Stu Cncl; JV Bsktbl; Var Crs Cntry; JV Trk; 1st Trphy Essy Spnsrd Litry Vlntrs Amer; Pep Ortrcl Cont 1st & 2nd; Stanford U; Med.

LAWTON, SONIA R; Oceanside HS; Oceanside, CA; (4); Var Crs Cntry.

LAWTON, TINA M.; Canyon Springs HS; Moreno Valley, CA; (4); Art Clb; Church Yth Grp; Cmnty Wkr; SADD; Teachers Aide; Off Jr Cls; Capt Pom Pon; Hon Roll; CA Schlsp Fed Life Mem; Mst Spirited Sr Girl; Riverside CC.

LAWTON, WILLIAM D; Lower Lake HS; Clearlake, CA; (3); 25/103; Am Leg Boys St; Hon Roll; Business Administration.

LAWYER, JORINE K; University HS; Irvine, CA; (2); 98/508; 4-H; Teachers Aide; 4-H Awd; Hon Roll; Pres Acad Fit Awd; U Of San Deigo; Bus.

LAXAGUE, ISABELLE A; Notre Dame HS; Burlingame, CA; (2); Debate Tm; Hosp Aide; Hostess Clb; Statespersons Of Am.

LAXINA, ROMULO; Southwest HS; San Diego, CA; (4); 36/478; Dance Clb; ROTC; Cit Awd; SD ST U; Health Sci.

LAY, IRENE; Oakland HS; Oakland, CA; (3); Dance Clb; French Clb; Key Clb; Prfct Atten Awd; CA ST-HAYWARD.

LAY, KENNETH L; East Bakersfield HS; Bakersfield, CA; (4); School Play; Ed Nwsp; JV Stat Bsbl; Var Stat Bsktbl; L Var Ftbl; JV Var Mgr(s); JV Var Score Keeper; L Var Trk; Hon Roll; Hstry Clb; Rank Am Mrt Cert Cmmnctns; ANPA Fndtn Val Staff, Schltc Jrnlstic Awd; Bakersfield Coll; Lib Arts.

LAY, ROMANIRAVI N; University HS; Irvine, CA; (3); English Clb; Key Clb; Nwsp; Rptr Yrbk; Ed Lit Mag; Off Sr Cls; French Hon Soc; Featured Poet Schl Mag; Intl Relations.

LAY, THOMAS; Brea-Olinda HS; Brea, CA; (1); Band; Mrchg Band; Pep Band; School Musical; Trk; Hon Roll.

LAYDEN, CHRIS; Liberty Union HS; Oakley, CA; (1); 97/447; Ftbl; Parish Cncl; Yth Ministry Rep; Bishops Dioceson; Reach; Yth Rep.

LAYER, ROBERT B; Ukiah HS; Ukiah, CA; (2); Boy Scts; Cmnty Wkr; Red Cross Aide; SADD; Color Guard; Drill Tm; Flag Corp; UCLA; Archeology.

LAYFIELD, NELSON E; Homestead HS; Sunnyvale, CA; (1); Church Yth Grp; Mrchg Band; Pep Band; Hon Roll; US Naval Acad; Intelligence.

LAYMAN, BOBBIE JEAN; Lincoln HS; Stockton, CA; (1); Pres Sec 4-H; Ed Nwsp; JV Swmmng; Cit Awd; 4-H Awd; Kiwanis Awd; Cnty Wnnr Cmmnty Pride; Scholars UC Davis Ldrshp Conf; Scholars CA Focus Pgm; Mdlst Club Nwsp & Rptr; Delta JC; Child Psych.

LAYMAN, DENISE K; Barstow HS; Barstow, CA; (1); Cmnty Wkr; Teachers Aide; Flag Corp; Mrchg Band; High Hon Roll; Hon Roll; Pediatrician.

LAYNE, JEFF; Santa Teresa HS; San Jose, CA; (2); JV Bsbl; JV Ftbl; Var Trk; Wt Lftg; Coached Bsbl & Ftbl.

LAYSON, SHERILL B; St Patrick-St Vincent HS; Vallejo, CA; (2); French Clb; Office Aide; JV Bsktbl; JV Vllybl; Hon Roll; Nrsng.

LAYTON, BECKY L; Indio HS; Indio, CA; (2); 93/365; Church Yth Grp; High Hon Roll; Hon Roll; CSF; Ped.

LAYTON, CARRIE A; Mater Dei HS; Los Alamitos, CA; (3); Church Yth Grp; Cmnty Wkr; Rep GAA; Hosp Aide; Spanish Clb; Rep Frsh Cls; Off Sr Cls; JV Var Vllybl; High Hon Roll; NHS; Natl Charity Leag Vlntr; CA JRS Clb Vlybl; Phys Thrpy.

LAYTON, ESTHER OUTA; Monache HS; Porterville, CA; (3); 12/353; Art Clb; Church Yth Grp; Math Tm; Stat Ice Hcky; Var Swmmng; Gov Hon Prg Awd; High Hon Roll; Presdntl Phys Ftnss Awd; Golden St Exam Alg High Hnrs; Certfd Lifeguard; CA ST U; Chem.

LAYTON, MEGAN; Foothill HS; Santa Ana, CA; (3); Cmnty Wkr; Pep Clb; Var Cheerldng; Var Gym; Chrmn Asst Teen; Asst Leag Santa Ana; USGF Rnkd Gym; 2nd ST Class,Uneven Par; Mem Cheerleading Team.

LAYTON, MIKE; West HS; Bakersfield, CA; (1); Band; Mrchg Band; Pep Band; Bsbl; Bsktbl; Golf; Tennis; High Hon Roll; Stanford U; Engrng.

LAYUG, MARLON D; George Washington HS; San Francisco, CA; (3); Chess Clb; Church Yth Grp; Cmnty Wkr; Var JV Ftbl; Var Vllybl; High Hon Roll; Hon Roll; Jr NHS; NHS; Aviation.

LAZAR, ROBYN A; Ocean View HS; Huntington Bch, CA; (4); Crs Cntry; Trk; Hon Roll; Costa Mesa Plc Assn Schlrshp; Orange Coast Coll; Frgn Lang.

LAZARIN, EMILIO; Schurr HS; Norwalk, CA; (4); Key Clb; Pres SADD; Band; Drm Mjr(t); Jazz Band; Sec Mrchg Band; Pep Band; Hon Roll; Trnmnt Of Roses Parade Band 90; Intl Relations.

LAZARIT JR, CRISPIN; Crenshaw HS; Los Angeles, CA; (2); Cmnty Wkr; Debate Tm; Office Aide; Speech Tm; School Play; Rptr Nwsp; High Hon Roll; Sal; Survival Club; Knights & Ladies; Campng Club; Comp Sci.

LAZARO, MARCY A; Lincoln HS; Lincoln, CA; (3); 40/146; Church Yth Grp; GAA; Office Aide; SADD; Teachers Aide; Temple Yth Grp; Var Bsktbl; JV Powder Puff Ftbl; Var Sftbl; Var Vllybl; U Of S CA; Ind Psych.

LAZAROWICH, KAMIL D; Liberty Baptist HS; San Jose, CA; (4); Church Yth Grp; FCA; Letterman Clb; Math Clb; Teachers Aide; Yrbk; Var Bsbl; Var Bsktbl; Capt Socr; Swmmng; Soccer In England; Aero Engr.

LAZARRE, PAUL E; Huntington Beach HS; Huntington Beach, CA; (2); Aud/Vis; Model UN; Ski Clb; Lit Mag; Wt Lftg; Wrstlng; Pres Acad Fit Awd; Amer Mdl Assn; Chlsy Awd-Media Prodctns; Comm.

LAZCANO, INAKI; Oak Park HS; Agoura Hills, CA; (1); JV Bsbl; JV Socr.

LAZENBY, SUSAN MURRAY; Woodbridge HS; Irvine, CA; (3); 90/450; AFS; Cmnty Wkr; Hosp Aide; SADD; Var Swmmng; Hon Roll; Water Polo Vrsty Capt; Pre-Med.

LAZEWSKI, NATHANAEL K; Calistoga HS; Calistoga, CA; (3); 2/40; Am Leg Boys St; Letterman Clb; Varsity Clb; Rep Frsh Cls; Rep Jr Cls; Intrml Bsbl; JV Var Bsktbl; JV Var Ftbl; Var L Tennis; High Hon Roll; St Rcgntn Gldn St Geom Exam; Santa Barbara U; Engrng.

LAZIER, MATT T; Templeton HS; Templeton, CA; (2); Drama Clb; Treas Jr Cls; High Hon Roll; Hon Roll; CSF Pres; Ldrshp Cls; U CA Santa Barbara; Jrnlsm.

LAZO, ESTELA; Fontana HS; Fontana, CA; (4); 25/801; Cmnty Wkr; FBLA; Office Aide; Service Clb; Rptr Yrbk; Cit Awd; High Hon Roll; Hon Roll; Prfct Atten Awd; Pres Acad Fit Awd; CSF Secy; Z Club Hstrn; U Of CA Riverside; Scl Sci.

LAZO, JEREMIAH D; Seaside HS; Marina, CA; (1); JV Ftbl; Arch.

LAZO, MADONNA SHIELA RAMOS; Alta Loma HS; Rancho Cucamonga, CA; (2); GAA; Spanish Clb; Teachers Aide; Sec Stu Cncl; JV Var Bsktbl; JV Var Sftbl; JV Var Vllybl; Cit Awd; High Hon Roll; Hon Roll; Air Force Acad; Med.

LE, ALAN H; Lowell HS; San Francisco, CA; (2); SADD; Teachers Aide; Temple Yth Grp; Band; Orch; School Musical; Gym; Score Keeper; Pres Acad Fit Awd; CSF; Solo/Ensemble-Superior Hnr; U CA-BERKELY; Dentristry.

LE, ANH CAM; University HS; Irvine, CA; (2); Model UN; Var Fld Hcky; High Hon Roll; UCLA; Bus.

LE, ANH D H; Torrance HS; Torrance, CA; (2); 43/441; Boy Scts; VP JA; Science Clb; Band; Mrchg Band; Pep Band; Civil Air Patrol; US St Fencing Assn; U Of Uppsala; Poly Sci.

LE, AU LANG N; Westminster HS; Westminster, CA; (3); Girl Scts; JCL; Latin Clb; Library Aide; Drill Tm; UCSD; Bus.

LE, BAO; Tustin HS; Santa Ana, CA; (1); Church Yth Grp; FCA; Vllybl; Gov Hon Prg Awd; Hon Roll; Pres Acad Fit Awd; UCI; Medcl.

LE, CAMLAN; San Gabriel HS; Rosemead, CA; (2); Cit Awd; Hon Roll.

LE, CATARINA H; Grant Union HS; Sacramento, CA; (3); Intnl Clb; Key Clb; Science Clb; Teachers Aide; Hon Roll; Asian America; Sacramento ST U; Psych.

LE, CHAU; Los Amigos HS; Santa Ana, CA; (2); 35/367; High Hon Roll; NHS; UCI; Comp Sci.

LE, CHAU T; Arlington HS; Riverside, CA; (2); Cmnty Wkr; ROTC; Teachers Aide; Prfct Atten Awd; UCLA; Bus.

LE, CHI; Highlands HS; Sacramento, CA; (3); 24/400; Trk; 89-90 Hghlnds Hgh Schl Scots Mdl Awd; 89-90 Wrtrs Sptlght Cert; 1988 Prncpl Awd Cert; Sac City; Ba Rgstr Nrs.

LE, CHRISTINE; Dana Hills HS; Laguna Beach, CA; (1); Spanish Clb; Dolphin Of The Month Frgn Lang; Achvt Awd Spanish; Achvt Awd Frshmn Engl.

LE, CUONG HUY; Herbert Hoover HS; Glendale, CA; (3); Library Aide; Math Tm; Science Clb; School Play; Stage Crew; Mgr Variety Show; Rep Frsh Cls; Rep Soph Cls; Rep Jr Cls; Trk; Gldn St Exam, Geo, Hnr Roll; UCLA; Astro Aerodynamic Engr.

LE, DANG H; Fontana HS; Moreno Valley, CA; (2); Rep Nwsp; Rep Yrbk; Crs Cntry; Ftbl; Wt Lftg; Cit Awd; High Hon Roll; Hon Roll; Prfct Atten Awd; UCLA; Stock Broker.

LE, DANIELLE K; La Sierra HS; Riverside, CA; (1); Rptr Nwsp; Var Tennis; Hon Roll; Prfct Atten Awd; Mock Trial Tm; Harvard; Law.

LE, DAO Q; Galileo HS; San Francisco, CA; (4); 35/400; JA; Acad Ltrs 88 & 89; San Francisco ST U; Nrsng.

LE, DIEM; Independence HS; San Jose, CA; (3); Art Clb; Math Clb; Science Clb; Temple Yth Grp; French Hon Soc; High Hon Roll; Prfct Atten Awd; CSF; Vietnms PTA Santa Clara Cnty; SJ ST; Biochem.

LE, DIEM; Westminster HS; Westminster, CA; (3); Art Clb; Hosp Aide; Rep Jr Cls; Bsbl; Bsktbl; Socr; Swmmng; Tennis; Vllybl; Wt Lftg.

LE, DIEM THANH; Encinal HS; Alameda, CA; (1); 44/195; Band; Asian Club; UC Riverside; Pediatrics.

LE, DINH; Edison SR HS; Stockton, CA; (3); Church Yth Grp; FCA; French Clb; SADD; Church Choir; Socr; Tennis; French Hon Soc; High Hon Roll; Hon Roll; UC Davis.

LE, DUC N; Tustin HS; Tustin, CA; (2); JA; Quiz Bowl; Scholastic Bowl; Science Clb; High Hon Roll; Prfct Atten Awd; Amnsty Intl Clb; OCAD Team; UCSD; Advrtsng.

LE, DUC Q; Schurr HS; La Puente, CA; (4); 25/532; Church Yth Grp; Cmnty Wkr; Computer Clb; Teachers Aide; Nwsp; Tennis; High Hon Roll; Hon Roll; Jr NHS; Loyola-Marymount U; Bus.

LE, DUYEN; Silver Creek HS; San Jose, CA; (2); Hon Roll; Prfct Atten Awd; UC Berkeley; Phrmcy.

LE, ELAINE L T; Oakland HS; Oakland, CA; (2); 34/600; Church Yth Grp; Library Aide; Tennis; Cit Awd; Hon Roll; Pres Acad Fit Awd; Upward Bound Pgm; Schlstc Achvt Awd; Drafting.

LE, GIAO-ANH H; Monterey HS; Marina, CA; (2); High Hon Roll; Pre-Med.

LE, HAI; Pioneer HS; San Jose, CA; (4); Vietnamese Club; Mech.

LE, HAN N; San Diego HS; San Diego, CA; (4); 1/339; Math Clb; Science Clb; Varsity Clb; Cit Awd; Pres Acad Fit Awd; Val; Var Badminton; U CA San Diego; Chemcl Engrng.

LE, HIEN B; Mira Mesa HS; San Diego, CA; (2); Chess Clb; Math Clb; Model UN; Orch; High Hon Roll; Kiwanis Awd; Lion Awd; Prfct Atten Awd; Pres Acad Fit Awd; CSF; Med.

LE, HIEN T; Grace Davis HS; Modesto, CA; (2); French Clb; FBLA; Hon Roll.

LE, HIEN T; Mira Mesa HS; San Diego, CA; (2); 71/797; Chess Clb; Intnl Clb; Math Clb; Math Tm; Model UN; Chorus; Church Choir; Cit Awd; NHS; Peer Cnslng Clb; UC Berkeley; Med.

LE, HOA; Abraham Lincoln HS; San Francisco, CA; (3); San Francisco ST; Pharm.

LE, HOA Q; Cordova SR HS; Rancho Cordova, CA; (4); 4/478; Art Clb; Cmnty Wkr; Library Aide; Model UN; Spanish Clb; Temple Yth Grp; Ed Yrbk; Rep Soph Cls; Treas Jr Cls; Treas Stu Cncl; CA Schlrshp Fdrtn; Natl Hlprs Peer Grp Cnslng; Spcl Friends Clb; U Of CA, San Diego,Pre-Med.

LE, HOA T; Edison HS; Fresno, CA; (1); Hon Roll.

LE, HUAN; Cordova HS; Rancho Cordova, CA; (3); 1/460; FBLA; Model UN; Yrbk; Var Ftbl; Intrml Trk; Cit Awd; High Hon Roll; NHS; CSF; UC Davis; Acctng.

LE, HUNG C; San Bernardino HS; San Bernardino, CA; (3); Cit Awd; NEDT Awd; UCLA; Mech Engrng.

LE, HUNG T; Escondido HS; Escondido, CA; (1); Nwsp; Var Tennis; Mst Imprvd Doubles Awd.

LE, HUNG V; Mira Loma HS; Sacramento, CA; (4); Art Clb; Computer Clb; Intnl Clb; Pres Acad Fit Awd; Art Schlrshp, Awd; CSU Sacramento; Civl Engrng.

LE, HUONG; Westmonster HS; Westminster, CA; (3); Royal Bnqt Purcuit Of Excllnc; Gldn West Coll; Bus.

LE, HUONG T; Tustin HS; Tustin, CA; (3); Cit Awd; Hon Roll; JETS Awd.

LE, HUY; Oakland HS; Oakland, CA; (3); JV Bsbl; Hon Roll; UCSH; Comp Sci.

LE, HUY M; Woodrow Wilson HS; Long Beach, CA; (3); Library Aide; Math Tm; Quiz Bowl; Teachers Aide; JV Socr; High Hon Roll; Hon Roll; NHS; Prfct Atten Awd; Pres Acad Fit Awd; Golden ST Exam For Algbra & Geomtry; Math Bowl; Princpl Awd 1987; Civil Engr.

LE, HUY Q; Santiago HS; Santa Ana, CA; (4); Sec Church Yth Grp; Computer Clb; JV Tennis; Var Vllybl; Hon Roll; Jr NHS; Prfct Atten Awd; Pres Acad Fit Awd; Badminton Var; Vietnamese Clb VP; Cal ST Poly Pomona; Comp Sci.

LE, JOHN N; Bakersfield HS; Bakersfield, CA; (3); 9/718; Key Clb; Math Clb; Math Tm; Science Clb; Orch; Vllybl; Hon Roll; CSF; Elec Engrng.

LE, JOHN N; Saddleback HS; Santa Ana, CA; (1); Spanish Clb; Speech Tm; Var Tennis; Elks Awd; UC Berkeley; Engrng.

LE, JON; Kingsburg HS; Kingsburg, CA; (2); Chess Clb; Computer Clb; Mu Alpha Theta; Pres Frsh Cls; JV Socr; Var Tennis.

LE, KIM HONG; Rancho Cotate HS; Rohnert Park, CA; (4); French Clb; Library Aide; Pep Clb; Spanish Clb; Teachers Aide; Yrbk; Prfct Atten Awd; Exc Wrkr Awd; Santa Rosa JC.

LE, KIM LAN T; J Eugene Mc Ateer HS; San Francisco, CA; (2); Hon Roll; Intl Bus.

LE, LAN N; John Glenn HS; Norwalk, CA; (4); 30/298; French Clb; Key Clb; Math Clb; Teachers Aide; Cit Awd; High Hon Roll; Hon Roll; CSF Schlrshp Awd; A P Clb; Mystery Bk Clb; U Of CA-IRVINE; Bio Sci.

LE, LAN T; Modesto HS; Modesto, CA; (4); Dance Clb; Sec Intnl Clb; Library Aide; Teachers Aide; Church Choir; Rptr Nwsp; JV Var Socr; Cit Awd; Hon Roll; Prfct Atten Awd; Medicine.

LE, LELAN; Lowell HS; San Francisco, CA; (3); Boy Scts; Church Yth Grp; French Clb; Varsity Clb; Ed Nwsp; Var Crs Cntry; Trk; Jr NHS; San Francisco Ballet For 10 Yrs; Mens Varsity Crew Coxswain; Commercial Actress; Coll; Orthodontics.

LE, LIEM; Gahr HS; Cerritos, CA; (2); Comp Engrng.

LE, LIEM T; Santiago HS; Tamerlane, CA; (3); Boy Scts; School Musical; Bsktbl; Swmmng; Trk.

LE, LINDA; Redlands HS; Loma Linda, CA; (2); French Clb; Spanish Clb; Rep Stu Cncl; Hon Roll; NHS; Pres Acad Fit Awd; Anesthesiologist.

LE, LISA; Arlington HS; Riverside, CA; (4); 16/400; Cmnty Wkr; FBLA; Key Clb; Spanish Clb; Varsity Clb; Tennis; High Hon Roll; Hon Roll; NHS; UC Irvine; Bus Admin.

LE, LOC P; Fresno HS; Fresno, CA; (3); 1/500; FFA; English Clb; Pres Acad Fit Awd; UCLA; Pre-Dentistry.

LE, LU; Saddleback HS; Santa Ana, CA; (2); Boy Scts; Church Yth Grp; NHS; Pres Acad Fit Awd; Saddleback Karate Clb; UCI Partnership; UCI; Medcl Doctor.

LE, MAI ANH; Live Oak HS; San Jose, CA; (3); Dance Clb; Pres French Clb; Sec Pep Clb; Pres SADD; Rptr Nwsp; Rep Stu Cncl; JV Var Cheerldng; Intrml JV Pom Pon; Hon Roll; Prfct Atten Awd; Princpals Awd; UCLA; Commnctns.

LE, MAI-TRAM; C K Mc Clatchy HS; Sacramento, CA; (2); 1/546; French Clb; Math Tm; Temple Yth Grp; Color Guard; Hon Roll; Prfct Atten Awd; CSF Clb, CA Schltc Fdrtn; Hnr CA Gldn St Ex Geom; Engr.

LE, MATT T; Kingsburg HS; Kingsburg, CA; (4); 1/140; Am Leg Boys St; VP Chess Clb; Sec Computer Clb; English Clb; Math Clb; Mu Alpha Theta; Var Socr; Var Tennis; High Hon Roll; Val; UC Santa Barbara; Elec Engrng.

LE, MIKE M; Santiago HS; Santa Ana, CA; (2); 32/541; Church Yth Grp; Treas Drama Clb; SADD; Church Choir; School Play; Variety Show; Pres Soph Cls; Bsktbl; Ftbl; Mgr(s); Ldrshp & Church Camp:SADD; Santiago Spirit; ASB; UCI; Psych.

LE, MINH V; Pioneer HS; San Jose, CA; (4); 14/200; Church Yth Grp; Pres French Clb; FBLA; Math Clb; Red Cross Aide; Capt Var Ftbl; Capt Var Trk; Capt Var Wrstlng; Hon Roll; NHS; UC Davis; Biochem.

LE, NGAN T; Fremont HS; Milpitas, CA; (2); Chess Clb; Debate Tm; Speech Tm; Tennis; High Hon Roll; Envrmntl.

LE, NGOC; Monte Vista HS; Spring Valley, CA; (4); Dance Clb; Hosp Aide; Key Clb; Teachers Aide; Rep Frsh Cls; Hon Roll; Jr NHS; NHS; Ntl Merit Ltr; Prfct Atten Awd; CSF 87-90; Natl Teenager 88; Sci Merit Ltr 86; CA U; Obstrcn.

LE, NGUYEN; Don Antonio Lugo HS; Chino Hills, CA; (3); 18/600; Cit Awd; 4-H Awd; High Hon Roll; Class Of 91 Clb; Prom Cmmnty; Cal Poly; Aero Engrng.

LE, NHUNG; C K Mc Calatchy HS; Sacramento, CA; (2); 29/485; Aud/Vis; French Clb; ROTC; High Hon Roll; HISP At Mcclatchy; Stanford; Law.

LE, NHUNG D; Livermore HS; Livermore, CA; (3); VP FBLA; Office Aide; Varsity Clb; Var Vllybl; Hon Roll; UC Davis; Fash Mktg.

LE, PHUC; Ocean View HS; Fountain Valle, CA; (3); 2/381; Computer Clb; Key Clb; Math Clb; Rptr Nwsp; Ntl Merit Ltr; Pres Acad Fit Awd; Vrsty Badminton-Mst Imprvd Player/Lttr; Asian Clb-Pres 89-90; Golden Hawk Wnnr-Math Mdl; CA Tech; Robotics.

LE, PHUONG D; Los Amigos HS; Santa Ana, CA; (2); High Hon Roll; Hon Roll; St Schlr; U Berkeley; Comp Pgm.

LE, ROSE P; Roosevelt HS; Fresno, CA; (1); Cit Awd; 4-H Awd; Gov Hon Prg Awd; High Hon Roll; Hon Roll; Prfct Atten Awd; Art; Bus.

LE, SERENA L; Notre Dame HS; San Jose, CA; (3); Hosp Aide; JA; Science Clb; Service Clb; Teachers Aide; Vllybl; High Hon Roll; Hon Roll; Jr NHS; Cngrsnl Yth Ldrshp Cncl; San Jose ST U; Physcn.

LE, SON; Galileo HS; San Francisco, CA; (2); Cit Awd.

LE, SON K; Edison HS; Stockton, CA; (2); Hon Roll; NHS; Vietnamese Clb; Chem Clb; UCD Clb; Badminton Tm; UC Davis; Phy.

LE, SUNNY M; Eisenhower HS; Rialto, CA; (4); 40/400; Boy Scts; Chess Clb; French Clb; Model UN; Ski Clb; Color Guard; Treas Stu Cncl; Cit Awd; Pres Acad Fit Awd; Lt Plc Explr Sctng; Mck Trl Co Fnls Mst Outstndng Wtnss; Robert Cable Mem Schlrshp; CSF; UCLA; Bio.

LE, TAM T; Buena Park HS; Fullerton, CA; (3); 10/400; French Clb; GAA; Treas Intnl Clb; Varsity Clb; Var Tennis; High Hon Roll; Hon Roll; Prfct Atten Awd; Vrsty Badmntn; CSF; City Of Fullertons Outstndg Citizn 90; UC Los Angeles; Bio.

LE, TAM T; Chula Vista HS; Chula Vista, CA; (3); 1/535; Art Clb; Computer Clb; Math Tm; Spanish Clb; Lit Mag; Hon Roll; Prfct Atten Awd; CA Schlstc Fed; Pan Asian Clb; Med.

LE, THANH; Hervert Hoover HS; San Diego, CA; (3); 1/32; Vllybl; Cit Awd; High Hon Roll; Prfct Atten Awd; Gldn St Exm Awds; Math.

LE, THAO JOANNA T; Bolsa Grande HS; Huntington Beach, CA; (3); #60 In Class; French Clb; VP Pres Latin Clb; Spanish Clb; Hon Roll; CA ST Long Beach; Nrs.

LE, THAO T; Irvin HS; Irvine, CA; (3); Intnl Clb; Key Clb; Ski Clb; Tennis; Vllybl; Cit Awd; High Hon Roll; Heritage Awd In Engl & Math; UCI; Dr.

LE, THERESA T; Gardena HS; Gardena, CA; (2); Church Yth Grp; NFL; Spanish Clb; Speech Tm; Church Choir; Stanford; Law.

LE, THERESE; San Ramon Valley HS; Alamo, CA; (4); FBLA; Key Clb; Teachers Aide; Chorus; School Musical; School Play; Karate Brwn Belt; CSF; Outstndng Acad Achvt Awd; U Of CA Davis; Mass Cmmnctns.

LE, THOA K; Saddleback HS; Santa Ana, CA; (1); Prfct Atten Awd; UCI; Engr.

LE, THUY; Oakland Tech; Oakland, CA; (4); Intnl Clb; Math Clb; Math Tm; SADD; Phtg Yrbk; Hon Roll; Kiwanis Awd; Gldn St Exmntn 87 & 88; Japanese Clb Scrtry; U Of CA Davis; Intl Bus.

LE, THUY T; Los Amigos HS; Santa Ana, CA; (2); French Clb; Library Aide; Office Aide; Church Choir; High Hon Roll; Hollywood Ballet Stry Cont Lost & Find; Orange Cnty Regstr Cont; CA ST Long Beach; Elem Educ.

LE, TINA; Baldwin Park HS; Baldwin Park, CA; (4); Art Clb; Spanish Clb; Lit Mag; Cit Awd; High Hon Roll; NHS; Prfct Atten Awd; USC; Med.

LE, TRANG; Los Amigos HS; Fountain Valley, CA; (3); French Clb; Teachers Aide; Band; Chorus; Hon Roll; Med.

LE, TRI DINH; Los Amigos HS; Santa Ana, CA; (2); 94/406; Drama Clb; French Clb; Key Clb; Stu Cncl; Crs Cntry; Var Tennis; Hon Roll; High Hnr Gldn St Exam Algebra; CA Schlrshp Fed; Orange Cnty Of Acad Decthln; U Of CA Irvine; Teacher.

LE, TRI T; Anaheim HS; Anaheim, CA; (3); Church Yth Grp; French Clb; Math Clb; Science Clb; JV Tennis; Hon Roll; NHS; CSF; U Irvine; Med.

LE, TRUC-LINH T; Hawthorne HS; Hawthorne, CA; (3); Sprt Ed Yrbk; Hon Roll; CSF.

LE, TRUNG; Baldwin Park HS; Baldwin Park, CA; (1); Chess Clb; FBLA; Science Clb; Cit Awd; Hon Roll; Prfct Atten Awd; Mech Engrng.

LE, TRUNG; Valley HS; Sacramento, CA; (4); Art Clb; Math Clb; School Play; Trk; Vllybl; High Hon Roll; Hon Roll; Cert Of Art Proficiency; Athl Hnrs; Hnr Rl Awd; Math Awd; Sci Awd; Cosumnes River Coll.

LE, TUAN D; Leuzinger HS; Lawndale, CA; (2); Church Yth Grp; Key Clb; Stu Cncl; JV Capt Ftbl; JV Vllybl; Cit Awd; Hon Roll; Vlybl Clb; CSF; Youth In Govt; UCLA; Bus.

LE, TUAN G; Hawthorne HS; Hawthorne, CA; (3); Church Yth Grp; Office Aide; JV Crs Cntry; JV Vllybl; High Hon Roll; Hon Roll; Centinela Valley HS Dist Outstndng Achvt; HS Achvt Cert; Martin Luther King Wrtng Cont Wnnr; UC Irvine; Dntl.

LE, TUAN H; Skyline HS; Oakland, CA; (2); Var Wrstlng; High Hon Roll; Hon Roll; Prfct Atten Awd; Student Of The Month At Skyline; Mathematics Awd; 9th Place Metal In Wrestling At Oakland; UC WA Or UC Berkeley; Engrng.

LE, TUNG B; Hawthorne HS; Hawthorne, CA; (4); Math Clb; Math Tm; Sec Science Clb; Hon Roll; Invlmnt Prgm Northrop HIP Trnng Crse; Prfct Attndnce Awd Northrop HIP Trng Crse; Cal Poly; Aero Engr.

LE, TUNG T; Sanger HS; Sanger, CA; (2); Model UN; ROTC; Science Clb; Prfct Atten Awd; Cvl Engrng.

LE, TUNG-QUAN H; Dos Pueblos HS; Goleta, CA; (2); Math Clb; JV Tennis; NHS; Pres Acad Fit Awd; Med.

LE, TUONG A; Canoga Park HS; Los Angeles, CA; (4); Church Yth Grp; FBLA; FFA; Science Clb; Intrml Bsktbl; High Hon Roll; Hon Roll; Prfct Atten Awd; Outstndng Sci Stu Awd; Chinese Schl Awds; UCLA; Bus.

LE, TUYEN K; Leuzinger HS; Hawthorne, CA; (3); French Clb; Science Clb; Spanish Clb; Chorus; JV Tennis; Vietnamese Clb; Korean Clb; UC Davis.

LE, UYEN; Wilcox HS; Santa Clara, CA; (4); Art Clb; French Clb; SADD; Deanza; Nrsng.

LE, VAN T; Oceanview HS; Westminster, CA; (1); Law.

LE, VAN T; San Marcos HS; San Marcos, CA; (3); French Clb; Hon Roll.

LE, VI-NHUAN; Monta Vista HS; Cupertino, CA; (4); 34/390; Cmnty Wkr; French Clb; Pep Clb; Service Clb; Teachers Aide; Var Cheerldng; High Hon Roll; NHS; Pres Acad Fit Awd; Hnr Guard; Badminton JV V MVP Capt; Mst Imprvd In Spirit Squad; UC Berkeley.

LE, VINH; Herbert Hoover HS; San Diego, CA; (1); 1/32; French Clb; Sftbl; Tennis; Vllybl; Cit Awd; High Hon Roll; Pres Acad Fit Awd; Top Mark Clb.

LE, VU X; University City HS; San Diego, CA; (3); 6/380; Chorus; Intrml Wt Lftg; Cit Awd; Hon Roll; U Of CA San Diego; Med.

LE, XUAN H; Santiago HS; Garden Grove, CA; (1); #16 In Class; Church Yth Grp; Computer Clb; Church Choir; Socr; Tennis; U CA Berkley; Physcs.

LE, YEN M; Grace M Davis HS; Modesto, CA; (3); French Clb; Intnl Clb; Library Aide; Teachers Aide; Hon Roll; Ntl Merit Ltr; Prfct Atten Awd; Coll Club; CSF; Bus.

LE BARON, MATT W; Monterey HS; Monterey, CA; (1); Church Yth Grp; Hon Roll; Gldn St Math Exm; Berkeley; Physicist.

LE BARRON, SANDY E; Antelope Valley HS; Lancaster, CA; (3); Church Yth Grp; Mssnry Wrk Mex 89; Awanas Ldr 89-90; Hstry.

LE BAUDOUR, RAQUEL M; Red Bluff Union HS; Red Bluff, CA; (4); Cmnty Wkr; GAA; Key Clb; Model UN; Ski Clb; SADD; Chorus; Off Jr Cls; JV Bsktbl; Var Trk; Ide Adobe Docent For Prk In Ctry Hstrcl William B Ide Adobe Prk; Fri Nite Live Membr; FR SO JR SR; Chco ST U; Policital Sci Engl.

LE BLANC, CHARLES A; South San Francisco HS; South San Francis, CA; (3); Am Leg Boys St; Hist FBLA; Stu Cncl; Hon Roll; VP MESA; Asst Drctr For Video Yrbk; Cal Poly; Elec.

LE BOUF, JAMES P; Leuzinger HS; Hawthorne, CA; (3); Boy Scts; Key Clb; Chorus; Wrstlng; Hon Roll; Order Of Arrow; Boy Scts; Law.

LE DUFF, ERICA; Canyon Springs HS; Moreno Valley, CA; (3); Cmnty Wkr; Hosp Aide; High Hon Roll; UCLA; Med.

LE FEVER, DAMON; Avalon HS; Avalon, CA; (2); 1/30; Var Bsbl; Cit Awd; High Hon Roll; Pres Soph Cls.

LE GORRETA, MARTHA; Western HS; Tulare, CA; (2); Acad Awd; Outstndng Achvt Frgn Lang; Acad Excllnce; USC; Math.

LE MAR, NATALIE; Cupertino HS; San Jose, CA; (4); GAA; Varsity Clb; Var Capt Fld Hcky; Var Sftbl; Hon Roll; San Jose ST; Nrs.

LE MAY, BRENDA; Simi Valley HS; Simi Valley, CA; (2); 236/781; Debate Tm; SADD; Chorus; School Play; Variety Show; Chrty Fund Rsr March Of Dimes; U Santa Barbara; Psych.

LE PAGE, JEREMY N; Del Oro HS; Loomis, CA; (2); 46/257; Church Yth Grp; Hon Roll.

LE VEAU, BETINA L; San Dieguito HS; San Diego, CA; (4); Church Yth Grp; Cmnty Wkr; FCA; GAA; Science Clb; Varsity Clb; Sec Frsh Cls; Rep Soph Cls; Rep Jr Cls; Rep Stu Cncl; Athletic Acad Awd; Revelle Coll UCSD; Psych.

LE-NGOC, UYEN-PHONG; San Gorgonio HS; Highland, CA; (3); 8/350; Cmnty Wkr; GAA; Hosp Aide; Pres Key Clb; Math Tm; Office Aide; Service Clb; VP Spanish Clb; Teachers Aide; JV Bsktbl; Lang.

LE-VU, NGUYET Q; Los Amigos HS; Santa Ana, CA; (2); 87/360; Church Yth Grp; Capt Drill Tm; Ed Nwsp; Stu Cncl; Var JV Swmmng; JV Tennis; Var Trk; NHS; Prfct Atten Awd; Pres Acad Fit Awd; Vietnamese Clb; Engl Commnctns.

LEA, SHANNON S; Paradise HS; Paradise, CA; (1); 2/306; JV Var Score Keeper; Stat Wrstlng; Hon Roll; Sec/Recptnst, Babysitting; UCLA; Law.

LEABHARD, STACEY M; San Marcos HS; Santa Barbara, CA; (2); Drama Clb; Acpl Chr; Chorus; School Musical; Stage Crew; Variety Show; Vocal Music Ltr; UC Santa Cruz; Eng.

LEACH, GWENDOLYNN R; Burlingame HS; Hillsborough, CA; (3); Church Yth Grp; Debate Tm; Teachers Aide; Rep Frsh Cls; Rep Soph Cls; Rep Jr Cls; Rep Stu Cncl; Cheerldng; Swmmng; Hon Roll; Work For San Francsico Marriott; PA ST; Hotel Management.

LEACH, JACKIE J; Bloomington HS; Bloomington, CA; (3); Boy Scts; Drama Clb; Thesps; School Play; Variety Show; Hon Roll; Fontana Sheriff Explorers; Cal ST; Law.

LEACH, KIEDI T; James Logan HS; Union City, CA; (3); Teachers Aide; Ed Nwsp; Law.

LEACHE, ADAM D; Huntington Beach HS; Huntington Beach, CA; (2); Boy Scts; Cit Awd; High Hon Roll; Hon Roll; Pres Acad Fit Awd; Surf Tm; Body Boarding; USC.

LEADINGHAM, STACY A; Mountain View HS; Mountain View, CA; (3); Dance Clb; Color Guard; Mrchg Band; Bus.

LEAF, CARRIE A; El Camino HS; Oceanside, CA; (3); Debate Tm; JA; Speech Tm; Band; Mrchg Band; Phtg Nwsp; Yrbk; Off Soph Cls; Off Jr Cls; Off Sr Cls; Photo; Piano; Film.

LEAHY, JORDAN M; Santa Cruz HS; Santa Cruz, CA; (3); Teachers Aide; Stage Crew; Score Keeper; Capt Vllybl; Wt Lftg; Santa Cruz Vllybl Leag All Leag Tm 90; Bosy USVBA Coaches Awd 90; Sci.

LEAK, SHAMATAYE; Sunset HS; Thomasville, NC; (2); French Clb; Hon Roll; Black Student Union; NC A&T; Hstry Tchr.

LEAKE, ROBERT; Liberty HS; Brentwood, CA; (1); FCA; Letterman Clb; L Var Wrstlng; Hon Roll; 105 Lb Leag Chmp; Brntwd News Athl Wk.

LEAL, ARIYN; Castle Park HS; Chula Vista, CA; (1); French Clb; Drill Tm; Avid; UCLA; Law.

LEAL, BURT H; Tulare Union HS; Tulare, CA; (2); Church Yth Grp; Rep Frsh Cls; JV Bsbl; Bsktbl; Hon Roll; Co MVP Bsbl Team; UCLA; Bus.

LEAL, CAROLINA; John F Kennedy HS; Los Angeles, CA; (3); FTA; Math Clb.

LEAL, CLAUDIA; Calexico HS; Calexico, CA; (3); Church Yth Grp; Spanish Clb; Teachers Aide; Church Choir; Mrchg Band; Imperial Valley Coll; Accntng.

LEAL, DANIELA A; San Dieguito HS; Encinitas, CA; (3); Girl Scts; Pep Clb; Varsity Clb; Chorus; Var Cheerldng; High Hon Roll; Hon Roll; Chicano Latino Schlrshp; UCLA; Bus Admin.

LEAL, EVAN; Sonoma Valley HS; Sonoma, CA; (2); High Hon Roll; Pres Schlr; SCF; Interact; UC Berkley; Med Engrng.

LEAL, JEFF; Portola HS; Portola, CA; (2); Spanish Clb; SADD; Teachers Aide; Sprt Ed Yrbk; Var Bsbl; Var Bsktbl; JV Ftbl; Var Golf; Hon Roll; Prfct Atten Awd; U CA.

LEAL, JOSE A; San Gorgonio HS; San Bernardino, CA; (3); French Clb; Science Clb; JV Socr; Jr NHS; Electrncs Engrng.

LEAL, JOSEPH; Beaumont HS; Beaumont, CA; (2); French Clb; Band; Bsktbl; Am Leg Aux Girls St; Wt Lftg; Elctrncs.

LEAL, MELISSA I; Rowland HS; Rowland Hts, CA; (1); Biola U; Social Studies.

LEAL, MICHAEL; Bishop Amat HS; San Gabriel, CA; (3); Hon Roll; Slvr Scrn Clb; Cty Leag Bsbl; Bsbl Sprtsmnshp Awd; USC; Engrng.

LEALAIMATAFAO, FAAALU; Roosevelt HS; Fresno, CA; (1); Church Yth Grp; Orch; Hon Roll; Mecha Clb; Chrch Choir; Stanford U.

LEAM, SAVOEURN; Modesto HS; Modesto, CA; (1); Chess Clb; DECA; Band; Ftbl; UTI; Mechanic.

LEANDRO, ALARCON J; San Gabriel HS; San Gabriel, CA; (2); Band; Jazz Band; Mrchg Band; Orch; Socr; Wt Lftg; UCLA; Musician.

LEANO, SHARON; Saint Francis HS; Folsom, CA; (3); NHS; High Hon Roll; Opt Clb Awd; Vllybl; Stu Cncl; Nwsp; Debate Tm; Cmnty Wkr; Intnl Clb; Speech Tm; Young Mens Inst Essay Fnlst; Sacramentos Hstry Day Essay Cont Semi-Finlst; Pre-Med.

LEAP, KOSAL; Crawford HS; San Diego, CA; (1); 31/407; JV Tennis; Cit Awd; Hon Roll; NHS; Prfct Atten Awd; U Of CA San Diego; Doctor.

LEAP, SOPHAL; Calvin Simmons JR HS; Oakland, CA; (3); High Hon Roll; Hon Roll; Elec Engr.

LEAR, MATTHEW J; Huntington Beach HS; Huntington Beach, CA; (2); Model UN; Var Tennis; Hon Roll; Bus.

LEARD, JEFFREY S; Hoover HS; Glendale, CA; (3); Church Yth Grp; Band; Church Choir; Jazz Band; Orch; Phtg Nwsp; Bsktbl; Capt L Crs Cntry; Var L Trk; Prfct Atten Awd; Orch 89; Photo & Dsgn; Golden St Exam Hnrs Geom & Alg; Elizabethtown Coll; Arch.

LEARD, LORRIANA E; Abraham Lincoln HS; San Jose, CA; (4); 1/230; Sec Frsh Cls; Sec Stu Cncl; Off Soph Cls; Off Jr Cls; Off Sr Cls; Cmnty Wkr; Debate Tm; Science Clb; Service Clb; Ski Clb; Intnl Order Of Jobs Daughters; CSF Life Mem; Stanford U; Intnl Rel.

LEAS, EDWARD B; El Cajon Valley HS; El Cajon, CA; (2); 17/469; JV Trk; JV Wrstlng; Cit Awd; High Hon Roll; Young Life; OR ST; Elec Engr.

LEATHERY, DAVID F; Arcadia HS; Arcadia, CA; (3); Church Yth Grp; Red Cross Aide; Service Clb; Band; Mrchg Band; Var Trk; Hon Roll; Pres Acad Fit Awd; Outstndng JR Awd Concert Band; Gold Sear Grad; UC Riverside; Bus.

LEAVITT, ALLISON; Palisades HS; Los Angeles, CA; (2); Office Aide; Rep Frsh Cls; Rep Stu Cncl; Vllybl; Revere Anti-Vivisection Soc; Lwyr.

LEAVITT, CARY L; Gridley Union HS; Gridley, CA; (3); Art Clb; Boy Scts; Church Yth Grp; Drama Clb; Spanish Clb; Varsity Clb; JV Var Ftbl; Var Ftbl; Hon Roll; Brigham Young U; Mgt.

LEAVITT, RONALD; University HS; Irvine, CA; (2); Intnl Clb; JA; Chinese Clb.

LEAVITT, THOMAS V; Santa Monica HS; Santa Monica, CA; (4); JA; Ed Lit Mag; Rep Sr Cls; NHS; Ntl Merit SF; Master Cnclr L C Kelley Chptr Intl Ordr De Molay; De Molay Of Term 88-89; Jr Statesmen Of Amer; Humanities.

LEBEAUF, JEANDRA; Immaculate Heart HS; Los Angeles, CA; (1); Church Yth Grp; Computer Clb; Dance Clb; Drama Clb; Service Clb; Spanish Clb; Stage Crew; Score Keeper; Elect Engrng.

LEBOWITZ, DANIEL J; Saratoga HS; Saratoga, CA; (1); Drama Clb; Chorus; School Musical; School Play; Hon Roll.

LEBRECHT, ELIZABETH A; Lutheran HS Of Orange County; Brea, CA; (3); Pres Church Yth Grp; Band; Chorus; Church Choir; Var JV Bsktbl; Var Sftbl; Var JV Vllybl; Hon Roll.

LEBRON, JEANETTE; William Workman HS; West Covina, CA; (3); Chorus; Hon Roll.

LEBRUN, LYNESE A; El Dorado HS; Brea, CA; (2); Church Yth Grp; Hosp Aide; Band; Mrchg Band; Pep Band; High Hon Roll; Hon Roll; Church Music Group Play & Sing; USD.

LEBRUN, MIKE J; Huntington Beach HS; Huntington Beach, CA; (1); Socr; Wt Lftg; Cit Awd; Hon Roll; Prfct Atten Awd; Pres Acad Fit Awd; U CA.

LECCE, JENNIE; Carmel HS; Carmel, CA; (3); Church Yth Grp; Cmnty Wkr; Sec Jr Cls; Stat Bsktbl; Score Keeper; Intl Mktg.

LECHLEITNER, ERIN; Vallejo SR HS; Vallejo, CA; (3); Drama Clb; Teachers Aide; JV Trk; Hon Roll; U Of San Francisco; Fash Des.

LECHUGA, ANALISA; Central Union HS; El Centro, CA; (3); Hosp Aide; Teachers Aide; Varsity Clb; Mgr Bsktbl; Mgr(s); Sftbl; Vllybl; Indocronology.

LECKBEE, ROBYN; Ventura HS; Oak View, CA; (4); Church Yth Grp; Girl Scts; SADD; Drill Tm; Pep Band; High Hon Roll; Prfct Atten Awd; Boy Scts; Cmnty Wkr; Library Aide; Rgnl Occptnl Pgm Prfct Atten Cert Of Prfcncy; Prof Secys Intl Schlrshp; Oakview Wmns League Schlrshp; Brigham Young U; Bus.

LECLAIR, NICOLE L; San Dimas HS; San Dimas, CA; (3); Hon Roll; Hnrs Cls Engl & Chem; Mt Sac; Psycht.

LEDBETTER, CARLO W; Ramona HS; Ramona, CA; (3); Var L Ftbl; Intrml JV Socr; Intrml Trk; Surfing; JR Coll; Bus Adm.

LEDBETTER, MATTHEW; Chestnut Ave Baptist Acad; Clovis, CA; (4); 1/17; Rep Church Yth Grp; Drama Clb; Teachers Aide; Chorus; Pep Band; School Musical; School Play; Var Capt Bsktbl; Var Capt Ftbl; Vllybl; Lynchburg VA Liberty U.

LEDBETTER, MICHAEL; Mt Whitney HS; Visalia, CA; (4); Art Clb; SADD; Teachers Aide; Var Ftbl; Var Trk; Var JV Wrstlng; Sequoias Coll; Sprts Med.

LEDBETTER, WOODY T; Ramona HS; Ramona, CA; (2); 31/345; Intrml Bsbl; L Var Ftbl; Intrml Socr; Surfing; SDSU; Ed.

LEDESMA, ERICA; St Joseph HS; Cerritos, CA; (3); 45/180; Church Yth Grp; Cmnty Wkr; Debate Tm; Drama Clb; French Clb; JA; Ski Clb; SADD; School Play; Stage Crew; Csf; Religion I Award; French Award; Loyola Marymount U; Lawyer.

LEDESMA, JANETTE E; James Logan HS; Union City, CA; (3); 241/972; Church Yth Grp; Cmnty Wkr; Intnl Clb; Science Clb; Teachers Aide; Mrchg Band; Powder Puff Ftbl; FCA; Prfct Atten Awd; UC Davis; Cmptr Sci.

LEDESMA, LISA; St Joseph HS; Cerritos, CA; (3); 29/180; Church Yth Grp; Cmnty Wkr; Debate Tm; Drama Clb; Sec French Clb; GAA; Ski Clb; SADD; School Play; Stage Crew; 2 Engl Awds; Frnch Clb Schlrshp; UCLA; Med.

LEDESMA, RALENA A; San Juan HS; Citrus Heights, CA; (4); 51/268; Church Yth Grp; Chorus; JV Powder Puff Ftbl; High Hon Roll; Csmtlgy; Real Estate.

LEDESMA, ROCHELLE M; Alta Loma HS; Upland, CA; (2); Church Yth Grp; Yrbk; Score Keeper; Sftbl.

LEDESMA, SANDY; Woodland HS; Woodland, CA; (4); 43/450; Art Clb; Drama Clb; English Clb; 4-H; French Clb; SADD; Thesps; School Musical; School Play; Stage Crew; CA St Art Scholar 89; CA Coll Of Arts; Art Educ.

LEDEZMA, CARLOS J; Pater Noster HS; Los Angeles, CA; (2); 4/67; Chorus; Nwsp; VP Frsh Cls; Sec Soph Cls; Var Crs Cntry; Var Capt Socr; Var Trk; Hon Roll; CSF; Chrsian Svc; AYSO Sccr; Stanford; Doctor.

LEDEZMA, EVA B; Portola JR SR HS; Portola, CA; (2); Cmnty Wkr; Library Aide; Band; Mrchg Band; Swing Chorus; Pres Frsh Cls; Rep Soph Cls; JV Bsbl; JV Vllybl; Hon Roll; Gold Hnr Soc; UC Davis; Doctor.

LEDEZMA, MARTIN R; Tulare Western HS; Tulare, CA; (4); Church Yth Grp; Cmnty Wkr; Rep Letterman Clb; Rep Sr Cls; Rep Stu Cncl; Var Capt Ftbl; Hon Roll; Lion Awd; Hefflefinger Schlrshp; Home Ec Awd; Coll Of Sequoias; Bus.

LEDGERWOOD, JEFFERSON S; Rio Mesa HS; Camarillo, CA; (3); Church Yth Grp; FCA; Math Clb; Church Choir; JV Var Bsktbl; JV Var Swmmng; JV L Vllybl; High Hon Roll; Hon Roll; Super Spartan Awd; CA Schlrshp Fed; Mnstr.

LEDUFF, EVA; Philip & Sala Burton HS; San Francisco, CA; (3); Dance Clb; VP French Clb; Sec Intnl Clb; Pep Clb; Treas Ski Clb; Church Choir; School Play; Trk; Hon Roll; Pres Black Stu Unio; GA Inst Tech; Engrng.

LEE, AARON; Tustin HS; Tustin, CA; (1); Band; Mrchg Band; JV Tennis; Stanford; Med.

LEE, ADA; San Leandro HS; San Leandro, CA; (3); 12/361; Cmnty Wkr; Math Tm; Orch; JV Swmmng; High Hon Roll; Prfct Atten Awd; Pres Acad Fit Awd; CSF.

LEE, ADLAND; South San Francisco HS; South San Francis, CA; (2); Math Clb; Prfct Atten Awd; Vlntr Smmr Day Camp Cnslr; San Francisco ST U; Comp Sci.

LEE, AE; Clovis HS; Fresno, CA; (3); French Clb; Intnl Clb; High Hon Roll; Asian Club; UC Santa Cruz; Dcrtng.

LEE, ALBERT; Walnut HS; Walnut, CA; (2); Ed Nwsp; Rep Frsh Cls; Rep Soph Cls; JV Ftbl; Var L Trk; Wt Lftg; Var L Wrstlng; Cit Awd; Hon Roll; Prfct Atten Awd; Karate; Accordian; Recrtn Advsr Chrch; US Naval Acad; Pilot.

LEE, ALBERT S; Buena HS; Ventura, CA; (3); 27/488; Trk; High Hon Roll; Hon Roll; Prfct Atten Awd; Prncpls Hnr Awd; Hnrs Math Awd; Stanford; Surgeon.

LEE, ALDRIN; Bullard HS; Fresno, CA; (3); 1/450; German Clb; Key Clb; Sec Math Clb; Math Tm; Sec Science Clb; SADD; Cit Awd; Hon Roll; Prfct Atten Awd; Val; Odyssey Of Mind; Comp Tm; UC Berkeley.

LEE, ALEXANDRE; Independence HS; San Jose, CA; (1); Math Tm; Hon Roll; JCLA; Comp Sci.

LEE, ALICE S; Arcadia HS; Arcadia, CA; (3); 20/639; Var Bsktbl; High Hon Roll; Prfct Atten Awd; Pres Acad Fit Awd; Hgh Hnrs Gldn St Exm Geom; Adv.

LEE, ALISON K; Homestead HS; Sunnyvale, CA; (3); Debate Tm; NFL; Teachers Aide; Band; Mrchg Band; Nwsp; Socr; French Hon Soc; High Hon Roll; NHS; Var & Jr Var Badminton; CSF Soc Act Mgr; Pianist; Sci.

LEE, ALLAN M; Arcadia HS; Arcadia, CA; (3); Church Yth Grp; Computer Clb; Math Clb; Red Cross Aide; Orch; Pasadena Yng Muscns Orchestra; Intl Buddhst Progrss Soc Transltns Cmmtt; 2nd Pl Awd SYMF Viola Plyng; Bus.

LEE, ALLEN; George Washington HS; San Francisco, CA; (4); 51/500; Cmnty Wkr; Key Clb; NFL; Speech Tm; Teachers Aide; Band; Ed Nwsp; JV Golf; High Hon Roll; Hon Roll; UC Davis; Psych.

LEE, ALLISON; Culver City HS; Culver City, CA; (1); Church Yth Grp; Girl Scts; Letterman Clb; Spanish Clb; Band; Rep Frsh Cls; Bsktbl; JV Var Swmmng; Hon Roll; Stu Leag; Anml Actvtst; Sailing; CA Berkley; Photo.

LEE, AMIE M; Pioneer HS; San Jose, CA; (4); 1/308; French Clb; Sec FFA; Math Clb; Service Clb; High Hon Roll; Ntl Merit SF; Pres Acad Fit Awd; Tech Asst Evergreen Vet Clnc; U CA Davis; Bio Sci.

LEE, AMY; Lowell HS; San Francisco, CA; (3); Office Aide; High Hon Roll; Hon Roll; Alg-Gldn St Exam Hnrs Awd 88; Geom Gldnstate Exam Hgh Hnrs Awd 89; U C Davis; Med.

LEE, AMY; Oakland HS; Pinole, CA; (3); French Clb; Service Clb; Treas SADD; Teachers Aide; Score Keeper; JV Capt Vllybl; Keywanettes; San Jose ST U; Bus Mgmt.

LEE, AMY S; Torrance HS; Torrance, CA; (3); French Clb; German Clb; Hosp Aide; Office Aide; Service Clb; School Play; Swmmng; LA Stu Coalition Club; Music Club; Press Club; Comp.

LEE, ANGEL S; Wallenberg Traditional HS; San Francisco, CA; (2); French Clb; Intnl Clb; Rptr Nwsp; Hon Roll; Blue & White Club; Law.

LEE, ANGELA; Laguna Hills HS; Laguna Hills, CA; (3); 13/400; Drama Clb; Key Clb; SADD; Teachers Aide; Yrbk; Var Tennis; Var Trk; High Hon Roll; Piano; Bus.

LEE, ANITA; Torrey Pines HS; San Diego, CA; (1); Bsktbl; Hon Roll; Doc.

LEE, ANITRA NICOLE; Luther Burbank HS; Sacto, CA; (3); 38/306; ROTC; Drill Tm; Bsktbl; Sftbl; Trk; Hon Roll; Prfct Atten Awd; Sac City; English Teacher.

LEE, ANNE; Edison HS; Stockton, CA; (3); #3 In Class; Computer Clb; Latin Clb; Math Clb; Science Clb; Teachers Aide; High Hon Roll; Hon Roll; NHS; Rotary Awd; Sci Fair; Sci Olympiad; Acad Decathlon; Phy.

LEE, ARLINDA A; San Marino HS; San Marino, CA; (4); 17/248; Cmnty Wkr; VP Treas JCL; Math Clb; Model UN; Q&S; Science Clb; Teachers Aide; Mrchg Band; Ed Yrbk; Stu Cncl; Med.

LEE, BARRON N; Bella Vesta HS; Orangevale, CA; (2); 5/406; Art Clb; FBLA; Math Tm; Spanish Clb; Tennis; High Hon Roll; NHS; Prfct Atten Awd; Spanish NHS; Cal Poly; Architecture.

LEE, BECKY; Rim Of The World HS; Lake Arrowhead, CA; (3); 29/280; Am Leg Aux Girls St; Church Yth Grp; Cmnty Wkr; Teachers Aide; Rptr Nwsp; VP Frsh Cls; VP Soph Cls; Off Sr Cls; JV Socr; Var L Tennis; Schlstc All Amer Awd; Schlr Athl 88; Golden St Exam Recog Alg; House Of Reps; Grad Hnr Grd; Cmmnctns.

LEE, BEN; Washington HS; Fremont, CA; (3); 6/306; JV Crs Cntry; JV Tennis; 1st Pl In Schl CAML 90 Precalculus; Phy.

LEE, BERTHA C; Long Beach Polytechnic HS; Long Beach, CA; (3); Dance Clb; Hosp Aide; Library Aide; Math Clb; Chorus; Orch; School Musical; Hon Roll; NHS; Long Beach Playhouse Vol; Jonathan Jacques Cancer Fair Vol; Rensselaer Medal Math & Sci.

LEE, BETTY; Nogales HS; La Puente, CA; (2); Church Yth Grp; FCA; Church Choir; Diving; Hon Roll.

LEE, BETTY; San Leandro HS; San Leandro, CA; (3); 45/361; Service Clb; High Hon Roll; Hon Roll; Ntl Merit Ltr; Prfct Atten Awd; Pres Acad Fit Awd; Mural Art Cmtpn 2nd Pl.

LEE, BINGHAM; Alhombra HS; Monterey Park, CA; (4); FBLA; Key Clb; Pep Clb; Spanish Clb; Varsity Clb; Rep Soph Cls; Rep Stu Cncl; Var JV Bsktbl; Var JV Ftbl; Alhambra Prnt Tchr Ass 90 Schlrshp Wnnr; Invlvmnt In Dj Grp; Prt Time Wrkr; U C Riverside; Medi Fld.

LEE, BONNIE; San Gabriel HS; San Gabriel, CA; (4); 53/721; Church Yth Grp; Sec Debate Tm; FBLA; JA; Sec Spanish Clb; Sec Speech Tm; Var Bsktbl; Hon Roll; Pres Acad Fit Awd; UC Irvine; Biolgcl Sci.

LEE, BRIAN; El Camino Real HS; Woodland Hills, CA; (2); Math Clb; Yrbk; Trk; Wrstlng; Hon Roll; Golden St Exam Hnrs; Korean/Amer Clb; UCLA; Med.

LEE, BRIAN J; Grace M Davis HS; Modesto, CA; (2); FBLA; Hon Roll; St Schlr; UOP; Corp Law.

LEE, BRIAN M; Fort Bragg HS; Fort Bragg, CA; (3); Treas VP 4-H; Treas Frsh Cls; Treas Soph Cls; Treas Jr Cls; Var JV Crs Cntry; Var JV Trk; 4-H Awd; High Hon Roll; Hon Roll; Jr NHS; Remote Control Airplanes, Cars, Boats; Botany; Ultra Lights, Planes, Aero Sp Tech; UC Davis; Lndscp Arch.

LEE, BRIAN Y; Bonita HS; La Verne, CA; (4); Art Clb; Computer Clb; FBLA; JCL; SADD; Teachers Aide; High Hon Roll; Pres Acad Fit Awd; CSF; Humanities On Campus; Order Of Merit Awd; U Of CA Irvine; Bio.

LEE, CAMILLA; Villanova Prep; Ojai, CA; (3); Debate Tm; Model UN; JV Socr; Var Tennis; Hon Roll; CSF; UCSB; Law.

LEE, CARISA A; Bishop O'dowd HS; Oakland, CA; (2); Cmnty Wkr; JV Swmmng; JV Tennis; High Hon Roll; NEDT Awd; Schlr Athlt Awd; CSF Mem; Deans List.

LEE, CARL M; James Logan HS; Union City, CA; (3); 79/750; Computer Clb; Intnl Clb; Hon Roll; CSF; Leo Club; UCSF; Med.

LEE, CAROLYN; Whitney HS; Cerritos, CA; (3); Girl Scts; JA; Church Choir; Drill Tm; Flag Corp; Yrbk; Var Sftbl; JV Swmmng; Vllybl; Church Yth Grp; Piano & Organ; UC Berkeley; Optometry.

LEE, CARRIE A; Notre Dame HS; Salinas, CA; (4); 2/93; Church Yth Grp; SADD; Cheerldng; Trk; NHS; Pres Acad Fit Awd; Sal; Bank Am Plaque Sci & Math; Tandy Tech Schlr; CA Schlrshp Fed Life Mem; Santa Clara U; Mech Engrng.

LEE, CECILIA E; Mater Dei HS; Santa Ana, CA; (2); Church Yth Grp; German Clb; Hosp Aide; Spanish Clb; Band; Mrchg Band; Pep Band; High Hon Roll; Hon Roll; NHS; Concert Choir Symphonci Band Sewing Clb; CSF; Standford U; Pre Med.

LEE, CHANG; Apple Valley HS; Lucerne Valley, CA; (3); Spanish Clb; Band; Mrchg Band; Pep Band; Tennis; Cit Awd; High Hon Roll; Pres Acad Fit Awd; UC Santa Barbara; Crmnl Law.

LEE, CHARLEEN E; Sunny Hills HS; Fullerton, CA; (4); Church Yth Grp; Cmnty Wkr; Spanish Clb; Church Choir; Var L Swmmng; High Hon Roll; NHS; Rotary Awd; UC Berkeley.

LEE, CHARLES; Whitney HS; Cerritos, CA; (1); Hon Roll; Pres Acad Fit Awd.

LEE, CHESTER K; Garden Grove HS; Garden Grove, CA; (1); German Clb; Hon Roll; Prfct Atten Awd; UC Berkeley; Acctng.

LEE, CHEUK HUNG; San Leandro HS; San Leandro, CA; (2); 8/399; High Hon Roll; Hon Roll; Opt Clb Awd; Prfct Atten Awd; CSF; Gldn ST Exam; Arch.

LEE, CHEUK-MAN; San Leandro HS; San Leandro, CA; (3); 18/361; Var Tennis; High Hon Roll; CSF; Chem Engr.

LEE, CHI-CHUN DAVID; Diamond Bar HS; Walnut, CA; (4); 3/455; VP Pres Chess Clb; Intnl Clb; Pres VP Science Clb; Ed Nwsp; Lit Mag; High Hon Roll; NHS; Ntl Merit Schol; Debate Tm; Math Tm; Acad Decathalon; Citizen Bee; Omaha Woodsmen Soc Amer Hstry Awd; Columbia U; Law.

LEE, CHIEH-JU; South Hills HS; West Covina, CA; (3); 17/250; Computer Clb; Debate Tm; Math Tm; Science Clb; Teachers Aide; High Hon Roll; Sci.

LEE, CHIEH-SHIN; Artesia HS; Cerritos, CA; (2); Intnl Clb; Spanish Clb; Diving; Tennis; Bus Mgmt.

LEE, CHONG S; Rancho Alamitos HS; Stanton, CA; (3); 5/35; Church Yth Grp; High Hon Roll; Hon Roll; Acadmc Exclinc Awd; Korean Club; UCLA; Doc.

LEE, CHONG STEVE; Beyer HS; Modesto, CA; (3); Key Clb; Nwsp; Off Jr Cls; Intrml Bsktbl; JV Tennis; JV Trk; Cit Awd; Hon Roll; Acad Decathlon; Philosophy Clb; CSF; Berkeley; Econ.

LEE, CHONG WOO; John F Kennedy HS; La Palma, CA; (4); Computer Clb; FBLA; Band; Mrchg Band; JV Tennis; Hon Roll; Golden St Exam Alge, Geom; Acctg.

LEE, CHRISTINA M; Ramona HS; Ramona, CA; (3); 66/280; Church Yth Grp; Off Dance Clb; Pep Clb; Spanish Clb; Drill Tm; School Play; Stu Cncl; Stat Bsktbl; Cit Awd; Church Pianist; Ballet Teacher; Dance Concert Prods; Valparaiso U; Music.

LEE, CHRISTINE SO-YUN; Eisenhower HS; Rialto, CA; (4); 7/662; Art Clb; Pres Church Yth Grp; 4-H; French Clb; FBLA; German Clb; Key Clb; Latin Clb; Spanish Clb; Church Choir; CSF; Korean Clb; Recvd 4 Schlrshps; Outstndng Achvt Engl; Prncpls Hnr Rll 87-90; UCLA; Biochmstry.

LEE, CHUN M; Rosemead HS; San Gabriel, CA; (3); Computer Clb; Math Clb; Science Clb; Acpl Chr; School Musical; School Play; Tennis; Gov Hon Prg Awd; Hon Roll; CSF; U Of CA Berkeley; Bus Mgmt.

LEE, CHUN YING MARIA; Artesia HS; Cerritos, CA; (3); Latin Clb; JV Tennis; CA ST U; Bus.

LEE, CLAIRE H; Mount Pleasant HS; San Jose, CA; (4); Art Clb; Church Yth Grp; Cmnty Wkr; Debate Tm; Pres French Clb; Sec FBLA; Rep Stu Cncl; High Hon Roll; Hon Roll; NHS; Mock Trl Tm; CSF; CA Golden St Math Awd; U CA Davis; Psych.

LEE, COLIN; El Toro HS; El Toro, CA; (3); 8/550; Sec Pres Key Clb; JV Crs Cntry; High Hon Roll; Hon Roll; Ntl Merit Ltr; Martial Arts Black Blt; Natl Mem Of Piano Gld; CSF Mem.

LEE, CORA HO; Palm Springs HS; Palm Springs, CA; (3); 15/570; Spanish Clb; Cit Awd; DAR Awd; High Hon Roll; CSF; Engl Dept Silvr Sand Awd; Natl Date Fest 1st Pl Art Awd; Graphics.

LEE, CRISTINA; E K Mc Clatchy HS; Sacramento, CA; (2); 1/535; Key Clb; Service Clb; High Hon Roll; Hon Roll; Crtv Wrtng Club & Asian Club; Amnstry Intl Clb; Lbrl Arts.

LEE, DANA E; Whitney HS; Cerritos, CA; (2); 92/120; Church Yth Grp; Drama Clb; Spanish Clb; Teachers Aide; Band; Church Choir; Mrchg Band; Orch; Variety Show; UC Berkeley; Liberal Arts.

LEE, DANIEL; Santa Monica HS; Santa Monica, CA; (1); Church Yth Grp; FBLA; Ski Clb; Ftbl; JV Vllybl; French Hon Soc; High Hon Roll; Pres Acad Fit Awd; CA Tech; Engrng.

LEE, DANIEL H; Villa Park HS; Villa Park, CA; (3); French Clb; Key Clb; SADD; Teachers Aide; Var Tennis; Hon Roll; NHS; Medicine.

LEE, DANIEL T; Esperanza HS; Yorba Linda, CA; (2); 20/500; German Clb; High Hon Roll; CA Schlrshp Fed; Top 25 Awd Acad Achvt.

LEE, DANNY; Kennedy HS; La Palma, CA; (3); Church Yth Grp; Teachers Aide; Bsktbl; JV Ftbl; JV Tennis; Hon Roll; Tutor; UCLA; Bus.

LEE, DANNY; South San Francisco HS; South San Francis, CA; (4); 1/250; Am Leg Boys St; Treas Math Clb; Rptr Nwsp; Treas Jr Cls; Stu Cncl; Ntl Merit SF; Pres Acad Fit Awd; Val; Badmntn; Stu Scl Sci Clb Pres; CSF Treas; Concrnd Stu Clb; Stanford U; Engrng.

LEE, DANNY L; San Clemente HS; Capistrano Bch, CA; (1); Teachers Aide; Intrml Mgr Bsktbl; Score Keeper; Bsktbl Vrsty Mgr; Sprts Med.

LEE, DARRIN C; Del Campo HS; Fair Oaks, CA; (3); Church Yth Grp; JV Socr; Capt Var Wrstlng; CA Schlrshp Fed; Wrestling Coach; CA Poly San Luis Obispo; Arch.

LEE, DARYL; Edison HS; Huntington Beach, CA; (3); Church Yth Grp; Key Clb; Math Clb; Model UN; Quiz Bowl; Scholastic Bowl; Spanish Clb; Orng Co Spllng Champ 88-89; St Cnsltn Champ 89; Orng Co Acad Decthln; Smmr Pre-Coll Prog UCI.

LEE, DAVID; Casa Roble Fundamental HS; Orangevale, CA; (3); 13/392; AFS; Treas 4-H; 4-H Awd; High Hon Roll; Hon Roll; NHS; St Schlr; Schl Rep HOBY Conf; Green Peace; Graphic Engr.

LEE, DAVID ALLEN; Rio Mesa HS; Camarillo, CA; (1); Boy Scts; Church Yth Grp; Band; Wt Lftg; L Wrstlng; Hon Roll.

LEE, DAVID S; El Camino Real HS; Woodland Hills, CA; (2); Boy Scts; Church Yth Grp; Band; Mrchg Band; Rep Soph Cls; JV L Bsktbl; JV L Socr; JV L Vllybl; Hon Roll; Sthrn CA Music Tchrs Assn Cert Mrt, Plyd Hnr Rctl.

LEE, DEBBIE C; Westlake HS; Thousand Oaks, CA; (2); Church Yth Grp; Hon Roll; Asn Clb; CSF; Tchr.

LEE, DEBBIE G; Canyon HS; Canyon Country, CA; (4); 84/500; FBLA; Spanish Clb; Swmmng; Spanish NHS; CSUN; Bus.

LEE, DEBORAH; Santa Catalina Schl; Hanford, CA; (1); Hosp Aide; JV Swmmng; Piano Cert Mrt; UCLA; Med.

LEE, DENNY; George Washington HS; San Francisco, CA; (3); Church Yth Grp; Key Clb; Service Clb; Hon Roll; Engr.

LEE, DEREK; Whitney HS; Cerritos, CA; (1); Boy Scts; JV Bsktbl; Var Trk; High Hon Roll; Prfct Atten Awd; Pres Acad Fit Awd; CJSF.

LEE, DESPINA; Lemoore Union HS; Lemoore, CA; (3); Church Yth Grp; Cmnty Wkr; Law.

LEE, DEWEY E; Bellarmine College Prep; San Jose, CA; (4); Cmnty Wkr; Phtg Nwsp; Ed Yrbk; JV Var Crs Cntry; Pres Acad Fit Awd; UC Berkeley; CPA.

LEE, DIANA; San Gabriel HS; Rowland Heights, CA; (3); Cmnty Wkr; Hosp Aide; Key Clb; Varsity Clb; Stu Cncl; Swmmng; Vllybl; Cit Awd; Hon Roll; Pres Acad Fit Awd; Courtesy Cmmtte VP; Girls League Pres; U CA San Diego; Bio.

LEE, DIANE A; San Marcos HS; San Marcos, CA; (4); 2/348; Dance Clb; Key Clb; Model UN; Pep Clb; Quiz Bowl; Spanish Clb; Teachers Aide; Rep Stu Cncl; Var Tennis; High Hon Roll; CA Schrshp Fed; Soroptimist Intl Awd; Fed-Mart Foundation Schlrshp Awd; CA U San Diego; Attorney.

LEE, DICK S; Bellarmine College Prep; San Jose, CA; (3); 65/300; Cmnty Wkr; Letterman Clb; Varsity Clb; Intrml Ftbl; Intrml Sftbl; Var L Wrstlng; 2 Yr Lg Champ Wrstlng & Sctn Qlfr; MI Wrstlr 88-89; Chrstn Athltc Assn Sftbl, Sccr & Bsktbl.

LEE, DICKSON D; Thousand Oaks HS; Thousand Oaks, CA; (4); Art Clb; Church Yth Grp; English Clb; Key Clb; Math Tm; NFL; Office Aide; Science Clb; Hon Roll; Opt Clb Awd; Gldn St Exams Geom & Alg II High Hnrs; CSF; Spch Trnmts; Moorpark CC; Bus Econ.

LEE JR, DIONISIO; Redondo Union HS; Manhattan Beach, CA; (4); 35/416; Computer Clb; FBLA; Key Clb; Office Aide; Band; Cit Awd; Prfct Atten Awd; Pres Acad Fit Awd; CSF; U Southern CA; Finance.

LEE, DO J; Bellarmine HS; Los Altos, CA; (1); Tae Kwon Do; Stanford; Engr.

LEE, DONESHA; Pittsburg HS; Pittsburg, CA; (3); Dance Clb; Drama Clb; SADD; Teachers Aide; Thesps; Church Choir; School Play; Intrml Bsktbl; Var Trk; Hon Roll; U CA Berkeley; Sci.

LEE, DONG JOO; Montclair HS; Montclair, CA; (2); Wrstlng; Hon Roll; Prfct Atten Awd; Montclair; Air Force Pilot.

LEE, DONNA; South San Francisco HS; South San Francis, CA; (4); 1/250; Treas Computer Clb; French Clb; Pres VP Math Clb; Math Tm; Science Clb; Var L Trk; Bausch & Lomb Sci Awd; High Hon Roll; Hon Roll; Ntl Merit SF; Asian-Amer Club; CSF; Sec Stu Soc Sci Club; UC-BERKELEY; Med.

LEE, DORA; Downey HS; Downey, CA; (2); FBLA; Science Clb; Tennis; Hon Roll; Prfct Atten Awd; Keywannettes; Yng Envrnmntlst Clb; Med.

LEE, DORA; Encinal HS; Alameda, CA; (3); 21/259; Church Yth Grp; Cmnty Wkr; FBLA; Pres Key Clb; ROTC; Spanish Clb; Color Guard; Yrbk; Var Swmmng; Hon Roll; Amer Lgn Mltry Excllnc Mdl; Var Rifle Tm; Bst Sqd & Bst Clr Guard Mdl; Bus Mgmnt.

LEE, DORIS; Aragon HS; San Mateo, CA; (3); Hon Roll.

LEE, DORIS; University HS; Irvine, CA; (4); 52/486; French Clb; Math Clb; French Hon Soc; High Hon Roll; Hon Roll; CSF; Acad Booster Clb; Golden St Exam Acad Excllnc Awd; U Of S CA; Bus Mgmt.

LEE, DOUA; Hoover HS; San Diego, CA; (3); 40/449; Church Yth Grp; French Clb; FTA; Intnl Clb; Library Aide; Chorus; Church Choir; Pom Pon; Socr; Sftbl.

LEE, DU-CHAN A; Downey HS; Downey, CA; (3); Church Yth Grp; Intnl Clb; Key Clb; Library Aide; JV Ftbl; Capt Var Wrstlng; UCLA; Elec Engr.

LEE, EDWARD B; Whitney HS; Cerritos, CA; (2); Church Yth Grp; JA; Spanish Clb; JV Swmmng; High Hon Roll; Prfct Atten Awd; JV Water Polo; Corp Sec & Personnel Of A Jr Achvt Co; CSF.

LEE, ELAINE; Lincoln HS; Stockton, CA; (3); Key Clb; Spanish Clb; Hon Roll; Medcl.

LEE, ELENA A; Mark Keppel HS; Alhambra, CA; (3); AFS; Church Yth Grp; Girl Scts; Q&S; Ed Nwsp; High Hon Roll; Hon Roll; Friendship Club; Brotherhood Sisterhood Club & Camp; CSF.

LEE, ELISA; Skyline HS; Oakland, CA; (2); Intnl Clb; Chorus; Stage Crew; Yrbk; Lit Mag; Treas Frsh Cls; Gym; Vllybl; Hon Roll; CSF; Intl Bus.

LEE, ELLEN; Sacramento HS; Sacramento, CA; (3); 63/342; Chrmn Church Yth Grp; Key Clb; Teachers Aide; Church Choir; Capt JV Gym; Hon Roll; Sec Treas NHS; Mexico Outreach Pgm; Bio.

LEE, ELLENITA; North HS; Torrance, CA; (2); French Clb; Cit Awd; Hon Roll; Chinese, Japanese & Saxon Clbs; Arch.

LEE, EMILIANO S; Abraham Lincoln HS; San Francisco, CA; (2); Office Aide; Pres Acad Fit Awd; Acad Finance; Bus.

LEE, ERIC; Clovis West HS; Fresno, CA; (3); Church Yth Grp; Cmnty Wkr; 4-H; Letterman Clb; SADD; Varsity Clb; Band; Church Choir; Drm Mjr(t); Jazz Band; WA Focus; Bst Shw CA-EXPO; Hghst Band Awd CA & AZ; Fresno ST U; Music.

LEE, ERIC C; College Park HS; Martinez, CA; (2); Church Yth Grp; Letterman Clb; Math Clb; Var Vllybl; Var Wrstlng; High Hon Roll; Bus.

LEE, ERICA; San Gorgonio HS; San Bernardino, CA; (3); Key Clb; Letterman Clb; Pep Clb; Stu Cncl; JV Var Cheerldng; Var Powder Puff Ftbl; Mock Trial Outstndng Prfrmnce; Yth To Yth Mayor Awd; Black Stu Union; Crmnlgy.

LEE, ERICA L H; La Canada HS; La Canada, CA; (4); 174/252; German Clb; Intnl Clb; Math Clb; SADD; Hon Roll; NHS; Pres Acad Fit Awd; Rotary Awd; Outstndng Advncd Art II Stu Of Yr; Scripps Coll.

LEE, ERIN; Santa Rosa HS; Santa Rosa, CA; (4); 30/585; Am Leg Aux Girls St; Pep Clb; Spanish Clb; SADD; Teachers Aide; Phtg Yrbk; Off Jr Cls; Off Sr Cls; JV Var Cheerldng; Var L Trk; CSF; Comptve Ice Skater; U Of San Diego; Span Instr.

LEE, ERIN A; Redlands SR HS; Redlands, CA; (3); Cmnty Wkr; Dance Clb; Pres Hosp Aide; Library Aide; Office Aide; Teachers Aide; Hon Roll; Nursing.

LEE, ESTHER S; North Hollywood HS; North Hollywood, CA; (1); Teachers Aide; Chorus; CSUN; Bus Admin.

LEE, EUN; Carson SR HS; Carson, CA; (3); Church Yth Grp; French Clb; Office Aide; Teachers Aide; Drill Tm; Flag Corp; Orch; Bsbl; Bsktbl; Ftbl; Brwn Blt Tae Kwon Do; UCLA; Rn.

LEE, EUN H; Sunny Hill HS; Fullerton, CA; (2); Color Guard; Rptr Nwsp; Cit Awd; High Hon Roll; Hon Roll; Prfct Atten Awd; Band Cncl VP; CCPC Hnrb Mntn Piano Div IIIA; Math Cert Of Mrt; Lwyr.

LEE, EUN J; University HS; Irvine, CA; (3); Church Yth Grp; Cmnty Wkr; French Clb; Key Clb; Church Choir; French Hon Soc; Hon Roll; UCLA.

LEE, EUNICE; John F Kennedy HS; La Palma, CA; (1); Key Clb; Intrml Capt Vllybl; High Hon Roll; Hnr Soc; Alg Gldn St Exm Awd; JV Bdmtn; Brkly; Arch.

LEE, EUNICE P; Cornelia Connelly Schl; Fullerton, CA; (3); 1/65; Church Yth Grp; Cmnty Wkr; GAA; Sec Hosp Aide; Intnl Clb; Model UN; Sec Science Clb; Sec Service Clb; Spanish Clb; Orch; Michael L Roston Creative Wrtng Cont Hnrbl Mntn; Korean Speech Wrtng Cont 1st Pl; USC Alumni Awd; Med.

LEE, EVANDRO T; Westmoor HS; Daly City, CA; (2); Cert Grtst Pnt Averg; U Of CA Berkley; Comp Engr.

LEE, FANNIE S; Galileo HS; San Francisco, CA; (4); Hon Roll; San Francisco ST U; Accntnt.

LEE, FENG-TING; Northview HS; Covina, CA; (2); Science Clb; Spanish Clb; Treas Jr Cls; JV Tennis; Var Trk; High Hon Roll; Floyd Myrick Awd Sci & Frgn Lang; Gldn St Exam Hnrs For Alg, Hgh Hnrs Geom; Acctng.

LEE, FINNY M; Turlock HS; Turlock, CA; (4); 3/500; Treas Letterman Clb; NFL; VP Service Clb; Treas Stu Cncl; Capt Crs Cntry; Kiwanis Awd; Sal; Rep Key Clb; Speech Tm; Mgr(s); Turlock Jr Miss 90; Qlfr To St Spch Trnmt 2 Yrs; Camp Royal Delg; UC Davis; Mgmt Econ.

LEE, FRANCES; John F Kennedy HS; La Palma, CA; (2); Treas Church Yth Grp; FBLA; Key Clb; High Hon Roll; Hon Roll; CSF; PTSA Undergrad Bio Awd; UCLA; Film.

LEE, FRANCIS YU HANG; George Washington HS; San Francisco, CA; (3); Boy Scts; Cmnty Wkr; Computer Clb; Sec Math Clb; Sec Science Clb; Service Clb; High Hon Roll; Schl Spon Bdmntn Team Vrsty Plyr; CA Schltc Fed; High Hnrs 1st Yr Alb & Geom Gldn St Exams; Engrng.

LEE, FRANK; Upland HS; Upland, CA; (4); 4/577; Chrmn AFS; Sec Treas Computer Clb; Pres VP Hosp Aide; Scholastic Bowl; Ed Nwsp; Stu Cncl; High Hon Roll; Kiwanis Awd; NHS; Church Yth Grp; Rgnl & Cnty Sci Fair Trphy Wnnr; Mayor & City Cncl Yth Ctznshp Awd; Most Outstndng Jr Vlntr; Duke U; Bio.

LEE, FRANK C; San Marino HS; San Marino, CA; (3); 9/260; Church Yth Grp; Cmnty Wkr; FBLA; Hosp Aide; Math Clb; Science Clb; Teachers Aide; Huntington Meml Hosp Volunteer Awd 89; CSF 89-90; ; Uture Physicians Club Vp; Harvard U; Med.

LEE, GENHSING; Fountain Valley HS; Fountain Valley, CA; (3); Computer Clb; Intnl Clb; JA; Key Clb; Red Cross Aide; Science Clb; Spanish Clb; UCLA; Math.

LEE, GEORGE; Bell Gardens HS; Bellgarden, CA; (3); FFA; Letterman Clb; Varsity Clb; Stu Cncl; Var Bsktbl; Var Ftbl; Var Trk; Law Enfrcmnt.

LEE, GEORGE C; Mission San Jose HS; Fremont, CA; (1); 1/466; Church Yth Grp; Cmnty Wkr; Library Aide; JV Crs Cntry; Gldn St Exam High Hnrs; MIT; Physics.

LEE, GERALD M; Bishop O'dowd HS; Oakland, CA; (2); Chorus; School Musical; School Play; Intrml Crs Cntry; Hon Roll; Pres Acad Fit Awd; CA ST Berkeley; Physics.

LEE, GINA G; Crossroads School For Arts And Sciences; Malibu, CA; (2); Orch; School Musical; Amer Clscl Leag, Natl Jr Clscl Leag; Plyng Violin; Music.

LEE, GINA M; Cupertino HS; Cupertino, CA; (2); Chorus; Nwsp; Cheerldng; Score Keeper; Socr; Vllybl; Hon Roll; All League Awd JV Sccr, De Anza Athltc; UC Santa Barbara; Sls.

LEE, GRACE; El Dorado HS; Yorba Linda, CA; (2); Intnl Clb; Math Clb; Math Tm; Church Choir; High Hon Roll; Calligraphy Clb Pres; Eclgy Clb; Outstndng Schlrs Awd; Pharmacy.

LEE, GRACE J; Fountain Valley HS; Fountain Valley, CA; (1); Cmnty Wkr; JV Bsktbl; UCI; Obstetrician.

LEE, GRACE K; El Toro HS; El Toro, CA; (3); Pres Church Yth Grp; Pres French Clb; Var Co-Capt Pep Clb; Var Co-Capt Cheerldng; High Hon Roll; Pr Advsr & Tutor; Tutr Handcppd Chldrn; UCLA; Bus.

LEE, GRACE S; John F Kennedy HS; La Palma, CA; (3); Church Yth Grp; Intnl Clb; Key Clb; Teachers Aide; Hon Roll; Pre Med.

LEE, HAE-YON; John F Kennedy HS; Granada Hills, CA; (4); Church Yth Grp; Teachers Aide; Church Choir; UC Irvine.

LEE, HANK C; Saint Ignatius College Prep; Daly City, CA; (4); Aud/Vis; Church Yth Grp; Cmnty Wkr; Science Clb; Church Choir; Yrbk; Vllybl; Wt Lftg; Stwd Math Awd; San Jose ST U; Comp Engrng.

LEE, HANS; Alhambra HS; Alhambra, CA; (4); 182/700; Science Clb; Intrml Bsktbl; JV Ftbl; JV Var Trk; Intrml Vllybl; Cert Of Achvt Comp Acctng; CA ST U Long Beach; Cvl Engr.

LEE, HAROLD T; Lowell HS; San Francisco, CA; (3); Teachers Aide; Band; Stat Bsktbl; Mgr(s); Var Capt Wrstlng; Chemathon 3rd Pl; Korean Club; UCLA; Law.

LEE, HEATHER; Canyon HS; Canyon Country, CA; (3); 2/500; Church Yth Grp; Spanish Clb; Var L Cheerldng; Cit Awd; High Hon Roll; NHS; Spanish NHS; CSF; Stanford U; Law.

LEE, HEATHER A; River City HS; W Sacramento, CA; (3); 1/215; Treas Key Clb; SADD; Sec Soph Cls; Sec Treas Jr Cls; Sec Stu Cncl; JV Var Bsktbl; Var Sftbl; JV Var Vllybl; High Hon Roll; CSF; Schltc Awd Math, Spnsh, Hstry & Sci; Mck Trl; U Of CA Berkeley; Engrng.

LEE, HEATHER H; Villa Park HS; Orange, CA; (2); Church Yth Grp; Cmnty Wkr; Key Clb; Nwsp; Tennis; High Hon Roll; Hon Roll; NHS; Bus Law.

LEE, HEIDI M; Mariposa County HS; Midpines, CA; (4); Sec FHA; Office Aide; Teachers Aide; DAR Awd; Hon Roll; Prfct Atten Awd; Bank Of Amer Achvt Awd-Appld Arts Plq; Rdng Fulfllmnt Reqrmnts Awd 86-87; U Of CA Berkeley; Bus.

LEE, HELEN; Fountain Valley HS; Fountain Valley, CA; (3); 2/700; Art Clb; Drama Clb; French Clb; Hosp Aide; Science Clb; Thesps; Acpl Chr; Chorus; Drill Tm; School Musical; Vlntr.

LEE, HELEN Y; Mount Eden HS; Hayward, CA; (3); Pres Church Yth Grp; Office Aide; Sec Sr Cls; Var Tennis; High Hon Roll; Hon Roll; Coll Club Secy; AHSME Math Cmptn 3rd Pl 89; UCLA; Psych.

LEE, HELENA H; Villa Park HS; Orange, CA; (2); Church Yth Grp; German Clb; Key Clb; Latin Clb; Ed Rptr Nwsp; Bsktbl; High Hon Roll; NHS; 1st Pl CA Essay "my Placce In Amer" Amer Lgn Essay Cont; Piano 9 Yrs; Svrl Awds Barquoe Fstvl; Stanford U; Law.

LEE, HENRY H; Warren HS; Downey, CA; (3); Treas Pres Computer Clb; Capt FBLA; Key Clb; Mu Alpha Theta; Spanish Clb; Prfct Atten Awd; Golden ST Exam Alg I & Geom High Hnrs; Acad Ltr Cert.

LEE, HOLTON L; Skyline HS; Oakland, CA; (3); 4/600; Boy Scts; Chess Clb; Debate Tm; Key Clb; Math Clb; Capt Math Tm; Capt ROTC; Color Guard; Drill Tm; Hon Roll; ROTC Ldrshp Mdls & Certs; RPI Medal Math/Sci; UC Berkeley; Med.

LEE, HUI-TING; Cajon HS; San Bernardino, CA; (3); Bus Math Schlrshp; Outstndng Achvt Algebra; IL; MBA.

LEE, HYO S; Warren HS; Downey, CA; (3); Art Clb; French Clb; FBLA; Key Clb; Math Clb; Mu Alpha Theta; Science Clb; Gldn St Exams Hnrs 1st Yr Alg, Geom.

LEE, JACKIE; Buena Park HS; Buena Park, CA; (3); Church Yth Grp; Dance Clb; Pres Debate Tm; JA; Math Tm; NFL; Band; Yrbk; Var Swmmng; Var Vllybl; Bnk Of Amer Awd; Mock Trl Outstndng Wtns Awd; UC Davis; Poli Sci.

LEE, JAMES; Oakland SR HS; Oakland, CA; (3); French Clb; German Clb; Key Clb; Math Clb; Ed Nwsp; Tennis; Hon Roll; Kiwanis Awd; Comp; Wrtng; Comp Sci.

LEE, JAMES; Poway HS; Poway, CA; (3); Math Clb; Orch; NHS; Fresh Acad Leag.

LEE, JAMES H; University HS; Irvine, CA; (4); 37/500; Church Yth Grp; Spanish Clb; Intrml Bsktbl; JV Vllybl; High Hon Roll; Pres Acad Fit Awd; UCLA; Elec Engrng.

LEE, JANE P; Santa Clara HS; Santa Clara, CA; (2); Hon Roll.

LEE, JANET; George Washington HS; San Francisco, CA; (2); Hosp Aide; Key Clb; Office Aide; Service Clb; Band; JV Tennis; Hon Roll; CSF; Genl Svc Soc; Med.

LEE, JANG C; El Toro HS; Irvine, CA; (4); 74/540; Art Clb; Church Yth Grp; German Clb; Intnl Clb; High Hon Roll; Hon Roll; Geographical Survey, Agricultural Club; Mothers Day Awd; Korean Lit Awd; Engrng Club; UC Irvine; Comp Sci.

LEE, JASON; George Washington HS; San Francisco, CA; (2); Chess Clb; Teachers Aide; Hon Roll.

LEE, JASON; Homestead HS; Sunnyvale, CA; (3); 2/89; Bus Profs of Am; Cmnty Wkr; Debate Tm; FBLA; JA; NFL; Service Clb; Speech Tm; SADD; Nwsp; CSF; Vlntrng Pblc Lbrary; U Of CA Berkeley; Engrng.

LEE, JASON T; Berkeley HS; Oakland, CA; (3); Cmnty Wkr; Speech Tm; Pres Variety Show; Nwsp; Var L Trk; Cit Awd; Prfct Atten Awd; Pres Yth Ldrshp & Development Club; Stu Exchng Pgm; UC Santa Barbara; Bus.

LEE, JEAN; Pacifica HS; Garden Grove, CA; (1); Church Yth Grp; Band; Mrchg Band; Pep Band; Tennis; Hon Roll; CSF; Schlr Of Qrtr 89-90; Teacher.

LEE, JEANNIE S; John F Kennedy HS; Sacramento, CA; (2); 45/530; Treas Art Clb; Chess Clb; Church Yth Grp; Sec Computer Clb; Library Aide; Math Clb; Hon Roll; CSF; High Hnrs-Gldn St Exam; Law.

LEE, JEANNIE Y; Berkeley HS; El Cerrito, CA; (3); Pres Church Yth Grp; Cmnty Wkr; Key Clb; Var Vllybl; Hon Roll; Sec St Schlr; Jr Statesman Amer; Clb Vllybl; CSF; Commnctns.

LEE, JEFF C; University HS; Irvine, CA; (2); 45/508; Intnl Clb; Math Clb; Science Clb; Bus.

LEE, JEFFREY; George Washington HS; San Francisco, CA; (2); Boy Scts; High Hon Roll; Hon Roll; Chinese Amer Club; CSF; U Of The Pacific; Dntstry.

LEE, JENNIFER; Francis W Parker HS; San Diego, CA; (1); Pres Frsh Cls; Var Socr; Var Trk; JV Vllybl; High Hon Roll; Hon Roll; Var Prfct Atten Awd; Excalibur Club; Natl Spanish Exam 10th Rank; Interact Club; Cal Poly SLO; Arch Engrng.

LEE, JENNIFER; Los Altos HS; Hacienda Heights, CA; (3); 11/376; Church Yth Grp; Var Swmmng; Var Vllybl; Hon Roll; Mst Insprtnl Awd Vrsty Vllybl; Piano.

LEE, JENNIFER K; University HS; Irvine, CA; (3); 181/551; Dance Clb; Speech Tm; Nwsp; Hon Roll; Natl Chrty Leag Tcktckrs 1st-2nd VP; Share Orslvs Clb Pres; Engl Lit.

LEE, JENNIFER Y; Whitney HS; Cerritos, CA; (1); Church Yth Grp; Drama Clb; FBLA; Key Clb; Library Aide; Model UN; JV Cheerldng; Cit Awd; High Hon Roll; Pres Acad Fit Awd; Mdcn.

LEE, JENNY; Arcadia HS; Arcadia, CA; (3); 17/639; Sec Church Yth Grp; French Clb; FBLA; Pres Math Clb; VP Science Clb; Speech Tm; Treas Orch; Rep Stu Cncl; NHS; Pres Acad Fit Awd.

LEE, JENNY; Chino HS; Chino, CA; (3); Teachers Aide; Band; Mrchg Band; Silver Spur, Band & Algbra II Awds; Mst Imprvd Band; Acctng.

LEE, JENNY; Fairfax HS; Los Angeles, CA; (3); FHA; Library Aide; Cit Awd; Hon Roll; Prometheans; College.

LEE, JENNY; Franklin SR HS; Stockton, CA; (2); Sec Frsh Cls; Hon Roll; Delta; Rgstrd Nrsng.

LEE, JENNY J; Central Union HS; El Centro, CA; (2); Church Yth Grp; JV Cheerldng; JV Tennis; Pres Acad Fit Awd; CSF; Interact Clb; UC Berkeley; Pre-Law.

LEE, JENNY J; Poway HS; Poway, CA; (4); VP Sec Church Yth Grp; Key Clb; Church Choir; Color Guard; Hon Roll; CSF; U CA-IRVINE; Soc Eclgy.

LEE, JEREMY J; Mater Dei HS; Anaheim, CA; (4); 1/425; ROTC; Ski Clb; VP Band; Jazz Band; Mrchg Band; Pep Band; Golf; Swmmng; Trk; High Hon Roll; Outstndng Band Awd 87 & 90; Rancho Santgo Coll Jazz Band; U Of CA Los Angeles; Atrophysc.

LEE, JERRY; Temple City HS; Temple City, CA; (2); Church Yth Grp; Key Clb; Spanish Clb; Spanish Clb; Church Choir; Yrbk; Intrml Bsktbl; JV Trk; Hon Roll; Phrmcy.

LEE, JESSIE J; Glendale HS; Glendale, CA; (2); Sec Church Yth Grp; Drill Tm; VP Frsh Cls; Sec Jr Cls; Cit Awd; High Hon Roll; NHS; Prfct Atten Awd; Pres Acad Fit Awd; Amer Lgn Awd; Julliard; Music.

LEE, JIM P; John F Kennedy HS; La Palma, CA; (1); Boy Scts; Church Yth Grp; Med.

LEE, JIMMY; Garfield Computer Sci Magnet HS; Los Angeles, CA; (2); Ed Nwsp; High Hon Roll; Prfct Atten Awd; Engrng.

LEE, JIMMY D; Kennedy HS; Buena Park, CA; (3); Var Ftbl; Wt Lftg; JV Wrstlng; Electrician.

LEE, JIMMY T; Skyline HS; Oakland, CA; (2); Computer Clb; Key Clb; Math Tm; Band; Orch; Cit Awd; Hon Roll; Prfct Atten Awd; Pres Acad Fit Awd; Sci.

LEE, JOANNE S; Walnut HS; Walnut, CA; (3); Intnl Clb; Spanish Clb; Cit Awd; Hon Roll; UCLA.

LEE, JOAQUINA M; Merced HS; Merced, CA; (2); Band; Flag Corp; Mrchg Band; Pep Band; Rep Frsh Cls; Rep Soph Cls; JV Sftbl; Hon Roll; U CA Davis; Lawyer.

LEE, JODI; Shasta HS; Redding, CA; (2); Acpl Chr; School Musical; Cheerldng; Hon Roll; Ballet, Tap & Piano; U C Berkeley; Psych.

LEE, JOE Y; Brea-Olinda HS; Brea, CA; (3); Ftbl; Trk; Wt Lftg.

LEE, JOHN; Buena Park HS; Buena Park, CA; (3); 44/374; Chess Clb; Computer Clb; Intnl Clb; Key Clb; Letterman Clb; Treas Math Clb; Varsity Clb; Treas Sr Cls; Var L Crs Cntry; Var Trk; Korean Club; Stu Mnth Spnsh Cls; UC Berkeley; Elec Engrng.

LEE, JOHN C; San Marino HS; San Marino, CA; (3); Art Clb; Bus Profs of Am; Cmnty Wkr; FBLA; Hosp Aide; Math Clb; NFL; Science Clb; Service Clb; Ntl Merit SF; Future Physcn Clb Pres & Fndr; Cambridge U Englnd Smmr Pgm; Columbia U; Bio.

LEE, JOHN C; Servite HS; Huntington Beach, CA; (2); 15/160; Ski Clb; Sec Frsh Cls; Ftbl; Hon Roll; UCLA; Bus.

LEE, JOHN E; J Eugene Mc Ateer HS; San Francisco, CA; (4); Church Yth Grp; Office Aide; Teachers Aide; Yrbk; Hon Roll; Dance Grp; Disc Jockey; San Jose ST U; Elec Engrng.

LEE, JONGHUI; Glendale HS; Glendale, CA; (4); 6/695; Cmnty Wkr; German Clb; NHS; Prfct Atten Awd; Pres Acad Fit Awd; CSF; Outstndng Stu Awd By Indstry Educ Cncl; Fdlty Fdrl Bnk Dstngshd Stu Awd; U Of CA San Diego; Moleclr Bio.

LEE, JOO-HYUNG; Leuzinger HS; Hawthorne, CA; (3); Cmnty Wkr; Sec Rep Jr Cls; Pres Treas Stu Cncl; Var JV Crs Cntry; Intrml Tennis; JV Trk; Hon Roll; AFS; Blck Blt Mrtl Arts; Yth Govt Pgm Bll Proponent, Assmblymn.

LEE, JOOYOUNG; Brea Olinda HS; Brea, CA; (3); 3/300; Sec Church Yth Grp; Cmnty Wkr; NFL; VP Service Clb; Var Speech Tm; Ed Nwsp; JV Tennis; Treas NHS; Rotary Awd; CA Brd Of Ed Stu Rep Semifnlst.

LEE, JOSEPH; Baldwin Park HS; Baldwin Park, CA; (2); Chess Clb; Science Clb; JV Swmmng; High Hon Roll; Dist Acdmc Ltr; Physcs.

LEE, JOSEPH; Piedmont Hills HS; San Jose, CA; (4); Church Yth Grp; Computer Clb; French Clb; Red Cross Aide; Orch; School Musical; Ed Nwsp; Ed Yrbk; Stu Cncl; Supers Stu Advsry Comm; Mayors Blue Ribbon Cncl; Chinese Club; Bus Psych.

LEE, JOSEPHINE C; Pius X HS; South Gate, CA; (3); Red Cross Aide; Stage Crew; Rptr Nwsp; Treas Frsh Cls; Sec Soph Cls; Sec Jr Cls; VP Stu Cncl; NHS; CSF; Interact Clb Pres; U San Francisco; Psych.

LEE, JOSEPHINE L; Canyon Springs HS; Moreno Valley, CA; (2); Pep Clb; Teachers Aide; Bsktbl; Cit Awd; High Hon Roll; Hon Roll; Bsktbl MIP Of Yr 88-89; Comp Sci.

LEE, JOSHUA EUN J; Sunny Hills HS; Fullerton, CA; (3); 20/470; Church Yth Grp; French Clb; Math Tm; Science Clb; Socr; Hon Roll.

LEE, JOYCE; Crescenta Valley HS; La Crescenta, CA; (3); Pres Sec Church Yth Grp; French Clb; Treas Math Clb; Treas Mu Alpha Theta; Sec Service Clb; Orch; Ed Lit Mag; JV Bsktbl; JV Capt Vllybl; Peer Tutoring; Med.

LEE, JOYCE Y; Lowell HS; San Francisco, CA; (2); French Clb; Red Cross Aide; SADD; Sec Orch; Mgr Tennis; Violin; Archt.

LEE, JUDITH; John A Rowland HS; Rowland Heights, CA; (2); Church Yth Grp; Cmnty Wkr; French Clb; Tennis; Trk; High Hon Roll; Hon Roll; Art; UCLA; Art.

LEE, JULIA C; Alameda HS; Alameda, CA; (4); 7/331; Red Cross Aide; Science Clb; Rptr Nwsp; Var Capt Vllybl; High Hon Roll; Hon Roll; NHS; Socty Womn Engrs Hghst Hnr; Art Awd; UC Berkeley Gftd Prog 86-89; Jack Clark Awd; Aerosp Engrng.

LEE, JULIA J; Herbert Hoover HS; Los Angeles, CA; (4); Church Yth Grp; Debate Tm; VP French Clb; Acpl Chr; Orch; Rep Frsh Cls; Rep Soph Cls; Sec Stu Cncl; High Hon Roll; Ntl Merit SF; CA Schlrshp Fedrtn 87-89; Biolgcl Scis.

LEE, JULLY H; Montebello HS; Montebello, CA; (4); 13/450; Am Leg Aux Girls St; Rep Key Clb; Sec SADD; Rep Sr Cls; Var Bsktbl; Powder Puff Ftbl; Var Capt Tennis; High Hon Roll; Pres Acad Fit Awd; Rotary Awd; U CA-SANTA Barbara; Bus Mgmt.

LEE, JUN S; Burbank HS; Burbank, CA; (3); Stage Crew; Capt JV Tennis; Hon Roll; U Of CA Los Angeles; Engnr.

LEE, JUNG-HWA; Gahr HS; Cerritos, CA; (3); 30/462; Intnl Clb; Spanish Clb; Tennis; Hon Roll; Engl Dept Blue & Gold Awd; Century 2000 Clb; UCLA; Phy.

LEE, KAREN; Thousand Oaks HS; Thousand Oaks, CA; (3); 18/598; Treas Key Clb; Pres NFL; Sec SADD; Off Frsh Cls; Var Trk; Peer Cnslr; Tn Ctr Advsry Cmmtte Pres; Yth To Yth; CA Schlrshp Fed Mem.

LEE, KATHERINE Y; John F Kennedy HS; Sacramento, CA; (1); 1/559; Chess Clb; Computer Clb; Latin Clb; Cit Awd; High Hon Roll; Prfct Atten Awd; Odyssey Of Mind 3rd Pl Tm CA; Math.

LEE, KATHY; Lincoln HS; San Francisco, CA; (3); Library Aide; CSU; Interior Dsgn.

LEE, KATHY C; Santa Fe Christian Schl; San Diego, CA; (3); Art Clb; French Clb; Girl Scts; JV Vllybl; Cit Awd; High Hon Roll; Doctor.

LEE, KATRICIA; Dana Hills HS; Laguna Niguel, CA; (3); Cmnty Wkr; Pep Clb; Yrbk; Capt JV Vllybl; Interact Clb Co-Pres; US Hstry Achvt Awd; Commnctns.

LEE, KEN W; Orosi HS; Orosi, CA; (3); 2/250; FFA; Math Clb; Intrml Bsktbl; Var Golf; Kiwanis Awd; Prfct Atten Awd; UCLA; Aerosp Engrng.

LEE, KENNETH; Irvine HS; Irvine, CA; (1); 40/650; Chess Clb; Key Clb; JV Tennis; NHS; U CA Berkeley; Poly Sci.

LEE, KENNETH; Oakland HS; Oakland, CA; (3); JV Swmmng; JV Vllybl; Hon Roll; Asian Club Pres; Hong Kong Stu Club Treas; Goal Club; UC Davis; Mech Engrng.

LEE, KENNETH K; Crescenta Valley HS; La Crescenta, CA; (2); French Clb; Letterman Clb; Mu Alpha Theta; Var Swmmng; CSF; Goldn St Exm Hgh Hnrs Geom; Water Polo.

LEE, KERMAN W; Edison HS; Stockton, CA; (2); French Hon Soc; Hon Roll.

LEE, KEUN H; Downey HS; Downey, CA; (4); VP Church Yth Grp; Key Clb; Library Aide; Science Clb; Treas Spanish Clb; Church Choir; JV Vllybl; Hon Roll; Pres Acad Fit Awd; U Of CA San Diego; Biochem.

LEE, KEVIN; Marina HS; Huntington Bch, CA; (4); Rep Key Clb; Treas Math Clb; NFL; Scholastic Bowl; Treas Speech Tm; Rptr Nwsp; High Hon Roll; Ntl Merit Ltr; Prfct Atten Awd; Acad Dcthln 88-90; 4th Pl Essay; Hgh Hnrs Geomtry; Soc Stds/Hstry Cert; Bus.

LEE, KHAMSI; Edison Computech HS; Fresno, CA; (2); Debate Tm; NFL; Speech Tm; Band; Mrchg Band; Pep Band; Hon Roll; OM; CSF; Berkley; Law.

LEE, KRYSTAL; Garey HS; Pomona, CA; (3); Art Clb; JV Bsktbl; JV Tennis; Prfct Atten Awd.

LEE, KYONG H; Gardena HS; Gardena, CA; (3); Pres Church Yth Grp; Sec Service Clb; Church Choir; Ed Lit Mag; Sun Schl Tchr.

LEE, LANA H; Redwood Christian HS; Castro Valley, CA; (3); 5/47; Band; Orch; Treas Frsh Cls; Treas Soph Cls; Treas Jr Cls; High Hon Roll; CSF; Chrch Orch; Hnr Math; Engrng.

LEE, LARRY C; Rim Of The World HS; Crestline, CA; (1); Cmnty Wkr; Prfct Atten Awd; YABA Bowling; UC San Bernardino; Engrng.

LEE, LEON; Irvine HS; Irvine, CA; (3); German Clb; Key Clb; Latin Clb; Ski Clb; Spanish Clb; Var L Vllybl; Kiwanis Awd; Ethnic Advisory Forum; Stu For Soc Responsibility; Amnesty Inlg; Key Clubber Of Month; Phys Thrpy.

LEE, LILLIAN; Abraham Lincoln HS; San Francisco, CA; (4); Yrbk; Mgr(s); Sftbl; Tennis; Hon Roll; CSF; Acad Of Finance; San Jose ST U.

LEE, LINDA K; La Canada HS; La Canada-Flint, CA; (3); 16/250; Church Yth Grp; English Clb; Hosp Aide; Key Clb; Math Clb; Mu Alpha Theta; Chorus; Vllybl; NHS; Ntl Merit SF.

LEE, LINDA M; San Gabriel HS; Alhambra, CA; (2); French Clb; Var Tennis; Hon Roll; Courtsy Cmmttee; UCLA; Engr.

LEE, LINDA S; Schurr HS; Montebello, CA; (1); Drill Tm; Prfct Atten Awd; CSF; SADD.

LEE, LISA S; Buena Park HS; Buena Park, CA; (3); Church Yth Grp; French Clb; Sec Science Clb; Speech Tm; Rptr Nwsp; Rep Stu Cncl; Mgr(s); Stat Score Keeper; Var L Swmmng; Cit Awd; Mock Trial; Sci Club Ofcr; Stu Mnth For Speech & Frnch; UC San Diego; Pdtrcn.

LEE, LONG; Clovis HS; Fresno, CA; (3); Band; Nwsp; Var Bsktbl; Socr; Var Trk; Var Vllybl; Var Wt Lftg; Fresno ST U; Phrmcy.

LEE, LOR; Duncan Polytechnical HS; Fresno, CA; (1); Intnl Clb; Chorus; Teachers Awd; Bus.

LEE, LORETTA; Fountain Valley HS; Fountain Valley, CA; (3); Church Yth Grp; JA; Latin Clb; Red Cross Aide; Science Clb; Off Jr Cls; Cit Awd; Hon Roll; Prfct Atten Awd; PALS; Bdmntn.

LEE, LOUIS; West Covina HS; West Covina, CA; (3); 7/440; Chess Clb; Computer Clb; German Clb; Treas Science Clb; Service Clb; SADD; Ed Yrbk; Rep Stu Cncl; High Hon Roll; CA Schlrshp Fed; German Hnr Soc; MIT; Comp Prog.

LEE, LYDIA; Galileo HS; San Francisco, CA; (4); 28/350; Intrml Vllybl; Hon Roll; Ntl Merit Ltr; Prfct Atten Awd; Pres Acad Fit Awd; Silver Seal Soc; Scl Stds Hnr; Practical & Voc Arts Hnr; CA Schlrshp Fed; Japanese Clb; San Francisco ST U; Nrsng.

LEE, LYNETTE; Gridley HS; Oroville, CA; (4); Drama Clb; Pep Clb; Ski Clb; Teachers Aide; Chorus; Cheerldng; Powder Puff Ftbl; Trk; Hon Roll; Friday Night Live; Butte Coll; Sociology.

LEE, LYNETTE; Woodrow Wilson HS; San Francisco, CA; (1); Church Yth Grp; ROTC; Hon Roll; Prfct Atten Awd; Mgr; Pres Acadc Ftns Awd; Ctznshp Awd; Stanford U; Med.

LEE, MAEVONNE; Marina HS; Huntington Beach, CA; (3); JA; Sec Key Clb; Spanish Clb; Band; Drm Mjr(t); Mrchg Band; Orch; School Musical; Rptr Lit Mag; Hon Roll; Schltc All Amer Awd; Arch.

LEE, MAGGIE W; Granada Hills HS; Los Angeles, CA; (2); Vllybl; Hon Roll; Prfct Atten Awd; Cert Achvt Spelling; Music Awd; Cert Accmplshmnt Prjct Bus; Bus.

LEE, MAI XI; Edison HS; Stockton, CA; (3); Library Aide; SADD; Orch; Var Socr; Var Vllybl; High Hon Roll; Hon Roll; NHS; Pres Acad Fit Awd; Var Bdmntn; CSF; Stanford; Law.

LEE, MARGARET; Sierra Vista HS; Baldwin Park, CA; (3); Hosp Aide; Badmntn; Mt Sac; Med Admin.

LEE, MARGARET M; Bridgemont HS; Alameda, CA; (3); Variety Show; Yrbk; Rep Frsh Cls; Pres Stu Cncl; Var Vllybl; Hon Roll; Rotary Awd; Org Wrt Dir JR Chapel; Prfmd Deut At 1990 Grdtn; Won Wmns Badmiton Intram; Business.

LEE, MARGARET S; Whittier Christian HS; Whittier, CA; (4); 1/180; Church Yth Grp; VP Soph Cls; Var Powder Puff Ftbl; Var L Trk; Hon Roll; Prfct Atten Awd; Val; CSF Pres; Hosp Vol; Invstmnt Clb; UCLA; Pre Med.

LEE, MATTHEW; El Cajon Valley HS; El Cajon, CA; (1); Pilot.

LEE, MEE; Saugus HS; Saugus, CA; (2); 30/500; Church Choir; Hon Roll; UCLA; Med.

LEE, MELANIE; Glen A Wilson HS; Hacienda Hts, CA; (3); Church Yth Grp; Debate Tm; Hosp Aide; Key Clb; SADD; Band; Church Choir; Mrchg Band; Nwsp.

LEE, MELISSA C; Poway HS; Poway, CA; (3); German Clb; Model UN; Varsity Clb; JV Crs Cntry; JV Gym; JV Socr; Var Trk; Intrml Wt Lftg; USD; Bus Admin.

LEE, MICHAEL; Bishop Amat Memorial HS; Hacienda Heights, CA; (4); 1/390; Cmnty Wkr; JV Var Socr; High Hon Roll; NHS; Acad Decath; Gld Mdls Overall Scr & Scl Sci LA Prvt Schls Acad Decath/Schlstc Lvl 89; Med.

LEE, MICHAEL A; Carlmont HS; San Mateo, CA; (2); Cmnty Wkr; Library Aide; Office Aide; Teachers Aide; Stage Crew; Hon Roll; Prfct Atten Awd; Bus.

LEE, MICHAEL A; Rio Mesa HS; Camarillo, CA; (1); Boy Scts; Church Yth Grp; Drama Clb; Band; Church Choir; Jazz Band; Mrchg Band; School Play; Hon Roll; Ventury All Cty Hnr Band; 1st Pl Canejo Plyrs Talnt Cmptn; Drama.

LEE, MICHAEL M; Oakland HS; Oakland, CA; (3); Computer Clb; Key Clb; Math Clb; Science Clb; Vllybl; Hon Roll; UC Davis; Civil Engr.

LEE, MICHAEL T; Independence HS; San Jose, CA; (3); Church Yth Grp; Cmnty Wkr; Math Tm; Science Clb; Yrbk; JV Tennis; Intrml Vllybl; Hon Roll; CA Schlrshp Fed; 1st Pl Awd Commercial Art Dsgn Eastridge Art Fr; UCLA; Adv.

LEE, MICHAEL Y; Servite HS; Anaheim, CA; (3); 9/160; Church Yth Grp; Quiz Bowl; Service Clb; Ski Clb; Stage Crew; Ed Lit Mag; Socr; JV Vllybl; Hon Roll; NHS; JR Statesmen Of Amer; CA Schlrshp Fed; Soferides; Med.

LEE, MICHELLE; Righetti HS; Santa Maria, CA; (1); Drill Tm; Flag Corp; Weight Lifting Clb; Strawberry Fstvl Qn 2nd Rnnr Up; UCLA; Advertising.

LEE, MICHELLE L; Abraham Lincoln HS; San Francisco, CA; (2); Church Yth Grp; Teachers Aide; Church Choir; Tennis; Hon Roll; LINS; Soph Clb; Outdoors Clb; UCLA; Marine Bio.

LEE, MICHELLE S; Ramona Convent Secondary Schl; Monterey Park, CA; (3); Art Clb; VP Church Yth Grp; Hosp Aide; Model UN; VP Frsh Cls; VP Soph Cls; Pres Stu Cncl; Var Co-Capt Tennis; High Hon Roll; NHS; CSF; CJSF; UCLA; Corporate Law.

LEE, MIMI; Abraham Lincoln HS; San Francisco, CA; (2).

LEE, MIN-AN L; Palmdale HS; Lancaster, CA; (3); JA; Spanish Clb; CSF; Keywanettes Clb; GATE; Bus Mgmt.

LEE, MING F; Lowell HS; San Francisco, CA; (2); Cmnty Wkr; Drama Clb; NFL; Speech Tm; Pres Soph Cls; Pres Jr Cls; Rptr Nwsp; St Fnlst Goldn Gate Speech Assn; UCLA; Jrnlsm.

LEE, MIRANDA; Newport Harbor HS; Costa Mesa, CA; (4); AFS; Church Yth Grp; Key Clb; Spanish Clb; Hon Roll; Girls Leag Sec; Chinese Clb; Fshn Inst Of Dsgn & Merch.

LEE, MITCHELL J; Skyline HS; Oakland, CA; (4); 21/580; Service Clb; SADD; Varsity Clb; Band; Orch; Var Golf; High Hon Roll; Hon Roll; Jr NHS; NHS; Marcus A Foster Clorox Co Schlrshp; Marcus A Foster Educational Inst Achvt Awd; Vlntr; U Of CA Davis; Bus Admin.

LEE, MORGAN B; St Marys HS; Stockton, CA; (2); Boy Scts; Church Yth Grp; Ski Clb; JV Ftbl; Wt Lftg; Hon Roll; Awd For Achvt World Regnl Studies.

LEE, MORGAN W; Lowell HS; San Francisco, CA; (3); Cmnty Wkr; Intnl Clb; Intrml Sftbl; Prfct Atten Awd; Pres Acad Fit Awd; CSF; Engrng.

LEE, NADIA M; San Marino HS; San Marino, CA; (2); 83/238; Art Clb; French Clb; JCL; Latin Clb; Math Clb; Red Cross Aide; Service Clb; Band; Mrchg Band; Tennis; CSF; Jazz Dance Company; UCLA; Law.

LEE, NELSON; Cerritos HS; Cerritos, CA; (3); Band; Mrchg Band; Tennis; UC Santa Barbara; Bus.

LEE, NENG; Edison Computech HS; Fresno, CA; (2); Church Yth Grp; French Clb; Hon Roll; Edison-Amer Hnong Clbs; Se Asian Clbs; Upward-Bound; Step Pgm; IRS Volunteer; Fresno ST U; Nrsng.

LEE, NICOLE; Central HS; Fresno, CA; (4); 3/150; Treas Science Clb; SADD; Rptr Nwsp; Treas Soph Cls; Treas Stu Cncl; Var Capt Cheerldng; Pom Pon; Elks Awd; High Hon Roll; Lion Awd; UC Santa Cruz; Psych.

LEE, NICOLE; Roosevelt HS; Fresno, CA; (1); Church Yth Grp; Drama Clb; FCA; GAA; Girl Scts; Library Aide; Office Aide; Teachers Aide; Chorus; Church Choir; MVP Awd Vllybl Trnmnt; Coaches Awd Vrsty Trck; UC Davis; Ped.

LEE, NORMAN W; George Washington HS; San Francisco, CA; (3); Cmnty Wkr; JA; Service Clb; Jazz Band; Rptr Nwsp; JV Bsbl; Var Trk; JV Vllybl; Hon Roll; NHS; UCLA; Advert.

LEE, PAO C; Mc Lane HS; Fresno, CA; (4); 4-H; French Clb; Teachers Aide; Socr; Fresno City Coll; Criminology.

LEE, PAT S; South HS; Torrance, CA; (4); 6/365; French Clb; German Clb; VP Math Clb; Sec Service Clb; Ed Nwsp; Ntl Merit SF; CSF Ofcrs; Cert Of Mrt; Stu Leag Ofcrs.

LEE, PATRICK; Hillsdale HS; San Mateo, CA; (4); 1/296; Pres Church Yth Grp; French Clb; VP Pres Math Clb; Capt Math Tm; Pres Science Clb; Church Choir; Ed Nwsp; Ed Lit Mag; High Hon Roll; Val; Piano; Bible Study Ldr; CSF; UC Berkeley; Comp Sci.

LEE, PATRICK G; George Washington HS; San Francisco, CA; (2); High Hon Roll; Hon Roll; CSF; Cert Of Achvt; Acctng.

LEE, PEGGY; Rosemead HS; El Monte, CA; (2); Church Yth Grp; Computer Clb; Drill Tm; Tennis; Cit Awd; Hon Roll; Prfct Atten Awd; Intnl Clb; Mrchg Band; Sec Keywanettes; Hse Of Reps; CSF; Med.

LEE, PETER J; Don Bosco Technical Inst; San Gabriel, CA; (3); Boy Scts; Church Yth Grp; Cmnty Wkr; Drama Clb; Church Choir; Nwsp; Trk; 1st Pl Schl Sci Fair; Crrnt Enrlmnt Arch Dsgn Cls; Cal Poly Pomona; Arch Dsgn.

LEE, RAYMOND; Webb School Of Calif; Apple Valley, CA; (3); Art Clb; Treas Spanish Clb; Acpl Chr; Orch; Ed Yrbk; Rep Jr Cls; L Tennis; Prfct Atten Awd; Pres Acad Fit Awd; Schlor Athlete; OH Heartland Conf Leader; Dorm Prefect; Bus.

LEE, RAYMOND S; Lincoln HS; San Francisco, CA; (1); Trk; Hon Roll; UC Berkeley.

LEE, REBA C; University Of San Diego HS; Oceanside, CA; (4); Church Yth Grp; Hon Roll; Peer Cnslng; Psych.

LEE, REBECCA J; Vacaville HS; Vacaville, CA; (3); Church Yth Grp; Drama Clb; Band; Chorus; Mrchg Band; School Musical; Hon Roll; Jr NHS; Sacramento ST; Cnslng.

LEE, REBEKAH E; University City HS; San Diego, CA; (3); 23/373; Church Yth Grp; Pres Intnl Clb; Orch; Rep Sr Cls; Capt Cheerldng; Cit Awd; NHS; Rotary Awd; Piano; Close Up; Miss Ntl Teenager Pageant.

LEE, RENEE; Miramonte HS; Orinda, CA; (4); 30/278; Church Yth Grp; Cmnty Wkr; French Clb; Hosp Aide; Intnl Clb; JCL; Latin Clb; Rep Sr Cls; Rep Stu Cncl; People To People Stu Ambsdr Soviet Union; Envrnmntl Club & Pblcty Offcr; Pomona Coll.

LEE, REX B; Herbert Hoover HS; Glendale, CA; (2); Teachers Aide; Bsbl; Hon Roll; Good Coll; Mjr Leag Bsbl Plyr.

LEE, RICHARD S; Warren HS; Downey, CA; (2); Computer Clb; Sec Key Clb; JSA Prlmntrn; FBLA; CSF; UC Berkeley.

LEE, ROBERT; George Washington HS; San Francisco, CA; (2); JV Swmmng; High Hon Roll; Hon Roll; CSF; HS Swimming All City Finals 1st Pl 2nd Pl 89-90.

LEE, ROBERT H; Hoover HS; Glendale, CA; (3); Church Yth Grp; JCL; Key Clb; Latin Clb; Letterman Clb; Red Cross Aide; ROTC; Scholastic Bowl; Varsity Clb; Orch; Marine Bio.

LEE, ROBERT W; La Canada HS; La Canada, CA; (3); Church Yth Grp; Math Clb; Variety Show; Intrml Bsktbl; Intrml Ftbl; High Hon Roll; NEDT Awd; Math Dept 1st Hnrs; Sunday Schl Tchr; Ntl Sci Olympd Physcl Sci Awd; Biomed Engr.

LEE, ROBYN ANN; Fountain Valley HS; Fountain Valley, CA; (1); Pep Clb; Ski Clb; Drill Tm; Hon Roll; College.

LEE, ROGER P; Irvine HS; Irvine, CA; (1); 2/520; Chess Clb; Jr NHS; Pres Acad Fit Awd; Geom Heritage Awd & Mdlln; Orng Cty Acad Dcthln Team Altrnt; Chinese Schl Kung Fu; Johns Hopkins U; Med.

LEE, ROLAND; Lowell HS; San Francisco, CA; (3); JV Bsbl; Var Crs Cntry; Var Trk; Phrmcy.

LEE, ROSALIE; Lowell HS; San Francisco, CA; (4); 134/630; Church Yth Grp; Q&S; Rep Sr Cls; Crs Cntry; Co-Capt Pom Pon; Trk; Ntl Merit SF; Pres Acad Fit Awd; Daycamp Cnslr; CSF; Big Bro Big Sis; UC Berkeley; Bus.

LEE, RUTH K; Walnut HS; Diamond Bar, CA; (4); 30/360; Treas Church Yth Grp; FBLA; Letterman Clb; Teachers Aide; Lit Mag; Off Frsh Cls; Off Soph Cls; Off Jr Cls; Sec Sr Cls; Bsktbl; Peer Counseling; U Of San Diego; Math/Teaching.

LEE, RYAN B; El Camino HS; So San Francisco, CA; (3); Am Leg Boys St; Intnl Clb; Math Tm; Service Clb; Ed Nwsp; Stu Cncl; Ntl Merit Ltr; CA Math Leag Schl Wnnr; Overall Stu Month 88; Stu Yr Engl & Soc Stud; UC Berkeley; Engr.

LEE, RYAN K; De La Salle HS; Walnut Creek, CA; (3); Teachers Aide; Stage Crew; High Hon Roll; Hon Roll; UC-BERKELEY; Arch.

LEE, SABING; Irvine HS; Irvine, CA; (4); 1/500; Treas Intnl Clb; Key Clb; Math Tm; Scholastic Bowl; Science Clb; Service Clb; Band; Mrchg Band; Ed Yrbk; High Hon Roll; Mth, Spnsh, Engl & Chem Hrtg Awds; Clsscl Music; U Of CA Los Angeles; Engnrng.

LEE, SAMMY; Downey HS; Downey, CA; (1); Art Clb; Key Clb; JV Tennis; Cit Awd; Pres Acad Fit Awd; Boy Scouts Of Amer Past Asst Patrol Leader; Stanford; Engrng.

LEE, SAMUEL C; El Dorado HS; Yorba Linda, CA; (2); 8/362; French Clb; Intnl Clb; Band; Jazz Band; Mrchg Band; Pep Band; Cit Awd; High Hon Roll; Hon Roll; NHS.

LEE, SANDRA; Alhambra HS; Alhambra, CA; (3); VP Treas Service Clb; Pres Service Clb; Treas Frsh Cls; VP Soph Cls; Sec Jr Cls; Off Sr Cls; Stu Cncl; Intrml Bsktbl; Hon Roll; Pres Acad Fit Awd; Theatre Svc Guild; Laule'a Soc Clb; Beast Mstr Awd; Bus.

LEE, SANDRA; Sunny Hills HS; Fullerton, CA; (3); 34/430; Spanish Clb; High Hon Roll; NHS; Vrsty Bdmntn Ltr; Dnc Prdctn; CA Schlstc Fed; Mktng.

LEE, SANDY; Burbank HS; Burbank, CA; (4); 26/439; Church Yth Grp; Cmnty Wkr; NFL; Pres Service Clb; Speech Tm; SADD; Teachers Aide; Chorus; Variety Show; Rep Stu Cncl; HOPE; Schlrshp From Rotry Clb, Parent Teacher Assn; UC Irvine.

LEE, SANDY; Irvine HS; Irvine, CA; (1); French Clb; Intnl Clb; JV Bsktbl; Hon Roll.

LEE, SANG Y; Hamilton Hummanities HS; Panorama City, CA; (3); Cmnty Wkr; Debate Tm; Varsity Clb; Orch; JV Var Vllybl; High Hon Roll; Hon Roll; NHS; Bus Admin.

LEE, SANG Y; Hoover HS; Glendale, CA; (2); JCL; Latin Clb; JV Vllybl; Ice Hockey Burbank Golden Bears; UC; Bus.

LEE, SANG-MIN; Gretchen A Whitney HS; Cerritos, CA; (3); Boy Scts; Hosp Aide; Key Clb; Var Capt Swmmng; Hon Roll; S W Yth Music Fstvl 89; Latin II Awd 88-89; Jr Guard Of Hnr.

LEE, SEAN H; Claremont HS; Claremont, CA; (3); Cit Awd; Hon Roll; Prfct Atten Awd; Outstndng Accntng Awd; Goldn St Exam Geom Hnr; CSU Fullerton; Accntng.

LEE, SEMISA; John F Kennedy HS; Buena Park, CA; (2); 2/35; Church Yth Grp; FBLA; Key Clb; Badminton; Future Philosophy Clb; UCLA; Optometrist.

LEE, SHANNIN; Canyon HS; Canyon Country, CA; (2); Drama Clb; Pep Clb; Ski Clb; Spanish Clb; Chorus; Cheerldng; Gym; Trk; Pres Acad Fit Awd; St Fnlst Gymnstcs CA; USC; Law.

LEE, SHANNON T; St Marys HS; Stockton, CA; (2); 2/180; Key Clb; Model UN; SADD; Varsity Clb; Stage Crew; Rep Soph Cls; Rep Jr Cls; Var Trk; Hon Roll; Pres Acad Fit Awd; CSF; CROP Cmmnty Svc Grp.

LEE, SHANNY J; Brea-Olinda HS; Brea, CA; (3); 16/290; Cmnty Wkr; Debate Tm; NFL; Quiz Bowl; Service Clb; Speech Tm; Intrml Crs Cntry; Var Trk; Pres Acad Fit Awd.

LEE, SHELL W; Bassett HS; La Puente, CA; (2); Stage Crew; Rep Stu Cncl; Capt Vllybl; Hon Roll; Prfct Atten Awd; Badmenton.

LEE, SHIRLEY X; Galileo HS; San Francisco, CA; (2); Church Yth Grp; School Musical; Hon Roll; Gldn St Exam Acad Excllnc Awd.

LEE, SIA; Fresno HS; Fresno, CA; (2); Church Yth Grp; Math Clb; ROTC; Science Clb; Color Guard; Drill Tm; Off Soph Cls; Bsbl; Sftbl; Cit Awd; Sci Fair Awd; Fresno City Coll; Nrsng.

LEE, SIRENA M; Franklin HS; Stockton, CA; (4); 10/350; Cmnty Wkr; GAA; Pep Clb; Ed Yrbk; JV Var Sftbl; JV Var Vllybl; High Hon Roll; Hon Roll; Bowlng All ST Awd Wnnr; Bank Of Am Achvt Awd; CSV Sacramento; Bus Admin.

LEE, SONG WOOK; Etiwanda HS; Etiwanda, CA; (2); 2/30; Church Yth Grp; JCL; Latin Clb; Church Choir; Hon Roll; Prfct Atten Awd; Badminton; UCLA; Pre-Med.

LEE, SOYEON SUNNY; Bloomington HS; Bloomington, CA; (2); Pres Sec Church Yth Grp; Drama Clb; Rep Frsh Cls; Sec Soph Cls; JV Cheerldng; JV Sftbl; High Hon Roll; NHS; CA Schlrshpo Fed; Mock Trials Outstndng Prfrmnc Awd; Grls Lg; Friday Night Live; HOBY Ambssdr; Eng.

LEE, STACEY; San Gabriel HS; San Gabriel, CA; (2); Rep Pep Clb; Red Cross Aide; Spanish Clb; Varsity Clb; Rep Stu Cncl; Var Crs Cntry; Var Trk; Ming Yuan Clsscl Dance Troupe Ldr; Mayor Of Montery Pk Awd Bst Performance; UC Berkly; Arch.

LEE, STANTON W; Hayward HS; Hayward, CA; (2); 18/237; Band; Jazz Band; Mrchg Band; Pep Band; Off Frsh Cls; Off Soph Cls; Hon Roll.

LEE, STEPHANIE; George Washington HS; San Francisco, CA; (3); Church Yth Grp; Math Clb; Office Aide; Science Clb; Teachers Aide; Cit Awd; High Hon Roll; Hon Roll; Chinese Speech Team 3rd Pl; San Francisco ST; Chemistry.

LEE, STEPHANIE A; John F Kennedy HS; Sacramento, CA; (1); 1/564; Ski Clb; Var Sftbl; High Hon Roll; Sacramento United Soccer Clb; Asian Clb; Prideshp Cmmtte; Odyssey Of The Mind.

LEE, STEPHEN C; South San Francisco HS; South San Francis, CA; (3); 1/250; Computer Clb; French Clb; Math Clb; Spanish Clb; Phtg Yrbk; Intrml Bsktbl; Mgr(s); Score Keeper; Hon Roll; Badmington Var; Comp Engr.

LEE, STEPHEN F; Lowell HS; San Francisco, CA; (3); Chess Clb; Computer Clb; Orch; Med.

LEE, STEVE C; Brea Olinda HS; Brea, CA; (3); 110/300; Intnl Clb; Tennis; Trk; Wt Lftg; Prfct Atten Awd; Bus.

LEE, STEVE M; Upland HS; Upland, CA; (3); Treas Computer Clb; FBLA; Math Tm; Spanish Clb; JV Tennis; High Hon Roll; Cngrssnl Schlr; Natl Yng Ldrs Conf; Cnty Sci Fr 2nd Pl; CA St Sci Fr; Stu Achvt Awds; Acad Dectlhn; Physics.

LEE, STEVEN; Carson HS; Carson, CA; (2); Chess Clb; Computer Clb; Teachers Aide; Tennis.

LEE, STEVEN H; Homestead HS; Sunnyvale, CA; (3); 1/383; FBLA; NFL; Yrbk; Rep Stu Cncl; French Hon Soc; Treas NHS; Ntl Merit Ltr; Opt Clb Awd; Natl Beta Clb; Nwsp; Envrnmntl Clb Treas; Stanford U; Aerospace Engrng.

LEE, STEVEN J; Lowell HS; San Francisco, CA; (3); Latin Clb; Library Aide; Tennis; Vllybl; Gov Hon Prg Awd; Ntl Merit Ltr; Amer Inst Archtcts Dsgn Comptn 3rd Pl; Bridge Club; Peanut Bttr & Jelly Club; U Of OR; Arch.

LEE, SUNG; Canoga Park HS; Los Angeles, CA; (3); Church Yth Grp; Band; Church Choir; Tennis; Prfct Atten Awd; Indvl Athltc Bst Sngls Plyr Vrsty Tnns; Engrng.

LEE, SUNG YOP; Hawthorne HS; Hawthorne, CA; (2); Church Yth Grp; Math Clb; Math Tm; Quiz Bowl; Science Clb; Service Clb; Hon Roll; Aerospace Engrng.

LEE, SUSAN; Downey HS; Downey, CA; (2); Church Yth Grp; French Clb; Science Clb; Service Clb; SADD; Acpl Chr; Chorus; CSF; Golden St Exam Geom Honors; U CA Berkeley.

LEE, SUSAN; El Rancho HS; Pico Rivera, CA; (2); Cmnty Wkr; Dance Clb; Hosp Aide; Intnl Clb; Key Clb; School Musical; Nwsp; JV Tennis; Hon Roll; Congrssnl Awd; 3rd Pl Essay Cont; Cmnty Spotlight; American U Paris; Actress.

LEE, SUSAN H; El Camino Real HS; La, CA; (3); Am Leg Aux Girls St; Pres Sec Church Yth Grp; Cmnty Wkr; Hosp Aide; Library Aide; NFL; Service Clb; Church Choir; Sec Rep Stu Cncl; JV Tennis; FOM; U Of CA; Phy.

LEE, SUSAN K; Granada Hills HS; Northridge, CA; (3); Church Yth Grp; Spanish Clb; SADD; JV Tennis; Hon Roll; Jr NHS; Prfct Atten Awd; Pres Acad Fit Awd; CSF; JR Statesmen Of Amer; UC Berkeley; Med.

LEE, SYLVIA P; Whitney HS; Cerritos, CA; (2); JA; Sftbl; JV Capt Vllybl; Tomodachi Kai Japanese Club.

LEE, SYNG; Saugus HS; Saugus, CA; (3); 40/400; Chorus; Hon Roll; UCLA; Med.

LEE, TANYA L; Hiram Johnson HS; Sacramento, CA; (2); FBLA; Nwsp; Cit Awd; Hon Roll; Friday Night Live; Culture Clb; ROP; UC Davis; Comp Prgmng.

LEE, TARA KRISTINA; St Francis HS; Mountain View, CA; (4); Sec Treas Band; Ed Yrbk; VP Frsh Cls; JV Crs Cntry; Var Sftbl; High Hon Roll; NHS; Tandy Tech Schlr & CSF; St Francis Sbjct Area Plq Math & Sci; Santa Clara Yth Hall Of Fam Schlrshp; U Of CA; Pre Med.

LEE, TARICK; Westhcester HS; Los Angeles, CA; (1); Aud/Vis; Bus Profs of Am; Church Yth Grp; Computer Clb; FCA; JA; Math Clb; Spanish Clb; Speech Tm; SADD; Ctznshp Awd; SC U; Engrg.

LEE, TERESA M; Lowell HS; San Francisco, CA; (2); Church Yth Grp; Hosp Aide; Science Clb; Teachers Aide; Gourmet Food Clb; Vllybl Clb; Tennis Cl!fmovie Clb.

LEE, THEODORE J; University HS; Irvine, CA; (3); Boy Scts; English Clb; Key Clb; Treas Jr Cls; Stu Cncl; French Hon Soc; Gov Hon Prg Awd; High Hon Roll; Ntl Merit Schol; Pres Acad Fit Awd; Brown U Bk Awd; Outstndng Sci Prjct Awd Irvine Dist; Golden St Exam High Hnrs Alg & Geom; Medcl.

LEE, THERESA; St Lawrence Acad; San Jose, CA; (1); 1/46; Math Clb; Chorus; Treas Frsh Cls; High Hon Roll; Hon Roll; Jr NHS; MIT; Engrng.

LEE, THERESA I; George Washington HS; San Francisco, CA; (2); Key Clb; Service Clb; Rep Soph Cls; Hon Roll; Chinese Amer Clb; Irwin Memrl Blood Bnk Vlntr.

LEE, TIFFANI Y; Chaminade College Prep; West Hills, CA; (3); 11/256; Debate Tm; Hosp Aide; Key Clb; Model UN; Chorus; Lit Mag; Hist Stu Cncl; NHS; Pres Acad Fit Awd; Amnesty Intl Fndr Schl Chapter/Pres; Humnts.

LEE, TIMOTHY SEAN-DAVID; Atascadero HS; Atascadero, CA; (4); 4/277; Church Yth Grp; Letterman Clb; Teachers Aide; Variety Show; JV Bsktbl; Var L Crs Cntry; Var L Trk; Cit Awd; High Hon Roll; Pres Acad Fit Awd; Winners Cir Chem; Schl Spelling Champ; Top 10 Sr Awd; Tandy Tech Schlr Awd; CA Polytech ST U; Elec Eng.

LEE, TOM H; Santa Clara HS; San Jose, CA; (1); JV Tennis; High Hon Roll; Prfct Atten Awd; Pres Acad Fit Awd; UC Berkeley; Elec Engrng.

LEE, TON V; Irvine HS; Irvine, CA; (3); 15/510; Chess Clb; Hosp Aide; JA; CSF; U Of CA San Diego; Pre Med.

LEE, TRACI A; Lowell HS; San Francisco, CA; (3); Church Yth Grp; Cmnty Wkr; Teachers Aide; Ed Yrbk; Stat Score Keeper; Crisis Intervention; Social Work.

LEE, TRICIA; Los Alamitos HS; Seal Beach, CA; (4); Sec FBLA; Model UN; Spanish Clb; Band; Capt Sec Color Guard; Mrchg Band; Rep Stu Cncl; VP CSF; Lit Vlntrs Of Amer; Jr Hnr Grd.

LEE, TRULEE M; Whitney HS; Cerritos, CA; (1); Var Church Yth Grp; Key Clb; Rep Nwsp; JV Swmmng; Hon Roll; Shaolin Kung-Fu; Business Admin & Mngmnt.

LEE, VANESSA A; Ygnacio Valley HS; Concord, CA; (1); Dance Clb; High Hon Roll; Stanford.

LEE, VANG; Merced HS; Merced, CA; (4); Merced Coll; Diesel Mechanic.

LEE, VIVIAN; John F Kennedy HS; Buena Park, CA; (3); Cmnty Wkr; Key Clb; Hon Roll; CA Schlrshp Fdrtn; Jr House; Acctng.

LEE, VIVIAN E; John F Kennedy HS; Sacramento, CA; (2); 54/525; Art Clb; Church Yth Grp; Treas Computer Clb; Sec German Clb; Math Clb; JV Tennis; Hon Roll; CSF; MTAC Music Pgm; UCLA; Pedtrcs.

LEE, VUE; A A Stagg HS; Stockton, CA; (4); Hon Roll; Heald Bus Coll; Comp.

LEE, WA; Clevis HS; Clovis, CA; (2); High Hon Roll; Fresno City Coll; Nrsng.

LEE, WAI K; Helix HS; La Mesa, CA; (4); 4/360; Church Yth Grp; Cmnty Wkr; Hosp Aide; Intnl Clb; Treas Key Clb; Math Tm; JV Tennis; Kiwanis Awd; Acad Dcthln; UCLA; Phrmcy.

LEE, WARREN W; Abraham Lincoln HS; San Francisco, CA; (2); Band; UC Davis; Bus.

LEE, WAYNE H; Edison HS; Huntington Beach, CA; (3); JA; Key Clb; Model UN; NFL; Spanish Clb; Rep Stu Cncl; Var Trk; NHS; Spanish NHS; Dstngshd Schlr; Pre Med.

LEE, WAYNE S; Hawthorne HS; Hawthorne, CA; (3); Key Clb; Ed Nwsp; Phtg Yrbk; JV Bsktbl; Var L Vllybl; Intrml Wt Lftg; Cit Awd; Hon Roll; CSF; New Life Clb; Ed.

LEE, WEI-CHIA; Woodside Priory HS; Hillsborough, CA; (3); 2/20; Boy Scts; Chess Clb; Computer Clb; Intnl Clb; Library Aide; Math Clb; Math Tm; Science Clb; Service Clb; Spanish Clb; Stu Wk Awd; Stu Fllwshp Chem San Jose ST U; Mdcl Sci.

LEE, WILLIAM; Schurr HS; Montebello, CA; (1); Intrml Wrstlng; Hstry & Bicycling Club; Stanford U.

LEE, WILMA; South San Francisco HS; San Bruno, CA; (2); Computer Clb; Math Clb; Mgr(s); JV Tennis; Hon Roll; CSF; Asian Am Clb; UC.

LEE, WILSON; Lowell HS; San Francisco, CA; (3); Science Clb; Teachers Aide; Varsity Clb; JV Var Crs Cntry; JV Var Trk; High Hon Roll; Crss Cntry Mst Imprvd Awd; Trck Mst Dedctd Awd; Bus.

LEE, WINDA; International Studies Acad; Daly City, CA; (4); San Francisco ST U.

LEE, XUE; Mc Lane HS; Fresno, CA; (4); 5/400; Church Yth Grp; School Musical; Cit Awd; High Hon Roll; Prfct Atten Awd; Asian Club; Human Relation; Project Alpha; Fresno State U; Surveying Engnr.

LEE, YAN; Mark Keppel HS; Monterey Park, CA; (2); Dance Clb; Treas Debate Tm; Math Clb; Office Aide; Teachers Aide; Gym; Score Keeper.

LEE, YOOJIN; Torrance HS; Torrance, CA; (3); Church Yth Grp; French Clb; Letterman Clb; Pep Clb; Science Clb; Service Clb; SADD; Church Choir; Hist Jr Cls; Stu Cncl; Spec Awds-Acad, ASB, Achvt Awds, Acad Ltr.

LEE, YOON H; John F Kennedy HS; Buena Park, CA; (4); Computer Clb; Swmmng; CSF; Prncpls Hnr Rl; Chem Engr.

LEE, YOON S; University HS; Irvine, CA; (1); 24/496; Off Church Yth Grp; Key Clb; Math Clb; Spanish Clb; Intrml Tennis; Hon Roll.

LEE, YOON SUN; Los Altos HS; Hacienda Hgts, CA; (4); Church Yth Grp; Band; Church Choir; Hon Roll; Handball; Poltcl Sci.

LEE, YOON Y; George Washington HS; San Francisco, CA; (2); Church Yth Grp; Varsity Clb; JV Bsktbl; Varsity Crew; Stanford U; Pre-Med.

LEE, YOUNG A; Herbert Hoover HS; Glendale, CA; (3); Church Yth Grp; JA; Key Clb; Spanish Clb; Cit Awd; Hon Roll; CSF; Med.

LEE, YOUNG J; Magnolia HS; Stanton, CA; (1); Intrml Bsktbl; Intrml Ftbl; Intrml Var Trk; Hon Roll; Cal Tech; Engr.

LEE, YU; Mount Eden HS; Hayward, CA; (3); 20/300; Chess Clb; Church Yth Grp; Cmnty Wkr; Debate Tm; FHA; German Clb; JA; Ski Clb; SADD; Teachers Aide; Stu Of Yr; Hmcmng Court; Stu Athl Of Yr; UCLA; Orthodontist.

LEE, YUN K; Seaside HS; Marina, CA; (2); Teachers Aide; Natural Helpers; Peer Ed; FNL; Med.

LEE, YVONNE H; J E Mc Ateer HS; San Francisco, CA; (4); Church Yth Grp; Science Clb; Teachers Aide; High Hon Roll; Hon Roll; DOGA Vancouver Schlrshps; 2nd Pl Sci Lesson Plan Cont; UCLA; Biochem.

LEECH III, WALTER A; Atwater HS; Atwater, CA; (3); Boy Scts; Church Yth Grp; French Clb; JV Var Ftbl; Intrml JV Socr; Intrml Trk; Var Wt Lftg; High Hon Roll; Jr NHS; Falcon Crest Awd 87-88; All League All-St Acad 89-90 Awd Ftbl; Elec Engr.

LEEDS, ROBERT LEE; Trabuco Hills HS; Santa Ana, CA; (3); Boy Scts; Computer Clb; Drama Clb; High Hon Roll; Hon Roll; Naval Acad; Air Traffic Cntrlr.

LEEDS, TINA M; Fairfax HS; Los Angeles, CA; (3); Cmnty Wkr; Hosp Aide; Letterman Clb; SADD; Varsity Clb; VP Frsh Cls; Pres Sr Cls; Var Socr; Var Tennis; Cit Awd; UC Santa Barbara; Bus Admin.

LEEDY, JENNIFER M; Bret Harte HS; Arnold, CA; (2); Church Yth Grp; Band; Church Choir; Pep Band; Pres Soph Cls; JV Bsktbl; Var Tennis; JV Vllybl; Hon Roll; Azuza Pacific; Teachr.

LEELAND, SHEA H; Abraham Lincoln HS; San Jose, CA; (3); Dance Clb; Drama Clb; French Clb; Speech Tm; Thesps; School Play; Stage Crew; Variety Show; Hon Roll; Acadmc Decthln; Congrssnl Yth Ldrshp Cncl 90; NASA Ames Research Ctr Lab Wrkr 89-90; Math.

LEEMANN, ERIKA L; University HS; Irvine, CA; (4); 9/496; Church Yth Grp; French Clb; Chorus; School Musical; Lit Mag; French Hon Soc; Hon Roll; Ntl Merit SF; Amnsty Intl.

LEEPER, SHERRAH; Hemet HS; Hemet, CA; (2); Sec Band; Mrchg Band; Pep Band; Powder Puff Ftbl; Stat Wrstlng; Bus.

LEER, DENISE Y; Modesto HS; Modesto, CA; (3); 4-H; Band; Chorus; Jazz Band; Pep Band; Var Socr; Var Swmmng; 4-H Awd; Prfct Atten Awd; Turlock Musi Cadets Alumni Band; Prfrmng Arts.

LEER, ERICA A; Escalon HS; Escalon, CA; (2); 4/131; Sec German Clb; Key Clb; Band; Jazz Band; Mrchg Band; Pep Band; School Musical; High Hon Roll; Pres Acad Fit Awd; CSF; PIT; HOBY; U Of Pacific; Music.

LEERAHAVANIT, TOM H; Lowell HS; San Francisco, CA; (3); Band; Gldn St Exam Alg Hnrs; Elec Engrng.

LEESMANN, KATHY; Vallejo SR HS; Vallejo, CA; (4); Science Clb; Varsity Clb; Band; Drm Mjr(t); Jazz Band; Mrchg Band; Orch; Pep Band; High Hon Roll; Rotary Awd; Northridge; Music Ed.

LEFAIVE, JEREMY W; Golden West HS; Visalia, CA; (2); Church Yth Grp; FCA; Band; Jazz Band; Mrchg Band; Orch; JV Bsbl; Ftbl; Wt Lftg; High Hon Roll; CSF; Young Life; Smmr League Vrsty Bsbl; Aeronautical Engr.

LEFEBVRE, KIM S; Grossmont HS; La Mesa, CA; (2); 114/429; Dance Clb; Hosp Aide; Intnl Clb; Pep Clb; SADD; Powder Puff Ftbl; JV Sftbl; UCLA; Psych.

LEFELSTEIN, CHERYL; Ygnacio Valley HS; Concord, CA; (4); 64/364; Teachers Aide; Color Guard; Orch; School Musical; Law Explorers Post; Humboldt ST U; Law.

LEFEVRE, DENNIS A; Torrance HS; Torrance, CA; (2); 106/454; Var Bsbl; Var Ftbl; Wt Lftg; Ice Hcky S CA Jr Kings 3rd Nation; Ice Hcky Bay Harbor Red Devils Capt, 2nd St; Denver U; Law.

LEFFLER, JONATHAN M; Trinity HS; Junction City, CA; (2); Church Yth Grp; Ski Clb; VP Bsbl; JV Bsktbl; JV Ftbl; Socr; Hon Roll; 1st Pl Mtrcrss Race 90; Coll Prep.

LEFLER, JULIE; Villa Park HS; Orange, CA; (3); French Clb; German Clb; Spanish Clb; JV Bsktbl; High Hon Roll; Hon Roll; CSF; U Of CA Irvine; Hstry.

LEFLER, SCOTT R; Enterprise HS; Palo Cedro, CA; (4); 24/330; Church Yth Grp; Model UN; Mu Alpha Theta; Science Clb; Stu Cncl; Capt Crs Cntry; Trk; Hon Roll; Pres Acad Fit Awd; CA Polytech; Biochem.

LEGASPI, JORGE; Paramount HS; Bellflower, CA; (2); Ftbl; Trk; Armed Forces.

LEGASPI, JOSEFINA L; Lemoore HS; Kettleman City, CA; (3); Cmnty Wkr; Drama Clb; English Clb; FBLA; FHA; Intnl Clb; Spanish Clb; Speech Tm; Teachers Aide; Chorus; Congressional Scholar In Wash DC; 1st Pl Local Nwsppr Mothers Day Essay; 1st Pl Business Awd; MA Inst Tech; Intl Business.

LEGASPI, JOY; Montgomery HS; San Ysidro, CA; (2); Girl Scts; Office Aide; Teachers Aide; Nwsp; UCSD; Law.

LEGASPI, MOISES G; King City HS; King City, CA; (3); FFA; Spanish Clb; Teachers Aide; Band; Chorus; Church Choir; Mrchg Band; School Musical; Wt Lftg; Hartnell Coll; Carpentry.

LEGER, CHODI; Davis SR HS; Davis, CA; (3); 256/450; Church Yth Grp; Pep Clb; Bsktbl; Powder Puff Ftbl; Art Fr; Cuesta JC; Arch Dsgn.

LEGER, SHERRI J; Pioneer HS; Whittier, CA; (4); 17/365; Church Yth Grp; French Clb; FTA; Intnl Clb; Pep Clb; SADD; Cheerldng; Swmmng; Hon Roll; U Of NV.

LEGG, CHRISTINA D; San Rafael HS; San Rafael, CA; (1); Church Yth Grp; Debate Tm; French Clb; Speech Tm; Band; Church Choir; Orch; Pep Band; School Play; Swmmng; Cnty Mock Trl Cont.

LEGGETT, HOLLI M; North HS; Bakersfield, CA; (4); 21/400; Church Yth Grp; Key Clb; Spanish Clb; Lit Mag; Hon Roll; NHS; Pres Acad Fit Awd; Pres Spanish NHS; Gottschalks Hi-Debs; Zora Briley Schlrshp; Outstndng Span Stu; Bakersfield JC; Phys Thrpst.

LEGLER, ANTHONY J; Mt Carmel HS; San Diego, CA; (1); Arch.

LEGORRETA, MAGDALENA; Western HS; Tulare, CA; (1); Acad Excll; USC; Math.

LEGRAND, ALICIA H; St Monica HS; Los Angeles, CA; (4); 12/125; Sec French Clb; Pep Clb; Ski Clb; Hon Roll; NHS; Homecoming Field Commissioner 89; Natl Hnr Soc Mem/Sel Beaver; CA Schlrshp Fed Mem; MI ST U; Jrnlsm.

LEGTERS, MARIANNE M; Foothill HS; Sacramento, CA; (3); Var L Sftbl; Hon Roll; Gldn St Exam, Geo Hnr Awd; Enrlld In Flight Ground Schl.

LEHMAN, BRENT J; Irvine HS; Irvine, CA; (2); 104/560; Boy Scts; Church Yth Grp; Letterman Clb; Math Tm; Chorus; School Play; Tennis; Wt Lftg; Cit Awd; Hon Roll; Physicist.

LEHMAN, CATHERINE R; Magnolia HS; Anaheim, CA; (3); 11/304; Church Yth Grp; Cmnty Wkr; Intnl Clb; Off Frsh Cls; Off Soph Cls; Off Jr Cls; Off Sr Cls; Intrml Sftbl; Var L Swmmng; JV Tennis; Stat For H20 Polo & Play H20 Polo; CS Schlstc Fed; Acad Dcthln & Mock Trial; Air Force Acad; Astrphycs.

LEHMAN, CHARITY M; Gahr HS; Boulder City, NV; (2); Var Mgr(s); UNLV; Court Reprtr.

LEHMAN, JEFF D; Arcata HS; Arcata, CA; (1); Boy Scts; Church Yth Grp; 4-H; Band; Mrchg Band; Hon Roll.

LEHMANN, JULIE A; Livermore HS; Livermore, CA; (3); 38/411; Drama Clb; FBLA; JA; SADD; Thesps; School Play; Stage Crew; Variety Show; Yrbk; Intrml Powder Puff Ftbl; Stanford; Jrnlsm.

LEHMANN, MICHELLE N; La Mirada HS; La Mirada, CA; (2); Church Yth Grp; French Clb; Rptr Nwsp; Hon Roll; Var Bsktbl; Var Score Keeper; JV Vllybl; Fnlst Miss Teen Amer Pageant; Poem Published; Psych.

LEHR, KELLIE M; 29 Palms HS; 29 Palms, CA; (2); VP Dance Clb; Drama Clb; SADD; School Musical; School Play; Stage Crew; Co-Ed Yrbk; Rptr Lit Mag; Rep Frsh Cls; Bk Photo Edtr; Jazz, Tap, Ballet Dancer; Boston U; Child Psycht.

LEHR, PAMELA J; La Jolla HS; San Diego, CA; (2); Church Yth Grp; Model UN; Spanish Clb; Var Socr; JV Swmmng; Var Trk; Var Vllybl; Hon Roll; Acad Leag Novice Tm; Smnr Pgm; Coca-Cola Awd Scct Tm.

LEHTO, JASON; North Tahoe HS; Tahoe Vista, CA; (3); Spanish Clb; Var L Crs Cntry; Hon Roll; Golden ST Exam 1st Yr Alg, Geom Hnrs; Bus.

LEI, EDWARD; Los Altos HS; Hacienda Hgts, CA; (2); Bsktbl; Ftbl; Trk; Vllybl; Wt Lftg; High Hon Roll; Golden St Exam; Elctrnc Engr.

LEI, HSIEN-HSIEN; Acalanes HS; Lafayette, CA; (4); 10/290; Hosp Aide; Math Clb; Model UN; Science Clb; Pres Spanish Clb; Jazz Band; Orch; School Musical; Yrbk; Trk.

LEI, LIXING JONATHAN; Garfield Computer/Sci Magnet HS; Los Angeles, CA; (3); Chess Clb; Science Clb; Band; Orch; Gym; JV Tennis; Hon Roll; Prfct Atten Awd; CSF; Duracell NSTA Schlrshp Cmptn Fntlst 90; Math Dept Awd 88; Electronic Engrng.

LEI, TONY; Abraham Lincoln HS; San Francisco, CA; (4); City Clg Of San Francisco; Engr.

LEI, WENDY W; Downey HS; Downey, CA; (4); Art Clb; Math Clb; Science Clb; Service Clb; Orch; Cit Awd; Kiwanis Awd; CA ST Ply Pomona.

LEI, ZHONG J; Oakland Technical HS; Oakland, CA; (2); Chess Clb; French Clb; Intnl Clb; Math Clb; Math Tm; High Hon Roll; Pres Acad Fit Awd; Engrng.

LEIBEE, DOMINIQUE C; San Dieguito HS; Encinitas, CA; (3); Church Yth Grp; Hon Roll; UCSF; Psych.

LEIBEE, SKYE J; Taft Union HS; Taft, CA; (3); 38/150; Church Yth Grp; Varsity Clb; Var Bsbl; L Capt Ftbl; Var Wt Lftg; Hon Roll; Lion Awd; Prfct Atten Awd; Friday Night Live; Explorers; Crmnl Jstc.

LEIBENSON, CARYN; St Margarets HS; Mission Viejo, CA; (2); Pres JCL; Latin Clb; Var Socr; High Hon Roll; Hon Roll; NHS; JV Sccr Team-Asst Coach.

LEIDREITER, NATHAN M; Pioneer HS; San Jose, CA; (3); 89/392; Church Yth Grp; JA; Ed Nwsp; Hon Roll; FL ST; Art.

LEIDY, JONATHAN D; Novato HS; Novato, CA; (3); Boy Scts; French Clb; Ski Clb; Band; VP Soph Cls; JV Ftbl; Var Tennis; High Hon Roll; Pres Acad Fit Awd; Cal Poly; Arch.

LEIGAN, JASMYN A; Atascadero HS; Atascadero, CA; (1); Church Yth Grp; Sftbl; Tennis; Cit Awd; Hon Roll; Arch Engr.

LEIGH, TARA J; Willits HS; Willits, CA; (2); Hon Roll; Math.

LEIJA, ENRIGUE; Artesia HS; Hawaiian Gardens, CA; (3); CA Poly Sn Luis Obispo; Arch.

LEIJA, ROSE MARIE B; Thomas Downey HS; Modesto, CA; (4); Office Aide; Service Clb; Teachers Aide; Stat Wrstlng; Cit Awd; Peer Asst; Modesto JC.

LEIMER, RON G; Colfax HS; Applegate, CA; (2); Ski Clb; Var Capt Bsbl; Var Capt Ftbl; Wt Lftg; Cit Awd; Hon Roll; Pres Acad Fit Awd; Running Bck Of Yr Ftbl 88-89, 89-90; Awds Supr Crftmnshp, Ctznshp Drftng; Arch.

LEIMGRUGER, RICKY; Holtville HS; Holtville, CA; (3); 2/120; 4-H; Math Tm; Mrchg Band; Pep Band; Ftbl; Wrstlng; Bausch & Lomb Sci Awd; 4-H Awd; High Hon Roll; Rotary Awd; Elec Engr.

LEININGER, GIDGET C; Southern Trinity HS; Zenia, CA; (2); Church Yth Grp; 4-H; GAA; Math Tm; VP Soph Cls; Bsktbl; Trk; Vllybl; Hon Roll; HS Rodeo; Chico ST U; Chldhd Dvlpmnt.

LEININGER, RYAN T; Ygnacio Valley HS; Pleasant Hill, CA; (2); Boy Scts; Varsity Clb; Var L Swmmng; Acad Achvt 89-90; NCS Schlr Athlt 89-90; NCS Distngshd Schltc Tm Vrsty Swmmng 90; Envrnmntl Engrng.

LEISER, CHRIS; Encina HS; Sacramento, CA; (3); 9/212; Church Yth Grp; Spanish Clb; Teachers Aide; Stu Cncl; JV Cheerldng; High Hon Roll; Hon Roll; V Songleading; Friday Night Live.

LEISER, CHRISTINA M; Encina HS; Carmichael, CA; (3); 10/211; Church Yth Grp; Spanish Clb; Teachers Aide; Church Choir; Stu Cncl; JV Cheerldng; High Hon Roll; Hon Roll; Songldng Var.

LEISING, MATT M; Glendale HS; Glendale, CA; (3); Drama Clb; Var Tennis; Hon Roll; Ntl Merit Schol; Pres Acad Fit Awd.

LEISTER, ZACK B; Clovis West HS; Fresno, CA; (3); Boy Scts; Church Yth Grp; Debate Tm; NFL; Hon Roll; Pres Acad Fit Awd; DECA; Eagle Scout; BYU; Sports Broadcasting.

LEISY, MICHELLE; Willow Glen HS; San Jose, CA; (2); Church Yth Grp; SADD; Var Capt Cheerldng; Var L Trk; Hon Roll; Pres Acad Fit Awd; CSF; Amnesty Intl.

LEITCH, KELLY J; El Cajon Valley HS; El Cajon, CA; (1); Church Yth Grp; Chorus; Drama Chrch; Biola U; Spec Educ Tchr.

LEITH, STACY; Savanna HS; Anaheim, CA; (1); Teachers Aide; Rptr Yrbk; Var Swmmng; Ltr In Water Polo & Swmmng; Acad Sports Awd; Plaque Mst Vlbl Var Swmmr.

LEITNER, DAVID C; Calaveras HS; Valley Springs, CA; (3); Drama Clb; Office Aide; Teachers Aide; Chorus; School Play; Cit Awd; Hon Roll; For The Love Of Chldrn Tlnt Show; Ucsc; Prfrmng Arts.

LEITNER, TAMMY; Grossmont HS; El Cajon, CA; (4); 79/381; NFL; Ski Clb; Speech Tm; Ed Yrbk; Treas Jr Cls; Treas Sr Cls; Var L Socr; Var L Tennis; Var L Trk; Hon Roll; Daisy Chain; Present SR Grad; Law.

LEITZ, CHRISTOPHE; Los Alamitos HS; Seal Beach, CA; (4); 23/502; Cmnty Wkr; French Clb; Hosp Aide; Math Clb; Quiz Bowl; Scholastic Bowl; Service Clb; JV Tennis; Intl Law.

LEIVAS, TIGE ROBERT; Rio Mesa HS; Oxnard, CA; (4); High Hon Roll; Hon Roll; Pres Acad Fit Awd; Indstrl & Trade Awd; Pres Fitness Awd; Schlstc Awd; Ambssdr Soviet Union; Bus.

LEIVO, KIRSTEN; Rancho Cotate HS; Rohnert Park, CA; (3); Pres Church Yth Grp; Cmnty Wkr; Drama Clb; German Clb; Intnl Clb; Teachers Aide; Chorus; Church Choir; School Play; Hon Roll; Sonoma ST U; Psych.

LEKAS, KIMBERLEE ANN; Lodi HS; Lodi, CA; (4); 63/399; Chess Clb; Sec German Clb; Teachers Aide; Hon Roll; Cert Mrt Piano; Frgn Lang Clb Treas; Humboldt ST U; German.

LEM, WASHINGTON; James A Garfield HS; Los Angeles, CA; (3); Sec Treas Church Yth Grp; Math Clb; Quiz Bowl; Scholastic Bowl; Science Clb; VP Service Clb; Church Choir; High Hon Roll; Ntl Merit Ltr; Prfct Atten Awd.

LEMA, JOSE; Foothill HS; Tustin, CA; (4); 20/350; Church Yth Grp; Key Clb; Math Tm; Office Aide; SADD; Crs Cntry; Socr; Trk; High Hon Roll; Hon Roll; 11th Natnwde Jnr Jugglrs; UC Berkeley; Bio.

LEMASTERS, THOMAS C; Chino HS; Ontario, CA; (2); High Hon Roll; Mck Trl; Poltcs.

LEMBACH, CAROLYN L; North Monterey County HS; Salinas, CA; (2); AFS; Church Yth Grp; Drama Clb; FBLA; SADD; School Play; Stu Cncl; Hon Roll; Amnsty Intl.

LEMBERGER, BETH L; Westlake Schl For Girls; Tarzana, CA; (3); Debate Tm; French Clb; Hosp Aide; Pres Model UN; NFL; Speech Tm; Thesps; Chorus; School Musical; Stage Crew; Natl Frnch Excam Grnad Concours 1st St, 3rd Rgnl, 5th Natl; Poly Sci.

LEMELIN, LORI A; Ontario HS; Ontario, CA; (4); 25/310; Church Yth Grp; Letterman Clb; Thesps; School Musical; School Play; Nwsp; Sec Sr Cls; Stat Bsktbl; Var L Socr; JV Var Vllybl; Cal ST San Bernardino; Theatre.

LEMERY, STEVE A; Torrey Pines HS; San Diego, CA; (2); JV Bsktbl; High Hon Roll.

LEMKE, MARK; St Lawrence Acad; San Jose, CA; (2); 22/62; Hon Roll; Sci Fictn Clb; Tlnt Srch John Hopkins U; Sci Fair Awd Slvr Medl Santa Clara Cnty; Chch Aide; Aeron Engr.

LEMMONS, BLAKE L; Modesto HS; Modesto, CA; (2); Ski Clb; Frosh Ftbl & Bsbl; Physcn.

LEMMONS, KATHRYN; Beyer HS; Modesto, CA; (3); Church Yth Grp; Debate Tm; Hosp Aide; NFL; Pep Clb; Spanish Clb; Speech Tm; Mrchg Band; JV Cheerldng; Hon Roll; Soroptomist Clb; Brigham Young U; Spch Path.

LEMOINE, MARK A; Sanger HS; Sanger, CA; (2); Science Clb; Spanish Clb; JV Vllybl; Water Polo Team Mvp; Aquatics Clb; Orthodontist.

LEMONS, JACKLINE L; Paramount HS; Paramount, CA; (3); Computer Clb; SADD; Teachers Aide; Drill Tm; Cit Awd; Hon Roll; Pres Acad Fit Awd; CSLB; Comp.

LEMONS, KIMBERLY A; St Joseph HS; Long Beach, CA; (3); GAA; Ski Clb; SADD; Var Powder Puff Ftbl; JV Swmmng; Hon Roll; Yth & Gvrnmnt; Vet Med.

LEMOS, JENNIFER A; Bullard HS; Fresno, CA; (1); SADD; Hon Roll; Pediatrician.

LEMOS, MICHELLE D; Arroyo Grande HS; Arroyo Grande, CA; (1); 68/589; JV Capt Bsktbl; JV Sftbl; Hon Roll; Pres Acad Fit Awd; MVP JV Bsktbl CIF, Holiday Trnmt; Most Inspirational JV Sftbl 89-90; U NV Las Vegas.

LEMOS, OLGA; San Fernando HS; Sylmar, CA; (3); Cit Awd; Hon Roll; Prfct Atten Awd; Tchng.

LEMOS, SUSIE I; Dos Palos HS; Dos Palos, CA; (3); FHA; JV Sftbl; JV Var Vllybl; Hon Roll; Pr Hlprs; Grls Athltc Clb Secy; Bus.

LEMPERLE, TRENT J; Patrick Henry HS; San Diego, CA; (2); Boy Scts; Ski Clb; JV Ftbl; Natl Eagle Soc Assn; Eagle Rnk; Bus Mgmt.

LEMPERT, BENJAMIN R; Lowell HS; San Francisco, CA; (2); Temple Yth Grp; Band; Var L Bsktbl; Hon Roll; Cmnty Prjcts Vlntr; Northern CA Maccabi Bsktbl Team.

LEMUS, DIANA; San Gabriel Mission HS; Alhambra, CA; (3); 19/115; Cmnty Wkr; Drama Clb; FBLA; GAA; Spanish Clb; Hon Roll; Hnrs CSF; Encore Clb; Bus.

LEMUS, FERNANDO; El Rancho HS; Pico Rivera, CA; (4); 16/650; Office Aide; Var Ftbl; Var Vllybl; Natl Hspnc Schlrshp Smfnlst; UCLA; Social Sci.

LEMUS, LUZ MARIA H; Hueneme HS; Oxnard, CA; (3); Drill Tm; Cit Awd; High Hon Roll; Hon Roll; Prfct Atten Awd; Ventura Coll; Nrsng.

LEMUS, ROSANA M; Colton Christian Schl; Colton, CA; (3); Church Yth Grp; Computer Clb; Drama Clb; Library Aide; School Musical; School Play; Sec Jr Cls; Bsktbl; Cheerldng; Hon Roll; Loma Linda U; Psych.

LEMUS, SANDRA B; Bell HS; Bell, CA; (2); Church Yth Grp; Child Cnslng.

LENABURG, KEITH; Dos Pueblos HS; Goleta, CA; (3); 52/320; Boy Scts; JV Tennis; Hon Roll; NHS; Marine Bio Club; Golden St Exam Alg & Geom Received Honors; CSF Mem.

LENCE, HOLLY; Granada HS; Livermore, CA; (4); 17/400; Art Clb; Church Yth Grp; Pep Clb; Teachers Aide; Cheerldng; Var Sftbl; High Hon Roll; Pres Acad Fit Awd; Bk Of America Dprtmntl Plq Awd; Dist Awd GAP Excllnc; Gd Ctznshp Crd Yellstaff Excllnc; UC Davis; Vet.

LENGER, STACIA; Santa Ynez Valley Union HS; Santa Ynez, CA; (2); 54/216; Church Yth Grp; Cmnty Wkr; 4-H; Service Clb; SADD; Teachers Aide; Rep Frsh Cls; Rep Soph Cls; JV Capt Sftbl; Trk; Intl Order Rainbow Girls; Real Estate.

LENGLE, BRADLEY; Skyline HS; Oakland, CA; (2); Boy Scts; Computer Clb; Debate Tm; Temple Yth Grp; Varsity Clb; Nwsp; Off Frsh Cls; Rep Stu Cncl; JV Var Lcrss; JV Tennis; JSA Treas; UCLA; Lw.

LENHART, MICHAEL A; Mountain Empire HS; Boulevard, CA; (3); 5/100; Art Clb; Church Yth Grp; Drama Clb; Pep Clb; Spanish Clb; Lit Mag; High Hon Roll; CSF; Outstndng Achvmnt Awd Coll-Rdy Wrtrs Prjct; Annapolis; Plt.

LENIHAN, BRIAN D; Lindsay HS; Lindsay, CA; (1); 1/200; Boy Scts; Ski Clb; Spanish Clb; Rep Frsh Cls; JV Bsbl; JV Ftbl; Var Socr; Intrml Vllybl; High Hon Roll; Hon Roll; Aerntcl Engrng.

LENIHAN, KATHLEEN M; Louisville HS; Sherman Oaks, CA; (2); Church Yth Grp; Hosp Aide; Science Clb; Ski Clb; Stage Crew; JV Tennis; JV Vllybl; Gov Hon Prg Awd; High Hon Roll; UCSB; Psych.

LENNING, TODD J; Hemet HS; Hemet, CA; (4); Computer Clb; FFA; Socr; De Vry Tech Schl; Comp.

LENNON, BRIDGET C; Grossmont HS; El Cajon, CA; (3); 124/385; Varsity Clb; Var Socr; Var Trk; Var Vllybl; 2nd Tm All League, Jr Yr, Vrsty Soccer; Sprts Med.

LENON, MICHELLE J; Fontana HS; Fontana, CA; (3); Bsktbl; Trk; Hon Roll.

LENOS, HOWARD A; Orange Glen HS; Valley Center, CA; (3); 30/458; Spanish Clb; NHS; CSF; San Diego ST U; Elctrnc.

LENTZ, JOSHUA J; Viewpoint Schl; Thousand Oaks, CA; (2); Spanish Clb; Stage Crew; JV Bsktbl; Crs Cntry; Ftbl; Var Swmmng; JSA; His Awd; Law.

LENTZ, RACHEL S; Rio Americano HS; Sacramento, CA; (3); 88/290; Debate Tm; Science Clb; Spanish Clb; Speech Tm; Teachers Aide; Thesps; School Play; Stage Crew; Crs Cntry; Socr; Wrkng Bckstg Cmnty Theater; Vlntr Vet Hosp; Santa Cruz U; Vet Med.

LENTZNER, BENJAMIN J; Rio Americano HS; Carmichael, CA; (4); 1/250; Pres Key Clb; Spanish Clb; SADD; Band; Jazz Band; Orch; Pep Band; NHS; Pres Acad Fit Awd; Val; U Of CA Los Angeles; Physcn.

LENZ, JESSICA; Vanden HS; Suisun City, CA; (2); 13/175; Art Clb; Drama Clb; French Clb; Sec Latin Clb; VP Soph Cls; Capt JV Cheerldng; Trk; High Hon Roll; Lion Awd; Rotary Awd; Wld Lf Vlntr; UC Santa Barbara; Artist.

LENZ, MARSHA; Tamalpais HS; Bolinas, CA; (4); Drama Clb; School Play; High Hon Roll; Hon Roll; Stu For Justice Clb; Inverness Garden Clb Awd; Cal Grant Awd; Humboldt ST U; Ntrl Resrc Pres.

LEO, MARIE; Monte Vista HS; Spring Valley, CA; (3); 167/396; Intnl Clb; SADD; Teachers Aide; Chorus; Grp Peer Guidnc Cnslng; Peaceful Amer Cert Prtcptn; Grossmont CC; Vet.

LEO, SANDRA; La Sierra HS; Riverside, CA; (3); Church Yth Grp; Drama Clb; Thesps; School Play; Bsktbl; Riverside CC; Bus.

LEOBARDO, MARQUEZ; C K Mcclatchy HS; Sacramento, CA; (2); 225/442; Dance Clb; ROTC; Spanish Clb; Wt Lftg; Sac ST; Justice FBI.

LEON, ALEX; Pioneer HS; Whittier, CA; (4); Church Yth Grp; Science Clb; Spanish Clb; Stage Crew; Yrbk; Rio Hondo Coll.

LEON, ANGELICA M; Sanger HS; Sanger, CA; (2); Church Yth Grp; Intnl Clb; Model UN; ROTC; Science Clb; Ski Clb; Spanish Clb; Teachers Aide; Chorus; Stu Cncl; Chicano Yth Clb; Armenian Clb; Crmnl Law.

LEON, BRANDY D; Indio HS; La Quinta, CA; (2); 33/550; GAA; Letterman Clb; Speech Tm; Varsity Clb; Treas Soph Cls; Treas Jr Cls; Var Sftbl; Var Vllybl; Hon Roll; Stu Ambssdr; Simons Rock; Lawyer.

LEON, CATHI; Adolf Camarillo HS; Camarillo, CA; (2); VP Frsh Cls; JV Cheerldng; Var Sftbl; U Of CA Berkeley; Psych.

LEON, DANNY K; Washington HS; Fremont, CA; (3); English Clb; Spanish Clb; Arch.

LEON, FRANK; Saint Anthony HS; Carson, CA; (3); 5/130; Church Yth Grp; Cmnty Wkr; Sec French Clb; Letterman Clb; Spanish Clb; SADD; Pres Sr Cls; JV Crs Cntry; Var Trk; Treas NHS; CA Schlrshp Fed; Campus Ministry.

LEON, GULMARO; Gardena HS; Gardena, CA; (3); French Clb.

LEON, HOLLANDA A; Whitney HS; Artesia, CA; (4); Church Yth Grp; Cmnty Wkr; Drama Clb; Key Clb; Spanish Clb; Color Guard; Flag Corp; Score Keeper; Hon Roll; Prncss City Norwalk 90; Vlntr Optcl Lab Hosp; U Of CA Irvine; Optmtrst.

LEON, KAREN; John A Rowland HS; Walnut, CA; (4); Letterman Clb; Science Clb; Spanish Clb; Var Bsktbl; Hon Roll; Quest Clb; Grls Leag; U Of San Diego.

LEON JR, MANUEL C; Mater Dei HS; Santa Ana, CA; (3); Office Aide; Band; Mrchg Band; Ftbl; Wrstlng; DAR Awd; High Hon Roll; Hon Roll; Engineering.

LEON, MARIA; James Logan HS; Union City, CA; (3); Latin Clb; Office Aide; Cls Rep; San Jose ST U; Comp Engr.

LEON, MARIA ISABEL; Centennial HS; Corona, CA; (3); Church Yth Grp; Cmnty Wkr; Dance Clb; FBLA; Office Aide; Var Socr; Var Mgr Trk; High Hon Roll; MECHA VP Mex Amer Hrtge Pgnt Awd 88; MECHA Clb Awd Hon 88; MVP Sccr 89; Cinco De Mayo Queen 89; Woodbury U; Bus Adm.

LEON, MARICELA; Bonita Vista HS; Bonita, CA; (3); Pep Clb; Tennis; Cit Awd; Hon Roll; U San Diego; Bus.

LEON, MARICELA; Garfield HS; Los Angeles, CA; (2); UCLA.

LEON, MARIO F; Artesia HS; Lakewood, CA; (1); Church Yth Grp; Cmnty Wkr; Office Aide; Hon Roll; Rainbow Leag.

LEON, MYRTLE; Loretto-Conaty HS; Los Angeles, CA; (3); Cmnty Wkr; JA; Ed Nwsp; VP Soph Cls; Stu Cncl; NHS; Pres Acad Fit Awd; Bus Ldrs Future Clb; Campus Ministry; Ambssdr Loretto; Mech Engr.

LEON, RICHARD M; Palmdale HS; Littlerock, CA; (3); JV Ftbl; Wt Lftg; Pierle Coll; Grphc Cmmnctns.

LEONANO, VIVIENNE; Glen A Wilson HS; Hacienda Hts, CA; (1); Band; Mrchg Band; Pep Band; Variety Show; Prfct Atten Awd; Band Lttr; 1st Ambassadors To Asia Comp Achvt Cert; UCSB; Med.

LEONARD, AMY; Fall River JR/Sr HS; Mc Arthur, CA; (2); Hon Roll; Healds Bus Schl; Bus.

LEONARD, BRIAN E; Antelope Valley HS; Lancaster, CA; (4); 72/488; Boy Scts; Church Yth Grp; JA; Teachers Aide; Varsity Clb; Stage Crew; L Ftbl; Golf; Hon Roll; Deptmntl Hons Sci & Math; BYU; Engr.

LEONARD, BRYAN S; Garden Grove HS; Garden Grove, CA; (3); 126/318; JV Ftbl; Hon Roll; 1st Prz Art Cntst; Comp & Sprts; Cmmrcl Arts.

LEONARD, CELERE; Cordova SR HS; Sacramento, CA; (2); Church Yth Grp; Cmnty Wkr; SADD; Band; Pep Band; Hon Roll; Jr NHS; Northbay Hnr Band; Ftr Prblm Slvrs Of Amer; Friday Night Live; Stanford; Phy.

LEONARD, COLLEEN M; San Dieguito HS; Encinitas, CA; (2); Teachers Aide; DAR Awd; High Hon Roll; Prfct Atten Awd; CA SCHLRSHP Fdrtn; UC Davis; Vet Med.

LEONARD, DEBBIE S; Adolpho Camarillo HS; Camarillo, CA; (3); 21/504; Church Yth Grp; Cmnty Wkr; Intnl Clb; Service Clb; Off Frsh Cls; Hist Soph Cls; Off Jr Cls; Stu Cncl; L Var Crs Cntry; Intrml Var Swmmng; Prncss; Mst Spirited Swmmng; Ltr Stu Govt; Stanford; Bus.

LEONARD, IAN J; Willow Glen Educ Park HS; San Jose, CA; (1); Hon Roll; CSF; Frgn Lang Achvt Awd; U CA Berkeley.

LEONARD, JAMIE L; Colfax HS; Gold Run, CA; (3); 3/152; L GAA; Pres Girl Scts; Rep Service Clb; SADD; Teachers Aide; Capt Varsity Clb; Pres Soph Cls; Off Sr Cls; Sec Treas Stu Cncl; Capt Var Bsktbl; Coach For Grls Bsktbl Camp; ROP Careers With Chldrn; Friday Night Live-VP; CA ST Coll; Chld Psych.

LEONARD, JANNY; Arrowhead Christian Acad; Twin Peaks, CA; (2); 1/20; Church Yth Grp; Scholastic Bowl; Spanish Clb; School Musical; School Play; Pres Jr Cls; L Var Bsktbl; L Var Sftbl; L Var Vllybl; High Hon Roll; Medicine.

LEONARD, JONATHON S; Gilroy HS; Gilroy, CA; (3); VP FFA; Letterman Clb; Red Cross Aide; Teachers Aide; VICA; JV Var Trk.

LEONARDINI, MARISA A; Loretto HS; Sacramento, CA; (2); Ski Clb; Yrbk; Swmmng; High Hon Roll; Ital Cath Fed Schlrshp 89.

LEONCAVALLO, DAVID R; Hueneme HS; Oxnard, CA; (3); 115/380; Ed Nwsp; Var Hon Roll; Masonic Awd; Ntl Merit Ltr; Cnty Sci Fair; Jrnlsm.

LEONE, JAMES R; Vallejo SR HS; Vallejo, CA; (2); Teachers Aide; JV Wrstlng; Hon Roll; U CA Sacramento; Aviatn.

LEONE, KERI; Carondelet HS; Clayton, CA; (3); 10/159; Church Yth Grp; Debate Tm; Intnl Clb; Service Clb; Rep Spanish Clb; Rep Sr Cls; Rep Stu Cncl; Cheerldng; High Hon Roll; NHS; Ice Skatng; UCLA; Sports Med.

LEONG, ALYSSA L; Cornelia Connelly Schl; Whittier, CA; (3); 1/46; Cmnty Wkr; Pres Library Aide; Red Cross Aide; Science Clb; Spanish Clb; School Play; High Hon Roll; NHS; Pres Acad Fit Awd; Val; 2nd Pl Wnnr Orange Cty Sci & Engrng Fair 90; 1st Pl Wnnr Intl Piano Recording Cmptn 87; Assisteen Awd.

LEONG, DANIEL C; Bishop Amat HS; West Covina, CA; (3); High Hon Roll; NHS; NEDT Awd; San Gabriel Chinese Cltrl Assn Yth Grp Teas; Spec Olympcs Coach; Cmnctns.

LEONG, JASMINE W; Encinal HS; Alameda, CA; (3); 28/233; Key Clb; Office Aide; ROTC; JV Tennis; JV Trk; Hon Roll; Rifle Team Capt; Comp Engrng.

LEONG, JASON; James Lick HS; San Jose, CA; (4); 22/257; Ed Nwsp; Rep Stu Cncl; Var L Crs Cntry; Var L Trk; Hon Roll; NHS; CSF; Law Rltd Ed Cmmttee Cmmndtn; Golden St Exam Geom Awd Hnrs; San Jose ST U; Aerosp Engrng.

LEONG, JOANNA; Mission San Jose HS; Fremont, CA; (2); Cmnty Wkr; Drama Clb; Hosp Aide; Library Aide; Pep Clb; Science Clb; Service Clb; JV Bsktbl; Hon Roll; Natl Wnnr Natl Piano Plyng Audtns; U Of CA; Engrng.

LEONG, LAUREL L; Casa Roble Fundamental HS; Orangevale, CA; (4); 4/374; AFS; Spanish Clb; School Musical; Stage Crew; Var Socr; High Hon Roll; Treas NHS; Ntl Merit SF; Acad Dcthln; CA Yth Sccr; Dstngshd Schlr.

LEONG, NICOLE; Agoura HS; Westlake Village, CA; (2); 1/480; Pep Clb; SADD; JV Capt Cheerldng; Hon Roll; Lat Hnr Soc; Natl Charity League; Medicine.

LEONG, STEVEN M; Skyline HS; Oakland, CA; (2); Computer Clb; Intnl Clb; Key Clb; Science Clb; Teachers Aide; High Hon Roll; Hon Roll; Aerosp Engrng.

LEONI, TINA; Dublin HS; Dublin, CA; (2); 5/224; Rptr Nwsp; Var L Socr; Var L Swmmng; DAR Awd; High Hon Roll; Hon Roll; Pres Acad Fit Awd; City Leag Sccr; CSF; Gldn St Exam Hnrs Awd Geom; UC Davis; Zoology.

LEONTAS, CHRIS; Hesperia Christian Schl; Hesperia, CA; (2); Band; Rep Chess Clb; Var Bsbl; JV Bsktbl; Var Ftbl; Sprts Med.

LEONTI, KRISTEN A; Branham HS; San Jose, CA; (1); GAA; Pres Frsh Cls; JV Fld Hcky; Var Socr; Var Sftbl; Hon Roll; Prfct Atten Awd; Fld Hockey MVP; Santa Clara.

LEOPOLDT, NIKKI; Yucaipa HS; Calimesa, CA; (4); Debate Tm; French Clb; Office Aide; Pep Clb; Speech Tm; Varsity Clb; Cheerldng; Opt Clb Awd; CSU San Bernardino; Psych.

LEOS, VICTORIA; Orosi HS; Cutler, CA; (3); Spanish Clb; SADD; Chorus; Mgr(s); JV Tennis; JV Capt Vllybl; High Hon Roll; Hon Roll; UCLA; Law.

LEOW, RICHARD M; Palmdale HS; Littlerock, CA; (3); Ftbl; Wt Lftg; Grphc Cmmnctns.

LEPALE, JOANN L; Bassett HS; La Puente, CA; (3); Cmnty Wkr; JV Tennis; Church Yth Grp; Friend To Friend 3yrs, Sec & Cmmtte Chairman; People To People HS Stu Ambssdr Northern Europe; Comp Sci.

LEPE, MONICA; Novato HS; Novato, CA; (3); Drama Clb; French Clb; School Play; Stage Crew; Hon Roll; Partial Schlrshp Exchnge USSR; Intl Rltns.

LEPE, PEDRO; Grant HS; Sacramento, CA; (3); Science Clb; Elks Awd; High Hon Roll; Prfct Atten Awd; Bio.

LEPF, ALEX N; Cloverdale HS; Cloverdale, CA; (3); Library Aide; Teachers Aide; Nwsp; Yrbk.

LEPPER, MICHELE M; Simi Valley HS; Simi Valley, CA; (4); Cmnty Wkr; Hosp Aide; Key Clb; Pep Clb; Ski Clb; Spanish Clb; Sec SADD; Variety Show; Treas Sr Cls; Stu Cncl; Cert Athltc Trnr; Soroptmst Awd High Acad; U CA-IRVINE; Bio.

LERCH, JOANNA C; Oakdale HS; Oakdale, CA; (3); JV Socr; JV Sftbl; JV Hon Roll.

LERMA, MISTI M; Dana Hills HS; Dana Point, CA; (2); Church Yth Grp; Cmnty Wkr; Spanish Clb; Drill Tm; Flag Corp; Nwsp; Stu Cncl; Amnesty Intl; CSF; Interact Rotary Intl Sec; Safe Rides; U Sidney; Intl Rel.

LERMAN, DAVID; El Camino Real HS; Reseda, CA; (2); 10/300; Computer Clb; Varsity Clb; Var Tennis; Stanford; Bus Mgmt.

LERNER, BRIAN G; Cajon HS; San Bernardino, CA; (1); 20/800; Boy Scts; Spanish Clb; Temple Yth Grp; L Swmmng; Elks Awd; High Hon Roll; Order Of The Arrow-Hnr Scout Awd; Law.

LERNER, MATTHEW; Ygnacio Valley HS; Concord, CA; (4); Pres Band; Mrchg Band; Pep Band; School Musical; High Hon Roll; Hon Roll; CSF Seal Bearer; Eclgy Clb; BGA Pres; Srptmst Ingl Svc Awd; CA Poly Tech ST U; Bus Admin.

LERNER, MICHAEL; Cajon HS; San Bernardino, CA; (2); 11/594; Boy Scts; Chess Clb; Rep Key Clb; Spanish Clb; L Var Swmmng; High Hon Roll; Hon Roll; Advncd Dungeons & Dragons Clb Of Cajon, Founder/Pres; Peer Cnslng Clb; Eagle Scout; Yale; Psych.

LERTYAOVARIT, VALERIE; Schurr HS; Montebello, CA; (1); Hon Roll.

LESCH, KRISTIN D; Monterey HS; Marina, CA; (3); Church Yth Grp; German Clb; Office Aide; Band; Mrchg Band; Orch; Pep Band; Var Crs Cntry; JV Trk; Hon Roll; Natrl Hlpr; Pr Eductr; Pepperdine U; Bus.

LESCHLY, MIKALA; Claremont HS; Claremont, CA; (4); 10/384; Science Clb; Teachers Aide; Chorus; Stat Bsktbl; Gym; Pres Acad Fit Awd; Vlntr Lcl Schl Orthpdclly Hndcppd Chldrn; UCLA Almni Bk Awd; CSF Lftm Stu; U CA Davis; Math.

LESEA, JENNIFER A; Pinole Valley HS; Rodeo, CA; (2); Debate Tm; Drama Clb; NFL; Teachers Aide; Stage Crew; JV Bsktbl; Var Vllybl; Hon Roll; CSF; UC; Health Sci.

LESH, JENNIFFER L; Delano HS; Delano, CA; (4); Art Clb; Church Yth Grp; Library Aide; VICA; Lit Mag; JV Trk; Hon Roll; Acad Decathlon Tm 90; Campus Life; Peer Cnclr; UC Berkeley; Engl.

LESHER, RICHARD W; Salinas HS; Salinas, CA; (3); Boy Scts; Teachers Aide; Band; Drm Mjr(t); Jazz Band; Mrchg Band; Orch; Pep Band; Hon Roll; Santa Clara Vanguard Cadets Drum & Bugle Corps 88; Drum Major 89; Santa Clara Vanguard A Corps 90; San Jose ST; Music.

LESLE, JACOB E; Serrano HS; Wrightwood, CA; (2); Church Yth Grp; French Clb; JV Bsbl; Var Bsktbl; Hon Roll; Elect Engr.

LESLIE, ANGELA M; Nevada Union HS; Nevada City, CA; (2); 1/535; SADD; Chorus; JV Capt Socr; High Hon Roll; CSF; U Of CA San Diego; Med.

LESLIE, LAWRENCE W; Burney HS; Burney, CA; (3); 12/56; Aud/Vis; Boy Scts; Church Yth Grp; SADD; Var Crs Cntry; Var Trk; Eagle Scout; Camp Royal 90; OR ST; Civil Engr.

LESLIE, MARINDA R; Norte Vista HS; Riverside, CA; (2); Church Yth Grp; Teachers Aide; Church Choir; Hon Roll; St Sci Fair Fnlst 89; Envrmntl Prtctn.

LESLIE, SHANNON M; Vanden HS; Vacaville, CA; (4); Church Yth Grp; Drama Clb; Chorus; JV Bsktbl; Hon Roll; Span 4 Yrs; Simpson Coll; Tchng Missions.

LESO, JOHN P; Francis Polytechnic HS; N Hollywood, CA; (4); Band; Jazz Band; Mrchg Band; Pep Band; Hon Roll; Band-Outstndng Brass; Music Department Awd; San Diego ST U.

LESSER, HADRIAN D; Beverly Hills HS; Beverly Hills, CA; (4); Office Aide; Yth & Hlth Issues Reprtr; Los Angeles KGK Am 1260; Santa Monica Coll; Radio Brdcst.

LESSLEY, SHANNON; Rim Of The World HS; Lake Arrowhead, CA; (2); Rep Frsh Cls; Rep Soph Cls; Var Trk; JV Vllybl; High Hon Roll; Prfct Atten Awd; Schlr/Athl Awd 88-90; Acad Ltr Awd; Sci.

LESTER, AUGUST M; Orange Glen HS; Valley Center, CA; (3); 33/520; Boy Scts; Church Yth Grp; 4-H; Hon Roll; Rotary Awd; Math Awd; Rotry Yth Ldrshp Awd; UCSB; Medcl.

LESTER, BRIAN; Moorpark HS; Moorpark, CA; (4); 15/150; Am Leg Boys St; Drama Clb; FCA; School Play; Stage Crew; Nwsp; Yrbk; Var Capt Bsktbl; Cit Awd; Hon Roll; All-Leag-Tri-Vly Bsktbl; 2nd Team All Ventura Cnty; Rnnr-Up Boys St; Accntnt.

LESTER, CRYSTAL R; Sherman Ind HS; Mescalero, NM; (3); FHA; JA; Ed Nwsp; Var Bsktbl; Trk; Wt Lftg; Cit Awd; High Hon Roll; GA Antonio Awd Native Amer W/Hghst Pt AVG; Mst Imprvd Female Stu; Outstndng Accmplshmnt NM Hstry; USAF.

LESZKAY, BLYTHE; Moorpark HS; Simi Valley, CA; (2); Debate Tm; Girl Scts; Teachers Aide; Acpl Chr; Band; Chorus; Flag Corp; School Musical; School Play; Stage Crew; Equestrian 1st Pl Awds Wstrn Jmp, Engl Rdng, Hntr Hack, Trl; Cmmrcls, TV, Film; Music-Piano,Horn; Davis U; Vet.

LETELIER, EDUARDO A; Santa Teresa HS; San Jose, CA; (3); Spanish Clb; Tutoring For Spnsh; Davis-San Diego U; Vet.

LETLOW, TINA; Firebaugh HS; Firebaugh, CA; (3); 7/80; Teachers Aide; Treas Jr Cls; Treas Stu Cncl; Var Bsktbl; Var Sftbl; Var Trk; High Hon Roll; Yng Ldrs Orgnztn San Jaquine Vly; UC Santa Barbara.

LETSON, BRIAN G; Mountain View HS; Los Altos, CA; (3); 55/300; Church Yth Grp; French Clb; JV Bsbl; Var L Ftbl; Var L Socr; Hon Roll; Arch.

LETT, MICHELLE; Burlingame HS; Belmont, CA; (3); Boy Scts; Cmnty Wkr; Hosp Aide; Intnl Clb; Spanish Clb; Band; Mrchg Band; Orch; Pep Band; JV Tennis; Sherriffs Offc Srch & Rescue; Peninsula Law Enfrcmnt Explr Acad Awd; UCLA; Bus.

LETTS, G STEPHEN C; Hart HS; Newhall, CA; (1); Boy Scts; Chess Clb; JV Swmmng; Eagle Scout.

LEUNG, ALVIN K; Abraham Lincoln HS; San Francisco, CA; (2); San Jose ST; Math.

LEUNG, ANITA K; Davis SR HS; Davis, CA; (4); Intnl Clb; U Of CA Davis.

LEUNG, ANNA; Mountainview HS; El Monte, CA; (2); FBLA; Princpls Hnr Roll; Comp.

LEUNG, ANNA; Oakland HS; Oakland, CA; (3); Cantonsese Clb; Bus Mgmnt.

LEUNG, CAMILLE M; Notre Dame HS; San Carlos, CA; (2); Church Yth Grp; French Clb; Library Aide; Math Clb; Science Clb; Stage Crew; Rptr Nwsp; Hon Roll; CA Schlrshp Fed; Bus.

LEUNG, CARESSE S; Notre Dame HS; San Carlos, CA; (2); Church Yth Grp; French Clb; Library Aide; Rptr Nwsp; Hon Roll; Prfct Atten Awd; Ballet; Piano.

LEUNG, CARMEN K; Phillip & Sala Burton Acdmc HS; Daly City, CA; (4); 18/157; Church Yth Grp; Teachers Aide; Rptr Nwsp; Rptr Lit Mag; Rep Sr Cls; Cit Awd; Hon Roll; Outstndng Perfrmnc In Ldrshp Awd 1990; San Francisco ST U; Bus Mgr.

LEUNG, CHRISTEL Y; Notre Dame HS; San Carlos, CA; (2); Rep Church Yth Grp; French Clb; Library Aide; Math Clb; Science Clb; Rptr Nwsp; Ed Lit Mag; Hon Roll; CA Schlrshp Fed; Sprt Awd; Hstss Clb; Parsons Schl Of Dsgn; Bio.

LEUNG, GRACE; Piedmont Hills HS; San Jose, CA; (3); 14/300; Drama Clb; French Clb; Variety Show; Lit Mag; Rep Stu Cncl; JV Var Cheerldng; High Hon Roll; Hon Roll; Piano; CA Schlrshp Fed; Stu Activist Clb; UCLA; Fshn Mrktng.

LEUNG, HERMAN; Pater Noster HS; Los Angeles, CA; (2); 6/70; Hon Roll; Stanford; Comp Sci.

LEUNG, JOSEPH; Culver City HS; Culver City, CA; (1); Church Yth Grp; Math Tm; Band; Orch; Ed Yrbk; Rep Frsh Cls; Rep Stu Cncl; Bsktbl; Cit Awd; High Hon Roll; Stu Of Yr; Harvard; Bus.

LEUNG, KAM M; George Washington HS; San Francisco, CA; (2); Computer Clb; Varsity Clb; Bsbl; Ftbl; Trk; Hon Roll; Pres Acad Fit Awd; Capt Ftbl Tm; Golden St Exam; Comp & Cars; UC Davis; Engrng.

LEUNG, KEVIN G; Amos Alonzo Stagg HS; Stockton, CA; (1); Church Yth Grp; Cmnty Wkr; Orch; NHS; Prfct Atten Awd; Edtr Mnthly Communication; Highst Hnr Rl; UC Berkeley; Electrnc Engr.

LEUNG, LANNY G; American HS; Fremont, CA; (3); JV Var Bsktbl; Intrml Ftbl; Hon Roll; Stu Of Mnth 88-89; Chrch Bsktbl MVP 3 Times; Bus.

LEUNG, LIANE L; Mercy HS; San Francisco, CA; (4); 52/156; Sec Service Clb; Teachers Aide; Hon Roll; Piano With Theory & Harmony For 8 Years; U Of San Francisco; Bus Field.

LEUNG, LUCINDA; Vacaville HS; Vacaville, CA; (4); 1/561; Chess Clb; Pres Var German Clb; Key Clb; Math Clb; Quiz Bowl; Treas Stu Cncl; JV Trk; Cit Awd; DAR Awd; High Hon Roll; U Of CA Berkeley; Bus.

LEUNG, MAY; Arroyo HS; San Leandro, CA; (3); 7/300; Church Yth Grp; Debate Tm; Vllybl; High Hon Roll; Voice Dem Awd; Var Badminton 3 Yrs; Asian Club 3 Yrs; Vp Jr Statesman; Engr.

LEUNG, MICHAEL H; Walnut HS; Walnut, CA; (2); 20/470; German Clb; Key Clb; Letterman Clb; Band; Yrbk; Off Frsh Cls; Off Soph Cls; Crs Cntry; Swmmng; Hon Roll; Prncpls Summa Cum Laude Awd; Ca Schlstc Fdrtn; Jr Olympics; UC Berkeley; Aero Engr.

LEUNG, PATRICK M; Le Grand Union HS; Planada, CA; (2); French Clb; Elec Engrng.

LEUNG, RAYMOND; Marina HS; Huntington Bch, CA; (3); Boy Scts; JA; Math Clb; Cit Awd; Hon Roll; Jr NHS; Aikido Brwn Blt; UCI; Elctrcl Engr.

LEUNG, RICKY; Luther Burbank HS; Sacramento, CA; (2); 5/389; Debate Tm; French Clb; Math Tm; Speech Tm; Orch; Var Vllybl; High Hon Roll; Hon Roll; Lion Awd; Opt Clb Awd; Hnr Piano; Hnr Orch; Stanford; Bus.

LEUNG, SANDY Y; Lowell HS; San Francisco, CA; (3); Pep Clb; Red Cross Aide; Service Clb; Variety Show; Intrml Vllybl; Orient Express Pres; Big Bros & Sisters; Wave 2000 Rep; Proj Star Essay Cont Wnnr; Ny U; Law.

LEUNG, SOPHIA SOO F; Oakland HS; Oakland, CA; (4); 23/405; Computer Clb; Key Clb; Math Clb; Sec Science Clb; Pres Spanish Clb; Ed Yrbk; Cit Awd; High Hon Roll; Pres Acad Fit Awd; Vrsty Badminton; U CA Berkeley; Med.

LEUNG, STEPHEN W; John F Kennedy SR HS; Sacramento, CA; (3); 21/422; German Clb; Math Clb; Teachers Aide; Mrchg Band; High Hon Roll; Hon Roll; Odyssy Mind Capt St Fnls; Sci.

LEUNG, VICKI W; Wallenberg Traditional HS; San Francisco, CA; (1); Orch; Hon Roll; Sci, Music & Law; Sci.

LEUNG, WILSON; George Washington HS; San Francisco, CA; (3); Pres Key Clb; Service Clb; Church Choir; Var Tennis; Hon Roll; Tennis Ace Clb Pres; Chrch Youth Fllwshp Chrprsn; Cal Poly; Arch Engrng.

LEUTE, ERIC J; Mountain View HS; Mountain View, CA; (3); Band; Jazz Band; Mrchg Band; Var Crs Cntry; JV Trk; High Hon Roll; Ntl Merit Ltr; Bicycle Rcng; Skiing; Brown Belt Karate.

LEUTY, JENNIFER; El Cajon Valley HS; El Cajon, CA; (2); Fld Hcky; Human Relations Clb; Teach.

LEV-ON, TOPAZ; Thousand Oaks HS; Thousand Oaks, CA; (3); 8/541; Var Debate Tm; French Clb; Hosp Aide; Intnl Clb; Math Tm; NFL; VP Speech Tm; SADD; Ed Lit Mag; Cit Awd; 1st Pl Ventura Cty Sci Fair 88; 4th Pl CA St Speech Assn Impromptu Speaking; Best Defense Pre-Trial; Medicine.

LEVAN, CHRISTY; Roseville HS; Rocklin, CA; (3); 78/407; Drama Clb; Library Aide; Office Aide; Pep Clb; Spanish Clb; SADD; Teachers Aide; School Play; Stage Crew; Off Jr Cls; Sir Thomas J Lipton Awd; Sprtsmnshp Awd; Soft All All Stars; All Star Indoor Soccer/Hot Shots Bsktbl; Crmnl Jstc.

LEVAN, MICHAEL; Valley HS; Elk Grove, CA; (3); Cit Awd; High Hon Roll; Hon Roll; Prfct Atten Awd; US Hstry Hnr Cls & Clb; Asian Clb; CSF; CA ST Sacramento; Crmnl Jstc.

LEVANGER, ANGELIQUE R; Woodland HS; Woodland, CA; (3); Pres Church Yth Grp; French Clb; SADD; VP Pres Jr Cls; Powder Puff Ftbl; Trk; Hon Roll; Jr NHS; NHS; Literary Club; Medicine.

LEVATO, JASON C; Ontario HS; Buena Park, CA; (2); German Clb; Hon Roll; Golden St Exam High Hnrs Geom Frosh Yr; Cert Achvmt Stu Of Month; U NE Las Vegas; Elec Tech.

LEVENSALER, KURT H; Golden West HS; Visalia, CA; (2); Church Yth Grp; Var Swmmng; St Schlr; JV Water Polo Capt; Ensenada MX Mission Trips; CA Schltc Fed.

LEVENSON, ERIKA; El Toro HS; El Toro, CA; (3); Key Clb; VP Temple Yth Grp; Stat Swmmng; Stat Trk; High Hon Roll; Prtcpnt Mock Trail.

LEVERETT, DAWN R; Sutter Union HS; Yuba City, CA; (3); 6/79; Am Leg Aux Girls St; Drama Clb; Girl Scts; Library Aide; Teachers Aide; Pres Band; Church Choir; Ed Yrbk; JV L Sftbl; Hon Roll; Heartsong Touring Drama/Musical Grp; Outstndng Musician Awd; CSF Cmmty Svc Rep; U Of Pacific; Music.

LEVESQUE, SANDRA R; William Workman HS; Valinda, CA; (2); Ed Nwsp; Var L Swmmng; CA Poly Pomona; Acctng.

LEVIN, KIM; Los Alamitos HS; Seal Beach, CA; (3); Cmnty Wkr; Chorus; School Musical; Hon Roll; Orange Cnty HS Of The Arts; Safe Rides; Mgr Of Kids Next Door Tour Group; UC Riverside; Psych.

LEVIN, LANCE A; Redlands HS; Redlands, CA; (2); Pres Acad Fit Awd; Accntnt.

LEVIN, LEAH; Gunn SR HS; Palo Alto, CA; (4); 12/299; Art Clb; JV Crs Cntry; High Hon Roll; Ntl Merit SF; Frnshp Proj; Peer Cnslng; Oberlin.

LEVINS, TONYA; Capital Christian HS; Sacramento, CA; (2); Art Clb; Church Yth Grp; Pep Clb; Rptr Nwsp; Sec Soph Cls; Var L Bsktbl; JV Vllybl; Hon Roll; UC Davis; Vet.

LEVIS, BAILEY; Albany HS; Berkeley, CA; (3); People To People Soviet Amer Yth Exchng; Gldn St Exam Hnrs In Alg & Geom.

LEVITT, STEPHANIE JEAN; Westlake HS; Thousand Oaks, CA; (2); 23/432; Debate Tm; Drama Clb; Math Tm; Speech Tm; SADD; High Hon Roll; Hon Roll; CA Schlrshp Fed; Peer Counseling; U Of CA San Diego; Psycht.

LEVREAU, ELAINE L; Clovis HS; Fresno, CA; (2); Cmnty Wkr; German Clb; Teachers Aide; Yrbk; Hon Roll; Ecology Clb; Fresno ST; Math.

LEVY, ALLISON; Simi Valley HS; Simi Valley, CA; (3); 167/666; Drama Clb; Girl Scts; Office Aide; Color Guard; School Play; Cit Awd; Bnai Brith Girls.

LEVY, BIANCA T; Pittsburg HS; Pittsburg, CA; (3); Hon Roll.

LEVY, BRIAN; Homestead HS; Los Altos, CA; (3); Ski Clb; JV Var Socr; Ntl Merit SF; CSF; Golden St Exam Geom High Hnrs; Stanford; Chem Engrng.

LEVY, DANA L; University HS; Irvine, CA; (3); School Musical; School Play; Stu Cncl; JV Cheerldng; High Hon Roll; Natl Charity League Reprtr, Recrdng Sec.

LEVY, DAVID D; Lowell HS; San Francisco, CA; (2); Teachers Aide; Temple Yth Grp; Var Capt Ftbl; Forensics Comptn; U Of WA Grinnell; Drama.

LEVY, DVIR; Taft HS; Tarzana, CA; (1); Tennis; Stanford; Sports.

LEVY, ERICA ROBIN; Valhalla HS; El Cajon, CA; (4); 31/412; Cmnty Wkr; Pres Intnl Clb; Key Clb; Pep Clb; Ski Clb; Temple Yth Grp; Chorus; Sec Sr Cls; Rep Stu Cncl; JV Swmmng; Japanese Studies; Comptv Figure Skating; UCSD; Intl Relations.

LEVY, ESTHER T; University City HS; San Diego, CA; (3); Teachers Aide; Temple Yth Grp; High Hon Roll; Piano; Karate Brown Blt; Grtr San Diego Sci Fr Awd; U Of CA San Diego; Bio.

LEVY, FERNANDA; Bonita Vista HS; Chula Vista, CA; (2); Office Aide; High Hon Roll; Hon Roll; Classical Ballet; Numerous Royal Acad Of Dncng Exams; Atty.

LEVY, GWEN A; South San Francisco HS; South San Francis, CA; (2); Cmnty Wkr; Library Aide; Band; Hon Roll; County Spcl Olympcs; Library Sci.

LEVY, HELEN; Dos Pueblos HS; Goleta, CA; (3); 1/338; Sec Math Clb; Pres Science Clb; Capt Flag Corp; NHS; CSF.

LEVY, JOSH Y; S Pasadena HS; S Pasadena, CA; (4); 9/270; Pres Debate Tm; Sec German Clb; Treas Math Clb; Pres Band; Jazz Band; Mrchg Band; Orch; Pep Band; School Musical; JV Wrstlng; Acad Decath Tm Top Scorer.

LEVY, MIKE; San Marcos HS; Carlsbad, CA; (3); Science Clb; VICA; Sci Fiction Club; AZ Arch Inst; Arch.

LEW, ALEX J; Don Antonio Lugo HS; Chino, CA; (3); 3/700; Key Clb; Science Clb; SADD; JV Trk; High Hon Roll; NHS; Ntl Merit SF; Prfct Atten Awd.

LEW, CATHY C; Hayward HS; Castro Valley, CA; (2); Spanish Clb; High Hon Roll; Hon Roll; CA St Senate Crtfct Recgntn Golden St Exam; Crtfct Achvt Excllnc Prfrmnc Span II.

LEW, DANNY A; Fairfield HS; Fairfield, CA; (2); Drama Clb; Acpl Chr; Chorus; School Play; Stage Crew; Diving; Gym; Swmmng; Hon Roll.

LEW, DERRICK J; St Ignatius College Prep; San Francisco, CA; (3); Cmnty Wkr; French Clb; SADD; Phtg Yrbk; Intrml Bsktbl; Wt Lftg; High Hon Roll; Hon Roll; Pres Acad Fit Awd; Elem Bsktbl Coach; Engl.

LEW, JAMES G; San Leandro HS; San Lorenzo, CA; (4); 3/350; Computer Clb; Math Tm; Service Clb; Tennis; High Hon Roll; Ntl Merit SF; U Of CA Berkeley Acclrtd HS Stds Pgm; CA Schlstc Fdrtn; Aerontcl Engrng.

LEW, MARK W; Leuzinger HS; Hawthorne, CA; (3); Sec Key Clb; Var L Crs Cntry; JV Trk; CA Schlrshp Fdrtn; VP Chinese Clb & Tnns Clb; Drftng.

LEW, MICHAEL A; Woodside HS; Redwood City, CA; (2); 7/502; Boy Scts; JV Crs Cntry; Var Swmmng; Goldn St Exam Algb With Hnrs; Bus.

LEW, PATTY Y; Gonzales HS; Soledad, CA; (2); SADD; Hon Roll; CSF; FBLA; Prin Hnr Rl.

LEW, RAYMOND J; John F Kennedy HS; Sacramento, CA; (2); 1/547; Computer Clb; Math Clb; Science Clb; Hon Roll; Pres Acad Fit Awd; High Hnrs Geom Golden St Exam; UC Berkeley; Engrng.

LEW, WILSON S; Carlmont HS; Belmont, CA; (2); 21/350; Pres Chess Clb; Math Clb; Var Bsktbl; JV Tennis; Wt Lftg; CSF; Asian-Amer Clb; Pre-Med.

LEW, WYMAN W; Hayward HS; Castro Valley, CA; (3); French Clb; Lit Mag; Off Frsh Cls; Off Soph Cls; Off Jr Cls; Hon Roll; CA Schlrshp Fed; Martin Luther King Jr Pstr Cntst; Hayward Zucchini Fstvl Pstr Cmptn; Anmtn.

LEWANDOWSKI, GREGORY; Daniel Murphy HS; Los Angeles, CA; (2); Quiz Bowl; Teachers Aide; JV Bsktbl; Mgr(s); Score Keeper; JV Trk; High Hon Roll; Gmtry Hnr Tutor; Arspc Engr.

LEWANDOWSKI, ROBBY R; Hart HS; Valencia, CA; (1); Boy Scts; Cit Awd.

LEWELLEN, ALLEGRA; Fresno Christian HS; Fresno, CA; (4); Church Yth Grp; Teachers Aide; Nwsp; Sec Frsh Cls; Rep Soph Cls; Stu Cncl; Cit Awd; High Hon Roll; Pres Acad Fit Awd; CA ST U Fresno; Bus Adm.

LEWICKI, KAREN S; Marymount HS; Sherman Oaks, CA; (2); Cmnty Wkr; DECA; Speech Tm; Chorus; Yrbk; Lit Mag; Var Swmmng; Tennis; High Hon Roll; Hon Roll; Mock Trial; Outward Bound; YMCA Yth Clb/Caravans; Berkeley; Lit.

LEWIS, AARON S; Oakmont HS; Roseville, CA; (4); Church Yth Grp; Ski Clb; Spanish Clb; SADD; Teachers Aide; Varsity Clb; Stat Cheerldng; Var Socr; Var Trk; Hon Roll; Yng Life; BYU; Mgnt.

LEWIS, AMBER; Mira Loma HS; Sacramento, CA; (2); 4/296; Math Clb; Science Clb; Rep Soph Cls; JV Bsktbl; Scrkpr Crs Cntry; Var Trk; High Hon Roll; Prfct Atten Awd; Pres Acad Fit Awd; Sci Olympiad Natl Team; Space Camp, Academy & Young Astronauts Pgm; Cal-Tech; Aeronautical Engr.

LEWIS, AMY; Villa Park HS; Villa Park, CA; (3); Key Clb; Rep Stu Cncl; Var Socr; JV Sftbl; JV Vllybl; Hon Roll; MVP Soccer; CA ST Fullerton; Supv.

LEWIS, ANDREW S; Palmdale HS; Acton, CA; (4); VP Spanish Clb; Phtg Yrbk; Soc Svc Club Senator; CA ST U; Teacher.

LEWIS, ANETRIC L; Cordova SR HS; Rancho Cordova, CA; (2); Gym; Trk; Vllybl; Hon Roll; Prfct Atten Awd.

LEWIS, ANN MARIE; Encinal HS; Alameda, CA; (1); Drama Clb; English Clb; French Clb; FBLA; Key Clb; ROTC; Spanish Clb; Band; Chorus; Mrchg Band; Bus & Prof Women; San Francisco ST; Comp Tech.

LEWIS, BARBARA; Arlington HS; Riverside, CA; (3); SADD; Acpl Chr; Chorus; Color Guard; Flag Corp; School Musical; Cit Awd; Hon Roll; Pres Acad Fit Awd; Jrnlsm.

LEWIS JR, BARRY H; Leucinger HS; Lawndale, CA; (3); Aud/Vis; Church Yth Grp; Drama Clb; Teachers Aide; School Play; Hon Roll; Little Leag; CA ST-BAKERSFIELD; Lawyer.

LEWIS, BRIAN A; North Salinas HS; Salinas, CA; (4); Boy Scts; Jazz Band; Mrchg Band; JV Var Bsktbl; Var Trk; Hon Roll; Plumbing.

LEWIS, CHAD E; San Dimas HS; San Dimas, CA; (2); Teachers Aide; School Play; Bsbl; Ftbl; Cit Awd; High Hon Roll; Hon Roll; Prfct Atten Awd; Roses Awd; Bus.

LEWIS, CHRISTA L; Hayward HS; Hayward, CA; (3); Church Yth Grp; Acpl Chr; Band; Church Choir; Mrchg Band; Vllybl; Hon Roll; Brigham Young U; Dntl Asst.

LEWIS, CRAIG; Antelope Valley Union HS; Lancaster, CA; (4); Hon Roll; U Northridge; Hist.

LEWIS, CYNTHIA A; Enterprise HS; Redding, CA; (2); Church Yth Grp; Cmnty Wkr; Dance Clb; Hosp Aide; Acpl Chr; Chorus; Church Choir; School Musical; Davis U; Med.

LEWIS, CYNTHIA K; Lincoln HS; Stockton, CA; (3); Cmnty Wkr; French Clb; Hosp Aide; SADD; JV Fld Hcky; Intrml Tennis; Psych.

LEWIS, DAVID A; Bellarmine College Prep; Gilroy, CA; (1); Boy Scts; Church Yth Grp; Cmnty Wkr; Var Debate Tm; NFL; Red Cross Aide; Speech Tm; BSA Eagle Scout, Lfgrd; Frgn Exch Stu France 89; Stanford U; Intl Law.

LEWIS, DAVID W; Wasco Union HS; Wasco, CA; (4); Church Yth Grp; Letterman Clb; Teachers Aide; Varsity Clb; Bsktbl; Ftbl; Capt Tennis; Wt Lftg; SSL Tnns Chmp & Capt; Fresno ST; Prfssnl Tnns Plyr.

LEWIS, DENEATRICE; La Puente HS; La Puente, CA; (3); Dance Clb; GAA; Varsity Clb; Drill Tm; Ed Yrbk; Drill Tm Asst Military Ldr & Squad Ldr; 89-90 Harvard Prize Book Recipient; USC; Writer.

LEWIS, DOMINIQUE M; Notre Dame Acad; Los Angeles, CA; (3); Cmnty Wkr; Spanish Clb; Yrbk; Cit Awd; Hon Roll; Bus.

LEWIS, DON V; Lower Lake HS; Clearlake, CA; (3); Band; Mrchg Band; Orch; Pep Band; Bsbl; Bsktbl; Score Keeper; Wrstlng; Gov Hon Prg Awd; CA Arts Schlr 89; Faces Intl 89; Faces Acting Workshop ACT Instrctr 88; Humboldt ST U; Music.

LEWIS, DYLAN B; Grossmont HS; El Cajon, CA; (3); 58/385; AFS; Intnl Clb; Hon Roll.

LEWIS, ELIZABETH A; El Camino Real HS; Woodland Hills, CA; (3); NFL; Speech Tm; SADD; Thesps; Acpl Chr; Swing Chorus; Lit Mag; Stu Cncl; Hon Roll; Debate Tm; Hstry.

LEWIS, ERIC S; Fullerton HS; Fullerton, CA; (1); FFA; Bsktbl; Powder Puff Ftbl; Trk; Rotary Awd; Work Drive In Dairy; OK ST U; Arch.

LEWIS, ERIC S; Newbury Park HS; Newbury Park, CA; (4); 64/380; Math Clb; Band; Jazz Band; Mrchg Band; High Hon Roll; Ham Radio Club; CSF; U Of CA Santa Barbara; Eng.

LEWIS, ERICA SUSAN ELIZABETH; San Pasqual HS; Escondido, CA; (3); 47/353; Pres Art Clb; French Clb; Intnl Clb; L Var Crs Cntry; L JV Trk; Prfct Atten Awd; 89-90 HS Outstndng Achvt Paintng Awd; 1st Pl Awd Assoctd Sr Artsts San Diego 88; Medcl Illustratr.

LEWIS, HEATHER A; El Toro HS; El Toro, CA; (4); 247/517; Pres Church Yth Grp; Drama Clb; Key Clb; Pep Clb; School Play; Yrbk; Hon Roll; CA Assn Stu Cncls Rgn Secy; Girls Leag Spirit Wk Chrmn; Grad Cmmtte; CA ST U; Long Beach; Fshn Mrch.

LEWIS, HOLLY R; North HS; Bakersfield, CA; (2); Drama Clb; Library Aide; School Play; Hon Roll; Cheerleader; Teacher Schl Counselor.

LEWIS, IAN R; Clovis West HS; Clovis, CA; (3); Band; Jazz Band; Mrchg Band; Orch; Hon Roll; CA All St Hnr Band 89-90; CA Music Eductrs Assn All St Hnr Band 89-90; Hnr Band & Orch Fresno-Madera; CA ST U Fresno; Music.

LEWIS, ISAAC J; Helix HS; La Mesa, CA; (3); 67/423; Varsity Clb; Yrbk; Capt Var Socr; Hon Roll; San Diego ST U; Comp.

LEWIS, J DEREK; Casa Roble HS; Citrus Heights, CA; (2); 16/485; Cit Awd; High Hon Roll.

LEWIS II, JAMES W; Paraclete HS; Lancaster, CA; (2); Drama Clb; Key Clb; SADD; JV Socr; Hon Roll; UCLA; Med.

LEWIS, JAMYE T; Washington Preparatory HS; Los Angeles, CA; (3); Church Yth Grp; Computer Clb; Office Aide; Pep Clb; Church Choir; School Play; High Hon Roll; Hon Roll; Attndnc; Mst Supprtv; TX Southern U; Acctng.

LEWIS, JAN C; Diamond Bar HS; Diamond Bar, CA; (2); German Clb; VP Key Clb; Science Clb; SADD; VP Golf; JV Var Tennis; Hon Roll; Pres Acad Fit Awd; Varsity Clb; JV Bdmntn; CSF; Harvard; Lw.

LEWIS, JANETE M; Turlock HS; Turlock, CA; (2); Church Yth Grp; Drama Clb; Avalon Model; Jazz/Tap/Portuguese Folklore Dnc Stu; MIC; Child Psych.

LEWIS, JENNIFER A; Garces Memorial HS; Bakersfield, CA; (3); Cmnty Wkr; Science Clb; Service Clb; Varsity Clb; School Play; High Hon Roll; Hon Roll; JV Sftbl; JV Var Vllybl; Wrkr Salvation Army; Asisteens Leag; Shop, Trvl, Hangout W/Friends.

LEWIS, JERNEA M; Canyon Springs HS; Moreno Valley, CA; (3); Teachers Aide; JV Bsktbl; Var Trk; Var Vllybl; High Hon Roll; Hon Roll; CIF Awd Vllybl & Trk; All Leag Team Vllybl MVP 89-90; CIF Sthrn Sctn Girls Vllybl Team 89-Athl Awd; Med.

LEWIS, JOHNNY; Berkeley HS; Berkeley, CA; (4); Chorus; School Play; Treas Soph Cls; Treas Jr Cls; Treas Sr Cls; Rugby Club; Malcolm X Awd; Math Engrng Sci Achvt Pgm Awd; Navy; Cmmnctns.

LEWIS, JONATHAN WILLIAM; Pacific Union College Prep; Angwin, CA; (3); Drama Clb; English Clb; French Clb; Hosp Aide; Chorus; School Musical; Off Jr Cls; Bsktbl; Ftbl; San Francisco ST U; Comm Adv.

LEWIS, JOYA MONIQUE; Sunset HS; Hayward, CA; (2); 58/237; JV Bsktbl; Hon Roll; Black Stu Union Secy; Grambling U; Accntng.

LEWIS, JULIE ANN; Pacific Union College Prep Schl; Angwin, CA; (2); Drama Clb; French Clb; Office Aide; Ski Clb; Speech Tm; Varsity Clb; Chorus; School Play; Phtg Yrbk; Diving; Pacific Union Coll; Prfrmng Art.

LEWIS, KALI; Thomas Downey HS; Modesto, CA; (1); 1/550; Church Yth Grp; Pep Clb; Nwsp; Rep Soph Cls; Cheerldng; Pom Pon; NHS; Downey Knight Achvt Awd; Brigham Young U.

LEWIS, KARI; Arroyo HS; San Lorenzo, CA; (4); Church Yth Grp; Letterman Clb; Teachers Aide; Varsity Clb; Stat Ftbl; Var Capt Socr; Var Capt Sftbl; Var Capt Vllybl; High Hon Roll; Hon Roll; Plyr Of Yr Sftbl 90; Athl Yr Sftl 88-89; All E Bay & All S Cnty Sftbl 88-89; Miami U Of OH; Med.

LEWIS, KIM A; Folsom HS; Folsom, CA; (3); Drill Tm; Sec Stu Cncl; Tennis; Cit Awd; Art.

LEWIS, KIRSTIN; Valley Christian Acad; Santa Maria, CA; (4); 1/18; Church Yth Grp; Band; Church Choir; School Play; Capt Cheerldng; Var Sftbl; Var Vllybl; Hon Roll; Lion Awd; Prfct Atten Awd; Pnscla Chrstn Coll; Sectrl Sci.

LEWIS, LA DONNA; South Bay Lutheran HS; Inglewood, CA; (4); 3/17; Am Leg Aux Girls St; Cmnty Wkr; Hosp Aide; Office Aide; Teachers Aide; School Play; JV Var Vllybl; Cit Awd; High Hon Roll; Hon Roll; San Diego ST U; Elem Ed.

LEWIS, LARA R; Mission Bay HS; La Mesa, CA; (4); Drama Clb; SADD; Chorus; School Musical; School Play; Stage Crew; Variety Show; Off Jr Cls; Off Sr Cls; Score Keeper; Humboldt; Wildlife Bio.

LEWIS, LATYANA V; Bishop O Dowd HS; Oakland, CA; (4); 105/226; Church Yth Grp; Band; Church Choir; High Hon Roll; Hon Roll; Ntl Achvmnt Schlrshp; UC San Diego; Mrne Bio.

LEWIS, MEDEA A; Armijo HS; Fairfield, CA; (3); Drama Clb; SADD; Teachers Aide; School Play; Rptr Nwsp; Cheerldng; Crs Cntry; Trk; DAR Awd; Hon Roll; NAPA Coll; Srgn.

LEWIS, MELANIE A; Fairfield HS; Fairfield, CA; (1); Sec Church Yth Grp; Hosp Aide; Church Choir; Cit Awd; High Hon Roll; NHS; Chrch Svc Prjcts; Tchrs Ade Vctn Bible Schl; Christ Coll Irvine.

LEWIS, MICHELLE D; Tokay HS; Lodi, CA; (2); Drama Clb; Library Aide; SADD; Teachers Aide; Hon Roll; Library Work; UC Davis; Lawyer.

LEWIS, MONICA C; Oak Ridge HS; El Dorado Hills, CA; (2); 30/300; Church Yth Grp; JV Cheerldng; High Hon Roll; Jacket Lttr-Hgh CSF Hnr Roll; Jacket Patch-Acad Hnrs; CA ST U-Sacramento; Sci.

LEWIS, REBECCA J; Mira Mesa HS; San Diego, CA; (2); 1/797; Church Yth Grp; JV Var Bsktbl; JV Sftbl; JV Trk; JV Var Vllybl; Hon Roll; NHS; Pres Acad Fit Awd.

LEWIS, ROBERT B; Buena HS; Ventura, CA; (4); 35/455; Church Yth Grp; French Clb; JV Bsktbl; Var Capt Crs Cntry; Var Trk; High Hon Roll; Pres Acad Fit Awd; UC Davis; Bio.

LEWIS, ROBERT M; Bonita HS; La Verne, CA; (4); Pres Aud/Vis; Pres Debate Tm; Hist Drama Clb; Model UN; Thesps; School Play; Stage Crew; JV Bsktbl; Hon Roll; 3rd Pl Thomas Jefferson Spch Cont 89; CA ST Fullerton; Theatre Art.

LEWIS, STEPHEN P; Pinole Valley HS; Hercules, CA; (2); Lit Mag; JV Bsktbl; Hon Roll; CSF; N Coast Sctn Schlr Athlte Awd; Coachs Awd JV Bsktbl; Commnctns.

LEWIS, SUSAN R; Huntington Park HS; Huntington Park, CA; (3); Teachers Aide; Flag Corp; Rep Soph Cls; Rep Jr Cls; Var Cheerldng; Var Powder Puff Ftbl; Score Keeper; Cty Chrldng Chmps 89; MESA.

LEWIS, TAMI E; Monache HS; Porterville, CA; (3); Church Yth Grp; Cmnty Wkr; Acpl Chr; Chorus; Church Choir; Color Guard; Var Swmmng; High Hon Roll; Hon Roll; CA ST Hnr Choir; Cert Hnr Excllnc Schlrshp; Portervl Ed Fndtn Plaq Acad Achvt Math; Brigham Young U Provo UT; Math.

LEWIS, TARA A; Ramona HS; Ramona, CA; (2); 8/350; Key Clb; Scholastic Bowl; Pres Chorus; Swing Chorus; Variety Show; Rep Frsh Cls; Cit Awd; Hon Roll; Pres Acad Fit Awd; People To People Stu Amb 1990; Voice Choir; UCSD; Prof Singer.

LEWIS, TASHANDA L; Mesa Verde HS; Citrus Heights, CA; (3); Bsktbl; Var Trk; Vrsty Bsktbl 3 Yrs; Track-St; Engrng.

LEWIS, THERESA; Lincoln Preparatory HS; San Diego, CA; (3); ROTC; Drill Tm; Cit Awd; Hon Roll; Med Asst.

LEWIS, TRACEY L; Victor Valley SR HS; Victorville, CA; (2); 33/605; Key Clb; Spanish Clb; Stat Bsktbl; Stat Crs Cntry; Stat Vllybl; High Hon Roll; Hon Roll; CSF; Marine Bio.

LEWIS, YVONNE M; Will C Wood HS; Vacaville, CA; (2); Spanish Clb; JV Bsktbl; High Hon Roll; NHS; Will C Wood Outstndng Acad Achvt 90; Sacramento ST; Law.

LEX, JENNIFER A; Ramona Convent Secondary Schl; Montebello, CA; (3); Cmnty Wkr; French Clb; GAA; Ed Yrbk; Pres Acad Fit Awd; Ecology Clb; CSF; Philamathion Soc; Accntnt.

LEXA, SHILO S; Clayton Valley HS; Clayton, CA; (1); 53/412; Color Guard; Hon Roll; Prfct Atten Awd; Scripts Inst; Mrne Zoolgy.

LEXING, ARICA R; Leuzinger HS; Hawthorne, CA; (1); JV Socr; Hon Roll.

LEYNES, EMMELINE A; Lowell HS; San Francisco, CA; (2); SADD; Hon Roll; UC Berkeley; Comp Sci.

LEYRAN, MARIE T; Saint Joseph HS; Cerritos, CA; (2); Church Yth Grp; Cmnty Wkr; Hosp Aide; Library Aide; SADD; Chorus; Church Choir; Hon Roll; Chrldng, Sftbl & Vllybl, Tennis; Loyola Mary Mount; Med.

LEYRETANA, ANNE C; Mater Dei HS; Anaheim, CA; (2); Cmnty Wkr; Hosp Aide; Spanish Clb; Band; Mrchg Band; Orch; High Hon Roll; NHS; German Clb; CA Schlstc Fed 88-90; Partnership Pgm; UCLA; Med.

LEYS, JOHN; Cardinal Newman HS; Penngrove, CA; (3); 7/78; JA; Spanish Clb; Mrchg Band; Variety Show; JV Tennis; Hon Roll; Pres Acad Fit Awd; Play Scottish Bagpipes; Berkeley; Engrng.

LEYSON, JENNIFER M; Emerson HS; Orange, CA; (3); Orch; School Play; Ed Yrbk; NEDT Awd; Head-Prom Cmmttee; Promethean Soc Awd; Accntng.

LEYTE-VIDAL, TODD; Junipero Serra HS; Belmont, CA; (4); 36/203; Church Yth Grp; Varsity Clb; Chorus; Var Capt Socr; Hon Roll; Ntl Merit SF; Statesman Am; Cath Yth Orgnztns Retreat Ldr & CSF; Bus Admin.

LEYUA, SERGIO; Chino HS; Chino, CA; (3); Church Yth Grp; Spanish Clb; Hon Roll; Prfct Atten Awd; Badmntn Tm; San Bernardino ST Coll; Arch.

LEYVA, ARACELI; Bell Gardens HS; Bell Gardens, CA; (3); Church Yth Grp; Cmnty Wkr; French Clb; Teachers Aide; Band; Mrchg Band; Pep Band; Hon Roll; Prfct Atten Awd; Congrssl Yth Ldrshp Cncl; CSF; Educ.

LEYVA, ISABEL; Calexico HS; Calexico, CA; (2); Intnl Clb; Spanish Clb; Teachers Aide; School Play; Cit Awd; Hon Roll; Prfct Atten Awd; Pres Acad Fit Awd; S Club VP 89-90; Imperial Valley Coll.

LEYVA, JOSE A; Pasadena HS; Pasadena, CA; (2); Chess Clb; Spanish Clb; Bsbl; Ftbl; Socr; Tennis; UCLA; Archtct.

LEYVA, MARIO A; Indio HS; Indio, CA; (3); 150/450; Church Yth Grp; Lit Mag; Trk; Wt Lftg; Wrstlng; MECHA Clb; Erly Otrch Prgm; U CA Riverside; Chrprctr.

LEYVA, RAMON; Saddleback HS; Santa Ana, CA; (3); Church Yth Grp; Band; Jazz Band; Mrchg Band; Pep Band; Bsbl; Math, Engrng, Sci Achvts; ITT Tech Inst; Elec Engr.

LEYVAS, CYNTHIA E; Calexico HS; Calexico, CA; (3); Church Yth Grp; French Clb; Girl Scts; Pres Key Clb; Flag Corp; Var L Bsktbl; Capt Powder Puff Ftbl; Var Sftbl; Var Swmmng; Var L Trk; Treas CA Schlrshp Fed Clb.

LEYYA, JESUS I; Artisia HS; Cerritos, CA; (3); Science Clb; Spanish Clb; Var L Swmmng; PAL Club; Engrng.

LEZADA, DIANE; Channel Islands HS; Oxnard, CA; (3); Church Yth Grp; DECA; Pep Clb; SADD; Flag Corp; Mrchg Band; Rep Stu Cncl; Cheerldng; Short Flags; All Am Girl; UCSB; Pediatrician.

LGALLEGOS, LANCE L; San Marcos HS; San Marcos, CA; (3); 104/367; Var Bsktbl; Var Ftbl; Hon Roll; Arch.

LI, ALEX C; San Gabriel HS; San Gabriel, CA; (2); Hon Roll.

LI, AMY E; Lowell HS; San Francisco, CA; (2); Orch; UC Davis; Vet Med.

LI, ELLIE Y; International Studies Acad; San Francisco, CA; (2); Cmnty Wkr; School Play; Lit Mag; Cit Awd; High Hon Roll; Prfct Atten Awd; Japnese Clb Treas; CSF; Fash Dsgn.

LI, EVAN W; Galileo HS; San Francisco, CA; (2); Church Yth Grp; Cmnty Wkr; ROTC; Color Guard; Hon Roll; Prfct Atten Awd; Cameron Hse Cmnty Ctr Bi Lngl Aftr Schl Pgm Club Pres.

LI, GUOYAO; Galileo HS; San Francisco, CA; (3); Yrbk; Off Jr Cls; Var Bsbl; Bsktbl; Tennis; Vllybl.

LI, HENRY; George Washington HS; San Francisco, CA; (4); Church Yth Grp; Computer Clb; Off Sr Cls; City Coll San Francisco; Engr.

LI, HENRY; George Washington HS; San Francisco, CA; (4); Church Yth Grp; Math Clb; Off Frsh Cls; San Francis CC; Elec Engr.

LI, HOGAN H; Abraham Lincoln HS; San Francisco, CA; (4); School Play; Rptr Nwsp; San Francisco ST U; Engr.

LI, JENNIFER; Louisville HS; Tarzana, CA; (2); Art Clb; Science Clb; Service Clb; School Musical; School Play; Stage Crew; VP Jr Cls; High Hon Roll; Hon Roll; Prfct Atten Awd; CSF; Span,Wrld His,Religion Awds; Frosh Welcome Wk Co-Chairperson; UCSD; Bio-Chem.

LI, JENNY Y; Homestead HS; Sunnyvale, CA; (1); FBLA; Hon Roll; GATE Clb; Asian Amer Assn; UC Riverside; Law.

LI, JIAN FENG; International Studies Acad; San Francisco, CA; (2); Art Clb; Computer Clb; Math Tm; Science Clb; Speech Tm; SADD; School Musical; Swing Chorus; Yrbk; Bsbl; Tchr.

LI, JIN L; Edison HS; Stockton, CA; (2); Key Clb; Math Clb; Office Aide; Science Clb; Hon Roll; NHS; Prfct Atten Awd; U Fo Pafic; Phrmscis.

LI, KEN Y; Mission HS; San Francisco, CA; (4); Church Yth Grp; Office Aide; Chorus; Act Table Tnns; TOP Awd; Algebra II Awd; San Francisco ST U; Comp Sci.

LI, KITTY K; Sierra Vista HS; Baldwin Park, CA; (1); Art Clb; Orch; Var Trk; Intrml Vllybl.

LI, LORRENA; Mission HS; San Francisco, CA; (1); Art Clb; Girl Scts; Library Aide; Cit Awd.

LI, MARY ZHI YAN; Abraham Lincoln HS; San Francisco, CA; (3); Boy Scts; Bausch & Lomb Sci Awd; St Schlr; Best Stu Sci Awd; Tennis, Vllybl, Reading; Upward Bound Pgm U San Francisco; UC Berkeley; Med.

LI, MICHAEL C; Fountain Valley HS; Fountain Valley, CA; (4); 30/625; German Clb; Model UN; Off Frsh Cls; Off Soph Cls; Off Jr Cls; Off Sr Cls; Stu Cncl; Var L Bsktbl; Capt Var Tennis; Hon Roll; CSF; Naval ROTC; U CA Los Angeles; Pol Sci.

LI, NHAN T; Alhambra HS; San Gabriel, CA; (3); FBLA; Intnl Clb; School Musical; NHS; Gldn St Awd Algebra; UCLA; Acctnt.

LI, SHU H; Live Oak HS; Morgan Hill, CA; (3); French Clb; FBLA; Teachers Aide; Chorus; School Musical; School Play; High Hon Roll; Hon Roll; Badminton; Amnesty Intl Club; Achvt Awd; CA Math League Cert Of Mrt; Outstndng Achvt; Gold Hnr Rl; U CA Davis; Math.

LI, SU-EN; West Covina HS; W Covina, CA; (4); 11/463; Treas Art Clb; Church Yth Grp; Computer Clb; Science Clb; Treas Service Clb; Spanish Clb; SADD; JV Tennis; High Hon Roll; Hon Roll; Amrcn Chmcl Scty S CA Sctn Otstndg Achvmnt Awd; Bnk Of Amrca Achvmnt Awd Bus; Bus & Chmstr Awds; U Of CA; Biochmstry.

LI, XING Y; J E Mc Ateer HS; San Francisco, CA; (4); Boy Scts; Computer Clb; Math Tm; Science Clb.

LI, YAYING; International Studies Acad; San Francisco, CA; (3); French Clb; Cit Awd; Hon Roll; Prfct Atten Awd; Acad Of Finance; CA Schlrshp Fed; Sch Stu Store Accntnt; Accntng.

LI, YI Y; Oakland Technical HS; Oakland, CA; (2); Computer Clb; Dance Clb; Debate Tm; English Clb; Model UN; Teachers Aide; Yrbk; Off Frsh Cls; Off Soph Cls; Swmmng; HOBY St Ldrshp Smnr Rep; Rep CA HOBY Intl Ldrshp Smnr; Schlrshp World Affrs Cncl; Stanford; Med.

LIAMSITHISACK, SOURIYO; Edison HS; Stockton, CA; (2); French Clb; Var Swmmng; Hon Roll; Bus.

LIANG, ALVIN J; International Studies Acad; San Francisco, CA; (3); German Clb; Rptr Lit Mag; High Hon Roll; Hon Roll; UC Berkeley.

LIANG, BETTY Y; Galileo HS; San Francisco, CA; (3); Girl Scts; Hosp Aide; Pep Clb; ROTC; Drill Tm; Treas Jr Cls; Treas Sr Cls; Tennis; DAR Awd; High Hon Roll; Acad Exel 88-90; Stu Of Month 88-89; Cert Merit High Hnr Soc Of Women Engrs; U CA Davis; Med.

LIANG, CHRISTINA T; University City HS; San Diego, CA; (4); 1/350; AFS; Church Yth Grp; Cmnty Wkr; Hosp Aide; SADD; Rptr Nwsp; Rep Stu Cncl; Powder Puff Ftbl; Cit Awd; Val; UC Berkeley.

LIANG, DALIA RI-GUI; George Washington HS; San Francisco, CA; (3); Library Aide; ROTC; Speech Tm; Teachers Aide; Hon Roll.

LIANG, EUGENE J; J Eugene Mc Ateer HS; San Francisco, CA; (3); Teachers Aide; High Hon Roll; CSF; Hmrm Rep; Chinese Club; Civil Engrng.

LIANG, JINTAN S; International Studies Acad; San Francisco, CA; (3); Church Yth Grp; Computer Clb; German Clb; Lit Mag; High Hon Roll; Hon Roll; Exclint Achvt German; Math In Cont; San Francisco ST U.

LIANG, MENG; Pioneer HS; Whittier, CA; (4); JA; School Musical; Bsktbl; Socr; Cit Awd; Hon Roll; Cal ST Los Angeles; Bus Admin.

LIANG, MICHAEL; Sacramento HS; Sacramento, CA; (2); 28/500; Math Engr.

LIANG, TONY W; University HS; Laguna Hills, CA; (4); 132/434; JCL; Off Science Clb; Intrml Bsktbl; Orange Cnty Acad Decthln; Natl Latin Hnr Soc; Chinese Cultre Awrnss Clb, Offcr, Cnslr & Cabnt Mem; Boston U; Bio.

LIAO, ELLEN E; Saratoga HS; Saratoga, CA; (1); Debate Tm; Intnl Clb; NFL; Red Cross Aide; Hon Roll; Treble Choir; Chrtrs Hnr Recital Plyd Piano; UCLA; Law.

LIAO, HELEN; Whitney HS; Cerritos, CA; (3); Church Yth Grp; Cmnty Wkr; FBLA; Hosp Aide; Key Clb; Orch; Yrbk; Ed Lit Mag; NHS; Sal; Prin Hnr Roll; Pres Acad Ftns Awd; Bus.

LIAO, JIMMY; Granada Hills HS; Sepulveda, CA; (2); VP Church Yth Grp; Cmnty Wkr; English Clb; FBLA; Math Clb; Math Tm; Science Clb; Service Clb; SADD; Teachers Aide; UCLA; Bus.

LIAO, LIANG; Santiago HS; Garden Grove, CA; (2); 5/498; Computer Clb; Science Clb; Socr; Tennis; High Hon Roll; Schlr Athl Of Yr; Acad Excllnc Awd Golden St Exam; Stanford; Bus.

LIAO, MAGGIE; Arcadia HS; Arcadia, CA; (2); Art Clb; Debate Tm; Math Clb; Red Cross Aide; Spanish Clb; Drill Tm; Yrbk; JV Tennis; Hon Roll; NHS; CSF; Gold Seal Grad; MVP Tennis; UCLA; Bus.

LIAO, SHIRLEY; Torrance HS; Torrance, CA; (3); 11/414; Church Yth Grp; Sec Intnl Clb; Chorus; Church Choir; Cit Awd; High Hon Roll; CSF; Acad Decathlon; UCLA.

LIAO, YULAN; Lowell HS; San Francisco, CA; (2); Chess Clb; Science Clb; Chorus; Church Choir; School Musical; High Hon Roll; CA Invtnl Chmthn 90; CLTAC Mandrn Spch Cont 89; Chinese Clb VP; CSF; Math.

LIAPES, SAMANTHA; Culver City HS; Culver City, CA; (3); Cmnty Wkr; Debate Tm; NFL; Speech Tm; Teachers Aide; School Musical; School Play; Off Frsh Cls; Off Soph Cls; Off Jr Cls; Youth & Govt Awd; Stu League; GATE; Los Angeles Stu Coalition; Lawyer; Psych.

LIAUTAUD, VALERIE M; Bishop Amat Memorial HS; Diamond Bar, CA; (2); Drill Tm; Art; Skiing; U Of Paris; Arch.

LIBAL, ELIZABETH L; El Camino HS; Sacramento, CA; (3); 115/366; Church Yth Grp; Rep French Clb; Key Clb; Var JV Swmmng; Camp Fire Boys And Girls; Friday Night Live; Wilderness Club.

LIBATIQUE, DAVID J; Ontario HS; Ontario, CA; (3); #6 In Class; Art Clb; Church Yth Grp; Key Clb; Math Clb; Science Clb; Spanish Clb; Stu Cncl; Hon Roll; Hnr Ushr; Hnrs Gldn St Exm; CSF; Jr Statsmn Amer Chptr VP.

LIBBY, PAULA L; Saint Anthony HS; Long Beach, CA; (3); 35/135; Church Yth Grp; GAA; Letterman Clb; SADD; Varsity Clb; Var Bsktbl; Var Socr; Var Sftbl; Var Capt Vllybl; Hon Roll; Cmmnctns.

LIBERTO, LISA CAMILLE; Liberty Christian HS; Newport Beach, CA; (3); Hosp Aide; Scholastic Bowl; Ski Clb; Spanish Clb; Chorus; Yrbk; JV Bsktbl; Var Cheerldng; JV Trk; High Hon Roll; Asstnc Leag; Best Rookie Yrbk; Pepperdine; Bus.

LICEA, PATRICIA; Sierra Vista HS; Baldwin Park, CA; (1); Teachers Aide; Cit Awd; Hon Roll; Pres Acad Fit Awd; Chem Engrng.

LICHT, MONICA; Escondido HS; Escondido, CA; (2); German Clb; SADD; High Hon Roll; Hon Roll; CSF; FBLA; NCAL; Tchr.

LICHTMAN, JAMES; Hilmar JR-SR HS; Hilmar, CA; (4); 5/108; Spanish Clb; Varsity Clb; Stu Cncl; Var L Ftbl; Var L Trk; Var L Wrstlng; High Hon Roll; Hon Roll; Pres Acad Fit Awd; CSF VP & Pres; Hnrs Gldn St Exmntn Geomtry; UC Santa Barbara; Comp Sci.

LICUANAN, TIFFANY C; St Joseph HS; Orange, CA; (2); Key Clb; Spanish Clb; Var Tennis; Hon Roll; Perfrmr Yr Tnns; MVP Tnns; 4th Pl Angelus Leag Singls; U Of CA Irvine; Pre-Med.

LIDDICOAT, MICHELLE C; Calaveras HS; Valley Springs, CA; (4); Sec AFS; Church Yth Grp; Pres Drama Clb; French Clb; School Play; Stage Crew; Yrbk; Lit Mag; Sec Jr Cls; Pres Sr Cls; U Of The Pacific; Phys Thrpy.

LIDDLE, REBECCA; Independence HS; San Jose, CA; (3); Cmnty Wkr; Debate Tm; Drama Clb; Office Aide; Service Clb; Chorus; Church Choir; Variety Show; Cit Awd; Prfct Atten Awd; BYU; Psych.

LIDDY, SHANNON M; Eltoro HS; El Toro, CA; (3); Yrbk; Capt L Crs Cntry; Capt L Trk; High Hon Roll; Pres Acad Fit Awd; ETHS Cross Cntry 87-89; All Orange Cnty Cross Cntry 87-88; Schlr Athelete Troch Awd 87-90.

LIEBBE, SHAYNA C; Laguna Hills HS; Laguna Hills, CA; (2); Debate Tm; Drama Clb; English Clb; French Clb; Key Clb; Model UN; SADD; Thesps; School Musical; School Play; US Cngrssnl Schlr; Soph OCAD Team; Georgetown U; Poly Sci.

LIEBEL, CHRISTOPHER J; St Michaels Prep; San Clemente, CA; (2); 1/34; Nwsp; Bsbl; Jr NHS; Orange Cnty Acad Dcthln Awd Rcpnt; Roneer Vlntrs Clb; Stanford.

LIEBER, KATHERINE STEWART; Monte Vista HS; Danville, CA; (2); Hosp Aide; Library Aide; Nwsp; Hon Roll; NHS; Natl Chrty Lg; CSF; Scl Stds Dept Awd.

LIEBER, KURT M; Torrey Pines HS; Del Mar, CA; (4); 150/475; French Clb; Teachers Aide; DAR Awd; Hon Roll; U Of WA; Psych.

LIEBERS, CHRISTOPHER M; Chula Vista HS; Chula Vista, CA; (1); 1/203; JV Socr; Cit Awd; High Hon Roll; Masonic Awd; Prfct Atten Awd; Pres Acad Fit Awd; Off Frsh Cls; CSF; Golden St Exam Geom High Hnrs; Asiaon Fllwshp Clb; Jnr Statesmn America; Stanford U; Biochem.

LIEMTHONGSAMOU, ATTAPHONE; John F Kennedy HS; Sacramento, CA; (2); 77/530; Cit Awd; High Hon Roll; Hon Roll; Prfct Atten Awd; Sacramento City Coll; Acctnt.

LIEMTHONGSAMOUT, ATTAPHONE; John F Kennedy HS; Sacramento, CA; (2); 77/530; Sacramento Cty Coll; Prof Bkkpr.

LIEN, JENNIFER; Clovis West HS; Fresno, CA; (2); Scholastic Bowl; Rptr Nwsp; Stat Bsktbl; Hon Roll; Pres Schlr; Mem Peer Cnslng Clb; Assist Sec Elem Smmr Sch; Violin Charity Funds; Stanford U; Pre-Med.

LIEN, PETER; Willow Glen Ed Park HS; San Jose, CA; (2); 1/400; Math Clb; Math Tm; Quiz Bowl; Var Tennis; CSF; CA Invtnl Chemathon 90; Stanford; Bus.

LIEN, RICHARD; Corona HS; Corona, CA; (3); 32/400; Cit Awd; Hon Roll; Prfct Atten Awd; Enjoy-Read Hstry Of US, Cllct Bsbl Cards & Equipmnt; Wnnr Svrl Awds Karate Trnmts; UCI; Surgeon.

LIEN, TIMOTHY J; Troy HS; La Habra, CA; (2); 53/400; Church Yth Grp; JCL; Latin Clb; Nwsp; Bsktbl; Trk; High Hon Roll; Hon Roll; Prfct Atten Awd; Advrtsng.

LIEN, TOM; Willow Glen HS; San Jose, CA; (3); 1/539; Am Leg Boys St; Cmnty Wkr; Drama Clb; Math Clb; Math Tm; Q&S; Science Clb; School Musical; School Play; Nwsp; Xerox Awd Hum, Social Studies; Santa Clara Vly Sci & Engrng Fair 2nd Pl; Brown U Bk Awd; Stanford; Med.

LIESMAN, TANTI; Gahr HS; Cerritos, CA; (2); High Hon Roll; Blue & Gold Awds; PTSA Achvt; Bus Admin.

LIETZKE, JENNIFER A; Livermore HS; Livermore, CA; (4); 10/372; Pres Church Yth Grp; Cmnty Wkr; German Clb; Hosp Aide; Speech Tm; Var Tennis; High Hon Roll; Ntl Merit SF; 3rd Pl N CA Amer Assn Tchrs Grmn 89; CA Schlrshp Fdrtn 86-89; Fri Nght Lv-Agnst Tn Drnkng; U Of CA Davis; Bio Sci.

LIETZOW, ERIC; John F Kennedy HS; La Palma, CA; (4); Boy Scts; Band; Jazz Band; Mrchg Band; Hon Roll; CA ST Long Beach; Acntng.

LIETZOW, MICHAEL T; John F Kennedy HS; La Palma, CA; (4); Boy Scts; Band; Jazz Band; Mrchg Band; Orch; Hon Roll; Pres Acad Fit Awd; CA ST Long Beach; Bus.

LIEU, BINH C; Bolsa Grande HS; Garden Grove, CA; (3); #3 In Class; French Clb; Science Clb; Bsktbl; Hon Roll; NHS.

LIEU, KIET V; Nogales HS; W Covina, CA; (2); Science Clb; High Hon Roll; Badmington; CSF; UCLA; Engrng.

LIEU, NHI T; Rosemead HS; Baldwin Park, CA; (4); 2/375; VP Key Clb; VP Science Clb; Pres Spanish Clb; JV Var Bsktbl; High Hon Roll; Kiwanis Awd; Opt Clb Awd; Sal; CSF, Gold Seal Bearer; Scl Sci Stu Yr 90; U Of CA San Diego; Pedtrcn.

LIEU, PHUONG V; Mark Keppel HS; Rosemead, CA; (3); Chorus; Hon Roll; Pasadena City Coll; Fashion.

LIEU, THY; Serra HS; San Diego, CA; (3); French Clb; Math Clb; Cit Awd; Hon Roll; Prfct Atten Awd; Pres Acad Fit Awd; CSF; Golden St Exmn Awd Geom; Outstanding Frnch Stu Awd; Med.

LIEU, TRUONG Q; Oceanside HS; Oceanside, CA; (4); 1/275; Chess Clb; Math Tm; Scholastic Bowl; Teachers Aide; Intrml Ftbl; JV Socr; Intrml Sftbl; Hon Roll; Val; UC Davis; Bio.

LIEU, VAN C; Montclair HS; Montclair, CA; (2); FBLA; Science Clb; School Play; Trk; Hon Roll; GATE Club; Best Spprtng Actor Awd 89-90; MIT; Aerospc Engr.

LIEW, JEFFREY C; Abraham Lincoln HS; San Francisco, CA; (3); Acpl Chr; Band; Orch; Var Trk; Hon Roll; World Affairs Club Treas; Interact Club VP & Treas; California Scholarship Federation; U C Davis; Dentistry.

LIFONZO, ERIKA V; St Genevieve HS; Sun Valley, CA; (2); Drama Clb; Spanish Clb; Intl Thespian Soc; Pediatric Nrs.

LIGHSTON, HEATHER; Immaculate Heart HS; Los Angeles, CA; (3); GAA; Spanish Clb; Hon Roll; UCLA; Film Dirctng.

LIGHT, DON E; Oakdale HS; Oakdale, CA; (2); Office Aide; ROTC; Band; Drill Tm; Drm Mjr(t); Orch; Pep Band; School Musical; Hon Roll; Doc.

LIGHT, KAREN M; Los Angeles Lutheran HS; Van Nuys, CA; (2); Cmnty Wkr; Drama Clb; Letterman Clb; Pep Clb; School Play; Stage Crew; Cheerldng; Cit Awd; High Hon Roll; Prfct Atten Awd; CSF; HOBY Ldrshp Fndtn; Jr Stmn Fndtn.

LIGHT, RON E; Oakdale HS; Oakdale, CA; (2); Dance Clb; Office Aide; ROTC; Teachers Aide; Band; Stage Crew; Hon Roll; Outstndng Achvt Awd; Yale; Comp Tech.

LIGHTBOURN, JEANNE ANN; Royal HS; Simi Valley, CA; (3); Church Yth Grp; Library Aide; Cit Awd; High Hon Roll; Chrch Athltcs; CSU Northridge; Elem Ed.

LIGON, BEAU JAMES G; Bellarmine-Jefferson HS; Los Angeles, CA; (1); JV Church Yth Grp; JV Vllybl; USC; Med.

LIGON, R JASON; Bonita Vista HS; Bonita, CA; (3); Church Yth Grp; Debate Tm; Key Clb; Model UN; Pep Clb; SADD; Acpl Chr; Chorus; Church Choir; Off Frsh Cls; Music Mach-Assist; Yale; Corp Law.

LIGOURI, MICHELLE; Concord HS; Concord, CA; (3); Cmnty Wkr; Drama Clb; SADD; Teachers Aide; Thesps; Chorus; Drm Mjr(t); Mrchg Band; School Musical; School Play; UCLA; Theatre Arts.

LIKENS, J ELIZABETH; Vivian Webb HS; Claremont, CA; (3); 4/46; Cmnty Wkr; Debate Tm; Ed Nwsp; Ed Lit Mag; Var Bsktbl; Var Sftbl; Stat Vllybl; High Hon Roll; Cum Laude; Math Awd; CSF.

LIKINS, MARY; Royal HS; Simi Valley, CA; (2); 2/643; Church Yth Grp; FCA; Rep Soph Cls; JV Capt Cheerldng; Var Swmmng; Cit Awd; High Hon Roll; NHS; Am Legn Awd; Swmmng Var MVP, All Leag, Schlr Athlt; Geom Golden ST Hnrs; Engrng.

LILES, APRIL L; Fresno Christian HS; Fresno, CA; (1); Church Yth Grp; Band; Mrchg Band; Pep Band; Rep Frsh Cls; JV Vllybl; Hon Roll; CA ST U-Fresno.

LILES, HEATHER NICOLE; Canyon HS; Plano, TX; (2); Church Yth Grp; Pep Clb; JV Cheerldng; Intrml Gym; Cit Awd; Hon Roll; CSF; Stu Of Month; Bus.

LILES, TAWNI L; Fort Dick Bible Acad; Brookings, OR; (3); 1/3; Church Yth Grp; School Play; Yrbk; Var L Bsbl; Var L Bsktbl; Var L Vllybl; Hon Roll; U Of OR; Intr Dsgn.

LILJEGREN, CRYSTAL M; Hemet HS; Aguanga, CA; (2); 196/740; Speech Tm; JV Trk; Lion Awd; Explorer Scouts VP & Pres; UC Irvine; Writer.

LILJENQUIST, MARY LYNN; Oakdale HS; Oakdale, CA; (2); Church Yth Grp; FHA; Socr; Swmmng; Trk; Cit Awd; High Hon Roll; Hon Roll; Brigham Young U; Elem Ed.

LILLARD, ANDREA K; Temecula Valley HS; Temecula, CA; (2); 28/590; Church Yth Grp; Cmnty Wkr; Ski Clb; High Hon Roll; Hon Roll; Grphc Dsgn.

LILLEY, REBECCA; Mission College Prep; Atascadero, CA; (3); Am Leg Aux Girls St; Sec Key Clb; Sprt Ed Yrbk; Stu Cncl; Var Crs Cntry; Var Socr; Var Trk; Hon Roll; Girls Nation Senator 90; HOPES Environmntl Clb Co-Founder; Poltcl Sci.

LILLIE, DANIEL F; Desert Christian HS; Acton, CA; (1); Band; High Hon Roll; Hon Roll; Stu Of Month; 2nd Pl ACSI Sci Fair; 2nd Pl Math Cmptn; Acctng.

LILLIE, DUSTIN M; Francis Parker HS; San Diego, CA; (2); Boy Scts; Ed Nwsp; Var Crs Cntry; Var Trk; Natl Latin Exam Cum Laude; Med.

LILLIG, ELIZABETH; Maranatha HS; Monrovia, CA; (4); Boy Scts; Treas Church Yth Grp; Drama Clb; Office Aide; Spanish Clb; Stage Crew; Rptr Nwsp; Phtg Rptr Yrbk; DAR Awd; Hon Roll; Salt Shaker Clb; Play Piano; CA ST Polytech U; Chrstn Ed.

LILLIGREN, THEODORE T; Turlock HS; Turlock, CA; (3); Church Yth Grp; Key Clb; Pres Letterman Clb; Var Capt Swmmng; Hon Roll; Rotry Camp Royal; Swmmng All Conf; Water Polo All Conf, All Section; Acctng.

LILLMAN, JEFFREY M; Encina HS; Sacramento, CA; (3); SADD; Teachers Aide; JV Var Ftbl; JV Var Wt Lftg; Engl.

LILLY, CORINA L; Norte Vista HS; Riverside, CA; (1); GAA; Teachers Aide; Var Sftbl; JV Vllybl; High Hon Roll; Hon Roll; Mtn View 1st Tm All Leag Stfbl; UCLA; Sports Med.

LIM, ADORIA; Lowell HS; San Francisco, CA; (4); 21/650; Orch; Var JV Tennis; Ntl Merit SF; U CA-BERKELEY; Bus Admin.

LIM, ADRIANNE S; Galileo HS; San Francisco, CA; (2); French Clb; Pep Clb; Trk; Hon Roll.

LIM, ALBERT I; Chaminade HS; Northridge, CA; (3); Church Yth Grp; Cmnty Wkr; Debate Tm; Drama Clb; Key Clb; Model UN; Speech Tm; Stage Crew; High Hon Roll; T-Ball & Bsktbl Coach; Ped.

LIM, ALLEN; Crescenta Valley HS; Glendale, CA; (4); 19/400; Boy Scts; Cmnty Wkr; FBLA; Intnl Clb; Key Clb; Mu Alpha Theta; Science Clb; Mgr Yrbk; Cit Awd; French Hon Soc; Sprts For Undrstndng & Cyclng Holland & France; Cyclng Natl Champs 88; Montrose Cyclng Team; Ctzn Bee; UC-DAVIS; Sprts Med.

LIM, BETTY; Fairfield HS; Fairfield, CA; (3); Art Clb; Boy Scts; German Clb; Key Clb; Service Clb; Band; Mrchg Band; Rep Frsh Cls; Rep Soph Cls; Rep Jr Cls; Most Dedicated Tennis 88-89; Var Ltr 88-89; Band Ltr 88-89; UC Davis; Art.

LIM, BRIAN SE HOON; Irvine HS; Irvine, CA; (2); Church Yth Grp; French Clb; Key Clb; Church Choir; Mrchg Band; Orch; Rptr Nwsp; Trk; JV Vllybl; Hon Roll; CSF; All Southern CA Hnr Orch & All ST Hnr Orch; GSE Gmtry High Hnr; Med.

LIM, CHERYLL A; John Marshall Fundamental HS; Pasadena, CA; (3); Key Clb; Service Clb; Teachers Aide; VP Stu Cncl; Mgr(s); Socr; Tennis; Cit Awd; Hon Roll; NHS; Intl Bus.

LIM, CHHON; San Gabriel HS; Monterey Park, CA; (2); JA; Spanish Clb; Cit Awd; Hon Roll; UCLA; Sci.

LIM, DAMON; George Washington HS; San Francisco, CA; (2); High Hon Roll; Hon Roll; Eagle Srvc Soc; UC Davis; Engrng.

LIM, DEREK H; California HS; San Ramon, CA; (3); Church Yth Grp; Capt Var Bsktbl; Hon Roll; Pres Acad Fit Awd; Law.

LIM, DONALD; Lowell HS; San Francisco, CA; (3); Library Aide; Tennis; Wt Lftg; High Hon Roll; Hon Roll; Prfct Atten Awd; Art Commissioner For Korean Club; U Of San Francisco; Pharm.

LIM, JAY; San Gabriel Acad; Whittier, CA; (3); Chorus; Off Frsh Cls; VP Soph Cls; Off Jr Cls; Intrml Bsktbl; Intrml Capt Ftbl; Intrml Socr; Intrml Sftbl; Intrml Tennis; Intrml Capt Vllybl; USC Semifnlst Sci Fr Rgnls; PUC; Pre-Med.

LIM, JEANNETTE B; Granada Hills HS; Northridge, CA; (2); Pres Church Yth Grp; Cmnty Wkr; SADD; Teachers Aide; Church Choir; L Intrml Trk; Cit Awd; Hon Roll; Prfct Atten Awd; Pres Acad Fit Awd; Jr Statesmn Amer Chptr Treas; CA Jr Schlrshp Fed Hnr Awd; CA Schlrshp Fed; Engl.

LIM, JENNIFER K; San Dimas HS; San Dimas, CA; (3); 2/300; Aud/Vis; GAA; SADD; Sec Frsh Cls; Pres Soph Cls; Stu Cncl; Var Bsktbl; Var Trk; High Hon Roll; ASB Ldrshp Clb; UC Berkeley; Bio.

LIM, JION; Gardena HS; Gardena, CA; (3); Library Aide; VP Service Clb; Prfct Atten Awd; Tutor Elem Schl Chldrn; Hnrble Mntn ACE Essy Cont; Skirball Inst Amer Values Hnrble Mntn; UC Berkeley.

LIM, JOHNNY; Kennedy HS; Los Angeles, CA; (2); Debate Tm; Bsktbl; CSUN; Bus.

LIM, JOYCE; Universtiy HS; Irvine, CA; (2); Science Clb; Orch; High Hon Roll; Cert UCI Pgm Otstndng HS Chem Stu.

LIM, KATHLEEN SUN; Flintridge Preparatory Schl; La Canada, CA; (3); Church Yth Grp; Cmnty Wkr; Key Clb; Math Clb; Spanish Clb; School Play; Stage Crew; Treas Frsh Cls; Var Tennis; Cit Awd; Spnsh Hnr Soc 2 Yrs; CROP Walk-A-Thon; Prom Cmmtte; Occidental Coll; Pre-Med.

LIM, KENNETH; Lowell HS; San Francisco, CA; (3); Teachers Aide; JV Crs Cntry; JV Tennis; Hon Roll; Jr NHS; Prfct Atten Awd; Pres Acad Fit Awd; VP Tennis Club; High Hnrs GSE Alg & Geo; Proj Bus; Engrng.

LIM, KENNETH; University HS; Irvine, CA; (2); 176/508; Spanish Clb.

LIM, KIMSIENG; Polytechnic HS; Long Beach, CA; (3); Church Choir; School Play; Var Tennis; Var Vllybl; Hon Roll; NHS; Val; Church Yth Grp; Math Clb; Math Tm; 2nd Pl N Long Bch Wmns Clb Art Shw; Portia Welfare Clb Long Bch; Mural Pgm Long Bch 88.

LIM, LEIGH C; Woodside HS; Sunnyvale, CA; (3); French Clb; FBLA; JV Tennis; High Hon Roll; Hon Roll; CSF; Spellng Tm; Bk Awds; Bus Admin.

LIM, MARGARET; Skyline HS; Oakland, CA; (2); Church Yth Grp; Cmnty Wkr; German Clb; Intnl Clb; Key Clb; Orch; Hon Roll; Jr NHS; Prfct Atten Awd; Asu-Asian Stu Union; Yth Ending Honger; Keywannettes; Yale; Lawyer.

LIM, MAUREEN G; Hamilton Music Acad; Los Angeles, CA; (2); School Play; Rep Frsh Cls; Var Swmmng; High Hon Roll; Bus.

LIM, MELANIE; Galileo HS; San Francisco, CA; (3); French Clb; JCL; Orch; Bsbl; Bsktbl; Tennis; Vllybl; Cit Awd; Hon Roll; Prfct Atten Awd; Badminton; Comp Prgm; Acntng; Secretary.

LIM, MIKE M; Etiwanda HS; Alta Loma, CA; (2); Church Yth Grp; JA; Hon Roll; Pres Acad Fit Awd; Physicist.

LIM, NOEL S; James Logan HS; Union City, CA; (3); 14/800; Church Yth Grp; Math Clb; NFL; High Hon Roll.

LIM, PANSY M; Amos Alonzo HS; Stockton, CA; (1); Church Yth Grp; Church Choir; Orch; Cit Awd; Hon Roll; Prfct Atten Awd; Churchs Monthly Nws Ltr Cmmnctn Staff; 3rd Pl Sci Fair; Athletic Awd; UC Coll; Med.

LIM, PATRICK; University HS; Irvine, CA; (1); JCL; Latin Clb; Orch; School Musical; High Hon Roll; Hon Roll; Pres Acad Fit Awd; All Southrn Hnr Orch; Hnrble Mrt Natl Latin Exmn Maxima Cum Laude.

LIM, PETER K; Whitney HS; Cerritos, CA; (3); Church Yth Grp; Rep Key Clb; Varsity Clb; Hist Soph Cls; Hist Jr Cls; Stu Cncl; JV Bsktbl; Var Trk; Hon Roll; NHS; UCLA; Poltcl Sci.

LIM, PHALEN; Orange HS; Orange, CA; (3); Key Clb; Math Clb; Tennis; Hon Roll; NHS; CFS; UCLA; Grphc Art.

LIM, PICOR; Millikan HS; Long Beach, CA; (4); Boy Scts; Church Yth Grp; Library Aide; Teachers Aide; Church Choir; Hon Roll; Ntl Merit Schol; Eagle Scout Awd; BYU; Electrcn Engr.

LIM, ROGER S; Montebello HS; Montebello, CA; (2); Church Yth Grp; Key Clb; Acpl Chr; Church Choir; Variety Show; High Hon Roll; Prfct Atten Awd; Culture Vultures Fine Arts Appreciation Club; Most Valbl Choir Mem; UCLA; Dntstry.

LIM, SEUNG Y; Abraham Lincoln HS; San Francisco, CA; (3); CSF; UC Davis; Teaching.

LIM, SIM H; A A Stagg HS; Stockton, CA; (4); U Pacific; Pharmacy.

LIM, SOPHOAT; Modesto HS; Modesto, CA; (3); Math Clb; Math Tm; Mu Alpha Theta; Hon Roll; Jr NHS; Medicine.

LIM, STANLEY L; Walnut HS; Walnut, CA; (3); Deans List; CSF; Comp Sci.

LIM, STEVE M; Lakewood SR HS; Long Beach, CA; (3); Off ROTC; Chorus; Color Guard; Drill Tm; Trk; Vllybl; Elks Awd; Daedalian Soc/Achvt Mdl; Fleet Reserve Assn/Smart Sailor Mdl; Dstngshd Cadet Awd; W Point Mltry Acad; Mltry Sci.

LIM, SUSIE; Carlmont HS; San Carlos, CA; (4); Church Yth Grp; Math Clb; Band; Church Choir; Orch; Stu Cncl; 1st Pl Congressnl Human Rights Cont; Golden St Exam; Honor Band; Health Sci.

LIM, TRICIA D; Valley View HS; Moreno Valley, CA; (2); High Hon Roll; CSF; U Of CA Irvine; Engr.

LIM, VERONICA; Breza-Olinda HS; Brea, CA; (1); Church Yth Grp; Tennis; UC Berkley; Psycht.

LIM, YEEKAI; Mira Loma HS; Rancho Cordova, CA; (3); 77/291; Chess Clb; Key Clb; Tennis; Jr NHS; UC LA; Chem Engrng.

LIM, YIN ONG JULIE; John F Kennedy HS; Sacramento, CA; (3); 42/422; French Clb; FBLA; FTA; Hon Roll; CA Schlrshp Fed; Pre-Med.

LIMA, ERIC G; Dos Palos HS; Dos Palos, CA; (3); Pres Frsh Cls; Intrml Soph Cls; JV Bsbl; Hon Roll; Bsbl; CA Schlstc Fed; Rcrtnl Coord.

LIMA, NANCY E; Carson HS; Carson, CA; (3); French Clb; FTA; Teachers Aide; Yrbk; Var Tennis; Hon Roll; Psych.

LIMA, NIKKI A; Abraham Lincoln HS; San Jose, CA; (3); Teachers Aide; Var Socr; Var Sftbl; Santa Teresa Athl Leag All Leag Awd; Humboldt ST; Teaching.

LIMBAGA, ARIES J; California HS; Whittier, CA; (2); Chess Clb; Spanish Clb; High Hon Roll; UC Riverside; Pre Med.

LIMBASUTA, NICOLE A; Pasadena HS; Pasadena, CA; (1); French Clb; Ski Clb; Band; Mrchg Band; Pep Band; Vllybl; Cit Awd; Most Creative; Best Girl Musician; FL ST U.

LIMBO, FRANCESCO C; Gahr HS; Cerritos, CA; (3); Hon Roll.

LIMBO, JOHN C; Gahr HS; Cerritos, CA; (1); Hon Roll; Electrncs.

LIMON, CRISTINA A; Thomas Downey HS; Modesto, CA; (4); Church Yth Grp; Teachers Aide; Otstndng Essay On Drug & Alcohol Abuse Awd; MJC; Bus Admin.

LIMON, XAVIER; Fremont Christian HS; Fremont, CA; (1); Church Yth Grp; Quiz Bowl; Ed Yrbk; Off Frsh Cls; Bsbl; Hon Roll; US Hstry, Govt Awd; Phys Thrpst.

LIMPOCO, FE D; Arroyo Grande HS; Grover City, CA; (4); 23/409; Key Clb; Hon Roll; Pres Acad Fit Awd; CSF; CA Poly ST U; Arch.

LIN, ALBERT S; Miraleste HS; Rancho Palos Verd, CA; (4); 1/170; Pres Math Clb; Model UN; Sec Service Clb; Pres Jr Cls; Var Capt Crs Cntry; Var Trk; Bausch & Lomb Sci Awd; Pres French Hon Soc; Pres NHS; Ntl Merit SF; Engrng.

LIN, ALEX; Edison HS; Huntington Beach, CA; (1); Church Yth Grp; Church Drama Grp; Vacatn Bible Schl Tchrs Aide; U Of CA; Doc.

LIN, ANDREW P; Villa Park HS; Anaheim, CA; (3); Key Clb; SADD; School Play; Rep Jr Cls; JV Socr; Var Trk; Hon Roll.

LIN, ANGEL Y; El Camino Fundamental HS; Citrus Heights, CA; (4); 3/341; Church Yth Grp; Pres Key Clb; Pres Math Clb; Math Tm; Pres Mu Alpha Theta; VP Science Clb; Pres Spanish Clb; NHS; Ntl Merit Schol; Pres Acad Fit Awd; Sacramento Cnty Acad Dcthln; Mdcl Explrers Treas; Bk Of Amer Sci/Math Awd; UC San Diego; Mdcl Rsrch.

LIN, ANGELA P; Arcadia HS; Arcadia, CA; (3); 2/639; French Clb; Sec FBLA; Hosp Aide; Sec Math Clb; Red Cross Aide; NHS; Ntl Merit Ltr; Prfct Atten Awd; Pres Acad Fit Awd; Bio Clb Sec; Kiowas Hon Srvc Clb; Ivy League Col; Med.

LIN, ANGIE; Irvine HS; Irvine, CA; (1); Key Clb; Var Tennis; Pres Acad Fit Awd; 13th Annual Heritage Awds; Chinese/Japanese Clbs; CSF; Soc Of Asian Stu; John Hopkins; Biomed.

LIN, ANNIE; Irvine HS; Irvine, CA; (1); 2/580; Key Clb; Band; Pres Acad Fit Awd; S Coast Chinese Cultural Assn Schlrshp; Chinese/Japanese Clb; CSF; Harvard; Poltcl Sci.

LIN, BELINDA T; Hayward HS; Hayward, CA; (2); 20/226; Church Yth Grp; German Clb; Church Choir; Sec Soph Cls; Sec Jr Cls; Var Tennis; High Hon Roll; Sci Fr 3rd Pl Schl, 4th Pl Cnty; Var Badminton 2 Yrs.

LIN, BRIAN B; Milpitas HS; Milpitas, CA; (3); Boy Scts; Spanish Clb; Acpl Chr; Band; Jazz Band; Orch; Pep Band; School Musical; School Play; Variety Show; CA Poly; Arch.

LIN, CHRISTINE CHIA-JUNG; Miramonte HS; Moraga, CA; (4); 6/278; Church Yth Grp; Cmnty Wkr; Church Choir; Orch; School Musical; Cit Awd; High Hon Roll; Ntl Merit SF; Youth Educator; Acad Decathlon; Engnrng.

LIN, CINDY; El Camino Real HS; West Hills, CA; (4); SADD; Teachers Aide; Off Frsh Cls; Off Soph Cls; Off Jr Cls; Tennis; Cit Awd; Prfct Atten Awd; Peer Cnslng; Jr Stsmn Amer; Acad Dcthln; Hands Acrs Cmps; LA Times Schlrshp Art Hist; Los Angeles Coll Pierce; Soc Sc.

LIN, DAVID; Monte Vista HS; Walnut Creek, CA; (4); Pres VP Church Yth Grp; Sec Computer Clb; Hosp Aide; Ski Clb; Tennis; Wt Lftg; Treas NHS; Ntl Merit SF; Piano Ntl Adtns & CA Music Assoc Awd; CA Schlrshp Fed; Pre Med.

LIN, DAVID P; Homestead HS; Sunnyvale, CA; (3); Church Yth Grp; Debate Tm; JA; Speech Tm; Teachers Aide; Church Choir; Tennis; Vllybl; High Hon Roll; Hon Roll; U C Davis; Psych.

LIN, DOCAS Y; Los Angeles County HS For The Arts; Arcadia, CA; (3); Band; Chorus; Orch; School Musical; MTAC Hnr Recital On Piano Solo; Intl Piano Cmptn; Juliard; Prfssnl Pianist.

LIN, EDDIE; Marina HS; Huntington Beach, CA; (2); Latin Clb; Pres Lit Mag; Hon Roll; Engrng.

LIN, ELAINE; Whitney HS; Cerritos, CA; (1); Tennis; Cit Awd; High Hon Roll; Hon Roll; Prfct Atten Awd; Schl Congress; Cert Mrt Exam Lvl VII Piano; Stu For Ethical Treatment Of Animals Clb.

LIN, ELLEN; Marina HS; Huntington Bch, CA; (4); Aud/Vis; Computer Clb; French Clb; Key Clb; Math Clb; Math Tm; Hon Roll; Pres Acad Fit Awd; U Of CA Irvine; Social Ecology.

LIN, ELTON L; Clovis West HS; Fresno, CA; (3); 108/530; Church Yth Grp; Cmnty Wkr; English Clb; FCA; FBLA; Intnl Clb; Key Clb; Letterman Clb; Math Clb; Math Tm; Cnty Sci Fair Awd Wnnr; 4th Indvl Rankings Cntrl CA Patrons Tenns Assn; Mem, Treas JR Statsmn Of Am; Civil Engrg.

LIN, EUNICE M; Washington HS; Fremont, CA; (3); 1/328; Letterman Clb; Scholastic Bowl; Treas Sr Cls; Off Stu Cncl; JV Var Tennis; Var Trk; Vllybl; High Hon Roll; California Scholarship Federation; High Honors Golden State Exam Geometry; Visual Arts.

LIN, FIONA Y; Los Gatos HS; Mt Sereno, CA; (4); 1/374; Cmnty Wkr; Dance Clb; DECA; NFL; Pres Service Clb; Speech Tm; Band; Chorus; Drill Tm; Mrchg Band; CA Yth Symphny; Miller Oratrcl & JR Citznshp Cups.

LIN, FRANK; Piedmont HS; Piedmont, CA; (3); Boy Scts; Debate Tm; Math Clb; Math Tm; Model UN; Science Clb; Spanish Clb; JV Var Socr; JV Swmmng; Var Tennis; St Wide Chemathon 7th 89; Golden St Xm Algebra Hi Hnrs; Golden St Xm Geometry Hi Hnrs; UC Berkeley.

LIN, HAN; Saratoga HS; Los Gatos, CA; (3); 19/216; Spanish Clb; Band; Jazz Band; Mrchg Band; Orch; School Musical; Nwsp; Hon Roll; Ntl Merit Ltr; SFRDS Treas; Natl Piano Plyng Audtns; Cngrssnl Yth Ldrshp Cncl 90; Columbus Schlrs Prgm; UC Berkeley.

LIN, HSI-SHAN; San Marcos HS; Santa Barbara, CA; (2); French Clb; Letterman Clb; Teachers Aide; Hon Roll; #1 Clb; CA Schlstc Fed; Art.

LIN, I-FAN F; Los Altos HS; Hacienda Hts, CA; (1); High Hon Roll; Prfct Atten Awd; JV Bdmntn; Schls Sci Fair Grand Prz; CSF.

LIN, JACK C; University HS; Irvine, CA; (2); 293/508; German Clb; Orch; JV Socr; U CA Irvine; Dntstry.

LIN, JASON C; North Hollywood HS; North Hollywood, CA; (3); Math Clb; Science Clb; Service Clb; Spanish Clb; Church Choir; Ed Nwsp; Cit Awd; High Hon Roll; Hon Roll; Prfct Atten Awd; Bilingual Cncl; Gldn St Exam High Hnr Geom; U Of CA Irvine; Biochem.

LIN, JEFFREY; San Ramon HS; Danvilla, CA; (3); Church Yth Grp; FBLA; Med.

LIN, JENNY; St Lawrence Acad; Milpitas, CA; (3); 5/30; Church Yth Grp; Cmnty Wkr; Hosp Aide; Math Clb; Math Tm; Science Clb; Service Clb; Temple Yth Grp; Chorus; Church Choir; CA Hnr Soc; 1st Awd Art Prjct; Santa Clara U; Bus.

LIN, JERSHI M; Schurr HS; Monterey Park, CA; (1); Church Yth Grp; Dance Clb; JV Crs Cntry; JV Trk; JV Wrstlng; Hon Roll; JV Leag Chmpns Wrstlng; Hstry Clb; Cyclng Clb; Chrch Choir; JV 2nd Pl Leag Chmpns Track; UCLA; Bus Mgmt.

LIN, JOHN; Arcadia HS; Arcadia, CA; (3); 35/639; AFS; Art Clb; Hosp Aide; Math Tm; Science Clb; Orch; JV Tennis; NHS; Ntl Merit Ltr; Pres Schlr; Biochem.

LIN, JOSEPH M; Hillsdale HS; San Mateo, CA; (3); Chess Clb; French Clb; Math Tm; Science Clb; Orch; School Musical; Hon Roll; Asian Clb; Badminton Team.

LIN, JUDITH; Brea Olinda HS; Brea, CA; (2); Cmnty Wkr; Key Clb; Ed Nwsp; Pres Acad Fit Awd; Rotary Awd; Spotlight Yth Awd; 2nd Pl Cnty Hstry Day 90; UCLA; Pedtrcn.

LIN, JUDY H; Woodbridge HS; Laguna Hills, CA; (4); 20/373; Church Yth Grp; Cmnty Wkr; SADD; Acpl Chr; Chorus; Church Choir; Jazz Band; Orch; School Musical; Variety Show; Heartsong-Teen Mnstry Choir; Piano; Prfsnl Muscn.

LIN, JULIA; Brea Olinda HS; Brea, CA; (4); 15/300; Sec Key Clb; Sec Service Clb; Ed Nwsp; Ed Yrbk; High Hon Roll; Jr NHS; NHS; Pres Acad Fit Awd; CA Schlrshp Fed; U CA Irvine.

LIN, KENNY S; Aragon HS; San Mateo, CA; (2); Boy Scts; Computer Clb; Nwsp; Crs Cntry; Trk; High Hon Roll; Actvts Commsn.

LIN, LARRY; Leuzinger HS; Gardena, CA; (3); AFS; Computer Clb; French Clb; Science Clb; Hon Roll; Prfct Atten Awd; CSF; Pr Tutorng Clb; UCLA.

LIN, LENNA; Galileo HS; San Francisco, CA; (3); Engl Literacy/Lifeskills Pgm.

LIN, LIN; Santa Ana Valley HS; Santa Ana, CA; (3); Art Clb; Scholastic Bowl; Stage Crew; Rptr Nwsp; DAR Awd; Hon Roll; NHS; Pres Acad Fit Awd; Pres Schlr; Sal; Engl Gold Mdl; Art.

LIN, LINDA; Garces Memorial HS; Bakersfield, CA; (2); Rep Frsh Cls; Rep Soph Cls; Sec Jr Cls; JV L Sftbl; Hon Roll; Sftbl Coachs Awd 89; Piano; Med.

LIN, LINDA J; Oxnard HS; Oxnard, CA; (1); High Hon Roll; Gldn St Exam Hgh Hnrs Alg; CSF; Berkeley; Med Rsrch.

LIN, LOUIS; Arcadia HS; Arcadia, CA; (2); Math Clb; School Play; Yrbk; Off Soph Cls; Tennis; Hon Roll; Stanford U; Dr.

LIN, LOUISA Y; Westmoor HS; Daly City, CA; (3); Church Yth Grp; Band; Rptr Soph Cls; Hon Roll; JV Song Girl.

LIN, MICHAEL; Mt Carmel HS; San Diego, CA; (4); 1/750; Q&S; Capt Scholastic Bowl; Ed Nwsp; VP Frsh Cls; Hon Roll; Ntl Merit SF; Val; Acad Dcthln; Interact Clb Pres; CSF; Bio.

LIN, MICHAEL; Wallenberg HS; San Francisco, CA; (3); Red Cross Aide; Orch; School Musical; School Play; Bsktbl; Socr; Sftbl; Swmmng; Tennis; Hon Roll; Schl Outstndng Keybrdng; Bus.

LIN, MING-CHANG; Marshall Fundamental HS; Pasadena, CA; (3); Chess Clb; Science Clb; Tennis; Prfct Atten Awd; UCLA; Elect Engrng.

LIN, NANCY; Westlake HS; Westlake Vlg, CA; (2); 1/431; Sec French Clb; Math Tm; Science Clb; Stat Swmmng; High Hon Roll; Hon Roll; Piano Cert Mrt Lvl 7; Stu Schlrshp Fndtn; CA Schlrshp Fndtn; Asian Culture Clb; Interact Rotary Clb.

LIN, NANCY D; Valencia HS; Placentia, CA; (3); Boy Scts; Cmnty Wkr; French Clb; FBLA; German Clb; Hosp Aide; Science Clb; Spanish Clb; Orch; Tennis; Acad Dcthln; Social Sci Stu Of Mnth; Pre Med.

LIN, NANCY W; Villa Park HS; Villa Park, CA; (3); Sec Church Yth Grp; Key Clb; JV Trk; Hon Roll; NHS.

LIN, PATRICIA; Glen A Wilson HS; Hacienda Hts, CA; (3); 15/428; VP Art Clb; Church Yth Grp; Office Aide; Band; Church Choir; Mrchg Band; Ed Nwsp; Socr; High Hon Roll; Hon Roll; Wind Ensemble, Sect Ldr; CSF.

LIN, PATRICK; Burlingame HS; Burlingame, CA; (3); 1/330; Church Yth Grp; Debate Tm; Math Clb; Math Tm; Service Clb; Rep Stu Cncl; JV Crs Cntry; JV Tennis; High Hon Roll; Svc Cmmssn.

LIN, ROBERT K; Glen A Wilson HS; Hacienda Hgts, CA; (3); Treas German Clb; Ed Nwsp; Intrml Mgr Golf; High Hon Roll; Hon Roll; History Day Awds 88 & 90; Dist Schlr; Eastern Los Angeles Jrnlsm Write Off 1st Pl News.

LIN, SALLIE; Corona Del Mar HS; Corona Del Mar, CA; (3); Mgr Cmnty Wkr; Drama Clb; Treas French Clb; Intnl Clb; NFL; Speech Tm; Var Tennis; JV Trk; High Hon Roll.

LIN, SANDOR T; Riverside Poly HS; Riverside, CA; (4); FBLA; Key Clb; SADD; Ftbl; Trk; Wt Lftg; Hon Roll; Prfct Atten Awd; Pres Acad Fit Awd; Santa Clara U; Elect Engrng.

LIN, SCOTT; International Studies Acad; San Francisco, CA; (3); Bausch & Lomb Sci Awd; High Hon Roll; Prfct Atten Awd; Hnr Gldn ST Exm-Alg, Geom; UC Berkeley; Comp Sci.

LIN, SEAN M; Miramonte HS; Moraga, CA; (3); 1/175; Hosp Aide; JCL; Latin Clb; Letterman Clb; Varsity Clb; Orch; Ed Yrbk; JV Bsktbl; VP Capt Tennis; Hon Roll.

LIN, SERENA P; University HS; Irvine, CA; (2); French Clb; Key Clb; Orch; School Musical; French Hon Soc; High Hon Roll; Hon Roll; Ballet; Med.

LIN, SHINE; Los Altos HS; Hacienda Hgts, CA; (2); Key Clb; Trk; Hon Roll.

LIN, STEVEN; Foothill HS; Santa Ana, CA; (3); 2/350; German Clb; Pres Key Clb; Pres Math Clb; Math Tm; Quiz Bowl; JV Crs Cntry; Var JV Trk; High Hon Roll; NEDT Awd; Acad Dcthln Team; Med.

LIN, STEVEN D; University HS; Irvine, CA; (1); Intnl Clb; Band; Mrchg Band; Orch; Variety Show; Off Soph Cls; Swmmng; Wrstlng; Cit Awd; Hon Roll; Ironman Wrestling Awd; UCI; Med.

LIN, TIM C; Cerritos HS; Cerritos, CA; (1); Key Clb; Model UN; Pacific Asn Clb; UCLA.

LIN, TING-YAO; Davis SR HS; Davis, CA; (3); 34/405; AFS; Intnl Clb; Key Clb; Office Aide; Pep Clb; Teachers Aide; Pres Acad Fit Awd; CA Hstry Day 3rd Pl 89; CSF; Badminton Team 89-90; Bus.

LIN, TOMMY; James Logan HS; Union City, CA; (3); 30/911; Computer Clb; French Clb; FBLA; German Clb; Intnl Clb; Library Aide; Math Clb; Service Clb; Spanish Clb; Teachers Aide.

LIN, TOMMY C; Alhambra HS; Alhambra, CA; (2); Trk; Doctor.

LIN, VICTOR; Arcadia HS; Arcadia, CA; (4); Math Clb; Science Clb; Service Clb; Orch; Cit Awd; High Hon Roll; NHS; Prfct Atten Awd; Pres Acad Fit Awd; UCLA; Bio.

LIN, WAI MUN; Abraham Lincoln HS; Daly City, CA; (2); Intnl Clb; Var Sftbl; CSF; Gldn St Exam Schlr; S F ST U; Bus.

LIN, WENDY; Mills HS; Burlingame, CA; (3); Math Tm; Badminton Tm; CA Schlrshp Fed; Accntng.

LIN, WENDY W; Villa Park HS; Villa Park, CA; (2); Church Yth Grp; Key Clb; Hon Roll; NHS; UC Berkeley; Bus.

LIN, XIONG; Mark Keppel HS; Los Angeles, CA; (2); Pep Clb; Cit Awd; High Hon Roll; Hon Roll; NHS; Golden ST Awd/Geometry; Golden ST Awd/Algebra II; Varsity Certificate In Cross Country; Coll; Science/Medicine.

LIN, YONG; Mt Whitney HS; Visalia, CA; (4); 1/367; Pres Chess Clb; French Clb; Latin Clb; Pres Math Clb; Pres Math Tm; Spanish Clb; Orch; Ntl Merit SF; Pres Acad Fit Awd; Val; Med Careers Club VP; VFW Speech 1st Pl; Soroptomist Yth Speech Forum; Stanford U; Bio.

LIN, YUIN; Valley HS; Santa Ana, CA; (3); Art Clb; School Play; Stage Crew; Rptr Nwsp; OCAD; Math Tutrng Pgm; Flm Clb; Art.

LINARES, JOE; William Howard Taft HS; Los Angeles, CA; (3); Chorus; Navy; Tech.

LINARES, LISA M; Saint Monica Catholic HS; Culver City, CA; (3); Treas Drama Clb; Key Clb; Latin Clb; Pep Clb; Thesps; Chorus; School Musical; School Play; Swing Chorus; Yrbk; CSF; Loyola Marymount U; Drama.

LINAYAO, ERNESTO C; James Lick HS; San Jose, CA; (1); Hon Roll; Naval Ofcr.

LINCH, LAVINIA; Clayton Valley HS; Concord, CA; (3); Church Yth Grp; Drama Clb; SADD; Varsity Clb; School Play; Off Sr Cls; Var Sprt Ed Socr; Var Sprt Ed Trk; Var Sprt Ed Art Clb; Jr Cls Prncss; 2nd Pl North Cst Sccr; St Trk Relay; SCI.

LINCOLN, DAVID; Cardinal Newman HS; Windsor, CA; (1); Church Yth Grp; Wt Lftg; Var Wrstlng; High Hon Roll; Freestyle Wrestling Olympic; Doctor.

LINCOLN, FELICIA J; Los Alamitos HS; Los Alamitos, CA; (3); Spanish Clb; Band; Mrchg Band; Pep Band; High Hon Roll; NHS; UCI; Prelaw.

LINCOLN, JENNIFER S; Enterprise HS; Redding, CA; (3); FBLA; Intnl Clb; Office Aide; Rptr Nwsp; Rep Soph Cls; Rep Stu Cncl; JV Bsktbl; Var Tennis; Hon Roll; Forgn Exch Stu Australia 89; Peer Adv Stu Cnslr; Hnrs Cls; CO ST U; Advrtsng.

LINCOLN, LALAINIA M; St Paul HS; Whittier, CA; (3); UCSB.

LINCOLN, MICHELLE L; Casa Roble Fundamental HS; Orangevale, CA; (4); 19/325; AFS; French Clb; Swmmng; High Hon Roll; Campus Life; UC Davis; Psych.

LINCOLN, SARAH L; Skyline HS; Oakland, CA; (2); Church Yth Grp; Teachers Aide; Band; Lit Mag; Bsktbl; Hon Roll; UCLA; Psych.

LINCOLN, SHANNON; Yosemite HS; Oakhurst, CA; (2); JV Bsktbl; JV Sftbl; JV Vllybl; High Hon Roll; Prfct Atten Awd; Law.

LIND, JENNIFER A; Woodland HS; Woodland, CA; (4); French Clb; SADD; Band; Swmmng; Hon Roll; Jr NHS; NHS; Sea Scouts; Amnesty International; CA Maritime Acad; Bus Admin.

LINDBERG, NICOLE H; Grace M Davis HS; Modesto, CA; (3); Art Clb; Teachers Aide; Hon Roll; Spel Olympcs; Close Up Washington DC; Engl.

LINDEBOOM, JULIE; El Toro HS; Dana Point, CA; (2); Key Clb; Swmmng; Hnr Rl; Mst Insprtnl Swmmr; CA ST U Fullerton; Commnctns.

LINDEMAN, LUKE; Winters HS; Winters, CA; (3); 3/90; Am Leg Boys St; Debate Tm; Scholastic Bowl; Ski Clb; SADD; Varsity Clb; School Play; Yrbk; Stu Cncl; JV Bsktbl; Acad Decathlon; US Air Frc Acad; Aviation.

LINDEN, BRYAN K; Covina HS; Covina, CA; (3); Boy Scts; Church Yth Grp; Letterman Clb; Band; Var L Ftbl; Var L Golf; Prfct Atten Awd; Pres Acad Fit Awd; Eagle Scout Awd.

LINDER, CAROLINE; Tulare Union HS; Tulare, CA; (2); Church Yth Grp; Band; Church Choir; Mrchg Band; Pep Band; Hon Roll.

LINDER, JODIE; Cloverdale HS; Cloverdale, CA; (3); Cmnty Wkr; FHA; Office Aide; SADD; Teachers Aide; Band; Cheerldng; Hon Roll; Santa Rosa JC; Prfrmng Arts.

LINDERMAYR, NICOLE E; Chadwick Schl; Redondo Beach, CA; (3); Cmnty Wkr; GAA; Teachers Aide; Chorus; JV Socr; Var Capt Swmmng; JV Var Vllybl; Hon Roll; Ntl Merit Ltr; Piano Cert Mrt Awd; Placed Rgnly In Natl Fr Cont; Stanford; Intl Bus.

LINDEROTH, ANNIE L; Piedmont HS; Piedmont, CA; (2); Dance Clb; SADD; Acpl Chr; JV Cheerldng; Ghldrn Of Amer Revltn; US Rowing Assn.

LINDGREN, GARY S; Portola JR/Sr HS; Portola, CA; (3); Church Yth Grp; Teachers Aide; Treas Frsh Cls; Rep Jr Cls; Ftbl; Trk; Wt Lftg; Prfct Atten Awd.

LINDGREN, JENNIFER L; Valhalla HS; El Cajon, CA; (2); 33/467; Church Yth Grp; Cmnty Wkr; SADD; Off Soph Cls; Swmmng; Wrstlng; Jazz Enzmble, Solst Awd Outstndng Prfrmce 89-90; Water Polo Grls; Spirtes Org; Pblcty Music Dept; Stanford; Sports Med.

LINDLEAF, STACIE L; Temple City HS; Temple City, CA; (2); Church Yth Grp; Dance Clb; Debate Tm; Pep Clb; School Play; VP Jr Cls; Capt Cheerldng; Trk; High Hon Roll; Nominee Attend Congressnl Yth Ldrshp Cncl; Nal Yng Ldrs Confrnc Wash DC; UCLA; Cmmnctns.

LINDLEY, BRANDON; Los Alamitos HS; Seal Beach, CA; (4); Drama Clb; German Clb; Ski Clb; Mrchg Band; Orch; Ed Yrbk; High Hon Roll.

LINDLEY, JOANNA MARIE; St Patrick - St Vincent HS; Vallejo, CA; (4); 1/141; Church Yth Grp; Teachers Aide; Ed Lit Mag; Rep Stu Cncl; High Hon Roll; NHS; Ntl Merit Ltr; Val; Coca-Cola Schlrs Prgm Natl Semifnlst; Pres Campus Mnstry; Dominican Coll; Math.

LINDNER, ROSALINDA L; Vallejo SR HS; Vallejo, CA; (3); Art Clb; Church Yth Grp; French Clb; SADD; Church Choir; Lit Mag; Hon Roll; Pres Acad Fit Awd; 3rd Pl Dist Wide Art Cntst; Artist Of Mnth 88-89; Art.

LINDQUIST, JOSHUA; Victor Valley Christian HS; Barstow, CA; (3); Yrbk; High Hon Roll.

LINDQUIST, LARRY A; Poway HS; Poway, CA; (2); Math Clb; Ski Clb; Intrml Bsbl; Var Trk; High Hon Roll; Hon Roll; Tnns; UCLA; Med.

LINDSAY, CHRIS; Hesperia HS; Hesperia, CA; (2); Boy Scts; French Clb; FFA; Science Clb; Wrstlng; Hon Roll; Sci Fair Awd; High Ltr Acad Achvt; Cal Poly Pamona; Vet.

LINDSAY, HEATHER J; Burroughs HS; Ridgecrest, CA; (3); 32/432; Pep Clb; Ski Clb; Teachers Aide; Ed Nwsp; Sec Treas Soph Cls; Pres Sr Cls; Rep Stu Cncl; JV Cheerldng; Powder Puff Ftbl; Co-Capt Var Socr; Level 8 Cmptn Gymnast; Tap; Ballet; Jazz Dancer; Mtn Biking; Interested In Envir Imprvmt; U CA; Bus.

LINDSAY, JON R; Grossmont HS; La Mesa, CA; (3); 15/385; Church Yth Grp; Scholastic Bowl; Chorus; School Musical; Ed Nwsp; Rptr Yrbk; Ed Lit Mag; Off Jr Cls; Stu Cncl; Hon Roll; Aerosp Engrng.

LINDSAY, KRISTA; Encinal HS; Alameda, CA; (4); 29/210; Pep Clb; Ski Clb; Sec Frsh Cls; VP Jr Cls; Stu Cncl; Var Capt Cheerldng; Var Capt Socr; Var Trk; High Hon Roll; NHS; WA ST U; Bus.

LINDSAY, LIZ A; Louisville HS; Pacific Palisades, CA; (3); Church Yth Grp; FHA; GAA; Ski Clb; SADD; Varsity Clb; Sec Stu Cncl; JV Trk; Var Vllybl; DAR Awd; Close-Up; Grls Athl Assoc-Historian; Yth Grp On Mission To Mexico.

LINDSAY, TERRI J; Hueneme HS; Oxnard, CA; (3); Library Aide; Teachers Aide; Stu Cncl; Socr; Sftbl; Hon Roll; Prfct Atten Awd; Mock Trial; BYU; Law.

LINDSEY, CHRISTY R; Carson HS; Carson, CA; (4); Church Yth Grp; Teachers Aide; Band; Chorus; Mrchg Band; Hon Roll; Dental Tech.

LINDSEY, DEREK P; Burroughs HS; Ridgecrest, CA; (3); Spanish Clb; Var Bsktbl; JV Crs Cntry; Var Trk; High Hon Roll; Pres Acad Fit Awd; Golden St Exam Geom High Hnrs; CSF.

LINDSEY, EDWARD S; St Bernard HS; Los Angeles, CA; (3); Church Yth Grp; Cmnty Wkr; JV Bsbl; JV Ftbl; L Vllybl; Cit Awd; Law Enforcement Explorer LAPD; Jr Knight Of St Peter Claver; Altar Boy St Malachs Catholic Church; CA ST U Dominguez Hls; Law.

LINDSEY, JENNIFER; Fred C Beyer HS; Modesto, CA; (4); 51/500; Am Leg Aux Girls St; Church Yth Grp; Cmnty Wkr; SADD; Teachers Aide; Acpl Chr; Chorus; Church Choir; School Musical; Swing Chorus; Peer Cnslng; Madrigal Sngrs; CSF; Brigham Young U; Educ.

LINDSEY, JOANN M; Seaside HS; Ft Ord, CA; (2); Band; Mrchg Band; Orch; Rep Stu Cncl; Mgr(s); Score Keeper; Var Swmmng; CCS Hnr Band; Friday Night Live Sober & Drug Free; Outstndng Cntrbtn Band; Accntng.

LINDSEY, LYNN; Tulelake HS; Tulelake, CA; (2); Office Aide; Chorus; Sec Frsh Cls; JV Capt Bsktbl; JV Cheerldng; Capt Vllybl; High Hon Roll; Hon Roll; Law.

LINDSEY, ROBIN R; Marina HS; Trabuco Canyon, CA; (4); 156/472; Letterman Clb; Spanish Clb; Teachers Aide; Varsity Clb; Var Bsbl; Wt Lftg; High Hon Roll; Hon Roll; Bsbl Won CIF St Champ; MVP Bsbl Tm; All Sunset Leag; Rancho Santiago; Bus.

LINDSEY, SHANNON; Beyer HS; Modesto, CA; (1); Debate Tm; German Clb; Girl Scts; Ski Clb; SADD; Rep Frsh Cls; Capt Cheerldng; Var L Swmmng; Hon Roll; Church Acts; Stanford; Doctor.

LINDSLEY, KRISTI; Rio Lindo Adventist Acad; Heddsburg, CA; (2); Church Yth Grp; Drama Clb; Chorus; School Play; Phtg Yrbk; VP Stu Cncl; Capt Bsktbl; Capt Vllybl; High Hon Roll; Hstry.

LINDSTRAND, CHRISTINE L; North Salinas HS; Salinas, CA; (3); Am Leg Aux Girls St; French Clb; SADD; Teachers Aide; Off Jr Cls; JV Fld Hcky; Var Swmmng; Trk; Cit Awd; High Hon Roll; Yth-Yth Drug Free Soc; Rotary Clb Top 100 Stu Awd; MBL Field Hcky Champ 89; Salinas Vly Aquatrics Clb; UNLV; Pysch.

LINDSTROM, BRETT C; Orange Glen HS; Escondido, CA; (1); 81/635; Drama Clb; School Play; Var Socr; Trk; Hon Roll; VA St Cup Soccer Champ 85-86; CA St Cup Soccer Champ 88; Intl Soccer Boys Games Tokoyo Japan 88; Prof Athlete.

LINDSTROM, CHRIS; Lincoln HS; Stockton, CA; (4); 8/513; Spanish Clb; Capt Crs Cntry; Trk; Cit Awd; High Hon Roll; Masonic Awd; Ntl Merit Ltr; Val; Bio Stu Of Yr 88-89; Tutrng Math And Span; Bank Of Am Achvt Awd; U CA Davis; Mech Engrng.

LINDSTROM, KIMBERLY T; Foothill HS; Tustin, CA; (3); Church Yth Grp; Letterman Clb; SADD; Varsity Clb; Acpl Chr; Chorus; Church Choir; Orch; School Musical; Swmmng; Sthrn CA Hnr Choir/All St Hnr Choir; Awd Excllnce 89 & 90 Vocal Music; Toured W/Musical Theatre Grp; Music.

LINENBERGER, MIKE; Mt View HS; Burney, CA; (3); Cmnty Wkr; Teachers Aide; Hon Roll; Wrkd For Barney Fire Dept 88; Srkd For Schl 89; Navy.

LINFOOT, ANDY J; Paraclete HS; Lancaster, CA; (3); 24/111; Debate Tm; Library Aide; Scholastic Bowl; High Hon Roll; Hon Roll; Engrng.

LING, ANNA; Independence HS; San Jose, CA; (3); 28/1078; Cmnty Wkr; German Clb; Ed Yrbk; Off Frsh Cls; Treas Soph Cls; VP Jr Cls; High Hon Roll; Hon Roll; NHS; Hnrs Recogntn For Golden St Exam For Alg; Stanford U; Pol Sci.

LING, LISA J; Del Campo HS; Carmichael, CA; (3); Debate Tm; FBLA; Q&S; Speech Tm; Rptr Nwsp; Stu Cncl; NHS; Aud/Vis; Bus Profs of Am; Church Yth Grp; KXTV TV Show Host Scratch; KXTV Intrnshp; 1st Pl Sacto Cnty Law Related Debate; UCLA; Natl Brdcstng.

LING, MILLIE; Galileo HS; San Francisco, CA; (2); Church Yth Grp; Pep Clb; Spanish Clb; Teachers Aide; Hon Roll; Span Club Officer; Slvr Seal Soc Mem; Stu Body Secy & Treas St Marys Chinese Sch 88-90; UCLA; Fshn Dsgn.

LING, QI-LING; Theodore Roosevelt HS; Los Angeles, CA; (3); Math Clb; Hon Roll; Stu Month 89; Outstndg Achvt Awd Chem; AP Clb; CSF.

LING, SANDRA S; Mtn View HS; Mountain View, CA; (4); Cmnty Wkr; French Clb; Intnl Clb; Scholastic Bowl; Service Clb; Spanish Clb; Orch; School Musical; UC San Diego; Sociology.

LING, TAMARA J; George Washington HS; San Francisco, CA; (3); Cmnty Wkr; Office Aide; Chorus; Church Choir; Off Jr Cls; Bsbl; Bsktbl; Trk; Cit Awd; Hon Roll; Coll Of Marin; Langs.

LINGAFELTER, KERRIE A; Clayton Valley HS; Zionsville, IN; (2); Church Yth Grp; Dance Clb; Drama Clb; GAA; Letterman Clb; SADD; Teachers Aide; Variety Show; Lit Mag; L Var Trk; CA All ST Gymnstcs Team 88; City Of Clayton Outstndng Teenager Awd; CSF; UC Irvine; Art/Dance.

LINGENFELTER, STEVEN M; Oak Ridge HS; Cameron Park, CA; (1); Hon Roll.

LINGLE, KRISTEN S; Valley Christian HS; Dublin, CA; (2); Church Yth Grp; Hist Jr Cls; Hon Roll.

LINGO, JULIE; Turlock HS; Turlock, CA; (2); 21/570; High Hon Roll; Hon Roll; Guitar Club; Biological Sci Awd; Bus.

LINGUA, ANDREW D; Los Angeles Lutheran HS; Glendale, CA; (3); Ski Clb; Acpl Chr; Band; Chorus; Jazz Band; Rep Frsh Cls; Var L Bsbl; Stat Bsktbl; Var L Ftbl; High Hon Roll; CA Schlrshp Fed.

LINH, RICKY H; El Cajon Valley HS; El Cajon, CA; (4); 10/278; Vllybl; Wt Lftg; Hon Roll; Pres Acad Fit Awd; CSF; San Diego ST U; Elec Engr.

LINHART, GRANT W; Notre Dame HS; Murrieta, CA; (1); 100/165; ROTC; School Musical; JV Ftbl; Outstndg Male Stu Alg; US Naval Acad; ROTC.

LININGER, STACIE M; Saugus HS; Saugus, CA; (3); Church Yth Grp; Variety Show; Sftbl; Hon Roll; Engrng.

LINK, CORY M; North Hollywood HS; North Hollywood, CA; (2); Temple Yth Grp; VP Stu Cncl; Hon Roll; Awd Acad Ecllnce.

LINLEY, CHARMAINE; North County Christian HS; Atascadero, CA; (3); School Play; Phtg Nwsp; Rptr Yrbk; Stu Cncl; Sftbl; Vllybl; Hon Roll; Church Yth Grp; Debate Tm; Drama Clb; Mst Insprtnl Vlybl 2 Yrs, Sftbl 1 Yr; CA Baptist Coll; Schl Admin.

LINN III, ELIAS; Central Union HS; El Centro, CA; (3); Var Bsktbl.

LINN, MARC; Riverbank HS; Oakdale, CA; (2); 12/105; Church Yth Grp; FCA; Teachers Aide; Frsh Cls; Soph Cls; VP Bsbl; VP Ftbl; VP Wt Lftg; VP Wrstlng; Hon Roll; Church Youth Group Musicals; 2 Yr Coach,Powder Pufffftbl; Sacramento St; Sports Medicine.

LINNELL, JENNIFER S; Temple City HS; Temple City, CA; (3); Drama Clb; Office Aide; Teachers Aide; Chorus; School Play; Stage Crew; Var Bsktbl; Hon Roll; Johnson Cnty CC; Chld Abs.

LINNERT, ALI; Mater Dei HS; Anaheim, CA; (4); 78/527; Church Yth Grp; Cmnty Wkr; Drama Clb; Office Aide; School Play; Score Keeper; Trk; Hon Roll; NHS; Secy Orange Cst Plmbg; Tnns; Racqtbl Clb; Boise ST U; Nurse.

LINNES, PHYLLIS L; Hanford HS; Hanford, CA; (2); Church Yth Grp; Church Choir; Flag Corp; Stat Bsktbl; Hon Roll; ID Unit-Co Capt; Jrnlsm.

LINSAO, DEBBIE; Monterey HS; Seaside, CA; (3); Teachers Aide; Var Capt Cheerldng; Powder Puff Ftbl; Natural Hlprs Clb; Sci Fair; U Of CA Santa Cruz Early Outrch Prtnrshp Pgm.

LINSDAU, AARON; Southwest HS; San Ysidro, CA; (2); Boy Scts; Science Clb; Intrml Vllybl; Pres Acad Fit Awd; Excllnc-Mth ST Of CA 89; Mth.

LINSON, ADAM D; Irvine HS; Irvine, CA; (1); Math Tm; Temple Yth Grp; Jazz Band; Mrchg Band; Orch; UCB; Music.

LINSTAD, MICHELLE L; Vintage HS; Napa, CA; (3); Girl Scts; Teachers Aide; Karate 2nd Deg Brwn Blt; Author.

LINSTAD, SHANNON; Pinole Valley HS; Pinole, CA; (1); Church Yth Grp; Gym; Hon Roll; St Mary's Coll; Lawyer.

LINTAG, GERMAINE; St Genevieve HS; Sun Valley, CA; (2); Hon Roll; Prfct Atten Awd; Latin Awd Magna Cum Laude; Medcl.

LINTHICUM, JAMES W; Yucaipa HS; Yucaipa, CA; (2); Boy Scts; JV Crs Cntry; JV Trk; High Hon Roll; Prfct Atten Awd; Golden St Exam Awd.

LIO, ALBERTO A; Calexico HS; Calexico, CA; (3); Treas Intnl Clb; Math Tm; JV Tennis; Hon Roll; Engr.

LIO, FRANCISCO M; Calexico HS; Calexico, CA; (1); Drama Clb; FBLA; Key Clb; Math Tm; School Play; Wt Lftg; Hon Roll; San Diego Sci Fair Cmptn 3rd Pl Physics.

LIONETTI, SARAH L; Louisville HS; Tarzana, CA; (1); Church Yth Grp; School Musical; Hon Roll; CSF.

LIOU, CINDY; Baldwin Park HS; Baldwin Park, CA; (3); Church Yth Grp; FBLA; Math Clb; Spanish Clb; Lit Mag; Stu Cncl; Tennis; Hon Roll; Social Work.

LIOU, JADDA; Richmond HS; San Pablo, CA; (3); Treas Church Yth Grp; FCA; Intnl Clb; Teachers Aide; Church Choir; Sec Jr Cls; Sec Sr Cls; Tennis; Gov Hon Prg Awd; Hon Roll; UC Davis; Business Admin.

LIOU, JENNIFER H C; Monterey HS; Pebble Beach, CA; (2); Sec German Clb; Sec Intnl Clb; Model UN; Band; Mrchg Band; Orch; JV Capt Fld Hcky; Trk; High Hon Roll; German Natl Soc.

LIOU, JOE JIA-KAE; Thousand Oaks HS; Thousand Oaks, CA; (3); Church Yth Grp; Intnl Clb; Math Clb; Math Tm; JV Bsbl; Hon Roll; Glnd St Geom Exam High Hnrs 89; CSF 89-90; Bsbl Sr Al Stars Sthrn CA Chmpns 89; Furman U; Bus Admin.

LIOU, SHIN-JYE; Baldwin Park HS; Baldwin Park, CA; (3); FBLA; Math Clb; Spanish Clb; Lit Mag; Stu Cncl; JV Tennis; High Hon Roll.

LIPMAN, MELISSA G; A A Stagg HS; Stockton, CA; (3); Cmnty Wkr; 4-H; Key Clb; Band; Mrchg Band; Pep Band; 4-H Awd; High Hon Roll; Bnd Lbrn; Cnflct Mgmt Team; U C Davis Treas; Vlntr Hlth Faire; Yth Govt For Camp Ryl & Grls St; San Francisco ST; Med.

LIPPY, BROOKE; East Bakersfield HS; Bakersfield, CA; (3); 16/423; Church Yth Grp; Drama Clb; Girl Scts; Chorus; School Musical; Variety Show; Hon Roll; Hstry Club; CSF; Northern AZ U; Music.

LIPSIT, KYLENE; Armijo HS; Fairfield, CA; (2); ROTC; Chorus; Color Guard; Mrchg Band; Pep Band; Cheerldng; Sacramento ST; Probation.

LIQUETE, ALAN; South San Francisco HS; South San Francis, CA; (2); Computer Clb; Math Clb; Science Clb; Aeronautcl Engrng.

LIQUEZ, VERONICA; Sierra Vista HS; Baldwin Park, CA; (3); Drill Tm; Variety Show; JV Var Cheerldng; Stat Wrstlng; Hon Roll; Prfct Atten Awd; Mt Sac; Pediatric Nrs.

LIQUIGAN, ANNA MAYBELLE S; John H Francis Polytechnic HS; N Hollywood, CA; (4); Dance Clb; Spanish Clb; Stu Cncl; Hon Roll; CSF Sealbearer; CA ST Los Angeles; Nrsng.

LIRA, ARLENE; Garfield HS; Los Angeles, CA; (4); School Play; Gym; Cit Awd; Hon Roll; Prfct Atten Awd; Most Imprvd In Algbra II; Cert Of Schlstc Achvmnt; Cert F/Outstndng Achvmnt In Englsh; Theatre Arts.

LIRA, GLORIA A; Saddleback HS; Santa Ana, CA; (3); Spanish Clb; Acad Ltr 88-89; Math-Engrng Clb; MECHA Clb; CA ST U Fullerton; Acctng.

LISIECKI, PHILIP A; University HS; Irvine, CA; (2); Math Tm; Spanish Clb; Swmmng; Pres Acad Fit Awd; Comp Sci.

LISLE, DEBORAH M; Whittier Christian HS; Whittier, CA; (3); 2/188; Church Yth Grp; Q&S; Capt Drill Tm; School Play; Nwsp; Drill Team 87-88,Ldr,Capt; CSF88-90; I Dare You Ldrshp Awd 89-90.

LIST, MANDIE J; Lowell HS; San Francisco, CA; (2); NFL; Speech Tm; Teachers Aide; Pres Acad Fit Awd; Keremesse Worker; Amer Heart Asso Jump-O-Thon; IN U; Sports Broadcaster.

LIST, SUSAN E; Etiwanda HS; Etiwanda, CA; (2); 77/782; Church Yth Grp; French Clb; Library Aide; Ed Yrbk; Hon Roll; Journ.

LISTER, BRYANT S; Corona HS; Corona, CA; (4); 21/540; Letterman Clb; SADD; Stu Cncl; Var Crs Cntry; High Hon Roll; Kiwanis Awd; Lion Awd; Pres Acad Fit Awd; Sorptmst Yth Ctznshp Awd; UCR; Biomed.

LISTON, JENNIFER M; Mission San Jose HS; Fremont, CA; (3); 68/435; Cmnty Wkr; Science Clb; Service Clb; Teachers Aide; Yrbk; Hon Roll; CA Schlrshp Fndtn; Hnrs Awd Golden St Exam Alg Geom; Bus.

LITERATUS, BELINDA R; Fontana HS; Fontana, CA; (3); Art Clb; Church Yth Grp; Cit Awd; High Hon Roll; Hon Roll; Prfct Atten Awd; Pres Acad Fit Awd; Val; Vrsty Badminton; CSF; UCLA.

LITROWNIK, ALLISON B; Grossmont HS; La Mesa, CA; (3); 39/385; Cmnty Wkr; French Clb; Lit Mag; Var Gym; Hon Roll.

LITT, NATASHA E; Lowell HS; San Francisco, CA; (3); Hosp Aide; Temple Yth Grp; Band; Stage Crew; Intrml Socr; Jnr Statesmn America Chptr VP; Hstry.

LITTFIN, JENNIFER L; Serra HS; San Diego, CA; (2); Church Yth Grp; Cmnty Wkr; JV Cheerldng; Cit Awd; Hon Roll; Opt Clb Awd; UCSB.

LITTLE, ANNALISA E; Bishop Montgomery HS; San Pedro, CA; (3); Sec Debate Tm; Girl Scts; Key Clb; NFL; Sec Speech Tm; Band; Chorus; School Musical; Stage Crew; JV L Crs Cntry; Envrnmntl Awrnss Clb Co-Fndr & Co-Pres.

LITTLE, BETHANY; Gridley HS; Gridley, CA; (4); 5/108; Drama Clb; Sec FHA; Sec Spanish Clb; School Musical; School Play; Ed Nwsp; Sec Sr Cls; Pom Pon; Tennis; High Hon Roll; Brigham Young U; Educ.

LITTLE, BRANDEN J; John F Kennedy HS; Sacramento, CA; (2); Art Clb; Aud/Vis; Church Yth Grp; German Clb; Var Crs Cntry; Stat Diving; Score Keeper; Stat Swmmng; Wt Lftg; Naval Acad Annapolis; Bus.

LITTLE, DAVID; Merced HS; Merced, CA; (3); Church Yth Grp; FCA; Church Choir; School Play; Var L Ftbl; Var L Socr; Var L Trk; Wt Lftg; Embry-Riddle Aeronautical U.

LITTLE, ERIC B; Foothill SR HS; Sacramento, CA; (2); German Clb; Yrbk; Hon Roll; U Of TN.

LITTLE, F SHANON; Beaumont HS; Calimesa, CA; (3); Sec Jr Cls; Sec Stu Cncl; JV Var Bsktbl; Var Cheerldng; JR Hnr Escort; Bus.

LITTLE, GREGORY H; Mojave HS; Mojave, CA; (1); JV Bsbl; Ftbl; Hon Roll.

LITTLE, JESSICA N; College Park HS; Pleasant Hill, CA; (1); Chorus; Variety Show; Rptr Phtg Nwsp; Lit Mag; JV Swmmng; SSU; Music.

LITTLE, KORI D; Corona SR HS; Corona, CA; (2); Church Yth Grp; GAA; Yrbk; Rep Stu Cncl; Var Bsktbl; Var Vllybl; ASB Athltc Comssnr; Ltrmn Clb Schlr Athl Awd; Brigham Young U.

LITTLE, LALAYNIA M; Princeton HS; Butte City, CA; (3); Sec FFA; Letterman Clb; Varsity Clb; Band; Sec Frsh Cls; Sec Soph Cls; Sec Jr Cls; Var Capt Bsktbl; Var Capt Sftbl; Var Capt Vllybl; Psych.

LITTLE, LISA; Louisville HS; Canoga Park, CA; (2); Church Yth Grp; Drama Clb; Hosp Aide; Nwsp; Yrbk; CPA.

LITTLE, MEGAN; Grossmont HS; El Cajon, CA; (3); 25/420; SADD; Teachers Aide; Var Socr; JV Sftbl; JV Tennis; Hon Roll; Amer Coll Musicians NPPA Dist; Jobs Dghtrs; Accptd UCSD Hnrs Early Admssn Prgm; Med.

LITTLE, SETH A; Antelope Valley HS; Lancaster, CA; (3); Church Yth Grp; Quiz Bowl; JV Trk; Hon Roll; Student Wk Spnsh, Geometry; Rep Frgn Langs; Frgn Lang.

LITTLE, STACIE A; Thousand Oaks HS; Westlake, CA; (2); Church Yth Grp; Girl Scts; Teachers Aide; Stage Crew; Hon Roll; UCSB; Bus.

LITTLE, TONJA N; Mesa Verde HS; Citrus Heights, CA; (2); Church Yth Grp; FTA; Teachers Aide; Orch; Hon Roll; Church Sftbl Tm.

LITTLEJOHN, TY RAESHA; Oakland Tech; Oakland, CA; (4); Church Yth Grp; Cmnty Wkr; Math Clb; Math Tm; Office Aide; ROTC; Church Choir; Drill Tm; Drm Mjr(t); Stu Cncl; MESA Pres 89-90; CA ST Poly U Pmna; Ptrlm Engr.

LITTLEJOHN, TYRAESHA D; Oakland Technical HS; Oakland, CA, (4); Church Yth Grp; Math Clb; Math Tm; Office Aide; ROTC; Church Choir; Drill Tm; Drm Mjr(t); Stu Cncl; Var L Trk; MESA Pgm Pres 89-90; Most Outstndng Stu Awd; Promise Awd; CA ST Poly U Pomona; Engrng.

LITTLEJOHNS, PENELOPE A; Dana Hills HS; San Juan Capistra, CA; (2); Church Yth Grp; Cmnty Wkr; Spanish Clb; Pres Frsh Cls; Treas Soph Cls; Stu Cncl; Trk; Hon Roll; Pres Acad Fit Awd; UCSD; Med.

LITTLEPAGE, EVELYN L; Vanden HS; Vacaville, CA; (1); 16/205; JV Bsktbl; JV Sftbl; JV Wt Lftg; High Hon Roll; Harvard Law Schl; Bus Law.

LITTLETON, RONDA SHALON; Eden Christian Acad; Oakland, CA; (2); Church Yth Grp; Computer Clb; Debate Tm; English Clb; Hosp Aide; Office Aide; Teachers Aide; Temple Yth Grp; VP Soph Cls; Sec Stu Cncl.

LITTLEWOOD, OLIVIA; Rim Of The World HS; Lake Arrowhead, CA; (2); 33/355; Church Yth Grp; Drama Clb; Stu Cncl; Var L Trk; Hon Roll.

LITTRELL, JENNIFER N; Del Oro HS; Loomis, CA; (2); 70/300; Office Aide; SADD; Teachers Aide; JV Crs Cntry; Var Powder Puff Ftbl; Var Sftbl; Hon Roll; UC Davis; Accntng.

LITZ, TINA; Poway HS; Poway, CA; (3); Intnl Clb; SADD; Band; Mrchg Band; Sftbl; NHS; Prfct Atten Awd; Hnry Mntn Del Mar Art Fair; Band; Med Lab Tech.

LIU, ALAN BARRY; Miramonte HS; Orinda, CA; (4); 3/278; Am Leg Aux Girls St; Science Clb; Spanish Clb; Yrbk; VP Frsh Cls; Treas Jr Cls; Rep Sr Cls; Var L Swmmng; Hon Roll; Lion Awd; MIT.

LIU, AMY; Berkeley HS; Berkeley, CA; (2); Art Clb; Church Yth Grp; ASU Clb; UC Berkeley; Math.

LIU, BETTY; Westminster HS; Westminster, CA; (2); Spanish Clb; CA Schlrshp Fed & Acad Boost Clb; HS Royal Banquet Nominee; Sign Lang Clb; UCLA; Bus.

LIU, CATHY; Arcadia HS; Arcadia, CA; (3); 106/639; Church Yth Grp; French Clb; Hosp Aide; Math Clb; Teachers Aide; High Hon Roll; Hon Roll; NHS; Prfct Atten Awd; CSF; U C-Santa Barbara; Ec.

LIU, CHIA; Schurr HS; Montery Park, CA; (1); Tennis; Trk; Hon Roll; Prfct Atten Awd; CA Schlrshp Fdrtn; CSF Frshmn Tutor; UCLA; Bus Mgmt.

LIU, CHIA-MIN; Rosemead HS; Rosemead, CA; (4); 1/390; Pres Debate Tm; FBLA; Pres Key Clb; Math Clb; Office Aide; Teachers Aide; Bsktbl; JV Var Trk; Pres Acad Fit Awd; Val; Pres Acad Dcthln; Gld Sl Wnnr CSF; U Of CA-BERKELEY; Engrng.

LIU, CINDY; American HS; Fremont, CA; (3); 8/310; Pres Church Yth Grp; French Clb; Spanish Clb; Church Choir; Ed Nwsp; Var Tennis; Hon Roll; Vrsty Badminton; Natl Piano Playing Audistions; Academic Block; Music.

LIU, CRAIG C; Palos Verdes HS; Rancho Palos Verd, CA; (4); 100/400; Church Yth Grp; Cmnty Wkr; Model UN; Service Clb; Spanish Clb; SADD; Nwsp; Var Trk; Lion Awd; S Bay Chinese Schl Pres; Cigna Hlthplan Lab Aide; UCSD; Bio.

LIU, DAVID; Edison HS; Huntington Bch, CA; (2); Key Clb; Quiz Bowl; JV Tennis; High Hon Roll; Soph Acdmc Decath Team Capt; Acdmc Comptn Lit Medalist; Cert UCI Prgm; JV Tnns Achvt Awd; Johns Hopkins; Med.

LIU, DAVID; Whitney HS; Cerritos, CA; (2); 17/190; JA; Orch; Swmmng; High Hon Roll; CJSF; Golden St Exam Awd; Medcl.

LIU, DAVID R; Poly HS; Riverside, CA; (4); 1/397; Latin Clb; Capt Quiz Bowl; Orch; Nwsp; Lit Mag; Bausch & Lomb Sci Awd; Cit Awd; High Hon Roll; NHS; Ntl Merit SF; Natl Merit Scholar Fnlst 90; London Intl Yth Sci Fortnight US Rep; Westinghouse Sci Tlnt Srch Wnnr 90; Harvard U; Physics.

LIU, DEANN; Fremont HS; Sunnyvale, CA; (3); 28/440; Debate Tm; DECA; NFL; Q&S; Service Clb; Drill Tm; Ed Nwsp; Sec Jr Cls; Pres Sr Cls; Var Bsktbl; Natl Hnr Soc; CSF; Sch Site Cncl; UC San Diego; Bus Mgmt.

LIU, DIANE K; Fremont HS; Sunnyvale, CA; (2); Church Yth Grp; Cmnty Wkr; Debate Tm; NFL; Service Clb; Speech Tm; VP Frsh Cls; Pres Soph Cls; JV Socr; JV Tennis; CSF; CA Poly; Arch.

LIU, DONG J; Skyline HS; Oakland, CA; (2); Math Clb; Acctng.

LIU, EDMOND C; Burbank HS; Burbank, CA; (3); JV Tennis; JV Trk; Hon Roll; Prfct Atten Awd; Pres Acad Fit Awd; Acad Decathlon 89-90; CSF 88-90.

LIU, EDMOND L; Lowell HS; San Francisco, CA; (2); Science Clb; Trk; Hon Roll; WA U; Sci.

LIU, EMILY; Temple City HS; San Gabriel, CA; (2); Off Church Yth Grp; Key Clb; SADD; Ed Nwsp; Stu Cncl; Cheerldng; Crs Cntry; Var Trk; High Hon Roll; NHS; CSF; Slctd Cngrssnl Schlr Rprsntng CA Natl Yng Ldrs Cnfrnc; Psych.

LIU, ERIC C; St Michaels Prep; Orange, CA; (2); Service Clb; Rptr Nwsp; Hon Roll; Jr NHS; Orange Cnty Acad Decthln; Harvard; Law.

LIU, EUGENIA L; Villa Park HS; Orange, CA; (2); Church Yth Grp; French Clb; Key Clb; Mgr(s); Tennis; High Hon Roll; NHS; CSF; Stnaford; Bus.

LIU, GLENDY; University HS; Irvine, CA; (4); 50/492; Church Yth Grp; Intnl Clb; Key Clb; VP Spanish Clb; Teachers Aide; Church Choir; Ed Nwsp; Var Trk; UC San Diego; Bio.

LIU, GRACE; Villa Park HS; Orange, CA; (2); Church Yth Grp; Intnl Clb; Latin Clb; Science Clb; Spanish Clb; Rptr Yrbk; High Hon Roll; NHS; Sci Olympd; Mock Trl; Med.

LIU, HELEN; San Dimas HS; Walnut, CA; (4); 1/270; Drama Clb; English Clb; GAA; Science Clb; SADD; Rep Frsh Cls; Var Capt Tennis; High Hon Roll; Masonic Awd; Ntl Merit Ltr; CSF Sec, Hstrn, VP; Interact Rep, Treas; Bank Of Amer Achvt Awd, Liberal Arts; UC Berkeley; Envrnmntl Sci.

LIU, HOWARD HO-CHI; George Washington HS; San Francisco, CA; (2); High Hon Roll; U Of CA; Engr.

LIU, I-CHUAN; Torrey Pines HS; Solana Beach, CA; (2); JV Bsbl; Prfct Atten Awd; 1st Del Mar Fair Mech Drftng Cont.

LIU, JENNY; San Ramon Valley HS; Danville, CA; (4); 6/397; Church Yth Grp; Cmnty Wkr; Hosp Aide; Key Clb; Math Tm; Model UN; Mu Alpha Theta; Science Clb; SADD; JV Swmmng; CSF; Acad Lttr; Chinese Schl; Cornell; Med.

LIU, JEREMY CHI-MING; Berkeley HS; Berkeley, CA; (4); Art Clb; Latin Clb; Science Clb; Ed Yrbk; Treas Soph Cls; NHS; Ntl Merit SF; Stu Dir Brd Educ; Fencing Tm; Envrnmntl Clb, Pgm Dir; Tufts U; Envrnmntl Stds.

LIU, JO JO C; Walnut HS; Diamond, CA; (2); 1/500; Debate Tm; Key Clb; Spanish Clb; Ed Yrbk; Rep Frsh Cls; Off Soph Cls; JV Crs Cntry; Var L Trk; High Hon Roll; Pres Acad Fit Awd; Jr Statesmen Of Amer; Crossfire; Ed.

LIU, JOHN; Granada Hills HS; Los Angeles, CA; (2); Arch.

LIU, JOYCE F; Lowell HS; San Francisco, CA; (3); NFL; Service Clb; Pres SADD; Chorus; Lit Mag; Sec Frsh Cls; Stat Bsktbl; Vllybl; Ntl Merit Ltr; Pres Acad Fit Awd; CSF; Shield & Scroll Hon Soc; Bd Of Schl & Cmmnty Svcs; Psych.

LIU, KATE; West Torrance HS; Torrance, CA; (2); Pep Clb; Chorus; School Musical; JV Cheerldng; JV Pom Pon; Hon Roll; Bus.

LIU, KENT XUAN J; Oakland HS; Oakland, CA; (2); Cmnty Wkr; Computer Clb; Math Clb; Science Clb; Ski Clb; Spanish Clb; Tennis; UCLA; Comm.

LIU, KUOVONNE A; Cajon HS; San Bernardino, CA; (3); 5/473; AFS; Chess Clb; Scholastic Bowl; Speech Tm; High Hon Roll; NHS; Ntl Merit Ltr; Voice Dem Awd; Acad Dcthln; Mock Trial.

LIU, LIANG Q; George Washington HS; San Francisco, CA; (2); 15/35; Cmnty Wkr; Computer Clb; Office Aide; Nwsp; Off Soph Cls; Bsktbl; Trk; Vllybl; Hon Roll; Prfct Atten Awd; Typist U S Dept Of Labor Smmr Yth Prog; PG&E Worker This Smmer Schl Yr; San Francisco City Coll.

LIU, LILLIAN A; Mills HS; Burlingame, CA; (2); Debate Tm; French Clb; Rptr Nwsp; Rep Frsh Cls; Rep Soph Cls; Mgr(s); JV Tennis; DAR Awd; High Hon Roll; Hon Roll; Peer Hlpng Prog:Impact Team.

LIU, LU CHENG; Mission San Jose HS; Fremont, CA; (4); Chess Clb; Computer Clb; Science Clb; Hon Roll; UC Santa Cruz; Cmptr Engrng.

LIU, LU-CHENG; Mission San Jose HS; Fremont, CA; (4); Chess Clb; Computer Clb; Science Clb; CSF; UC Santa Cruz; Comp Engrng.

LIU, LUIS F; John A Rowland HS; Rowland Heights, CA; (2); 1/600; Spanish Clb; Wrstlng; High Hon Roll; Prfct Atten Awd; MA Inst Of Tech; Aerontcl Engr.

LIU, MANH A; Rosemead HS; Rosemead, CA; (2); Hon Roll; Prfct Atten Awd; Elctrnc Engr.

LIU, MARY; South Pasadena HS; S Pasadena, CA; (3); Debate Tm; Drama Clb; Speech Tm; SADD; Teachers Aide; Thesps; Chorus; Stage Crew; High Hon Roll; Hon Roll; Salute Exc Acad Awd; U C Santa Barbara; Bus.

LIU, MICHELLE S; University HS; Irvine, CA; (4); 5/500; Sec Debate Tm; Math Tm; NFL; Speech Tm; Teachers Aide; Mrchg Band; JV Var Bsktbl; High Hon Roll; Ntl Merit SF; Sal; Newcomers Clb Secy; Amnesty Intl.

LIU, NANCY Y; Oakland HS; Oakland, CA; (3); CA ST U Hayward; Bus Acctng.

LIU, NUOMING; Phillip & Sala Burton Acad HS; San Francisco, CA; (2); Red Cross Aide; High Hon Roll; Prfct Atten Awd; Pres Acad Fit Awd.

LIU, PAROUSIA; Van Nuys HS; Los Angeles, CA; (4); 33/534; Teachers Aide; Ed Nwsp; Ntl Merit SF; Pres Acad Fit Awd; Lausd Comp Sci Comptn 2nd Pl.

LIU, PAUL; Oakland HS; Oakland, CA; (4); Chess Clb; Cmnty Wkr; Computer Clb; French Clb; Library Aide; Science Clb; SADD; Stage Crew; Stu Cncl; Tennis; Preston Bi-Lingual Schlrshp 90; Gareth Fong Acadmc Tnns Schlrshp 90; UC Los Angeles; Archtctr.

LIU, PAUL; Schurr HS; Montery Park, CA; (3); Chess Clb; Church Yth Grp; Computer Clb; Math Clb; Math Tm; Phtg Yrbk; Var L Trk; Schl Art Show 2 1st Plcs; LA Cnty Fr 1 1st & 1 Hnrbl Mntn; City Coll Art Show 1 2nd Pl; Robotic Engr.

LIU, PAUL F; Live Oak HS; Morgan Hill, CA; (3); 16/530; FBLA; Spanish Clb; Band; Mrchg Band; Orch; Pep Band; High Hon Roll; Hon Roll; Vrsty Badmntn; CSF; UCLA; Engrng.

LIU, PETER S; Brea Olinda HS; Brea, CA; (3); 1/288; Debate Tm; Treas Key Clb; Sec Letterman Clb; NFL; Service Clb; Speech Tm; Nwsp; Yrbk; L Crs Cntry; L Tennis; 1st Pl Orange Cnty Sci & Engrng Fr Mth; Acad Dcthln Tm.

LIU, POLLY P; Los Altos HS; Hacienda Hts, CA; (2); Color Guard; Hon Roll; Dist Schlr; CSF.

LIU, RAYMOND C; Kennedy HS; Artesia, CA; (2); Computer Clb; FBLA; Key Clb; JV Tennis; Hon Roll; Prfct Atten Awd; UCLA; Law.

LIU, ROCKSON C; Mark Keppel HS; S San Gabriel, CA; (3); 3/800; VP Key Clb; Math Clb; Mu Alpha Theta; Science Clb; Var Vllybl; Prfct Atten Awd; Math Medallion Awd; USC; Comp Sci.

LIU, STEPHENIE Y; Westchester HS; Los Angeles, CA; (4); 1/400; VP Hosp Aide; Intnl Clb; Office Aide; Red Cross Aide; Service Clb; Teachers Aide; Var Capt Tennis; High Hon Roll; Ntl Merit SF; Williams Coll; Envrnmntl Bio.

LIU, TRISHA; Salinas HS; Salinas, CA; (3); 1/350; Ski Clb; Pres Spanish Clb; Speech Tm; Capt Color Guard; Capt Flag Corp; Orch; School Musical; High Hon Roll; Church Yth Grp; Cmnty Wkr; Stanford Smmr Sch; Ft Ord Ski Tm; Brdcst Jrnlsm.

LIU, VIVIAN C; Pinole Valley HS; Hercules, CA; (2); French Clb; Teachers Aide; Hon Roll; CSF Club; UC Berkeley; Bus Adm.

LIU, WEN-HUI; Abraham Lincoln HS; San Francisco, CA; (4); 25/444; Church Yth Grp; French Clb; Math Clb; Math Tm; Office Aide; Science Clb; Teachers Aide; Varsity Clb; Acpl Chr; Chorus; Slvr Mdlst Acad Decthln Cmptn; 3rd Pl Wnnr Schl Sci Fr; 1st Prz Wnnr Chinese Brdcstng Radio Anncr; UC Berkeley; Chemistry.

LIU, WENDY G.; Cupertino HS; Cupertino, CA; (3); Sec Treas Key Clb; Service Clb; Sec Frsh Cls; JV Var Cheerldng; Var Pom Pon; JV Var Trk; NHS; JCL; Stu Cncl; Bsktbl; Kiwanis Clb Schlrshp; 2nd Pl Optimist Oratorical Awd; ASB Elect/Rally Cmmssnrs/Sec; Broadcstng.

LIU, WENDY WEI; A Lincoln HS; San Francisco, CA; (4); 2/444; Church Yth Grp; Cmnty Wkr; Science Clb; Sal; St Schlr; Acad Decthln Hnr Tm; CSF; Schl Sci Dept Awd; UC Berkeley; Bio Chem.

LIU, YUEH-SE; Abraham Lincoln HS; San Francisco, CA; (4); 1/444; Church Yth Grp; Math Clb; Science Clb; Acpl Chr; Church Choir; Hon Roll; Val; UC Berkeley; Chem.

LIU, ZHIQIN; International Studies Acad; San Francisco, CA; (2); Hon Roll; Ed.

LIVE, CONNIE F; Fontana HS; Fontana, CA; (1); Hon Roll; Phy.

LIVELY, PENNY; Hillcrest Christian Schl; Mission Hills, CA; (1); 2/22; Church Yth Grp; Ed Yrbk; Treas Stu Cncl; Sftbl; Trk; Vllybl; Cit Awd; Hon Roll.

L!VERMORE, DANIEL G; La Quinta HS; Fountain Valley, CA; (3); 5/333; Var Capt Ftbl; Hon Roll; NEDT Awd; Hlth Prfssn.

LIVINGSTON, ADAM J; Oak Ridge HS; El Dorado Hills, CA; (2); 1/250; Var Crs Cntry; Var Trk; High Hon Roll; Hon Roll; Ntl Merit Ltr; SCF; San Joaquin Sctn Cntry Meet; UCB; Sci.

LIVINGSTON, DANIEL B; Torrey Pines HS; Rancho Santa Fe, CA; (3); 122/456; Boy Scts; Church Yth Grp; Key Clb; Rep Soph Cls; Rep Jr Cls; Capt JV Bsbl; L Var Ftbl; Var Wt Lftg; JV Wrstlng; Pre-Law.

LIVINGSTON, TIFFINY L; Turlock HS; Turlock, CA; (2); 75/300; Church Yth Grp; Drama Clb; FTA; SADD; Thesps; Church Choir; School Musical; School Play; Variety Show; Intrml Sftbl; Ed.

LIZAK, JENNY; Tomales HS; Pt Reyes Sta, CA; (3); 4-H; Ski Clb; Spanish Clb; Var Stat Bsbl; Var Stat Ftbl; 4-H Awd; Hon Roll; Pres Acad Fit Awd; Pres Jr Cls; High Point Wnnr Horses Evnt; Cake Decrtng Tchr 4-H; Davis Coll; Counslr.

LIZALDE, ERIK; Lynwood HS; Lynwood, CA; (2); Teachers Aide; JV Bsbl; Long Beach ST; Med.

LIZARDO, AMYBELLE MAGLABE; Vallejo SR HS; Vallejo, CA; (3); Church Yth Grp; Office Aide; Teachers Aide; Sec Soph Cls; Sec Jr Cls; Sec Stu Cncl; JV Tennis; Hon Roll; Jr NHS; NHS; Assoctd Stu Body Secy; U Of Davis; Med.

LIZARRAGA, ALVARO; Calexico HS; Calexico, CA; (2); Spanish Clb; Chorus; Intrml Bsbl; JV Wrstlng; Life Sci Hnr Stu; World Hstry Hnr Stu; UCLA; Law.

LIZARRAGA, LOURDES; Fillmore HS; Fillmore, CA; (2); Drill Tm; Flag Corp; Sftbl; Cit Awd; High Hon Roll; Prfct Atten Awd; Migrant Clb; Renaissnce Prgrm; Archaelgy.

LIZER, TOBY K; Don Antonio Lugo HS; Chino, CA; (2); Church Yth Grp; Drama Clb; VP Thesps; School Musical; School Play; VP Swmmng; High Hon Roll; Water Polo JV Capt; HOBY Amb; UCLA; Bus.

LJUBIC, STEPHANIE; Mary Star HS; San Pedro, CA; (3); GAA; Math Clb; Flag Corp; Nwsp; Ed Yrbk; Off Sr Cls; Hon Roll; NHS; Capt Flag Tm; CA ST Dominguez; Ed.

LLAMAS, DIONICIO; Mountain View HS; Baldwin Park, CA; (1); Math Tm; NFL; Spanish Clb; Band; Hon Roll; UCLA; Engrng.

LLAMAS, EVA BEATRIZ; James Monroe HS; Panorama City, CA; (2); Band; Tennis; Hon Roll; Pres Acad Fit Awd; CSF; S CA U; Comp Sci.

LLAMAS, JOSE; Roosevelt HS; Los Angeles, CA; (2); Cmnty Wkr; Varsity Clb; Hon Roll; Prfct Atten Awd; Hlth Career Clb; USC; Sci Tech.

LLAMAS, MONICA; Pius X HS; Downey, CA; (1); Hon Roll; Nature Poem Published; Readng & Wrtng Poems; Hnrs Classes; Harvard; Math.

LLAMAS, SERGIO; Cajon HS; San Bernardino, CA; (2).

LLAMERA, EUGENE R; Amos Alonzo Stagg HS; Stockton, CA; (4); 7/340; Church Yth Grp; Key Clb; Math Clb; NFL; Science Clb; Nwsp; Off Jr Cls; Stu Cncl; Socr; NHS; Acad Dcthln; Asian Clb; De Molay; UC Davis; Psych.

LLAMIDO, MARIJO A; Sierra Vista HS; Baldwin Park, CA; (1); Church Choir; Hon Roll; Lamp Of Learning Awd Acad Excllnc; Music; Wrtng; Med.

LLANILLO, LORI SPRING; Elk Grove HS; Elk Grove, CA; (2); #26 In Class; Powder Puff Ftbl; Var L Trk; L High Hon Roll; CSF Stu 2 Sems; U Of CA Davis Outreach Pgm Stu Minority Schlrs; Grls Vrsty Delta Lg Triple Jmp Champ; U Of CA Davis; Marine Bio.

LLANOS, SARAH M; Desert HS; Edwards, CA; (2); Dance Clb; San Diego ST; Art.

LLANTERO, RICHARD F; Long Beach Polytechnic HS; Long Beach, CA; (3); Science Clb; Spanish Clb; High Hon Roll; Math & Sci Excllnc Awds; 4.0 Stu Awd; Cal Poly San Luis Obispo; Engr.

LLAUSAS, ESTER; Temple Christian HS; Perris, CA; (1); Sec Frsh Cls; Var Bsktbl; Var Cheerldng; JV Vllybl; Hon Roll; Ed.

LLAVE, BERNARD; Channel Islands HS; Oxnard, CA; (2); FBLA; JV Bsktbl; Intrml Trk; High Hon Roll; Prfct Atten Awd; Acad Awd Acctng; CSF; FBLA CA St Conf; CSUN; Acctng.

LLAVORE, EMILY J; Holy Family HS; Glendale, CA; (3); Art Clb; Cmnty Wkr; Office Aide; Service Clb; Chorus; Church Choir; Sec Rep Frsh Cls; Pres Soph Cls; VP Jr Cls; Stu Cncl; Jeffrey Ballet Smmr Wrkshp Schlrshp 88; I Dare You Ldrshp Awd; CSF 88; Bus Mgmt.

LLERA, JESSE D; Monterey HS; Seaside, CA; (3); FCA; Teachers Aide; Yrbk; JV Ftbl; Var Capt Socr; Var Trk; Hon Roll; San Diego ST; Bus.

LLEWELLYN, LISA M; El Dorado HS; Placentia, CA; (2); Church Yth Grp; Band; Church Choir; Mrchg Band; High Hon Roll; Hon Roll; Jr NHS; HS Band Outstndng Grl Of Yr 89 & 90; Chld Dvlpmnt.

LLOSA, JENNIFER; Andrew P Hill HS; San Jose, CA; (2); French Clb; CSF; MESA; Peer Cnslr.

LLOSA, LORENA; Andrew Hill HS; San Jose, CA; (4); Dance Clb; French Clb; Math Tm; Hon Roll; NHS; Pres Acad Fit Awd; Supreme Court Justc; CSF; Math Tutor; Santa Clara U; Arts, Sci.

LLOYD, CASEY; Palo Verde HS; Blythe, CA; (4); #2 In Class; Pres Church Yth Grp; Drama Clb; 4-H; Key Clb; Pep Clb; Service Clb; School Musical; School Play; Bsktbl; Gym; Rotary 4 Way Tst Spch Cont; Schl Site Cncl; Pediatrics.

LLOYD, DANELLE M; Mira Costa HS; Hawthorne, CA; (2); Office Aide; Chorus; High Hon Roll; Hon Roll; Pres Acad Fit Awd; Schl Rec Golden ST Alg Exam; Jrnlst.

LLOYD, DEANNA S; Mont Clair HS; Claremont, CA; (3); Church Yth Grp; CHSPE Passed; Chaffey; Teach Frgn Lang.

LLOYD, JASON; Palo Verde HS; Blythe, CA; (2); Boy Scts; Church Yth Grp; Computer Clb; 4-H; JA; Letterman Clb; Pep Clb; Quiz Bowl; SADD; Var Ftbl; CSF; Interact; Photo; CA Inst Tech; Robotic Engrng.

LLOYD, JODIE L; Diamond Bar HS; Diamond Bar, CA; (1); Church Yth Grp; Model UN; Teachers Aide; Acpl Chr; Chorus; Church Choir; School Musical; Cit Awd; Hon Roll; Music.

LLOYD, KARA; Granada Hills HS; Northridge, CA; (3); Debate Tm; Drama Clb; Speech Tm; Sec Thesps; School Musical; School Play; Capt Cheerldng; Tennis; Jr NHS; USC; Brdcst Jrnlsm.

LLOYD, RENEA; West HS; Torrance, CA; (4); Office Aide; SADD; Teachers Aide; Cheerldng; Powder Puff Ftbl; Capt JV Vllybl; NHS; Rep Frsh Cls; Rep Soph Cls; VP Jr Cls; 1st Mascot; Cheer Trainer Torrance Pop Warner Ftbl; CSU Long Beach; Accntng.

LLOYD, STACEY; Arroyo Grande HS; Arroyo Grande, CA; (2); Cheerldng; Swmmng; Chld Psych.

LLUIS, CHRISTINE; Westridge Schl; Arcadia, CA; (4); Cmnty Wkr; French Clb; Model UN; School Musical; School Play; JV Vllybl; Natl Hispanic Schlr; Peer Cnslr; Law.

LO, A NIEN; Oakland HS; Oakland, CA; (2); Computer Clb; Key Clb; Spanish Clb; Teachers Aide; Vllybl; Hon Roll; U Of Hayward.

LO, AILEEN; Lincoln HS; Stockton, CA; (3); Art Clb; Hosp Aide; Latin Clb; Mu Alpha Theta; Speech Tm; SADD; Teachers Aide; High Hon Roll; CSF; Bio Sciences.

LO, AMY; San Gabriel HS; San Gabriel, CA; (2); Red Cross Aide; Spanish Clb; Speech Tm; Rep Frsh Cls; JV Vllybl; Famille Des Amies; Keywanettes; Courtesy Cmmtte; Boys Vllybl Stats; Peer Cnslng; U Of CA San Diego; Sociology.

LO, CARRIE A; C K Mc Clatchy HS; Sacramento, CA; (2); 1/400; Church Yth Grp; Cmnty Wkr; Key Clb; SADD; Powder Puff Ftbl; Hon Roll; Prfct Atten Awd; JV Bsktbl; JV Sftbl; JV Vllybl; Asian Stu Union; Harvard; Bus.

LO, DANNY S H; Galileo HS; San Francisco, CA; (4); 14/350; Math Clb; High Hon Roll; Hon Roll; NHS.

LO, DENNY Y; Arcadia HS; Arcadia, CA; (3); Hosp Aide; JA; Office Aide; High Hon Roll; NHS; Prfct Atten Awd; UC, Irvine; Phrmclgy.

LO, DICKINSON K; Irvine HS; Irvine, CA; (2); Chess Clb; Hon Roll; Lacrosse; MIT; Comp Prgmr.

LO, HAY L; Granada Hills HS; Los Angeles, CA; (2); Library Aide; Pep Clb; Hon Roll; Prfct Atten Awd.

LO, JANE MEI JUN; Fountain Valley HS; Fountain Valley, CA; (1); Church Yth Grp; Cit Awd; High Hon Roll; CSF Secy; Chinese Club Rep; Bowling Club; GSE 1st Yr Alg High Honors; UC Berkeley; Med.

LO, JANIE F; Alameda HS; Alameda, CA; (4); 15/331; Church Yth Grp; Girl Scts; VP Science Clb; Teachers Aide; St Schlr; 1st Pl Maritime Essy Wnnr; Rcgntn By Soc Of Women Engrs For 3 Yrs Acadmc Excllnc; Chem Trophy; UC Davis; Med.

LO, JEFF M; San Marino HS; San Marino, CA; (3); Math Clb; Science Clb; Teachers Aide; Stat Bsktbl; SR Advsry Brd; Tnns Clb; Arch/Intr Dsgn Clb; Golden St Exam Awd.

LO, KAREN; San Ramon Valley HS; Danville, CA; (3); 1/420; NFL; Speech Tm; Capt Color Guard; Orch; High Hon Roll; NHS; Acad Dcthln Awds; CSF; Engrg.

LO, MICHELLE C; J F Kennedy HS; La Palma, CA; (3); German Clb; Teachers Aide; Yrbk; Treas Sr Cls; Sec Treas Stu Cncl; Bsktbl; JV Tennis; PETA; Bus Mgmt.

LO, MITH; Tokay HS; Lodi, CA; (1); Hmong Club 2nd VP; UCLA; Accntnt.

LO, NANA; San Gabriel HS; San Gabriel, CA; (1); Vllybl; Hon Roll; Psych.

LO, TAC Q; Oakland HS; Oakland, CA; (2); French Clb; Key Clb; JV Bsbl; JV Ftbl; JV Trk; Wt Lftg; Hon Roll; CA ST U Hayward; Contrctr.

LO, TERRI S; Mark Keppel HS; Rosemead, CA; (3); FBLA; Key Clb; Rep Math Clb; Rep Mu Alpha Theta; Teachers Aide; VP Band; Mrchg Band; Orch; Pep Band; Nwsp; U CA Los Angeles; Pharm Engr.

LO, THAO; Grant HS; Sacramento, CA; (3); Var Socr; Hon Roll; Frnch I, One Chevron Certs Of Hnr.

LO, THERESA R; Saint Francis HS; Los Altos, CA; (1); Intnl Clb; SADD.

LO, TRICIA; J Eugene Mc Ateer HS; San Francisco, CA; (2); Teachers Aide; Hon Roll; Bus Mgmt.

LO, WAMENG; Dos Pueblos HS; Goleta, CA; (2); 98/299; JV Bsbl.

LOAN, NGUYEN T; A A Stagg HS; Stockton, CA; (3); High Hon Roll; Prfct Atten Awd; Pres Acad Fit Awd; CSF; Nrs.

LOBAO, CHRISTINA D; Thomas Downey HS; Modesto, CA; (2); Drama Clb; French Clb; Service Clb; Orch; JV Swmmng; Hon Roll; Prfct Atten Awd; Modesto Stanislaus Symph Yth Orch; Mst Imprvd Player; Mst Inspirtnl; CSF; U CA-BERKELEY; Ed.

LOBATO, ALFONSO; Watsonville HS; Watsonville, CA; (2); Math Clb; JV Socr; Hon Roll; Prfct Atten Awd; Engr.

LOBE, SACIA Y; Serrano HS; Phelan, CA; (1); Church Yth Grp; Rep Frsh Cls; High Hon Roll; CSF; BYU HI; Mdcl Prfssn.

LOBO, GILLIAN; Whitney HS; Cerritos, CA; (2); Key Clb; Yrbk; Ed Lit Mag; High Hon Roll; CA Schlrshp Fed; Mr Sun Pgm; Golden St Exam Alg Hnrs.

LOCATELLI, JASON; Kingsburg HS; Selma, CA; (2); Church Yth Grp; 4-H; Varsity Clb; Band; Mrchg Band; School Musical; Var Ftbl; Var Trk; JV Wrstlng; 4-H Awd; Vrsty Crs Cntry Team; U CA Fresno; Physcl Thrpy.

LOCK, CORINNE; Wallenberg HS; San Francisco, CA; (2); 4-H; Hon Roll.

LOCKE, JULIA A; Baker Valley HS; Baker, CA; (3); Pep Clb; SADD; School Play; Nwsp; Yrbk; Pres Frsh Cls; VP Jr Cls; Treas Stu Cncl; Var Bsktbl; Var Cheerldng; Cal Poly San Luis Obispo; Acctn.

LOCKETT JR, JAMES F; St Joseph HS; Santa Maria, CA; (3); 14/121; Boy Scts; Chess Clb; Science Clb; Stage Crew; Ed Lit Mag; Hon Roll; Excllnc Svrl Subj Areas; Natl Merit Schlr; Med.

LOCKHART, JASON; Forest Lake Christian HS; Meadow Vista, CA; (2); 1/23; Church Yth Grp; Var L Bsbl; JV Stat Bsktbl; Hon Roll; Have 2 Jobs; Rcntly Purchsd Own Comp & Enjoy Prog; Air Force Acad; Engr.

LOCKHART, KELLI; Fresno HS; Fresno, CA; (3); 150/500; Math Clb; Science Clb; Drill Tm; Var JV Cheerldng; JV Mgr(s); JV Score Keeper; JV Sftbl; Hon Roll; Ntl Merit Ltr; CSF; U CA-DAVIS; Law.

LOCKHART, KELLY C; Etiwanda HS; Alta Loma, CA; (2); Drama Clb; Pep Clb; Ski Clb; Spanish Clb; Cheerldng; Crs Cntry; Trk; High Hon Roll; Prfct Atten Awd; Etiwanda Base Mgmt Tm; Bio.

LOCKHART, KIMBERLY; Thousand Oaks HS; Thousand Oaks, CA; (4); 60/530; Intnl Clb; SADD; Teachers Aide; Ed Nwsp; Pres Acad Fit Awd; Spanish NHS; Natl Leag Amer Pen Wmn Schlrshp; Pepperdine U; Jrnlsm.

LOCKIE, ADAM S; Apple Valley HS; Apple Valley, CA; (3); German Clb; Band; High Hon Roll; Hon Roll; NE U; Mch Enrng.

LOCKIE, SHAWN; Homestead HS; Sunnyvale, CA; (4); Bus Profs of Am; Drama Clb; Band; Chorus; Drill Tm; Mrchg Band; School Play; Yrbk; Treas Frsh Cls; Treas Soph Cls; UCLA; Bus.

LOCKLIN, DUHON S; Susan Miller Dorsey HS; Los Angeles, CA; (2); 2/23; Math Clb; Spanish Clb; Band; Mrchg Band; USC; Marines.

LOCKWOOD, PAUL D; Shasta HS; Redding, CA; (2); Church Yth Grp; FCA; Church Choir; School Musical; School Play; Nwsp; Bsbl; Bsktbl; High Hon Roll; Prfct Atten Awd; Stanford U; Engr.

LOCKWOOD, SCOTT L; St Bernard HS; Inglewood, CA; (3); Church Yth Grp; Rep Jr Cls; Capt Var Ftbl; Var Trk; Hon Roll; Schlr Athltc; CSF; Sports Med.

LOCZI, MAGDA; Moorpark HS; Moorpark, CA; (4); 39/255; Model UN; Ski Clb; Pres Soph Cls; JV Capt Cheerldng; High Hon Roll; Stu Brd Rep; Cmmssnr Of Spirit; Blood Drive; CASC Rep; Cmmnctns.

LOEB, ELISSA SHARON; Poway HS; Poway, CA; (1); Chorus; Hon Roll; Pres Local Bhai Brith Girls; Ice Dancing; Literature Tchr.

LOEFFELBEIN, GRETA KAREN; Ponderosa HS; Shingle Springs, CA; (4); 14/286; Chorus; Hon Roll; Pres Acad Fit Awd; Human Activists Orgnztn-HS Peace, Liberation & Envrnmntl Clb; Organic Gardening; Ltr Wrtng For Causes; OR ST U; Vegan Nutrition.

LOEFFLER, BRIGITTE L; Arlington HS; Riverside, CA; (2); Teachers Aide; Phys Thrpst.

LOEFKE, JENNIFER M; Temecula Valley HS; Temecula, CA; (4); Church Yth Grp; Letterman Clb; Teachers Aide; Mgr(s); Score Keeper; L Vllybl; Hon Roll; Palomar JC; Bus.

LOEHR, STACEY; St Lucys HS; Pomona, CA; (3); Drama Clb; Red Cross Aide; Thesps; School Play; Var Capt Cheerldng; Elks Awd; High Hon Roll; Ntl Merit Ltr; Pep Clb; Prfct Atten Awd; CA Schlrshp Fed; NEDT Awd; Pepperdine; Psych.

LOEPFE, MARCEL A; Grossmont HS; La Mesa, CA; (1); French Clb; German Clb; Cit Awd; Hon Roll; U Of Zurich Switzerland; Comp.

LOERA, FELIPE E; Bishop Amat HS; La Puente, CA; (3); JV Bsbl; JV Bsktbl; Bus.

LOERA, GISEL; St Genevieve HS; North Hollywood, CA; (3); Church Yth Grp; JV Vllybl; Bus.

LOERA, JOSEPH A; William Workman HS; Valinda, CA; (3); 65/250; Key Clb; Band; Drm Mjr(t); Jazz Band; Mrchg Band; Pep Band; Powder Puff Ftbl; Hon Roll; Tri-M Pldgmstr Chptr 1917; Stu Mnth Jan 89; 1st Pl Mace Drm Mjr Corono Chrstmas Parade 89; U Of Southern CA; Music Perfrm.

LOERA, MARISOL; San Jose High Acad; San Jose, CA; (4); Office Aide; Teachers Aide; Off Frsh Cls; Off Soph Cls; Off Jr Cls; Off Sr Cls; JV Cheerldng; Var Crs Cntry; JV Pom Pon; Var JV Score Keeper; Evergreen Vly Clg; Bus Admin.

LOESCH, DAWN; Arcadia HS; Arcadia, CA; (4); 28/620; Church Yth Grp; Band; Mrchg Band; Orch; Pep Band; NHS; Ntl Merit Ltr; Pres Acad Fit Awd; Rotary Awd; Sal; CA ST U Fresno; Animal Sci.

LOESCH, PHILLIP; Reedley HS; Galt, CA; (2); 11/268; Computer Clb; Math Clb; Math Tm; Band; Mrchg Band; Pep Band; Var Golf; JV Wrstlng; Jr Engrng Tech Soc; Golf Clb; Engrng.

LOESER, MEGAN B; Wilson HS; Long Beach, CA; (3); 92/820; Cmnty Wkr; Drama Clb; Speech Tm; Church Choir; Drill Tm; Stu Cncl; JV Swmmng; Hon Roll; NHS; Church Yth Grp; Yth Vlntr Of Yr 90.

LOEURM, SAY; Andrew P Hill HS; San Jose, CA; (3); French Clb; San Jose ST U; Med Tech.

LOEWEN, GENEVA; Chico SR HS; Chico, CA; (2); Church Yth Grp; FFA; Pep Clb; SADD; Capt Cheerldng; Trk; Hon Roll.

LOEWEN, SHAUNA D; Fresno Christian HS; Fresno, CA; (4); Church Yth Grp; Office Aide; Spanish Clb; Band; Color Guard; Mrchg Band; Variety Show; Yrbk; Tennis; High Hon Roll; Vrsty Awd Tennis; Hi Debs Mdlng; Miss Teenage Pageant; Fresno Pacific Coll; Psych.

LOEWENTHAL, CHOLENA; Petaluma HS; Petaluma, CA; (1); Debate Tm; Cheerldng; UCSB; Lwyr.

LOFLIN, DAVID J; Trabuco Hills HS; Trabuco Canyon, CA; (2); Claremont Mc Kenna; Tchr.

LOFSTEDT, INGRA L; Gahr HS; Cerritos, CA; (3); Church Yth Grp; AFS; Rep French Clb; JA; Church Choir; Ed Nwsp; Var Capt Cheerldng; Cit Awd; Hon Roll; John Robert Powers Model & Tlnt Wnnr & Schrshp.

LOFTIS, JENNIFER C; Burlingame HS; Burlingame, CA; (2); UC Davis; Zoologist.

LOFTIS, SHARA; Los Alamitos HS; Los Alamitos, CA; (3); Intnl Clb; Amnsty Intl; Intrct.

LOFTON, JEFFREY A; Hilmar HS; Turlock, CA; (3); FFA; Letterman Clb; Teachers Aide; VICA; Var Capt Bsktbl; Var L Trk; Hon Roll; Fresno ST; Auto Tech.

LOFTUS, BRANDY N; Burbank HS; Burbank, CA; (3); Debate Tm; Office Aide; School Play; Var Swmmng; Hon Roll; Pres Acad Fit Awd; HOPE; UC Santa Barbara; Pedtrcn.

LOGAN, BENJAMIN L; Vintage HS; Vallejo, CA; (2); Church Yth Grp; Key Clb; Pres Soph Cls; Rep Stu Cncl; JV Bsktbl; Var L Swmmng; Intrml Vllybl; Basic Life Club 89-90; Ldrshp Awd; Schl Rcgntn Status Golden St Exam Algebra.

LOGAN, CHRIS; Woodcrest Christian HS; Moreno Valley, CA; (1); Church Yth Grp; Drama Clb; Letterman Clb; Stage Crew; Intrml Var Bsbl; Intrml JV Bsktbl; Intrml Crs Cntry; Intrml Capt Socr; JV Capt Vllybl; Prfct Atten Awd; KLUB Torch; Westmont Coll; Prfrmng Arts.

LOGAN, ISRAEL; St Bernard HS; Los Angeles, CA; (3); Science Clb; Jazz Band; Schl Rock Band Guitarist; UCLA; Law.

LOGAN, LEIGH A; Saint Joseph HS; Lakewood, CA; (2); French Clb; Key Clb; Rptr Nwsp; Hon Roll; CSF; Teachers Aide Prsh CCD Pgm; Jrnlsm.

LOGAN, WILLIAM P; St Ignatius College Prep; San Francisco, CA; (3); Spch & Dbte Tm; CSF; Sound Crew; Cmptr Sci.

LOGEMANN, DIETRA D; Troy HS; Fullerton, CA; (2); 30/350; Church Yth Grp; FCA; VP Key Clb; Letterman Clb; Ski Clb; Spanish Clb; Drill Tm; Pres Soph Cls; Var Capt Bsktbl; Var Tennis; Mgr Bus.

LOGOLUSO, MICHELLE; Madera HS; Madera, CA; (2); Church Yth Grp; Dance Clb; Girl Scts; Pep Clb; SADD; Variety Show; VP Frsh Cls; Sec Stu Cncl; JV Capt Bsktbl; Intrml Capt Cheerldng; JR Vrsty Stu Athlt Awd; 1st Pl Clovis Pep Clssc; Top 10 Of Class 1988-90; Fresno ST U; Bus.

LOGRIP, ALISON; Notre Dame Acad; Los Angeles, CA; (3); 2/120; Cmnty Wkr; Dance Clb; SADD; Acpl Chr; Chorus; Ed Yrbk; Cit Awd; High Hon Roll; NHS; Campus Mnstry Of Schl; Bus.

LOGSDON, EDDIE N; W T Ellis HS; Olivehurst, CA; (3); Cmnty Wkr; Dance Clb; Drama Clb; Library Aide; Office Aide; Pep Clb; SADD; Teachers Aide; School Play; Stage Crew; Sutter Yuba Assn Of Realtors Schlrshp; Athletic Capt Athlt Of Yr; Top Model; Harvard U; Lwyr.

LOGUE, MELISSA D; Bear River HS; Auburn, CA; (2); Color Guard; Yrbk; Trk; Cit Awd; Hon Roll; Show-Pop Choir.

LOH, CINDY; San Gabriel Acad; Montebello, CA; (2); Ski Clb; Teachers Aide; Orch; Yrbk; Rep Frsh Cls; Rep Soph Cls; Socr; Sftbl; Vllybl; Hon Roll; Outstdng Relgn Awd; Bible Achvmt Awd; Sccr, Sftbl 1st Pl; Speed Typng Awd; U Of Southern CA; Med.

LOH, JUNE D; Lowell HS; San Francisco, CA; (4); 23/626; French Clb; Hosp Aide; Model UN; Teachers Aide; Chorus; School Play; Ed Nwsp; NHS; Ntl Merit Ltr; Pacific Musical Soc Piano Cmptn 1st Pl; UC Berkeley; Med.

LOHMAN, KRISTEN; Mills HS; Millbrae, CA; (3); Girl Scts; Band; Rep Jr Cls; JV Bsktbl; Var Swmmng; Hon Roll; Ntl Merit Ltr; People To People Initv Understndng Svt-Amer Yth Exchng.

LOHR JR, JOHN; 29 Palms HS; Twentynine Palm, CA; (4); 20/132; Boy Scts; Church Yth Grp; Debate Tm; Spanish Clb; Varsity Clb; Rep Frsh Cls; VP Soph Cls; Pres Jr Cls; VP Sr Cls; Rep Stu Cncl; Northern AZ U; Law.

LOHR, PAMELA C; San Dieguito HS; Carlsbad, CA; (3); Office Aide; Speech Tm; Teachers Aide; School Play; Humbolt; Tchr.

LOHRUNGRUANG, JAMIE; Mark Keppel HS; Monterey Park, CA; (3); Math Clb; Chorus; Prfct Atten Awd; UCLA; Comp Sci.

LOHSAWAT, DAN; Whitney HS; Cerritos, CA; (1); High Hon Roll.

LOI, DANNY B; Phillip And Sab Academic HS; San Francisco, CA; (2); High Hon Roll; Hon Roll; NEDT Awd; Gldn St Exm 89; Pre-Med.

LOI, LAC K; Ocean View HS; Huntington Bch, CA; (4); 30/500; Key Clb; Math Clb; Varsity Clb; Cit Awd; 4-H Awd; Hon Roll; Prfct Atten Awd; Vrsty Bdmntn Plyr; CA Schlrshp Fed; Bank Of Amer Awd In Math; CA Poly Pomona; Mech Engrn.

LOI, WINNY; St Elizabeth HS; Oakland, CA; (4); GAA; Yrbk; Vllybl; Hon Roll; NHS; Pres Acad Fit Awd; Csmtcs Mrchndsng.

LOK, AVON V; Garey HS; Pomona, CA; (2); Key Clb; Drill Tm; NHS; Mst Outstndng Bio, Spnsh & Wrld Cvlztn; CSF; Stanford; Pediatrics.

LOK, LEY; Millikan HS; Norwalk, CA; (3); Teachers Aide; CA ST U; Comp Prgmr.

LOK, YIT F; Mark Keppel HS; Monterey Park, CA; (3); 20/700; Boy Scts; Library Aide; Math Clb; Science Clb; Swmmng; UCLA; Elec Engrng.

LOKEY, RICHARD A; Calaveras HS; San Andreas, CA; (2); 4-H; FFA; Band; Mrchg Band; JV Ftbl; Var Capt Swmmng; 4-H Awd; Hon Roll; Prfct Atten Awd; Cattle Penning At Fair; Brk 2 Schl Swm Rcrds & Won Trophy MVP Swmmr; Drum Corp.

LOKKEN, KRISTI; Vacaville HS; Vacaville, CA; (2); Church Yth Grp; Drama Clb; Speech Tm; Thesps; Church Choir; School Musical; School Play; Stage Crew; Stu Cncl; Hon Roll; Youth Dir Girls Youth Camp; Pres Youth Church Group; BYU; Law.

LOMAS, M CHRISTINE; Arroyo Grande HS; Decatur, AL; (3); 10/448; Art Clb; Church Yth Grp; Drama Clb; French Clb; Key Clb; Teachers Aide; Varsity Clb; Var L Trk; Hon Roll; Acad Excllnc Awds 87-90; Congressional Schlr 90; CSF 88-90; HOBY Ambssdr; Yale; Instructnl Systems Dsgnr.

LOMAX, LAMONT; Skyline HS; Oakland, CA; (2); Dance Clb; Pres Spanish Clb; JV Bsktbl; Wt Lftg; Hon Roll; Sal; Block Ltr Awd Dance; CA ST U Hayward; Prfssnl Danc.

LOMBARDI, MIKE R; Piedmont HS; Piedmont, CA; (3); Boy Scts; Church Yth Grp; Art Clb; JV Crs Cntry; JV Trk; High Hon Roll; Hon Roll; St Schlr; Hgh Hnrs Golden St Exm Alg, Geom, Alg II/Trig; Treas Italian Clb; U Of CA Davis; Hotel Mgmt.

LOMBARDI, PAUL M; Mt Shasta HS; Mount Shasta, CA; (2); Church Yth Grp; Band; Chorus; Church Choir; Jazz Band; JV Bsktbl; Var Trk; DAR Awd; High Hon Roll; Music.

LOMBARDO, KRISTEN L; Montgomery HS; Santa Rosa, CA; (3); 4-H; Sec Treas French Clb; Treas FBLA; VP Key Clb; SADD; Band; Mrchg Band; Ed Yrbk; Stu Cncl; Var Bsktbl; Lamp Of Knowledge Schlstc Awd; Schlr Athl Awd; Cmp Cnslr Bennett Vly Outdoor Ed; Stu Of Week; Psych.

LOMELI, APRIL C; Sanger HS; Sanger, CA; (2); Church Yth Grp; Computer Clb; ROTC; Chorus; Drill Tm; Prfct Atten Awd; CSUF; Business.

LOMELI, CRISTINA R; Modesto HS; Patterson, CA; (3); Church Yth Grp; Var Dance Clb; Capt Color Guard; Var Cheerldng; Psych.

LOMELI, DALIA V; Bell Gardens HS; Commerce, CA; (3); Art Clb; Dance Clb; Drama Clb; Spanish Clb; Pres Acad Fit Awd; Simmons Coll; Pre-Med.

LOMELI, ELIZABETH C; Fillmore HS; Fillmore, CA; (4); Church Yth Grp; GAA; Office Aide; Aud/Vis; Varsity Clb; Church Choir; Yrbk; Lit Mag; Bsktbl; Socr; Ventura JC.

LOMELI, FAVIOLA; Skyline HS; Oakland, CA; (3); Hon Roll; Prfct Atten Awd; U Of CA Berkeley.

LOMELI, JOHN M; Montebello HS; Montebello, CA; (3); Church Yth Grp; French Clb; Teachers Aide; VICA; Hon Roll; Elec & Comp & Bike Riding; Comp Engr.

LOMELI, JOSE LUIS; Fillmore HS; Fillmore, CA; (2); Church Yth Grp; Bsbl; Ftbl; Socr; Hon Roll; Stu Acad Inst; U Santa Barbara; Engr.

LOMELI, JUDITH T; Garfield HS; Los Angeles, CA; (2); French Clb; Orch; Cit Awd; Hon Roll; Prfct Atten Awd; Schlrshp Clb.

LOMELI, MARIBELLE; Mar Vista HS; National City, CA; (3); Dance Clb; Drama Clb; Chorus; Yrbk; Mgr(s); Trk; Tchrs Asst At Boys & Girls Club Of Amer 87; San Diego ST U; Adm Of Justice.

LOMELI, MICHELLE; Cupertino HS; Cupertino, CA; (3); Church Yth Grp; Cmnty Wkr; Key Clb; Chorus; Color Guard; School Musical; Stu Cncl; Cheerldng; Powder Puff Ftbl; Sftbl; Coachs Awd Sftbl Bst Attitude; Gldn St Exm Alg I Hnrs; Excllnce Awds BOC & Mythlgy; Psych.

LOMELI, TRINI; Sacred Heart HS; Los Angeles, CA; (2); 17/123; Church Yth Grp; VP GAA; Letterman Clb; Rptr Lit Mag; Treas Soph Cls; JV Bsktbl; Var Crs Cntry; Sftbl; Hon Roll; NHS; Ill Be Representing Ca As A Congressional Scholar In The Natl Young Leaders Conf; Member Of Ca Schlsp; Loyola Marymount; Corporate Law.

LOMELIN, MAURICIO; University City HS; San Diego, CA; (4); 9/400; Computer Clb; French Clb; Math Tm; Model UN; Teachers Aide; Varsity Clb; Var Tennis; Cit Awd; High Hon Roll; Hon Roll; Ranked Tennis Player S CA; Galaxy Awd High Hnrs Golden St Exam; Best Schlr Schlrshp & Awd; CSF Mem; MA Inst Of Tech; Elec Engrng.

LOMENICK, TIFFANY A; Simi Valley HS; Simi Valley, CA; (2); 37/753.

LOMMORI, CAROL D; Upper Lake HS; Upper Lake, CA; (3); 4/37; Am Leg Aux Girls St; Chorus; Yrbk; Treas Soph Cls; VP Jr Cls; Sec Sr Cls; Var Cheerldng; Var Sftbl; Var Capt Vllybl; Hon Roll; CSF; Jr Statesmen Of Amer; Humboldt ST; Bus.

LONDON, GALEN A; East Bakersfield HS; Bakersfield, CA; (2); Rep Drama Clb; Thesps; Chorus; School Play; Yrbk; Bst Supporting Actor Drama Play; Collectr Comic Bks; Drama.

LONDONO, JOHN; St Francis HS; Glendale, CA; (4); Art Clb; Cmnty Wkr; Letterman Clb; Mu Alpha Theta; Spanish Clb; JV L Bsktbl; JV Var Ftbl; Wt Lftg; Hon Roll; Spanish NHS; CSF; Hall Of Fame; Schlr/Athlt.

LONDRE, JUSTIN T; Las Lomas HS; Walnut Creek, CA; (3); Varsity Clb; Stu Cncl; Var L Bsktbl; Var L Golf; Chemathon Bay Area; Bsktbl Coaches Awd 89-90; Bus.

LONEY, MATTHEW T; Las Lomas HS; Walnut Creek, CA; (3); Boy Scts; French Clb; Teachers Aide; Var Capt Crs Cntry; Var Trk; Hon Roll; Bay Area Chemathon; US Naval Acad; Bus.

LONG, BRAD A; Hoover HS; Fresno, CA; (1); Qtr Midget Racing; Radio Control Car Racing; Mech Eng.

LONG, CHAD M; Grace Davis HS; Modesto, CA; (3); French Clb; Math Tm; Science Clb; Varsity Clb; Var Crs Cntry; Var Trk; Var Wrstlng; High Hon Roll; 1st Pl Metric Estmtn ST Sci Olympiad 88; Scrd 800 Math Sctn SAT; 3rd Pl Tm Sctn Cross Cntry; Engrng.

LONG, CHARETTA A; Encinal HS; Alameda, CA; (1); Band; Mrchg Band; Pep Band; Pres Frsh Cls; Cheerldng; Pom Pon; Georgetown U; Interior Dsgn.

LONG, CHRISTINA L; Antelope Valley HS; Lancaster, CA; (3); 12/631; Church Yth Grp; Pres French Clb; Treas Intnl Clb; Math Tm; Quiz Bowl; High Hon Roll; Hon Roll.

LONG, CHRISTOPHER A; Salinas HS; Salinas, CA; (3); Boy Scts; Church Yth Grp; Ski Clb; Treas Band; Jazz Band; Mrchg Band; Pep Band; Trk; High Hon Roll; Pres NHS; Engrng.

LONG, DENISE D; Palmdale HS; Palmdale, CA; (2); 29/813; Treas Band; Mrchg Band; Orch; Lbrn Pep Band; Hon Roll; Intract Secy; CSF; Pre-Law.

LONG, DIANE; Lincoln HS; Los Angeles, CA; (4); 17/400; Key Clb; JV Vllybl; Hon Roll; CSF Gld Sl Bearer; UC Irvine; Fine Arts.

LONG, JERRED; Bakersfield HS; Bakersfield, CA; (2); Church Yth Grp; Letterman Clb; Pep Clb; SADD; Teachers Aide; Varsity Clb; Mrchg Band; Bsbl; Bsktbl; Crs Cntry; Olympc Dvlpmnt Prgrm Sccr Natl Lvl; Sprts Med.

LONG, JESSICA L; Simi Valley HS; Simi Valley, CA; (2); 1/753; Church Yth Grp; Intnl Clb; Band; Drill Tm; Powder Puff Ftbl; JV Score Keeper; Hon Roll; Jr NHS; Med.

LONG, JOHNNY; John Glenn HS; Norwalk, CA; (2); Am Leg Boys St; Cmnty Wkr; Computer Clb; FBLA; FTA; Intnl Clb; Key Clb; Nwsp; Bsktbl; Wt Lftg; CA U Long Beach; Elctrnc Tech.

LONG, KASAUNDRA L; Clovis HS; Clovis, CA; (2); Library Aide; Office Aide; SADD; Teachers Aide; Chorus; Church Choir; Cit Awd; Hon Roll.

LONG, LEA ELLEN; Chico SR HS; Chico, CA; (4); 17/350; Cmnty Wkr; Debate Tm; Drama Clb; Intnl Clb; Key Clb; Office Aide; Spanish Clb; Hon Roll; Lion Awd; Voice Dem Awd; CA Poly; Law.

LONG, MARIA LOURDES; Poway HS; Poway, CA; (4); 46/728; Church Yth Grp; SADD; Ftbl; Mrchg Band; High Hon Roll; Jr NHS; NHS; Kiwanis Yth Salute; Jr Hnr Chair; Stu Venture; UCSB; Pre-Med.

LONG, MOLLY B; Paradise HS; Paradise, CA; (2); Church Yth Grp; French Clb; GAA; Hosp Aide; Var Crs Cntry; Var Trk; Hon Roll; Fri Night Live Clb; Braille Bk Binders Clb; Med.

LONG, PATRICK; Hoover HS; Fresno, CA; (2); Letterman Clb; JV Socr; JV Var Swmmng; High Hon Roll; Hon Roll; Jr Var & Var Water Polo; Achvt In Scl Sci Top 5% Of Cls; Med.

LONG, ROOSEVELT A; Morningside HS; Inglewood, CA; (3); 5/80; Church Yth Grp; Church Choir; Bsbl; Ftbl; Trk; Wt Lftg; Wrstlng; Grambling; Bus.

LONG, TALINA L; Red Bluff Union HS; Mineral, CA; (3); Teachers Aide; Friday Night Live; Sr Steerng Cmmtte; Bus Mgmt.

LONG, TAYLER; Whitney HS; Cerritos, CA; (4); Drama Clb; Thesps; School Play; Rptr Nwsp; L Var Bsktbl; L Var Trk; NHS; Val; Acad Acad Achvt Hnr Stu; Jnr Statesmn America; Stanford U; Bio Sci.

LONG, TRACY; George Washington HS; San Francisco, CA; (2); Sec Red Cross Aide; School Musical; Rep Frsh Cls; High Hon Roll; Hon Roll; CSF; Vietnamese Clb; Chinese-Amer Clb; UC Davis; Phrmcy.

LONG, TRAVIS J; Victor Valley HS; Oro Grande, CA; (2); 14/604; Key Clb; SADD; High Hon Roll; VP Fencing Team; Rowdy Rabbit Rooters; Booster Club; Teaching TV, Radio Prodctn.

LONG, TYREE J; Morningside HS; Inglewood, CA; (3); Boy Scts; Drama Clb; Color Guard; School Play; Stage Crew; Intrml Bsbl; Intrml Ftbl; Hon Roll; Law Enforcement Explorer; El Camino; Fire Sci.

LONG, WENDY F; Armijo HS; Fairfield, CA; (2); Ski Clb; Sftbl; Swmmng.

LONGACRE, DEBBIE D; Paraclete HS; Lancaster, CA; (2); Drama Clb; SADD; Socr; Hon Roll; ST U Of NY Plattsbrgh; Jrnlsm.

LONGACRE, LIZETTE R; Savanna HS; Buena Park, CA; (3); Letterman Clb; Varsity Clb; Rep Soph Cls; Bsktbl; Powder Puff Ftbl; Score Keeper; Var Capt Vllybl; Hon Roll; NHS; 89 Vrsty Vlybl MVP; La Verne U; Jrnlsm.

LONGACRE, MIKE; St Marys College HS; Richmond, CA; (3); Church Yth Grp; Cmnty Wkr; Intnl Clb; Math Tm; Teachers Aide; Chorus; Stage Crew; Yrbk; Rep Stu Cncl; Intrml Bsktbl; Specl Recog Awd Athltc Acadmc Achvt; Specl Achvt Awd Geom I, II; Cert Of Awd Natl Yth Conf Yth Govt; U CA Berkeley; Arch.

LONGAZO, TERESA G; Norco SR HS; Norco, CA; (3); Church Yth Grp; Pep Clb; Science Clb; Spanish Clb; Band; Color Guard; Mrchg Band; Pres Acad Fit Awd; Cvl Air Ptrl; Acad Dcthln 90-91; Plntry Astrnmy.

LONGEST, JEFFREY S; Foothill HS; Sacramento, CA; (2); High Hon Roll; Arch Drafting.

LONGLEY, JOY; Southbay Christian HS; Sunnyvale, CA; (1); Church Yth Grp; Chorus; School Musical; High Hon Roll; Hon Roll; De Anza Comm Coll.

LONGNECKER, DARREN W; Redlands SR HS; Redlands, CA; (3); Boy Scts; Band; Mrchg Band; Pep Band; Phtg Yrbk; Bicyclng Tm; CA ST San Bernardino; Dentist.

LONGO, ELIZABETH; Saratoga HS; Saratoga, CA; (4); 30/274; Intnl Clb; Sec Spanish Clb; Teachers Aide; Color Guard; Flag Corp; DAR Awd; Hon Roll; Ntl Merit Ltr; Natl Cncl Tchrs Of Engl Wrtng Achvt Awd; U Durham; Russian.

LONGORIA, ANGEL R; Oakdale HS; Oakdale, CA; (2); Dance Clb; Pep Clb; Variety Show; Intrml JV Bsktbl; Intrml JV Ftbl; Stat Score Keeper; Var Swmmng; Intrml Wt Lftg; Cit Awd; Prfct Atten Awd; Arts & Crfts; Mdlng; Modesto JC; Arch.

LONGORIA, STEPHANIE D; Casa Roble HS; Citrus Heights, CA; (2); 140/461; AFS; Church Yth Grp; VP Pres Drama Clb; German Clb; Teachers Aide; Thesps; School Play; UC Berkley; Prof Mod Art.

LONTOC, FREDERICK; Bonita Vista HS; Bonita, CA; (4); Church Yth Grp; Ski Clb; Ed Nwsp; Cit Awd; High Hon Roll; Hon Roll; Prfct Atten Awd; UCSD; Engr.

LOO, JENNIFER A; Edison HS; Huntington Beach, CA; (1); Band; Mrchg Band; Orch; Chinese Clb; Comp.

LOO, MICHAEL C; South San Francisco HS; South San Francis, CA; (2); Computer Clb; FBLA; Math Clb; Sec Jr Cls; Capt L Swmmng; JV Capt Wrstlng; High Hon Roll; Prfct Atten Awd; Paino; Typing Awd; CSF; Concerned Stu Club; Water & Snow Skiing & Swimming; Stanford; Bus.

LOOC, MI; Oakland HS; Oakland, CA; (2); Cit Awd; Hon Roll; Close Up Club; Freshwing Club.

LOOKABAUGH, SCOTT M; Clairemont HS; San Diego, CA; (4); Ed Yrbk; L Bsbl; L Gym; Var Sftbl; Var Swmmng; Cit Awd; Hon Roll; Pres Acad Fit Awd; AZ ST U; Bus.

LOOMER, RUTH M; Buena HS; Ventura, CA; (3); Church Yth Grp; FCA; Var Capt Socr; Var Trk; Cit Awd; Hon Roll; Pres Acad Fit Awd; Elem Ed.

LOOMIS, JULIE; Armijo HS; Fairfield, CA; (3); Ski Clb; Gym; Cit Awd; Hon Roll; UC Davis; Vet.

LOOPER, AGAPE; S F University HS; San Francisco, CA; (4); Cmnty Wkr; JV Var Bsktbl; JV Var Fld Hcky; Sftbl; Ntl Merit SF; 1st Pl Track Youth Build Activities Cmte; Law.

LOOPER, KIMBERLY S; Norte Vista HS; Riverside, CA; (3); Cmnty Wkr; Sec FBLA; Capt Pep Clb; Q&S; VP SADD; Varsity Clb; Ed Yrbk; Treas Stu Cncl; Capt Cheerldng; High Hon Roll; Coreographed Dances; U CA-RIVERSIDE; Psychlgy.

LOOPER, TANUA S; Antelope Valley HS; Lancaster, CA; (3); Church Yth Grp; FFA; FHA; Office Aide; Teachers Aide; Church Choir; Cit Awd; High Hon Roll; Hon Roll; San Diego ST Coll; Intr Design.

LOOPSTRA, JONATHAN A; Saddleback HS; Santa Ana, CA; (3); Boy Scts; Pres Church Yth Grp; Band; Lit Mag; Prfct Atten Awd; Pres Acad Fit Awd; RPG Sec; Crtv Wrtng Clb; CSF.

LOPATKA, KEITH A; Chaminade College Prep; West Hills, CA; (2); Cmnty Wkr; High Hon Roll; Jr NHS; Jr Ambssdr People To People Exchng Russia 88; Hist Clb; Rocket Clb; Notre Dame; Lawyer.

LOPATKA, SHELBY L; Thousand Oaks HS; Thousand Oaks, CA; (3); Spanish Clb; Mgr Ed Nwsp; JV Trk; NHS; Math.

LOPER, APRIL A; Fred C Beyer HS; Modesto, CA; (3); FFA; Teachers Aide; Gym; Swmmng; Vllybl; High Hon Roll; Hon Roll; Zoology.

LOPER, ERIC M; Point Loma HS; San Diego, CA; (3); 127/431; Key Clb; JV Var Bsktbl; JV Ftbl.

LOPES, LOREN F; Turlock HS; Turlock, CA; (4); 118/500; Church Yth Grp; Drama Clb; Pres FFA; Letterman Clb; Ftbl; Hon Roll; CA Hlstn Assoc Dstngshd Jr Boy 90; Buck Clsn Awd Outstndng FFA Dairy Stu; FFA Parli Pro Team; Modesto JC; Dairy Sci.

LOPES, TONY A; College Park HS; Martinez, CA; (3); 11/317; Var L Bsbl; Bsktbl; Ntl Merit Ltr; CSF; USCB; Bus.

LOPES, WAYNE P; Lincoln HS; Stockton, CA; (2); 158/568; Church Yth Grp; Trk; Hon Roll; Podiatry.

LOPEZ, ADRIAN; University HS; Los Angeles, CA; (2); Math Tm; Office Aide; Teachers Aide; Var Bsbl; Intrml Bsktbl; Capt Ftbl; Intrml Vllybl; Wt Lftg; Cit Awd; Hon Roll; UCLA; Med.

LOPEZ, ADRIANA; Calexico HS; Calexico, CA; (1); French Clb; Math Tm; Hon Roll.

LOPEZ, ADRIANA; Santiago HS; Garden Grove, CA; (2); French Clb.

LOPEZ, ADRIANA S; Village Christian HS; Sun Valley, CA; (3); 4/123; English Clb; Letterman Clb; Math Clb; Mu Alpha Theta; Spanish Clb; Sec Jr Cls; Rep Stu Cncl; JV Var Vllybl.

LOPEZ, AGUSTIN F; Torrey Pines HS; Del Mar, CA; (1); Aud/Vis; Off Frsh Cls; JV Ftbl; San Diego ST U; Pediatrician.

LOPEZ, ALBERTO; Providene HS; North Hollywood, CA; (2); Art Clb; Church Yth Grp; French Clb; Engr Artist.

LOPEZ, ALEJANDRA M; Mission San Jose HS; Fremont, CA; (3); Rptr Nwsp; Ed Yrbk; Treas Soph Cls; Mgr Stu Cncl; JV Gym; Var Trk; REACH Amer Pres; CSF Secy; Peer Counseling.

LOPEZ, ALEJANDRO; Garey HS; Pomona, CA; (2).

LOPEZ, ALEX J; Brawley Union HS; Brawley, CA; (3); JETS Awd; Comp.

LOPEZ, ALFREDO A; St John Bosco HS; Bellflower, CA; (2); Church Yth Grp; Drama Clb; French Clb; Thesps; Varsity Clb; Band; Mrchg Band; School Play; Swmmng; Hon Roll; Water Polo; Med.

LOPEZ, ALICE M; Upland HS; Upland, CA; (2); Church Yth Grp; Key Clb; SADD; Stage Crew; Sec Stu Cncl; Var Crs Cntry; Var Trk; Cit Awd; Hon Roll; Upland Police Explrr Post 606; CA Schlr Fed; Hstry Mnth Poster Cmptn; 2nd San Bernardina Cnty; UC San Diego; Elec Engr.

LOPEZ, ALMA L; Coalinga HS; Huron, CA; (3); FTA; Hosp Aide; Office Aide; Ed Yrbk; Bsktbl; Tennis; Hon Roll; Prfct Atten Awd; Smmr Schl Laney Coll, W Hlls Coll & UCB; Stanford; Med.

LOPEZ, AMICA; San Benito HS; San Juan Bautista, CA; (2); AFS; Church Yth Grp; Intnl Clb; Teachers Aide; School Play; Hon Roll; St Schlr; AFS Summer Homestay Prgm 90; Child Psych.

LOPEZ, ANDREA MICHELLE; Walnut HS; Walnut, CA; (4); 131/346; Dance Clb; Key Clb; Red Cross Aide; Service Clb; SADD; Chorus; Church Choir; Stage Crew; Variety Show; Lit Mag; Walnut Valley Saferides Vp & Sec; Girls Lge Treas; Grad With Hnrs; Mt San Antonio; Lit.

LOPEZ, ANDRES A; Pasadena HS; Pasadena, CA; (2); Var Socr.

LOPEZ, ANDREW R; John Glenn HS; Buena Park, CA; (3); Office Aide; Teachers Aide; Ftbl; Wt Lftg; Wrstlng; Cit Awd; Exclnc In Electrncs; CA ST U Fullerton; Elec Engr.

LOPEZ, ANGELA; Lompoc SR HS; Lompoc, CA; (2); Cmnty Wkr; Dance Clb; FFA; FHA; Pep Clb; SADD; Lit Mag; Rep Frsh Cls; Capt JV Cheerldng; Masonic Awd; UCLA; Comp Tech.

LOPEZ, ANGELA M; Oakland HS; Oakland, CA; (3); Drama Clb; Library Aide; Pep Clb; ROTC; SADD; Teachers Aide; Chorus; Color Guard; Nwsp; Yrbk; Mills Coll Upward Bound 4.0 Awd; Vars Acadmc Achvt Awds; Howard Coll; Psych.

LOPEZ, ANGELICA P; Walnut HS; Walnut, CA; (2); Key Clb; Office Aide; Spanish Clb; Teachers Aide; Lit Mag; Trk; Wt Lftg; Hon Roll; CA Schlrshp Fed; Engrng.

LOPEZ, ANITA; Atwater HS; Winton, CA; (3); Cmnty Wkr; FCA; Red Cross Aide; Var Socr; Var JV Tennis; Var Trk; High Hon Roll; Champns Track; Ntl Peace Essay Cntst 3rd Awd; Aeronutcl Engr.

LOPEZ, ANNA L; La Puente HS; La Puente, CA; (3); Drama Clb; GAA; Pres JA; Letterman Clb; Spanish Clb; Thesps; Varsity Clb; School Play; Stage Crew; Pres Jr Cls; Sigma Banquet; Dance; Drama; U Of Santa Barbara; Drama.

LOPEZ, ANNA M; St Genevieve HS; Van Nuys, CA; (3); French Clb; JV Vllybl; Mktng.

LOPEZ, ANNABEL P; Pittsburg HS; Pittsburg, CA; (2); Church Yth Grp; Cmnty Wkr; Off Soph Cls; High Hon Roll; Hon Roll; Prfct Atten Awd; Engrng.

LOPEZ, ANTHONY A; Dos Palos HS; Dos Palos, CA; (3); AFS; Office Aide; SADD; Stu Cncl; JV Var Trk; Hon Roll; Play Guitar & Draw & Paint; Tchr.

LOPEZ, ANTHONY T; Leuzinger HS; Lawndale, CA; (3); Church Yth Grp; Cmnty Wkr; Computer Clb; Math Clb; SADD; Wt Lftg; Cit Awd; High Hon Roll; Hon Roll; Prfct Atten Awd; Kaiser Permanent Hosptl Smmr Yth 89; UCLA; Sci/Math.

LOPEZ, ARACELI; Fontana HS; Fontana, CA; (2); Socr; Sftbl; Law.

LOPEZ, ARLENE E; Warren HS; Downey, CA; (2).

LOPEZ, ARMANDO X; El Dorado HS; Placentia, CA; (3); 117/317; Var Ftbl; Hon Roll; Aeronautical Engr.

LOPEZ, BEATRICE; Montebello HS; Montebello, CA; (2); FCA; SADD; Varsity Clb; Acpl Chr; Var Vllybl; Hon Roll; UCLA; Bus.

LOPEZ, BLANCA; George Washington Prep; Los Angeles, CA; (4); Orch; Var Crs Cntry; Var Trk; Hon Roll; Knights & Ladies Hnrs Clb; UC Irvine; Accntng.

LOPEZ, BLANCA A; Santa Monica HS; Santa Monica, CA; (3); Var L Socr; Bst Dfnsv Plyr 87-88; JV Sccr; MIP Of Yr 88-89 Vrsty Sccr; Scnd Tm Bay Leg 89-90 Vrsty Sccr; Accntng.

LOPEZ, BOB; Cajon HS; San Bernardino, CA; (3); #25 In Class; Key Clb; Spanish Clb; Ed Lit Mag; Pilot.

LOPEZ, BRANDI L; Azusa HS; Azusa, CA; (2); 19/304; Sec SADD; Pres Jr Cls; Fld Hcky; Hon Roll; Represent Hugh Obrian Yth Conf; Mock Trail Tm; JR Class Pres 90-91; USC; Dentistry.

LOPEZ, BRENDA; Bell Gardens HS; Bell Gardens, CA; (1); Chess Clb; Temple Yth Grp; Church Choir; Swmmng; Wt Lftg; Prfct Atten Awd; CA ST; Pediatrician.

LOPEZ, CARLOS; Selma HS; Selma, CA; (3); 42/256; Rptr FFA; Teachers Aide; Chorus; Rptr Nwsp; Hon Roll; Lion Awd; Mem Schl Based Coordinate Prgm; Fresno ST U; Ag Educ.

LOPEZ, CESAR; Central Union HS; El Centro, CA; (3); 76/543; Var Socr; Cit Awd; Hon Roll; CA ST U; Ag.

LOPEZ, CHRISTINA M; Gladstone HS; Covina, CA; (3); SADD; Band; Mrchg Band; Pep Band; Sec Jr Cls; Stu Cncl; Score Keeper; Swmmng; Hon Roll; Prfct Atten Awd; Music.

LOPEZ, CHRISTINE B; Lodi HS; Stockton, CA; (4); 122/399; French Clb; Hon Roll; San Joaquin Delta; Crimnl Admin.

LOPEZ, CHRISTINE E; Fresno HS; Fresno, CA; (3); 16/550; French Clb; Intnl Clb; Science Clb; Rptr Yrbk; Var Tennis; French Hon Soc; High Hon Roll; Hon Roll; Prfct Atten Awd; Rcvd A Varsity Letter For Tennis; Rcvd An Academic Letter; Member Of CA Scholarship Federation; Cal Poly; Engineering.

LOPEZ, CHRISTY F; Kingsburg HS; Kingsburg, CA; (3); Church Yth Grp; SADD; Teachers Aide; Band; Mrchg Band; Pep Band; Trk; Prfct Atten Awd; VROP; Chrstn Ldrshp Inst.

LOPEZ, CLARA; Northview HS; Azusa, CA; (2); Dance Clb; Pep Clb; Pom Pon; Girls Leag; Invlvd In My Church; Azusa Pacific U; Math.

LOPEZ, CLAUDIA; Pomona HS; Pomona, CA; (3); Computer Clb; German Clb; Spanish Clb; Sftbl; Wt Lftg; Hon Roll; Mecha Clb; LULAC; Mt Sac; Eclgyst.

LOPEZ, CLAUDIA M; Fremont HS; San Carlos, CA; (2); Pres Soph Cls; Stu In Media Acad; Oklnd All Cty Cncl; Law.

LOPEZ, CRISTINA; El Rancho HS; Pico Rivera, CA; (2); FTA; Key Clb; Spanish Clb; SADD; Teachers Aide; Hon Roll; UCSD; Sch Supt.

LOPEZ, CYNTHIA V; Colton HS; Colton, CA; (2); Key Clb; Yrbk; Sec Soph Cls; Rep Stu Cncl; Hon Roll; Mem Of Future Ldrs Of Amer; UCLA; Pre Law.

LOPEZ, DANIEL A; Sweetwater HS; National City, CA; (4); Drama Clb; Pres JA; Thesps; School Play; Variety Show; JV Trk; Wt Lftg; Cit Awd; Hon Roll; MECHA Dir Publcty; UCLA; Theatr Arts.

LOPEZ, DANIEL D; Madera HS; Madera, CA; (2); Dance Clb; Intrml Crs Cntry; JV Var Socr; Hon Roll; FBLA; Latin Clb; Stu Of Yr 89-89; Hnrs Alg II Awd; HS Folklrc Dance Grp; MIT; Bus.

LOPEZ, DAVID M; Glendora HS; Glendora, CA; (3); Science Clb; High Hon Roll; Hon Roll; Treas Frsh Cls; Pres Soph Cls; Pres Jr Cls; Pres Stu Cncl; Var JV Ftbl; Bus.

LOPEZ, DENISE G; John Burroughs HS; Burbank, CA; (4); Church Yth Grp; Dance Clb; Office Aide; Red Cross Aide; Drill Tm; Orch; Cheerldng; High Hon Roll; Watterson Coll; Law.

LOPEZ, DIANA L; Paraclete HS; Lancaster, CA; (3); Cmnty Wkr; Hosp Aide; Intnl Clb; JV Vllybl; Hon Roll; Rotary Awd; Hnrs Spnsh; CSF; Phys Thrpy.

LOPEZ, DOMINGO; Roosevelt HS; Fresno, CA; (2); JV Socr; Hon Roll; Med.

LOPEZ, DOROTHY E; Santa Ana HS; Santa Ana, CA; (3); Intnl Clb; Cit Awd; ROP Cert 90; CA ST Fullerton; Comp.

LOPEZ, ELIZA; Strathmore Union HS; Strathmore, CA; (3); 9/90; School Play; Rptr Nwsp; Ed Yrbk; Pres Soph Cls; Pres Jr Cls; Sftbl; Tennis; Vllybl; Cit Awd; High Hon Roll; Mock Trial; Ldrshp Yth Conf Pepperdine U; Ten-2nd Pl Girls Dbls-East Sierra League; Porterville Coll; Law.

LOPEZ, ELIZABETH; Dos Palos HS; Firebaugh, CA; (4); FHA; Office Aide; Teachers Aide; Rptr Nwsp; Phtg Yrbk; Hmcmg Queen 89-90; JCG Pres; Poem Published In Book; Merced Coll.

LOPEZ, ELIZABETH R; Sweetwater HS; National City, CA; (3); Sec VP Church Yth Grp; Teachers Aide; Cit Awd; Hon Roll; Prfct Atten Awd; Culture Clb; Intl Schl Of Bus Pgm Schlrshp Awd; Comps.

LOPEZ, ELIZABETH S; Balboa HS; San Francisco, CA; (3); Pres Soph Cls; Rep Stu Cncl; Var Bsktbl; Var Capt Crs Cntry; Var Sftbl; Var Capt Trk; Var Vllybl; Hon Roll; VP Schl; Publicity Mgr 88-89; 100 Buc VP; Cmptr Analyst.

LOPEZ, ELVIRA; Manteca HS; Lathrop, CA; (2); 1/500; Treas Intnl Clb; Key Clb; JV Bsbl; Bsktbl; High Hon Roll; Hon Roll; Dance Grp Ballet Fklrco De Lathrap; CA Schlrshp Fed; Acad Dcthln; Envrnmntlst.

LOPEZ, ERICCA; Gahr HS; Cerritos, CA; (2); Co-Capt Pep Clb; Varsity Clb; Co-Capt Drill Tm; Cheerldng; Pom Pon; Cit Awd; Spanish NHS; Dance.

LOPEZ, ERICK G; North Hollywood HS; North Hollywood, CA; (2); Letterman Clb; Teachers Aide; Arch.

LOPEZ, ERNEST L; Bell HS; Maywood, CA; (3); Band; Mrchg Band; Cit Awd; Hon Roll; UCLA; Comp.

LOPEZ, ESTELLA; River City HS; W Sacramento, CA; (3); Treas Spanish Clb; Hon Roll; Prfct Atten Awd; MESA; Multicltr Clb Treas; Peer-Engrng & Comp Sci; UCD.

LOPEZ, ESTHER ALICIA; Mount Diablo HS; W Pittsburg, CA; (1); French Clb; VP Frsh Cls; Hon Roll; CSF; Pop Warner Chrldng Coach; GATE.

LOPEZ, EVELYN PAOLA; Highlands HS; North Highlands, CA; (2); 24/400; Hon Roll; MESA; U S-Davis; Comp Sci Engrng.

LOPEZ, FAITH L; El Dorado HS; Placentia, CA; (3); 182/317; Church Yth Grp; Rptr Nwsp; Var JV Crs Cntry; JV Socr; Var JV Trk; Hon Roll; Track Awd-Mst Insprtnl; Wrtng & Drwng/Art; Fullerton JC; Wrtng.

LOPEZ, FAVIAN A; Don Bosco Technical Inst; Whittier, CA; (4); Cmnty Wkr; Amer Soc Of Mtls Intl; Big Bro Pgm; Amer Soc Non-Destructive Tstng; U CA Irvine; Film Prod.

LOPEZ, FELIPE H; Fontana HS; Fontana, CA; (4); 67/790; Church Yth Grp; Spanish Clb; Band; Jazz Band; Mrchg Band; School Musical; High Hon Roll; Hon Roll; Pres Acad Fit Awd; John Philip Sousa Awd; Semper Fidelis Awd; Musical Schlrshp To Grmny; Music.

LOPEZ, FRANCIS C; Seaside HS; Seaside, CA; (2); AFS; High Hon Roll; Upward Bound MPC; Airline Pilot.

LOPEZ, FRANCISCO T; Salinas HS; Salinas, CA; (2); Band; High Hon Roll; Prfct Atten Awd; Early Outreach Pgm Of U Of CA Santa Cruz; Sheriff Explorers; Acad Gold Card.

LOPEZ, FRANK A; Don Antonio Lugo HS; Chino, CA; (3); Band; Mrchg Band; Orch; JV Trk; High Hon Roll; Hon Roll; Pres Acad Fit Awd; Won Music Schlrshp; Lttred Acad & Band; Engrng Bus.

LOPEZ, FRANKIE; Roseville HS; Roseville, CA; (1); Church Yth Grp; JA; Red Cross Aide; Spanish Clb; Hon Roll; Davis; Doctor.

LOPEZ, GABRIEL; Tustin HS; Tustin, CA; (1); Intrml Bsbl; Intrml Bsktbl; Hon Roll; Prfct Atten Awd; U NV Las Vegas; Bsbl.

LOPEZ, GERMAN L; Calexico HS; Calexico, CA; (1); Socr; Hon Roll; UCSD.

LOPEZ, GINA M; Eisenhower HS; San Bernardino, CA; (2); Phtg Yrbk; Sftbl; Hon Roll; Bus.

LOPEZ, GLENN A; Ontario HS; Ontario, CA; (3); Teachers Aide; Varsity Clb; JV Var Bsktbl; Prfct Atten Awd; Schltc Awd 89-90; Play Golf; Wrk Comps; Cal Poly Pomona; Real Est.

LOPEZ, GRACIELA; Santa Clara HS; Oxnard, CA; (2); Church Yth Grp; French Clb; JV Bsktbl; High Hon Roll; NHS; UCLA; Bus.

LOPEZ, HENRY; Bell HS; Cudahy, CA; (3); Cit Awd; CSF; Elec Techncn.

LOPEZ, IGNACIO R; Gonzales HS; Greenfield, CA; (3); Church Yth Grp; Cmnty Wkr; Varsity Clb; Chorus; Crs Cntry; Socr; Trk; Wt Lftg; Hon Roll; Prfct Atten Awd; UCSD; Law.

LOPEZ, IRIS S; James Lick HS; San Jose, CA; (4); Church Yth Grp; Intnl Clb; Math Clb; SADD; Teachers Aide; Sftbl; Tennis; Hon Roll; Prfct Atten Awd; Evergreen Coll; Engrng.

LOPEZ, IRMA Y; East Bakersfield HS; Bakersfield, CA; (2); JA; Math Clb; SADD; Bsktbl; Sftbl; High Hon Roll; Loma Linda U; Obstrcs.

LOPEZ, J DIEGO; Grosssmont HS; Spain; (4); Church Yth Grp; Intnl Clb; Acpl Chr; Var L Socr; JV L Swmmng; Water Polo; Rugby; Madrid U; Law.

LOPEZ, JEANNIE; Fairfield HS; Fairfield, CA; (2); Rep Soph Cls; JV Cheerldng; JV Sftbl.

LOPEZ, JENNY C; Tustin HS; Tustin, CA; (1); 197/461; Church Yth Grp; Var Sftbl.

LOPEZ, JESSICA; Upper Lake HS; Upper Lake, CA; (2); Office Aide; Spanish Clb; SADD; Band; Chorus; Pres Frsh Cls; JV Bsktbl; JV Capt Cheerldng; JV Capt Pom Pon; Score Keeper; Bus.

LOPEZ, JESUS; Nogales HS; West Covina, CA; (2); Cit Awd; Hon Roll; Merit Awd Fall Semester 89-90; Merit Awd Fall Semester 88; UCLA; Engrng.

LOPEZ, JOHN P; Glendora HS; Glendora, CA; (4); SADD; Teachers Aide; Band; JV Rep Mrchg Band; School Play; Variety Show; Rptr Yrbk; Treas Frsh Cls; Pres Sr Cls; Hon Roll; Stu Mont 89; Acad Yr 89-90; Outstndng SR 90; Organized Fund Raiser Hlp Lukemia Patient Cmnty; S CA U; Bus Admin.

LOPEZ, JOSE B; Warren HS; Downey, CA; (3); JV Bsbl; JV Bsktbl; Prfct Atten Awd; Math.

LOPEZ, JOSE LUIS; Le Grand Union HS; Planada, CA; (4); Dance Clb; Score Club; UC ST Sacramento; Criminology.

LOPEZ, JUAN J; Venice HS; Los Angeles, CA; (2); German Clb; MESA; Jr Club; MA Inst Of Tech; Engrng.

LOPEZ, JULIANNA; Oak Grove HS; San Jose, CA; (2); Sec SADD; JV Vllybl; MESA; Bowlng; Cal Poly San Luis; Arch Engrng.

LOPEZ, KARLA; Marian Catholic HS; San Diego, CA; (3); Cmnty Wkr; Debate Tm; Drama Clb; NFL; Pep Clb; Spanish Clb; Speech Tm; SADD; Thesps; Varsity Clb; Jack Nolan Speech Fnst; Miss Teen San Diego Finlst; Med.

LOPEZ, LAURA; St Genevieve HS; Sylmar, CA; (2); Dance Clb; French Clb; Letterman Clb; Pep Clb; JV Bsktbl; JV Sftbl; French Hon Soc; UCLA.

LOPEZ, LEONORA; Live Oak HS; San Martin, CA; (3); Church Yth Grp; Dance Clb; Pep Clb; SADD; Pres Jr Cls; Rep Stu Cncl; Var Cheerldng; Var Fld Hcky; JV Trk; Yth Diocese Awd 1st Rnnr Up; Santa Clara; Ed.

LOPEZ, LETICIA; Eisenhower HS; Rialto, CA; (4); 10/622; Church Yth Grp; French Clb; FBLA; Spanish Clb; Teachers Aide; High Hon Roll; Hon Roll; Jr NHS; NHS; Cal ST U; Bus Admin.

LOPEZ, LISA M; Apple Valley HS; Apple Valley, CA; (2); FCA; Temple Yth Grp; Off Frsh Cls; Victor Valley Chrstn.

LOPEZ, LISSETTE X; Ygnacio Valley HS; Pittsburg, CA; (1); Latin Clb; Pres Frsh Cls; Bsktbl; High Hon Roll; Schl Site Cncl Vice Chrmn; UC Berkeley Prtnrshp Pgm; Ptsa Awd; UC Berkeley; Engr.

LOPEZ, LONNIE R; North HS; Bakersfield, CA; (2); Cmnty Wkr; Treas Drama Clb; School Play; Stage Crew; Rptr Nwsp; Ed Yrbk; High Hon Roll; CA Schlrshp Fed; Video News Clb; Reported For Local Nwspaper; Jrnlsm Psych.

LOPEZ, LOURDES; Northview HS; Covina, CA; (3); Teachers Aide; Hon Roll; Principals Hnr Roll Cert; Legal Sec.

LOPEZ, LOURDES; Ribet Acad; Glendale, CA; (4); Dance Clb; Latin Clb; Math Clb; Ski Clb; Varsity Clb; Chorus; Drill Tm; Ed Yrbk; Rep Frsh Cls; Glendale Coll; Bus.

LOPEZ, LUCIA L; Glen A Wilson HS; Hacienda Hts, CA; (2); Girl Scts; Band; Mrchg Band; Hon Roll; Prfct Atten Awd; Bus.

LOPEZ, LUPE; Livingston HS; Livingston, CA; (2); FBLA; Yrbk; Off Frsh Cls; Bsbl; Bsktbl; Cheerldng; Crs Cntry; Ftbl; Powder Puff Ftbl; Score Keeper; Doctor.

LOPEZ, LUZ M; Roosevelt HS; Los Angeles, CA; (2); Key Clb; Library Aide; Office Aide; Chorus; Church Choir; Cit Awd; Hon Roll; Jr NHS; Phys Ed Awd; Spelling Awd; Active Mem Key Club; Bus.

LOPEZ, MARBY; Corona HS; Corona, CA; (3); Drama Clb; German Clb; Flag Corp; Hon Roll; Appalachian ST U; Jrnlsm.

LOPEZ, MARCO A; San Dimas HS; San Dimas, CA; (2); Bsktbl; Var L Crs Cntry; Var L Trk; Cit Awd; High Hon Roll; Hon Roll; Kiwanis Awd; Prfct Atten Awd; Pres Acad Fit Awd; Perseverance Awd; Roses Awd; Royal Star Awd; Law Enfrcmnt.

LOPEZ, MARCOS A; Canyon HS; Canyon Country, CA; (2); JV Vllybl; Hon Roll; U Southern CA; Chem.

LOPEZ, MARIA; Silver Creek HS; San Jose, CA; (2); Church Yth Grp; Cmnty Wkr; Dance Clb; Stu Cncl; Swmmng; Hon Roll; Pres MESA; San Juan Obispo; Arch.

LOPEZ, MARIA A.; Orland HS; Orland, CA; (3); 1/125; VP Key Clb; Spanish Clb; Ed Nwsp; Pres Frsh Cls; Pres Soph Cls; Pres Jr Cls; Pres Sr Cls; Var Capt Cheerldng; Powder Puff Ftbl; JV Var Sftbl; Fri Night Live; Gftd & Tlntd Ed; CSF; Sociology.

LOPEZ, MARIA CARMEN; Sanger HS; Sanger, CA; (3); Vllybl; Police Clb.

LOPEZ, MARIA I; Nogales HS; W Covina, CA; (4); 35/582; Aud/Vis; Church Yth Grp; Drama Clb; Pres German Clb; School Play; Stage Crew; Lit Mag; Cit Awd; High Hon Roll; Amnesty Intl; Photo Club; UCLA; Prfssnl Filmmaker.

LOPEZ, MARIA J; Castle Park HS; Chula Vista, CA; (3); 43/422; Hon Roll; Bllt Folklorico-Prfrmng Mxcn Dncs; Exec Sec.

LOPEZ, MARIA J; Granada Hills HS; Sylmar, CA; (3); NFL; ROTC; Treas Speech Tm; Chorus; Orch; Cit Awd; High Hon Roll; NHS; Prfct Atten Awd; Pres Acad Fit Awd; PETA People Ethical Treatmnt Anmls; Photogrphy; Psych.

LOPEZ JR, MARIO; Sierra Vista HS; Baldwin Park, CA; (1); Chess Clb; Band; Mrchg Band; High Hon Roll; Hon Roll; Pres Acad Fit Awd; UCLA; Music.

LOPEZ, MARISA; El Toro HS; El Toro, CA; (4); 7/536; Var JV Tennis; High Hon Roll; Interact Clb-Treas; CA Schlstc Fdrtn; Saferides-Boardmember; U C Berkeley; Arch.

LOPEZ, MARISOL A; Pinole Valley HS; Pinole, CA; (2); Church Yth Grp; Rptr Nwsp; Hon Roll; Interact Club; CSF; Amnesty Intl; City Yth Comm; Contra Costa Coll Smmr Hnr Theatere 88 & 89; Anml Rghts.

LOPEZ, MARIVEL; Bonita Vista HS; Bonita, CA; (2); Flag Corp.

LOPEZ, MARTHA C; Santa Ana HS; Santa Ana, CA; (2); Computer Clb; Dance Clb; Hosp Aide; Office Aide; Stage Crew; Off Frsh Cls; Kiwanis Awd; UCLA; Crmnl Jstc.

LOPEZ, MARTIN; San Benito HS; Hollister, CA; (2); French Clb; VP FBLA; JV Socr; Wt Lftg; Stanford; Bus Lw.

LOPEZ, MARTIN V; King City HS; King City, CA; (3); FFA; Teachers Aide; Hon Roll; Bus.

LOPEZ, MARY JANE P; St Genevieve HS; Gasylmar, CA; (3); French Clb; Hon Roll; CSUN; Bus Admin.

LOPEZ, MERRICK R; Glendale Adventist Acad; Palmdale, CA; (1); Band; Hon Roll; Pres Acad Fit Awd; Loma Linda; Med.

LOPEZ, MICHAEL A; Indio HS; Indio, CA; (4); Color Guard; Gym; USFSA Icesktng; ISIA.

LOPEZ, MIGUEL A; Calexico HS; Calexico, CA; (2); Spnsh AP Clb; Imperial Vly Coll; Tchr.

LOPEZ, MIGUEL A; South San Francsisco HS; South San Francis, CA; (2); Hon Roll; Law.

LOPEZ, MIKE T; Wasco Union HS; Wasco, CA; (2); JV Ftbl; Capt JV Trk; JV Wt Lftg; GATE Pgm; Engr.

LOPEZ, MIRIAM; Sacred Heart Of Mary HS; Los Angeles, CA; (3); Cmnty Wkr; GAA; Hosp Aide; Chorus; School Play; Rep Soph Cls; Rep Jr Cls; Rep Stu Cncl; Hon Roll; NHS; Mother Butler Cum Laude Scts; Yth Gov Prog; Loyola Marymount U; Law.

LOPEZ, MIRNA; El Rancho HS; Pico Rivera, CA; (2); Church Yth Grp; Cmnty Wkr; Intnl Clb; Math Clb; Math Tm; Science Clb; Var L Trk; Cit Awd; High Hon Roll; Hon Roll; CA ST Long Beach; Med.

LOPEZ, MONICA; Norwalk HS; Norwalk, CA; (2); Pep Clb; SADD; Teachers Aide; Drill Tm; Var Capt Cheerldng; Var Trk; Cit Awd; High Hon Roll; Hon Roll; Prfct Atten Awd; Stanford; Engineering.

LOPEZ, MYRA; Beyer HS; Modesto, CA; (3); Latin Clb; Cit Awd; Hon Roll; Hnrs Golden St Exam Geom; Patriot Awd For Frgn Lang; Mech Engnr.

LOPEZ, NEA C; North Salinas HS; Salinas, CA; (4); Church Yth Grp; Office Aide; Spanish Clb; SADD; Teachers Aide; Acpl Chr; Chorus; Church Choir; Nwsp; Wt Lftg; U; Psychology.

LOPEZ, NELSON X; San Fernando HS; Pacoima, CA; (4); Var Socr; Cit Awd; CSUN; Comp.

LOPEZ, NENA M; Chino HS; Chino, CA; (3); Church Yth Grp; Socr; Hon Roll; Music Video Prdctn.

LOPEZ, NORA ALICIA; Castle Park HS; Chula Vista, CA; (2).

LOPEZ, NORA M; Alisal HS; Salinas, CA; (4); Scrkpr Drama Clb; Library Aide; Office Aide; Teachers Aide; High Hon Roll; Hon Roll; Prfct Atten Awd; Pres Acad Fit Awd; Acadc Achvt Gld Card; Hartnell Coll; Comp Engr.

LOPEZ, NORMA; El Rancho HS; Pico Rivera, CA; (2); Church Yth Grp; Intnl Clb; Science Clb; Crs Cntry; Trk; Hon Roll; Sports; CA ST U Long Beach; Ed.

LOPEZ, OCTAVIO P; Pater Noster HS; Los Angeles, CA; (4); 10/53; Cmnty Wkr; FBLA; Letterman Clb; Office Aide; Service Clb; Varsity Clb; Church Choir; Treas Jr Cls; Var Bsktbl; JV Crs Cntry; U CA Santa Barbara; Sprts Med.

LOPEZ, PATRICIA A; Downey HS; Downey, CA; (2); FCA; Spanish Clb; Drill Tm; Var Crs Cntry; Intrml Powder Puff Ftbl; Var Trk; Latino Clb; Hwarang-Do; Northwestern; Med.

LOPEZ, PATRICK R; Glendale Adv Acad; Palmdale, CA; (3); 9/59; Teachers Aide; Treas Soph Cls; Intrml Mgr Bsktbl; Intrml Mgr Ftbl; Hon Roll; NHS; Awd Merit Gemetry 89 & Alg Ii 90; Cal Poly San Luis Obispo; Engr.

LOPEZ, PEDRO L; Richard HS; Artesia, CA; (3).

LOPEZ, PEDRO N; San Gorgonio HS; San Bernardino, CA; (3); 80/700; Church Yth Grp; French Clb; Latin Clb; Library Aide; Spanish Clb; Teachers Aide; School Play; Powder Puff Ftbl; Prfct Atten Awd; Spanish NHS; U Of Southern CA; Math.

LOPEZ, RALPH; Saddleback HS; Santa Ana, CA; (3); Cmnty Wkr; Spanish Clb; SADD; Var Capt Bsbl; Wrstlng; Cit Awd; Hon Roll; Prfct Atten Awd; Pres Acad Fit Awd; Stu Of Month-Wall Of Fame; Bus.

LOPEZ, RAMIRO; Gardena HS; Gardena, CA; (3); Teachers Aide; Yrbk; Bsbl; Cit Awd; Prfct Atten Awd; USC Med Cor Pgm Med Pgm; USC; Doctor.

LOPEZ, RAMON P; Servite HS; La Palma, CA; (3); Debate Tm; Var Ftbl; Var Socr; Var Wt Lftg; CSF.

LOPEZ, REBECCA L; Hemet HS; Hemet, CA; (3); 238/475; Church Yth Grp; Office Aide; Teachers Aide; Acpl Chr; Chorus; Rep Sr Cls; Rep Stu Cncl; JV Powder Puff Ftbl; Prfct Atten Awd.

LOPEZ, RENE O; Escondido HS; Escondido, CA; (1); Spanish Clb; Var Socr; Sportsman Award; Jim Humphrey Memorial Award; U C L A; Sports Medicine.

LOPEZ, ROBERTO; Hayward HS; Hayward, CA; (3); Var Bsbl; Bsktbl; Var L Ftbl; Socr; Wt Lftg; Var Hon Roll; Firefighter; Mrns & Army.

LOPEZ, ROBERTO; North Hollywood HS; N Hollywood, CA; (4); Math Clb; Chorus; Crs Cntry; Trk; High Hon Roll; Rnsslr Plytech Inst Mdl Awd-Mth & Sci Excllnc; Mst Outstndng Sci JR Stu 88-89; Outstndng Achvt-Mdrs; U Of CA Los Angeles; Biochem.

LOPEZ, ROBERTO; San Pedro HS; San Pedro, CA; (3); English Clb; JA; Service Clb; Teachers Aide; Color Guard; Wt Lftg; Prfct Atten Awd; Navy; Comp Engr.

LOPEZ, ROGELIO; Salesian HS; Los Angeles, CA; (3); 6/87; VP Letterman Clb; Nwsp; Capt Bsktbl; VP Crs Cntry; JV Trk; Hon Roll; Univ.

LOPEZ, ROY; Eagle Rock HS; Los Angeles, CA; (3); Chess Clb; Jazz Band; Mrchg Band; Crs Cntry; Trk; Ntl Merit Ltr; Prfct Atten Awd; Pres Acad Fit Awd; Close Up Fndtn Ctzn Bee; Harvard.

LOPEZ, RUBEN; Lynwood HS; Lynwood, CA; (2); Teachers Aide; Wt Lftg; Arch.

LOPEZ, RUBY L; Tomales HS; Inverness, CA; (3); Cmnty Wkr; Ski Clb; Pres Spanish Clb; Teachers Aide; Flag Corp; Stu Cncl; JV Var Cheerldng; High Hon Roll; Hon Roll; Jr NHS; Bus.

LOPEZ, SALVADOR; Gonzales Union HS; Soledad, CA; (2); Ftbl; High Hon Roll; Prfct Atten Awd; CA Schlrshp Fed.

LOPEZ, SOCORRO A; Saddleback HS; Santa Ana, CA; (3); French Clb; FBLA; Intnl Clb; Pep Clb; SADD; Acpl Chr; Chorus; Variety Show; Stu Cncl; Vllybl; Peace Clb; Pre-Law.

LOPEZ, SONIA A; Selma HS; Selma, CA; (3); Church Yth Grp; Dance Clb; FHA; Girl Scts; Pep Clb; Spanish Clb; Teachers Aide; Cheerldng; Pom Pon; Hon Roll; Cert Of Achvt; Frsno Pcfc Coll; Psych.

LOPEZ, SONIA L; Sweetwater Union HS; National City, CA; (2); Hon Roll; SDSU; Cmptr Pgmmr.

LOPEZ, STEFANIE; Glen A Wilson HS; Hacienda Hts, CA; (2); Art Clb; Rep Band; Mrchg Band; Orch; Off Frsh Cls; Off Soph Cls; Rep Stu Cncl; Trk; Mst Outstndng Band Stu; Jeff Briggs Memrl Awd; Mst Promising Band Stu; 2nd Pl Writing Awd; UC Berkeley; Commnctns.

LOPEZ, STEVEN RONNIE; Don Bosco Tech Inst; Monterey Park, CA; (1); 28/244; JV Bsktbl; Grphc Comm.

LOPEZ, SUZANNA; Bishop Amat HS; S El Monte, CA; (3); Girl Scts; Spanish Clb; Hon Roll; NHS; U Southern CA.

LOPEZ, TAMI; Downey HS; Downey, CA; (1); Church Yth Grp; Cmnty Wkr; Pep Clb; Cheerldng; High Hon Roll; St Schlr; Assisteens; Dance Grp Cmptns; Stanford; Law.

LOPEZ, TESSA; Richard Gahr HS; Artesia, CA; (3); Chess Clb; Cmnty Wkr; Drama Clb; GAA; Intnl Clb; Office Aide; SADD; Teachers Aide; Varsity Clb; School Play; Pr Cnslr 3 Yrs; CA ST; Law.

LOPEZ, THERESA; Chaffey HS; Ontario, CA; (4); 6/250; Church Yth Grp; Band; Mrchg Band; Ed Yrbk; Powder Puff Ftbl; High Hon Roll; Hon Roll; CA Schlrshp Fed Clb VP; Keywannette Clb; Ivy Chain; CAL Poly San Luis Obispo; Arch.

LOPEZ, VALERIE; St Genevieve HS; Arleta, CA; (3); Art Clb; Office Aide; Spanish Clb; Teachers Aide; Chorus; Flag Corp; Orch; Bsktbl; Hon Roll; UCLA; Educ.

LOPEZ, VERNA; Arroyo HS; El Monte, CA; (2); Key Clb; Pep Clb; Chorus; School Musical; Variety Show; Cheerldng; Cit Awd; Hon Roll; Friday Nght Live; JV Cheer 1990-91; JR Clas Secy 1990-91; Cal ST Fullerton; Advtsng Agcy.

LOPEZ, VERONICA A; Mt Carmel HS; San Diego, CA; (4); DECA; Off FBLA; Psych.

LOPEZ, VIRGINIA; Fillmore HS; Fillmore, CA; (4); Library Aide; Teachers Aide; Prfct Atten Awd; Tchr.

LOPEZ, WILLIAM D; Hueneme HS; Oxnard, CA; (3); JV Socr; Hon Roll; Prfct Atten Awd; Engr.

LOPEZ, XOCHITL; Southwest HS; San Ysidro, CA; (2); Jazz Band; Hon Roll; ASB.

LOPEZ LIZARDO, MANUEL; Moorpark HS; Moorpark, CA; (3); Latin Clb; Crs Cntry; Trk; Hon Roll; Mst Vlbl Rnnr Crss Cntry; Nature, Reading; Mech Engr.

LOPEZ LIZARDO, MARIA ESTHER; Moorpark HS; Moorpark, CA; (3); Latin Clb; Var Crs Cntry; Var Trk; Hon Roll; Moorpark Coll; Attrny.

LOPUHOVSKY, WENDY; Highlands HS; North Highlands, CA; (1); JV Capt Bsktbl; Powder Puff Ftbl; JV Vllybl; CSUS; Elem Tchr.

LOR, KOU; Roosevelt HS; Fresno, CA; (2); Hon Roll; Fresno ST; Air Craft Mech.

LOR, MAO; Grant HS; Sacramento, CA; (2); Intnl Clb; Science Clb; Stu Cncl; Tennis; High Hon Roll; Stu Rchng Out; Kybd Clb; Pacr Prd Clb; Kybdst.

LOR, SOPHIN; Paramount HS; Paramount, CA; (2); Lit Mag; Var Crs Cntry; Intrml Trk; Cit Awd; Prfct Atten Awd; Pres Acad Fit Awd; CSF Schlrshp Fed Club & Coll Club; Principal Achvt List; MVP Cross Country 89-90.

LOR, TEVY; Lincoln HS; Stockton, CA; (4); Church Yth Grp; Teachers Aide; School Musical; Intrml Crs Cntry; JV Tennis; Hon Roll; Vrsty Bdmttn; CA Schlstc Fed Clb; Davis; Gen Srgn.

LOR, XEE; Lindhurst HS; Marysville, CA; (2); Doc.

LOR, YANG; Hoover HS; Fresno, CA; (1); Hon Roll.

LORBIECKI, JEREMY; Beyer HS; Modesto, CA; (3); Bsktbl; Ftbl; Hon Roll; College; Business/Accounting.

LORCA, HERMINIA S; Eagle Rock HS; Los Angeles, CA; (3); Sec Key Clb; SADD; Hon Roll; Frndshp Intl Assn; U Of CA Riverside; Biomed Sci.

LORD, BEVERLIE; Saint Michaels HS; Los Angeles, CA; (2); 5/300; Pres Church Yth Grp; Cmnty Wkr; Drama Clb; 4-H; Sec FHA; School Play; Ed Nwsp; Var Cheerldng; JV Vllybl; Hon Roll; Ms Debutante 89; Stu Month; Mt St Marys Coll; CPA.

LORD, BRADLEY; Bishop Amat HS; West Covina, CA; (4); 45/415; Var Trk; Hon Roll; Cal Poly Pomona; Corp Law.

LORD, DAWN M; Arlington HS; Riverside, CA; (3); Teachers Aide; Bsktbl; Trk; Trk; San Diego ST U; Marine Bio.

LORD, ELI; Hamilton HS Academy Of Music; North Hollywood, CA; (4); Band; Jazz Band; Mrchg Band; School Musical; School Play; Wt Lftg; Hon Roll; CA ST Northridge; Music.

LORD, KEVIN T; Clovis HS; Clovis, CA; (4); 102/536; Debate Tm; Science Clb; Teachers Aide; Var Tennis; Wt Lftg; Hon Roll; Pres Acad Fit Awd; Fresno ST U; CPA.

LORENAT, JEAN; San Mateo HS; Foster City, CA; (3); Church Yth Grp; German Clb; VP Soph Cls; Pres Jr Cls; JV Capt Socr; JV Capt Tennis; Var L Trk; High Hon Roll; City Yth Advsry Cncl 9-11, Vice Chrmn; Gldn St Math Awds-Alg Hi Hnrs, Geom Hnrs; Track Outstndng Awd.

LORENTZ, CHRISTINA V; Pinole Valley HS; Pinole, CA; (1); German Clb; Gym; Trk; UC Berkeley; Ped.

LORENZ, CHRIS; Victor Valley HS; Victorville, CA; (1); Aviation.

LORENZ, GEORGE W; Oakdale HS; Oakdale, CA; (2); Chess Clb; Science Clb; Ski Clb; Rep Stu Cncl; JV Bsbl; Capt Var Socr; Hon Roll; Prfct Atten Awd; UCLA; Marketing.

LORENZ, ROBERT B; Mountain View HS; El Monte, CA; (1); ROTC; Yrbk; Bsbl; Bsktbl; Ftbl; Socr; Sftbl; Vllybl; Wt Lftg; Cit Awd; Probation Officer.

LORENZANA, VERONICA; Whitney HS; Cerritos, CA; (1); Var JV Cheerldng; Opt Clb Awd.

LORENZINI, RYAN A; Mission San Jose HS; Fremont, CA; (1); Church Yth Grp; Ski Clb; Guitar, Music, Keyboards; Bus.

LORENZO, HOLLY; Tulare Western HS; Waukena, CA; (4); 2/230; Am Leg Aux Girls St; Church Yth Grp; 4-H; Off Stu Cncl; Sec Jr Cls; Off Sr Cls; Stu Cncl; Cheerldng; Vllybl; High Hon Roll; Soroptimist Intl Girl Of Month 89; Tulare Co Jr Fair Bd Secy; CA ST U Fresno; Accntng.

LORENZO, IDA A; Warren HS; Downey, CA; (2); School Play.

LORENZO, JOSIE; Mills HS; Redwood City, CA; (2); CA Schlrshp Fed 89 90; Acad Achvt Awd 88-89; Principals Awd 90; Acctng.

LORETTA, ANDREW E; University Of San Diego HS; San Diego, CA; (2); Church Yth Grp; Cmnty Wkr; JV Bsktbl; Stat Score Keeper; Cit Awd; Athl Trng.

LORIE, GEORGIA; Los Gatos HS; Monte Sereno, CA; (4); 50/374; NFL; Speech Tm; Orch; Yrbk; Stu Cncl; High Hon Roll; Hon Roll; Ntl Merit SF; Ice Skate Cmptns 9 Yrs; CSF Pres; Drama Awd For Speech & Debate; Bus.

LORINCZ, AIMEE G; San Benito Joint Union HS; Hollister, CA; (2); Church Yth Grp; 4-H; GAA; Var Tennis; 4-H Awd; Hon Roll; CSF; UCSB.

LORRABAQUIO, ALBERT; Redlands HS; San Bernardino, CA; (2); Aud/Vis; Cmnty Wkr; Computer Clb; Library Aide; Scholastic Bowl; Teachers Aide; Intrml Bsbl; Intrml JV Bsktbl; Intrml Ftbl; Wt Lftg; Coll Prep Courses; USC; Arch.

LORTIE, JENNIFER L; Flintridge Preparatory Schl; La Canada Flintri, CA; (3); Latin Clb; School Play; Stage Crew; Variety Show; JV Bsktbl; JV Var Swmmng; JV Var Vllybl; Cit Awd; Hon Roll; NHS; Natl Ltn Hnr Soc; Crmnlgy.

LOS, CHRIS W; Trabuco Hills HS; Mission Viejo, CA; (1); 42/360; Boy Scts; Intrml Vllybl; Hon Roll; Rotary Awd; CA Poly; Vet Sci.

LOSEE, MICHELE L; Victor Valley SR HS; Victorville, CA; (2); Church Yth Grp; Teachers Aide; Hon Roll; Engl Awd; Brigham Young U; Dance Chrgrphr.

LOSEE, SAM; Sierra HS; Tollhouse, CA; (2); FFA; Bsbl; Socr; Trk; Hon Roll; Fresno ST; Bus; Landscaping.

LOSEY, MATT W; Paraclete HS; Lancaster, CA; (2); Debate Tm; Drama Clb; JA; Key Clb; Quiz Bowl; School Play; Yrbk; Var Golf; High Hon Roll; NHS.

LOSH, JASMINE A; Bullard HS; Fresno, CA; (2); Band; Hon Roll; Bio, Phys Sci & Bullard Acad Awds; CA ST U Of Fresno; Bus.

LOSKOT, KELLY S; St Bernard HS; Los Angeles, CA; (2); Hon Roll; Hrsbck Rdng & Hrse Show; HS Diploma 90; Entrnmnt Indstry.

LOSS, ELIZABETH R; Villa Park HS; Villa Park, CA; (4); 2/487; Key Clb; SADD; Rptr Yrbk; Var Capt Cheerldng; High Hon Roll; NHS; Pres Acad Fit Awd; Sal; Mock Trial Team; Math Medallion; CSF Treas; UCLA; Lang.

LOSS, RICK; Villa Park HS; Villa Park, CA; (3); Key Clb; SADD; Stu Cncl; Var Swmmng; Hon Roll; Vrsty Water Polo.

LOTAKOV, ANETA M; Birmingham HS; Tarzana, CA; (3); Art Clb; Computer Clb; Dance Clb; Rep Ski Clb; School Musical; Sec Frsh Cls; Var Swmmng; Gov Hon Prg Awd; High Hon Roll; Earth Rights Clb; UCLA; Medcl.

LOTHRINGER, JENNIFER; Ocean View HS; Huntington Bch, CA; (4); Dance Clb; Pep Clb; Teachers Aide; Drill Tm; Var Cheerldng; CSF; Westminstr Mall Fash Panel; Cmnty Serv Aids Walk; CA ST U Fullerton; Intl Bus.

LOTINO, MARIO T; Carson HS; Carson, CA; (3); German Clb; Off Jr Cls; CSF; Chem Clb; Interact; UC Irvine; Surgeon.

LOTT, HEATHER A; Ramona HS; Riverside, CA; (3); 35/400; Drama Clb; French Clb; Chorus; School Musical; Rptr Nwsp; Ntl Merit SF; Natl Engl Mrt Awd; 1st Pl Sr Poetry Div; CA St San Bernadino Creatvie Wrtng Cont; Engl.

LOTTIE, SHONDI A; Washington Prep HS; Los Angeles, CA; (3); Cmnty Wkr; JA; Pres Math Clb; Office Aide; Teachers Aide; Jazz Band; Ed Yrbk; Rep Jr Cls; Stu Cncl; JV Pom Pon; Schlstc Acad Dcthln; Knights & Ladies; Mesa VP; USC; Pre Med.

LOUCH, LORI A; San Juan HS; Orangevale, CA; (4); 34/268; Church Yth Grp; Library Aide; Sec SADD; Band; Church Choir; Capt Flag Corp; Pep Band; Hon Roll; Bk Amer Plaq Wnr; CA ST U Sacramento; Elem Ed.

LOUCKS, DARIN; Beyer HS; Modesto, CA; (3); German Clb; Ski Clb; Ed Yrbk; L Capt Crs Cntry; L Var Trk; Cit Awd; Hon Roll; Sports Med.

LOUGEAY, GREGG C; San Dieguito HS; Encinitas, CA; (3); Var Vllybl; Golden St Exam Hnrs; Aerospc Engrng.

LOUGEE, AMY; Palmdale HS; Palmdale, CA; (3); 21/644; Church Yth Grp; Pep Clb; SADD; Teachers Aide; Off Sr Cls; JV Cheerldng; Powder Puff Ftbl; Hon Roll; Keywanettes; Bus.

LOUGHRAN II, EDMUND; Wheatland Union HS; Wheatland, CA; (1); FBLA; German Clb; JA; Letterman Clb; Varsity Clb; JV Bsktbl; Var L Crs Cntry; Var L Trk; Hon Roll; Air Force Acad; Engl.

LOUGHRY, BROOKS S; El Toro HS; El Toro, CA; (3); 98/484; Bsktbl; Ftbl; Hon Roll.

LOUI, ALBERT; Alameda HS; Alameda, CA; (2); 7/290; Chess Clb; Science Clb; JV Tennis; High Hon Roll; Hon Roll; Prfct Atten Awd; Astrophyscs.

LOUI, APRIL W; Pinole Valley HS; Pinole, CA; (3); Pres Debate Tm; French Clb; Math Clb; Pres NFL; Science Clb; Ski Clb; Pres Speech Tm; Teachers Aide; Rep Jr Cls; High Hon Roll; Best Debate Team 89-90; 1st Pl Showstopper Natl Tlnt Cmptn; 2nd Pl Exchange Clb Tlnt Show; Cty Yth Comm; Cornell; Medicine.

LOUI, RACHEL; Alameda HS; Alameda, CA; (4); 17/325; Art Clb; Church Yth Grp; English Clb; Science Clb; Var Tennis; Var Trk; High Hon Roll; Hnrs Awd Gldn St Exm Geom 87; Acad Awd 89 4 Smstrs 4.0 GPA Mth, Frgn Lang; CA Schlrshp Fdrtn; U CA Davis.

LOUIE, BRIAN G; Phillip & Sala Burton HS; San Francisco, CA; (3); Cmnty Wkr; Drama Clb; Red Cross Aide; Teachers Aide; School Play; Stage Crew; Bsbl; Score Keeper; Vllybl; Wt Lftg; Principals Hnr Roll; Free Throw Awd; Pres Awd; San Francisco ST; Bus Mgmt.

LOUIE, CELESTE; Lowell HS; San Francisco, CA; (3); Office Aide; Red Cross Aide; Hon Roll; Pres Acad Fit Awd; Bus Admin.

LOUIE, DENNIS; Irvine HS; Irvine, CA; (2); 120/553; Church Yth Grp; Ski Clb; Band; Mrchg Band; JV Bsbl; JV Socr; UCLA; Bus.

LOUIE, EDWARD; Edison SR HS; Stockton, CA; (3); Boy Scts; Math Clb; Science Clb; VICA; Hon Roll; NHS; Mech Engr.

LOUIE, ERIN A; Villa Park HS; Villa Park, CA; (3); Treas French Clb; Key Clb; SADD; Teachers Aide; High Hon Roll; Hon Roll; NHS; Pres Acad Fit Awd; UC Santa Barbara; Advrtsng.

LOUIE, FRANCINE; Mc Ateer HS; San Francisco, CA; (2); Mgr Vllybl; Cit Awd; Prfct Atten Awd; Pres Acad Fit Awd; Bus.

LOUIE, GINA M; Pittsburg HS; Pittsburg, CA; (4); 3/288; Sec Mu Alpha Theta; Sec Science Clb; Treas Service Clb; Var Tennis; High Hon Roll; CSF; Acad Decath; Centra Costa Cnty Spelling Bees 1989-90; U CA-LOS Angeles; Bus.

LOUIE, KRISTINA D; Lowell HS; San Francisco, CA; (2); German Clb; Pres Intnl Clb; Jr Statesmn America; Juniata Coll; Bio.

LOUIE, LESLIE; Schurr HS; Montebello, CA; (3); Office Aide; SADD; Varsity Clb; JV Sftbl; JV Tennis; Var Trk; CA Schlrshp Fed; Interact Club Incmng Pres 90-91; U Of CA; Bus Admin.

LOUIE, NICOLE A; College Park HS; Pleasant Hill, CA; (2); Church Yth Grp; Drama Clb; Spanish Clb; JV Cheerldng; Hon Roll; Pedtrn.

LOUIE, SHARIANNE G; Lowell HS; San Francisco, CA; (3); Cmnty Wkr; Hosp Aide; Office Aide; Q&S; Science Clb; Service Clb; Teachers Aide; Orch; Gov Hon Prg Awd; High Hon Roll; Pre-Med Clb Sec & Publcty Mgr; CSF; UC Davis; Chem.

LOUIE, TAMMY; Raoul Wallenberg Traditional HS; San Francisco, CA; (2); Boy Scts; Sec Intnl Clb; Library Aide; Math Clb; Math Tm; Red Cross Aide; Temple Yth Grp; Chorus; Orch; Nwsp; CSF 1989-90; Gldn St Exam High Hnrs-Alg; Gallo Salame Ldrshp Awd; Suprior-Solo Ensmbl Fstvl; U Of CA Berkeley; Genetcs.

LOUIE, TIM; San Marino HS; San Marino, CA; (3); 80/260; Boy Scts; Chess Clb; Computer Clb; JCL; Treas Latin Clb; Stage Crew; JV Crs Cntry; Var Trk; DAR Awd; High Hon Roll; Loyola Marymount U; Elec Engrng.

LOUIS, ELHAM J; Saratoga HS; Los Gatos, CA; (1); Drama Clb; Chorus; School Musical; Rep Stu Cncl; Hon Roll; Interact Clb; VP, Secy Chorus; Bio.

LOUIS, EMILY G; Edison HS; Huntington Beach, CA; (1); Boy Scts; Church Yth Grp; GAA; Intrml Vllybl; High Hon Roll; Pres Acad Fit Awd; Phys Ed Acad Imprvmnt Awd; U CA; Sprts Med.

LOUIS, LATRICIA D; Chino HS; Chino, CA; (2); Bsktbl; Trk; Vllybl; Prfct Atten Awd; Ebony Excllnc Clb; Law.

LOUISA, STEPHANIE ANN; San Leandro HS; San Leandro, CA; (4); Var Cheerldng; High Hon Roll; Hon Roll; Rally Squad Schlrshp; CSU; Adv.

LOUKOS, MELISSA; Hesperia HS; Phelan, CA; (4); Church Yth Grp; Cmnty Wkr; Key Clb; SADD; Stu Cncl; Trk; Hon Roll; CA ST San Diego; Crtve Writ.

LOUREIRO, ALBERTO; Palo Verde HS; Blythe, CA; (2); Letterman Clb; Spanish Clb; Bsbl; Bsktbl; Ftbl; Hon Roll; U CA San Diego; Bus Mgmt.

LOUREIRO, MICHAEL D; East Union HS; French Camp, CA; (1); 1/500; Bsbl; Bsktbl; Ftbl; Wt Lftg; Hon Roll; Gate; Stanford; Arch.

LOUTSCH, AARON P; Casa Grande HS; Petaluma, CA; (2); Band; Jazz Band; Mrchg Band; Var Bsbl; JV Crs Cntry; Var Wrstlng; High Hon Roll; Hon Roll; NHS; Hgh Hnrs Golden St Exm Geom, Hnrs Alg I; CA Poly; Aerospace Engr.

LOUTZENHISER, MARK S; Casa Roble Fundamental HS; Orangevale, CA; (4); Boy Scts; Math Tm; Science Clb; JV Socr; Var Trk; Cit Awd; High Hon Roll; NHS; Ntl Merit SF; Prfct Atten Awd; U CA Berkeley; Chem Engr.

LOUX, SHARON M; Castro Valley HS; San Leandro, CA; (3); Church Yth Grp; Acpl Chr; Church Choir; School Musical; Variety Show; VP Jr Cls; Intrml Ftbl; JV Swmmng; JV Tennis; High Hon Roll; Madrigals Stu Dir.

LOVAN, LESLIE J; Clovis West HS; Clovis, CA; (3); Church Yth Grp; Drama Clb; Intnl Clb; Spanish Clb; Teachers Aide; Band; Mrchg Band; High Hon Roll; Hon Roll; Spnsh Ed.

LOVATO, JOHNNY; Adolfo Camarillo HS; Camarillo, CA; (4); 17/450; Cmnty Wkr; FBLA; Ski Clb; SADD; Yrbk; Intrml JV Bsbl; Intrml JV Ftbl; JV Golf; Hon Roll; Counselor At Childrens YMCA Camps; UC Santa Barbara; Bus Econ.

LOVATO, JOSE L; Ontario HS; Ontario, CA; (3); Computer Clb; Math Tm; Speech Tm; Var Tennis; High Hon Roll; Honors In Alg Gldn St Exam; HLOP; UCLA; Law.

LOVATO, JUAN L; Eagle Rock HS; Los Angeles, CA; (3); Pres Chess Clb; Varsity Clb; Chorus; Stage Crew; Var Bsktbl; Var Vllybl; Cit Awd; Hon Roll; Engr.

LOVE, ANGELA E; Samuel F B Morse HS; San Diego, CA; (2); Drama Clb; Chorus; Drill Tm; School Musical; Variety Show; Trk; Cit Awd; Hon Roll; Art Club In Sydney Australia; Engrng.

LOVE, BARBARA Y; Skyline HS; Oakland, CA; (3); German Clb; Hosp Aide; Key Clb; SADD; Band; Socr; High Hon Roll; Gldn St Merit Schlr Algbr & Hnrb Mntn Geom; CJSF; CSF; Pre-Med.

LOVE, CARALEE; Trabuco Hills HS; Mission Viejo, CA; (2); 42/415; Church Yth Grp; Dance Clb; Drama Clb; Chorus; Church Choir; School Musical; School Play; Swing Chorus; Variety Show; Rep Frsh Cls; Brigham Young U.

LOVE, CYDNEY; Palo Verde HS; Blythe, CA; (3); Cmnty Wkr; GAA; JA; Key Clb; Teachers Aide; JV Bsktbl; JV Vllybl; Hon Roll.

LOVE, DAVID A; Torrey Pines HS; Rancho Santa Fe, CA; (2); Boy Scts; Office Aide; Bsktbl; Ftbl; Lcrss; 1st Pl Cyling Comptn; Econ.

LOVE, DONALD R; Montclair HS; Montclair, CA; (3); 70/204; Bus Profs of Am; Dance Clb; Drama Clb; Math Clb; Math Tm; Teachers Aide; Varsity Clb; Chorus; Jazz Band; VP Jr Cls; USC; Engr.

LOVE, EDDIE H; Workman HS; Valinda, CA; (1); Bsbl; Bsktbl; Ftbl; Wt Lftg; Cit Awd; Hon Roll; Prfct Atten Awd; MVP Bsktbl & Ftbl; Stu Mnth For Math & Home Ec; Trophy Mst Pts & Mst Rebounds Bsktbl; Prfssnl Athlt.

LOVE, JAIME E; Lowell HS; San Francisco, CA; (3); Church Yth Grp; Cmnty Wkr; Teachers Aide; Church Choir; Goldn St Exam Alg Hnrs.

LOVE, JENNIFER; Fred C Beyer HS; Empire, CA; (1); SADD; Cheerldng; UC Berkeley; Corp Law.

LOVE, JESSIE C; John F Kennedy HS; Sacramento, CA; (2); 157/525; Church Yth Grp; FHA; GAA; SADD; Bsktbl; Sftbl; Prnts For Black Stu Achvt Schlrshp; Mst Vlubl Jv Offnsve Plyr Bskbl; Mst Vlubl Defnsve Plyr Jr Sftbl; Social Worker.

LOVE, JULIE M; Valhalla HS; El Cajon, CA; (2); 17/450; Hosp Aide; Rptr Nwsp; Stu Cncl; High Hon Roll; Jrnlsm.

LOVE, KACI; Westchester HS; Los Angeles, CA; (3); Church Yth Grp; Cmnty Wkr; Hosp Aide; Rep Soph Cls; Rep Jr Cls; Hon Roll; Debutante Schlrshp Ball-Ms Personality; 170 Volunteer Svc Hrs; Grambling ST U; Psych.

LOVE, MELANIE; Lodi Acad; Stockton, CA; (1); Church Yth Grp; Drama Clb; Ski Clb; Band; Off Frsh Cls; Bsbl; Capt Bsktbl; Gym; Vllybl; Hon Roll; La Sierra; Psych.

LOVE, ROSE M; Fremont HS; Oakland, CA; (2); Drama Clb; GAA; Office Aide; Teachers Aide; Var Bsktbl; Var Sftbl; Cit Awd; High Hon Roll; Hon Roll.

LOVE, SUMMER; Lynbrook HS; San Jose, CA; (3); Church Yth Grp; Pep Clb; Rep Stu Cncl; Cheerldng; Socr; JV Vllybl; Westmont Santa Barbara; Bus.

LOVE, TARA; Oak Hill HS; Sylmar, CA; (4); Dance Clb; Drama Clb; School Play; Stage Crew; Ed Yrbk; Off Sr Cls; Capt Cheerldng; Var Sftbl; Var Vllybl; Hon Roll; 1st Team All Leag CIF Sftbl; UCLA; Pre-Law.

LOVE, TONISE; Luther Burbank HS; Sacramento, CA; (2); 120/389; Bsbl; Tennis; Obstetrcs.

LOVEJOY, ADRIENNE M; La Puente HS; La Puente, CA; (4); Teachers Aide; Variety Show; Rep Stu Cncl; Var L Bsktbl; Powder Puff Ftbl; Hon Roll; Black Stu Union VP; Dept Area Awd Excllnc Drftng; Specl Olympcs Vol Hacienda Schl Dist; CA Polytechnic ST U; Arch.

LOVEJOY, GINA; Fred C Beyer HS; Modesto, CA; (3); Church Yth Grp; Hosp Aide; Service Clb; SADD; Hon Roll; CSF; Sci.

LOVEJOY, REBECCA L; Atwater HS; Atwater, CA; (3); Church Yth Grp; Sec FHA; SADD; Band; Mrchg Band; Pep Band; Hon Roll; Peer Cnslr; Fri Night Live; Outstndng Stu Cert; Fresno ST; Psych.

LOVELAND II, MARK R; Monte Vista HS; Spring Valley, CA; (2); 18/422; Hon Roll; U CA-SAN Diego.

LOVELESS, TIMOTHY M; Yucca Valley HS; Yucca Valley, CA; (3); Quiz Bowl; Rptr Nwsp; Golf.

LOVELESS, TOM W; Tustin HS; Tustin, CA; (3); Church Yth Grp; JA; Church Choir; Mgr Stage Crew; Off Sr Cls; Ftbl; Golf; Hon Roll.

LOVELL, ANN C; El Camino HS; Oceanside, CA; (1); Debate Tm; NFL; Scholastic Bowl; Speech Tm; JV Tennis; Hon Roll; Opt Clb Awd; Commnctns.

LOVELL, JENNIFER A; Ramona HS; Ramona, CA; (2); 75/350; Church Yth Grp; Dance Clb; 4-H; 4-H Awd; Prfct Atten Awd; Fshn Mrch.

LOVELL, JENNIFER M; Mar Vista HS; Imperial Beach, CA; (1); 15/530; Yrbk; JV Socr; JV Sftbl; Hon Roll; Prfct Atten Awd; CSF; ASA Sftbl; UCLA; Sci.

LOVELL, JOHN; Oakmont HS; Roseville, CA; (1); Cmnty Wkr; 4-H; German Clb; Teachers Aide; JV Socr; JV Trk; 4-H Awd; Hon Roll.

LOVELL, MATT W; Ramona HS; Ramona, CA; (3); 59/294; Boy Scts; Church Yth Grp; 4-H; VP FBLA; Crs Cntry; Trk; Arch.

LOVELY, LOUELLA; Bellarmine Jefferson HS; Los Angeles, CA; (2); French Clb; Hosp Aide; Varsity Clb; Hon Roll; NHS; Pres Acad Fit Awd; VP Frsh Cls; Sec Treas Jr Cls; JV Var Sftbl; Var Vllybl; All Leg San Fernando Vly Vrsty Vlybl; Vlybl Clb Team, Cptrd Vlybl Mnthy Jr Cup Title; MVP Sftbl; Corp Law.

LOVETT, CRYSTAL L; Clovis HS; Clovis, CA; (3); Church Yth Grp; Ski Clb; SADD; Hon Roll; Class Of 91 Clb; Dance Prog; Fresno ST.

LOVETT, ERICK P; Central Union HS; El Centro, CA; (2); Boy Scts; Church Yth Grp; FFA; Bsbl; Ftbl; Socr; Swmmng; Hon Roll; Pres Schlr; CA Poly Pomona; Engr.

LOVEWELL, KIMBERLY; Helix HS; La Mesa, CA; (4); 119/367; Key Clb; Prfct Atten Awd; Cert Outstndng Achvt Creative Wrtng Site Write Off 90; Cert Of Outstndng Achvt Creative Wrtng; Grossmont CC; Med.

LOVGREN III, KENNETH; Shasta HS; Redding, CA; (4); 69/423; Church Yth Grp; Model UN; Acpl Chr; School Musical; School Play; Nwsp; Bsbl; Powder Puff Ftbl; Hon Roll; Music; Shasta CC; Engl.

LOVIE, MARK D; Westminster HS; Westminster, CA; (3); Ski Clb; Outstndng Prfrmnce Indstrl Technlgy; CA Poly; Arch.

LOVRIC, KRISTINA; St Genevieve HS; Northridge, CA; (3); French Clb; High Hon Roll; Med.

LOW, ALBERT S; Whitney HS; Cerritos, CA; (1); JV Swmmng; Hon Roll; Prfct Atten Awd; Pres Acad Fit Awd; CJSF; Law.

LOW, BRIAN; Antioch SR HS; Antioch, CA; (3); Church Yth Grp; Letterman Clb; Var Bsbl; Bsktbl; Hon Roll; UC Davis; Aeronautical Engr.

LOW, CHRISTOPHER M; Monte Vista HS; Spring Valley, CA; (4); 87/496; Pres Church Yth Grp; Var JV Trk; Hon Roll; Police Athl Leag; Amnesty Intl; UC San Diego; Arch.

LOW, CLARINDA; Alhambra HS; Alhambra, CA; (3); Church Yth Grp; Cmnty Wkr; Pep Clb; Sec Science Clb; Off Soph Cls; Off Jr Cls; Stat Bsbl; Co-Capt Cheerldng; Ntl Merit Ltr; CSF; Pep Squad VP & Treas.

LOW, GARRETT S; South San Francisco HS; S San Francisco, CA; (4); Cmnty Wkr; French Clb; Math Clb; Science Clb; L Bsktbl; Var Tennis; High Hon Roll; NHS; Pres Acad Fit Awd; Asian Amer Clb; UC Davis; Mech Engrng.

LOW, JENNIFER J; Ygnacio Valley HS; Concord, CA; (1); CSF; CA U.

LOW, KEVIN Y; Alhambra HS; Monterey Park, CA; (3); Am Leg Boys St; Cmnty Wkr; Computer Clb; Debate Tm; Hosp Aide; Math Clb; Math Tm; VP Model UN; NFL; Red Cross Aide; Various Debate Awds; Various Math Awds & Hnrs; U S CA; Med.

LOW, KIMBERLY A; South San Francisco HS; South San Francis, CA; (3); Church Yth Grp; Cmnty Wkr; Computer Clb; FBLA; Math Clb; Science Clb; Rptr Yrbk; NHS; Soc Sci Clb Scrtry; CA Schlrshp Fdrtn Life Mbr.

LOW, KRISTIN; South San Francisco HS; South San Francis, CA; (3); Rep Church Yth Grp; Computer Clb; FBLA; Math Clb; Science Clb; Church Choir; Soc Of Woman Engrs; CSF.

LOW, LISA M; Westmoor HS; Daly City, CA; (4); 10/326; Library Aide; Teachers Aide; Chorus; Church Choir; Jazz Band; Cit Awd; High Hon Roll; Hon Roll; Masonic Awd; Prfct Atten Awd; CA Schltc Fed; Tri-M Sec; Achvt Hall Of Fame Westmoor Frgn Lang; UC Davis; Landscp Arch.

LOW, MIKE J; Whitcomb HS; Glendora, CA; (4); Art Clb; Office Aide; Ed Nwsp; VP Stu Cncl; L Sftbl; L Vllybl; Prfct Atten Awd; Amer Lgn Schl Awd; Sprt Whitcomb Awd; Citrus Coll.

LOW, ROSEMARY; Casa Grande HS; Petaluma, CA; (2); Church Yth Grp; Drama Clb; Intnl Clb; School Play; Variety Show; Var Vllybl; 4-H Awd; High Hon Roll; Hon Roll; NHS.

LOWAS, CHUCK; River City HS; W Sacramento, CA; (1); French Clb; JV Bsktbl; Crs Cntry; High Hon Roll; Hon Roll; Pres Schlr; Coaches Awd Bsktbl; Schlstc Ltr Sci; Friday Night Live Club-Similar To SADD; UNLV; Arch.

LOWE, DANIEL J; Don Bosco HS; San Gabriel, CA; (3); Church Yth Grp; Var Bsktbl; Computer Engrng.

LOWE JR, DENNIS E; Apple Valley SR HS; Apple Valley, CA; (1); Spanish Clb; Hon Roll; Teacher.

LOWE, JENNIE A; Tustin HS; Santa Ana, CA; (2); 16/400; Church Yth Grp; Off Frsh Cls; Rep Soph Cls; JV Crs Cntry; Var Swmmng; High Hon Roll; Hon Roll; NEDT Awd; Swm Sthrn CA Aquatics Clb; Pre-Med.

LOWE, RICK; Lassen HS; Halong, CA; (4); 5/160; Am Leg Boys St; Pres 4-H; Treas Letterman Clb; Pres Jr Cls; Pres Stu Cncl; Var L Ftbl; Var Capt Wrstlng; Cit Awd; High Hon Roll; Pres NHS; USAF Acad; Aero Sp Engrng.

LOWE, SARAH; Bret Harte HS; Vallecito, CA; (1); AFS; Church Yth Grp; Drama Clb; Girl Scts; Math Tm; Band; Mrchg Band; Pep Band; School Musical; School Play; Sea Explorer Post; Math.

LOWE, STEVEN C; Palmdale HS; Pear Blossom, CA; (2); 42/800; Capt JV Bsbl; Hon Roll; Pres Acad Fit Awd; AZ ST U; Bus.

LOWE, WILLETTE C; Fairfield HS; Fairfield, CA; (3); Computer Clb; Key Clb; Math Tm; Science Clb; Spanish Clb; Band; Mrchg Band; Socr; Wt Lftg; Cit Awd; U; Linguist.

LOWELL, ASHLEIGH H; Livermore HS; Livermore, CA; (3); French Clb; School Musical; Rep Soph Cls; Rep Jr Cls; JV Var Tennis; High Hon Roll; Interact Co-Head; Sociology.

LOWENTHAL, TRACY; Maricopa HS; Frazier Park, CA; (2); 1/52; Cmnty Wkr; Drama Clb; GAA; Spanish Clb; School Play; Stage Crew; Pres Frsh Cls; Stu Cncl; JV Capt Bsktbl; Powder Puff Ftbl; CSF Pres; UCLA; Thtr.

LOWMILLER, JENNIFER M; Del Campo HS; Carmichael, CA; (3); Friday Night Live; UC Davis; Equine Vet.

LOWN, BRIAN L; Elk Grove HS; Sacramento, CA; (4); #2 In Class; Computer Clb; Math Tm; Scholastic Bowl; Science Clb; Variety Show; Rep Sr Cls; Var L Wrstlng; High Hon Roll; Ntl Merit SF; Pres Acad Fit Awd; Outstndg Top 10 Awd; SAT Schlrshp Awd Hgst Score In Schl; Bk Of Amer Plq Wnnr & AF Acadc Awd Mth-Sci; U Of CA Berkeley; Electrcl Eng.

LOWRY, ASHLEY; Bullard HS; Fresno, CA; (3); Church Yth Grp; FCA; Pep Clb; SADD; Teachers Aide; Pom Pon; Vllybl; Fine Arts.

LOWRY, BRENDA; Arlington HS; Riverside, CA; (4); 26/320; Church Yth Grp; Cmnty Wkr; Drama Clb; School Play; Ed Nwsp; Var Tennis; High Hon Roll; NHS; Pres Schlr; U San Francisco; Comm.

LOWRY, CHRISTINE M; Kingsburg HS; Kingsburg, CA; (1); JV Tennis; Hon Roll; Acadc Blck K Fro Schlstc Excllnce; Law.

LOWRY, MICHAEL E; Mission Bay HS; San Diego, CA; (4); 1/300; Key Clb; Sec Letterman Clb; School Musical; Capt Var Bsbl; Cit Awd; High Hon Roll; Kiwanis Awd; Prfct Atten Awd; Val; 1st Tm Western Leag Bsbl Awd, All Star Tm; UC San Diego; Accntng.

LOYA, DIEGO; Los Altos HS; Hacienda Hgts, CA; (2); Church Yth Grp; Cmnty Wkr; Band; Jazz Band; Mrchg Band; Orch; Pep Band; Hon Roll; Prfct Atten Awd; All Southern California Junior Honor Band; UCSD; Radio Communications.

LOYA, ELIDA; La Sierra HS; Riverside, CA; (2); Treas Soph Cls; Sftbl; Capt Vllybl; Hon Roll; Prfct Atten Awd.

LOYA, JASON L; Walnut HS; Walnut, CA; (2); Ski Clb; JV Var Ftbl; Cit Awd; High Hon Roll; Hon Roll; Sci Fair Awd 1st Pl.

LOYAL, AUDRA; Santa Ynez Valley Union HS; Santa Ynez, CA; (3); 6/162; Art Clb; Church Yth Grp; Socr; Swmmng; High Hon Roll; Hon Roll; Stu Action Team Drug-Freen Orgnztn Co-Pres; Peer Cnslng; Applause Art Cont Visual Arts Wnnr 89; Zoology.

LOYD, BRIDGETTE S; North HS; Bakersfield, CA; (2); Dance Clb; Office Aide; Service Clb; Ski Clb; Spanish Clb; Treas Jr Cls; JV Bsktbl; Intrml Sftbl; Intrml JV Vllybl; High Hon Roll; Performing Arts.

LOYD, D YVETTE; Sierra Joint Union HS; Tollhouse, CA; (2); Church Yth Grp; Cmnty Wkr; Hosp Aide; SADD; Chorus; Stage Crew; Stat Bsktbl; Score Keeper; Stat Swmmng; Stat Trk; Fresno ST U; Med.

LOYO, SEAN L; Gardena HS; Gardena, CA; (3); FFA; Hon Roll; Cal Poly San Luis Obspo; Engr.

LOYOLA, MARIA LILY S; Morse SR HS; San Diego, CA; (4); Dance Clb; Hon Roll; Consistncy Awd; CA Grant B; Nurse.

LOYOLA, ROWELL; Western HS; Anaheim, CA; (4); Pres Chess Clb; Computer Clb; French Clb; Speech Tm; Var Socr; Var Tennis; High Hon Roll; Var NHS; CA Schltc Fdrtn VP; Frgn Lang Clb; GATE; Biomed Sci.

LOZA, ALBERTO; San Fernando HS; Pacoima, CA; (3); Hon Roll; Math Teacher.

LOZA, ANGELICA S; Montclair HS; Ontario, CA; (2); Science Clb; Var Tennis; High Hon Roll; Hon Roll; GATE Clb Pres; Intl Law.

LOZA, ARACELI; Araceli Loza HS; Hayward, CA; (4); Church Yth Grp; Drama Clb; Latin Clb; Spanish Clb; Varsity Clb; Acpl Chr; Chorus; Church Choir; Variety Show; Var Vllybl; Cal ST Hayward; Nrsg.

LOZA, ESMERALDA E; Corona HS; Corona, CA; (2); 192/427; Science Clb; Var Mgr(s); Mgr Sftbl; CA ST Fullerton; Law.

LOZA, LEEANN; Mt Pleasant HS; San Jose, CA; (3); 196/400; Church Yth Grp; Yrbk; Off Jr Cls; Stu Cncl; Art Clb; JV Cheerldng; Intrml Crs Cntry; Capt Socr; Capt Sftbl; High Hon Roll; San Jose ST; Pre Law.

LOZA, SUSANA I; Carlmont HS; Belmont, CA; (4); 21/350; Cmnty Wkr; Debate Tm; Drama Clb; Math Clb; Speech Tm; Ed Nwsp; Ed Yrbk; Off Frsh Cls; Off Soph Cls; Off Jr Cls; Harvard U; Psych.

LOZANO, ALBERT; Don Bosco Technical Inst; West Covina, CA; (4); Church Yth Grp; Service Clb; NHS; Pres Acad Fit Awd; Screen Printing Clb; Medallion Awd; Schlrshps L A Litho Clb, GATF; Art Ctr Coll Of Design; Art.

LOZANO, AMY E; San Gabriel Mission HS; Los Angeles, CA; (2); 28/124; FBLA; Hon Roll; CSF; USC; Acctng.

LOZANO, BELISA; Tulare Union HS; Tulare, CA; (3); Art Clb; Church Yth Grp; GAA; Varsity Clb; Band; Var Capt Diving; JV Swmmng; Wt Lftg; Hon Roll; Hnr Band; JR All Amer Hall Of Fame Band Hnrs; San Francisco ST U; Psych.

LOZANO, DONNABEL B; Encinal HS; San Leandro, CA; (3); 5/259; FBLA; Pep Clb; SADD; Off Frsh Cls; Off Jr Cls; Stu Cncl; JV Cheerldng; Var Pom Pon; High Hon Roll; CSF; Vrsty Badminton; Gldn St Exam Hnrb Mntn; UC Berkeley; Comp Sci.

LOZANO, ELIDIA; San Benito HS; Hollister, CA; (3); 24/370; Treas Spanish Clb; Hon Roll; Santa Clara U; Comp Repair.

LOZANO, EVA D; Montebello HS; Pico Rivera, CA; (2); Dance Clb; Variety Show; Hon Roll; Prfct Atten Awd.

LOZANO, GRISELDA; Hamilton Union HS; Hamilton City, CA; (3); Church Yth Grp; Cmnty Wkr; GAA; Office Aide; Spanish Clb; SADD; Teachers Aide; Church Choir; Var Sftbl; Var Trk; Mecha Pres; Taught Catechism; Cmnty Work; CA ST U Chico; Bus.

LOZANO, LISA I; North HS; Bakersfield, CA; (2); Church Yth Grp; Letterman Clb; Chorus; JV Swmmng; Vllybl; High Hon Roll; Hon Roll; UC San Francisco; Phrmcy.

LOZANO, LYDIA; Chula Vista Christian HS; Imperial Beach, CA; (4); 1/4; Church Yth Grp; Office Aide; Teachers Aide; School Play; Yrbk; Rep Soph Cls; VP Jr Cls; Pres Sr Cls; Cit Awd; Hon Roll; J Swaggart Bible Coll; Bus Admn.

LOZANO, MARC; La Serna HS; Whittier, CA; (3); 73/350; Intrml Ftbl; Intrml Golf; Hon Roll; Comp Sci.

LOZANO, STEVEN J; River City HS; W Sacramento, CA; (3); 4/215; Am Leg Boys St; Pres Key Clb; Thesps; School Musical; School Play; Pres Stu Cncl; Swmmng; Trk; High Hon Roll; Pres Acad Fit Awd; MESA; Friday Night Live; Bus.

LOZANO, SYLVIA; Mayfair HS; Long Beach, CA; (3); English Clb; VP Sec JA; Stat Bsktbl; Var Cheerldng; Var Pom Pon; Hon Roll; Peer Counseling; Psychology.

LOZANO, VERONICA; John H Francis Polytechnic HS; Sun Valley, CA; (3); Cmnty Wkr; Pres Spanish Clb; VP SADD; Teachers Aide; School Play; VP Pres Frsh Cls; Rep Stu Cncl; Powder Puff Ftbl; Hon Roll; LAPD Law Enfrcmnt Explorer; Woodbury U; Inter Dsgn.

LOZIER, NATHAN S; Novato HS; Novato, CA; (2); Band; Orch; Lit Mag; Hon Roll.

LOZINSKI, GRACE M; Live Oak HS; Morgan Hill, CA; (4); 4/505; Church Yth Grp; VP FBLA; Ski Clb; Spanish Clb; Speech Tm; SADD; Rptr Nwsp; Rep Soph Cls; Off Sr Cls; Var Vllybl; San Francisco Press Clb 3rd Pl News Wrtng; CA Schlrshp Fed; Jr Miss Pgm 1st Alt & Schlstc Awd; UC San Diego; Pre-Med.

LPE, NORA M; Alisal HS; Salinas, CA; (4); Dance Clb; Library Aide; Office Aide; Teachers Aide; High Hon Roll; Hon Roll; Pres Acad Fit Awd; Acadc Achvt Gld Card; Hartnell Coll; Comp.

LU, AMY B; Ocean View HS; Westminster, CA; (1); Intrml Vllybl; Keywanettes; U CA Irvine; Pediatrician.

LU, BING; Phillip And Sala Burton HS; San Francisco, CA; (4); 5/178; Computer Clb; Math Clb; Ski Clb; Teachers Aide; Vllybl; High Hon Roll; GSE Hgh Hnr Alg 87; GSE Hgh Hnr Geom 88; UCLA; Bio-Chem.

LU, CHIH CHUN M; Rosemead HS; Rosemead, CA; (3); Treas Computer Clb; Treas FBLA; Key Clb; Math Clb; Spanish Clb; Off Frsh Cls; JV Tennis; High Hon Roll; Prfct Atten Awd; Acad Decthln Team-Hnrs; CSF.

LU, CHIH-HSIEN; Arcadia HS; Arcadia, CA; (3); Art Clb; Cmnty Wkr; FBLA; Intnl Clb; Red Cross Aide; Service Clb; Ski Clb; Spanish Clb; SADD; Yrbk; Kiowas Cmmnty Srvc Clb Semi Finlst; Amnesty Intl; 3rd Pl Art Cont Womens Clb; Cal Poly Pomona; Archtctr.

LU, CHRISTOPHER; Rolling Hills HS; Rolling Hills, CA; (3); 16/326; Cmnty Wkr; French Clb; Science Clb; Service Clb; Spanish Clb; SADD; Lit Mag; Intrml Crs Cntry; Var JV Trk; JV Wrstlng; CSF; Bus Admin.

LU, DAVID V; Lowell HS; San Francisco, CA; (2); Chess Clb; Science Clb; Teachers Aide; Regstry Secy; Hgh Hnrs Gldn St Exam; CSF; Engrng.

LU, GRACE K; Carlmont HS; Belmont, CA; (3); 13/325; Church Yth Grp; Cmnty Wkr; Hosp Aide; Math Clb; Church Choir; Orch; Yrbk; Off Sr Cls; Hon Roll; Modeling; Acad Decathlon; Santa Barbara U; Med.

LU, HA T; Lowell HS; San Francisco, CA; (2); Office Aide; Chinese Club; Agape Fllwshp; Psych.

LU, HAI H; Rosemead HS; Rosemead, CA; (3); Computer Clb; Library Aide; Science Clb; Teachers Aide; High Hon Roll; Hon Roll; CA Schltc Fed; Sign Lang Club; Art; Cal Poly Pomona; Elec Engrng.

LU, HANH C; Marshall Fundamental HS; Alhambra, CA; (3); Science Clb; Phtg Yrbk; Vllybl; Psych.

LU, HUY Q; John Marshall Fundamental HS; Pasadena, CA; (4); 28/160; Pres Chess Clb; Church Yth Grp; Church Choir; Orch; Stu Cncl; Var Trk; Hon Roll; NHS; Won Trophy; Pasadena Boys Club Cmmty Svc; Gold Seal Bearer; UCLA; Mech Eng.

LU, HUY T; Herbert Hoover HS; San Diego, CA; (1).

LU, JENNIFER Y; George Washington HS; San Francisco, CA; (4); High Hon Roll; Hon Roll; Engl Clb; Pharmacy.

LU, JOSEPH; George Washington HS; San Francisco, CA; (3); Red Cross Aide; Teachers Aide; Band; Bsbl; Socr; Tennis; Cit Awd; High Hon Roll; Hon Roll; Gldn St Exam Hnrs Alg, Geo & Hstry; UC Berkeley; Arch.

LU, LILY; Calexico HS; Calexico, CA; (3); Church Yth Grp; FBLA; Math Tm; Church Choir; Rep Soph Cls; Hon Roll; CSF; UC Berkeley; Bus Admin.

LU, LINDA P; Diamond Bar HS; Diamond Bar, CA; (2); Cmnty Wkr; French Clb; Intnl Clb; Hist Key Clb; Math Clb; Science Clb; SADD; Rep Frsh Cls; Off Soph Cls; Trk; Intl Relations.

LU, LINH; Hawthorne HS; Hawthorne, CA; (4); Cmnty Wkr; Hosp Aide; Drill Tm; UC Irvine; Ped.

LU, LINH K; Mark Keppel HS; Monterey Park, CA; (3); FBLA; Hosp Aide; Key Clb; VP Pres Math Clb; Science Clb; Service Clb; Off Jr Cls; Chrmn Sr Cls; High Hon Roll; NHS; Gldn St Exam High Hnrs Geom & Alg; Crown & Sceptre; Engrng.

LU, MICHAEL W; Homestead HS; Sunnyvale, CA; (1); German Clb; JV Trk; Soccer; Clairnet; Bsbl Cards; Doctor.

LU, PAMELA W; Marina HS; Huntington Beach, CA; (4); JCL; Latin Clb; Pres Math Clb; Quiz Bowl; Lit Mag; JV Tennis; Ntl Merit SF; Math.

LU, PAUL; Edison HS; Huntington Beach, CA; (3); VP Church Yth Grp; Model UN; Ski Clb; Var Socr; Var L Tennis; High Hon Roll; Pres Schlr; CSF; Med.

LU, PHONG T; La Quinta HS; Westminster, CA; (3); Key Clb; Math Clb; Science Clb; Spanish Clb; JV Bsktbl; Var Vllybl; High Hon Roll; Hon Roll; Jr NHS; NHS; UC Irvine; Bio.

LU, RITHY; University HS; Irvine, CA; (3); JCL; Quiz Bowl; UC Irvine; Pediatrics.

LU, TAN; Mc Ateer HS; San Francisco, CA; (3); Chess Clb; Computer Clb; VP FBLA; Teachers Aide; Swmmng; Tennis; High Hon Roll; Stu Conservation Pgm, Volunteer Work; Eng Explorer Post; Worked Full Scale Tech Noe Vly Comp/Micro-Com; Stanford; Comp Sci.

LU, TU T; Independence HS; San Jose, CA; (4); 83/825; FBLA; Hosp Aide; JA; Science Clb; Teachers Aide; Var Crs Cntry; Var Trk; Hon Roll; CA Schlrshp Fed Lf Mem; Magna Cum Laude; Chinese Club Schlrshp; UC Berkeley; Bio Sci.

LU, VINH T; John A Rowland HS; Rowland Hts, CA; (3); Debate Tm; Math Clb; Science Clb; Speech Tm; Varsity Clb; Var Trk; Cit Awd; High Hon Roll; Prfct Atten Awd; Pres Acad Fit Awd; GATE; CSF; UC Davis; Med.

LU, WEI-YUEH; Valencia HS; Placentia, CA; (1); Chess Clb; German Clb; Science Clb; Hon Roll; Natl Space Soc; UC Berkeley; Astrophysics.

LU, YU-LIN JEFF; Rosemead HS; Rosemead, CA; (2); Computer Clb; FBLA; Key Clb; Math Clb; JV Tennis; High Hon Roll; Prfct Atten Awd; CSF Mem; Acdmc Decathlon Tm 89; JV Mst Vlble Plyr 90.

LU BIEN, MATTHEW T; Orange Glen HS; Valley Center, CA; (4); 20/500; Church Yth Grp; 4-H; SADD; Cit Awd; French Hon Soc; 4-H Awd; Hon Roll; NHS; Pres Acad Fit Awd; UC Santa Barbara; Bus.

LUA, MARIA E; Santiago HS; Garden Grove, CA; (2); French Clb; Sec Jr Cls; JV Trk; Hon Roll; Med.

LUANGRATH, SENGMANY C; Highlands HS; North Highlands, CA; (3); Church Yth Grp; French Clb; Off Jr Cls; Powder Puff Ftbl; Socr; Cit Awd; High Hon Roll; Hon Roll; Prfct Atten Awd; UCLA; Bus Admin.

LUANGRATH, TONH; Modesto HS; Modesto, CA; (4); Accntnt.

LUANGVISETH, TYLER P; Will C Crawford HS; San Diego, CA; (2); 37/383; French Clb; Key Clb; Cit Awd; Hon Roll; 4-H; Jr NHS; NHS; Acad Tm; CA Schlstc Fed; U Of San Dieog; Tchr.

LUBENSKY, MICAH; Arlington HS; Riverside, CA; (4); 10/339; Art Clb; Teachers Aide; Temple Yth Grp; Chorus; High Hon Roll; Pres Acad Fit Awd; Mst Insprtnl Awd Concert Choir; Asst Coach Acad Decthln; Cmmnded Stu Natl Achvt Schlrshp Pgm Negro Stu; UC Berkeley.

LUBI, DOREEN FRANCES; Nogales HS; W Covina, CA; (2); Dance Clb; Pep Clb; Science Clb; Teachers Aide; Rep Stu Cncl; JV Cheerldng; JV Pom Pon; Hon Roll; Prfct Atten Awd; Med.

LUBIC, BRYAN J; Poway HS; Poway, CA; (3); 187/696; Math Clb; SADD; JV Swmmng; High Hon Roll; Hon Roll; Bus.

LUC, BAT; San Gabriel HS; Rosemead, CA; (2); Church Yth Grp; Tennis; Hon Roll; Accntnt.

LUC, HELEN V; Gahr HS; Norwalk, CA; (3); 1/327; Spanish Clb; High Hon Roll; Century 2000 Club Mem; Yrbk Section Edition; Acad Dcthln; CSF; Tennis Club; Berkeley; Ped.

LUC, VAN Y; Tustin HS; Tustin, CA; (2); 3/275; Science Clb; Tennis; High Hon Roll; Hon Roll; Libr Vlntr; Pre Law.

LUCAN, TERESA M; Bellarmine Jefferson HS; Sunland, CA; (2); Church Yth Grp; French Clb; Church Choir; Rep Soph Cls; Stat Ftbl; Score Keeper; Var Sftbl; Var Vllybl; Hon Roll; Vllybl & Sftbl; Sci.

LUCAS, BLAKE EDWARD; El Cajon Valley HS; El Cajon, CA; (4); 19/379; Letterman Clb; Band; Pep Band; Ed Yrbk; Stu Cncl; Var Cheerldng; Var Swmmng; Hon Roll; Leo Club-Pres/VP; Water Polo-Var; 2nd Tm All Lg Water Polo; Grphc Comm.

LUCAS, BRYAN P; Laguna Beach HS; Laguna Beach, CA; (4); 45/180; Church Yth Grp; Computer Clb; Treas Drama Clb; Pres FBLA; Library Aide; Scholastic Bowl; Science Clb; Treas Thesps; Mgr Stage Crew; Stat Ftbl; Gldn St Exm Hgh Hnrs; Cptlst Soc Pres; Natl Mck Trl Cmptn; Law.

LUCAS, CASSANDRA L; Rubidoux HS; Riverside, CA; (4); 79/578; French Clb; Teachers Aide; Off Band; Rep Color Guard; Flag Corp; Mrchg Band; Hon Roll; Prfct Atten Awd; RCC; Mar Zoolgy.

LUCAS, COLLEEN; Edison HS; Stockton, CA; (2); Church Yth Grp; Latin Clb; Math Tm; Church Choir; JV Crs Cntry; Var Swmmng; Hon Roll; Vrsty Water Polo; Air Force Acad; Aeron Engrng.

LUCAS, MONICA U; Mesa Verde HS; Citrus Heights, CA; (2); Cmnty Wkr; JV Bsktbl; Cit Awd; Hon Roll; Prfct Atten Awd; Honorary Engl Awd; Writing Awd; UC Davis; Med.

LUCAS, ROE; Tranquillity HS; Tranquillity, CA; (2); Boy Scts; Church Yth Grp; Cmnty Wkr; Spanish Clb; SADD; Acpl Chr; Church Choir; Jazz Band; Mrchg Band; Pep Band; Humboldt; Vet.

LUCAS, SALLY A; Arcadia HS; Arcadia, CA; (3); Chrmn Church Yth Grp; Cmnty Wkr; Girl Scts; Hosp Aide; Hist Band; Chorus; Church Choir; Mrchg Band; Orch; Pep Band; Commnctns.

LUCAS, SASKIA; Dos Pueblos HS; Goleta, CA; (3); Am Leg Aux Girls St; Church Yth Grp; Ski Clb; JV Bsktbl; JV Vllybl; High Hon Roll; Hon Roll; NHS; Student Volunteer At Raphael House For Battered Women; Member Friends Of Amnesty; Cal ST; Social Work & Politics.

LUCAS, SCHANNAE; Gahr HS; Cerritos, CA; (3); Church Yth Grp; Cmnty Wkr; Church Choir; Trk; Vllybl; High Hon Roll; Black Hstry Makers Of Tomorrow; UCI Schlrs In Training; Knowldg/Ecl Responsblty Pgm-UCI; Sci.

LUCAS, SHELLYMARIE C; Monte Vista HS; Spring Valley, CA; (3); Church Yth Grp; SADD; Planet Awrnss Clb Pres; U GA; Wrtng.

LUCATERO, ARCELIA R; Lincoln HS; Lincoln, CA; (4); 11/139; Drama Clb; English Clb; Spanish Clb; Rep Frsh Cls; VP Soph Cls; Gym; Vllybl; Hon Roll; U Guadfalajara Mexico; Lawyer.

LUCATERO, VERONICA; Woodlake Union HS; Woodlake, CA; (3); Key Clb; Science Clb; Stu Cncl; Cit Awd; High Hon Roll; Hon Roll; Kiwanis Awd; Prfct Atten Awd; Maya Club; CSF; Counseling.

LUCCHESE, MARY; Sonoma Valley HS; Sonoma, CA; (4); Cmnty Wkr; SADD; Yrbk; Hon Roll; NHS; Ldrshp Cls Coordinates Schl, Cmnty Scl Actvts; Mrtktng Asstnt For Wine Industry; UC Davis; Bio.

LUCCHESI, JODI; Tomales HS; Petaluma, CA; (3); #14 In Class; Sec 4-H; French Clb; FFA; SADD; Teachers Aide; Sec Frsh Cls; Stat Bsbl; Var Cheerldng; High Hon Roll; Hon Roll; Frnch Achvt Awd; 4-H Showmnshp 1st Pl Awd; Linfield; Dentstry.

LUCCHESI, JOEL N; Casa Grande HS; Petaluma, CA; (2); JV Ftbl; JV Trk; JV Wt Lftg; Hon Roll; Cal Poly; Arch.

LUCENA, LAURA A; Fontana HS; Fontana, CA; (1); Band; Mrchg Band; Pep Band; Hon Roll; Vet.

LUCERO, DANA C; Louisville HS; West Hills, CA; (1); Church Yth Grp; Cmnty Wkr; Dance Clb; Office Aide; High Hon Roll; Pres Acad Fit Awd; Basllet & Jazz Co; Teach Dance; U Of Santa Barbara.

LUCERO, FRANK L; Daniel Murphy HS; Los Angeles, CA; (2); French Clb; Teachers Aide; Nwsp; Ed Yrbk; Pres Jr Cls; Bsktbl; Var JV Ftbl; Var Socr; Wt Lftg; Coach Bsktbl Elem Schl, Undefeated Season; Psych.

LUCERO, MARY; Mountain View HS; S El Monte, CA; (1); GAA; Pep Clb; JV Sftbl; Hon Roll; Prfct Atten Awd; Sftbl Athltc Achvt Cert; Typing Proficiency Cert; Schl Yr Mrt Cert 89-90; Pepperdine; Psych.

LUCERO, SABRINA R; Baldwin Park HS; Baldwin Park, CA; (2); Band; Mrchg Band; Pep Band.

LUCERO, SHELLY A; Vacaville HS; Vacaville, CA; (3); SADD; Teachers Aide; Chorus; High Hon Roll; Hon Roll; Arch.

LUCERO, WILLIE D; Red Bluff Union HS; Red Bluff, CA; (1); FFA; JV Bsbl; Bsktbl; Ftbl; Wt Lftg; Hon Roll; Schl Imprvmnt Cmmttee; Industrial Tech.

LUCEY, STEPHEN M; St Ignatius College Prep; San Francisco, CA; (3); 32/244; Church Yth Grp; Cmnty Wkr; Letterman Clb; Pep Clb; Varsity Clb; JV Var Ftbl; JV Var Trk; Hon Roll.

LUCHT, DANIEL; Bret Harte Union HS; Murphys, CA; (4); 3/120; Church Yth Grp; Ski Clb; Speech Tm; School Musical; VP Sr Cls; High Hon Roll; Ntl Merit Schol; Rotary Awd; St Schlr; Boy Scts; Eagle Sct; U Of CA San Diego; Engrng.

LUCHT, LAURA E; Bret Harte Union HS; Murphys, CA; (2); Church Yth Grp; Ski Clb; Church Choir; School Musical; Sec Stu Cncl; JV Vllybl; Hon Roll; Peer Cnslng Pres; 1st Pl Arnold Rotary Clb Speech Cont 89-90; Golden St Math Exam High Hnrs; Psych.

LUCIA, JOSEPH P; Poway HS; Poway, CA; (1); Church Yth Grp; Trk.

LUCIO, DENISE M; Bishop Amat Memorial HS; West Covina, CA; (3); Church Yth Grp; Swmmng; Hon Roll; U Of Redlands; Psych.

LUCIO, MARIO F; Bishop Amat HS; Covina, CA; (3); Church Yth Grp; Letterman Clb; Varsity Clb; Capt Socr; Hon Roll; Engrng.

LUCK, CHAD W; Village Christian HS; Van Nuys, CA; (3); Church Yth Grp; Drama Clb; Letterman Clb; School Musical; Stage Crew; Variety Show; Pres Frsh Cls; Rep Stu Cncl; Crs Cntry; JV Trk; Top 10 Rnnr Crss Cntry; Pilot.

LUCK, CHEYENNE; Glendale HS; Glendale, CA; (3); Library Aide; Ski Clb; Teachers Aide; Band; Jazz Band; VP L Swmmng; Trk; Hon Roll; JV & Vrsty Ltr Water Polo; CSF; U Of CA Snta Barb; Aeronautics.

LUCK, JAMIE W; Sir Francis Drake HS; San Anselmo, CA; (2); School Play; Hon Roll; CA U; Jrnlsm.

LUCK, KERRY A; Grossmont HS; La Mesa, CA; (2); Dance Clb; Hosp Aide; Teachers Aide; Cheerldng; Gym; Swmmng; Prfct Atten Awd; Dcng.

LUCKETT, MICHAEL D; Beaumont HS; Beaumont, CA; (4); 1/150; Church Yth Grp; Treas French Clb; Math Clb; Model UN; Quiz Bowl; School Play; High Hon Roll; NHS; Ntl Merit SF; Prfct Atten Awd; Space Acad Level I; Rotary Yth Ldrshp Awds Camp; Natl Yng Ldrshp Conf; Engrng.

LUCKINBILL, SUSAN R; Beyer HS; Modesto, CA; (3); Computer Clb; Debate Tm; Ski Clb; Cit Awd; Hon Roll; Comp Accntng; Bus.

LUCZAK, MELISSA L; Paraclute HS; Lancaster, CA; (3); Church Yth Grp; Drama Clb; Hon Roll; San Diego ST; Phys Thrpy.

LUCZAK, RICHARD D; Paraclete HS; Lancaster, CA; (2); JA; JV Socr; Pilot.

LUDDINGTON, TRACY A; Buena Park HS; Buena Park, CA; (3); 2/350; Sec Drama Clb; Science Clb; Thesps; School Musical; School Play; Stage Crew; High Hon Roll; Pres Acad Fit Awd; CA Schlrshp Fed; U Of MN.

LUDI, NANCY P; La Mirada HS; La Mirada, CA; (3); NFL; JV Sftbl; JV Tennis; Hon Roll; Prfct Atten Awd; CSF; Astromny Clb; Ed.

LUDIN, JOYCE E; Morro Bay HS; Morro Bay, CA; (4); 4/200; Dance Clb; French Clb; Teachers Aide; Varsity Clb; Capt Var Socr; High Hon Roll; NHS; Pres Acad Fit Awd; Asst Dir Perf Cntrl Coast Jazz; U CA-SANTA Barbara; Dance.

LUDLOW, LAURA A; Thomas Downey HS; Modesto, CA; (1); Church Yth Grp; Art Clb; Bsktbl; Var L Swmmng; JV Vllybl; Hon Roll; Brigham Young U; Acctg.

LUDOVICO, JENNIFER D; Oak Ridge HS; El Dorado Hills, CA; (2); SADD; Var Swmmng; JV Var Vllybl; Cit Awd; High Hon Roll; Hon Roll; Jr NHS; NHS; Pres Schlr; MVP Varsity Swimming; MVP Varsity Volleyball; MVP Inspirational Varsity Swimming; Mental Health Counselor.

LUDWICK, NATALIE M; Emerson HS; Orange, CA; (1); Orch; School Play; DAR Awd; High Hon Roll; NEDT Awd; Prfct Atten Awd; Asst Tchr Japanese Smmr Schlr Prgm; UCSF; Med.

LUDWICKZAK, JOHN F; Bishop Amat HS; Hacienda Hghts, CA; (3); 130/399; Church Yth Grp; Cmnty Wkr; Letterman Clb; Varsity Clb; JV Bsbl; JV Capt Ftbl; Var Capt Trk; Var Capt Wt Lftg; Cit Awd; Hon Roll.

LUDWIG, AUDRA L; Casa Roble HS; Orangevale, CA; (2); Church Yth Grp; Pep Clb; Drill Tm; Ed Nwsp; Cit Awd; High Hon Roll; Hon Roll; Attorney.

LUDWIG, HOLLY; Paraclete HS; Palmdale, CA; (3); Letterman Clb; Var L Crs Cntry; Var L Trk; High Hon Roll; NEDT Awd; CSF Tres; Z Club; Music.

LUDWIG, ILOFF CLINT; Liberty HS; Benicia, CA; (3); Teachers Aide; Var Bsktbl; Var Golf; Var Sftbl; Var Vllybl; Hon Roll; Awd Achvt Voctnl Child Care & Bldng & Ground Maintnc; Child Psych.

LUDWIG, JOSHUA J; Ventura HS; Ventura, CA; (4); SADD; Teachers Aide; JV Bsktbl; Intrml Ftbl.

LUDWIG, MICHAEL J; Pioneer HS; San Jose, CA; (2); Am Leg Boys St; Bsbl; Bsktbl; Crs Cntry; Hon Roll; Chico ST; Aerospc Engr.

LUDY, JENNIFER C; Wasco Union HS; Wasco, CA; (1); Band; Mrchg Band; Orch; Pep Band; JV Capt Sftbl; JV Vllybl; Wt Lftg; High Hon Roll; Hon Roll; Pres Acad Fit Awd; Dstngshd Schlr Pgm; CSF; Hnr Soc; UCLA; Med.

LUDY, MARIE; Wasco HS; Wasco, CA; (3); Art Clb; Letterman Clb; Rep Frsh Cls; Var Sftbl; Var Vllybl; Wt Lftg; High Hon Roll; Hon Roll; Pres Acad Fit Awd; All League Pitcher, Hnrb Mntn & All Area Pitcher; Dstngshd Schlr Pgm; CSF Gold Card Hldr; Cal Poly San Luis Obispo; Archt.

LUE, PETER C; Huntington Beach HS; Huntington Beach, CA; (2); Chess Clb; Key Clb; Math Clb; Crs Cntry; Hon Roll; Orange Cnty Acad Decthln; Gldn St Exam, Algebra I Hgh Hnrs; Schl Twr Awd Medallion In Hist; UC Berkeley; Astrophysics.

LUECHA, ANN; Diamond Bar HS; Diamond Bar, CA; (4); 9/460; Hosp Aide; Rptr Nwsp; Lit Mag; JV Tennis; High Hon Roll; Kiwanis Awd; Lion Awd; Pres Acad Fit Awd; Vrsty Badminton Tm; Jr Statesman Of Amer Chapt Pres; UCLA; Bio.

LUECK, JOEL E; West HS; Bakersfield, CA; (2); Church Yth Grp; Science Clb; Teachers Aide; Band; Jazz Band; Mrchg Band; Pep Band; Var Swmmng; Hon Roll; GATE & Hnrs/Advncd Plcemnt Classes; Cyclng Clb; UCLA.

LUECK, TRACY A; Paradise HS; Magalia, CA; (3); 12/236; Drill Tm; Pom Pon; Hon Roll; CA Schlrshp Fdrtn; Pblshd Poetry Anthology; Pblshrs Choice Awd.

LUEDDECKE, MARK A; Cajon HS; San Bernardino, CA; (2); Computer Clb; German Clb; Bsktbl; Wt Lftg; Stu Cncl; Comp.

LUEDER, SUZANNE; Archbishop Mitty HS; San Jose, CA; (4); 5/225; Cmnty Wkr; French Clb; Math Tm; Science Clb; VP Service Clb; SADD; Ed Yrbk; JV Socr; High Hon Roll; NHS; CSF Commnty Svc Coordinator; Amnesty Intl; Independant Aging; U CA San Diego; Physics.

LUEDERS, DANA S; Santa Margarita HS; Mission Viejo, CA; (3); 6/227; Church Yth Grp; Treas Key Clb; Model UN; Rptr Nwsp; Yrbk; L Var Tennis; High Hon Roll; NHS.

LUEDTKE, BRAD M; California Lutheran HS; Santa Ana, CA; (3); Church Yth Grp; School Play; Ed Nwsp; Sec Jr Cls; L Var Bsbl; L Var Ftbl; Hon Roll; Pres Acad Fit Awd; Val; Congrssnl Yth Ldrshp Cncl; Pre Law.

LUEHR, SONJA ANNE; Corona SR HS; Corona, CA; (3); GAA; Intrml Bsbl; Intrml Bsktbl; Intrml Sftbl; Intrml Trk; Var Vllybl; Automtv Techn; RCC; Comp Techn.

LUEVANO, BRENDA C; Central Union HS; El Centro, CA; (2); Church Yth Grp; Hosp Aide; VICA; Pep Clb; Flag Corp; Sec Frsh Cls; Trk; Hon Roll; GATE; Stanford; Bus.

LUEVANO, JESSE D; Trabuco Hills HS; Mission Viejo, CA; (2); 130/415; Spanish Clb; SADD; Var Bsbl; Ftbl; Var Wt Lftg; JV Wrstlng; Acctnt.

LUEVANO, MARCOS D; Turlock HS; Turlock, CA; (3); 17/500; Church Yth Grp; Letterman Clb; Var L Bsktbl; Var L Trk; MVP Trck; PTSA Achvt Awd; Rotary Stu Mnth; Commnctns.

LUEVANO, MELISSA; Whitney HS; Cerritos, CA; (1); Church Yth Grp; Spanish Clb; Color Guard; Hon Roll; Pres Acad Fit Awd; UCSD; Educ.

LUEVANO, MIQUEL D; Lompoc SR HS; Lompoc, CA; (2); Letterman Clb; Sec Spanish Clb; Teachers Aide; Crs Cntry; Trk; Prncpls List; Engl Achvt Awd; UCLA; Cmmnctns.

LUFT, JULIE D; Marina HS; Huntington Beach, CA; (2); Spanish Clb; SADD; Varsity Clb; Capt Bsktbl; Sftbl; Capt Vllybl; Cit Awd; Hon Roll; Prfct Atten Awd; Pres Acad Fit Awd; Athletes Agnst Substance Abuse; Bus.

LUGINBILL, KERRY R; Torrey Pines HS; Del Mar, CA; (2); VP Soph Cls; JV Cheerldng; Mgr(s); DAR Awd; Hon Roll; CSF; HOBY; San Diego U; Home Ec.

LUGO, ANNA L; Fillmore HS; Piru, CA; (2); Church Yth Grp; JV Stat Sftbl; Cit Awd.

LUGO, CHANTAL A; Immaculate Heart HS; Los Angeles, CA; (4); Church Yth Grp; GAA; Mu Alpha Theta; Spanish Clb; L Capt Bsktbl; JV Cheerldng; Hon Roll; NEDT Awd; Spanish NHS; 90 Natl Hispanic Schlr Awds Pgm Semi Fnlst; Engr.

LUGO, GLORIA E; Central Union HS; El Centro, CA; (3); 9/500; Debate Tm; Speech Tm; Orch; Lit Mag; Hon Roll; Mck Trl Defnse Attrny; Bst Spkr Awd; Psych.

LUGO, MARIBEL; Milpitas HS; Milpitas, CA; (3); 22/487; Spanish Clb; Var Tennis; Prncpls Honor Roll 89; Schlr Athl Awd; 3rd Pl Egg Drop And Trig St Cmptn; Outstndng Stu Span; Arch.

LUGO, MARIVEL; Locke HS; Los Angeles, CA; (3); Church Yth Grp; Cmnty Wkr; French Clb; Office Aide; Church Choir; Cheerldng; Paid Stu Wrkr; Latin Choir Ascersion Cath Church Vol Teacher Chldn In Bible Stud; Claremont Mc Kenna; Cinamatic.

LUGO, MONICA L; Hemet HS; Hemet, CA; (2); Church Yth Grp; Drama Clb; Teachers Aide; School Play; Rep Frsh Cls; Stat Ftbl; Tennis; Hstry Ed.

LUGUE, RONALD M; Balboa HS; San Francisco, CA; (2); ROTC; Band; Nwsp; High Hon Roll; Hon Roll; Youth Court; Arch.

LUHNOW, JOHN C; Valhalla HS; Jamul, CA; (3); 58/408; JV Ftbl; Var Wt Lftg; Cit Awd; Hon Roll; Kiwanis Awd.

LUHRSEN, KURT F; Villa Park HS; Orange, CA; (4); 21/425; Var Capt Bsbl; Elks Awd; High Hon Roll; NHS; UC San Diego; Strctrl Engrng.

LUI, ALVIN W; James Logan HS; Union City, CA; (2); Church Yth Grp; Yrbk; Hon Roll; Chinese Bible Chrch; UC Davis; Lawyer.

LUI, BRENNA; Saugus HS; Valencia, CA; (4); 85/450; Girl Scts; SADD; GLADD Guidance Ldrs Agnst Drnkng & Drugs; Safe Rides; Peer Cnslng; Psych.

LUI, GEORGE; Hesperia HS; Hesperia, CA; (3); 46/637; Computer Clb; Math Tm; Spanish Clb; Hon Roll; CA Schlrshp Fed; CA Poly U; Elen Engrng.

LUI, MARIA JOAN; John Marshall HS; Los Angeles, CA; (4); 2/670; Pres Church Yth Grp; VP Spanish Clb; SADD; Trk; Capt Vllybl; Pres VP NHS; Ntl Merit Ltr; Pres Acad Fit Awd; Sal; Church Choir; Ephebian Society; Tandy Technology Scholar; Dartmouth College.

LUI, NANCY S; Pittsburg HS; Pittsburg, CA; (3); Church Yth Grp; JV Capt Bsktbl; JV Sftbl; JV Vllybl; Hon Roll.

LUI, SAMUEL; Maranatha HS; Rowland Heights, CA; (4); 4/120; Church Yth Grp; Spanish Clb; Chorus; Nwsp; Trk; Schl Rlgs Grp; CSF; Dartmouth Coll; Educ.

LUI, SIMON; Maranatha HS; Rowland Heights, CA; (4); Church Yth Grp; Spanish Clb; Chorus; Nwsp; JV Crs Cntry; Var Mgr(s); JV Var Trk; High Hon Roll; CSF; ACSI Mst Distinguished Stu; Cornell U; Arch.

LUIS, ALICIA; Santa Monica HS; Santa Monica, CA; (1); Band; Inter Desgnr.

LUIS, ESTHER; Long Beach Poly HS; Long Beach, CA; (2); VP Sec FBLA; VP Soph Cls; Stu Cncl; High Hon Roll; Hon Roll; NHS; MECHA Sec; CA Schlrshp Fed; Clb Latino; Bus.

LUIS, LISA A; Watsonville HS; Freedom, CA; (3); 75/400; Ed Nwsp; Hon Roll; Feature Editor Sch Newspaper; Awds Jrnlsm Acad; Helped Teach Religious Ed 1st Grade; San Jose ST; Jrnlsm.

LUISI, LISA A; Redwood HS; Visalia, CA; (3); Church Yth Grp; French Clb; Key Clb; Office Aide; Teachers Aide; Cheerldng; Pom Pon; Hon Roll.

LUIZ, CHRISTINA I; Galt HS; Acampo, CA; (2); Church Yth Grp; 4-H; Spanish Clb; Teachers Aide; 4-H Awd; Hon Roll; Prfct Atten Awd; Spirit Clb; UOP; Lawyer.

LUIZZO, PATRICK A; Wallenberg Traditional HS; Newton Lower Fls, MA; (1); Orch; Socr; Sftbl; Hon Roll; Tutorial Pgm; UC Berkeley; Law.

LUJAN, CONRAD L; Leuzinger HS; Lawndale, CA; (3); Church Yth Grp; Stat Bsktbl; Stat Ftbl; Intrml Gym; Stat Sftbl; Stat Vllybl; Cit Awd; Hon Roll; Presdntl Phys Fitness Awd; CSF; BYU.

LUJAN, ESTAN M; Lowell HS; San Francisco, CA; (2); Spanish Clb; JV Ftbl; Var Wrstlng; Gldn ST Exm Acad Excllnc Awd; Math Engrng Sci Achvt Clb; UC Berkeley; Mech Engrng.

LUJAN, JENNY; San Bernardino HS; San Bernardino, CA; (3); Cmnty Wkr; FBLA; SADD; Teachers Aide; Cheerldng; Capt Var Pom Pon; High Hon Roll; Hon Roll; MESA; Phoenix Pgm; Bsktbl Hmcmng Swthrt; Chmbr Commerce Awd; Accntng.

LUJAN, KRISTIE; Valley HS; Sacramento, CA; (4); Church Yth Grp; Cmnty Wkr; SADD; Varsity Clb; VP Soph Cls; VP Jr Cls; VP Sr Cls; VP Stu Cncl; Var Capt Socr; Cit Awd; Natl Hspnc Schlr Semi-Nflst; Hmcmng Princess; GATE Clb; UC Davis; Poltcl Sci.

LUJAN, LEILA A; Pamona Convent HS; Altadena, CA; (3); 31/98; Debate Tm; GAA; Letterman Clb; Model UN; Red Cross Aide; Phtg Rptr Nwsp; Phtg Rptr Yrbk; Pres Jr Cls; Var Bsktbl; Var Capt Trk; Sprts Med.

LUJAN, MARY HELEN; Sierra Vista HS; Baldwin Park, CA; (4); French Clb; School Musical; Phtg Yrbk; Stu Cncl; Hon Roll; Poms Published; Guitar Piano; Golden Poet Awd; Ml Sac JC; Photo.

LUJAN, ROBERT V; Yucaipa SR HS; Yucaipa, CA; (3); Spanish Clb; SADD; Capt JV Bsbl; Var Bsktbl; Lion Awd; Pres Acad Fit Awd; Congrssnl Schlr Congrssnl Yth Ldrshp Cncl; Phrmcy.

LUJAN, ROSEMARIE; Pius X HS; Compton, CA; (3); Latin Clb; Pep Clb; Spanish Clb; Varsity Clb; Chorus; Flag Corp; Variety Show; Var Cheerldng; Powder Puff Ftbl; JV Sftbl; U Of CA Riverside; Sociology.

LUJANO, ANNA; Brawley HS; Westmorland, CA; (2); FHA; Office Aide; Pep Clb; JV Sftbl; JV Sftbl & KKIS 89.

LUK, ALAN HING TUNG; Lowell HS; San Francisco, CA; (2); Church Yth Grp; Science Clb; Movie Clb; Stanford.

LUKASIEWICZ, REBECCA; L A Baptist HS; Granada Hills, CA; (2); 1/140; Drill Tm; School Play; Hon Roll; CA Schlrshp Fed; Vol VA Hosp; Doctor.

LUKEI, ANDY A; Woodbridge HS; Irvine, CA; (2); AFS; Church Yth Grp; Cmnty Wkr; Red Cross Aide; Rep Soph Cls; Score Keeper; JV Capt Vllybl; Hon Roll; Jr NHS; Pres Acad Fit Awd; CSF; Water Polo & Surf Clb; CA Berkley; Bus.

LUKENBILL, JULIE A; Poway HS; Poway, CA; (3); Church Yth Grp; Pep Clb; SADD; Ed Yrbk; Stu Cncl; Powder Puff Ftbl; JV Swmmng; Prfct Atten Awd; Peer Cnslng; CSULB; Elem Sch Tchr.

LUKENS, REGINA M; Saint Paul HS; La Mirada, CA; (3); Hon Roll; NHS; CA Schlrshp Fed; Bus.

LUKKONEN, KATHRYN L; San Gorgonio HS; Highland, CA; (3); AFS; Girl Scts; SADD; Ed Nwsp; JV Sftbl; JV Tennis; Rotary Awd; Sftbl Club; Friday Night Live; Interact; CA ST U San Bernardino; Comm.

LULL, MARY J; Whitney HS; Cerritos, CA; (2); Church Yth Grp; Dance Clb; English Clb; Key Clb; Teachers Aide; Church Choir; Variety Show; Lit Mag; Hon Roll; CA ST Long Beach; Phrmcy.

LUM, BELINDA C; Lowell HS; San Francisco, CA; (2); Cmnty Wkr; GAA; NFL; Speech Tm; JV Stat Bsktbl; Mgr(s); Stat Score Keeper; Trk; Lion Awd; Volunteer Coach For Basketball At Elementary School; Tutor At Elementary; Psychology.

LUM, CATHERINE L; Fremont HS; Sunnyvale, CA; (2); 1/421; Church Yth Grp; Debate Tm; Speech Tm; Socr; Tennis; Mock Trl Tm; Astras; CA Yth Smyphny.

LUM, CATHY; Fremont HS; Sunnyvale, CA; (2); 1/400; Church Yth Grp; Debate Tm; NFL; Speech Tm; JV Cheerldng; Var Socr; Var Tennis; CA Yth Symphny; ASTRAS Grls Srvc Clb.

LUM, CYNTHIA L; Carlmont HS; Belmont, CA; (2); 1/526; Orch; High Hon Roll; Treas St Schlr; Amnesty Intl; Asian Amer Club; Soph Bd; Stanford U; Sci.

LUM, CYNTHIA M; Downey HS; Downey, CA; (2); VP French Clb; Hosp Aide; Sec Key Clb; Letterman Clb; Treas Math Clb; VP Science Clb; Church Choir; Var Tennis; High Hon Roll; Hnrb Mntn CA-NV-HI Keywanettes Oratory Cmptn; DARE; Young Envrnmntlsts Pres & Fndr; MIT; Aeronautical Engrng.

LUM, GRACE; Lowell HS; San Francisco, CA; (3); French Clb; GAA; Varsity Clb; Orch; French Hon Soc; Vrsty Bdmntn Team 90-91; Ed.

LUM, KAREN; Eagle Rock SR HS; Los Angeles, CA; (2); GAA; JA; Key Clb; Var Score Keeper; JV Tennis; Hon Roll; Hands Across Campus HAC; E Clb; Ocadental Coll; Archaeology.

LUM, KRISTY M; Armijo HS; Suisun City, CA; (1); Band; Mrchg Band; Pep Band; Frsh Cls; Stu Cncl; JV Bsktbl; JV Vllybl; U CA-DAVIS; Pediatrcs.

LUM, LAMBERT; Mt Eden HS; Hayward, CA; (4); 20/300; Chess Clb; Church Yth Grp; Computer Clb; Math Clb; Science Clb; Hnrbl Mntn Alameda Cnty Faire Photo; CSFHONORED UC Davis Chncllrs Schlr; Hi Hnrs Golden ST Gmtry Ex; UCLA; Comp Sci Engr.

LUM, LORI L; John F Kennedy HS; Sacramento, CA; (4); Art Clb; Church Yth Grp; Debate Tm; Spanish Clb; Speech Tm; Off Sr Cls; Cit Awd; Hon Roll; Bank Of Amer Art; UC Santa Cruz; Law.

LUM, MAY SUE; Phillip & Sala Burton Academic HS; San Francisco, CA; (3); Band; High Hon Roll; Bus.

LUM, MICHAEL N; South HS; Bakersfield, CA; (3); Cmnty Wkr; Pres Intnl Clb; Key Clb; Ski Clb; Rep Jr Cls; L Trk; Hon Roll; NHS; Bus Mgmt.

LUM, RAYMOND F; Hogan SR HS; Vallejo, CA; (3); Chess Clb; Computer Clb; SADD; Teachers Aide; Nwsp; High Hon Roll; Med.

LUM, SHARON; Lowell HS; San Francisco, CA; (3); Library Aide; Hon Roll; High Hnrs For Algebra, Geom; CSF; Hon Mntn 21st Annual Arch Dsgn Cmptn; CA Polytech; Arch.

LUM, WENDY ALICIA; Phillip And Sara Burton Acad HS; San Francisco, CA; (4); 84/177; Cmnty Wkr; Service Clb; Ed Yrbk; Rep Off Frsh Cls; Rep Off Soph Cls; Rep Off Jr Cls; VP Sr Cls; Stu Cncl; Vllybl; Prfct Atten Awd; Prncpls Awd & Svc Awd & Hmrm Rep Awd; San Frncisco City Coll; Bus Mgr.

LUMALANG, CHARLENE M; Immaculate Heart HS; Los Angeles, CA; (3); GAA; JA; Mgr Swmmng; Critics Choice Club VP & Pres.

LUMANLAN, ROY; Montebello HS; Montebello, CA; (2); Key Clb; Letterman Clb; SADD; Acpl Chr; Church Choir; Rep Frsh Cls; Var Golf; Northrop U; Aeronaut Engrng.

LUMBI, TANYA R; Herbert Hoover HS; Fresno, CA; (2); Var Diving; Var Socr; JV Vllybl; Peer Cnlsr; Mst Imprvd JV Soccer Plyr; Fine Arts.

LUMSDEN, NEIL G; San Dieguito HS; Encinitas, CA; (2); Quiz Bowl; Scholastic Bowl; Teachers Aide; Bsktbl; Cit Awd; Prfct Atten Awd; Pres Acad Fit Awd; UCSD; Zoology.

LUN, SAROEUN; Roosevelt HS; Fresno, CA; (3); Church Yth Grp; Church Choir; Hon Roll; ASIAN Club; SADD Club; Ed.

LUNA, ADRIANA G; Moreno Valley HS; Moreno Vly, CA; (3); Teachers Aide; Hon Roll; RCC Coll; Law Enfrcmnt.

LUNA, AGUSTIN F; San Pedro HS; San Pedro, CA; (3); Band; Drm Mjr(t); Jazz Band; Mrchg Band; Orch; Pres Jr Cls; Crs Cntry; Cit Awd; High Hon Roll; Prfct Atten Awd; Croatian Clb; Louis Armstrong Jazz Awd; Arch.

LUNA, ANTHONY; Don Bosco Technical Inst; West Covina, CA; (4); Boy Scts; Chess Clb; Church Yth Grp; Varsity Clb; Var Capt Bsbl; Amer Soc Metls Intl; Semifnlst Natl Hspnc Hnrs Pgm; Cal Poly; Matrls Sci.

LUNA, BLANCA ESTELA; Baldwin Park HS; Baldwin Park, CA; (3); FBLA; Key Clb; Math Clb; High Hon Roll; Prfct Atten Awd; Badminton Var; Bus.

LUNA, CARLOS A; St Ignatius College Prep; San Francisco, CA; (4); Cmnty Wkr; JV Ftbl; Var Lcrss; Hon Roll; UC Berkeley.

LUNA, CARLOS S; Blair HS; Pasadena, CA; (1); JV Socr; Cit Awd.

LUNA, CARMEN; Pasadena HS; Altadena, CA; (2); Spanish Clb; Hon Roll; Badminton Team V; MESA; Stu Of Yr Awd; USC; Engrng.

LUNA, CATHY; Mountain View HS; El Monte, CA; (1); Drill Tm; Vllybl; High Hon Roll; Hon Roll; Lawyr.

LUNA, ELIZABETH; Calipatria HS; Calipatria, CA; (3); Spanish Clb; Karate; IVC; Scl Sci.

LUNA, ELSA; Dana Hills HS; San Juan Capistra, CA; (2); Debate Tm; Drama Clb; Model UN; Science Clb; Spanish Clb; Orch; School Play; Swmmng; High Hon Roll; Lion Awd; Mock Trial; SAVE; CSF; Bus.

LUNA, FLORENCE C; Samuel F B Morse HS; San Diego, CA; (2); 70/764; Chorus; Med Asst.

LUNA, INEZ B; Vacaville HS; Vacaville, CA; (2); Church Yth Grp; Office Aide; Crs Cntry; Hon Roll; Pwr Of Postv Stu Awd 88-89; Cert Achvt Gldn St Exam 90; UC San Diego; Biomdcl Physic.

LUNA, JANET H; Bishop Amat HS; La Puente, CA; (2); Chorus; School Musical; Hon Roll; NHS; CSF; 5th Pl Natl Spanish Exam; Amer Sign Lang; USC; Med.

LUNA, JULIE; Selma HS; Fresno, CA; (4); 47/189; Debate Tm; Drama Clb; English Clb; Spanish Clb; Speech Tm; SADD; VICA; Chorus; Hon Roll; Lion Awd; Gottschalks Hi Deb Model 89-90; Fresno City Clg; Engl Tchr.

LUNA, JUSTIN J; Gladstone HS; Covina, CA; (3); Wt Lftg; Hon Roll; Law.

LUNA, MARIA P; Mark Keppel HS; Monterey Park, CA; (3); Pres Latin Clb; Teachers Aide; VP Treas Mrchg Band; Pep Band; Employee Month; 6th Pl Natl Spnsh Exam; Score 5 Spnsh Lang AP Exam; Psych.

LUNA, MARIA S; Kingsburg HS; Traver, CA; (3); #10 In Class; Pres Church Yth Grp; Cmnty Wkr; FTA; Math Clb; Math Tm; Pres Spanish Clb; Pres SADD; Church Choir; Mrchg Band; Pep Band; Nrsng.

LUNA, MARY; Nogales HS; La Puente, CA; (2); Church Yth Grp; Hon Roll; Acad Achvmnt Excllnc Phys Ed Merit Awd; CA ST Fullerton; Accntng.

LUNA, MICHELE L; Gilroy HS; Gilroy, CA; (4); Am Leg Aux Girls St; Church Yth Grp; Drama Clb; Sec Speech Tm; School Musical; School Play; Treas Soph Cls; Pres Stu Cncl; Stat Bsbl; Powder Puff Ftbl; CSF; Little Leag Scorekeeper; UCLA; Intl Bus.

LUNA, MONICA G; Santa Paula Union HS; Santa Paula, CA; (2); 118/344; Boy Scts; FTA; Spanish Clb; Temple Yth Grp; Spanish NHS; UCSB; Tchr.

LUNA, SONIA; St Genevieve HS; Arleta, CA; (3); Spanish Clb; Stu Cncl; Var Bsktbl; Var Sftbl; Sftbl & Bsktbl All-Acad Awd; Pgm Sftbl Acad Awds; CSUN; Bus.

LUNA, TRINA M; Duncan Polytechnical HS; Fresno, CA; (1); Church Yth Grp; SADD; Outstndng Achvt Fmly/Soc Lvng, Tech Crfts Awds; San Diego St U; Accntnt.

LUNCEFORD, CARLTON D; David Starr Jordan HS; Long Beach, CA; (3); Church Yth Grp; Math Tm; Var JV Ftbl; JV Trk; Hon Roll; Jr NHS; Schltc All-Amer; Accntng.

LUNCEFORD, CHRISTY J; Trabuco Hills HS; Trabuco Canyon, CA; (2); 28/450; Church Yth Grp; Socr; Sftbl; Hon Roll; Dstnghsd Schlr; 1st Tm All Leag Sccr 89-90 & Sftbl 88-89; Jr Olympic Sftbl; Psych.

LUNCEFORD, JEFFREY D; Rim Of The World HS; Running Springs, CA; (4); 45/200; Drama Clb; Thesps; School Play; Ed Nwsp; Cit Awd; High Hon Roll; Lion Awd; Pres Acad Fit Awd; Rotary Awd; 3.0 GPA; CA ST U-San Bernardino; Med.

LUND, ERICA; Paraclete HS; Lancaster, CA; (4); 16/130; Debate Tm; Drama Clb; JA; Drill Tm; Stat Mgr Ftbl; High Hon Roll; NHS; CSF; Schlstc All Am; Pepperdine U; Finance.

LUND, LARK K; Nevada Union HS; Grass Valley, CA; (1); Chorus; Bsktbl; High Hon Roll.

LUNDBERG, SARALYNN; Redwood Christian HS; Castro Valley, CA; (2); Church Yth Grp; Vllybl; High Hon Roll; Pres Acad Fit Awd; Selected Voice Honor Choir; Certificate Of Merit Piano Competition 3 Yrs; Christian Schl Tchr.

LUNDBERG, SCOTT R; Los Gatos HS; Los Gatos, CA; (4); 1/374; Debate Tm; Math Tm; Speech Tm; Var L Bsbl; Var L Ftbl; Hon Roll; Ntl Merit SF; NEDT Awd; Rnsslr Top Physics Stu Medal; Ftbl 2nd Team All-League; Stanford U.

LUNDBERG, SHAWN; Alhambra HS; Martinez, CA; (2); Boy Scts; Church Yth Grp; Drama Clb; Hosp Aide; Phtg Nwsp; Hon Roll; Photography Club; Academic Decathalon; Diabetes Camp Counselor At Bearskin Meadow; History/Medical Field.

LUNDBOM, KRISTIN; Livermore HS; Livermore, CA; (1); Church Yth Grp; Dance Clb; Band; Mrchg Band; JV Cheerldng; Stat Score Keeper; High Hon Roll; CSF; Music Awd; UC Davis; Educator.

LUNDBOM, PATRICK D; Livermore HS; Livermore, CA; (3); 46/499; Boy Scts; Church Yth Grp; SADD; Color Guard; Var Wrstlng; High Hon Roll; Hon Roll; JV Crs Cntry; Wrld Boy Sct Jamboree Australia; U Of CA Riverside; Bio.

LUNDBORG, MONA S C; Bolsa Grande HS; Garden Grove, CA; (4); Art Clb; Drama Clb; German Clb; JV Tennis; Var L Trk; Hon Roll; Athl Of Mnth Apr Trk; MVP Trk; Mst Outsntdng Stu Awd Comp Sci; CA Schlrshp Fed; Exchange Stu Germany; Intl Bus.

LUNDE, CHARLIENNE R; Kingsburg HS; Kingsburg, CA; (2); 2/150; Church Yth Grp; GAA; Letterman Clb; SADD; Varsity Clb; Treas Frsh Cls; Bsktbl; Crs Cntry; Trk; High Hon Roll; Hugh O'brian Yth Ldrshp Smnr; MVP Cross Cntry Club; Rotary Top 40; Lawyer.

LUNDE, CHRISTOPHER S; Claremont HS; Claremont, CA; (4); 28/383; Boy Scts; Church Yth Grp; Ski Clb; JV Var Socr; High Hon Roll; Vllybl Clb Pres; UC Santa Cruz; Environment.

LUNDE, GARRETT C; Kingsburg Jt Union HS; Kingsburg, CA; (4); 1/183; Am Leg Boys St; Church Yth Grp; Letterman Clb; Math Clb; Math Tm; VP Mu Alpha Theta; Teachers Aide; Varsity Clb; Lit Mag; Bsbl; CSF; Hnrs Awd Goldn St Exam; Aerospace Engrng.

LUNDY, DENNIS R; East Bakersfield HS; Bakersfield, CA; (1); Boy Scts; Hosp Aide; Teachers Aide; Band; Mrchg Band; Ftbl; Wrstlng; Hon Roll; Dctr.

LUNDY, STEFFANI A; Cajon HS; San Bernardino, CA; (3); AFS; Cmnty Wkr; GAA; Key Clb; Spanish Clb; SADD; Yrbk; Var Swmmng; Var Vllybl; Peer Cnslng; Child Psych.

LUNDY, WILLIAM B; Mc Ateer HS; San Francisco, CA; (3); Boy Scts; Band; Jazz Band; Pep Band; School Musical; JV Bsbl; JV Ftbl; JV Wrstlng; Hon Roll; Cert Opn Wtr Diver; Envrnmntl Camp Cnslr; U CA Santa Cruz; Comp Sci.

LUNETTA-BROWN, MELISSA; Pomona Catholic HS; Ontario, CA; (2); GAA; Model UN; Spanish Clb; Treas Frsh Cls; Rep Stu Cncl; Cheerldng; JV Sftbl; Hon Roll; NHS; Outstndng All Around Stu 88-89; Sci Fair 2nd Pl Bio Awd 89-90; UCLA; Dentistry.

LUNGREN, KELLY; St Francais HS; Roseville, CA; (1); Church Yth Grp; Drama Clb; GAA; JA; Ski Clb; Band; School Play; Stage Crew; Var Trk; Cit Awd; Naval Acad; Naval Cmmndr.

LUNN, SUSAN R; Coalinga HS; Coalinga, CA; (3); AFS; Pres Debate Tm; Drama Clb; Pres FTA; SADD; School Play; Stage Crew; Rep Sec Stu Cncl; JV Sftbl; Var Trk; Grls League; Frdy Nght Live; CA ST U Fresno; Bus Admin.

LUNSFORD, ROBYN M.; Del Oro HS; Penryn, CA; (4); 20/250; French Clb; GAA; Pep Clb; Ski Clb; Band; Jazz Band; Mrchg Band; Pep Band; JV Bsktbl; Var Bsktbl; John Philip Sousa Awd; TX A&M U; Intl Bus.

LUNSTAD, KARA L; Hanford HS; Hanford, CA; (1); 4-H; FFA; Pep Clb; Teachers Aide; Sec Frsh Cls; JV Cheerldng; JV Diving; JV Swmmng; JV Wt Lftg; High Hon Roll; Dntl.

LUO, CHIA CHI KELLY; Alhambra HS; Alhambra, CA; (4); Computer Clb; Office Aide; Teachers Aide; Temple Yth Grp; Chorus; Church Choir; Badmntn Coaches Awd; Adventurers Club Pres; CPA.

LUO, DAVID H L; George Washington HS; San Francisco, CA; (2); Church Yth Grp; Key Clb; Math Clb; Red Cross Aide; Science Clb; Service Clb; Teachers Aide; Mgr(s); Vllybl; High Hon Roll; CA Schlrshp Fdrtn; Cert Of Achvmnts-Chem & Engl; Prfrm Lab Experiments; U C Davis; Sci/Math.

LUONG, AI THAI Q; Santa Clara HS; Santa Clara, CA; (4); Yrbk; Peace Clb; Amnsty Intl; U CA Santa Barbara; Englsh.

LUONG, BINH; Mission HS; San Francisco, CA; (3); Cmnty Wkr; Girl Scts; Intnl Clb; Latin Clb; Teachers Aide; School Musical.

LUONG, CUONG P; Mark Keppel HS; Rosemead, CA; (2); Bsktbl; Cit Awd.

LUONG, DUNG; Fountain Valley HS; Fountain Valley, CA; (2); Computer Clb; Key Clb; Tchr.

LUONG, DUONG; John F Kennedy HS; Buena Park, CA; (4); Computer Clb; FBLA; Key Clb; Ed Yrbk; High Hon Roll; NHS; St Schlr; CSF; Bdmntn Vrsty; Phrmcst.

LUONG, HUONG; C K Mc Clatchy HS; Sacramento, CA; (2); 17/487; French Clb; Hosp Aide; Math Clb; Math Tm; High Hon Roll; Hon Roll; Prfct Atten Awd; Arch.

LUONG, JULIE Y; Rosemead HS; Rosemead, CA; (3); Service Clb; SADD; Judicial Brd Clb; CA Poly Pomona; Bus.

LUONG, KELLY HA A; John F Kennedy HS; Los Angeles, CA; (3); Key Clb; Library Aide; Office Aide; Teachers Aide; Cit Awd; Hon Roll; San Diego ST; Schl Tchr.

LUONG, KHAI THUC; W C Overfelt HS; San Jose, CA; (4); 7/352; Math Clb; Math Tm; Science Clb; Var Socr; Hon Roll; NHS; CA Schlrshp Fdrtn-VP-PRES; Bdmnt; U C Davis; Physics.

LUONG, KIEU V; Mark Keppel HS; Rosemead, CA; (1); Debate Tm; FBLA; Key Clb; Math Clb; Band; Cit Awd.

LUONG, LIEN K; Cordova SR HS; Rancho Cordova, CA; (2); 13/540; Tennis; Hon Roll; Jr NHS; Bio Chem.

LUONG, LILA T; Skyline HS; Oakland, CA; (3); Library Aide; Cit Awd; Hon Roll; Asian Stu Union; Schlrshp Mdl; UC Davis; Bus Mgmt.

LUONG, MAY T; San Gabriel HS; San Gabriel, CA; (2); French Clb; Pep Clb; Red Cross Aide; Hon Roll; Pres Acad Fit Awd; Interact Club.

LUONG, MIA C; Skyline HS; Oakland, CA; (2); Computer Clb; Teachers Aide; Cit Awd; Hon Roll; Prfct Atten Awd; Asian St Union; Bus.

LUONG, MINDY; Independence HS; San Jose, CA; (3); Science Clb; High Hon Roll; Police Ofcr.

LUONG, MINH-NGUYET THI; Santa Ana Valley HS; Santa Ana, CA; (4); 16/325; Drama Clb; FBLA; Key Clb; School Play; Variety Show; High Hon Roll; Prfct Atten Awd; Service Clb; Rptr Nwsp; Lit Mag; SAVVY Secy & Vp; CSF Seal Bearer; Bst Effortg Awd, Positive Attitude & Silver Medal For Math; UC Irvine; Bio Sci.

LUONG, TAI N; Andrew Hill HS; San Jose, CA; (2); Viet Clb; San Jose ST U; Comp Pgmr.

LUONG, TAYLOR; La Quinta HS; Alhambra, CA; (2); Socr; Trk; Hon Roll; Vietnamese Club; Chef.

LUONG, THANH T; Santa Clara HS; Santa Clara, CA; (2); French Clb; JV Var Socr; Hon Roll; CSF; Soroptomist; U Of Stanford; Psych.

LUONG, THAO C; San Marcos HS; Santa Barbara, CA; (2); Math Clb; Math Tm; ROTC; Hon Roll; Sppllng Cmpptn Cnty Champp 2nd ST Comppp; Elect Engrng.

LUONG, THUY; John W North HS; Riverside, CA; (2); Church Yth Grp; Church Choir; UC Irvine; Nrsng.

LUONG, TIEN T; Independence HS; San Jose, CA; (3); Bus.

LUONG, TOAN; Alhambra HS; Alhambra, CA; (4); 42/690; Cmnty Wkr; Letterman Clb; Red Cross Aide; Service Clb; Yrbk; Var L Bsktbl; High Hon Roll; Hon Roll; Golden St Exam Algebra & Geo Hnrs Bsktbl MVP Awd Yrbk Cover Dsgnr 90; Bio.

LUONG, TUAN A; Alhambra HS; Alhambra, CA; (3); Cal ST; Acctnt.

LUONG, TUYEN; San Bernardino HS; San Bernardino, CA; (2); 3/600; Chess Clb; Letterman Clb; Math Clb; Math Tm; Speech Tm; Varsity Clb; Tennis; Cit Awd; High Hon Roll; Hon Roll; U Of CA Irvine; Med.

LUONG, TUYET HA; William C Overfelt HS; San Jose, CA; (4); 2/300; Treas Math Clb; Math Tm; VP Science Clb; High Hon Roll; NHS; CSF; Dist Math Cont 4th Pl Trphy Calculus; Santa Clara U; Acctng.

LUONG, VICTORIA; Pomona HS; Pomona, CA; (4); 1/250; Intnl Clb; JA; Scholastic Bowl; Stu Cncl; Vllybl; Cit Awd; Pres Acad Fit Awd; Rotary Awd; Val; Occidental Coll; Bio.

LUONG, YEN LOAN; East Union HS; Manteca, CA; (4); 16/271; Key Clb; Science Clb; Temple Yth Grp; Cit Awd; Hon Roll; Sci & Math Conf; Sci Olympiad Awd; UC Davis; Civil Engrng.

LUQMAN, KHADIJAH; King/Drew Med Magnet HS; Los Angeles, CA; (3); Drama Clb; English Clb; Girl Scts; Intnl Clb; Chorus; School Play; Variety Show; Lit Mag; Cit Awd; High Hon Roll; Outstndng Span Awd; Engl Dept Awd; Linguistics.

LUQUE, DEANNA M; East Bakersfield HS; Bakersfield, CA; (1); VP Frsh Cls; Var L Socr; Var L Sftbl; L Vllybl; Hon Roll; GATE Prgm; UCLA; Med.

LUQUE, PAUL; Rowland HS; Rowland Heights, CA; (2); Letterman Clb; Spanish Clb; Ftbl; Var Capt Socr; Hon Roll; Prfct Atten Awd; Animtn Film Awd; CA ST Fullerton; Med.

LUQUIN, JOSE ENRIQUE; Channel Island HS; Oxnard, CA; (2); Boy Scts; Science Clb; JV Wrstlng; Hon Roll; Pres Acad Fit Awd; Stu Athlte Schlr Awd; Doctor.

LURIE, KEVIN P; Woodside HS; Redwood City, CA; (2); French Clb; Ski Clb; Treas Temple Yth Grp; Rep Frsh Cls; Rep Soph Cls; JV Tennis; High Hon Roll; Hon Roll; UC Davis; Vet Med.

LURIE, PETRA; San Mateo HS; Foster City, CA; (3); Cmnty Wkr; Dance Clb; Debate Tm; Latin Clb; Spanish Clb; Variety Show; Gym; Powder Puff Ftbl; High Hon Roll; Hon Roll; Fstr Cty Yth Advsry Cncl; Pr Cnslr; Jr Statsmn Amer.

LUSARDI, CLINTON S; Arroya Grande HS; Arroyo Grande, CA; (3); Hon Roll; Water Polo; Moorpark; Animal Trng.

LUSBY, SHANE G; Edison Computech HS; Fresno, CA; (3); Computer Clb; Hon Roll; Dist Comp Dept Awd; 3 Gldn St Awds-Math; Comp Sci AP Tst Qlfd Scr; UC Berkeley; Chem Engrng.

LUSE, MICHELLE; St Genevieve HS; North Hollywood, CA; (3); 15/169; French Clb; High Hon Roll; CA ST U Northbridge.

LUSHER, LAURA; S D S C P A HS; San Diego, CA; (2); Church Yth Grp; Dance Clb; English Clb; Spanish Clb; SADD; Band; Jazz Band; School Musical; Paralegl.

LUSHINSKY, MICHAEL A; Brea Olinda HS; Brea, CA; (1); Boy Scts; High Hon Roll; Hon Roll; Engr.

LUSIANI, NICOLE; San Lorenzo HS; San Lorenzo, CA; (4); 34/220; Am Leg Aux Girls St; Drama Clb; School Musical; Co-Ed Nwsp; Pres Stu Cncl; Hon Roll; Outstndng Sr Perf Arts; Jostens Bst Sr AwdROTARY Speech Wnnr; St Marys Coll; HS Tchr.

LUSTER, LA TASHA R; Galileo HS; Oakland, CA; (2); Church Yth Grp; Cmnty Wkr; Teachers Aide; Church Choir; School Musical; Cit Awd; UC Berkeley; Law Enfrcmnt.

LUSTIG, FRANCESCA M; Miramonte HS; Orinda, CA; (1); JV Cheerldng; Hon Roll; U Of WA; Advrtsng.

LUTHER, CONNIE I; Connie Isabelle Luther HS; Mission Viejo, CA; (2); #29 In Class; Church Yth Grp; Cmnty Wkr; French Clb; Key Clb; High Hon Roll; Mrt Crt Frnch Camp 90; Acad Awd 3.93 GPA; Awd Outstndng Achv Frnch I & II.

LUTHER, JENNIFFER; Enterprise HS; Redding, CA; (3); 27/435; Church Yth Grp; Intnl Clb; Mu Alpha Theta; Acpl Chr; Chorus; Church Choir; Swing Chorus; Hon Roll; Pledge Dr Vlntr Local PBS; Mst Outstndng Jazz Solst Nava Jazz 87-88; Dance Cls Ballet, Tap Mdrn Dnc; Crmnl Lawyer.

LUTMAN, TARA L; Live Oak HS; San Jose, CA; (3); 26/530; Church Yth Grp; Dance Clb; Sec Key Clb; Teachers Aide; Ed Lit Mag; JV Var Vllybl; High Hon Roll; Hon Roll; Prfct Atten Awd; Pres Acad Fit Awd; Badmntn #3 Grls Dbls; Santa Clara U; Psych.

LUTRICK, LARA A; Enterprise HS; Redding, CA; (3); 11/427; Drama Clb; Intnl Clb; Science Clb; Thesps; School Play; Stage Crew; Yrbk; Mgr Vllybl; Hon Roll; Photog Clb.

LUTSKY, HANNAH M; Casa Grande HS; Petaluma, CA; (2); Temple Yth Grp; Chorus; Crs Cntry; Hon Roll; Socr; Piano.

LUTTON, BARTON G; Arcadia HS; Temple City, CA; (3); 401/658; Boy Scts; Drama Clb; Teachers Aide; School Play; Stage Crew; Yrbk; Var L Socr; Var L Trk; Hon Roll; Masonic Awd; Bus.

LUTTRELL, MAXIMILIAN H; Lowell High; San Francisco, CA; (3); Rep Stu Cncl; Gov Hon Prg Awd; CA Schlrhp Fed; Music Appreciation Soc; Bowling Leag; Comp Sci.

LUTZ, BRIAN J; Paraclete HS; Lancaster, CA; (2); Key Clb; SADD; JV Var Bsktbl; High Hon Roll; Hon Roll; CSF; UCLA; Sports Med.

LUTZ, ELIZABETH A; Patrick Henry HS; San Diego, CA; (2); Lit Mag; Cit Awd; Hon Roll; Jr NHS; 1st Pl Microbio In Sci Fair; Marine Bio.

LUTZ, ELIZABETH M; John F Kennedy HS; La Palma, CA; (4); Church Yth Grp; Band; Jazz Band; Mrchg Band; School Play; Mgr Nwsp; Sut Mnth Nov; Acad Dcthlm Tm; UC Riverside; Psych.

LUTZI, JULIANA BETH; Terra Linda HS; San Rafael, CA; (4); Cmnty Wkr; Debate Tm; Flag Corp; School Musical; Yrbk; Stu Cncl; Capt Cheerldng; Var Pom Pon; Var Trk.

LUTZOW, DEBORAH J; Del Oro HS; Loomis, CA; (4); 1/229; Val; NHS; Lion Awd; Pres Church Yth Grp; Drm Mjr(t); Jazz Band; Pep Band; Chorus; Drama Clb; Sec Stu Cncl; Host Intl Awrd Marchng Band; B & A Achvmnt Awrd Fine Arts; Schlrshp,Lorene Lobner Keena & Aburn Exchng; Sierra; Photography.

LUU, CATHY; George Washington HS; San Francisco, CA; (3); JA; Teachers Aide; Variety Show; Score Keeper; Cit Awd; High Hon Roll; Hon Roll; Prfct Atten Awd; Teachers Assistance; USF; Marketing.

LUU, CO K; Hoover HS; San Diego, CA; (3); JA; Math Clb; Cit Awd; High Hon Roll; NHS; UCSD; Strctrl Engr.

LUU, CUONG; Oakland HS; Oakland, CA; (4); Computer Clb; Math Clb; Math Tm; Science Clb; Teachers Aide; Lit Mag; Bsbl; Bsktbl; Swmmng; Vllybl; Bank Of Amer Achvt Awd Frgn Lang; UCLA; Bus.

LUU, CUONG Q; Prospect HS; San Jose, CA; (3); 17/277; Chess Clb; Cmnty Wkr; Computer Clb; Math Clb; Crs Cntry; Trk; Wrstlng; High Hon Roll; Prfct Atten Awd; CA Goldn St Exam Goem Hnr; CA Poly; Arch.

LUU, HELEN; Santa Teresa HS; San Jose, CA; (1); Church Yth Grp; Intnl Clb; Model UN; SADD; Rep Stu Cncl; High Hon Roll; Peer Grp Cnslng; Tutor Voc Subjects; Fellowshp Clb; Bus Mgmt.

LUU, HOA T; Lowell HS; San Francisco, CA; (2); UCSF Vlntr; UC Berkeley; Arch Dsgn.

LUU, HUNG; Fairfield HS; Suisun City, CA; (3); Chess Clb; French Clb; Key Clb; Cit Awd; French Hon Soc; High Hon Roll; Hon Roll; Jr NHS; NHS; Highest Frnch Hnrs; UC Berkeley; Elect Engrng.

LUU, HUY C; Oakland HS; Oakland, CA; (3); French Clb; School Musical; Cit Awd; St Schlr; 3rd Pl Perf Trophy Africa Map Contest; Excllnt Achvmt Piano Trophy; Cal ST U Hayward; Geog.

LUU, LAN; Burroughs HS; Anaheim, CA; (4); Debate Tm; Drama Clb; Spanish Clb; SADD; Teachers Aide; Variety Show; Hon Roll; Cal State Fullerton; Business.

LUU, LINH K; Birmingham HS; Los Angeles, CA; (1); FBLA; Hon Roll; Prfct Atten Awd; U Of Ca Los Angeles; Astrnmy.

LUU, LOANNE; Bullard HS; Fresno, CA; (1); Math Clb; Math Tm; SADD; Cit Awd; High Hon Roll; Hon Roll; Prfct Atten Awd; Pres Acad Fit Awd; Stanford; Med.

LUU, LONG; Ontario HS; Ontario, CA; (2); Art Clb; Math Clb; Spanish Clb; Teachers Aide; Off Soph Cls; Hon Roll; Prfct Atten Awd; Asian Club; 3rd Pl Poetry Cont; UCLA; Zoologist.

LUU, MY TRINH; Phillip & Sala Burton HS; San Francisco, CA; (4); 2/180; High Hon Roll; Prfct Atten Awd; Davis Coll; Med.

LUU, NHON T; Fullerton Union HS; Fullerton, CA; (1); 50/408; JV Tennis; Jr NHS; NHS; Prfct Atten Awd; Intl Baccalaureate; CA ST U Fullerton; Engr.

LUU, PHONG K; San Gabriel HS; San Gabriel, CA; (3); Cit Awd; Hon Roll; Prfct Atten Awd.

LUU, PHONG-HIEN; Mira Mesa HS; San Diego, CA; (2); Boy Scts; Chess Clb; Cmnty Wkr; Computer Clb; Intnl Clb; Key Clb; Math Clb; Science Clb; Spanish Clb; Temple Yth Grp; Badminton; CJSF; 4.0 Clb; UCSD; Microbio.

LUU, PHUOC; Mark Keppel HS; Monterey Park, CA; (3); Hon Roll.

LUU, TAM; Ontario HS; Ontario, CA; (1); German Clb; Pep Band; Trk; Hon Roll; Prfct Atten Awd; Peforming Arts Band; Sch Musicale; Teacher.

LUU, TUAN M; Leuzinger HS; Hawthorne, CA; (2); Art Clb; Chess Clb; French Clb; Key Clb; Math Tm; Science Clb; Ski Clb; Spanish Clb; Teachers Aide; Band.

LUU, VINH T; George Washington HS; San Francisco, CA; (2); AFS; Boy Scts; Hosp Aide; Library Aide; Office Aide; Quiz Bowl; Service Clb; Service Clb; Off Soph Cls; Bsbl.

LUX, ANDREW J; Servite HS; Cypress, CA; (2); Church Yth Grp; Cmnty Wkr; Intrml Bsktbl; JV Golf; Hon Roll; Jr Statesman Of Amer; CA Schltc Fed; Engr.

LUYEN, VINH N; Independence HS; San Jose, CA; (3); 29/956; Chess Clb; Pres Acad Fit Awd; Supt Hnrs Lst; San Jose ST U; Elec Engr.

LUZ, ANDRE R; Don Antonio Lugo HS; Chino, CA; (2); 4/1200; Cit Awd; Hon Roll; CSF; Gldn St Exam Hnr Awd; Gldn Cnqst Awds Frgn Lang 88-89, Sci 89-90; Med.

LUZON, ROSEMARY; O Farrell School-Creative Arts; San Diego, CA; (1); Orch; Tennis; Hon Roll.

LWADE, STACI L; Pinole Valley HS; San Pablo, CA; (4); Office Aide; Teachers Aide; Var Powder Puff Ftbl; Var Swmmng; Hon Roll; Interact Clb; Var Water Polo; CSU Sacramento; Sociology.

LY, ANGELA; Abraham Lincoln HS; San Francisco, CA; (3); Teachers Aide; Chorus; Ed Yrbk; Off Jr Cls; Hist Stu Cncl; UCLA; Bus Mgmt.

LY, ANH QUOC; Tustin HS; Tustin, CA; (2); Sec Treas German Clb; Latin Clb; Math Tm; Quiz Bowl; Science Clb; High Hon Roll; Hon Roll; JV Vllybl; Acad Decathlon; Booster Club Math Stu; MIT; Engr.

LY, BERNICE Q; Lowell HS; San Francisco, CA; (2); Hosp Aide; Office Aide; ROTC; Prfct Atten Awd; Pres Acad Fit Awd; CA Schlrshp Fdrtn; Hnrs GSE Algebra; U; Medi/Psych.

LY, BINH; Baldwin Park HS; Baldwin Park, CA; (1); Bsktbl; Ftbl; Bdmntn; Princeton; Arch.

LY, CHHING K; Fontana HS; Fontana, CA; (4); Art Clb; VP Chess Clb; High Hon Roll; Pres Acad Fit Awd; Bdmntn 3 Yrs Vrsty; CSF; Ushers Cls 89; UCLA; Biochem.

LY, DAVID; Independence HS; San Jose, CA; (3); 58/962; Debate Tm; Math Tm; NFL; Science Clb; Speech Tm; CSF; Golden St Exam Hnrs Awd Geom; UC Davis; Aeronautical Engr.

LY, DAVID H; Galileo HS; San Francisco, CA; (4); 2/35; French Clb; JA; Library Aide; Red Cross Aide; ROTC; Spanish Clb; Drill Tm; Hon Roll; NHS; Pres Acad Fit Awd; U CA Davis; Bus.

LY, EILEEN LINH-MY; Lincoln HS; Los Angeles, CA; (3); Cmnty Wkr; Sec FBLA; Hon Roll; CSF; NALEO; Pacific Asian Clb; Bus.

LY, GEORGE TRI NHON; San Gabriel HS; Alhambra, CA; (3); Computer Clb; Tennis; Cit Awd; Hon Roll; Wnnr Beginning Typwrtng/Kybrd Stu Cont 89; Cert Achvt Typng I; UCLA.

LY, HIEU; Valley HS; Sacramento, CA; (4); 3/482; Pres French Clb; Pres Math Clb; Pres Math Tm; Pres Science Clb; Hon Roll; Semi Fnlst Schl Annual Mock Trial Tm; Stu Coach Schl Acad Decathlon Tm; Bank Am Awd Math & Sci; UC Davis; FBI Agent.

LY, HUE MY; John F Kennedy HS; Granada Hills, CA; (2); Key Clb; Math Clb; Cit Awd; High Hon Roll; Secy Math Clb; CSF; Edtr Schl Lit Mag; UCLA; Pedtrcn.

LY, HUY T; Lodi HS; Stockton, CA; (2); Var Tennis; High Hon Roll; 2nd Chemathn Cmptn; Boys, Girls Clb SE Asn Hnr Roll Stu; CSF; UC Davis; Med.

LY, JACKIE; Pasadena HS; Pasadena, CA; (2); Girl Scts; Pep Clb; Quiz Bowl; Spanish Clb; Orch; School Play; Rptr Nwsp; Off Soph Cls; Sec Stu Cncl; JV Vllybl; Design Fashionable Outfits; Work With Children; Partcpnt In Pasadena Historical Soc; UCLA; Fshn Designer.

LY, JULIE; Downtown Business Magnet HS; Los Angeles, CA; (2); Cit Awd; Hon Roll; Prfct Atten Awd; Cert Excllnc Typing, Span; 66th Annual Model Yacht Regatta Cert; UCLA; Law.

LY, JULIE QUAN B; Mission HS; San Francisco, CA; (4); Spllng Chmpn; Acctnt.

LY, KEN; Oakland HS; Oakland, CA; (3); JV Bsbl; JV Bsktbl; JV Trk; JV Wt Lftg; Alameda Coll; Electrncs.

LY, KHANH S; Mark Keppel HS; Monterey Park, CA; (1); Mu Alpha Theta; Hon Roll; Prfct Atten Awd; United For Peace; Peer Cnslng; Jrnlsm.

LY, LAM; Rosemead HS; Rosemead, CA; (3); Computer Clb; Key Clb; Math Clb; Spanish Clb; Prfct Atten Awd; CA Schlrshp Fed; Badminton Tm Jr Var & 2 Yrs Var; Pasadena CC; Auto Mech.

LY, LE BICH; Gardena HS; Gardena, CA; (3); Service Clb; CSF; UCI; Math.

LY, LEE; Downey HS; Bellflower, CA; (2); Church Yth Grp; JV Tennis; Cit Awd; High Hon Roll; Prfct Atten Awd; UCLA; Engr.

LY, LIEN N; Irvine HS; Irvine, CA; (3); Teachers Aide; Tennis; Hon Roll; Cmmnty Wrk; CA ST Fullerton; Bus.

LY, LINDA N; Wallenberg Traditional HS; San Francisco, CA; (4); French Clb; Science Clb; Service Clb; Varsity Clb; Band; Var Vllybl; High Hon Roll; Hon Roll; Pres Acad Fit Awd; U Of CA Los Angeles; Bio.

LY, LOAN C; San Gabriel HS; San Gabriel, CA; (3); FBLA; Office Aide; Pep Clb; Teachers Aide; Cit Awd; High Hon Roll; Hon Roll; Jr NHS; Prfct Atten Awd; Garvey Schl Schltc Awd & Trophy; Ust Pl Essay My Teacher & Trophy; Gold Medal March Dimes Rdng Champ; CA ST U LA; Flight Attend.

LY, LONG; Abraham Lincoln HS; Rosemead, CA; (3); 7/30; Hon Roll.

LY, MAN MAY P; San Gabriel HS; Alhambra, CA; (1); Spanish Clb; Drill Tm; Yrbk; Cit Awd; Hon Roll; Mck Trl Cmptn; CSF; UCLA; Psych.

LY, MARY; Slater JR HS; Santa Rosa, CA; (1); Sec Letterman Clb; Pres Pep Clb; Drill Tm; Ed Yrbk; Cheerldng; Trk; Var Vllybl; High Hon Roll; Spanish Clb; VP Frsh Cls; UCSB; Bus Acctnt.

LY, MAY K; Edison HS; Fresno, CA; (1); Hon Roll; Vita TCE Cert Rcgntn; UCSC; TV.

LY, MINHCHAU T; Monterey HS; Seaside, CA; (2); High Hon Roll; CSF; UCLA; Bus.

LY, NAM D; Mark Keppel HS; Rosemead, CA; (4); FBLA; Key Clb; Mu Alpha Theta; Hon Roll; Cert Of Excellence Foreign Lang; NC Riverside.

LY, NGHI V; William Workman HS; La Puente, CA; (1); Intnl Clb; Science Clb; Band; Mrchg Band; Tennis; High Hon Roll; Prfct Atten Awd; 2nd Pl Speak-Up Cont; Math.

LY, NGHIA M; Temple City HS; Arcadia, CA; (2); Science Clb; Teachers Aide; Trk; Vllybl; CA Schlrshp Fed; UCLA; Med.

LY, NGHIA Q; George Washington HS; San Francisco, CA; (1); High Hon Roll; Hon Roll.

LY, OAI; Saddleback HS; Santa Ana, CA; (4); Art Clb; Chess Clb; Mu Alpha Theta; Spanish Clb; JV Tennis; JV Trk; Hon Roll; Prfct Atten Awd; CA Schlrshp Fdrtn; Dept Awd Gld Mdlst Spnsh; Cert Vlntrng Cambodn Fmly Agncy; UC Berkeley; Arch.

LY, PHAN ELAINE; San Gabriel HS; Rosemead, CA; (2); Bsktbl; Tennis; Vllybl; Hon Roll; Swmmng; Bowling; Pharmacy.

LY, PHUONG H; Leuzinger HS; Lawndale, CA; (1); Cit Awd; Hon Roll; Renssnc Prgm-Hrn Stus; APPI Prgm; Berkeley U; Law.

LY, RANDY; Galileo HS; San Francisco, CA; (2); High Hon Roll; Hon Roll; Stu Mnth; Acadc Block G; UC Berkeley; Engr.

LY, SENGSAVANG; Clouts HS; Clovis, CA; (3); Debate Tm; French Clb; Pres Intnl Clb; NFL; Speech Tm; Vllybl; High Hon Roll; Hon Roll; CA Schltc Fed; Peer Cnslr; Fresno Cnty Sch Asian Bd Mem; UC Santa Barbara; Bus Atty.

LY, SENH D; Mark Keppel HS; Rosemead, CA; (3); Var Bsktbl; Var Socr; Cit Awd; Hon Roll; Pasadena City Coll; Jewelry.

LY, SINH; Mark Keppel HS; Monterey Park, CA; (1); Bsktbl; Peer Cnslng; U Of CO; Bus.

LY, SIOV KHENG; Skyline HS; Oakland, CA; (2); Intnl Clb; Math Tm; Yrbk; Treas Frsh Cls; Sftbl; Vllybl; Cit Awd; High Hon Roll; Pres Acad Fit Awd; UC Berkeley; Hlth.

LY, STEVE; George Washington HS; San Francisco, CA; (3); Ftbl; Wt Lftg; Cit Awd; Hon Roll; Hotel Mgmt.

LY, THONG; Saddleback HS; Santa Ana, CA; (1); Tennis; Engrng.

LY, TOU VU; C K Mc Clatchy HS; Sacramento, CA; (2); 200/487; French Clb; ROTC; SADD; Drill Tm; Rptr Nwsp; JV Ftbl; JV Tennis; Hmong Clb; UC Davis; Bus Mgmt.

LY, TRAN M; Alhambra HS; Alhambra, CA; (2); Rep Stu Cncl; UCLA; Med.

LY, TRANG T; Orange Glen HS; Escondido, CA; (4); Art Clb; Bsbl; Sftbl; Trk; Wt Lftg; Yrbk; Med Asst.

LY, TU H; Washington HS; San Francisco, CA; (3); Hosp Aide; Intnl Clb; Key Clb; Treas Math Clb; Office Aide; Treas Red Cross Aide; Treas Science Clb; Sec Service Clb; Teachers Aide; Chorus; CSF Brd Dir 87-90; Vrsty Badminton Team; Gldn St Exam Hmrs 88-89; UC Davis; Pediatrics.

LY, UYEN H; Gunderson HS; San Jose, CA; (2); Debate Tm; High Hon Roll; Hon Roll; Pres Schlr.

LY, UYEN K; Hamilton High Music Acad; Los Angeles, CA; (3); Chess Clb; Church Yth Grp; Cmnty Wkr; Spanish Clb; Band; Mrchg Band; Tennis; Hon Roll; Med.

LY, VANG; Modesto HS; Modesto, CA; (3); CA ST U.

LY, VINH; Rosemead HS; Rosemead, CA; (2); Chess Clb; Debate Tm; Intnl Clb; Key Clb; Wrstlng; Wrstlng-Victor Vly Trnmnt, Fastest Fall Pin Awd, Coaches Awd, Vrsty Ltr; Acess Hghr Educ Achvt Awd; Naval Acad; Bus Mgmt.

LY, VINH Q; Rosemead HS; San Gabriel, CA; (2); High Hon Roll; Prfct Atten Awd; GSE High Hnrs; Rio Hondo Coll Cert Of Achvt Drftng Cmptn; CA Poly Tech; Mech Engrng.

LY, YENGNONG; Clovis HS; Fresno, CA; (3); Science Clb; High Hon Roll; Hon Roll; US Naval Sea Cadet Corps; Aviation.

LYALL, RENEE E; Acalanes HS; Lafayette, CA; (4); Dance Clb; Pep Clb; Spanish Clb; SADD; Teachers Aide; Powder Puff Ftbl; Sftbl; Swmmng; High Hon Roll; Hon Roll; Daphne; Assisteens; Yth Educator; UCLA; Law.

LYBECK, STACEY R; John F Kennedy HS; Sacramento, CA; (2); 65/530; SADD; Yrbk; Rep Frsh Cls; Sec Soph Cls; VP Jr Cls; Socr; Hon Roll; CSF.

LYBRAND, KIMBERLY A; El Capitan HS; Lakeside, CA; (2); 2/455; Church Yth Grp; Math Tm; Quiz Bowl; Var Mgr(s); High Hon Roll; Hon Roll; Leos Clb Sectry; Aquatics Clb; Chrch Lector; Commnctns.

LYELTON, RENEE L; Concord HS; Concord, CA; (3); Teachers Aide; Intrml Bsktbl; JV Vllybl; High Hon Roll; Hon Roll; SADD; Hayward ST; Acctnt.

LYEW, STEVE C; San Gabriel HS; San Gabriel, CA; (2); JA; Spanish Clb; Off Soph Cls; Stu Cncl; Bsktbl; JV Stat Tennis; Hon Roll; Jr NHS; KTEMA ES AEI YMCA HI Y Clb; Stretcher Crew; Worked On Parade Float For Merril Lynch; UC San Diego; Bus Mngmnt.

LYFORD, RICHELLE L; Eisenhower HS; Rialto, CA; (4); 29/655; Girl Scts; Hist Spanish Clb; Band; Mrchg Band; Variety Show; Capt Cheerldng; Hon Roll; NHS; Pres Acad Fit Awd; Friday Night Live VP & Histrn; CSU San Bernardino; Elem Ed.

LYKINS, AMY; Foothill HS; Pleasanton, CA; (2); Church Yth Grp; FBLA; Hosp Aide; Hon Roll; Nrsng.

LYKINS, MARY LEE; Foothill HS; Pleasanton, CA; (2); 51/356; Church Yth Grp; Mgr FBLA; JV Yrbk; Hon Roll; CSF; Chrstn Spprt Grp; Covenanto Cll; Hstry Ed.

LYLE, CYBELE K; Pasadena HS; Sierra Madre, CA; (3); Ski Clb; Spanish Clb; Phtg Nwsp; VP Jr Cls; VP Stu Cncl; JV Sftbl; Var Tennis; Hon Roll; Z Clb; Greenpeace; UCSC; Envrnmntl Stds.

LYLE, REBECCA E; Troy HS; Fullerton, CA; (2); Church Yth Grp; French Clb; Key Clb; Capt Drill Tm; Cit Awd; DAR Awd; High Hon Roll; Jr NHS; NHS; Pres Acad Fit Awd; Dance Act III Acad Prfrmng Arts; Future Earth Clb; UC Santa Barbara; Med.

LYLES, JOY E; Berean Christian HS; Oakley, CA; (3); Church Yth Grp; Library Aide; Office Aide; Church Choir; School Play; Stage Crew; Var L Crs Cntry; High Hon Roll; Hon Roll; ACSI Distinguished Stu; Bus.

LYMAN, HEATHER T; Rubidoux HS; Riverside, CA; (2); Church Yth Grp; Speech Tm; JV Swmmng; Var L Vllybl; Pres Acad Fit Awd; Law.

LYMAN, JENNIFER; Bellarmine-Jefferson HS; Los Angeles, CA; (4); JA; Pep Clb; School Musical; VP Sr Cls; JV Var Cheerldng; Var Tennis; Hon Roll; CA Schlrshp Fed; Ntl Hspnc Schlr Aws Semi Finlst; UC Berkeley; Psych.

LYMAN, JESSICA; Mira Costas HS; Manhattan Beach, CA; (2); Key Clb; Rep Soph Cls; JV Crs Cntry; JV Trk; Hon Roll; S-Clb Cls Rep; Yth Undrstndng.

LYN, EVY; Palisades HS; Pacific Palisades, CA; (4); School Musical; Stu Cncl; Var Cheerldng; NHS; Pres Acad Fit Awd; Dance Clb; Drama Clb; JA; Office Aide; Cngssnl Yth Ldrshp Cncl; CA Schlrshp Fdrtn; Palisades Dancers; Heal Bay Clb; Peace Clb; Task Force; U Of CA, Santa Barbara.

LYNCH, AIMEE S; Laguna Hills HS; Laguna Hills, CA; (1); Sec French Clb; Hist Key Clb; Hist Model UN; SADD; Cheerldng; High Hon Roll; St Schlr; MUN Awd; Mock Trial; Ballet Classes; Perf Ballet Pacifica.

LYNCH, BEN J; Analy HS; Sebastopol, CA; (3); 9/234; Letterman Clb; Teachers Aide; Nwsp; Rep Stu Cncl; Var L Ftbl; Wt Lftg; High Hon Roll; CSF; 1st Team All-League Ftbl; Bus.

LYNCH, HEATHER A; Mt View HS; Los Altos, CA; (3); 29/319; Service Clb; Nwsp; Pres Soph Cls; Pres Jr Cls; Var Tennis; Var Trk; High Hon Roll; Hon Roll; Pres Acad Fit Awd; Multicltrl Task Frc; HOBY Ldrshp Conf Ambsdr; Hmcmng Chrmn 90; Comm.

LYNCH, JENNA M; Academy Of Our Lady Of Peace; San Diego, CA; (1); High Hon Roll; Hon Roll; CSF.

LYNCH, JILL E; Mt Whitney HS; Visalia, CA; (2); Key Clb; Spanish Clb; Tennis; Hon Roll; CSUF; Tchr.

LYNCH, KATHLEEN L; St Bernard HS; Eureka, CA; (2); Ed Sprt Ed Nwsp; Pres Frsh Cls; Pres Soph Cls; Pres Jr Cls; Rep Stu Cncl; JV Bsktbl; Var Sftbl; JV Vllybl; High Hon Roll; Hon Roll; Humboldt Del Norte Intschlstc Assn Rep; Mem Schls Srptmst Clb.

LYNCH, KERIN L; San Dimas HS; San Dimas, CA; (3); Var Fld Hcky; Cit Awd; Hon Roll; Prfct Atten Awd; Amer Heritage Club; CA Schlrshp Fed; Roses Awds & Ctznshp Awds; Vet.

LYNCH, MISTY D; Napa HS; Napa, CA; (1); GAA; Key Clb; JV Bsktbl; JV Sftbl; JV Vllybl; Cit Awd; High Hon Roll; Hon Roll; Pres Acad Fit Awd; Pres Schlr; Kiwanis Sftbl; UCLA; Bus.

LYNCH, RAQUEL C; Mira Mesa HS; San Diego, CA; (3); 32/777; Cmnty Wkr; Dance Clb; JA; Library Aide; Office Aide; Teachers Aide; Chorus; Pres Soph Cls; Rep Stu Cncl; Capt Cheerldng; Law.

LYNCH, ROBERT J; El Dorado HS; Placentia, CA; (4); Am Leg Boys St; Boy Scts; ROTC; Band; Mrchg Band; High Hon Roll; NHS; Ntl Merit Schol; Eagl Sct Boy Scts Of Am; Cert Of Meritorious Svc; U CA Riverside; Poltícl Sci.

LYNCH, THERESA Y; Mayfair HS; Elmore, MN; (1); Church Yth Grp; Sec English Clb; JA; Key Clb; Teachers Aide; Chorus; Cit Awd; High Hon Roll; Hon Roll; Schl Site Cncl; U Of Santa Cruz; Marine Bio.

LYNES, KIM; Elk Grove HS; Elk Grove, CA; (2); 1/531; Church Yth Grp; JV Cheerldng; High Hon Roll; Hon Roll; CSF 88-90; Acad Ltr 89-90; Cal Poly SLO; Inter Dsgn.

LYNES, KRISSY; Elk Grove HS; Elk Grove, CA; (3); 7/609; Church Yth Grp; Chorus; Church Choir; Drill Tm; High Hon Roll; Hon Roll; Acadmc Ltr; CSF; Toastmstrs Intl Yth Ldrshp Pgm; Art.

LYNETT, KRISTI S; Vacaville HS; Vacaville, CA; (3); Band; Stu Cncl; Var Bsktbl; Var Crs Cntry; Var Socr; Var Trk; High Hon Roll; Rotary Awd; Church Yth Grp; FCA; All-Sectnl Soccer Team, Crss Cntry Team; IL St Soccer Team.

LYNN, CHRISTOPHER MATTHEW; Calaveras HS; San Andreas, CA; (2); 23/200; 4-H; Ski Clb; JV Socr; JV L Trk; Hon Roll; Am Foreign Exchng Stud Clb; Fldat Comm 9th; CA Schlstc Fed Clb; NASA Space Camp 1990; Coll; Pilot Armed Forces.

LYON, CAMILO; Bellarmine College Prep; Woodside, CA; (1); Church Yth Grp; Spanish Clb; JV Ftbl; JV Socr; Intrml Wt Lftg; Stanford; Doctor.

LYON, CHRIS S; John F Kennedy HS; Sacramento, CA; (1); 77/559; Art Clb; ROTC; SADD; Color Guard; Drill Tm; Ftbl; Sftbl; Cit Awd; Hon Roll; Mltry Ordr Of Wrld Wars Awd; Friday Nght Live Clb; Dvl Dogs Rfl Team; Military Acad; Pilot.

LYON, GREG S; Los Amigos HS; Fountain Valley, CA; (3); Science Clb; Spanish Clb; Phtg Yrbk; Hon Roll; U CA Santa Barbara; Bio Sci.

LYON, JERRY; Hesperia HS; Hesperia, CA; (3); Boy Scts; Pres Church Yth Grp; Science Clb; Spanish Clb; Bsktbl; Hon Roll; Wrk With Crpt; Typng Cls 65 Wrds Per Min; :Byu; Study Sci.

LYON, LAURA; Trinity Union HS; Trinity Center, CA; (1); FTA; Ski Clb; Spanish Clb; School Musical; High Hon Roll; Envrnmntl Awrnss Trip; Tchr.

LYON, TINA L; Thomas Downey HS; Modesto, CA; (3); Church Yth Grp; SADD; Chorus; Mgr Ftbl; Var Sftbl; JV Vllybl; Stat Wrstlng; Inter Desgnr.

LYONS, AMY M; Leland HS; San Jose, CA; (2); Church Yth Grp; GAA; Church Choir; JV Fld Hcky; JV Socr; Azusa Pacific; Bus.

LYONS, CLINT J; Foothill HS; Bakersfield, CA; (2); Debate Tm; German Clb; NFL; Hon Roll; Aerospc Engr.

LYONS, DONALD; La Puente HS; La Puente, CA; (4); Art Clb; Chess Clb; Letterman Clb; Pep Clb; Varsity Clb; Variety Show; Pres Jr Cls; Rep Stu Cncl; Var Bsbl; JV Bsktbl; Brd Rep; PEP Sec; All Leag Wide Rcvr 2nd Tm; All Vly Outstndng Stu Awd; Ceramics Clb Pres; USC; Actr.

LYONS, JENNIFER L; Oxnard HS; Oxnard, CA; (3); Color Guard; Stat Swmmng; Acadmcs, Color Guard & Swim Stats Ltrs; CSF; Peer Hlprs.

LYONS, JEREMIAH; Redlands HS; Redlands, CA; (3); JA; Office Aide; Teachers Aide; Orch; JV Crs Cntry; Socr; 2 Outstndng Schlrshp Awds Math; Arrow Of Light Awd, Eagle Sct; Forestry.

LYONS, LATRICE; Washington Preparatory HS; Gardena, CA; (2); Church Yth Grp; GAA; Varsity Clb; Church Choir; Sftbl; Vllybl; Cit Awd; High Hon Roll; Hon Roll; Prfct Atten Awd; Sunday Schl Tchr; UCLA; Acctnt.

LYONS, MEGAN; Delano HS; Delano, CA; (4); 17/375; Letterman Clb; Pep Clb; Nwsp; Lit Mag; Stu Cncl; Var Cheerldng; Var Swmmng; High Hon Roll; Sec NHS; CA Assn Stu Cncls Rgn 11 Pres; UC Santa Barbara; Bus.

LYONS, NICOLE A; Grace M Davis HS; Modesto, CA; (4); 128/425; Art Clb; Dance Clb; Drama Clb; Thesps; School Play; JV Cheerldng; Var Swmmng; Hnr Stu; Pblshd Poetry; Dance Clb; Chico ST U; Engl.

LYONS, SHAWN M; Point Loma HS; San Diego, CA; (2); 30/482; JV Bsbl; Hon Roll; Prfct Atten Awd; Pres Schlr.

LYUBARSKY, INNA MICHELLE; U S Grant HS; Encino, CA; (4); 120/ 692; Cmnty Wkr; Intnl Clb; SADD; Cit Awd; Hon Roll; Stu Leag Pres & VP; CSF; United Way Chairperson; U Southern CA; Bus.

MA, ANGELA; Cerritos HS; Cerritos, CA; (1); French Clb; FHA; JCL; Model UN; Service Clb; Cheerldng; Hon Roll; FHA Rgnl Comptn 1st Pl Inter Dsgn & 3rd Pl Semi-Fnls; Princeton; Bus Law.

MA, AUDREY; Lowell HS; San Francisco, CA; (3); Chess Clb; Red Cross Aide; Science Clb; SADD; Intrml Tennis; CSF; Bio Clb; Pre-Med Clb; U CA Davis; Doc.

MA, BIN; Skyline HS; Oakland, CA; (4); Hon Roll; CSF; SF ST U; Bus Admin.

MA, BINH; San Gabriel HS; San Gabriel, CA; (3); Office Aide; Spanish Clb; Cit Awd; Hon Roll; Intercultrlc Clb; Interact; Yth In Govt Awd; Med.

MA, CHRISTINA; Abraham Lincoln HS; San Francisco, CA; (4); 6/400; Art Clb; Math Clb; Var Trk; Hon Roll; CA Schrlshp Fed VP; Acad Of Finance; Burmese Clb; Engl Dept & Frgn Lang Dept Awds; UC Berkeley; Bio Sci.

MA, HOUSTON; Berkeley HS; Berkeley, CA; (3); Chess Clb; Computer Clb; Math Clb; Math Tm; Rep Frsh Cls; Rep Soph Cls; Rep Jr Cls; Rep Sr Cls; Rep Stu Cncl; Var Trk; Stu Body VP; Hmcmng King 1st Rnnrup; Cadid Rpblcns Club VP; Elec Engrng.

MA, JIANGUO; George Washington HS; San Francisco, CA; (2); Hon Roll; San Francisco City Coll.

MA, KATHY; Lincoln HS; Stockton, CA; (3); 28/592; JCL; Latin Clb; Math Clb; Mu Alpha Theta; SADD; Var Trk; High Hon Roll; Hon Roll; St Schlr; 2 Marrs Assn Schlrshps; Acad Ltr; UC; Film Stds.

MA, KIMBERLY; Edison HS; Stockton, CA; (4); Teachers Aide; Tennis; Fash Dsgn.

MA, LAURA; Mark Keppel HS; Monterey Park, CA; (2); #1 In Class; Key Clb; Mu Alpha Theta; Stage Crew; Lit Mag; High Hon Roll; 7th Natl Math Leag Alg II; Tutor Math Clb; Peer Tutor Pgm; 2nd Annl Rainbow Refrnc Rally.

MA, LULU; Garden Grove HS; Garden Grove, CA; (2); Hon Roll; GATE Art Prgm; Intr Dsgn; Dsgn; Dsgnr.

MA, MARGARET H; Notre Dame Acad; Santa Monica, CA; (3); 18/112; Church Yth Grp; Spanish Clb; Hon Roll; NHS; Vol Santa Monica Lib Literacy Prgm; CSF.

MA, NGOC; Narbonne Math/Science Magnet HS; Carson, CA; (3); French Clb; Hosp Aide; Key Clb; Math Clb; Service Clb; Teachers Aide; Pres Orch; Var Tennis; Hon Roll; Prfct Atten Awd; CSF; PAL Pres; Biomed Engnrng.

MA, PAULINE H; Lowell HS; San Francisco, CA; (2); 10/35; 4-H; Spanish Clb; U CA Davis; Med.

MA, PHONG Q; Lincoln HS; San Francisco, CA; (1); Comp Pgm.

MA, RICKY; Tokay HS; Stockton, CA; (3); Math Clb; Science Clb; Comp.

MA, STELLA K; Oakland HS; Oakland, CA; (4); 1/400; French Clb; Hosp Aide; VP Soph Cls; VP Jr Cls; Treas Stu Cncl; Var L Tennis; High Hon Roll; Pres Acad Fit Awd; Val; Harvard Coll; Bus.

MA, STEVEN F; Galileo HS; San Francisco, CA; (3); Math Clb; Science Clb; Hon Roll; UC Davis; Math.

MA, THERESA; Taft HS; Tarzana, CA; (2); Prfct Atten Awd; Knighrs & Ladies; Stanford U.

MA, VINH T; Lowell HS; San Francisco, CA; (2); Science Clb; Hnrs Golden St Exm Alg; 3rd Pl Mandarin Spch Cont; Vllybl Clb; Engrng.

MAALI, KAHRAMAN; Fountain Valley HS; Fountain Valley, CA; (2); Bus Profs of Am; Computer Clb; Spanish Clb; Teachers Aide; VICA; Acpl Chr; School Musical; Bsbl; Bsktbl; Ftbl; Bus Law 1 Yr Ernd Cert; Hm Econ 2 Yrs; Vocatnl Cultrs; Dntl Radiolgst.

MAANI, ALAN; Beyer HS; Modesto, CA; (3); Ed Yrbk; Fri Nght Lv Clb; CA Schlrshp Fdrtn.

MAAS, ANGELA; Ramona HS; Ramona, CA; (2); 20/345; Church Yth Grp; 4-H; Letterman Clb; Pep Clb; Sec Frsh Cls; Capt Var Cheerldng; Var Trk; Cit Awd; 4-H Awd; Hon Roll.

MAAS, BRIAN J; Edison HS; Huntington Beach, CA; (4); 4/495; French Clb; Model UN; Church Choir; Jazz Band; Trk; Ntl Merit SF; Rock Band; Elec Engrng.

MAASCH, CRAIG; Valhalla HS; El Cajon, CA; (2); 164/451; Aud/Vis; Church Yth Grp; Band; Mrchg Band; Orch; Pep Band; Variety Show; U Of Sthrn CA; Scrnwrtr.

MAASS, ELEANOR K; Alameda HS; Alameda, CA; (1); 20/300; Rptr Nwsp; Var Trk; High Hon Roll; Stu Of Wk.

MABABA, MELANIE; Carson HS; Carson, CA; (2); Nwsp; Sec Frsh Cls; Rep Soph Cls; Rep Stu Cncl; Capt Ftbl; Var Swmmng; Cit Awd; Hon Roll; Jr NHS; Pres Acad Fit Awd; Girls Flag Ftbl MVP; Phys Educ Dept Awd; 6 Semstrs Schlrshp Plque; Aeronautcl Engrng.

MABALOT, ROSS O; Bonita Vista HS; Bonita, CA; (3); Office Aide; JV Crs Cntry; Var Trk; Cit Awd; Hon Roll; Prfct Atten Awd; Pres Acad Fit Awd; Assoctd Std Bdy Wrkr; Archtr.

MABASA, JOSEPH LEONARD; Don Bosco Technical Inst; Los Angeles, CA; (1); 31/224; Band; Jazz Band; Mrchg Band; Orch; School Musical; NEDT Awd; Engrng.

MABREY, MONICA A; Rio Linda SR HS; Sacramento, CA; (3); Church Yth Grp; English Clb; German Clb; Girl Scts; Quiz Bowl; Ed Yrbk; Hon Roll; CA Cadet Corps; Vrsty Rifle Tm 2 Yrs; Omaha Woodman Awd Amer Hstry; CSUS; History.

MAC, KIET G; Lincoln HS; Los Angeles, CA; (1); Church Yth Grp; FCA; Bsktbl; Hon Roll.

MAC, TERESA NIEM T; San Gabriel HS; Rosemead, CA; (3); Church Yth Grp; Debate Tm; FBLA; Key Clb; NFL; Spanish Clb; Band; JV Var Swmmng; High Hon Roll; Hon Roll; Mock Trl Cmptn 4th Pl; Philosophy.

MAC ADAM, WADE; Folsom HS; Folsom, CA; (3); Model UN; Rep Sr Cls; JV Ftbl; Var JV Trk; High Hon Roll; Hon Roll; Jr NHS; Friday Night Live; CA Poly San Luis Obispo; Arch.

MAC CARTNEY, HEATHER L; Los Angeles County HS For The Arts; San Dimas, CA; (4); Dance Clb; Debate Tm; Drama Clb; French Clb; Hosp Aide; Office Aide; Pep Clb; SADD; Teachers Aide; Thesps; CA Arts Schlr; Music Prfrmnc.

MAC COMB, DOUGLAS R; Las Lomas HS; Walnut Creek, CA; (2); Archt.

MAC DONALD, ALETHA; Victor Valley HS; George Afb, CA; (3); Pep Clb; Chorus; Church Choir; Reg Nurse.

MAC DONALD, BRYCE C; St Vincent De Paul HS; Sebastopol, CA; (2); Boy Scts; Office Aide; Rep Frsh Cls; Rep Soph Cls; JV Bsbl; JV Bsktbl; JV Ftbl; Golf; Tennis; Opt Clb Awd; Capt Ftbl Tms; Golf Profssnl.

MAC DONALD, DANA L; Point Loma HS; San Diego, CA; (2); 1/482; Girl Scts; High Hon Roll; Hon Roll; CSF; Gold Mrt Awd.

MAC DONALD, ERIN C; East Bakersfield HS; Bakersfield, CA; (1); French Clb; Off Frsh Cls; Intrml L Bsktbl; L Var Swmmng; Intrml L Vllybl; High Hon Roll; Hon Roll; Pres Acad Fit Awd; Creative Wrtng; CSF; Santa Catalina; Math.

MAC DONALD, JENNIFER; Westwood HS; Westwood, CA; (2); Art Clb; Spanish Clb; Band; Mrchg Band; VP Frsh Cls; Pres Soph Cls; JV L Bsktbl; Var L Trk; JV L Vllybl; High Hon Roll; Chico St Incntve Grant 2 Yrs; Frshmn & Soph Top Grl Awd; Top Span Stu Awd; Chico ST U; Inter Decrtng.

MAC DONALD, JENNIFER E; Yucaipa HS; Calimesa, CA; (1); 1/530; Church Yth Grp; Tennis; High Hon Roll.

MAC DONALD, JENNY J; Westwood HS; Westwood, CA; (2); Art Clb; Spanish Clb; Band; Mrchg Band; VP Frsh Cls; Pres Soph Cls; JV L Bsktbl; Mgr(s); Var L Trk; JV L Vllybl; Chico St Incntv Grant Wnnr; Top Girl Awd; Outstndng Spnsh II Stu; U Of CA Davis; Inter Dcrtr.

MAC DONALD, JEREMY D; El Camino Real HS; Woodland Hills, CA; (3); Church Yth Grp; Cmnty Wkr; Teachers Aide; Acpl Chr; Chorus; School Musical; Variety Show; Tennis; Bus.

MAC DONALD, JOSH P; University HS; Irvine, CA; (1); Band; Jazz Band; Mrchg Band; Orch; Pep Band; School Musical; Bass Section Ldr All-Sthrn CA Hnr Orch; Aeron.

MAC DONALD, KATHLIENE; Norwalk HS; Norwalk, CA; (4); 1/284; Am Leg Aux Girls St; Letterman Clb; Service Clb; Ed Yrbk; VP Sr Cls; Var Capt Crs Cntry; Var Capt Trk; Ntl Merit Ltr; Val; CA Schlrshp Fed; Whittier Coll; Engl Ed.

MAC DONALD, SEAN DAVID; Bishop O'dowd HS; San Leandro, CA; (4); 8/220; Cmnty Wkr; Drama Clb; SADD; Band; School Musical; Stage Crew; Rep Frsh Cls; Pres Jr Cls; Pres Sr Cls; Stu Cncl; Vassar Coll; Indstrl Psych.

MAC DOWELL, MATTIAS J; Dana Hills HS; Laguna Niguel, CA; (3); Srfng; Bus.

MAC ISAAC, JOHN L; Apple Valley HS; Apple Valley, CA; (2); Church Yth Grp; Key Clb; St Thomas Aquinas; Liberal Arts.

MAC IVER, KELLY; Foothill HS; Pleasanton, CA; (4); 6/311; Church Yth Grp; Treas Soph Cls; Off Sr Cls; Rep Stu Cncl; JV Cheerldng; Pom Pon; High Hon Roll; Hon Roll; Math, Draftng & Work Expernce GPA Acad Awds; Cal Poly; Interior Dsgn.

MAC KAY, ALLIE; Louisville HS; Westlake Vlg, CA; (3); Drama Clb; GAA; Pep Clb; Ski Clb; Acpl Chr; Chorus; Yrbk; Cheerldng; Tennis; High Hon Roll; Most Insprtnl JV Tennis; Capt Vrsty Chrldng; Humboldt; Tchng.

MAC KENZIE, JOANNE K; Lemoore HS; Lemoore, CA; (2); Var Crs Cntry; Var Trk; Grls X-Country MI; Girls Trck MI; Int Design.

MAC KINNAN, JULENE; Concord HS; Concord, CA; (3); 69/250; SADD; Chorus; Hon Roll; Outstndng Acad JR Awd 90; Schl Acad Prgm 1st Acad Cls; Diablo Valley JC; Singing.

MAC LAIRD, MISHA; Berkeley HS; Oakland, CA; (3); Letterman Clb; Crs Cntry; Swmmng; CSF; Math/Sci.

MAC LAUGHLIN, GERI A; Forest Lake Christian Schl; Penn Valley, CA; (2); Church Yth Grp; Phtg Yrbk; Teacher.

MAC LAUGHLIN, KAREN M; La Sierra Acad; Riverside, CA; (2); Drama Clb; School Musical; Pres Yrbk; Hon Roll; NHS; Pathfinder Cnslr Clb Dsgnd Dev Ldrshp Ability; U CA Berkely; Architect.

MAC MILLAN, SHANNON A; San Pasqual HS; Escondido, CA; (2); French Clb; Var Socr; JV Sftbl; Var Trk; Scer/Al-Avocado Leag 1st Tm, Co-Plyr Yr, CIF Plyr Of Yr; Tchr.

MAC MILLAN, VIRGINIA; Palm Desert HS; Yucca Valley, CA; (4); 26/319; Teachers Aide; High Hon Roll; Hon Roll; Restaurant.

MAC MULLEN, KASEY L; Cupertino HS; San Jose, CA; (2); 89/298; Teachers Aide; Nwsp; Lit Mag; Stu Cncl; Pom Pon; Interact; Commnctns.

MAC NEIL, THOMAS J; Saint Genevieve HS; Canoga Park, CA; (3); Drama Clb; Thesps; School Play; Stage Crew; High Hon Roll; Comp Engrng.

MAC PHERSON, HEATHER; Crescenta Valley HS; Glendale, CA; (4); 26/370; French Clb; Mu Alpha Theta; Teachers Aide; Drill Tm; Stu Cncl; NHS; Pres Acad Fit Awd; Delegtn Pres, Bill Author/Sponser CA Yth & Gov; Ldrshp Development Pgm; CA Lutheran U; Bus.

MAC PHERSON, JOHN M; Santa Rosa HS; Santa Rosa, CA; (4); 12/500; Speech Tm; Ed Nwsp; Crs Cntry; Hon Roll; Masonic Awd; Ntl Merit Schol; Pres Acad Fit Awd; Val; Stu Of Yr; Princeton Outstndng Achievemnt Awd; Acad Olympiad Gold Medalist; Uc Berkeley; English.

MACAIAS, NOEL Z; Daniel Murphy HS; Los Angeles, CA; (2); Bsktbl; Wt Lftg; UCLA; Elec Engr.

MACALA, RICK; Artesia HS; Lakewood, CA; (3); JA; Science Clb; Cit Awd; Hon Roll; Aeronautical Engnr.

MACAM, MARIA; Southwest HS; San Diego, CA; (4); 32/482; Am Leg Aux Girls St; Cmnty Wkr; Debate Tm; Drama Clb; JA; NFL; ROTC; Scholastic Bowl; SADD; Thesps; Cmmnctns.

MACARAEG, ULYSSES; Sweetwater HS; San Diego, CA; (4); 17/388; Computer Clb; Office Aide; Sec Science Clb; Off Sr Cls; Mgr(s); Var Tennis; Mgr Trk; Hon Roll; Prfct Atten Awd; CSF; Asian Intl Assn; U Of CA San Diego; Comp Engrng.

MACARANAS, CAROLYN A; Lowell HS; Sacramento, CA; (2); Church Yth Grp; Chorus; Church Choir; School Musical; Alg Hons Golden St Exam; Red Cross Clb.

MACASERO, MICHAEL C; Don Bosco Technical Inst; Pasadena, CA; (3); Hon Roll; NHS; Logo Desgn Gym Floor & Cover Of 89-90 Yrbk; Patch Dsgn For Schl Class Jckts; Sheridon Coll Applied Arts; Art.

MACASPAC, JANETTE; La Puente HS; La Puente, CA; (3); Drama Clb; VP Service Clb; Nwsp; Treas Jr Cls; JV Tennis; High Hon Roll; Hon Roll; Vrsty Bdmntn; Frnd-2-Frnd Secy; Girls Leag.

MACATUNO, ANNA KRISTINE O; Abraham Lincoln HS; Los Angeles, CA; (3); Art Clb; Debate Tm; Drama Clb; English Clb; Speech Tm; School Musical; U Of CA Los Angeles; Hotl Mgmt.

MACAULEY, DAVE; San Ramon Valley HS; Danville, CA; (2); Band; JV Bsbl; Prfct Atten Awd; UC Berkley; Bus.

MACCARTHY, STACY A; University City HS; San Diego, CA; (3); Office Aide; SADD; Variety Show; Yrbk; Junior Lifeguards; Golden State Exam Honors-Geometry.

MACCHIA, MARGARET A; Edison HS; Huntington Beach, CA; (2); Church Yth Grp; Flag Corp; CSF; Keywanettes Club; Jrnlsm.

MACCIONI, LORENA K; John Burroughs HS; Burbank, CA; (4); Teachers Aide; Drill Tm; Nwsp; Hon Roll; Beautician.

MACDONALD, JENNIFER; Dixon HS; Dixon, CA; (3); FBLA; Letterman Clb; Teachers Aide; Stu Cncl; Var Cheerldng; High Hon Roll; Rotary Clb Ldrshp Camp; Bus Admin.

MACDONALD, REED A; San Dieguito HS; Encinitas, CA; (3); Boy Scts; Pres Church Yth Grp; Cmnty Wkr; JV Var Socr; High Hon Roll; Hon Roll; NHS; Pres Acad Fit Awd; CSF; San Diego Schlr Athl Awd; Mustang Press Grphcs Club; Brigham Young U; Engrng.

MACEDO, DANIEL; Webb School Of Calif; Los Angeles, CA; (1); Cmnty Wkr; JV Crs Cntry; JV Socr; JV Trk; Latino Recruitment Cmmtte.

MACEDO, GEORGE C; Gilbert HS East; Anaheim, CA; (2).

MACEDO, JACELYN G; East Union HS; Manteca, CA; (1); 30/439; L Var Sftbl; JV Vllybl; Hon Roll.

MACFARLANE, DANA; Monta Vista HS; Cupertino, CA; (2); 70/342; French Clb; Ski Clb; Chorus; Drill Tm; Hon Roll; The Earth Savers Club; Interact Club; College.

MACH, CUONG T; San Gabriel HS; Rosemead, CA; (2); High Hon Roll; Hon Roll; Prfct Atten Awd; CSF; UCLA; Elec Engr.

MACH, JIMMY; George Washington HS; San Francisco, CA; (2); Band; JV Bsbl; Hon Roll; Pres Acad Fit Awd; 2nd Pl Bsbl Tm Mdls; San Francisco City Coll.

MACHADO, GISELLE; Bishop Alemany HS; Van Nuys, CA; (4); 67/290; Church Yth Grp; SADD; Chorus; Hon Roll; NHS; CSF; Boston U; English.

MACHADO, GRACIE; Lincoln HS; Lincoln, CA; (4); 2/160; Am Leg Aux Girls St; French Clb; Scholastic Bowl; Pres SADD; Phtg Nwsp; Phtg Yrbk; Ed Lit Mag; Pres Frsh Cls; Pres Soph Cls; Stu Cncl; UOP Summer Honors Prgm; Bank Of America Awd For Sci & Math; U CA Berkeley Alumni Schlrsp; U CA Berkeley; Med.

MACHADO, LYNDA P; Bishop Montgomery HS; Lawndale, CA; (2); Spanish Clb; Drill Tm; JV Var Score Keeper; CSF; Smmr League Bsktbl; Job Monsoon Lagoon Water Park; Dsgnr.

MACHADO, MICHAEL J; So San Francisco HS; South San Francis, CA; (2); Spanish Clb; Hon Roll; Hnrs Gldn St Exam Algebra; Cinematogrphy.

MACHADO, RUSTY R; Mater Dei HS; Huntington Beach, CA; (2); Ice Hcky; Socr; Hon Roll; Santa Barbara; Art.

MACHADO, STACY; San Dieguito HS; Encinitas, CA; (4); 232/512; Teachers Aide; Yrbk; Sec Jr Cls; Accntng.

MACHADO, STEPHANIE A; Tulare Union HS; Tulare, CA; (2); 35/461; Church Yth Grp; Hosp Aide; Band; Mrchg Band; Hon Roll; Prfct Atten Awd; CSF; Bakersfield ST Coll; Nrsng.

MACHEN, JENNIFER K; Tokay HS; Lodi, CA; (3); Teachers Aide; Cit Awd; High Hon Roll; Hon Roll; Bus Coll; Acctnt.

MACHKOFF, JEFF C; Irvine HS; Irvine, CA; (3); 13/570; Varsity Clb; Var Tennis; Wt Lftg; High Hon Roll; Hon Roll; Heritage Awd Excllnc Engl Lit 89; Athletic Excllnc Awd Ten 89; Martial Arts Blackbt; Cmmnctns.

MACHUCA, MARIA; Roosevelt HS; Los Angeles, CA; (4); 16/750; Teachers Aide; Var L Socr; Var L Swmmng; High Hon Roll; Hon Roll; Tandy Schlr Awd; Bank Of Am Awd Soc Stud; Ephebian Soc; Mount St Marys Coll; Bio.

MACIAS, BEATRIZ; El Sereno JR HS; El Paso, TX; (1); Chorus; Jrnlsm, Dance, Comp Prog & Art; Comps.

MACIAS, CARMELA H; San Pedro HS; San Pedro, CA; (3); Church Yth Grp; Cmnty Wkr; Office Aide; Red Cross Aide; Sec Service Clb; Temple Yth Grp; Orch; Prfct Atten Awd; Acadmc All Stars Slvr Div Schltc Excllnc Awd; Commodores Awd; Teen Advocate Trng Compltn Awd; Bio Chem.

MACIAS, ELOY G; Chaffey HS; Ontario, CA; (3); Hosp Aide; Math Clb; Variety Show; Yrbk; Off Jr Cls; Bsbl; Ftbl; Wt Lftg; Hon Roll.

MACIAS, GABY; St Joseph HS; Lakewood, CA; (3); GAA; Rep Soph Cls; Capt JV Cheerldng; Powder Puff Ftbl; Hon Roll; Loyola Marymount U.

MACIAS, GINGER L; John Glenn HS; Norwalk, CA; (3); 3/128; Church Yth Grp; Dance Clb; French Clb; Key Clb; Math Clb; Science Clb; JV Cheerldng; Trk; High Hon Roll; Earthwatch Grant; Med.

MACIAS, HILDA; Valley HS; Elk Grove, CA; (4); Cmnty Wkr; Office Aide; Prfct Atten Awd; MESA Club; Consumenes River Coll; Comp Sci.

MACIAS, JENNIFER N; Alverno HS; Monrovia, CA; (3); 13/67; Church Yth Grp; Cmnty Wkr; Hosp Aide; Model UN; Science Clb; Chorus; Rptr Yrbk; Lit Mag; Off Jr Cls; Off Sr Cls; A P US Hstry; Schl Govt; UC Santa Cruz; Phy.

MACIAS, JENNIFER R; Cupertino HS; Cupertino, CA; (4); Pep Clb; Drill Tm; Sec Soph Cls; JV Co-Capt Cheerldng; NHS; Peer Cnslng; Nom Bank Of Amer Awd Engl; CA Poly San Luis Obispo; Engl.

MACIAS, JESSICA; Hemet HS; Lakeview, CA; (3); Church Yth Grp; Sec Science Clb; Spanish Clb; SADD; Hon Roll; Prfct Atten Awd; Future Ldrs Of Amer; Bullpup Awd 86-88; Frgn Lang Acad; Engl Achvt; Loma Linda U; Dentistry.

MACIAS, JOSE; Bell HS; Huntington Park, CA; (3); Stage Crew; JV Crs Cntry; JV Var Tennis; MESA; Aero Engrng.

MACIAS, LETICIA; Fremont HS; Oakland, CA; (2); Library Aide; Pres Nwsp.

MACIAS, LORI K; Cupertino HS; Cupertino, CA; (3); Cmnty Wkr; Service Clb; Peer Cnslng; Interact; Altruettes; Water Polo Club.

MACIAS, LORI M; Central Union HS; El Centro, CA; (3); 40/543; Cmnty Wkr; Pep Clb; Ed Rptr Nwsp; Hon Roll; Spanish Awd; Awd For Camp Cnslr; Acad Lttr; Jrnlsm.

MACIAS, LUCILA; Nogales HS; West Covina, CA; (3); 42/628; Church Yth Grp; Treas Chorus; Church Choir; Variety Show; High Hon Roll; Hon Roll; Pres Acad Fit Awd; Trphy For Most Dedicated In Choir; CA ST Fullerton; Acctng.

MACIAS, MARTINA; Lemoore Union HS; Lemoore, CA; (2); 74/342; Church Yth Grp; Var Speech Tm; Church Choir; Powder Puff Ftbl; Score Keeper; JV Tennis; High Hon Roll; Hon Roll; CA Hstry Day; Spch Team Var Spkr.

MACIAS, MARY E; Calaveras HS; Wallace, CA; (2); AFS; Var Trk; Cit Awd; 3rd Pl Mdl Trk Leag Fnls; Heald Bus Coll; Legal Asst.

MACIAS, NORA L; Sweetwater HS; San Diego, CA; (4); 28/426; Spanish Clb; Teachers Aide; Drill Tm; Yrbk; Hon Roll; CA Schlrshp Fed; Part Time Job; UCSD; Psych.

MACIAS, PABLO; Calexico HS; Calexico, CA; (2); 4-H; Pep Clb; AVID Clb; Law.

MACIAS, RAGUEL; Sierra Vista HS; Baldwin Park, CA; (4); Church Yth Grp; Math Clb; Rptr Nwsp; Pres Jr Cls; VP Sr Cls; Var Pom Pon; JV Sftbl; High Hon Roll; Prom Qn; U Of CA Los Angeles; Med.

MACIAS, ROSABEL; Castle Park HS; Chula Vista, CA; (3); 5/422; Church Yth Grp; Dance Clb; School Play; Hon Roll; Drama Prfrmng Schl Ply; Prfmng Ballet Folklorico; Photo.

MACIAS, SAMUEL; John Glenn HS; Norwalk, CA; (2); Church Yth Grp; French Clb; Key Clb; Science Clb; Band; Drm Mjr(t); Jazz Band; Mrchg Band; Pep Band; High Hon Roll; MESA; CSF; Pepperdine U; Pre-Med.

MACIEL, BRENDA E; Hanford Joint Union HS; Hanford, CA; (2); Church Yth Grp; FFA; Teachers Aide; Bsktbl; Score Keeper; Swmmng; Hon Roll; Chptr Farmer Deg.

MACIEL, BRION A; C K Mc Clatchy HS; Sacramento, CA; (3); 65/390; Cmnty Wkr; French Clb; Rptr Nwsp; Yrbk; Chrmn Stu Cncl; JV Var Bsbl; JV Bsktbl; Hnrs Gldn St Math Exm; Friday Night Live; UC Santa Barbara; Dntstry.

MACIEL, CANDACE Y; Eagle Rock HS; Los Angeles, CA; (3); Drill Tm; Yrbk; Pres Frsh Cls; Rep Jr Cls; JV Vllybl; Hon Roll; Kabanokas Schl Svc Clb VP; Commissioner Religious Affairs; Corp Law.

MACIEL, GILBERT; North Monterey County HS; Salinas, CA; (3); Hon Roll; Auto Body.

MACIEL, JOSE J; Huntington Park HS; Huntington Park, CA; (3); Boy Scts; Church Yth Grp; Socr; Cerritos.

MACIEL, MARTHA L; Santa Paula HS; Santa Paula, CA; (3); JA; Hon Roll; Prfct Atten Awd; Migrant Ed Stu; Ventura Coll; Nrsg.

MACIEL, SUSANA; Garfield HS; Los Angeles, CA; (3); Mrchg Band; Hon Roll; Prfct Atten Awd; Coll; Comp Pgmr Word Prccsng.

MACIN, ALLYSON; Del Campo HS; Fair Oaks, CA; (3); 68/410; Debate Tm; French Clb; Q&S; Speech Tm; Ed Nwsp; Cit Awd; Hon Roll; Pianst; Spec Olympcs Coach/Vlntr; Recgnzd Nwsp Artcls; U Of CA Berkeley; Pre-Med.

MACISAAC, SANDRA J; Montgomery HS; Santa Rosa, CA; (2); Church Yth Grp; Teachers Aide; Yrbk; Hon Roll; Santa Rosa JC; Health.

MACIUJEC, ARIADNA G; John Glenn HS; Norwalk, CA; (2); Library Aide; Office Aide; Teachers Aide; Church Choir; Nwsp; JV Tennis; Var Trk; High Hon Roll; Hon Roll; Prfct Atten Awd; Project Interdependence Club Offcr; CSF; Phys Thrpy.

MACIULA, NORAH C; Marina HS; Huntington Beach, CA; (3); Art Clb; Church Yth Grp; French Clb; VP JA; Thesps; Chorus; Church Choir; School Musical; School Play; Stage Crew; Quality Review Commtte Stu Rep; Fshn Design.

MACK, BRIAN HARRIS; Eden Christian Acad; Oakland, CA; (3); Church Yth Grp; Cmnty Wkr; Debate Tm; English Clb; Science Clb; Teachers Aide; Temple Yth Grp; Church Choir; Orch; Pres Frsh Cls; Alameda Coll Comp Sci Cls; Alameda Coll; Bus Law.

MACK, GREG; Los Alamitos HS; Los Alamitos, CA; (3); Science Clb; High Hon Roll; CA Schlrshp Fed; Intgrct & Eclgy Clbs; Bus Fnc.

MACK, JANELL; Adolfo Camarillo HS; Camarillo, CA; (3); 45/430; Church Yth Grp; Band; Drm Mjr(t); Mrchg Band; Orch; High Hon Roll; Hon Roll; Cal Poly SLO; Engnrng Sci.

MACK, JEANETTA L; Oakland HS; Oakland, CA; (3); Band; High Hon Roll; Rptr Nwsp; L Trk; Kewanettes; Law.

MACK, RACHEL; Fort Bragg HS; Willits, CA; (3); Drama Clb; FBLA; SADD; Teachers Aide; School Musical; School Play; Yrbk; Stat Bsktbl; JV Vllybl; Hon Roll; Sonoma ST; Ed.

MACK, RHONDA M; Huntington Beach HS; Huntington Beach, CA; (3); Letterman Clb; Teachers Aide; Varsity Clb; Var Capt Crs Cntry; Var Trk; Cngrssnl Yth Ldrshp Cncl; Sprts Med.

MACK, SHERYL A; Carlmont HS; San Carlos, CA; (3); Key Clb; Rep Frsh Cls; Rep Soph Cls; Rep Jr Cls; Var Mgr(s); CSF; Merry Moppet Preschl Tchrs Aide; Tchr.

MACK, TAMIKA L; Abraham Lincoln HS; San Francisco, CA; (2); San Francisco ST; Nrsng.

MACK, TASHIMA A; Bishop Montgomery HS; Compton, CA; (3); Letterman Clb; Treas Soph Cls; Stu Cncl; Var Bsktbl; Trk; US Clb; CSF; Deans List; Acctng.

MACKAY, KAREN S; Indio HS; Indio, CA; (4); Church Yth Grp; Mat Maids-Capt; Bus Acad Letter; Christ Coll Irvine; Ed.

MACKAY, MARC C; Oak Ridge HS; Shingle Springs, CA; (1); 6/300; JV Bsbl; High Hon Roll; Hon Roll; Jr NHS; NHS; Bsbl Ponderosa Ltl Leag; Auto Racing Midget Car Cmptns; Cmpltd Hunter Safety Clss & Avid Hunter; UC Davis; Cmptr Engr.

MACKEN, CHRISTOPHER M; Brawley Union HS; Brawley, CA; (1); Art Clb; Church Yth Grp; Bsktbl; Hon Roll; U NV Las Vegas; Bus.

MACKEY, JASON M; Fairfax HS; Los Angeles, CA; (3); Boy Scts; Church Yth Grp; FCA; Band; Bsktbl; Trk; UCLA; Arch.

MACKH, MEGAN E; Aptos HS; Aptos, CA; (1); Service Clb; Var Bsktbl; JV Sftbl; JV Vllybl; Inter-Club Cncl Rep Assoc Stu Body; Zenith Club Secy; Gftd & Tlntd Ed Prgm Mem; CSF Mem.

MACKIE, STEVE P; Woodland HS; Woodland, CA; (3); Boy Scts; Church Yth Grp; Quiz Bowl; Teachers Aide; Band; Mrchg Band; Orch; Pep Band; Variety Show; Ftbl; Brigham Young U; Phys Therapy.

MACKLIN, TAMMY; Ceres HS; Modesto, CA; (2); Church Yth Grp; Intnl Clb; VP Key Clb; SADD; Rptr Nwsp; Rep Jr Cls; Rep Sr Cls; Stat Swmmng; High Hon Roll; Stanislaus ST U; Med.

MACKLIN, ZACH T; Marina HS; Huntington Beach, CA; (2); Var Swmmng; Schlr Athl Awd.

MACKULIAK, STACIE; Fort Bragg HS; Fort Bragg, CA; (2); Church Yth Grp; Rep Frsh Cls; Var JV Bsktbl; Var Crs Cntry; Var Trk; Med.

MACO, BRIAN; Mountain View HS; El Monte, CA; (1); Bsktbl; Psych.

MACON, JEFF A; Redwood HS; Visalia, CA; (3); 22/350; Var L Ftbl; Var L Trk; JV Wrstlng; High Hon Roll; Hon Roll; Sci, Math Coll Of Sequoias Enrchmnt Pgm; Cngrssnl Yth Ldrshp Cncl.

MACUNE, CYNTHIA S; Thousand Oaks HS; Thousand Oaks, CA; (4); 12/540; Church Yth Grp; 4-H; French Clb; Girl Scts; Science Clb; Pres Sec Service Clb; Church Choir; Bsktbl; 4-H Awd; Hon Roll; Safe Rides For Drunken Teens; Vet Asst; CSF; Vet Sci.

MACY, BRIAN EUGENE; Ponderosa HS; El Dorado, CA; (4); 1/289; Church Yth Grp; 4-H; Math Tm; Band; Chorus; Church Choir; Jazz Band; Mrchg Band; School Musical; Hon Roll; Bnk Of Amrca Awd Sci; Cert Otstndng Achvmnt Sci; Schlrshp Peace Ofcr Rsrch & Ed FDN; CSU San Luis Obispo; Indst Eng.

MADANI, ALICE; Mater Dei HS; Huntington Beach, CA; (1); Drama Clb; Spanish Clb; JV Cheerldng; CSF; UCLA; Psychiatrist.

MADARANG, EMILY L; Castle Park HS; Chula Vista, CA; (2); 39/473; GAA; Socr; Tennis; Masonic Awd; Music Sci/Bio; U Of CA San Diego; Nrsng.

MADARANG, RUBY S; Chula Vista HS; National City, CA; (1); Cit Awd; Hon Roll; 1st Pl Sci Fair 88; CSF; Vlntr Wrkr Paradise Vly Hosp; UCSD; Med.

MADDELA, JOSEPH A; Delano HS; Delano, CA; (3); 23/500; Drama Clb; French Clb; German Clb; Quiz Bowl; Scholastic Bowl; Chorus; JV Tennis; Hon Roll; NHS; Med.

MADDEN JR, CLAYTON P; South HS; Bakersfield, CA; (3); 58/351; Teachers Aide; Stu Cncl; Capt Bsktbl; Var Ftbl; Trk; High Hon Roll; Kiwanis Awd; Lion Awd; Prfct Atten Awd; All-League & Area Ftbl & Bsktbl; Poltcl Sci.

MADDEN, LLOYD E; Southwest HS; San Diego, CA; (3); Am Leg Boys St; Cmnty Wkr; Key Clb; Teachers Aide; Var Capt Socr; Rotary Awd; Athltcs Cmmssnr-Assoctd Stu Body; MVP Sccr Team; Chemcl Engrng.

MADDEN, NICK M; A A Stagg HS; Stockton, CA; (3); Boy Scts; Spanish Clb; SADD; Orch; School Musical; Rptr Nwsp; VP Sr Cls; JV Var Socr; Vllybl; High Hon Roll; UC Davis; Medieval Stud.

MADDEN, TIMOTHY B; Hogan SR HS; Vallejo, CA; (2); Church Yth Grp; Cmnty Wkr; Trk; Hon Roll; Law.

MADDI, PRASANTHI; Downey HS; Downey, CA; (2); French Clb; Library Aide; Service Clb; Trk; Prfct Atten Awd; UCLA; Med.

MADDOCK, JENNIFER L; Orange Lutheran HS; Corona, CA; (3); VP Church Yth Grp; Pep Clb; Chorus; JV Cheerldng; Var Pom Pon; Trk; JV Vllybl; Hon Roll; Chrldr Of Yr 89-90; Ed.

MADDOX, JILL; Burbank HS; Burbank, CA; (4); 1/425; Cmnty Wkr; Hosp Aide; NFL; Sec Science Clb; Speech Tm; Hist Temple Yth Grp; Rep Stu Cncl; JV Var Swmmng; Pres Acad Fit Awd; CSF Sealbearer; Candy Stripers Candy Co Schlrshp Awd; Brown U.

MADDOX, TONYA L; Hesperia HS; Hesperia, CA; (3); Church Yth Grp; Teachers Aide; Socr; Sftbl; Hon Roll; AZ ST U; Bus Exec.

MADDOX, TRACY; Gilroy HS; Gilroy, CA; (4); 10/356; Letterman Clb; SADD; Stage Crew; Ed Nwsp; Yrbk; Rep Stu Cncl; Var Bsktbl; Powder Puff Ftbl; High Hon Roll; Opt Clb Awd; CA Schlrshp Fed Life Mem; Vrsty Badminton; CIF Schlr Athlete Of Yr; San Jose ST; Bus Admin.

MADDUX, JOHN T; Thousand Oaks HS; Thousand Oaks, CA; (3); 1/600; Math Tm; SADD; Pres Band; Jazz Band; Mrchg Band; Pep Band; School Musical; High Hon Roll; Gold Seal CSF; Natl Mrt Commnded Schlr; Outstndng Jr Band Mem; Engrng.

MADEO, LORA; Clairemont HS; San Diego, CA; (3); 34/212; Rptr Nwsp; Hon Roll; Musician.

MADER, BRIAN J; St Francis HS; Los Altos, CA; (2); 34/356; Intrml JV Bsktbl; DAR Awd; Backpacking; Golf; Fishing; Environmentalist.

MADERA, CRISTINA; Basse HS; La Puente, CA; (2); Church Yth Grp; Band; Phtg Yrbk; Hon Roll; UCLA; Poltcl Sci.

MADERA, EDWIN; Bellflower HS; Bellflower, CA; (3); 10/343; Cmnty Wkr; Rep JA; Library Aide; Math Clb; Mu Alpha Theta; Quiz Bowl; Teachers Aide; Ed Nwsp; Rep Frsh Cls; High Hon Roll; Bio High Hnrs Awd; John Hopkins U; Med.

MADIA, ERIC; Cardinal Newman HS; Rohnert Park, CA; (3); 3/100; Church Yth Grp; Spanish Clb; Intrml JV Bsbl; Intrml Bsktbl; Cit Awd; High Hon Roll; Rotary Awd; Newman Ldrshp Schlrshp; UCLA; Bus Mgmt.

MADISON, MILES C; Sonora HS; Sonora, CA; (3); 2/300; Rep Frsh Cls; Rep Soph Cls; Treas Jr Cls; Treas Sr Cls; Rep Stu Cncl; JV Bsktbl; Capt Var Socr; JV Wt Lftg; High Hon Roll; Hon Roll; Engl.

MADISON, TAMMY CAMILLE; Victor Valley SR HS; Victor Ville, CA; (3); Dance Clb; Varsity Clb; Drill Tm; Lit Mag; Gym; Trk; Pres Acad Fit Awd; FL A&M; Model.

MADOLE, KERRY S; Chino HS; Chino, CA; (3); Treas FHA; Treas Pep Clb; Ski Clb; Treas SADD; Bsktbl; Var Cheerldng; Mgr(s); Powder Puff Ftbl; Score Keeper; High Hon Roll; CA ST Fullerton; Elem Tchr.

MADRAS, DANIELLE D; Yucca Valley HS; Joshua Tree, CA; (3); 3/146; Intnl Clb; Math Clb; High Hon Roll; Histry Stu Yr Awd; UC Riverside; Pre-Law.

MADRID, ARMANDO; Cantwell HS; Alhambra, CA; (4); Drama Clb; Science Clb; Spanish Clb; School Play; Off Sr Cls; Trk; High Hon Roll; Hon Roll; NHS; Spanish Ii Outstndng Achvt Awd; Hosp Vlntr Work; Ucls; Astrophysics.

MADRID, GINA D; Moorpark HS; Moorpark, CA; (4); Spanish Clb; Nwsp; Sec Frsh Cls; Sec Jr Cls; Off Sr Cls; Hon Roll; Bank Of Amer Achvt Awd; Moorpark CC; Bilingual Speech.

MADRID, JOANNA R; San Pedro HS; San Pedro, CA; (2); Church Yth Grp; Cmnty Wkr; Dance Clb; Drama Clb; GAA; JA; Pep Clb; Teachers Aide; Drill Tm; School Play; All St Sftbl Tm 87; Miss Teenage Pgnt Nov 89; Accntnt.

MADRID, LAURA; Theodore Roosevelt HS; Los Angeles, CA; (3); Proyerto Hermano; Lib Vlntr; Cal ST; Elem Educ.

MADRID, MARIA C; Notre Dame Acad; Inglewood, CA; (3); 33/112; Library Aide; Service Clb; SADD; Yrbk; Cit Awd; Hon Roll; NHS; Queens Cncl; Campus Mnstry Secy Treas.

MADRID, MARINETTE B; Hogan SR HS; Vallejo, CA; (2); Rep Spanish Clb; SADD; Teachers Aide; Rep Stu Cncl; JV Vllybl; High Hon Roll; Hon Roll; Pres Acad Fit Awd; Vrsty Bdmntn Tm; U Of CA Davis; Eductr.

MADRID, MICHAEL R; Poway HS; Poway, CA; (2); Jazz Band; UCSD; Med.

MADRID, MYLENE; Hogan SR HS; Vallejo, CA; (3); Church Yth Grp; Teachers Aide; JV Var Vllybl; Hon Roll; Vrsty Badmntn; JV Vllybl MVP Plq; Vrsty Vllybl Mst Imprvd Plq; Sacramento ST U; Nrsng.

MADRID, SAMANTHA L; Simi HS; Simi Valley, CA; (3); Church Yth Grp; Debate Tm; Drama Clb; Speech Tm; Rptr Nwsp; High Hon Roll; NHS; Natl Modeling Cmptns; CSUN; Bus Law.

MADRIGAL, AMERICO G; St Francis HS; E Palo Alto, CA; (2); 194/356; Ftbl; Hon Roll; Tae Kwon Doe; Sccr; Mech Engr.

MADRIGAL, ARMANDO; Red Bluff Union HS; Red Bluff, CA; (2); Ftbl; Trk; Wt Lftg; Wrstlng; Hon Roll; Prfct Atten Awd; Mst Insprtnl Trk; Natl Chmpn Wrstlng; Columbia NY; Bus.

MADRIGAL, CLAUDIA; O'farrell SCPA; San Diego, CA; (3); Dance Clb; Teachers Aide; High Hon Roll; Hon Roll; Prfct Atten Awd; Math.

MADRIGAL, ELIZABETH; Palo Verde HS; Blythe, CA; (2); JV Cheerldng; Hon Roll.

MADRIGAL, ELIZABETH R; Woodcrest Christian Schl; Perris, CA; (3); 1/60; Church Yth Grp; Dance Clb; Model UN; Chorus; Church Choir; School Musical; School Play; Variety Show; Yrbk; Rep Soph Cls; Phys Thrpy.

MADRIGAL, JAVIER; Oakdale HS; Oakdale, CA; (2); Spanish Clb; Cal ST U.

MADRIGAL, MARIA D; Paramount HS; Paramount, CA; (2); 9/666; Hosp Aide; Band; Mrchg Band; Crs Cntry; Trk; High Hon Roll; Hon Roll; Pres Acad Fit Awd; Good Ctznshp Awd; Law.

MADRIGAL, ROSENDO J; Garfield HS; Los Angeles, CA; (2); Art Clb; Boy Scts; Drama Clb; Spanish Clb; Varsity Clb; Band; Jazz Band; Mrchg Band; Stage Crew; Frsh Cls; CA ST Long Beach; Engrng.

MADRIGAL, SONIA M; William Workman HS; La Puente, CA; (2); Drama Clb; GAA; Letterman Clb; Varsity Clb; Acpl Chr; Chorus; School Play; Variety Show; Bsktbl; Pom Pon; Fshn Show Modeling Most Photogenic Awd; Perf Arts.

MADRIGAL, SUZANNE A; Mater Dei HS; Fountain Valley, CA; (3); Church Yth Grp; Treas Spanish Clb; Rep Stu Cncl; JV Capt Bsktbl; Hon Roll; NHS; Spcl Olympcs; CSF; WASC Cmmtte; USD; Nrsng.

MADRIGAL, VICTOR; San Pasqual HS; Winterhaven, CA; (2); Treas Letterman Clb; Treas Band; Pres Soph Cls; Var Bsbl; Capt Var Bsktbl; Score Keeper; High Hon Roll.

MADRIL, HECTOR A; Calexico HS; Calexico, CA; (1); Avid Club; Sci.

MADRIZ, GLORIA; Brawley Union HS; Sacramento, CA; (4); 28/300; AFS; FBLA; Pep Clb; SADD; Prfct Atten Awd; CSF; Frgn Lang Clb; Migrant Clb; CSU Sacramento; Accntng.

MADRIZ, MARCELA; Cajon HS; San Bernardino, CA; (1); Dance Clb; French Clb; Math Clb; Teachers Aide; Band; Chorus; Drill Tm; School Musical; School Play; Variety Show; Physician.

MADRONA, SORREL R; Berkeley HS; Berkeley, CA; (3); Dance Clb; Chorus; Yrbk; High Hon Roll; Psych.

MADRUGA, BECKY J; Hanford HS; Hanford, CA; (2); Church Yth Grp; Drama Clb; Spanish Clb; School Musical; School Play; Bsbl; Bsktbl; Crs Cntry; Trk; Vllybl; MVP Vllybl Tm; Billengual Stu Hanford Sec; COS; Cartooning.

MADRUGA, KIMBERLY A; Hanford Union HS; Hanford, CA; (1); FHA; Tennis; Hon Roll; FHA 1st Pl JR Div St Champ.

MADRUGA, MICHELLE; Redwood HS; Visalia, CA; (4); Pep Clb; Spanish Clb; Band; Mrchg Band; School Musical; JV Var Cheerldng; Var Pom Pon; Var Sftbl; Hon Roll; Pres Acad Fit Awd; Coll Of The Sequoias; Chd Psych.

MADRY, MONA N; Victor Valley HS; George AFB, CA; (3); 24/416; Hosp Aide; Pres Key Clb; Capt Drill Tm; Var L Cheerldng; Environmntl Clb; Med.

MADSEN, AIMEE E; Apple Valley SR HS; Apple Valley, CA; (3); Key Clb; Teachers Aide; Hon Roll; Peer Cnslng; Teen Asstnce Guidnce; Safe & Sober Task Frce Teen Theatr; Ob/Gyn Nrsng.

MADSEN, BRENDA; Marina HS; Huntington Beach, CA; (4); 57/535; AFS; JCL; Key Clb; Latin Clb; JV Var Tennis; High Hon Roll; Hon Roll; Pres Acad Fit Awd; Tennis Schlr Athlt Awd; Coach Awd; U CA Irving; Info Sci.

MADSEN, CRAIG W; American HS; Fremont, CA; (1); 90/430; Church Yth Grp; Hon Roll; Prfct Atten Awd.

MADSEN, JENNIFER L; Palmdale HS; Palmdale, CA; (3); Girl Scts; Band; Mrchg Band; Orch; Pep Band; Stage Crew; Nwsp; High Hon Roll; Hon Roll; Engl.

MADSEN, JILL; Bloomington Christian Schl; Bloomington, CA; (2); Letterman Clb; Var Capt Bsktbl; Var Score Keeper; Var Sftbl; Var Capt Vllybl; Lttle League Bsbll SR Div Ptchr; Vllybll All Vctry League 89; Sprtswmn Yr 89; Sftbll All Vctry League; Point Loma Nazarene Coll; Med.

MADSEN, MIKE; Adolpho Camarillo HS; Moorpark, CA; (3); Ftbl; Trk; Prfct Atten Awd; Vrsty Ftbl Coachs Trophy; Cal ST U Northridge; Accntng.

MADSEN, NATHAN J; Salinas Union HS; Salinas, CA; (2); Boy Scts; Church Yth Grp; JV Wrstlng.

MADSEN, STEVE H; Canyon Springs HS; Moreno Valley, CA; (3); Boy Scts; Church Yth Grp; German Clb; Teachers Aide; Band; Music.

MADU, FRANK; Mc Ateer HS; San Francisco, CA; (3); Office Aide; Teachers Aide; Bsktbl; Ftbl; Trk; Wt Lftg; Wrstlng; Cit Awd; High Hon Roll; Hon Roll; UCLA; Bus.

MADUAKOLAM, JOHNETTA; Willits HS; Willits, CA; (3); Am Leg Aux Girls St; SADD; School Musical; Pres Frsh Cls; Sec Soph Cls; Treas Jr Cls; Pres Sr Cls; Var Cheerldng; JV Vllybl; Hon Roll; Jobs Dghtrs Hnrd Qn 89-90; Peer Cnslng; U Of San Francisco; Pre Med.

MADUENA, ANDY; Coalinga HS; Coalinga, CA; (2); JV Crs Cntry; West Hills Coll.

MADUENA, PEGGY; San Benito HS; Hollister, CA; (4); 55/252; Art Clb; Aud/Vis; Church Yth Grp; Cmnty Wkr; Computer Clb; Dance Clb; English Clb; Office Aide; Spanish Clb; Teachers Aide; Miss Teen In Amer; Stage Techniques; Sacramento U; Cnslng.

MADUENA, RAUL; Wasco Union HS; Wasco, CA; (3); FFA; Spanish Clb; Crs Cntry; Trk; Wt Lftg; Hon Roll; Trk Clb; Mecha Clb; Migrant Clb; Fresno ST U; Indstrl Tech.

MADUENO, HILDA; Fred C Beyer HS; Modesto, CA; (1); Computer Clb; Dance Clb; Cit Awd; Hon Roll; UC Davis; Bus Admin.

MADUENO, VICTOR; Hueneme HS; Oxnard, CA; (1); UCSB; Music.

MADULI, GEMMA DY; Galt HS; Galt, CA; (4); 8/159; FHA; Hosp Aide; Intnl Clb; Service Clb; Cit Awd; High Hon Roll; Pres Acad Fit Awd; CSF; St Lukes Epscpl Chrch Nrsng Schlrshp; Cal Grant A; Pell Grant; Sacramento ST U; Nrsng.

MAEBARA, LIZA; Notre Dame Acad; Los Angeles, CA; (3); Spanish Clb; Trk; HOPE Clb; Berkeley U; Chld Psych.

MAEDA, KARI J; Clovis HS; Clovis, CA; (2); Hosp Aide; Band; Mrchg Band; Pep Band; High Hon Roll; Hon Roll; CSF; Bus.

MAEDA, KEVIN H; Westmoor HS; Daly City, CA; (4); 2/326; Treas Sr Cls; Crs Cntry; Trk; High Hon Roll; Masonic Awd; NHS; Pres Acad Fit Awd; Sal; Coll Entrance Clb Treas; U Of CA Berkeley; Mech Engrng.

MAEDA, KIM Y; Foothill HS; Santa Ana, CA; (4); 5/326; Church Yth Grp; Spanish Clb; SADD; Church Choir; High Hon Roll; NHS; Ntl Merit Schol; JV Crs Cntry; JV Co-Capt Socr; Top Schlr; All A's; U Of CA Rgnts Schlrshp; U Of CA Berkeley.

MAEDA, STACY ANN; Sacramento Waldorf Schl; Wilton, CA; (2); Orch; School Musical; Yrbk; Equine Artist; Trning & Shwng Amercn Miniatr Horses; Amernc Miniatr Horse Assn; Art.

MAEHR, MIKE; Damien HS; Alta Loma, CA; (2); 89/269; Cmnty Wkr; JA; Ski Clb; Var Golf; JV Socr; Most Imprvd-Soccer; Coaches Awd-Golf; Bankng/Finance.

MAES, KART; Millikan HS; Long Beach, CA; (2); Church Yth Grp; Ftbl; Vllybl; Cit Awd; Hon Roll; Pres Acad Fit Awd; Bus.

MAES, PAULETTE E; Novato HS; Novato, CA; (1); Debate Tm; Drama Clb; French Clb; Hosp Aide; SADD; Lit Mag; Diving; High Hon Roll; Pres Schlr; Cornell U; Cltrl Anthropology.

MAESTAS, ANTHONY B; Santa Clara HS; Port Hueneme, CA; (3); Pres Church Yth Grp; Treas Letterman Clb; Pep Clb; Mgr Stage Crew; Stu Cncl; Var Bsbl; Capt Var Bsktbl; Hon Roll; Altar Boy Pres Of Parish; Stu Senate A Class Rep; Ref Yth Bsktbl; CA ST Long Beach; Bio.

MAGADAN, OBDULIA; Palo Verde HS; Blythe, CA; (3); Spanish Clb.

MAGALLANES, ERNESTINA; Gladstone HS; Azusa, CA; (3); FBLA; SADD.

MAGALLANES, EVA; Santa Ana HS; Santa Ana, CA; (3); Bus.

MAGALLANES, LISA G; Pius X HS; South Gate, CA; (4); Flag Corp; Variety Show; Rptr Yrbk; Powder Puff Ftbl; JV Vllybl; Hon Roll; NHS; CSF; Legn Essay Cont-3rd Pl; Loyola Marymount U.

MAGALLANES, TOM J; Thousand Oaks HS; Thousand Oaks, CA; (2); Letterman Clb; Varsity Clb; Intrml Bsbl; Intrml Bsktbl; JV Capt Ftbl; Intrml Socr; Var Wt Lftg; JV Ftbl Plyr Of Week.

MAGALLANES, VERONICA; Etna Union HS; Fort Jones, CA; (3); Drama Clb; Pep Clb; Spanish Clb; SADD; Teachers Aide; Band; Mrchg Band; School Play; Variety Show; Friday Night Live & Stu Cncl Actvty Chrmn; UTEP; Commnctns.

MAGALLON, CELIA S; Dos Palos HS; Mendota, CA; (4); Latin Clb; Teachers Aide; Frgn Lang Dept Awd; CSU Stanislaus; Liberal Stds.

MAGALLON, DAVID; Oxnard HS; Oxnard, CA; (2); Cmnty Wkr; Rep Stu Cncl; JV Bsbl; JV Bsktbl; Var Score Keeper; High Hon Roll; Crmnl Sci.

MAGALLON, VICTOR; Henry T Gunderson HS; San Jose, CA; (4); 6/443; Cmnty Wkr; Intrml Bsktbl; Intrml Var Swmmng; Var L Trk; Ntl Merit Ltr; Natl Hispanic Schlr Awds Prog Semi-Fnlst; CSF; Schl Climate Cmmttee; Stanford U; Elec Engrg.

MAGALONG, JENNIFER G; Mira Mesa HS; San Diego, CA; (2); 60/850; Treas Church Yth Grp; French Clb; Church Choir; Rptr Nwsp; Off Frsh Cls; Sec Soph Cls; VP Jr Cls; Pres Acad Fit Awd; CSF; Intl Order Jobs Dghtrs; Medcl.

MAGANA, AMALIA; Gardena HS; Gardena, CA; (2); Church Yth Grp; Cit Awd; JETS Awd; MESA; CSF; U Of CA Los Angeles.

MAGANA, ARMANDO M; Palm Springs HS; Cathedral City, CA; (3); Chess Clb; Var Ftbl; JV Tennis; Hon Roll; CA Poly; Arch.

MAGANA, GABRIELA; Santa Paula HS; Santa Paula, CA; (2); Church Yth Grp; Letterman Clb; SADD; CA Schlrshp Fdrtn; Migrant Stu Ldrshp Cmmtte Pres; Educ.

MAGANA, JENNIFER B; Ramona HS; Riverside, CA; (2); 39/447; FBLA; Intnl Clb; Bsktbl; Hon Roll; Admin Asst 89; Vol Packer For Courses At Set Free Ministries 88; Stanford U; Comp Sci Engrng.

MAGANA, JESUS; Mtn View HS; South El Monte, CA; (2); Ftbl; Hnr Roll; UCLA; Engrng.

MAGANA, JESUS; Patterson HS; Westley, CA; (4); 3/85; Am Leg Boys St; Art Clb; Letterman Clb; Spanish Clb; SADD; Varsity Clb; Pres Stu Cncl; Var JV Ftbl; Var JV Trk; JV Wrstlng; Trans Vly Leag Outstndng Schl Athl Of Yr; Bank Of Amer Cert Sci; CA Schlrshp Fed; Cal Poly San Luis Obispo; Engr.

MAGANA, JOEL; Rio Vista HS; Walnut Grove, CA; (3); Science Clb; Trk; High Hon Roll; Hon Roll; Prfct Atten Awd; Latnos Unidos Club; CA Schlshp Fed; Engrg.

MAGANA, LILIANA; South Tahoe HS; South Lake Tahoe, CA; (3); 24/214; Service Clb; JV Sftbl; CA Schlrshp Fdrtn.

MAGANA, ROSA A; Modesto HS; Modesto, CA; (2); Church Yth Grp; Girl Scts; Office Aide; Teachers Aide; Band; Chorus; Church Choir; School Play; Yrbk; Bsbl; MJC Acad; Plc Offcr.

MAGANA, SANDRA; Fairfax HS; Los Angeles, CA; (2); Hon Roll; LASA; Comp Prgmr.

MAGANA, SYLVIA A; Ontario HS; Ontario, CA; (3); Art Clb; Church Yth Grp; Key Clb; Science Clb; Spanish Clb; Var Crs Cntry; Var Trk; Hon Roll; Ivy Chain; Cal Poly Polynet; CSF; Cal Poly; Med.

MAGARIN, MARIBEL; Orosi HS; Orosi, CA; (3); Drama Clb; Math Clb; Spanish Clb; SADD; Chorus; Flag Corp; Jazz Band; Mrchg Band; Hon Roll; Hnr Band; Bus.

MAGARO, MATT A; Grace M Davis HS; Modesto, CA; (3); FFA; SADD; High Hon Roll; Hon Roll; U C Davis; Mrn Blgst.

MAGAZZU, NICOLE; Casa Roble HS; Oangeville, CA; (2); Library Aide; Teachers Aide; Acpl Chr; Chorus; Church Choir; Score Keeper; Swmmng; UCLA; Jrnlsm.

MAGBANUA, ELAYNE H; Lemoore Union HS; Lemoore, CA; (3); Church Yth Grp; Pep Clb; Spanish Clb; JV Cheerldng; JV Var Mgr(s); Hon Roll; Jobs Dghtrs; Confirmation; Lunch Buddies; Coll Of Seqouias; Reg Nrs.

MAGBANUA, VANESSA D; Montclair HS; Montclair, CA; (2); JV Vllybl; Stu Of Mnth.

MAGBUAL, RICHARD S; Ramona HS; Riverside, CA; (2); 22/500; Band; Jazz Band; Mrchg Band; Orch; Pep Band; Hon Roll; Bus.

MAGCAUAS, JENNY L; Pinole Valley HS; Hercules, CA; (1); Church Yth Grp; Hon Roll; UC Berkeley.

MAGDALENO, DUSTIN; Santa Paula Union HS; Santa Paula, CA; (3); 8/260; Letterman Clb; Var JV Bsbl; Var JV Ftbl; Var Capt Socr; High Hon Roll; Hon Roll; Ntl Merit Ltr; CSF; MVP Vrsty Ftbl & Sccr Awds 89-90; 1st Tm All Leag Stu Athlte Awd Sccr; All Leag Ftbl & Sccr88-90.

MAGDALENO, JOHN AMMON; Trinity HS; Salyer, CA; (4); AFS; Am Leg Boys St; French Clb; Intnl Clb; Letterman Clb; Scholastic Bowl; Stu Cncl; JV Var Bsktbl; JV Var Trk; Hon Roll; Acad Dcthln Tm Cnty & St; Wn Cnty Mth Cont; AFS France; Comp Sci.

MAGDALENO, JUDITH R; El Cajon Valley HS; El Cajon, CA; (3); 37/431; Bsktbl; Hon Roll; AVID Clss; UC LA; Pilot.

MAGDALENO, MARISSA R; J F Kennedy HS; Granada Hills, CA; (3); Key Clb; Off Jr Cls; Stu Cncl.

MAGDALENO, ROSA I; Hueneme HS; Port Hueneme, CA; (2); FBLA; SADD; Socr; High Hon Roll; Engr.

MAGDALENO, VICTOR; Moorpark HS; Moorpark, CA; (4); 52/180; Stu Cncl; Var Ftbl; Var Socr; Var Trk; Wt Lftg; High Hon Roll; Hon Roll; ASB Cmmssnr Of Athltcs; Mecha Club; Athltc Club; Cal Lutheran U; Educ.

MAGDALENO III, VINCENT G; Dos Palos HS; Dos Palos, CA; (2); Spanish Clb; Ftbl.

MAGDANGAL, ROCHELLE; Immaculate Conception Acad; San Francisco, CA; (4); Rep GAA; Q&S; Service Clb; Rptr Nwsp; VP Frsh Cls; Sec Soph Cls; Pres Sr Cls; Stu Cncl; Hon Roll; Prfct Atten Awd; Block Soc; CLC; Spirit Awd; FIDM; Fash Merch.

MAGDATO, GLENN D; Fontana HS; Fontana, CA; (2); High Hon Roll; Hon Roll; Prfct Atten Awd; HS Achvt Awd; Doctor.

MAGEE, ALLISON; San Luis Obispo SR HS; San Luis Obispo, CA; (2); 27/250; Intnl Clb; School Play; Stage Crew; Var Crs Cntry; Var L Trk; High Hon Roll; Gldn Tgr Awd; Outdoor Clb; Hnr Achvt Gldn St Exam Geom; Zoology.

MAGEE, DONNA L; El Camino Real HS; Los Angeles, CA; (3); CAL ST; Bus Admin.

MAGELSSEN, HANS E; Hilmar HS; Hilmar, CA; (1); Church Yth Grp; VICA; Intrml Bsktbl; Var Trk; Hon Roll; Pres Acad Fit Awd; MVP Bsktbl Tm; CA Poly; Arch.

MAGER, AMANDA LEE; Arcata HS; Blue Lake, CA; (3); Rptr Yrbk; Var Bsktbl; Var Sftbl; Var Vllybl; Cit Awd; High Hon Roll; Yurok Indian Tribe; Top 10 Per Cnts JR Cls; Humboldt ST U; Tchng/Coach.

MAGER, JOHN C; Arcata HS; Blue Lake, CA; (2); Var Bsbl; Bsktbl; Hon Roll; Lttrfd Bsbl; Yurok Indian Tribe; AZ ST; Coaching.

MAGERSEN, SHELBY; Etiwanda HS; Alta Loma, CA; (1); Church Yth Grp; Cmnty Wkr; Var Cheerldng; Modeling; UCLA; Phy.

MAGGARD, JENNIFER; Capistrano Valley Christian HS; Mission Viejo, CA; (4); 2/61; Pres Church Yth Grp; Pres Pep Clb; Spanish Clb; Yrbk; Rep Stu Cncl; Var Capt Cheerldng; Elks Awd; Hon Roll; Pltcl Sci.

MAGGARD, JENNIFER; Capistrano Valley Christian HS; Mission Viejo, CA; (4); 2/62; Pres Church Yth Grp; Spanish Clb; Yrbk; Rep Stu Cncl; Capt Cheerldng; Elks Awd; Pres Acad Fit Awd; Sal; Soroptmst Yth Ctznshp Awd; CSF; Bnk Of Amer Achvt Awd; Wstmnt Coll; Pltcl Sci.

MAGGARD, MICHELLE; Capistrano Valley Christian HS; Mission Viejo, CA; (3); 1/47; Church Yth Grp; Var Cheerldng; High Hon Roll.

MAGGART, MONA M; Palmdale HS; Palmdale, CA; (3); Teachers Aide; Var Mgr Socr; Art.

MAGGINI, JASON M; Riverdale HS; Burrel, CA; (3); Computer Clb; Science Clb; Yrbk; High Hon Roll; Outstndng Stu Awd Comp Sci; Comp Sci.

MAGGS, MICHAEL; Immanuel Christan HS; Ridgecrest, CA; (3); Varsity Clb; Var Ftbl; Intrml Golf; Intrml Lcrss; Var Mgr(s); Intrml Socr; Var Swmmng; Intrml Tennis; Intrml Vllybl; Hon Roll; Notre Dame; Engrng.

MAGHINAY, MARY ANN S; Edison HS; Stockton, CA; (2); High Hon Roll.

MAGLAN, CELESTE; Andrew P Hill HS; Milpitas, CA; (4); 17/280; Dance Clb; Off Dance Clb; French Clb; Math Tm; Chorus; Nwsp; Lit Mag; Sec Soph Cls; Rep Jr Cls; Stu Cncl; CSF; Peer Cnslng; Indepndnt Aging Pgm Vlntr; UC Santa Barbara; Mrktng.

MAGLAQUI, JANEL BARBARA S; Woodrew Wilson HS; Long Beach, CA; (4); 30/788; Computer Clb; Intnl Clb; High Hon Roll; NHS; Pres Acad Fit Awd; CSULB; Comp Sci.

MAGLAYA, JENNIFER; Brethren JR/Sr HS; Long Beach, CA; (1); 40/90; Church Yth Grp; Pep Clb; VP Frsh Cls; JV Cheerldng; Trk; High Hon Roll; Hon Roll; Pres Acad Fit Awd; Tutor 7th Grdrs Eng; Stanford; Bus.

MAGLAYA, MAHLANIE L; St Patrick St Vincent HS; Vallejo, CA; (1); Hon Roll; UC Berkeley; Nrsng.

MAGLIO, COURTNEY J; San Gabriel Mission HS; Pasadena, CA; (2); 9/144; Church Yth Grp; Cmnty Wkr; FBLA; GAA; Spanish Clb; Swmmng; High Hon Roll; Hon Roll; CSF; Hghst Candy Seller 1st Pl 90; Retreat Ldr; Youth Grp; U CA Santa Barbara; Bus.

MAGLIO, PETER; Edison HS; Fresno, CA; (2); JV Bsbl.

MAGNER, SHANNON E; Montgomery HS; Santa Rosa, CA; (2); Church Yth Grp; French Clb; FFA; Office Aide; Teachers Aide; Yrbk; Vlntr Humane Soc; Christ Coll Irvine; Advrtsng.

MAGNO, CHERIE; Workman HS; Valinda, CA; (2); Intnl Clb; Band; Mrchg Band; Hon Roll; Plyd Piano; Plyd Clarinet; RN.

MAGNO, GREG G; Central Union HS; El Centro, CA; (4); 19/498; Am Leg Boys St; Letterman Clb; Math Tm; Red Cross Aide; School Play; Var L Swmmng; Bausch & Lomb Sci Awd; High Hon Roll; Ntl Merit Ltr; Pres Acad Fit Awd; UC San Diego; Ocean Engrng.

MAGNO, NOLA; Bishop Amat HS; La Puente, CA; (4); 34/390; GAA; Sec Soph Cls; Rep Stu Cncl; JV Var Bsktbl; JV Var Vllybl; High Hon Roll; Hon Roll; VP NHS; CSF; Coaches Awd Vllybl; Advertising.

MAGOCH, EDWARD; Antelope Valley HS; Lancaster, CA; (4); Debate Tm; French Clb; Key Clb; Math Tm; Pep Clb; Scholastic Bowl; Pres Band; Drill Tm; Jazz Band; Mrchg Band; San Diego ST; Law.

MAGOULAS, ANNA M; Ukiah HS; Ukiah, CA; (2); 2/554; Debate Tm; French Clb; Spanish Clb; School Musical; Treas Jr Cls; Stu Cncl; Tennis; High Hon Roll; Pres Acad Fit Awd; Coll Band; UC Davis; Frgn Lang.

MAGPANTAY, MARIA C; Edison SR HS; Stockton, CA; (2); Computer Clb; Dance Clb; 4-H; Tennis; Hon Roll; Samuel Merrit Coll; RN.

MAGSIG, MARLA; Clovis West HS; Fresno, CA; (3); Capt Church Yth Grp; Band; Mrchg Band; Pep Band; Var Capt Bsktbl; Var Swmmng; JV Vllybl; Hon Roll; Hnrs Awd Gldn St Exam Alg; Athl Trng.

MAGUEN, SHIRA; Westlake Schl; Los Angeles, CA; (3); Cmnty Wkr; Dance Clb; French Clb; Service Clb; Temple Yth Grp; Ed Nwsp; Lit Mag; French Hon Soc; Articles Publshed LA Times; 1st Frnch Write-Off; Dance Co; Cmmnty Svcs; Psych.

MAGUIRE, BARBARA J; Del Oro HS; Loomis, CA; (2); 48/267; Drama Clb; Sec Treas SADD; Chorus; School Play; Cit Awd; Hon Roll; Friday Night Live Secy & Treas; U CA Davis; Med.

MAGYAR, MICHELLE; Lincoln HS; Stockton, CA; (4); Church Yth Grp; Sec Latin Clb; Pres Letterman Clb; Var Swmmng; Var Vllybl; Hon Roll; Sports Psych.

MAGZANYAN, ANAHIT; St Bellarmine-Jefferson HS; Los Angeles, CA; (2); Dance Clb; Math Clb; Science Clb; Spanish Clb; Rep Frsh Cls; JV Var Tennis; High Hon Roll; Hon Roll; NHS; Piano; CSF; Tnns Awds 1st Pl, Mst Imprvd; Northridge; Phy.

MAH, FRANCINE J; Phillip & Sala Burton Academic HS; San Francisco, CA; (4); 64/158; Cmnty Wkr; Computer Clb; French Clb; Girl Scts; JA; Ski Clb; Teachers Aide; Chorus; Yrbk; Rep Frsh Cls; JETS Clb; CA Polytech St U; Comp Sci.

MAH, JANNIFER L; Central Union HS; El Centro, CA; (1); Orch; Hon Roll; Ballet; Piano; UCSD; Jrnlsm.

MAH, RICHARD KEITH; Santa Paula Union HS; Santa Paula, CA; (2); Var Tennis; High Hon Roll; CSF; CA Inst Tech; Elect Engrng.

MAHAL, JENNIFER K; Chula Vista HS Creatve/Prfmng Arts; Chula Vista, CA; (3); 125/535; Church Yth Grp; Library Aide; Speech Tm; Acpl Chr; Chorus; School Musical; Mgr Stage Crew; Ed Nwsp; Off Soph Cls; Cit Awd; Theatre Arts.

MAHAL, LARA; Bonita Vista HS; Chula Vista, CA; (3); 21/556; Church Yth Grp; Drama Clb; JV Quiz Bowl; Var Scholastic Bowl; Speech Tm; Chorus; School Musical; School Play; Stage Crew; Variety Show; 1st Pl Tianamen Sq Writing Cont; Pacific Yrly Meeting Vigil Cmmttee Clerk; Soc Sci.

MAHAL, TEJI P; Clovis HS; Fresno, CA; (3); Spanish Clb; SADD; Dntl.

MAHAN, CAMILLE N; Stagg HS; Stockton, CA; (2); Cmnty Wkr; Church Choir; Drill Tm; Mrchg Band; Crs Cntry; Trk; NHS; BSU; Alnateen; Social Wrkr.

MAHAN, CHANTAL M; Carlsbad HS; Carlsbad, CA; (2); Sec AFS; Drama Clb; Service Clb; Chorus; Stage Crew; Var Trk; Hon Roll; Lancer Day Homecoming Cmmtte; UCLA; Sports Thrpst.

MAHAN, MARCUS; Arlington HS; Riverside, CA; (2); Varsity Clb; Var Ftbl; JV Wrstlng; USC; Engineer.

MAHAR, JESSICA D; Tustin HS; Tustin, CA; (2); 60/400; Church Yth Grp; Pep Clb; Red Cross Aide; Spanish Clb; Rep Frsh Cls; Off Jr Cls; Stu Cncl; Cheerldng; JV Crs Cntry; Hon Roll; Principals Hnr Roll; CSF; Dsgn.

MAHARAJ, YUGESH; Fred C Beyer HS; Modesto, CA; (1); Stu Cncl; Var Socr; Intrml Cit Awd; Intrml Hon Roll; Intrml Prfct Atten Awd; Bus.

MAHBOOB, RAY; Dos Pueblos HS; Goleta, CA; (3); 117/320; Letterman Clb; Varsity Clb; JV Bsktbl; Var Capt Crs Cntry; JV Tennis; Var Trk; UCSB; Lwyr.

MAHBOUBIAN, ROYA; University City HS; San Diego, CA; (3); Cit Awd; High Hon Roll; CSF; Ldrshp Grp; ONC; UCSD; Med.

MAHBOUBIAN, SHERLY; Taft HS; Woodland Hills, CA; (3); Drama Clb; Ski Clb; Spanish Clb; Teachers Aide; Thesps; Jazz Band; School Play; Stage Crew; Yrbk; Gym; CSF; Knights & Ladies; Jewish Clb; UCLA; Bio.

MAHEDA, LUIGI S; Bonita Vista HS; San Diego, CA; (1); Church Yth Grp; JV Ftbl; JV Trk; Chula Vista Police Explrer; CA ST U Davis; Vet.

MAHER JR, MICHAEL; St Patrick-St Vincent HS; Vallejo, CA; (3); Church Yth Grp; Debate Tm; Sec Soph Cls; JV Socr; Var Tennis; High Hon Roll; CSF; Stanford; Bus.

MAHER, WENDY L; Sierra Vista HS; Baldwin Park, CA; (1); Color Guard; Mrchg Band; Rep Frsh Cls; Cit Awd; Hon Roll; Cal St Fullerton; Tchr.

MAHETA, MEGHVI M; Irvine HS; Irvine, CA; (1); Church Yth Grp; French Clb; Key Clb; CSF; Indian Clb; Actvsts Poltcl Awrnss.

MAHMOOD, JAMSHED R; Tustin HS; Tustin, CA; (4); Chess Clb; Ftbl; Swmmng; Vllybl; Wt Lftg; Anti Drug Cmpgn; Orange Coast CC; Film Dir.

MAHMOOD, MUJAHID; Clovis HS; Clovis, CA; (4); Debate Tm; Hosp Aide; Math Tm; Model UN; Science Clb; Speech Tm; High Hon Roll; Ntl Merit Ltr; Pres Acad Fit Awd; US Cycling Fed Mem; Acad Decathln Mem; Intl Baccalaureate Full Diploma; U CA San Diego; Med.

MAHMOUD, JINAN; Mercy HS; San Francisco, CA; (1); 23/120; Art Clb; Intnl Clb; Stage Crew; Hon Roll; Photo Clb.

MAHMOUDI, JALAL M; Eureka HS; Flagstaff, AZ; (3); Chess Clb; Rptr Nwsp; Var Crs Cntry; Hon Roll; Physics & Drafting Awds.

MAHMOUDI, MITRA L; San Dieguito HS; Leucadia, CA; (4); 10/540; Cmnty Wkr; SADD; Ed Nwsp; High Hon Roll; NHS; Ntl Merit SF; Interact; Jr Hnr Guard; Bahai Yth Grp; Enviro Sci.

MAHMOUDI, RAMIN M; San Dieguito HS; Encinitas, CA; (2); High Hon Roll; Dingo Boingo Sec Soc; San Diego U; Bus Mgmt.

MAHNKE, MELINDA E; Fountain Valley HS; Fountain Valley, CA; (3); German Clb; Acpl Chr; Chorus; School Musical; School Play; Stage Crew; JV Tennis; Var L Trk; Piano; Sonoma ST U; Scndry Engl Ed.

MAHNKEN, EARL JASSON; Bishop Amat HS; La Puente, CA; (2); 84/418; Church Yth Grp; Cmnty Wkr; JV Trk; Hon Roll; Friday Night Live; Spcl Olympics Volunteer; Poltcl Sci.

MAHNOVSKI, SERGEJ; Flintridge Preparatory Schl; Glendale, CA; (3); Spanish Clb; JV Var Bsktbl; Var Socr; Var Capt Swmmng; Cit Awd; High Hon Roll; Hon Roll; Jr NHS; NHS; Ntl Merit Ltr; Vrsty Water Polo Hnrb Mntn Most Dedicated Awds; Brnz Mdl CSF; Brown Bk Awd; Bio.

MAHOLLAND, SHAWN; Eneinal HS; Alameda, CA; (4); 8/250; Teachers Aide; Varsity Clb; Golf; High Hon Roll; Jr NHS; Prfct Atten Awd; Heald Bus Coll; Bus Mgmt.

MAHOME, TONI M; Roosevelt HS; Los Angeles, CA; (2); Chorus; Church Choir; Variety Show; JV Bsktbl; Trk; Hon Roll; Mst Imprvd Bsktbl Plyr 89-90, All Eastern Leag 2nd Tm; Psych.

MAHON, LAUREN E; Walnut HS; Walnut, CA; (2); Girl Scts; Spanish Clb; Teachers Aide; JV L Swmmng; High Hon Roll; Off Soph Cls; JV MVP Swm; 2-Yr Spllng Bee Wnr; GATE; CSF; Sci Fctn Clb; Socratc Clb; Sci Fair 3rd Pl; Pblshd Poetry.

MAHONE, MARK; Marina HS; Huntington Beach, CA; (2); JA; JV Socr; JV Trk.

MAHONEY, PHIL; Coronado HS; Coronado, CA; (3); 30/150; Drama Clb; Teachers Aide; Thesps; School Musical; School Play; Stage Crew; Variety Show; Hon Roll; Liberal Arts.

MAHR, ERIC M; John W North HS; Riverside, CA; (1); Church Yth Grp; Var L Crs Cntry; JV Trk; JV Wrstlng; Hon Roll; CA Schltc Fed; Aerosp Eng.

MAHR, JENNIFER J; Sunny Hills HS; Fullerton, CA; (3); 71/430; French Clb; Nwsp; DAR Awd; High Hon Roll; Advncd Plcmnt Art Pgm; Comic Bk Clb Treas; Art.

MAHRU, LORRAINE A; Villa Park HS; Anaheim Hills, CA; (2); Drama Clb; Temple Yth Grp; School Play; High Hon Roll; NHS; Acad Ltr; Fine Arts.

MAHZOON, SHABNAM; Westmont HS; Campbell, CA; (2); French Clb; Math Clb; French Hon Soc; High Hon Roll; NHS; Rotary Awd; CSF; Bio.

MAI, BRIAN P; Montgomery HS; Santa Rosa, CA; (2); JA; Key Clb; Science Clb; Treas Spanish Clb; Cit Awd; High Hon Roll; Hon Roll; Jr NHS; V Badinton; Yth Sccr; Traveled To Frgn Countries; Engr.

MAI, CHI; Southern California Christian HS; Tustin, CA; (3); Cmnty Wkr; Hosp Aide; Teachers Aide; Nwsp; High Hon Roll; NHS; Prfct Atten Awd; Wrote Column L A Times HS Stu Section; U Of CA Irvine; Med.

MAI, HIEU T; Nogales HS; West Covina, CA; (3); 130/650; Science Clb; Cit Awd; Hon Roll; Prfct Atten Awd; CSF; Embassy Intl; Chem.

MAI, LELE; Independence HS; San Jose, CA; (2); Art Clb; French Clb; Science Clb; Hon Roll; CA Schlshps Fed.

MAI, LIEN T; Leuzinger HS; Hawthorne, CA; (3); Computer Clb; French Clb; Hon Roll; Vietnamese Club; Bus Accntng.

MAI, LOAN; Oakland HS; Oakland, CA; (4); 3/28; Hon Roll; Vietnamese Clb; Outstndg Acadc Achvt; Prsdntl Acadc Ftnss Awd; Cert Awd Math; Ceramics; CA ST U Hayward; Comp Sci.

MAI, MAX; Millikan HS; Long Beach, CA; (4); Boy Scts; Office Aide; Orch; Off Sr Cls; Vllybl; Schlrhsp LBD Bd Of Realtors; CA ST Long Beach; Math.

MAI, NGOE; Santa Teresa HS; San Jose, CA; (3); Church Yth Grp; French Clb; Girl Scts; Church Choir; San Jose ST U; Ed.

MAI, PHUONG; San Lorenzo HS; San Leandro, CA; (1); Church Yth Grp; Computer Clb; English Clb; FCA; Office Aide; SADD; Teachers Aide; Church Choir; Orch; JV Tennis; UC Berkeley.

MAI, STACI T; Mark Keppel HS; Monterey Park, CA; (1); Math Clb; Drill Tm; Hon Roll; UCLA; Chem.

MAI, THAO T; Edison Computech HS; Fresno, CA; (2); French Clb; JV Swmmng; JV Vllybl; Cit Awd; Gov Hon Prg Awd; High Hon Roll; Hon Roll; Engl.

MAI, THUAN T; Nogales HS; W Covina, CA; (2); Hon Roll; Intrml Tennis; Intrml Trk; CSF; Mech Engr.

MAI, TINA H; Temple City HS; Temple City, CA; (4); 5/375; Sec AFS; VP Church Yth Grp; French Clb; Hosp Aide; Treas Key Clb; Ed Nwsp; Ed Yrbk; Stu Cncl; L Capt Crs Cntry; L Trk; Cls Hnr Grd; High Achvrs Bio Pgm; HOBY Fnlst; Med.

MAIALE JR, ENRICO MARIO; Sherman Oaks CES HS; Canoga Park, CA; (3); VP Sr Cls; Var Bsbl; JV Var Bsktbl; Var Cheerldng; Var Capt Ftbl; Var Wt Lftg; Bowling; Athl Yr Frshmn; MVP Bsbl; Bus.

MAIDEN, MARY BETH; Southern California Christian HS; Tustin, CA; (2); 3/70; Church Yth Grp; Dance Clb; Drama Clb; Pep Clb; Spanish Clb; Speech Tm; Teachers Aide; Chorus; School Musical; School Play; Missionary Trips; Law.

MAIDENS, AIMEE M; Sierra Joint Union HS; Shaver Lake, CA; (2); Drama Clb; Chorus; School Musical; Stage Crew.

MAIENSCHEIN, ERICA; Poway HS; Poway, CA; (4); 170/728; AFS; SADD; Lit Mag; Pres Frsh Cls; Rep Stu Cncl; High Hon Roll; Interact VP; CA Schlrshp Fed; Peer Cnslr; UCSD; Commnctns.

MAIER, JENNIFER; Orestimba HS; Newman, CA; (1); Drama Clb; Pep Clb; Spanish Clb; SADD; Band; Jazz Band; Mrchg Band; Pep Band; School Musical; Pres Frsh Cls; Med.

MAIER, MIKE C; Orestimba HS; Newman, CA; (3); SADD; Hon Roll; Motorcylcing; Weight-Lftng; CSF; Modesto JC; Arch.

MAILANGKAY, RINI N; West Covina HS; West Covina, CA; (2); JV Vllybl; Badmntn JV; CA ST Fullerton; Med.

MAILLIARD, JEFF J; Saint Francis HS; Menlo Park, CA; (2); 111/360; Var Ftbl; Var Golf; High Hon Roll; Hon Roll; Pres Acad Fit Awd; SADD.

MAIN, BRAD A; Paradise HS; Paradise, CA; (3); 29/233; Teachers Aide; JV Var Bsbl; L Bsktbl; JV Ftbl; Intrml Socr; Intrml Trk; Hon Roll; Kiwanis Awd; Athl Of Mnth; CIF; Var Bsbll; Masters Coll Newhall; Educ.

MAIO, AMY SUSAN; Pittsburg HS; Pittsburg, CA; (1); 7/489; Church Yth Grp; Band; Mrchg Band; Hon Roll; UC Davis; Vet.

MAIORANA, JENIFER; Pacific Grove HS; Pacific Grove, CA; (4); Church Yth Grp; Drama Clb; Key Clb; Teachers Aide; Stu Cncl; JV Var Cheerldng; Var Pom Pon; JV Wt Lftg; High Hon Roll; Hon Roll; Mtry Penninsula Coll; Comm.

MAIORANA, JENNIFER; Pacific Grove HS; Pacific Grove, CA; (1); Church Yth Grp; Drama Clb; Key Clb; Teachers Aide; Off Soph Cls; Off Sr Cls; Stu Cncl; Capt Cheerldng; Pom Pon; Wt Lftg; Rally Coord; Chico ST; Commnctns.

MAIR-RICHARDSON, STACIE; Elk Grove HS; Sacramento, CA; (4); Dance Clb; JV Gym; 5 Yrs Span; Waitress/Courtesy Clerk; Csus; Teaching Elem Ed.

MAIRENA, JENNY; Bishop Amat HS; Pomona, CA; (3); Treas Church Yth Grp; Band; Mrchg Band; Var Bsktbl; Hon Roll; NHS; NEDT Awd; Law.

MAISONNEUVE, KRISTEN; Bakersfield HS; Bakersfield, CA; (2); Church Yth Grp; Ski Clb; Stage Crew; JV Swmmng; Hon Roll; UCLA; Psych.

MAISTERRENA, MAITE; St Joseph HS; South Gate, CA; (3); 33/198; Office Aide; Spanish Clb; SADD; High Hon Roll; Hon Roll; Loyola Marymount U; Linguisties.

MAITHEL, SHISHIR K; Whitney HS; Cerritos, CA; (2); 1/150; JA; Key Clb; Spanish Clb; JV Socr; JV Tennis; High Hon Roll; Prfct Atten Awd; CSF; CJSF; Golden St Exam-Hghst Hnrs; Ping Pong Clb-Founder; Med.

MAJAM, MELISSA AURORA; West Covina HS; W Covina, CA; (4); 6/250; Dance Clb; German Clb; Science Clb; Rptr Nwsp; High Hon Roll; Hon Roll; Prfct Atten Awd; CSF; Grmn Hnr Soc; PTSA Schlrshp; Cal Poly Pomona; Psych.

MAJANO, MAYRA; Culver City HS; Culver City, CA; (3); Church Yth Grp; Church Choir; French Hon Soc; Hon Roll; Airline Pilot.

MAJARIAN, MICAH B; Edison HS; Fresno, CA; (1); Computer Clb; Ski Clb; Cheerldng; Swmmng; Tennis; Hon Roll; NHS; CSF; Water Polo; UC Davis.

MAJIED-MUHAMMAD, JAMILLAH M; Marshall Fundamental HS; Altadena, CA; (3); Sec Drama Clb; Science Clb; Band; Mrchg Band; Orch; Pep Band; Capt Var Bsktbl; Var Sftbl; Var Tennis; Var Trk; USC; Arch.

MAJOR, ERIC D; Dana Hills HS; Laguna Beach, CA; (2); Drama Clb; School Play; Off Frsh Cls; JV Var Ftbl; JV Socr; JV Var Wt Lftg; Prof Actor; Saddleback JC; Sprts Med.

MAJOR, JON; Ambassador Baptist HS; Rialto, CA; (1); Var Bsbl; Var Bsktbl; JV Ftbl; Hon Roll; MVP Awd JV Ftbl; SDSU; Prof Bsbl Player.

MAJOR, YVETTE SHANTA; Burroughs HS; Ridgecrest, CA; (3); VP Church Yth Grp; Treas Key Clb; SADD; Band; Church Choir; Rep Soph Cls; Rep Jr Cls; Rep Stu Cncl; Stat Bsktbl; Prfct Atten Awd; Fashion Designer.

MAJORS, CRAIG W; Oak Park HS; Agoura Hills, CA; (1); JV Ftbl; Var L Trk; Intrml Pres Acad Fit Awd; Rookie Of Yr Trck & Fld; CSUN Northridge; Phys Thrpy.

MAK, HEBRON H; Central Union HS; El Centro, CA; (1); Church Yth Grp; Church Choir; Orch; Comp Engr.

MAK, JOAN Y; North Salinas HS; Salinas, CA; (2); Treas VP German Clb; Key Clb; Math Tm; Science Clb; Cit Awd; Elks Awd; High Hon Roll; NHS; Prfct Atten Awd.

MAK, POLLY P; George Washington HS; San Francisco, CA; (3); Dance Clb; JA; Pep Clb; Teachers Aide; School Play; Var Pom Pon; High Hon Roll; Hon Roll; Chinese Amer Club-Svc To Club, Selling Candies, Car Wash, Help Recycle Papers/Aluminium Sch & Home; Pharm.

MAK, WEIBIN; Woodrow Wilson HS; San Francisco, CA; (3); FBLA; Science Clb; Var Tennis; Intrml Trk; Intrml Vllybl; Hon Roll; NHS; Pres Acad Fit Awd; USF; Bus.

MAK, WINNIE W; Alhambra HS; Alhambra, CA; (3); Sec FBLA; Math Clb; Red Cross Aide; Science Clb; Lit Mag; Election Cmmtte; Medcl Clb; Psych.

MAKADA, SAMEER H; Las Lomas HS; Walnut Creek, CA; (3); 25/273; Rep Soph Cls; Var Crs Cntry; Var Tennis; Var Wrstlng; Big Brother; UCLA; Biochem.

MAKADIA, KIRAN D; Irvington HS; Fremont, CA; (3); 13/261; Art Clb; Hon Roll; Stu Mnth; CSF; Bus Accntg.

MAKAM, KIRAN N; Alameda HS; Alameda, CA; (2); Science Clb; High Hon Roll; Hon Roll; Law.

MAKAY, MORAYMA M; St Monica Catholic HS; Santa Monica, CA; (2); Rep Art Clb; Thesps; Chorus; School Musical; Lit Mag; Rep Soph Cls; Sec Jr Cls; High Hon Roll; Hon Roll; CSF; Animal Rights Group; Yale U; Arch.

MAKHINSON, MICHAEL; Burbank HS; Burbank, CA; (2); Hosp Aide; Teachers Aide; Prfct Atten Awd; CSF; Natl Acad Decathlon; Med.

MAKJAVICH, LYNN M; Bret Harte HS; Arnold, CA; (2); Church Yth Grp; Chorus; Intrml Wt Lftg; Hon Roll; CSF; UC Santa Cruz; Marine Bio.

MAKRES, TRACY; Capuchino HS; San Bruno, CA; (4); Letterman Clb; Drill Tm; Mrchg Band; Variety Show; Hon Roll; NHS; Prfct Atten Awd; Distnctn Math; CSF Life Membrshp; Yth In Govt Essay Wnnr 90; San Francisco ST U; Cvl Engrng.

MAKRIS, NIKKI M; Fairfield HS; Fairfield, CA; (2); Church Yth Grp; Girl Scts; Church Choir; Hon Roll; NHS; Elem Schl Vlntr Srvce.

MAKSRIVORAWAN, BHOHATHAI; Schurr HS; Los Angeles, CA; (3); Am Leg Aux Girls St; Hosp Aide; Key Clb; Q&S; Nwsp; Rep Frsh Cls; Rep Soph Cls; Treas Sr Cls; Ntl Merit Ltr; Outstndng Jrnlst Schl Paper; Jrnlsm.

MAKSRIVORAWAN, JAILUK O; Schurr HS; Monterey Park, CA; (2); French Clb; Rptr Nwsp; Hon Roll; CSF; Fresh Rep; Jr Statesmn Of Amer; Leg Invlmnt Officer; Ecology Club; Bio.

MAKWANA, ANITA; Burbank SR HS; Burbank, CA; (2); Drama Clb; Teachers Aide; Chorus; School Play; Stage Crew; High Hon Roll; Hon Roll; Jr NHS; NHS; Pres Acad Fit Awd; San Diego ST U; Arch.

MAL, VAN V; Milpitas HS; Milpitas, CA; (3); 6/487; French Clb; Badminton V&JV; Medcl.

MALAK, DAN R; Redlands HS; Redlands, CA; (3); Letterman Clb; Varsity Clb; Var Bsktbl; Var Socr; Var Trk; Cit Awd; Vlntr YMCA; All Cnty Sccr Plyr; Bus.

MALAMANIG, CHRISTINE; Kerman HS; Kerman, CA; (3); 3/130; Math Tm; Ed Nwsp; Ed Lit Mag; Pres Stu Cncl; JV Sftbl; JV Tennis; Hon Roll; JETS Awd; Acdmc Dcthln Hnrs Tm; Gottschalks Hi-Deb Pgm Bd Rep.

MALANGA, KELLEY; Christian HS; San Diego, CA; (4); 1/99; Church Yth Grp; VP Ski Clb; Chorus; School Musical; Var Sftbl; High Hon Roll; NHS; Prfct Atten Awd; Val; FCA; El Cajon Rotary Schlrshp; CSF Sealbearer; Wheaton Coll; Medcl.

MALBOEUF, LAFLECHE; Warren HS; Downey, CA; (2); JV Bsktbl; Var Sftbl; Bus.

MALCOLM, ANDREA; Arlington HS; Riverside, CA; (2); Church Yth Grp; FTA; Letterman Clb; Pep Clb; Church Choir; Cheerldng; Hon Roll; Acteens Qn Regent In Svc, Natl Convention; Musicalifornia Musical Perf 89-90; Elem Educ.

MALCOLM, CHARISMA; Canyon Springs HS; Moreno Valley, CA; (3); Church Yth Grp; Letterman Clb; Varsity Clb; Pres Frsh Cls; JV Sftbl; Var Trk; Var Vllybl; Cmnty Wkr; Hon Roll; CSF; Black Stu Union; U PA; Cardiology.

MALCOLM, JANINE L; Bishop O'down HS; Oakland, CA; (3); 24/240; GAA; Math Clb; Math Tm; Ski Clb; Chorus; Phtg Ed Yrbk; Intrml Var Vllybl; High Hon Roll; Psychlgy.

MALCOLM II, NATHANIEL ERIC; Mater Dei HS; Irvine, CA; (3); Am Leg Boys St; Church Yth Grp; Cmnty Wkr; Stu Cncl; Bsktbl; Ftbl; Trk; High Hon Roll; NHS; Cit Awd; Athltc Cmmssnr; Med.

MALCOMSON, CHRISTINE S; Fremont Christian HS; Fremont, CA; (4); Church Yth Grp; Church Choir; School Play; Mgr Stage Crew; Ed Yrbk; Var Bsktbl; Co-Capt Tennis; Var Trk; Pres Acad Fit Awd; AAU/Mars-Milky Way Bar HS All Amer Awd; Acadc Champ Tm Capt 90; Pilot.

MALDIA, EMMYLOU J; Rosemead HS; Fontana, CA; (3); Computer Clb; FCA; French Clb; FBLA; Intnl Clb; Spanish Clb; Teachers Aide; Off Jr Cls; Off Sr Cls; Capt Bsktbl; Hnr Roll; Most Imprvd Plyr Sftbl; U Of S CA; Law.

MALDONADO, ADRIANA; Arvin HS; Lamont, CA; (3); 100/350; Spanish Clb; Sftbl; CA ST Coll; Bus.

MALDONADO, BEATRIZ A; Abraham Lincoln HS; Los Angeles, CA; (1); Capt Cheerldng; Drill Team; Chrldr; MESA; Upward Bound; NASA Engr.

MALDONADO, CATARINO M; Indio HS; Indio, CA; (3); Off Jr Cls; Socr; Wt Lftg; Wrstlng; Cit Awd; High Hon Roll; Prfct Atten Awd; Arch.

MALDONADO, DAISY M; Irvine HS; Irvine, CA; (1); Church Yth Grp; Debate Tm; Latin Clb; Spanish Clb; Crs Cntry; Mgr(s); Sftbl; JV Trk; Cit Awd; Kababian Clb; Afro Amer Clb; Noter Dame; Attorney.

MALDONADO, DIANNA; Cabrillo HS; Lompoc, CA; (3); Cmnty Wkr; Spanish Clb; Teachers Aide; Drill Tm; Mrchg Band; Score Keeper; Sftbl; Hon Roll; Stu Of Mnth April 90; PA ST; Psych.

MALDONADO, ESTELA M; Alisal HS; Salinas, CA; (3); Hon Roll.

MALDONADO, HILDA; Carson HS; Carson, CA; (3); Intnl Clb; Spanish Clb; Cit Awd; Hon Roll; Prfct Atten Awd; Bus Admin.

MALDONADO, LILIA; Gahr HS; Artesia, CA; (1); Hon Roll; Intl Clb; Blu-Gld Awd Spnsh III; Bus Admin.

MALDONADO, MAYBELLINE F; Glendale HS; Glendale, CA; (3); Church Yth Grp; Cmnty Wkr; Yrbk; Cit Awd; Prfct Atten Awd; Clothing Schlrshp Awd; Honor E Awd; Law.

MALDONADO, MAYRA; Channel Islands HS; Oxnard, CA; (2); Spanish Clb; Hon Roll; Prfct Atten Awd; Acad Achvt Awd.

MALDONADO, NANCY G; Orangewood Adventist Acad; Santa Ana, CA; (4); Church Yth Grp; Library Aide; Spanish Clb; Varsity Clb; Church Choir; VP Sr Cls; Var Vllybl; Walla Walla Coll; RN.

MALDONADO, ROSA V; Chula Vista HS; Imperial Beach, CA; (3); 103/493; SADD; Chorus; Stage Crew; Cit Awd; UCSD; Pre-Law.

MALDONADO, SOFIA; Carson HS; Carson, CA; (2); FTA; Latin Clb; Cit Awd; Hon Roll; Pres Acad Fit Awd; Goldn St Exam Algbra Hnrs; Acctng.

MALDONADO, STEPHANIE L; Mt Pleasant HS; San Jose, CA; (1); San Jose ST; Prof Dancer.

MALDONADO, VERONICA; James Logan HS; Union City, CA; (3); Powder Puff Ftbl; Trk; Hon Roll; Trvl Clb; Close-Up; Psych.

MALDONDO, ROBERT R; Richard Gahr HS; Artesia, CA; (3); Dance Clb; French Clb; Latin Clb; Spanish Clb; JV Socr; Var Trk; Cit Awd; Hon Roll; Prfct Atten Awd; Bus.

MALED, KATIE; Bakersfield HS; Bakersfield, CA; (3); Dance Clb; Office Aide; Ski Clb; Teachers Aide; Off Jr Cls; Capt Cheerldng; JV Powder Puff Ftbl.

MALEK, ERIC F; Villa Park HS; Villa Park, CA; (4); 11/500; Computer Clb; Sec 4-H; Key Clb; Math Clb; Science Clb; Pres Spanish Clb; SADD; High Hon Roll; NHS; Pres Acad Fit Awd; Gale W Pattison Yth Ldrshp Schlr; 3rd Pl Engrng Orange Cty Sci/Engrng Fr 90; Spel Awd Amer Inst Chem; U Of San Diego; Elec Engrng.

MALEK, JANET H; Villa Park HS; Villa Park, CA; (2); Cmnty Wkr; 4-H; Hosp Aide; Key Clb; VP Spanish Clb; SADD; Cit Awd; 4-H Awd; High Hon Roll; Hon Roll; CSF; Oceanogrphy Clb; UC San Diego; Medcl.

MALEK, SIAMAK; San Dimas HS; La Verne, CA; (4); Computer Clb; English Clb; Var L Crs Cntry; Var Trk; Elks Awd; High Hon Roll; Pres Interact Clb; VP Dead Physcsts Soc; VP Ecology Clb; UC San Diego; Neuro Srgn.

MALERVY, MICHAEL J; Laguna Hills HS; Aliso Viejo, CA; (4); 7/328; Mrchg Band; Ntl Merit Ltr; Pres Acad Fit Awd; CSF; U CA San Diego.

MALESKY, EDMUND; Redlands HS; Redlands, CA; (2); Debate Tm; Letterman Clb; NFL; Spanish Clb; Speech Tm; Varsity Clb; Nwsp; Socr; Tennis; Cit Awd; CSF.

MALIJEWSKI, KATIE M; Roseville HS; Rocklin, CA; (2); Hosp Aide; Science Clb; Sierra Coll; Teacher.

MALIK, CRAIG L; Sherman E Burroughs HS; Ridgecrest, CA; (4); Boy Scts; Ski Clb; Variety Show; Yrbk; JV Socr; Var Trk; Hon Roll; Pres Acad Fit Awd; U CA Davis; Mech Engr.

MALIK, FAISAL H; Artesia HS; Cerritos, CA; (2); Boy Scts; Science Clb; JV Bsktbl; Cit Awd; High Hon Roll; Hon Roll; Sci Cont; Citizenship/Schlrshp Awd 9 Times; CA Schlrshp Fed; Aerontcl Engr.

MALIK, YASSER; American HS; Fremont, CA; (3); Bsktbl; Tennis; High Hon Roll; Bsbl, Drwng/Mech & Crtnng; Arch.

MALIKYAR, EDDRIS; College Park HS; Pleasant Hill, CA; (3); AFS; Debate Tm; French Clb; Tennis; Intl Bus.

MALKI, JULIET P; South Pasadena HS; S Pasadena, CA; (4); 82/295; Church Yth Grp; Treas French Clb; Service Clb; Teachers Aide; Ed Nwsp; JV Bsktbl; Pres Acad Fit Awd; CSF; U Of La Verne; Bus Admin.

MALKIN, SCOTT R; Marina HS; Huntington Beach, CA; (1); JCL; Latin Clb; High Hon Roll; UCLA; Med.

MALLALLY, ERIN E; Louisville HS; Tarzana, CA; (2); School Play; High Hon Roll; Explorers Club VP; CA Schltc Fed; Med.

MALLARI, CHRISTOPHER E; Independence HS; San Jose, CA; (3); Cmnty Wkr; Var L Tennis; Hon Roll; Prfct Atten Awd; Pres Acad Fit Awd; CSF; CA Poly Tech; Elec Engrng.

MALLARI, NEIL A; Bishop Amat HS; Diamond Bar, CA; (2); High Hon Roll; NHS; NEDT Awd; Chrstn Svc.

MALLEK, ANNE E; Edison HS; Fresno, CA; (1); Hosp Aide; High Hon Roll; Hon Roll; Outstndg Achvt Awds Soc Stud & Comp Sci; Smmr Swm Tchr; Play Piano; Ed.

MALLEN, JAMIE R; Louisville HS; Calabasas, CA; (1); GAA; Var Cheerldng; High Hon Roll; Pres Acad Fit Awd; Acad Schlrshp; Keybrdng Excllnce Awd; Cathlc Schlrshp Fed.

MALLERY, DOUGLAS R; Cupertino HS; Santa Clara, CA; (1); Boy Scts; Church Yth Grp; FBLA; NFL; Speech Tm; Nwsp; Yrbk; Ed Lit Mag; High Hon Roll; Hon Roll; Make A Real Chnge For Kids-Ldr; Peer Cnslng; Japanese Anmtn Clb; Intl Affrs.

MALLEY, LAURA E; Bella Vista HS; Fair Oaks, CA; (2); 3/400; FBLA; Math Tm; Pep Clb; Spanish Clb; School Musical; Var L Cheerldng; Var L Diving; High Hon Roll; Hon Roll; NHS; CA Cngrssnl Schlr Natl Young Ldrs Conf; Engl, Math, Spnsh, Photo & Sci Awds; Stu Reachng Out; Duke U; Bus.

MALLI, JESSY; Tulare Union HS; Tulare, CA; (2); 3/480; Science Clb; Band; Mrchg Band; Pep Band; Off Frsh Cls; Off Soph Cls; Var Socr; Var Tennis; High Hon Roll; Pres Acad Fit Awd; CSF; Stanford; Med.

MALLICK, PROJIT; Canoga Park HS; Canoga Park, CA; (4); 1/383; Cmnty Wkr; Service Clb; Ed Nwsp; High Hon Roll; Hon Roll; Pres Acad Fit Awd; Val; CSF Pres & Seymour Fnlst; CA Acad Decathlon Tm; UC Berkeley; Econ.

MALLINSON, JEFFREY C; Trabuco Hills HS; Mission Viejo, CA; (2); Church Yth Grp; Cmnty Wkr; Spanish Clb; Church Choir; Wt Lftg; Hon Roll; Delphi Pgm; Golden St Exam; Biola U; Chrstn Educ.

MALLINSON, MICHAEL S; Bakersfield Adventist Acad; Bakersfield, CA; (4); Church Yth Grp; Drama Clb; Band; Chorus; Church Choir; Color Guard; Jazz Band; Orch; School Play; Swing Chorus; John Phillips Sousa Music Awd; ALT Schlrshp; Pcfc Un Coll; Music Pre-Med.

MALLON, AMY L; Lakewood HS; Lakewood, CA; (4); Cmnty Wkr; Office Aide; Spanish Clb; Sec Sr Cls; Stat Bsbl; Stat Ftbl; JETS Awd; Finance.

MALLON, JOSEPH; Arroyo HS; San Lorenzo, CA; (3); 9/270; Church Yth Grp; Cmnty Wkr; Debate Tm; FCA; JA; Service Clb; Speech Tm; Varsity Clb; Bsbl; Bsktbl; Parish Cncl Of St Johns Church; AZ Wrk At Apache Indian Camp; CSF; UC Santa Barbara; Engr.

MALLON, ROBIN K; Norte Vista HS; Riverside, CA; (2); 95/492; French Clb; FFA; Hon Roll.

MALLON, TISHA M; Skyline HS; Oakland, CA; (3); Cmnty Wkr; Girl Scts; Library Aide; Office Aide; Chorus; School Musical; Socr; Cit Awd; Horsebck Rdng; Envrnmntl Issues; U Of Pacific; Sci.

MALLOY, BRIAN P; Irvine HS; Irvine, CA; (2); 1/550; French Clb; Rep Key Clb; Math Tm; Science Clb; Lit Mag; JV Tennis; Cit Awd; High Hon Roll; Hon Roll; Pres Acad Fit Awd; JETS Sci Comptn 90; Sci Olympd Team 90; CSF Offcr; Amer Chemical Soc Test Chem Team.

MALMQUIST, KRISTA; Watsonville HS; Watsonville, CA; (3); Pep Clb; Varsity Clb; Variety Show; Off Jr Cls; Var Cheerldng; Cabrillo Coll; Graphic Dsgn.

MALMSTROM, KELDA J; Berkeley HS; Berkeley, CA; (3); French Clb; Var Crs Cntry; Var Trk; Vlntr Aide Jr Rangers Pgm Tilden Pk; Graphic Arts.

MALONE, BRIAN J; Capistrano Valley HS; Mission Viejo, CA; (3); Church Yth Grp; Cmnty Wkr; Pep Clb; Ski Clb; Varsity Clb; Variety Show; Pres Soph Cls; Stu Cncl; Bsbl; Ftbl; HOBY; GATE Pgm; Engrng.

MALONE, BRYCE P; Rim Of The World HS; Running Springs, CA; (3); 69/259; Boy Scts; Chess Clb; Letterman Clb; Scholastic Bowl; Varsity Clb; Rptr Nwsp; Ed Yrbk; JV Var Bsbl; JV Wrstlng; Hon Roll; Acad Dcthln; Cal ST; Jrnlsm.

MALONE, COLLEEN E; Louisville HS; Woodland Hills, CA; (1); Church Yth Grp; Cmnty Wkr; Drama Clb; Hosp Aide; Service Clb; Hon Roll; HS Hnrs Entrnc; Chrstn Svc Core; CA Schlrsp Fed.

MALONE, JENNIFER M; Bishop Amat Memorial HS; West Covina, CA; (3); Friday Night Live; Amnesty Intl; Lacidem; Cal Poly Pomona; Ed.

MALONE, LAURIE A; Poway HS; Poway, CA; (3); Church Yth Grp; Band; Mrchg Band; Orch; Pep Band; Hon Roll; Environmental Awareness Club; UCLA; Music.

MALONE, MAUREEN; Mercy HS; Daly City, CA; (3); Mgr GAA; Chorus; Ed Nwsp; Mgr(s); JV Trk; JV Var Vllybl; High Hon Roll; Hon Roll; CSF; U Of CA Davis; Engr.

MALONE, MAUREEN M; Livermore HS; Livermore, CA; (3); Drama Clb; VP 4-H; German Clb; Hosp Aide; Orch; School Musical; School Play; Stage Crew; 4-H Awd; Hon Roll; Stage Mgr Touring Opera Co; Danc For Modern & Ballet Danc Co; Tch Piano.

MALONEY, JODI; San Diego Acad; San Diego, CA; (1); Church Yth Grp; Computer Clb; Teachers Aide; Chorus; Ftbl; Socr; Sftbl; Hon Roll; Comptrs.

MALONEY, LAURA A; Lowell HS; San Francisco, CA; (3); Service Clb; Pres Soph Cls; Pres Jr Cls; L Swmmng; Ntl Merit Ltr; Law.

MALONEY, MARY; Palos Verdes HS; Palos Vrds Pen, CA; (4); 51/371; Latin Clb; Teachers Aide; Var Capt Bsktbl; Hon Roll; NHS; Pres Acad Fit Awd; U Of CA-SANTA Barbara.

MALONEY, MEGHAN H; Apple Valley HS; Apple Valley, CA; (2); Church Yth Grp; Key Clb; Spanish Clb; High Hon Roll; Hon Roll; Doctor.

MALONEY, MOLLY; Porterville HS; Porterville, CA; (4); Am Leg Aux Girls St; Pres Church Yth Grp; Drama Clb; French Clb; Letterman Clb; Teachers Aide; Thesps; Band; Church Choir; Mrchg Band; Brigham Yng Y Ldrshp Awd; Baughman Grphy Schlrshp; Cntrl CA Grocers Awd; Brigham Young U; Elem Ed.

MALONEY, WILLIAM T; Manteca HS; Manteca, CA; (3); Sec Boy Scts; Sec French Clb; Rotary Camp Royal; PTA CA St Brd Of Mgrs.

MALONY, SCOTT J; Redwood HS; Visalia, CA; (3); Church Yth Grp; Spanish Clb; Varsity Clb; Rep Stu Cncl; Tennis; Hon Roll; UC Berkeley; Commnctns.

MALOOF, STAN D; Warren HS; Downey, CA; (2); Cmnty Wkr; Service Clb; Ski Clb; Var Swmmng; Water Polo JV Capt; Peer Counselor; Golden Bear Awd; CA ST Fullerton; Fireman.

MALOUF, WALID E; Lowell HS; San Francisco, CA; (3); French Clb; French Hon Soc; Amer Assn Of Frnch Teachers Hnr Cert; Bus.

MALOVOS, MARK M; Del Campo HS; Sacramento, CA; (3); 80/450; Ed Yrbk; Var Capt Crs Cntry; Var Capt Trk; Hon Roll; Cross Cntry Sac-Joaquin Sec Champ 88-89; Stanford Yrbk Camp Hnrbl Mntn Dsgn & Copy Wrtg; Law.

MALOY, CHRIS; Chaffey HS; Ontario, CA; (1); Boy Scts; Math Clb; Ftbl; Wrstlng; Hon Roll; Math Hnrs; UCLA; Med.

MALPHURS, REGINA M; Homestead HS; Sunnyvale, CA; (1); 50/300; Drama Clb; Spanish Clb; School Play; Stage Crew; Diving; Gym; Swmmng; Trk; Cit Awd; High Hon Roll; San Diego ST; Marine Bio.

MALQUIST, VAUGHN; North HS; Bakersfield, CA; (1); Boy Scts; Church Yth Grp; Hon Roll.

MALRAY, JULIET; University HS; Los Angeles, CA; (2); Drama Clb; Drill Tm; School Play; Rep Stu Cncl; Cheerldng; Cit Awd; Hon Roll; Write Short Stories & Poems; Acting; Play Guitar & Piano; Psych.

MALSTEAD, ALLISON N; Clairemont HS; San Diego, CA; (2); French Clb; Model UN; Quiz Bowl; Service Clb; School Play; Rptr Nwsp; Ed Lit Mag; JV Sftbl; Hon Roll; Opt Clb Awd; Amnesty Intl Urgnt Actn Coord; Poly Sci.

MAM, JACQUELINE P; A A Stagg HS; Stockton, CA; (1); Cmnty Wkr; Dance Clb; Debate Tm; Drama Clb; Key Clb; NFL; Service Clb; Speech Tm; School Play; Stage Crew; CSF; Asian Advisory Cmmtte; Conflict Mgmt; Boston U; Bus.

MAMARIL, DENNIS; Bishop Amat HS; West Covina, CA; (4); 20/400; Var Tennis; High Hon Roll; Hon Roll; NHS; Prfct Atten Awd; Amnsty Intl Clb; Chrstn Svc; CSF; Bio.

MAMARIL, JENNIFER L; Saint Joseph HS; Buena Park, CA; (2); Dance Clb; Spanish Clb; Hon Roll; CA Schlrshp Fed; Berkeley; Art Dsgn.

MAMARIL, JOEL R; Cleveland HS; Canoga Park, CA; (2); Hon Roll; Pierce Clg; Arch.

MAMMANO, LINDA C; La Mirada HS; La Mirada, CA; (2); Sec Drama Clb; Hosp Aide; NFL; Speech Tm; School Play; Tennis; High Hon Roll; Pres Acad Fit Awd; HOBY Ambssdr; CSF; Lwyr.

MAMSA, ABDUR R; Anaheim HS; Anaheim, CA; (3); Church Yth Grp; Math Clb; Science Clb; Spanish Clb; Cit Awd; High Hon Roll; Hon Roll; NHS; Prfct Atten Awd; Pres Acad Fit Awd; Natl Hnr Soc; Philosophy Clb; USC; Bus Admin.

MAN, KARENA K; Lowell HS; San Francisco, CA; (2); Cmnty Wkr; Hosp Aide; Orch; Rep Stu Cncl; DAR Awd; S F Bay To Brkrs Race Vlntr 89-90; Jrnlsm.

MAN, THERESA; Edison HS; Huntington Bch, CA; (2); Church Yth Grp; Key Clb; Model UN; Flag Corp; Yrbk; Kiwanis Awd; Soph OCAD Team Mgr; Church Youth Group Hospitality Chairperson; Piano; Tennis; Stamp Collecting; Dance; UCLA; Med.

MAN, WAI; St Joseph Notre Dame HS; Oakland, CA; (4); 12/97; Cmnty Wkr; School Play; High Hon Roll; Hon Roll; NHS; Bk Amer Cert Math; Tandy Tech Schls Awd; Math Comptn SF; Engr.

MANABAT, JHON P; Sweet Water HS; National City, CA; (3); Off Soph Cls; Bsktbl; Ftbl; Socr; Vllybl; Hon Roll.

MANAHAN, JONATHAN; Loyola HS; Los Angeles, CA; (2); Hon Roll; NEDT Awd; CA Schlrshp Fed; Pre-Law Clb; Violin; Harvard; Law.

MANALANG, MARY ROSE R; Paraclete HS; Palmdale, CA; (2); 2/145; Drama Clb; Sec Key Clb; Office Aide; Pres Service Clb; Sec SADD; Stage Crew; High Hon Roll; Hon Roll; NHS; CSF; Zonta Clb.

MANALO, ARIEL; South Tahoe HS; S Lake Tahoe, CA; (3); Key Clb; Yrbk; Pres Soph Cls; Pres Jr Cls; JV Bsktbl; Var Trk; High Hon Roll; Prfct Atten Awd; Ldrshp Clss; CSF VP; U Of San Diego.

MANALO, CAROLYN; Bonita Vista HS; Bonita, CA; (4); 5/531; Art Clb; Church Yth Grp; Intnl Clb; Var Letterman Clb; Teachers Aide; Nwsp; Off Frsh Cls; Stu Cncl; Hon Roll; Scty Women Engrs Cert Mrt; CSF; Interntl Bacclrte Pgm; CA Poly San Luis Obispi; Arch.

MANALO, EILEEN; Encinal HS; Alameda, CA; (4); 11/220; VP FBLA; Rep JA; Rep Stu Cncl; Var JV Vllybl; High Hon Roll; 1st Pl FBLA Advncd Keybrdng; Mst Inspirational Vllybl Player 88; San Fran ST U; Bus.

MANALO, MICHAEL G; West Covina HS; West Covina, CA; (3); Cmnty Wkr; Debate Tm; Drama Clb; Library Aide; Office Aide; Pres Service Clb; Pres SADD; Rep Frsh Cls; Rep Soph Cls; Off Jr Cls; Friday Night Live Pres; Teenwork Rep 90.

MANALO, NOREEN; South Tahoe HS; So Lake Tahoe, CA; (3); 1/215; SADD; Orch; JV Sftbl; Var Tennis; High Hon Roll; Prfct Atten Awd; CSF; Soroptomist S Club.

MANANSALA, CLARISSA D; St Genevieves HS; Sun Valley, CA; (3); Chorus; Drill Tm; Rptr Nwsp; Mgr Yrbk; Hon Roll; UCLA; Nrsng.

MANANSALA, DOMINIC B; Lowell HS; San Francisco, CA; (3); Library Aide; Hnrs Golden State Exams Geometry; Helped Clean Up San Franciscos Ocean Beach; San Jose ST U; Electronics.

MANAOIS, ANTHONY A; Wallenberg HS; San Francisco, CA; (2); Band; Jazz Band; Cit Awd; High Hon Roll; Hon Roll; Bio, Frnch & Band Acadmc Awds; Amer Israel Exchng Pgm; Berklee Schl Music; Music.

MANAOIS, TEODOR A; Lowell HS; San Francisco, CA; (3); Band; Church Choir; JV Crs Cntry; JV Trk; Intrml Vllybl; General Denistry.

MANCA, PETER J; Fremont HS; Sunnyvale, CA; (2); Debate Tm; Math Tm; NFL; Speech Tm; School Musical; JV Socr; High Hon Roll; Hewlett Packard Excllnc Math & Sci Awd; 3rd Pl Santa Clara Valley Math Field Day.

MANCERA, JOSE JUAN; Gonzales HS; Chualar, CA; (4); 3/170; Math Tm; Science Clb; Teachers Aide; Band; Chorus; Socr; Cit Awd; High Hon Roll; Prfct Atten Awd; St Schlr; CSF Sealbearer; Mem Musical Band Soldados Del Amor; Block G Awd; Stanford U; Bus Admin.

MANCEWICZ, ERIN N; Savanna HS; Buena Park, CA; (2); Pep Clb; Cheerldng; Hon Roll; Pres Acad Fit Awd; Writing Poetry; Envrnmnt; Surfing; U Of Southern CA; Chld Psych.

MANCHESTER, ALLISON P; Santa Barbara HS; Santa Barbara, CA; (2); #22 In Class; Church Yth Grp; Cmnty Wkr; Acpl Chr; Trk; Hon Roll; Pres Acad Fit Awd; UC Davis; Pre Med.

MANCHESTER, ANDREA; Amador Valley HS; Pleasanton, CA; (3); Boy Scts; Church Yth Grp; Hosp Aide; Intnl Clb; Color Guard; Mrchg Band; Capt Of ID Sqd & Received Lttr 89-90; Outstndg Prfrmr ID Unit 89-90; Prfrmnd At Aloha Bowl 89; Physcl Thrpy.

MANCHESTER, BECKY J; Lincoln HS; San Jose, CA; (3); Var Bsktbl; Var Trk; Var JV Vllybl; Mock Trial; Yth & Govt; Acad Decathlon; UC Santa Barbara; Anthropology.

MANCILLA, ADALIZ; Gompers Secondary HS; Spring Valley, CA; (3); 1/90; Pres French Clb; Drill Tm; Ed Lit Mag; Sec Jr Cls; Rep Stu Cncl; Var Crs Cntry; Var Trk; High Hon Roll; CA Scholastic Federation; Rensselaer Math Science Award; Architect Editor.

MANCILLA, CLAUDIA I; Gompers Secondary HS; Spring Valley, CA; (1); 25/270; Church Yth Grp; Pres French Clb; Rptr Soph Cls; Crs Cntry; Hon Roll; VP Jr NHS; Prfct Atten Awd.

MANCILLA, JESUS; Gompers Secondary HS; Spring Valley, CA; (4); Pres French Clb; Pres Math Clb; Pres Math Tm; Mrchg Band; Off Soph Cls; Off Jr Cls; Var Socr; Caltech; Chem Engrng.

MANCILLA JR, ROBERT L; Eagle Rock HS; Los Angeles, CA; (3); School Play; Var Bsbl; Capt Var Ftbl; Var Trk; Hon Roll; NHS; Bus Club; UCLA; Bus.

MANCINI, ANDREA; Lakewood HS; Lakewood, CA; (4); Art Clb; Cmnty Wkr; Science Clb; Speech Tm; Teachers Aide; Drill Tm; Stage Crew; Yrbk; Rep Frsh Cls; Rep Soph Cls; High Hnrs Grad; LBCC.

MANCUSO, MICHAEL J; Chino HS; Chino, CA; (3); Science Clb; Spanish Clb; Teachers Aide; Hon Roll; Comp Sci.

MANDAC, JANIS BEE; East Union HS; Lathrop, CA; (3); 4/315; JA; Letterman Clb; Sec Science Clb; SADD; Var L Vllybl; Cit Awd; High Hon Roll; Prfct Atten Awd; Nor-Cal Jr Statesmn Conf 88-89; Asian Clb VP 89-90; Stanford U; Ped.

MANDAC, LELANI R; San Pedro HS; San Pedro, CA; (2); Cmnty Wkr; Drama Clb; Letterman Clb; Pep Clb; Drill Tm; Orch; School Musical; Pres Soph Cls; Capt Cheerldng; Future Leaders Of San Pedro.

MANDEL, BRYAN; Los Alamitos HS; Los Alamitos, CA; (3); Intnl Clb; Letterman Clb; Model UN; Science Clb; Spanish Clb; Teachers Aide; Varsity Clb; Rep Stu Cncl; JV Bsktbl; Var Capt Tennis; Ecology Club; UCLA; Invest Bnkg.

MANDEL, DAN A; Esperanza HS; Yorba Linda, CA; (3); Intnl Clb; Temple Yth Grp; Var Swmmng; Wt Lftg; High Hon Roll; Hon Roll; NHS; Gldn St Exam Geom Hgh Hnrs; Bus Admin.

MANDEL, SELINA S; Torrance HS; Torrance, CA; (2); JV Socr; JV Trk; JV Vllybl; Hon Roll.

MANDELL, JASON; San Dieguito HS; Cardiff, CA; (2); SADD; Jazz Band; Phtg Yrbk; Safe Rides Comm Of Pblcty; Outstndng Acad Achvt Prac Arts; Prncpls Awd For Svc.

MANDEVILLE, AMY C; Bret Harte Union HS; Murphys, CA; (2); Church Yth Grp; Drama Clb; SADD; School Musical; School Play; Stage Crew; Hon Roll; Friday Nite Live Membrshp Chm; Stu Dir Drama Prod; UCSB; Film Dir.

MANDIGO, KRISTINA I; John Muir HS; Altadena, CA; (2); Orch; Marchng Band Pagntry; Mrchng Dynmcs Drum Circuit; Lit Arts.

MANDRELL, STACY; Chowchilla Union HS; Chowchilla, CA; (4); 21/114; Church Yth Grp; Letterman Clb; Band; Jazz Band; Mrchg Band; Pep Band; JV Bsktbl; JV Var Sftbl; High Hon Roll; John Philip Sousa Awd; Sftbl Coachs Awd 3 Yrs; Outstndng Band Jr; Merced Coll; Aviation.

MANDRY, MICHAEL D; Rubidoux HS; Riverside, CA; (4); JA; Teachers Aide; Var Golf; Electrcn.

MANDT, ANDREA S; Antioch SR HS; Antioch, CA; (4); 34/582; French Clb; Spanish Clb; Varsity Clb; JV Sftbl; JV Var Swmmng; Var Tennis; JV Vllybl; High Hon Roll; Hon Roll; Pres Acad Fit Awd; Soc Women Engr Merit Hnr; USS Kiska Schlrshp; Most Imprvd Swmr; CSU; Elect Engr.

MANDT, GAYLE E; Antioch HS; Antioch, CA; (2); 141/721; Cmnty Wkr; Letterman Clb; Spanish Clb; Ed Nwsp; Sec Frsh Cls; Sec VP Soph Cls; Pres Jr Cls; Tennis; Hon Roll; Pres Acad Fit Awd; Am Leg Awd 89; Stu Mentor 88-89; CA Schlrshp Fedrtn 90; Nrsng.

MANEESUT, SAREENA; San Fernando HS; N Hollywood, CA; (2); Key Clb; High Hon Roll; Hon Roll; UCSD; Doctor.

MANES, MARGARET S; The Bishops Schl; San Diego, CA; (3); Church Yth Grp; Cmnty Wkr; Latin Clb; Varsity Clb; Var Crs Cntry; Var Socr; Var Swmmng; Var Trk; Kiwanis Awd; Painting; Jewelry Making; Piano.

MANES, NATHAN P; Athenian Schl; Brentwood, CA; (3); Cmnty Wkr; Hosp Aide; Var Swmmng; 200 Hr Clb Awd; Cb Sct, Comp Rm Vlntr; Gntcs.

MANES, TAMMIE L; Marysville HS; Marysville, CA; (3); 3/160; Off Soph Cls; Treas Jr Cls; Stat Swmmng; Cit Awd; High Hon Roll; Hon Roll; Jr NHS; Lion Awd; Prfct Atten Awd; Rotary Awd; CSF; Fri Night Live Pres; U Of Santa Barbara; Ed.

MANESE, MARIE C; Aquinas HS; Highland, CA; (2); Church Yth Grp; Church Choir; Sec Frsh Cls; Cheerldng; High Hon Roll; Hon Roll; USC; Corp Law.

MANESS, STACY L; March Mountain HS; Moreno Valley, CA; (3); Computer Clb; Drama Clb; Office Aide; Chorus; Comp Pgmmg.

MANETTA, KATY; Foothill HS; Santa Ana, CA; (3); Cmnty Wkr; Debate Tm; Chorus; Stage Crew; JV Fld Hcky; High Hon Roll; Hon Roll; Acad Excllnc Awd Goldenst Exam Geo With Hnrs.

MANETTI, XHANA C; El Molino HS; Guerneville, CA; (4); Art Clb; Computer Clb; Drama Clb; FFA; JA; Teachers Aide; Acpl Chr; Chorus; Color Guard; Drill Tm; San Francisco Cnsrvtry Music.

MANFREDI, KENNETH J; Rio Americano HS; Sacramento, CA; (3); 62/288; Pres Frsh Cls; JV Var Bsbl; JV Var Bsktbl; All Lg Bsktbl; Hnbl Mntn All City Bsktbl; Phys Ed.

MANFREDI, TASHA A; Madera HS; Madera, CA; (2); 4-H; Swmmng; 4-H Awd; Hon Roll; Rotary Awd; UC Davis; Vet Sch.

MANFUT, KISSEL E; International Studies Acad; San Francisco, CA; (4); Teachers Aide; High Hon Roll; San Francisco ST U; Astrophysc.

MANGACCAT, JENNIFER A; James Logan HS; Union City, CA; (3); Church Yth Grp; Powder Puff Ftbl; Hon Roll; Nrsng.

MANGAHAS, ANA CECILIA O; South San Francisco HS; San Bruno, CA; (2); Drama Clb; Sec French Clb; School Musical; School Play; Sec Soph Cls; French Hon Soc; Hon Roll; Amnesty Intl; Asian-Amer Club; Exploring Psts BSA; Art Hist.

MANGANDI, CHRIS S; Burbank SR HS; Burbank, CA; (2); French Clb; School Musical; School Play; Swing Chorus; Variety Show; Pres Frsh Cls; Bsktbl; Ftbl; Trk; Cit Awd; Med.

MANGINDIN, ANGELICA P; Mt Pleasant HS; San Jose, CA; (3); Math Clb; Acpl Chr; Band; Var Swmmng; Hon Roll; NHS; CSF; Sing For Mt Pleasant Jazz Singers Rcgnzd No 1 In Nation By Downbeat Mag; UC Davis; Psych.

MANGINI, ELIZABETH A; Notre Dame HS; Redwood City, CA; (2); Church Yth Grp; Debate Tm; Hosp Aide; Teachers Aide; School Musical; Rptr Nwsp; Pres Soph Cls; Var Cheerldng; JV Swmmng; NEDT Awd; Bus.

MANGINI, KELLIE L; Lodi HS; Stockton, CA; (2); Pres Church Yth Grp; Cmnty Wkr; Acpl Chr; Hon Roll; Erly Mnrng LDS Semnry; Pacific U; Music.

MANGIONA, AIMEE N; Palos Verdes HS; Palos Verdes Est, CA; (2); Church Yth Grp; German Clb; Rptr Nwsp; Rep Frsh Cls; Rep Soph Cls; Score Keeper; Vllybl; Pres Acad Fit Awd; JR Catholic Daughters Of Ameicas; Tutoring Handicapped Chldrn; Loyola Marymount U.

MANGOLD, JENNIFER L; Diamond Bar HS; Walnut, CA; (3); SADD; Acpl Chr; Chorus; Variety Show; Vocal Jazz Choir; Ed.

MANGRUM, LEANNE M; Fortuna Union HS; Scotia, CA; (3); 20/169; SADD; Ed Yrbk; NHS; CSF; Alg Stu Mth; Yth Edctr/Drgs, Alchl; U Of OR; Intr Dsgn.

MANGUM, DEBORAH; Southwest HS; San Diego, CA; (3); #3 In Class; Key Clb; Drill Tm; Cit Awd; High Hon Roll; Pres Acad Fit Awd; Explr Scts & Pan Asian Clb & CSF; Sci.

MANGUM, TANYA; Palo Verde Valley HS; Blythe, CA; (4); 14/154; Drama Clb; Pep Clb; Teachers Aide; Stage Crew; Yrbk; Treas Sr Cls; Cheerldng; Mgr(s); Sftbl; Vllybl; S Clb Pres; CSF; Asst Mgr Popeyes; Stanislaus ST U.

MANIALUNG, ALLAN S; Grant Union HS; Sacramento, CA; (3); Art Clb; FFA; Intnl Clb; Band; Jazz Band; Mrchg Band.

MANIES, LAURA; Lowell HS; San Francisco, CA; (3); Band; Orch; Var Gym; Mst Insprtnl Awd Novice Girls Team Rowng; Israeli Alliance & Adventres Alliance Clbs; Temple Yth Grp.

MANIFOLD, JENNIFER; Berean Christian HS; Concord, CA; (3); 7/70; Church Yth Grp; French Clb; Office Aide; Teachers Aide; Temple Yth Grp; Stat Var Bsktbl; Var Cheerldng; Sftbl; JV Vllybl; High Hon Roll; CSF; Outstndng Engl Awd; Westmont; Political Sci.

MANIGO, TYESHA; Garey HS; Pomona, CA; (3); Church Yth Grp; JA; Pep Clb; Off Jr Cls; Stu Cncl; Bsktbl; Cheerldng; MESA; Black Stu Union VP; Clark U.

MANIO, SHEILA M; Mater Dei HS; Anaheim, CA; (3); Spanish Clb; Var Bsktbl; Hon Roll; Pro Life; Cal Poly Pomona; Engr.

MANION, KRISTI L; Cordova SR HS; Rancho Cordova, CA; (3); Pep Clb; Science Clb; Pres Frsh Cls; JV Bsktbl; Var Socr; Wt Lftg; Hon Roll; Acad Achvt Weight Trng; Frnsc Sci.

MANION, RANDY J; Tustin HS; Tustin, CA; (2); Cmnty Wkr; JA; Var Ftbl; Var Wt Lftg; JV Wrstlng; Cit Awd; Hon Roll; NEDT Awd; Pres Acad Fit Awd; Stanford U; Corp Law.

MANISAP, SOMPHONE S; Highlands HS; Sacramento, CA; (2); French Hon Soc; High Hon Roll; Hon Roll; Compostn Awd; Prncpls Hnr Roll; U Of CA Irvine; Med.

MANISCALCO, RACHEL; George Washington HS; San Francisco, CA; (2); Var JV Mgr(s); Var Sftbl; JV Swmmng; Bus Comp Acad; Law Enfrcmnt.

MANIT, EDDY C; Serra HS; Redwood City, CA; (2); 1/208; Church Yth Grp; German Clb; JA; Math Clb; Ski Clb; Intrml Sftbl; JV Tennis; High Hon Roll; CSF; JSA; Stanford U; Chem Engr.

MANITTA, CHRISTINE; Oakmont HS; Roseville, CA; (1); Math Tm; JV Socr; Hon Roll; Acadmc Tlnt Srch; Asilomar Organ Comptn; Engrng.

MANIVONE, AMONEXAY; San Pasqual HS; Escondido, CA; (2); French Clb; Comp Sci.

MANJAL, SUKHBIR S; Alisal HS; Salinas, CA; (4); 6/262; French Clb; Science Clb; Cit Awd; High Hon Roll; Prfct Atten Awd; Pres Acad Fit Awd; UC David; Bio.

MANJRA, ZAREEN; Gharr HS; Cerritos, CA; (1).

MANK, ROBERT; John F Kennedy HS; Sacramento, CA; (4); VP AFS; Ed Yrbk; Rep Frsh Cls; VP Pres Soph Cls; VP Pres Jr Cls; Pres Sr Cls; VP Stu Cncl; Var JV Socr; Hon Roll; Opt Clb Awd; Rugby Tm Cptn, Treas & All City; Grnd Rnnr Up Sci Fair; AFS Exch Stu Greece; U OR; Arch.

MANKARIOUS, MICHAEL; Brea-Olinda HS; Brea, CA; (3); 35/292; Cmnty Wkr; Service Clb; Swmmng; Wt Lftg; Interact Clb Cert Svc Awd; Athltc Awd Swmmng; Goldn St Exm Awd CA Legsltre; Secy/Treas CSF; Elec Engrng.

MANKARIOUS, PETER A; Santa Monica HS; Santa Monica, CA; (1); Hon Roll; Prfct Atten Awd; Acad Decathlon; Delians; Amer HS Math Exam; Doctor.

MANKOTIA, PANKAJ; Abraham Lincoln HS; San Francisco, CA; (3); Art Clb; Aud/Vis; Computer Clb; SADD; Chorus; High Hon Roll; Outstndng Stu Awd-PAL; Outdoor Pioneer Awd; Outstndng Ldrshp.

MANKOTIA, SHRUTI; Abraham Lincoln HS; San Francisco, CA; (2); Girl Scts; Teachers Aide; Stage Crew; High Hon Roll; Prfct Atten Awd; Outstndng Service Awd; Outstndng Acadmc Achvt Awd; Abraham Lincoln; Sci.

MANLAPAZ, MARIEL; Lincoln HS; Stockton, CA; (3); 1/592; Cmnty Wkr; FBLA; Hosp Aide; Key Clb; Latin Clb; Mu Alpha Theta; Office Aide; Spanish Clb; SADD; Lit Mag; Med.

MANLEY, AARON T; Los Amigos HS; Fountain Valley, CA; (4); German Clb; Key Clb; Science Clb; Intrml Crs Cntry; JV Var Golf; Hon Roll; CA Soc CPAS Schlrshp; USC; Acctng.

MANLEY, KIMBERLY; Antelope Valley HS; Rosamond, CA; (4); JA; Treas Acpl Chr; Chorus; Swing Chorus; Hon Roll; Pres Acad Fit Awd; Antelope Valley CC; Fshn Mrch.

MANLEY, LOGAN P; Valley HS; Sacramento, CA; (1); Boy Scts; FBLA; FFA; Red Cross Aide; Swmmng; Hon Roll; Most Imprvd Swmmng; Greenhand FFA; Swine Prdctn; Humboldt ST U; Forestry.

MANLEY, TARA; Dana Hills HS; Sumter, SC; (1); Church Yth Grp; Flag Corp; Stage Crew; Davis Coll CA; Vet.

MANLEY, THOMAS N; Anderson Union HS; Redding, CA; (4); 8/200; Church Yth Grp; FCA; Teachers Aide; Crs Cntry; Cit Awd; Hon Roll; Pres Acad Fit Awd; Voice Dem Awd; Liscensed Bicycling Racer USCF; CSF Life; Golden St Schlr-Geom & Alg; U CA Davis; Bio Sci.

MANN, ANNE N; Casa Grande HS; Petaluma, CA; (4); French Clb; German Clb; Science Clb; Ski Clb; Teachers Aide; Yrbk; Hon Roll; NHS; Ntl Merit Ltr; Pres Acad Fit Awd; U Of CA Santa Cruz; Marine Bio.

MANN, BRIAN J; Escondido Union HS; Escondido, CA; (1); Church Yth Grp; Socr; JV Vllybl; Prfct Atten Awd; U CA SB.

MANN, DEREK; Newport Harbor HS; Newport Beach, CA; (2); 6/313; AFS; Sec VP Jr Cls; Tennis; CSF.

MANN, ERIC W; Elliot Pope Preparatory Schl; Yucca Valley, CA; (4); 11/70; U Of CA, Riverside; Comp Sci.

MANN, ERIK LIVINGSTON; Benicia HS; Benicia, CA; (4); 3/243; Church Yth Grp; Computer Clb; Service Clb; SADD; High Hon Roll; Hon Roll; Lion Awd; NHS; Prfct Atten Awd; Pres Acad Fit Awd; Benicia Sea Scts; Young Lfe Mem; Bank Of Amer Achvmnt Awd Comp Sci; Gldn Sst Exm Awd In Algbra; CA ST U; Comp Sci.

MANN, JESSICA; Westlake HS; Westlake Village, CA; (4); 23/435; VP JA; VP Stu Cncl; L Var Cheerldng; Hon Roll; NHS; Pres Acad Fit Awd; Dance; CSF; Student Senate; UCSB; Psych.

MANN, LINDA S; Amercian Christian Acad; Anderson, CA; (2); 1/3; Church Yth Grp; School Play; Stage Crew; Pres Frsh Cls; Pres Soph Cls; L Var Bsktbl; Score Keeper; Var L Vllybl; Snack Bar Asst; Shasta Coll.

MANN, MARIA; Mark Keppel HS; Monterey Park, CA; (2); Spanish Clb; Drill Tm; Cit Awd; Hon Roll.

MANN, MATTHEW H; Sherman E Burroughs HS; Ridgecrest, CA; (3); 42/425; Art Clb; Church Yth Grp; Cmnty Wkr; Spanish Clb; Teachers Aide; Rep Nwsp; VP Soph Cls; VP Sr Cls; Rep Stu Cncl; Bsktbl; CJSF Pres; James Monroe Jr Schl Prncpls Acad Excllnc & Ldrshp Awd; Mntr Stu Wrkng Engrng Dept; UC Davis; Arch.

MANN, NIKKI; Tustin HS; Tustin, CA; (2); Church Yth Grp; Debate Tm; Band; Jazz Band; Mrchg Band; Orch; Pep Band; Off Jr Cls; Cit Awd; High Hon Roll; CSF; UC Irvne; Psych.

MANN, RUPINDER; Grace M Davis HS; Modesto, CA; (3); Sec AFS; Hosp Aide; Math Tm; VP Science Clb; VP Spanish Clb; SADD; High Hon Roll; Ucla; Math.

MANN, SARA A; American Christian Acad; Anderson, CA; (4); 1/8; Church Yth Grp; Teachers Aide; School Play; Pres Jr Cls; Pres Sr Cls; Capt L Bsktbl; Capt L Vllybl; Cit Awd; DAR Awd; Val; Simpson Coll; Elem Educ.

MANN, TERRY P; Sunny Hills HS; Fullerton, CA; (2); 5/450; Intnl Clb; Pres Soph Cls; VP Jr Cls; Var L Bsktbl; JV Ftbl; Var L Trk; High Hon Roll; NHS; Rotary Awd; Outstndng Soph Stu Awd, Citizenship Awd; All Freeway Leag Bsktbl Tm; Law.

MANNAN, MELISSA Y; Napa HS; Napa, CA; (1); Trk; Psych.

MANNARD, ERICA J; San Luis Obispo SR HS; San Luis Obispo, CA; (2); 29/150; Church Yth Grp; Intnl Clb; Ski Clb; Stage Crew; Var Swmmng; Hon Roll; CSF; Law.

MANNEH, BASEM N; Balboa HS; San Francisco, CA; (2); Aud/Vis; Cmnty Wkr; Library Aide; Office Aide; Teachers Aide; Varsity Clb; Stage Crew; Off Soph Cls; Stu Cncl; Bsktbl; Schl, Cmnty Ldrshp; SFSU; Poli Sci.

MANNING, ANDREW E; Orange HS; Orange, CA; (4); Church Yth Grp; FCA; Math Clb; Model UN; Acpl Chr; School Musical; Rptr Nwsp; VP Frsh Cls; VP Capt Ftbl; Var Wt Lftg; Southern Methodist U; Intl Law.

MANNING, BILL W; Temecula Valley HS; Temecula, CA; (2); Church Yth Grp; Office Aide; U CA Davis; Vet Med.

MANNING, HEATHER M; Los Gatos HS; Los Gatos, CA; (4); 48/374; JV Trk; Hon Roll; Ntl Merit SF; After Schl Job For 2 Yrs; Active Outside Schl In Areas Of Dance & Horseback Rdng; Zoology.

MANNING, JASON M; Vacaville SR HS; Vacaville, CA; (3); Chess Clb; Cmnty Wkr; French Clb; Key Clb; SADD; Teachers Aide; Hon Roll; Prfct Atten Awd; Voice Dem Awd; Soroptomist Clb-VP; U CA-DAVIS; Med.

MANNING, JEREMY D; South HS; Bakersfield, CA; (3); Hon Roll; Mobile Oil Excl Club; Gldn St Exam Acad Excl Awd-Geom With Honors; Engrng.

MANNING, JONAH B; Huntington Beach HS; Huntington Beach, CA; (2); Model UN; VP Jr Cls; Intrml Socr; Intrml JV Tennis; Hon Roll; Pres Acad Fit Awd; JR Statesmen Of Amer; UC Davis; Engrng.

MANNING, MANDY; Christian Life HS; Fortuna, CA; (3); 1/6; Church Yth Grp; Church Choir; Yrbk; Pres Jr Cls; Hon Roll; Pres Acad Fit Awd; Elem Ed.

MANNING, MARK L; Vacaville HS; Vacaville, CA; (4); 13/560; Boy Scts; Church Yth Grp; Band; Jazz Band; Orch; Pep Band; School Musical; Mgr Bsktbl; High Hon Roll; Pres Acad Fit Awd; Christ Coll; Math.

MANNING, MELISSA J; Alameda HS; Alameda, CA; (4); Ski Clb; Spanish Clb; School Play; Ed Lit Mag; Rep Jr Cls; Stu Cncl; JV Swmmng; JV Vllybl; High Hon Roll; Bud Brnch; Bicnntnl Constituional Comptn Tm Ldr; U Of CA San Diego; Law.

MANNING, NIKKI; Tustin HS; Tustin, CA; (2); Rep Frsh Cls; Var L Socr; Var L Trk; Sccr Mst Imprvd & All League Hnrb Mntn; San Diego ST.

MANNING, PAUL MATTHEW; John A Rowland HS; Rowland Hts, CA; (4); 131/558; VP Aud/Vis; Boy Scts; French Clb; Science Clb; Rep Stu Cncl; Hon Roll; Prfct Atten Awd; 2nd Pl Intl Flm Fstvl; The Bill Scott Awd; Bank Of Amer Awd-Art; CA ST U; Radio.

MANNING, SHANNON M; Bakersfield HS; Bakersfield, CA; (3); 51/718; Sec Church Yth Grp; Key Clb; Teachers Aide; Sec Band; Mrchg Band; Orch; Rep Sr Cls; Var Crs Cntry; Var Powder Puff Ftbl; Var Trk; Mock Trial; CSF.

MANNING, SHEILA; Corona HS; Corona, CA; (4); 6/484; Church Yth Grp; Mrchg Band; Orch; Bsktbl; Swmmng; High Hon Roll; Pres Acad Fit Awd; Val; Sndry Schl Tchr; Lfgrd, Swim Instr; U Of CA Davis; Spnsh.

MANNION, BRACKEN; Christian Brothers HS; Sacramento, CA; (2); Church Yth Grp; German Clb; Math Tm; High Hon Roll; CSF; Brigham Young U.

MANNION, THOMAS J; San Rafael HS; San Rafael, CA; (2); Key Clb; Jazz Band; JV Bsbl; JV Capt Bsktbl; JV Ftbl; High Hon Roll; CSF; Schlr Athl Awd; U Of CA; Coaching.

MANNS, JOHN; South HS; Bakersfield, CA; (4); Wt Lftg; Engrng.

MANNY, DESIREE; Eisenhower HS; Rialto, CA; (2); Letterman Clb; Flag Corp; Var Trk; JV Vllybl; Hon Roll; USC; Chirprctr.

MANOLOS, JOHN ZUNG; Walnut HS; Walnut, CA; (3); FBLA; Trk; Hon Roll; Cal Poly Pomona; Eng.

MANONGDO-LLAMAS, CHIARA MAY; South San Francisco HS; South San Francis, CA; (4); Drama Clb; JA; Office Aide; Spanish Clb; Chorus; School Musical; School Play; Stage Crew; High Hon Roll; Hm Ec Stu Mnth Dec & Yr 87-88; Bus Mgmt.

MANOPHINIVES, TANAYOOS; St Bernard HS; Los Angeles, CA; (3); JV Var Ftbl; UCLA; Eng.

MANOUK, KHOURIN; Hoover HS; Fresno, CA; (1); French Clb; Math Clb; Ski Clb; Rptr Nwsp; JV Ftbl; Var JV Socr; JV Swmmng; JV Vllybl; Fashn Desgn.

MANOUS, CYNTHIA JEAN; Pius X HS; Lynwood, CA; (4); Drama Clb; Capt Flag Corp; School Play; Sec Frsh Cls; Sec Sr Cls; High Hon Roll; NHS; Church Yth Grp; Red Cross Aide; Band; CA Schlrshp Fed; Prom Qn 90; Voice Of Democracy Essay Cont Wnnr; UCLA; Engl.

MANOUX, CHRISTINE; San Marcos HS; Santa Barbara, CA; (2); School Musical; Yrbk; JV Capt Cheerldng; Hon Roll; St Schlr.

MANRING, SHANNON M; James Logan HS; Union City, CA; (3); Teachers Aide; Band; Mrchg Band; Hon Roll; Prfct Atten Awd; Music; Nrs.

MANRIQUEZ, BERTHA; Hueneme HS; Port Hueneme, CA; (2); Mrchg Band; L Socr; JV Soccer MVP; UCSB; Comp.

MANRIQUEZ, JANETH E; Castle Park HS; Chula Vista, CA; (3); French Clb; VP MECHA Club; MECHA Club Award; SDSU; Psychology Or Bus Admin.

MANSEL, DOUGLAS; Berean Christian HS; Alamo, CA; (4); 1/70; High Hon Roll; Hon Roll; Pres Acad Fit Awd; Val; CSF; Bnk America Achvt Awd Math/Sci; Tandy Technlgy Schlr; Distngshd Christian HS Stu Acad/Ldrshp; UC Berkeley; Aviation.

MANSFIELD, CHARLES; Canyon HS; Canyon Country, CA; (1); Pres Letterman Clb; SADD; School Play; Bsktbl; Crs Cntry; Trk; Cit Awd; Prfct Atten Awd; U Of NV Los Vegas; Comp.

MANSFIELD, DANIEL N; Poway HS; San Diego, CA; (4); 47/730; Varsity Clb; Var Lcrss; High Hon Roll; Kiwanis Awd; NHS; CSF; U Of CA.

MANSINI, JENNIFER S; Novato HS; Novato, CA; (3); Church Yth Grp; Key Clb; Teachers Aide; Band; Mrchg Band; Capt Var Cheerldng; JV Pom Pon; JV Socr; Hon Roll; Lfgrd.

MANSKE, NOEL R; Irvine HS; Irvine, CA; (2); Church Yth Grp; Debate Tm; Office Aide; Speech Tm; Intrml Swmmng; Activist For Poltcl Awrnss; Spur Awd; Christ Coll-Irvine; Poly Sci.

MANSKER, ROBERT L; Del Campo HS; Citrus Heights, CA; (3); 76/446; FBLA; Office Aide; Spanish Clb; Crs Cntry; Trk; CA ST U Sacramento; Intl Bus.

MANSMITH, MICHAEL J; San Benito HS; San Juan Batsta, CA; (3); Church Yth Grp; 4-H; JV Bsktbl; Var Ftbl; Wt Lftg; 4-H Awd; Hon Roll; VP Mansmith Entrprses; Bus.

MANSOLINO, DAVID M; Villa Park HS; Villa Park, CA; (2); Church Yth Grp; JV Bsbl; Var L Bsktbl; Hon Roll; NHS; CSF; Guitar; Envrmntl Sci.

MANSON, CARLA D; Mojave HS; California City, CA; (2); High Hon Roll; Attorney.

MANSOUR, ASMA A; Leuzinger HS; Gardena, CA; (3); Art Clb; Treas French Clb; Science Clb; Cit Awd; Hon Roll; APPI Membrshp Awd; Stu Of Yr Awd; CSF; Cmmty Svc Awd; Cal-Tech; Engrng.

MANSOURI, SHIDEH; Palisades HS; Los Angeles, CA; (3); VP Cmnty Wkr; JA; Library Aide; Math Clb; Math Tm; Service Clb; Yrbk; Rep Stu Cncl; Crs Cntry; High Hon Roll; Mrksmn Hnr Scty Treas; Piano; RAND Dist Schlr; UCLA; Med.

MANSUBI, SHERWIN P; Bellarmine HS; Saratoga, CA; (3); Cmnty Wkr; Debate Tm; NFL; Speech Tm; Stat Bsktbl; JV Trk; Physician.

MANTEUFFEL, MISCHA; University HS; Marina Del Rey, CA; (4); Art Clb; Santa Monica Collfgraphic Arts.

MANTYLA, CARL J; Troy HS; Yorba Linda, CA; (2); 79/230; Drama Clb; German Clb; Wt Lftg; Wrstlng; Hon Roll; Water Actvts; Pepperdine; Law.

MANTZ, KIM; Livermore HS; Livermore, CA; (1); 28/427; Pres 4-H; Co-Capt Cheerldng; Score Keeper; 4-H Awd; High Hon Roll; Hon Roll; Project Alert.

MANUEL, ALICIA L; Hilltop HS; Chula Vista, CA; (2); Dance Clb; SADD; Drill Tm; Crs Cntry; Cit Awd; Hon Roll; Pres Acad Fit Awd; U Santa Barbara; Fshn Bus.

MANUEL, EUGENE M; La Canada HS; La Canada Flintri, CA; (3); 129/250; Pres Band; Pres Mrchg Band; Jrnlsm.

MANUEL, EZRA L; Bret Harte Union HS; Angels Camp, CA; (2); FHA; Var Socr; JV Tennis; Hon Roll; Friday Night Live; Voc Olympics; Humboldt ST U; Forest Rcrtn.

MANUEL, LEILANI S; San Gorgonio HS; San Bernardino, CA; (3); Church Yth Grp; Computer Clb; Gym; Powder Puff Ftbl; Sftbl; Var Trk; Indstrl Engrng.

MANUEL, MISTY C; Pasadena HS; Pasadena, CA; (2); Debate Tm; Drama Clb; French Clb; GAA; Pep Clb; Speech Tm; Sec Acpl Chr; Pres Chorus; School Musical; School Play; Asian-Amer Clb, Pres; Bus.

MANUEL, ROMMEL A; Eagle Rock HS; Los Angeles, CA; (3); VP Intnl Clb; Jazz Band; Mrchg Band; Off Jr Cls; Hist Sr Cls; Intrml Bsktbl; Var Capt Cheerldng; Mgr(s); Score Keeper; Intrml Trk; Outstndng Solo Awd 88-89; USC; Music.

MANUEL, TANEIA D; Ganesha HS; Pomona, CA; (3); Off Jr Cls; JV Cheerldng; Var Trk; Hon Roll; Active Member MESA Program; Active Member Early Outreach Program; Chosen As Coronet For Grad & Baccl; Medicine/Obstetrician/Gyn.

MANUKAY, ROSALYNE MERIDITH; St Bernard HS; Los Angeles, CA; (3); Church Yth Grp; Cmnty Wkr; Drama Clb; Hosp Aide; Library Aide; Service Clb; Speech Tm; Teachers Aide; Thesps; Varsity Clb; HOBY Conf; Outstndng Achvt Schl Svc; Outstndng Achvt Theatre; U Of La Verne; Lawyer.

MANUS, JOSHUA E; Delta HS; West Sacramento, CA; (2); FBLA; SADD; JV Ftbl; Hon Roll; Comp Prgmng.

MANVILLE, ADAM; Ocean View HS; Huntington Beach, CA; (2); Boy Scts; Church Yth Grp; Ftbl; Wrstlng.

MANZANILLA, RHODORA; James Lick HS; San Jose, CA; (3); #2 In Class; Sec Church Yth Grp; Cmnty Wkr; Church Choir; Sec Frsh Cls; Sec Soph Cls; VP Jr Cls; Sec Stu Cncl; High Hon Roll; Hon Roll; NHS; CA Schlrshp Fed; VAR Badminton Tm; Asian Club Sec; UC Berkley; Optometrty.

MANZANO, LUIS A; Borrego Springs HS; Borrego Springs, CA; (1); Art Clb; Latin Clb; Spanish Clb; School Musical; Bsbl; Police Acad.

MANZANO, NATALIE; East Bakersfield HS; Bakersfield, CA; (2); Church Yth Grp; Cmnty Wkr; Varsity Clb; Key Clb; Office Aide; SADD; Teachers Aide; Chorus; Hon Roll; Bakersfield Coll; Phy.

MANZANO, VIRGINIO JOSE; Fresno Adventist Acad; Fresno, CA; (3); 3/23; Church Yth Grp; Off Jr Cls; Socr; Trk; Cit Awd; NHS; ASB Secy.

MANZO, EDUARDO; Saddleback HS; Santa Ana, CA; (1); FBLA; Bsktbl; Tennis; Fresh Bsktbl Coachs Awd; Kiwanis Bowl; CA Schlrshp Fed; Bus.

MANZO, ELIZABETH; David Starr Jordan HS; Long Beach, CA; (4); Am Leg Aux Girls St; Key Clb; Teachers Aide; Cit Awd; Hon Roll; Prfct Atten Awd; Cert Rcgntn Shrthnd Awd; Acad Ltr Awd; Cal ST U Long Bch; Mdcn.

MANZO, HEATHER; Clovis HS; Clovis, CA; (3); SADD; Kings River CC; Kindrgdn Tchr.

MANZO, MARTHA L; Sonoma Valley HS; Sonoma, CA; (1); AFS; Santa Barbara U; Cmptr Pgmmng.

MANZO, VERONICA; Southwest HS; San Diego, CA; (2); Teachers Aide; Prfct Atten Awd; Chrldrs For Sccr; Southwestern Coll.

MANZOLI, VICKI C; Loretto HS; Roseville, CA; (3); 2/50; Intnl Clb; Service Clb; Ed Nwsp; Hon Roll; NEDT Awd; Mock Triam Tm; CSF; Cultural Pursuits; Corrspndnt For Sidetracks; Sons Of Italy Lodge.

MANZON, FRANCHESCA; March Mountain HS; Mountain Home, ID; (4); GAA; Stu Cncl; Var Sftbl; Var Vllybl; High Hon Roll; Manch AFB Teen Ldrshp Rep; Outstndng Teen Rep Strategic Air Cmmnd; Teen Mthr; Stenogrphr.

MAO, ANNE A; Mater Dei HS; Fountain Valley, CA; (3); French Clb; JCL; Latin Clb; NHS; UCLA; Bus.

MAO, VINCENT K; Cerritos HS; Cerritos, CA; (1); JCL; Science Clb; Wt Lftg; UCLA; Vet.

MAPALO, FRANCESCA L; San Benito HS; Hollister, CA; (1); 69/464; Church Yth Grp; Cmnty Wkr; FCA; GAA; JA; Key Clb; Pep Clb; Ski Clb; Cheerldng; Vllybl.

MAPANAO, MARITES D; Escondido HS; Escondido, CA; (1); Band; Chorus; Mrchg Band; French Hon Soc; Hon Roll; Prfct Atten Awd; Am Musical Fdtn Band Honors; Directors Awd; Med.

MAPEL, AMY K; Mira Mesa HS; San Diego, CA; (3); Church Yth Grp; Cmnty Wkr; Key Clb; Chorus; Color Guard; Yrbk; Cit Awd; High Hon Roll; Hon Roll; Pres Acad Fit Awd; Intl Bus.

MAPES, KATHERINE E; Brawley Union HS; Brawley, CA; (3); AFS; Church Yth Grp; SADD; Church Choir; Rptr Nwsp; High Hon Roll; Water Skiing; Horseback Riding; Chrch Drama Grp; Liberal Arts.

MAPLES, MANDY; North HS; Vacaville, CA; (2); French Clb; Hosp Aide; Math Clb; Office Aide; Ski Clb; Teachers Aide; Acpl Chr; Swing Chorus; Nwsp; Hon Roll; Pianst; CSF; UC Davis; Sci.

MAPLES, MICHELE A; Moor Park HS; Moorpark, CA; (3); Drill Tm; Flag Corp; Off Sr Cls; Drftng.

MAPSON, ANGELA M; Lowell HS; San Francisco, CA; (2); SADD; Band; Hon Roll; Big Bros & Sisters Org.

MAQPUSAO, MECHELE C; Armijo HS; Fairfield, CA; (2); Church Yth Grp; Hon Roll; Jr NHS; NHS; Pres Acad Fit Awd; Fil-Am Clb; Asian-Amer Clb VP; Pacific Islndrs Assn Sec; UC Davis; Dermtlgy.

MAQUIRE, CHRISTINE M; Los Gatos HS; Los Gatos, CA; (3); Art Clb; Service Clb; Hon Roll; Envrnmntl Clubs & Actvts; Pltcl Sci.

MAR, CHRISTINE; Bishop O'dowd HS; Piedmont, CA; (2); Cmnty Wkr; Ski Clb; Sec Frsh Cls; High Hon Roll.

MAR, DAVID D; John F Kennedy HS; Los Angeles, CA; (3); Church Yth Grp; FTA; Math Clb; Teachers Aide; Intrml Bsktbl; Cit Awd; Hon Roll; Prfct Atten Awd; Math Awd Algbr II 2nd Pl JFK Math Meet; JFK Math Tutor Awd 90; UCLA; Engr.

MAR, DAVID T; Fremont HS; Sunnyvale, CA; (3); 1/387; Debate Tm; NFL; Bausch & Lomb Sci Awd; NHS; Ntl Merit Ltr; Opt Clb Awd; Founded Envrnmntl Clb Pres; German I,II & III; Bio AP,Phys & Drftng I Awds; CSF.

MAR, GLENN KEVIN; Sunset HS; Hayward, CA; (4); 4/193; Treas Am Leg Boys St; Cmnty Wkr; Ski Clb; Treas Frsh Cls; Treas Soph Cls; Treas Jr Cls; Treas Sr Cls; JV Var Tennis; Vllybl; Army Schlr/Athlete Awd; Hayward Firefghtrs Athlete Schlrshp; CSF-LIFE Mem; CA ST U-Hayward; Bus Admin.

MAR, GLORIA; Schurr HS; Montebello, CA; (4); 17/580; Chess Clb; Church Yth Grp; Cmnty Wkr; French Clb; Hosp Aide; Sec Intnl Clb; Spanish Clb; SADD; High Hon Roll; Prfct Atten Awd; Cal Tech Inst Sci Prgm; CSF Life-Time; U Of Southern CA.

MAR, KENFORD T; Hoover HS; San Diego, CA; (3); FBLA; Math Clb; Office Aide; Science Clb; Cit Awd; NHS; Pres Acad Fit Awd; Hnrs Goldn St Exm Alg; Hgh Hnr Goldn St Exm Geom.

MARA- COE, SHEILA L; River City HS; W Sacramento, CA; (2); Debate Tm; French Clb; Key Clb; SADD; Cit Awd; French Hon Soc; Frnch Outstndng Achvt Awd; Corporate Lawyer.

MARAMBA, WENDY C; Sweetwater Union HS; National City, CA; (4); 2/396; Church Yth Grp; Cmnty Wkr; Intnl Clb; Science Clb; Ed Yrbk; Tennis; Trk; High Hon Roll; Rotary Awd; Assoc Stu Bdy; Soclgy.

MARANDA, TOM P; Saint Josephs HS; Santa Maria, CA; (3); Church Yth Grp; Debate Tm; Red Cross Aide; Color Guard; JV Golf; Civil Air Patrol-Staff Sgt; Aerospace Engrng.

MARANTAL, EMMANUEL S; St Ignatius College Prep; San Francisco, CA; (3); Church Yth Grp; Cmnty Wkr; Crs Cntry; CSF; Asian Stu Coaltn; Med.

MARASCO, STEVE R; Covina HS; Covina, CA; (4); 25/235; Pres Band; Pres Jazz Band; Pres Mrchg Band; Hon Roll; John Philip Sousa Awd; Band Booster Schrlshp; Dirs Awd Mst Insprtnl Sr; Citrus Coll; Music Bus.

MARASHIAN, JULIANNE R; Bullard HS; Fresno, CA; (1); French Clb; Key Clb; Off Frsh Cls; High Hon Roll; Pres Acad Fit Awd; Bio.

MARASIGAN, FRANK R; Elk Grove HS; Elk Grove, CA; (3); 8/548; Cmnty Wkr; Jazz Band; Mrchg Band; Orch; Var Tennis; Gov Hon Prg Awd; Ntl Merit Ltr; Asian-Pacific Islndr Clb Treas; Mabuay Leo Cmmnty Clb Srgnt At Arms; CSF; Aerosp Engrng.

MARASSE, DONALD R; Mojave HS; Cantil, CA; (1); Boy Scts; Spanish Clb; SADD; Teachers Aide; Chorus; School Musical; School Play; Stage Crew; Yrbk; Trk; Loyala Marymount U; Engr.

MARAVILLA, MIRNA J; Garfield HS; Los Angeles, CA; (3); Chorus; Cit Awd; Prfct Atten Awd; Census 90 Awd; Tchr.

MARAVILLA, VICTORIO A; Skyline HS; Oakland, CA; (2); Latin Clb; Spanish Clb.

MARBELLO, MAY CONCEPCION; Marian Catholic HS; San Diego, CA; (4); 10/100; Am Leg Aux Girls St; Pres Drama Clb; Capt Speech Tm; Church Choir; Capt Var Cheerldng; Var JV Socr; Opt Clb Awd; Church Yth Grp; French Clb; NFL; Miss Southbay Filipino Amer Cmmnty San Diego 89; San Diegos Yng Woman Yr 90; Bank Amer Plq Awd 90; Fordham U; Jrnlsm.

MARBLESTONE, KAREN; Antioch HS; Oakley, CA; (4); Treas Spanish Clb; Letterman Clb; JV Diving; Jr NHS; Pres Schlr; Golden St Awd Alg & Geom; U Of CA Irvine; Bio.

MARC, RACHEL; Valley Christian HS; San Jose, CA; (3); Church Yth Grp; French Clb; Orch; School Musical; School Play; Sftbl; Hon Roll; CSF.

MARCANO, MICHELLE L; West Covina HS; W Covina, CA; (3); Art Clb; Church Yth Grp; Drama Clb; SADD; School Play; Stage Crew; Law Tchr.

MARCARIO, KIM M; Colton HS; Colton, CA; (3); FFA; Teachers Aide; Hon Roll; Ofcr FFA Scrty & Hstrn; Prncpls Hnr Rll; Chptr Frmr Dgree FFA; Cal Poly Pomona; Ag Bus.

MARCEL, J R; Bellarmine Coll Prep; Pleasanton, CA; (3); Drama Clb; Speech Tm; School Musical; School Play; Stage Crew; Variety Show; L Cheerldng.

MARCELENO, ANA L; Herbert Hoover HS; San Diego, CA; (4); Cmnty Wkr; Teachers Aide; Hon Roll; NHS.

MARCELES, HERNANDO M; Yucaipa HS; Yucaipa, CA; (1); Crs Cntry; Hon Roll; Pres Acad Fit Awd; Arch.

MARCELIN, ALEXANDER D; Serra HS; Los Angeles, CA; (3); 10/65; Church Yth Grp; Dance Clb; JA; Letterman Clb; Varsity Clb; VP Frsh Cls; VP Soph Cls; VP Jr Cls; JV Bsbl; Var Bsktbl; Bus.

MARCELO, FLORABEL V; Galileo HS; San Francisco, CA; (2); Church Yth Grp; Pep Clb; Church Choir; School Musical; Lit Mag; Off Soph Cls; Cheerldng; Cit Awd; Hon Roll; San Francisco State U; Nurse.

MARCHAIS, VALERIE; Santa Clara HS; Oxnard, CA; (3); Library Aide; Office Aide; Pep Clb; Chorus; Hon Roll; Compu Literacy Awd; Consumer Math Awd; RN.

MARCHAND, TARA R; Casa Roble Fundamental HS; Citrus Heights, CA; (4); Am Leg Aux Girls St; French Clb; Teachers Aide; High Hon Roll; Hon Roll; NHS; Ntl Merit SF; Co-Fndr/Pres Stdnt Bttr Future/Interact; Outstndng Engl Stdnt; CSF; Outstng Hist Stdnt; U CA Davis; Psych.

MARCHESE, JENNIFER; Villa Park HS; Orange, CA; (4); Art Clb; Church Yth Grp; French Clb; Pep Clb; Ed Nwsp; Hon Roll; Amnesty Intl Villa Park Chapt Pres; Cuesta Coll; Jrnlsm.

MARCHESI, GIANCARLO V; Armijo HS; Fairfield, CA; (1); Socr; Wrstlng; Hon Roll; Med.

MARCHETTI, BRIAN ANDREW; La Jolla HS; La Jolla, CA; (4); Church Yth Grp; Intnl Clb; Service Clb; Band; School Play; JV Ftbl; JV Trk; Savannah Coll Art/Dsgn Schlrshp; Cal Poly Ponoma; Urban Planning.

MARCHIANO, JASON; Colton HS; Grand Terrace, CA; (2); Boy Scts; Church Yth Grp; Letterman Clb; Var Socr; Hon Roll; Jr NHS; NHS; Water Polo Vrsty Co-Capt; Eagle Sct; Optometry.

MARCHILLO, LISA N; Summerville HS; Twain Harte, CA; (3); Dance Clb; Drama Clb; French Clb; Library Aide; Ski Clb; Chorus; Swing Chorus; Hon Roll; Long Beach ST; Jrnlsm.

MARCHMAN, LEVEL S; So Bay Lutheran HS; Los Angeles, CA; (3); Var Bsktbl; High Hon Roll; UNLV; Comps.

MARCIAL, MARIETA T; Salinas HS; Salinas, CA; (3); JV Cheerldng; Hon Roll; Job Experience Retail Sales J C Penneys; Christian Catholic Dev; San Jose ST; Nrsg.

MARCIONE, NICOLE A; Rim Of The World HS; Cedar Glen, CA; (1); 1/473; Art Clb; Spanish Clb; Sftbl; High Hon Roll; Hon Roll; CSF; Chiro.

MARCONI, ABBIE; Florin HS; Sacramento, CA; (2); 100/800; Church Yth Grp; Drama Clb; German Clb; Girl Scts; Key Clb; SADD; Drill Tm; Pres Stu Cncl; JV Cheerldng; Var Trk; Stanford U; Lwyr.

MARCONNET, JENNIFER L; Hayward HS; Hayward, CA; (2); 34/237; Church Yth Grp; Chorus; Hon Roll.

MARCOTTE, LISA K; Yuba City HS; Yuba City, CA; (4); Church Yth Grp; Key Clb; Ski Clb; SADD; Varsity Clb; Phtg Yrbk; Swmmng; Hon Roll; Wmns Vrsty Ath Soc; Mary Aaron Schlrshp; Yuba Coll; Bus.

MARCOTTE, MARIALENA; Redondo Union HS; Redondo Bch, CA; (2); Drama Clb; Spanish Clb; Teachers Aide; JV Crs Cntry; Var Socr; High Hon Roll; Hon Roll; Amnsty Intl Clb; Envrnmntl Stds.

MARCOTTE, TRACEE J; Paraclete HS; Lancaster, CA; (3); GAA; Powder Puff Ftbl; Var Capt Sftbl; Hon Roll; Sci Awd 90.

MARCOTTE, WILLIE C; Mission Viejo HS; Mission Viejo, CA; (3); 25/430; Treas French Clb; Spanish Clb; School Musical; High Hon Roll; Prfct Atten Awd; Metric Assn; Math.

MARCOUX, SIONAINN; Foothill HS; Orange, CA; (4); 16/346; Cmnty Wkr; Red Cross Aide; Var Capt Swmmng; High Hon Roll; Acadmc All Amer & All Amer Swmmng; Math Tutor; Stanford U.

MARCOVSKY, DAVID S; Downtown Business Magnet HS; Burbank, CA; (2); Aud/Vis; Computer Clb; Hosp Aide; Teachers Aide; Nwsp; Yrbk; VP Frsh Cls; Stat Bsktbl; JV Var Score Keeper; Stat Sftbl; UCLA; Comp Cnsltnt.

MARCUM, CORYNN M; Del Campo HS; Fair Oaks, CA; (3); 7/449; Church Yth Grp; Cmnty Wkr; Ed Nwsp; Stu Cncl; Var Stat Ftbl; JV Socr; Var Tennis; NHS; Ntl Merit Ltr; Pres Acad Fit Awd; Stu Govt Svc Awd; Stu Rchng Out; Stu Advsry Cncl Chm; Hlth.

MARCUS, BENJAMIN L; El Camino Real HS; Woodland Hills, CA; (2); SADD; Hon Roll; Hse Of Rep 89; Ted Wittenberg Cup; All Around Swmmr 89; Sr Swmmng Awd 89.

MARCUS, DARLA FAITH; Glendale HS; Glendale, CA; (2); Church Yth Grp; Drama Clb; Office Aide; Service Clb; Drill Tm; School Play; VP Stu Cncl; Cit Awd; Hon Roll; Photo.

MARCY, DAVID A; Silver Valley HS; Daggett, CA; (3); Aud/Vis; Chess Clb; FFA; Wt Lftg; Hon Roll; FFA Mrt Awd; Minstry.

MARCY, NATHAN R; El Camino HS; Oceanside, CA; (2); Yrbk; Pres Jr Cls; JV Socr; Var Swmmng; Cit Awd; Hon Roll; Wildcat Wnnr; Pepperdine U; Telecommnctns.

MARES, ANN; Chester HS; Chester, CA; (4); Letterman Clb; Science Clb; Spanish Clb; Varsity Clb; Chorus; L Var Gym; Sr Proj Clss Chairmn; Prncpl Hnr Roll; Rgnl Occuptn Pgm; Nrsng.

MARES, GABRIEL; Chino HS; Chino, CA; (2); JV Bsktbl; Govt.

MARGALITH, TAL; Torrey Pines HS; Solana Beach, CA; (2); Var JV Swmmng; Hon Roll; CSF; Spc Sci.

MARGETTA, KIM; Coast Union HS; San Simeon, CA; (4); AFS; Church Yth Grp; Drama Clb; FBLA; Office Aide; Chorus; Sec Jr Cls; Crs Cntry; Var Sftbl; Hon Roll; Cuesta Coll; Spcl Ed.

MARGETTS, HEATHER; Chula Vista SR HS; Chula Vista, CA; (3); 12/535; Church Yth Grp; Cmnty Wkr; Pep Clb; Yrbk; Pres Frsh Cls; Pres Soph Cls; VP Sr Cls; Stu Cncl; JV Var Cheerldng; Var Trk; The Amer Lgn Cert Of Schl Awd Post 434; VFW Of US Awd Hnr; Attnd Wrld Affrs Smr U Of WI Whitewater; Psych.

MARGILETH, JEFF D; Tustin HS; Santa Ana, CA; (1); 11/466; Boy Scts; Math Tm; Pres Speech Tm; Crs Cntry; Trk; Hon Roll; Judo Blue Belt; Orange Cty Acad Dcthln Frosh Team 5th Cty; Harvey Mudd; Eng.

MARGOSIAN, GABRIEL J; Venice HS; Los Angeles, CA; (2); Wt Lftg; Hon Roll; Achvt Awd Ind Arts; CA Jr Schlrshp Fed; Marksmen Hnr Roll Soc; Prncpls Awd; W Los Angeles CC; Engr.

MARGULIS, STEVEN A; San Diego HS; San Diego, CA; (3); 5/415; Quiz Bowl; Science Clb; Var L Tennis; High Hon Roll; Pres Acad Fit Awd; Hgh Hnrs Gldn St Exam Geo; Arch.

MARIA, KATIE; Notre Dame HS; San Jose, CA; (3); 6/90; Church Yth Grp; Drama Clb; Hosp Aide; Treas Science Clb; Service Clb; SADD; Capt Varsity Clb; Var Capt Vllybl; High Hon Roll; NHS; CSF Tutor Undrclsmn; CA St Plytch; Aero Engr.

MARIANI, MOLLY L; Saint Francis HS; Los Altos, CA; (1); 85/400; Cmnty Wkr; Dance Clb; GAA; SADD; JV Socr; Stat Vllybl; Hon Roll; Outstndng 1st Yr Artist; Bus.

MARIANI, NANCY A; St Francis HS; Los Altos, CA; (3); 88/290; Service Clb; SADD; Var Mgr(s); JV Powder Puff Ftbl; Intrml JV Vllybl; High Hon Roll; Hon Roll; Natl Charity Leag.

MARIANO, CLARIBEN; Southwest HS; San Diego, CA; (2); #1 In Class; Intnl Clb; Key Clb; Letterman Clb; Model UN; Scholastic Bowl; SADD; Stu Cncl; Mgr(s); Socr; Tennis; CSF; Sci Olympd; Peace Clb; Bus Mgmt.

MARIANO, EDWARD R; St Vincent HS; Petaluma, CA; (3); 1/60; Aud/Vis; Pres Debate Tm; NFL; Pres Speech Tm; Rep Stu Cncl; Var Tennis; Bausch & Lomb Sci Awd; Cit Awd; Elks Awd; High Hon Roll; Natl Span Exam Awds Lvl 1 3rd In US & Lvl 2 4th In US; Lvl 3 Ust In US Natl Span Exam; Med.

MARIANO, MICHELLE B; Andrew P Hill HS; San Jose, CA; (3); 1/445; Cmnty Wkr; FBLA; Math Tm; VP SADD; Treas Sr Cls; JV Var Vllybl; High Hon Roll; Pres NHS; Vrsty Badminton; CSF; Bus Info Systems.

MARIANO, MICHELLE M; Dowell HS; San Francisco, CA; (2); Hosp Aide; Library Aide; Office Aide; SADD; Hon Roll; MESA; Kermesse Clb; Svc Prjct Soph Clss; UCSF; Nrs.

MARIANO, RHEA G; St Joseph HS; Bellflower, CA; (2); Drama Clb; Hosp Aide; Science Clb; Spanish Clb; SADD; High Hon Roll; NEDT Awd.

MARIANO, ROSE M; Bridgemont HS; South San Francis, CA; (3); Yrbk; Ed Lit Mag; Pres Soph Cls; VP Stu Cncl; Var Intrml Bsktbl; Intrml Var Vllybl; High Hon Roll; Hon Roll; NHS; Rotary Awd; U Of CA; Accntng.

MARICHALAR, JOSEPH D; Cupertino HS; Santa Clara, CA; (2); Church Yth Grp; Letterman Clb; Ed Nwsp; Var Crs Cntry; JV Trk; Spanish NHS.

MARIETTA, PETER; Trabuco Hills HS; Mission Viejo, CA; (1); Church Yth Grp; Thesps; JV Bsktbl; JV Trk; Hon Roll; Acad Decathlon; U CA; Lit.

MARIFAT, YAMA; Washington HS; Fremont, CA; (3); 25/330; Cmnty Wkr; German Clb; Quiz Bowl; Scholastic Bowl; Bsktbl; Gov Hon Prg Awd; High Hon Roll; Hon Roll; Prfct Atten Awd; Pres Acad Fit Awd; CSF; Berkeley; Pre-Med.

MARIN, BEATRIZ; Moreno Valley HS; Moreno Vly, CA; (3); 87/520; Treas French Clb; Science Clb; Spanish Clb; Rotary Awd; Dentist.

MARIN, CARLOS A; Los Amigos HS; Santa Ana, CA; (3); Band; Jazz Band; Mrchg Band; Orch; Pep Band; Swmmng; Hon Roll.

MARIN, HAROLD J; Fontana HS; Fontana, CA; (2); Hon Roll; Jr NHS; Air Force; Psych.

MARIN, MARIA A; Gladstone HS; Azusa, CA; (3); Var Cheerldng; Hon Roll; Mesa Clb; Comp.

MARIN, MARIA LORETO; North Monterey County HS; Salinas, CA; (3); FBLA; SADD; Rep Soph Cls; JV Bsktbl; JV Crs Cntry; Hartnell Coll; Arch.

MARIN, MONIQUE M; La Puente HS; La Puente, CA; (3); Yrbk; Cit Awd; Hon Roll; Badminton; ROP; Vet.

MARIN, PAULA R; Garfield HS; Los Angeles, CA; (3); Church Yth Grp; Office Aide; Var Crs Cntry; Var Trk; Cit Awd; Prfct Atten Awd; Schlr Athlete Awd 89; Mst Dedicated Runner 89; Fash Dsgnr.

MARIN, PETER; Las Lomas HS; Walnut Creek, CA; (3); Art Clb; Spanish Clb; Acpl Chr; Chorus; School Play; Stage Crew; Variety Show; Off Frsh Cls; Stu Cncl; Socr; Graphic Dsgn.

MARIN, SANDRA; Bellarmine Jefferson HS; North Hollywood, CA; (2); Church Yth Grp; Hon Roll.

MARIN, STEVEN F; Hesperia HS; Hesperia, CA; (3); Boy Scts; Cmnty Wkr; ROTC; High Hon Roll; CA Poly Pomona; Art.

MARINAS, LARISA TRINA; Liberty Baptist HS; San Jose, CA; (4); Church Yth Grp; Cmnty Wkr; Red Cross Aide; Church Choir; School Musical; VP Stu Cncl; Capt Cheerldng; Score Keeper; Capt Sftbl; Vllybl; Hmcmng, Prm Cmmtte; Ms TEEN Cntst; San Francisco Inst Of Dsgn.

MARINERO, OSCAR ALEXIS; Hamilton HS Academy Of Music; North Hollywood, CA; (2); Chess Clb; Debate Tm; French Clb; Math Tm; Jazz Band; Orch; School Play; Pres Soph Cls; Trk; Hon Roll; CSF; Hamilton Music Acad; High Hnrs Achvmnt Awd Fldn ST Exam; Harvard U; Poli Sci.

MARINESCU, MICHELLE; El Toro HS; Lake Forest, CA; (3); Church Yth Grp; Dance Clb; Drama Clb; French Clb; Intnl Clb; Chorus; Church Choir; School Play; Variety Show; High Hon Roll; Intrct Clb; Grls Leg; Mock Trl 90-91; Bus.

MARINEZ, DAVID; Los Altos HS; Industry, CA; (3); 53/370; Cmnty Wkr; Key Clb; Science Clb; Hon Roll; Prfct Atten Awd; UCLA; Medcl.

MARINEZ, DAVID A; Rowland HS; Rowland Hts, CA; (2); Church Yth Grp; JV Ftbl; JV Socr; JV Wt Lftg; Hon Roll; Prfct Atten Awd; Bus Mgmt.

MARINI, ASHLIE M; Gompers Secondary Schl; San Diego, CA; (1); 1/413; Cmnty Wkr; Girl Scts; Var Crs Cntry; Hon Roll; Jr NHS; Prfct Atten Awd; Pres Acad Fit Awd; Russian Clb.

MARINO, ANTHONY; Paraclete HS; Lancaster, CA; (3); Key Clb; Letterman Clb; JV Var Socr; High Hon Roll; Hon Roll; Prfct Atten Awd; CA Schlrshp Fed; Bus.

MARINO, JON; Mater Dei HS; Fountain Valley, CA; (3); School Musical; School Play; Pres Stu Cncl; JV Capt Ftbl; Mem Of CA Schlrshp Fed; Mem Campus Yth Chrstn Mnstry; Eng Lit.

MARINO, KIMBERLY; Granada HS; Livermore, CA; (3); 44/278; Dance Clb; Letterman Clb; Ski Clb; Teachers Aide; Ed Nwsp; Var JV Cheerldng; JV Diving; Gym; Var Trk; High Hon Roll; Cmpfr Cnslr; Chrldr Coach; Chllng Day; Chrldng Amer Fnlst; Hygnst.

MARINO, MORGAN L; Newport Harbor HS; Palm Desert, CA; (2); Church Yth Grp; Cmnty Wkr; Drama Clb; Girl Scts; Hosp Aide; Drill Tm; Pep Clb; Red Cross Aide; Ski Clb; Teachers Aide; Debutantes; Mtls & Awds For Trck Races; Bus.

MARINO, NAYIBE Z; Saddleback HS; Santa Ana, CA; (3); Pep Clb; Science Clb; Spanish Clb; SADD; Rep Stu Cncl; Var Capt Tennis; Hon Roll; ESL Stu Mth, Pres; MANA Orange Cnty; Acad Awd.

MARINO, ZACHARY A; Vacaville HS; Vacaville, CA; (4); 94/562; Cmnty Wkr; Library Aide; Quiz Bowl; SADD; Stu Cncl; Ftbl; Golf; Mgr(s); Wt Lftg; Cit Awd; Stu Schl Brd; U Of Chicago; Hstry.

MARION, CHRISTOPHER; Benicia HS; Benicia, CA; (4); 46/240; Math Clb; SADD; JV Var Socr; JV Var Wt Lftg; High Hon Roll; Hon Roll; JETS Awd; Pres Acad Fit Awd; Achvt Awd Benicia Ycht Clb 87-89; Cmnty Bt Sfty; US Cst Grd Axlry; US Pwr Sqdrns; CA Polytech U; Engrng.

MARIS, OTHA S; El Dorado HS; Placerville, CA; (2); Math Tm; JV Crs Cntry; JV Trk; High Hon Roll; Prfct Atten Awd; Outstndng Math Stu Awd 89-90; Gold Seal Golden St Exm.

MARISA, PEREZ L; St Joseph HS; Cerritos, CA; (2); Church Yth Grp; Debate Tm; Drama Clb; JA; Ski Clb; Pres Soph Cls; Off Jr Cls; Stu Cncl; Crs Cntry; Hon Roll; UCLA; Nws Brdcstng.

MARISCAL, LUIS A; Alisal HS; Salinas, CA; (3); Cmnty Wkr; FBLA; Math Tm; Var Bsktbl; Var Capt Golf; Score Keeper; Cit Awd; Hon Roll; Prfct Atten Awd; Calculus Awd; CSF; Us Acad Decathlon; Comp Engr.

MARJI, REEMA; Central Union HS; El Centro, CA; (1); Hon Roll; Kiwanis Awd; Pres Acad Fit Awd; UCLA; Child Psych.

MARK, KAREN; John Marshall HS; Los Angeles, CA; (4); 5/675; Cmnty Wkr; VP French Clb; Sec NFL; Rep Stu Cncl; NHS; Pres Acad Fit Awd; Acad Decthln Mst Dsrvng Mem; Bank Amer Achvt Awd Sci; Centry III Ldrs Pgm Alt; U Of WA; Aerntcs.

MARKARIAN, THOMAS F; Sherman E Burroughs HS; Ridgecrest, CA; (3); 5/350; Pep Clb; Spanish Clb; Varsity Clb; Ed Nwsp; JV Bsktbl; Var Golf; Var Tennis; High Hon Roll; NHS; Pres Acad Fit Awd; Amer Lgn Sch Awd; 1st Pl Rgnl Sci & Engrng Fair; Athletic Hnr Roll; CA ST U Fresno; Elec Engrng.

MARKEY, JENNIFER; Nevada Union HS; Rough And Ready, CA; (2); Sec Soph Cls; Rep Stu Cncl; Friday Night Live; Child Psych.

MARKHAM, BETH; Redwood HS; Visalia, CA; (2); Church Yth Grp; Drama Clb; German Clb; Thesps; School Play; Rptr Nwsp; High Hon Roll; NHS; Acad Ltr; CSF; Sequoias Coll; Library Sci.

MARKHAM, CATHY J; Presentation HS; San Jose, CA; (4); 6/137; Art Clb; Spanish Clb; SADD; Nwsp; Lit Mag; Ntl Merit Ltr; Pres Acad Fit Awd; CSF; Robert C Byrd Schlrshp; U C Davis Cal Aggie Alumni Schlrshp; U C Davis; Writer.

MARKMAN, GREGORY W; Miraleste HS; Rolling Hls Ests, CA; (3); Cmnty Wkr; Key Clb; Model UN; Ski Clb; Spanish Clb; SADD; Stu Cncl; Capt Var Golf; Hon Roll; U Of Southern CA; Med.

MARKMAN, JACOB; J E Mc Ateer HS; San Francisco, CA; (2); VA U Gftd Smmr Enrchmnt; Hnrs Prgm Engl, Bio & Geom.

MARKO, RICHARD; Agoura HS; Westlake Vill, CA; (4); 66/442; Var Capt Bsktbl; Hon Roll.

MARKS, CHRISTAL DAWN; Tehachapi HS; Tehachapi, CA; (2); Church Yth Grp; Dance Clb; Drama Clb; Pep Clb; SADD; Teachers Aide; School Play; Mgr Stage Crew; Variety Show; Ed Yrbk; Prod Asstnt Tv Movie AFI; Asst Dir Two Cmmnty Prods; UCLA; Perf Arts.

MARKS, CRAIG S; Bellarmine College Prep; San Jose, CA; (3); 10/300; Debate Tm; NFL; Service Clb; Speech Tm; Teachers Aide; Temple Yth Grp; School Play; Ntl Merit Ltr; Opt Clb Awd; Outstndng Yth Of San Jose Mayors Awd 90; St Ambssdr To USSR 89; Schl Theatre Arts Dept Bus Mgr.

MARKS, JEFF A; San Bernardino HS; San Bernardino, CA; (3); Var Bsbl; Var Ftbl; Mst Outstndg Athlete; Acctg.

MARKS, KAI L; Nevada Union HS; Penn Valley, CA; (2); 4-H; School Play; 4-H Awd; High Hon Roll; Friday Night Live Clb Drug & Alcohol Prvtn; Spec Olympics Gold Mdlst.

MARKS, KRISTY A; San Gorgonio HS; San Bernardino, CA; (3); Cmnty Wkr; Ski Clb; Spanish Clb; Varsity Clb; Yrbk; JV Var Socr; JV Var Tennis; Hon Roll; NHS; Doctor.

MARKS, SANDRA R; Artesia HS; Cerritos, CA; (2); Dance Clb; Office Aide; School Musical; Score Keeper; Hon Roll; Pet Asst Leag; Pepperdine; Law.

MARKUSSEN, REBECKA LYNN; Hemet HS; Midway City, CA; (4); Office Aide; Teachers Aide; Var Bsktbl; Var Powder Puff Ftbl; Score Keeper; Var Sftbl; Wt Lftg; Long Beach ST; Air Force.

MARKWALD, DANIELLE M; Edison HS; Huntington Beach, CA; (2); JV Sftbl.

MARKWORT, JEROMY; Morro Bay HS; Los Osos, CA; (1); Aud/Vis; Church Yth Grp; Letterman Clb; Spanish Clb; Varsity Clb; Bsktbl; Cheerldng; Score Keeper; Hon Roll; San Luis Obisbo Bsktbl Cmp Bst Dfnsv Plyr 89; Mock Rock Cmptn Var Awds; Cuesta Tech; Electrncs.

MARKWYN, ABIGAIL M; Montgomery HS; Santa Rosa, CA; (3); 1/450; Church Yth Grp; French Clb; Girl Scts; Church Choir; Yrbk; Var L Swmmng; Cit Awd; High Hon Roll; Jr NHS; Pres Acad Fit Awd; Harvard Bk Awd; CA Schlstc Fed; Swim Tm, Mst Vlbl Swmmr 89 & 90.

MARLATT, ANGEL J; Hesperia HS; Hesperia, CA; (3); Drama Clb; Office Aide; Spanish Clb; Teachers Aide; Thesps; School Musical; School Play; Stage Crew; Variety Show; JV Bsktbl; Coll; Psycholoty.

MARLATT, JENNIFER T; Norte Vista HS; Riverside, CA; (1); Letterman Clb; Varsity Clb; Var Swmmng; High Hon Roll; Hon Roll; Marine Bio.

MARLEAU, PETER A; Manteca HS; Manteca, CA; (2); 8/420; SADD; Cit Awd; High Hon Roll; Prfct Atten Awd; Pres Acad Fit Awd; Pres Schlr; Outstndng Math Stu Cert; Outstndng Spnsh Stu Awd; UCLA; Film & Special Effects.

MARLETTE, BRIAN T; Oak Ridge HS; El Dorado Hills, CA; (2); 59/290; Band; Pep Band; Var L Ftbl; JV Trk; Var Wt Lftg; Var L Wrstlng; Hon Roll.

MARLEY, JEREMY P; Livermore HS; Livermore, CA; (2); 36/415; Boy Scts; Church Yth Grp; Drama Clb; Latin Clb; Orch; School Musical; High Hon Roll; Pres Acad Fit Awd; Cum Laude, Maxima Cum Laud Ntn Ltn Exm 89 & 90; Diablo Yth Symphny Orch; UC Santa Cruz; Marine Bio.

MARLIN, APRIL; Escalon HS; Escalon, CA; (3); 4-H; Bsktbl; Cheerldng; Sftbl; Trk; Vllybl; 4-H Awd; Hon Roll; Pres Acad Fit Awd; Life Guard Cerif; Teach Handicap Children To Swim; SR Yr 1/2 Day Modesto JR Coll; Business.

MARLIN, PASCHA; Santa Rosa HS; Santa Rosa, CA; (3); Math Tm; Acpl Chr; Orch; School Musical; Yrbk; Hist Sr Cls; Var L Swmmng; High Hon Roll; Opt Clb Awd; Pres Acad Fit Awd; Marthin Luther King Jr Spch Cntst 1st Pl Sch, 1st Rnnr-Up Cty; Stu For Soc Rspnsblty Secy, Publcty; Genetic Rsrch.

MARLOW, JEFFREY K; Poway HS; Poway, CA; (1); Church Yth Grp; Band; Mrchg Band; High Hon Roll; Stu Recgntn Awd.

MARLOW, PAUL A; Lutheran H S Of Orange County; Corona, CA; (2); Boy Scts; Church Yth Grp; JV Ftbl; Boy Scout Of The Yr 90.

MARLOW, RENEE; Poway HS; Poway, CA; (3); Church Yth Grp; Band; Jazz Band; Mrchg Band; JV Bsktbl; JV Swmmng; High Hon Roll; NHS.

MARLOW, SCOTT A; Turlock HS; Turlock, CA; (2); 81/400.

MARMITO, JEFFERY L; Bonita Vista HS; Chula Vista, CA; (3); Cmnty Wkr; Hosp Aide; Pep Clb; JV Capt Ftbl; JV Trk; Hon Roll; Med.

MARMOLEJO, PATRICK H; Don Bosco HS; Maywood, CA; (3); JV Bsbl; Mr Salazar Printing Schlrshp Awd; GATF Printing Awd; Grphc Cmmnctns.

MARMON, S M; Cate Schl; Los Angeles, CA; (4); Dance Clb; School Musical; School Play; Variety Show; Socr; Trk; Ntl Merit Ltr; Resdntl Advsr Dormtry & Peer Cnsclr; Chem.

MARNATI, TAMMERA; Bloomington HS; Fontana, CA; (4); Office Aide; Capt Bsktbl; Powder Puff Ftbl; Sftbl; Phillips Coll; Travel Agnt.

MAROOT, MICHELLE ANN; Bullard HS; Fresno, CA; (3); Sec Church Yth Grp; Teachers Aide; VP Band; Mrchg Band; Pep Band; Ed Yrbk; Rep Stu Cncl; Bsktbl; Photo Jrnlsm.

MAROTO, DORIS Y; Saint Joseph HS; Lakewood, CA; (2); Library Aide; Hon Roll; Prfct Atten Awd; Cert Of Achvt Spanish III 89-90; Vet.

MAROUSEK, KEVIN P; Corona SR HS; Corona, CA; (2); Church Yth Grp; Debate Tm; Drama Clb; Office Aide; Speech Tm; School Play; Stage Crew; Nwsp; Lit Mag; Pres Acad Fit Awd; CA Mock Trial; UNLV; Hotel Mgmt.

MAROVICH, JACKIE L; Coronado HS; Coronado, CA; (4); 52/142; Cmnty Wkr; Pres French Clb; Hosp Aide; Intnl Clb; Model UN; Service Clb; Teachers Aide; Flag Corp; School Play; Var Sftbl; U Of San Diego.

MARPLE, TERRI L; Valhalla HS; El Cajon, CA; (1); Church Yth Grp; Flag Corp; Bsktbl; U TN; Pedtrcn.

MARQUES, JEANETTE M; Notre Dame HS; Menlo Park, CA; (3); School Play; Ed Yrbk; Lit Mag; Var Trk; High Hon Roll; Hon Roll; Libary Clb; Mst Outstndng Art 88; Hstss Clb; Campus Ministry; Poetry Cont Wnnr; UC Santa Cruz; Art.

MARQUESS, KEVIN D; El Camino Fundamental HS; Sacramento, CA; (3); Chess Clb; Computer Clb; Latin Clb; Math Clb; Science Clb; Band; Cit Awd; Hon Roll; NHS; St Schlr; Sci Olympd Team Plcd 3rd In ST; Friday Night Line VP; Bio Engr.

MARQUETTE, MICHELE D; Strathmore HS; Lindsay, CA; (3); 8/85; SADD; Teachers Aide; Stage Crew; Ed Nwsp; Ed Yrbk; Lit Mag; Rep Frsh Cls; Rep Soph Cls; VP Jr Cls; Var Tennis; 2 Yrs Prfct 4.0 GPA Plq Wnnr; Outstndg Stu Awd Span,Engl,Wrld Hist & US Hist; SADD Rep Cnty; Envrnmntl Sci.

MARQUETTE, RENE; Granada HS; Alameda, CA; (4); French Clb; Var Socr; Vllybl; Jnr Olympc Tryouts CO; Wstrn Rgnl Sccr Trnmn NM; All Con Sccr Tm; Mst Outstndng Awd Sccr; Regis Coll; Socialogy.

MARQUEZ, ADRAIN B; Adison Computech HS; Fresno, CA; (1); Church Yth Grp; Dance Clb; FCA; Band; Drm Mjr(t); Jazz Band; Mrchg Band; Orch; Pep Band; Tennis; AZ Indian Rsrvtns Mission Work; UCLA; Med.

MARQUEZ, ANAFE; San Gabriel Acad; Glendora, CA; (2); Church Yth Grp; Library Aide; Teachers Aide; Orch; Nwsp; Off Soph Cls; Ftbl; Sftbl; Swmmng; Vllybl; Art,Music & Flgbll; Med.

MARQUEZ, APRIL J; Garfield HS; Los Angeles, CA; (2); Law.

MARQUEZ, BERNABE; Kingsburg HS; Kingsburg, CA; (3); ROTC; Engine Prfrmnc.

MARQUEZ, ELIZABETH; Castle Park HS; Chula Vista, CA; (1); French Clb; Yrbk; Off Soph Cls; Cit Awd; Ballet Folkorico; Southwestern Coll; Cmptr Prgm.

MARQUEZ, ERNESTO; Artesia HS; Hawaiian Gardens, CA; (3); 1/30; Art Clb; Cmnty Wkr; Spanish Clb; Varsity Clb; Bsbl; Ftbl; Socr; Hon Roll; GATE Pgm; Cal ST Long Beach; Mdcn.

MARQUEZ, ESPERANZA; James Lick HS; San Jose, CA; (4); 53/257; Church Yth Grp; Cmnty Wkr; Sec Treas Intnl Clb; Sec Band; Church Choir; Mrchg Band; Pep Band; JV Bsktbl; Hon Roll; Natl Hnr Roll; JV V Badminton; Wntr Grd Co-Cptn; San Jose ST U; Nrsng.

MARQUEZ, ESTELLA; St Monica Catholic HS; Santa Monica, CA; (2); Spanish Clb; Sftbl; Sftbl Coach Awd; 2nd Hnrs; Key Clb Treas; Lwyr.

MARQUEZ, FABIOLA; San Gabriel Mission HS; Los Angeles, CA; (2); 13/124; Drama Clb; GAA; Letterman Clb; Varsity Clb; JV Capt Bsktbl; Var Gym; Var Mgr(s); Var Sftbl; JV Vllybl; Hon Roll; ITESM; Med.

MARQUEZ, FRANCES M; Rubidoux HS; Mira Loma, CA; (4); Spanish Clb; Hon Roll; Prfct Atten Awd; RCC; Dentistry.

MARQUEZ, FRANK H; Bishop Amat Memorial HS; Covina, CA; (2); JV Bsktbl; Dance.

MARQUEZ, JACKIE; Saint Monica HS; Santa Monica, CA; (2); Pres Sec Key Clb; Spanish Clb; JV Sftbl; Hon Roll; NHS; CSF; Coachs Awd; Physician.

MARQUEZ, JENNIFER S; Westmoor HS; Daly City, CA; (3); Church Yth Grp; Sec Drama Clb; VP German Clb; Model UN; School Play; Stage Crew; Rep Jr Cls; Rep Sr Cls; Hon Roll; People To People Yth Sci Exch Schlrshp To Travel USSR; Intl Thespian Soc Hnr Thespian Awd; Med.

MARQUEZ, JONATHAN; Sierra Vista HS; Baldwin Park, CA; (2); Chess Clb; Band; Mrchg Band; JV Var Wrstlng; Hon Roll; Concert/Symphonic Band; Percussion Ensemble.

MARQUEZ, LAWRENCE; Don Bosco Tech Inst; Walnut, CA; (3); NEDT Awd; Prin Lst.

MARQUEZ, LORENA; Edison HS; Fresno, CA; (2); FBLA; Hon Roll; MECHA; Lions Clb; UC-BERKELEY; Bus.

MARQUEZ, LUZ MARIA; St Genevieve HS; Van Nuys, CA; (2); Church Yth Grp; Hon Roll; CA Schlrshp Fed; Latin Natl Ex; Play The Piano; CA ST U Northridge; Teacher.

MARQUEZ, LYDIA; Baldwin Park HS; Valinda, CA; (4); 4/400; Key Clb; Science Clb; Spanish Clb; Ed Lit Mag; Treas Soph Cls; JV Fld Hcky; Var Tennis; High Hon Roll; NHS; Prfct Atten Awd; Gldn ST Exam Hnrs Algbr; Yale Book Awd; Vrsty Bdmntn; Pre Law.

MARQUEZ, MARC T; Woodland HS; Woodland, CA; (3); Wrstlng; NHS; Prfct Atten Awd; MESA Mem; Acctg.

MARQUEZ, MARIA; Kingsburg HS; Kingsburg, CA; (2); Teacher.

MARQUEZ, MARIBEL; Castle Park HS; Chula Vista, CA; (1); French Clb; Yrbk; Off Soph Cls; Ballet Folkloriko; Southwestern Coll; Cmptr Prgm.

MARQUEZ, MARTINA C; Clovis HS; Clovis, CA; (2); Color Guard; Hon Roll; Hawaiian Dncng & Perfmng; Mexican Amer Clovis High Orgn; Berkley U; Pedtrcn.

MARQUEZ, NASH; Southest Lutheran HS; Huntington Park, CA; (3); 2/10; Nwsp; Ed Yrbk; Var L Ftbl; Cit Awd; Hon Roll; Prfct Atten Awd; Pro Deo Et Schola Awd; 1st Team All Leaguq CIF Ethtmn Ftbl Awd; Outsndng Lnmn Awd; CA Inst Of Arts; Cartoonist.

MARQUEZ, OLGA; Sacred Heart Of Mary HS; Montebello, CA; (3); Cmnty Wkr; Computer Clb; French Clb; School Musical; School Play; Variety Show; Ed Yrbk; Rep Sr Cls; Stu Cncl; Cit Awd; Cum Laude; CSF; USC; Arch.

MARQUEZ, PANFILO; Fontanan HS; Fontana, CA; (3); 41/1090; Church Yth Grp; Intnl Clb; Spanish Clb; School Play; High Hon Roll; Hon Roll; Pres Acad Fit Awd; Campus Life; Acad Pentathalon, Decatlon; Azusa Pacific; Ed.

MARQUEZ, ROSALINA; Kingsburg HS; Kingsburg, CA; (2); Wt Lftg; Hon Roll.

MARQUEZ, SANDRA; Santa Cruz HS; Santa Cruz, CA; (1); Spanish Clb; Teachers Aide; Off Frsh Cls; Socr; Hon Roll; UCBA.

MARQUEZ, SANDRA P; California HS; San Ramon, CA; (3); Art Clb; Intnl Clb; Spanish Clb; High Hon Roll; Awd Art Outstndng Achvt; Sunset HS Awd Advncd Art Outstndng Achvt; Phys Educ Outstndng Achvt; U Of CA Berkeley; Engrng.

MARQUEZ JR, SANTIAGO; Edison HS; Stockton, CA; (1); Hon Roll; UC Davis Erly Outrch Prgm, Davis JASRAP; Bowlng; Sci.

MARQUEZ, SILVIA E; Tracy Joint Union HS; Tracy, CA; (3); 33/401; Spanish Clb; SADD; JV Var Vllybl; High Hon Roll; Hon Roll; Med.

MARQUEZ, SONYA MARIE; Bella Vista HS; Fair Oaks, CA; (2); 34/406; Drama Clb; Spanish Clb; School Musical; School Play; Treas Soph Cls; Cheerldng; Spanish NHS; Friday Night Live; Dance Co; U CA; Jrnlsm.

MARQUEZ, SUSANA; Chino HS; Chino, CA; (3); Bilingl Sec.

MARQUEZ, VALERIE K; St Joseph HS; Santa Maria, CA; (3); Key Clb; SADD; Stat Swmmng; JV Trk; Jr NHS; Hancock.

MARQUEZ, VERONICA; Ernest Righetti HS; Guadalupe, CA; (1); Upward Bound; Erly Acad Outreach; GATE; Med.

MARR, HEATHER D; Greenville JR-SR HS; Greenville, CA; (3); Drama Clb; FBLA; VP Service Clb; Teachers Aide; Band; Chorus; School Play; Stage Crew; Variety Show; Rptr Nwsp; Won Schl Spelling Bee 89, Cnty 90; Writing.

MARR, JULIE; Granite Hills HS; Alpine, CA; (2); 42/530; Hosp Aide; Model UN; Chorus; Hon Roll; Jobs Dghtrs Offcr; Outsndng Jobs Dghtr; Bus.

MARR, KIMIKO N; Casa Roble Fundemental HS; Orangevale, CA; (3); Chorus; Cit Awd; Hon Roll; Kiwanis Awd; Prfct Atten Awd.

MARR, SAMANTHA M; Irvine HS; Irvine, CA; (3); Debate Tm; Speech Tm; Teachers Aide; JV Swmmng; Pres Acad Fit Awd; Spch Shw; Spch Trnmnt; Spch Tm Capt 90 & 91; U Of CA Santa Barbara; Pre-Law.

MARRA, MELANNIE L; Live Oak HS; Morgan Hill, CA; (3); 280/580; FBLA; Office Aide; Spanish Clb; SADD; Teachers Aide; Stu Cncl; Bsktbl; Socr; Sftbl; Hon Roll; Heald Bus Coll; Bus.

MARRACINO, PAMELA Y; Clayton Valley HS; Clayton, CA; (3); Drama Clb; Hosp Aide; SADD; School Play; Sec Jr Cls; Var Crs Cntry; Var Trk; Hon Roll; Syracuse NY.

MARRANATE, ATIPOL C; Bullard HS; Fresno, CA; (2); UC San Francisco; Phrmcy.

MARROQUIN, MARITZA; Downey HS; Downey, CA; (3); French Clb; FBLA; JA; Ski Clb; Rep Nwsp; Off Sr Cls; Cit Awd; Hon Roll; Rprsnt CA As Cngrssnl Schlr; Dwny Intrct Clb Secy; Rtry Yth Ldrshp, Kiwanis Ldrshp Cnfrnce; UCSB; Bus.

MARROW, STEPHANIE; Paramount HS; Los Angeles, CA; (1); 234/940; Church Yth Grp; Teachers Aide; Yrbk; Hon Roll; Pediatrician.

MARS, CAROLE; Valhalla HS; El Cajon, CA; (4); 16/415; Church Yth Grp; Cmnty Wkr; Dance Clb; Girl Scts; Letterman Clb; Varsity Clb; Lit Mag; JV Var Bsktbl; Stat Var Trk; UA Tucson; Envrnmntl Stds.

MARSCHALL, JEFFREY J; Clearlake HS; Minneapolis, MN; (1); Hon Roll.

MARSH, AMY N; Woodside HS; Redwood City, CA; (2); 14/280; Church Yth Grp; Dance Clb; Drama Clb; Teachers Aide; Church Choir; School Musical; School Play; JV Tennis; Cit Awd; High Hon Roll; Schl Mascot; Mexicali Mission Trip; Mem CSF.

MARSH, ANTHONY S; Culver City HS; Culver City, CA; (1); Intrml Bsktbl; Intrml Trk; Cit Awd; Hon Roll; Scott Newmann Ctr Cert Of Prtcptn; NSF Young Schlrs Pgm; Club-Animal Activists.

MARSH, BROCK; Poway HS; San Diego, CA; (3); Church Yth Grp; Letterman Clb; Teachers Aide; VP Jr Cls; Var Bsbl; Var Bsktbl; High Hon Roll; NHS; MVP Bsbl; Capt Bsktbl JV; Outstndng Art Stdt Awd 90.

MARSH, DAVID W; J F Kennedy HS; Buena Park, CA; (3); Var Wrstlng; Hon Roll; UCLA; Engrng.

MARSH, ELIZABETH; North Hollywood HS; No Hollywood, CA; (2); Church Yth Grp; Computer Clb; Rep Frsh Cls; Var Capt Cheerldng; Hon Roll; CA Poly; Arch Engr.

MARSH, KELLI; San Jose High Acad; San Jose, CA; (2); Pep Clb; Var Cheerldng; Mgr(s); Score Keeper; Stat Sftbl; Hon Roll; CSF; Recvd Many Awds In Chrldng; Berkley Coll; Comp Prgmr.

MARSH, KEVIN A; Dos Pueblos HS; Goleta, CA; (3); Boy Scts; Golf; Athl Rnd Tbl Golfr Of Yr; Athl Of Wk; AZ ST; Prfssnl Golfr.

MARSH, KIMBERLEE; Golden West HS; Visalia, CA; (2); Church Yth Grp; Sec FCA; Intnl Clb; VP Frsh Cls; Var Capt Bsktbl; Var Sftbl; Var Vllybl; High Hon Roll; Hon Roll; Chrch Yth Grp Cmmtte; CSF; UCLA; Dermtlgst.

MARSH, MATT F; Valhalla HS; El Cajon, CA; (3); 92/450; Key Clb; Letterman Clb; Ski Clb; Teachers Aide; Varsity Clb; Stu Cncl; Bsktbl; High Hon Roll; Hon Roll; Pres Acad Fit Awd; 2nd Team All Leag-Bsktbl 88-90; Schlr-Athlete Awd; Loyola Marymount U; Bus.

MARSH, MELISSA G; Oak Park HS; Agoura Hills, CA; (1); Girl Scts; Key Clb; School Musical; JV Bsktbl; Var Tennis; Hon Roll; Pres Acad Fit Awd; Peer Cnslng; Sci.

MARSH, SARAH L; Palos Verdes HS; Palos Verdes Ests, CA; (4); Pres Key Clb; JV Crs Cntry; Var Diving; Var Socr; California Scholarship Federation; Assembly 4 Yr Queen; High School All America; 2 A & 3 A Diving CIF; Southern Methodist U; Finance.

MARSH, SHARON L; Apple Valley HS; Apple Valley, CA; (2); Drama Clb; Drill Tm; Rptr Nwsp; Hon Roll; Writing Club VP; CSF; Law.

MARSH, TRACY D; Vacaville HS; Vacaville, CA; (4); 91/536; Var L Sftbl; Solano CC; CPA.

MARSHALL, AMY; Oxnard HS; Oxnard, CA; (1); Church Yth Grp; French Clb; Church Choir; Sec Treas Soph Cls; JV Cheerldng; High Hon Roll; Hon Roll; NHS; Covenant Plyrs Intrnl Reptry Theater Wn Grps Meteor Awd; Harvard; Philosphy.

MARSHALL, AMY A; University HS; Irvine, CA; (3); JCL; Drill Tm; Orch; Rptr Nwsp; Ed Lit Mag; Ntl Merit SF; Ntl Latin Hnr Soc; Princeton Price For Poetry; Engl Teacher.

MARSHALL, ANDREA L; Imperial HS; Imperial, CA; (2); FFA; GAA; Math Tm; Varsity Clb; VICA; Stat Bsktbl; Cheerldng; Golf; Var Vllybl; High Hon Roll; CSF 89-90; Bus.

MARSHALL, CHELSEA D; Ramona HS; Ramona, CA; (3); 2/294; Scholastic Bowl; Spanish Clb; High Hon Roll; CSF; CA Polytech ST U; Arch.

MARSHALL, COURTNEY; Hanford HS; Hanford, CA; (1); Church Yth Grp; FFA; Office Aide; Pep Clb; Pep Band; Cheerldng; Pom Pon; Wt Lftg; Hon Roll; NHS; Rally Club; Tchr.

MARSHALL, CRYSTAL D; El Toro HS; El Toro, CA; (3); Teachers Aide; High Hon Roll; Hon Roll; Keywanettes.

MARSHALL, JASON R; Delta HS; Clarksburg, CA; (2); 1/70; Boy Scts; Pres Soph Cls; Stat Bsbl; Var Bsktbl; Var Score Keeper; Hon Roll; US Air Force Acad; Pilot.

MARSHALL, JENNIFER L; Sequoia HS; San Carlos, CA; (4); Pep Clb; Acpl Chr; Band; Chorus; Drm Mjr(t); Phtg Yrbk; Var Bsktbl; Long Beach ST; Speech Tchr.

MARSHALL, JENNIFER M; Boron HS; North Edwards, CA; (2); Church Yth Grp; Math Tm; Teachers Aide; Chorus; Drill Tm; Sftbl; Vllybl; Sr Leag-Bsbl; Dental Asst.

MARSHALL, KARY L; Hilltop HS; Chula Vista, CA; (2); Intnl Clb; Office Aide; Rep SADD; Cit Awd; Hon Roll; Rep Stu Cncl; JV Var Socr; Capt JV Sftbl; Outstndng Achvt Spansh; Renaissnce Clb; San Diego ST; Psych.

MARSHALL, KIMBERLY A; University HS; Irvine, CA; (1); Letterman Clb; Band; Mrchg Band; Orch; School Musical; Lit Mag; Hon Roll; Pres Acad Fit Awd; Laureate Awd Outstndng Achvt Chinese; Dist Sci Fair Fnlst; Artwrk Pblsh Literary Mag; Music.

MARSHALL, KIMBERLY C; Lassen Union HS; Susanville, CA; (4); 29/159; Office Aide; Teachers Aide; Band; Score Keeper; High Hon Roll; Hon Roll; Masonic Awd; Pres Acad Fit Awd; Post Hnrd Queen Intl Ord Of Jobs Dtrs; Mem CA Schlrshp Fed; Psych.

MARSHALL, MARCUS C; Dos Palos HS; Dos Palos, CA; (2); Letterman Clb; Mrchg Band; Bsktbl; Ftbl; Trk; Hon Roll; Black Stu Union; Bus Adm.

MARSHALL, MARGARET; Polytechnic HS; Long Beach, CA; (2); Church Yth Grp; Dance Clb; FTA; Intnl Clb; Teachers Aide; Acpl Chr; Chorus; Church Choir; Drill Tm; Pom Pon; Pursuit Of Excellence Awd Bus, Math; Smith Coll.

MARSHALL, MIKE C; Sunny Hills HS; Buena Park, CA; (4); Cmnty Wkr; Letterman Clb; Ftbl; Fullerton Coll; Bus.

MARSHALL, MILA A; Morningside HS; Inglewood, CA; (3); FBLA; JA; Math Clb; Office Aide; Pep Clb; SADD; Teachers Aide; Stu Cncl; Co-Capt Cheerldng; Cit Awd; 87-88 Math Fair 1st Pl; OH ST; Med.

MARSHALL, MONICA R; Lincoln Prep HS; San Diego, CA; (2); Girl Scts; Letterman Clb; Pep Clb; Varsity Clb; Band; Mrchg Band; Variety Show; Rep Frsh Cls; Rep Soph Cls; Var Trk; Young Ladies Leag & Project STEP; Span & Hstry Wrtng Contests; Schltc Achvmnt Awd; Spelman U; Med.

MARSHALL, NICHOLAS K; Eureka HS; Eureka, CA; (3); Aud/Vis; High Hon Roll; Ntl Merit SF; Cmpsng Music; Piano; Visl Arts; Pomona Coll; Physcs.

MARSHALL, SHAKTI F; Fremont HS; Sunnyvale, CA; (1); Orch; Crs Cntry; Trk; De Anza Coll; Teacher.

MARSHALL, SONYA M; Eureka HS; Eureka, CA; (1); Drama Clb; Intnl Clb; High Hon Roll; Outside Of Sch Chorus; Soured Soviet Union & Romania; Plyd Piano 5 Yrs.

MARSHALL, STEPHANIE; Grant Union HS; Sacramento, CA; (3); Bsktbl; Mgr(s); Sftbl; Tennis; Vllybl; High Hon Roll; Hon Roll; German Clb; Crs Cntry; Score Keeper; Academic Dcthln; Mock Trial; Knowledge Bowl; Premed.

MARSHALL, STEPHANIE K; Selma HS; Selma, CA; (2); FFA; Swmmng; Hon Roll; Fresno ST; Psych.

MARSHALL, STEVEN A; Napa HS; Napa, CA; (3); Boy Scts; Ftbl; Swmmng; Hon Roll.

MARSHALL, SUMMER L; Notre Dame Acad; Santa Monica, CA; (3); Art Clb; Rep Spanish Clb; JV Bsktbl; JV Vllybl; Cit Awd; Hon Roll; Amicae Justicae Clb Schl Envrnmntl Awareness & Social Just; Amnesty Intl Clb; Loyola Marymount U; Educ.

MARSHALL, SUPANEE T; Armijo HS; Fairfield, CA; (3); AFS; ROTC; Teachers Aide; Drill Tm; Hon Roll; ROTC Sports-Sftbl/Bowlng/Vllybl/Bsktbl; UCLA; Psych.

MARSHALL, TANYA M; El Camino HS; Oceanside, CA; (2); Dance Clb; Color Guard; Drill Tm; Variety Show; JV Gym; JV Socr; JV Vllybl; Hon Roll; Manuf Rep.

MARSHALL, TIM C; University HS; Irvine, CA; (3); Computer Clb; Bsktbl.

MARSTELLER, BRIAN D; Hesperia HS; Hesperia, CA; (3); Spanish Clb; Var L Bsbl; Var L Ftbl; High Hon Roll; Bus.

MARSTON, TIMAREE F; Marysville HS; Brownsville, CA; (1); Art Clb; German Clb; Intnl Clb; SADD; Band; Mrchg Band; Pep Band; JV Tennis; High Hon Roll; Hon Roll; Camp Fire Board Mem; Camp Fire Outdoor Progression Award Highest Level; Completed CIT Prgm With Hnrs; University; Child Psychology.

MARTANEZ, LEON M; Mar Vista HS; San Ysidro, CA; (3); JV Socr; Aerospace Engr.

MARTASIAN, SARAH; Encina HS; Sacramento, CA; (2); Cmnty Wkr; Pep Clb; SADD; Lit Mag; JV Cheerldng; Hon Roll.

MARTEL, RENEE; Antelope Valley HS; Lancaster, CA; (3); 13/817; Letterman Clb; Pep Clb; Spanish Clb; SADD; Yrbk; High Hon Roll; Hon Roll; Pres Acad Fit Awd; CSF; Cls Treas; Yrbkr Of Yr Outstndng Achvt In Yrbk Cls; Brdcst Jrnlst.

MARTELL, GRACIELA; Mountain View HS; S El Monte, CA; (4); GAA; Teachers Aide; JV Bsktbl; Stat Sftbl; Var L Tennis; Hon Roll; Tennis MIP 88-89; Tennis Coaches Awd 89-90; Mt St Marys Clg; Child Devt.

MARTELL, JEANETTE; Rosary HS; Anaheim, CA; (4); 28/140; French Clb; Science Clb; Hon Roll; Sci.

MARTELLI, JOSHUA F; Helix HS; La Mesa, CA; (1); Key Clb; Treas Frsh Cls; VP Soph Cls; JV Bsktbl; JV Ftbl; JV Socr; JV Trk; Cit Awd; Hon Roll; CSF; Notre Dame; Psych.

MARTEN, MARGRET; Archbishop Mitty HS; Los Gatos, CA; (2); 22/209; Art Clb; French Clb; SADD; JV Swmmng; High Hon Roll; Hon Roll; NHS; Santa Clara U; Commercl Art.

MARTENS, DONALD; San Pedro HS; San Pedro, CA; (4); 6/544; Treas NFL; School Musical; Stu Cncl; Intrml Bsktbl; High Hon Roll; Jr NHS; Prfct Atten Awd; Pres Acad Fit Awd; Congressional Schlr; Gold Sealbearer CA Schlrshp Fed; USC; Engrng.

MARTENSON, CHRISTOPHER J; Village Christian HS; Burbank, CA; (3); Church Yth Grp; Martial Arts; Chiropractic.

MARTIN, AARON; Capistrano Valley Christian HS; Mission Viejo, CA; (4); 6/63; FCA; Stu Cncl; Var L Bsbl; Capt L Ftbl; Var L Socr; Pres Acad Fit Awd.

MARTIN, AARON R; Don Antonio Lugo HS; Chino, CA; (3); #8 In Class; Var Swmmng; High Hon Roll; V Water Polo; Hiking, Cycling Clb; Golden Conqst Awds Comp Sci, Humerous Hnr.

MARTIN, ALEJANDRA; Montclair HS; Montclair, CA; (3); Hon Roll; Prfct Atten Awd; Awds In Reading,ESL,Homemaking,French I & French II,Stu Of Mnth 90; Cal Poly Pomona; Translator.

MARTIN, AMI; Amador HS; Ione, CA; (3); Drama Clb; Pep Clb; Spanish Clb; School Play; JV Cheerldng; High Hon Roll; Hon Roll; Acad Hall Of Fame For Amador HS Chrtr 89; Amrcn River Coll; Rsprtry Thrps.

MARTIN, ANDY J; Helix HS; Lemon Grove, CA; (3); 19/600; High Hon Roll; UCSD; Comp Sci.

MARTIN, ANGELA M; Montclair HS; Ontario, CA; (1); Teachers Aide; Prfct Atten Awd; Consvtml Forstr.

MARTIN, BECKY; Serra HS; San Diego, CA; (2); 1/460; Church Yth Grp; Hosp Aide; Pep Clb; Yrbk; JV Cheerldng; High Hon Roll; Hon Roll; Acad Leag; CA Schrlshp Fed; Medcl.

MARTIN, BENJAMIN; University HS; Los Angeles, CA; (2); AFS; Ed Yrbk; Pres Frsh Cls; Crs Cntry; Intrml Trk; High Hon Roll; Hon Roll; Nxt Yr Italy AFS; English.

MARTIN, BENJAMIN D; Red Bluff Union HS; Red Bluff, CA; (4); 33/340; Boy Scts; Letterman Clb; Mu Alpha Theta; Band; Mrchg Band; School Musical; School Play; JV Ftbl; JV Var Wrstlng; Hon Roll; Sons Am Revolution Eagle Sct Schlrshp; CA ST U Chico.

MARTIN, BRENDA R; Fontana HS; Fontana, CA; (2); Hon Roll; UCR; Psych.

MARTIN, BRIAN D; Bishop Montgomery HS; Hermosa Beach, CA; (3); FBLA; JA; Ski Clb; Varsity Clb; Bsktbl; Golf; Vllybl; U S CA; Invstmt Banker.

MARTIN, BRIAN W; Gunn HS; Palo Alto, CA; (2); Boy Scts; SADD; Var Crs Cntry; JV Socr; JV Swmmng; Jr Natl Luge Tm Candidate; CYSA Soccer Referee; Phys Sci.

MARTIN, CARLOS B; El Camino Fundamental HS; Carmichael, CA; (3); Latin Clb; VP Frsh Cls; Var Ftbl; Var Wrstlng; UC Davis; Bus Admin.

MARTIN, CARRIE L; Mt Whitney HS; Visalia, CA; (4); Teachers Aide; Var L Bsktbl; Var L Sftbl; Var L Vllybl; All Leag & All Area Sftbl 88-90; All Cntrl Sctn Sftbl 88-89; Fresno ST; Phys Thrpy.

MARTIN, CHAD R; Grossmont HS; San Diego, CA; (4); Teachers Aide; Rep Stu Cncl; JV Var Ftbl; San Diego ST U.

MARTIN, CHANDRA L; Etiwanda HS; Rancho Cucamonga, CA; (2); Church Yth Grp; JA; Cit Awd; Hon Roll; Prfct Atten Awd; Stu Of Mnth Awd; Outstndng Acadmc Achvt Awd; Engl Cert Achvt.

MARTIN, CHRIS W; Silver Valley HS; Fort Irwin, CA; (2); Hon Roll; Engrng.

MARTIN, CHRISTINA L; Alverno HS; Pasadena, CA; (4); Church Yth Grp; Girl Scts; Model UN; Rep Frsh Cls; Rep Soph Cls; Off Jr Cls; Stu Cncl; Hon Roll; NHS; Polish Folkdance Ensmble; U Southern CA; Bus.

MARTIN, CHRISTINE A; Abraham Lincoln HS; San Francisco, CA; (3); Church Yth Grp; Cmnty Wkr; Band; Church Choir; Hghly Invlvd War On Drugs; Outrchs & Positve Alternative Rppng; Yng People Peer Pressure & Drugs; Stanford U; Nrs.

MARTIN, CRYSTAL; Mission Viejo HS; Laguna Beach, CA; (4); 43/479; Sec Church Yth Grp; Pres German Clb; Key Clb; Model UN; Scholastic Bowl; SADD; Teachers Aide; VP Pres Church Choir; Variety Show; Treas Jr Cls; Deans Schlrshp USC; U Of Sthrn CA; Psych.

MARTIN, DANIEL P; Rancho Alamitos HS; Garden Grove, CA; (3); French Clb; Varsity Clb; Bsktbl; Ftbl; Socr; Vllybl; Wt Lftg; Hon Roll; Pres Acad Fit Awd; Capt & MVP Vllybll Team; Co-Capt JV Teams; Golden West Coll; Arch.

MARTIN, DOUGLAS; Lincoln HS; Stockton, CA; (3); Sec Aud/Vis; Church Yth Grp; Ski Clb; Church Choir; School Play; Stage Crew; High Hon Roll; Hon Roll; Spcl Effcts Makeup; Microbio.

MARTIN, ELYSIA K; Mayfield SR HS; Pasadena, CA; (3); Church Yth Grp; Cmnty Wkr; Library Aide; Teachers Aide; Chorus; Rptr Yrbk; Hon Roll; NHS; CA Schlrshp Fed; Religion Awd; U Of CA; Envrnmntl Stds.

MARTIN, ERIN E; Arvin HS; Lamont, CA; (2); Band; Color Guard; Hon Roll; Rdng; Wrtng Poetry; Lawyer.

MARTIN, FLORINDA G; Carson HS; Carson, CA; (3); German Clb; Library Aide; High Hon Roll; Nrsg.

MARTIN, HANS C; Bishop O'dowd HS; Oakland, CA; (3); 7/250; High Hon Roll; CSF.

MARTIN, HEIDI D; Eureka SR HS; Eureka, CA; (3); FBLA; Girl Scts; Teachers Aide; Cheerldng; Powder Puff Ftbl; Profeciency Chld Care & Guidance Cert; Humboldt ST U; Phys.

MARTIN, HOPE; Rosary HS; Mission Viejo, CA; (4); 4/138; Debate Tm; NFL; Chorus; Stage Crew; Nwsp; Cit Awd; High Hon Roll; Ntl Merit SF; Peer Tutoring; CA Schlrshp Fed; Schl Chptr Of Stu Against Drug Abuse; Poltcl Sci.

MARTIN, J JASON; Sonoma Valley HS; Sonoma, CA; (3); 1/300; High Hon Roll; Prfct Atten Awd; CA Schlrshp Fdrtn; Sr Cnslr In Trng Cmp For Diabetic Chldrn.

MARTIN JR, JAMES A; Fresno HS; Fresno, CA; (2); Ski Clb; JV Ftbl; Var Wt Lftg; High Hon Roll; Hon Roll; Prfct Atten Awd; MESA; MECHA Mexican Amer Spnsh Club; Amer Inst Arch Awd; USC; Arch.

MARTIN, JANET; North HS; Torrance, CA; (4); 195/468; Drama Clb; Teachers Aide; Chorus; Flag Corp; Trk; Cit Awd.

MARTIN, JENNIFER L; Golden West HS; Visalia, CA; (1); Church Yth Grp; Band; JV Socr; L Var Trk; High Hon Roll; Hon Roll; Acad Ltr; City Bobby Sox Sftbl; AAU City Trk; CA Poly San Obspo; Photojrnlst.

MARTIN, JESSACA D; Grave Davis HS; Modesto, CA; (3); French Clb; FTA; Teachers Aide; Trk; Sheriff Cadets; U Of San Francisco; Elem Educ.

MARTIN, JOHN J; Vacaville HS; Vacaville, CA; (3); JV Var Bsbl; JV Var Ftbl; JV Trk; JV Var Wt Lftg; JV Wrstlng; Cit Awd; Hon Roll; Prfct Atten Awd; CA St U Sacramento; Math.

MARTIN, JOSEPH M; Abraham Lincoln HS; San Jose, CA; (3); 82/407; Spanish Clb; Mgr(s); Var Swmmng; Hon Roll; Vrsty Badmntn; Homecmng Cmmttee; Ln Timer-Grls Swmmng; San Diego ST U; Bio Sci.

MARTIN, JULIA; Moreau HS; San Lorenzo, CA; (4); 9/295; SADD; Rep Frsh Cls; Stat Bsktbl; JV Var Powder Puff Ftbl; JV Trk; High Hon Roll; NHS; Pres Acad Fit Awd; Police & Firemans Ins Assn Schlrshp Wnnr; CSF; Sum Cum Laud Grad; U Of CA Santa Barbara; Law.

MARTIN, JULIE; Lodi HS; Lodi, CA; (4); 20/399; Letterman Clb; Office Aide; Varsity Clb; Var L Socr; Var L Sftbl; Var L Vllybl; High Hon Roll; Lodi-Tokay Rotary, Lodi Womens Clb & CSEA Schlrshps; CSF; UOP; Bus Admin.

MARTIN, JULIE; Los Angeles Baptist HS; Sepulveda, CA; (3); Church Yth Grp; Teachers Aide; Chorus; Co-Capt Drill Tm; JV Cheerldng; Gym; Stu Mntr Pgm; Staff Servent; Big Sister Pgm; CA ST U; Pre-Schl Tchr.

MARTIN, JULIE C; Redwood HS; Visalia, CA; (3); Church Yth Grp; Pres FHA; JCL; Latin Clb; Pep Clb; Band; Mrchg Band; Pep Band; JV Vllybl; NHS; Cmnty Musical Stop The World.

MARTIN, JULIE E; Southern California Christian HS; Orange, CA; (3); Church Yth Grp; GAA; Office Aide; Ed Yrbk; Powder Puff Ftbl; Var Sftbl; Var Vllybl; High Hon Roll; Hon Roll; NHS; Biola U.

MARTIN, KAI S; Arcadia HS; Temple City, CA; (2); Art Clb; Aud/Vis; Church Yth Grp; English Clb; 4-H; Science Clb; Rptr Nwsp; 4-H Awd; Jr Navy Pgm; Maritime Acad; Mrchnt Marine.

MARTIN, KAREN; Mt Carmel HS; San Diego, CA; (4); Church Yth Grp; Dance Clb; DECA; Office Aide; Pep Clb; Mesa JC; Art.

MARTIN, KATHERINE L; Oakmont HS; Roseville, CA; (3); 8/400; Cmnty Wkr; Drama Clb; Scholastic Bowl; Service Clb; SADD; Teachers Aide; Variety Show; Ed Yrbk; Swmmng; High Hon Roll; Water Polo; Gold Awd; Sci.

MARTIN, KERRIE L; Santana HS; Santee, CA; (3); 21/290; San Diego ST; Child Care.

MARTIN, KIMBERLY; Faith Baptist HS; Canoga Park, CA; (4); 5/40; Drama Clb; VP Soph Cls; VP Jr Cls; VP Sr Cls; Var L Bsktbl; Var L Cheerldng; Var L Trk; Hon Roll; U CA San Diego; Biomedl Engrng.

MARTIN, KRISTA M; Huntington Beach HS; Huntington Beach, CA; (1); Cmnty Wkr; Girl Scts; Ski Clb; Bsktbl; Trk; Vllybl; Hon Roll; Ice Sktng; Tower Awd; Wrtng; UCSB; Write Chldrns Books.

MARTIN, KRISTINA M; Chino HS; Chino, CA; (4); Church Yth Grp; Cmnty Wkr; Office Aide; High Hon Roll; Hon Roll; 3rd Pl Wnnr Cnty Wine Pstr Cntst; Chaffey Coll; Cmmrcl Art.

MARTIN, KRISTY M; La Reina HS; Thousand Oaks, CA; (3); Church Yth Grp; Cmnty Wkr; Hosp Aide; NFL; Service Clb; Speech Tm; SADD; Rptr Nwsp; Rep Soph Cls; Rep Jr Cls; Fnlst Spch Cmptn; Cmmnctns.

MARTIN, LANCE K; Oakmont HS; Roseville, CA; (3); 80/400; Boy Scts; Var Letterman Clb; JV Var Ftbl; JV Var Trk; Wt Lftg; Hon Roll; Gldn St Exm 1st Yr Alg & Geomtry Hnrs Awds; CA ST U Sacramento; Acctng.

MARTIN, LAUREN G; Faith Baptist HS; Canoga Park, CA; (4); 3/46; Pres Soph Cls; Pres Jr Cls; Pres Sr Cls; Pres Stu Cncl; Var Capt Bsktbl; Var Cheerldng; Var Capt Trk; Var Capt Vllybl; High Hon Roll; Ntl Merit SF; UCSD; Premed.

MARTIN, LAURIE A; Modesto HS; Modesto, CA; (3); Teachers Aide; JV Var Sftbl; Hon Roll; Stu Ambssdr To USSR; Explrer For Fire Dept; AF Acad; Airlne Plt.

MARTIN, LEANNA R; Santa Barbara HS; Santa Barbara, CA; (3); Church Yth Grp; Cmnty Wkr; Reading; Bike Riding; CPA.

MARTIN, LEWIS C; Taft HS; Taft, CA; (2); #31 In Class; Hon Roll; Prfct Atten Awd; Pilot.

MARTIN, LIBERTY; San Rafael HS; San Rafael, CA; (2); Chess Clb; Math Clb; Ski Clb; Socr; Trk; High Hon Roll; Hon Roll; Golden St Exm Hnrs Math; Spectlr Stu Sci; Robtcl Eng.

MARTIN, LISA; Central Catholic HS; Oakdale, CA; (2); Art Clb; Drama Clb; Ski Clb; Spanish Clb; Pom Pon; Var Trk; Hon Roll.

MARTIN, LORI; Rosary HS; Yorba Linda, CA; (2); L Var Swmmng; High Hon Roll; Notre Dame.

MARTIN, LORI D; Cabrillo HS; Bellevue, NE; (3); Letterman Clb; Scholastic Bowl; JV L Bsktbl; JV Socr; Var L Swmmng; Var L Vllybl; Acad Decathlon; Cabrillo Aquarium Club; Purdue U; Med.

MARTIN, MARTHA M; Fontana HS; Fontana, CA; (4); Key Clb; Hon Roll; Word Prcssng.

MARTIN, MATT C; Bellarmine College Prep; Los Gatos, CA; (3); 5/300; Boy Scts; Cmnty Wkr; Service Clb; Teachers Aide; Varsity Clb; Pep Band; Var Crs Cntry; Var L Trk; Jr Statesmen Of Amer.

MARTIN, MELISSA M; Irvington HS; Fremont, CA; (2); Drama Clb; FCA; Math Clb; Office Aide; Teachers Aide; School Play; Treas Soph Cls; Var Socr; JV Var Sftbl; JV Var Vllybl; Stanford U; Med.

MARTIN, MELISSA S; San Benito HS; Hollister, CA; (2); Drama Clb; Office Aide; Science Clb; School Play; Cmps Life Clb; Ballet Grad Awd; Love Wrkng With Chldrns; Acting.

MARTIN, MICHELLE; Springs Of Living Water Acad; Chico, CA; (2); Church Yth Grp; Drama Clb; Speech Tm; Teachers Aide; Acpl Chr; Chorus; School Musical; Variety Show; Hon Roll; Prfct Atten Awd; Stanford U; Psych.

MARTIN, MILTON; S E Gompers Secondary Schl; San Diego, CA; (4); Church Yth Grp; VP FTA; Teachers Aide; Band; Chorus; Church Choir; Rptr Nwsp; Stu Cncl; Cit Awd; Hon Roll; San Diego City Schls Schlrshp Wnnr; Bnk Of Amer Plaque Wnnr In Fine Arts; Point Loma Nazarene Coll; Elem.

MARTIN, MONIQUE L; Skyline HS; Oakland, CA; (2); ROTC; Chorus; Church Choir; School Musical; Variety Show; Sec Frsh Cls; Blck Stu Union Pres; Skyline Gospel Choir; Oakland Yth Chorus; Mdl Gov Arts Schlr.

MARTIN, NIKOLE; Cypress HS; Cypress, CA; (1); JV Cheerldng; Church Yth Grp; Drama Clb; Pep Clb; School Play.

MARTIN, NOE D; Antelope Valley HS; Lancaster, CA; (3); Graphic Art.

MARTIN, PATRICIA; Mc Ateer HS; San Francisco, CA; (3); Girl Scts; Pres Latin Clb; Off Sr Cls; Hon Roll; UCSF Nrsng Explorers; UC Davis; Nrsng.

MARTIN, PATRICK; Edison Computech HS; Fresno, CA; (1); FBLA; Teachers Aide; JV Ftbl; Mgr(s); Score Keeper; Socr; Wt Lftg; Cit Awd; Hon Roll; Prfct Atten Awd; Stu Of Wk/Stu Of Mnth; Accntnt.

MARTIN, PATRICK T; Servite HS; Anaheim, CA; (2); Var Bsbl; Var Bsktbl; High Hon Roll; NHS; CSF; Notre Dame; Engr.

MARTIN, PEGGY M; Oxnard HS; Oxnard, CA; (4); Pres Church Yth Grp; Church Choir; Masonic Awd; ROP; Acctng.

MARTIN, QIANYA SAMOANE; Inglewood HS; Inglewood, CA; (1); Dance Clb; Drama Clb; Flag Corp; School Play; Variety Show; JV Swmmng; Cit Awd; Hon Roll; Ladies & Knights Clb; #10,000 Schlrshp Wnnr, Eckerd Coll; $4,000 Schlrshp Wnnr, Millikin U; Harvard.

MARTIN, REBECCA B; Claremont HS; Claremont, CA; (4); 65/417; Debate Tm; French Clb; Q&S; VP Ski Clb; Ed Nwsp; Sec Treas Soph Cls; JV Socr; Hon Roll; Ntl Merit SF; US Acad Decthln; Amnesty Intl; Lions Clb Intl Yth Exchng; Pol Sci.

MARTIN, ROBERT J; Orange Glen HS; Escondido, CA; (3); Church Yth Grp; Drama Clb; Teachers Aide; Yrbk; Hon Roll; Modeling Major Hair & Clthng Sponsors; UCSD; Bus.

MARTIN, RONNIE A; Wilcox HS; Santa Clara, CA; (1); JV Bsbl; JV Ftbl; Intrml Mgr Wt Lftg; Hon Roll; All League In Baseball; AZ ST U.

MARTIN, RUBEN; Mark Keppel HS; Rosemead, CA; (3); Teachers Aide; Varsity Clb; Bsbl; Ftbl; Wrstlng; Mount San Antonio Coll; Bus.

MARTIN, RYAN J; Mater Dei HS; Huntington Bch, CA; (3); 1/500; Church Yth Grp; Cmnty Wkr; Intrml Bsktbl; Socr; JV Capt Vllybl; High Hon Roll; NHS; Pres Acad Fit Awd; CSF; Congrsnl Yth Ldrshp Cncl; Envrmntl Awareness Comm; U Notre Dame; Prep Stud.

MARTIN, SANDY F; Tulare Union HS; Tulare, CA; (1); Church Yth Grp; Speech Tm; Hon Roll; Prtguese Clb; Ct Rprtr.

MARTIN, SEAN R; Viewpoint HS; Northridge, CA; (1); Aud/Vis; Key Clb; Crs Cntry; Ftbl; Wt Lftg; Kiwanis Awd; Headmasters List For 3 Quarters; Bus.

MARTIN, SETH J; Vacaville HS; Vacaville, CA; (3); Yrbk; Wrstlng; Bus.

MARTIN, SYBIL; Hayfork HS; Hyampom, CA; (4); Am Leg Aux Girls St; Art Clb; Aud/Vis; Church Yth Grp; Drama Clb; Pep Clb; Thesps; Acpl Chr; Chorus; School Musical; Walt Disney Dreamers/Doers Awd; Bank F Amer Fine Arts Awd; Art Dept Awd; Shasta Coll; Art.

MARTIN, TAMI C; Mater Dei HS; Anaheim, CA; (3); Cmnty Wkr; Sec German Clb; GAA; Intnl Clb; School Play; Hon Roll; NHS; Pres Acad Fit Awd; Sci, German, Liberal Arts & Engl Hnrs; Vlntr Work; U CA Irvine.

MARTIN, TANISHIA S; Dorsey HS; Los Angeles, CA; (2); Church Yth Grp; Drama Clb; Girl Scts; Drill Tm; Hon Roll; Grambling U; Pedtrcs.

MARTIN, TANJAREEN C; St Bernard Catholic HS; Inglewood, CA; (3); Church Yth Grp; Latin Clb; Pep Clb; SADD; Church Choir; Drill Tm; School Musical; School Play; Rep Stu Cncl; JV Bsktbl; Show Team Co-Capt; Palm Sun Pilgrimage-Walk For Homeless; Black Cultrl Awrnss Clb-Asst VP; Mass Cmmnctns.

MARTIN, TEMESHIA M; Amos Alonzo Stagg HS; Stockton, CA; (3); Church Choir; Yrbk; Powder Puff Ftbl; Prfct Atten Awd; BSU; Ldrshp Cls; Heald Bus Coll; Word Proc.

MARTIN, THOMAS; Bell HS; Maywood, CA; (3); #6 In Class; Cmnty Wkr; Math Tm; High Hon Roll; Hon Roll; NHS; St Schlr; MESA-MATH Engrng Sci Achvt-Pres; Outstndng MESA Stu 89-90; Acad Decathln; CA Inst Of Tech; Physics.

MARTIN, TINA M; O'farrell SCPA; San Diego, CA; (4); 9/107; Church Yth Grp; Girl Scts; Letterman Clb; Chorus; Church Choir; Orch; School Musical; Stage Crew; Hon Roll; Prfct Atten Awd; Girl Scout Gold Awd Hghst Achvt; Pres CSF; Peer Cnslng.

MARTIN, TOM; Dana Hills HS; Laguna Beach, CA; (4); 20/500; JCL; Latin Clb; Science Clb; Ntl Merit Ltr; Pres Acad Fit Awd; U CA Irvine; Biolgcl Chem.

MARTIN, TRACIE M; El Toro HS; Laguna Beach, CA; (3); Office Aide; Teachers Aide; High Hon Roll; Hon Roll; Girls League; UCSB; Maine Bio.

MARTIN, TRACY L; Chino HS; Chino, CA; (3); Dance Clb; Teachers Aide; JV Var Trk; High Hon Roll; Jr NHS; NHS; Prfct Atten Awd; Part-Time Wrk.

MARTIN, VALENCIA M; George Washington Prep; Los Angeles, CA; (3); Church Yth Grp; Hosp Aide; Church Choir; JV Var Cheerldng; Score Keeper; High Hon Roll; Hon Roll; Tuskegee U; Poly Sci.

MARTIN, WENDY M; Napa HS; Vallejo, CA; (3); Chorus; Hon Roll; Bus Awd; Retl Oprtns Awd Outstndng Sklls; Chrprctr.

MARTIN, WESTI B; Sierra Joint Union HS; N Fork, CA; (2); FHA; GAA; Spanish Clb; SADD; Intrml JV Bsktbl; JV Sftbl; Intrml JV Vllybl; Fresno City Coll; Dental Hygnst.

MARTINDALE, GREG; Sonoma Valley HS; Sonoma, CA; (4); 5/277; Cmnty Wkr; Letterman Clb; Service Clb; Var L Bsbl; JV L Bsktbl; JV L Ftbl; Intrml Vllybl; High Hon Roll; Hon Roll; 1st 2 Yrs 4.0 Grd Pt Avg; Plyr Rep Bsbl Coach Slctn 89; 2 Yrs Var Bsbl Tm; CA Schlrshp Fed Lftm; CA U Santa Barbara; Chem Engrg.

MARTINDALE, TODD E; Bolsa Grande HS; Garden Grove, CA; (2); Band; Mrchg Band; Orch; Pep Band; Brass Choir; Berkeley Coll Of Music.

MARTINDELCAMPO, GABRIEL; Fontana HS; Fontana, CA; (3); Chess Clb; Math Clb; Science Clb; Lit Mag; Cit Awd; Gov Hon Prg Awd; High Hon Roll; Hon Roll; Prfct Atten Awd; CSF; Math Awd; Religion Awd; JR Gold Medal; U Of CA Riverside; Pre Med.

MARTINELLI, CINDY M; Liberty Union HS; Brentwood, CA; (1); Pep Clb; SADD; Acpl Chr; Band; Cheerldng; Trk; Prfct Atten Awd; Pres Acad Fit Awd; JFK Law Sch; Law.

MARTINELLI, KRISTA J; Mills HS; S San Francisco, CA; (3); Am Leg Aux Girls St; Church Yth Grp; Cmnty Wkr; Letterman Clb; Rep Soph Cls; Rep Jr Cls; Rep Sr Cls; Var Capt Cheerldng; Trk; High Hon Roll; Peer Cnslr; Comm.

MARTINEZ, ADRIAN A; John F Kennedy HS; Buena Park, CA; (1); Acpl Chr; School Play; Trk; Wrstlng; USC Berkly; Arch.

MARTINEZ, ADRIANA Z; Coachlla Valley HS; Mecca, CA; (3); 30/395; Teachers Aide; Hon Roll; Advanced Placemnt/Humanities Clb.

MARTINEZ, AIDA; Ramona HS; Ramona, CA; (3); 7/280; Latin Clb; Teachers Aide; Prfct Atten Awd; CSF; Svrl Stu Of Month Awds; Jr Daisy Chain; Palomar Coll; Biling Tchr.

MARTINEZ, ALEJANDRO; Pasadena HS; Pasadena, CA; (3); Cmnty Wkr; Spanish Clb; Hon Roll; Prfct Atten Awd; Prom Cmmtte 91; Treas MESA; CSF; Elect Engrng.

MARTINEZ, ALFRED E; Notre Dame HS; Moreno Valley, CA; (1); 73/150; JV Ftbl; Hon Roll; US Naval Acad; Naval Pilot.

MARTINEZ, ALICIA; Lindsay HS; Lindsay, CA; (1); Church Yth Grp; Vllybl.

MARTINEZ, AMALIA; Richard Gahr HS; Cerritos, CA; (3); Spanish Clb; Band; Mrchg Band; Crs Cntry.

MARTINEZ, ANA; Alexander Hamilton HS; Los Angeles, CA; (2); Teachers Aide; Church Choir; Mrchg Band; Var Bsbl; Comp Prgmr.

MARTINEZ, ANA E; Castle Park HS; Chula Vista, CA; (3); 47/422; Church Yth Grp; French Clb; German Clb; Band; Church Choir; Mrchg Band; Pep Band; Bst Frshmn & Soph Musician; SDSU; Aeronau Engrng.

MARTINEZ, ANNA LIZA R; Carson HS; Carson, CA; (2); Ed Nwsp; Ed Lit Mag; Off Frsh Cls; Stu Cncl; JV Tennis; High Hon Roll; Prfct Atten Awd; SIPA; 1st Pl Bring In Cont SW Regnl Cont For Jrnlsm; Harvard; Engrg.

MARTINEZ, APRIL GARNETT E; Samuel F B Morse HS; Spring Valley, CA; (3); SADD; Chorus; School Play; Lit Mag; Var Cheerldng; Cit Awd; French Hon Soc; Hon Roll; CSF; Writers Clb.

MARTINEZ, ARLENE; San Pedro HS; San Pedro, CA; (2); Hosp Aide; Drill Tm; Cit Awd; Acad All Stars; Art & Ballet; Psych.

MARTINEZ, ARMANDO; Baldwin Park HS; Baldwin Pk, CA; (2); Chess Clb; Scholastic Bowl; Science Clb; Spanish Clb; Band; Jazz Band; Mrchg Band; Pep Band; Var Bsbl; 1st & 2nd Pl Womens Clb Poetry Cont; Bsbl Awd.

MARTINEZ, BARBARA N; Bullard HS; Madera, CA; (3); 1/500; Hosp Aide; Intnl Clb; Key Clb; Hon Roll; Prfct Atten Awd; Italian Clb; JR Larcs Clb; Sch Recognition Alg I Golden St Exam.

MARTINEZ, BEN F; Madera HS; Madera, CA; (3); Cmnty Wkr; Speech Tm; SADD; Mgr Jr Cls; JV Vllybl; Madera Cnty Alcohol, Drug Advsry Brd 88-91; VFW 3rd Pl Speech Awd; Mock Trial Team; Woodbury U; Bus Mgmt.

MARTINEZ, BLAINE B; Carson HS; Carson, CA; (2); U Of Guan; Elec Engr.

MARTINEZ, BRIAN K; Alpaugh Unified School Dist; Earlimart, CA; (3); Drama Clb; Letterman Clb; Band; Mrchg Band; Sec Frsh Cls; VP Soph Cls; VP Jr Cls; Rep Stu Cncl; Var Bsbl; Var Bsktbl; Mst Outstndng Acad Stu; Mst Imprvd Crss Cntry; Bakersfield City Coll; Brdcstng.

MARTINEZ, BRYAN J; Huntington Beach HS; Huntington Bch, CA; (3); Boy Scts; Church Yth Grp; Ski Clb; Spanish Clb; Bsktbl; Vllybl; Pres Acad Fit Awd; Al Reboin Awd; U CA-SANTA Barbara; Aerosp Sci.

MARTINEZ, BRYAN M; Bellarmine HS; Morgan Hill, CA; (2); Bsbl; Ftbl; Wt Lftg; Stanford; Med.

MARTINEZ, CARLOS A; W C Overfelt HS; San Jose, CA; (2); Pres Science Clb; School Play; Var Swmmng; Bus.

MARTINEZ, CARLOS M; Saint Anthony HS; Long Beach, CA; (3); Capt Bsbl; JV Bsktbl; Ftbl; Hon Roll; Phys Thrpy.

MARTINEZ, CARMEN E; Rosemead HS; Rosemead, CA; (1); SADD; CA ST; Psych.

MARTINEZ, CAROLINE LEILANI; Woodland HS; Woodland, CA; (4); School Musical; Rptr Yrbk; Stu Cncl; Var Capt Cheerldng; Gym; Var Capt Pom Pon; NHS; Pres Acad Fit Awd; Sthrn CA Yth Ctznshp Sem 89; PDK Prspctv Tchrs Inst Camp 89; All-Star Chrldng Squad Coach; UCLA; Cinematogrphy.

MARTINEZ, CESAR H; Nogales HS; La Puente, CA; (2); 99/2000; Var Ftbl; Var Trk; Cit Awd; Hon Roll; Pres Acad Fit Awd; Ftbl Capt; Miami U; Dietician.

MARTINEZ, CHRISTINA; Mountain View HS; El Monte, CA; (1).

MARTINEZ, CHRISTINA A; Fremont HS; Sunnyvale, CA; (3); 28/380; VP Service Clb; School Play; Ed Nwsp; Rep Stu Cncl; JV Var Cheerldng; NHS; Rotary Awd; Exec Cncl, CSF; Pr Cnslr; Stu Mnth; Rally Commssnr; Red/White Awd Jrnlsm; Harvard Almni Awd Outstndng Jr; U Of CA San Diego; Phy.

MARTINEZ, CHRISTINA C; Turlock HS; Turlock, CA; (1); Band; Mrchg Band; Pep Band; Bsktbl; Sftbl; Trk; Vllybl; Intrstd Drwng, Pntng & Wdwrk.

MARTINEZ, CHRISTINA E; Sacred Heart HS; Los Angeles, CA; (3); 5/100; Cmnty Wkr; GAA; Chorus; Church Choir; School Play; High Hon Roll; Hon Roll; NHS; Sci Pin; Jr Statesman; Devry Tech Inst; Comp Tech.

MARTINEZ, CHRISTINA Y; Woodrow Wilson HS; Los Angeles, CA; (4); Debate Tm; NFL; Pep Clb; Ed Nwsp; 90 Bicentennial Team 1st Pl Regionals & 9th In St In Natl Bicntnl Competition On Constn & Bl Of Rts; UC Riverside.

MARTINEZ, CHRISTOPHER; Hesperia HS; Hesperia, CA; (4); Boy Scts; Church Yth Grp; Teachers Aide; Drm Mjr(t); Mrchg Band; Var Cheerldng; Hon Roll; Golden St Geom Awds; AR Tech U; Nuclear Physicist.

MARTINEZ, CHRISTOPHER L; Carpinteria HS; Carpinteria, CA; (4); Cmnty Wkr; JV Var Bsbl; JV Var Ftbl; JV Var Mgr(s); Hon Roll; 280 Credits In HS; Sant Barbara City Coll; Acctnt.

MARTINEZ, CINDY K; Anaheim HS; Anaheim, CA; (3); Pres German Clb; Var Sftbl; Var Vllybl; CA ST Fullerton.

MARTINEZ, CLAUDIA M; Covina HS; West Covina, CA; (3); Hon Roll; CSF; CA ST U Los Angeles; Ped.

MARTINEZ, CRYSTAL C; Oak Ridge HS; Cameron Park, CA; (1); Church Yth Grp; Cmnty Wkr; Var L Trk.

MARTINEZ, DAMIAN; Glen A Wilson HS; Hacienda Hts, CA; (4); Debate Tm; Spanish Clb; Rptr Nwsp; Var JV Socr; Var Trk; Spanish NHS; Acad Decthln LA Cnty No 1 Wnnrs; Mock Trial Defnse Lawyer; Chptr Pres Jr Statesmn Amer; Engl.

MARTINEZ, DAMIAN S; San Marcos HS; San Marcos, CA; (1); Scholastic Bowl; Var Swmmng; High Hon Roll; Swim Tm; Lifeguard; Phy.

MARTINEZ, DANA; La Habra HS; La Habra, CA; (3); 20/414; Pep Clb; Quiz Bowl; Color Guard; Treas Soph Cls; Off Jr Cls; VP Sr Cls; Powder Puff Ftbl; High Hon Roll; Hon Roll; Flag Tm Co-Capt; Stu Govt Day; Psych.

MARTINEZ, DANAE; Western Christian HS; Pomona, CA; (4); Church Yth Grp; Cmnty Wkr; Model UN; Pep Clb; Teachers Aide; Chorus; Church Choir; School Play; Stu Cncl; Score Keeper; Hd Chrldr 3 Yrs; Gymnst; US CA Davis; Phys Thrpy.

MARTINEZ, DANIEL; Sanger HS; Sanger, CA; (2); Prfct Atten Awd; Pres Acad Fit Awd; Golden ST Exam Schl Rcgntn; Fresno ST U.

MARTINEZ, DANIEL R; Hawthorne HS; Hawthorne, CA; (2); JV Bsbl; Var Socr; JV Vllybl; Var Wt Lftg; Knight Clb; Engrng.

MARTINEZ, DAVID; San Ramon Valley HS; Danville, CA; (2); Varsity Clb; Var Socr; JV Trk; Hon Roll; Mst Outstndng Stu Engl, Spnsh, Advncd Math & Hstry; U Pacific; Bus Finance.

MARTINEZ, DAVID; Sanger HS; Sanger, CA; (2); ROTC; Cit Awd; Military Police.

MARTINEZ, DAVID A; Rio Linda SR HS; Sacramento, CA; (2); Cit Awd; Hon Roll.

MARTINEZ, DAVID A; St Francis HS; Alhambra, CA; (2); Church Yth Grp; Cmnty Wkr; Math Clb; JV Bsbl; U CA Berkeley.

MARTINEZ, DAWN M; Richard Gahr HS; Artesia, CA; (3); Hon Roll; Blue & Gold Awd 88-90; Span II 88-89; Span III & Chem 89-90; U Berkeley; Sci.

MARTINEZ, DENEISE; Soquel HS; Aptos, CA; (3); Church Yth Grp; FFA; Chorus; Stu Cncl; Var Cheerldng; Var Pom Pon; Var Trk; Fresno; Vet.

MARTINEZ, DIANA; Pasadena HS; Pasadena, CA; (1); Church Yth Grp; French Clb; Me CHA.

MARTINEZ, DIANA V; North HS; Bakersfield, CA; (2); Band; Mrchg Band; Pep Band; Hon Roll; Bus.

MARTINEZ, EDITH C; Bell HS; Maywood, CA; (3); Rep Frsh Cls; Rep Jr Cls; Cit Awd; Hon Roll; Arch.

MARTINEZ, ELISA M; Sutter Union HS; Loma Rica, CA; (3); 17/75; FFA; Rptr Nwsp; Hon Roll; Auto Body Painter.

MARTINEZ, ELIZABETH; El Cajon Valley HS; El Cajon, CA; (2); Law.

MARTINEZ, ELMER R; Birmingham HS; Los Angeles, CA; (4); 61/425; Var Socr; Cit Awd; Hon Roll; Stu Of Mnth Frgn Lng; CA ST U Los Angls; Pltcl Sci.

MARTINEZ, EMILIANO Z; Del Campo HS; Sacramento, CA; (3); Varsity Clb; JV Var Ftbl; JV Trk; JV Wrstlng.

MARTINEZ, ERIKA R; Bolsa Grande HS; Garden Grove, CA; (3); Drama Clb; Office Aide; SADD; Band; Mrchg Band; Trk; Hon Roll; Prodcr.

MARTINEZ, ESMERALDA; Saddleback HS; Santa Ana, CA; (1); French Clb; Yrbk; U Of CA Fullerton; Nrsng.

MARTINEZ, ESTHER; Sierra Vista HS; Baldwin Park, CA; (1); JV Bsktbl.

MARTINEZ, FRACIA S; Castle Park HS; Chula Vista, CA; (3); Var Tennis; Amer-Asian Clb; Comp Sci.

MARTINEZ, GERARDO; Fremont HS; Oakland, CA; (2); Church Yth Grp; Latin Clb; Math Clb; ROTC; Drill Tm; Bsbl; Bsktbl; Ftbl; Swmmng; Wt Lftg; Upward Bound Pgm; Partnershp Pgm; Math/Engrng/Sci/Achvt-MESA; U CA-SANTA Barbara; Civil Engr.

MARTINEZ, GLORIA; Montebello HS; Montebello, CA; (2); Spanish Clb; SADD; Acpl Chr; Lbrn Chorus; Stat Bsktbl; Hon Roll.

MARTINEZ, GLORIA N; Sacred Heart Prep; Menlo Park, CA; (2); JV Cheerldng; Var Crs Cntry; JV Swmmng; Var Trk; Hon Roll.

MARTINEZ, GREG; Victory Christian HS; Placerville, CA; (3); Church Yth Grp; FCA; Yrbk; Off Sr Cls; Bsktbl; Ftbl; High Hon Roll; Hon Roll; NHS; School Musical; Supvr Awd; Biola U; Comp Sci.

MARTINEZ, IVAN; Robert A Millikan HS; Long Beach, CA; (4); 15/759; Boy Scts; Pres Computer Clb; Sec Key Clb; Quiz Bowl; Science Clb; Rep Jr Cls; Rep Sr Cls; Stu Cncl; Var L Swmmng; High Hon Roll; Waterpolo Ltr & Chmps; Hispnc Edctrs Schlr; CSF; Slide Show Photogrphr; Wharton Schl; Bus Adm.

MARTINEZ, JAIME; Modesto HS; Modesto, CA; (3); Boy Scts; Teachers Aide; Little League Bsbl Team Asstnt Coach.

MARTINEZ, JAIME F; Santa Maria HS; Santa Maria, CA; (3); Intrml Bsktbl; Var Ftbl; Intrml Wt Lftg; Drftg Articultn Cert.

MARTINEZ, JASON A; Lemoore HS; Lemoore, CA; (3); FBLA; Spanish Clb; SADD; Stage Crew; Bsbl; Ftbl; Socr; Wrstlng; High Hon Roll; Outstndng Work Hnrs Engl; Jr Var Bsbl Capt; UC Davis; Bus.

MARTINEZ, JAVIER; Saddleback HS; Santa Ana, CA; (1); Orange Coast Coll.

MARTINEZ, JEREMY R; Hesperia HS; Hesperia, CA; (2); Boy Scts; Pres Church Yth Grp; ROTC; Church Choir; Var Socr.

MARTINEZ, JESSE; Calexico HS; Calexico, CA; (1); JV Wrstlng; High Hon Roll; Commnctns.

MARTINEZ, JESUS; Mt Whitney HS; Farmersville, CA; (2); SADD; JV Ftbl; Car Audio Systems; Exotic Cars; UCSC; Bus.

MARTINEZ, JOHN R; Damien HS; Upland, CA; (4); 78/188; Ski Clb; Nwsp; Rep Frsh Cls; JV Bsbl; JV Tennis; Hon Roll; Biking Club; Kairos Retreat Ldr; Tijuana Project; U S CA; Entrprnrshp.

MARTINEZ, JOHNNY F; Fillmore HS; Fillmore, CA; (2); Bsbl; Socr; Wt Lftg.

MARTINEZ, JONATHAN E; Rosemead HS; San Gabriel, CA; (3); FBLA; JV Trk; Hon Roll; Pres Acad Fit Awd; Gun Clb VP; Wrld Hstry & Geogphy Hnrs Cls; US Hstry Adv Plcmnt Cls; Cal Tech; Aerospc.

MARTINEZ, JORGE; Oakland HS; Oakland, CA; (4); 108/405; Band; Chorus; Jazz Band; Orch; School Musical; Crs Cntry; Socr; Yng Musicians Pgm UC Brkly; Natl Hspnc Schlrshp Pgm Semi-Fnlst; All-City Jazz Band & Orchstra; US Intl U; Bus.

MARTINEZ, JOSE A; Sweetwater HS; National City, CA; (1); Math Tm; Bio Hnrs; UCSD; Cmptrs.

MARTINEZ, JOSE L; Lynwood HS; Lynwood, CA; (2); Var Crs Cntry; Var Tennis; JV Trk; Long Beach ST; Educ.

MARTINEZ, JOSE L; Mount Pleasant HS; San Jose, CA; (4); Teachers Aide; Close-Up Pgm; Plyd PAL Ftbl/Bsbl; Dist Atty.

MARTINEZ, JUAN I; Cantwell HS; Los Angeles, CA; (3); Letterman Clb; Yrbk; Var Bsbl; Var Bsktbl; Var Ftbl; Var Socr; Hon Roll; CA ST Los Angeles; Bus.

MARTINEZ, JUAN J; Garfield HS; Los Angeles, CA; (3); Teachers Aide; Varsity Clb; Var Crs Cntry; Var Ftbl; Score Keeper; Var Sftbl; Var Trk; Var Vllybl; Wt Lftg; Prfct Atten Awd; Rock Climbing Clb.

MARTINEZ, JUAN M; Gonzales Union HS; Gonzales, CA; (1); Cit Awd; Hon Roll; Prfct Atten Awd; Cmptr Tech.

MARTINEZ, JUANA M; Alisal HS; Salinas, CA; (3); Girl Scts; Hosp Aide; Hon Roll; USC Santa Cruz; Pre Med.

MARTINEZ, JULIAN M; Hoover HS; Fresno, CA; (3); English Clb; Math Clb; Science Clb; Spanish Clb; Variety Show; Congrsnl Schlr Natl Young Ldrsh Conf; Photo; SDSU; Eng.

MARTINEZ, JULIE N; Riverbank HS; Riverbank, CA; (2); Church Yth Grp; Drama Clb; Thesps; School Play; Mgr Stage Crew; Phtg Yrbk; Powder Puff Ftbl; Hon Roll; Mock Trial Comptn 88-90; Bus Mgmt.

MARTINEZ, JULIETTE V; Lowell HS; San Francisco, CA; (3); Church Yth Grp; Spanish Clb; Band; Orch; Pep Band; Rep Stu Cncl; Rep JV Socr; Intrml Vllybl; Viking Soccer Lge 1st Pl; Georgetown; Aerospace Dynamics.

MARTINEZ, JULIO E; Mayfair HS; Cerritos, CA; (1); Cmnty Wkr; English Clb; Spanish Clb; Rptr Nwsp; Crs Cntry; Cit Awd; High Hon Roll; Hon Roll; Key Clb; Awd For All A In Spnsh; Med.

MARTINEZ, KARLA G; Glendale HS; Glendale, CA; (3); Church Yth Grp; Teachers Aide; Cit Awd; Prfct Atten Awd; Badmntn JV; Stu Mnth Awd; Lang.

MARTINEZ, KARLA P; Chino HS; Chino, CA; (3); Spanish Clb; Prncpl Hnr Rl; Stu Excl Rcgntn; Cal Poly U; Arch.

MARTINEZ, KATRINA L; Theodore Roosevelt HS; Fresno, CA; (4); 63/605; Cmnty Wkr; Dance Clb; VP Letterman Clb; Service Clb; School Play; Stage Crew; Var Capt Socr; Gottschalks Hi Deb; Tri 12 Svc Club; Acadmc Excllnc In Bio Awd; CA ST U Fresno; Phys Thrpy.

MARTINEZ, LA VONNE C; Highlands HS; North Highlands, CA; (3); French Clb; Powder Puff Ftbl; Hon Roll; Ftbl Mgr; Psych.

MARTINEZ, LAURA M; Fillmore HS; Fillmore, CA; (4); Church Yth Grp; FFA; SADD; Teachers Aide; Band; Mrchg Band; Ed Yrbk; Sftbl; Cit Awd; Varsity Clb; Helper To Down Syndrom Person & Lrng More About Them; Paralegal.

MARTINEZ, LAURIE M; Norte Vista HS; Riverside, CA; (1); #72 In Class; Church Yth Grp; Cmnty Wkr; Church Choir; Color Guard; High Hon Roll; Hon Roll; Prfct Atten Awd; Funniest In Color Guard; Bus.

MARTINEZ, LEE B; Saddleback HS; Santa Ana, CA; (3); Boy Scts; Band; JV Ftbl; JV Trk; Var Wrstlng; Karate; Med.

MARTINEZ, LETICIA; Calipatria HS; Calipatria, CA; (3); Math.

MARTINEZ, LINDA M; Fairfield HS; Suisun City, CA; (2); Church Yth Grp; GAA; High Hon Roll; CSF Secy; SADD; Drl Tm; Stanford U.

MARTINEZ, LISA; Alder JR HS; Fontana, CA; (1); Office Aide; Cheerldng; Sftbl; Hon Roll; Cal ST Fullerton; Bus.

MARTINEZ, LISA; St Josephs HS; Anaheim, CA; (3); 9/180; Cmnty Wkr; Drill Tm; High Hon Roll; CSF; CA ST Fullerton; Bus Mgmt.

MARTINEZ, LISA M; Paraclete HS; Lancaster, CA; (3); Debate Tm; Spanish Clb; SADD; Flag Corp; CA ST Northridge; Bus.

MARTINEZ, LIZETTE MARIE; La Reina HS; Moorpark, CA; (3); 19/67; GAA; Letterman Clb; Pep Clb; Service Clb; Spanish Clb; Teachers Aide; Varsity Clb; Var L Cheerldng; Cit Awd; Hon Roll; Mst Outstndng JV Chrldr 88-89.

MARTINEZ, LORENA; Riverdale Joint Union HS; Five Points, CA; (4); FTA; Intnl Clb; Pep Clb; SADD; Chorus; Cheerldng; Hon Roll; MECHA Clb; Fresno ST U.

MARTINEZ, LORENA A; Chula Vista HS; San Diego, CA; (2); 85/203; Chess Clb; Debate Tm; Cit Awd; UCSD; Dentist.

MARTINEZ, LOURDEZ; Edison HS; Fresno, CA; (1); Teachers Aide; CSU Fresno; Tchr.

MARTINEZ, LUCIA; Montgomery HS; San Diego, CA; (2); French Clb; Band; Flag Corp; Mrchg Band; Pep Band; Rep Frsh Cls; Rep Soph Cls; Sftbl; Cit Awd; Hon Roll; Banner Team; Berkeley; Lawyer.

MARTINEZ, LUIS A; Orosi HS; Orosi, CA; (3); 18/177; Church Yth Grp; Office Aide; Spanish Clb; Teachers Aide; Var Bsbl; Hon Roll; Fresno ST; Teacher.

MARTINEZ, MANUEL E; Garfield HS; Pico Rivera, CA; (3); Chess Clb; Science Clb; Mst Outstndng Stu Awd; Awd Excllnce; Outstndng Stu Adv Math & Chem; Bus.

MARTINEZ, MARCO A; Alisal HS; Salinas, CA; (2); Drama Clb; JV Socr; Engrng.

MARTINEZ, MARIA; King City HS; Greenfield, CA; (3); Computer Clb; French Clb; FFA; Hon Roll; Sacramento Acad; Bus.

MARTINEZ, MARIA D; Alisal HS; Salinas, CA; (2); AFS; Drama Clb; Pres Frsh Cls; VP Soph Cls; Stu Cncl; High Hon Roll; Pres Acad Fit Awd; Rotary Awd; CSF; Asian Exchange; GATE; ADAPT Sec; Acad Decathlon Tm.

MARTINEZ, MARIA D; Cajon HS; San Bernardino, CA; (2); Yrbk; Gym; Prfct Atten Awd; One Of Bst Bilingual Stu; Valley Coll; Doctor.

MARTINEZ, MARIA E; Bell Gardens HS; Commerce, CA; (2); Drill Tm; JV Socr; JV Trk; JV Vllybl; U Of S CA; Bus Admin.

MARTINEZ, MARIA E; Francis Polytechnic HS; Sun Valley, CA; (3); Hon Roll.

MARTINEZ, MARIA S; Bellarmine-Jefferson HS; North Hollywood, CA; (3); 40/150; Church Yth Grp; Spanish Clb; Var Tennis; Hon Roll; Guard Pride Rcgnt Awd 89 & 90; Prom Cmmtte 90; Nrs.

MARTINEZ, MARIBEL M; Warren HS; Downey, CA; (3); Ski Clb; Teachers Aide; Trk; CA ST U; Real Estate.

MARTINEZ, MARIO; Menlo Atherton HS; East Palo Alto, CA; (3); Art Clb; Church Yth Grp; Cmnty Wkr; Dance Clb; Latin Clb; Office Aide; Spanish Clb; Chorus; School Musical; Swing Chorus; Cycling; CA Poly San Luis Obispo; Engr.

MARTINEZ, MELANIE A; Eisenhower HS; San Bernardino, CA; (3); High Hon Roll; NHS; CSF; Grls Acad Clb-Sobobans, Svc Clb Azurettes; Usc; Bus.

MARTINEZ, MELISSA; Shafter HS; Shafter, CA; (4); Church Yth Grp; Office Aide; Color Guard; Ed Nwsp; Mgr Yrbk; Sec Jr Cls; Sec Sr Cls; L Tennis; Hon Roll; Shafter Jr Miss Pgm 88-89; Phrmcst Clerk; U Pacific-Stockton; Phrmcy.

MARTINEZ, MELISSA J; Rubidoux HS; Riverside, CA; (4); AFS; Church Yth Grp; Science Clb; Acpl Chr; Swing Chorus; Treas Soph Cls; Tennis; NHS; Aeronautcs.

MARTINEZ, MONICA L; El Camino HS; Oceanside, CA; (3); Dance Clb; Pep Clb; Teachers Aide; Drill Tm; Variety Show; Yrbk; JV Socr; Hon Roll; Wildcat Wnnr; Candt Yrbk Edtr In Chf; Jrnlsm.

MARTINEZ, PATRICIA; Downtown Business Magnet HS; Los Angeles, CA; (3); Cmnty Wkr; French Clb; Latin Clb; Library Aide; Spanish Clb; Teachers Aide; High Hon Roll; Hon Roll; Ntl Merit Schol; Prfct Atten Awd; Cal Poly Pomona; Engrng.

MARTINEZ, PATRICIA G; Ontario HS; Ontario, CA; (2); German Clb; Htl Mgmt.

MARTINEZ, POPPY; Modoc HS; Alturas, CA; (3); VP Spanish Clb; Hon Roll; Scholastic Bowl; CSF; CA St Acad Decthln Tm; Rainbow Grls; Astrophysics.

MARTINEZ, RACHEL; Bonita Vista HS; Chula Vista, CA; (2); Intnl Clb; Mgr(s); Cit Awd; UC Berkeley; Writer.

MARTINEZ, RAMIRO M; Arvin HS; Mettler, CA; (2); Var Ftbl; Hon Roll.

MARTINEZ, RAMONA; Modesto HS; Modesto, CA; (4); 34/450; Spanish Clb; Teachers Aide; Color Guard; Cit Awd; Hon Roll; Wntr Grd; MASA Clb; Awd Clr Grd; CSU; Bus Admin.

MARTINEZ, RAOUL; Saddleback HS; Irvine, CA; (3); Debate Tm; Letterman Clb; Science Clb; Speech Tm; Chorus; High Hon Roll; Outstndng Achvt Engl 87-88; Acad Achvt Hnrs Entrnce 87; Bronze Mdl Engl 88-89; Novice Trophies Spch 89; Yale; CPA.

MARTINEZ, RAQUEL; Edison HS; Stockton, CA; (3); Teachers Aide; Stu Cncl; Var Cheerldng; Score Keeper; Hon Roll; USC; Psych.

MARTINEZ, RAUL; Skyline HS; Oakland, CA; (2); Science Clb; Hon Roll; Prfct Atten Awd; Cal ST Hayward; Law.

MARTINEZ, REGINA K; Rio Mesa HS; Oxnard, CA; (1); Hon Roll; Wrtr.

MARTINEZ, RENE J; Bell Gardens HS; Bell Gardens, CA; (1); Hon Roll; Prfct Atten Awd; Ftbl; Wt Lftg; Frosh Top 10 Awd; Soc Stud Best Boy; Most Imprvd Orch Musician; Miami; Arch.

MARTINEZ, RICK; North Salinas HS; Salinas, CA; (4); 18/350; L Var Bsktbl; Var L Ftbl; High Hon Roll; NHS; Pres Acad Fit Awd; Natl Ftbl Fndtn Schlr/Athlte Fnlst; CA Polytech ST; Nutrtnl Sci.

MARTINEZ, RICK J; Fillmore HS; Fillmore, CA; (2); 32/317; Office Aide; SADD; Rptr Lit Mag; JV Ftbl; JV Trk; Wrstlng; High Hon Roll; Hon Roll; Ftr Ldrs Amer; Northridge; Elec Engr.

MARTINEZ, ROBERTO C; Central Union HS; El Centro, CA; (2); Church Yth Grp; FBLA.

MARTINEZ, ROCHELLE; Cajon HS; San Bernardino, CA; (4); GAA; Stu Cncl; Var Cheerldng; Riverside CC.

MARTINEZ, ROSA; Sierra Vista HS; Baldwin Park, CA; (3); Teachers Aide; Bsbl; Bsktbl; Sftbl; Swmmng; Tennis; Vllybl; Wt Lftg; Cit Awd; Hon Roll; Fshn Mrch.

MARTINEZ, RUTH N; Grant HS; Sacramento, CA; (3); Church Yth Grp; Dance Clb; Intnl Clb; Vllybl; Cit Awd; Hon Roll; CSF; Upward Bond Proj; Bus.

MARTINEZ, SARA; Edison HS; Fresno, CA; (4); 29/225; Church Yth Grp; SADD; Band; Mrchg Band; Orch; Var Swmmng; Stat Vllybl; High Hon Roll; Natl Hispanic Schlr; Mesa; UC San Diego; Reg Nurse.

MARTINEZ, SERGIO; Bolsa Grande HS; Garden Grove, CA; (1); Boy Scts; Spanish Clb; JV Crs Cntry; JV Socr; JV Trk; Police Sci.

MARTINEZ, SERGIO A; John F Kennedy HS; Buena Park, CA; (2); Var L Crs Cntry; Var L Trk; JV Capt Wrstlng; High Hon Roll; Hon Roll; Golden St Exam Geom Schl Hnrs; JV Wrstlng MVP; Kaiser Permanente Teen Clinic Teen Advsr Grp; Comp Prgmr.

MARTINEZ, SHEILA; Montgomery HS; San Diego, CA; (3); Cmnty Wkr; Hosp Aide; Church Choir; Mrchg Band; Cit Awd; Hon Roll; Prfct Atten Awd; Pres Acad Fit Awd; Gldn St Exm Achvt Awd Geom; CSF; UCSD; Engrng.

MARTINEZ, SILVIA M; John Muir HS; Altadena, CA; (3); Latin Clb; Spanish Clb; Variety Show; Off Soph Cls; JV Vllybl; Cit Awd; Hon Roll; Ntl Merit Ltr; Opt Clb Awd; Upward Bound Pgm; Law.

MARTINEZ, SONIA; Huntington Park HS; Huntington Park, CA; (3); Dance Clb; Office Aide; Teachers Aide; Drill Tm; High Hon Roll; MESA; Cls Rep; Bus Admin.

MARTINEZ, SONIA B; Gompers HS; San Diego, CA; (2); 67/145; JV Vllybl; Prfct Atten Awd; MESA; Pan Asian.

MARTINEZ, STEVIE M; Arlington HS; Riverside, CA; (3); Var Bsbl; JV Ftbl; Am Leg Bsbl; Riverside Agnst Drgs; Casa Blanca Hm Nghbrly Svc; Arlington HS Outstndng Achvt Awd; CVL Engrng.

MARTINEZ, SYLVIA; Lowell HS; San Francisco, CA; (4); Church Yth Grp; Stu Cncl; Var JV Cheerldng; Upward Bound Coll Prep Program; Registry VP; UC Davis; English.

MARTINEZ, TERESA M; Atascadero HS; Atascadero, CA; (1); Church Yth Grp; Drill Tm; Cal Poly; Engl.

MARTINEZ, TINA M; Kingsburg HS; Kingsburg, CA; (1); Hon Roll; Fresno ST U; Nrsng.

MARTINEZ, VERONICA; St Paul HS; Pico Rivera, CA; (4); Am Leg Aux Girls St; Red Cross Aide; Spanish Clb; Rptr Nwsp; Var Socr; Var Trk; JV Vllybl; Hon Roll; NHS; Spanish NHS; March For Hunger; Vlntr; Amer Red Cross Blood Drive Chairperson; UCLA; Pre-Med.

MARTINEZ, VERONICA B; Fresno HS; Fresno, CA; (1); Church Yth Grp; Band; Mrchg Band; Cit Awd; Fresno ST; Acctnt.

MARTINEZ, VIOLETA S; Butte Valley HS; Dorris, CA; (4); 2/19; Cmnty Wkr; Drama Clb; French Clb; Pres FHA; Library Aide; Office Aide; Ski Clb; Spanish Clb; SADD; Teachers Aide; OR Inst Tech; Phys Thrpy.

MARTINEZ-JASSO, ANGELES; Our Lady Of Loretto Bishop HS; Los Angeles, CA; (3); 6/100; GAA; Rep Stu Cncl; Var Bsktbl; High Hon Roll; Hon Roll; NHS; Amb Clb; Loyola Marymount; Law.

MARTINI, FAYNE M; Portola JR/Sr HS; Portola, CA; (1); Var Sftbl; JV Vllybl; Whitworth Coll; Marine Archelgy.

MARTINI, LAURENT A; Lycee Francais HS; San Francisco, CA; (2); School Play; Stage Crew; Rptr Yrbk; Stu Cncl; Music; Art; Bilingual Engl, Frnch; Acad Of Art Coll; Advrtsmnt.

MARTINI, MICHAEL T; Arcata HS; Arcata, CA; (2); Library Aide; Intrml Bsktbl; Var Socr; Hon Roll; Amer Lgn Bsbl Team.

MARTINS, LISA; Fred C Beyer HS; Modesto, CA; (3); Spanish Clb; Stat Bsktbl; Stat Vllybl; Hon Roll; Secy Fri Ngt Live; Patriot Awd Math; CSF; U Of MA Amhurst; Intr Desgn.

MARTINSEN, CARLENE; Christian HS; El Cajon, CA; (4); 6/96; Church Yth Grp; Teachers Aide; Pres Frsh Cls; Rep Jr Cls; Rep Stu Cncl; Var L Socr; Var Capt Tennis; Var L Vllybl; High Hon Roll; VP Soph Cls; Distngshd Stu; Outstndng Stu 3 Yrs; Hnr Sctu; The Masters Coll; Phys Educ.

MARTINSON, NICHOLE M; Alameda HS; Alameda, CA; (4); 109/357; Drama Clb; Thesps; School Musical; School Play; Stage Crew; Pom Pon; Hon Roll; Cable/TV Media Island City Limits; Bank Of Amer Awd Outstndng Achvt Drama; Acad A Eng, Fine Arts; San Francisco ST U; Radio.

MARTIR, GRACIELA; Benjamin Franklin HS; Los Angeles, CA; (4); Band; Drill Tm; Yrbk; Cit Awd; Psych.

MARTON, TRACY R; Gahr HS; Norwalk, CA; (1); Speech Tm; Teachers Aide; Yrbk; Off Frsh Cls; High Hon Roll; Hon Roll; Pres Schlr; UC Long Beach; Eng Teacher.

MARTSH, CARMEN T; Etiwanda HS; Fontana, CA; (2); Church Yth Grp; JA; High Hon Roll; Prfct Atten Awd; U Of NM; Tchng.

MARUKO, SUSAN E; Edison HS; Fresno, CA; (1); Temple Yth Grp; Orch; High Hon Roll; Fresno Yth Philharmonic Orch; Yth Perf Awds Keybd Cncrts Piano, 3rd Pl; MTAC St Music Cnvntn.

MARUN, ELIZABETH ERIKA; Torrey Pines HS; Rancho Santa Fe, CA; (2); Ed Nwsp; Hon Roll; Helen Woodward Animal Ctr Vlntr, Thrptc Riding For Handicapped; UCSD; Anthropology.

MARUYAMA, EMI; Bonita Vista HS; Chula Vista, CA; (4); 43/521; Intnl Clb; ROTC; Band; Cit Awd; Hon Roll; Pres Acad Fit Awd; Outstndng Stu Accntng Clss, Wrld Cultures Clss; Geom Clss; Bus Adm.

MARVILLE, ONITSHA J; Norte Vista HS; Riverside, CA; (1); 17/492; Hon Roll; Dance; Sftbl; Hnrs Awds 4 Qrtrs; Dentist.

MARVIN, ERIC; Kings Christian HS; Hanford, CA; (1); 1/20; Church Yth Grp; Cmnty Wkr; Nwsp; Rep Frsh Cls; Stu Cncl; High Hon Roll; Hon Roll; CA Schlrshp Fed.

MARVIN, JENNIFER A; Bonita Vista HS; Chula Vista, CA; (3); Church Yth Grp; Cmnty Wkr; FBLA; Drill Tm; Variety Show; Yrbk; Crs Cntry; Trk; Bus Mgmt.

MARVIN, STEVE; Kings Christian HS; Hanford, CA; (3); 1/20; Church Yth Grp; Letterman Clb; Treas Stu Cncl; Cit Awd; High Hon Roll; Hon Roll; Cmnty Wkr; School Play; Nwsp; Yrbk; Hmcmng King; CSF; Stu Ldrshp Awd.

MARX, THOMAS P; Corona SR HS; Corona, CA; (2); Church Yth Grp; Pres Computer Clb; Debate Tm; Letterman Clb; Science Clb; Speech Tm; Stage Crew; Ed Lit Mag; JV Swmmng; Hon Roll; CSF; KC Altar Srvr Awd; US Naval Acad; Aerosp Engrng.

MARZAN, JOEL; Santa Fe HS; Santa Fe Spgs, CA; (4); 4/330; Cmnty Wkr; Computer Clb; Key Clb; Library Aide; Math Clb; Office Aide; Science Clb; Service Clb; Spanish Clb; Teachers Aide; LA Rip Statue Liberty Fstvl 86; LA Mayors Cmmndtn; LA Yth Anti-Drug Spkr; 1st Soroptomist Clb 90; UCLA; Poltcl Sci.

MARZAN, LEAH MAY; Bishop Montgomery HS; Gardena, CA; (4); 130/358; Service Clb; Ed Yrbk; Ed Lit Mag; Rep Frsh Cls; Hon Roll; Prfct Atten Awd; Asian Cltr Clb; Hnrb Mntn Annl Sci Fair-Physcs Div; Lcl CC Drng Snr Yr-Accmltng Credits; U Of Southern CA; Biomdcl Engr.

MARZEC, JESSICA A; El Camino HS; Oceanside, CA; (1); Scholastic Bowl; High Hon Roll; Pres Acad Fit Awd; Engl Dept Stu Yr; MIT; Aerospace Engrng.

MARZETTE, CANDICE A; Bullard HS; Fresno, CA; (3); Key Clb; SADD; Band; Mrchg Band; Pep Band; Accounting.

MARZIANO, ANDRA M; El Cerrito HS; El Cerrito, CA; (2); Thesps; Acpl Chr; Flag Corp; School Musical; School Play; Stage Crew; Swmmng; Drama Schl Camps Cnslr.

MARZILIANO, TINA D; Clovis HS; Clovis, CA; (3); FFA; NFL; SADD; Rptr Lit Mag; JV Bsktbl; Var Powder Puff Ftbl; Sign Lang Clb; USC; Pre-Med.

MARZILLIER, NICOLE A; Kennedy HS; Granada Hills, CA; (3); Teachers Aide; Hon Roll; Acad Pentathalon; Sci.

MARZOLF, CURT H; Woodland HS; Woodland, CA; (3); Cmnty Wkr; French Clb; JV Var Crs Cntry; JV Trk; Hon Roll; Coach; Little Dribblers; Soccer; Clarkson U; Aerospace Engrng.

MARZULLO, SARA F; San Clemente HS; San Juan Capistra, CA; (1); Church Yth Grp; 4-H; German Clb; Science Clb; Orch; 4-H Awd; Pres Acad Fit Awd; Violin Cert Mrt Level 5; Super Ratng Solo Fest; UC Davis; Vet Med.

MARZWELL, DESIREE; Claremont HS; Claremont, CA; (1); Temple Yth Grp; Drill Tm; Gym; Swmmng; Harvard; Law.

MASALAYSAY, LEILA M; Mercy HS; San Francisco, CA; (1); Dance Clb; GAA; Rep Frsh Cls; Var Sftbl; JV Vllybl; Hon Roll; CSF; UC Davis; Med.

MASANGCAY, GINA G; Pittsburg HS; Pittsburg, CA; (1); Sec Frsh Cls; Stat Bsktbl; Stat Trk; JV Vllybl.

MASANGCAY, MAUREEN F; Irvington HS; Fremont, CA; (3); High Hon Roll; Hon Roll; Prfct Atten Awd; Peroming Arts Dept Club; Engl Awd; Vocational Sch; Bus Admin.

MASCARINA, JANICE; Castle Park HS; Chula Vista, CA; (4); 4/328; Hosp Aide; Tennis; Cit Awd; Hon Roll; Prfct Atten Awd; Rotary Yth Ldrshp Awd; Grls, Wmn Sprts Day Rcgntn; Stu Bdy VP; Bus.

MASCARINAS, NORMAN C; Seaside HS; Fort Ord, CA; (3); AFS; Spanish Clb; High Hon Roll; Hon Roll; Jr NHS; DYA Ftbl & Soccer; Cal Poly; Mech Engr.

MASCARO, KELLY R; Pinole Valley HS; Hercules, CA; (1); Church Yth Grp; Ski Clb; Bsktbl; Sftbl; Hon Roll.

MASCORRO, MARISA; Mary Star Of The Sea HS; Long Beach, CA; (4); Church Yth Grp; Math Clb; Pep Clb; Var JV Cheerldng; JV Sftbl; Hon Roll; NHS; Ntl Merit SF; CSF; JR Stsmn Assoc; Engr.

MASHARO, ANN; Huntington Beach HS; Huntington Beach, CA; (4); French Clb; Office Aide; Tennis; Trk; Pres Acad Fit Awd; Tower Awd-Excl French; Orange Coast Coll; Frgn Lang.

MASIAS, ROSA J; Nogales HS; La Puente, CA; (2); Band; Mrchg Band; Pep Band; Hon Roll; Prfct Atten Awd; CA ST Los Angeles; Psych.

MASIH, ANUPAMA; Parallete HS; Palmdale, CA; (3); Church Yth Grp; Cmnty Wkr; Drama Clb; Hosp Aide; Key Clb; Service Clb; Teachers Aide; Chorus; Church Choir; Hon Roll; Princpls Awd; CSF; Svc Awd; Zee Clb; UCLA; Physician.

MASINAS, AISA M; John A Rowland HS; Rowland Hts, CA; (3); French Clb; Office Aide; Science Clb; Drill Tm; Stage Crew; Rep Stu Cncl; Powder Puff Ftbl; High Hon Roll; NHS; Prfct Atten Awd; Superior Achvt Drama; CA Schlrshp Fed; Loyola Marymount; Pre-Law.

MASLOWSKI, SANDY; Bonita HS; La Verne, CA; (2); Band; Color Guard; Mrchg Band; Majorette; USC.

MASON, CANEYA C; Luther Burbank HS; Sacramento, CA; (2); 128/598; Art Clb; Church Yth Grp; Dance Clb; FTA; Girl Scts; ROTC; SADD; Church Choir; Drill Tm; School Play; ROTC Hnr Awd; Prep Squad; Track Awd; MI ST; Med.

MASON, CARRIE R; Apple Valley HS; Apple Valley, CA; (3); Church Yth Grp; Drill Tm; Trk; Hon Roll; Lion Awd; Prfct Atten Awd; Pres Acad Fit Awd; Air Force Military Acad; Math.

MASON, CHRISTINE D; La Sierra HS; Riverside, CA; (3); Girl Scts; Math Clb; SADD; Sec Band; Jazz Band; Mrchg Band; Stage Crew; High Hon Roll; Hon Roll; CSF; RCC.

MASON, DAMIEN M; Casa Grande HS; Petaluma, CA; (2); Varsity Clb; Variety Show; JV Bsbl; Var Ftbl; Var Capt Wrstlng; Hon Roll; Friday Night Live; UC Berkeley; Bus Admin.

MASON, DANIEL E; Redwood HS; Visalia, CA; (2); Treas FBLA; German Clb; Math Clb; Mrchg Band; Hon Roll; FBLA Conf 3rd Pl Math, Voctnl Ed Olympics 3rd Pl Accntng 90; UC Riverside; Biochem.

MASON, ELLIOTT; Beverly Hills HS; Los Angeles, CA; (4); Boy Scts; Science Clb; Ed Nwsp; Var L Crs Cntry; Var L Trk; Ntl Merit Ltr; Pres Acad Fit Awd; Egl Sct; Bnk Of Amer Plq Wnnr In Sci & Math; Elec Engrng.

MASON, GILBERT; Avalon JR/Sr HS; Avalon, CA; (4); 2/21; Am Leg Boys St; Yrbk; Rep Stu Cncl; Wt Lftg; High Hon Roll; Coin & Stamp Cllctn; Martial Arts; Drawing, Art; Golden West; Psych.

MASON, ISAAC A; Mabel E O'farrell SCPA HS; San Diego, CA; (3); Stage Crew; Yrbk; Sec Jr Cls; Hon Roll; Pres Acad Fit Awd; Acctng.

MASON, JAMES F; Yucca Valley HS; Yucca Valley, CA; (2); Church Yth Grp; Computer Clb; Math Clb; Var JV Ftbl; Cit Awd; High Hon Roll; Hon Roll; Prfct Atten Awd; Golden St Exam Hnrs.

MASON, KRISTEN M; Fountain Valley HS; Fountain Valley, CA; (1); JV Trk.

MASON, LISA D; Casa Roble Fundamental HS; Citrus Heights, CA; (2); 62/461; Spanish Clb; Rep Stu Cncl; Mgr(s); Score Keeper; Stat Swmmng; Hon Roll; U CA; Chld Psych.

MASON, MICHELLE L; Chino HS; Ontario, CA; (2); Church Yth Grp; Stu Cncl; Cit Awd; High Hon Roll; Hon Roll; Prfct Atten Awd; Pres Acad Fit Awd; Science Clb; Teachers Aide; Stat Ftbl; Spirit Clb; Badminton Team; CSF; BYU; Child Psych.

MASON, NICHOLE T; John F Kennedy HS; Richmond, CA; (3); Church Yth Grp; Dance Clb; Drama Clb; Science Clb; Chorus; Church Choir; VP Frsh Cls; Rep Ftbl; Rep Jr Cls; Cheerldng; Long Beach ST U; Pharm Studies.

MASON, RHYS; Damien HS; Claremont, CA; (2); 46/269; Chess Clb; Debate Tm; Speech Tm; Teachers Aide.

MASON, SANDRA D; Santa Paula HS; Santa Paula, CA; (3); 14/235; Drama Clb; Key Clb; SADD; School Musical; School Play; Stage Crew; Swmmng; Hon Roll; Acad Ltr.

MASON, SARA; Eagle Rock HS; Los Angeles, CA; (2); Gym; Hon Roll; U Of S CA; Spec Ed.

MASON, TERRY A; Montgomery HS; Santa Rosa, CA; (3); Spanish Clb; Teachers Aide; Hon Roll; Prfct Atten Awd; Stu Of Week 3 Times In One Semester; Badminton Var; Most Imprvd Span Awd; Cal Poly; Aeronautics.

MASON, TINA M; Valley HS; Elk Grove, CA; (3); Church Yth Grp; Office Aide; SADD; Teachers Aide; Chorus; Mgr(s); Powder Puff Ftbl; Score Keeper; Hon Roll; NHS; UC Davis; Pre Law.

MASON, ZACHARY J; Woodside HS; Redwood City, CA; (4); Chess Clb; Church Yth Grp; Computer Clb; Latin Clb; Math Clb; Math Tm; Nwsp; Hon Roll; Fencing; Korote; Boy Area Thulhoid Support Grp; Simons Rock Coll; Al R & D.

MASRI, TARIQ M; Oak Ridge HS; Cameron Park, CA; (3); 12/280; Teachers Aide; Band; Chorus; Orch; School Musical; Stu Cncl; Hon Roll; El Dorado Union Outstndng Sci Achvt 90; San Francisco Yth Orch; Tanglewood Music Inst 90; Music.

MASSEE, JAMES W; Lassen HS; Susanville, CA; (2); 4-H; Band; Jazz Band; Mrchg Band; Pep Band; Ftbl; Swmmng; 4-H Awd; Chico ST U; Comp Prgmr.

MASSEY, JASON E; Edison HS; Huntington Beach, CA; (1); German Clb; Model UN; Tennis; Distngshd Schlr; Orthopedics.

MASSEY, JILL M; Bishop Montgomery HS; Redondo Beach, CA; (2); GAA; Ski Clb; JV Speech Tm; SADD; Varsity Clb; Yrbk; JV Bsktbl; Score Keeper; Var JV Vllybl; UCSD; Marine Bio.

MASSEY, KEVIN R; Lindsay HS; Lindsay, CA; (1); Church Yth Grp; Key Clb; Var L Swmmng; Var L Vllybl; Hon Roll; Water Polo Lttr; Aeron Engrng.

MASSEY, MARY A; Hoover HS; Fresno, CA; (1); Church Yth Grp; Dance Clb; Chorus; Church Choir; Cit Awd; Hon Roll; UCLA; Performing Arts.

MASSEY, SHANNON; Mc Farland HS; Mcfarland, CA; (1); Church Yth Grp; Dance Clb; Debate Tm; Chorus; Var Cheerldng; Var Sftbl; High Hon Roll; Wrld Hstry/Cultres/Geog Awd Wnnr; Fresno ST U; Medcl Care.

MASSEY, TAJAI D; Bishop O'dowd HS; Oakland, CA; (2); Church Yth Grp; Lit Mag; JV Ftbl; JV Trk; High Hon Roll; NEDT Awd; Pres Acad Fit Awd; Blck Stu Union; Gamma Phi Alpha Frat Inc; Stanford; Ped Cardlgst.

MASSIE, JEREMIAH B; Corning Union HS; Corning, CA; (3); Am Leg Boys St; 4-H; Intnl Clb; Letterman Clb; Ski Clb; Spanish Clb; Teachers Aide; Stage Crew; Phtg Yrbk; Intrml JV Bsktbl; Ldrshp Cls; Peer Tutor Math; UCSD; Bio.

MASSOLETTI, CHRISTINE N; Calistoga JR/Sr HS; Calistoga, CA; (2); Church Yth Grp; Ski Clb; Sec Frsh Cls; Rep Soph Cls; JV Var Bsktbl; JV Var Cheerldng; JV Var Pom Pon; Var L Sftbl; Cit Awd; High Hon Roll.

MASSON, SAMUEL T; San Marcos HS; Santa Barbara, CA; (3); 110/350; Drama Clb; School Musical; Variety Show; Ed Nwsp; Rep Frsh Cls; Rep Soph Cls; Rep Jr Cls; Stu Cncl; Prfct Atten Awd; Rotary Awd; Politics.

MAST, ALOUN; Eureka HS; Eureka, CA; (1); Intnl Clb; Teachers Aide; Bsktbl; Socr; Trk; Hon Roll; Stud Of Yr 89; Letter In Eureka Trk Tm; Law.

MAST, THERESA K; Loretto HS; Sacramento, CA; (3); Hosp Aide; Science Clb; Bsktbl; Vllybl; Special Interest-Piano; Voice; Friday Night Live Club; Chruch Youth Group; SAC ST.

MASTAGNI, MICHAEL; Beyer HS; Modesto, CA; (4); 15/512; Var Bsbl; Var Bsktbl; High Hon Roll; Hon Roll; CSF; Bus Admin.

MASTERS, KIMBERLY; Christian HS; Lakeside, CA; (3); Church Yth Grp; 4-H; Hosp Aide; Key Clb; SADD; Teachers Aide; JV Capt Socr; JV Var Sftbl; Stat Var Vllybl; DAR Awd; Masters Coll; Ed.

MASTERSON, LUCY A; Samuel F B Morse HS; San Diego, CA; (4); 85/583; Pres FTA; Var Socr; Var Sftbl; Var Vllybl; Hon Roll; US Army Reserve National Scholar Athlete Award; Sw Coll; Liberal Studies.

MASTON, COLBY J; Southbay Christian HS; Sunnyvale, CA; (2); Spanish Clb; Var Bsbl; San Jose ST; Mech Engr.

MASTON, ERICA; Valley Christian HS; San Jose, CA; (4); Church Yth Grp; Cmnty Wkr; FCA; Mrchg Band; Stage Crew; Treas Jr Cls; Stu Cncl; Var Capt Cheerldng; Var Pom Pon; Hon Roll; All Amer Awd 1990; Hewlett Packard Schlrshp; Ldrshp Awd 1990; Biola U; Bus Admin.

MASTRO, DENISE M; Whittier Christian HS; Fullerton, CA; (2); Church Yth Grp; Ski Clb; JV Var Cheerldng; Powder Puff Ftbl; High Hon Roll; Flag Corp; CA Schltc Fdrtn.

MASTROCINQUE, DENA M; Louisville HS; Van Nuys, CA; (3); 15/66; Church Yth Grp; FHA; Chorus; High Hon Roll; Hon Roll; NHS; St Schlr; UCLA; Law.

MASUDA, AIKO L; Hanford HS; Hanford, CA; (1); VP Frsh Cls; Cheerldng; JV Swmmng; Hon Roll; Peer Cnslng; Child Psych.

MASUDA, MATTHEW C; Atwater HS; Atwater, CA; (2); Service Clb; JV Crs Cntry; Var Trk; Hon Roll; Cal Poly SLO; Cmptr Engrng.

MASUDA, SANDRA Y; Ramona Convent HS; Monterey Park, CA; (3); Art Clb; Cmnty Wkr; GAA; Library Aide; Math Clb; Model UN; Chorus; Nwsp; JV Tennis; Hon Roll; Econ.

MASUDA, YOKO MAYDEEN; Schurr HS; Rosemead, CA; (3); Am Leg Aux Girls St; Cmnty Wkr; French Clb; Hosp Aide; Key Clb; Bsktbl; Bausch & Lomb Sci Awd; Hon Roll; Treas NHS; Japanese Schl Grad.

MASUMURA, YOKO; Gardena SR HS; Gardena, CA; (3); Chrmn Church Yth Grp; Intnl Clb; Spanish Clb; Teachers Aide; Hon Roll; Prfct Atten Awd; High Hnrs Golden St Exmntn Geomtry 88; Bus Admin.

MASUR, SHAWNA C; Lower Lake HS; Clearlake, CA; (3); Church Yth Grp; FBLA; Teachers Aide; Church Choir; Trk; Cit Awd; High Hon Roll; Hon Roll; CA Schlrshp Fed; Bus.

MASUSHIGE, MICHAEL Y; Hawthorne HS; Hawthorne, CA; (1); Pres Chess Clb; Quiz Bowl; Hon Roll; Acad Decathalon; Pepperdine; Comp Engr.

MATA, ABE; John F Kennedy HS; Sacramento, CA; (4); 20/407; Church Yth Grp; Cmnty Wkr; Dance Clb; Office Aide; Capt ROTC; Drill Tm; Var Capt Wrstlng; High Hon Roll; Pres Acad Fit Awd; Pres Schlr; Sacramento Bee Silver Cert; Schlr Athlt Trophy; Tae Kwon Do Black Belt Champ; Sacramento ST U; Med.

MATA, ALEX; Sanger HS; Sanger, CA; (2); Intrml Var Ftbl; Var Wt Lftg; Bio.

MATA, ROBERT J; St Paul HS; Whittier, CA; (3); 102/277; Hon Roll; March For Hunger; Tijuana Baja CA Orpha N Trip; Engrng.

MATA, YOLANDA; Gladstone HS; Azusa, CA; (4); Church Yth Grp; SADD; Var Tennis; Prfct Atten Awd; Badminton; Ed.

MATAELE, VILIAMI; West HS; Lawndale, CA; (4); Pres Church Yth Grp; Cmnty Wkr; Computer Clb; Debate Tm; FCA; JA; Band; Jazz Band; Pep Band; Cit Awd; U CA Santa Cruz; Scl Ecology.

MATAESE, SAOFAGA; Skyline HS; Oakland, CA; (3); Church Yth Grp; Dance Clb; GAA; Varsity Clb; Church Choir; Nwsp; Yrbk; Score Keeper; Sftbl; Vllybl; CSF; BYU; Bus Mgmt.

MATAI, SEEMA; San Marcos HS; Santa Barbara, CA; (2); Cmnty Wkr; Pres Service Clb; Hon Roll; #1 Clb Awd; Pres Of Outstndng Clb Of Yr; Cmnty Service Vlntr; U CA; Med.

MATALON, RENAT; El Camino Real HS; Woodland Hills, CA; (2); SADD; Teachers Aide; Tennis; Cit Awd; Hon Roll; Peer Cnslng; Karate; U San Diego; Med.

MATAS, SANDRA; Bishop Amat HS; Covina, CA; (4); 37/401; Church Yth Grp; Cmnty Wkr; Ed Yrbk; High Hon Roll; NHS; Civil Air Patrl; Latin Am Stu Org Sec; Part Time Employment; Harvard; Bus Admn.

MATCHETT, BRIAN; Taft HS; Topanga, CA; (3); Var L Gym; Prfct Atten Awd; Pres Acad Fit Awd; All Star Tm 89; Rgnl Comptr 3 Yrs; Aeronautics.

MATEJCIK, JOE; Sonoma Valley HS; Kenwood, CA; (3); Hon Roll; CSF; Commnctns.

MATEO, QUEENCY D; Sweetwater HS; National City, CA; (3); 1/364; Dance Clb; VP English Clb; Pres French Clb; Church Choir; Flag Corp; Jazz Band; Yrbk; Cit Awd; High Hon Roll; Prfct Atten Awd; Outstndng Math Plaque; Publcty Cmmssnr Asian Intl Assn; UCSD; Med.

MATHAI, PAUL; Clovis HS; Clovis, CA; (4); Church Yth Grp; Computer Clb; Debate Tm; Math Clb; Math Tm; Science Clb; Bsbl; Tennis; Hon Roll; JETS Awd; Acad Decathalon.

MATHAY, STEVE H; Folsom HS; Folsom, CA; (3); 42/190; Ski Clb; JV Socr; JV Tennis; Ski Team Nastar; Arch.

MATHENEY, BRYAN S; Ventura HS; Ventura, CA; (3); 4/500; Var Swmmng; Hon Roll.

MATHERLY, SHAWNA; Mount Whitney HS; Visalia, CA; (4); 28/373; Sec Capt FFA; Office Aide; SADD; Teachers Aide; Drm Mjr(t); Hon Roll; CSF; FFA Chptr Sweetheart; Sr Pacesetter; UC Davis; Vet Med.

MATHERS, CHRISTOPHER; Antioch HS; Mokelumne Hill, CA; (4); 138/585; Bus Profs of Am; Computer Clb; FBLA; Hon Roll; Cert Profcncy Comp Acctng, Regnl Occptnl Pgm Comp Acctng; Antioch Animanl Hosp Schlrshp; CA ST U Sacramento; Bus Admin.

MATHERSHED, GENE L; Edison HS; Fresno, CA; (4); 90/200; Letterman Clb; Teachers Aide; Var Powder Puff Ftbl; Hon Roll; Libr Asst; Psych.

MATHES, ASHLEIGH D; Academy Of Our Lady Of Peace HS; San Diego, CA; (3); 30/110; GAA; School Musical; Rep Jr Cls; Stu Cncl; Var L Bsktbl; JV Cheerldng; Var L Trk; Var L Vllybl; Hon Roll; NEDT Awd; Jr HS Bsktbl Coach 2 Yrs; Bio.

MATHESON, CAMERON S; Agoura HS; Westlake Village, CA; (4); 3/435; Pres Drama Clb; Acpl Chr; Chorus; School Musical; NHS; Ntl Merit SF; Dartmouth; Law.

MATHESON, ERIK M; Culver City HS; Culver City, CA; (3); French Clb; Varsity Clb; Var Capt Swmmng; Cit Awd; Hon Roll; Waterpolo Team V Capt; Gldn St Acad Excllnc Awd Alg, Geom; Bus.

MATHESON, KEVIN; Del Oro HS; Penryn, CA; (1); Boy Scts; Church Yth Grp; Hon Roll; Musician.

MATHESON, SUSIE M; Kerman HS; Kerman, CA; (4); German Clb; Intnl Clb; Letterman Clb; Varsity Clb; Chorus; School Musical; School Play; Stage Crew; Swing Chorus; Variety Show; Brisane Rock Eistedfod Grp Dance Comptn; YFU Exchng Pgm Stu; Brisbane Coll; Tourism.

MATHEWS, ALEXIS M; C K Mc Clatchy HS; Sacramento, CA; (2); Church Yth Grp; 4-H; FBLA; Girl Scts; Office Aide; Red Cross Aide; ROTC; SADD; Church Choir; Drill Tm; Blck Schlrs; MESA; Cltr Clb; Bus.

MATHEWS, CHRYSTAUNIA; West Covina HS; West Covina, CA; (2); German Clb; Pep Clb; SADD; Drill Tm; Var JV Cheerldng; High Hon Roll; CSF; German Hnr Soc; Friday Night Live.

MATHEWS, COREY L; Atwater HS; Merced, CA; (1); Boy Scts; Intrml Bsktbl; JV Crs Cntry; UCLA; Bus.

MATHEWS, JIM; Irvine HS; Irvine, CA; (3); 5/800; Temple Yth Grp; Band; Mrchg Band; Ftbl; Wt Lftg; Wrstlng; Hon Roll; Northwestern Coll; Med.

MATHEWS, MEGAN A; Venice HS; Venice, CA; (2); Gym; Mgr(s); Cit Awd; High Hon Roll; Pres Acad Fit Awd; HS Peace Clb VP; Peer Cnslr; Psych.

MATHEWS, MICHAEL C; Mater Dei HS; Tustin, CA; (4); Cmnty Wkr; Service Clb; Rptr Yrbk; Pres Sr Cls; Hon Roll; NHS; Pres Acad Fit Awd; Rotary Awd; October Young Man Of The Month; Principals Advisory Board; Social Studies Dept Award; U Of Notre Dame; Amer History.

MATHEWS, MINDY; Needles HS; Needles, CA; (2); 2/90; FHA; Key Clb; Rptr Nwsp; Phtg Yrbk; Rep Soph Cls; JV Bsktbl; Var Cheerldng; Var Sftbl; Var Tennis; High Hon Roll.

MATHEWS, SOBY M; Whitney HS; Cerritos, CA; (3); JA; Key Clb; Church Choir; Var L Trk; High Hon Roll; Hon Roll.

MATHEWS, THERESA M; Paraclete HS; Lancaster, CA; (2); Cmnty Wkr; FTA; GAA; Bsktbl; High Hon Roll; Lrng Disabled Chldrn Tutor; Loyola Marymount; Teacher.

MATHIAS, ALEX L; Gahr HS; Norwalk, CA; (1); Bsktbl; Cit Awd; High Hon Roll; Prfct Atten Awd; Blue & Gold Awd.

MATHIAS, JENNI; Canyon HS; Canyon Country, CA; (1); Dance Clb; Chorus; Rptr Yrbk; JV Gym; JV Vllybl; Cit Awd; COC; Choreogrphr.

MATHIESEN, DAN; Marina HS; Huntington Bch, CA; (4); 107/480; Boy Scts; Cmnty Wkr; JA; JCL; Key Clb; Latin Clb; Letterman Clb; Ski Clb; Spanish Clb; SADD; Eagle Sct; Ad Altare Dei Cathlc Svc Awd; Vigil Hnr; Ophthlmlgy.

MATHIESEN, DAVID L; Fresno HS; Fresno, CA; (2); 1/1000; Cmnty Wkr; Crs Cntry; Trk; High Hon Roll; Hon Roll.

MATHIESON, JOHN C; Alameda HS; Alameda, CA; (2); 18/290; Boy Scts; Var Swmmng; Let V Wtrpolo; Hnrs In Gldn ST Gmtry Exam.

MATHIEU, FOREST; Bishop Union HS; Bishop, CA; (4); Am Leg Boys St; Church Yth Grp; FFA; Teachers Aide; Stage Crew; Phtg Nwsp; Rep Jr Cls; Rep Sr Cls; Crs Cntry; High Hon Roll; High Sierra Pioneer Awd-Vocatnl Ldrshp; Vocatnl Ldrshp Hnr Cert; 1st Interst Bank-1st Pl Div 2; CA Polytech-Sn Luis Obispo; Ag.

MATHIS, JARED; Maxwell HS; Maxwell, CA; (4); 2/30; Am Leg Boys St; Treas FBLA; Pres FFA; Pres Spanish Clb; SADD; Pres Band; Pres Frsh Cls; Pres Soph Cls; Pres Stu Cncl; Var Bsbl; Govt.

MATHIS, KARLA M; Victor Valley HS; Victorville, CA; (3); Church Yth Grp; Drama Clb; Sec French Clb; Service Clb; Spanish Clb; Orch; Gym; Prfct Atten Awd; Girls League Clb; Airline Stewardess.

MATHIS, SAMANTHA R; Marysville HS; Marysville, CA; (3); 9/150; Am Leg Aux Girls St; Art Clb; Church Yth Grp; Debate Tm; Pres VP 4-H; Stu Cncl; JV Swmmng; Var JV Vllybl; 4-H Awd; Hon Roll; Acadmc Dcthln Hghst Score Intervws; HOBY Fndtn Delg 89; Chrch Drama Prdctns & Wrshp Teams; Yuba Coll; Pre Med.

MATHIS, STEPHANIE C; Mariposa County HS; Hornitos, CA; (2); French Clb; Girl Scts; Ski Clb; VP Soph Cls; JV Bsktbl; Var Golf; JV Vllybl; High Hon Roll; Soph Schlshp; Bsktbl Hghst GPA & Spec Dedication Awd; Most Dedicated Vlybl; CSF; UC Davis; Vet.

MATHOT, JEAN C; El Toro HS; El Toro, CA; (3); 69/493; French Clb; Swmmng; Hon Roll; Var Water Polo; Jr Natl Yth Tm Water Polo; Back To Back CIF Champs Water Polo; Air Force; Sports Med.

MATIAN, ARASH D; William Howard Taft HS; Woodland Hills, CA; (3); Debate Tm; JA; NFL; Speech Tm; Temple Yth Grp; Lit Mag; Off Jr Cls; Hon Roll; Lion Awd; Pres Acad Fit Awd; UCLA; Med.

MATIAS, CHRISTINA; Acad Of Our Lady Of Peace; San Diego, CA; (4); Cmnty Wkr; Key Clb; Spanish Clb; Sftbl; Hon Roll; Grls Athltc Assn; Mesa JC.

MATIC, ANGELINA; John F Kennedy HS; La Palma, CA; (3); Varsity Clb; Chorus; Yrbk; Sec Frsh Cls; Sec Soph Cls; Sec Jr Cls; Stu Cncl; Socr; Tennis; Tennis Team Capt; Prom Cmmtte; Bus.

MATIJASEVIC, JEANNE I; Holy Family HS; Glendale, CA; (2); Church Yth Grp; Library Aide; Rep Frsh Cls; Sec Stu Cncl; Var Capt Bsktbl; Var Vllybl; Prfrmd For Popes Visit St Anthonys Croation Kolo Grp 88; Hugh O Brien Ldrshp Smnr Stu Embssdr; USC; Law.

MATINEZ, KATHY E; Mt Pleasant HS; San Jose, CA; (3); CCOC Cert Of Completion; Real Estate.

MATIONG, ROGER C; Irvine HS; Irvine, CA; (2); Math Tm; Band; Jazz Band; Mrchg Band; Orch; Pep Band; School Musical; Stage Crew; Pres Acad Fit Awd; Engrng.

MATLACK, BRANDY; Lake Elisnore HS; Lake Elsinore, CA; (3); 177/472; Teachers Aide; Chorus; Hnr Awrd Comp Cert; RDP Retl Merch; Cert Comp ROP Floral Desgn; Fullton JC; Retail Bus Mngmnt.

MATLEY, WENDY; Monte Vista Christian HS; Watsonville, CA; (4); Church Yth Grp; School Play; Treas Stu Cncl; Var Cheerldng; Var Socr; JV Swmmng; High Hon Roll; NHS; CA Schlrshp Fed; Readers Theatre; Spirit Commissionar.

MATLOCK, ELIZABETH A; Bishop Amat HS; Walnut, CA; (3); Church Yth Grp; Pep Clb; Flag Corp; Psych.

MATLOCK, GLENN; Fremont Christian HS; Fremont, CA; (2); VP Soph Cls; Var Bsbl; Var Socr; Hon Roll; CSF; Astronautical Engr.

MATLOCK JR, GLENN RAY; Fremont Christian HS; Fremont, CA; (2); Teachers Aide; Yrbk; VP Soph Cls; Var L Bsbl; Var Socr; High Hon Roll; HOBY Ldrshp Smnr Ambssdr; CSF; Jr Var Sccr Coaches Awd; Numerous Cls Awds & Hnrs; Military Awcad; Engl.

MATLOCK, JEREMY R; Don Antonio Lugo HS; Chino, CA; (2); 1/800; Church Yth Grp; Church Choir; Golf; Tennis; High Hon Roll; Hon Roll; CA Schlrshp Fnd; Biola U; Tchr.

MATLOCK, JOSHUA G; Don Lugo HS; Chino, CA; (2); 1/800; Church Yth Grp; Church Choir; Golf; Tennis; Cit Awd; High Hon Roll; Hon Roll; CA Schlrshp Fnd; Biola U.

MATLOSZ, MELISSA A; Louisville HS; Chatsworth, CA; (4); Church Yth Grp; Cmnty Wkr; Dance Clb; Drama Clb; GAA; School Musical; School Play; Treas Soph Cls; VP Jr Cls; Trk; Retrt Ldrs Sr Yr; Lousiville Schlrshp; Ecnmcs Awd; Gold Seal & Close Up; CA Poly Tech U; Spch Commnctns.

MATNEY, MICHAEL J; Irvington HS; Fremont, CA; (4); 32/241; Teachers Aide; Hon Roll; Econ Dept Awd; Close-Up 90; Ihlone Coll; Admin Of Justice.

MATNEY, STEVEN D; Taft Union HS; Mc Kittrick, CA; (3); #13 In Class; Pres 4-H; Letterman Clb; Varsity Clb; Phtg Yrbk; Stu Cncl; Var L Ftbl; Var L Trk; Wt Lftg; High Hon Roll; Prfct Atten Awd; Bus Admin.

MATOS, CHRISTINA; Oakdale HS; Oakdale, CA; (1); Secy.

MATOS, JENNIFER; Archbishop Mitty HS; Santa Clara, CA; (2); 1/225; Dance Clb; Math Tm; School Musical; Treas Frsh Cls; High Hon Roll; Hon Roll; Civic Clb; HOBY Ldrshp Essy Semi Fnlst; Sphmr Yr Hmrm Rep; Santa Clara U; Law.

MATSON, DANIELA J; Notre Dame HS; Salinas, CA; (3); Debate Tm; Science Clb; SADD; Pres Frsh Cls; Off Soph Cls; Stu Cncl; JV Bsktbl; Var Tennis; High Hon Roll; Hon Roll; Amnesty Intl Secy; Notre Dame Awds Engl, Phys Educ & Econ.

MATSON, JENNIFER L; Analy HS; Sebastopol, CA; (2); Art Clb; Drama Clb; French Clb; Stage Crew; High Hon Roll; Skakespeare Clb; Cert Of Merit Frnch; Clsscl Piano.

MATSON, KARRIE L; Mc Kinleyville HS; Mckinleyville, CA; (1); Var Capt Bsktbl; Var L Sftbl; Var L Tennis; Phys Ed Tchr.

MATSON, MICHAEL D; Artesia HS; Hawaiian Gardens, CA; (1); JV Var Socr; Hon Roll; Engrng.

MATSUDA, JAYNE M; Prospect HS; San Jose, CA; (1); 75/178; Band; Mrchg Band; Kendo-Jpnese Fncng; UC Davis; Vet.

MATSUDA, MICHAEL T; Apple Valley HS; Apple Valley, CA; (2); Boy Scts; Church Yth Grp; Key Clb; Spanish Clb; Nwsp; Off Jr Cls; JV Crs Cntry; JV Socr; Jnr Statsmn Of Amer; CSF; Sprts Med.

MATSUDA, WENDY; Skyline HS; Oakland, CA; (4); 32/580; Cmnty Wkr; German Clb; SADD; NHS; Opt Clb Awd; Prfct Atten Awd; Pres Acad Fit Awd; Schltc Achvt Art Awds; Howard Zacchini Fest Poster Cont Hnrb Mntn; UC Davis; Psych.

MATSUDA, YUKI; John F Kennedy HS; Cypress, CA; (3); Church Yth Grp; Intnl Clb; Key Clb; Letterman Clb; Pep Clb; SADD; Swing Chorus; Rep Frsh Cls; Rep Soph Cls; Stu Cncl; UCSB; Optometry.

MATSUKUMA, KAREN E; Lowell HS; San Francisco, CA; (2); French Clb; NFL; Speech Tm; Orch; Opt Clb Awd; Koto Japnse Strng Instrmnt; Sccr Police Actvts Leag/Viking Sccr Leag; CA Music Edctrs Assoc 89 & 90; Sci.

MATSUMOTO, AKIHISA; Athenian Schl; Danville, CA; (3); Stage Crew; Bsbl; Arch.

MATSUMOTO, LYNLY R; John F Kennedy HS; La Palma, CA; (1); Varsity Clb; Rep Soph Cls; Var L Bsktbl; Stat Score Keeper; JV Vllybl; Hon Roll.

MATSUMOTO, NAOMI; Ontario HS; Ontario, CA; (4); Church Yth Grp; Sec Dance Clb; German Clb; Letterman Clb; Science Clb; Teachers Aide; Varsity Clb; Capt Drill Tm; Variety Show; Var Tennis; Riverside CC; Radiology.

MATSUMOTO, NOZOMI; The Athenian Schl; Japan; (3); Stage Crew; Off Sr Cls; Var Socr; JV Vllybl; Wt Lftg.

MATSUMOTO, TARISA A; Gardena HS; Gardena, CA; (3); 1/500; Church Yth Grp; Drama Clb; Hosp Aide; Library Aide; School Play; Phtg Yrbk; Hist Frsh Cls; Var L Bsktbl; Var L Sftbl; Kiwanis Awd; CSF; Voice Recitals.

MATSUMURA, SANDRA YOSHIKO; Gridley Union HS; Gridley, CA; (4); 2/107; Drama Clb; FHA; Spanish Clb; Teachers Aide; School Play; Yrbk; Tennis; High Hon Roll; Hon Roll; NHS; Acad Decathln Team; U Of CA-BERKELEY.

MATSUNAGA, AYUMI KIKI; Capital Christian HS; Elk Grove, CA; (2); Church Yth Grp; Computer Clb; Debate Tm; Church Choir; Sec Frsh Cls; JV Cheerldng; High Hon Roll; Church Drama Grp; CSF 88-90; Stanford U; Med.

MATSUO, DIANE; John F Kennedy SR HS; Sacramento, CA; (4); 36/408; Am Leg Aux Girls St; Pres Frsh Cls; Treas Soph Cls; Pres Jr Cls; Pres Stu Cncl; Socr; Tennis; Opt Clb Awd; Church Yth Grp; Debate Tm; Yng Lf; Stu Body Pres; Camp Ten Tm; Stu Store Mgr; Stu Advsry Cncl; CA U San Diego; Cmmntns.

MATSUO, NOBORU; Rio Mesa HS; Camarillo, CA; (1); Aud/Vis; Church Yth Grp; High Hon Roll; GATE; 1st Degree Balck Belt; Medicine.

MATSUURA, MAGGY K; Bullard HS; Fresno, CA; (1); French Clb; Vllybl; Hon Roll; Pres Acad Fit Awd; Plyng Piano Seven Yrs; MVP Frshmn Vllybll Tm; Amnesty Intrntl Clb 89-90.

MATSUYAMA, DUKE; La Habra HS; La Habra, CA; (3); Rep Jr Cls; VP L Trk; Pres Acad Fit Awd; CA ST U Fullerton; Elec Engr.

MATSUZAKI, CAROL; Garfield Computer Sci Magnet HS; Los Angeles, CA; (3); Computer Clb; Capt Math Tm; Service Clb; Teachers Aide; School Play; Stage Crew; Variety Show; Rptr Nwsp; Var L Bsktbl; Capt Powder Puff Ftbl; CSF 1st Pl Svc Hours; Golden St Exam Geom Hnrs; Bsktbl & Tennis MVP, All Leag; Natl Yng Leaders Conf; MA Inst Of Tech; Sci.

MATTA, HEBA A; Arcadia HS; Arcadia, CA; (3); 200/600; Sec Church Yth Grp; Debate Tm; Drama Clb; NFL; Thesps; Ed Nwsp; Amnsty Intl VP; Greenpeace; UC Berkeley.

MATTA, MARIA V; Redwood HS; Visalia, CA; (3); 47/300; Pres Church Yth Grp; Pep Clb; Band; Mrchg Band; JV Var Score Keeper; Var L Socr; Var L Sftbl; Hon Roll; Jr NHS; CSF.

MATTAR, RAFIK S; Royal HS; Simi Valley, CA; (2); Chess Clb; Computer Clb; Bsktbl; Socr; Tennis; Wt Lftg; CSUN; Dntl.

MATTERI, ROBIN CHRISTINE; Williams HS; Williams, CA; (1); Church Yth Grp; Pres FFA; Pep Clb; Band; Pep Band; JV Var Cheerldng; Sftbl; Trk; Hon Roll; Yuba JC; Eng.

MATTERN, NOEL D; Irvington HS; Fremont, CA; (2); 23/330; Church Yth Grp; Drama Clb; School Play; Stu Cncl; JV Crs Cntry; Var Socr; High Hon Roll; N Coast Sctn Sccr & NCS Schlr Athlete; N Coast Sctn Crss Cntry; Drama Awd-Bst Actor & Schlr Actr Bdmn; Sci.

MATTES, SEAN R; Corcoran HS; Corcoran, CA; (4); 6/115; Church Yth Grp; Varsity Clb; Ftbl; Golf; U CA Davis; Cmptr Sci.

MATTESON, CHRISTOPHER PEREZ; Done Pine HS; Lone Pine, CA; (3); 2/30; Am Leg Boys St; Letterman Clb; SADD; Pres Stu Cncl; Var L Bsktbl; Var Capt Ftbl; Var L Trk; Hon Roll; Sal; Al-CIF 89; Boys ST; Phys Thrpy.

MATTESON, DAWN M; Etiwanda HS; Alta Loma, CA; (2); Computer Clb; Girl Scts; Key Clb; Latin Clb; SADD; Pres Acad Fit Awd; Med.

MATTEUCCI, MIKE J; San Luis HS; San Luis Obispo, CA; (3); Mgr Boy Scts; Varsity Clb; VICA; Swmmng; High Hon Roll; Hon Roll; Eagle Sct; CA Poly San Luis Obispo; Bus.

MATTHESON, KATHLEEN M; Apple Valley HS; Apple Valley, CA; (3); Hon Roll; World Of Poetry Cont Hnrbl Mntn; Poems Published; Photojrnlst.

MATTHEW, DAWN M; Sonora Union HS; Groveland, CA; (3); Church Yth Grp; Teachers Aide; Church Choir; Stu Cncl; Hon Roll; Brn Agn Chrstn-Sndy Sch Tchr; Sgn Lang; Columbia JC; Tchr.

MATTHEWS, BRIAN; Oxnard HS; Oxnard, CA; (4); 2/400; Boy Scts; Pres Church Yth Grp; Treas French Clb; Math Tm; Var Socr; Var Trk; Elks Awd; High Hon Roll; Prfct Atten Awd; Pres Acad Fit Awd; CSF Pres; UC Berkeley.

MATTHEWS, CRESCENT N; Bonita Vista HS; Imperial Beach, CA; (2); Church Yth Grp; Cit Awd; Hon Roll; Modeling Clb; Cornell U.

MATTHEWS, CYNTHIA; Lynwood HS; Lynwood, CA; (3); #45 In Class; Debate Tm; JA; Library Aide; Office Aide; Teachers Aide; Phtg Yrbk; Church Yth Grp; NHS; Campus Lf; UCLA; Nrsng.

MATTHEWS, DAMISHA R; Antelope Valley HS; Lancaster, CA; (3); Church Yth Grp; Library Aide; Teachers Aide; Church Choir; Hon Roll; Howard U; Pre Med.

MATTHEWS, DEWAYNE A; Modoc HS; Alturas, CA; (3); FFA; Letterman Clb; Bsbl; Wrstlng; Rotary Awd; Rotarian Stu Of Mnth; Mural Project; Comp Service Tech.

MATTHEWS, DOUG; Notre Dame Schl; Chico, CA; (1); Boy Scts; Church Yth Grp; Drama Clb; Church Choir; School Play; VP Stu Cncl; JV Bsktbl; Hon Roll; U CA Berkley; Bio.

MATTHEWS, JOSHUA T; Southern California Christian HS; Orange, CA; (3); Church Yth Grp; Cmnty Wkr; Pep Clb; Science Clb; High Hon Roll; NHS; Prfct Atten Awd; Aviation-Private Pilot-Flght Schl Cmplted Smmr 90; CA ST Fullerton; Intrntl Bus.

MATTHEWS, KERI L; Don Antonio Lugo HS; Chino, CA; (3); Am Leg Aux Girls St; Church Yth Grp; Letterman Clb; JV Swmmng; JV Vllybl; Hon Roll; Clss Of 91 Clb; Azusa Pacific U; Liberal Arts.

MATTHEWS, MICHAEL; Covina HS; West Covina, CA; (3); Am Leg Boys St; Treas Model UN; Treas Soph Cls; Off Sr Cls; Var Bsbl; Cit Awd; Prfct Atten Awd; CSF; CA Golden ST Exam Awds; Hustle & Heart Awds Bsbl; Soc Sci.

MATTHEWS, MIRIAM J; Southern California Christian HS; Orange, CA; (1); Art Clb; Church Yth Grp; Spanish Clb; Variety Show; Hon Roll; Ice Capades Chalet Sktg Schl; ISIA; Westmont; Psych.

MATTHEWS, SHARON M; San Dieguito HS; Encinitas, CA; (3); English Clb; School Play; Stage Crew; Yrbk; JV Gym; JV Tennis; High Hon Roll; Golden St Exam-High Hnrs; Environmntl Sci.

MATTHEWS, TARA; Los Lomas HS; Walnut Creek, CA; (4); 34/260; Hosp Aide; Temple Yth Grp; Band; Jazz Band; Rep Stu Cncl; Cheerldng; Pom Pon; Powder Puff Ftbl; Trk; St Schlr; All Amer Sprstr NCA 89; John Muir Hosp Vlntr; Yth Ed For Intrmdt Sch Stu 89; Eagle Aloho Bowl 89; U CA Davis; Biolgcl Sci.

MATTHIE, SUZANNE S; Bishop Union HS; Bishop, CA; (3); Church Yth Grp; Cmnty Wkr; Math Tm; Spanish Clb; Chorus; School Play; Gym; Hon Roll; Save The Bay Envrimtl Club; Yth To Yth; Marine Biology.

MATTHIES, HEIDI L; Whittier Christian HS; Norwalk, CA; (3); German Clb; Bsktbl; Powder Puff Ftbl; Trk; Hon Roll; CSF; CA ST Fullerton.

MATTHIES, TAMSEN M; Banning HS; Banning, CA; (2); Sec Drama Clb; Sec Intnl Clb; Library Aide; Pres Speech Tm; School Play; Hon Roll; Lion Awd; Acadmcs Ltr; N Shore Animal Leag & Humane Frmng Assn; Elem Schl Tchr.

MATTHYS, JENNIFER R; Livingston HS; Delhi, CA; (1); Chorus; High Hon Roll.

MATTI, RONE; Granite Hills HS; El Cajon, CA; (1); JV Var Bsktbl; Hon Roll; MI ST; Bsktbl.

MATTINGLY, CHRISTINE S; Lassen HS; Janesville, CA; (4); 48/166; Girl Scts; Letterman Clb; Teachers Aide; Sec Treas Chorus; Stu Cncl; JV Var Trk; Elks Awd; NHS; Pres Acad Fit Awd; Lassen Coll; CPA.

MATTISON, DENNIS W; Bonita Vista HS; Chula Vista, CA; (2); Capt Church Yth Grp; Computer Clb; Math Clb; Science Clb; Teachers Aide; Church Choir; Nwsp; Hon Roll; Prfct Atten Awd; Chula Vista Police Explrs Post 831 Patrlmn; Cafeteria Aide; ROHR Indstrs Comp Explr Post 2681 Pres; UCSD; Law Enfrcmnt.

MATTISON, JEANEY; Pacific Palisades HS; West Los Angeles, CA; (1); 50/450; Church Yth Grp; Science Clb; Cheerldng; Swmmng; Prfct Atten Awd; UC Berkeley; Mech Engr.

MATTISON, JON; Rio Lindo Adventist Acad; Turlock, CA; (4); Church Yth Grp; Spanish Clb; Acpl Chr; Chorus; Co-Ed Nwsp; DAR Awd; Pacific Union Clg; Graphcs Tech.

MATTIX, BRENT S; Roseville HS; Roseville, CA; (3); 9/460; Spanish Clb; Capt Ftbl; Swmmng; Intrml Vllybl; High Hon Roll; Prfct Atten Awd; Pres Acad Fit Awd; CSF; Coaches Awd Ftbl; USC; Govt.

MATTMILLER, ALEX; Oxnard HS; Oxnard, CA; (3); Computer Clb; French Clb; Nwsp; Rep Stu Cncl; Swmmng; UCSB; Comp.

MATTS, CHRISTINA; Oak Park HS; Bakerfield, CA; (2); Teachers Aide; High Hon Roll; Hon Roll; Jazz Dance; Karate; Stanford; Lwyr.

MATTSON, DENISE C; East Bakersfield HS; Bakersfield, CA; (1); Girl Scts; Key Clb; Var Trk; Vllybl; Hon Roll; CA Schlstc Fed; Friday Night Live.

MATTY, CARMEN; Lincoln HS; Stockton, CA; (4); 13/513; Church Yth Grp; Cmnty Wkr; Sec FBLA; JV Socr; High Hon Roll; Sal; Peer Cnslg/ Conflct Mgmt; Soc Sci.

MATUBANG, PHILLIP V; Corona SR HS; Corona, CA; (3); 5/402; Latin Clb; Rptr Nwsp; Bsktbl; High Hon Roll; NHS; NEDT Awd; Mock Trl Team 2nd Pl Riverside Cty; CA Schlrshp Federation Mbr; Sci Fair Part; Honrl Ment Dist Levl; U Of CA Berkeley; Law.

MATULIK, KRISTIN J; Don Antonio Lubo HS; Chino, CA; (4); 53/556; Church Yth Grp; GAA; SADD; Varsity Clb; Var Socr; Var Sftbl; High Hon Roll; Hon Roll; NHS; Gldn Cnqst Awrd Englsh Soph Yr; UT ST U; Busi Finance.

MATUNNO, NORMA; Carlsbad HS; Carlsbad, CA; (2); Swmmng; Vllybl.

MATUSKA, MICHAEL D; Lincoln HS; Stockton, CA; (3); 126/592; Church Yth Grp; Library Aide; JV Var Bsbl; JV Bsktbl; JV Var Ftbl; Var Wt Lftg; Hon Roll; Pres Acad Fit Awd; Pres Schlr; CSF.

MATYAS, JASON M; Yucaipa HS; Yucaipa, CA; (1); Church Yth Grp; Spanish Clb; JV Wrstlng; Cit Awd; High Hon Roll; Engr.

MATZ, JENNIFER; Birmingham HS; Encino, CA; (2); FBLA; Hosp Aide; Key Clb; Letterman Clb; SADD; Stu Cncl; JV Swmmng; High Hon Roll; Ntl Merit Schol; Opt Clb Awd; Psych.

MATZEN, TANYA T; Colton HS; Colton, CA; (1); Pep Clb; Vllybl; Wrtng Songs, Poems & Shrt Stories; UCLA; Bus Mgmt.

MAUCH, DENNIS R; Elk Grove HS; Sacramento, CA; (2); 70/592; FFA; JV Bsbl; JV Bsktbl; Fresno ST; Bus.

MAUCH, HEIDI L; Moorpark HS; Moorpark, CA; (2); Sftbl; High Hon Roll.

MAUCHLEY, STEPHEN; Oakdale HS; Oakdale, CA; (3); Boy Scts; Bsktbl; Brigham Young U; Tchr.

MAUGA, TAFI JUNIOR; Carlsbad HS; Carlsbad, CA; (1); 72/450; Church Yth Grp; Intrml Bsbl; Capt Bsktbl; Capt Ftbl; Capt Socr; JV Trk; JV Var Wrstlng; Cit Awd; Opt Clb Awd; Prfct Atten Awd; Booster Clb Awd; Coaches Awd Ftbl Wrstlng; Bst Field Track; Ldrshp Awd; CO U; Phy.

MAULDIN, ALYSSON; Sutter Union HS; Sutter, CA; (4); 4/80; Am Leg Aux Girls St; Pres Stu Cncl; JV Var Cheerldng; Powder Puff Ftbl; JV Sftbl; Var Trk; Cit Awd; High Hon Roll; Pres Schlr; Rotary Awd; Acad Dcthln For CA; Cty Champs 90; Exch Stu Japan; Lions Club Intnl Exch; Pres Ldrshp Awd 90; CA ST U Chico; Intnl Bus.

MAULDIN, AMANDA D; Antelope Valley HS; Lancaster, CA; (3); Church Yth Grp; Pres French Clb; Pep Clb; Red Cross Aide; VP Service Clb; SADD; Stu Cncl; Hon Roll; Pres Acad Fit Awd; Cmpltd Girls Camp Sumiteer Prgm; Jr Ldr Girls Camp 2 Yrs; Brigham Young U; Interior Dsgn.

MAULHARDT, ANN E; La Reina HS; Oxnard, CA; (3); 21/69; Sec SADD; Ed Yrbk; Rep Stu Cncl; Cit Awd; Hon Roll; NHS; Cnty Acad Decathlon Tm; Natl Charity League; CSF; Amer Soviet Yth Exch; Math Teach.

MAULHARDT, STACY L; Santa Clara HS; Oxnard, CA; (2); 13/200; NFL; Speech Tm; High Hon Roll; NHS; CSF.

MAUNES, CHRISTINE R; Alhambna HS; Martinez, CA; (2); Art Clb; Teachers Aide; Hon Roll; Record Sec For Business Club; Cert Of Merit Mt Diablo Med Ctr; Friday Night Live; Cert Merit Am Assoc W; Archaeology.

MAUNEY, LINDA EMILY R; San Pedro HS; San Pedro, CA; (3); Church Yth Grp; Spanish Clb; Rep Jr Cls; Hon Roll; Jr NHS; Prfct Atten Awd; Lndr Coll; Elem Ed.

MAUNEY, MICHELLE N; El Toro HS; El Toro, CA; (3); Teachers Aide; Treas Sr Cls; JV Var Bsktbl; JV Var Vllybl; Hon Roll; Vllybl-MVP, Mst Imprvd, Mst Offnsv Plyr Of Yr & 1st Team All Leag 88, 89, 90; Bsktbl Mst Imprvd 88; U Of WA; Advrtsng Dsgn.

MAUNG, KYAW; Abraham Lincoln HS; Daly City, CA; (3); Chess Clb; Math Clb; Bsktbl; High Hon Roll; San Francisco ST U; Elec Engr.

MAUNZ, MATTHEW C; Santa Barbara HS; Santa Barbara, CA; (3); Varsity Clb; Swmmng; Vllybl; Water Polo V Awds.

MAUPIN, BARRY T; Artesia HS; Lakewood, CA; (2); Church Yth Grp; Rep Jr Cls; Hist Stu Cncl; JV Bsbl; JV Ftbl; JV Var Wrstlng; Hon Roll; Prfct Atten Awd; Pres Acad Fit Awd; Arch.

MAURANTONIO, MICHAEL S; North Monterey County HS; Prunedale, CA; (2); Intnl Clb; Letterman Clb; SADD; Varsity Clb; Stu Cncl; JV Capt Ftbl; Trk; Var Capt Wrstlng; Hon Roll; Frshmn Ftbl MVP; ASU; Pro-Football.

MAUREAS, ELLENI MARIE; Huntington Beach HS; Huntington Beach, CA; (1); Model UN; Teachers Aide; Band; Mrchg Band; Pep Band; Model United Nations; Chamber Of Commerce Womans Div Yth Art Fair Awd; Stanford; Psych.

MAURER, JENNIFER A; Pittsburg HS; Pittsburg, CA; (1); FBLA; Chorus; Julliard; Music.

MAURER, MATTHEW J; Santa Barbara HS; Santa Barbara, CA; (3); 80/475; Jazz Band; Intrml Socr; Intrml Tennis; Hon Roll; Pres Acad Fit Awd.

MAURICIO, MARITESS; Hoover HS; San Diego, CA; (4); 1/362; Model UN; NFL; ROTC; Ed Nwsp; Sec Jr Cls; High Hon Roll; VP NHS; Pres Acad Fit Awd; Val; Stu Of Year; Natl Sci Mrt Awd; Natl Convention On Ldrshp Delg; UCSD; Engrng.

MAURICIO, PHOEBE; International Studies Acad; San Francisco, CA; (3); French Clb; Ed Yrbk; Pres Soph Cls; VP Stu Cncl; Hon Roll; Peer Cnslr; Acad Of Fnanc; Nrdsmns Brass Plum Fshn Bd; Brdcstng.

MAURO, KATIE; Lincoln HS; Stockton, CA; (3); Key Clb; Teachers Aide; Ed Nwsp; JV Var Crs Cntry; JV Var Trk; High Hon Roll; Jr NHS; Mu Alpha Theta; Ski Clb; High Hon Roll; CSF Offcr; Bee Zee Svc Orgnztn Stu; Journlsm Eductrs; Assn Stu 88-89; Hnr Recital Wnr 88-89; Span Awd.

MAURO, MICHELLE; Mt Shasta HS; Mt Shasta, CA; (3); Church Yth Grp; French Clb; Chorus; Hon Roll; Pres Frsh Cls; Recrtnl Sccr; Lions Clb Speech Cont; Recrtnl Gym Asst Coach; Genetics.

MAUTINO, KEVIN J; Saint Anthony HS; Long Beach, CA; (2); Church Yth Grp; Cmnty Wkr; Letterman Clb; JV Var Bsbl; JV Ftbl; JV Var Socr; Hon Roll; Var Sccr Tm B Avg Awd; JV Bsbl MVP Awd; Art.

MAUTNER, MARK C; Vintage HS; Napa, CA; (2); Treas Key Clb; Service Clb; Acpl Chr; Chorus; School Musical; School Play; Swing Chorus; Variety Show; Cit Awd; Napa Chapt Order Of Demolay; Napa JC; Theater Arts.

MAWLAOUI, DANIELLE G; Miramonte HS; Orinda, CA; (1); Vllybl; Hon Roll; Prfct Atten Awd; Stanford; Business.

MAXA, STACY L; Ramona HS; Ramona, CA; (3); 20/342; Church Yth Grp; Dance Clb; Hon Roll; Kiwanis Awd; San Diego ST U; CPA.

MAXEY, RACHAEL; Highlands HS; North Highlands, CA; (3); NFL; Ski Clb; Speech Tm; Church Choir; L Mgr(s); Socr; High Hon Roll; Lion Awd; Voice Dem Awd; Odd Fllws Untd Natns Pilgrmge Yth Delg; BYU; Frgn Lang.

MAXFIELD, CHRISTINE; North HS; Bakersfield, CA; (2); Hon Roll; CSF; Gftd & Tlntd Educ; U AK Anchorage; Zoologist.

MAXWELL, AMY; San Bernardino HS; San Bernardino, CA; (3); 12/500; Church Yth Grp; Cmnty Wkr; Band; Color Guard; Mrchg Band; High Hon Roll; NHS; Mock Trial 87-90; CA Schlrshp Fed; Ivy Chain Hnr Guard 87-90; CA ST U San Bernardino.

MAXWELL, BRENDA; Los Altos HS; Hacienda Hgts, CA; (3); Church Yth Grp; Pep Clb; Ed Nwsp; Off Jr Cls; Stu Cncl; Capt Co-Capt Cheerldng; Hon Roll; Prfct Atten Awd; Goldn St Exam Alg Hnrs; Schl Schlr; Jr Hnr Awd; Pediatrics.

MAXWELL, CASADY; Irvine HS; Carlsbad, CA; (3); Cmnty Wkr; Teachers Aide; JV Vllybl; Hon Roll; Pres Acad Fit Awd; Cmptv Srfng; San Diego ST; Intr Dsgn.

MAXWELL, IRENE F; Newark Memorial HS; Newark, CA; (3); 19/512; Pres Sr Cls; Rep Jr Cls; Crs Cntry; High Hon Roll; French Clb; SADD; VP Chess Clb; Cmnty Wkr; Yrbk; FBLA; Newark Yth Congress; CA Assn Of Stu Cncls; Capital Focus; Poly Sci.

MAXWELL, JEFF; Cardinal Newman HS; Santa Rosa, CA; (1); Hon Roll; USC; Electronics.

MAXWELL, RYAN A; Chaffey HS; Ontario, CA; (3); JV Bsbl; JV Ftbl; High Hon Roll; Hon Roll; Actvts Brd; UCSD; Ed.

MAXWELL, TISA L; Washington Prep HS; Los Angeles, CA; (3); Co-Capt Drill Tm; School Musical; Variety Show; Rep Soph Cls; Rep Jr Cls; Hon Roll; Prfct Atten Awd; Empress Clb; Peace Clb; Tuskegee U; Bus.

MAY, ALLISON M; Mater Dei HS; Orange, CA; (3); 1/600; Am Leg Aux Girls St; Church Yth Grp; Cmnty Wkr; Drama Clb; Hosp Aide; Ski Clb; Spanish Clb; SADD; Teachers Aide; School Play; Orange Cnty Miss TEEN 89; Cnty & St Schlstc Awds 89; Ldrshp Awd 90; St Cmmnty Svc Awd 90.

MAY, CARRIE A; Newbury Park HS; Newbury Park, CA; (3); 47/347; Church Yth Grp; Church Choir; Sec Frsh Cls; Sec Soph Cls; Sec Jr Cls; Rep Stu Cncl; Hon Roll; St Schlr; CA Luth U; Elem Teacher.

MAY, DAWN M; East Bakersfield HS; Bakersfield, CA; (4); 74/398; Intnl Clb; Hon Roll; Physics Olympcs; Mock Trial; Constitutional Convention; CA ST U-Bakersfield; Med.

MAY, JANNETTE; Pasadena HS; Pasadena, CA; (2); Dance Clb; Tennis; Miss US Teen Pgnt 1990; PCC; CPA.

MAY, JOANN J; St Bernard HS; Eureka, CA; (2); 2/52; Service Clb; Hon Roll; Redwood Cncrt Ballet; Coll Of Redwoods.

MAY, MELANIE R; Hanford Union HS; Hanford, CA; (2); Art Clb; Crs Cntry; Mgr(s); Trk; CSF; Envrnmntlst.

MAY, ROXANNE C; Escondido HS; Escondido, CA; (1); Band; Mrchg Band; Pep Band; Hon Roll; Prfct Atten Awd; Educ.

MAY, SHANE W; Thousand Oaks HS; Thousand Oaks, CA; (3); 75/580; Church Yth Grp; Math Tm; Spanish Clb; SADD; Var JV Bsktbl; Var L Golf; Hon Roll; Jr NHS.

MAYA, PATRICIA; Notre Dame HS; San Jose, CA; (3); Intnl Clb; JV Var Swmmng; Outstndng Achvt Typing 1 & II; San Jose ST U; Teaching.

MAYBEE, STEPHANIE A; Grace M Davis HS; Modesto, CA; (2); Band; Mrchg Band; Pep Band; Phys Thrpy.

MAYBERRY, SCOTT C; St Ignatius College Prep; San Francisco, CA; (1); Aud/Vis; Nwsp; Var JV Bsbl; Var JV Bsktbl; Var JV Ftbl; Athltc Dept Svc Awd; OH U.

MAYBIN, CHAD; Palmdale HS; Pearblossom, CA; (4); 6/600; Am Leg Boys St; Church Yth Grp; Science Clb; Ski Clb; JV Tennis; Cit Awd; Hon Roll; Lion Awd; Masonic Awd; Ntl Merit Schol; Local & Rgnl Speech Cont Wnnr; Lions Clb; US Military Acad; Engrng.

MAYEDA, AKEMI; Palisades HS; Pacific Palisades, CA; (4); 9/450; Temple Yth Grp; Hon Roll; Pres Acad Fit Awd; Dharma Schl Tchr W LOS Angeles Buddhst Temple; Kinnara Gagaku Music Of Imprl Crt Japan; Taiko; East Asian Stds.

MAYER, HEATHER; Independence HS; San Jose, CA; (4); Church Yth Grp; GAA; SADD; Stu Cncl; Co-Capt Var Cheerldng; L Swmmng; Trk; Chico ST; Educ.

MAYER, JENNIFER; Elsinore HS; Elsinore, CA; (2); 58/589; Flag Corp; JV Bsktbl; Vllybl; Prfct Atten Awd; Sci.

MAYER, KIMBERLY; Marina HS; Huntington Bch, CA; (1); Hosp Aide; Diving; Cit Awd; High Hon Roll; Pres Acad Fit Awd; Peer Asstnc League; UCLA; Director.

MAYER, NICHOLE; John F Kennedy HS; Sacramento, CA; (3); 54/515; Var Swmmng; Hon Roll; Med.

MAYERICH, SANDRA; Presentation HS; Apo New York, NY; (4); French Clb; German Clb; JA; Key Clb; Mu Alpha Theta; Science Clb; SADD; High Hon Roll; NHS; UC San Diego; Pre-Med.

MAYES, JENNIFER; Simi Valley HS; Simi Valley, CA; (2); 33/706; Drill Tm; Nwsp; Hon Roll; CSF; U Of CA; Psych.

MAYES, KEITH L; Fresno Christian HS; Fresno, CA; (3); 2/45; Church Yth Grp; Chorus; Var Socr; Var Tennis; High Hon Roll; CMC Natl Motocross Racing Trans-Cal Winner 89.

MAYES, MONICA; Orange Glen HS; Valley Center, CA; (3); 10/458; Church Yth Grp; Spanish Clb; Church Choir; Rep Stu Cncl; JV Stat Bsktbl; JV Sftbl; Hon Roll; NHS; Nrth Cnty Acadmc Leag; CSF; Bus Admin.

MAYES, NICOLE; Orange Glen HS; Valley Center, CA; (3); 10/458; Church Yth Grp; Spanish Clb; Church Choir; Rep Stu Cncl; JV Stat Bsktbl; JV Sftbl; NHS; NCAL; CSF; Bus Admin.

MAYFIELD, ALISHYA N; Sacred Heart Prep; Portola Valley, CA; (2); Drama Clb; High Hon Roll; Hon Roll; Showjumping Horses.

MAYFIELD, MELINDA R; Enterprise HS; Redding, CA; (3); 21/170; Drama Clb; Spanish Clb; Flag Corp; Powder Puff Ftbl; High Hon Roll; NHS; Gate Pgm.

MAYFIELD, SCOTT A; Nevada Union HS; Rough And Ready, CA; (3); 66/551; Church Yth Grp; Cmnty Wkr; Acpl Chr; Chorus; Church Choir; School Musical; Rep Stu Cncl; JV Var Bsktbl; JV Var Trk; Hon Roll; JR Natl Bsktbl Tm; Med.

MAYFIELD, SYDNIA; Oceanside HS; Oceanside, CA; (1); Church Yth Grp; School Play; GATE; UCSD; Law.

MAYGREN, LAEL K; Rio Mesa HS; Camarillo, CA; (1); Church Yth Grp; Flag Corp; High Hon Roll; Hon Roll; NHS; Opt Clb Awd; Pres Acad Fit Awd; CSF; Stanford; Lwyr.

MAYHEW, JAMIE A; Mater Dei HS; Orange, CA; (2); 1/550; Hosp Aide; Teachers Aide; Lbrn Chorus; School Musical; School Play; Stage Crew; Variety Show; High Hon Roll; NHS; Pres Acad Fit Awd; CS Schlrshp Fed; Campus Mnstry; 4th Runner-Up Orange Cnty Miss TEEN; Stanford; Med.

MAYHEW, MATT J; Mater Dei HS; Costa Mesa, CA; (2); Church Yth Grp; French Clb; Varsity Clb; Rep Soph Cls; Var Vllybl; French Hon Soc; High Hon Roll; NHS; Ntl Merit Schol; CA Schlrshp Fed; Pianist; Dartmouth.

MAYHEW, RICK A; South Fork HS; Redway, CA; (3); Boy Scts; FHA; SADD; Varsity Clb; Band; Mrchg Band; Var Bsbl; JV Var Bsktbl; Hon Roll; Prfct Atten Awd; Engl Awd; Television Broadcasting.

MAYLAD, MARIA; Covina HS; Covina, CA; (4); Hon Roll; Asian Clb; CAL ST; Nursing.

MAYNARD, SHAKIMA N; Diamond Bar HS; Diamond Bar, CA; (1); Art Clb; Church Yth Grp; Chorus; Trk; High Hon Roll; Hon Roll; Spellman; Lawyr.

MAYNER, CHRIS M; Canyon HS; Duarte, CA; (4); Church Yth Grp; Cmnty Wkr; Rep Nwsp; Intrml Mgr Bsktbl; Intrml Mgr Ftbl; Intrml Mgr Tennis; Best Defensv Plyr Bsktbl; Most Imprvd Plyr Bsktbl; De Vry; Electronic Engrg.

MAYO, ANN; College Park HS; Pleasant Hill, CA; (3); Drama Clb; French Clb; Hosp Aide; Mem Of Yth Educators; Psych.

MAYO, KATHLEEN ELIZABETH; Poway HS; Poway, CA; (3); 19/760; Girl Scts; Model UN; Band; Co-Ed Yrbk; Lit Mag; Rep Frsh Cls; Var L Crs Cntry; Intrml Tennis; Var L Trk; Cit Awd; Fml Schlr Athlete 87-88; PTSA Cert Mrt Hnrs Engl 89-90; TX U Austin; Cmmctns.

MAYO, MICHELE ANN; Chatsworth HS; Chatsworth, CA; (3); Cmnty Wkr; Dance Clb; Hosp Aide; Office Aide; Gym; Cit Awd; Hon Roll; Equestrian Team Ldr; UCLA; Neonatal Nrs.

MAYOR, STEPHANIE D; Valencia HS; Placentia, CA; (3); Church Yth Grp; Band; Mrchg Band; Ed Yrbk; Off Jr Cls; High Hon Roll; NHS; Pres Acad Fit Awd; CSF; Distngshd Schlr 88-90; U CA; Med.

MAYORAL, MIRIAM E; Mission Bay HS; San Diego, CA; (3); 77/307; Treas DECA; German Clb; DECA Awds; USD; Bus.

MAYORGA, EMILY; Notre Dame HS; San Jose, CA; (2); Church Yth Grp; Drama Clb; Hosp Aide; Cheerldng; Trk; JV Vllybl; Hon Roll; CSF; Med.

MAYORGA, GRACE A; Independence HS; San Jose, CA; (2); Latin Clb; JV Bsktbl; Pres Acad Fit Awd; Art.

MAYORQUIN, VICTOR G; Moreau HS; Hayward, CA; (4); Chess Clb; Cmnty Wkr; Wrstlng; Bank Amer Achvt Awd Frgn Lang; San Jose ST U; Aerospc Engrng.

MAYOU, MICHELLE R; Milpitas HS; Milpitas, CA; (3); 146/487; French Clb; Hon Roll; Prfcncy Accntng Awd; Amnsty Intl; Accntng.

MAYRHOFER, THOMAS B; The Chadwick Schl; Rancho Pls Vrds, CA; (4); Cmnty Wkr; Letterman Clb; Teachers Aide; Var Capt Bsbl; JV Bsktbl; Var Ftbl; Hon Roll; Ntl Merit Ltr; Prep League Bsbl-All League 1st Tm 89-90; Daily Breeze/South Bay Athl Clb All-Star Bsbl Tm 90; Coll/William & Mary; Intl Bus.

MAYS, BILLI JO; Lodi HS; Stockton, CA; (4); Cmnty Wkr; Dance Clb; Drama Clb; Key Clb; SADD; Thesps; Drill Tm; School Musical; School Play; French Clb; Stu In Prvntn Peer Edctr; Bnk Amer Drama Achvt Awd; Candystrppr; Berkeley; Bus Admin.

MAYS, EBONY L; Riverside Poly HS; Riverside, CA; (4); 38/389; Church Yth Grp; Key Clb; SADD; Teachers Aide; Rptr Nwsp; Bsktbl; Sftbl; Vllybl; High Hon Roll; Pres Acad Fit Awd; UCLA; Mtrls Engrng.

MAYS, EUGENE W; Richard Gahr HS; Cerritos, CA; (3); Hosp Aide; Var Bsktbl; Hon Roll; Morehouse; Med.

MAYS, LACHRECIA; St Bernard HS; Los Angeles, CA; (3); Girl Scts; Pep Clb; Cit Awd; Sci Fair Awd; Stanford; Pre-Med.

MAYS, NATHAN C; Torrance HS; Torrance, CA; (3); 43/425; Church Yth Grp; Cmnty Wkr; Science Clb; JV Capt Vllybl; Cit Awd; High Hon Roll; Hon Roll; Specl Awd Recog Of Outstndng Achvt 90; UC Irvine; Comp Sci.

MAYUGA, JOSEPH R; Carson HS; Carson, CA; (3); Service Clb; Teachers Aide; Band; Mrchg Band; Hon Roll; Acad Pentathlon Tm; Acad Awd Comp Prgrmg.

MAYWEATHER, BERTRAM C; Sunny Hills HS; Fullerton, CA; (3); Aud/Vis; Church Yth Grp; Drama Clb; Pres Frsh Cls; VP Soph Cls; Off Jr Cls; Var Sr Cls; Var Bsktbl; Var Ftbl; High Hon Roll.

MAZANET, JENNIFER L; Tustin HS; Tustin, CA; (1); 25/450; Church Yth Grp; Key Clb; Band; Mrchg Band; Sftbl; High Hon Roll; Hon Roll; Acad Achvt Awd Wnnr; CSF Sealbearer; Piano Lssns; Elem GATE Tchr.

MAZARIEGOS, OLGA L; Lynwood HS; Lynwood, CA; (3); Church Yth Grp; German Clb; Teachers Aide; Color Guard; Drill Tm; Prfct Atten Awd; Young Marines Ftnss & Basic Awds; U CA Fullerton; Med Cardiolgst.

MAZE, GARRETT W; Mt Whitney HS; Visalia, CA; (3); 17/300; Church Yth Grp; Teachers Aide; Church Choir; Yrbk; Diving; Swmmng; Hon Roll; Water Polo; Biking; Math.

MAZER, CATHRYN; University HS; Los Angeles, CA; (2); Chorus; School Musical; School Play; Crs Cntry; Socr; Hon Roll; Psych.

MAZI, TONIJO; Cabrillo HS; Lompoc, CA; (2); Church Yth Grp; Cmnty Wkr; Girl Scts; SADD; Drill Tm; Pep Band; Var L Crs Cntry; Var JV Socr; Var L Trk; Hon Roll; Acadmc Dcthln Team 90-91; Tchng.

MAZLER, MILANA; Stephens Wise Einstein Acad; Studio City, CA; (1); Nwsp; Yrbk; Stu Cncl; Sftbl; Vllybl; UCLA; Lawyer.

MAZMANIAN, AVETIS E; Montebello HS; Montebello, CA; (2); Swmmng; Hon Roll; Rgnl Occptnl Prgm; Pltcs.

MAZNER, JEREMY S; Palo Alto HS; Palo Alto, CA; (2); Stage Crew; Rptr Nwsp; Phtg Ed Yrbk; L Trk; Hon Roll; Pres Schlr.

MAZUR, ANGELA C; The Athenion Sch; Pleasant Hill, CA; (3); Ed Lit Mag; High Hon Roll; Ntl Merit SF; Choreograph & Perform Dances At Sch; Sch Envrnmntl Group; Writing Poetry; Publ In Lit Mag; Ireland; Envrnmntl Studies.

MAZUR, STEVE D; Escondido HS; San Marcos, CA; (3); FFA; Office Aide; Cit Awd; Pres Acad Fit Awd; Surfing; Bsktbll; Arch; Comp Drftsmn.

MAZZA, JAMIE; Mountain Empire HS; Alpine, CA; (4); 1/102; Am Leg Boys St; Letterman Clb; Pep Clb; Variety Show; Pres Frsh Cls; Treas Stu Cncl; Var Capt Bsbl; Var Capt Bsktbl; Var Ftbl; High Hon Roll; Army Schlr-Athl; Suter/Mazza Schlr Athl Of Yr; Hmcmg Ct; Long Beach ST U; Elec Engrng.

MAZZA, KIMBERLY M; Yuba City HS; Yuba City, CA; (2); Cmnty Wkr; Pep Clb; Orch; Ed Yrbk; Davis U; Pediatrician.

MAZZACAVALLO, BRANDON; Dana Hills HS; Laguna Niguel, CA; (3); Letterman Clb; Math Tm; Quiz Bowl; SADD; Rep Frsh Cls; Rep Soph Cls; Rep Jr Cls; Rep Sr Cls; Stu Cncl; Var L Vllybl; CA YMCA Yth Mdl Lgsltr, Ct, Bll Athr, Assmblymn; 2nd Pl Sci Fair Bichem; Aerntcl Engr.

MAZZARINO, VITO; Dana Hills HS; San Juan Capistra, CA; (2); Boy Scts; Sprt Ed Nwsp; Jrnlsm.

MAZZELA, RORY L; Herbert Hoover HS; Fresno, CA; (4); 51/391; Cmnty Wkr; Pep Clb; Sec Ski Clb; Pres Spanish Clb; Band; Color Guard; Flag Corp; Jazz Band; Mrchg Band; Orch; Mc Donalds All Am HS Band; CSF; NSOA All Natl Hnrs Orch; U Southern CA; Concrt Muscn.

MAZZI, FELICIA A; Pinole Valley HS; Pinole, CA; (3); Church Yth Grp; Off Cmnty Wkr; Ski Clb; Spanish Clb; Ed Nwsp; Ed Yrbk; Lit Mag; Off Jr Cls; Sec Sr Cls; Rep Stu Cncl; Prin Advisory Brd; Jr Prom Qn 90; CA St Smmr Schl For Arts Stu; Conflict Mgmt Mgr 2 Yrs.

MC ADAM, DANIEL G; Fontana HS; Fontana, CA; (2); High Hon Roll; Hon Roll; Pres Acad Fit Awd; Cmptr Prgmr.

MC ADAMS, JENNY M; Placer HS; Auburn, CA; (2); Pep Clb; SADD; JV Cheerldng; JV Pom Pon; Intrml Mgr Wt Lftg; Hon Roll; Pres Acad Fit Awd; Arbcs; Trvlng; Stnfrd; Bus.

MC ADAMS, TIFFANY M; Cloverdale HS; Cloverdale, CA; (2); 3/67; Church Yth Grp; Pep Clb; Band; Church Choir; Jazz Band; Mrchg Band; Pep Band; Variety Show; Rep Soph Cls; JV Var Cheerldng; CA Schlrshp Fed; Mexican Amer Yth Orgnztn; Wasc Cmmtte; U Pacifica; Music Bus.

MC ALEECE, ERIN; Mission Bay HS; San Diego, CA; (2); 43/380; FTA; Scholastic Bowl; Var Swmmng; JV Vllybl; Cit Awd; High Hon Roll; Prfct Atten Awd; SADD; Teen Inst; CSF; Govt In Motion.

MC ALEXANDER, KIMBERLY; Garden Grove HS; Garden Grove, CA; (3); 27/300; Church Yth Grp; Intnl Clb; Science Clb; Ski Clb; Sec Frsh Cls; VP Soph Cls; Pres Jr Cls; Pres Sr Cls; Var Crs Cntry; Var Capt Trk.

MC ALISTER, DUSTIN H; Atascadero HS; Atascadero, CA; (3); FFA; CA Poly Sn Luis Obispo; Admin.

MC ALISTER, JASON P; Washington HS; Fremont, CA; (3); 81/304; Church Yth Grp; Quiz Bowl; Voice Dem Awd; Hnrs Geo On Gldn ST Exam; Hnrb Mntn Photo 2(Cnty Fair; Comp Sci.

MC ALISTER, SHANNON; Hanford Union HS; Hanford, CA; (1); Church Yth Grp; FBLA; Hon Roll; Cal Poly; Law.

MC ALISTER, TRACEY KATHRYN; La Serna HS; Whittier, CA; (3); Church Yth Grp; Debate Tm; Drama Clb; Spanish Clb; Acpl Chr; School Musical; School Play; Variety Show; Hon Roll; NHS; Engl.

MC ALISTER, TRACIE C; East Bakersfield HS; Bakersfield, CA; (2); Band; Mrchg Band; Var L Crs Cntry; Var L Trk; High Hon Roll; CA Schltc Fed Clb; Math,Engrng & Sci Achvt Clb; Hugh Obrian Yth Conf; Most Insprtnl Awd Cross-Cnty; Writer.

MC ALLASTER, MARK M; Bonita HS; La Verne, CA; (1); Cmnty Wkr; JV Socr; High Hon Roll; Order Or Merit; Arch.

MC ALLISTER, ANDREW C; San Diego HS; San Diego, CA; (3); 45/415; Chess Clb; Math Clb; Math Tm; Pep Clb; Quiz Bowl; Scholastic Bowl; VP Science Clb; Varsity Clb; Band; Jazz Band; Aerospace Engr.

MC ALLISTER, JOHN M; North HS; Bakersfield, CA; (4); JA; Powder Puff Ftbl; Score Keeper; Bakersfield Coll; Arch.

MC ALLISTER, SHIRLEY; Eisenhower HS; Rialto, CA; (2); Church Yth Grp; Key Clb; Band; Color Guard; Drill Tm; Mrchg Band; High Hon Roll; Hon Roll; Jr NHS; NHS; CSF; Friday Night Live; Principals Hnr Roll; UCLA; Pediatrics.

MC ALLISTER, TINA; Needles HS; Needles, CA; (2); Chorus; Pres Soph Cls; Stat Bsktbl; Var Mgr(s); Powder Puff Ftbl; Var Score Keeper; Var Sftbl; JV Vllybl; Hon Roll; Sftbl Al-Leag NIAA; Psych.

MC ALOON, DIANA L; Newport Harbor HS; Costa Mesa, CA; (2); Drama Clb; Latin Clb; Thesps; Band; Mrchg Band; School Play; Stage Crew; High Hon Roll; Physics.

MC ANALLY, STEPHANIE L; La Reina HS; Agoura Hills, CA; (3); 44/67; Church Yth Grp; GAA; Office Aide; SADD; Church Choir; Yrbk; Var L Socr; Stat Sftbl; JV Var Vllybl; Cit Awd; CSF; CA Hnr Soc; ASU; Adv.

MC ANELLY, STEVE; Vail HS; Huntington Park, CA; (4); Aud/Vis; Cmnty Wkr; Library Aide; Office Aide; Teachers Aide; Stage Crew; Rep Stu Cncl; Cit Awd; High Hon Roll; Hon Roll; Athletic Activities; Spcl Hnr Awd-Hgh Scores On CA Achvt Test; Spcl Hnr Awd-Rcpnt Of Cal-Grant B; Siskiyous; Forestry.

MC ARTHUR, JEN-E; Westminster HS; Midway City, CA; (3); AFS; Church Yth Grp; Pep Clb; Service Clb; Ski Clb; Teachers Aide; Cheerldng; Score Keeper; Swmmng; Trk; Acad Lttr/Pin; Clss Cmmttee; U Of HI; Span.

MC ARTHUR, KATHRYN A; Loretto HS; Loomis, CA; (3); 17/70; Office Aide; Service Clb; Teachers Aide; JV Tennis; Hon Roll; Cal Poly San Luis Obispo; Vet.

MC ARTHUR, NISHA G; North HS; Bakersfield, CA; (3); 46/368; Spanish Clb; Teachers Aide; Powder Puff Ftbl; Hon Roll; Phys Thrpy.

MC ARTHUR, SHAMEKA L; Saint Bernard Catholic HS; Los Angeles, CA; (3); Church Yth Grp; Yrbk; JV Var Bsktbl; Score Keeper; Vllybl; Pediatrics.

MC AULAY, MICHAEL J; So Cal Christian HS; Placentia, CA; (3); JV Bsbl; High Hon Roll; MVP Bsbl; Chapman; Wrtng.

MC AULIFFE, JODY ANN C; Serrano HS; Oak Hills, CA; (3); Office Aide; Band; Vet.

MC AULIFFE, RYANE G; Milpitas HS; Milpitas, CA; (3); 32/487; Drama Clb; French Clb; Hosp Aide; School Play; JV Swmmng; High Hon Roll; NHS; Amnesty Intl VP; Explorers Med Post VP; UC Santa Barbara; Intl Studies.

MC AVOY, HOLLY A; Montgomery HS; Santa Rosa, CA; (2); Yrbk; Rep Frsh Cls; VP Soph Cls; VP Jr Cls; Cheerldng; Var Swmmng; Var Tennis; Var Vllybl; NHS; Hnrs Clb Pres.

MC BAIN, CHRISTOPHER D; Montgomery HS; Santa Rosa, CA; (2); Church Yth Grp; Pep Clb; Band; School Musical; Var Golf; Mgr(s); High Hon Roll; Hon Roll; Spanish NHS; Uc.

MC BRAYER, MARY B; Desert JR/Sr HS; Edwards, CA; (2); Church Yth Grp; Math Tm; Q&S; Drill Tm; Ed Nwsp; L Var Tennis; Cit Awd; High Hon Roll; Hon Roll; CSF.

MC BRIDE, DANA C; Fillmore HS; Fillmore, CA; (2); Church Yth Grp; Drill Tm; Hon Roll; 3 Gld Seals Fillmore Unifd Englsh Awds; Mem Of Jobs Dghtrs; Crt Rcrdr.

MC BRIDE, HEATHER; Thomas Downey HS; Modesto, CA; (3); Art Clb; Church Yth Grp; Drama Clb; Key Clb; Letterman Clb; SADD; Varsity Clb; Crs Cntry; Trk; Wt Lftg; BYU.

MC BRIDE, JACOB M; Central Union HS; El Centro, CA; (2); Wrstlng; High Hon Roll; Hon Roll; UCSD; Marine Bio.

MC BRIDE, JUSTIN; Marina HS; Huntington Bch, CA; (4); Church Yth Grp; Computer Clb; Model UN; Varsity Clb; JV Bsbl; Var Bsktbl; Var Crs Cntry; Var Trk; Hon Golden ST Exam Geom; Bldng Comp; Bus Mrktng.

MC BRIDE, KARI L; Apple Valley HS; Apple Valley, CA; (4); Am Leg Aux Girls St; Church Yth Grp; Drama Clb; Girl Scts; Chorus; School Musical; Hon Roll; Pres Acad Fit Awd; Show Choir; Physcl Thrpy.

MC BRIDE, KEVIN L; Apple Valley HS; Apple Valley, CA; (2); Church Yth Grp; Spanish Clb; Hon Roll; Vlybl; Little League Umpire; Notre Dame; Meteorology.

MC BRIDE, LEAH A; San Pasqual HS; Escondido, CA; (3); Debate Tm; Drama Clb; German Clb; NFL; Speech Tm; Chorus; Church Choir; School Play; Variety Show; Yrbk.

MC BRIDE, LEO; Palo Verde HS; Blythe, CA; (3); 4-H; Hon Roll; Art; Drafting; ROP Printing; Draftsman.

MC BRIDE, MEREDITH A; San Pedro HS; Slidell, LA; (2); Girl Scts; Hon Roll; Bus.

MC BRIDE, SHANE; Sutter HS; Sutter, CA; (3); Computer Clb; FFA; Math Clb; Office Aide; Spanish Clb; Varsity Clb; Yrbk; Off Frsh Cls; Bsbl; Bsktbl; Pilot-USAF Aero Clb; Mst Imprvd Athl; Fresno ST ROTC; Pilot.

MC BRIDE, TIFFINY; Santa Cruz HS; Soquel, CA; (2); Aud/Vis; Cmnty Wkr; Girl Scts; Gym; Swmmng; Vllybl; Wt Lftg; Hon Roll; Bike Rdng; Rnng; Sprntng; Photo; Cabrillo Coll; Pk Rngr.

MC CABE, BRIAN J; Mount Diablo HS; Missoula, MT; (1); Ftbl; Wrstlng; High Hon Roll; Aviation.

MC CABE, MICHAEL J; Artesia HS; Lakewood, CA; (3); Stu Cncl; Var Capt Crs Cntry; Var Capt Trk; Prfct Atten Awd; Intl Sports Exchng With Germany; Engl.

MC CABE, THOMAS P; Skyline HS; Oakland, CA; (3); Boy Scts; Lcrss; Ntl Merit Ltr; Pres Acad Fit Awd; Stu Conservtn Assn; Forestry.

MC CAFFERTY, GEORGE J; Forest Lake Christian Schl; Auburn, CA; (2); Boy Scts; Church Yth Grp; Teachers Aide; Var Bsbl; JV Bsktbl; Hon Roll; Exchnge Stu Brazil; Point Loma Coll; Bus.

MC CAFFERY, APRIL D; Los Angeles County HS For The Arts; Los Angeles, CA; (4); Acpl Chr; Chorus; Jazz Band; Variety Show; Rptr Nwsp; Sec Sr Cls; Hon Roll; Prfct Atten Awd; Prfrmd Frqntly Aids Bnfts; CA ST U Long Bch; Theatre Art.

MC CAFFERY, CATHERINE; Pacific Grove HS; Pacific Grove, CA; (3); Am Leg Aux Girls St; Office Aide; School Play; Ed Nwsp; Sec Soph Cls; JV Bsktbl; Mgr(s); Score Keeper; JV Swmmng; Stu Of Mnth.

MC CAFFERY, MEGHAN K; Seaside HS; Ft Ord, CA; (3); Cmnty Wkr; Hosp Aide; High Hon Roll; Hon Roll; Monterey Bay Aquarium Vol; AZ U; Psych.

MC CAGE, SHANNON D; Nevada Union HS; Grass Valley, CA; (3); Church Yth Grp; Chorus; JV Powder Puff Ftbl; JV Sftbl; Hon Roll; Math.

MC CAIN, TAMEKA; San Gorgonio HS; San Bernardino, CA; (3); Letterman Clb; Pep Clb; Spanish Clb; Teachers Aide; Stu Cncl; JV Bsktbl; Var Trk; Blck Future Ldrs; Bsu; Day Trippers; Asian Clb; Mecha; NYU; Commnctns.

MC CALESTER, GREGORY C; Sherman E Burroughs HS; Ridgecrest, CA; (3); Teachers Aide; Gym; Hon Roll.

MC CALIP, ILEANA A; Chula Vista HS; Chula Vista, CA; (2); 133/558; Dance Clb; Service Clb; Flag Corp; Yrbk; John Hopkins; Pre-Med.

MC CALL, CATHERINE A; Irvine HS; Irvine, CA; (1); JV Trk; Hon Roll; Psychlgst.

MC CALL, DARREN E; Coronado HS; Coronado, CA; (3); Stu Cncl; Swmmng; Coll U Of Redlands.

MC CALLEY, MATTHEW T; Bakersfield HS; Bakersfield, CA; (2); Boy Scts; German Clb; Letterman Clb; Rptr Nwsp; JV Swmmng; High Hon Roll; Hon Roll; Prfct Atten Awd; Eagle Scout-Order Of Arrow; CSF; Music Tchrs Assn Of CA Mrt Cert Pgm.

MC CALLUM, JENNIFER; Analy HS; Sebastopol, CA; (4); Am Leg Aux Girls St; Aud/Vis; Rep Frsh Cls; VP Soph Cls; Mgr Stu Cncl; Stat Ftbl; Lion Awd; Crew Daily Bulletin; Santa Rosa JC; Comm.

MC CAMAN, DAVID; Carlmont HS; Belmont, CA; (3); 18/376; Cmnty Wkr; Key Clb; CSF; Friends Of Millard Fillmore; Outstndng Achvtmnt Awds Algbr & Algbr II; Bus.

MC CAMMON, TAWNYA D; Redwood HS; Visalia, CA; (4); Church Yth Grp; Math Clb; Math Tm; Band; Mrchg Band; Intrml JV Tennis; Intrml Vllybl; Hon Roll; NHS; Pres Acad Fit Awd; 4.0 GPA; Cert Rcgntn Bus Div; CSF; CA Polytech ST; Arch.

MC CANCE, SEAN B; Millikan HS; Long Beach, CA; (3); ROTC; Color Guard; Co-Ed Yrbk; Rep Stu Cncl; Rep Crs Cntry; Cit Awd; Jr NHS; Prfct Atten Awd; Pres Acad Fit Awd; Superior Jr Cadet Decoration Awd; Play On Clb Sccr Teams; ROTC Rifle Team; Astro.

MC CANN, JOHN; San Joaquin Memorial HS; Fresno, CA; (3); Off Church Yth Grp; Cmnty Wkr; Debate Tm; Off Key Clb; Letterman Clb; Model UN; NFL; Science Clb; Ski Clb; Spanish Clb; Rotary Camp Royal; ACT Clb; Stanford; Med.

MC CANN, NICHOLE; Rosary HS; Walnut, CA; (3); French Clb; Ski Clb; Pres Jr Cls; High Hon Roll; Acad Decthln Tms; CSF; U Of CA Irvine; Med.

MC CANN, STEVE M; Polytechnic HS; Arleta, CA; (3); Cmnty Wkr; Var Capt Bsktbl; UCLA; Brdcstng.

MC CANTS, TANISHA D; Richmond HS; San Pablo, CA; (1); Church Yth Grp; Hon Roll; U AZ; Psych.

MC CARROLL, MICHAEL P; Los Altos HS; Los Altos, CA; (3); 3/313; Capt Debate Tm; Latin Clb; Chorus; Ed Nwsp; Pres Jr Cls; Capt Var Bsktbl; High Hon Roll; Ntl Merit SF; Rotary Awd; Spanish NHS; NCTE Nominee.

MC CARTEN, RYAN M; Novato HS; Novato, CA; (3); Boy Scts; Latin Clb; Intrml Vllybl; Hon Roll; NHS; CA Schlsp Fed; Sci.

MC CARTHY, BRIAN J; Washington HS; Fremont, CA; (2); 67/238; Ski Clb; Spanish Clb; Nwsp; JV Crs Cntry; JV Tennis; JV Trk; Hon Roll; Amnesty Intl; U Of San Diego.

MC CARTHY, BRONWYN A; Cornelia Connelly HS; Cypress, CA; (3); Pres German Clb; VP Pres Intnl Clb; Stage Crew; VP Capt Vllybl; Dnfth Awd; High Hon Roll; NHS; Auxlry Of Natl Assistnc Leag Assisteens Chrmn; Congrssl Schlrnatl Yth Ldrshp Merit Cert; Vet Med.

MC CARTHY, CHRIS E; Live Oak HS; Morgan Hill, CA; (3); 62/595; GAA; JA; Pep Clb; Off Frsh Cls; Off Sr Cls; Var L Bsktbl; Var L Fld Hcky; Powder Puff Ftbl; Var L Sftbl; Hon Roll; Athlete Of Week, Mnth & Yr; Fresno ST; Pre Vet.

MC CARTHY, CLIFFORD A; La Habra HS; Whittier, CA; (4); 3/341; Sec FBLA; Quiz Bowl; Science Clb; Band; Jazz Band; Mrchg Band; High Hon Roll; NHS; Ntl Merit SF; Fil Club VP; Orange Cnty Acadmc Dec; Harvey Mudd; Engrg.

MC CARTHY, EMILY; San Leandro HS; San Leandro, CA; (2); Cmnty Wkr; Drama Clb; Girl Scts; Pep Clb; Ski Clb; Teachers Aide; Chorus; Sec Frsh Cls; Rep Soph Cls; Rep Stu Cncl; Ed.

MC CARTHY, GREGORY M; St Ignatius College Prep; Daly City, CA; (4); 154/310; Boy Scts; Cmnty Wkr; Letterman Clb; Red Cross Aide; Teachers Aide; Varsity Clb; Var Swmmng; Eagle Sct Awd; Ldrshp Awd 90; San Francisco ST U; Elec Engr.

MC CARTHY, JESSICA; Hanford HS; Hanford, CA; (2); Church Yth Grp; FBLA; Stat Swmmng; Hon Roll; Frgn Exch Clb; Bus.

MC CARTHY, K AMBER; Hemet HS; Hemet, CA; (4); 80/518; Pres AFS; Pres Church Yth Grp; Key Clb; SADD; Chorus; Church Choir; Stage Crew; Swmmng; Pres Acad Fit Awd; Pres Schlr; BYU; Econ.

MC CARTHY, KATHLEEN; Sequoia HS; San Carlos, CA; (2); Church Yth Grp; Cmnty Wkr; Treas Debate Tm; Rep Soph Cls; Hon Roll; Amnsty Intl Clb Pres; CSF; Earth Dy Clb; Stu Ambssdr USSR.

MC CARTHY, LEE S; Torrey Pines HS; Rancho Santa Fe, CA; (3); Aud/Vis; VICA; Phtg Nwsp; Rep Stu Cncl; Scuba Diving; Skiing; Comp Construction; Engrng.

MC CARTHY, MECHELLE; St Lawrence Acad; San Jose, CA; (1); Chorus; Var Bsktbl; Hon Roll; Jr NHS; Sci Fctn Clb-Sec; Clb Sccr; Santa Clara U; Tchr.

MC CARTHY, MICHAEL W; R A Millikan HS; Long Beach, CA; (4); 160/726; Aud/Vis; Hosp Aide; Math Clb; Pep Clb; Scholastic Bowl; Teachers Aide; Rep Jr Cls; Crs Cntry; Trk; Ntl Merit SF.

MC CARTHY, SHELLY R; Kingsburg HS; Kingsburg, CA; (1); Church Yth Grp; FTA; Math Tm; Band; Chorus; Church Choir; Mrchg Band; Pep Band; Var Sftbl; JV Vllybl; Volleyball Club; Fresno City JC; Nursing.

MC CARTHY, THOMAS; El Toro HS; El Toro, CA; (2); 121/520; JV Socr; Var L Wrstlng; Hon Roll; MVP Wrstlng; Engr Drftg, Body Boarding; Arch.

MC CARTNEY, JASON A; Downieville HS; Downieville, CA; (2); 1/4; Letterman Clb; Model UN; Pres Frsh Cls; VP Soph Cls; Var L Bsktbl; CSF; Comp Engr.

MC CARTNEY, KELLY B; Del Notre HS; Crescent City, CA; (2); Boy Scts; Church Yth Grp; 4-H; JV Ftbl; 4-H Awd; High Hon Roll; Hon Roll; Surfing, Bowling, Biking; Arch Dsgn.

MC CARTY, MELISSA; Rosary HS; Fullerton, CA; (4); 19/135; Drama Clb; French Clb; Pep Clb; SADD; Thesps; Chorus; School Musical; School Play; High Hon Roll; Debate Tm; CA Schlrshp Fed; Jr Statesmen Of Amer; Theatre.

MC CASLIN, STEVE A; El Toro HS; El Toro, CA; (3); German Clb; Teachers Aide; Intrml Bsktbl; Var L Crs Cntry; Var L Trk; Hon Roll; Engrng Clb Treas; Arch.

MC CAULEY, STACY C; Arlington HS; Riverside, CA; (3); Var Capt Socr; Var Trk; Stat Vllybl; Hon Roll; All CIF 3rd Team Girls Sccr; UCLA.

MC CAW, ROBIN L; Beaumont HS; Beaumont, CA; (3); Pep Clb; Varsity Clb; Band; Mrchg Band; Var Cheerldng; Var Pom Pon; Hon Roll; Prfct Atten Awd; Optometry.

MC CHESNEY, SONNET; South Tahoe HS; South Lake Tahoe, CA; (3); French Clb; Key Clb; Powder Puff Ftbl; Sftbl; Wt Lftg; Hon Roll; UC Davis; Ped.

MC CLAIN, BRIAN L; Lincoln HS; Lincoln, CA; (4); 7/150; School Play; Yrbk; Rep Stu Cncl; JV Bsktbl; Var L Ftbl; Var Capt Trk; Bausch & Lomb Sci Awd; Cit Awd; High Hon Roll; NHS; Sacramento ST U; Chem Tchr.

MC CLAIN, LORRIE; Sunset HS; Oakland, CA; (3); Church Yth Grp; Cmnty Wkr; Key Clb; Acpl Chr; Chorus; Church Choir; Cit Awd; Hon Roll; Ecology Clb; CMEA Fest Chorus; March Of Dimes Vlntr; Howard U; Design Arch.

MC CLAIN, ROSLYN; Valley HS; Sacramento, CA; (4); 25/450; Key Clb; Cit Awd; Hon Roll; GATE; MESA; CSF; CA ST U.

MC CLAIREN, PATRICIA YVETTE; William Workman HS; Bloomington, CA; (4); 46/246; Science Clb; Ski Clb; Ed Yrbk; Capt Trk; Cit Awd; Hon Roll; Prfct Atten Awd; Copy Edtr Yrbk; Acadc Dcthln; Mdl Wnng 2nd Pl Super Quiz Dcthln; Roses Of Hnr; Awd Excel CA Intrschlstc; San Diego ST U; Pre Med.

MC CLANAHAN, SUSAN N; San Rafael HS; San Rafael, CA; (2); Cmnty Wkr; Debate Tm; Hosp Aide; Library Aide; Band; Mrchg Band; Hnrs Eng Top 5 Pct Of Class; Stanford; Phy.

MC CLANANAN, SANDRA E; Manteca HS; Manteca, CA; (2); Hosp Aide; SADD; Color Guard; Rep Frsh Cls; Hon Roll; Cmpltd & Passed EMT; UC Davis; Ped.

MC CLASKEY, DANNY T; Bella Vista HS; Fair Oaks, CA; (2); 32/406; JV Bsbl; JV Ftbl; Wt Lftg; Hon Roll; Schlstc Achvt Awds; Orthodontist.

MC CLASKEY, JENNIFER; Shasta HS; Redding, CA; (4); 13/328; Sec SADD; Rptr Yrbk; Var Capt Cheerldng; JV Var Swmmng; High Hon Roll; Hon Roll; Pres Acad Fit Awd; Pres Schlr; Key Clb; Science Clb; Grotefund Schlrsp; Redding Womens Club Scchlrsp; Amer Assn Of Univ Women Awd; U CA Davis; Human Dev.

MC CLAUGHRY, CORINNE M; Los Gatos HS; Los Gatos, CA; (3); 22/333; Church Yth Grp; Debate Tm; Hosp Aide; Spanish Clb; Speech Tm; Rep Jr Cls; Capt Powder Puff Ftbl; JV Tennis; High Hon Roll; Gldn St Exam High Hnrs; Span Achvt Excllnc Awd; Piano; UC System; Doctor.

MC CLAURY, SCOTT D; Yucaipa HS; Yucaipa, CA; (3); 13/356; Church Yth Grp; Debate Tm; French Clb; NFL; Speech Tm; JV Bsbl; Intrml Mgr Ftbl; Cit Awd; High Hon Roll; South CA Ylth Ctznshp Seminar Pepperdine U 90.

MC CLEARY, DANIELLE N; Castlemont HS; Oakland, CA; (2); Math Clb; Science Clb; Rep Frsh Cls; VP Soph Cls; High Hon Roll; Hon Roll; Math/Engr/Sci Achvt; Big Bros/Big Sis; Elect Engr.

MC CLELLAN, BRYCE C; Mount Pleasant HS; San Jose, CA; (3); Math Clb; SADD; Bsbl; Evergreen CC; Auto Mchnc.

MC CLELLAN, JERRY E; South Bay Lutheran HS; Los Angeles, CA; (3); Church Yth Grp; Yrbk; VP Stu Cncl; Var Bsbl; Var Ftbl; Hon Roll; Ftbl.

MC CLELLAN, JODY E; Cordona SR HS; Rancho Cordova, CA; (3); 23/535; Church Yth Grp; Model UN; SADD; Band; Orch; Var L Trk; High Hon Roll; Jr NHS; CA Schlrshp Fed; Quiz Team Sci Plympd; CA Poly SLO; Arspc Engrng.

MC CLELLAN, LEE J; Upland HS; Upland, CA; (3); VP Acpl Chr; Chorus; Sec Swing Chorus; Cheerldng; Crs Cntry; Outstndng Soloist Fullerton Fstvl; Wrld Chair Of Yr Bournemouth Eng Intl Fstvl; UCLA; Music.

MC CLELLAN, LINDY; Mission Viejo HS; Mission Viejo, CA; (3); Church Yth Grp; Drama Clb; Office Aide; Thesps; Acpl Chr; Chorus; Church Choir; School Musical; School Play; Variety Show; Musicl Theatre.

MC CLELLAN, NICOLE M; Turlock HS; Turlock, CA; (2); 38/600; AFS; Letterman Clb; Science Clb; JV Crs Cntry; Var L Socr; JV Trk; High Hon Roll; Hon Roll; Acad All Conf Tm.

MC CLELLAN-NESS, TRACI L; Poway HS; Poway, CA; (4); 49/728; Treas AFS; Church Yth Grp; Drama Clb; Pres Treas FBLA; SADD; School Play; Yrbk; JV Swmmng; Hon Roll; Kiwanis Awd; Outstndng Stu Mnth Busnss 89; Miss Teen CA 1st Rnnr Up 89; UC Bereley; Intl Bus.

MC CLENAHAN, CHRISTINA M; North HS; Bakersfield, CA; (1); Drama Clb; ROTC; Spanish Clb; Teachers Aide; Color Guard; Drill Tm; Top 10 Natl Phys Ftnss; Military.

MC CLENDON, ANTQUENETTE; Castlemont HS; Oakland, CA; (2); High Hon Roll; Fashion; Math; MIT; Comp Sci.

MC CLENDON, KENDRA L; Rim Of The World HS; Running Springs, CA; (1); 54/500; Sec Spanish Clb; Teachers Aide; Rptr Nwsp; Rep Frsh Cls; JV Socr; Hon Roll; Rotary Awd; VP-JSA; Caterer.

MC CLENDON, RICHARD; Bellarmine HS; San Jose, CA; (2); Latin Clb; Ski Clb; Intrml Bsktbl; JV Ftbl; Intrml Sftbl; JV Trk; Intrml Vllybl; JV Wrstlng; Irish Club; San Jose Hstrcl Museum Vlntr.

MC CLENDON, SUSAN R; Terra Linda HS; San Rafael, CA; (3); Intrml Bsktbl; French Hon Soc; Frnch.

MC CLIMANS, MELISSA D; Corona Heights Christian HS; Riverside, CA; (3); Church Yth Grp; Key Clb; Library Aide; Pep Clb; SADD; Ed Yrbk; Var JV Tennis; High Hon Roll; JR Stsmn Of Amer; Riverside CC; Photo.

MC CLISH, KRISTIN A; Dana Hills HS; Laguna Niguel, CA; (2); SADD; Rep Frsh Cls; Rep Soph Cls; Rep Stu Cncl; High Hon Roll; Hon Roll; Youth In Govt; CSF; Schl Recognition Algebra For Golden St Exam; USC; Bus.

MC CLORY, MARINA S; Paso Robles HS; Templeton, CA; (1); Dance Clb; GAA; Pep Clb; Spanish Clb; Cheerldng; Sftbl; High Hon Roll; Hon Roll; NEDT Awd; MVP Chrldng; UCSB; Fshn Mrchndsng.

MC CLOSKEN, AMY A; Saint Francis HS; Los Gatos, CA; (3); Church Yth Grp; SADD; Yrbk; DAR Awd; High Hon Roll; NHS; Opt Clb Awd; Independent Aging Pgm; Yth Advisory Commission; Vet Med.

MC CLOUD, BRIAN B; Sonora HS; Sonora, CA; (3); JV Ftbl; Sierra JC; Poltcl Sci.

MC CLOUD, MICHAEL M; Coalinga HS; Coalinga, CA; (2); FCA; Yrbk; Yrbk; JV Bsbl; JV Bsktbl; JV Var Ftbl; JV Var Wt Lftg; Military Offcr.

MC CLUNG, CARRAH M; Los Angeles Baptist HS; Van Nuys, CA; (3); 17/100; Church Yth Grp; Teachers Aide; Chorus; Off Jr Cls; Hon Roll; Big Brthr/Big Sistr Pgm; CA Baptist Coll.

MC CLURE, BRIAN D; Arlington HS; Riverside, CA; (2); Computer Clb; Socr; Motorcycle Racing.

MC CLURE, JOHN M; Alisal HS; Jalinas, CA; (4); Computer Clb; Varsity Clb; Mrchg Band; Pep Band; Off Soph Cls; JV Var Bsktbl; JV Var Ftbl; Var Golf; Hon Roll; Prfct Atten Awd; Syracuse U; Pre Med.

MC CLURE, KASSANDRA; Torrey Pines HS; Del Mar, CA; (3); 43/469; Pep Clb; Science Clb; Ski Clb; Stu Cncl; JV Var Gym; JV Var Pom Pon; High Hon Roll; Hon Roll; UNC Chapel Hill; Aviation.

MC CLURE, YARRA; Arcata HS; Arcata, CA; (1); French Clb; SADD; Rptr Yrbk; Off Frsh Cls; Interact; SECS; Corp Law.

MC CLURKIN, COLLEEN; Righetti HS; Santa Maria, CA; (4); 2/400; Aud/Vis; Church Yth Grp; GAA; JA; Office Aide; Varsity Clb; Var L Tennis; High Hon Roll; Jr NHS; Dale Carnegie Grad Cmnctns; CA Schlrshp Fdrtn Life; CIF-SS Fnlst Grls Tnns; Westmont Coll; Bus.

MC CLUSKEY, JEFF A; Carlsbad HS; Carlsbad, CA; (1); Pep Clb; Hon Roll; U Of CA San Diego; Dntstry.

MC COLLOM, NATALIE R; Escondido HS; Escondido, CA; (1); Church Yth Grp; Key Clb; Science Clb; Varsity Clb; Var Swmmng; Wt Lftg; Cit Awd; Hon Roll; Prfct Atten Awd; Pres Acad Fit Awd; UCSD; Phy.

MC COLLUM, JENIFER D; Edison HS; Stockton, CA; (3); Church Yth Grp; Latin Clb; Pres SADD; Teachers Aide; Acpl Chr; Band; Rptr Yrbk; Rep Stu Cncl; Hon Roll; City Sftbl; Human Relations Club Pres; Delta Coll; Sci.

MC COLLUM, PHILIP; Bakersfield HS; Bakersfield, CA; (3); 21/700; Church Yth Grp; Cmnty Wkr; Band; Mrchg Band; Pep Band; Hon Roll; Band Offcr 89-90 90-91; Abilene Chrstn U; Grphc Engrng.

MC COMB, CRISSY RENEE; Lutheran HS; Chino, CA; (4); 1/23; ROTC; Yrbk; Pres Stu Cncl; Var Bsktbl; L Trk; Var Vllybl; High Hon Roll; NHS; Val; Bank Amer Awd Appld Arts; Jr Statsmn; Gold Seal Bearer CSF; U Of CA Irvine; Scl Sci.

MC COMBER, DEBI L; Tracy HS; Tracy, CA; (4); 88/400; FFA; FHA; GAA; Bsktbl; Sftbl; Hon Roll; CA ST; Criminal Jstc.

MC COMBS, LAURA R; San Luis Obispo HS; San Luis Obispo, CA; (2); Church Yth Grp; German Clb; Letterman Clb; Chorus; Church Choir; Var L Bsktbl; JV Tennis; Var L Trk; Med.

MC CONNELL, ANGELA G; Victor Valley HS; Victorville, CA; (3); 11/450; Drama Clb; Key Clb; Ed Nwsp; Hon Roll; Fencing; Lit Club; Chaffey Coll; Crt Rprtng.

MC CONNELL, CHRISTINE; Hemet HS; Hemet, CA; (2); Cmnty Wkr; Capt Flag Corp; Stat Wrstlng; Fashion.

MC CONNELL, KERRY A; Desert Christian HS; Bermuda Dunes, CA; (3); 1/8; Church Yth Grp; Teachers Aide; Chorus; Church Choir; VP Soph Cls; Pres Jr Cls; Pres Stu Cncl; Bsktbl; Cheerldng; Powder Puff Ftbl; Dstngshd Chrstn HS Stu; All Leag Vllybl 2 Yrs, Bsktbl 3 Yrs, Sftbl 2 Yrs; Chrldng Co-Capt 2 Yrs; Biola U; Elem Educ.

MC CONNELL, MARY F; Vacaville HS; Muscatine, IA; (3); Model UN; SADD; Rptr Yrbk; Hon Roll; SPCA Vlntr; Capri Cosmetology Coll; Make-Up.

MC CONNELL, MICHELE L; Eagle Rock HS; Los Angeles, CA; (3); Trk; FIDM; Fshn Dsgn.

MC CONNELL, TRACY L; Acalanes HS; Lafayette, CA; (1); AFS; SADD; Chorus; Powder Puff Ftbl; Radio Club DJ; Horseback Riding Ranked In ST; UCSB; Marine Bio.

MC CONNELL, WILLIAM S; Alta Loma HS; Alta Loma, CA; (4); Boy Scts; Church Yth Grp; Jazz Band; Crs Cntry; Trk; Wrstlng; High Hon Roll; Hon Roll; Cum Laude Soc; Chaffey Coll; Engl Lit.

MC CONOLOGUE, KELLY; Mesa Verde HS; Citrus Heights, CA; (2); 70/257; Dance Clb; Girl Scts; Cheerldng; Score Keeper; Vrsty Song Ldr; Slvr Awd Grl Scts; Anml Care Tech.

MC CONVILLE, JESSICA L; Los Angeles County HS For The Arts; Valencia, CA; (4); 20/148; Treas French Clb; FBLA; SADD; School Musical; School Play; High Hon Roll; Hon Roll; Dance.

MC COOL, REGINA C; Serra HS; San Diego, CA; (2); Var Capt Cheerldng; UCLA; Bus Mgmnt.

MC CORD, JENNIFER M; San Dieguito HS; Carlsbad, CA; (2); Teachers Aide; Hon Roll; Pres Acad Fit Awd; CSF; Pre-Med.

MC CORKELL, DAVID; Liberty Union HS; Byron, CA; (3); 6/323; Debate Tm; NFL; Speech Tm; Chorus; School Musical; School Play; Stage Crew; Hon Roll; Lion Awd; Ntl Merit SF; Theatre.

MC CORMAC, WENDY M; John F Kennedy HS; Sacramento, CA; (2); 15/525; High Hon Roll; CSF.

MC CORMACK, BRANDON L; Cajon HS; San Bernardino, CA; (3); Church Yth Grp; Chorus; Sftbl; New Life Clb Pres; CA ST Sn Bernadrno; Ocngrphr.

MC CORMACK, ROSE B; Whitney HS; Artesia, CA; (2); Girl Scts; Key Clb; Band; Mrchg Band; Rptr Nwsp; JV Bsktbl; Var Crs Cntry; Var Trk; High Hon Roll; Opt Clb Awd; Hnrb Mntn Natl Essy Cmptn Skirball Inst Amer Values.

MC CORMACK, SHANNON C; Canyon Springs HS; Moreno Valley, CA; (3); Office Aide; Stage Crew; Bsktbl; Hon Roll; TV Prdctn; Dbt Tm & Pr Ldrshp; US Navy; Tech Fld.

MC CORMICK, LAUREN K; Rim Of The World HS; Lake Arrowhead, CA; (4); Drama Clb; Teachers Aide; Co-Capt Drill Tm; Rptr Yrbk; Tch Dnc Clss-Bllt, Tap & Jazz; CSU San Bernardino; Sprts Med.

MC CORMICK, LORI; Irvington HS; Fremont, CA; (3); Drama Clb; Key Clb; Office Aide; Stage Crew; Yrbk; Stat Ftbl; Stat Swmmng; Hon Roll; UC Santa Cruz; Accntng Bus.

MC CORMICK, MARCIA L; Milpitas HS; Milpitas, CA; (4); 16/390; Church Yth Grp; Spanish Clb; Speech Tm; Rep Stu Cncl; Cheerldng; Swmmng; Elks Awd; Hon Roll; NHS; Pres Acad Fit Awd; U Of CA Davis; Ntrl Sci.

MC CORMICK, REBECCA J; Desert Christian HS; Palmdale, CA; (1); Church Yth Grp; Girl Scts; Church Choir; Phtg Yrbk; Ed Lit Mag; Off Frsh Cls; Rep Stu Cncl; Hon Roll; Girl Sct Slvr Awd; Piano Singing Solos.

MC COSH, DEBORAH; East Union HS; Manteca, CA; (2); 4/411; Church Yth Grp; Sec 4-H; Band; Church Choir; Mrchg Band; Pep Band; Cit Awd; 4-H Awd; High Hon Roll; Prfct Atten Awd; CMTA ST Hnrs Piano Rctl; CA Schlrshp Fdrtn.

MC COSKEY, STEPHANIE; Fred C Beyer HS; Modesto, CA; (3); Church Yth Grp; Dance Clb; Pep Clb; Ski Clb; SADD; Acpl Chr; Band; Chorus; Church Choir; Color Guard; Schlrshp Fed; Engrng.

MC COUBREY, HEATHER; Fred C Beyer HS; Modesto, CA; (3); Church Yth Grp; French Clb; Pep Clb; Service Clb; Ski Clb; SADD; Ed Yrbk; Var Golf; Var Vllybl; Hon Roll; UGANC Secy; Adv.

MC COVEY, JESSE C; Hoopa HS; Hoopa, CA; (3); Var Bsbl; JV Bsktbl; JV Var Ftbl; Var Wt Lftg; JV Wrstlng; Hon Roll; Lassen JC; Constrctn.

MC COVEY, MICHELLE M; Hoopa Valley HS; Hoopa, CA; (4); 3/50; Church Yth Grp; Sec Key Clb; Pep Clb; Scholastic Bowl; SADD; Ed Yrbk; VP Frsh Cls; Off Jr Cls; VP Stu Cncl; Stat Bsktbl; CA Yth Cncl; CSF Pres IN Clb; James B Black PG&E Spnsrd Schlrshp; Cal Poly San Luis Obispo; Archt.

MC COWIN, CHARLES E; Notre Dame HS; Rialto, CA; (3); 47/140; Boy Scts; JA; Variety Show; Capt Var Bsktbl; Capt Var Trk; Hon Roll; Bus Mgmt.

MC COWIN, ROBERT; Ramona HS; Ramona, CA; (3); Teachers Aide; Civil Air Patrol Cadet Cmmndr; Civil Air Patrol Cmmndrs Cmmndtn Awd & Billy Mitchell Awd; Air Force; Aeronautics.

MC COWN, ARTHUR J; Magnolia HS; Anaheim, CA; (3); Church Yth Grp; Teachers Aide; Varsity Clb; Var Ftbl; Var Wrstlng; Surfing; Qlfd For Southern CA Masters Wrstlng Trnmt; AZ ST U; Bus.

MC COY, BRIAN J; Desert HS; Edwards, CA; (3); Am Leg Boys St; FBLA; Pres Jr Cls; JV Var Bsktbl; JV Ftbl; Var Golf; JV Trk; Treas NHS; HOBY; Acad Decthln; Bank Amer Achvt Awd.

MC COY, CHAD C; Clovis HS; Clovis, CA; (2); VICA; Eclgy Clb; Engrng.

MC COY, CORRINA M; Eugene Mc Ateer HS; San Francisco, CA; (3); Drama Clb; Teachers Aide; School Play; Rptr Nwsp; Phtg Yrbk; Vllybl; Cit Awd; Hon Roll; CA ST Coll; Adv.

MC COY, DEMETRIUS D; James Monroe HS; Los Angeles, CA; (3); Dance Clb; SADD; Band; Chorus; Jazz Band; Rptr Nwsp; Phtg Yrbk; Rep Frsh Cls; Rep Stu Cncl; Hon Roll; CSF; Hmnts; Electrncs.

MC COY, DERON T; Irvine HS; Irvine, CA; (3); 32/520; JV Var Bsktbl; JV Var Ftbl; High Hon Roll; Hon Roll; NHS; Pres Acad Fit Awd; Pres Schlr; Academic Excl Awd; Geometry With High Honors; Heritage Awd Math; Scholar Athlete Awd; UCLA.

MC COY, JANEEN; Herlong HS; Herlong, CA; (3); Church Yth Grp; FBLA; Pres SADD; Yrbk; VP Frsh Cls; Sec Stu Cncl; JV Var Score Keeper; JV Vllybl; Hon Roll; NHS; Teenwork Attender; Wnr HOBY Cont; Fine Arts Stu; Psych.

MC COY, JAY K; Yosemite HS; Coarsegold, CA; (3); Church Yth Grp; Debate Tm; VP FFA; Band; Jazz Band; Mrchg Band; Pep Band; FFA Spvsd Occptnl Ed Prgm; Gold Awd Natl; Hghst Achvt Awd FFA Welding; Elec Engrng.

MC COY, JEANNETTE E; Colfax HS; Colfax, CA; (2); 11/180; French Clb; Math Tm; Ski Clb; JV Bsktbl; JV Socr; JV Sftbl; JV Swmmng; High Hon Roll; Hon Roll; Pres Acad Fit Awd; Alpha Omega Awd; Heart Surgeon.

MC COY, KANE P; Bellarmine College Pre; San Jose, CA; (2); Church Yth Grp; NFL; Service Clb; JV Swmmng; JV Wrstlng; Pres Acad Fit Awd; Wtr Polo; 1st Tm All STAL Hnrs; UCLA; Pltcs.

MC COY, KRISTEN K; Desert HS; Edwards, CA; (2); Church Yth Grp; Ed Nwsp; Rep Stu Cncl; JV Bsktbl; JV Trk; JV Vllybl; High Hon Roll; HOBY Ldrshp Smnr; CSF; Acad Xclnc Cmmtte.

MC COY, SCOTT; California HS; Danville, CA; (3); Teachers Aide; Acpl Chr; Chorus; Piano; Cert Of Merit St Of CA; 2 Consecutive Yrs Spelling Bee Finals Contre Costa County; U Of The Pacific; Prfrmng Arts.

MC COY, TANYA I; Tulare Union HS; Tulare, CA; (3); Drama Clb; Treas French Clb; Speech Tm; Stage Crew; Treas Frsh Cls; Stu Cncl; Lion Awd; Acadmc Dec Team; Mock Trial Team; Friday Night Live; Sad Pres; Ldrshp Class Spon; W TX ST U; Psych.

MC COY, TIM; Carlsbad HS; Carlsbad, CA; (4); 15/300; Varsity Clb; Ftbl; Socr; Trk; Wt Lftg; Cit Awd; Hon Roll; NHS; Prfct Atten Awd; Palomar JC; Firemn.

MC CRACKEN, TAWNYA L; Winters HS; Winters, CA; (3); AFS; German Clb; GAA; Letterman Clb; Library Aide; Office Aide; Pep Clb; SADD; Teachers Aide; Drill Tm; UCLA; Comp Prgmr.

MC CRANK, SUSAN L; Westmoor HS; Daly City, CA; (3); 15/325; VP Service Clb; SADD; Chorus; Rep Frsh Cls; Stat Bsktbl; Hon Roll; Friday Night Live Club Vp; Amnesty Intl Club; Comm.

MC CRAW, DUSTIN J; Manteca HS; Manteca, CA; (2); 31/420; Computer Clb; VICA; Var Swmmng; High Hon Roll; Hon Roll; De Molay; Cal Poly; Arch Engrng.

MC CRAY, LLEWELLYN L; Fontana HS; Fontana, CA; (3); Art Clb; Science Clb; Bsktbl; ITT; Comp Tech.

MC CREADY, MATT E; Los Amigos HS; Fountain Valley, CA; (3); Ski Clb; Var Bsbl; JV Bsktbl; Var Ftbl; Hon Roll; Photo.

MC CREESH, MIKE P; Victor Valley HS; Victorville, CA; (3); Var Ftbl; Var Trk; Wt Lftg; MI U; Comp Sci.

MC CUAN, ANNA L; De Anza HS; El Sobrante, CA; (3); Church Yth Grp; Girl Scts; Pep Clb; Red Cross Aide; Ski Clb; Ed Yrbk; JV Bsktbl; Var Cheerldng; Var Pom Pon; High Hon Roll; Yth Educator.

MC CUENN, DUSTIN; Mc Farland HS; Delano, CA; (3); Church Yth Grp; FFA; JV Bsbl; Var Ftbl; Var Socr; Var Trk; Hon Roll.

MC CUISTION, JENNIFER; Simi Valley HS; Simi Valley, CA; (4); Dance Clb; Key Clb; Speech Tm; SADD; Teachers Aide; Drill Tm; March Of Dimes; Moorpark JC; Math.

MC CULLEN, MONICA L; Napa HS; Napa, CA; (2); Hon Roll; Art Awds; Fshn Buyer.

MC CULLEY, DAWN; Mt View HS; Fall River Mlls, CA; (3); Art Clb; Church Yth Grp; Dance Clb; 4-H; FHA; Ski Clb; Teachers Aide; Band; Chorus; Nwsp; Shasta Coll; Police Offcr.

MC CULLOCH, SCOTT A; Gilroy HS; Gilroy, CA; (3); Boy Scts; Letterman Clb; Teachers Aide; Rep Frsh Cls; Ftbl; JV Var Swmmng; Wrstlng; Hon Roll; JV & Var Wtrpl; San Jose St U.

MC CULLOUGH, BONNIE; Hoover HS; Fresno, CA; (4); 32/390; Church Yth Grp; Science Clb; CSF; Powder Puff Ftbl; Young Life; Church Sftbl Tm; U CA Davis; Bio.

MC CULLOUGH, CAREY J; Huntington Beach HS; Huntington Beach, CA; (2); Church Yth Grp; Model UN; Teachers Aide; JV Socr; JV Trk; Pedtrc Nrs.

MC CULLOUGH, LANA K; Fontana HS; Fontana, CA; (4); Church Yth Grp; Debate Tm; 4-H; Library Aide; Pep Clb; Teachers Aide; Var Bsktbl; JV Sftbl; 4-H Awd; Hon Roll; Upward Bound Coll Pgm, Cal St, San Bernardino; Cal ST San Bernardino; Pre Law.

MC CULLOUGH, LESLEY; Valley Christian Acad; Santa Maria, CA; (3); 1/17; Church Yth Grp; Chorus; Rep Jr Cls; Stu Cncl; Stat Bsktbl; Score Keeper; JV Sftbl; Cit Awd; High Hon Roll; Bible Quiz Team; Pensacola Chrstn Coll; Accntng.

MC CULLOUGH, MARY; Mater Dei HS; Orange, CA; (3); Hosp Aide; Spanish Clb; Chorus; School Musical; High Hon Roll; NHS; Pres Acad Fit Awd; Outstndng Choral Stu Awd; 100 Hr Hosp Volunteer Awd; GPA Awd; Jrnlsm.

MC CULLOUGH, MEGAN; Flintridge Prep; La Canada Flintri, CA; (3); Church Yth Grp; French Clb; Key Clb; Chorus; Orch; School Musical; School Play; Variety Show; Treas Sr Cls; Var Bsktbl; BYU.

MC CULLOUGH, MICHELE; Los Angeles Center For Enrichd Studies; Los Angeles, CA; (4); 17/120; Sec Church Yth Grp; Science Clb; Sec Service Clb; Teachers Aide; School Musical; School Play; Variety Show; Nwsp; Sec Jr Cls; Sec Sr Cls; Peer Cnslng Group; Young Black Schlrs; Performing Arts Stearing Cmmtte; Spelman Coll; Dramatic Arts.

MC CULLOUGH, TOSHA; Liberty Union HS; Oakley, CA; (2); 26/360; Chorus; Ed Nwsp; Swmmng; Hon Roll; Pres Acad Fit Awd; Sal; UC Berkeley; Law.

MC CUNE, ADAM M; Northview HS; Covina, CA; (3); Boy Scts; Church Yth Grp; SADD; Nwsp; Off Soph Cls; Bsktbl; Hon Roll; UCLA; Writer.

MC CURDY, AMBER R; Fairfield HS; Fairfield, CA; (2); JV Bsktbl; Var Crs Cntry; Hon Roll; Fcomp.

MC CURDY, KARLA D; Shafter HS; Bakersfield, CA; (3); 44/204; Church Yth Grp; 4-H; SADD; Band; Mrchg Band; Pep Band; Var L Bsktbl; Powder Puff Ftbl; Hon Roll; Teacher.

MC CUSKER, AMY L; Dana Hills HS; Dana Point, CA; (1); Church Yth Grp; Pep Clb; Rep Stu Cncl; JV Cheerldng; JV Gym; Intrml Wt Lftg; Cit Awd; Gymnastics Awd Most Inspirational; Surfing Tm; Math.

MC DANIEL, CANDICE; Rio Mesa HS; Camarillo, CA; (2); 10/450; Church Yth Grp; Drama Clb; 4-H; Letterman Clb; Varsity Clb; Band; Drm Mjr(t); Mrchg Band; Pep Band; School Musical; 4-H Guide Dogs For Blind Prgrm; Stanford; Sci.

MC DANIEL, CARLA; San Gorgonio HS; Highland, CA; (2); ROTC; Teachers Aide; Bsktbl; Hon Roll; Stanford; Civil Rights Atty.

MC DANIEL, ELIZABETH; Santa Ana HS; Santa Ana, CA; (3); Dance Clb; Debate Tm; Pep Clb; Science Clb; Flag Corp; School Musical; School Play; Cheerldng; Gym; Vllybl; Reg Sci Olympiad 2nd Pl; GATE Stu Of Month; Fnlst Yth Expo Tlnt Search; Top 10 Perf Arts Dept Awd; Fr.

MC DANIEL, JACKIE; Fremont HS; Oakland, CA; (2); Art Clb; Church Yth Grp; Cmnty Wkr; Drama Clb; Math Clb; ROTC; Science Clb; Ed Nwsp; Ed Lit Mag; Sec Frsh Cls; Cal ST Hayward; Comp Engr.

MC DANIEL, JEROD L; Herbert Hoover HS; San Diego, CA; (2); JV Ftbl; JV Trk; Var Wrstlng; Police Officer.

MC DANIEL, LORI A; San Clemente HS; San Clemente, CA; (4); Church Yth Grp; Debate Tm; FBLA; Pep Clb; Spanish Clb; SADD; Acpl Chr; Rep Sr Cls; JV Cheerldng; Var Socr; Vrsty Soccer Most Insprtnl; Vocal Arts Club Treas; Acad & Ctnzshp Cmmndtn 88; Brown U; Engl.

MC DANIEL, TONIKA; Senior HS; Los Angeles, CA; (3); Church Yth Grp; Cheerldng; Hon Roll; Prfct Atten Awd; Howard U; Med.

MC DERMOTT, BRIAN L; Colton HS; Colton, CA; (4); Church Yth Grp; Office Aide; Stage Crew; High Hon Roll; Hon Roll; Bldrs Clb; Lawyer.

MC DEVITT, DAVID; Channel Islands HS; Littleton, CO; (2); 87/679; JV Bsbl; JV Bsktbl; Hon Roll; Prfct Atten Awd; Bio Lab Acad Awd & Stu Month; JV Bsbl & Bsktbl Coachs Awd; Aero Engr.

MC DILL, ERIN; Moorpark HS; Moorpark, CA; (2); 7/244; Church Yth Grp; 4-H; Pres Intnl Clb; Stat Bsbl; High Hon Roll; Hon Roll; Horse Trng/Shwng Eqtn Saddleseat; Yth Horse Judgng; CSF; Pepperdine U.

MC DONALD, AMANDA H; Red Bluff Union HS; Red Bluff, CA; (3); Art Clb; Aud/Vis; Cmnty Wkr; Computer Clb; Dance Clb; FHA; Hosp Aide; JA; SADD; Teachers Aide; Jr Steering Cmmtte; F-N-L; Laudbauch Tutoring Staff; UCLA; Audio-Visual Production.

MC DONALD, C T; Pacifica HS; Cypress, CA; (3); 77/275; Var L Ftbl; Var Wt Lftg; US Hstry; Mltry.

MC DONALD, CAROLINE E; Clayton Valley HS; Concord, CA; (3); Church Yth Grp; Girl Scts; Intnl Clb; Letterman Clb; SADD; Stage Crew; Crs Cntry; Trk; Hon Roll; Acadc Lttr; U C Santa Cruz; Law.

MC DONALD, CHRISTIAN M; Bakersfield HS; Bakersfield, CA; (3); 69/718; Science Clb; Var Capt Swmmng; Mst Imprvd Swmmr; Schlstc Achvt Awd; UC San Diego; Bio.

MC DONALD, DILLON S; Oak Ridge HS; Shingle Springs, CA; (3); 25/261; JV Bsbl; High Hon Roll; Gldn St Exam, Geo, Hnrs Awd; Cal Poly; Engr.

MC DONALD, JAKE D; Nevada Union HS; Nevada City, CA; (3); Cmnty Wkr; Pep Clb; ROTC; Stage Crew; Bsktbl; Cheerldng; Var Capt Ftbl; Var Capt Trk; Capt Wt Lftg; High Hon Roll; USMC; Teach.

MC DONALD, KATHERINE P; North Monterey County HS; Watsonville, CA; (2); Church Yth Grp; French Clb; SADD.

MC DONALD, KERI; Rosary HS; Buena Park, CA; (3); Hon Roll.

MC DONALD, KIMBERLY; Bonita HS; La Verne, CA; (1); Cmnty Wkr; Hosp Aide; Office Aide; Pep Clb; SADD; Rptr Nwsp; Phtg Yrbk; Masonic Awd; Miss La Verne; UC Santa Barbara; Bus.

MC DONALD, KRIS; Eureka HS; Arcata, CA; (1); Cit Awd; High Hon Roll; Pres Acad Fit Awd; CA Tech; Engrng.

MC DONALD, LISA C; Louisville HS; Santa Monica, CA; (2); GAA; Science Clb; JV Vllybl; Hon Roll; Jrnlsm.

MC DONALD, MARCY L; North HS; Bakersfield, CA; (3); 12/368; Church Yth Grp; FCA; Spanish Clb; Teachers Aide; Band; Drm Mjr(t); Mrchg Band; Pep Band; Bsktbl; Crs Cntry; CA Schlrshp Fed; Bakersfield JC; Phys Thrpy.

MC DONALD, MELISSA A; Mater Dei HS; Santa Ana, CA; (3); 50/499; Church Yth Grp; Letterman Clb; Varsity Clb; Bsktbl; Trk; Wt Lftg; 3rd Natn Hgh Jump; Bst Mark CA Hgh Jmp 90; 8th Bst CA Long Jmp 90; Forestry.

MC DONALD, MIKELE M; Mc Ateer J Eugene HS; San Francisco, CA; (2); School Musical; School Play; Stage Crew; Hon Roll; Outdoors Clb; Directors Apprentice Work Prog; Ceramics.

MC DONALD, SHANDRA L; Paramount HS; Long Beach, CA; (4); 65/479; Church Yth Grp; FCA; SADD; Rptr Nwsp; Ed Lit Mag; Var Trk; Hon Roll; Prfct Atten Awd; Treas Letterman Clb; JV Crs Cntry; Bank Of Amer Fnlst; Trk & Fld Top Fund Raiser; CSU Long Beach; Crmnl Jstc.

MC DONALD, SHAY; Mt Whitney HS; Visalia, CA; (3); AFS; Art Clb; Sec Church Yth Grp; Drama Clb; French Clb; Hosp Aide; SADD; School Play; Off Jr Cls; JV Tennis; Nrsng.

MC DONALD, TIMOTHY P; Cajon HS; San Bernardino, CA; (3); Band; Mrchg Band; Var Swmmng; Hon Roll; Water Polo, Bowling; Mar Bio.

MC DONALD, TONJA L; Apple Valley HS; Apple Valley, CA; (3); Pres FHA; Key Clb; Teachers Aide; Band; Mrchg Band; Pep Band; High Hon Roll; Hon Roll; Pres Acad Fit Awd; CSF; Chmbr Cmmrc Stu Mth; CA ST U; Elem Tchr.

MC DONALD, TRICIA L; San Dieguito HS; Leucadia, CA; (3); Cmnty Wkr; Var L Crs Cntry; JV Socr; Var L Trk; Hon Roll; Algebra I High Hnrs; Palomar; Sports Med.

MC DONALD, YVONNE M; Argonaut HS; Jackson, CA; (2); VP FBLA; Key Clb; Ski Clb; Band; Mrchg Band; Pep Band; JV Sftbl; High Hon Roll; Hon Roll; Jr Princess Of Intl Order Of Jobs Daughters; Math.

MC DONELL, MATTHEW T; Hillcrest Christian Schl; Camarillo, CA; (3); Church Yth Grp; Drama Clb; School Musical; Var L Bsktbl; Hon Roll; Ntl Merit SF; Med.

MC DONNELL, ANNE B; Vista HS; Vista, CA; (3); 6/464; Church Yth Grp; Sec Key Clb; Flag Corp; Rep Jr Cls; Cit Awd; High Hon Roll; CA Schlrsp Fed; Coll; Commun.

MC DONNELL, BRIAN D; Servite HS; La Habra, CA; (2); Ski Clb; Bsktbl; Golf; Hon Roll; Cmptv Divng; USD U Of San Diego; Law.

MC DONNELL, TRACEY F; Calvary Baptist Schl; Crockett, CA; (1); Church Yth Grp; Pep Clb; Bsktbl; Hon Roll.

MC DONOUGH, SHEILA J; California HS; Whittier, CA; (3); 26/369; FBLA; Girl Scts; JCL; Latin Clb; Spanish Clb; Teachers Aide; Stat Bsktbl; Stat Sftbl; Hon Roll; CSF; Page, Los Angeles Cnty Library.

MC DOUGAL, JEFF N; Riverdale HS; Riverdale, CA; (2); 14/250; Church Yth Grp; FFA; Letterman Clb; Science Clb; Rep Pep Band; Treas Soph Cls; Rep Stu Cncl; Capt Bsktbl; Var Ftbl; L Trk; Fresno ST U; Cvl Engrng.

MC DOUGALL, TIMOTHY J; Granada HS; Livermore, CA; (4); 15/306; Teachers Aide; Band; Var L Bsktbl; Capt Vllybl; High Hon Roll; Pres Acad Fit Awd; Rotary Awd; St Schlr; US Naval Acad Cngrssnl Appt; US Naval Acad; Pilot.

MC DOWELL, CAROLINE; South Tahoe HS; S Lake Tahoe, CA; (4); 19/206; Band; Orch; Variety Show; Hon Roll; NHS; Soroptimist Awd; Sonoma ST U.

MC DOWELL, DEKETRA; Ambassador HS; San Benardino, CA; (2); Church Yth Grp; Drill Tm; Bsktbl; Cheerldng; Hon Roll; Law.

MC DOWELL, HEATH; Wasco HS; Wasco, CA; (3); Boy Scts; 4-H; FFA; Band; Mrchg Band; Pep Band; Rep Yrbk; Var Golf; Var Socr; 4-H Awd; Ed Sci.

MC DOWELL, JENNIFER L; Mission Viejo HS; Mission Viejo, CA; (4); Spanish Clb; Color Guard; Hon Roll; Pres Acad Fit Awd; Interntnl Baccalrt Diploma Cert; Tutoral Asst Prg; Peer Adv; Loyola Marymount U.

MC DOWELL, LETITIA M; Castlemont HS; Oakland, CA; (3); Pres Church Yth Grp; Pres Computer Clb; JA; Library Aide; Spanish Clb; Teachers Aide; Church Choir; Stage Crew; Variety Show; Rptr Yrbk; CA ST Hayward.

MC DOWELL, MIKA; Alta Loma HS; Alta Loma, CA; (1); JV Socr; Var Sftbl; Cert Athltc Awd JV Sccr; Athltc Emblm Vrsty Sftbl; CA Intrschlstc Fdrtn Awd Sftbl; Al-Bsln Leag Awd; Chaffey Coll; Police Sci.

MC DOWELL, NAKEESHA L; Richard Gahr HS; Cerritos, CA; (1); Off Frsh Cls; High Hon Roll; Hon Roll; Blue & Gold Awrd Spnsh; Gahr H Schl-PTSA Awrd; Tchrs Apprctn Awrd; Howard U; Entrepreneur.

MC ELFISH, CLINTON M; Hueneme HS; Port Hueneme, CA; (3); Boy Scts; Church Yth Grp; Rep Stu Cncl; JV Bsktbl; VP Socr; Cit Awd; Hon Roll; Pres Acad Fit Awd; Eagle Sct & Acad Excllnc Awd; 3 Yr Lttrmn; Law.

MC ELHENY, KIM; Calvary Chapel HS; Costa Mesa, CA; (2); Art Clb; Church Yth Grp; Computer Clb; Library Aide; Office Aide; Pep Clb; Spanish Clb; L Cheerldng; Stat Ftbl; Var Powder Puff Ftbl; Interior Dsgn.

MC ELHENY, KIMBERLY; Calvary Chapel HS; Costa Mesa, CA; (2); Art Clb; Church Yth Grp; Library Aide; Office Aide; Spanish Clb; Teachers Aide; Var Cheerldng; Var Stat Ftbl; Powder Puff Ftbl; Hon Roll; Interior Dsgn.

MC ELHINNEY, ELIZABETH C; Torrey Pines HS; Rancho Santa Fe, CA; (1); Church Yth Grp; JV Bsktbl; Hon Roll; CSF; Arts.

MC ELHINNEY, RACHEL E; Morro Bay HS; Los Osos, CA; (3); 9/170; AFS; Drama Clb; French Clb; School Musical; School Play; Yrbk; High Hon Roll; Hon Roll; Ntl Merit Ltr; CSF; GATE; Acad Dcthln Team; Engl/Teacher.

MC ELHONE, PAMELA; Ponderosa HS; Shingle Springs, CA; (1); Office Aide; Teachers Aide; Drm Mjr(t); Rptr Nwsp; UCLA; Jrnlst.

MC ELLIGOTT, MICHAEL; Summerville Union HS; Mi-Wuk, CA; (3); French Clb; FBLA; Crs Cntry; Bausch & Lomb Sci Awd; Hon Roll; Natl Mrt Schlrshp Fnlst; CA Santa Barbara; Elec Engr.

MC ELRATH, ANAMARIA; California HS; Whittier, CA; (2); Church Yth Grp; Cmnty Wkr; Pep Clb; SADD; Sec Frsh Cls; Pres Soph Cls; Var Crs Cntry; JV Trk; Hon Roll; Prfct Atten Awd; U CA-IRVINE; Med.

MC ELRATH, DIANA R; California HS; Whittier, CA; (2); Church Yth Grp; Cmnty Wkr; Pep Clb; Rep Frsh Cls; Rep Soph Cls; Rep Jr Cls; Stat Mgr(s); Var Swmmng; Hon Roll; Prfct Atten Awd; Phy.

MC ELREE, TRACEY J; Davis SR HS; Richland Center, WI; (4); Church Yth Grp; Office Aide; Pep Clb; Band; Chorus; Pep Band; School Musical; JV Bsktbl; Var Powder Puff Ftbl; JV Sftbl; Peer Helping; U Of N IA; Bus.

MC ELROY, HEATHER A; Paraclete HS; Lancaster, CA; (2); SADD; Bsktbl; High Hon Roll; CSF; Z-Clb; Chld Psych.

MC ELROY, MELISSA I; John Burroughs HS; Burbank, CA; (2); Teachers Aide; Drill Tm; Flag Corp; Nwsp; Yrbk; Off Frsh Cls; Cheerldng; Swmmng; Hon Roll; NHS; CA JR Schlrshp Fdrtn.

MC ELROY, MICHELE K; Torrey Pines HS; San Diego, CA; (2); 1/500; Trk; DAR Awd; Hon Roll; Pres Acad Fit Awd; Actvst Clb TPHS; Alumni CO Outward Bound Schls; Pr Cnclng; Berkely; Med.

MC ELVAIN, KRISTINE L; Canyon HS; Anaheim, CA; (2); 5/37; FBLA; FHA; School Musical; High Hon Roll; Hon Roll; Jr NHS; NHS; Pres Acad Fit Awd; Euro Clb; Auburn U; Intl Bus Mgmt.

MC EVOY, KENNETH J; St Michaels Coll Prep; Mission Viejo, CA; (2); Art Clb; Computer Clb; School Play; Stage Crew; Rptr Nwsp; Pres Rptr Yrbk; Var Bsbl; Var Bsktbl; Hon Roll; Jr NHS; Wght Lftng; Yng Mrns; JR Life-Grd; Annapolis Nvl Acad; Aerontcs.

MC EWEN, ANGELA E; Washington HS; Fremont, CA; (2); Sec Pres Church Yth Grp; Var Stat Vllybl; 2nd Pl Essay Cont; Brigham Young U; Psych.

MC FADDEN, CHRISSY D; Orange Glen HS; Valley Center, CA; (2); Church Yth Grp; Ski Clb; JV Swmmng; Cit Awd.

MC FADDEN, ELENA O; Mc Clatchy HS; Sacramento, CA; (4); 38/444; Math Clb; Math Tm; Mrchg Band; Ed Nwsp; Rep Soph Cls; Off Jr Cls; JV Sftbl; Var Swmmng; Ntl Merit SF; Econ.

MC FADEN, ROBERT M; Sweetwater HS; National City, CA; (2); Church Yth Grp; Jazz Band; Off Frsh Cls; Cit Awd; Prfct Atten Awd; Schlrshp Awd; Votd Mst Lkly Sccd; Schl Tchr.

MC FADYEN, BRIAN N; Casa Roble HS; Orangevale, CA; (2); Drama Clb; School Musical; School Play; Stage Crew; Tennis; Cit Awd; Best Supporting Actor Awd; Eagle Awd.

MC FALL, DESIRAY; Hayward HS; Hayward, CA; (2); 63/237; GAA; Office Aide; Pep Clb; Spanish Clb; Teachers Aide; Drill Tm; Cheerldng; Pom Pon; Powder Puff Ftbl; Cit Awd; Spnsh Club Secy; Harvard; Law.

MC FARLAND, CANDICE A; Carlsbad HS; Carlsbad, CA; (1); Key Clb; Speech Tm; Acad League; Dance,Drama Classes; Tchr.

MC FARLAND, HOLLY; Roseville HS; Roseville, CA; (3); 23/500; AFS; Church Yth Grp; German Clb; Cheerldng; Crs Cntry; High Hon Roll; Hon Roll; Pres Acad Fit Awd; CA Poly San Louis Obispo; Arch.

MC FARLAND, JANELLE M; Rim Of The World HS; Running Springs, CA; (3); 63/259; Church Yth Grp; Drama Clb; Spanish Clb; Teachers Aide; Var Intrml Tennis; Hon Roll; Prfct Atten Awd; CA ST-SAN Bernardino; Lib Stu.

MC FARLAND, JOSH A; Bret Harte HS; Avery, CA; (2); Ski Clb; Hon Roll.

MC FARLAND, SEAN A; Santa Clara HS; Oxnard, CA; (2); 22/198; Boy Scts; Church Yth Grp; Cmnty Wkr; School Play; High Hon Roll; Hon Roll; NHS; Altar Boy; Yth Grp Govt Finance Cmmsnr; Bio.

MC FARLAND, SHELLEY L; Eureka SR HS; Eureka, CA; (4); 13/303; SADD; Orch; Yrbk; Powder Puff Ftbl; Socr; Tennis; Var L Trk; Cit Awd; High Hon Roll; Golden St Exam Algebra High Hnrs 87, Geometry 88; CSF; CSU; Visual Comm.

MC FARLAND, SONJIA K; Mercy HS; South San Francis, CA; (3); GAA; Latin Clb; SADD; Varsity Clb; Pres Acad Fit Awd; Pres Frsh Cls; Rep Soph Cls; Rep Jr Cls; Pres Stu Cncl; Var Socr; HS Schlrshp; Black Stu Union; Prfrmng Arts Assn; Commnctns.

MC FARLANE, NOLAN W; Monroe HS; Sepulveda, CA; (2); Computer Clb; Drama Clb; English Clb; Intrml Bsktbl; Intrml Trk; CSF; DARE; Stanford; Crm Law.

MC GAUTHA, VANESSA; Washington HS; Fremont, CA; (3); Church Yth Grp; Church Choir; Drill Tm; Capt Bsktbl; Pom Pon; Capt Powder Puff Ftbl; Wt Lftg; Jr Usher Brd; South/Alameda Cnty Young Woman Yr 1st Rnnr Up; T V Brdcstng.

MC GEE, CHRIS W; Point Loma HS; San Diego, CA; (4); 38/442; Aud/Vis; UC Berkeley; Bus Econ.

MC GEE, DAVID W; Miramonte HS; Orinda, CA; (1); Boy Scts; Church Yth Grp; JCL; Latin Clb; Band; Pep Band; Hon Roll; Maxima Cum Laude JCL Natl Exam; Jr Ldr Of Yr BS Troop; Sr Patrol Ldr BS Troop.

MC GEE, HEATHER M; Montclair HS; Montclair, CA; (4); 54/256; Church Yth Grp; Ski Clb; Treas Sr Cls; Stu Cncl; Var Cheerldng; Var Capt Swmmng; Hon Roll; Cal Poly Pomona.

MC GEE, MELINDA V; Berkeley HS; Berkeley, CA; (3); Sec Church Yth Grp; Grambling ST U; Law.

MC GEE, MICHELLE; North Highlands HS; Sacramento, CA; (3); Var L Vllybl; Wt Lftg; Var L Bsktbl; Var L Sftbl; Hon Roll; Comp Pgmng.

MC GEE, RAMONA N; St Anthony HS; Carson, CA; (2); Dance Clb; Girl Scts; Pep Clb; Chorus; Cheerldng; Powder Puff Ftbl; UCLA; Sci.

MC GEE, RENEE; Valley Christian HS; Livermore, CA; (3); Church Yth Grp; Drama Clb; Thesps; Church Choir; Rep Stu Cncl; Stat Bsbl; Stat Bsktbl; Var Cheerldng; Var Sftbl; Hon Roll; CSF; Litry Mag Awd; Biola.

MC GHEE, RAYCHELLE L; Morningside HS; Inglewood, CA; (3); Church Yth Grp; Math Tm; Office Aide; Sec Church Choir; Rep Stu Cncl; Cheerldng; Cit Awd; High Hon Roll; YES To Job; Images K-Nay Yth Grp; UC Berkeley; Law.

MC GILL, HOPE CHERE; Piedmont Hills HS; San Jose, CA; (3); Debate Tm; Hosp Aide; NFL; Pep Clb; Spanish Clb; Speech Tm; Cheerldng; Swmmng; High Hon Roll; Hon Roll; CSF; Psych.

MC GILL, KATHLEEN A; Loretto HS; Citrus Heights, CA; (2); Church Yth Grp; Cheerldng; Crs Cntry; Swmmng; Tennis; Stanford U; Med.

MC GILL, MELANIE A; Gompers Secondary HS; San Diego, CA; (2); 105/159; Cmnty Wkr; Computer Clb; Pres English Clb; FTA; Pres Girl Scts; Pres Science Clb; Treas Spanish Clb; SADD; Chorus; Color Guard; Bwlng Tm Capt 1st Pl Natl Tourny; Engl Tchr.

MC GINLEY, SCOTT D; Garden Grove HS; Garden Grove, CA; (3); VP Frsh Cls; Treas Soph Cls; Treas Jr Cls; VP Sr Cls; Rep Stu Cncl; JV Trk; High Hon Roll; Hon Roll; NHS; HS Ambssdr Orient; Yth Govt Cty Mgr; ASB Cmps Info Cmmssn; CSF; UNLV; Htl Mgmt.

MC GINTY, DANIEL M; Bellarmine College Prep; Gilroy, CA; (3); 11/300; Church Yth Grp; Letterman Clb; Intrml Mgr Bsbl; Intrml Mgr Bsktbl; Intrml Mgr Ftbl; L Socr; Intrml Mgr Sftbl; Hon Roll.

MC GLOIN, MARY C; Casa Grande HS; Petaluma, CA; (3); Drama Clb; French Clb; SADD; Thesps; Acpl Chr; Chorus; School Musical; School Play; Stage Crew; Variety Show; Petaluma Yth Sccr Leag; Petaluma Yth Sftbl Assoc CSF; Theater Arts.

MC GLOTHLIN, BENJAMIN B; Antelope Valley HS; Lancaster, CA; (3); Pres German Clb; Hosp Aide; Band; Mrchg Band; Orch; Pep Band; Rep Soph Cls; High Hon Roll; Ntl Merit Ltr; CSF; Natl German Test St Fnlst; Pres/VP German-Amer Prtnrshp Prgm; Jr Hnr Line; Rcgntn Golden St Alg; Med.

MC GLOTHLIN, MELISSA A; Nevada Union HS; Nevada City, CA; (3); 58/535; Spanish Clb; SADD; Chorus; Sec Jr Cls; VP Sr Cls; Rep Stu Cncl; Powder Puff Ftbl; Sftbl; Trk; Hon Roll; Peer Tutoring; Chrldr Coach; Elem Teacher.

MC GLOTHLIN, TAMARA L; Sherman E Burroughs HS; Ridgecrest, CA; (4); Ski Clb; JV Trk; Cthlc Yth Grp Asst Ldr; IWV Swm Tm; GOLD Randburg Plyrs; Cal Poly,San Louis Obisbo; Engr.

MC GLYNN, MICHAEL J; Quincy HS; Quincy, CA; (2); Cmnty Wkr; FBLA; Spanish Clb; Phtg Yrbk; Rep Soph Cls; JV L Bsbl; JV L Ftbl; Var L Wrstlng; Hon Roll; Kids Soccer Coach; Little League Ump; Butte Coll; Wildlife Bio.

MC GOLDRICK, JOHN T; Santa Monica HS; Malibu, CA; (3); Church Yth Grp; French Clb; Var Trk; Hon Roll; Pre-Med.

MC GOLDRICK, NATHAN; Santa Fe Christian HS; Oceanside, CA; (3); 5/35; Church Yth Grp; JV Bsbl; JV Bsktbl; JV Socr; High Hon Roll; Rotary Awd.

MC GONAGLE, SEAN D; Dublin HS; Dublin, CA; (3); Computer Clb; French Clb; JA; JV Bsbl; JV Bsktbl; Hon Roll; Gldn St Hnr Alg 88 & Gmtry 89; CA St Hnr Outstndng Acdmc Prfrmnc 89; U Of Notre Dame; Cmmrcl Art.

MC GOUGH, SHERRY A; Rosamond HS; Rosamond, CA; (3); Drama Clb; School Play; Score Keeper; Cit Awd; Hon Roll.

MC GOURTY, DANIEL; Marysville HS; Oregon House, CA; (2); Ski Clb; JV Bsbl; JV Capt Ftbl; Hon Roll; Prfct Atten Awd; Chrch, City Tm Bsktbl; U Of Sthrn CA.

MC GOVERN, CATHY; Holy Names HS; Berkeley, CA; (4); Am Leg Aux Girls St; Drama Clb; Acpl Chr; School Musical; School Play; Variety Show; VP Frsh Cls; VP Soph Cls; Rep Jr Cls; Rep Sr Cls; Choral Hnr Soc; Yth Understndng Intl Exchng Spain; Cls Svc Awd 87-88; CA U Davis.

MC GOVERN, SHAWN; Moorpark HS; Moorpark, CA; (2); 35/62; Rep Soph Cls; JV Bsbl; JV Var Ftbl; JV Socr; Ml; Engrng.

MC GOWAN, ELYSSIA; Coast Christian Schls; Hawthorne, CA; (3); Church Yth Grp; Computer Clb; English Clb; French Clb; Hosp Aide; Math Tm; Science Clb; Teachers Aide; Varsity Clb; Yrbk; MVP-VRSTY Sftbl Trophy; Congrssnl Yth Ldrshp Cncl; U Of S CA; Med.

MC GOWAN, KERRY E; Thomas Downey HS; Modesto, CA; (3); 1/600; Cmnty Wkr; German Clb; Letterman Clb; Service Clb; Spanish Clb; Band; Drm Mjr(t); Jazz Band; Pep Band; School Musical; Summr Camp Cnslr; Am Lung Assn Vlntr; Hugh O Brian Yth Fndtn Ldrshp Conf; CA Schlrshp Assn; UC Davis; Envrnmntl Rsrc Engrg.

MC GOWAN, MELISSA ANNE; Chico SR HS; Chico, CA; (4); #1 In Class; Key Clb; Spanish Clb; Sec SADD; Rep Frsh Cls; Stu Cncl; Stat Bsktbl; Mgr(s); VP Tennis; JV Vllybl; Cit Awd; CSF Jr Rep & Pres; Instrctnl Cncl; Dorothy B Ramon Awd For Spnch Achvt; CSU; Med.

MC GOWAN, MYISHA D; Diamond Bar HS; Diamond Bar, CA; (2); Church Yth Grp; Chorus; Church Choir; Drill Tm; Cit Awd.

MC GOWAN, SEAN; Cardinal Newman HS; Sonoma, CA; (2); Var Crs Cntry; JV Trk; Hon Roll; Hon Roll; CSF Clb; Engr.

MC GOWEN, TAMMY; Highlands HS; N Highlands, CA; (3); Color Guard; Drill Tm; Cit Awd; Hon Roll; American River Coll; Elem Tchr.

MC GRANAHAN, DEVON K; Troy HS; Fullerton, CA; (2); Church Yth Grp; Cmnty Wkr; Key Clb; Drill Tm; Variety Show; Swmmng; High Hon Roll; Hon Roll; NHS; UCLA; Law.

MC GRATH, JASON S; Montgomery HS; Santa Rosa, CA; (3); Band; Mrchg Band; Orch; Var L Ftbl; Hon Roll; Trailblazers Ride Asst; U CA Berkeley; Engrng.

MC GRATH, KIMBERLY J; Folson HS; Pulaski, NY; (4); 10/200; SADD; Teachers Aide; Band; Mrchg Band; Rep Stu Cncl; High Hon Roll; VP NHS; Ntl Merit Ltr; Pres Acad Fit Awd; St Lawrence U; Bio.

MC GRATH, LAURA A; Ocean View HS; Huntington Beach, CA; (1); Church Yth Grp; Key Clb; Key Clb; JV Bsktbl; Ftbl; JV Swmmng; 1st Female Ftbl Plyr; 2 Gavels Hnr; Most Insprtnl Girls Bsktbl; Pltcl Sci.

MC GRATH, MOLLY; Berkeley HS; Berkeley, CA; (3); Cmnty Wkr; Hosp Aide; Stage Crew; Lit Mag; Schl Rcgntn Golden St Exam Algebra & Geom; Piano; Santa Cruz; Eng.

MC GRATH, PAT J; Ramona HS; Riverside, CA; (1); Cit Awd; Pres Acad Ftnss Awd; U Of CA Riverside; Chef.

MC GRATH, ROLAND; Maybeck HS; Oakland, CA; (4); Ntl Merit SF.

MC GRATH, SARA; San Luis Obispo HS; San Luis Obispo, CA; (1); Art Clb; JV Crs Cntry; Powder Puff Ftbl; JV Socr; JV Trk; Hon Roll; Amnesty Intl Clb; Friends Of Earth Sec Treas; Earth Day Coalition.

MC GRATH, SEAN T; Buena HS; Ventura, CA; (4); 12/471; FBLA; JA; Capt Quiz Bowl; Ed Nwsp; High Hon Roll; NHS; Ntl Merit SF; Pres Acad Fit Awd; Mem Of Acad Dcthln Tm; Mem Of Mock Trl Tm; CA ST U; Bus Admin.

MC GRAW, HOLLY; Bonita Vista HS; Bonita, CA; (1); 28/400; Art Clb; Hosp Aide; Model UN; Office Aide; Cit Awd; French Hon Soc; High Hon Roll; Prfct Atten Awd; Schlrshp Awd; U Of San Diego.

MC GRAW, MATTHEW A; Los Angeles Lutheran HS; Sepulveda, CA; (2); Art Clb; Boy Scts; Church Yth Grp; Drama Clb; Letterman Clb; Ski Clb; Chorus; School Musical; School Play; Yrbk; Cal ST U; Cinematography.

MC GREGOR, PAT; Mt Shasta HS; Mt Shasta, CA; (4); 1/78; Boy Scts; Band; Chorus; School Musical; Swing Chorus; Var Bsbl; Var Bsktbl; JV Ftbl; JV Tennis; Bausch & Lomb Sci Awd; Bank Of Amer Awd Wnnr, Math & Sci; Bus.

MC GREGOR, TAMMY M; Norte Vista HS; Riverside, CA; (1); Church Yth Grp; Dance Clb; High Hon Roll; Hon Roll; Prfct Atten Awd; RCC; Childhood Dev.

MC GREW, ROSE S; Grace M Davis HS; Modesto, CA; (1); Nwsp; Hon Roll; CA Schlrst Fed; UCLA; Jrnlsm.

MC GRIFF, COLETTE E; Paso Robles HS; Paso Robles, CA; (2); Band; Mrchg Band; Orch; Pep Band; Trk; High Hon Roll; Math, Engr, Sci Achvt; UCLA; Jrnlsm.

MC GROUTHER, WILLIAM W; Bishop O'dowd HS; Oakland, CA; (3); Art Clb; Boy Scts; Debate Tm; Varsity Clb; Phtg Nwsp; Phtg Yrbk; Lcrss; High Hon Roll; Hon Roll; YMCA Red Ragger, Camp Cnslr.

MC GRUDER, MARK G; Morningside HS; Los Angeles, CA; (4); JA; Varsity Clb; Nwsp; Yrbk; Stu Cncl; Bsbl; Ftbl; Hon Roll; Yng Blck Schlrs; Yth In Govtmnt; Angel Cty Link Achvr Prog; Engr.

MC GUINESS, MEGAN E; Saint Anthony HS; Long Beach, CA; (3); 12/130; Church Yth Grp; Cmnty Wkr; Drama Clb; SADD; School Musical; School Play; Yrbk; Stat Bsktbl; Stat Crs Cntry; Stat Vllybl; CA Schlrshp Fed; Engl Ed.

MC GUIRE, CORINNE A; John A Rowland HS; Rowland Hts, CA; (2); Church Yth Grp; Dance Clb; Letterman Clb; Pep Clb; Varsity Clb; Var Cheerldng; Hon Roll; UCSB; Law.

MC GUIRE, JENNIFER; Tulare Western HS; Tulare, CA; (1); Treas Science Clb; Cheerldng; Hon Roll; Marine Bio.

MC GUIRE, JERRY TYSON; Gahr HS; Bellflower, CA; (2); Red Cross Aide; JV Bsbl; JV Ftbl; JV Wrstlng; Hon Roll; Lion Awd; Pres Acad Fit Awd; Rio Hondo Coll 14th Annual HS Drafting Cmptn 6th Pl; CA Polytech Coll Pomona; Arch.

MC GUIRE, LAURIE A; Patterson HS; Patterson, CA; (3); FCA; FBLA; FHA; Office Aide; Ski Clb; Spanish Clb; Bsktbl; Sftbl; Vllybl; High Hon Roll; Miss Patterson 90; Miss Congeniality 91; Soclgy.

MC GUIRE, PATSY J; Lowell HS; San Francisco, CA; (2); Cmnty Wkr; Teachers Aide; Chorus; Off Frsh Cls; Off Soph Cls; French Hon Soc; Hon Roll; Uc Santa Barbara; Child Psych.

MC GUIRE JR, RICHARD A; West HS; Bakersfield, CA; (1); Boy Scts; Band; Mrchg Band; Tennis; Hon Roll; Explr Sct Bkrsfld Fire Dept; Engrng.

MC GUIRE, SHELBY D; Oxnard HS; Oxnard, CA; (4); Church Yth Grp; Ed Yrbk; Hon Roll; Intrnshp Assmblymns Office; Bus Admin.

MC GUIRE, STACEY L; Burbank HS; Burbank, CA; (4); 24/450; Cmnty Wkr; GAA; Hosp Aide; Letterman Clb; Science Clb; Service Clb; Speech Tm; Chorus; Stu Cncl; Var Capt Crs Cntry; UC Berkeley; Bus Admin.

MC GUIRE, TARA D; Foothill HS; Sacramento, CA; (2); Church Yth Grp; Dance Clb; Teachers Aide; Band; Flag Corp; Mrchg Band; Hon Roll; Pres Acad Fit Awd; GATE; Swmmng Club; Cal Poly; Engrng.

MC GUNNIGLE, STEPHEN; Manteca HS; Manteca, CA; (2); 40/400; Hon Roll; CA St Indstrl & Tech Ed 3rd; Cmmrcl Art.

MC HALE, BRYCE S; Garden Grove HS; Garden Grove, CA; (1); JV Bsbl; Hon Roll; Pitched Prfct Game CGGLL All-Star Tourn 90; Bsbl.

MC HENRY, JACK K; Barstow HS; Barstow, CA; (1); Ftbl; Chem Engr.

MC HENRY, TAMARA D; Mt Whitney HS; Visalia, CA; (3); Hon Roll; COS; Elem Tchr.

MC HUGH, KRISTIANNE M; Newark Memorial HS; Hayward, CA; (3); Drama Clb; French Clb; Acpl Chr; Chorus; School Musical; School Play; Stage Crew; Cal ST Hayward; Comp.

MC ILROY, DARIN M; Los Angeles Baptist HS; El Segundo, CA; (3); Boy Scts; Church Yth Grp; JV Crs Cntry; JV Var Socr; JV Trk; Var Vllybl; Outdoor Actvts; Aviation; Photo.

MC INNES, CARYN G; Mira Mesa HS; San Diego, CA; (2); 111/797; GAA; Office Aide; JV Socr; JV Trk; San Diego ST U; Orthdntst.

MC INNES, MATTHEW R; Pacifica HS; Cypress, CA; (3); Church Yth Grp; Elect Engr.

MC INTIRE, KATHRYN F; La Reina HS; Thousand Oaks, CA; (3); 13/70; Art Clb; Church Yth Grp; Church Choir; Off Soph Cls; Cit Awd; High Hon Roll; Hon Roll; Jr NHS; NHS; Ntl Merit SF; Schlrshp; Sec Schl Office; CSF; U Of CA Santa Barbara; Engl.

MC INTOSH, DENISE M; Trinity HS; Burnt Ranch, CA; (2); Church Yth Grp; Drama Clb; Swmmng; Hon Roll; Alpine Club; CSF; Bus.

MC INTOSH, JASON R; West Covina Hills SDA HS; Walnut, CA; (1); Church Yth Grp; Teachers Aide; School Musical; School Play; Stage Crew; Yrbk; Off Frsh Cls; Hon Roll; Prfct Atten Awd; Loma Linda U; Orthodntcs.

MC INTOSH, JUSTIN C; Corona HS; Corona, CA; (2); Church Yth Grp; French Clb; Band; School Musical; Bsktbl.

MC INTOSH, MARTHA; Indio HS; Indio, CA; (4); 5/388; Var Capt Pep Clb; Teachers Aide; Var Capt Cheerldng; Hon Roll; CSF; Press Enterprise Riverside Mrt Schlr; Pepperdine; Law.

MC INTOSH JR, ROBERT C; Junupa Valley HS; Riverside, CA; (2); Boy Scts; Pres Soph Cls; Pres Stu Cncl; Var Swmmng; UCLA; Medcl.

MC INTOSH, RONALD F; Redwood HS; Visalia, CA; (3); Church Yth Grp; Math Clb; Math Tm; Jazz Band; JV Ftbl; Hon Roll; CA Schlrshp Fed.

MC INTOSH, SOPHIA; John F Kennedy HS; Sacramento, CA; (4); 131/388; Church Yth Grp; Computer Clb; Dance Clb; GAA; Girl Scts; Library Aide; Church Choir; Cit Awd; Hon Roll; Pres Acad Fit Awd; Black Stu Union Athl Ability & Acad Achvts; Sacramento City Coll; Med.

MC INTYRE, ANDREW S; El Toro HS; El Toro, CA; (3); 7/500; Treas Am Leg Boys St; Pres German Clb; Model UN; Var L Swmmng; High Hon Roll; Water Polo 2 CIF Champs; Jr Natl Tm; Most Imsprntl Awd; Vrsty Ltrs; Excllnc Awd Advncd Math; CSF; Comm.

MC INTYRE, HEATHER; Loara HS; Anaheim, CA; (3); French Clb; Sec Color Guard; Mgr Jazz Band; Mrchg Band; Pep Band; Hon Roll; Flag Sec, Mst Dependable, Oustndng Acad 89-90; Psych.

MC INTYRE, JENNIFER M; Hemet HS; Hemet, CA; (2); JV Bsktbl; JV Crs Cntry; JV Powder Puff Ftbl; JV Socr; JV Vllybl; Hon Roll; Attorney.

MC INTYRE, MELIA A; Montgomery HS; Santa Rosa, CA; (4); 8/402; Art Clb; Church Yth Grp; French Clb; JA; Letterman Clb; Library Aide; Office Aide; SADD; Teachers Aide; Church Choir; U Of La Verne; Paralegal.

MC INTYRE, PETER J; St Francis HS; Glendale, CA; (3); Cmnty Wkr; Math Clb; Mu Alpha Theta; Pep Clb; Ski Clb; Spanish Clb; Mgr Yrbk; Hon Roll; NHS; Spanish NHS; 4th Pl Nation, 1st Pl Sch Geom Natl Math Leag; S CA Mtnrs Assn; U Of PA; Bus.

MC IVER, LINDA K; North Montery County HS; Castroville, CA; (2); FBLA; Hosp Aide; SADD; Hon Roll; Fresno ST; Schl Tchr.

MC JONES, HEATHER J; Rincon Valley Christian HS; Santa Rosa, CA; (2); Church Yth Grp; Cmnty Wkr; Capt Flag Corp; Stat Bsktbl; Misnry Kid Deputn.

MC KAY, JOHN S; Vahalla HS; El Cajon, CA; (3); Letterman Clb; Office Aide; Ski Clb; SADD; Varsity Clb; Ftbl; Wt Lftg; Wrstlng; 3 Time League Wrestling Champ; State Qualifier; Power Lifting Champ.

MC KAY, JULIE; Lincoln HS; Stockton, CA; (3); 53/592; Church Yth Grp; Cmnty Wkr; JCL; Latin Clb; SADD; Teachers Aide; Var Vllybl; High Hon Roll; Stu In Preventn; CSF; Educ.

MC KAY, MARTIN J; Sonoma Valley HS; Sonoma, CA; (2); 63/244; Church Yth Grp; Letterman Clb; Acpl Chr; Band; Chorus; Church Choir; Mrchg Band; Pep Band; School Musical; School Play; Gldn St Exam Achvt Geom; Med.

MC KEE, AMBER; Kearny HS; Albany, OR; (2); Cmnty Wkr; Hon Roll; AYSSO Sccr; Girls Sftbl; Royal Servants Intl 3 Yrs In Europe; Drama Tm; Southern CA Chrstn Coll; Ed.

MC KEE, BRADLEY R; Marin Catholic HS; San Francisco, CA; (4); 7/200; Ed Lit Mag; High Hon Roll; Pres Acad Fit Awd; Acad Dcthln Cnty & St Cmptn; U CA Los Angeles; Engr.

MC KEE, CHRIS E; Berkeley HS; Berkeley, CA; (3); Swmmng; Hon Roll; PROBE Envrnmntl Grp; Video Club; UCLA; Bus.

MC KEE, D STEPHEN; Liberty Christian Acad; Fountain Valley, CA; (2); Aud/Vis; Church Yth Grp; School Musical; Stage Crew; Nwsp; Var JV Bsbl; Var JV Bsktbl; Var JV Ftbl; Cit Awd; High Hon Roll; Ftbl & Bsbl Awd 89-90; Movies.

MC KEE, EMILY A; Pescadero HS; Loma Mar, CA; (1); Var Frsh Cls; JV Bsktbl; Score Keeper; Hon Roll; Math.

MC KEE, FELICIA A; Carlmont HS; Palo Alto, CA; (2); Stat Trk; Hon Roll; Math Engr Sci Achvmnt Clb; CA Schlrshp Fedrtn Mem; Engr.

MC KEE, PATRICK S; Marina HS; Huntington Beach, CA; (3); AFS; Treas Spanish Clb; Rptr Nwsp; High Hon Roll; Frgn Exchng Stu Smmr 89; Went To Honduras With AFS; Tutor Acad Clss; Span, Math, Engl, Social Studies; Librl Arts.

MC KEEVER, DANIEL M; North Hills Christian Schl; Benicia, CA; (3); 1/5; Church Yth Grp; Rptr Nwsp; Ed Yrbk; Sec Treas Soph Cls; Var Bsktbl; High Hon Roll; Prfct Atten Awd; Prin Awd.

MC KEIGHEN, JENNIFER; Sierra Joint HS; Clovis, CA; (4); 27/175; Chess Clb; Debate Tm; Ski Clb; SADD; Varsity Clb; Treas Frsh Cls; Rep Jr Cls; Sec Stu Cncl; JV Var Bsktbl; Var Crs Cntry; Rdng ATC; Azusa Pacific; Fmly & Mrtl Thrp.

MC KELLIGON, CARRIE E; Del Campo HS; Carmichael, CA; (3); 27/490; Cmnty Wkr; Ski Clb; Varsity Clb; Variety Show; Rep Jr Cls; Stu Cncl; Stat Ftbl; JV Socr; Var Swmmng; Coach Recreatnl Soccer Tm.

MC KELLIGON-HILL, GERALD; Sonoma Valley HS; Sonoma, CA; (3); Drama Clb; French Clb; Intnl Clb; Letterman Clb; School Play; Stage Crew; Variety Show; Yrbk; VP Jr Cls; VP Stu Cncl; Sister Cities Exchange Stu Italy; Singles Tennis Chmpn 89; USC; Cinematography.

MC KELVY, MELINDA K; Red Bluff Union HS; Red Bluff, CA; (2); Church Yth Grp; Dance Clb; Drama Clb; French Clb; Girl Scts; SADD; Teachers Aide; Band; Mrchg Band; Orch; Dance Tm; Prfrmng Arts Ldrshp Tm; CA ST U; Dance.

MC KENNA, DENISE N; Grossmont HS; El Cajon, CA; (1); Capt JV Pom Pon.

MC KENNA, LAURALEI; Valley Christian Acad; Santa Maria, CA; (4); 3/18; Church Yth Grp; Teachers Aide; Chorus; Pep Band; Sec Stu Cncl; Var Capt Bsktbl; Var Cheerldng; Capt L Sftbl; Capt L Vllybl; Hon Roll; MVP Vlybl Leg; Band Dir Awd 88; Northland Bptst Bible; Coaching.

MC KENNON, JOHN E; Bishop Amat HS; Walnut, CA; (1); Writer.

MC KENZIE, BONNIE; Sherman E Burroughs HS; Ridgecrest, CA; (3); Drama Clb; Thesps; Acpl Chr; Chorus; Orch; School Musical; School Play; High Hon Roll; CA Orch Dir Assoc; CSF; Music Ed.

MC KENZIE, GREGG W; Cupertino HS; Cupertino, CA; (3); Var Ftbl; Hon Roll; Schlr Athl Awd; Boston Coll; Bus.

MC KENZIE, JULIE A; La Reina HS; Simi Valley, CA; (2); Cmnty Wkr; Variety Show; Cit Awd; Mock Trial Team; YMCA Camp Cnslr; U Of CA; Elem Schl Tchr.

MC KENZIE, KARMEN B; Woodland HS; Woodland, CA; (3); Cmnty Wkr; French Clb; FBLA; Key Clb; SADD; Teachers Aide; Swmmng; Hon Roll; NHS; Jr NHS; All Amer Meddley Relay; UC Santa Barbara; Sports Med.

MC KENZIE, KATHLEEN; Cajon HS; San Bernardino, CA; (2); 19/592; Treas Church Yth Grp; Cmnty Wkr; Hosp Aide; Band; Drm Mjr(t); Jazz Band; Mrchg Band; Var Socr; NHS; Natl Charity Leag; Dartmouth; Sci.

MC KENZIE, KELLY M; La Reina HS; Simi Valley, CA; (3); Cmnty Wkr; Dance Clb; Drama Clb; Hosp Aide; NFL; Speech Tm; SADD; Variety Show; Cit Awd; Hon Roll; Mock Trials Cnty Champs 90; YMCA Day Camp Vlntr; CA Poly San Luis Obispo; Vet.

MC KENZIE, MICHAEL; North Valley Christian HS; Redding, CA; (3); Church Yth Grp; Sec Computer Clb; Chorus; Church Choir; Var Bsktbl; Hon Roll; Comp.

MC KENZIE, PAULETTE B; George Washington Prep HS; Los Angeles, CA; (2); Nurse.

MC KENZIE, SARAH KRYN; Elk Grove HS; Elk Grove, CA; (2); Church Yth Grp; Dance Clb; FFA; Drill Tm; Hon Roll; Otstndng Eng Awd; CA Schlrshp Fdrtn; Acad Lttr Rcpnt; Santa Barbara; Spch Pthlgy.

MC KENZIE, STACI L; Livermore HS; Livermore, CA; (2); 124/424; Latin Clb; Stat Vllybl; Hon Roll; People To People Stu Amb Prog; St Marys; Comp Sci.

MC KEON, JODI; Middletown HS; Marysville, CA; (4); 7/59; Am Leg Aux Girls St; FBLA; Office Aide; Teachers Aide; School Musical; Ed Nwsp; Ed Yrbk; Treas Frsh Cls; Treas Soph Cls; Sec Treas Jr Cls; UC Davis; Comp Sci.

MC KINLAY, JULIA E; San Pasqual HS; Escondido, CA; (3); 103/353; Hosp Aide; Var Tennis; Cit Awd; Hon Roll; Prfct Atten Awd; Jrnlsm.

MC KINLEY, ERIC HEATH; Canyon HS; Canyon Country, CA; (3); Church Yth Grp; Cmnty Wkr; FCA; French Clb; JA; Science Clb; SADD; Band; Church Choir; Jazz Band; Chrch Of Canyons Yth Grp.

MC KINLEY, MICHELLE D; Hesperia Christian Schl; Hesperia, CA; (3); 9/40; Acpl Chr; Chorus; School Musical; School Play; Rptr Nwsp; Var Bsktbl; Var Crs Cntry; JV Vllybl; Hon Roll; Prfct Atten Awd; Public Rltns.

MC KINLEY, ONEISHA; Skyline SR HS; Oakland, CA; (2); Comp Engrng.

MC KINLEY, TRUDY R; Nevada Union HS; Nevada City, CA; (3); Pres Art Clb; Pres Chess Clb; Pres Church Yth Grp; Teachers Aide; Church Choir; High Hon Roll; CSF VP Of Tutorng; Spcl Olympcs Coach; Crftd Lifeguard; Humboldt ST U; Scndry Tchr.

MC KINNEY, CINDY K; Arroyo Grande HS; Oceano, CA; (1); 31/580; Church Yth Grp; Church Choir; Color Guard; Hon Roll; Civil Air Patrol; USAF Acad; Space Sci.

MC KINNEY, CLEMINATU; Mira Mesa HS; Poway, CA; (4); 21/819; Cmnty Wkr; Key Clb; Teachers Aide; Drill Tm; Var L Mgr(s); Stat Score Keeper; Cit Awd; Hon Roll; NHS; CPA.

MC KINNEY, JOE A; Thomas Downey HS; Modesto, CA; (3); SADD; Teachers Aide; JV Wt Lftg; UC Davis; Engr.

MC KINNEY, MATT R; Atascadero HS; Santa Margarita, CA; (3); Sec FFA; Letterman Clb; Math Tm; Office Aide; Rep Frsh Cls; Rep Stu Cncl; L Var Ftbl; L Var Trk; JV Wrstlng; Cit Awd; FFA Pblc Spkng & Prlmntry Prcdr Tm; CA Polytech ST U; Anml Sci.

MC KINNEY, MICAH G; Cajon HS; San Bernardino, CA; (4); Church Yth Grp; Cmnty Wkr; Debate Tm; Teachers Aide; Hon Roll; Ntl Merit SF; San Diego ST U; Bus.

MC KINNEY, TARA LYNN; Ramona HS; Riverside, CA; (3); 51/232; Dance Clb; French Clb; Pep Clb; Teachers Aide; Color Guard; Cheerldng; Pom Pon; Bus.

MC KINNEY, TRISHA A; Ramona HS; Ramona, CA; (3); 52/242; Church Yth Grp; Dance Clb; SADD; Flag Corp; Stat Ftbl; Hon Roll; Peom Published In Bk; Stanilaus ST U; Psych.

MC KINNON, CINDY L; Thousand Oaks HS; Thousand Oaks, CA; (3); Church Yth Grp; GAA; Office Aide; Teachers Aide; Rptr Nwsp; Var L Vllybl; Plays For Zuma Bay Vllybl Clb; Pepperdine U; Wrtr.

MC KINNON, MALANEE; Paradise HS; Paradise, CA; (2); JV Fld Hcky; Powder Puff Ftbl; Var Socr; JV Trk; Cit Awd; High Hon Roll; Hon Roll; Pres Acad Fit Awd; Phys Ed Awd 88-89; Outstndng Stu Hnrb Mntn; Outstndng Stu Engl; Chico ST; Law Enfrcmnt.

MC KINSEY, WENDY; Oxnard HS; Oxnard, CA; (1); Church Yth Grp; Bsktbl; Var Trk; JV Vllybl; CSF; Stanford; Med.

MC KIRDY, AIMEE; San Ramon Valley HS; Diablo, CA; (1); 4-H; Band; Mrchg Band; Trk; UC Davis; Bus.

MC KITRICK, JOLINE M; Apple Valley HS; Apple Valley, CA; (3); Drama Clb; FHA; Girl Scts; Key Clb; Spanish Clb; JV Capt Bsktbl; Trk; High Hon Roll; Pres Acad Fit Awd; Intr Dsgn.

MC KNIGHT, KEITH M; Bret Harte HS; Arnold, CA; (3); SADD; Varsity Clb; School Play; Bsktbl; Crs Cntry; Ftbl; Trk; Hon Roll; Green Belt; Mtn Clmbng; U C Berkeley; Lawyr.

MC KNIGHT, MICHELL D; George Washington HS; San Francisco, CA; (3); ROTC; Teachers Aide; Drill Tm; Mgr(s); Hrsbck Rdng & Wrkng With Chldrn; UC Davis; Vet.

MC KNIGHT, SPONTANEOUS R; Chino HS; Ontario, CA; (3); 18/561; Church Yth Grp; Ski Clb; Sec Frsh Cls; Var Swmmng; JV Tennis; Bausch & Lomb Sci Awd; High Hon Roll; Natl Achvmnt Semi Fnlst; CA Schlrshp Fdrtn; Bio-Med.

MC KNIGHT, ZILLIARY M; John F Kennedy HS; Sacramento, CA; (3); JCL; Office Aide; Drill Tm; Variety Show; Off Frsh Cls; Off Soph Cls; Off Jr Cls; Cit Awd; Hon Roll; BSU; Sac City Clg; Nrsng.

MC KOLSKEY, MARTY L; Carlmont HS; Belmont, CA; (3); 8/241; Pres Latin Clb; School Play; Stu Cncl; Hon Roll; Ntl Merit SF; Yth Empwrmnt Sys Stu Rep; SHOUT; Kids Day; Eng.

MC KOWN, AARON M; Newport Harbor HS; Newport Beach, CA; (2); 25/309; Var Bsbl; Bsktbl; JV Ftbl; Pres Acad Fit Awd.

MC KOY, JEANNETTE E; Montclair HS; Montclair, CA; (3); Church Yth Grp; Cmnty Wkr; Dance Clb; Drama Clb; Girl Scts; Pep Clb; Band; Chorus; Church Choir; Drill Tm; Sign Lang Clb; Mt San Antonio Coll; Intrepretr.

MC LACHLAN, RYAN J; Serra HS; San Diego, CA; (2); 21/490; Pep Clb; Var Tennis; Cit Awd; High Hon Roll; Hon Roll; Varsity Waterpolo Lettered Most Dedicated; MVP Tennis; Business.

MC LAIN, TONJA K; Marina HS; Huntington Beach, CA; (3); Church Yth Grp; Drama Clb; Pres FHA; Spanish Clb; Speech Tm; Pres SADD; Teachers Aide; Mgr School Musical; School Play; Intrml Bsktbl; OK ST U; Dramatic Arts.

MC LAREN, SHANE; San Bernardino HS; San Bernardino, CA; (4); 79/365; Art Clb; Cmnty Wkr; Intnl Clb; Model UN; ROTC; Drill Tm; Off Frsh Cls; Stu Cncl; Intrml Bsktbl; Var Socr; St Natl Bicntnnl Cmptn Cnstitn & Bill Of Rghts; Vice Chr CSUSB Mdl UN; CA ST Fullerton; Bio.

MC LAUCHLAN, SHANNON K; Helix HS; San Diego, CA; (2); 32/449; Quiz Bowl; School Play; Sec Soph Cls; JV Swmmng; Hon Roll; Spirit Club; Fshn & Self Image Club; UCLA; Psych.

MC LAUGHLIN, BLAINE; West HS; Torrance, CA; (4); 20/425; VP JA; Service Clb; Ski Clb; Ftbl; Wt Lftg; Wrstlng; High Hon Roll; Hon Roll; Pres Acad Fit Awd; Pres Schlr; Scuba Dvng Naui OPII Certfd; Photo; UCSD; Intl Bus.

MC LAUGHLIN, EMILY J; Dixon HS; Dixon, CA; (1); JV Sftbl; Modeling-Spitz Ritter Modeling Agcy, Look Agency; Snow Skiing; UCLA; Sci.

MC LAUGHLIN, GIOVANNA M; Torrey Pines HS; Rancho Santa Fe, CA; (1); Church Yth Grp; JV Tennis; Psych.

MC LAUGHLIN, IAN J; Morro Bay HS; Los Osos, CA; (3); 15/238; SADD; Teachers Aide; Band; JV Bsktbl; Var L Crs Cntry; Var Capt Trk; High Hon Roll; CA U Snta Crz; Marine Bio.

MC LAUGHLIN, JEREMY; Victor Valley SR HS; Victorville, CA; (2); Math Tm; JV Bsktbl; Var Ftbl; Wt Lftg; Cit Awd; Hon Roll.

MC LAUGHLIN, MICHELLE; Chatsworth HS; Chatsworth, CA; (3); Church Yth Grp; Hosp Aide; SADD; Teachers Aide; Chorus; Drill Tm; Ed Yrbk; Hon Roll; Pres Acad Fit Awd; Psych.

MC LAUGHLIN, ROBIN S; Oxnard HS; Oxnard, CA; (2); #13 In Class; Church Yth Grp; Spanish Clb; Jazz Band; Mrchg Band; School Play; Yrbk; Socr; Hon Roll; Most Team Spirit Soccer Awd; CSF; Drama.

MC LAUGHLIN, STEVE B; Serra HS; Hillsborough, CA; (4); Church Yth Grp; Letterman Clb; Rptr Phtg Nwsp; Phtg Ed Yrbk; Var Crs Cntry; Var Trk; High Hon Roll; Mst Outstndng Track Athl V 90; Engl Acad Awd 89-90; Svc Awd 90; Sant Clara U; Hstry.

MC LAUGHLIN, VERONICA L; Cajon HS; San Bernardino, CA; (3); Church Yth Grp; Nrs.

MC LAURIN, CORRINE M; Coronado HS; Coronado, CA; (3); VP French Clb; Hist Model UN; Ed Yrbk; Ed Lit Mag; Crs Cntry; Trk; Hon Roll; Rotary Awd; Wkly HS Clmnst Local Paper Coronado Jrnl; U CA; Corp Law.

MC LEAN, KATHRYN A; Del Campo HS; Citrus Heights, CA; (3); 16/446; Teachers Aide; High Hon Roll; CSF; Friday Night Live Co-Pres; Sci.

MC LEAN, KATHRYN M; Antioch HS; Pittsburg, CA; (2); Church Yth Grp; Library Aide; Chorus; Church Choir; Orch; Stage Crew; Hon Roll; Natl JR Hgh Hnr Choir 89; Frgn Exchange Stu 90-91; U Of CA, Santa Cruz; Mrne Bio.

MC LEAN, LACY D; Silver Valley HS; Fort Irwin, CA; (2); JV Var Ftbl; Hon Roll; Did Well On Golden St Exam Algebra 89; Arch.

MC LEAN, MARYBETH; Academy Of Our Lady Of Peace; San Diego, CA; (3); Cmnty Wkr; Model UN; Spanish Clb; Variety Show; Stu Cncl; Var L Tennis; Hon Roll; NHS; NEDT Awd; Spanish NHS; Natl Bicentennial US Constitution Cmptn; Prer Camp Enterprise; Liberal Arts.

MC LEAN, SCOTT C; Flintridge Preparatory Schl; Monrovia, CA; (3); Phtg Yrbk; Off Jr Cls; Pres Sr Cls; Pres Stu Cncl; Var L Socr; Cit Awd; High Hon Roll; NHS; JCL; Key Clb; Natl Ltn Hnr Soc; Xerx Awd; Middlebury Coll; Engl.

MC LEAN, SCOTT T; Tracy HS; Tracy, CA; (4); 47/355; High Hon Roll; Hon Roll; Acad Ltr; Humboldt ST U; Biogst.

MC LELLAN, JASON; James Madison HS; San Diego, CA; (4); 55/347; Church Yth Grp; Yrbk; VP Stu Cncl; Bsktbl; High Hon Roll; Hon Roll; Ntl Phys Ed Awd; Dominican Coll; Intl Bus.

MC LELLAN, MARY; Oakmont HS; Roseville, CA; (2); 106/447; German Clb; Stat Score Keeper; Cit Awd; Hon Roll; U Of CA Santa Cruz; Marine Bio.

MC LEMORE, EARNEST J; John F Kennedy HS; Sacramento, CA; (2); German Clb; Math Clb; Band; Mrchg Band; Pep Band; JV Bsktbl; Intrml Crs Cntry; Intrml JV Trk; Cit Awd; Hon Roll; Urban League; Georgetown U; Comp Engrng.

MC LENNAN, LAURA L; Alverno Heights Acad; Arcadia, CA; (3); 21/67; Girl Scts; Varsity Clb; Stage Crew; Sec Soph Cls; VP Jr Cls; VP Stu Cncl; Stat Bsktbl; Var L Sftbl; JV Var Vllybl; Hon Roll; CSF; NHS 2 Yrs; Athl Dir 90; Schl ASU Vp 90-91; U Of San Diego; Law.

MC LEOD, JENNIFER; Trubuco Hills HS; Mission Viejo, CA; (1); 19/353; Girl Scts; Spanish Clb; Swmmng; Hon Roll; NHS; Girl Sct Slvr Awd; Mission Viegjo Nadadores; U Of CA San Diego; Vet.

MC LIN, JESSE R; Trinity HS; Lewiston, CA; (1); Art Clb; Ski Clb; SADD; Rep Stu Cncl; Hon Roll; 90 CA Art Schlr; Alpine Clb; Frgn Exchng Stu-To Switzerland; Peer Helper; Grphc Arts.

MC LINTOCK, MONIQUE; Vista Migm HS; Vista, CA; (4); 14/443; Cmnty Wkr; Dance Clb; 4-H; Girl Scts; Pep Clb; Service Clb; SADD; School Musical; Variety Show; Treas Jr Cls; Blck Blt-Karate; Yth Cmmssn Chrprsn; Jnr Miss Prgm-Sprt Of Jnr Miss Awd 90; Cal Poly; Bus.

MC MAHAN, HENRY J; Corona HS; Corona, CA; (3); Debate Tm; VP Drama Clb; School Musical; School Play; Stage Crew; Pres Sr Cls; Debate Team Was Mock Trial Finished 2nd In Div.

MC MAHAN, JEFF J; Alta Loma HS; Cucamonga, CA; (2); JV L Ftbl; Wt Lftg; Prfct Atten Awd; Mst Val Lineman Ftbl Awd 88.

MC MAHAN, SONIA L; Los Angeles Baptist HS; Granada Hills, CA; (4); Church Yth Grp; French Clb; Chorus; Var L Crs Cntry; Var L Trk; Hon Roll; NHS; Pres Schlr; CA Schlrshp Fed Gold Seal Bearer; CSU Northridge.

MC MAHON, AMY M; King City HS; Bradley, CA; (3); 4-H; FFA; L Var Bsktbl; L Var Vllybl; High Hon Roll; MVP Vlybl & Bsktbl Leags; CSF; St Fash Show St 4-H Cnvtn; Bus.

MC MAHON, CLAIRE L; Mater Dei HS; Santa Ana, CA; (2); Cmnty Wkr; Hosp Aide; Ed Nwsp; Rep Frsh Cls; Rep Soph Cls; JV Trk; High Hon Roll; Hon Roll; NHS; Dance; CA Schlrshp Fdrtn.

MC MAHON, FORREST D; Abraham Lincoln HS; San Francisco, CA; (2); Var Wrstlng; Hon Roll; UC Berkeley; Bus.

MC MAHON, GINA M; Will C Crawford HS; San Diego, CA; (3); 7/332; Mgr(s); Vllybl; Hon Roll; Law.

MC MAHON, KATHLEEN A; Antioch SR HS; Antioch, CA; (3); Drama Clb; Girl Scts; Letterman Clb; School Play; Swmmng; Hon Roll; Sprts; Crtv Wrtng; Read; Sacramento St U; Tchng.

MC MAHON, MATTHEW P; Loyola HS; Manhattan Beach, CA; (2); Debate Tm; Latin Clb; JV Bsktbl; JV Vllybl; Hon Roll; Amnesty Intl; Clb Vllybl; Loyola Clssc Leag; Georgetown; Hstry.

MC MAHON, MEGHAN C; Marina HS; Huntington Beach, CA; (3); Church Yth Grp; Hosp Aide; Pep Clb; Service Clb; Spanish Clb; High Hon Roll; Songleading Capt; Dance Tm; Schl Site Cncl; UC Santa Barbara.

MC MAHON, NOAH; Calvary Chapel HS; Santa Ana, CA; (2); Church Yth Grp; Speech Tm; VP Soph Cls; JV Vllybl; Cit Awd; Hon Roll; Pres Acad Fit Awd; Sal; Bst Wrtr U Of CA At Irvine Wrtrs Prjct; Bst Chrstn Example Awd; Near Prfct Attndnce Awd; U Of CA; Pblc Rltns.

MC MAHON, RYAN T; Valhalla HS; El Cajon, CA; (1); JV Bsktbl; JV Crs Cntry; JV Tennis; Mst Effrt Germn; UCSD; Lawyer.

MC MAKEN, ROMY A; Monteray Bay Acad; Atascadero, CA; (4); Church Yth Grp; Church Choir; Drill Tm; School Play; Rptr Nwsp; VP Soph Cls; Hon Roll; Psych.

MC MANIGAL, MELISSA; Rio Americano HS; Carmichael, CA; (3); Aud/Vis; Church Yth Grp; Service Clb; Spanish Clb; Pres SADD; Capt Drill Tm; Mgr Stage Crew; High Hon Roll; Hon Roll; Lion Awd; Friday Nght Live; Jr Statsmn Amer; Miss Ten Schlrshp, Rcgntn Pgm; Nordstrom Brass Plum Fshn Brd; ROP; Commnctns.

MC MANUS, JESSE T; Chula Vista HS; Chula Vista, CA; (2); 239/300; Treas Church Yth Grp; Thesps; School Musical; Stage Crew; Co-Ed Nwsp; Prfct Atten Awd; Prdctn Drama; SPEAK; Main Attraction; Berkeley; Drama.

MC MANUS, SUSAN L; Grossmont HS; El Cajon, CA; (3); #10 In Class; Am Leg Aux Girls St; Cmnty Wkr; Sec Treas Key Clb; VP Pep Clb; Speech Tm; SADD; Teachers Aide; Varsity Clb; School Play; Rep Frsh Cls; ASB Comssnr Svc.

MC MASTER, CHASE; Tracy HS; Tracy, CA; (2); 134/483; Church Yth Grp; Bsbl; Bsktbl; Hon Roll; Sports Anlyst.

MC MASTER, HEATHER J; Dana Hills HS; Laguna Niguel, CA; (1); Church Yth Grp; Thesps.

MC MATH, KENDAL J; Chino HS; Chino, CA; (3); Church Yth Grp; Spanish Clb; Teachers Aide; Chorus; Church Choir; Pres Acad Fit Awd; Overall Dir Chrch Missn Outreach; Christians Campus; Elem Schl Teacher.

MC MENAMIN, SARA B; Torrey Pines HS; Del Mar, CA; (2); 14/503; JV Fld Hcky; JV Socr; Hon Roll.

MC MILLAN, KYLA KYM; Palm Springs HS; Palm Springs, CA; (3); Cmnty Wkr; Active Frndshp Network; Peer Cnslng Pgm; Grossmont JR Coll; Psych.

MC MILLAN, LORI A; Merced HS North; Merced, CA; (2); Church Yth Grp; Swmmng; Hon Roll; Keywanettes Club; Merced JC; Teacher.

MC MILLEN, JEFF S; Bonita Vista HS; Bonita, CA; (1); Computer Clb; Model UN; Cit Awd; Hon Roll; Masonic Awd; Pres Schlr; Boy Scts Comp Explorer Post; Space Engrng; CA Tech; Space Engr.

MC MILLIN, KEIKI M; Sierra HS; Prather, CA; (2); Art Clb; Ski Clb; Spanish Clb; Var Cheerldng; Var Pom Pon; JV Var Tennis; JV Vllybl; Hon Roll; NHS; Congrssnl Yth Ldrshp Awd; Sierra Pacific Club Vllybl; CSF; Art.

MC MILLIN, KEIKILANI M; Sierra Joint Union HS; Prather, CA; (2); Art Clb; Ski Clb; Spanish Clb; SADD; VP Frsh Cls; Var Cheerldng; JV Var Tennis; JV Vllybl; Hon Roll; NHS; Sierra Pacific Vlybl Club; Biola; Art Teacher.

MC MILLIN, VANESSA; El Capitan HS; Lakeside, CA; (4); 44/429; Math Clb; Office Aide; Red Cross Aide; Spanish Clb; Teachers Aide; School Play; Off Frsh Cls; JV Bsktbl; Intrml Swmmng; JV Tennis; Vaquero Mnth Jan Wrk Exprnc; San Diego ST; CPA.

MC MINDES, AMBER L; Vacaville HS; Vacaville, CA; (3); Pres Church Yth Grp; 4-H; Band; Chorus; Church Choir; School Musical; School Play; Stat Bsktbl; Var Tennis; Var Trk; Fnlsh Media Essay Cont U CA Davis; Congrssnl Yth Cncl; Brigham Young U; Hstry.

MC MULLEN, CHRISTOPHER D; Downtown Business Magnet HS; Burbank, CA; (4); #6 In Class; Chess Clb; Var Capt Golf; Gov Hon Prg Awd; Natl Bus Merit Awd; Golden St Ex Geo W/Hons; CSF; Astrophysics.

MC MULLEN, DESIREE L; Hemet HS; Hemet, CA; (4); 89/517; Art Clb; Hosp Aide; Key Clb; Teachers Aide; Hon Roll; Ntl Merit Ltr; Western ST Coll CO; Reg Nurse.

MC MULLEN, SCOTT A; Rim Of The World HS; Blue Jay, CA; (3); Bsktbl; Var L Tennis; Cit Awd; Prfct Atten Awd; Bus.

MC MURRAY, EDDIE D; John F Kennedy HS; Sacramento, CA; (2); French Clb; JV Var Vllybl; Hon Roll; Arch.

MC MURRAY, MAUREEN; John F Kennedy HS; Sacramento, CA; (4); 37/452; French Clb; Worked For Schl; Pre Law.

MC MURRAY, TREVOR R; North HS; Salinas, CA; (2); Wt Lftg; Hartnell; Police Officer.

MC NABB JR, RICHARD S; Manteca HS; Manteca, CA; (2); 11/450; Var Crs Cntry; Var Socr; Var Tennis; Hon Roll; California Scholastic Federation; College; Engineering.

MC NACK, ANISA; Sunset HS; Hayward, CA; (3); Math Clb; Mrchg Band; Sec Frsh Cls; JV Var Bsktbl; Var Sftbl; Cit Awd; High Hon Roll; Hon Roll; Black Stu Union Sec; Prtnrshp Pgm Hlp Get Coll; Dancing & Singing; Howard U; Bus.

MC NAIRN, JANA D; John W North HS; Riverside, CA; (1); Church Yth Grp; Hon Roll; Pro Intnl Baccalaureate; Int Dsgn.

MC NALL, SONYA L; Armijo HS; Fairfield, CA; (1); Church Yth Grp; Key Clb; Band; Color Guard; Mrchg Band; Pep Band; Cit Awd; Hon Roll; U Of CA Davis; Vet.

MC NALLEY, CODY P; Ocean View HS; Huntington Beach, CA; (1); FBLA; Key Clb; Model UN; Intrml Tennis; U CA Berkeley.

MC NALLY, PATRICK S; Edison HS; Huntington Beach, CA; (3); Capt Debate Tm; JA; Key Clb; Model UN; Quiz Bowl; Capt Speech Tm; SADD; JV Crs Cntry; AFS; Church Yth Grp; Mock Trial Capt; Sister City Yth Group; Stu Ambassador To Japan 89; UC Berkeley; Law.

MC NAMARA, ANNA; San Lorenzo Valley HS; Felton, CA; (2); Pep Clb; Red Cross Aide; Varsity Clb; Chorus; VP Frsh Cls; Pres Soph Cls; Pres Jr Cls; Rep Stu Cncl; JV Var Trk; Hon Roll; Cadet Firefighter; Pre Elect Color Guard Tm; HI U; Phys Therapy.

MC NAMARA, JENNIFER L; Granada Hills HS; Northridge, CA; (3); High Hon Roll; Hon Roll; Prfct Atten Awd; Rotary Awd; CSF; Interact Clb; Arch.

MC NAMEE III, GEORGE ALLEN; Bonita Vista HS; Chula Vista, CA; (4); 14/523; Office Aide; VP Sr Cls; Var L Bsbl; Var L Bsktbl; Var L Ftbl; Var Socr; High Hon Roll; Hon Roll; Jr NHS; Atty.

MC NATT, ANGELO C; Mt Pleasant HS; San Jose, CA; (3); Cmnty Wkr; Math Clb; Math Tm; Science Clb; Nwsp; Sec Sr Cls; NHS; CSF; Jrnlsm.

MC NATT, JENNIFER E; Don Antonio Lugo HS; Chino, CA; (2); Var Socr; Var Sftbl; Var Vllybl.

MC NAUGHTON, JASON L; Fairfield HS; Fairfield, CA; (2); ROTC; Band; Jazz Band; Mrchg Band; Pep Band; Ftbl; Wt Lftg; Wrstlng; Cit Awd; Jazz Choir; UC Davis; Police Offcr.

MC NAUGHTON, LORI A; Kingsburg HS; Kingsburg, CA; (3); 24/178; Church Yth Grp; Rep Drama Clb; Band; Mrchg Band; Pep Band; School Play; Var Bsktbl; Var Trk; Hon Roll; Selma Girls Bsktbl Trnmt MVP; BYU.

MC NEAL, CUSHONDRA; Mojave HS; California City, CA; (2); Church Yth Grp; Band; Church Choir; Mrchg Band; Pep Band; High Hon Roll; Hon Roll; Black Schlstc Awd; Law.

MC NEALY, ERIC M; Grant HS; Sacramento, CA; (4); Aud/Vis; Computer Clb; French Clb; Office Aide; Pep Clb; SADD; Teachers Aide; Sec Bsktbl; Mgr(s); Var Score Keeper; San Diego ST U; Accntng.

MC NEAR, SHANNON; Turlock HS; Turlock, CA; (2); Computer Clb; Dance Clb; Gym; Sftbl; Wt Lftg; Bnkr.

MC NEIL, GREGORY P; George Dewey HS; San Francisco, CA; (4); 15/65; Pres Intnl Clb; Scholastic Bowl; Spanish Clb; SADD; Chorus; School Musical; Rep Stu Cncl; Tennis; Hon Roll; Pres Acad Fit Awd; Outstndng Achvt Awds; Hnrs Grad; U MD; Scndry Ed.

MC NEIL, JENNIFER L; Montgomery HS; Santa Rosa, CA; (3); Cmnty Wkr; Dance Clb; Office Aide; Teachers Aide; Band; High Hon Roll; Hon Roll; Jr NHS; Pres Acad Fit Awd; Golden St Exam Outstndng Achvt 1st Yr Alg W/Hnrs Awd 87; San Francisco U; Law.

MC NEIL, KEILY L; Seaside HS; Seaside, CA; (3); Art Clb; Stat Bsktbl; Mgr(s); Score Keeper; High Hon Roll; Hon Roll; Mst Imprvd Stu; Socl Wrk.

MC NEIL, KRISTIA L; Livermore HS; Livermore, CA; (3); Church Yth Grp; 4-H; Pep Clb; Teachers Aide; JV Bsktbl; 4-H Awd; Hon Roll; San Jose ST U; Intr Dsgn.

MC NEIL, LA QUINZIA S; Technical HS; Oakland, CA; (1); Church Yth Grp; Band; Church Choir; Cit Awd; Hon Roll; Essay Awd; Oakland Trffc Resrv Hrnbl Dschrg.

MC NEIL, RAFFIANNE; The Acad Of Our Lady Of Peace; Santa Barbara, CA; (1); Church Yth Grp; Cmnty Wkr; Variety Show; Hon Roll; Notre Dame; Pre-Med.

MC NEIL, SHELBY P; Morningside HS; Inglewood, CA; (3); Church Yth Grp; FCA; FBLA; Girl Scts; Hosp Aide; Math Clb; Science Clb; Teachers Aide; Church Choir; School Play; Peer Cnslg; Debutant Ball Alpha Kappa Alpha; Fisk; Bio.

MC NEILL, CHRISTINA; Diamond Bar HS; Walnut, CA; (4); 43/463; Rep Acpl Chr; Rep Chorus; Mrchg Band; Orch; Swing Chorus; Rptr Nwsp; Stat Ftbl; High Hon Roll; Pres Acad Fit Awd; Miss Teen CA Pgnt; CA ST U Fullerton; Med.

MC NEILL, KENNETH W; Clear Lake HS; Lakeport, CA; (3); Am Leg Boys St; Boy Scts; Band; Jazz Band; Pep Band; School Musical; VP Frsh Cls; VP Soph Cls; Rep Jr Cls; JV Var Bsktbl; Bsktbl Foreign Exch To Australia Smmr 90; Sonoma ST U; Med Bio.

MC NEILL, KIMBERLY I; Arcadia HS; Arcadia, CA; (3); 174/646; Drama Clb; Ski Clb; Teachers Aide; School Musical; School Play; VP Frsh Cls; Off Jr Cls; Off Sr Cls; Stu Cncl; JV Mgr Crs Cntry; Liberal Arts.

MC NEILLY, HEATHER A; Burlingame HS; San Bruno, CA; (3); SADD; Hon Roll; Davis; Tchr.

MC NEILLY, JOE; Sonoma Valley HS; Boyes Hot Springs, CA; (2); Model UN; Hon Roll; CSF.

MC NERNEY, SUSAN; Arcata HS; Bayside, CA; (3); Drama Clb; Science Clb; Spanish Clb; Speech Tm; Teachers Aide; School Play; Mgr Stage Crew; Variety Show; Ed Lit Mag; St Fnlst CA Hstry Day 90; Linfield Coll; Engl/Spnsh Tchr.

MC NICHOLS, BRIAN T; Clayton Valley HS; Clayton, CA; (2); German Clb; Letterman Clb; Teachers Aide; JV Wrstlng; Cit Awd; Hon Roll; Acad Ltr; 3rd Yr German; CSF; CA Berkely; Genrl Contractor.

MC NOWN, JEFF; San Benito Hollister HS; Hollister, CA; (3); 25/370; Am Leg Boys St; Church Yth Grp; Cmnty Wkr; FCA; Letterman Clb; Pep Clb; Red Cross Aide; Ski Clb; Teachers Aide; Varsity Clb; Most Val Wrstlr; CSF; Ftbl Coaches Awd; MVP Track; All Leag Track; Pre-Med.

MC NULTY, TIMOTHY P; Arlington HS; Riverside, CA; (2); Teachers Aide; JV Ftbl; Wt Lftg; Soph King; Coll Of The Desert; Accntng.

MC NUTT, SHANNON; Enterprise HS; Redding, CA; (4); Math Clb; Mu Alpha Theta; JV Bsktbl; Intrml Cheerldng; Intrml Gym; Intrml Sftbl; JV Vllybl; Hon Roll; Pres Acad Fit Awd; CA Poly; Envrnmntl Dsgn.

MC PARTLAND, KELLY M; Oak Ridge HS; Cameron Park, CA; (1); Church Yth Grp; Socr; High Hon Roll; CSF.

MC PEAK, GLENNA J; Bishop Amat HS; Walnut, CA; (3); Hosp Aide; Drill Tm; Stu Cncl; JV Capt Cheerldng; Powder Puff Ftbl; High Hon Roll; NHS; Bio.

MC PEEK, TANYA L; El Capitan HS; El Cajon, CA; (4); 43/404; VP SADD; Teachers Aide; Lit Mag; Trk; Cit Awd; Hon Roll; El Capitan High Outreach Prgm; Peer Listening; UC-RIVERSIDE; Sociology.

MC PETERS, CHRISTIAN D; Edison Computech HS; Fresno, CA; (1); Ftbl; Mrt List; USC; Comp Prgmr.

MC PHEETERS, MELISSA; Village Christian Schl; Lakeview Terrace, CA; (2); Church Yth Grp; Library Aide; Service Clb; Spanish Clb; Church Choir; JV Var Cheerldng; Stat Ftbl; Tchr.

MC PHERSON, ERIKA; Harbor HS; Santa Cruz, CA; (4); French Clb; JA; Model UN; Drill Tm; School Musical; School Play; High Hon Roll; Pres Acad Fit Awd; Theatre Movement; French III-HIGH Hnrs; Hrns-Grphc Arts; U CA; TV.

MC PHERSON, NATHAN; Woodrow Wilson HS; Los Angeles, CA; (3); Capt Chess Clb; ROTC; Color Guard; Stage Crew; Acad Dcthln Cmptn; Bicntnnl Tm Cmptn; ROTC Ldrshp Camp Vandenburg AFB; ROTC Drll Tm; U S CA; Med.

MC PHERSON, SHANNON; Big Bear HS; Big Bear City, CA; (4); 13/105; Am Leg Aux Girls St; Girl Scts; Science Clb; Var Capt Bsktbl; Var Capt Sftbl; Var Capt Tennis; Pres Schlr; Schlstc All Amer; CSF Seal Bearer; CA Baptist Coll; Phys Educ.

MC PHETERS, JON P; San Dieguito HS; Encinitas, CA; (2); Boy Scts; JV Socr; Hon Roll; CSF; San Diego ST U.

MC QUEEN, DANIEL; Simi Valley HS; Simi, CA; (3); Debate Tm; NFL; Speech Tm; SADD; Rep Jr Cls; Pres Acad Fit Awd; Sctry CSF; Acad Decthln; Mck Trl; Social Sci.

MC QUEEN, THOMAS G; Foothill HS; Bakersfield, CA; (2); Church Yth Grp; 4-H; German Clb; Ski Clb; 4-H Awd; Hon Roll; Cal Poly ST U; Arch.

MC QUEEN-SMITH, TAMMI; Hilltop HS; Bonita, CA; (3); Drama Clb; Renaissance Clb; UCLA; Psych.

MC QUILKIN, AMY; Moorpark HS; Moorpark, CA; (3); 2/255; FBLA; Key Clb; Band; Mrchg Band; Sec Soph Cls; Rep Sec Stu Cncl; Stat Bsktbl; JV Sftbl; Var JV Vllybl; High Hon Roll; Key Clb Stu Of Month; UCLA; Psych.

MC QUILLAN, HOLLY J; Tehachapi HS; Tehachapi, CA; (2); 1/200; Church Yth Grp; FFA; Rep Jr Cls; Var Tennis; High Hon Roll; NHS; Play Piano; Bio Stu Of Yr Awd 89-90; Acadmc Ltr; Stanford U; Teachng.

MC QUIRK, DAWN; Orland HS; Orland, CA; (4); 15/111; Church Yth Grp; English Clb; FCA; School Play; Rep Frsh Cls; Var Bsktbl; Vllybl; High Hon Roll; NHS; Pres Acad Fit Awd; Chico ST; Teacher.

MC QUITTY, ALISSA A; Piedmont HS; Piedmont, CA; (4); VP AFS; SADD; Powder Puff Ftbl; Socr; High Hon Roll; CSF-LIFE Time Stu; Jr Statesmn Of Am-VP; U CA-BERKELEY.

MC ROBERTS, SHERI L; Tulare Western HS; Tulare, CA; (3); JV Bsktbl; JV Sftbl; JV Vllybl; Bobby Soxs; ASA; Coll Of Sequoias; Sports Med.

MC SHANE, KANDIE; Bellflower HS; Bellflower, CA; (2); 67/341; Off Frsh Cls; Rep Stu Cncl; Var Capt Cheerldng; Mgr(s); Stat Trk; Hon Roll; Cypress Coll; Court Reprtr.

MC SHANE, KENNETH; Monterey HS; Monterey, CA; (4); Boy Scts; Church Yth Grp; Cmnty Wkr; Letterman Clb; Library Aide; Yrbk; Golf; Score Keeper; JV Wrstlng; 1st Pl Monterey Cty Sci Fair 89; CSF; Vlntr Guide Monterey Bay Aquarium; Monterey Peninsula Col6; Bio.

MC SHANE, MICHAEL J; Vanden HS; Vacaville, CA; (4); 20/143; Church Yth Grp; VP Ski Clb; Rep Frsh Cls; L Var Bsbl; Capt Var Socr; L Var Wrstlng; High Hon Roll; Kiwanis Awd; Pres Acad Fit Awd; Sch Rally Cmmssnr; TX A&M U; Petro Engrng.

MC SHANE, TERESA A; West HS; Bakersfield, CA; (3); French Clb; Phys & Mental Hlth That Deal With Chldrn; Bakersfield Coll; Pediatrician.

MC SHERRY, JENNIFER R; Sacramento Adventist Acad; Rancho Cordova, CA; (2); Church Yth Grp; Band; School Musical; VP Frsh Cls; Off Soph Cls; Fld Hcky; Band Tours; Med.

MC SWAIN, MELISSA N; School Age Mothers HS; Westminster, CA; (2); House Commons 89-90.

MC SWANE, MITCHELL M; Hiram Johnson HS; Sacramento, CA; (3); Boy Scts; School Play; Nwsp; Hon Roll; Theatre.

MC SWEENEY, KAYTE; Crescenta Valley HS; La Crescenta, CA; (1); Church Yth Grp; Hosp Aide; Drill Tm; U Of CA Davis; Med.

MC TIGHE, JENNIFER H; Grossmont HS; El Cajon, CA; (3); 25/520; Spanish Clb; SADD; Rep Soph Cls; Rep Jr Cls; Rep Stu Cncl; Var Capt Swmmng; Hon Roll; UC Santa Barbara; Tchr.

MC WHERTER, TODD P; Aptos HS; Aptos, CA; (2); JV Bsbl; JV Bsktbl; High Hon Roll; NHS.

MC WHORTER, MIKE L; Anderson Union HS; Redding, CA; (3); Art Clb; FFA; Teachers Aide; Var L Bsbl; JV Bsktbl; Fishing, Skiing, Bsbl; Bsbl Plyr.

MC WILLIAMS, AMY R; Exeter Union HS; Exeter, CA; (2); 1/250; FHA; Letterman Clb; Sec Soph Cls; JV L Tennis; Capt Var Vllybl; High Hon Roll; Russ Weems Enterprises Yth Of Mth Awd.

MC YOUNG, SHANNON L; Yreka HS; Montague, CA; (3); 14/174; German Clb; Ski Clb; High Hon Roll; CSF; Marine Bio.

MEACHAM, SONYA A; Antelope Valley HS; Lancaster, CA; (4); 99/743; Hist 4-H; VP Intnl Clb; Spanish Clb; Teachers Aide; Off Frsh Cls; Off Soph Cls; Capt JV Bsktbl; Yth Bsktbl Coach; San Diego ST; Chld Dvlpmnt.

MEAD III, JOHN W; Moorpark HS; Moorpark, CA; (2); Church Yth Grp; Cmnty Wkr; JV Bsbl; JV Capt Bsktbl; Hon Roll; Psych.

MEADER, MATTHEW J; University City HS; San Diego, CA; (3); 131/373; Church Yth Grp; School Musical; School Play; Stage Crew; Hon Roll; Cert Of Perf In Stage Craft; Bus.

MEADOR, ALYSON E; Ocean View HS; Quantico, VA; (2); Cmnty Wkr; Model UN; Yng Rpblcns Secy; Schl St Cncl Frosh Rep; Mdl Untd Ntns Bst Dlgt Awds; U Of S CA; Law.

MEADOWS, AMY E; Tomales HS; Petaluma, CA; (3); Pres FFA; Spanish Clb; Treas Soph Cls; Treas Sec Jr Cls; Var Bsktbl; Var Capt Bus Profs of Am; Treas 4-H; SADD; Varsity Clb; School Play; CSF Sec; Princpls List; All League Vlybl & Bsktbl; Interior Dsgn.

MEADOWS, DYNL J; Herbert Hoover HS; Glendale, CA; (2); Church Yth Grp; Spanish Clb; Band; Jazz Band; Mrchg Band; Pep Band; Cit Awd; Hon Roll; Band Lttrman; USC; Law.

MEADOWS, JEREMY E; Poway HS; Poway, CA; (3); Varsity Clb; Var Socr; Hon Roll; SDSU; Crmnl Jstc.

MEADOWS, JUSTIN D; Arvin HS; Arvin, CA; (2); Rptr Nwsp; Golf; High Hon Roll; Engl.

MEAGHER, DAN T; Davis SR HS; Davis, CA; (2); 4-H; JV Ski Clb; JV Golf; Hon Roll; U Of CA San Diego; Comp Sci.

MEAGHER, KELLY; Valley Christian HS; San Jose, CA; (3); Church Yth Grp; Chorus; School Play; Ed Nwsp; Treas Jr Cls; JV Cheerldng; Intrml Powder Puff Ftbl; Var Tennis; Var Trk; Hon Roll; Lived In Paris France 2 Yrs; Cls Homcmng Princss 90; Assn Of Chrstn Schls Intl As Distgshd Chrstn Stu; Sports Med.

MEANEY, LARRY; King City HS; King City, CA; (4); 3/175; Treas Am Leg Boys St; Church Yth Grp; Quiz Bowl; Science Clb; Treas Service Clb; Treas SADD; Teachers Aide; Chorus; Rptr Yrbk; Treas Sr Cls; 2nd In Class; Cal Poly; Elec Engr.

MEANS, MARY EV L; Thomas Downey HS; Modesto, CA; (3); AFS; Church Yth Grp; Dance Clb; Hosp Aide; NFL; Speech Tm; Band; Socr; Swmmng; Hon Roll; U Of CA.

MEAR, DONALD MICHAEL; Western HS; Anaheim, CA; (3); Boy Scts; Varsity Clb; Band; Jazz Band; Mrchg Band; Pep Band; Capt Swmmng; Hon Roll; NHS; Spirit Of Amer Mrchng Band Tour Of Europe 90; Vrsty Water Polo; 1st Pl Arch Yth Expo; Arch Drftng.

MEASE, CAMERON L; Ramona HS; Riverside, CA; (4); 34/274; Aud/Vis; Drama Clb; Thesps; Jazz Band; Mrchg Band; School Musical; School Play; Stage Crew; Hon Roll; Pres Acad Fit Awd; Hnr Thespian Intl Thespian Soc; Riverside Cmmty Plyrs Outstndg Drama Stu; Schl Dist Vis & Perf Art Awd; Riverside CC.

MEASE, SARA L; El Cajon Valley HS; El Cajon, CA; (3); 5/390; Church Yth Grp; Letterman Clb; Science Clb; Sprt Ed Yrbk; VP Jr Cls; Var Capt Bsktbl; Var Capt Sftbl; Var Trk; Var Capt Vllybl; High Hon Roll; San Diego Tribune All-Acad Sftbl Tm 90; All-Lg Bsktbl, Sftbl; Sprts Med.

MEASELLE, LISA C; Hoover HS; Fresno, CA; (2); Hon Roll; Mock Trial; CA Yng Writers Conf; U Of London; Engl Lit.

MECHAM, KEVIN T; Fairfield HS; Fairfield, CA; (1); Church Yth Grp; Ftbl; Hon Roll; Bowling; WA ST U; Mech.

MECKFESSEL, SHON G; Rio Americano HS; Sacramento, CA; (3); Art Clb; Church Yth Grp; Cmnty Wkr; Science Clb; Acpl Chr; Jazz Band; Lit Mag; Lbrl Arts.

MEDDINGS, C TODD; CVC 5 HS; Mission Viejo, CA; (3); Boy Scts; Church Yth Grp; Cmnty Wkr; Drama Clb; Office Aide; Teachers Aide; Band; Yrbk; Rep Frsh Cls; Stu Cncl; Eagle Scout; Nice Person; Baylor; Bus.

MEDDOCK, BUDDY F; Madera HS; Madera, CA; (2); Art Clb; English Clb; Nwsp; JV Var Bsbl; JV Var Ftbl; Wt Lftg; Hon Roll; Coyotee Man Awd Awd; Best Offensive Lineman Awd; Ftbl Pgm Cover Picture 2nd Pl Awd 90; CA ST U Fresno; Commercl Art.

MEDEIROS, DINA M; Oak Ridge HS; El Dorado Hills, CA; (1); Ski Clb; Capt Vllybl; Hon Roll; US Ski Assn; Far West Hnr Roll.

MEDEIROS, ERIN K; Troy HS; Yorba Linda, CA; (2); Drill Tm; Hon Roll; Future Earth Fndr; Spcl Educ.

MEDEIROS, GORETTI M; Mount Shasta HS; Mount Shasta, CA; (2); Chorus; Pres Frsh Cls; VP Soph Cls; Capt Powder Puff Ftbl; Amer Coll For Applied Arts.

MEDEIROS, JESSICA M; Rim Of The World HS; Blue Jay, CA; (2); Cmnty Wkr; Drama Clb; Girl Scts; Spanish Clb; Teachers Aide; Stage Crew; Hon Roll; Acad Lttr; Vrsty Lttr Trk & Bsktbl; OH ST U; Psych.

MEDEIROS, JOANNE B; Ontario HS; Ontario, CA; (2); Art Clb; Computer Clb; Ski Clb; SADD; Crs Cntry; Vet.

MEDEIROS, KATHERINE M; Turlock HS; Turlock, CA; (3); 119/600; Church Yth Grp; Cmnty Wkr; Church Choir; Hon Roll; Ply Keybrd In Band; Piano Recitals; Fshn Dsgn.

MEDEIROS, LISA A; Cloverdale HS; Cloverdale, CA; (3); 5/68; Church Yth Grp; FHA; Office Aide; Lit Mag; VP Soph Cls; Sec Treas Jr Cls; Treas Stu Cncl; Hon Roll; Spanish Clb; Math/Sci Awds; Ballet Stu; U Of UT; Ballet.

MEDEIROS, MARY S; Independence HS; San Jose, CA; (3); 44/1000; Church Yth Grp; German Clb; High Hon Roll; Hon Roll; High Achvment German Awd; Psych.

MEDEL, TOMMY R; Carpinteria HS; Carpinteria, CA; (2); 30/167; Church Yth Grp; Cmnty Wkr; Office Aide; Teachers Aide; JV Bsbl; JV Ftbl; Wt Lftg; Hon Roll; Kiwanis Awd; Pres Acad Fit Awd; UC Berkeley.

MEDELLIN, FELISA S; South HS; Bakersfield, CA; (3); 72/424; Church Yth Grp; Cmnty Wkr; Library Aide; Teachers Aide; High Hon Roll; Hon Roll; Prfct Atten Awd; CSU Bakersfield; Bio.

MEDELLIN, SUSAN; Sonora HS; La Habra, CA; (4); Hon Roll; Mid Term Jan 90; Cal ST Fullerton; Accntng.

MEDENILLA, LULU; Apple Valley HS; Apple Valley, CA; (3); 24/765; Church Yth Grp; Pep Clb; Spanish Clb; VP Frsh Cls; VP Jr Cls; VP Sr Cls; High Hon Roll; Hon Roll; Rotary Awd; Jr Statesmn Amer, VP; Med.

MEDFORD, CHERYL; Deanza TES; Richmond, CA; (3); Art Clb; Computer Clb; Hosp Aide; Office Aide; Cit Awd; Law.

MEDHURST, BRUCE; Ygnacio Valley HS; Pleasant Hill, CA; (3); Boy Scts; Varsity Clb; Capt Ftbl; L Trk; Wt Lftg; Elks Awd; Engrng.

MEDIATI, CHRISTINE L; St Joseph Notre Dame HS; Alameda, CA; (3); Service Clb; Teachers Aide; Sec Frsh Cls; Var Sftbl; Hon Roll; NHS; Nrsng.

MEDINA, AIDA L; Nogales HS; La Puente, CA; (3); Church Yth Grp; Chorus; Variety Show; High Hon Roll; Hon Roll; Prfct Atten Awd; ASB Cmmtte.

MEDINA, ANDREW; Bishop Montgomery HS; Carson, CA; (3); Varsity Clb; Intrml Capt Vllybl; Long Beach ST U; Ed.

MEDINA, ARACELI G; Laguna Hills HS; Laguna Hills, CA; (1); Model UN; Hon Roll.

MEDINA, BRENDA; San Jacinto HS; San Jacinto, CA; (3); Sec Church Yth Grp; VP French Clb; FBLA; Bus Econ.

MEDINA, CARMEN A; Regina Caeli HS; Los Angeles, CA; (3); French Clb; Pep Clb; Chorus; School Musical; Hon Roll; MED Doctor.

MEDINA, CHERINA; Alexander Hamilton Acad Of Music; Santa Monica, CA; (3); Service Clb; School Play; Stage Crew; JV Bsktbl; Intrml Sftbl; Cit Awd; High Hon Roll; Rotary Awd; CA ST Prfrmng Arts Prgm For GATE; Sci Awd; Stanford.

MEDINA, CLAUDIA; Mc Farland HS; Mc Farland, CA; (3); Church Yth Grp; Drama Clb; School Play; Hon Roll; CA ST U; Hstry.

MEDINA, CYNTHIA J; Bonita HS; La Verne, CA; (2); Treas FBLA; SADD; JV Bsktbl; Var Trk; Hon Roll; Prfct Atten Awd; SAVE Club & Yng Musicians Club; Acctng Awd; Trk Ltr; U Of La Verne; Bus Admin.

MEDINA, DENISE; Corcoran HS; Corcoran, CA; (2); Cmnty Wkr; FFA; Pep Clb; Red Cross Aide; Band; Mrchg Band; Pep Band; JV Cheerldng; JV Pom Pon; Var Sftbl; Cty Swm Team-Corcoran Blu Dlphns 10 Yrs; Fresno ST U; Bus.

MEDINA, EDGAR V; North Monterey County HS; Castroville, CA; (4); Ftbl; Hon Roll; Vica Drafting Clb; Cal Poly; Arch.

MEDINA, ENEDILIA; Fontana HS; Fontana, CA; (2); Church Yth Grp; Acad Slvr Mdl; Church Lctr; Bus Admin.

MEDINA, ERIC A; Arlington HS; Riverside, CA; (2); Rptr FFA; Varsity Clb; FFA Equestrian Team; Breeding, Raising Swine; Showing Swine At Fairs; Landscpng At Fairs; Greenhand; Cal Poly; Horse & Swine Prod.

MEDINA, ESTEBAN; Orosi HS; Orosi, CA; (2); Ftbl; Fresno ST; Hstry.

MEDINA, FLOR DE MARIA; Woodrow Wilson HS; San Francisco, CA; (3); Church Yth Grp; Cmnty Wkr; Dance Clb; Hosp Aide; Spanish Clb; Chorus; Variety Show; Advncd Plcmnt Spanish; Dentist.

MEDINA, HEATHER; Fullerton Union HS; Fullerton, CA; (4); Sec Drama Clb; FFA; Thesps; Phtg Yrbk; Elks Awd; High Hon Roll; Pres Acad Fit Awd; Vet Asst; Orange Cnty Centennial Schlrshp; Rotary Top 100; Moorpark Coll; Wildlife Mgmt.

MEDINA, HECTOR; Los Banos HS; Los Banos, CA; (2); Latin Clb; Spanish Clb; Wt Lftg; Cit Awd; Hon Roll; UC Davis; Arch.

MEDINA, JAIME; Sweetwater Union HS; National City, CA; (1); 2/100; Lit Mag; Prfct Atten Awd; Phtgrphy; Poetry; San Diego ST U; Phtgrphy.

MEDINA, JAN CAMILLE; Workman HS; Valinda, CA; (1); Intnl Clb; Cit Awd; Hon Roll; Prfct Atten Awd; Achvt Awd; Cal Poly Pomona; Music Tchr.

MEDINA, JAVIER; Southwest HS; San Diego, CA; (2); Pres Acad Fit Awd; Golden St Exam; Comp Engr.

MEDINA, JOSE B; Golden West HS; Visalia, CA; (1); Boy Scts; Band; Ftbl; Hon Roll; Stanford; Med.

MEDINA, JOSE M; Leuzinger HS; Hawthorne, CA; (2); Elect Engr.

MEDINA, JULIA M; O'farrel SCPA HS; San Diego, CA; (1); 13/227; Hon Roll.

MEDINA, KARISSA; Ramona Convent Secondary Schl; Monterey Park, CA; (3); 12/97; Cmnty Wkr; Treas French Clb; Model UN; Stu Cncl; High Hon Roll; Hon Roll; NHS; Hon Roll; Natl Hnr Soc Pres 90-91; CSF & Tutor Fellow Stus 88; Ecology Club 87; Fine Arts Club 89-90; Lawyer.

MEDINA, LORENA; Bell Gardens HS; Bell Gardens, CA; (2); Drama Clb; Psych.

MEDINA, MARIA ESTHER; Woodrow Wilson HS; San Francisco, CA; (3); Church Yth Grp; Cmnty Wkr; Dance Clb; Hosp Aide; Spanish Clb; Teachers Aide; Chorus; Variety Show; Bsbl; Bsktbl; Advance Placement Spnsh; Bus.

MEDINA, MICHELLE; Whitney HS; Cerritos, CA; (4); Hist Key Clb; Color Guard; Rep Soph Cls; Rep Jr Cls; Stu Cncl; High Hon Roll; NHS; Pres Acad Fit Awd; Sal; CSF Rep; UCLA; Pltcl Sci.

MEDINA, MIRAFLOR C; Carson HS; Carson, CA; (4); Speech Tm; Band; Co-Ed Yrbk; Stu Cncl; Tennis; High Hon Roll; NHS; Opt Clb Awd; Pres Acad Fit Awd; Departmental Award-Science; Bank Of America Award-Soc Stud; CA Schlrshp Fed-Gold Bearer Lifetime Mem; Calpoly Pomona; Physics.

MEDINA, MYRA; Silver Creek HS; San Jose, CA; (4); Cmnty Wkr; English Clb; GAA; Varsity Clb; Rptr Nwsp; Off Jr Cls; Off Sr Cls; Var Tennis; Cit Awd; High Hon Roll; CSF; Snr Schlrshp; Natl Hnr Soc; Magna Cum Laude; Schlr Athl; UC Santa Cruz; Psych.

MEDINA, NATHAN; Western HS; Anaheim, CA; (4); 17/200; Chess Clb; Church Yth Grp; Cmnty Wkr; Computer Clb; Drama Clb; FBLA; Socr; Tennis; Trk; Cit Awd; Disnelnd Chllng Art; Goldn ST Exm Hnbl Recog Adv Geom; Smmr Ldrshp Acad 89; Spc Arch.

MEDINA, OLGA V; Saddleback HS; Santa Ana, CA; (3); Spanish Clb; SADD; Aid Cath Church; Girls Leag & Hspnc Scty Club; U Irvine; Fshn Dsgnr.

MEDINA, PROTACIO N; Indio HS; Indio, CA; (1); AFS; Intrml Ftbl; USC; Ftbl Plyr.

MEDINA, REBECA C; Casa Grande HS; Chicago, IL; (3); 63/288; Spanish Clb; Hon Roll; Acctg.

MEDINA, ROBERT; Cantwell HS; Monterey Park, CA; (3); Science Clb; Spanish Clb; Rptr Nwsp; Rep Frsh Cls; Treas Stu Cncl; JV Bsktbl; Hon Roll; NHS; CSF; Bus.

MEDINA, ROMMEL R; St Ignatius College Prep HS; San Bruno, CA; (3); Orch; Hon Roll; Stanford U; Comp Sci.

MEDINA, SALLY MIRANDA; Quartz Hill HS; Quartz Hill, CA; (4); FHA; Office Aide; Spanish Clb; Teachers Aide; Elks Awd; Hon Roll; Pres Acad Fit Awd; Voc Ed Stu Mnth; Stu Yr Chld Care 90; Slvr Mdlln Stu Yr; Mills Coll; Chld Psych.

MEDINA, SANDRA; Richard Gahr HS; Artesia, CA; (2); 129/600; Bus Profs of Am; Office Aide; SADD; Teachers Aide; High Hon Roll; Dntl Asst.

MEDINA, SOPHIA L; Gahr HS; Artesia, CA; (2); 121/490; Score Keeper; Hon Roll; Blue & Gld Awd In Math; CA ST Flrtn; Engr.

MEDINA, VILMA Z; Pasadena HS; Pasadena, CA; (1); Church Yth Grp; Cit Awd; Hon Roll; Prfct Atten Awd; Pres Acad Fit Awd; Spanish NHS; Law.

MEDLER, JOHN J; Downey HS; Downey, CA; (2); Church Yth Grp; Spanish Clb; Band; Prfct Atten Awd.

MEDLEY, TAMEKA; So San Francisco HS; San Francisco, CA; (4); 72/283; FBLA; Stu Cncl; Cheerldng; Pom Pon; Hon Roll; Black Stu Union Treas; MESA; San Jose ST U; Child Devl.

MEDNICK, SAMANTHA; Torrey Pines HS; San Diego, CA; (3); 62/475; Drama Clb; Hosp Aide; Pep Clb; SADD; Thesps; Drill Tm; School Musical; School Play; Rptr Nwsp; Lit Mag; Del Mar Actors Theatre; Publshd Athr; Vlntr Salvation Army; Smith Coll; Theatre.

MEDRANO, BERTHA MARLENE; Bell HS; Maywood, CA; (3); Teachers Aide; Rep Jr Cls; High Hon Roll; NHS; MESA Secy; Mem CA Schlrshp Fed; UCSB; Med.

MEDRANO, CARMEN; Lowell HS; San Francisco, CA; (3); Church Yth Grp; Latin Clb; SADD; Teachers Aide; Chorus; JV Bsktbl; Home Registry Rep To Class Govt; Club Rep To Schl Govt; Coll; Psych.

MEDRANO, CYNTHIA M; San Gabriel Mission HS; Whittier, CA; (3); Sftbl; Law.

MEDRANO, GAY R; Tokay HS; Stockton, CA; (4); 98/614; Church Yth Grp; Drill Tm; Rep Stu Cncl; JV Crs Cntry; JV Var Trk; Hon Roll; Hmcmng Prncss; CSF Gold Seal Bearer; Delta Coll; Phys Thrpy.

MEDRANO, KATHERINE; Hanford Union HS; Hanford, CA; (2); Vllybl; Psych.

MEDRANO, MARTIR MARTIN; Highland HS; Bakersfield, CA; (4); 22/291; French Clb; Spanish Clb; Hon Roll; Pres Acad Fit Awd; Rotary Awd; Intramurals Capt; CSF Gold Seal; Mst Outstndng Bus Stu; CSU Bakersfield; Bus.

MEDRANO, MOSES; Tranquillity Union HS; San Joaquin, CA; (3); 15/200; French Clb; FBLA; Ski Clb; Teachers Aide; Varsity Clb; Mrchg Band; Crs Cntry; Vllybl; Wrstlng; Hon Roll.

MEDRANO, TIFFANY ROXANNE; Hanford HS; Hanford, CA; (2); Intnl Clb; High Hon Roll; Hon Roll; CA Schlrshp Fed; Math Engrng & Sci Achvt; Cert Awd Schltc Achvt; CA ST U Fresno; Arch.

MEDSKER, ADRIENNE; West Covina Hills HS; La Puente, CA; (2); Church Yth Grp; Office Aide; Teachers Aide; Chorus; School Musical; Variety Show; Yrbk; Treas Soph Cls; Hon Roll; Loma Linda U; Doctor.

MEEH, WANDA J; Apple Valley HS; Apple Valley, CA; (3); Pres Church Yth Grp; Ed Yrbk; Stat L Trk; Stat Wrstlng; Hon Roll; 1st & 3rd Pl Oil Pntng Cnty Fair; UCSD; Psych.

MEEHAN, AIMEE C; Huntington Beach HS; Huntington Beach, CA; (2); Model UN; Red Cross Aide; Spanish Clb; Ski Clb; Var Socr; JV Trk; JV Vllybl; Hon Roll; CSF; Jr Statesmen Of Amer; Al Reboin Awd; CS Jr Vlybl Club 87-89; U Of CA; Law.

MEEHAN, MELISSA LEIGH; Poway HS; Poway, CA; (4); Church Yth Grp; Dance Clb; SADD; Capt Co-Capt Color Guard; High Hon Roll; Hon Roll; Pres Acad Fit Awd; UC Santa Barbara.

MEEHAN, SEAN M; Arroyo Grande HS; Grover City, CA; (1); Bsbl; Socr; GATE; Arch.

MEEHAN, WENDY; Santa Fe Christian College Prep; Escondido, CA; (3); 1/35; Pres English Clb; French Clb; Ed Lit Mag; JV Cheerldng; Powder Puff Ftbl; JV Stat Vllybl; High Hon Roll; NHS; Hghst Achvr ; Hghst Achvr Wrld Hstry; Hghst Achvr Biol; Pepperdine U; Bus.

MEEKER, RON A; Elk Grove HS; Elk Grove, CA; (3); 1/600; Am Leg Boys St; Boy Scts; Church Yth Grp; SADD; Teachers Aide; Varsity Clb; Bsktbl; Tennis; High Hon Roll; Pres Acad Fit Awd; Hgh Hnrs Geo Gldn St Exam; Brigham Young U; Pre-Dntstry.

MEEKS, ALICIA; Lakewood HS; Lakewood, CA; (3); Drill Tm; Pres Soph Cls; Pres Jr Cls; Stu Cncl; Cheerldng; Pres Acad Fit Awd; Amer Lgn Awd; Mst Oustndng Stu Wrld Stds II; Law.

MEEKS, ANGELIQUE D; Tracy HS; Tracy, CA; (3); Church Yth Grp; Acpl Chr; Chorus; School Musical; School Play; Variety Show; Socr; Trk; Hon Roll; Lion Awd; Acad Arts Awd & Music Schlrshp; Accntng.

MEEKS, BRENDA L; Portola JR SR HS; Portola, CA; (3); 12/45; Yrbk; High Hon Roll; Hon Roll; Prfct Atten Awd; Pres Acad Fit Awd; Rep Stu Cncl; Var Bsktbl; JV Gym; Var Sftbl.

MEEKS, JEFF A; Arlington HS; Riverside, CA; (2); Computer Clb; JV Capt Bsktbl; Hon Roll; CSF; Arch.

MEEKS, ROBYNN HAZEL; St Michaels HS; Los Angeles, CA; (1); GAA; Var Trk; JV Vllybl; Hon Roll; UCLA Minority Pre-Engrng Pgm; U CA; Math.

MEFFORD, JOEL; Fairfield HS; Fairfield, CA; (4); 1/500; German Clb; Math Clb; Scholastic Bowl; Science Clb; Hist Jr Cls; Hist Sr Cls; Crs Cntry; Trk; Bausch & Lomb Sci Awd; Cit Awd; UC Davis; Gentcs.

MEFFORD, LINDA E; San Gorgonio HS; San Bernardino, CA; (3); 2/400; Ski Clb; Spanish Clb; JV Powder Puff Ftbl; Stat Score Keeper; JV Tennis; NHS; Spanish NHS; CSF; Aces Sec; Hnr Guard; U Of Redlands; Engr.

MEFFORD, RANDI; Bakersfield HS; Bakersfield, CA; (1); FCA; Pep Clb; Ed Nwsp; Stu Cncl; Pom Pon; High Hon Roll; Hon Roll; NHS; Pom Pon Sqd NCA Natl Chmps; OIPA Awd Stry Schl Nwspr; Obstrcn.

MEGAB, TARIC A; Arcadia HS; Arcadia, CA; (2); Quiz Bowl; Science Clb; Hon Roll.

MEGINNESS, CHRISTINE A; Mission San Jose HS; Fremont, CA; (3); 21/420; Cmnty Wkr; Drama Clb; French Clb; Science Clb; Thesps; Chorus; School Musical; School Play; Stage Crew; Swing Chorus; Amnsty Intl; CA Schlrshp Fed; Fr Awd; U CA; Eng.

MEGLEMRE, JENNIFER; Western Christian HS; Pomona, CA; (3); Church Yth Grp; Service Clb; Yrbk; Treas Soph Cls; Rep Jr Cls; Var L Bsktbl; JV Vllybl; High Hon Roll; NHS; Sunday Schl Nwsp Edtr; Azusa Pacific U Mexicali Outreach; Sec Educ.

MEGO, DIANA P; Bell Gardens HS; Bell Gardens, CA; (4); 20/520; French Clb; Teachers Aide; Trk; High Hon Roll; Hon Roll; Prfct Atten Awd; CSF; MECHA; Cert Of Accmplshmnt Comp Sys Rockwell Div; UC Irvine; Bio Sci.

MEHANY, ALBERT E; Hawthorne HS; Hawthorne, CA; (3); Church Yth Grp; Cmnty Wkr; Key Clb; Var Vllybl; Bausch & Lomb Sci Awd; High Hon Roll; Pres Acad Fit Awd; Pres Schlr; The Harvard Prize Book; Pres CSF; Med.

MEHAS, ALETHEA C; Clovis West HS; Fresno, CA; (3); Letterman Clb; Office Aide; Teachers Aide; Diving; Gym; Vllybl; High Hon Roll; Pres Acad Fit Awd; Hsit Day 1st St; Hist Day 88 5th Natl; CA Intrschlstc Fed; All Arnd Gymnstcs Chmp 88; Sci.

MEHEEN, TIFFANY; Carmel HS; Carmel, CA; (2); Var L Sftbl; Var L Tennis; Hon Roll; GATE.

MEHER, MICHELLE M; Saint Bonaventure HS; Camarillo, CA; (4); Church Yth Grp; Cmnty Wkr; Drama Clb; Pep Clb; Quiz Bowl; Teachers Aide; Church Choir; School Musical; School Play; Stage Crew; Bank Amer Achvt Awd Frnch; Natl Hnr Soc; Vars Schl Sbjct Achvt Awds; Las Patronas Deb 90; Cal Poly San Luis Obispo; Jrlsm.

MEHL, DEREK J; Golden West HS; Visalia, CA; (1); Boy Scts; Band; Hon Roll; CSF; Acadc Ltr.

MEHL, STEFFEN; Oroville HS; Oroville, CA; (3); Am Leg Boys St; Church Yth Grp; Capt Socr; High Hon Roll; Sci Stu Of Month.

MEHRTEN, JOSEPH L; Lodi HS; Clements, CA; (3); Church Yth Grp; Science Clb; 4-H Awd; High Hon Roll; Hon Roll; NHS; Prfct Atten Awd; 4-H; Gld, Slvr, Bronze Mdls Sci Olympd; Gld Slvr Bronze Mdls Various Evnts NRA Postal Shoot 89; US Naval Acad; Systems Engr.

MEHTA, JULIE; Oak Grove HS; San Jose, CA; (4); 1/450; Drama Clb; Math Tm; School Play; Lit Mag; NHS; Ntl Merit Schol; Prfct Atten Awd; Pres Acad Fit Awd; Val; 1st Pl Amer Ed Week Essay Contest 88; 1st Pl FL St Regn XI Sci Fair 87; 1st Pl Spelng Bee 87.

MEHTA, MANISH H; Central Union HS; El Centro, CA; (1); Art Clb; Computer Clb; Math Tm; Tennis; Hon Roll; 2nd Pl County Math Cyphering Cmptn; Tnns Trophy.

MEHTA, NIRAJ; Leuzinger HS; Hawthorne, CA; (4); 13/600; Sec Hist AFS; Pres Chess Clb; Pres VP French Clb; Hon Roll; High Hon Roll; Pres Acad Fit Awd; CSF Sealbearer; USC; Aerospace Engr.

MEHTA, PARAS P; Cerritos HS; Cerritos, CA; (4); 1/555; Pres Model UN; Science Clb; VP Stu Cncl; Elks Awd; Ntl Merit Schol; Pres Schlr; Rotary Awd; Val; CA St Brd Of Ed; 1st Pl Untd Nations Natl Essay Contest; USA Today Acadmc Top 20; Harvard U; Physics.

MEHTA, PRITI P; California HS; San Ramon, CA; (4); Sec Debate Tm; NFL; Office Aide; Science Clb; Ski Clb; Speech Tm; Ed Lit Mag; Mgr(s); Swmmng; High Hon Roll; CSF; UC Berkeley.

MEIDINGER, HEATHER A; Lowell HS; San Francisco, CA; (2); Variety Show; Rptr Nwsp; Rep Frsh Cls; JV Crs Cntry; Var L Tennis; Var L Trk; CSF; Adventure Alliance Club.

MEIER, AMY C; John Muir HS; Altadena, CA; (3); French Clb; Hosp Aide; Treas Jr Cls; JV Vllybl; Hon Roll; Girl Scts; Treas Pres Service Clb; Off Soph Cls; Pediatrics.

MEIGIDE, JULIE R; Ramona HS; Riverside, CA; (2); #16 In Class; Yrbk; VP Jr Cls; Var L Swmmng; CSF; JV Water Polo; USC; Psych.

MEIGS, TAMMIE; Yucca Valley HS; Morongo Valley, CA; (3); Church Yth Grp; VP Jr Cls; Capt Var Cheerldng; Var L Gym; Powder Puff Ftbl; High Hon Roll; Hon Roll; Prfct Atten Awd; UC Santa Cruz; Accntng.

MEIKLE, JENNIFER; Bret Harte HS; Murphys, CA; (2); High Hon Roll; Hon Roll; Pres Acad Fit Awd; Piano; Nrsng.

MEILE, CARI L; Brea-Olinda HS; Brea, CA; (3); 10/292; Church Yth Grp; Cmnty Wkr; Pres Rep GAA; Nwsp; Mgr Yrbk; Stat Sftbl; Var Trk; Capt L Vllybl; VP NHS; Ntl Merit Ltr; CSF; Acad Booster Clb; Safe-Rides.

MEIN, JANIS; Modesto HS; Modesto, CA; (3); Orch; Hon Roll; Prfct Atten Awd; CSF; U Of Pacific; Phrmclgy.

MEINERS, CAROLYN L; Bishop Montgomery HS; Torrance, CA; (3); Church Yth Grp; Cmnty Wkr; Letterman Clb; Var Bsktbl; Powder Puff Ftbl; Var Trk; Intrml Wt Lftg; Chrch Ldrshp Grp.

MEISENHEIMER, BRENT L; Oak Park HS; Agoura Hills, CA; (1); Crs Cntry; AYSO Soccer; Mbr Civil Air Patrol; GSE Academic Excellence Awd For First-Year Algebra Honors.

MEISER, JENNIFER L; Alhambra HS; Martinez, CA; (4); 1/200; Church Yth Grp; Cmnty Wkr; Dance Clb; Drama Clb; SADD; Variety Show; Stu Cncl; Swmmng; Wt Lftg; Hon Roll; Christian Clwng; Jr Statesmn Poly-Sci SF Sympsm; UC Santa Cruz; Socal Wrk.

MEISER, REBECCA A; Alhambra HS; Martinez, CA; (2); Church Yth Grp; Dance Clb; Hosp Aide; Cheerldng; Swmmng; Tennis; High Hon Roll; Hon Roll; Golden St Math Awd; Amer Assn U Of Women Of Merit Cert In Algebra, Bio, Engl; UC Santa Cruz; Pediatrician.

MEISNER, GREG; Kerman HS; Kerman, CA; (3); #1 In Class; German Clb; Letterman Clb; Math Tm; Science Clb; Chorus; Variety Show; Capt Ftbl; Bausch & Lomb Sci Awd; Hon Roll; JETS Awd; Astronomy Club; Engrng.

MEISS, ANGELA S; Tustin HS; Tustin, CA; (1); Church Yth Grp; Science Clb; Rptr Nwsp; Insterested In Art, Mucis, Human Rights, & Envrnmntl Issus; Lcl Amnsty Intl Grp & Sierra Clb; Poly Sci.

MEISTER, DOUGLAS W; Fountain Valley HS; Fountain Valley, CA; (1); Bsktbl.

MEISTER, ERIKA S; Redlands HS; Redlands, CA; (2); German Clb; Key Clb; Yrbk; Prfct Atten Awd; Interact Club; CSF; Arch.

MEISTER, MARCUS R; John F Kennedy HS; Buena Park, CA; (3); Boy Scts; Church Yth Grp.

MEITER, JOHN S; La Habra HS; Whittier, CA; (4); 8/300; VP Church Yth Grp; Drama Clb; VP FBLA; Key Clb; Pres VP NFL; Quiz Bowl; School Play; Capt Wrstlng; NHS; Aeronautical Engrng.

MEITH, KARISSA A; Irvine HS; Irvine, CA; (2); 135/553; AFS; JV Capt Bsktbl; Var Sftbl; JV Var Vllybl; Hon Roll; All League Stbl; Sftbl & Bsktbl Vsty Ltr; Al Tourn Team Wdbrdg & Corona Tourney.

MEITZ, GILLIAN I; Grossmont HS; El Cajon, CA; (3); Church Yth Grp; Dance Clb; French Clb; Cit Awd; Awd For Frnch Speaking FLES Natl Frnch Cont; Ed.

MEJIA, AGHAM-SILANGAN; Milpitas HS; Milpitas, CA; (1); JV Trk; Bsktbl Asst Coach; Amateur BMX Freestyler; Auto Engrng.

MEJIA, ALVARO J; El Toro HS; Trabuco Canyon, CA; (3); Boy Scts; Letterman Clb; Teachers Aide; Varsity Clb; Ftbl; Socr; Wt Lftg; Hon Roll; Prfct Atten Awd; Excllnce Awd; Law.

MEJIA, ANGELINA G; Saddleback HS; Santa Ana, CA; (1); French Clb; SADD; Variety Show; Var Bsktbl; Sftbl.

MEJIA, ARACELY; Santa Ynez HS; Buellton, CA; (3); 4/180; Rptr 4-H; Treas FBLA; Yrbk; Var Cheerldng; Elks Awd; Bus.

MEJIA, BOBBI E; East Union HS; Lathrop, CA; (1); Hon Roll; Radio Brdcst.

MEJIA, CLAUDIA; Bell HS; Cudahy, CA; (4); French Clb; Var Crs Cntry; Var Trk; ELAC.

MEJIA, CORINA I; Senior HS; Dos Palos, CA; (2); FHA; Pep Clb; SADD; Band; Mrchg Band; Pep Band; Merced JC; Advrtsng.

MEJIA, DAYSI; Hawthorne HS; Hawthorne, CA; (2); Hon Roll; Pres Acad Fit Awd; Piano Playing; Fash Desgng; UCLA; Bus Mgmt.

MEJIA, DIANE B; La Puente HS; La Puente, CA; (3); Church Yth Grp; Color Guard; Cit Awd; High Hon Roll; Hon Roll; Prfct Atten Awd; 1st Liet Tall Flags; SR Cls Delg; Pre-Law.

MEJIA, ESPERANZA; Schurr HS; Los Angeles, CA; (2); 30/39; Hon Roll; Schl Spirt; UCLA; Doctor.

MEJIA, FIDEL M; Roseville HS; Roseville, CA; (2); 8/445; German Clb; Ftbl; High Hon Roll; UC Davis; Acctng.

MEJIA, FRANCISCO; Mountain View HS; S El Monte, CA; (2); Wt Lftg; METAS VP; Biking Viking Bicycling Clb; Juvenile Clb; U Southern CA; Psych.

MEJIA, GLORIA; Nogales HS; La Puente, CA; (2); Court Secy.

MEJIA, IRENE; Los Altos HS; Hacienda Hgts, CA; (3); Church Yth Grp; Acpl Chr; Chorus; JV Powder Puff Ftbl; Score Keeper; Hon Roll; Bell Choir; Sci Fr; Awd For Mst Imprvd In Bell Choir; UCSD; Fshn Dsgnr.

MEJIA, LYDIA; Patterson HS; Vernalis, CA; (3); GAA; Spanish Clb; SADD; Chorus; Var Capt Crs Cntry; Var Trk; Hon Roll; Anim Hlth Tech.

MEJIA, MARIA M; Newport Harbor HS; Santa Ana, CA; (3); Church Yth Grp; Dance Clb; Hosp Aide; SADD; Teachers Aide; UCLA; Crmnl Law.

MEJIA, OSVALDO; John Muir HS; Altadena, CA; (3); Treas Key Clb; Band; Mrchg Band; Pep Band; JV Var Bsbl; Engrng.

MEJIA, RENEE; Woodrow Wilson HS; Long Beach, CA; (4); Church Yth Grp; English Clb; Math Tm; Office Aide; Science Clb; Band; Stage Crew; Hon Roll; NHS; Pres Acad Fit Awd; Cert Achvmt Span 3-4; Hosp Volunteer; Phi Beta Kappa Outstndng Schltc Achvmt; San Diego ST U.

MEJORADO, HUMBERTO; Pater Noster HS; Los Angeles, CA; (1); 6/50; Sec Soph Cls.

MEKA, MAMATHA; Gahr HS; Cerritos, CA; (4); Prfct Atten Awd; Span Acad Achvt; Poli Sci.

MEKDARA, ALAN; Bellflower HS; Bellflower, CA; (3); 6/264; FBLA; Hosp Aide; JA; Letterman Clb; Sec Math Clb; Sec Mu Alpha Theta; Varsity Clb; Ed Nwsp; Var Capt Ftbl; Wt Lftg; CSF; Bus Admin.

MEKIKIAN, TIGRAN; Bellarmine Jefferson HS; Burbank, CA; (2); Cmnty Wkr; JV Capt Ftbl; Var Trk; Var Wt Lftg; Hon Roll; Most Insp Plyr Ftbll; UC-BERKLEY; Law.

MEKJAVICH, ELLEN C; Amos Alonzo Stagg HS; Stockton, CA; (1); Church Yth Grp; Cmnty Wkr; Hosp Aide; Intnl Clb; Key Clb; Stu Cncl; Socr; High Hon Roll; NEDT Awd; Swmmng; Began Schl Pltcl Actn Clb; Intrn St Sntr John Garamendis Ofc; Rep Schl Bd; Stanford; Govt Wrk.

MEKURIA, TEWODROS; El Dorado HS; Placentia, CA; (1); Band; Bsktbl; High Hon Roll; Marching & Field Tournament Trophies; U CA Berkeley; Arch.

MEKY, MUNA S; Moreau HS; Fremont, CA; (3); Dance Clb; Office Aide; Hon Roll; Sec Black Stu Union; Shelter For Abused Families; Yng Eritreans; Howard; Acctng.

MELAMED, SETH; Berkeley HS; Berkeley, CA; (3); Boy Scts; Ed Nwsp; Var Capt Wrstlng.

MELANIE, FLOWERS S; Antelope Valley HS; Lancaster, CA; (3); Rptr Nwsp; Rep Jr Cls; Stu Cncl; Hon Roll; Jr NHS; Modeling Club; Blck Stu Union; Jr Senate.

MELANSON, RICHARD R; Ontario HS; Ontario, CA; (2); Band; Mrchg Band; Cit Awd; High Hon Roll; Prfct Atten Awd; CSF; Outstndng/Most Imprvd Band Stu; San Diego ST; Psych.

MELARA, ALEXIA C; Burbank HS; Burbank, CA; (2); Cmnty Wkr; JV Bsktbl; UCLA; Med.

MELARA, LUIS A; Hoover HS; Glendale, CA; (3); Treas Church Yth Grp; French Clb; Teachers Aide; Sprt Ed Yrbk; French Hon Soc; Hon Roll; Prfct Atten Awd; Outstndng Jr Frnch Dept; CSF; Christian Clb; UCLA; Dentistry.

MELCHOR, ALBERTO R; Venice HS; Los Angeles, CA; (3); Latin Clb; JV Ftbl; Var Socr; Intrml Wt Lftg; Cit Awd; Hon Roll; UC Berkeley; Jrnlsm.

MELCHOR, ARACELI; Calvin Simmons HS; Oakland, CA; (1); Spanish Clb; Vllybl; Prfct Atten Awd; U CA Berkeley; Teacher.

MELCHOR, CHERYL ANN V; Whitney HS; Cerritos, CA; (1); Dance Clb; Key Clb; Rptr Nwsp; Yrbk; Music Actvts; CA Jr Schlstc Fed; Music.

MELCHOR, CHRIS V; St Joseph Notre Dame HS; Oakland, CA; (3); Cmnty Wkr; Teachers Aide; L Var Socr; Hon Roll; NHS; Prfct Atten Awd; Aviation.

MELE, STEPHANIE L; Moonpark HS; Moorpark, CA; (2); Socr; Trk; Wt Lftg; High Hon Roll; Hon Roll; Scr Mst Mprvd; Sccr All Leag 1st Tm; Dnc.

MELEEN, MARNI K; Del Mar HS; San Jose, CA; (2); Church Yth Grp; Cmnty Wkr; Intnl Clb; Church Choir; Sec Frsh Cls; JV Fld Hcky; Hon Roll; Photojrnlsm.

MELENA, JENNY; Westwood HS; Westwood, CA; (4); Church Yth Grp; Drama Clb; Teachers Aide; School Play; Hon Roll; Lassen CC; Nrs.

MELENDEZ, DANIEL R; Nogales HS; Walnut, CA; (2); 6/800; Church Yth Grp; Science Clb; Band; Jazz Band; Mrchg Band; Nwsp; Tennis; High Hon Roll; Prfct Atten Awd; CSF; Stanford U; Bio.

MELENDEZ, LIZ J; Bell HS; Bell, CA; (3); JV Sftbl; Hon Roll; NHS; Psycht.

MELENDEZ, MARGIE B; Coachella Valley HS; Thermal, CA; (4); 13/365; Band; Jazz Band; Mrchg Band; JV Crs Cntry; Stat Ftbl; JV Score Keeper; JV Sftbl; Cit Awd; Hon Roll; John Philip Sousa Awd; Dir Awd; UCLA; Crmnl Law.

MELENDEZ, MARIA C; Canoga Park HS; Canoga Park, CA; (3); Cit Awd; Prfct Atten Awd; Pierce Coll; Engrng.

MELENDEZ, MICHELLE L; Las Plumas HS; Oroville, CA; (3); Church Yth Grp; Dance Clb; Office Aide; Spanish Clb; Up-Ward Bound Chico St; Karate; Chico ST; Bus.

MELENDEZ, NOEMI; Oakland HS; Oakland, CA; (3); Church Yth Grp; Teachers Aide; Cit Awd; Hon Roll; CA ST-HAYWARD; Ed.

MELENDREZ, ALVARO M; Capuchino HS; San Bruno, CA; (1).

MELENDREZ, BLANCA; Castle Park HS; Chula Vista, CA; (3); Church Yth Grp; French Clb; Latin Clb; Chorus; Cit Awd; Hon Roll; U San Diego; Law.

MELENDREZ, ERICK; Whittier Christian HS; Pomona, CA; (2); Church Yth Grp; Ftbl; Poem Published; World Of Poetry Golden & Silver Awd; Smithsonian Inst; Bus.

MELENDREZ, JENNY C; Thomas Downey HS; Modesto, CA; (2); Teachers Aide; Nmodesto JC; Lawyer.

MELENDREZ, ROGELIO; Senior HS; Chula Vista, CA; (4); School Musical; Off Soph Cls; Var Ftbl; Wt Lftg; Law.

MELER, ALISON B; University HS; Irvine, CA; (3); JCL; L Var Fld Hcky; JV Swmmng; Hon Roll; Spanish NHS; JCL Housing Cmmssnr; Mst Imrpvd Swmmng; Sci.

MELGAR, BARBARA E; Colton HS; Colton, CA; (2); Bsktbl; Hon Roll; Law.

MELGAR, CLAUDIA E; Bakersfield HS; Bakersfield, CA; (2); Dance Clb; FBLA; Hon Roll; Prfct Atten Awd; MESA; Cal Poly San Luis Obispo; Engr.

MELGOZA, JUAH; Sunset HS; Hayward, CA; (2); Computer Clb; FBLA; Spanish Clb; Varsity Clb; Bsbl; Score Keeper; Socr; Cit Awd; Hon Roll; Hayward U.

MELGOZA, MONICA; Los Amigos HS; Santa Ana, CA; (3); Church Yth Grp; Latin Clb; High Hon Roll; Hmcmng Princess; FIDM Fashion Inst; Design.

MELGOZA, TERESA; Lompoc HS; Lompoc, CA; (3); Spanish Clb; Teachers Aide; Var Socr; Prfct Atten Awd; Athltc Awd Sccr 89-90; Schlr Athl Awd 89-90; Upward Bound Pgm; Estudiantes Unidos Club.

MELILLI, DAVID; Capostrano Valley Christian HS; Laguna Hills, CA; (2); Church Yth Grp; Dance Clb; Drama Clb; Library Aide; Spanish Clb; Band; Chorus; Church Choir; School Musical; School Play; Boy Yr; Coaches Awd JV Soccer; Stanford; Bus Lawyer.

MELILLI, DAVID H; Capostrano Valley Christian Schl; Laguna Beach, CA; (2); Church Yth Grp; Spanish Clb; SADD; Band; Church Choir; School Play; JV Bsbl; Var Socr; Hon Roll; Boy Of Yr; Amer Lgn Awd; Bus.

MELILLO, NICHOLAS J; Riverdale HS; Clovis, CA; (4); Am Leg Boys St; Treas FHA; VP Letterman Clb; Office Aide; Pep Clb; Science Clb; Ski Clb; Varsity Clb; Rep VP Stu Cncl; Var Capt Tennis; Sonora Ldrshp Conf 88-89; MVP Tnns 89; Cal ST U Fresno; Bus Admin.

MELIM, SUZY M; Downieville HS; Downieville, CA; (1); Aud/Vis; Girl Scts; Letterman Clb; Ski Clb; Phtg Yrbk; Sec Treas Frsh Cls; Var Bsktbl; Golf; Var Vllybl; Hon Roll; CSF; Jrnlsm.

MELINA, PAULETTE D; El Camino Real HS; Woodland Hills, CA; (2); Dance Clb; GAA; Pep Clb; Varsity Clb; Variety Show; Off Frsh Cls; Off Soph Cls; Off Jr Cls; Stu Cncl; Bsktbl; Sch Achvt/Schlrsp Awds; Cmmnty Svc; Elem Sch Athltcs Coach; Citywide Essay Awds; U Of Santa Barbara; Psych.

MELKA, DENNIS; Saint Ignatius College Prep; Larkspur, CA; (3); 18/245; Boy Scts; Debate Tm; Service Clb; Speech Tm; Nwsp; Bausch & Lomb Sci Awd; High Hon Roll; Lion Awd; Opt Clb Awd; Voice Dem Awd; Intnl Bus.

MELKONIAN, LIZA; Abraham Lincoln HS; San Francisco, CA; (3); Church Yth Grp; Teachers Aide; Rep Stu Cncl; Mgr(s); Top 10% Of Frshmn Cls; CA ST U Sn Frncsc; Bus.

MELLEM, JEFFREY A; West Covina HS; W Covina, CA; (3); Church Yth Grp; Letterman Clb; Science Clb; Rptr Nwsp; Var Crs Cntry; Var Trk; Hon Roll; Prfct Atten Awd; Goldn St Awd Geom; Catalina Island Marine Inst; Engrng.

MELLEN, BRANDIE D; Whitney HS; Cerritos, CA; (2); 136/168; Cmnty Wkr; Treas JA; Key Clb; JV Swmmng; Golden St Exam High Hnrs Algbra I; Acctnt.

MELLGREN, NAOMIE D; Sonora Union HS; Columbia, CA; (2); Church Yth Grp; SADD; Band; Mrchg Band; Pep Band; Art.

MELLIN, SCARLETT A; Victor Valley HS; Victorville, CA; (4); 3/313; NFL; Pep Clb; Teachers Aide; Varsity Clb; Color Guard; Vllybl; High Hon Roll; Kiwanis Awd; Val; Cal Poly Pomona; Zoolgy.

MELLO, BRANDEN; Bullard HS; Fresno, CA; (4); 17/450; Cmnty Wkr; Debate Tm; French Clb; Key Clb; Model UN; NFL; School Play; Rep Frsh Cls; Pres Soph Cls; VP Jr Cls; Bullard HS Boy Of Yr; FUSD Cnslng Awd Outstndng Stu; Santa Clara U; Pre Law.

MELLO, JENA; Napa HS; Napa, CA; (4); Church Yth Grp; Key Clb; Letterman Clb; Pep Clb; VP Jr Cls; VP Stu Cncl; Var Capt Bsktbl; Var Capt Powder Puff Ftbl; Var Capt Sftbl; Var Capt Vllybl; Brd Of Ed Stu Rep; Sacramento ST; Phys Therapist.

MELLO, JOE V; Livingston HS; Delhi, CA; (3); French Clb; Math Tm; ROTC; SADD; Teachers Aide; JV Var Bsbl; JV Var Ftbl; Wt Lftg; Cit Awd; High Hon Roll; Cal Poly; Comp Engr.

MELLO, SCOTT A; Escalon Unifed School Dist; Escalon, CA; (3); 42/125; JV Ftbl; Acad Awd.

MELLO, TARA D; Modesto HS; Modesto, CA; (4); 4-H; FFA; GAA; Pep Clb; Spanish Clb; Teachers Aide; JV Bsbl; Cheerldng; Gym; Lion Awd; Hmcmng Qn Ftbl 88; MVP Bsbl 88; Fresno; Dental Hyg.

MELLON, KRISTINA; Ontario HS; Ontario, CA; (4); German Clb; Teachers Aide; Band; Mrchg Band; School Musical; Variety Show; Lit Mag; Tennis; Prfct Atten Awd; Pres Acad Fit Awd; CSF; Prncpls Hnr Rl; Band Clb Treas; U Of Southern CA; Creatv Wrtng.

MELLOS, CHRIS S; Mission Bay HS; San Diego, CA; (1); Church Yth Grp; JA; Math Clb; Science Clb; Spanish Clb; JV Bsbl; JV Bsktbl; Cit Awd; 4-H Awd; High Hon Roll; Sci.

MELO, ERNIE S; Turlock HS; Turlock, CA; (2); Pres FFA; FFA Awds; Cal Poly; Ag Bus.

MELO, LUIS G; Chino HS; Chino, CA; (4); 39/541; 4-H; Letterman Clb; Library Aide; Spanish Clb; Teachers Aide; Off Sr Cls; Off Stu Cncl; High Hon Roll; Hon Roll; School Site Council; Student Senate; Spirit Club; CA ST; Accounting.

MELONI, ADRIAN; Oxnard HS; Oxnard, CA; (3); Boy Scts; Varsity Clb; Bsbl; Wt Lftg; Cit Awd; High Hon Roll; Hon Roll; Ventura Coll; Law.

MELOTTE, AMY; Saddleback HS; Santa Ana, CA; (2); Drill Tm; Black Stu Union; Bus Exec.

MELOTTI, SUZANNE M; Poway HS; Poway, CA; (2); 6/834; German Clb; Key Clb; Ski Clb; Band; Jazz Band; Mrchg Band; Orch; JV Swmmng; High Hon Roll; Pres Acad Fit Awd; CSF; U Of CA Los Angeles; Med.

MELROSE, MICHELLE L; Oak Ridge HS; El Dorado Hills, CA; (2); Spanish Clb; Varsity Clb; Tennis; CSF; Principals Hons Schl Lttr 4.0 GPA; Most Insprtnl Tnns Team Awd; Pepperdine U; Commnctns.

MELTON, CHRISTOPHER M; Dixon HS; Vacaville, CA; (4); 10/127; AFS; FBLA; Intnl Clb; Treas Jr Cls; Treas Stu Cncl; JV Ftbl; JV Trk; High Hon Roll; Pres Acad Fit Awd; Rotary Awd; UC Berkeley; Intrntl Banking.

MELTON, JEANNE A; Liberty Christian HS; Huntington Bch, CA; (2); Church Yth Grp; Chorus; Yrbk; Cit Awd; High Hon Roll.

MELTON, JENNIFER R; Troy HS; Yorba Linda, CA; (2); Dance Clb; Office Aide; Teachers Aide; Chorus; Color Guard; Cit Awd; High Hon Roll; Hon Roll; Bg Sistr Pgm; Bus.

MELTON, NATHAN L; Warren HS; Downey, CA; (2); Boy Scts; Var Trk; Crmnlgy.

MELVILLE, RYAN J; Ramona HS; Ramona, CA; (2); Boy Scts; VP Church Yth Grp; Drama Clb; French Clb; School Musical; Stu Cncl; Bsktbl; Crs Cntry; Mgr(s); Vllybl; Hnry Rec Geom & Alg Golden ST Exam; Troop Ldr & Eagle Scout Awd; Piano 8 Yrs; Air Force Acad; Pilot.

MEMBRERE, JOHN J; Holtville HS; Holtville, CA; (3); FFA; JV Ftbl; Intrstd Law Enfrcmnt & Wrk Prt Time; Imperial Vly Coll; Law.

MEN, CHANMALIN; Lakewood HS; Long Beach, CA; (3); Prfct Atten Awd; Pride Clb; Sec Pam M.

MENA, BRAULIO; Gardena HS; Gardena, CA; (2); Art Clb; French Clb; Opt Clb Awd; MESA Clb; Arch.

MENARD, IVY; Coast Joint Union HS; Cambria, CA; (2); Spanish Clb; Sec Jr Cls; JV Sftbl; Hon Roll.

MENDELL, MIKE R; Huntington Beach HS; Huntington Beach, CA; (2); Letterman Clb; Varsity Clb; Socr; Var Wrstlng.

MENDELSSOHN, DENISE M; Huntington Beach HS; Huntington Beach, CA; (3); Church Yth Grp; Red Cross Aide; Spanish Clb; Trk; Vllybl; High Hon Roll; CSF; Arch.

MENDENHALL, GREGORY D; Poway HS; Poway, CA; (1); Boy Scts; Church Yth Grp; Varsity Clb; Var Swmmng; Water Polo; Med.

MENDENHALL, TABITHA N; Mission Viejo HS; Mission Viejo, CA; (1); 21/400; Mrchg Band; Orch; School Musical; Hon Roll; Swmmg; Intl Baccalaureate; Brigham Young U; Tchr.

MENDES, KRISTINA M; Fortuna Union HS; Fortuna, CA; (3); Church Yth Grp; Drama Clb; Speech Tm; VP Band; Drm Mjr(t); VP Mrchg Band; Rep Stu Cncl; SADD; Teachers Aide; Acpl Chr; VFW Conductress; Rhododendron Yth Ambassador Fortuna Female Rep; Humboldt ST; Music.

MENDES, LINO JAMES; Hanford Union HS; Hanford, CA; (1); Church Yth Grp; FFA; Band; Jazz Band; Hon Roll; Jr NHS; NHS; Centenial Cmmnty Yth Band; FFA Meat Jdgng Team; Chrch Yth Of Yr Awd; Coll Of Sequoias; CPA.

MENDES, VICTOR; Ceres HS; Modesto, CA; (3); Ftbl; Wt Lftg; Hon Roll; Pres Acad Fit Awd; Stanislaus ST; Teacher.

MENDEZ, ALEXANDER; Calexico HS; Calexico, CA; (2); Treas FBLA; Pres Intnl Clb; Treas Soph Cls; 1st Pl Cnty & 6th Pl St Rgnl Natl Frnch Exam 88-90; UC San Diego; Pltcl Sci.

MENDEZ, ALINA L; San Luis Obispo HS; Los Osos, CA; (2); 40/319; Chorus; Variety Show; Hon Roll; Pres Acad Fit Awd; Cmnty Theater; CA Schlrshp Fed; Dance; Psych.

MENDEZ, ANGELIQUE; Upland HS; Upland, CA; (3); Church Yth Grp; Cmnty Wkr; Rep Pep Clb; Drill Tm; JV Math Tm; Var Capt Pom Pon; Powder Puff Ftbl; Dance Team 9-10 Lieutenant 11 Capt 12 Capt.

MENDEZ, EDUARDO; Pasadena HS; Pasadena, CA; (1); Hon Roll.

MENDEZ, EDWARD; Damien HS; Diamond Bar, CA; (2); Church Yth Grp; Cmnty Wkr; Drama Clb; School Play; Drma.

MENDEZ, ENRIQUE R; Lindsay HS; Lindsay, CA; (3); Spanish Clb; Hon Roll; Acad Decathlon Mdl 89-90; Golden St Exam Geom High Hnrs 88; Engrng.

MENDEZ, HAROLD Y; Workman HS; Salem, NH; (2); Spanish Clb; JV Bsbl; JV Wrstlng; JV Basebl MVP; Corp Law.

MENDEZ, JAY MARTIN M; Los Amigos HS; Fountain Valley, CA; (3); Var Ftbl; Hon Roll; Golden ST Exam Alg & Geom Hnrs; Robotics Engrng.

MENDEZ, JOEY A; Schurr HS; Montebello, CA; (3); Key Clb; Band; Jazz Band; Mrchg Band; Pep Band; Stu Cncl; Var Wrstlng; Hon Roll; Surf Clb; USC; Bus.

MENDEZ, KIRA A; Academy Of Our Lady Of Peace; La Mesa, CA; (1); Church Yth Grp; GAA; Hosp Aide; School Musical; Rep Frsh Cls; Hon Roll; CSF.

MENDEZ, LAURA; Parlier HS; Parlier, CA; (2); Drama Clb; FTA; Stage Crew; Off Soph Cls; Stu Cncl; Vllybl; Hon Roll; Spanish NHS; Migrant Clb; Vllybl Clb; Rally Clb; Sftbl Clb; EOP; Sci Clb; Drama Clb; UC Santa Barbara; Marine Bio.

MENDEZ, MARIA; Thomas Downey HS; Modesto, CA; (3); Church Yth Grp; Office Aide; Teachers Aide; Gym; Cit Awd; Sec.

MENDEZ, MARISOL; Aragon HS; San Mateo, CA; (4); 121/356; Hosp Aide; Spanish Clb; SADD; Cheerldng; Var Gym; Trk; Cit Awd; Prfct Atten Awd; Pres Acad Fit Awd; Block A; Hayward ST; Nrsng.

MENDEZ, MARY ROSE; Yosemite HS; Raymond, CA; (2); Office Aide; Yrbk; Cit Awd; Hon Roll; Prfct Atten Awd; Spnsh Tutor; Sec.

MENDEZ, MISTALA T; Saddleback HS; Santa Ana, CA; (4); FBLA; JA; Spanish Clb; Speech Tm; Teachers Aide; Ed Nwsp; Stat Bsbl; Stat Ftbl; JV Sftbl; Hon Roll; CA ST U Fullerton; Comm News.

MENDEZ, NORMA; San Dieguito HS; Encinitas, CA; (3); 97/570; Church Yth Grp; Cmnty Wkr; Library Aide; Office Aide; Teachers Aide; Fld Hcky; Hon Roll; Pres Acad Fit Awd; Presdntl Acad Fit Awd Prgm; UCLA; Word Prcsng.

MENDEZ, RAUL L; Riverbank HS; Riverbank, CA; (4); 2/90; Math Tm; Band; Jazz Band; Mrchg Band; Pep Band; Bsktbl; Tennis; Cit Awd; Dnfth Awd; High Hon Roll; Schlr Athlete Awd; Rvrbk Chmbr Of Cmmnc Bus Schlrshp; B & M Mauley Mem Rotary Club Schlrshp; CSU; Bus.

MENDEZ, SANDRA E; Montgomery HS; Santa Rosa, CA; (2); JA; Latin Clb; Pep Clb; Drill Tm; Yrbk; Sftbl; Cit Awd; Hon Roll; Bus.

MENDEZ, SHANNON; Hawthorne HS; Lennox, CA; (1); Church Yth Grp; Dance Clb; English Clb; Latin Clb; JV Score Keeper; Loyola Marymount; Real Estate.

MENDEZ, SUSAN; Santa Ana HS; Santa Ana, CA; (3); GAA; Pep Clb; Pep Band; Off Jr Cls; Var Bsktbl; Var Cheerldng; Var Swmmng; Var Vllybl; Hon Roll; Prncpls Hnr Rl; U Southern CA; Sprts Med.

MENDEZ, VIRGINIA G; Pomona HS; Pomona, CA; (2); Church Yth Grp; Chorus; Cit Awd.

MENDEZ, VIVIAN; Roosevelt HS; Fresno, CA; (1); Band; Sftbl; Vllybl; Hon Roll; UCLA; Law.

MENDIA, MELANIE M; California HS; Whittier, CA; (2); Church Yth Grp; Cmnty Wkr; Drama Clb; SADD; Thesps; Band; Sec Church Choir; Jazz Band; School Musical; Off Frsh Cls; All St, All Southern Hnr Band; Music.

MENDIBLES, PETE D; Firebaugh HS; Firebaugh, CA; (2); Computer Clb; SADD; Varsity Clb; Ftbl; Swmmng; Wt Lftg; Wrstlng; Cit Awd; High Hon Roll; Hon Roll; Natl Yng Ldrs Conf; UCLA; Acctng.

MENDIBURU, JOHN G; East Bakersfield HS; Bakersfield, CA; (3); 65/441; Key Clb; Office Aide; SADD; Teachers Aide; High Hon Roll; Hon Roll; CSF 87-88 & 89-90; Fri Night Live; CA ST U; Elem Educ.

MENDIOLA, GUSTAVO R; Wilson HS; Los Angeles, CA; (3); 10/500; Key Clb; Math Tm; ROTC; Color Guard; Stage Crew; Masonic Awd; Rifle Tm; All City ROTC Command Sgt Mjr; Sons Amer Rev; Mil Order Of World Wars; Arch.

MENDIVIL, TERRIN; Bishop Montgomery HS; Lomita, CA; (2); Key Clb; SADD; High Hon Roll; CSF; Numerous Subject Awds; Prin Hnr Roll; Sci.

MENDOZA, ALICIA; Orestimba HS; Crows Landing, CA; (3); Treas Spanish Clb; SADD; Color Guard; Yrbk; Hon Roll; CA ST U; Teacher.

MENDOZA, ALICIA I; Sutter Union HS; Robbins, CA; (4); Debate Tm; FBLA; FHA; Office Aide; Science Clb; Spanish Clb; Yrbk; Cheerldng; Wt Lftg; High Hon Roll; Rcvd Lcl Schlrshps; Thnk Tank; Chrch Actvts; Sra; Fnl; Chico ST U; Pltcl Sci/Pre Law.

MENDOZA JR, ALMARIO G; Valley View HS; Moreno Valley, CA; (2); Var Bsktbl; Hon Roll; Prfct Atten Awd; Interact Clb; Early Acad Outreach Pgm; CSF; Stanford; Phy.

MENDOZA, ANN C; Pinole Valley HS; Pinole, CA; (1); Spanish Clb; JV Trk; High Hon Roll; GSE Hgh Hnrs Awd; CSF; Stanford.

MENDOZA, ARACELI; Fresno HS; Fresno, CA; (4); 20/450; Debate Tm; FBLA; Chorus; Church Choir; Off Sr Cls; Var Crs Cntry; JV Socr; Var Trk; Gov Hon Prg Awd; MESA; Upwrd Bnd Pgm Pres & Schl Rep; Grl Of Yr Awd; GSE Alg I Hnrs; Bofa Plack Awd; Acad Decthln; Fresno City Coll.

MENDOZA, ARMIE V; Monterey HS; Seaside, CA; (3); Hon Roll; Acad Exllnc Awd; CA Schlrshp Fed Clb; Upward Bnd Prgm; Monterery Peninsula; Nrsng.

MENDOZA, BARBARA; La Mirada HS; La Mirada, CA; (2); Church Yth Grp; NFL; Speech Tm; Stu Cncl; Hon Roll; Cls Secy 90-91; CSF.

MENDOZA, CARMELA D; Sunny Hills HS; Fullerton, CA; (3); 153/430; Hon Roll; Prfct Atten Awd; CA ST Fullerton; CPA.

MENDOZA, CAROL; Ganesha HS; Pomona, CA; (3); French Clb; Hosp Aide; Office Aide; Science Clb; Off Jr Cls; MESA; Bio.

MENDOZA, CESAR A; Castle Park HS; Chula Vista, CA; (3); 70/422; French Clb; Band; Arch.

MENDOZA, CHERYL; Mercy HS; S San Francisco, CA; (3); GAA; Sec Spanish Clb; Variety Show; Off Jr Cls; Var Tennis; High Hon Roll; Prfct Atten Awd; CA Schlrshp Fdrtn; Pblcty Offcr Of JR Stsmn Of Amer Clb; Stus Awr Of Absd Sbstncs Clb Treas; Comp Sci.

MENDOZA, CIPRIANA; Arroyo Grande HS; Nipomo, CA; (4); Church Yth Grp; Library Aide; Spanish Clb; SADD; Teachers Aide; Chorus; Church Choir; School Musical; School Play; Cit Awd; Outstndng Upwrd Bndr; Miss Co-Ed St Fnlst; Bld Dr, Spcl Olympcs Vlntr; Oceano Wmns Clb Grnt; Smmr Inst; Cal Poly; Bus Admin.

MENDOZA, DENES F; Princeton HS; Colusa, CA; (4); 1/10; Butte Coll; Sci.

MENDOZA, DIANA; Calexico Union HS; Calexico, CA; (3); Boy Scts; Color Guard; Crs Cntry; Vllybl; San Diego ST U; Crmnl Just.

MENDOZA, DIANA I; Valley HS; Santa Ana, CA; (4); 17/240; Spanish Clb; Hon Roll; Pres Acad Fit Awd; St Schlr; CSF Sealbearer; Efren Herrera, Orange Cnty Mexcn Am Bar Assn Awd; Asst Leag Santa Ana Inc Awd; U CA Irvine; Bilingl Ed.

MENDOZA, DUANE; Princeton HS; Colusa, CA; (3); 2/18; Am Leg Boys St; Cmnty Wkr; FFA; Red Cross Aide; Pres Frsh Cls; Pres Jr Cls; Rep Stu Cncl; JV Var Bsbl; JV Var Socr; JV Var Trk; CSF; Davis; Intl Relations.

MENDOZA, EDWARD M; San Marcos HS; Santa Maria, CA; (3); Church Yth Grp; Off ROTC; Band; Jazz Band; Mrchg Band; Pep Band; School Musical; Physcs.

MENDOZA, ESTELA B; Academy Of Our Lady Of Peace; National City, CA; (4); 21/123; Church Yth Grp; French Clb; Hosp Aide; Key Clb; SADD; Teachers Aide; School Musical; Yrbk; Treas Soph Cls; Treas Jr Cls; Hnrs Awd Pepsi Ldrshp Schlrshp; CSF; Natl Yng Ldrs Conf Dlgt; Congrsnl Intern; Old Globe Theatre Vlntr; Georgetown U; Frgn Svc.

MENDOZA, FERNANDO F; Channel Islands HS; Oxnard, CA; (2); English Clb; FBLA; Math Clb; Science Clb; Spanish Clb; Var Crs Cntry; Var Trk; High Hon Roll; Hon Roll; Prfct Atten Awd; Vet.

MENDOZA, HECTOR R; St Genevieve HS; Sun Valley, CA; (2); Office Aide; Teachers Aide; Chorus; JV Bsbl; Hon Roll; CJSF.

MENDOZA, IMELDA G; Kearny SR HS; San Diego, CA; (3); JA; Phy.

MENDOZA, JENNIFER; Selma HS; Selma, CA; (1); Drama Clb; Flag Corp; Hon Roll; Mexican Dance.

MENDOZA, JENNIFER D; Abraham Lincoln HS; San Francisco, CA; (2); Band; U Of San Francisco; Nrsng.

MENDOZA, JOEY D; Walnut HS; Walnut, CA; (3); Church Yth Grp; Cmnty Wkr; FCA; JA; Capt Var Ftbl; Capt Var Wrstlng; High Hon Roll; Hon Roll; Jr Hnr Guard; Athl Of Yr 87-88; Psych.

MENDOZA, JOSE; Santa Ana Valley SR HS; Santa Ana, CA; (3); U Of CA At Irvine; Law.

MENDOZA, JOSE I; Sweet Water HS; National City, CA; (2); Cit Awd; Hon Roll; Prfct Atten Awd; Weight Lifting; Law Enfrcmnt.

MENDOZA, JUAN A; Glendale Adventist Acad; North Hollywood, CA; (3); Boy Scts; Church Yth Grp; Cmnty Wkr; Pthfndrs Club; Andrews U; Electrncs.

MENDOZA, JUANITA; Indio HS; Coachella, CA; (2); Office Aide; Pep Clb; Stu Cncl; Var L Cheerldng; Var Pom Pon; Cit Awd; Hon Roll; Prfct Atten Awd; Dance, Swmmng; Barbizon Modelng Grad; UC Santa Barbara.

MENDOZA, JULIETA; J H Polytechnic HS; Sun Valley, CA; (3); French Clb; Office Aide; Teachers Aide; Hon Roll; Prfct Atten Awd; Acadc Dcthln; CSF; Ldies Clb; Bio-Med Engr.

MENDOZA, JULIETA; Woodland HS; Woodland, CA; (4); Church Yth Grp; Church Choir; HERO; Outstndng Achiever; CSU Sacramento; Bus.

MENDOZA, LAURA; William Workman HS; La Puente, CA; (2); Spanish Clb; Hon Roll; Prfct Atten Awd; CSF; Achvt Awd; Dist Schlr Awd; Engrng.

MENDOZA, LIDUBINA; Channel Islands HS; Oxnard, CA; (4); FBLA; Key Clb; Office Aide; Spanish Clb; Teachers Aide; VICA; Var L Crs Cntry; Var Trk; Cit Awd; 4-H Awd; MECHA Clb Pres 88-90; Cmmnty Chrch Chorus; US Navy; Archt.

MENDOZA, LIZA; Warren HS; Downey, CA; (3); Chorus; Pres Frsh Cls; Pres Soph Cls; Pres Jr Cls; Cheerldng; Bible Club; Peer Cnslr; UCLA; Bus.

MENDOZA, LUIS A; Central Union HS; El Centro, CA; (2); Intrml Bsbl; High Hon Roll; Hon Roll; CSC; Early Outreach Pgm; USAF Acad; AF Pilot.

MENDOZA, MABEL; Fresno HS; Fresno, CA; (1); MESA; UC Santa Barbara.

MENDOZA, MARICRUZ; Coachella Valley HS; Thermal, CA; (4); FBLA; Hon Roll; Prfct Atten Awd; Acad Excllnc In Bus Mchns & Spnsh III 1989-90; CA ST U; Elem Ed.

MENDOZA, MARK M; Diamond Bar HS; Diamond Bar, CA; (2); Bus Profs of Am; Pres Key Clb; Spanish Clb; SADD; Tennis; Hon Roll; Kiwanis Awd; U Of S CA; Dnstry.

MENDOZA, MARLIES D; Santa Barbara HS; Santa Barbara, CA; (3); 31/475; GAA; SADD; Pres Sr Cls; Socr; Vllybl; High Hon Roll; Hon Roll; CA Schlrshp Fed; Stu Govt; Jr Statesmen Assn; U Of CA; Law.

MENDOZA, MELVIN T; Don Bosco Technical Inst; Alhambra, CA; (2); Hon Roll.

MENDOZA, MONICA; Pomona HS; Chino, CA; (1); French Clb; JV Vllybl; Hon Roll.

MENDOZA, MONICA L; Saint Anthonys HS; Long Beach, CA; (2); Dance Clb; Drama Clb; School Musical; Variety Show; High Hon Roll; Hon Roll; NHS; CSF; UC Irvine; Med.

MENDOZA, NOREEN; Ribet Acad; Glendale, CA; (4); 3/28; Pep Clb; Ski Clb; Varsity Clb; Yrbk; Cheerldng; Prfct Atten Awd; Mbr Stu Accreditation Cmmtte; Homecomng Princess; Outstndng Comp Stu; Loyola Marymount U UCLA; Dr.

MENDOZA, RICHARD; Bellarmine College Prep; San Jose, CA; (4); Boy Scts; Teachers Aide; Ntl Merit SF; Bus.

MENDOZA, ROGELIO G; Saddleback HS; Santa Ana, CA; (3); FBLA; Spanish Clb; Tm Stu Orange Cnty Acad Cmptn Sddlbck; MESA; Medical.

MENDOZA, ROSA; Orestimba HS; Crows Landing, CA; (2); Spanish Clb; JV Bsktbl; San Jose ST U; Elect Engrng.

MENDOZA, SANDRO; Crenshaw SR HS; Los Angeles, CA; (3); Art Clb; Church Yth Grp; Computer Clb; Latin Clb; Library Aide; Spanish Clb; Stage Crew; Score Keeper; Socr; Cit Awd; Knights & Ladies; Math Class Advsr; Psych.

MENDOZA II, SERGIO H; Temple City HS; Temple City, CA; (2); Church Yth Grp; Cmnty Wkr; Intrml Bsbl; Var Wrstlng; Judo; Vrsty Coachs Awd For Wrstlng 89-90; Hnrary Vrsty Wrstlr Of Wk; UCLA; Law.

MENDOZA, TERESA C; Villa Park HS; Orange, CA; (3); Church Yth Grp; Key Clb; Letterman Clb; Spanish Clb; SADD; Rep Soph Cls; Var Socr; Var Trk; Hon Roll; NHS; San Diego ST U; Bus Admin.

MENDOZA, TRACY S; Lemoore Union HS; Lemoore, CA; (3); FCA; French Clb; SADD; Crs Cntry; Powder Puff Ftbl; Hon Roll; Outstndng Achvt In Art & Bus Sklls; CSF; CSU-FRESNO; Jrnlsm.

MENDOZA, TRINA G; Bolsa Grande HS; Garden Grove, CA; (3); 27/335; Acpl Chr; Stat Bsktbl; Cit Awd; Hon Roll; Jr NHS; U CA-RIVERSIDE; Bio.

MENENDEZ, AMY A; Ukiah HS; Ukiah, CA; (1); 41/625; Drama Clb; School Musical; Pres Frsh Cls; JV Bsktbl; Var Socr; Var Swmmng; Pres Acad Fit Awd; Safe Riders; Schlr Athlt; ASB Treas; UCLA; Artist.

MENENDEZ, INGRID; Chaminade Coll Prep; Canoga Park, CA; (2); Art Clb; Church Yth Grp; Drama Clb; Stage Crew; Hon Roll; UCLA; Lawyer.

MENES, JUANITA; Rio Mesa HS; Camarillo, CA; (1); Library Aide; Office Aide; Church Choir; School Play; Cheerldng; Phys Ed.

MENESES, ELIA E; Pasadena HS; Pasadena, CA; (3); Church Yth Grp; FCA; Hosp Aide; Spanish Clb; Cit Awd; CA ST La; Tchng.

MENESES, NORMA M; Etiwanda HS; Alta Loma, CA; (2); Hosp Aide; Latin Clb; JV Tennis; JV Trk; Hon Roll; Prfct Atten Awd; Cum Laude Natl Latin Exam Awd; UCLA; Med.

MENEZ, FREDELIX O; Irvine HS; Irvine, CA; (1); Chess Clb; Math Tm; High Hon Roll; Hon Roll; Pres Acad Fit Awd; HS Heritage Awd; Acad Dcthln.

MENEZ, THERESE C; Providence HS; Glendale, CA; (2); VP Art Clb; Hosp Aide; Pep Clb; Chorus; Sec Frsh Cls; Sec Jr Cls; Cheerldng; Var Trk; JV Vllybl; Hon Roll; CSF; 2nd Hnrs; Travel; Med.

MENEZES, AMY; Monterey HS; Seaside, CA; (3); German Clb; Var Cheerldng; Hon Roll; Prfct Atten Awd.

MENG, DAVID; Ramona HS; Ramona, CA; (2); Chess Clb; Varsity Clb; JV Trk; Var Wrstlng; Hon Roll; Phrmcst.

MENG, OLIVER; Santa Monica HS; Santa Monica, CA; (3); JV Crs Cntry; JV Trk; MECHA Clb; Cancer Research Lab; UCLA; Cancer Research.

MENGEL, KIM; Temple City HS; San Gabriel, CA; (4); 79/348; Dance Clb; English Clb; Pep Clb; Stu Cncl; JV Var Cheerldng; Tennis; Kiwanis Awd; Chrldng Awd Most Spirited,Invlvd & Insprntl; CA Poly-Pomona; Bus.

MENINI, THOMAS J; Apple Valley HS; Apple Valley, CA; (2); Mrchg Band; High Hon Roll.

MENNING, GENEVIEVE L; Modoc HS; Canby, CA; (3); 9/68; Am Leg Aux Girls St; Letterman Clb; Pres Pep Clb; Science Clb; Sec Mrchg Band; VP School Play; Sec Frsh Cls; Sec Stu Cncl; Capt Cheerldng; High Hon Roll; Bio.

MENSING, TARA; Mission College Prep; Atascadero, CA; (3); Church Yth Grp; 4-H; Office Aide; Ski Clb; Rptr Yrbk; Treas Soph Cls; Treas Jr Cls; Var Cheerldng; 4-H Awd; Hon Roll; 4-H Treas/JR Ldr; Help Our Planet Earth Survive Clb; CA Lutheran; Acctng.

MENVIELLE, DAWN M; Central Union HS; El Centro, CA; (2); Pep Clb; Speech Tm; Rep Stu Cncl; JV Var Pom Pon; Var Swmmng; Hon Roll; Rotary Awd; Jobs Dghtrs; Mock Trial; Psych.

MENVILLE, CHAD B; Santa Monica HS; Malibu, CA; (1); Ski Clb; Swmmng; Hon Roll; Opt Clb Awd; Pres Acad Fit Awd; Spartn Awd 89; NCCJ Poetry Fnlst 88 & 89; U Of CA Los Angeles; Dntst.

MENYHAY, CAROLYN S; Madera HS; Madera, CA; (2); Church Yth Grp; Band; Mrchg Band; Pep Band; Rep Frsh Cls; Swmmng; Cit Awd; Hon Roll; Marimba Band; JR Young Ladies Inst; Mst Vlbl Vrsty Swmmr.

MENZEL, THIJS I; Santa Clara HS; Oxnard, CA; (3); Office Aide; Teachers Aide; Rptr Frsh Cls; Chrmn Soph Cls; Rptr Jr Cls; Rptr Stu Cncl; Cit Awd; High Hon Roll; Hon Roll; Pres Acad Fit Awd; Arch.

MENZL, ADRIAN C; Serra HS; Laguna Niguel, CA; (3); Church Yth Grp; Cmnty Wkr; FCA; French Clb; German Clb; Varsity Clb; Var Cheerldng; Var Ftbl; Pres Acad Fit Awd; AR Coll; Arch.

MEONO, JAMES; Notre Dame HS; Granada Hills, CA; (4); 9/249; Pres Intnl Clb; Letterman Clb; Varsity Clb; Var Bsbl; Var Ftbl; Var Socr; Var Trk; NHS; NEDT Awd; Dartmouth Clg; Engrng.

MERA, VICTOR R; Bishop Montgomery HS; Lomita, CA; (3); Crs Cntry; Hon Roll; Engrng.

MERAZ, EDGAR; Dos Palos HS; Dos Palos, CA; (3); Nwsp; Yrbk; VP Bsbl; VP Wt Lftg; Fresno Coll; Drftng.

MERAZ, EFREN; Dos Palos Joint Union HS; South Dos Palos, CA; (3); FHA; Library Aide; Hon Roll; Art Dsgn.

MERAZ, MARGARET; Arvin HS; Arvin, CA; (2); Ski Clb; Band; Mrchg Band; Treas Jr Cls; Var Tennis; Hon Roll; U Irvine; Bacterialgy.

MERAZ, MARTHA; Kingsburg HS; Kingsburg, CA; (3); Teachers Aide.

MERCADO, ADOLFO; Christian Brothers HS; Sacramento, CA; (2); Cmnty Wkr; FHA; Science Clb; Sec Spanish Clb; Stage Crew; Lit Mag; Hon Roll; MESA; UC Outrch; CA U; Pedtrcn.

MERCADO, LUIS A; Herert Hoover HS; San Diego, CA; (3); Church Yth Grp; Cmnty Wkr; Intnl Clb; Key Clb; Elec Engr.

MERCADO, MANUEL; Livingston HS; Delhi, CA; (3); Prfct Atten Awd; B Hnr Roll; X-Ray Tech.

MERCADO, RENE; Orosi HS; Orosi, CA; (3); Hon Roll; Acad Awd; Reedley JC; Auto Mech.

MERCADO, SARA; Dixon HS; Dixon, CA; (2); 4-H; Letterman Clb; Library Aide; Math Clb; Office Aide; Teachers Aide; Rep Stu Cncl; JV Cheerldng; Score Keeper; Var Trk; Sacramento ST Coll; Arch.

MERCADO, TANYA M; Abraham Lincoln HS; San Jose, CA; (3); Church Yth Grp; Band; Mrchg Band; School Musical; JV Var Bsktbl; Crs Cntry; JV Sftbl; Trk; High Hon Roll; Hon Roll; Mathmtcs,Engr,Sci Achvt MESA VP; U CA; Pre Med.

MERCADO, VERONICA; Sacred Heart Of Jesus HS; Los Angeles, CA; (2); GAA; Hon Roll; NHS; Chrstn Actn Mvmnt; UCLA; Law Enfrcmnt.

MERCER, JODI M; Mission Viejo HS; Mission Viejo, CA; (2); 98/496; Church Yth Grp; GAA; Key Clb; JV Sftbl; Med.

MERCER, LYN ANNE; El Toro HS; El Toro, CA; (2); JCL; Band; Jazz Band; Mrchg Band; Orch; Pep Band; School Musical; Stage Crew; Hon Roll; Jr NHS; Scripps Coll; Bio.

MERCER, MELISSA G; Yucaipa HS; Yucaipa, CA; (3); French Clb; JA; Letterman Clb; Crs Cntry; Trk; High Hon Roll; NHS; Jr Hnr Usher; Schlr Athlte Trck & Crs Cntry; Acad Ltr Recvng 3.5 GPA; Bus.

MERCER, MICHAEL J; El Toro HS; El Toro, CA; (4); 40/530; High Hon Roll; Hon Roll; JETS Awd; Pres Acad Fit Awd; Engnrng Clb; CSF Seal Bearer; Embry Riddle; Engnrng.

MERCER, NICOLE M; Troy HS; Yorba Linda, CA; (2); French Clb; Teachers Aide; Band; Mrchg Band; Pep Band; Nwsp; High Hon Roll; NHS; Rotary Awd; Wrtng/Poetry; Animal Rghts; Outstndng Achvt Merit Awd Math & Lang; Lang Instrctr.

MERCER, SHELLEY M; Central Catholic HS; Modesto, CA; (3); Church Yth Grp; Key Clb; Letterman Clb; Service Clb; Ski Clb; SADD; Powder Puff Ftbl; Sftbl; St Marys Coll; Scl Worker.

MERCER, SHERI A; Central Catholic HS; Modesto, CA; (3); 20/58; Church Yth Grp; GAA; Letterman Clb; Service Clb; Ski Clb; SADD; Yrbk; Bsktbl; Powder Puff Ftbl; Trk; Cal Poly San Luiso Bispo; Hlth.

MERCHAN, HERMAN C; El Camino Real HS; Canoga Park, CA; (4); Letterman Clb; Spanish Clb; Varsity Clb; Var JV Bsbl; JV Socr; Pres Acad Fit Awd; Pierce Coll; Engrng.

MERCHANT, LESLIE; Foothill HS; Santa Ana, CA; (4); 8/300; Cmnty Wkr; Spanish Clb; Teachers Aide; Crs Cntry; Tennis; Trk; High Hon Roll; Ntl Merit SF; NEDT Awd; UC Berkeley; Bio.

MERCHANT, LISA CAROLE; Los Altos HS; Hacienda Hgts, CA; (4); Church Yth Grp; Letterman Clb; Chorus; Church Choir; Swing Chorus; Cheerldng; Powder Puff Ftbl; Socr; Capt Var Swmmng; Wt Lftg; Hmcmg Prncss; JR Prom Qn; Pepperdine U; Advtg.

MERCHANT, SANJAY; Mission Viejo HS; Mission Viejo, CA; (2); 7/400; Model UN; Ftbl; Trk; Wt Lftg; High Hon Roll; Jr NHS; Pres Acad Fit Awd; Pres Schlr; CSF; MUN Delg Awds; Tp 25; Ftbl Outstndng Dfnsv Plyr Awd; Stanford; Comp Tech.

MERCIER, KATE A; Trinity HS; Helena, CA; (2); Drama Clb; Ski Clb; Yrbk; JV Trk; High Hon Roll; Hon Roll; Peer Cnslng Tm; UCSD; Engl.

MERCURIO, CHRISTIAN; Bonita HS; Glendora, CA; (3); French Clb; Model UN; School Musical; Variety Show; Var Trk; Frnch Clb, VP; Musician.

MERCY, BRANDON L; Calvary Baptist HS; San Dimas, CA; (3); Church Yth Grp; Stage Crew; Off Frsh Cls; Var Vllybl; Outstndng Art Awd; CA Polytchnc Pomona; Chem.

MERCY, KRIS; Calvary Baptist HS; San Dimas, CA; (1); Var Vllybl; Pres Acad Fit Awd.

MEREDITH, MELANIE L; Carlmont HS; San Carlos, CA; (3); Girl Scts; Temple Yth Grp; Band; Rep Frsh Cls; Rep Soph Cls; Rep Jr Cls; Var L Sftbl; JV Var Vllybl; Ntl Merit Ltr; Rensselaer Mdl Acad Excllnc-Math & Sci; CA Schlrshp Fed; Amnsty Intl-Treas; Enrgrng.

MEREDITH, STEVEN P; Bonita Vista HS; Bonita, CA; (1); 82/537; Boy Scts; Church Yth Grp; Cit Awd; Drwng; Tnns & Racktbl; Medcl.

MEREZKO, NATASHA; Mc Kinleyville HS; Mckinleyville, CA; (4); Sec Drama Clb; Sec Spanish Clb; School Play; Cit Awd; Amer Bus Women Assn Schlrshp; Bnk America Achvt Awd Sci; Redwoods Coll; Bio.

MERIAM, ALICE; Silver Creek HS; San Jose, CA; (3); 32/650; Pep Clb; School Play; Stage Crew; Sec Sr Cls; Var Cheerldng; High Hon Roll; CSF; Jr Hmcmng Prncss; Archlgst.

MERICAL, SONJA R; Fremont Christian HS; Newark, CA; (3); Hosp Aide; Hon Roll; Music Awd Piano; Star Stu Awd; Bus Awd Typng; Stanford U; Med.

MERILLANA, CECILIA A; Alisal HS; Salinas, CA; (4); Office Aide; Teachers Aide; Yrbk; Score Keeper; Hon Roll; GATE Clb; Princpals Hnr Roll; Hartnell; Psych.

MERINO, DENNIS C; Pasadena HS; Pasadena, CA; (2); Letterman Clb; SADD; Yrbk; Tennis; Tchr.

MERIWETHER, MARGO; Rio Americano HS; Sacramento, CA; (4); Aud/Vis; French Clb; Hosp Aide; Mgr Bsktbl; Trk; Hon Roll; Sacramento Chldrsn Comm Yth Bd Mem; Sassiest Girl America Fnlst; 17 Magazine Cover Girl Semi-Fnlst; U CA Los Angeles; Comm.

MERLO, CHRISTINA; Holy Family HS; Los Angeles, CA; (2); Church Yth Grp; Office Aide; Speech Tm; Chorus; School Musical; Intrml Sftbl; Intrml Tennis; Intrml Vllybl; Jr NHS; Opt Clb Awd; Crt Rptr.

MERLOS, MOISES M; Eisenhower HS; Rialto, CA; (3); Var Crs Cntry; Var Trk; Hon Roll; Doctor.

MERON, BRANDI; San Dieguito HS; Encinitas, CA; (2); Church Yth Grp; Var L Bsktbl; Var L Gym; Wt Lftg; Cit Awd; Prfct Atten Awd; Pres Acad Fit Awd; Cornell; Bus Mgr.

MERRIFIELD, CHARLES D; Pomway HS; Poway, CA; (2); Model UN; JV Socr; Coll.

MERRILL, CHRISTOPHER; Casa Roble HS; Citrus Heights, CA; (4); 56/325; French Clb; Ed Yrbk; Tennis; Best All Arnd Sr Clss; Sr Ball Prince; Writers Fari 1st & 2nd Pl; UC Santa Cruz; Physics.

MERRILL, JEFF; Lindsay HS; Lindsay, CA; (2); FFA; Letterman Clb; Bsktbl; Ftbl; Golf; Vllybl; Wt Lftg; Hon Roll; Cal Poly; Ag Bus.

MERRILL, MATTHEW S; Newbury Park HS; Newbury Park, CA; (4); VP Art Clb; Boy Scts; Church Yth Grp; Letterman Clb; Church Choir; L JV Bsktbl; L Var Ftbl; Var Sftbl; L Var Wt Lftg; Cit Awd; Eagle Boyscouts Of Amer; Illustration Design.

MERRILL, SHAWNA; Woodland HS; Woodland, CA; (2); SADD; U Of CA Davis.

MERRITT, CARRIE; Ursuline HS; Santa Rosa, CA; (4); 20/98; Am Leg Aux Girls St; Church Yth Grp; Cmnty Wkr; JA; Pres Soph Cls; Pres Jr Cls; Pres Stu Cncl; Var Swmmng; Var Capt Tennis; Cit Awd; Girl Awd; Japan Ambssdr; Santa Rosa Rotarian Lsrshp Awd; Syracuse U; Brdcst Jrnlsm.

MERRITT, JANINE; Washington HS; Los Angeles, CA; (3); Pres VP Church Yth Grp; Dance Clb; Girl Scts; Pep Clb; Teachers Aide; Church Choir; Var Cheerldng; JV Crs Cntry; JV Trk; Hon Roll; Delta Phi Teens; Comp Sci.

MERRITT, LARRY; Gardena HS; Los Angeles, CA; (4); Stu Cncl; Var Ftbl; Var Capt Trk; Yng Black Schlrs Awd Of Achvt; Cert Of Appreciation Schl Ldrshp; CSU Dominguez Hills.

MERRIWEATHER, NICOLE; Tulare Union HS; Tulare, CA; (3); 23/400; Speech Tm; Mrchg Band; High Hon Roll; Lion Awd; Capt Ltrgirl Squad; Lions Club Spch Cntst Wnnr; Cmmnctns.

MERRYMAN, LESLIE N; Riverdale HS; Riverdale, CA; (3); Church Yth Grp; Drama Clb; Pep Clb; SADD; Church Choir; School Play; JV Var Bsktbl; Mgr(s); Score Keeper; Var Trk; Fresno ST; Art.

MERSEREAU, KATIE M; San Dominico HS; Novato, CA; (2); Art Clb; Cmnty Wkr; French Clb; Hosp Aide; Speech Tm; Cit Awd; High Hon Roll; CSF Awd; Bio Hnrs; Drwng & Pntng Hnrs.

MERSEREAU, KRISTIE A; San Domenico HS; Novato, CA; (2); Aud/Vis; French Clb; Girl Scts; Speech Tm; Sec Soph Cls; Gym; Var Socr; Cit Awd; High Hon Roll; NHS; Medicine; Jornalism.

MERSON, NOELLE A; Hoover HS; Fresno, CA; (3); Var Swmmng; Hon Roll; Fresno ST; Accntnt.

MERSY, MELISSA A; Vista HS; Vista, CA; (3); 4/464; Hosp Aide; Intnl Clb; Key Clb; Ski Clb; Var Fld Hcky; Var Swmmng; High Hon Roll; CA Schlrshp Fed; Bio.

MERTENS, MICHAEL; Ponderosa HS; Placerville, CA; (1); JV Bsbl; Hon Roll; UCLA; Econmcs.

MERTINS, AMY L; St Joseph HS; Santa Maria, CA; (3); 38/135; Church Yth Grp; Key Clb; SADD; Band; Swmmng; New Horizons; Swim Team Awd; Allan Hancock Coll.

MERTZ, ELIZABETH A; Sir Francis Drake HS; San Anselmo, CA; (4); 2/140; Church Yth Grp; Drama Clb; Ski Clb; SADD; Varsity Clb; School Play; Variety Show; Pres Soph Cls; JV Var Bsktbl; JV Cheerldng; Photo; U S CA; Soclgy.

MERVINE, NOAH G; Ukiah HS; Ukiah, CA; (3); VICA; Band; Mrchg Band; Var L Socr; Elec Engr.

MERZ, JENNIFER A; Valhalla HS; El Cajon, CA; (3); Dance Clb; Drama Clb; 4-H; Girl Scts; Key Clb; Model UN; Pep Clb; ROTC; Ski Clb; SADD.

MESA, DARLENE S; Arlington HS; Riverside, CA; (3); Church Yth Grp; FFA; Girl Scts; Hosp Aide; Cit Awd; Hon Roll; Artists Schl Pride Lion; Stu Mnth Awd FFA; UC Davis; Vet.

MESA, DEBORAH L; Immanuel HS; Selma, CA; (4); 22/67; Church Yth Grp; Church Choir; Hon Roll; Latin Am Bible Inst; Ministry.

MESA, SAGI M; Mater Dei HS; Huntington Beach, CA; (2); Church Yth Grp; Spanish Clb; Drill Tm; Hon Roll; Loyola Marymount; Family Law.

MESALLEM, IBRAHIM; Abraham Lincoln HS; San Francisco, CA; (3); JV Socr; Acad Of Fin; Bus.

MESERVY, DAISY L; Tracy Joint Union HS; Tracy, CA; (2); 43/500; SADD; Var Crs Cntry; Var Trk; Hon Roll; Pres Acad Fit Awd; Schlr Athlete Awd; Sci.

MESERVY, LONDON; Chula Vista HS; Chula Vista, CA; (2); Boy Scts; Pres Church Yth Grp; Dance Clb; Drama Clb; School Play; Variety Show; Stat Bsbl; JV Ftbl; Prfct Atten Awd; Pres Acad Fit Awd; Eagle Scout; Scripps Cmmnty Svc Awd.

MESKELL, MATTHEW W; Chaminade College Prep; Tarzana, CA; (3); Boy Scts; Church Yth Grp; Color Guard; Var Socr; Var Vllybl; High Hon Roll; Jr NHS; NHS; Pres Acad Fit Awd; CSF; Law.

MESSER, ADAM W; Bret Harte HS; Murphys, CA; (3); 4-H; FHA; Teachers Aide; School Play; JV Var Ftbl; JV Var Trk; 4-H Awd; Hon Roll; Wildlife Law Enfrcmnt.

MESSER, ANGELA; Corona SR HS; Corona, CA; (4); Debate Tm; French Clb; Band; Color Guard; Mrchg Band; Orch; Pep Band; Stat Bsktbl; JV Swmmng; JV Tennis; Riverside Cmmnty; Educ.

MESSER, LAURIE; Palm Desert HS; Palm Desert, CA; (2); 1/402; Cmnty Wkr; Spanish Clb; Var Tennis; High Hon Roll; Prfct Atten Awd; Nabisco Jnr Tnns Tourn High Pnt Earnr 88-89; Outstndng Engl Awd 89; Prncpls Awd 89; Attrny.

MESSERLY, MARGO M; Pioneer HS; San Jose, CA; (3); 90/392; Office Aide; Spanish Clb; Teachers Aide; Stu Cncl; Hon Roll; Interact Clb.

MESSINA, ANTHONY A; Don Antonio Lugo HS; Chino, CA; (2); Church Yth Grp; German Clb; Prfct Atten Awd; Ballrm Dncng; Wghtlftng; Guitar Plyng; Kybrd; Yth Cnslng; Biola U.

MESSINA, LISA; North Hollywood HS; North Hollywood, CA; (3); Spanish Clb; Cit Awd; High Hon Roll; Hon Roll; Engl.

MESSINA, LISA; St Patrick-St Vincent HS; Vallejo, CA; (2); Science Clb; Rep Soph Cls; JV Vllybl; High Hon Roll; NHS; CSF.

MESSINA, MICHAEL H; Hilltop HS; Chula Vista, CA; (3); Boy Scts; Debate Tm; Office Aide; Quiz Bowl; Speech Tm; SADD; Teachers Aide; Socr; Swmmng; UCSD; Tchr.

MESSNER, CYNTHIA M; Hoopa HS; Salyer, CA; (3); Drama Clb; Key Clb; Thesps; Band; Chorus; Mrchg Band; School Play; Bsktbl; Vllybl; Hon Roll; Schltc All Amer; Med.

MESSNER, MIQUELLE C; Pinole Valley HS; Hercules, CA; (3); Intnl Clb; Ski Clb; Flag Corp; Hon Roll; U Of Santa Barbara.

MESTAS, NADALIE; West Covina HS; West Covina, CA; (3); Ski Clb; Drill Tm; JV Var Cheerldng; JV Score Keeper; USC; Accntnt.

METCALF, CARRIE; Oroville HS; Oroville, CA; (2); Pres Church Yth Grp; SADD; Stu Cncl; Stat Bsktbl; JV Cheerldng; Stat Vllybl; Hon Roll; UC Sacramento ST; Marine Bio.

METCALF, CURT A; North HS; Bakersfield, CA; (2); Church Yth Grp; Computer Clb; Ftbl; Mgr(s); US Naval Acad; Aerontcl Engrng.

METCALF, DAWNA D; Glendale HS; Glendale, CA; (3); Church Yth Grp; Var Sftbl; Jr NHS; NHS; PALS Peer Counselors 1989-90; Forming Of The Glendale Teen Support Center; CSUN; Physical Therapy.

METCALF, MARLA GALE; Los Angeles Baptist HS; Granada Hills, CA; (4); 31/90; Church Yth Grp; School Play; Phtg Rptr Nwsp; Phtg Rptr Yrbk; Phtg Rptr Lit Mag; Sec Frsh Cls; Capt JV Cheerldng; Capt Sftbl; Vllybl; Hon Roll; Azusa Pacific U; Athl Trng.

METCALF, SHERRY L; Summerville HS; Sonora, CA; (1); Church Yth Grp; Pep Clb; JV Cheerldng; JV Sftbl; High Hon Roll; Hon Roll; CSF; AFS; Prsctr.

METCALFE, JOHN J; Victor Valley HS; Victorville, CA; (2); Chess Clb; Computer Clb; Key Clb; Ed Nwsp; JV Socr; Cit Awd; Hon Roll; CSF; Med.

METCHIKOFF, DENISE; Huntington Beach HS; Huntington Beach, CA; (3); Church Yth Grp; Var Swmmng; JV Vllybl; Hon Roll; Sunday Schl Teacher; Psych.

METOYER, DELIA M; Mission Viejo HS; Rancho Santa Marg, CA; (3); Church Yth Grp; Intnl Clb; Key Clb; Science Clb; Spanish Clb; School Play; NHS; Cmnty Wkr; Drama Clb; Pep Clb; Tutor; Sunday Schl Teacher; Safe Rides; Law.

METROYANIS, JENNIFER; Mount Carmel HS; San Diego, CA; (2); Cit Awd; Prfct Atten Awd; Pres Acad Fit Awd; Chrldrs Coach 1st Pl Cheer, 5th Pl Dance 89; Rec Leag Sftbl; UCSD.

METSIOU, TONY M; Granite Hills HS; El Cajon, CA; (2); 31/444; Hon Roll; Musicn.

METTLER, DARREN L; Mission Viejo HS; Mission Viejo, CA; (3); Church Yth Grp; Band; Jazz Band; Mrchg Band; Orch; School Musical; Westmont; Music.

METTLER, ERIC G; Woodside HS; Portola Valley, CA; (2); Teachers Aide; Band; Jazz Band; Mrchg Band; Yrbk; Off Jr Cls; JV Capt Bsbl; Hon Roll; Remote Control Car Racing.

METZ, JULIE D; Fremont Christian HS; Union City, CA; (1); Church Yth Grp; Speech Tm; Acpl Chr; Band; School Musical; Chrmn Frsh Cls; High Hon Roll; Hon Roll; Hmcmng Prncss; Chld Dvlpmnt.

METZ, KRIS E; Armijo HS; Fairfield, CA; (2); Socr; Hon Roll; Film Production.

METZGER, AUDRA P; Miramonte HS; Moraga, CA; (3); 43/182; Church Yth Grp; Cmnty Wkr; Science Clb; JV Bsktbl; Var Capt Socr; Var L Sftbl; Var L Vllybl; High Hon Roll; Hon Roll; Drama Clb; Natl Charity League Awd; Friday Night Live; Young Life; Med.

METZGER, DONNA; Cypress HS; Buena Park, CA; (2); JV Cheerldng; NHS; RN.

METZGER, ULEAF GORDON; Calaveras HS; San Andreas, CA; (3); Boy Scts; Church Yth Grp; Cmnty Wkr; Ski Clb; Var Golf; Var Mgr(s); Mgr Socr; Var Tennis; Hon Roll; SEED Pgm 90; Zoology.

MEUX, MICHAEL; Edison Computech HS; Fresno, CA; (3); 36/350; Church Yth Grp; JA; Latin Clb; Varsity Clb; Var Ftbl; Var Capt Trk; Capt Wt Lftg; Cit Awd; Ftbll & All Amer; U CA Davis; Pre Med.

MEW, MATTHEW; Tustin HS; Tustin, CA; (2); Church Yth Grp; VP German Clb; Latin Clb; Science Clb; Ski Clb; Church Choir; JV Bsktbl; High Hon Roll; Hon Roll; Schl Recgntn Golden St Exm Alg; Hgh Hnrs Gldn St Exm Geom; Hosptl Admin.

MEYER, ALICIA M; Santa Clara HS; Oxnard, CA; (3); 32/145; Hosp Aide; Pep Clb; Spanish Clb; Fld Hcky; Hon Roll; NHS; CSF.

MEYER, ANN J; El Cajon Valley HS; El Cajon, CA; (3); 48/320; Teachers Aide; Hon Roll; Med.

MEYER, ARIANA D; Foothill HS; Santa Ana, CA; (2); French Clb; Flag Corp; 3 Yrs Actng Classes; UCLA; Psych.

MEYER, BRIAN J; Simi Valley HS; Simi Valley, CA; (3); Teachers Aide; Var L Bsbl; JV Var Bsktbl; JV Var Ftbl; Hon Roll; Pres Acad Fit Awd; Bst Dfnsv Plyr JV Bsktbl 89-90; Bus.

MEYER, BRYAN P; Don Lugo HS; Chino, CA; (2); 6/800; Church Yth Grp; FCA; Ftbl; Trk; Wt Lftg; High Hon Roll; Prfct Atten Awd; Penn ST; Teaching.

MEYER, CAROLE; Glendale HS; Glendale, CA; (2); Dance Clb; Hosp Aide; Service Clb; Variety Show; Cit Awd; Pres Acad Fit Awd; CSF; Natl Educl Dvlpmnt Test Super Achvt Cert; Gldn St Exam Hnrs Awd Alg; UCLA; Psych.

MEYER, DANA R; Junipero Serra HS; San Diego, CA; (3); 109/391; Hon Roll; Letterettes-Mgr; AZ ST U; Acctng.

MEYER, DANIEL L; Norte Vista HS; Riverside, CA; (1); Church Yth Grp; Ftbl; High Hon Roll; Intrvwd Peer Asstnc Ldrshp.

MEYER, ERIKA A; Hayward HS; Hayward, CA; (3); 18/180; Church Yth Grp; German Clb; Office Aide; Mrchg Band; Ed Nwsp; Lit Mag; Hon Roll; Mass Commnctns.

MEYER, JAKE M; Mar Vista HS; San Diego, CA; (1); Scholastic Bowl; Intrml Bsktbl; JV Ftbl; Intrml Wt Lftg; JV Wrstlng; Golden St Exam Algebra High Awd 89-90; UCSD; Med.

MEYER, JENNIFER E; Santa Clara HS; Oxnard, CA; (3); 42/145; Varsity Clb; Var L Vllybl; Hon Roll; Right To Life Org; Ventura Coll; Arch.

MEYER, KARIN E; Notre Dame HS; Salinas, CA; (3); Church Yth Grp; JV Var Bsktbl; Var Trk; JV Var Vllybl; Hon Roll; St Schlr; Bus.

MEYER, KELLY; Mc Kinleyville HS; Mc Kinleyville, CA; (3); AFS; SADD; Yrbk; Var Capt Bsktbl; Var Sftbl; Var Tennis; Hon Roll; CSF; Hnrs Golden St Exams Alg I.

MEYER, KELLY M; Los Altos HS; Los Altos, CA; (3); Church Yth Grp; Teachers Aide; Var Powder Puff Ftbl; Capt Var Swmmng; High Hon Roll; Psych.

MEYER, LISA; Encina HS; Sacramento, CA; (4); Cit Awd; Hon Roll; ROP Child Care Achvmnt Ser.

MEYER, MICHELLE E; Burney JR/Sr HS; Anderson, CA; (2); Stage Crew; Yrbk; Mgr Bsktbl; Mgr Vllybl; Hon Roll; CSF; Teen Ldrs Secy; US Air Force; Aerospc Engrng.

MEYER, MIKE L; Yucca Valley HS; Joshua Tree, CA; (4); Teachers Aide; Hon Roll; Masonic Awd; Regnl Occupational Pgm Awd & Cert; ITT Tech Inst; Elect.

MEYER, PAUL D; San Dieguito HS; Encinitas, CA; (2); Boy Scts; Church Yth Grp; Red Cross Aide; JV Bsbl; JV Socr; Cit Awd; High Hon Roll; Engrng.

MEYER, RODRICK H; Eureka SR HS; Eureka, CA; (4); 7/300; Church Yth Grp; Cmnty Wkr; Key Clb; Ski Clb; Jazz Band; Rep Frsh Cls; Treas Jr Cls; Var Bsbl; Var Bsktbl; Var Capt Socr; Stanford U; Bio.

MEYER, TARAH T; Clovis West HS; Fresno, CA; (3); 400/560; Cmnty Wkr; Var Cheerldng; Gym; VP MESA; Sgt At Arms BSU; Greenpeace; Indian Clb; Amnesty Intl; Mst Vlbl Jr Schlrshp Awd; UCLA; Medcl Sci.

MEYER, THERESA A; St Joseph HS; Downey, CA; (4); 3/170; JV Bsktbl; High Hon Roll; Ntl Merit Ltr; Pres Acad Fit Awd; CSF 87-90; Relgs Ed Volntr Tchrs Aide-Pre-Schl Levl; U Of CA Berkeley; Arch.

MEYER, TINA M; Etiwanda HS; Etiwanda, CA; (2); Latin Clb; Pep Clb; SADD; Drill Tm; Cheerldng; Phy.

MEYERS, BETTY J; Baldwin Park HS; Baldwin Park, CA; (3); Dance Clb; Teachers Aide; Sec Chorus; Variety Show; Stat Score Keeper; Stat Swmmng; Hon Roll; Acctng.

MEYERS, CARMIN C; Mira Mesa HS; San Diego, CA; (3); FHA; Natl Beta Clb; Spanish Clb; Rep Stu Cncl; Top 100 Stndts Mira Mesa; Whos Who; Stndt Of Mnth Englsh Dpt; U Of CA; Biology Medi.

MEYERS, GARY D; Herbert Hoover HS; Fresno, CA; (2); Debate Tm; NFL; Speech Tm; Temple Yth Grp; Acad Dcthln; CSF; Pltcl Sci.

MEYERS, KAMI; Madison HS; San Diego, CA; (2); Church Yth Grp; Drama Clb; GAA; Hosp Aide; Chorus; Church Choir; School Musical; School Play; Variety Show; JV Cheerldng; CA Yth Chorale; CA St Comptn JV Cheer Sqd 2nd Pl; USC; Educ.

MEYERS, LISA; Analy HS; Sebastopol, CA; (3); Dance Clb; Pep Clb; Band; Mrchg Band; Pep Band; Cheerldng; High Hon Roll; Hon Roll; Med.

MEYET, COURTNEY E; Helix HS; La Mesa, CA; (1); Band; Mrchg Band; Orch; Pep Band; Hon Roll; Prfct Atten Awd; Sthrn CA Hnr Band/Orch; San Diego Cnty Hnr Band; Wildwood Music Camp Schlrshp; Instrmntl Music.

MEYETTE, KELLY F; Burbank HS; Burbank, CA; (3); Drill Tm; Var Swmmng; Hon Roll; Pres Acad Fit Awd; Rgnl Occptn Pgm Achvt Awd Cmmrcl Art; CJSF; Humboldt ST U; Forestry.

MEYETTE, RICHARD; St Monica HS; Culver City, CA; (3); Am Leg Boys St; VP Chess Clb; Rep Soph Cls; Rep Jr Cls; VP NHS; Acadmc Dcthln; Teenwork 89; CSF; Elec Engrng.

MEYLOR, HEATHER A; La Quinta HS; Westminster, CA; (3); 27/333; Treas Jr Cls; Var Fld Hcky; Vllybl; High Hon Roll; NHS; Atten Southern CA Yth Ctznshp Smnr; CSF; Rcvd Xerox Awd.

MEZA, DIANA; Glen A Wilson HS; Hacienda Hts, CA; (1); Church Yth Grp; French Clb; Band; Mrchg Band; Pep Band; Variety Show; JV Cheerldng; Prfct Atten Awd; Pediatrics.

MEZA, FERNANDO L; Bishop Amat Memorial HS; La Puente, CA; (4); 40/400; Church Yth Grp; Crs Cntry; Trk; Wt Lftg; NHS; Latin Amer Stu Orgnztn Pres; CSF; Spcl Olympcs Vlntr; Lbrl Stds.

MEZA, GILBERT; Cantwell HS; Rosemead, CA; (3); Letterman Clb; Science Clb; Varsity Clb; JV Var Bsbl; JV Var Crs Cntry; JV Trk; Hon Roll; Chess Clb; Bus.

MEZA, JAVIER; Dos Palos Brancos HS; Dos Palos, CA; (2); Computer Clb; Office Aide; Spanish Clb; Crs Cntry; Ftbl; Mgr(s); Trk; Wt Lftg; Wrstlng; Prfct Atten Awd; Law Enfrcmnt.

MEZA, JOEL A; Indio HS; Indio, CA; (3); 51/443; Var Socr; Var Tennis; Hon Roll; Prfct Atten Awd; Palm Desert Coll.

MEZA, LUIS B; Canoga Park HS; Canoga Park, CA; (1); JV Bsbl; JV Ftbl; JV Wrstlng; Prfct Atten Awd; UCLA; Engr.

MEZA, MARCIE; Calexico HS; Calexico, CA; (3); FBLA; Math Tm; Teachers Aide; Stu Mnth Accntng Bus Dept; 89 Goldn St Exm Geom W/Hnrs; Kelsey Jenny; Bus.

MEZA, MARIO L; Bishop Amat HS; La Puente, CA; (3); Letterman Clb; School Play; Var L Trk; Hon Roll; Natl Spnsh Exam; Latin Am Stud Organ; Tutor; Law Enfrcmnt.

MEZA, PATRICIA; Saint Genevieve HS; Arleta, CA; (3); Church Yth Grp; Cmnty Wkr; Dance Clb; Debate Tm; Drama Clb; Model UN; Pep Clb; Spanish Clb; SADD; Teachers Aide; Taekwondo; UCLA; Dentstry.

MEZA, ROSA E; Academy Of Our Lady Of Peace; San Diego, CA; (2); Church Yth Grp; Cmnty Wkr; Spanish Clb; Church Choir; Stu Cncl; Hon Roll; Spcl Rcgtn Excllnc In Astronomy; Spcl Hnr Old Testament, Frnch II & Intro Phys Sci; USD; Arch.

MEZA, ROZANNA L; Montgomery HS; San Diego, CA; (3); Yrbk; Mgr(s); Var Co-Capt Trk; Aztec Lg; San Diego Tribunes All Acad Tms; Most Inspirational Track; U San Diego; Bus.

MEZA, SUSY; Calexico HS; Calexico, CA; (3); Am Leg Aux Girls St; Rep Church Yth Grp; VP Pres Key Clb; Math Tm; Service Clb; Rep Frsh Cls; Stu Cncl; Var Cheerldng; Powder Puff Ftbl; Trk; HOBY Fndtn Awd.

MEZA, VICTOR M; Fontana HS; Fontana, CA; (2); Wt Lftg; Hon Roll; Pres Acad Fit Awd; Constrctn Engrng.

MEZACK, ERIK P; Norco SR HS; Norco, CA; (2); Church Yth Grp; Model UN; Var Swmmng; Hon Roll; Vrsty Swmmng Coaches Awd; Prncpls Awd Mnth Feb; Mtn Vw Acad All Leag Tm; Open Water Scuba Cert; UC Davis; Vet Med.

MEZACK, PAUL S; Norco HS; Norco, CA; (4); Church Yth Grp; Computer Clb; Math Clb; Science Clb; SADD; Acpl Chr; Chorus; Church Choir; Stage Crew; St Schlr; CA Poly Pomona; Engr.

MEZHISKY, JULIA; Brea-Olinda HS; Brea, CA; (2); 17/344; Dance Clb; Drama Clb; Speech Tm; School Play; Jr NHS; Law.

MEZQUITA, EDUARDO M; St Genevieve HS; Sepulveda, CA; (2); Temple Yth Grp; Variety Show; JV Ftbl; Hon Roll; Arch.

MEZULIS, AMY H; Santa Rosa HS; Santa Rosa, CA; (4); 1/500; Cmnty Wkr; Treas Drama Clb; VP JA; VP Service Clb; Pres SADD; L Var Swmmng; L Var Tennis; Cit Awd; High Hon Roll; Masonic Awd; Peer Cnslng; Harvard; Pre-Med.

MGUYEN, DAI P; San Bernardino HS; San Bernardino, CA; (2); German Clb; Math Clb; UCLA; Med.

MIANA, EMANUEL; Granger JR HS; National, CA; (1); 4/268; Nwsp; Yrbk; JV Vllybl; High Hon Roll; Hon Roll; Prfct Atten Awd; ASB Rep; AIA Rep; Books/Beyond; ASU; Psycht.

MIANI, SHANNON M; Palmdale HS; Palmdale, CA; (2); 29/813; Church Yth Grp; Chorus; Rep Stu Cncl; JV Mgr(s); Hon Roll; UCLA; Law.

MIAO, CHENG L; Clovis West HS; Fresno, CA; (1); Boy Scts; Church Yth Grp; FBLA; Math Clb; Math Tm; High Hon Roll; Eng.

MIAO, ED; Fairfield HS; Fairfield, CA; (4); 3/550; Pres German Clb; Pres Science Clb; Band; Mrchg Band; Rep Sr Cls; Stu Cncl; Crs Cntry; Trk; VP NHS; Intramrl Vllybl; Acad Decathln; UC Davis; Genetics.

MIAO, SHELLY H; La Sierra Academy Of SDA; Riverside, CA; (2); Spanish Clb; Teachers Aide; Cit Awd; Hon Roll; NHS; Harvard; Law.

MICANEK, RICHARD J; Alhambra HS; Martinez, CA; (3); 9/214; Boy Scts; Band; Stu Cncl; L Ftbl; L Trk; High Hon Roll; Hon Roll; Rotary Awd; Stanford; Physics.

MICHAEL, CORRINA E; Las Plumas HS; Oroville, CA; (3); 6/120; Dance Clb; Science Clb; JV Tennis; Cit Awd; High Hon Roll; Prfct Atten Awd; Cultural Club Pres; Fri Night Live; Bus.

MICHAEL, ERIK E; Downey HS; Downey, CA; (3); Library Aide; Science Clb; Ski Clb; Ftbl; Vllybl; Yng Astronauts; Clb Vllybl; Rookie Of Yr Vllybl; Hstry.

MICHAEL, STEVEN J; Thousand Oaks HS; Thousand Oaks, CA; (3); Math Clb; Math Tm; NFL; Science Clb; Spanish Clb; Treas Speech Tm; Ntl Merit Ltr; Acad Decthln Tm 89-90; CSF 87-90.

MICHAEL, YUKIKO; Convent Of The Sacred Heart; San Francisco, CA; (4); Drama Clb; Mgr(s); Pres Socr; Ntl Merit Ltr; Crw; Hspnc Schlrshp Semi-Fnlst.

MICHAELIS, MICHELLE LYNN; Pioneer HS; San Jose, CA; (4); 23/268; French Clb; Spanish Clb; Teachers Aide; Var Crs Cntry; Var Trk; Hon Roll; Pres Acad Fit Awd; Amnesty Intl; Earth Day Clb; Honorary Serv Awd; U Of OR; Psych.

MICHAELS, PHILIP E; San Ramon Valley HS; Danville, CA; (4); 9/402; Am Leg Boys St; Church Yth Grp; FBLA; Key Clb; Speech Tm; Teachers Aide; School Musical; School Play; Variety Show; Nwsp; CSF; Bsktbl Announcer; Acad Decathalon; U CA San Diego; Jrnlsm.

MICHAELS, RENEE C; J C Fremont HS; Los Angeles, CA; (4); Art Clb; Church Yth Grp; Dance Clb; Office Aide; Teachers Aide; Chorus; Church Choir; Rptr Nwsp; Sec Jr Cls; Stu Cncl; El Camino Coll; Law.

MICHAELS, SHELLY L; Castle Park HS; Chula Vista, CA; (2); Drill Tm; Pres Frsh Cls; Pres Soph Cls; Pres Jr Cls; JV VP Cheerldng; Girls Lg; UCLA; Lawyer.

MICHAELS, STEPHANIE; Los Alamitos HS; Los Alamitos, CA; (3); Spanish Clb; SADD; Temple Yth Grp; Varsity Clb; Var L Swmmng; Hon Roll; NHS; St Schlr.

MICHAELSEN, ERIK N; Montgomery HS; Santa Rosa, CA; (2); Cmnty Wkr; French Clb; JA; Band; Trk; Cit Awd; High Hon Roll; Jr NHS; NHS; Hstry.

MICHAELSON, DELHA S; Anacapa HS; Santa Barbara, CA; (1); Church Yth Grp; Cmnty Wkr; Coordinator Yth Cnfrnce Unitarian Unvrslst Pacfc Sthwst Dstrct Mini-Cnfrnce 70 Yth.

MICHALAK, MELISSA L; Santa Clara HS; Santa Clara, CA; (3); Church Yth Grp; Chorus; Church Choir; Mrchg Band; Variety Show; Score Keeper; Hon Roll; Stu Imprvmnt Prgrm Awd Music; Engl.

MICHALESKI, REBECCA A; El Camino Fundamental HS; Carmichael, CA; (4); Church Yth Grp; Key Clb; Spanish Clb; Teachers Aide; Chorus; Church Choir; NHS; Pres Acad Fit Awd; El Camino Bus Awd; Stu Of Mnth Bus Accmplshmnts; Amer River CC; Acctng.

MICHALIK, DAVID EDWARD; Mater Dei HS; Newport Beach, CA; (3); Church Yth Grp; German Clb; Latin Clb; Spanish Clb; Rep Sr Cls; Var Swmmng; Hon Roll; NHS; CSF 89-90; UC-BERKELEY; Med.

MICHALOPOULOS, CHLOE; El Dorado HS; Placentia, CA; (2); Drama Clb; Intnl Clb; Science Clb; School Play; Swmmng; High Hon Roll; NHS; Acad Decthln Tm; Mck Trl Tm; Invlmnt Poltcl Cmpgns; Med.

MICHALSKI, TOM P; Ontario HS; Ontario, CA; (2); Chess Clb; Spanish Clb; JV Ftbl; Var Socr; Gov Hon Prg Awd; Hon Roll; Prfct Atten Awd; Bst Soph Comp Applctns Stu Awd; USC; Comp Engrng.

MICHALSKI, TONY P; Huntington Beach HS; Huntington Beach, CA; (3); Hon Roll; UCLA; Med.

MICHAUD, CATHERINE M; Raney JR HS; Corona, CA; (1); 173/475; Church Yth Grp; Chorus; Variety Show; CA ST Fullerton; Prof Singer.

MICHAUD, KELLY M; Atascadero HS; Atascadero, CA; (2); Church Yth Grp; SADD; Tennis; Hon Roll; Pres Acad Fit Awd; Piano, Karate; Bus.

MICHAUD, MIKE B; Oak Park HS; Agoura Hills, CA; (2); 15/115; JV Bsbl; Var L Socr; Hon Roll.

MICHEL, ALI; Capital Christian HS; Gold River, CA; (1); Church Yth Grp; Sec Frsh Cls; JV Cheerldng; Var Tennis.

MICHEL, ARTHUR J; Vista HS; Vista, CA; (4); 22/445; Ed Church Yth Grp; Science Clb; Service Clb; Ski Clb; Spanish Clb; Teachers Aide; Stage Crew; Natl Hspnc Schlr Awds Semi Fnlst; U Of CA; Engr.

MICHEL, CYNTHIA; Center HS; North Highlands, CA; (1); 1/241; Drama Clb; Stage Crew; High Hon Roll; CSF; Ped.

MICHEL, MONIQUE; Sacred Heart Of Mary HS; Pico Rivera, CA; (3); Aud/Vis; Church Yth Grp; Cmnty Wkr; Dance Clb; Girl Scts; JA; Office Aide; SADD; Varsity Clb; School Musical; Ballet; UC Santa Cruz; Psych.

MICHELENA, MAGDALEN; Central Catholic HS; Patterson, CA; (4); 2/75; Treas Art Clb; Key Clb; VP Soph Cls; Treas Stu Cncl; Var Capt Socr; Var Sftbl; Pres Acad Fit Awd; Sal; Outstndng Schlr Athlete Awd; Camp Royal; Decathln Team; Modesto JC; Liberal Arts.

MICHELETTI, JESSICA; Pacific Grove HS; Pacific Grove, CA; (3); Church Yth Grp; Var Cheerldng; Hon Roll; Pres Acad Fit Awd; SDSU; Bus.

MICHELI, CORINNE L; Clovis HS; Clovis, CA; (1); Spanish Clb; SADD; High Hon Roll; CA Schlstc Fdrtn; Friday Night Live; CA St U Fresno; Zoolgy.

MICHELLI, MARIAH; Capistrano Valley Christian HS; San Jn Capistrano, CA; (1); Church Yth Grp; Dance Clb; Pep Clb; JV Cheerldng; Gym; Dscplshp; Wrshp Tm; Pryr Grp; Lawyer.

MICHELS, JESSICA L; Hanford Union HS; Westwood, CA; (2); Drama Clb; Chorus; Var Crs Cntry; Var Trk; Hon Roll; Vrsty Ltr Crs Cntry Trphy Mst Imprvd; Vrsty Ltr Track Trphy Mst Outstndng Middle Distance; Sci.

MICHELS, JOHN L; Servite HS; Fountain Valley, CA; (3); Church Yth Grp; Cmnty Wkr; Debate Tm; Service Clb; SADD; Rptr Yrbk; Lit Mag; Rep Stu Cncl; JV Socr; High Hon Roll; Teen Vlntr Fntn Vly Pblc Lbry 88; Vlntr Stff Mem Assoc Catholic Stu Cncls 87; CA Schlrshp Fed; Pre-Law Bus Admin.

MICHELSON, JULIE A; Fountain Valley HS; Fountain Valley, CA; (1); Key Clb; CSF; PALS Clb; Sign Lang Clb; UCLA.

MICHELSON, KERITH; La Jolla Country Day Schl; La Jolla, CA; (4); 1/52; VP Sec Key Clb; Acpl Chr; School Musical; School Play; Lit Mag; Sec Frsh Cls; Var Cheerldng; French Hon Soc; Cum Laude Hnr Soc; Vlntr At La Casa De Los Pobres Tijuana Mx; 3rd & 4th Pls Natl Frnch Exam; Phy.

MICHELSTEIN, RUTH A; Louisville HS; Tarzana, CA; (1); Church Yth Grp; Drama Clb; High Hon Roll; CA Schlrshp Fed; UCLA; Phy.

MICHNO, JEAN; South San Francisco HS; S San Francisco, CA; (4); Church Yth Grp; Red Cross Aide; Sacramento Spon Capitol Focus Trip; Cities Prspctvs Mem; Sierra Mtns Camp Trip 1 Wk; San Mateo Coll; Arch.

MICKEL, DREW W; Piedmont HS; Piedmont, CA; (4); French Clb; School Musical; Stu Cncl; Var Ftbl; Var Golf; Var Capt Socr; Var Tennis; Pres Acad Fit Awd; CA Schlrshp Fed 100% Member; CA Interschlstc Fed Top Ten Male Schlr/Athl; SADD Pres; Princeton.

MICKELSON-REAY, ALEXIS H; Sacramento HS; Sacramento, CA; (1); 84/683; Drama Clb; Band; Mrchg Band; Pep Band; School Play; Hon Roll; Braggin Dragon; Vsl/Prfrmng Arts Centre; Sutter Gen Hsptl Axlry Vlntr; Tradtnl Jazz Soc Vlntr; Drama.

MICKLE, SCOTT; Mission Bay HS; San Diego, CA; (2); Band; Jazz Band; Pep Band; JV Wrstlng; Prfct Atten Awd; Christ Lutheran Chrch; Cyclst Clb; 1st & 3rd Awds Arch Del Mar Fr 89 & 90; North TX ST; Arch.

MICKLE, STACY C; Willits HS; Willits, CA; (4); 7/116; Math Tm; SADD; Teachers Aide; VICA; Band; Chorus; Jazz Band; Orch; School Musical; Sec Sr Cls; Pr Cnslng; Big Brothers/Big Sisters; UC Davis.

MICKLIN, MISTI M; Selma HS; Selma, CA; (3); 18/211; Cmnty Wkr; Pep Clb; SADD; Chorus; Stu Cncl; JV Cheerldng; Var Pom Pon; High Hon Roll; Chrldng Awds-Mst Imprvd, Mst Vlubl, Coach 87-88, 88-89, 89-90.

MICUCCI, BONNIE; North Torrance HS; Torrance, CA; (2); 131/410; Church Yth Grp; Drill Tm; Cit Awd; Hon Roll; SDSU; Bus.

MIDDLEDITCH, ANDREW J; University HS; Irvine, CA; (3); 19/550; JCL; JV Socr; Var Trk; High Hon Roll; Spanish NHS; STAAND; Natl Latin Hnr Soc; UC Santa Barbara Coll Creative Stds Math Exam; Bio Sci.

MIDDLETON, BILL M; Santa Rosa HS; Santa Rosa, CA; (3); Church Yth Grp; Teachers Aide; Wrstlng; Cit Awd; High Hon Roll; Hon Roll; Santa Rosa JC; Law Enfrcmnt.

MIDDLETON, KATHY M; Colton HS; Grand Terrace, CA; (4); Church Yth Grp; FHA; Girl Scts; SADD; Teachers Aide; Church Choir; Cit Awd; Hon Roll; NEC; Acctnt.

MIDDLETON, KEITA T; Mater Dei HS; Huntington Beach, CA; (1); Church Yth Grp; Band; Mrchg Band; Pep Band; Trk; Harvard Law Schl; Law.

MIDGLEY, ANDREW R; El Camino HS; Carmichael, CA; (3); 17/366; Aud/Vis; Boy Scts; German Clb; Ski Clb; VP L Swmmng; Pres Acad Fit Awd; Varsity Letter Water Polo; Wilderness Club Team Leader; Eagle Scout; Pre-Med.

MIDGLEY, MICHELLE L; Gahr HS; Norwalk, CA; (1); Pres Church Yth Grp; Drama Clb; School Play; High Hon Roll; Opt Clb Awd; CSU Long Beach.

MIEDEMA, RYAN M; Valley View HS; Moreno Valley, CA; (1); Band; Bsbl; JV Ftbl; Wt Lftg; High Hon Roll; Sci.

MIEKE, TANIA S; Mission Viejo HS; Mission Viejo, CA; (1); 1/455; Model UN; Hon Roll; Ind Study Sprt Equestrn Jmpng & Showng; Spk Fr, Ger, Span; Top Percntl Natl Ger Exam; Med.

MIEL, ELIZABETH E; Palmdale HS; Palmdale, CA; (2); Spanish Clb; Red Cross Aide; School Play; Nwsp; Sec Frsh Cls; JV Var Vllybl; Cit Awd; High Hon Roll; Hon Roll; Prfct Atten Awd; CJSF-CSF; AADAP; APC; Mdcl.

MIERNIK, PAUL J; La Sierra HS; Riverside, CA; (1); Intrml Socr; JV Tennis; High Hon Roll; Drftng.

MIGNANO, JOE J; Ygnacio Valley HS; Concord, CA; (3); Boy Scts; Church Choir; HS Achvt Awd; Cal ST Hayward.

MIGUEL, JENNIFER C; Caruthers Union HS; Fresno, CA; (4); Computer Clb; FBLA; Library Aide; Yrbk; Mgr Bsktbl; Stat Sftbl; Hon Roll; Pres Acad Fit Awd; Ftbl Hmcmng Qn 89; Fresno City Coll; Bio.

MIGUEL, RANDY R; Bellarmine Coll Prep; San Jose, CA; (3); Church Yth Grp; Cmnty Wkr; Service Clb; Varsity Clb; Intrml Bsbl; Intrml Bsktbl; Intrml Ftbl; Intrml Trk; Wt Lftg; Var Wrstlng; Dsc Jcky; Sprts Car Drvng; Mbr Blck B Bellarmine Stu; Acad Stndng; UC Berkeley; Engnrng.

MIHAILOFF, LAURA; Lowell HS; San Francisco, CA; (4); 68/626; French Clb; GAA; Pres JA; Elks Awd; Pres Acad Fit Awd; CSF; Gldn St Hnrs Awd; Hnr Soc; UC Berkeley; Hstry.

MIHALKO, KRISTIN S; Lowell HS; San Francisco, CA; (2); French Clb; SADD; Variety Show; Off Frsh Cls; Rep Soph Cls; Gym; Vlntr At Explorotorium; Advntr Clb.

MIHOK, ALISON L; Central Catholic HS; Oakdale, CA; (1); 7/75; Art Clb; Church Yth Grp; Debate Tm; Key Clb; Science Clb; School Play; Sftbl; High Hon Roll; Piano Plyng; Dance; UC Santa Cruz; Spanish.

MIHRAM, KELLY C; Lutheran HS; Anaheim, CA; (2); Church Yth Grp; Thesps; Band; Pep Band; School Musical; School Play; Phtg Yrbk; JV Capt Cheerldng; Trk; Certfd Scuba Divr.

MIJARES, GEANNINE; Christian Ctr; Pittsburg, CA; (1); 2/16; Church Yth Grp; Drama Clb; Letterman Clb; Chorus; Church Choir; School Play; Variety Show; JV Bsbl; JV Cheerldng; Hon Roll; Hmcmng Princess; Bethany Bible Coll; Drama.

MIKA, SUZANNE; Seaside HS; Ft Ord, CA; (3); French Clb; Speech Tm; Teachers Aide; Church Choir; School Musical; School Play; High Hon Roll; Hon Roll; Monterey Bay Opera Soc; U Of TX; Child Psych.

MIKE, KEISHA L; Garey HS; Phillips Ranch, CA; (4); 3/292; Church Yth Grp; Cmnty Wkr; Hosp Aide; Service Clb; Band; Mrchg Band; Cit Awd; Hon Roll; VP NHS; CA Schltc Fed Pres 86-90; Math, Engrng, Sci Achvt Club MESA; Stu Frgn Exch Club; U SCA; Biochem.

MIKELS, JEFF; Apple Valley Christian Schl; Victorville, CA; (1); Church Yth Grp; Pres Frsh Cls; Rep Stu Cncl; L Bsbl; L Bsktbl; L Vllybl; High Hon Roll; Prfct Atten Awd; Chrch Mnstr.

MIKELS, JODI; Apple Valley Christian Schl; Victorville, CA; (4); 1/15; Church Yth Grp; School Musical; School Play; Yrbk; Treas Jr Cls; Sec Stu Cncl; Capt Bsktbl; Capt Cheerldng; L Vllybl; Val.

MIKHAIL, MAGED S; Nogales HS; West Covina, CA; (2); Church Yth Grp; German Clb; Bsktbl; High Hon Roll; CSF; Chrch Plays; Med.

MIKI, JENNIFER S; Schurr HS; Los Angeles, CA; (4); 61/220; Teachers Aide; Mgr Band; Mrchg Band; Pep Band; Ed Yrbk; Hon Roll; CSF; Rgnl Occptnl Prog Flrstry Cls; Intr Dsgn.

MIKITA, LIZ; Salinas HS; Salinas, CA; (3); Scl Work.

MIKLUSAK, COURTNEY R; Flintridge Prep; La Canada Flintri, CA; (3); French Clb; Key Clb; Math Clb; Mgr Bsktbl; JV Var Swmmng; High Hon Roll; Hon Roll; NHS; 8 Hnrs/AP Crses; Vlntr Wrker Absd Chldrn; Bus.

MIKULA, MICHAEL W; Ocean View HS; Huntington Beach, CA; (1); Band; Jazz Band; Mrchg Band; Outstndng FRSHMN Band Jazz & Mrchng; Coach Awd Bowlng & Cert & Awds; Yth Mnstry.

MIKULASEK, LAURIE; Livermore HS; Livermore, CA; (3); Church Yth Grp; 4-H; Hosp Aide; Stage Crew; 4-H Awd; High Hon Roll; Hon Roll; 2 1st Pl & 1 3rd Pl Artwork Alemeda Cnty Fr; Animal Rights Rep 89 Lawrence Hall Sci Sympsm; Professor Of Philosphy.

MIKULSKI, CHRISTINA; Don Lugo HS; Chino Hills, CA; (4); Dance Clb; Ski Clb; Drill Tm; Yrbk; JV Cheerldng; JV Socr; Hon Roll; NHS; FIDM Fshn Insti; Intr Dsgnr.

MILANEY, JENNIFER M; Louisville HS; Westlake, CA; (3); 13/64; FHA; Hosp Aide; Hon Roll; French II And III Awds; Mem Of Ca Schlshp Fedrtn; Medical Doc.

MILANEY, KIRSTEN A; Louisville HS; Westlake, CA; (3); 17/69; CSF; Vet.

MILANO, CHANTAL; Rim Of The World Ca; Running Springs, CA; (1); Teachers Aide; Drill Tm; Police Force.

MILAS, NICOLE C; Pacifica HS; Garden Grove, CA; (1); Computer Clb; Band; Mrchg Band; Orch; Pep Band; Hon Roll; CSF; Ecology Clb; Chem.

MILAZZO, JENNIFER I; Louisville HS; Reseda, CA; (3); 6/67; Church Yth Grp; Cmnty Wkr; FHA; GAA; Chorus; School Musical; School Play; JV Trk; High Hon Roll; Hon Roll; CSF; Emmaus Rtrt; Loyola Marymount U.

MILES, ANGELA; Providence HS; Sherman Oaks, CA; (3); GAA; Letterman Clb; Pep Clb; Ski Clb; Varsity Clb; Chorus; Var Capt Cheerldng; Sftbl; CA ST Northridge; Elem Educ.

MILES, BRADLEY E; Fremont Christian HS; Fremont, CA; (2); ROTC; Varsity Clb; Socr; Tennis; Hon Roll; Engrng.

MILES, HEATHER; Aptos HS; Aptos, CA; (3); Church Yth Grp; Speech Tm; School Musical; School Play; Stu Cncl; Var Pom Pon; High Hon Roll; Ntl Merit SF; Am Leg Aux Girls St; JV Bsktbl; Cngrss-Bundestag Schlrshp; Smith Bk Awd.

MILES, HEATHER J; San Diego HS; San Diego, CA; (3); Church Yth Grp; Drama Clb; Hosp Aide; Intnl Clb; Key Clb; Science Clb; Thesps; Varsity Clb; School Musical; School Play; Traveled To Russia 90; U CA Los Angeles; Drama.

MILES, ROSE OF SHARON; Grant SR HS; Sacramento, CA; (3); Church Yth Grp; Computer Clb; Debate Tm; Drama Clb; English Clb; German Clb; Math Clb; Math Tm; Office Aide; Pep Clb; African Amer Club VP; Gospel Choir Pres & VP; Berkley U; Pathlgy.

MILES, SARA S; Acalanes HS; Lafayette, CA; (3); Church Yth Grp; French Clb; GAA; Girl Scts; Hosp Aide; Service Clb; Teachers Aide; Varsity Clb; Ed Nwsp; Var Crs Cntry; Sftbl Vrsty Coachs Awd, Mst Vlble; Crs Cntry Mst Imprvd; Vlybl Coaches Awd.

MILES, SHAWNDRA; Crenshaw HS; Los Angeles, CA; (4); 20/300; Cmnty Wkr; Girl Scts; Office Aide; Drill Tm; Sec Sr Cls; Hon Roll; Pres Acad Fit Awd; Ephebian Soc; Yng Blck Schlr; Kngths/Ladies; U CA Santa Barbara; Law.

MILES, TEREESA L; Turlock HS; Turlock, CA; (3); 20/550; Church Yth Grp; Drama Clb; Key Clb; NFL; Speech Tm; Stat Bsktbl; Score Keeper; Stat Socr; Var Trk; Stat Vllybl; Bus Admin.

MILES, VANISHA; Fontana HS; Fontana, CA; (2); #11 In Class; GAA; Office Aide; Chorus; Bsktbl; Tennis; Trk; Pediatrics.

MILEY, THOMAS J; Servite HS; Cypress, CA; (3); 2/170; Lit Mag; JV Ftbl; JV Golf; JV Trk; Ntl Merit SF; Jr Statesmen Of Am; CSF; NHS.

MILFORD, JOHN; Novato HS; Novato, CA; (3); Latin Clb; Hon Roll; Pres Acad Fit Awd; Cum Laude Awd Ntl Latin Ex 89; Mech Engr.

MILGRAM, JOHN; Clovis West HS; Fresno, CA; (4); 61/530; Aud/Vis; Pres Treas Chess Clb; FBLA; Math Clb; Math Tm; Science Clb; Rep Stu Cncl; Wt Lftg; High Hon Roll; Hon Roll; Sci Olympiad Wnnr 1st Pl 88-90; Golden St Exam Awd Of Excllnc Geom 88; Fresno Fair 1st & 2nd Art Show; Northwestern U; Biochem.

MILICI, ANGELA M; Norco HS; Norco, CA; (3); 1/400; Art Clb; Hosp Aide; Model UN; JV Swmmng; Cit Awd; High Hon Roll; Pres Acad Fit Awd; Var Mck Trl; CSF; Acad Dcthln; Med.

MILINIC, MARA T; Pioneer HS; San Jose, CA; (2); Drill Tm; Stat Bsktbl; JV Capt Vllybl; Hon Roll; Masonic Awd; Intl Order Jobs Daughters; 3 Yrs Line Officer; Piano 7 Yrs; Asst Coach 6th Gr Girls Bsktbl; Elementary Education.

MILLAR, ETHAN D; Bishop O'dowd HS; Oakland, CA; (3); 1/250; Art Clb; Teachers Aide; Nwsp; High Hon Roll; Hon Roll; Ntl Merit Ltr; Rotary Awd; Val; Schl Art Calendar Cont Wnnr; Engl Writing Awds; Harvard; Comp Sci.

MILLAR, JOSH V; Westlake HS; Thousand Oaks, CA; (2); 1/400; Stu Cncl; Var L Swmmng; High Hon Roll; Hon Roll; Jr Var Water Polo MVP; Var Swmg Most Imprvd; CSF Mem; Interact Club Mem; Twice Reflections Fnlst Music.

MILLARD, ANN M; Rio Linda SR HS; Rio Linda, CA; (1); Church Yth Grp; Girl Scts; Band; Church Choir; Mrchg Band; JV Bsktbl; JV Swmmng; JV Vllybl; Hon Roll; UC Berkeley; Engrng.

MILLARD, PAMELA D; Casa Roble Fundamental HS; Citrus Heights, CA; (4); 32/344; Church Yth Grp; Cmnty Wkr; SADD; Church Choir; Rep Frsh Cls; Pres Soph Cls; Off Sr Cls; VP Stu Cncl; Hon Roll; Campus Cleanup Cmmtte; Accrediation Cmmtte; Sierra CC; Music Technlgy.

MILLDRUM, ANDY J; Burney JR SR HS; Burney, CA; (1); Band; School Musical; Trk; Pres Acad Fit Awd; CA ST U; Life Sci.

MILLDRUM, BRITTANY H; Thomas Downey HS; Modesto, CA; (1); Church Yth Grp; Dance Clb; Teachers Aide; School Musical; Off Frsh Cls; Sec Treas Stu Cncl; CSF; Dance, Jazz, Ballet, Modern; Fresno U; Dancer.

MILLER, ADAM S; Acalanes HS; Lafayette, CA; (2); Spanish Clb; Rptr Nwsp; Pres Soph Cls; VP Jr Cls; Var Swmmng.

MILLER, ADRIENNE M; Arcadia HS; Arcadia, CA; (2); 25/599; Sec Church Yth Grp; Dance Clb; Hosp Aide; Ski Clb; Drill Tm; School Play; Yrbk; Sec Frsh Cls; Bsktbl; Sftbl; Assisteens; U C System.

MILLER, ALLISON S; Encinal HS; Alameda, CA; (3); 2/230; Church Yth Grp; Key Clb; Math Tm; School Musical; Ed Yrbk; Sec Soph Cls; Sec Jr Cls; Treas Stu Cncl; High Hon Roll; CSF Secy & Pres; Bdmntn Team Ltr; Mktng.

MILLER, AMY; Paso Robles HS; Paso Robles, CA; (3); 50/350; Teachers Aide; Drill Tm; Pep Band; Hon Roll; Acad Dcthln; Hstry Day; Dance Show.

MILLER, AMY E; Lee Vining HS; Lee Vining, CA; (3); 2/7; Am Leg Aux Girls St; School Play; Nwsp; Yrbk; Sec Stu Cncl; Var Cheerldng; Var Powder Puff Ftbl; Var Sftbl; Var Vllybl; Hon Roll; Audubon Soc Schlrshp Camp.

MILLER, ANDREA L; Whittier Christian HS; Whittier, CA; (2); Church Yth Grp; Bsktbl; Sftbl; Pres Church Yth Grp; Boston U; Psych.

MILLER, ANGEL M; Ganesha HS; Pomona, CA; (3); Pep Clb; JV Cheerldng; Hon Roll; Cal Poly Pomona; Psych.

MILLER, ANTHONY E; Gahr HS; Norwalk, CA; (2); Teachers Aide; Band; Color Guard; Mrchg Band; Bsktbl; JV Ftbl; Var Tennis; Wt Lftg; Hon Roll; USC; Music Ed.

MILLER, ARIA R; George Washington HS; San Francisco, CA; (3); Art Clb; Church Yth Grp; Cmnty Wkr; Dance Clb; Intnl Clb; JA; Office Aide; Red Cross Aide; Ski Clb; SADD; Chrch Yth Deacon.

MILLER, BECKY M; San Gabriel HS; San Gabriel, CA; (3); Sec Church Yth Grp; French Clb; Red Cross Aide; Science Clb; Varsity Clb; Church Choir; Rep Stu Cncl; Var L Bsktbl; Var L Sftbl; Hon Roll; Pnt Loma Nazarene Coll; Bio.

MILLER, BENJAMIN G; Modesto Christian HS; Modesto, CA; (3); Church Yth Grp; Letterman Clb; Scholastic Bowl; Teachers Aide; VP Jr Cls; Treas Stu Cncl; Bsbl; Crs Cntry; Ftbl; Trk; Arch.

MILLER, BENSON; Miramonte HS; Oakland, CA; (2); Boy Scts; Letterman Clb; VICA; JV Bsbl; JV Ftbl; Var L Wrstlng; Hon Roll; Pres Acad Fit Awd.

MILLER, BRENDAN; Clovis HS; Clovis, CA; (4); 30/536; Church Yth Grp; Computer Clb; FBLA; Math Clb; Math Tm; Science Clb; Band; Mrchg Band; JETS Awd; Ntl Merit Schol; Intl Sci & Engrng Fair 4th Pl; CA ST Polytech U; Cmptr Sci.

MILLER, BRIAN; Skyline HS; Oakland, CA; (3); Var L Socr; Hon Roll; All City Sccr Select Oakland; Olympic Dvlpmnt Tm; CA Yth Sccr Assn Dist 4; U Of CA; Engrng.

MILLER, BRIAN K; Sanger HS; Sanger, CA; (3); Ski Clb; Intrml Ftbl; Var L Socr; Trk; NHS; Gldn ST Math Schlr In Geo; Awd Acad Schvmnt; Fresno ST; Engr.

MILLER, CASSANDRA N; Tulare Western HS; Tulare, CA; (2); Church Yth Grp; Color Guard; Hon Roll; UCLA; Ed.

MILLER, CEDRIC; Mckinleyville HS; Arcata, CA; (4); 2/125; Am Leg Boys St; Pres Drama Clb; 4-H; School Musical; School Play; Ed Nwsp; Var L Wrstlng; Elks Awd; High Hon Roll; Lion Awd; U CA Santa Barbara; Engl.

MILLER, CHAD; Boron JR/Sr HS; Boron, CA; (3); 7/35; Math Tm; Varsity Clb; Yrbk; Var L Bsktbl; High Hon Roll; Hon Roll; NHS; CSF; Outstndng Yrbk Stu; Cal Poly San Luis Obispo; Engr.

MILLER, CHERI L; Newark Memorial HS; Newark, CA; (4); SADD; Teachers Aide; Ed Yrbk; Var JV Cheerldng; JV Gym; Hon Roll; Prfct Atten Awd; Schlrshp W Cst Tae Kwon Doe; Law.

MILLER, CHRIS M; Lakewood SR HS; Lakewood, CA; (4); 172/750; Var Capt Bsbl; High Hon Roll; Lion Awd; Prfct Atten Awd; Pres Acad Fit Awd; Loyola Marymount U; Bus.

MILLER, CHRISTAL; Riverbank HS; Oakdale, CA; (2); 1/200; Church Yth Grp; Hosp Aide; SADD; Band; Rep Frsh Cls; Sec Soph Cls; Cheerldng; Stat Ftbl; L Tennis; Vllybl; CSF CA Schlrshp Fdrtn; Air Force Acad; Med.

MILLER IV, CHRISTIAN J; Foothill HS; Pleasanton, CA; (4); Boy Scts; Drama Clb; FBLA; SADD; Stage Crew; Nwsp; Off Sr Cls; Rep Stu Cncl; Var Crs Cntry; Ntl Merit SF; Golden St Exam-High Hnrs; Sci Stu Of Mnth-Sci; Aerospc Engr.

MILLER, CHRISTOPHER A; Oakdale HS; Oakdale, CA; (3); French Clb; Crs Cntry; Trk; Rgnl Occptnl Pgm Cert Merit Comp; Hist.

MILLER, COLIN M; Aragon HS; Hillsborough, CA; (3); Var Gym; Var Capt Wrstlng; High Hon Roll; Pres Acad Fit Awd.

MILLER, CONNIE; Pacific Union College Prep Schl; Angwin, CA; (1); Office Aide; Band; Variety Show; Stu Cncl; Wmns Ensmble; Woodwind Quintet; Pacific Union Coll.

MILLER, DANIEL C; Imperial HS; Pasadena, CA; (3); Aud/Vis; Q&S; Chorus; Nwsp; Yrbk; VP Frsh Cls; VP Jr Cls; Cit Awd; Educ.

MILLER, DAVID S; West Covina HS; W Covina, CA; (4); Letterman Clb; Ski Clb; Teachers Aide; Varsity Clb; JV Socr; Capt Swmmng; High Hon Roll; Hon Roll; Acad Ltr; CSF; Swim Tm MVP; Cal Poly Pomona.

MILLER, DAWN M; Lone Pine HS; Lone Pine, CA; (4); French Clb; Rep Sr Cls; Rep Stu Cncl; Capt Sftbl; Hon Roll; Comp Tech Awd; Mst Imprvd Plyr; Comp Oper.

MILLER, EDI M; Roosevelt School Of The Arts; Fresno, CA; (2); Chorus; Mrchg Band; Orch; Stage Crew; Ed Yrbk; Pres Frsh Cls; Var Cheerldng; Cit Awd; Hon Roll; Friday Night Live; Fresno ST U; Law.

MILLER, EDWARD J; Servite HS; Buena Park, CA; (3); Debate Tm; Math Tm; Spanish Clb; Stu Cncl; DAR Awd; Hon Roll; NHS; Green Belt Karate; Jr Statesmn Of Amer; USD; Bus.

MILLER, ELENI K; John Burroughs HS; Burbank, CA; (3); Drama Clb; Office Aide; Teachers Aide; Chorus; School Musical; Nwsp; Yrbk; Treas Stu Cncl; Bsbl; Bsktbl.

MILLER, ERIC; Orosi HS; Cutler, CA; (3); French Clb; FFA; JV Ftbl; JV Trk; Wt Lftg; Hon Roll; Kings River JC; Criminology.

MILLER, ERIN D; Salinas HS; Salinas, CA; (3); Cmnty Wkr; Red Cross Aide; Sec Frsh Cls; Rep Soph Cls; Rep Jr Cls; Sec Sr Cls; Powder Puff Ftbl; Swmmng; Trk; High Hon Roll; Ldrshp Club; Hmcmng Cmmttee; Golden Buddies, Sr Citizen/Crippled Work; FNL Rep, Friday Night Live; UC Davis; Med.

MILLER, GRETCHEN H; El Cerrito HS; El Cerrito, CA; (4); Hon Roll; Karate 3 Yrs; Law Enfrcmnt Explr 1 Yr; CSF Life Time Mbr; Contra Costa Coll; Law Enfrcmnt.

MILLER, H PETER R; Dos Palos HS; Dos Palos, CA; (3); Am Leg Boys St; Boy Scts; Church Yth Grp; FBLA; Letterman Clb; Rep Jr Cls; JV Var Ftbl; Var Tennis; Pres Acad Fit Awd; Rotary Awd; Camp Royal Rtry Ldrshp Camp; 1st Pl Nrth Sequoia Leag Vrsty Tnns; Brigham Young U; Doctor.

MILLER, HEATHER; Yucaipa HS; Yucaipa, CA; (4); 30/294; Pres Church Yth Grp; Treas DECA; FHA; SADD; Teachers Aide; Flag Corp; DAR Awd; High Hon Roll; Rotary Awd; St Fnlst FHA-HERO Cmptn; 3rd Pl Orng Cnty Fair Voc Olympc Swng/Mdlng; CSF; Grad Hnrs; Ricks Coll; Fshn Dsgn.

MILLER, JAMES; Cajon HS; San Bernardino, CA; (3); 51/393; Hon Roll; CA Schlstc Fed; 222 Prgrm; CA-SOAP; Hstry.

MILLER, JANET; Hanford Joint Union HS; Hanford, CA; (2); Church Yth Grp; FHA; Chorus; Cit Awd; High Hon Roll; Early Outrch Prgm; Frgn Exchng; UC Irvine; Pediatrics.

MILLER, JASON B; River City HS; W Sacramento, CA; (2); Boy Scts; Chess Clb; High Hon Roll; Prfct Atten Awd; Upward Bound; Mech Engr.

MILLER, JASON D; Camarillo HS; Camarillo, CA; (3); Phtg Yrbk; Vllybl; Chem.

MILLER, JASON E; San Diego Acad; National City, CA; (3); 1/40; Church Yth Grp; Teachers Aide; Phtg Yrbk; Rep Jr Cls; High Hon Roll; Hon Roll; NHS; Yth Ambassador HUBY Fndtn; Jobs Wendys Hamb, Del Taco Fast Food Rest; Bus.

MILLER, JASON S; Portola JR-SR HS; Portola, CA; (2); Emblm For Good Grds; ROP Prgm; Comp Prgmng.

MILLER, JENNA N; Huntington Beach HS; Huntington Bch, CA; (4); 120/493; Model UN; Teachers Aide; Score Keeper; Hon Roll; Pres Acad Fit Awd; Tower Awds Engl 87, Hstry 88-89; Golden St Exam Academio Awd 86; OCC; Ed.

MILLER, JENNIFER; Faith Christian HS; Yuba City, CA; (3); Church Yth Grp; Yrbk; Rep Soph Cls; Sec Treas Stu Cncl; Hon Roll; Bethany Bible Coll; Chldrns Mns.

MILLER, JENNIFER; Woodbridge HS; Irvine, CA; (4); 81/391; Drama Clb; Ski Clb; Teachers Aide; Sftbl; Hon Roll; Pres Acad Fit Awd; San Diego ST U; Bus.

MILLER, JENNIFER A; Canyon Springs HS; Moreno Valley, CA; (4); 1/575; Mgr Cmnty Wkr; VP Math Clb; NFL; Ed Lit Mag; Rep Soph Cls; JV Vllybl; Sec Pres NHS; Val; Ckap US Acad Decathlon; Stu Model Cngrss Cmmtte Chair; CA Inst Of Tech; Appld Physics.

MILLER, JENNIFER C; Yteshiva University Of Los Angeles; Los Angeles, CA; (4); School Play; Nwsp; Ed Yrbk; Hon Roll; Ntl Merit SF; Pres Of Schl Spirit Cmmtte; VP Of Educ Jewish Yth Grp; Psych.

MILLER, JENNY; Rosary HS; Placentia, CA; (2); Cmnty Wkr; Service Clb; Stage Crew; Off Frsh Cls; JV Tennis; High Hon Roll; Hon Roll; Yorba Linda Rec Dept Vlntr; Jr Statesmn Of Amer; Cls Decthln Tm 90.

MILLER, JERRY L; Mat Carmel HS; San Diego, CA; (3); Church Yth Grp; SADD; Variety Show; Var Tennis; Var Wrstlng; Hon Roll; VP Jr NHS; Prfct Atten Awd; Class Senator; AZ ST U; Microbiologist.

MILLER II, JOHN RICHARD; Granada HS; Livermore, CA; (4); 18/300; Cmnty Wkr; Pres Science Clb; Service Clb; Spanish Clb; Orch; Rptr Nwsp; JV Var Swmmng; High Hon Roll; Hon Roll; Pres Acad Fit Awd; CSF Outstndng Mem; UC Davis; Bio Sci.

MILLER, JON C; Oakmont HS; Roseville, CA; (1); Boy Scts; Church Yth Grp; Debate Tm; Quiz Bowl; Spanish Clb; Speech Tm; Ftbl; Wt Lftg; BYU; Law.

MILLER, KARA R; Rim Of The World HS; Running Springs, CA; (1); Art Clb; Debate Tm; Drama Clb; Model UN; School Play; Rep Stu Cncl; JV Socr; Hon Roll; Ntl Merit Ltr; Pres Acad Fit Awd; Swm Tm.

MILLER, KAREN J; East Bakersfield HS; Bakersfield, CA; (2); French Clb; Band; Mrchg Band; Pep Band; Hon Roll; U Calif San Diego; Surgeon.

MILLER, KASHA M; Savanna HS; Anaheim, CA; (3); Am Leg Aux Girls St; Drama Clb; Hosp Aide; Teachers Aide; School Play; Nwsp; JV Var Powder Puff Ftbl; JV Sftbl; Var Trk; Wrstlng; Sftbl MVP 89; Accntng.

MILLER, KEITH L; Bella Vista HS; Fair Oaks, CA; (3); 18/363; Ski Clb; Spanish Clb; JV Bsktbl; JV Var Socr; Spanish NHS.

MILLER, KERI F; Mission Viejo HS; Mission Viejo, CA; (3); French Clb; Hosp Aide; Intnl Clb; Key Clb; CA St Schlrshp Fed 89-90; Spirit Of Diablos Awd 89.

MILLER, KIMBERLY; Del Campo HS; Carmichael, CA; (2); 7/460; Band; Mrchg Band; Pep Band; Fri Night Live.

MILLER, KIMBERLY D; Mt Whitney HS; Visalia, CA; (4); 63/336; Church Yth Grp; Sec Debate Tm; JCL; Pres Key Clb; Latin Clb; SADD; Church Choir; High Hon Roll; Brigham Young U.

MILLER, KIRSTEN; Foothill HS; Santa Ana, CA; (4); Pep Clb; Chorus; Rep Frsh Cls; Intrml JV Cheerldng; JV Swmmng; Hon Roll; Kids In Need; Safe Rides; Knight Singers; U Pacific; Elem Ed.

MILLER, KRISTEN; Clairemont HS; San Diego, CA; (2); Church Yth Grp; SADD; Teachers Aide; Yrbk; VP Frsh Cls; Treas Soph Cls; Sec Jr Cls; Hon Roll; CSF; BYU.

MILLER, KURTIS M; St Bernard HS; Los Angeles, CA; (3); Church Yth Grp; Varsity Clb; Orch; JV Var Bsbl; JV Var Ftbl; Cit Awd; Hon Roll; Deans Hnr Roll; Blck Cultural Awrnss Club; All Conf Plyr Ftbl 89-90; U Of S CA; Sports Med.

MILLER, LARA J; Sutter HS; Sutter, CA; (2); 1/75; Church Yth Grp; Band; Mrchg Band; Pep Band; School Play; Variety Show; Rep Soph Cls; Stat Bsktbl; Mgr(s); Score Keeper; CSF; Music.

MILLER, LISA; North Monterey County HS; Salinas, CA; (2); Ski Clb; SADD; Hon Roll.

MILLER, LISA M; Tehachapi HS; Tehachapi, CA; (4); Church Yth Grp; FHA; Teachers Aide; Chorus; Sftbl; High Hon Roll; Hon Roll; Prfct Atten Awd; CIF; Masters Coll; Elem Ed.

MILLER, LORI A; North HS; Bakersfield, CA; (2); Church Yth Grp; Cmnty Wkr; FCA; Teachers Aide; JV Bsktbl; Var L Crs Cntry; Var L Trk; Wt Lftg; Hon Roll; MVP Cross Cntry & Track; Gottschalks Hi-Debs; UC Irvine; Arch.

MILLER, LUCRETIA M; Nevada Union HS; Nevada City, CA; (3); Cmnty Wkr; Girl Scts; Teachers Aide; Pres Jr Cls; Rep Frsh Cls; JV Crs Cntry; Var Socr; Golden St Exam Hnrs Alg; Editor Video Magazine; Editor Video Yrbk; Work Deli & Caterer; Comm.

MILLER, LYNN K; Abraham Lincoln HS; San Francisco, CA; (3); GAA; Intnl Clb; Temple Yth Grp; Yrbk; Score Keeper; Trk; Hon Roll; Masonic Awd; Vrsty Fencing Team; Intlorder Of Jobs Daughter-Queen.

MILLER, MARC H; Fred C Beyer HS; Modesto, CA; (3); Hist 4-H; Cit Awd; 4-H Awd; High Hon Roll; HS Patriot Awd Exmplry Stu Sci Dept; Gldn St Math Ex Hnrs; Arch.

MILLER, MARK A; Paraclete HS; Leona Valley, CA; (3); Drama Clb; Key Clb; Letterman Clb; Ski Clb; Varsity Clb; Bsbl; Bsktbl; Golf; Socr; Hon Roll; Explorers Los Angeles Cnty Fire Dept; Fire Sci.

MILLER, MARY E; Foothill HS; Pleasanton, CA; (4); 102/300; Church Yth Grp; Cmnty Wkr; Debate Tm; Drama Clb; Service Clb; SADD; Thesps; School Play; Stage Crew; Yrbk; Congressional Yth Ldrshp Awd; Sr Princess Intl Order Of Jobs Dghtrs; Las Positas JC.

MILLER, MATTHEW J; Atwater HS; Winton, CA; (2); Church Yth Grp; Spanish Clb; Score Keeper; Wrstlng; Hon Roll; Teacher.

MILLER, MATTHEW K; Poway HS; Poway, CA; (3); Letterman Clb; Varsity Clb; Capt Var Lcrss; Swmmng; High Hon Roll; Jr NHS; A-Team; Peer Cnslng; CSF.

MILLER, MC KEENA; Cazadero Acad; Jenner, CA; (4); Art Clb; Cmnty Wkr; Dance Clb; Drama Clb; Ski Clb; Chorus; Drill Tm; School Musical; School Play; Variety Show; Art Awds; Interior Dsgn.

MILLER, MICHAEL; Biggs HS; Gridley, CA; (4); 2/50; Cmnty Wkr; Library Aide; Pep Clb; Pres Band; Jazz Band; Mrchg Band; Pep Band; Off Jr Cls; Off Sr Cls; VP Stu Cncl; Acad Dec; KCPM Chnnl 24 Bst & Brghtst; Butte Coll; Math.

MILLER, MICHAEL A; Monte Vista HS; Spring Valley, CA; (3); Aud/Vis; Drama Clb; Hist Thesps; Pres Chorus; School Musical; School Play; Stage Crew; Variety Show; Prfct Atten Awd; TV News Bulltn Dir 90; Outstndng Choral Awd 89-90; Grossmont Coll; Tlcmmnctn.

MILLER, MICHAEL A; Vanden HS; Vacaville, CA; (3); 45/175; Boy Scts; Church Yth Grp; Ski Clb; JV Ftbl; JV Tennis; Hon Roll; BYU; Aircraft.

MILLER, MICHAEL P; La Habra HS; La Habra, CA; (3); 9/400; Spanish Clb; Teachers Aide; Stu Cncl; Var Bsktbl; Var Ftbl; Powder Puff Ftbl; Var Trk; High Hon Roll; Great Books Club; Powder Puff Vlybl & Coach.

MILLER, MICHELLE E; La Reina HS; Thousand Oaks, CA; (3); Cmnty Wkr; GAA; Teachers Aide; Cit Awd; French Hon Soc; Hon Roll; Ntl Merit Schol; Amnesty Intl Treas Cntry Coord; Intl Equestrian League MVP; Davis.

MILLER, MICHELLE L; Valhalla HS; El Cajon, CA; (4); 116/412; Sftbl; Grossmont Coll; Math.

MILLER, NANCY; Soquel HS; Santa Cruz, CA; (2); Church Yth Grp; Cheerldng; Hon Roll; Intensive Engl Clss; Cal Poly; Bus.

MILLER, NATHAN H; Ramona HS; Ramona, CA; (3); 80/294; Boy Scts; VICA; Wrstlng; Eagle Scout; Natl Soc Sons Of Amer Revolution Achvt Awd; NRA Pro Marksman; USAF Acad; Pilot.

MILLER, PAMELA S; Paraclete HS; Lancaster, CA; (2); Cmnty Wkr; Drama Clb; Key Clb; Rep Frsh Cls; Sec Jr Cls; High Hon Roll; NHS; Stu Aginst Drunk Drvng; CSF; Z Clb; Stanford U; Sci.

MILLER, RHONDA; Christian HS; Santee, CA; (4); 8/98; Church Yth Grp; Girl Scts; Key Clb; Pep Clb; SADD; Teachers Aide; Band; Chorus; Capt Color Guard; Mrchg Band; San Diego ST; Educ.

MILLER, RICHARD E; Arroyo Grande HS; Grover City, CA; (2); Church Yth Grp; Dance Clb; Church Choir; JV Var Ftbl; JV Var Trk; JV Wrstlng; OK U; Anesthesiologist.

MILLER, ROBERT A; Owens Valley United HS; Independence, CA; (2); Boy Scts; Bsbl; Bsktbl; Ftbl; Mechanic.

MILLER, ROBERT D; San Pasqual Valley Inified HS; Winterhaven, CA; (2); 1/45; SADD; VP Frsh Cls; Stu Cncl; JV Var Bsktbl; High Hon Roll; Prfct Atten Awd; Friday Night Live; U Of Redlands.

MILLER, ROBIN C; Poway HS; Poway, CA; (3); Varsity Clb; Mgr Nwsp; Sftbl; Trk; Capt Sec Vllybl; Athlt Wk; CIF Vllybl; San Dego Tribune Achvt All Acadmc Team; Jrnlsm.

MILLER, ROBYN L; Hawthorne HS; Hawthorne, CA; (3); Sec Key Clb; Pep Clb; Ski Clb; Treas Frsh Cls; Treas Soph Cls; Hist Jr Cls; Rep Stu Cncl; Var Capt Cheerldng; 4-H Awd; High Hon Roll; Mem CA Schlrshp Fed; UC Santa Barbara; Elem Ed.

MILLER, RONDEE; Orange Glen HS; Escondido, CA; (2); JV Var Swmmng; Water Polo; Math Achvt Awd; Robotic.

MILLER, RYAN A; Santa Monica HS; Santa Monica, CA; (2); Teachers Aide; Rep Frsh Cls; Stu Cncl; Var Vllybl; Hon Roll; Pres Acad Fit Awd; Pres Schlr; Yth/Govt; Anti Grafitti Cmpgn.

MILLER, SABINA G; Rio Mesa HS; Camarillo, CA; (1); Drama Clb; School Play; Stage Crew; Swmmng; Writer.

MILLER, SARAH; San Clemente HS; San Clemente, CA; (4); Church Yth Grp; FBLA; VP Science Clb; JV Crs Cntry; JV Sftbl; Bausch & Lomb Sci Awd; High Hon Roll; NHS; Prfct Atten Awd; Val; Orange Co Jugglers Club; UC Berkeley; Chem.

MILLER, SARAH A; Nevada Union HS; Nevada City, CA; (3); JV Capt Bsktbl; Powder Puff Ftbl; JV Var Vllybl; Hon Roll; UCSB.

MILLER, SHANLEY R; Chino HS; Chino, CA; (2); FFA; Teachers Aide; Parliamentary Procedure Team Secy; Livestock Judging; Ag.

MILLER, SHANNON N; Whittier Christian HS; Chino, CA; (2); Church Yth Grp; Chorus; Church Choir; Treas Frsh Cls; Treas Soph Cls; Var Trk; JV Vllybl; Hon Roll; CA Schlrshp Fed; Amer Lit.

MILLER, SHAYLA; Canyon Springs HS; Moreno Vly, CA; (3); Church Yth Grp; Intnl Clb; Hon Roll; Teens Against Drugs Sec; Home Ec Awd; Animal Rights Clb; UC Riverside; Psych.

MILLER, SHELBI; Diamond Bar HS; Diamond Bar, CA; (3); 165/486; Church Yth Grp; SADD; Color Guard; High Hon Roll; Hon Roll; Sr Cls Cmmtte; Color Grd Actvy Dir; UCI; Pre-Med.

MILLER, SHELLEY A; Branham HS; San Jose, CA; (2); Art Clb; Girl Scts; Hon Roll; Sadd; Brwn Grl Scout Co-Ldr; Grnd Prz Rnr Up San Jose Mrcry Nws Dsgn An Ad Cnt; CA Schlrshp Fed; Sports Jrnlsm.

MILLER, SHEMIA M; Venice HS; Los Angeles, CA; (3); Office Aide; Wrtng Poetry & Stories; Blk Stu Union; Drwng Cartoon Chrctrs For Cmnty Clb; Law.

MILLER, STACY D; Antelope Valley HS; Lancaster, CA; (3); 5/631; Church Yth Grp; Cmnty Wkr; Math Clb; Math Tm; Quiz Bowl; Ski Clb; Spanish Clb; Var L Swmmng; High Hon Roll; Hon Roll; Swim Instr; Z-Club Pres; CSF Reporter Hstrn; Genetics.

MILLER, STEPHANIE; Casa Roble HS; Orangevale, CA; (2); Church Yth Grp; Spanish Clb; Church Choir; Drill Tm; Pres Rep Soph Cls; Stu Cncl; High Hon Roll; Friday Night Live; U Of CA; Brdcstg.

MILLER, STEPHANIE; Valley Christian HS; San Jose, CA; (3); Church Yth Grp; Cmnty Wkr; Hosp Aide; Chorus; Sec Frsh Cls; VP Soph Cls; Pres Jr Cls; Stat Bsktbl; Var Trk; JV Var Vllybl; All Leag Vllybl; Hnrbl Mntn All Leag Utility Plyr; JR Class Hall Prncs.

MILLER, STEPHANIE ANN; Modesto HS; Modesto, CA; (2); JV Var Sftbl; High Hon Roll; Hon Roll; CSF; Penn ST; Economics.

MILLER, STEPHANIE R; Live Oak HS; Morgan Hill, CA; (3); 7/530; FBLA; Hosp Aide; Band; Chorus; Jazz Band; Mrchg Band; Pep Band; Ed Lit Mag; High Hon Roll; Hon Roll; CSF Treas; Band & Color Grd; Supr Hosp Vol; UC Santa Barbara; Psych.

MILLER, STEVE K; Orange HS; Orange, CA; (3); Am Leg Boys St; Church Yth Grp; Cmnty Wkr; FCA; ROTC; Teachers Aide; Varsity Clb; Nwsp; Treas Sr Cls; Stu Cncl; Bio.

MILLER, STEVEN DALE; Kearny HS; San Diego, CA; (4); 1/320; Am Leg Boys St; Drama Clb; Letterman Clb; SADD; Teachers Aide; School Play; Stage Crew; Rptr Nwsp; Yrbk; Off Frsh Cls; Piano Cmptn/Cmpstn; UCSD; Bioengrng.

MILLER, SUSAN; East Union HS; Manteca, CA; (3); 9/315; French Clb; Hosp Aide; Science Clb; VP SADD; Thesps; School Play; Stage Crew; High Hon Roll; Jr NHS; Masonic Awd; Intl Ordr Rnbw Grls Chrty; Natl Yth Ldrshp Schlr; Stu Mth; Dominican Coll; Bhvr Pedtrcs.

MILLER, SUSAN; Willows HS; Willows, CA; (4); 5/112; Sec Church Yth Grp; FBLA; Key Clb; Letterman Clb; Office Aide; Sec Frsh Cls; Treas Soph Cls; Rep Jr Cls; Pres Sr Cls; Stat Bsbl; Div 4 St Champs Grls Bsktbll 88; CSF; Westmont Coll; Bus Admin.

MILLER, TANYA; Hueneme HS; Oxnard, CA; (2); Church Yth Grp; Drama Clb; SADD; School Play; Stage Crew; Wt Lftg; Law.

MILLER, TANYA; St Mary's Acad; Los Angeles, CA; (4); 4/84; Church Yth Grp; Girl Scts; Church Choir; School Musical; Powder Puff Ftbl; Hon Roll; NHS; Sal; Spanish NHS; Outstndng Afro-Amer UC Davis; Cal ST Northridge; Engrng.

MILLER, TIFFANY; Pomona Catholic HS; Montclair, CA; (4); Sec Stu Cncl; NHS; Bank Of Am Achvt Awd; Chapman Coll; Chld Psych.

MILLER, TIFFANY A; Del Campo HS; Citrus Heights, CA; (3); Church Yth Grp; Pep Clb; Ski Clb; Teachers Aide; Band; Mrchg Band; Pep Band; Socr; Wt Lftg; Girl Scts; Amer River.

MILLER, TINA L; Thomas Downey HS; Modesto, CA; (2); Church Yth Grp; Stat Bsktbl; Hon Roll; Friday Night Live; Galen Coll; Medcl Asst.

MILLER, TOM B; San Rafael HS; San Rafael, CA; (3); 14/225; Var Tennis; Hon Roll; Surfing.

MILLER, VERONICA N; Notre Dame HS; Salinas, CA; (4); Pep Clb; Hon Roll; NHS; US Hstry & Govt Awd.

MILLER, WENDY E; Santa Barbara HS; Santa Barbara, CA; (2); FTA; Acpl Chr; Band; Chorus; Mrchg Band; Orch; Pep Band; Violin, Alto Sax, Flute, Piano; Windsurfing; Acapella Choir, Madrigals; Phys Thrpy.

MILLER, WILLIAM L; Coast Joint Union HS; Cambria, CA; (3); 1/60; AFS; Am Leg Boys St; Boy Scts; Church Yth Grp; Spanish Clb; Ed Nwsp; Pres Sr Cls; Stat Bsktbl; Mgr(s); Score Keeper; Wghtlftng Mdl Clb; Cnty Wide Essy Cntst; Hnrs Glden ST Exm Geo Div; Fresno Sst U; Crmnlgy.

MILLET, KEVIN J; Apple Valley HS; Lucerne Valley, CA; (2); Ftbl; Hon Roll; Civil Engr.

MILLHEIM, KASEY P; Mariposa County HS; Mariposa, CA; (4); 19/103; Sec FBLA; Office Aide; Teachers Aide; Band; Chorus; Mrchg Band; Pep Band; Variety Show; Var Bsktbl; Var Vllybl; Bank Of Amer Awd Music; Conductors Awd Choir 89 90; Herman Saenger Memrl Music Schlrshp 90; Berklee Coll Of Music; Music.

MILLIGAN, CHRISTOPHER S; University City HS; San Diego, CA; (3); Var Socr; Var Vllybl; Ntl Merit Ltr; 2nd Pl Schl Lip Sync Contest; Commissioner Of Athltcs; Villa AAA Soccer Tm.

MILLIGAN, ELAINE J; Upland HS; Upland, CA; (2); Key Clb; Varsity Clb; Sec Frsh Cls; VP Soph Cls; Treas Jr Cls; Var Socr; Var Trk; High Hon Roll; Hon Roll; MIP Sccr Tm 89; MV Offnsv Plyr Sccr Tm 90; All Bsln Lg Sccr Tm 90; MV Trck 89.

MILLIGAN, JENNIFER; Gajon HS; San Bernardino, CA; (2); 46/595; VP Frsh Cls; Pres Soph Cls; Tennis; Treas NHS; Mock Trial Team, Bst Defns Attorney Awd; Tnns Singles Plyr; Stanford U; Law.

MILLIGAN, REGGIE; J E Mc Ateer HS; San Francisco, CA; (3); Aud/Vis; Computer Clb; Teachers Aide; Varsity Clb; Church Choir; Rptr Yrbk; JV Bsbl; JV Var Bsktbl; JV Var Mgr(s); JV Var Score Keeper; Brdcstng; Refering; Commnctns; UCSB; Coaching.

MILLIKAN, KEVIN R; Crescenta Valley HS; La Crescenta, CA; (2); Church Yth Grp; French Clb; Key Clb; Math Clb; Mu Alpha Theta; Stu Cncl; JV L Bsbl; L Bsktbl; JV L Vllybl; Sports Med.

MILLIKAN, MARCELLA A; St Joseph HS; Lakewood, CA; (3); 22/350; Church Yth Grp; Cmnty Wkr; Hosp Aide; Spanish Clb; High Hon Roll; Hon Roll; Alg & Frnch Awds; Untd Clrs St Joseph Clb; CA ST Long Beach; Nurse.

MILLIKEN, ALLISON C; Bella Vista HS; Fair Oaks, CA; (1); 24/500; Cit Awd; High Hon Roll; Friday Night Live.

MILLIKEN, TAWNY MARIE; La Serna HS; Whittier, CA; (4); 26/354; Church Yth Grp; Library Aide; Teachers Aide; Church Choir; Stage Crew; Hon Roll; NHS; CA Schlrshp Fed Life Mem; Prin List; Dstngshd Schlr; Biola U; Lbrl Stds.

MILLINGTON, KIMBERLY; Capistrano Valley HS; Mission Viejo, CA; (3); Science Clb; Var Sftbl; Hon Roll; CSF; Hstrcl Soc Actvts Chrprs; Achvt Awd.

MILLINGTON, PETER; Monroe HS; Panorama City, CA; (3); 10/23; Church Yth Grp; Jazz Band; School Play; Rep Frsh Cls; Rep Soph Cls; Rep Jr Cls; Var Bsktbl; Var Ftbl; Hon Roll; Engrng.

MILLION, BECKY; Mt Whitney HS; Visalia, CA; (4); 60/318; FBLA; Hosp Aide; Spanish Clb; SADD; Teachers Aide; Band; Jazz Band; JV Vllybl; Hon Roll; Pres Acad Fit Awd; CSF; Coll Of Sequoias; Art.

MILLIS, KURT E; Moorpark HS; Moorpark, CA; (4); Drama Clb; Letterman Clb; Rptr Phtg Nwsp; L JV Bsbl; Capt Var Ftbl; L Var Trk; Wrstlng; High Hon Roll; Hon Roll; Lion Awd; Moorpark JC; Med.

MILLNER, TONYA L; John W North HS; Riverside, CA; (1); Cmnty Wkr; Spanish Clb; Teachers Aide; High Hon Roll; Hon Roll; Golden St Exam Albegra I Awd; Teacher.

MILLS, ALEXANDER G; Servite HS; Westminster, CA; (3); Letterman Clb; Red Cross Aide; Varsity Clb; JV Bsktbl; Var Ftbl; OSC; Bus Mgmnt.

MILLS, AUDRA K; S C P A HS; San Diego, CA; (4); Church Yth Grp; Hosp Aide; Letterman Clb; Office Aide; SADD; Teachers Aide; Chorus; Church Choir; Cit Awd; High Hon Roll; Sec-CSF; Pt Loma Nazarene Coll; Music.

MILLS, CHRISTINE L; San Benito HS; Joplin, MO; (1); 38/200; Church Yth Grp; Mgr(s); Score Keeper; Trk; High Hon Roll; Pedtrcn.

MILLS, CLAIRE M; San Rafael HS; San Rafael, CA; (2); 7/200; Church Yth Grp; Intnl Clb; Spanish Clb; Chorus; School Musical; Variety Show; CA Local Educ Reform Network Rep; CSF.

MILLS, DANNY L; Paso Robles HS; Paso Robles, CA; (4); 60/220; Art Clb; Church Yth Grp; Office Aide; Teachers Aide; Bsbl; Bsktbl; Socr; Cit Awd; Hon Roll; Police Officer.

MILLS, DENA L; Southport Christian Acad; El Cajon, CA; (3); Church Yth Grp; Drama Clb; Teachers Aide; Church Choir; School Musical; Yrbk; High Hon Roll; AZ ST; Med.

MILLS, JASON S; Yucaipa HS; Yucaipa, CA; (2); 47/454; Boy Scts; Key Clb; Letterman Clb; Varsity Clb; Var JV Ftbl; JV Capt Socr; Var L Trk; Wt Lftg; Prfct Atten Awd; Pres Acad Fit Awd; Schlstc Ltr; Engrng.

MILLS, LARA; Independence HS; Fremont, CA; (2); Church Yth Grp; Cmnty Wkr; 4-H; Hosp Aide; Teachers Aide; Bsktbl; Cheerldng; Trk; 4-H Awd; Hon Roll; Chrldr Rally; AF Acad; Pilot.

MILLS, LUANA B; Culver City HS; Culver City, CA; (3); Church Yth Grp; Spanish Clb; Varsity Clb; Stage Crew; Off Soph Cls; Off Jr Cls; Var Socr; JV Swmmng; Var Vllybl; Spanish NHS; Brigham Young U; Cmmnctns.

MILLS, NICOLE D; Lemoore HS; Lemoore, CA; (4); 25/293; French Clb; Pep Clb; Ed Lit Mag; Rep Jr Cls; Var Sr Cls; Var Stu Cncl; Var Swmmng; Hon Roll; NHS; CSF; Ltr 3 Yrs Vrsty Swmmng; CA ST U Fresno; Indstrl Arts.

MILLS, RANDALL S; Notre Dame HS; Riverside, CA; (2); 6/190; JV Bsktbl; Var Ftbl; High Hon Roll; Spanish NHS; Cmptv Roller Sktng Artistc; UCLA.

MILLS, SHERRI L; Pinole Valley HS; Pinole, CA; (2); Gym; JV Sftbl; Water Polo Jv; Diablo Vly Coll; Bus Adm.

MILLS, TENA; Piedmont Hills HS; San Jose, CA; (3); 75/430; Spanish Clb; Cheerldng; Crs Cntry; Gym; Trk; MESA Vp 89, Pres 90; Most Outstndng MESA Stu 90; KCIU TV Talnt Srch 1st Pl; Talnt Show 1st Pl Dance; U CA Los Angelos; Engrng.

MILLS, TINA M; Sonora HS; Sonora, CA; (3); Church Yth Grp; Office Aide; Ski Clb; School Musical; Off Frsh Cls; Off Soph Cls; JV Var Cheerldng; Var Trk; High Hon Roll; Honors In Golden State Exam In Algebra; Honorable Mention In Golden State Exam In Geometry; Cal Poly; Graphic Design.

MILNER, TERRI K; Bishop Montgomery HS; Torrance, CA; (2); Church Yth Grp; English Clb; GAA; Pep Clb; Ski Clb; Cheerldng; Crs Cntry; Gym; Ice Hcky; Score Keeper; Jr Lifegrds 3 Yrs; UC Santa Barbara; Engl Lit.

MILNER, TIFANY E; Ramona HS; Ramona, CA; (3); 3/324; Church Yth Grp; Score Keeper; High Hon Roll; San Vicente Pony Clb; CSF; Amnesty Intl; U Of CA Riverside; Animal Gen.

MILTON, ANDREA D; Viewpoint HS; Agoura Hills, CA; (3); Drama Clb; Key Clb; Model UN; Chorus; School Play; Yrbk; Lit Mag; Rep Frsh Cls; Sec Soph Cls; VP Sr Cls; Brdcst Jrnlsm.

MILTON, KIMBERLY; C K Mc Clatchy HS; Sacramento, CA; (3); Church Yth Grp; Cmnty Wkr; German Clb; Girl Scts; Office Aide; Band; Church Choir; Mrchg Band; School Musical; Swmmng; CEDA All St Honor Band; Summer Frgn Exchange Pgm; U CA San Diego; Intl Relations.

MIM, KUN; Davis HS; Modesto, CA; (2); Boy Scts; Tennis; Hon Roll; Armed Forces; Physician.

MIM, THOEUNG; Grace M Davis HS; Modesto, CA; (1); 3/30; Hon Roll; Pediatrician.

MIMOUN, RINA; Santa Monica HS; Santa Monica, CA; (3); Drama Clb; SADD; School Play; Stage Crew; Ed Nwsp; Actng.

MIMRAN, RONNIE I; Saugus HS; Saugus, CA; (3); 5/456; Am Leg Boys St; Quiz Bowl; Red Cross Aide; Varsity Clb; Pres Frsh Cls; Rep Soph Cls; VP Jr Cls; Off Sr Cls; VP Stu Cncl; Capt L Socr; U Of CA LA; Sports Med.

MIN, ANTHONY S; Richard Gahr HS; Cerritos, CA; (1); Off Frsh Cls; High Hon Roll; Water Polo Team; UCLA; Phrmcy.

MIN, CHRISTINA Y; Sunny Hills HS; Fullerton, CA; (1); Key Clb; Model UN; Spanish Clb; JV Swmmng; JV Tennis; High Hon Roll; Cmptv Piano 11 Yrs; Intl Rltns.

MIN, DON; Sunny Hills HS; Fullerton, CA; (3); 91/450; Cmnty Wkr; Teachers Aide; Hon Roll; JR Vrsty Badmntn; Engr.

MIN, HWA YOUNG; Hiram Johnson HS; Sacramento, CA; (2); Treas Church Yth Grp; Cmnty Wkr; JV Capt Vllybl; High Hon Roll; NHS; Mathletes.

MIN, JEFFREY K; San Ramon Valley HS; Danville, CA; (3); 4/420; Speech Tm; School Musical; Stage Crew; Stat Bsktbl; JV Tennis; JV Trk; High Hon Roll; Rensselaer Mdl; Scl Stds Outstndng Achvt; AHSSP-HNRS Pgm-U CA Berkeley; U CA-BERKELEY; Bioengrng.

MIN, JOON Y; Alta Loma HS; Alta Loma, CA; (4); Mgr Intnl Clb; Key Clb; High Hon Roll; Hon Roll; Pres Acad Fit Awd; Cum Laude Soc; Badminton Jr Var Mst Inspirational Player; Acad Decathlon; Cal Poly Pomona; Arch.

MIN, LILY; John A Rowland HS; Upland, CA; (2); Math Clb; Spanish Clb; Band; Mrchg Band; Pep Band; High Hon Roll; Prfct Atten Awd; GSE Hgh Hnrs; 4.0 Awd; Bst Geom Stu; UC System.

MINA, CHARLENE D; Pinole Valley HS; Hercules, CA; (2); French Clb; NFL; Speech Tm; Chorus; Pres Frsh Cls; VP Soph Cls; Rep Stu Cncl; Hon Roll; CSF; U CA-BERKELEY; Geology.

MINA, MIRIAM V; Trona HS; Trona, CA; (2); Capt Math Tm; Rep Frsh Cls; Pres Soph Cls; JV Bsktbl; Var L Sftbl; Var L Vllybl; High Hon Roll; NHS; Medals Chem & Cp Engl; 2nd Leag Hgh Scr Mth; CSF; UCR; Med.

MINASSIAN, PATRICK; Glendale HS; Glendale, CA; (3); Hon Roll; Prfct Atten Awd; Word Proc Awd; Math.

MINATISKAN, ALICE; Glendale HS; Glendale, CA; (2); Library Aide; Office Aide; Teachers Aide; Band; Jazz Band; Mrchg Band; Orch; Pep Band; Nwsp; Cit Awd; UCLA; Sci.

MINCHIN, MARTHA E; Bakersfield HS; Bakersfield, CA; (3); 7/718; Church Yth Grp; VP JA; Spanish Clb; Ed Nwsp; Ed Lit Mag; Hon Roll; Ntl Merit Ltr; CSF; Interact Clb Treas; Commnctns.

MINDORO, ALWYN; Glendale Adventist Acad; Tujunga, CA; (1); 10/64; Church Yth Grp; FCA; Hosp Aide; Varsity Clb; Acpl Chr; Band; Chorus; Church Choir; JV Bsktbl; Hon Roll; Kidsafe & The Great Amer Smokeout; UCLA; Mech Engr.

MINEO, HEATHER K; John A Rowland HS; Rowland Hgts, CA; (4); 65/566; Dance Clb; Letterman Clb; Q&S; Science Clb; Varsity Clb; Rptr Yrbk; Rep Stu Cncl; JV Socr; JV Var Sftbl; High Hon Roll; U Of San Diego; Marine Bio.

MINER, JENNIFER; El Toro HS; El Toro, CA; (2); 25/557; Church Yth Grp; French Clb; German Clb; Chorus; Church Choir; School Musical; High Hon Roll; Chrch Camp Cnslr; CSF.

MINER, SANDRA K; Modesto HS; Modesto, CA; (3); AFS; Key Clb; GATE Prgm; Stanislaus ST.

MINER, SHANNON; Alameda HS; Alameda, CA; (4); 83/357; Cmnty Wkr; Dance Clb; Pres Drama Clb; Sec French Clb; Letterman Clb; Red Cross Aide; Pres Thesps; School Musical; School Play; Stage Crew; Bnk Amer Plq Fine Arts; Acad A Awds; Outstndng Stu Perfmng Arts; Muscl Theatre.

MINER, TRISTA M; Lincoln HS; Stockton, CA; (3); 96/592; Church Yth Grp; Chorus; School Musical; High Hon Roll; Hon Roll; Prfct Atten Awd; Photogrphy, Photo Cntsts; CA Jr Schlstc Fdrtn; Nrsng.

MINERVA, MICHELLE; Fred C Beyer HS; Modesto, CA; (4); 29/520; Church Yth Grp; Hosp Aide; Pep Clb; Service Clb; Ski Clb; SADD; Cit Awd; Hon Roll; NHS; CSF; Modesto JC; Psych.

MINET, HEATHER DIANE; Helix HS; San Diego, CA; (3); 50/420; Church Yth Grp; Library Aide; Office Aide; Teachers Aide; Chorus; School Musical; Variety Show; Hon Roll; Law.

MING, CARIN; So Cal Christian HS; Orange, CA; (3); Church Yth Grp; Office Aide; Spanish Clb; Chorus; Church Choir; Cheerldng; Gym; High Hon Roll; Ntl Merit Ltr; Early Childhood Ed.

MINGUET, MICHAEL R; Loyola HS; Los Angeles, CA; (2); Hon Roll; NEDT Awd; Prfct Atten Awd; 9th Pl CA Ntl Frnch Cntst 89; Geolpgy-Plntlgy Clb.

MINIOR, JENNIFER A; Turlock HS; Turlock, CA; (2); 146/570; Advncd Optnl Gymnst; U Of UT; Bus.

MINIUM, LARA M; Santa Cruz HS; Santa Cruz, CA; (3); GAA; Key Clb; Teachers Aide; JV Sftbl; JV Var Tennis; Danny O'Connell Sprtsmnshp Awd 87-88; Achvt Pin Geom, Pre-Calculus, Bio, Chem; Awd Math/Sci/Soc Stud; UC Davis; Vet.

MINKLER, BETH; Yosemite HS; Oakhurst, CA; (1); Boy Scts; Church Yth Grp; Cmnty Wkr; Drama Clb; Pep Clb; SADD; School Play; JV Cheerldng; JV Pom Pon; JV Sftbl; Med.

MINNICK, CHRISTINE G; Glendale Adventist Acad; Glendale, CA; (3); 3/60; FCA; Chorus; Yrbk; VP Frsh Cls; VP Treas Soph Cls; Rep Sr Cls; Stu Cncl; Var Intrml Bsktbl; Var Intrml Vllybl; NHS; Outstndng Schlts Achvt 87-89; USC; Engrng.

MINNIS, AARON P; Ceres HS; Modesto, CA; (3); 2/300; Am Leg Boys St; FBLA; Pres Key Clb; Model UN; SADD; Treas Jr Cls; Pres Sr Cls; Swmmng; High Hon Roll; Hon Roll; CSF; Friday Night Live; Santa Clara; Law.

MINO, JENNIFER E; Santa Margarita HS; Laguna Beach, CA; (3); 4-H; French Clb; Band; Mrchg Band; Pep Band; School Musical; Stage Crew; Stu Cncl; Swmmng; Hon Roll; Living Hstry; U OH ST; Pre-Med.

MINOOEE, OMEDE; San Dieguito HS; Carlsbad, CA; (2); Cmnty Wkr; French Clb; Intnl Clb; Office Aide; Cit Awd; Hon Roll; Prfct Atten Awd; Med.

MINOR, CHERI E; Summerville HS; Sonora, CA; (3); Church Yth Grp; Chorus; Church Choir; Ed Yrbk; Cit Awd; Hon Roll; Interior Design.

MINOR, DONNY; Sacramento HS; Sacramento, CA; (2); JV Ftbl; JV Wrstlng; Hon Roll; UC Berkeley.

MINOR, KIMBERLY M; California HS; San Ramon, CA; (3); 48/400; Cmnty Wkr; Hosp Aide; Service Clb; Spanish Clb; Off Soph Cls; VP Jr Cls; Pres Sr Cls; L Var Bsktbl; High Hon Roll; NHS; Schl Site Cncl Mem; Chld Psych.

MINOR, OSCAR; Garey HS; Pomona, CA; (3); Spanish Clb; Wt Lftg; Cit Awd; Mt San Antonio Coll; Mech Engr.

MINOW, JASON A; Marina HS; Huntington Beach, CA; (1); Temple Yth Grp; High Hon Roll.

MINTERS, KARIEM M; St Bernards HS; Compton, CA; (3); Cmnty Wkr; Library Aide; JV Var Bsktbl; Pres 89-90 Blck Awrns Clb; Howard U; History.

MINTEY, PIPER J; Saint Bernard HS; Eureka, CA; (4); Pres Church Yth Grp; Cmnty Wkr; Dance Clb; Drama Clb; English Clb; Hosp Aide; Intnl Clb; Letterman Clb; NFL; Service Clb; Hgh Rank Fornscs; Hgh Chrch Awds; Natl Yng Ldrs Conf; Ricks Coll; Sci.

MINTON, CHRISTINE PIILANI; Kaimuki HS; La Habra, CA; (4); 31/334; Drama Clb; Color Guard; School Play; Lit Mag; High Hon Roll; Hon Roll; Ntl Merit Ltr; Golden State Exam; Algebra I; High Honors; Amnesty International; Newspaper Reporter; Page Editor; Fashion Design.

MINTY, FARZANA M; Savanna HS; Buena Park, CA; (2); Key Clb; Pep Clb; Science Clb; Service Clb; Rep Frsh Cls; Rep Soph Cls; Swmmng; High Hon Roll; Hon Roll; Jr NHS; VIA Swm Ctr.

MINTZ, KARYN B; Thousand Oaks HS; Thousand Oaks, CA; (4); 1/540; Math Tm; Spanish Clb; Speech Tm; SADD; Temple Yth Grp; Treas Band; Pres Mrchg Band; Pep Band; Rep Soph Cls; NHS; HOBY Fndnt Ambssdr 88; John Philip Sousa Band Awd 90; Ventura Cnty Hnr Bnd 88 & 90; UC Berkeley.

MIRABAL, LESLIE M; Hayward HS; Hayward, CA; (1); Church Yth Grp; Band; Mrchg Band; Sec Frsh Cls; VP Soph Cls; Score Keeper; Var Socr; Var Sftbl; Var Vllybl; Hon Roll; Acctng.

MIRALLES, MARLA L; St Joseph HS; Bellflower, CA; (2); GAA; SADD; Chorus; Variety Show; JV Capt Cheerldng; Hon Roll; St John Bosco Tlnt Shw 1st & 3rd Pl Sining; St Joseph Tlnt Shw 1st & 2nd Pl Singing.

MIRAMONTES, LOUIS M; Bishop Amat HS; West Covina, CA; (3); Hon Roll; Silver Screen Clb; Photo Clb; USC.

MIRAMONTES, OLGA V; Irvington HS; Fremont, CA; (3); GAA; Rep Frsh Cls; Rep Soph Cls; Rep Jr Cls; Treas Sr Cls; Var Capt Socr; Var Sftbl; High Hon Roll; Hon Roll; Pres Acad Fit Awd; Athl Yr Awd 89-90; Fresno ST; Phys Thrpy.

MIRAMONTES, ROBERT; Merced HS North; Merced, CA; (2); Hon Roll; Prfct Atten Awd.

MIRANDA, ABIGAIL; Southwest HS; San Diego, CA; (3); 4/498; Sec Key Clb; Office Aide; SADD; Ed Nwsp; Ed Yrbk; Sec Jr Cls; Var Tennis; Hon Roll; Prfct Atten Awd; Pres Acad Fit Awd; Pan-Asian Clb Treas; Assoc Stu Bdy Cncsns Cmsnr; CSF; Stnfrd; Pdtrc Med.

MIRANDA, ADRIANA M; Sacred Heart Of Jesus HS; Los Angeles, CA; (2); Church Yth Grp; Cmnty Wkr; Dance Clb; Yrbk; Hon Roll; NHS; Columbia Coll Hollywood; Music.

MIRANDA, ALMA R; Roosevelt HS Magnet; Los Angeles, CA; (3); Service Clb; Drill Tm; School Play; Stage Crew; Yrbk; Var Bsktbl; Capt Cheerldng; Capt Powder Puff Ftbl; Sftbl; Capt Vllybl; CA Poly-Pomona; Med.

MIRANDA, BARBIE; Southwest HS; San Diego, CA; (2); 26/673; Key Clb; SADD; Ed Yrbk; Var Tennis; Cit Awd; Hon Roll; Prfct Atten Awd; ASB Storemgr; Pan Asian Sgt Arms; Sword & Shields Concessns; Bus.

MIRANDA, CYNTHIA; Bloomington HS; Bloomington, CA; (3); Color Guard; Drill Tm; Mrchg Band; Ed Yrbk; Mgr(s); Powder Puff Ftbl; Hon Roll; Pres Jr NHS; Chrch Mnstr; Cthlc Rlgs Pgm; US Navy; Cmmnctns.

MIRANDA, DAMARIS; Andrew P Hill HS; San Jose, CA; (3); Sec Jr Cls; VP Sr Cls; Tennis; Var Vllybl; Hon Roll; Rotary Awd; GATE Hnrs; Camp Enterprse 90; Stanford; Psych.

MIRANDA, DAVID; South San Francisco HS; S San Francisco, CA; (3); Drama Clb; FBLA; Spanish Clb; Chorus; School Musical; Stu Mnt Prfrmng Arts; CSF; Prncpls Awd 88-90; UC Davis; Accntnt.

MIRANDA, DENISE A; Charter Oak HS; Covina, CA; (4); 94/365; Church Yth Grp; Cmnty Wkr; Dance Clb; Latin Clb; Pep Clb; Service Clb; VP Spanish Clb; Sec Treas SADD; Teachers Aide; Varsity Clb; Badmntn; Prom Cmmttes; Stu Leag; Pblcty Clb; Amer Poetry Anthlgy; UCLA; Poltcl Sci.

MIRANDA, FERNANDO; St Bernard HS; Culver City, CA; (3); Church Yth Grp; Latin Clb; Capt JV Bsbl; Capt JV Ftbl; Hon Roll; All-Amer Schlr & Athlt; Dfnsv MVP Soph Ftbl; UCLA; Engrng.

MIRANDA, HENEDINA E; Amos Alonso Stagg HS; Stockton, CA; (3); High Hon Roll; Prfct Atten Awd; JV Bdmntn; Delta; Nrse.

MIRANDA, JAMES; Beyer HS; Modesto, CA; (3); Var Crs Cntry; Var Trk; Var Wrstlng; Cit Awd; Hon Roll; St Schlr; Hosp Volunteer; Med.

MIRANDA, JAMES V; Sunset HS; Hayward, CA; (3); Church Yth Grp; Treas Jr Cls; Bsktbl; Golf; Socr; Hon Roll; Law Enfrcmnt.

MIRANDA, JOSEPH A; Damien HS; Irwindale, CA; (3); Church Yth Grp; Cmnty Wkr; Red Cross Aide; JV Bsbl; Ftbl; Bsbl Card Clb; U Of Southen CA; Bus.

MIRANDA, LETICIA C; Southwest HS; San Diego, CA; (1); 63/546; Prfct Atten Awd; Bowling Awds; ABC Stu; Prfct Ftns; SDSU; Pedtrcn.

MIRANDA, MANUEL O; King City HS; King City, CA; (2); 19/230; Church Yth Grp; Cmnty Wkr; JA; VP Sr Cls; JV Bsbl; JV Var Bsktbl; Ftbl; Cit Awd; High Hon Roll; Hon Roll; Sacramento ST; Bus Admin.

MIRANDA, MANUELA; North Hollywood HS; North Hollywood, CA; (2); Church Yth Grp; Teachers Aide; JV Sftbl; Los Angeles Valley Coll; Bnkng.

MIRANDA, MARILYN B; Leuzinger HS; Lawndale, CA; (2); Office Aide; Teachers Aide; Drill Tm; Mrchg Band; UCLA.

MIRANDA, MARVIN E; Lynwood HS; Lynwood, CA; (3); 9/700; Intnl Clb; Math Clb; Pres Stu Cncl; High Hon Roll; MESA; Bus.

MIRANDA, MAUREEN O; Bishop Montgomery HS; Hawthorne, CA; (2); SADD; High Hon Roll; Hon Roll; Prfct Atten Awd; CSF; Concordia; Asian Culture Club; Med.

MIRANDA, MICHAEL L; Pasadena HS; Pasadena, CA; (3); Boy Scts; Church Yth Grp; JV Var Bsbl; JV Vllybl; Hon Roll; Par Villi Dei Relgs Chtlc Awd Cub Scts; Ad Altare Dei Rlgs Chtlc Awd Boy Sct.

MIRANDA, RAFAEL A; St Francis HS; San Jose, CA; (2); 60/356; Church Yth Grp; Cmnty Wkr; Intnl Clb; Service Clb; SADD; Color Guard; JV Bsktbl; JV Trk; High Hon Roll; Pres Acad Fit Awd; US Naval Sea Cadet Corp; CSF; Aerospace Engrng.

MIRANDA, RICHARD T; Bell Gardens HS; Bell Gardens, CA; (2); Q&S; Ed Nwsp; Co-Ed Lit Mag; Ftbl; Hon Roll; Norwich Military Acad; Pilot.

MIRANDA, ROSA M; Anaheim HS; Anaheim, CA; (4); French Clb; Science Clb; Spanish Clb; Hon Roll; NHS; Mecha Club; CSF; Arch Cont 2nd Pl; Cal ST Fullerton; Civil Engr.

MIRANDA, TEANA R; Lowell HS; San Francisco, CA; (3); Cmnty Wkr; Hosp Aide; Red Cross Aide; Service Clb; SADD; Nwsp; Ntl Merit Ltr; CSF; Goldn St Exam Alg & Geom Awds; Arch/Engrng Clb Rep.

MIRCH, CASEY K; Bridgemont HS; Brisbane, CA; (4); 1/10; Church Yth Grp; Chorus; Rptr Yrbk; Ed Lit Mag; Rep Soph Cls; Rep Jr Cls; Pres Stu Cncl; Var Bsbl; Var Bsktbl; L Crs Cntry; Cvl Air Ptrl; St Assmblywmn Stu Advsry Cmmttee.

MIRELES, MONICA; San Jose HS Acad; San Jose, CA; (3); Bsbl; Bsktbl; Crs Cntry; Swmmng; Tennis; Vllybl; Wt Lftg; San Jose ST U.

MIROCHNIK, LINA; Hillsdale HS; Belmont, CA; (4); 18/400; French Clb; Nwsp; Ed Lit Mag; Ntl Merit SF; Jnr Clsmn Amer; Amnstry; Wrld Affrs Clb; CSF; 4 Englsh Hnrs Awds AP Hstry Awd; UCLA; Marketing.

MIRPURI, SHALINI A; Chaminade College Prep; Granada Hills, CA; (3); 78/185; Dance Clb; Hosp Aide; Key Clb; Letterman Clb; Chorus; Drill Tm; Var Cheerldng; Hon Roll; Dance Ballet,Jazz,Tap.

MIRZA, ASIF A; Galileo HS; Daly City, CA; (4); 10/325; VP JA; Pep Clb; VP Science Clb; Spanish Clb; Teachers Aide; VP Sr Cls; Cit Awd; High Hon Roll; Hon Roll; Sec NHS; Block Gr VP; Medal Top Stu; Plaque Top Stu; U C Davis.

MIRZA, SAJEDA; Phillip & Sala Burton Academic HS; Daly City, CA; (3); JA; Spanish Clb; School Musical; Yrbk; Pres Rep Frsh Cls; Pres Rep Soph Cls; Pres Rep Jr Cls; High Hon Roll; Hon Roll; Hghst GPA Cert Acadmc Achvt; Top Stu US Hstry Hnrs Cert Merit; Bus.

MIRZADEH, DARYA; Santa Teresa HS; San Jose, CA; (2); German Clb; Spanish Clb; SADD; Yrbk; Score Keeper; St Schlr; Close Up Fndtn; Goldn St Exm Recgntn Alg I; Mount Holyoke; Bio.

MISAJONM, LEILANI K; St Anthony HS; Long Beach, CA; (2); Church Yth Grp; Dance Clb; Drill Tm; High Hon Roll; NHS; Congrssnl Mdl Of Hnr; Soph Crt; Contessa Di Napoli; Asst Dir Intl Childrens Choir; Med.

MISCH, DEBBIE; Napa HS; Napa, CA; (3); 12/351; Church Yth Grp; Key Clb; Pep Clb; Acpl Chr; Chorus; Swing Chorus; Sec Jr Cls; Pres Sr Cls; Var Capt Cheerldng; JV Sftbl; Napanee Awd 3 Yrs; Cal Poly; Intl Bus.

MISCHELL, JEFF S; Bishop Union HS; Bishop, CA; (3); Boy Scts; Ski Clb; Band; Ftbl; Hon Roll; Cycling; Water Skiing; Embry-Riddle U; Aircraft Engr.

MISEMER, GERALD P; Buena HS; Ventura, CA; (4); Church Yth Grp; Pep Clb; SADD; Chorus; School Musical; Rep Stu Cncl; Mgr Vllybl; Mock Trial Team; Ventura Coll.

MISHELOFF, ROBERT A; Dublin HS; Dublin, CA; (3); 18/220; Band; Ed Nwsp; Pres Sr Cls; Var L Crs Cntry; Var L Swmmng; Var L Wrstlng; High Hon Roll; Hon Roll; Poem Pblshd Treasured Poems Of Amer 90; Lesher Cmmnctns Schltc Jrnlsm Awd 90; Pre Med.

MISHRA, PREETI; Homestead HS; Sunnyvale, CA; (4); Debate Tm; German Clb; NFL; Sec Service Clb; Speech Tm; Teachers Aide; Nwsp; Yrbk; NHS; Ntl Merit SF; Pr Cnslng Ofcr; CA Schlsrhp Fdrtn; Bus.

MISIC, MARGARET; Poly HS; Riverside, CA; (1); Drama Clb; Intnl Clb; Key Clb; SADD; Stage Crew; JV Swmmng; High Hon Roll; Prfct Atten Awd; Girls Leag Fresh Rep; Stanford U; Psych.

MISIOWIEC, PHILIP; Poway HS; San Diego, CA; (3); 20/775; Hist FBLA; Model UN; Science Clb; Rptr Nwsp; JV Swmmng; High Hon Roll; Hon Roll; Cert Merit Engl Awd PTS Assn; Concours Natl Frnch Awd; Outstndng Delg Awd Mdl UN Conf; Stanford U; Mdcn.

MISIUK, CATHY A; Calvary Chapel HS; Costa Mesa, CA; (4); Socr; Office Aide; Teachers Aide; Stage Crew; Stu Cncl; JV Var Sftbl; Hon Roll; Val; Geom Golden St Exam Hnrs; S CA Coll; Sec Tchr.

MISKEY, TOM S; Chico SR HS; Chico, CA; (4); 9/368; Art Clb; Library Aide; Spanish Clb; SADD; Yrbk; Lit Mag; Vllybl; Cit Awd; Hon Roll; Pres Acad Fit Awd; CSUC Hnrs Pgm; Schl Clbs T-Shirt Dsgnr; CA ST U Chico; Illus.

MISKIMIN, AMY; Maranatha Christian HS; Pasadena, CA; (1); Church Yth Grp; SADD; Drill Tm; Yrbk; Cheerldng; Mgr(s); Sports Med.

MISLANG, ROBERT D; Santa Barbara HS; Santa Barbara, CA; (3); JV Bsbl; Hon Roll; Golden St Exam; Comp Sci.

MISQUEZ, MARK; Libery Union HS; Brentwood, CA; (4); 20/360; Am Leg Boys St; Letterman Clb; Off Jr Cls; Off Sr Cls; Stu Cncl; Var Bsbl; JV Var Ftbl; Hon Roll; NHS; Schlr Athl, Bsbl & Ftbl; Bus Mgmt.

MISSETT, BRIAN; Palo Alto HS; Palo Alto, CA; (2); Church Yth Grp; Cmnty Wkr; Band; Ed Nwsp; Rep Frsh Cls; Rep Soph Cls; Rep Jr Cls; Stu Cncl; JV Tennis; High Hon Roll; Cycle Ride Weekly; Piano; Aviation Lssns; Health Surgeon.

MISTRETTA, BARBARA J; Orange Glen HS; Escondido, CA; (4); Library Aide; Teachers Aide; Pres Acad Fit Awd; Bus.

MISTRIEL, STEPHEN D; Brawley Union HS; Brawley, CA; (1); Aud/Vis; Band; Church Choir; Mrchg Band; Hon Roll; Prfct Atten Awd; Telecommnctns.

MISTRY, BHAVESH; Sequoia HS; Redwood City, CA; (2); Service Clb; JV Bsktbl; High Hon Roll; Hon Roll; Prfct Atten Awd; Comp Application Awd.

MISTRY, HITENDRA S; Mount Pleasant HS; San Jose, CA; (4); 10/360; SADD; Varsity Clb; Var Socr; Intrml Trk; High Hon Roll; NHS; Ntl Merit Ltr; Badminton Vrsty Mbr 2 Yrs; CSF; San Jose ST U; Aerospace Engr.

MISTRY, SHAILEN; Sunny Hills HS; Fullerton, CA; (2); 7/454; Chess Clb; FBLA; Intnl Clb; Key Clb; Spanish Clb; Intrml Crs Cntry; Intrml Trk; High Hon Roll; Coaches Awd Track; 3rd Pl St Parliamntry Proc Comptn; 9th Pl Ecnmcs St FBLA; U CA; Bus Admin.

MISTRY, SONIA P; Herbert Hoover HS; Fresno, CA; (3); 50/430; French Clb; Treas Science Clb; Treas SADD; Orch; Rptr Nwsp; CA Schlrshp Fed; Amnesty Intl; CA ST U Orch.

MISTRY, SUNIT D; Pilgrim Schl; Los Angeles, CA; (3); 1/13; Model UN; Stage Crew; Pres Jr Cls; Var Bsktbl; Var Ftbl; Var Vllybl; Cit Awd; Hon Roll; Jr NHS; NHS; Hghst Acadmc Achvt; MVP Awd Vllybl; 2nd Team All Heritage Leag Vllybl 90; Med.

MITCHAM, KELLY; Los Alamitos HS; Seal Beach, CA; (3); FCA; Band; Mrchg Band; Pep Band; Hon Roll; CA Schltc Fdrtn; CA ST Irvine; Soc Sci.

MITCHELL, ANDRE T; Bellarmine College Prep; San Jose, CA; (3); 73/296; Pep Clb; Teachers Aide; Var Wrstlng; Bellarmine Blck B Clb; Jack & Jill Of Amer Inc; NAACP; Howard U; Elec Engr.

MITCHELL, BARBARA; St Marys Acad; Los Angeles, CA; (3); 5/84; Cmnty Wkr; Girl Scts; Spanish Clb; Stage Crew; Yrbk; High Hon Roll; Spanish NHS; California Scholarship Federation; Accounting.

MITCHELL, CARLO J; Hoover HS; North Fork, CA; (2); 33/535; Church Yth Grp; German Clb; Ski Clb; Rptr Nwsp; JV Tennis; High Hon Roll; Prfct Atten Awd; Frshmn Tennis; CSF; Frgn Exch Stu To Germany 90; Tech.

MITCHELL, CAROLYN A; Sweetwater HS; National City, CA; (3); Office Aide; SADD; Nwsp; Lit Mag; Off Sr Cls; Stu Cncl; Cit Awd; Hon Roll; CSF; ASB; Asian Intl Assn; Stanford U; Jrnlsm.

MITCHELL, CYNTHIA; Morningside HS; Long Beach, CA; (4); 16/175; Library Aide; Speech Tm; Teachers Aide; Rptr Nwsp; Yrbk; Hon Roll; Bnk America Achvt Awd; Cert Mrt Awd; Outstndng Awd Engl & Scl Stds; Cal ST Dominguez Hills; Jrnlsm.

MITCHELL, DAVID B; Mira Costa HS; Redondo Beach, CA; (1); Church Yth Grp; Pep Clb; ROTC; Science Clb; Intrml Bsktbl; Var Cheerldng; Cit Awd; ROTC Bulldog Awd; Sci.

MITCHELL, DOUGLAS E; Glendora HS; Glendora, CA; (4); 45/377; Key Clb; Spanish Clb; Speech Tm; Band; Jazz Band; Mrchg Band; Pep Band; Hist Sr Cls; JV Socr; Pres Acad Fit Awd; Span Medallion; Coll Of Wooster; Intl Relations.

MITCHELL, EDWARD M; Saint Ignatius Coll Prep; San Francisco, CA; (3); 31/255; Ed Nwsp; Yrbk; Var Swmmng; Hon Roll; St Ignatius Block Club; Stu Talent Search Merit Awd From Johns Hopkins U; U CA Davis; Structural Engrng.

MITCHELL, FATEAMA A; Poly HS; Long Beach, CA; (2); Church Yth Grp; Dance Clb; English Clb; GAA; Latin Clb; Math Clb; Office Aide; ROTC; SADD; Teachers Aide; Cal ST U; Fshn Dsgnr.

MITCHELL, GINA L; Independence HS; San Jose, CA; (3); 1/962; Pres Church Yth Grp; Cmnty Wkr; Service Clb; Church Choir; Var Swmmng; NHS; Ntl Merit Ltr; CSF; Peer Cnslng Cnslr; Outstndng Yng Womn Awd; BYU; Librl Arts.

MITCHELL, JASON E; Narbonne HS; Carson, CA; (3); Church Yth Grp; Band; Jazz Band; Var Wt Lftg; Cit Awd; High Hon Roll; Hon Roll; Prfct Atten Awd; UCLA; Bus Mgmt.

MITCHELL, JASON P; Rio Lindo Adventist Acad; Redding, CA; (4); 26/96; Church Yth Grp; Spanish Clb; Varsity Clb; Acpl Chr; Band; Chorus; School Play; Yrbk; Off Frsh Cls; Off Soph Cls; Pacific Union Coll; Biochem.

MITCHELL, JENNIFER S; Palm Springs HS; Cathedral City, CA; (3); JV Capt Bsktbl; Var Swmmng; Hon Roll; Waterpolo; Cmmty Church Work; UCSD; Bus.

MITCHELL, JENNY; South San Francisco HS; So San Francisco, CA; (2); Pep Clb; SADD; Var Cheerldng; Bus.

MITCHELL, JOAN; Arlington HS; Riverside, CA; (3); 11/418; Quiz Bowl; SADD; Chorus; School Musical; Stage Crew; Swing Chorus; Var L Bsktbl; Var L Trk; Golden St Exam Algebra & Geom Hnrs; Mech Engr.

MITCHELL, JOHN D; Antelope Valley HS; Lancaster, CA; (3); 95/900; Computer Clb; Hon Roll; Golden St Exam Geom Hnrs; GATE; UC Berkeley; Comp Engr.

MITCHELL, JOI L; Huntington Park HS; Inglewood, CA; (1); Rep Frsh Cls; Hon Roll; CSF; MESA; Biola U; Med.

MITCHELL, KENNETH A; Liberty Union HS; Oakley, CA; (3); 78/368; Boy Scts; Church Yth Grp; Cmnty Wkr; FCA; Chorus; Church Choir; School Play; Variety Show; High Hon Roll; Outstndng Math; Arts/Drawngs Hnrs Show; Drama.

MITCHELL, KIMBERLY S; Senior HS; Fort Irwin, CA; (3); Cmnty Wkr; Hosp Aide; Red Cross Aide; Band; Jazz Band; Mrchg Band; Pep Band; High Hon Roll; Hon Roll; Hnr Band; UCLA; Med.

MITCHELL, KRISTEN D; Abraham Lincoln HS; San Jose, CA; (3); Church Yth Grp; Teachers Aide; Var Sftbl; JV Var Vllybl; MVP Vlybl & 1st Tm All Leag JV Tm 87-88; Chiropractic.

MITCHELL, KRISTINE; St Vincents HS; Rohnert Park, CA; (3); Church Yth Grp; French Clb; Pep Clb; SADD; Church Choir; School Play; JV Bsktbl; Var Cheerldng; Crs Cntry; Var Pom Pon; Santa Rosa JR Coll; Intr Dsgn.

MITCHELL, LEIGH R; Redwood HS; Visalia, CA; (2); Church Yth Grp; FBLA; German Clb; Chorus; Church Choir; School Musical; Hon Roll; Rdng; Playing The Piano; Fresno Pacific Coll; Music.

MITCHELL, LORI; Del Campo HS; Carmichael, CA; (2); Church Yth Grp; Debate Tm; Drama Clb; French Clb; Speech Tm; School Play; Lion Awd; Rotary Awd; 1st Pl Sacramento Law Ed Cnfrnc; Oxford; Law.

MITCHELL, MELODY A; Silver Valley HS; Ft Irwin, CA; (1); 306/514; Church Yth Grp; German Clb; Piano Lssns.

MITCHELL JR, MICHAEL P; Rio Mesa HS; Camarillo, CA; (2); Church Yth Grp; Varsity Clb; Rep Sr Cls; Var Bsbl; Var Bsktbl; Bus.

MITCHELL, MICHAEL S; Tustin HS; Tustin, CA; (2); 1/470; Boy Scts; Church Yth Grp; Math Tm; Quiz Bowl; Science Clb; Rep Stu Cncl; Swmmng; High Hon Roll; NEDT Awd; Water Polo; Acad Dcthln; Brigham Young U; Law.

MITCHELL, MICHELLE; Hoover HS; Fresno, CA; (2); 69/690; JV Capt Socr.

MITCHELL, MICHELLE; Regina Caeli HS; Compton, CA; (1); English Clb; Spanish Clb; Var Cheerldng; Hon Roll; Prfct Atten Awd; UCLA; Gynecology.

MITCHELL, MONICA M; Norco SR HS; Corona, CA; (2); FBLA; Office Aide; Pep Clb; SADD; Band; Mrchg Band; Peer Cnslng; Riverside CC; Early Chldhd.

MITCHELL, MONIQUE R; Fairfield HS; Fairfield, CA; (2); Church Yth Grp; Cmnty Wkr; Girl Scts; Teachers Aide; Chorus; Church Choir; Cit Awd; Prfct Atten Awd; Sucess Consortium Prg/Attnd Smmr Rsdntl Prgm; BSU African-Amer Stu Union; Sec Of New Beginning Choir; Hampton Inst; Sociology.

MITCHELL, NICOLE L; Coast Joint Union HS; Morro Bay, CA; (2); #5 In Class; AFS; Church Yth Grp; French Clb; FHA; Girl Scts; SADD; Ed Nwsp; Hon Roll; 3rd Pl Cnty Essay Cont; Hmcmng Cmmtte; Bus Mgmt.

MITCHELL, NINA A; Westlake Schl; Santa Monica, CA; (1); Drama Clb; French Clb; Math Tm; NFL; Speech Tm; Thesps; School Play; Rptr Nwsp; Ed-In-Chief Westlake Smmrtms; 2nd Pl Nationally In Le Grand Concours French Cntst.

MITCHELL, OZZIE; Central HS; Carrollton, GA; (2); Art Clb; Spanish Clb; Trk; De Vry U; Electrnc Engrng.

MITCHELL, RYAN G; Mission Viejo HS; Mission Viejo, CA; (1); Model UN; Ftbl; Socr; 2nd Pl MUN Conf At Stanford U.

MITCHELL, SHANNON; Fresno Christian HS; Fresno, CA; (1); Church Yth Grp; Chorus; Church Choir; Rep Yrbk; Sec Soph Cls; Cheerldng; Cit Awd; High Hon Roll; Hon Roll; Pres Acad Fit Awd; Fresno ST; Sci.

MITCHELL, SHAWNDA J; Trabuco Hills HS; Coto De Caza, CA; (2); Cmnty Wkr; French Clb; Key Clb; Sec Pep Clb; High Hon Roll; Hon Roll; NHS; Prfct Atten Awd; Religious Cmnty Svc.

MITCHELL, SUZANNE M; St Marys HS; Stockton, CA; (2); Band; Drm Mjr(t); Mrchg Band; Pep Band; Stage Crew; Var Tennis; Hon Roll.

MITCHELL, TANYA L; Capistrano Valley HS; Mission Viejo, CA; (3); Girl Scts; Letterman Clb; Math Tm; Stu Cncl; Stat Bsktbl; L Var Sftbl; JV Var Vllybl; Cit Awd; High Hon Roll; Pres Acad Fit Awd.

MITCHELL, TIMIKA; Vanden HS; Trvis A F B, CA; (1); 42/211; Hon Roll; Ethnic Clb; Chess, Swmmng, Gymnstcs; Dance Team; Acctnt.

MITCHELL, TIMOTHY S; Westmoor HS; Daly City, CA; (4); Church Yth Grp; Ftbl; Trk; Georgetown; Bus Admin.

MITCHELL, TOBY C; Rio Lindo Adventist Acad; Redding, CA; (2); Church Yth Grp; Yrbk; Lit Mag; Intrml Bsbl; Intrml Sftbl; Hon Roll; Rio Lindo Acad; Jrnlsm.

MITCHELL, TODD L; Newport Harbor HS; Newport Beach, CA; (2); DAR Awd; Hon Roll; Pres Acad Fit Awd.

MITCHELL, YVONNE L; Redlands SR HS; Redlands, CA; (4); Hon Roll; Intl Ordr Jbs Dghtrs; Crafton Hills Coll.

MITO, KATHLEEN N; L A Baptist HS; West Hills, CA; (3); 40/105; Church Yth Grp; Drama Clb; Office Aide; Teachers Aide; Drill Tm; School Play; Phtg Yrbk; VP Soph Cls; Off Sr Cls; Var Mgr(s); Pepperdine; Law.

MITSCHAN, JENNIFER M; Casa Grande HS; Petaluma, CA; (4); 42/269; German Clb; Office Aide; Teachers Aide; Hon Roll; NHS; Prfct Atten Awd; Wildlife, Forestry & Engl Achvt Awds; Santa Rosa JC.

MITSUHASHI, ALISON A; Del Campo HS; Carmichael, CA; (3); Church Yth Grp; French Clb; Pep Clb; Teachers Aide; Band; Drill Tm; Stat Bsktbl; Hon Roll; CSF Acad Club Sci Awd; Bus.

MITSUI, PAUL; Montclair College Prep; Reseda, CA; (4); Computer Clb; Math Clb; Science Clb; Yrbk; Ed Lit Mag; Var Tennis; Bausch & Lomb Sci Awd; Hon Roll; NHS; NEDT Awd; Aerosp Engrng.

MITSUNAGA, JONATHAN K; Los Gatos HS; Los Gatos, CA; (3); 47/341; Boy Scts; Band; Mrchg Band; Pep Band; School Musical; Stage Crew; JV Var Ftbl; JV Var Trk; Hon Roll; Rotary Awd; Outside Band Jobs; NAVI Scuba Diver; UC San Diego; Medcn.

MITTAN, MARK C; Fillmore HS; Fillmore, CA; (1); 64/237; Church Yth Grp; VP FCA; SADD; JV Bsktbl; JV Ftbl; JV Trk; Coaches Awd; Young Life; UCLA; Comp.

MITTIE, KIM GERALD; Sierra Joint Union HS; Clovis, CA; (2); Art Clb; 4-H; Yrbk; Cit Awd; 4-H Awd; Hon Roll; Pres Schlr; St Schlr; Spcl Awd Art Fresno Dist Fair; Crtd Yrbk Cvr; CJSF.

MITZEV, VASSIL; John Marshall HS; Los Angeles, CA; (4); 20/850; Am Leg Boys St; Cmnty Wkr; Letterman Clb; Natl Beta Clb; NFL; Ski Clb; Speech Tm; SADD; Varsity Clb; Nwsp; U Chicago; Engl.

MIU, JOHNNY; Antioch SR HS; Antioch, CA; (4); Letterman Clb; Teachers Aide; Ftbl; Trk; Wt Lftg; Hon Roll; Prfct Atten Awd; Schlr Athlt 88-90; MVP Awd 87-89; Most Outstndng Hrdlr Awd 90; Most Outstndng Stu Awd 86-87; Capt 89-90.

MIX, BERT J; Canyon Springs HS; Moreno Valley, CA; (3); Bsbl; Bsktbl; High Hon Roll; Riverside CC.

MIXON, DAWN; Taft Union HS; Taft, CA; (2); Church Yth Grp; Cmnty Wkr; Key Clb; Pep Clb; VP Frsh Cls; VP Soph Cls; Pres Jr Cls; Var Cheerldng; Hon Roll; Pres Acad Fit Awd; Chrstn Clb.

MIYAGISHIMA, GREGORY M; Whitney HS; Norwalk, CA; (2); Aud/Vis; JV Bsbl; JV Bsktbl; Disk Jcky Bus 1st Degree Prodctns; Humane Soc US; Mercy Crusade; CAT Care Clb; U CA Los Angeles; Rcrdng Ind.

MIYAHARA, PENNIE C; Bishop Montgomery HS; Hawthorne, CA; (2); Ski Clb; SADD; Prfct Atten Awd; Loyola Marymount; Schl Tchr.

MIYAKE, ALICE; Crescenta Valley HS; La Canada Flint, CA; (3); Hosp Aide; Sec Key Clb; VP Mu Alpha Theta; Ed Nwsp; Cheerldng; Var Gym; JV Tennis; Pres NHS; CA Schlrshp Fed; Bio Chem.

MIYAMOTO, BRENDA S; James A Garfield HS; Monterey Park, CA; (4); 5/650; Cmnty Wkr; Hosp Aide; VP SADD; Ed Nwsp; Stu Cncl; High Hon Roll; Pres Acad Fit Awd; Rotary Awd; CSF Pres; Acadmc Dcthln Team; Loyola Marymount U; Engl.

MIYAMOTO, CHRISTOPHER; Notre Dame HS; Burbank, CA; (4); Church Yth Grp; Cmnty Wkr; Debate Tm; Pres JA; Mrchg Band; Var L Swmmng; High Hon Roll; NEDT Awd; CSF; Awd Excllnc Wrtng-Engl Dept 90; Magna Cum Laude-Gradtn; Occidental Coll; Engl.

MIYAMOTO, HOLLY K; Clayton Valley HS; Concord, CA; (1); 1/374; FBLA; Band; Color Guard; Mrchg Band; Cit Awd; Hon Roll; Acad Lttr; Music/Colorguard Lttr; CSF; UCLA; Bus.

MIYASAKA, JENNIFER J; Newbury Park HS; Nepwbury Park, CA; (2); 1/270; Church Yth Grp; Girl Scts; SADD; Drm Mjr(t); Mrchg Band; Orch; High Hon Roll; Hon Roll; Pres Acad Fit Awd; Prncpls Schlr Athl Awd; Reed Coll; Math.

MIYASHIRO, ANSON S; Eagle Rock HS; Los Angeles, CA; (2); JV Tennis; High Hon Roll; Jr CSF; Acad Dcthln.

MIYASHIRO, EDWARD; Glen A Wilson HS; Hacienda Hts, CA; (4); Pres Church Yth Grp; VP Band; Mrchg Band; Socr; Trk; Hon Roll; Pres Acad Fit Awd; Hstry Day 3rd In LA Cnty; UC Riverside; Pharmacy.

MIYATA, EUGENE S; Mills HS; Millbrae, CA; (2); Band; Pep Band; Lit Mag; UCLA; Econ.

MIYOSHI, AMY; Washington Union HS; Fresno, CA; (2); FCA; FBLA; Nwsp; VP Soph Cls; VP Jr Cls; Stu Cncl; Var Tennis; Piano.

MIYOSHI, HENRY HIROAKI; Fowler HS; Fowler, CA; (4); 1/88; Boy Scts; Church Yth Grp; Capt Math Clb; Pres Spanish Clb; Drm Mjr(t); Pres Stu Cncl; Capt Tennis; Elks Awd; Ntl Merit Ltr; Pres Acad Fit Awd; Biomedical Resch Intern/Uc Valley Medical Ed Fndt; Capt Acad Decathlon/Sci Olympiad; Natl JACL Schol; Stanford U; Physician.

MIYOSHO, MICHAEL; Washington Union HS; Fresno, CA; (4); Am Leg Boys St; FBLA; VP Science Clb; Rep Stu Cncl; Stat Ftbl; Var Tennis; High Hon Roll; Hon Roll; Lion Awd; Sec NHS; U Sthrn CA; Math.

MIZE, DANIELLE M; Arroyo Grande HS; Pismo Beach, CA; (3); Cmnty Wkr; Rep Sr Cls; JV Var Cheerldng; JV Sftbl; U; Marine Biolgist.

MIZERAK, ANDY J; Escondido HS; Escondido, CA; (1); Church Yth Grp; JV L Vllybl; Hon Roll; UCSD; Doctor.

MIZINIAK, MIKOLAJ; Canyon HS; Canyon Country, CA; (3); 43/501; JV Socr; Jr Air Force ROTC.

MIZUGUCHI, STACEY E; Pioneer HS; San Jose, CA; (1); Spanish Clb; JV Vllybl; Interact Clb; Art.

MIZUMOTO, LISA; Edison Computech HS; Fresno, CA; (3); 1/240; Church Yth Grp; French Clb; Sec FBLA; Hosp Aide; JCL; Ski Clb; Band; Mrchg Band; JV Swmmng; 89 Sci Olympd 1st Pl Rgnl & 2nd Pl St; 90 Odyssy Mnd 1st Pl Rgnl & 4th St; Fresno Gumyo Taiko Grp; Stanford U; Intl Bus.

MKHITARIAN, ANNA A; Village Christian Schls; Shadow Hills, CA; (2); English Clb; Math Clb; Mu Alpha Theta; Spanish Clb; Teachers Aide; Stage Crew; Parsons; Fshn Dsgn.

MKRTCHIAN, SARA; Montebello HS; Montebello, CA; (1); Church Yth Grp; Orch.

MKRTCHYAN, HARUTYUN; Hollywood HS; Los Angeles, CA; (3); Chess Clb; Church Yth Grp; FCA; Math Clb; Church Choir; School Play; Yrbk; Off Sr Cls; Bsbl; Bsktbl; USC.

MO, CUINI; Independence HS; San Jose, CA; (1); Church Yth Grp; French Clb; Science Clb; Orch; Hon Roll; Pres Acad Fit Awd; Chinese Club.

MO, SOCHETRA; Mc Lane HS; Fresno, CA; (3); 14/30; Drama Clb; FTA; Model UN; Science Clb; Ski Clb; Spanish Clb; SADD; Stage Crew; Ed Phtg Yrbk; Sec Sr Cls; Interact Clb Treas; CSF VP; MESA & Sci Olympiad; CSUF Fresno ST; Psych.

MOALA, ILAISAANE T; Mt Diablo HS; W Pittsburg, CA; (1); Church Choir; Sec Frsh Cls; JV Sftbl; Trk; Hon Roll; Cnflct Rsltn Prgm; CSF; DVC; Lawyer.

MOATS, MEGAN; Tehachapi HS; Tehachapi, CA; (3); 5/225; Am Leg Aux Girls St; Church Yth Grp; Treas FBLA; Pep Clb; Treas Soph Cls; Stu Cncl; Var Cheerldng; Intrml Gym; Var Trk; High Hon Roll; Friday Night Live Clb; Stu Forum; CSF; USCS; Marine Bio.

MOBECK, CRAIG M; Bellarmine College Prep; San Jose, CA; (3); 53/308; Church Yth Grp; Cmnty Wkr; Service Clb; Teachers Aide; JV Bsbl; Stat Trk.

MOBERG, KIRSTEN E; Davis SR HS; Davis, CA; (3); Band; Pep Band; Yrbk; Rep Frsh Cls; Capt Cheerldng; Var JV Fld Hcky; Peer Counselor.

MOBERT, BRENDAN Y; Point Arena HS; Gualala, CA; (2); School Play; Stage Crew; Nwsp; Hon Roll; Sonoma ST U Pre-Coll Upwrd Bound Prm; Poems Pblshd Lnd Six Seasns; Coll; Physics.

MOBLEY, DORENA E; Enterprise HS; Redding, CA; (3); Girl Scts; Teachers Aide; Nwsp; Hon Roll; Pres Acad Fit Awd.

MOBLEY, JEFF C; Modoc HS; Alturas, CA; (3); FFA; Yrbk; Hon Roll; Carpentry 1st Pl Awd 90; Carpentry.

MOBLEY, JENNIFER ANNE; Eisenhower HS; Rialto, CA; (4); 83/655; Model UN; Pres Frsh Cls; Rep Soph Cls; Rep Jr Cls; Rep Sr Cls; Stu Cncl; Capt Cheerldng; High Hon Roll; Hon Roll; CA Assn Of Stu Cncls Rgnl Pres; CA Assn Of Stu Cncls St Cncl; Azurettes; UC San Bernardino; Poltcl Sci.

MOBLEY, TANISHA L; Antelope Valley HS; Lancaster, CA; (3); Church Yth Grp; JA; Cit Awd; Hon Roll; Blk Stu Union; Bus Ed Commndtn; Spelman; Perfrmng Arts.

MOBLEY, WENDY D; Riverbank HS; Riverbank, CA; (2); Church Yth Grp; SADD; Swmmng; Tennis; Modesto JC; Comp Pgmr.

MOCHEL, GLENN E; Delta HS; We Sacramento, CA; (1); JV Bsbl; West Sacramento Police Cadet; Archtctre.

MOCHIZUKI, LISA MARI; San Joaquin Memorial HS; Hanford, CA; (1); Pres French Clb; Math Clb; CSF; Shotokan Karate; Frdy Nght Live; Genrl Acad Excllnc Awd.

MOCK, CYNTHIA J; John F Kennedy HS; Sacramento, CA; (1); 25/559; Church Yth Grp; FCA; Rep Frsh Cls; JV Bsktbl; Var Sftbl; Cit Awd; High Hon Roll; Berkeley; Pharm.

MOCK, DAVE P; California HS; San Ramon, CA; (3); High Hon Roll; Hon Roll; Ntl Merit Ltr; San Diego ST.

MOCK, JUDY; Mark Keppel HS; Monterey Park, CA; (4); High Hon Roll; Hon Roll; CA ST U; Bus Admin.

MOCK, LINDA; Chinese Christian Schls; Union City, CA; (3); Chrmn Church Yth Grp; Church Choir; Mrchg Band; Orch; Nwsp; Intrml Vllybl; High Hon Roll; Hon Roll; San Francisco Bay Area Sci Fair 4th Pl; Contintl Math Leag Achvmt Cert; Chrysler Fund AAU Cert.

MOCSNY, TARA F; George Washington HS; San Francisco, CA; (2); Speech Tm; Band; Hon Roll; Opt Clb Awd; Coaches Cup; Webster Cup; 1st Alt St Chmpnshps Speech 89-90.

MOCTEZUMA, ANA L; Montebello HS; Los Angeles, CA; (2); Church Yth Grp; Teachers Aide; Acpl Chr; VP Chorus; Mrchg Band; Var JV Bsktbl; JV Vllybl; Cit Awd; Hon Roll; UCLA Mariposa Prog; Psych.

MODANLOU, BIJAN S; Corona Del Mar HS; Corona Del Mar, CA; (2); AFS; Key Clb; SADD; Lit Mag; Ftbl; Wrstlng; PAJ; UCLA; Bus.

MODARRESS, KATAYOON; Miraleste HS; Ranchos Palos Ver, CA; (3); 63/175; Service Clb; Spanish Clb; Powder Puff Ftbl; JV Socr; JV Sftbl; Hon Roll; Pres Acad Fit Awd; Girls Athltc Clb; Math.

MODESTO JR, RUBEN; A A Stagg HS; Stockton, CA; (1); Band; Mrchg Band; Var Wrstlng; High Hon Roll; Hon Roll; Georgetown; Lwyr.

MODGLIN, KEVIN D; St Bernard Catholic HS; Los Angeles, CA; (3); Church Yth Grp; Pres Computer Clb; Hon Roll; NEDT Awd; CSF; Natl Pk Svc Vlntr Yosemite Natl Pk; UCSB; Elctrnc Engrng.

MODUGNO, LETITIA; Canyon HS; Cyn Cntry, CA; (4); 2/474; Am Leg Aux Girls St; Church Yth Grp; Pres Drama Clb; Treas FBLA; Intnl Clb; Ed Nwsp; VP Frsh Cls; Treas Jr Cls; JV Crs Cntry; JV Stat Trk; Safe Rides; CSF; Acadmc Ltr; U Of CA San Diego; Educ.

MODUGNO, MARIKA A; William S Hart HS; Newhall, CA; (2); Treas Church Yth Grp; Girl Scts; JV Bsktbl; CA Schlrshp Fed; JV Knwldg Mstrs Open.

MOELTER, SHANNON; Santana HS; Santee, CA; (4); 6/557; Church Yth Grp; GAA; Varsity Clb; Var L Swmmng; Var L Vllybl; High Hon Roll; Hon Roll; Jr NHS; Lifgrd/Swm Instr; Golden St Alg-Hnrs Geom; Tribune All Acad Swmmr; SDSU; Math Teacher.

MOEN, SHAWN; St Joseph HS; Westminster, CA; (4); Church Yth Grp; GAA; Letterman Clb; Office Aide; Pep Clb; Spanish Clb; SADD; Varsity Clb; Drill Tm; Powder Puff Ftbl; U Of Southern CA; Phys Thrpy.

MOENCH, SARA; Lemoore HS; NAS Lemoore, CA; (1); Band; Mrchg Band; Pep Band; Rep Frsh Cls; Var Cheerldng; Mgr(s); Score Keeper; Mgr Vllybl; Hon Roll; All Stars Sftbl; Penn ST.

MOERK, KIRSTIN C; Bullard HS; Fresno, CA; (3); 1/600; Cmnty Wkr; German Clb; Hosp Aide; Key Clb; SADD; School Play; High Hon Roll; Hon Roll; Ntl Merit SF; Amnesty Intl; Big Brothers/Big Sisters; Ylae U; Psych.

MOES, KELLY; Millikan HS; Long Beach, CA; (4); 57/750; Church Yth Grp; Cmnty Wkr; Dance Clb; Key Clb; Pep Clb; Teachers Aide; Capt Drill Tm; School Musical; Var Cheerldng; Var Pom Pon; CSULB; Chld Psych.

MOESTA, JULIE A; Temecula Valley HS; Murrieta, CA; (4); 1/360; Church Yth Grp; Teachers Aide; Crs Cntry; Trk; Prfct Atten Awd; Pres Acad Fit Awd; Val; CSF Seal Bearer; John Brown U; Bio.

MOFFAT, BLAINE L; Hueneme HS; Port Hueneme, CA; (2); 182/504; JV Ftbl; Draftsman.

MOFFAT, KARI L; Rio Mesa HS; Camarillo, CA; (1); Church Yth Grp; Drama Clb; School Play; Stage Crew; Off Frsh Cls; JV Vllybl; Cit Awd; High Hon Roll; Pres Acad Fit Awd; Fst Ptch Sftbl; BYU; Lawyer.

MOFFAT, SUSAN M; El Toro HS; El Toro, CA; (2); Orch; School Musical; Elem Teacher.

MOFFAT, TINA N; El Camino HS; Sacramento, CA; (4); 89/366; JV Bsktbl; Var JV Socr; Var Tennis; Vllybl; Awd Hnr For Consistnt & Outstndng Schlrshp; UC Davis; DVM.

MOFFETT, WHITNEY K; Tulare Union HS; Tulare, CA; (2); Letterman Clb; Flag Corp; Mrchg Band; JV Var Bsktbl; JV Sftbl; Hon Roll; Cosmetologist.

MOFFITT, ANDREA; Indio HS; Indio, CA; (2); 91/536; French Clb; Cheerldng; Trk; Wt Lftg; Cit Awd; Hon Roll; UCLA; Vet.

MOFFITT, DIANE; Central Union HS; El Centro, CA; (2); 7/900; Drama Clb; German Clb; Speech Tm; School Play; UC Berkley; Scl Sci.

MOFFITT, HILLARY; Biggs HS; Biggs, CA; (3); 3/52; Am Leg Aux Girls St; 4-H; Am Leg Boys St; Treas Stu Cncl; Stat Bsktbl; 4-H Awd; High Hon Roll; NHS; Pres Acad Fit Awd; CSF; Prom Co-Chairman; Pharmacy.

MOFID, GOLAFARID; Corona HS; Corona, CA; (2); Cmnty Wkr; Dance Clb; English Clb; French Clb; Intnl Clb; Library Aide; Ski Clb; Rptr Nwsp; JV Bsktbl; Tennis; Save Clb VP; Bst Recycler Awd; PCR Clb Pres; Loma Linda U; Med.

MOGANNAM, BISHARA A; Abraham Lincoln HS; San Francisco, CA; (3); Boy Scts; Church Yth Grp; Ed Nwsp; Swmmng; Trk; UC Berkeley; Mech Engr.

MOGANNAM, FREIDA N; Lowell HS; San Francisco, CA; (3); Cmnty Wkr; Latin Clb; Red Cross Aide; SADD; JV Crs Cntry; Pres Acad Fit Awd; Artwork Displayed De Young Museum; Premed Club.

MOGEN, MICHAEL J; Indio HS; Indio, CA; (4); 10/367; Temple Yth Grp; Band; Mrchg Band; Var JV Trk; Prfct Atten Awd; UC Riverside; Math.

MOGGIA, ELLEN; Dos Pueblos HS; Goleta, CA; (3); Church Yth Grp; Drama Clb; Intnl Clb; School Play; Variety Show; Ed Nwsp; Hon Roll; Jr NHS; NHS; Psych Clb, VP & Co-Fndr.

MOGHADAM, MONIREH M; Chaffey HS; Ontario, CA; (4); 11/436; Pres Sec Service Clb; SADD; Yrbk; Stu Cncl; Powder Puff Ftbl; Var Trk; Var Vllybl; High Hon Roll; Kiwanis Awd; CSF; Pitzer Coll; Econ.

MOGHTADERI, KAMRAN; Saint Ignatius College Prep; San Francisco, CA; (3); Service Clb; Spirit Clb; Statesmen Of Amer; CSF; Bus.

MOGUEL, ROBERT; St John Bosco HS; Norwalk, CA; (4); 67/200; SADD; Varsity Clb; Crs Cntry; Trk; Hon Roll; Spanish NHS; MVP Cross Cntry; Outstndg Achvt Spnsh; Cal Poly Pomona; Comptr Sci.

MOGULL, ROBIN L; Del Campo HS; Carmichael, CA; (3); 186/446; Dance Clb; SADD; Temple Yth Grp; Band; Drill Tm; Capt Flag Corp; Mrchg Band; Pep Band; Capt Idntfctn Unit Marching Band; Long Beach ST; Liberal Arts.

MOH, TIM; Andrew Hill HS; San Jose, CA; (3); Math Clb; Math Tm; JV Bsbl; High Hon Roll; Hon Roll; Prfct Atten Awd; Bdmtn Team; Supv List; U C Davis; Med.

MOHAJERANI, LADAN; Oak Park HS; Agoura, CA; (2); Key Clb; CSF; Stu Govt Hstrn.

MOHAMMAD, SUHILA; George Washington HS; San Francisco, CA; (2); Stage Crew; Hon Roll; UC Berkley.

MOHAMMED, HANIF; Warren HS; Downey, CA; (3); Yrbk; Off Jr Cls; Rgnl Occptnl Trng; Outstndng Cls Awds; Stu Mnth Awd ROP; UCLA; Electrnc Engr.

MOHAMMED, SARAH; Wilson HS; San Francisco, CA; (3); FBLA; Hon Roll; Cert Mrt Soc Of Wmn Engrs; Gldn St Exam Awd; Cert Amer Soc Cell Bio, Amer Soc Biochem, Moleclr Bio; U Of San Francisco; Nrsng.

MOHAMOUD, ABDI MOHAMED; Crawford HS; San Diego, CA; (4); JV Bsktbl; Mgr(s); Score Keeper; Hon Roll; San Diego Chapt Links Mst Outstndng Black Male In Cty; Project STEP; Congrssnl Dstngshd Svc Awd; San Diego ST U; Comp Sci.

MOHANAN, SVETA; Quartz Hill HS; Lancaster, CA; (2); Debate Tm; Hosp Aide; Key Clb; SADD; High Hon Roll; Envrnmntl Intrsts Grnpc Earth Islnd; UCLA; Med.

MOHME, STEPHEN A; Santa Barbara HS; Santa Barbara, CA; (3); Boy Scts; Cmnty Wkr; VP SADD; Rep Stu Cncl; Var Tennis; Hon Roll; Lion Awd; St Schlr; HOBY; CIF Southern Sectn 5 A Boys Tnns Chmpns 88-90; Engrng.

MOHR, CORY R; Beaumont HS; Beaumont, CA; (1); Church Yth Grp; Teachers Aide; Trk; Masonic Awd; USC; Bus.

MOHR, SANDRA; Willows HS; Willows, CA; (2); Sftbl; High Hon Roll; Hon Roll; CSF; FNL; Chico ST U; Bus Mngmnt.

MOHTASHAMIAN, ARASH; Ontario HS; Ontario, CA; (3); German Clb; Math Clb; Hon Roll; St Schlr; Snt CA Lgsltr Schlstc Accmplshmt Gldn ST Exm; Hnr Ushr Awd; Cert Mrt Math, Frgn Lang; Mdcl Dr; Pre-Med.

MOITE, ROBERT; Parlier HS; Parlier, CA; (2); Boy Scts; Cmnty Wkr; Band; Mrchg Band; Pep Band; Off Soph Cls; JV Bsbl; JV Capt Ftbl; Var Wrstlng; Top Offnsve Ftbl Plyr Awd; Avcad Achvt Awds; Band Awd; Phys Ed Teacher.

MOK, APOLLO P; California HS; San Ramon, CA; (4); Chess Clb; Cmnty Wkr; Library Aide; Teachers Aide; Var Mgr(s); High Hon Roll; Prfct Atten Awd; Rotary Awd; California High School Student Of The Month May 1990; Cal ST; Finance.

MOK, GILBERT W; Gretchen Whitney HS; Cerritos, CA; (3); Drama Clb; Hosp Aide; Key Clb; Library Aide; Nwsp; Hist Sr Cls; High Hon Roll; NHS; French Clb; Service Clb; Hmrm Rep Of Schl Cngrss; CA Schlrshp Fed Mem.

MOK, MANITH; Woodrow Wilson HS; Long Beach, CA; (4); Math Clb; Math Tm; Science Clb; Orch; DAR Awd; High Hon Roll; NHS; Pres Acad Fit Awd; Rotary Awd; Yth Vol Svc Awd; Math Dept Awd; Best Math Stu 89-90; CA ST Long Beach; Comp Sci.

MOK, PATRICIA P; Skyline HS; Oakland, CA; (3); German Clb; Sec Key Clb; SADD; Band; Jazz Band; Orch; Hon Roll; Math.

MOK, PLATO A; California HS; San Ramon, CA; (3); 23/381; Cmnty Wkr; Computer Clb; Debate Tm; NFL; High Hon Roll; Contra Costa Cnty Spllng Chmpnshp; SPA Clb; Wew Crew; Law.

MOK, SIMON; Westmoor HS; Daly City, CA; (3); Vrsty Badmntn; San Mateo Coll.

MOK, YURIKA; Crossroads Schl; Santa Monica, CA; (4); Cmnty Wkr; Orch; Ntl Merit Ltr; Oberlin Coll.

MOLACEK, JENNIFER; Hemet HS; Hemet, CA; (3); 68/535; Hosp Aide; JA; Office Aide; Science Clb; High Hon Roll; Hon Roll; ROP Nrs Asst; CSF; Top Engl Awd; Pediatrician.

MOLENDYK, MINDY M; Mt Diablo HS; Concord, CA; (4); Cmnty Wkr; Hon Roll; CA Schlrshp Fed; Diablo Valley Clg; Zoolgy.

MOLENKAMP, WILLIE C; Livermore HS; Livermore, CA; (2); Church Yth Grp; Debate Tm; Band; JV Ftbl; Var Wrstlng; Hon Roll; CSF.

MOLER, SEAN; Aptos HS; Aptos, CA; (1); Yrbk; L Intrml Bsktbl; L Var Crs Cntry; L JV Tennis; Hon Roll; Bus Clb; CSF; Bus.

MOLGARD, VALORIE; Mesa Verde HS; Citrus Heights, CA; (1); High Hon Roll; Hon Roll; Bus.

MOLHO, JOSHUA; El Dorado HS; Placerville, CA; (3); 6/350; Am Leg Boys St; Key Clb; Science Clb; School Play; Var Socr; High Hon Roll; NHS; Ntl Merit Ltr; CA Schltc Fed Pres 89-90; Engrng.

MOLICA, STEPHEN R; Nevada Union HS; Nevada City, CA; (3); 68/550; JV Bsbl; JV Capt Bsktbl; Var Capt Ftbl; Hon Roll; Bus.

MOLIN, ALLISON P; Marysville HS; Forbestown, CA; (3); Sec Art Clb; Debate Tm; Drama Clb; NFL; Spanish Clb; Hon Roll; CA Arts Schlr 90; Intrsts Invrmntl Prtctn; San Francisco Art Inst; Art.

MOLINA, ANA V; San Bernardino HS; San Bernardino, CA; (3); 7/35; Chorus; Drill Tm; Rotary Yth Ldrshp Awd; Poetry; Work Part Time; Child Psych.

MOLINA, CARIE A; Dinuba HS; Dinuba, CA; (3); Band; Jazz Band; Mrchg Band; Pep Band; Hon Roll; Band Awds; Acad Achvt Awds; Bio Physics.

MOLINA, CARLOS A; Copuchino HS; San Bruno, CA; (3); Church Yth Grp; Rep Stu Cncl; Ftbl; Phys Ftnss; Coll Of San Mateo; Radio DJ.

MOLINA, CAROL L; Canyon Springs HS; Moreno Valley, CA; (3); Var Swmmng; Hon Roll; Sci Fair 2nd Pl; UC Davis; Intl Bus.

MOLINA, EDWIN; Baldwin Park HS; Baldwin Park, CA; (2); U Of CA Berkeley; Amer Hstry.

MOLINA, FRANCISCO A; Manual Arts HS; Los Angeles, CA; (2); Office Aide; ROTC; Teachers Aide; Color Guard; Drill Tm; Rep Frsh Cls; Cit Awd; WA U; Bus Mgmt.

MOLINA, KARLA M; Yucca Valley HS; Joshua Tree, CA; (3); Intnl Clb; Math Clb; Capt Color Guard; Mrchg Band; Trk; Vllybl; High Hon Roll; Hon Roll; Scuba Dvng; Mock Trial; Geom Gldn St Awd High Hnrs; Harvey Mud U; Engrng.

MOLINA, KRISTYNLORETH; Fremont HS; Oakland, CA; (2); Nwsp; Cit Awd; High Hon Roll; Hon Roll; Doctor.

MOLINA, LIZA; St Genevieve HS; Canoga Park, CA; (3); Dance Clb; Pep Clb; Drill Tm; Yrbk; VP Frsh Cls; High Hon Roll; NEDT Awd; Prfct Atten Awd; Nwsp; Stu Cncl; Miss Spr Snstnl Santa Barbara USA Camp Routine B; CA Polytechnic In SLO; Arch.

MOLINA, MARY SANTOS; King City HS; Greenfield, CA; (3); Church Yth Grp; Drama Clb; Thesps; Drill Tm; Flag Corp; School Play; Stage Crew; Sftbl; Acting.

MOLINA, MICHELLE; Madera HS; Madera, CA; (3); Church Yth Grp; Trk; Hon Roll; Woodbury U; Intnl Bus.

MOLINA, MONIQUE; Foothill HS; Bakersfield, CA; (3); Teachers Aide; Hon Roll; CA ST U; Fashion Design.

MOLINA, NORMAN; Palisades HS; Los Angeles, CA; (2); Spanish Clb; Prfct Atten Awd; Bus Educ.

MOLINA, ROSA ELENA; Los Altos HS; Hacienda Hts, CA; (4); 36/375; Drama Clb; Var Capt Crs Cntry; Var Trk; High Hon Roll; Pres Schlr; CSF; Jr Hon Grd; Cal Poly Pomona; Liberal Arts.

MOLINA, SERVANDO; Reedley HS; Orange Cove, CA; (4); 1/330; Computer Clb; FTA; Science Clb; Teachers Aide; JV Capt Bsktbl; JV Crs Cntry; Var L Vllybl; High Hon Roll; Val; Peer Tutor Prgm; JETS; Schlr Athlte; Stanford; Math.

MOLINARI, CHRISTIAN M; St Ignatius College Prep; San Francisco, CA; (3); 3/251; Am Leg Boys St; Letterman Clb; Service Clb; Spanish Clb; Speech Tm; VP Soph Cls; VP Jr Cls; VP Stu Cncl; JV Bsktbl; Var Socr; Co-Pres Christian Life Cmnty; Big Brothers; CSF.

MOLINARI, MONICA C; Ramona Convent; Montebello, CA; (3); Church Yth Grp; Cmnty Wkr; GAA; Latin Clb; Var Letterman Clb; Spanish Clb; Varsity Clb; School Play; Stu Cncl; Var Swmmng; Co-Chrmn SMARTI Yth Grp South Montebello Area Rsdnts; Cal Poly Pomona; Vet.

MOLINELLI, AMY; Burlingame HS; Hillsborough, CA; (2); Church Yth Grp; Debate Tm; 4-H; French Clb; Treas Soph Cls; JV Tennis; Hon Roll; Law.

MOLLENKAMP, AMY; Chadwick HS; Rolling Hills Est, CA; (1); Cmnty Wkr; Debate Tm; Drama Clb; Hosp Aide; Speech Tm; Chorus; Nwsp; Var Socr; JV Tennis; Wt Lftg; Young Poets Soc; Writer Of Mnth Schl Nwsp; CA Interschltc Fed Acad Tm Hnrb Mntn; Childrens Theatre; Cardiologist.

MOLLICA, LAWSON C; Edison HS; Huntington Beach, CA; (4); Debate Tm; Model UN; SADD; Var L Ftbl; Var L Trk; Var Wt Lftg; Hon Roll; Mdl UN Gavel Awd; All Cnty, St Ftbl; Gldn Key Acad Athltc Awd; Outstndng Linemna Yr; Track Hall Fame; U Of Pittsburgh; Sports Med.

MOLLICA, MIKE D; Las Lomas HS; Walnut Creek, CA; (1); Church Yth Grp; Rptr Nwsp; JV Bsbl; Hon Roll; Az St U; Sport Psychology.

MOLLOT, SCOT J; Foothill HS; Santa Ana, CA; (3); 19/316; Boy Scts; Temple Yth Grp; JV Vllybl; JV Var Wrstlng; Hon Roll; Gldn St Exam Hnrs Alg & Geom; Berkeley; Advtsng.

MOLON, NOEL P; Montgomery HS; San Diego, CA; (3); Church Yth Grp; FBLA; Service Clb; Band; Church Choir; Mrchg Band; School Play; Nwsp; Cit Awd; Hon Roll; UCSD Coll Rdy Wrtrs Proj Cert Outstndng Achvt 90; Peer Cnslr 89-90; Cmnty Svc Agncy Vol; U CA San Diego; Ec.

MOLWAY, HOLIDAY; University HS; Irvine, CA; (2); Church Yth Grp; AFS; GAA; Letterman Clb; Science Clb; Ski Clb; Varsity Clb; Sec Soph Cls; Off Jr Cls; Stu Cncl; Mst Insprtnl Grl Vrsty Trck 1990; GIF In Trck; Sci.

MOMAND, WAHID; American HS; Fremont, CA; (1).

MOMII, MACHIKO; Salinas HS; Seattle, WA; (4); 107/300; Sec Church Yth Grp; Cmnty Wkr; VP French Clb; Intnl Clb; Key Clb; Spanish Clb; Teachers Aide; Ed Yrbk; Stu Cncl; Hon Roll; Jpn Am Ctzns Leag Schlrshp Awd; Mexicali-Mssnry Work; Whitworth Coll-Spokane.

MONA, A-ONG; Edison HS; Fresno, CA; (2); Church Yth Grp; FTA; Church Choir; JV Sftbl; Tennis; Cit Awd; Hon Roll; VITA Vlntr; Fresno ST; Dntst.

MONACO, WINIFRED; Costa Mesa HS; Costa Mesa, CA; (4); Am Leg Aux Girls St; Church Yth Grp; Ski Clb; Spanish Clb; VP Soph Cls; Treas Jr Cls; Off Sr Cls; Stu Cncl; Var JV Cheerldng; JV Trk; SDSU; Pre-Med.

MONAHAN, LISA; Arlington HS; Riverside, CA; (4); 22/340; Chorus; Color Guard; School Musical; Lit Mag; Var Pom Pon; High Hon Roll; Chamber Singers; Treas Of Yth To Yth; U CA; Vet.

MONARES, ADRIANA; Turlock HS; Turlock, CA; (3); Church Yth Grp; Latin Clb; Library Aide; Spanish Clb; Cit Awd; Hon Roll; Prfct Atten Awd; Pres Acad Fit Awd; CA ST U Stanislaus.

MONARRES, ADDA I; Saint Michael HS; Los Angeles, CA; (2); Spanish Clb; Hon Roll; Sal; Stu Of Mnth; Ucla; Engrng.

MONARREZ, ALVARO ADRIAN; Montclair HS; Montclair, CA; (4); Key Clb; Math Clb; VICA; Intrml Bsktbl; Intrml Socr; Intrml Swmmng; Intrml Swmmng; Hon Roll; CSF; GATE; CA ST Polytechnic U; Mech Eng.

MONARREZ, SANDRA; Notre Dame HS; Salinas, CA; (2); Var Crs Cntry; JV Sftbl; Hon Roll; A Team; Chico ST; Dentist.

MONASTERIO, CLAUDIA; Bullard HS; Fresno, CA; (2); English Clb; FCA; Intnl Clb; Math Clb; Math Tm; Science Clb; Spanish Clb; Teachers Aide; School Play; Lit Mag; CSF.

MONCADA, JERARDO H; John A O'connell HS; San Francisco, CA; (2); Hon Roll; San Francisco Boys Clb Mssn Brnch 8 Yrs; Mission Keystone Clb 2 Yrs; CA Polytech ST U; Strctl Drft.

MONCADA, SUSIE; Santa Teresa HS; San Jose, CA; (3); Spanish Clb; Band; Mrchg Band; Var Socr; JV Trk; Wt Lftg; Stu Of Wk-Frgn Lang; Outstndng Span Stu; UCLA; Med.

MONCAYO, OSCAR; North Salinas HS; Salinas, CA; (1); Arch.

MONCLOVA, TINA; Alvin HS; Lamont, CA; (1); Church Yth Grp; Spanish Clb; Pres Frsh Cls; Sftbl; Vllybl; Hon Roll; MESA; CSF; Cal Poly Coll; Arch.

MONCRIEF, JULIE R; Don Antonio Lugo HS; Chino Hills, CA; (3); Drama Clb; Pep Clb; Ski Clb; Powder Puff Ftbl; Swmmng; Trk; Hon Roll; San Diego ST; Bus Admin.

MONCUR, JARON C; Shafter HS; Shafter, CA; (3); Boy Scts; Church Yth Grp; Letterman Clb; Bsktbl; Ftbl; Wt Lftg; BYU; Bus.

MONDAY, KLAY W; Cordova SR HS; Rancho Cordova, CA; (3); 1/460; Pres German Clb; Model UN; SADD; Teachers Aide; High Hon Roll; Hon Roll; Jr NHS; NHS; Ntl Merit SF; Cngrss Bundestag Yth Exchng Schlrshp; UC Berkeley.

MONDRAGON, JUAN E; Baldwin Park HS; Baldwin Park, CA; (2); Drama Clb; Science Clb; Variety Show; JV Bsbl; JV Bsktbl; JV Ftbl; Hon Roll.

MONDRAGON, JULIE; Hawthorne HS; Inglewood, CA; (3); Teachers Aide; Drill Tm; Trk; Prfct Atten Awd.

MONDRAGON, ROXANNE R; East Bakersfield HS; Bakersfield, CA; (4); Church Yth Grp; Debate Tm; JA; Science Clb; High Hon Roll; Hon Roll; Treas MESA Clb 89; Pres MESA Clb 90; 4th Pl Natl Bicentl Constnl; Art Awd Bank Of Am; Schlrshp La Tolt; Bakersfield JC; Arch.

MONERIEF, DEBBIE A; Montclair HS; Upland, CA; (2); Drm Mjr(t); Mrchg Band; Orch; Pep Band; Cit Awd; Prfct Atten Awd; Cert Achvt; Boston U; Music.

MONES, CRYSTAL M; Huntington Beach HS; Huntington Bch, CA; (3); Church Yth Grp; Dance Clb; German Clb; Red Cross Aide; Church Choir; Variety Show; Pres Jr Cls; Hon Roll; HOBY Ambssdr; Prom Orgnzr; Bus.

MONFREDINI, LAURA N; Notre Dame HS; San Mateo, CA; (2); Church Yth Grp; Debate Tm; Math Clb; Science Clb; School Play; Cheerldng; JV Tennis; Hon Roll; NEDT Awd; CSF; Jr Statesman Of America; Summer Swim Tm; Bus Law.

MONG, FRANK Y; St Ingatius College Prep; San Francisco, CA; (2); Cmnty Wkr; Dance Clb; JA; Latin Clb; Science Clb; Varsity Clb; Var L Vllybl; Hon Roll; CA Schlrshp Fdr; Med Fld.

MONGE, MANUEL LUIS; Don Bosco Tech Inst; Los Angeles, CA; (2); 40/212; Debate Tm; Drama Clb; Trk; NHS; Campus Mnstry; Intrmrl Flr Hockey; CA Poly Pomona; Aerosp Engr.

MONGE, MELANIE R; Mater Dei HS; Santa Ana, CA; (2); Church Yth Grp; GAA; Church Choir; Var Crs Cntry; JV Mgr(s); Var JV Score Keeper; Var Trk; High Hon Roll; Acctng.

MONGE, SONNY; El Camino Real HS; West Hills, CA; (2); Thesps; Envrnmntl Club; UC San Diego.

MONGRAIN, JASON; Brawley Union HS; Brawley, CA; (3); Tennis; Wt Lftg; UCSD; Psych.

MONGUIA, RAMON; Chaffey HS; Ontario, CA; (1); Art Clb; Church Yth Grp; Teachers Aide; Chorus; High Hon Roll; Hon Roll; Outstndng Stu; Mst Imprvd Stu; Cartoonist.

MONIA, VANESSA N; Saratoga HS; Saratoga, CA; (3); Dance Clb; Drama Clb; SADD; Chorus; Church Choir; Color Guard; School Musical; School Play; Variety Show; Vlntr Am Vets; Humbolt; Actrss.

MONIZ, JENNIFER; Santa Rosa HS; Santa Rosa, CA; (4); Dance Clb; JA; Pep Clb; Variety Show; Cheerldng; Score Keeper.

MONIZ, KAREN; Oakdale HS; Oakdale, CA; (3); Letterman Clb; SADD; Teachers Aide; Rptr Yrbk; Bsktbl; Powder Puff Ftbl; Sftbl; Vllybl; Wt Lftg; Cit Awd; ASVAB Exam; Bst Offnsv Plyr Sftbl; Chld Psych.

MONJACK, KRISTIE MARIE; Paraclete HS; Quartz Hill, CA; (2); Church Yth Grp; Cmnty Wkr; Office Aide; Service Clb; VP SADD; Yrbk; Hon Roll; SADD VP; Z Clb; Service Awd; U C; Child Psych.

MONK, GRANT; Yucaipa HS; Mentone, CA; (4); Pres Chess Clb; Sec FBLA; German Clb; NFL; Speech Tm; School Play; Ed Lit Mag; Tutrd Govt, Ec; Acad Dcthln Tm; Acad Excllnc Awd, Acad Ltr; Pamona Coll; Grmn.

MONKRESS, MATTHEW W; Fred L Beyer HS; Modesto, CA; (3); Boy Scts; Drama Clb; School Play; Variety Show; Cit Awd; High Hon Roll; Hon Roll; UCLA; Hstry.

MONLEY, ERIKA J; Woodland HS; Woodland, CA; (3); Church Yth Grp; Band; Yrbk; Capt Bsktbl; JV Sftbl; Var Sftbl; JV Vllybl; Hon Roll; Ahtl Of Yr; Ed.

MONNIER, MATT B; Woodland HS; Woodland, CA; (2); Church Yth Grp; FFA; SADD; Hon Roll; Jr NHS; Prfct Atten Awd; UCD; Engrng.

MONNIN, LAURIE A; San Marcos HS; San Marcos, CA; (3); 4-H; FFA; Girl Scts; JV Var Tennis; Hon Roll; Mesa Coll; Vet.

MONNINGER, ROBERT M; Arlington HS; Riverside, CA; (2); L Ftbl; Hon Roll; USC; Pro Ftbl.

MONPONBANUA, AILEEN H; Palm Springs HS; Palm Springs, CA; (3); 13/600; Cmnty Wkr; Treas Spanish Clb; Hon Roll; Jr Statesmn Of Amer; CSF; U Of CA San Diego; Math.

MONROE, AARON N; Homestead HS; Sunnyvale, CA; (1); Church Yth Grp; Dance Clb; Drama Clb; Pep Clb; Thesps; School Play; Stage Crew; JV Wrstlng; Actng.

MONROE, HEATHER S; Don Antonio Lugo HS; Chino, CA; (4); 21/474; Pres Church Yth Grp; Cmnty Wkr; Drama Clb; French Clb; Thesps; School Play; Stage Crew; Stat Bsktbl; High Hon Roll; NHS; Yng Wmnhd Medallion; Vol Chuck Badar Cmpgn; U CA Riverside; Pol Sci.

MONROE, JENNIFER D; Oak Ridge HS; Rescue, CA; (3); FBLA; JA; Office Aide; Acpl Chr; School Play; Stage Crew; Gym; Cit Awd; High Hon Roll; Hon Roll; Sq Dancing/Diploma; Childrens Plays; Am River; Bus.

MONROE, JONATHAN E; Don Antonio Lugo HS; Chino, CA; (2); JV Bsbl; Var Bsktbl; Hon Roll; UNLV; Pro Athl.

MONROE, LAURA; University HS; Los Angeles, CA; (4); Teachers Aide; Chorus; Co-Capt Flag Corp; Rptr Yrbk; Off Sr Cls; JV Bsktbl; Hon Roll; Blck Stu Union Pres; U MD Baltimore; Corp Law.

MONROE, MELISSA S; Fairfield HS; San Antonio, TX; (2); GAA; SADD; French Hon Soc; Jrnlsm.

MONROE, PERRY; Alameda HS; Alameda, CA; (2); 10/290; Boy Scts; Var Swmmng; High Hon Roll; Order Of Th Arrow Vice Chief; Water Polo V Ltrmn.

MONROE, TARA L; Central HS; El Centro, CA; (3); Var Swmmng; Hon Roll; Physcl Thrpst.

MONROY, CARLOS A; Santa Barbara HS; Santa Barbara, CA; (3); Computer Clb; Rptr Ed Nwsp; Off Sr Cls; Socr; Hon Roll; Union Latina Club Fndr & 1st VP; Bilingual Comp Wrkshp; Stu Of Wk; Outstndng ESl Stu; Law.

MONROY, JANET G; Brawley Union HS; Brawley, CA; (1); Church Yth Grp; Hon Roll; Early Acad Outreach Pgm; UCSD; Poltcl Sci.

MONROY, LAURA P; King City Joint Union HS; Greenfield, CA; (3); Drama Clb; FBLA; SADD; School Play; Trk; High Hon Roll; Grad From Yo Puedo 87; Adv Ldrshp Trng 3 Yrs; :Csf; Org For Raza Achvmnt; Amer Soc Cell Bio Pgm; UCSB; Psychiatry.

MONSALVE, OLGA R; Bonita Vista HS; Bonita, CA; (3); 89/559; Church Yth Grp; Rptr Nwsp; Yrbk; Rep Soph Cls; Rep Stu Cncl; Score Keeper; L Var Swmmng; Cit Awd; High Hon Roll; Pres Acad Fit Awd; Task Force-Soph & Jnr; Socl Sci.

MONSON, ANGELA M; Atascadero HS; Atascadero, CA; (3); Church Yth Grp; Church Choir; Rptr Nwsp; Yrbk; Var L Bsktbl; Var L Vllybl; Marine Bio.

MONTAGUE, KATHERINE; Troy HS; Fullerton, CA; (2); Teachers Aide; Band; Church Choir; Mrchg Band; Off Frsh Cls; Stu Cncl; JV Sftbl; Cit Awd; Hon Roll; Harvard; Law.

MONTALTO, LEIGH; Helix HS; La Mesa, CA; (4); 27/368; Color Guard; Church Yth Grp; FTA; VP Sec Key Clb; Service Clb; Ed Yrbk; Stu Cncl; High Hon Roll; Cal ST Northridge; Eng.

MONTALVO, PATRICIA R; Washington Union HS; Fresno, CA; (4); 56/148; French Clb; Library Aide; Model UN; Science Clb; Teachers Aide; Band; Jazz Band; Fresno City Coll; Chem.

MONTALVO, SABRINA R; Gilroy HS; Gilroy, CA; (1); Church Yth Grp; Dance Clb; Chorus; Church Choir; JV Cheerldng; Hon Roll; Pres Acad Fit Awd; Ranbow Grls Choirs, Musician; Spec Olmpcs Vlntr; Cmnty Theater; Azusa Pacific U; Music.

MONTAMO, EMILIA; Central Union HS; El Centro, CA; (3); CA Schlstc Federation; Med.

MONTANEZ, ELIZABETH A; Santa Clara HS; Oxnard, CA; (2); JV Bsktbl; JV Sftbl; JV Vllybl; Hon Roll; Fshn Dsgn.

MONTANEZ, JULIE C; Edison Computech HS; Fresno, CA; (3); Church Yth Grp; FBLA; Var Sftbl; MESA; U Of CA Riverside; Acctng.

MONTANEZ, MARGARITA; Valley HS; Santa Ana, CA; (3); Spanish Clb; Church Choir; Cit Awd; Hon Roll; Stdy Jb; U Of CA.

MONTANO, GUADALUPE; Central Union HS; El Centro, CA; (3); Math Tm; CSF; Stu Of Mnth; Engrng.

MONTANO, GUADALUPE R; Hueneme HS; Oxnard, CA; (2); Key Clb; Socr; Cit Awd; Hon Roll; Prfct Atten Awd; USB; Med.

MONTANO, JULIO C; Bell Gardens HS; Bell Gardens, CA; (2); JV Ftbl; Var Tennis; Prfct Atten Awd; Berkeley U; Gynecologist.

MONTANO, MIKE T; Bellacmine College Prep; San Jose, CA; (3); 100/300; Church Yth Grp; Intrml Bsbl; Intrml Bsktbl; Intrml Ftbl; Intrml Sftbl; Intrml Vllybl; Bowling; Arch.

MONTE, MICHAEL; Richmond HS; San Pablo, CA; (3); Cmnty Wkr; French Clb; Gym; Hon Roll; UC Berkeley; Med.

MONTEGNA, CANDICE; Point Loma HS; San Diego, CA; (3); Cmnty Wkr; Drama Clb; Key Clb; SADD; Ed Yrbk; Var Capt Cheerldng; U Of WI Madison; Psychlgy.

MONTEITH, STACIA; Etiwanda HS; Alta Loma, CA; (3); Drama Clb; French Clb; Poetry Clb.

MONTELLANO, DANIEL A; Bishop Amat HS; West Covina, CA; (3); Intrml Crs Cntry; Natl Sci Olympiad; UCLA; Law.

MONTELLANO, LIDIA; Schurr HS; Los Angeles, CA; (1); Hon Roll; UCLA; Fshn Desgnr.

MONTELONGO, ANGELICA S; Fillmore HS; Fillmore, CA; (1); Treas Frsh Cls; Cit Awd; Future Ldrs Of Am; U CA Santa Barbara Partnershp Pgm; Migrant Pgm; U CA Santa Barbara; Psych.

MONTELONGO, BEATRICE; Bell Gardens HS; Bell Gardens, CA; (3); French Clb; Dnfth Awd; CSF; Bus Admin.

MONTELONGO, DOMINIC J; Bishop Amat HS; Alhambra, CA; (3); Cmnty Wkr; Crs Cntry; Tennis; Amnesty Intl; Chrstn Svcs; Natl Hnrs Soc.

MONTELONGO, JENNIFER; Mayfield SR HS; Temple City, CA; (3); AFS; Cmnty Wkr; GAA; Library Aide; Ski Clb; Varsity Clb; Rptr Nwsp; Var Crs Cntry; Var Socr; Var Trk; Ahmonson Schlr; Friday Night Live Stu Against Drunk Driving Grp; Stanford U; Psych.

MONTEMAYOR, JON JAY E; Bonita Vista HS; Bonita, CA; (3); Band; Yrbk; Cit Awd; Hon Roll; Jr NHS; Amnsty Intl; Stu For Envrnmntl Awrnss; Engrng.

MONTEMAYOR, MARSHA; Cornelia Connelly HS; Hacienda Heights, CA; (3); Cmnty Wkr; GAA; Intnl Clb; School Play; Capt Cheerldng; High Hon Roll; Elem Educ.

MONTEMAYOR, MARYGRACE N; Los Alamitos HS; Los Alamitos, CA; (3); Intnl Clb; Spanish Clb; Teachers Aide; High Hon Roll; Cert Of Hnr; Children Of Mary; Cal Poly Pomona; Accntng.

MONTEMAYOR, RAYMOND; Loyola HS; Torrance, CA; (2); Cmnty Wkr; Yrbk; Stat Bsktbl; Hon Roll; NEDT Awd; SAT Prepartns Clss; MSA Minrty Stu Asso; Engr.

MONTENEGRO, BRENDA; Central Union HS; El Centro, CA; (3); Church Yth Grp; Prfct Atten Awd; Loma Linda; Law.

MONTENEGRO, CHRISTY A; John F Kennedy HS; Buena Park, CA; (1); Drama Clb; Chorus; Church Choir; Variety Show; Cmnctns.

MONTENEGRO, RAVI R; Troy HS; Placentia, CA; (2); 8/323; Chess Clb; Treas Math Clb; Math Tm; Treas Frsh Cls; JV Crs Cntry; JV Trk; High Hon Roll; Rotary Awd; Bible Bowl 6th Pl Test In Nation; Elec Engr.

MONTEON, ANGELICA V; Carlmont HS; Redwood City, CA; (1); Bsktbl; Sftbl; Swmmng; Stanford; Dr.

MONTERMOSO, JUAN R; Saint Francis HS; Sunnyvale, CA; (4); Cmnty Wkr; Ed Bus Profs of Am; Ed Yrbk; JV Var Crs Cntry; JV Var Golf; High Hon Roll; NHS; Ntl Merit SF; Jr Statesmn Of Amer; Pres Of Ntl Hnr Soc Chptr; Robert J Urban Awd; Yale U; Pltcl Sci.

MONTERO, CARLOS; Brawley HS; Westmorland, CA; (3); FTA.

MONTERO, CLAUDIA; Montgomery HS; San Ysidro, CA; (3); JV Sftbl; Southwestern Coll; Comp Sci.

MONTERO, PABLO; Madera HS; Madera, CA; (2); Boy Scts; French Clb; FFA; SADD; USC.

MONTERROZO, ELIDA; Van Nuys HS; Van Nuys, CA; (4); Church Yth Grp; Library Aide; Office Aide; Teachers Aide; Data Entry; Pierce Coll; Med.

MONTERRUBIO, JORGE; Fairfield HS; Fairfield, CA; (4); 14/495; Chess Clb; Math Clb; Science Clb; Var Tennis; French Hon Soc; High Hon Roll; NHS; Geneology Clb VP; #1 Hispanic; U Of CA Davis; Intl Rltns.

MONTES JR, FRANCISCO; Lindsay HS; Lindsay, CA; (3); Art Clb; Boy Scts; Church Yth Grp; Latin Clb; Spanish Clb; Temple Yth Grp; Band; Church Choir; Mrchg Band; Swing Chorus; Amer Leg Aux Awd; Calendar Art Schlorshp Pgrm; Walt Disney Dreamers/Doers Awd.

MONTES III, JOSE A; Balboa HS; San Francisco, CA; (2); Rep Stu Cncl; Var Ftbl; Mgr(s); Score Keeper; JV Trk; Hon Roll; 100 Buc Mem.

MONTES, JOSEPHINE M; Leuzinger HS; Hawthorne, CA; (2); Vllybl; Hon Roll; Loyola Maramount.

MONTES, JUDITH; Fontana HS; Fontana, CA; (2); Chorus; Capt Vllybl; Prfct Atten Awd; Bus.

MONTES, MICAELA; Garfield HS; Los Angeles, CA; (3); Chess Clb; ROTC; Treas SADD; Band; Nwsp; Hon Roll; Prfct Atten Awd; Pres Acad Fit Awd; UC Berkeley; Astronmy.

MONTES, MICHAEL; Bellarmine College Prep; San Jose, CA; (3); 1/300; Cmnty Wkr; Teachers Aide; Band; Jazz Band; Pep Band; School Musical; Rptr Yrbk; Stat Score Keeper; Genrl Excllncd Awd; Holy Cross Coll Bk Awd; Intrnshp NASA Sharp Pgm Smmr 90; U Of CA; Economics.

MONTES DE OCA, ANGELICA; Sweetwawter HS; National City, CA; (3); 35/429; Dance Clb; Drama Clb; Pep Clb; Spanish Clb; School Play; Yrbk; Stu Cncl; ASB Treas; ASB Finance Cmmssnr; Mdlgn Club VP; MECHA VP; Psych.

MONTES DE OCA, JOEL; Azusa HS; Azusa, CA; (2); #1 In Class; Crs Cntry; Trk; CSF.

MONTES-GIOVE, CARLOS M; El Cajon Valley HS; El Cajon, CA; (4); JV Var Ftbl; Hon Roll; Assis Coach Pop Warner Footbal 1989; Sacremento Cty Coll; Teacher.

MONTEZ, BERNADETTE O; San Benito Joint Union HS; Hollister, CA; (2); Cmnty Wkr; French Clb; Hosp Aide; Pep Clb; Red Cross Aide; JV Tennis; High Hon Roll; Hon Roll; Ldrshp; Frgn Exchng Clb; Heart Surgeon.

MONTEZ, DENETIA M; Carson HS; Carson, CA; (3); FTA; Drill Tm; School Play; Stage Crew; Stu Cncl; Cheerldng; Hon Roll; Phy.

MONTEZ, MICHELLE; Oxnard HS; Oxnard, CA; (2); 66/604; Church Yth Grp; French Clb; Cheerldng; Prfct Atten Awd; Undrgrnd Shakespeare Soc; Super Soph; U Of CA Berkeley; Engl Tchr.

MONTGOMERY, ANN MARIE; Riverdale Joint Union HS; Riverdale, CA; (4); 8/64; Church Yth Grp; FFA; FHA; GAA; VP Letterman Clb; Office Aide; Pep Clb; Science Clb; Ski Clb; Pres SADD; Pop Wrnr Chldr Coach; Buckingham Mdlng Schl; Vtd All Arnd SR; CA ST U Fresno; Cmmnctns.

MONTGOMERY, BETH; J W North HS; Riverside, CA; (2); Acpl Chr; Chorus; School Musical; Swing Chorus; Variety Show; Mgr(s); Tennis; Cit Awd; Hon Roll; Ltrd Jazz, Concert Choir; U Of CA Riverside; Vet.

MONTGOMERY, BETHANY L; John W North HS; Riverside, CA; (2); 95/510; Hon Roll; Pres Acad Fit Awd; Vocal Jazz Choir.

CALIFORNIA MORA/243

MONTGOMERY, DEBBIE; Bakersfield HS; Bakersfield, CA; (2); Church Yth Grp; Teachers Aide; Chorus; High Hon Roll; Hon Roll; Acadc Dcthln; Supr Rnkng Stu Piano; CSF; U San Diego.

MONTGOMERY, JESSICA; Sonoma Valley HS; Sonoma, CA; (3); Model UN; Service Clb; Stu Cncl; Stat JV Bsbl; JV Cheerldng; JV Pom Pon; Powder Puff Ftbl; High Hon Roll; Hon Roll; 2nd Pl In UNA USA Nation Essay Cntst CSF; Pltcl Sci.

MONTGOMERY, KEITH S; Holtville HS; Holtville, CA; (3); 16/100; Church Yth Grp; FBLA; Pep Clb; Chorus; Treas Frsh Cls; Ftbl; Wrstlng; Hon Roll; Marines.

MONTGOMERY, KELLY; Loyalton HS; Loyalton, CA; (3); Art Clb; Church Yth Grp; Dance Clb; Drama Clb; 4-H; Letterman Clb; Ski Clb; Spanish Clb; SADD; Drill Tm; Chico ST; Bio.

MONTGOMERY, KIM; Alhambra HS; Martinez, CA; (2); Church Yth Grp; Cmnty Wkr; Dance Clb; Drama Clb; English Clb; French Clb; Hosp Aide; Pep Clb; Service Clb; SADD; Yth Ftbl Chrldng Coach; Friday Nite Live Clb; Kiwanis Fld Rep To Japan; Congrssnl Cmmtte For Yth 90; U CA San Diego; Intl Relations.

MONTGOMERY, MARK A; Lynwood HS; Lynwood, CA; (3); 203/671; Church Yth Grp; Cmnty Wkr; Variety Show; Bsktbl; Var L Ftbl; Var L Trk; Prfct Atten Awd; Top 15 High Jumpers In Southern CA; Ran 8x200 Sunkist Invt Indoor Trk Meet Plcd 2nd; DJ Svc Part Own; U Of Southern CA; Comp Sci.

MONTGOMERY, MARKITA L; Castlemont HS; Oakland, CA; (3); Intnl Clb; Math Clb; Math Tm; Quiz Bowl; Spanish Clb; Yrbk; Cit Awd; High Hon Roll; Hon Roll; NHS; US House Rep Page; Bike & Ski Club; UC Berkeley; Math.

MONTGOMERY, MEGAN; Los Alamitos HS; Los Alamitos, CA; (4); Spanish Clb; Socr; High Hon Roll; Hon Roll; CSF.

MONTGOMERY, TAMI; Antioch HS; Antioch, CA; (3); Church Yth Grp; FHA; SADD; Band; Mrchg Band; Pres Acad Fit Awd; Maint Auto Club; Stu Mnth; Cert Achvt Indpndnt Lvng; Pre Med.

MONTICALVO, ROSASITA C; Andrew Hill HS; San Jose, CA; (1); Church Yth Grp; Plc Acad CPR Crs; Frshmn Clb; FYO.

MONTIEL, MARTHA S; Robert A Millikan HS; Long Beach, CA; (3); AFS; Pres Math Clb; Teachers Aide; Stu Cncl; Cit Awd; Retl/Fshn Mrchng; Exec Shdw Pgm; Jnr Optmst Clb; Accntng.

MONTIEL, RICHARD G; Fontana HS; Fontana, CA; (2); Quiz Bowl; Scholastic Bowl; Chorus; Ftbl; Socr; Friday Night Live; Acad Dcthln; UCLA; Sci.

MONTOYA JR, ALBERT; El Rancho HS; Pico Rivera, CA; (2); Debate Tm; Key Clb; ROTC; Spanish Clb; JV Trk; Hon Roll; Yng Mrns Cmmndng Offcr Of Unit; MESA; Tae Kwon Do; US Naval Acad; Pltcl Sci.

MONTOYA, ANN M; Rowland HS; Rowland Heights, CA; (2); 241/620; Art Clb; Church Yth Grp; Acpl Chr; School Musical; Variety Show; Guitar Clss; Guitar Rctls; Grphc Art.

MONTOYA, DANIEL; Arcata HS; Arcata, CA; (4); Pres Church Yth Grp; Math Tm; SADD; Teachers Aide; Stage Crew; Stu Cncl; Capt Crs Cntry; Capt Trk; Cit Awd; Exchnge Clb Stu Mnth; Bank Amer Cert Math; Hoby Ambssdr; Humboldt ST; Math.

MONTOYA III, JOSEPH; Bishop Amat HS; Whittier, CA; (3); Church Yth Grp; Varsity Clb; Rep Frsh Cls; Rep Soph Cls; Rep Jr Cls; JV Crs Cntry; Var Tennis; Hon Roll; Arch.

MONTOYA, LISA M; Foothill HS; Santa Ana, CA; (2); 178/326; JV Var Bsktbl; Hon Roll; Grphc Arts.

MONTOYA, MARITESS; Southwest HS; San Diego, CA; (4); Hosp Aide; SADD; Teachers Aide; Flag Corp; Variety Show; Hon Roll; Prfct Atten Awd; San Diego ST U.

MONTOYA, OLIVER DY; Carson HS; Carson, CA; (3); Computer Clb; FFA; Cit Awd; Hon Roll; NHS; Prfct Atten Awd; Cert Of Recgntn; Cal Poly Pomono; Sci.

MONTOYA, RAQUEL L; Montgomery HS; Santa Rosa, CA; (3); Ed Nwsp; NHS; Pres Acad Fit Awd; Crtve Wrtng; UCLA; Hist.

MONTOYA, VERONICA; Southwest HS; San Ysidro, CA; (2); Office Aide; Off Frsh Cls; Socr; Vllybl; Prfct Atten Awd; ASB Treas.

MONTZ, INES M; Apple Valley HS; Apple Valley, CA; (3); Cmnty Wkr; Sec Key Clb; Teachers Aide; Rptr Nwsp; Stat Bsktbl; Stat Tennis; JV Trk; Hon Roll; TAG; Bio.

MONUGIAN, SCARLETT; Pioneer HS; Whittier, CA; (4); Church Yth Grp; Girl Scts; Band; Flag Corp; Mrchg Band; Girls Leag VP; Paralegal.

MONZON, CHRISTINA E; Milpitas HS; Milpitas, CA; (1); ROTC; Band; Mrchg Band; Pep Band; High Hon Roll; Hon Roll; Ballet; USC; Sci.

MONZON, CYNTHIA; Santa Clara HS; Santa Clara, CA; (3); Hosp Aide; Pep Clb; Stu Cncl; Co-Capt Cheerldng; Powder Puff Ftbl; JV Trk; Acad Dcthln Tm; Rotary Interact Clb Ofc Pblcty Dir; Amnesty Intl.

MOODY, JAMES L; Vanden HS; Suisun City, CA; (1); 16/210; Latin Clb; VP Frsh Cls; JV Bsbl; JV Bsktbl; High Hon Roll; UC Davis; Law.

MOODY, JOEL S; Fortuna Union HS; Loleta, CA; (3); Church Yth Grp; SADD; Teachers Aide; High Hon Roll; Co-Pblshd Artcl Brtsh Cactus-Succlnt Jrnl; Humboldt ST; Envrnmt Rsrc Engr.

MOODY, MICHAEL; Adolfo Camarillo HS; Camarillo, CA; (2); SADD; Pres Frsh Cls; Pres Jr Cls; Rep Stu Cncl; JV Crs Cntry; JV Trk; High Hon Roll; Hon Roll; Opt Clb Awd; Carmen Camarillo Jones Awd; Peer Helper; Phy.

MOON, DANIEL H; Lutheran HS Of Orange County; Anaheim, CA; (2); Quiz Bowl; Band; Church Choir; Pep Band; School Musical; Off Frsh Cls; Hon Roll; Lion Awd; Orange Cty Acad Decathalon; Elem Ed.

MOON, JENNIFER; Los Alamitos HS; Los Alamitos, CA; (3); Drama Clb; Ski Clb; Teachers Aide; Chorus; JV Tennis; Hon Roll; Poetry Club; Amnesty Intl; CSF; Ecology Club.

MOON, JENNY; Garces HS; Bakersfield, CA; (3); Intnl Clb; Key Clb; Science Clb; Powder Puff Ftbl; Var Tennis; High Hon Roll; Hon Roll; CA Schlrshp Fed; Stu Orgnzd Svc; Pr Cnslng; Intl Bus.

MOON, MONIKA; Carlsbad HS; Carlsbad, CA; (3); 158/370; Cit Awd; Hon Roll; Acad Imprvmnt Awd; UCSD; Commnctns.

MOON, SUERIE; University HS; Irvine, CA; (2); 3/500; Church Yth Grp; Cmnty Wkr; JCL; Latin Clb; JV Bsktbl; JV Trk; High Hon Roll; NHS; Pres Acad Fit Awd; STAAND; ECO Crew; Bus.

MOON, TINA; Glendale HS; Glendale, CA; (2); Drill Tm; CSUN; Bus.

MOON, TOBY G; Pittsburg HS; Pittsburg, CA; (3); Boy Scts; Pep Clb; Ed Nwsp; Bsbl; Bsktbl; Crs Cntry; Bus.

MOON, TRACI; Chico SR HS; Chico, CA; (2); Church Yth Grp; Hosp Aide; Pep Clb; SADD; Teachers Aide; JV Bsktbl; JV Cheerldng; JV Fld Hcky; Var Sftbl; Pres Acad Fit Awd; Tchr.

MOONEY, ERIN L; Huntington Beach HS; Huntington Bch, CA; (3); Hosp Aide; Vrsty Ftbl Stat Grl; Rd Crss Clb; Sistr Cities Assn Sec; CSF; Engl Lit.

MOONEY, MEGAN; Huntington Beach HS; Huntington Beach, CA; (1); Red Cross Aide; School Musical; Stat Score Keeper; Sister Cities Assn-Exchng Stu Pgm; Tower Awd-Acad Achvt; U CA-SB; Vet Med.

MOONSAMY, NEIL; El Cerrito HS; El Cerrito, CA; (4); AFS; Church Yth Grp; German Clb; VP Intnl Clb; Pres SADD; Acpl Chr; School Musical; Off Soph Cls; Crs Cntry; Tennis; Bay Area Anti-Apartheid Ntwrk; UC Berkeley; Biolgcl Sci.

MOORE, ALLISON E; Saratoga HS; Saratoga, CA; (2); Pep Clb; Acpl Chr; Sec Frsh Cls; Stu Cncl; JV Bsktbl; JV Capt Cheerldng; Hon Roll; City Yth Cmmssnr; Natl Chrty Leag Rec Secy.

MOORE, AMY B; Roseville HS; Roseville, CA; (3); German Clb; Key Clb; Office Aide; Pep Clb; Science Clb; Spanish Clb; Mrchg Band; Bus.

MOORE, AMY NICOLE; Bear River HS; Grass Valley, CA; (4); 1/160; Church Yth Grp; Science Clb; Rptr Yrbk; Treas Jr Cls; Treas Sr Cls; Var Capt Trk; Var Capt Vllybl; Cit Awd; High Hon Roll; CA Schltc Fdrtn 4 Yrs; Sprtsmnsp Awd Trk; All Leag Hnrb Mntn Vllybl; Grphc Dsgn.

MOORE, ANDREA; Whittier Union HS; Whittier, CA; (3); Teachers Aide; Variety Show; Ed Nwsp; Wt Lftg; Cit Awd; DAR Awd; Stu Of Mnth 90; 2nd Pl Bst Crtn Whittier Union HS Dist Jrnlsm; Otis/Parsons Smmr Prgm Art Clss; Otis/Parsons Inst Dsgn; Cmrl Ar.

MOORE, ANGIE; Lower Lake HS; Clearlake Oaks, CA; (4); 5/110; Am Leg Aux Girls St; Pres Church Yth Grp; Cmnty Wkr; VP ROTC; Treas Jr Cls; Capt Sftbl; Cit Awd; Elks Awd; High Hon Roll; Lion Awd; CSF; Future Historians Of Amer; Sacramento ST U; Englsh.

MOORE, ANINA; Santa Ynez Valley HS; Santa Ynez, CA; (3); 11/164; Cmnty Wkr; Drama Clb; Teachers Aide; School Play; Variety Show; Lit Mag; Ntl Merit SF; Greenpeace; CA Schlrshp Fed; Animal Rights Clb VP; Envrnmntl Sci.

MOORE, BETRINA; Channel Islands HS; Oxnard, CA; (4); 20/486; Drama Clb; Church Choir; Pres Frsh Cls; VP Stu Cncl; Capt Bsktbl; Capt L Trk; Cit Awd; High Hon Roll; Hon Roll; Acad Ltr Awd; United Black Studs CA Schlrshp Awd; Alpha Kappa Alpha Schlrshp; CA U; Comm.

MOORE, BRENDA; Armijo HS; Suisun, CA; (3); Var L Bsktbl; U Of Sacramento; Child Psych.

MOORE, BRET D; Shasta HS; Redding, CA; (2); 126/442; Church Yth Grp; Drama Clb; School Play; Nwsp; Ftbl; Hon Roll; Phys Ftnss Awd 89; Shasta Coll; Real Estate.

MOORE, CARLA L; Colfax HS; Applegate, CA; (2); 26/197; Art Clb; Church Yth Grp; Drama Clb; 4-H; Bsktbl; Trk; Hon Roll; Alpha Omega Society.

MOORE, CHERESE S; North HS; Bakersfield, CA; (4); 42/467; Church Yth Grp; Varsity Clb; JV Bsktbl; JV Var Sftbl; Hon Roll; CSF; Bakersfield Coll; Bus Admin.

MOORE, CHRISTINA; Merced HS; Merced, CA; (3); Art Clb; Cmnty Wkr; Model UN; Pep Clb; Stu Cncl; Cheerldng; Hon Roll; Art Schlrs Awds Art Shws 89-90; 2 2nd Pl Hnrs Merced Gottschalks Hi-Deb Modl Bst All Yr Hi Deb Trphy; San Diego ST Long Bch; Tchr.

MOORE, CHRISTOPHER; Escondido HS; Escondido, CA; (4); Church Yth Grp; Office Aide; Ski Clb; Stu Cncl; Ftbl; Tennis; High Hon Roll; Hon Roll; Hocky; Rollr Blading; Chico ST; Marktng.

MOORE, CRAIG A; Redlands JR Acad; Redlands, CA; (2); Chorus; Stage Crew; Ed Nwsp; Score Keeper; Cit Awd; Hon Roll; Mesa Grande; Law.

MOORE, DANA; Del Oro HS; Loomis, CA; (3); 8/275; Art Clb; Cmnty Wkr; Science Clb; Ski Clb; Teachers Aide; Var L Bsktbl; Var L Crs Cntry; Var L Trk; High Hon Roll; NHS; Boys St 1st Rnnrup; Outstndng Stu Of Yr Awd Drftng; Stanford; Arch.

MOORE, DANA E; San Rafael HS; San Rafael, CA; (2); 8/256; GAA; Var Bsktbl; Var Socr; Var Vllybl; Hon Roll; 2nd Pl Awd Cnty Sci Fair.

MOORE, DARRYLL J; Chino HS; Ontario, CA; (3); Church Yth Grp; Rep Stu Cncl; Var Trk; Hon Roll; I Enjoy Playing Beach Volleyball; Reading; Tennis As A Hobby; Business.

MOORE, DARRYLL J; Chino HS; Rialto, CA; (3); Church Choir; Stu Cncl; Powder Puff Ftbl; Var Trk; Hon Roll; Bus.

MOORE, DAVIA; J F Kennedy HS; Granada Hills, CA; (2); SADD; Teachers Aide; Vllybl; Hon Roll; NHS; Prfct Atten Awd; UCLA; Acctng.

MOORE, DAVID R; Kern Valley HS; Lake Isabella, CA; (2); Pep Clb; Spanish Clb; Varsity Clb; JV Bsktbl; Var Crs Cntry; Var Tennis; Hon Roll; Engrng.

MOORE, DENISE R; Luther Burbank SR HS; Sacramento, CA; (3); French Clb; Girl Scts; Band; Drm Mjr(t); Mrchg Band; Nwsp; Cit Awd; High Hon Roll; Prfct Atten Awd; Coll; Paralegal.

MOORE, DOMENIQUE D; Rim Of The World HS; Twin Peaks, CA; (3); 48/250; Church Yth Grp; Dance Clb; Drama Clb; Teachers Aide; Acpl Chr; Chorus; Stats For Football And Wrestling; Friday Night Live Member; Crafton; Firefighting.

MOORE, DOUGLAS A; Atascadero HS; Atascadero, CA; (3); #25 In Class; Am Leg Boys St; Boy Scts; Church Yth Grp; FBLA; Teachers Aide; Temple Yth Grp; Varsity Clb; Treas Sr Cls; Socr; High Hon Roll; Music; Art; Sports; CA Poly; Intl Mrktng.

MOORE JR, EDWARD L; Victor Valley HS; George Afb, CA; (3); 74/424; Art Clb; Boy Scts; Church Yth Grp; Red Cross Aide; Chorus; Yrbk; Hon Roll; Korean Tea Kwon Do; Gymnastics; U Of CA Snta Barbara Comp Sci.

MOORE, GAYLE E; Vacaville HS; Vacaville, CA; (3); Church Yth Grp; French Clb; Sec Key Clb; Office Aide; Score Keeper; High Hon Roll; Hon Roll; Prfct Atten Awd; Gldn St Xm Hi Hnrs; CSF; Cal Poly; Engrng.

MOORE III, HUDSON L; Pinole Valley HS; Pinole, CA; (3); Rep Stu Cncl; Var L Ftbl; Var L Trk; Var L Wt Lftg; Yth Educator (Yth Educator Pgm); Cnflct Mngr (Conflict Mngmnt); Criminal Law Fttbll.

MOORE, JAMES J; Cabrillo HS; Vandenberg AFB, CA; (4); Debate Tm; Math Tm; Church Choir; High Hon Roll; Jr NHS; NHS; Pres Acad Fit Awd; CA Acadmc Dcthln; Bnk Amer Achvt Awd Comp Stds; Rensselaer Polytech Inst Math & Sci Awd; CA Polytech ST U; Comp Sci.

MOORE, JANINE R; Del Mar HS; San Jose, CA; (1); Hosp Aide; Orch; School Play; Var Tennis; NHS; Music; Badminton; Bus.

MOORE, JENNIFER M; Will C Wood HS; Vacaville, CA; (1); Hon Roll; Dlphn Trnr.

MOORE, JEREL E; Mc Lane HS; Fresno, CA; (2); School Musical; School Play; Swing Chorus; High Hon Roll; Hon Roll; U Of Southern CA; Acctnt.

MOORE, JOHN M; Clovis HS; Clovis, CA; (4); 139/540; Boy Scts; Church Yth Grp; FBLA; Chorus; Mgr(s); JV Socr; JV Vllybl; Hon Roll; Serve A 2 Year Mission For My Church; Brigham Young U; A F ROTC.

MOORE, KANDI; Hoover HS; Fresno, CA; (2); Church Yth Grp; Pep Clb; Cheerldng; Swmmng; Fresno ST U; Tchng.

MOORE, KATRINA A; Clovis West HS; Clovis, CA; (1); French Clb; Intnl Clb; Bsktbl; Crs Cntry; Hon Roll; CSUF; Poet.

MOORE, KENNY E; San Marcos HS; Santa Barbara, CA; (3); 37/380; JV Ftbl; L Var Trk; Mock Trial.

MOORE, KIMBERLY; Ferndale Union HS; Ferndale, CA; (2); SADD; Band; Chorus; Sftbl; Cit Awd.

MOORE, LEANNA E; Santa Ynez HS; Solvang, CA; (3); Church Yth Grp; FBLA; Teachers Aide; JV Var Sftbl; JV Tennis; Campus Chrstn Fellowshp Clb; Animal Rights Clb; Med.

MOORE, LESLIE; Del Campo HS; Fair Oaks, CA; (2); 40/460; Pep Clb; Speech Tm; SADD; JV Capt Cheerldng; JV Swmmng; NHS; Opt Clb Awd; CSF; Stu Reachng Out; Pre-Law.

MOORE, LISA R; Downey HS; Downey, CA; (3); Church Yth Grp; Drama Clb; SADD; School Play; Variety Show; Powder Puff Ftbl; Hon Roll; Student Of The Month In Drama; Mission America Tour Of 7 States In Drama; Pt Loma Nazarene Coll; Nursing.

MOORE, MASON M; C K Melatchy HS; Sacramento, CA; (1); JCL; Mrchg Band; JV Ftbl; Var Golf; Var Wt Lftg; USC; Comp Sci.

MOORE, MEGAN K; Irvine HS; Irvine, CA; (1); Church Yth Grp; Cmnty Wkr; Pep Clb; Ski Clb; Cheerldng; Swmmng; Hnrs Class Hstry; UCSD; Psychologist.

MOORE, MICHAEL A; La Sierra HS; Riverside, CA; (1); JV Ftbl; Intrml Wt Lftg; Intrml Wrstlng; Notre Dame; Pilot.

MOORE, MICHELLE C; Fountain Valley HS; Fountain Valley, CA; (3); Variety Show; Hon Roll; Engl.

MOORE, MICHELLE M; St Paul HS; Whittier, CA; (3); Church Yth Grp; Girl Scts; Tennis; Law.

MOORE, MIKE W; Colfax HS; Weimar, CA; (2); 1/178; FBLA; VP Math Clb; JV Tennis; High Hon Roll.

MOORE, NECHOLE L; Montclair HS; Ontario, CA; (2); FHA; Teachers Aide; Co-Capt Var Cheerldng.

MOORE III, PAUL A; Monte Vista HS; Walnut Creek, CA; (3); Teachers Aide; Variety Show; Var Bsbl; Ftbl; Bus.

MOORE, PETER J; Costa Mesa HS; Costa Mesa, CA; (3); Church Yth Grp; Chorus; Church Choir; School Musical; Stage Crew; JV Bsktbl; Intrml Ftbl; Cit Awd; Hon Roll.

MOORE, REGAN A; Roseville HS; Colfax, CA; (3); 30/411; German Clb; Science Clb; Spanish Clb; Rep Frsh Cls; Var Bsktbl; JV Var Swmmng; Var Tennis; Var Vllybl; High Hon Roll; Hon Roll; CSF.

MOORE, ROSALIE ANN; Surprise Valley HS; Cedarville, CA; (4); 2/16; Pres 4-H; Treas FBLA; FFA; Treas GAA; Office Aide; Sec Pep Clb; Nwsp; Hon Roll; Sec Treas Yrbk; Pres Frsh Cls; CSF; Supt Ldrshp Awd; Sierra CC; Acctnt.

MOORE, RUTH; Valley HS; Santa Ana, CA; (4); Computer Clb; French Clb; Intrml Score Keeper; Intrml Vllybl; Assist Legue Santa Ana Schlrshp; Cmptr Applctn Spclst Cert; Academy Pgm Awd; Cmptr Tech.

MOORE, SAMUEL ROBERT; Don Bosco Technical Inst; La Habra, CA; (2); High Hon Roll; Hon Roll.

MOORE, SARAH; Thomas Downey HS; Modesto, CA; (2); Key Clb; Spanish Clb; Speech Tm; Tennis.

MOORE, SHARONIA L; Academy Of Our Lady Of Peace; San Diego, CA; (3); Church Yth Grp; Dance Clb; Hosp Aide; Spanish Clb; SADD; School Musical; Pres Jr Cls; Pres Sr Cls; Cheerldng; JV Var Vllybl; Miss San Diego, Cand Miss CA TEEN Pgnt; 4 Yr HS Schlrshp; Pre-Med.

MOORE, SONOYA D; St Marys Acad; Inglewood, CA; (2); Church Yth Grp; Debate Tm; French Clb; Church Choir; School Musical; Sec Frsh Cls; Rep Soph Cls; Var Cheerldng; Cit Awd; Hon Roll; Hampton U; Attorney.

MOORE, STEPHANIE; Aquinas HS; Redlands, CA; (4); 34/90; Church Yth Grp; Cmnty Wkr; Girl Scts; Pep Clb; Teachers Aide; Var Cheerldng; Var Pom Pon; Hon Roll; Cal ST Fullerton; Spch Pathlgy.

MOORE, STEPHANIE; Taft Union HS; Taft, CA; (3); 10/200; Church Yth Grp; Yrbk; Stat Bsbl; Stat Bsktbl; High Hon Roll; Hon Roll; BYU; Pre-Med.

MOORE, STEPHANIE J; San Marcos HS; San Marcos, CA; (3); Church Yth Grp; Library Aide; SADD; Teachers Aide; Score Keeper; Hon Roll; Stat Bsktbl; Stat Sftbl; Stat Trk; Bio.

MOORE, STEPHEN; Downey HS; Norwalk, CA; (3); 99/500; Church Yth Grp; JA; Key Clb; Red Cross Aide; Spanish Clb; SADD; Rep Frsh Cls; Rep Jr Cls; Stu Cncl; Trk; CA Boys St Alt; Outstndng Frshmn Awd; Goldn St Awd; UCI; Law.

MOORE, TERESA S; Argonaut HS; Ione, CA; (4); 7/85; Band; Jazz Band; Yrbk; Hon Roll; Bank Of American Award In Foreign Language; Sierra JR Coll; Forensic Det.

MOORE, TIMOTHY J; Bolsa Grande HS; Garden Grove, CA; (3); 2/330; Church Yth Grp; Cmnty Wkr; Latin Clb; Math Clb; Office Aide; Scholastic Bowl; Science Clb; Teachers Aide; JV Socr; JV Var Tennis; CSF; Acad Decathalon Tm; 2nd Pl Orange Cty Sci Fair; Dntstry.

MOORE, TRACIE E; Victor Valley SR HS; Victorville, CA; (3); 17/365; VP Pres Band; Drm Mjr(t); Jazz Band; Sec Mrchg Band; Pep Band; High Hon Roll; Hon Roll; Mst Imprvd Bnd; Outstndng Achvt Bnd; Acad Excllnc Awd Gldn St Exam Alg Hnrs; CA ST U; Music.

MOORE, WALIDAH; Armijo HS; Fairfield, CA; (2); Church Yth Grp; Dance Clb; Drama Clb; Girl Scts; Pep Clb; Chorus; Church Choir; School Musical; School Play; JV Cheerldng; Coll; Acting Singing.

MOOREHEAD, EMIL O; Morningside HS; Inglewood, CA; (3); Rep Stu Cncl; Var Bsbl; Var Bsktbl; Var Ftbl; Var Trk; Psych.

MOOREHEAD, JENNIFER B; Del Mar HS; San Jose, CA; (4); 34/222; Pres German Clb; Key Clb; Math Clb; Phtg Yrbk; Tennis; Pres Schlr; CSF; Bio Club VP & Pres; West Valley; Arch.

MOORHEAD, JOHN; Polytechnic HS; N Hollywood, CA; (3); Aud/Vis; Chess Clb; Drama Clb; SADD; Tennis; Pres Acad Fit Awd; Hnr Soc; UCLA; TV Prodcr.

MOORMAN, TAMI; Granite Hills HS; El Cajon, CA; (4); 14/470; Am Leg Aux Girls St; Church Yth Grp; Debate Tm; GAA; Service Clb; Speech Tm; SADD; Varsity Clb; Var Powder Puff Ftbl; Var L Socr; Bank Of Amer Cert Wnnr; CA Poppy Algebra & Geom High Hnrs; Pepperdine U; Comp Sci.

MOORS, CHARLENE J; Canyon Springs HS; Moreno Vly, CA; (3); Sec Treas FBLA; Teachers Aide; Band; Sec Mrchg Band; High Hon Roll; Hon Roll; CSF; CA Ctr Music Arts Riverside Pops X-L Band; Elem Educ.

MOORTHY, GEETHA V; Westlake Schl For Girls; Los Angeles, CA; (4); Art Clb; Cmnty Wkr; Dance Clb; French Clb; Red Cross Aide; Jazz Band.

MOORTY, SHYAMALA P; Monterey HS; Seaside, CA; (3); Art Clb; Dance Clb; German Clb; VP Thesps; Chorus; School Musical; School Play; Stage Crew; Ed Lit Mag; High Hon Roll; CA Arts Schlr 90; Dance.

MOOTZ, JOANA; Western HS; Stanton, CA; (2); Church Yth Grp; Pep Clb; Church Choir; Orch; High Hon Roll; SOS Clb; Frgn Lang Clb; Grls Leag; CSF; UCLA; Med.

MORA, ANGELICA; St Joseph HS; Lakewood, CA; (3); 15/175; GAA; Spanish Clb; SADD; Drill Tm; Cheerldng; Pom Pon; Hon Roll; Prfct Atten Awd; Long Beach ST; Bus Admin.

MORA, ANGELINA T; Schurr HS; Rosemead, CA; (2); Church Yth Grp; Cmnty Wkr; Girl Scts; SADD; Chorus; U SC; Medical Tech.

MORA, ARACELI; Selma HS; Selma, CA; (1); 32/310; School Play; Cheerldng; Teacher.

MORA, CYNTHIA Y; Polytechnic HS; Sun Valley, CA; (2); Church Yth Grp; GAA; Letterman Clb; Pep Clb; Chorus; Drill Tm; Treas Frsh Cls; Stu Cncl; Var Crs Cntry; Var Trk; Interior Dsgn.

MORA, ERIC; Valley Christian HS; San Jose, CA; (3); Varsity Clb; School Musical; School Play; Tennis; High Hon Roll; Church Yth Grp; Debate Tm; Drama Clb; Red Cross Aide; Santa Clara Co Hnr Band; CA St Hnr Band; Interntl Tae Kwon Do Fllswshp; Red Crs Lf Grd & Instrctr; Stanford U; Poltcl Sci.

MORA, FABIAN; Gonzales HS; Soledad, CA; (1); Church Yth Grp; JV Ftbl; Var Trk; Hon Roll; Pres Acad Fit Awd.

MORA, HENRY L; Nathaniel Narbonne HS; Torrance, CA; (2); Chess Clb; Crs Cntry; Trk; Vllybl; Martial Arts Hapkido; UCSD; Aero Engr.

MORA, INGRID C; Bishop Amat HS; Valinda, CA; (4); Special Olympcs; Friday Night Club.

MORA, JENNIFER; Westminster HS; Westminster, CA; (3); Band; Jazz Band; Mrchg Band; Pep Band; Var L Swmmng; Star Certificate Performing Arts; Most Valuable Player Girls Swim Team; Sterling Coll; Environmentalist.

MORA, MARGARET M; Lincoln HS; Stockton, CA; (4); 177/513; SADD; Acpl Chr; Chorus; School Musical; Powder Puff Ftbl; Stat Wrstlng; Hon Roll; Beyond War; Choir Cncl Sec; Jr Var Badminton; Sonoma ST U; Art.

MORA, MARIA; Balboa HS; San Francisco, CA; (2); Off Jr Cls; Sftbl; Vllybl; Cit Awd; Hon Roll; Jr NHS; 390 Pts Phys Ftnss Awded; 2nd Pl Rdng Comprhnsn; City Coll San Fran; Astrnmy.

MORA, MARIA G; East Bakersfield HS; Bakersfield, CA; (3); Teachers Aide.

MORA, NORMA; San Dieguito HS; Encinitas, CA; (3); Church Yth Grp; Cmnty Wkr; Office Aide; Prfct Score A P Span Exm; UCLA; Accntnt.

MORA, OSCAR R; North Monterey County HS; Castroville, CA; (2); Church Yth Grp; Teachers Aide; Crs Cntry; JV Trk; Cit Awd; High Hon Roll; Schlstc Awd Wrld Cultrs.

MORA, SILVIA; Pasadena HS; Pasadena, CA; (4); French Clb; JA; Spanish Clb; Teachers Aide; Hon Roll; CSF; NW Coll; Optmtry.

MORABE, DANTE J; Alhambra HS; Martinez, CA; (3); Teachers Aide; Pres Frsh Cls; JV Intrml Bsktbl; Capt Var Ftbl; Var JV Trk; Var JV Wt Lftg; High Hon Roll; Hon Roll; Alhambra Stu Bdy Treas; DFAL Stu Exchng Pgm; Schlr Athlte; Med.

MORABITO, MARISA A; Lincoln HS; Stockton, CA; (3); 187/538; VP French Clb; SADD; Sftbl; Tennis; Hon Roll; San Joaquin Delta Coll; Electro.

MORAES, CINDY; Notre Dame HS; San Jose, CA; (3); 5/90; Church Yth Grp; Drama Clb; JA; SADD; Acpl Chr; School Play; Stage Crew; Rep Nwsp; Ed Lit Mag; Tennis; CSF; San Joses Mayors Yth Honoree; Piano Plyng Fashion Shows & Schl Functions.

MORAINE, MAIA; Sacramento Waldorf HS; Fair Oaks, CA; (1); Church Yth Grp; Orch; Clb Peer Hlpng.

MORALES, ADOLFO G; Saint John Bosco HS; Huntington Park, CA; (3); 72/200; Spanish Clb; Varsity Clb; Intrml Mgr Bsktbl; Intrml Mgr Church Yth Grp; Var Socr; Hon Roll; Soccer Bst Offnsve Plyr; All-Del Rey League 1st Team; Cal ST Los Angeles; Psycht.

MORALES, ADRIAN; Burlingame HS; Hillsborough, CA; (3); Spanish Clb; Teachers Aide; School Play; Ed Yrbk; Var Ftbl; Var Swmmng; Wt Lftg; Var Capt Wrstlng; High Hon Roll; Hon Roll; Dentistry.

MORALES, ANA C; Estancia HS; Costa Mesa, CA; (3); Swmmng; Capt Vllybl; Cit Awd; Hon Roll; Ntl Merit Schol; NEDT Awd; Prfct Atten Awd; Hlth Clb; Dance Awd; Golden West Coll.

MORALES, ANGELA M; St Joseph HS; Lakewood, CA; (3); Cmnty Wkr; DECA; Drama Clb; Varsity Clb; Var Crs Cntry; Cit Awd; Hon Roll; Prfct Atten Awd; Acad Dcthln; Loyola Marymount; Law.

MORALES, ANN M; Independence HS; San Jose, CA; (3); 191/962; Dance Clb; Band; Mrchg Band; NHS; Bus.

MORALES, ANTONIO; River City HS; W Sacramento, CA; (3); Cmnty Wkr; Spanish Clb; Socr; Wt Lftg; Hon Roll; Prfct Atten Awd; Gldn St Exam Geom Rcgntn; Sci Super Test 2nd Pl; UC Davis; Electrnc Engrn.

MORALES, ARNOLD; Rio Mesa HS; Oxnard, CA; (3); 66/369; Art Clb; English Clb; Lit Mag; Cit Awd; Hon Roll; Boys Bsktbl Club; Law.

MORALES, BECKY; J W North HS; Riverside, CA; (2); Pep Clb; Rptr Yrbk; Rep Soph Cls; JV Socr; Stat Swmmng; Hon Roll; SAVE; U Of CA; Psych.

MORALES, BRYAN J; Summerville Union HS; Twain Harte, CA; (3); 1/150; AFS; Art Clb; Pres French Clb; High Hon Roll; Hon Roll; UC Berkeley; Design Engr.

MORALES, CYNTHIA L; Thomas Downey HS; Modesto, CA; (2); Church Yth Grp; Dance Clb; Drama Clb; Spanish Clb; Teachers Aide; Thesps; School Play; Stage Crew; Variety Show; Phtg Rptr Yrbk; Azteca Clb; Engl.

MORALES, DANIEL; Valley HS; Sacramento, CA; (4); 67/446; Band; Jazz Band; Mrchg Band; Pep Band; JV Bsbl; JV Capt Wrstlng; Hon Roll; Musical Excel Awd; Louis Armstrong Jazz Awd; Sacramento City Coll; Sprts Med.

MORALES, DELFINA M; Mc Farland HS; Mc Farland, CA; (3); Stat Wrstlng; CA ST U; Paralegal.

MORALES, DIANA; Independence HS; San Jose, CA; (2); Church Yth Grp; Girl Scts; Latin Clb; Spanish Clb; Church Choir; Hon Roll; Prfct Atten Awd; UCO; Early Outreach Pgm; Stanford U; Poltcl Sci.

MORALES, EDDIE; Kingsburg HS; Kingsburg, CA; (2); Ftbl; Auto Mchnc.

MORALES, EDWIN E; Saint Genevieve HS; Arleta, CA; (2); JV Capt Bsktbl; French Hon Soc; USC; Lawyer.

MORALES, EILEEN M; Fontana HS; Fontana, CA; (2); Yrbk; Off Soph Cls; Cheerldng.

MORALES, ELIZABETH; Buena Park HS; Anaheim, CA; (4); Dance Clb; Drama Clb; Intnl Clb; Office Aide; Spanish Clb; Teachers Aide; School Play; Pres Frsh Cls; Pres Soph Cls; Intrml Bsktbl; MISS Pan Amer CA Trophy Cntrys Best Costume; CA ST Fullerton; Intl Bus.

MORALES, ELIZABETH; Hueneme HS; Oxnard, CA; (2); 32/369; Church Yth Grp; Stu Cncl; Capt Bsktbl; Score Keeper; High Hon Roll; Hon Roll; Prfct Atten Awd; Future Ldrs Of Amer; Smmr Acad Insti; Frmrs Ins Sctry; U CA Davis; Med.

MORALES, ELIZABETH M; Don Antonio HS; Chino, CA; (3); 208/493; Church Yth Grp; Chorus; School Play; Tennis; Trk; Vllybl; Cit Awd; NHS; Fullerton Coll; Bus Admin.

MORALES, JESUS; Sweetwater HS; National City, CA; (2); 48/481; Cit Awd; Hon Roll; Prfct Atten Awd; UCLA; Bus Mgt.

MORALES, JORGE; Gonzales HS; Soledad, CA; (4); 5/170; Am Leg Boys St; VP Stu Cncl; Intrml Var Ftbl; JV Trk; Elks Awd; High Hon Roll; Rotary Awd; CSF; Interact Club; Santa Clara U; Mech Engrng.

MORALES, JOSE A; Bell HS; Cudahy, CA; (2); Boy Scts; French Clb; Pres Sr Cls; Var Crs Cntry; Var Trk; High Hon Roll; CSF; UCLA; Comp Svc Tech.

MORALES, JOSEPH L; Nogales HS; La Puente, CA; (2); Pres Soph Cls; JV Ftbl; Wt Lftg; Var Wrstlng; High Hon Roll; Hon Roll; Pres Acad Fit Awd; UCLA; Obstetrcs.

MORALES, JULIO; Garfield HS Magnet; Anaheim, CA; (2); Varsity Clb; Var Bsbl; Bsktbl; Trk; Cit Awd; Hon Roll; Prfct Atten Awd; 1st Pl Mdl Rgn B Spllng Bee 84; Highly Gftd Stu; Arch.

MORALES JR, JUSTO; Hamilton HS Academy Of Music; Bell, CA; (2); Chess Clb; Jazz Band; Mrchg Band; Orch; Brass Ensmble 2nd Trombone & 2nd Baritone; Los Angeles All Cty All Dist Mrchng Band 3rd Trombone; USC; Music.

MORALES, LAURA O; Woodrow Wilson HS; Los Angeles, CA; (3); French Clb; FTA; Pep Clb; Teachers Aide; Hon Roll; Spnsh Lang Advncd Plcmnt Exam 5; Gftd & Tlntd Club; Pasadena City Coll; Tchr.

MORALES, LISA M; Garey HS; Pomona, CA; (3); 4/256; Hosp Aide; Spanish Clb; Temple Yth Grp; Treas Jr Cls; Treas Stu Cncl; Co-Capt Cheerldng; Pom Pon; Cit Awd; High Hon Roll; Hon Roll; Frgn Exchng Clb; Engr Clb-Mesa VP & Sec; UC Berkeley; Phys.

MORALES, MARLON; St Monica HS; Los Angeles, CA; (2); Art Clb; Boy Scts; Drama Clb; Thesps; Chorus; School Musical; Off Frsh Cls; Off Soph Cls; Stu Cncl; Bsktbl; Commrcl Pilot.

MORALES, MARTHA A; Hueneme HS; Oxnard, CA; (1); Rep Frsh Cls; Migrant Prog; Future Scholars Northridge U; Northridge U; Trvl & Tourism.

MORALES, MARTHA A; Roosevelt HS; Los Angeles, CA; (3); Hon Roll; Prfct Atten Awd; CA ST Los Angeles; Nrsng.

MORALES, MICHAEL B; San Diego HS; San Diego, CA; (3); 40/415; JV Ftbl; JV Swmmng; JV Trk; JV Wrstlng; Cit Awd; Hon Roll; Mech Engrng.

MORALES, NOEL I; Grananda Hills HS; Los Angeles, CA; (2); Bsbl; Bsktbl; UCLA; Bus.

MORALES, NORA A; Eisenhower HS; Rialto, CA; (3); JV Capt Bsktbl; JV Sftbl; JV Vllybl; Cit Awd; Athltc Cert; Spnsh Awd; Engl Acad Achvt Medal; Cal ST U; Chld Psych.

MORALES, NORA M; Manual Arts HS; Los Angeles, CA; (2); Church Yth Grp; FTA; Hon Roll; Tchr.

MORALES, NORMA A; San Pasqual HS; Escondido, CA; (3); 22/353; Cmnty Wkr; French Clb; Hosp Aide; Intrml Tennis; JV Intrml Vllybl; Hon Roll; Prfct Atten Awd; Chicano Latino Yth Ldrshp Conf; Stanford; Scl Sci.

MORALES, OLIVIA; Warren HS; South Gate, CA; (2); Church Yth Grp; Cmnty Wkr; Church Choir; Prfct Atten Awd; PTA Svcs Regogntn; FL Intl U; Bus Law.

MORALES, PATRICIA; Lincoln HS; Lincoln, CA; (1); Hon Roll.

MORALES, ROBERT; Southbay Christian Schl; Sunnyvale, CA; (4); 3/27; Church Yth Grp; Computer Clb; Letterman Clb; Math Clb; Science Clb; Spanish Clb; Varsity Clb; Acpl Chr; Chorus; School Musical; All Leag Bsktbl; Astrophyscs.

MORALES, SHENYELL A; Washington Prep HS; Los Angeles, CA; (2); Hon Roll; Pres Acad Fit Awd.

MORALES, STEPHANIE; Rubidoux HS; Riverside, CA; (4); 24/578; Teachers Aide; Treas Jr Cls; Off Soph Cls; Mgr(s); Var L Sftbl; Cit Awd; Hon Roll; Prfct Atten Awd; Prom Cmmtte; Chrstn Club; U Of CA-BERKLEY; Bus Admin.

MORALES, SYLVIA; Gonzales Union HS; Soledad, CA; (1); Church Yth Grp; Dance Clb; Drama Clb; Hosp Aide; Model UN; Red Cross Aide; SADD; Bsktbl; Vllybl; Hon Roll.

MORALES, WALTER; Don Bosco Technical Inst; Los Angeles, CA; (3); Drftn, Dsgn 2nd Pl Sch Yrly Awd; Prncpls List; Amer Soc Of Engrs, Arch; Art, Woodworking S; UC Berkeley; Arch.

MORALEZ, LORRAINE M; Tulare Western HS; Tulare, CA; (1); Church Yth Grp; SADD; Color Guard; Hon Roll; Hspnc Yth Ldrshp; Acadc Excel; Trip UC Davis; Fresno ST U; Elem Tchr.

MORAN, ALLISYN; Dos Pueblos HS; Santa Barbara, CA; (4); 2/303; Church Yth Grp; Off Debate Tm; Treas Math Clb; VP Service Clb; Teachers Aide; Orch; Rep Stu Cncl; Var L Swmmng; Bausch & Lomb Sci Awd; Elks Awd; Mock Trial Clb Fndr & Treas, Cnty Champs, 3rd In St 90; Bank Of Amer Librl Arts Plaque Wnnr; Tufts U; Intl Relations.

MORAN, AMANDA O; Grossmont HS; La Mesa, CA; (4); 32/350; VP Cmnty Wkr; FBLA; Service Clb; Ski Clb; Varsity Clb; Lit Mag; Rep Stu Cncl; Powder Puff Ftbl; Var Socr; JV Tennis; Med.

MORAN, ANNA K; San Gorgonio HS; Highland, CA; (3); AFS; Pres Treas Church Yth Grp; Pep Clb; Treas Spanish Clb; Cheerldng; Swmmng; NHS; Prfct Atten Awd; Treas Spanish NHS; CA ST San Bernardino; Advrtsn.

MORAN, DALE; Mojave HS; Mojave, CA; (2); School Play; JV L Ftbl; Hon Roll; Comp Tech.

MORAN, JACOB M; Oak Park HS; Agoura Hills, CA; (2); 17/119; Dungeons/Dragons Clb.

MORAN, JESSICA A; Holtville HS; Holtville, CA; (3); FHA; Office Aide; Pep Clb; UN Reno.

MORAN, JON W; Dos Pueblos HS; Santa Barbara, CA; (2); 11/285; Water Polo; Surf Club; Engrng.

MORAN, KATHY A; Carondelet HS; Danville, CA; (3); Church Yth Grp; Cmnty Wkr; Latin Clb; Stu Cncl; Oaklnd Stu Ldrshp Conf Cnslr; Loyola Marymount; Zoology.

MORAN, KELLY L; Grossmont HS; Spring Valley, CA; (1); Dance Clb; Hosp Aide; JV Swmmng; SD ST U; Nrsng.

MORAN, PATRICIA A; Carondelet HS; Danville, CA; (3); Church Yth Grp; Dance Clb; Drama Clb; Latin Clb; SADD; School Musical; School Play; Stage Crew; Rep Frsh Cls; Rep Jr Cls; Cnslr Ldrshp Conf 4 Yrs Oakland CA; CVO Camp Involvement 10 Yrs; Communications.

MORAN, RHONDALYN E; St Francis HS; Sacramento, CA; (2); Church Yth Grp; Latin Clb; NFL; Science Clb; Chorus; Church Choir; School Musical; Var Trk; Hon Roll; JR Statesmen Of Amer; Bell Choir VP; U CA Santa Cruz; Music.

MORAN, ROSA L; Schurr HS; Los Angeles, CA; (4); Office Aide; Teachers Aide; Swim Team 88; E Los Angeles; Gynecology.

MORAN, SUSANA E; St John HS; San Francisco, CA; (4); 8/39; Art Clb; French Clb; Varsity Clb; Church Choir; Yrbk; Crs Cntry; Trk; Care Bear Awd Dscpln; Frgn Lang Awd; Art & Music Apprctn Awd; San Francisco Citty Coll; Arch.

MORANTE, EDUARDO; Helix HS; La Mesa, CA; (4); Science Clb; Hon Roll; Golden ST Exam Alg Honors; Perf Arts; CSF; US Intl U; Bus.

MORAZZINI, ZACHERY P; Delta HS; West Sacramento, CA; (3); Drama Clb; SADD; School Play; VP Frsh Cls; Rep Sr Cls; JV Bsktbl; JV Var Crs Cntry; JV Var Ftbl; JV Tennis; JV Var Trk; 75 Point Awd/Ltr; UCSD; Hstry.

MORCHI, RAVI S; Whitney HS; Cerritos, CA; (2); 1/150; Art Clb; Key Clb; Engrng.

MORCILLO, GERALDINE; Seaside HS; Fort Ord, CA; (3); AFS; Cmnty Wkr; Stu Cncl; Var Cheerldng; Friday Night Live Against Drinking And Driving And Drugs; UC Santa; Public Relations.

MORDECAI, JOHNNY R; Monterey HS; Seaside, CA; (2); Wt Lftg; High Hon Roll; Hon Roll.

MORDHORST, DENISE; Edison HS; Huntington Beach, CA; (2); Socr; Campfire; UCI; Dntl Hygnst.

MOREAU, AMY R; Cornelia Connelly HS; Anaheim, CA; (1); Cmnty Wkr; Science Clb; Teachers Aide; Temple Yth Grp; Chorus; School Play; JSA; Connelly Plyrs Acting Troupe; Lib Clb; Engnrng.

MOREAU, NADIA A; Encina HS; Sacramento, CA; (3); Cmnty Wkr; French Clb; GAA; Teachers Aide; Varsity Clb; JV Var Bsktbl; JV Gym; Var Socr; JV Tennis; SRO-ANTI Drg Pgm; Sprtscstr.

MOREFIELD, CHERYL; Herbert Hoover HS; San Diego, CA; (2); 1/530; Church Yth Grp; Cit Awd; High Hon Roll; Hon Roll; Yng Orgnsts Cmptn 89 & 93; Cert Awd 3.3 Hghr GPA; Writing.

MOREHOUSE, REBECCA K; Norco HS; Corona, CA; (1); Church Yth Grp; JV Tennis; Prfct Atten Awd; Tennis Mst Imprvd Awd; Outstndng Stu Awd; Law.

MORELAND, DAMON R; Pittsburg HS; Pittsburg, CA; (1); Pep Clb; Arch.

MORELOCK, HEATHER; Palo Verde HS; Blythe, CA; (2); Drama Clb; Pep Clb; Hon Roll; CSF; NSH; Pedtrcn.

MORELOS, MARCIA; San Joaquin Memorial HS; Fresno, CA; (4); 15/110; GAA; Letterman Clb; Science Clb; Spanish Clb; Sftbl; Hon Roll; Pres Acad Fit Awd; Intl Frgn Lang Awd; Schlstc All Amer; U CA Davis; Chem.

MORELOS, MARCIE E; San Joaquin Memorial HS; Fresno, CA; (4); 15/110; GAA; Letterman Clb; Science Clb; Spanish Clb; Sftbl; Hon Roll; Pres Acad Fit Awd; Intl Frgn Lang Awd; Schlstc All Amer; U CA Davis; Chem.

MORELOS, SEAN; Tracy Joint Union HS; Tracy, CA; (2); 56/483; Church Yth Grp; Cmnty Wkr; Debate Tm; Pres 4-H; VP FFA; Letterman Clb; Office Aide; JV Capt Ftbl; Var Wrstlng; 4-H Awd; Stanford; Law.

MORENO, AARON; Christian Brothers HS; Sacramento, CA; (3); 20/108; Math Tm; Pres Jr Cls; JV Var Crs Cntry; Var Capt Socr; JV Var Trk; High Hon Roll; Hon Roll; St Schlr; CA St Soccer Tm; Bsktbl Announcer For Schl Games; St Marys College; History.

MORENO, ANTHONY C; Grant Union HS; Sacramento, CA; (3); 25/250; Cmnty Wkr; Red Cross Aide; JV Bsbl; JV Var Bsktbl; Sftbl; Invlvd Cmmnty Ctrs; Police Athltc Lg Sftbl; U Of NC; Accntng.

MORENO, BESSY C; San Gabriel Acad; El Monte, CA; (3); Pres Church Yth Grp; GAA; Teachers Aide; Acpl Chr; Church Choir; Var Bsbl; JV Bsktbl; Capt Sftbl; Cit Awd; High Hon Roll; Scl Worker.

MORENO, BLANCA S; Montclair HS; Pomona, CA; (2); Art Clb; English Clb; Hosp Aide; Office Aide; Teachers Aide; Nwsp; Cit Awd; High Hon Roll; PSAT Hnr; Engl II Jrnlsm; Sci; Dr.

MORENO, CARLOS; Christian Brothers HS; Sacramento, CA; (2); German Clb; Var Socr; Hon Roll; UCLA; Mech Engr.

MORENO, CHRISTINA; Rubidoux HS; Riverside, CA; (4); 17/578; Dance Clb; Teachers Aide; Color Guard; Treas Mrchg Band; Pep Band; Rep Jr Cls; Sec Sr Cls; Powder Puff Ftbl; Stat Wrstlng; High Hon Roll; Prncpls Advsry Cncl; CA Schltc Fdrtn VP, Pres; Amer Music Fndtn Band Hnrs; CA ST Fullerton; Music.

MORENO, CYNTHIA; Pomona Catholic Girls HS; Montclair, CA; (2); GAA; Varsity Clb; Sftbl; Hon Roll.

MORENO, DENISE; Tulare Joint Union HS; Tulare, CA; (4); Var Socr; Hon Roll; Co-Op Club; Coll Of Sequoias; Legal Secy.

MORENO, ELIZABETH; Woodrow Wilson HS; Los Angeles, CA; (3); Church Yth Grp; Stage Crew; Vllybl; LIFE Pgm.

MORENO, FELICITAS; Dinuba HS; Dinuba, CA; (3); 25/200; Pres Soph Cls; Hon Roll; Sci.

MORENO, FLORENTINA R; Amos Alonzo Stagg HS; Stockton, CA; (3); Dance Clb; Office Aide; Pep Clb; Teachers Aide; Hon Roll; NHS; HOSA Secy; HOSA Top 10 St Fnlst Job Sklls; Reg Nurse.

MORENO, FRANCINE; Chino HS; Chino, CA; (2); FFA; Var Bsktbl; Intrml Swmmng; MVP BCI Itnl 88; MVP Intl 89; Bsktbl Clssc Trny Chmpns 88; 89 Annandale VA & BCI Consltn; Tchng.

MORENO, HELKA L; Highlands HS; Sacramento, CA; (2); Engrng.

MORENO, IRENE M; Santa Teresa HS; San Jose, CA; (2); SADD; Chorus; Peer Cnslng Pgm; Psych.

MORENO, JAMES M; Hueneme HS; Oxnard, CA; (2); Oxnard Coll; Arch.

MORENO, JENNIE; Chino HS; Ontario, CA; (2); JV Capt Cheerldng; Var Pom Pon; Hon Roll; Pres Acad Fit Awd.

MORENO, JENNIFER; Rosary HS; La Mirada, CA; (2); Science Clb; Rptr Nwsp.

MORENO, JESSICA; Moorpark HS; Moorpark, CA; (3); French Clb; Office Aide; Trk; Hon Roll; U Of Santa Barbara; Lwyr.

MORENO, JUSTIN; Carpinteria HS; Carpinteria, CA; (4); 6/158; French Clb; School Play; Rptr Nwsp; Var JV Bsktbl; Var L Ftbl; Var L Tennis; Hon Roll; Masonic Awd; CSF; Mock Trl; Elec Engrng.

MORENO, LEONARD; Chino HS; Chino, CA; (3); Spanish Clb.

MORENO, LETICIA; Hueneme HS; Oxnard, CA; (2); High Hon Roll; Hon Roll; Ed.

MORENO, LINDA G; Chaffey HS; Ontario, CA; (1); French Hon Soc; Hon Roll; Keywanettes Clb; CA Poly; Civil Engr.

MORENO, LISA R; Costa Mesa HS; Costa Mesa, CA; (3); Chorus; Variety Show; Sftbl; Trk; Capt Vllybl; Hon Roll; U Of Southern CA; Marketing.

MORENO, MARIA C; Schurr HS; Monterey Park, CA; (2); Drama Clb; Key Clb; Varsity Clb; Off Soph Cls; Cheerldng; Socr; Sftbl; Vllybl; Hon Roll; UC Santa Cruz; Cmmrcl Art.

MORENO, MARISA; Pomona Catholic Girls HS; Fontana, CA; (2); Church Yth Grp; Cmnty Wkr; GAA; Hosp Aide; Pep Clb; Spanish Clb; Rptr Nwsp; Lit Mag; Rep Frsh Cls; JV Cheerldng; CSF; Med.

MORENO, MARITZA; Bell Gardens HS; Bell Gardens, CA; (2); Spanish Clb; Orch; Crs Cntry; Trk; Immgrtn Offcr.

MORENO, MICHAEL J; Oak Ridge HS; Cameron Park, CA; (4); 10/232; Art Clb; Pres Church Yth Grp; Intnl Clb; Var Swmmng; Hon Roll; Ntl Merit SF; JV Ski Tm; Aerospc Clb; Aerontcl Engr.

MORENO, PATRICK M; Bishop Amat HS; Covina, CA; (1); Boy Scts; JV Vllybl; NYU; Law.

MORENO, RENATO; St Monicas HS; Santa Monica, CA; (3); Church Yth Grp; Cmnty Wkr; Office Aide; Teachers Aide; JV Bsbl; Var Crs Cntry; High Hon Roll; CA Schlrshp Fed; Bus.

MORENO, ROSA M; Santiago HS; Santa Ana, CA; (2); 6/490; Hon Roll; Span Club; Tour Guide.

MORENO, RUBEN NICOLAS; Don Bosco Technical Inst; Rosemead, CA; (1); 44/244; Boy Scts; Drama Clb; Trk; NEDT Awd; Hnrs Entrnc; Outstndg Effort & Imprvmnt Elects; Successfully Srpssng Challenges Wrld Hist, Engl & Span.

MORENO, SONYA M; Modesto HS; Modesto, CA; (3); Art Clb; Dance Clb; Latin Clb; Spanish Clb; SADD; Teachers Aide; Chorus; JV Cheerldng; Var Trk; Cit Awd; Trophie In Math; Spec Interest Music; Awds Spanish,History,Music; Student Of Themonth; Honor Roll; San Francisco ST U; Engineer.

MORENO, TANYA K; Imperial HS; Glendale, CA; (3); Church Yth Grp; Varsity Clb; Chorus; Church Choir; Swing Chorus; Intrml Bsktbl; Intrml Fld Hcky; Intrml Socr; Var L Sftbl; Var Trk; Yth Group Gold Level Art Awd; Graphic Art.

MORENO, YAMAIRA M; Victor Valley HS; Victorville, CA; (1); Drill Tm; Prfct Atten Awd; Inter Dsgnr.

MORENO, YOLANDA; Oak Ridge HS; Cameron Park, CA; (2); Drama Clb; Spanish Clb; School Play; Hon Roll; OR ST; Psych.

MORENO-TORROBA, JOSE T; Torrey Pines HS; San Diego, CA; (2); Spanish Clb; Hon Roll; CSF; Intl Relations.

MORETON, JULIA; Trabuco Hills HS; Trabuco Canyon, CA; (2); 30/420; Church Yth Grp; Cmnty Wkr; Pep Clb; Wt Lftg; Hon Roll; NHS; Commrcl Art.

MORETTI, STEPHEN; Benicia HS; Benicia, CA; (2); Church Yth Grp; Ski Clb; SADD; Band; Church Choir; Jazz Band; Mrchg Band; Orch; Pep Band; Golf; Muscl Fndtn Band Hnrs; CMEA Hnrs; 2 Supr & 1 Commnd Perfrmnc Duet/Solo; Supr Muscnshp; Music.

MORETTO, CHRISTINE; Napa HS; Napa, CA; (3); Cmnty Wkr; Spanish Clb; Chorus; School Musical; Yrbk; Tennis; Cit Awd; High Hon Roll; CSF; CA Girls St Rep Cntst Semifnlst; Northwestern U; Med.

MOREY, ALI J; Chino HS; Chino, CA; (3); Am Leg Aux Girls St; Church Yth Grp; Pres Chorus; School Musical; Var JV Vllybl; Cit Awd; High Hon Roll; Rotary Awd; Azusa Pacific U; Vcl Music.

MOREY, STACEY D; Workman HS; Valinda, CA; (3); FFA; Cit Awd; Hon Roll; Prfct Atten Awd; Perfrmng Arts Dance; Span Club; Rgnl Occupation Pgm Photo, FFA; MTSAC; Ag.

MOREY, TIM; Julian Union HS; Julian, CA; (4); 5/45; Church Yth Grp; Spanish Clb; Varsity Clb; Yrbk; Rep Frsh Cls; Var Vllybl; Hon Roll; Pres Acad Fit Awd; Rotary Awd; San Diego ST U; Bus.

MORFIN, FIDEL; Red Bluff Union HS; Red Bluff, CA; (1); Hon Roll; Prfct Atten Awd; Med.

MORFORD, JONI; Aptos HS; Aptos, CA; (4); 11/275; Math Clb; Q&S; Teachers Aide; Ed Nwsp; Ed Yrbk; Bsktbl; Powder Puff Ftbl; JV Var Vllybl; High Hon Roll; Pres Acad Fit Awd; California Scholarship Federation Lifetime Member; Cabrillo JC; Communications.

MORGA, MARIA J; San Dimas HS; San Dimas, CA; (4); Aud/Vis; Cmnty Wkr; VP English Clb; GAA; Speech Tm; SADD; School Play; Stu Cncl; Capt Sftbl; Tennis; Co-Founder SADD & Saferide Prgm In Cmmnty; 1st Pl 90 Lions Clb Speech Fnls; Cal ST U; Lawyer.

MORGAN, ABRAM E; Newark Memorial HS; Newark, CA; (3); JV Ftbl; JV Wrstlng; Hon Roll; Prfct Atten Awd; Kung Fu; Crmnlgy.

MORGAN, AMY; Ocean View HS; Huntington Bch, CA; (2); Church Yth Grp; Cmnty Wkr; Debate Tm; Model UN; Color Guard; Cit Awd; Hon Roll; Masonic Awd.

MORGAN, ANJEANETTE; Torrance HS; Torrance, CA; (4); Church Yth Grp; French Clb; Pep Clb; Teachers Aide; Church Choir; Flag Corp; Tennis; Cit Awd; El Camino Coll Accntng Cls 89-90; El Camino Coll; Bus Admin.

MORGAN, BERNADINE R; Summerville Union HS; Twain Harte, CA; (3); 56/141; ROTC; Chorus; Barbazon; Model.

MORGAN, CARLIE R; Lindhurst HS; Marysville, CA; (3); Debate Tm; Drama Clb; ROTC; Color Guard; Drill Tm; Ed Nwsp; Hon Roll; Amer Legion-Schlstc Excllnc Awd; UC Davis; Aeronaut Engr.

MORGAN, CECILIA M; St Bernard HS; Los Angeles, CA; (3); Church Yth Grp; Hosp Aide; Pep Clb; Trk; Cit Awd; Cal ST Northridge; Bus Admin.

MORGAN JR, DAVID L; Thomas A Edison HS; Stockton, CA; (3); Cmnty Wkr; Latin Clb; Teachers Aide; Stu Cncl; Hon Roll; Giftd Talntd Ed; Bus Admn.

MORGAN, ELIZABETH W; Hayward HS; Hayward, CA; (1); Church Yth Grp; Girl Scts; Band; Mrchg Band; Orch; High Hon Roll; Sch Sci Fir 1st Pl Phys Sci Div; CMEA Excclnc Rtng.

MORGAN, ERIC EUGENE; Wheatland Union HS; Yuba City, CA; (3); 8/109; Art Clb; German Clb; Scholastic Bowl; Ski Clb; Var JV Bsbl; JV Bsktbl; Var JV Ftbl; Var Socr; High Hon Roll; Hon Roll; Engl, Chem & German Awd; Engr.

MORGAN, GLORIA A; Wasco Union HS; Wasco, CA; (3); FTA; Rptr Nwsp; Lit Mag; Powder Puff Ftbl; High Hon Roll; Mock Trial; CA Schlrshp Fed; Ed.

MORGAN, HEATHER A; Irvine HS; Irvine, CA; (3); Church Yth Grp; Dance Clb; Key Clb; SADD; Teachers Aide; Chorus; JV Crs Cntry; Hon Roll; NHS; Heritage Award In Home-Arts; Dance 7 Years; CSF; Education/Elem Schl Teacher.

MORGAN, JARROD S; Del Campo HS; Fair Oaks, CA; (3); Boy Scts; Church Yth Grp; Drama Clb; FHA; Acpl Chr; Chorus; Church Choir; Variety Show; Hist Frsh Cls; Pres Acad Fit Awd; All St Hnr Choir; BYU; Psych.

MORGAN, JEFFREY P; Lincoln HS; Stockton, CA; (3); School Play; Golf; Hon Roll; UCLA; Anthrplgy.

MORGAN, KELLY J; Santa Barbara HS; Santa Barbara, CA; (2); Church Yth Grp; Drama Clb; French Clb; Letterman Clb; Acpl Chr; Chorus; School Musical; School Play; Stage Crew; Variety Show; Theatrical.

MORGAN, LAURA A; El Dorado HS; Pollock Pines, CA; (4); 4-H; Science Clb; Speech Tm; Teachers Aide; Mrchg Band; Cit Awd; 4-H Awd; High Hon Roll; NHS; Pres Acad Fit Awd; CA ST U Sacramento; Med.

MORGAN, NICK S; Sutter HS; Sutter, CA; (2); 1/70; FBLA; Intnl Clb; Science Clb; SADD; Teachers Aide; Pres Frsh Cls; Accntng.

MORGAN, ROBYN N; Woodrow Wilson HS; Long Beach, CA; (3); JV Bsktbl; Long Beach City Coll; Mod Mgmt.

MORGAN, RYAN E; Oak Ridge HS; Shingle Springs, CA; (3); FBLA; Intnl Clb; Letterman Clb; Math Tm; Lit Mag; Var L Tennis; JV Wrstlng; High Hon Roll; Hon Roll; U CA-IRVINE; Psycht.

MORGAN, SCOTT W; Fallbrook Union HS; Menifee, CA; (3); Letterman Clb; Office Aide; Ski Clb; SADD; Varsity Clb; JV Ftbl; Ice Hcky; Var Trk; Var Wrstlng; Hon Roll; HI ST U; Bus.

MORGAN, SEAN A; Skyline HS; Oakland, CA; (3); Church Yth Grp; Var L Trk; Hon Roll; Crss Cntry.

MORGAN, SHAWN M; Vallejo SR HS; Vallejo, CA; (3); French Clb; SADD; Varsity Clb; Capt Golf; Capt Socr; Hon Roll; Sccr League; Police Act League; Elec Engrng.

MORGAN, SHIREEN; Calipatria HS; Niland, CA; (3); Art Clb; Cmnty Wkr; 4-H; Off Soph Cls; Sftbl; 4-H Awd; High Hon Roll; Hon Roll; Bass Guitar; Imperial Vly Coll; RN.

MORGAN, STEVE A; Rim Of The World HS; Running Springs, CA; (2); Boy Scts; Church Yth Grp; Band; Church Choir; Mrchg Band; Orch; School Musical; Hon Roll; Pres Acad Fit Awd; Julliard Schl Of Music.

MORGAN, TAMARA L; Oak Ridge HS; Shingle Springs, CA; (1); Church Yth Grp; Var Debate Tm; FBLA; Math Tm; Var Speech Tm; SADD; Rep Frsh Cls; Rep Stu Cncl; Cit Awd; High Hon Roll; CSF; CA Assn Stu Cncls; Cal Poly; Engrng.

MORGAN, TIFFANY C; Alverno HS; Arcadia, CA; (2); Off Frsh Cls; Var Sftbl; JV Var Vllybl; Occidental Coll; CPA.

MORI, AISHA K; Venice HS; Los Angeles, CA; (1); Hon Roll; UCLA; Engl.

MORI, MICHELE A; Venice HS; Los Angeles, CA; (4); Hosp Aide; Treas Pres Service Clb; Teachers Aide; Drill Tm; Yrbk; Rep Stu Cncl; Cit Awd; Hon Roll; Prfct Atten Awd; Santa Monica CC.

MORI, RICHARD K; South San Francisco HS; South San Francis, CA; (2); Spanish Clb; Tennis; Cit Awd; High Hon Roll; CSF; Tnns Clb; UC Berkeley; Engrng.

MORIARTY, PAT; St Ignatius HS; San Francisco, CA; (2); Service Clb; Nwsp; Var Tennis; Hon Roll; CSF; Irish Club.

MORICONI, RACHEL J; Sacred Heart Prep; San Jose, CA; (2); Church Yth Grp; Cmnty Wkr; Model UN; Chorus; School Musical; School Play; Phtg Yrbk; Var Socr; Var Trk; Hon Roll; Cmpng Club Pres; U MI; Math.

MORIMOTO, JAN C; Gardena HS; Gardena, CA; (4); 6/433; Hosp Aide; JCL; NFL; Speech Tm; Nwsp; Sec Frsh Cls; Var Tennis; High Hon Roll; Hon Roll; Kiwanis Awd; UCLA.

MORIN, MONIQUE F; Schurr HS; Los Angeles, CA; (4); 55/580; Key Clb; Speech Tm; SADD; Chorus; Yrbk; Hist Stu Cncl; Stat Bsbl; JV Sftbl; Hon Roll; Ntl Merit SF; Grls League VP; CA Schlrshp Fdrtn; Chrch Vol Wrk; Ucla; Bus Adv.

MORING III, RICHARD T; Santa Rosa HS; Santa Rosa, CA; (4); 36/535; Church Yth Grp; Computer Clb; Math Tm; Speech Tm; Teachers Aide; Var Wrstlng; High Hon Roll; Hon Roll; Pres Acad Fit Awd; U Of CA LA; Aerospc Engrng.

MORISAKI, GREGG; Kennedy HS; La Palma, CA; (3); Teachers Aide; Bsktbl; Bus.

MORITA, JENNIFER K; Mesa Verde HS; Citrus Heights, CA; (2); 3/300; Math Clb; Math Tm; Sec Spanish Clb; Orch; Nwsp; Lit Mag; High Hon Roll; Hon Roll; Friday Night Live Sec/Treas; Sacra Yth Spymph; CSF; Stu Reaching Out; Lit Club; Mesa Verde Wrtng Cont.

MORITA, MAYUKO E; Sacramento Country Day Sch; Woodland, CA; (3); Art Clb; Cmnty Wkr; Red Cross Aide; SADD; Chorus; Orch; Rep Frsh Cls; Var Bsktbl; DAR Awd; Prfct Atten Awd; Cmptns Held Across CA Classical Music; Write Stories & Plays Since 4th Grade; Eastman; Med.

MORK, PAULINE J; Antioch SR HS; Antioch, CA; (2); Church Yth Grp; Drama Clb; Teachers Aide; School Musical; School Play; Hon Roll; Write Creatv Stories; Stanford U; Law.

MORLAN, CHRISTIE M; Ontario HS; Ontario, CA; (3); 12/443; Church Yth Grp; German Clb; Key Clb; Church Choir; Ed Yrbk; High Hon Roll; Azusa Pacific U; Bio.

MORLEDGE, JAMES E; West HS; Bakersfield, CA; (1); Debate Tm; NFL; Spanish Clb; Speech Tm; School Play; Rptr Nwsp; Hon Roll; GATE; Bakersfield Comp Club; AZ ST U; Comp Prgmr.

MORLEY, CHRISTINA M; St Genevieve HS; Canoga Park, CA; (4); Girl Scts; JA; Letterman Clb; Pep Clb; SADD; Varsity Clb; Band; Ed Yrbk; Rep Frsh Cls; Rep Soph Cls; Mst Sesrvng Stu Awd Gvn Mike Antonovich 5th Dist 90; Marion & Gold Awd GSA; Hmcmng Qn & St Fnlst Pgnt; San Diego ST U.

MORLEY, JENNY S; Santa Barbara HS; Santa Barbara, CA; (2); 22/450; Church Yth Grp; Hosp Aide; Acpl Chr; Score Keeper; Stat Vllybl; High Hon Roll; Hon Roll; Santa Barbara Madrigal Sngrs.

MORO, JOHN; Paraclete HS; Lancaster, CA; (3); 8/128; Cmnty Wkr; JA; Letterman Clb; JV Var Crs Cntry; JV Var Socr; JV Trk; High Hon Roll; NHS; CA Schlrshp Fed; 7 Yrs Altar Boy; Build Mdl Airplaines; USAF Acad; Arspc Engr.

MOROAICA, ANDRA; Downey HS; Downey, CA; (4); 5/500; French Clb; NFL; Speech Tm; Ed Nwsp; Hon Roll; NHS; Pres Acad Fit Awd; Studied Ballet 10 Yrs Capt Of Cmpttn Team; UCI; Lit.

MOROAK, VARINDER K; Lindhurst HS; Marysville, CA; (3); Am Leg Aux Girls St; Drama Clb; Intnl Clb; Key Clb; SADD; Thesps; School Play; Stage Crew; Off Frsh Cls; Pres Soph Cls; Pre-Med.

MORONEY, COURTNEY; Notre Dame HS; San Carlos, CA; (3); Cmnty Wkr; Debate Tm; Varsity Clb; Pres Frsh Cls; Var Socr; Var JV Tennis; High Hon Roll; Hon Roll; NHS; Co-Chrprsn Chrstms Frml, Org Frml Dance Natl Hnr Soc; Bobby Sox Sftbl Cty; CYSA Sccr Cty.

MORPHEW, MICHELLE; La Jolla HS; San Diego, CA; (4); 1/350; Model UN; Science Clb; Service Clb; Variety Show; Ed Yrbk; Var L Bsktbl; Ntl Merit SF; Var L Swmmng; Interact Clb; Spcbrdg/Intl Frndshp Clb; Natl Spanish Exam; Harvard U; Intl Stds.

MORPHIS, ANGIE; Troy HS; Fullerton, CA; (1); Church Yth Grp; Office Aide; CA ST U Long Beach; Bus.

MORRICAL, KRISTIN; San Mateo HS; Foster City, CA; (3); Library Aide; Office Aide; Teachers Aide; Band; Color Guard; Flag Corp; Mrchg Band; Stage Crew; Gym; Hon Roll; Chld Dvlpmnt; Transportn; Hotel/Restrnt Mgmt; CA ST Schl; Chld Dvlpmnt.

MORRICE, ALLYSON D; Westmoor HS; Daly City, CA; (1); Church Yth Grp; Hosp Aide; SADD; Score Keeper; High Hon Roll; Pres Acad Fit Awd; USS Carl Vinson Clb; Close-Up Clb; U Of CA San Francisco; MD.

MORRIS, AARON; Torrance HS; Torrance, CA; (4); 4-H; Letterman Clb; Service Clb; VP Temple Yth Grp; Rep Sr Cls; Var L Crs Cntry; Var L Trk; Hon Roll; Blck Blt Karate 88; Japan Airlines Sponsrd Intl Origami Cmptns 4 Yrs; UC Santa Barbara; Bio.

MORRIS, ALYCIA; Marshall Fundamental HS; Altadena, CA; (3); Drama Clb; Key Clb; Teachers Aide; Chorus; Orch; Stat Bsktbl; Stat Sftbl; JV Tennis; Var Trk; Var Vllybl; Med.

MORRIS, ANGELA A; Modesto HS; Modesto, CA; (1); Orch; Hon Roll; Prfct Atten Awd; Chrch Yth Grp; Bus.

MORRIS, ANGIE; Gidden West HS; Visalia, CA; (2); Cmnty Wkr; French Clb; FHA; Intnl Clb; Natl Beta Clb; Color Guard; Bsktbl; Diving; Elks Awd; High Hon Roll; Dance Line; Acad Ltr; UC Irvine; Physics.

MORRIS, AUNQUISE; Mc Clymonds HS; Oakland, CA; (3); Church Yth Grp; Cmnty Wkr; ROTC; Teachers Aide; Church Choir; Rptr Nwsp; Yrbk; Stu Cncl; Co-Capt Cheerldng; High Hon Roll; UC Davis; Vet.

MORRIS, BRANDIE; Helix HS; San Diego, CA; (3); 33/470; Treas Sec Church Yth Grp; Treas Sec Cmnty Wkr; NFL; Speech Tm; Pres Frsh Cls; Rep Soph Cls; Rep Jr Cls; Stu Cncl; Var Capt Cheerldng; Mgr(s); CSF; Golden St Exam Hnrs; Speech Team Most Inspiratnl Spkr; USD; Law.

MORRIS, BUFFY; South Tahoe HS; Tahoe Paradise, CA; (4); ROTC; Service Clb; Spanish Clb; SADD; Teachers Aide; Powder Puff Ftbl; Sftbl; Hon Roll; Northridge U; Vet.

MORRIS, CAROL A; Davis SR HS; Davis, CA; (2); Church Yth Grp; Band; Gym; Mgr(s); UCLA; Chld Psych.

MORRIS, CHRISTOPHER J; Notre Dame HS; Hemet, CA; (1); 18/165; Church Yth Grp; JV Ftbl; High Hon Roll; Lima Lama An Amer-Polynesion For Martial Art; Frsh Ftbl Coaches Awd; Vrsty Awd For PE; Sprts Med.

MORRIS, CHRISTOPHER L; Silver Valley HS; Daggett, CA; (2); Church Yth Grp; Yrbk; Cit Awd; High Hon Roll; Prfct Atten Awd; Outstndng Band Achvt Awd; Acad Decathlong; Marine Aquarist Club; Santa Cruz; Marine Bio.

MORRIS, DESEREE A; Mt Pleasant HS; San Jose, CA; (2); Church Yth Grp; GAA; JV Bsktbl; JV Cmnty Wkr; UCLA; Phy.

MORRIS, DUSTIN; Bullard HS; Fresno, CA; (2); Tennis; Prfct Atten Awd; USAR Acad CO Sprngs; Pilot.

MORRIS, DUSTY; Bloomington HS; Fontana, CA; (3); JV Tennis; JV Trk; Hon Roll; Pres Acad Fit Awd; CA HS Rodeo Chmpn, 90 Chmp Goat Tyer; Fresno ST U; Phys Thrpy.

MORRIS, ELENA M; Montclair HS; Montclair, CA; (3); #29 In Class; Var Trk; Hon Roll; Phys/Erth Sci Of Coll Prep Achvmnt Awd 88; Cert Of Excl Hnrs Chem 90; Yng Schlr Prgm Ca Poly Pomona; Chaffey Coll; Pre-Med.

MORRIS, ERIC W; Monte Vista HS; Spring Valley, CA; (2); 39/461; Band; Golf; Hon Roll.

MORRIS, FRANKIE M; Hogan SR HS; Vallejo, CA; (3); Service Clb; Spanish Clb; Rptr Nwsp; Wrstlng; Cit Awd; High Hon Roll; Hon Roll; Jr NHS; NHS; Stat-Wrestling Team; San Francisco ST U; Cmmnctn.

MORRIS, HEATHER J; Skyline HS; Oakland, CA; (2); Church Yth Grp; Church Choir; Var L Cheerldng; Dance; Sociology.

MORRIS, HOLLY E; John F Kennedy HS; Sacramento, CA; (3); Cmnty Wkr; Dance Clb; ROTC; Ski Clb; Spanish Clb; Teachers Aide; School Musical; School Play; Variety Show; Rep Frsh Cls; CSU; Elem Tchr.

MORRIS, JEFF; California HS; San Ramon, CA; (3); 150/400; JA; Teachers Aide; Stu Cncl; JV Tennis; Sacramento ST Coll; Law Offcr.

MORRIS, JENNIFER; Delano HS; Delano, CA; (3); Pep Clb; Teachers Aide; Varsity Clb; Nwsp; Cheerldng; Hon Roll; NHS; Prfrmng Dance Co; Head Vrsty Chrldr 90-91; Lcl Beauty & Tlnt Show; Dance.

MORRIS, JERRY E; Mojave HS; California City, CA; (1); High Hon Roll; Engrng.

MORRIS, JILL E; Notre Dame HS; Salinas, CA; (4); Art Clb; Church Yth Grp; Dance Clb; FCA; Letterman Clb; Science Clb; SADD; Varsity Clb; Var Bsktbl; JV Var Sftbl; San Diego ST U; Dentstry.

MORRIS, KARIN; Charter Oak HS; Covina, CA; (3); Am Leg Aux Girls St; Sec Treas Cmnty Wkr; Sec Dance Clb; Pres Pep Clb; VP Frsh Cls; Pres Soph Cls; VP Jr Cls; VP Stu Cncl; JV Var Cheerldng; High Hon Roll; Attended UCLA Summer School 1989; Attended Boston College Summer School 1990.

MORRIS, KERRIE; Central Union HS; El Centro, CA; (2); Pep Clb; Co-Capt Cheerldng; Var Swmmng; JV Tennis; High Hon Roll; CSF; ASB Ast Commssnr; Med.

MORRIS, KIMBERLY L; Ferndale Union HS; Ferndale, CA; (3); Art Clb; Church Yth Grp; Cmnty Wkr; English Clb; 4-H; Sec FFA; Pep Clb; SADD; Rep Soph Cls; Sec Jr Cls.

MORRIS, KRISTIN; Carlmont HS; Belmont, CA; (3); 7/320; Band; School Musical; Var Vllybl; Ntl Merit Ltr; CSF; Amnsty Intl.

MORRIS, LILAH; Lincoln HS; Stockton, CA; (3); 44/592; Debate Tm; Key Clb; Mu Alpha Theta; NFL; Speech Tm; Pres Temple Yth Grp; Nwsp; JV Var Jr Cls; Var Trk; High Hon Roll.

MORRIS, LISA L; St Anthony HS; Lakewood, CA; (2); Drama Clb; French Clb; SADD; High Hon Roll; Hon Roll; NHS; Pres Acad Fit Awd; Schl Srv, Rdng, Spelling Awds.

MORRIS, MARC E; Monte Vista HS; Spring Valley, CA; (2); 46/461; Golf; Yng Republican Clb.

MORRIS, NEVA; Middletown HS; Cobb, CA; (4); 11/68; Cmnty Wkr; Dance Clb; Drama Clb; Intnl Clb; Pep Clb; Spanish Clb; Teachers Aide; Band; Mrchg Band; Pep Band; Lioness Clb Awd; U Of CA; Bio Sci.

MORRIS, NOAH J; Paradise HS; Paradise, CA; (1); Art Clb; Bsktbl; Ftbl; Frshmn Art Awd; Paradise Writing Project; Chico ST U; U Art Tchr.

MORRIS, REBECCA A; Beaumont HS; Cherry Valley, CA; (3); 4/200; JA; Teachers Aide; Var L Tennis; NHS; Stu Of CSF VP; Attnd HOBY Conf; Rcvd Acadc Awds In Wrld Hist, US Hist AP, & Hnrs Engl; Psych.

MORRIS, ROBERT P; Leuzinger HS; Hawthorne, CA; (2); JV Bsbl; JV Crs Cntry; Var Wrstlng.

MORRIS, RYAN; Chino HS; Chino, CA; (3); Drama Clb; FCA; JV Bsktbl; Var JV Ftbl; Var JV Wt Lftg; UCLA; Jrnlsm.

MORRIS, SANDRA; Sierra Viota HS; Baldwin Park, CA; (4); VP FBLA; Girl Scts; Pres Letterman Clb; Math Clb; Science Clb; Speech Tm; Teachers Aide; Off Stu Cncl; Var Bsktbl; Var Cheerldng; Gs Wider Opportunity Participant-Medical Observation/Educational Seminar; U Of CA Irvine; Pre Med.

MORRIS, SHAIRONDA R; El Camino Fundamental HS; Citrus Heights, CA; (3); 89/451; Spanish Clb; SADD; Acpl Chr; Tennis; Hon Roll; UCSF Early Outrch Residncy Prgm; UCSF; Med.

MORRIS, SHARI; Corning Union HS; Chico, CA; (4); Debate Tm; GAA; Intnl Clb; Science Clb; Ski Clb; Drill Tm; Vllybl; Butte Coll; Nrsng.

MORRIS, STEPHANIE; Taft Union HS; Fellows, CA; (4); 28/175; Key Clb; Teachers Aide; Band; Mrchg Band; Phtg Nwsp; Sec Jr Cls; Sec Sr Cls; Stat Bsktbl; Var Powder Puff Ftbl; Score Keeper; Bnk America Achvt Awd Frgn Lang; Taft Coll; Bus Admin.

MORRIS, TRACY; Foothill HS; Pleasanton, CA; (4); 11/325; Church Yth Grp; Sec Frsh Cls; Sec Soph Cls; Rep Jr Cls; Stu Cncl; Var JV Cheerldng; Capt JV Socr; High Hon Roll; Hon Roll; Ntl Merit Ltr; ASB Commissioner Of Publicity; Sunol Schlrshp; CSF; Cal Poly SLO; Biochem.

MORRIS, WILLIAM S; Turlock HS; Turlock, CA; (3); 47/603; JV Var Ftbl; JV Var Trk; Ftbl & Trk All Acad Conf Tm; Engrng.

MORRISETTE, DAHRYANOUS D; Magnolia HS; Anaheim, CA; (2); Cmnty Wkr; School Play; Stage Crew; Variety Show; VP Soph Cls; Var JV Ftbl; Var JV Trk; Wt Lftg; Hon Roll; Prfct Atten Awd; MVP Frshmn & JV Ftbl; Orange Lg Chmpng; Hmcmng Prnc Sphmr Yr & JR Mr Universe.

MORRISON, AKILAK C; San Bernardino HS; San Bernardino, CA; (2); Capt Drill Tm; Swmmng; Var Trk; Black Stu Union; Bus.

MORRISON, BRIAN L; Piedmont HS; Piedmont, CA; (2); Aud/Vis; Temple Yth Grp; JV Bsbl; JV Crs Cntry; Hon Roll; Confirmed Hnrs From Temple; Gardeng Bus; Golden St Alge Hnrs.

MORRISON, DANIEL; Los Angeles HS; Los Angeles, CA; (3); Boy Scts; Church Yth Grp; Math Clb; Church Choir; Off Jr Cls; Bsktbl; Score Keeper; Stat Sftbl; Tennis; Wt Lftg.

MORRISON, JANNIEN; Strathmore Union HS; Porterville, CA; (3); Art Clb; Church Yth Grp; Drama Clb; FHA; German Clb; Letterman Clb; Office Aide; SADD; Drill Tm; School Play; Nurse.

MORRISON, JESIA; Washington Prep; Los Angeles, CA; (3); Girl Scts; Hon Roll; CSF; UCLA; Organic Chem.

MORRISON, JULIE; Mt Carmel HS; San Diego, CA; (4); 16/732; Capt Color Guard; Capt Flag Corp; Hon Roll; Pres Acad Fit Awd; UC Santa Barbra; Bio.

MORRISON, KEVIN H; Warren HS; Downey, CA; (2); Boy Scts; Church Yth Grp; Service Clb; Ski Clb; Rptr Nwsp; Swmmng; Water Polo Tm; Hgh Hnrs GSE.

MORRISON, KEVIN P; Damien HS Prep; La Verne, CA; (4); Cmnty Wkr; Letterman Clb; Varsity Clb; Var Capt Bsktbl; JV Ftbl; Hon Roll; Kiwanis Awd; Young Blk Schlr Awd; NAACP Yth; Jack & Jill; U Of San Diego; Bus Admin.

MORRISON, LEE P; San Clemente HS; San Juan Capistra, CA; (1); Wrstlng; OR ST U; Bus.

MORRISON, OMAR H; Pasadena HS; Altadena, CA; (3); Science Clb; Yrbk; Bsktbl; Trk; Hon Roll; Math; Arch.

MORRISON, ROBERT A; Orange Glen HS; Escondido, CA; (2); Church Yth Grp; DECA; German Clb; ROTC; VP Soph Cls; Crs Cntry; Socr; Trk; NHS; Pres Acad Fit Awd; US Naval Acad; Aviation.

MORRISON, SHELLY A; Ventura HS; Ventura, CA; (1); 27/539; JV Bsktbl; JV Capt Vllybl; High Hon Roll; Frshmn Vllybl MVP Awd; Vrsty Ltr For Acad.

MORRISON, WESLEY L; Skyline HS; Oakland, CA; (3); Church Yth Grp; Ski Clb; Church Choir; Hon Roll; Pres Schlr; CSF; Engrng.

MORRISROE, DENNIS; Bret Harte HS; Murphys, CA; (1); Ski Clb; JV L Tennis; High Hon Roll; Rep Frsh Cls; CA Schltc Fed; Acad Block.

MORRISS, KIMBERLY J; Diamond Bar HS; Diamond Bar, CA; (3); Church Yth Grp; French Clb; Rep SADD; Color Guard; Hon Roll; Child Dev.

MORRISSETTE, ERIC J; San Dieguito HS; Encinitas, CA; (2); Bsbl; JV Socr; High Hon Roll; Pres Acad Fit Awd.

MORRISSETTE, MONIKA T; Norte Vista HS; Riverside, CA; (1); Church Yth Grp; Dance Clb; French Clb; FFA; Girl Scts; Trk; Hon Roll; Cert Merit Piano; Dist Histy Day 2nd Pl Rbbn; UCLA; Attrny.

MORROW, AMBER; Marina HS; Huntington Beach, CA; (4); JA; Key Clb; Pep Clb; Spanish Clb; Pres SADD; Ed Yrbk; Hon Roll; U CA Irvine.

MORROW, BRYAN W; Yucca Valley HS; Yucca Valley, CA; (2); Math Clb; Band; Jazz Band; Mrchg Band; Orch; School Musical; Var Wrstlng; Hon Roll; Gldn St Awd Alg I Schl Rec; Cal Tech; Engrng.

MORROW, STEPHANIE; Moorpark HS; Moorpark, CA; (4); 10/180; Am Leg Aux Girls St; Key Clb; Rep Sr Cls; Rep Stu Cncl; JV Var Cheerldng; JV Sftbl; JV Vllybl; High Hon Roll; Ivy Chain; Outstndng Acdmc Achvt Awd; Loyola Marymount U; Bus.

MORSE, JANIS L; Fowler HS; Fresno, CA; (3); 10/92; Church Yth Grp; Drama Clb; FCA; Letterman Clb; Spanish Clb; Var Sftbl; Var Trk; Var JV Vllybl; Hon Roll; Masonic Awd; Jobs Dghtrs; Friday Night Live; UC Santa Barbara; Pre-Med.

MORSE, KATHRYN; Foothill HS; Pleasanton, CA; (3); Boy Scts; Church Yth Grp; Cmnty Wkr; Computer Clb; French Clb; GAA; JA; JCL; Latin Clb; Ski Clb; Windsurfing Instructor; Cal Poly; Aerospc Engrng.

MORSE, KRISTIN M; Garden Grove HS; Garden Grove, CA; (2); Church Yth Grp; Drama Clb; Key Clb; Speech Tm; Thesps; Acpl Chr; School Play; Stage Crew; Variety Show; Ed Yrbk; Liberal Arts.

MORSE, SEAN A; Chino HS; Chino, CA; (1); Boy Scts; Church Yth Grp; Band; Jazz Band; Mrchg Band; Orch; Hon Roll; BYU; Med.

MORSHAUSER, TANJA; Escondido HS; Escondido, CA; (3); German Clb; Var Trk; Hon Roll; Lang German, Span, Typing, Rdng, Swmmng; SDSU; Lang.

MORSI, MARWA S; Downey HS; Downey, CA; (3); French Clb; Intnl Clb; Math Clb; Office Aide; Trk; Les Torcheres VP; Lib Clb Sec & Treas; Hnr Grd; USC; Chld Psych.

MORTARA, SCOTT; Arcadia HS; Arcadia, CA; (4); 344/642; Ski Clb; Hon Roll; Water Ski Clb; Grant Southern CA Edison; Bus.

MORTELA, CECILIA C; San Benito HS; Hollister, CA; (2); French Clb; JV Sftbl; U CA Davis; Phys Thrpy.

MORTENSEN, CAROL; Clovis HS; Fresno, CA; (4); Church Yth Grp; Dance Clb; Rptr Nwsp; Ed Lit Mag; Hon Roll; Ecology Club-Secretary/ Treasurer; Broadcasting; Fresno Cty Coll; Psychology.

MORTENSEN, HEATHER K; Hanford HS; Hanford, CA; (1); Teachers Aide; Yrbk; Tennis; Hon Roll; Pepperdine; Interior Dsgnr.

MORTENSEN, LITHIA D; Hesperia HS; Hesperia, CA; (4); Pres Church Yth Grp; Cmnty Wkr; FBLA; Hosp Aide; SADD; Drill Tm; Rptr Yrbk; Rep Stu Cncl; Hon Roll; Pres Acad Fit Awd; U Clb Pres; Outdr Educ Cnslr; BYU; Elem Educ.

MORTENSEN, MICHELLE; San Dieguito HS; Carlsbad, CA; (2); English Clb; Key Clb; Teachers Aide; Hon Roll; Prfct Atten Awd; CSF; Golden St Ex Hnrs Geo,Alg; Crmnlgy.

MORTHOLE, GREG ERROL; Del Campo HS; Fair Oaks, CA; (3); 37/446; Boy Scts; Band; Mrchg Band; Var Crs Cntry; Var Trk.

MORTON, ANDREA N; Hawthorne HS; Hawthorne, CA; (3); Stu Cncl; JV Crs Cntry; JV Trk; Hon Roll; New Life Club; CSF; Peer Cnslng; Intr Dsgn.

MORTON, ANGELA M; Skyline HS; Oakland, CA; (3); Drama Clb; Library Aide; Office Aide; Pep Clb; ROTC; Speech Tm; Teachers Aide; School Play; Rep Frsh Cls; Pres Jr Cls; Mills Coll Upward Bound; AK Fairbanks/ Occidental; Psych.

MORTON, JAMES C; Palm Springs HS; Cathedral City, CA; (3); Var Crs Cntry; JV Var Trk; JV Var Wrstlng; High Hon Roll; Hon Roll; Coachs Awd Wrstlng 89-90; Prin Awd Acdmc Achvmnt 88-90; Embry Riddle U; Engnrng.

MORTON, JOHN; Merced HS; Merced, CA; (3); Boy Scts; Church Yth Grp; Office Aide; Hon Roll; Engrng.

MORTON, KARRIE L; Canyon Springs HS; Moreno Vly, CA; (3); Church Yth Grp; Girl Scts; Science Clb; Ed Yrbk; L Stat Bsktbl; Mgr(s); Sftbl; Vllybl; Church Brd Yth Pgm; CPA.

MORTON, MICHELLE; Kingsburg HS; Kingsburg, CA; (4); 10/150; French Clb; FFA; Girl Scts; Letterman Clb; Gov Hon Prg Awd; High Hon Roll; Hon Roll; Astrnmy Clb; CSL; Amer Lgn Aux; Cal Poly San Luis Obispo; Anmls.

MORTON II, VICTOR A; St Francis HS; Redwood City, CA; (2); 126/358; Letterman Clb; SADD; Church Choir; Stage Crew; Var Bsktbl; Var JV Ftbl; High Hon Roll; Hon Roll; Engl Tchr.

MORTON, WILL H; Lowerlake HS; Lower Lake, CA; (3); 19/125; Boy Scts; Var Capt Ftbl; Tennis; Var Capt Wt Lftg; Hon Roll; Pres Acad Fit Awd; Odssy Mind; Cal Poly San Louis Obisbo; Arch.

MORTON-BOURS, EMMA C; Henry M Gunn HS; Portola Valley, CA; (4); 5/275; Cmnty Wkr; Intnl Clb; Service Clb; JV Crs Cntry; JV Trk; Ntl Merit SF; Yale Bk Awd; Rensselaer Math & Sci Awd; CSF.

MOSAQUITES III, NICOLAS; Damien HS; Montclair, CA; (1); 1/38; Ftbl; Wrstlng; Cit Awd; Hon Roll; Spanish NHS; Lwyr.

MOSCOSO, MARIEL; Belklarmine Jefferson HS; Burbank, CA; (2); Church Yth Grp; Cmnty Wkr; French Clb; SADD; Teachers Aide; Chorus; Church Choir; Color Guard; JV Bsktbl; JV Sftbl; Georgetown U; Bus Law.

MOSEANKO, TODD; San Gabriel Acad; Duarte, CA; (3); 4/42; Church Yth Grp; Cmnty Wkr; Drama Clb; French Clb; Spanish Clb; Band; Chorus; Church Choir; School Play; Stage Crew; Advncd Karate; Bodybldg; Amer Acad Drmtc Arts; Theatrcl.

MOSELEY, AMY; Ramona HS; Ramona, CA; (3); Church Yth Grp; French Clb; Off Stu Cncl; Var Bsktbl; Var Vllybl; Rpt.

MOSELEY, MELISSA; Ramona HS; Ramona, CA; (2); Cheerldng; Gym.

MOSEN, KHIRSTEN M; San Dieguito HS; Encinitas, CA; (3); 130/570; Boy Scts; Church Yth Grp; Dance Clb; SADD; Swmmng; Hon Roll; Saferides.

MOSER, HEATHER; Foothill HS; Bakersfield, CA; (2); Church Yth Grp; Cmnty Wkr; Dance Clb; Hosp Aide; JA; Ski Clb; Teachers Aide; Varsity Clb; Cheerldng; Pom Pon; Jr Achvt Most Sales Awd; Fine Arts Awd; Pediatrician.

MOSER, KIMBERLY; Apple Valley Christian HS; Hesperia, CA; (3); 1/18; Church Yth Grp; Drama Clb; Pres Frsh Cls; Pres Soph Cls; Off Pres Jr Cls; Treas Stu Cncl; Var Sftbl; Var Vllybl; High Hon Roll; Prfct Atten Awd.

MOSES, TAMARA; O'farrell SCPA HS; San Diego, CA; (1); Chorus; Cit Awd; Hon Roll; Scl Stds Outstndng Achvt Awd; Engl Dstnctn Awd; Acad Achvt Awd; Bus Mgmt.

MOSGOFIAN, ISAAC P; Mc Kinleyville HS; Mckinleyville, CA; (2); Church Yth Grp; SADD; School Play; Stage Crew; Yrbk; JV Bsktbl; Score Keeper; Tennis; Hnrb Mntn; Stanford Med; Dctr.

MOSHELL, MICHELLE T; Woodside HS; Woodside, CA; (3); FBLA; Teachers Aide; Socr; Tennis; Hon Roll; Ntl Merit Ltr; Piano; CA Schlrshp Fed; Cnfrssnl Schlr; Brown; Pre Med.

MOSHIMER, JULIE A; San Gorgonio HS; Highland, CA; (3); Girl Scts; Key Clb; Teachers Aide; Yrbk; Schlr Ltr 3.5 GPA; Silver Awd; UCR; Envrnmntl.

MOSHREFI, HOUTAN; Clovis HS; Clovis, CA; (4); French Clb; Library Aide; Math Clb; Office Aide; Teachers Aide; Varsity Clb; Var Bsktbl; Var Ftbl; JV Socr; Wt Lftg; Fresno City Coll; Med.

MOSIMAN, THOMAS C; Clovis HS; Clovis, CA; (3); Church Yth Grp; Tennis; Prfct Atten Awd; Cngrssnl Yth Ldrshp Cncl Cngrssnl Schlr; U Of CA; Med.

MOSKAL, MICHELE; St Genevieves HS; Arleta, CA; (3); Dance Clb; Drama Clb; French Clb; Pep Clb; Drill Tm; School Musical; Stat Bsktbl; Var Cheerldng; Hon Roll; Intl Thespian Soc Sec; UC Santa Barbara; Bus Admin.

MOSLER, LAYNE L; Troy HS; Yorba Linda, CA; (2); 1/335; FCA; JCL; Key Clb; Latin Clb; Nwsp; Cheerldng; Var Crs Cntry; Var Socr; Var Trk; Rotary Awd; Published Short Story & 3 Poems; HOBY Ambssdr; Natl Latin Exam Slvr Mdlst; Swarthmore; Wrter.

MOSLEY, CAPRICE D; Crenshaw HS; Compton, CA; (4); Speech Tm; Chorus; Church Choir; School Musical; School Play; Variety Show; Cit Awd; Hon Roll; Aud/Vis; JA; TV News Show, Cougar News; Cal ST-NORTH Ridge; Brdcstng.

MOSLEY, JENNY M; Victor Valley HS; Victorville, CA; (3); 6/350; Church Yth Grp; French Clb; Key Clb; Yrbk; High Hon Roll; Palm Beach Atlantic; Psych.

MOSLEY, MAYA L; Bishop O'dowd HS; Oakland, CA; (3); Var Crs Cntry; Var Trk; Envrnmntl Awareness Grp; Marine Bio.

MOSLEY, SHANNON M; Beaumont HS; Beaumont, CA; (1); Pep Clb; Spanish Clb; Yrbk; Thesps; High Hon Roll; Hon Roll; NHS.

MOSLEY, SHEILA K; Victor Valley HS; Victorville, CA; (4); 7/303; Key Clb; Color Guard; Treas Stu Cncl; JV Vllybl; High Hon Roll; Kiwanis Awd; Val; Mock Trial Tm; CA Schlrshp Fed VP & Sec; Western OR ST Coll; Math Ed.

MOSLEY, TRACY A; Mira Costa HS; Redondo Beach, CA; (2); Church Yth Grp; Office Aide; Teachers Aide; Phtg Yrbk; Score Keeper; Var Sftbl; Cit Awd; High Hon Roll; Hon Roll; Princpals Hnr Roll; San Diego ST; Bus.

MOSQUEDA, ANNA R; Elk Grove HS; Elk Grove, CA; (4); 9/496; Red Cross Aide; Color Guard; Flag Corp; Hon Roll; Prfct Atten Awd; Sci Olympd Clb; Photo, Math Dept Awds; Bk Amer Achvt Awd-Math; CSF Lf Mem; Sacramento City Coll; Nrsng.

MOSQUEDA, ENRIQUE; Roosevelt HS; Los Angeles, CA; (2); Math Clb; Office Aide; Spanish Clb; Tennis; Cit Awd; Hon Roll; Prfct Atten Awd.

MOSQUEDA, MARIA A; Dos Palos HS; South Dos Palos, CA; (2); Church Yth Grp; Dance Clb; Library Aide; Teachers Aide; Church Choir; Crs Cntry; Trk; Cit Awd; High Hon Roll; Hon Roll; Pres Acad Fit Awd.

MOSQUERA, GLENN P; John A O'connell HS; San Francisco, CA; (3); Vllybl; Wt Lftg; Wrstlng; San Francisco ST U.

MOSS, JAEVON A; Cajon HS; San Bernardino, CA; (2); Ftbl.

MOSS, JASON; San Ramon Valley HS; Danville, CA; (2); Key Clb; Temple Yth Grp; Acpl Chr; Chorus; Hon Roll; Hebrew U; Orthdntst.

MOSS, JEROMIE N; Arvin HS; Bakersfield, CA; (1); Aud/Vis; 4-H; Pep Clb; Ski Clb; Band; Jazz Band; Mrchg Band; Pep Band; 4-H Awd; Hon Roll; Project For Health-Study Through U C Davis, Ext; Duke; Stanfrd; Miami; Business Lw.

MOSS, MARK E; Capistrano Valley Christian Schl; Dana Point, CA; (2); Church Yth Grp; Var L Socr; JV Vllybl.

MOSS, RICHARD; Pasadena HS; Camarillo, CA; (1); Hon Roll.

MOSS, TODD A; Santa Barbara HS; Santa Barbara, CA; (3); Drama Clb; Ski Clb; School Play; Rptr Nwsp; JV Var Wrstlng; Hon Roll; HS Rowing Club; UC System; Bus.

MOSS, TONIA; Washington Prep HS; Los Angeles, CA; (3); Hosp Aide; Office Aide; Teachers Aide; Chorus; Church Choir; Drill Tm; School Play; Yrbk; Pom Pon; Nrsng.

MOSSADEGH, BEHZAD; International Studies Acad; San Francisco, CA; (3); Cmnty Wkr; French Clb; German Clb; Hosp Aide; Intnl Clb; Teachers Aide; Bsktbl; Socr; Sftbl; Trk; Internshp Pgm; Intl Actvts; San Francisco ST U; Chem.

MOSSBERG, KRISTEN; South HS; Torrance, CA; (4); Cmnty Wkr; French Clb; Pep Clb; SADD; Drill Tm; Cheerldng; Powder Puff Ftbl; Prncpls Hnr Roll; OSCAR Awd; Stu Leag; Int Dsgn.

MOSSER, ERIC D; Newport Harbor HS; Newport Beach, CA; (3); JV Socr; Peer Cnslng; Psych.

MOSSMAN, JOANNA M; Mayfair HS; Bellflower, CA; (2); 11/250; English Clb; JA; Jazz Band; Mrchg Band; Pep Band; High Hon Roll; Prfct Atten Awd; Long Beach Jr Concert Band; Music Excllnc Awd Jazz Band.

MOSTAFA, AMIRA S; Notre Dame HS; Salinas, CA; (2); High Hon Roll; Hon Roll; Outstndng Achvmnt Engl Awd; Anml Rghts; Crtve Wrtng.

MOSTAGO, MARIA S; Sweetwater HS; National City, CA; (4); Church Yth Grp; DECA; Varsity Clb; Church Choir; Variety Show; Bsktbl; Tennis; Cit Awd; High Hon Roll; Hon Roll; U Of SD; Bus Admin Accntnt.

MOSTAJO, MARIA V; Sweetwater HS; National City, CA; (4); 7/396; Church Yth Grp; Treas DECA; FBLA; Science Clb; Varsity Clb; Church Choir; Variety Show; Bsktbl; Tennis; Vllybl; UC Riverside; Bus Admin.

MOSTHAFF, CHRISTOPHER; Rubidoux HS; Rubidoux, CA; (4); FTA; SADD; Teachers Aide; Varsity Clb; Var Bsbl; JV Ftbl; Hnrb Mntn PTSA Reflctns Wrtng Cont; Sports Therapy.

MOTA, ALFREDO; Duarte HS; Duarte, CA; (3); JV Wrstlng; Engl Awd.

MOTA, BLANCA Y; Cajon HS; San Bernardino, CA; (1); Art Clb; Computer Clb; Girl Scts; Library Aide; Math Clb; Office Aide; Spanish Clb; Band; Mrchg Band; Modeling Cls I&II&III; Natl Guards; Chaffy Coll.

MOTA, CINDY R; Notre Dame HS; Hollister, CA; (2); Cmnty Wkr; Science Clb; Red Ribbon Wk Actvts & Plnng San Benito Cnty Drug Free Week; Plnng & Orgnzsng Notre Dame Hmcmng; Fresno ST U; Bus.

MOTA, NOBELIA MARIA; Hilmar JR/Sr HS; Livingston, CA; (3); Sec FFA; Letterman Clb; VP Spanish Clb; Acpl Chr; Band; Drm Mjr(t); Mrchg Band; Pep Band; Hon Roll; Law.

MOTA, THOMAS; Modesto HS; Salida, CA; (4); #17 In Class; Teachers Aide; JV Var Bsktbl; Intrml JV Ftbl; High Hon Roll; Hon Roll; MJC; Bus Admin.

MOTAMED, SOHEIL; Einstein Acad; Sherman Oaks, CA; (4); #1 In Class; Science Clb; Treas Soph Cls; Treas Jr Cls; Treas Sr Cls; Pres Stu Cncl; Var Bsbl; Var Capt Bsktbl; High Hon Roll; Val; UCLA.

MOTAWAKEL, OMAR; Chatsworth HS; Chatsworth, CA; (3); Art Clb; Chess Clb; Letterman Clb; Rep Frsh Cls; JV Var Bsktbl; Ftbl; JV Vllybl; Hon Roll; Bus.

MOTHERSHED, ERNAE L; Chaffey HS; Ontario, CA; (1); Church Yth Grp; Spanish Clb; Hon Roll; Lt Gov Keywanettes; Pres Top Teens Amer; USC; Financial Anylist.

MOTLEY, ANGELA; Central Union HS; El Centro, CA; (2); Pep Clb; Speech Tm; Church Choir; Var Trk; Hon Roll; Capitol Focus Pgm; American U; Jrnlsm.

MOTOHASHI, NAOMI E; Chaminade College Prep; Granada Hills, CA; (3); Cmnty Wkr; Rep Stu Cncl; Hon Roll; Asian Amer Club; Judo.

MOTTA, DARCI M; Concord HS; Concord, CA; (3); Girl Scts; Pres VP Model UN; Teachers Aide; Hon Roll; CSF; Soropimist Intl Concords Poetry Cont 1st Pl.

MOTTA, LUIS; John A Rowland HS; Rowland Heights, CA; (2); JV Swmmng; Cit Awd; Hon Roll; Law.

MOTTERN, KATIE; John Burroughs HS; Burbank, CA; (2); Church Yth Grp; Drill Tm; Capt Flag Corp; VP Frsh Cls; Var Cheerldng; High Hon Roll; Pres Acad Fit Awd; Val; CA JR Schlstc Fed Sealbearer; Faculty Memrl Awd; Geom Golden St Exam Hnrs.

MOTTON, CARMEN R; Washington Prep; Los Angeles, CA; (2); Dance Clb; Pep Clb; Nursing.

MOTUFAU, FAAFETAI; Fontana HS; Fontana, CA; (3); Computer Clb; FBLA; Office Aide; Acpl Chr; Chorus; Church Choir; School Musical; Yrbk; JV Bsktbl; Powder Puff Ftbl; Princeton; Bus Mgmt.

MOUA, GNIA; Atwater HS; Winton, CA; (2); Math Tm; Hon Roll; Prfct Atten Awd; UC Davis; Accntng.

MOUA, HANG; Clovis HS; Clovis, CA; (3); High Hon Roll; Hon Roll; CSF; Princpls Hnr Roll; UCSB; Bus.

MOUA, LEE; Nathaniel Narbonne HS; Torrance, CA; (2); Church Yth Grp; Prfct Atten Awd; Pres Acad Fit Awd; Peer Asst Leag Secy; CA JR Schlrshp Fed.

MOUA, PANHIA; Modesto HS; Modesto, CA; (1); Dance Clb; Intnl Clb; Math Clb; Math Tm; Office Aide; Orch; Cit Awd; High Hon Roll; Hon Roll; CA Music Educators Assoc/Honors Grp; CSF; Modesto Union WCJU Essay Cntst St Finals 3rd Pl; Pharmacy.

MOUA, TENG; Narbonne HS; Torrance, CA; (2); Church Yth Grp; Office Aide; Church Choir; Bsktbl; Hon Roll; Prfct Atten Awd; Sci.

MOUA, THOR P; Roosevelt HS; Fresno, CA; (4); Boy Scts; Church Yth Grp; Band; Church Choir; Socr; Wt Lftg; Cit Awd; High Hon Roll; Prfct Atten Awd; CSUF; Crmnlgy.

MOUCHESS, CARMEN LUZ; Downey HS; South Gate, CA; (4); 206/394; Church Yth Grp; Cmnty Wkr; French Clb; Office Aide; Medcl Occptns Cls Act; Cerritos Coll; Psych.

MOULD, GREG; Liberty HS; Oakley, CA; (4); Pep Clb; SADD; Teachers Aide; Ed Nwsp; Stat Bsktbl; Mgr(s); Stat Sftbl; Vllybl; Hon Roll; Cal ST Hayward; Bus.

MOULE, JASON; Bear River HS; Grass Valley, CA; (4); 13/150; Am Leg Boys St; Drama Clb; School Play; Sec Jr Cls; Pres Stu Cncl; JV Ftbl; Capt Var Wrstlng; Cit Awd; High Hon Roll; Pres Acad Fit Awd; Odysy Mind Fnlst; Ntl Young Ldrshp Conf; People To People Stu Amb Russia; CO U; Aerosp Engr.

MOUNSEY, CHRISTINE A; Robertson HS; Fremont, CA; (3); Rptr Nwsp; Hon Roll; Prfct Atten Awd.

MOUNT, CHRISTINE; East Union HS; Manteca, CA; (4); 14/296; Key Clb; SADD; Teachers Aide; Rptr Nwsp; Crs Cntry; Powder Puff Ftbl; Score Keeper; Trk; Cit Awd; Hon Roll; Envrnmntl Sci.

MOUNT, DAVID E; El Camino HS; Oceanside, CA; (3); 21/364; Debate Tm; Scholastic Bowl; JV Bsbl; JV Wrstlng; High Hon Roll; Hon Roll; Ntl Merit SF; Prfct Atten Awd; Golden St Exam Algebra & Geom Hnrs; Boston U; Aerospace Engrng.

MOUNT, TIM M; South HS; Bakersfield, CA; (3); 11/400; Chess Clb; Debate Tm; French Clb; Intnl Clb; Key Clb; NFL; Speech Tm; Hon Roll; Ntl Merit SF; St Forensics Trnmnt; Writer.

MOUNTSIER, DONDI L; Santa Rosa HS; Santa Rosa, CA; (3); Church Yth Grp; Dance Clb; Drama Clb; Key Clb; Pep Clb; Spanish Clb; Acpl Chr; School Play; Hon Roll; Prfct Atten Awd; Perf Arts.

MOURAD, CLAUDIA; Edison HS; Huntington Beach, CA; (2); Church Yth Grp; French Clb; Pep Clb; Var Cheerldng; Little Schlr Awd 89; UCI; Bus Admin.

MOUROUX, GREGORY; Live Oak HS; Morgan Hill, CA; (3); 45/560; FBLA; Spanish Clb; Teachers Aide; Rep Sr Cls; JV Crs Cntry; JV Tennis; Wt Lftg; Hon Roll; Ntl Merit Ltr; 1st Plce Chem Schl Sci Fair; Cal Poly; Pre-Law.

MOUROUX, JEFFREY P; Live Oak HS; Morgan Hill, CA; (4); Art Clb; Wt Lftg; JV Wrstlng; Cit Awd; Hon Roll; Pres Acad Fit Awd; Morgan Hill Unified Schl Dit Schlrshp Fund; San Jose ST U; Aninmation.

MOUSHIGIAN, ANDREA LORI; Hoover HS; Fresno, CA; (4); 37/400; Ski Clb; Mgr Nwsp; Prncpls Awd-Acad Excllnc; Jrnlsm Hnr Awd; CSF Life Member; Marine Bio.

MOUSSA, RITA R; Gahr HS; Norwalk, CA; (2); 74/490; Church Yth Grp; French Clb; Office Aide; Church Choir; 4-H Awd; High Hon Roll; Hon Roll; Engl Acad Excllnc Awd; U CA-IRVINE; Med.

MOUSTAFA, AMAL; Northgate HS; Walnut Creek, CA; (1); French Clb; Hosp Aide; Quiz Bowl; School Play; Rptr Nwsp; High Hon Roll; Hon Roll; Hmc Cmmty; UC Berkley; Cert Pblc Accnt.

MOUTTAPA, MICHELE M; Edison HS; Stockton, CA; (3); Church Yth Grp; Hosp Aide; Nwsp; Ed Yrbk; Intrml Tennis; Var Trk; High Hon Roll; Jr NHS; Ntl Merit Ltr; Pres Acad Fit Awd; CSF Pres.

MOUW, ALLISON J; Central Valley Christian HS; Tulare, CA; (3); 1/20; Church Yth Grp; Chorus; Rep Soph Cls; Pres Jr Cls; Pres Sr Cls; VP Stu Cncl; Var Bsktbl; Var Vllybl; High Hon Roll; CSF; Acad Dcthln Team; Cal Poly; Bus Mgmt.

MOWAT, ANDREW A; Piedmont HS; Piedmont, CA; (3); Am Leg Boys St; Boy Scts; Chess Clb; Cmnty Wkr; Key Clb; Science Clb; Yrbk; JV Crs Cntry; Var Golf; Var JV Socr; Econ.

MOWBRAY, ROBERT A; Central Union HS; El Centro, CA; (2); 4-H; Stage Crew; JV Ftbl; 4-H Awd; Fishng, Boating, Water Skiing, Horsebck Rdng; Engrng.

MOWER, SHERITY K; Casa Roble Fundamental HS; Citrus Heights, CA; (3); VP Church Yth Grp; Cmnty Wkr; French Clb; Hosp Aide; Science Clb; Dnfth Awd; Hon Roll; NHS; Prfct Atten Awd; Interact Clb; Friday Night Live; BYU; Anesthslgy.

MOXLEY JR, THOMAS; Artesia HS; Cerritos, CA; (1); Speech Tm; JV Var Bsbl; Ftbl.

MOY, LISA; Lowell HS; San Francisco, CA; (3); Hosp Aide; Speech Tm; Band; Ntl Merit Ltr; CSF; Gldn St Exm Alg & Geom Hgh Hnrs.

MOYA, ARTEMIO; Central Catholic HS; Modesto, CA; (1); #13 In Class; Pres Soph Cls; JV Tennis; Hon Roll; Chrstn Awd; Engl Awd; Arch.

MOYA, CATHERINE J; Woodland HS; Woodland, CA; (3); Pres English Clb; French Clb; Intnl Clb; Key Clb; Pres Ski Clb; SADD; Co-Ed Yrbk; Ed Lit Mag; Off Frsh Cls; Off Jr Cls; Afaa Certified Aerobics Instructor; Exercise Physiology.

MOYA, RACHEL C; Gladstone HS; Covina, CA; (3); Church Yth Grp; Drama Clb; Ski Clb; Thesps; Chorus; School Musical; School Play; Var Swmmng; Prfct Atten Awd.

MOYA, RENE; Loyalton HS; Loyalton, CA; (4); 3/33; Am Leg Boys St; Dance Clb; Drama Clb; FBLA; Hosp Aide; Yrbk; Pres Jr Cls; Rep Stu Cncl; High Hon Roll; NHS; Rtry Intl Yth Exchng; FBLA Mr FBL CA; Elk Natl Fndtn Schlrshp; U CA.

MOYDELL, MELANIE; Folsom HS; Folsom, CA; (1); Model UN; Cheerldng; Hon Roll; Med.

MOYE, ALISON M; Westside HS; Dos Palos, CA; (2); FHA; High Hon Roll; Stu Of Month & Yr; Cosmetology.

MOYEN-VAN SLIMMING, JANICE L; Cabrillo HS; Lompoc, CA; (4); 17/223; Pres Church Yth Grp; 4-H; SADD; Sec Treas Band; Drm Mjr(t); Mrchg Band; Pep Band; High Hon Roll; Ntl Merit Ltr; CSF-LIFE Mem; Semper Fidelis Awd-Musical Excllnc; Dollars For Schlrs Schlrshp; UCLA; Engl.

MOYER, AMBER; Kern Valley HS; Kernville, CA; (1); FFA; Math Clb; Math Tm; SADD; Powder Puff Ftbl; JV Sftbl; JV Vllybl; Wt Lftg; Cit Awd; Hon Roll; CA Schltc Fed; Vlybl Rookie Of Yr; U CA Davis; Vet.

MOYER, DEBORAH M; Gompers Secondary HS; San Diego, CA; (2); 20/145; Drill Tm; Hon Roll; CSF; Career Club Secy; Oceanogrphy Club; UC San Diego; Marine Bio.

MOYER, FREDERICK C; El Cerrito HS; El Cerrito, CA; (4); 2/600; Boy Scts; Teachers Aide; Band; Mrchg Band; School Musical; Lit Mag; High Hon Roll; Sal; UC Davis; Engnrng.

MOYER, JENNIFER J; Homestead HS; Sunnyvale, CA; (4); 192/400; Church Yth Grp; Cmnty Wkr; French Clb; Chorus; Church Choir; Color Guard; Drm Mjr(t); Stu Cncl; NHS; Camp Crtfctn & Tall Tree Uahoha Camp Chrch LDS; YW Awd Chrch; Brigham Young U; Brdcst Comm.

MOYER, JENNIFER L; Shasta HS; Redding, CA; (3); Debate Tm; Drama Clb; SADD; Thesps; School Play; Stage Crew; Lit Mag; Hon Roll; Intl Ordr Rainbow Girls; Yth To Yth; Envirnmntlst Club; Shasta Coll; Tchr.

MOYER, VICTOR M; Cupertino HS; Cupertino, CA; (2); Church Yth Grp; JV L Bsbl; Sr Leag Bsbl All Stars & Led Team & Hr's & Stln Bases 90; Stanford U; Comp Sci.

MOYERS, GEORGINA I; Nogales HS; West Covina, CA; (2); 4-H Awd; High Hon Roll; Hon Roll; UCLA; Anesthesiology.

MOYES, RICHARD S; Chino HS; Chino, CA; (2); Drama Clb; School Musical; School Play; Stage Crew; UCLA; Bus.

MOYLAN, JAMES F; St Ignatius HS; San Francisco, CA; (3); 17/244; Letterman Clb; Ftbl; Hon Roll.

MOYNAHAN, KELLY S; Santa Teresa HS; San Jose, CA; (2); Sec Church Yth Grp; JA; Ski Clb; SADD; Teachers Aide; Jazz Band; School Musical; Trk; High Hon Roll; San Jose ST U; Radio & TV.

MOYRON, SUSANA; Calexico HS; Calexico, CA; (2); Elem Ed.

MOZAFFARI, MARYAM; Santa Teresa HS; San Jose, CA; (4); 13/444; French Clb; Hon Roll; Math & Photo Conts Chert Hnr; CSF; 2 Poems Schls Frnch Magzne; San Jose ST U; Optometry.

MOZEYAN, ARAM; Holy Martyrs & Ferrahian HS; Santa Monica, CA; (3); Pres Jr Cls; Var Crs Cntry; Hon Roll; CSF; Acad All Amer; Genetics.

MOZZINI, MONICA; Orland HS; Orland, CA; (2); Drama Clb; Cheerldng; Chico ST; CPA.

MROZ, SUSAN; Del Mar HS; San Jose, CA; (4); 13/210; Church Yth Grp; Hon Roll; Pres Acad Fit Awd; Chrstn Clb Pres; NV Church Of God Advsry Cmmtte; San Jose ST; Nrsng.

MROZEK, JULIE; Righetti HS; Santa Maria, CA; (3); 1/400; Cmnty Wkr; Math Tm; Scholastic Bowl; School Play; Treas Frsh Cls; Treas Soph Cls; Treas Stu Cncl; JV Var Bsktbl; JV Sftbl; JV Var Vllybl; Chsn For Accrdtn Tm-Anaheim Schl; Mst Insprtnl Vllybl 89; Exprss Sftbl JRS 89; Stanford; Lwyr.

MU, PAULINE H; San Marino HS; San Marino, CA; (4); 30/265; NFL; Speech Tm; Band; Jazz Band; Mrchg Band; Orch; Treas Sr Cls; Treas Stu Cncl; Var Capt Bsktbl; Var Capt Sftbl; Yale U; Ec.

MUCETTI, ROSANNA GINA; Providence HS; Van Nuys, CA; (1); Intnl Clb; Varsity Clb; Chorus; Var Sftbl; Var Vllybl; High Hon Roll; Pres Acad Fit Awd; Media Tract; USC; Engl.

MUCK, SHAWNAE; Washington Prep HS; Los Angeles, CA; (3); Pep Clb; Red Cross Aide; SADD; Varsity Clb; Chorus; Drill Tm; Off Jr Cls; Stu Cncl; JV Cheerldng; Pom Pon; Peer Hall Cnslr; Gramblin; Law.

MUCKELROY, BEN; Ramona Unified Schl Dist; Carbondale, IL; (2); Boy Scts; Church Yth Grp; Band; Chorus; Socr; Tennis; Outstndng Male Tnns Plyr; Numerous Tnns Awds & Achvts; Pro Tnns Player.

MUE, LAWRENCE; Castro Valley HS; Castro Valley, CA; (3); 37/371; German Clb; Hon Roll; Prfct Atten Awd; CSF; UC Davis; Mech Engnrng.

MUECK JR, WERNER F; Marsyville HS; Marysville, CA; (1); Hon Roll; Princpls Schlr Acad Ltr; Goldn Schlr Star; U Pacific CA; Commercl Art.

MUELLER, CATHY J; Sonora Union HS; Sonora, CA; (2); 7/350; Church Yth Grp; Dance Clb; 4-H; Spanish Clb; Acpl Chr; Gym; Hon Roll.

MUELLER, DAN J; Coast Christian Schls; Torrance, CA; (2); Drama Clb; ROTC; Band; Chorus; Jazz Band; Mrchg Band; Pep Band; Var Bsktbl; Var Ftbl; JV Socr.

MUELLER, DANIEL H; Mater Dei HS; Los Alamitos, CA; (2); 1/499; Church Yth Grp; Bsktbl; NHS; CSF.

MUELLER, JEFF R; Valhalla HS; El Cajon, CA; (1); Church Yth Grp; Debate Tm; Band; Jazz Band; Mrchg Band; Pep Band; Prfct Atten Awd.

MUELLER, JENN; Yosemite HS; Coarsegold, CA; (2); JV Bsktbl; High Hon Roll; IRRA Indust Rltns Rsrch Assoc; FOBL Friends Oakhurst Brnch Library; Intllgnce Spec.

MUELLER, JON E; Sonora Union HS; Sonora, CA; (3); Church Yth Grp; Computer Clb; Office Aide; Ski Clb; Spanish Clb; Wt Lftg; Cit Awd; Hon Roll; Cmptr Syst Anal.

MUELLER, SUZIE; Placer HS; Auburn, CA; (4); Art Clb; Drama Clb; Pres 4-H; French Clb; FFA; Pres FHA; German Clb; Variety Show; 4-H Awd; High Hon Roll; Bnk America Plque Wnnr Lbrl Arts; Cnty & Rgnl Wnnr 4-H Horse, 5th Pl Rank St; Insurance.

MUELLER, TRACY; Downey HS; Downey, CA; (3); Church Yth Grp; Service Clb; Teachers Aide; Church Choir; Nwsp; Ed Yrbk; Stu Cncl; Var Capt Cheerldng; CA Schlstc Fed; Assisteens Svc Clb Crrspndng Secy; Jrnlsm.

MUELLNER, JENNIFER D; Valhalla HS; Spring Valley, CA; (2); 121/451; Sec German Clb; Intnl Clb; Key Clb; Band; JV Swmmng; Var L Vllybl; B Avrg; Rssn For 2 Yrs; Stu Of Mnth Wrld Studies; USAF Acad; Arntcl Engrng.

MUGGE, SARA E; Amador Valley HS; Pleasanton, CA; (4); 16/413; Church Yth Grp; Var Co-Capt Vllybl; French Hon Soc; Ntl Merit SF; Bus.

MUGHANNAM, RITA; Mills HS; Burlingame, CA; (3); 32/300; Church Yth Grp; Intnl Clb; Hon Roll; Lion Awd; CSF; Mills HS Prin Awd; Geom & Alg Golden ST Exam Awd; Bio.

MUHAMMAD, DESDEMONIA L; Bullard HS; Fresno, CA; (2); 4-H; Band; Church Choir; Mrchg Band; Pep Band; School Musical; Variety Show; Bsktbl; Medicine.

MUHAMMAD, MEDINAH; Sister Clara Muhammad HS; Los Angeles, CA; (2); Drill Tm; School Musical; School Play; Ed Yrbk; UCLA; OB/Gyn.

MUHAMMAD, RASHEEDAH; Sister Clara Muhammad HS; Los Angeles, CA; (3); Debate Tm; Drill Tm; School Musical; School Play; Ed Yrbk; Law.

MUHAMMAD, SHANA; Lincoln HS; San Diego, CA; (4); Church Yth Grp; Cmnty Wkr; Drama Clb; FTA; Office Aide; Pep Clb; Trk; Doc.

MUHLY, HEIDI M; Lodi HS; Lodi, CA; (1); Church Yth Grp; English Clb; Chorus; High Hon Roll; Concordia Lutheran Coll OR.

MUI, ANDREW T; Woodside HS; Redwood City, CA; (2); Church Yth Grp; JV Tennis; Hon Roll; CA Polytech ST U; Cmptr Sci.

MUI, ANNA M; Lowell HS; San Francisco, CA; (3); Church Yth Grp; Church Choir; Nwsp; CSF; Chem Engrng.

MUI, BRIAN Y; Nogales HS; Walnut, CA; (2); #4 In Class; Science Clb; JV Tennis; Cit Awd; High Hon Roll; Hon Roll; Prfct Atten Awd; Pres Acad Fit Awd; CSF; Med.

MUI, CECILY; Encinal HS; Alameda, CA; (3); 3/233; Church Yth Grp; Hosp Aide; VP Key Clb; Var Crs Cntry; Var Swmmng; High Hon Roll; CSF Treas; Peo/Peo Yuth Sci Exch; Gldn St Exm Geom/1st Hnrs Algb; Sci.

MUI, EDWIN W; Pasadena HS; Pasadena, CA; (2); Golden St Exam Schlr Yr 89; Cal ST Poly Pomona; Arch.

MUI, LIK; San Leandro HS; Alameda, CA; (4); 1/322; Chrmn Chess Clb; Computer Clb; Intnl Clb; Key Clb; Pres Math Clb; Capt Math Tm; Speech Tm; Off Jr Cls; Off Sr Cls; JV Tennis; UC Davis & Berkeley Rgnts Chncllrs Schlrshps; San Leandro Lions Club Stu Spkr Cntst 1st Pl 88; MA Inst Tech; Biomed Engr.

MUI, SILBEY S; Skyline HS; Oakland, CA; (4); 8/580; Cmnty Wkr; Hosp Aide; Key Clb; Math Clb; Teachers Aide; Lit Mag; Cit Awd; Elks Awd; High Hon Roll; Kiwanis Awd; UC Berkeley Accelerated HS Stu Pgm; PROMISE Awd; Walt Disney World Dreamer & Doers Awd; U CA Berkeley; Med.

MUI, STINA H; San Leandro HS; San Leandro, CA; (3); 1/361; Hosp Aide; Library Aide; Math Clb; Math Tm; Service Clb; Spanish Clb; Speech Tm; Teachers Aide; Var Capt Crs Cntry; Var Trk; CSF Pres; Octagon Clb VP; Genetic Engrng.

MUILENBURG, COREY W; Arcata HS; Arcata, CA; (4); Teachers Aide; Band; Church Choir; Jazz Band; Pep Band; JV Var Bsktbl; Var Golf; Cit Awd; Hon Roll; Middle Schl Bsktbl Team Coach; Humboldt ST U; Bio.

MUINCH, SHAWNA A; Mt Shasta HS; Mount Shasta, CA; (2); Church Yth Grp; Teachers Aide; Cheerldng; Powder Puff Ftbl; Socr; Cit Awd; Hon Roll; Real Estate.

MUINO, DANIEL P; Newark Memorial HS; Newark, CA; (3); 1/370; Boy Scts; Cmnty Wkr; Debate Tm; Pres Spanish Clb; SADD; Off Frsh Cls; Off Yrbk; High Hon Roll; NHS; Ntl Merit Ltr; CSF Treas; Spnsh V Frgn Lang Awd; Bio.

MUIRBROOK, KRISHA K; Hanford HS; Hanford, CA; (1); Off Church Yth Grp; VP Drama Clb; FBLA; FHA; School Musical; School Play; Cit Awd; High Hon Roll; 1st Pl Fnlst FHA St Cmptn; BYU; Educ.

MUKAE, KRISTEN; Capistrano Valley HS; Mission Viejo, CA; (3); Church Yth Grp; German Clb; Pep Clb; Drill Tm; Cheerldng; Hon Roll; UC San Diego.

MUKAI, CHRISSY L; Whitney HS; Lakewood, CA; (2); 55/168; Var L Bsktbl; Var L Sftbl; Var L Vllybl; Vet.

MUKASA, EKIRIYA; Newport Christian HS; Santa Ana, CA; (4); 7/13; Church Yth Grp; Scholastic Bowl; School Play; Hon Roll; Prt Tm Job-Day Cr Ctr; Full Tm Holidy Wrk; Med.

MULDROW, DANA; Washington Prep HS; Los Angeles, CA; (3); Hon Roll; Long Beach ST; Elec.

MULHALL, JENNIFER; Victor Valley HS; Apple Valley, CA; (4); Church Yth Grp; Cmnty Wkr; Drama Clb; Pep Clb; Ski Clb; Teachers Aide; JV Cheerldng; Var Score Keeper; Homcmng Qn 89; Miss Victorville 90; Victor Valley JC; Bus Mgmt.

MULHOLLAND, ANTHONY V; Don Antonio Lugo HS; Chino, CA; (2); VP Drama Clb; Thesps; School Play; Stage Crew; Variety Show; Hon Roll; U CA Davis; Vet Med.

MULHOLLAND, JULIE G; St Paul HS; La Habra, CA; (3); 54/300; Speech Tm; Var L Socr; Hon Roll; NHS; Mrch For Hngr; Psych.

MULHOLLAND, MICHELLE M; Chula Vista HS; Chula Vista, CA; (3); 28/535; Church Yth Grp; Drama Clb; Thesps; School Musical; School Play; Stage Crew; Variety Show; Hon Roll; Prfct Atten Awd; Piano & Singing; Tchr.

MULLANE, DONALD; Bishop Amat Memorial HS; Hacienda Heights, CA; (1); Ftbl; Hon Roll.

MULLEN, KATHARINA M; Vacaville HS; Vacaville, CA; (3); Drill Tm; Hon Roll; Attend Mdlng Schl Barbizon; Solano; Accntng.

MULLEN, TAMI; Foothill HS; Sacramento, CA; (3); SADD; Cheerldng; Gym; Powder Puff Ftbl; Trk; UNLC; Mktng.

MULLEN, TRACY M; Louisville HS; Woodland Hills, CA; (2); Church Yth Grp; Drama Clb; GAA; School Musical; Rep Stu Cncl; Var Vllybl; High Hon Roll; CSF; TACSC; Amnesty Intl; Engl.

MULLENDORE, JENNIFER E; Rim Of The World HS; Blue Jay, CA; (2); 1/329; Church Yth Grp; Model UN; Pres Spanish Clb; Var Bsktbl; Var Trk; Hon Roll; NHS; Pres-Jr Stsmn Of Amer; Dist Fnls Wnnr-Rotary 4 Way Spch Cntst; CA Schlstc Fed.

MULLENS, JUSTIN; Benicia HS; Benicia, CA; (3); Ski Clb; Band; Jazz Band; Pep Band; School Musical; Variety Show; Mst Outstndng Musician 89 Los Medanos Jazz Fstvl; Mstr Musician 88 Stanford Jazz Cmp; All-Str Jazz Bnd; NY Schl Music; Prof Musician.

MULLER, ALBERTA; St Genevieve HS; Panorama City, CA; (2); GAA; Model UN; Pep Clb; Spanish Clb; SADD; Varsity Clb; Pres Soph Cls; JV Var Bsktbl; Stat Sftbl; JV Var Vllybl; U Notre Dame; Nrse.

MULLER, AUDREY J; Aragon HS; San Mateo, CA; (2); Pres Church Yth Grp; Intnl Clb; Service Clb; SADD; Orch; Pep Band; Variety Show; Yrbk; Rep Frsh Cls; VP Rep Soph Cls; MVP Crosscntry/Julie Hurley Outstndng Perf Track; Comm Art.

MULLER, BRANDON T; Hesperia Christian Schl; Hesperia, CA; (3); 3/32; Quiz Bowl; Rptr Nwsp; JV Bsktbl; High Hon Roll; Hon Roll; Cmmnctns.

MULLER, BRIAN A; N Hollywood Highly Gifted Magnet; North Hollywood, CA; (2); Boy Scts; Chess Clb; French Clb; Service Clb; Orch; L Swmmng; Prfct Atten Awd; Pres Acad Fit Awd; Pres Schlr; Ecology Clb; Vet Med.

MULLER, CHRISTINA M; St Genevieve St HS; Panorama City, CA; (3); Cmnty Wkr; GAA; Pep Clb; Ski Clb; SADD; School Play; Pres Soph Cls; Pres Jr Cls; Pres Stu Cncl; Bsktbl; 1st Tm All Leag Bsktbl; U Of Notre Dame; Drama.

MULLER, ELIZABETH M; Montclair HS; Alta Loma, CA; (2); #4 In Class; Capt JV Socr; Sftbl; Ntl Merit Ltr; Natl Ltn Exm Slvr Mdl; Mck Trl; Engrng.

MULLER, HEIDI C; Notre Dame Belmont HS; Half Moon Bay, CA; (4); Church Yth Grp; Cmnty Wkr; Library Aide; Teachers Aide; Variety Show; Off Jr Cls; Off Sr Cls; Cheerldng; Tennis; Swiss Schlrshp; Cal Ply; Ag Bus.

MULLER, INGRID N; Glendale Adventist Acad; Glendale, CA; (4); 8/80; Church Yth Grp; School Musical; Ski Clb; Teachers Aide; Ed Nwsp; Treas Soph Cls; Sec Jr Cls; Var Vllybl; Hon Roll; NHS; Modeling; Nutrition.

MULLER, JEREMY M; Highlands HS; North Highlands, CA; (1); Church Yth Grp; French Clb; Off Frsh Cls; Bsktbl; Tennis; Cit Awd; Hon Roll; U Of CA Berkeley; Archtl Drwng.

MULLER, MICHELLE; Esparto HS; Esparto, CA; (3); AFS; Church Yth Grp; Drama Clb; SADD; School Play; Helpng Homelss & Hungry; Modlng; Amer Acad Dramatic Arts; Actng.

MULLER, TRUDY M; Notre Dame HS; Half Moon Bay, CA; (2); 8/110; Cmnty Wkr; Debate Tm; Library Aide; Service Clb; SADD; Teachers Aide; Variety Show; Off Frsh Cls; Off Soph Cls; Treas Stu Cncl; Schl Bio Stu Of Month; MVP PPSL Vrsty Tnns; Jr Statesmen Of Amer; CSF; U Notre Dame; Sports Med.

MULLERY, ROBIN S; Los Gatos HS; Monte Sereno, CA; (3); GAA; Key Clb; Office Aide; Spanish Clb; Varsity Clb; Var L Swmmng; Hon Roll; Yth Advsry Cmssn; 1st Pl In Santa Clara Vly Sci Fr; Amnsty Intl Treas; Leo Clb; HELP.

MULLET, SARA S; Beyer HS; Modesto, CA; (3); Debate Tm; Drama Clb; NFL; Spanish Clb; Speech Tm; School Play; Rptr Yrbk; Hon Roll; Pres Acad Fit Awd; U Of Sthrn CA; Lwyr.

MULLIGAN III, JAMES T; Selma HS; Selma, CA; (3); 140/300; Church Yth Grp; Cmnty Wkr; Debate Tm; French Clb; Pres FFA; FTA; Teachers Aide; FFA Rep Stu Cncl; Fresno ST U; Ag Ed.

MULLIGAN, RODNEY A; Mount Diablo HS; Pittsburg, CA; (1); Cit Awd; Hon Roll; Prfct Atten Awd; Comp.

MULLINGS, MICHAEL L; East Bakersfield HS; Bakersfield, CA; (4); 9/432; Boy Scts; Chess Clb; Church Yth Grp; French Clb; Intnl Clb; Off Key Clb; Office Aide; Teachers Aide; Band; Church Choir; CA Schlstc Fed Gold Seal Wnnr; Century III Rep; Walt Disney Dreamers & Doers Awd; Bakersfield Coll; Poltcl Sci.

MULLINS, CHRISTINE L; John F Kennedy HS; Granada Hills, CA; (4); Cmnty Wkr; Library Aide; Teachers Aide; Varsity Clb; Yrbk; Var L Tennis; High Hon Roll; Hon Roll; Masonic Awd; Outstndng Jobs Daughters Awd; Engrng Awd; Schlr Athl Awd; Cal ST U Northridge; Commnctns.

MULLINS, EDEN E; Redwood HS; Visalia, CA; (2); Church Yth Grp; Chorus; Church Choir; Tennis; High Hon Roll; Hon Roll; Pres Acad Fit Awd; Tylore Cnty Yth Orch 1st Chair 2nd Section; Private Violin Lessons Mth Schlrshp; Mst Insprtnl Tnnis; Psych.

MULLINS, KATHRYN; Hanford Joint Union HS; Hanford, CA; (2); Church Yth Grp; FBLA; JA; Varsity Clb; Sftbl; Vllybl; NHS; Prfct Atten Awd; Schlr Athlt Awd; Stu Of Mnth Sci; W Yosemit Leag 2nd Tm All Leag Sftbl; Battng Champ Trphy; Law.

MULLINS, MELODY; Alexander Hamilton HS; Santa Monica, CA; (3); Church Yth Grp; Hosp Aide; Acpl Chr; School Musical; Stage Crew; High Hon Roll; People/People HS Stu Ambssdr 90; CA ST U Los Angeles; Engl.

MULLINS, SCOTT L; Clovis West HS; Fresno, CA; (2); JV Vllybl; Hon Roll; Passd Goldn ST Exam Alge; USC; Arch.

MULOKAS, RIMA K; Chaminade College Prep; Chatsworth, CA; (3); Church Yth Grp; Cmnty Wkr; Girl Scts; Key Clb; Letterman Clb; Pep Clb; SADD; Sec Frsh Cls; Rep Soph Cls; Rep Jr Cls; CSF; UC Irvine; Math.

MULREAN, TAMARA; Mountain Empire HS; Campo, CA; (2); Drama Clb; 4-H; Letterman Clb; Spanish Clb; Teachers Aide; Band; Mrchg Band; School Play; Stage Crew; Variety Show; San Diego Union Tribune Schltc Jrnlst Awd; Jrnlsm.

MULVANEY, HEATHER M; Whitney HS; Cerritos, CA; (1); Church Yth Grp; Church Choir; High Hon Roll; Hon Roll; Teacher.

MULVANEY, RAMSEY A; Wilson Woodrow SR HS; Long Beach, CA; (2); Teachers Aide; School Play; Rep Soph Cls; Ftbl; JV Socr; Cit Awd; High Hon Roll; Hon Roll; NHS; MVP Sccr; UC Santa Barbara; Pre-Law.

MUMA, JULIE C; Mesa Verde HS; Citrus Heights, CA; (1); 2/279; Church Yth Grp; Church Choir; High Hon Roll; Dance Sue Geller Dance Studio; Bowl At Birdcage Lanes; Teacher.

MUMM, KATIE; Nevada Union HS; Camptonville, CA; (1); 1/450; Chorus; High Hon Roll; Val; Ballet; Piano, Singing; Ballet.

MUMMERT, GREG T; La Sierra HS; Riverside, CA; (3); Church Yth Grp; Teachers Aide; School Musical; School Play; Variety Show; JV Capt Bsktbl; High Hon Roll; Prfct Atten Awd; Pacific Christian Coll; Theolgy.

MUNAF, RUBINA K; San Leandro HS; San Leandro, CA; (2); Office Aide; Pep Clb; Teachers Aide; Off Soph Cls; Rep Stu Cncl; Sftbl; Vllybl; ASB Sntr 89-90.

MUNAR, MICHAEL; Warren HS; Downey, CA; (3); 20/456; JA; Key Clb; Mu Alpha Theta; JV Socr; Var Wrstlng; High Hon Roll; NHS; CSF; GSE 1st Yr Algbra Hnrs; GSE Geom Hgh Hnrs; UCLA; Med.

MUNAWEERA, NAYOMI U; Arcadia HS; Arcadia, CA; (3); AFS; Debate Tm; Hosp Aide; Library Aide; Teachers Aide; Temple Yth Grp; Flag Corp; High Hon Roll; Hon Roll; NHS.

MUNCADA, RHAMESIS; Fremont HS; Sunnyvale, CA; (2); Cmnty Wkr; Band; Mrchg Band; Alg I Gldn St Exam High Hnrs; UCLA; Med.

MUND, KERSTIN E; El Centro Union HS; Imperial, CA; (2); Futurist Clb; Stanford.

MUNDA, ANA V; Whitney HS; Cerritos, CA; (2); Cmnty Wkr; Key Clb; Teachers Aide; Variety Show; Rptr Nwsp; NHS; Filipino Clb Dance Troupe Coordntr; UC San Diego; Psych.

MUNDA, JENNY C; Village Christian Schls; Sunland, CA; (3); 13/123; Church Yth Grp; Drama Clb; Office Aide; Spanish Clb; Church Choir; Hon Roll; Jr NHS.

MUNDA, MICAELA V; Lowell HS; San Francisco, CA; (2); ROTC; Color Guard; VP Frsh Cls; Rep Soph Cls; Filipino-Amer Clb Offcr; San Francisco ST; Bus.

MUNDA, MICHELE; Mercy HS; Daly City, CA; (3); 24/130; Intnl Clb; School Musical; School Play; Stage Crew; Lit Mag; Vllybl; Hon Roll; Med.

MUNDAY, KAREN A; Hoover HS; Fresno, CA; (2); Band; Mrchg Band; Orch; JR Mets Clb; Marine Bio.

MUNDELL, WINFIELD A; Hesperia HS; Hesperia, CA; (2); 1/800; ROTC; Spanish Clb; Treas Stu Cncl; JV Tennis; High Hon Roll; Prfct Atten Awd; Univ Club; CSF; Boys Tnns Tm Treas; Aeronautical Engrng.

MUNDO, TANYA; Sierra Vista HS; Baldwin Park, CA; (1); Church Yth Grp; Color Guard; Mrchg Band; Redlands; Pediatrician.

MUNDY, KATE A; Bonita Vista HS; Bonita, CA; (3); 78/559; Art Clb; Model UN; Sec Chorus; Capt Var Crs Cntry; Capt JV Socr; Capt Var Trk; Cit Awd; Hon Roll; CYSA Soccer 90 AAA; Med.

MUNDY, MARCUS B; Rio Lindo Adventist Acad; Angwin, CA; (2); Aud/Vis; Church Yth Grp; Ed Rptr Nwsp; Wt Lftg; Prfct Atten Awd; Rio Lindo Adventist Acad.

MUNGAN, MOLLIE M; Coleville HS; Bridgeport, CA; (4); 1/12; Dance Clb; Drama Clb; School Play; VP Jr Cls; Pres Stu Cncl; Cheerldng; Sftbl; High Hon Roll; Opt Clb Awd; Val; CSF; CA St Summer Schl Of Arts; Santa Clara U; Dance.

MUNGO, PAOLO; St Anthonys HS; Long Beach, CA; (2); Church Yth Grp; Varsity Clb; Crs Cntry; Trk; 2nd Pl X Cntry; 2nd In League Trk & X Cntry JV; Frshmn Most Outstndng Athlt X Cntry; Irvin U; Robotic Engrg.

MUNGUIA, ERLIE C; Bell HS; Lynwood, CA; (4); 7/636; Computer Clb; French Clb; Math Clb; Nwsp; Ftbl; French Hon Soc; 4-H Awd; High Hon Roll; NHS.

MUNGUIA, FLORA; Coachella Valley HS; Thermal, CA; (3); Hon Roll; Nutricianist.

MUNI, JYOTI; Mills HS; San Francisco, CA; (3); Debate Tm; Ed Nwsp; High Hon Roll; Hnrs Rcgntn Golden St Exam Algebra I; Nwspr Articles/Local Papers; Distgsh Serviceawd/Jourlsm-Editor; U Of CA.

MUNIZ, CESAR; Bell Garden HS; Commerce, CA; (1); FCA; Ftbl; Wt Lftg; Wrstlng; Architecture/Engineering.

MUNIZ, ISABEL M; Oakdale HS; Farmington, CA; (3); FFA; Teachers Aide; JV Bsktbl; Hon Roll; Landscaping.

MUNIZ, ISAIAH S; Bell Gardens HS; Commerce, CA; (1); Columbia U; Archtct.

MUNIZ, JENNIFER S; Notre Dame HS; Pacific Grove, CA; (3); Church Yth Grp; Dance Clb; VP Drama Clb; VP Hosp Aide; Science Clb; Chorus; School Musical; School Play; Variety Show; Rptr Nwsp; Amnesty Intl; Sci Clb; Drama Clb; Med.

MUNIZ, JOSE J; Los Amigos HS; Santa Ana, CA; (1); Church Yth Grp; Drama Clb; FFA; Temple Yth Grp; School Play; Stage Crew; Bsktbl; Ftbl; Tennis; Trk; Hstry.

MUNIZ, MARISELA I; Richard Gahr HS; Cerritos, CA; (2); Church Yth Grp; Girl Scts; Teachers Aide; Rep Frsh Cls; Hist Soph Cls; Off Jr Cls; Var Stat Bsbl; Var Stat Bsktbl; Var Stat Ftbl; Var Mgr(s); UCLA; Chld Psych.

MUNIZ, ROSEMARY; Warren HS; South Gate, CA; (2); Spanish Clb; Teachers Aide; Cerritos Coll; Lab Tech.

MUNIZ, RUDY D; Savanna HS; Buena Park, CA; (2); Boy Scts; JA; JV Socr; JV Tennis; Life Sci Stu Of Yr; UCLA; Bus.

MUNJEE, KANEEZ M; Alexander Hamilton Acad Of Music; Encino, CA; (2); French Clb; Girl Scts; Math Tm; Natl Beta Clb; VP Service Clb; School Play; Music & Piano; Harvard.

MUNN, SIMMONE; Los Angeles HS; Los Angeles, CA; (3); Church Yth Grp; Hosp Aide; Chorus; Church Choir; Orch; Rptr Nwsp; Tp Teens Of Am; Hmcmng Brnss; Vw Pk Ctlln; Debutante 90; Btlln Escrt 90; Brdcst Jrnlsm.

MUNOZ, ANA M; Eisenhower HS; Rialto, CA; (2); Library Aide; Sftbl; Vllybl; Hon Roll; Track Team; Coachs Awd-Sftbl; Mst Insprtnl Plyr-Vllybl; MECHA Clb VP 89; HS Stu Cnslr.

MUNOZ, ANDREA; Glendora HS; Glendora, CA; (2); Pep Clb; Orch; JV Cheerldng; High Hon Roll; Hon Roll; Broadcasting.

MUNOZ, DANIEL; Highlands HS; Sacramento, CA; (3); 3/325; Quiz Bowl; Scholastic Bowl; Var L Ftbl; Var L Golf; Var Capt Socr; High Hon Roll; Pres Acad Fit Awd; St Schlr; European Sccr Clb; 1st Tm All Leag Sccr; Sports Med.

MUNOZ, DESIREE A; Sacramento HS; Sacramento, CA; (2); 154/500; Sftbl; MESA; College; Accounting Physician.

MUNOZ, DIANA; Mater Dei HS; Tustin, CA; (3); Church Yth Grp; Hosp Aide; Drill Tm; Treas Frsh Cls; Rep Stu Cncl; Cheerldng; Pom Pon; High Hon Roll; Hon Roll; Medcl.

MUNOZ, DIANA; Turlock HS; Turlock, CA; (2); Church Yth Grp; Pep Clb; Cheerldng; Sftbl; Wt Lftg; Dance Class 79-82; Sftbl Team; Chrldr 85; Powder Puff 85; Powder Pufftbl 86-87, Chrldr 88-89; Jr Hi Hnr; FL ST; Prof Dancer.

MUNOZ, ELAYNE F; Selma HS; Selma, CA; (3); Sftbl; Pr Cnslng; Fresno ST Berkeley; Psych.

MUNOZ, ESPERANZA D; Lincoln Prep HS; San Diego, CA; (2); GAA; Bsktbl; Sftbl; Hon Roll; Stu Against Animal Abuse; Helping Aide Convlsnt Home; MVP Bsktbl; Marine Bio.

MUNOZ, FRANCO D; Berkeley HS; Berkeley, CA; (4); Boy Scts; Latin Clb; Socr; Wt Lftg; Wrstlng; High Hon Roll; Hon Roll; Med.

MUNOZ, JOSEPH M; Santa Barbara HS; Santa Barbara, CA; (3); Ftbl; Hon Roll; MESA 4 Yr Mthmtcs Engr Sci Achr; Lttrd Ftbl Won CIF Chmpnshps; UCSD; Bus.

MUNOZ, MANUEL; Hueneme HS; Oxnard, CA; (3); 32/376; Church Yth Grp; Band; Hon Roll; Sun Schl Tchr; Cal Poly; Engrng.

MUNOZ, MARCO A; King City HS; King City, CA; (3); Intrml Var Bsbl; Intrml Ftbl; Fresno City Coll; Art.

MUNOZ, MARK J; International Studies Acad; San Francisco, CA; (2); ROTC; Philanthropy Club.

MUNOZ, MERCEDES A; Workman HS; La Puente, CA; (2); Hon Roll; Prfct Atten Awd; UCLA; Comp.

MUNOZ, MICHAEL D; East Bakersfield HS; Bakersfield, CA; (1); JV Crs Cntry; Athltc Booster Club Awd Outstndng Acadmc Achvt; Block E B Club Awd Most Insprtnl Crss Cntry 89-90.

MUNOZ, MONICA Z; Centro Union HS; El Centro, CA; (2); Cmnty Wkr; Drama Clb; Pep Clb; SADD; Cmptr Pgmmr.

MUNOZ, NICOLE L; Jefferson HS; Daly City, CA; (3); GAA; Office Aide; SADD; Teachers Aide; Cheerldng; Sftbl; Cit Awd; Psych.

MUNOZ, PAULINA; Chatsworth HS; Chatsworth, CA; (4); Treas FHA; Office Aide; Drill Tm; Var Cheerldng; Hon Roll; Teachers Aide; CSUN; Med.

MUNOZ JR, RAMON G; Atwater HS; Atwater, CA; (1); FFA; Bsbl; Ftbl; Socr; High Hon Roll; Hon Roll; Stanford U; Elec Engr.

MUNOZ, RAUL L; Bell Gardens HS; Bell Gardens, CA; (3); Office Aide; JV Socr; JV Trk; Hon Roll; Med Doc.

MUNOZ, ROSA H; Hanford HS; Visalia, CA; (3); Am Leg Aux Girls St; Spanish Clb; Teachers Aide; Fshn.

MUNOZ, ROXANA A; Nogales HS; W Covina, CA; (2); German Clb; Hosp Aide; Crs Cntry; Swmmng; Hon Roll; Prfct Atten Awd; Pres Acad Fit Awd.

MUNOZ, SERINA; East Bakersfield HS; Bakersfield, CA; (2); UCLA; Pharm.

MUNOZ, SUSANA; Palm Springs HS; Cathedral City, CA; (3); Drama Clb; Hist French Clb; Sec Treas Frsh Cls; JV Bsktbl; JV Sftbl; Hon Roll; Awd-Gldn St Exam; Hnrs Algebra & Geo; Mex-Amer Yth Assn; CSF; Aeronautcal Engrng.

MUNOZ, VERONICA; Lindhurst HS; Marysville, CA; (2); Latin Clb; Teachers Aide; Cit Awd; High Hon Roll; Phys Sci, Lindhurst Blazer Awds; Comp Sci.

MUNOZ, VERONICA A; Warren HS; South Gate, CA; (3); French Clb; Key Clb; Cit Awd; Vol-Vet Hosp; Davis U; Vet Med.

MUNOZ, WENDY; Montgomery HS; San Diego, CA; (2); Teachers Aide; Drill Tm; Cit Awd; Prfct Atten Awd.

MUNOZ, YESSICA; Saddleback HS; Santa Ana, CA; (4); FBLA; Pep Clb; Science Clb; Spanish Clb; SADD; Hon Roll; USC Schl Of Phrmcy; Phrmclgy.

MUNSELL, SHERRY L; Rubiodux HS; Mira Loma, CA; (4); Rptr Yrbk; Var Capt Bsktbl; Powder Puff Ftbl; Sftbl; Hon Roll; UCR; Psych.

MUNSER, MORTEN; Amador HS; Pleasanton, CA; (4); Trk; Wt Lftg; B Of A Inds Arts, Golden St Exam Awds; Cal Poly San Luis Obispo; Engr.

MUNSER, NINETT; Amador Valley HS; Pleasanton, CA; (1); School Play; Cheerldng; Graphic Dsgn.

MUNSHOWER, ANDREA L; Etiwanda HS; Rancho Cucamonga, CA; (3); Hosp Aide; Pres Key Clb; Library Aide; Teachers Aide; Hon Roll; CA ST U San Bernardino; Nrsng.

MUNSON, JOHN D; Livermore HS; Livermore, CA; (4); Boy Scts; Church Yth Grp; French Clb; Office Aide; Pres Ski Clb; Band; Jazz Band; Mrchg Band; School Musical; School Play; Dir Awd; U CA Santa Cruz; Marine Bio.

MUNSON, LEE; Palm Desert HS; Palm Desert, CA; (2); Model UN; Band; High Hon Roll; CA Schlrshp Fdrtncoll Of Desert Jazz Band, Symphnc Band; U Of CA Irvine Acad Talnt Srch 89; Stanford U; Econ.

MUNYAN, HANNAH; Chaffey HS; Rancho Cucamonga, CA; (4); 100/380; Pres Church Yth Grp; Rep Model UN; Thesps; Stage Crew; Ed Yrbk; Stu Govt Day Cnclwmn; Ricks Coll.

MUNZING, DANIELLE R; Hanford HS; Hanford, CA; (3); Cmnty Wkr; FFA; Teachers Aide; Band; Mrchg Band; Yth For Undrstndng, Smmr Exchng Pgm; Lib Arts.

MUONG, PHAL K; Lakewood HS; Long Beach, CA; (2); Intrml Vllybl; Var Wrstlng; Forest Ranger.

MURAI, MIHO; Huntington Beach HS; Huntington Beach, CA; (2); Church Yth Grp; Cmnty Wkr; Dance Clb; Debate Tm; GAA; Rep Treas Key Clb; Model UN; Red Cross Aide; Speech Tm; School Musical; X-Country Awds; Key Clb Awd; Stanford; Engl.

MURAI, NATSUKO; Huntington Beach HS; Huntington Bch, CA; (4); 7/450; Treas Key Clb; Math Clb; Math Tm; Spanish Clb; Teachers Aide; JV Tennis; High Hon Roll; Hon Roll; Ntl Merit Ltr; CA Schlrshp Fed Clb Treas; Ath Bdmntn Jr Vrsty; Tower Awd Math; U CA Berkeley; Math.

MURAI, WENDY K; John F Kennedy HS; Sacramento, CA; (3); 26/422; Am Leg Aux Girls St; Church Yth Grp; Var Debate Tm; NFL; Off Soph Cls; Sec Treas Jr Cls; Sec Sr Cls; High Hon Roll; Bus.

MURAKAMI, JUNE; Paramount HS; Paramount, CA; (3); 15/440; Computer Clb; FTA; Orch; Hon Roll; Pres Acad Fit Awd; CA Schlstc Fed 89-90; Schlrshp For Music Lessons 89.

MURAMOTO, DEAN T; Rubidoux HS; Mira Loma, CA; (4); Boy Scts; Chess Clb; Var Crs Cntry; JV Var Trk.

MURAMOTO, ERIK; John F Kennedy HS; Sacramento, CA; (2); 64/525; JV Bsktbl; Cit Awd; Hon Roll; Pres Acad Fit Awd; Asian Bsktbl Ttm; UC; Bus.

MURANO, RYAN W; Mammoth HS; Mammoth Lakes, CA; (3); Boy Scts; Band; Jazz Band; Pep Band; School Musical; Bsktbl; Crs Cntry; Socr; High Hon Roll; Hon Roll; Ski Race Team; Martial Arts; Snowbd Team; U NV Reno; Frst Mgmt.

MURAO, KIM T; Alhambra HS; Alhambra, CA; (3); JV Sftbl; San Diego ST; Acctng.

MURAOKA, TOMOKO; Sunny Hills HS; La Habra, CA; (3); Key Clb; Spanish Clb; Hon Roll; Dance Prodctn; Interior Desgnr.

MURATORE, JAY; Atwater HS; Merced, CA; (1); Cmnty Wkr; FCA; Intrml Ftbl; JV Tennis; JV Wt Lftg; JV Var Wrstlng; Hon Roll; Prfct Atten Awd; Interact.

MURAVEZ, RACHEL; Oxnard HS; Oxnard, CA; (4); 18/400; Church Yth Grp; Drama Clb; English Clb; Math Clb; Scholastic Bowl; Science Clb; Service Clb; SADD; Band; Jazz Band; Bank Of America Music Awd; U Of OR; Eng Tchrr.

MURAVIOV, LISA L; California HS; Whittier, CA; (3); Church Yth Grp; Sec Treas SADD; Ed Yrbk; Biola; Lawyer.

MURDOCK, BRETT M; Brea Olinda HS; Brea, CA; (3); 3/350; Boy Scts; Cmnty Wkr; Band; Drm Mjr(t); Orch; Capt Var Crs Cntry; JV Socr; JV Var Swmmng; Var L Trk; High Hon Roll; VP & Pres Guide Dogs For Blnd; Interact Clb Treas; Lifgrd; Sccr Coach; Ed.

MURDOCK, TRAVIS R; William S Hart HS; Valencia, CA; (4); Church Yth Grp; Math Clb; Swmmng; Brigham Young U; Bus.

MURGUIA, ABRAM; Ernest Righetti HS; Guadalupe, CA; (2); 8/461; Var Socr; High Hon Roll; Hon Roll; Upward Bound; CA Schlstc Fed; Dance; CA Poly Sn Luis Obispo; Engrng.

MURGUIA, ANGELICA; Polytechnic HS; Arleta, CA; (3); French Clb; Spanish Clb; SADD; Teachers Aide; Rptr Nwsp; Cit Awd; High Hon Roll; Hon Roll; YCS; MECHA; CSUN; Accntng.

MURGUIA, DOLORES; Ernest Righetti HS; Guadalupe, CA; (4); 20/372; Cmnty Wkr; Dance Clb; High Hon Roll; Upward Bond Prog; Multi-Culture Club; Cal Poly; Aminal Sci.

MURILLO, BERTHA; James A Garfield HS; Los Angeles, CA; (3); Orch; Cit Awd; Hon Roll; Prfct Atten Awd; Rotary Awd; Peer Counselor; CA Schlrshp Fed; Hnr Stu Of Mnth; USC; Bus.

MURILLO, CHRISTINA; Le Grand HS; Merced, CA; (3); Am Leg Aux Girls St; Dance Clb; Drama Clb; Spanish Clb; Teachers Aide; Varsity Clb; Drill Tm; School Play; Treas Frsh Cls; Treas Soph Cls; Block L; Santa Barbara U; Bus.

MURILLO, CYNTHIA V; Banning HS; Wilmington, CA; (3); Church Yth Grp; Cmnty Wkr; French Clb; JA; Latin Clb; Math Clb; Teachers Aide; Band; Church Choir; Drill Tm; U Of Santa Barbara.

MURILLO, DANIEL L; Central Catholic HS; Modesto, CA; (3); Art Clb; Science Clb; Ski Clb; SADD; JV Ftbl; Hon Roll; Bio.

MURILLO, ELIZABETH; Chino HS; Chino, CA; (3); Church Yth Grp; Spanish Clb; Powder Puff Ftbl; Hon Roll; Cmmnctns.

MURILLO, HORTENCIA B; Bullard HS; Fresno, CA; (1); Spanish Clb; Stanford; Acctnt.

MURILLO, IGNACIO; Cathedral HS; Los Angeles, CA; (4); 10/108; Math Clb; Red Cross Aide; Spanish Clb; VP Sr Cls; Var Socr; Hon Roll; NHS; Spanish NHS; Loyola Marymount U; Engrng.

MURILLO, LETICIA L; Escondido HS; Escondido, CA; (1); Spanish Clb; Teachers Aide; Band; Mrchg Band; U Of CA, San Diego; Music.

MURILLO, MELANIE; Ganesha HS; Diamond Bar, CA; (2).

MURILLO, PABLO; Baldwin Park HS; Baldwin Park, CA; (4); Pres Art Clb; Chess Clb; FBLA; Crs Cntry; Socr; Trk; Wt Lftg; Cit Awd; High Hon Roll; Hon Roll; Track Awds; Aerontcl Engr.

MURILLO, SUSIE; William C Overfelt HS; San Jose, CA; (1); Church Yth Grp; MI Coll; Lawyer.

MURILLO, VERA; Pius X HS; Compton, CA; (1); Temple Yth Grp; Hon Roll; Sal; U Of CA Los Angeles; Accntnt.

MURNIEKS, JOHN; Roseville HS; Rocklin, CA; (3); Art Clb; Boy Scts; Sec German Clb; Band; Mrchg Band; Var L Crs Cntry; Var L Tennis.

MURO, ADRIANA; San Gabriel HS; San Gabriel, CA; (2); Office Aide; Spanish Clb; High Hon Roll; Hon Roll; Maso Ltn Clb; Acad Achvt Awd; UC Berkely; Psycht.

MURPHIN, CHARITY; Troy HS; Battleground, WA; (1); Wrld Hstry Achvt Awd; Chld Dev Achvt Awd.

MURPHY, AILEEN O; Immaculate Conception Acad; Daly City, CA; (4); 12/55; Letterman Clb; Rptr Nwsp; Hon Roll; NHS; Prfct Atten Awd; Church Yth Grp; Cmnty Wkr; GAA; Office Aide; Service Clb; 1st Pl Vault Gymnstcs 87; Stu Cncl Awd; U Of San Francisco; Law.

MURPHY, AUDRA L; University HS; Irvine, CA; (4); 85/450; Drama Clb; Treas Intnl Clb; Quiz Bowl; Church Choir; Jazz Band; Mrchg Band; School Musical; Stage Crew; Rptr Nwsp; Rep Frsh Cls; 3rd Pl Sunrise Exchng Clb Tlnt Show; Chrch Pianist; Chiroprtc Asst; Chapman Coll; Music.

MURPHY, BILL J; Leland HS; San Jose, CA; (2); Aud/Vis; Rep Frsh Cls; Rep Soph Cls; Ftbl; Socr; Tennis; Wt Lftg; Cit Awd; Hon Roll; Mech Engrng.

MURPHY, BRETT A; Fairfield HS; Fairfield, CA; (2); Church Yth Grp; High Hon Roll; Prfct Atten Awd.

MURPHY, BRIAN K; San Dimas HS; San Dimas, CA; (3); Letterman Clb; Bsbl; Bsktbl; Ftbl; Wrstlng; High Hon Roll; Treas VICA; Accntng.

MURPHY, DAIMHIN P; Drew College Prep; San Francisco, CA; (3); VP Intnl Clb; High Hon Roll; Natl Sci Olympiad Awd Biology 89; Awd Biology 89; Envrnmntl Sci 88; Comp Sci 90; Tchr Asst Comp Sci 90; Engineering.

MURPHY, FRANCIS J; St Ignatius College Prep; San Francisco, CA; (3); Drama Clb; Science Clb; Service Clb; SADD; Stage Crew; Intrml Bsbl; Var Crs Cntry; JV Trk; High Hon Roll; Ntl Merit Ltr; Liturgy Grp; CSF Bk Schlrshp; Cmnty Svc Cmmendtn.

MURPHY, GREG M; St Francis HS; South Pasadena, CA; (2); 4/180; FCA; Math Clb; Mu Alpha Theta; Ed Yrbk; Var L Crs Cntry; JV L Trk; High Hon Roll; Hon Roll; Sec NHS; CSF; Acad Hall Of Fame; U Of Notre Dame; Poli Sci.

MURPHY, HEATHER; Canyon HS; Anaheim, CA; (1); GAA; JV Swmmng; Modeling; Ballet; Math/Sci.

MURPHY, JEANNE; Los Alamitos HS; Seal Beach, CA; (3); Math Tm; Spanish Clb; Chorus; Rep Stu Cncl; JV Crs Cntry; JV Trk; Cit Awd; Hon Roll; Pre-Med.

MURPHY, JENNIFER; Loara HS; Anaheim, CA; (3); Pep Clb; Teachers Aide; JV Var Cheerldng; Var Pom Pon; Var Swmmng; High Hon Roll; Hon Roll; Jr NHS; NHS; Prfct Atten Awd; ASB-SEC; Gldn St Exam-Geom & Algb; Disneyland 1st Annual Pigskin Clssc Pep Sqd; Bus.

MURPHY, JOSEPH; Trabuco Hills HS; Mission Viejo, CA; (3); 12/346; French Clb; School Play; Pres Frsh Cls; Pres Stu Cncl; Var Bsktbl; JV Ftbl; JV Golf; High Hon Roll; Hon Roll; Jr NHS; Bsktbl Coach Awd; CSF; Law.

MURPHY, KATHLEEN; Clovis West HS; Clovis, CA; (3); 62/650; Cmnty Wkr; 4-H; FBLA; Hosp Aide; Intnl Clb; SADD; Rep Frsh Cls; Rep Jr Cls; Cheerldng; Capt Powder Puff Ftbl; CSF; Big Bros Big Srs; Fresno Cty Yng Woman Of Yr Cmptn; U CA Irvine; Ped.

MURPHY, KERRY B; Palos Verdes HS; Rnch Palos Verdes, CA; (4); 118/337; Pres VP JA; Library Aide; Spanish Clb; Teachers Aide; School Musical; School Play; Stage Crew; Sftbl; Greek Club Pres; Oscar Awd; Outstndng Achvt Stage Mgt; CA ST U Chico; Bus Admin.

MURPHY, KERRY M; Corning Union HS; Corning, CA; (4); 1/120; Rep GAA; Yrbk; Sec Stu Cncl; Var Capt Bsktbl; Var Capt Fld Hcky; Stat Ftbl; JV Var Sftbl; Var Trk; Elks Awd; Kiwanis Awd; UC Davis; Biolgcl Sci.

MURPHY, LAURIE C; Mission Viejo HS; Mission Viejo, CA; (1); 49/455; Church Yth Grp; GAA; Var Trk; JV Vllybl; High Hon Roll; Hon Roll; Mst Versatile Awd In Trk; UCLA; Sports Med.

MURPHY, LENORE MARIE; Ygnacio Valley HS; Concord, CA; (2); Key Clb; Bsktbl; Pres Of Key Clb 90-91; Chrch Yth Grp.

MURPHY, MARY; Carlmont HS; Belmont, CA; (2); 1/400; Cmnty Wkr; GAA; JV Socr; JV Tennis; CSF; IDEX; Amnesty Intl; Stu For A Better Environment; Badminton JV; Med.

MURPHY, MELANIE K; Brea-Olinda HS; Brea, CA; (2); 17/300; GAA; Mgr(s); Score Keeper; JV L Socr; Var L Swmmng; High Hon Roll; Hon Roll; Jr NHS; Pres Acad Fit Awd; Pres Schlr; Natl Hstry ST Fnlst 90; Mst Imprvd Swmr 88-90; Med.

MURPHY, MELISSA K; Hayward HS; Hayward, CA; (1); Drama Clb; Stu Peer Cnslr.

MURPHY, MICHAEL; Foothill HS; Pleasanton, CA; (3); Cmnty Wkr; Red Cross Aide; Rep Frsh Cls; Rep Soph Cls; Rep Jr Cls; Rep Stu Cncl; Capt JV Crs Cntry; Capt JV Ftbl; Stat Score Keeper; Capt Var Trk; Gifted And Talented; Best In Trk; Peer Counselor; Lifeguard Of Year; CPR Awd; UCSC; Chld Dvlpmnt.

MURPHY, MICHELLE; Capital Christian Schl; Sacramento, CA; (2); Church Yth Grp; VP Frsh Cls; Bsktbl; Golf; Mgr(s); Tennis; Cit Awd.

MURPHY, NOELLE R; Bret Harte HS; Vallecito, CA; (2); Church Yth Grp; Cmnty Wkr; GAA; Service Clb; Ski Clb; Band; Pep Band; JV Bsktbl; JV Sftbl; JV Vllybl; Friday Night Live; CSF.

MURPHY, OWEN; Yosemite HS; Oakhurst, CA; (2); Letterman Clb; Hist Service Clb; Varsity Clb; VP Soph Cls; Var Crs Cntry; JV Socr; JV Tennis; High Hon Roll; Stu Of Mnth 89; Crs Cntry Fnlst 88 & 89.

MURPHY, RYAN; Los Alamitos HS; Los Alamitos, CA; (4); Church Yth Grp; Drama Clb; School Play; Capt Cheerldng; Cit Awd; Hon Roll; Ntl Merit Ltr.

MURPHY, RYAN R; Brea Olinda HS; Brea, CA; (1); Teachers Aide; Bsktbl; Hon Roll; Jr NHS; Pres Acad Fit Awd; Arch.

MURPHY, SARAH K; Mc Clatchy HS; Sacramento, CA; (1); Pep Clb; Ski Clb; Pres Frsh Cls; Powder Puff Ftbl; JV Socr; Cls Pres 90; U Of CA; Jrnlst.

MURPHY, SEAN S; Bullard HS; Fresno, CA; (4); 13/445; Model UN; Jazz Band; Orch; School Musical; Rep Stu Cncl; High Hon Roll; Ntl Merit SF; All ST Hnr Orch; Engrng.

MURPHY, SEDRIC; Fontana HS; Fontana, CA; (2); Bsbl; Ftbl; Wt Lftg; CO; Brdcstng.

MURPHY, STEVEN E; Coleville HS; Coleville, CA; (3); VP Frsh Cls; Rep Soph Cls; Var Bsbl; Var Bsktbl; Var Ftbl; Hon Roll; Pre-Med.

MURPHY, SUNNY; Mountain View HS; Sunnyvale, CA; (4); JA; Band; Mrchg Band; Orch; Pep Band; School Musical; JV Sftbl; Hon Roll; Stu Of Music Cncl As Photog 88-89; Band Camp Staff 89; Schlrshp San Jose GI Forum & Mtn Vw Rotary; UC San Diego; Elem Schl Tchr.

MURPHY, TAMARA; Serrano HS; Phelan, CA; (1); Acpl Chr; Band; Chorus; Church Choir; Mrchg Band; Orch; Swing Chorus; Rep Stu Cncl; JV Bsktbl; JV Vllybl; Amer Music Fndtn Band Hnr; Fullerton; Music.

MURPHY, WILLIAM L; North Monterey County HS; Salinas, CA; (2); Chess Clb; Drama Clb; SADD; Band; Jazz Band; Mrchg Band; Orch; Pep Band; Stage Crew; Wrkd Lights At Western Stage Theatre Co Of Hartnell Coll; Math.

MURR, AMY K; El Toro HS; El Toro, CA; (4); Church Yth Grp; Cmnty Wkr; Intnl Clb; Service Clb; Swmmng; Hon Roll; Masonic Awd; Intrntnl Order Of Rainbow For Girls; Chldrns Church Choir Drctr; Multiple Leadership Schlrshp Receipnt; U Of AL; Accounting.

MURRAY, DANIEL S; Pacifica HS; Garden Grove, CA; (2); 43/294; Var Bsbl; Var Bsktbl; JV Ftbl; Hon Roll; Bio Clb; Jv Ftbl Offnsv Plyr Of Yr Awd; MVP Fresh Bsktbl; UCSD; Vet.

MURRAY, HEATHER; King City HS; King City, CA; (2); Church Yth Grp; Cheerldng; Pom Pon; Trk; Hon Roll; Commercial Clb; Interact Clb; UC Santa Cruz; Jrnlsm.

MURRAY, JENNIFER L; El Toro HS; El Toro, CA; (3); Art Clb; Church Yth Grp; Cmnty Wkr; GAA; Girl Scts; Service Clb; Teachers Aide; Church Choir; JV Socr; High Hon Roll; Cptn JV Socr Tm; Socr Coach El Toro Clb Tm; Mst Insprtnl JV Socr Tm; Saddleback JC; Intr Decrtr.

MURRAY, LISA A; San Luis Obispo HS; San Luis Obispo, CA; (2); Key Clb; SADD; Powder Puff Ftbl; JV Swmmng.

MURRAY, LISA M; Cajon HS; San Bernardino, CA; (3); JA; Band; Rptr Yrbk; Cal ST; Accntnt.

MURRAY, MELINDA R; Victor Valley HS; Victorville, CA; (2); Church Yth Grp; Band; Church Choir; Drill Tm; Mrchg Band; Cit Awd; Hon Roll; U WA; Lawyer.

MURRAY, MICHAEL BRIAN; Mt Carmel HS; San Diego, CA; (3); 120/700; Church Yth Grp; Drama Clb; NFL; Speech Tm; Thesps; School Musical; School Play; Pres Stu Cncl; Cit Awd; Hon Roll; Maureen O Connors Yth Advsry Cncl San Diego; Pres Just Say No Club; Georgetown; Intl Relations.

MURRAY, MICHELLE; Newbury Park HS; Newbury Park, CA; (4); 35/400; Church Yth Grp; Cmnty Wkr; French Clb; Math Tm; Pep Clb; Church Choir; Var JV Cheerldng; Powder Puff Ftbl; Hon Roll; Moorpark Coll; Comm.

MURRAY, MIKE B; Grossmont HS; El Cajon, CA; (2); Aud/Vis; Boy Scts; Church Yth Grp; German Clb; Key Clb; Ski Clb; SADD; Nwsp; Swmmng; Vllybl; BYU; Vet.

MURRAY, PATRICK V; Montclair HS; Montclair, CA; (3); JV Bsbl; Var JV Bsktbl; JV Ftbl; High Hon Roll; Hon Roll.

MURRAY, RICHARD M; Thousand Oaks HS; Thousand Oaks, CA; (3); 29/541; Boy Scts; Var Tennis; High Hon Roll; Pres Acad Fit Awd; Acadmc Excllnc Awd Geom; Prncpls Hnr Roll; CSF; MVP Dbls Mrmnte Leag Tnns; Bsbl All Star Team; US Air Force; Aeronaut Engr.

MURRAY, ROBERT C; Westlake HS; Westlake Vlg, CA; (4); 69/440; Office Aide; Teachers Aide; Capt Socr; Hon Roll; Pres Acad Fit Awd; 1st Tm All Lg, MVP, Coaches Awd Soccer; Moorpark Coll; Admin.

MURRAY, TANYA; Saddleback HS; Santa Ana, CA; (4); AFS; Debate Tm; English Clb; Spanish Clb; Speech Tm; Stat Swmmng; High Hon Roll; Pres Acad Fit Awd; CSF; AZ U; Pharmacy.

MURRAY, TANYA M; Santa Monica HS; Santa Monica, CA; (3); Ski Clb; Rep Soph Cls; JV Socr; JV Trk; Yth & Govt 89-90; Fund Raising Cmmtte Head; UC.

MURRAY, TASHARA N; Norte Vista HS; Riverside, CA; (2); 132/445; Church Yth Grp; SADD; Varsity Clb; Var Bsktbl; Var Trk; JV Vllybl; Hon Roll; Black Stu Union Sec 89-90; UC Partners 89-90; CIF Bsktbl 89-90 3rd Pl; Hampton; Financial Analyst.

MURRAY, TODD S; Ventura HS; Ventura, CA; (2); Debate Tm; Science Clb; Cit Awd; High Hon Roll; Hon Roll; Prfct Atten Awd; Yth Sci Ambssdr To Russia-People To People Ambssdr Prgrms; Chem Delgtn; Rdng & Wrtng Sci Fictn; Fresno ST U; Sci.

MURRAY, TOMMY; Washington HS; Los Angeles, CA; (3); Band; Stu Cncl; Bsktbl; Swmmng; Trk; Wt Lftg; Brthrs Jahi; Engr.

MURRELL, GEORGETTE S; Westminster HS; Westminster, CA; (2); Latin Clb; Teachers Aide; Var L Vllybl; Jr NHS; Pres Acad Fit Awd; Interact; CSF; Psych.

MURRELL, ZURI A; Pacific Palisades HS; Los Angeles, CA; (2); Pres Computer Clb; Ski Clb; Church Choir; Var Tennis; High Hon Roll; Prfct Atten Awd; Fulfillment Fund Schlrshp Pgm; Bio.

MURREY, CAROLINE; Upland HS; Upland, CA; (2); 30/750; Ed Phtg Nwsp; Hon Roll; Jr NHS; Friday Night Live Clb VP & Co-Pres; Mock Trial Tm; CA Schlrshp Fed; UCLA; Phy.

MURRIETA, DENISE B; San Bernardino HS; San Bernardino, CA; (4); Library Aide; Off Jr Cls; Hon Roll; S B Valley Coll; Acctng.

MURRY, ASABI O; Culver City HS; Culver City, CA; (3); Cmnty Wkr; Dance Clb; Science Clb; Variety Show; Rep Soph Cls; JV Var Mgr(s); JV Var Trk; Ntl Merit SF; Pres Acad Fit Awd; Write Ptry & Draw; Mrktng.

MURRY, DAVID J; Junipero Serra HS; Hawthorne, CA; (2); Boy Scts; Science Clb; JV Bsbl; VP Socr; Cit Awd; Hon Roll; Bird Clb; Vet Med.

MURVINE, LARRY D; Bell Gardens HS; Cudahy, CA; (3); Tri-Cty Yth Grp; U Of CA Davis; Vet.

MUSCHENETZ, ROLAND I; Morro Bay HS; Los Osos, CA; (2); 8/220; French Clb; German Clb; Treas Key Clb; Band; Jazz Band; Mrchg Band; Pep Band; Yrbk; High Hon Roll; Comp-Aided Grphc Illstrtr.

MUSED, ANWAR M; Richmond HS; Richmond, CA; (4); Bsbl; Socr; Comp Prgmr.

MUSELLA, STEPHANIE J; St Bernard HS; Los Angeles, CA; (3); Pep Clb; Spanish Clb; Varsity Clb; Var L Swmmng; Cit Awd; High Hon Roll; Prfct Atten Awd.

MUSIC, MICHAEL; Central Valley Christian HS; Rosamond, CA; (4); 3/22; Church Yth Grp; Drama Clb; School Play; Nwsp; Ed Yrbk; Stu Cncl; JV Bsktbl; Intrml Vllybl; Hon Roll; Opt Clb Awd; Sthrn CA Coll; Mnstry.

MUSIC, ROBERT LEE; Oroville HS; Oroville, CA; (3); 39/193; Church Yth Grp; Var L Bsbl; Capt L Bsktbl; Capt L Ftbl; Hon Roll; Accntng.

MUSICANT, ANDREA; Valhalla HS; La Mesa, CA; (4); 17/480; Am Leg Aux Girls St; Pres Cmnty Wkr; VP Ski Clb; Ed Nwsp; Pres Jr Cls; Var Tennis; Cit Awd; Bank Of Amer Plaque For Outstndng Liberal Arts Stu; Jr State Club Pres; UC Berkeley; Poltcl Sci.

MUSSELMAN, TODD; Hemet HS; Hemet, CA; (4); 67/578; Church Yth Grp; German Clb; Teachers Aide; JV Bsbl; Var Crs Cntry; JV Ftbl; Var Trk; Hon Roll; Jr NHS; CSF; U KS; Poltcl Sci.

MUSTION, CHRIS; Escondido HS; Oceanside, CA; (3); 14/450; Church Yth Grp; Stage Crew; Intrml JV Bsbl; High Hon Roll; NHS; Ntl Merit Ltr; California Scholarship Federation.

MUTH, ERIN M; Kolbe Acad; Napa, CA; (2); Church Yth Grp; Debate Tm; Drama Clb; School Play; Variety Show; Rptr Nwsp; Treas Frsh Cls; Treas Soph Cls; Stu Cncl; High Hon Roll; Extracurrical City Spon Sftbl; Jean Baptiste De La Salle Awd, Our Schls Top Awd; Dale Evans Poetry Awd; Jrnlsm.

MUTH, KETHY; Artesia HS; Lakewood, CA; (3); Intnl Clb; Drill Tm; JV Tennis; Camodian Clb; CSULB; Bus.

MUTH, KEVIN J; Oakmont HS; Roseville, CA; (4); 8/390; Spanish Clb; SADD; Band; Mrchg Band; Pres Soph Cls; VP Jr Cls; Var Capt Swmmng; High Hon Roll; Vrsty Water Polo Capt; CA Polytech San Luis Ob; Bus.

MUTHER, ANN C; Atascadero HS; Atascadero, CA; (2); 9/350; Church Yth Grp; JV Bsktbl; JV Sftbl; JV Vllybl; Cit Awd; High Hon Roll; Hon Roll; MVP Vllybl, Bsktbl, Sftbl; Art Hnrs; Lbrl Art.

MUUSERS, FRANNIE; Silver Creek HS; San Jose, CA; (3); Intnl Clb; Speech Tm; JV Var Tennis; Cit Awd; High Hon Roll; SCAD; Law.

MUZSEK, SHELLEY; Irvington HS; Fremont, CA; (4); Dance Clb; Drama Clb; Ski Clb; School Musical; School Play; Variety Show; Stu Cncl; Capt Cheerldng; Hon Roll; Rotary Awd; DARE Project; Jr Miss Schlrshp Pageant; Viking Awd; San Diego ST U.

MYADA, ELAINE L; John Muir HS; Pasadena, CA; (2); Church Yth Grp; Acpl Chr; School Musical; JV Vllybl; Church Cheerleading; Track And Volleyball.

MYER, PAMELA A; Monte Vista HS; Spring Valley, CA; (3); 22/373; Treas Church Yth Grp; Key Clb; Chorus; JV Gym; Hon Roll; CSF; Amnsty Intl Clb; Mth.

MYERS, ALAN A; Monte Vista HS; Spring Valley, CA; (2); Aud/Vis; Church Yth Grp; Cmnty Wkr; DECA; Drama Clb; FBLA; Spanish Clb; Varsity Clb; Var Bsbl; Var Ftbl; Marine Corp; Wrtr.

MYERS, APRIL A; Poway HS; Poway, CA; (1); Church Yth Grp; Key Clb; High Hon Roll; UCSD; Teacher.

MYERS, CHAD W; Arroyo Grande HS; Nipomo, CA; (2); JV Bsbl; JV Bsktbl; Hon Roll; UCLA.

MYERS, ELIZABETH A; Torrance HS; Torrance, CA; (2); Girl Scts; Hist Frsh Cls; Treas Jr Cls; Swmmng; U CA Irvine; Bus.

MYERS, EVE; Morro Bay HS; Los Osos, CA; (2); Church Yth Grp; French Clb; VP SADD; Capt Cheerldng; Pres Acad Fit Awd; BYU; Jrnlsm.

MYERS, JACQUELYN F; Paraclete HS; Lancaster, CA; (2); Hosp Aide; JA; Key Clb; Service Clb; SADD; Drill Tm; Treas Frsh Cls; JV Bsktbl; JV Trk; Archaeology.

MYERS, JENNIFER L; Morro Bay HS; Los Osos, CA; (4); 30/200; Var Capt Bsktbl; Var Capt Vllybl; Elks Awd; San Luis Cnty Plyr Of Yr 89-90; MVP Vlybl Season 89; MVP For Bsktbl Season 89-90; Cuesta Coll; Sprts Med.

MYERS, JOSH; El Cerrito HS; El Cerrito, CA; (1); Church Yth Grp; JV Bsktbl.

MYERS, KARA C; El Camino Fundamental HS; Sacramento, CA; (3); 6/366; French Clb; Cit Awd; High Hon Roll; NHS; Yrbk Frnch Sprstr & Eng.

MYERS, KARIN L; Lemoore HS; Lemoore, CA; (4); 17/294; Church Yth Grp; Drama Clb; Teachers Aide; Chorus; School Play; Stage Crew; Variety Show; Lit Mag; JV Var Gym; Var Swmmng; Prdctn Felix Awds Show; Capt V Gymnastics, Mst Vlbl JV Gymnstcs; Bnk Amer Cert Awd Achvt Drama; Sonoma ST; Math.

MYERS, MARCUS S J; Ramona HS; Ramona, CA; (3); 13/294; Phtg Nwsp; Ed Yrbk; Hon Roll; Capt Acad Team; Jostens/Canon Schl Pict Cont Hnrbl Mntn; CSF; People To People Yth Pgm; FL ST U; Hstry.

MYERS, MARK J; North Bakersfield HS; Bakersfield, CA; (2); Church Yth Grp; Cmnty Wkr; Ntl Merit Schol; Summer Job; CA Inst Tech; Envrnmntl Engr.

MYERS, MARLO R; Escondido HS; Escondido, CA; (4); Trk; Hon Roll; Yrbk; Reach Awd Schlstc Achvt; Palomar CC; Bus.

MYERS, MARTHA M; Hoover HS; Fresno, CA; (3); Church Yth Grp; 4-H; Teachers Aide; Sftbl; Vllybl; 4-H; Fresno ST; Lrg Anml Vet.

MYERS, RAY; Hoover HS; Fresno, CA; (2); 62/480; JV Ftbl; Var Wt Lftg; Var Wrstlng; Hon Roll; Fresno ST; Bus Law.

MYERS, REBEKAH L; Lutheran HS Of Orange County; Placentia, CA; (2); Var Crs Cntry; Var Socr; Var Trk; Lancer Pride Awd, Cross Cntry & Treas.

MYERS, STEPHANIE; Castro Valley HS; Castro Valley, CA; (2); 235/404; Acpl Chr; Variety Show; UC Santa Cruz; Sci.

MYERS, SUSAN; Ernest Righetti HS; Santa Maria, CA; (1); 1/350; Church Yth Grp; Pep Clb; Capt Cheerldng; Golf; High Hon Roll; Outstndng Achvt Awd.

MYERS, SUSAN L; Orange Glen HS; Escondido, CA; (1); Drama Clb; Stage Crew; Hon Roll; Cndstrpng Hosp Dist; SDSU; Spec Educ.

MYERS, THANE K; South Fork HS; Redway, CA; (3); Treas Am Leg Boys St; Art Clb; Intnl Clb; Math Clb; SADD; High Hon Roll; Kiwanis Awd; Prfct Atten Awd; Var Tennis; Tae Kwon Do; Fire Prtctn & Prvntn; UC San Diego.

MYHRE, STEVEN M; Bullard HS; Fresno, CA; (2); JV Var Bsbl; Jv Bsbl MVP; Grls Sftbl Coach 89 & 90; Arts; Arts.

MYLAR, BRANDON B; Oakdale HS; Oakdale, CA; (3); Drama Clb; Spanish Clb; J-Club; U Santa Barbara; Engl.

MYLES, LA SHON; Arlington HS; Riverside, CA; (3); Church Yth Grp; Office Aide; Pep Clb; Teachers Aide; Varsity Clb; Flag Corp; Mrchg Band; JV Var Cheerldng; JV Var Socr; Hon Roll; Black Stu Union Secy; Cal ST San Bernardino; Educ.

MYRICK, ALISSA B; Bishop O'dowd HS; Berkeley, CA; (2); Cmnty Wkr; Drama Clb; School Musical; School Play; High Hon Roll; Hon Roll; Most Outstndng Frshmn Girl; CSF; Ped Med.

MYTELS, LAURA; Palo Alto HS; Palo Alto, CA; (4); 69/319; Girl Scts; Nwsp; Rep Soph Cls; Rep Jr Cls; Stu Cncl; Intrml Socr; Hon Roll; Ntl Merit Ltr; Silver Seal Awd Contributng To Schl; Palo Alto Unified Schl Dist Distinguished Schlr; Amnesty Intl; Bates Coll.

MYUNG, EUNICE; University HS; Irvine, CA; (4); 28/500; Sec Church Yth Grp; Service Clb; VP Spanish Clb; Orch; School Musical; Lit Mag; Stu Cncl; Ntl Merit SF; Pres Acad Fit Awd; Spanish NHS.

MYUNG, JANE; University HS; Irvine, CA; (2); Church Yth Grp; Spanish Clb; High Hon Roll; Jr NHS; NHS; Pres Acad Fit Awd; High Hnr 1st Yr Algebra, Geom Golden St Exam; Bi.

NA, EUNYOUNG J; Pius X HS; Huntington Park, CA; (3); Pres Treas Math Clb; Spanish Clb; Church Choir; Jazz Band; Nwsp; Sec Sr Cls; High Hon Roll; NHS; Rotary Awd; CA Schlrshp Fed; Pre-Med.

NA, SUSAN S; Mira Costa HS; Manhattan Beach, CA; (2); Hosp Aide; Key Clb; Service Clb; Rep Pep Band; Rep Soph Cls; JV Trk; Hon Roll; Prfct Atten Awd; Girls Lg; Physlgy Club; CSF; Med.

NA-NAKORNPANOM, ARTHUR; Katella HS; Anaheim, CA; (4); 7/350; Computer Clb; JA; Key Clb; Letterman Clb; Math Clb; Math Tm; Quiz Bowl; Scholastic Bowl; Science Clb; Varsity Clb; Gldn ST Exm-Geom Hgh Hnrs; CSF Gld Seal Bear; S Cal Jr Glf Assn Schlrshp; UCLA; Aerospc Engr.

NABAVI, MARYAM D; Irvine HS; Irvine, CA; (3); Church Yth Grp; French Clb; Hosp Aide; Teachers Aide; Swmmng; Tennis; Vllybl; High Hon Roll; Hon Roll; CA Schlrshp Fed 3 Yrs; UCI; Sci.

NABAVI-NOORI, SKARLETE; Palm Desert HS; Palm Desert, CA; (4); 36/319; High Hon Roll; Hon Roll; Ntl Merit Ltr; Prfct Atten Awd; Math Awd; Law.

NACARIO, MICHELLE; Southwest HS; San Diego, CA; (2); Key Clb; Drill Tm; Stu Cncl; CSF; UCLA; Bus.

NACEY, JOHN; Damien HS; Claremont, CA; (2); Letterman Clb; Var Capt Golf; Hon Roll.

NACK, ADINA; Los Alamitos HS; Rossmoor, CA; (4); Spanish Clb; Temple Yth Grp; Nwsp; JV Var Bsktbl; JV Capt Crs Cntry; JV Var Trk; Ntl Merit SF; Acad Dcthln 3rd Pl Orange Cntry; UCLA; Soc Sci.

NACNAC, WENDELL D; Pittsburg HS; Pittsburg, CA; (2); Hon Roll; UCLA; Bus.

NADAL, JOYCE ANN; Notre Dame HS; San Jose, CA; (2); 30/94; Drama Clb; Intnl Clb; Library Aide; Pep Clb; SADD; Chorus; Stage Crew; VP Jr Cls; Cheerldng; Hon Roll; Peer Cnslg; ASB Publicity Secy 90-91.

NADON, KIMBERLY R; Mt Whitney HS; Visalia, CA; (2); Church Yth Grp; French Clb; Band; Mrchg Band; Pep Band; Swmmng; Hon Roll; Scicon Cnslr; Spch Thrpst.

NAEEM, AYESHA; West HS; Bakersfield, CA; (1); Hosp Aide; Key Clb; Poetry Awd Silver Poet Awd 89; Harvard; Med.

NAEIMI, PANY; Hillsdale HS; San Mateo, CA; (3); JV Office Aide; Science Clb; Teachers Aide; Yrbk; Hon Roll; CSF; Spanish Awd; World Affrs Clb; Dentstry.

NAEVE, TRENT; Hesperia HS; Hesperia, CA; (3); 63/613; Church Yth Grp; German Clb; Ski Clb; Teachers Aide; Bsbl; Ftbl; Wt Lftg; High Hon Roll; Hon Roll; Calculus.

NAFTULIN, RYAN E; Palos Verdes HS; Palos Vrds Pen, CA; (4); 15/337; Model UN; Spanish Clb; Ed Nwsp; Var Capt Swmmng; NHS; Pres Acad Fit Awd; Interact Club; Sci Dept Awd; Stu Act League Pres; Amer Acad Of Achvt; U Of MI.

NAFTZGER, MARK P; Redlands HS; Redlands, CA; (2); Socr; Hon Roll; Pres Acad Fit Awd; Frgn Lang Qrtly Dept Awd.

NAGAI, LENA; Rowland HS; Rowland Heights, CA; (2); Cmnty Wkr; Dance Clb; 4-H; French Clb; Science Clb; Drill Tm; Cit Awd; Hon Roll; Prfct Atten Awd; GSE Hnrs; Awd For 4.0 GPA; Comm Art.

NAGAR, NANDINI RAO; Tamalpais HS; Tiburon, CA; (2); SADD; Chorus; Church Choir; Hon Roll; Friday Nght Live Club; UC Davis; Chld Psych.

NAGASAWA, MAKO A; Whitney HS; Cerritos, CA; (4); 2/169; Church Yth Grp; Hosp Aide; Stu Cncl; Var Capt Swmmng; Sec NHS; Ntl Merit Schol; Opt Clb Awd; Sal; Soup Ktchn & Wldlf Fndrsng Dir; Stanford.

NAGATA, MICHELE L; Orosi HS; Orosi, CA; (4); 1/122; Church Yth Grp; Band; Pres Soph Cls; Pres Stu Cncl; Bausch & Lomb Sci Awd; Hon Roll; Val; Mock Trail Tm; Intl Order Of The Rainbow For Gilrs; Cutler/Orosi Chamber Of Commerce Jr Achvt Awd; Pepperdne U; Bus Admin.

NAGATA, STEVE T; Los Altos HS; Hacienda Hts, CA; (3); 75/367; VP Band; Sec Jazz Band; Sec Mrchg Band; Pep Band; Cit Awd; Hon Roll; Prfct Atten Awd; Trnmt Roses Hnr Band 90; SCSBOA Hnr Jazz Band; UCSD; Bio Sci.

NAGEL, MARK S; San Ramon Valley HS; San Ramon, CA; (3); 35/385; VICA; Off Soph Cls; Off Jr Cls; Stu Cncl; Var L Bsktbl; Hon Roll; Pres Acad Fit Awd; Golden St Alg Awd; Schlr Athlt Awd 3 Yrs; Bus Adm.

NAGI, OMAR A; Monache HS; Porterville, CA; (3); High Hon Roll; Lion Awd; Prfct Atten Awd; Srptmst Frm Dist Wnnr; Sci Olympd Tm; CSF; Engrng.

NAGLE, KIMBERLY J; Ygnacio Valley HS; Concord, CA; (1); Band; Mrchg Band; Var L Swmmng; High Hon Roll; CSF; Archaeology.

NAGPAL, AMRIT; Bellarmine College Prep; Los Altos, CA; (1); Intrml Ftbl; JV Var Golf; Intrml Sftbl.

NAGRA, JASWINDER; Washington Union HS; Fresno, CA; (2); FCA; FBLA; Intnl Clb; Sec Soph Cls; Tennis; High Hon Roll; CSF; Friday Night Live; Amnesty Intl Co-Actvts Dir.

NAGTALON, DENNIS G; Westmoor HS; Daly City, CA; (3); Math Clb; Thesps; Varsity Clb; School Play; Rep Jr Cls; Var Cheerldng; Var Swmmng; Var Vllybl; Hon Roll; Prfct Atten Awd; Amnesty Intl; Collegiate Schltc Fed; West Point; Med.

NAGUIAT, RAMON M; St John Bosco HS; Cerritos, CA; (2); Church Yth Grp; Cmnty Wkr; French Clb; Key Clb; High Hon Roll; CSF; Frnch Excllnce Awd; Jr Statesmn Assn; Berkeley; Corp Law.

NAGY, CHRISTINE A; Sacred Heart Prep; Menlo Park, CA; (1); Church Yth Grp; Hosp Aide; Service Clb; Chorus; Hon Roll; Photo; Med.

NAHAVANDI, KIOMARS; Corona HS; Corona, CA; (2); Office Aide; Bsktbl; Bus.

NAHORAI, GINA; University HS; Los Angeles, CA; (3); Rep Jr Cls; High Hon Roll; Hon Roll; CSF; Medical Careers Club VP; Doctor.

NAIDU, BERNARD N; Bishop O'dowd HS; Oakland, CA; (3); Church Yth Grp; Dance Clb; Cit Awd; Hon Roll; Prfct Atten Awd; San Jose ST; Elec Engrng.

NAIK, HURSH S; Calvary Christian Acad; El Sobrante, CA; (2); 2/15; Hosp Aide; Service Clb; Teachers Aide; Yrbk; Cit Awd; High Hon Roll; Hosp Volunteer; Med.

NAIMY, RICHARD; Oak Hill Prep; N Hollywood, CA; (3); Church Yth Grp; Cmnty Wkr; Drama Clb; FCA; Ski Clb; Teachers Aide; School Play; Stage Crew; Variety Show; Bsbl; Peer Grp Cnslr; UCLA; Bus.

NAJAFABADI, MARYAM A; Pasadena HS; Sierra Madre, CA; (1); French Clb; JA; Hon Roll; CSF; Badmntn Team; Creatv Wrtng Club; Cal Tech; Astronaut.

NAJERA, CYNTHIA; San Gabriel HS; Alhambra, CA; (4); 72/737; AFS; GAA; Hosp Aide; Service Clb; Spanish Clb; Chorus; School Play; Cheerldng; Crs Cntry; Hon Roll; Psych Clb; Acad Achvt Scl Stds; Amor Amici; PCC; Brdcst Jrnlsm.

NAJERA, GEROME R; Don Bosco Technical Inst; Pico Rivera, CA; (3); L Var Bsbl; Intrml Bsktbl; Intrml Vllybl; Med.

NAJIB, SENA; Savanna HS; Anaheim, CA; (2); Teachers Aide; Cal Poly Promona; Doctor.

NAJLIS, RAY J; James Logan HS; Hayward, CA; (3); JV Var Bsbl; JV Bsktbl; JV Var Ftbl; Hon Roll; UC Berkeley; Entrepreneur.

NAJUMI, MARY; Chaffey HS; Ontario, CA; (1); FHA; Prfct Atten Awd; Art Achvt Cert; Teacher.

NAKADA, GRACE; Venice HS; Los Angeles, CA; (4); Flag Corp; Yrbk; Off Frsh Cls; Cit Awd; Pres Acad Fit Awd; Nghbrhd Yth Assn Yth Cmnty Srvc Awd; UC Irvine; Bus.

NAKAHARA, STEVE R; Pacifica HS; Garden Grv, CA; (3); Spanish Clb; JV Var Socr; Skiing; Vllybl.

NAKAMOTO, LEANNE; Cypress HS; Cypress, CA; (3); Key Clb; Pep Clb; Service Clb; Varsity Clb; Yrbk; Var Capt Crs Cntry; Var Trk; Hon Roll; Yth Cmmssn Tsk Frc; Lib Vlntr; Crs Cntry Al-Empire Leag Jr Tm 89-90; Prncpls Hnr Rl; GATE Idntfd Stu; Optmtry.

NAKAMOTO, STACIE; Tustin HS; Tustin, CA; (3); Cmnty Wkr; Rep Frsh Cls; Rep Soph Cls; Off Jr Cls; Cheerldng; Crs Cntry; Hon Roll; Ntl Merit Ltr; Mem Of OCAD; Rustin HS Elec Cmmsr 1990-91; Mem Keywanettes Clb At Tustin HS.

NAKAMURA, LINDA R; Gardena HS; Gardena, CA; (3); Church Yth Grp; Intnl Clb; Library Aide; Sec Service Clb; Off Frsh Cls; Score Keeper.

NAKAMURA, MAGGIE M; Monterey HS; Monterey, CA; (3); Ed Yrbk; Pres Frsh Cls; VP Soph Cls; Sec Jr Cls; Treas Sr Cls; Var Fld Hcky; Var Capt Trk; Var Vllybl; High Hon Roll; Pres NHS.

NAKAMURA, MAILE M; Glen A Wilson HS; Hacienda Hgts, CA; (4); Key Clb; Science Clb; Stat Bsktbl; Score Keeper; Stat Socr; JV Swmmng; JV Var Tennis; High Hon Roll; Hon Roll; Pres Acad Fit Awd; Numerous Tnns Awds & Hnrs; CA ST Fullerton U; Bus.

NAKAMURA, MIRI; Marina HS; Huntington Bch, CA; (1); Var Swmmng; UCLA; Interprtr.

NAKAMURA, YOSHIKO J; Alhambra HS; Alhambra, CA; (4); 220/690; Pep Clb; Treas Service Clb; Band; JV Bsktbl; JV Swmmng; Grls Leag Art Chrprsn; Water Polo Statscn; Pasadena City Coll; Japanese.

NAKANISHI, STACEY; University HS; Irvine, CA; (2); Church Yth Grp; Drama Clb; JCL; Spanish Clb; JV Crs Cntry; JV Socr; Tennis; JV Trk; Latin Clb; Ski Clb; Club Soccer Team Capt; Natl Charity League Hstrn, Recrdng Sec Reprtr; UCI; Med.

NAKANO, ANGELA T; Wilcox HS; Sunnyvale, CA; (1); 1/400; Church Yth Grp; Spanish Clb; Sec Frsh Cls; JV Bsktbl; Var L Tennis; High Hon Roll; Amnsty Intl.

NAKAO, KEITH S; Don Bosco Technical Inst; Whittier, CA; (3); Church Yth Grp; Cmnty Wkr; Intrml Vllybl; U Of HI; Bus Admin.

NAKAO, SUSAN M; Fountain Valley HS; Fountain Valley, CA; (2); JV Bsktbl; JV Trk; Hon Roll; Mst Imprvd Athltc Awd Trk; Cert Mrt Awd Piano.

NAKASONE, LINDA; Fairfax Magnet Of Visual Arts; N Hollywood, CA; (4); 9/60; French Clb; Office Aide; Prfct Atten Awd; RI Schl Dsgn Annl Art Awd; Vsl Arts Mgnt Ctr Mst Artstc Awd; Dept Awd Art; Otis Art Inst Of Parsons Sch.

NAKATANI, GRANT M; Bonita Vista HS; Chula Vista, CA; (2); 1/600; Model UN; JV Trk; DAR Awd; Pres Acad Fit Awd; Hghst Male For Bonita Vista PSAT; Law.

NAKAZAWA, SHINO; George Washington HS; San Francisco, CA; (4); Church Yth Grp; Varsity Clb; Pres Soph Cls; Chrmn Stu Cncl; Tennis; High Hon Roll; Hon Roll; Table Tnns; Achvt Awds; Vlntr Acvtvs Mntlly Defcnt People; San Francisco ST U; Intl Rltns.

NAKAZONO, CHIHARU; San Marcos HS; La Costa, CA; (3); French Clb; Intnl Clb; Key Clb; Spanish Clb; High Hon Roll; Hon Roll; CSF; UC San Diego.

NAKHAM, SANH; Grant HS Dist; North Highlands, CA; (3); SADD; Teachers Aide.

NAKHLA, PHILIP; Valley Christian HS; La Mirada, CA; (2); Band; Jazz Band; Mrchg Band; Pep Band; School Musical; Var Crs Cntry; JV Socr; JV Trk; JV Vllybl; Hon Roll.

NALIBOFF, TENLAY J; Santa Monica HS; Santa Monica, CA; (1); Ski Clb; Tennis; Retail Sales Store; UCSD; Mrktng.

NALLE, MARIDI T; South Pasadena HS; South Pasadena, CA; (2); Drama Clb; Chorus; School Musical; Yrbk; Cheerldng; Sftbl; CA Chldrns Choir Colburn Schl Of Perf Arts; Peace Club Core Facilitator; U CA.

NAM, ARTHUR; Earl Warren HS; Downey, CA; (4); 11/435; FBLA; Letterman Clb; Quiz Bowl; Var Trk; Cit Awd.

NAM, GEORGE A; Monterey HS; Monterey, CA; (3); FCA; Letterman Clb; JV Ftbl; Var Swmmng; Wt Lftg; JV Capt Wrstlng; Hon Roll; Acad Decathelon; UC Santa Barbara; Envrnmnt Eng.

NAM, JULI; A Lincoln HS; San Francisco, CA; (3); Library Aide; Church Choir; Stu Cncl; Mgr(s); Hon Roll.

NAM, SANG CHUN; Grant HS; Los Angeles, CA; (4); 5/650; Service Clb; Hon Roll; U CA Berkeley; Econ.

NAMBIAR, SANJAY; Torrance HS; Torrance, CA; (2); 1/454; Latin Clb; JV Vllybl; High Hon Roll; Hon Roll; Reflectns Essay Cont Wnnr; UCLA.

NAMBOUN, SANYA; Bassett HS; La Puente, CA; (3); Cit Awd; Hon Roll; Treas Jr NHS; NHS; Prfct Atten Awd; Peer Cnslng; UC Riverside; Bus.

NAMEKATA, JAMES S; Ramona HS; Riverside, CA; (3); 2/450; Scholastic Bowl; JV Bsbl; High Hon Roll; Jr Sho-Dan Ho Karate; Schl, Dist, Inland & St Sci Fair Wnnr; PTA Reflection Cont Schl & Cnty Wnnr; Ramona; Comp Sci.

NAMGOONG, JUHNGHA; Pasadena HS; Sierra Madre, CA; (2); #1 In Class; Chess Clb; French Clb; Red Cross Aide; Spanish Clb; School Play; Yrbk; Bsktbl; Sftbl; Tennis; Vllybl; Badminton Player Var No 1 Dbl; Achvmt Awd; Most Imprvd Player Badminton Trophy; UCLA; Law.

NAMLIK, DAWN D; Poway HS; Poway, CA; (3); 348/728; VP SADD; Hosp Aide; Debate Tm; Church Yth Grp; Cert Mrt Amer Lit; Amnesty Intl; Grossmont Coll; Wrk People.

NAMMACHANTHY, KERK; Grace M Davis HS; Modesto, CA; (3); Boy Scts; Church Yth Grp; FFA; Intnl Clb; Intrml Ftbl; Var Socr; Prfct Atten Awd.

NANCE, JAMES D; St Franics HS; Sunnyvale, CA; (3); Boy Scts; Ntl Merit Ltr; Arch.

NANCE, JASON; El Camino Real HS; West Hills, CA; (2); 40/450; Church Yth Grp; Teachers Aide; Drm Mjr(t); Jazz Band; Mrchg Band; UCLA; Music.

NANCE, JENNIFER L; Grossmont HS; La Mesa, CA; (2); 55/460; Cmnty Wkr; German Clb; Hosp Aide; Ski Clb; Stu Cncl; Trk; Hon Roll; Brdcst Jrnlst.

NANDINO, DANNY; Garfield HS; Los Angeles, CA; (3); Computer Clb; Math Clb; Orch; High Hon Roll; Hon Roll; Prfct Atten Awd; Pres Schlr; Cngresnl Yth Ldrshp Cncl Awd; UC Berkeley; Mchncl Engrng.

NANES, DEVRA; Troy HS; Fullerton, CA; (3); 40/330; Cmnty Wkr; Drama Clb; Pep Clb; Ski Clb; Spanish Clb; Temple Yth Grp; Drill Tm; School Play; Variety Show; JV Cheerldng; TALIT.

NANGIN, LINDA; Saddleback HS; Orange, CA; (4); 65/520; FBLA; Humnts.

NANQUIL, JOSEPHINE C; Notre Dame HS; San Jose, CA; (3); 16/90; Cmnty Wkr; Intnl Clb; Science Clb; Hon Roll; NHS; Girl Scts; VP Stu Cncl; Charity Of Stu Fed Vol; VP Sci Club; Cath Yth Org; San Jose ST U; Med Tech.

NANTHA, PHOUSYDAO; Arlington HS; Riverside, CA; (3); FBLA; Yrbk; Wrstlng; High Hon Roll; Pres Acad Fit Awd; Cal Poly Pomona; Engrng.

NAPENAS, GINA J; Notre Dame Acad; Los Angeles, CA; (3); Hosp Aide; Rep Yrbk; Rep Soph Cls; Rep Jr Cls; VP Sr Cls; Hon Roll; NHS; Med.

NAPIZA, MARIA BELINDA R; Vallejo SR HS; Vallejo, CA; (4); Sec Science Clb; Acpl Chr; Chorus; Hon Roll; Merit Awd Engl; Human Rghts Essy Cntst Wnnr; Asian Am Clb; Succs Consrtm Awd High Grade Pt Avrg; Golden Gate U; Hotl Mgmt.

NAPOLES, DANTE; Inglewood HS; Inglewood, CA; (2); Jazz Band; Orch; Play Classical & Blues Guitar; Enjoy Rdng His Books; USC; His.

NAPPER, MONIQUE D; Irvine HS; Irvine, CA; (3); 111/512; Church Yth Grp; Cmnty Wkr; Key Clb; Teachers Aide; Chorus; Treas Sr Cls; Rep Stu Cncl; Var Bsktbl; JV Trk; Jack & Jill Amer Pres; Blck Stu Union VP; Johnson C Smith; Psych.

NAQUIN, THERESA M; St Joseph HS; Long Beach, CA; (2); Church Yth Grp; GAA; Office Aide; Drill Tm; JV Tennis; Hon Roll; Dnc Prfrmnc; CA Schlrshp Fed; Smll Dnc Tm; UCSD; Pre Law.

NARANJO, JORGE; Hueneme HS; Oxnard, CA; (2); Key Clb; Church Choir; Yrbk; Off Soph Cls; Socr; Hon Roll; Karate Comptn Kickboxing Intl Trnmt.

NARANJO, MARGARITA; Sequoia HS; Redwood City, CA; (1); Cmnty Wkr; JA; AFS; Ed Yrbk; Cit Awd; Hon Roll; Maiso Club-Human Relations Officer; CA Schlrshp Fed Member; Evening Of Excellence-Awd Acad Achvt; Coll Of Notre Dame; Bus Adminst.

NARANJO, RAQUEL; San Fernando HS; San Fernando, CA; (3); Library Aide; Science Clb; Off Sr Cls; Stu Cncl; Sftbl; Hon Roll; Future Schlrs Pgm; I Love To Read Bk Clb; Keywanettes; Kndgtn Tchr.

NARAYANAN, KARTHIK R; Whitney HS; Cerritos, CA; (2); JA; Latin Clb; Band; Rptr Nwsp; Hon Roll; U Of SC.

NARDELLO III, JOHN R; Aptos HS; Aptos, CA; (1); Boy Scts; Prfct Atten Awd; Pres Acad Fit Awd; MIT; Comp Prgmr.

NARDINELLI, JONATHAN A; El Camino Fundamental HS; Citrus Heights, CA; (4); 88/341; SADD; JV Var Tennis; Cit Awd; Hon Roll; Hnr Can Bearer Grad Cls 89; CA ST Sacramento; Bus.

NAREDO, TONY; Oroville HS; Oroville, CA; (3); 1/193; Letterman Clb; Varsity Clb; Rptr Nwsp; Rep Jr Cls; Var JV Ftbl; Var Socr; Var Tennis; Var Trk; High Hon Roll; Prfct Atten Awd.

NAREDO III, TONY J; Oroville HS; Oroville, CA; (3); 1/193; Letterman Clb; Rptr Nwsp; Rep Soph Cls; JV Var Ftbl; High Hon Roll; Prfct Atten Awd; Pres Acad Fit Awd; Var Socr; Var Tennis.

NARH, WINFRED; Junipero Serra HS; Gardena, CA; (2); Dance Clb; Pres Soph Cls; Capt JV Bsktbl; Cit Awd; Hon Roll; Acad Awds; Mst Insprtnl JV Bsktbl Plyr Awd; Comp Engr.

NARIDO II, EULALAE; Los Angeles HS; La Puente, CA; (4); Office Aide; Teachers Aide; Hon Roll; Prfct Atten Awd; Filipino Clb; Ephebian Soc; Cal ST Los Angeles; Comp Sci.

NARIKAWA, AUDRA; Whitney HS; Cerritos, CA; (2); Church Yth Grp; Cmnty Wkr; Key Clb; Phtg Yrbk; JV Swmmng; Cit Awd; Hon Roll; Pres Acad Fit Awd; Prom Cmmtte; Cls Photo; Japanese Clb; UCLA; Educ.

NARIO, PATRICIA G; St Francis HS; Sacramento, CA; (3); VP Service Clb; SADD; Chorus; Rizal Leo Club Of Sacramento Sec; Cultrl Dnc; CSF; Latin Hnr Soc; Law.

NARITA, KIMBERLY M; Grace Davis HS; Modesto, CA; (4); 113/450; Teachers Aide; JV Var Diving; Powder Puff Ftbl; Var Sftbl; Var Capt Vllybl; Cit Awd; Hon Roll; Pres Acad Fit Awd; Diving-Sectnls-16th/13th Pl-88/89; Vllybl-KLOC Trnmnt-MVP Team 1st; Modesto JC.

NARONG, KETSADA; Hoover HS; San Diego, CA; (2).

NARTATEZ, MARK L; Don Bosco Tech Inst; Walnut, CA; (3); Service Clb; Hon Roll; JETS Awd; NHS; Prfct Atten Awd; Wharton; Bus.

NARULA, GURPREET S; Santa Clara HS; Santa Clara, CA; (3).

NARVAEZ, ALICIA G; St Paul HS; Pico Rivera, CA; (3); Intnl Clb; Spanish Clb; Hon Roll; NHS; Spanish NHS; Sister Cities Club; Campus Mnstry Club; CSF; Pre Med.

NARVAEZ, JACQUELINE; St Genevieve HS; Canoga Park, CA; (2); Spanish Clb; SADD; Civil Air Patrol Air Force; Bus.

NARVARTE, VIVIAN B; Thomas A Edison HS; Stockton, CA; (3); Debate Tm; Sec NFL; Speech Tm; Sec Soph Cls; Var Tennis; High Hon Roll; Hon Roll; NHS; Mdcl Fld.

NARVASA, DELILAH; Leuzinger HS; Lawndale, CA; (1); Prfct Atten Awd; Prncpls List Awd For 4.0 GPA; Earth Envrnmntlst Clb.

NASCIMENTO, DANIELA; San Ramon Valley HS; Danville, CA; (2); 12/400; Band; Jazz Band; School Musical; School Play; JV Bsktbl; JV Vllybl; High Hon Roll; UCLA; Engrng.

NASH, AMZIE; Monterey HS; Seaside, CA; (3); Letterman Clb; Teachers Aide; L Bsktbl; Hon Roll; Ntl Merit Ltr; Loyola-Marymount; Bus.

NASH, ANGIE; Calvary Chapel HS; Santa Ana, CA; (2); Church Yth Grp; Drama Clb; Var Capt Cheerldng; Hon Roll.

NASH, EMILY; Big Valley HS; Adin, CA; (2); Church Yth Grp; 4-H; FFA; Church Choir; JV Bsktbl; JV Cheerldng; 4-H Awd; Hon Roll; UC Davis; Med.

NASH, ERIK B; Cupertino HS; San Jose, CA; (1); JV Ftbl; De Anza; Bnkng.

NASH, JON D; Golden West HS; Visalia, CA; (2); Church Yth Grp; JV Bsbl; JV Bsktbl; Intrml Wt Lftg; NHS; Prfct Atten Awd; Pres Acad Fit Awd; Ntre Dm U; Engrng.

NASH, KAREN M; Upper Lake HS; Upper Lake, CA; (3); Art Clb; GAA; SADD; Bsktbl; Trk; Pres Acad Fit Awd; Nrsng.

NASH, MARGARET; Tokay HS; Lodi, CA; (1); Dance Clb; School Play; Cheerldng; Pom Pon; Hon Roll; CSF.

NASH, MATT E; Orange Glen HS; Escondido, CA; (3); Church Yth Grp; FCA; German Clb; Key Clb; Quiz Bowl; Band; Mrchg Band; Orch; Pep Band; Rptr Nwsp; Acad Dcthln; Work; Multnomah Schl Of Bible; Mnstry.

NASH, MELINDA; Calvary Chapel HS; Santa Ana, CA; (1); Dance Clb; Girl Scts; Library Aide; Teachers Aide; Variety Show; Yrbk; Cheerldng; UCSB; Jrnlst.

NASH, NATHANIEL H; Escalon HS; Escalon, CA; (1); 11/154; German Clb; Varsity Clb; JV Bsbl; JV Capt Ftbl; JV Wt Lftg; Var Wrstlng; Hon Roll; Prfct Atten Awd; Pres Acad Fit Awd; U OR; Sprts.

NASH, SEAN L; Skyline HS; Oakland, CA; (3); Thesps; School Play; Stage Crew; Hon Roll; Art.

NASH, STEPHANIE; Big Valley HS; Adin, CA; (4); Art Clb; Church Yth Grp; Debate Tm; Drama Clb; FCA; 4-H; FFA; GAA; Library Aide; Pep Clb; Phys Educ Teacher.

NASIR, LISA J; Bridgemont HS; Pacifica, CA; (2); Church Yth Grp; Yrbk; Sec Treas Soph Cls; Stu Cncl; High Hon Roll.

NASR, ROSHANAK; Dana Hills HS; Laguna Niguel, CA; (3); Save Clb; UCI; Psych.

NASRAWI, SWETLANA E; Orange HS; Orange, CA; (3); Sec Treas Church Yth Grp; Rep Drama Clb; Key Clb; School Musical; School Play; Co-Ed Yrbk; Var Bsktbl; JV Vllybl; CA ST Fullerton; Advrtsng.

NASSANEY, JOSEPHINE; Le Lycee Francais De L A HS; Harbor City, CA; (2); Church Yth Grp; Dance Clb; Drama Clb; French Clb; Hosp Aide; Pep Clb; Ski Clb; Spanish Clb; Acpl Chr; Chorus; Bard; Psych.

NASSAR, TAREK; San Marin HS; Novato, CA; (3); Chess Clb; Intnl Clb; JV Var Trk; CA Golden Bell Exam Awd Algebra, Geom; CA Schlrshp Fed Jr Rep; Comp Engrng.

NASSER, ANNA M; Villa Park HS; Orange, CA; (3); Sec VP Church Yth Grp; French Clb; Church Choir; Score Keeper; Hon Roll; Tchng.

NASSIROGHLI, LAYLA; Torrey Pines HS; Solana Beach, CA; (3); 54/457; Var Fld Hcky; JV Var Socr; Hon Roll; Hnrble Mntn Palamar Leag Glrs Sccr; Hnrs CA Gldn St Exm; CSF; 2nd Tm Palamar Leag Grls Sccr; U Of OR.

NASTASI, DIONNE; Birmingham HS; Van Nuys, CA; (2); Dance Clb; FBLA; Pep Clb; SADD; Capt Drill Tm; School Musical; Off Frsh Cls; Off Soph Cls; Mgr Swmmng; Hon Roll; Bus.

NASTAV, LEANDRA M; Mountain Empire SR HS; Campo, CA; (2); Art Clb; Spanish Clb; Band; Mrchg Band; Hon Roll; Hnr Soc Clb; Acad Ltr Jr Var.

NATESUWON, NAVAPORN N; Clovis West HS; Clovis, CA; (3); Church Yth Grp; French Clb; Intnl Clb; Crs Cntry; Trk; High Hon Roll; Hld Job All Through HS; UC Davis; Orthpdc Srgry.

NATI, CHRISTINE R; Hogan SR HS; Vallejo, CA; (2); Church Yth Grp; Science Clb; Spanish Clb; SADD; Church Choir; Rptr Nwsp; Cit Awd; Hon Roll; NHS; Cert Of Mrt In Sci & Music; U CA Davis; Med.

NATION, SETH; Redlands HS; Redlands, CA; (2); 220/1600; Var JV Ftbl; Notre Dame; T V Brdcstng.

NATION, TRACI J; Foothill HS; Santa Ana, CA; (3); Drama Clb; Thesps; Flag Corp; School Musical; School Play; Stage Crew; High Hon Roll; Hon Roll; PFO Awd; Pepperdine; Theatre.

NATIUK, JULI-ANN R; Newbury Park Adventist Acad; Thousand Oaks, CA; (4); 2/34; Church Yth Grp; Ski Clb; VP Spanish Clb; Band; School Play; Yrbk; Treas Stu Cncl; High Hon Roll; Pres Acad Fit Awd; Blue Blt Krte; Pacific Union Coll.

NATIVIDAD, AVELIZA; Highlands HS; N Highlands, CA; (3); Church Yth Grp; Church Choir; Yrbk; Treas Frsh Cls; Treas Soph Cls; Treas Jr Cls; Var Cheerldng; Var Socr; High Hon Roll; Outstndng Jnr UCSB Hnrs Day 90; Sctry MESA; Sctry/Treas CSF; Engrng.

NATIVIDAD, LEE R; Whitney HS; Cerritos, CA; (3); Dance Clb; SADD; Rep Frsh Cls; Bsktbl; Ftbl; Swmmng; Tennis; Vllybl; Wt Lftg; Cit Awd; Club Kaibigan Pilipino Club; Prom Cmmtte; CA ST Long Beach; Nrsng.

NATVIG, SHERI E; Enterprise HS; Redding, CA; (4); Pres Church Yth Grp; Mu Alpha Theta; Sec Stu Cncl; JV Bsktbl; Powder Puff Ftbl; Cit Awd; High Hon Roll; Hon Roll; U Of CA Davis; Math.

NATWICK, LAURA M; Nevada Union HS; Nevada City, CA; (2); Church Yth Grp; Band; JV Fld Hcky; High Hon Roll; Hon Roll; Thanks For Being You Awd; French Concours Awd; Stanford; Actress.

NAUCK, STEVE F; John F Kennedy HS; Buena Park, CA; (4); Boy Scts; Church Yth Grp; Cmnty Wkr; Computer Clb; Debate Tm; FBLA; NFL; Red Cross Aide; Speech Tm; School Musical; FBLA 1st Chapter In Nation & Schlr; Stu Of Month; CA ST Fullerton; Commnctns.

NAUGHTON, CHARLENE R; Santa Margarita HS; Mission Viejo, CA; (3); Aud/Vis; Band; Pep Band; Phtg Yrbk; Rep Sr Cls; Var Capt Socr; Var Capt Trk; Hon Roll; Mst Vlbl Vrsty Sccr; Mst Vlbl Fld Vrsty Trc; All CIF Sthrn Sctn Sccr; U Of San Francisco; Advtsng.

NAUGHTON, MAEVE K; Saint Francis HS; Santa Clara, CA; (3); 110/292; Church Yth Grp; NFL; Pep Clb; Varsity Clb; Nwsp; Ed Yrbk; JV Sftbl; L Var Tennis; Intrml Vllybl; High Hon Roll.

NAUGLER, DE ANNE M; Seaside HS; Marina, CA; (2); Church Yth Grp; Church Choir; Swmmng; Hon Roll; Lab Tech.

NAUMANN, LAURIE J; Eureka HS; Eureka, CA; (3); AFS; Church Yth Grp; Hosp Aide; Service Clb; Pres Ski Clb; Pres Soph Cls; Pres Jr Cls; Pres Sr Cls; Stu Cncl; Intrml Socr; Exchng Stu Costa Rica; Global Confrnc Taos NM; Tennis 2 Cnty Dbls Chmpn 88-89; Span.

NAUTA, CARMELLITA R; Silver Valley HS; Fort Irwin, CA; (2); Library Aide; Sec SADD; Teachers Aide; Temple Yth Grp; Sec Chorus; Church Choir; School Musical; Sftbl; Capt Vllybl; Hon Roll; Bwlng Capt; Real Est.

NAUYEH, TRI D; Edison HS; Huntington Beach, CA; (2); Scuba Dvng; Law.

NAVA, MICHELLE; St Patrick-St Vincent HS; Vallejo, CA; (1); High Hon Roll; Ice Sktng, Jrnlsm; Stanford U; Medcl Genetic Engr.

NAVACH, JEFF M; Carlmont HS; San Carlos, CA; (3); Var JV Bsbl; Var Crs Cntry; Var JV Socr; High Hon Roll; Hon Roll; CSF.

NAVAL, GARRY; Earl Warren HS; Downey, CA; (4); 19/395; FBLA; Key Clb; Teachers Aide; JV Var Tennis; JV Trk; Cit Awd; Opt Clb Awd; Stu Mnth FBLA; 1st Pl Bus Orgnztn Comptn; CSF; UC Berkeley; Bus Admins.

NAVALTA JR, ILDEFONSO L; San Benito HS; Hollister, CA; (3); 38/343; Yrbk; Hon Roll; Peer Ldrshp; UCSD; Acctng.

NAVALTA, NORMAN G; San Benito HS; Hollister, CA; (2); 114/270; Boy Scts; Chess Clb; Computer Clb; Letterman Clb; Science Clb; Spanish Clb; Bsbl; Ftbl; Wt Lftg; Wrstlng; Comp Pgmr.

NAVAR, CATARINA; King/Drew Medical Magnet HS; Los Angeles, CA; (3); Hosp Aide; Math Tm; Spanish Clb; Flag Corp; Stu Cncl; Vllybl; Hon Roll; Prfct Atten Awd; Acad Pentathalon & Decathalon; Sci Project; Biochem.

NAVAR, VERONICA; Roosevelt HS; Los Angeles, CA; (3); Treas Church Yth Grp; Cmnty Wkr; Red Cross Aide; Teachers Aide; School Play; Stage Crew; Cit Awd; Hon Roll; Prfct Atten Awd; Coll Core Curr Acad Cncl Rep Awd; Cert Merit; Hnr Rl Cum Laude Cert; Loyola Marymount U; Elem Tchr.

NAVARRETE, ESTEBAN M; Kingsburg HS; Hanford, CA; (2).

NAVARRETE, GUILLERMO; Manor Baptist Christian Schl; Hayward, CA; (3); 1/3; Church Yth Grp; Office Aide; Speech Tm; Band; School Musical; Phtg Yrbk; VP Jr Cls; Var Bsktbl; Socr; High Hon Roll; Civil Air Patrol; Principals Awd; Coachs Awd; Bus.

NAVARRETE JR, GUILLERMO S; Manor Baptist Christian Schl; Hayward, CA; (3); Church Yth Grp; Library Aide; Office Aide; Speech Tm; Band; School Musical; School Play; Stage Crew; Rptr Nwsp; Yrbk; Cvl Air Patrol; Christian Character Awd; Coachs Awd; Bus.

NAVARRETE, JOSE A; Westside Alternative Schl; Santa Fe Springs, CA; (4); 1/12; Teachers Aide; Mgr Yrbk; Rep Frsh Cls; Rep Jr Cls; Treas Sr Cls; Var JV Bsktbl; Var JV Sftbl; Cit Awd; Val; U CA Irvine; Engl.

NAVARRETE, JOSE L; Central Union HS; El Centro, CA; (2); 107/665; JV Wrstlng; Hon Roll; San Diego ST U; Arch.

NAVARRETE, LUISA; Orosi HS; Cutler, CA; (1); Pre-Harvest Qn Fstvl 2nd Pl; Secy.

NAVARRETE, MARIA; Los Angeles HS; Los Angeles, CA; (4); Yrbk; Off Sr Cls; Hon Roll; De Vry Inst Tech; Acctng.

NAVARRETE, RAQUEL; Alverno Heights Academy For Girls; Pasadena, CA; (3); 14/67; Church Yth Grp; Off Soph Cls; Var Bsktbl; Hon Roll; CA Schlrshp Fed; Athl Cmmssn; Ed.

NAVARRETTE, VERONICA; Redwood HS; Visalia, CA; (4); 2/350; Church Yth Grp; Cmnty Wkr; Math Clb; Office Aide; Spanish Clb; Ed Nwsp; Pres Jr Cls; Var Diving; Hon Roll; NHS; Cmnty To Cmmndad Cross Cltural Ethnic Actvty W/Mexico; Visalia Cty 90; Ideal Miss Chrmgrl-Beauty Wnnr; Santa Crz CA U; Pltcl Sci.

NAVARRO, APOLONIA; Central HS; Fresno, CA; (4); #13 In Class; GAA; Latin Clb; Science Clb; JV Var Bsktbl; Var Sftbl; Lion Awd; Fresno ST; Arch.

NAVARRO, AURELIE; Hogan SR HS; Vallejo, CA; (3); Church Yth Grp; Cmnty Wkr; Hist FHA; Office Aide; Spanish Clb; Teachers Aide; Drill Tm; VP Jr NHS; Prfct Atten Awd; Pres Acad Fit Awd; U CA-BERKELEY; Acctng.

NAVARRO, AZUCENA; Abraham Lincoln HS; Los Angeles, CA; (2); FTA; Hon Roll; Prfct Atten Awd; Pres Acad Fit Awd; MESA Outstndng Stu 89-90; Aerospace Engrng.

NAVARRO, BILLIE JO; Las Plumas HS; Palermo, CA; (1); 40/249; Church Yth Grp; FFA; Girl Scts; Office Aide; Band; Mrchg Band; Butte Coll; Kndgrdn Tchr.

NAVARRO, BLANCA D; Alisal HS; Salinas, CA; (3); Crs Cntry; Prfct Atten Awd; Optometry.

NAVARRO, CARLOS; St Genevieve HS; Sepulveda, CA; (4); Pep Clb; Spanish Clb; Hon Roll; UCLA; Podiatrist.

NAVARRO, CARTER; St Lawrence Acad; Sunnyvale, CA; (1); Chess Clb; Math Clb; Hon Roll; Jr NHS; Pres Acad Fit Awd; Video Games; Role Plyng Games; Drwng.

NAVARRO, CHERYL; Paramount HS; Paramount, CA; (4); Capt Pep Clb; Capt Pep Band; Pres Frsh Cls; Pres Soph Cls; Pres Jr Cls; Pres Stu Cncl; Capt Cheerldng; JV Sftbl; Clg, Svc Clb; Loyola Marymount U; Comm.

NAVARRO, CLAIRE J; Diamond Bar HS; Diamond Bar, CA; (2); 1/400; Church Yth Grp; Cmnty Wkr; French Clb; Intnl Clb; Treas Key Clb; Math Tm; Hon Roll; U Of San Diego; Aerospc Engr.

NAVARRO, DENISE; Bellflower HS; Bellflower, CA; (3); 49/276; JV Cheerldng; Var Capt Pom Pon; Hon Roll; Most Dedicated Squad Chrldng; Long Beach City JC; Cnslng.

NAVARRO, DIANA O; Modesto HS; Modesto, CA; (3); Orch.

NAVARRO, DULCE P; Modesto HS; Modesto, CA; (3); Church Yth Grp; Mac Acad; Achvt Awd Frgn Lang; Sacramento ST U; Law.

NAVARRO, ELIZABETH; San Benito HS; Hollister, CA; (3); Church Yth Grp; Office Aide; Church Choir; Mgrnt Grp; Biola U.

NAVARRO, ELVIA; James A Garfield HS; Los Angeles, CA; (2); Office Aide; Teachers Aide; Hon Roll; Elem Tchr.

NAVARRO, ENRIQUE; George Washington HS; San Francisco, CA; (3); Speech Tm; Pol Sci.

NAVARRO, FERNANDO; Orestimba HS; Newman, CA; (3); Med.

NAVARRO, JENNIFER; Monte Vista HS; Spring Valley, CA; (3); 14/377; Cmnty Wkr; Hosp Aide; Drill Tm; Yrbk; Treas Frsh Cls; Off Sr Cls; Hon Roll; Dance Co; CSF; Pacific Islanders Vp; Nrsng.

NAVARRO, JESSICA M; Southwest HS; San Diego, CA; (3); Church Yth Grp; Hosp Aide; Office Aide; SADD; Teachers Aide; Chorus; Drill Tm; San Diego ST U; Englsh.

NAVARRO, JESUS; King City HS; Greenfield, CA; (3); Drama Clb; Latin Clb; Thesps; Peer Cnslr Natrl Hlprs; Cal Arts; Actng.

NAVARRO, LETICIA E; Palo Verde HS; Blythe, CA; (2); VP Pep Clb; Spanish Clb; Flag Corp; Sec Soph Cls; Stat Trk; Stat Wrstlng; Hon Roll.

NAVARRO, LILIANA; Hueneme HS; Port Hueneme, CA; (1); UCLA; Nrsng.

NAVARRO, MARIA; Modesto HS; Modesto, CA; (2); Church Yth Grp; Sacramento ST; Psych.

NAVARRO, MARISOL; Sierra Vista HS; Baldwin Park, CA; (3); Bus Profs of Am; Lit Mag; Mdlng; Bus Adm.

NAVARRO, MARTHA L; Our Lady-Laretto Bishop Conaty HS; Los Angeles, CA; (3); 89/95; FBLA; Treas Soph Cls; Treas Stu Cncl; Hon Roll; NHS; Prfct Atten Awd; Ambassadors Club; Bus Industry Schl; French Awd; Comp Sci.

NAVARRO, MONTANIEL S; Valley HS; Sacramento, CA; (3); 17/600; Teachers Aide; High Hon Roll; Hon Roll; GATE Club; CSF Life Mem; A P Physics Club; A P US Hstry Club Mem; U Of CA Davis; Premed.

NAVARRO, OSCAR; Cantwell HS; Huntington Park, CA; (1); Spanish Clb; JV Bsbl; JV Ftbl; Hon Roll; Notre Dame; Med.

NAVARRO, RAQUEL; John Muir HS; Pasadena, CA; (3); JV Swmmng; Upward Bound Prjct CA St LA; Stu Svc Cmmtte; Friday Nite Live; CA ST LA; Lawyer.

NAVARRO, ROMMEL P; Whitney HS; Cerritos, CA; (2); JA; Key Clb; JV Bsbl; High Hon Roll; CSF; Med Club; City Rcrtnl Bsktbl Lg; UCLA; Med.

NAVARRO, RUBEN; Pioneer HS; San Jose, CA; (1); Teachers Aide; School Play; Wrstlng; Cit Awd; Hon Roll; Prfct Atten Awd; San Jose ST; Indstrl Engr.

NAVASCA, JOANNA L; Wilcox HS; Santa Clara, CA; (1); JV Tennis; Hon Roll; Asian Clb; Art; Dentistry.

NAVEA, MAITA R; St Genevieve HS; Canoga Park, CA; (3); Dance Clb; French Clb; Drill Tm; CSF; Liturgy Clb.

NAVO, CHRIS L; Bear River HS; Grass Valley, CA; (2); Cmnty Wkr; Band; Pep Band; Fri Night Live; Spcl Olypmcs-Coordntr; Comp Pgmr.

NAWATA, AMY; Contra Costa Christian HS; Walnut Creek, CA; (3); 2/30; Rep Drama Clb; Chorus; School Play; Pres Frsh Cls; Var Cheerldng; Var Socr; High Hon Roll; Cert Of Merit; ACSI Distngshd Stu; NCS Schlr Athl Chrldng.

NAYAK, MAHESH N; Acalanes HS; Lafayette, CA; (4); U Of CA Los Angls; Biolgcl Sci.

NAYLOR, JODI L; Antelope Valley HS; Lancaster, CA; (3); Office Aide; Teachers Aide; Variety Show; Hon Roll; CSU Long Beach; Ed.

NAYLOR, W JASON; Palisades HS; Los Angeles, CA; (4); 28/445; Chorus; Rptr Nwsp; Ntl Merit SF; Pres Acad Fit Awd; Space Settlmnt Dsgn Comptn; Outward Bnd; The Pro Choice Coalition; CA U; Csmlgy.

NAZARENO, GENEVIEVE; Bishop Amat HS; Pomona, CA; (4); 30/400; Cmnty Wkr; Drama Clb; School Musical; School Play; Stu Cncl; Stat Socr; Hon Roll; Sec NHS; Rlgs Affrs Cmmsnr; Comp Pgmr.

NAZARIAN, ADRIN; Holy Martyrs Ferrahian HS; Canoga Park, CA; (3); Yrbk; Rep Soph Cls; Rep Stu Cncl; Var Crs Cntry; Var Socr; AYF Since 88; AYSO 89-90; Soccer Coach In Armenian Scouts And Athlete Organization; Electronics Engineering.

NAZARIAN, ANNA; John Muir HS; Pasadena, CA; (2); Cmnty Wkr; Red Cross Aide; ROTC; Yrbk; Hon Roll; Kiwanis Awd; Edtr, Rptr, Advc Clmnst AFJROTC Nwsltr; Mem Upward Bnd; Impact Cnslr; UCLA; Psych.

NAZARIAN, NANCY C; Bishop Montgomery HS; Gardena, CA; (3); 67/413; Pres Debate Tm; Rep JA; Treas Key Clb; NFL; Pres Speech Tm; Teachers Aide; Chorus; School Musical; Stage Crew; Ed Nwsp; Dance Ballet Co Pacific Amer Ballet; Dancer 54th East Band; Intl Relations.

NAZARIAN, TAMAR N; Armenian Mesrobian HS; Whittier, CA; (4); Church Yth Grp; Church Choir; Hon Roll; CSF; CSU Fullerton; Pharmacy.

NAZEMI, PEZHMAN; El Camino Real HS; West Hills, CA; (3); VP FBLA; Key Clb; Band; Mrchg Band; Pep Band; Intrml Bsktbl; High Hon Roll; Mst Imprvd Plyr-Bnd Awd; Mst Imprvd Mrchr-Bnd Awd; Ldrshp Skills; U In CA; Dr.

NDUATI, ROBIN W; Upland HS; Upland, CA; (2); 32/688; Color Guard; Drill Tm; Rep Stu Cncl; High Hon Roll.

NEAGOE, FLAVIUS O; College Park HS; Pleasant Hill, CA; (3); French Clb; Math Clb; Socr; Wrk Bank Of America; 6th Pl Natl Math Leag 88-89; Hgh Hnrs Golden St Exam 88; Cmptr Sci.

NEAL, JULIE; Saddleback HS; Santa Ana, CA; (3); VP Spanish Clb; JV Bsktbl; Var L Cheerldng; JV Score Keeper; CSF; Brdcstng.

NEAL, JULIE K; Escondido HS; Escondido, CA; (3); Pres Church Yth Grp; Dance Clb; Drama Clb; VP FBLA; Quiz Bowl; School Play; Ed Yrbk; Var L Cheerldng; Hon Roll; Prfct Atten Awd; Phys Thrpy.

NEAL, LATASHA D; Dorsey HS; Los Angeles, CA; (4); Pep Clb; Hon Roll; Pres Acad Fit Awd; In Knights & Ladies Hnr Soc; Humboldt ST U; Nrsng.

NEAL, LIZA MARIA; SD Schl/Creative & Performing Arts; San Diego, CA; (3); 9/123; Church Yth Grp; Cmnty Wkr; Dance Clb; Church Choir; School Musical; Variety Show; Ed Yrbk; Cit Awd; High Hon Roll; Ntl Merit Ltr; Hnrs Gldn St Exm Alg & History; Dept Hnrs Engl & Ballet; Brd Mem Sierra Svc Prjct; Literature.

NEAL, MARY ELLEN; Valley Christian HS; San Jose, CA; (1); Church Yth Grp; Cheerldng; High Hon Roll; San Jose ST U; Elem Tchr.

NEAL, REBECCA; Del Norte Indepndnt Study Prgm HS; Gasquet, CA; (3); Cmnty Wkr; FFA; SADD; Drill Tm; Bsktbl; Cheerldng; Sftbl; Trk; Cit Awd; High Hon Roll; CA Indpndnt Study Pgm; Cmmnctns.

NEAL, RIQUEL A; Project Grasp & Pittsburg HS; Pittsburg, CA; (2); Church Yth Grp; Girl Scts; Library Aide; Pep Clb; Ski Clb; Acpl Chr; Chorus; Church Choir; School Musical; School Play; Hayward ST; Prfrmng Music.

NEAL, TOBY; Paradise Adventist Schl; Paradise, CA; (2); Art Clb; Church Yth Grp; FCA; Ski Clb; Band; Ftbl; Sftbl; Vllybl; Hon Roll; Union Coll; Med.

NEAL, VICKI L; El Camino HS; Oceanside, CA; (3); 24/338; Church Yth Grp; Flag Corp; Hon Roll; Stu Of Mnth Bus Educ; Typng Hnrs; Alg & US Hstry Wildcat Wnnr; Mira Costa; Bus.

NEANDER, CINDY; Vacaville HS; Vacaville, CA; (2); Cmnty Wkr; Spanish Clb; Church Choir; Vllybl; Cit Awd; High Hon Roll; NHS; Church Yth Grp; Quiz Bowl; Teachers Aide; Var Badminton; CSF; Amer Legion God And Country Awd; Sacramento ST; Ecnmcs.

NEARY, SHANNON L; El Camino HS; Sacramento, CA; (3); 16/366; Teachers Aide; Chorus; High Hon Roll; Friday Night Live.

NEAT, MELANIE; Lakewood HS; Lakewood, CA; (1); Church Yth Grp; Drama Clb; Stage Crew; Off Frsh Cls; Vllybl; Miss Amer Coed Pgnt St Fnlst; Oxford; Theatre Arts.

NEBEL, DIANA L; Montclair HS; Montclair, CA; (2); Church Yth Grp; JV Capt Socr; CA Poly Summer Day Camp-Jr Cnslr; U CA-SAN Diego; Psych.

NEBERGALL, AMY; Liberty Union HS; Brentwood, CA; (1); 14/430; FCA; French Clb; Letterman Clb; Pep Clb; Ski Clb; SADD; Phtg Yrbk; Var Tennis; Hon Roll.

NEBYELUL, ZURYASH; Lincoln HS; San Diego, CA; (3); Spanish Clb; Crs Cntry; Trk; Cit Awd; Hon Roll; Prfct Atten Awd; Trk & Crss Cntry Awds.

NECE, JOELL J; Rim Of The World HS; Blue Jay, CA; (2); 127/359; Art Clb; Church Yth Grp; Spanish Clb; Teachers Aide; Church Choir; JV Sftbl; Hon Roll; Dist Art Show 1st Pl Wnnr; Photojrnlsm.

NEEDHAM, JAMIE S; Santa Ynez HS; Buellton, CA; (3); Var Bsbl; Var Ftbl; Wrstlng; Bus.

NEELEY, AMANDA M; Vacaville HS; Vacaville, CA; (2); Church Yth Grp; Girl Scts; Intnl Clb; Office Aide; Hon Roll; Nrsng.

NEELY, BEN; South San Francisco HS; South San Francis, CA; (3); VP Drama Clb; FBLA; Thesps; School Musical; School Play; Stage Crew; JV Ftbl; San Mateo; Brdcstng Engr.

NEELY, BRANDY L; Rosamond HS; Rosamond, CA; (3); Office Aide; Teachers Aide; Bsktbl; Cheerldng; Hon Roll; AV Coll; Bus Mgmt.

NEELY, BRYAN B; San Benito HS; Hollister, CA; (3); 66/370; Ski Clb; Spanish Clb; Stu Cncl; Ftbl; High Hon Roll; Hon Roll; Bike Clb; ROMP; Chem Engrng.

NEELY, KAREN LYNN; Bear River HS; Grass Valley, CA; (2); 19/248; Intnl Clb; Library Aide; Rep Soph Cls; JV Capt Bsktbl; Stat Ftbl; Elks Awd; High Hon Roll; Pres Acad Fit Awd; Coast Guard Acad.

NEEM, JOHANN N; College Park HS; Pleasant Hill, CA; (2); AFS; Debate Tm; French Clb; German Clb; Model UN; Hon Roll; CSF; Fri Nght Live; U PA; Law.

NEER, JENNY D; Beaumont HS; Cherry Valley, CA; (3); 15/180; Church Yth Grp; FCA; Letterman Clb; Quiz Bowl; Teachers Aide; Varsity Clb; Church Choir; Stat Bsbl; Var L Bsktbl; JV Vllybl; Jr Statesman; Lib.

NEESE, ERIK R; Wood Land HS; Woodland, CA; (2); Boy Scts; Service Clb; Spanish Clb; Mrchg Band; Pep Band; Rptr Phtg Yrbk; Gym; Hon Roll; Jr NHS; Prfct Atten Awd; Gymnastics Coach; Life Sct 90; Law.

NEFF, ANDREA M; Mayfield SR Schl; Pasadena, CA; (3); Var Trk; Var Vllybl; Equestrian Actvts; AZ ST U.

NEFF, DEBRA M; Redlands HS; Redlands, CA; (2); Cmnty Wkr; Chrmn Hosp Aide; Library Aide; Model UN; Pep Clb; Teachers Aide; JV Trk; Cit Awd; Sci.

NEFF, KEVIN; Tustin HS; Tustin, CA; (3); Varsity Clb; Acpl Chr; Chorus; Ftbl; Trk; Wt Lftg; Wrstlng; Hon Roll; Pre-Med.

NEGASH, DANIEL; Washington HS; Fremont, CA; (3); JV Bsktbl; JV Trk; Lets Tough The Future Together; Pre-Law.

NEGASH, EDEN; Washington HS; Fremont, CA; (4); Cmnty Wkr; Dance Clb; Pep Clb; Teachers Aide; Varsity Clb; Crs Cntry; Powder Puff Ftbl; Trk; CSF; Fleet Rsrve Assn Essay Wnnr; Lets Touch Future Togther Clb; UC Berkeley; Arch.

NEGISHI, MAYUMI; El Toro HS; El Toro, CA; (4); 5/545; Key Clb; Rptr Nwsp; High Hon Roll; Ntl Merit SF; 2nd Pl Piano Prfrmnc 88; Schlrshp To Atnd Ross Math Prgm OSU; 1st Pl Jpns Essay In Japan 88; Prnctn; Hmnts.

NEGLEY, MICHAEL P; Del Campo HS; Carmichael, CA; (3); 41/448; Am Leg Boys St; Chess Clb; Computer Clb; Debate Tm; Drama Clb; FCA; FBLA; Key Clb; Math Tm; Scholastic Bowl; Duke U; Math.

NEGRETE, ADELAIDE; Hilltop HS; Chula Vista, CA; (4); French Clb; Assn Of Latn Am Spnsh Spkng Stus Sec; CSF; CA ST Los Angeles; Med.

NEGRETE, ALEJANDRO D; Montclair HS; Ontario, CA; (2); Cmnty Wkr; Jazz Band; Mrchg Band; Pep Band; Ftbl; USAF Acad; Law.

NEGRETE, DAISY C; Warren HS; South Gate, CA; (2); Cit Awd; 90 Essay Writng Cont Wnnr; Psych.

NEGRETE, IMELDA; San Benito HS; Hollister, CA; (2); 41/356; French Clb; Hon Roll; Prfct Atten Awd; CSF; MECHA; Sacramento ST; Law.

NEGRETE, KATHRYN L; Kern Valley HS; Kernville, CA; (2); Pep Clb; Spanish Clb; Varsity Clb; Yrbk; Stat Bsktbl; Powder Puff Ftbl; JV Sftbl; Var Vllybl; High Hon Roll; Hnrs Engl.

NEGRETE, MATT T; Clayton Valley HS; Clayton, CA; (2); Varsity Clb; Var Wrstlng; Water Polo JV; CSF; Surfing; CA Poly; Engrng.

NEGRETE, NOE; St Paul HS; La Mirada, CA; (3); 6/286; French Clb; Var L Bsbl; JV Bsktbl; Var L Crs Cntry; Stat Ftbl; Intrml Sftbl; French Hon Soc; Hon Roll; NHS; Religion Awd Jr; Bsbl Coaches Awd; Prin Hnr Rl Jr/Soph; Stanford; Engrng.

NEGRETE, OLGA; Hueneme HS; Oxnard, CA; (4); Intnl Clb; Key Clb; Drill Tm; Kiwanis Awd; Intl Clb Treas; Prfct Atten 4 Yrs; Lamp Bearers; UCLA; Med.

NEGRON, ADAM J; Gladstone HS; Azusa, CA; (3); FBLA; Office Aide; Cyclng; Swmmng; Bus.

NEGRON, ISAURA; Pittsburg HS; Pittsburg, CA; (2); Hon Roll; San Francisco ST; Bus.

NEGRON, JUAN; Bellarmine Jefferson HS; North Hollywood, CA; (3); 25/275; Church Yth Grp; Math Clb; Science Clb; Socr; Wt Lftg; Hon Roll; Svrl Art Awds; Child Lit Cont.

NEGRON, MICHELLE; Cordova SR HS; Rancho Cordova, CA; (2); Church Yth Grp; Hosp Aide; Speech Tm; Mem M E S A; Intrnatl Order Of Jobs Daughters; U C Davis; Obstetrics.

NEGRON, ROBERTO C; Bellarmine Jefferson HS; North Hollywood, CA; (1); Church Yth Grp; Math Clb; Science Clb; Bsktbl; High Hon Roll.

NEHER, ANDREA L; Las Plumas HS; Palermo, CA; (4); French Clb; Intnl Clb; Library Aide; Flag Corp; Phtg Rptr Nwsp; Stat Bsbl; Stat Bsktbl; Stat Ftbl; Stat Trk; Hon Roll; Golden St Exm Geometry; Peer Tutor; Usaf.

NEHRING, SETH M; Clovis HS; Fresno, CA; (2); L Var Swmmng; Water Polo Tm; CA ST U Fresno.

NEIBEL, TRACY D; Mission Viejo HS; El Toro, CA; (3); 43/450; Church Yth Grp; Drama Clb; Model UN; Thesps; Color Guard; School Musical; School Play; Stage Crew; Hon Roll; Pres Acad Fit Awd; Drama Troup; Tutor Math, Chem, Spnsh; HIGH AP Test Scores; UC Irvine; Chem.

NEIDER, ANNA M; Galt HS; Galt, CA; (3); FHA; Poetry; Music; Cosmetologist.

NEIGHBORS, DAWN R; Cajon HS; Devore, CA; (3); Church Yth Grp; Cmnty Wkr; Girl Scts; Church Choir; Color Guard; Yrbk; Swmmng; Girl Sct Slvr Awd; Delg GS Natl Conv; UC Santa Cruz; Marine Bio.

NEIGHBORS, JENNY L; Cordova HS; Mather A F B, CA; (3); 15/464; Var Cheerldng; Hon Roll; Ntl Merit SF; Tp Frnch II Stu Awd; Hstry.

NEIL, ERIN K; College Park HS; Pleasant Hill, CA; (2); Bsktbl; High Hon Roll; Hon Roll; U CA; Arch.

NEILEY, CLEMENCIA E; Enterprise HS; Whitmore, CA; (3); Acpl Chr; Chorus; CA Horse Assn Gymkhanas; U Of Santa Barbra; Acctng.

NEILL, JERUSHA; Del Campo HS; Fair Oaks, CA; (1); JV L Cheerldng; JV Sftbl; Stanford U; Crmnl Law.

NEILSEN, AARON G; Mayfair HS; Lakewood, CA; (3); Vllybl.

NEILSEN, AMIE J; Brethren HS; Lakewood, CA; (2); Pres Frsh Cls; Var Socr; JV Vllybl.

NEILSEN, JULIE L; Ponderosa HS; El Dorado, CA; (3); 40/277; Am Leg Aux Girls St; Debate Tm; Speech Tm; Var Trk; Hon Roll; 2nd Pl Native Sons Of CA Spch Cntst; 2nd Pl Lions Club Spch Cntst; Pol Sci.

NEILSEN, MICHAEL; Mt Whitney HS; Visalia, CA; (3); Art Clb; Boy Scts; SADD; Var Crs Cntry; Var Trk.

NEIMAN, ARWEN WENDI F; Whitney HS; Cerritos, CA; (2); 65/150; Dance Clb; Debate Tm; Drama Clb; French Clb; Intnl Clb; JA; Pep Clb; Speech Tm; Band; School Play; Jr Statesmn Bst Debator; Illumination Clb Cmmssn Pblcty; Jr Statesmn Amer Photo/Asst Hstrn; Harvard; Poltcs.

NEIPP, ELISA; Apple Valley Christian HS; Apple Valley, CA; (2); Church Yth Grp; Chorus; Stat Bsbl; Bsktbl; Score Keeper; Stat Sftbl; Cit Awd; Hon Roll; Pblshd Ptry Ptry Anthology; Advrtsing.

NEISWENDER, CARYN; Tri-City Christian Schl; Carlsbad, CA; (1); 1/30; Art Clb; Church Yth Grp; Drama Clb; Letterman Clb; Stu Cncl; Var Bsktbl; Vllybl; Cit Awd; High Hon Roll; Hon Roll; Discipleshp Awd Bsktbl & Vlybl; Hghst Acadmc Hnr Hstry & Bible; Marine Bio.

NEITZEL, RICHARD L; Apple Valley HS; Apple Valley, CA; (2); Boy Scts; Band; Mrchg Band; JV Trk; High Hon Roll; Jr NHS; San Bernandino Cty Hnr Band; Cal Poly Pomona; Pilot.

NEIVELT, SABRA; Berkeley HS; Berkeley, CA; (3); Hon Roll; Smmr Exchng/Study Pgm In Spain; Psych.

NEKAIEN, SEENA; Encinal HS; Alameda, CA; (3); Math Tm; Cit Awd; Hon Roll; Prfct Atten Awd.

NELLY, KRISTINA M; Lowell HS; San Francisco, CA; (3); Aud/Vis; Rep Intnl Clb; Red Cross Aide; Service Clb; SADD; Teachers Aide; Off Yrbk; Fil-Am Clb; Depeche Mode & Mozart Skateboarding.

NELMS, WENDY L; Monache HS; Porterville, CA; (4); 28/291; Rptr Nwsp; Rep Soph Cls; Rep Sr Cls; L Crs Cntry; L Trk; Wt Lftg; Hon Roll; Voice Dem Awd; Sci Olympd Team; CSF; Point Loma Nazarene Coll; Med.

NELSEN, CHRISTA; San Gabriel HS; San Gabriel, CA; (4); French Clb; German Clb; Library Aide; Pep Clb; Hist SADD; Yrbk; Rep Stu Cncl; Var Cheerldng; Hon Roll; Jr Divitan Awd; Stu Of Mnth ; Bd Of Ed Rep; Citrus Coll.

NELSEN, SARAH ELAINE; Branham HS; San Jose, CA; (2); Church Yth Grp; 4-H; SADD; Hon Roll; CSF; Raised Guide For Blind; UC Davis; Vet.

NELSON, ALBERT R; University HS; Irvine, CA; (2); Church Yth Grp; Cmnty Wkr; Teachers Aide; Band; Jazz Band; Mrchg Band; Orch; Pep Band; Stage Crew; Variety Show; 1BA Pony Leag Bsbl 90-Mgr; Band Exec Cncl; U AR; Bus Admin.

NELSON, ALLYSON G; Wm S Hart HS; Valencia, CA; (3); Mu Alpha Theta; Red Cross Aide; Band; Stage Crew; Rep Frsh Cls; JV Var Cheerldng; Var Diving; Var Trk; NHS; CSF; Microbio.

NELSON, ALYSSA A; Rosamond HS; Rosamond, CA; (3); 4/100; Rptr Pres 4-H; Letterman Clb; Math Tm; Treas Frsh Cls; Treas Soph Cls; Treas Jr Cls; Treas Sr Cls; Stu Cncl; Var L Bsktbl; High Hon Roll; Engrng.

NELSON, AMY E; Tustin HS; Tustin, CA; (1); 11/466; Church Yth Grp; High Hon Roll; Acad Achvt Awd; U VA; Med.

NELSON, BECKY; Benicia HS; Benicia, CA; (2); Church Yth Grp; Cmnty Wkr; Debate Tm; Drama Clb; Key Clb; Pep Clb; SADD; Teachers Aide; VP Capt Cheerldng; Gym; Police Cadet; Sftbl Bst Sprtsmn Awd; UCA All St Chsn Perfrmn London 90; Police.

NELSON, BETH E; Rio Americano HS; Carmichael, CA; (3); Acpl Chr; Chorus; Recgntn CSSSA Excllnc Music; San Francisco Symphny Yth Orchstra; Chmbr Music Perfmnr; Cellist.

NELSON, BRANDON; Oxnard HS; Oxnard, CA; (2); Art Clb; Boy Scts; Computer Clb; Am Leg Aux Girls St; Varsity Clb; Stu Cncl; Swmmng; Wrstlng; Marine Bio.

NELSON, BRYAN J; Capistrano Valley HS; Mission Viejo, CA; (3); Var L Swmmng; Varsity Ltrmn Water Polo; Schltc Achvt Awd Alg Cls, Swmng Banquet; Cal Poly; Engrng.

NELSON, CANDICE Y; Don Antonio Lugo HS; Chino, CA; (3); #5 In Class; JV Bsktbl; JV Socr; Var Tennis; Var Trk; Hon Roll; Arch.

NELSON, CATHERINE P; La Habra HS; Whittier, CA; (2); Color Guard; School Play; Var L Swmmng; Coll; Chld Psych.

NELSON, CHRIS J; Elk Grove HS; Elk Grove, CA; (4); FHA; Office Aide; Band; Hon Roll; Cosumnes River Coll.

NELSON, COLLEEN R; St Genevieve HS; Sepulveda, CA; (2); Church Yth Grp; GAA; Letterman Clb; Pep Clb; Spanish Clb; Chorus; JV Bsktbl; JV Sftbl; JV Vllybl; High Hon Roll; Jrnlsm.

NELSON, CYA; Immanuel HS; Sanger, CA; (2); Cheerldng; Powder Puff Ftbl; Hon Roll; Cmmrcl Art.

NELSON, DANIELLE; Moorpark HS; Moorpark, CA; (3); 18/245; Key Clb; Pep Clb; Variety Show; Treas Jr Cls; Treas Sr Cls; Var Capt Cheerldng; High Hon Roll; Lion Awd.

NELSON, DAWN; Winters HS; Winters, CA; (4); Church Yth Grp; Hist FBLA; Office Aide; SADD; JV Bsktbl; Score Keeper; Stat Swmmng; Stat Vllybl; Hon Roll; Pres Acad Fit Awd; Life Bible Coll; Ed.

NELSON, DENNIS T; Apple Valley HS; Apple Valley, CA; (3); 26/850; Church Yth Grp; Drama Clb; Letterman Clb; Pep Clb; Spanish Clb; Varsity Clb; Var L Tennis; High Hon Roll; Grls Tennis Var Stat; UC Santa Barbara; Bus Admin.

NELSON, ERIKA; St Helena HS; Angwin, CA; (3); Key Clb; Ski Clb; SADD; Teachers Aide; JV Var Cheerldng; Var Pom Pon.

NELSON, GREGORY K; El Toro HS; El Toro, CA; (3); 19/481; Boy Scts; Church Yth Grp; French Clb; Treas Key Clb; Var L Crs Cntry; JV Capt Socr; Var L Trk; High Hon Roll; Hon Roll; Kiwanis Awd; Erth Sci Acad Excel Awd; Med.

NELSON, HILARY D; Downey HS; Downey, CA; (2); Var L Bsbl; Var L Bsktbl; JV L Vllybl; San Diego ST; Med.

NELSON, JASON D; Lindsay HS; Lindsay, CA; (3); Church Yth Grp; VP Key Clb; Letterman Clb; Teachers Aide; Sec Jr Cls; Intrml JV Bsktbl; Intrml L Ftbl; Intrml L Tennis; Hon Roll; Mst Imprvd Tennis Plyr Awd; 98% All Areas Combined Impact Score 89; Landscape Arch.

NELSON, JENNIFER; O W Holmes JR HS; Davis, CA; (1); CA Schlrshp Fed; UC Stanford; Corp Lawyer.

NELSON, JENNIFER; St Joseph HS; Cerritos, CA; (2); 19/196; Debate Tm; Ski Clb; Spanish Clb; SADD; High Hon Roll; Hon Roll; Pres Acad Fit Awd; Outstndng Achvt Awd Span I & II; Outstndng Achvt Awd Geom; CSF; Math.

NELSON, JEROME; Placer HS; Auburn, CA; (2); Cmnty Wkr; Key Clb; Ski Clb; Pres Jr Cls; JV Bsbl; Var Crs Cntry; Var Sftbl; Var Trk; JV Wt Lftg; Var Wrstlng; MVP Bsbl All Star Tm; Spec Olympcs Coach; Orthopdcs.

NELSON, JESSICA ANNE; Robert Louis Stevenson Schl; Salinas, CA; (4); Sec AFS; Church Yth Grp; Ski Clb; Spanish Clb; Varsity Clb; Nwsp; JV Fld Hcky; JV L Tennis; High Hon Roll; Hon Roll; AFS Spain 88-89; Wellesley Coll; Lbrl Arts.

NELSON, JON-MICHAEL; Santa Paula Union HS; Santa Paula, CA; (1); Boy Scts; Church Yth Grp; SADD; Band; Jazz Band; Mrchg Band; Pep Band; JV Var Bsbl; JV Var Socr; Hon Roll; CSF; BYU; Law.

NELSON, JULIA L; Monte Vista HS; Danville, CA; (2); Church Yth Grp; Pep Clb; Science Clb; Spanish Clb; Chorus; JV Crs Cntry; Var L Trk; High Hon Roll; HOBY; Math.

NELSON, KELLY J; Bishop Montgomery HS; Harbor City, CA; (2); Girl Scts; Letterman Clb; SADD; Sftbl; Slvr Awd Grl Scts; Chld Psych.

NELSON, KEN; Benicia HS; Benicia, CA; (4); Cmnty Wkr; Band; Jazz Band; Mrchg Band; Pep Band; Wrstlng; Hon Roll; Hg Hnrs Geom; Awds CMEA Music; Command Prfrmnc Awds; Schlrshp Silverlake Band Camp; CA Poly; Engrng.

NELSON, KIMBERLY A; Apple Valley HS; Apple Valley, CA; (1); Church Yth Grp; French Clb; JA; Ed Yrbk; Stat Ftbl; Tennis; Hon Roll; Writing; AZ ST U; Teaching.

NELSON, KIMBERLY A; Rio Lindo Acad; Santa Rosa, CA; (3); FFA; Spanish Clb; Chorus; School Play; Nurse.

NELSON, KRISTYN NOEL; Antioch SR HS; Antioch, CA; (4); 27/582; Letterman Clb; Office Aide; Service Clb; Varsity Clb; Acpl Chr; Chorus; Nwsp; JV Bsktbl; Var Crs Cntry; JV Sftbl; CSF; U CA Davis; Sclgy.

NELSON, LAWRENCE K; Yosemite Union HS; Coarsegold, CA; (3); Computer Clb; Office Aide; Teachers Aide; Acpl Chr; Chorus; JV Wt Lftg; Taught Bus Comp Class; U Of CA; Bus.

NELSON, LEAH L; San Jaun HS; Orangevale, CA; (4); Pep Clb; Badmittn; Data Entry.

NELSON, LORRI J; Arroyo Grandea HS; Arroyo Grande, CA; (2); 28/625; Church Yth Grp; Pep Clb; JV Capt Cheerldng; JV Tennis; High Hon Roll; Hon Roll.

NELSON, MARQUETTE L; Downtown Business Magnet HS; Hawthorne, CA; (3); Off Jr Cls; Off Sr Cls; Stu Cncl; Hon Roll; Acad Of Finance; Fund Schlr; Fashn Merch.

NELSON, MICHAEL TORRE; Modoc HS; Alturas, CA; (4); 12/50; Boy Scts; FBLA; FFA; Pres Stu Cncl; Elks Awd; Hon Roll; Kiwanis Awd; Rotary Awd; Lab Aide; Rotary Intl Frgn Exchange Stu; Pre-Med.

NELSON, MICHELE L; North Tahoe HS; Kings Bch, CA; (3); 3/69; Band; Jazz Band; Stage Crew; Rep Soph Cls; Sec Jr Cls; Mgr Crs Cntry; Hon Roll; Opt Clb Awd; JSA JR Statesmen Of Amer; Acad Decathlon; Peer Cnslr; Bus Adm.

NELSON, NATALIE A; Marymount HS; Los Angeles, CA; (3); Church Yth Grp; Hosp Aide; Trk; CSF; Stu Support Peer Cnslng; Retreat Team.

NELSON, NATICA P; Liberty Union HS; Oakley, CA; (1); 82/430; Chorus; Friday Night Live; OR ST; Interior Dsgns.

NELSON, PAUL A; Servite HS; La Habra, CA; (2); Var Crs Cntry; JV Socr; Intrml Trk; Jr Statesmen Amer Chptr Sec, VP; Acad Decathlon Tm 90-91; Mech & Aerospc Engrng, Arch, Poltcl Sci.

NELSON, ROSE; Immaculate Heart HS; Los Angeles, CA; (4); Math Clb; Model UN; Mu Alpha Theta; Service Clb; Yrbk; Var JV Swmmng; High Hon Roll; Dance Clb; NEDT Awd; CSF Seal Bearer; USC Smmr Hnrs Prog; Psych.

NELSON, SALIHA; Crawford HS; San Diego, CA; (3); 60/332; Cmnty Wkr; Dance Clb; Intnl Clb; Letterman Clb; Spanish Clb; Teachers Aide; Varsity Clb; Drill Tm; Variety Show; Sec Sr Cls; ASB Commssnr Race/ Human Rltns; Alpha Kappa Alpha Debutante 90; Howard U; Law.

NELSON, SARA; Cupertino HS; Cupertino, CA; (4); 1/220; Mrchg Band; VP Soph Cls; Mgr Jr Cls; Stu Cncl; Capt Cheerldng; DAR Awd; Elks Awd; NHS; Ntl Merit SF; Pres Acad Fit Awd; Interact Clb Pres; Robert C Byrd Schlrshp; Princeton U.

NELSON, SARA R; Trinity HS; Burnt Ranch, CA; (2); Rptr Ed Nwsp; Rep Frsh Cls; Rep Soph Cls; Rep Stu Cncl; Var JV Bsktbl; Var L Crs Cntry; Var L Trk; High Hon Roll; Hon Roll; Kiwanis Awd; CA ST Smmr Schl For Art; AFS Prgm; Pacific U; Grphc Art.

NELSON, SCOTT D; Rim Of The World HS; Crestline, CA; (3); Church Yth Grp; Quiz Bowl; Bsktbl; JV Tennis; High Hon Roll; NHS; Christian Svc Brigade; Amer Lgn Env Confrnc; Ski Tm; Env Sci.

NELSON, SHERI; Salinas HS; Salinas, CA; (4); Church Yth Grp; Computer Clb; Drama Clb; English Clb; Speech Tm; Teachers Aide; School Play; Hon Roll; NHS; Prfct Atten Awd; Eng & Hnrs Eng Awds; UC-SANTA Cruz; Author.

NELSON, STACIE L; Rim Of The World HS; Crestline, CA; (1); Church Yth Grp; JV Socr; Var Trk; JV Vllybl; Hon Roll.

NELSON JR, STEVEN DALE; Willow HS; Apple Valley, CA; (4); Boy Scts; Ftbl; Wt Lftg; Wrstlng; Cit Awd; High Hon Roll; Hon Roll; Ctznshp Awds.

NELSON, SUZANNA L; Quartz Hill HS; Lancaster, CA; (2); Church Yth Grp; Dance Clb; French Clb; Drill Tm; Hon Roll; BYU; Psych Tchr.

NELSON II, SYLFORD; San Pasqual Acad; Spring Valley, CA; (4); Church Yth Grp; Cmnty Wkr; Band; VP Jr Cls; Intrml Bsktbl; Intrml Ftbl; U CA San Diego; Robotic Engrng.

NELSON, TAMMI L; San Lorenzo HS; San Lorenzo, CA; (2); 13/200; FBLA; Yrbk; Sec Frsh Cls; Sec Soph Cls; Var L Bsktbl; Stat Sftbl; JV Capt Vllybl; High Hon Roll; Acadmc Excllnce Awd Soc Sci; Invited To Cngrssnl Yth Ldrshp Cncl Conf; CSF; San Jose ST U; Lib Art Instr.

NELSON, TANISHA ROCHELLE; Fremont HS; Oakland, CA; (4); 103 Track; Gramblin U; Law Pre Law.

NELSON, TIFFANY R; St Joseph HS; Cerritos, CA; (3); Church Yth Grp; Cmnty Wkr; GAA; Pep Clb; Ski Clb; SADD; Chorus; Rep Sr Cls; Stu Cncl; Capt Cheerldng; Vrsty Dance Tm.

NELSON, TIM; Calvary Chapel HS; Anaheim, CA; (2); Church Yth Grp; Speech Tm; Rptr Nwsp; Yrbk; Stu Cncl; Var Trk; Var Vllybl.

NELSON, TODD C; Clovis HS; Clovis, CA; (2); Boy Scts; Church Yth Grp; Spanish Clb; Band; Church Choir; Lit Mag; Tennis; High Hon Roll; St His Day 89; Church Sport Teams Vlybl Sftbl Bsktbl; Work For Dad; Brigham Young U; Acct.

NELSON, TOM; Winters HS; Winters, CA; (3); FHA; Letterman Clb; Pep Clb; Chorus; VP Soph Cls; Var Cheerldng; Cmp Tyl Rtry/Ldrshp Camp; Yth Day Stu Prd Chm; Yth Cncl Pres City Of Winters; Winters Warriros Msct 89; Chcio St U.

NELSON, TYLER; Edison HS; Huntington Beach, CA; (3); Boy Scts; Church Yth Grp; Drama Clb; Quiz Bowl; Scholastic Bowl; VP Stu Cncl; JV Crs Cntry; JV Swmmng; High Hon Roll; Spanish NHS; BYU; Med.

NELSON, VIRGINIA; Hemet HS; Hemet, CA; (4); 56/518; Church Yth Grp; Acpl Chr; JV Crs Cntry; Var Capt Socr; Hon Roll; Lion Awd; CA Schlrshp Awd; Brigham Yng U; Elem Ed.

NELSON, VIVIAN; Adolfo Camarillo HS; Camarillo, CA; (1); 15/556; Pep Clb; SADD; School Play; Cheerldng; Hon Roll; Zoologist.

NEMEC, ELIZABETH; Palm Springs HS; Cathedral City, CA; (1); Color Guard; Flag Corp; Mrchg Band; Orch; Cit Awd; Hon Roll; Slvr Snds Awd Outstndng Achvt; 1 Ptry Contst Awd; Comp Sci.

NEMEC, PHILIP A; Bellarmine College Prep; Saratoga, CA; (3); Aud/Vis; Church Yth Grp; Computer Clb; 4-H; Ski Clb; Church Choir; 4-H Awd; Comp Sci.

NEMETH, JOHN D; Paradise HS; Magalia, CA; (1); Ftbl; Pilot.

NEMETH, KIMBERLEY A; La Sierra HS; Riverside, CA; (3); Church Yth Grp; Girl Scts; Teachers Aide; Chorus; Hon Roll; Prfct Atten Awd; CSF; Acad Decathalon; UCI; Cmptrs.

NEMIROVSKY, IRINA; The College Preparatory Schl; Concord, CA; (3); Dance Clb; Debate Tm; Variety Show; NHS; Math/Sci.

NENADOV, SUZY L; Yosemite HS; Madera, CA; (2); Sec Church Yth Grp; Sec Ski Clb; Rptr Yrbk; Hon Roll; Rotary Intl Stu Of Mnth Plaque 88; Fresno ST U; Psych.

NEO, CHRISTINA X; Hawthorne HS; Hawthorne, CA; (1); Dance Clb; Pres Frsh Cls; Pres Soph Cls; Stu Cncl; JV Cheerldng; Hon Roll; Centinela YMCA Yth/Govt Pgm; Hnrs Engl & Alg; Pres Alg 1 Hnrs Cls; U Of Southern CA; Bus.

NEPOMUCENO, MARYLOU S; Mesa Verde HS; Citrus Heights, CA; (2); 4/259; Art Clb; English Clb; Math Tm; Trk; Hon Roll; Prfct Atten Awd; Fri Nght Live; Art Portfolio Pgm; Acadmc Awd.

NERELL, JODI A; Los Banos HS; Los Banos, CA; (3); AFS; Church Yth Grp; 4-H; GAA; Letterman Clb; Pep Clb; SADD; Teachers Aide; Varsity Clb; Cheerldng; AFS, VP Of Intrct, CSF Prtpnt Natl Hnr Scty; Sci Clb; Davis; Med.

NERELL, SCOTT A; Los Banos HS; Los Banos, CA; (1); Church Yth Grp; JV Bsktbl; JV Trk; High Hon Roll; Umpire; Phys Therapist.

NERI, ALBERT; Garfield HS; Los Angeles, CA; (3); Spanish Clb; Band; ELAC HS Extension Pgm.

NERI, DANIEL E; St Monica Catholic HS; Los Angeles, CA; (3); 4/120; Church Yth Grp; Drama Clb; Pep Clb; Thesps; School Musical; School Play; Swing Chorus; High Hon Roll; NHS; Xerox Awd For Achvt Hmnts & Scl Sci; Obstetrician.

NERI, SABRINA R; Foothill HS; Bakersfield, CA; (3); Spanish Clb; Teachers Aide; CA ST U Bkersfld; Bus.

NERIDA, TEYANNA M; Vacaville Union HS; Vacaville, CA; (3); Drama Clb; SADD; Chorus; Stage Crew; High Hon Roll; Hon Roll; Peer Cnclng; Spec Intrst In Helping Chldrn Cope With Prblms; Solano Coll; Fshn Coordntr Dsgn.

NERLAND, PAUL R; Clovis HS; Clovis, CA; (3); Debate Tm; Drama Clb; Speech Tm; High Hon Roll; Hon Roll; Church Usher-Lay Speaker-Leader Of Prayers & Songs; Enjoy Outdoors; Sci.

NERSISS, POLET P; John F Kennedy HS; Granada Hills, CA; (3); Drama Clb; French Clb; SADD; School Play; Cmmnctrs Awd; CSUN; Bus.

NERVAIZ, ERIC; Piedmont Hills HS; San Jose, CA; (4); Math Clb; U Of San Francisco; Dntl.

NESBITT, CHRISTOPHER R; Hawthorne HS; Hawthorne, CA; (3); Key Clb; L Var Ftbl; Var Trk; Var Vllybl; Wrstlng; Hon Roll; Law Enfrcmnt.

NESBITT, JOAN F; North Monterey County HS; Salinas, CA; (2); FBLA; SADD; Band; Mrchg Band; Pep Band; Stat Bsktbl; JV Var Cheerldng; Hon Roll; Dance Clb; Drama Clb; Dance; Chrldr Of Yr Awd 89; Dance.

NESS, GENEVIEVE R; Grossmont HS; El Cajon, CA; (2); 36/430; Church Yth Grp; Dance Clb; Treas French Clb; Intnl Clb; Key Clb; JV Crs Cntry; JV Gym; Var Sftbl; Var Vllybl; Hon Roll; Most Outstndng Chemm,Frnch Stu; UCLA; Med.

NESS, STEPHANIE L; Etiwanda HS; Alta Loma, CA; (2); Girl Scts; High Hon Roll; Hon Roll; Interior Dsgn.

NESSI, HEATHER L; Gridley HS; Gridley, CA; (4); Off Church Yth Grp; Drama Clb; French Clb; FHA; Office Aide; Var Cheerldng; Hon Roll; U Pacific; Pharmacy.

NESSLAGE, ZACK R; Oakdale HS; Waterford, CA; (2); Jazz Band; School Musical; Stage Crew; Cit Awd; High Hon Roll; Hon Roll; Modesto JC; Pipe Fttr.

NEST, ANNE MARIE; Carlsbad HS; Carlsbad, CA; (1); 11/352; School Play; Stage Crew; Gym; High Hon Roll; Hon Roll; Jr NHS; Prfct Atten Awd; CSF; Acad Leag; Phy.

NESTMAN, KRISTIN E; Torrey Pines HS; Solana Beach, CA; (1); JV Sftbl; Hon Roll; CA Schlst Fed; Sftbl Clb.

NETA, ITAY; Monterey HS; Monterey, CA; (2); Model UN; Temple Yth Grp; High Hon Roll; Jr NHS; Stu Tutoring Pgm.

NETHERTON, DAWN; El Dorado HS; Yerba Linda, CA; (3); 4/250; Cmnty Wkr; Intnl Clb; Pep Clb; Ski Clb; Teachers Aide; Var Capt Cheerldng; High Hon Roll; NHS; CSF.

NETHERTON, DREW P; Glen A Wilson HS; Hacienda Heights, CA; (3); 180/500; Drama Clb; German Clb; Letterman Clb; Ski Clb; Teachers Aide; Varsity Clb; Stage Crew; Stu Cncl; Var Capt Swmmng; Pres Acad Fit Awd; All-Amer, 2(d Team, All CIF Water Polo; All San Gabriel Vly Team Swimming; USC; Law.

NETKA, KRYSTINE; St Joseph HS; Cerritos, CA; (4); 27/180; Dance Clb; GAA; Pep Clb; SADD; Varsity Clb; Drill Tm; Pom Pon; High Hon Roll; Hon Roll; NEDT Awd; Cmnty Svc Preschl Tchr; Loyola Marymount U; Poli Sci.

NETT, CRAIG R; Woodcrest Christian HS; Menifee Valley, CA; (1); High Hon Roll; Piano; Perf Arts.

NETTLES, BRIAN C; Ramona HS; Riverside, CA; (2); 51/447; Church Yth Grp; Bsbl; Bsktbl.

NETTLETON, CERISE K; Folsom HS; Folsom, CA; (3); Intnl Clb; Model UN; Band; Mrchg Band; High Hon Roll; Hon Roll; Opt Clb Awd; Pres Acad Fit Awd; Stu Rchng Out; CSF; Excllnt Work & Longty At Awd; CA Poly; Engr.

NETTLETON, MELISSA D; Thomas Downey HS; Modesto, CA; (1); Church Yth Grp; Band; Var JV Sftbl; JV Vllybl; Hillsdale Free Baptist; Teach.

NETTO, CHRISTY; North Monterey County HS; Salinas, CA; (2); Dance Clb; Crs Cntry; Socr; Sftbl; Fresno ST; Acctnt.

NETTO, ISADORE O; Duarte HS; Duarte, CA; (3); 1/152; Church Yth Grp; Key Clb; Science Clb; Stat Trk; High Hon Roll; Hon Roll; Val; Harvard Book Awd; AP Bio Awd; AP Chem Awd; UCLA; Elec Engrng.

NEUBERG, JENNIFER L; San Benito HS; Hollister, CA; (3); 4-H; French Clb; FFA; FHA; Ski Clb; Color Guard; Powder Puff Ftbl; Socr; 4-H Awd; Hon Roll.

NEUDECK, CARLENE M; Lowell HS; San Francisco, CA; (3); Church Yth Grp; Cmnty Wkr; German Clb; SADD; Teachers Aide; Varsity Clb; Band; Badminton.

NEUDECKER, LORI K; Laguna Hills HS; Laguna Hills, CA; (4); 20/330; SADD; Var L Socr; Hon Roll; Pres Acad Fit Awd; CA Schlrshp Fed Gold Seal Bearer & Life Mem; Medallion Schlr; Acad Ltrmn; U CA Irvine; Socl Eclgy.

NEUENDORF, KEN; Seaside HS; Duncan, OK; (1); Boy Scts; Hon Roll; Dsgn.

NEUENSCHWANDER, SCOTT M; Concord HS; Pittsburg, CA; (4); Church Yth Grp; Cmnty Wkr; Drama Clb; FCA; JA; Letterman Clb; Model UN; Ski Clb; SADD; Teachers Aide; Los Medanos JC.

NEUFELD, JENNIFER LYNN; Monterey Bay Acad; Columbia, CA; (3); 1/90; Church Yth Grp; Ski Clb; Band; Chorus; Orch; School Musical; School Play; Ed Yrbk; Pres Frsh Cls; VP Soph Cls; Pacific Union Coll; Med.

NEUFELD, NETTIE L; Dos Palos HS; Dos Palos, CA; (1); Church Yth Grp; FHA; Color Guard; CSF; Fshn Dsgnr.

NEUFELD, STEPHEN P; Wasco Union HS; Wasco, CA; (3); Church Yth Grp; Cmnty Wkr; Var Capt Golf; High Hon Roll; Fresno Pcfc Coll; Arch.

NEUHAUS, BRANDI N; Ponderosa HS; Shingle Springs, CA; (4); Church Yth Grp; 4-H; FBLA; Ski Clb; Spanish Clb; Stat Bsktbl; Score Keeper; 4-H Awd; Hon Roll; Peer Cnslng Assn Of Am; Am River; Psych.

NEUHAUS, CAROLINE E; St Bonaventure HS; Camarillo, CA; (4); 35/135; Church Yth Grp; Pres Drama Clb; Sec Speech Tm; Chorus; Church Choir; School Musical; Mgr Stage Crew; Capt Cheerldng; NHS; Bnk Amer Drama Awd; CS; Natl Forensic Leag Emerald Awd; Loyola Marymount U; Engl.

NEUHAUS, JENNIFER L; Venice HS; Venice, CA; (2); Church Yth Grp; Service Clb; Band; School Play; Sec Frsh Cls; Stu Cncl; L Trk; JV L Vllybl; Cit Awd; Hon Roll; Cathy Moraga Freebird Schlrshp; Fri Night Live Co-Chrmn; Elem Tchr.

NEUMANN, CHRISTINA; Rancho Cotate HS; Rohnert Park, CA; (3); JV Sftbl; JV Trk; Envrionmental Clb 89-90; Sonoma ST; Advertising.

NEUMANN, GILAD; Einstein Acad; North Hollywood, CA; (1); Boy Scts; Quiz Bowl; Temple Yth Grp; Pres Frsh Cls; Var Bsbl; Var Bsktbl; UCLA; Cardiosurgery.

NEUMANN, KATHRYN A; Edison HS; Huntington Beach, CA; (4); Church Yth Grp; Model UN; Var Fld Hcky; JV Swmmng; Var Tennis; Hon Roll; Pres Acad Fit Awd; Alg Golden St Exam Hnrs; Bank Of Amer Achvt Awd; U CA Santa Barbara.

NEUMANN, KIMBERLY A; San Ramon HS; Danville, CA; (2); 114/567; Church Yth Grp; Library Aide; School Play; High Hon Roll; Hon Roll; Law.

NEUMANN, LINDA R; Polytechnic HS; Riverside, CA; (1); 30/600; Church Yth Grp; Cmnty Wkr; Drama Clb; Key Clb; Service Clb; SADD; Chorus; Church Choir; Swing Chorus; High Hon Roll; Debate; Chrch Soloist; Actng; Cosmtlgy.

NEUMANN, STEFFEN; Saint Monica HS; Los Angeles, CA; (3); Bsbl; Swmmng; Trk; Wt Lftg; Hon Roll; Water Polo; Engr.

NEUMAYR, THOMAS P; Burlingame HS; Hillsborough, CA; (3); JA; Teachers Aide; Crs Cntry; Hon Roll.

NEUMEYER, CHRIS F; Esperanza HS; Anaheim, CA; (2); 1/500; Cmnty Wkr; Debate Tm; Intnl Clb; NFL; Speech Tm; High Hon Roll; NHS; Pres Soph Cls; VP Stu Cncl; Mock Trial; Stu Union For Pol Awrnss; UC Berkeley; Pol Sci.

NEUMEYER, MARK J; Willits HS; Willits, CA; (3); JV Socr; JV Trk; Hon Roll; Pres Acad Fit Awd; Pres Schlr; Peer Cnslr; Art.

NEUNKIRCH, ROBERT L; Tracy HS; Tracy, CA; (2); 17/540; Church Yth Grp; German Clb; SADD; Rptr Nwsp; Lit Mag; JV Bsbl; Hon Roll; Acad Ltr; Arch Engrng.

NEUYEN, AMANDA; Irvine HS; Irvine, CA; (2); Art Clb; Aud/Vis; Chess Clb; Drama Clb; French Clb; School Musical; School Play; Stage Crew; Variety Show; Swmmng; Crop Cls; Bst Dress; Shiniest Hair; Mst Poised; Theatre, Films, Model; UCLA; Theatre.

NEVAREZ JR, ARTHUR M; Selma HS; Selma, CA; (3); Church Yth Grp; Debate Tm; Math Clb; SADD; Bsbl; Cit Awd; MESA Club; Engr.

NEVAREZ, LISA A; Saint Francis HS; San Jose, CA; (2); 17/356; Cmnty Wkr; Intnl Clb; Library Aide; Service Clb; Nwsp; Ed Yrbk; High Hon Roll; Shakespeare Clb Brd Mem; Envrnmnt Clb; Lit.

NEVAREZ, LUZMARIA G; Modesto HS; Modesto, CA; (3); Office Aide; Prfct Atten Awd; Chrldng Berryessa Cougars; San Jose City Coll; Bus.

NEVAREZ, SONIA L; Willow Glen HS; San Jose, CA; (1); VP Frsh Cls; JV Fld Hcky; JV Socr; Cit Awd; San Diego; Pediatrics.

NEVE, KELLY J; Morro Bay HS; Los Osos, CA; (2); Church Yth Grp; Pep Clb; SADD; Church Choir; Drill Tm; Bsktbl; Powder Puff Ftbl; Score Keeper; Hon Roll; Baton Twirling-Cmmnty Perfrmncs; Sun Schl Tchr/Keyboardist; CA Polytech Coll; Photo Ed.

NEVES JR, DAVID; Linden HS; Lockeford, CA; (3); 12/151; Pres 4-H; Teachers Aide; Band; Mrchg Band; Pep Band; Var L Ftbl; Score Keeper; Var Trk; 4-H Awd; Hon Roll; U Of Pacific; Elec Engr.

NEVES, JANELLE; Hanford HS; Hanford, CA; (1); Dance Clb; Drama Clb; 4-H; FBLA; Math Clb; Pep Clb; Ski Clb; Spanish Clb; School Play; Off Frsh Cls; Pepperdine; Lawyer.

NEVILLE, ANGELA; Mt Carmel HS; San Diego, CA; (3); 39/745; AFS; Rep Stu Cncl; Var Cheerldng; NHS; Spanish NHS; Vrsty Crew Cocahes Awd; E%clgy Clb; Grp Ldr Sundevil Ldrshp Tretret; CA Schlrshp Fed.

NEVILLE, LISA; La Habra HS; La Habra, CA; (3); Church Yth Grp; Pres Key Clb; Teachers Aide; Chorus; Church Choir; Hon Roll; Figure Skater; Fullerton Coll; Envrnmntl Sci.

NEVILLE, TRICIA A; East Bakersfield HS; Bakersfield, CA; (3); 54/441; Church Yth Grp; Chorus; Church Choir; Orch; School Play; Var Socr; Sftbl; JV Swmmng; Var JV Vllybl; Hon Roll; MVP Sftl, JV Vllybl, Sccr & All Area Sccr; Hnr Orch & Choir; Most Vlbl Cncrt Choir Singer; Bakersfield Coll; Elem Tchr.

NEVIN, JASON S; Santa Cruz HS; Santa Cruz, CA; (1); Church Yth Grp; JV Bsktbl; Capt JV Ftbl; JV Var Trk; Wt Lftg; Hon Roll; Sprtsmnshp Awd Ftbl; MOST Vlvl Trk.

NEVIN, MICHELLE; El Dorado HS; Placentia, CA; (1); Church Yth Grp; Cheerldng; Diving; Sports Med.

NEW, AARON; Tracy Joint Union HS; Tracy, CA; (2); 82/483; Bus Profs of Am; FBLA; Ski Clb; SADD; Cit Awd; Hon Roll; NEDT Awd; Spec Work Exper Bus Training; Bus Sales.

NEW, STEVEN T; Downey HS; Downey, CA; (4); Church Yth Grp; Jazz Band; Mrchg Band; Orch; Pep Band; Golden St Exam Alg 88, Geom 89; CSU Long Beach; Elec Engrng.

NEW, TINA; Modesto HS; Modesto, CA; (3); Drama Clb; 4-H; FBLA; FHA; SADD; Teachers Aide; School Play; Stage Crew; Ltr Grl; CA ST U Stanford; Bio Tchr.

NEWBERN, AUTUMN D; Hesperia HS; Hesperia, CA; (3); Computer Clb; FBLA; FFA; FHA; Girl Scts; VP Pres Key Clb; SADD; Chorus; Hon Roll; The Writing Celebration 1st Pl Poetry; Dist Poetry Achvt Awd; Victor Valley; Sign Lang Ed.

NEWBERRY, JASON AARON; San Juan HS; Citrus Heights, CA; (1); JV Bsbl; JV Ftbl; Hnr Natl Turkey Fed; Miami U; Sports.

NEWBERRY, KIMBERLEY K; Bella Vista HS; Orangevale, CA; (3); 97/403; Spanish Clb; Pres Acad Fit Awd.

NEWBERRY, REBECCA E; Immaculate Heart HS; Burbank, CA; (4); 1/124; Church Yth Grp; Model UN; Ed Nwsp; High Hon Roll; Hon Roll; Ntl Merit Ltr; NEDT Awd; Amnesty Intl; Coalition For Peace/Jstc Fndr; Macalester Coll; Anthrplgy.

NEWBOLD, DANIEL E; Grossmont HS; El Cajon, CA; (1); Boy Scts; Church Yth Grp; Memb San Diego Herpetological Soc; Memb Ord Of The Arrow Bsa.

NEWBORN, MARILYN M; San Pedro HS; Los Angeles, CA; (3); Teachers Aide; Var Sprt Ed Bsktbl; Var Sprt Ed Trk; Cit Awd; Prfct Atten Awd; Schltc Excllnce Cert Regntn 88 & 89; Engl/Elem Ed.

NEWBROUGH, WILLIAM J; Berean Christian HS; Concord, CA; (4); 5/76; Chorus; High Hon Roll; Hon Roll; Piano- Pepsi Cmptn 1st Prz,Fnlst, 17/GM Cmptn; Palo Alto Cncrto; Beethovan Young Pianst Cmptn; Julliard Schl Of Music; Piano.

NEWBY, HELEN L; Bella Vista HS; N Highlands, CA; (4); 72/341; Church Yth Grp; Cmnty Wkr; Debate Tm; Library Aide; Science Clb; Service Clb; SADD; Teachers Aide; Chorus; Hon Roll; Golden St Supr Wrtg Awd; Wells Coll; Physician.

NEWCOMB, ANGIE R; South HS; Bakersfield, CA; (3); 98/458; Library Aide; Office Aide; SADD; Teachers Aide; Natl Jr Hnr Soc; Petroleum Engr.

NEWCOMBE, ROBERT M; Etiwanda HS; Cucamonga, CA; (2); UCLA.

NEWELL, DEBBIE L; University HS; Santa Ana, CA; (4); 103/477; Church Yth Grp; French Clb; Chorus; Swing Chorus; Worthy Stu Awd 89-90; Girls Clb; Clark Coll; Music.

NEWELL, JAKE J; Shasta Union HS; Redding, CA; (2); Mu Alpha Theta; Ftbl; Trk; Wt Lftg; Hon Roll; Hgh Hnrs CA Gldn St Exm Algbr & Geom; CA Polytech ST U; Arch.

NEWELL, JULIE S; Chester JR/Sr HS; Lake Almanor, CA; (4); 7/60; Art Clb; Church Yth Grp; Cmnty Wkr; Spanish Clb; Band; Rptr Yrbk; JV Var Gym; Powder Puff Ftbl; Stat Score Keeper; JV Var Vllybl; CA Arts Schlr 89; Century III Ldrs Certfcct Merit 89; Candt Girls St 89; AP Engl; Loyola Marymount U; Art.

NEWELL, NICOLE; J F Kennedy HS; Anaheim, CA; (4); Knotts Berry Frm 88-89; CVS Phrmcy 90; UCLA; Biochem.

NEWELL, SARINDA; Mendocino Community HS; Mendocino, CA; (4); 1/9; Cmnty Wkr; Math Clb; Teachers Aide; Band; Chorus; Mrchg Band; School Musical; School Play; Stage Crew; Ntl Merit SF; Fncng Clb; MIT; Elec Engnrng.

NEWELL, WENDY; Chester JR/Sr HS; Lake Almanor, CA; (2); 1/48; Art Clb; Church Yth Grp; Library Aide; Math Clb; Ski Clb; Spanish Clb; SADD; Teachers Aide; VP Chorus; Trk; Gldn ST Awd Hnrs Alg I; Schlr Athlt Awd-Trck & Ski Tm; CSF Secy; U Of CA Berkeley; CPA.

NEWEY, RICHARD C; Indio HS; Bermuda Dunes, CA; (1); Church Yth Grp; Cmnty Wkr; Drill Tm; Cit Awd; Hon Roll; Sports; AZ ST U; Archeology.

NEWGENT, MATTHEW A; Highlands HS; North Highlands, CA; (4); French Clb; Pres Ski Clb; Band; Yrbk; Var L Crs Cntry; Var L Socr; JV Trk; Hon Roll; Law Tm Defnse Lawyer; Stu Ambssdr Soviet Union; Defense Language Inst; Intl Law.

NEWLOVE, NOELLE; Valley Christian Acad; Santa Maria, CA; (3); Church Yth Grp; Teachers Aide; Chorus; Var Cheerldng; Hon Roll; Prfct Atten Awd; Jr Statesmn Of Amer; Most Outstdng Std; Pensacola Christian Coll; Educ.

NEWMAN, BECKY L; Sonora Union HS; Sonora, CA; (4); 47/254; Church Yth Grp; 4-H; Teachers Aide; Acpl Chr; Band; Chorus; Church Choir; Mrchg Band; Pep Band; School Musical; Bk Of Amer Achvt Awd In Music; Stanislaus ST; Music.

NEWMAN, CORI; Adolfo Camarillo HS; Camarillo, CA; (1); School Play; Cheerldng; U CA Los Angeles; Chld Psycht.

NEWMAN, DEANNA L; Corona HS; Corona, CA; (2); 27/400; FBLA; GAA; Ski Clb; Spanish Clb; Ed Yrbk; Sftbl; Vllybl; Hon Roll; Pres Acad Fit Awd; Snow & Water Skiing; Long Beach ST; Athl Trnr.

NEWMAN, GAYLE; Elk Grove HS; Elk Grove, CA; (3); Church Yth Grp; Teachers Aide; Church Choir; Drill Tm; Ed Yrbk; Hon Roll; BRIGHAM Young U.

NEWMAN, HUNTER C; Carlsbad HS; Oceanside, CA; (3); 105/450; High Hon Roll; Hon Roll; Horse Bck Rdng; Vet.

NEWMAN, JANA M; Ramona HS; Riverside, CA; (3); 55/403; Church Yth Grp; FHA; Hosp Aide; JA; Red Cross Aide; SADD; Teachers Aide; Hon Roll; Prfct Atten Awd; Pres Acad Fit Awd; New Kid On The Block Fan Clb Capt; Loma Linda Med Schl; Med.

NEWMAN, JENNIFER L; Petaluma HS; Petaluma, CA; (3); 19/267; High Hon Roll; Hon Roll; UCSF; Pre-Med.

NEWMAN, JILL K; San Diequito HS; Encinitas, CA; (2); Speech Tm; School Play; Stage Crew; Ed Nwsp; JV Sftbl; JV Vllybl; Advncd Clas Jr Theatre; Modeling Class; Read, Write, Sports; TX Tech; Commctns.

NEWMAN, JULIE; St Marys HS; Stockton, CA; (2); Church Yth Grp; Cmnty Wkr; 4-H; Hosp Aide; Key Clb; Service Clb; Speech Tm; School Play; High Hon Roll; Hon Roll; Oil Painting; Coll For Summer Sch; USD; Phys Thrpst.

NEWMAN, LAURIE L; Serra HS; San Diego, CA; (2); FTA; Key Clb; Pep Clb; Ski Clb; SADD; Cheerldng; Cit Awd; Hon Roll; U Of Santa Barbara.

NEWMAN, MEGAN; South HS; Redondo Bch, CA; (2); 70/372; FTA; Pep Clb; Service Clb; Teachers Aide; JV Cheerldng; Elem Ed.

NEWMAN, MICHAEL K; Granada Hills HS; Northridge, CA; (2); Ski Clb; Rep Frsh Cls; Rep Soph Cls; JV Ftbl; Cit Awd; High Hon Roll; Hon Roll; Pres Acad Fit Awd; Med Doc.

NEWMAN, NATALIE D; El Cerrito HS; Kensington, CA; (2); Band; Flag Corp; Stat Bsbl; Asian Stu Union; CSF; UCLA; Chem Engr.

NEWMAN, S TODD; Saint Margarets Episcopal Schl; Laguna Hills, CA; (3); 1/32; Debate Tm; Drama Clb; Speech Tm; Stage Crew; Yrbk; Pres Stu Cncl; Var Bsbl; Var Bsktbl; JV Crs Cntry; Var Ftbl; Bus.

NEWMAN, WENDY; Greenville JR/Sr HS; Greenville, CA; (2); 1/48; Ski Clb; Band; Chorus; Variety Show; VP Frsh Cls; Pres VP Soph Cls; Capt Cheerldng; Var Sftbl; JV Vllybl; High Hon Roll; GSE Alg-High Hnrs.

NEWSON, DEADTRICK R; Montclair HS; Montclair, CA; (2); Bsktbl; Wt Lftg; Wrstlng; Typing & Job Sklls Outstndng Achvt Awd.

NEWTON, CARYL; The Academy Of Our Lady Of Peace; San Diego, CA; (1); Church Yth Grp; Cmnty Wkr; High Hon Roll; NEDT Awd; Bst Engl Stu Awd 89-90; Co Wrtr Script Annual Vrty Shw 90; Aftr Schl Asst To Disabled Cmmnty; Law.

NEWTON, DONTE L; Carson HS; Carson, CA; (2); Rep Frsh Cls; Trk; Cit Awd; Real Estate.

NEWTON, ELIJAH J; Fresno Christian HS; Fresno, CA; (1); Church Yth Grp; Ftbl; Golf; Hon Roll; Elec Engrng.

NEWTON, EREK A; Dana Hills HS; Laguna Niguel, CA; (2); Bsktbl; U Of S CA; Bus.

NEWTON, LA TRES A; San Gorgonio HS; San Bernardino, CA; (2); Cmnty Wkr; Hosp Aide; Red Cross Aide; SADD; CA ST; Cmptr.

NEWTON, RICHARD S; Montgomery HS; Santa Rosa, CA; (3); Boy Scts; Pres Church Yth Grp; Science Clb; Spanish Clb; Crs Cntry; Trk; Hon Roll; Jr NHS; Pres Acad Fit Awd; Eagle Sct; BYU; Mech Engrng.

NEWTON, SARAH; Saratoga HS; Saratoga, CA; (2); Debate Tm; NFL; Chorus; Church Choir; School Musical; Sec Jr Cls; Capt Swmmng; Trk; Hon Roll; Law.

NEWTON, SARAH C; Tracy HS; Tracy, CA; (2); 25/483; Church Yth Grp; 4-H; FFA; SADD; High Hon Roll; Friends Of Spec Olympics; CA Schlrshp Fed; Hiking Clb; Stanslaus; Vet.

NEWTON, SCOTT R; Apple Valley HS; Apple Valley, CA; (3); Letterman Clb; Teachers Aide; Capt Var Socr; Wt Lftg; Hon Roll; Phys Trnr.

NG, AIMEE E; Concord HS; Concord, CA; (3); SADD; Teachers Aide; Hon Roll.

NG, AMY S; Coalinga HS; Coalinga, CA; (4); AFS; SADD; Teachers Aide; Band; Stu Cncl; Hon Roll; Pres Acad Fit Awd; CSF; Acad Enrchmnt Decthln; UC Irvine; Dental.

NG, ANDY; Don Bosco Tech HS; Montebello, CA; (3); Computer Clb; Var Hon Roll; NHS; CA Poly.

NG, BRENDA; Lowell HS; San Francisco, CA; (2).

NG, BURTON K; Lowell HS; San Francisco, CA; (3); Church Yth Grp; FCA; Varsity Clb; JV Var Bsktbl; Comp.

NG, CHRISTINA Y; Drew College Prep; San Francisco, CA; (4); Phtg Yrbk; VP Stu Cncl; Var JV Vllybl; Pepperdine U; Bus.

NG, CHRISTINE K; Montebello HS; Montebello, CA; (3).

NG, DAVID; Don Bosco Technical Inst; Monterey Park, CA; (2); Computer Clb; Hosp Aide; Nwsp; High Hon Roll; NHS.

NG, DAVID; Sky Line HS; Oakland, CA; (1).

NG, DEMETRIA; Lowell HS; San Francisco, CA; (3); Varsity Clb; Var L Bsktbl; Var L Trk; Var L Vllybl; 89-90 All City Bsktbl/Vllybl.

NG, ELISA M; Ramona Convent HS; Monterey Park, CA; (3); Art Clb; Church Yth Grp; Cmnty Wkr; GAA; Hosp Aide; Model UN; Office Aide; SADD; Var Crs Cntry; Stat Tennis; Med.

NG, FELICIA Y; Mark Keppel HS; Monterey Park, CA; (2); Library Aide; Math Clb; Mu Alpha Theta; Band; Mrchg Band; Pep Band; Leos Clb 89-90; UCLA; Law.

NG, FRANCES; Mark Keppel HS; Monterey Park, CA; (3); 6/680; FBLA; Math Clb; Math Tm; Mu Alpha Theta; Cit Awd; High Hon Roll; Opt Clb Awd; Prfct Atten Awd; CSF; Octagon Svc Club Treas; Math.

NG, GRACE; Arcadia HS; Arcadia, CA; (4); 13/620; Am Leg Aux Girls St; Sec Rptr FBLA; VP Hosp Aide; Treas Science Clb; Treas Spanish Clb; NHS; Pres Acad Fit Awd; Sal; Natl Bicntnnl Cmptn Constitution & Bill Of Rights 1st Pl 22nd Cngrssnl Dist & 3rd Pl St CA; UCLA; Economics.

NG, JEFFREY; Phillip S Sala Burton HS; San Francisco, CA; (3); Chess Clb; Computer Clb; Office Aide; Orch; Lit Mag; Hon Roll; Elect Engr.

NG, JULIE Y; Phillip & Salaburton Academic HS; San Francisco, CA; (4); Computer Clb; French Clb; Office Aide; Ski Clb; Phtg Yrbk; Hon Roll; San Francisco ST U; Bus Adm.

NG, KARMAN; Acalanes HS; Orinda, CA; (2); 50/243; AFS; Spanish Clb; SADD; Hon Roll; Radio Clb; Stu Rep; CA Schlrshp Fdrtn.

NG, KINGSLEY; Mark Keppel HS; Monterey Park, CA; (4); 9/667; Debate Tm; Math Clb; Mu Alpha Theta; NFL; VP Science Clb; Cit Awd; High Hon Roll; Hon Roll; Pres Acad Fit Awd; 6th Oratry Novice Chmpnshps 86-87; CSF; 88-89 Sci Fr Coord; U Of CA Irvine; Comp Sci.

NG, LAM-WING; Mark Keppel HS; Monterey Park, CA; (2); JV Tennis; Hon Roll; Girls Leag Clb.

NG, LAWRENCE Y; Phillip & Sala Burton HS; San Francisco, CA; (3); Hon Roll; Bus Mgmt.

NG, LOUIS; Glen A Wilson HS; Hacienda Hts, CA; (2); Church Yth Grp; Teachers Aide; Band; Mrchg Band; Orch; Hon Roll; Asian Amer Hacienda Hts Tenns Tournmnnt 3rd Pl; Golden St Exams Hnrs Algb; Industry Hills Aquatc Clb; Med.

NG, MAE Y; Alameda HS; Alameda, CA; (4); 10/325; Treas Science Clb; Var Trk; Var Vllybl; Hon Roll; Asian, EBS Tutrng (Sec), & Lions Clbs; UC Berkeley; Mchncl Engrng.

NG, MARGARET S; Montclair HS; Montclair, CA; (4); 8/174; Hosp Aide; Yrbk; Var Crs Cntry; Var Trk; Elks Awd; Hon Roll; NHS; Prfct Atten Awd; Congressman Dreiers Outstndng Svc Cmmnty; Hosp Svcs Regnl Occuptnl Prgm; Retail Store Job; UC-IRVINE.

NG, MIKE A; California HS; San Ramon, CA; (3); Letterman Clb; Red Cross Aide; Teachers Aide; Var L Swmmng; Hon Roll; Var, Ltr Water Polo; Swim Instr & Lifeguard; First Aide & CPR; Law.

NG, NANCY; Abraham Lincoln HS; San Francisco, CA; (3); Cmnty Wkr; Teachers Aide; VP Jr Cls; VP Stu Cncl; Cheerldng; Tennis; Chico Ag Exchng Stu; Yth Edctr Pgm; Acad Of Fin; Jr Club; Bus.

NG, NORMAN; Lowell HS; San Francisco, CA; (2); Chess Clb; Science Clb; Bio.

NG, PAUL C; Pinole Valley HS; Hercules, CA; (3); AFS; Art Clb; Chess Clb; Computer Clb; Debate Tm; French Clb; Math Clb; Math Tm; NFL; Science Clb; Engrng.

NG, PRENTICE Y; Marina HS; Huntington Beach, CA; (1); JCL; Latin Clb; JV Tennis; High Hon Roll; Yale U; Bus.

NG, ROXANNA J; Schurr HS; Monterey Park, CA; (2); Spanish Clb; SADD; Band; Mrchg Band; Orch; Hon Roll; Prfct Atten Awd; Grls Leag; Jr Statesmn Amer; Piano; U Of Southern CA.

NG, RUDY J; Lowell HS; San Francisco, CA; (2); Teachers Aide; CSF.

NG, SAPPHIRA; Lowell HS; San Francisco, CA; (3); Office Aide; Var Trk; Chemathon 4th Pl; Bus.

NG, SUN T; Nogales HS; Walnut, CA; (4); 11/557; Science Clb; Teachers Aide; Rptr Yrbk; High Hon Roll; Vrsty Bdmnt; Olympc Clb; CA Schlrshp Fed; U CA Los Angeles; Mech Engrng.

NG, TINA; Abraham Lincoln HS; San Francisco, CA; (2); ROTC; Drill Tm; Rep Soph Cls; Bus.

NG, WENCY W; Skyline HS; Oakland, CA; (2); Sec German Clb; Hosp Aide; Key Clb; Math Clb; Math Tm; High Hon Roll; Hon Roll; U CA Berkeley.

NG, WILLIAM; Lowell HS; San Francisco, CA; (3); Hosp Aide; Latin Clb; Orch; Rptr Nwsp; Pres Acad Fit Awd; UC Davis; Orthopedics.

NG, WILLIAM; San Clemente HS; San Clemente, CA; (1); German Clb; Hon Roll; Pres Acad Fit Awd; CSF.

NG, WING N; George Washington HS; San Francisco, CA; (2); High Hon Roll; Hon Roll; Vrsty Badmntn; ST U San Jose; Accntng.

NGAN, PRUDENCE; Milipitas HS; Milpitas, CA; (1); Spanish Clb; Hon Roll; Spnsh Clb Treas; Stanford; Lwyr.

NGAN, TAI; Orange HS; Garden Grove, CA; (2); Key Clb; Math Clb; Science Clb; Tennis; Cit Awd; High Hon Roll; Hon Roll; NHS; Acad Decathalon; Asian Club; Bus.

NGANN, SACCARA; Villa Park HS; Orange, CA; (3); Spanish Clb; Prncpls Hnr Rl; CSF; Asian Clb.

NGARIYAN, SUMENA; Abraham Lincoln HS; San Francisco, CA; (2); Acpl Chr; CSF; UC Berkeley; Hotel Mgmt.

NGHIEM, CINDY; Patrick Henry HS; San Diego, CA; (2); Sec French Clb; Lit Mag; High Hon Roll; NHS; Prfct Atten Awd; Pres Acad Fit Awd; Outstndng Engl & Sci Stu; Kiwanis Bldrs Clb; UC San Diego; Med.

NGHIEM, QUAN; Oakland HS; Oakland, CA; (2); 19/669; Spanish Clb; Teachers Aide; Var Tennis; Cit Awd; Hon Roll; Golden St Exam Acad Excllnc Awd; Golden St Schlrs 88; Marcus A Foster Educl Inst Achvt Awd; U CA Berkeley; Civil Engrng.

NGIN, PITOU; Artesia HS; Lakewood, CA; (2); JA; High Hon Roll; Prfct Atten Awd; Pres Acad Fit Awd; Conestoga; Gate Prgm; UCLA; Aero Engr.

NGO, ANH; Lowell HS; San Francisco, CA; (2); Band; JV Var Bsbl; JV Bsbl Chmpnshp 90; UC Berkeley; Doc.

NGO, BICH; Seaside HS; Marina, CA; (2); French Clb; Medicine.

NGO, BOBBY D; Glendale HS; Glendale, CA; (4); Drama Clb; Chorus; School Musical; School Play; Variety Show; Rptr Nwsp; Crs Cntry; Vlybl & Bsktbl; PTSA Achvmnt Schlrshp; CA ST Northridge; Bus.

NGO, CHANH V; Luther Burbank HS; Sacramento, CA; (3); Var Vllybl; Hon Roll; VP Prodctn Econmcs Cls; Sacramento CC; Mech Engr.

NGO, CUONG; John F Kennedy HS; Cypress, CA; (3); Chess Clb; Computer Clb; FBLA; Key Clb; Rep Yrbk; Bsktbl; Var Tennis; Hon Roll; NHS; UCLA; Arch.

NGO, DAVID; Galileo HS; San Francisco, CA; (4); Computer Clb; JA; Math Clb; Red Cross Aide; Science Clb; Hon Roll; CSF; U CA Davis.

NGO, DIANE A; Independence HS; San Jose, CA; (3); Sec Debate Tm; Teachers Aide; Chorus; CA Schlrshp Fed; I-Pride; Acctng.

NGO, DIANE B; San Gabriel HS; San Gabriel, CA; (2); Service Clb; Spanish Clb; SADD; Rep Frsh Cls; Rep Soph Cls; Stat Tennis; Hon Roll; CSF; UCLA; Psych.

NGO, DU K; Skyline HS; Oakland, CA; (2); Chess Clb; Intnl Clb; Math Clb; Math Tm; Off Frsh Cls; Stu Cncl; Wrstlng; UC Berkley.

NGO, DUYEN K; Hawthorne HS; Lawndale, CA; (4); AFS; Aud/Vis; Hosp Aide; Ski Clb; Ed Nwsp; Hon Roll; Acadmc Dcthln; Diaconians; TV Reporter.

NGO, HANH T; Pasadena HS; Pasadena, CA; (3); Am Leg Aux Girls St; French Clb; Teachers Aide; Var JV Vllybl; French Hon Soc; Vietnamese Clb; Asian-Am Clb; Greenpeace; Amnesty Intl; CA ST Los Angeles; Bus Mgmt.

NGO, HIEN V; La Quinta HS; Westminster, CA; (1); Cmnty Wkr; JV Tennis; High Hon Roll; Hon Roll; Jr NHS; NHS; UCI; Comp.

NGO, HOA; Bassett HS; La Puente, CA; (3); Tennis; Acad Achvt Engl; Outstndng Excllnc Chem, Typng; Physcn.

NGO, HOANG; Bellarmine College Prep; San Jose, CA; (3); 50/300; Dance Clb; Science Clb; JV Socr; Hon Roll; Hnr Pin St Peters Prep; JV Soccer St Petera Prep; Oriental Clb St Peters Prep; UC Davis; Elec Engr.

NGO, HOWARD H; Lowell HS; San Francisco, CA; (2); Church Yth Grp; NFL; Office Aide; Speech Tm; Teachers Aide; Chorus; School Musical; School Play; VP Kermesse Fnd Rsr; Chns Schl Vllybl Tm Cptn 1st Pl 89; High Hnr Roll Chns Schl; Harvard; Law.

NGO, HUNG M; Chaffe HS; Ontario, CA; (3); French Clb; Church Choir; Yrbk; Off Frsh Cls; Socr; CA Tech; Electrnc Drftng.

NGO, HUONG M; Alhambra HS; Alhambra, CA; (3); Red Cross Aide; Band; Mrchg Band; Orch; JV Swmmng; Hon Roll; Spanish NHS.

NGO, JENNY B; Rosemead HS; Rosemead, CA; (1); Math Clb; Cit Awd; High Hon Roll; Hon Roll; Prfct Atten Awd; Actvts-Sign Lang & Poetry Clubs; Achvts-1st & 3rd Pl Hstry Day, Stu Mnth, Wnnr Indo-Chinese Schlrshp; UC Davis; Medical Field.

NGO, KIET; Saddleback HS; Santa Ana, CA; (1); French Clb; FBLA; JV Var Wrstlng; USC; Bio.

NGO, LAM Q; Lowell HS; San Francisco, CA; (2); Office Aide; Red Cross Aide; Chinese Clb; Golden St Exam 1st Yr Alg Hgh Hnrs 89; UC Berkeley; Pre-Med.

NGO, LINH KIEU; Van Nuys HS; Reseda, CA; (4); Cmnty Wkr; French Clb; Teachers Aide; Varsity Clb; Off Soph Cls; Off Jr Cls; Vllybl; Cit Awd; High Hon Roll; Hon Roll; CSF; Chinese Clb; UCSD; Medcl.

NGO, LISA; Galileo HS; San Francisco, CA; (2); Dance Clb; Chinese Culture Clb; Chinese Bilingual Clb; Piano; Dermatology.

NGO, LOC; San Bernardino HS; San Bernardino, CA; (1); Socr; San Bernardino HS Outstanding Athlete; Math Academic Excellence; College; Air Plane Mechanical.

NGO, LUONG T; San Diego HS; San Diego, CA; (3); 30/415; Math Tm; Teachers Aide; NHS; Prfct Atten Awd; Erly Otrch Prgrm; ROP Clss Tllr Trngn; CSF.

NGO, MAI PHUONG; Chino HS; Chino, CA; (2); Science Clb; Spanish Clb; SADD; Band; Mrchg Band; High Hon Roll; Prfct Atten Awd; Pres Acad Fit Awd; Spanish NHS; Badminton; Silver Spur Awd; CSF; UCLA; Med.

NGO, NHI H; Schurr HS; Montebello, CA; (2); Spanish Clb; High Hon Roll; Hon Roll; Prfct Atten Awd; SADD; Chinese & Intl Clb; Accntng.

NGO, NHIEN; James Madison HS; San Diego, CA; (4); 1/368; Cmnty Wkr; Hosp Aide; JA; Math Clb; Math Tm; Mu Alpha Theta; Teachers Aide; Var L Tennis; Cit Awd; High Hon Roll; Robert C Byrd Hnrs Schlrshp; UCSD Erly Adm Hnr Prgm; Salk Inst Intrnshp; Hlth Career/Yth Ldrshp Awds; UCSD; Pre-Med.

NGO, NHUT M; Hoover HS; San Diego, CA; (3); 36/365; French Clb; Nwsp; Cit Awd; Hon Roll; NHS; Gldn St Exam Alg & Geom; Top Of Mark Club; ROP Grphc Arts; CA Poly ST U SLO; Cmmnctns.

NGO, PHUOCLUONG D; Wilcox HS; Santa Clara, CA; (1); Cit Awd; Hon Roll; Prfct Atten Awd; Alg I Golden St Awd; Dermatology.

NGO, PHUONG P; Skyline HS; Oakland, CA; (2); Hosp Aide; Key Clb; Temple Yth Grp; Lit Mag; Hon Roll; Val; Latin Clb; Math Clb; Math Tm; Orch; Asian Advsry Cmmtte Grome Essay Awd; Vietnamese Stu Union Secy; CA Schlrshp Fed; Stanford; Srgn.

NGO, PINKY; Casa Roble Fundamental HS; Orangevale, CA; (2); 47/461; AFS; FBLA; Spanish Clb; Cit Awd; High Hon Roll; Hon Roll; NHS; Prfct Atten Awd; Pres Acad Fit Awd; Med.

NGO, TAM MINH; Hoover HS; San Diego, CA; (1); #1 In Class; Math Clb; Cit Awd; French Hon Soc; High Hon Roll; NHS; Acadmc Leag Club; NHS Club; Gldn St Exam Awd; UCSD; Arch Drftng.

NGO, THANH; Westminster HS; Midway, CA; (1); Cit Awd; U Of Irvine.

NGO, THAO M; Edison HS; Fresno, CA; (1); Var Tennis; Hon Roll; Vol Incm Tax Asst; UC Berkeley.

NGO, THI; Leuzinger HS; Lawndale, CA; (1); Kiwanis Awd; Swmg; Vlybl; Pres Acad Ftnss Awd; U CA Irvine.

NGO, THINH; La Sierra HS; Riverside, CA; (4); 20/350; Art Clb; Chess Clb; Science Clb; High Hon Roll; Hon Roll; Prfct Atten Awd; Aeronautic.

NGO, THUC X; Mountain View HS; El Monte, CA; (3); VP FBLA; Tennis; Hon Roll; Engrng.

NGO, TRAN M; Saddleback HS; Santa Ana, CA; (2); FBLA; Spanish Clb; SADD; Cit Awd; Hon Roll; Acad Ltr; Love Writing; Teacher Selection For Earth Watch Schlrshp; USC; Med.

NGO, TRANG T; Castle Park HS; San Diego, CA; (4); 17/328; Cmnty Wkr; Hosp Aide; Intnl Clb; JA; Service Clb; Ed Nwsp; Rep Jr Cls; Rep Sr Cls; Rep Stu Cncl; Cit Awd; Cert Spec Congrssnl Recgntn From Jim Bates; Cert Outstndng Achvt Cnty Wide Subjct; UCSD; Bio.

NGO, TRANG-AIME; Tokay HS; Stockton, CA; (3); 10/600; French Clb; Speech Tm; SADD; Temple Yth Grp; Orch; Stat Bsktbl; Var Trk; High Hon Roll; Prfct Atten Awd; CSF; Cmmnctn Imprvmnt Assn; Stu In Prevention Drugs & Alcohol; U San Diego-Pre Med.

NGO, TUNG T; San Bernandino HS; San Bernardino, CA; (3); 27/400; AFS; French Clb; FBLA; Var Tennis; High Hon Roll; NHS; Prfct Atten Awd; Pres Acad Fit Awd; Bowling; Fishing; UCR; Intl Bus.

NGO, UYEN THI-CHAU; Poway HS; Poway, CA; (3); 46/761; Cit Awd; High Hon Roll; Hon Roll; NHS; Amnesty Intl Ofcr; Keywannetts; Environmntl Awarenss; CSF; U Of CA San Diego; Med.

NGO, VINH; Alameda HS; Alameda, CA; (3); Varsity Clb; JV Bsktbl; JV Var Ftbl; Var Tennis; Hon Roll; Jujitsu Clb 1st Pl; Judo Cntst 85 & 87; All Lg Crnr Bck Ftbl Tm; Bst Back Awd; Lg Champs Tennis Tm; UCLA; Sports Med.

NGO, VY T; Milpitas HS; Milpitas, CA; (1); High Hon Roll; Hon Roll; Piano; Arch Engr.

NGO, VYRIO; Santa Ana HS; Santa Ana, CA; (3); Chess Clb; Math Clb; Science Clb; Stu Cncl; Var Tennis; Gov Hon Prg Awd.

NGOC, NGUYEN K; Santiago HS; Santa Ana, CA; (2); 20/498; Art Clb; French Clb; German Clb; Math Tm; Awd Stu Of The Qrtr; UCI; Pre-Med.

NGOV, PRAUS L; Madison HS; San Diego, CA; (3); Var Crs Cntry; Var Trk; Cit Awd; Hon Roll; Prfct Atten Awd; San Diego Tribunes All Acad Tm; Martial Arts; USD; Chem.

NGOV, SENG V; Oxnard HS; Van Nuys, CA; (4); 14/400; Computer Clb; Drama Clb; Spanish Clb; Teachers Aide; School Play; Stage Crew; Nwsp; Cit Awd; High Hon Roll; Hon Roll; CA ST Northridge; Accntng.

NGOYEN, QUYEN V; La Quinta HS; Santa Ana, CA; (4); 15/340; French Clb; Key Clb; Hon Roll; Schlr Of The Qrtr; Viet Clb CSF; UCT; Pharm.

NGU, ANH H; Mira Mesa HS; San Diego, CA; (2); 4-H; Math Clb; Math Tm; Science Clb; Trk; Cit Awd; 4-H Awd; NHS; CJSF & CSF; Project Prevent Clb; Peer Cnslg Clb; Arch.

NGU, HAO; Bakersfield HS; Bakersfield, CA; (3); Church Yth Grp; Debate Tm; Key Clb; Speech Tm; Hon Roll; Interact Club; Stu For Wrld Cnsrvtn; Bus.

NGU, PHUONG; San Marcos HS; Santa Barbara, CA; (2); French Clb; USCD; Intr Dsgn.

NGUY, CYNDI T; Mark Keppel HS; Monterey Park, CA; (2); FBLA; Key Clb; Math Clb; Bsktbl; Vllybl; CSF-CA Schlrshp Fed; UCLA Of CA ST; Bus Admin.

NGUY, HOA TU; Hoover HS; San Diego, CA; (2); 1/538; FTA; Office Aide; Hon Roll; SDSU Stu Svc Awd; SDSU; Fashn Merch.

NGUY, HUNG; Westminster HS; Garden Grove, CA; (1); Yrbk; Var Bsktbl; Capt Var Ftbl; Var Tennis; Bus.

NGUY, LAN TU; Hoover HS; San Diego, CA; (3); FTA; Hon Roll.

NGUY, MY THANA; George Washington HS; San Francisco, CA; (2); Drama Clb; Chorus; Variety Show; Rep Soph Cls; JV Swmmng; High Hon Roll; Hon Roll; Cert Prtcptn Pblc Schls Wk; Cert Achvt Engl; UCLA; Bus.

NGUY, THOMSON DAVID; Moorpark HS; Moorpark, CA; (2); 1/247; Band; Jazz Band; Mrchg Band; Pep Band; School Play; Variety Show; Rptr Nwsp; Rptr Yrbk; JV Crs Cntry; JV Trk; US Nvl Acad; Physcs.

NGUYEN, ALEX P; Bassett HS; Valinda, CA; (3); French Clb; Letterman Clb; Varsity Clb; Bsktbl; Tennis; Wt Lftg; French Hon Soc; Hon Roll.

NGUYEN, ALISON; Wilcox HS; Santa Clara, CA; (1); Chorus; High Hon Roll; Vietnamese Club; Outstndng Achvmnt Wrld Hist; UC Stanford; Lwyr.

NGUYEN, ALLEN; James Lick HS; San Jose, CA; (4); 18/257; French Clb; Intnl Clb; Math Tm; Var Crs Cntry; Var Tennis; Hon Roll; NHS; San Jose ST U; Acctng.

NGUYEN, AN; Edison HS; Stockton, CA; (2); French Clb; Teachers Aide; Band; Lit Mag; Off Jr Cls; Bsktbl; Ftbl; Tennis; Vllybl.

NGUYEN, ANDERSON; Lowell HS; San Francisco, CA; (3); Am Leg Boys St; ROTC; Teachers Aide; Color Guard; Wt Lftg; High Hon Roll; Prfct Atten Awd; Pres Acad Fit Awd; Cornell U; Sci/Math.

NGUYEN, ANDREW M; Bullard HS; Fresno, CA; (2); German Clb; Hosp Aide; SADD; Tennis; Trk; Cinematography.

NGUYEN, ANGELA T; Santana HS; Santee, CA; (4); 49/557; High Hon Roll; Hon Roll; Vietnamese Yth Mem; Rcvd Sprts Awd; Grossmont Coll; Comp Engr.

NGUYEN, ANH; Edison HS; Stockton, CA; (2); Hon Roll; NHS; Comp Engr.

NGUYEN, ANH; Valencia HS; Placentia, CA; (2); Science Clb; Spanish Clb; High Hon Roll; Pres Acad Fit Awd; Spanish NHS; Dstngshd Schlr Awd; Med.

NGUYEN, ANH QUAN QUOC; Orange HS; Orange, CA; (4); 12/425; Hosp Aide; Pres Key Clb; Sec Drm Mjr(t); Quiz Bowl; Scholastic Bowl; VP Science Clb; Service Clb; Varsity Clb; Ftbl; Tennis; Karate Blck Blt; U Of CA San Diego; Pedtrcn.

NGUYEN, ANH T; Lincoln HS; Stockton, CA; (2); Temple Yth Grp; Orch; High Hon Roll; Hon Roll; Pres Acad Fit Awd; Students In Prevention; Coll Schltc Fed; Pediatrician.

NGUYEN, ANH T; Milpitas HS; Milpitas, CA; (2); French Clb; Service Clb; Stu Cncl; Mgr(s); Stat Score Keeper; Cit Awd; High Hon Roll; NHS; Med.

NGUYEN, ANN T; Westminster HS; Westminster, CA; (3); Latin Clb; School Musical; High Hon Roll; Prfct Atten Awd; St Schlr; Cal ST Fullerton; Nrsng.

NGUYEN, ANTU; Westminster HS; Westminster, CA; (4); Sec Church Yth Grp; VP German Clb; Pres Key Clb; Teachers Aide; Church Choir; Ed Nwsp; Kiwanis Awd; Pres Schlr; CSF; Orng Cty Acad Decthln Team; Stu Of Mnth-Feb; U Of CA Los Angeles; Physcs.

NGUYEN, BANG C; Buena Park HS; Buena Park, CA; (3); Computer Clb; Key Clb; Math Clb; Tennis; High Hon Roll; Prfct Atten Awd; Physcn.

NGUYEN, BAO QUOC; Washington HS; San Francisco, CA; (2); Chess Clb; German Clb; Math Clb; Red Cross Aide; Science Clb; Hon Roll; Achvmnt Awrd In Grmn Gemtry & Wrld Cvlztn; Schl Rcgntn Awrd In Gldn St Exam; UC School System.

NGUYEN, BAOCHAU D; Escondido HS; Escondido, CA; (1); Cit Awd; Hon Roll; Prfct Atten Awd; CSF; Polomar Coll; Arch.

NGUYEN, BAOKIEM; Fremont HS; Sunnyvale, CA; (2); French Clb; Model UN; Lcrss.

NGUYEN, BECKY; North Hollywood HS; North Hollywood, CA; (3); Treas Church Yth Grp; GAA; JA; Natl Beta Clb; Spanish Clb; Chorus; Church Choir; Var Capt Vllybl; High Hon Roll; Hon Roll; CJSF; CSF.

NGUYEN, BEE; Escondido HS; Evista, CA; (4); Dance Clb; Key Clb; Sec Treas Pep Clb; Ski Clb; Rep Jr Cls; Rep Sr Cls; Rep Stu Cncl; Var Capt Cheerldng; Var Capt Pom Pon; JV Var Powder Puff Ftbl; Daisy Chain; Coaches & Advsr Awds-Chrldng; Palomar; Med.

NGUYEN, BESSIE; Pittsburg HS; Pittsburg, CA; (1); Church Yth Grp; Cmnty Wkr; Office Aide; Teachers Aide; Chorus; Church Choir; Hon Roll; U O Pacific; Bus.

NGUYEN, BICH LOAN N; Ganesha HS; Pomona, CA; (3); 3/260; Pres French Clb; VP Math Clb; Var Tennis; Cit Awd; High Hon Roll; Hon Roll; CA Schlrshp Fed; UC Irvine; Civil Engrng.

NGUYEN, BICH TY N; Ramona HS; Riverside, CA; (3); 14/403; French Clb; Temple Yth Grp; Varsity Clb; Var L Tennis; Hon Roll; U Of Riverside; Dentistry.

NGUYEN, BICHNGA; Lincoln HS; Stockton, CA; (3); 1/592; Church Yth Grp; Mu Alpha Theta; Spanish Clb; High Hon Roll; CSF; Intl Bus.

NGUYEN, BICHNGOC T; Tustin HS; Tustin, CA; (4); Girl Scts; Chorus; High Hon Roll; Vietnamese Club; Piano; Hiking; USC Long Bch; Bio.

NGUYEN, BINH VUONG; Rancho Alamitos HS; Stanton, CA; (4); 2/245; Church Yth Grp; Cmnty Wkr; French Clb; Science Clb; Teachers Aide; Orch; Elks Awd; High Hon Roll; Hon Roll; Sal; Svc Hand Awd; Math & Hstry Tutor; Girls League; UCI; Med.

NGUYEN, CAM TU; Mc Clymond HS; Oakland, CA; (1); Art Clb; Church Yth Grp; French Clb; FBLA; Hosp Aide; Intnl Clb; Math Clb; Model UN; ROTC; Band; Multi-Cltrl Clb; Mdcl Dctr.

NGUYEN, CAMLINH THI; Edison HS; Stockton, CA; (3); French Clb; Hon Roll; Outstndng Acac Hnrs Awd; Frnch Cls 3/4 Hnr; Nrsng.

NGUYEN, CAROLINE T; Mission Viejo HS; Mission Viejo, CA; (1); 6/450; Mrchg Band; Hon Roll; Intl Baccalaureate Pgm.

NGUYEN, CAROLYN N; Bonita HS; La Verne, CA; (1); Church Yth Grp; Drama Clb; FBLA; SADD; School Play; Var Tennis; High Hon Roll; Hon Roll; Ntl Merit Ltr; Stu Agnst The Violation Of Earth; CSF.

NGUYEN, CASSIE T; Jordan HS; Long Beach, CA; (3); English Clb; Key Clb; Math Clb; Band; School Play; Vllybl; Kiwanis Awd; Opt Clb Awd; Pres Acad Fit Awd; Val; Schlrshp Prvt Lssns On Clrnt; Miss US Teen CA Pgnt; Bdmnt Team, Asian Clb; Vlybl Clb; CATP; USC; Actng.

NGUYEN, CATHY; Skyline HS; Oakland, CA; (3); Key Clb; Math Clb; Teachers Aide; Yrbk; Hon Roll; ASU; VSU VP; Internl Clb; Med.

NGUYEN, CATHY A; J F Kennedy HS; Sacramento, CA; (4); Art Clb; Cmnty Wkr; Computer Clb; French Clb; Math Clb; Speech Tm; Band; Nwsp; Cert Awd-Outstndng Achvt 87-88; Hnrs-Geom Gldn ST Exm; Med.

NGUYEN, CHARLES; University HS; Irvine, CA; (3); 41/580; Boy Scts; French Clb; Intnl Clb; Math Clb; Science Clb; Nwsp; JV Trk; French Hon Soc; Hon Roll; NHS; VP Vietnamese Club 88-90; BSA Eagle Candidate; Project Ngoc Or Proj Pearl; UCI Helps Refugees; UCI; Bio-Chem.

NGUYEN, CHAU H; Irvine HS; Tustin, CA; (3); Boy Scts; Cmnty Wkr; Ftbl; Trk; Gov Hon Prg Awd; High Hon Roll; Pres Acad Fit Awd; UCI; Med.

NGUYEN, CHAU Q; Estancia HS; Costa Mesa, CA; (2); CA ST Long Beach; Word Proc.

NGUYEN, CHI; Siver Creek HS; San Jose, CA; (4); 89/420; Office Aide; Teachers Aide; Hon Roll; Certfct Recogntn; Certfft Achvt Crtfct Merit; PE Hon; Mission Coll.

NGUYEN, CHI D; Mark Keppel HS; Alhambra, CA; (4); French Clb; FBLA; Key Clb; Pres Math Clb; Rep Math Tm; Science Clb; Cit Awd; High Hon Roll; Pres Acad Fit Awd; YMCA Clb; Yth Govt; Elizabeth Habar Schlrshp Fund; UC Irvine; Bio.

NGUYEN, CHI DIEM; Hoover HS; San Diego, CA; (2); Cit Awd; High Hon Roll; Hon Roll; NHS; Prfct Atten Awd; Astronomy.

NGUYEN, CHI L; Costa Mesa HS; Costa Mesa, CA; (4); 4/233; Church Yth Grp; Cmnty Wkr; Computer Clb; JCL; Sec Latin Clb; Math Clb; Math Tm; Pres Science Clb; Ed Nwsp; Cit Awd; JV Badmntn; CSF Sealbrer; U Intrschltc Leag; U Of CA Irvine; Langs.

NGUYEN, CHI P; Huntington Beach HS; Huntington Beach, CA; (2); Red Cross Aide; UC Irvine; Med.

NGUYEN, CHIEN; Hoover HS; San Diego, CA; (1).

NGUYEN, CHINH T; Santiago HS; Garden Grove, CA; (2); Art Clb; Computer Clb; French Clb; GAA; Yrbk; Mgr(s); JV Tennis; JV Trk; High Hon Roll; Hon Roll; CSF; GA Tech; Theatre.

NGUYEN, CHINH V; Fremont HS; Oakland, CA; (3); Computer Clb; Math Clb; Band; JV Tennis; Cit Awd; High Hon Roll; Hon Roll; Ntl Merit Ltr; Poly ST U CA; Arch.

NGUYEN, CHRIS; Lowell HS; San Francisco, CA; (3); Science Clb; Band.

NGUYEN, CHRIS T; Magnolia HS; Orange, CA; (3); Hosp Aide; High Hon Roll; Ntl Merit Ltr; Smmr Ldrshp Acad Nwsp Stff; Natl Hnr Soc; CSF; Gate Club; Intl Club Schlrshp; Med.

NGUYEN, CHRISTINA P; Southwest HS; San Diego, CA; (3); Church Yth Grp; SADD; High Hon Roll; Hon Roll; Amer Lit Awd; 3-D Dsgn Awd; Interact Club; Bus.

NGUYEN, CINDY QUYNH-TRANG; Costa Mesa HS; Costa Mesa, CA; (4); 7/239; Cmnty Wkr; French Clb; Quiz Bowl; Pres Service Clb; Variety Show; Ed Nwsp; Ed Yrbk; Sec Soph Cls; VP Stu Cncl; High Hon Roll; Exchng Club Yth Of The Yr; CA Schlrshp Fed; Vlntr Tchr Vietnamese Lang Ctr; Stanford U; Englsh.

NGUYEN, CUC H; Andrew Hill HS; San Jose, CA; (3); 22/444; French Clb; Math Tm; Hon Roll; CSF; Natvie Amer Club; U CA Santa Cruz; Accntng.

NGUYEN, CUONG; Leuzinger HS; Hawthorne, CA; (2); Church Yth Grp; Computer Clb; Frsh Cls; Stu Cncl; Crs Cntry; Trk; Cit Awd; YMCA Fairhurst Awd; Karate Plq; Bsktbl, Ftbl Trphys; Comp Sci.

NGUYEN, CUONG P; Mountain View HS; El Monte, CA; (4); Debate Tm; Drama Clb; FBLA; JV Tennis; Cit Awd; Cycling Clb; Creative Wrtng Clb; CA ST Los Angeles; Bus Fnance.

NGUYEN, CUONG Q; Andrew Hill HS; San Jose, CA; (3); 4/30; Church Yth Grp; Math Clb; Teachers Aide; JV Var Bsktbl; High Hon Roll; Hon Roll; Cal Poly; Comp Engrng.

NGUYEN, CUONG T; Bolsa Grande HS; Westminster, CA; (2); Church Choir; Intrml Bsktbl; Intrml Ftbl; Intrml Swmmng; Intrml Trk; Intrml Vllybl; Hon Roll.

NGUYEN, CYNTHIA HOAITRAN; Santa Clara HS; San Jose, CA; (4); Cmnty Wkr; Hosp Aide; Red Cross Aide; Science Clb; Spanish Clb; Teachers Aide; Temple Yth Grp; VICA; Chorus; Church Choir; Help The Boat People Pgm; Explorers Clb; San Jose ST U; Optometrist.

NGUYEN, DAI; San Bernardino HS; San Bernardino, CA; (3); German Clb; Math Clb; High Hon Roll; Prfct Atten Awd; UCLA; Med.

NGUYEN, DAI T; Costa Mesa HS; Costa Mesa, CA; (4); 74/233; Sec German Clb; Library Aide; Science Clb; Teachers Aide; Var Tennis; AP Chem Club; AP Physics Club; Vietnamese Club; Cal ST Pomona; Bus Admin.

NGUYEN, DAL P; Andrew Hill HS; San Jose, CA; (3); Art Clb; French Clb; Math Tm; Vietnms Clb; UC Davis; Mktg.

NGUYEN, DANG M; San Diego HS; San Diego, CA; (2); French Clb; Rptr Nwsp; Rep Frsh Cls; Var Socr; JV Trk; Jr NHS; Aerospace Engrng.

NGUYEN, DANH; Fred C Beyer HS; Modesto, CA; (3); Art Clb; SADD; Hon Roll; Psychology.

NGUYEN, DANH H; Bonita HS; La Verne, CA; (3); Art Clb; FBLA; SADD; JV Tennis; High Hon Roll; Hon Roll; Ntl Merit Ltr; CSF; Goldn St Exam Alg & Geom Acad Excllnce Hnrs Awd; Arch.

NGUYEN, DANNY; La Quinta HS; Fountain Valley, CA; (2); 5/46; Chess Clb; Key Clb; Bsktbl; Socr; Tennis; Vllybl; Bus.

NGUYEN, DAO; Andrew Hill HS; San Jose, CA; (4); 37/293; French Clb; Math Tm; Hon Roll; Pres Acad Fit Awd; Native Am Club; CSF; UC Santa Cruz; Dntstry.

NGUYEN, DAT; Hoover HS; San Diego, CA; (2); French Clb; Nwsp; Yrbk; Hon Roll; Badmntn; Hnr Awd Congrss; Golden St Exm Awd; Comp Pgmmr.

NGUYEN, DAT; Saddleback HS; Santa Ana, CA; (4); 46/520; Chess Clb; Cmnty Wkr; French Clb; Mu Alpha Theta; Science Clb; Tennis; Prfct Atten Awd; Outwrd Bnd Awd; U Of CA Irvine; Comp Sci.

NGUYEN, DAT D; Los Amigos HS; Fountain Valley, CA; (2); 1/365; Quiz Bowl; Scholastic Bowl; High Hon Roll; Hon Roll; Aikido-Blue Blet Japn Mrtl Arts; CSF; UCI; Comp Engrng.

NGUYEN, DAT H; Poway HS; San Diego, CA; (1); JV Ftbl; JV Vllybl; JV Wrstlng; Cit Awd; High Hon Roll; Hon Roll; Prfct Atten Awd; Pres Acad Fit Awd; Fresh Of Yr; Mst Outstndng Wrestler; Stu Of Mnth Nov 89, March 90; Stanford; Med.

NGUYEN, DAWN; Katella HS; Anaheim, CA; (3); Key Clb; Pep Clb; Teachers Aide; School Play; Pres Frsh Cls; Pres Soph Cls; Cheerldng; Tennis; Cit Awd; Hon Roll; UC Santa Barbara; Psych.

NGUYEN, DENNIS; San Diego HS; San Diego, CA; (3); Debate Tm; French Clb; Intnl Clb; Tennis; UCSD; Med.

NGUYEN, DIANA T; Mater Dei HS; Garden Grove, CA; (2); Vllybl; UCI; Psych.

NGUYEN, DIEM L; Costa Mesa HS; Costa Mesa, CA; (4); 4/233; Church Yth Grp; Cmnty Wkr; Computer Clb; Latin Clb; Math Clb; Math Tm; Science Clb; Church Choir; Rptr Nwsp; High Hon Roll; UIL Typing; Jr Var Badminton; CA Schlrshp Fed; U Of CA Irvine; Comp Sci.

NGUYEN, DIEN; Baldwin Park HS; Baldwin Park, CA; (2); Cit Awd; High Hon Roll; Fri Night Live Club; CA ST Pomona; Comp Sci.

NGUYEN, DIEP; La Quinta HS; Westminster, CA; (3); 27/338; Chess Clb; French Clb; Key Clb; SADD; Cit Awd; High Hon Roll; Hon Roll; NHS; Ntl Merit Ltr; CSF 2 Yrs; Vietnamese Clb; Natl Hnr Soc 7 Yrs; Silver Aztec 89-90; UCLA; Bio.

NGUYEN, DIEP N; Los Amigos HS; Fountain Valley, CA; (3); 11/294; Teachers Aide; High Hon Roll; Goldn St Acad Excllnce Awd; Keywanettes Clb; Rgnl Sci Olympd; UC Irvine; Comp Sci.

NGUYEN, DIEP T; Grant HS; Sacramento, CA; (1); Cit Awd; High Hon Roll; Hon Roll; Real Est.

NGUYEN, DOAN K; Villa Park HS; Orange, CA; (2); Capt Church Yth Grp; Key Clb; Math Clb; Office Aide; Hist Science Clb; Variety Show; High Hon Roll; Sweepstakes Wnnr Of Schl Sci Fair Best Of The Fair 90; U Of CA Irvine; Preventv Med.

NGUYEN, DOI; Bolsa Grande HS; Garden Grove, CA; (3); Arch.

NGUYEN, DONALD Q; Milpitas HS; Milpitas, CA; (4); 17/500; Capt Debate Tm; Drama Clb; 4-H; French Clb; Mgr JA; Math Tm; Capt Speech Tm; School Play; Ed Nwsp; Stu Cncl; Spk Fr,Engl,Vietnamese & Japanese; Spch Dbate Champ Lincoln-Douglas Tourney; U CA Los Angeles; Law.

NGUYEN, DOROTHY H; Santa Teresa HS; San Jose, CA; (1); Rep French Clb; Hosp Aide; Model UN; Hon Roll; CSF; Amnesty Intl; Hokubei Manichi Math Cnst 3rd Pl 90.

NGUYEN, DUC B; Los Amigos HS; Fountain Valley, CA; (2); 52/423; French Clb; Key Clb; Hon Roll; Mock Trl Tm; Nom Stu Ambssdr Pgm; Law.

NGUYEN, DUC T; Mount Pleasant HS; San Jose, CA; (2); Engrng.

NGUYEN, DUCQUAN P; Don Bosco Technical Inst; Downey, CA; (3); Chess Clb; Church Yth Grp; JV Crs Cntry; Hon Roll; JETS Awd; NHS; Outstndng Awd; Acad Awds; 4th Pl-Advncd Mech Drafting Cmptn-Rio Hondo Coll; Cal Poly-Ramona; Mech Engr.

NGUYEN, DUNG; Mira Mesa HS; Seattle, WA; (3); Drama Clb; Key Clb; School Play; U Of Washington; Physcology.

NGUYEN, DUNG; San Gorgonio HS; San Bernardino, CA; (4); Library Aide; Science Clb; Prfct Atten Awd; San Bernardino Vly Coll; Acctng.

NGUYEN, DUNG; Westminster HS; Huntington Beach, CA; (2); Church Yth Grp; Bsktbl; Vllybl; Cit Awd; Prfct Atten Awd.

NGUYEN, DUNG B; Mount Pleasant HS; San Jose, CA; (4); Math Clb; Math Tm; Teachers Aide; Hon Roll; Magna Cum Laude; Acctg.

NGUYEN, DUNG N; Herbert Hoover HS; San Diego, CA; (3); 3/365; Drama Clb; French Clb; Church Choir; School Play; Cit Awd; Hon Roll; Prfct Atten Awd; U Of CA; Medcl Fld.

NGUYEN, DUNG T; Bolsa Grande HS; Garden Grove, CA; (3); 11/338; French Clb; Math Clb; Math Tm; Science Clb; Church Choir; JV Bsktbl; Cit Awd; Hon Roll; Prfct Atten Awd; Peer Tutoring; Vietnamese Club; Phrmcy.

NGUYEN, DUSTY CAUH; La Quinta HS; Westminster, CA; (1); Chess Clb; German Clb; Spanish Clb; Church Choir; Tennis; Hon Roll; Pres Acad Fit Awd; Read And Write; Vietnamese Club.

NGUYEN, DUY; Loara HS; Anaheim, CA; (4); Am Leg Boys St; Pres Key Clb; Stu Cncl; Crs Cntry; Elks Awd; High Hon Roll; Kiwanis Awd; NHS; Pres Acad Fit Awd; Anaheim Yth Of Yr Awd; CALI-NEV-GA Key Clb Dist Outstndng Pres & Top Ten Lt Gov Awds; UCLA; Bus.

NGUYEN, DUY NHAT; Don Bosco Technical Inst; San Gabriel, CA; (3); 5/200; Dance Clb; Debate Tm; Ed Nwsp; Rptr Yrbk; JV Bsktbl; High Hon Roll; NHS; Stanford; Pre-Med.

NGUYEN, DUY Q; Los Amigos HS; Santa Ana, CA; (2); Intnl Clb; Key Clb; Spanish Clb; Off Soph Cls; Capt Bsktbl; Var Tennis; JV Vllybl; Hon Roll; NHS; Cert Of Achvt For Ambssadors To Asia; Bus.

NGUYEN, DUY-MINH H; Fremont HS; Sunnyvale, CA; (2); 98/400; French Clb; Speech Tm; Orch; JV Trk.

NGUYEN, EDDY; Saddleback HS; Costa Mesa, CA; (2); Church Yth Grp; Cmnty Wkr; Math Clb; Mu Alpha Theta; Science Clb; Speech Tm; Nwsp; High Hon Roll; Hgh Hnr Algb Gldn St Exam & Hgh Hnr CA-GEOM Exam; Kiwanis Bowl; Mock Trial; Knwldg Mstrs; Bridge Clb; Sci.

NGUYEN, EMILY; Fremont HS; Sunnyvale, CA; (2); 48/435; Am Leg Aux Girls St; Debate Tm; Hosp Aide; NFL; Speech Tm; Orch; Crs Cntry; Trk; Med Research Sci.

NGUYEN, FRANCE; Montgomery HS; San Diego, CA; (2); 5/594; Aud/Vis; VP Am Leg Boys St; Treas Spanish Clb; Capt Flag Corp; Ed Yrbk; VP Soph Cls; Pres Jr Cls; Var Trk; High Hon Roll; Aud/Vis; ASB Senate; FAD; Spnsh I & II Awds; Pediatrics.

NGUYEN, FRED C; Homestead HS; Sunnyvale, CA; (3); Mgr Art Clb; French Clb; Var JV Ftbl; High Hon Roll; NHS; Acad Green & White Awd-Arch Drftg; Write Poems & Songs; CA Poly SLO; Arch Dsgn.

NGUYEN, GASTON; Irvine HS; Irvine, CA; (2); Key Clb; VP Ftbl; Wt Lftg; Wrstlng; CA Schlrshp Fed; Usc; Arch.

NGUYEN, GIANG; Fremont HS; Sunnyvale, CA; (2); 57/421; Church Yth Grp; NFL; Opt Clb Awd; CA Schlrshp Fed; Psych.

NGUYEN, GINA ANN; Saddleback HS; Costa Mesa, CA; (3); Am Leg Aux Girls St; Church Yth Grp; Cmnty Wkr; FBLA; Intnl Clb; Mu Alpha Theta; Red Cross Aide; Spanish Clb; Chorus; Sec Treas Frsh Cls; Natl Frat Stu Musicians Dist Hnr; Princeton; Intl Bus.

NGUYEN, GINA T; Trabuco Hills HS; El Toro, CA; (2); 45/411; Church Yth Grp; French Clb; Service Clb; SADD; Hon Roll; NHS; Pres Acad Fit Awd; CSF; Play Piano; UCSD; Psych.

NGUYEN, GUYNH; Los Amigos HS; Fountain Valley, CA; (2); 1/365; Drama Clb; Pres French Clb; German Clb; School Play; Stu Cncl; JV Tennis; High Hon Roll; Prfct Atten Awd; Pres Acad Fit Awd; CSF; Korean Club Secy; Keywanettes Club; UCLA; Corp Law.

NGUYEN, HA D; Cordova SR HS; Rancho Cordova, CA; (3); Spanish Clb; Cit Awd; High Hon Roll; Prfct Atten Awd; Art & Math Awds; UCLA; Travel/Tourism.

NGUYEN, HA H; Pacifica HS; Stanton, CA; (2); Spanish Clb; Intrml Bsktbl; Cit Awd; Bio Club, Ecology Club, Comp Club; USC; Dentist.

NGUYEN, HA H; Sweetwater HS; National City, CA; (3); 33/605; FTA; Office Aide; Pep Clb; Spanish Clb; SADD; Flag Corp; Bsktbl; Cit Awd; Hon Roll; Prfct Atten Awd; Gnrl Effct Corgrphy; UC Riverside; Rsgtr Nrs.

NGUYEN, HAI C; Edison HS; Stockton, CA; (3); French Clb; Science Clb; Stage Crew; Hon Roll; UC Davis; CPA.

NGUYEN, HAI MINH T; Trabuco Hills HS; Mission Viejo, CA; (4); 58/328; Spanish Clb; SADD; Sprt Ed Nwsp; Var Crs Cntry; Var Trk; Hon Roll; NHS; Prfct Atten Awd; Keywanettes Bst New Membr; CSF; UC Irvine; Optometry.

NGUYEN, HAI V; Eagle Rock HS; Los Angeles, CA; (2); Library Aide; Acpl Chr; Band; Chorus; Mrchg Band; Orch; Hon Roll; Music.

NGUYEN, HAL; Crawford HS; San Diego, CA; (2); Opt Clb Awd; U Coll Of San Diego:Medicine.

NGUYEN, HANG T; Mira Mesa HS; San Diego, CA; (2); French Clb; Trk; Cit Awd; NHS; Prfct Atten Awd; Asia Acad Comptn Ambassadors; UCSD; Bio.

NGUYEN, HANH T; Escondido HS; Vista, CA; (1); French Clb; German Clb; Hon Roll; Cert Schlstc Achvt Frnch I; CSF; Math.

NGUYEN, HANH T; Ocean View HS; Fountain Valley, CA; (1); Math Clb; Service Clb; SADD; Tennis; Cit Awd; High Hon Roll; Badminton Team; Pals; Asian Club; U Of CA Irvine; Pediatrician.

NGUYEN, HANH T; Westminster HS; Westminster, CA; (2); Spanish Clb; Acpl Chr; Church Choir; JV Tennis; JV Trk; JV Vllybl; High Hon Roll; U Of CA Irvine; Med.

NGUYEN, HAU T; Glendora HS; Glendora, CA; (4); Art Clb; Dance Clb; Hon Roll; Cal Poly Pomona; Intl Bus.

NGUYEN, HELLEN C; Bonita HS; La Verne, CA; (2); Drama Clb; French Clb; SADD; School Play; Hon Roll; Prfct Atten Awd; Pres Acad Fit Awd; CSF.

NGUYEN, HIEN; Hawthorne HS; Hawthorne, CA; (2); Quiz Bowl; Stu Cncl; Capt Bsktbl; Hon Roll; CA ST Long Beach; Arch.

NGUYEN, HIEN HEATHER; Mark Keppel HS; Monterey Park, CA; (2); Key Clb.

NGUYEN, HIEN THI; Montgomery HS; San Diego, CA; (2); FBLA; Church Choir; Off Frsh Cls; Accntng.

NGUYEN, HIEP; Hawthorne HS; Hawthorne, CA; (2); Hon Roll; NHS; Long Beach ST; Jrlsm.

NGUYEN, HIEU D; Laguna Hills HS; Laguna Hills, CA; (4); 36/320; Church Yth Grp; Key Clb; Math Clb; SADD; Teachers Aide; Pres Frsh Cls; Crs Cntry; Tennis; Wrstlng; CSF; Creative Writing Club; Global Awareness Club; U Of CA Irvine; Bio Sci.

NGUYEN, HIEU H; Savanna HS; Anaheim, CA; (3); Band; Var Ftbl; FBI.

NGUYEN, HIEU N; Nogales HS; W Covina, CA; (2); Science Clb; Tennis; High Hon Roll; UC Berkeley; Phy.

NGUYEN, HOAN; Bolsa Grande HS; Westminster, CA; (3); 6/1200; Math Clb; Science Clb; Hon Roll; CSF; UCLA; Bio.

NGUYEN, HOANG; Andrew Hill HS; San Jose, CA; (4); Math Tm; Teachers Aide; Nwsp; Davis; Med.

NGUYEN, HONG; West HS; Bakersfield, CA; (3); Hon Roll; Cal ST U; Nrsng.

NGUYEN, HONG N; Gardena HS; Gardena, CA; (2); Church Yth Grp; French Clb; Library Aide; Var Vllybl; Cit Awd; Hon Roll; Opt Clb Awd; CA Schlrshp Fed; Viet Nam Cltr Clb Pres; Oscr Awd; Loyola Marymount U; Phys Thrpy.

NGUYEN, HOUBI TUNG T; Dana Hills HS; Laguna Niguel, CA; (1); Math Clb; Math Tm; Orch; Hon Roll; Irvine Soccer Clb; Stanford; Med.

NGUYEN, HUNG; Bolsa Grande HS; Garden Grove, CA; (2); Spanish Clb; Hon Roll.

NGUYEN, HUNG; Skyline HS; Oakland, CA; (3); German Clb; Key Clb; Cit Awd; Prfct Atten Awd; Vietnamese Union; Asian Stu Union; Contractor.

NGUYEN, HUNG DINH; Wilson HS; Long Beach, CA; (3); UCI; Dentist.

NGUYEN, HUNG N; Leuzinger HS; Lawndale, CA; (4); 36/500; Varsity Clb; Var Socr; Var Capt Vllybl; CA ST U Long Beach; Mech Engr.

NGUYEN, HUNG QUOC; Vanden HS; Fairfield, CA; (4); 1/143; Chess Clb; Model UN; Var Capt Tennis; Elks Awd; High Hon Roll; Lion Awd; Ntl Merit Ltr; Pres Acad Fit Awd; Val; Voice Dem Awd; U CA Santa Barbara; Comp Sci.

NGUYEN, HUNG-ANH P; La Quinta HS; Fountain Valley, CA; (3); 8/336; Chess Clb; French Clb; Key Clb; Science Clb; Tennis; High Hon Roll; Prfct Atten Awd; Pres Acad Fit Awd; Pres Schlr.

NGUYEN, HUONG; Tennyson HS; Hayward, CA; (4); 11/278; Debate Tm; French Clb; Rptr Nwsp; Sec Jr Cls; JV Vllybl; Hon Roll; Bnk Amer Frgn Lang Awd; UC Davis; Bio.

NGUYEN, HUONG KATE; Valley HS; Santa Ana, CA; (4); 1/341; Art Clb; Chess Clb; Church Yth Grp; Computer Clb; VP Key Clb; Scholastic Bowl; Stage Crew; Rptr Nwsp; Lit Mag; High Hon Roll; Vietnamese Clb VP; Orange Cnty Sci Fair 1st Pl; Orange Cnty Acad Decathlon 1st Pl Sci & Engl; MA Inst Of Tech; Engrng.

NGUYEN, HUONG T; Hueneme HS; Port Hueneme, CA; (3); 16/578; Pres Computer Clb; Drama Clb; Cit Awd; High Hon Roll; Prfct Atten Awd; Pres Acad Fit Awd; Cty Sci Fair 2nd Pl; CA St Sci Fair Fnlst; UC Santa Barbara; Comp Sci.

NGUYEN, HUY; James Lick HS; San Jose, CA; (2); High Hon Roll; Hon Roll; NHS; Santa Barbara; Engrng.

NGUYEN, HUY K; Pacifica HS; Garden Grove, CA; (1); Spanish Clb; JV Tennis; Cit Awd; Hon Roll; Prfct Atten Awd; CA Schlrshp Fed; UCI; Pre-Med.

NGUYEN, HUY T; Los Amigos HS; Santa Ana, CA; (3); 68/301; French Clb; Intrml Swmmng; Hon Roll; Karate; Embry-Riddle; Comp Sci.

NGUYEN, HUY T; Tustin HS; Tustin, CA; (2); #16 In Class; Key Clb; Science Clb; Hon Roll; Kiwanis Awd; Pres Acad Fit Awd; VP Soph Cls; JV Crs Cntry; JV Trk; Bus.

NGUYEN, HUYEN H; Orange HS; Orange, CA; (4); 2/380; Hosp Aide; Varsity Clb; Ed Nwsp; Rep Jr Cls; Vllybl; High Hon Roll; NHS; Pres Acad Fit Awd; Sal; 1st Pl Wnnr Rockwell Intrntl AFE Essy Cont; U Of CA Los Angeles.

NGUYEN, HUYEN L; Mira Mesa HS; San Diego, CA; (4); 1/750; Church Yth Grp; Cmnty Wkr; Key Clb; Math Tm; Office Aide; Scholastic Bowl; Science Clb; Off Jr Cls; Stu Cncl; High Hon Roll; ASB Mem; 2nd Pl Schl Sci Fair; Achvd High Hnrs Gldn ST Exam; UCSD; Bio.

NGUYEN, HUYEN T; Anaheim HS; Anaheim, CA; (3); Church Yth Grp; Math Clb; Science Clb; Teachers Aide; Variety Show; High Hon Roll; NHS; Prfct Atten Awd; CSF Clb; Asian Clb; UCLA; Nrsng.

NGUYEN, JAMES; Monterey HS; Seaside, CA; (2); Bsktbl; Hon Roll; Bus.

NGUYEN, JAMES GIANG; Don Antonio Lugo HS; Chino, CA; (3); Cit Awd; High Hon Roll; Prfct Atten Awd; Recrtn Ldr; Stu Of Wk; CA ST Polytech Pomona; Recrtn.

NGUYEN, JEANNIE H; Bolsa Grande HS; Garden Grove, CA; (2); French Clb; Hosp Aide; Science Clb; Service Clb; Teachers Aide; Bsbl; Swmmng; Tennis; Vllybl; Wt Lftg; UCI; Phrmcy.

NGUYEN, JENNIFER ANH DAO; John Marshall HS; Pasadena, CA; (1); Drama Clb; Math Clb; Science Clb; Cit Awd; Hon Roll; Origami; U Of CA Berkeley; Engr.

NGUYEN, JENNY; El Cajon Valley HS; El Cajon, CA; (2); Art Clb; Acpl Chr; NEDT Awd; Grossmont; Grphc Dsgnr.

NGUYEN, JOHN B; Santa Clara HS; Santa Clara, CA; (1); Hon Roll; Engr.

NGUYEN, JON D; Mt Carmel HS; San Diego, CA; (3); Prfct Atten Awd; CSF.

NGUYEN, JOSEPH H; Santa Clara HS; Santa Clara, CA; (2); Boy Scts; Hon Roll; Golden ST Exam Alg I; UC Berkeley; Bus.

NGUYEN, JOSEPH M; Newbury Park Adventist Acad; Newbury Park, CA; (3); Church Yth Grp; Computer Clb; Ski Clb; Spanish Clb; Band; Phtg Yrbk; Off Jr Cls; Intrml Sftbl; Intrml Vllybl; Presidential Physical Fitness Awd 87-88; Martial Arts Enthvsiast 88-89; Natl Physical Fitns Awd 88-89; Pacific Union Coll; Photography.

NGUYEN, KALY M; Mission Viejo HS; Mission Viejo, CA; (1); 1/600; Church Yth Grp; Color Guard; Hon Roll; Psych.

NGUYEN, KATHY A; Wilcox HS; Santa Clara, CA; (1); 15/400; Orch; Hon Roll.

NGUYEN, KATIE; Redwood HS; Visalia, CA; (4); #1 In Class; Hosp Aide; Math Clb; Spanish Clb; Rptr Nwsp; Ed Lit Mag; JV Cheerldng; JV Var Swmmng; Rep Stu Cncl; Mck Trl Team; CSF; Gtschlks Hi-Deb Mdl; Blgcl Sci.

NGUYEN, KHAI C; Bolsa Grande HS; Westminster, CA; (3); 9/377; Math Clb; High Hon Roll; Hon Roll; NHS; Prfct Atten Awd.

NGUYEN, KHANG H; San Marcos HS; Santa Barbara, CA; (2); French Clb; Yrbk.

NGUYEN, KHANG N; Tustin HS; Tustin, CA; (3); 9/446; Church Yth Grp; JA; Key Clb; Science Clb; JV Vllybl; High Hon Roll; Hon Roll; JV Vllybl Coaches Awd; CSF Clb; Acad Achvt Awd; Cal Poly; Arspc Engr.

NGUYEN, KHANH; Mt Eden HS; Hayward, CA; (3); 3/296; Computer Clb; Var Tennis; High Hon Roll; Hon Roll; Prfct Atten Awd; Pres Acad Fit Awd; CSF; Hnrs Gld St Exm 89; Badmntn Vrsty; UC Berkeley; Pre-Med.

NGUYEN, KHANH; Piedmont Hills HS; San Jose, CA; (1); Drama Clb; Bsbl; Ftbl; Wrstlng; High Hon Roll; Prfct Atten Awd; Stanford; Dentistry.

NGUYEN, KHANH; Valley HS; Santa Ana, CA; (4); 70/300; French Clb; Tennis; Cal ST Long Bch; Fin.

NGUYEN, KHANH K P; Adrian C Wilcox HS; Santa Clara, CA; (2); FHA; Girl Scts; Red Cross Aide; Church Choir; Hon Roll; Prfct Atten Awd; Amnesty Intl; 5 Yrs Piano; U CA Santa Barbara; Bus.

NGUYEN, KHANH T; El Capitan HS; Lakeside, CA; (2); 22/455; French Clb; JV Vllybl; Hon Roll; Coord Invent Am; Acad Bowl; Leos Club; UC Berkeley; Intl Relations.

NGUYEN, KHANH T; El Toro HS; El Toro, CA; (1); Intnl Clb; High Hon Roll; Keywanettes Clb; Interact Clb; Engl Excllnce Awd; Stanford; Pediatrics.

NGUYEN, KHANH X; Saddleback HS; Santa Ana, CA; (1); Boy Scts; Ftbl; Trk; U Of CA Los Angeles; Doctor.

NGUYEN, KHOA; Mira Costa HS; Hawthorne, CA; (2); Cit Awd; UCLA; Math.

NGUYEN, KHOA; Rountain Valley HS; Fountain Valley, CA; (2); Elect Engrng.

NGUYEN, KHOA D; Woodbridge HS; Irvine, CA; (4); 3/400; Math Tm; Science Clb; Ski Clb; Var Tennis; Var Wrstlng; High Hon Roll; Hon Roll; NHS; Ntl Merit SF; Pres Acad Fit Awd; Blck Belt Tae Kwondo; Mock Trl; U CA San Diego; Engrng.

NGUYEN, KHOA V; Milpitas HS; Milpitas, CA; (4); French Clb; Red Cross Aide; ROTC; Drill Tm; JV Tennis; Hon Roll; Pres Acad Fit Awd; CA Schrlshp Fed Scrtry & VP; Vrsty Schlr; Supt Hnr Roll; U Of CA; Pre Med.

NGUYEN, KHOI; Milpitas HS; Milpitas, CA; (2); 2/570; Debate Tm; Math Tm; Model UN; Science Clb; Band; Jazz Band; Tennis; Cit Awd; High Hon Roll; Jr NHS; 3rd Pl Sci Olympiad 1989.

NGUYEN, KHOI V; Kearny HS; San Diego, CA; (2); Service Clb; Cit Awd; Hon Roll; Med.

NGUYEN, KHUONG; Milpitas HS; Milpitas, CA; (2); 86/559; ROTC; Drill Tm; Schl Hnr Roll; Vietnmese & Astrnmy Clb; UCLA; Bus.

NGUYEN, KIEN-QUOC; Costa Mesa HS; Costa Mesa, CA; (3); 50/260; Spanish Clb; Varsity Clb; JV Swmmng; Varsity Badminton; Varsity Waterpolo-JV Capt; AZ ST; Aerospace Engr.

NGUYEN, KIET; Rancho Alamitos HS; Stanton, CA; (2); Vllybl; High Hon Roll; Hon Roll; U Of CA Irvine; Dr.

NGUYEN, KIEU; Garden Grove HS; Garden Grove, CA; (3).

NGUYEN, KIM A; Los Amigos HS; Santa Ana, CA; (2); Church Yth Grp; Drama Clb; French Clb; German Clb; Key Clb; Pep Clb; School Play; Off Frsh Cls; Off Jr Cls; Tennis; UCLA; Bus.

NGUYEN, KIM HONG T; Cypress HS; Cypress, CA; (3); Church Yth Grp; FBLA; Intnl Clb; Key Clb; Chorus; Church Choir; Cit Awd; High Hon Roll; Diati Clb; CA Schlrshp Fed; Engl Awd; Phrmcst.

NGUYEN, KIM LOAN T; Marina HS; Huntington Beach, CA; (3); Church Yth Grp; Key Clb; Office Aide; Spanish Clb; Yrbk; Cit Awd; Hon Roll; Jr NHS; Bus.

NGUYEN, KIM-CHI; Norte Vista HS; Riverside, CA; (2); 17/452; FBLA; JA; Science Clb; Score Keeper; Sftbl; Tennis; Vllybl; High Hon Roll; Prfct Atten Awd; Hstry Day; High Score Natl Math Test; UCI; Doctor.

NGUYEN, KIM-MOT T; San Gorgonio HS; San Bernardino, CA; (3); English Clb; Math Tm; Var Crs Cntry; Cit Awd; Ntl Merit Schol; JV Badminton; Math Field Day Cert; CSF; Cal Poly Pomona; Math.

NGUYEN, KIMBERLY T; Irvington HS; Fremont, CA; (2); 16/326; French Clb; Spanish Clb; Stu Cncl; JV Vllybl; Frshmn JV & Vrsty Badmntn; Mem REACH Amern Drug & Alcohol Pgm; Mem Prfrmng Arts Dept; UCLA; Elec Engr.

NGUYEN, KY; Montclair HS; Montclair, CA; (2); Latin Clb; Math Clb; Chorus; School Musical; JV Tennis; JV Wrstlng; Natl Latin Mrt Soc; UCLA; Bus.

NGUYEN, KY P; Riverside Ramona HS; Riverside, CA; (2); 4/450; French Clb; Varsity Clb; Var L Tennis; Cit Awd; French Hon Soc; High Hon Roll; Prfct Atten Awd; CSF; Cal Tech; Aerospc Engnrng.

NGUYEN, LAM T; Santiago HS; Garden Grove, CA; (3); Computer Clb; French Clb; Hon Roll; CA Poly Pomona; Mech Engr.

NGUYEN, LANH; Lincoln HS; Stockton, CA; (3); Hon Roll; UC San Diego; Aerntcl Engrng.

NGUYEN, LE Q; Santa Ana HS; Santa Ana, CA; (1); JV Vllybl; UCI; Engr.

NGUYEN, LENNY; St Lawrence Acad; San Jose, CA; (4); 3/26; Teachers Aide; Chorus; School Play; Variety Show; VP Sr Cls; Capt Cheerldng; Var Socr; Var JV Vllybl; NHS; CSF; Santa Clara U; Psych.

NGUYEN, LIEM T; Royal HS; Simi Valley, CA; (4); 5/30; Pres Acad Fit Awd; Dept Awd-Engl & Sec Lang; CA St U Bakersfield/Admission Wth Hnrs; CA ST U; Comp Sci.

NGUYEN, LIEN; La Quinta HS; Santa Ana, CA; (1); 44/344; Hon Roll; USC; Acctng.

NGUYEN, LIEN CHAU; Montgomery HS; Santa Rosa, CA; (2); Pep Clb; Spanish Clb; Teachers Aide; Cit Awd; Hon Roll; NHS; Prfct Atten Awd; Coll Bound Prgm; Stu Of Mnth/Wk; Outstndng Stu Hnr Awd 87-89; U CA Davis; Med.

NGUYEN, LIEN T; Edison HS; Stockton, CA; (1); 2/30; French Clb; JV Socr; French Hon Soc; Hon Roll; UCO Clb; UC Davis Upwrd Bnd.

NGUYEN, LIEU; Westminster HS; Westminster, CA; (3); CA ST Fullerton; Reg Nrs.

NGUYEN, LILY K; Costa Mesa HS; Costa Mesa, CA; (4); Spanish Clb; Teachers Aide; Yrbk; Hist Stu Cncl; Tennis; USC; Bus Admin.

NGUYEN, LINDA ANH B; Los Amigos HS; Fountain Valley, CA; (2); 1/340; Key Clb; Scholastic Bowl; Spanish Clb; Var Bsktbl; Var Swmmng; Var Trk; JV Vllybl; Cit Awd; Jr NHS; Smith Coll; Bio.

NGUYEN, LINDA MINH; Saddleback HS; Santa Ana, CA; (3); FBLA; Science Clb; Rptr Nwsp; Rptr Lit Mag; Prfct Atten Awd; Pres Acad Fit Awd; CSF 87-91; UCL Partners & STEP; Vol At Orange County Interfaith Shelter 88-89; UCLA; Dentistry.

NGUYEN, LINH D B; Montclair HS; Montclair, CA; (2); Church Yth Grp; Model UN; Var Tennis; Prfct Atten Awd; Poetry San Bernadino Cnty Wrtng Clbrtn; Mock Congrss; Mock Trial; Outstndng Pre-Trial Attorney; Comp Sci.

NGUYEN, LINHTRANG N; Leuzinger HS; Hawthorne, CA; (3); French Clb; Science Clb; Teachers Aide; Rep Stu Cncl; JV Crs Cntry; JV Socr; Cit Awd; Hon Roll; CSF; Outstndng Prfmnce Cert; Lyla Mrymnt U; Intl Bus.

NGUYEN, LISA Q; Milpitas HS; Milpitas, CA; (4); 6/400; Science Clb; Spanish Clb; Hon Roll; NHS; Pres Acad Fit Awd; Badmntn Tm Var; UC Davis; Doctor.

NGUYEN, LISAHUONG T; Chaffey HS; Ontario, CA; (2); 4-H; FBLA; Key Clb; Drill Tm; Cit Awd; Hon Roll; Prfct Atten Awd; Acctg.

NGUYEN, LOAN; Santa Clara HS; Santa Clara, CA; (4); French Clb; Capt JV Cheerldng; High Hon Roll; CSF; San Jose ST U; Bus.

NGUYEN, LOAN P; Magnolia HS; Anaheim, CA; (3); Intnl Clb; Library Aide; Teachers Aide; Cit Awd; UCI; Pharmacist.

NGUYEN, LOAN T; Leuzinger HS; Hawthorne, CA; (3); Computer Clb; Pres Science Clb; Chorus; Church Choir; High Hon Roll; Hon Roll; Prfct Atten Awd; CSF Secy; Principle List.

NGUYEN, LOAN T; Tokay HS; Stockton, CA; (3); Chess Clb; German Clb; Intnl Clb; Pres Key Clb; Cit Awd; High Hon Roll; Prfct Atten Awd; No 1 Single Player On The Badminton Team; Stanford U; Business.

NGUYEN, LOC; Bakersfield HS; Bakersfield, CA; (3); 10/749; Debate Tm; VP JA; NFL; Pres Service Clb; Variety Show; Nwsp; JV Bsktbl; JV Swmmng; NHS; Rotary Awd; Intl Econ.

NGUYEN, LOC T; Livermore HS; Livermore, CA; (4); French Clb; FBLA; Latin Clb; Teachers Aide; High Hon Roll; Hon Roll; Bank Of America Vocational Awd; Golden State Honor Awd; Nat Lat I Bronze Awd; San Jose St; Business/Accntnt.

NGUYEN, LOI; Tokay HS; Stockton, CA; (3); Orch; Hon Roll; Sacramento ST; Social Wrkr.

NGUYEN, LOI N; Costa Mesa HS; Santa Ana, CA; (3); Bsktbl; Vllybl; Wt Lftg; Orange Coast Coll; Optcl Engr.

NGUYEN, LONG; Andrew Hill HS; San Jose, CA; (3); 4/350; Boy Scts; Cmnty Wkr; Math Tm; School Play; Variety Show; Vllybl; Cit Awd; High Hon Roll; Hon Roll; Prfct Atten Awd; Stu Of Wk Awd; De Anza.

NGUYEN, LONG; Edison HS; Stockton, CA; (1); Debate Tm; Math Clb; NFL; Speech Tm; UC Davis; Pediatrics.

NGUYEN, LONG; Oakland HS; Oakland, CA; (2); Chess Clb; Computer Clb; Math Clb; Science Clb; High Hon Roll; UC Berkeley; Psych.

NGUYEN, LUA T; C K Mc Clatchy SR HS; Sacramento, CA; (2); 70/442; Phrmcst.

NGUYEN, LUCY M; Marina HS; Westminster, CA; (2); Cit Awd; Hon Roll; Harvard; Physcn.

NGUYEN, LUM; Clovis HS; Clovis, CA; (2); Intnl Clb; ROTC; Teachers Aide; High Hon Roll; Hon Roll; Fresno ST; Tchng.

NGUYEN, LUYEN DINH; Saddleback HS; Santa Ana, CA; (3); VP Chess Clb; Pres Computer Clb; FBLA; Math Clb; Hon Roll; U Of CA Irvine; Comp Sci.

NGUYEN, LY; Raoul Wallenberg HS; San Francisco, CA; (1); VP Frsh Cls; Var Vllybl; Hon Roll; U CA Berkeley; Bus.

NGUYEN, LYLY; Westminster HS; Westminster, CA; (2); French Clb; Hosp Aide; Pep Clb; Service Clb; Off Frsh Cls; Off Soph Cls; Cheerldng; JV Swmmng; High Hon Roll; Jr NHS; Pepperdine U; Marine Bio.

NGUYEN, MACHUY; Gahr HS; Cerritos, CA; (2); 5/463; Spanish Clb; JV Capt Vllybl; Hon Roll; Prfct Atten Awd; Tennis Club; California Scholarship Federation; Cal Poly; Engineering.

NGUYEN, MAI LINH; Ganyon Springs HS; Moreno Vly, CA; (3); FBLA; Ski Clb; SADD; Rep Frsh Cls; VP Soph Cls; Rep Jr Cls; Mgr(s); Socr; Swmmng; Tennis; ASB VP; CSF.

NGUYEN, MAI NGOC; Costa Mesa HS; Costa Mesa, CA; (4); 4/298; Church Yth Grp; French Clb; GAA; Girl Scts; Chrmn Hosp Aide; Pres Science Clb; Service Clb; Spanish Clb; Teachers Aide; Lit Mag; Asian Clb Pres & VP; Hghst Hnr Aws CA Schlstc Fndtn; U CA Irvine; Med.

NGUYEN, MAI T; Fountain Valley HS; Fountain Valley, CA; (2); Church Yth Grp; Hon Roll; Orange Coast Coll; Cmptr Sci.

NGUYEN, MAI T; Trabuco Hills HS; Mission Viejo, CA; (2); 14/415; Computer Clb; French Clb; Girl Scts; Spanish Clb; SADD; JV Bsktbl; JV Tennis; High Hon Roll; Hon Roll; Jr NHS; CSF; Natl Ftnss Awd; UC Berkeley; Intl Bus.

NGUYEN, MAI T; Westminster HS; Westminster, CA; (2); Church Yth Grp; Office Aide; Spanish Clb; Bsbl; Vllybl; Interact Clb; Berkeley; Law.

NGUYEN, MAO B; Corona HS; Corona, CA; (4); GAA; Var Capt Bsktbl; Hon Roll; Cal Poly Pomona; Finance.

NGUYEN, MARIE N; James Lick HS; San Jose, CA; (3); Cmnty Wkr; Intnl Clb; Math Tm; Treas Jr Cls; Var Swmmng; High Hon Roll; Hon Roll; NHS; Rotary Awd; CSF; Vietnamese PTA Awd; Medicine.

NGUYEN, MARK; Skyline HS; Oakland, CA; (3); Pres German Clb; Key Clb; Hon Roll; VSU Judge; ASU VP; CSF; UC Berkeley; Pre-Med.

NGUYEN, MARY T; Orange Glen HS; Escondido, CA; (2); 1/586; Church Yth Grp; Cmnty Wkr; VP Key Clb; Yrbk; Var Socr; JV Tennis; High Hon Roll; NHS; Schlr Athlte Scc 89-90 & Tnns 88-89.

NGUYEN, MICHELLE; Marina HS; Midway City, CA; (4); 9/484; JCL; Key Clb; Rptr Nwsp; Rep Jr Cls; Capt Var Crs Cntry; JV Trk; High Hon Roll; Math Clb; Office Aide; Varsity Clb; Jnr Vlntr St Josephs Hosp; Vlntr Stndrd Cmmtte Hosp; Stu Advsry Cmmtte Rep HS; UCLA; Bio.

NGUYEN, MIMI; Lowell HS; San Francisco, CA; (3); Hosp Aide; Latin Clb; Red Cross Aide; SADD; Orch; Rep Jr Cls; CSF; Golden St Exam Awds.

NGUYEN, MINH; Westmont HS; Campbell, CA; (4); Prfct Atten Awd; Pres Acad Fit Awd; UC Davis; Med.

NGUYEN, MINH-TRAM; Santa Teresa HS; San Jose, CA; (3); Cmnty Wkr; VP Pres French Clb; Q&S; Varsity Clb; School Musical; Rptr Ed Nwsp; Pres Stu Cncl; JV Var Vllybl; NHS; CSF; Med.

NGUYEN, MITZI T; Mt Pleasant HS; San Jose, CA; (3); Vllybl; High Hon Roll; Hon Roll; Vietnamese Club; Asian Club; CSF; Berkely; Optometry.

NGUYEN, MY; Costa Mesa HS; Costa Mesa, CA; (3); French Clb; Office Aide; Science Clb; Teachers Aide; UCI; Pharmacy.

NGUYEN, MY K; Mira Mesa HS; San Diego, CA; (2); #1 In Class; FBLA; Intnl Clb; Key Clb; Model UN; NHS; Pres Acad Fit Awd.

NGUYEN, NAM A; Costa Mesa HS; Costa Mesa, CA; (3); Intrml Bsktbl; Intrml Swmmng; Intrml Wt Lftg; Golden St Exam Hnrs Alg & Geom; Cngrssnl Schlr; Bus.

NGUYEN, NANCY K; Fountain Valley HS; Huntington Bch, CA; (4); 6/600; VP Drama Clb; Pres Science Clb; High Hon Roll; CA Schlrshp Fed; Bdmntn; Bank Of Amer Achvt Awd; UC Irvine; Bio Sci.

NGUYEN, NANCY N; Wilcox HS; Santa Clara, CA; (1); Orch; JV Swmmng; JV Trk; Hon Roll; Music Piano; Cert Of Achvt Bio; Art; Stanford U; Sci.

NGUYEN, NGA; Reseda HS; Reseda, CA; (4); French Clb; Sec FBLA; CSF; CSU Northridge; Acctng.

NGUYEN, NGA; University City HS; San Diego, CA; (3); 49/373; Church Yth Grp; Intnl Clb; High Hon Roll; CSF; 3rd Pl Frnch Cont Local Wnnr 1st Yr Frnch; 3rd Pl Scl Stds Essay Cont; U San Diego; Bus Law.

NGUYEN, NGA LAUREN; Troy HS; Fullerton, CA; (2); 19/334; French Clb; Key Clb; JV Vllybl; French Hon Soc; High Hon Roll; Rotary Awd.

NGUYEN, NGA P; Fountain Valley HS; Huntington Beach, CA; (2); Church Yth Grp; Science Clb; NHS; UCLA; Pediatrician.

NGUYEN, NGHI H; Homestead HS; Sunnyvale, CA; (2); 74/408; Stanford U; Bus.

NGUYEN, NGOC; Santa Clara HS; Santa Clara, CA; (4); DECA; French Clb; JA; Teachers Aide; Score Keeper; Socr; Trk; High Hon Roll; Pres Acad Fit Awd; Assn CA Schl Admin Awd; Santa Clara Police Offcr Assn Bob Avina Memrl Awd; U Santa Cruz; Psycht.

NGUYEN, NGOC VAN; Valley HS; Santa Ana, CA; (4); 5/300; Chess Clb; Church Yth Grp; Quiz Bowl; Rptr Nwsp; Lit Mag; Var JV Tennis; High Hon Roll; Prfct Atten Awd; Vietnamese Clb; Coll Partnership; Boston U; Phys Thrpy.

NGUYEN, NGOC-DUNG; Andrew Hill HS; San Jose, CA; (2); DECA; French Clb; Rep Stu Cncl; Bsktbl; Swmmng; Tennis; Vllybl; Hon Roll; Vietnamese Clb; CSF; U Of CA Davis; Phrmcy.

NGUYEN, NGOC-LAN C; Silver Creek HS; San Jose, CA; (3); 32/589; Service Clb; Stu Cncl; High Hon Roll; Rotary Awd; St Schlr; Futr Med Workrs Clb; UCLA; Orthdntst.

NGUYEN, NGOCDUNG T; Homestead HS; Sunnyvale, CA; (1); Orch.

NGUYEN, NGUC QUYEN T; San Gorgonio HS; San Bernardino, CA; (3); #67 In Class; Asian Clb 3 Yrs; Vrsty Badminton; CA ST San Bernrdno; Comp Sci.

NGUYEN, NGUYEN Q; Costa Mesa HS; Santa Ana, CA; (3); 3/226; French Clb; Math Clb; Math Tm; Teachers Aide; High Hon Roll; Hon Roll; Orange Coast Coll HS Math Awd; HS Math Awd 89; Math Assn America Clb; UC Berkeley; Engrng.

NGUYEN, NGUYET A; Notre Dame HS; Campbell, CA; (3); Church Yth Grp; Cmnty Wkr; Girl Scts; Intnl Clb; Pep Clb; Science Clb; Service Clb; SADD; Chorus; Church Choir; Svc Clb/Volunteer/Sport Awds; San Jose ST U; Bus.

NGUYEN, NHIEN; Novato HS; Novato, CA; (1); Dance Clb; French Clb; Office Aide; Crs Cntry; Gym; Cit Awd; Hon Roll; Berkley U; Nurse.

NGUYEN, NHUHA T; Silver Creek HS; San Jose, CA; (2); Math Tm; High Hon Roll; Ntl Merit Schol; Prfct Atten Awd; Pres Acad Fit Awd; Amer Merit Awd; Gldn ST Exam 1st Yr Algbr & Gmtry Hnrs; U CA Davis; Phrmcst.

NGUYEN, NHUNG; Monterey HS; Marina, CA; (2); High Hon Roll; Hon Roll; Kiwanis Awd; Tennis; Ping Pong; Achvmt & Hnr For Outstndng Acad Excl; Clothes Dsgng; San Jose U ST; Secy.

NGUYEN, NICK; Cypress HS; Cypress, CA; (3); Hosp Aide; Teachers Aide; VP Frsh Cls; Var Ftbl; Intrml Ice Hcky; JV Trk; Var L Vllybl; High Hon Roll; Prfct Atten Awd; Med.

NGUYEN, NIKKI LE UT THI; Bolsa Grande HS; Westminster, CA; (4); 1/323; Math Clb; Red Cross Aide; Science Clb; Spanish Clb; Speech Tm; Teachers Aide; Stu Cncl; Cit Awd; NHS; Prfct Atten Awd; Yth Advisory Cmmtte; Golden Voices; U S CA; Bus Admin.

NGUYEN, OANH; Anaheim HS; Anaheim, CA; (3); Drama Clb; Thesps; Band; Jazz Band; Mrchg Band; Orch; Pep Band; School Play; Variety Show; NHS; Theater In The Attic; Theater.

NGUYEN, PAT M; Rosemead HS; Rosemead, CA; (1); Bsktbl; UCLA; Med.

NGUYEN, PETER H; Mesa Verde HS; Citrus Heights, CA; (2); Spanish Clb; Bsktbl; Ftbl; Tennis; Trk; Wt Lftg; Cit Awd; Hon Roll; Prfct Atten Awd; U CA Davis; Med.

NGUYEN, PHAN M; Santa Clara HS; Sunnyvale, CA; (4); Boy Scts; Teachers Aide; Lit Mag; Gym; Swmmng; Trk; Vllybl; Wt Lftg; San Jose ST U; Psych.

NGUYEN, PHAT; La Serna HS; Whittier, CA; (3); Boy Scts; Chess Clb; Math Clb; Science Clb; Off Sr Cls; Socr; Swmmng; Hon Roll; NHS; UCLA; Engr.

NGUYEN, PHONG; Sunny Hills HS; Fullerton, CA; (2); Church Yth Grp; JCL; Latin Clb; Capt Bsktbl; Hon Roll; JV Badminton; Latin St Convntn Awds; CA ST Fullerton; Bus.

NGUYEN, PHONG C; San Gorgonio HS; San Bernardino, CA; (3); Key Clb; Engr.

NGUYEN, PHONG H; San Clemente HS; Capistrano Bch, CA; (1).

NGUYEN, PHU; Orange HS; Orange, CA; (3); JV Var Bsktbl; Davis; Vet.

NGUYEN, PHUC T; Pioneer HS; San Jose, CA; (3); Art Clb; Boy Scts; French Clb; Intnl Clb; Math Clb; Socr; High Hon Roll; Hon Roll; Prfct Atten Awd; Var Badminton 3 Yrs; Vietnamese Clb Sec & Pres; UCLA; Dentistry.

NGUYEN, PHUNG K; Pioneer HS; San Jose, CA; (1); Hon Roll; CA Schlrshp Fed; Jrnlsm; UC Berkeley; Math.

NGUYEN, PHUONG; W C Overfelt HS; San Jose, CA; (3); Math Clb; Math Tm; Science Clb; Spanish Clb; SADD; Teachers Aide; Off Jr Cls; Gym; High Hon Roll; UC Davis; Bus.

NGUYEN, PHUONG D; James Lick HS; San Jose, CA; (1); High Hon Roll; Jr NHS; Pres Acad Fit Awd; Golden ST Exam Geom High Hnrs; UC-SANTA Cruz; Comm Ad.

NGUYEN, PHUONG T; Lincoln HS; San Jose, CA; (3); 7/407; French Clb; Math Tm; Spanish Clb; Teachers Aide; Intrml Bsktbl; Intrml Socr; Intrml Tennis; Intrml Vllybl; High Hon Roll; Hon Roll; UC Davis; Engr.

NGUYEN, PHUONG T; Westminster HS; Westminster, CA; (3); Church Yth Grp; French Clb; Capt Girl Scts; Teachers Aide; Hon Roll; Jr NHS; JR Bdmntn; VP Sgn Lang Clb; Pep Sqd.

NGUYEN, PHUONG-DAO; Marina HS; Garden Grove, CA; (4); 3/484; JCL; Sec Key Clb; Latin Clb; Sec Treas Math Clb; Ed Lit Mag; Lit Mag; VP Frsh Cls; Hon Roll; Ntl Merit SF; Yrbk-Edtr In Chief, Actvtsd Ed & Index Ed; Math Clb-1st Pl Alg II Div & 2nd Pl Anlys Div; Math.

NGUYEN, PHUONGTHAO C; James Logan HS; Union City, CA; (3); Teachers Aide; Hon Roll; Cal ST; Med.

NGUYEN, QUANE; Santiago HS; Santa Ana, CA; (4); Spanish Clb; Hon Roll; California Scholarship Federation Club; CA ST; Mechanical Engineer.

NGUYEN, QUEEN A; Notre Dame HS; San Jose, CA; (3); 10/90; Cmnty Wkr; Hosp Aide; Intnl Clb; JA; Pres Sec Science Clb; Treas Frsh Cls; Off Soph Cls; High Hon Roll; Jr NHS; NHS; Biochem.

NGUYEN, QUEENIE D; San Gabriel Mission HS; Alhambra, CA; (2); 1/130; Cmnty Wkr; VP French Clb; FBLA; Math Clb; Science Clb; Rptr Nwsp; Phtg Yrbk; St Schlr; Stanford; Dermatology.

NGUYEN, QUOC H; Durham HS; Durham, CA; (2); 1/75; FFA; Trk; Hon Roll; CSF; GATE; CA ST U Chico; Bus.

NGUYEN, QUOC H; San Diego HS; San Diego, CA; (2); 1/400; French Clb; Var Socr; High Hon Roll; Pres Acad Fit Awd; Amer Leg Schl Awd; Vietnamse Amer PTA San Diego; Oustndng Awd 89; UCLA; Cardiologyu.

NGUYEN, QUYEN H; Venice HS; Culver City, CA; (2); French Clb; Hosp Aide; Red Cross Aide; Cit Awd; Hon Roll; Prfct Atten Awd; Gldn St Exam Alg I High Hnr; Engrng.

NGUYEN, QUYEN V; Silver Creek HS; San Jose, CA; (3); Band; Cit Awd; Hon Roll; San Jose ST U; Elctrncs.

NGUYEN, QUYNH H; Roosevelt HS; Los Angeles, CA; (2); 1/30; Computer Clb; VP Math Clb; Math Tm; Science Clb; Teachers Aide; Varsity Clb; Church Choir; School Play; Treas Frsh Cls; Var Golf; Comm Svc Awd; Stu Of Mnth Awd; League Champs In Golf; Cal Poly; Aeronautic Engr.

NGUYEN, QUYNH K; Garden Grove HS; Garden Grove, CA; (3); Church Yth Grp; French Clb; Intnl Clb; Spanish Clb; Natl Hnr Soc 2 Yrs; CSF; UCI; Med.

NGUYEN, QUYNHCHAU T; Norco HS; Corona, CA; (3); 6/399; Hosp Aide; Model UN; Science Clb; Spanish Clb; High Hon Roll; Pres Jr NHS; NHS; Ntl Merit Ltr; Pres Acad Fit Awd; Val; Japan Smmr Exchng Stu; Acadmc Decathlon Silver Mdl Speech & Bronze Mdl Interview; GATE-PAC Awds; UC Riverside; Bio Med.

NGUYEN, RICKY; Monterey HS; Marina, CA; (3); Church Yth Grp; Nwsp; Yrbk; JV Capt Bsktbl; Tennis; High Hon Roll; NHS; Bus Admin.

NGUYEN, ROSANNA T; Del Campo HS; Citrus Heights, CA; (1); 24/461; Stu Reaching Out; Piano.

NGUYEN, ROSIE B; Rowland HS; Rowland Heights, CA; (3); Cmnty Wkr; Science Clb; Spanish Clb; High Hon Roll; CSF.

NGUYEN, SCOTT H; Canyon HS; Anaheim, CA; (1); JV Trk; UCLA; Med.

NGUYEN, SI; La Puente HS; La Puente, CA; (2); Art Clb; Math Clb; Off Soph Cls; Hon Roll; Prfct Atten Awd; Elec; Elec Engr.

NGUYEN, SISSI A; Fountain Valley HS; Fountain Valley, CA; (4); 17/632; French Clb; Pep Clb; Speech Tm; Ed Yrbk; Off Sr Cls; Var Swmmng; High Hon Roll; Ntl Merit Ltr; Pres Acad Fit Awd; U Of CA San Diego; Bio.

NGUYEN, SON; Beyer HS; Modesto, CA; (4); 35/506; FBLA; Intnl Clb; SADD; Cit Awd; Hon Roll; Prfct Atten Awd; Modesto JC.

NGUYEN, SON; Pioneer HS; San Jose, CA; (2); Church Yth Grp; FBLA; Math Clb; Spanish Clb; Yrbk; Score Keeper; Vllybl; Wrstlng; Hon Roll; CSF; Asb Rep; Asb Cmmssnr.

NGUYEN, SON H; Marina HS; Huntington Beach, CA; (3); Boy Scts; Bsktbl; Swmmng; Water Polo; UCI; Bus.

NGUYEN, SON H; South HS; Bakersfield, CA; (3); 5/516; Am Leg Boys St; Debate Tm; Hosp Aide; Intnl Clb; JA; Pres Key Clb; NFL; Science Clb; Speech Tm; Var Tennis; Pre-Med.

NGUYEN, SON V; Mt Pleasant HS; San Jose, CA; (2); Ftbl; Trk; Hon Roll; Stanford; Bus Mgmt.

NGUYEN, SONG NGOC L; San Gabriel HS; San Gabriel, CA; (3); Cmnty Wkr; Hosp Aide; Key Clb; Sec Treas Red Cross Aide; Service Clb; Spanish Clb; Rep Jr Cls; Rep Stu Cncl; High Hon Roll; Pres Acad Fit Awd; Interact Clb Pres; Indstry Educ Cncl Medallion Achvt Plaque; Acad Decathlon Team; U CA Los Angeles; Pediatrics.

NGUYEN, STACEY; Edison HS; Huntington Beach, CA; (1); Church Yth Grp; Treas Intnl Clb; Spanish Clb; Lit Mag; UCI; Bus.

NGUYEN, TAI D; Monterey HS; Marina, CA; (3); Computer Clb; Teachers Aide; Orch; JV Crs Cntry; JV Trk; Hon Roll; UCSC Yo Puedo Pgm 88; CA St Yth Ldrshp Conf VP 89; Vietnamese Club Pres; UC Berkeley; Engrng.

NGUYEN, TAM; Lowell HS; San Francisco, CA; (3); Sec Treas Art Clb; Office Aide; Q&S; Red Cross Aide; Science Clb; SADD; Teachers Aide; French Hon Soc; CA Schlrshp Fed; Golden St Exam Algebra, Geom High Hnrs; Poltcl Sci.

NGUYEN, TAM T; Estancia HS; Costa Mesa, CA; (2); Cmnty Wkr; Sec Key Clb; Treas VP NFL; Service Clb; VP Treas Speech Tm; Yrbk; Lit Mag; Hon Roll; Lion Awd; Opt Clb Awd; Top 10 Outstndng Witness Mock Trial Cmptn; Peer Cnslr HS.

NGUYEN, TAM T; Galileo HS; San Francisco, CA; (3); Pep Clb; Spanish Clb; Cit Awd; Hon Roll; Chinese Bilngl Clb Histrn; Acad Excllnc Awd; Stu Of Mnth; San Francisco ST; Secy.

NGUYEN, TAM T; La Sierra HS; Riverside, CA; (3); Math Clb; Cit Awd; Hon Roll; Prfct Atten Awd; UC Irvine; Med.

NGUYEN, TAM T; Saddleback HS; Santa Ana, CA; (1); Debate Tm; Mu Alpha Theta; Speech Tm; Var Trk; Opt Clb Awd; Prfct Atten Awd; Pres Acad Fit Awd; Orange Cty Acad Decathlon 3rd Pl; Saddleback Karate Team 3rd Pl Natl; CSF; Stanford U; Med.

NGUYEN, TAM V; Cajon HS; San Bernardino, CA; (4); Boy Scts; Cmnty Wkr; Drama Clb; Intnl Clb; Electrnc.

NGUYEN, TAMMY; Hoover HS; San Diego, CA; (1); Engr.

NGUYEN, TAMMY; Santa Teresa HS; San Jose, CA; (3); French Clb; Hosp Aide; Spanish Clb; Speech Tm; Church Choir; Nwsp; Yrbk; NHS; CA Shlrshp Fed; Span Stu Of Wk.

NGUYEN, TAN M; Bolsa Grande HS; Westminster, CA; (1); Chess Clb; Vietnamese Club; Bus.

NGUYEN, TEMY; Nogales HS; Walnut, CA; (2); Science Clb; Band; Mrchg Band; High Hon Roll; Pres Acad Fit Awd; UCI.

NGUYEN, THACH; Montclair HS; Montclair, CA; (2); Math Tm; Teachers Aide; Varsity Clb; Tennis; Trk; Wrstlng; Cal Poly; Elec Engr.

NGUYEN, THAI; Edison HS; Huntington Beach, CA; (4); JA; JV Wrstlng; Hon Roll; Pres Acad Fit Awd; Goldn St Exam Awd; Golden Key Awd; U Of CA Irvine; Mech Engrng.

NGUYEN, THAI; Hoover HS; San Diego, CA; (2); Hon Roll; Jr NHS; NHS; Pres Acad Fit Awd; Elec Engrng.

NGUYEN, THAI; Westminster HS; Westminster, CA; (2); Church Yth Grp; Hosp Aide; Spanish Clb; Wrstlng; High Hon Roll; Hon Roll; Pres Schlr; Rotary Awd; Med.

NGUYEN, THAI QUOC; Herbert Hoover SR HS; San Diego, CA; (2); 1/600; Boy Scts; French Clb; JA; Math Clb; Cit Awd; High Hon Roll; Hon Roll; Jr NHS; NHS; Prfct Atten Awd; UCLA; Aerospace Engrng.

NGUYEN, THAIPHUONG H; Irvine HS; Tustin, CA; (2); Debate Tm; French Clb; Girl Scts; Key Clb; Science Clb; Temple Yth Grp; Tennis; Trk; Cit Awd; Hon Roll; Med.

NGUYEN, THANH; Mater Dei HS; Fountain Valley, CA; (1); Band; Mrchg Band.

NGUYEN, THANH DINH; Tokay HS; Stockton, CA; (3); 1/650; Chess Clb; German Clb; Treas Key Clb; JV Tennis; High Hon Roll; Prfct Atten Awd; CSF; CIA; Vietnamese Clb Treas; UC-BERKELEY; Med.

NGUYEN, THANH H; Tokay HS; Stockton, CA; (1); 67/600; Intnl Clb; Hon Roll; Pres Acad Fit Awd; Vietnamese Clb; Asian Clb; UC Davis; Med.

NGUYEN, THANH NGOC; Hoover Herbert HS; San Diego, CA; (3); Hon Roll; NHS; Top Mark Clb; San Diego ST U; Teach.

NGUYEN, THANH T; Chaffey HS; Ontario, CA; (1); Elec Engrng.

NGUYEN, THANH-LE; Pasadena HS; Pasadena, CA; (2); 1/430; Intnl Clb; Nwsp; Yrbk; Stu Cncl; High Hon Roll; Vietnamese Club Pres; Acadmc Dcthln; U Of CA Irvine; Law.

NGUYEN, THANH-THAO HO; Westminster HS; Westminster, CA; (1); Girl Scts; Spanish Clb; Teachers Aide; Rep Soph Cls; Bk Clb & Sgn Lang Clb; CSF; UCLA; Pharm.

NGUYEN, THANHDAO; Artesia HS; Artesia, CA; (3); JA; Science Clb; Nwsp; Tennis; Wt Lftg; Cit Awd; High Hon Roll; Hon Roll; UCI; Drftng Engrng.

NGUYEN, THANHTRANG; Polytechnic HS; Riverside, CA; (3); 1/40; Art Clb; Church Yth Grp; Cmnty Wkr; DECA; FCA; FTA; Girl Scts; Intnl Clb; JCL; Math Clb; Riverside Cnty Indstrl Educ 1st Pl Awd; Hnrble Mntn CAROC/P Food Shw; Phy Ftns 1st Pl; Dentistry.

NGUYEN, THAO D; Valley View HS; Moreno Valley, CA; (1); Rptr Nwsp; Cit Awd; Gov Hon Prg Awd; High Hon Roll; Jr NHS; UC Riverside; Psych.

NGUYEN, THAO N; Sunset HS; Hayward, CA; (1); Bsbl; Tennis; Hon Roll; Stanford.

NGUYEN, THAO P; La Sierra HS; Riverside, CA; (2); Hon Roll; Prfct Atten Awd; CSF; L A Sierra.

NGUYEN, THERESA D; Notre Dame HS; San Jose, CA; (3); Church Yth Grp; Cmnty Wkr; Intnl Clb; SADD; Drill Tm; School Play; JV Swmmng; High Hon Roll; Hon Roll; NHS; UCLA; Child Psych.

NGUYEN, THERESA T; El Toro HS; El Toro, CA; (2); 23/565; Dance Clb; High Hon Roll; Gymnstcs Cmptn; CSF; Phys Thrpy.

NGUYEN, THIEN; Mt Eden HS; Hayward, CA; (2); NHS; Coll Club; Harvard; Med.

NGUYEN, THIEN-VAN; La Quinta HS; Westminster, CA; (2); 2/362; French Clb; Key Clb; Pep Clb; JV Fld Hcky; JV Sftbl; Jr NHS; NEDT Awd; Rotary Awd; CSF; Vietnamese Clb; UCLA; Engl.

NGUYEN, THITRAM NGOC; J Eugene Mc Ateer HS; San Francisco, CA; (3); Office Aide; Teachers Aide; Hon Roll; Wellesley Coll HS Hnrs Seminar In Sci; Close-Up Fndtn Pgm; San Francisco ST U; Pharmacy.

NGUYEN, THO D; Buena Park HS; Fullerton, CA; (3); 35/390; Computer Clb; Letterman Clb; Teachers Aide; Varsity Clb; Var JV Bsbl; Var JV Bsktbl; JV Ftbl; Var Tennis; Prfct Atten Awd; Acad Decathlon; UC Irvine; Dental Hygiene.

NGUYEN, THOA T; Wilson HS; Long Beach, CA; (4); Library Aide; Teachers Aide; JV Tennis; JV Vllybl; Cit Awd; DECA Treas; ROP-OUTSTNDNG Stu Rcgntn Cmptn; Fshn Dsgnr.

NGUYEN, THOAI D; Saddleback HS; Santa Ana, CA; (3).

NGUYEN, THOMAS; Azusa HS; Pomona, CA; (4); 3/233; Church Yth Grp; FCA; Letterman Clb; Band; Church Choir; Crs Cntry; Cit Awd; High Hon Roll; NHS; Prfct Atten Awd; U CA San Diego; Bio.

NGUYEN, THOMAS; Rancho Alamitos HS; Laguna Hills, CA; (4); Am Leg Boys St; Church Yth Grp; Ed Yrbk; Rep Stu Cncl; Var Capt Socr; Var Tennis; NEDT Awd; Yth Commssn Chrmn; CIF Schlr/Athlte; Seal Bearer.

NGUYEN, THU M; Andrew Hill HS; San Jose, CA; (1); Swmmng; Tennis; San Jose ST U; Bus.

NGUYEN, THU M; Independence HS; San Jose, CA; (3); 29/962; VP Science Clb; Ed Nwsp; Ed Lit Mag; CSF Treas.

NGUYEN, THU TRANG; Poly Technic HS; Riverside, CA; (3); Church Yth Grp; Cmnty Wkr; FTA; Girl Scts; JA; Math Clb; Math Tm; NFL; Teachers Aide; Temple Yth Grp; UCR; Business.

NGUYEN, THU TRANG T; Bolsa Grande HS; Garden Grove, CA; (4); 65/323; Art Clb; Teachers Aide; CSU Fullerton; Acctnt.

NGUYEN, THUY; Orange HS; Orange, CA; (3); Key Clb; Math Clb; Math Tm; Office Aide; Science Clb; Ed Nwsp; Score Keeper; Trk; Hon Roll; NHS; Scats; UCLA; Sci.

NGUYEN, THUY D; Mission Viejo HS; Ranch Santa Marg, CA; (1); 1/415; JV Tennis; Hon Roll; Intl Baccalureate Prgm; UCLA; Med.

NGUYEN, THUY H; Ramona HS; Riverside, CA; (1); 1/582; Intnl Clb; Chorus; Tennis; Hon Roll; Prfct Atten Awd; Pres Acad Fit Awd; Golden St Exam-Alg Hnrs; Reflections Cont-2nd Pl-Lit/Poem.

NGUYEN, THUY N; Costa Mesa HS; Costa Mesa, CA; (4); 1/238; Science Clb; Service Clb; Spanish Clb; Teachers Aide; Nwsp; Var Capt Bsktbl; Var Capt Vllybl; High Hon Roll; Jr NHS; Kiwanis Awd; Bdmntn JV, Var, Co-Capt & Let; Army Rsrv Schlr Athlt Awd; Costa Mesa Mustang Yr; U CA Irvine; Comp Sci.

NGUYEN, THUY T; Silver Creek HS; San Jose, CA; (3); 225/650; Church Yth Grp; Dance Clb; FBLA; Church Choir; Gym; Hon Roll; San Jose ST U; Intl Bus.

NGUYEN, THUY THI THANH; Edison HS; Stockton, CA; (2); French Clb; High Hon Roll; Hon Roll; Math.

NGUYEN, THUY VAN; Bolsa Grande HS; Garden Grove, CA; (3); 40/360; French Clb; GAA; Red Cross Aide; Teachers Aide; Rep Frsh Cls; Rep Soph Cls; Rep Jr Cls; JV Bsktbl; Var Tennis; JV Vllybl; 4th Tnns Dbls Leag; CIF; Cal ST Fullerton; Bus Admin.

NGUYEN, THUYTRANG VICTORIA; Bolsa Grande HS; Garden Grove, CA; (2); Chess Clb; Church Yth Grp; Spanish Clb; Church Choir; CA ST U Long Beach; Law.

NGUYEN, THY C; Tustin HS; Tustin, CA; (1); 11/466; Key Clb; Science Clb; Swmmng; Hon Roll; Ethnc Advsry Cncl; Vietnamese Clb; UCI; Bio.

NGUYEN, TIEN D; Bolsa Grande HS; Westminster, CA; (2); Chess Clb; Math Clb; Science Clb; Spanish Clb; Yrbk; Var JV Ftbl; JV Tennis; Cit Awd; Hon Roll; Jr NHS; Vietnamese Club; Chinese Club; CSF; UC Irvine; Med.

NGUYEN, TIEN X; Pioneer HS; San Jose, CA; (2); Spanish Clb; Vietnamese Clb; UC Berkeley; Drafting.

NGUYEN, TINA; California HS; Whittier, CA; (3); #4 In Class; Art Clb; French Clb; FBLA; German Clb; Spanish Clb; High Hon Roll; Hon Roll; Top 100 Stus; Stu Of Mnth Span III, Eng II; UCLA; Ped.

NGUYEN, TINH; Monterey HS; Seaside, CA; (3); Cit Awd; High Hon Roll; Pres Acad Fit Awd; AFS & CSF; Intl Stds Prgrm Outstndng Achvmnt Frgn Lng Schlrshp; UC Davis; Optmtrst.

NGUYEN, TINNY T; Independence HS; San Jose, CA; (4); 14/800; Church Yth Grp; Girl Scts; Red Cross Aide; Church Choir; Orch; Ed Yrbk; High Hon Roll; NHS; Yth Fllwshp Chrstn Club Treas, Secy; CA Schlrs Fed Secy; UC Davis; Biochem.

NGUYEN, TOAN B; Leuzinger HS; Hawthorne, CA; (4); Pres Math Clb; VP Science Clb; Capt Crs Cntry; Var Trk; Pres Acad Fit Awd; Schlrshp Awd; Math.

NGUYEN, TOAN V; Bolsa Grande HS; Westminster, CA; (2); 2/377; Science Clb; Spanish Clb; Temple Yth Grp; JV Vllybl; Hon Roll; NHS; Varsity Badminton; UCI; Bio.

NGUYEN, TOM; Milpitas HS; Milpitas, CA; (2); Boy Scts; Letterman Clb; Pep Clb; Spanish Clb; Varsity Clb; Rep Frsh Cls; Rep Soph Cls; Crs Cntry; Score Keeper; Trk; Schlr Athlt Awd; Frosh Var Athlt; CA CCS Champ Track & Cross-Cntry; Arch Dsgn.

NGUYEN, TOMMY; Mc Lane HS; Fresno, CA; (4); Cmnty Wkr; Math Clb; Model UN; Quiz Bowl; Scholastic Bowl; Science Clb; High Hon Roll; Hon Roll; Prfct Atten Awd.

NGUYEN, TONGA T; Mountain View HS; El Monte, CA; (3); Church Yth Grp; Sftbl; FBLA; Intnl Clb; Science Clb; School Play; Lit Mag; Hon Roll; 1st Sci Fr; Grad Northwest Coll Med Asst; U Of Pacific; Pharmacy.

NGUYEN, TRA T; Modesto HS; Modesto, CA; (3); Intnl Clb; Cit Awd; Hon Roll; Prfct Atten Awd; Sacramento ST U; Psych.

NGUYEN, TRAM; Garden Grove HS; Garden Grove, CA; (2); 22/402; Math Tm; Speech Tm; Chorus; Church Choir; Hon Roll; Math.

NGUYEN, TRANG; Moorpark HS; Moorpark, CA; (4); Drama Clb; French Clb; Treas Intnl Clb; Sec Key Clb; High Hon Roll; Hon Roll; Kiwanis Awd; NHS; Pres Acad Fit Awd; CA Scholorshp Fed; Stud Of The Mo 88; UCLA; Soc Sci.

NGUYEN, TRANG; Westminster HS; Westminster, CA; (3); Comp Engr.

NGUYEN, TRANG M; Silver Creek HS; San Jose, CA; (4); 25/490; Math Clb; NFL; Speech Tm; Rptr Yrbk; Stu Cncl; Var Tennis; High Hon Roll; NHS; Vrsty Badmnt, Mst Insprtnl Plyr Tnns; CSF Schlrshp Rcpnt; Stu Mnth 6 90; UC Davis; Bio.

NGUYEN, TRANG P; Saddleback HS; Santa Ana, CA; (3); Drama Clb; French Clb; FBLA; Science Clb; School Play; Stage Crew; Yrbk; Cit Awd; Hon Roll; Yrbk Wrtr; Stu Lf Edtr; UCI Treas; Step Clb Pres; UCI; Socl Wrkr.

NGUYEN, TRANG T; Leuzinger HS; Hawthorne, CA; (3); Science Clb; Teachers Aide; Tennis; VP Vllybl; Cit Awd; Hon Roll; Prfct Atten Awd; CSF; Art Awd.

NGUYEN, TRANG T; Magnolia HS; Anaheim, CA; (3); Natl Hnr Soc Clb; CSF; CA ST Long Beach; Nurse.

NGUYEN, TRANG T; Pasadena HS; Pasadena, CA; (2); French Clb; Yrbk; Sec Stu Cncl; Hon Roll; St Schlr; CSF; JV Plyr Badmington Team; Creative Wrtng Club; UCLA; Med.

NGUYEN, TRANG T; Roosevelt HS; Fresno, CA; (1); Hon Roll; Piano; Voice; Pdtrcn.

NGUYEN, TRANG T; St Patrick-St Vincent HS; Vallejo, CA; (3); Church Choir; Pres Soph Cls; JV Vllybl; High Hon Roll; NHS; CA Schlrshp Fed.

NGUYEN, TRAVIS; Leuzinger HS; Lawndale, CA; (4); 20/400; Pres French Clb; VP Science Clb; Band; Tennis; Cit Awd; Hon Roll; Pres Acad Fit Awd; CSF; Cal St Dominguez Hill; Bus.

NGUYEN, TRI; Garden Grove HS; Garden Grove, CA; (3); Boy Scts; Church Yth Grp; Cmnty Wkr; Computer Clb; Drama Clb; Intnl Clb; Math Clb; Stage Crew; Variety Show; High Hon Roll; Robotics.

NGUYEN, TRI M; Saddleback HS; Santa Ana, CA; (3); 1/500; Debate Tm; French Clb; Math Clb; Math Tm; Mu Alpha Theta; Speech Tm; Gld Medl Math 87-89; Cal-Tech; Engrng.

NGUYEN, TRINH; Rancho Alamitos HS; Stanton, CA; (3); French Clb; Science Clb; Teachers Aide; Cit Awd; High Hon Roll; Hon Roll; Prfct Atten Awd; Pres Acad Fit Awd; UCI; Pharmacy.

NGUYEN, TRINH; Valley HS; Santa Ana, CA; (3); Key Clb; Pep Clb; Cheerldng; High Hon Roll; Pres Acad Fit Awd; Girls St; Smith Coll; Psych.

NGUYEN, TRINH M; Valley HS; Sacramento, CA; (4); 23/485; Debate Tm; Drama Clb; English Clb; French Clb; NFL; Science Clb; Speech Tm; Sec Pres SADD; Teachers Aide; Thesps; Spch Comptn Mdls; Mock Trial Dfns Atty; 1st Pl Art Cntst; Jr Statesman Rep; Lenea Fstvl; Pltcl Sci.

NGUYEN, TRONG; San Gabriel HS; Rosemead, CA; (2); Sec Cmnty Wkr; Treas Debate Tm; JA; Treas NFL; Spanish Clb; Treas Speech Tm; SADD; Off Jr Cls; Vllybl; High Hon Roll; Crtsy Cmmtte VP; Stu Congress; Berkeley U; Med.

NGUYEN, TRONG V; Rosemead HS; Rosemead, CA; (1); Chess Clb; Debate Tm; High Hon Roll; CSF; UCLA; Bus.

NGUYEN, TRUC V; Pasadena HS; Pasadena, CA; (2); Church Yth Grp; Hon Roll; CSF.

NGUYEN, TRUNG; Corona HS; Corona, CA; (4); 63/485; Math Clb; Math Tm; Prfct Atten Awd; Pascal Awd; U Of CA Riverside; Biomdcl Sci.

NGUYEN, TRUNG; Saddleback HS; Santa Ana, CA; (3); Boy Scts; French Clb; FBLA; Science Clb; Cit Awd; Hon Roll; Pres Acad Fit Awd; Acadc Lttr.

NGUYEN, TRUNG H; Alexander Hamilton HS; Los Angeles, CA; (3); 2/40; Church Yth Grp; French Clb; Library Aide; Math Tm; Bsktbl; U Of CA; Phrmcy.

NGUYEN, TRUONG M; San Gabriel HS; Rosemead, CA; (3); 3/700; FBLA; Math Clb; Math Tm; Quiz Bowl; Red Cross Aide; Scholastic Bowl; Service Clb; Spanish Clb; Stu Cncl; High Hon Roll; Acad Decthln Team; Indstry Ed Cncl Mdl Awd Wnnr-Math; Math.

NGUYEN, TU-LAN; Fountain Valley HS; Huntington Beach, CA; (1); Church Yth Grp; Computer Clb; Teachers Aide; High Hon Roll; UC Irvine; Designing Engr.

NGUYEN, TU-UYEN N; University HS; Irvine, CA; (4); 14/468; Debate Tm; Hosp Aide; Pres Service Clb; Speech Tm; Lit Mag; Var Bsktbl; High Hon Roll; Ntl Merit Ltr; Spanish NHS; Sci Fair Awds; CROP Cls Trng Preschl Aide; CSF Gold Seal Bearer; U Of CA Irvine; Bio.

NGUYEN, TUAN H; Irvington HS; Fremont, CA; (2); 12/450; Art Clb; Boy Scts; Chess Clb; Computer Clb; French Clb; Math Clb; Science Clb; JV Bsktbl; JV Tennis; JV Vllybl; Med.

NGUYEN, TUAN T; Edison HS; Stockton, CA; (4); 12/400; Aud/Vis; Chess Clb; English Clb; Math Clb; Science Clb; Spanish Clb; Teachers Aide; High Hon Roll; Hon Roll; NHS; Acad Decathlon Pres; Hmcmng King Fnlst; Martial Arts; UC Davis; Psycht.

NGUYEN, TUAN-ANH P; La Quinta HS; Fountain Valley, CA; (2); Chess Clb; French Clb; Bsktbl; Tennis; Hon Roll; Ntl Merit Schol; Prfct Atten Awd; Pres Schlr.

NGUYEN, TUONG B; Costa Mesa HS; Costa Mesa, CA; (3); 15/230; Math Clb; Math Tm; Var Tennis; High Hon Roll; Hon Roll; CSF; Pre Med.

NGUYEN, TUONG D; Bolsa Grande HS; Garden Grove, CA; (3); 21/338; Cmnty Wkr; Math Clb; Science Clb; Bsktbl; Tennis; Hon Roll; Jr NHS; NHS; CSF; Berkley; Law.

NGUYEN, TUYET T; Stagg HS; Stockton, CA; (4); Art Clb; Vllybl; Cit Awd; High Hon Roll; Hon Roll; Fshn Inst Dsgn & Merch; Fshn.

NGUYEN, UINH; Tustin HS; Tustin, CA; (1); Intrml Bsktbl; Hon Roll; Robotic Engr.

NGUYEN, UYEN L; Costa Mesa HS; Costa Mesa, CA; (3); Spanish Clb; Chorus; Orch; Hon Roll; Vietnamese Clb; UCI; Optometry.

NGUYEN, UYEN T; Indio HS; Indio, CA; (1); VP French Clb; Sec Frsh Cls; Sec Stu Cncl; Sftbl; Cit Awd; High Hon Roll; Hon Roll; Prfct Atten Awd; CSF; Project Pursuit; UCLA; Dermatology.

NGUYEN, UYEN T; Yerba Buena HS; San Jose, CA; (3); Church Yth Grp; Cmnty Wkr; French Clb; Key Clb; Math Clb; Office Aide; Teachers Aide; Rptr Yrbk; Rep Stu Cncl; JV Tennis; U Of CA; Doctor.

NGUYEN, VAN; La Quinta HS; Garden Grove, CA; (3); French Clb; Key Clb; Hon Roll; CSF; Petrolm Engrng.

NGUYEN, VAN T; University HS; Irvine, CA; (4); 14/500; Cmnty Wkr; Dance Clb; Debate Tm; English Clb; Girl Scts; Hosp Aide; Key Clb; Math Clb; Math Tm; NFL; Orange Cty Acad Dcthln; Music Piano; U CA Berkeley; Med.

NGUYEN, VAN-CUONG; Bella Vista HS; Sacramento, CA; (4); Computer Clb; French Clb; FBLA; Intnl Clb; Math Clb; Science Clb; Trk; Cit Awd; French Hon Soc; Hon Roll; CSF; Indochina Assn Awd; UC Davis; Phrmcy.

NGUYEN, VI; John Marshall Fund HS; Pasadena, CA; (4); Key Clb; ROTC; Science Clb; Spanish Clb; Chorus; JV Tennis; Cit Awd; Hon Roll; Prfct Atten Awd; Art Center HS Pgm Schlrshp; Rowe & Gayle Giesen Trust Fund Art Schlrshp; Art Center Dsgn; Envrnmntl Dsgn.

NGUYEN, VIET H; James Logan HS; Union City, CA; (3); High Hon Roll; Airplane Mech.

NGUYEN, VINH; Poway HS; Poway, CA; (2); 31/808; Church Yth Grp; Intnl Clb; Model UN; Science Clb; High Hon Roll; Hon Roll; NHS; Prfct Atten Awd; Pres Acad Fit Awd; Achiever Of Mnth; PTSA Cert Of Mrt; CA Jr Schrshp Fed Hnr Awd; Engrng.

NGUYEN, VINH THY; Saddleback HS; Santa Ana, CA; (4); 45/508; Cmnty Wkr; FBLA; Spanish Clb; Hon Roll; Prfct Atten Awd; Stu Tchr Ed Prgm; UCI Prtnrshp; UC; Biomed.

NGUYEN, VU; Edison HS; Fresno, CA; (1); Computer Clb.

NGUYEN, VU ANDREW; Saint Ignatius College Prep; San Francisco, CA; (3); Debate Tm; Model UN; Speech Tm; Hon Roll; Pres Acad Fit Awd; Rptr Nwsp; Boston Coll; Bus.

NGUYEN, VUONG D; Bolsa Grande HS; Westminster, CA; (3); Yrbk; Off Sr Cls.

NGUYEN, VY T; Downey HS; Norwalk, CA; (4); Cmnty Wkr; JA; Science Clb; Service Clb; Temple Yth Grp; Chorus; Kiwanis Awd; CA Ply Pomona; Cvl Engr.

NGUYEN, XUAN; Lincoln HS; Stockton, CA; (3); High Hon Roll.

NGUYEN, YEN KHANH; Arlington HS; Riverside, CA; (3); 6/400; FBLA; Ed Nwsp; High Hon Roll; Stu Mo Bus; Petry, Writing & Drawing; CSF; Daisy Chain Escort Grad Ceremony; U Of South CA; Pediatrician.

NGUYEN, YEN P; Chaffey HS; Ontario, CA; (4); FBLA; Office Aide; Teachers Aide; Rep Jr Cls; Rep Stu Cncl; Cit Awd; High Hon Roll; Hon Roll; NHS; Prfct Atten Awd; ROP Sshn Mrchndsng; Eng Stu Of Mnth 1989-90; Inst Desgn Mrchng; Fshn Mrktng.

NGUYEN, YUONG; Westminster HS; Westminster, CA; (2); Bsktbl; Arch.

NGUYEN-VO, PHUNG M; Tustin HS; Tustin, CA; (2); Cmnty Wkr; Library Aide; Science Clb; Hon Roll; Prfct Atten Awd.

NGUYENSOVAN, LUCIE H; John Marshall Fundamental HS; Pasadena, CA; (3); Sec Key Clb; Science Clb; Spanish Clb; Teachers Aide; Stu Cncl; JV Tennis; Hon Roll; Sec NHS; CA Schlrshp Soc; Inter Schl Dist Union; Herodotus Clb; Poltcl Sci.

NGYUEN, DIEM; Costa Mesa HS; Costa Mesa, CA; (4); 4/233; Church Yth Grp; Cmnty Wkr; Computer Clb; Latin Clb; Math Clb; Math Tm; Science Clb; Ed Nwsp; Cit Awd; DAR Awd; Vrsty Bdmntn; U Interschlstc League Typewriting; CA Schlrshp Fed; U Of CA; Comp Sci.

NHAM, CUONG B; Cordova HS; Rancho Cordova, CA; (3); Church Yth Grp; Model UN; Spanish Clb; Jr NHS; Outstndng Englsh, Spnsh & Hstry Stu Of Yr 87-88; Sacramento ST U.

NHAM, MINH V; Andrew Hill HS; San Jose, CA; (3); Computer Clb; FBLA; Lit Mag; Bsbl; Swmmng; Hon Roll; San Jose ST U; Engr.

NHAN, CAU T; Galileo HS; San Francisco, CA; (3); Art Clb; Computer Clb; Math Clb; Swmmng; Tennis; Vllybl; Hon Roll.

NHEK, ARUNNY; Independence HS; San Jose, CA; (3); JV Bsktbl; Var Sftbl; JV Vllybl; Cambodian Clb; San Jose ST; Engrng.

NHEK, MOM R; Wilson HS; Long Beach, CA; (3); French Clb; JA; Red Cross Aide; Chorus; Yrbk; Cit Awd; Voice Dem Awd; U Of CA Irvine; Phy.

NHIEU, MARY; South Pasadena HS; Los Angeles, CA; (4); French Clb; Hosp Aide; Math Tm; Spanish Clb; Teachers Aide; Nrs.

NHIEU, TRUNG L; Andrew Hill HS; San Jose, CA; (2); Math Clb; Math Tm; San Jose ST U; Comp Opertns.

NHOK, MAP N; Mc Clymonds Academy HS; Oakland, CA; (3); Var Vllybl; Hon Roll; Prfct Atten Awd; UC Berkeley Upwrd Bnd; UC Berkeley.

NIAZI, SURKHAB A; Pacific Palisades HS; Los Angeles, CA; (2); Chess Clb; Computer Clb; Ed Nwsp; Prfct Atten Awd; MIT; Cmptr Sci.

NIBLEY, HOLLY D; Durham HS; Durham, CA; (2); 31/73; Drama Clb; GAA; Mrchg Band; School Play; Stage Crew; JV L Bsktbl; Var L Trk; JV L Vllybl; Hon Roll; Pres Acad Fit Awd; JV Vlybl Ms Hstl Awd 1988-89; JV Trk Mst Outstndng Fld Athlt 1989-90; JV Bsktbl-Ms Dfns Awd 1989; Prfsnl Photo.

NICASSIO, JOSEPHINE N; Polytechnic HS; N Hollywood, CA; (3); Church Yth Grp; Office Aide; Spanish Clb; Teachers Aide; Ed Nwsp; Yrbk; Rep Stu Cncl; Hon Roll; Jrnlsm Awd; Engl Awd; Prncpls List; Hnr Roll; Educ.

NICDAO, ANDRE VINCENT; Cantwell HS; Rosemead, CA; (2); 1/26; Church Yth Grp; Math Tm; Science Clb; High Hon Roll; NHS; 1st Pl Ahsme Tst; Wrkrs Exp Prog; Princeton U; Med.

NICHOLAS, AYLA G; South Coast HS; Gualala, CA; (3); Teachers Aide; High Hon Roll; Hon Roll; Photo; Drftng; Photo.

NICHOLAS, ROBERT T; Oakridge HS; Cameron Park, CA; (1); High Hon Roll; Hon Roll; CFS Pgm; Outstndng Awd Alg; Stanford; Law.

NICHOLES, KATRINA; Granada HS; Livermore, CA; (2); Church Yth Grp; Intnl Clb; Drill Tm; Powder Puff Ftbl; UC Davis; Vet.

NICHOLLS, SAMANTHA N; Louisville HS; Woodland Hills, CA; (3); Church Yth Grp; Band; Church Choir; Orch; Stage Crew; Hon Roll; Sociology.

NICHOLS, AMENAH K; Merced HS; Merced, CA; (4); Church Yth Grp; Cmnty Wkr; Drama Clb; Teachers Aide; Church Choir; Drill Tm; Rep Stu Cncl; Trk; Cit Awd; Hon Roll; BSU VP & Dir Of Publicity; Merced CC; Teacher.

NICHOLS, AMY; Hughson Union HS; Modesto, CA; (4); 13/119; Am Leg Aux Girls St; Pres Treas FFA; GAA; Yrbk; Treas Frsh Cls; Treas Soph Cls; Pres Jr Cls; JV Var Sftbl; Pres Acad Fit Awd; Trans Valley Leag Outstndng Schlr Athl Vrsty Ftbl 90; HS Faculty Lrdshp Awd; Cal Poly San Luis Obispo; Ag.

NICHOLS, BRENDA; Placer HS; Auburn, CA; (4); English Clb; 4-H; French Clb; Ski Clb; Teachers Aide; Var L Vllybl; French Hon Soc; 4-H Awd; Pres Acad Fit Awd; U S Vlybl Clb, Coach; UC Davis; Forestry.

NICHOLS, CHRISTINE L; Venice HS; Los Angeles, CA; (2); Church Yth Grp; Service Clb; Mrchg Band; Nwsp; Hist Soph Cls; JV Cheerldng; Crs Cntry; Cit Awd; Hon Roll; Photo Club; Chatelains; Athenians Hnr Soc; Woodbury U; Int Dsgn.

NICHOLS, CINDY; James Madison HS; San Diego, CA; (3); Church Yth Grp; Cmnty Wkr; Drama Clb; Pep Clb; Church Choir; Drill Tm; Rptr Yrbk; Var Cheerldng; Prfct Atten Awd; Pres Acad Fit Awd; Intrntl Ordr Rnbw Grls; Jrnlsm.

NICHOLS, DIANE H; Las Plumas HS; Oroville, CA; (2); 47/284; Church Yth Grp; Debate Tm; Rptr 4-H; Pres FFA; Key Clb; SADD; Band; Mrchg Band; Sec Frsh Cls; 4-H Awd; Upward Bound; Harvard U; Lawyer.

NICHOLS, JASON L; Turlock HS; Turlock, CA; (2); 190/645; Church Yth Grp; Cmnty Wkr; Rep Soph Cls; Var Swmmng; Var Trk; Water Polo Vrsty; CA Berkely; Attorney.

NICHOLS, JENNIFER A; Casa Roble Fundemental HS; Orangevale, CA; (2); 79/800; French Clb; Drill Tm; Cheerldng; Diving; Gym; Cit Awd; Hon Roll; Univrsal Dance Star Awd UDA; 2 Drawings Publshd Mag; Piano; BYU; Graphic Art.

NICHOLS, KATHERINE E; Newport Christian HS; Corona Del Mar, CA; (2); Latin Clb; Scholastic Bowl; Ski Clb; Chorus; School Musical; Var Capt Bsktbl; Var Sftbl; Var Vllybl; High Hon Roll; Prfct Atten Awd; VP Hiking Clb; Jobs Dghtrs; U CA Irvine; Med.

NICHOLS, KENA; Oakland Technical HS; Oakland, CA; (1); 30/250; VP Church Yth Grp; Dance Clb; Hosp Aide; Speech Tm; Drill Tm; Ed Nwsp; Rep Frsh Cls; JV Trk; Hon Roll; Prfct Atten Awd; Many Awds Trck; M L King Awd Trophy; Upward Bound; Finalist N Miss Natl Teen Pagnt; UC Berkely; Surgn.

NICHOLS, MATT A; Valley Christian HS; Hawaiian Gardens, CA; (1); Stage Crew; JV Bsktbl; JV Ftbl; Surfing; Waterskiing; USC; Arch.

NICHOLS, NICOLE R; Edison HS; Huntington Beach, CA; (1); Teachers Aide; Vllybl; Preserve Envrnmnt; UCLA.

NICHOLS, REGINA; Strathmore HS; Strathmore, CA; (3); Church Yth Grp; SADD; Band; Church Choir; Drill Tm; Flag Corp; Hon Roll; Friday Nite Live; Point Loma Nazarene Coll; Psych.

NICHOLS, TAMMY L; Clovis West HS; Clovis, CA; (3); High Hon Roll; Hon Roll.

NICHOLSON, AMY M; Monache HS; Porterville, CA; (3); 7/300; Pres Church Yth Grp; Church Choir; Mrchg Band; Sec Soph Cls; Rep Jr Cls; Stu Cncl; Stat Bsktbl; Var JV Tennis; High Hon Roll; Voice Dem Awd; CSF; Point Loma Nazarene Coll.

NICHOLSON, BRANDI; George Washington Preparatory HS; Los Angeles, CA; (3); Church Yth Grp; Math Clb; Science Clb; Service Clb; SADD; Temple Yth Grp; Church Choir; Variety Show; Lit Mag; Hon Roll; Acad Decathlon Tm 89-90; St Anthony Grand Lodge; U Of Southern CA; Comp Sci.

NICHOLSON, KEVIN S; Laguna Beach HS; Laguna Beach, CA; (3); Office Aide; Ski Clb; SADD; Teachers Aide; Hon Roll; Pres Acad Fit Awd; Var Bsbl; JV Ftbl; Var Wt Lftg; Safe Conduct Cncl; Bus.

NICHOLSON, RACHEL A; Modesto HS; Modesto, CA; (3); Art Clb; Spanish Clb; Rally Clb; Bio Sci.

NICHTER, TRACY; Rosary HS; Anaheim, CA; (3); Church Yth Grp; Speech Tm; Variety Show; Var Vllybl; Hon Roll; VP Pressure Free Assoc; Co-Pres Safe Rides; USCUBA Vlybl; HOBY Awd; Bus.

NICKEL, HEIDI K; Garces Memorial HS; Bakersfield, CA; (2); #2 In Class; JA; Math Clb; Pres Frsh Cls; Stu Cncl; Var L Crs Cntry; Intrml Powder Puff Ftbl; Intrml Sftbl; Var L Trk; High Hon Roll; Hon Roll.

NICKEL, JAMES C; Garces Memorial HS; Bakersfield, CA; (3); Church Yth Grp; Letterman Clb; Ski Clb; Var Ftbl; Intrml Golf; JV Tennis; Var Trk; Intrml Wrstlng; Kayaking; Hunting; Skiing; UCSD; Ag Law.

NICKELL, APRIL; Valley Christian HS; San Jose, CA; (1); Church Yth Grp; Drama Clb; JV Bsktbl; Hon Roll; JV Chrldng Ldrshp Awd.

NICKELL, MISTY A; Alpaugh Unified HS; Alpaugh, CA; (2); Church Yth Grp; Band; Pres Frsh Cls; Sec Pres Stu Cncl; Capt Bsktbl; Cheerldng; Sftbl; Vllybl; Hon Roll; Stu Cncl Pres 90-91; MVP Vlybl; 1st Tm All Leag Sftbl; Mst Outstndng Athlt Awd; Mst Insprtnl Vly/Bsktbl; Pepperdine U; Telecmmnctns.

NICKELS, THOMAS; St Genevieve HS; Arleta, CA; (3); Letterman Clb; JV Var Bsbl; JV Var Ftbl; NEDT Awd; Comp Engrng.

NICKERSON, APRIL A; Granada HS; Granada Hills, CA; (2); Church Yth Grp; Debate Tm; Drama Clb; Girl Scts; Pep Clb; Science Clb; Chorus; School Play; Variety Show; Rep Soph Cls; Actress.

NICKOLS, LA TASHA N; Eisenhower HS; Rialto, CA; (3); Spanish Clb; Teachers Aide; Rep Stu Cncl; Var Trk; Hon Roll; NHS; Prfct Atten Awd; Howard U; Lwyr.

NICOLAI, PETER T; San Rafael HS; San Rafael, CA; (2); French Clb; Cit Awd; Grand Prz Behavrl Sci Cnty Sci Fair & 2nd Pl Bay Area Sci Fair; Golden ST Exmntn Acadmc Excllnc Awd; Cal Poly; Arch.

NICOLAS, ANNA ZARINA M; Hogan SR HS; Vallejo, CA; (3); Church Yth Grp; Science Clb; Spanish Clb; SADD; Teachers Aide; Church Choir; Hon Roll; Badminton; FNL; UC Davis.

NICOLAS, DONABELLE RODRIGO; St Joseph Catholic HS; Bellflower, CA; (2); Hosp Aide; Rep Frsh Cls; Treas Soph Cls; Rep Jr Cls; Hon Roll; USSJ; U Of Irvine; Med.

NICOLAS, JOHN A; Tokay HS; Stockton, CA; (2); Bsbl; Bsktbl; Capt Ftbl; Hon Roll; Babe Ruth Bsbl Leag; Natl Young Leaders Congrssnl Schlr; ID ST; Dentistry.

NICOLAS JR, MABINI P; Carson HS; Carson, CA; (2); Sec Service Clb; Teachers Aide; Rptr Nwsp; Off Frsh Cls; Intrml Bsktbl; Intrml Sftbl; Var Tennis; Prfct Atten Awd; Pres Acad Fit Awd; GPA Plaq; Bruce Carpenter Awd; Outstndng Athl.

NICOLAS, PIA MARIE; George Washington HS; San Francisco, CA; (4); Art Clb; Cmnty Wkr; SADD; Teachers Aide; Rep Soph Cls; Rep Jr Cls; Rep Sr Cls; Rep Stu Cncl; Stat Bsktbl; Mgr Ftbl; Vlntr Spcl Olympics; Photo Clb; Fncng; Arch.

NICOLAYSEN, PAULA C; Poway HS; Poway, CA; (3); 163/714; Teachers Aide; High Hon Roll; Hon Roll; Amnesty Intl; Outstndng Achvt Awd In Child Care; U CA; Ed.

NICOLETTI, KRISTEN C; Dos Palos HS; Dos Palos, CA; (3); 5/140; AFS; Church Yth Grp; GAA; Letterman Clb; Math Clb; Spanish Clb; SADD; Varsity Clb; Band; Mrchg Band; Acad Decathlon; CA Thoroughbred Breeders Assn; Chrstphrs Chrch Grp; Engl.

NICOLETTI, MICHELLE L; Dos Palos HS; Dos Palos, CA; (2); AFS; GAA; Band; Drm Mjr(t); Mrchg Band; Orch; Pep Band; Stu Cncl; Var L Sftbl; Hon Roll; CSF; Bronco Band Outstndng Stu Clss Awd 90; Head Majorette Awd; CSU Fresno; Accntng.

NICOLL, STEVE; Valley Torah HS; Long Beach, CA; (4); 1/19; Temple Yth Grp; Rptr Nwsp; Ed Yrbk; Treas Pres Stu Cncl; Var Bsbl; Var Capt Bsktbl; Pres Acad Fit Awd; Val; Schlrshps Bobtin, Cong Mogen David Moren Family; L A Times Outstndng Stu Citizen; Stu Store Mgr; U Of PA; Biomedcl Sci.

NICORA, JEFFREY A; Cordova SR HS; Rancho Cordova, CA; (2); 40/540; Am Leg Boys St; Intrml Bsbl; JV Ftbl; Cit Awd; High Hon Roll; Hon Roll; Pres Acad Fit Awd; Cert Superior Achvmnt & Excllnc Of Prfrmnc In Sci; Biologist Oceanographer.

NICOSIA, MIKE P; Katella HS; Anaheim, CA; (2); JV Wrstlng; Cit Awd; Hon Roll; Arch.

NIEBALA, CHRIS B; Irvine HS; Irvine, CA; (1); Boy Scts; Computer Clb; Sea Scts; Sci.

NIEDIEK, DIANE; Corona SR HS; Victorville, CA; (2); 117/473; JV Bsktbl; Var Stat Mgr(s); JV Vllybl; Off Road Rcng; Modeling; Water, Jet Skiing; UC Santa Barbara; Bus Mgmt.

NIEDNAGEL, MIRIAM R; Monte Vista HS; Alamo, CA; (1); 36/400; Church Yth Grp; Orch; Var L Trk; CA Schlrshp Fed Mem; YMCA Yth & Gov Mem; Studied Piano 9 Yrs & Won 3rd Pl Contra Costa Perf Arts.

NIEDZIELSKI, ALEX P; Sunset HS; Hayward, CA; (3); Hon Roll; Bus.

NIEFFENEGGER, TRENT R; Woodland HS; Woodland, CA; (2); Boy Scts; Church Yth Grp; FFA; Socr; Wrstlng; Hon Roll; Farm Mgmt.

NIEGA, XYLENE J; Bellarmine Jefferson HS; North Hollywood, CA; (2); Spanish Clb; Teachers Aide; Hon Roll; NHS; CSF.

NIEHAUS, ANGIE L; Hilltop HS; Chula Vista, CA; (2); Yrbk; Pres Jr Cls; Girls Leag Rep; ASB Pres; ASB Outstndng Svc Awd; UCSB.

NIELD, SUNDAY C; Torrey Pines HS; Solana Beach, CA; (3); Band; Jazz Band; Pep Band; Off Jr Cls; JV Sftbl; Var Trk; JV Vllybl; Hon Roll; SDSU.

NIELSEN, ANA MARIE; Clayton Valley HS; Concord, CA; (4); 15/415; Art Clb; Church Yth Grp; GAA; Pep Clb; Service Clb; Acpl Chr; Band; Chorus; Church Choir; Variety Show; BYU; Art.

NIELSEN, DEBBIE; Archbishop Mitty HS; San Jose, CA; (3); Cmnty Wkr; Spanish Clb; SADD; Teachers Aide; Chorus; Var Cheerldng; High Hon Roll; NHS; Spnsh Cultr Clb Sec; CSF; Psych.

NIELSEN, ERIK K; Rio Americano HS; Sacramento, CA; (3); 66/290; Art Clb; Key Clb; Yrbk; JV Bsktbl; Var Swmmng; Hon Roll; CVC Chmpnshp In Water Polo; Bus.

NIELSEN, HANA; Analy HS; Sebastopol, CA; (2); Debate Tm; Science Clb; Acpl Chr; Stu Cncl; Trk; Aviation Club Mem; CSF Mem; Outstndng Achvt Geom; Purdue U; Aviation.

NIELSEN, JULIANNE G; Estancia HS; Costa Mesa, CA; (2); Church Yth Grp; Drama Clb; Latin Clb; Spanish Clb; Speech Tm; Church Choir; Bsktbl; Score Keeper; Sftbl; Vllybl; Speak Fluent Spanish; UCLA; Atty.

NIELSEN, KRISTA A; Providence HS; Burbank, CA; (3); Church Yth Grp; Cmnty Wkr; Drama Clb; Girl Scts; Hosp Aide; Red Cross Aide; Chorus; Hon Roll; CSF; Psych.

NIELSEN, PAUL M; Serra HS; San Diego, CA; (3); Boy Scts; Church Yth Grp; Debate Tm; Speech Tm; Trk; Hon Roll; Prfct Atten Awd; Ad Tarie Dei; Parlevu Dei; Articles Pblshd; SDSU; Acctng.

NIELSEN, SUSAN K; Washington Union HS; Fresno, CA; (2); Church Yth Grp; FCA; FBLA; Intnl Clb; Tennis; Vllybl; Hon Roll; CSF; Block W-Acad; Ed.

NIELSEN, WENDY; Rolling Hills HS; Rolling Hills, CA; (4); 27/316; German Clb; Mrchg Band; Orch; School Musical; Ed Lit Mag; High Hon Roll; NHS; Pres Acad Fit Awd; CSF; German Hnr Soc; UC San Diego; Engl.

NIELSON, ADAM; Clovis West HS; Clovis, CA; (3); Church Yth Grp; Letterman Clb; Ski Clb; Speech Tm; JV Bsbl; JV Bsktbl; Ftbl; Socr; Var Tennis; Wt Lftg; Devil Pups Camp For Yng Marines; Mexicali Yth Outreach Mssn Mexico; San Diego ST; Bus.

NIEM, TU; Hiram Johnson West Campus HS; Sacramento, CA; (2); 25/182; JV Wrstlng; Hon Roll; Vol Tutoring; Comp; Electrncs; Comp.

NIEMACK, ELISA J; Westridge Schl For Girls; Altadena, CA; (2); Art Clb; Church Yth Grp; GAA; Var Socr; Var Sftbl; JV Vllybl; Wt Lftg; Outstndng Stu Health; MVP Var Sccr; UCSD; Elem Ed.

NIEMANN, ELYSE; Vintage HS; Napa, CA; (3); Am Leg Aux Girls St; Pres VP Church Yth Grp; Scholastic Bowl; Band; Church Choir; Mrchg Band; JV Bsktbl; Score Keeper; Var Socr; Var JV Vllybl; Engl Schlr Awd; HS Envrnmntl Conf Washington DC; Pple To Pple Ambssdr Soviet Union; Envrnmntl Clb; U CA; Intl Rltns.

NIEMANN, ERIKA; Modesto HS; Modesto, CA; (3); Pres AFS; Art Clb; Church Yth Grp; 4-H; SADD; School Play; JV Trk; JV Var Vllybl; 4-H Awd; Hon Roll; Acad Decathlon Tm; Girls St Delg 90.

NIEMEYER, NICOLE; John F Kennedy HS; Sacramento, CA; (3); 93/476; AFS; French Clb; Teachers Aide; Diving; Biolgcl Sci.

NIEMIEC, MARK; Rim Of The World HS; Crestline, CA; (2); 2/252; Church Yth Grp; Spanish Clb; JV Capt Bsktbl; Socr; Hon Roll; Prfct Atten Awd; Cal ST San Bernardino; Sci.

NIERE, FARR V; Carson HS; Carson, CA; (3); 5/636; Church Yth Grp; Science Clb; Service Clb; Church Choir; Off Jr Cls; Stu Cncl; Var Rotary Awd; Nw-Lf Clb; CSF; Squrs; Johns Hopkins; Nero-Srgry.

NIERVA, CHRISTY P; Samuel F B Morse HS; San Diego, CA; (2); 43/764; Intnl Clb; SADD; Variety Show; Rep Nwsp; Lit Mag; Hon Roll; Jr NHS; Northridge; Phys Thrpy.

NIES, ANNE M; Rio Hondo Preparatory Schl; Covina, CA; (1); Church Yth Grp; Cmnty Wkr; Stu Cncl; Var Bsktbl; JV Cheerldng; JV Capt Sftbl; JV Vllybl; Hon Roll; Pep Clb; Chorus; Coach 2nd & 3rd Grd Grls Vlybl, Bsktbl, Sftbl & Kick Ball.

NIETES, KATRINA R; Abraham Lincoln HS; San Francisco, CA; (2); Var Capt Cheerldng; Cit Awd; Far East Chrldng Cmptn-3rd Pl; Drug/Alcohol Clss Completion Cert; U S CA; Intl Mrktng.

NIETO, ANGELA L; Pasadena HS; Pasadena, CA; (3); Yrbk; Hon Roll; Blck Stu Union.

NIETO, GABRIELLE; San Gabriel Mission HS; Montebello, CA; (3); Church Yth Grp; Office Aide; Pep Clb; Red Cross Aide; Service Clb; School Musical; School Play; Hon Roll; Medallion Awd 90; Friends Of The Sea Otter; UC Santa Cruz; Marine Bio.

NIETO, JOSE M; St Bernard HS; Los Angeles, CA; (2); Church Yth Grp; Hosp Aide; Letterman Clb; Spanish Clb; Varsity Clb; Var Crs Cntry; JV Socr; Var Vllybl; High Hon Roll; Hon Roll; CSF; Tae Kwon Do; Med.

NIETO, LENORA M; St Anthony HS; Paramount, CA; (2); Aud/Vis; Church Yth Grp; Hosp Aide; School Musical; School Play; Var Trk; Hon Roll; Drama, Logistics; U Of Southern CA; Theatre Arts.

NIETO, STEFANIE; Mercy HS; San Francisco, CA; (4); 7/167; Cmnty Wkr; Dance Clb; GAA; Sec Treas Spanish Clb; Variety Show; Cheerldng; Hon Roll; Chrstn Ldrshp-Advncd Smnr; Santa Clara U; Psych.

NIEVARES, LYNNETTE C; Santa Clara HS; Santa Clara, CA; (3); 53/382; JA; Spanish Clb; Teachers Aide; Intrml Vllybl; Cit Awd; Hon Roll; Prfct Atten Awd; Dean Witter Stock Market Cont Top 10 2 Times; CSF Clb; UCSB; Bus.

NIEVES, DAISY; Hueneme HS; Oxnard, CA; (3); Letterman Clb; SADD; Drill Tm; Socr; Hon Roll; Prfct Atten Awd; Pres Acad Fit Awd; Nurse.

NIEVES, GLENN G; Bloomington HS; Bloomington, CA; (2).

NIEVES, PHILLIP R; Newark Memorial HS; Newark, CA; (3); 24/355; Spanish Clb; SADD; Teachers Aide; High Hon Roll; Hon Roll; JV Trk; Intrml Wt Lftg; Life Sci Outstndng Stu Awd; Psych Hnr Awd; UC Davis; Psych.

NIGRO, ANGELA V; Carondelet HS; Walnut Creek, CA; (3); 1/162; Hosp Aide; Pres Latin Clb; Ed Nwsp; Sec Treas Soph Cls; Stu Cncl; Var L Crs Cntry; Var L Swmmng; Var L Trk; High Hon Roll; VP NHS; Pres Of CSF; Xerox Awd; Intl Wnnr Piano Plyng Audtns; Stanford; Med.

NIJJAR, SERVJIT; Yuba City HS; Yuba City, CA; (3); 21/450; High Hon Roll; Aisan Clb; CSF; Friday Night Live; Optometry.

NIKKHESSAL, ARASH; Santa Monica HS; Malibu, CA; (1); High Hon Roll; Pres Acad Fit Awd; UCLA; Med.

NIKNAFS, NEGIN; La Habra HS; La Habra, CA; (4); 20/365; Am Leg Aux Girls St; Bus Profs of Am; Cmnty Wkr; Treas FBLA; Key Clb; Q&S; Science Clb; Spanish Clb; Yrbk; Lit Mag; Stu Leag Treas/Secy/Home Ec Rep; Cal ST U Fullerton; Bus Admin.

NIKRAVAN, ASHKAAN; San Gabriel HS; San Gabriel, CA; (1); Church Yth Grp; Rep Frsh Cls; Stu Cncl; Cit Awd; Hon Roll; UCLA; Med.

NIKRAVESH, BITA; Notre Dame HS; Foster City, CA; (3); Cmnty Wkr; Dance Clb; Debate Tm; Drama Clb; French Clb; Library Aide; Pep Clb; SADD; Teachers Aide; Drill Tm; Crs Cntry Hnr; CSF; Trk Hnrs; Drama Hnrs; Comm.

NILES, AMY C; Los Gatos HS; Los Gatos, CA; (2); 26/342; Church Yth Grp; Sec VP 4-H; Service Clb; JV Var Bsktbl; JV Swmmng; 4-H Awd; Hon Roll; Raise Guide Dogs For Blind; UC Davis; Vet Med.

NILES, DARBY; Fortuna Union HS; Fortuna, CA; (4); Cmnty Wkr; 4-H; FHA; Math Tm; Office Aide; SADD; Stu Cncl; Powder Puff Ftbl; Tennis; Hon Roll; JOBS Daughters; Cal Poly San Luis Obispo; Math.

NILES, SCOTT C; Righetti HS; Santa Maria, CA; (2); Aud/Vis; Drama Clb; Ski Clb; Hon Roll; UCLA; Film Stud.

NILMEYER, JESSICA J; Grace M Davis HS; Modesto, CA; (2); Spanish Clb; SADD; Band; Jazz Band; Mrchg Band; Powder Puff Ftbl; Vllybl; Boston U; Marine Bio.

NILO, MARICELA; Huntington Park HS; Maywood, CA; (2); Tennis; High Hon Roll.

NILSSON, LINDA M; Kingsburg Joint JR HS; Fresno, CA; (3); FFA; Vet.

NIMO, ELAINE E; Gahr HS; Norwalk, CA; (2); 38/468; Rptr Nwsp; Var Tennis; Hon Roll; Prfct Atten Awd; Century 2000 & Tennis Clbs; GAHR Talent Show 3rd Pl; USC.

NIMO, ROSANNA E; Whitney HS; Norwalk, CA; (3); Key Clb; Latin Clb; High Hon Roll; Hon Roll; CSF; U Southern CA; Med.

NING, STANLEY S; Flintridge Prep Schl; Pasadena, CA; (3); JCL; Latin Clb; Variety Show; JV Var Tennis; High Hon Roll; Hon Roll; NHS; UC San Diego; Plstc Surgeon.

NINH, DOMINIC; Adolfo Camarillo HS; Camarillo, CA; (3); Church Yth Grp; Cmnty Wkr; French Clb; FBLA; Intnl Clb; Office Aide; Pep Clb; SADD; Variety Show; Rptr Nwsp; UC Irvine; Med.

NINO, ALAN P; Bellarmine-Jefferson HS; Los Angeles, CA; (2); Trk; UCLA; Law.

NIPAY, WENNIE; Patten Acad Of Christian Eductn; Union City, CA; (4); 1/6; Church Yth Grp; Cmnty Wkr; Debate Tm; Letterman Clb; Natl Beta Clb; Pep Clb; Teachers Aide; Band; Chorus; Church Choir; Band VP 86-87; Band Pres 87-89; Percussion Sect Leader 86-90; Choir Vp 87-88; Patten Symphonette; Intl Bus Financing.

NIPPER, DUSTIN C; Foothill HS; Pleasanton, CA; (3); 125/400; Drama Clb; Girl Scts; Teachers Aide; School Play; Stage Crew; Grn Club Protctn Of Our Planet; UCLA; Law.

NISEWANER, KARNA; Mills HS; Millbrae, CA; (2); Church Yth Grp; Math Clb; Math Tm; JV L Socr; Var L Trk; JV L Vllybl; Masonic Awd; Rainbow Girl; Prncpls Awd; High Hon Geom Golden St Exam; Earth; CSF; Math/Hstry.

NISHANIAN, CHRISTINA; Bolsa Grande HS; Garden Grove, CA; (1); Cit Awd; High Hon Roll; Hon Roll; Law.

NISHI, CHRIS S; Buena Park HS; Fullerton, CA; (3); Chess Clb; Cmnty Wkr; Key Clb; Treas Science Clb; JV Var Wrstlng; Cit Awd; High Hon Roll; Prfct Atten Awd; CSF; Chiropractor.

NISHI, JULIAN; Buena Park HS; Fullerton, CA; (3); Chess Clb; Key Clb; Letterman Clb; Science Clb; Var L Wrstlng; High Hon Roll; Hon Roll; Prfct Atten Awd; Vlntr City Of Fullerton; Bus.

NISHI, MAO; Canyon HS; Anaheim, CA; (3); Cmnty Wkr; Math Clb; Band; Mrchg Band; Cit Awd; High Hon Roll; NHS; CSF; Amnsty Intl.

NISHIKAWA, S PHILIP; Castro Valley HS; Castro Valley, CA; (4); 11/320; Pres Acad Fit Awd; CSF; Dept Awds Alb, Elem Functn, Geo, Chem, Trig, Calcus, Hist, Photogrphy; U CA-DAVIS; Chem Engr.

NISHIMOTO, LISA S; Adrian C Wilcox HS; Sunnyvale, CA; (1); 1/413; 4-H; Temple Yth Grp; JV Bsktbl; CSF; Amnsty Intl; JV Badmntn; Jrnlsm.

NISHIMOTO, MAYUMI; Westminster HS; Midway City, CA; (3); Cmnty Wkr; Key Clb; Latin Clb; Speech Tm; Chorus; Treas Jr Cls; Stat Bsktbl; Mock Trial; California Scholastic Federation; Advanced Placement Club; International Business.

NISHIMOTO, MEGUMI; Westminster HS; Midway City, CA; (2); 4/700; JCL; Latin Clb; Service Clb; Chorus; Treas Frsh Cls; Rotary Awd; People To People HS Stu Ambssdr; Outstng Stu Nominee; Martin Music Cntr Accrdn Jazz Combo Mbr; Intl Bus.

NISHIMOTO, STEVE T; Davis SR HS; Davis, CA; (3); 1/400; Church Yth Grp; Letterman Clb; Spanish Clb; Var Golf; Stat Vllybl; Off Pres Acad Fit Awd; Hrns & Hgh Hnrs For Gldn St Exam; Lftm Mem Of CA Schlrshp Fdrtn.

NISHITA, JEFFREY; Pioneer HS; San Jose, CA; (4); Boy Scts; Treas FBLA; Service Clb; Var Capt Bsktbl; JV Var Tennis; Pres NHS; CSF; Acad Dcthln Team Hnr Stu; UCSB; Bus Econ.

NISHITA, KIMI A; Pioneer HS; San Jose, CA; (3); Church Yth Grp; Cmnty Wkr; Math Clb; Q&S; Spanish Clb; Varsity Clb; Yrbk; Rep Stu Cncl; JV Bsktbl; Var Trk.

NISSEN, ALLISON; Colfax HS; Weimar, CA; (3); 26/152; Teachers Aide; Crs Cntry; Trk; Hon Roll.

NITAO, JANET N; Tustin HS; Tustin, CA; (4); 25/377; Church Yth Grp; Cmnty Wkr; Hosp Aide; Rep Soph Cls; Off Jr Cls; VP Sr Cls; Bsktbl; High Hon Roll; Opt Clb Awd; Pres Acad Fit Awd; Chrtr Pres Octagon Clb; UC Berkeley.

NITSCHKE, MARY A; Roosevelt HS; Fresno, CA; (3); 7/680; JCL; Quiz Bowl; Pres Acpl Chr; Band; School Musical; School Play; Stage Crew; Rep Soph Cls; Hon Roll; Outstndng Awds-Bio & Alg II 89, Trig, AP Hstry & Xerox Humnts Stu Cntrl CA 90; Fresno Civic Ballet; Performing Arts.

NITSCHKE, RIKA K; Clovis HS; Fresno, CA; (3); Church Yth Grp; FCA; Pres Hist FFA; Capt Cheerldng; Gym; Trk; Hon Roll; Natl Chrldrs Assn Natl Chmpns 88-89; FFA Frm Rcrd Tm 2nd Hgh Ind St Fnls; Eqstrn-Thrghbrd-Lvstck Shws; Vet.

NITZEL JR, DONALD L; Samuel F B Morse HS; San Diego, CA; (3); 18/641; Church Yth Grp; Bsbl; Ftbl; Mgr(s); Score Keeper; High Hon Roll; Prfct Atten Awd; Pres Acad Fit Awd; Golden St Math Test Hnrs 89; Sprts Med.

NIU, MARK L; Homestead HS; Sunnyvale, CA; (4); 29/384; Church Yth Grp; VP FBLA; VP JA; NFL; SADD; Band; Co-Ed Nwsp; Yrbk; Off Jr Cls; Mgr Stu Cncl; CSF-PRES; U CA-BERKELEY; Indstrl Engr.

NIX, JENNIFER R; Lindsay HS; Lindsay, CA; (2); Church Yth Grp; Church Choir; Hon Roll; CA St Mock Trial Comptn; Law.

NIX, KEVIN S; San Dimas HS; San Dimas, CA; (3); Letterman Clb; Varsity Clb; VICA; Bsbl; Swmmng; Wrstlng; High Hon Roll; Hon Roll; Engrng.

NIX, NICOLE M; Sanger HS; Fresno, CA; (3); Science Clb; Ski Clb; Teachers Aide; Pres Sr Cls; Bsktbl; Score Keeper; Var Swmmng; Waterpolo/Sccr/Bsktbl Coach; Armenian Clb; Aquatics Clb; Fresno ST; Orthopedics.

NIX, TRACI L; Mc Farland HS; Mc Farland, CA; (3); Acad Excllnc Awds In Engl, Math, Sci; UC Davis; Med.

NIXON, JOHN T; Warren HS; Downey, CA; (3); Church Yth Grp; Church Choir; Var Capt Bsbl; Var Capt Ftbl; Natl Chmpn Am Amateur Bsbl Team 87; Freedom From Drugs Art Cont Grnd Prz Wnnr; CA ST-FULLERTON; Cmmrcl Art.

NIXON, KELLY; Yucca Valley HS; Joshua Tree, CA; (2); Church Yth Grp; French Clb; GAA; Model UN; Yrbk; Bio Tutor Awd; Engl Tchr.

NIYOGI, RUMA; Simi Valley HS; Simi Valley, CA; (3); 29/670; Debate Tm; Drama Clb; French Clb; Math Clb; Math Tm; NFL; Quiz Bowl; Spanish Clb; Speech Tm; Thesps; Speech & Debate CA St Fnlst 90; Intl Relations.

NOBLE, ALISON R; Adrian C Wilcox HS; Santa Clara, CA; (1); 14/412; Church Yth Grp; Band; Church Choir; Jazz Band; Mrchg Band; Pep Band; Rptr Yrbk; JV Bsktbl; High Hon Roll; CSF.

NOBLE, CARRIE M; Alto Loma HS; Alta Loma, CA; (1); 3/30; GAA; Spanish Clb; Bsktbl; Score Keeper; Sftbl; Hon Roll; Peer Cnslng; Cal Poly; Psych.

NOBLE, DAWN M; Washington HS; Fremont, CA; (3); Hon Roll; Rep Assmbly Clsrm Rep; Art.

NOBLE, ERIN T; Antelope Valley HS; Lancaster, CA; (3); 61/631; Church Yth Grp; German Clb; Sec Band; Mrchg Band; Pep Band; Off Jr Cls; High Hon Roll; Hon Roll; Stu Week & Silver Antelope Dedctn Awds; UC Santa Barbara; Intl Bus.

NOBLE, JUNE E; Watsonville HS; Watsonville, CA; (2); 246/545; Church Yth Grp; Church Choir; Hon Roll; Vet Assistance.

NOBLE, LAVON; Serrano HS; Pinon Hills, CA; (3); Capt Drill Tm; Capt Flag Corp; Stage Crew; High Hon Roll; Hon Roll; Victor Vly JC; Math.

NOBLES, RYAN M; Apple Valley HS; Apple Valley, CA; (2); Teachers Aide; Nwsp; JV Bsbl; Hon Roll; AZ ST; Pro Bsbl.

NOCAR, HELEN; Paradise HS; Magalia, CA; (1); Church Yth Grp; Bsktbl; Cheerldng; Powder Puff Ftbl; Swmmng; Hon Roll; Chico ST U; Nursing.

NOCELLA, KIRSTEN A; Tustin HS; Tustin, CA; (2); JV Crs Cntry; JV Trk; Hon Roll; Excllnt Achvt Engl; FBI Agent.

NOCKER, CORINNA P; Santa Barbara HS; Santa Barbara, CA; (2); Church Yth Grp; German Clb; ROTC; Science Clb; SADD; Band; Color Guard; Mrchg Band; Orch; Pep Band; Rifle/Drill Team; Med.

NOCOM, SHEREEN C; John Burroughs HS; Burbank, CA; (4); English Clb; L Vllybl; Hon Roll; Accntng.

NODLAND, DANIELLE M; Temecula Valley HS; Temucula, CA; (2); Indus Engr.

NOE, ANGELA; Christian HS; San Diego, CA; (4); 1/90; Church Yth Grp; Key Clb; Pep Clb; Spanish Clb; Teachers Aide; Orch; Yrbk; Treas Stu Cncl; Hon Roll; Ntl Merit Ltr; Accntng.

NOE, TINA; Whittier Christian HS; Hacienda Heights, CA; (1); Church Yth Grp; Dance Clb; Girl Scts; Color Guard; Drill Tm; Score Keeper; Prfct Atten Awd.

NOEL, LISA; La Sierra HS; Riverside, CA; (4); 10/275; Pres Church Yth Grp; French Clb; VP Pep Clb; VP Frsh Cls; Cheerldng; Co-Capt Pom Pon; Swmmng; High Hon Roll; Cmmssnr Pblcty, Rep To Bd Of Educ-Stu Govt; Brigham Young U.

NOEL, MARK D; La Sierra HS; Riverside, CA; (2); Boy Scts; Church Yth Grp; Spanish Clb; Var L Swmmng; High Hon Roll; Hon Roll; Med.

NOFAL, TINA; Ramona HS; Ramona, CA; (2); 1/345; Dance Clb; FBLA; Key Clb; Scholastic Bowl; Sec Stu Cncl; Amnesty Intl; Stu Senate; CSF; Oxford; Law.

NOFLIN, WADE; Leuzinger HS; Hawthorne, CA; (3); Letterman Clb; Library Aide; Teachers Aide; Varsity Clb; JV Var Ftbl; JV Var Trk; Cit Awd; Hon Roll; Prfct Atten Awd; Psych.

NOGOSEK, JOSEPH G; Santa Teresa HS; San Jose, CA; (2); Varsity Clb; JV Capt Bsbl; Socr; Hon Roll; Sccr, St Cp Chmpns 88, Dist Tms 88 & 89; Bsbl All Star 84-89; Trple A Bsbl Tm Smmr 90; AZ ST U; Bsbl.

NOGUCHI, AKIKO; Concord HS; Concord, CA; (3); Cmnty Wkr; Drama Clb; Teachers Aide; School Play; Swmmng; Hon Roll; Pres Acad Fit Awd; Nordestrom Brass Plum Fshn Bd; Hist Club; CSF; UC Santa Cruz; Club Mgr.

NOH, SUNG J; Whitney HS; Cerritos, CA; (2); Church Yth Grp; DECA; Intnl Clb; Letterman Clb; Science Clb; Varsity Clb; Band; Var Bsbl; JV Swmmng; High Hon Roll; Water Polo Jr Vrsty; Med.

NOKHAM, BOUNTHIENG; Arlington HS; Riverside, CA; (3); 4/458; FBLA; Quiz Bowl; Teachers Aide; High Hon Roll; Opt Clb Awd; Pres Acad Fit Awd; Pres Schlr; Coll Bowl; Astrnmy Club; UC Irvine; Banking.

NOLAN, KELLY D; Torrey Pines HS; Solana Beach, CA; (2); Church Yth Grp; Girl Scts; Letterman Clb; Varsity Clb; JV Var Socr; JV Var Sftbl; Hon Roll; UCLA; Doctor.

NOLAN, MICHAEL J; San Ramon Valley HS; Danville, CA; (2); 49/400; Cmnty Wkr; School Play; Stu Cncl; JV Capt Trk; Hon Roll; Jack Box Sclr Athelete Awd; Arch Engr.

NOLAND, MARK E; Mountain Empire HS; Campo, CA; (3); 8/106; Pres German Clb; Letterman Clb; Varsity Clb; Var Bsktbl; Cit Awd; High Hon Roll; Hon Roll; Hotel Managment.

NOLAND, WILLIAM H; Lemoore Union HS; Lemoore, CA; (2); Church Yth Grp; Cmnty Wkr; Off Frsh Cls; Pres Soph Cls; Stu Cncl; JV Bsktbl; Powder Puff Ftbl; Var Swmmng; Hon Roll; Intrml Vllybl; Little League Ump; CA Assn Stu Cncls Ldrshp Camp Rep.

NOLASCO, DELILAH S; Wasco Union HS; Wasco, CA; (3); Hon Roll; Hnrs Soc.

NOLASCO, ROSELLE; Phineas Banning HS; Los Angeles, CA; (3); Church Yth Grp; Office Aide; Pep Clb; Spanish Clb; School Play; Rptr Nwsp; Ed Yrbk; Treas Frsh Cls; Rep Soph Cls; Rep Jr Cls; Stu Leag; NY U; Law.

NOLEN, CRISTINA M; Antelope Valley HS; Lancaster, CA; (3); Sec Drama Clb; FHA; VP German Clb; Office Aide; Bsktbl; Powder Puff Ftbl; Swmmng; Plc Offcr.

NOLEN III, JAMES O; Serrano HS; Phelan, CA; (1); Church Yth Grp; Chorus; Crs Cntry; JV L Trk; Hon Roll; Pres Acad Fit Awd; Track 2 Mile Brnz Medal; 10k Will Rogers Race Gold Medal.

NOLEN, LISA; Alhambra HS; Lafayette, CA; (2); Church Yth Grp; Dance Clb; Band; Drm Mjr(t); Jazz Band; Mrchg Band; Pep Band; JV Sftbl; Int Decorator.

NOLES, TREMAYNE; Westchester HS; Los Angeles, CA; (2); Scholastic Bowl; Var Bsbl; JV Ftbl; Cit Awd; High Hon Roll; NHS; Prfct Atten Awd; Sal; Stu Of Month Awd; Schlr Athl Awd; U AZ; Elect Engrng.

NOLL, TRACEY; Hanford Union HS; Hanford, CA; (3); Church Yth Grp; FBLA; FHA; Office Aide; Teachers Aide; Crs Cntry; Hon Roll; Prfct Atten Awd; Stat Wrstlng; Career Ctr Aide; Outstndng Stu Awd; Fshn Dsgn.

NOLTE, DEREK S; King City HS; King City, CA; (3); Art Clb; Scholastic Bowl; Teachers Aide; High Hon Roll; Hon Roll; UC Santa Barbara; Mrktng.

NOLTENSMEIER, ROBYN L; Kern Valley HS; Lake Isabella, CA; (1); Bsktbl; Powder Puff Ftbl; Score Keeper; Trk; Wt Lftg; Barbizon; Modeling.

NOMA, NAMIO A; Casa Roble Fundamental HS; Orangevale, CA; (2); 47/461; French Clb; Stat JV Bsktbl; Stat Var Ftbl; Var Mgr(s); Cit Awd; Hon Roll; Elem Schl Libr Vlntr; Comp Sci.

NOMACHI, AMY; Palisades HS; Los Angeles, CA; (3); Sec Church Yth Grp; Math Clb; JV Capt Bsktbl; JV Sftbl; Hon Roll; Prfct Atten Awd; Pres Acad Fit Awd; Business.

NOMI, SHARON M; Cerritos HS; Cerritos, CA; (1); Science Clb; Pres Acad Fit Awd; Involved In Japanese Natl Hnr Soc & CA Schlrshp Fed; Won Numerous Prizes, Schlrshps Piano Study; Music.

NONG, VOTHA; Yerba Buena HS; San Jose, CA; (4); VP Math Clb; Red Cross Aide; Variety Show; Rep Stu Cncl; Crs Cntry; Vllybl; U Of CA Davis; Physlgy.

NONMAN II, RICHARD K; Edison HS; Fresno, CA; (1); Church Yth Grp; Cmnty Wkr; Church Choir; Drill Tm; JV Trk; Sci Olympcs CA ST Champs Qualifier Trk; USAF Acad; Arspc Engr.

NOOKER, JENNIFER L; Wasco Union HS; Wasco, CA; (2); Church Yth Grp; Ski Clb; Chorus; Church Choir; Stage Crew; JV Bsktbl; VP Capt Swmmng; JV Vllybl; Wt Lftg; Mst Insprtnl Bsktbl; Mst Imprvd V Swmmng; Athltc Trainer.

NOONAN, TIFFANY H; Bonita HS; La Verne, CA; (3); 35/300; Treas Church Yth Grp; Rep GAA; Letterman Clb; Var L Fld Hcky; Var Swmmng; High Hon Roll; Order Of Mrt; Bus Admin.

NOONIS, FELICIA C; Pinole Valley HS; San Pablo, CA; (2); Acpl Chr; Hon Roll; Jr NHS; Pres Acad Fit Awd; CSF; UC Davis; Pediatrics.

NOOR, YASMIN; Mira Mesa HS; San Diego, CA; (2); French Clb; Library Aide; Math Clb; Math Tm; Science Clb; Speech Tm; Yrbk; Stu Cncl; Trk; High Hon Roll; 4.0 Clb; Library Monitor Of Yr Awd; CJSF; UCSD; Law.

NOORZAY, FARZANA; Birmingham HS; Van Nuys, CA; (1); Hon Roll; Bus.

NORBROTHEN, CHRISTINE S; Mission Viejo HS; Mission Viejo, CA; (3); Church Yth Grp; Girl Scts; Key Clb; Red Cross Aide; Band; Mrchg Band; NHS; Safe Rides; CA ST Long Beach; Nurse.

NORBROTHEN, KAREN S; Mission Viejo HS; Mission Viejo, CA; (2); Girl Scts; Band; Mrchg Band; Hon Roll; Med.

NORBURY, SHERI L; Del Oro HS; Loomis, CA; (2); 5/175; Chess Clb; VP Drama Clb; Pep Clb; SADD; School Play; Cheerldng; Pom Pon; Trk; Cit Awd; High Hon Roll; TV Brdcstng.

NORD, JULIE A; East Bakersfield HS; Bakersfield, CA; (4); 25/412; Church Yth Grp; Intnl Clb; Key Clb; Teachers Aide; High Hon Roll; Pres Schlr; CSU Bakersfield; Envrmntl Engr.

NORD, KIRSTEN; Del Mar HS; San Jose, CA; (2); 10/325; Church Yth Grp; Girl Scts; Orch; Fld Hcky; High Hon Roll; CSF; Tchrs Aid; Myrs Yth Conf Peer Cnslr; 1st Pl Crmcs, Hnrbl Mntn Stnd Gls Dist Art Shw; Stanford; Aerntcs.

NORD, LISA K; Immanuel HS; Reedley, CA; (4); 13/57; Church Yth Grp; Library Aide; Co-Ed Yrbk; Var L Tennis; Mst Inspirational-Tennis 90; Coaches Awd 87/89; Rotary Awd; Kings River CC; Elem Ed.

NORDBLOM, MICHELLE L; Antelope Valley HS; Lancaster, CA; (4); 107/570; Cmnty Wkr; Treas Service Clb; Pres Spanish Clb; Rep Sr Cls; Stat Wrstlng; Elks Awd; Kiwanis Awd; Church Yth Grp; Intnl Clb; Red Cross Aide; Bnk Of Amer Achvt Awd Frgn Lang; Golden St Exam Geom Hnrs Awd; A P US Hstry, Span, Engl, Govt Exams; Loyola Marmount U; Frgn Lang.

NORDEN, ANDY B; Anderson Union HS; Anderson, CA; (4); Teachers Aide; JV Var Ftbl; Var L Wrstlng; Hon Roll; Pres Acad Fit Awd; Jr Olympcs Natl Chmpn Wrstlng; Sacramento ST Coll; Phys Thrpy.

NORDGREEN, GRACE; Highlands HS; North Highlands, CA; (3); Church Yth Grp; Computer Clb; Chorus; Church Choir; Hon Roll; Bus, Pers Comp & Word Prcssng Awds; Amer River Coll; Comp.

NORDSTROM, KAROLYN; Thousand Oaks HS; Thousand Oaks, CA; (3); Pres Church Yth Grp; Ski Clb; Band; Mrchg Band; Variety Show; Gym; Trk; Cit Awd; Hon Roll; Pres Acad Fit Awd; USGF Ntl Gymn 8 Yrs; High Jump Champ Var 90; Stake Rep Yth Prgm LDS Church; Vol Hlpr Spec Olympics; Med Field.

NORDYKE, MICHELLE L; Tulare Union HS; Tulare, CA; (4); 66/352; Color Guard; Drill Tm; Hon Roll; COS; Bus.

NORDYKE, WAYNE A; Duncan Polytechnical HS; Fresno, CA; (3); Law Enfrcmnt.

NOREM, JOSH S; Grace M Davis HS; Modesto, CA; (3); Key Clb; Ski Clb; SADD; Rep Soph Cls; VP Jr Cls; Rep Stu Cncl; Socr; Var Swmmng; Cit Awd; Hon Roll.

NORGARD, LISA H; South Valley HS; Ukiah, CA; (4); 4-H; Sec FFA; Office Aide; Teachers Aide; Cit Awd; FFA Color Guard; Horticulture.

NORGREN, MARC; Canoga Park HS; Los Angeles, CA; (2); Boy Scts; ROTC; Awd Of Mrt; Arln Plt.

NORIEGA, CHRISTINA; San Benito HS; Hollister, CA; (2); 18/370; French Clb; High Hon Roll; Prfct Atten Awd; Sccr Club Secy; Mecha Club; Frgn Exchng Club; Berkely; Bus Admin.

NORIEGA, KEN; Bishop Amat HS; Pomona, CA; (2); English Clb; Hosp Aide; Socr; Cit Awd; High Hon Roll; Japanese Schl; UC Berkeley; Sci.

NORIEGA, MARCO C; Santa Clara HS; Oxnard, CA; (2); 3/220; Varsity Clb; VP Jr Cls; JV Capt Bsbl; JV Capt Ftbl; Var Capt Socr; High Hon Roll; Hon Roll; NHS; Prfct Atten Awd; Pres Acad Fit Awd; CSF; Partnership Pgm; Stanford; Sci.

NORIEGA, MIA; Bishop Amat HS; Pomona, CA; (4); 15/350; English Clb; Spanish Clb; Chorus; Tennis; Cit Awd; High Hon Roll; Japanese Schl; UC Berkeley; Corp Law.

NORIEGA, RUFO; Servite HS; Anaheim, CA; (4); Art Clb; Boy Scts; Cmnty Wkr; Drama Clb; Library Aide; Quiz Bowl; Spanish Clb; SADD; Church Choir; School Musical; Loyola; Liberal Arts.

NORITAKE, ADAM; Whittier Christian HS; Montebello, CA; (2); Band; Mrchg Band; Orch.

NORLAND, AMY; Huntington Beach HS; Huntington Beach, CA; (2); Rep Frsh Cls; JV Stat Ftbl; Queen Of Cts Prncss; Happy Clb; U Of CA; Vet.

NORLING, JOHN ACE W; Los Amigos HS; Fountain Valley, CA; (3); Aud/Vis; Boy Scts; Church Yth Grp; Sailing Clb; 4th In St In Soling 89; Orange Coast Coll; Aviation.

NORMAN, BRYAN A; Arlington HS; Riverside, CA; (2); L Band; L Jazz Band; L Mrchg Band; JV Bsktbl; Var L Ftbl; Var L Trk; Wt Lftg; Mock Trial; Outstndng Awd Jazz Band Cmptn; Fnlst Leag Trk Chmpnshps-Discus; U Of AZ; Prfssnl Ftbl.

NORMAN, CAROLYN M; Notre Dame HS; San Jose, CA; (3); 9/90; Church Yth Grp; Pres Sec 4-H; Rptr Nwsp; Rep Jr Cls; Pres Sr Cls; JV Var Bsktbl; 4-H Awd; High Hon Roll; NHS; CSF; SADD; Cal Poly San Luis Obispo; Sci.

NORMAN, CARRIE R; El Toro HS; El Toro, CA; (4); 28/530; French Clb; High Hon Roll; Ntl Merit Ltr; Pres Acad Fit Awd; CSF; Sonoma ST U; Mgmt.

NORMAN, CHERYL L; Don Antonio Lugo HS; Chino, CA; (3); Church Yth Grp; Drama Clb; German Clb; School Play; Powder Puff Ftbl; Vllybl; High Hon Roll; Pres Acad Fit Awd.

NORMAN, HOLLY D; Chula Vista HS; San Diego, CA; (2); 66/581; High Hon Roll; Hon Roll; Christian Coll.

NORMAN, JAHA F; Pittsburg HS; Pittsburg, CA; (2); 10/250; Mrchg Band; Bsktbl; Var JV Sftbl; JV Vllybl; High Hon Roll; Hon Roll; CSF; SEPIA Secy; BSU VP; Spelman; Law Enfrcment.

NORMAN, MICHAEL C; Lassen HS; Standish, CA; (4); Boy Scts; Pres Drama Clb; Teachers Aide; School Play; Trk; Hon Roll; Rotary Awd; Explorer Post 2nd Lt; CSF; U S CA; Drama.

NORMAN, ZORA; Oroville HS; Oroville, CA; (4); Mgr Yrbk; Mgr(s); Score Keeper; Hon Roll; Blck Stu Union Pres; Barry K Brookter Schlrshp; Butte Coll; Dietetics.

NORMINGTON, VICTORIA A; Del Campo HS; Citrus Heights, CA; (3); Church Yth Grp; Cmnty Wkr; Debate Tm; French Clb; FBLA; SADD; Teachers Aide; VP Jr Cls; High Hon Roll; NHS; Sacrento Ballet Co-Dancer/ Full Schlrshp; San Fran Ballet Schl Training; Rotary Ldrshp Awd; Arch.

NORNG, PHEAKDEY; Edison Computech HS; Fresno, CA; (4); FHA; Spanish Clb; SADD; High Hon Roll; Prfct Atten Awd; Spnsh Club Pres; IRS Awds & Certs; Achvt Awd Spnsh Club, Bio Aid & Comp Aid; Pepsi Awds Vllybl; CA ST U Fresno; Family Prac.

NORRED, RODGER; Firebaugh HS; Madera, CA; (4); Letterman Clb; Office Aide; Teachers Aide; Ftbl; Wt Lftg; Wrstlng; Lion Awd; MVP Vrsty Ftbl & Wrstlng; Rotary Nrth Sth All Star Ftbl Game; Fresno City Cnty All Star Ftbl Game; Fresno City COLL; Educ.

NORRIS, CHRISTIAN W; Irvine HS; Irvine, CA; (3); Var Vllybl; Irvine Valley Coll.

NORRIS, ERIN; Tomales HS; Tomales, CA; (4); 1/35; Drama Clb; Spanish Clb; Band; Church Choir; Jazz Band; Orch; School Play; Sec Jr Cls; Sec Sr Cls; Rep Stu Cncl; Holy Names Coll; Music.

NORRIS, JAMES M; Mt Diablo HS; Concord, CA; (3); 40/290; Boy Scts; Letterman Clb; Teachers Aide; Varsity Clb; School Play; Ed Nwsp; Pres Jr Cls; Pres Stu Cncl; Var Bsbl; Var Capt Bsktbl; USMA; Pre-Med.

NORRIS, KARIN; Sherman Oaks C E S HS; Reseda, CA; (3); French Clb; Office Aide; Service Clb; Spanish Clb; Rptr Yrbk; Rep Sr Cls.

NORRIS, MICHAEL D; Oak Grove HS; San Jose, CA; (2); Var L Bsbl; Var L Ftbl; Fresh Athlt Of Yr; Soph Athlt Of Yr; Var Bsktbl; Soph Of Yr Mount Hamilton Athltc Leag.

NORRIS, SEAN; Sierra Joint Union HS; Prather, CA; (4); 8/190; Letterman Clb; SADD; Var L Crs Cntry; Var L Trk; High Hon Roll; JETS Awd; NHS; Pres Acad Fit Awd; CSF; CA Poly San Luis Ob; Engrng.

NORRIS, SUZANNE; Leigh HS; Los Gatos, CA; (4); 1/250; Art Clb; French Clb; Pres Frsh Cls; Off Soph Cls; Sec Jr Cls; VP Sr Cls; Var Pom Pon; Hmcmng Queen 89-90; Bnk Of Amer Plque In Fine Arts; Cmpbl Union HS Dist Schrshp; U C Santa Barbara; Art.

NORRIS, THOMAS; Cajon HS; San Bernardino, CA; (2); Church Yth Grp; Cmnty Wkr; JV Tennis.

NORRIS, TOM P; Cajon HS; San Bernardino, CA; (2); Church Yth Grp; JV Tennis.

NORTH, DUSTI; Campbell Hall HS; Tarzana, CA; (4); 4/68; Boy Scts; Dance Clb; French Clb; Girl Scts; Pep Clb; Red Cross Aide; Service Clb; Sec Yrbk; Lit Mag; Off Soph Cls; CSF; UCLA Alumni Schlr; Girl Sct Gold Awd; Bnk America Math Awd; Cum Laude Soc; UCLA; Film/T V.

NORTH, STACEY L; Mission Viejo HS; Mission Viejo, CA; (4); Drama Clb; Office Aide; Teachers Aide; School Play; Rep Stu Cncl; Capt Pom Pon; Miss Teen Schlsp & Recog Pgnt; U AZ; Psych.

NORTHCUTT, TAMARA; Mira Mesa HS; San Diego, CA; (2); 111/834; Church Yth Grp; Model UN; Ytping Awd; Hrnbl Mntn-Lttr To Edtr; Piano 10 Yrs; BYU; Home Ec.

NORTHUP, NINA R; Marysville HS; Dobbins, CA; (4); 18/194; Art Clb; Pres Church Yth Grp; Treas NHS; NFL; SADD; Church Choir; Flag Corp; Mrchg Band; School Play; Off Sr Cls; Frgn Lang Apprctn Club; Bank Of America Awd Engl; Exchng Club Stu Qtr/Dist Fnlst; U Of CA Irvine; Psych.

NORTHWAY, CHRIS; Reignierd HS; Benicia, CA; (1); Office Aide; Speech Tm; Teachers Aide; Ed Nwsp; Teacher.

NORTON, BECKY; Las Lomas HS; Walnut Creek, CA; (1); Church Yth Grp; Drama Clb; Acpl Chr; School Musical; Rep Frsh Cls; JV Diving; JV Gym; High Hon Roll; Natl Chrldng & Pom Pon Chmpns; CSF; UC Hmblt; Peace Corps.

NORTON, JABARI H; Bishop O'dowd HS; Hayward, CA; (2); Aud/Vis; JV Var Ftbl; Var Tennis; Var Wt Lftg; Red Crss Vlntr Wk; Stanford; Bus Mgmt.

NORTON, JEFF T; San Dieguito HS; Encinitas, CA; (2); Ski Clb; Spanish Clb; Band; School Play; Bsbl; Ftbl; Wt Lftg; Hon Roll; St Schlr; CA Golden St Awd Hnrs Geom; Hnrs Engl 7 Yrs; Hnrs Geom 3 Yrs; Hnrs Algebra 3 Yrs; Spnsh 3 Yrs; US Air Force Acad; Engrng.

NORTON, JILL; Redwood HS; Visalia, CA; (3); Church Yth Grp; Band; Mrchg Band; Hon Roll; Hand Bell Chr; CSF; Invlvd Stu.

NORTON, KENDRA J; Samuel E Gompers HS; San Diego, CA; (2); 78/ 154; Cmnty Wkr; Dance Clb; Key Clb; Spanish Clb; Drill Tm; Treas Frsh Cls; Treas Soph Cls; Cit Awd; Hon Roll; Jr NHS; Outstndng Stu Awd MESA; Spelman Coll; Law.

NORTON, KIERSTEN; Lincoln HS; Stockton, CA; (3); Church Yth Grp; Cmnty Wkr; USC; Advrtsng.

NORTON, MICHAEL A; Sir Francis Drake HS; San Anselmo, CA; (2); French Clb; Ski Clb; Intrml Ftbl; Var Tennis; French Hon Soc; High Hon Roll; Hon Roll; CSF Hgh Hnrs Awd-Alg/Geom.

NORTON, MICHELLE R; Casa Grande HS; Petaluma, CA; (2); Letterman Clb; JV Bsktbl; Var Sftbl; JV Vllybl; Otstndng Stu In PE; Ctznshp Awd; Bus.

NORTON, NATHAN E; Rio Mesa HS; Camarillo, CA; (3); 8/369; Church Yth Grp; Quiz Bowl; Varsity Clb; School Play; Intrml Bsktbl; Var L Trk; Cit Awd; Hon Roll; CSF Treas 89-90; Acad Letter; Aero Engrg.

NORTON, SHANNON; Ponderosa HS; Shingle Springs, CA; (4); 1/289; Rep Am Leg Aux Girls St; Ed Church Yth Grp; Cmnty Wkr; Treas Stu Cncl; Capt Var Sftbl; Capt Var Tennis; Cit Awd; Hon Roll; NHS; Pres Acad Fit Awd; CSF; Northwestern U; Intl Eco.

NORTON, TANYSSA M; Thomas Downey HS; Modesto, CA; (2); SADD; Wt Lftg; Part-Time Wrk After Schl; Guitar Lessons; Uop; Accntnt.

NORTON, TRACIE; Modesto HS; Modesto, CA; (4); Pep Clb; Teachers Aide; Var Swmmng; Hon Roll; ROP Merit Awd; Greenpeace Club; Statistician Water Polo Tm; Modesto JC; Educ.

NORUM, JENNIE; Brea Olinda HS; Brea, CA; (2); 25/375; Dance Clb; Spanish Clb; Color Guard; Yrbk; Stat Bsbl; JV Socr; High Hon Roll; Grls Leag Caminet Mem; CSF.

NORWOOD II, SAMUEL; Livermore HS; Byron, CA; (4); 50/300; Church Yth Grp; Cmnty Wkr; Debate Tm; Latin Clb; Rptr Nwsp; Var Bsktbl; Var Capt Golf; Elks Awd; Hon Roll; Stu Of Mnth; Boosters Awd; Lttrmn On Glf Tm; Jackson Sst; Pre Med.

NORWOOD, VINCENT O; William Workman HS; W Covina, CA; (1); Church Yth Grp; Drama Clb; School Play; Hon Roll; Hnrs Englsh Soc; PACE Coll Stu At Cal ST; Stanford; Bio.

NOTARO, SEAN; California HS; Dublin, CA; (4); Bus Profs of Am; Church Yth Grp; FBLA; Letterman Clb; Spanish Clb; Vllybl; Hon Roll; Maui JC; Engrng.

NOTLEY, LISA D; Huntington Beach HS; Huntington Beach, CA; (3); Flag Corp; High Hon Roll; Prfct Atten Awd; U CA San Diego; Bus.

NOTT, MELAINE R; Don Lugo HS; Chino, CA; (2); San Diego ST U; Psych.

NOUHI, SEPEIDEH; California HS; Whittier, CA; (4); 1/363; Am Leg Aux Girls St; Cmnty Wkr; JCL; Pres Latin Clb; Pep Clb; Q&S; SADD; Teachers Aide; Varsity Clb; Ed Nwsp; Fri Night Live Pres; UCLA; Biomed.

NOUVONG, EKARATH B; Buena HS; Ventura, CA; (3); Off FBLA; SADD; Teachers Aide; Var JV Trk; Medicine.

NOUVONGSA, PHEN; Edison Computech HS; Fresno, CA; (2); Var Trk; Vllybl.

NOUYEN, YEN T; Marina HS; Huntington Beach, CA; (3); Math Clb; Table Tnns; Viet Clb.

NOV, SAVANG; Edison HS; Stockton, CA; (3); FTA; Science Clb; Teachers Aide; Sftbl; Cit Awd; Hon Roll; Prfct Atten Awd; Photography & Chem Clubs; Delta CC; Bus Mgmt.

NOVAK, JENNIFER; Helix HS; Lemon Grove, CA; (3); Church Yth Grp; Cmnty Wkr; Dance Clb; Drama Clb; French Clb; Key Clb; Pep Clb; SADD; Drill Tm; Rptr Nwsp; SAAC; Ldrshp Stu Cncl.

NOVAK, ROBERT S; Notre Dame HS; Norco, CA; (1); 29/200; Cmnty Wkr; Rptr Nwsp; Bsktbl; Ftbl; Wt Lftg; Hon Roll; Karate; Acad Of Model Aeronautics Club; USAF Acad.

NOVAK, WENDIE; Fountain Valley HS; Fountain Valley, CA; (4); Boy Scts; Girl Scts; SADD; Teachers Aide; Chorus; School Play; Mgr(s); Var Powder Puff Ftbl; Video Yearbook Staff; Communications Arts & Technology; Polynesian Music & Dance; Pierce College; Cinematography.

NOVAKOVICH, NADA L; Berkeley HS; El Cerrito, CA; (3); Cmnty Wkr; Debate Tm; Latin Clb; Swmmng; Natl Latin Exm Magna Cum Laude; CSF; Berkeley; Med.

NOVELL, ELISHA J; Sierra Joint Union HS; North Fork, CA; (4); 17/163; Var Crs Cntry; Var Trk; Mock Trial; Cmnty Theatre Grp; CSF; Law Enfrcmnt.

NOVERO, DAVID; Liberty Union HS; Oakley, CA; (2); 1/392; Church Yth Grp; VP Sec 4-H; Stage Crew; Rptr Yrbk; Rep Soph Cls; Var Swmmng; Hon Roll; CSF; REACH Yth On The Move; UCLA; Tv Jrnlsm.

NOVILLA, MARITES; Montgomery HS; San Diego, CA; (4); FBLA; Hosp Aide; JA; Ed Yrbk; Var Tennis; Hon Roll; French Dept Awd; San Diego Tribune Achvt Awd; U Of CA-SAN Diego; Bio.

NOVOA, CLAUDIA; Victor Valley HS; Adelanto, CA; (2); Chorus; Med.

NOVOTNY, SANGHEE C; Winters HS; Winters, CA; (2); Church Yth Grp; Cmnty Wkr; Letterman Clb; Chorus; Rep Frsh Cls; Bsktbl; Vllybl; Cit Awd; Hon Roll; Friday Night Live; Early Outreach Prgm; Sacramento ST; Acctg.

NOWAKOWSKA, KATHRINE L; Rancho Alamitos HS; Stanton, CA; (3); Teachers Aide; Mrchg Band; Hon Roll; Reading Awd; Cypryss Coll; Intl Merch.

NOWATNICK, BILLY A; Yucaipa HS; Yucaipa, CA; (2); Spanish Clb; Ftbl; Wt Lftg; Wrstlng; Hon Roll; Prfct Atten Awd.

NOWATNICK JR, MICHAEL D; Yucaipa HS; Yucaipa, CA; (3); Hon Roll; Arch.

NOWDEN, APRIL; Lincoln Prep HS; San Diego, CA; (4); Church Yth Grp; Church Choir; Drill Tm; Cheerldng; Trk; Cit Awd; Hon Roll; Grambling; Bus Admin.

NOWICKI, MICHELE M; Poway HS; Poway, CA; (3); 154/717; SADD; Hon Roll; Intl Order Jobs Daughters; Marine Bio.

NOWLAND, JOHN; Western HS; Buena Park, CA; (4); Boy Scts; Church Yth Grp; Teachers Aide; Varsity Clb; Var Socr; Var Swmmng; NHS; Cypress JC.

NOWROOZANI, CYRUS; Canoga Park HS; Canoga Park, CA; (3); Church Yth Grp; Treas Key Clb; Mrchg Band; Pres Frsh Cls; VP Jr Cls; Trk; Jr NHS; Pres Acad Fit Awd; PTSA Schlrshp 89-90; All Dist Hnr Band 87-90; Homecmng Prnc 87-90; UCSD; Pre Law.

NOY, LAM YONG; Oakland HS; Oakland, CA; (2); Church Choir; School Play; Yrbk; Cit Awd; Hon Roll; Elem Educ.

NOY, SOTHAL; Thomas Edison HS; Stockton, CA; (1); Intrml Bsbl; Hon Roll; Astronomy; Geography; Comp Tech; UC Davis; Sci.

NOYER, DAN E; Clovis HS; Clovis, CA; (1); Dance Clb; Drama Clb; Chorus; School Musical; School Play; Prncpls Hnr Roll; Fresno ST U; Geologist.

NOYES, HEATHER; South San Francisco HS; Daly City, CA; (4); Pres FBLA; Pres JA; Pep Clb; Hon Roll; San Francisco ST U; Bus Admin.

NOYES, JULIE A; El Cajon Valley HS; El Cajon, CA; (2); Church Yth Grp; Dance; Acctg.

NUBLA, ANNE; Hillsdale HS; S San Francisco, CA; (4); 51/299; Church Yth Grp; Cmnty Wkr; Latin Clb; Teachers Aide; Varsity Clb; Stu Cncl; Var Capt Cheerldng; Hon Roll; Prjct Cars ; CSF; Pals F/Plsy; Sci.

NUCKLES, DANNY A; Casa Grande HS; Petaluma, CA; (2); 12/30; Debate Tm; French Clb; Speech Tm; Tennis; Trk; High Hon Roll; Jr NHS; NHS; Pres Acad Fit Awd; Poltcl Sci.

NUDELMAN, GRIGORY; George Washington HS; San Francisco, CA; (4); Computer Clb; Debate Tm; Math Clb; Math Tm; Science Clb; Speech Tm; Band; Ed Nwsp; Capt Diving; Stat Socr; San Francisco ST U; Chmstry.

NUESSLE, LISA R; Monterey Bay Acad; Port Orchard, WA; (4); Church Yth Grp; Teachers Aide; Intrml Bsktbl; Intrml Sftbl; Intrml Vllybl; High Hon Roll; GPA Schlrshp Awd; Walla Walla Coll; Bus Mgmt.

NUFFER, COURTNAY K; Oak Ridge HS; Cameron Park, CA; (2); Church Yth Grp; Ski Clb; Band; Hon Roll; U Of Davis CA; Vet.

NUFFER, KARINA N; Oak Ridge HS; Cameron Park, CA; (1); Church Yth Grp; Ski Clb; Band; Hon Roll; Sci.

NUGENT, ERIN; Mt Shasta HS; Mt Shasta, CA; (3); GAA; Quiz Bowl; Ski Clb; Band; Chorus; School Musical; JV Var Bsktbl; Var Sftbl; Var Swmmng; High Hon Roll; Golden St Math Comptn; MVP Bsktbl; CA U; Intl Law.

NUGYEN, ANDREW H; John A Rowland HS; Rowland Heights, CA; (3); Service Clb; Spanish Clb; Off Sr Cls; Var Swmmng; Var Tennis; High Hon Roll; NHS; Sci.

NUKI, CHRISTIE; Salinas HS; Salinas, CA; (3); Thesps; Acpl Chr; Chorus; School Musical; School Play; Stage Crew; Variety Show; Yrbk; Cheerldng; Swmmng; Renaissance Club; Stenbck Sngrs; Monterey Peninsula Opera Co; Voice.

NULL, DAWN M; Oakdale HS; Waterford, CA; (3); AFS; Church Yth Grp; Hosp Aide; Ski Clb; Church Choir; School Play; Stage Crew; Vllybl; Hon Roll; Med.

NULL, JEFF; Benicia HS; Benicia, CA; (4); 8/248; Key Clb; Stage Crew; Var Socr; Var Trk; Var Capt Wrstlng; High Hon Roll; NHS; Pres Acad Fit Awd; US Army Reserve Natl Schlr/Athl Awd; Sacramento ST U; Engrng.

NULL, KARA R; Calvary Christian Acad; Stockton, CA; (2); Church Yth Grp; Library Aide; Chorus; Church Choir; Cit Awd; High Hon Roll; Hon Roll; NHS; Daycamp Cnslr & Tchr; Accmpnst; Singng Ensmbl; Cnslng.

NULL, LANCE L; Hanford HS; Hanford, CA; (3); 12/452; Teachers Aide; Rep Frsh Cls; Rep Sr Cls; JV Bsktbl; Ftbl; Var Socr; Var Swmmng; Wtrpolo 89 & 90; Schlr Athlt 88-89; Lyons Clb Rep Wrld Affrs Smnr 90; Pilot.

NULL, SCOTT; Clovis HS; Clovis, CA; (3); Church Yth Grp; Science Clb; Band; Church Choir; Jazz Band; Mrchg Band; Orch; Pep Band; School Musical; Hon Roll; Mst Dedicated Brass 88-89; Chrch Orch; Biola U; Psych.

NUNAG, RENY D; Abraham Lincoln HS; San Francisco, CA; (2); Bsbl; Bus.

NUNCZ, EVELYN; Irvine HS; Irvine, CA; (2); Latin Clb; Office Aide; Swmmng, Sccr, Pool, Comp; Egngr.

NUNES, ANGELA; Chino HS; Chino, CA; (3); Dance Clb; Pep Clb; Band; Rep Stu Cncl; JV Bsktbl; Var Vllybl; Cit Awd; High Hon Roll; Hon Roll; Rotary Awd; Acctng.

NUNES, BRIAN E; Bellarmine HS; San Jose, CA; (3); Cmnty Wkr; Service Clb; Varsity Clb; Var Bsbl; JV Crs Cntry; Amer Leag Bsbl; Chrstn Life Cmnty Clb; Retreat Ldr.

NUNES, DEVIN G; Tulare Union HS; Pixley, CA; (3); 35/401; 4-H; FFA; Intrml Bsktbl; 4-H Awd; Hon Roll; Pres Acad Fit Awd; Sal; St Chmpn 4-H Dairy Jdgng Tm 90; Holstein Assn; Select Sires Instr Artfcl Insmntn; CA Poly; Dairy Sci.

NUNES, JENNIFER; Garden Grove HS; Garden Grove, CA; (4); Hist Latin Clb; VP Pep Clb; Science Clb; SADD; Flag Corp; Rptr Yrbk; Stu Cncl; Var Trk; Hon Roll; Garden Grove Rotary Clb Stu Voctnl Awd 90; LA Music Ctr Spotlight Awd Cmptn Rnnr Up; Dance.

NUNES, LARRY F; San Benito HS; Hollister, CA; (2); Church Yth Grp; Letterman Clb; Varsity Clb; VICA; Var Capt Ftbl; JV Var Trk; Wt Lftg; JV Var Wrstlng; Hon Roll; Pres Acad Fit Awd; Ftbl Fresh MVP Lineman/ Sophmr MVP Backer/Capt Fresh; Wrestling-Jr 2nd League/3 Trnmnts 1 Places; Fresno ST; Sports Medicine.

NUNES, LISA A; Redwood HS; Corte Madera, CA; (4); Hon Roll; CSF; Peer Cnslng; UCSB; Bus.

NUNES, MAE F; Sutter Union HS; Yuba City, CA; (3); 16/69; Art Clb; Church Yth Grp; Computer Clb; French Clb; FBLA; FFA; FHA; SADD; Church Choir; Stu Cncl; Completion Of Comp & Accntng Cls Certs; Yuba Clg; Child Care.

NUNES, MICHAEL A; Pittsburg HS; Pittsburg, CA; (1); Math Clb; Teachers Aide; Cit Awd; High Hon Roll; Prfct Atten Awd; Pres Schlr; Mth.

NUNES, NICOLE; East Nicolaus HS; Rio Oso, CA; (3); Church Yth Grp; Office Aide; Pep Clb; Ski Clb; Treas Frsh Cls; Rep Soph Cls; Sec Stu Cncl; Bsktbl; Powder Puff Ftbl; Trk; Amer River Coll.

NUNES, SANDRA S; Manteca HS; Manteca, CA; (3); 8/358; Key Clb; Letterman Clb; SADD; Pres Frsh Cls; Pres Soph Cls; Pres Jr Cls; Pres Sr Cls; Stu Cncl; JV Bsktbl; Capt Var Sftbl; Tnns Vrsty Most Imrpvd & Insprtnl; Sftbl JV Capt & MVP Best Ofsnv; CSF; Bsktbl JV Capt Best Dfnsv; Fresno ST; Civil Engrng.

NUNEZ, ALMA R; Saint Joseph HS; Paramount, CA; (3); Church Yth Grp; French Clb; Spanish Clb; Rep Frsh Cls; Rep Sec Soph Cls; Rep Sr Cls; Powder Puff Ftbl; Hon Roll; Loma Linda U; Med.

NUNEZ, ANASTACIO; Modesto HS; Modesto, CA; (3); Band; Mrchg Band; Var Trk; JV Var Wrstlng; Cit Awd; Hon Roll; Muscle Cars; Motorcycles; Modesto JC; Math.

NUNEZ, BRENT M; Torrance HS; Moreno Vly, CA; (4); Cmnty Wkr; Office Aide; Var JV Ftbl; Var JV Vllybl; Wt Lftg; City Of Torrance Firemans Mem Schlrshp 90; El Camino CC; Fire Tech.

NUNEZ, ERICKA P; Orange Glen HS; Escondido, CA; (1); Church Yth Grp; Cmnty Wkr; Drama Clb; Chorus; Church Choir; JV Stat Score Keeper; Cit Awd; Teenage Cerebral Palsy Spprt Grp-Fndr.

NUNEZ, G CHRIS; Damien HS; Claremont, CA; (3); Cmnty Wkr; JV Var Ftbl; Intrml Wrstlng; High Hon Roll; Mexican Amer Clb; Black Stu Union; Psych.

NUNEZ, GRACIE S; Central Union HS; El Centro, CA; (2); 149/600; Church Yth Grp; Office Aide; Teachers Aide; Hon Roll; Hnr Roll; Crmnl Jstc.

NUNEZ, HILDA; Saddleback HS; Santa Ana, CA; (3); Cmnty Wkr; Drama Clb; FHA; Teachers Aide; Bsktbl; Rancho Santiago; Nrsng.

NUNEZ, JASON B; Hogan SR HS; Vallejo, CA; (3); Chess Clb; Science Clb; Spanish Clb; SADD; Pres Jr Cls; Var Ftbl; Var Swmmng; Var Wt Lftg; Rotary Awd; Cls Nwsltr Edtr; Physcst.

NUNEZ, JUAN F; Dos Palos HS; Dos Palos, CA; (3); AFS; Church Yth Grp; FCA; 4-H; FHA; Letterman Clb; Office Aide; SADD; Teachers Aide; Varsity Clb; ASB Pres; San Diego ST; Journ.

NUNEZ, LOUISE; Cypress HS; Cypress, CA; (3); Church Yth Grp; Drama Clb; Pep Clb; Teachers Aide; Swmmng; Vllybl; Dancing; Modeling; Cypress Clg; Dancing.

NUNEZ, LUPITA; Dos Palos HS; Dos Palos, CA; (1); Hon Roll; Univ Teacher.

NUNEZ, MARIA ELENA; Tranquillity Union HS; Mendota, CA; (2); French Clb; Hon Roll; Frnch Mrt Cert; CSF Clb; UC Santa Cruz; Med.

NUNEZ, MARIA G; San Pasqual HS; Yuma, AZ; (3); 6/30; Latin Clb; Office Aide; SADD; VP Jr Cls; Rep Stu Cncl; AZ Western Coll; Reg Nurse.

NUNEZ, MONICA; North Salinas HS; Salinas, CA; (2); French Clb; JV Fld Hcky; JV Powder Puff Ftbl; JV Tennis; JV Vllybl; High Hon Roll; Hon Roll; Rotary Awd; Peer Ldrshp Fri Night Live; Cnflct Rsltn Team; Psych.

NUNEZ, NORBERTO; John Glenn HS; Norwalk, CA; (4); 1/300; Am Leg Boys St; Church Yth Grp; Cmnty Wkr; Pres FBLA; Key Clb; Office Aide; Treas Stu Cncl; Var L Crs Cntry; Var L Trk; High Hon Roll; Harvey; Envrnmntl Engrng.

NUNEZ, OSCAR; Andrew P Hill HS; San Jose, CA; (2); Bsbl; Bsktbl; Ftbl; Socr; Sftbl; Swmmng; Tennis; Vllybl; Wt Lftg; San Jose ST U; Civil Engr.

NUNEZ, PATRICIA M; Point Loma HS; San Diego, CA; (3); 62/431; Intnl Clb; Hon Roll; MECHA Club Secy; Art Recognition Awd; Obstetrician.

NUNEZ, RIGOBERTO; Palo Verde HS; Blythe, CA; (4); Latin Clb; JV Bsbl; JV Bsktbl; Var Crs Cntry; Var JV Socr; Sftbl; Swmmng; Tennis; Intrml Trk; Var Wt Lftg; 5 Trophies & 1 Medal Boxing; 3 1st Pl Trophies Soccer; MVP Bsbl; Palo Verde CC; Welding.

NUNEZ, RODEN H; Independence HS; San Jose, CA; (3); Varsity Clb; Bsktbl; Socr; UCLA; Med.

NUNEZ, VICKI M; Arroyo Grande HS; Oceano, CA; (2); 120/630; Church Yth Grp; Cmnty Wkr; Key Clb; JV Vllybl; Hon Roll; Alan Hancock Coll; Acctnt.

NUNEZ-ROCHA, GERALDINA; Will C Crawford HS; San Diego, CA; (4); 104/320; Stu Cncl; JV Var Bsktbl; Var L Tennis; Var L Trk; Var L Vllybl; Hon Roll; U Of CA San Diego; Bus Admin.

NUNGARAY, JOSIE; California HS; Whittier, CA; (2); Pep Clb; VP Frsh Cls; JV Bsktbl; JV Tennis; Hon Roll; Masonic Awd; UCLA; Acctnt.

NUNN, CHUAN E; Orange Glen HS; Escondido, CA; (1); 15/451; French Clb; Scholastic Bowl; Varsity Clb; Chorus; Powder Puff Ftbl; Vllybl; High Hon Roll; NHS; Pres Acad Fit Awd; CSF Life; Sci Stu Of Yr; CA Poly SLO; Hmn Devlpmnt.

NUNN, LISA M; Carlsbad HS; Carlsbad, CA; (1); Chorus; Var Sftbl; Hon Roll.

NUNN, LISI; Monta Vista HS; Cupertino, CA; (3); Dance Clb; Pep Clb; Band; Drill Tm; Mrchg Band; Cheerldng; Pom Pon; Med.

NUNN, MICHELE S; Clovis HS; Clovis, CA; (3); Cmnty Wkr; Teachers Aide; Fresno City Coll; Photo.

NUNNEMAKER, STEPHEN N; Willits HS; Willits, CA; (3); AFS; Key Clb; Teachers Aide; Phtg Yrbk; VP Jr Cls; JV Bsktbl; High Hon Roll; Hon Roll; 2nd Pl Mendocino Cnty Accntng Comptn; CPA.

NUNNES, DANIEL A; Oak Ridge HS; Folsom, CA; (1); ASU; Physics.

NUNO, DIANA; Southwest HS; San Ysidro, CA; (3); 75/493; Intnl Clb; Spanish Clb; Chorus; Pep Band; Rep Jr Cls; Rep Stu Cncl; High Hon Roll; MECHA Clb; Psycht.

NUNO, ELENA; Edison-Computech HS; Fresno, CA; (4); Letterman Clb; Pres Science Clb; Hist Service Clb; SADD; VP Frsh Cls; Treas Jr Cls; Off Sr Cls; Rep Stu Cncl; Var Socr; JV Var Sftbl; Stanford U; Eng.

NUNO, ELIZABETH R; Coachella Valley HS; Coachella, CA; (2); GAA; Girl Scts; Drill Tm; Treas Soph Cls; Bsbl; Bsktbl; Mgr(s); Sftbl; Trk; Vllybl; Cosmtlogy.

NUNO, JANIS; Garfield HS; Los Angeles, CA; (3); Cmnty Wkr; Library Aide; Co-Capt Drill Tm; Jazz Band; Orch; Co-Capt Cheerldng; Hon Roll; Moniachi; LA JR Philhamonic; Commissioner Publicity Band & Drill Tm.

NUNO, JESUS A; Estancia HS; Santa Ana, CA; (2); Ftbl; CA ST Fullerton; Crmnl Law.

NUNO, RODRIGO A; Sacred Heart Cathedral Prep; San Francisco, CA; (2); Drama Clb; Spanish Clb; Thesps; School Play; Stage Crew; Yrbk; Var Hon Roll; Awd Best Grade Alg; Thespian Awd 1 Star; U Of The Pacific; Publc Rltns.

NURSALIM, SUSANTO; San Marino HS; San Marino, CA; (3); French Clb; FBLA; Ntl Merit Ltr; Ardent Golf Player; MBA.

NURSE-FINDLAY, STEPHEN; Van Nuys HS; Panorama City, CA; (4); 50/534; Key Clb; Office Aide; Hnr Scty; U CA Los Angeles; Med.

NURU, TOFIK; Colton HS; Colton, CA; (2); Intrml Bsktbl; Cit Awd; Hon Roll; NHS; UCLA; Mgmt.

NUSS, ELAINE M; Hesperia HS; Hesperia, CA; (3); Church Yth Grp; VP Spanish Clb; High Hon Roll; Hon Roll; Prfct Atten Awd; Chrch Drama Team; Kindergarden Tchr.

NUSSBAUM, JOHN; Davis SR HS; Novato, CA; (3); 87/408; Boy Scts; Church Yth Grp; Office Aide; Spanish Clb; Thesps; Varsity Clb; Band; Chorus; School Musical; JV Bsktbl.

NUSSBAUM, TERRY; Mount Diablo HS; Martinez, CA; (4); 63/250; Cmnty Wkr; Office Aide; School Play; Off Jr Cls; Socr; Swmmng; Wt Lftg; Hon Roll; Images Of Hope; Crosfire Drama Grp; UC Berkeley; Psych.

NUSSER, THOMAS P; Campolinda HS; Moraga, CA; (4); 1/225; AFS; Hosp Aide; Var Capt Crs Cntry; Var Capt Trk; High Hon Roll; Hon Roll; Pres Acad Fit Awd; Val; Dist Art Cntst 1st Pl; Friends; UCSD.

NUTH, SAMPHORS; Oakland HS; Oakland, CA; (2); Computer Clb; French Clb; Vllybl; Cit Awd; Tutor Cambodia; Bus.

NUVYEN, TAM V; Bolsa Grande HS; Westminster, CA; (2); Spanish Clb; Bsktbl; Cit Awd; Hon Roll; CSF; WASC Stu Cmmtte; Chinese Clb; UCI.

NUYTTEN, HEIDI NOEL; Bear River HS; Auburn, CA; (3); Church Yth Grp; Cit Awd; High Hon Roll; Hon Roll; Prfct Atten Awd; Masons Deserving Youth Awd; U Of CA; Intr Dsgn.

NUZZI, JAMES M; Oxnard HS; San Diego, CA; (2); Debate Tm; Math Clb; Math Tm; Red Cross Aide; Spanish Clb; Speech Tm; Score Keeper; Socr; Trk; Hon Roll; MIT; Physics.

NY, PHIBUN; Norwalk HS; Norwalk, CA; (4); 4/286; VP Art Clb; Pres French Clb; Sec Service Clb; Rptr Nwsp; Var Tennis; Var Vllybl; Cit Awd; High Hon Roll; Kiwanis Awd; Pres Acad Fit Awd; CSF Schl Chptr Pres; UC San Diego; Engl Prfssr.

NYBERG, SARAH M; Orange Glen HS; Escondido, CA; (3); 30/458; Am Leg Aux Girls St; Key Clb; Spanish Clb; Band; Mrchg Band; Ed Yrbk; Hon Roll; NHS; Rotary Awd; Educ.

NYBO, JOY; Bakersfield HS; Bakersfield, CA; (4); 12/669; Debate Tm; NFL; Speech Tm; Band; Orch; Lit Mag; High Hon Roll; Pres Schlr; CSF; CA Poly U; Nutritional Sci.

NYE, NICOLE S; Clovis West HS; Fresno, CA; (3); 57/560; Church Yth Grp; Girl Scts; Chorus; High Hon Roll; Hon Roll; Prfct Atten Awd; Ed.

NYGREN, DAVID A; Skyline HS; Oakland, CA; (3); Key Clb; Orch; School Play.

NYHAN, KATIE; Paraclete HS; Lancaster, CA; (1); Church Yth Grp; Drama Clb; School Play; VP Frsh Cls; JV Cheerldng; High Hon Roll; Foreign Lang Awd Span 1 Tchrs Awd; Chef.

NYITRAI, DENNIS; Bellarmine College Prep; Santa Clara, CA; (3); Var Co-Capt Swmmng; V Waterpolo 2x Jr Natl Qlfr; 1st, 2nd Pl Finish In CCS; Natl Rcrd Relay Team; Block B Svc Membr; Med.

NYKOLUK, MONTY J; Trinity HS; Weaverville, CA; (1); Boy Scts; Church Yth Grp; Cmnty Wkr; Ski Clb; Band; Chorus; Pres Frsh Cls; Stu Cncl; Var Bsbl; JV Bsktbl; Peer Helper; Coachs Awd Bsktbl; Rookie Awd Bsbl; Pro Bsbl.

NYLANDER, JASON D; Golden West HS; Visalia, CA; (2); 42/300; Intnl Clb; Frsh Cls; Hon Roll; CSF; Envrnmntl Clb; Princeton; Govrnmnt.

NYLANDER, KURT; Placer HS; Auburn, CA; (2); Church Yth Grp; Key Clb; JV Bsbl; Var JV Ftbl; Wt Lftg; Hon Roll.

NYRE, MICHAEL A; Victor Valley HS; Victorville, CA; (3); 30/605; Boy Scts; Church Yth Grp; Service Clb; High Hon Roll; Hon Roll; Pres Acad Fit Awd; Eagle Scout Awd; Physcn.

NYSTROM, TRACY M; La Reina HS; Thousand Oaks, CA; (3); 1/70; Service Clb; Yrbk; Sec Frsh Cls; Rep Soph Cls; Sec VP Stu Cncl; High Hon Roll; Jr NHS; NHS; Pres Acad Fit Awd; Spanish NHS; Cmnty Stu Cncl.

O, DAO M; La Quinta HS; Fountain Valley, CA; (3); Cmnty Wkr; Key Clb; Treas Math Clb; Office Aide; Science Clb; SADD; Teachers Aide; Hon Roll; NHS; Rotary Awd; Badmntn.

O, TAE KEUM; Gahr HS; Artesia, CA; (2); 61/490; Hon Roll; UCLA; Med.

O BALLES, JAY; Leuzinger HS; Hawthorne, CA; (3); Art Clb; Boy Scts; Computer Clb; French Clb; Key Clb; Science Clb; Chorus; Ntl Merit Ltr; Cal Tech; Physicist.

O BERLIN, SHELLEY R; Cajon HS; San Bernardino, CA; (2); Pep Clb; SADD; Var Capt Cheerldng; Recgntn Awd Acad Frnch I & World Hstry; UCLA; Adv Acctnt.

O BOSKY, CARRIE L; Modesto HS; Modesto, CA; (3); Dance Clb; Color Guard; Cheerldng; High Hon Roll; Hon Roll; UC Davis; Law.

O BRADOVICH, MICHAEL DAVID; Covina HS; West Covina, CA; (3); Drama Clb; Stage Crew; JV Var Tennis; CA ST Fullerton; Bus Admin.

O BRANOVICH, AMY D; Armijo HS; Suisun, CA; (2); AFS; Ski Clb; Rep Soph Cls; Gym; Tennis; Hon Roll; Psych.

O BRIEN, BRENDA A; Whittier Christian HS; La Mirada, CA; (4); Church Yth Grp; Band; Mrchg Band; Pep Band; Pre Med.

O BRIEN, DAVID D; El Toro HS; El Toro, CA; (3); 92/502; JV Swmmng; Hon Roll; Pres Acad Fit Awd; Jr Var Water Polo.

O BRIEN, ERIN; Terra Nova HS; Pacifica, CA; (2); Pres Drama Clb; VP French Clb; Thesps; School Musical; School Play; JV Vllybl; Hon Roll; Gse Hnrs.

O BRIEN, JENNIFER D; St Francis HS; San Jose, CA; (4); Drama Clb; Intnl Clb; Speech Tm; Thesps; High Hon Roll; Hon Roll; UC Santa Barbara.

O BRIEN, MARK P; Borrego Springs HS; Ranchita, CA; (3); 1/23; Key Clb; Rptr Nwsp; Ed Yrbk; Pres Stu Cncl; Var L Bsbl; Var L Bsktbl; Var L Ftbl; Hon Roll; Ftbl Bst Dfnsve Back Awd; Engrng.

O BRIEN, MARNIE D; Tustin HS; Tustin, CA; (2); 8/423; Debate Tm; FHA; JA; Letterman Clb; Scholastic Bowl; Science Clb; Stu Cncl; Bsktbl; Score Keeper; Var L Swmmng; FOHR; OCAD Team; Engl Stu Yr Awd; Harvard; Colonial Amer Hstry.

O BRIEN, MICHAEL P; Artesia HS; Lakewood, CA; (2); Hon Roll; Grade Acad Ltr.

O BRIEN, MIKE D; Fort Bragg HS; Fort Bragg, CA; (3); Sec VICA; JV Var Ftbl; JV Var Golf; NHS; Santa Rosa JC; Crmnlgy.

O BRIEN, NATHAN L; Eureka HS; Eureka, CA; (4); 28/303; Chess Clb; Computer Clb; Drama Clb; Intnl Clb; Ski Clb; School Play; Nwsp; Edtr In Chf Of Edtn In Nwspr; Mjr Contrb & Wrtr For Sr Cls Nght.

O BRIEN, PAUL; Bishop Amat HS; Covina, CA; (3); 10/400; English Clb; Math Clb; Red Cross Aide; Service Clb; Lit Mag; Hon Roll; NHS; Adopt A Grandparent; Specl Olympcs Coach; Summr Camp Cnslr; U San Francisco; Profssr.

O BRIEN, SEAN M; Davis SR HS; Davis, CA; (3); SADD; Teachers Aide; Ldr Spprt Blnd Olympcs; Resrc Elem Schl Anti-Drnk/Drg Pgm; Amer River JC; Nrsng.

O BRIEN, SHARLENE E; Casa Roble HS; Penryn, CA; (3); 20/250; GAA; JA; Letterman Clb; Spanish Clb; Teachers Aide; Varsity Clb; Yrbk; Rep Frsh Cls; Rep Treas Soph Cls; Rep Sec Stu Cncl; Sci.

O BRIEN, TIM W; Ramona HS; Riverside, CA; (2); Boy Scts; JV Tennis; Var L Wrstlng; UCSD; Math.

O BRYAN, NICOLE M; Huntington Beach HS; Huntington Bch, CA; (3); Dance Clb; German Clb; High Hon Roll; Hon Roll; Hgh Hnr Golden St Exam Alg; Orange Coast; Engrng.

O CALLAGHAN, SHANNON; San Ramon Valley HS; Alamo, CA; (1); Teachers Aide; JV Var Bsktbl; JV Sftbl; Hon Roll; Pres Acad Fit Awd; Al Caffodio Sccr.

O CAMPO, BERENICE; Hilltop HS; Chula Vista, CA; (2); French Clb; Intnl Clb; Teachers Aide; Frgn Lang & Global Stds.

O CONNELL, ALLISON L; Bishop O'dowd HS; Alameda, CA; (2); Church Yth Grp; Ski Clb; Stage Crew; Nwsp; Stu Cncl; JV Crs Cntry; High Hon Roll; NEDT Awd; Pres Schlr; Jr Statesmen Of Amer; Med.

O CONNELL, LARA M; Mater Dei HS; Orange, CA; (3); Cmnty Wkr; VP Debate Tm; Treas French Clb; Sec Spanish Clb; Teachers Aide; Drill Tm; JV Crs Cntry; Cit Awd; Hon Roll; Vlntr 2 Yrs Rehab Inst Orange; Psych/Sociology.

O CONNOR, JOSEPH; El Cajon Valley HS; El Cajon, CA; (3); 40/455; VP Key Clb; Library Aide; Office Aide; Q&S; Teachers Aide; Ed Nwsp; Hon Roll; Jrnlsm.

O CONNOR, KATHRYN L; Los Amigos HS; Fountain Valley, CA; (2); 25/365; Church Yth Grp; Band; Jazz Band; Mrchg Band; Pep Band; Var L Crs Cntry; Var Capt Trk; High Hon Roll; Hon Roll; Pres Acad Fit Awd; Vrsty Trk Coaches Awd.

O CONNOR, KELLEEN L; El Toro HS; El Toro, CA; (4); 37/522; Teachers Aide; High Hon Roll; Hon Roll; NEDT Awd; Pres Acad Fit Awd; Mock Trial; CSF Sealbearer; LA Police Protective Leag Schlrshp; U Of CA-IRVINE; Elem Ed.

O CONNOR, MICHAEL R; Fall River JR SR HS; Mc Arthur, CA; (2); 4-H; FFA; Teachers Aide; JV Bsktbl; JV Ftbl; JV Wrstlng; Hon Roll; Ag-Bus.

O CONNOR, ORIELE; La Jolla HS; La Jolla, CA; (2); Cmnty Wkr; Key Clb; SADD; Cheerldng; Trk; Hon Roll; Prfct Atten Awd; UCSD.

O CONNOR, SHAWN M; Del Campo HS; Fair Oaks, CA; (2); 69/460; Science Clb; Bsktbl; Ftbl; JV Trk; NHS; Sci Olympd; West Point; Physics.

O DANIEL, LAURIE; Hanford HS; Hanford, CA; (4); Church Yth Grp; Cmnty Wkr; Dance Clb; Drama Clb; FBLA; Office Aide; Thesps; Band; Drill Tm; Mrchg Band; Body Bldng; Band Boosters; Cmnty Theater; Awds Dance; Lettr Grl; Nutritionist.

O DONNELL, MELANIE E; Clovis West HS; Clovis, CA; (3); Drama Clb; Pres English Clb; Key Clb; Stage Crew; Ed Lit Mag; Tennis; High Hon Roll; Ntl Merit Ltr; Pres Acad Fit Awd; Acad Decthln; Young Playwrights Clb; Crtv Wrtg.

O DONNELL, MOIRA; Mercy HS; Pacifica, CA; (4); 16/104; Church Yth Grp; Variety Show; Mgr Nwsp; Rep Soph Cls; Pres Jr Cls; Pres Stu Cncl; High Hon Roll; NHS; Ntl Merit Ltr; Jr Stsmn Amer-Fnded Chptr At Schl, Srvd Regnl, St Cbnt; CA Schlrshp Fdrtn; Amnsty Intl; Phys.

O DONNELL, PEGGY M; Monte Vista HS; Spring Valley, CA; (1); SDSU.

O DONNELL, SHAUNA L; Las Plumas HS; Oroville, CA; (2); Ski Clb; Rptr Nwsp; Off Frsh Cls; Off Soph Cls; Bsktbl; Score Keeper; Sftbl; Trk; Vllybl; Wt Lftg; Jrnlsm.

O DONNELL, TOBIN M; George Washington HS; San Francisco, CA; (3); Nwsp; JV Bsktbl; Var Ftbl; Var Lcrss; JV Capt Socr; High Hon Roll; Hon Roll; Envrnmntl Clb; GEO; Guitar Plyr; Prfssr Bio.

O FARRELL, KIMBERLY; Redwood HS; Corte Madera, CA; (4); Math Clb; Scholastic Bowl; Science Clb; SADD; Ed Nwsp; Var Crs Cntry; Var Diving; Var Swmmng; Hon Roll; CSF; UC Santa Cruz; Psych.

O GARA, CHRIS C; Atwater HS; Atwater, CA; (3); FFA; Hon Roll; FFA Green Hand Awd, Chaptr Farmr Awd, ST Frmr Awd; Cal Poly; Ag Bus.

O GORMAN, AMY; Sonoma Valley HS; Sonoma, CA; (3); Dance Clb; Intnl Clb; Model UN; Pep Clb; Spanish Clb; SADD; Stu Cncl; Stat Bsbl; Var Cheerldng; Var Pom Pon.

O GRIFFIN, MOSE; Galileo HS; San Francisco, CA; (2); Hon Roll; Front Running Amateur Sprinter-Runner; Piano; Japanese Lang Stu.

O HAGAN, JENNIE R; Salinas HS; Salinas, CA; (3); Church Yth Grp; Cmnty Wkr; Drama Clb; VP English Clb; JA; Teachers Aide; Thesps; Chorus; Church Choir; School Musical; Golden St Schlr U S Histry; Westmont Coll CA; Brdcstng.

O HAGAN, MAUREEN; Thousand Oaks HS; Thousand Oaks, CA; (3); Pres Debate Tm; Drama Clb; Pres NFL; Pres Speech Tm; SADD; Teachers Aide; Stage Crew; Lit Mag; Stat Bsktbl; Powder Puff Ftbl.

O HALLORAN, MOLLIE; Pomona Catholic HS; Cucamonga, CA; (4); SADD; Chorus; Nwsp; Co-Capt Yrbk; Lit Mag; Sec Sr Cls; Treas Stu Cncl; Sthrn CA Area Mdrn Physcs Inst; Clown Mnstry; CSF; U AZ; Arspc Engrng.

O HANLON, MICHELLE X; Willow Glen SR HS; San Jose, CA; (1); Hosp Aide; Latin Clb; Office Aide; SADD; Teachers Aide; Band; Jazz Band; Diving; Swmmng; Cit Awd; Photo.

O HARA, PATRICIA K; Fremont HS; Sunnyvale, CA; (2); #1 In Class; Church Yth Grp; Debate Tm; Math Tm; NFL; Service Clb; Speech Tm; SUSAN Clb; Astras Grls Svc Clb; CSF; Math.

O LAUGHLIN, J J; Glendora HS; Glendora, CA; (4); Service Clb; Pres Jr Cls; Var L Bsbl; Var L Bsktbl; Var L Ftbl; High Hon Roll; Pres Acad Fit Awd; Qtrbk Ftbl All-America & All-St; CIF Player Of Yr; Tm MVP; Baseline Lg Outstndng Sr & Schlr-Athlt; U IL; Bus Adm.

O LEARY, CHRISTOPHER M; El Camino Fundamental HS; Carmichael, CA; (3); 5/400; Off Chess Clb; Thesps; School Musical; School Play; Rptr Nwsp; JV Bsktbl; Intrml Vllybl; High Hon Roll; NHS; Math.

O MALLEY, CHRISTOPHER JAMES; Bear River HS; Grass Valley, CA; (3); Speech Tm; Var Wrstlng; Cit Awd; Hon Roll; Lion Awd; Cert NAUI Scuba Diver; UC Pepperdine; Marine Bio.

O MALLEY, CORY D; Valley Christian HS; Los Alamitos, CA; (2); Church Yth Grp; Letterman Clb; Varsity Clb; JV Ftbl; Var Var Socr; All Olympic League Soccer Tm 90; Jrnlsm.

O MALLEY, DENNIS ROBERT; Ballarmine HS; Morgan Hill, CA; (3); 38/365; Church Yth Grp; Cmnty Wkr; Debate Tm; Letterman Clb; Library Aide; Office Aide; Varsity Clb; Ftbl; Trk; Wt Lftg; Cngrssnl Schlr Awd; All Cnfrnc Ftbll; Engnrng.

O MALLEY, SEAN C; Bellarmine College Prep; San Jose, CA; (4); 1/305; Debate Tm; Service Clb; Speech Tm; SADD; Crs Cntry; Socr; Swmmng; Trk; Elks Awd; Pres Schlr; PG & E Schlrshp Fnlst; GI Forum Schlrshp; Stanford U.

O MARA, COLLEEN; Dos Pueblos HS; Goleta, CA; (3); Cmnty Wkr; Dance Clb; Drill Tm; Stu Cncl; Var Cheerldng; High Hon Roll; Hon Roll; NHS; UCSB Jr Pgm; Pediatric Med.

O MEARA, ERIN K; Thomas Downey HS; Modesto, CA; (2); JV Var Sftbl; JV Vllybl; Coll Clb; CSF; Knight Of Wk Awd-3 Times Vllybl/2 Times Sftbl; MVP-VLLYBL/Sftbl; Stanford; Phrmcy.

O MEARA, ROBERT W; La Sierra HS; Riverside, CA; (2); Church Yth Grp; Yrbk; Swmmng; Wt Lftg; Wrstlng; Cit Awd; High Hon Roll; Hon Roll; NHS; UCLA; Engl.

O NEAL, ALLISON; Oakdale HS; Waterford, CA; (2); Church Yth Grp; Band; Mrchg Band; Pep Band; Cit Awd; Outstndng Band Awds; Chrch Sftbl & Vlybl; Modedto JC; Tchr.

O NEAL, JENNIFER S; El Camino Fundamental HS; Sacramento, CA; (3); 1/375; Chess Clb; Var JV Crs Cntry; Var JV Trk; NHS; Ntl Merit SF; Debate Tm; French Clb; Math Tm; Ski Clb; Jazz Band; Moot Court; Wilderness Club Founding Pres; Capitol Crew; UC Berkeley; Sci.

O NEAL, JULIE M; Chula Vista HS; Chula Vista, CA; (4); Treas Pres Service Clb; SADD; Teachers Aide; Cit Awd; High Hon Roll; Opt Clb Awd; Pres Acad Fit Awd; Creative & Performing Arts Schl; San Diego ST U; Sci Sci.

O NEAL, LORI; Montgomery HS; Santa Rosa, CA; (3); Teachers Aide; Band; Mrchg Band; Stu Of Mnth Twice; Typing Trophy 1st Pl; Santa Rosa JC; Bus Mgmt.

O NEAL, RUBEN A; Barstow HS; Barstow, CA; (4); Church Yth Grp; Drama Clb; School Play; Wt Lftg; Wrstlng; High Hon Roll; Hon Roll; Electrncs.

O NEAL, STEPHANIE D; Sanger HS; Fresno, CA; (3); Church Yth Grp; Chorus; Sftbl; Cit Awd; Bus.

O NEIL, DARCIE; Fairbanks Country Day HS; Leucadia, CA; (3); 1/8; Nwsp; Yrbk; Rep Frsh Cls; Treas Jr Cls; Cheerldng; High Hon Roll; Engl Spkng Union Shkspr Comptn; Educ.

O NEIL, DYLAN M; North Monterey County HS; Castroville, CA; (2); AFS; Church Yth Grp; FBLA; Ski Clb; Band; Jazz Band; JV Bsktbl; JV Trk; High Hon Roll; NHS; USA Slct Sccr Tm Europn Tr; Outstndng Jzz Musicnshp Spcl Rcgntn Cuesta Col Jzz Fstvl; Music Achvt Awd; UCLA; Intl Bus.

O NEIL, ELIZABETH A; Serrano HS; Wrightwood, CA; (2); 9/248; FBLA; JV Vllybl; Hon Roll; Stu For Stu Peer Cnslng; Bus.

O NEILL, AUDEENE; Ramona HS; Riverside, CA; (2); 20/447; Church Yth Grp; Band; Drm Mjr(t); Mrchg Band; Var Bsktbl; Hon Roll; Annapolis Naval Acad.

O NEILL, CRAIG A; Rancho Cotate HS; Rohnert Park, CA; (4); 19/250; Drama Clb; JA; School Play; Variety Show; VP Sr Cls; Stu Cncl; Trk; Wt Lftg; Hon Roll; CSF; Top 20 Stu 90; 90 Sonoma Cnty Acad Decthln 5 Mdls; Stu Mnth Dec; U Of CA San Diego; Economics.

O NEILL, RENEE J; Armijo HS; Suisun City, CA; (2); Certif Of Achievement/Excellence In Math By State Of Calif; UCLA; Child Psychologist.

O QUINN, SHANE; Rio Del Sol HS; Sacramento, CA; (3); Rptr Yrbk; American River JC; Hstry.

O RAM, CRYSTAL L; Paramount HS; Paramount, CA; (1); Church Yth Grp; Band; Mrchg Band; Cit Awd; Hon Roll; Pediatrics.

O RILEY, TANYA; Lompoc HS; Lompoc, CA; (4); FBLA; FFA; Pep Clb; SADD; Sftbl; Prfct Atten Awd; Allan Hancock; Photo.

O RIORDAN, C DABNEY; Chadwick HS; Rancho Palos Verd, CA; (2); Cmnty Wkr; Library Aide; Model UN; Orch; School Musical; Lit Mag; JV Capt Bsktbl; Var Cheerldng; Var L Sftbl; Hon Roll.

O RORKE, REBECCA L; Lassen HS; Standish, CA; (2); 29/244; Treas Hist 4-H; JV Fld Hcky; 4-H Awd; Hon Roll; CA Schlrshp Fed; Lassen Co Sci Fair Achvt Awd; Bst Ovrll Exhbt; Dntl.

O ROURKE, JASON S; Marina HS; Huntington Beach, CA; (4); 6/484; Computer Clb; Pres Debate Tm; Rep Math Clb; Nwsp; Var Crs Cntry; JV Trk; High Hon Roll; Ntl Merit SF; YMCA-YOUNG Mens Cleanup Assoc.

O ROURKE, SEAN T; Bullard HS; Fresno, CA; (3); Debate Tm; FCA; German Clb; NFL; SADD; School Play; JV Socr; JV Capt Vllybl; Hon Roll; NHS; High Hnrs On Golden St Hstry Test; U Of Santa Barbara; Psych.

O SHEA, HEATHER K; Louisville HS; Calabasas, CA; (1); High Hon Roll; Eng Awd; CSF; Stanford U; Psych.

O SHEA, PATRICK J; Montgomery HS; Santa Rosa, CA; (3); VP Frsh Cls; Var Bsktbl; High Hon Roll; Hon Roll; N Coast Section CIF Schlr Athl; N CA Ldrshp Conf; Sports Med.

O SHEA, SEAN; Los Altos HS; Hacienda Hts, CA; (2); 111/396; Church Yth Grp; Science Clb; School Play; JV Capt Ftbl; JV Capt Vllybl; Cit Awd; Hon Roll; Prfct Atten Awd; Pres Acad Fit Awd; Teens For Life; Yng Repblcns-Teens For Ken Manning.

O SULLIVAN, BRIDGETT E; South Fork HS; Garberville, CA; (3); Pres 4-H; FHA; JA; Pep Clb; 4-H Awd; Hon Roll; Rotary Awd; Sec Frsh Cls; Pres Soph Cls; Pres Jr Cls; Acctnt.

O SULLIVAN, IAN; San Dieguito HS; Encinitas, CA; (3); 60/570; Lit Mag; L Var Crs Cntry; Var Swmmng; Intrml Tennis; L Var Trk; Intrml Vllybl; JV Wrstlng; Hon Roll; Pres Acad Fit Awd; St Rep Natl HS Triathlon Chmpnshp 90; 2nd Pl Microbio Rgnl Sci/Engrng Fr 88; Vlntr Of Yr Awd; CA Poly; Recreation & Leisure.

O SULLIVAN, TRACIE A; Lodi HS; Stockton, CA; (1); Chorus; VP Frsh Cls; Sec Soph Cls; High Hon Roll; Hon Roll; GATE Cert; Yth Chrle.

O TOOLE, KEVIN L; Concord HS; Concord, CA; (4); JA; Teachers Aide; Tennis; Bausch & Lomb Sci Awd; Hon Roll; CSF; Bank Of Amer Achvt Awd; Tandy Technlgy Schlr; U CA Berkeley; Civil Engrng.

OAK, MARGARET F; Vista HS; Shelley, ID; (3); 28/480; Pres Church Yth Grp; Key Clb; Chorus; Church Choir; Drill Tm; Flag Corp; Swing Chorus; Cit Awd; Ntl Merit SF; Opt Clb Awd; Church Camp Ldr 89 & 90; ASB Convntn 89-90; ASB Fclty Commssnr & Communctns Commssnr; Pre-Med.

OAKES, ANGELA R; Venice HS; Encino, CA; (1); JV Vllybl; Forgn Lang Magnet; Excllnc Wrk Habits Cooprtn 89-90.

OAKES, BRENDON J; Bolsa Grande HS; Garden Grove, CA; (2); Spanish Clb; Rep Frsh Cls; Rep Soph Cls; Var Swmmng; Hon Roll; Vrsty Wtr Polo; Surf Clb; Marine Bio.

OAKES, KERI; Del Campo HS; Carmichael, CA; (2); 115/460; Drama Clb; Acpl Chr; Band; Chorus; Mrchg Band; Pep Band; School Musical; School Play; Stage Crew; Variety Show; Peace Yth Ambssdr Of Soviet Union; Juliard; Brdway Prfrmr.

OAKES, MARTIN E; North Coast Alternative HS; Del Mar, CA; (2); Intrml Crs Cntry; U Of Bath England; Aero Engr.

OAKEY, ANDREA M; North Monterey County HS; Salinas, CA; (2); Pep Clb; Rptr Soph Cls; Rep Stu Cncl; Capt Mgr(s); Var Trk; Hon Roll; Jr NHS; Pres Acad Fit Awd; Ldrshp Cls; UCLA; Law.

OAKLAND, BRYCE; Calvary Chapel HS; Santa Ana, CA; (2); Boy Scts; Ski Clb; Wt Lftg; Hon Roll; Comp.

OAKLAND, WADE; Calvary Chapel HS; Santa Ana, CA; (2); Boy Scts; Church Yth Grp; Ski Clb; Teachers Aide; Band; Yrbk; JV Var Ftbl; Var Trk; Var Wrstlng; Hon Roll; Bus.

OAKLEY, LAURA M; Modesto HS; Modesto, CA; (1); Art Clb; Church Yth Grp; Church Choir; Tchr.

OANH, PHAM T; Rosemead HS; Rosemead, CA; (3); Cit Awd; High Hon Roll; Hon Roll; CSF; Sgn Lang Clb; Med.

OATES, FAWN A; Grace Davis HS; Modesto, CA; (2); Art Clb; Drama Clb; French Clb; FTA; SADD; Notre Dame; Law.

OATMAN, LORI A; Tracy Joint Union HS; Tracy, CA; (3); 176/401; Church Yth Grp; Office Aide; SADD; Teachers Aide; Chorus; Yrbk; Hon Roll; U OR; Chld Psych.

OBA, STEPHANIE; Marina HS; Huntington Bch, CA; (3); Spanish Clb; Band; Mrchg Band; Var Capt Bsktbl; Trk; High Hon Roll; All Star Seyo Bsktbll Trnmnt; Engrng.

OBAID, MOSI AISHA; Sister Clara Muhammad HS; Compton, CA; (1); Debate Tm; Drill Tm; Yrbk; Vllybl; Cncl Cmnty Clbs Inc; Cert Of Commendation From Mayor; Fshn Dsgnr.

OBASI, CHINYERE; Los Angeles Ctr For Enriched Studies; Los Angeles, CA; (3); Church Yth Grp; Church Choir; Drill Tm; Rep Jr Cls; VP Sr Cls; Var Capt Bsktbl; Var Capt Vllybl; Riordan Schlr; Fulfillment Fund Schlr; CSF Secy; Comp Engrng.

OBEDIAH, REENA; Los Angeles Baptist HS; Northridge, CA; (3); 17/100; Art Clb; Church Yth Grp; Drama Clb; Intrml Var Trk; High Hon Roll; Hon Roll; Jr NHS; Ntl Merit Ltr; Rotary Awd; CSF; U Of CA Davis; Pre Med.

OBENSKI, STEVEN M; Gompers Secondary HS; San Diego, CA; (1); Math Clb; Math Tm; Pres Spanish Clb; High Hon Roll; Hon Roll; CSF; Hnr Smnrs Of San Diego 89-90; Brd Of Educ Of SDUSD Hnrs; Psych.

OBER, ZEPHA; Lowell HS; San Francisco, CA; (2); Drama Clb; French Clb; Red Cross Aide; Gym; Socr; Coll.

OBERG, PONTUS B H; Newport Harbor HS; Newport Beach, CA; (3); Boy Scts; Crs Cntry; JV Socr; JV Var Tennis; High Hon Roll; CSF; Princeton Book Award; Rensselear Math & Science Award; UCI; Pre Med.

OBERING, KANDI A; Norco HS; Norco, CA; (3); 23/399; Spanish Clb; High Hon Roll; Hon Roll; Showing Horses; Bus.

OBERLE, JEFF; Westminster HS; Westminster, CA; (3); 126/416; Crs Cntry; Trk; Vllybl.

OBERLE, JULIE L; Westminster HS; Westminster, CA; (4); 136/450; Spanish Clb; Yrbk; Rep Soph Cls; Var L Crs Cntry; Var L Socr; Var L Sftbl; Cls-Up Clb; Wtr Polo Statstcn; CSF.

OBERLIN, BRIDGET; Providence HS; Glendale, CA; (2); GAA; Model UN; Pep Clb; Stage Crew; Pres Frsh Cls; Sec Stu Cncl; Var Bsktbl; Var Cheerldng; Var Crs Cntry; Var Trk; Brdcst Jrnlsm.

OBERMAN, AMY L; Palm Springs HS; Rancho Mirage, CA; (3); Cmnty Wkr; Debate Tm; FTA; Hosp Aide; Chorus; Color Guard; Flag Corp; Mrchg Band; Treas Stu Cncl; Hon Roll; CSF; JR Statesmen Of Amer; Mock Trial Team; U CA Irvine; Sci.

OBERMANN, KRISTI; Desert JR/Sr HS; San Antonio, TX; (4); Church Yth Grp; Office Aide; Teachers Aide; Varsity Clb; Band; Mrchg Band; Hon Roll; Kiwanis Awd; NHS; Bnk Amer Awd Bus; Athl Of Yr; Schlr Athl; W TX ST; Bus.

OBESTER, MISTY L; Cornelia Connelly HS; Garden Grove, CA; (1); School Play; Hon Roll; Frnch Awd Hnrb Mntn 90; Vet.

OBILLO, BRENT; Narbonne HS; Harbor City, CA; (4); Church Yth Grp; Math Tm; Phtg Yrbk; Stu Cncl; Capt Var Crs Cntry; Capt Var Trk; Hon Roll; Ntl Merit Ltr; Opt Clb Awd; Mst Outstndng Srvce Awd; DARE; Ephebians; Pepperdine U; Math Ed.

OBILLO, FELINO S; Montgomery HS; San Ysidro, CA; (2); Band; Drm Mjr(t); Jazz Band; Mrchg Band; Swing Chorus; Rptr Nwsp; JV Var Ftbl; Var Golf; Cit Awd; Prfct Atten Awd; Schlrshp Awd; Ftbl Player Of Yr; Bio-Chem Engr.

OBREGON, EVANGELINA; Our Lady Of Peace HS; Chula Vista, CA; (3); French Clb; ROTC; School Musical; Air Force; Sci.

OBRIEN, HEATHER L; Lincoln HS; Stockton, CA; (2); 145/568; JV Socr; JV Trk; Hon Roll; Pres Acad Fit Awd.

OBRIEN, SCOT; Silver Valley HS; Yermo, CA; (2); JV Ftbl; Cit Awd; Hon Roll; Barstow Coll; Hwy Patrol.

OBST, CHRISTINE M; Rim Of The World HS; Crestline, CA; (3); 20/260; Drama Clb; Teachers Aide; Co-Capt Color Guard; Rep Jr Cls; Rep Stu Cncl; Stat Wrstlng; Hon Roll; Jnr Statsmn Of Amer; Arch.

OCA, GHANDI S; Jefferson HS; Daly City, CA; (4); 2/274; Model UN; Science Clb; Chorus; Stage Crew; Nwsp; Stu Cncl; High Hon Roll; NHS; Prfct Atten Awd; Pres Acad Fit Awd; CA Schlrshp Fed Mem; Bank Of Amer Achvt Awd Eng; Daly City Rotary Club Schlrshp Awd; U CA Davis.

OCAMPO, CHARLES R; Valley HS; Sacramento, CA; (4); Church Yth Grp; Cmnty Wkr; French Clb; Intnl Clb; Office Aide; Teachers Aide; High Hon Roll; Hon Roll; U Of CA-DAVIS; Soclgy.

OCAMPO, EVERARDO L; Wasco Union HS; Wasco, CA; (2); Cmnty Wkr; Latin Clb; JV Crs Cntry; JV Socr; Cit Awd; High Hon Roll; Hon Roll; Typing Cert Of Proficiency; Comp.

OCAMPO, KIMBERLY; Mira Mesa HS; San Diego, CA; (2); Drill Tm; Modeling; CA Jr Schlstc Fed; U CA San Diego.

OCAMPO, MARISELA; Notre Dame Acad; Los Angeles, CA; (3); VP Mgr Hosp Aide; Rep Science Clb; Spanish Clb; SADD; Ed Yrbk; Cit Awd; High Hon Roll; Hon Roll; U CA-BERKELEY; Bio.

OCAMPO, MARISOL R; Notre Dame Acad; Los Angeles, CA; (3); VP Hosp Aide; Science Clb; Spanish Clb; Ed Yrbk; Cit Awd; High Hon Roll; Hon Roll; Lion Awd; Cmps Mnstry; UCLA; Engl.

OCAMPO, RONALD C; Mills HS; Millbrae, CA; (3); Am Leg Boys St; Boy Scts; Church Yth Grp; Cmnty Wkr; Dance Clb; Intnl Clb; Variety Show; Rep Frsh Cls; Sec Soph Cls; Treas Stu Cncl; Filipino Ply Prfrmd Palace Of Five Arts; Strtd Filipino Armcn Alliance FAA HS; Cal Poly; Archt.

OCAMPO, XENA V; Immaculate Heart HS; Glendale, CA; (2); Church Choir; Prfct Atten Awd; Arch.

OCASION, LOUISE; Hilltop HS; National City, CA; (2); 11/530; Var Cheerldng; Pep Clb; Ski Clb; SADD; Nwsp; Stu Cncl; Hon Roll; Ntl Merit Ltr; CSF; Stanford; Law.

OCH, GARY; Pasadena HS; Pasadena, CA; (4); 7/433; VP French Clb; Key Clb; Ski Clb; VP Spanish Clb; Ed Nwsp; VP Frsh Cls; VP Jr Cls; Xerox Humanities Soc Sci Awd; Water Polo.

OCHIQUI, CHARLOTTE; Sweetwater HS; National City, CA; (3); 48/422; Computer Clb; Dance Clb; French Clb; Pep Clb; Science Clb; Band; Drill Tm; Variety Show; Stu Cncl; Cheerldng; Advanced Choreography; CALIFORNIA Scholastic Federation Potential Lifetime Member; Honors Program; Coll; Aerospace Engr.

OCHOA, ADRIANA; Alisal HS; Salinas, CA; (1); High Hon Roll; Bill Gate Clb; Comp Engr.

OCHOA, ADRIANA; Sunset HS; Hayward, CA; (2); Latin Clb; Hon Roll; Mills Coll.

OCHOA, ALFONSO; Liberty Union HS; Brentwood, CA; (3); Socr; Trk; Hon Roll; Elecs.

OCHOA, CANDY M; Turlock HS; Turlock, CA; (3); Spanish Clb; CA Art Ed Assn Yth Art Mnt Awd 87; Rtry Clb Stu Of Mnth Awd; Modesto JC; Art.

OCHOA, CLAUDIA; Savanna HS; Anaheim, CA; (2); Spanish Clb; Cosmetology.

OCHOA, DANIEL L; Central Union HS; Seeley, CA; (2); Church Yth Grp; Cmnty Wkr; FCA; Service Clb; SADD; Chorus; Church Choir; Var Mgr(s); Santa Barbara ST U; Const.

OCHOA, FABIAN; Junipero Serra HS; Compton, CA; (3); Church Yth Grp; French Clb; Spanish Clb; Hon Roll; Cal ST Long Beach; Comp Sci.

OCHOA, JANEL L; William Workman HS; Valinda, CA; (1); Cit Awd; Cmptr Tech Prgms; Mt San Antonio Coll; Word Proc.

OCHOA, JORGE G; Hesperia HS; Hesperia, CA; (3); 81/605; Computer Clb; FBLA; Spanish Clb; Hon Roll; CSU San Bernardino; Bus.

OCHOA JR, JUVENTINO; Fowler HS; Fowler, CA; (3); 4/90; Math Tm; Spanish Clb; Ed Nwsp; Rptr Yrbk; VP Sr Cls; Var JV Tennis; Cit Awd; Hon Roll; Pres Acad Fit Awd; Golden St Exam, Geo Hnrs; Schl Rep Camp Royal 90.

OCHOA, KATINA GONZALEZ; Chula Vista HS; Chula Vista, CA; (3); 183/493; Church Yth Grp; Cmnty Wkr; Dance Clb; Debate Tm; Drama Clb; Office Aide; Pep Clb; Spanish Clb; Drm Mjr(t); Rep Soph Cls; 1 Of 66 Chsn To Work In Nations Capitol As Page Smmr 90; Teen Miss San Diego 87; Teen Miss South By 88; Harvard; Lawyer.

OCHOA, LIZETH; East Union HS; Manteca, CA; (2); Church Yth Grp; Latin Clb; Spanish Clb; Cit Awd; High Hon Roll; Hon Roll; Joaquin Clb Treas; Comp.

OCHOA, LUCY; Winters HS; Winters, CA; (3); Church Yth Grp; Cmnty Wkr; GAA; Letterman Clb; SADD; Varsity Clb; JV Bsktbl; Stat Var Sftbl; JV Var Vllybl; Hon Roll; Fri Night Live Secy; Youth Cmmssn Secy; Notre Dame; Intr Dsgn.

OCHOA, LYNNA H; Alexander Hamilton HS; Los Angeles, CA; (3); Church Yth Grp; Cmnty Wkr; Dance Clb; Drama Clb; French Clb; Yrbk; Sftbl; Cit Awd; Hon Roll; NHS; Prtcptd Celebratn Papal Visit; Vol Chldrns Museum; Yth Ldrshp Actn Yth Cmmnty Srvc; Georgetown; Intl Relations.

OCHOA, MARIA ELENA; Liberty Union HS; Brentwood, CA; (4); 4/307; Hon Roll; Stu Of Mnth-Bus Dept & PE; Los Medanos CC; Med.

OCHOA, OCTAVIO; Bell Gardens HS; Bell Gardens, CA; (2); 10/1000; JV Swmmng; Var Tennis; Prfct Atten Awd; JV Water Polo; USC; Elec Engr.

OCHOA, RENEE R; Tulare Western HS; Tulare, CA; (3); 30/250; Church Yth Grp; VP 4-H; Science Clb; Ski Clb; Teachers Aide; Band; Mrchg Band; Pep Band; Hon Roll; Prfct Atten Awd; John Philip Sousa Band Awd; U S Collegiate Wind Band European Tour; Coll Of The Sequoias; Ed.

OCHOA JR, RICARDO; Bonita Vista HS; Bonita, CA; (4); Pres Key Clb; Quiz Bowl; Scholastic Bowl; Ed Nwsp; Stu Cncl; JV Trk; JV Wrstlng; Hon Roll; Ntl Merit SF; Opt Clb Awd; UC San Diego; Law.

OCHOA, SONIA; Sylmar HS; Sylmar, CA; (3); JA; Letterman Clb; SADD; Temple Yth Grp; Varsity Clb; JV Diving; Var Gym; Cit Awd; Hon Roll; Prfct Atten Awd; Cls Cabinet; Woodbury U; Int Dsgn.

OCHS, DANIEL E; Simi Valley HS; Simi Valley, CA; (3); 45/666; Boy Scts; Band; Jazz Band; Mrchg Band; Hon Roll; Engrng.

OCHS, SHANDA L; Casa Grande HS; Petaluma, CA; (2); Teachers Aide; Band; NHS; CSF; Drivers Ed Achvt Awd; Marine Bio.

OCKERBERG, KENNETH P; Arcata Union HS; Blue Lake, CA; (2); Var Crs Cntry; Var Trk; CSF; Engrng.

OCKERMAN, JEFF M; J Eugene Mc Ateer HS; San Francisco, CA; (4); Pres Chess Clb; Debate Tm; Math Tm; Quiz Bowl; Science Clb; Teachers Aide; Band; Capt Swmmng; Hon Roll; St Schlr; Russian Clb Sec; Acad Dcthln Mdl Wnnr; Astronomy.

OCONER, ELLEN O; Sherman Oaks CES HS; Los Angeles, CA; (4); 3/98; NFL; VP Spanish Clb; Drill Tm; Rep Hist Stu Cncl; Vllybl; Cit Awd; Hon Roll; CSF-VP 88-89/Pres 89-90; Peer Coll Cnslr; Finance Cmmttee; Bus Acctng.

ODA, SUSAN; Wilcox HS; Sunnyvale, CA; (4); French Clb; FTA; Model UN; Teachers Aide; Sec Stu Cncl; Var Cheerldng; High Hon Roll; Pres Acad Fit Awd; PTSA Schlrshp; Dads, Grads & Moms Schlrshp; CSF; UCLA; Bus.

ODDO, ANGELA S; San Gabriel Mission HS; Monrovia, CA; (3); Cmnty Wkr; FBLA; Pep Clb; Service Clb; Hon Roll; Stu Schlrshp; CA Schlrshp Fed; Cal Poly Pomona; Bus.

ODDONE, KIM K; Village Christian HS; Sun Valley, CA; (3); Church Yth Grp; Drama Clb; Powder Puff Ftbl; Var Stat Ftbl; HS Missns Clb; Woodbarry Coll; Interior Dsgn.

ODDY, ROBIN M; Carlsbad HS; Carlsbad, CA; (4); 42/345; Church Yth Grp; Pep Clb; Ski Clb; SADD; Chorus; Off Frsh Cls; JV Var Cheerldng; Gym; Elks Awd; Hon Roll; Pr Advct Pres; UC Santa Barbara; Commnctns.

ODELL, NINA; Roseville HS; Rocklin, CA; (3); 9/411; Science Clb; Teachers Aide; Band; Mrchg Band; Pep Band; Var Trk; High Hon Roll; CSF; Vetrns Of Frgn Wars Ladies Auxlry; CA ST U Sacramento; Tchr.

ODEN, RITA M; Rio Linda HS; Sacramento, CA; (2); Spanish Clb; School Play; High Hon Roll; Hon Roll; Mst Imprvd Stu; Envrnmntl Awrns; Poltcs; USC; Envrnmntl Bio.

ODIO, REGINA; Canyon HS; Santa Clarita, CA; (1); Girl Scts; Pep Clb; Red Cross Aide; Cheerldng; Hon Roll; Pres Acad Fit Awd; Doctor.

ODOM, MELINDA A; Redwood HS; Visalia, CA; (3); Sec Church Yth Grp; Chorus; Hon Roll; Peer Cummunicator; Point Loma Nazarene Coll.

ODUM, JENNIFER M; Lone Pine Unified HS; Independence, CA; (2); 3/40; Am Leg Aux Girls St; Math Tm; Office Aide; Spanish Clb; Band; Nwsp; Var L Bsktbl; JV Var Score Keeper; Var L Vllybl; High Hon Roll; Sober Grad-Fndr/Pres; County Acad Achvt Awd; Schl Site Cncl; Span Ed.

ODY, YAYA; Los Altos HS; Hacienda Hgts, CA; (2); Stu Cncl; JV Bsktbl; JV Swmmng; High Hon Roll; Hon Roll; Prfct Atten Awd; Berkley; Pre Med.

ODZAK, TANJA I; Watsonville HS; Watsonville, CA; (3); 16/500; Ed Nwsp; Var Swmmng; High Hon Roll; Hon Roll; Prfct Atten Awd; CSF.

OEDING, MATTHEW R; Ukiah HS; Ukiah, CA; (4); Boy Scts; Church Yth Grp; Cmnty Wkr; Treas JA; Stu Mnth; Egle Sct Awd; Rlgn Cls Grad; BYU HI.

OEI, IVAN K; Servite HS; Cypress, CA; (3); 5/181; Boy Scts; Service Clb; Teachers Aide; Jazz Band; Orch; Hon Roll; NHS; NEDT Awd; Outstndng Chem Stu Awd Orange Cnty Amer Chem Soc; VP CA Schlrshp Fed 90-91; Accrdnst 82.

OELSCHIG, TREVOR H; Troy HS; Fullerton, CA; (2); 9/450; Boy Scts; Intrml Bsbl; JV Bsktbl; High Hon Roll; Rotary Awd.

OFFEL, KEVIN D; El Dorado HS; Placentia, CA; (3); 76/317; Letterman Clb; Math Clb; Spanish Clb; Teachers Aide; Varsity Clb; Band; Stage Crew; Rep Jr Cls; JV Bsbl; Var L Ftbl; USAF Acad; Bus Admn.

OFFEN, STEPH J; Woodside HS; Woodside, CA; (2); Teachers Aide; Stage Crew; Rep Soph Cls; JV Capt Socr; Var Capt Trk; Hon Roll; Horses.

OFFENBERG, K C; Don Bosco Technical Inst; Montebello, CA; (3); Intrml Bsktbl; Intrml Var Trk; High Hon Roll; Hon Roll; Lion Awd; NHS; St Schlr; Indstry Educ Cncl Medallion Awd 89-90; Acad & Schl Spirit Awd 87-89; Model Legisltr/Crt VP Of Delgtn; Econ.

OFFERMANN, TONYA J; San Luis Obispo HS; San Luis Obispo, CA; (2); #1 In Class; Church Yth Grp; Treas SADD; Chorus; JV Var Vllybl; High Hon Roll; CSF; Club Vllybl; CIF 2a Vllybl Chmpns 89-90; Christ Coll Irvine; Ed.

OFFILL, JOSHUA J; Morro Bay HS; Cayucos, CA; (4); Yrbk; Bsktbl; Hon Roll; Cuesta Coll; Gen Educ; Mortician.

OFFNER, JENNIFER L; James Logan HS; Union City, CA; (3); Color Guard; Nw Haven Unfd Schl Dist Show; FL For Color Guard Sqd & Hs Band Compete; San Diego ST; Marine Bio.

OFRASIO, MYRA; Mercy HS; S San Francisco, CA; (3); Service Clb; Spanish Clb; Yrbk; VP Frsh Cls; Sec Jr Cls; Var Cheerldng; High Hon Roll; NHS; Spanish NHS; Excllnc Rgls Stds; Soc Women Engrs Math, Sci; Chem Olympiad Fnlst; UCLA; Pre-Med.

OGARD, KAARY; Mt Whitney HS; Visalia, CA; (3); AFS; Spanish Clb; SADD; Band; Mrchg Band; Pep Band; Diving; Sftbl; Hon Roll; Instrmntlst Mgzn Merit Awd; Stu Of Mnth Nov 89.

OGATA, MIYE; Hoover HS; Fresno, CA; (4); 46/400; Am Leg Aux Girls St; French Clb; Letterman Clb; Nwsp; Var Capt Bsktbl; Var Trk; Var Capt Vllybl; High Hon Roll; Coaches Awd Vrsty Bsktbl; Gldn St Math Awd; HOBY Ldrshp Camp; City Cnty All Star Bsktbl Game.

OGBORN, DAVID W; Hesperia HS; Hesperia, CA; (2); ROTC; JV Ftbl.

OGBUNAMIRI, NGOZI; Pilgrim Schl; Los Angeles, CA; (4); 2/24; Ed Nwsp; Pres Stu Cncl; Var Capt Bsktbl; Var Capt Vllybl; Cit Awd; DAR Awd; NHS; Ntl Merit Schol; Pres Acad Fit Awd; All-St Plyr Vllybl & Bsktbl; Soc Wmn Engrs Awd; Los Angeles All-Str Tm Bsktbl; Harvard U; Bio.

OGDEN, CYNTHIA; Apple Valley SR HS; Wichita, KS; (4); 103/441; Church Yth Grp; Pep Clb; Band; Mrchg Band; Cmptr Tech.

OGDEN, SELENE; Carmel HS; Carmel, CA; (3); Key Clb.

OGDEN, STEVEN GRANT; West Valley HS; Cottonwood, CA; (4); 9/152; French Clb; Math Tm; Teachers Aide; Var L Bsbl; Var L Ftbl; Wt Lftg; High Hon Roll; NHS; Ntl Merit Ltr; Pres Acad Fit Awd; CA Schlstc Fed; Golden St Exam Hgh Hnrs Alg & Geom; Schlr Athl Shield; UC Davis; Engrng.

OGI, JEFFREY; Poway HS; Poway, CA; (3); Computer Clb; FBLA; German Clb; Math Clb; SADD; JV Swmmng; High Hon Roll; NHS; Treas CSF; Intract Clb; UCLA; Engrng.

OGLE, CHRISTINA L; Poly HS; Riverside, CA; (3); Church Yth Grp; Cmnty Wkr; Drama Clb; FBLA; GAA; Hosp Aide; Key Clb; Office Aide; SADD; Bsbl; Blac Comm Art; Artst.

OGLE, JAMES A; Fountain Valley HS; Fountain Valley, CA; (3); Drama Clb; Chorus; Church Choir; Capt Ftbl; Marine Bio; Writng; Art; Westmont; Drftng.

OGLESBY, HEATHER J; Mar Vista HS; Imperial Beach, CA; (2); Cmnty Wkr; ROTC; Band; Jazz Band; Mrchg Band; Bsktbl; JV Crs Cntry; Med.

OGLESBY, JANE; Cornelia Connelly HS; Garden Grove, CA; (3); 1/42; Cmnty Wkr; Drama Clb; GAA; Intnl Clb; Pres Science Clb; Service Clb; School Play; Stage Crew; Lit Mag; Rep Stu Cncl; Soc Wmn Engrs Cert Merit; 2nd Orng Cnty Sci Fair Chem 89; Renssalaer Club Orng Cnty Awd Sci Fair 89; Pomona Coll.

OGLESBY, KATHERYN E; Cornelia Connelly HS; Garden Grove, CA; (1); 1/30; GAA; Hosp Aide; Pres Science Clb; School Play; Var L Socr; Var Sftbl; High Hon Roll; Pres Acad Fit Awd; Jr Statesmen Of Amer; Library Club; Pamona Coll; Med.

OGLETREE, DAVID J; Summerville HS; Mi Wuk Village, CA; (3); Ski Clb; Spanish Clb; Stu Cncl; Tennis; UC; Bus.

OH, ALBERT; Sunny Hills HS; Orange, CA; (3); 5/420; Sec Church Yth Grp; Debate Tm; VP Model UN; Sec Sr Cls; Rep Stu Cncl; Var Golf; High Hon Roll; NHS; Ntl Merit Ltr; Rotary Awd; Brnz Mdl Outstndng Achvt U S Hstry & Eng; Gld Mdls Outstndng Achvt Sthrn CA Jnr Golf Assn 86-88.

OH, CATHERINE M; John A Rowland HS; Rowland Heights, CA; (2); Cmnty Wkr; French Clb; Science Clb; Off Frsh Cls; Tennis; High Hon Roll; Badminton; CSF; Interact Club; UCLA; Law.

OH, DANNY; Servite HS; Orange, CA; (2); Church Yth Grp; Ski Clb; Phtg Yrbk; VP Jr Cls; Var Bsktbl; Var Swmmng; Hon Roll; Water Polo; Bicyclng Clb; CSF; U Of CA Irvine; Med.

OH, HEIDI M; Artesia HS; Hawaiian Gardens, CA; (2); Church Yth Grp; Science Clb; Ski Clb; Spanish Clb; SADD; Band; Chorus; Church Choir; Socr; Sftbl; Music; Intl Clb; Korean Clb; CSF; Phy.

OH, HYONG H; Gahr HS; Cerritos, CA; (2); Chess Clb; Computer Clb; Math Clb; JV Vllybl; Hon Roll; Prfct Atten Awd; CSF; Tnns Clb; CA Tech U; Engrng.

OH, INSIK; Skyline HS; Oakland, CA; (2); Church Yth Grp; Band; Orch; Tennis; Pres Acad Fit Awd; U CA-BERKELEY; Mech Engr.

OH, JENNIFER M; J Eugene Mc Ateer Schl Of The Arts; San Francisco, CA; (2); 4-H; School Play; VP Frsh Cls; Pres Soph Cls; Hon Roll; Russian Exchng Stu; Mc Ateer Coll Scty; Close Up Clb; HOBY.

OH, JIN; Armijo HS; Fairfield, CA; (3); Var Bsbl; Var Bsktbl; Hon Roll; UC Santa Barbara.

OH, KYUNG S; Paramount HS; Paramount, CA; (2); 15/599; Var Tennis; Cit Awd; High Hon Roll; Acad Excllnc Awd; UCLA; Engrng.

OH, LINDA; El Toro HS; El Toro, CA; (3); VP Church Yth Grp; Cmnty Wkr; Intnl Clb; Church Choir; Yrbk; Stat Trk; Cit Awd; High Hon Roll; Hon Roll; JETS Awd; Orange County Arch Yth Expo Excllnc Awd.

OH, PETER B; Monte Vista HS; Danville, CA; (4); Treas Church Yth Grp; Cmnty Wkr; Pres Debate Tm; Pres Key Clb; NFL; Pres Speech Tm; VP Jr Cls; JV Trk; Intrml Vllybl; Lion Awd; Police Dept Yth Div Svc; Acadc Dcthln; Achvmnt Awds German; Sierra Club; Pltcl Sci.

OH, PETER C; Carson HS; Carson, CA; (4); Boy Scts; JV Ftbl; Var Swmmng; Wt Lftg; Hon Roll; Prfct Atten Awd; Powerlifting Tm; CSU Long Beach; Elect Engr.

OH, SAMUEL; Kennedy HS; Sepulveda, CA; (3); Church Yth Grp; Cmnty Wkr; Math Clb; Church Choir; Bsbl; Cit Awd; Hon Roll; Prfct Atten Awd; Karate; Kickboxing, Boxing; UCLA; Med.

OH, STACEY; Crescenta Valley HS; La Crescenta, CA; (2); Church Yth Grp; French Clb; Key Clb; Pep Clb; Chorus; Church Choir; Drill Tm; Korean Clb Tutor; Sec Korean Clb; Grls Glee Sec; Dentist.

OH, STEPHEN; Fountain Valley HS; Fountain Valley, CA; (2); Science Clb; Band; Jazz Band; Mrchg Band; Orch; Pep Band; Bsbl; High Hon Roll.

OH, SUMI; San Gabriel HS; San Gabriel, CA; (4); 17/737; Computer Clb; VP Sec German Clb; Library Aide; Band; School Play; Rep Stu Cncl; High Hon Roll; CSF; U Of CA Riverside; Pedtrcn.

OH, SUN M; John Glenn HS; Norwalk, CA; (4); 15/430; Church Yth Grp; Dance Clb; GAA; Church Choir; Nwsp; Off Sr Cls; Gym; Tennis; Trk; High Hon Roll; UCLA; Elec Engrng.

OH, SUZIE Y; Glendale HS; Glendale, CA; (3); Hosp Aide; Spanish Clb; Drill Tm; Rep Stu Cncl; Trk; Cit Awd; NHS; Pres Acad Fit Awd; Korean Clb Pres; Med Exlprs Clb VP; Vrsty Pep Squad; Montrose Fire Dept Vlntr; Obstetrtian.

OHANESIAN, CECELIA M; Clovis HS; Clovis, CA; (2); Band; Jazz Band; Mrchg Band; Pep Band; School Musical; High Hon Roll; Hon Roll; Sign Lang; Rdng Horses; CSF; Teach.

OHANESIAN, STEWART E; Sunny Hills HS; La Mirada, CA; (2); Spanish Clb; Band; Jazz Band; Mrchg Band; High Hon Roll; Jr NHS; U Of Santa Clara; Sci.

OHARA, LISA M; John F Kennedy HS; Sacramento, CA; (3); 91/422; AFS; FBLA; Spanish Clb; Japanese Schl Grad; Japan Studies Schlrshp Awd; Sacramento City Coll; Envrmntls.

OHGI, JENNIFER N; Ocean View HS; Westminster, CA; (1); Church Yth Grp; French Clb; Model UN; Service Clb; JV Swmmng; Swin Team MVP; Water Polo; Japanese Lang Schl 9th Grade Grad Progress Awd.

OHLE, ALLISON M; West HS; Torrance, CA; (1); 44/400; Church Yth Grp; JA; Flag Corp; Hon Roll; Pres Acad Fit Awd; Sal; UCSD Med Schl; Ped.

OHLE, MELISSA; West HS; Torrance, CA; (4); 45/480; Office Aide; Band; Yrbk; Var Cheerldng; Hon Roll; NHS; San Diego ST U; Child Dev.

OHLFEST, STEVEN; University City HS; San Diego, CA; (3); 131/373; Aud/Vis; Church Yth Grp; Model UN; Church Choir; JV Golf; Hon Roll; CA Jr Schlrshp Fed Awd; Pres Acad Ftns Awd; Hardest Wrkr U City Dance Co Awd 89; TV Prod.

OHLSON, AMY L; Baptist Christian Hemet HS; Idyllwild, CA; (3); Teachers Aide; Band; Stu Cncl; Hon Roll; Biola U.

OHLSON, BRIGHTSTAR; Mt Madonna HS; Watsonville, CA; (2); 2/15; Cmnty Wkr; Drama Clb; Variety Show; Ed Yrbk; Sec Frsh Cls; Pres Soph Cls; High Hon Roll; Supvr/Mgr Sch Run Store; Peer Tutoring; Span Hon; Med.

OHLSON, LILY; Mant Madonna Schl; Watsonville, CA; (4); Art Clb; Drama Clb; Ski Clb; Chorus; School Play; Stage Crew; Nwsp; Yrbk; Off Soph Cls; Bsktbl; Comm Svc; Coll Lvl Spnsh, Drwng ,Comptns, & Prntmkng Clss; UC Davis; Art.

OHR, PAUL; Servite HS; Cerritos, CA; (2); Church Yth Grp; Debate Tm; Pres Frsh Cls; VP Soph Cls; Capt Bsktbl; NHS; CSF; MVP Bsktbl.

OHRT, KIRSTIN R; St Bonaventure HS; Ventura, CA; (4); Church Yth Grp; Cmnty Wkr; Sec Debate Tm; Intnl Clb; Letterman Clb; NFL; Ski Clb; Sec Speech Tm; SADD; Varsity Clb; Interact Clb VP; Stu Of Mnth; Athl Of Wk 3 Times; Jr Statesmen Of Amer; UCSB; Engl.

OHSHIMA, KAREN M; Marina HS; Huntington Beach, CA; (3); Dance Clb; JCL; Latin Clb; Pep Clb; Ski Clb; Var Capt Cheerldng; Hon Roll; Business Major.

OHSHIMA, PAUL H; Marina HS; Huntington Beach, CA; (1); Hon Roll.

OHTA, JASON M; La Quinta HS; Westminster, CA; (1); Key Clb; Bsbl; Bsktbl; Ftbl; Wt Lftg; NEDT Awd Super Prfrmnc; SEYO Bsktbl Leag; Stanford.

OIEN, KATHRYN; Brethren SR HS; Long Beach, CA; (2); Band; Mrchg Band; Var Socr; JV Sftbl; Var Vllybl; Hon Roll; Prtcptd ACSI Hnr Bnd 89; U Of Sthrn CA; Engr.

OJEDA, ALISHA M; Paradise HS; Paradise, CA; (2); Cmnty Wkr; Girl Scts; Key Clb; SADD; Chorus; Butte U; Lwyr.

OJEDA, ESMERALDA; Arroyo Grande HS; Nipomo, CA; (3); Spanish Clb; Upward Bound.

OJEDA, JESUS F; Colton HS; Colton, CA; (2); Ftbl; Wt Lftg; Hon Roll; Stanford U; Accntng.

OJEDA, JORGE A; St Paul HS; Pico Rivera, CA; (3); Hon Roll; Dentist.

OJEDA, KALEEN S; Nevada Union HS; Nevada City, CA; (3); 46/551; High Hon Roll; Hon Roll.

OJEDA, STACY; Clayton Valley HS; Concord, CA; (1); Church Yth Grp; Pep Clb; Cheerldng; Hon Roll; Commnty Chrldng Team Diablo Vlly Hawks; UC Davis; Doctor.

OJHA, RAJESH P; Luther Burbank HS; Sacramento, CA; (3); 6/276; Off Math Clb; Red Cross Aide; ROTC; Spanish Clb; Ed Yrbk; Treas Stu Cncl; Bsktbl; Co-Capt Trk; High Hon Roll; Salvation Army Angel Tree Vlntr; UCLA; Doctor.

OKA, CALVIN KOJI; St Ignatius College Prep; South San Francis, CA; (3); 64/260; Boy Scts; Church Yth Grp; Cmnty Wkr; Service Clb; JV Bsktbl; JV Ftbl; Var Vllybl; Hon Roll; Dycmp Cnslr; Piano; UC Berkeley Acad Tlnt Dvlpmnt Prgrm.

OKADA, DANIEL T; Hilltop HS; San Ysidro, CA; (4); 87/444; Boy Scts; Church Yth Grp; French Clb; JA; Teachers Aide; Varsity Clb; Var Capt Ftbl; Wrstlng; Cit Awd.

OKAMOTO, DARLENE T; Montgomery HS; Santa Rosa, CA; (2); Spanish Clb; Drill Tm; School Play; Nwsp; Rep Stu Cncl; JV Capt Cheerldng; Hon Roll; Jr NHS; Prfct Atten Awd; Pres Acad Fit Awd; Golden St Exam High Honors In Alg & Geo; Shirly Ann Knight Awd Drama; Sonoma St U Coll Bound; Stanford; Bus.

OKAMOTO, KATHLEEN K; Los Altos HS; Hacienda Hts, CA; (3); Church Yth Grp; Pep Clb; Teachers Aide; Varsity Clb; Pres Rep Frsh Cls; Rep Soph Cls; Rep Jr Cls; Pres Stu Cncl; Co-Capt Cheerldng; Hon Roll; Spg Games For Exceptional Chldrn Coach/Instr 89; Engl.

OKAMURA, BRENT T; Whitney HS; Cerritos, CA; (2); 95/170; Key Clb; JV Capt Bsbl; JV Capt Bsktbl; JV Capt, MVP Wtrpolo; Jpnese Clb; Orthdntst.

OKAMURA, CINDY M; John W North HS; Riverside, CA; (1); German Clb; Key Clb; Rptr Nwsp; Hon Roll; Pres Acad Fit Awd; JSA Secy; Asian Stu Union Treas; Liberal Arts.

OKAMURA, JEFF A; Marysville HS; Marysville, CA; (4); Band; Jazz Band; Mrchg Band; Bsktbl; Ftbl; Powder Puff Ftbl; Wt Lftg; Woodleaf Counselor; Spirit Club VP; Chico; Accntng.

OKAMURA, SONIA S; Rio Mesa HS; Somis, CA; (1); Drama Clb; Intnl Clb; School Play; Rep Frsh Cls; JV Swmmng; JV Tennis; Hon Roll; CSF; UCSB; Psych.

OKANO, SUNSHINE M; Hoover HS; Fresno, CA; (3); 49/543; Band; Mrchg Band; CSF; GSE Hnrs; CYLC; Psych.

OKASAKI, CATHLEEN; Schurr HS; Monterey Park, CA; (3); Intnl Clb; SADD; Rptr Nwsp; Hon Roll; Prfct Atten Awd; Vlntr At Monterey Park City Hll; Jrnlsm.

OKAZAKI, JASON A; Mission Viejo HS; Mission Viejo, CA; (1); 1/455; Math Tm; Model UN; Ski Clb; Bsbl; Bsktbl; Ftbl; High Hon Roll; Most Imprvd Awd-Bsktbl; Outstndng Ptchr Awd-Bsbl.

OKELLEY-LEWIS, REBEKAH R; Palmdale HS; Palmdale, CA; (3); Pres Church Yth Grp; Hon Roll; BYU; Interior Decor.

OKERSTROM, LESLIE; Western HS; Anaheim, CA; (3); Pep Clb; SADD; Color Guard; Nwsp; Stu Cncl; Cheerldng; Prfct Atten Awd; Girls Leag; Wrestlerette Clb; San Diego ST U; Psych.

OKI, KEITH S; Nogales HS; Walnut, CA; (2); 33/800; Letterman Clb; Science Clb; Capt Socr; Tennis; High Hon Roll; CSF; Bus Mgmt.

OKIMURA, HEIDI; Woodcrest Christian HS; Grand Terrace, CA; (2); Church Yth Grp; FCA; Chorus; Variety Show; JV Bsktbl; Var L Crs Cntry; Cit Awd; Hon Roll; NHS; U Of HI; Psych.

OKLAND, HEATHER I; Los Amigos HS; Fountain Valley, CA; (3); 36/293; French Clb; Science Clb; High Hon Roll; Hon Roll; Gymnstcs St Chmpnshp Tm 88, 89 & 90; Indvdl Chmpn Intl Invtnl Meet England 90; Sci.

OKROJEK, AGNIESZKA M; Abraham Lincoln HS; San Francisco, CA; (3); Office Aide; Var Swmmng; Vrsty Swmmr Brnz Mdl 89-90 Cty Fnls; UC Berkeley; Comp Prgmr.

OKSEN, CHRISTINE M; Apple Valley SR HS; Apple Valley, CA; (2); Aud/Vis; Church Yth Grp; Cmnty Wkr; Library Aide; SADD; Chorus; Cit Awd; Hon Roll; MPC; Art.

OKU, LYNN N; Venice HS Foreign Language Magnet; Venice, CA; (1); Church Yth Grp; Girl Scts; Prfct Atten Awd; Delphians; Silver Awd.

OKUBO, TANYA; Andrew P Hill HS; San Jose, CA; (2); Math Tm; Color Guard; JV Cheerldng; Hon Roll; Prfct Atten Awd; Lfsklls Stu Of Yr 88-89; Anti Grafiti Prog; Var Cheer Capt 90-91; Educ.

OKUHARA, TOHRU; Burlingame HS; San Mateo, CA; (4); Intnl Clb; Math Clb; Science Clb; Service Clb; Ski Clb; Teachers Aide; School Musical; Ed Nwsp; Ed Yrbk; Sec Soph Cls; Srvce Cmssn; CSU Long Beach; Bus Admin.

OKUTOMO, JUNKO; Prospect HS; Saratoga, CA; (1); 16/251; Dance Clb; Orch; Off Jr Cls; Math Cmptn.

OLAGUE, CLAUDIA; Mission HS; Monrovia, CA; (2); Church Yth Grp; GAA; Hosp Aide; Var Capt Swmmng; Hon Roll; Prfct Atten Awd; Arcadia Swim Clb; Vet.

OLALIA, SHELLA MARIE F; Channel Islands HS; Oxnard, CA; (2); Hosp Aide; Rep Stu Cncl; Hon Roll; Prfct Atten Awd; Med.

OLAMIT, JUSTIN N; Sacramento HS; Sacramento, CA; (2); Boy Scts; Orch; Var Socr; NHS; Asst Principal Sacramento Yth Symphony; Julliard; Music.

OLANDER, HEATHER P; Poway HS; San Diego, CA; (2); 4/790; Sec FBLA; Key Clb; Pep Clb; SADD; JV Sftbl; JV Tennis; Pres Acad Fit Awd; Pr Cnslng; CSF; Ivy League Schl; Mngmnt.

OLAVARRI, MICHAEL R; Branham HS; San Jose, CA; (1); School Play; JV Socr; Hon Roll.

OLAY, MARIEFE VILA; Skyline HS; Oakland, CA; (2); Church Yth Grp; Intnl Clb; Key Clb; ROTC; Color Guard; Drill Tm; Ed Yrbk; VP Stu Cncl; DAR Awd; Hon Roll; Var Rifle Tm; CSF; Lector St Jarlath Parish; Aerosp Engrng.

OLDEEN, DANE C; Apple Valley HS; Apple Valley, CA; (3); Wt Lftg; High Hon Roll; Hon Roll; Pres Acad Fit Awd; Welding, Fabricating; Victorville CC; Welding.

OLDEN, ROBIN JOY; La Serna HS; Whittier, CA; (4); #6 In Class; Church Yth Grp; Acpl Chr; Church Choir; Drill Tm; Variety Show; Cit Awd; High Hon Roll; Hon Roll; NHS; Ntl Merit Ltr; Hnrb Mntn Jessamyn West Wrtng Cntst; Wellesley Bk Awd; Westmont Coll; Tchng.

OLDENBURGER, JOHN W; El Camino HS; Sacramento, CA; (3); 1/366; Church Yth Grp; Var Bsbl; Intrml Wt Lftg; NHS; Engr.

OLDFIELD, ALICIA; Fred C Beyer HS; Modesto, CA; (3); Pep Clb; Service Clb; SADD; Yrbk; Rep Soph Cls; Rep Jr Cls; Cheerldng; Trk; Cit Awd; Hon Roll; Cnty Prayer Brkfst Yth Rep.

OLDHAM, CHRISTOPHER; San Ramon Valley HS; San Ramon, CA; (3); 25/420; High Hon Roll; Prfct Atten Awd; Acadmc Achvt Awd Sci; Crfctn Cmmdtn Outstng Acadmc Achvt; Achvt Golden St Examntn Geo Hgh Hons; Aerospace Engr.

OLDHAM, TODD M; Edison HS; Huntington Beach, CA; (3); Cadet Staff Sgt Civl Air Patrol; Gld Key Social Studies.

OLDS, JULIE A; Arcata HS; Arcata, CA; (3); Treas Drama Clb; Speech Tm; Band; School Musical; Stage Crew; Variety Show; Lit Mag; Cit Awd; French Hon Soc; High Hon Roll; Golden St Exam Alg Hgh Hnrs; UC Davis; Phys Thrpst.

OLEA, SABINA; Bassett HS; La Puente, CA; (3); Day Care Center Employment; Kindergarden Teacher.

OLEKSOW, KATHLEEN D; Monte Vista HS; Spring Valley, CA; (2); Key Clb; Letterman Clb; Pep Clb; Var L Socr; Var L Vllybl; Pres Acad Fit Awd; Schlrshp Ply San Diego Clb Vllybl.

OLERICH, ERIKA A; Santa Barbara HS; Santa Barbara, CA; (3); 74/472; Ski Clb; JV Diving; Var Tennis; Vllybl; Bio.

OLESEN, PATRICIA; Fremont Christian HS; Hayward, CA; (2); Letterman Clb; Socr; Sftbl; Veterinarian.

OLESEN, PATTY J; Fremont Christian HS; Hayward, CA; (3); Var Socr; Var Sftbl; JV Vllybl; Hon Roll; Vet.

OLESKA, JOHN; El Camino Real HS; West Hills, CA; (4); Hon Roll; JETS Awd; Acad Excllnc Math; UC Davis; Engrng.

OLGUIN, CURTIS; Orange Glen HS; Temecula, CA; (4); Var Trk; JV Wrstlng; Hnry Cert Write Off; U CA-SAN Diego; Comm.

OLGUIN, JASON J; Hanford Joint Union HS; Hanford, CA; (2); Art Clb; FBLA; Science Clb; Teachers Aide; JV Tennis; Berkeley; Bus Admin.

OLGUIN, LETICIA; Burbank HS; Sun Valley, CA; (3); Office Aide; Rptr Nwsp; Hon Roll; CA ST Northridge; Bus Mgmt.

OLGUIN, SILVIA L; Oxnard HS; Oxnard, CA; (3); 36/479; Drama Clb; Hon Roll; Uxmal Clb; Math Clb Spc Intrsts; Hosp Aide; Oxnard Coll.

OLHEISER, MICHELE E; Homestead HS; Sunnyvale, CA; (3); French Clb; Capt Color Guard; Advncd Plcmnt Frnch & Engl; Santa Clara U; Law.

OLITO, TIFFANY D; Victory Christian HS; Sacramento, CA; (2); Church Yth Grp; Cmnty Wkr; Pep Clb; Science Clb; Rptr Yrbk; Rep Soph Cls; Var Bsktbl; Var Sftbl; Var Vllybl; Hon Roll; Soph Princess; Sacramento ST; Cmmnctns.

OLIVA, ARMANDO L; Bellarmine Jefferson HS; Burbank, CA; (3); Spanish Clb; Speech Tm; JV Bsktbl; Var Ftbl; Var Tennis; Var Wt Lftg; Walk Amer Muscular Distrphy; Enumerator US Census Bureau; Bus.

OLIVA, CHRISTINA MARIE; Bloomington Christian HS; Bloomington, CA; (2); Church Yth Grp; Church Choir; Stu Cncl; Capt Cheerldng; Hon Roll; CA ST U; Bus Admin.

OLIVA, ELISEO M; St John Bosco HS; South Gate, CA; (2); 4/220; Boy Scts; Computer Clb; French Clb; Bsbl; Socr; Trk; Hon Roll; Masonic Awd; Bsktbl; CA Schlrshp Fed; Bus; Accntng.

OLIVA, KRISTEN; Canyon Springs HS; Moreno Valley, CA; (2); Letterman Clb; Teachers Aide; Varsity Clb; Sec Jr Cls; Var Socr; Var Tennis; Hon Roll; ASB; Coaches Awd Sccr; Mst Imprvd Awd Tnns; UCI; Med.

OLIVA, M MICHELLE; Rosary HS; Villa Park, CA; (4); 15/140; Church Yth Grp; Cmnty Wkr; Ski Clb; VP Spanish Clb; School Play; High Hon Roll; NHS; Prfct Atten Awd; Pres Acad Fit Awd; Gold Team Capt Schl Prdctn; CA Poly San Luis Obispo; Chem.

OLIVA, MARVIN R; John A Rowland HS; Rowland Heights, CA; (2); Bsbl; Socr; Comp Sci.

OLIVA JR, RICARDO; Santa Ana HS; Santa Ana, CA; (2); Science Clb; Crs Cntry; Socr; Trk; Hon Roll; MESA Math, Engr & Sci Achvmnt Club; Engr.

OLIVAR, ANTHONY M; Pater Noster HS; Los Angeles, CA; (2); 1/30; Chess Clb; Computer Clb; Math Clb; Science Clb; Nwsp; Hon Roll; NHS; Sal; Physiology.

OLIVARES JR, JOEL A; South San Francisco HS; San Bruno, CA; (3); Latin Clb; Stu Cncl; JV Ftbl; Capt Var Wrstlng; Amer Lgn Boys St Awd Fnlst; 1st Lt Patriot Ldrs Of U S Clb; Fresno ST; Phys Thrpy.

OLIVARES, MARIA L; Oxnard HS; Oxnard, CA; (2); French Clb; Vllybl; Hon Roll; MESA Club.

OLIVARES, RAQUEL; Roosevelt HS; Los Angeles, CA; (2); Church Yth Grp; Spanish Clb; Drill Tm; School Play; Stu Cncl; Gym; Sftbl; Swmmng; Cit Awd; High Hon Roll; UCLA Prtnrshp Pgm; ELAC Upward Bound; Law.

OLIVAREZ, SONIA; Palm Desert HS; La Quinta, CA; (3); Cmnty Wkr; JA; Rep Stu Cncl; High Hon Roll; Prfct Atten Awd; CSF; UC Berkeley; Pre-Med.

OLIVAS, ANGELA R; Santa Maria HS; Santa Maria, CA; (3); Pep Clb; Teachers Aide; Drill Tm; Cheerldng; Powder Puff Ftbl; Socr; Bus.

OLIVAS, CLARA; Calexico HS; Calexico, CA; (1); Key Clb; Rep Stu Cncl; JV Score Keeper; French Hon Soc; Hon Roll; Be Great Wrtr & Nxt Shakespeare; Song Recorded; UC Davis; Animl Hsbndry.

OLIVAS, JULIE M; Fontana HS; Fontana, CA; (2); Cit Awd; High Hon Roll; Prfct Atten Awd; UCR; Accntng.

OLIVAS, OLGA L; Bell Gardens HS; Bell Gardens, CA; (3); French Clb; JV Tennis; Hon Roll; Prfct Atten Awd; CSF; Golden St Exam Alg 1-2; USC; Phy.

OLIVAS, VICTOR M; Bell Gardens HS; Bell Gardens, CA; (4); 31/500; Drama Clb; Hon Roll; Prfct Atten Awd; MECHA Club; CSF; SAT Vocabulary Cert Of Imprvmnt Awd; UCI; Physics.

OLIVE, LOUKISHA N; Redlands SR HS; Loma Linda, CA; (3); Church Yth Grp; Teachers Aide; Chorus; Church Choir; Variety Show; Bsktbl; Trk; Prfct Atten Awd; Miss Black Awrns, Young Hill 88-86; Most Outstndng Voclst 88; Soclgy.

OLIVEIRA, ANNA M; Portola JR-SR HS; Graeagle, CA; (3); 2/53; Am Leg Aux Girls St; Church Yth Grp; Teachers Aide; Varsity Clb; Band; Pres Soph Cls; JV Var Cheerldng; Tennis; High Hon Roll; Hon Roll; Yth To Yth; Plumas Cty Voc Olympics; Yth Forum; Western ST Yth To Yth Conf; Eng.

OLIVEIRA, CHRIS J; Manteca HS; Manteca, CA; (2); 22/430; Socr.

OLIVEIRA, JANEA R; Lemoore HS; Lemoore, CA; (2); 1/332; Church Yth Grp; Spanish Clb; Yrbk; Bsktbl; Powder Puff Ftbl; Vllybl; CA Schlrshp Fed; Soph Cls Homcmng Princess; Outstndng Freshman Girl 88-89.

OLIVEIRA, JULIE R; Lemoore HS; Lemoore, CA; (3); 14/293; Spanish Clb; SADD; Sec Frsh Cls; Bsktbl; Powder Puff Ftbl; Trk; Vllybl; Jr Cls Homcmng Princess; Jr Escort; CA Schlrshp Fed.

OLIVEIRA, LISA; Hilmar JR/Sr HS; Hilmar, CA; (2); Art Clb; Church Yth Grp; Sec FFA; Sec Office Aide; Bsktbl; Swmmng; Vllybl; Hon Roll; Jr Coll; Ag.

OLIVEIRA, SERENA S; Oakmont HS; Greenwood, CA; (2); 113/425; Drama Clb; German Clb; School Musical; Stage Crew; Score Keeper; Vllybl; Cit Awd; Hon Roll; Drama.

OLIVER, CARIANN E; Rio Linda SR HS; Sacramento, CA; (2); Church Yth Grp; Spanish Clb; Church Choir; High Hon Roll; CA Schlrshp Fed; CA Poly; Arch Engr.

OLIVER, CHRISTINA L; California HS; San Ramon, CA; (3); 20/368; Dance Clb; Teachers Aide; Rep Soph Cls; NHS.

OLIVER, DIANA T; Leuzinger HS; Hawthorne, CA; (3); Pres Spanish Clb; Ed Nwsp; Sec Jr Cls; Rep Sr Cls; Stu Cncl; Cit Awd; Hon Roll; Camp Cnslr; CSF; Jrnlst.

OLIVER, DIANE; Thomas Downey HS; Modesto, CA; (1); Pep Clb; Band; Mrchg Band; Pep Band; Hon Roll; Knight Achvt Awd; Friday Night Live; Marine Bio.

OLIVER, ERIC A; Woodside HS; Portola Valley, CA; (2); Ski Clb; Capt Ftbl; The Times Stu Jrnlsm Awd; Most Inspirational.

OLIVER, ERICA H; Granada Hills HS; Northridge, CA; (2); Dance Clb; Girl Scts; SADD; Stage Crew; Rep Stu Cncl; High Hon Roll; Pres Acad Fit Awd; Histry & Sci Deptmntl Awds; Silver Seal Awd Engl; Harvard; Law.

OLIVER, JULEE ELIZABETH; Clayton Valley HS; Brentwood, CA; (3); Church Yth Grp; Teachers Aide; Hon Roll; People To People Yth Sci Exch Russia Yth Ambass 90; World Peace; Pre-Vet Med.

OLIVER, KATHLEEN A; Woodcrest Christian HS; Canyon Lake, CA; (2); Church Yth Grp; Band; Church Choir; Jazz Band; Orch; Variety Show; Yrbk; Rep Soph Cls; Cit Awd; High Hon Roll; Wildwood Music Camp; City Concert Band; Music.

OLIVER, KEVIN CAMPBELL; Helix HS; La Mesa, CA; (3); 3/487; Key Clb; Swmmng; High Hon Roll; Hon Roll; Pres Acad Fit Awd; Water Polo; Stanford; Math.

OLIVER, KRISTY; Central Valley Christian HS; Visalia, CA; (2); Church Yth Grp; Acpl Chr; Chorus; Stat Bsbl; JV Var Cheerldng; Var Pom Pon; Hon Roll; Youth Ambassador Trip To Russia; Law.

OLIVER, KURT; Damien HS; Upland, CA; (3); 89/231; Letterman Clb; Spanish Clb; SADD; Varsity Clb; Var L Ftbl; Var L Wt Lftg; Hon Roll; Pres Acad Fit Awd; USC; Bus.

OLIVER, LAURA L; Escondido HS; Escondido, CA; (1); Church Yth Grp; Ski Clb; Hon Roll.

OLIVER, LAURIE A; Bella Vista HS; Folsom, CA; (2); 95/406; German Clb; Phtg Yrbk; Schltc Achvt Soc Sci; Congrsnl Schlr Natl Yth Ldrshp Cert Merit; Stu Against Drugs & Alc Abuse; USAFA; Pilot.

OLIVER, MARK; San Marcos HS; San Marcos, CA; (3); Key Clb; Ski Clb; Intrml Var Ftbl; JV Vllybl; Intrml Wrstlng; High Hon Roll; Hon Roll; Pres Acad Fit Awd; Proclmtn Prom; CO ST U; Math.

OLIVER, MELINDA A; San Leandro HS; San Leandro, CA; (2); Church Yth Grp; Drama Clb; Q&S; Teachers Aide; Phtg Nwsp; Off Jr Cls; Hon Roll; Abilene Christian U TX; Photo.

OLIVER, REBECCA E; Branham HS; San Jose, CA; (2); Church Yth Grp; French Clb; GAA; SADD; JV Swmmng; French Hon Soc; Hon Roll; Bus.

OLIVER, SHANNON; Mother Lode Christian Schl; Soulsbyville, CA; (1); 4/15; Teachers Aide; Flag Corp; Cheerldng; Sftbl; Vllybl; Law.

OLIVER, STACI L; Mater Dei HS; Westminster, CA; (3); Cmnty Wkr; Hosp Aide; Ed Yrbk; Rep Jr Cls; Stu Cncl; JV Sftbl; DAR Awd; Hon Roll; Outstndng Achvt Awd; Chrstn Svc Awd; CO ST U; Psych.

OLIVER, VICTORIA M; Glendora HS; Glendora, CA; (4); 1/375; Sec VP Computer Clb; Sec VP Math Clb; SADD; Teachers Aide; Hon Roll; Pres Acad Fit Awd; Val; U Of CA Riverside; Biolgcl Sci.

OLIVER, ZACHARY; St Michaels College Prep HS; San Clemente, CA; (2); Art Clb; School Play; Rptr Stage Crew; Rptr Yrbk; Pres Soph Cls; Hon Roll; Jr NHS; NHS; Orange Cnty Acad Decthln; U Of CA Santa Barbara.

OLIVERI, TOM; Damien HS; Upland, CA; (2); 2/250; Debate Tm; NFL; Speech Tm; Chorus; Sec Frsh Cls; Sec Soph Cls; Hon Roll; NHS; CSF; Frshmn Yr; UC Davis; Vet.

OLIVEROS, CATHERINE; Don Antonio Lugo HS; Chino, CA; (3); Church Yth Grp; Hosp Aide; Spanish Clb; Teachers Aide; Sec Sr Cls; Hon Roll; Translator For Yth Grp To Help Needy In Mexico; Med.

OLIVO, GABRIEL; Leuzinger HS; Lawndale, CA; (3); Science Clb; Medieval Hstry Europe & Japan; Villoation Mst Ordered Systms; Roman Empire Stud; UCLA.

OLIVO, GEORGE; Bell Gardens HS; Bell Gardens, CA; (2); Letterman Clb; Var Capt Bsbl; Var Ftbl; Hon Roll.

OLKOWSKI, BRIAN; Desert HS; North Edwards, CA; (2); Boy Scts; FBLA; Var Math Tm; Band; Mrchg Band; Co-Ed Nwsp; Sec Frsh Cls; Sec Soph Cls; Sec Jr Cls; Var JV Trk; MVP JV Trk; CSF.

OLKOWSKI, STEVEN M; Desert HS; North Edwards, CA; (3); FBLA; Library Aide; Math Tm; Var Ftbl; High Hon Roll; Hon Roll; CSF; Mathletes Ltr; Pres Clsrm; Bnk Amer Awd Math; UC Santa Barbara; Mech Engrng.

OLLANO, OLIVER H; Bishop Amat Memorial HS; Chino Hills, CA; (3); Church Yth Grp; Cmnty Wkr; Dance Clb; Band; Jazz Band; Mrchg Band; Pep Band; Variety Show; Intrml Trk; Intrml Vllybl; 3rd & 1st Pl Awds Schl Tlnt Shows 89, 90; UC Irvine; Math/Sci.

OLLAR, BRIAN; Orestimba HS; Newman, CA; (3); Pres Church Yth Grp; Treas SADD; Treas Frsh Cls; Treas Soph Cls; Pres Jr Cls; JV Ftbl; Hon Roll; ROP Stdt Advsry; JR Ldrshp; Peer Hlpg Prog; Chld Psych.

OLLOM, JASON; Redlands HS; Redlands, CA; (2); Letterman Clb; Varsity Clb; Var L Ftbl; Var L Socr; Var L Trk; Var Wt Lftg; Hon Roll; Fireman.

OLMEDA, GUILLERMINA; San Pedro HS; San Pedro, CA; (4); Science Clb; Knights Hnor Soc; Sex Equity Essy Cntst Wnnr; Art Wrk In USC Art Show; U Southern CA; Frnsc Sci.

OLMOS, CAROLINA; Roosevelt HS; Los Angeles, CA; (3); Lawyer.

OLMOS, HILARIA; Hiram Johnson HS; Sacramento, CA; (3); 26/120; Drama Clb; Latin Clb; Office Aide; ROTC; Science Clb; Spanish Clb; MESA; Crmnl Just.

OLMSTED, CHRISTINE; Fred C Beyer HS; Modesto, CA; (3); SADD; Hon Roll; Bus.

OLOMI, GHANI; Itiwanda HS; Rancho Cuccamonga, CA; (2); Bsktbl; Swmmng; Hon Roll; Med.

OLOW, JENNIFER C; Mount Miguel HS; Lemon Grove, CA; (4); 29/452; Church Yth Grp; Cmnty Wkr; GAA; Hosp Aide; Office Aide; Pep Clb; Orch; Lit Mag; Capt Var Sftbl; Capt Var Tennis; CSFLCA Schlrshp Fndtn; Rep US Tour Of Scotland England 88; FL ST U; Bus.

OLPOC, RICHARD; Redlands HS; Loma Linda, CA; (3); Band; JV Ftbl; Var Wt Lftg; JV Wrstlng; Hon Roll; Prfct Atten Awd; Automotive/Mechanic; Audio; Elec Engrng.

OLSA, SUEANN; La Serna HS; Whittier, CA; (1); 108/400; Church Yth Grp; Girl Scts; Latin Clb; Math Clb; Pep Clb; Drill Tm; JV Cheerldng; Stat Gym; Var Score Keeper; Cit Awd; Jobs Dghtrs; USC; Acctng.

OLSEN, AMY C; East Union HS; Manteca, CA; (2); Band; Mrchg Band; Pep Band; VP Frsh Cls; JV Bsbl; Peace Officer.

OLSEN, AVERY APRIL; Helix HS; Lemon Grove, CA; (2); 37/461; Church Yth Grp; Hosp Aide; JV Diving; JV Swmmng; BYU; Fshn Dsgn.

OLSEN, BRETT C; Bonita HS; La Verne, CA; (4); 9/302; Art Clb; Model UN; Cit Awd; Hon Roll; Jr NHS; Pres Schlr; Natl Yng Ldrs Conf 90; Bank Of Amer Achvt Awd Soc Stud 90; Acadc Dcthln 88-89; CA ST U Chico; Intl Rltns.

OLSEN, CARA; Hemet HS; Hemet, CA; (4); 3/518; Am Leg Aux Girls St; Church Yth Grp; French Clb; Quiz Bowl; VP Frsh Cls; Rep Soph Cls; DAR Awd; High Hon Roll; Ntl Merit Ltr; Opt Clb Awd; Royl Acad Dancing Ballet Exmntns; Sndy Schl Teacher; CA Poly San Luis Obispo; Art.

OLSEN, CHAD; Merced HS; Merced, CA; (3); Sec Drama Clb; Service Clb; Thesps; Treas Orch; School Musical; School Play; Lit Mag; Sec Stu Cncl; High Hon Roll; Natl Guild Piano Teacher Stu Auditions Super Rtng Natl Wnnr; Merced Symphony Orch Schlrshp Awd; U Of CA; Commnctns.

OLSEN, DANIEL S; Poly HS; Riverside, CA; (1); Band; Jazz Band; Mrchg Band; Pep Band; Hon Roll; Pres Acad Fit Awd; Comps.

OLSEN, JENNIFER D; Casa Grande HS; Petaluma, CA; (2); 47/295; Church Yth Grp; Ski Clb; Church Choir; Var Crs Cntry; Stat Vllybl; Hon Roll; NHS; UC Davis; Horticulture.

OLSEN, JESSE DALE; Monte Vista HS; Lemon Grove, CA; (3); Boy Scts; Church Yth Grp; Math Clb; Math Tm; Mu Alpha Theta; Science Clb; Elks Awd; High Hon Roll; Hon Roll; Eagle Sct; BYU; Comp Prgmr.

OLSEN, JOSHUA D; Monterey HS; Monterey, CA; (3); Boy Scts; Teachers Aide; Yrbk; Hon Roll; Cal Poly San Luis; Arch.

OLSEN, KERRY L; Orestimba HS; Newman, CA; (2); Pep Clb; SADD; Color Guard; Flag Corp; VP Frsh Cls; VP Soph Cls; JV Cheerldng; JV Score Keeper; JV Vllybl; Hon Roll; Modesto JC; Psych.

OLSEN, KRIS R; Temecula Valley HS; Rancho, CA; (2); 3/370; Boy Scts; Pres Church Yth Grp; Ski Clb; Varsity Clb; Hon Roll; JV Bsbl; JV Bsktbl; JV Var Ftbl; Wt Lftg; Hnrs The Golden St Exam Geo; Sch Ath Of Yr; UC Berkeley; Math.

OLSEN, KRISTIN; Modesto HS; Modesto, CA; (2); Pres Church Yth Grp; Cmnty Wkr; Acpl Chr; Church Choir; Nwsp; Vllybl; High Hon Roll; Mock Trial Piano-Cert Of Merit State Cnvntn Natl Guild CSF; Law.

OLSEN, NICOLE; Mojave HS; California City, CA; (3); #4 In Class; Church Yth Grp; German Clb; Letterman Clb; Office Aide; Teachers Aide; Temple Yth Grp; Chorus; Var Sftbl; JV Var Vllybl; Jr NHS; CA Schrlshp Fed; Bus.

OLSEN, SANDRA D; Analy HS; Sebastopol, CA; (3); Band; Jazz Band; Mrchg Band; Pep Band; Var JV Bsktbl; Var Socr; JV Var Sftbl; JV Vllybl; Hon Roll; Math Awd; MVP Bsktbl; 2nd Pl SCL Soccr; Aviatn.

OLSEN, TROY V; Rio Linda SR HS; Rio Linda, CA; (3); Boy Scts; Cmnty Wkr; Computer Clb; FFA; ROTC; Hon Roll; Color Guard; Drill Tm; CA Cadet Corps CA ST Commander; Civil Air Patrol; Rifle Team; Hnr Guards; Drill Teams; USMA; Sci.

OLSKY, GREGORY N; Arcadia HS; Arcadia, CA; (2); Office Aide; Teachers Aide; JV Bsbl; JV Socr; Hon Roll.

OLSON, AMANDA J; Canyon HS; Canyon Country, CA; (1); Church Yth Grp; Hon Roll; Babysitting; Swimming.

OLSON, AMY S; Analy HS; Sebastopol, CA; (2); Church Yth Grp; Varsity Clb; Nwsp; JV Bsktbl; JV VP Sftbl; JV VP Vllybl; Hon Roll; Wrkng With Hndcppd Chldrn; CSF; CIF Schlr Athl; OR ST U; Chld Dev.

OLSON, EARL T; Capistrano Valley HS; Mission Viejo, CA; (3); Church Yth Grp; Letterman Clb; Science Clb; Ski Clb; Score Keeper; Vllybl; Wt Lftg; Cit Awd; Hon Roll; Jr Hnr Escort; Arch.

OLSON, ELIZABETH D; Coast Union HS; Cambria, CA; (2); AFS; Church Yth Grp; Ski Clb; Spanish Clb; Var Bsktbl; JV Sftbl; JV Vllybl; High Hon Roll; Cert Excl Art/Math Awd.

OLSON, ERIC C; Grossmont HS; La Mesa, CA; (3); Off Debate Tm; Pres Drama Clb; Key Clb; NFL; Capt Quiz Bowl; Off Speech Tm; School Play; Rptr Nwsp; Rep Stu Cncl; Hon Roll; Theatre.

OLSON, ERICA C; Nevada Union HS; Nevada City, CA; (1); Church Yth Grp; Chorus; JV Bsktbl; JV Socr; Hon Roll; Prncpls Schlr Athl Awd; Stock Brkr.

OLSON, EVAN D; Morro Bay HS; Los Osos, CA; (3); 17/238; Church Yth Grp; Band; Jazz Band; Mrchg Band; Pep Band; Intrml Bsbl; JV Socr; JV Tennis; High Hon Roll; Csf.

OLSON, JENNIFER N; Magnolia HS; Anaheim, CA; (1); Band; Color Guard; Flag Corp; Mrchg Band; Orch; Atty At Law.

OLSON, JOHN D; Bishop O'dowd HS; Oakland, CA; (4); 6/226; Pres Stu Cncl; JV Ftbl; High Hon Roll; Ntl Merit SF; St Schlr; Chptr Pres Jr Stsmn Amer; Princetn Bk Awd-Acadc Excllnc, Extrcrrclr Achvt, Prsnl Chrctr; Euchrst Mnstr; U Of Chicago; Law.

OLSON, JULIE; Santana HS; El Cajon, CA; (4); 132/560; Letterman Clb; Office Aide; Teachers Aide; Varsity Clb; Nwsp; JV Var Bsktbl; Hon Roll; Del Mar 4 Photo Awd 1st, 3rd, 2 4th Places; Outstndng Achvt Photo 2 Yrs; Mission Bay Career Ctr; Trvl.

OLSON, KARA D; East Union HS; Richland, WA; (3); Church Yth Grp; Temple Yth Grp; Variety Show; High Hon Roll; Hon Roll; Prfct Atten Awd; Piano; Brigham Yng U; Math.

OLSON, KAREN; Ponderosa HS; Shingle Springs, CA; (4); 2/280; Church Yth Grp; Speech Tm; Band; Church Choir; Drm Mjr(t); Mrchg Band; Gov Hon Prg Awd; High Hon Roll; Lion Awd; Opt Clb Awd; Oxnard Coll; Law.

OLSON, KATHERINE; Summerville Union HS; Sonora, CA; (2); Church Yth Grp; 4-H; Teachers Aide; 4-H Awd; High Hon Roll; Hon Roll; Pres Acad Fit Awd; FIRE Inst Christn Disciple Ship Trng; Bethany Bible Coll.

OLSON, KENT; Le Lycee Francais De L A HS; Los Angeles, CA; (3); 1/15; German Clb; Spanish Clb; Hnrs Engl, Bio; Adv Plcmnt French; UC Berkley; Bus Adm.

OLSON, KIMBERLY D; Mission Viejo HS; Mission Viejo, CA; (1); Boy Scts; Model UN; Color Guard; Flag Corp; Hon Roll; Intl Baccalaurte; MUN Awd Good Delg ADHOC Cmmtte; CA ST Davis; Vet.

OLSON, KRISTEN; Woodbridge HS; Irvine, CA; (1); 86/427; French Clb; Off Drill Tm; JV Cheerldng; Hon Roll; Dance Jazz Perfrmng Grp, Natl Title Wnnr; Drill Officrs Cmptn 1st Pl.

OLSON, KRISTIN A; Concord HS; Concord, CA; (3); Am Leg Aux Girls St; Mgr Band; Mrchg Band; Var Trk; JV Vllybl; Hon Roll; CSF; Yth Eductr; Dist Hnr Band; San Francisco ST; Bus.

OLSON, LYNETTE C; San Pedro HS; San Pedro, CA; (4); 34/522; Am Leg Aux Girls St; Cmnty Wkr; Rptr Nwsp; Off Jr Cls; Stu Cncl; Var JV Cheerldng; High Hon Roll; Yth & Govt; DARE Speaker; AZ ST U; Commnctns.

OLSON, MARK; Grossmont HS; El Cajon, CA; (1); Bsbl; Socr; 4-H; AZ ST; Arch.

OLSON, MEREDITH L; Aptos HS; Salem, OR; (1); Church Yth Grp; Rep Frsh Cls; Hon Roll; CSF; Piano; Ed.

OLSON, MIKELE C; Hogan HS; Vallejo, CA; (2); Girl Scts; Spanish Clb; Ed Nwsp; Swmmng; Hon Roll; Vrsty Grls MEL Leag Chmpns 88-89 & 89-90; Jrnlsm.

OLSON, MIRA R; El Camino HS; Carmichael, CA; (3); 33/366; Off German Clb; Ski Clb; Var JV Swmmng; Cit Awd; NHS; Var Water Polo; El Caminos Grmn Stu Yr; UCSD; Mrn Bio.

OLSON, PETER A; Redwood Christian HS; Castro Valley, CA; (2); Chess Clb; Church Yth Grp; Chorus; Church Choir; Pres Frsh Cls; JV Bsktbl; JV Socr; JV Trk; Hon Roll; Collect Bsbl Cards; U Of CA Davis; Bio-Chem.

OLSON, RYAN; Francis Parker HS; La Mesa, CA; (1); Church Yth Grp; Cmnty Wkr; Math Tm; VP Frsh Cls; Stu Cncl; JV Bsktbl; JV Ftbl; JV Wrstlng; Hon Roll.

OLSON, SCOTT A; Portola JR SR HS; Portola, CA; (2); Boy Scts; Ftbl; Trk; Wt Lftg; Wrstlng; Hon Roll; USAF Acad; Pilot.

OLSON, SUZANNE M; Grace M Davis HS; Modesto, CA; (4); 6/425; Church Yth Grp; Drama Clb; Science Clb; Cit Awd; Elks Awd; Interact Clb Pres; Acad Dcthln; Sci Olympd; UC Davis; Educ.

OLSON, WILLIAM H; Bellarmine College Prep; San Mateo, CA; (4); 19/306; NFL; Speech Tm; School Musical; School Play; Stage Crew; Ntl Merit SF; Cmmnty Thtre; Theater.

OLSTER, TODD; Edison HS; Huntington Beach, CA; (3); English Clb; Key Clb; Model UN; Science Clb; Off Frsh Cls; Off Jr Cls; Stu Cncl; Bsbl; High Hon Roll; Pres Acad Fit Awd; Stu Envrnmntl Asso SEA Clb.

OLSZEWSKI, DAN M; Poway HS; Poway, CA; (3); Church Yth Grp; Varsity Clb; Bsbl; Ftbl; Wt Lftg; Hon Roll; Fnlst AC Timed Wrtng Cntst; Psych.

OLSZEWSKI, PAUL K; Tomales HS; Tomales, CA; (2); FFA; SADD; Varsity Clb; Off Soph Cls; Bsktbl; Ftbl; Trk; Wt Lftg; MI St; Art.

OLVERA, CESAR O; Mc Farland HS; Mc Farland, CA; (4); 7/130; Am Leg Boys St; Church Yth Grp; FBLA; VICA; Yrbk; Stu Cncl; Cit Awd; Hon Roll; CA ST U Bakersfield; Educ.

OLVERA, KRISTINA; Madera HS; Madera, CA; (2); Intnl Clb; Band; Color Guard; Drm Mjr(t); Jazz Band; Mrchg Band; Pep Band; Variety Show; Hon Roll; Marimba Bnd; Santa Cruz U; Stckbrkng.

OLVERA, LESLEY; Reedley HS; Reedley, CA; (3); Cmnty Wkr; German Clb; Speech Tm; Drm Mjr(t); Pep Band; Pres Frsh Cls; Rep Jr Cls; Score Keeper; High Hon Roll; Pres Acad Fit Awd; HOBY Ldrshp Conf; Schl Rep; Dncr 12 Yrs; Presdntl Clssrm Yng Amer Grad; UC Santa Barbara; Mar Bio.

OLVERA, LUPE; Fontana HS; Fontana, CA; (2); Teachers Aide; Awd Outstndng-Math 90; 3 Poems Pblshd In Schl Bk-From The Heart; Mgr Clthng Store.

OLVERA, TRISTANA; Valley HS; Sacramento, CA; (4); Church Yth Grp; Dance Clb; Science Clb; Rptr Yrbk; Var Capt Cheerldng; JV Var Sftbl; Hon Roll; Math Clb; Mrchg Band; Stds Rchng Out Std Coord; Most Insprtnl Awd Chrldng; Ldrshp Awd; U Of CA Los Angeles.

OMAN, JEANNA R; St Mary's HS; Jacksonville, FL; (2); Church Yth Grp; Cheerldng; Diving; Sftbl; Wt Lftg; Hon Roll; Host Intl Ed Frm Stu From France 90; Ballet Stu & Prfrmr 81-90; U N FL; Comp Sci.

OMAPAS, JUDY; Lemoore HS; Lemoore, CA; (3); Art Clb; Church Yth Grp; Pep Clb; Sec Spanish Clb; Sec Soph Cls; Sec Jr Cls; Sec Sr Cls; JV Var Cheerldng; Var Trk; Hon Roll; Miss Filipino-Amer Kings Cnty 88-90.

OMER, LEAH A; Granada Hills HS; Granada Hills, CA; (4); 112/650; Church Yth Grp; Pres VP Girl Scts; Capt L Bsktbl; JV Var Sftbl; DAR Awd; Hon Roll; Ephebian Soc; Alilene Christian U; Bus Admin.

OMO, JENNIFER; Mojave HS; California City, CA; (2); Girl Scts; Spanish Clb; Band; Flag Corp; Mrchg Band; Pep Band; High Hon Roll; Hon Roll; Pres Acad Fit Awd.

OMS, THERESA M; St Genevieve HS; Van Nuys, CA; (2); Computer Clb; GAA; Letterman Clb; Pep Clb; School Play; Rep Soph Cls; JV Sftbl; High Hon Roll; Hon Roll; U Of CA San Diego; Psych.

OMURA, THAD; Los Altos HS; Los Altos, CA; (3); 18/530; High Hon Roll; Off Jr Cls; VP Sr Cls; Var Wrstlng; Intl Karate Wnnr 2nd Pl 88, 1st Pl 89; Stanford; Engrng.

ON, MARINA; Homestead HS; Sunnyvale, CA; (3); 1/383; Art Clb; Church Yth Grp; Computer Clb; FBLA; Hosp Aide; Intnl Clb; Sec Math Clb; Treas Red Cross Aide; Service Clb; Teachers Aide; Green & White Awd In Comp; CA Schlrshp Fed.

ONA, OLIVER A; Bonita Vista HS; Bonita, CA; (1); JV Bsbl; Cit Awd; Jr NHS; Prfct Atten Awd; Comp; Comp Engr.

ONDO, JENNI; Antioch HS; Antioch, CA; (4); 33/630; Drama Clb; Letterman Clb; Mu Alpha Theta; Pep Clb; Teachers Aide; Drill Tm; School Play; Sec Stu Cncl; Cheerldng; Hon Roll; 2nd Pl Essay Cont; Tutor; U CA Davis; Teaching.

ONG, ADELINE; Redlands HS; Loma Linda, CA; (2); Key Clb; Spanish Clb; Chorus; High Hon Roll; Pres Acad Fit Awd; Rotary Awd.

ONG, ARNELA F; Valley View HS; Moreno Valley, CA; (2); Yrbk; Cit Awd; High Hon Roll; Prfct Atten Awd; Pres Acad Fit Awd.

ONG, ASHLEY C; Montgomery HS; San Diego, CA; (2); 37/594; Chorus; Variety Show; Prfct Atten Awd; Pres Acad Fit Awd; Southwestern Coll; Med Doc.

ONG, BENSON; Woodrow Wilson HS; San Francisco, CA; (3); ROTC; Band; Drill Tm; Tennis; Hon Roll; Elec Engrng.

ONG, CATHERINE Y; Galileo HS; San Francisco, CA; (3); French Clb; Pep Clb; Chorus; Phtg Nwsp; Off Frsh Cls; Off Soph Cls; Off Jr Cls; Hist Sr Cls; DAR Awd; Hon Roll; Emerson Boston MA; Commnctns.

ONG, CUONG D; San Gabriel HS; Monterey Park, CA; (4); 202/737; FBLA; Key Clb; Office Aide; Varsity Clb; Bsktbl; Crs Cntry; Score Keeper; Swmmng; Cit Awd; Hon Roll; Cal ST Poly Pomony.

ONG, DAO; Sierra Vista HS; Baldwin Park, CA; (1); Math Clb; Hon Roll; Prfct Atten Awd; UCLA; Nrs.

ONG, DAT V; Mark Keppel HS; San Gabriel, CA; (3); Debate Tm; VP French Clb; Key Clb; Math Clb; Science Clb; Chorus; Tennis; Cit Awd; French Hon Soc; High Hon Roll; Fltwd Assn Awd; CA U Sn Fran; Med.

ONG, DAVID H; Mount Diablo HS; Concord, CA; (3); 1/273; FBLA; Ski Clb; Spanish Clb; Var Tennis; High Hon Roll; Prfct Atten Awd; CSF; Asian Club Treas; UC Davis; Plstc Srgn.

ONG, ELISA; John F Kennedy SR HS; Sacramento, CA; (4); Rptr Sec FBLA; Sec Treas Math Clb; Math Tm; Spanish Clb; Speech Tm; Teachers Aide; Sec Lit Mag; Hon Roll; Ntl Merit SF; Solo Wth Scrmnto Sypmny-Wnnr-Yng Artst 88-89; Solo Wth Chico Symphny-Wnnr-Yng Artst 87.

ONG, ELIZABETH S; Workman HS; West Covina, CA; (3); Church Yth Grp; Cmnty Wkr; Computer Clb; Dance Clb; Drama Clb; French Clb; GAA; Intnl Clb; Key Clb; Letterman Clb; Comp.

ONG, ERIC; Rosemead HS; Rosemead, CA; (3); 2/40; UCLA; Bio.

ONG, JANE; San Pedro High Marine Sci Magnet; Carson, CA; (4); #16 In Class; Cmnty Wkr; Sec Science Clb; Lbrn Chorus; Variety Show; Var Tennis; Wt Lftg; Cit Awd; High Hon Roll; Prfct Atten Awd; Gld Seal Bearer; Merit Awd Outstndg Achvt Marine Sci Studies; Outstng Stu Ctznshp Annl Rcgntn; CSU Dominguez Hills; Bus Admin.

ONG, JOHANNA; Ulysses S Grant HS; Palmdale, CA; (4); 1/611; Cmnty Wkr; Debate Tm; Service Clb; Speech Tm; Temple Yth Grp; VP Frsh Cls; High Hon Roll; Hon Roll; Pres Acad Fit Awd; CA Schlrshp Fe Sec; Knights & Ladies Sec SR Hnr/Svc Club; Mock Trial Tm; UCLA; Engl.

ONG, KATHY L; Lowell HS; San Francisco, CA; (3); Q&S; Rep Red Cross Aide; Science Clb; High Hon Roll; Swmmng; Ice Sktng; Goldn St Exm Hgh Hnrs Math, Alg & Geom; U Of CA; Bio.

ONG, LEE-SHYAN; Mira Mesa HS; San Diego, CA; (3); French Clb; Science Clb; Powder Puff Ftbl; Cit Awd; Hon Roll; Peer Cnslng; Teens Helping Other Teen Clb; CSF; UCSD; Pharmacy.

ONG, NEWTON W; Saint Ignatius College Prep; San Francisco, CA; (3); 126/260; Cmnty Wkr; Ed Yrbk; Hon Roll; Recycling Clb; U CA Davis; Civil Engrng.

ONG, PHAT V; Edison HS; Huntington Beach, CA; (2); Quiz Bowl; Scholastic Bowl; JV Tennis; NHS; CSF; Orange Cty Acad Decathlon; Geom Golden Key Nom; U CA Irvine; Medcl.

ONG, SHARON B; Oakland HS; San Leandro, CA; (3); French Clb; Pres SADD; Ed Nwsp; VP Soph Cls; Sftbl; Co-Capt Swmmng; Vllybl; Hon Roll; Japan Town Asian Short Story Cmptn 1st Pl 88; Golden St Schlr; Jrnlsm.

ONG, WINSON; Woodrow Wilson HS; San Francisco, CA; (3); ROTC; Band; Drill Tm; Tennis; High Hon Roll; Golden St Exam Alg High Hnrs, Geom Hnrs; UC Davis; Med.

ONGACO, ALEXIS; Bishop Amat Memorial HS; Whittier, CA; (4); Cmnty Wkr; Teachers Aide; Trk; High Hon Roll; Hon Roll; NHS; Prfct Atten Awd; Rcgntn For Wrk Done In Spcl Olympics 87; Cmnty Wrk For Delhaven Cmnty Ctr Awd 86; CA Schlrshp Fed 89; U C Riverside; Med.

ONGWISETH, NIPITH; Western Christian HS; Walnut, CA; (3); Rep Frsh Cls; Var Crs Cntry; Var Swmmng; JV Tennis; Var JV Trk; Hon Roll; Arch.

ONGYOD, ALVIN D; Willow Glen Educational Park HS; San Jose, CA; (2); Hon Roll; Pres Acad Fit Awd; Natl Geog Reporter.

ONISHI, MARC; Christian Brothers HS; Sacramento, CA; (3); 2/110; Pres Computer Clb; German Clb; Math Clb; School Play; Treas Soph Cls; Treas Jr Cls; Stat Bsktbl; High Hon Roll; NHS; Signum Fidei; CA Schlrshp Fdrtn; Deptmntl Hnrs-Mthmtcs; Sci.

ONISHI, SCOTT; Christian Brothers HS; Sacramento, CA; (3); 15/100; Computer Clb; German Clb; Math Tm; Red Cross Aide; SADD; School Play; Sec Jr Cls; Var Stat Bsktbl; Hon Roll; NHS; Engrng.

ONKEN, MATTHEW S; Las Plumas HS; Oroville, CA; (1); 16/249; Church Yth Grp; Ski Clb; Mrchg Band; Orch; Pep Band; Tennis; Hon Roll; Nazarene Bible Quiz Team; Civil Air Ptrl; USAF Acad; Prfssnl Engr.

ONKHAM, YUON; Wilson HS; Long Beach, CA; (2); JV Socr; JV Prfct Atten Awd; Asian Club; Elec Tech.

ONO, TAKUMA; Bonita Vista HS; Bonita, CA; (2); Ftbl; Wt Lftg; FBLA; Wt Lftg; Wrstlng; Cit Awd; Vet.

ONSTOT, JUSTIN; Springs Of Living Water Acad; Chico, CA; (4); VP Church Yth Grp; Band; Chorus; Yrbk; Var Bsktbl; Trk; High Hon Roll; Prfct Atten Awd; Pres Acad Fit Awd.

ONSUM, SHALOME; Fort Bragg HS; Fort Bragg, CA; (3); Art Clb; Church Yth Grp; Pep Clb; GAA; SADD; Sec Jr Cls; Rep Stu Cncl; JV Crs Cntry; JV Sftbl; Hon Roll; Peer Cnslng & Latchkey Vol For Daycare; Jr Partner Big Bro/Sisters & Bowl For Kids Sake; Swim Team; Boulder U Denver; Schl Pysch.

ONTIVEROS, DIANA; Lincoln HS; Los Angeles, CA; (3); Church Yth Grp; Church Choir; Drill Tm; Cit Awd; High Hon Roll; Hon Roll; Educ.

ONTIVEROS, ELSA; El Cajon Valley HS; El Cajon, CA; (3); Spnsh Club; Gymnstcs.

ONTIVEROS, JOSE A; Canyon HS; Monrovia, CA; (4); Art Clb; Drama Clb; Nwsp; Yrbk; Rep Sr Cls; Stu Cncl; Ftbl; Rotary Awd; ITT Tech Inst; Comp.

OOSTERHUIS, ROBERT J; Santa Barbara HS; Santa Barbara, CA; (2); 1/450; Math Tm; Intrml Bsbl; JV Capt Bsktbl; Var Capt Golf; High Hon Roll; Pro Golfer.

OPENA, MARILEN T; Arlington HS; Riverside, CA; (2); Art Clb; Teachers Aide; Cit Awd; Hon Roll; Prfct Atten Awd; Comp Sci.

OPHASO, PHITHOUN; Buena Park HS; Fullerton, CA; (3); Computer Clb; High Hon Roll; Hon Roll; Span Cert Of Rcgntn; Prfct Attnd; Distngshd Schlrs Awd.

OPPELT, SARAH D; Dana Hills HS; San Juan Capistrn, CA; (1); Stu Cncl; JV Crs Cntry; JV Trk; Law.

OQUENDO, VICTOR S; Colton HS; Colton, CA; (1); Ftbl; Intrml Wt Lftg; JV Wrstlng; Riverside CC.

ORAM, SUZY Y; Alameda HS; Alameda, CA; (4); 46/325; Cmnty Wkr; Ski Clb; School Musical; Nwsp; Rep Frsh Cls; Pres Soph Cls; Off Jr Cls; Pres Sr Cls; Stu Cncl; Cheerldng; HOBY Fndtn Schl Ldrshp Rep; CASC; Prncpls Ldrshp Awd 90; DAR Awd 90; Sci.

ORANGES, CANDACE C; St Mary's HS; Stockton, CA; (2); Church Yth Grp; Dance Clb; Key Clb; SADD; Drill Tm; School Musical; School Play; High Hon Roll; Hon Roll; CSF; Awd Of Achvt Frnch; Acadmc Hnrs Awd.

ORAVETZ, PAULA M; Yucca Valley HS; Morongo Valley, CA; (3); Church Yth Grp; Office Aide; Band; Jazz Band; Mrchg Band; Orch; Pep Band; School Musical; Stage Crew; Vllybl; Univ Clb; John Philip Sousa Awd; Natl Pioneer Ministries Awd, Awana Timothy Awd; San Diego ST U; Music.

ORAYANI, CECILIA; St Joseph HS; Long Beach, CA; (4); 46/173; Cmnty Wkr; Drama Clb; Key Clb; Science Clb; Service Clb; Spanish Clb; SADD; Chorus; School Musical; Hon Roll; CA ST U-Long Beach; Nrsng.

ORBAI, ALEXANDRU; Grace Davis HS; Modesto, CA; (2); Band; Physician.

ORBE, PHILIPP T; Gardena HS; Gardena, CA; (3); JA; Service Clb; Essay Cont Hnr Mntn-Imprtnce Values In Amer Soc, 1st Pl -An Ideal Education; Acad Clb Of Excel; U Of Sthrn CA; Aeronaut Engrng.

ORBEGOSO, MARCOS L; Boron HS; Boron, CA; (3); Letterman Clb; Varsity Clb; Rptr Yrbk; Var L Ftbl; High Hon Roll; Hon Roll; CSF 88-90; AZ ST.

ORCHANIAN, LARA A; Pasadena HS; Pasadena, CA; (2); Church Yth Grp; SADD; Church Choir; Bsktbl; Hon Roll; AYF; Youth Choir; ACSI; Speech Meet 1st Pl Dramatic Poetry; UCLA; Pediatrician.

ORCHOLSKI, KYMBERLY A; Bishop Amat Memorial HS; Hacienda Hts, CA; (4); Cmnty Wkr; Drama Clb; School Play; Rptr Nwsp; Var Tennis; Mem Nture Cnsrvncy 2 Yrs; Englsh.

ORCUTT, LORENA R; Hoopa HS; Hoopa, CA; (3); Cmnty Wkr; Key Clb; Science Clb; SADD; Band; Var Bsktbl; JV Powder Puff Ftbl; Var Sftbl; Var Trk; Cit Awd; Stus Exhibiting Common Sense-SECS Clb; CA Maritime Acad; Mech Engrng.

ORDANZA, GERALD F; Mt Pleasant HS; San Jose, CA; (2); SADD; Tennis; Var Wrstlng; Hon Roll; NHS; Cycling; Radio Cntrl Cars; San Jose ST U; Elec Engr.

ORDAZ, EDGAR; Mountain View HS; El Monte, CA; (1); Intrml Trk.

ORDAZ, SERAFINA; Andrew P Hill HS; San Jose, CA; (2); Acpl Chr; Stage Crew.

ORDENANA, M EILEEN; Moreau HS; Newark, CA; (4); Church Yth Grp; Cmnty Wkr; Key Clb; SADD; Stat Bsktbl; Hon Roll; UC Santa Barbara.

ORDINOLA, GINA; San Gabriel HS; Rosemead, CA; (2); Teachers Aide; Mgr(s); Score Keeper; Hon Roll.

ORDIZ, MELEAH V; Blair HS; Pasadena, CA; (3); Chess Clb; Church Yth Grp; Cmnty Wkr; JA; Office Aide; Service Clb; Chorus; Rptr Lit Mag; Var Socr.

ORDONEZ, ARIEL M; Servite HS; Cypress, CA; (3); Church Yth Grp; Cmnty Wkr; Debate Tm; Letterman Clb; Red Cross Aide; Ski Clb; Varsity Clb; Var Ftbl; NHS.

ORDONEZ, DAHLIA A; Southwest HS; San Diego, CA; (3); Library Aide; Teachers Aide; Vllybl; Hon Roll; CSF; A-Team; Cmnty Vllybl; UCSD; Bus.

ORDONEZ, MARGARET; Vista HS; Vista, CA; (4); Var JV Fld Hcky; Hon Roll; Ntl Merit SF; Natl Frnch Exam Lvls I & II Hnrbl Mntn; U Of CA Berkeley.

ORDUNA, JOSE; Saddleback HS; Santa Ana, CA; (4); 44/500; Latin Clb; Spanish Clb; Band; Mrchg Band; VP Swmmng; Var Capt Water Polo; UC Berkeley; Psych.

ORDUNA, RODRIGO; Saddleback HS; Santa Ana, CA; (3); Church Yth Grp; Band; Mrchg Band; Pep Band; School Musical; Hon Roll; CSF Clb; UCI Partners Clb; Math, Engrng, Sci & Arts Clb; UC Berkeley; Arch.

ORDUNO, JOSE; South West HS; San Diego, CA; (4); 7/498; JA; Teachers Aide; Church Choir; Cit Awd; Hon Roll; Prfct Atten Awd; Rotary Awd; U Of San Diego; Crmnl Law.

ORDUNO, LIBRADO; Southwest HS; San Diego, CA; (3); History Fr; USD; Law.

OREFICE, ANGELA C; Arroyo Grande HS; Arroyo Grande, CA; (2); Church Yth Grp; Key Clb; Crs Cntry; Var L Crs Cntry; L Var Trk; Wt Lftg; Cit Awd; Hon Roll; Vet.

OREFICE, GINA M; Arroyo Grande HS; Arroyo Grande, CA; (2); Church Yth Grp; Key Clb; Var Bsktbl.

OREGEL, CESAR; Leuzinger HS; Inglewood, CA; (2); Band; Jazz Band; Mrchg Band; Spanish NHS; Law Enfrcmnt.

OREGON, CECILIA; San Gabriel Mission HS; Los Angeles, CA; (4); 23/108; Art Clb; GAA; Stage Crew; VP Stu Cncl; Var Crs Cntry; Var Trk; Cit Awd; Hon Roll; NHS; Prfct Atten Awd; U CA-BERKELEY; Bio.

ORELLANA, JOHANNA K; Holy Family Girls HS; Los Angeles, CA; (3); Art Clb; Drama Clb; School Play; Stage Crew; U Of S CA; Engr.

ORELLANA, LESLIE L; Westmoor HS; Daly City, CA; (3); Debate Tm; French Clb; SADD; Hon Roll; Treas Frsh Cls; Pres Sr Cls; Stu Cncl; Amnesty Intl Grp Ldr Of HS Chapter; Westmoors Interest Saving Habitat; Coll Centrnc Clb.

ORENYAK, KIMBERLY L; Chino HS; Chino, CA; (1); Hon Roll; Schl Flag Team; Psych.

OREWYLER, CHRISTINE R; Mayfair HS; Lakewood, CA; (1); Church Yth Grp; GAA; VP Soph Cls; JV Tennis; Hon Roll; Eng Hndbll Choir Natl Fine Arts; Supr Rtng Fest 89; UC-IRVINE; Psych.

ORGAN, MARLEE S; Schurr HS; Monterey Park, CA; (1); Church Yth Grp; Band; Church Choir; Mrchg Band; JV L Bsktbl; Hon Roll; Maccabi Jr Olympics; CA Girls Bsktbl Tm Mem; Bass Clarinet-Marching Band; Rookie Of Yr Girls Bsktbl; Long Beach ST; Phys Thrpy.

ORGIS, LORI; Cypress HS; Seaside, CA; (3); Computer Clb; Library Aide; Office Aide; Ed Nwsp; Stu Cncl; High Hon Roll; Teen Outreach Pgm; Teen Parents Grp; Peer Cnslr.

ORITI, LAURA E; Analy HS; Sebastopol, CA; (4); French Clb; Teachers Aide; Acpl Chr; Band; Chorus; Jazz Band; Mrchg Band; Pep Band; School Musical; Variety Show; Cal ST Northridge; Music.

ORLANDI, GIUSEPPE L; George Washington HS; Giuseppe, CA; (3); Church Yth Grp; German Clb; Chorus; Hon Roll; Elec Music; Fencng, Archery, Hunting; Comp Tech; San Francisco City Coll; Bus.

ORLANDO, KRISTIN E; Louisville HS; Canoga Park, CA; (1); Church Yth Grp; Drama Clb; Chorus; Stage Crew; Hon Roll; Phys Sci Awd; UCLA; Dr.

ORLANDO, TABITHA E; Woodside HS; Woodside, CA; (2); Rep Soph Cls; Pres Acad Fit Awd.

ORMAN, BRANDON H; Orange Lutheran HS; Santa Ana, CA; (2); Var L Ftbl; Var L Trk; Wt Lftg; Var L Wrstlng; Prfct Atten Awd; Bus.

ORMEROD, JENNIFER; Monterey Bay Acad; Santa Cruz, CA; (3); Art Clb; Church Yth Grp; Drama Clb; Teachers Aide; Acpl Chr; Chorus; School Musical; School Play; Variety Show; Phtg Yrbk; CA Poly-Tech; Arch.

ORMONDE, CLAIRE D; Irvington HS; Fremont, CA; (2); 32/400; Church Yth Grp; Var Socr; Var Sftbl; Var Vllybl; Advrtsmt Chrch Yth Grp; U Of Pacific; Phrmcst.

ORMONDE, TONY; Hilmar HS; Hilmar, CA; (1); Intrml Art Clb; Intrml Ftbl; Intrml Wt Lftg; Var Wrstlng; Hon Roll.

ORMSBEE, MIKI F; College Park HS; Pleasant Hill, CA; (3); Cmnty Wkr; VP French Clb; Intnl Clb; Hon Roll; Attnd Japanese Schl 4 Yrs; UC Davis; Intl Rel.

ORMSETH, SARA R; Irvine HS; Irvine, CA; (3); 34/624; Church Yth Grp; Capt Dance Clb; Drama Clb; Ski Clb; Capt Chorus; School Musical; Variety Show; Rep Stu Cncl; Hon Roll; UCI; Prfrmng Arts.

ORNDORFF, JILL D; Don Lugo HS; Chino, CA; (3); Teachers Aide; High Hon Roll; Hon Roll.

ORNELAS, JEANNINE; Sequoia HS; San Mateo, CA; (4); 27/350; CA Poly-San Luis Obispo; Arch.

ORNELAS, LENEL H; Ventura HS; Fillmore, CA; (3); 60/431; L Socr; L Swmmng; High Hon Roll; Hnr Court; Dsgnr.

ORNTA, VONG P; Fresno HS; Fresno, CA; (2); Church Yth Grp; Math Tm; Church Choir; Cit Awd; Prfct Atten Awd; Fresno City Coll; Elec Engrng.

ORONA, CYNTHIA; Bassett HS; Los Angeles, CA; (4); Dance Clb; Off Sr Cls; Cit Awd; Hon Roll; Jr NHS; NHS; Spanish NHS; Mt St Marys Coll; Psych.

ORONA, MARTIN; San Gabriel HS; San Gabriel, CA; (1); Church Yth Grp; Temple Yth Grp; Bsktbl; Vllybl; Athl Awd Of Honor; Peer Cnslr; Medicine.

ORONA, NICHOLE R; Analy HS; Sebastopol, CA; (4); 129/215; Library Aide; Spanish Clb; Band; Cheerldng; JV Powder Puff Ftbl; Var Tennis; Hon Roll; Grad Modelng Schl; Santa Rosa JC; Law.

OROPEZA, ARCELIA; Artesia HS; Hawaiian Gardens, CA; (1); Police Ofcr.

OROPEZA, DEBORAH; Brethren HS; Bellflower, CA; (4); 3/70; Church Yth Grp; Math Tm; Orch; Nwsp; Elks Awd; High Hon Roll; Sal; Robert C Byrd Hnrs Schlr; Biolo U.

OROPEZA, PATRICIA D; Needles HS; Needles, CA; (2); Chorus; JV Var Sftbl; Cit Awd; CA Schlstc Fdr; Psychlgy.

OROPILLA, VICKYMAY V; Mira Mesa HS; San Diego, CA; (2); Church Yth Grp; Cmnty Wkr; French Clb; Hosp Aide; Chorus; Church Choir; U Of CA San Diego; Pdtrcn.

OROS, LISSA A; Willow Glen HS; San Jose, CA; (4); Boy Scts; Church Yth Grp; JA; Key Clb; Quiz Bowl; Science Clb; Varsity Clb; Tennis; Trk; YMC Yth In Govt; Mesico Mssnry; SJSU; Molecular Bio.

OROSCO, MARK L; Hanford Union HS; Hanford, CA; (3); FBLA; VP Jr Cls; Bsbl; Bsktbl; Ftbl; Socr; Trk; High Hon Roll; Hon Roll; Jr NHS; MESA Pres.

OROSZ, ANGELINA; Rosemead HS; Rosemead, CA; (3); Intnl Clb; Hon Roll; Ntl Merit Ltr; New Encounters; Cal Poly Pomona; Bus.

OROSZ, STEPHANIE; St Lawrence Acad; Milpitas, CA; (4); 8/26; Cmnty Wkr; Band; Chorus; Rep Soph Cls; Pres Jr Cls; L Var Bsktbl; Var Cheerldng; Var Capt Vllybl; NHS; Rotary Awd; Whittier Coll; Music.

OROZCO, ARACELI; Nogales HS; La Puente, CA; (3); Cit Awd; Hon Roll; Prfct Atten Awd; Nrsng.

OROZCO, BERNADETTE; Montebello HS; Montebello, CA; (4); Drama Clb; Office Aide; Pep Clb; Teachers Aide; Ed Nwsp; JV Var Cheerldng; Hon Roll; 3rd Plc Ftr Wrtng ELA-JEA Write Offs; Stu Of Mnth Eng; Cert Rcgntn Bst Ftr Wrtr; Loyola Marymount U; Cmmnctns.

OROZCO, CLAUDIA; Norte Vista HS; Riverside, CA; (2); Rep Stu Cncl; Cit Awd; Hon Roll; Partnrshp Prgm; U CA Riverside.

OROZCO, GABRIELA; El Rancho HS; Pico Rivera, CA; (2); Drama Clb; Crs Cntry; Trk; Parsons Schl Design; Fashn Dsgn.

OROZCO, LAURA E; Notre Dame Acad; Los Angeles, CA; (3); Cit Awd; Core-Cmps Mnstry; USC; Poly Sci.

OROZCO, LETICIA; Venice HS; Venice, CA; (2); Orch; Yrbk; Vllybl; Athenian; Cathy Moraga Schlrshp; Hnrs In Music & Fr; Boston U; Music.

OROZCO, LUZ M; Sacred Heart Of Jesus HS; Los Angeles, CA; (3); Church Yth Grp; Library Aide; Office Aide; Quiz Bowl; Spanish Clb; Stage Crew; Sec Soph Cls; Pres Jr Cls; VP Stu Cncl; Trk; Attnded Yth Ctznshp Smnr Pepperdine U; Hlth.

OROZCO, MARCOS; Calipatria HS; Calipatria, CA; (3); Am Leg Boys St; Pres Sec Church Yth Grp; Pres FBLA; Speech Tm; SADD; Pres Frsh Cls; Treas Soph Cls; Rep Jr Cls; Rep Stu Cncl; High Hon Roll; Bus.

OROZCO, MARIA D; Castle Park HS; Chula Vista, CA; (1); French Clb; Cit Awd; Pres Acad Fit Awd; GATE Cert; U S Intl U; Intl Bus.

OROZCO, MARIA D; Sierra Vista HS; Baldwin Park, CA; (2); Band; Mrchg Band; Pep Band; CA ST Fullerton; Music.

OROZCO, MIREYA O; Phineas Banning HS; S Gate, CA; (3); Church Yth Grp; Office Aide; Mrchg Band; Variety Show; Rptr Nwsp; Hist Sr Cls; Stu Cncl; B Avg-Hghr Cert, Pin; Chrgrphy; UCLA; Psycht.

OROZCO, MONICA M; Corona HS; Corona, CA; (3); 51/430; Rep Stu Cncl; High Hon Roll; Hon Roll; Pres Acad Fit Awd; Hourando A Nuestras Estrellas; Mecha Club; UC San Diego; Law.

OROZCO, PEDRO; John Glenn HS; Norwalk, CA; (2); 1/300; French Clb; Band; Mrchg Band; Pep Band; Ed Nwsp; Cit Awd; High Hon Roll; NEDT Awd; Prfct Atten Awd; Sci Olympd; Chicano-Latino Yth Ldrshp Conf; Norwalk All-City Yth Band; Carleton Coll.

OROZCO, SONNY R; Alisal HS; Salinas, CA; (2); Ftbl; Wrstlng; High Hon Roll; Hon Roll; Coll Core Currclm; Stu Mnth; Karate; San Jose ST; Tech Engr.

OROZCO, SVEN; Chula Vista HS; Eugene, OR; (2); Boy Scts; Chess Clb; Swmmng; Hon Roll; Upward Bound; Sword & Shld; Hgh Hnrs Gldn ST Rcgntn Geom; OSU; Law.

OROZCO, VALERIE A; Calipatria HS; Calipatria, CA; (4); 2/72; Am Leg Aux Girls St; Pres Church Yth Grp; Treas Drama Clb; FBLA; Math Tm; Treas Pep Clb; Speech Tm; SADD; Sec Frsh Cls; Elks Awd; Assoctd Stu Body-VP, Bus Mgr & Secy; CSF Pres; Volntr-Share Cmmdts Dstrbtr; U Of San Diego; Poly Sci.

ORPHANOS, KATE M; San Marcos HS; San Marcos, CA; (2); Church Yth Grp; Cmnty Wkr; French Clb; Key Clb; Scholastic Bowl; Service Clb; Church Choir; Ed Nwsp; L Var Trk; High Hon Roll; Girls JV Trk MVP; Stu Of Yr Frgn Lang Frnch; North Cnty Acad League Avocado JC Chmpns; Sci.

ORPILLA, JENNIFER; Robert D Edgren HS; Folsom, CA; (4); 12/275; Church Yth Grp; Cmnty Wkr; Computer Clb; Dance Clb; Intnl Clb; Letterman Clb; Office Aide; Pep Clb; Red Cross Aide; Science Clb; Discover Japan Club; Sci Sympsm; U Of CA Berkeley; Aerospc Engr.

ORR, CHRISTIE L; Norte Vista HS; Riverside, CA; (1); Pres Church Yth Grp; Pep Clb; Church Choir; Sec Treas Soph Cls; Co-Capt Cheerldng; Var Swmmng; High Hon Roll; Hon Roll; Swmmr Mnth-Aprl.

ORR, CHRISTOPHER; Tulelake HS; Tulelake, CA; (4); 2/32; School Play; VP Frsh Cls; Pres Soph Cls; Treas Jr Cls; Stu Cncl; L JV Bsbl; L JV Ftbl; High Hon Roll; Sal; Val; CA Polytech Inst; Marine Bio.

ORR, ERICA; San Ramon Valley HS; Alamo, CA; (2); Drill Tm; High Hon Roll; St Schlr.

ORR, JARROD E; Yuba City HS; Yuba City, CA; (4); 5/516; Church Yth Grp; Teachers Aide; Orch; Vllybl; High Hon Roll; Pres Acad Fit Awd; Sal; CA Schlrshp Federation Life Mem; Tandy Schlr; Ambassador Coll; Bus.

ORR, JEFFERY R; Apple Valley HS; Apple Valley, CA; (3); Hon Roll; Opt Clb Awd.

ORR, JODI L; Burroughs HS; Ridgecrest, CA; (3); Church Yth Grp; FBLA; Treas SADD; High Hon Roll; Hon Roll; Dental.

ORR, KATRINA S; San Gorgonio HS; Redlands, CA; (4); VP Computer Clb; FBLA; Office Aide; Chorus; Peer Cnslng; DARE Schlrshp; Smmr Solofest Awd; Child Psych.

ORR, KYMBERLY; El Toro HS; El Toro, CA; (3); 38/470; French Clb; Phtg Yrbk; Intrml Mgr Vllybl; High Hon Roll; World Hstry Excllnce Awd Medal Wnnr; USC; Bus.

ORR, NATHAN; Santa Paula Union HS; Santa Paula, CA; (4); Office Aide; Tennis; High Hon Roll; US Vllybl Assn Team Ojai Vllybl Clb; Surfing; U CA.

ORR, RICHARD C; Hesperia HS; Hesperia, CA; (3); Ftbl; Socr; Hon Roll; CA Jr Schlstc Fed; Law Enfrcmnt.

ORSI, ELIZABETH; University HS; Tiburon, CA; (3); Debate Tm; GAA; Letterman Clb; Service Clb; Spanish Clb; Capt Varsity Clb; Sec Frsh Cls; Sec Soph Cls; Sec Stu Cncl; Capt Var Bsktbl; CSF; Stanford U; Sci.

ORSI, TERRY; Lincoln HS; Stockton, CA; (3); Boy Scts; Key Clb; Science Clb; Spanish Clb; JV Var Socr; JV Trk; Hon Roll; Pres Acad Fit Awd; Annpls Nvl Acad; Avtn.

ORSO, ALBERT; Riverside Poly HS; Riverside, CA; (2); 20/500; Sec Key Clb; School Play; Ed Yrbk; Chrmn Jr Cls; JV Socr; Hon Roll; Kiwanis Awd; Pres Acad Fit Awd; Drama Clb; SADD; CA ST U San Bernandino Poetry Cont Hnrs; Spanish Hnr Soc.

ORT, ALISON R; Poway HS; San Diego, CA; (2); Church Yth Grp; Hosp Aide; Key Clb; Stage Crew; Stat Trk; Hon Roll; Prfct Atten Awd; Pres Acad Fit Awd; Hosp/Spcl Olympcs Volunteer; Bst Typing Stu; Med.

ORTA, ENRIQUE; Cantwell HS; Los Angeles, CA; (4); Cmnty Wkr; Letterman Clb; Library Aide; Spanish Clb; Varsity Clb; Nwsp; JV Var Crs Cntry; JV Trk; Hon Roll; Wopn A To Z Shakespeare Quiz 1st Pl; Ranked 2nd Spanish Class; Christman Party; UCLA; Pre Med.

ORTEGA, ADAN G; Brawley Union HS; Westmorland, CA; (3); Church Yth Grp; Var Bsktbl; Ftbl; Hon Roll; Comp Pgmr.

ORTEGA JR, AGUSTIN; Inglewood HS; Inglewood, CA; (1); Drama Clb; ROTC; Acting.

ORTEGA, ALMA CONCEPCION; Huntington Park HS; Huntington Park, CA; (3); Teachers Aide; Mrchg Band; PREP; Spcl Achvt Awd Bio Cls Fair; Intl Relatns.

ORTEGA, ANTONIO; Hanford Joint Union HS; Hanford, CA; (1); Hon Roll; U CA Berkeley; Ecnmst.

ORTEGA, ANTONIO S; Southwest HS; San Diego, CA; (3); Arch.

ORTEGA, CARLOS; Roosevelt HS; Los Angeles, CA; (4); L Ftbl; L Tennis; Stat Trk; Hon Roll; Schlr Athlt Awd; Alumni Assn Schlrshp & Genesis Wnnr; CSU; Sociolgy.

ORTEGA, CARLOS G; Sunset HS; Hayward, CA; (2); Church Yth Grp; Key Clb; Ftbl; Wt Lftg; Cit Awd; Hon Roll; Pre-Coll Acad UC Brkly; Cvl Air Ptrl Airfrce Axllry; Prtnrshp Pgrm; San Jose ST; Engnrng.

ORTEGA, CHRIS P; Monroe HS; Northridge, CA; (2); Computer Clb; Teachers Aide; Ftbl; Wt Lftg; Hon Roll.

ORTEGA, FLEURDELINE S; Holy Family HS; North Hollywood, CA; (2); Drama Clb; Hon Roll; Med.

ORTEGA, FRANZISKA; Huntington Beach HS; Huntington Beach, CA; (2); Church Yth Grp; Model UN; Service Clb; Hon Roll; Prfct Atten Awd; Psycht.

ORTEGA, GEORGE M; Colton HS; Colton, CA; (1); Aud/Vis; FBLA; Scholastic Bowl; Jazz Band; Nwsp; JV Ftbl; JV Wt Lftg; JV Wrstlng; Hon Roll; NHS; USC; Jrnlsm.

ORTEGA, IMELDA; Sacred Heart HS; Los Angeles, CA; (3); 13/115; Pres Church Yth Grp; Drama Clb; Chorus; School Play; Hon Roll; Prfct Atten Awd; CCD Tchr & Aide; Cal ST; Stwrdss.

ORTEGA, IRENE; Brethren HS; Long Beach, CA; (3); Church Yth Grp; Sec Frsh Cls; Sec Soph Cls; JV Var Sftbl; JV Var Vllybl; Jnr Vrsty Sftbl MVP; Mech Engrng.

ORTEGA, ISABEL M; Eisenhower HS; Rialto, CA; (3); Teachers Aide; Band; Jazz Band; Mrchg Band; Pep Band; Ed Nwsp; Off Sr Cls; Swmmng; Cit Awd; Hon Roll; Miss Interst Natl 1st Rnnr Up 88; Cal ST U; Paralegal.

ORTEGA, JACKIE; San Mateo HS; Foster City, CA; (3); Model UN; Pres Spanish Clb; Color Guard; Flag Corp; Var Bsktbl; JV Gym; JV Socr; JV Var Swmmng; Hon Roll; Amigos De Las Amer Volunteer; Genetic Engrng Clb.

ORTEGA, JAIME; Cantwell HS; Rosemead, CA; (4); 16/53; Art Clb; Drama Clb; Sec Treas Spanish Clb; Thesps; Chorus; School Musical; Rptr Yrbk; Lit Mag; Hon Roll; NHS; CSF; Kairos Retreat Ldr & Asst Dir 90; Gold Seal Bearer; Woodbury U; Int Dsgn.

ORTEGA, JESSICA; Victor Valley HS; Victorville, CA; (3); Church Yth Grp; Office Aide; Red Cross Aide; Drill Tm; UCLA; Comp Pgmng.

ORTEGA JR, JESUS; Hueneme HS; Port Hueneme, CA; (1); Key Clb; JV Ftbl; JV Wt Lftg; Bsktbl; Mth.

ORTEGA, JESUS A; Bell HS; Cudahy, CA; (3); Pres Sr Cls; Ftbl; Hon Roll; Engl.

ORTEGA, JOJET; Hayward HS; Hayward, CA; (2); 69/237; Spanish Clb; Sec Frsh Cls; Stu Cncl; Stat Bsktbl; Hon Roll; Filipino Amer Cncl Of Union Cty; Hayward HS Sci Fr 4th Pl; Santa Clara U.

ORTEGA, JOWELL MANDE; Pinole Valley HS; Hercules, CA; (2); Dance Clb; Spanish Clb; SADD; Band; Color Guard; School Musical; Hon Roll; NHS.

ORTEGA, K NICOLE; Casa Rdde Fundamental HS; Citrus Heights, CA; (3); 61/370; AFS; Church Yth Grp; Drama Clb; School Musical; School Play; Variety Show; Var Swmmng; Cit Awd; Hon Roll; German Clb; Fri Nite Lv; Intract.

ORTEGA, KIMBERLEY K; Capistrono Valley HS; Mission Viejo, CA; (3); Dance Clb; Drama Clb; Thesps; School Musical; School Play; Stage Crew; Hon Roll; Pres Acad Fit Awd; Law.

ORTEGA, MIGUEL E; Channel Islands HS; Oxnard, CA; (1); Church Yth Grp; Cmnty Wkr; Key Clb; Science Clb; Church Choir; Stage Crew; Rep Stu Cncl; Intrml Crs Cntry; Intrml Trk; Hon Roll; Future Ldrs Of Am; Schlr Athlete; Participation Awds; U CA-SANTA Barbara; Arch.

ORTEGA, NICOLE M; Chino HS; Chino, CA; (3); Church Yth Grp; Drama Clb; Ski Clb; Spanish Clb; Teachers Aide; Yrbk; JV Score Keeper; Hon Roll; Foods Cls Natl Cntst 2nd Pl; Psych.

ORTEGA, RAUL; St Ignatius College Prep; San Francisco, CA; (4); 32/288; Church Yth Grp; VP Spanish Clb; Ed Yrbk; Intrml Ftbl; Intrml Sftbl; Intrml Vllybl; High Hon Roll; Spanish NHS; Comp Engrng.

ORTEGA, ROSA M; Huntington Park HS; Huntington Park, CA; (2); Key Clb; Math Clb; Science Clb; Chorus; Drill Tm; School Play; Stu Cncl; Cit Awd; Gov Hon Prg Awd; Hon Roll; MESA; USC Smmr Schl; Law.

ORTEGA, TITO; Orange Glen HS; Escondido, CA; (2); AFS; Am Leg Boys St; Bus Profs of Am; Math Tm; Off Frsh Cls; Engrng.

ORTEGA REFUGIO, JOE A; Coalinga HS; Huron, CA; (4); Art Clb; Boy Scts; Bsbl; Ftbl; Socr; Trk; W Hills Coll; Art Tchr.

ORTEGASO, RAYMOND L; Don Bosco Technical Inst; West Covina, CA; (3); Letterman Clb; Var Capt Bsktbl; Hon Roll; Goldn Tiger Awd; Accntng.

ORTEGON, TONY; Le Grand Union HS; Planada, CA; (2); FFA; JV Var Bsbl; JV Var Ftbl.

ORTGIESEN, TODD; Mira Mesa HS; San Diego, CA; (2); Math Tm; Science Clb; Off Soph Cls; Rep Stu Cncl; JV Crs Cntry; JV Trk; High Hon Roll; Hon Roll; Prfct Atten Awd; Pres Acad Fit Awd; Acad Leag; PHYSICS.

ORTHMEYER, PAIGE; Poway HS; Poway, CA; (3); Church Yth Grp; Pep Clb; NHS; CSF; Notre Dame; Sci.

ORTIZ, ALMA ROSA; Sweetwater HS; National City, CA; (2); Law.

ORTIZ JR, ANTONIO; Gonzales HS; Chualur, CA; (1); Bsbl; Bsktbl; Ftbl.

ORTIZ, BONNIE B; Delano HS; Delano, CA; (4); 12/355; Church Yth Grp; Rptr FHA; Library Aide; Band; Church Choir; Mrchg Band; JV Sftbl; JV Vllybl; High Hon Roll; NHS; CSF; MESA; Cal ST U Bakersfield; Bus Mgr.

ORTIZ, CIRO; Patterson HS; Patterson, CA; (4); 16/117; Am Leg Boys St; Drama Clb; Letterman Clb; Ski Clb; Spanish Clb; School Play; Stage Crew; JV Var Bsbl; JV Var Bsktbl; JV Var Ftbl; Camp Royal Ldrshp Camp Rnr Up; Mens Hnr Soc Club; CA ST U.

ORTIZ, CORINA M; Chaparral HS; El Cajon, CA; (2); Teachers Aide; Band; Chorus; Stu Cncl; Wt Lftg; Prfct Atten Awd; Law.

ORTIZ, DAVID; Ernest Righetti HS; Santa Maria, CA; (4); Treas FBLA; Teachers Aide; Var Trk; Cit Awd; High Hon Roll; Hon Roll; CA Interschlstc Fed Awd Trck Champs; Stdt Of Semstr; Mst Imprvd Trck & Fld; Fresno ST U; Acctnt.

ORTIZ, DENISE A; Antioch HS; Antioch, CA; (4); 125/625; Var Bsktbl; Var Mgr(s); Cit Awd; Hon Roll; Hstry Hnr; Odem Cnstr Schlrshp; U San Francisco Grant; U Of San Francisco; Crdlgy.

ORTIZ, DIANNA J; Hesperia HS; Hesperia, CA; (3); Pres SADD; Acpl Chr; School Play; Nwsp; Rep Frsh Cls; Hist Soph Cls; VP Stu Cncl; Phtg Ftbl; JV Trk; HOBY Ambssdr; Stu Shrff Advsry Cncl; U Of CA Irvine; Med.

ORTIZ JR, EDWARD; Edison HS; Fresno, CA; (1); Cit Awd; Hon Roll; Caltech; Comp Pgmr.

ORTIZ, ELIZABETH; Sacred Heart HS; Los Angeles, CA; (2); Church Yth Grp; Cmnty Wkr; Dance Clb; Teachers Aide; Chorus; School Play; Ed Yrbk; Rep Frsh Cls; Cit Awd; Prfct Atten Awd; CA ST Los Angeles; Chld Psych.

ORTIZ, ENRIQUE G; St Paul HS; Cerritos, CA; (3); Letterman Clb; SADD; Varsity Clb; Var Bsbl; Var Ftbl; Var Wt Lftg; Cit Awd; Hon Roll; U Of S CA; Arch.

ORTIZ, ERIC T; Loyola HS; Pasadena, CA; (2); 6/290; JV Bsbl; Hon Roll; CSF; Stanford; Corp Law.

ORTIZ, GRACE; Morro Bay HS; Los Osos, CA; (3); Hosp Aide; Chorus; Drill Tm; Sftbl; Hon Roll; Fresno U; Nrs.

ORTIZ, JULIA D; St Genevieve HS; Arleta, CA; (4); Art Clb; Church Yth Grp; Cmnty Wkr; Off Girl Scts; Off JA; Off Pep Clb; Science Clb; Drill Tm; Hon Roll; Mt Saint Marys College.

ORTIZ, LILIA; Bell Gardens HS; Commerce, CA; (3); Church Yth Grp; Dance Clb; FCA; FHA; Prfct Atten Awd; Bus.

ORTIZ, LIZETH; St Michael's HS; Los Angeles, CA; (2); Ed Nwsp; Pres Frsh Cls; Hon Roll; Started Own Majorette Group Clb; Psych.

ORTIZ, MARCO; Redwood HS; Visalia, CA; (3); Am Leg Boys St; Church Yth Grp; JV Ftbl; High Hon Roll; Bus.

ORTIZ, MARIA; Palo Verde HS; Blythe, CA; (2); Church Yth Grp; JV Vllybl; Hon Roll; Air Force Acad; Aviation.

ORTIZ, MARIA A; California HS; Whittier, CA; (3); 34/328; Teachers Aide; Cmptrs; ROP; CSU; Bus.

ORTIZ, MARIA G; Calipatria HS; Calipatria, CA; (2); Off Soph Cls; Bsktbl; Powder Puff Ftbl; Score Keeper; Vllybl; Hon Roll; Mst Imprvd Bsktbll; Bsktbll Hmcmng Royalty; UCSD; Bus Admin.

ORTIZ, MARIA I; Gladstone HS; Azusa, CA; (3); Church Yth Grp; GAA; SADD; Varsity Clb; Bsktbl; Sftbl; Tennis; Prfct Atten Awd; Trvl Srvc Occptns.

ORTIZ, MARIA J; Leuzinger HS; Lawndale, CA; (2); Art Clb; Teachers Aide; Sftbl; Rotary Awd; Advncd Ceremics Cls; Hnrb Mtns 1st Pl Awd; UCLA; Comp.

ORTIZ, MIGUEL A; Baldwin Park HS; Baldwin Park, CA; (3); Ftbl; Hon Roll; Woodchucks.

ORTIZ, ODILON; Kingsburg Joint Union HS; Kingsburg, CA; (3); Socr; Acad Block K Awd; Engrng.

ORTIZ, OMAR; St John Bosco HS; La Mirada, CA; (2); Drama Clb; JV Crs Cntry; Var Capt Vllybl; High Hon Roll; Hon Roll; Cvl Air Ptrl; Kokoro Vllybl Clb; Cycling; Stanford U; Mltry.

ORTIZ, PHILIP; George Washington HS; San Francisco, CA; (1); Aud/Vis; Cmnty Wkr; Library Aide; Band; Chorus; Church Choir; School Play; Mgr Bsktbl; Crs Cntry; Ftbl.

ORTIZ JR, RAMIRO; St John Bosco HS; Downey, CA; (2); French Clb; Key Clb; Pep Clb; Sec Frsh Cls; JV Bsktbl; Var Trk; Hon Roll; Duke; Law.

ORTIZ, RICHARD; Redwood HS; Visalia, CA; (2); Pres Church Yth Grp; Band; Chorus; Mrchg Band; Pep Band; Var Crs Cntry; Var Trk; Hon Roll; Hnr Band; Ldrshp Intern Pgm; Medcl Doctor.

ORTIZ, RUTH; Chaffey HS; Ontario, CA; (4); Church Yth Grp; Office Aide; Co-Capt Color Guard; Co-Capt Flag Corp; Hon Roll; Spanish.

ORTIZ, SANDRA; San Fernando HS; Pacoima, CA; (2); Cmnty Wkr; VP FBLA; Library Aide; Office Aide; Service Clb; Teachers Aide; Drill Tm; Ed Yrbk; Pres Frsh Cls; Stu Cncl; Desrvng Stu Awd; Keywanettes Pres; Futre Ldrs America Pgm; Law.

ORTIZ, SHIRLEY D; Chaparral HS; Phelan, CA; (4); Sftbl; Elks Awd; Hon Roll; Lion Awd; UC Riverside; Acctng.

ORTIZ, SOPHIA; Alverno HS; Pasadena, CA; (3); 6/67; Rep Frsh Cls; Sec Soph Cls; Off Jr Cls; Off Sr Cls; Cit Awd; Hon Roll; NHS; Sophomore Yr I Helped Write Our Class Constitution; Worked Parttime After School; CSF; Business Administration.

ORTIZ, SYLVIA R; Sacred Heart Of Jesus; Los Angeles, CA; (2); Cmnty Wkr; GAA; Sec Frsh Cls; Sec Jr Cls; JV Crs Cntry; JV Trk; Hon Roll; NHS; Frnch II Excllnce Awd; Chrstn Actve Movemnt Clb Rep; Newmn Fndtn Acknwldgmnt Awd; Bus.

ORTIZ, TRAVIS; Covenant Christian HS; Chula Vista, CA; (3); 1/3; Treas Church Yth Grp; School Play; JV Bsbl; Var Capt Ftbl; High Hon Roll; Hon Roll; Pres Frsh Cls; Pres Soph Cls; Sci Awd Midway Bptst Schl; Plyng Guitar; Bus.

ORTIZ, VALERIE; Sonoma Valley HS; Glen Ellen, CA; (4); 68/280; Debate Tm; Sec VP FFA; NFL; Speech Tm; 4-H Awd; Hon Roll; UC Berkeley; Teacher.

ORTIZ, VICTOR A; San Clemente HS; Capistrano Beach, CA; (1); Math Tm; Ftbl; Pres Acad Fit Awd; Mst Imprvd Plyr Awd; GATE Pgm Evltn Cmmtte; Law.

ORTIZ, VIRGINIA C; Culver City HS; Culver City, CA; (2); Spanish Clb; Band; Cit Awd; Ctznshp Hnr Rl; Air Force Acad; Aerosp Engr.

ORTIZ, YVETTEH; Bell HS; Bell, CA; (4); 8/639; Church Yth Grp; Cmnty Wkr; Key Clb; Math Tm; Quiz Bowl; Tennis; Cit Awd; High Hon Roll; NHS; Ntl Merit SF; Junior Statemen Of Amer; Stanford U; Civil Engrng.

ORTLINGHAUS, PAUL R; Rancho Cotate HS; Rohnert Park, CA; (3); Am Leg Boys St; Pres Church Yth Grp; Cmnty Wkr; Teachers Aide; JV Var Ftbl; Wt Lftg; Hon Roll; NHS; Tchr Hessel Union Church Bible Schl 90; Biola U; Yth Pstr.

ORTMANN, HEIDI M; Fremont HS; Sunnyvale, CA; (3); Church Yth Grp; Debate Tm; DECA; NFL; Office Aide; Opt Clb Awd; Stanford; Brdcst Jrnlsm.

ORTON, AMANDA; Silver Valley HS; Newberry Spgs, CA; (4); 1/70; Church Yth Grp; Cmnty Wkr; Letterman Clb; Church Choir; VP Stu Cncl; Var Cheerldng; Var JV Powder Puff Ftbl; Var Capt Vllybl; Var DAR Awd; Var Hon Roll; Miss Nwbry Spgs 87; Hmcmng Ct 89; Rep US Vllybl Tm Australia 89; Biola U; Phys Thrpy.

ORTON, CHAD S; Woodland HS; Woodland, CA; (2); SADD; Hon Roll; Jr NHS; Excllnc Awd Frgn Lang, Wrld Hstry; Stu Mth 88-90; UC Davis; Pdtrcn.

ORTUNO, ERIKA; Calexico HS; Calexico, CA; (2); Math Clb; Spanish Clb; SADD; Cheerldng; Vllybl; Comp Pgm.

ORVANANOS, LAURA; Coronado HS; Coronado, CA; (3); 19/136; Art Clb; Cmnty Wkr; French Clb; JV Socr; L Stat Tennis; Hon Roll; NHS; Yth To Yth Clb; Girls Svc Clb; Booster Clb; Law.

ORVIS, MICHELLE; Barstow HS; Barstow, CA; (4); 96/613; Church Yth Grp; Cmnty Wkr; Key Clb; Spanish Clb; Band; Mrchg Band; Yrbk; Cit Awd; High Hon Roll; Hon Roll; Barstow CC; Prllgl.

ORWAT, DIANE M; Paraclete HS; Lancaster, CA; (2); Church Yth Grp; Hosp Aide; Key Clb; SADD; Yrbk; JV Trk; JV Vllybl; Hon Roll; Z-Clb; Chrstn Svc Awd; Teaching.

OSAKO, MARY M; Venice HS; Culver City, CA; (3); Church Yth Grp; 4-H; Hosp Aide; Varsity Clb; Drill Tm; Orch; Treas Frsh Cls; VP Cheerldng; VP Tennis; Jr NHS; CA Jr Schlrshp Fed Top Hnr Awd; UCLA.

OSAWA, RIE; Arcadia HS; Arcadia, CA; (3); Pasadens City Coll; Bus.

OSBORN, ANN MARIE; Merced HS; Austin, TX; (4); French Clb; Teachers Aide; JV Tennis; JV Trk; High Hon Roll; Hon Roll; Cert Achvt Draftng Tech; Austin CC; Reg Nurse.

OSBORN, ANTHONY J; Saint Anthony HS; Lakewood, CA; (2); Church Yth Grp; Cmnty Wkr; Letterman Clb; Spanish Clb; Band; Jazz Band; Mrchg Band; Orch; Pep Band; Notre Dame; Arch.

OSBORN, BETH J; Bretheren JR/Sr; Lakewood, CA; (1); Church Yth Grp; Band; Church Choir; Color Guard; Flag Corp; Mrchg Band; Off Frsh Cls; Cheerldng; Swmmng; Hon Roll; ST Finalist Amer Ican Teen Pageant; Grapic Art Interior Design.

OSBORN, KATHRYN E; Napa HS; Napa, CA; (1); 1/400; Drama Clb; Supt Schlr; CA Golden ST Exam; UC Berkely; Arch.

OSBORNE, HEATHER L; Amos Alonzo Stagg HS; Stockton, CA; (2); Church Yth Grp; Drama Clb; Teachers Aide; Thesps; Chorus; Church Choir; Stage Crew; High Hon Roll; Hon Roll; 2 Tms Wnnr Bst Tec Awd Drama; Wnnr Bst Thspn Drama; Set/Light Desgn.

OSBORNE, HEATHER M; Torrey Pines HS; San Diego, CA; (2); Chorus; Drill Tm; School Musical; Stage Crew; CA Schlrshp Fed; Law.

OSBORNE, HOLLY M; Burlingame HS; Hillsborough, CA; (1); Debate Tm; Drama Clb; Nwsp; JV Socr; JV Tennis; Hon Roll; Pres Acad Fit Awd; Bay Area Stu For Envrnmnt Grp; Northwestern; Nwsp Jrnlst.

OSBORNE, JEFFREY M; Apple Valley HS; Apple Valley, CA; (2); JV Bsktbl; Sccr.

OSBORNE, JENNIFER; St Patricks-St Vincents HS; Fairfield, CA; (3); 2/150; Church Yth Grp; Pep Clb; Service Clb; VP Jr Cls; Var Capt Vllybl; High Hon Roll; CSF; U Of CA Davis; Pre-Law.

OSBORNE, KAITLIN; Mtn View HS; Mountain View, CA; (1); Trk; Vllybl; Hon Roll.

OSBORNE, LESLIE A; Burney HS; Burney, CA; (3); 3/55; Am Leg Aux Girls St; FBLA; Red Cross Aide; Teachers Aide; VP Jr Cls; Pres Sr Cls; JV Var Bsktbl; JV Var Vllybl; High Hon Roll; Pres Acad Fit Awd; Bus Admin.

OSBORNE, MUHSIN K; Mountain View HS; Mountain View, CA; (3); Cmnty Wkr; Teachers Aide; Jazz Band; Mrchg Band; Pep Band; Var Bsktbl; Howard U; Arch Desgn.

OSCARSON, RON S; Roseville HS; Rocklyn, CA; (2); Spanish Clb; SADD; Ftbl; Swmmng.

OSDALE, LONNA; Western HS; Stanton, CA; (3); Pres Pep Clb; Varsity Clb; VP Frsh Cls; Treas Soph Cls; Rep Stu Cncl; Var Cheerldng; Var Sftbl; Cit Awd; NHS; Prfct Atten Awd; CA ST Fullerton; Engl Ed.

OSEGUERA, DAVID G; San Dieguito HS; Encinitas, CA; (2); JV Bsbl; Hon Roll; Bio Stu Yr; UCLA; Engrng.

OSENBAUGH, SHANNON L; Dana Hills HS; Laguna Niguel, CA; (2); Spanish Clb; SADD; Socr; Trk; UCSB; Bus.

OSGOOD, KELLY M; St Joseph HS; Cypress, CA; (2); Cmnty Wkr; GAA; Hosp Aide; Var Drill Tm; Dance Concert 89 90; St Marys Of IN; Phys Thrpy.

OSGOOD, KEVIN; Mabel O'farrell Schl For C&P Arts; San Diego, CA; (2); 1/152; School Musical; School Play; Variety Show; High Hon Roll; Pres Acad Fit Awd; Mousketeer On Mickey Mouse Clb On Disney Chnnl; Mbr CA JR Schlrshp Fed; Hnr For Acad Exclnc; Perf Arts.

OSHER, JASON; Encina HS; Sacramento, CA; (4); 15/163; Spanish Clb; High Hon Roll; Hon Roll; Gldn St Exm Alg I 87; U Of CA Santa Barbara.

OSHEROFF, STEPHANIE; Los Amigos HS; Fountain Valley, CA; (2); Drama Clb; SADD; Thesps; School Musical; School Play; Variety Show; Pres Frsh Cls; Hon Roll; Var Lttr-Drama; 1st Pl Fntn Vly Exchng Clb Tlnt Shw; 2nd Pl Rgnl Exchng Clb Tlnt Shw; UCSD; Prfrmng Arts.

OSHIDARI, ALLYSON T; Amos Alonzo Stagg HS; Stockton, CA; (4); 2/400; Key Clb; NFL; Speech Tm; Orch; Pres Sr Cls; Capt Bsktbl; High Hon Roll; Kiwanis Awd; Pres Acad Fit Awd; Sal; Stanford U; Humanities.

OSHIMA, JENNI; Oakmont HS; Roseville, CA; (2); 6/435; Drama Clb; German Clb; Ski Clb; SADD; Drill Tm; High Hon Roll; Pres Acad Fit Awd; CSF; Global Impact; UC San Diego; Marine Bio.

OSHIRO, CORINNE NOELANI; North HS; Gardena, CA; (1); 1/490; Drama Clb; Spanish Clb; Rep Frsh Cls; Cit Awd; High Hon Roll; NHS; Pres Acad Fit Awd; Outstndng Schlstc Ctzns; OSCAR Awd-Outstndng Ctznshp Awd Of Rcgntn; UCLA; Bus.

OSHIRO, MARK M; Couina HS; West Covina, CA; (3); Office Aide; Asian Club; Badminton; SADD; Cal ST Fullerton; Accountant.

OSHITA, DAMON T; Foothill HS; Santa Ana, CA; (3); 60/316; Boy Scts; Church Yth Grp; Acpl Chr; Band; Church Choir; School Musical; Var L Crs Cntry; Intrml JV Trk; High Hon Roll; Hon Roll; 2nd Pl UCI Yng Singer Of Yr, Rotary Intl; PFO Awds, Vocal; Ed Doyle Vocal Music Awd; U Penn; Bus.

OSIAS, ALEXANDER M; Serra HS; San Mateo, CA; (4); 5/160; German Clb; Math Clb; Chorus; Church Choir; School Musical; School Play; Nwsp; Yrbk; Hon Roll; Ntl Merit Ltr; Comp Engrng.

OSKIN, MICHAEL E; Edison HS; Huntington Beach, CA; (3); High Hon Roll; Hon Roll; Dstnctn Vrbl, Math; Gldn ST Exm-Geom Hgh Hnrs; Geolgy.

OSMANI, FARIBA; Gladstone HS; Asuza, CA; (3); Hon Roll; UCLA; MD.

OSMANSKI, KIMBERLY J; Amos Alonzo Stagg HS; Stockton, CA; (3); Church Yth Grp; Pep Clb; Spanish Clb; Var Capt Cheerldng; High Hon Roll; Psych.

OSMOND, AMIE C; Apple Valley HS; Apple Valley, CA; (1); 60/700; Church Yth Grp; French Clb; JA; Pep Clb; Teachers Aide; Stat Bsbl; Stat Sftbl; JV Tennis; Cit Awd; High Hon Roll; Yale; Bus.

OSNAYA, ALICE; El Rancho HS; Pico Rivera, CA; (4); Dance Clb; Drama Clb; Sec Stu Cncl; Score Keeper; UCLA; Law.

OSNER, BLYTHE M; Thomas Downey HS; Modesto, CA; (2); Church Yth Grp; Drama Clb; SADD; Thesps; Acpl Chr; Chorus; Church Choir; Orch; School Musical; School Play; Music.

OSORIO, ANGELA T; South HS; Bakersfield, CA; (3); Church Yth Grp; Sec Service Clb; Hon Roll; Hi Deb-Gottschalks Cmnty Svc; Psych.

OSPITAL, FRANCENE; Bret Harte Union HS; Murphys, CA; (3); Church Yth Grp; Teachers Aide; Rptr Nwsp; JV Score Keeper; JV Sftbl; Hon Roll; Fri Night Live; Interact Club; SAVE Envrnmntl Club; U Of Pacific; Bus.

OSSI, NICOLE M; Presentation HS; San Jose, CA; (4); Art Clb; Church Yth Grp; Cmnty Wkr; Drama Clb; French Clb; Math Clb; Service Clb; Spanish Clb; Teachers Aide; High Hon Roll; CSF; Bnk Amer Scl Stds Cert; Tandy Awd; Gen Excllnc Math Awd; Svc Club Awd; Outstndng Spnsh Stu; Santa Clara U; Bus.

OSSINALDE, CELINE; Washington Union HS; Fresno, CA; (4); Church Yth Grp; French Clb; FBLA; FHA; FTA; Pep Clb; Teachers Aide; Yrbk; VP Capt Cheerldng; JV VP Tennis; Hi-Deb Prgrm Rep; U Of CA Santa Cruz; Psych.

OSTASHAY, AMY; Huntington Beach HS; Huntington Beach, CA; (3); Dance Clb; School Musical; JV Sftbl; JV Vllybl; San Diego ST; Math.

OSTASHAY, GREG; Damien HS; La Verne, CA; (2); 29/269; Boy Scts; Church Yth Grp; Spanish Clb; High Hon Roll; USAF Acad; Pilot.

OSTER, ELIZABETH A; Buena HS; Ventura, CA; (3); Cmnty Wkr; FBLA; Hosp Aide; Letterman Clb; SADD; Teachers Aide; Nwsp; Hon Roll; Cmptv Irish Stp-Dncng; Natl Chrty League Tcktckr.

OSTER, HEATHER R; Ramona HS; Ramona, CA; (3); 51/294; Treas German Clb; Band; Mrchg Band; Pep Band; School Musical; Stage Crew; Cit Awd; Playd Pit Orch; Amnsty Intl; Pres Sch Anml Rights Clb; Intl Rels.

OSTERBERG, LINNEA A; Edison-Computech HS; Fresno, CA; (1); JCL; JV Tennis; Capt Vllybl; Hon Roll; CA Schlrshp Fed; Miami U; Prof Of Latin.

OSTERBERG, TANYA; Oxnard HS; Oxnard, CA; (2); 30/604; Church Yth Grp; VP Computer Clb; French Clb; Flag Corp; High Hon Roll; Hon Roll; Ntl Merit Ltr; Prfct Atten Awd; Photo Clb; CSF; Gftd/Tlntd Educ.

OSTERIA, KAREN; Saint Joseph HS; Cerritos, CA; (3); JA; Ski Clb; SADD; Rep Jr Cls; Stu Cncl; Capt Powder Puff Ftbl; Intl Soc; Phys Thrpy.

OSTERODE, ERIC K; Arlington HS; Riverside, CA; (3); Chess Clb; Computer Clb; Quiz Bowl; Rptr Yrbk; High Hon Roll; Hon Roll; CSF; Acad Dcthln; UCR; Comp Prgmr.

OSTINI, GINA; Davis SR HS; Davis, CA; (3); 57/405; Dance Clb; Pep Clb; Var Capt Cheerldng; Powder Puff Ftbl; Hon Roll; Dance; Horse Actvts; UC Davis; Bio.

OSTLE, SHANDA; Foothill HS; Pleasanton, CA; (3); 8/296; Pres 4-H; JCL; Latin Clb; Pres Service Clb; SADD; Church Choir; Cit Awd; 4-H Awd; High Hon Roll; Voice Dem Awd; US-USSR Smnr Clbl Wrmng; US Scotland Exchng.

OSTRANDER, ALISON M; West Covina HS; West Covina, CA; (1); Church Yth Grp; SADD; Hon Roll; Most Prmsng Frosh Artist; Career Ed; Visage Mdlng Clb; Cal Poly U; Art Ed.

OSTRANDER, KIRSTEN; Sanger HS; Sanger, CA; (2); Model UN; ROTC; Ski Clb; Teachers Aide; JV Cheerldng; Var L Crs Cntry; Var L Swmmng; Creative Writing Cont; USD; Ariline Pilot.

OSTROVSKAYA, YELENA; J Washington HS; San Francisco, CA; (3); Math Tm; Yrbk; Tnns; Music; Comp; Berkley Schl; Comp Prog.

OSTROW, JENNIFER S; Bullard HS; Fresno, CA; (1); JV Capt Tennis; High Hon Roll; CSF; Tutor Algebra; UCSB; Bus Mngmnt.

OSTROW II, RICK D; Artesia HS; Hawaiian Gardens, CA; (3); Intnl Clb; Pres JA; Science Clb; Intrml JV Bsbl; Cit Awd; Hon Roll; Eclgy Clb; CSF; Frshmn Bsebl Dfnsv Plyr Of Yr; CA ST Fullerton.

OSTROWSKI, JULIE; Terra Linda HS; San Rafael, CA; (4); 50/153; Am Leg Aux Girls St; Cmnty Wkr; French Clb; Ed Yrbk; Lit Mag; Recrdr/Treas Ch 195 Intl Order Of Rainbow Girls; Sonoma ST U; Poly Sci.

OSTROWSKY, NATHAN A; Dos Pueblos HS; Goleta, CA; (3); Boy Scts; Chess Clb; Band; Mrchg Band; Orch; Pep Band; Ntl Merit Ltr; High Hnrs Gldn St Geometry Exam.

OSUNA, JOANNA; Southwest JR HS; San Diego, CA; (1); Office Aide; Teachers Aide; Band; Stage Crew; UCSD; Comp Tech.

OSUNA, LAURA; Garfield HS; Los Angeles, CA; (2); Library Aide; Math Tm; Office Aide; Science Clb; Var Crs Cntry; Var Sftbl; Var Trk; Cit Awd; Hon Roll; Pres Acad Fit Awd; Outstndng Achvt Mdls Frnch & Engl 89; Outstndng 10th Grader Plq & Trphy Crss Cntry, Track & Field; Yale; Medcl.

OSUNA, LUIS A; Southwest HS; San Ysidro, CA; (3); Var Socr; San Diego ST U; Brdcstng.

OSUNA, MARCO; Mar Vista HS; San Ysidro, CA; (4); 134/285; Teachers Aide; Mecha Clb; Southwestern Coll; Telemedia.

OSUNA, MARICELA; Workman HS; Valinda, CA; (2); Cit Awd; Hon Roll; San Antonio Coll; Immigrtn Ofcr.

OSUNA, MARTHA; Calexico HS; Calexico, CA; (1); Sec Frsh Cls; JV Bsktbl; JV Sftbl; JV Vllybl; Early Outrch Pgm; SDSU; Elem Tchr.

OSWALD, ANTHONY L; Santa Clara HS; Oxnard, CA; (4); 30/180; Church Yth Grp; JV Bsktbl; Wt Lftg; High Hon Roll; NHS; Karate Stu; Cuesta Coll; Natrl Rsrce Mngmnt.

OSWALD, RYAN A; Trabuco Hills HS; Mission Viejo, CA; (1); Church Yth Grp; Crs Cntry; Trk; Freshman MVP Award For Cross Country; Set New School Record For Freshman Mile; MIP Award; Washington State.

OSWALT, ELIZABETH; Montgomery HS; San Diego, CA; (3); Chorus; Rep Frsh Cls; Rep Soph Cls; Rep Jr Cls; Mgr(s); Score Keeper; Cit Awd; Prfct Atten Awd; Law.

OSWOLD, JENNIFER L; Saint Francis HS; Sunnyvale, CA; (2); Pep Clb; JV Capt Cheerldng; Swmmng; Hon Roll; Radio Club; Hlth.

OTA, JEFF; James Lick HS; San Jose, CA; (4); 1/250; Church Yth Grp; Intnl Clb; Math Clb; Math Tm; Ed Nwsp; Sec Soph Cls; VP Jr Cls; Sec Stu Cncl; Var Capt Bsktbl; Var Golf; Century III Ldrshp Pgm St Fnlst & Schlrshp Wnnr; Model Stu Of J Lick HS 88; J Lick HS Announcer; Engrs.

OTA, RONALD L; Fresno HS; Fresno, CA; (2); Church Yth Grp; Debate Tm; NFL; Speech Tm; Band; Mrchg Band; Rep Stu Cncl; 2 Vrsty Lttrs Acad; Mck Trl Tm; Poltcl Sci.

OTANES, ARLENE V; Mission Viejo HS; Mission Viejo, CA; (3); 96/445; Color Guard; Ed Nwsp; CA Schlrshp Fed; Child Psych.

OTERO, DAVID M; Monte Vista HS; Spring Valley, CA; (2); Band; Jazz Band; Mrchg Band; School Musical.

OTERO, JOSEPHINE EMBRO; Mt View HS; El Monte, CA; (2); SADD; Acpl Chr; Chorus; Kiwanis Awd; Pres Acad Fit Awd; Woodbury U; Int Des.

OTERO, MARK; Hiram Johnson HS; Sacramento, CA; (3); Boy Scts; Stage Crew; Wt Lftg; JV Wrstlng; Hon Roll; Art Awd; Comp Pgm.

OTLANG, LIZZETTE C; Woodrow Wilson HS; San Francisco, CA; (3); FBLA; Hon Roll; Friday Nght Live; Hnr Soc; CA Schlrshp Fed; Filipino Clb; San Francisco ST U; Law.

OTLEY, KIMBERLY S; Del Oro HS; Loomis, CA; (2); 6/267; Pep Clb; Drill Tm; Bsktbl; Cheerldng; Swmmng; High Hon Roll; MVP Swmmng 90; CSF 90; Cum Laude Acad Distnctn Recpnt 90; OR ST; Sports Med.

OTREMBA, MICHELLE; Righetti HS; Santa Maria, CA; (3); 4-H; Treas FFA; 4-H Awd; High Hon Roll; Santa Maria Vly Rdng Clb All Around Hi Point Yth 89; Sanrais Qtr Hrse Assn All Arnd Nvc Yth 89; Cal Poly San Luis Obispo; Ag.

OTT, AARON K; Las Plumas HS; Berry Creek, CA; (1); 11/290; Treas 4-H; Rptr VICA; Band; Mrchg Band; Pep Band; JV Bsbl; 4-H Awd; Hon Roll; Amer Rabbit Breeders Assn; Strctrl Engr.

OTT, BRENT S; Hesperia HS; Hesperia, CA; (2); CSF; University Club; Bus Accntng.

OTT, CHRISTINA; West Hills HS; Santee, CA; (3); Computer Clb; Dance Clb; Math Tm; SADD; Drill Tm; Hon Roll; Church Yth Grp; Office Aide; Pep Clb; Spanish Clb; Dance; Ice Sktng; Grossmont JC; Fashn Retail.

OTT, CHRISTY L; Fairfield HS; Fairfield, CA; (2); Church Yth Grp; Drama Clb; School Musical; School Play; Stage Crew; Natl Coast Sctn-Schlr/Athlt; Mdlng/Actng; U C Davis; Sci.

OTTE, JENNIFER L; Bishop Montgomery HS; Gardena, CA; (2); Key Clb; DAR Awd; Hon Roll; Pres Acad Fit Awd; CSF; Interact Club.

OTTMANN, WENDI; Masa Verde HS; Citrus Heights, CA; (2); 20/257; French Clb; VP Soph Cls; Pres Jr Cls; Var Cheerldng; JV Var Sftbl; Wt Lftg; High Hon Roll; Hon Roll; UCSB; Bus.

OTTN, KARIN A; Kings Christian HS; Lemoore, CA; (3); Church Yth Grp; FHA; Ski Clb; Teachers Aide; Chorus; School Play; Stage Crew; JV Var Cheerldng; JV Gym; High Hon Roll; Cal Baptist; Psych.

OTTO, BRIAN S; Foothill HS; Santa Ana, CA; (3); 66/328; High Hon Roll; Hon Roll; 3rd Pl Div Womens Clb Amer Heritage Essay Cont; Parent Faculty Org Awd Of Excllnc; Outstndng Soph Bus; Cal Poly San Luis Obisop; Comp.

OTTOBONI, JULIE T; Saint Francis HS; Monte Sereno, CA; (1); 55/396; Church Yth Grp; Rptr Yrbk; JV Sftbl; High Hon Roll; Grd Schl Vllybl Team Coach; Santa Clara U; Med.

OTTOMANYI, STEVEN; California HS; Whittier, CA; (3); German Clb; Math Tm; High Hon Roll; Acad Deca; Golden St Ex High Hnrs Alg, Geo, Hstry; CA ST-FULLERTON; Intl Bus.

OU, JUDY H; Fremont Christian Schl; Hayward, CA; (1); Church Yth Grp; FCA; Church Choir; Trk; Vllybl; High Hon Roll; Art.

OU, MALA K; Lincoln HS; Stockton, CA; (3); 70/538; Teachers Aide; Cit Awd; Hon Roll; Pres Acad Fit Awd; Delta Coll; Bnktllr.

OU, PENG L; Venice HS; Los Angeles, CA; (2); Computer Clb; FTA; Yrbk; Trk; Cit Awd; Hon Roll; Prfct Atten Awd; Proj Upward Bound; UCLA; Mechncl Engr.

OU, SALLY; Lowell HS; San Francisco, CA; (2); Sec Church Yth Grp; French Clb; Teachers Aide; Church Choir; Orch; Golden St Exam High Hnrs; U CA Berkeley; Life Sci.

OU, SAM W; Crossroads Schl; Culver City, CA; (3); Church Yth Grp; Cmnty Wkr; Math Tm; Service Clb; Teachers Aide; Chorus; Orch; Trk; High Hon Roll; Jr NHS; Gvrnrs Schlr FL.

OU, SERENA J; Westmoor HS; Daly City, CA; (1); Hosp Aide; Chorus; High Hon Roll; Giftd & Tlntd Educ; Med.

OU, VICTOR W; Palm Desert HS; Bermuda Dunes, CA; (2); JV Trk; High Hon Roll; CA Schlrshp Fdrtn; Piano; Jr Vlntr Eisenhower Med Ctr Auxiliary; Hgh Hnrs Gldn St Exam-Geom; Pre-Med.

OU YANG, JIAN P; Edison HS; Stockton, CA; (2); Math Clb; Hon Roll; Prfct Atten Awd; U Pacific; Phrmcy.

OU YANG, MEI X; Edison HS; Stockton, CA; (3); Math Tm; Science Clb; Hon Roll; Prfct Atten Awd; Gldn St Exam Alg & Geom High Hnrs; Chem-Thon Chem Cntst 1st Pl; A P Stu; U Of The Pacific; Phrmcy.

OUANO, ANNE E; Lowell HS; San Francisco, CA; (3); Treas Church Yth Grp; Red Cross Aide; Orch; Goldn St Exam Math Awd; Christian Ldrshp Inst Pgm; Fil-Am Clb; UC Davis; Nrsng.

OUANO, JOAN; Notre Dame HS; San Jose, CA; (3); 26/95; Hosp Aide; Science Clb; Cheerldng; Hon Roll; NHS; CSF; Fshn Dsgn.

OUBRE, ANGEL D; Bishop Montgomery HS; Carson, CA; (3); Dance Clb; JA; Letterman Clb; Drill Tm; Hon Roll; Jack & Jill Of Amer Inc; U Of CA Berkeley; Pre-Med.

OUCH, CHET; Tokay HS; Stockton, CA; (1); 1/742; High Hon Roll; Prfct Atten Awd; CSF.

OUCH, KARONA; Modesto HS; Modesto, CA; (3); French Clb; FHA; Intnl Clb; Teachers Aide; Orch; Hnr Excel 90; UCLA Berkeley; Acctnt.

OUCHIDA, JENNIFER N; Rio Americano HS; Carmichael, CA; (4); 6/265; Sec Church Yth Grp; Service Clb; Spanish Clb; Teachers Aide; Treas Soph Cls; VP Jr Cls; Pres Sr Cls; Var Tennis; Var Trk; Gov Hon Prg Awd; Stu Reaching Out Spkr; Claremont Mckenna Schlr Awd; Badminton; Claremont Mckenna Coll; Psych.

OUELLETTE, ERIN; Los Alamitos HS; Cypress, CA; (3); Teachers Aide; Chorus; Color Guard; Crs Cntry; Trk; Long Beach ST.

OUELLETTE, JACQUELINE M; Alemany HS; Simi Valley, CA; (4); 11/312; Church Yth Grp; SADD; Co-Ed Lit Mag; Hon Roll; NHS; Pres Acad Fit Awd; CA Schlrshp Fed; Gymnastics; CA ST U Sacramento; Bio.

OUGH, FAITH M; Berkeley HS; Berkeley, CA; (3); French Clb; Key Clb; High Hon Roll; Hon Roll; Crew Tm Rowing; Water Polo Tm; GSE Alg Hgh Hnrs, Geom Hnrs.

OUK, CHRISTOPHER VIRAK; Lincoln HS; Stockton, CA; (2); 99/568; Cit Awd; High Hon Roll; Hon Roll; UC Davis; Comp Sci.

OUK, MAUV; T Roosevelt HS; Fresno, CA; (3); Art Clb; English Clb; Science Clb; JV Var Tennis; JETS Awd; Prfct Atten Awd; Math Engrng Sci Achvmt; Asian Club Secy; Early Outrch Pgm; CA Polytechnic Inst; Archtr.

OUK, VANNA; Edison SR HS; Stockton, CA; (3); French Clb; JA; Teachers Aide; Hon Roll; Cambodian Clb Sec; UC Davis:Ed.

OUNDJIAN, JENNIFER L; John Burroughs HS; Burbank, CA; (3); Acpl Chr; Chorus; Variety Show; Rep Frsh Cls; Hon Roll; Prfct Atten Awd; CA Jr Schlstc Fed; Music.

OUNJIAN, MICHAEL Z; La Serna HS; Whittier, CA; (2); 1/450; Latin Clb; JV Bsktbl; Var L Tennis; High Hon Roll; Hon Roll; NHS; Prfct Atten Awd; Tp 100 Stu; Prncpls Lst; CSF.

OURIQUE, JENNIFER A; St Joseph HS; Artesia, CA; (3); Church Yth Grp; GAA; Letterman Clb; Varsity Clb; Rep Jr Cls; Treas Stu Cncl; Capt Var Bsktbl; Var JV Sftbl; JV Co-Capt Vllybl; Hon Roll; Walt Disney Drmrs & Doers Awd; Elem Educ.

OUSE, KRISTI; Gustine HS; Newman, CA; (1); 10/84; Church Yth Grp; Treas VP 4-H; FBLA; Treas Frsh Cls; JV Cheerldng; Stat Score Keeper; Sacrameto ST; Dntl Hygne.

OUYANG, JASON; Lincoln HS; San Francisco, CA; (1).

OVALLE, ERICKA; Belmont HS; Los Angeles, CA; (4); Library Aide; Office Aide; Pep Clb; Speech Tm; Teachers Aide; Co-Capt Cheerldng; Swmmng; Hon Roll; Hnr Stu; Arch.

OVALLE, GUADALUPE; Fresno HS; Fresno, CA; (3); SADD; Tennis; Hon Roll; Prfct Atten Awd; Mathmtcl,Engr,Sci Achvt MESA Pres; Jr Larcs,Mecha,UC Santa Cruz,Outrch Prog,CSF; Asian Amer Clb; UC Davis; Astronaut.

OVALLES, KAREN; Sweetwater Union HS; National City, CA; (2); Church Choir; Rep Frsh Cls; Rep Soph Cls; Rep Stu Cncl; Stat Bsktbl; JV Vllybl; Cit Awd; High Hon Roll; Prfct Atten Awd; UCSD; Med.

OVENEPHET, DOUANGCHAY B; Clovis HS; Clovis, CA; (3); Fresno ST Coll; Bus.

OVERACKER, RON E; Tulare Union HS; Tulare, CA; (3); 24/401; Church Yth Grp; Cmnty Wkr; Drama Clb; Rep Soph Cls; Rep Jr Cls; Stu Cncl; JV Ftbl; JV Var Trk; Hunting; Umpire; Cal Poly; Arch.

OVERHAUSER, CHANDRA BLYTHE; Harbor HS; Santa Cruz, CA; (4); Letterman Clb; Service Clb; Ski Clb; Sftbl; High Hon Roll; Hon Roll; Young Schlrs Pgm 89; CSF; Cal Poly SLO; Animal Sci.

OVERHOLER, GRACIE; Analy HS; Sebastopol, CA; (3); Math Tm; Teachers Aide; Varsity Clb; Pres Jr Cls; Var Socr; Var Trk; Hon Roll; Pres Acad Fit Awd; Immnlgy.

OVERHOLT, SHERI; San Gorgonio HS; San Bernardino, CA; (4); 1/450; Church Yth Grp; Pep Clb; Chorus; School Musical; Var L Vllybl; High Hon Roll; NHS; Bk Am Achvt Awd Fine Arts; U CA-RIVERSIDE; Biomed Sci.

OVERHOLT, STEFANI R; Roseville HS; Roseville, CA; (3); 7/412; Am Leg Aux Girls St; Church Yth Grp; French Clb; German Clb; Key Clb; Science Clb; Co-Ed Yrbk; Sec Frsh Cls; VP Soph Cls; Rep Jr Cls; CSF; Rprsnt Sch In Rotary Youth Ldrshp Cnfrnce; Pres Sci Clb; Secy Prin Advsry Cmmtte; Bus Psych.

OVERHULS, HOLLY; Valley Christian HS; Cerritos, CA; (3); Church Yth Grp; Drama Clb; JA; Teachers Aide; Varsity Clb; Church Choir; Drill Tm; School Musical; Trk; Hon Roll.

OVERN, KAREN M; Walnut HS; Walnut, CA; (1); 1/469; Yrbk; Score Keeper; Stat Swmmng; High Hon Roll; CSF; GATE; Golden St Exam Geom.

OVERSON, PETER; Norwalk HS; Norwalk, CA; (4); 2/270; Chess Clb; Church Yth Grp; Pres Math Clb; Math Tm; Model UN; Service Clb; Speech Tm; Co-Capt Tennis; Bausch & Lomb Sci Awd; High Hon Roll; Co-Scholar Athlt Of Yr; Eagle Scout; Seagull Awd; Cerritos Coll; Bus.

OVERTON, JAMES L; Thomas Downey HS; Modesto, CA; (3); JV Wrstlng.

OVERTON, JENELL; El Segundo HS; El Segundo, CA; (4); 29/148; French Clb; Key Clb; Pres Capt Pep Clb; Pres Acpl Chr; School Musical; Swing Chorus; JV Bsktbl; Capt JV Cheerldng; Capt Var Pom Pon; JV Sftbl; Bank Of Amer Plaque Wnnr For Fine Arts; Principls Advisory Cncl; Hmcmng Qn; Chico ST U; Liberal Stds.

OVERTON, LISA; King/Drew Medical Mag HS; Carson, CA; (3); VP Church Yth Grp; Cmnty Wkr; Hosp Aide; Service Clb; Treas Church Choir; Drill Tm; Ed Yrbk; High Hon Roll; Hon Roll; Prfct Atten Awd; Cngrsnl Schlr Awd; Sprtl Excllnc Awd; Stu Mnstry Achvt Awd; Oral Roberts U; Psych.

OVERTURF, DEIRDRE L; Eisenhower HS; Rialto, CA; (4); Church Yth Grp; French Clb; Key Clb; Office Aide; SADD; High Hon Roll; Hon Roll; Jr NHS; NHS; Acad Decthln; Acad Awds Grmn & Frnch; Neurosurgeon.

OVERTURF, RAMONA L; Amos Alanzo Stagg HS; Stockton, CA; (1); Church Yth Grp; Crs Cntry; Mgr(s); High Hon Roll; Hon Roll; Prfct Atten Awd; Young Authors Fair Wnr; Highest Scorer Eng Camp Tests; Drama/Speech Stu; UCLA; Intr Decorator.

OVIATT, TAMARA K; San Marcos HS; San Marcos, CA; (3); Church Yth Grp; VP French Clb; Pep Clb; Varsity Clb; Band; Mrchg Band; Stu Cncl; Var Capt Bsktbl; Cheerldng; Var Fld Hcky; Vrsty Bsktbl-MVP,1st Tm All Lge,All Lge Hnrb Mntn; Band Cncl Rep; Lang Achvt Awd; 1st Tm All Acad/Schl; UCLA; Med.

OVIEDO, MICHAEL G; Kearny HS; San Diego, CA; (3); 13/322; Nwsp; Ed Yrbk; Rep Frsh Cls; VP Jr Cls; Pres Sr Cls; Rep Stu Cncl; Var JV Bsktbl; Var Vllybl; Jr NHS; Mntl Hlth Coverage 88; Jr Male Of Yr 90; JV Bsktbl MVP; Phys Thrpy.

OW, JULIA; George Washington HS; San Francisco, CA; (3); Hon Roll; Pharm.

OW, MARY K; Kerman HS; Kerman, CA; (2); 4/174; VP German Clb; Math Tm; Quiz Bowl; Chorus; JV Bsktbl; Var Tennis; JV Vllybl; High Hon Roll; Pres Acad Fit Awd; Astrnmy Clb; U C-Santa Barbara; Physics.

OW YANG, GISELLE; Carlmont HS; Belmont, CA; (4); 1/300; Math Clb; Phtg Nwsp; Ed Yrbk; Off Frsh Cls; Off Soph Cls; Off Jr Cls; Ntl Merit SF; Pres Acad Fit Awd; Val; Bank Of Amer Achvt-Liberal Arts Fnlst; Harvard Book Prize; MIT Ldrshp Awd; Pomona Coll; Chem.

OWCARZ, ELIZABETH A; El Toro HS; El Toro, CA; (3); French Clb; VP Chorus; High Hon Roll; Phys Thrpy.

OWEN, CANDICE; Home HS; Paso Robles, CA; (1); The Cousteau Soc & Greenpeace; UNLV; Fshn Mrchndsng.

OWEN, JON E; Fowler HS; Fowler, CA; (4); Boy Scts; FCA; FFA; Letterman Clb; Bsbl; Bsktbl; Ftbl; Bank Of Am Cert Awd 90; Sci Olympiad Team 90; FFA St Vine Pruning Team; Kings River CC; Sci.

OWEN, MATTHEW N; Martin Luther King HS; Davis, CA; (4); Church Yth Grp; Cmnty Wkr; Teachers Aide; Hon Roll; Rotary Awd; Vrs Outdoor Actvts; CA ST San Diego; Scl Svc.

OWEN, SARAH M; Nova Independent Study HS; Novato, CA; (3); Church Yth Grp; Office Aide; SADD; Cheerldng; NEDT Awd; Coll Of Marin; Nrsng.

OWEN, STEPHANIE E; Redwood JR Acad; Santa Rosa, CA; (4); 6/9; Church Yth Grp; Drama Clb; Scholastic Bowl; Teachers Aide; Chorus; School Play; Treas Soph Cls; Treas Jr Cls; Sec Treas Stu Cncl; Intrmrls; PUC; Dental Hygnst.

OWEN, STEVE J; Los Angeles County HS For The Arts; W Covina, CA; (3); Band; Jazz Band; Orch; Music.

OWEN, TAFT C; Pasadena HS; Pasadena, CA; (3); Cmnty Wkr; Q&S; Spanish Clb; Teachers Aide; Ed Nwsp; Phtg Yrbk; Stu Cncl; Var Capt Ftbl; Var Capt Socr; Intrml Wt Lftg; Bus.

OWEN, VALERIE K; Hoover HS; Fresno, CA; (2); Church Yth Grp; Office Aide; Fresno City Coll; Engl Tchr.

OWENS, AMY E; Los Amigos HS; Fountain Valley, CA; (2); Church Yth Grp; Drama Clb; German Clb; Key Clb; Pep Clb; Thesps; School Musical; School Play; Var Swmmng; Hon Roll; Water Polo Stats; Equestrian Jmpng; UC Davis; Vet.

OWENS, ANDY; Mira Costa HS; Manhattan Beach, CA; (3); Art Clb; Key Clb; Letterman Clb; Yrbk; Var Capt Bsbl; JV Bsktbl; Cit Awd; High Hon Roll; Hon Roll; Ntl Merit Ltr; Outstndng Achvt Fine Art Trophy 89-90; All-Ocean Lg Tm Bsbl 90; Schlr Athlete Awd Bsbl, Bsktbl 87-90; UC.

OWENS, BRENDA; John Marshall Fund Secondary Schl; Pasadena, CA; (3); Church Yth Grp; Drama Clb; Teachers Aide; Church Choir; Drill Tm; Cit Awd; Stat Trk; Rop Childcare; Glitter Ave Clb; Pres The Voices Of Praise Chrch Yth Choir; Howard U; Pediatrcl Nurse.

OWENS, DANIELLE L; Summerville HS; Soulsbyville, CA; (3); Aud/Vis; Drama Clb; French Clb; Ski Clb; Chorus; School Play; Rptr Yrbk; Powder Puff Ftbl; Swmmng; JV Vllybl; Close-Up Pgm Washington DC; Cal Poly San Luis Obispo; Nutrn.

OWENS, DAVID R; Fresno Christian HS; Fresno, CA; (3); Church Yth Grp; Cmnty Wkr; 4-H; Chorus; Sec Treas Frsh Cls; JV Crs Cntry; Var Ftbl; High Hon Roll; Life Mbr CA Schlrshp Fdr; Choir Ensemble; Dnstry.

OWENS, DIANA C; Santa Clara HS; Oxnard, CA; (3); 22/145; Girl Scts; Varsity Clb; Var L Bsktbl; Var L Trk; Hon Roll; NHS; Fshn Merch.

OWENS, HEATHER M; Sierra H Union HS; Tollhouse, CA; (4); Sec Church Yth Grp; VP Service Clb; SADD; Teachers Aide; Acpl Chr; Chorus; Church Choir; School Musical; Bsktbl; Gym; Modeling Mrt; Girls Leag-VP; Vllybl Chmpnshp Wnnr; Fresno City.

OWENS, HOLLY C; Torrance HS; Torrance, CA; (4); Church Yth Grp; Pep Clb; Service Clb; Chorus; Church Choir; Cit Awd; Hon Roll; El Camino.

OWENS, JENESHIA K; Ingelwood HS; Los Angeles, CA; (1); Flag Corp; Mrchg Band; Ed Rptr Nwsp; Ed Rptr Yrbk; Swmmng; Mdlng Club; Stanford.

OWENS, JENNIFER; South Tahoe HS; S Lake Tahoe, CA; (3); 1/211; Treas Key Clb; Band; Treas Frsh Cls; JV Cheerldng; Var Crs Cntry; Var Swmmng; Var Trk; NHS; Prfct Atten Awd; Pres Acad Fit Awd; Reno Piano Fest Supr Awds; Life Sci.

OWENS, JESSICA; Red Bluff HS; Red Bluff, CA; (1); GAA; Key Clb; Science Clb; SADD; Bsktbl; JV Sftbl; Hon Roll; Chico ST U; Ocngrphr.

OWENS, JOHN P; Sierra Joint Union HS; Tollhouse, CA; (2); Boy Scts; Church Yth Grp; Drama Clb; SADD; Varsity Clb; Band; Chorus; Church Choir; Jazz Band; Mrchg Band; Golden St Exm High Hnrs; BYU; Comp Prgmr.

OWENS, JON; Capo Valley Christian HS; Mission Viejo, CA; (3); Church Yth Grp; Letterman Clb; Varsity Clb; Pres Jr Cls; Stu Cncl; L Bsktbl; Var Crs Cntry; High Hon Roll; Hon Roll; Ntl Merit Ltr; Hugh O'brien Yth Ambrsdr; Mission Clb; Law.

OWENS, KELLI N; Live Oak HS; Live Oak, CA; (4); FFA; Nwsp; Yrbk; Pres Jr Cls; Pres Stu Cncl; Bsktbl; Sftbl; Vllybl; DAR Awd; Hon Roll; Ftbl Hmcmng Qn 89; Rep Distngshd Schls Cnvntn 90; HS Prin Hiring Cmmtte 89; Yuba Coll; Nrsng.

OWENS, KRISTINA R; Hawthorne HS; Lennox, CA; (2); Church Yth Grp; Rptr Yrbk; Stat Bsktbl; Black Hstry Mnth Rep; New Life Club; Stu Ministry Awds; Psych.

OWENS, LISA L; Caruthers Union HS; Dinuba, CA; (4); Office Aide; Teachers Aide; Flag Corp; Bsktbl; Mgr(s); Score Keeper; Vllybl; Cit Awd; High Hon Roll; Block C; Fresno City Coll; Law Enfrcmnt.

OWENS, SANDRA R; Livermore HS; Livermore, CA; (3); Church Yth Grp; Debate Tm; Latin Clb; Library Aide; NFL; Speech Tm; Teachers Aide; Church Choir; Var Crs Cntry; Var Trk; Brigham Young U.

OWENS, SHEA; Selma HS; Selma, CA; (3); 64/200; Debate Tm; FFA; Teachers Aide; Hon Roll; Outstndng Pres Debate Tm 88; Outstndng Rptr Debate Tm 89; St Farmer Degree 90; UC Davis; Vet.

OWENS, XANATH; St Joseph HS; Long Beach, CA; (4); 36/173; Cmnty Wkr; Dance Clb; French Clb; Drill Tm; Cheerldng; High Hon Roll; Hon Roll; NHS; NEDT Awd Outstndng Acad Perf; Natl Hispanics Semi Fnlst; 1220 SAT Score; UCLA; Law.

OWER, DAVID W; St Francis HS; Pasadena, CA; (2); Cmnty Wkr; Letterman Clb; Var L Ftbl; Var L Trk; Var Wt Lftg; Del Rey League 2nd Pl Shotput; Trophy Most Imprvd Vrsty Trck; UCLA; Astronomy.

OWSKEY, ROBERT T; Fremont HS; Sunnyvale, CA; (2); Church Yth Grp; JV Capt Socr; Var Swmmng; Hon Roll; Pres Acad Fit Awd; Water Polo Capt All Leg Plyr MVP; GATE Clb; Annapolis Naval Acad; Chem.

OWSLEY, HOLLI; Edison HS; Lebanon, MO; (1); Dance Clb; Model UN; Stat Ftbl.

OWSLEY, KARI M; San Pasqual HS; Escondido, CA; (2); Church Yth Grp; Pep Clb; Pediatrics.

OXENDINE, VALERIE; Edison HS; Fresno, CA; (2); FTA; Hon Roll; CA Schlrshp Fed; USC.

OXFORD, SCOTT D; West HS; Bakersfield, CA; (2); 4-H; Letterman Clb; Ski Clb; Phtg Yrbk; Bsbl; Ftbl; Socr; Phys Ftns Awd; Sit-Up Recrd 89; CA Poly.

OXLEY, JENNIFER C; Glendale Adventist Acad; Pasadena, CA; (2); 2/56; Cmnty Wkr; FCA; Teachers Aide; Varsity Clb; Acpl Chr; Band; VP Frsh Cls; Intrml Bsbl; Var Intrml Bsktbl; Hon Roll; UC-BERKELEY; Med.

OYLER, CAMI L; Southern Calif Christian HS; Orange, CA; (3); Church Yth Grp; Office Aide; Spanish Clb; Teachers Aide; Yrbk; Var Capt Bsktbl; Var Sftbl; Hon Roll; Graphic Layout Artist.

OYLER, CANDICE L; Southern California Christian HS; Orange, CA; (2); Church Yth Grp; Office Aide; Teachers Aide; Var Sftbl; High Hon Roll; Hon Roll; Chrch Leag Vllybl, Ldr For Yng Children; Chld Psych.

OYOLA, JOSE J; John Burroughs HS; Burbank, CA; (3); Spanish Clb; JV Socr; Hon Roll.

OYTAS, NOMER R; Chula Vista HS; Bonita, CA; (3); 7/493; VP Pres Band; Jazz Band; Mrchg Band; Pep Band; Var Tennis; Cit Awd; Prfct Atten Awd; Pres Acad Fit Awd; CSF; Music Awds; Aerospace Engrng.

OZAETA, JERE S; Fresno Adventist Acad; Fresno, CA; (2); 1/23; Church Yth Grp; Teachers Aide; Off Soph Cls; Fld Hcky; Church Yth Grp; Hon Roll; NHS; Fresno Adventist Acad; Bio.

OZAETA, RIANAN A; Yucca Valley HS; Landers, CA; (2); Pres Church Yth Grp; Debate Tm; FBLA; Intnl Clb; Math Clb; Var Trk; Cit Awd; High Hon Roll; Hon Roll; Pres Acad Fit Awd; High Hnrs On The Golden St Exam; Top 10 Pct Of Stu Nationally; Comp Sci.

OZAWA, ALISON J; John Burroughs HS; Burbank, CA; (2); Rptr Nwsp; Rptr Phtg Yrbk; Lit Mag; Pres Jr Cls; Var Swmmng; JV Vllybl; High Hon Roll; Pres Acad Fit Awd; Yrbk Photo; Psych.

OZAWA, EDDIE; Culver City HS; Los Angeles, CA; (1); Teachers Aide; Rptr Yrbk; Rep Frsh Cls; Rep Soph Cls; JV Bsbl; JV Bsktbl; Elks Awd; Hon Roll; UCSD; Engr.

OZOA, DARA DIANA N; Notre Dame HS; San Jose, CA; (3); Church Yth Grp; JV Swmmng; Hon Roll; Drawing, Taking Photos, Dance; UC Santa Cruz; Bus Admin.

OZOLS, ALEX; Lowell HS; San Francisco, CA; (3); Cmnty Wkr; Dance Clb; German Clb; Model UN; Office Aide; Var L Tennis; Vrsty Badmitton Team; Law.

OZSVATH, RITA; Moorpark HS; Moorpark, CA; (2); High Hon Roll; Hon Roll; CSU Northridge; Tchr.

OZUNA, SELENA; Villa Park HS; Anaheim, CA; (3); Cmnty Wkr; Key Clb; Pres Pep Clb; SADD; Art Clb; Stu Cncl; Var JV Cheerldng; High Hon Roll; NHS; Aerospace Engr.

PABALINAS, ROMMEL T; Vallejo SR HS; Vallejo, CA; (3); Chess Clb; Hon Roll; Prfct Atten Awd; Pres Acad Fit Awd; Top Chem Stu; Bio.

PABLA, HARPEET; Dublin HS; Dublin, CA; (2); #1 In Class; JV Tennis; High Hon Roll; Pres Acad Fit Awd; Med.

PABLO, EILEEN P; Holy Family HS; Los Angeles, CA; (3); Cmnty Wkr; Chorus; Rptr Nwsp; Co-Ed Yrbk; Off Soph Cls; Sec Jr Cls; Stu Cncl; JV Bsktbl; JV Vllybl; Hon Roll; CSF; U CA-LOS Angeles; Math.

PABUSTAN, JOSEPHINE T; Newbury Park HS; Newbury Park, CA; (3); Dance Clb; FBLA; Key Clb; Drill Tm; Hon Roll; Deans List Acad GPA; Awd Mst Outstndng Soph; Filipino Clb; Grls Leag; Corp Law.

PACAL, ADAM R; Birmingham HS; Encino, CA; (3); 1/700; FBLA; Hosp Aide; Math Clb; SADD; Bsktbl; JV Trk; Hon Roll; Ntl Merit SF; Val; Med.

PACE, JAMES; Monte Vista Christian HS; Morgan Hill, CA; (4); 2/100; Math Clb; Math Tm; Treas Frsh Cls; Treas Soph Cls; Treas Jr Cls; Treas Sr Cls; Mgr Bsktbl; JV Golf; Var Socr; High Hon Roll; U CA Davis; Comp Sci.

PACE, KIMBERLEY; Sierra Joint Union HS; North Fork, CA; (3); Art Clb; Cmnty Wkr; Model UN; SADD; Teachers Aide; Yrbk; Rep Soph Cls; VP Jr Cls; Hon Roll; Art Awds; Comm Art & Gallery Showings; Fresno ST; Art.

PACE, LISA; Poway HS; San Diego, CA; (3); SADD; Teachers Aide; Trk; High Hon Roll; NHS; CSF; UCSD.

PACHECO, ANA C; Etiwanda HS; Etiwanda, CA; (2); High Hon Roll; Hon Roll; Prfct Atten Awd; Bus.

PACHECO, ARTHUR; St Anthony HS; Long Beach, CA; (3); Am Leg Boys St; Spanish Clb; Variety Show; Ed Nwsp; Var JV Bsbl; JV Bsktbl; Hon Roll; Prfct Atten Awd; Bus.

PACHECO, CHRISTINE M; Mt Pleasant HS; San Jose, CA; (4); 57/289; Church Yth Grp; FBLA; Teachers Aide; Varsity Clb; Yrbk; JV Var Tennis; French Hon Soc; Hon Roll; NHS.

PACHECO, CLAUDIA; Calexico HS; Calexico, CA; (3); Church Yth Grp; Cmnty Wkr; Treas FBLA; Office Aide; Spanish Clb; Teachers Aide; Flag Corp; Mrchg Band; Flag Sqd 3 Yrs; Teacher.

PACHECO, ELIZABETH; Garfield HS; Los Angeles, CA; (3); Bus Profs of Am; Cmnty Wkr; Flag Corp; Off Jr Cls; Bsktbl; Cheerldng; Prfct Atten Awd; ELA Coll; Bus.

PACHECO, ELIZABETH; John H Francis Polytechnic HS; North Hollywood, CA; (3); Drama Clb; Letterman Clb; Spanish Clb; Sec SADD; Teachers Aide; Rptr Nwsp; Phtg Yrbk; Rep Stu Cncl; Powder Puff Ftbl; Hon Roll; Ladies & Squires-Treas; CJSF; CSF; Obstetrcs.

PACHECO, JANNETTE G; John Muir HS; Los Angeles, CA; (3); Church Yth Grp; Cmnty Wkr; Teachers Aide; Stage Crew; VP Frsh Cls; Pres Soph Cls; Pltcl Clb Founder; HOBY Soph Cls Rep; CA ST U Los Angeles; Lwyr.

PACHECO, JOSE J; Long Beach Plytechnic HS; Long Beach, CA; (4); 101/789; Church Yth Grp; Drama Clb; FBLA; Intnl Clb; Key Clb; Math Tm; SADD; School Play; Pres Frsh Cls; Tennis; MA Inst Of Tech; Bio Sci.

PACHECO, JUAN C; Los Altos HS; Industry, CA; (3); Science Clb; Hon Roll; Robotics; Robotics.

PACHECO, VERONICA; St Michaels HS; Los Angeles, CA; (2); GAA; Spanish Clb; Flag Corp; JV Vllybl; Hon Roll.

PACHO, JOANNE; Independence HS; San Jose, CA; (3); Cmnty Wkr; Hosp Aide; Thesps; School Musical; School Play; JV Var Pom Pon; High Hon Roll; Hon Roll; NHS; Treas Frsh Cls; Rookie Yr Awd Annl Theatre Awds; Harvard; Pre-Law.

PACK, CATHERINE Y; Poway HS; Poway, CA; (2); 3/834; Church Yth Grp; JV Crs Cntry; JV Trk; High Hon Roll; Env Clb; Golden St Awd Geo.

PACK, HEIDI K; Gompers Secondary Schl; San Diego, CA; (2); 8/145; Pres Church Yth Grp; JV Vllybl; High Hon Roll; Hon Roll; Acad Ltr; 3rd Pl Rgnl Sci Fair & Astrnmy Assn Awd.

PACK, KRISTINA L; San Bernardino HS; San Bernardino, CA; (4); 19/365; Church Yth Grp; Letterman Clb; Scholastic Bowl; Church Choir; Variety Show; Ed Yrbk; Co-Capt Cheerldng; Var Swmmng; High Hon Roll; Pres Acad Fit Awd; Brigham Young U; Microbio.

PACK, LINDA S; Canyon Springs HS; Moreno Valley, CA; (3); Church Yth Grp; Treas FBLA; Pep Clb; Drill Tm; Mrchg Band; Yrbk; Lit Mag; Rep Jr Cls; Acad Achvt Awd; Brigham Young U.

PACK, LISA; Mater Dei HS; Westminster, CA; (4); 1/540; Ski Clb; Chorus; Rep Frsh Cls; Stu Cncl; Stat Bsktbl; High Hon Roll; NHS; Pres Acad Fit Awd; CSF; Soroptomist Intl Santa Ana; Tustin Girl Of Mnth; 100 Hrs Comm Svc; UCLA; Law.

PACKARD, BRENT ALBERT; Lutheran HS; Santa Ana, CA; (3); 1/120; Stat Bsktbl; Hon Roll; Acad Decath; CA Schlrshp Fed; Achvt Awds-Phys Sci Chem Algb II Physcs & Spnsh I & III; U CA Irvine; Biotech.

PACKER, LYNN T; Kearny SR HS; San Diego, CA; (4); 14/297; Office Aide; SADD; Varsity Clb; Yrbk; Var L Bsbl; Hon Roll; Jr NHS; NHS; Pres Acad Fit Awd; San Diego Cnty Med Scty Awd 1st Pl; Cty Cnfrnc All Acad Tm Bsebl 1989-90; UCSD; Engr.

PACLEB, JOANNE M; Hogan HS; Vallejo, CA; (3); Church Yth Grp; Cmnty Wkr; Science Clb; Spanish Clb; SADD; Yrbk; Treas Frsh Cls; Ftbl; Powder Puff Ftbl; Vllybl; UC Berkeley; Phrmcy.

PADACA, MELISSA D; Vacaville HS; Vacaville, CA; (3); Cmnty Wkr; Science Clb; Spanish Clb; Band; Cit Awd; High Hon Roll; NHS; Prfct Atten Awd; Pres Acad Fit Awd; Pres Schlr; Gldn St Exam Awd Alg; Solono Cnty Lit Awd Shrt Stry; VP SPCA Clb; UCLA; Psych.

PADADAN, JIMMY T; Balboa HS; San Francisco, CA; (3); Debate Tm; Drama Clb; ROTC; Temple Yth Grp; Acpl Chr; Chorus; School Play; High Hon Roll; Hon Roll; Lit Mag; De La Salle U; Music.

PADAYHAG, SUSIE N; Edison HS; Stockton, CA; (2); Key Clb; Service Clb; Stat Bsbl; Hon Roll; Piano; UOP; Music.

PADDEN, RYAN J; Del Campo HS; Citrus Heights, CA; (3); 1/446; Boy Scts; ROTC; Scholastic Bowl; Treas Stu Cncl; Intrml Bsktbl; Var Ftbl; Capt Sftbl; JV Swmmng; Capt Vllybl; JV Wrstlng; Air Force Assn Awd; Amer Lgn Schltc Excllnce; Intl Law.

PADDEN, TIMOTHY J; Del Campo HS; Citrus Heights, CA; (1); 92/460; Boy Scts; Church Yth Grp; Cmnty Wkr; ROTC; Drill Tm; Rep Frsh Cls; Intrml Vllybl; Cit Awd; ROTC Mltry Ordr Wrld Wrs Awd; Bsa Ad Altr Dei Rlgs Emblm; USAF; Arch.

PADDOCK, BRIDGET S; El Dorado HS; Placentia, CA; (3); GAA; Intnl Clb; Science Clb; Varsity Clb; Rep Stu Cncl; Var Socr; Var Swmmng; Var Tennis; High Hon Roll; Jr NHS; Bus.

PADDOCK, DEANNA C; Alpaugh Unified HS; Alpaugh, CA; (4); 3/9; Science Clb; Ed Nwsp; Ed Yrbk; VP Soph Cls; Sec Jr Cls; VP Sr Cls; Var Cheerldng; Var Sftbl; Var Vllybl; Hon Roll; Alace Skeen Awd; Cls Hstrn; Riverside; Athletic Tranner.

PADGETT, BARBARA A; Manteca HS; Manteca, CA; (4); 1/326; Church Yth Grp; Pres FBLA; Letterman Clb; Spanish Clb; Ed Yrbk; VP Stu Cncl; 4-H Awd; NHS; Val; Poem Pblshd In Poetic Vcs Of Amer; Coca-Cola Schlrshp Semi-Fnlst; Bnk Of Amer Plq Awd Wnnr-Lbrl Arts; Hstry.

PADGETT, CARISSA N; Beaumont HS; Cherry Valley, CA; (1); Church Yth Grp; FCA; French Clb; Church Choir; Flag Corp; Variety Show; Treas Soph Cls; Hon Roll; Hand Identification Shields; Indpndnt Drama Grp; Pepperdine U; Engl.

PADGETT, LISA; Willows HS; Willows, CA; (4); 24/100; FBLA; Office Aide; Teachers Aide; Var Cheerldng; Score Keeper; Var Sftbl; JV Vllybl; Hon Roll; Block W; Vocational Olympcs; Butte Coll; Acctng.

PADGETT, MARIA; Chula Vista HS; Chula Vista, CA; (2); Office Aide; Pep Clb; Chorus; Drill Tm; JV Var Cheerldng; Gym; Cit Awd; Hon Roll; Pres Acad Fit Awd; UC-BERKELEY; Psych.

PADGETT, SPENCER; St Michaels College Prep Schl; Lake Forest, CA; (2); Art Clb; Stat Bsktbl; High Hon Roll; NHS; US Naval Acad.

PADGETT, TIFFANY; Luther Burbank HS; Sacramento, CA; (2); 43/315; SADD; Stage Crew; Score Keeper; Hon Roll; Spellma Coll; Electrncs.

PADILLA, ABEL M; Aragon HS; Foster City, CA; (2); Church Yth Grp; Cmnty Wkr; Teachers Aide; Band; Earth Day; Dance Decortng Cmmttee.

PADILLA, ANGELICA M; Sunset HS; Hayward, CA; (2); Rep Frsh Cls; Rep Soph Cls; Var Cheerldng; Hon Roll; Broadcasting.

PADILLA, CINDY Z; Santa Cruz HS; Santa Cruz, CA; (2); Hon Roll; Law.

PADILLA, DANETTE; Sonora HS; Springerville, AZ; (3); Art Clb; Dance Clb; GAA; Ski Clb; Gym; JV Sftbl; JV Vllybl; Female Phys Ftnss Awd.

PADILLA, DANIEL V; Loyola HS; Glendale, CA; (2); Art Clb; Drama Clb; Intnl Clb; Letterman Clb; Science Clb; Orch; School Musical; Variety Show; Ed Lit Mag; JV Crs Cntry; CSF; Yng Musicians Fndtn Chambr Music Schlrshp Opers Stgrng Quartet.

PADILLA, DEREK SHANE; El Camino HS; Daly City, CA; (3); 11/343; Math Tm; Varsity Clb; Ed Rep Nwsp; Lit Mag; Pres Jr Cls; JV Var Ftbl; Mgr(s); JV Var Trk; High Hon Roll; Jr NHS; Acad Ltr 87-88; Vlntr Tutor; Golden Puet Awd 88-89; Multi-Cultural Club; CA Schlrshp Fed; Amnsty Intl; UC Davis; Englsh.

PADILLA, DUANE J; Loyola HS; Glendale, CA; (2); Art Clb; Drama Clb; Intnl Clb; Letterman Clb; Science Clb; Orch; School Musical; Variety Show; Ed Lit Mag; JV Crs Cntry; CSF; Yng Muscns Fndtn; Chambr Musc Schlrshp Awd Wnnr.

PADILLA, EDGAR B; Servite HS; Buena Park, CA; (2); Varsity Clb; Var Tennis; MVP Tenns Var Awd 89-90; UCI; MD.

PADILLA, EFREN; Rio Mesa HS; Oxnard, CA; (1); Bsbl; Cal Lutheran U Upwrd Bnd Pgm; Stanford; Neurology.

PADILLA, GRACIELA; Southwest HS; San Diego, CA; (3); 10/493; Dance Clb; Latin Clb; Spanish Clb; Hon Roll; Mexican Rodeos; UCSD; Vet.

PADILLA, JOAHNNA A; Mater Dei HS; Huntington Beach, CA; (3); Cmnty Wkr; Ed Yrbk; High Hon Roll; NHS; CSF; Stanford U; Bio.

PADILLA, JOCELYN; Paraclete HS; Lancaster, CA; (1); JV Vllybl; CA Schlrshp Fdrtn; Prncpls Hnr Roll.

PADILLA, JOSEPH V; Paraclete HS; Lancaster, CA; (3); Yrbk; Treas Jr Cls; JV Crs Cntry; Var Socr; JV Trk; NHS; NEDT Awd; CSF; Principals List Awd; MIT; Engr.

PADILLA, LORENA R; Norco HS; Norco, CA; (2); Dance Clb; FBLA; Church Choir; Rptr Nwsp; Lion Awd; Rotary Awd; Excllnce Referal Math; Journlsm.

PADILLA, LYNN A; Valley HS; Sacramento, CA; (2); 71/280; SADD; Drill Tm; Hon Roll; Psych.

PADILLA, MARIA G; Lincoln Prep HS; San Diego, CA; (2); 62/272; Computer Clb; Teachers Aide; Cit Awd; Bus Admin.

PADILLA, MARIBEL; Sweetwater HS; National City, CA; (3); Church Yth Grp; French Clb; Teachers Aide; Trk; Cit Awd; French Hon Soc; Hon Roll; Hnrs Club; UCLA; Law.

PADILLA, MICHAEL; Calvin Simmons JR HS; Oakland, CA; (1); ROTC; Drill Tm; Cit Awd; Hon Roll; Aeronaut Engr.

PADILLA, MICHAEL T; North Hollywood HS; Sunland, CA; (3); Band; Var L Tennis; High Hon Roll; Hon Roll.

PADILLA, NAOMI R; William Workman HS; Valinda, CA; (1); #93 In Class; Drama Clb; Crsss Stitchng; Aerbcs; Band; Bus.

PADILLA, PATRICIA A; Roosevelt HS; Los Angeles, CA; (3); Dance Clb.

PADILLA, RAYMOND L; Escalon HS; Escalon, CA; (1); Debate Tm; German Clb; JV Ftbl; JV Tennis; UC Berkeley; Law.

PADILLA, RONNIE; San Gabriel Acad; Huntington Park, CA; (4); Yrbk; Pres Frsh Cls; Loma Linda U Mrt Schlrshp; Pacific Union Coll.

PADILLA, SANDIA S; Roosevelt HS; Fresno, CA; (4); Library Aide; CA ST U Fresno.

PADILLA, TERESA; Victor Valley HS; Victorville, CA; (2); Church Yth Grp; Office Aide; Sftbl; Vllybl.

PADMORE, LORI; St Patricks/St Vincent HS; Vallejo, CA; (4); 13/150; Letterman Clb; Pep Clb; Drill Tm; Var L Bsktbl; Var L Cheerldng; Var L Pom Pon; Var L Sftbl; High Hon Roll; Ntl Merit Ltr; Bio.

PADOVICH, SAMANTHA; Saugus HS; Saugus, CA; (4); 62/440; Church Yth Grp; Office Aide; Pep Clb; Teachers Aide; Church Choir; Stu Cncl; Var Cheerldng; Hon Roll; Chrch Awds; UT Vly CC; Law.

PADUA, EZRA P; Glendale HS; Glendale, CA; (2); Art Clb; Computer Clb; French Clb; Capt Vllybl; Cit Awd; Prfct Atten Awd; CA ST Los Angeles; Cmmrcl Art.

PADUA, JERILYN; Bonita Vista HS; Bonita, CA; (4); 50/532; Church Yth Grp; Office Aide; Drill Tm; Flag Corp; Mrchg Band; Rep Nwsp; Yrbk; Hon Roll; Maria Clara De Pilipinas Sorority Bus Mgr; San Diego U; Bus.

PADUA, RACHELLE; Lemoore HS; Lemoore, CA; (3); Pep Clb; Spanish Clb; SADD; Var Cheerldng; Powder Puff Ftbl; High Hon Roll; San Diego ST; Bus Mgmt.

PAECK, JOANN; Chatsworth HS; Northridge, CA; (3); Church Yth Grp; Ski Clb; Off Frsh Cls; Stu Cncl; Cheerldng; UC Santa Barbara; Int Dsgn.

PAET, ANDREA A; Chamindade Coll Prep; Northridge, CA; (3); Science Clb; Rptr Nwsp; Cmnty Wkr; Campus Ministry; Astronomy Club Pres; Bio Club; Asian-Am Club; Radio Club; Sci Fair; Sp Acad Levle I/Ii; Med.

PAET, BEVERLY T; Independence HS; San Jose, CA; (2); Band; Color Guard; Mrchg Band; Hon Roll; U/Coll Opportunity Pgm; Battle Of The Classes Schl Rallies; Acad Achvt Awds; U CA-BERKELEY; Engr.

PAEZ, ANARELLA C; Nogales HS; La Puente, CA; (2); Pep Clb; Chorus; Var Cheerldng; JV Sftbl; Hon Roll; Prfct Atten Awd; Show Choir; Cert Recgntn Excllnce Engl; Vet Med.

PAEZ, FABIAN; Blair HS; Pasadena, CA; (3); Computer Clb; JA; ROTC; Drill Tm; Wt Lftg; Cit Awd; High Hon Roll; Prfct Atten Awd; Mrksmnshp Clv; ROP Mchncs; LSR Tech.

PAEZ, GILBERT; Mark Keppel HS; Monterey Park, CA; (1); Church Yth Grp; Band; Mrchg Band; Pep Band; JV Swmmng; Play Trumpet In Christian Music Ministry Group; USC; Computer Field.

PAEZ, JOSE; John H Francis Polytechnic HS; Pacoina, CA; (3); Spanish Clb; Teachers Aide; Band; Cit Awd; High Hon Roll; Hon Roll; Prfct Atten Awd; Indstrl Ed Mdlln Awd; Electronics Tech.

PAEZ, KATHIA C; Nogales HS; La Puente, CA; (3); 34/544; Dance Clb; French Clb; Office Aide; Pep Clb; Var Cheerldng; Hon Roll; Cert Rcgntn Excllnc Frnch III; Mt St Marys Coll; Med.

PAEZ JR, NELSON M; Walnut HS; Walnut, CA; (3); Bus Profs of Am; Chess Clb; Church Yth Grp; FBLA; Hosp Aide; Key Clb; Latin Clb; Spanish Clb; JV Bsktbl; Var Tennis; U Of CA L A; Med.

PAFFORD, LAURA C; Dos Palos Joint Union HS; Dos Palos, CA; (2); 9/125; AFS; Church Yth Grp; 4-H; GAA; Pep Clb; Mrchg Band; Bsktbl; Sftbl; Tennis; Vllybl; CSF; Fresno ST U; Teacher.

PAFFORD, REBECCA L; Bret Harte HS; Copperopolis, CA; (2); Church Yth Grp; FHA; Pep Clb; School Play; Sec Jr Cls; Stat Bsktbl; Cheerldng; Pom Pon; 2nd Pl St Cmptn FHA Energy Cnsrvtn; Peer Cnclng; Chico.

PAGADUAN, JOANN S; Mt Carmel HS; San Diego, CA; (3); Band; Mrchg Band; Pediatrcs.

PAGALING, ANTHONY; Southwest HS; San Diego, CA; (3); 31/400; FBLA; JA; Letterman Clb; Varsity Clb; Rep Frsh Cls; Var JV Bsbl; Var JV Ftbl; Cit Awd; Hon Roll; San Diego ST U; Bus.

PAGALING, MARIANO; Southwest HS; San Diego, CA; (3); FBLA; Rep Frsh Cls; Stu Cncl; Var Bsbl; JV Ftbl; Hon Roll; U Of CA Los Angeles; Bus Admin.

PAGAN, MARIA; Enterprise HS; Shingletown, CA; (4); Dance Clb; Drill Tm; Var Pom Pon; Mgr Stat Trk; Hon Roll; U Of Berkely CA; Opomtry.

PAGE, AMY K; Apple Valley HS; Apple Valley, CA; (3); FFA; GAA; JV Var Bsktbl; Capt Var Sftbl; JV Var Vllybl; Hon Roll; Var Sftbl All Leag 1st Tm; Var Vlybl Dist Champs 89; Comm.

PAGE, CARISTA L; San Bernardino HS; San Bernardino, CA; (4); Teachers Aide; Band; Cit Awd; Hon Roll; CSUSB; Psych.

PAGE, CYNTHIA D; Twenty Nine Palms HS; Twentynine Palms, CA; (3); Pep Clb; Teachers Aide; Acpl Chr; Band; Chorus; Church Choir; Jazz Band; Mrchg Band; Pep Band; School Musical.

PAGE, DI ANDRE L; Hilmar JR-SR HS; Stevinson, CA; (3); 1/111; JV Var Bsktbl; Var Trk; Hon Roll; CSF; Acad All Amer Schlr; UC Irvine; Comp Sci.

PAGE, KIMI; San Pedro HS; San Pedro, CA; (2); Dance Clb; Debate Tm; NFL; Pep Clb; Capt Cheerldng; UCLA; Law.

PAGE, LAURA CATHERINE; West Valley HS; Cottonwood, CA; (4); Church Yth Grp; English Clb; Office Aide; Spanish Clb; SADD; Teachers Aide; Church Choir; Sec Jr Cls; Var Cheerldng; George Grotefund Schlrshp; Anderson Union HS Dist Cmmnty Schlrshp; BYU; Vocal.

PAGE, LAWRENCE A; Arroyo Grande HS; Grover City, CA; (3); Hon Roll; Lang Arts Awd; 2nd Pl Hstry Day; Kung Fu; San Francisco ST U; Intl Bus.

PAGE, LETECIA; Barstow HS; Barstow, CA; (3); 10/330; Rep Jr Cls; JV Cheerldng; JV Trk; High Hon Roll; Hon Roll; Acadc Dcthln 89-90; Secy Blck Stu Union 88-89; Pres Black Stu Union 89-90; Engl.

PAGE, PATRICK; Shafter HS; Bakersfield, CA; (4); 9/230; Boy Scts; JV Ftbl; Var Swmmng; JV Wrstlng; Ntl Merit SF; CSF Life Mem; USJA Judo HS Natls 2nd P-89; Bank Of Am Achvt Awd-Sci; San Diego ST U; Mech Engrng.

PAGE, RACHEL L; Carlsbad HS; Carlsbad, CA; (1); Church Yth Grp; Key Clb; Chorus; Church Choir; VP Stu Cncl; Cit Awd; DAR Awd; Hon Roll; Prfct Atten Awd; Pres Acad Fit Awd; Bobby Sox Sftbl; Brigham Young U; Ed.

PAGE, REGINA; Senior HS; Oakland, CA; (4); 2/6; Pres Church Yth Grp; Computer Clb; Office Aide; Spanish Clb; Teachers Aide; Chorus; School Musical; School Play; Rptr Nwsp; Ed Yrbk; Yth Cnslr Volunteer; Nrsng.

PAGE, RENEE M; Del Notre HS; Auburn, MI; (2); Church Yth Grp; Drama Clb; School Play; Stage Crew; Variety Show; Ed Rptr Yrbk; Cit Awd; Hon Roll; Prfct Atten Awd; Reading; Law.

PAGE, ROBYN A.; Woodside HS; Redwood City, CA; (3); AFS; Church Yth Grp; Cmnty Wkr; Teachers Aide; Ed Rptr Nwsp; Rep Stu Cncl; Cheerldng; Harvard Book Awd; Interact Clb Pres; Spirit Cmmssr; Intl Rltns.

PAGE, SHAUNA L; Sonora HS; Sonora, CA; (3); 22/277; VP Frsh Cls; Rep Soph Cls; Stu Cncl; Capt Var Bsktbl; Capt Var Vllybl; UC Santa Barbara; Psycht.

PAGE, SHERRI R; Valhalla HS; El Cajon, CA; (4); 3/433; Drama Clb; Pres French Clb; Scholastic Bowl; Thesps; School Play; Var L Bsktbl; High Hon Roll; Ntl Merit SF; Acad Decathlon 2 Gld Mdls Lit & Interview 88; Yth Ldrshp Awd-Natl Yth Ldrs Conf.

PAGE, TINA A; San Gabriel Mission HS; Monterey Park, CA; (3); Church Yth Grp; GAA; Letterman Clb; Pep Clb; Varsity Clb; Var Cheerldng; Var Sftbl; Sftbl Horizon All Leag Awd; Bus.

PAGE, TONYA FAY; Patten Acad Of Christian Ed; Oakland, CA; (3); 2/6; Pres Church Yth Grp; Cmnty Wkr; Pres Debate Tm; VP Speech Tm; Teachers Aide; Rep Chorus; School Musical; School Play; Rptr Nwsp; Ed Yrbk; Spnsh Hnrs; Hstry Hnr; Hstry Prfssr.

PAGPAGUITAN, FRITZIE; Sunset HS; Hayward, CA; (3); English Clb; Girl Scts; Math Clb; Science Clb; Variety Show; Sec Jr Cls; Cheerldng; Vllybl; Hon Roll; Excllnc Awd; Typing; Comp.

PAGSANJAN JR, RODOLFO G; Hanford Joint Union HS; Hanford, CA; (2); Art Clb; FBLA; JV Crs Cntry; Hon Roll; CSF; Bio.

PAGTAKHAN, JORI BAYANI G; Stagg SR HS; Stockton, CA; (1); High Hon Roll.

PAHAL, BINDERJIT; Livingston HS; Livingston, CA; (1); Cit Awd; Hon Roll; Prfct Atten Awd.

PAHAL, CHARANJIT; Livingston HS; Livingston, CA; (2); French Clb; Cit Awd; Hon Roll; Kiwanis Awd; Prfct Atten Awd; Perfect Attendance Since 6th Grd; RN.

PAHL, MOLLY J; Carlsbad HS; Carlsbad, CA; (1); Pep Clb; SADD; Pres Chorus; VP Frsh Cls; JV Capt Socr; Var L Swmmng; Hon Roll; NCA Swm Tm; Music Dir.

PAHWA, SANDHYA; Washington HS; Fremont, CA; (4); FCA; French Clb; Key Clb; Library Aide; Service Clb; Color Guard; Flag Corp; Mrchg Band; School Musical; Nwsp; Badminton Tm; Bus Clb; Indian Youth Grp; UC Berkeley; Med.

PAI, EDWIN P; John W North HS; Riverside, CA; (4); 3/317; JV Var Tennis; Opt Clb Awd; Pres Acad Fit Awd; Spanish NHS; Val; Ceramics; California Scholarship Federation; U Of Calif; Biomedical Science.

PAI, JENNIFER S; Bolsa Grande HS; Garden Grove, CA; (1); VP Church Yth Grp; Computer Clb; Intnl Clb; Key Clb; Spanish Clb; Church Choir; Orch; School Musical; High Hon Roll; Hon Roll; Fine Arts Clb; Acad Decath; U C Irvine; Med.

PAI, KEVIN SUN; Montclair HS; Mira Loma, CA; (2); JV Capt Ftbl; JV Trk; JV Wt Lftg; Ftbl; Construction.

PAIGE, CHRISTOPHER M; Manteca HS; Manteca, CA; (1); 17/430; SADD; Band; Mrchg Band; JV Tennis; High Hon Roll; Math.

PAIGE, MATT; Lincoln HS; Stockton, CA; (3); 79/592; JV Bsbl; JV Var Bsktbl; JV Var Ftbl; JV Socr; Hon Roll; Pltcl Clb; CSF; Arch.

PAIGE, MATTHEW J; Cardinal Newman HS; Sebastopol, CA; (2); Service Clb; JV Bsbl; JV Bsktbl; JV Golf; Wt Lftg; High Hon Roll; Pres Acad Fit Awd; Sprts Jrnlst.

PAIK, ANDREA; Saint Ignatius HS; San Bruno, CA; (2); Crs Cntry; Hon Roll; Math.

PAIK, RENE; Alameda HS; Alameda, CA; (4); 56/331; Church Yth Grp; French Clb; Orch; Ed Nwsp; Lit Mag; Sec Soph Cls; Sec Jr Cls; Off Sr Cls; Sec Stu Cncl; Oakland Yth, San Francisco Yth Orch; UC Berkeley.

PAINE, EVAN L; South Fork HS; Miranda, CA; (3); 6/65; SADD; School Musical; Bsktbl; Ftbl; High Hon Roll; Prfct Atten Awd; CSF; HROP; Rotary Awd; Engrng.

PAINTER, CHARITY; Mt Whitney HS; Visalia, CA; (2); Church Yth Grp; Hon Roll; Dance, Ballet, Tap, Jazz; Amer Lgn Awd; Pres Awd Outstndng Acad Achvt; Int Decorator.

PAINTER, GREG R; Mt Shasta HS; Mount Shasta, CA; (3); Engrng.

PAINTER, TARA; Fairfield HS; Fairfield, CA; (4); Orch; High Hon Roll; Hon Roll; U Of CA; Psych.

PAISLEY, SUZANNE N; Foothill HS; Santa Ana, CA; (4); 58/346; Church Yth Grp; Cmnty Wkr; Pep Clb; Red Cross Aide; School Musical; Var Capt Cheerldng; Var Capt Gym; High Hon Roll; Lion Awd; NHS; Central Orange Cnty Panhellenic Schlrshp; U AZ Alumni Schlrshp; U AZ; Ed.

PAISTE, JANE; Samuel F B Morse HS; San Diego, CA; (4); Art Clb; Treas DECA; French Clb; Office Aide; Teachers Aide; Capt Flag Corp; Nwsp; Off Frsh Cls; Piano 9 Yrs; Bank Of Amer Achvt Awd-Bus; USA Awds & Ribbons; San Diego ST U; Nrsng.

PAIT, RONNIELO; Southwest HS; San Diego, CA; (2); 44/673; SADD; Stu Cncl; Hon Roll; ASB Comm; Peace Clb; UC Berkley; Corp Law.

PAJELA, ROSELYNN T; Salinas HS; Salinas, CA; (2); Band; Color Guard; Jazz Band; Mrchg Band; Orch; Pep Band; JV Bsktbl; JV Trk; Hon Roll; San Jose ST; Engrng.

PAJO, VOLTAIRE A; Gladstone HS; Azusa, CA; (4); Science Clb; SADD; JV Var Tennis; High Hon Roll; Prfct Atten Awd; Rotary Awd; CA Poly Pomona; Mech Engrng.

PAK, CHONG NAM; Fairfax HS; Los Angeles, CA; (3); Library Aide; Drill Tm; Art; UCLA; Art.

PAK, HYEMI; Wasco Union HS; Wasco, CA; (3); 3/200; Church Yth Grp; VP Cmnty Wkr; FHA; Math Clb; Rptr Nwsp; Sec Soph Cls; Pres Jr Cls; Pres Sr Cls; Rep Stu Cncl; Var Tennis; Mock Trial-Dfns Atty; Acad Decthln Hnrs; CSF-GOLD Card/Pres; Bus Admin.

PAK, JOON; Rancho Alamitos HS; Garden Grove, CA; (2); FCA; Spanish Clb; Ftbl; Wrstlng; High Hon Roll; Hon Roll; UCLA.

PAK, KYU H; Granada Hills HS; Northridge, CA; (4); 53/550; Cmnty Wkr; Computer Clb; Science Clb; Mrchg Band; Tennis; Prfct Atten Awd; Pres Acad Fit Awd; UCLA; Elec Engrng.

PAK, MARIO; Abraham Lincoln HS; San Francisco, CA; (2); Acad Of Finance; UCSF; Doc.

PAK, MIHUI; Santa Monica HS; Santa Monica, CA; (4); 17/620; Drama Clb; Stage Crew; Rptr Nwsp; High Hon Roll; Ntl Merit SF; Chch Vlntr; UCLA Hnr Schlr; Delian Hnr Socty Secy.

PAK, SOYUNG; Palo Alto HS; Palo Alto, CA; (2); Cmnty Wkr; German Clb; Intnl Clb; Band; Mrchg Band; Pep Band; Rptr Mgr Nwsp; Swmmng; Hon Roll.

PAK, SUNNY K; Lowell HS; San Francisco, CA; (3); Boy Scts; Chess Clb; Cmnty Wkr; Hosp Aide; Science Clb; Orch; Ed Nwsp; Med Explr Post VP Vlntrng; Bio Club Pres; CA Music Educ Assn; CSF; Shield & Scroll Hnr Soc; Pre Med.

PAL, SANGEETA; Arcadia HS; Arcadia, CA; (3); 55/643; Chrmn Hosp Aide; Red Cross Aide; Band; Mrchg Band; Phtg Yrbk; Hon Roll; NHS; Pres Acad Fit Awd; Acad Dcthln Team.

PALACIOS, DANIEL; Mt Carmel HS; San Diego, CA; (4); Boy Scts; VP Chess Clb; Church Yth Grp; Pres Computer Clb; Golden St Exam Geom Hnrs; Aerosp Engrng.

PALACIOS, GINA; Burlingame HS; Millbrae, CA; (3); Church Yth Grp; Spanish Clb; Lit Mag; Var Crs Cntry; Var Trk; Search & Rescue.

PALACIOS, JOSE RAFAEL; Burlingqme HS; San Francisco, CA; (4); Coll Of San Mateo; Arch.

PALACIOS, JULIE A; Canyon Springs HS; Moreno Valley, CA; (2); Church Yth Grp; Stage Crew; Trk; Child Dvlpmnt & Cnslr; Chld Dvlpmnt.

PALACIOS, STEPHANIE; Fall River JR-SR HS; Fall River Mills, CA; (4); 20/50; FBLA; Office Aide; Teachers Aide; Yrbk; Sec Sr Cls; Hon Roll; Yrbk Medal Jr; Heald Evergreen Coll; Accntnt.

PALANCA, ANJANETTE G; St Joseph HS; Cerritos, CA; (3); 47/200; Cmnty Wkr; Drama Clb; GAA; Varsity Clb; School Play; JV Var Tennis; High Hon Roll; Hon Roll; Prfct Atten Awd; Outstndng Stu Awd-Peace & Just Cls & Intro To Comp Cls; Explorers Club Career Awareness; Tnns Tm Awd; Graphic Dsgn.

PALANCA, GEORGIANA V; University HS; Los Angeles, CA; (3); Latin Clb; Teachers Aide; Rep Frsh Cls; JV Cheerldng; Hon Roll; Amnsty Intl; Illstrtn Awd; Peer Cnslng Pgm.

PALANCA, MONA L; Bishop Amat Memorial HS; West Covina, CA; (1); Drill Tm; Filipino Dance Clb; Med.

PALAZZO, CAMILLE R; Savanna HS; Anaheim, CA; (3); FBLA; Pep Clb; Rep Frsh Cls; Rep Soph Cls; Rep Jr Cls; Pres Sr Cls; Stu Cncl; Stat Bsktbl; Powder Puff Ftbl; Var JV Vllybl; Vlntr Spcl Olympcs; March Of Dimes Walk-A-Thon; Vlntr Cystic Fibrosis; Bus.

PALEMBAS, JENNIFER L; Corona HS; Corona, CA; (1); Church Yth Grp; Drama Clb; Chorus; School Musical; Pres Acad Fit Awd; CSF; Choir Ltr; Theatre Arts.

PALENSCHAT, SARAH; Bonita Vista HS; Bonita, CA; (4); SADD; Chorus; Sec Frsh Cls; Sec Soph Cls; Sec Jr Cls; Capt Cheerldng; Trk; Stat Wrstlng; Hon Roll; Hmcmng Qn; UC Davis; Nutrition.

PALIGUTAN, ADRIAN W R; Southwest HS; San Diego, CA; (4); #1 In Class; Am Leg Boys St; Cmnty Wkr; Drama Clb; English Clb; Math Tm; SADD; School Play; Stage Crew; Swing Chorus; Variety Show; U C Berkley; Civil Engnr.

PALLO, LORI; Tomales HS; Petaluma, CA; (3); 4-H; FFA; Ski Clb; Varsity Clb; Cheerldng; 4-H Awd; Hon Roll; Sonoma ST; Acctng.

PALM, DARREN M; Kingsburg HS; Kingsburg, CA; (2); Bsktbl; CSF.

PALM, RYAN S; Kingsburg HS; Kingsburg, CA; (4); Chess Clb; SADD; Ftbl; Trk; Val; CA ST U; Agbus.

PALMA, CARLOS E; Leuzinger HS; Inglewood, CA; (4); 87/517; Spanish Clb; Var Bsbl; JV Ftbl; Var Tennis; Wt Lftg; CSU Dominquez Hills; Finance.

PALMA, CLAUDIO; Sacred Heart Prep; Redwood City, CA; (2); High Hon Roll; NHS; Tnns; Stanford; Doctor.

PALMA, KLEBER J; West Torrance HS; Torrance, CA; (3); 150/403; Cmnty Wkr; JV Socr; Cit Awd; Envrnmntl Clb; Ganadores Del Futuro Pepsi Schlrshp; Exploration Of Arch Schlrshp 90; Arch.

PALMA, NIDIA L; Nathaniel Narbonne HS; Torrance, CA; (3); Teachers Aide; Cit Awd; Home Ec Merit Awd; Long Beach ST; Bus.

PALMA, RENEE K; Chino HS; Chino, CA; (2); Mgr(s); JV Var Socr; Var L Sftbl; Hon Roll; USC; Bus.

PALMA, SHEILA LYNN E; Tokay HS; Stockton, CA; (4); Spanish Clb; Capt Drill Tm; Variety Show; Hon Roll; Pres Acad Fit Awd; CA Schlrshp Fed Slbr; Asian Clb; UC Davis.

PALMATIER, ALEX M; Escondido HS; Escondido, CA; (3); 45/480; Ski Clb; Var Socr; Hon Roll; Principals Hnr Roll; Golden St Exam Geom Hnrs; Bus Mgmt.

PALMER, BENJAMIN S; Athenian HS; Pleasanton, CA; (3); SADD; Mgr Stage Crew; Off Jr Cls; Bsktbl; Socr; Tennis; Hon Roll; Prfct Atten Awd; Athenian Wildrnss Expernc-Emergncy Grp Ldr; Lawrence Berkeley Sci Awd.

PALMER, CHARLES; Damien HS; Diamond Bar, CA; (3); 52/217; Cmnty Wkr; Debate Tm; NFL; JV Bsbl; Hon Roll; NHS; UC San Diego; Mrn Bio.

PALMER, ELIZABETH A; Testimonial Christian Schl; Los Angeles, CA; (1); Chess Clb; Chorus; Church Choir; School Musical; School Play; JV Cheerldng; Hon Roll; Karate; Stu Of Mth Awd; Outstndng Stu Awd; USC; Police Ofcr.

PALMER, ERIN; Marina HS; Huntington Bch, CA; (3); AFS; JCL; Latin Clb; Var L Bsktbl; JV Trk; High Hon Roll; Athlts Agnst Substance Abuse; Ca Schlstc Fed; 2 Silver Mdls For Achvt On The Natl Latin Exam; Pltcl Sci.

PALMER, JAMES L; Ramona HS; Riverside, CA; (4); Chess Clb; Latin Clb; Letterman Clb; Varsity Clb; Stage Crew; Swmmng; Hon Roll; Water Polo; UCR; Bio.

PALMER, JOE; Saint Francis HS; Altadena, CA; (2); Ski Clb; Ed Yrbk; Var Tennis; Intrml Trk; Hon Roll; NHS; Spanish NHS; CA Schlrshp Fed; Hall Of Fame 4.0 GPA; Outstndng Score NEDT Tsts; UCLA; Phy.

PALMER, LYNN A; Mayfair HS; Lakewood, CA; (3); Church Yth Grp; Drama Clb; JA; Ski Clb; SADD; Thesps; Mrchg Band; Pep Band; School Play; Powder Puff Ftbl; Long Bch City Coll; Psych.

PALMER, NEAL A; Branham HS; San Jose, CA; (2); Boy Scts; Chess Clb; Acpl Chr; Chorus; Church Choir; School Musical; High Hon Roll; Hon Roll; 4th Pl Intl Comp Prblm Slvng Cont; High Pt Swmmng 89; Outstndng Phys Educ Stu 89; Comp Prgmr.

PALMER, ROXANNE; Elk Grove HS; Sacramento, CA; (2); Dance Clb; 4-H; GAA; Pep Clb; SADD; Rep Jr Cls; Var Cheerldng; Var Gym; 4-H Awd; Pres Acad Fit Awd; Dental Hyg.

PALMER, STEPHANIE; Le Lycee Francais HS; Encino, CA; (4); Var Sftbl; Var Swmmng; USC; Bio.

PALMERTREE, CHRISTINA L; Rio Mesa HS; Camarillo, CA; (3); Church Yth Grp; Wt Lftg; Cit Awd; Hon Roll; Mock Trl; Super Sprtn Awd; Scrtry Of Bsebl Card Clb; Renaissance Excllnc Awd.

PALMORE, JENNIFER A; Clovis West HS; Fresno, CA; (2); Church Yth Grp; Key Clb; Ski Clb; Var Diving; Var Gym; High Hon Roll; Pres Acad Fit Awd; GATE; CSF; Peer Cnslng; U Of CA; Educ.

PALNO, KATIE L; Corona HS; Corona, CA; (2); 7/473; Church Yth Grp; Pep Clb; Science Clb; Rep Frsh Cls; Rep Stu Cncl; Cheerldng; High Hon Roll; Pres Acad Fit Awd; CSF; Prncpls Awd.

PALOMARES, ALICIA; Indio HS; Indio, CA; (4); 9/390; Church Yth Grp; Dance Clb; VP Sec Hosp Aide; Var Crs Cntry; Var Trk; Sec Rep NHS; Spanish NHS; Natural Helpers; Jr Statesmen Of Amer; Soroptimist Schlrshp; UC Irvine; Psych.

PALOMARES, SUSANA G; Bishop Amat HS; La Puente, CA; (3); Church Yth Grp; Cmnty Wkr; Spanish Clb; JV Trk; JV Vllybl; Cit Awd; Hon Roll; Pres Acad Fit Awd; Silver Screen Club; Work Experience Pgm; UCLA; Math.

PALOMAREZ, TRINA; San Marcos HS; Santa Barbara, CA; (3); Aud/Vis; Drama Clb; Teachers Aide; Phtg Yrbk; JV Bsktbl; JV Trk; Hon Roll; UCLA; Film.

PALOMAREZ, YOLANDA H; Norte Vista HS; Riverside, CA; (1); SADD; JV Bsktbl; Cit Awd; Elks Awd; High Hon Roll; Lion Awd; Pres Acad Fit Awd; Psych.

PALOMINO, STACI; Hesperia HS; Hesperia, CA; (2); Church Yth Grp; FBLA; ROTC; Spanish Clb; Drill Tm; Hon Roll; San Diego ST Coll; Accntng.

PALOR, SHERYL; Franklin JR HS; Vallejo, CA; (1); Church Yth Grp; French Clb; Teachers Aide; Ed Yrbk; Off Frsh Cls; Stu Cncl; High Hon Roll; Sec NHS; UC Berkeley; Chld Psych.

PALOS, PAUL; Gladstone HS; Azusa, CA; (3); Drama Clb; FBLA; Letterman Clb; Science Clb; Ski Clb; SADD; School Play; Stage Crew; Crs Cntry; Trk; Jr Civitans Clb; Film Drctng.

PALOUTZIAN, MARK A; Santa Barbara HS; Santa Barbara, CA; (3); Math Tm; Acpl Chr; Band; Jazz Band; Mrchg Band; High Hon Roll; Pres Acad Fit Awd; Physcs.

PALOUTZIAN, ROBERT E; Kingsburg HS; Kingsburg, CA; (2); Church Yth Grp; Computer Clb; FFA; Mu Alpha Theta; Rptr Nwsp; Hon Roll; Gldn St Exam Alg & Geom; Natl FFA Fndtn Awd Nrsry Oprtns.

PALTER, LORI; Irvine HS; Irvine, CA; (2); 34/545; Key Clb; Pep Clb; Hon Roll; Heritage Awd; CA ST Fullerton; Engrng.

PALTIEL, STEPHEN; Hillsdale HS; Foster City, CA; (4); 35/296; Boy Scts; Church Yth Grp; Cmnty Wkr; Math Tm; Science Clb; Rptr Nwsp; Ed Lit Mag; Elks Awd; Hon Roll; Masonic Awd; Exploring, Post 830, Srch & Rescue Shp Acad 89; Explr Of Yr 88; Squadldr, Top Stu; MIT; Civil Engrng.

PALUSKA, BARBARA E; St Josephs HS; Lakewood, CA; (4); 3/183; Church Yth Grp; Treas GAA; Q&S; Ed Yrbk; Var Capt Bsktbl; Var Capt Crs Cntry; Gym; Swmmng; JV Vllybl; High Hon Roll; Schlr Athl Yr Hall Fame 89; CSF Sealbearer 90; CA ST Fullerton.

PAMINIANO, ERWIN; International Studies Acad; San Francisco, CA; (2); Church Yth Grp; Treas Frsh Cls; Pres Soph Cls; Hon Roll; Tennis; Track; Volleyball; Poetry; Berkeley; Business Management.

PAMINTUAN, DULCE A; Redlands SR HS; Loma Linda, CA; (2); Church Yth Grp; Church Choir; Loma Linda Acad; Pdtrc Nrs.

PAMPHILE, JANE A; Concord HS; Concord, CA; (3); Church Yth Grp; Cmnty Wkr; Letterman Clb; VP Jr Cls; Var Tennis; Rotary Awd; St Mary's Coll; Acctng.

PAMPLONA, JANETH M; Norwalk HS; Norwalk, CA; (4); #21 In Class; Sec Art Clb; French Clb; Math Clb; Service Clb; Chorus; Cit Awd; Hon Roll; Ntl Merit Schol; Prfct Atten Awd; CSF; Trig, Geom, Alg I & Spansh 1 & 2 Awds; Interact Clb 89-90; UCLA; Comp Sci.

PAN, ELIZABETH; Westlake HS; Westlake Vlg, CA; (2); Church Yth Grp; Hosp Aide; SADD; Hon Roll; Photo Cert Of Mrt; Bus.

PAN, MARK HSIAO-HWA; Capistrano Valley HS; Mission Viejo, CA; (4); Chess Clb; German Clb; Letterman Clb; Math Tm; Science Clb; Varsity Clb; JV Crs Cntry; Mgr(s); Capt Wrstlng; Kiwanis Awd; Wrstlng Leag Champ 88-89; Chem Stu Of Yr 89; UCI; Psych.

PAN, RONG; Woodrow Wilson HS; San Francisco, CA; (3); Spanish Clb; Hon Roll; CA Schlrshp Fed; UC Santa Cruz; Chem Engrng.

PAN, ROXANNE S; Huntington Beach HS; Huntington Beach, CA; (2); Church Yth Grp; Hosp Aide; Key Clb; Model UN; Red Cross Aide; Drill Tm; JV Swmmng; Bapt Voice Chldrns Chorus; CSF; Dance Ballet & Gym; Med.

PAN, TOM C; Cupertino HS; Cupertino, CA; (3); 42/235; High Hnr Gldn St Geom Exam; Badminton Var; Chinese Club; Engr.

PANABANG, EMELITA W; Orosi HS; Orosi, CA; (2); Chorus; Score Keeper; Cit Awd; Hon Roll; Kings River CC; Nrs.

PANANGANAN, MARK D; Hogan SR HS; Vallejo, CA; (3); Computer Clb; SADD; Hon Roll; CSF; UC Davis; Mech Engrng.

PANCHAL, JITESH G; North Salinas HS; Salinas, CA; (4); Science Clb; Spanish Clb; Cit Awd; High Hon Roll; Hon Roll; Prfct Atten Awd; U C Berkeley; Law.

PANDEY, ANNAROSE; Thousand Oaks HS; Camarillo, CA; (3); #13 In Class; French Clb; Science Clb; Speech Tm; VP Frsh Cls; High Hon Roll; Ntl Merit Ltr; Conejo Valley Youth Symphny; Vlntr Stud Conservtn Assoc; Equestrian Actvtes; U; Zoology Wildlife Mngmnt.

PANDEY, VATSALA; Paso Robles HS; Paso Robles, CA; (1); Med.

PANDIAN, ANAND SANKAR; Harvard Schl; Encino, CA; (4); Cmnty Wkr; Debate Tm; Model UN; NFL; Service Clb; Speech Tm; High Hon Roll; Hon Roll; Ntl Merit SF; Opt Clb Awd; Pltcl Sci.

PANDO, ALBERT T; Fresno Christian HS; Sanger, CA; (2); Church Yth Grp; Acpl Chr; Chorus; Church Choir; School Musical; Off Frsh Cls; Bsktbl; Ftbl; High Hon Roll; Hon Roll; Amer Chrstn Yth Chorale; Azusa Pacific U; Med.

PANDO, CYNTHIA; Ontario HS; Ontario, CA; (3); Art Clb; Church Yth Grp; Science Clb; Spanish Clb; SADD; Drill Tm; Pres Sr Cls; Cit Awd; Hon Roll; Cal ST Long Bch; Phys Thrpy.

PANDO, MARCOS I; Sonora HS; Brea, CA; (3); Ski Clb; Teachers Aide; Var L Bsbl; Ftbl; Powder Puff Ftbl; Var Socr; Hon Roll; Co Bst Defnsve Plyr 89-90 Vrsty Bsbl; 89-90 Slctd All Leag Tm 2nd Tm.

PANDYA, AMISHA; Moorpark HS; Moorpark, CA; (2); 11/256; Church Yth Grp; Dance Clb; Girl Scts; Intnl Clb; Library Aide; Variety Show; Sec Soph Cls; Cit Awd; High Hon Roll; Masonic Awd; CSF; Cmpttve Figure Skater, Have Won Mdls & Trphys; Play Piano; UCLA; Pediatrician.

PANELLA, DOMINIQUE; Encina HS; Sacramento, CA; (3); 5/211; Church Yth Grp; 4-H; Sec Spanish Clb; Orch; Lit Mag; Treas Jr Cls; Pres Sr Cls; L Capt Socr; L Var Vllybl; High Hon Roll; Canned Food Dr Orgnzr & Head; Biola U; Phys Educ.

PANER, FLORMELINE; Franklin JR HS; Vallejo, CA; (1); Co-Capt Drill Tm; Ed Nwsp; Rptr Yrbk; Off Frsh Cls; Stu Cncl; Hon Roll; Hnr Soc VP; Jrnlsm & Sci Awds.

PANER, PERLITA DOLORES; Dr James J Hogan SR HS; Vallejo, CA; (3); Spanish Clb; Band; Mrchg Band; Rptr Nwsp; Ed Yrbk; JV Cheerldng; Hon Roll; Var Badmntn; CA Schlrshp Fed; Cncrt Band; UOP; Sprts Med.

PANG, ALICE M; San Gabriel HS; San Gabriel, CA; (3); Dance Clb; FBLA; Var Capt Pom Pon; JV Swmmng; Hon Roll; CSF; Yrbk Tlntd Jr; Indstry Educ Cncl Medlln Awd In Bus Educ 90; UCLA; Bus Admin.

PANG, ALLEN C; Willow Glen HS; San Jose, CA; (2); Letterman Clb; Q&S; Quiz Bowl; Varsity Clb; Ed Nwsp; Var L Tennis; High Hon Roll; Hon Roll; Ivy League Coll.

PANG, CINDY; Mission San Jose HS; Fremont, CA; (1); 1/466; Church Yth Grp; Intnl Clb; Performing Arts.

PANG, ELAINE C; San Gabriel HS; San Gabriel, CA; (2); Dance Clb; Service Clb; Spanish Clb; SADD; JV Pom Pon; Hon Roll; San Marino Dance Acad; CSF; Acad Achvt Awd Bus Ed, Sci; UCLA; Medcn.

PANG, KAREN H; Lodi HS; Lodi, CA; (2); 215/587; Church Yth Grp; JA; Key Clb; Spanish Clb; Teachers Aide; Temple Yth Grp; Acpl Chr; Chorus; Sec Treas Jr Cls; Soph Track A Dist 1 Representative; Close-Up Club; Teaching.

PANG, LYNETTE; Edison HS; Stockton, CA; (4); 4/200; Pres VP Aud/Vis; Sec Latin Clb; DAR Awd; High Hon Roll; Hon Roll; Treas Hist NHS; Sec Jr Cls; CSF; Acadmc Dcthln Tm; Bus Adm.

PANG, SUSIE L; Liberty Baptist Schl; San Jose, CA; (4); Chorus; Church Choir; Nwsp; Yrbk; Sec Stu Cncl; Stat Bsktbl; Score Keeper; Trk; Vllybl; Hon Roll; Bank Of Amer Achvt Awd Sci/Math; Pianist; Santa Claira Yth Hall Of Fame; U Of CA; Engrng.

PANG, TAMMY RENA; Ygnacio Valley HS; Walnut Creek, CA; (4); Cmnty Wkr; Model UN; Service Clb; Sec Frsh Cls; Rep Stu Cncl; JV Pom Pon; Var Score Keeper; Hon Roll; NHS; Acad All Amer; Achvt Awd; Outstndng Acad Achvt; UCSF; Nrsng.

PANG, TONY H; Lodi HS; Lodi, CA; (4); 100/200; Chess Clb; Dance Clb; 4-H; Hosp Aide; Library Aide; Math Clb; Math Tm; Quiz Bowl; Color Guard; Stage Crew; Physics Tutor; Microbio Lab Asst; Russian Stu Ambssdr; Mills Coll; Jrnlst.

PANGAN, KRISTINA A; Nogales HS; W Covina, CA; (2); Dance Clb; Science Clb; JV Tennis; Hon Roll; Prfct Atten Awd; Badminton JV; Modern Dance Perfmng Arts JV&V; Psych.

PANGANIBAN, MARY; Southwest HS; San Diego, CA; (2); Socr; Vllybl; Cit Awd; Hon Roll; Prfct Atten Awd; Pres Acad Fit Awd; Art Inst Schl Stu; ASB For 9t Grade-My Pstn Was Trust Funds Cmssnr- I Was Also In Pan-Asian Clb; Bus Mgmt.

PANGBORN, FRANCINE M; Los Angeles Lutheran HS; Los Angeles, CA; (2); Church Yth Grp; Hon Roll; Prfct Atten Awd; Pres Frsh Cls; Brwnfld Memrl Schlshp Lthrn HS; Med.

PANGELINAN, MICHELLE T; North HS; Bakersfield, CA; (2); Church Yth Grp; Office Aide; Teachers Aide; Mrchg Band; Off Frsh Cls; Hon Roll; U Of HI; Bus Admin.

PANGILINAN, ELAINE S; Whitney HS; Cerritos, CA; (1); Drama Clb; French Clb; Key Clb; Pep Clb; Rptr Nwsp; JV Cheerldng; Hon Roll; Med.

PANGILINAN, GINA B; J Eugene Mc Ateer HS; San Francisco, CA; (3); Girl Scts; Cheerldng; Sftbl; Tennis; Hon Roll; Close Up; Filipino Club; Oakland Athl Leag Awd; UC Berkeley; Fashion Dsgn.

PANGILINAN, JOY B; Westmoor HS; Daly City, CA; (2); Hon Roll; Med.

PANGILINAN, RUEL J; Hamilton HS; Los Angeles, CA; (2); JA; Bsktbl; Cert Merit Acadmc Achvt Hstry; Conditioning Pgm; UCLA; Med.

PANGLE, PAMELA; Hesperia HS; Hesperia, CA; (3); Art Clb; Church Yth Grp; SADD; Chorus; Hon Roll; Prfct Atten Awd; Awd Hardest Wrkr In Class; Intr Dsgn.

PANGMAN, BRANDON W; Downieville HS; Downieville, CA; (4); 2/8; Cmnty Wkr; Pres Dance Clb; Drama Clb; German Clb; VP Sec Model UN; Capt Ski Clb; Speech Tm; School Play; Stage Crew; Ed Yrbk; Pepperdine U; Land Dvlpmnt.

PANIAGUA, ELKA; Downtown Business Magnet HS; Bell, CA; (2); Cmnty Wkr; Debate Tm; Office Aide; Spanish Clb; Speech Tm; Teachers Aide; Band; Hon Roll; Prfct Atten Awd; Awds Of Achvt Grphic Arts, Hnr Engl & Hnr Geom; Medalist Hnr Soc; Engrng.

PANIAGUA, SUZETTE; Holy Family HS; Sierra Madre, CA; (3); Church Yth Grp; Cmnty Wkr; FCA; Letterman Clb; Varsity Clb; Var Capt Vllybl; High Hon Roll; Hon Roll; Prfct Atten Awd; Citrus Coll.

PANINYAMA, SHARON L; Escondido HS; Escondido, CA; (3); Art Clb; Church Yth Grp; FBLA; Key Clb; Pep Clb; Cheerldng; Sftbl; Recognition In Art; BYU; Art.

PANITCHUPHON, LEE ADINA; Mark Keppel HS; Monterey Park, CA; (1); Drama Clb; JV Swmmng; Hon Roll; Prfct Atten Awd; 1st Pl Wnnr Backstroke Swmmng Fnls; MVP JV Swmmng; Mark Keppel Ltr Awd Swmmng; USC; Pediatrician.

PANKEY, KAREN E; Fallbrook HS; Bonsall, CA; (4); 17/379; Jazz Band; L Mrchg Band; School Musical; Variety Show; Lit Mag; High Hon Roll; Ntl Merit SF; Wind Ensmbl; Music Ed.

PANKRATZ, SPRING; University City HS; Santa Barbara, CA; (4); 52/331; Church Yth Grp; Pep Clb; SADD; Chorus; Church Choir; Co-Capt Drill Tm; Hon Roll; Pres Acad Fit Awd; Bank Amer Awd Music; CSF Life Awd; Pres Schlrshp Westmont Coll; Westmont Coll; Biol.

PANLILIO, MICHELLE; Western Christian HS; Upland, CA; (4); Office Aide; Service Clb; Teachers Aide; Chorus; Ed Yrbk; Treas Jr Cls; Treas Stu Cncl; High Hon Roll; NHS; Acadmc Decathln; Claremont Mc Kenna Coll; Bio.

PANNELL, WESTLY H; San Benito HS; Hollister, CA; (2); Church Yth Grp; Cmnty Wkr; Hon Roll; Explorer Scts; Aeronautical Engr.

PANOS, NICOLE; Christian HS; El Cajon, CA; (3); 2/79; Drama Clb; Key Clb; Teachers Aide; School Play; Var Tennis; Hon Roll; NHS; Bus.

PANOS, PETE G; Willow Glen HS; San Jose, CA; (2); 7/300; Church Yth Grp; Cmnty Wkr; Ftbl; Wrstlng; High Hon Roll; Hon Roll; Prfct Atten Awd; Pres Acad Fit Awd; Super Qz Chmps 88-89&89-90; Chemathon 89-90; Chrch Bsktbl Tm 89-90; Brkly; Pedtrcs.

PANSE, ROBERT B; Enterprise HS; Redding, CA; (3); Boy Scts; Church Yth Grp; Drama Clb; FBLA; Chorus; School Play; Rep Jr Cls; Var L Score Keeper; Hon Roll; Cert Wrd Prfct Spel Comp Course; Shasta Coll; Radio DJ.

PANTOJA, CARLA M; Santa Clara HS; Santa Clara, CA; (2); Church Yth Grp; Drama Clb; German Clb; Service Clb; Spanish Clb; Speech Tm; Chorus; Variety Show; Cit Awd; Hon Roll; Santa Clara JR Theatr; UC Davis; Vet Med.

PANTOJA, JOSE S; Clovis West HS; Pinedale, CA; (3); Church Yth Grp; Spanish Clb; SADD; Peer Cnslng; Elem Tutr; VP Mayo Clb/Hs Reps; Rep Fri Nght Lv; Psychp.

PAOLI, AARON L; Nova HS; Big Bend, CA; (1); Church Yth Grp; Cmnty Wkr; FFA; JV Bsktbl; JV Trk; Friday Night Live; Engrng.

PAOLI, ARLENE; Shasta HS; San Bruno, CA; (4); Church Yth Grp; Drama Clb; FBLA; Office Aide; School Play; Hon Roll; Math Awd; 5th Pl Sect Fnls FBLA Acctng; Skyline Coll; Acctng.

PAOLI, GREG G; Pinole Valley HS; Pinole, CA; (2); Ski Clb; Phtg Yrbk; Hon Roll; Prfct Atten Awd; Pres Acad Fit Awd; Pres Schlr; 1st Pl AHSME 88-89; Photo.

PAOLINELLI, SONIA; Mercy HS; San Mateo, CA; (3); Hosp Aide; Var Cheerldng; Var Pom Pon; JV Tennis; High Hon Roll; Hstss Club; Itln Club; UC Davis; Bus.

PAOLO, DOMENIC; Santa Teresa HS; San Jose, CA; (4); JV Var Bsbl; Mst Imprvd Bsbl Player; West Valley JC; Econ.

PAPA, ANTHONY L; Warren HS; South Gate, CA; (2); Ski Clb; JV Var Bsktbl; JV Var Ftbl; Wt Lftg; Hon Roll; Cal ST Long Beach; Bus.

PAPA, ERIC F; Monte Vista HS; Spring Valley, CA; (3); 30/373; Intnl Clb; Key Clb; Cit Awd; Prfct Atten Awd; Pacific Islanders Clb; San Diego ST U; Acctng.

PAPA, LORENE E; Las Plumas HS; Oroville, CA; (2); 12/257; Church Yth Grp; French Clb; FHA; SADD; Church Choir; Pres Frsh Cls; Pres Soph Cls; Trk; Ricks JC.

PAPAY, HEATHER D; Adolfo Camarillo HS; Camarillo, CA; (3); 34/430; Church Yth Grp; Spanish Clb; High Hon Roll; Sciences.

PAPAZIAN, SHAWN; St Bernards HS; Los Angeles, CA; (3); Art Clb; Ski Clb; Spanish Clb; Varsity Clb; Rep Frsh Cls; Rep Jr Cls; Var Ftbl; Var Socr; Vllybl; USC; Movie Dir.

PAPE, RANDALL A; Del Campo HS; Fair Oaks, CA; (3); Boy Scts; Letterman Clb; Spanish Clb; JV Var Ftbl; CA ST U Sacramento; Hstry.

PAPENDICK, ANGELA; Red Bluff Union HS; Red Bluff, CA; (3); 43/358; Cmnty Wkr; Rep Stu Cncl; Powder Puff Ftbl; Hon Roll; Pvctnl Stu Of Mnth 90; Sacramento St; Bus.

PAPER, LISA L; Hoopa Valley HS; Salyer, CA; (3); High Hon Roll; Hon Roll; CSF; Heald Bus Coll; Pblc Accntnt.

PAPIERNIAK, ERIC S; De La Salle HS; Diablo, CA; (4); Library Aide; Ed Yrbk; Chrstn Invlvmnt-Cmnty Svc; U Of CA Davis; Pre-Med.

PAPIN, ANNETTE; Cajon HS; San Bernardino, CA; (3); Aud/Vis; Church Yth Grp; Girl Scts; Ski Clb; Nwsp; Sftbl; Swmmng; CA ST; Jrnlsm.

PAPPAS, BASIL D; Carmel HS; Carmel, CA; (3); Church Yth Grp; Computer Clb; Debate Tm; Key Clb; Math Tm; Spanish Clb; Nwsp; High Hon Roll; Ntl Merit Ltr; Rotary Awd; Math Tutor; Monterey Peninsula Yacht Clb.

PAPPAS, JENNIFER L; St Genevieve HS; Sherman Oaks, CA; (2); Drama Clb; French Clb; Thesps; Stage Crew; Hon Roll; UCLA; Arch.

PAPPAS, KALIOPI; Lincoln HS; Stockton, CA; (1); Church Yth Grp; 4-H; Girl Scts; Key Clb; Ed Nwsp; Lit Mag; 4-H Awd; High Hon Roll; Kiwanis Awd; Pres Acad Fit Awd; Sportswriter.

PAPPAS-VESCERA, KIM; Hayward HS; Hayward, CA; (2); Trk; Hon Roll; Trck Lttr; N Coast Sctn CIF Dstngshd Schlstc Tm Awd Trck 89-90; CA ST Hayward; Bus.

PAPPOUS, ELPINIKE; Oak Grove HS; San Jose, CA; (4); 13/490; Sec Church Yth Grp; Cmnty Wkr; Computer Clb; Rep Stu Cncl; JV Bsktbl; Hon Roll; NHS; Pres Acad Fit Awd; Acropolis Dancer; Magna Cum Laude; Unergrad Awd Scl Sci; Santa Clara U; Math.

PAQUET, PAUL E; Bonita HS; La Verne, CA; (1); Hon Roll; Order Of Merit Hnr; Accntng.

PARADA, CHRIS A; Placer HS; Auburn, CA; (2); Art Clb; Spanish Clb; Socr; Hon Roll; AZ ST; Tchr.

PARADA, GREGORY; Baldwin Park HS; Baldwin Pk, CA; (1); Scholastic Bowl; Cit Awd; High Hon Roll; Stanford; Phy.

PARADA, OLINDA; Grant HS; Los Angeles, CA; (4); Outstndng Phys Ed Awd; Pierce Coll; Scl Wrkr.

PARAGAS, DANIEL C; Independence HS; San Jose, CA; (2); High Hon Roll; Comp.

PARAS, LAMBERTO K; St Ignatius College Prep; South San Francis, CA; (3); 12/244; Rptr Nwsp; Ed Yrbk; Intrml Trk; Bay Area & Schl Sci Fair 1st Plcs; Civil Engrng.

PARAYNO, CHERYL B; Nogales HS; Walnut, CA; (4); Church Yth Grp; Office Aide; Teachers Aide; JV Vllybl; Chrch Chrldng-Yth Opprtnts United; Chrch Track & Fld; Bus Mgt.

PARAYNO, KRISTINE B; Nogales HS; West Covina, CA; (2); Lit Mag; Cit Awd; High Hon Roll; Prfct Atten Awd; CA Ambssdrs Pgm; USC; Nrsng.

PARDE, MICHAEL C; Bishop Amat HS; Diamond Bar, CA; (3); NHS; NEDT Awd.

PARDINI, AARON; Chico SR HS; Chico, CA; (3); 1/364; Cmnty Wkr; Letterman Clb; Quiz Bowl; VICA; Var Crs Cntry; L Trk; High Hon Roll; Hon Roll; Pres Acad Fit Awd; Ambassador People To People Youth Sci Exchange USSR; Best Biology Stu Of Year; Best Chem Stu Of Smstr; University; Marine Biology.

PARDO, ADRIANA; Roosevelt HS; Los Angeles, CA; (2); Cmnty Wkr; Intnl Clb; School Play; Ed Nwsp; Hon Roll; Prfct Atten Awd; MESA; Folklorico Awd; WA U; Elec Engr.

PARDO, ANDRES; Anaheim HS; Anaheim, CA; (3); Bsbl; Elec Engrng.

PARDUE, BRENT L; East Bakersfield HS; Bakersfield, CA; (2); Band; Mrchg Band; Pep Band; Rep Stu Cncl; JV Bsktbl; Var Tennis; Hon Roll.

PAREAS, PHILIP L; Ygnacio Valley HS; Pleasant Hill, CA; (2); Boy Scts; JV Crs Cntry; JV Socr; L Trk; Schlr Athlte.

PAREDES, ALICIA B; Paramount HS; Paramount, CA; (2); Orch; Hon Roll; Prfct Atten Awd; College Clb; Marine Bio.

PAREDES, FLORENCE; Kingsburg HS; Kingsburg, CA; (2); Church Yth Grp; Teachers Aide; Church Choir; Mrchg Band; Tennis; Hon Roll.

PAREDES, KATRINKA K; Magnolia HS; Anaheim, CA; (2); Swmmng; High Hon Roll; CSF; Comm Art.

PAREDES, MARIA I; Fontana HS; Fontana, CA; (3); Teachers Aide; JV Vllybl; Prfct Atten Awd; Arch.

PAREDES, STEVE E; Eagle Rock HS; Los Angeles, CA; (3); Math Clb; Science Clb; Variety Show; Off Jr Cls; Off Sr Cls; Stat JV Bsktbl; Var Golf; Hon Roll; JETS Awd; Prfct Atten Awd; CSF Current Pres; Natl Sci Olympiad St Fnlst Rgnl Gold Mdlst; Schlr Athlt Gulf & Track.

PAREKH, ASHISH R; Sonora HS; La Habra, CA; (2); 11/350; JA; Math Clb; Spanish Clb; Temple Yth Grp; Variety Show; JV Tennis; High Hon Roll; Hon Roll; Jr NHS; Pres Acad Fit Awd; CSF; Gldn St Exam Math; Johns Hopkins; Genetic Engr.

PAREKH, MONA; Homstead HS; Sunnyvale, CA; (1); French Clb; Hosp Aide; UCLA; Med.

PARENO, JOEL S; St Anthony HS; Long Beach, CA; (3); Band; Mrchg Band; Orch; Pep Band; JV Vllybl; Eng Awd 88; Vol Svcs 90; CSF; CA ST Fullerton; Bus Adm.

PARENT, PAULETTE M; Pasadena HS; Sierra Madre, CA; (2); French Clb; Band; Mrchg Band; Swmmng; Green Peace; Amnesty; Drum Line; UCSD; Marine Bio.

PARENTE, VICTORIA R; Laguna HS; Laguna Hills, CA; (4); Cmnty Wkr; Drama Clb; Hosp Aide; Treas Thesps; School Musical; Ed Yrbk; Stu Cncl; Hon Roll; CA Assn Of Stu Cncls Exec Cabinet; U Southern CA.

PARERO, DOMINIC L; Saint Genevieve HS; Arleta, CA; (3); Letterman Clb; Pep Clb; Varsity Clb; Var Bsktbl; Var Crs Cntry; Var Vllybl; Hon Roll; All Acad Awd Vllybl, Bsktbl; Arch.

PARIDES, DANIEL; Channel Island HS; Oxnard, CA; (4); Socr; Sftbl; Swmmng; Wt Lftg; Hon Roll; Bus.

PARIKH, ANIT A; Savanna HS; Anaheim, CA; (2); Intnl Clb; Key Clb; Pep Clb; Science Clb; Rptr Nwsp; Off Frsh Cls; Off Soph Cls; JV Tennis; CA Schlrshp Fed; Acad Decathlon Tm; JV MVP Tnns.

PARIKH, NITA C; Mayfair HS; Lakewood, CA; (2); English Clb; JA; Treas SADD; Treas Mrchg Band; High Hon Roll; Prfct Atten Awd; Asian Clb; Bus.

PARIKH, RUJUTA; Los Alamitos HS; Seal Beach, CA; (4); Math Clb; Math Tm; Science Clb; Rptr Nwsp; JV Vllybl; Cit Awd; High Hon Roll; Hon Roll; UC Berkeley; Chem.

PARIKH, SHAILI; Bishop Amat HS; Diamond Bar, CA; (1); UCLA; Law.

PARILLO, HEATHER M; Mayfield SR HS; Alhambra, CA; (2); Church Yth Grp; GAA; Scholastic Bowl; Ski Clb; SADD; Varsity Clb; Rep Jr Cls; Var Sftbl; Elks Awd; High Hon Roll; Stanford; Law.

PARIS, TANYA IRINA; Saratoga HS; Saratoga, CA; (4); 1/280; French Clb; Key Clb; Service Clb; High Hon Roll; Ntl Merit Schol; Val; T J Watson Memorial Scholarship; NASA Fellowship Award; Pomona Coll; Biology.

PARISI, KRISTEN A; Carlsbad HS; Carlsbad, CA; (1); Church Yth Grp; Science Clb; Ski Clb; SADD; Treas Frsh Cls; VP Soph Cls; Bsktbl; Sftbl; Tennis; High Hon Roll; Berkeley; Law.

PARISIO, ALEX W; Willows HS; Willows, CA; (2); 18/91; Church Yth Grp; Key Clb; Letterman Clb; SADD; Varsity Clb; Var JV Ftbl; Golf; Ntl Merit Ltr; Pres Acad Fit Awd.

PARISOTTO, SARA; Shasta HS; Redding, CA; (2); 56/300; Rep Soph Cls; JV Cheerldng; High Hon Roll; Dancing.

PARK, ANDREW C; Etiwanda HS; Alta Loma, CA; (4); Pres Church Yth Grp; Key Clb; Ski Clb; Rptr Yrbk; JV Tennis; High Hon Roll; Prfct Atten Awd; CSF; Acad Decathlon Tm; Natl Bicentennial Comptn Semi-Fnlst; UC Berkeley; Mech Engrng.

PARK, ANDREW K; Dana Hills HS; Laguna Niguel, CA; (1); Church Yth Grp; Cmnty Wkr; JCL; Latin Clb; Church Choir; Orch; Stu Cncl; Hon Roll; Acad Decathlon Tm; All-Southern Hnr Orch; Stanford; Med.

PARK, ANNE; Campbell Hall HS; Van Nuys, CA; (3); Church Yth Grp; Cmnty Wkr; Dance Clb; French Clb; Service Clb; Ski Clb; SADD; Ed Yrbk; Hon Roll; NCA All Amer Songleader Fnlst; Var Songleader 2 Yrs Capt.

PARK, BIK-NA; Ocean View HS; Huntington Beach, CA; (2); Cmnty Wkr; Math Clb; Chorus; High Hon Roll; CSF; Hgh Hnrs Golden St Geom Exam; Art; Tnns; Santa Cruz U; Intl Rltns.

PARK, CELINE J; Louisville HS; Calabasas, CA; (2); 13/90; Art Clb; Church Yth Grp; Girl Scts; Nwsp; JV Tennis; Cit Awd; High Hon Roll; Hon Roll; Rcvd Algebra Awd & Religion Awd; CSF; Cert Of Merit 7 Yrs; Korean Sch 2 Semesters Rcvd Highest Honor.

PARK, CHAN; Bellflower HS; Bellflower, CA; (3); Art Clb; FBLA; JA; Math Clb; Mu Alpha Theta; Spanish Clb; Rptr Nwsp; JV Sftbl; High Hon Roll; CSF; Golden St Awd; Air Force; Air Traffic Cntrllr.

PARK, CINDY J; Sunny Hills HS; Fullerton, CA; (1); FBLA; Key Clb; Spanish Clb; JV Sftbl; Vllybl; High Hon Roll; Prfct Atten Awd; Rotary Awd; MVP Vlybl; Cls VP; UCLA; Law.

PARK, CLINTON H; Escondido Adventist Acad; Escondido, CA; (3); VP Church Yth Grp; Ski Clb; Teachers Aide; Varsity Clb; Band; Chorus; Orch; School Musical; Bsktbl; Ftbl; Tae Kwon Doe Trnmnt Chmpn; U CA Berkeley; Med.

PARK, DANIEL M; Los Amigos HS; Fountain Valley, CA; (3); Church Yth Grp; German Clb; Off Stu Cncl; JV Bsbl; JV Var Ftbl; L Var Wrstlng; High Hon Roll; Pres Acad Fit Awd; Gldn W Col Wrstlng Cnslr; San Diego ST U; Acctng.

PARK, DAVID; Arcadia HS; Arcadia, CA; (4); 1/640; Pres Church Yth Grp; Pres Red Cross Aide; Treas Spanish Clb; Orch; Treas Sr Cls; JV Tennis; Cit Awd; High Hon Roll; Hon Roll; NHS; Spcl Olympcs Vlntr; Union Station Vlntr CA Soup Kitchen; Arcadia Red Cross Bd Of Dir; MIT; Med.

PARK, DAVID Y; West HS; Torrance, CA; (3); Church Yth Grp; JA; Service Clb; Temple Yth Grp; Rptr Yrbk; JV Crs Cntry; JV Ftbl; Var Tennis; Hon Roll.

PARK, DENISE H; Sunny Hills HS; Fullerton, CA; (3); 7/430; Cmnty Wkr; Key Clb; Spanish Clb; Yrbk; Var Tennis; Var Trk; High Hon Roll; NHS; Piano; Tutor; Med.

PARK, ELAINE; Benicia HS; Benicia, CA; (3); 1/200; Sec French Clb; FBLA; VP Band; VP Mrchg Band; Stu Cncl; Var Tennis; Hon Roll; Jr NHS; Acad Decathlon.

PARK, ELIZABETH D; Los Altos HS; Hacienda Hgts, CA; (3); Flag Corp; Yrbk; JV Tennis; High Hon Roll; Keywannettes; Badminton; Litry Clb.

PARK, EUGENE; College Park HS; Walnut Creek, CA; (3); Pres Church Yth Grp; Service Clb; Spanish Clb; Var Socr; JV Trk; High Hon Roll.

PARK, EUNJOO; Hart HS; Newhall, CA; (2); Church Yth Grp; Acpl Chr; Chorus; Church Choir; Swmmng; Hon Roll; Golden St Exam Hnr; U Of CA; Music.

PARK, GIWOONG; Whitney HS; Cerritos, CA; (2); 1/168; Church Yth Grp; JA; JV Bsbl; High Hon Roll; CSF; Stanford U.

PARK, GLORIA; Rio Americano HS; Sacramento, CA; (3); Art Clb; German Clb; Math Tm; Science Clb; SADD; Rptr Phtg Nwsp; Yrbk; Cit Awd; High Hon Roll; Hon Roll; Tutrng Stu; JR Statesman Of Amer; CSF; Southern CA; Grphc Dsgn.

PARK, GRACE H; Chaminade College Prep; Northridge, CA; (3); Church Yth Grp; FCA; Intnl Clb; Pep Clb; JV Cheerldng; JV Tennis; JV Trk; Intrml Vllybl; High Hon Roll; Hon Roll; San Diego CA U; Spcl Ed.

PARK, HYUNG UK; John F Kennedy HS; La Palma, CA; (3); Church Yth Grp; Var Ftbl; Hon Roll; PTA Rep; Natl Yng Ldrs Conf, Cngrssnl Schlr; U Chicago; Pre-Med.

PARK, JAE HYUN; Victor Valley HS; Apple Valley, CA; (3); Cmnty Wkr; Prfct Atten Awd; UC Riverside; Dentstry.

PARK, JANE J; University HS; Irvine, CA; (3); 87/537; Key Clb; Spanish Clb; Treas Speech Tm; Orch; Capt Gym; JV Tennis; JV Trk; High Hon Roll; Ntl Merit Ltr; Pres Acad Fit Awd; Key Clb Mem; Speech Debate; Dramatic Interpretation.

PARK, JASON H; University HS; Irvine, CA; (3); 99/600; Church Yth Grp; Cmnty Wkr; Hosp Aide; Intnl Clb; JCL; Latin Clb; Ski Clb; Spanish Clb; Church Choir; Intrml Flag Corp; UC-BERKLEY; Med.

PARK, JASON J; Granada Hills HS; Granada Hills, CA; (2); Church Yth Grp; Cmnty Wkr; Hosp Aide; Ski Clb; SADD; Var Wt Lftg; Var Wrstlng; Cit Awd; Hon Roll; St Schlr; Wrstlng 2nd Lg 4th City; Wght Lftng 1st CA Clean Jerk Cmptn; JSA Jr Statesmn Am Clb; Ucla; Drmtlgst.

PARK, JAY; Trabuco Hills HS; El Toro, CA; (2); Drama Clb; Quiz Bowl; Spanish Clb; Var Lcrss; UCLA; Med.

PARK, JAY H; John F Kennedy HS; Sepulveda, CA; (3); Boy Scts; Church Yth Grp; Band; Orch; Off Jr Cls; JV Ftbl; JV Capt Vllybl; Sci Olympd Medals.

PARK, JI JI J; San Marino HS; San Marino, CA; (4); 1/245; Hosp Aide; Math Clb; Model UN; Var Bsktbl; Var Vllybl; Hon Roll; Ntl Merit SF; Pres Acad Fit Awd; Rotary Awd; Val; Scty Of Women Engrs Cert Of Achvt; CO Schl Mines Mdl; USC Summer Hnr Prgm; Harvard-Radcliffe U; Bio Engrng.

PARK, JIHAE; Chino HS; Ontario, CA; (3); 17/500; Sec Church Yth Grp; FCA; Church Choir; JV Var Vllybl; High Hon Roll; Prfct Atten Awd; Badminton All-Lg Tm; Cert Merit Piano; Stanford; Med.

PARK, JIN; Granada Hills HS; Northridge, CA; (3); Computer Clb; Science Clb; Hon Roll; Prfct Atten Awd.

PARK, JOE; San Gabriel Acad; Walnut, CA; (3); Church Yth Grp; Off Jr Cls; Vllybl; Hon Roll; NHS; Pacific Union Coll; Engrng.

PARK, JOHNNY; Los Altos HS; Hacienda Hgts, CA; (4); Hosp Aide; Key Clb; Tennis; Hon Roll; Ntl Merit Ltr; Johns Hopkins U; Bio.

PARK, JONG H; Sunny Hills HS; Fullerton, CA; (4); Pres Church Yth Grp; Key Clb; Var Tennis; High Hon Roll; Rotary Awd; Spanish NHS; Johns Hopkins U; Pre-Med.

PARK, JONG-SOO; Canyon HS; Newhall, CA; (4); 14/500; Chorus; Church Choir; Var Socr; Cit Awd; NHS; St Schlr; UC Irvine; Orthodontist.

PARK, JOON; Sunny Hills HS; Fullerton, CA; (2); 21/463; VP FBLA; Intnl Clb; Treas Key Clb; Spanish Clb; Nwsp; Var Crs Cntry; Var Trk; DAR Awd; High Hon Roll; Rotary Awd.

PARK, JULIE H; Whitney HS; Cerritos, CA; (1); Key Clb; Sec Model UN; Rptr Nwsp; Pres Acad Fit Awd; VP CA Jr Schlrshp Fed; Vlntr Lib.

PARK, JULIE S; Whitney HS; Cerritos, CA; (3); Church Yth Grp; Hosp Aide; JA; Key Clb; Teachers Aide; Color Guard; Flag Corp; Variety Show; Nwsp; Sndy Schl Tchr; Outstndng Acad Achvt Engl Spnsh Wrld Hstry; 2nd Pl Mdlst Drill Down; UCLA; Med.

PARK, JUN K; El Camino Real HS; West Hills, CA; (2); Church Yth Grp; Band; Mrchg Band; JV Vllybl; High Hon Roll; Hon Roll; Jr Statesman Of Amer; CA Schlrshp Fed; Steering Cmmtte; Med.

PARK, JUN T; De Anza HS; Richmond, CA; (3); Cmnty Wkr; Hosp Aide; Math Clb; Math Tm; Spanish Clb; Teachers Aide; Phtg Nwsp; Var Tennis; Cit Awd; DAR Awd; Spelling Bee Wnr; MVP Ten Tm, Most Improved Plague 89; Play Violin/Piano/Harmonica/Flte Vibraphone; Bio.

PARK, JUNG; Los Angeles HS; Los Angeles, CA; (4); 2/30; French Clb; High Hon Roll; NHS; Prfct Atten Awd; Bus.

PARK, JUNKO S; Notre Dame Acad; Culver City, CA; (3); 28/120; Church Yth Grp; Spanish Clb; Chorus; Yrbk; HOPE Clb.

PARK, KARYN M; Monrovia HS; Monrovia, CA; (3); Church Yth Grp; SADD; Band; Mrchg Band; Pep Band; Trk; Hon Roll; Drm Mjr(t); Scholorship Society; Girls League; GSE-ALGEBRA I-SCHOOL Recognition Award; Business.

PARK, KWAN H; John A Rowland HS; Rowland Hts, CA; (3); JV Ftbl; JV Wt Lftg; Hon Roll; Prfct Atten Awd; Accntng.

PARK, MEE K; Buena Park HS; Cypress, CA; (4); 13/304; Church Yth Grp; Cmnty Wkr; Intnl Clb; Teachers Aide; Chorus; High Hon Roll; High Hnr Mark & Acad Stds On Diploma Grad; CSF; Dstngshd Schlr Cert; Scl Sci Stu Of Month; Govt Hnr Pin; U Sthrn CA; Phys Thrpst.

PARK, MIN H; Chula Vista HS; Chula Vista, CA; (3); 6/493; Computer Clb; Math Tm; Prfct Atten Awd; UCSD.

PARK, MYEONG-JOO; El Camino Real HS; Los Angeles, CA; (2); Cmnty Wkr; Drill Tm; Var Cheerldng; Stu League; Soph Steerng Cmmtte.

PARK, NANCY; Los Altos HS; Hacienda Hts, CA; (1); Church Yth Grp; Intnl Clb; Key Clb; Swmmng; Wt Lftg; Cit Awd; High Hon Roll; Prfct Atten Awd; Tutor Friends & Cousins; Johns Hopkins U; Obstetrician.

PARK, PETER; Bellarmine College Prep; San Jose, CA; (2); Cmnty Wkr; Service Clb; Off Frsh Cls; Ftbl; Tennis; Wt Lftg; High Hon Roll; Hon Roll; NHS; Prncpls Hnr Rl Hghst Acad Achvt; JV Mst Insprtnl Player; UC Berkeley; Engrng.

PARK, PETER; Ft Bragg HS; Fort Bragg, CA; (2); JV Var Ftbl.

PARK, PETER Y; Gretchen Whitney HS; Cerritos, CA; (4); Church Yth Grp; French Clb; Nwsp; Hon Roll; Ntl Merit SF; Intrct Clb-Dir Of Actvts; Korean Clb-Treas.

PARK, RICHARD J; James A Garfield HS; Los Angeles, CA; (3); Science Clb; Sprt Ed Nwsp; Pres Sr Cls; JV Bsktbl; Var Ftbl; Var Trk; Cit Awd; Hon Roll; Prfct Atten Awd; Pres Acad Fit Awd; Cardiology.

PARK, RICHARD S; Mira Mesa HS; San Diego, CA; (2); Cmnty Wkr; French Clb; Off Soph Cls; Intrml Bsktbl; Ftbl; Pres Acad Fit Awd; Schl Rep For Moose Lodge Convntn San Diego Chptr; Capt Yth Bsktbl Tm; Med.

PARK, SCOTT S; Van Nuys HS; Los Angeles, CA; (3); Mgr Church Yth Grp; Key Clb; Math Clb; SADD; Church Choir; Stu Cncl; Var Capt Tennis; Cit Awd; Hon Roll; Prfct Atten Awd; Korean Clb-Treas; Church Yth Grp Sports Cmmttee-Ldr.

PARK, SO HYUN; Glendale HS; Glendale, CA; (2); Church Yth Grp; Spanish Clb; Hon Roll; Prfct Atten Awd; Capt Marjorette Tm; Bilingual Tutor For Spnsh Peers; Grad In Cum Laude; Law.

PARK, SONYA S; Irvine HS; Irvine, CA; (4); 60/550; Church Yth Grp; Pres Girl Scts; Key Clb; Church Choir; Orch; Hon Roll; Heritage Awds Dept Math 89-90; CA U San Diego; Bio-Chem.

PARK, STANLEY S; Artesia HS; Cerritos, CA; (4); Church Yth Grp; Cmnty Wkr; Pres French Clb; Model UN; Red Cross Aide; Sec Science Clb; Service Clb; Speech Tm; Teachers Aide; Rptr Lit Mag; Interact Clb Res/Treas; Rainbow Leag Facilitator; Swim Tm Var & Capt; CA ST U Long Beach; Bus.

PARK, SUNG W; Irvine HS; Irvine, CA; (3); 35/512; Hon Roll; Heritage Awd; Spcl Interests In Music & Tnns; Awd Achvt-Esl; Berleley U; Comp Sci.

PARK, SUNG W; Sunny Hills HS; Fullerton, CA; (3); 29/429; Church Yth Grp; Cmnty Wkr; JCL; Latin Clb; Band; Crs Cntry; Trk; High Hon Roll; Ntl Merit Ltr; CA Schlrshp Federation; U Of CA Berkeley; Arch.

PARK, TAEHWAN; Monterey HS; Fort Ord, CA; (3); Hon Roll; CSF Clb; U Of WA; Astrnmy.

PARK, TERRY J; Whittier Christian HS; Fullerton, CA; (3); Hosp Aide; Library Aide; Ed Yrbk; Treas Jr Cls; Var Tennis; Prfct Atten Awd; Piano; Dartmouth; Bio.

PARK, TIMOTHY H; Eagle Rock HS; Los Angeles, CA; (3); VP Pres Church Yth Grp; Service Clb; VP Orch; Stu Cncl; JV Capt Bsktbl; Var Capt Vllybl; Cit Awd; High Hon Roll; Prfct Atten Awd; Val; Engrng.

PARK, TONY; Pacifica HS; Cypress, CA; (2); Mrchg Band; CA Schlr Fed; Schlr Qtr Awd; Engrng.

PARK, YON; Grossmont HS; El Cajon, CA; (4); 1/381; Church Yth Grp; Debate Tm; VP Math Clb; NFL; Speech Tm; Church Choir; Lit Mag; JV Var Cheerldng; Powder Puff Ftbl; Bausch & Lomb Sci Awd; Grad Hnr Grd 89; SOFFA; Hgh Hnrs Geo Gldn St Exam; Med.

PARK, YOUNG S; Buena Park HS; Cypress, CA; (4); 42/304; Church Yth Grp; Cmnty Wkr; Intnl Clb; Teachers Aide; Chorus; High Hon Roll; CSF; Distngshd Schlr Cert 90; U Southern CA; Dntl Hygne.

PARKE, KRISTINA; Rosary HS; Fullerton, CA; (4); 6/150; Cmnty Wkr; Hosp Aide; Spanish Clb; Stage Crew; High Hon Roll; NHS; Pres Acad Fit Awd; CSF; UC Santa Barbara; Envrnmntl St.

PARKER, AARON L; Hoover HS; Fresno, CA; (3); 43/480; Boy Scts; Pres Church Yth Grp; French Clb; Ski Clb; Diving; Swmmng; Hon Roll; Pres Acad Fit Awd; Water Polo; Eagle Sct; Brigham Young U; Med.

PARKER, AMY M; Roseville HS; Roseville, CA; (1); Spanish Clb; JV Bsktbl; High Hon Roll; Trvlg; UCLA; TV.

PARKER, ANDY; Redwood HS; Visalia, CA; (3); 1/400; Pres Latin Clb; Math Tm; Science Clb; Service Clb; JV Frsh Cls; Var L Tennis; Hon Roll; Jr NHS; NHS; Var Ltr Water Polo; MVP JV Water Polo; No 1 Tnns Rank Cntrl Cal Smmr Leag USTA; Engrng.

PARKER, APRIL; Hillsdale HS; San Mateo, CA; (4); 46/380; Cmnty Wkr; NFL; Treas Spanish Clb; Speech Tm; Ed Nwsp; Ed Lit Mag; Rep Stu Cncl; French Clb; Math Clb; Math Tm; Wrld Affrs Clb VP & Scrtry; San Mateo Cty Yth Advsry Cncl Cmmssnr & Scrtry; Vlntr Ctr Stu Brd; U CA; TV News Brdcstng.

PARKER, CAROLEE; Valley HS; Elk Grove, CA; (4); 1/485; Teachers Aide; JV Bsktbl; Powder Puff Ftbl; Var L Socr; High Hon Roll; Ntl Merit Ltr; Prfct Atten Awd; Ntl Achvt Semiflnst; MESA; CSF; Harvey Mudd Coll; Elec Engrng.

PARKER, CARRIE; Alameda HS; Alameda, CA; (2); 19/285; Church Yth Grp; Teachers Aide; Church Choir; School Play; Treas Soph Cls; Var L Swmmng; Cit Awd; Hon Roll; JV Water Polo; Schlr Athlt; Chldrns Hosp Inc Bud Branch; Sprts Med.

PARKER, CHAD E; Cordova SR HS; Rancho Cordova, CA; (3); Library Aide; Model UN; Teachers Aide; School Play; Var L Bsbl; Var L Bsktbl; Intrml L Ftbl; Mgr(s); Cit Awd; Elks Awd; Athletic Clb Pres; Outstndng Athlete; Outstndng Stu; Phys Ed.

PARKER, CHRISTOPHER D; Buena HS; Ventura, CA; (4); Pres Church Yth Grp; German Clb; School Musical; Nwsp; JV Trk; Pres Acad Fit Awd; Acad Decathlon; Mock Trial; CSF Gold Seal Bearer; San Francisco ST U; TV/Radio.

PARKER, DENISE N; La Habra HS; La Habra, CA; (2); 25/382; Cmnty Wkr; Drama Clb; Letterman Clb; Ski Clb; Rptr Nwsp; Rep Frsh Cls; Var Crs Cntry; Var Trk; High Hon Roll; Rotary Awd; Stu Leag Rep & Sec; Interact Club; Acad Decathon 3rd Pl Mdl Hlth Category; CA ST Fullerton; Envrnmtl Law.

PARKER, DIANE M; Armijo HS; Fairfield, CA; (2); AFS; Key Clb; Ski Clb; Rep Jr Cls; Hon Roll; Ldrshp; Cntrl Cmmtte; Boston U; Psych.

PARKER, ELIZABETH; Crescent Valley HS; La Crescenta, CA; (1); Church Yth Grp; Chorus; Church Choir; Drill Tm; Korean Clb; Girls Leag; Legal Secy.

PARKER, FRANCES E; Del Campo HS; Lansdale, PA; (3); 122/420; ROTC; Swmmng; Sons Of Amer Rvltn Medl; Natl Sojrnrs Awd Medl; Amer Lgn Genl Military Excllnc Awd-Medl; Usaf; Psych.

PARKER, JASON D; Monache HS; Porterville, CA; (3); Cmnty Wkr; FBLA; Letterman Clb; Office Aide; SADD; Varsity Clb; Stage Crew; JV Bsbl; Var Ftbl; Var Golf; Fresno ST U; Bus.

PARKER, JASON W; Norco SR HS; Norco, CA; (3); 12/432; Church Yth Grp; Model UN; Teachers Aide; Variety Show; Var Bsktbl; Var Golf; High Hon Roll; Pres Acad Fit Awd; Lg Fnlst Golf MVP 89-90; Psych.

PARKER, JEFF; San Clemente HS; San Clemente, CA; (4); Church Yth Grp; Cmnty Wkr; Computer Clb; German Clb; Office Aide; Teachers Aide; JV Socr; Cit Awd; Work At Boys & Girls Club; Saddleback Coll; Bus Mgt.

PARKER, JENNIFER L; Livermore HS; Livermore, CA; (3); Church Yth Grp; Cmnty Wkr; Pres 4-H; Hosp Aide; Pep Clb; Ski Clb; Band; 4-H Awd; Hon Roll; Augustana Coll; Home Ec Tchr.

PARKER, JOEL A; Moreau HS; Union City, CA; (4); 132/267; Boy Scts; Cmnty Wkr; 4-H; Trk; 4-H Awd; Hon Roll; People/People Stu Ambssdr; Pole Vltr; Pilots Lcsnce; ASU; Aerntcl Engrng.

PARKER, JONI; Mission Viejo HS; Laguna Hills, CA; (4); 42/380; Pres Model UN; Pep Clb; Spanish Clb; SADD; Rep Stu Cncl; JV Var Cheerldng; Hon Roll; NHS; Pres Acad Fit Awd; UC Berkeley; Bus.

PARKER, KEVIN M; Clayton Valley HS; Clayton, CA; (4); 78/444; Ski Clb; Varsity Clb; Nwsp; Stu Cncl; JV Bsbl; JV Var Ftbl; Hon Roll; 2nd Tm All Leag BVAL Offnsve Grd 1990; Chico ST; Bus.

PARKER, LESLIE H; Roseville HS; Roseville, CA; (2); 87/454; Church Yth Grp; Letterman Clb; Spanish Clb; Acpl Chr; Church Choir; JV Bsktbl; JV Socr; Var Capt Tennis; DAR Awd; CSUS; Span Tchr.

PARKER, MANDY B; Sonoma Valley HS; Sonoma, CA; (1); Church Yth Grp; Hon Roll.

PARKER, MELISSA; Palo Verde HS; Blythe, CA; (4); 6/175; Drama Clb; Sec Treas Pep Clb; Service Clb; School Musical; School Play; Stage Crew; High Hon Roll; Hon Roll; NHS; CA ST U Fullerton; Acctng.

PARKER, MICHAEL J; Mayfair HS; Lakewood, CA; (2); JA; Intrml Bsktbl; Intrml Socr; Intrml Wt Lftg; Intrml Wrstlng; Hon Roll; Arch.

PARKER, MORGAN H; William H Taft HS; Tarzana, CA; (3); Spanish Clb; Teachers Aide; Spanish NHS; CA Schlrshp Fed.

PARKER, RICHARD A; Palmdale HS; Palmdale, CA; (3); 23/644; High Hon Roll; Engr.

PARKER, ROBIN; Elk Grove HS; Elk Grove, CA; (2); Church Yth Grp; Dance Clb; JV Pom Pon; Var Trk; Intl Order Of Rainbow Girls Chrty Line Offcr; U CA; Mrktng.

PARKER, SADIE; Cajon HS; San Bernardino, CA; (3); Pep Clb; Teachers Aide; Variety Show; JV Cheerldng; Var Crs Cntry; Score Keeper; Cit Awd; French Hon Soc; Hon Roll; Cal ST; Acctnt.

PARKER, SARA I; Thomas Downey HS; Modesto, CA; (1); Modesto JC; Chld Psych.

PARKER, SCOTT A; Monte Vista HS; Walnut Creek, CA; (2); 160/400; Yth & Govt; Cal Poly; Arch.

PARKER, SHANNON; Grace M Davis HS; Modesto, CA; (2); AFS; GAA; SADD; Var Socr; Var Swmmng; Cit Awd; High Hon Roll; Vrsty Wtr Polo Tm; Psych.

PARKER, SHAWNA C; Notre Dame HS; Salinas, CA; (2); Church Yth Grp; Hon Roll; Dance Recital; Cal Poly; Hstry Tchr.

PARKER, THEO G; Hemet HS; Hemet, CA; (2); Teachers Aide; Powder Puff Ftbl; Trk; Wrstlng; Cal Tech; Engr.

PARKER, TREMAYNE A; Pasadena HS; Pasadena, CA; (2); Church Yth Grp; Hosp Aide; JA; Church Choir; School Musical; Var Bsktbl; Var Trk; U Las Vegas; Med.

PARKER, WYATT L; Arcata HS; Bayside, CA; (1); Boy Scts; Church Yth Grp; French Clb; JV Ftbl; JV Trk; JV Wrstlng; French Hon Soc; High Hon Roll; Military.

PARKER, ZACHARY B; Clovis West HS; Fresno, CA; (2); VP Debate Tm; Drama Clb; ROTC; VP Speech Tm; Ed Lit Mag; Hon Roll; Intl Baccaleaurate; St Ambassador; Comp.

PARKES, TERRIE D; Fresno HS; Fresno, CA; (2); Church Yth Grp; Dance Clb; Pep Clb; Teachers Aide; Church Choir; Variety Show; JV Cheerldng; JV Swmmng; UCSB; Int Dsgn.

PARKHURST, DARCY B; Arcata HS; Arcata, CA; (2); Sec Jr Cls; Var Powder Puff Ftbl; Var Sftbl; Humboldt ST; Bus.

PARKHURST, STACY A; Fairfield HS; Fairfield, CA; (4); Girl Scts; Rptr Nwsp; French Hon Soc; San Jose ST; Graphic Dsgn.

PARKHURTRS, MELISSA D; Bonita Vista HS; Chula Vista, CA; (3); 20/600; Band; Swing Chorus; Ed Nwsp; Ed Yrbk; Rep Jr Cls; Rep Sr Cls; Sec Stu Cncl; Var Cheerldng; Var Tennis; High Hon Roll; Music Mchne Shw Choir; Cal Poly; Envrnmntl Engrng.

PARKINSON, BRETT; Indio HS; Bermuda Dunes, CA; (1); 10/629; Church Yth Grp; Swmmng; Wt Lftg; High Hon Roll; Hon Roll; Waterpolo; BYU; Math.

PARKINSON, KRISTA; Indio HS; Bermuda Dunes, CA; (3); 12/451; Pres Church Yth Grp; Off Drama Clb; FTA; NFL; Spanish Clb; Speech Tm; School Play; Stage Crew; Var Capt Cheerldng; Var Trk; Circle Theater Actng Co; CSF Hstrn; Rnkd 3rd Citrus Blt Dramatic Intrprtn; BYU; Commnctns.

PARKINSON, TRACY L; Tustin HS; Tustin, CA; (1); 129/460; Hosp Aide; Var Pep Clb; UCLB; Nrsng.

PARKS, AARON; Thomas Downey HS; Modesto, CA; (2); FFA; CA ST U; Comp Prog.

PARKS, ALEX BENJAMIN; Southwestern Acad; Pasadena, CA; (3); Boy Scts; Church Yth Grp; English Clb; Math Clb; Teachers Aide; Yrbk; VP Jr Cls; Golf; Vllybl; Mst Imprvd Math Stu; Fl Schlrshp Stu; Willamette U.

PARKS, AMBER; Gunderson HS; San Jose, CA; (1); Ski Clb; JV Fld Hcky; Var JV Score Keeper; Wt Lftg; Young Life; Vlntr Work YMCA; Lawyer.

PARKS, BRANDY; Indio HS; Indio, CA; (2); Church Yth Grp; Drama Clb; Pep Clb; School Play; JV Cheerldng; Var Gym; Good Attndnc Awd; Real Est Agnt.

PARKS, CANDYCE; Dinuba Union HS; Dinuba, CA; (3); Pep Clb; Teachers Aide; Acpl Chr; Chorus; Var Co-Capt Cheerldng; Pom Pon; Capt Powder Puff Ftbl; Hon Roll; Madrigal Grp Won Slvr Medal Intl Music Fstvl Toronto; CA ST U Fresno; Music.

PARKS, CARRIE M; Wasco Union HS; Wasco, CA; (3); Varsity Clb; Band; Jazz Band; Pep Band; Bsktbl; Sftbl; Vllybl; Hon Roll; Prfct Atten Awd; CSF Mem; Phys Thrpy.

PARKS, ERIK M; Tomales HS; Valley Ford, CA; (4); Debate Tm; 4-H; FFA; Ski Clb; SADD; Teachers Aide; Varsity Clb; Band; Sec Soph Cls; Capt Bsbl; Santa Monica City; Crmnl Invstg.

PARKS, HEATHER A; Rim Of The World HS; Blue Jay, CA; (3); Church Yth Grp; Pres FCA; Chorus; Sec Church Choir; School Play; Variety Show; Treas Frsh Cls; Rep Soph Cls; Rep Jr Cls; Sec Sr Cls; UC Santa Cruz; Chld Dev.

PARKS, HOLLY L; Modera HS; Madera, CA; (2); Church Yth Grp; VP 4-H; SADD; Varsity Clb; Rep Stu Cncl; Var Socr; JV Sftbl; Var Vllybl; 4-H Awd; Hon Roll; 4-H Vet Sci Rcrds Comptn Wnnr; Fresno ST; Rgstrd Nrs.

PARKS, JANE; Fairfield HS; Fairfield, CA; (1); Drama Clb; School Musical; School Play; Stage Crew; Hon Roll; USC; Psych.

PARKS, JOHN P; De Anza HS; Richmond, CA; (4); 2/268; Math Tm; Var L Bsktbl; L Capt Crs Cntry; JV Ftbl; Var L Trk; Ntl Merit SF; Pres Acad Fit Awd; Sal; CSF Lifetime Mem; Natl Achvmt Schlsp; Army Reserve Natl Schlr-Athlt Awd; CA Inst Of Tech; Mech Eng.

PARKS, JOHN-SCOTT; Thomas Downey HS; Modesto, CA; (4); Drama Clb; Letterman Clb; Thesps; Band; VP Chorus; Jazz Band; Mrchg Band; Pep Band; Stage Crew; Cit Awd; Stage Asst City Schls, Perfmng Arts; Modesto JC; Cmmctns.

PARKS, JOSHUA A; The Bishops Schl; Del Mar, CA; (3); Pres Varsity Clb; Pres Jr Cls; Var L Bsbl; Var L Ftbl; Var L Socr; Hon Roll; Ntl Merit Ltr; Rotary Awd; Church Yth Grp; Latin Clb; Sccr CIF Champs 88-89 & 89-90; Advncd Plcmnt Bio, Chem, Physics, European Hist & US Hist.

PARKS, KATHY; Community Christian HS; Bakersfield, CA; (4); Office Aide; SADD; Teachers Aide; Nwsp; VP Stu Cncl; Powder Puff Ftbl; Sftbl; Acadmc Dcthln; City Teen Govt Day; Bakersfield JC; Psych.

PARKS, KEVIN W; Bakersfield HS; Bakersfield, CA; (3); 1/711; Boy Scts; Church Yth Grp; Science Clb; Jazz Band; Orch; Rep Jr Cls; VP Stu Cncl; JV Capt Bsbl; JV Bsktbl; JV Capt Ftbl; Hmnts & Soc Sci Awd; Stu For Wrld Cnsrvtn; BYU; Frst Engr.

PARKS, SHAWNA D; Antioch HS; Antioch, CA; (3); Church Yth Grp; Cmnty Wkr; Pep Clb; Teachers Aide; Bsktbl; Vllybl; Hon Roll; CJSF Clb.

PARKS, TODD; Rio Linda SR HS; Rio Linda, CA; (2); Ftbl; Art.

PARLATO, KATRINA; Fortuna Union HS; Fortuna, CA; (4); Ed Nwsp; Stat Bsbl; Var Capt Bsktbl; Elks Awd; Kiwanis Awd; Lion Awd; Pres NHS; Pres Schlr; Jobs Daughters Past Hnrd Qn; CSF; U San Francisco; Bus.

PARLET, ANGELA D; Burroughs HS; Columbus, GA; (4); Cmnty Wkr; FHA; Ski Clb; Teachers Aide; Nwsp; JV Bsktbl; Var Trk; High Hon Roll; Hon Roll; History Prof.

PARMELY, SHANE S; San Diegvito HS; La Costa, CA; (2); Rep Frsh Cls; Rep Soph Cls; Var L Gym; Var L Socr; JV Vllybl; High Hon Roll; Hon Roll; Pres Acad Fit Awd; Gldn ST Exm/Alg Hgh Hnrs, Geom Hnrs; Amnsty Intl; Prdcd TV Tlk Shw; Flm Wrtng.

PARMLEY, JENNIFER A; Whittier Christian HS; Whittier, CA; (3); Chess Clb; Church Yth Grp; Letterman Clb; Spanish Clb; Teachers Aide; Off Band; Chorus; Church Choir; Off Mrchg Band; Pep Band; TX Chrstn U; Bus Mgmt.

PARNELL, CRYSTAL; Righetti HS; Santa Maria, CA; (3); Church Yth Grp; French Clb; Hon Roll; Modelng; Acting; BYU.

PARNELL, TAMMY; San Rafael HS; San Rafael, CA; (1); Church Yth Grp; School Play; Bsktbl; Cit Awd; Poem Publshd Anthology; Actress.

PARODI, CARLOS; Saint Francis HS; Glendale, CA; (2); JA; Math Clb; Spanish Clb; Varsity Clb; Crs Cntry; Socr; High Hon Roll; Hon Roll; Pres Acad Fit Awd; AP Geom; Ingles Hnr; Homer Hstry; AP Spnsh; V Crss Cntry; V Sccr; All Star Bsbl.

PARODI, JOHN J; Central Catholic HS; Modesto, CA; (3); 5/59; Art Clb; Cmnty Wkr; Service Clb; Ski Clb; Treas Stu Cncl; Var JV Bsbl; Var JV Socr; High Hon Roll; St Schlr; Vet Sci.

PARODI, MICHELLE; Soquel HS; Soquel, CA; (4); JA; Ski Clb; Chorus; Rep Frsh Cls; Rep Soph Cls; Rep Pres Jr Cls; Rep Sr Cls; Rep Stu Cncl; Elks Awd; High Hon Roll; Organizer Toys Tots Toy Collection; CCS Hnr Choir; CSF; UC Berkeley; Envrnmntl Sci.

PARQUER, DARCY A; Loretto HS; Sacramento, CA; (3); 19/62; Church Yth Grp; Cmnty Wkr; Science Clb; Service Clb; JV Bsktbl; JV Var Crs Cntry; Var Trk; Hon Roll; Guitar Awds; Wmns Div Rocklin Jubilee Fun Run 89 2nd, 90 1st; Peer Mnstry; CSF; Spirit & Sport Club; CA ST U Sacramento; Psych.

PARR, AARON M; Skyline HS; Oakland, CA; (3); Church Yth Grp; Letterman Clb; Red Cross Aide; Var Crs Cntry; Var Trk; UC Berkeley; Sci Jrnlsm.

PARR, JENNIFER J; Palmdale HS; Palmdale, CA; (3); 12/640; Library Aide; Sec Service Clb; SADD; Hon Roll; Gymnstcs Coach; Gymnst-Pvt Clb; UC Davis; Chrprctc.

PARRA, BLANCA I; King City Joint Union HS; Greenfield, CA; (4); FFA; Teachers Aide; Capt Drill Tm; Mxcn Amrcn Yth Assn; HS Chr; Fresno St U; Nrsng.

PARRA, JOSEPH D; Don Bosco Technical Inst; Rosemead, CA; (3); Yrbk; Campus Ministry; LA San Gabriel Valley Srch; Comm.

PARRA, MAGDALENA; Baldwin Park HS; Baldwin Park, CA; (3); Spanish Clb; Teachers Aide; Nwsp; Yrbk; VP Jr Cls; Cit Awd; Hon Roll; Part-Time Job; San Diego ST U; Bilingual Lwyr.

PARRA, MARTHA D; King City Union HS; Greenfield, CA; (3); 9/215; Drama Clb; Drill Tm; School Play; MAYA Clb VP; CSF; CLYLC Prtcpnt; UCLA; Actress.

PARRA, SUSANA; Sierra Vista HS; Baldwin Park, CA; (3); Church Yth Grp; Hon Roll; CA Poly Pomona.

PARRALES, RONALDO; Bishop Amat Memorial HS; Chino Hills, CA; (4); 120/401; Church Yth Grp; Cmnty Wkr; Debate Tm; Office Aide; Speech Tm; Bsktbl; Cit Awd; Hon Roll; Pres Speech Clb; Pro-Life Awd; UCLA; Commnctns.

PARRAZ, MARIO R; Live Oak HS; Morgan Hill, CA; (3); Boy Scts; Teachers Aide; ROP Cert Elec; Grn Hnr Soc Cert Rcgntn In Schlrshp.

PARRINO, KRISTINE; Sunny Hills HS; Fullerton, CA; (3); Dance Clb; Pep Clb; Spanish Clb; Chorus; Pom Pon; Cit Awd; Hon Roll; U Of CA Santa Barbara.

PARRIS, JESSICA; Mira Mesa HS; San Diego, CA; (3); 2/777; Church Yth Grp; VP Pres Thesps; Acpl Chr; School Musical; School Play; Rep Soph Cls; Hon Roll; Pres Acad Fit Awd; Coll; Musical Theatre.

PARRISH, REBECCA C; Davis SR HS; Davis, CA; (3); Cmnty Wkr; Dance Clb; Key Clb; Chorus; Hon Roll; Peace Clb; Special Ed.

PARRISH, ROBERT; Morse HS; San Diego, CA; (2); 289/764; Boy Scts; Service Clb; Teachers Aide; Hon Roll; Jr NHS; CSF; Arch Engr.

PARROTT, DANIELLE; Lincoln HS; Stockton, CA; (3); Latin Clb; Chorus; High Hon Roll; Hon Roll; Handbell Choir; UC U; Med.

PARRY, BRIAN; Carlsbad HS; Carlsbad, CA; (4); SADD; Teachers Aide; School Play; Yrbk; Cit Awd; Hon Roll; VP Frsh Cls; CSF; Pepperdine U; Humanities.

PARRY, SHANNON; Acalanes HS; Lafayette, CA; (1); Church Yth Grp; Drama Clb; Hosp Aide; Chorus; Church Choir.

PARSEKYAN, DIKRAN; Ferrahian HS; Sherman Oaks, CA; (2); School Play; Trk; Phrmcst.

PARSELL, LLEWELYN M; Amos Alonzo Stagg HS; Stockton, CA; (1); School Musical; Hon Roll.

PARSLOW, RICK T; Don Antonio Lugo HS; Lucerne Valley, CA; (2); Trk; JV Wrstlng; Hon Roll; Golden Conquest Achvtmnt Awd; Track Vrsty Ltr; Annapolis Naval Acad; Navy Plt.

PARSON, JAMES B; La Sierra HS; Los Alamitos, CA; (2); Crs Cntry; Wt Lftg; Civil Air Patrol.

PARSON, JAMES M; Anaheim HS; Anaheim, CA; (3); Quiz Bowl; Stu Cncl; Ftbl; Score Keeper; Wt Lftg; Wrstlng; Pres Acad Fit Awd; Pres Schlr; Gldn St Math Exam-Agl & Geo Hnrs; 2nd Team All Orng Leag Defsnv Linemn; U S Air Force Acad; Pilot.

PARSONAGE, DENISE R; Atascadero HS; Atascadero, CA; (2); Sec Frsh Cls; Sec Soph Cls; Hon Roll; ASB Secy 90-91; Ldrshp Cls; Psych.

PARSONS, CHRIS; Mira Loma HS; Carmichael, CA; (2); 2/283; Math Clb; Science Clb; Band; Jazz Band; Mrchg Band; Bsktbl; Sci Olympiad; Stanford; Med.

PARSONS, DARRELL B; Rio Americano HS; Sacramento, CA; (3); 47/290; Boy Scts; Church Yth Grp; Sec Key Clb; Band; Church Choir; Jazz Band; Orch; JV Var Socr; JV Trk; Cit Awd; Scer Tm 8th Pl St; 1st Pl Jazz Cmptn; UC Davis; Pdtrtn.

PARSONS, GRETA; Rio Mesa HS; Camarillo, CA; (1); 1/490; Church Yth Grp; Cmnty Wkr; SADD; JV Swmmng; High Hon Roll; NHS; UCLA; Med.

PARSONS, JASON M; Apple Valley SR HS; Apple Vly, CA; (1); Chess Clb; Computer Clb; Math Tm; Spanish Clb; High Hon Roll; Prfct Atten Awd; Golden ST Exam Geom Hnrs; Geom Hnrs; Air Force.

PARSONS, KATHERINE A; Thomas Downey HS; Modesto, CA; (2); Office Aide; Spanish Clb; School Play; Rptr Nwsp; Cit Awd; Hon Roll; Prfct Atten Awd; Nursing.

PARSONS, SONIA; Sherman Indian HS; Peach Springs, AZ; (4); 1/47; Treas Sr Cls; Sec Stu Cncl; High Hon Roll; Hon Roll; NHS; Opt Clb Awd; Val; MESA; RSI George Washington U Smmr 89; Riverside CC; Bus Admin.

PARSONS, STEFANIE K; Thomas Downey HS; Modesto, CA; (2); Church Yth Grp; Drama Clb; NFL; Church Choir; Var Socr; Coll Clb; UC Davis; Sci.

PARSONS, STEPHANIE; Cordova SR HS; Sacramento, CA; (3); Cmnty Wkr; Science Clb; Spanish Clb; Yrbk; Rep Stu Cncl; Bsktbl; Vllybl; Hon Roll; Jr NHS; Wt Lftg; Coaches Awd; Vlntr Wrk; Bowling Tm; UCLA; Med.

PARSONS, TANIA D; Liberty HS; Brentwood, CA; (2); Band; Hon Roll; Law.

PARSONS, TROY; Fred C Beyer HS; Modesto, CA; (4); 13/506; Chess Clb; Math Clb; Math Tm; Science Clb; SADD; Teachers Aide; Mgr Nwsp; Mgr Yrbk; Mgr Bsktbl; Hon Roll; Sci Patriot Awd; CSF; CA ST U; Math Teacher.

PARTAIN, JENNIFER K; Beaumont HS; Beaumont, CA; (3); Ed Yrbk; JV Tennis; Hon Roll; Rotary Awd.

PARTCH, JONATHAN T; Bishop O'dowd HS; Alameda, CA; (2); Var Swmmng; All Amer Relay 88-89; North Coast Sect Swmmng Fnlst; East Shore Athltc Lgue Swm Rcrd.

PARTEE, JASON R; Canyon HS; Canyon Country, CA; (1); English Clb; Band; Mrchg Band; Orch; Pep Band; Hon Roll; Intrml Bsktbl.

PARTIER, JUSTIN A; J Eugene Mc Ateer/Schl Of The Arts; San Francisco, CA; (2); Boy Scts; Hon Roll; Actvly Involved In Theatre Tech In Schl Of The Arts 2 Yrs; U Of CA Santa Cruz; Film Dir.

PARTRIDGE, MARCUS D; Beaumont HS; Beaumont, CA; (1); Church Yth Grp; Var FCA; Letterman Clb; Var Crs Cntry; JV Trk; Wt Lftg; Hon Roll; Alive Clb-Brd Ofcr; Point Loma Nazarene Coll; Pastr.

PARTRIDGE, SIDNEY; Granada Hills HS; Sylmar, CA; (3); Church Yth Grp; Drama Clb; FCA; Bsbl; Var L Ftbl; Var Trk; Amer Lit Hnrs; OK U; Law.

PARUCCI, SUELLY V; Holy Family HS; Sun Valley, CA; (2); Church Yth Grp; Hosp Aide; Library Aide; Var Sftbl; JV Trk; Prfct Atten Awd; Loyola Marymount U; Chld Psych.

PARWIZ, SULAIMAN S; Clayton Valley HS; Concord, CA; (4); Church Yth Grp; Model UN; Teachers Aide; Intrml Ftbl; Intrml Wrstlng; UCIV; MD.

PARY, ANA-MARIA; Saddleback HS; Santa Ana, CA; (2); Chorus; Hon Roll; Prfct Atten Awd; MESA Math Engr & Sci Achvt Clb; UCI Partners Clb; Certfct Achvt Bio; CSF; U CA Irvine; Frgn Lang Tchr.

PARYSEK, AMY K; Santa Clara HS; Santa Clara, CA; (2); 28/412; Sec Treas Church Yth Grp; Drama Clb; German Clb; Chorus; Church Choir; School Play; Wildrnss Advnturers Clb; San Jose ST.

PASCARELLA, NICOLE; Torrey Pines HS; San Diego, CA; (2); 97/503; Church Yth Grp; Pres SADD; Acpl Chr; Chorus; Tennis; Hon Roll; Pres Acad Fit Awd; Cmnty Theatre/Choir; Italian Clb; Hghst Score Possible In Math At CAT Test; UCSD; Math.

PASCHAL, NINA D; Fontana HS; Bloomington, CA; (2); Church Yth Grp; Rep Frsh Cls; Rep Stu Cncl; Var Cheerldng; Stat Mgr(s); Score Keeper; JV Sftbl; Cit Awd; Hon Roll; Prfct Atten Awd; UC Irvine; Psych.

PASCO, JESSICA; Ambassador Baptist HS; Rialto, CA; (2); Var Bsbl; Var Sftbl; High Hon Roll; Hon Roll.

PASCOE, TRISHA A; Woodland HS; Woodland, CA; (3); Church Yth Grp; Church Choir; HEROES Awd; Prayer Warriors; Yth Grps Blooper Ball Games; Radiology Tech.

PASCUA, ARLENE B; Mt Pleasant HS; San Jose, CA; (1); Church Yth Grp; Church Choir; JV Cheerldng; Hon Roll; UC Davis; Bus.

PASCUA JR, ELEANOR J; Hawthorne HS; Hawthorne, CA; (4); Church Yth Grp; Sec Intnl Clb; Hist Science Clb; Service Clb; Nwsp; Ed Yrbk; Hist Jr Cls; Sec Stu Cncl; Rotary Awd; Chmbr Cmmrc Vlntr Apprctn Day; CA ST U Long Beach; Nrsng.

PASCUA, JOSEPH A; Saint Monicas Catholic HS; Los Angeles, CA; (3); Thesps; Acpl Chr; Chorus; School Musical; Stage Crew; Swing Chorus; Variety Show; Var Swmmng; NHS; Asian-Pacific Clb; Prfrmng Arts Awds; Bio.

PASCUA, SIMONETTE V; Santa Clara HS; Sunnyvale, CA; (3); Math Tm; Spanish Clb; Chorus; Cit Awd; 4-H Awd; Hon Roll; Santa Clara U; Nrsng.

PASCUAL, ALEXANDER A; Warren HS; Downey, CA; (2); Debate Tm; FBLA; Nwsp; Bsktbl; Law.

PASCUAL, EILEEN; Bishop Amat HS; West Covina, CA; (3); Cmnty Wkr; Teachers Aide; School Play; Hon Roll; CSF; Filipino Clb; Nrsng.

PASCUAL, GABRIEL; Chula Vista Christian HS; Chula Vista, CA; (2); 1/20; Church Yth Grp; Computer Clb; Trk; High Hon Roll; Piano; Boxing; Grossmont; Vet Sci.

PASCUAL, GERARD L; Hogan SR HS; Vallejo, CA; (3); Spanish Clb; Yrbk; JV Wrstlng; Cngrssnl Schlr Oct 90; U Of CA Davis; Med.

PASCUAL, JOSEPH Q; San Leandro HS; San Leandro, CA; (2); 20/399; Bsktbl; JV Ftbl; JV Trk; Hon Roll; Prfct Atten Awd; Pres Acad Fit Awd; CA JR Schlrshp Fed; CA Schltc Fed; "A Poly Tech ST; Engrng.

PASCUAL, KATHLEEN; Herbert Hoover HS; Glendale, CA; (4); 1/524; Hosp Aide; Sec Key Clb; Drill Tm; Ed Nwsp; Lit Mag; VP Stu Cncl; Mgr(s); Cit Awd; High Hon Roll; Ntl Merit SF; Math & Sci Mdl; CSF; Chem Engrg.

PASCUAL, RICHARD; Foothill HS; Pleasanton, CA; (3); 7/190; Debate Tm; Hosp Aide; JCL; Latin Clb; Service Clb; Lit Mag; Var Crs Cntry; JV Trk; CA Schlrshp Fed; U Of CA San Diego; Medcl Dctr.

PASCUZZI, JOHN; San Ramon Valley HS; Danville, CA; (3); 13/420; Intnl Clb; Speech Tm; Band; Tennis; High Hon Roll; Johns Hopkins; Intl Rltns.

PASELK, DEBORAH A; Arcata HS; Bayside, CA; (3); Church Yth Grp; Drama Clb; Treas Spanish Clb; SADD; Chorus; Stage Crew; Variety Show; Rep Frsh Cls; Interact Club Treas; Humbolt ST U.

PASETES, GEORGE; San Ramon Valley HS; Danville, CA; (2); 21/400; Art Clb; Intnl Clb; JV Tennis; High Hon Roll; Hon Roll; Pres Acad Fit Awd; CA Golden St Exam High Hnrs Geom; Attended Acad Arts Specl Smmr Art Course; Achvt Awd Frgn Lang Span; UCLA; Arch.

PASH, ALLISON; Monte Vista HS; Danville, CA; (3); Dance Clb; Chorus; Variety Show; Powder Puff Ftbl; Var Swmmng; N Coast Sec Schlr Athltc.

PASHA, HALIMAH; Skyline HS; Oakland, CA; (2); Dance Clb; Debate Tm; Drama Clb; Girl Scts; Thesps; Co-Ed Nwsp; Hon Roll; Literary Clb; Jr Statesmn America; Hilman; Writr.

PASHAYAN, SHAHE; Reseda HS; Canoga Park, CA; (3); Boy Scts; Chess Clb; FBLA; Key Clb; Natl Beta Clb; Off Jr Cls; Off Sr Cls; Var Tennis; High Hon Roll; Dentstry.

PASION, ANABELLA B; Hogan SR HS; Vallejo, CA; (2); SADD; Drill Tm; Yrbk; Hon Roll; Piano.

PASQUAL, SHARON L; Redwood Acad; Forestville, CA; (3); 1/6; Church Yth Grp; Drama Clb; Library Aide; Office Aide; Quiz Bowl; Scholastic Bowl; Chorus; School Play; Rep Nwsp; Ed Yrbk; Amer U; Intl Bus.

PASQUINELLI, ALYSSA D; St Joseph HS; Cypress, CA; (3); 50/180; Cmnty Wkr; GAA; Ski Clb; SADD; Stage Crew; Rep Soph Cls; Rep Jr Cls; Rep Sr Cls; Rep Stu Cncl; Powder Puff Ftbl; Cypress Coll.

PASRICH, PUNEET; Santa Barbara HS; Santa Barbara, CA; (4); 15/450; Boy Scts; Scholastic Bowl; Nwsp; JV Crs Cntry; High Hon Roll; NHS; Pres Acad Fit Awd; Comp Lab Admin; Library Technen; CSF; U Of CA Los Angeles; Elec Engr.

PASSEY, JENNALEE; Liberty Union HS; Oakley, CA; (3); 29/339; Pres Church Yth Grp; Treas French Clb; Acpl Chr; Church Choir; School Musical; Swing Chorus; Rptr Yrbk; High Hon Roll; Hon Roll; BYU; Tchr.

PASSNO, NICOLE; Crescenta Valley HS; Glendale, CA; (1); 25/300; Church Yth Grp; Pep Clb; Drill Tm; Nwsp; Cheerldng.

PASTEN, SORAYA; Sweetwater HS; Chula Vista, CA; (3); Dance Clb; Hawaiian Dance Diploma; UCSD; Dance Instructor.

PASTIS, JAMES; Edison HS; Huntington Bch, CA; (4); 186/511; Teachers Aide; Mrchg Band; Pep Band; U CA Irvine; Cmptr.

PASTOR, MARILOU; Chowchilla Union HS; Madera, CA; (2); 6/142; Church Yth Grp; FBLA; Pep Clb; Variety Show; JV VP Cheerldng; VP Pom Pon; Score Keeper; High Hon Roll; Prfct Atten Awd; Gottschalks Hi-Deb.

PASTOR, PETER A; Chowchilla Union HS; Madera, CA; (4); 6/125; Co-Ed Nwsp; Rptr Yrbk; Treas Jr Cls; Sec Sr Cls; Wrstlng; High Hon Roll; Pres Acad Fit Awd; CSF; ST Chpn Comp Tm; Acad Dcthln; CA ST U Fresno.

PASTORE, GRISEL E; Lowell HS; San Francisco, CA; (3); Cmnty Wkr; German Clb; Hosp Aide; Office Aide; Orch; Trk; Stu Exchng Pgm In Italy; Tae Kwon Do.

PASTORE, NICHOLAS; St Joseph HS; Santa Maria, CA; (4); 3/117; Ski Clb; SADD; Vllybl; Cit Awd; High Hon Roll; Luso-Amer & Italian Cathlc Fed Schlrshps; Santa Barbara Fndtn Grant; Cal Poly San Luis Obispo; Arch.

PASTRAN, PATRICIA A; American HS; Fremont, CA; (3); Med.

PASTRANA, MELISSA J; Huntington Beach HS; Huntington Beach, CA; (2); Hosp Aide; Model UN; Red Cross Aide; Spanish Clb; Stu Cncl; JV Socr; JV Trk; High Hon Roll; Jr Statesmen Of America; Coach AYSO Soccer Team; Tower Awd 2 Yrs Engl; Safe Rides; Harvawrd; Biological Sci.

PATACSIL, ILA; San Diego HS; San Diego, CA; (2); Chorus; Church Choir; Drill Tm; Flag Corp; Chld Psych.

PATAIL, OMAR A; Huntington Beach HS; Huntington Beach, CA; (2); AFS; Boy Scts; Chess Clb; Computer Clb; High Hon Roll; Badmntn; Physcn.

PATAKI, HELEN M; Hayward HS; Castro Valley, CA; (3); VP German Clb; Hist Q&S; Science Clb; Teachers Aide; Acpl Chr; Band; Orch; Var Socr; Var JV Vllybl; Hon Roll; Bdmntn Capt All Leag Team; Yth Orch; Nrthrn CA Jr Bdmntn Chmpnshps Mxd Dbls Open 1st Pl 90.

PATANE, BRENDAN A; Pittsburg SR HS; Pittsburg, CA; (4); 40/277; Church Yth Grp; FBLA; Ski Clb; SADD; Teachers Aide; JV Ftbl; Hon Roll; Delta Brd Realtrs Schlrshp; Sacramento ST U; Bus Admin.

PATANELLA, LISA M; Loara HS; Anaheim, CA; (4); French Clb; Band; Jazz Band; Mrchg Band; Pep Band; Bsktbl; Sftbl; Vllybl; Hon Roll; NHS; SEDS Clb; CSU Fullerton; Music.

PATAPOFF, BENJAMIN W; Huntington Beach HS; Huntington Beach, CA; (1); Church Yth Grp; Teachers Aide; JV Capt Crs Cntry; JV Golf; JV Trk; Engr.

PATCHE, MICHELE N; Encina Academy Of Science And Tech; Sacramento, CA; (3); 25/212; Drama Clb; Key Clb; Pep Clb; SADD; Teachers Aide; Band; Jazz Band; Pep Band; Hon Roll; UC Davis; Vet.

PATE, BRYAN L; Coronado HS; Coronado, CA; (3); 3/150; Ski Clb; VP Frsh Cls; Pres Soph Cls; Pres Stu Cncl; JV Bsbl; Var Ftbl; Capt Var Socr; JV Trk; Hon Roll; NHS.

PATE, SEAN C; St Ignatius College Prep; Daly City, CA; (3); Art Clb; Letterman Clb; Pep Clb; Varsity Clb; Var L Ftbl; Var L Trk; Jr Statesmen Amer; Loyola Marymount U; Grphc Dsgn.

PATEL, AJIT; Tri City Christian Schl; Oceanside, CA; (3); Boy Scts; Ed Yrbk; Swmmng; High Hon Roll; Hon Roll; Bus.

PATEL, AMISH R; Bellarmine College Prep; San Jose, CA; (3); Hosp Aide; Teachers Aide; Yrbk; UC Berkeley; Pre-Med.

PATEL, ANAND; Apple Valley HS; Apple Valley, CA; (3); Band; Mrchg Band; Socr; Tennis; High Hon Roll; Med.

PATEL, ANITA; Carlmont HS; Belmont, CA; (3); CSM; Music.

PATEL, ANITA R; Troy HS; Fullerton, CA; (2); Girl Scts; Intnl Clb; JCL; Key Clb; Latin Clb; Spanish Clb; Band; Mrchg Band; Nwsp; Stu Cncl.

PATEL, ANJLEE; South San Francisco HS; South San Francis, CA; (2); Soccer; Med.

PATEL, APOOR K; Poly HS; Riverside, CA; (1); FBLA; Band; Jazz Band; Mrchg Band; Pep Band; High Hon Roll; Pres Acad Fit Awd; Hnr Band; Phy.

PATEL, ASHISHKUMAR A; Millikan HS; Long Beach, CA; (2); Cit Awd; High Hon Roll; Harvard; Dr.

PATEL, ASMITA; S Tahoe HS; S Lake Tahoe, CA; (3); 17/211; SADD; Hon Roll.

PATEL, AVANI R; Etiwanda HS; Fontana, CA; (3); Key Clb; Spanish Clb; High Hon Roll; UC Riverside.

PATEL, CHANDRAHAS B; South HS; Bakersfield, CA; (3); Cmnty Wkr; Intnl Clb; Key Clb; Teachers Aide; Var Socr; Var Tennis; Cit Awd; Hon Roll; NHS; Med.

PATEL, DARSHANA R; Apple Valley HS; Apple Valley, CA; (2); Math Tm; Spanish Clb; Intrml Tennis; High Hon Roll; Mock Trial Team; CSF; Envrnmntl Sci.

PATEL, DEENA; Marin Catholic HS; San Rafael, CA; (4); 17/198; Cmnty Wkr; French Clb; JA; Yrbk; Lit Mag; High Hon Roll; Hon Roll; NHS; Ntl Merit Schol; Watercolor & Oil Pntng Sketching; Travel Europe, India, Japan; Writing/Rdng; CA U Santa Barbara; Engl.

PATEL, DEVANGI; Brea-Olinda HS; Brea, CA; (3); Church Yth Grp; Intnl Clb; Temple Yth Grp; Hon Roll; Prfct Atten Awd; Acad Booster & Interact Clbs; Pre Schl Teacher & Print Shop Aide; Intl Law.

PATEL, DEVINDRA; Alhambra HS; Alhambra, CA; (3); Cmnty Wkr; Pep Clb; Service Clb; Variety Show; JV Cheerldng; Le Aikanes Tri-Hi-Y; Svc Clb; Frshmn Fundrsr; 2 Yr Lgsltre Rep; Grls Leag Hstrn; Law.

PATEL, DHAVAL; Narbonne HS; Torrance, CA; (2); JV Capt Vllybl; Hon Roll; Schlr Ath Awd; Prncpls List; Elec Engr.

PATEL, DIPTI T; Montgomery HS; Santa Rosa, CA; (4); 42/402; Computer Clb; Model UN; Science Clb; Off Jr Cls; High Hon Roll; NHS; Prfct Atten Awd; GPA 3.60 Awd; Sonoma St U; Chem.

PATEL, GAYATRI D; Cajon HS; San Bernardino, CA; (4); Cmnty Wkr; Tennis; Vllybl; Badminton Cert; Math Cert; CA ST; Med.

PATEL, HANNON R; Bellarmine College Prep; Milpitas, CA; (2); Debate Tm; Hosp Aide; Math Clb; NFL; Science Clb; Service Clb; Speech Tm; Stage Crew; Nwsp; JV Golf; NASA Ames Resrch 1st Pl; Cnty Sci Fair 2nd Pl; NASA Wrk Fllwshp; Johns Hopkins U; Med.

PATEL, HEENA B; Valley HS; Sacramento, CA; (3); English Clb; Office Aide; Teachers Aide; Cit Awd; High Hon Roll; Hon Roll; Prfct Atten Awd; UC Davis; Phy.

PATEL, HEMA; Bellflower HS; Bellflower, CA; (3); Am Leg Aux Girls St; Art Clb; English Clb; FBLA; JA; Key Clb; Math Clb; Mu Alpha Theta; Spanish Clb; High Hon Roll; FBLA; Cls Rep Self-Esteem Conf; Cerritos Coll; CPA.

PATEL, HITEN; Valencia HS; Yorba Linda, CA; (2); 1/400; FBLA; Intnl Clb; Science Clb; Tennis; High Hon Roll; Jr NHS; NHS; Prfct Atten Awd; Pres Acad Fit Awd; Stanford; Medicine.

PATEL, JAY; Marina HS; Huntington Bch, CA; (3); JCL; Latin Clb; Math Clb; JV Tennis; High Hon Roll; Golden Shield Nominatn Mthmtcs; Med.

PATEL, JITESH; Huntington Beach HS; Huntington Beach, CA; (2); Key Clb; Hon Roll; CSF; Peer Cnslr; UCI; Law.

PATEL, KAILASH R; Live Oak HS; Morgan Hill, CA; (3); 150/450; FBLA; GAA; Library Aide; Teachers Aide; Bsktbl; Cit Awd; San Jose ST; Bus.

PATEL, KALPESH; Cajon HS; San Bernardino, CA; (2); Chess Clb; Key Clb; French Hon Soc; High Hon Roll; NHS; Prfct Atten Awd; Harvard; Dentist.

PATEL, KAPESH V; Irvine HS; Irvine, CA; (1); Intnl Clb; JV Tennis; JV Trk; Wt Lftg; Cit Awd; Hon Roll; UC Davis; Med Sci.

PATEL, KRINA; Nova HS; Summit City, CA; (1); Band; Mrchg Band; Cheerldng; Trk; Hon Roll; Stanford; Med.

PATEL, LINA A; Katella HS; Anaheim, CA; (4); Hosp Aide; Key Clb; SADD; Nwsp; High Hon Roll; Hon Roll; NHS; Pres Acad Fit Awd; U Of Irvine.

PATEL, MAHESH KANTILAL; Fremont HS; Sunnyvale, CA; (2); NFL; Hon Roll; Badminton Tm; Red & White Awd.

PATEL, MAHESH P; Long Beach Polytechnic HS; Long Beach, CA; (3); High Hon Roll; Hon Roll; USC; Acctng.

PATEL, MALHAR; Ganesha HS; Diamond Bar, CA; (2); Boy Scts; Math Clb; Teachers Aide; Orch; Socr; Cit Awd; High Hon Roll; Excellency In Geomtry Golden ST Exam; Medical Field.

PATEL, MANISHA S; El Toro HS; El Toro, CA; (1); 92/500; French Clb; GAA; Sec Key Clb; Service Clb; JV Tennis; Hon Roll; Kiwanis Awd; Awd Jr Leag Vlntr Ctr; Plq Outstndng Offcr Keywanette; UCI.

PATEL, MEGHNA; William S Hart HS; Valencia, CA; (1); FBLA; Intnl Clb; Stanford U; Lawyer.

PATEL, MITAL; Willows HS; Willows, CA; (4); Cit Awd; High Hon Roll; CSF Treas; Elec Engr.

PATEL, MONIKA K; San Dimas HS; San Dimas, CA; (3); Hosp Aide; Temple Yth Grp; School Play; Cit Awd; Gov Hon Prg Awd; Hon Roll; CA ST-FULLERTON; Med Doc.

PATEL, MRUNAL; Hart HS; Valencia, CA; (1).

PATEL, NEEL; Menlo Schl; Redwood City, CA; (3); Cmnty Wkr; Chorus; School Musical; School Play; Variety Show; Rptr Nwsp; Ed Yrbk; Treas Sr Cls; Crs Cntry; Socr; VP/Pres Schl Cmnty Svc Clb; Co Chrmn Of San Mateo Cnty Vlntr Cntr; Stu Bd.

PATEL, NEHAL G; Whitney HS; La Mirada, CA; (3); Boy Scts; Church Yth Grp; JA; Spanish Clb; Var Trk; High Hon Roll; Pres Acad Fit Awd; Indian Sri Lankan Clb; Eagle Sct; Scrty Pacific Natl Bank Tllr; Doctor.

PATEL, NILA C; Grant Union HS; Sacramento, CA; (4); 2/286; Computer Clb; English Clb; Intnl Clb; Spanish Clb; School Musical; Variety Show; Hon Roll; Prfct Atten Awd; Rotary Awd; Sal; Achvt & Outstndng Stu Certs; Cnslr Outstndng Achvt Chevron; Bank Of Amer Achvt Awd; CSU Sacramento; Pharmacy.

PATEL, NIRAJ D; Burbank HS; Burbank, CA; (2); Spanish Clb; Yrbk; Cit Awd; Hon Roll; Jr NHS; Prfct Atten Awd; Mech Engr.

PATEL, NISHA; Franklin JR HS; Vallejo, CA; (1); Nwsp; Yrbk; VP Frsh Cls; High Hon Roll; Hon Roll; Prfct Atten Awd; DVC; Bus.

PATEL, NISHA; Gretchen Whitney HS; Cerritos, CA; (3); Hosp Aide; Key Clb; Latin Clb; SADD; Color Guard; High Hon Roll; Ntl Merit Ltr; Stanford; Bus.

PATEL, NISHA; Santa Cruz HS; Santa Cruz, CA; (3); Key Clb; VP Spanish Clb; Rep Stu Cncl; Hon Roll; Secy Womns Hnr Soc; ASB VP; Pedtrcn.

PATEL, PARAG S; Willits HS; Willits, CA; (3); Key Clb; Library Aide; Teachers Aide; Treas Sr Cls; Var Capt Bsktbl; JV Var Score Keeper; Cit Awd; High Hon Roll; Hon Roll; Chem Awd; Bsktbl Awds; Geography & US/Amer Wrld Hstry Awd; Stanford U; Med.

PATEL, PRAVEEN; Polytechnic HS; Long Beach, CA; (2); Chess Clb; Cit Awd; Prfct Atten Awd; UCLA.

PATEL, PREETY R; San Lorenzo HS; Oakland, CA; (2); Dance Clb; Fashion Dsg.

PATEL, PRITI; Monte Vista HS; Alamo, CA; (3); French Clb; Office Aide; Pep Clb; Ski Clb; SADD; Flag Corp; Mrchg Band; Powder Puff Ftbl; High Hon Roll; Hon Roll; Graphc Desgn.

PATEL, PURVI B; Buena Park HS; Buena Park, CA; (4); French Clb; GAA; Intnl Clb; Key Clb; Math Clb; Red Cross Aide; Varsity Clb; JV Var Tennis; Hon Roll; NHS; Acad Decathlon; JV Badminton; Tnns Trnmnt Semi-Fnlst, Fnlst & Qtr Fnlst; Indian Amer Club; CA ST Fullerton; Bus.

PATEL, PURVI P; Bonita HS; La Verne, CA; (2); Science Clb; JV Bsktbl; Pres Acad Fit Awd; Envrnmntl Protection; UCLA; Marine Bio.

PATEL, RADHA; Mills HS; Burlingame, CA; (3); Cmnty Wkr; Debate Tm; Intnl Clb; Model UN; Yrbk; Stu Cncl; Mgr(s); Mgr Socr; U CA.

PATEL, RAJU R; Mt View Schl; Los Altos, CA; (3); Chess Clb; Cmnty Wkr; Computer Clb; French Clb; JA; Library Aide; Math Clb; Math Tm; Science Clb; Ski Clb; CSF; GATE Stu; Physician.

PATEL, RAJUL A; John F Kennedy HS; Granada Hills, CA; (4); 7/560; Hist Debate Tm; Hosp Aide; Treas Key Clb; Ed Nwsp; Off Sr Cls; Capt Bsktbl; High Hon Roll; Pres Acad Fit Awd; DECA; NHS; CSF Membrshp Secy; Schl Accrdtn Cmmttee; Ephebians; UCLA; Med.

PATEL, RITU; Cajon HS; San Bernardino, CA; (3); Cmnty Wkr; Hosp Aide; Key Clb; SADD; Sec Stu Cncl; Cit Awd; High Hon Roll; Jr NHS; NHS; Rotary Awd; Challenge Bowl; Mock Trial; Acad Decathalon; Pre-Med.

PATEL, SAFALI; University HS; Irvine, CA; (4); Sec Treas French Clb; Key Clb; Spanish Clb; Mgr Yrbk; French Hon Soc; Hon Roll; SABE; U Of CA Irvine; Social Sci.

PATEL, SAMIR A; East Bakersfield HS; Bakersfield, CA; (4); 17/477; Church Yth Grp; Cmnty Wkr; Hosp Aide; VP Intnl Clb; VP Key Clb; Pres Jr Cls; Pres Sr Cls; Var Capt Tennis; Hon Roll; Acad Ltr GPA Tow Semesters; Homecoming Float Chairperson 2 Yrs; UCLA; Undeclared Life Sci.

PATEL, SAMIR R; Washington HS; Fremont, CA; (2); 30/325; JA; Ski Clb; Lit Mag; Off Soph Cls; Intrml Tennis; Hon Roll; Prfct Atten Awd; Amnsty Intl VP.

PATEL, SANJAY B; Mission HS; San Francisco, CA; (4); Sprt Ed Nwsp; JV Wrstlng; Elec Engrng.

PATEL, SHARMILA A; Notre Dame HS; San Carlos, CA; (2); Math Clb; Science Clb; Church Choir; Cit Awd; High Hon Roll; NEDT Awd; Exclnc In Span I & II; UC Berkeley; Pre-Med.

PATEL, SNEHAL I; Redwood HS; Visalia, CA; (2); Computer Clb; FBLA; German Clb; Math Clb; Math Tm; Science Clb; SADD; Hon Roll; CSF; U Southern CA; CPA.

PATEL, SONAL R; Warren HS; Downey, CA; (3); 10/460; Cmnty Wkr; Dance Clb; Mu Alpha Theta; Science Clb; Service Clb; Temple Yth Grp; High Hon Roll; Opt Clb Awd; Rotary Awd; St Schlr; Bio.

PATEL, SWATI R; Artesia HS; Lakewood, CA; (3); French Clb; JA; Red Cross Aide; Science Clb; Spanish Clb; Sec Jr Cls; Rep Sr Cls; Stu Cncl; High Hon Roll; Conestoga Awd; Hnr Guard Cls 90; U Of Irvine; Med.

PATEL, TARANG B; Lincoln HS; Stockton, CA; (3); 85/538; Mu Alpha Theta; High Hon Roll; Hon Roll; CSF; Golden St Exam-Alg I Hnrs; Span I/Ii Hnrs; U CA Davis; Med.

PATEL, URVASHI R; Mira Costa HS; Redondo Beach, CA; (2); Var Bsktbl; Var Sftbl; Var Trk; Cit Awd; Hon Roll; Prfct Atten Awd; Pres Acad Fit Awd; Yth Clb.

PATEL, YOGESHKUMAR K; Don Bosco Technical Inst; Compton, CA; (2); 8/252; Computer Clb; Drama Clb; Math Tm; School Play; Stage Crew; Nwsp; Hon Roll; NHS; Prfct Atten Awd; CA Schlrshp Fed; Bus/Engrng.

PATERNA, JULLEE M; Mt Shasta HS; Mount Shasta, CA; (2); Hosp Aide; Teachers Aide; Trk; Cit Awd; High Hon Roll; Hon Roll; Vlntr Sisson Elem Math Field Day; Set-Up Halloween Hntd House.

PATERSON, ERIN E; Dos Pueblos HS; Goleta, CA; (2); Color Guard; Flag Corp; Yrbk; Hon Roll; Prfct Atten Awd; UCSB; Pediatric Nurse.

PATES, WENDY; Montclair HS; South Bend, IN; (2); SADD; Teachers Aide; Chorus; Ed Yrbk; Hon Roll; Prfct Atten Awd; Cert Exclnc In Bio/Health; Psych.

PATHAK, ANJALI P; Whitney HS; Cerritos, CA; (2); Intnl Clb; JA; Model UN; Phtg Yrbk; JV Tennis; Hon Roll; Pres Acad Fit Awd; Hstry Day LA 2nd Prz; U Of CA; Marine Bio.

PATINO, ALMA A; San Marcos HS; Santa Barbara, CA; (3); 133/380; Acpl Chr; Chorus; Flag Corp; Swing Chorus; Variety Show; Yrbk; Hon Roll; Treas MESA; Ltr 3 Tms; Hnr Soc CSF; UCSB; Med.

PATINO, KURT R; Bellarmine Jefferson HS; N Hollywood, CA; (4); Am Leg Boys St; Drama Clb; Band; Variety Show; Ed Nwsp; Pres Sr Cls; Var L Bsbl; Cit Awd; NHS; Pepperdine U; Theatr Arts.

PATIO, ANNA MARIA L; Franklin JR HS; Vallejo, CA; (2); Drama Clb; Thesps; Drill Tm; School Play; Off Frsh Cls; High Hon Roll; Hon Roll; Accntnt.

PATRICIO, PONCECA ANNE N; Milpitas HS; Milpitas, CA; (2); ROTC; Drill Tm; Nwsp; Yrbk; Hon Roll; UC San Francisco; Medcl.

PATRICK, GAVIN; Irvington HS; Fremont, CA; (3); 64/251; Church Yth Grp; Rep Stu Cncl; Var Crs Cntry; Var Ftbl; Var Socr; Var Trk; Hon Roll; Rotary Awd; Fremont Police Detp Explrs; Rotarian Yth Ldrshp Awd Schlrshp; DARE; Crimnl Law.

PATRICK, KATHLEEN J; Hemet HS; Hemet, CA; (3); 36/500; Church Yth Grp; Cmnty Wkr; JA; Key Clb; Spanish Clb; SADD; Nwsp; Var Trk; Cit Awd; Hon Roll; Humboldt ST U; Marine Bio.

PATRICK, KEVIN J; North HS; Bakersfield, CA; (2); French Clb; Math Tm; ROTC; Crs Cntry; Trk; High Hon Roll; NHS; CSF; Stu Plts Lcns; Aerntcl Engrng.

PATRICK, MARY KATHLEEN; Highlands HS; North Highlands, CA; (3); Church Yth Grp; French Clb; Chorus; Ed Nwsp; Yrbk; Treas Jr Cls; Var Vllybl; Cit Awd; High Hon Roll; Hon Roll; 1st Pl Black Hstry Essay Cont; CA ST U Sacramento; Hstry.

PATRICK, REBECCA J; Oak Ridge HS; El Dorado Hills, CA; (1); Church Yth Grp; High Hon Roll; Pres Acad Fit Awd; Friday Night Live; CSF; BYU; Arch.

PATRICK, ROY L; Monte Vista HS; Spring Valley, CA; (1); Chess Clb; Computer Clb; Intrml Bsktbl; Intrml Ftbl; Intrml Tennis; Intrml Vllybl; Cit Awd; Scba Dvng; Avtn; Avtn.

PATRICK, TERI L; Victor Valley HS; Newmanstown, PA; (2); 12/675; FBLA; Girl Scts; Key Clb; Trk; Hon Roll; NHS; Tutor-Algb & Geom; Gldn St Exam Hnrs Geom; Indp Dolphin Swmm Tm; Purdue; Fin Anlyst.

PATRIKYAN, ARTASHES; Herbert Hoover HS; Glendale, CA; (2); Var Bsktbl; UCLA; Dentist.

PATRON, ELIZABETH; Calexico HS; Calexico, CA; (2); Hon Roll.

PATRON, MORYAH T; Mayfield SR HS; Glassell Park, CA; (2); Chorus; Hon Roll; Hnr Awe Bio; Amnesty Intl; Campus Guides.

PATRON, REBECCA MARIE; Mar Vista HS; Imperial Beach, CA; (1); AFS; Church Yth Grp; Hosp Aide; Latin Clb; Office Aide; Spanish Clb; SADD; Teachers Aide; Church Choir; Swing Chorus; Hstry & Eng Gate Prgm Awd; Art Awd; Journlsm.

PATRY, IRENE; Fred C Beyer HS; Modesto, CA; (3); Church Yth Grp; Treas French Clb; Hist FBLA; Cit Awd; High Hon Roll; CSF 87-89; Ptrt Awd 89; Gldn ST Exm Geo Hnrs 89; Mktg.

PATSKO, STACEY; Christian HS; El Cajon, CA; (3); 2/105; Key Clb; Pep Clb; SADD; Teachers Aide; Var Capt Bsktbl; Var Capt Sftbl; JV Capt Vllybl; Hon Roll; Prfct Atten Awd; Math.

PATTEN, BENJAMIN A; Don Antonio Lugo HS; Chino, CA; (3); Church Yth Grp; Drama Clb; German Clb; Hon Roll; CSF Public Rltns Ofcr; Biomed Engrng.

PATTEN, JASMINE; Palm Springs HS; Palm Springs, CA; (4); Cmnty Wkr; French Clb; JV Var Cheerldng; Var Powder Puff Ftbl; Cit Awd; High Hon Roll; Pres Acad Fit Awd; Envrnmnt; Poetry; UC Santa Cruz; Envrnmntl Stds.

PATTERSON, CAMILLE; Arroyo HS; San Lorenzo, CA; (4); 18/268; Church Yth Grp; Ski Clb; Church Choir; Ed Nwsp; Var Swmmng; JV Var Vllybl; High Hon Roll; Hon Roll; Bk Of Amer Achvt Awd Engl; San Lorenzo Educ Assn Schlrshp; Azusa Pacific U Deans Schlrshp; Azusa Pacific U; Lib Studies.

PATTERSON, ELISABETH C; Serrano HS; Wrightwood, CA; (2); 2/248; Church Yth Grp; Treas VP FBLA; Girl Scts; JA; Letterman Clb; Band; Mrchg Band; Hist Frsh Cls; Var L Vllybl; High Hon Roll; 4th Pl Slalom Jr Olympics Snow Ski Rcng; 2nd Princess Miss Wrightwood Pgnt; 1st Pl Wrtng Celebration; US System; Med Fld.

PATTERSON, ERIN N; Chaffey HS; Cucamonga, CA; (3); 23/400; Dance Clb; French Clb; Teachers Aide; Var L Swmmng; JV Var Tennis; High Hon Roll; Hon Roll; NESC Clb; CSF; Sonoma ST U CA; Teacher.

PATTERSON II, GREGORY; Lincoln Prep HS; San Diego, CA; (4); JA; Model UN; SADD; Varsity Clb; Var Trk; Hon Roll; Rotary Awd; Links Inc; MESA; Morehouse Coll; Engrng.

PATTERSON, HEATHER L; Dixon HS; Dixon, CA; (2); AFS; Church Yth Grp; Var Sec 4-H; Intnl Clb; JV Bsktbl; 4-H Awd; Hon Roll; Prfct Atten Awd; Hrsbck Rdng; 4-H Cmp Cnslr; U Of CA Davis.

PATTERSON, JERAD S; Bella Vista HS; Orangevale, CA; (3); 10/390; Church Yth Grp; French Clb; Science Clb; Ski Clb; Varsity Clb; Var Golf; JV Var Socr; French Hon Soc; High Hon Roll; CSF; Econ & Engl Awds; Bus.

PATTERSON, LEISA; Turlock HS; Turlock, CA; (4); AFS; Pres DECA; Key Clb; Office Aide; Science Clb; SADD; Teachers Aide; Yrbk; JV Var Score Keeper; Hon Roll; Bus Mgmt.

PATTERSON, MARISA E; Savanna HS; Anaheim, CA; (4); 5/283; Dance Clb; Drama Clb; Girl Scts; JA; Teachers Aide; Drill Tm; Ed Nwsp; Treas Jr Cls; NHS; Pres Acad Fit Awd; Girl Scout Gold Awd; Yth Commission; Yth Task Force; CA ST U Fullerton; Psych.

PATTERSON, MICHELLE D; Eisenhower HS; Rialto, CA; (3); Office Aide; Drill Tm; Treas Jr Cls; Off Sr Cls; Stu Cncl; Stat Bsktbl; Cit Awd; Hon Roll; Sci Dept Awd; Azurettes Pres; Med.

PATTERSON, MICHELLE L; Independence HS; San Jose, CA; (4); Art Clb; Treas Church Yth Grp; Var JV Sftbl; Var Swmmng; Hon Roll; Advanced Plcmnt Art; San Fran Acad Of Art; Art.

PATTERSON, OMARI O; Bishop O'dowd HS; Oakland, CA; (4); Drama Clb; School Play; Yrbk; Ftbl; Trk; Thtr Arts.

PATTERSON, PRISCILLA; Presentation HS; San Jose, CA; (2); 5/92; Debate Tm; Spanish Clb; Speech Tm; Hon Roll.

PATTERSON, REBECCA T; Poway HS; Poway, CA; (2); 38/826; Capt Debate Tm; Service Clb; Temple Yth Grp; Thesps; Chorus; JV Swmmng; High Hon Roll; Amnesty Intl; CSF.

PATTERSON, SHON TEL M; Ganesha HS; Diamond Bar, CA; (3); Bsktbl; Sftbl; Trk; Vllybl; MESA Prgm 87; Atten Harvey Mudd Coll; MVP Bstkbl 86-87; Sftbl MVP 89; Vrsty Bsktlbl Coachs Awd 89-90; Central ST CAL ST; Law.

PATTERSON, THOMAS S; Rincon Valley Christian HS; Santa Rosa, CA; (2); 1/30; VP Church Yth Grp; Yrbk; Rep Frsh Cls; Rep Soph Cls; VP Stu Cncl; Var Bsktbl; Cit Awd; High Hon Roll; Pres Acad Fit Awd; Bicycle Racing; Biola U; Theology.

PATTERSON, WILLIAM C; El Camino Fundamental HS; Sacramento, CA; (3); Church Yth Grp; German Clb; Ski Clb; SADD; Intrml Bsbl; Intrml Bsktbl; JV Ftbl; Intrml Var Score Keeper; Intrml Socr; Intrml Tennis; Outstndng Art Awds; Outstndng Ath Awd Bsktbl; GSE Awd Alg; UC.

PATTISON, KIRSTEN N; Norte Vista HS; Riverside, CA; (2); Dance Clb; Girl Scts; Stat Trk; RAD; Interior Dsgn.

PATTISON, MARK W; Poway HS; San Diego, CA; (3); Teachers Aide; High Hon Roll; Hon Roll; Peer Cnslng; Just Say No; U San Diego.

PATTON, ANDREA L; Santa Clara HS; Santa Clara, CA; (4); Bsktbl; Cheerldng; Pom Pon; Score Keeper; Trk; Sectry Blck Stu Union; De Anza JC; Bus Admin.

PATTON, BRENDA L; St Joseph HS; Norwalk, CA; (2); Drama Clb; GAA; Key Clb; Science Clb; Spanish Clb; SADD; Yrbk; Var Crs Cntry; High Hon Roll; Hon Roll; CSF; Acad Awds; YMCA Vlntr; Marine Bio.

PATTON, DAVID L; Irvington HS; Fremont, CA; (4); 19/241; Church Yth Grp; Science Clb; Var Crs Cntry; Var Trk; Var Vllybl; High Hon Roll; Pres Acad Fit Awd; CSF; Hiking Clb; Chemathon Bay Area Rnkd 165 Of 700 88-89; Physcs Olympcs 89-90; UC Davis; Mech Engrng.

PATTON, ERSKINE L; South Fork HS; Redway, CA; (3); Chorus; Jazz Band; Rptr Ed Nwsp; JV Trk; Hon Roll; Rotary Music Awd 89-90; Schl Achvt Awds Music & Sci; Music Production.

PATTON, HEATHER M; Davis SR HS; Davis, CA; (2); Church Yth Grp; Teachers Aide; Band; Pep Band; Var Diving; Bus Mgr.

PATTON, KAYATT S; Mc Clymonds HS; Oakland, CA; (2); ROTC; Varsity Clb; Band; Chorus; Off Frsh Cls; Var Bsktbl; Var Sftbl; Hon Roll; Hnr Platoon; Gramblin ST; Jrnlsm.

PATTON, KERCHINA L; Fremont HS; Oakland, CA; (3); Cmnty Wkr; Model UN; Pep Clb; Drill Tm; Drm Mjr(t); Mrchg Band; Pep Band; School Play; Variety Show; Gym; Model.

PATTON, KIM; Taft HS; Fellows, CA; (4); 16/179; AFS; Drama Clb; French Clb; Teachers Aide; Band; Jazz Band; Mrchg Band; Orch; Pep Band; High Hon Roll; Acad Decthln; Mck Trl; Friday Night Live; U Of CA Santa Cruz; Comp Sci.

PATTON, KIMBERLY L; Pittsburg HS; Pittsburg, CA; (3); FBLA; Hon Roll; High Hon Roll; Awd Acad Achvt 89; Plaq Concord Nvl Wpns Sta Mst Outstndng Smmr Wkr 88; San Francsico ST U; Comp Sci.

PATTON, SHAREEN L; University HS; Irvine, CA; (3); Crs Cntry; JV Socr; Var Capt Sftbl; Hon Roll; Litry Shrts Club; Recycl Club; Schlr Athlete Awd; Arch.

PATU, LELE LISA; Phillip & Sala Burton Academic HS; Seattle, WA; (3); 21/745; Church Yth Grp; Cmnty Wkr; Dance Clb; English Clb; GAA; Library Aide; Office Aide; SADD; Teachers Aide; Chorus; VP Chrch Yth Choir; Seattle U; Law.

PATUGAN, ROLLENCE Y; Sierra Vista HS; Baldwin Park, CA; (4); Drama Clb; Math Clb; Speech Tm; Teachers Aide; Thesps; School Play; Variety Show; Bsktbl; Trk; High Hon Roll; CA ST Poly Pomona; Elect Comp.

PATWARDHAN, ASHISH V; John F Kennedy HS; La Palma, CA; (2); JV Crs Cntry; JV Trk; Cit Awd; High Hon Roll; Pres Acad Fit Awd; CSF; UCR; Vet.

PATZ, STEPHANIE H; Concord HS; Concord, CA; (3); Var Bsktbl; JV Sftbl; Var Tennis; Hon Roll; CSF; Schlr/Athl Awd.

PATZER, E BRETT; Miramonte HS; Orinda, CA; (1); JV Ftbl; JV Swmmng; JV Wrstlng; Hon Roll.

PAUGH, LEE A; Valley Christian HS; Long Beach, CA; (3); Boy Scts; Church Yth Grp; Cmnty Wkr; Church Choir; Ftbl; USC; Bus.

PAUL, BAMBI E; Eisenhower HS; Rialto, CA; (4); 3/655; Church Yth Grp; Key Clb; Speech Tm; Ed Lit Mag; Cit Awd; High Hon Roll; Hon Roll; Jr NHS; Kiwanis Awd; NHS; CSF; Sobobans Clb; Spnsh Clb VP; San Diego ST U; Spch Comm.

PAUL, JOCELYN I; Leuzinger HS; Hawthorne, CA; (1); Law.

PAUL, MELISSA DAWNELLE; Poway HS; San Diego, CA; (4); 28/677; VP Cmnty Wkr; Drama Clb; Sec German Clb; Intnl Clb; Key Clb; School Play; Ed Yrbk; High Hon Roll; Kiwanis Awd; 3rd Rnnr Up Miss TEEN CA Pgnt; Peer Counseling Pgm; Peer Tutoring; U Of AR; Jrnlsm.

PAUL, MICHELLE; North County Christian Schl; Templeton, CA; (4); 2/8; Teachers Aide; Chorus; Sec Frsh Cls; Rep Soph Cls; VP Stu Cncl; Capt Bsktbl; NHS; 88 John Hancock Schlr In Reinactment Of Signing Of US Constitution; Elem Educ.

PAUL, SHERRY; Alameda HS; Alameda, CA; (4); Church Yth Grp; Dance Clb; Drama Clb; FCA; Library Aide; Chorus; School Musical; Stage Crew; Hon Roll; Outstndng Makeup Crew Stage Awd Schl Musical; Davis; Chld Psych.

PAUL, YOLANDA; St Michael's HS; Los Angeles, CA; (2); VP Soph Cls; Hon Roll; Aerospc Engr.

PAULE, ANGELINA; Southwest HS; San Diego, CA; (2); #56 In Class; Pep Clb; SADD; Drill Tm; Pres Frsh Cls; Rep Stu Cncl; JV Cheerldng; Cit Awd; Hon Roll; Pres Acad Fit Awd; Cal Poly San Luis Obispo; Arch.

PAULEY, JULIE; East Bakersfield HS; Bakersfield, CA; (1); JV Cheerldng; Hon Roll; Cal Poly; Child Ed.

PAULIN, GERALDINE M; Norwalk HS; Norwalk, CA; (3); French Clb; Math Clb; Hon Roll; Prfct Atten Awd; Frnch Clb Sec & Actvts Commssnr; UC Irvine; Phy.

PAULINO, CARLA J; Downey HS; Downey, CA; (3); Church Yth Grp; Cmnty Wkr; Library Aide; Math Clb; Science Clb; VICA; Band; Mrchg Band; Hon Roll; Kywntts; Dy Cmp Cnslr; Bio.

PAULINO, ERWIN C; De Anza HS; El Sobrante, CA; (3); AFS; Cmnty Wkr; Debate Tm; Math Clb; NFL; Office Aide; Science Clb; Speech Tm; SADD; Teachers Aide; W Contra Costa Costa Sci Fair 3rd Pl; Mst Spirited Sccr Plry 89; U San Francisco; Bus Mgmt.

PAULINO, JANICE; Yucca Valley HS; Yucca Valley, CA; (3); Church Yth Grp; Office Aide; Drill Tm; Off Soph Cls; Cit Awd; Hon Roll; Wrkng Eldrly; Loma Linda U; Pdtrcn.

PAULINO, SANDRA; King Drew Med Mag HS; Los Angeles, CA; (3); Church Yth Grp; Dance Clb; Drama Clb; French Clb; Pep Clb; Band; Drill Tm; School Musical; School Play; VP Frsh Cls; UC Berkley; Pdtrcn.

PAULO, ANNALEE J; St Joseph HS; Whittier, CA; (3); 64/180; Drama Clb; Red Cross Aide; School Play; Yrbk; Var Cheerldng; High Hon Roll; Hon Roll; Art; Video Prodctn; Piano; Media.

PAULO, GEMMA L; Lemore Union HS; Lemoore, CA; (2); 1/400; Church Yth Grp; Spanish Clb; Var Bsktbl; JV Vllybl; High Hon Roll; CA Schlstc Fed; Play Organ For Church.

PAULOS, VERA; Glendale HS; Glendale, CA; (3); Art Clb; Dance Clb; Library Aide; Treas Science Clb; Hon Roll; Prfct Atten Awd; Glendale Coll; Bus Law.

PAULSEN, ERIC C; Victor Valley HS; Victorville, CA; (2); Intrml Fld Hcky; VP L Ftbl; VP L Socr; Intrml Wt Lftg; Cit Awd; High Hon Roll; Hon Roll; Prfct Atten Awd; Jrnlsm.

PAULSEN, KRIS; Serrano HS; Phelan, CA; (4); 39/213; French Clb; FBLA; Chorus; Capt Var Flag Corp; High Hon Roll; Hon Roll; Leos Stu For Stu; People To People Stu Ambassador; Child Psych.

PAULSON, ALICIA C; Clovis HS; Clovis, CA; (3); Church Yth Grp; Model UN; Office Aide; Teachers Aide; Hon Roll; Cross Stitch Club; 6 Yrs Tutoring, Chld Dev, Soc Cls; Fresno ST U; Engl.

PAULSON, BECKY; College Park HS; Pleasant Hill, CA; (2); Sec Frsh Cls; Sec Soph Cls; Stu Cncl; Bsktbl; Var Swmmng; High Hon Roll; Golden St Exam Alg Hnrs; UC Santa Barbara; Medcl.

PAVAO, EARL J; Manteca HS; Manteca, CA; (1); 76/457; Church Yth Grp; Drm Mjr(t); Rep Frsh Cls; Intrml Bsktbl; Hon Roll.

PAVICH, STEVE M; Elk Grove HS; Elk Grove, CA; (4); 3/580; Office Aide; JV Bsbl; High Hon Roll; Hon Roll; U CA Irvine; Ec.

PAVLAK, BETH A; Canyon Springs HS; Moreno Valley, CA; (4); 63/580; Pep Clb; Var Cheerldng; Var Socr; Var Swmmng; Hon Roll; Natl Yng Ldrs Assoc; Dancng Images Perfmng Grp; 3 Natl Titles & 5 ST Titles Dance; Riverside CC; Physcl Thrpy.

PAVLAK, STEPHANIE T; Canyon Springs HS; Moreno Valley, CA; (3); ROTC; Varsity Clb; Var L Crs Cntry; Var L Socr; JV Sftbl; Var L Trk; High Hon Roll; Hon Roll; NHS; Civil Air Patrol, Blue Baret Hnr Cadet & Grp Hnr Cadet; Emply Of Mnth Mc Donalds; UC Davis; Vet.

PAVLINAC, CHRISTINA M; San Dimas HS; Glendora, CA; (4); Church Yth Grp; Dance Clb; Drama Clb; Office Aide; Teachers Aide; Chorus; Church Choir; Variety Show; Yrbk; Pres Church Choir; Pres Schl Choir 88-89; Citrus; Dental.

PAVLOV, VESELINA; Tustin HS; Tustin, CA; (3); 5/468; AFS; Hosp Aide; Swmmng; High Hon Roll; Hon Roll; Pres Acad Fit Awd; Orange Cnty Acad Decthln Tm; Literary Clb Secty; CSF; Bus Admin.

PAWLACK, JENNIFER LYNN; Brea-Olinda HS; Brea, CA; (3); Church Yth Grp; Cmnty Wkr; VP Dance Clb; School Musical; Sec Soph Cls; VP Jr Cls; VP Sr Cls; JV Var Cheerldng; Hon Roll; NHS; CSF; Sf Rds SADD; Rd Rbbn Wk Agnst Drgs; Whittier Coll; Elem Schl Tchr.

PAWLOSKI, ADINE M; Santa Margarita HS; Laguna Niguel, CA; (3); 51/227; Ski Clb; Var Vllybl; High Hon Roll; NHS; Hmcmng Queen 89; Acad Hnrs-Engl II & III, Geom, Painting, Chem, US Hstry.

PAXTON, NATASHA R; Sacramento Adventist Acad; Sacramento, CA; (2); Church Yth Grp; Ski Clb; Band; Chorus; Gym; Elks Awd; Backpacking Clb; Med.

PAXTON, SHARLENE; Immanuel Christian Schl; Ridgecrest, CA; (1); Ski Clb; Spanish Clb; High Hon Roll; Hon Roll.

PAY, STACEY M; Paraclete HS; Palmdale, CA; (2); 15/145; Cmnty Wkr; Drama Clb; JA; VP Key Clb; Office Aide; Pres SADD; Yrbk; JV Trk; Cit Awd; High Hon Roll; Z-Clb; Mission Club; CSF; Amer Sign Lang Clb; Psych.

PAYAN, MARISOL; Roosevelt HS; Los Angeles, CA; (4); Cmnty Wkr; Hosp Aide; Library Aide; SADD; Yrbk; Lit Mag; French Hon Soc; Hon Roll; Pres Acad Fit Awd; Century III Ldrs Awd; U S Govt/Econ Hnr Mdlln; UC Santa Cruz; Psych.

PAYAN, MAYRA L; Arroyo HS; El Monte, CA; (4); Church Yth Grp; Dance Clb; French Clb; Key Clb; Teachers Aide; Chorus; JV Crs Cntry; Var Trk; CA ST U LA.

PAYAQUI, PHOEBE; Bonita Vista HS; Bonita, CA; (4); 1/500; Church Yth Grp; Hosp Aide; Quiz Bowl; Yrbk; Stu Cncl; Hon Roll; Fine Arts Clb; CA Schlrshp Fdr; Acad Dcthln.

PAYASLIAN, MELISSA; Armijo HS; Fairfield, CA; (2); Band; Mrchg Band; Bsktbl; Sftbl.

PAYE, STEPHANIE L; Nevada Union HS; Grass Valley, CA; (3); 5/551; Church Yth Grp; SADD; Sec Stu Cncl; High Hon Roll; Gymnastics; Golden St Exam Hnrs Alg I; Stu Of Mnth Apr 90; CA Poly San Luis Obispo.

PAYNE, AMANDA; Serrano HS; Wrightwood, CA; (2); Church Yth Grp; GAA; JV Bsktbl; Mgr Ftbl; Mgr(s); Brigham Yng U; Chldrn.

PAYNE, ANDREA C; Mt Carmel HS; San Diego, CA; (4); 51/764; Treas Debate Tm; JA; NFL; Speech Tm; Teachers Aide; Rptr Nwsp; Hon Roll; Pres Acad Fit Awd; Rotary Awd; Ranked 9th In CA For The Debate; High Honors Golden State Exam-Algebra & Geometry; Spoke At Grad; UCLA; English.

PAYNE, ASHLEY L; John Muir HS; Pasadena, CA; (3); GAA; Letterman Clb; Service Clb; Ski Clb; Speech Tm; Varsity Clb; Nwsp; Treas Soph Cls; VP Jr Cls; Pres Sr Cls; Capt Grls Soccer Team 89-90; USC; Advrtsng.

PAYNE, CYNTHIA; Mt Carmel HS; San Diego, CA; (3); Drama Clb; GAA; Var Bsktbl; Trk; Wt Lftg; Cit Awd; Kiwanis Awd; Prfct Atten Awd; San Diego Tribune All Acad Team Bsktbl; CA St Chmpnshp Qlfr; Pacific U; Grphc Dsgnr.

PAYNE, DANNIELLE; Corcoran HS; Corcoran, CA; (3); Church Yth Grp; Cmnty Wkr; Drama Clb; French Clb; FFA; FHA; Flag Corp; Powder Puff Ftbl; Trk; Hon Roll; Aerospace.

PAYNE, ELLEN; Canyon HS; Canyon Country, CA; (4); 11/450; Sec Debate Tm; Girl Scts; Intnl Clb; Band; Jazz Band; Pres Mrchg Band; Orch; Pep Band; High Hon Roll; NHS; Bank Of Amer Plaque; Geom & Alg Golden St Exams; Bahai Peace Awd; Semper Fidelis Music Awd; U CA San Diego; Bio.

PAYNE, HEIDI E; La Sierra HS; Riverside, CA; (1); Pres Church Yth Grp; Cmnty Wkr; Computer Clb; Drama Clb; Pres SADD; Teachers Aide; Church Choir; Nwsp; Cit Awd; Hon Roll; Brigham Young U; Cnslr.

PAYNE, JAMES; Redlands HS; Redlands, CA; (2); Church Yth Grp; Cit Awd.

PAYNE, JASON A; Roseville HS; Rocklin, CA; (2); Church Yth Grp; Computer Clb; Electronics.

PAYNE, JENNIFER R; Clairemont HS; San Diego, CA; (2); 1/236; Girl Scts; Model UN; Band; L Var Mrchg Band; Pep Band; L Var Swmmng; Hon Roll; Pres Acad Fit Awd; Girl Scout Silver Awd; San Diego Outrigger Canoe Club; Waterpolo Vrsty Lttr; UC San Diego; Med.

PAYNE, KELLEY C; Grossmont HS; El Cajon, CA; (3); Dance Clb; Spanish Clb; Variety Show; Treas Frsh Cls; Stu Cncl; Swmmng; Los Angeles Schl Of Art.

PAYNE, KENNA KAY; Notre Dame HS; Riverside, CA; (3); 7/143; Art Clb; Hosp Aide; Flag Corp; Rptr Nwsp; Var Swmmng; High Hon Roll; Xerox Awd For Humanities/Scl Sci; Numerous Awds For Outstndng Schlrshp 2 Yrs; Camp Cnslr; Pre-Med.

PAYNE, KRISTEN J; Nevada Union HS; Grass Valley, CA; (3); SADD; Teachers Aide; Drill Tm; Flag Corp; Socr; High Hon Roll; CSF; Santa Cruz; Mawrine Bio.

PAYNE, LAURA L; Atascadero HS; Atascadero, CA; (2); Drama Clb; Socr.

PAYNE, MATT S; North HS; Bakersfield, CA; (2); Church Yth Grp; Hosp Aide; Band; Mrchg Band; Pep Band; Yrbk; Kiwanis Awd; Masonic Awd; Pacific Union; Elem Educ.

PAYNE, MICHAEL J; Clovis HS; Clovis, CA; (2); Church Yth Grp; FCA; SADD; Off Frsh Cls; Off Soph Cls; Sec Treas Jr Cls; Var Bsktbl; Cit Awd; High Hon Roll; Hon Roll; Notre Dame.

PAYNE, NISSA R; Calipatria HS; Laredo, TX; (4); 12/68; Art Clb; Drama Clb; Math Clb; Math Tm; Pep Clb; Science Clb; SADD; Mgr Sr Cls; Stat Bsktbl; Hon Roll; Friday Night Live; U Of CA Santa Cruz; Genetics.

PAYNE, PAM L; North HS; Oildale, CA; (3); 21/396; FHA; Teachers Aide; Hon Roll; Kiwanis Awd; GATE Pgm; CSUB; Art.

PAYSEN, WAYNE T; Colton HS; Grand Terrace, CA; (1); Boy Scts; Socr; Waterpolo; UCR; Electrophysicst.

PAYSINGER, ESTELLE MARIE; John F Kennedy HS; Richmond, CA; (4); 11/243; Hosp Aide; Science Clb; Spanish Clb; Teachers Aide; Rptr Nwsp; Hon Roll; CSF; Bank Of Am Achvt Awd Frgn Lang; UC Davis; Med.

PAYTASH, STEPHEN E; South Fork HS; Redway, CA; (3); 3/90; Art Clb; Math Tm; Pep Clb; Scholastic Bowl; VP SADD; Teachers Aide; Ed Rptr Nwsp; Crs Cntry; Var Wrstlng; High Hon Roll; Schlstc Achvt Awd In Amer Hstry 90; Rotary Scl Sci Awd 89, Accntng Awd 88; North Coast Schlr/Athl 88.

PAYTON, COURTNEY D; Sherman E Burroughs HS; Ridgecrest, CA; (2); Drama Clb; Pres Pep Clb; Thesps; Chorus; School Play; Rptr Ed Nwsp; Rep Soph Cls; JV Powder Puff Ftbl; VP Socr; VP Sftbl; HOBY Fdtn; San Diego St U; Comm.

PAYTON, JULIE A; Fresno HS; Fresno, CA; (2); 1/350; Pres FHA; JCL; Latin Clb; Color Guard; Flag Corp; Hon Roll; Pres Acad Fit Awd; Rcvd Acad Ltr & Emblem 89-90; Med.

PAYTON, NIKKI J; Leuzinger HS; Hawthorne, CA; (2); Dance Clb; Girl Scts; School Play; High Hon Roll; Hon Roll.

PAZ, FABIOLA; Bellflower HS; Bellflower, CA; (2); Library Aide; Office Aide; Spanish Clb; Teachers Aide; Hon Roll; Prfct Atten Awd.

PAZ, OLIVIA M; William Workman HS; La Puente, CA; (1); Church Yth Grp; Cmnty Wkr; Drama Clb; School Play; Stage Crew; UCLA; Law.

PAZ, PATRICIA V; Hueneme HS; Oxnard, CA; (1); Band; Mrchg Band; Cit Awd; High Hon Roll; Hon Roll; U Of CA Santa Barbara; Med.

PAZ, RODOLFO G; Gahr HS; Lakewood, CA; (3); Church Yth Grp; Band; Mrchg Band; Var L Crs Cntry; Var L Trk; Hon Roll; MVP Crss Cntry 1988-89; MIR Crss Cntry 1989-90; CSULB; Math.

PAZMINO, CATHERINE; Fontana HS; San Bernardino, CA; (1); Church Yth Grp; Cheerldng; Tennis; Scl Wrkr.

PEABODY, TRICIA M; Foothill HS; Orange, CA; (1); Hon Roll; Pres Acad Fit Awd; Pres Schlr; Orange Coast Coll; Airln Attndt.

PEACH, JO ANN M; Notre Dame HS; San Jose, CA; (3); FFA; Girl Scts; Hosp Aide; Intnl Clb; Nwsp; Yrbk; Cheerldng; Sftbl; Hon Roll; 1st Prz Poetry Cont; Stu Goodwill Ambssdr-People To People Pgm; Santa Clara U; Law.

PEACOCK, DIXYE D; Silver Valley HS; Yermo, CA; (3); Drama Clb; School Play; Nwsp; Pres Jr Cls; Rep Stu Cncl; Stat Bsktbl; Var Vllybl; Cit Awd; Hon Roll; Mck Trl; Mst Supprtve Vrsty Vllybl Plyr; Excllnce Awd; Theatrical Arts.

PEACOCKE, ADAM; Cardinal Newman HS; Santa Rosa, CA; (4); 7/78; Church Yth Grp; Cmnty Wkr; 4-H; Letterman Clb; Service Clb; Spanish Clb; Varsity Clb; Church Choir; Rep Sr Cls; JV Var Bsktbl; UCLA; Commnctns.

PEACOCKE, RACHEL A; Montgomery HS; Santa Rosa, CA; (2); Church Yth Grp; High Hon Roll; Ed.

PEAKS, KAMMI; George Washington Preparatory HS; Los Angeles, CA; (3); Church Yth Grp; Math Clb; Pep Clb; Ed Nwsp; Sec Frsh Cls; Stu Cncl; Hon Roll; Jr NHS; Pres Acad Fit Awd; Sal; UCLA Partnershp Pgm; Knights & Ladies Ldrshp Clb; Pre-Med.

PEARCE, JOANNA D; Miraleste HS; Rolling Hls Ests, CA; (3); 20/160; German Clb; SADD; Ed Nwsp; JV Bsktbl; High Hon Roll; Hon Roll; Pres Acad Fit Awd; U Of Sthrn CA; Arch.

PEARCE, KENNETH W; St Francis HS; Mountain View, CA; (2); Var Bsbl; Capt JV Bsktbl; Ftbl; Varsity Clb; Hon Roll; Athl Of Yr; MVP Offnsv Ftbl; Mountain View Babe Ruth Bsbl Triple Crown Wnnr, Lowest ERA 89.

PEARCE, RICHARD G; Rancho Alamitos HS; Garden Grove, CA; (4); 18/245; Teachers Aide; Band; Mrchg Band; Pep Band; Bsktbl; Vllybl; High Hon Roll; Hon Roll; Orch; 2 Yrs 1st Tm All-Lg Vlybl All Cty Hnrbl Mntn; Sr Athlete Of Yr; M&M Mars All-Amer Athlete; CA ST Long Bch; Cmptr Sci.

PEARCE, SABRINA; Ayala HS; Chino Hills, CA; (1); L Chorus; Var Bsktbl; Hon Roll; Child Psych.

PEARCE, SALLY; Acalanes HS; Lafayette, CA; (3); AFS; Church Yth Grp; Cmnty Wkr; Service Clb; SADD; Teachers Aide; Varsity Clb; Band; JV Var Sftbl; Ntl Merit Ltr; Natl Charity Leag; UC Santa Barbara; Law.

PEARCY, KERI L; Moorpark HS; Moorpark, CA; (2); 13/300; Intnl Clb; Treas Band; Treas Jazz Band; Treas Mrchg Band; Treas Pep Band; JV Sftbl; High Hon Roll; Hon Roll; CSF; Yth Church Grp; UC Davis; Vet.

PEARLMUTTER, NEIL; Santa Rosa HS; Santa Rosa, CA; (2); School Musical; School Play; Stage Crew; Stat Bsktbl; Mgr(s); Make-Up Effects Movies; Acting.

PEARSE, DEVON E; Santa Cruz HS; Santa Cruz, CA; (2); Hon Roll; Bio.

PEARSON, DAVID; Tri-City Christian HS; Vista, CA; (2); Church Yth Grp; Vllybl; High Hon Roll; Biola U.

PEARSON, HEATHER N; El Toro HS; El Toro, CA; (3); Church Yth Grp; Var Debate Tm; French Clb; Speech Tm; JV Crs Cntry; JV Trk; High Hon Roll; Lion Awd; Ntl Merit Ltr; Top 20 Awd; Excllnce Awds Engl; Westmont Coll; Law.

PEARSON, JAMES; Los Alamitos HS; Los Alamitos, CA; (3); Boy Scts; Chess Clb; Science Clb; Spanish Clb; High Hon Roll.

PEARSON, JENNIFER R; Yreka HS; Yreka, CA; (3); 42/179; Spanish Clb; SADD; Yrbk; Hon Roll; CSF-CALIFORNIA Scholarship Federation; U Of OR; History Professor.

PEARSON, JESSICA; Maxwell HS; Maxwell, CA; (4); 1/23; Church Yth Grp; Drama Clb; Spanish Clb; SADD; Jazz Band; Treas Sr Cls; Var Sftbl; Vllybl; Pres Acad Fit Awd; Peer Cnslng; Chairprsn & PR Officer; Eng.

PEARSON, KAYCEE L; Indio HS; Indio, CA; (2); 55/551; Church Yth Grp; Hon Roll; Fresh Creative Wrtng Cntst 1st Pl Essay Catergory.

PEARSON, MATTHEW JAMES COLLINS; East Bakersfield HS; Bakersfield, CA; (4); 1/416; Intnl Clb; VP Key Clb; Pres Math Clb; JV Socr; Intrml Vllybl; High Hon Roll; Cngrssnl Dist Hrngs On Constitn 1st Pl; Acad Decthln; Goldn St Exam Hnrs; U Of CA Santa Barbara; Engrng.

PEARSON, NICOLE R; College Park HS; Concord, CA; (3); Spanish Clb; Var Crs Cntry; Var Trk; Hon Roll; Pres Acad Fit Awd; UC Davis; Bus.

PEARSON, REBECCA L; Lutheran HS Of Orange County; Santa Ana, CA; (2); Church Yth Grp; Bsktbl; Vllybl; Hon Roll.

PEARSON, SERENA J; Grossmont HS; El Cajon, CA; (1); Intnl Clb; Gym; Hon Roll; San Diego Cty Team Penning Assn; Law.

PEARSON, TAMMY LYNN; Lower Lake HS; Clearlake, CA; (4); 8/108; Office Aide; Pep Clb; Elks Awd; High Hon Roll; Friday Nite Live; Elem Aide; CSF; Sonoma ST U; Elem Educ.

PEARTREE, KENNETH A; Bellarmine College Prep; Morgan Hill, CA; (3); 40/300; Cmnty Wkr; Ski Clb; Jazz Band; Pep Band; Rptr Nwsp; Var Crs Cntry; CA Schlrshp Fed; Natl Space Soc Achvt Awd; Natl Semiconductor Corp Awd; UC Berkeley; Mech Engrng.

PEASE, DAVID M; Gompers Secondary HS; San Diego, CA; (2); Sec Chess Clb; JV Ftbl; JV Wt Lftg; City Vol Library Aide.

PEASE, MEGAN M; Rio Hondo Prep; Duarte, CA; (1); Chorus; School Musical; JV Bsktbl; JV Cheerldng; JV Sftbl; JV Vllybl; Hon Roll; Girls Sprts Coach; Vet.

PEASE, SHAWNA LEE; Taft Union HS; Taft, CA; (1); 1/300; Church Yth Grp; Drama Clb; School Play; Rep Frsh Cls; Var Cheerldng; Var Diving; High Hon Roll; Pres Acad Fit Awd; Friday Night Live Clb; ASF.

PEASE, TIFFANY M; Montclair HS; Montclair, CA; (1); Church Yth Grp; Church Choir; GATE; Ballet; Int Design.

PEASE, TRACI L; Paradise HS; Paradise, CA; (2); Hon Roll; Csmtlgy.

PEASLEY, ERICKA B; Oakdale HS; Oakdale, CA; (3); 2/250; Sec AFS; Sec Chess Clb; Pres Debate Tm; Math Tm; Sec Science Clb; Pres Speech Tm; Ed Yrbk; Rep Stu Cncl; Var Swmmng; Little People Am Co-Natl Teen Coord; Acad Decathion Hnrs Gold Medal Lang & Lit; CA Schlrshp Fed; Pre-Med.

PEAVY, CARMEN M; Southwest HS; San Ysidro, CA; (2); 526/627; Sec Church Yth Grp; Cmnty Wkr; Girl Scts; Key Clb; Var Cheerldng; Var Trk; Intrml Wt Lftg; Hon Roll; Prfct Atten Awd; Peace Clb; Humboldt ST U; Med.

PEAVY, CYNTHIA; Southwest HS; San Ysidro, CA; (4); Drama Clb; Key Clb; SADD; Capt Cheerldng; Humboldt ST U; Lbrl Arts.

PECACHE, ANNE C; South San Francisco HS; South San Francis, CA; (3); FBLA; Math Clb; Pres Frsh Cls; Off Sr Cls; Var Bsktbl; Var Sftbl; Var Vllybl; Golden St Exam High Hnr Geom.

PECANIC, ANDY J; Santa Clara HS; Santa Clara, CA; (2); Trk; High Hon Roll; Hon Roll; Cert In Bio; USC; Arch.

PECHAN, STACEY J; Brea Olinda HS; Brea, CA; (1); Library Aide; Stage Crew; Yrbk; Off Soph Cls; Vllybl; Jr NHS; Prfct Atten Awd; Pres Acad Fit Awd; Rotary Awd; Girls League.

PECK, CHRISTIE; Granada HS; Livermore, CA; (4); 43/247; Pep Clb; Teachers Aide; Var Pom Pon; JV Score Keeper; High Hon Roll; Hon Roll; Outstndng Achvt Awd; Las Positas JC Livermore; Nrsg.

PECK, DIONNE M; Ramona HS; Ramona, CA; (3); SADD; Teachers Aide; Varsity Clb; Nwsp; Var Gym; Amer Sign Lang; Chldrns Med.

PECK, PAUL J; Montclair HS; Ontario, CA; (2); JV Bsbl; Bsktbl; L Ftbl; Hon Roll; Colt Bsbl; Prof Bsbl Plyr.

PECK, REBECCA I; Enterprise HS; Shingletown, CA; (3); 14/400; Mu Alpha Theta; Var Bsktbl; Stat Trk; High Hon Roll; Outstndng Awds-Geog, Bus, Alg & Frnch; Golden ST Exam Recog; Spcl Olympcs Vlntr; Bus Mgmt.

PECK, RYAN J; Centennial HS; Corona, CA; (3); 22/440; Sprt Ed Nwsp; Rep Stu Cncl; Var Ftbl; Wt Lftg; Reporter CA Schlrshp Fed; UCLA; Jrnslm.

PECKHAM, ROBERT L; John Marshall Fundamental HS; Altadena, CA; (3); Chess Clb; Science Clb; Chorus; Crs Cntry; Trk; Hon Roll; NHS; Acadmc Dcthln; Fri Nght Live Treas; HOBY Ambssdr; Engrng.

PECTOL, SARA L; Chino HS; Chino, CA; (2); 1/800; Church Yth Grp; Science Clb; Spanish Clb; Teachers Aide; Church Choir; Bsktbl; JV Vllybl; Hon Roll; Engl & PE Silver Spur Awd; Phys Ftnss Awd; BYU; Spcl Educ.

PEDERSEN, BRANT E; Bullard HS; Fresno, CA; (2); 62/550; Jr Natl Windsurfing Champ US; Board Sailing Assn 89; JETS 89-90; Sail Maker.

PEDERSEN, DOUG A; Burbank HS; Burbank, CA; (2); Church Yth Grp; Cmnty Wkr; Stage Crew; Ftbl; Hon Roll; U Southern CA; Lwyr.

PEDERSEN, JILL M; Montgomery HS; Santa Rosa, CA; (2); Teachers Aide; Yrbk; Vllybl; Hon Roll; Prfct Atten Awd.

PEDERSEN, ROBERT J; Clovis HS; Clovis, CA; (3); Boy Scts; Church Yth Grp; Drama Clb; Nwsp; Pres Frsh Cls; Sec Soph Cls; JV Var Ftbl; Var Sftbl; High Hon Roll; Hon Roll; Law Enforcement Explorers; Aeronautical Engrng.

PEDERSON, GRANT D; Apple Valley HS; Apple Valley, CA; (1); Mrchg Band; ASU; Art Hist.

PEDERSON, MICHAL L; Marina HS; Huntington Beach, CA; (3); VP AFS; Rep Church Yth Grp; JCL; Latin Clb; Spanish Clb; Band; Mrchg Band; Orch; Pep Band; School Musical; Luthern Bible Inst.

PEDRAJA, JENETTE B; Eagle Rock HS; Los Angeles, CA; (2); Church Yth Grp; Drill Tm; Var Mgr(s); Var Score Keeper; JV Vllybl; Hon Roll; Prfct Atten Awd; Store Reps Cmmttee; Schlrshp, Acad Exclnc Awd; Outstdng Achvmt Awd Socl Stds; Outstdng Phy Ed Std Of Yr; Comp Analysis.

PEDRAZA, DIANA; Alverno HS; Pasadena, CA; (3); 17/70; Multicultrl Clb; Geo Awd; CSF; Engrng.

PEDRIOL, JONNA J; Livermore HS; Livermore, CA; (3); Cmnty Wkr; VP 4-H; Library Aide; Yrbk; JV Var Swmmng; 4-H Awd; High Hon Roll; Friday Night Live; Peer Asst Listeners; CA Schlrshp Fed.

PEDRIQUEZ, LAREINA R; University City HS; San Diego, CA; (4); 24/334; Dance Clb; Pep Clb; Spanish Clb; SADD; Capt Drill Tm; Variety Show; Off Jr Cls; Off Sr Cls; Stu Cncl; Cit Awd; Queen Philippine Faire 89-90; CSF Life Membr; Golden St Math Exam-Hnrs; U Of CA-LOS Angeles; Pediatric.

PEDROSA, CATHERINE A; Carson HS; Carson, CA; (2); Teachers Aide; Varsity Clb; Band; Orch; Var Bsktbl; Score Keeper; Hon Roll; Pres Acad Fit Awd; Faculty Outstndng Stu Awd; Band Dir Awd.

PEDROSA, MONICA A; El Camino HS; Oceanside, CA; (3); 35/364; Dance Clb; Pep Clb; SADD; Teachers Aide; Drill Tm; Rep Jr Cls; Treas Stu Cncl; Cit Awd; Hon Roll; Prfct Atten Awd; Accounting/Business.

PEDROZA, ALBERT J; Bishop Mora Salesian HS; Los Angeles, CA; (3); 2/97; VP Computer Clb; Treas Letterman Clb; Varsity Clb; Rptr Nwsp; Var Crs Cntry; Var Socr; Var Trk; High Hon Roll; Hon Roll; NHS; Volunteer CCD Teacher Salesian Boys & Girls Club; MVP Cross Cntry & Lg Champ; Letterman Soc Treas; Berkeley.

PEDROZA, DAVID; Bishop Mora Salesian HS; Los Angeles, CA; (3); Cmnty Wkr; Varsity Clb; Var Crs Cntry; JV Trk; Hon Roll; Lettermen Soc.

PEDROZA, JOHNNY; Claremont HS; Westminster, CA; (4); Yrbk; Var L Bsbl; Var L Bsktbl; Var Capt Ftbl; Var Capt Vllybl; All CIF Team Ftbl 89; Lg Ftbl 88-89; Highest Hnr Geom Awd; Long Beach ST Coll; Pre-Med.

PEDROZA, JULIO C; Montebello HS; Montebello, CA; (1); JV Socr.

PEDROZA, LORENA; Southwest HS; San Ysidro, CA; (4); Dance Clb; Library Aide; Model UN; Office Aide; SADD; Teachers Aide; Stage Crew; Variety Show; Stu Cncl; Hon Roll; Ed.

PEEBLES, JUDITH; Helix HS; La Mesa, CA; (2); 60/449; FTA; Yrbk; Rep Soph Cls; Hon Roll; Opt Clb Awd; Cinematography Club; San Diego ST U; Teacher.

PEEFF, DAN T; Ygnacio Valley HS; Walnut Creek, CA; (1); Varsity Clb; Crs Cntry; Trk; Army; DEA.

PEEL, SHERI R; Mira Mesa HS; San Diego, CA; (3); 83/777; Rep Soph Cls; Cit Awd.

PEEL, TEMRE R; Robert A Millikan HS; Long Beach, CA; (3); Church Yth Grp; Drama Clb; JA; School Play; Rptr Nwsp; Sprt Ed Yrbk; JV Bsktbl; Sftbl; VP Trk; Hon Roll; Long Beach ST; Law.

PEELER, AMY; Loyalton HS; Loyalton, CA; (4); 2/34; Sec Drama Clb; FBLA; Ski Clb; School Play; Ed Yrbk; Treas Stu Cncl; Var L Cheerldng; Var Sftbl; JV Var Vllybl; High Hon Roll; UC Davis; Psych.

PEELLE, JOHN R; Poway HS; San Diego, CA; (2); Boy Scts; Chorus; JV Tennis; Pres Acad Fit Awd.

PEER, LORNA; Garcis Memorial HS; Bakersfield, CA; (1); 2/160; Key Clb; Lit Mag; High Hon Roll; Psychology.

PEESADAT, SUMA; Bonita Vista HS; Chula Vista, CA; (2); Model UN; Band; Cit Awd; Ntl Merit Ltr; CSF Secy; San Diego Lelegu Assn; Sci.

PEET, RAMONA C; St Bonaventure HS; Ojai, CA; (3); 22/122; Var Sftbl; High Hon Roll; CSF.

PEEVYHOUSE, CHAD M; Santa Teresa HS; San Jose, CA; (2); 24/487; Hgh Hnrs Gldn ST Alg Exm; Embry-Riddle; Engrng Physcs.

PEEVYHOUSE, KEITH T; Santa Teresa HS; San Jose, CA; (2); 13/487; Spanish Clb; Hon Roll; Chrstn Fllwshp Clb; Acad Mdl Arntcs; Embry-Riddle; Arntcl Engr.

PEFFER, MONICA K; San Pasqual HS; Escondido, CA; (2); French Clb; German Clb; Intnl Clb; JV Tennis; CSF; SAVE; Med.

PEGARELLA, ANDREA D; Thomas Downey HS; Modesto, CA; (4); Key Clb; NFL; Spanish Clb; Speech Tm; SADD; Ed Yrbk; Sec Treas Soph Cls; Pres Schlr; CSF Sealbearer; Knight Achvt Sci Awd; U Of Pacific; Pharmacy.

PEGEESE, KESHONEA M; Bassett SR HS; La Puente, CA; (2); Church Yth Grp; FBLA; Drill Tm; Variety Show; Nwsp; Parlgl.

PEGG, JAMES T; Gardena HS; Gardena, CA; (3); Church Yth Grp; JA; Service Clb; Var Ftbl; Wrk At Marukai Whlsle Mart; Bus.

PEGG, LISA J; Cupertino HS; San Jose, CA; (3); Drama Clb; Teachers Aide; Acpl Chr; Flag Corp; Mrchg Band; School Play; Ed Lit Mag; Var JV Gym; JV Swmmng; Grappler Grls-Wrstlng Spprt Tm; Chico; Bus Mktng.

PEGUES, KERRIE A; St Bernard HS; Gardena, CA; (3); Cmnty Wkr; Hosp Aide; Letterman Clb; Varsity Clb; VP Frsh Cls; L Var Trk; Yng Gftd & Black Honoree; Bus Adm.

PEI, JOHN; Upland HS; Upland, CA; (2); Boy Scts; Letterman Clb; Varsity Clb; Crs Cntry; Trk; Hon Roll; Claremont Mc Kenna U; Bus.

PEI, PETER; Arcadia HS; Arcadia, CA; (4); Chess Clb; Computer Clb; Service Clb; Yrbk; Prfct Atten Awd; 1st Arcadia Sch Dist Art Exhibt; Principal Recogntn Roll; U C Riverside; Bus.

PEIMBERT, ERNESTO ALONSO; Don Bosco Technical Inst; West Covina, CA; (1); 29/244; JV Bsktbl; NEDT Awd; Principals List.

PEINEMANN, MILO A; Valhalla HS; La Mesa, CA; (3); 19/430; Boy Scts; Church Yth Grp; Debate Tm; German Clb; SADD; Ed Nwsp; Var Crs Cntry; Var Trk; Ntl Merit SF.

PEIRCE, JESSICA L; San Marcos HS; San Marcos, CA; (3); Church Yth Grp; Spanish Clb; Church Choir; JV Socr; Var Trk; High Hon Roll; The Masters Coll; Missions.

PEIZNER, DAVID M; Mills HS; Burlingame, CA; (3); Intnl Clb; JA; Treas Sr Cls; Trk; High Hon Roll; Hon Roll; Pres Acad Fit Awd.

PELACHE, KRISTINA A; Pioneer HS; San Jose, CA; (2); JV Crs Cntry; JV Socr; Hon Roll; Pres Earthday Club; CSF; UC Santa Barbara; Jrnlsm.

PELAVO, MARISSA M; Notre Dame HS; Morgan Hill, CA; (3); 11/100; Hosp Aide; Intnl Clb; Rep Science Clb; Rep Frsh Cls; Hon Roll; NHS; CSF; Retreat Ldr/Aide 90; Spcl Olympc Vlntr 90; Outstndng Achvt Frnch I&III; Mrktng.

PELAYO, BEATRIZ A; Mayfield SR Schl; Alhambra, CA; (2); Church Yth Grp; Library Aide; School Play; VP Soph Cls; Hon Roll; NHS; CSF.

PELAYO, CARMEN J; Garden Grove HS; Garden Grove, CA; (1); Var L Socr; JV Sftbl; Vllybl; High Hon Roll; Harvard; Med.

PELAYO, CLAUDIA; Garfield HS; Los Angeles, CA; (4); Drama Clb; SADD; Teachers Aide; Band; Orch; Ed Yrbk; Rep Jr Cls; Rep Sr Cls; Bsktbl; Prfct Atten Awd; Mecha; Stu Affrs Cmmtte Offcr; UC Anta Barbara; Psych.

PELAYO, JAIME; Saint Genevieve HS; Pacoima, CA; (2); 2/150; Model UN; High Hon Roll; Mock Trial Comptn.

PELAYO, LETICIA; Roosevelt HS; Huntington Park, CA; (3); Church Yth Grp; Variety Show; Pres Frsh Cls; Rep Stu Cncl; JV Var Bsktbl; Var Capt Trk; JV Var Vllybl; Cit Awd; Hon Roll; A P Clb; Sci Fr; Law.

PELAYO, MANUEL N; Wasco Union HS; Wasco, CA; (3); School Play; Stage Crew; Co-Capt Nwsp; Summer Jrnlism Camp 90; Jrnlst.

PELCMAN, JASON P; Enterprise HS; Redding, CA; (1); Church Yth Grp; Pres Acad Fit Awd; UCLA; Draftng.

PELES, TAL TOVA; Norco HS; Corona, CA; (4); 2/465; Cmnty Wkr; Dance Clb; FBLA; Model UN; Pep Clb; Sec Temple Yth Grp; Swing Chorus; Rptr Nwsp; Rep Stu Cncl; Cheerldng; Mock Trials Attny; CSF Pres; Coca Cola Rgnl Schlr; Coronas Jr Miss/Young Woman Of Yr 90; UCLA; Commnctns.

PELLEG, TAL; El Camino HS; Woodland Hills, CA; (2); Teachers Aide; Pres Jr Cls; Stu Cncl; Ski Clb; Stat Golf; Stat Tennis; Psych.

PELLEGRINI, LISA M; Oak Ridge HS; Cameron Park, CA; (3); 9/225; Church Yth Grp; Cmnty Wkr; FBLA; Hosp Aide; SADD; Teachers Aide; Cit Awd; Elks Awd; High Hon Roll; NHS; 2nd Pl Acctng I FBLA Nrthrn Sect; Fri Nght Lv; CSF; Sacramento ST; Acctng.

PELLERIN, SONIA M; Skyline HS; Oakland, CA; (3); Aud/Vis; Church Yth Grp; FCA; JA; Chorus; Church Choir; School Musical; Var Bsktbl; Var Vllybl; Opt Clb Awd; Paiten Acad Bsktbl MVP; Cls Jdg; UC Berkeley; Ophthlmc Ped Srgn.

PELLETIER, SABRINA; Liberty Union HS; Brentwood, CA; (4); 24/225; Church Yth Grp; FCA; Letterman Clb; Office Aide; Pep Clb; Teachers Aide; Varsity Clb; Rep Frsh Cls; Rep Soph Cls; Rep Jr Cls; All Trnmt Plyr; Italian Cthlc Fdrtn Schlrshp; Schl Gen Schlrshp; CSU Sacramento; Biolgcl Sci.

PELLETIER, STACIE; University HS; Irvine, CA; (3); Teachers Aide; Chorus; Hon Roll; Principals Awd; Broadcasting.

PELLETT, FRANK A; Lassen Unified HS; Susanville, CA; (2); Boy Scts; Band; Church Choir; U CA Sacramento; Math.

PELONIS, PETER T; Downey HS; Downey, CA; (4); Church Yth Grp; Cmnty Wkr; Dance Clb; French Clb; Intnl Clb; SADD; Thesps; Socr; Trk; French Hon Soc; CA ST-FULLERTON; Bus Econ.

PELONIS, SOTIRIOS T; Downey HS; Downey, CA; (3); Church Yth Grp; Cmnty Wkr; Dance Clb; French Clb; Intnl Clb; SADD; Thesps; Var Socr; Var Trk; French Hon Soc.

PELSTER, JENNIFER R; Orange HS; Santa Ana, CA; (3); Hosp Aide; Teachers Aide; Band; Jazz Band; Mrchg Band; Pep Band; Hon Roll; UC Davis; Vet Med.

PELTIER, CURT J; Livingston HS; Delhi, CA; (1); Spanish Clb; Teachers Aide; Chorus; Tennis; Hon Roll; CA ST U; Dentstry.

PELTIER II, THOMAS A; North HS; Bakersfield, CA; (3); Church Yth Grp; Computer Clb; French Clb; Math Tm; Science Clb; Ski Clb; Teachers Aide; Rptr Nwsp; Swmmng; Hon Roll; Freedoms Fndtn; Phileo Club Pres.

PELTON, JODY L; Calipatria HS; Niland, CA; (3); Drama Clb; SADD; Friday Night Live; Non Confrmst Music Soc; Criminlgst.

PELTONEN, MICHELLE; Moorpark HS; Moorpark, CA; (4); 9/203; Teachers Aide; Sec Sr Cls; Rep Stu Cncl; Capt Var Socr; Var Vllybl; High Hon Roll; Hon Roll; Athltc Clb; Tri-Vly Leag MVP; Hmcmng Queen; Chico ST U; Bus Admin.

PEMBERTON, CHARAN K; Apple Valley SR HS; Apple Valley, CA; (1); Intrml Bsktbl; JV Trk; Cit Awd; U Of A.

PEMBERTON, JOE E; Burroughs HS; Burbank, CA; (3); Ftbl; Trk; Hon Roll; Cal Poly; Dsgn Engr.

PEMPEJIAN, MARLENE; Armenian Mesrobian HS; Pasadena, CA; (3); Girl Scts; Teachers Aide; Var Socr; Cit Awd; Hon Roll; Civil Law.

PEMPER, ERIC M; Livermore HS; Livermore, CA; (3); Ski Clb; Speech Tm; JV Trk; Wt Lftg; Gov Hon Prg Awd; Hon Roll; Bus.

PENA, CARLOS E; San Rafael HS; San Rafael, CA; (2).

PENA, CAROLINA E; Saddleback HS; Santa Ana, CA; (2); Med.

PENA, CHRISTOPHER; Canyon HS; Anaheim, CA; (4); JCL; Latin Clb; Ed Lit Mag; Var Bsbl; CSF; 3rd Pl Ayn Rand Essy Cntst; Acadc Ltr Top 50 3 Yrs; VC Santa Barbara; Pltcl Sci.

PENA, DENNISE N; Hawthorne HS; Lawndale, CA; (3); Model UN; Spanish Clb; Cit Awd; Acad Dcthln; Hnrs Spansh; Law.

PENA, DIANA P; Andrew Hill HS; San Jose, CA; (3); GAA; Teachers Aide; Yrbk; Socr; Partnership Pgm; Spell Out; Mesa Clb Mem; Comp Sci.

PENA, EDNA G; Calexico HS; Calexico, CA; (2); Cmnty Wkr; Rep Pep Clb; Spanish Clb; Mrchg Band; Math Awd In Algebra 89; Natl Spnsh Exam Fplma Of Hnr 89; Natl Gldn St Exam Dplma Of Hnr 89; UCSD; Ophthalmologist.

PENA, IRENE; Shafter HS; Shafter, CA; (1); Key Clb; Pep Clb; Ski Clb; Cheerldng; Tennis; Hon Roll; UCLA; Med.

PENA, LUZ M; Lincoln HS; San Diego, CA; (2); 2/238; Hon Roll; Prfct Atten Awd; VP La Raza Clb; Rptr "el Gzito" Hispnc Nwsp; Girard Pgm; Psych.

PENA, MICHAEL V; James Logan HS; Union City, CA; (3); Church Yth Grp; NFL; Speech Tm; Powder Puff Ftbl; High Hon Roll; Hon Roll; Ldrshp Cls; San Francisco ST; Pediatrcn.

PENA, MICHELLE FELISA; Bell Gardens HS; Commerce, CA; (2); Band; Crs Cntry; Sftbl; Swmmng; Girls Leag; Cert Appreciation; Ltr Awd; Police Woman.

PENA, PERLA M; Fresno HS; Fresno, CA; (2); Church Yth Grp; Dance Clb; FBLA; Key Clb; Office Aide; ROTC; SADD; Cit Awd; High Hon Roll; Hon Roll; Sci.

PENA, ROSEMARIE; California HS; Whittier, CA; (3); Teachers Aide; Band; Chorus; Mrchg Band; Pep Band; Stage Crew; Chamber Singers; Music.

PENA, RUTH; Liberty Union HS; Knightsen, CA; (1); Church Yth Grp; Office Aide; Band; Yrbk; Stu Cncl; Bsbl; Sftbl; Vllybl; Hon Roll; Prfct Atten Awd; Airline Stewardss.

PENA, SHANNON M; Colfax HS; Colfax, CA; (4); 28/150; Art Clb; Red Cross Aide; Science Clb; Service Clb; Ski Clb; SADD; Teachers Aide; Phtg Yrbk; Hon Roll; Golden St Awd Hnrs In Geom; Service Clb Sr Rep; CA Poly San Luis Obispo; Arch.

PENA, SINFOROSA A; Saint Anthony HS; San Pedro, CA; (2); Dance Clb; Girl Scts; Hosp Aide; Letterman Clb; Spanish Clb; SADD; Band; Jazz Band; Mrchg Band; Pep Band; ExclInc In Chrstn Srv Outstndng 88-89, Super 89-90; AZ ST U; Poltcl Sci.

PENAFIEL, MICHAEL S; Fontana HS; Fontana, CA; (2); Cit Awd; High Hon Roll; U Of CA Riverside.

PENAFLOR, THERESE M; Lowell HS; San Francisco, CA; (3); ROTC; Color Guard; Drill Tm; Prfct Atten Awd; JROTC Acad Achvt Awd; Filam Clb.

PENALOZA, LORENA; Cotton HS; San Bernardino, CA; (4); 1/350; Am Leg Aux Girls St; Key Clb; Q&S; Ed Nwsp; Sec Stu Cncl; Kiwanis Awd; NHS; Val; Church Yth Grp; JA; FLA; Chicano Latino Yth Ldrshp Prjct; U Of CA Berkeley; Intl Ecnmcs.

PENALVER, JESUS; Rancho Alamitos HS; Garden Grove, CA; (4); Church Yth Grp; Church Choir; Val; CA ST Fullerton; Comp Engr.

PENATE, CLAUDIA S; Bell HS; Bell, CA; (3); Pep Band; Rptr Nwsp; JV Vllybl; Cit Awd; High Hon Roll; 2nd Pl Awd; AZ ST U; Arch.

PENCE, HEATHER T; Palm Valley Schl; Cathedral City, CA; (3); Teachers Aide; Band; Orch; Ed Yrbk; Var Bsktbl; Socr; Sftbl; Hon Roll; Ntl Merit SF; Sndy Schl Secy; Palm Vlly Schl Fclty Awd 87-88; Physics.

PENCE, NICOLE S.; Temecula Valley HS; Temecula, CA; (2); 3/590; Capt Drill Tm; Cit Awd; High Hon Roll; Pres Acad Fit Awd; Val; Jr Exch Club; EARTH Club; U Of CA; Envrnmntlst.

PENDERGAST, NATHAN; Fremont Christian HS; Fremont, CA; (4); Ski Clb; Spanish Clb; Teachers Aide; NHS; CSF Pres 89-90; Hist Tchr.

PENDERGRAFT, JULIE; Leland HS; San Jose, CA; (3); Church Yth Grp; Key Clb; Math Clb; Spanish Clb; SADD; Drill Tm; Stu Cncl; Cheerldng; CSF; Cmmnty Comptv Leag Swim Team; Nrsng.

PENDERGRAFT, JULIE A; Etwanda HS; Alta Loma, CA; (2); Polytechnic U; Arch.

PENDERGRAFT, RUTH JEAN; Castle Park HS; Chula Vista, CA; (2); 39/473; Church Yth Grp; Drama Clb; Speech Tm; School Play; JV Var Ftbl; JV Var Mgr(s); Zlgst.

PENDERGRAFT, THERESA R; Narbonne HS; Lomita, CA; (2); Church Yth Grp; Hosp Aide; Math Tm; Hon Roll; Prfct Atten Awd; Goldn St Exam High Hnrs Alg I; Bus.

PENDLETON, JUSTUS J; Eureka SR HS; Eureka, CA; (1); Key Clb; Hon Roll; Pres Acad Fit Awd; CA Inst Of Tech; Astronomy.

PENDLETON, MICHAEL S; Galileo HS; San Francisco, CA; (2); Hon Roll; Hnr Rl Cert; Clark Atlanta U; Jrnlsm.

PENFIELD, AMY; Del Campo HS; Rancho Cordova, CA; (2); Psych.

PENFIELD, MATTHEW W; The Bishops Schl; Escondido, CA; (4); Cmnty Wkr; Model UN; Scholastic Bowl; Service Clb; SADD; School Musical; School Play; Rptr Nwsp; Lit Mag; VP Sr Cls; Natl Cncl Tchrs Engl Writing Awd.

PENG, DENNIS; Lowell HS; San Francisco, CA; (2); Boy Scts; Church Yth Grp; Red Cross Aide; JV Var Bsbl; Swimming Instructor For Red Cross; Collect Baseball Football & Basketball Cards; UC Berkeley; Medical/Business.

PENG, JEANIFER; Richard Gahr HS; Artesia, CA; (2); Hon Roll; PTSA Cert Achvt; Cerritos Coll; Acctnt.

PENG, JUDY; Bullard HS; Fresno, CA; (3); Church Yth Grp; French Clb; Math Clb; Math Tm; Science Clb; French Hon Soc; JETS Awd; GSE Geom Hgh Hnr; Natl Comp Mnth Cont-Hnrbl Mntn; Engr.

PENG, MY LIN; Orange HS; Garden Grove, CA; (3); Math Clb; Science Clb; JV Tennis; Vllybl; Hon Roll; Treas NHS; CSF; Amer Chem Soc Fnlst In Chem For Orange Hgh; Bus.

PENG, SHIH-HSIN; Edison HS; Huntington Beach, CA; (2); Key Clb; Math Tm; Lit Mag; Tennis; Orange Cnty Acad Cmptn; Chinese Clb; Engrng.

PENG, YUJANG MARGRET; C K Mc Clatchy HS; Sacramento, CA; (3); Orch; Stat Bsktbl; Var Trk; Var Vllybl; CA Poly; Arch.

PENILLA, CARLOS GABRIEL; Schurr HS; Montebello, CA; (3); Aud/Vis; Boy Scts; Church Yth Grp; Letterman Clb; Library Aide; SADD; Teachers Aide; Varsity Clb; VICA; Intrml JV Ftbl; 1st Pl Arch-Art Show; 9th Pl Arch Drftg Rio Hondo Coll; 3rd Pl Arch MUSD VICA Cmptn; Arch.

PENIX, JOSHUA E; John F Kennedy HS; Sacramento, CA; (2); 54/525; Sec Computer Clb; Debate Tm; NFL; ROTC; Temple Yth Grp; Hon Roll; Masonic Awd; Prfct Atten Awd; CA Schlrshp Fed; Comp Sci.

PENJOYAN, JUDY L; Ocean View HS; Huntington Beach, CA; (1); Rep Model UN; Treas Soph Cls; Stat Bsktbl; Stat Vllybl; Hon Roll; Pres Acad Fit Awd; Bus.

PENN, BRANDON M; Dos Pueblos HS; Goleta, CA; (2); School Play; Rep Stu Cncl; Socr; Trk; Wrstlng; Gov Hon Prg Awd; Hon Roll; Ntl Merit Ltr; Pres Acad Fit Awd; Set New Rcrd Lng Jmp, Dist Chmpn Lng Jmp & Jvln; Natl Title Spokane-1st Lng Jmp, 2nd Dcthln, 3rd Jvln; Chem Engr.

PENN, LYNIQUE; Whitney HS; Cerritos, CA; (4); Key Clb; Pep Clb; Teachers Aide; Varsity Clb; Var Cheerldng; JV Score Keeper; Cit Awd; Hon Roll; Yng Blk Schlrs 86-90; Pres Of Essence Clb 89-90- VP 88-89; Dir Of Actvties Key Clb 86-87; Howard U; Bus Mgmt.

PENN, U TOPIA K; Lincoln Prepatory HS; San Diego, CA; (4); Debate Tm; FTA; Pep Clb; Ed Yrbk; Hon Roll; Long Beach ST; Bus Mgmt.

PENNACCHIO, LILLIAN E; Analy HS; Sebastopol, CA; (2); Church Yth Grp; Spanish Clb; Rep Frsh Cls; JV Bsktbl; Var Trk; High Hon Roll; Hon Roll; OGIT; Bus.

PENNE, RACHEL; Norwalk HS; Norwalk, CA; (1); 23/271; Sec Church Yth Grp; Library Aide; Spanish Clb; Teachers Aide; Color Guard; Trk; Student Of The Year For Spanish Ii; Student Of The Quarter 2nd Quarter Of Schl Yr; Cerritos Coll; Psychologist.

PENNELL, ADAM D; Oakdale HS; Oakdale, CA; (2); Engr.

PENNELL, RAINBOW E; Angels Gate HS; San Pedro, CA; (3); Girl Scts; Office Aide; Chorus; Evnt Orgnzr; Hd Dcrtns Cmmtte; Psych.

PENNER, CARLOS M; Edison/Computech HS; Fresno, CA; (1); Ski Clb; Spanish Clb; Teachers Aide; Vllybl; Hon Roll; NASA Sci Prjct Cert; CA Enrgy Educ Forum Enrgy Rsrch Excllnce Awd; Stanford; Doctor.

PENNER, ERION E; Fontana HS; Fontana, CA; (4); 23/800; Teachers Aide; High Hon Roll; Prfct Atten Awd; Pres Acad Fit Awd; CSF; Chaffey CC; Nrsng.

PENNER, SONDRA J; Clovis HS; Clovis, CA; (3); Church Yth Grp; FCA; JV Var Vllybl; High Hon Roll; Hon Roll; CSF; Sign Lang Stu Intrprtr.

PENNEY, GREGORY A; Benicia HS; Benicia, CA; (2); Spanish Clb; School Musical; Bsbl; Bsktbl; Crs Cntry; Swmmng; Trk; Hon Roll.

PENNEY, JOHN; Edison HS; Huntington Beach, CA; (2); Model UN; Band; Mrchg Band.

PENNEY, LAURA J; Edison HS; Huntington Bch, CA; (4); 12/503; Cmnty Wkr; French Clb; JA; Key Clb; Band; Mrchg Band; French Hon Soc; High Hon Roll; Opt Clb Awd; Pres Acad Fit Awd; Orange Cnty Tall Clb Schlrshp; Golden St Exam Geom Hnrs; Bryn Mawr Coll PA; Teacher.

PENNINGTON, TRAVIS LEE; Rubidoux HS; Riverside, CA; (2); Teachers Aide; JV Bsktbl; JV Trk.

PENNINO, CINDY A; Bonita HS; La Verne, CA; (2); French Clb; SADD; Capt JV Sftbl; JV Var Vllybl; Hon Roll.

PENNY, PRENTICE J; St Bernard HS; Los Angeles, CA; (3); Aud/Vis; Boy Scts; Church Yth Grp; Cmnty Wkr; Letterman Clb; Office Aide; Nwsp; Bsbl; Ftbl; Trk; Jack And Jill Far West Regn VP; Angel City Links Achvr 91; 1st Pl Black Stu Un Art Prz; Howard U; Film Wrtng.

PENRICE, CELAYOA M; Arlington HS; Riverside, CA; (3); Church Yth Grp; Cmnty Wkr; Dance Clb; Hosp Aide; Pep Clb; Chorus; School Musical; Variety Show; Rptr Yrbk; Drctrs Awd Choir; Reg Nrs.

PENROD, JULIE J; Victor Valley HS; George A F B, CA; (2); JV Var Trk; Hon Roll; Vet Med.

PENROD, JUSTIN R; Victorville HS; Gafb, CA; (3); Spanish Clb; Hon Roll; Kiwanis Awd; NHS; Rptr Nwsp; Var L Crs Cntry; Var L Trk; Var Capt Wrstlng; Engrng.

PENTA, ERIC J; Sunny Hills HS; Fullerton, CA; (3); Cmnty Wkr; JA; Teachers Aide; JV Bsbl; Var Tennis; Hon Roll; Vp Of Yth N Govt; Vp Of Portuguese Club; Masonic Demolay; Yth Ldrshph Toastmaters Pres; CA ST Fullerton; Bus.

PENTEK, JOZSEF R; Whitney HS; Cerritos, CA; (1); Church Yth Grp; Computer Clb; Drama Clb; French Clb; Model UN; Lit Mag; High Hon Roll; Pres Acad Fit Awd; Astrophysics.

PENTERMAN, AMBER L; Faith Christian HS; Yuba City, CA; (2); Church Yth Grp; Var Sftbl; Var Vllybl; Hon Roll; Soc Wrkr.

PENTOPOULOS, ANALENE J; Las Lomas HS; Walnut Creek, CA; (1); 1/245; Hosp Aide; Model UN; Var Socr; Var Tennis; Var Trk; Undergrad Achvt Awd; Pre Med.

PENTOPOULOS, MARC A; Las Lomas HS; Walnut Creek, CA; (3); Treas Intnl Clb; Model UN; SADD; Rptr Nwsp; JV Socr; Var L Tennis; NHS; Acadmc Decthln Hnr Div; Katate Black Belt.

PEOPLES, JENNIFER; Antioch SR HS; Oakley, CA; (4); Cmnty Wkr; Key Clb; Service Clb; Chorus; Variety Show; Rptr Yrbk; BYU Frgn Lang Fair Awd Supr Rtng Ger; Stu Of Mnth Prin Awd; Diablo Vly Coll; Art.

PEOPLES, TANISHA L; Gardena HS; Gardena, CA; (4); Office Aide; Capt Drill Tm; Treas Sr Cls; Rep Stu Cncl; Hon Roll; Pres Acad Fit Awd; CA Schlrshp Fed; Tribe Clb; U Of CA Irvine; Sociology.

PEPPARD, MICHAEL A; Bellarmine Jefferson HS; Glendale, CA; (2); Church Yth Grp.

PEPPER, DEANNA E; Woodcrest Christian Schl; Riverside, CA; (1); Church Yth Grp; Treas 4-H; Var L Crs Cntry; Var L Sftbl; 4-H Awd; High Hon Roll; CIF Chmpnshps Sftbl & Cross Cntry; Athl Awd, Chrstn Service & Acad Awd For Annual High Hnrs; Teaching.

PEPPER, RICHARD L; Woodcrest Christian HS; Riverside, CA; (3); 4-H; JV Var Vllybl; 4-H Awd; High Hon Roll; Hnr Soc Rep; Coachs Awd JR Vlybl; UC Irvine; Engrng.

PEPPER, SASHA; Livermore HS; Livermore, CA; (1); Pep Clb; Cheerldng; Stat Wrstlng; Hon Roll; U Of Santa Barbara; Law.

PERA, MICHELLE A; Oak Ridge HS; Cameron Park, CA; (1); Church Yth Grp; SADD; JV Sftbl; JV Vllybl; High Hon Roll; Hon Roll; CSF; Engrng.

PERALES, CARLY; Lindsay HS; Lindsay, CA; (3); 2/140; Church Yth Grp; Key Clb; Letterman Clb; Spanish Clb; Rep Jr Cls; VP Capt Bsktbl; Capt Ftbl; Var L Tennis; Hon Roll; CSF; Golden St Exam Hnrs Geom; Phys Educ.

PERALES, EMILY NICHOLE; Tulare Western HS; Tulare, CA; (2); Church Yth Grp; Cmnty Wkr; GAA; Pep Clb; Spanish Clb; Color Guard; Flag Corp; Var Cheerldng; Var Pom Pon; JV Sftbl; Tulare Bobby Sox Sftbl All Stars; U Of CA Los Angeles; Psych.

PERALTA, CAREYNA; Santa Clara HS; Santa Clara, CA; (3); 12/430; Service Clb; Spanish Clb; Teachers Aide; Flag Corp; Mrchg Band; Variety Show; Hon Roll; Prfct Atten Awd; CSF.

PERALTA, ERICA; Montgomery HS; San Diego, CA; (3); Sec Church Yth Grp; Hosp Aide; Drill Tm; Orch; Nwsp; Rep Jr Cls; Rdy Wrtrs Prjct; Outstndng Achvt 89-90; Sunday Schl Tchr Grace Allaince Chrch 89-90; UCSD; Optmtry.

PERALTA, JASON R; Pinole Valley HS; Hercules, CA; (1); AFS; Computer Clb; French Clb; Wt Lftg; Friday Night Live; Amnsty Intl; CA Berkeley; Comp Prgmr.

PERALTA, JOSELYN; North Salinas HS; Salinas, CA; (1); Church Yth Grp; Key Clb; Spanish Clb; Band; Mrchg Band; Off Soph Cls; Cit Awd; Hon Roll; Prfct Atten Awd; Phy.

PERALTA, RICARDO; El Camino Fundamental HS; Sacramento, CA; (3); 40/366; Chess Clb; Debate Tm; FTA; JV Swmmng; Wt Lftg; 4-H Awd; NHS; Water Polo JV, Vrsty; Early Outrch Pgm Schlrshp; CA Fed Schlrshps; Natl Yth Ldrsp Awd 90; Optmtry.

PERALTA, SHERRY A; Abraham Lincoln HS; San Francisco, CA; (2); Church Yth Grp; ROTC; Teachers Aide; Drill Tm; Mltry Ordr Of Arrow Wrs; San Fran ST U; Acctng.

PERALTA, VERONICA P; Workman HS; La Puente, CA; (2); Church Yth Grp; Letterman Clb; Mrchg Band; JV Cheerldng; Var Swmmng; Hon Roll; Bus Admin.

PERALTA, VICKEY L; William Workman HS; La Puente, CA; (4); 19/150; Key Clb; Mrchg Band; Var L Swmmng; Hon Roll; Spanish NHS; Modern Music Masters Secy 2 Yrs VP; Drumline Cptn 2 Yrs; U Of La Verne; Bus Admin.

PERAZA, PABLO A; North Hollywood HS; North Hollywood, CA; (2); Church Yth Grp; Teachers Aide; Bus.

PERCE, LEANNE K; Atascadero HS; Atascadero, CA; (2); Church Yth Grp; 4-H; Speech Tm; Band; Mrchg Band; Pep Band; School Musical; JV Tennis; JV Trk; Hon Roll; Pat Jacksons Amer Dnce; Won Dist & Cty Wrtng Conts; Squad Ldr Marching Band.

PERCIFIELD, JOLENE S; Mesa Verde HS; Citrus Heights, CA; (3); 10/275; VP Jr Cls; VP Sr Cls; JV Var Bsktbl; JV Sftbl; JV Var Vllybl; Pres Acad Fit Awd; Stu Rchng Out; CSF; 1C Santa Barbara; Bus Mgmt.

PERCIVAL, KRISTA L; Palm Desert HS; Palm Desert, CA; (4); 5/250; Spanish Clb; Swing Chorus; VP Jr Cls; Sec Stu Cncl; Var Capt Bsktbl; Var L Trk; Var L Vllybl; 4-H Awd; High Hon Roll; NHS; Coll Of The Desert; Gen Ed.

PERDOMO, YVETTE L; Bellflower HS; Bellflower, CA; (3); 2/280; JA; Key Clb; Letterman Clb; Treas Math Clb; Sec Jr Cls; Sec Sr Cls; Var Bsktbl; Var Vllybl; Kiwanis Awd; Pres Acad Fit Awd; CSF; Physcn.

PERDUE, JESSICA R; Bonita Vista HS; Bonita, CA; (2); 79/517; Key Clb; Varsity Clb; Off Frsh Cls; Off Jr Cls; Var L Fld Hcky; JV Capt Socr; Var Trk; Cit Awd; Hon Roll; Masonic Awd; San Diego Union Tribunes All Acad Team; UC Santa Barbara; Engl.

PEREA, DOLLY R; John Glenn HS; Norwalk, CA; (4); GAA; Letterman Clb; Office Aide; Speech Tm; SADD; Teachers Aide; Varsity Clb; School Play; Off Jr Cls; Off Sr Cls; Sftbl, Bsktbl, Bsbl Stats; Tm Sftbl Mgr; Tm Bsbl Mom; Cerritos Coll; Law.

PEREA, PEDRO; Alian Leroy Locke HS; Los Angeles, CA; (3); ROTC; Mach Oper.

PEREDNIK, ANNA; George Washington HS; San Francisco, CA; (2); Nwsp; Off Frsh Cls; UC Berkeley; Comp Prgmr.

PEREDO, MARIA B; Rio Linda SR HS; Sacramento, CA; (2); Church Yth Grp; English Clb; Spanish Clb; Var Cheerldng; High Hon Roll; Hon Roll; CSF; SS Teacher; U CA; Sci.

PEREIDA, EMMA; Arvin HS; Arvin, CA; (2); Church Yth Grp; Computer Clb; Letterman Clb; Math Clb; Science Clb; Ski Clb; Treas Soph Cls; Var Cheerldng; Var Tennis; Hon Roll; U CA-SANTA Cruz; Med Chem.

PEREIRA, CELINA M; San Jose HS Acad; San Jose, CA; (3); Church Yth Grp; Cmnty Wkr; Drama Clb; Office Aide; Teachers Aide; Chorus; School Play; JV Tennis; High Hon Roll; Hon Roll; CSF; Santa Clara U; Pre Law.

PEREIRA, LAILA M; Loretto HS; Roseville, CA; (1); 1/80; Intnl Clb; Science Clb; SADD; Nwsp; High Hon Roll; NEDT Awd; CSF 89-90; Cal St U Of Sac Tlnt Srch Schlrshp; Hghst GPA Cls; Sci.

PEREIRA, LIZABETH; Hanford HS; Hanford, CA; (3); Church Yth Grp; FBLA; Hosp Aide; Intnl Clb; Acpl Chr; School Musical; Hon Roll; CA Schlrshp Fed; Med.

PEREIRA, NELIA; Riverdale HS; Riverdale, CA; (3); Church Yth Grp; Drama Clb; Office Aide; Flag Corp; Nwsp; Ed Yrbk; Sec Jr Cls; Stu Cncl; High Hon Roll; Bus.

PEREIRA, ROGER; Armigo HS; Fairfield, CA; (3); Latin Clb; Math Tm; Yrbk; Off Soph Cls; Bsbl; Ftbl; Socr; Sftbl; Swmmng; Trk; Stanford U; Econ.

PEREIRA, ROSARIO L; Notre Dame HS; San Martin, CA; (3); Drama Clb; Treas SADD; Chorus; Off Stu Cncl; Var Co-Capt Bsktbl; Var Socr; Var Sftbl; Var Co-Capt Vllybl; Hon Roll; Scrd 5 Of 5 On Spanish Ap Test; Hnrs Engl British & Eurpn Lit; Indvdlzd Math Class (2); US San Diego; Ped/Pre-Med.

PEREIRA, ROSEMARY S; Notre Dame HS; San Jose, CA; (3); Church Yth Grp; Intnl Clb; Science Clb; Teachers Aide; Chorus; Rptr Nwsp; Treas Soph Cls; Intrml Bsktbl; Intrml Vllybl; High Hon Roll; Blue Ribbon Delegate Mayors Yth Conf 88-90; Yth Forum 89-90; CA Schlrshp Fed Mem; Santa Clara U; Eng.

PERELSTEIN, ILYA; Bel-Air Prep Schl; Los Angeles, CA; (4); 2/35; Office Aide; Teachers Aide; Stage Crew; Ed Nwsp; Ed Yrbk; High Hon Roll; Hon Roll; Sal; Barpy Freedman Svc Awd; 1st Pl Sci Fair 88-90; Stu Of Month 89; U Southern CA; Med.

PERERA, KISHANI A; Whitney HS; Cerritos, CA; (1); Church Yth Grp; Drama Clb; Hon Roll; Animal Rights Clb-Founder; Natl Piano Playng Auditions; Music Tchrs Assn Of CA-MRT Cert Level 1/2; U Of CA; Bus.

PERES, TERESA D; El Camino Fundemental HS; Sacramento, CA; (3); 67/366; Church Yth Grp; Cmnty Wkr; 4-H; Latin Clb; Library Aide; Varsity Clb; Lit Mag; Var JV Swmmng; Intrml Wt Lftg; Cit Awd; Friday Night Live; Early Outreach Prgm; Mesa.

PEREYRA, MINERVA; Chula Vista HS; Chula Vista, CA; (4); 155/505; Pep Clb; Yrbk; Bsktbl; Vllybl; ASB Cmmssnr Fnanc 89-90; San Diego ST U; Bus.

PEREZ, ABELAM; Oxnard HS; Oxnard, CA; (2); Art Clb; Ftbl; Tennis; Prfct Atten Awd; UCSB; Acting.

PEREZ, ADRIANA; Mater Dei HS; Santa Ana, CA; (3); Drama Clb; Sec Hosp Aide; Spanish Clb; Campus Minstry; Statesmen Of Amer; Berkeley; Law.

PEREZ, AGAPITO; Gonzales Union HS; Gonzales, CA; (3); Varsity Clb; Nwsp; Off Frsh Cls; Off Jr Cls; Ftbl; Wt Lftg; Hon Roll; Prfct Atten Awd; High Tech Inst; Arch.

PEREZ, ALEJANDRA C; Whittier HS; Whittier, CA; (3); Hosp Aide; Teachers Aide; Band; Hon Roll; Nrsng.

PEREZ, ALISA M; Aptos HS; Freedom, CA; (2); 75/341; Frm Rep.

PEREZ, ALISHA C; Escondido HS; Escondido, CA; (3); Cmnty Wkr; JV Socr; Cert Schltc Achvt; Cert Mrt.

PEREZ, ALMA; Gladstone HS; Azusa, CA; (4); Nwsp; Hon Roll; CSF; E San Gabriel Regnl Occptnl Prog; Fashion Merchndsng; Mexico U Autonoma De Guadalaja.

PEREZ, AMARANTA; International Studies Acad; San Francisco, CA; (1); Phtg Yrbk; High Hon Roll; Asian Clb; ESL Awd; UC Berkeley.

PEREZ, ANA R; Bell Gardens HS; Commerce, CA; (2); 5/813; SADD; Color Guard; Mrchg Band; Trk; Hon Roll; Prfct Atten Awd; Spec Interest; Top Ten; NYU; Med.

PEREZ, ANGEL; Ontario HS; Ontario, CA; (3); Capt Socr; ; Psych.

PEREZ, ANNA L; La Jolla HS; San Diego, CA; (2); Drama Clb; Library Aide; School Play; Rep Soph Cls; JV Fld Hcky; Bus Mgmt.

PEREZ, ANTHONY; Kerman HS; Kerman, CA; (3); Chorus; JV Wrstlng; Pride Awd Life Sci & US Histry; ROP Landscaping; U Southern CA; Accntng.

PEREZ, BEN R; North Salinas HS; Salinas, CA; (2); Spanish Clb; Bsbl; Socr; Hon Roll; Var Mst Imprvd Plyr Sccr 89-90; Fresno ST U; Law Enfrcmnt.

PEREZ, CARLOS; Nogales HS; La Puente, CA; (2); 42/827; Tennis; Hon Roll; CSF; Berkeley; Engrng.

PEREZ III, CARLOS A; Hamilton HS; Sepulveda, CA; (2); Boy Scts; Church Yth Grp; Office Aide; Band; Jazz Band; Nwsp; Bsktbl; Gym; Vllybl; High Hon Roll; UC Brkly; Music.

PEREZ, CECILIA; Sweetwater HS; National City, CA; (2); High Hon Roll; Hon Roll; AVID; UCSD; Phy.

PEREZ, CELESTE N; Brawley Union HS; Brawley, CA; (3); Fash Dsgnr.

PEREZ, CHRISTIAN A; Tracy Joint Union HS; Tracy, CA; (2); 16/483; Math Clb; Spanish Clb; SADD; Hon Roll; Intl Bacclurt Prog; CSF; US Achvt Acad; Med.

PEREZ, CLAUDIA; Bonita Vista HS; Chula Vista, CA; (3); Dance Clb; Model UN; Teachers Aide; Varsity Clb; Acpl Chr; Chorus; Variety Show; Off Jr Cls; Cit Awd; Song & Dance Ensmble; Vol For Homeless; Choir Awd; Varsity Ltrs In Acad; Elem Ed.

PEREZ, CLAUDIA; Central Union HS; El Centro, CA; (3); 26/543; Teachers Aide; Cit Awd; Hon Roll; U Of Santa Barbara; Spch Thrpst.

PEREZ, CLAUDIA; Marvista HS; Imperial Beach, CA; (1); Dance Clb; Clothes Dsgnr.

PEREZ, CLAUDIA; St Paul HS; Norwalk, CA; (3); Intnl Clb; Red Cross Aide; Spanish Clb; Crs Cntry; Tennis; High Hon Roll; Hon Roll; Jr NHS; NHS; Spanish NHS; CSF; UCLA; Med.

PEREZ, CLAUDIA T; John Burroughs HS; Burbank, CA; (3); Dance Clb; Library Aide; Chorus; Variety Show; VP Frsh Cls; Hon Roll; Fresh Cls Treas; Valley Coll; Travel/Trsm.

PEREZ, DANNY; Canyon Springs HS; Moreno Valley, CA; (2); Ftbl; Wrstlng; Hon Roll; Arch.

PEREZ, DARLENE R; Lindsay HS; Lindsay, CA; (1); Church Yth Grp; Latin Clb; Office Aide; Science Clb; Spanish Clb; SADD; Teachers Aide; Church Choir; Nwsp; Swmmng; RN.

PEREZ, DEBORAH; Maricopa HS; Maricopa, CA; (4); 7/34; Am Leg Aux Girls St; Pres Church Yth Grp; Drama Clb; GAA; Sec Science Clb; Spanish Clb; Yrbk; Var L Bsktbl; Powder Puff Ftbl; Var Capt Sftbl; US Am Legn Schlr Awd; US Army Reserve Natl Schlr/Athlete Awd; Cuesta CC; Cnslr.

PEREZ, DIANNE; Workman HS; W Covina, CA; (4); 164/269; Teachers Aide; Stu Cncl; Powder Puff Ftbl; Hon Roll; Awd Engl 4 Tchr Outstndng Wrk; Fashn Merch.

PEREZ, EDNA J; Bishop Amat HS; Walnut, CA; (3); Spanish Clb; Spanish NHS; Silver Screen Clb; UC San Diego; Comptr Sci.

PEREZ, EDUARDO; Coachella Valley HS; Thermal, CA; (3); Library Aide; Math Clb; Spanish Clb; Teachers Aide; Trk; Hon Roll; Advanced Placemen Span Test Received A 5; Bakersfield; Bilingual Ed.

PEREZ, ENRIQUE; Arroyo HS; San Lorenzo, CA; (4); 30/267; Church Yth Grp; Speech Tm; Var Ftbl; Var Trk; Var Wt Lftg; High Hon Roll; Hon Roll; Lion Awd; St Schlr; Italian Cathlc Schlrshp; San Lorenzo Dist Schlrshp; Engrs Week Outstndng Stu Awdfschlr Athl V Ftbl; CA Polytech ST U; Arch Engrng.

PEREZ, ENRIQUE; Mar Vista HS; San Ysidro, CA; (2); 63/467; Co-Ed French Clb; ROTC; JV Var Socr; Englsh Hnrs; Wrld Cltrs Hnrs; UCLA; FBI Agnt.

PEREZ, ERIKA; Artesia HS; Cerritos, CA; (3); Science Clb; Spanish Clb; Rep Frsh Cls; VP Soph Cls; Off Jr Cls; Pres Stu Cncl; Var Bsktbl; Var Cheerldng; Var Sftbl; Var Vllybl; High Hnr Roll; Pet Asst Lgue; Vet.

PEREZ, ERNESTO C; Tehachapi HS; Tehachapi, CA; (3); #4 In Class; VP FBLA; Spanish Clb; Rptr Nwsp; Lit Mag; High Hon Roll; Lion Awd; Acad Decathlon; CA Schlstc Fed; Acctng.

PEREZ, EVELIA; Pinole Valley HS; Hercules, CA; (2); Church Yth Grp; Debate Tm; French Clb; Amnesty Intl; Pltcl Sci.

PEREZ, GABRIEL C; Palmdale HS; Palmdale, CA; (1); Intrml Bsbl; Stanford U; Hwy Patrol.

PEREZ, GENOVEVA; Fremont HS; Oakland, CA; (3); Church Yth Grp; Lit Mag; Tennis; High Hon Roll; Hon Roll; Mesa Club; San Francisco ST; Ped.

PEREZ, GERARDO; Bell Gardens HS; Commerce, CA; (3); FCA; JV Bsbl; JV Bsktbl; JV Ftbl; Prfct Atten Awd.

PEREZ, GIESELLE; Immaculate Heart HS; Los Angeles, CA; (2); 35/99; Drama Clb; GAA; Service Clb; Stage Crew; Off Soph Cls; High Hon Roll; CSF; Loyala Marymount; Bus Mgt.

PEREZ, GINA; South West HS; San Ysidro, CA; (2); Art Clb; Computer Clb; Dance Clb; Office Aide; Varsity Clb; School Play; Nwsp; Rep Soph Cls; JV Bsktbl; JV Ftbl; San Diego ST U; Soc Psycht.

PEREZ, GUADALUPE; Artesia HS; Hawaiian Gardens, CA; (1); Church Yth Grp; Photo Clb; UCLA; Lwyr.

PEREZ, GUADALUPE; Calexico HS; Calexico, CA; (3); Var Cheerldng; Hon Roll; Our Ldy Gudlp Cthlc Yth Grp.

PEREZ, GUADALUPE; Sacred Heart Of Mary HS; Los Angeles, CA; (3); 1/85; Aud/Vis; GAA; Church Choir; School Play; Variety Show; Rep Soph Cls; Rep Jr Cls; Stu Cncl; Hon Roll; NHS; 1st, 2nd Pl Natl Span Exams.

PEREZ, HECTOR R; Daniel Murphy HS; Los Angeles, CA; (3); French Clb; Rep Frsh Cls; JV Ftbl; Cit Awd; Hon Roll; UCLA; Engrng.

PEREZ, HERMINIA; Halminton HS; Los Angeles, CA; (2).

PEREZ, IDMELDA; Holy Family HS; Los Angeles, CA; (4); Library Aide; Teachers Aide; Chorus; Off Soph Cls; Cheerldng; Score Keeper; Kiwanis Awd; Cal Poly Pomona; Civil Engr.

PEREZ, IMELDA; Hemet HS; Winchester, CA; (2); Dance Clb; English Clb; Math Tm; Spanish Clb; SADD; Teachers Aide; Off Soph Cls; Bsktbl; Ftbl; Sftbl; Attorney.

PEREZ, ISABEL; Arlington HS; Riverside, CA; (4); Off Sr Cls; Hon Roll; Comp.

PEREZ, JEANETTE I; South Bay Junior Acad; Inglewood, CA; (2); Church Yth Grp; Office Aide; Teachers Aide; Church Choir; School Musical; Yrbk; VP Frsh Cls; Sec Soph Cls; Vllybl; Cit Awd; ASB VP; Obstetrician.

PEREZ, JERRY; Mt Whitney HS; Visalia, CA; (3); DECA; Key Clb; Letterman Clb; SADD; VP Frsh Cls; Off Soph Cls; Rep Stu Cncl; Var JV Bsbl; Hon Roll; CSF; Assoc Stu Body Cmmssnr Clbs; U C Santa Barbara; Bus Adm.

PEREZ, JOE L; Daniel Murphy Catholic HS; Los Angeles, CA; (2); JV Bsktbl; Var Crs Cntry; Var Mgr(s); Var Socr; Var Trk; 2nd Hnr Roll; Bus.

PEREZ, JOSE R; Workman HS; Valinda, CA; (2); Computer Clb; Ftbl; Socr.

PEREZ, JOSEPH; West Covina HS; West Covina, CA; (3); Boy Scts; Cmnty Wkr; W Covina Police Explrer; Devil Pups Prgm; Azusa Pacific U; Police Admin.

PEREZ, JOYCE P; Notre Dame Acad; Los Angeles, CA; (4); Drama Clb; SADD; Acpl Chr; School Play; Variety Show; Ed Yrbk; Cit Awd; Hon Roll; Prfct Atten Awd; Campus Mnstry Retreat Chairperson; U Southern CA; Bus.

PEREZ, JUAN C; Orosi HS; Cutler, CA; (2); Letterman Clb; Spanish Clb; Band; Mrchg Band; VP Frsh Cls; JV Capt Bsbl; JV Ftbl; DAR Awd; Hon Roll; Pres Acad Fit Awd; Fresno ST U; Microbio.

PEREZ, JUDITH; San Fernando HS; Arleta, CA; (4); Church Yth Grp; Cmnty Wkr; FBLA; Band; Church Choir; Drm Mjr(t); Jazz Band; Mrchg Band; Pep Band; School Musical; U CA Santa Barbara; Educ.

PEREZ, JUDY A; Southern CA Christian HS; Fullerton, CA; (1); Church Yth Grp; Teachers Aide; Church Choir; School Musical; Stage Crew; Sec Soph Cls; Bsktbl; Hon Roll; Pres Acad Fit Awd; Missionettes; Biola U; Interprtr.

PEREZ, JULIO; Inglewood HS; Inglewood, CA; (4); 15/426; Am Leg Boys St; Latin Clb; Yrbk; Var Socr; Swmmng; Var Tennis; Hon Roll; Prfct Atten Awd; Pres Acad Fit Awd; Acad Decath; MESA Math Engrng Sci Assoc; TRW Sci Fair; USC; Bus Admn.

PEREZ, KAREN A; Grace M Davis HS; Modesto, CA; (3); AFS; Drama Clb; Hosp Aide; NFL; Pres Science Clb; Sec Treas Service Clb; Spanish Clb; Speech Tm; SADD; Camp Royal; Music Tchrs Cert Of Mrt Piano, Hnrs Recital, MTA St Cnvntn; Sci Olympiad; CSF.

PEREZ, KATHRYN; St Joseph HS; Diamond Bar, CA; (3); Capt GAA; Ski Clb; Flag Corp; Mrchg Band; Phtg Ed Yrbk; Sec Rep Frsh Cls; Sec Rep Stu Cncl; Var Capt Crs Cntry; JV Swmmng; Hon Roll; People To People Ambssdr Pgm; S Gate City Yth Band; Cross-Cntry Coaches Awd; UCLA.

PEREZ, KRISTINA J; La Quinta HS; Fountain Valley, CA; (3); French Clb; Key Clb; Treas SADD; Teachers Aide; Yrbk; Hon Roll; Mock Trl; Law.

PEREZ, LA SHARON; El Camino HS; Oceanside, CA; (2); 213/400; Church Yth Grp; Cmnty Wkr; FCA; FFA; ROTC; Drill Tm; Stu Cncl; Cit Awd; DAR Awd; Kiwanis Awd; ROTC Drill Tapout 4th In Nation; ASB Mdl Of Accomplishment; Harvard; Poltcl Sci.

PEREZ, LEONARD D; Irvine HS; Irvine, CA; (2); 51/546; Spanish Clb; JV Tennis; Cit Awd; Hon Roll; Pres Acad Fit Awd; CSF; Berkeley; Med Doc.

PEREZ, LEOPOLDO; Indio HS; Indio, CA; (1); Fld Hcky; Cit Awd; Prfct Atten Awd; Boys Clb Of Amer Cert Of Awd; Keystone Clb; Coll Of The Desert; Elec Engr.

PEREZ, LETICIA; Indio HS; Indio, CA; (1); Office Aide; Bsktbl; Crs Cntry; Trk; Prfct Atten Awd; Pres Acad Fit Awd.

PEREZ, LISA; West HS; Bakersfield, CA; (2); Spanish Clb; Cheerldng; Hon Roll.

PEREZ, LISA A; Hilmar HS; Turlock, CA; (3); Art Clb; Drama Clb; Pres FFA; GAA; Letterman Clb; Speech Tm; SADD; Teachers Aide; School Play; Ed Nwsp; Outstndng Animal Sci Awd-FFA; MVP Sftbl; CA ST U-Stanislaus; Acctng.

PEREZ, LUPE; Avenal HS; Kettleman City, CA; (3); Church Yth Grp; Pep Clb; Church Choir; L Cheerldng; High Hon Roll; Hon Roll; CSF; Camp Counselor; Ed.

PEREZ, MANUEL; Coachella Valley HS; Coachella, CA; (4); 18/286; Church Yth Grp; Cmnty Wkr; Teachers Aide; Band; Mrchg Band; Variety Show; Rep Frsh Cls; Sec Soph Cls; Rep Jr Cls; Off Sr Cls; U C Riverside; Pol Sci.

PEREZ, MANUEL A; Sanger HS; Sanger, CA; (2); JV Bsktbl; JV Tennis; Psych.

PEREZ, MARCELLA V; John A Rowland HS; Rowland Hts, CA; (4); 67/558; Cmnty Wkr; Office Aide; Teachers Aide; Cit Awd; High Hon Roll; Hon Roll; Prfct Atten Awd; Pres Acad Fit Awd; Whittier Coll; Ed.

PEREZ, MARGARITA; Paramount HS; Paramount, CA; (3); SADD; Chorus; Color Guard; Orch; Interior Designer.

PEREZ, MARIA; Abraham Lincoln HS; San Francisco, CA; (2); Ski Clb; Chorus; Variety Show; Treas Frsh Cls; Treas Soph Cls; Bsktbl; Swmmng; Art & Drama; Brdcstng; CSU Coll.

PEREZ, MARIA E; Santa Ana HS; Santa Ana, CA; (3); Rancho Santiago Coll; Elec Engr.

PEREZ, MARIO A; Hesperia HS; Hesperia, CA; (2); 31/650; Church Yth Grp; Dance Clb; Spanish Clb; Rptr Nwsp; JV Trk; High Hon Roll; Outstndng Span Stu Awd; Dist Sci Fr Hnrs; Sci Internship UC Riverside.

PEREZ, MARISOL; Santa Teresa HS; San Jose, CA; (2); Church Yth Grp; Cmnty Wkr; French Clb; Latin Clb; Church Choir; Variety Show; Hon Roll; Stu Of Week Frgn Lang Dept; Sec Laino Stu Union; Tutor Spnsh, Engl Spkng Stu; Santa Barbara U; Psych.

PEREZ, MARISSA E; Carson HS; Carson, CA; (3); FFA; JA; Teachers Aide; Hon Roll; Prfct Atten Awd; Splling Cont; Acad Achvmt; CA ST U; Sociology.

PEREZ, MECHELLE L; El Rancho HS; Pico Rivera, CA; (4); High Hon Roll; Hon Roll; Bank Of Amer Plaque Wnnr; CSF; Rainer Funds Art Schlrshp; Bryans Coll; Ct Rprtr.

PEREZ, MELISA R; Turlock HS; Turlock, CA; (2); 8/600; Church Yth Grp; Sec Rep FFA; Rep Nwsp; Off Jr Cls; JV Bsktbl; JV Vllybl; High Hon Roll; Hon Roll; Stu Of Month.

PEREZ, MELISSA; Kerman HS; Kerman, CA; (2); 6/170; Yrbk; Ftbl; JV Sftbl; JV Vllybl; Hon Roll; CSF; Untd Mxcn Amer Soc; Law.

PEREZ, MICHELLE; Kingsburg HS; Kingsburg, CA; (2); Spanish Clb; Kings River Coll; Comp.

PEREZ, MIRNA; Inglewood HS; Inglewood, CA; (3); Latin Clb; ROTC; Hon Roll; USC; Bus Management.

PEREZ, MOISES; Orange Glen HS; Valley Center, CA; (3); 229/458; Teachers Aide; Hon Roll; CA Poly Pomona; Lndscpng.

PEREZ, NAIN J; Nogales HS; Walnut, CA; (3); Var Ftbl; Var Trk; Wt Lftg; High Hon Roll; Hon Roll; Deans List; Sch High Jump Record Breaker; Merit Awd; Jrnlst.

PEREZ, NORMA; Arvin HS; Arvin, CA; (3); French Clb; Latin Clb; Spanish Clb; SADD; Hon Roll; MECHA Clb; Ecology Clb; Law.

PEREZ, ODETTE N; Los Gatos HS; Los Gatos, CA; (2); Hon Roll; San Fran Ballet Schl Smr Stu; Piano; Stanford; Med.

PEREZ, PATRICK; Glen A Wilson HS; Hacienda Hts, CA; (4); Church Yth Grp; Key Clb; Ski Clb; Nwsp; Yrbk; DAR Awd; Hon Roll; NHS; Pres Acad Fit Awd; Rep Jr Cls; Statesmen Of Amer Chptr Treas, VP, S CA St Spkr; Natl Hspnc Schlr Semi Fnlst; Amnesty Intl Co-Pres; UC Berkeley; Poltcl Sci.

PEREZ, PAUL J; Marshall Fundamental HS; Pasadena, CA; (3); Am Leg Boys St; Key Clb; Var L Tennis; Var L Trk; Hon Roll; Pasadena Sci Fair-Botany 3rd Pl; Photo; Los Angeles Cnty Sci Fari-Botany-Hnrb Mntn; SEED Pgm.

PEREZ, RAFAEL B; Mission Bay HS; San Diego, CA; (1); 63/413; Computer Clb; Cit Awd; Hon Roll; Pres Schlr; Played On Sftbl Team; UCSD; Med.

PEREZ, RAMIL; Daniel Murphy HS; Los Angeles, CA; (3); 17/79; Art Clb; Chess Clb; Quiz Bowl; Scholastic Bowl; Rep Soph Cls; Hon Roll; USC Walkathon; Asian Club; 2nd Pl Sci Fair 88; Phrmcy.

PEREZ, RAYMOND E; Arcadia HS; Arcadia, CA; (2); Church Yth Grp; Ski Clb; Rep Soph Cls; Ftbl; JV Vllybl; Hstrn; Sprts Med.

PEREZ, RENE; Pater Noster Catholic HS; Los Angeles, CA; (2); Church Yth Grp; English Clb; Bsktbl; Ftbl; Score Keeper; Wt Lftg; Hon Roll; NHS; St Schlr; UCLA; Pharm.

PEREZ, RICK; West HS; Bakersfield, CA; (3); Art Clb; Church Yth Grp; Math Clb; Math Tm; Ski Clb; Band; Bsbl; Bsktbl; Ftbl; Mgr(s); U Of AZ; Elec Engr.

PEREZ, ROBERT; Saddleback HS; Santa Ana, CA; (3); Boy Scts; Band; Mrchg Band; Pep Band; JV Crs Cntry; JV Trk; Eagle Sct; Pre-Med.

PEREZ, ROBIN; Fountain Valley HS; Fountain Valley, CA; (4); Spanish Clb; Capt Varsity Clb; Capt Socr; L Capt Swmmng; Spanish NHS; CSF Clb; JV & Vrsty Wtr Polo-MIP 88; UCI; Engrng.

PEREZ, SAMIRA; San Fernando HS; Arleta, CA; (3); Church Yth Grp; Cmnty Wkr; Teachers Aide; Band; Jazz Band; Mrchg Band; Cit Awd; Hon Roll; Prfct Atten Awd; Pres Acad Fit Awd; Vol Santa Rosa Cmnty Ctr Wrkg With Chldrn; Law.

PEREZ, SANDRA; San Gorgonio HS; San Bernardino, CA; (3); Boy Scts; Church Yth Grp; English Clb; Latin Clb; Q&S; Service Clb; Nwsp; Lit Mag; Prfct Atten Awd; Writng Celebratn 1st Pl Prose; Upwrd Bnd; Jrnlsm.

PEREZ, SANDRA D; Corona HS; Corona, CA; (2); Spanish Clb; Drill Tm; Prfct Atten Awd; CA ST Fullerton; Bus.

PEREZ, SCOTT C; University HS; Irvine, CA; (1); Intrml Crs Cntry; JV Socr; Intrml Trk; Hon Roll; Mst Vlbl Sprntr Trk; Law.

PEREZ, SELENE; St Bonaventure HS; Camarillo, CA; (4); 22/145; Pres Speech Tm; Band; Church Choir; School Musical; Variety Show; Ed Yrbk; Hon Roll; NHS; Future Latino Ldrs Of Amer Speaker Of Week; Natl Hispanic Schlr Semi Fnlst; U CA Santa Cruz; Bio.

PEREZ, SONIA; St Bonaventure HS; Santa Paula, CA; (4); 10/137; Band; Church Choir; Pep Band; Yrbk; Hon Roll; NHS; CSF; Ntl Hispanic Schlrshp Semi-Fnlst; Engr.

PEREZ, SONIA A; Sacramento Adventist Acad; Sacramento, CA; (2); 7/50; Drama Clb; Ski Clb; Band; Chorus; Sec Frsh Cls; VP Soph Cls; Prfct Atten Awd; Assocd Stu Body Srgnt At Arms; Pacific Union Coll; Law.

PEREZ, SONIA A; William C Overfelt HS; San Jose, CA; (3); Science Clb; Superintendents Hnr Roll; MESA Awd Mst Otstndng Jr; CA Schlrshp Fed.

PEREZ, THERESA P; Don Antonio Lugo HS; Chino, CA; (2); Girl Scts; Hon Roll; Trvl Sftbl.

PEREZ, TRANQUILINA; Butte Valley Unified HS; Macdoel, CA; (2); Computer Clb; Pep Clb; Teachers Aide; Sec Stu Cncl; JV Bsktbl; High Hon Roll; Hon Roll; CSF.

PEREZ, VIRGINIA; Castle Park HS; Chula Vista, CA; (3); Rptr Nwsp; Yrbk; Cit Awd; UCSD; Marine Bio.

PEREZ, WILIAM M; Bellarmine College Prep; San Jose, CA; (4); Cmnty Wkr; Pres Acad Fit Awd; U Dallas; Philosophy.

PEREZ, YURIEN S; Homestead HS; Sunnyvale, CA; (1); Air Force; Pilot.

PEREZ, ZARIT I; San Gabriel Mission HS; Pasadena, CA; (3); 13/127; Cmnty Wkr; Drama Clb; French Clb; FBLA; GAA; Spanish Clb; Var Trk; JV Vllybl; High Hon Roll; Hon Roll; LA MADD 1st Pl Cntst Wnr, Natl Hnry Mntn Awd; Trk-Fld Fnls Awd; Corp Lwyr.

PEREZCHICA, ANNIE; Mc Farland HS; Mcfarland, CA; (2); Letterman Clb; Pep Clb; Chorus; Sec Soph Cls; VP Jr Cls; Stu Cncl; Var Cheerldng; Var Tennis; Hon Roll; Friday Night Live.

PERI, SHARON A; Taft HS; Tarzana, CA; (2); Art Clb; High Hon Roll; Hon Roll; A P Tst Bio; Achvt Tst Bio; CA Poly Tech; Arch.

PERIAS, MELCHIOR; Garces Memorial HS; Delano, CA; (3); 6/120; Letterman Clb; Math Tm; Var L Swmmng; High Hon Roll; Engrng.

PERICH, LEAH J; East Bakersfield HS; Bakersfield, CA; (2); Ed Nwsp; Hon Roll; Chsn Natl Yng Ldrs Conf DC 90; Mem Kern Cnty Horse Shw Assn Wnnr Ovr 100 Awds & Rbbns; Jrnlsm.

PERICONI, CAROLYN; Leuzinger HS; Lawndale, CA; (4); Church Yth Grp; GAA; Pep Clb; Bsktbl; Cheerldng; Sftbl; Hon Roll; Bus Mgmt.

PERINE, MOLLY L; Woodside HS; Woodside, CA; (2); Ski Clb; Teachers Aide; Phtg Yrbk; Bsktbl; Sftbl; Athlete Of Week; MVP Bsktbl Tm.

PERKES, COURTNEY A; Golden West HS; Visalia, CA; (2); 36/400; Church Yth Grp; Debate Tm; FCA; Sec Intnl Clb; Sec NFL; Speech Tm; Rptr Nwsp; Rep Frsh Cls; JV Bsktbl; JV Sftbl; Wnnr Lyons Spch Cntst; Awded Degree Of Mrt, Hnr, Excllnc & Dstnctn By Natl Forensics Leg; Lawyer.

PERKINS, APRIL; Trinity HS; Douglas City, CA; (1); Church Yth Grp; 4-H; Sec Frsh Cls; 4-H Awd; High Hon Roll; Hon Roll.

PERKINS, CRISTI A; Lincoln Preparatory HS; San Diego, CA; (3); 20/200; Drill Tm; JV Bsktbl; Crs Cntry; Hon Roll; Schlshp & Spcl Training San Diego Unifd Schl Dist; Ltrmn Jckt Acad Excllnc; U Of CA San Diego; Med.

PERKINS, JENNIFER K; Livermore HS; Livermore, CA; (3); Drama Clb; Intnl Clb; Flag Corp; Rptr Nwsp; JV Swmmng; Hon Roll; U Of CA-BERKELEY; Psych.

PERKINS, JEREMY D; Paraclete HS; Lancaster, CA; (2); Church Yth Grp; Debate Tm; SADD; Rep Stu Cncl; JV Capt Socr; Hon Roll; NHS.

PERKINS, KRISTA M; Mills JR HS; Rancho Cordova, CA; (1); 15/261; Model UN; Speech Tm; Stu Cncl; Cheerldng; Cit Awd; High Hon Roll; Hon Roll; Jr NHS; Opt Clb Awd; Law.

PERKINS, LETICIA; Colton HS; Colton, CA; (3); Church Yth Grp; Church Choir; Off Jr Cls; Off Sr Cls; Swmmng; Hon Roll; Jr NHS; NHS; UC Riverside; Psych.

PERKINS, MELISSA A; Novato HS; Novato, CA; (3); GAA; Spanish Clb; Band; Mrchg Band; Ed Lit Mag; Var L Bsktbl; Var L Socr; High Hon Roll; Pres Acad Fit Awd; CSF Life-Time Stu; All Lg Sccr & Bsktbl.

PERKINS, STEVE; Beacon Christian HS; Foster City, CA; (1); Drama Clb; School Play; Socr; Hon Roll; Drama.

PERKINS, TIM; Biggs HS; Biggs, CA; (4); 1/48; Am Leg Boys St; Church Yth Grp; 4-H; Letterman Clb; Library Aide; Band; School Play; Pres Soph Cls; Pres VP Stu Cncl; JV Var Bsktbl; Fnlst Stu Rep CA St Brd Educ; Hnr Stu Amer Acad Achvt Wkend Excllnc; CA St Trck Mt Fnls; Cornell U; Ecnmcs.

PERKOV, MIA NICOLE; Bishop Montgomery HS; Rancho Palos Verd, CA; (2); Drama Clb; Service Clb; SADD; Cit Awd; High Hon Roll; Hon Roll; U SC; Acting.

PERKS, BRIAN DEAN; Culver City HS; Granada Hills, CA; (2); Band; Mrchg Band; Pep Band; School Musical; Cit Awd; Hon Roll; Stage Band; UCLA; EMT.

PERLAS, DENNIS O; Eagle Rock HS; Los Angeles, CA; (3); Pres Intnl Clb; Office Aide; Ski Clb; SADD; Teachers Aide; Temple Yth Grp; Band; Jazz Band; Variety Show; Ed Yrbk; SADD Poster Cont 1st Pl Wnnr; UCLA; Spcl Effcts Engr.

PERLAS, MARLO V; Notre Dame San Jose HS; San Jose, CA; (3); 20/100; Drama Clb; SADD; School Play; Rptr Nwsp; Rep Jr Cls; Var JV Bsktbl; Teachers Aide; High Hon Roll; NHS; Myrs Yth Conf; Athltc Blck; Loyola Marymount; Intl Cmnctns.

PERLEE, SUZANNE W; Sonora HS; Groveland, CA; (3); Girl Scts; Band; Sec Stu Cncl; Bsktbl; Powder Puff Ftbl; Sftbl; Vllybl; CSF; SFF; Bus.

PERLICHEK, JEFF; Liberty Union HS; Oakley, CA; (3); 34/400; Church Yth Grp; FCA; Letterman Clb; Ski Clb; SADD; Varsity Clb; Acpl Chr; Rep Stu Cncl; JV Socr; Var Swmmng; UC Santa Cruz; Pre-Medcl.

PERLIS, AMY H; San Rafael HS; San Rafael, CA; (2); JA; Temple Yth Grp; High Hon Roll; Muscl Theater; Lawyr.

PERLMAN, KENNETH S; Buena HS; Ventura, CA; (4); 26/500; Ed Nwsp; Var Swmmng; Pres Acad Fit Awd; Vrsty Water Polo; CSF Gold Sealbearer; David B Graham-Stella Brittingham Schlrshp; Demske Writing Awds; U Of CA San Diego.

PERLOVICH, YELENA; J F Kennedy HS; Granada Hills, CA; (3); English Clb; Key Clb; Library Aide; Teachers Aide; JV Swmmng; Hon Roll; Engl Achvt Awd; UCLA; Ed.

PERLROTH, JOSHUA D; Woodside HS; Portola Vly, CA; (3); 1/350; Intnl Clb; Var Crs Cntry; Var Trk; Bausch & Lomb Sci Awd; Med.

PERNARELLI, JENNIFER; Mammoth HS; Mammoth Lakes, CA; (3); 4/75; SADD; JV Var Tennis; Hon Roll.

PERONE JR, NESTOR LUIS; Mater Dei HS; Costa Mesa, CA; (4); 1/500; Drama Clb; ROTC; Intrml Socr; High Hon Roll; Jr NHS; NHS; Rotary Awd; Campus Mnstry; CSF; Air Force Assn JROTC Mdl; US Air Force Acad; Navigation.

PERONO, LEMUEL R; Ramona HS; Ramona, CA; (2); Church Yth Grp; JV Ftbl; Var Trk; Wt Lftg; High Hon Roll; Triple Superior-S W Musical Festvl; UNI; Engrng.

PEROSSIO, PILAR; Saddleback HS; Mission Viejo, CA; (4); Church Yth Grp; French Clb; FBLA; JA; Letterman Clb; Pep Clb; Drill Tm; Cheerldng; Gym; Score Keeper; Hmcmng Prncs; Prom Qn; Frnch Awds; UCLA; Lwyr.

PEROZZI, JEFF W; Greenville JR-SR HS; Taylorsville, CA; (3); 4-H; Yrbk; Var Bsbl; JV Var Ftbl; 4-H Awd; Mecn Engrng.

PERRAULT, JEFFREY M; Thousand Oaks HS; Thousand Oaks, CA; (2); 175/534; Rep Frsh Cls; Var Bsktbl; Wt Lftg; Hon Roll; Prfct Atten Awd; CYBA Bsktbl Team Coach; Bsktbl Smmr Camps Worker; Pro Hoopsters Clb; Phys Ed.

PERRETTA, JENNIFER N; Idyllwild Schl Of Music & The Arts; Idyllwild, CA; (4); Chorus; High Hon Roll; Hon Roll; Illustrated The Bk Undrstndng The Life Of Birds; Humboldt ST; Ornithology.

PERRI, JENNIFER; Irvine HS; Irvine, CA; (3); 92/512; Band; Mrchg Band; L Var Diving; JV Socr; Intrml Vllybl; Hon Roll; Pres Acad Fit Awd; Stu Math Tutor; Math.

PERRON, CELESTE; Santa Monica HS; Malibu, CA; (3); Church Yth Grp; French Clb; FBLA; Service Clb; Ed Nwsp; Hon Roll; Wellesley Book Awd; Natl Charity Leag 50 Hr Awd; Jrnlst.

PERRON, STEPHANIE F; Chaminade College Prep; Malibu, CA; (2); Church Yth Grp; Cmnty Wkr; Model UN; Pres Frsh Cls; VP Soph Cls; JV Swmmng; Hon Roll; Jr NHS; NHS; Georgetown.

PERRY, AMY; Orestimba HS; Crows Landing, CA; (2); Sec 4-H; SADD; Color Guard; Stat Trk; Vllybl; 4-H Awd; Hon Roll.

PERRY, CHRISTINA L; Tulare Western HS; Tulare, CA; (1); Art Clb; Church Yth Grp; Dance Clb; English Clb; FCA; GAA; Math Clb; Pep Clb; Science Clb; SADD; Arch.

PERRY, DANIEL E; Hayward HS; Hayward, CA; (3); VP German Clb; Teachers Aide; Acpl Chr; Band; Drm Mjr(t); Mrchg Band; Lit Mag; JV Crs Cntry; JV Tennis; Hon Roll; CSF; Exchnge Stu Germany.

PERRY, DAWANNA; Pinole Valley HS; Hercules, CA; (2); Hon Roll; The CA Schlrshp Fed.

PERRY, DENA M; Nevada Union HS; Nevada City, CA; (1); 64/589; Var L Cheerldng; Var L Pom Pon; Hon Roll; U CA Davis; Pediatrician.

PERRY, DORIT; California HS; San Ramon, CA; (2); 1/450; Cmnty Wkr; Drama Clb; Treas Intnl Clb; Service Clb; Temple Yth Grp; Thesps; School Play; Rptr Nwsp; Diving; High Hon Roll.

PERRY, DWIGHT E; Washington Prep HS; Los Angeles, CA; (3); Church Yth Grp; Teachers Aide; Church Choir; Color Guard; Bsktbl; Cit Awd; Chem Hnrs Awds; Hnr Rl; Oral Robert U; Bus.

PERRY, GINA M; Santa Clara HS; Santa Clara, CA; (3); Office Aide; JV Var Score Keeper; JV Sftbl; JV Swmmng; Cit Awd; Hon Roll; W Valley JC; Law Enfrcmnt.

PERRY, JEFF W; Hilmar HS; Hilmar, CA; (3); 10/90; Church Yth Grp; 4-H; FFA; Letterman Clb; Quiz Bowl; Spanish Clb; Bsbl; Ftbl; Wt Lftg; 4-H Awd; Jr CA Holstein Clb; CA Poly San Luis Obispo.

PERRY, JENNIFER; Borrego Springs HS; Borrego Springs, CA; (4); 2/26; Key Clb; Pres Frsh Cls; Pres Soph Cls; VP Jr Cls; Pres Sr Cls; Pres Stu Cncl; Bsktbl; Cheerldng; Sftbl; Pres Acad Fit Awd; U San Diego; Anthrplgy.

PERRY, JILL; Hillsdale HS; Foster City, CA; (4); 19/296; French Clb; Treas VP Soph Cls; VP Jr Cls; JV Swmmng; Hon Roll; Annesty Intl Pres; JR ST Men Of Amer; CA Schlrshp Fndtn; UC Berley; Bus.

PERRY, KATHLEEN M; Mission College Prep; Atascadero, CA; (3); Drama Clb; Chorus; School Play; Ed Yrbk; Sec Frsh Cls; JV Bsktbl; Score Keeper; JV Trk; JV Stat Vllybl; High Hon Roll; CSF.

PERRY, MARY K; Etiwanda HS; Alta Loma, CA; (2); Church Yth Grp; French Clb; Church Choir; High Hon Roll; Hon Roll; MO U Columbia; Fshn Mrchndsng.

PERRY, MATTHEW; Poway HS; Poway, CA; (3); Math Clb; Band; Mrchg Band; Pep Band; School Play; High Hon Roll; NHS; U Of C; Bus.

PERRY, MICHAEL J; Ukiah HS; Ukiah, CA; (3); Boy Scts; Chess Clb; Church Yth Grp; German Clb; SADD; JV Swmmng; Hon Roll; Pres Acad Fit Awd; Intl Karate Assn; Explorers Arcadia Police Dept; U CA-LOS Angeles; Law.

PERRY, NEELIA R; Orestimba HS; Gustine, CA; (3); Church Yth Grp; Office Aide; Pep Clb; ROTC; Teachers Aide; Bsktbl; Cheerldng; Trk; Hon Roll; Modesto JR Coll; Dental Asstg.

PERRY, RENEE; Fall River JR SR HS; Cassel, CA; (2); Art Clb; Church Yth Grp; Math Clb; Ski Clb; Band; VP Soph Cls; Stat Bsktbl; Crs Cntry; Score Keeper; JV Var Trk; Youth To Youth Teen Ldr; HOBY Alt; UCSB.

PERRY, ROCHELLE R; Warren HS; La Mirada, CA; (3); Teachers Aide; Band; Mrchg Band; Pep Band; Stat Bsktbl; JV Mgr(s); JV Var Trk; Hon Roll; NHS; Teaching.

PERRY, ROGER; Highlands HS; Sacramento, CA; (3); VP Soph Cls; Capt L Ftbl; Var L Golf; Powder Puff Ftbl; High Hon Roll; Hon Roll; Pres Acad Fit Awd; CSF; UC Davis; Elec Engrng.

PERRY, RYAN W; Pinole Valley HS; Hercules, CA; (1); Church Yth Grp; FCA; Swmmng; Hon Roll; Waterpolo; Mst Vlble Swmmr Pgm 89; Stanford U; Law.

PERRY, STEPHANIE D; Escalon HS; Linden, CA; (1); 2/158; Church Yth Grp; Pres Debate Tm; VP Pres 4-H; FFA; German Clb; SADD; Cit Awd; 4-H Awd; High Hon Roll; Hon Roll; Horse Showing; U C Davis; Vet.

PERRY, TIFFANY R; Hiram W Johnson HS; Sacramento, CA; (2); 27/182; Bus Profs of Am; Church Yth Grp; Red Cross Aide; Church Choir; Orch; Swmmng; Tennis; High Hon Roll; Hon Roll; Lifeguard; BYU.

PERRY, ZANNETTE A; Point Loma HS; San Diego, CA; (4); 1/442; ROTC; Drill Tm; DAR Awd; High Hon Roll; Hon Roll; NHS; Ntl Merit SF; Rotary Awd; Elec Engr.

PERRY THISTLE, NATHANIEL R; Nevada Union HS; Grass Valley, CA; (3); Cmnty Wkr; NFL; Pres Thesps; Acpl Chr; Chorus; Church Choir; School Musical; School Play; Stage Crew; Swing Chorus; Overseas Choir Tour Poland & USSR; Foothill Theater Co; Prfrmng Arts.

PERRYMAN, JOHNATHAN L; N Monteray County Unified Schl Dist; Castroville, CA; (2); SADD; Teachers Aide; Bsktbl; Ftbl; Trk; Wt Lftg; Cit Awd; Hon Roll; Pres Acad Fit Awd; Iron Man Awd Trck; MVP Ftbl; U NV-RENO; Pro Ftbl.

PERSONS, CHUCK; Cordova SR HS; Rancho Cordova, CA; (3); 103/462; Cmnty Wkr; Model UN; JV Bsbl; Capt Var Ftbl; JV Wrstlng; High Hon Roll; Hon Roll; NHS; Top 10 Stu Yr; Natl Hnr Soc Offcr; Bus.

PERSSON, SAMANTHA; Tracy Joint Union HS; Tracy, CA; (2); 89/264; Church Yth Grp; Drama Clb; French Clb; Girl Scts; Intnl Clb; Math Clb; Science Clb; SADD; Orch; School Musical; CSF; Goldn St Exam Alg I High Hnrs, Geom Hnrs; Crmnl Law.

PERVA, MARY A; Mclane HS; Fresno, CA; (1); Yrbk; Cit Awd; Prfct Atten Awd; Journ; Track; Chrldg; Wrtr.

PESH, SHAWN P; Beacon Christian HS; Foster City, CA; (1); Teachers Aide; Chorus; Stage Crew; Stu Cncl; Bsbl; Bsktbl; Socr; Tennis; Hon Roll; Pres Acad Fit Awd; UCLA; Med.

PESNILIAN, HAGOP; Schurr HS; Montebello, CA; (3); Chess Clb; Intnl Clb; Letterman Clb; Math Clb; Office Aide; Teachers Aide; Bsktbl; Wt Lftg; Wrstlng; Hon Roll; Bio.

PESTA, MICHELLE L; Porterville HS; Terra Bella, CA; (4); GAA; Library Aide; Band; Mrchg Band; Pep Band; Nwsp; Rptr Nwsp; Hon Roll; Uniform Clrk Band; Cap Mentor; Fnancl Scrtry Band; Vlntr At Rest Home; Fresno City Coll; Rdlgc Technen.

PESTANA, JOHN R; Serrano HS; Wrightwood, CA; (3); Boy Scts; Church Yth Grp; Band; Mrchg Band; Variety Show; Cit Awd; Hon Roll; Skiing Snow & Wtr; Comps; Snowbrdng; BYU Provo.

PESUTICH, JASON P; Bishop Montgomery HS; Harbor City, CA; (3); Art Clb; JA; Ftbl; Graphic Dsgn.

PETAGARA, MINETTE; Western HS; Anaheim, CA; (4); Drama Clb; Teachers Aide; School Play; Cit Awd; Hon Roll; Dramatcs Achvt Awd; Acad Achvt Awd; Med.

PETCHPOO, SUNISA; Los Amigos HS; Fountain Valley, CA; (2); Drama Clb; Teachers Aide; Thesps; School Play; Stage Crew; Hon Roll; Best Actress In A 1 Act Play; Travel Club; Educational Tour In France And England; Theatre Arts.

PETER, LAURA; Vintage HS; Napa, CA; (2); 37/500; Hosp Aide; Teachers Aide; Acpl Chr; Chorus; School Musical; Pom Pon; Cit Awd; 4-H Awd; Hon Roll; UCLA; Med.

PETERS, ANGELA M; Santa Barbara HS; Santa Barbara, CA; (3); Ed Nwsp; Rep Stu Cncl; High Hon Roll; Childcare Prog; Parent Clb Treas; Coll; Accntng.

PETERS, CHRISTINE M; Clear Lake HS; Lakeport, CA; (3); SADD; Teachers Aide; Pres Frsh Cls; Pres Soph Cls; Pres Jr Cls; Pres Sr Cls; Stu Cncl; Fld Hcky; Tennis; Trk; Stu Of Mnth Awd; Accntng.

PETERS, CHRISTOPHER M; Bishop O'dowd HS; Oakland, CA; (3); Church Yth Grp; Rep Frsh Cls; JV Var Bsktbl; JV Var Trk; Cit Awd; Hon Roll; Morehouse.

PETERS, CHRISTY S; Torrey Pines HS; Solana Beach, CA; (3); 89/457; Church Yth Grp; Score Keeper; Socr; Vllybl; High Hon Roll; Hon Roll; CSF; Sccr-1st Team Palomar League/CIF/Co-MVP League.

PETERS, DANIEL J; Kingsburg HS; Kingsburg, CA; (1); Chess Clb; Church Yth Grp; Band; Mrchg Band; Orch; Pep Band; Hon Roll; Pres Acad Fit Awd; Pres Schlr; AUC; Engrng.

PETERS, ELIZABETH C; Garles Memorial HS; Bakersfield, CA; (3); Church Yth Grp; Cmnty Wkr; Pep Clb; Science Clb; Service Clb; SADD; Rptr Nwsp; Hon Roll; Enterprise Clg; U Of San Diego; Bus.

PETERS, ERICA R; Hilmar HS; Hilmar, CA; (1); Church Yth Grp; Drama Clb; 4-H; FFA; Girl Scts; Pep Clb; SADD; Cheerldng; Sftbl; 4-H Awd; FFA Awds.

PETERS, ERIN K; Quincy HS; Quincy, CA; (2); Drama Clb; Ski Clb; Spanish Clb; Teachers Aide; School Play; VP Frsh Cls; VP Soph Cls; Rep Stu Cncl; JV Crs Cntry; JV Trk; Law.

PETERS, ERIN M; Ramona HS; Riverside, CA; (3); 92/403; Teachers Aide; Chorus; Sftbl; Hon Roll; Ntl Merit Ltr; UCR; Bus.

PETERS, JAMES R; Serrano HS; Phelan, CA; (1); JV Capt Bsbl; JV L Bsktbl; JV Var Ftbl; Wt Lftg; Hon Roll; Pres Acad Fit Awd; JV Ltr Ftbl & Bsbl; Notre Dame; Phys Ed.

PETERS, JENNIFER L; Eureka HS; Eureka, CA; (1); Cmnty Wkr; Dance Clb; Service Clb; Ski Clb; Chorus; Drill Tm; Orch; JV Cheerldng; Masonic Awd; Bowl-A-Thon Big Brthrs Big Sistrs; Sacramento ST; Math.

PETERS, JENNIFER L; Valhalla HS; El Cajon, CA; (1); Church Yth Grp; Speech Tm; Sec Frsh Cls; JV Cheerldng; JV Gym; Hon Roll; Psych.

PETERS, KATIE LYNN; Needles HS; Needles, CA; (2); 3/95; Church Yth Grp; FHA; Pres Key Clb; Band; Rep Soph Cls; Var Cheerldng; High Hon Roll; Kiwanis Awd; St Schlr; Voice Dem Awd; Eastern Star & Does For Pblc Solo Piano Perfmnc; UCSD; Commnctns.

PETERS, KELLY J; El Cajon HS; El Cajon, CA; (2); 4-H; Key Clb; Gym; Trk; Wt Lftg; Wrstlng; US SR Judo Champnshp 2nd Pl Womens Div 90; JR Olympic Judo Natl Champnshps 1st Pl 90; Toki U Japan; Zoology.

PETERS, LAURIE J; Liberty Union HS; Brentwood, CA; (3); 26/339; JV Pres Church Yth Grp; Rptr Debate Tm; VP French Clb; Treas FFA; Ed Yrbk; Pres Frsh Cls; Rep Stu Cncl; JV Bsktbl; JV Sftbl; Var Swmmng; CSF; FFA Chptr Swthrt; Brigham Young U.

PETERS, MICHAEL W; Napa HS; Napa, CA; (3); Computer Clb; Rptr Nwsp; Ed Lit Mag; St Schlr; RENS Comptn; U CA Berkeley; Music.

PETERS, RACHELLE; Brethren HS; La Palma, CA; (3); 1/60; Church Yth Grp; Math Tm; Acpl Chr; Band; Mrchg Band; Pep Band; School Play; High Hon Roll; CA Schlrshp Fed Six-Teens.

PETERS, REBECCA S; Willow Glen Educational Park HS; San Jose, CA; (2); Hosp Aide; SADD; Gym; Trk; UC Davis; Animal Sci.

PETERS, TINA A; Carlmont HS; Belmont, CA; (3); Chorus; Pres Acad Fit Awd.

PETERSEN, CARLEEN A; Ramona HS; Ramona, CA; (2); Treas 4-H; GAA; Pep Clb; Capt Socr; Vllybl; Cit Awd; 4-H Awd; Hon Roll; Prfct Atten Awd; Bst Dfnsv Awd-JV Socr 89-90; Ambssdr Clb; Raise Guide Dogs For Blind; U CA-SANTA Barbara; Orthpdcs.

PETERSEN, ERIC P; Torrey Pines HS; Encinitas, CA; (2); Scholastic Bowl; Ski Clb; High Hon Roll; Hon Roll; Yng At Art San Diego Museum Of Art 90.

PETERSEN, HENRY S; Eureka HS; Eureka, CA; (2); High Hon Roll; Med.

PETERSEN, JULI A; Ferndale HS; Loleta, CA; (2); Church Yth Grp; GAA; Math Tm; SADD; Treas Soph Cls; Pres Jr Cls; JV Bsktbl; JV Vllybl; Cal Poly.

PETERSEN, JULIE N; Durham HS; Oroville, CA; (2); Sec 4-H; GAA; Ski Clb; Rptr Yrbk; Rep Frsh Cls; VP Soph Cls; VP Jr Cls; JV Var Bsktbl; JV Var Trk; JV Var Vllybl; CSF Pres.

PETERSEN, KRISTIN; Flintridge Preparatory Schl; Pasadena, CA; (1); Pep Clb; Yrbk; VP Frsh Cls; JV Cheerldng; Var L Trk; Art.

PETERSON, AARON B; Indio HS; Indio, CA; (1); Aud/Vis; Computer Clb; FFA; Science Clb; Spanish Clb; Nwsp; High Hon Roll; JETS Awd; UC Berkeley; Comp Engrng.

PETERSON, AMANDA N; Miramonte HS; Orinda, CA; (1); JCL; Latin Clb; NFL; Speech Tm; Sec Frsh Cls.

PETERSON, ANNE M; Redwood Christian HS; Castro Valley, CA; (2); Church Yth Grp; Temple Yth Grp; Off Frsh Cls; Off Jr Cls; JV Capt Bsktbl; JV Stat Vllybl; Hon Roll; People To People HS Stu Ambassador Northern Europe 90; Bus.

PETERSON, APRIL J; Tustin HS; Tustin, CA; (2); Church Yth Grp; Pep Clb; Cheerldng; Gym; Trk; High Hon Roll; Hon Roll; New Life Clb; Wellesley; Med.

PETERSON, BECKY J; Redlands HS; Redlands, CA; (3); Letterman Clb; Varsity Clb; Bsktbl; Socr; Sftbl; Trk; Vllybl; Hon Roll; Acad Awds; Ed.

PETERSON, BRANDON E; Palma HS; Monterey, CA; (2); Var Bsbl; JV Bsktbl; High Hon Roll; NHS; Scholastic Athlete Award.

PETERSON, BRENT; Atascadero HS; Atascadero, CA; (3); Var Trk; Atty.

PETERSON, BRIAN A; Granada Hill HS; Northridge, CA; (3); Computer Clb; Debate Tm; JA; JV L Bsktbl; Var L Swmmng; High Hon Roll; Hon Roll; Yng Black Schlr; CSF; Peer Assistance Ctr Peer Cnslr; Med.

PETERSON, CARLA K; Saint Joseph Notre Dame HS; Alameda, CA; (3); JV Var Bsktbl; Var Sftbl; Var Tennis; Hon Roll; NHS; Prfct Atten Awd; St Schlr; Ed/Teacher.

PETERSON, CHRISTINE LYNN; Academy Of Our Lady Of Peace; San Diego, CA; (3); Hosp Aide; Chorus; School Musical; Rep Stu Cncl; Hon Roll; Treas NHS; Prfct Atten Awd; Acad Decathlon; Acad Leag; CSF.

PETERSON, CHRISTOPHER K; Apple Valley SR HS; Apple Valley, CA; (2); FBLA; German Clb; High Hon Roll; Jr Statesmen Of Amer; HS Wrtng Clb; Lawyer.

PETERSON, DANIEL C; Redwood Christian HS; San Lorenzo, CA; (4); Church Yth Grp; Office Aide; Teachers Aide; Band; Var Crs Cntry; Var Trk; High Hon Roll; Hon Roll; Ntl Merit SF.

PETERSON, DANIEL JAMES; Orland HS; Orland, CA; (4); 14/111; Boy Scts; Key Clb; Band; Ed Nwsp; Treas Sr Cls; Cit Awd; Elks Awd; Hon Roll; Egl Sct; CSF; Snta Clra U; Cmmctns.

PETERSON, DAVID; Marysville HS; Marysville, CA; (2); Treas Art Clb; Debate Tm; German Clb; SADD; Cit Awd; High Hon Roll; Hon Roll; Rotary Awd; Fri Night Live; CA ST U-Chico; Law.

PETERSON, ELAINE M; College Park HS; Pleasant Hill, CA; (3); 3/296; AFS; Am Leg Aux Girls St; Drama Clb; Letterman Clb; Chorus; School Musical; School Play; Lit Mag; Treas Soph Cls; Sec Rep Stu Cncl; Outstndng Soph & Jr Grl Awds; St PTA Bd Mgrs; Harvard Prz Bk Awd; PTSA Hlth Coord; Engl Curr Assoc; U Of CA; Law.

PETERSON, ERICKA D; Highlands HS; North Highlands, CA; (3); SADD; Teachers Aide; Band; Mrchg Band; Var JV Swmmng; Comp Sci.

PETERSON, GEORGE; Palo Verde Valley HS; Blythe, CA; (2); Church Yth Grp; FFA; Ed Nwsp; JV Wrstlng; Church Council; Aero Engr.

PETERSON, GLEN; Faith Christian HS; Yuba City, CA; (3); 1/20; Chess Clb; Church Yth Grp; 4-H; Quiz Bowl; Ski Clb; Pres Jr Cls; Sec Stu Cncl; Var Bsbl; Var Capt Bsktbl; Var Socr; CSF; Aerosp Engrng.

PETERSON, HEATHER E; Ventura HS; Ventura, CA; (2); Office Aide; JV Socr; JV Var Vllybl; Hon Roll; Natl AYSO Soccer Games Div II Grls 1st Pl.

PETERSON, JAMEY M; Montgomery HS; Santa Rosa, CA; (2); Spanish Clb; JV Var Wrstlng; Hon Roll; Jr NHS; Pres Acad Fit Awd; Santa Rosa Babe Ruth Bsbl; Santa Rosa JC.

PETERSON, JANEEN R; Pinole Valley HS; Hercules, CA; (3); Debate Tm; French Clb; NFL; Sftbl; Hon Roll; Boston U; Law.

PETERSON, JENNIFER CHRISTINE; Petaluma HS; Petaluma, CA; (2); Church Yth Grp; Cmnty Wkr; Pep Clb; Capt JV Cheerldng; JV Pom Pon; Hon Roll; U Of CO; Communctions.

PETERSON, JIM; James Logan HS; Union City, CA; (2); JV Bsbl; JV Bsktbl; Sr Babe Ruth; Airplane Mech.

PETERSON, JULIE; Rosary HS; Brea, CA; (3); French Clb; VP Soph Cls; Var Bsktbl; Var Vllybl; Pres Acad Fit Awd; Pres Schlr; Rotary Awd; Bus.

PETERSON, KARINA; Bonita Vista HS; Bonita, CA; (4); Art Clb; Intnl Clb; Chorus; Rcvd Various Schlrshp & Ctznshp Awds Flag Escort; UCSD; Bus.

PETERSON, KATIE A; Sacred Heart Prep; Menlo Park, CA; (2); Model UN; Service Clb; Thesps; Chorus; School Musical; School Play; Ed Lit Mag; Var JV Cheerldng; Hon Roll; Millord Fillmore Trivia Clb; Amnesty Intl; Writer.

PETERSON, KRISTA; El Rancho HS; Whittier, CA; (4); 7/450; Am Leg Aux Girls St; Drama Clb; Pep Clb; Capt Drill Tm; School Play; Variety Show; Rep Frsh Cls; Treas Stu Cncl; Co-Capt Pom Pon; High Hon Roll; UC Santa Barbara.

PETERSON, KRISTIN; Capistrano Valley Christian HS; Mission Viejo, CA; (4); 1/69; Church Yth Grp; Cmnty Wkr; Yrbk; Var Socr; JV Trk; Dnfth Awd; High Hon Roll; Pres Acad Fit Awd; CA Schlrshp Fed Treas; Discipleship; Bio Ped.

PETERSON, LEAH; Louisville HS; Westlake Village, CA; (3); Cmnty Wkr; French Clb; FHA; Hosp Aide; Key Clb; Stage Crew; High Hon Roll; NHS; Frnch Plys Wn Awds; Camp Cnslr.

PETERSON, LYNN M; Redwood Christian HS; San Lorenzo, CA; (2); Church Yth Grp; Teachers Aide; School Play; Sec Frsh Cls; Sec Jr Cls; JV Bsktbl; Var Tennis; Var Trk; High Hon Roll; Pltcl Sci.

PETERSON, MATTHEW N; Villa Park HS; Orange, CA; (3); Key Clb; High Hon Roll; NHS; CSF; Marine Bio.

PETERSON, MICAH R; Valley Christian HS; Downey, CA; (1); Church Yth Grp; Hon Roll; CAL ST U; Music.

PETERSON, MICHAEL B; Armona Union Acad; Hanford, CA; (3); Church Yth Grp; Rptr Nwsp; Yrbk; VP Soph Cls; Ftbl; Socr; Sftbl; Vllybl; Hon Roll; Prfct Atten Awd; Pacific Union Coll.

PETERSON, MICHELLE; Grossmont HS; Andover, MN; (1); Dance Clb; Cit Awd; Hon Roll; Prfct Atten Awd.

PETERSON, MIKE; Mammoth HS; Mammoth Lakes, CA; (2); 1/61; Cmnty Wkr; Drama Clb; Hosp Aide; Math Tm; Scholastic Bowl; Thesps; Band; Chorus; Jazz Band; School Musical; Ice Hockey; Cmnty Drama & Music Productions; Dstngshd Schlr All Acad Areas; Brown; Med.

PETERSON, MIKE D; Bonita HS; La Verne, CA; (3); 24/296; Church Yth Grp; German Clb; Office Aide; Varsity Clb; Var Bsktbl; Var Crs Cntry; Var Ftbl; Var Trk; Pres Acad Fit Awd; Brigham Young U.

PETERSON, MORGAN A; Nevada Union HS; Grass Valley, CA; (3); 8/550; Ski Clb; School Musical; School Play; Rep Jr Cls; JV Powder Puff Ftbl; Var Trk; High Hon Roll; Pre Med.

PETERSON, NIKKI; Christian HS; El Cajon, CA; (3); Church Yth Grp; Cmnty Wkr; Key Clb; Library Aide; Pep Clb; Ski Clb; Orch; Ed Yrbk; VP Swmmng; High Hon Roll; Counslng.

PETERSON, PAIGE K; Torrey Pines HS; Del Mar, CA; (3); 144/457; SADD; Rptr Nwsp; Var Tennis; CSF; Commnctns.

PETERSON, RAYMOND; Bishop Amat Memorial HS; West Covina, CA; (3); Am Leg Boys St; Boy Scts; Band; Mrchg Band; High Hon Roll; NHS; Ntl Merit SF; Prfct Atten Awd; Amateur Radio Tech Class License; Law.

PETERSON, REBECCA A; Santiago HS; Garden Grove, CA; (2); Color Guard; Drm Mjr(t); Mrchg Band; Var Crs Cntry; JV Fld Hcky; Var Trk; Schlr Athlete; Aeronautics.

PETERSON, RENA; Rio Vista HS; Isleton, CA; (3); FHA; Pep Clb; Science Clb; Chorus; JV Var Cheerldng; High Hon Roll; Hon Roll; Friday Night Live Clb; Bus Admin.

PETERSON, STEPHEN L; Burbank HS; Burbank, CA; (3); Var JV Tennis; Pres Acad Fit Awd; Teachers Aide; Cmptr Sci.

PETERSON, SVEA K; Clovis HS; Clovis, CA; (2); Church Yth Grp; Drama Clb; FCA; Chorus; Church Choir; School Musical; Swing Chorus; High Hon Roll; Pres Acad Fit Awd; ACDA Western Div Hnr Choir; Fresno Cnty Hnr Choir; VCC Yth Grp Ldrshp 2 Yrs; Wheaton; Perf Arts.

PETERSON, TAMARA L; Palm Springs HS; Desert Hot Spring, CA; (3); 3/533; Church Yth Grp; Cmnty Wkr; Varsity Clb; Var L Bsktbl; Var L Crs Cntry; Var L Trk; Cit Awd; Elks Awd; High Hon Roll; Prfct Atten Awd; Acad Awds 4.0 GPA; Prncpls Awds-Hghst GPA Vrsty Bsktbl; Chrch Vlntr Mexico; UC Davis; Envrnmntl Txclgy.

PETERSON, TERESA; Palmdale HS; Acton, CA; (2); 52/870; Church Yth Grp; Pep Clb; Ski Clb; Flag Corp; Stu Cncl; JV Capt Cheerldng; Gym; Sftbl; Wt Lftg; Hstrn Keynettes Club; San Diego; Pub Rel.

PETERSON, TRACI; Palo Verde HS; Blythe, CA; (2); Church Yth Grp; Dance Clb; Drama Clb; School Musical; School Play; Cheerldng; Golf; High Hon Roll; Kiwanis Awd; NHS; CA Schlstc Federation; Brigham Young U.

PETERSON-TURNER, MELISSA; Serrano HS; Apple Valley, CA; (4); Boy Scts; Church Yth Grp; DECA; FCA; FBLA; FFA; FHA; Pep Clb; SADD; Teachers Aide; MS ST U; Brdcstng Commnctns.

PETIKIAN, MARIAM A; Armenian Mesrobian HS; Montebello, CA; (2); Drama Clb; Bus Mgmt.

PETREQUIN, BRYAN J; Santa Teresa HS; San Jose, CA; (2); French Clb; JA; Science Clb; High Hon Roll; Jr NHS; Hgh Hnrs Alg I Gldn St Exam; CSF; UCLA; Bus.

PETRIG, HEATHER D; Lemoore Union HS; Lemoore, CA; (3); 1/323; Church Yth Grp; VP Sec FCA; Spanish Clb; School Play; Var Crs Cntry; Var Capt Diving; High Hon Roll; Physcs Clb; Photo Clb; CSF; Med Doc.

PETROCELLI, BRIAN R; Sunny Hills HS; Fullerton, CA; (3); Church Yth Grp; Pep Clb; Ski Clb; Spanish Clb; Phtg Yrbk; Rep Stu Cncl; Diving; DAR Awd; Hon Roll; ASB Rep Outstndng Achvt Awd 89-90; CA Poly-San Luis; Bus Mgmt.

PETROSSIAN, VAHE; Crescenta Valley HS; La Crescenta, CA; (3); Boy Scts; Chess Clb; Computer Clb; French Clb; Letterman Clb; Math Clb; Mu Alpha Theta; JV L Crs Cntry; Var L Trk; Pres Acad Fit Awd; UCLA; Physics.

PETROSYAN, HERMINE; Burbank HS; Burbank, CA; (3); Bio.

PETROW, REGINA M; Bishop Manogue HS; Sacramento, CA; (1); High Hon Roll; Hon Roll; Jr NHS; NHS; Prfct Atten Awd; Gen Excllnc Awd World Hstry, Span I; Hnr Rl Cert; CA ST U; Ed.

PETRUCCI, STEFANIE; Madera HS; Madera, CA; (2); Sec 4-H; SADD; School Musical; Variety Show; Sec Soph Cls; Cheerldng; 4-H Awd; Hon Roll; Interact Club; Fresno ST U; Interior Decrtng.

PETRY, ANDREA L; Newport Harbor HS; Santa Ana, CA; (2); Drill Tm; Ed Nwsp; Whos Who Among Amer Hs Stdnts Last Yr; U Of CA; Ed.

PETTEE, MARTIN; Wm S Hart HS; Newhall, CA; (4); FBLA; Yrbk; Intrml JV Ftbl; JV Var Swmmng; Ftbl Capt; Cal Poly SLO; Constructn Mgmt.

PETTEWAY, KENYA D; A Hamilton HS; Los Angeles, CA; (2); Church Yth Grp; Dance Clb; Drill Tm; Variety Show; Prfct Atten Awd; Music Adad; UC Santa Barbara; Bus Econ.

PETTEY, STEVE R; Branham HS; San Jose, CA; (4); Var L Lcrss; JV Bsktbl; Var L Ftbl; High Hon Roll; NHS; Booster Clb Schlrshp; PTA Schlrshp; All-League Ftbl & Bsbl; U Of AZ; Bus.

PETTEYS, GLENN D; Santa Barbara HS; Santa Barbara, CA; (2); 50/450; VP German Clb; Stage Crew; Yrbk; JV Swmmng; Intrml Wt Lftg; Hon Roll; Music; UCSC; Frgn Lang.

PETTIBON, KRISTINA L; Clovis West HS; Fresno, CA; (3); SADD; Drill Tm; Powder Puff Ftbl; Hon Roll; Tap & Jazz Dance; Fresno Jazz Co 2 Perfromances 89; Bus.

PETTIBONE, CAROLYN N; Cupertino HS; Cupertino, CA; (2); Church Yth Grp; Cmnty Wkr; Debate Tm; Drama Clb; School Play; Hon Roll; CA Schlrshp Fdrtn; Intrct Clb; Bio.

PETTIGREW, MICHAEL; Valhalla HS; El Cajon, CA; (2); JV Bsbl; JV Bsktbl; Law.

PETTIGREW, MICHAEL A; Roseville HS; Roseville, CA; (1); Church Yth Grp; Math Clb; Math Tm; Office Aide; Socr; High Hon Roll; Sacramento ST; Engrng.

PETTINGILL, BARBARA A; Dublin HS; Dublin, CA; (3); Rep Frsh Cls; Pres Soph Cls; Off Sr Cls; Capt Var Bsktbl; Socr; Var Sftbl; Var Tennis; Hon Roll; Teachers Aide; Jnr Vrsty Bsktbl MVP; Golden St Exam Alg Hnrs; Phys Thrpst.

PETTIT, AUDRA; Santa Rosa HS; Santa Rosa, CA; (1); Pep Clb; Spanish Clb; Band; School Musical; School Play; Rptr Yrbk; Cheerldng; Cit Awd; Hon Roll; Honor Soc; Optimist Clb.

PETTIT, ERICA J; Pacific HS; San Bernardino, CA; (1); Church Yth Grp; Cmnty Wkr; Church Choir; Swmmng; Won Writing Celebrtn; San Diego ST U; Marine Bio.

PETTIT, GINGER L; Paraclete HS; Lancaster, CA; (2); Church Yth Grp; Drama Clb; French Clb; Hosp Aide; SADD; School Play; Variety Show; Vllybl; Hon Roll; Fshn Inst Of Dsgn; Intr Dec.

PETTIT, RYAN; Monte Vista HS; Diablo, CA; (2); Boy Scts; Church Yth Grp; French Clb; Science Clb; SADD; Bsbl; Ftbl; Wt Lftg; Hon Roll; Pres Acad Fit Awd; U CA; Bus.

PETTITT, SCOTT R; Santa Teresa HS; San Jose, CA; (3); Pres Science Clb; Spanish Clb; Stu Cncl; Var Ftbl; Var Bausch & Lomb Sci Awd; Cit Awd; Hon Roll; Pres Acad Fit Awd; Bus Adm.

PETTUS, CHRYSTAL; Lower Lake HS; Lower Lake, CA; (3); Am Leg Aux Girls St; English Clb; VP French Clb; GAA; Ed Nwsp; Sec Frsh Cls; Sec Soph Cls; Sec Jr Cls; JV Var Bsktbl; Score Keeper; Schlr Athl; Bch Vllybl Team Coordinator; Estrn Carolina U; Forestry.

PETTUS, TOBY; Apple Valley Christian HS; Hesperia, CA; (1); 1/25; Var Bsbl; Var Bsktbl; Cit Awd; High Hon Roll; Finish Carpentry, Many Const Trades; Aviation; Aviation.

PETTWAY, DOUGLAS; Cajon HS; San Bernardino, CA; (2); Church Yth Grp; Church Choir; Playing Piano & Guitar; Aero Engrng.

PETTY, RENAE M; San Marcos HS; Santa Barbara, CA; (1); Church Yth Grp; SADD; JV Vllybl; Yth Vllybl Assn 1st Tm; Statscn Var Vllybl Tm; Friday Night Live; CA Poly; Acctnt.

PETTY, SHAWN G; Fontana HS; Fontana, CA; (2); Ftbl; Mgr(s); Wt Lftg; Bus.

PETUNIS, JOE M; Del Campo HS; Fair Oaks, CA; (3); 96/446; Var L Trk; Trpl A Awd Trck.

PETZOLDT, ERIC E; Valencia HS; Placentia, CA; (3); Cmnty Wkr; Science Clb; Var L Bsbl; Var L Bsktbl; Cit Awd; Hon Roll; Lion Awd; Civil Air Patrol C/Tsgt; US Space Camp Acad II Rght Stuff Awd; Placentia Political Cmpgn Wrkr; Wichita ST U; Aviation Mgmt.

PEWITT, JANITH M; Vacaville HS; Vacaville, CA; (4); Church Yth Grp; French Clb; VP JA; Model UN; Golf; High Hon Roll; Dist Awd Natl Fr Test; Rotary Intl Exch Stu France; Work.

PHILLIPS, TIFFANY N; Apple Valley HS; Apple Valley, CA; (1); Drama Clb; Speech Tm; Drill Tm; Swing Chorus; Cit Awd; Hon Roll; Opt Clb Awd; Optimist Speech Comptn 1st Pl; Drill Tm & Choral Awds; Long Beach U; Mktg.

PHILLIPS, TIPHANIE J; Valley View HS; Moreno Valley, CA; (1); 1/550; Church Yth Grp; Co-Ed Yrbk; Lit Mag; Rep Stu Cncl; Var Capt Bsktbl; Var L Crs Cntry; Var L Trk; High Hon Roll; Gldn St Exam-1st Algebra; CSF; Mst Vlble Plyr Cross-Cntry & Bsktbl; Division I U; Bio.

PHILLIPS, TODD A; Victor Valley HS; Las Vegas, NV; (2); 39/605; Hon Roll; Intrmrl Hcky Leag; Schl Recgntn Goldn St Exm Alg; Geom St Hnrs Gldn St Exm; UCLA; Engrng.

PHILLIPS, TRISHA; Locke HS; San Pedro, CA; (4); 1/168; Am Leg Aux Girls St; Scholastic Bowl; Teachers Aide; Church Choir; Drill Tm; School Play; Sec Sr Cls; Stu Cncl; Capt Trk; Val; Stanford U; Pre-Med.

PHILLIPS, VICKI L; Hiram W Johnson HS; Sacramento, CA; (2); 52/180; Girl Scts; ROTC; Teachers Aide; Color Guard; Hon Roll; ROTA Natl Awd Dghtrs Of Fndrs Patriots Amer; Tchr.

PHILLIPS-WING, JASON R; Hoover HS; Fresno, CA; (1); Band; Jazz Band; Orch; JV Bsbl; JV Ftbl; High Hon Roll; Pres Acad Fit Awd; Golden St Schlr Hnrs; U Of TX; Math.

PHILLIPSEN, ERICA L; Alameda HS; Alameda, CA; (4); 8/340; Band; Mrchg Band; Var Capt Socr; Var Swmmng; Water Polo Tm; Acad Clb CSF; U CA.

PHILPOTT, MICHAEL J; University Of San Diego HS; San Diego, CA; (3); Ski Clb; Archetecture Schl; Arch.

PHIMISTER, ANDREW J; Oakridge HS; Shingle Springs, CA; (3); 2/256; Debate Tm; Spanish Clb; Ftbl; Wt Lftg; High Hon Roll; U Of San Diego; Med.

PHIMMASONE, DAVANH; Mission HS; San Francisco, CA; (1); Wrld Civilztn Hnr.

PHIMPASATH, KHANHKEO; A A Stagg HS; Stockton, CA; (4); Dance Clb; Drama Clb; English Clb; FBLA; Office Aide; Temple Yth Grp; Band; Bsktbl; Vllybl; High Hon Roll.

PHIMSIPASOM, PHAINGEUN C; San Bernardino HS; San Bernardino, CA; (3); Art Clb; Intnl Clb; JA; Math Clb; SADD; JV Ftbl; JV Tennis; High Hon Roll; Hon Roll; Jr NHS; Natl Hon Art Clb; Asion Clb; Hunger Buster Clb; UCR; Pediatrcn.

PHINEAS, CARRIE; Phineas Banning HS; Lomita, CA; (3); Dance Clb; Ski Clb; Rep Nwsp; Yrbk; Pres Frsh Cls; Var Capt Cheerldng; Var Sftbl; High Hon Roll; Close-Up; Most Imsprtnl Sftbl; Syracuse U NY; Bus.

PHIPPS, ANTHONY M; De La Salle HS; Concord, CA; (3); Cmnty Wkr; Office Aide; Service Clb; Ski Clb; Rep Frsh Cls; Rep Sr Cls; JV Bsktbl; Var Vllybl; High Hon Roll; NHS; Bus.

PHIPPS, BRENDA C; Moorpark HS; Moorpark, CA; (2); FHA; Hosp Aide; Yrbk; Bsktbl; Sftbl; Hon Roll; Bst Offnse Bsktbl; Mst Dedctd Plyr Bsktbl; Bst Defnsve Plyr Sftbl; Pres FHA; Moorpark JC; Reg Nurse.

PHIPPS, DAVE M; Strathmore HS; Strathmore, CA; (3); 18/83; Church Yth Grp; FFA; Var Bsktbl; Cit Awd; High Hon Roll; Forestry Svc.

PHIPPS, RON L; Elsinore HS; Canyon Lanke, CA; (3); Cmnty Wkr; Letterman Clb; Math Clb; ROTC; Teachers Aide; Varsity Clb; Var L Ftbl; L Capt Golf; JV Var Tennis; Wt Lftg; Top 10% Schl Acad; Vlntry Cmnty Svc; Pre-Med.

PHISTER, BECKY L; Davis SR HS; Davis, CA; (2); Church Yth Grp; Pres Stu Cncl; Var Tennis; JV Trk; Hon Roll; Pres Acad Fit Awd; Rotary Awd; Cmnty Wkr; Ski Clb; Spanish Clb; Mayors Drug Task Force; Holland Tennis Exchng; City Yth Entertainment Brd; Schl Advsry Cmmttee-Stu Rep; Atty.

PHLAUM, JASON; Palm Desert HS; La Quinta, CA; (2); Church Yth Grp; High Hon Roll; Hon Roll; Club Proj Pursuit Awd For Desert Beautiful Awd; UCLA.

PHO, HOEUY S; Lincoln HS; Stockton, CA; (3); #104 In Class; Hon Roll; Delta Clg; Comp Prgrmr.

PHO, LING; George Washington HS; San Francisco, CA; (2); Service Clb; Ski Clb; Hon Roll; Chinese Amer Club; Vlybl Clb; U CA Davis.

PHOMMACHALY, BOUNHAK T; A A Stagg HS; Stockton, CA; (4); Church Yth Grp; Office Aide; Teachers Aide; High Hon Roll; Hon Roll; Prfct Atten Awd; Indo-Chinese Club; Delta Coll San Joaquin; Nrsg.

PHOMMASY, CHANPASONG; Sweetwater HS; National City, CA; (3); Cit Awd; Hon Roll; Prfct Atten Awd; Acad Awd & Hnr Rl Soph.

PHOMSOPHA, BOUNLAHONG M; Orestimba HS; Newman, CA; (2); 1/96; Church Yth Grp; VP Science Clb; Band; Band; Pep Band; Treas Soph Cls; JV Capt Crs Cntry; Var Tennis; Hon Roll; CSF; UC Davis; Pre-Med.

PHOMSOPHA, JAMES C; River City HS; West Sacramento, CA; (3); Church Yth Grp; Cmnty Wkr; Key Clb; Natl Beta Clb; Ftbl; Socr; Vllybl; High Hon Roll; JETS Awd; Prfct Atten Awd; CSF Secy; Math Engrng Sci Achvt Club; Acadmc Dcthln; Engrng.

PHOMVONGSA, NOURATH; Lodi HS; Stockton, CA; (3); Church Yth Grp; FBLA; Temple Yth Grp; Ftbl; Trk; Hon Roll; UC Davis; Bus.

PHONGMANY, XAY; Foothill HS; N Highlands, CA; (2); French Clb; JV Socr; Asian Club; CSF; Science Club; CSUS; Teacher; Comp Programmer.

PHONGSAIPHONH, PAULEE; River City HS; West Sacramento, CA; (3); Key Clb; Hon Roll; Prfct Atten Awd; Multi-Cultural Club; Bus.

PHONGSAMRAN, PAULA; St Genevieve HS; Sun Valley, CA; (3); French Clb; Socr; Unity Clb; CSF; Biolgcl Sci.

PHONTHONGSY, PAM; Santa Ynez Valley Union HS; Buellton, CA; (3); 17/160; FBLA; Pep Clb; Spanish Clb; Drill Tm; Yrbk; Pom Pon; Sign Lang Clb; UCSB; Accntnt.

PHONTHONGSY, SIPHOUANGKHAM P; Santa Ynez Valley HS; Goleta, CA; (3); 17/106; VP FBLA; Pep Clb; Yrbk; Var Co-Capt Cheerldng; Pom Pon; Lang Clb; UCA All Star Chrldr; Piano; SBCC; Lang.

PHOTINOS, NICHOLAS; College Park HS; Concord, CA; (2); Model UN; Band; Jazz Band; Mrchg Band; Hon Roll; Pres Acad Fit Awd; Diablo Yth Symphny; Oakland Yth Symphny; Music.

PHOUANGPHET, MALAI; Hoover HS; Fresno, CA; (1).

PHOUTHARATH, VANECHAY; Modesto HS; Modesto, CA; (2); Dance Clb; French Clb; Intnl Clb; Teachers Aide; Orch; Bsktbl; Cit Awd; Hon Roll; Prfct Atten Awd; San Jose ST; Law Enfrcmnt.

PHOUTHAVONG, PHOULAMNAO; Duncan Polytech HS; Fresno, CA; (2); Hon Roll; Prfct Atten Awd; Comp Anlys.

PHU, KIET M; Eagle Rock HS; Los Angeles, CA; (2); Pres Key Clb; Band; Hon Roll; Fshn.

PHU, LINH M; Baldwin Park HS; Baldwin Park, CA; (4); Spanish Clb; SADD; Yrbk; Stu Cncl; Hon Roll; Keywanettes; Hnr Soc; Upward Bound; U Of CA Irvine; Psych.

PHU, MINH N; Eagle Rock HS; Los Angeles, CA; (3); Sec Key Clb; Sec SADD; Mrchg Band; Ed Yrbk; Hon Roll; CSF; Tchr.

PHU, PHAN T; Lowell HS; San Francisco, CA; (2); Science Clb; High Hon Roll; Fest Vlntr; Arch.

PHUNG, ANN H; San Gabriel HS; S San Gabriel, CA; (2); Hon Roll; Prfct Atten Awd; CSF; UC Irvine; Pdtrcn.

PHUNG, HARRISON H; Galileo HS; San Francisco, CA; (4); Cit Awd; Hon Roll; St Schlr; OSU.

PHUNG, JACQUELINE H; Don Antonio Lugo HS; Chino, CA; (2); Church Yth Grp; German Clb; Key Clb; SADD; Teachers Aide; Rep Frsh Cls; JV Crs Cntry; Var Mgr(s); JV Trk; World Civilztns Clss Cls Rep; Ldrshp Invlmnt; Law.

PHUNG, JOHN O; Cleveland Humanities HS; Canoga Park, CA; (3); Boy Scts; Chess Clb; Cmnty Wkr; Ski Clb; VICA; JV Ftbl; Var Swmmng; JV Vllybl; Hon Roll; Natl VICA Rep CA Ldrshp; Aviation.

PHUNG, LIEM; Rosemead HS; Rosemead, CA; (1); Chorus; Swmmng; High Hon Roll; Tennis; Governrs Hnr Pgm; Devt Test Awd; Secy.

PHUNG, LINH M; San Gabriel HS; Alhambra, CA; (2); Hon Roll; UCLA; Medcl Tech.

PHUNG, LISA T; Saddleback HS; Santa Ana, CA; (3); Chess Clb; English Clb; Sec Treas French Clb; Science Clb; High Hon Roll; Slvr Mdl Frgn Lang; Acad Awds.

PHUNG, PHAN T; Mark Keppel HS; Monterey Park, CA; (2); Math Clb; Stage Crew; Lit Mag; Stat Bsktbl; Cit Awd; High Hon Roll; Prfct Atten Awd; Badminton,Mbr CA Schlrshp Fdrtn; UCLA; Education.

PHUNG, SON P; Luezinger HS; Hawthorne, CA; (3); Computer Clb; 4-H; Treas Key Clb; Science Clb; L Var Crs Cntry; L Var Trk; 4-H Awd; Gov Hon Prg Awd; High Hon Roll; Pres Acad Fit Awd; Cross-Cntry & Track Boys Var Acad Athlete 90; Jr Class Spelling Bee Champ 90; Peer Tutorer; UCLA; Mechncl Engrng.

PHUNG, THAI K; Fremont HS; Sunnyvale, CA; (4); DECA; Spanish Clb; Teachers Aide; Gov Hon Prg Awd; NHS; U CA Irvine; Comp Sci.

PHUNG, THANH; Saddleback HS; Santa Ana, CA; (3); Drama Clb; Spanish Clb; Thesps; School Play; Var Tennis; William & Mary Coll; Bus.

PHUNG, VAN; Saddleback HS; Santa Ana, CA; (1); Spanish Clb; Var Tennis; Elks Awd; CSF.

PHUONG, LUCY O; Mt Pleasant HS; San Jose, CA; (1); Math Clb; Rep Stu Cncl; High Hon Roll; Stanford; Med.

PHUONG, PATTY; Helix HS; La Mesa, CA; (3); 58/448; Drama Clb; French Clb; Hosp Aide; VP Intnl Clb; Key Clb; Speech Tm; Var Tennis; Var Trk; Hon Roll; Fashion & Self-Image Club; CSF; Astronomy/Sci; U Of CA Irvine; Medical.

PHUONG, SUZANNE H; George Washington HS; San Francisco, CA; (3); Teachers Aide; Rep Frsh Cls; Rep Soph Cls; 4-H Awd; High Hon Roll; Hon Roll; Chinese Clb Secy 88; Hmerm Rep 88 & 89; Long Beach; Bus.

PHUONG, TRACY; Saddleback HS; Santa Ana, CA; (2); French Clb; Tennis; Art; Vietnamese Clb; Badminton.

PIASECKI, DEREK A; San Marcos HS; Santa Barbara, CA; (2); Aud/Vis; Computer Clb; Math Clb; Math Tm; Band; Jazz Band; Mrchg Band; Orch; Pep Band; School Musical; Comp Prgmmng; Music; Elec Engr.

PICAR, EMILY I; Bakersfield HS; Bakersfield, CA; (2); Orch; Cal Poly U; Med Tech.

PICAZO, MARLENE; Hanford Union HS; Hanford, CA; (2); 17/521; FBLA; English Clb; FCA; Math Engrng Sci Achvt; CSF; Acad Awd; U CA Davis; Bus Mgmt.

PICAZO, ROSEMARY R; Hanford Joint Union HS; Hanford, CA; (3); 38/452; Library Aide; Rptr Nwsp; Prfct Atten Awd; Hnr Roll 88-90; High Hnr Roll 89-90; Acadmc Ltr & Awd 88-90; CSF; Cert Awd Outstndng Sci 89; Psych.

PICENO, ABIGAIL; San Jose High Acad; San Jose, CA; (3); ROTC; Hon Roll; Word Processor.

PICENO, LEYLAN; Calexico HS; Calexico, CA; (2); French Clb; Drill Tm; Cit Awd; Hon Roll; Imperial Valley Coll; Law Enfcm.

PICHARDO, ANTHONY R; Amos Alanzo Stagg HS; Stockton, CA; (1); Drama Clb; Treas Key Clb; NFL; Spanish Clb; Speech Tm; Thesps; School Musical; School Play; Stage Crew; Kiwanis Awd; Delta Coll; Lawyer.

PICHARDO, DORIS B; Richard Gahr HS; Artesia, CA; (3); FBLA; Spanish Clb; Hon Roll.

PICHARDO, LISSETT D; Hawthorne HS; Hawthorne, CA; (3); Am Leg Aux Girls St; Pres Key Clb; Pres Stu Cncl; Stat Bsktbl; Stat Sftbl; JV Vllybl; Hon Roll; Kiwanis Awd; YMCA Yth In Govt; Peer/Tutoring Cnsl; Key Clbbr Of Yr 89; Outstndng Soph Of Stu Cncl; Atty.

PICHARDO, PAUL M; A A Stagg HS; Stockton, CA; (3); FBLA; Key Clb; NFL; Spanish Clb; Thesps; Stage Crew; Ed Nwsp; Off Sr Cls; Hon Roll; Kiwanis Awd; Co Found & Pres Anime Club; Tech Work & Light Deltz Coll Musical; Stagg High Acad Decathlon Team; Cornell U; Physics.

PICHELMAYER, CATHERINE B; Samuel F B Morse HS; San Diego, CA; (4); 116/583; Library Aide; Lit Mag; Hon Roll; Jr NHS; NHS; Med.

PICK, CHRISTOPHER J; Carlmont HS; Belmont, CA; (2); Chess Clb; Computer Clb; Acad Excllnce Awd; Comp Prgmr.

PICKEL, JED M; Mission Viejo HS; Mission Viejo, CA; (2); Church Yth Grp; Cmnty Wkr; Intnl Clb; Key Clb; Model UN; Spanish Clb; SADD; Var Crs Cntry; Var L Trk; High Hon Roll; CSF.

PICKEL, JENNY E; Mission Viejo HS; Mission Viejo, CA; (4); Church Yth Grp; Cmnty Wkr; French Clb; Model UN; SADD; Chorus; Crs Cntry; Trk; Hon Roll; NHS; Intl Baccalourate; U CA Davis.

PICKENS, CLAIRE; Sonoma Valley HS; Glen Ellen, CA; (1); 4-H; JV Bsktbl; Var Crs Cntry; Var Trk; High Hon Roll; MVP Trk; Arch.

PICKENS, HEATHER; Jordan HS; Long Beach, CA; (2); Church Yth Grp; Drama Clb; Thesps; Church Choir; Capt Drill Tm; School Play; Var Gym; DAR Awd; Pres Acad Fit Awd; Fairfield YMCA Awd; Teacher.

PICKENS, JOSEPH A; Tehachapi HS; Keene, CA; (3); Church Yth Grp; Key Clb; Letterman Clb; Band; Orch; JV Var Bsktbl; JV Var Crs Cntry; Var Trk; Hon Roll; Friday Night Live, Drug & Alcohol Awareness Club; Acad Teacher.

PICKENS, MARKISE D; Baldwin Park HS; Baldwin Park, CA; (2); Boy Scts; Letterman Clb; ROTC; Teachers Aide; Band; Jazz Band; Mrchg Band; Pep Band; Rep Stu Cncl; JV Bsktbl; USC.

PICKENS, SUZANNE L; Liberty Christian HS; Huntington Bch, CA; (2); 1/27; Church Yth Grp; Chorus; Church Choir; School Musical; Var Bsktbl; Sftbl; Cit Awd; High Hon Roll; Prfct Atten Awd; Athl Of God Awd; 1st Pl Piano Cmptn PC Extravaganza; Liberty; Teacher.

PICKEREL, VENESSA; Mt Shasta HS; Mt Shasta, CA; (4); Pep Clb; Band; Jazz Band; Var Cheerldng; Hon Roll; Masonic Awd; CA ST U Chico; Biolgcl Sci.

PICKETT, ANANDA; Lower Lake HS; Clearlake, CA; (3); 18/160; Am Leg Aux Girls St; Drama Clb; School Play; Stage Crew; Variety Show; Crs Cntry; Trk; Hon Roll; Rotary Intl 90-91 Exchnge Stu Chile; Conservatn Clb.

PICKETT, CARTER; Redlands HS; Mentone, CA; (4); FBLA; Ski Clb; Spanish Clb; Princeton; Law.

PICKETT, CYNTHIA; Mt Carmel HS; San Diego, CA; (4); 8/764; AFS; Rep Stu Cncl; JV Var Gym; JV Vllybl; Kiwanis Awd; NHS; Ntl Merit SF; Stanford U; Comm.

PICKETT, ROBERT S; Simi Valley HS; Simi Valley, CA; (3); 81/675; High Hon Roll; NHS; Pres Acad Fit Awd; Computers Jr Yr Hs; Computers Teachers Aide Sr Yr; Computer Science Coll; CA St U; Computer Science.

PICKETT, SUSAN; Phineas Banning HS; Los Angeles, CA; (4); 89/551; Sec Service Clb; Pres Chorus; Church Choir; Drill Tm; Sec Stu Cncl; Stat Bsktbl; Hon Roll; World Of Curls Awd; Yng Black Schlrs; Howard U; Bus Mgmt.

PICKETT, TIMOTHY J; Ontario HS; Claremont, CA; (3); 23/446; Art Clb; Key Clb; Spanish Clb; Hon Roll; Prfct Atten Awd; Jr Statesmn Of America Secy; GATE Club; GLOBAL Poli Awrnss Treas; UC Berkeley; Arch.

PICONE, LOUIE J; Liberty Union HS; Oakley, CA; (1); 17/450; Chorus; Gov Hon Prg Awd; Hon Roll; Pres Acad Fit Awd; USC; Dentstry.

PICTON, CORY M; St Ignatius HS; Alamo, CA; (3); 27/225; Am Leg Boys St; Service Clb; Stage Crew; Capt Stu Cncl; JV Bsktbl; Var Capt Cheerldng; Var L Crs Cntry; Var L Golf; JV Trk; High Hon Roll; CSF; Minstry Grp.

PIEL, SUZANNE; Northview HS; Covina, CA; (4); Cmnty Wkr; GAA; Pep Clb; Teachers Aide; Chorus; Drill Tm; Cheerldng; Hon Roll; Bnk Of Amer Plaq Wnnr Music; Valley Vista 5 Awd; Mt San Antonio Coll Jazz Band Singer; CA St Long Beach; Music.

PIERATT, BILLY B; Schurr HS; Monterey Park, CA; (1); Church Yth Grp; Key Clb; JV Wrstlng; Chrch Sftbl Tm; UCLA; Bus.

PIERCE, ALEXANDER J; San Dieguito HS; Encinitas, CA; (2); Chess Clb; Church Yth Grp; Computer Clb; Scholastic Bowl; Teachers Aide; Crs Cntry; Trk; Hon Roll; Golden St Exam High Hnrs Algbra, Geomtry; CA Jr Schlrshp Fndtn; John Hopkins Univ Math Vbrk Search.

PIERCE, BRIAN O; La Sierra HS; Riverside, CA; (2); Drama Clb; Sec French Clb; Thesps; School Musical; School Play; Off Jr Cls; Cheerldng; JV Tennis; High Hon Roll; Hon Roll; CA Schlrshp Fdrtn-4 Yrs; Gldn St Exam Schlr; UCLA; Cmnctns.

PIERCE, CECILY A; Washington Prep; Los Angeles, CA; (4); Dance Clb; Office Aide; ROTC; Chorus; Church Choir; Drill Tm; High Hon Roll; Hon Roll; Acad Schlr; Psych.

PIERCE, HOLLYANN; Roseville HS; Citrus Heights, CA; (2); 26/445; French Clb; VP Math Clb; Hon Roll; Prfct Atten Awd; Acad Mrt Awd; Dancing; Horseback Rdng; BYU; Bus.

PIERCE, KYLE; San Ramon Valley HS; Danville, CA; (2); Boy Scts; Band; High Hon Roll; Mustang Soccer.

PIERCE, RICHEL Y; Rubidoux HS; Mira Loma, CA; (4); 105/578; Rep Drama Clb; Capt Color Guard; School Play; Stage Crew; Rptr Yrbk; Co-Capt Flag Corp; Hon Roll; Prfct Atten Awd; Tech.

PIERCE, SARA M; Morro Bay HS; Los Osos, CA; (2); Var L Bsktbl; Var L Crs Cntry; Hon Roll; Bsktbl All Leag All Cnty, All CIF 89-90; Crs Cntry All Leag; Chrch Yth Grp.

PIERCE, SHAWNA L; Claremont HS; Garden Grove, CA; (2); Letterman Clb; Lit Mag; Rep Stu Cncl; Stat Bsbl; Stat Bsktbl; Stat Ftbl; Mgr(s); Score Keeper; Cit Awd; High Hon Roll; Philosophy Awd; Stu Cncl Awd; CA Poly-Tech; Robotics.

PIERCE, VICKI I; Calaveras HS; Mountain Ranch, CA; (3); 28/176; Chorus; Hon Roll; Intl Order Of Rainbow For Girls; Vlntr; San Joaquin Delta Coll; Bus.

PIERCE, WENDY S; Brea-Olinda HS; Brea, CA; (3); 13/300; Church Yth Grp; Cmnty Wkr; French Clb; Hosp Aide; Intnl Clb; Hist Service Clb; Ed Yrbk; JV Bsktbl; Score Keeper; JV Tennis; Pres CSF; Pres Jr Guild Friendly Hills Rgnl Med Ctr; Del Sister-City Itanno Japan; Point Loma Nazarene Coll; Dntl.

PIERCEALL, JUSTINE; Highlands HS; Sacramento, CA; (3); Sec Church Yth Grp; Girl Scts; Pep Clb; Science Clb; Ski Clb; Band; Flag Corp; Score Keeper; Hon Roll; Chapman Coll; Int Dcrtng.

PIERCY, CARRIE; Apple Valley Christian Schl; Apple Valley, CA; (1); 1/23; Church Yth Grp; Hosp Aide; Teachers Aide; Church Choir; Sftbl; High Hon Roll; VBS Tchr; Tchg.

PIERPOINT, ELIZABETH; Christian HS; Pine Valley, CA; (4); Church Yth Grp; Drama Clb; Sec 4-H; Key Clb; Pep Clb; SADD; School Play; Yrbk; Var Cheerldng; L Sftbl; Masters Coll; Hm Econ.

PIERSON, BRADLEY J; Mar Vista HS; Imperial Beach, CA; (1); Drama Clb; Bsbl; Bsktbl; Ftbl; Vllybl.

PIERSON, CHRISTOPHER A; Golden West HS; Visalia, CA; (2); Chess Clb; DECA; Math Clb; JV Swmmng; High Hon Roll; CSF; Gldn St Exam Geom Hnrs; Water Polo Team; Stanford.

PIERSON, JOELLE; Willows HS; Willows, CA; (4); 1/108; Pres Church Yth Grp; Ed Nwsp; Ed Yrbk; Treas Stu Cncl; Rotary Awd; Val; CA Schlrshp Fed-VP; Acad Decath 1st Pl; Brigham Young U; Ec.

PIERSON, MARC E; Maranatha HS; Altadena, CA; (2); Church Yth Grp; Drama Clb; French Clb; Speech Tm; Band; Chorus; Church Choir; School Play; 3rd Pl Readers Theater Cmptn; Point Loma Nazarene; Drama.

PIERUCCINI, BELLE; Notre Dame HS; Salinas, CA; (1); 1/100; Church Yth Grp; Treas Frsh Cls; Stu Cncl; Vllybl; High Hon Roll; Tutor; UCLA; Med.

PIETERS, STEPHANNIE J; Edison HS; Huntington Beach, CA; (1); Dance Clb; Crs Cntry; Socr; Law; UCLA; Law.

PIETRANTONIO, ENRICO; Sunny Hills HS; Fullerton, CA; (3); 15/420; Spanish Clb; Var L Socr; High Hon Roll; Prfct Atten Awd; Rotary Awd; Natl Span Exm Hnr Cert; Engrng.

PIETRO, HEATHER R; Atwater HS; Atwater, CA; (2); French Clb; Swmmng; Long Beach U; Psych.

PIETZ, ERIK C; Marysville HS; Browns Valley, CA; (3); #3 In Class; Debate Tm; 4-H; German Clb; Jazz Band; JV Var Bsktbl; JV Ftbl; High Hon Roll; Eagle Scout; All-Star Bsktbll Tour Sweden.

PIGNATELLI, ROBERTA J; Poway HS; Poway, CA; (4); 8/800; Drama Clb; Sec Jr Cls; Sec Stu Cncl; JV Tennis; High Hon Roll; NHS; Rotary Awd; Pr Cnslng; CSF; Arch.

PIKE, HOLLY J; Silver Valley HS; Newberry Spgs, CA; (2); Church Yth Grp; Pres Jr Cls; Sec Stu Cncl; JV Cheerldng; JV Sftbl; Miss Nwbrry Spgs 89; Pepperdine U; Bus Admin.

PIKE, JENNIFER M; Riverdale HS; Riverdale, CA; (2); GAA; Pep Clb; SADD; Teachers Aide; Var Tennis; High Hon Roll; Hon Roll; Wlrd Hstry Acad Achvt Awd; Kybrd Skills Acad Achvt Awd; Girls PE Acad Achvt Awd; Cal Poly; Educ.

PIKE, JULIE E; Oak Ridge HS; El Dorado Hills, CA; (2); Hosp Aide; High Hon Roll; Hon Roll; CSF; U CA; Med.

PIKE, ROBERT J; Santana HS; Santee, CA; (2); English Clb; Letterman Clb; Ski Clb; Varsity Clb; Nwsp; Yrbk; VP Frsh Cls; VP Stu Cncl; JV Bsbl; JV Ftbl; Photo; UCLA; Debate.

PIKUL, KRISTEN; Edison HS; Huntington Beach, CA; (1); Church Yth Grp; Band; Jazz Band; Mrchg Band; Pep Band; Gov Hon Prg Awd; High Hon Roll; Jr NHS; Math Tutor; Pediatrician.

PILANDE, MELANIE M; San Jose High Acad; San Jose, CA; (4); 3/150; Drama Clb; Spanish Clb; Yrbk; Ed Lit Mag; JV Bskbtl; JV Socr; JV Vllybl; Hon Roll; Pres Acad Fit Awd; Badminton Var; Acad Decathon; San Jose ST.

PILGRIM, JONATHAN D; San Gorgonio HS; Highland, CA; (3); 7/450; VP Church Yth Grp; Cmnty Wkr; French Clb; Key Clb; Pep Clb; Sec Service Clb; JV Tennis; Treas NHS; Rotary Awd; ACES Acad Clb VP; Golden St Exam Awd Wnnr; U CA; Bus.

PILKINGTON, LAURIE; Channel Islands HS; Oxnard, CA; (3); Rep Frsh Cls; Rep Soph Cls; JV Cheerldng.

PILLARS, ROSALYN; Santa Cruz HS; Felton, CA; (3); GAA; Band; Mrchg Band; Rptr Nwsp; Rep Jr Cls; Capt Trk; Vllybl; Hon Roll; BSU; Achvt Awd.

PILLE, NICOLE; Ocean View HS; Huntington Beach, CA; (4); 12/450; Church Yth Grp; Spanish Clb; Drill Tm; Vllybl; Pres Acad Fit Awd; Dstngshd Schlr; CSF Sealbearer; CA ST Fullerton; Intl Bus.

PILLY, VIKAS K; Nogales HS; W Covina, CA; (2); 20/300; Debate Tm; Hosp Aide; Science Clb; JV Bskbtl; JV Tennis; High Hon Roll; Prfct Atten Awd; Pres Acad Fit Awd; CSF; Stanford; Med.

PILOTIN, PAMELA A; St Genevieve HS; Panorama City, CA; (3); Dance Clb; Scholastic Bowl; Church Choir; Drill Tm; Socr; Hon Roll; UCLA; Pre Med.

PILTZ, BRIAN L; Tustin HS; Tustin, CA; (2); 35/432; Computer Clb; JA; Gov Hon Prg Awd; High Hon Roll; Jr NHS; NHS; Prfct Atten Awd; Sci & Scl Sci Spcl Rcgntn Awd; Biochem.

PIMENTEL, MICHELLE ALISON; Central Catholic HS; Riverbank, CA; (3); Cmnty Wkr; Service Clb; Ski Clb; Yrbk; Var L Cheerldng; Var Powder Puff Ftbl; Var L Socr; Intrml Sftbl; Var Tennis; Hon Roll; Stu Of Qrtr Jr; Bus.

PIMENTEL, PAULINE F; Whitney HS; Cerritos, CA; (3); Hosp Aide; Sec Mrchg Band; Sec Orch; Nwsp; Rep Ed Sr Cls; Var Capt Swmmng; High Hon Roll; NHS; Frsh Soph JV Water Polo JV Capt MVP; CA Schlrshp Fed CSF Sr Cls Rep.

PIN, HOUY; A A Stagg HS; Stockton, CA; (4); Off Sr Cls; Hon Roll; Prfct Atten Awd; Schlstc Achvt Awd; Secretarial.

PIN, MONICA; Almos Alonzo Stagg HS; Stockton, CA; (4); Am Leg Aux Girls St; Art Clb; Pres Aud/Vis; Sec FBLA; Rptr Nwsp; Stu Cncl; High Hon Roll; Hon Roll; Prfct Atten Awd; Indo-Chinese Clb VP; 3 Yrs Vrsty Badmntn; UCSA Conflct Mgmt Team; Cambodian Clb; CSU Sacramento; Bus Admin.

PINA, ALAYNA; Palmdale HS; Little Rock, CA; (3); Drama Clb; Speech Tm; SADD; Teachers Aide; Chorus; Church Choir; School Musical; School Play; Hon Roll; Prfct Atten Awd; Columbia Coll; Radio Brdcst.

PINA, MARGARITA; Sweetwater HS; San Diego, CA; (4); VP Spanish Clb; Teachers Aide; Drill Tm; Ed Yrbk; VP Frsh Cls; Hon Roll; Jr NHS; Pres Acad Fit Awd; MECHA Asst Hstrn; UC Irvine; Pre-Law.

PINA, XAVIER; Hanford HS; Hanford, CA; (3); Sec Treas Church Yth Grp; JV Var Crs Cntry; Var Capt Golf; Cross Country Freshmn Most Valuable Runner; Most Inspirational Var Golf; Bilingual Students Of Hanford; COS; Secondary Teacher.

PINA, YADIRA; Sweetwater HS; National City, CA; (2); 31/524; Teachers Aide; Cit Awd; Prfct Atten Awd; Future Teacher Clb; UCSD; Teacher.

PINARD, JASON; Highlands HS; North Highlands, CA; (2); Boy Scts; Church Yth Grp; SADD; VP Frsh Cls; VP Stu Cncl; Socr; Cit Awd; Hon Roll; Prfct Atten Awd; Pres Acad Fit Awd; PA ST; Math.

PINCUS, MEGAN D; Irvine HS; Irvine, CA; (3); Dance Clb; Off Drama Clb; Thesps; Chorus; School Musical; School Play; Schlr Athl Awd; Irvine Singers; Heritage Awd, Best Actress & Best Supprtng Actress Drama/Theatre Arts.

PINDER, JADA; Moorpark HS; Moorpark, CA; (2); Treas FHA; Spanish Clb; Variety Show; Hon Roll; Dance Co Studio One; Howard U; Pre Med.

PINE, SUSAN Y; Cordova HS; Sacramento, CA; (2); Grphc Arts Dsgn.

PINEAULT, JILL SUZANNE; Poway HS; Poway, CA; (4); 45/728; Church Yth Grp; Thesps; Chorus; Church Choir; School Musical; School Play; Swmmng; High Hon Roll; Kiwanis Awd; NHS; Stu Vntr; UCSB; Nrsng.

PINEDA, ALDINE J; Glendale HS; Glendale, CA; (3); Aud/Vis; Teachers Aide; Chorus; AZ ST U; Arch.

PINEDA, ALEX M; Hollywood HS; Los Angeles, CA; (3); Am Leg Boys St; Latin Clb; Rep Jr Cls; Hon Roll.

PINEDA, ANA Y; Sacred Heart Of Jesus HS; Los Angeles, CA; (3); Bus Profs of Am; Teachers Aide; Hon Roll; NHS; Natl Spanish Exam 10th Pl; Rgstrd Nrsng.

PINEDA, DIANA; Schurr HS; Los Angeles, CA; (3); Am Leg Aux Girls St; French Clb; Key Clb; Treas Spanish Clb; Varsity Clb; Acpl Chr; Off Sr Cls; Capt Var Crs Cntry; JV Var Trk; Hon Roll; USC; Psych.

PINEDA, EARL; Ulysees S Grant HS; Van Nuys, CA; (2); Cmnty Wkr; French Clb; Service Clb; Teachers Aide; CSF; Hnr Soc; Filipino Clb; Essay Awd.

PINEDA, ERENDIRA E; San Pedro SR HS; San Pedro, CA; (2); Church Yth Grp; Teachers Aide; Sftbl; Prfct Atten Awd; El Camino JC.

PINEDA, ESPERANZA C; Alisal HS; Salinas, CA; (2); Church Yth Grp; Cmnty Wkr; SADD; Band; Mrchg Band; Pep Band; High Hon Roll; Hon Roll; Prfct Atten Awd; ORALE; CSF; Comp Accntng.

PINEDA, ISABEL; Redlands HS; Redlands, CA; (2); Office Aide; Pres Spanish Clb; Teachers Aide; Cit Awd; Hon Roll; CSU San Bernardino; Teacher.

PINEDA, MARISA; Buena HS; Ventura, CA; (4); 28/471; Church Yth Grp; SADD; Mrchg Band; JV Bskbtl; JV Swmmng; Vllybl; Pres Acad Fit Awd; CA Schlrshp Fed God Seal Brer; Yth Opptnty Fndtn Excptnl Schlr Rnnr Up; USC; Exrcs Sci.

PINEDA, MICHAEL A; Christian Ctr; Pittsburg, CA; (4); 3/9; Church Yth Grp; Letterman Clb; Pep Clb; Variety Show; Rep Frsh Cls; VP Stu Cncl; Var Capt Bskbtl; Var Capt Vllybl; Var Capt Wrstlng; Hon Roll; Most Imprvd Acadmclly Awd; Outstndng Sprtsmnshp Awd; CIF Schltc Achvt Awd; CA ST U Long Beach; Psych.

PINEDA, MIGUEL; Warren HS; Downey, CA; (4); Lit Mag; Off Jr Cls; U Of Southern CA; Phys Therapy.

PINEDA, MYRIAM; Robert A Millikan HS; Long Beach, CA; (3); French Clb; Office Aide; Teachers Aide; Cit Awd; Hon Roll; Mdl Mrt Engl; LEAP.

PINEDO, JORGE M; Patterson HS; Westley, CA; (2); FFA; Ski Clb; Bsbl; Bsktbl; Hon Roll; Modesto JC; Law Enfrcmnt.

PINEDO, PATRICIA S; Santa Ana HS; Santa Ana, CA; (2); Dance Clb; Chorus; Swing Chorus; Variety Show; SAC; Social Svc.

PINEO, WARREN K; Arroyo Grande HS; Arroyo Grande, CA; (2); JV Bsktbl; Var Ftbl; Var Golf; 1st Tm All Leag Golf; Coachs Awd; U AZ; Engl Ed.

PINERO, ISAGANI M; Etiwanda HS; Alta Loma, CA; (3); Ski Clb; JV Socr; Hon Roll; Industrial Dsgn.

PING, ELMER M; El Camino Fundamental HS; Sacramento, CA; (3); 37/376; Chess Clb; Computer Clb; Math Clb; Science Clb; VICA; High Hon Roll; NHS; Ntl Merit Ltr; Pres Acad Fit Awd; Sci Bowl; Physics.

PINGEL, MAILE R; Salinas HS; Salinas, CA; (3); Hosp Aide; Service Clb; Ed Nwsp; Hon Roll; Golden Buddies; Ldr & Orgnzr Frshmn Orientations 89-90; Cert Of Achvt French; CA ST Campus; Int Dsgn.

PINGEL, SARAH; Mt Whitney HS; Visalia, CA; (3); 11/356; Pep Clb; Cheerldng; Diving; High Hon Roll; Jr Stsmn; Keywntts; CSF.

PINKARD, MICHELLE; Capuchino HS; San Bruno, CA; (3); Church Yth Grp; GAA; Red Cross Aide; Teachers Aide; School Play; Stage Crew; Pres Sr Cls; Swmmng; Tennis; Hon Roll; Achvt Awd; UC Davis; Law.

PINKAS, SARAH M; Los Lomas HS; Walnut Creek, CA; (2); French Clb; Service Clb; SADD; Band; Jazz Band; Rep Stu Cncl; JV Bsktbl; Hon Roll; Cornell; Hotel Mgmt.

PINKHAM, MICHAEL J; Pinole Valley HS; Pinole, CA; (2); Drama Clb; Thesps; Acpl Chr; Chorus; School Musical; School Play; Stage Crew; Gym; Drama Awds; Theatre.

PINKNEY, STEPHANIE; John Muir HS; Altadena, CA; (2); Church Yth Grp; Church Choir; Var Trk; Hon Roll; Black Stu Union; Corp Law.

PINLAC, LORNA A; Santa Clara HS; Oxnard, CA; (2); 2/173; Church Yth Grp; Pep Clb; Church Choir; Variety Show; Rep Stu Cncl; Cit Awd; High Hon Roll; NHS; CSF; Acad Excllnce Awd; U CA; Pediatrics.

PINLAC, MARIE G; Whitney HS; Cerritos, CA; (2); Drama Clb; Hon Roll; CSF; CA Jr Schlrshp Fund; Builders Club; UCLA; Med.

PINNEY, KELLIE S; El Camino Fundamental HS; Sacramento, CA; (3); Teachers Aide; JV Var Vllybl; Cit Awd; Hon Roll; USVBA; Early Outreach Pgm; Sacramento ST U; Psych.

PINNO, MERCEDES; Alemany HS; Northridge, CA; (4); 1/289; Am Leg Aux Girls St; Cmnty Wkr; Hosp Aide; Red Cross Aide; Pres Sec SADD; Stu Cncl; Cit Awd; High Hon Roll; Hon Roll; NHS; Acad Dcthln Tm Brnz & Gld Mdls; Bnk Of Amer Achvmnt Awd & HS Awd Engl; CA Poly Pomona; Aerspc Engr.

PINON, JOSEPH P; San Diego HS; San Diego, CA; (3); 5/415; Chess Clb; Intnl Clb; Var Capt Swmmng; JV Wrstlng; Ntl Merit Ltr; Vlntr; Archaeology.

PINSON, PAUL A; Atwater HS; Atwater, CA; (2); Var Ftbl; Cal ST Schl; Graphic Art.

PINTANE, HEATHER; Piner HS; Santa Rosa, CA; (4); 17/400; Am Leg Aux Girls St; JA; Speech Tm; Orch; VP Soph Cls; Off Sr Cls; VP Stu Cncl; Var Capt Pom Pon; DAR Awd; Hon Roll; Harvard Book Recipient; 1st Pl Golden Gate Speech; U Cal Santa Barbara.

PINTEA, SILVIO R; Loyola HS; Los Angeles, CA; (2); Church Yth Grp; Cmnty Wkr; German Clb; Church Choir; School Play; Stage Crew; Pres Acad Fit Awd; Karate Clb; German Bk Awd; UCLA; Doctor.

PINTELLO, BRIAN S; Chula Vista HS; Chula Vista, CA; (2); Boy Scts; Chess Clb; Cmnty Wkr; Computer Clb; Varsity Clb; Var Golf; Mgr(s); Score Keeper; Cit Awd; Tutor; Pudget Sound; Aerospace.

PINTO, MONICA L; American HS; Fremont, CA; (3); 56/300; Spanish Clb; Trk; Hon Roll; CSF; Santa Barbara; Med.

PINZON, RUBEN A; Chula Vista HS; Chula Vista, CA; (2); Science Clb; Flag Corp; Bsbl; Bsktbl; Socr; Tennis; Cit Awd; Engr.

PIOL, CAREEN L; Notre Dame Acad; Los Angeles, CA; (4); Science Clb; Service Clb; Rptr Yrbk; Cit Awd; Hon Roll; Badminton Team; Music Clb; U Of CA Santa Cruz; Legal Stds.

PIORECKI, PIOTR; Narbone HS; Harbor City, CA; (4); Service Clb; Off Sr Cls; Ftbl; Gym; Swmmng; Air Spc Engrng.

PIOTROWSKI, JULIE S; Escondido HS; Escondido, CA; (4); Church Yth Grp; Cmnty Wkr; Dance Clb; FBLA; Hosp Aide; Letterman Clb; Crs Cntry; Gym; Trk; Elks Awd; CSF; US Air Force Recruiting Svc Math & Sci Achvt Awd; Schlr Athl Awds; U Of The Pacific; Biolgcl Sci.

PIOWHITE, ANNA LUISA M; Watsonville HS; Watsonville, CA; (2); 38/545; Hon Roll; Prfct Atten Awd; JR CA Schlrshp Fed Clb; Lawyer.

PIPER, SUSAN; San Marcos HS; Santa Barbara, CA; (4); Key Clb; Pep Clb; Ski Clb; Var Co-Capt Cheerldng; Swmmng; Hon Roll; NHS; Pres Acad Fit Awd; Sealbearer.

PIPITONE, TINA MARIE; Inland Christian HS; San Bernardino, CA; (4); Church Yth Grp; Teachers Aide; Mgr Yrbk; Pres Jr Cls; Ed Stu Cncl; Var Cheerldng; Var Crs Cntry; Hon Roll; Val; Christian Character Awd; Soph, Jr, & Sr Hmecmng Princess; Natl Phys Fit Awd; Prsdntl Phys Fit Awd; Ca Baptist Coll; Cnslng.

PIPKIN, AUGUST; Dinuba HS; Dinuba, CA; (2); 3/250; VP Church Yth Grp; Math Tm; Band; Chorus; Church Choir; Jazz Band; Mrchg Band; Pep Band; JV Capt Cheerldng; JV Powder Puff Ftbl; Sci, Engl, Hstry Schlstc Ltrs; Engrng Smmr Inst On Full Schlrshp; 2 Rock Metal Milltia; Engrng.

PIPKIN, MELISSA; Immanuel HS; Fresno, CA; (2); Cheerldng; Trk; High Hon Roll; Hon Roll; Med.

PIPOLO, REBEKAH M; Bella Vista HS; Sacramento, CA; (2); 100/412; Drama Clb; Office Aide; Chorus; School Musical; School Play; Stage Crew; Variety Show; Church Musical Pageant; UCSB; Corp Law/Theater Arts.

PIPP, JENNIFER; University HS; Irvine, CA; (3); 135/551; Church Yth Grp; VP Cmnty Wkr; Capt Color Guard; Drill Tm; 100 Hrs Cmnty Srvc Awd; Clrguard Ltr & 2nd & 3rd Yr Pins; Engl Lit.

PIPPENGER, TIFFANI C; Kern Valley HS; Lake Isabella, CA; (2); Church Yth Grp; Drama Clb; GAA; Letterman Clb; Pep Clb; Spanish Clb; Speech Tm; SADD; Thesps; Varsity Clb; VFW Spch Cont Awd 1st Pl; VFW Spch Awd Dist 3rd Pl; UCLA; Dramatic Art.

PIPPER, PAUL H; Palmdale HS; Palmdale, CA; (2); 37/720; Chess Clb; Church Yth Grp; FFA; Intnl Clb; JA; Ski Clb; Var Golf; Hon Roll; Mtrlgy.

PIR, PERVEZ P; Norco SR HS; Corona, CA; (2); Debate Tm; Drama Clb; Model UN; Teachers Aide; School Play; Stage Crew; JV Crs Cntry; JV Socr; JV Trk; Cit Awd; UCLA; Med.

PIRA, ELIZABETH; Cajon HS; San Bernardino, CA; (3); 19/356; Rep Intnl Clb; Office Aide; NHS; Ctzn Bee; CSF; Accntng.

PIRKL, BENJAMIN A; San Marcos HS; Goleta, CA; (2); Ski Clb; Var L Swmmng; Water Polo Tm Vrsty Let; UCSB; Marine Bio.

PIRNIK, LACYNE; Fremont Christian HS; Fremont, CA; (3); Church Yth Grp; Letterman Clb; Ski Clb; Teachers Aide; Church Choir; Rep Soph Cls; Off Jr Cls; Var Cheerldng; Var Sftbl; Mst Insprtnl Vrsty Sftbl Blyr; Azusa; Elem Tchr.

PIROOZFAR, AHTOSSA; Mills HS; Millbrae, CA; (4); Debate Tm; Drama Clb; Hosp Aide; Intnl Clb; Letterman Clb; Pep Clb; Thesps; School Play; Variety Show; Rep Frsh Cls; Bnk Of Amer Awd-Drama; Ms Millbrae; Mills Drama Lftm Pass Awd; San Francisco ST U; Theatre.

PIRRELL, IVY DEVRA; Ocean View HS; Huntington Bch, CA; (3); Ski Clb; Stat Score Keeper; JV Tennis; Hon Roll.

PISCATELLA, MATHEW STEVEN; Canyon Springs HS; Redlands, CA; (4); Cmnty Wkr; VP Debate Tm; Sec JA; NFL; Speech Tm; Hon Roll; CA ST Mck Trl Tm Dfns Atty; Moreno Vly City Yth Ct-Asst DA; UC Riverside; Law.

PISCAZZI, GIANNA; Rosary HS; Buena Park, CA; (2); Ski Clb; High Hon Roll; Hon Roll; UCLA.

PISHARODY, UMA K; Gunn HS; Palo Alto, CA; (4); #4 In Class; Church Yth Grp; Cmnty Wkr; JA; Spanish Clb; Band; HOBY Ldrshp Smnr; Music; Med.

PISZCZEK, TAMI; Oxnard HS; Oxnard, CA; (2); 14/654; Church Yth Grp; Church Choir; Variety Show; Nwsp; High Hon Roll; Prfct Atten Awd; Jazz Dance Tchr.

PITCHFORD, AYEESHA; Washington Preparatory HS; Los Angeles, CA; (2); Church Yth Grp; Cmnty Wkr; Dance Clb; Drama Clb; Church Choir; Orch; School Play; Off Jr Cls; Stu Cncl; JV Bsbl; Natl Music Assn Schlrshp; Profiency Engl Pgm Speech & Shakespearean Speech Awds; Xavier U LA; Speech Pathology.

PITCHFORD, DANIEL D; North Salinas HS; Salinas, CA; (3); Science Clb; Spanish Clb; Elks Awd; High Hon Roll; Hon Roll; Kiwanis Awd; Comp Sci.

PITCHFORD, MIA; Banning HS; Banning, CA; (3); Intnl Clb; Spanish Clb; SADD; Yrbk; Hon Roll; Grad Daisy Chain; CSF; Black Stu Assn Clb; U CA Riverside; Psych.

PITESKY, MAURICE; University HS; Los Angeles, CA; (3); Orch; Rptr Nwsp; JV Bsbl; Hon Roll; Temple Yth Grp; Vet.

PITMAN, CYNTHIA A; Redwood HS; Visalia, CA; (3); 8/313; Cmnty Wkr; German Clb; Hosp Aide; Math Tm; Q&S; Band; Rptr Nwsp; High Hon Roll; Witns And Lwyr Mock Trial Tm; Quill And Scroll; Engrng.

PITT, DANA L; Granada Hills HS; Los Angeles, CA; (3); Boy Scts; Church Yth Grp; Library Aide; Church Choir; School Play; Var Bsktbl; Cit Awd; Hon Roll; Prfct Atten Awd; CA Tech Poly; Elect Engrng.

PITT, ERIC S; Bellarmine College Prep; San Jose, CA; (4); 140/300; Cmnty Wkr; Letterman Clb; Varsity Clb; Var L Bsbl; Intrml Bsktbl; Intrml Ftbl; JV L Socr; Chrisitin Life Cmmnty Clb; Bus.

PITT, KATHRYN E; Yuba City HS; Yuba City, CA; (4); Church Yth Grp; GAA; Pep Clb; SADD; Teachers Aide; Temple Yth Grp; Varsity Clb; Chorus; Church Choir; Yrbk; MVP Var Hockey Tm; Brigham Young U; Elem Ed.

PITTALUGA, BONNIE; El Toro HS; El Toro, CA; (3); #5 In Class; Key Clb; Var Crs Cntry; Capt JV Socr; Capt Var Trk; High Hon Roll; Ntl Merit Ltr; Excllnc Awds; CSF; Psych.

PITTERS, NIGEL B; Golden Gate Acad; Vallejo, CA; (3); Church Yth Grp; Acpl Chr; Band; Church Choir; Stat Rep Yrbk; Stu Cncl; Bsktbl; Soc Sci.

PITTMAN JR, H MAURICE; Saint Monica Catholic HS; Los Angeles, CA; (3); 5/124; Boy Scts; Cmnty Wkr; Drama Clb; Thesps; Var Varsity Clb; Chorus; School Musical; School Play; Stage Crew; Rep Frsh Cls; Adult CPR; Blck Cultural Soc; Standard 1st Aid; Life Grd Training; Loyola Marymount U; Clncl Psych.

PITTMAN, MONIQUE S; Moreau HS; Castro Valley, CA; (3); 2/300; Cmnty Wkr; High Hon Roll; Cngrssnl Schlr Natl Yng Ldrs Conf 90; CSF; Pres African Amer Stu Union; Gift Of Blackness Awd 90; Stanford; Polit Sci.

PITTMAN, NICOLE D; Narbonne HS; Carson, CA; (3); Service Clb; Drill Tm; Yrbk; Cit Awd; High Hon Roll; Hon Roll; Pres Acad Fit Awd; Dept Awd-Outstndng Chem Achvt; Cmmnctns.

PITTNER, BRIAN J; Desert JRSR HS; Edwards, CA; (2); JV Bsbl; JV Bsktbl; Teen Learship Forum; UC Davis; Veterinarian.

PITTS, JASON; Manteca HS; Manteca, CA; (2); 36/385; SADD; Bsbl; Bsktbl; High Hon Roll; Hon Roll; Mst Insprtnl Bsbl Plyr; Engr.

PITTS, MICHAEL S; Thomas Downey HS; Modesto, CA; (3); Church Yth Grp; Debate Tm; Key Clb; NFL; Speech Tm; Pres Jr Cls; JV Socr; JV Swmmng; St Qualifying Acadmc Decthln Team; Qualfr St Stu Congrss Trnmnt; Law.

PITTS, SHAWN A; North HS; Oildale, CA; (3); 43/361; Church Yth Grp; French Clb; Chorus; Swing Chorus; Rptr Nwsp; Hon Roll; Masonic Awd; Intl Supreme Cncl Order Of Demolays; Kern Leag Intl Supreme Cncl Pres; Aeronautical Engr.

PITTSENBARGER, JUSTIN E; Davis SR HS; Davis, CA; (3); 18/405; Restoring Old Cars; Saleman.

PITTSER, VELMA; Del Norte HS; Fort Dick, CA; (2); Pres 4-H; FFA; Drill Tm; 4-H Awd; Hon Roll; Prfct Atten Awd; Humboldt; Tchr.

PITZER, THOMAS S; Liberty Union HS; Brentwood, CA; (2); 9/402; Church Yth Grp; FCA; Hon Roll; Pres Acad Fit Awd; Schl Indstrl Arts Awd; CSF; Drafting.

PIXTON, SANDRA G; Woodland HS; Woodland, CA; (3); Church Yth Grp; Teachers Aide; Hon Roll; Yuba Coll Marysville; X-Ray.

PIYASIL, FAWN; Clovis HS; Clovis, CA; (3); Dance Clb; Teachers Aide; Variety Show; Lit Mag; Hon Roll; MESA; Cnty, St Sci Fair 88; Bus.

PIZZICA, JOSHUA; Paradise HS; Magalia, CA; (2); Boy Scts; Letterman Clb; Var Crs Cntry; Socr; Var Swmmng; Var Wrstlng; Hon Roll; Eagle Sct; Arch.

PIZZO, MATTHEW J; Warren HS; Downey, CA; (1); Debate Tm; Speech Tm; Hon Roll; Lion Awd; Jr Statesmen Of Amer; U S CA; Poltcn.

PLACE, DAVID C; Rio Mesa HS; Camarillo, CA; (1); Church Yth Grp; SADD; Renaissance Cmmttmnt To Excllnc; YUGO; Coast Guard.

PLACENTI, PHILLIP M; Edison/Computech HS; Fresno, CA; (1); Hosp Aide; Orch; JV Swmmng; Hon Roll; Piano; Fresno Yth Symphony; Music.

PLACIDE, GEHANNE; Mount Diable HS; Concord, CA; (1); Bsktbl; Stat Ftbl; UCLA; Law.

PLACIDE, HOWARD D; Atwater HS; Atwater, CA; (3); French Clb; Hon Roll; Pres Acad Fit Awd; Bus Admin.

PLACILLA, CHRISTINA D; Sunny Hills HS; Buena Park, CA; (2); 189/486; Church Yth Grp; French Clb; Orch; Lit Mag; Intrml Tennis; Russian Trnsltr.

PLAGEMAN, ELIZABETH K; Bishop O'dowd HS; Oakland, CA; (2); 6/250; Drama Clb; Girl Scts; Thesps; School Play; Rptr Frsh Cls; Off Soph Cls; High Hon Roll; NHS; Pres Acad Fit Awd.

PLAHY, CHERIE; Hilltop HS; Chula Vista, CA; (3); Cmnty Wkr; Pep Clb; Var Cheerldng; SDSU; Bus.

PLAISTED, JASON E; Patrick Henry HS; San Diego, CA; (4); Church Yth Grp; Cmnty Wkr; Letterman Clb; Varsity Clb; Var Ftbl; Wt Lftg; Var Wrstlng; Hon Roll; Bus.

PLAMANN, CHRIS R; La Canada HS; La Canada Flintri, CA; (3); 74/240; Cmnty Wkr; Debate Tm; Letterman Clb; Speech Tm; Intrml JV Bsbl; Var L Bsktbl; Var L Ftbl; Powder Puff Ftbl; Pres Acad Fit Awd; MVP JV Ftbl Qrtrbck; John Wooden Awd Sccss JV Bsktbl; ROP Paralgl Course Jnr; U Of CO Boulder; Pre-Law.

PLANK, NICOLE; Marina HS; Huntington Bch, CA; (4); VP AFS; Church Yth Grp; Drama Clb; Key Clb; Spanish Clb; SADD; Teachers Aide; Nwsp; Swmmng; Pres Acad Fit Awd; CSU Long Beach; Bus Acctg.

PLANT, OWEN M; Veiwpoint HS; Newbury Park, CA; (2); Chess Clb; Drama Clb; Key Clb; School Play; Hon Roll; Pres Acad Fit Awd; Rptr Yrbk; JV Bsktbl; Var Crs Cntry; Var Swmmng.

PLANTE, VERONICA L; Yucca Valley HS; Yucca Valley, CA; (3); Bsktbl; Powder Puff Ftbl; Trk; Wt Lftg; Hon Roll; Doctor.

PLANTILLA JR II, ALBERTO B; Bishop Amat Memorial HS; Hacienda Heights, CA; (2); Church Yth Grp; French Clb; Intnl Clb; Band; Chorus; Church Choir; Jazz Band; Mrchg Band; Pep Band; School Musical; Doctor.

PLAPPERT, MONICA L; Lincoln HS; Stockton, CA; (2); 44/568; Church Yth Grp; GAA; Latin Clb; SADD; Teachers Aide; Sftbl; Hon Roll; Pres Acad Fit Awd; Golden St Exam Awd; Natl Latin Exam Awd; Safe Rides; Psych.

PLARSKI, ROBERT G; Poway HS; Poway, CA; (3); SADD; Varsity Clb; Stu Cncl; JV Var Bsbl; Hon Roll; CSF; West Point.

PLASCENCIA, ANTONIO; Garfield HS; Los Angeles, CA; (3); Wt Lftg; Elec Engrng.

PLASCENCIA, BLANCA E; Downey HS; Downey, CA; (2); Cmnty Wkr; Rep Frsh Cls; JV Sftbl; Cit Awd; High Hon Roll; Hon Roll; Jr NHS; Pres Acad Fit Awd; Sftbl Mst Imprvd; Real Estate.

PLASCENCIA, TERESSA M; Clovis HS; Clovis, CA; (3); Church Yth Grp; GAA; Spanish Clb; JV Bsktbl; Var Sftbl; Hon Roll; MACHO Clb; Bsktbl & Sftbl Coachs Awd; CA ST U Fresno.

PLASCENCIA, VERONICA; Andrew Hill HS; San Jose, CA; (2); Cmnty Wkr; Teachers Aide; Vllybl; Supreme Crt Mem 90-91; Latin Amer Stu Org Secy 90-91; MESA Pgm; Psych.

PLATA, EVELYN; Reseda HS; Los Angeles, CA; (4); FBLA; Spanish Clb; Speech Tm; Cit Awd; Prfct Atten Awd; CA ST U Northridge.

PLATA, MONICA E; Sierra Vista HS; Baldwin Park, CA; (1); Band; Mrchg Band; Arch.

PLATIS, SAM; Los Alamitos HS; Los Alamitos, CA; (3); Church Yth Grp; Intnl Clb; Office Aide; Chorus; Ftbl; Socr; Wt Lftg; Sons Of Pericles Natl Grk Mens Frat; Altar Boy; Grk Orthdx Yth Amrca; U Of Southern CA; Crmnl Law.

PLATO, CARI L; Carlmont HS; San Carlos, CA; (4); Art Clb; Cmnty Wkr; Dance Clb; 4-H; Girl Scts; Yrbk; Off Jr Cls; Cheerldng; Socr; 4-H Awd; Mrt In Art; Fshn Dsgn.

PLATO, JESSECA; Carlmont HS; San Carlos, CA; (2); Capt Cheerldng; Capt Pom Pon; Swmmng; Wt Lftg; Stu For Better Environment Clb; Bus.

PLATONI, KARA A; Irvine HS; Irvine, CA; (1); 2/500; Drama Clb; French Clb; Key Clb; Chorus; School Musical; Stage Crew; Kiwanis Awd; CSF; Ethnc Advsry Forum; Soc Wrkr.

PLATT, TODD; Los Alamitos HS; Cypress, CA; (3); Church Yth Grp; Chorus; Ftbl; Socr.

PLATTER, AMY; Gridley Union HS; Biggs, CA; (2); Dance Clb; French Clb; FFA; FHA; Pep Clb; Chorus; School Play; Variety Show; JV Var Cheerldng; JV Var Pom Pon; FFA Lvstck Jdgng Team St Comptn; Dupree & Tremaine Dance Expose; Boston U; Theatre.

PLAXEN, KAREN T; Louisville HS; Encino, CA; (2); Church Yth Grp; Cmnty Wkr; Drama Clb; Library Aide; Office Aide; School Musical; School Play; 2nd Pl Harvard Lang Speak Off; U Of CA San Diego; Chld Psych.

PLAXTON, CHARITY A; Yucaipa HS; Yucaipa, CA; (2); Sec Church Yth Grp; Drama Clb; FTA; Pep Clb; Spanish Clb; Chorus; Church Choir; School Musical; School Play; Variety Show; Acad Ltr; Music Ltr.

PLAXTON, TRINA M; Ponderosa HS; Placerville, CA; (1); Church Yth Grp; 4-H; Bsktbl; Part Time Job; Vlntr Wrk Wolf Mntn Camp Grass Vly; Cmptd Math Stplchs Math Cmptn; Chico ST.

PLAZA, ARLENE I; John Glenn HS; Norwalk, CA; (2); Church Yth Grp; Dance Clb; Hon Roll; U CA Santa Barbara.

PLAZA, DANNY B; Francis Polytechnic HS; Arleta, CA; (3); Spanish Clb; Nwsp; Hlpng Hand & Outstndng Prfrmnce Engl Awds; Bus Mgmt.

PLAZA, SANDRA M; Chatsworth HS; Los Angeles, CA; (4); 14/600; Library Aide; Office Aide; Spanish Clb; Teachers Aide; Var Gym; Trk; Cit Awd; High Hon Roll; Prfct Atten Awd; Rotary Awd; Coll Schlrshp; Loyola Marymount U; Film Prod.

PLEASANTS, HILLARY A; Antioch HS; Antioch, CA; (3); German Clb; Teachers Aide; Rptr Nwsp; JV Sftbl; JV Vllybl; Hon Roll; East Clb; Sonoma ST U; Marine Bio.

PLEAU, KRISTEN; Davis HS; Davis, CA; (1); Church Yth Grp; Cmnty Wkr; SADD; Chorus; School Musical; Sec Stu Cncl; Intrml Bsktbl; JV Cheerldng; NEDT Awd; Pres Acad Fit Awd; Azusa Pacific; Child Psychlsgy.

PLECNIK, CHRISTINE E; St Josephs HS; Long Beach, CA; (2); 2/289; SADD; CSF; CA ST U Long Beach; Chemist.

PLEMONS, JAMIE A; Bullard HS; Fresno, CA; (1); SADD; JV Socr; Var Sftbl; UCLA; Orthodontist.

PLESCIA, BRIAN J; Nevada Union HS; Grass Valley, CA; (3); Am Leg Boys St; Boy Scts; Jazz Band; Phtg Nwsp; Var L Socr; Var L Tennis; Var L Vllybl; Hon Roll; St Schlr; Friday Night Live St & Cnty Lvl Ldrshp; Prin Schlr/Athl Awds; U Of CA; Motion Picture Indus.

PLETTNER, RICHARD J; Edison HS; Clovis, CA; (1); Church Yth Grp; Hosp Aide; Band; Mrchg Band; High Hon Roll; Hon Roll.

PLICK, LEONARD; Damien HS; Montclair, CA; (4); 16/192; Cmnty Wkr; Drama Clb; School Musical; Treas Stu Cncl; Var L Bsktbl; Hon Roll; Pres Acad Fit Awd; MVP Bsktbl 2 Yrs; Jim George Awd; Yng Gftd Black Awd; Yng Natl Schlstc Ldrs Awd; Pitzer Coll; Recording Arts.

PLUCKHAN, BRADLEY J; California Lutheran HS; Los Gatos, CA; (3); 2/18; Latin Clb; Pres Frsh Cls; VP Jr Cls; Rep Stu Cncl; Var L Bsbl; Var L Bsktbl; Var L Ftbl; High Hon Roll; Pres Acad Fit Awd; Med.

PLUFF, DEBORAH; Santa Clara HS; Santa Clara, CA; (2); Stat Score Keeper; Hon Roll; Cal Poly; Engrng.

PLUM, JANELLE; Gretchen Whitney HS; Temecula, CA; (3); Drama Clb; FTA; Pres VP JA; Key Clb; Drill Tm; Stage Crew; Rptr Nwsp; Rep Stu Cncl; High Hon Roll; CSF; Pre-Med.

PLUMB, ALEC; Edison-Computech HS; Fresno, CA; (4); Computer Clb; Model UN; Ed Lit Mag; JETS Awd; Ntl Merit Schol; UC San Diego; Comp Engrng.

PLUMB, DANIEL P; Yucca Valley HS; Yucca Valley, CA; (3); Pres Rptr Nwsp; Hon Roll; Pres Acad Fit Awd; ASU; Physics.

PLUMB, STEVE W; Dos Pueblos HS; Santa Barbara, CA; (2); 93/299; JV Swmmng; Santa Barbara Bus Coll; Bus.

PLUMLEY, JENNIFER L; Novato HS; Novato, CA; (2); ROTC; Teachers Aide; Cheerldng; Pom Pon; Sftbl; Hon Roll; Pres Acad Fit Awd; UCSC.

PLUMLEY, LAURA L; Edison HS; Huntington Beach, CA; (3); VP Dance Clb; French Clb; Ski Clb; Teachers Aide; Score Keeper; Hon Roll; Acad Schvmnt Awd In Sci Sphmr Yr; Acad Achvmnt Awd In Home Ec & Gldn Key Nmne Voct Tech JR Yr; Long Beach ST; Psychlgy.

PLUMMER, BRIAN KEITH; San Gabriel Acad; Covina, CA; (3); 5/53; Church Yth Grp; Teachers Aide; Band; Yrbk; Off Frsh Cls; High Hon Roll; NHS; Prfct Atten Awd; ROP Hosp Ofc Wrk; Journlsm.

PLUNKETT, BRANDY; Fillmore HS; Piru, CA; (3); Teachers Aide; Yrbk; Law.

PLYMALE, SHANNON M; Atwater HS; Atwater, CA; (1); Drama Clb; SADD; School Play; High Hon Roll; Hon Roll; CSF; Falcon Crest Awd-Hghst Acad Stndng Engl Cls; Hgh Scorer PSAT/Nmsqt; U Of CA; Prfrmng Arts.

PO, TIN V; Galileo HS; San Francisco, CA; (3); French Clb; Science Clb; Var Vllybl; Hon Roll; Pres Sci Clb & French Clb; UC Davis.

POARCH, TANEKA L; Testimonial Christian Schl; Los Angeles, CA; (3); Church Choir; School Play; Hon Roll; Prfct Atten Awd; Fashin Designing, Cooking & Modeling; Brooks Coll; Fashn Design.

POBJOY, TRICIA E; Granada Hills HS; Granada Hills, CA; (3); Debate Tm; Rep Frsh Cls; Rep Jr Cls; Rep Sr Cls; Stu Cncl; Intrml Ftbl; JV Var Swmmng; Intrml Vllybl; Cit Awd; High Hon Roll; Stu To Stu Rltns; Peer Cnslr; Jr Statesman Of Amer; Berkely; Bus.

POBLACION, AILEEN J; Monterey Bay Acad; Madera, CA; (1); Church Yth Grp; Chorus; Church Choir; School Musical; Off Frsh Cls; High Hon Roll; Prfct Atten Awd; Filipino Folk Dncs; Handels Messiah Prfrmr; Grls Clb Pianist.

POBLETE, NICHOLAS E; St Ignatius College Prep; Daly City, CA; (3); Boy Scts; School Play; Bsbl; Ftbl; Sci.

POCHOP, SARAH K; Will C Wood HS; Vacaville, CA; (2); Church Yth Grp; Hosp Aide; Band; Mrchg Band; Hon Roll; Flght Attndnt.

POCZULP, JESSI L; Del Oro HS; Loomis, CA; (2); 21/270; GAA; Pres Frsh Cls; Stu Cncl; JV Bsktbl; Var Socr; Hon Roll; Law.

PODESTA, TARA; Linden HS; Linden, CA; (2); 5/153; FFA; Math Tm; Spanish Clb; JV Var Sftbl; JV Var Vllybl; High Hon Roll; Hon Roll; Stockton Vlybl Clb; Soc Sci Awd; CSF.

PODESTA, WILLIAM J; De La Salle HS; Lafayette, CA; (4); AFS; Boy Scts; Band; South America 90-91; Yth Educator; St Marys Coll; Bio.

POE, RACHEL; Los Angeles Baptist HS; Northridge, CA; (4); Church Yth Grp; Library Aide; Pep Clb; Drill Tm; Yrbk; Lit Mag; VP Jr Cls; Var Capt Cheerldng; Sftbl; Hon Roll; JV Bsbl Stats; Jr-Sr Banquet Cmmtte; HS Fshn Show; Art Show; Cheer Awds Most Sprtd, Insprtnl Coach Awd; CSU Of Northridge.

POE, TONIA C; Centennial HS; Compton, CA; (3); Teachers Aide; Band; Mrchg Band; Pep Band; School Musical; Rptr Nwsp; Rep Jr Cls; Rep Stu Cncl; Powder Puff Ftbl; Hon Roll; Stu Mnth Awd; Brdcst Jrnslm.

POEMOCEAH, JOSEPH M; Anaheim HS; Anaheim, CA; (3); 340/399; Quiz Bowl; Band; Lbrn Mrchg Band; Pep Band; Stu Cncl; JV Ftbl; JV Var Wrstlng; Gldn St Exm Math Schlr; JR Hgh Pnt Awd Wnnr Service Pnt Bnqt; Outstndng Soph Bandsman; Aeronautical Engr.

POESTHORST, HELGE; Washington Union HS; Fresno, CA; (4); Church Yth Grp; Drama Clb; French Clb; FBLA; Intnl Clb; School Play; Tennis; Vllybl; Hon Roll; JETS Cmptn Achvt; CSF Awd; Lttr Outstndng Acad Awds; Prfssr Bio.

POGAN, CARI; Norco SR HS; Norco, CA; (3); 23/397; Church Yth Grp; GAA; Model UN; L Var Crs Cntry; Score Keeper; JV Intrml Sftbl; Intrml Trk; Intrml JV Vllybl; Hon Roll; Pres Acad Fit Awd; Altrnt Grls ST; Cal Poly Pomona; Bio.

POGGEMANN, FELIX G; Morro Bay HS; Morro Bay, CA; (3); 11/239; English Clb; French Clb; Letterman Clb; Math Tm; Science Clb; Ski Clb; Teachers Aide; Varsity Clb; Ed Yrbk; VP Frsh Cls; Geom Gldn St High Hnrs Awd; Most Vlbl Swmmr; Davis U; Gntc Engrng.

POGGI, GINA; Dana Hills HS; Laguna Niguel, CA; (1); Trk; Vllybl; Reading; Engl.

POGLEDICH, PHILIP J; Napa HS; Napa, CA; (4); 62/341; Cit Awd; Hon Roll; Prfct Atten Awd; Creative Writing-Non-Fiction/Prose Fiction-Excllnc Awds; U Of CA-DAVIS; Engl.

POGUE, JENNIFER K; Inglewood HS; Los Angeles, CA; (4); Debate Tm; French Clb; Pep Clb; Science Clb; Speech Tm; Ed Yrbk; Stu Cncl; High Hon Roll; Yng Black Schlrs, MESA, NAACP Acad Excllnc Awd; UCLA Alumni JR Of Yr Awd; Prncpls Advsry Cmmttee; Intl Rltns.

POGUE, JODY D; Sacramento Adventist Acad; Roseville, CA; (2); Church Yth Grp; Ski Clb; Band; Chorus; Pres Soph Cls; Hon Roll; Sacramento Advntst Acad.

POHLE, JILL; Montclair HS; Montclair, CA; (2); 77/499; JV Cheerldng; Prfct Atten Awd.

POHLEN, ANDY J; Pius X HS; Downey, CA; (3); 10/150; Intnl Clb; Letterman Clb; Varsity Clb; Yrbk; Bsktbl; Crs Cntry; Golf; Score Keeper; High Hon Roll; Hon Roll; Art.

POHLEN, CHRISTINE; Pius X HS; Downey, CA; (3); 1/200; GAA; Capt JV Pep Clb; Service Clb; Var L Golf; High Hon Roll; Hon Roll; NHS; St Schlr; Interact Svc Club; 3 Wk Engrng Camp At U Of Notre Dame; U Of Notre Dame; Engrng.

POHLMAN, BRYAN H; Downey HS; Downey, CA; (4); VP Key Clb; Yrbk; JV Bsbl; JV Bsktbl; JV Ftbl; Var Capt Vllybl; High Hon Roll; Hon Roll; NHS; Long Beach; Pol Sci.

POHLMAN, NAOMI I; Dana Hills HS; Laguna Niguel, CA; (2); Hon Roll; Ntl Merit Schol; Harvard U; Bus.

POIDL, DAGMAR; Leland HS; San Jose, CA; (2); French Clb; FFA; Trk; U Of HI Manoa; Intl Bus.

POINDEXTER, RONALD D; Norte Vista HS; Riverside, CA; (4); 56/350; Church Yth Grp; Letterman Clb; Teachers Aide; Varsity Clb; Var L Bsbl; JV Bsktbl; Var Capt Ftbl; Wt Lftg; High Hon Roll; Hon Roll; Acad Achvmnt Awd; 2nd Tm All Leag Ftbl; Pepsi Mle Athlt Of Yr Awd; Riverside CC; Bus Mngmt.

POINDEXTER, SARAH M; Bella Vista HS; Orangevale, CA; (2); Church Yth Grp; Pep Clb; Cheerldng; Swmmng; UC Santa Barbara; Pblc Rltns.

POINTER, DAN E; Independence HS; Kelsey, CA; (4); 16/100; SADD; Stage Crew; Rep Sr Cls; Rep Stu Cncl; Hon Roll; Prfct Atten Awd; St Of Wk; Top Crdts For Smstr; USAF; Aviator.

POITZ, ADINDA A; Nevada Union HS; Grass Valley, CA; (3); Church Yth Grp; 4-H; SADD; Teachers Aide; Color Guard; Intrml Mrchg Band; Var Powder Puff Ftbl; 4-H Awd; Frgn Exchange Stu-Germany; Traveling Clb Sec; Long Bch ST; Psych.

POKORNY, JASON; San Leandro HS; Oakland, CA; (2); Boy Scts; Church Yth Grp; Key Clb; Rep Frsh Cls; Rep Soph Cls; JV Bsktbl; Pres Acad Fit Awd; Mst Imprvd Bkstbl 89-90.

POKORSKI, MICHELLE; St Joseph HS; South Gate, CA; (2); 69/196; Church Yth Grp; Drama Clb; GAA; Teachers Aide; Drill Tm; Hon Roll; Dance Team; Keywanette Clb; Sci.

POL, CHAN; A A Stagg HS; Stockton, CA; (3); Off Frsh Cls; Off Soph Cls; Off Jr Cls; Hon Roll; Prfct Atten Awd; Young Authors Faire; Delta Coll; Accntng.

POLANCO, CLARA E; Our Lady Loreito-Bishop Conaty HS; Los Angeles, CA; (3); 7/147; FBLA; Intnl Clb; Spanish Clb; Rep Frsh Cls; Rep Soph Cls; Treas Jr Cls; Treas Stu Cncl; JV Capt Vllybl; Hon Roll; NHS; Vlntrs Of Amer Upward Bound; Ambssdrs Clb.

POLCHOWSKI, LISA M; Burlingame HS; Burlingame, CA; (3); Church Yth Grp; Debate Tm; Teachers Aide; Lit Mag; Tennis; Trk; Hon Roll; Ten World Outreach; Vocation Bible Sch Tchr; CSF; Biotech.

POLDER, JASON; Lemoore HS; Lemoore, CA; (4); 2/300; Treas Jr Cls; Pres Sr Cls; Pres Stu Cncl; Capt Socr; Tennis; NHS; Ntl Merit Schol; Sal; CSF; Alternate Boys St; Cal Poly San Luis Obispo; Engr.

POLETTI, AMY L; Arroyo Grande HS; Oceano, CA; (1); 70/589; Church Yth Grp; VP Chrch Yth Grp; Awd Home Ec Dept; Tchng.

POLFER, RYAN K; Huntington Beach HS; Huntington Beach, CA; (2); Boy Scts; Church Yth Grp; Letterman Clb; Surf Club; Meteorology.

POLGAR, VANESSA I; Lowell HS; San Francisco, CA; (3); Latin Clb; Library Aide; Office Aide; Teachers Aide; Band; Orch; Tennis; NHS; Piano.

POLHEMUS, LAUREN A; Galt HS; Galt, CA; (2); Hon Roll; Friday Night Live; Harvard; Law.

POLICICCHIO, MELBA E; Lowell HS; San Francisco, CA; (2); Church Yth Grp; Teachers Aide; Church Choir; School Musical; School Play; Bsktbl; Trk; Hmerm Secy; Bsktbl Coach; Psych.

POLICICCHO, NICOLE; John Marshall HS; Los Angeles, CA; (4); Debate Tm; GAA; Spanish Clb; Lit Mag; Rep Frsh Cls; Rep Soph Cls; Rep Jr Cls; Rep Sr Cls; Intrml Ftbl; Var Sftbl; Wn Mc Collum Schlrshp Jrnlsm; USC Smmr Hnr Pgm 89; U Of Southern CA; Brdcst Jrnls.

POLINO, DARREN S; Eisenhower HS; Rialto, CA; (3); Boy Scts; Rptr Nwsp.

POLITZER, BENJAMIN E; San Dieguito HS; Encinitas, CA; (4); 3/543; Boy Scts; Nwsp; Pres Frsh Cls; L Var Bsktbl; Hon Roll; NHS; Westingshouse Sci Tlnt Srch Hnrs Group.

POLK, BRIDGETTE M; Lynwood HS; Lynwood, CA; (3); Bsktbl; Bus.

POLK, CORINNA B; Walnut HS; Walnut, CA; (3); Key Clb; Teachers Aide; JV Swmmng; Hon Roll; Pres Acad Fit Awd; Nwsp; Pwr Club Chrmn Of Rcylcng Cmmtte; Pre Law.

POLK, GARLAND R; Westmoor HS; Daly City, CA; (2); Boy Scts; Church Yth Grp; FCA; Varsity Clb; L JV Bsbl; L Var Socr; Christ Coll Irvine; Pastor.

POLK, LORI M; San Bernardino HS; San Bernardino, CA; (2); 90/715; Model UN; NFL; Speech Tm; Early Child Dev.

POLK, MARA K; Rio Vista HS; Rio Vista, CA; (3); AFS; Hist FHA; Hosp Aide; Science Clb; Chorus; School Musical; High Hon Roll; Acad Dcthln; CA Sect Amer Chemcl Soc; HS Chem Awd; Psych.

POLKINGHORNE, REX; Mills HS; Burlingame, CA; (3); Service Clb; VP Frsh Cls; Rep Stu Cncl; JV Crs Cntry; Var Mgr(s); JV Tennis; Lbrl Arts.

POLLACK, JENNIFER; Arroyo Grande HS; Arroyo Grande, CA; (2); Dance Clb; JV Vllybl; San Francisco U; Costume Dsgn.

POLLACK, SUZY T; Del Oro HS; Auburn, CA; (2); 8/248; Drama Clb; Sec Treas Service Clb; School Play; Sec Treas Frsh Cls; Pres Soph Cls; JV Swmmng; High Hon Roll; Recog Alge Golden St Exam; CSF; Princeton; Law.

POLLAND, TAMY; University HS; Los Angeles, CA; (3); Art Clb; Teachers Aide; Temple Yth Grp; Rep Jr Cls; Off Sr Cls; Ldrshp Mrt Awd; HOBY; CA Saratoga Yth Ldrshp Conf Schlrshp; Amnsty Intl; Linden Ctr Resdntl Vlntr; Psych.

POLLARD, LEONARD M; Serra HS; Los Angeles, CA; (3); 13/50; Art Clb; Boy Scts; Dance Clb; JA; Letterman Clb; Nwsp; Var L Ftbl; Var L Socr; Var Wt Lftg; Hon Roll; CA ST Northridge; Bus Mgmt.

POLLARD, LISA C; Fresno Christian HS; Fresno, CA; (3); Church Yth Grp; Cmnty Wkr; Chorus; Color Guard; Tennis; Vllybl; Hon Roll; Hi-Deb Prog; Fresno Pacific Coll; Tchng.

POLLARD, MARIE; Brea-Olinda HS; Brea, CA; (4); 50/300; Rep Church Yth Grp; Pres Sec 4-H; Speech Tm; Chorus; Church Choir; Stage Crew; 4-H Awd; NHS; Ntl Merit SF; Rotary Awd; TX Womans U; Fashion Dsgn.

POLLARD, RUSSELL G; Fresno Christian HS; Fresno, CA; (1); Church Yth Grp; FCA; Varsity Clb; Band; Mrchg Band; Pep Band; Bsktbl; High Hon Roll; Point Loma Nazarene Coll; Bus.

POLLEY, TODD; Brethron HS; Downey, CA; (1); Boy Scts; Church Yth Grp; Sec Frsh Cls; JV Bsbl; JV Ftbl; Intrml Wt Lftg; Hon Roll; Eagle Sct; UCLA; Marine Bio.

POLLICINO, ALEXANDER N; Hamilton HS; Los Angeles, CA; (3); Var Crs Cntry; Var Diving; JV Ftbl; Var Trk; Bus.

POLLINGER, RUTH S; Antelope Valley HS; Lancaster, CA; (2); Dance Clb; Drama Clb; Office Aide; School Play; Yrbk; Hon Roll; CSF; Theatre Arts.

POLLITT, AMBER L; Barstow HS; Barstow, CA; (1); Church Yth Grp; French Clb; Church Choir; Hon Roll; Cert Achvt Beginning Amer Sign Lang; Natl Piano Plyng Audtns Guild Super Rtng; Chrstn Achvt Pgnt; SW Baptist Coll; Deaf Tchr.

POLLMAN, TERESA; Clovis West HS; Clovis, CA; (3); Church Yth Grp; Acpl Chr; Chorus; Color Guard; Swing Chorus; Hon Roll; Arabian Horse Comp Rgnl & Intl Lvl; Clovis W Winterguard Plcd 3rd At Intl Comp Mrch 90; UC Santa Barbara; Fild Of Law.

POLLNER, TANIA; Los Alamitos HS; Los Alamitos, CA; (4); Church Yth Grp; Office Aide; Spanish Clb; Orch; JV Bsktbl; Var L Crs Cntry; Var L Trk; Hon Roll; Pres Acad Fit Awd; U CA Riverside; Englsh.

POLLOCK, BRYAN R; Savanna HS; Buena Park, CA; (2); Boy Scts; Band; Mrchg Band; Orch; Pep Band; Pres Acad Fit Awd; Law Enfrcmnt.

POLLY, SAM; M Ckinleyville HS; Arcata, CA; (3); Boy Scts; Church Yth Grp; FFA; Crs Cntry; High Hon Roll; Hon Roll; Prfct Atten Awd; Golden ST Exam Awd Geom; Humboldt ST U; Forestry.

POLONI, LORI M; Bella Vista HS; Fair Oaks, CA; (2); 40/406; French Clb; FBLA; JV Swmmng; French Hon Soc; Stu Reaching Out; Friday Night Live; U CA Davis; Vet.

POLOVINA, ANDREA; Sierra Joint Union HS; Tollhouse, CA; (4); Church Yth Grp; Math Clb; Math Tm; Scholastic Bowl; Science Clb; SADD; Church Choir; Variety Show; Tennis; High Hon Roll; Menlo Park Coll; Bio.

POLTA, DAN; Escondido HS; Escondido, CA; (4); 7/300; Scholastic Bowl; Band; Drm Mjr(t); Mrchg Band; Pep Band; Var Capt Golf; Cit Awd; High Hon Roll; Dartmouth Coll; Engl.

POLUCHA, MICHEAL I; Brea Olinda HS; Brea, CA; (1); Church Yth Grp; JV Tennis; Hon Roll; Handicapped Ministry At Church.

POLYAKOV, VLADISLAV; Van Nuys HS/Ms Magnet; Reseda, CA; (4); 53/530; Chess Clb; Hosp Aide; Ed Nwsp; JV Crs Cntry; JV Trk; Prfct Atten Awd; Pres Acad Fit Awd; Pres Schlr; 4th Pl Stock Mkt Cmptn; UCSD; Bio.

POMAR, ROXANA R; Acadamy Of Our Lady Of Peace; San Diego, CA; (3); Cmnty Wkr; Spanish Clb; School Musical; Variety Show; Var Trk; Hon Roll; Spanish NHS; Big/Little Sister Cmmtte; Jr Unity Cmmtte; CSF; UCSD; Bus.

POMILIA III, FRANK A; Ukiah HS; Ukiah, CA; (2); JV Bsbl; JV Ftbl; JV Wrstlng; Redwood Empire Champ 175 Lb Clss Wrestling; Coaches Awd Ftbl; MI Bsbl; Drafting.

POMOZZI, LINDA; John A Rowland HS; Chino, CA; (3); 132/560; Church Yth Grp; Teachers Aide; Band; Drill Tm; Mrchg Band; Stat Var Bsbl; Stat Ftbl; Cit Awd; Hon Roll; Capt Of Auxiliary; Riverside CC; Dance.

POMPOSO, EDITH G; Louisville HS; Woodland Hills, CA; (2); Hon Roll; Harvard Spnsh Comp; Law.

PON, COLLEEN A; George Washington College Prep; San Francisco, CA; (2); Q&S; Speech Tm; Nwsp; Lit Mag; Sec Frsh Cls; Sec Soph Cls; Cit Awd; Gov Hon Prg Awd; Hon Roll; 1st Pl Invest In Amer Press Confrnc 89; CSF 89-90; Hnrs Golden St Exam; Commnctns.

PON, CYNTHIA; Piedmont Hills HS; San Jose, CA; (4); 13/361; French Clb; Math Tm; Service Clb; Teachers Aide; Stage Crew; Co-Ed Nwsp; Lit Mag; High Hon Roll; Hon Roll; Black Belt Tae Kwon Do; Martial Arts Outstndng Instr Awd 88; CSF Gold Seal Bearer & Life Mem; U CA Santa Barbara; Comm.

PON, PAMELA; Woodrow Wilson HS; San Francisco, CA; (3); FBLA; Hon Roll; Int Dcrtng.

PONCE, ANDREW; Del Oro HS; Penryn, CA; (4); Art Clb; U NV Reno; Chem Engrng.

PONCE, ANTHONY; Roosevelt HS; Fresno, CA; (4); 28/565; Church Yth Grp; Science Clb; Chorus; Vllybl; Hon Roll; Step To Coll Pgm; Smmr Jr Pgm; UC Davis; Rsrch Sci.

PONCE, JOEL C; Pater Noster HS; Glendale, CA; (2); 1/30; Bsktbl; Hon Roll; UCLA; Bus Adm.

PONCE, JUAN M; Moorpark HS; Moorpark, CA; (4); 22/173; Pres Acad Fit Awd; CSF Secy; Law Enforcement Explorers; CA Lutheran U; Justice Admin.

PONCE, LETICIA R; Grant HS; Sacramento, CA; (3); Aud/Vis; Science Clb; Stu Cncl; Var Powder Puff Ftbl; Cit Awd; Hon Roll; MESA Clb; People To People Sci Exchng Pgm; Berkeley; Archaeology.

PONCE, LUIS; Bakersfield HS; Bakersfield, CA; (2).

PONCE, MARGARITA; Kerman HS; Kerman, CA; (3); Chorus; Var Sftbl; JV Vllybl; Var Sprts Ltr; Goals For Yth Prgm.

PONCE, MICHAEL U; Bellarmine College Prep; San Jose, CA; (4); San Jose ST U; Elect Engrng.

PONCE, MIGUEL; Mt Carmel HS; San Diego, CA; (4); 100/750; Debate Tm; Stat Band; Jazz Band; Mrchg Band; Pep Band; Kiwanis Awd; Ntl Merit Ltr; Natl Hispanic Schlr Semi-Fnlst; Civil Engrng.

PONCE, SANDRA E; Immaculate Heart HS; Hollywood, CA; (3); Pres French Clb; GAA; Math Clb; Science Clb; Service Clb; Spanish Clb; Frnch II Awd; CSF & Wilderness Clubs; USC; Arch.

PONCELET, JANET K; San Luis Obispo HS; San Luis Obispo, CA; (4); Church Yth Grp; FHA; Hon Roll; Pres Acad Fit Awd; Finalist For Central Coast HS Art Competition; CA Polytech U; Graphic Design.

POND, SAMUEL E; Brawley Union HS; Brawley, CA; (1); Science Clb; Band; Mrchg Band; IVC; Marine Bio.

PONDER, GWENDOLYN; San Gorgonio HS; Highland, CA; (4); 1/460; VP Treas Debate Tm; Model UN; NFL; Quiz Bowl; Scholastic Bowl; Service Clb; Pres SADD; Ed Nwsp; Off Jr Cls; Stu Cncl; S CA Edison Schlrshp; Smithsonian Inst Intrnshp 90; Rgnts Schlrhsp UCB; U CA Berkeley; Law.

PONG, KEVIN; J E Mc Ateer HS; San Francisco, CA; (3); Computer Clb; JA; Letterman Clb; Math Tm; Quiz Bowl; Scholastic Bowl; Spanish Clb; Teachers Aide; Yrbk; Rep Stu Cncl; Bio.

PONG, KIT; Willow Glen HS; San Jose, CA; (2); 14/431; Var JV Vllybl; Hon Roll; UCLA; Nrsng.

PONGBANDITH, THEPPHARACK; Orestimba HS; Newman, CA; (3); Hon Roll; Prfct Atten Awd; CSU Stanislaus; Tchr.

PONGKHAMSING, CHAN; Casa Grande HS; Petaluma, CA; (2); 38/297; French Clb; JV Var Ftbl; JV Var Trk; Hon Roll; NHS; Prfct Atten Awd; Pres Acad Fit Awd; CA Schlrshp Fed; Upward Bound Pgm; Stanford; Phy.

PONSEN, ZACHARY J; San Clemente HS; San Clemente, CA; (4); Science Clb; Sports; San Diego U; Engrng.

PONSFORD, JULIE; John F Kennedy HS; Sacramento, CA; (4); 68/388; AFS; Church Yth Grp; VP Dance Clb; FBLA; VP FTA; Pres VP Spanish Clb; Color Guard; School Musical; Variety Show; Rptr Nwsp; U CA Davis.

PONTELLE, BOBBY D; Taft HS; Tarzana, CA; (2); Rptr Nwsp; Rptr Yrbk; Rptr Lit Mag; UCLA; Bus.

PONTERES, AGNES S; Bolsa Grande HS; Garden Grove, CA; (3); French Clb; Orch; School Musical; Off Jr Cls; JV Tennis; JR Coll Then UCLA; OR Nurse.

PONTERIO, KATHRYN E; Monte Vista HS; Spring Valley, CA; (3); 61/373; Church Yth Grp; Teachers Aide; JV Cheerldng; Var Diving; Socr; Sftbl; Hon Roll; Goldn St Exam 1st Yr Alg Hnrs Acad Excllnce Awd; San Diego Tribunes All-Acad Team; Elem Ed.

PONTILLAS, MARIANO B; Alisal HS; Salinas, CA; (3); JV Var Bsbl; Stat Score Keeper; Cit Awd; High Hon Roll; Hon Roll; U Of Southern CA; Pre-Med.

PONTIN, MICHAEL G; Taft Union HS; Taft, CA; (3); 1/200; Boy Scts; Var Crs Cntry; JV Trk; High Hon Roll.

PONTIS, TAMRA R; Morro Bay HS; Morro Bay, CA; (3); Treas AFS; Cmnty Wkr; GAA; Girl Scts; Speech Tm; Yrbk; Stu Cncl; Powder Puff Ftbl; JV Trk; Var Trk; St Wide Ldrshp Camps With CA Assn Of Stu Cncls; Selected By Rotary Club Attnd Dist Ldrshp Camp; William & Mary; Govt.

POOL, JENNIFER L; Woodcrest Christian HS; Moreno Valley, CA; (1); Church Yth Grp; Church Choir; Var Bsktbl; Var Vllybl; High Hon Roll; NHS; Bus.

POOLE, CAPRECIA M; Madison HS; San Diego, CA; (4); 31/368; Latin Clb; Chorus; Yrbk; Var Sftbl; Cit Awd; High Hon Roll; Hon Roll; Pres Acad Fit Awd; CSF; U CA Berkeley; Comp Sci.

POOLE, CARRIE; San Joaquin Memorial HS; Fresno, CA; (4); 3/118; Am Leg Aux Girls St; VP Pres GAA; VP Science Clb; VP Jr Cls; VP Sr Cls; Var Capt Bsktbl; Var Capt Crs Cntry; Cit Awd; Elks Awd; NHS; U CA Davis; Med.

POOLE, JENNIFER J; Rio Mesa HS; Camarillo, CA; (3); Church Yth Grp; FCA; FTA; School Play; Ed Lit Mag; Var JV Score Keeper; JV Trk; Hon Roll; Sgt At Arms; Math Teach.

POOLE, JESSICA; Oxnard HS; Port Hueneme, CA; (3); 28/479; French Clb; Intrml Cheerldng; High Hon Roll; Hon Roll; Golden St Exam Algebra & Geom; Outstndng Achvt Math/Sci & Geom.

POOLE, MEDEA; Liberty Union HS; Oakley, CA; (2); 1/448; Cmnty Wkr; Letterman Clb; NFL; Speech Tm; Varsity Clb; Band; Mrchg Band; Pep Band; Var L Trk; High Hon Roll; Athltc Dir Awd Acdmc Achvt Vrsty Trck; Stu Of Mnth Achvt Awd Math Dept; CIF Schlr Ath; UC Davis; Med.

POOLE, OCTAVIA; Liberty Union HS; Oakley, CA; (3); 1/450; FCA; Pres Sec French Clb; Intnl Clb; Letterman Clb; NFL; Pep Clb; Sec Hist Speech Tm; Varsity Clb; Band; Drm Mjr(t); CA Schlsrhp Fed; Stu Rep To The Schl Brd; N Coast Section Cif Schlr Athlt Track; UC Davis; Med.

POOMEE, ANNE W; Modesto HS; Modesto, CA; (3); 1/540; AFS; Hosp Aide; Intnl Clb; Treas Key Clb; Spanish Clb; Mrchg Band; Cit Awd; High Hon Roll; 89-90 Mock Trial Cmptn Mdl & Cert Outstndng Achvt; Stanford; Med.

POON, ADAM; Rosemead HS; Rosemead, CA; (3); Computer Clb; Key Clb; Science Clb; Cit Awd; Hon Roll; Prfct Atten Awd; Chem Engrng.

POON, WILBURG; Rosemead HS; Rosemead, CA; (4); 20/398; Cmnty Wkr; Computer Clb; FBLA; JA; Treas Key Clb; Treas Math Clb; Science Clb; Spanish Clb; Thesps; Treas Stu Cncl; Futurist Club Pres & Fndr 90; CA ST U Pomona; Engrng.

POONI, KULBIR; Yuba City HS; Yuba City, CA; (3); 99/400; Hon Roll; Asian Clb; Accntng.

POOR, STACEY L; Lassen Union HS; Susanville, CA; (3); Art Clb; Church Yth Grp; Bsktbl; JV Trk; Hon Roll; CSF; 1st & 3rd Pl Voctnl Olympcs Drftng Comptn 89-90; Grphc Dsgnr.

POPE, AMY; Chico SR HS; Chico, CA; (4); 1/368; Pres Church Yth Grp; Cmnty Wkr; French Clb; Teachers Aide; Acpl Chr; Chorus; Church Choir; Stu Cncl; Stat Bsktbl; Var JV Cheerldng; Piano Stu; Rgnl Sci Fair Wnnr; BYU; Engl.

POPE, ELIZABETH; North Valley Christian Schl; Central Valley, CA; (3); Church Yth Grp; Chorus; School Musical; Rep Soph Cls; Sec Jr Cls; Cheerldng; Capt Sftbl; Hon Roll; Shasta Coll; Elem Educ.

POPE, ERIN; Central Catholic HS; Manteca, CA; (3); 18/54; Art Clb; Sec French Clb; Sec Intnl Clb; Science Clb; Sec Sr Cls; Bsktbl; Cheerldng; Powder Puff Ftbl; Score Keeper; Otdrs Clb; Chrstn Svc Awd; Eng III Acad Achvmnt Awd; Pre-Med.

POPE, ERIN L; Santana HS; Santee, CA; (2); 14/379; Var L Bsktbl; L Var Sftbl; Hon Roll; Golden St Algebra Exam High Hnrs.

POPE, JENNIFER A; Yucca Valley HS; Yucca Valley, CA; (1); Church Yth Grp; Sftbl; Hon Roll; Acadmc Awd 4.0 GPA; Vrsty Stbl Lttr & Acdmc Lttr; Stu Month All A's 90; Law.

POPE, KEVIN F; San Joaquin Memorial HS; Fresno, CA; (4); Aud/Vis; French Clb; Key Clb; Library Aide; Science Clb; Spanish Clb; Intrml Mgr Bsktbl; High Hon Roll; Hon Roll; CSF; Friday Night Live; St Marys Coll; Finance.

POPE, KUEN; Marina HS; Huntington Bch, CA; (4); 18/505; AFS; Am Leg Aux Girls St; JA; Key Clb; Spanish Clb; Treas Frsh Cls; Rep Soph Cls; Rep Jr Cls; High Hon Roll; Pres Acad Fit Awd; CA Poly; Bus.

POPKES, SHERI; Modesto HS; Modesto, CA; (2); Church Yth Grp; Acpl Chr; Church Choir; Sec Soph Cls; Hon Roll; CSF.

POPKES, SUSAN; Modesto HS; Modesto, CA; (4); 16/471; Church Yth Grp; Scholastic Bowl; Science Clb; Sec Acpl Chr; Ed Yrbk; Sec Stu Cncl; High Hon Roll; Yng Repblcns, Pres; Bethel Coll; Ed.

POPP, SYLVIA R; College Park HS; Martinez, CA; (3); Church Yth Grp; Teachers Aide; Var Sftbl; High Hon Roll; Hon Roll; Tchr.

POPPE, KELLY L; Gahr HS; Artesia, CA; (3); 436/468; Church Yth Grp; Hosp Aide; Office Aide; Teachers Aide; Ed Nwsp; Stu Cncl; Cit Awd; High Hon Roll; Spec Awds Span Lvl II; U Of Santa Barbara.

POPPLETON, EMILY ANN; Redlands HS; Mentone, CA; (4); Church Yth Grp; Drama Clb; JV L Swmmng; High Hon Roll; Hon Roll; Cal Poly Pomona; Psych.

POPPLEWELL, KRISTINA A; Clovis HS; Clovis, CA; (1); Drama Clb; School Musical; Cheerldng; Hon Roll; UCLA; Actress/Teacher.

POPULIN, ARIEL; Highland HS; Bakersfield, CA; (2); JV Capt Bsktbl; JV Capt Ftbl; Hon Roll; Spanish NHS; MVP Bsktbl; UCLA; Bus.

POQUE, MICHELE; Princeton HS; Princeton, CA; (4); 2/10; Am Leg Aux Girls St; FBLA; FFA; FHA; GAA; Pep Clb; Cit Awd; DAR Awd; Gov Hon Prg Awd; Chico ST U; Law.

POR ROS, THARITH; Sanger HS; Sanger, CA; (4); Intnl Clb; Teachers Aide; Phrmcst.

PORCH, PATRICIA ANN; Pasadena HS; Pasadena, CA; (2); Greenpeace Interest; PCC; Marine Bio.

PORCHER, OMEGA H; San Gorgonio HS; San Bernardino, CA; (3); English Clb; Chorus; Var L Ftbl; JV Var Trk; Sprts Med.

PORCIUNCULA, RENELYNNE I; Chula Vista HS; San Diego, CA; (2); 25/535; Church Yth Grp; Pep Clb; Church Choir; Ed Nwsp; Cheerldng; L Mgr(s); JV Sftbl; JV Tennis; Cit Awd; Hon Roll; Asian Club Pres & Secy; Gldn St Exam Hnrs Geom; Peer Mnstry; U Of CA San Diego; Psych.

PORNBANLUELAP, JARAN; Chaminade College Prep; Northridge, CA; (3); Hon Roll; NHS; USC; Bus.

PORRAS, MARIA J; Notre Dame HS; Riverside, CA; (3); 32/140; Church Yth Grp; Debate Tm; French Clb; Hosp Aide; School Musical; Powder Puff Ftbl; French Hon Soc; Hon Roll; Medicine.

PORRATA, ALEXANDRA M; Tomales HS; Inverness, CA; (4); Cmnty Wkr; Drama Clb; Letterman Clb; Service Clb; Ski Clb; Spanish Clb; School Play; VP Frsh Cls; VP Soph Cls; Var Tennis; Bank Of Amer Plaq Wnnr Frgn Lang; Puerto Rito Colegio Rosa Bell; Dominican Coll; Nrsng.

PORRES, LUIS E; Ganesha HS; Pomona, CA; (3); Aud/Vis; Nwsp; Bsbl; Var JV Ftbl; Wt Lftg; High Hon Roll; Hon Roll; Prfct Atten Awd; Fullerton; Graphic Arts.

PORTACIO, ELEANOR LYNN; James Logan HS; Union City, CA; (3); Church Yth Grp; Var Color Guard; Treas Frsh Cls; Rep Stu Cncl; JV Cheerldng; JV Pom Pon; Powder Puff Ftbl; JV Tennis; Ldrshp 87; Marching On 90; Excllnc In Ldrshp Awd 87-88; Commercial Art.

PORTEOUS, JUSTIN E; Arcata HS; Arcata, CA; (2); Cit Awd; High Hon Roll; Hon Roll; Prfct Atten Awd; Grnblt Jujitsu; Peer Cnslng; UC Davis; Med Doctor.

PORTER, AMY K; Mira Loma HS; Carmichael, CA; (4); 7/257; French Clb; Office Aide; Teachers Aide; Band; Mrchg Band; Pep Band; Cit Awd; High Hon Roll; Hon Roll; Pres Acad Fit Awd; CSF Lf; Humboldt ST; Envrnmntl Bio.

PORTER, APRIL C; Fontana HS; Fontana, CA; (3); Drama Clb; Chorus; Stage Crew; Hon Roll; Badminton Tm; Acad Decathlon Tm; CA Schlrshp Fndtn; Math.

PORTER, BRANDON D; Hiram W Johnson HS; Sacramento, CA; (3); 8/150; FBLA; Ftbl; Vllybl; High Hon Roll; Hon Roll; NHS; OK U; Arch.

PORTER, BRIAN A; Fontana HS; Fontana, CA; (3); FBLA; Band; Mrchg Band; Var Ftbl; Intrml Tennis; Intrml Trk; Intrml Wrstlng; Hon Roll; Econ.

PORTER, DANA; Folsom HS; Folsom, CA; (2); Model UN; Teachers Aide; Flag Corp; Rptr Nwsp; High Hon Roll; Opt Clb Awd; Stu Reaching Out; Friday Night Live; Natural Hlprs; Med.

PORTER, DANIELLE L; Chino HS; Chino, CA; (2); Hon Roll; Silver Spur Awd.

PORTER, DAWN M; North HS; Bakersfield, CA; (3); 24/400; Drama Clb; JA; Ski Clb; Spanish Clb; Teachers Aide; Stage Crew; Rptr Nwsp; Var Tennis; Hon Roll; Spanish NHS; Intl Bus.

PORTER, JENNIFER; El Cajon Valley HS; El Cajon, CA; (3); Church Yth Grp; Cmnty Wkr; German Clb; SADD; Chorus; Church Choir; Color Guard; Drill Tm; Swing Chorus; Letterman Clb; Asusa Pacific U; Med.

PORTER, JULIE M; Washington HS; Fremont, CA; (2); French Clb; Pep Clb; Stu Cncl; JV Gym; Var Trk; Hon Roll; Hgh Hnrs Gldn St Exm Algbr; GSE Geom Hnrs; Piano; UCLA; Pblc Rltns.

PORTER, JUSTIN D; Tracy Joint Union HS; Tracy, CA; (2); Church Yth Grp; SADD; JV Bsbl; High Hon Roll; Hon Roll; Kiwanis Awd; Stanford U; Sprts Jrnlsm.

PORTER, LARA R; North HS; Bakersfield, CA; (2); Fld Hcky; English Clb; FCA; Sec French Clb; Ski Clb; Teachers Aide; Band; Var Crs Cntry; Var Trk; Hon Roll; Azuza Pacific U; Psych.

PORTER, LISA N; Olathe S/Temecula HS; Murrieta, CA; (2); Drama Clb; Office Aide; School Play; Stage Crew; Variety Show; High Hon Roll; Hon Roll; UCLA Syracuse; Soc Sci.

PORTER, RACHELE F; Downtown Business Magnet HS; Wilmington, CA; (2); Intrml Drill Tm; Intrml Cheerldng; Var Sftbl; Cit Awd; Hon Roll; Prfct Atten Awd; Spellman; Bus Law.

PORTER, SAMANTHA; Arcadia HS; Arcadia, CA; (4); Hosp Aide; Red Cross Aide; Hist Band; Hist Mrchg Band; Orch; Var Swmmng; Hon Roll; NHS; Prfct Atten Awd; Pasadena City Coll; Psych.

PORTER, SCOTT S; Del Campo HS; Fair Oaks, CA; (2); 3/460; Teachers Aide; Var Ftbl; Var Trk; High Hon Roll; CSF; Med.

PORTER, SEAN; Damien HS; Pomona, CA; (2); Drama Clb; School Play; Hon Roll; Fishing,Drama & Baseball Card Club; CA Polytech; Bus Admin.

PORTER, SEAN J; Colton HS; Colton, CA; (1); UCLA; Med.

PORTER, STEVE A; Victor Valley HS; Victorville, CA; (4); Office Aide; ROTC; SADD; School Play; Bsktbl; Trk; Wt Lftg; Hon Roll; Police Ofcr.

PORTIGAL, SHANA E; Calabasas HS; Woodland Hills, CA; (1); Service Clb; Thesps; Rep Stu Cncl; Hon Roll; Pres Schlr; Golden St Exam Geom; 1st Pl Intermediate Music Recital; CA Hnrs Soc; UCLA; Law.

PORTILLO, DELMY E; Westmoor HS; Daly City, CA; (3); Church Yth Grp; Computer Clb; Drama Clb; Office Aide; Spanish Clb; SADD; Teachers Aide; Drill Tm; Stage Crew; San Diego ST; Comp.

PORTILLO, EILEEN R; Gladstone HS; Azusa, CA; (3); Sec FBLA; SADD; Drill Tm; Jr Civitan; Bus.

PORTILLO, OSCAR D; Ramona HS; Riverside, CA; (3); 18/403; Ed Nwsp; Var Crs Cntry; Var Trk; Boston U; Aerospace.

PORTILLO, REYMUNDO H; Kingsburg HS; Kingsburg, CA; (3); Church Yth Grp; Spanish Clb; Hon Roll; JC.

PORTILLO, STEPHANIE MARIE; Modesto Christian HS; Waterford, CA; (4); Boy Scts; Church Yth Grp; Cmnty Wkr; Hosp Aide; Pres Clb; SADD; Teachers Aide; Variety Show; Phtg Rptr Yrbk; Crs Cntry; Peer Cnslr; Point Loma Nazarene Coll; Phy.

PORTLOCK, KERI LIN; Atwater HS; Atwater, CA; (3); Drama Clb; FCA; 4-H; FFA; FHA; Key Clb; SADD; JV Cheerldng; JV Swmmng; JV Tennis; Hi Deps; Tchr.

PORTNOY, ANDREW F; Loyola HS; Culver City, CA; (2); Drama Clb; Pep Clb; Chorus; School Musical; School Play; Stage Crew; Variety Show; Nwsp; Var Cheerldng; High Hon Roll; CSF; Amer Nusimatic Assn Schlrshp; Yale; Bus.

PORTO, DONALD; Miramonte HS; Orinda, CA; (1).

PORTUGAL, GABRIEL; St Genevieve HS; North Hollywood, CA; (2); Church Yth Grp; Ski Clb; Band; High Hon Roll; Hon Roll; Prfct Atten Awd; Certfcte Outstndng Achievement; Cal S U; Elec Technology.

PORTUGAL IV, RAMON A; Leuzinger HS; Hawthorne, CA; (3); Art Clb; Teachers Aide; Chorus; School Musical; Trk; Cit Awd; Prfct Atten Awd; Straight A Awd; Med.

PORUP, JENS MATTHEW; Casa Roble Fundamental HS; Orangevale, CA; (2); 3/461; Church Yth Grp; Debate Tm; French Clb; Math Tm; Science Clb; Jazz Band; Mrchg Band; High Hon Roll; Pres Acad Fit Awd; VP Interact Clb.

POSARD, MARK; Buena HS; Ventura, CA; (1); Boy Scts; Temple Yth Grp; Var Bsbl; Var Bsktbl; Hon Roll; Pres Acad Fit Awd; U AZ; Pro Athlete.

POSAS, RUTH T; Hill Top HS; Chula Vista, CA; (4); 14/439; AFS; Sec Art Clb; Intnl Clb; Pep Clb; Phtg Nwsp; Hon Roll; Prfct Atten Awd; Pres Acad Fit Awd; CSF; San Diego ST U; Nrsng.

POSEY, COLLEEN E; Monte Vista HS; Casa De Oro, CA; (2); Church Yth Grp; Cmnty Wkr; SADD; Orch; Bible Study Tchr; UCLA; Pediatrician.

POSEY, MARLA L; Valley HS; Sacramento, CA; (2); 39/431; Drama Clb; Service Clb; Var Tennis; Hon Roll; Mock Trial Awd; CSF; Stu Rchng Out Cert Vnltrng; Acadmc Olympcs Awd; Spellman; Bus Admin.

POSEY, RACHEL; Nogales HS; Walnut, CA; (3); UC Berkeley.

POSEY, VIC E; Taft Union HS; Taft, CA; (4); 41/239; French Clb; Key Clb; Letterman Clb; Pep Clb; Service Clb; SADD; Varsity Clb; Band; Jazz Band; Mrchg Band; Bank Of Am Achvt Awd-Music; John Philip Sousa Awd; Firestone ET Drag Racing Series-Schl Rep; Fresno ST U; Arch.

POSHARD, DEAN G; Del Mar HS; San Jose, CA; (3); 75/250; Letterman Clb; Bsktbl; Var Vllybl; Hon Roll; Marine Bio.

POSS, DAVID MICHAEL; Rubidoux HS; Moreno Valley, CA; (4); 35/700; Letterman Clb; Teachers Aide; Varsity Clb; Socr; High Hon Roll; Hon Roll; Pres Acad Fit Awd; Mrtl Arts-Taijutsu-1st Degree Blk Blt; Wrk 20-30 Hrs Wkly At Stater Bros; Plyd Sccr Snc Age 6-Goal Kpr; UCR; Bus Admin.

POSSELT, THEO; Berkeley HS; Berkeley, CA; (4); Ntl Merit SF; Philosophy & Fine Arts Club; First STEP Peace Club.

POST, ALISON J; Redding Seventh-Day Adventist HS; Anderson, CA; (1); 2/8; Church Yth Grp; Office Aide; Ski Clb; Teachers Aide; Acpl Chr; Chorus; Color Guard; Drill Tm; School Musical; School Play; ASB Ofcr; Adventure Clb P; Rio Lindo Advntst Acad; Soc Wrk.

POST, AMANDA; Carlmont HS; San Carlos, CA; (2); 1/400; Temple Yth Grp; Orch; JV Tennis; CA Yth Symphony; Badminton; CSF.

POST, BETHANIE L; Milpitas HS; Milpitas, CA; (4); Sec Boy Scts; French Clb; ROTC; Jazz Band; Mrchg Band; Rep Stu Cncl; Hon Roll; NHS; Mock Trl Tm; All Amer Star Perf Tm; Brigham Young U; Music Cmpstn.

POST, CHARLENE A; Montclair HS; Ontario, CA; (4); Key Clb; Ski Clb; Band; Mrchg Band; Hon Roll; Ntl Merit Ltr; Prfct Atten Awd; Montclair Band Treas; Vet Asst; Vet.

POST, KAREN B; Oxnard HS; Oxnard, CA; (3); Dance Clb; French Clb; Office Aide; SADD; Teachers Aide; Stu Cncl; Var Swmmng; High Hon Roll; Hon Roll; Jr NHS; UC Davis; Genetics.

POST, LESLIE A; Sacred Heart Cathedral Prep; San Francisco, CA; (4); 50/189; Spanish Clb; Chorus; Stage Crew; Var Trk; Intrml Vllybl; Hon Roll; Humboldt ST U; Bus Adm.

POST, MICHELLE A; Mayfair HS; Lakewood, CA; (4); 2/160; Am Leg Aux Girls St; Key Clb; SADD; Co-Capt Color Guard; School Play; Lit Mag; Treas Frsh Cls; VP Jr Cls; Chrmn Stu Cncl; Sal; CSF Pres; Pr Cnslr; UCLA; Counslng.

POST JR, PAUL; Apple Valley HS; Apple Valley, CA; (3); French Clb; Trk; Hon Roll; CA Poly Pomona; Elec Engrng.

POST, THOMAS A; Bishop O'dowd HS; Alameda, CA; (2); 4/500; Service Clb; Tennis; Jr Statesman Amer; Law.

POST, WILLIAM; Bishop O'dowd HS; Alameda, CA; (2); 25/500; Church Yth Grp; Cmnty Wkr; Tennis; High Hon Roll.

POSTELL, BRANDY L; North HS; East Nicolaus, CA; (3); Drama Clb; French Clb; JA; Rep Band; Treas Chorus; Jazz Band; Mrchg Band; Pep Band; School Play; Stage Crew; UC David; Radiology.

POSTICH, MARK; Woodside Priory Schl; Portola Valley, CA; (2); 5/19; Computer Clb; JV Bsktbl; JV Tennis; Hon Roll.

POSTLE, JOEL; San Gorgorio HS; San Bernardino, CA; (3); Bsktbl; Var JV Trk; Cit Awd; Pres Acad Fit Awd.

POSTLETHWAITE V, HARTLEY; Hillsdale HS; San Mateo, CA; (4); 17/286; Am Leg Boys St; Boy Scts; Church Yth Grp; Service Clb; Stage Crew; Rptr Nwsp; Rptr Yrbk; Stat Crs Cntry; JV Var Socr; Capt Var Swmmng; Eagle Scout; Svc Commssn Pres; CSF; Golden St Math Exam Hnrs Alg; Naval Acad; Commrcl Pilot.

POSTMA, ANDREA J; Tustin HS; Santa Ana, CA; (2); Church Yth Grp; Cmnty Wkr; GAA; Intnl Clb; SADD; Teachers Aide; Var Tennis; Var Trk; High Hon Roll.

POSTMA, NIKI; Tustin HS; Tustin, CA; (3); Church Yth Grp; German Clb; Latin Clb; Office Aide; Pep Clb; Church Choir; Orch; Off Frsh Cls; Capt Cheerldng; Hon Roll; Westmont Coll.

POSTON, RENEE A; Ramona HS; Ramona, CA; (2); 19/350; Drill Tm; Hon Roll; CSF; U Of CA Santa Barbara.

POSTOVOIT, RACHEL M; Bishop Amat HS; West Covina, CA; (3); Drama Clb; Teachers Aide; School Musical; School Play; Rptr Nwsp; JV Trk; Opt Clb Awd; Cmmnty Vlntr Lanterman St Hosp; Camp Cnslr Recreation In San Diego Post; CSUN; Theatre Arts.

POSTRADO, MARIE VIC M; Balboa HS; San Francisco, CA; (3); Hon Roll; Yth Crt Pgm; Schl 100 Buc Socty; Schl Ssci Educ Pgm; Med.

POTKONJAK, NICKI M; Mira Mesa HS; San Diego, CA; (2); 111/797; Drama Clb; Library Aide; School Play; Stage Crew; Yrbk; Cit Awd; Natl Hnrs Sem Prgm San Diego; St Fnlst Miss Amer Coed Pagnt; Fshn Mrchndsg.

POTKONJAK, STEVEN M; Mira Mesa HS; San Diego, CA; (4); 127/750; Church Yth Grp; Hon Roll; Black Belt Tae Kwon Do Asstnt Instr; Early Admssn Hnr Prgm; Private Pilot License 90; UCSD; Aerspc Engr.

POTOMAC, CHELSEA; Mission Bay HS; San Diego, CA; (2); 1/3800; Church Yth Grp; FTA; Math Clb; Math Tm; Quiz Bowl; Scholastic Bowl; SADD; Lit Mag; Var Swmmng; JV Vllybl; Karate; Tutor; Sci.

POTTER, CARRIE LYN; C K Mc Clatchy HS; Sacramento, CA; (3); 6/390; Cmnty Wkr; Science Clb; Math Tm; High Hon Roll; Ntl Merit SF; Mrchg Band; Church Choir; Treas French Clb; Church Yth Grp; Fnlst In Essay Cont; U Of CA Santa Cruz; Envrnmntl.

POTTER, ELIZABETH A; Central Catholic HS; Modesto, CA; (1); Dance Clb; Hosp Aide; SADD; Teachers Aide; Bsktbl; Cheerldng; Sftbl; Hon Roll.

POTTER, JENNY; Vintage HS; American Canyon, CA; (4); 5/430; Crs Cntry; Trk; Cit Awd; Hon Roll; NHS; Intrct Clb; Stu Exchnge; Dominican Coll; Math.

POTTER, KEVIN R; Paso Robles HS; Paso Robles, CA; (2); Pres Debate Tm; VP FFA; Speech Tm; JV Wrstlng; 4-H Awd; Hon Roll; CA St Wnning Livestck Judgng Team; Rgnl Creed Speakng Wnnr; Cal Poly San Luis Obispo; Ag.

POTTER, MICHELE R; Los Amigos HS; Santa Ana, CA; (3); Dance Clb; Drama Clb; Teachers Aide; Thesps; School Play; Stage Crew; Hon Roll; Kennedy Fndtn; Make A Wish Fndtn; UCI; Dance.

POTTER, PAUL; Santa Maria Joint Union HS; Santa Maria, CA; (2); FFA; JV Bsbl; Bsbl.

POTTER, REBECCA D; Rio Linda HS; Sacramento, CA; (4); German Clb; Spanish Clb; SADD; Teachers Aide; Ed Yrbk; Hon Roll; Medical Psychiatry.

POTTS, KRISTEN M; Corona HS; Corona, CA; (2); 5/473; Church Yth Grp; Letterman Clb; SADD; Rptr Nwsp; Ed Yrbk; Lit Mag; Mgr(s); Vllybl; High Hon Roll; Pres Acad Fit Awd; Sch Recgntn Geo Gldn St Exam; Sci Fair-1st Pl Phys Sci Sch Level, 5th Pl Dist Level & 2nd Overall.

POTTS, MICHELLE; Cope JR HS; Redlands, CA; (1); Church Yth Grp; Chorus; Drill Tm; Yrbk; Cit Awd; Hon Roll; Prfct Atten Awd; Intr Dsgnr.

POTTS, STEPHANIE LYNNE; Colfax HS; Meadow Vista, CA; (3); 23/165; Office Aide; SADD; Flag Corp; High Hon Roll; Hon Roll; Ed Yrbk; Yrbk Staff; UC Davis; Psych.

POTYONDY, GABE JAMES; Orange Lutheran HS; Villa Park, CA; (3); Ski Clb; SADD; Hon Roll; Pres Acad Fit Awd; Tnns; UC Irvine; Med.

POUEY, EDOUARD J; St Ignatius College Prep; San Francisco, CA; (3); Var JV Socr; Hon Roll; Liturgy Grp; Bus Admin.

POULATIAN, ADRINEH E; Burbank HS; Burbank, CA; (4); 35/429; Spanish Clb; SADD; Pres Acad Fit Awd; Smmr Medcl Career Pgm; Sign Lang; U Of CA San Diego; Comp Sci.

POULIN, RICHARD T; Dos Palos HS; Dos Palos, CA; (2); AFS; SADD; Band; JV Bsbl; Var Tennis; JV Wrstlng; Hon Roll; Author.

POULIOT, ANGELA; San Ramon Valley HS; Danville, CA; (4); 290/450; Church Yth Grp; Drama Clb; Office Aide; Pep Clb; Teachers Aide; School Musical; School Play; Stage Crew; Rep Soph Cls; Rep Jr Cls; CA All Stars Chrldng Squad Ntl Champs Both Pom Poms & Chrldng 89-90; Lk Merit Schl Nrsng; Nrsng.

POULOS, BRETT A; Trabuco Hills HS; Mission Viejo, CA; (1); 21/340; SADD; Bsktbl; Var Golf; High Hon Roll; Hon Roll.

POULOS, RENEE C; Banning HS; Banning, CA; (4); 15/143; Office Aide; Spanish Clb; Teachers Aide; Varsity Clb; Stu Cncl; Sftbl; Swmmng; Vllybl; Cit Awd; Hon Roll; CA ST San Bernardino; Accntng.

POULSEN, DANIELLE; Fort Dick Bible Acad; Brookings, OR; (1); 1/5; Church Yth Grp; School Musical; School Play; Bsktbl; Vllybl; Hon Roll; Schl Activities Piano Player; Point Loma Nazarene Coll; Nanny.

POULSEN, FREDRIK N; Point Loma HS; San Diego, CA; (2); 30/482; Library Aide; ROTC; Teachers Aide; Color Guard; Cit Awd; Hon Roll; Kiwanis Awd; Prfct Atten Awd; Toastmstrs Intl; Brnz Merit Awd; Rcgntn Awd-Schl Svc; U S Naval Acad; Math.

POULSEN, GREG A; Enterprise HS; Redding, CA; (3); JV Var Bsbl; JV Var Bsktbl; JV Ftbl; Var Golf; JV Score Keeper; Intrml High Hon Roll; BYU; Bus.

POULSEN, JESPER; Los Alamitos HS; Seal Beach, CA; (3); French Clb; Science Clb; Teachers Aide; Var Tennis; Hon Roll; Ntl Merit Ltr; Gldn St Exam Geom & Alg High Hnrs; Bus.

POULSEN, JESSICA S; Los Altos HS; Hacienda Hgts, CA; (2); Cmnty Wkr; Hosp Aide; Rptr Phtg Yrbk; Var Swmmng; Hon Roll; Ntnl Chrty League; U Of TX; Physcl Thrpst.

POULSON, LISA J; Burbank HS; Burbank, CA; (3); Pres Church Yth Grp; Office Aide; Pres VP Chorus; School Musical; Variety Show; Rep Stu Cncl; Stat Bsktbl; JV Sftbl; Pres Acad Fit Awd; CJSF; Most Tlntd; 3 Vocal Music Schlrshps; BYU; Vocal Music.

POULTER, CLINT H; Walnut HS; Walnut, CA; (2); 133/479; Church Yth Grp; Ski Clb; JV Var Bsktbl; Var L Ftbl; Var L Trk; Wt Lftg; Hon Roll; Bus.

POUND JR, WILL B; Carlmont HS; Redwood City, CA; (3); Wt Lftg; San Luis Obispo Cal Poly; Music.

POUNDS, JEFFREY R; Casa Grande HS; Petaluma, CA; (3); 57/288; Var Bsbl; Hon Roll; NHS; Phys Thrpy.

POURADIB, MERSEDEH; University Of San Diego HS; San Diego, CA; (4); 23/305; Cmnty Wkr; Hosp Aide; Intnl Clb; Math Clb; Science Clb; Service Clb; Ski Clb; Pres Frsh Cls; JV Tennis; High Hon Roll; CSF; Math, Frnch & Vlntr Awds; Tutorng Clb; UCSD; Bio.

POURHAMIDI, JALEH; Mt Carmel HS; San Diego, CA; (4); Drama Clb; French Clb; Key Clb; Math Clb; Math Tm; Science Clb; SADD; Band; School Play; Stage Crew; CSF Seal Bearer; U Of CA San Diego; Med.

POUX, CHRISTINE M; Silver Valley HS; Springfield, VA; (2); Church Yth Grp; Cmnty Wkr; Letterman Clb; Red Cross Aide; VP Frsh Cls; JV Bsktbl; Var Sftbl; JV Vllybl; High Hon Roll; Wntrfst Prncss 89; Outstndng Engl Stu 90; Hnrb Mntn Alg I GSE Test; VA Tech; Ed.

POWELL, ALANNA N; Trinity HS; Weaverville, CA; (1); FFA; GAA; Ski Clb; JV Bsktbl; Var Sftbl; High Hon Roll; Pres Acad Fit Awd; Agri Mgmt.

POWELL, ALEXANDRIA V; Vintage HS; Vallejo, CA; (1); Girl Scts; Key Clb; School Musical; School Play; Bsktbl; Cheerldng; Trk; Vllybl; Wt Lftg; Spelman Coll; Engl.

POWELL, CINDY; Mother Lode Christian Schl; Sonora, CA; (3); Pep Clb; Band; Chorus; Jazz Band; Mrchg Band; Pep Band; School Musical; School Play; Yrbk; VP Jr Cls; Phys Thrpy.

POWELL, COLLETTE K; Templeton HS; Templeton, CA; (2); Hosp Aide; Teachers Aide; Yrbk; Off Frsh Cls; Off Soph Cls; Var Score Keeper; Var Socr; JV Trk; High Hon Roll; Hon Roll; Sci Sci Hnr Cert; 89 Homcmng Ct Princss; Ct Reportng.

POWELL, DEANNA R; Chino HS; Chino, CA; (2); Church Yth Grp; FCA; Chorus; Church Choir; Stage Crew; Cit Awd; Hon Roll; Schlrshp Awd; Ebony Excllnc Clb; Chrch Yth Ldr; Long Beach ST U; Nrs.

POWELL, DIANA; Highlands HS; Sacramento, CA; (2); Treas Stu Cncl; Capt Cheerldng; Hon Roll.

POWELL, DOUGLAS E; Escondido HS; Escondido, CA; (1); Church Yth Grp; Cmnty Wkr; Quiz Bowl; Orch; Music Prfcnty Violin, Fddl, Orgn, Mndln, Bss Gtr & Piano; Stg Prfrmnc; Fddl Chmpnshp; Trvl.

POWELL, JENNIE G; Mt Diablo HS; Concord, CA; (3); FHA; SADD; Teachers Aide; Score Keeper; JV Vllybl; Cit Awd; High Hon Roll; Hon Roll; Tutored Stu Math & Other Sub 2 Yrs; Csf; Dixie JC; Bus Mgmt.

POWELL, LATASHA R; Stagg HS; Stockton, CA; (1); GAA; Letterman Clb; JV Bsktbl; Hon Roll; Summer League Bsktbl; Law.

POWELL, LINDEE S; Mt Whitney HS; Visalia, CA; (2); Pres Church Yth Grp; Cmnty Wkr; Drama Clb; Chorus; Church Choir; Stage Crew; Hon Roll; Spcl Olympics Vlntr 86-90; CSF; Brigham Young U; Advrtsng Mgmt.

POWELL, MONICA; Modesto Christian HS; Modesto, CA; (3); Boy Scts; Church Yth Grp; Pep Clb; Teachers Aide; Acpl Chr; Chorus; School Musical; Treas Jr Cls; Stat Bsktbl; Score Keeper; Teen Chptr Cncrnd Women For Amer Co-Ldr; Hi-Deb Modeling.

POWELL, NADINA; Ganesha HS; Diamond Bar, CA; (4); 5/200; FCA; GAA; JA; Office Aide; SADD; Varsity Clb; Church Choir; Pres Sr Cls; Stu Cncl; Capt Bsktbl; Alpha Kappa Alpha Schlrshp; Booster Clb; Math Eng & Sci Achvt; UC San Diego; Poltcl Sci.

POWELL, NICHOLE C; Pilgrim Schl; Los Angeles, CA; (2); 2/12; Chorus; VP Frsh Cls; Pres Soph Cls; Pres Jr Cls; Var L Bsktbl; Var L Vllybl; Cit Awd; NHS; Pres Acad Fit Awd; HOBY; UCLA; Law.

POWELL, RETTA; San Luis Obispo SR HS; San Luis Obispo, CA; (4); 46/289; Church Yth Grp; Dance Clb; 4-H; Intnl Clb; Key Clb; Office Aide; Pep Clb; Ski Clb; SADD; School Musical; Presdntl Clssrm; Black & Gold Schlrshp; Hmcmng & Cls Float Cmmttes; Prom Cmmtte; Golden Tiger Awd; CA Poly; Elem Educ.

POWELL, RYAN A; Capistrano Valley HS; Mission Viejo, CA; (3); CSF; Bus.

POWELL, SAMANTHA J; A A Stagg HS; Stockton, CA; (1); High Hon Roll; CSF.

POWELL, SARA M; Clovis West HS; Fresno, CA; (3); Church Yth Grp; Key Clb; Ski Clb; SADD; Powder Puff Ftbl; Sftbl; Trk; High Hon Roll; Hon Roll; UC San Diego; Orthodntcs.

POWELL, VANESSA JOY; Carson HS; Carson, CA; (3); Church Yth Grp; Drama Clb; FTA; Chorus; Church Choir; Rptr Yrbk; Rep Stu Cncl; Cit Awd; Hon Roll; Prfct Atten Awd; Interact Clb; CSF; Ftbl Tm Stats; Obstetrics.

POWER, ANN E; Apple Valley HS; Apple Valley, CA; (2); Church Yth Grp; Dance Clb; Math Tm; Spanish Clb; Drill Tm; Treas Frsh Cls; Treas Jr Cls; Cit Awd; High Hon Roll; Hon Roll; Span, Hstry, Math, Engl Hnrs; Apple Vly HS Dance Team; Jr Statesmn Amer; UNLV; Pdtrcs.

POWER, CHERYLE CELANE; Victor Valley SR HS; Victorville, CA; (2); Dance Clb; French Clb; SADD; Teachers Aide; Band; Jazz Band; Mrchg Band; Orch; Pep Band; School Musical; Peer Cnslng; U OR; Music.

POWER, CHRIS W; Woodcrest Christian HS; Corona, CA; (4); Church Yth Grp; Drama Clb; Teachers Aide; Acpl Chr; Variety Show; JV Var Bsktbl; JV Ftbl; Var Trk; Var Vllybl; Hon Roll; US Army Resrv Natl Schlr Athl Awd; Athltcs Awd; Svc Awd; Biola U; Psych.

POWER, ERIN T; Ukiah HS; Redwood Valley, CA; (2); Dance Clb; Diving; Gymnst Clb; UC Santa Cruz.

POWER, LISA; Villa Park HS; Villa Park, CA; (2); Hosp Aide; Intnl Clb; Key Clb; Spanish Clb; Off Frsh Cls; Off Soph Cls; JV Bsktbl; Mgr(s); JV Socr; JV Tennis; Mass Commnctns.

POWER, RAYMOND F; Antelope Valley HS; Lancaster, CA; (3); 78/600; JV Vllybl; Hon Roll; CSF.

POWERS, AMBER C; Oak Ridge HS; Camino, CA; (3); Pres 4-H; Intnl Clb; Var L Swmmng; 4-H Awd; High Hon Roll; Hon Roll; Golden St Exam-Geom High Hnrs; Hstry Day Wnnr; Environmntlst Clb; Col Of Arts & Crafts Csmmer Pgm; CSF; Art.

POWERS, AMY; Enterprise HS; Palo Cedro, CA; (3); Church Yth Grp; Intnl Clb; Thesps; Acpl Chr; Band; Church Choir; Orch; School Musical; School Play; Stage Crew; Ecology Club; Photo Club; Shasta JC; Theatre.

POWERS, AMY C; Foothill HS; Bakersfield, CA; (3); 121/356; FCA; Office Aide; Ski Clb; Teachers Aide; Stage Crew; Var Bsktbl; Var Powder Puff Ftbl; Var Sftbl; Var Vllybl; Hon Roll.

POWERS, COURTNEY; Taft Union HS; Taft, CA; (1); 1/245; Drama Clb; Key Clb; Pres Frsh Cls; Stu Cncl; Cheerldng; Tennis; Hon Roll; CA Schlstc Fed; Friday Night Live Brd; Poltcl Sci.

POWERS, DARCIE E; Branham HS; San Jose, CA; (1); VP Frsh Cls; Var Crs Cntry; High Hon Roll; Hon Roll; CSF.

POWERS, ERIN; Taft Union HS; Taft, CA; (4); 13/180; Ed Yrbk; VP Frsh Cls; Pres Soph Cls; Rep Jr Cls; Pres Stu Cncl; Var Cheerldng; DAR Awd; Bank Of Amer Plaque Awd; Sec Teacher.

POWERS, JEFFREY; Aptos HS; Watsonville, CA; (2); Letterman Clb; Teachers Aide; JV Bsktbl; Var L Golf; Golfer Of Year SCCAL; Golf Prof.

POWERS, JULIE E; San Juan HS; Citrus Heights, CA; (3); 11/284; Key Clb; Teachers Aide; Chorus; Intrml Sftbl; High Hon Roll; Kiwanis Awd; Prfct Atten Awd; Cert Of Excel Wrtng, Stand Of Prof Test; Grnd Rnnr Up CA Cent Vly Sci/Engr Fair; Natl Piano Plyng Aud; Bio.

POWERS, KRISTIN; Palo Verde HS; Blythe, CA; (4); Chorus; Variety Show; Ed Nwsp; Hon Roll; Natl Sci Mrt Awd; UCR; Jrnlsm.

POWERS, MICHAEL W; Chaminade College Prep; Northridge, CA; (4); Cmnty Wkr; Key Clb; Rep Frsh Cls; Var L Bsbl; Intrml JV Bsktbl; JV Var Ftbl; Wt Lftg; NHS; Pres Acad Fit Awd; Pres Schlr; U CA San Diego; Bus.

POWERS, PATRICIA; Antelope Valley HS; Lancaster, CA; (3); 53/635; Dance Clb; Teachers Aide; Chorus; Drill Tm; Off Soph Cls; Off Jr Cls; Gym; Hon Roll; Dnc Tm Ldr; Stu Agnst Gng Actvty Sec; Debnrs; Pallamar JC; Dnc.

POWERS, PATRICIA L; St Joseph HS; Artesia, CA; (3); 38/190; Church Yth Grp; Cmnty Wkr; GAA; JV Var Sftbl; Prfct Atten Awd; CSF; Vllybl & Slo-Ptch Sfbl; Anml Cr.

POWERS, SHARA T; Coalinga-Huron Unified HS; Coalinga, CA; (2); VP FFA; Treas Band; Sec Chorus; Jazz Band; Mrchg Band; Tennis; Hon Roll; Sect Proj Comp Gold Awd; Cow Palace Jr Grnd Natl Lvstck Expo Brnz Grp; ASU; Real Est.

POWERS, TINA J; James Lick HS; San Jose, CA; (1); Dance Clb; Office Aide; Rep Frsh Cls; High Hon Roll; Hon Roll; Prfct Atten Awd; CSF Clb; San Jose ST U; Med.

POWERS, TONI A; Sherman E Burroughs HS; Ridgecrest, CA; (2); Teachers Aide; Temple Yth Grp; Cit Awd; Hon Roll; Pres Acad Fit Awd; 2nd Pl Optmst Club Essay Cntst; Indstrl Arts Dept Awd; San Diego ST U; Pltcl Sci.

POWJEJEEN, SHERRY; John F Kennedy HS; Granada Hills, CA; (2); JV Vllybl; Hon Roll.

POY, VINCENT C; International Studies Acad; San Francisco, CA; (2); Band; Lit Mag; High Hon Roll; Hon Roll; Comp Prgmg; Electrncs; CA Inst Of Tech; Physcs.

POYTHRESS, PENNETHEIA L; Turlock HS; Turlock, CA; (3); 36/1200; Pep Clb; Spanish Clb; Band; Drill Tm; Mrchg Band; Pep Band; School Play; Variety Show; Sec Frsh Cls; Rep Stu Cncl; CA HS Rodeo Assn; Northern CA Jr Rodeo Assn; Womens Team Ropng Assn; Fresno ST U; Arch.

POYTHRESS, SOPHIA; International Studies Acad; San Francisco, CA; (2); Hon Roll; Musical Instruments; Pre Law.

POZNANSKY, KAREN; Irvine HS; Irvine, CA; (1); Hosp Aide; Temple Yth Grp; Nwsp; Tennis; Hon Roll; Ply Piano; Phtgrphy; Tennis; Med.

POZO, SANTIAGO P; Mark Keppel HS; Monterey Park, CA; (3); Var L Crs Cntry; Var L Trk; High Hon Roll; Hon Roll; Medallion Awd Wnnr; CIF Trk Qlfr 800 M Run; Aerospace Engrng.

POZOS, YOLANDA M; Albany HS; Rodeo, CA; (1); Flag Corp; JV Bsktbl; JV Vllybl; High Hon Roll; Jr NHS; Sci.

POZZI, LISA; Tomales HS; Valley Ford, CA; (4); 3/41; Am Leg Aux Girls St; Debate Tm; 4-H; FFA; Math Clb; Office Aide; Ski Clb; Pres Spanish Clb; Varsity Clb; Ed Yrbk; SUSDS Stu Mth 88; UC Davis; Eng.

PRABHAKAR, PAVITRA; Whitney HS; Cerritos, CA; (3); 1/176; Drama Clb; VP JA; Key Clb; Teachers Aide; School Play; Phtg Yrbk; Sec Jr Cls; High Hon Roll; Ntl Merit Ltr; CA Schlrshp Fed; Arch.

PRACK, LANG; Edison HS; Stockton, CA; (2); Spanish Clb; High Hon Roll; Hon Roll; Pedtrcn.

PRADD, MENDY L; J W North HS; Riverside, CA; (2); Treas Frsh Cls; JV Sftbl; Black Stu Union; Amer Legion Awd; San Diego ST U; Bus.

PRADITTAPHONH, INKHAM T; Oakland HS; Oakland, CA; (2); 70/620; Pres Church Yth Grp; Cmnty Wkr; Dance Clb; Church Choir; School Musical; Variety Show; Yrbk; Hon Roll; BYU; Psycht.

PRADO, ABIMAEL; Monache HS; Porterville, CA; (2); Art Clb; Latin Clb; JV Trk; JV Wrstlng; Mexican Amer Clb; Elec Engr.

PRADO, CHAD A; Hamilton Music Acad; Sylmar, CA; (1); Band; Orch; Intrml Bsktbl; Intrml Vllybl; Cit Awd; Hon Roll; USC; Law.

PRADO, CHERRIE MARIE; Alameda HS; Alameda, CA; (3); 26/287; High Hon Roll; Pre-Med.

PRADO, CYNTHIA A; St Joseph HS; Norwalk, CA; (2); 12/200; Cmnty Wkr; GAA; Hosp Aide; Chorus; Pres Nwsp; Var Crs Cntry; High Hon Roll; CSF; Harvard U; Med.

PRADO, ESPERANZA; Santiago HS; Santa Ana, CA; (2); Spanish Clb; Hon Roll; CSF; Early Outreach Pgm UCI; UCI; Bus Admin.

PRADO, MARQUETTA M; Sierra Vista HS; Baldwin Park, CA; (1); Band; Mrchg Band.

PRADO, PATRICIA; Leuzinger HS; Hawthorne, CA; (3); Church Yth Grp; Dance Clb; Var Capt Crs Cntry; Capt Trk; Girls Vrsty Trk Coachs Awd 89, 90; UCLA; Comp Prgmr.

PRADO, RITA; Vacaville HS; Vacaville, CA; (3); Science Clb; Spanish Clb; Pediatrics.

PRADO, ROSA MARIA; Holy Family HS; Glendale, CA; (3); Art Clb; Drama Clb; Library Aide; Stu Cncl; Hon Roll; CA Schlrshp Fed; Dance; CA ST Polytech U; Mgmt.

PRAHM, KELLY; St Francis HS; Los Altos, CA; (3); Church Yth Grp; Cmnty Wkr; Service Clb; SADD; Rep Frsh Cls; JV Cheerldng; Capt Powder Puff Ftbl; JV Var Vllybl; High Hon Roll; NHS; Natl Chmap Vlybl; Teen Bd.

PRANKE, LYNN MARIE; Dos Pueblos HS; Goleta, CA; (4); 23/281; Pres Debate Tm; High Hon Roll; Hon Roll; NHS; Pres Acad Fit Awd; Mock Trial Team Atty; UC San Diego; Pltcl Sci.

PRANOTO, DARWIN; Cerritos HS; Cerritos, CA; (2); Church Yth Grp; Trk; Hon Roll; UCLA; Elec Engr.

PRAPONG, WIJAN; Cajon HS; San Bernardino, CA; (2); 1/400; Chess Clb; Var Tennis; High Hon Roll; Scrd 800 On Math Sctn Of PSAT; John Hopkins Spnsrd Smmr Schl For Tlntd Yths; CA Schltc Fed; Med.

PRASAD, DENNIS; Rancho Cotate HS; Rohnert Park, CA; (4); Cmnty Wkr; SR JC; Comp Prgmr.

PRASAD, NEEL; Beyer HS; Modesto, CA; (3); Cit Awd; Hon Roll; Straight A Awd; CSF; Pharmacist.

PRASAD, PINKI; Washington HS; Fremont, CA; (2); Stu Cncl; Hon Roll; Opt Clb Awd; Pres Acad Fit Awd; Golden ST Awd; CSF; Med.

PRASAD, PRANEETA; Luther Burbank HS; South Sacramento, CA; (3); 29/276; Hon Roll; Prfct Atten Awd; Sci.

PRASAD, SHAILENDRA P; South San Francisco HS; South San Francis, CA; (3); French Clb; Math Clb; Science Clb; Var Crs Cntry; Mgr(s); Var Tennis; Wt Lftg; Jr NHS; Kiwanis Awd; Pres Acad Fit Awd; CSF Club; Tech.

PRAT, CHANTEL S; Manteca HS; Manteca, CA; (2); 11/400; Dance Clb; 4-H; Key Clb; SADD; Teachers Aide; JV Bsktbl; High Hon Roll; Hon Roll; Golden ST Exam Hnrs; Tchrs Awd In Hlth, Sfty, Spnsh & Geomtry; 4.0 Awd; Law.

PRATHER, DAVID; Fontana HS; Fontana, CA; (2); Boy Scts; Pep Band; Bsbl; Bsktbl; Ftbl; Trk; Wt Lftg; Wrstlng; Hon Roll; Law Enfrcmnt.

PRATHER, MICHELLE; Fontana HS; Grand Terrace, CA; (1); Church Yth Grp; Cit Awd; High Hon Roll; Hon Roll; Classcl Ballet/Piano Stu; Summer Camp Cnslr; Hl ST U; Marine Bio.

PRATT, CYNTHIA ELAINE; San Dimas HS; San Dimas, CA; (3); FBLA; Hosp Aide; Key Clb; SADD; Cit Awd; High Hon Roll; Hon Roll; Cmnty Wkr; Computer Clb; JA; Royal Star 89-90; Hosptl Cert 100 Hrs & Pin; ROSES Awd Atten & Schlrshp US Hstry; CA Poly; Engl Lit.

PRATT, JENNIFER M; Grace M Davis HS; Modesto, CA; (2); Church Yth Grp; SADD; Band; Mrchg Band; Peer Facilitating; Modern Dance; Brigham Young U; Psych.

PRATT, KATHERINE; Foothill HS; Pleasanton, CA; (4); 12/323; Drama Clb; Hosp Aide; School Play; Stage Crew; Ed Nwsp; Interact Clb Treas; Lewis/Clark Coll Portland OR.

PRATT, KIMBERLY M; Notre Dame HS; Northridge, CA; (4); 49/279; Cmnty Wkr; JA; Latin Clb; Red Cross Aide; SADD; Ed Yrbk; High Hon Roll; NEDT Awd; Amnesty Intnl; CSF Gold Sealbearer; Cmmnty Assts Homeless Youngsters; U CA-SAN Diego; Journls.

PRATT, MICHELLE; Granada HS; Memphis, TN; (3); Church Yth Grp; Hosp Aide; Teachers Aide; Socr; Var Trk; Hon Roll; Child Care; Ed.

PRATT, STEVEN J; University City HS; San Diego, CA; (3); 490/600; Boy Scts; Computer Clb; Key Clb; Teachers Aide; Rptr Lit Mag; Bus Cmptr Cnsltng.

PRATTO, GABRIELLE; Pinole Valley HS; Pinole, CA; (1); Spanish Clb; School Play; High Hon Roll; Hon Roll; CSF.

PRAUGHT, JEFFREY; Casa Grande HS; Petaluma, CA; (3); 4/285; Boy Scts; Spanish Clb; Pres Band; Jazz Band; Mrchg Band; Pep Band; Lit Mag; Var Golf; Hon Roll; NHS; Meteorology.

PRAUS, JULIANE M; A A Stagg HS; Stockton, CA; (3); JV Var Cheerldng; JV Var Vllybl; Hon Roll; Academic Decathalon Team.

PRAUSS, JENIFER; Del Norte HS; Crescent City, CA; (3); Church Yth Grp; Dance Clb; Drama Clb; Speech Tm; Thesps; School Musical; School Play; Stage Crew; Variety Show; Rep Soph Cls; 2nd Rnnr Up Jr Miss Pgnt; Spring Dance Concert; 3rd Pl 89 Cnty Wide Geom Tst; U Of CA; Drama.

PRAVONGVIENGKHAM, SONEPHETH; Huntington Beach HS; Huntington Bch, CA; (2); JV Bsktbl.

PRAYNSIRISAK, TANAVART; Savanna HS; Anaheim, CA; (2); Drama Clb; Rep Frsh Cls; Rep Soph Cls; Var Swmmng; Prfct Atten Awd; Jr Var Water Polo; CSF; Comp Sci.

PRAYTOR, JIM E; Thomas Downey HS; Modesto, CA; (4); Church Yth Grp; Spanish Clb; Chico ST; Constrctn Engr.

PREACH, AMY A; Folsom HS; Folsom, CA; (3); Intnl Clb; Band; Mrchg Band; Orch; Pep Band; School Musical; Var JV Tennis; High Hon Roll; NHS; Cty CA All St Hnr Band Bassoon; CSF; Stu Rechng Out; Hlth Sci.

PREADO, AMELIA; Mayfield SR HS; Los Angeles, CA; (2); Intrml Wt Lftg; Hon Roll; NHS; Campus Guide 89; U Of Southern CA; Med.

PRECIADO, ARACELY; Hueneme HS; Oxnard, CA; (3); #22 In Class; Cit Awd; High Hon Roll; Prfct Atten Awd; Accntnt.

PRECIADO, CYNTHIA; Piedmont Hills HS; San Jose, CA; (4); Pres French Clb; Math Tm; Red Cross Aide; Stage Crew; Rptr Nwsp; Treas Jr Cls; JV Bsktbl; Sec NHS; Schl Site Cncl Rep; U Of CA Berkeley; Bus Admin.

PRECIADO, MARIA A; Hueneme HS; Oxnard, CA; (2); 6/300; Dance Clb; Latin Clb; High Hon Roll; Prfct Atten Awd; MESA; Hnr Crcl; FLA; ESRP; Engrng.

PRECLARO, JODDI; Bishop Amat Memorial HS; Oceanside, CA; (3); Church Yth Grp; Cmnty Wkr; Drama Clb; Spanish Clb; JV Trk; UCSD; Cmptr Sci.

PREFTOKIS, ANASTASIA A; Skyline HS; Oakland, CA; (2); Church Yth Grp; Dance Clb; Pep Clb; Church Choir; Pres Acad Fit Awd; Church Vlybl & Bsktbl Team; Promise Schlr; Drug & Health Ed Awd.

PREGO, CARMEN A; John Glenn HS; Norwalk, CA; (2); Dance Clb; Office Aide; Band; Variety Show; Crs Cntry; Flmnco Dncng; U CA Santa Barbara; Bus.

PREHODA, SARAH M; Fontana HS; Fontana, CA; (2); Church Yth Grp; Drama Clb; Hosp Aide; Color Guard; School Musical; High Hon Roll; Pres Schlr; CSF; Outstndng Achvt Drama; Hnrbl Mntn San Bernadino Cnty Wrtng Celbtn; Jrnlsm.

PREISSLER, DEBBY; St Joseph HS; Cerritos, CA; (2); 49/196; Church Yth Grp; GAA; Service Clb; Drill Tm; Hon Roll; Darke U; Chld Psych.

PREITE, PAIGE L; Highland HS; Bakersfield, CA; (3); Church Yth Grp; JA; Key Clb; Pep Clb; Band; Off Stu Cncl; Hon Roll; Engrng.

PREMJEE, AYAZ; Santa Monica HS; Santa Monica, CA; (1); Boy Scts; Church Yth Grp; Cmnty Wkr; Library Aide; Office Aide; Teachers Aide; School Play; JV Bsktbl; JV Socr; Swmmng; Stu Month; Elec Engrng.

PRENTICE, SHELBY E; Simi Valley HS; Simi Valley, CA; (3); Yrbk; Sftbl; Moorpark CC.

PRESA, AURORA; Montgomery HS; San Diego, CA; (4); 4/390; Ed Nwsp; Capt JV Cheerldng; Tennis; Elks Awd; Hon Roll; Pres Acad Fit Awd; Assoctd Stu Body Cmmssnr Stu Actvts; Outstndng Schlr; U Of CA Riverside; Bus.

PRESA, PERCIVAL L; Irvington HS; Fremont, CA; (3); 5/308; Spanish Clb; JV Var Tennis; CSF Mem; Lang Dept Awd Span III; Indl Arts Dept Awd Drftg I; Cal Poly San Luis Obispo; Eng.

PRESCHER, LISA M; Antelope Valley HS; Lancaster, CA; (4); Boy Scts; Chess Clb; Natl Beta Clb; Science Clb; Band; Jazz Band; Mrchg Band; Orch; Pep Band; Hon Roll.

PRESCOTT, CAROLEE; Maranatha HS; Sierra Madre, CA; (4); 6/100; Church Yth Grp; Service Clb; Chorus; Church Choir; Nwsp; Var Crs Cntry; Var Trk; High Hon Roll; Bibl Memry Hnr Rl; Bio.

PRESCOTT, DERIC; Saint Augustine HS; Chula Vista, CA; (2); 16/189; Boy Scts; Pres Key Clb; Pres Model UN; Office Aide; Speech Tm; Church Choir; Rptr Frsh Cls; Ed Yrbk; Stat Bsbl; High Hon Roll; Rcvd Congrssnl Medla Of Hnr From Congrssmn Jim Bates; Stanford; Attorney.

PRESCOTT, JAMES J; Esperanza HS; Yorba Linda, CA; (2); 14/671; Art Clb; Church Yth Grp; Cmnty Wkr; Debate Tm; NFL; Speech Tm; Trk; Wt Lftg; High Hon Roll; NHS; Mock Trial Team Lawyer, 3rd In Cnty; Stu Union Of Poltcl Awrnss; U CA Berkeley; Politics.

PRESCOTT, LIBBIE; Esperanza HS; Yorba Linda, CA; (1); 1/627; Var Debate Tm; Drama Clb; NFL; Speech Tm; Chorus; Rep Frsh Cls; Sec Soph Cls; Cit Awd; High Hon Roll; Jr NHS; Jobs Daughters Bethel; Stu Union-Poltcl Awrnss-Publcty Cmmssnr; Mock Trial Team; Jrmiss Teen LA Co 90; Stanford.

PRESCOTT, ZAC A; Dana Hills HS; Dana Point, CA; (3); Church Yth Grp; JV Ftbl; JV Socr; Pres Acad Fit Awd; Sonoma ST.

PRESLER, CINDY LEE; Poway HS; Poway, CA; (4); 24/680; Pep Clb; SADD; Intrml Tennis; Cit Awd; High Hon Roll; NHS; Teen Repblcn; CA Schltc Fdrtn; U Of CA; Comp Sci.

PRESLEY, APRIL DAWN; Fontana HS; Fontana, CA; (2); 1/1400; Cmnty Wkr; Pep Clb; Quiz Bowl; Scholastic Bowl; Off Soph Cls; Cheerldng; High Hon Roll; Hon Roll.

PRESLEY, JASON; Lutheran HS; Norco, CA; (2); 29/135; Letterman Clb; Varsity Clb; Var L Bsbl; Intrml L Bsktbl; JV Capt Ftbl; Intrml Socr; Intrml Trk; Intrml Vllybl; Intrml Wt Lftg; Intrml Cit Awd; JV Sprtsmnshp Awd; MVP JV Ftbll, Var Bsbll Sprt Awd; Sci Awd 88-89; Fresno ST; Bus.

PRESLEY, KIMI L; San Pasqual HS; Escondido, CA; (1); Teachers Aide; Chorus; Variety Show; SDSU; Elem Schl Tchr.

PRESLEY III, MARION E; Poway HS; Columbia, SC; (1); Boy Scts; German Clb; Science Clb; Hon Roll; Prfct Atten Awd; Pres Acad Fit Awd; Acad Team Capt; Natl Lang Arts Olympiad.

PRESLEY, TAMEKA S; Sacramento HS; Sacramento, CA; (2); Cmnty Wkr; GAA; Var Socr; Hon Roll; Wrtng/Rdng; Chld Care; CIF SAC Joaquin Sctn Awd.

PRESSER, DAVID Z; San Marcos HS; Santa Barbara, CA; (3); 5/330; Debate Tm; Hosp Aide; Intnl Clb; Temple Yth Grp; Acpl Chr; School Musical; Yrbk; Treas Jr Cls; Treas Stu Cncl; Rennsaeler Math P Sci Awd; Med.

PRESSEY, KAREN M; Temecula Valley HS; Temecula, CA; (2); Drama Clb; Thesps; School Musical; School Play; Lit Mag; Jnr Exchnge Clb; U CA; Engl.

PRESSMAN, JESSICA B; Torrey Pines HS; Del Mar, CA; (1); Lit Mag; Sec Frsh Cls; Sec Soph Cls; Cheerldng; Hon Roll; Stanford U; Law.

PRESTON, CHAUCA A; Lindhurst HS; Olivehurst, CA; (3); Dance Clb; Drama Clb; Thesps; Band; Drm Mjr(t); Mrchg Band; Pep Band; School Play; Stage Crew; Var Swmmng; Secy Aquatics Club; Golden St Schlr Schl Recgntn Geom, Algebra I; Acad Decathalete; Bio.

PRESTON, CHRIS; San Marcos HS; San Marcos, CA; (4); Pres Computer Clb; Math Tm; Quiz Bowl; Scholastic Bowl; Science Clb; Variety Show; Ed Nwsp; High Hon Roll; Hon Roll; Ntl Merit Ltr; CA Schlrshp Fed; San Diego ST U; Sci.

PRESTON, ELIZABETH K; Torrey Pines HS; San Diego, CA; (1); Church Yth Grp; FCA; Hon Roll; Horseback Riding Engl Show Jmpng; UCLA; Chrstn.

PRESTON, INDIA A; Santa Clara HS; Oxnard, CA; (3); Pep Clb; Teachers Aide; Rep Jr Cls; Vllybl; Hon Roll; Interact Clb; U Davis; Vet.

PRESTON, JENNIFER M; Fresno HS; Fresno, CA; (2); Rptr Yrbk; Bsktbl; Hon Roll; Teaching.

PRESTON, MELISSA L; St Francis HS; San Jose, CA; (4); Church Yth Grp; Cmnty Wkr; Service Clb; Intrml Mgr Sftbl; Intrml Mgr Vllybl; Hon Roll; Cal Polytechnic ST U; Mech Eng.

PRESTON, MERLE E; Irvine HS; Irvine, CA; (3); German Clb; Spanish Clb; Off Sr Cls; JV Tennis; Intrml Trk; CSF; Natl Charity League Sec, 2nd VP; Accntng.

PRESTON, RICHARD R; Cajon HS; San Bernardino, CA; (3); 12/400; Rep Sr Cls; Rep Stu Cncl; Var L Bsbl; Var L Ftbl; High Hon Roll; Hon Roll; NHS; Wght Lftng; Hghst Cchs Awd Bsbl & Ftbl; Med.

PRESUTTI, ANNIE J; Marina HS; Huntington Beach, CA; (2); GAA; Varsity Clb; Var Bsktbl; Var Sftbl; Stat Vllybl; Hon Roll; Pres Acad Fit Awd; AASA; UCLA; Exotic Anml Trnr.

PRESZLER, DAVID M; Yreka Union HS; Gazelle, CA; (3); 13/198; Church Yth Grp; Pres 4-H; Q&S; Ed Nwsp; JV Bsktbl; Ftbl; Var Tennis; Top 100 Awd; Cmptr Prog.

PRETZER, JEFFREY M; Clovis HS; Clovis, CA; (2); JV Golf; Hon Roll; CA ST U Fresno; Bio.

PREUSS, RACHEL; Calavaras HS; Angels Camp, CA; (3); 3/180; AFS; VP Intnl Clb; Ski Clb; SADD; Teachers Aide; Ed Yrbk; Stat Trk; JV Vllybl; Hon Roll; Wrking At Presch.

PREWETT, JOE E; Mills HS; Burlingame, CA; (2); Orch; Nwsp; Rep Stu Cncl; JV Bsbl; JV Bsktbl; All-League Awd Bsbl & Bsktbl; CA Yth Symphny.

PREZ, MARTHA; Sweetwater HS; National City, CA; (3).

PREZ, NICHOLAS R; Pioneer HS; Whittier, CA; (4); Science Clb; Rep Ski Clb; Rep Spanish Clb; Var Golf; Var Tennis; High Hon Roll; United Hispanic Schlrshp Fndtn; Booster Clb Schlrshp Fndtn; UC Irvine; Dentistry.

PREZIOSO, KAREN; Casa Grande HS; Petaluma, CA; (3); 50/300; High Hon Roll; Hon Roll; NHS; Pres Acad Fit Awd; CSF; Nursing.

PRIBBLE, VANESSA L; Coast Union HS; Cambria, CA; (2); FHA; Pep Clb; SADD; Chorus; Cheerldng; Sftbl; Cit Awd; Hon Roll; Pres Acad Fit Awd; Cambrid Cnctn Plyrs Actng Grp; Hi Deb Mdlgn/Slf Conf Pgm; Tlnt Show Prtcpnt Mock Rock Wnnr 2nd Pl; San Jose ST; Vocal Music.

PRIBYL, JERALYN M; Mills HS; Burlingame, CA; (3); Church Yth Grp; Dance Clb; Drama Clb; Pep Clb; SADD; School Play; L Cheerldng; Var L Pom Pon; High Hon Roll; Hon Roll; Lang.

PRICE, AMBER D; Norte Vista HS; Riverside, CA; (2); 30/500; Church Yth Grp; Acpl Chr; Capt Cheerldng; DAR Awd; High Hon Roll.

PRICE, AMY N; College Park HS; Martinez, CA; (3); Teachers Aide; Hon Roll; Sacramento ST; Nrs.

PRICE, BERNARD J; Sun Set HS; Hayward, CA; (3); Sec Key Clb; Variety Show; Rep Frsh Cls; Rep Soph Cls; Rep Jr Cls; VP Stu Cncl; Var Golf; Hon Roll.

PRICE, BRENDA M; Orangewood Adventist Acad; Garden Grove, CA; (2); Church Yth Grp; Teachers Aide; Chorus; High Hon Roll; Hndbll Choir; Occptnl Thrpy.

PRICE, CAMERON S; Servite HS; Anaheim, CA; (3); 12/148; Debate Tm; Letterman Clb; Red Cross Aide; Varsity Clb; School Musical; Var Swmmng; Intrml Vllybl; Ntl Merit Ltr; Water Polo-Varsty Ltr; Engrng.

PRICE, CHRISTINE; John Burroughs HS; Burbank, CA; (2); Art Clb; High Hon Roll; Hon Roll; Share Schl Org Burbank; Instrmntlst.

PRICE, CHRISTOPHER J; Capistrano Valley HS; Mission Viejo, CA; (3); Boy Scts; JV Bsbl; Bsktbl; Var Crs Cntry; Prfct Atten Awd; Golden St Exam Geom Hnrs 87-88; CSF 88-89; Hstrcl Soc VP 88-89.

PRICE, CHRISTOPHER L; Yosemite HS; Coarsegold, CA; (2); FBLA; Band; Nwsp; Hon Roll; U Miami; Robotics.

PRICE, DANIEL R; Palo Alto HS; Palo Alto, CA; (2); Jazz Band; Mrchg Band; Pep Band; Nwsp; JV Tennis; French Hon Soc; High Hon Roll; Waterpolo; Asn Cult Exchng Clb.

PRICE, DERRICK DWAYNE; South Bay Lutheran HS; Inglewood, CA; (2); Boy Scts; Service Clb; Stu Cncl; Bsbl; Prfct Atten Awd; Loyola U; Cmmrcl Wrtr.

PRICE, ERIN; Birmingham HS; Van Nuys, CA; (3); Church Yth Grp; SADD; Rptr Yrbk; Rep Frsh Cls; Rep Jr Cls; Var Mgr Crs Cntry; Var Mgr Trk; High Hon Roll; CSF; Frgn Exchng Stu; Earth Rights Club; Med.

PRICE, EVAN P; Oakdale HS; Waterford, CA; (3); #10 In Class; JV Crs Cntry; JV Trk; High Hon Roll; Hon Roll; Law.

PRICE, GARY S; Liberty Union HS; Brentwood, CA; (1); Church Yth Grp; FCA; Band; Mrchg Band; Pep Band; Rep Frsh Cls; Intrml Ftbl; Intrml Wt Lftg; JV Wrstlng; Hon Roll; Leroy Geddes Awd; San Jose St; Chiroprctr.

PRICE, HEATHER M; Marysville HS; Marysville, CA; (1); Key Clb; Pep Clb; Sftbl; Hon Roll; Friday Night Live.

PRICE, JENNIFER J; Clayton Valley HS; Antioch, CA; (3); Church Yth Grp; Drama Clb; Speech Tm; School Musical; School Play; Hon Roll; Crossfire Campus Clb; Conflict Mngmnt VP; Youth Grp/Staff; CVHS; Bethel; Business.

PRICE, JENNY A; Laguna Hills HS; Laguna Hills, CA; (1); #33 In Class; Church Yth Grp; Bsktbl; Swmmng; CSF; Arch.

PRICE, JULIE; Del Campo HS; Carmichael, CA; (4); 52/429; Church Yth Grp; Cmnty Wkr; Debate Tm; Red Cross Aide; Speech Tm; Capt Tennis; Hon Roll; NHS; Voice Dem Awd; Pepperdine U; Psych.

PRICE, KELLI J; Rio Mesa HS; Camarillo, CA; (3); FTA; Teachers Aide; Rep Stu Cncl; Camp Cnslr; Spcl Olympc Hlpr; SDSU; Early Chldhd Educ.

PRICE, KEVIN; Montclair HS; Ontario, CA; (1); Church Yth Grp; JV L Ftbl; Var L Swmmng; Wt Lftg; Hon Roll; Healty Club; Marine Biologist.

PRICE, KEVIN S; Salinas HS; Salinas, CA; (2); AFS; Math Tm; Pres Band; Jazz Band; Mrchg Band; Orch; Pep Band; Ed Nwsp; Capt Var Bsktbl; Var Golf; Cntrl Coast Sctn Hnr Band; Schlr Athl Awd Bsktbl; Hghst GPA Bsktbl Team; U Of CA Davis; Music.

PRICE, KRECIA L; Barstow HS; Barstow, CA; (1); Vllybl; Hon Roll; Harvard U; Corp Law.

PRICE, KRISTI; Santana HS; Santee, CA; (3); Debate Tm; Sec Drama Clb; Girl Scts; Math Tm; Office Aide; Ski Clb; Speech Tm; SADD; Teachers Aide; School Play; Associated Stu Body Treas; Jrnlst.

PRICE, LAURA M; Cuyama Valley HS; Cuyama, CA; (2); School Play; Var Bsktbl; Var Cheerldng; Var Sftbl; Var JV Vllybl; High Hon Roll; Hon Roll; Pres Acad Fit Awd; Athlete Yr; Vet Med.

PRICE, LAUREN MIEL; St Helena HS; Saint Helena, CA; (4); Am Leg Aux Girls St; Cmnty Wkr; Key Clb; Var Tennis; High Hon Roll; Hon Roll; Pres Acad Fit Awd; CSF; Acad Dcthln; Amnsty Intl Sec; UC Davis.

PRICE, LIZ; Hemet HS; Hemet, CA; (2); Drama Clb; Spanish Clb; Thesps; School Musical; School Play; Stage Crew; Yrbk; Cit Awd; High Hon Roll; CSF; Author.

PRICE, MICHELLE C; North HS; Bakersfield, CA; (2); Drama Clb; German Clb; Intnl Clb; JA; Service Clb; Teachers Aide; Thesps; Swmmng; Hon Roll; Jr NHS; Bus Admin.

PRICE, RHONDA L; Grossmont HS; La Mesa, CA; (3); 46/392; Church Yth Grp; Dance Clb; French Clb; German Clb; Hosp Aide; Ski Clb; Hon Roll; Pres Acad Fit Awd; BYU; Accntng.

PRICE, ROBERT; Saddleback HS; Irvine, CA; (4); 3/500; Am Leg Boys St; Church Yth Grp; Pres English Clb; Var Capt Crs Cntry; Var Capt Trk; Ntl Merit SF; Pres Acad Fit Awd; Rotary Awd; Voice Dem Awd; Elec Engrng.

PRICE, SAMANTHA D; Orosi HS; Orosi, CA; (3); Church Yth Grp; Intnl Clb; Pep Clb; SADD; Rptr Nwsp; Yrbk; Hon Roll; International Order Of Rainbow For Girls Past Worthy Advisor.

PRICE, SHAWN A; Aptos HS; La Selva Beach, CA; (2); FFA; Office Aide; Socr; Comp Aided Dsgn.

PRICE, STEPHANIE E; Skyline HS; Oakland, CA; (2); Art Clb; Church Yth Grp; Cmnty Wkr; Debate Tm; GAA; Key Clb; Library Aide; Office Aide; Teachers Aide; Orch; 6th Annual Moot Ct Cmptn Prtcptn Awd; Spelman Coll; Law.

PRICE, SUMMER; Laguna Hills HS; Laguna Hills, CA; (1); Band; Jazz Band; Mrchg Band; Pep Band; Swmmng; JV Tennis; Hon Roll; GAIA; Creative Wrtng Clb; Music.

PRICE, WENDY NOELLE; Lincoln Preparatory HS; San Diego, CA; (4); 1/227; AFS; Aud/Vis; Church Yth Grp; Treas French Clb; FTA; Letterman Clb; Quiz Bowl; SADD; Varsity Clb; Band; Red Blt-Tang Soo Do-8th Prmtn; Piano-Cmpsng Sngs & Lyrcs; UC Santa Barbara; Educ.

PRICHARD, AMY E; Cajon HS; San Bernardino, CA; (2); Wrtng Celebrtn-Poetry Div Wnnr; Golden Lariat-Poetry Edtr.

PRICHARD, KATHLEEN M; San Juan HS; Citrus Heights, CA; (4); 93/268; French Clb; Girl Scts; Hon Roll; American River Coll; Landscpng.

PRICHARD, SHELLY D; Lutheran HS; Yorba Linda, CA; (3); Church Yth Grp; Teachers Aide; Band; JV Var Crs Cntry; Hon Roll; Cross Country Team Hgh Cumulative GPA Avg Awd; Arch.

PRIDE, MELETHIA L; Stagg HS; Stockton, CA; (2); Church Yth Grp; GAA; Teachers Aide; Band; Bsktbl; Powder Puff Ftbl; Trk; Cit Awd; Prfct Atten Awd; Med.

PRIEGO, CANDIDA; Garey HS; Pomona, CA; (3); Prfct Atten Awd; Law.

PRIEST, BECKY; Wasco Union HS; Wasco, CA; (2); Church Yth Grp; Drama Clb; Math Clb; School Play; Stage Crew; Treas Frsh Cls; Treas Soph Cls; High Hon Roll; Hon Roll; Prfct Atten Awd; Interact Clb; Golden Cert Awd.

PRIETO, HERMAN; Channel Islands HS; Oxnard, CA; (4); Art Clb; School Play; Nwsp; Yrbk; Socr; Oxnard Coll; Engr.

PRIETO, LA DAWN E; Sonora Union HS; Sonora, CA; (2); 58/375; Church Yth Grp; SADD; Acpl Chr; Chorus; School Musical; Variety Show; VP Soph Cls; JV Bsktbl; Var Trk; Hon Roll; U CA Davis; Pre Med.

PRIETO, MONIQUE; Moorpark HS; Moorpark, CA; (3); FBLA; Key Clb; Pep Clb; Treas Stu Cncl; Cheerldng; Pom Pon; Score Keeper; Hon Roll; Dance Cls; Waitress/Hostess; UCLA; Bus.

PRIETO, RACHEL G; Eisenhower HS; Rialto, CA; (2); Drill Tm; Hon Roll; NHS; Pres Acad Fit Awd; Pediatrics.

PRIGGE, LAURA L; Woodland HS; Woodland, CA; (3); Red Cross Aide; Band; Mrchg Band; Var L Bsktbl; Var L Sftbl; Elks Awd.

PRIJATEL, JEAN M; Huntington Beach HS; Huntington Beach, CA; (2); Church Yth Grp; Girl Scts; Model UN; Red Cross Aide; Ski Clb; High Hon Roll; Hon Roll; Pres Acad Fit Awd; Environmental Law.

PRILL, JOHN E; Bellflower HS; Bellflower, CA; (3); 49/200; Band; Jazz Band; Treas Mrchg Band; School Musical; School Play; Hon Roll; Science Clb; Teachers Aide; Orch; Pep Band; Most Superlative Player Drum Line; Louis Armstrong Awd Jazz Band; CAP Prgm; Outstndng Stu; Naval Acad; Engr.

PRILL, MILA M; Foothill SR HS; Sacramento, CA; (4); 1/280; Key Clb; Scholastic Bowl; Science Clb; Orch; Elks Awd; High Hon Roll; Val; CSF Pres; Sacramento Yth Symphny; All St Hnr Orchstra; Seymour Fnlst; Lawrence Hall Sci Biotech Sympsm; Stanford U; Molecular Bio.

PRIME, MARY; Fairfield HS; Fairfield, CA; (2); Cmnty Wkr; ROTC; Band; Mrchg Band; Rep Frsh Cls; Rep Stu Cncl; Sftbl; Cit Awd; Jr NHS; Drug Prvntn Sympsm-Prvntn 90; Booker T Washington Revised Cnfrnc; Air Force Acad; Aerospc.

PRIMO, PABLO C; South Bay JR Acad; Gardena, CA; (3); Boy Scts; Bsktbl; Socr; Wt Lftg; Cit Awd; Hon Roll; Engr.

PRIMOUS, DAWNEE M; Pasadena HS; Sierra Madre, CA; (3); Church Yth Grp; JA; Office Aide; Speech Tm; Teachers Aide; Acpl Chr; Chorus; Drill Tm; Mgr(s); Trk; Fnlst 19th Annual Natl Tnager Pgnt; Spelman; Music.

PRINCE, KEITH; Clovis HS; Clovis, CA; (4); Varsity Clb; Ftbl; Powder Puff Ftbl; Wt Lftg; Hon Roll; Ftbl 2nd Team All NYL; Fresno ST.

PRINCIPI IV, ANTHONY J; Torry Pines HS; Rancho Santa Fe, CA; (3); 150/400; Church Yth Grp; FCA; Key Clb; Letterman Clb; Varsity Clb; Ed Nwsp; Pres Frsh Cls; Var L Ftbl; Var L Lcrss; JV Wrstlng; MVP USAF Acad La Crosse Camp 90; San Diego Cty All Star La Crosse 89-90; USAFA; USAF.

PRINGLE, MEREDITH A; Casa Roble Fundamental HS; Citrus Heights, CA; (2); 10/461; Church Yth Grp; Spanish Clb; Church Choir; High Hon Roll; CSF; Stu Rchng Out; Fri Night Live; Duke U.

PRINS, LORA; John W North HS; Riverside, CA; (2); Cheerldng; Socr; Swmmng; Hon Roll; UCLA; Drama.

PRIOLO, WENDY L; Pioneer HS; San Jose, CA; (3); FHA; Girl Scts; Office Aide; Tennis; Interact Club; Vlntr Wrk; Camp Cnslr; ASB Cmmssnr; De Anza JC.

PRISCO, MARNI; Etiwanda HS; Alta Loma, CA; (4); 4/489; Debate Tm; Science Clb; Phtg Yrbk; Rep Sr Cls; Rep Stu Cncl; Swmmng; Tennis; High Hon Roll; Masonic Awd; NHS; CSF; Hillside Aquatic Team; U CA Davis; Anml Sci.

PRISK, ANDREA B; St Joseph HS; Long Beach, CA; (4); 3/173; Drama Clb; French Clb; Key Clb; Pres Science Clb; School Play; Stage Crew; High Hon Roll; Pres Acad Fit Awd; CA Schlrshp Fed Sealbearer; CA ST U Long Bch; Marine Bio.

PRITCHARD, RYAN A; Sac Adventist HS; Citrus Heights, CA; (2); Church Yth Grp; Ski Clb; Band; Chorus; Bsktbl; Ftbl; Score Keeper; Socr; Sftbl; Trk; Elec Engr.

PRITZKAU, DAVID; Newark Memorial HS; Newark, CA; (4); 2/370; Capt Quiz Bowl; SADD; High Hon Roll; Prfct Atten Awd; Pres Acad Fit Awd; Rotary Awd; Sal; Tandy Technlogy Schlr; Sci/Scl Sci & Math Deptmntl Hnrs; UCLA; Physics.

PROBST, LYNETTE; Charter Oak HS; Glendora, CA; (4); 5/363; Office Aide; Pres Science Clb; Spanish Clb; Speech Tm; SADD; Flag Corp; Rptr Nwsp; Stu Cncl; JV Swmmng; Var L Tennis; U Of CA Irvine; Psych.

PROBST, MONICA LYNNE; Christian HS; El Cajon, CA; (4); 3/100; Church Yth Grp; Pep Clb; Science Clb; Ski Clb; Spanish Clb; Teachers Aide; Yrbk; Hon Roll; CSF; Pt Loma Nazarene Coll; Elem Ed.

PROBSTFIELD, BRANDI; Douglass JR HS; Woodland, CA; (1); Band; Mrchg Band; Yrbk; Stu Cncl; Capt Cheerldng; High Hon Roll; VP Jr NHS; Prfct Atten Awd; Pres Acad Fit Awd; Vlntr Chrldng Instrctr CA Yth Ftbl Pgm; Make Porcelain Dolls; Stanford; Chld Psych.

PROCHAZKA, SIMONA; El Cajon Valley HS; El Cajon, CA; (3); 1/393; Letterman Clb; Yrbk; Var L Ftbl; Capt Socr; JV Sftbl; Trk; High Hon Roll; Condors Sccr Team-Capt; UC Santa Barbara; Chem.

PROCLIVO, ANDREW; Poway HS; San Diego, CA; (3); Rep Stu Cncl; Bsbl; JV Bsktbl; High Hon Roll; Hon Roll; NHS; Loyola Marymount; CPA.

PROCOPIO, GINA; Grossmont HS; La Mesa, CA; (4); 13/381; Church Yth Grp; Cmnty Wkr; Key Clb; Letterman Clb; Math Clb; Ski Clb; SADD; Teachers Aide; Varsity Clb; Church Choir; Stu Athltc Trnr Vrsty Ftbl Tm; Pre Med.

PROCTOR, BRANDIE D L; Santa Rosa HS; Larkfield, CA; (3); Cmnty Wkr; English Clb; French Clb; Office Aide; Ed Yrbk; Ed Lit Mag; Sec Treas Frsh Cls; High Hon Roll; Opt Clb Awd; Rotary Awd; Frgn Exch To France 90-91; Evergreen Olympia; Lib Arts.

PROCTOR, JENNIFER L; North HS; Bakersfield, CA; (1); Drama Clb; VP JA; Spanish Clb; Teachers Aide; School Musical; School Play; Stage Crew; High Hon Roll; Pres Acad Fit Awd; CSF.

PROCTOR, JENNY L; San Rafael HS; San Rafael, CA; (2); Aud/Vis; Cmnty Wkr; Drama Clb; School Musical; School Play; Stage Crew; High Hon Roll; Hon Roll; 1st Pl Proj 6 Video Fstvl Dir; 1st Pl W Proj 6 Video Fstvl 90; Eng Hnrs; Filmmaker.

PROCTOR, LOREN; Tracy Joint Union HS; Tracy, CA; (4); 58/355; FFA; Hon Roll; Intract Clb; Stu Wk; Pres Tracy Hstrcl Soc; CSU; Geology.

PROCTOR, VIRGINIA S.; San Pedro HS; San Pedro, CA; (3); Church Yth Grp; Office Aide; Teachers Aide; Cit Awd; Hon Roll; Comp Stu Of Yr 88; Accntng.

PROEHL, AIMEE; San Leandro HS; San Leandro, CA; (3); 78/1000; Scrkpr Cmnty Wkr; JV Ski Clb; Rep Frsh Cls; Rep Soph Cls; Rep Jr Cls; Rep Sr Cls; Stu Cncl; Var Bsktbl; Score Keeper; Capt Var Socr; Bronco Awd; EBAI All Leag; 1st Tm CT Vrsty Sccr Awd; Edgar Cerf Memrl Awd; 1st Pl Singles/Doubles Tnns; Dartmouth; Visual Arts.

PROKOP, JAMIE M; Manteca HS; Manteca, CA; (2); 48/420; Var Tennis; Hon Roll; ASB Commssnr Of Ralls & Essmbls; Vrsty Lttr Sophmr Yr In Ttns; Mem Drug & Alcohol Free Clb; Tchr.

PROKOP, LARRY E; Woodland HS; Woodland, CA; (2); Church Yth Grp; Hon Roll; Awds-Excllnt Math, Prfct Atten, HEROES; San Luis Obispo; Elec Engr.

PROLA, ELIZABETH I; Bishop O'dowd HS; San Leandro, CA; (3); 2/225; Treas Debate Tm; Ed Nwsp; Chrmn Stu Cncl; JV Var Bsktbl; High Hon Roll; NHS; Sal; Princeton Awd; Soc Women Engrs Math/Sci Awd; UC Berkeley; Bio.

PRONIN, MICHAEL; South Hills HS; W Covina, CA; (4); 16/245; VP Debate Tm; Hosp Aide; Pres Service Clb; Ed Nwsp; Rep Frsh Cls; Rep Soph Cls; Rep Jr Cls; Rep Sr Cls; Sec Stu Cncl; NHS; USC; Bus.

PRONK, LISA N; Grace M Davis HS; Modesto, CA; (2); Drama Clb; French Clb; Thesps; Orch; Hon Roll; CSF; Bio.

PROPSERI, JULIANE M; Red Bluff HS; Red Bluff, CA; (3); Teachers Aide; Bsktbl; Mgr(s); Score Keeper; JV Var Sftbl; Hon Roll; Prfct Atten Awd; JV Sftbl MVP Awd; Shasta Coll; Bus.

PROSSER, MELINDA L; Crescenta Valley HS; Glendale, CA; (4); 3/375; Church Yth Grp; Hosp Aide; Mu Alpha Theta; Church Choir; Mgr Nwsp; Var Capt Swmmng; DAR Awd; Pres NHS; Ntl Merit Ltr; Pres Acad Fit Awd; CSF; Natl Chrty Leag; 3rd Pl Bk Amer-Math, Sci; Stanford U; Law.

PROSYAK, MARGARITA; Birmingham HS; Reseda, CA; (3); FBLA; Key Clb; SADD; Chorus; Ed Yrbk; Cheerldng; Golf; High Hon Roll; Hon Roll; Fashion Dsgn Artst Mnth Awd; Yrbk Staff Achvmnt Awd; Natl Yth Ldrshp Cert Merit; UCSB; Advrtsng.

PROTACIO, JOYANNA C; Etiwanda HS; Alta Loma, CA; (3); Ed Yrbk; Hon Roll; Friday Night Live; Peer Cnslng; La Verne; Psych.

PROTZEL, ALEXANDER L; Albany HS; Albany, CA; (2); Science Clb; Spanish Clb; Teachers Aide; Intrml Bsbl; JV Capt Bsktbl; Var Crs Cntry; Intrml Var Score Keeper; Intrml Sftbl; Intrml Vllybl; Hon Roll; Hgh Hnrs Gldn St Exam-Math; Achvt Chemathon; Chem Tutor; Sci.

PROUDFOOT, MARK; Liberty Union HS; Brentwood, CA; (2); 6/402; Band; Jazz Band; Mrchg Band; Pep Band; UC Davis; Dentistry.

PROUDFOOT, THOMAS; Liberty Union HS; Brentwood, CA; (4); 9/225; Band; Jazz Band; Mrchg Band; Ed Nwsp; Rotary Awd; Mck Trl; Spllng Bee; U Of CA Berkeley; Immunology.

PROULX, JAMES C; Encinal HS; Alameda, CA; (3); 10/277; Hosp Aide; Key Clb; ROTC; Drill Tm; Jazz Band; Mrchg Band; Orch; JV Swmmng; High Hon Roll; CSF Pres, Sec; JSA Treas; Pre-Dentistry.

PROUTY, HEATHER; Turlock Christian HS; Turlock, CA; (4); 6/28; Church Yth Grp; Cmnty Wkr; Teachers Aide; Color Guard; Mrchg Band; School Musical; School Play; Cheerldng; Sftbl; Vllybl; Columbia JC; Forest Ranger.

PROUTY, KATIE; Northview HS; Covina, CA; (4); 1/206; Am Leg Aux Girls St; Cmnty Wkr; Pres GAA; Sec Band; School Play; Ed Yrbk; Off Sr Cls; JV Var Bsktbl; JV Var Sftbl; JV Var Vllybl; Bank Of Amer Plaque-Librl Arts; CA Schlrshp Fed Life Mem Pres; U CA Los Angeles; Engrng.

PROVOST, JENNELL; Albany HS; Albany, CA; (4); 34/207; French Clb; Service Clb; SADD; Teachers Aide; Lit Mag; Var Cheerldng; Capt Pom Pon; Intrml Sftbl; JV Intrml Vllybl; High Hon Roll; Baton Twrlng; Big Sis Grls Honorary Bike Club; Guitar; St Marys Coll; Educ.

PROVOST, THERESA J; Santa Clara HS; Santa Clara, CA; (4); French Clb; Spanish Clb; Teachers Aide; French Hon Soc; Hon Roll; Prfct Atten Awd; Pres Acad Fit Awd; Wilderness Adventures Clb; Mission Coll; Acctng.

PROWELL, ROY W; Antioch HS; Antioch, CA; (2); 26/707; Boy Scts; Letterman Clb; JV Crs Cntry; Intrml Tennis; JV Trk; Hon Roll; CJSF; CSF; U Of CA Davis.

PRUE, IVY; Paraclete HS; Quartz Hill, CA; (1); Church Yth Grp; Cmnty Wkr; SADD; Acpl Chr; High Hon Roll; Hon Roll; Pres Acad Fit Awd; Fshn Dsgn; Gourmet Cook; BYU; Fshn Dsgn.

PRUIS, JILL; Village Christian Schl; Sunland, CA; (4); Church Yth Grp; Drama Clb; English Clb; GAA; Mu Alpha Theta; Capt Var Bsktbl; CSF; Vrsty Bsktbl Mst Imprvd Plyr; Cal Poly SLO; Rec Admin.

PRUITT, CASH XAVIER; La Sierra HS; Riverside, CA; (1); Bus Profs of Am; Cmnty Wkr; Var Ftbl; Var Trk; Early Coll Outreach Prep; USC; Aerntcl Engrng.

PRUITT, LISA; Highlands HS; North Highlands, CA; (3); Acpl Chr; Hon Roll; Sacramento ST U; Law.

PRUITT, MARCUS W; Washington Preparatory HS; Los Angeles, CA; (3); Pres Frsh Cls; Rep Stu Cncl; High Hon Roll; Letterman Clb; CSF; Ldrshp & AE Pgm; Stanford U; Bus Admin.

PRUITT, MYEASHA; Lynwood Adventist Acad; Paramount, CA; (1); 1/30; Church Yth Grp; GAA; Church Choir; Pres Frsh Cls; Var Sftbl; Cit Awd; High Hon Roll; NHS; Pres Acad Fit Awd; Bible Bowl Tm; Phy.

PRUITT, SCARLET M; Monterey HS; Pebble Beach, CA; (3); Drama Clb; Key Clb; School Musical; School Play; Ed Lit Mag; High Hon Roll; UC; Psych.

PRUITT, SCOTT K; Rio Mesa HS; Camarillo, CA; (3); AFS; FCA; Teachers Aide; Rptr Nwsp; Stu Cncl; JV Bsbl; JV Bsktbl; Intrml Ftbl; Intrml Socr; Intrml Vllybl.

PRUITT, STACEY D; Clovis HS; Fresno, CA; (4); Church Yth Grp; Library Aide; Office Aide; High Hon Roll; Hon Roll; EMT Cert; Health Sci.

PRUM, PHYRUM; Ventura HS; Ventura, CA; (3); 156/431; GAA; SADD; Var Capt Socr; Var Sftbl; Hon Roll; Prfct Atten Awd; Spirit Club; UC Davis; Med Doc.

PRUNEAU, THERESA A; La Reina HS; Thousand Oaks, CA; (2); Drama Clb; GAA; Yrbk; Girls Sftbl Assn; Campus Mnstry; Mktg.

PRYOR, MATTHEW J; Bret Harte HS; Murphys, CA; (2); Church Yth Grp; Letterman Clb; SADD; Treas Jr Cls; JV Bsbl; JV Bsktbl; Var Socr; Hon Roll; W Coast Sccr Team Tour Europe; Ftchr.

PRYOR, MONICA; Montgomery HS; Santa Rosa, CA; (3); French Clb; Pep Clb; Hon Roll; Stu Week Awd; Nutritionlst.

PRYZE, ANN C; Redlands HS; Redlands, CA; (4); Church Yth Grp; Drama Clb; French Clb; Pep Clb; Nwsp; Pom Pon; Var JV Swmmng; Kimberly Jrs Yng Grls Etqtt Clb; Swm Tm; U Of AZ; Bus.

PRZYBYLSKI, JAMIE M; Grossmont HS; Santee, CA; (4); 40/400; Church Yth Grp; Lit Mag; Tennis; Pres Acad Fit Awd; Awd SC Hstry Fr Hghst Hnrs; Pacific Christian; Psych.

PSCHIRRER, KELLY J; Torrey Pines HS; San Diego, CA; (3); AFS; Art Clb; Dance Clb; Teachers Aide; Variety Show; Rptr Lit Mag; Hon Roll; Japanese Clb; Otis Parsons Sch Art Smr Pgr; UC-SANTA Barbara; Art.

PSYLLOS, ELENI V; Chaminade College Prep; Glendale, CA; (3); 16/184; Cmnty Wkr; Drama Clb; Key Clb; Model UN; VP SADD; Nwsp; Yrbk; Pres Frsh Cls; Rep Soph Cls; Sec Jr Cls; USC; Bus.

PUCCIARELLI, STEVE G; St John Bosco HS; Huntington Park, CA; (2); Computer Clb; French Clb; High Hon Roll; NHS; Pres Acad Fit Awd; CSF; Bus.

PUCCINELLI, KIM M; Liberty Union HS; Byron, CA; (3); 69/339; Am Leg Aux Girls St; Dance Clb; Drama Clb; Speech Tm; Acpl Chr; School Musical; Nwsp; Rep Stu Cncl; Gym; Hon Roll; Comp Horse Shows, Appaloosa Circuit; SADD; Stu Ldrshp; Sacramento ST; Bus Mgmt.

PUCHALSKI, ERIC N; Gompers Secondary HS; San Diego, CA; (3); Church Yth Grp; Office Aide; Drill Tm; School Musical; Vllybl; Hon Roll; Prfct Atten Awd; Pres Acad Fit Awd; Sea Acaets Color Guard, Drill, Tm; People-People Yth Sci Exchng; Military Pilot; Aviation.

PUCILLO, MEGAN; St Bernard HS; Eureka, CA; (4); 7/40; Am Leg Aux Girls St; Church Yth Grp; Cmnty Wkr; Teachers Aide; Rptr Nwsp; Yrbk; Ed Lit Mag; Sec Frsh Cls; Sec Soph Cls; Treas Jr Cls; Soroptmst Club Sr Dir & Treas; Safe & Sober Acknwldgmnt Chrprsn; Sonoma ST U; Elem Ed.

PUCKETT, SONIA; Liberty Union HS; Pittsburg, CA; (3); 4-H; Treas FFA; FHA; Speech Tm; Teachers Aide; Dnfth Awd; DAR Awd; 4-H Awd; Prncpls Advsty Cmmttee; Brentwood Rotary Ag Schlrshp; Make It Yourself W/Wool Dist 14 Wnnr; Fresno ST; Vet Sci.

PUDHNUM, VAHINI; Mira Loma HS; Sacramento, CA; (3); 18/284; Church Yth Grp; Cmnty Wkr; Math Clb; Office Aide; Science Clb; Teachers Aide; School Play; Yrbk; Cit Awd; High Hon Roll; CSF 89-90; Acad Awd Top 20 Cls 90; Peer Cnslr 89-90; Law.

PUDJAYANA, EDWARD; Walnut HS; Walnut, CA; (3); Boy Scts; Key Clb; Spanish Clb; Chorus; Hon Roll; Prfct Atten Awd; Sci Fiction Clb; Army Offcr.

PUENTE, LIDIA; Saddleback HS; Bakersfield, CA; (3); Boy Scts; Drama Clb; FBLA; German Clb; Hosp Aide; Spanish Clb; SADD; Rptr Nwsp; Prfct Atten Awd; Spanish NHS; Peers-In-Contact Sec; Boston U; Law.

PUENTE, MICHAEL A; St Ignatius Prep; San Francisco, CA; (3); Pres Science Clb; Orch; Sci Club Pres; Sci-Ffantasy Club Pres; Psych.

PUENTES, CLAUDIA; Point Loma HS; San Diego, CA; (3); Girl Scts; Chorus; Orch; Bsbl; FIDM; Fshn Dsgn.

PUENTES, ELOY; Mcfarland HS; Mc Farland, CA; (3); Church Yth Grp; Cmnty Wkr; Rptr FFA; Science Clb; Var Bsbl; Hist Bsktbl; JV Trk; Wt Lftg; Cit Awd; High Hon Roll; Engrng.

PUGA, GERARDO; Hanford HS; Hanford, CA; (1); Paramedic.

PUGH, ALICE L; University City HS; San Diego, CA; (3); Science Clb; High Hon Roll; Hon Roll; Prfct Atten Awd; Pres Acad Fit Awd; Pres Schlr; Gymnstcs & Dance Awds.

PUGH, BRENDA K; O Farrell SCPA; San Diego, CA; (3); 2/160; Letterman Clb; Teachers Aide; Yrbk; Hon Roll; Pres Acad Fit Awd; Pres Soph Cls; Treas Jr Cls; Academic Decathlon Team 89-90; Academic League Team 87-89; UCSD; Law Enfrcmnt.

PUGH, MEREDITH A; La Reina HS; Thousand Oaks, CA; (3); Dance Clb; Drama Clb; Speech Tm; SADD; Thesps; Chorus; School Musical; Variety Show; Yrbk; Cit Awd; Perfrmng Arts Awd; Stu Of Month; Dance Awds; Loyola Marymount CA; Dance.

PUGHE, ADAM S; Rubidoux HS; Riverside, CA; (4); Teachers Aide; JV Var Bsktbl; Hon Roll; CA ST San Bernadino; Psych.

PUGMIRE, KRISTIN; Concord HS; Concord, CA; (3); Church Yth Grp; Service Clb; Ski Clb; SADD; Teachers Aide; Sec Frsh Cls; VP Sr Cls; High Hon Roll; Pres Acad Fit Awd; Vlbyl; Bsktbl & Sftbl Chrch; Span Awd; BYU; Fash Desgn.

PUJOL, LUCIA; San Gabriel HS; Rosemead, CA; (2); Church Yth Grp; Latin Clb; Pep Clb; Spanish Clb; SADD; Yrbk; Cheerldng; Cit Awd; Hon Roll; UC Irvine; Child Psych.

PULANCO, THERESA MAZON; Lowell HS; San Francisco, CA; (4); ROTC; Chorus; Color Guard; Drill Tm; Rep Stu Cncl; JV Var Cheerldng; Dghtrs Fndng Fathers ROTC; Drl Div ROTC 1st Pl; Rdng; San Francisco ST U; RN.

PULIDO, AUDELIA T; Delta HS; Walnut Grove, CA; (1); Latin Clb; Spanish Clb; Rep Frsh Cls; Hon Roll; Prfct Atten Awd; U Of Pacific; Nrsng.

PULIDO, ONESIMA; Livingston HS; Livingston, CA; (1); Cit Awd; High Hon Roll; Hon Roll; Kiwanis Awd; Prfct Atten Awd; High Scores Math, PE, Hstry.

PULIDO, PEDRO; Southern California Christian HS; Fullerton, CA; (4); 13/60; Pres French Clb; Acpl Chr; Pres Band; Chorus; Rptr Yrbk; Var Bsbl; Var Ftbl; Hon Roll; NHS; Natl Hspnc Schlrs Awds Pgm Semifnlst; Azusa Pacific U; Biochem.

PULIDO, SAID URIEL; Westchester HS; Lennox, CA; (3); AFS; ROTC; Acpl Chr; Color Guard; Mrchg Band; School Musical; Yrbk; Crs Cntry; Cit Awd; High Hon Roll; Spks Eng, Romanian, Persian/Farsi, French & Span; Gymnstics; UCLA; Pilot.

PULIDO, TONY C; Downey HS; South Gate, CA; (2); Bsbl; Interact Clb.

PULIDO, VERONICA A; John H Francis Polytechnic HS; Sun Valley, CA; (3); Dance Clb; English Clb; Teachers Aide; Treas Frsh Cls; Rep Stu Cncl; Hon Roll; Outstndng Stu Awd; Cert Of Redgntn Sun Vlly Chmbr Of Commrc; Dept Awd Outstndng Achvmnt In Bus Ed; Woodbury U; Acctng.

PULIZZI, GARY J; James Lick HS; San Jose, CA; (3); 14/250; Band; Color Guard; Jazz Band; Mrchg Band; Pep Band; Hon Roll; Stu Week; Elec.

PULJAN, STACY L; Shasta HS; Redding, CA; (2); 95/442; JV Swmmng; U Portland; Bus Mgmt.

PULLEY, JEFFREY M; Contra Costa Christian HS; Lafayette, CA; (3); Church Yth Grp; Drama Clb; FCA; Band; Chorus; Church Choir; School Play; VP Treas Frsh Cls; Stu Cncl; L Var Socr; Cngrssnl Schlr-Natl Yng Ldrs Conf; Mssnry Mexico Sccr Team; DVTFL Cnty; US Air Force Acad; Cvl Engrng.

PULLIAM, ALISON R; Hayward HS; Hayward, CA; (2); 7/237; Church Yth Grp; Cmnty Wkr; Chorus; Var Capt Socr; Var Trk; High Hon Roll; Hon Roll; Pres Acad Fit Awd; NCS, CIF Schlr Athl; Black Stu Union; Prncss; Stanford; Sprts Med.

PULLIAM, TEELA M; Gunn HS; Palo Alto, CA; (4); 121/275; Drama Clb; School Play; Gym; Swmmng; Crtfd Scuba Dvr; UC-SANTA Cruz; Engrng.

PULLING, KATINA; Casa Roble HS; Citrus Heights, CA; (3); 28/370; Church Yth Grp; Drama Clb; Girl Scts; Scholastic Bowl; Spanish Clb; SADD; Church Choir; High Hon Roll; Hon Roll; NHS; Travel.

PULSIPHER, ROSEMARY; Paraclete HS; Leona Valley, CA; (3); Church Yth Grp; Cmnty Wkr; Key Clb; Service Clb; SADD; Chorus; Church Choir; Powder Puff Ftbl; Hon Roll; NHS; CA Schlrshp Fed; Brigham Young U; Dntl Hygiene.

PULVER, ANDREW P; Alta Loma HS; Cucamonga, CA; (3); Church Yth Grp; Cmnty Wkr; Teachers Aide; DAR Awd; High Hon Roll; Peer Counseling; Sunday Schl Teacher; Cal Poly Pomona; Elem Teacher.

PUMMILL, DANA L; Harbor HS; Riverbank, CA; (4); Church Yth Grp; VP SADD; Teachers Aide; Rptr Nwsp; Rep Soph Cls; Hon Roll; Pres Acad Fit Awd; Dancing,Tap, Jazz & Ballet; Cal Poly; Phy Ther.

PUNIA, HARKIRAN; Irvington HS; Fremont, CA; (3); 14/261; Art Clb; Girl Scts; Spanish Clb; Orch; Bsktbl; Hon Roll; Prfct Atten Awd; Cert Acad Achvt; Badminton, Soccer; Med.

PUNSIRI, CASSANDRA; El Camino Real HS; Woodland Hills, CA; (2); Pep Clb; Drill Tm; Mgr(s); Hon Roll; Black Awareness Mnth Awd 88-89; Athl Awd 89-90; Freshman Steering Cmmtte; Arch Engrng.

PUNT, STEVEN; Calvary Chapel HS; Fountain Valley, CA; (4); 4/28; Chess Clb; Church Yth Grp; Computer Clb; Acpl Chr; Chorus; Church Choir; School Musical; Rptr Nwsp; High Hon Roll; Calvary Chapel Bible; Biblical.

PUNYASAVATSUT, MICHELLE; Village Christian HS; Sun Valley, CA; (3); 5/123; English Clb; Hosp Aide; Math Clb; Mu Alpha Theta; Sec Spanish Clb; Teachers Aide; Rep Sr Cls; Stat Bsktbl; Var Vllybl; Med.

PUNZALAN, CRISTINA; Granada Hills HS; Northridge, CA; (2); JR Statesmen Of Amer; CSF; Algebra K Awd; Stanford U; Sci.

PURA, ALBERT A; Washington HS; San Francisco, CA; (3); Drama Clb; VP Treas JA; Office Aide; Treas Ski Clb; SADD; School Musical; School Play; Treas Soph Cls; Hon Roll; De Molay Sr Cnslr; Sports Admin.

PURCELL, ADAM H; Skyline HS; Oakland, CA; (3); Boy Scts; Church Yth Grp; Cmnty Wkr; Teachers Aide; Pres Frsh Cls; Stu Cncl; JV Bsktbl; Hon Roll; Bus Admin.

PURCELL, ANITA R; Chula Vista HS; National City, CA; (3); Math Tm; Varsity Clb; Church Choir; School Musical; Var Swmmng; Natl City Police Explorers Sargeant; CSF; Criminal Jstc.

PURCELL, JAMALLE M; Mission San Jose HS; Fremont, CA; (1); Church Yth Grp; GAA; Sftbl; Ldrshp Cncl; CSF; Med.

PURCELL, JASON M; Sunset HS; Hayward, CA; (2); 62/286; JV Tennis; Hon Roll; U C-Davis; Comp Sci.

PURCELL, JENNIFER A; Arroyo Grande HS; Nipomo, CA; (2); 118/580; Church Yth Grp; Dance Clb; Treas Rptr FFA; Var Cheerldng; Hon Roll; Outstndng Ag Stu 89-90; CA S Cst Rgnl Treas FFA; CA 90 St Dairy Prdcts Chmpn FFA; CA ST Northridge; Dance.

PURDON, PATRICK; Chula Vista HS; Chula Vista, CA; (2); 1/605; Computer Clb; Var Capt Swmmng; Water Polo Ltr; JR Statesman Of Amer; CA St Sci Fair Hnrb Mntn Biochem Div; CA Tech; Aerospace Engrng.

PURDY, DEREK; Santa Clara HS; Santa Clara, CA; (3); 1/420; Pres Chess Clb; High Hon Roll; Rotary Awd; Acadc Dcthln; Schl Site Cncl; Engr.

PURDY, EMILY S; Redlands HS; Redlands, CA; (3); 112/911; Band; Mrchg Band; Orch; Pep Band; Rptr Nwsp; Rptr Yrbk; Treas Frsh Cls; Cit Awd; Hon Roll; Jr NHS; 5th Pl Crtcl Revw Inland Jrnlsm Educ Assoc; Hnrb Mntn Poetry 90 Wrtng Clbrtn; 90 Chepulechi; Pacific Union Coll; Engl Teachr.

PURDY, MICHELLE; Hemet HS; Hemet, CA; (3); Girl Scts; JA; Teachers Aide; Rptr Nwsp; Cit Awd.

PURDY, TRICIA M; Notre Dame HS; San Jose, CA; (3); Var Bsktbl; Var Sftbl; Var Vllybl; Hon Roll; USVBA Clb Vlybl; Humboldt ST U; Phyl Ed Coach.

PUREFOY, TABITHA; Frisbie JR HS; San Bernardino, CA; (2); 1/480; Hosp Aide; Flag Corp; Capt Cheerldng; Trk; High Hon Roll; Intl Exch Club Stu Of Mnth; S Ca Edison Essay Cntst 1st Pl; Amer Leg Aux Stu Of Yr; Stanford U; Psych.

PUREWAL, CHANDEEP S; Selma HS; Selma, CA; (3); Letterman Clb; SADD; Teachers Aide; Varsity Clb; Jazz Band; Off Jr Cls; Stu Cncl; JV Var Bsktbl; JV Var Ftbl; JV Var Tennis; Cal Poly San Luis Obispo; Engr.

PURGANAN, ANITA M; Atwater HS; Atwater, CA; (2); Pres Acad Fit Awd; CSF; Fresno ST; Comp Tech.

PURIFICACION, DENNIS T; Milpitas HS; Milpitas, CA; (2); Church Yth Grp; Cmnty Wkr; ROTC; Science Clb; Church Choir; Drill Tm; Nwsp; Yrbk; Hon Roll; Toastmasters Intl Clb; Catechism Teacher; Amer Leg For Schltc Excllnce & Military Excllnce Awds; RN.

PURINTON, JOSH JORDAN; Laytonville HS; Laytonville, CA; (2); Jazz Band; School Play; JV Bsktbl; Var Crs Cntry; High Hon Roll; Peer Cnslr; Comp.

PURINTON, MICHELLE D; Newport Harbor HS; Costa Mesa, CA; (4); Yrbk; Stu Cncl; Bsktbl; Swmmng; Hon Roll; Orange Coast Coll; Chld Psych.

PURKEY, LEANNA M; Monache HS; Porterville, CA; (3); 3/300; Am Leg Aux Girls St; Art Clb; Church Yth Grp; Cmnty Wkr; Letterman Clb; Pep Clb; Red Cross Aide; Treas Spanish Clb; SADD; Teachers Aide; CSF; Point Loma Nazarene Coll.

PURNELL, TAMARA L; Fairfield HS; Fairfield, CA; (2); Spanish Clb; SADD; Variety Show; Cit Awd; Cls Candy Sales; San Diego ST; Marine Bio.

PURSE, TAMRA L; Santa Clara HS; Santa Clara, CA; (2); Art Clb; Debate Tm; Sec Pep Clb; Spanish Clb; Teachers Aide; Co-Capt Drill Tm; Sec Treas Frsh Cls; Sec Treas Soph Cls; VP Jr Cls; JV Co-Capt Cheerldng; Wldrnss Advtrs Clb; Educ.

PURUGGANAN, ROSELYN; St Joseph HS; Long Beach, CA; (3); 32/180; Drama Clb; Pres Hosp Aide; School Play; Stage Crew; Rptr Yrbk; High Hon Roll; NEDT Awd; Piano Study Cert Merit; UCLA; Bio.

PURVIS, LISA K; San Rafael HS; San Rafael, CA; (2); Spanish Clb; Band; Pep Band; Var Socr; JV Swmmng; Var Tennis; Hon Roll; NHS; 2nd Pl Martin Cnty Sci Fair; 3rd Pl San Francsco Bay Area Sci Fair; CSF; U Of CO Boulder.

PUSLOSKIE, DELORIS R; Banning HS; Cabazon, CA; (2); 21/200; Teachers Aide; Mgr(s); Vllybl; High Hon Roll; Hon Roll; CA Schltic Fed; Democrtc Rep Conv.

PUSTEJOVSKY, DEBRA; Chico SR HS; Chico, CA; (2); Church Yth Grp; SADD; JV Bsktbl; JV Vllybl; High Hon Roll; Prfct Atten Awd; Arch.

PUTMAN, CHRIS; University HS; Irvine, CA; (2); Church Yth Grp; Ftbl; Wt Lftg; Wrstlng; Engrng.

PUTMAN, LISA N; Clovis HS; Clovis, CA; (2); VP Church Yth Grp; Debate Tm; Hosp Aide; NFL; Speech Tm; Teachers Aide; Variety Show; Amer Ambulance Explorer Post 911 Sec; 2nd Pl Sierra Vly Forensics Lg Cmptn Oratory; CA ST Spch Fnlst; Bringham Young U; Pediatric.

PUTNAM, CHRISTINE L; South Beach HS; Burbank, CA; (4); 1/20; Drama Clb; Office Aide; Teachers Aide; School Play; VP Stu Cncl; High Hon Roll; Val; Beverly Seefeld Ltry Awd; S Bch HS Fndrs Awd; Grt Bks Pres Awd; CA St U Northridge; Jrnlsm.

PUTT, JAMES; Foothill HS; Pleasanton, CA; (4); 38/311; SADD; Hon Roll; Interact Clb; CA Schlrshp Fed; UC Davis; Commnctns.

PUTT, KEITH A; Washington HS; Fremont, CA; (3); 64/364; Boy Scts; French Clb; Intnl Clb; Letterman Clb; Ski Clb; Speech Tm; Variety Show; JV Ftbl; Var Golf; Eagle Sct; Rotary Intl Spch Cont Lcl Dist Wnnr; Bus.

PUTTERE, JENNIFER; Loretto HS; Sacramento, CA; (3); 16/65; Sci Club; CSF; Flute Playing; Cal Poly; Indl Eng.

PUYOL, JUAN-ANTONIO; St Francis HS; Sun Valley, CA; (2); 1/180; Debate Tm; Math Clb; Math Tm; Pep Clb; Ed Yrbk; JV Ftbl; JV Trk; High Hon Roll; VP NHS; Spanish NHS; CA Schlrshp Fed; Law.

PUZON, JAN-PAUL N; Palos Verdes HS; Palos Vrds Pen, CA; (3); 23/330; Church Yth Grp; Cmnty Wkr; Intnl Clb; Library Aide; Math Clb; Service Clb; Hon Roll; NHS; CSF; Jr Statesman Of Amer; CA St Exam Geom High Hnr Roll; Materials Engrng.

PYATT, CHAD J; Victor Valley HS; Victorville, CA; (3); Ocngrphy.

PYATT, WILLIAM L; Lee Vining HS; Lee Vining, CA; (2); School Play; Sec Frsh Cls; Sec Soph Cls; Var Bsktbl; Var Crs Cntry; Var Ftbl; Cit Awd; Hon Roll; Prfct Atten Awd; ROTC; Tchr.

PYEATT, GEORGINA M; Corning Union HS; Corning, CA; (3); Pres Church Yth Grp; Drama Clb; Intnl Clb; Science Clb; Chorus; Church Choir; School Musical; Sftbl; High Hon Roll; Prfct Atten Awd; Intl Relations.

PYKKONEN, HEIDI; Pacific Christian HS; Los Angeles, CA; (3); Church Yth Grp; School Play; Ed Yrbk; Treas Jr Cls; Co-Capt Var Bsktbl; Var Sftbl; Var Vllybl; Hon Roll; Hmcmng Prncss; ASB Offcr.

PYLE, JEREMY L; Redlands SR HS; Redlands, CA; (3); Treas AFS; Pres German Clb; Quiz Bowl; JV Trk; Sci Fair 88 1st Pl Schl, 3rd Pl Dist, 1st Pl Rgnl; Fndr & Pres HS Ecology Clb; Astrophysics.

PYLE, MELINDA M; Edison HS; Huntington Bch, CA; (4); 30/500; Drama Clb; Hosp Aide; Service Clb; Capt Color Guard; Flag Corp; Off Jr Cls; Off Sr Cls; Stat Bsktbl; Pres Acad Fit Awd; Spanish NHS; Member Of The Year-Tall Flags; Homecoming Nominee; Teaching.

PYLES, TRACY R; Diamond Bar HS; Diamond Bar, CA; (2); Cmnty Wkr; Stat Bsbl; Var L Tennis; CSF.

QASQUS, FIRAS A; Pomona HS; Pomona, CA; (4); Math Tm; Science Clb; Hon Roll; CA ST; Petrolm Engrng.

QAZI, ALI; Rio Linda HS; Sacramento, CA; (2); Chess Clb; Church Yth Grp; Quiz Bowl; Science Clb; SADD; High Hon Roll; Pres Aerntcs Clb; Awd NASA; Math Dept & Sci Awds; MIT; Aerospace Engrng.

QUACH, ANH H; Sunset HS; Hayward, CA; (3); Hon Roll; Comp.

QUACH, ANH T; Valley View HS; Moreno Valley, CA; (2); High Hon Roll; Hon Roll; CAP Wrtng Cntst Awd; UCLA; Mdcl Fld.

QUACH, CHI A; Lincoln HS; Los Angeles, CA; (4); Library Aide; Teachers Aide; Yrbk; Hon Roll; Prfct Atten Awd; UC Irvine; Math Ed.

QUACH, HA DAT; Mark Keppel HS; Monterey Park, CA; (3); Key Clb; Math Clb; Science Clb; Spanish Clb; Vrsty Badmntn; Grls Leag; CSF; Forgn Lang.

QUACH, HAI T; San Gabriel HS; Alhambra, CA; (4); 157/737; Computer Clb; French Clb; VP FBLA; Hon Roll; Chiness Club; Geolgy Club; Dramtc Interptn Frnch; UCLA; Frnch.

QUACH, HUY; Oakland HS; Oakland, CA; (3); CA ST Hayward; Real Est Brkr.

QUACH, LIEN N; Bolsa Grande HS; Westminster, CA; (3); 6/338; French Clb; Math Clb; Science Clb; Var JV Bsktbl; Var Tennis; JV Vllybl; Hon Roll; Yth Ldrshp For Action Constitutnl Rights Fndtn; Chinese Clb Pres; Orange Cnty Sci Awd Hnrble Mntn; CA U Of Riverside; Bus Admin.

QUACH, LINH; Bolsa Grande HS; Westminster, CA; (2); #2 In Class; French Clb; Letterman Clb; Math Tm; Science Clb; Spanish Clb; Var JV Bsktbl; Var Tennis; Var Vllybl; Hon Roll; USC; Pediatrics.

QUACH, NGAN T; Santa Cruz HS; Santa Clara, CA; (2); 1/455; French Clb; Spanish Clb; Hon Roll; S-Clb; CA Schlrshp Fndtn.

QUACH, PHUONG H; Alhambra HS; Alhambra, CA; (2); Service Clb; Teachers Aide; Var Crs Cntry; JV Swmmng; Spnsh Hnr Soc; Teen Clb; Alakai VP.

QUACH, PHUONG N; George Washington HS; San Francisco, CA; (2); Vllybl; Chinese Amer Club; CSF; US Davis Ag Ecchng Prgm; UC Davis; Landscape Dsgn.

QUACH, QUAN; Fremont HS; Oakland, CA; (3); 8/35; Church Yth Grp; Cmnty Wkr; Math Clb; Math Tm; Teachers Aide; Sftbl; Vllybl; Cit Awd; French Hon Soc; High Hon Roll; Aerospace Engr.

QUACH, TAI Q; William C Overfelt HS; San Jose, CA; (1); Intrml Trk; Hon Roll; Stanford; Doc.

QUACH, TAM T; Ganesha HS; Pomona, CA; (4); 28/269; Sec Pres French Clb; Math Clb; Sec Sr Cls; Var Tennis; Cit Awd; Hon Roll; Grad Cls 90 Sr Cls Spkr; CSF; CA ST U Fullerton; Psych.

QUACH, THU; Silver Creek HS; San Jose, CA; (1); Color Guard; Color Guard; Pres Soph Cls; High Hon Roll; Supreme Court Justice; Supts Stu Advisory Cmmtte; CSF; Ophthalmology.

QUACH, TRANG N; Fremont HS; Sunnyvale, CA; (4); 6/389; Teachers Aide; Hon Roll; NHS; CA Golden ST Alg Hnrs; CA Schlrshp Fed Awd; San Jose ST U; B S Bio.

QUACH, TUONG; Hiram W Johnson HS; Sacramento, CA; (2); 44/182; Church Yth Grp; Hon Roll; Prfct Atten Awd; Psycht.

QUACH, UYEN T; Mark Keppel HS; Monterey Park, CA; (1); Drama Clb; Math Clb; CSF; United For Peace.

QUADHAMER, DAVID A; San Pedro HS; San Pedro, CA; (2); Crs Cntry; Trk; Cit Awd; High Hon Roll; Prfct Atten Awd; CSF; Draftng Clb; Future Ldr San Pedro Awd; UCLA; Engrng.

QUADRI, SUFIA A; Hawthorne HS; Hawthorne, CA; (3); Cmnty Wkr; Hosp Aide; Intnl Clb; Key Clb; Service Clb; Hon Roll; Sci.

QUAID, CYNTHIA M; Eisenhower HS; Rialto, CA; (3); Key Clb; Ed Nwsp; Vllybl; High Hon Roll; Hon Roll; NHS; Prfct Atten Awd; Pres Acad Fit Awd; Outstndng Sci Stu; 4.0 GPA Trphy; Ltr R Awd; Fri Night Live VP; U Of CA Riverside; Bus Admin.

QUALLS, BRYAN D; Clovis West HS; Fresno, CA; (2); Church Yth Grp; Ski Clb; Var Tennis; High Hon Roll; Pres Acad Fit Awd; Engrg.

QUAN, ALBERT W; San Marino HS; San Marino, CA; (3); 75/260; FBLA; Math Clb; Red Cross Aide; Science Clb; JV Stat Bsbl; JV Var Mgr(s); JV Var Score Keeper; Gldn St Exm Awd Hgh Hnrs Algbr; Video Clb; Bsbl.

QUAN, ANDREW L; Schurr HS; Hacienda Heights, CA; (4); 1/580; Treas Key Clb; Pres Math Tm; Mrchg Band; Nwsp; Off Frsh Cls; Off Soph Cls; Off Sr Cls; Tennis; Ntl Merit SF; Opt Clb Awd; Ntl Hnr Soc; CSF; Asian Clb.

QUAN, BRIAN; James Lick HS; San Jose, CA; (4); 1/243; Intnl Clb; Math Tm; Teachers Aide; Bsktbl; Capt Tennis; High Hon Roll; NHS; Prfct Atten Awd; Pres Acad Fit Awd; Elec Engrng.

QUAN, ELAINE; San Gabriel HS; Rosemead, CA; (3); 4-H; JA; Pres Sec Band; Pres Mrchg Band; Orch; Rep Stu Cncl; Var Trk; Hon Roll; Elec; Strtchr Crw; CA Poly U; Chem Engr.

QUAN, EMERSON C; St Ignatius College Prep; South San Francis, CA; (3); 12/244; Cmnty Wkr; Science Clb; Service Clb; School Play; Capt Cheerldng; JV Ftbl; Var Trk; High Hon Roll; Pres Acad Fit Awd; CSF; Sci Fair Awd 90; Stanford; Pre-Med.

QUAN, JOSEPHINE; El Camino HS; S San Francisco, CA; (3); Intnl Clb; Math Tm; CSF & Spllng Bee Tm; Nmrs Awds Engl, Geom, Physics; Sthu Monty Bus, Sci; Piano Recital Music Tchr Assn; UC Berkeley; Acctng.

QUAN, KRISTINE A; La Quinta HS; Fountain Valley, CA; (3); 17/330; Church Yth Grp; Key Clb; VP Spanish Clb; Var Tennis; NHS; Girls League; CSF Secy.

QUAN, LUULY P; Bolsa Grande HS; Garden Grove, CA; (2); 2/377; Spanish Clb; Orch; Treas Soph Cls; Stu Cncl; Hon Roll; Jr NHS; Pres Acad Fit Awd; Bio.

QUAN, MARGARET; Pioneer HS; San Jose, CA; (3); 7/392; Pres Service Clb; Pres Spanish Clb; Pres Frsh Cls; VP Jr Cls; Var Capt Tennis; CA ST Dreamer & Doer 90; Yth Hnr For Dist San Jose Unity Brkfst 90; Exectv Wmn Intl Schlrshp Prgm; Santa Clara U; Bus.

QUANG, TONY; Lowell HS; San Francisco, CA; (2); Chess Clb; Cmnty Wkr; Science Clb; Hon Roll; Prfct Atten Awd; Chess Natl Team 2nd Pl 90; Neurology.

QUARLES, MARKEL; San Luis Obispo HS; San Luis Obispo, CA; (1); VP Church Yth Grp; Church Choir; Bsktbl; Ftbl; Var Trk; Hon Roll.

QUATROCHI, REBECCA M; Hesperia HS; Hesperia, CA; (4); 82/627; High Hon Roll; Hon Roll; Sons Of Italy Schlrshp; U Clb; HUSD Outdoor Ed; Victor Valley Coll; Vet.

QUAZI, TANIMA; San Dimas HS; San Dimas, CA; (3); Yrbk; Sec Treas Soph Cls; JV Tennis; High Hon Roll; Hon Roll; Pres Acad Fit Awd; CSF; Jr Statesman Assn; Lit Hnrs Soc; UCLA; Envrnmntl Law.

QUDDUS, MOHAMMAD OSMAN; Independence HS; San Jose, CA; (2); Library Aide; Teachers Aide; Ftbl; Wrstlng; UCLA; Pedtrcn.

QUE, BRIAN J; Vanden HS; Fairfield, CA; (3); 33/150; VP French Clb; Science Clb; SADD; Band; Church Choir; Jazz Band; Mrchg Band; Pep Band; Ftbl; Var Tennis; Kuk Sool Won, Korean Martial Art; Mem CA Schlrshp Fed; U CA Davis; Hmnties.

QUE, DARRELL; Coachella Valley HS; Coachella, CA; (2); Math Clb; Hon Roll; Karate; Arch.

QUEANO, MANUEL F; Baldwin Park HS; Baldwin Park, CA; (2); Chess Clb; JV Tennis; Hon Roll.

QUEBRAL, ROSEMARIE G; Canyon Springs HS; Moreno Valley, CA; (3); 1/700; Art Clb; Cmnty Wkr; Service Clb; Pres Sr Cls; Bausch & Lomb Sci Awd; High Hon Roll; NHS; Rotary Awd; State Science Fair Finalist; Numerous Art Awards; Acceptance Into CA St Summer School For The Arts.

QUEEN, JEANNE H; Placer HS; Newcastle, CA; (2); French Clb; School Musical; Rptr Nwsp; Hon Roll; Century Clb; Dance Co; UC Davis; Frgn Lang.

QUEEN, JENNIFER S; University City HS; San Diego, CA; (3); 7/388; Church Yth Grp; SADD; School Play; Rep Soph Cls; Rep Jr Cls; Rep Sr Cls; Rep Stu Cncl; Stat Bsktbl; Var Capt Swmmng; Var Vllybl; Pegasus Pgm Acadmclly Tlntd; Intl Educ Ntwrk Physics Stdy Trip USSR; US Naval Acad Sci Engrng Smnr.

QUEENER, JENNIFER A; El Toro HS; El Toro, CA; (2); Church Yth Grp; Church Choir; Rep Stu Cncl; Var Trk; Hon Roll; Keybrdst Chrch; Psych.

QUEJADA, GINA L; University HS; Los Angeles, CA; (3); Art Clb; GAA; Library Aide; Bsktbl; JV Capt Vllybl; Hon Roll; MVP Trphy 89; Schlr Awd Vllybl; Outstndng Plyr Plaq; Santa Monica Coll; Comp Occptn.

QUELIZA, EMILY JANE; Mercy HS; San Francisco, CA; (3); 10/135; Cmnty Wkr; Dance Clb; Sec Drama Clb; Math Clb; Spanish Clb; Speech Tm; School Musical; Stage Crew; Capt Stu Cncl; Cheerldng; Christian Ldrshp Awd; Theatre Dedication; Vlntr Work Handicapped Ctr; UCLA; Mktg.

QUESADA, ERIC; Glendora HS; Azusa, CA; (4); 22/375; Key Clb; Math Clb; Pres Spanish Clb; Speech Tm; Yrbk; Off Frsh Cls; JV Bsbl; Intrml Ftbl; Kiwanis Awd; Voice Dem Awd; GMI; Instrl Engrng.

QUESADA, ROXANA C; St Anthony HS; Long Beach, CA; (4); Church Yth Grp; Dance Clb; Spanish Clb; SADD; Hon Roll; NHS; CA Schlrshp Fed; Vlybl Parish Team; Wrk With Chldrn In Charis Mssns; Mount St Marys Coll.

QUESADES, JASON; San Bernardino HS; San Bernardino, CA; (2); Math Clb; High Hon Roll; Hon Roll; Prfct Atten Awd; 2nd Pl Math Olympics Lvl 2 MESA Day 90; Acad Schl Ltr GPA Hghr 3.50; UC Santa Barbara; Nuclear Engr.

QUESNETTE, NICOLE A; Woodside HS; Redwood City, CA; (2); Church Yth Grp; Cmnty Wkr; Var Gym; JV Tennis; Hon Roll; Pres Acad Fit Awd; St Schlr; CSF.

QUEVEDO, MARISSA; Porterville HS; Porterville, CA; (3); Debate Tm; Intnl Clb; Science Clb; Spanish Clb; Drill Tm; Sec Soph Cls; Sec Jr Cls; Rep Stu Cncl; Hon Roll; HS Commndtn Cert; MECHA 3 Yrs; Natural Helpr 2 Yrs; Cap Mentor; Law Enfrcmnt.

QUEZADA, ALEJANDRA; Regina Ceali HS; Compton, CA; (1); Church Yth Grp; Spanish Clb; Chorus; Hon Roll.

QUEZADA, ANA M; George Washington HS; San Francisco, CA; (2); Ski Clb; Var JV Bsktbl; Var Trk; Hon Roll; Mt St Marys; Med.

QUEZADA, CLAUDIA; Hamilton Union HS; Hamilton City, CA; (4); 1/35; FFA; Teachers Aide; Lit Mag; Treas Stu Cncl; Var L Trk; Cit Awd; DAR Awd; Elks Awd; High Hon Roll; Lion Awd; CA Schlrshp Fed; MECHA Span Club; CA Dept Of Educ Cert Recgntn; CA ST U Chico; Intl Bus.

QUEZADA, CLAUDIA E; Clairemont HS; San Diego, CA; (1); Spanish Clb; Teachers Aide; Vllybl; Hon Roll; CSF; UCSD; Law.

QUEZADA, ERICA; Immaculate Conception Acad; San Francisco, CA; (2); GAA; Varsity Clb; Pres Jr Cls; Bsktbl; Sftbl; Vllybl; High Hon Roll; NHS; CA Schlrshp Fed; Alumnae Awd Assn Schlrshp; Hoby Awd; Acting.

QUEZADA, JOSE L; Downey HS; South Gate, CA; (4); Church Yth Grp; JV Var Bsbl; JV Var Crs Cntry; Var Socr; Hon Roll; Pres Schlr; Schlr/Athl Awd; USC; Dntstry.

QUEZADA, MIQUEL; Dos Palos HS; Firebaugh, CA; (2); Band; Mrchg Band; Pep Band; JV Bsbl; JV Bsktbl; JV Ftbl; Bus.

QUEZADA, VERONICA S; Southwest HS; San Ysidro, CA; (2); Dance Clb; Model UN; Cit Awd; Hon Roll; Jr NHS; Prfct Atten Awd; SDSU; Psycht.

QUIAMBAO, CHERRY; Whitney HS; Cerritos, CA; (2); Teachers Aide; Varsity Clb; Color Guard; Flag Corp; Var Tennis; Clubkaibigan-Pilipino Clb Cabinet, Dance Troupe Coordinator; Royal Regiment Clb; UCI; Pediatrics.

QUIAMBAO, JENNIFER A; Valley HS; Sacramento, CA; (3); 41/420; SADD; High Hon Roll; Hon Roll; Sac ST; Med Tech.

QUIBELL, JULIAN; Montgomery HS; Santa Rosa, CA; (2); French Clb; SADD; Band; Jazz Band; Pep Band; Yrbk; JV Bsbl; Cit Awd; High Hon Roll; NHS.

QUICK, ERIC J; Artesia HS; Cerritos, CA; (3); JV Bsktbl; Var Ftbl; Var Socr; Var Vllybl; Var Wt Lftg; Hon Roll; Pres Acad Fit Awd; USC; Bus Mgmt.

QUIDOR, BRYCE E; Chino HS; Chino, CA; (3); Library Aide; Teachers Aide; Stu Who Excel Sci; Comp Pgmng.

QUIHUIS, GISELL; Calexico HS; Calexico, CA; (4); 2/440; Church Yth Grp; Math Clb; Math Tm; Service Clb; Rep Spanish Clb; SADD; Rep Jr Cls; Rep Stu Cncl; NHS; Sal; Migrant Clb Pres; Imperial Cnty Uniserve Schlrshp; CA Schlrshp Fed Rep; Stanford U; Math.

QUIJADA, CHRISTINA; John W North HS; Riverside, CA; (3); Sec Church Yth Grp; Teachers Aide; Church Choir; JV Tennis; French Hon Soc; Hon Roll; UCR; Bus.

QUIJADA, JESSIE M; John Burroughs HS; Burbank, CA; (2); Church Yth Grp; Drill Tm; Hon Roll; Valley Coll; Flght Attndnt.

QUIJADA, RENATA I; William Workman HS; Valinda, CA; (4); 25/264; Intnl Clb; Key Clb; Science Clb; Spanish Clb; Teachers Aide; Var Tennis; High Hon Roll; Pres Acad Fit Awd; Spanish NHS; Excllnc Achvt Awd; CA Schlrshp Fed; 2 Yr Schlr Silver Mdl; CA ST San Bernardino; Hstry.

QUIJANO, EDGAR; Calexico HS; Calexico, CA; (2); SDSU; Arch.

QUIJANO, GRACE A; Beyer HS; Modesto, CA; (4); Church Yth Grp; Intnl Clb; JA; Church Choir; Cit Awd; High Hon Roll; CSF; San Jose ST U; Bus.

QUILALA, FLORIZZA C; St Joseph HS; Cerritos, CA; (4); 1/173; Church Yth Grp; Debate Tm; VP Drama Clb; Math Tm; Stage Crew; Yrbk; Powder Puff Ftbl; High Hon Roll; Prfct Atten Awd; Val; Rgnts Schlrshp Rcpnt U Of CA; Phesela Schlrshp Rcpnt; Natl Yng Ldrs Cnfrnc In WQA DC; U Of CA Riverside; Bio Med.

QUILANTANG, DANNY L; Castle Park HS; Chula Vista, CA; (2); 128/473; Church Yth Grp; Intnl Clb; Letterman Clb; Varsity Clb; JV Bsktbl; Var Ftbl; Var Trk; Wt Lftg; Cit Awd; Elks Awd; SOSU; Socialogist.

QUILEZA, MICHAEL; Bishop Amat Memorial HS; Baldwin Park, CA; (3); English Clb; Math Clb; High Hon Roll; AMAT Cyclng Clb Pres; Xanadu Wrtrs Clb; US Cyclng Fedrtn Bcycl Rcr; U CA Santa Barbara; Med.

QUILLIN, MELISSA L; Lodi HS; Lodi, CA; (1); Church Yth Grp; Chorus; Church Choir; Hon Roll.

QUILOP, YVONNE; Loma Linda Acad; Loma Linda, CA; (2); Teachers Aide; Chorus; Off Soph Cls; NHS; Prfct Atten Awd.

QUIMBO, ERIC A; Mater Dei HS; Costa Mesa, CA; (3); Church Yth Grp; Hosp Aide; Letterman Clb; Spanish Clb; Stu Cncl; Bsktbl; Var Ftbl; JV Trk; Hon Roll; Pres Acad Fit Awd; Spcl Olympics Vlntr; Hnrb Mntn Compstn; Med.

QUIMBY, KRISTINA L; Apple Valley SR HS; Apple Valley, CA; (3); Chess Clb; Cmnty Wkr; Letterman Clb; Office Aide; Varsity Clb; Var Stat Bsbl; Var Capt Socr; Var Capt Trk; Hon Roll; Vrsty Sccr MVP; Olympc Dvlpmnt 1 St Try-Outs/Sccr; Cmptv Sccr Trvlng Tm; Chld Psychtrst.

QUIN, CYNTHIA JEAN; Canyon Springs HS; Moreno Valley, CA; (2); Church Yth Grp; Capt Pep Clb; Science Clb; Ski Clb; Spanish Clb; VP Jr Cls; JV Capt Cheerldng; Swmmng; Wt Lftg; Hon Roll; People To People Stu Ambssdr Russia 90; Prom Cmmtte 91-92; Psych.

QUINCANNON, EMILY A; University Of San Diego HS; Newport, RI; (2); Church Yth Grp; Intnl Clb; Service Clb; Varsity Clb; Rep Frsh Cls; Var Crs Cntry; Var Swmmng; Hon Roll; Pres Acad Fit Awd; Night To Feed Homeless-Volunteer.

QUINDO, MARILYN Z; Mira Mesa HS; San Diego, CA; (2); 1/797; Church Yth Grp; FBLA; Library Aide; Engl.

QUINLAN, BECKY K; Thomas Downey HS; Modesto, CA; (3); Pres AFS; Cmnty Wkr; Letterman Clb; NFL; Science Clb; Speech Tm; JV Var Crs Cntry; Var Socr; High Hon Roll; Kiwanis Awd; Congressional Awd For Cmnty Service 88; Modestos Yng Woman Of Yr 91; 5th Pl Natl Sci Olympiad Cmprn 90; UCLA; Television Commnctns.

QUINLAN, FOREST; Taft Union HS; Taft, CA; (3); 3/200; Boy Scts; Church Yth Grp; Key Clb; Band; Mrchg Band; Yrbk; Var Capt Crs Cntry; Trk; High Hon Roll; Pres Acad Fit Awd.

QUINLIN, RACHEL; Mother Lode Christian Schl; Sonora, CA; (2); 2/16; Church Yth Grp; Teachers Aide; Band; Chorus; Mrchg Band; Rep Stu Cncl; Var Score Keeper; Var Sftbl; JV Var Vllybl; Hon Roll; Sci.

QUINN, APRIL ADENA; Westminster HS; Westminster, CA; (2); Drill Tm; Hon Roll; Acad Letter; Long Beach ST; Cmmnctns.

QUINN, COLLEEN; Tustin HS; Tustin, CA; (1); #1 In Class; Key Clb; Math Tm; Science Clb; Speech Tm; Off Frsh Cls; High Hon Roll; Acad Decathlon; Literary Clb; Ethnic Advsry Cncl; Engl.

QUINN, COLLEEN C; Carondelet HS; Lisle, IL; (3); 30/162; Cmnty Wkr; Ski Clb; Spanish Clb; SADD; Yrbk; Var Crs Cntry; Var Trk; High Hon Roll; NHS; Spanish NHS; CSF; Lawpost Mem; 3rd-5th Grade Church Bsktbl Tm Co-Coach; UCLA; Crmnl Lawyer.

QUINN, GREGG; Taft HS; Woodland Hills, CA; (4); 45/830; Spanish Clb; Chorus; Bsktbl; Swmmng; Vllybl; Hon Roll; Jr NHS; Pres Acad Fit Awd; Statesmn Amer Orgnztn; U C Santa Barbara; Engl.

QUINN, JENNIFER D; Galt HS; Acampo, CA; (2); Band; Mrchg Band; Pep Band; JV Sftbl; JV Vllybl; Hon Roll; Bus.

QUINN, JILL M; St Francis HS; Sacramento, CA; (2); Cmnty Wkr; Latin Clb; Swmmng; Tennis; Hon Roll; Pres Acad Fit Awd; Politics.

QUINN, LAURIE A; Rancho Cotate HS; Rohnert Park, CA; (2); Church Yth Grp; Spanish Clb; SADD; Pres Soph Cls; Hon Roll; City Sftbl; Jr HS Math Teacher.

QUINN, LISA; Ukiah HS; Ukiah, CA; (2); 72/554; Church Yth Grp; Drama Clb; Chorus; School Musical; School Play; Variety Show; Var Stat Socr; Hon Roll; Athltc Awd; Bus Ed Dept Awd-Wrd Prcssng; Sacramento ST; Drma.

QUINN, MICHAEL T; Bellarmine College Prep; San Jose, CA; (3); Cmnty Wkr; Latin Clb; JV Var Bsbl; Intrml Bsktbl; Intrml Ftbl; Intrml Vllybl; JV Var Wrstlng; Ntl Merit SF; Mgr Little Leag Bsbl Tm.

QUINN, NICK G; St Bernards HS; Los Angeles, CA; (3); Art Clb; Church Yth Grp; Cmnty Wkr; Church Choir; JV Ftbl; Wt Lftg; Cit Awd; Altrst Soc Schlrshp Awd 1st Pl; Northrup U OSCAR Awd; Howard U; Poli Sci.

QUINN, REBECCA E; Pleasant Valley HS; Chico, CA; (4); 107/246; Aud/Vis; Church Yth Grp; GAA; Teachers Aide; Temple Yth Grp; Orch; Var L Bsktbl; Capt Var Crs Cntry; Var L Trk; Hon Roll; Butte Coll; Math Teacher.

QUINN, SHANNON; Tustin HS; Tustin, CA; (3); Cmnty Wkr; Key Clb; Letterman Clb; Var L Swmmng; Hon Roll; Natl Grls/Wmn Sprts Day Recgntn Outstndng Prtcptn Swmmng; Mst Vlbl Vrsty Swmmr 3 Yrs; Amer Cancer Vlnt; Bus.

QUINN, STACY L; San Benito HS; San Juan Bautista, CA; (3); 7/350; Church Yth Grp; Office Aide; SADD; JV Sftbl; High Hon Roll; CSF Treas.

QUINN, TARA D; Yuba City HS; Yuba City, CA; (4); 13/516; Rep Key Clb; Office Aide; SADD; Ed Yrbk; Off Frsh Cls; Off Soph Cls; Off Jr Cls; Off Sr Cls; High Hon Roll; Hon Roll; Schrlshp From Rideout Mem Aux; CA Schrlshp Fed Gold Bearer; Yuba Coll; Optmtry.

QUINN, THOMAS J; Antelope Valley HS; Lancaster, CA; (3); 1/620; Am Leg Boys St; Letterman Clb; Service Clb; VP Jr Cls; VP Stu Cncl; L Var Bsbl; L Var Crs Cntry; L Var Socr; High Hon Roll; NHS.

QUINNEY, ERIC A; Bonita Vista HS; Chula Vista, CA; (2); Boy Scts; Church Yth Grp; Computer Clb; Model UN; SADD; Score Keeper; Cit Awd; Hon Roll; Prfct Atten Awd; Outstndng Comp Achvt; ROP Trng; BYU; Bus Mgmt.

QUINONES, BENJAMIN; Redlands HS; Redlands, CA; (4); Treas Bus Profs of Am; Rep Soph Cls; Treas Jr Cls; Treas Sr Cls; Bsbl; Bsktbl; JV Var Ftbl; Trk; NHS; FLA Org; Cngrssnl Smnr Wash DC; 90 Natl Hspnc Schlrs Awds Pgm; UC San Diego; Psych.

QUINONES, MARIBEL; St Marys Acad; Los Angeles, CA; (2); Church Yth Grp; Cmnty Wkr; Latin Clb; Service Clb; Spanish Clb; Chorus; Stage Crew; Lawyer.

QUINONES, OMAR M; Central HS; Barstow, CA; (3); Yrbk; Altrntv Ind Synthszr Band; Music Compsr; Songwrtr; Pro Keybrdst.

QUINONEZ, ERIC J; Bonita Vista HS; National City, CA; (3); Band; Intrml Bsbl; Bsktbl; JV Ftbl; Var Wt Lftg; Pres Acad Fit Awd; Mst Imprvd Stu; VP & Sect Ldr Adv Band; San Diego ST U; Law.

QUINONEZ, FRANK; Santa Ana HS; Santa Ana, CA; (4); 2/400; Am Leg Boys St; JA; Pres Math Clb; Rptr Nwsp; Stu Cncl; Var Capt Crs Cntry; Var Trk; High Hon Roll; Pres Acad Fit Awd; Sal; Win Ganade El Futuro Con Pepsi Award; AAU All Amer Scholar Athlete ST Of CA; US Army Schlr Medl Wn; Georgetown U; Intl Relations.

QUINTAL, ABRIL I; St Genevieve HS; Sun Valley, CA; (3); Drama Clb; Thesps; Drill Tm; School Play; Stage Crew.

QUINTANA, CARLOS; Delano HS; Delano, CA; (4); 1/355; Letterman Clb; Band; Capt L Bsktbl; Var L Tennis; Hon Roll; NHS; Ntl Merit SF; Val; Acad Decathlon Tm Hnrs Div; Bank Of Amer Plaque Wnnr; Stanford; Engrng.

QUINTANA, INGRID E; Pius X HS; Lynwood, CA; (3); Hon Roll; NHS; Rotary Awd; CA Schlrshp Fed; Campus Mnstry; Psych.

QUINTANA, JEANNINE; Beyer HS; Riverbank, CA; (3); FHA; Rep Soph Cls; Var Stu Cncl; Swmmng; Nrs.

QUINTANA, LAURA L; Bell Gardens HS; Bell Gardens, CA; (2); 6/1000; French Clb; GAA; Stu Cncl; Var Sftbl; JV Vllybl; Hon Roll; Prfct Atten Awd; Mst Imprvd JV Vlybl; UCLA; Psycht.

QUINTANA, MARCO P; Homestead HS; Sunnyvale, CA; (3); SADD; Treas Jr Cls; Stu Cncl; JV Bsbl; Bsbl.

QUINTANA, MARIO A; Canyon Springs HS; Riverside, CA; (3); Church Yth Grp; Letterman Clb; Varsity Clb; JV Capt Socr; Var Trk; Bus Fncl Advisor.

QUINTANA JR, NICK; Selma HS; Selma, CA; (2); Var Capt Wrstlng; High Hon Roll; Hon Roll; Cntrl Sequoia Lg Champ & Freestyle Wrstlng St Champ 90; Cntrl Sctn Champ & 3rd CA St Wrstlng 89-90; AZ ST U; Phys Thrpy.

QUINTANA, TINA; Apple Valley HS; Apple Valley, CA; (1); Key Clb; Chorus; Church Choir; Swing Chorus; Hon Roll.

QUINTANAR, FRANCISCA; Calipatria HS; Calipatria, CA; (3); Art Clb; Drama Clb; Math Tm; Speech Tm; School Play; Ed Nwsp; Yrbk; High Hon Roll; CSF, Sec; UCSD; Latin Lit.

QUINTANAR, LUZ ELENA; Calipatria HS; Calipatria, CA; (4); 1/68; Art Clb; Drama Clb; Math Tm; Band; Co-Ed Yrbk; Hon Roll; Prfct Atten Awd; Val; CSF Vp & Lftm Mem; MENTE 89; Friday Nite Live; U CA San Diego; Math.

QUINTANILLA, ANELI G; William Workman HS; Valinda, CA; (3); 25/300; Treas Spanish Clb; Stat Vllybl; Hon Roll; Prfct Atten Awd; Pres Acad Fit Awd; Spanish NHS; Schl Schlr; Stu Of Mnth Frgn Lang & Home Ec; Outstndng Achvt Awd Chem; Med.

QUINTANILLA, MARITZA C; American HS; Fremont, CA; (4); 36/323; Bus Profs of Am; French Clb; Spanish Clb; SADD; Sec Frsh Cls; Off Soph Cls; Score Keeper; High Hon Roll; Spanish NHS; Most Outstng Span Stu 88; Bank Amer Awd Outstng Achvt Frgn Langs 90; UC Santa Barbara.

QUINTANILLA, VINCENT P; El Cajon Valley HS; El Cajon, CA; (2); 74/431; Comp Sci.

QUINTARD, KACEY R; Apple Valley HS; Apple Valley, CA; (2); Cmnty Wkr; Letterman Clb; SADD; Teachers Aide; Varsity Clb; Bsktbl; Socr; Sftbl; Hon Roll; Sports Med.

QUINTERO, DINA H; Downey HS; Downey, CA; (4); Treas Service Clb; Drill Tm; Rptr Nwsp; JV Bsktbl; Les Tourcheres His & Treas Svc Clb; Grls Leag Histn Svc Clb; Long Beach Clb; Englsh.

QUINTERO, REBECCA; Sacred Heart Of Jesus HS; Los Angeles, CA; (3); GAA; Girl Scts; Letterman Clb; Library Aide; Treas Frsh Cls; VP Jr Cls; Var Trk; JV Var Vllybl; Hon Roll; NHS.

QUINTERO, ROSA GUILL; Alisal HS; Salinas, CA; (2); Computer Clb; Spanish Clb; Yrbk; Off Soph Cls; Swmmng; Hon Roll; Prfct Atten Awd; Spanish NHS; Arch.

QUINTERO VILLEGAS, VICTOR H; Locke HS; Los Angeles, CA; (3); Art Clb; ROTC; Teachers Aide; Socr; USC; Arch.

QUINTEROS, JUAN CARLOS; Canoga Park HS; Canoga Park, CA; (3); Treas Church Yth Grp; Cler Clb; Church Choir; Mrchg Band; Orch; JV Bsktbl; Med.

QUINTEROS, TRACIE; Pinole Valley HS; Hercules, CA; (2); Church Yth Grp; Varsity Clb; Band; Color Guard; Flag Corp; Mrchg Band; JV Swmmng; Hon Roll; Water Polo Vrsty; USA Water Polo; Swimming Instrctr Aide; Lawyer.

QUINTNA, JENNIFER; Bear River HS; Auburn, CA; (3); Church Yth Grp; Cmnty Wkr; Nwsp; Pom Pon; Hon Roll; NC Exchnge Pgm; Azusa Pacific U; RN.

QUINTO, JEFFREY G; San Leandro HS; San Leandro, CA; (3); 4/361; Church Yth Grp; Cmnty Wkr; Band; Hon Roll; Pres Acad Fit Awd; CA Schlrshp Fed; Frgn Lang Awd; U CA Berkeley; Health Sci.

QUINTO, JOSEPH R; Alameda HS; Alameda, CA; (4); 6/325; Treas Soph Cls; VP Jr Cls; VP Stu Cncl; JV Var Bsktbl; JV Var Ftbl; Hon Roll.

QUINTOS, YESENIA; Mira Mesa HS; San Diego, CA; (4); 129/849; Spanish Clb; Var Capt Trk; Hon Roll; Pres Acad Fit Awd; HIP; San Diego Union/Tribunes All-Acad Team; Mesa JC; Arch.

QUINTRELL, JALAINE; Alhambra HS; Alhambra, CA; (3); Cmnty Wkr; Service Clb; Chorus; Stu Cncl; Med Clb; CSF; Cal ST LA; Engr.

QUIOCHO, EDWARD QUINOLA; College Park HS; Pleasant Hill, CA; (3); Aud/Vis; Band; Mrchg Band; JV Wrstlng; Muslim Stus Assn; Human Rghts & Frgn Affrs; Audio Engr.

QUIRANTE, JAEMA; Fairfield HS; Suisun City, CA; (2); Cheerldng.

QUIRANTE, JOY S; Academy Of Our Lady Of Peace; San Diego, CA; (3); 11/116; Key Clb; Pres Frsh Cls; Rep Soph Cls; Treas Jr Cls; Pres Sr Cls; Var Tennis; Hon Roll; NHS; Spanish NHS; Spanish NHS; CA Schlrshp Fed; CA Polytech Inst; Arch.

QUIRANTE, LAWRENCE R; Sierra Vista HS; Baldwin Park, CA; (3); French Clb; Ftbl; Swmmng; Tennis; Wrstlng; Opt Clb Awd; Pres Acad Fit Awd; US Judo Jr Natl Champ 88; Thomas J Lipton Sprtsmn Awd; E Vly Boys & Grls Clb Sprtsmn Of Yr 88; Civil Engrng.

QUIRAY, SHANA; Chaffey HS; Ontario, CA; (3); 3/550; Library Aide; Pep Clb; Variety Show; Lit Mag; Pom Pon; High Hon Roll; Hon Roll; NHS; Prfct Atten Awd; Cngrssnl Schlr.

QUIRK, COLLEEN; Santa Rosa HS; Santa Rosa, CA; (2); Dance Clb; Teachers Aide; Acpl Chr; Chorus; Pres Acad Fit Awd; Comptv Rllrsktng; Coll Bnd Pgm For Minority Stu; UC Davis; Bus.

QUIRK, MICHAEL; Garces Memorial HS; Bakersfield, CA; (3); Boy Scts; Lit Mag; Var Crs Cntry; JV Trk; High Hon Roll; CA Schltc Fed; Stanford U; Med.

QUIRK, TOM P; La Serna HS; Whittier, CA; (3); 90/393; Ski Clb; Stu Cncl; Var L Bsbl; JV Bsktbl; JV L Ftbl; CA Poly Sn Luis Obispo; Acctng.

QUIROZ, ALICIA G; St Anthony HS; Long Beach, CA; (2); Church Yth Grp; Cmnty Wkr; Office Aide; Spanish Clb; Teachers Aide; Bsktbl; Score Keeper; Swmmng; Trk; High Hon Roll; CSF; U Southern CA; RN.

QUIROZ, BELIA E; Calexico HS; Calexico, CA; (2); Church Yth Grp; SADD; Temple Yth Grp; Cit Awd; Hon Roll; Brigham Young U; Acctng.

QUIROZ, CARLOS U; Calexico Adventist Mission Acad; Calexico, CA; (2); Church Yth Grp; VP Frsh Cls; Prfct Atten Awd; Loma Linda U; Heart Srgn.

QUIROZ, IRENE; Palo Verde HS; Blythe, CA; (2); FFA; Pres Soph Cls; Rep Stu Cncl; High Hon Roll; Hon Roll; Kiwanis Awd; Lion Awd; NHS; Tech Engrng.

QUIROZ, JENNIE R; Clovis HS; Clovis, CA; (2); GAA; Spanish Clb; SADD; Off Jr Cls; Bsbl; Powder Puff Ftbl; Score Keeper; Sftbl; Var Swmmng; Var Trk; Fresno ST; Phy Ther.

QUIROZ, RAQUEL L; Colton HS; Colton, CA; (1); Church Yth Grp; Office Aide; Chorus; Church Choir; JV Capt Socr; JV Sftbl; Hon Roll; Phy.

QUIST, DON C; Rio Linda HS; Sacramento, CA; (2); Cmnty Wkr; French Clb; High Hon Roll; NHS; Prfct Atten Awd; Pres Acad Fit Awd; Delg Ioof; Gldn St Exam Outstndng Acad Achvt; Outstndng Achvt Awds 90; Harvard; Med.

QUITMEYER, DAVID; John Jenkins Christian Acad; Santa Paula, CA; (2); 1/20; Variety Show; Treas Stu Cncl; Var L Bsktbl; High Hon Roll; Pres Acad Fit Awd; Most Christian Character; DARE Spec Awd; Teachers Awd Twice Rcvd; Writing Awds & Pblctns Storys/Poems; UCLA; Film.

QUIZON, KENNETH P; Eagle Rock HS; Los Angeles, CA; (3); Chess Clb; Computer Clb; Hon Roll; Lion Awd; Prfct Atten Awd; Outstndng Achvt Comptr Sci & Sci 88-89; Schltc Achvt Hnrs Cert 88-89; MIT; Sci.

QUON, ANNA; Etiwanda HS; Fontana, CA; (2); Church Yth Grp; Treas French Clb; VP FBLA; JV Badminton; Ped.

QUON, LAWRENCE Y; Eagle Rock HS; Los Angeles, CA; (2); Cmnty Wkr; Key Clb; Ski Clb; Phtg Yrbk; JV Tennis; Pres Acad Fit Awd; Hnrs Pgm; Chinese Clb; Womens Hstry Wk Essay Cont-2nd Pl; Med.

QUON, LISA; Ben Franklin HS; Los Angeles, CA; (3); Art Clb; Church Yth Grp; Cmnty Wkr; Key Clb; Library Aide; Var Crs Cntry; Var Trk; Hmn Rghts Clb; Photo; Athenians Schlrshp Fed.

QUON, RICHARD P; Gunderson HS; San Jose, CA; (4); 1/450; Cmnty Wkr; Math Clb; Varsity Clb; Var L Tennis; High Hon Roll; Hon Roll; NHS; Ntl Merit SF; Val; SHARP Prog NASA Rsrch Ctr; Superintendents Awd; Elec Engr.

QUON, VIVIAN W; Etiwanda HS; Fontana, CA; (2); Church Yth Grp; Rptr FBLA; Band; Mrchg Band; Rptr Nwsp; Lit Mag; Hon Roll; IEJA St Qlfr; Columbia U; Engl.

QURA, JOHNNY; Abraham Lincoln HS; San Francisco, CA; (3); JV Bsbl; JV Bsktbl; JV Ftbl; Intrml Gym; Intrml Mgr(s); JV Pom Pon; Var JV Socr; Intrml Sftbl; Intrml Swmmng; Intrml Tennis.

RA, PHILIP; Fountain Valley HS; Fountain Valley, CA; (3); Boy Scts; Church Yth Grp; Key Clb; Spanish Clb; Bsktbl; JV Tennis; Cit Awd; Prfct Atten Awd; CA Poly San Luis Obispo; Arch.

RAAB, ALISON; St Joseph HS; Santa Maria, CA; (3); 7/134; Church Yth Grp; Drama Clb; SADD; Rptr Nwsp; Treas Stu Cncl; JV Swmmng; High Hon Roll; NHS; Ntl Merit SF; Jr Statesmen Of Amer; CA Schlrshp Fed; Intl Rltns.

RAABE, RUTH A; Davis HS; Davis, CA; (2); 1/328; Church Yth Grp; Hosp Aide; Band; Pep Band; Pres Acad Fit Awd; Young Life; Badminton Team; Princ Awd 89; Gldn ST Exam Alg & Geom Hnrs; U CA; Phys Ther.

RAANES, BILL; Antioch HS; Antioch, CA; (4); Forestry.

RABANERA, MARIVER L; Colton HS; Colton, CA; (1); Church Yth Grp; Cit Awd; Hon Roll; Prfct Atten Awd; JV Bsktbl; JV Tennis; Loma Linda U; Chemist.

RABBITT, JARRETT M; Oroville HS; Oroville, CA; (2); JV Bsktbl; Socr; JV Hon Roll; JV Prfct Atten Awd; Bsktbl Ltr; Coaches Awd Plq 89-90.

RABENAU, ANDREA J; Chino HS; Ontario, CA; (2); Dance Clb; FBLA; Library Aide; Math Clb; Math Tm; Teachers Aide; Band; Stage Crew; Nwsp; Lit Mag; Silver Spur Award; Harvard; Clinical Adolesc Psych.

RABIDEAU, AARON; Casa Grande HS; Petaluma, CA; (3); JV Wrstlng; Jr NHS; NHS; CA ST U; Bus Mgmt.

RABIN, MIRIAM; Los Alamitos HS; Long Beach, CA; (3); Capt Chess Clb; Drama Clb; Math Clb; NFL; Science Clb; Temple Yth Grp; Orch; Ed Nwsp; High Hon Roll; NHS; Hrsbck Rdr; Sccd Natl Lvl Cmptn-Natl Gld Piano; Ntnwd Frnch Cont Cmptn-Scrd Top 20 Pct.

RABINOVICH, LIYA; Lowell HS; San Francisco, CA; (2); SADD; Color Guard; Stage Crew; High Hon Roll; Russian Club PR; Big Brother/Big Sister; Bio.

RABINOVICI, MICHAEL; Taft HS; Woodland Hills, CA; (2); Service Clb; CSF; Tutoring Svc; Club Tnns Plyr; Sci.

RABO, NICOLE; Notre Dame Schl; Durham, CA; (2); Church Yth Grp; Dance Clb; Drama Clb; Science Clb; Church Choir; School Play; JV Bsktbl; Intrml Cheerldng; Intrml Pom Pon; Intrml Cit Awd; Actrss.

RABOURN, SAMANTHA S; Ramona HS; Santa Ysabel, CA; (2); Teachers Aide; Hon Roll; Earth Envrnmnt Awrnss Grp; Fair Trtmnt Anmls Grp; Film Ind.

RABY, LORRANE E; San Jacinto HS; San Jacinto, CA; (3); 2/200; Church Yth Grp; Model UN; Spanish Clb; Band; Mrchg Band; Pep Band; Tennis; Cit Awd; High Hon Roll; Mck Trl; U Of CA Riverside; Math.

RACEK, NICHOLE M; Academy Of Our Lady Of Peace; Chula Vista, CA; (1); 1/180; Church Yth Grp; Var Trk; High Hon Roll; NEDT Awd; Piano, Skiing; Harvard Medcl Schl; Dermtlgy.

RACH, JANICE; Millikan HS; Long Beach, CA; (3); Dance Clb; Pep Clb; Teachers Aide; Band; Drill Tm; Yrbk; Bsktbl; Capt Cheerldng; Capt Pom Pon; Capt Sftbl; Chiropractics.

RACH, JENNY; Millikan HS; Long Beach, CA; (4); 90/647; Pep Clb; Band; Drill Tm; Jazz Band; Sprt Ed Yrbk; Var Cheerldng; Hon Roll; USCLB; Elementary Schl Tchr.

RACHSHTUT, MICKEY; Einstein Acad; Encino, CA; (1); 1/24; Teachers Aide; School Play; Sec Frsh Cls; Bsktbl; Socr; High Hon Roll; Hon Roll; Med.

RACK, PAUL G; Whitney HS; Artesia, CA; (1); Boy Scts; High Hon Roll; CJSF; UC Santa Barbara; Marine Bio.

RACY, TARISE S; Mt Diablo HS; Pittsburg, CA; (1); Dance Clb; French Clb; FBLA; Band; Drill Tm; Var L Sftbl; Hon Roll; UCLA; Bus Econ.

RADDAVONG, AMMONE; Costa Mesa HS; Costa Mesa, CA; (2); Math Clb; Office Aide; Spanish Clb; Teachers Aide; Var Tennis; Hon Roll; Orange Coast Coll; Psych.

RADDEN, ROBERT J; Patrick Henry HS; San Diego, CA; (4); 50/501; Art Clb; Aud/Vis; Cmnty Wkr; Model UN; Office Aide; Science Clb; Service Clb; Ski Clb; Spanish Clb; Teachers Aide; Schl News Telecast; Sprts Anchr & Edtr; Cngrssnl Yth Ldrshp Cncl; Yth Opptrnts Fndtn; UCLA Los Angles; Flm.

RADEBAUGH, SHANNON; Irvine HS; Irvine, CA; (2); 4-H; 4-H Awd; Hon Roll; Art.

RADENBAUGH, DOULGAS L; Edison/Compu Tech; Fresno, CA; (2); 135/300; Boy Scts; Ftbl; Socr; Trk; Hon Roll; Jr Statesmen Of America; Cal Poly; Cmptr System Anlst.

RADER, ADRIENNE E; Palmdale HS; Palmdale, CA; (3); 46/644; Cmnty Wkr; FFA; Pep Clb; Yrbk; Off Sr Cls; Cheerldng; Powder Puff Ftbl; Hon Roll; CSF; Keywanette Clb; San Diego ST U; Med.

RADER, GINA LEA; Central Valley HS; Central Valley, CA; (2); Church Yth Grp; Cmnty Wkr; Letterman Clb; Office Aide; Band; Mrchg Band; Cheerldng; Socr; Swmmng; Wt Lftg; Friday Night Live; Yth To Yth; Reach Out Amer; Notre Dame; Psych.

RADER, JEREMY; Heritage Christian HS; Brea, CA; (3); 1/20; Church Yth Grp; Drama Clb; Math Tm; Science Clb; Church Choir; Bsbl; Capt Bsktbl; Hon Roll; St Schlr; Biola U; Crmnlgy.

RADI, RAMI R; Leuzinger HS; Hawthorne, CA; (3); Aud/Vis; Teachers Aide; Stage Crew; Video Prdctn; San Diego ST; Video Technon.

RADLEY, KRISTEN R; North HS; Bakersfield, CA; (2); Church Yth Grp; Chorus; Church Choir; Variety Show; High Hon Roll; Hon Roll; NHS; CSF; Interact Clb; Jazz Choir; Point Loma Nazarene Coll.

RADLEY, LAURA S; Irvine HS; Irvine, CA; (1); GAA; Key Clb; Ski Clb; Spanish Clb; JV Crs Cntry; JV Trk; High Hon Roll; Hon Roll; UCLA; Inter Dsgn.

RADMALL, HEATHER L; Ponderosa HS; Rescue, CA; (3); 27/278; Chess Clb; French Clb; Library Aide; Rptr Nwsp; High Hon Roll; Hon Roll; Prfct Atten Awd; Acad Letter; CA ST U; Bio.

RADOMSKI, KACIE; San Ramon Valley HS; Danville, CA; (2); 12/400; Church Yth Grp; Dance Clb; Teachers Aide; JV Cheerldng; High Hon Roll; Principals Scholar Athlete Award C S F; College.

RADTKE, KELSIE; Arrowhead Christian Acad; San Bernardino, CA; (4); 4/16; Teachers Aide; Chorus; Sec Jr Cls; VP Sr Cls; Var Crs Cntry; Var Sftbl; JV Tennis; NHS; Pres Acad Fit Awd; Azusa Pacific U; Nrsng.

RADTKE, SARAH; Poway HS; San Diego, CA; (3); Church Yth Grp; Band; Mrchg Band; Pep Band; Trk; High Hon Roll; Hon Roll; NHS; Pres Acad Fit Awd; PHS Envrmntl Clb; AZ ST; Math.

RAE, AMI; El Toro HS; El Toro, CA; (2); 20/550; Model UN; JV Socr; Sftbl; Stat Vllybl; High Hon Roll; CA Schlrshp Fed; Grls League; Adv.

RAE, JANET L; Francis W Parker HS; San Diego, CA; (2); Church Yth Grp; SADD; Var Socr; Var Sftbl; Hon Roll; Grls Leag; Interact; Amnsty Intl; Pedtrcn.

RAEL, ANDREA; Pius X HS; South Gate, CA; (4); 5/185; Church Yth Grp; Math Clb; Mu Alpha Theta; Stu Cncl; Var Crs Cntry; JV Var Trk; Hon Roll; NHS; Ntl Merit SF; Acad Decathln; U San Diego; Sociology.

RAFALOVICH, STEVE R; Corona Del Mar HS; Corona Del Mar, CA; (4); 64/315; JV Crs Cntry; High Hon Roll; Pres Schlr; Classcl Guitarist; U Of CO-BOULDER; Bus Admin.

RAFEEDIE, NIDAL I; Colton HS; Grand Terrace, CA; (1); Model UN; Socr; Swmmng; Hon Roll; Prfct Atten Awd; HS Stu Ambssdr Prgrm; Acad Cmptn; Constr.

RAFENSTEIN, ALI R; Bonita Vista HS; Bonita, CA; (1); 36/537; Church Yth Grp; Girl Scts; Library Aide; Ayso Soccer.

RAFF, SUSAN; Ukiah HS; Ukiah, CA; (2); 63/310; Church Yth Grp; Cmnty Wkr; English Clb; FBLA; Letterman Clb; Office Aide; SADD; Band; Variety Show; Rep Stu Cncl; Stat Girl Achvt Awd 88-90; Stat Girl Of Yr 89-90; UCLA; Law.

RAFFAELI, MICHAEL A; Saint Francis HS; Sunnyvale, CA; (4); Art Clb; English Clb; Math Clb; Science Clb; SADD; Phtg Nwsp; Phtg Yrbk; High Hon Roll; Jr NHS; NHS; Jnr Statesmn Assoc; Amnsty Intrntl; CSF; U Of CA San Diego; Bio.

RAFFAELLI, SAMANTHA A; Don Antonio Lugo HS; Chino, CA; (4); 27/689; Am Leg Aux Girls St; VP Office Aide; Stat Bsbl; High Hon Roll; NHS; Prfct Atten Awd; Golden Conquest Math Cert Wnnr, Phys Ed Plque Wnnr; Cal ST Fullerton.

RAFFEL, MICHELLE DIANE; Yucaipo HS; Yucaipa, CA; (4); 23/300; Church Yth Grp; German Clb; Teachers Aide; Nwsp; Capt Var Bsktbl; Powder Puff Ftbl; Var Score Keeper; High Hon Roll; Hon Roll; Lion Awd; Ambssdrs Pres; CA ST U San Bernardino.

RAGEL, STEVE C; Eisenhower HS; Colton, CA; (3); Teachers Aide; Var Trk; Cit Awd; Hon Roll; NHS; C Clb; Athl Schlr Awd; V Ltr Awd Track, Field; Stu Pilot Cert; Cert Awd Spnsh II; U Of SAN Diego; Aerntcl Engr.

RAGER, JASON M; San Pasqual HS; Escondido, CA; (3); Cit Awd; Hon Roll; Prfct Atten Awd.

RAGER, JEFF A; Torrey Pines HS; Solana Beach, CA; (1); Ftbl; Stanford; Intl Bus.

RAGHUNATHAN, SANGEETHA; Troy HS; Fullerton, CA; (2); #9 In Class; Key Clb; Spanish Clb; Ed Nwsp; JV Capt Bsktbl; Var L Crs Cntry; Var L Trk; DAR Awd; High Hon Roll; Jr NHS; Rotary Awd; 8 Yr Wnnr Natl Guild Piano Tchrs; Slctd Play Music Teachers Assoc Annl Music Cnvtn.

RAGLAND, CHARLES; El Camino HS; Oceanside, CA; (3); 35/364; Church Yth Grp; Pres FFA; Pres Jr Cls; Pres Sr Cls; JV Bsktbl; Gov Hon Prg Awd; Hon Roll; Prfct Atten Awd; 1 Of 40 Stu Attended Ron Packards Amer Govt Seminar Washington DC 90; Jr Ag Stu Of Yr 89; US Govt.

RAGLAND, MEISHAUNEE V; Carlmont HS; East Palo Alto, CA; (1); Cmnty Wkr; UCLA; Pediatrician.

RAGLAND, ROXANNE; Fallbrook Union HS; Fallbrook, CA; (4); 10/388; AFS; Church Yth Grp; JV Crs Cntry; JV Gym; Var Swmmng; High Hon Roll; Hon Roll; NHS; Pres Acad Fit Awd; Palomar Coll; Bio.

RAGLAND, SEAN A; Laguna Hills HS; Laguna Hills, CA; (4); 47/318; Cmnty Wkr; Math Clb; Office Aide; VP SADD; Variety Show; Pres Soph Cls; Pres Jr Cls; Pres Sr Cls; Ftbl; Wt Lftg; VP Yth Agnst Drugs; Exchng Clb Yth Of Yr Rnnr Up; Outstng Yng Ldr Awd; Grad Spkr; Exchng Stu Moscow; AZ ST U; Aerontcl Engr.

RAGLIN, SHERRELL; St Marys Acad; Los Angeles, CA; (2); French Clb; GAA; Variety Show; Yrbk; Var Bsktbl; Var Vllybl; Cit Awd; Hon Roll; 2nd Rnnr Up Homcmng Qn; CIF All Amer Leag Plyr Bsktbl; CA ST Long Beach; Lawyer.

RAGO, JOSEPH E; Bishop O'dowd HS; Castro Valley, CA; (2); Church Yth Grp; Ski Clb; Hon Roll; Karate; Poetry; Art; Engrng.

RAGUENEAU, VALERIE C; Lycee Francais Laperouse HS; San Francisco, CA; (2); Yrbk; Bsbl; Bsktbl; Gym; Socr; Swmmng; Visual Arts; Music; Design.

RAGUINDIN, RAYMOND J; South San Francisco HS; S San Francisco, CA; (3); Church Yth Grp; FBLA; Math Clb; Bus.

RAHEBI, BITA; San Ramon Valley HS; Danville, CA; (2); Office Aide; High Hon Roll; Friday Night Live; Law.

RAHHAL, ELLIS M; Eisenhower HS; Rialto, CA; (2); 1/800; Band; Jazz Band; Mrchg Band; Pep Band; Hon Roll; Jr NHS; NHS; Pres Acad Fit Awd; Golden St Exam Hgh Hnrs; Sci Dept Awd; Physics.

RAHIM, ZARGHOONA; Encinal HS; Alameda, CA; (4); 2/222; Debate Tm; Pres French Clb; Hosp Aide; Math Tm; NFL; Science Clb; Trk; Cit Awd; High Hon Roll; Hon Roll; Sal; Tlntd & Gftd Pgm; Able To Speak & Write Fluently Farsi, Arabie, Urdu & Pushtu; Biochem.

RAHIMIAN, JEANNINE; Palisades HS; Los Angeles, CA; (2); Debate Tm; Math Clb; Math Tm; Science Clb; Speech Tm; Orch; Rep Fld Hcky; Rep Stu Cncl; Var Tennis; Pres Acad Fit Awd; Pali Outreach-Fndr/Sec 89-90; Debate Superiority Cert 90; Outstndng Chem Achvt Awd 90.

RAHM, KIMBERLY R; Whittier Christian HS; Hacienda Heights, CA; (3); Teachers Aide; JV Capt Bsktbl; Powder Puff Ftbl; Var Sftbl; JV Capt Vllybl; Rcv Schlrshp To Pepperdine Ldrshp Camp; CA Schltc Fed; Invtd U Of CA Santa Barbara For Schlr Day.

RAHMAN, KATHLEEN S; Mc Ateer HS; San Francisco, CA; (3); Stage Crew; Hon Roll; Citywd Photo Awd; Stu For Envrnmnt Clb; MACS Clb; Bio.

RAHMAN, SALAH; Trabuco Hills HS; El Toro, CA; (3); Spanish Clb; Bsktbl; Ftbl; Orange Cnty Acad Decathlon-4th Pl Literature & 5th Pl Fine Arts Cmptn; Columbia U; Arch Engrng.

RAHN, DAVID B; Bellarmine College Prep; Menlo Park, CA; (3); 1/300; Chess Clb; Cmnty Wkr; Math Clb; Science Clb; Teachers Aide; Phtg Yrbk; Bausch & Lomb Sci Awd; Ntl Merit Ltr; 3rd Pl Santa Clara Vly Chem Cmptn; Aerosp Engrng.

RAI, DAVID A; Glendale Adventist Acad; Tujunga, CA; (2); Church Yth Grp; Cmnty Wkr; Computer Clb; FCA; Teachers Aide; Band; Yrbk; Vllybl; Hon Roll; NHS; Presidential Academic Fitness Award.

RAI, RAVINDERPAL S; Live Oak HS; Live Oak, CA; (3); 11/80; JV Var Bsktbl; Hon Roll; U Davis; Engrng.

RAILSBACK, RYAN J; Notre Dame HS; Riverside, CA; (1); 35/200; Church Yth Grp; SADD; JV Bsbl; Cit Awd; Hon Roll; Pres Acad Fit Awd; UCA Riverside; Law.

RAIMER, WENDY M; Red Bluff Union HS; Los Molinos, CA; (3); 11/350; Letterman Clb; Stu Cncl; Bsktbl; Golf; Gym; Trk; Vllybl; Wt Lftg; High Hon Roll; Hon Roll.

RAINALDI, JOSEPH P; Serra HS; Millbrae, CA; (3); 1/250; Chess Clb; Computer Clb; Math Clb; Mu Alpha Theta; Mgr Nwsp; High Hon Roll; Ntl Merit Ltr; Prfct Atten Awd; Pres Schlr; Millbrae Beutfctn Commsn; Comp Sci.

RAINE, MIKE L; Etiwanda HS; Etiwanda, CA; (3); Mrchg Band; VP Sr Cls; Var Wrstlng; Envrnmntl Sci.

RAINEY, JAMES B; Las Alamitos HS; Long Beach, CA; (2); Church Yth Grp; Cmnty Wkr; Teachers Aide; JV Crs Cntry; JV Trk; High Hon Roll; Hon Roll; CSF; PTSA; Psych.

RAINEY, NYCOLE; Galileo HS; San Francisco, CA; (2); Church Yth Grp; Dance Clb; Spanish Clb; Trk; High Hon Roll; USC; Defense Attorney.

RAINS, TOM F; Canyon HS; Canyon Country, CA; (2); Capt Bsktbl; Music.

RAISNER, JUSTIN R; Lowell HS; San Francisco, CA; (2); Boy Scts; Office Aide; Teachers Aide; Band; Rptr Nwsp; Part Time Inventory Taker With Rgis.

RAJA, ALEEM U; John F Kennedy HS; Sacramento, CA; (4); Chess Clb; Debate Tm; FBLA; German Clb; Math Clb; Math Tm; NFL; Speech Tm; Ed Lit Mag; Hon Roll; UC Berkeley; Poli Sci.

RAJAGOPAL, KANAKA; Torrance HS; Torrance, CA; (2); 18/454; JA; Pep Clb; Service Clb; SADD; Rep Frsh Cls; Hist Soph Cls; JV Co-Capt Cheerldng; Cit Awd; Hon Roll; High Hnrs-Gldn St Geom Exam; CSF; Jnr Statesmn Of Amer; Cvl Engr.

RAJAGOPALAN, VIDYA; Santa Clara HS; Santa Clara, CA; (3); Spanish Clb; UC Santa Cruz; Jrnlsm.

RAJALINGAM, RAJINA; Paraclete HS; Lancaster, CA; (4); Cmnty Wkr; Debate Tm; Hosp Aide; Key Clb; Letterman Clb; Teachers Aide; Crs Cntry; Trk; High Hon Roll; NHS; Bio & Constitution Achvt Awds; Doctor.

RAJKUMAR, KAMELA; Newport Harbor HS; Costa Mesa, CA; (2); Church Yth Grp; Debate Tm; Varsity Clb; Orch; Bsktbl; Tennis; Trk; Cit Awd; Hon Roll; Pres Acad Fit Awd; Loyala Marymount; CPA.

RAK, VANESSA L; Las Lomas HS; Walnut Creek, CA; (3); 63/270; Cmnty Wkr; French Clb; Intnl Clb; Teachers Aide; Sec Sr Cls; Rep Stu Cncl; Hon Roll; Rotary Awd; Yth Educator; Chemathon Awd Wnnr; Palladians; U Of CA; Intl Stds.

RAKOSKI, SCOTT K; Paraclete HS; Palmdale, CA; (2); Drama Clb; JA; Key Clb; Letterman Clb; SADD; School Play; JV Ftbl; Var Capt Socr; JV Var Trk; Hon Roll; Rlgn Awd; Frgn Lang Awd; Prncpls Awd; Lang Arts Awd; U Of CO Boulder; Vet Med.

RAKTHET, JAY; Covina HS; Couzna, CA; (4); 12/237; Math Clb; Model UN; JV Var Tennis; Hon Roll; Comp Sci.

RALSTEN, KELLY G; Mt Whitney HS; Visalia, CA; (3); FHA; Spanish Clb; Band; Mrchg Band; Pep Band; Hon Roll; Pres Acad Fit Awd; CSF; Mock Trial Team; UC Davis; Law.

RALSTON, ANNE; El Molino HS; Sebastopol, CA; (4); 24/203; Chrmn Church Yth Grp; Pres FFA; Science Clb; Spanish Clb; Speech Tm; Teachers Aide; Church Choir; Ed Yrbk; DAR Awd; High Hon Roll; Assctd Stu Bdy Schl Bd Rep; CA FFA Pblc Spkng Champ 89; N CA FFA VP; San Francisco U; Nrsng.

RAM, REETA L; Sunset HS; Hayward, CA; (3); Dance Clb; Debate Tm; Library Aide; Math Tm; Office Aide; Nwsp; High Hon Roll; Medcl.

RAM, YANIR; Paraclete HS; Lancaster, CA; (3); 12/128; Debate Tm; Key Clb; Letterman Clb; Nwsp; Yrbk; Var Ftbl; JV Socr; Var Wt Lftg; High Hon Roll; Hon Roll; CSF.

RAMALLO, JOSEPH; Damien HS; Pomona, CA; (4); 18/189; Cmnty Wkr; Office Aide; SADD; JV Bsktbl; JV Crs Cntry; Var Trk; Hon Roll; Pres Acad Fit Awd; MESA; Natl Hispanic Schlrshp Semi Fnlst; U Of Miami; Marine Bio.

RAMANI, TRIPTI; Fountain Valley HS; Huntington Beach, CA; (3); Cmnty Wkr; Hosp Aide; Science Clb; Spanish Clb; Ed Nwsp; Off Frsh Cls; Off Soph Cls; Off Jr Cls; High Hon Roll; Envrnmntlst Clb EPA; Pres Mdcl Explrers-Pacifica Hosp; Asst Chld Lf Spclst Kaiser Permanente; U Of CA; Psychbio.

RAMBO, BRIDGETTE; Polytechnic HS; Moreno Valley, CA; (2); Church Yth Grp; Church Choir; Drill Tm; High Hon Roll; UCLA; Engrng.

RAMBO, CARLA J; Ramona HS; Riverside, CA; (2); Church Yth Grp; GAA; Latin Clb; Mgr(s); Socr; Vllybl; Riverside CC; Psych.

RAMBO, DARCI L; Foot Hill HS; Bakersfield, CA; (2); Drama Clb; SADD; Chorus; School Musical; Natl Young Leaders Conf Congrssnl Schlr; Amer Lgn Essay Cont 2nd Pl; Intl Order Of Jobs Daughters; Spcl Ed.

RAMBONGA, BARRY C; Orosi HS; Orosi, CA; (3); SADD; Var Bsbl; Intrml Bsktbl; JV Ftbl; Intrml Vllybl; Hon Roll; Hi-Y Cls Rep 89; Kings River CC; Arch.

RAMBUS, SHEKELIA; Montgomery HS; San Diego, CA; (3); Cit Awd; Prfct Atten Awd; Fine Arts & 1st Yr Spanish Awds; UCLA; Bus.

RAMER, SANDRA L; Oakdale HS; Oakdale, CA; (3); Art Clb; Church Yth Grp; Ski Clb; Varsity Clb; Rptr Yrbk; Rep Stu Cncl; Var JV Swmmng; Hon Roll; Business.

RAMEY, HEATHER L; Armijo HS; Fairfield, CA; (2); AFS; Drama Clb; Ski Clb; SADD; School Musical; School Play; Stage Crew; Variety Show; VP Soph Cls; Off Jr Cls; Ldrshp; Prof Trngng-Acting; Voice; Dance; Piano; Perfrmng Arts.

RAMEY, TANA L; Yreka HS; Yreka, CA; (3); Cmnty Wkr; Ski Clb; Spanish Clb; Teachers Aide; Varsity Clb; VP Sr Cls; JV Var Sftbl; Sacramento ST Coll; Bus.

RAMEY, TRACEY D; Fort Bragg HS; Fort Bragg, CA; (2); 1/170; Hon Roll; Prfct Atten Awd; Pres Acad Fit Awd; CSF; Cert Achvmt Various Subjects; Golden St Exam Acad Excl Awd; Geom With Hnrs; Humboldt ST; Teach.

RAMEZZANO, DAVID C; San Rafael HS; San Rafael, CA; (3); 1/226; Am Leg Boys St; Debate Tm; French Clb; Rep Stu Cncl; Bsktbl; Bausch & Lomb Sci Awd; Acadc Dcthln; CA Schlrshp Fdrtn; UCLA; Sprts Brdcstr.

RAMIEREZ, RITA; Bishop Amat HS; Baldwin Park, CA; (3); Varsity Clb; Var Sftbl; JV Vllybl; U CA-SANTA Cruz; Chld Psych.

RAMIL, TRESSY; Mt Carmel HS; San Diego, CA; (3); Pep Clb; Teachers Aide; Off Jr Cls; Stu Cncl; JV Cheerldng; Mgr Ftbl; Stu Senate; Just Say No Clb; Convention Delg; U CA; Engl.

RAMILO, GETULIO I; Santa Maria HS; Santa Maria, CA; (3); 1/536; Am Leg Boys St; Church Yth Grp; Cmnty Wkr; Drama Clb; Hist FBLA; Math Clb; Math Tm; Q&S; Quiz Bowl; Scholastic Bowl; JEA 1st Pl Awd Excllnce Natl Sprtswrtng; HOBY Ldrshp Awd; Dir Spectlr Fnd Rsr; UCSD; Pre-Med.

RAMIREZ, ALFREDO; Corcoran HS; Corcoran, CA; (4); Am Leg Boys St; Church Yth Grp; VP Science Clb; Teachers Aide; Treas Varsity Clb; VP Band; Drm Mjr(t); Mrchg Band; Pep Band; Rep Frsh Cls; CSF Treas; MED.

RAMIREZ, ALFREDO; Modesto HS; Salida, CA; (3); JV Var Bsbl; JV Var Bsktbl; JV Var Ftbl.

RAMIREZ, ALICIA; Coachella Valley HS; Coachella, CA; (2); Church Yth Grp; Band; Mrchg Band; Hon Roll; Prfct Atten Awd; U Of CA Riverside; Dietcn.

RAMIREZ, AMANDA M; Hoover HS; Fresno, CA; (1); Color Guard; Flag Corp.

RAMIREZ, ANA LILIA; Southwest HS; San Ysidro, CA; (3); Tchr.

RAMIREZ, ANABEL; Fillmore HS; Fillmore, CA; (3); Teachers Aide; Var Socr; Hon Roll; Honors Spanish; Moorpark; Accounting.

RAMIREZ, ANDREA; Venice HS; Los Angeles, CA; (2); Band; Bsktbl; Gym.

RAMIREZ, ANGELA M; Armijo HS; Fairfield, CA; (1); Band; Mrchg Band; Pep Band; Cert Of Achvt Excllnce In Math 90; Bsbl & Bowling; Bus Math.

RAMIREZ, ANGELICA; Paramount HS; Hollydale, CA; (2); Cmnty Wkr; Hosp Aide; Cit Awd; High Hon Roll; Hon Roll; Phy.

RAMIREZ, ANNA I; Tomales HS; Point Reyes Stati, CA; (3); Library Aide; Office Aide; Spanish Clb; SADD; Stat Vllybl; Hon Roll; Home Ec Gold Plaque; Spnsh Awd; Marin Coll; Med Asst.

RAMIREZ, ANTHONY; King City HS; San Lucas, CA; (3); Treas Latin Clb; Pres Sr Cls; JV Capt Bsktbl; High Hon Roll; Hon Roll; CSF; Natl Young Ldrs Conf Cngrssnl Schlr; Camp Royal Rep; Bus Admin.

RAMIREZ, ARGELIA C; Hueneme HS; Port Hueneme, CA; (2); Church Yth Grp; Pep Clb; JV Cheerldng; Medcl.

RAMIREZ, ARMI-CLAUDINE E; Gardena HS; Carson, CA; (3); Drama Clb; Library Aide; Treas Service Clb; Speech Tm; School Play; Hon Roll; Jr NHS; Prfct Atten Awd; CSF; Fulfillment Fund Schlr.

RAMIREZ, BRIAN J; Capuchino HS; San Bruno, CA; (1); Var Capt Crs Cntry; JV Trk; Var Wrstlng; 1st Team Crss Cntry; 2nd Team Wrstlng; OK U; Wrstlng.

RAMIREZ, CARLOS A; Modesto HS; Riverbank, CA; (2); Red Cross Aide; Bsbl; Crs Cntry; Wt Lftg; Cit Awd; Police Ofcr.

RAMIREZ, CARRIE M; Edison HS; Huntington Bch, CA; (3); Model UN; Teachers Aide; Var Socr; Var Sftbl; Ath Trnr; Law.

RAMIREZ, CELIA; Oxnard HS; Oxnard, CA; (2); 43/126; Hon Roll; MESA Clb; Rdng Mrt; Ventura Coll; Rgstrd Nrsng.

RAMIREZ, CHERYL; Walnut HS; Walnut, CA; (2); 135/479; Key Clb; Letterman Clb; Spanish Clb; Off Soph Cls; Var JV Crs Cntry; Var JV Trk; High Hon Roll; Hon Roll; Spiked Mustangs Club; CSF; Crossfire; CA Poly Pamona; Arch.

RAMIREZ, CHRISTINA C; Central Union HS; El Centro, CA; (3); Rdng Wrtng Shrtstries & Ptry; Invld In Envrmntl Issues; UCSD; Engl.

RAMIREZ, CINDY E; Redlands SR HS; Redlands, CA; (4); Church Yth Grp; Cmnty Wkr; Hosp Aide; Letterman Clb; SADD; Teachers Aide; Sec Frsh Cls; Var L Bsktbl; Intrml Socr; Var L Trk; Kimberly Jrs; UC San Diego; Chld Psych.

RAMIREZ, CLAUDIA; King City HS; Greenfield, CA; (3); FFA; Hon Roll; Hartnell Coll; Bus.

RAMIREZ, CLAUDIA U; Calexico HS; Calexico, CA; (3); Math Tm; Hon Roll; 1st Yr Alg-High Hnrs; Natl Span Exam-4th 88/1st Pl 90; CA Math League Cert; AHSME; Math.

RAMIREZ, CORNELIO; Torrey Pines HS; Solana Beach, CA; (1); Bsbl; Bsktbl; Crs Cntry; Ftbl; Gym; Lcrss; Socr; Swmmng; Tennis; Vllybl.

RAMIREZ, CRISTIAN A; Fontana HS; Fontana, CA; (2); 143/1500; Pres FBLA; Quiz Bowl; Scholastic Bowl; Teachers Aide; Rptr Nwsp; Ed Yrbk; JV Ftbl; Socr; Trk; Wt Lftg; CA Schlrshp Fed; Futur Latino Ledr Of Amer; Berkley; Bus Admin.

RAMIREZ, CYNTHIA C; Saint Francis HS; Orangevale, CA; (4); 11/145; Cmnty Wkr; Hosp Aide; SADD; School Musical; Stage Crew; Hist Jr Cls; Hist Sr Cls; Sec NHS; Pres Acad Fit Awd; U WA.

RAMIREZ, DAVID A; Orange Glen HS; Escondido, CA; (3); Church Yth Grp; Spanish Clb; JV Socr; JV Swmmng; High Hon Roll; Hon Roll; JV V Water Polo; Cert Hnr Frgn Lang; Cal Poly; Engrng.

RAMIREZ, DELIA R; Calexico HS; Calexico, CA; (3); Key Clb; Teachers Aide; Migrant Clb; Ntrl Sci.

RAMIREZ, DESIREE R; Mater Dei HS; Irvine, CA; (3); Cmnty Wkr; Spanish Clb; Band; Mrchg Band; Pep Band; Tennis; High Hon Roll; NHS; CSF; UC Irving; Med.

RAMIREZ, EDGAR G; Chula Vista HS; Chula Vista, CA; (2); Letterman Clb; Library Aide; Varsity Clb; Bsbl; Ftbl; Trk; Wt Lftg; Dntstry.

RAMIREZ, EDUARDO; Rio Mesa HS; Oxnard, CA; (3); Var Crs Cntry; JV Trk; Hon Roll; CA Schlrshp Fed; Med.

RAMIREZ III, EDWARD B; El Camino HS; Oceanside, CA; (3); Spanish Clb; Speech Tm; SADD; Cit Awd; Hon Roll; Prfct Atten Awd; Med.

RAMIREZ, ENRIQUE A; Castle Park HS; Chula Vista, CA; (4); Ed Yrbk; Stu Cncl; JV Ftbl; Var JV Wrstlng; Hon Roll; SCF; San Diego ST U; Engrng.

RAMIREZ, EUGENIA; Sierra Vista HS; Baldwin Park, CA; (1); Badminton Jr Var; Sci.

RAMIREZ, EULALIA F; Garfield HS; Los Angeles, CA; (3); 2/35; French Clb; Girl Scts; Hosp Aide; Library Aide; Science Clb; Service Clb; Teachers Aide; Orch; Hon Roll; Prfct Atten Awd; CA Schlrshp Fed Clb; UCLA Prtnrshp Prog; Bio Sci.

RAMIREZ, FRANCISCO; San Jose HS; San Jose, CA; (3); Ftbl; Welding.

RAMIREZ, FRANCISCO J; Santa Ana Valley HS; Santa Ana, CA; (3); Key Clb; Office Aide; Teachers Aide; Prfct Atten Awd; Gld Mdl Ecnmcs; US Mrn Corp; Plt.

RAMIREZ, FRANK Y; East Bakersfield HS; Bakersfield, CA; (1); Band; Jazz Band; Mrchg Band; Pep Band; JV Wrstlng; Hon Roll; MESA, Math, Engr, Sci Achvt; Chem Engr.

RAMIREZ, FREDERICK R; Milpitas HS; Milpitas, CA; (1); UC Berkeley; Comp Pgmng.

RAMIREZ, GUADALUPE; Albraham Lincoln HS; Los Angeles, CA; (2); Church Yth Grp; Teachers Aide; Crs Cntry; Trk; Hon Roll; Prfct Atten Awd; Bllt; UCLA Prtnrshp Prgrm; Kndrgrtn Tchr.

RAMIREZ, GUADALUPE M; Compton HS; Compton, CA; (3); Hon Roll; ASB Sec 90-91.

RAMIREZ, HENRIETTA; Ontario HS; Ontario, CA; (3); Key Clb; Science Clb; Band; Jazz Band; Mrchg Band; School Musical; Cit Awd; Hon Roll; Sci Stu Of Yr 89-90; Hnb Mntn Walt Disney World Dreamers & Doers Schlrship; Med.

RAMIREZ, HIPOLITO; Wasco HS; Wasco, CA; (2); Hon Roll; Prfct Atten Awd; MECHA; Csf; Cal Poly; Electrnc Engr.

RAMIREZ, ISAAC J; Hesperia HS; Hesperia, CA; (3); Art Clb; Spanish Clb; High Hon Roll; Hon Roll; Prfct Atten Awd; Prncpls Hnr Roll; Deans List.

RAMIREZ, JESSE M; James Lick HS; San Jose, CA; (3); Drama Clb; Band; School Musical; School Play; Stage Crew; Hon Roll; NHS; Stu Of CSF; Acadc Decath; Deptmntl Hnrs In Drama; Advertising Design.

RAMIREZ, JESSICA; Baldwin Park HS; Baldwin Park, CA; (3); 18/465; VP Church Yth Grp; Spanish Clb; Church Choir; Off Frsh Cls; Off Soph Cls; Off Jr Cls; High Hon Roll; Hon Roll; Phtg Yrbk; Rep Stu Cncl; U Of Irvine; Arntcl Engrng.

RAMIREZ, JIMMY I; Washington Union-Easton HS; Fresno, CA; (2); FBLA; Teachers Aide; Hon Roll; Fri Night Live; Bus Clerk; Acctng.

RAMIREZ, JOAN; Balboa HS; San Francisco, CA; (2); Nwsp; Off Soph Cls; Stu Cncl; Sftbl; Hon Roll; UCLA.

RAMIREZ, JOAQUIN; Bell Gardens HS; Bell Gardens, CA; (3); Socr; Engrng.

RAMIREZ, JOEY; Santa Paula Union HS; Santa Paula, CA; (2); 17/350; Cmnty Wkr; SADD; JV Bsbl; JV Bsktbl; JV Ftbl; Cit Awd; Hon Roll; 16 Mnth Hnr Carrier Vntra Co ST Free Press; Two MVP Awds Frm Vntra Coll Bsktbll Cmp; Physcl Educ.

RAMIREZ, JOHN D; Villa Park HS; Orange, CA; (2); Boy Scts; Key Clb; Hon Roll; Mock Trial; Orange Cnty Acadmc Decath; Us His Prof.

RAMIREZ, JOHN P; Baldwin Park HS; Baldwin Park, CA; (3); 19/424; Art Clb; Aud/Vis; Boy Scts; Bus Profs of Am; Church Yth Grp; Cmnty Wkr; Dance Clb; Letterman Clb; ROTC; SADD; Devil Pup Pgm; Advanced ROP Pgm; Mt San Antonio CC; Law.

RAMIREZ, JOSE A; Montebello HS; Pico Rivera, CA; (4); 16/489; Key Clb; Var Ftbl; Var Capt Socr; JV Var Vllybl; Hon Roll; Lion Awd; NHS; Pres Acad Fit Awd; Yth Opportunity Fndtn Excptnl Schlr; U Of Notre Dame; Aerospace Engr.

RAMIREZ, JOSE R; North Hollywood HS; North Hollywood, CA; (2); FFA; Hon Roll; Tutor; Pilot.

RAMIREZ, JOY M; Kerman HS; Kerman, CA; (2); 19/224; FTA; Spanish Clb; Chorus; Color Guard; Hon Roll; Jazz Choir; Madrigal Choir; Psych.

RAMIREZ, JUAN J; Sunset HS; Hayward, CA; (2); Var Socr; Hon Roll.

RAMIREZ, JULIE A; James Logan HS; Union City, CA; (3); Band; Mrchg Band; Orch; Pep Band; Hon Roll; Mock Trial; CA ST Hayward.

RAMIREZ, KARLA; Marin Catholic HS; Novato, CA; (4); Cmnty Wkr; Spanish Clb; Variety Show; Sec Frsh Cls; Var JV Cheerldng; Var JV Pom Pon; JV Vllybl; High Hon Roll; Hon Roll; NHS; UC Irvine; Bio Sci.

RAMIREZ, LETICIA; Gonzales HS; Soledad, CA; (1); Jrnlsm.

RAMIREZ, LIZBETH; San Gabriel HS; Rosemead, CA; (3); JV Sftbl; MASO Clb; Math.

RAMIREZ, LIZBETH A; Calexico HS; Calexico, CA; (1); Upward Bound; Friday Night Live; Early Outreach; UCLA; Comp Engrng.

RAMIREZ, LUCIA A; Pacific Palisades HS; South Gate, CA; (3); Church Yth Grp; Church Choir; Outstndng Prfrmnc Comp Awd; Missionettes Prog Tchr; Grphc Dsgnr.

RAMIREZ, LUIS E; Bell Gardens HS; Commerce, CA; (1); Church Yth Grp; Cit Awd; Hon Roll; U CA-IRVINE; Comp Pgmmr.

RAMIREZ, LUIS E; Fontana HS; Fontana, CA; (2); Church Yth Grp; Band; Jazz Band; Mrchg Band; Pep Band; Phtg Yrbk; Cit Awd; Hon Roll; Prfct Atten Awd; Cal Ply Pomona; Civil Engrng.

RAMIREZ, MALIN A; International Studies Acad; San Francisco, CA; (2); Cmnty Wkr; Stus Against Animal Cruelty; Publicity Cmmtte Of Stu Govt; Run My Own Day Care Ctr; Film.

RAMIREZ, MARCELA; Sweetwater HS; National City, CA; (3); 39/481; Science Clb; Variety Show; Yrbk; Off Frsh Cls; Treas Soph Cls; High Hon Roll; Mecha; Danc Chorgrphy; CSF; Math.

RAMIREZ, MARGARITA G; Armijo HS; Suisun City, CA; (2); JV Vllybl; Hon Roll; Vllybl; Walk Amer, Walk A-Thon To Fight Birth Defects.

RAMIREZ, MARGIE G; Madera HS; Madera, CA; (2); Church Yth Grp; Band; Church Choir; Mrchg Band; Orch; Treas Frsh Cls; Crs Cntry; Cit Awd; Hon Roll; Prfct Atten Awd; Marimba Band Treas; Golden St Exam-Geom W/ Hnrs 89; Top 10 Awd; Hnrs Engl Awd; UCLA; Med.

RAMIREZ, MARIA E; G Washington Prep HS; Los Angeles, CA; (3); Treas Church Yth Grp; Cmnty Wkr; Debate Tm; Hosp Aide; Math Clb; Service Clb; Speech Tm; Band; Rptr Nwsp; Cit Awd; UCLA; Med.

RAMIREZ, MARIA R; Hawthorne HS; Lennox, CA; (2); Dance Clb; Drama Clb; Girl Scts; Spanish Clb.

RAMIREZ, MARICELA; Sierra Vista HS; Baldwin Park, CA; (1); Dance Clb; Orch; Hon Roll; JV Badminton; UCLA; Pedtrcn.

RAMIREZ, MARTHA; Modesto HS; Modesto, CA; (2); JA; Spanish Clb; Orch; Hon Roll; Prfct Atten Awd; Elem Tchr.

RAMIREZ, MARTHA A; Mc Farland HS; Mc Farland, CA; (3); Church Yth Grp; Cmnty Wkr; FBLA; Spanish Clb; SADD; Sec Sr Cls; Var Crs Cntry; Var Sftbl; Var Trk; Hon Roll; Interior Dsgn.

RAMIREZ, MARY L; San Gabriel HS; San Gabriel, CA; (1); Spanish Clb; Sftbl; Vllybl; UCLA; Law.

RAMIREZ, MATTHEW A; Bellarmine-Jefferson HS; Los Angeles, CA; (1); Stage Crew; Hon Roll; Aeronauical Engrng.

RAMIREZ, MAYTE; Orestimba HS; Crowslanding, CA; (2); Hon Roll; CA Sst U; Bilngl Tchr.

RAMIREZ, MIGUEL S; Notre Dame HS; Riverside, CA; (1); Church Yth Grp; Cmnty Wkr; CSF.

RAMIREZ, MIREYA; St Anthony HS; Garden Grove, CA; (2); Spanish Clb; JV Vllybl; Hon Roll; NHS; CSF.

RAMIREZ, MONICA NINA; Sacred Heart HS; Los Angeles, CA; (4); Church Yth Grp; GAA; Hosp Aide; JA; Spanish Clb; SADD; School Play; Stage Crew; Yrbk; Off Soph Cls; UC Santa Cruz; Pre-Law.

RAMIREZ, MONIKA M; Oxnard HS; Oxnard, CA; (3); 54/570; Church Yth Grp; Hosp Aide; Treas NFL; Spanish Clb; School Musical; School Play; Nwsp; Treas Stu Cncl; Var Crs Cntry; Doctorate; Art Psych.

RAMIREZ, NANCY A; Montgomery HS; San Diego, CA; (2); Church Yth Grp; French Clb; Band; Flag Corp; Vllybl; Cit Awd; Prfct Atten Awd; Law.

RAMIREZ, OFELIA; Pioneer HS; Whittier, CA; (2); JCL; Teachers Aide; Off Jr Cls; Var Socr; Var Trk; JV Vllybl; Kick Boxing; Tchrs Asst; Law Enfrcmnt.

RAMIREZ, PATRICIA; East HS; Bakersfield, CA; (2); Church Yth Grp; Teachers Aide; Chorus; Vllybl; Cit Awd; Hon Roll; Awrd Frndlst; CA Poly; Crrctn Offc.

RAMIREZ, PATRICIA; Our Lady/Loretto-Bishop Conaty HS; Los Angeles, CA; (3); Church Yth Grp; Cmnty Wkr; Library Aide; Hon Roll; UC Los Angeles; Teacher.

RAMIREZ, PATRICIA; Sanger HS; Sanger, CA; (2); Dance Clb; Latin Clb; ROTC; Swmmng; Cmptr.

RAMIREZ, PAULA; Laguna Hills HS; Laguna Hills, CA; (3); 19/321; French Clb; Math Clb; SADD; Stat Bsbl; L Co-Capt Cheerldng; JV Trk; CSF, Sec; Cardiology.

RAMIREZ, PAULINA; Lynwood HS; Lynwood, CA; (3); Dance Clb; Math Clb; Acad Decathlon; UCLA; Phys.

RAMIREZ, PRISCILLA C; Etiwanda HS; Cucamonga, CA; (2); Drama Clb; Intrml Vllybl; U CA San Diego; Crmnl Lawyer.

RAMIREZ, RAQUEL; Los Alamitos HS; Artesia, CA; (3); Art Clb; SADD; Teachers Aide; Stage Crew; Ed Nwsp; Orange Cnty HS Of Arts-Visual Arts Dept; Awd Of Cmndtn-Prnceton U Poetry Cntst; Amnesty Intl-Stu Leag; Art.

RAMIREZ, RICARDO; Culver City HS; Culver City, CA; (3); Intrml Ftbl; Hon Roll.

RAMIREZ, RICHARD; Monache HS; Porterville, CA; (3); Am Leg Boys St; Art Clb; Church Yth Grp; Spanish Clb; SADD; Rep Jr Cls; Rep Stu Cncl; Var Capt Crs Cntry; Var Capt Trk; Cit Awd; Interact Clb; Schlr Athlete Of Yr; Congrssnl Schlr; Poly Sci.

RAMIREZ, RICHARD D; Northview HS; Covina, CA; (4); Art Clb; Teachers Aide; Varsity Clb; Var Capt Tennis; Hon Roll; Prfct Atten Awd; Art; Outdoors; CA Poly Pomona; Arch.

RAMIREZ, ROBERTO; Live Oak HS; Live Oak, CA; (3); 7/70; Chess Clb; FTA; Spanish Clb; SADD; Teachers Aide; Variety Show; Pres Frsh Cls; Rep Stu Cncl; Bsktbl; Capt Tennis; All-Leag In Tnns; CSF CA Schlstc Fdrtn; Decathlon Team; Davis U; Engrng.

RAMIREZ, ROCIO; Andrew Hill HS; San Jose, CA; (3); Capt JV Bsktbl; Capt Var Trk; MESA; San Jose ST; Crmnlgy.

RAMIREZ, RUBY R; James Lick HS; San Jose, CA; (1); Dance Clb; JV Bsktbl; JV Vllybl; Hon Roll; Block Letter Clb; Stu Of The Week; Most Imprvd Vllybl; Advrtsmnt.

RAMIREZ, SAMUEL; Colton HS; Colton, CA; (2); Chess Clb; Intrml Bsbl; Hon Roll.

RAMIREZ, SAMUEL RICAFORTE; Richard Gahr HS; Cerritos, CA; (1); Dance Clb; Variety Show; Off Frsh Cls; Cit Awd; Cmmndtn Awd; Blue & Gold Achvt Awd Keybrdng; U Of CA Irvine; Med.

RAMIREZ, SANDRA; Roosevelt HS; Los Angeles, CA; (2); Dance Clb; French Clb; Key Clb; Math Clb; French Hon Soc; Comp Prog.

RAMIREZ, SANDY; Fontana HS; Fontana, CA; (3); Debate Tm; Spanish Clb; Hon Roll; Leo Clb Treas; Physiolgy.

RAMIREZ, SARA J; Pomona HS; Pomona, CA; (1); Hon Roll.

RAMIREZ, SHARLYN; St Genevieve HS; Van Nuys, CA; (2); French Clb; Rep Frsh Cls; VP Soph Cls; Stu Cncl; San Diego ST U; Ped Nurse.

RAMIREZ, SISTO G; San Clemente HS; Capistrano Bch, CA; (4); Computer Clb; UCI; Comp Sci.

RAMIREZ, SONIA; Arroyo HS; El Monte, CA; (4); Key Clb; Teachers Aide; Drill Tm; Ed Yrbk; Sec Frsh Cls; Sec Soph Cls; VP Jr Cls; VP Sr Cls; Var Capt Cheerldng; Hon Roll.

RAMIREZ, THERESA; Bell Gardens HS; Bell Gardens, CA; (3); Church Yth Grp; Dance Clb; FCA; Office Aide; Teachers Aide; Cheerldng; Powder Puff Ftbl; Deaf Stu Tchr.

RAMIREZ, VERONICA; Atwater HS; Atwater, CA; (3); FFA; Hon Roll; CSU Treas; ROP; Merced Coll; Vet.

RAMIREZ, VICTOR HUGO; Montclair HS; Montclair, CA; (2); 1/35; Dentist.

RAMIREZ, VICTOR T; Castle Park HS; Chula Vista, CA; (3); Church Yth Grp; Band; Color Guard; Mrchg Band; Orch; Pep Band; Off Jr Cls; Stu Cncl; Capt Swmmng; Var Wrstlng; Water Polo-Capt; AF Assn Citation; Cdt Capt Cvl Air Patrol Sqd 67; Aerosp.

RAMIREZ, YOSSA N; Calexico HS; Calexico, CA; (2); Math Tm; Stat Bsktbl; Hon Roll; Mascot; U Of CA San Diego.

RAMIREZ, ZALDY; Daniel Murphy HS; Los Angeles, CA; (2); Church Yth Grp; Cmnty Wkr; Nwsp; Yrbk; Hon Roll; Svc Awd 88-89; CSF; Law.

RAMIREZ, ZENAIDA M; St Genevieve HS; Van Nuys, CA; (3); Church Yth Grp; Hosp Aide; Spnsh Frgn Lang Awds; Los Angeles Pierce Coll; Bus.

RAMIRIOS, ESTHER; Hawthorne HS; Hawthorne, CA; (2); Sec Key Clb; Teachers Aide; Hist Frsh Cls; Vllybl; Cit Awd; Dance; USC; Aerosp Engrng.

RAMM, JOSH S; Righetti HS; Santa Maria, CA; (2); Church Yth Grp; JV Ftbl; High Hon Roll; Hon Roll; Ministry.

RAMON, CHRIS A; Hesperia HS; Hesperia, CA; (2); Boy Scts; ROTC; Engl.

RAMON, MARINA L; Mc Lane HS; Fresno, CA; (3); 28/427; Am Leg Aux Girls St; Church Yth Grp; Cmnty Wkr; FCA; SADD; Pres Sr Cls; Var Mgr(s); Var Sftbl; Var Vllybl; Hon Roll; Vrsty Vlybl Coachs Awd; ASB Pres; UC Santa Cruz; Marine Bio.

RAMOND, LISA A; Rio Vista HS; Rio Vista, CA; (3); 1/74; AFS; German Clb; Science Clb; Ed Nwsp; Ed Yrbk; Bsktbl; Socr; Tennis; High Hon Roll; Ntl Merit Ltr; CA Schlrshp Fed; UC David; Vet.

RAMONES, SEAN D; Walnut HS; Walnut, CA; (4); 50/320; Aud/Vis; Boy Scts; Chess Clb; Cmnty Wkr; Computer Clb; Debate Tm; Hosp Aide; Intnl Clb; JA; Library Aide; Citzn Bee Cntst Regnl Semi Fnlst; Invst, Collct, Sell Bsbl Cards; UC Riverside; Med.

RAMORINO, MONTI; St Genevieve HS; Panorama, CA; (2); Church Yth Grp; Treas Model UN; JV Bsbl; JV Bsktbl; High Hon Roll; Hon Roll; Prfct Atten Awd; Frosh Awd Frosh Bsktbl; Outstndng Achvmt Span II.

RAMOS, ALEGRE N; Providence HS; Los Angeles, CA; (2); Dance Clb; Debate Tm; Letterman Clb; Natl Beta Clb; NFL; Ski Clb; Chorus; School Musical; Nwsp; VP Jr Cls; Bus.

RAMOS, ALICIA NOEL; Alhambra HS; Martinez, CA; (2); Dance Clb; Drama Clb; School Play; Stage Crew; Hon Roll; Actress.

RAMOS, ALMA I; Fairfax HS; Los Angeles, CA; (2); Church Yth Grp; Hosp Aide; Library Aide; Spanish Clb; Orch; JV Bsktbl; Var Sftbl; JV Vllybl; Cit Awd; Hon Roll; UCLA; Med.

RAMOS, ANA R; Pasadena HS; Pasadena, CA; (4); JA; Latin Clb; Library Aide; Spanish Clb; Hon Roll; CA ST U-Los Angeles; Bus.

RAMOS, ARIES HERNANDEZ; Garces Memorial HS; Delano, CA; (2); JA; Key Clb; Letterman Clb; Church Choir; Bsktbl; JV Trk; High Hon Roll; NHS; UCLA; Med.

RAMOS, BERNADETTE; Garces HS; Delano, CA; (1); 2/150; Hosp Aide; Var Tennis; High Hon Roll; Awd Hghst Histry GPA Frshmn Cls; UCLA; Med.

RAMOS, BRENDA L; Chaffey HS; Ontario, CA; (3); French Clb; Key Clb; High Hon Roll; Hon Roll; Prfct Atten Awd; Acad Deca; Keywnets; Humnts; Frnch.

RAMOS, CATHERINE N; San Pasqual HS; Escondido, CA; (3); 55/369; Intnl Clb; SADD; Teachers Aide; Ed Yrbk; Powder Puff Ftbl; Hon Roll; Jr NHS; Prfct Atten Awd; Pres Acad Fit Awd; San Diego ST U; Comp Sci.

RAMOS, CLAUDIA; St Joseph HS; South Gate, CA; (2); 90/196; Cmnty Wkr; English Clb; Science Clb; Hon Roll; Prfct Atten Awd; UCLA; Pediatrcn.

RAMOS, ELISELDA; Lakewood HS; Long Beach, CA; (3); Office Aide; Cit Awd; Hon Roll; NHS; Prfct Atten Awd; Plaq Supr Alg, Spnsh Stu; Pin CJSF; LBCC; Bus.

RAMOS, ELIZABETH; Bishop Amat Memorial HS; San Dimas, CA; (3); Treas Spanish Clb; Yrbk; Hon Roll; Friday Night Live; Bus.

RAMOS, ELODIA M; Rio Mesa HS; Oxnard, CA; (3); Art Clb; Church Yth Grp; Cmnty Wkr; Drama Clb; JA; Service Clb; SADD; Thesps; Varsity Clb; Church Choir; Pres Chrch Yth Grp; Seminary Promotion 2 Yrs; Oxnard Coll; Aviation.

RAMOS, EULALIA; Palo Verde HS; Blythe, CA; (3); 18/263; Office Aide; Spanish Clb; Teachers Aide; Hon Roll.

RAMOS, FERLIE ANNE M; Carson HS; Carson, CA; (3); Drama Clb; German Clb; Hosp Aide; Church Choir; JV Tennis; Hon Roll; NHS; Acad Awd Span, Humanities; Qrtr Fnlst Tnns Trnmnt; CA ST Long Beach; Nrsng.

RAMOS, GABRIELA; Pius X HS; Huntington Park, CA; (3); Math Clb; Science Clb; Spanish Clb; Var Tennis; Hon Roll; Treas Rotary Awd; CSF; MESA; Travel Club; UC Berkeley; Med.

RAMOS, GARRETT A; Bishop Amat Memorial HS; Diamond Bar, CA; (3); Letterman Clb; Varsity Clb; Var Capt Vllybl; Slvr Screen Clb; Archaeolgy.

RAMOS, GERALDINE S; William Workman HS; West Covina, CA; (2); 7/340; Intnl Clb; Pres Soph Cls; Cit Awd; High Hon Roll; Pres Acad Fit Awd; Red Cross Aide; Science Clb; Band; Mrchg Band; Rep Stu Cncl; ASB; Parliamentarian; Dist Schlr; Inter Clb & Org Cncl; CA Schlrshp Fed; Campus Beautification; Stu Rltn; CA Poly Pomona; Arch.

RAMOS, GLORIA; San Gabriel Mission HS; San Gabriel, CA; (2); Church Yth Grp; Math Clb; Science Clb; Variety Show; Rep Frsh Cls; VP Soph Cls; Rep Stu Cncl; High Hon Roll; Prfct Atten Awd; Cmnty Wkr; Hnr Soc VP; LIFE Pgm; Schl & Cmnty Srvce Awd; Loyola Marymount U; Intl Bus.

RAMOS, GLORIA E; Galileo HS; San Francisco, CA; (2); French Clb; Spanish Clb; Hon Roll; Various Languages; Hlth; Comps; Comp Prgrmmr.

RAMOS, GOLDA G; Huntington Park HS; Huntington Park, CA; (3); Cmnty Wkr; Math Clb; Prtcptn Awd Math Fair 90; Cert Of Achvt Frnch 2; Cert For Spcl Rchntn Sci Prjct; Cert Of Supr Acad Excl; UCLA; Doctor.

RAMOS, JAIME; Don Bosco Technical Inst; San Gabriel, CA; (4); 16/231; Chess Clb; Church Yth Grp; Cmnty Wkr; Letterman Clb; Varsity Clb; VP Soph Cls; Stu Cncl; Var Crs Cntry; JV Trk; JV Capt Vllybl; JV Crss Cntry MVP; Golden Tiger Awd; UC Riverside; Bus.

RAMOS, JAVIER E; Schurr HS; Monterey Park, CA; (2); Var Ftbl; Var Trk; Wt Lftg; NHS; Prfct Atten Awd; San Diego U; Telecommnctns.

RAMOS, JINGLE MAYNIGO; South Tahoe HS; S Lake Tahoe, CA; (4); Girl Scts; Key Clb; Sec Science Clb; High Hon Roll; UCLA; Nrsng.

RAMOS, JOANNA; Liberty Union HS; Brentwood, CA; (4); Church Yth Grp; Office Aide; Teachers Aide; Chorus; Rep Stu Cncl; Hon Roll; Dental Assist.

RAMOS, JOSE; Wasco Union HS; Wasco, CA; (4); Art Clb; Church Yth Grp; Dance Clb; Drama Clb; Latin Clb; Hon Roll; Spanish NHS; Helen Sears Memrl Schlrshp; Public Spkng Awd; 1st Pl 7th Anl Poetry Cont; Fashion Inst; Inter Desgn.

RAMOS, JUAN; Theodore Roosevelt HS; Los Angeles, CA; (4); 1/762; JA; Math Clb; Orch; Treas Stu Cncl; Cit Awd; Hon Roll; Prfct Atten Awd; Val; Acad Decathlon Capt; Boys Clb; Harvard.

RAMOS, JUDY LYNN B; Santa Clara HS; Santa Clara, CA; (3); 33/389; GAA; Stat Bsktbl; Powder Puff Ftbl; Var Vllybl; Hon Roll; Prfct Atten Awd; CSF; Spansh Lang, Bus & Poetry Awds; San Jose ST; Nrsng.

RAMOS, KAREN MICHELE; D S Jordan HS; Long Beach, CA; (4); Dance Clb; Key Clb; Thesps; School Play; Ed Lit Mag; Pres Acad Fit Awd; Drama Clb; Math Tm; Office Aide; Teachers Aide; NCTE Wrtng Fnlst; Bank Amer Plaq Wnnr Liberal Arts; Drama Awds; Bst Lead 90; Dir Choice Outstndng Actng; LBCC; Engl.

RAMOS, LARISSA C; Westmoor HS; Daly City, CA; (2); High Hon Roll; Hon Roll; San Francisco ST U.

RAMOS, LIBBY M; Modesto HS; Waterford, CA; (2); Band; Mrchg Band; Var Bsktbl; Var Socr; Var Sftbl; Capt JV Vllybl; Hon Roll; Real Estate.

RAMOS, LINDA S; Alverno HS; Pasadena, CA; (3); 4/68; Intrml Mgr Pep Clb; Service Clb; Chorus; Church Choir; Rptr Lit Mag; Off Jr Cls; High Hon Roll; Hon Roll; CSF; Bio.

RAMOS, LIZ C; Tulare Western HS; Tulare, CA; (4); 3/230; Church Yth Grp; Rep Stu Cncl; JV Bsktbl; Var JV Tennis; Elks Awd; Lion Awd; Pres Schlr; Portugese Club; Assoc Stu Body; Girl Of Month; Cuesta Coll; Bus Admin.

RAMOS, MANDY; Arroyo Grande HS; Nipomo, CA; (1); 71/580; Church Yth Grp; Rep Stu Cncl; JV Bsktbl; JV Vllybl; Pepperdine; Dntstry.

RAMOS, MANUEL C; Central Union HS; Calexico, CA; (2); German Clb; Var Socr; Rookie Of Yr; Stu Of Mnth; U Of CA Los Angeles; Arch.

RAMOS, MARIA; Palo Verde HS; Ripley, CA; (2); Preschool Teacher.

RAMOS, MAURICIO; Birmingham HS; Arleta, CA; (4); Am Leg Boys St; Debate Tm; French Clb; FBLA; Key Clb; Latin Clb; NFL; SADD; Thesps; School Play; Pepperdine U; Dist Attorney.

RAMOS, NICOLE L; Etiwanda HS; Rancho Cucamonga, CA; (3); 41/606; Church Yth Grp; Cmnty Wkr; Intnl Clb; JCL; Latin Clb; Ski Clb; Band; Rptr Nwsp; Var Score Keeper; Hon Roll; USC; Bus Admin.

RAMOS, NORMA; Montebello HS; Pico Rivera, CA; (2); Church Yth Grp; Cmnty Wkr; Drama Clb; Acpl Chr; Chorus; School Musical; Variety Show; Stat Bsktbl; Cit Awd; High Hon Roll.

RAMOS, OCTAVIO; San Gabriel HS; Rosemead, CA; (2); Church Yth Grp; French Clb; JA; Key Clb; Spanish Clb; Off Soph Cls; Stu Cncl; Swmmng; Wt Lftg; Hon Roll; U Of CA Los Angeles; Phys Ed.

RAMOS, OSCAR; San Benito HS; Hollister, CA; (2); Church Yth Grp; Rep Soph Cls; Treas Stu Cncl; Var Capt Socr; High Hon Roll; Prfct Atten Awd; Pres Acad Fit Awd; League Of United Latin Amer Ctzns; Aftb Schl Job; Stanford; Pharm.

RAMOS, RODOLFO; Montclair HS; Montclair, CA; (2); 2/32; JV Socr; Prfct Atten Awd; Electroni Engrng.

RAMOS, ROSALBA; Brawley Union HS; Brawley, CA; (3).

RAMOS, SANDRA V; Bell HS; Cudahy, CA; (3); FTA; JA; Pep Clb; Teachers Aide; Drill Tm; Nwsp; Yrbk; Hon Roll; UC San Diego.

RAMOS, SELINA; Eisenhower HS; Rialto, CA; (2); Cheerldng.

RAMOS, SHELLY; Pierce HS; Arbuckle, CA; (4); 1/64; Am Leg Aux Girls St; VP Pres FHA; Rptr FHA; VP Chorus; Rep Stu Cncl; Var Co-Capt Vllybl; 4-H Awd; Val; Amer Acad Achvt; CA Farm Bureaus Teenager Of Yr; Gldn St FFA Degree; CA Polytech U; Plant Geneticst.

RAMOS, TERESA; Paramount HS; Paramount, CA; (2); Letterman Clb; Orch; Rep Soph Cls; Sec Jr Cls; Crs Cntry; Trk; Cit Awd; Hon Roll; Prfct Atten Awd; Hnr Orchestra; CSF.

RAMOWSKI, RUSSELL J; Capistrano Valley Christian HS; Oceanside, CA; (4); Church Yth Grp; Cmnty Wkr; Computer Clb; English Clb; Latin Clb; Math Clb; Red Cross Aide; Science Clb; Ski Clb; Spanish Clb; Point Long Nazarene; Bus.

RAMPOLDI, KRISTI L; Lincoln HS; Lincoln, CA; (3); 5/197; FBLA; GAA; Pep Clb; Treas Spanish Clb; SADD; Sec Jr Cls; JV Var Bsktbl; Capt Var Vllybl; Hon Roll; Acad Decthln.

RAMSEY, BRIAN; Redwood HS; Visalia, CA; (3); 31/387; Church Yth Grp; Varsity Clb; Jazz Band; Mrchg Band; Var Ftbl; Wt Lftg; Hon Roll; MVP-DFNSV Unit Var Ftbl; Acad Lttr; CA Schlrshp Fed; Engrng.

RAMSEY, DEVIN W; Fresno Christian HS; Clovis, CA; (2); Church Yth Grp; Letterman Clb; Varsity Clb; Band; Jazz Band; Mrchg Band; Var L Bsbl; JV Bsktbl; JV Capt Ftbl; Var L Socr; Judo Black Belt 81-; Judo Natl Cmptn; Pepperdine; Sports Med.

RAMSEY, LESLIE A; Clairemont HS; San Diego, CA; (3); 34/212; JV Var Cheerldng; AZ ST U; Mrktng.

RAMSEY, MARSHALETTE C; Los Amigos HS; Santa Ana, CA; (3); Church Yth Grp; Key Clb; Off Spanish Clb; SADD; Bsktbl; Tennis; Trk; Hon Roll; Blck Stu Union Clb; MESA; Orange Cnty Acad Dcthln; U CA Riverside; Bus Mgmt.

RAMSEY, MELLANIE D; Troy HS; Yorba Linda, CA; (2); 58/368; Church Yth Grp; Drama Clb; Key Clb; Chorus; School Play; Nwsp; High Hon Roll; Outstanding Achvt & Stu Engl Hnrs II, Drama II; Bst Support Actress & Bst Player Of Yr; Law.

RAMSEY, NICOLE MARIE; Edison HS; Huntington Bch, CA; (4); Cmnty Wkr; Debate Tm; Teachers Aide; School Play; High Hon Roll; Hon Roll; Pres Acad Fit Awd; CA Schlrshp Fed; Yng Repub-Treas; Musician-Organ; UCLA; Math.

RAMSEY, RAIN; Coast Union HS; Cambria, CA; (2); Humboldt ST U; Forest Ecology.

RAMSEY, REBECCA G; Santa Barbara HS; Santa Barbara, CA; (4); 10/466; Church Yth Grp; Sec Acpl Chr; Stu Cncl; Capt Vllybl; High Hon Roll; Hon Roll; Pres Acad Fit Awd; Vllybl Schlrshp; Madrigals; Northern IL U; Accntng.

RAMSEY, TINA D; Selma HS; Selma, CA; (4); 2/192; Dance Clb; French Clb; Service Clb; SADD; Band; Jazz Band; Mrchg Band; Pep Band; School Play; Stu Cncl; Semper Fidelis Awd; B Of A Achvt Plaq; Fresno ST U; Liberal Stds.

RAMSEYER, JOY D; Calvary Chapel HS; Fountain Valley, CA; (3); 60/365; Art Clb; Church Yth Grp; Score Keeper; JV Var Swmmng; Hon Roll; Jr NHS; Marine Bio Clb; Art Grphc Dsgn.

RANA, EILEEN M; Cornelia Connelly HS; Garden Grove, CA; (2); VP GAA; School Play; Lit Mag; Var Bsktbl; Var Sftbl; Var Capt Vllybl; Hon Roll; 1st All League-Vrst Bsbl; 2nd All League-Vllybl; MVP-JR Vllybl; Rookie Of Yr 88-89.

RANASINGHE, ROMA; Sacramento Adventist Acad; Orangevale, CA; (3); Church Yth Grp; Drama Clb; Ski Clb; Spanish Clb; Chorus; Rptr Nwsp; VP Frsh Cls; Pres Stu Cncl; Trk; NHS; Algebra & Engl Outstndng Effort Awds; Pacific Union Coll; Med.

RANCK, MICHELLE J; Apple Valley HS; Apple Valley, CA; (3); Church Yth Grp; Band; Church Choir; Jazz Band; Mrchg Band; Orch; Pep Band; Powder Puff Ftbl; High Hon Roll; U Denver; Ag.

RANDAL, JENNIFER L; Nevada Union HS; Nevada City, CA; (1); Church Yth Grp; SADD; Acpl Chr; Chorus; Church Choir; Swing Chorus; Cit Awd; Hon Roll; Hnr Choir; VP Friday Nght Live; CA ST U Sacramento; Advrtsng.

RANDALL, BONNIE L; Bella Vista HS; Orangevale, CA; (3); 1/430; Church Yth Grp; Math Clb; Spanish Clb; Cheerldng; Var Swmmng; Hon Roll; NHS; Spanish NHS; CSF Ways & Means Dir; Lions Club Spch Cntst Fnlst; Mock Trial Team.

RANDALL, FADRA D; Dinuba HS; Dinuba, CA; (2); Church Yth Grp; Chorus; Church Choir; Sec Frsh Cls; Var Tennis; Hon Roll; Hoby Ambssdr; Ntrl Hlprs; Fresno Pacific; Ed.

RANDALL, JENNETTE M; Cordova SR HS; Mather A F B, CA; (3); 14/454; German Clb; Natl Beta Clb; Band; Chorus; Mrchg Band; Orch; School Musical; School Play; Hon Roll; NHS; Music.

RANDALL, JENNIFER; Orangewood Acad; Torrance, CA; (4); 1/45; Church Yth Grp; Teachers Aide; School Musical; Rptr Nwsp; Ed Yrbk; Sec Sr Cls; High Hon Roll; Pres Acad Fit Awd; Val; Var Bsktbl; Andrews U; Med.

RANDALL, PETER W; Sonora HS; Sonora, CA; (4); 20/254; Boy Scts; Drama Clb; Teachers Aide; Thesps; Band; Chorus; Jazz Band; School Musical; Stage Crew; Hon Roll; Vlntr Firefighter & Fire Cadet; Emergency Medical Techn; Stu Of Tuolomne County Explorer Srch & Rescue; U Of CA At Davis; Bio Sci.

RANDALL, RACHEL; Bullard HS; Fresno, CA; (2); Church Yth Grp; Hosp Aide; Pep Clb; School Play; Cheerldng; Swmmng; Law.

RANDELL, SHANNON D; Monterey HS; Seaside, CA; (3); Chico ST U.

RANDHAWA, GURDEEP S; Selma HS; Selma, CA; (3); 67/200; JV Wrstlng; Acad Speech Awd; Fresno ST U.

RANDHAWA, HARDEEP K; Moreno Valley HS; Moreno Valley, CA; (2); Church Yth Grp; Intnl Clb; Science Clb; Church Choir; Hon Roll; Prfct Atten Awd; Interact Clb; Prin List; Math.

RANDLEMAN, ROBYN; Ponderosa HS; Shingle Springs, CA; (1); Pep Clb; Drill Tm; JV Cheerldng; High Hon Roll; Sacramento ST Coll; Law.

RANDOLPH, ALICIA D; John F Kennedy HS; Sacramento, CA; (2); Church Yth Grp; GAA; JV Sftbl; Accntng.

RANDOLPH, CHRISTOPHER D; Nevada Union HS; Nevada City, CA; (3); 84/551; Church Yth Grp; Var Bsbl; Bsktbl; Var Capt Socr; Hon Roll; Pres Acad Fit Awd; Soccer Club.

RANDOLPH, DEVON; Compton HS; Compton, CA; (3); Computer Clb; English Clb; Library Aide; Ski Clb; Teachers Aide; School Play; Off Sr Cls; Ftbl; Sftbl; Vllybl; Law.

RANDOLPH, ERNIE R; Hoover HS; Fresno, CA; (2); Var Capt Bsbl; JV Ftbl; JV Socr; Wt Lftg; Cit Awd; Hon Roll; Dentstry.

RANDOLPH, LAKISHA; Edison HS; Fresno, CA; (2); Church Yth Grp; Math Tm; Teachers Aide; Band; Chorus; Church Choir; Yrbk; Score Keeper; Sftbl; Vllybl; PREPS Club; Teaching.

RANDOLPH, SASHA L; Valley HS; Sacramento, CA; (3); Church Yth Grp; Hosp Aide; Office Aide; Var Socr; Cit Awd; Hon Roll; Asilomar Ldrshp; Denistry.

RANDOLPH, SHAWNELLE; Point Loma HS; San Diego, CA; (2); 81/482; Church Yth Grp; Dance Clb; Girl Scts; Church Choir; Drill Tm; Pom Pon; Cit Awd; Lawyer.

RANDRIAMAHEFA, RADO; La Sierra HS; Loma Linda, CA; (2); French Clb; Library Aide; JV Socr; Prfct Atten Awd; Airplane Spon; Airplane Pilot.

RANE, YOGESH; Santa Teresa HS; San Jose, CA; (3); JA; Science Clb; Spanish Clb; U Of CA Davis; Pre-Med.

RANESES, JANET C; North Salinas HS; Salinas, CA; (4); Computer Clb; French Clb; Prfct Atten Awd.

RANEY, AMBER M; Fontana HS; Fontana, CA; (3); Sec Treas Church Yth Grp; Ski Clb; Teachers Aide; Sec Stu Cncl; Bsktbl; Mgr(s); Score Keeper; Var Swmmng; Hon Roll; Jr Cncl; Hgh Point Ldr Swim Clb; Long Beach ST; Phys Ed.

RANEY, ATHENA; Barstow HS; Barstow, CA; (1); Church Yth Grp; Church Choir; Bsktbl; Hon Roll; Aztec Rifle Tm & Capt; Light Brigade; Criminology.

RANEY III, L V; Herbert Hoover HS; Fresno, CA; (4); Church Yth Grp; FCA; VP Letterman Clb; Office Aide; Scholastic Bowl; Teachers Aide; Capt Varsity Clb; Variety Show; Var Capt Ftbl; JV Capt Trk; CSF; N AZ U; Engrng.

RANEY, RENEE; Barstow HS; Barstow, CA; (2); Church Yth Grp; Church Choir; Mrchg Band; Pep Band; Off Soph Cls; JV Cheerldng; Var Trk; UCLB; Dist Attny.

RANEY, SHANNON L; Ceres HS; Ceres, CA; (3); Ski Clb; Band; Chorus; Nwsp; Hon Roll; Voctnl Acad Achvt Awd Newspapr/Indepndnt Livng; Comp Pgmng.

RANGARAJAN, VAIJAYANTHY; Glen A Wilson HS; Hacienda Hts, CA; (4); 1/380; Science Clb; Acpl Chr; Chorus; Variety Show; High Hon Roll; Ntl Merit SF; Pres Acad Fit Awd; Acad Decthn 1st Los Angeles Cnty; Piano 10 Yrs; Vcl Music.

RANGEL, ISAI L; Nogales HS; La Puente, CA; (2); 84/708; Church Yth Grp; Letterman Clb; Varsity Clb; Stage Crew; Var Swmmng; High Hon Roll; Hon Roll; Prfct Atten Awd; Var Waterpolo; Cal Poly; Aero Engr.

RANGEL, JORGE A; William H Taft HS; Los Angeles, CA; (2); JV L Ftbl; Arch.

RANGEL, LAURA A; Turlock HS; Turlock, CA; (3); #184 In Class; Spanish Clb; Fresno U; Engl.

RANGEL, LETICIA C; El Rancho HS; Pico Rivera, CA; (4); 78/550; Cmnty Wkr; Computer Clb; Debate Tm; Drama Clb; Pres German Clb; GAA; Hosp Aide; Letterman Clb; Library Aide; Office Aide; Pres Of German Club; Advncd Placement Chem Club Ofcr; Cal ST Long Beach; Chem Engrng.

RANGEL JR, NICK; Huntington Bch HS; Huntington Beach, CA; (4); Debate Tm; Key Clb; Model UN; Speech Tm; Intrml Trk; Ntl Merit Ltr; Pres Acad Fit Awd; JR Stsmn Of Amer; CA Poly; Comm.

RANGEL, RITA; Mtn Empire HS; Jacumba, CA; (4); Cmnty Wkr; GAA; Letterman Clb; Pep Clb; Spanish Clb; SADD; Teachers Aide; Variety Show; Rep Frsh Cls; Pres Soph Cls; AP Span Test; Congressnl Yth Ldrshp Conf; Span.

RANGEL, ROSALBA; Hesperia HS; Hesperia, CA; (2); Church Yth Grp; FHA; Girl Scts; Band; Church Choir; School Play; Nwsp; Cit Awd; Hon Roll; Prfct Atten Awd; UCLA; Lwyr.

RANGEL, TRISTIN F; Orestimba HS; Newman, CA; (3); Drama Clb; Letterman Clb; Pep Clb; SADD; Color Guard; Nwsp; Var JV Bsktbl; Var Cheerldng; Var Pom Pon; Var Powder Puff Ftbl; CSF; JV Bsktbl Mst Insprtnl Awd; 3 Sftbl Chmpnshps 88-90; Freso ST; Psych.

RANGEL, YESENIA; Arvin HS; Arvin, CA; (3); Church Yth Grp; Computer Clb; Office Aide; Teachers Aide; Color Guard; Vllybl; Hon Roll; Law Enfrcmnt.

RANGSITH, DON; Mark Keppel HS; Monterey Park, CA; (1); Bus.

RANIERI, ELIZABETH; Caustoga HS; Calistoga, CA; (4); Am Leg Aux Girls St; Cmnty Wkr; Office Aide; Pep Clb; Ski Clb; Teachers Aide; Yrbk; Rep Frsh Cls; Rep Soph Cls; Sec Jr Cls; Scroptomist Ctznshp Awd; Chico ST U; Psych.

RANIREZ, LETICIA A; Mc Farland HS; Mc Farland, CA; (3); FHA; SADD; Teachers Aide; Ed Lit Mag; Cert Hnr Alg I; Cert Cmpltn Mrktng, Merch; Nrsng.

RANK, SAMI K; Lowell HS; San Francisco, CA; (3); Sec Pres Boy Scts; English Clb; Band; Chorus; School Play; JV Socr; Karate Trnmt Trphys; U CA Santa Cruz; Acting.

RANKIN, CHAD G; Orosi HS; Orosi, CA; (3); Church Yth Grp; Cmnty Wkr; FFA; Letterman Clb; Teachers Aide; Mrchg Band; JV Bsktbl; Var Ftbl; Hon Roll.

RANKIN, ROBYN M; California HS; Whittier, CA; (3); Church Yth Grp; Cmnty Wkr; Dance Clb; Drama Clb; FBLA; Office Aide; Pep Clb; Red Cross Aide; ROTC; SADD; ASB Govt Pblcty Chrprsn; Gldn St Exam Hhg Hnrs Alb I & II & Geo; Ed.

RANKIN, SHANE M; Poway HS; Poway, CA; (4); Letterman Clb; Varsity Clb; Var Wrstlng; San Diego ST U; Bus Admin.

RANSOM, ELSA; Lowell HS; San Francisco, CA; (2); NFL; Fncng Team; Russian Clb; Short Stry Clb; Poltcl Sci.

RANSOM, RICHARD; Kingsburg HS; Kingsburg, CA; (2); Boy Scts; Church Yth Grp; Cmnty Wkr; FFA; Letterman Clb; Color Guard; JV Bsktbl; JV Ftbl; JV Wt Lftg; Pres Acad Fit Awd; Plc Explrer; Sequoias Coll; Law Enfrcmnt.

RANSOM, STACEY; Kingsburg HS; Kingsburg, CA; (4); 17/143; VP Art Clb; Church Yth Grp; Sec Debate Tm; Drama Clb; Sec FFA; FHA; JA; Mu Alpha Theta; Pep Clb; SADD; CA ST Champ Vine Judging; CA ST Champ Farm Rec; 1st/Schlrshp Kearney Ag Fut Essay Comp; CA ST U Fresno; Ag Bus.

RANSOM, TENAYA MILDRED; James Lick HS; San Jose, CA; (2); Cmnty Wkr; Intnl Clb; Church Choir; Pres Soph Cls; Stu Cncl; JV Cheerldng; Hon Roll; Prfct Atten Awd; Berkeley; Bus.

RANSTROM, COREY J; Independence HS; San Jose, CA; (3); Boy Scts; Lg Sccr; Crrntly Lf Sct/Wkng On Egl Sct; Law Enfrcmnt.

RAO, DAVE; Servite HS; Placentia, CA; (3); Boy Scts; Debate Tm; Hosp Aide; JV Tennis; Tri-Schl Safe Rides Pgm SADD; License Cert Nrs Asst; Exctv Bd Schls Jr Statesmen Amer Chapter; Pre-Med.

RAO, SHEELA; University HS; Irvine, CA; (2); JCL; Lit Mag; High Hon Roll; Pres Acad Fit Awd; Clsscl Indian Dance & Music, Ice Skating; Ntl Latin Hnr Soc 89-90 Gold Medals; Ornage Cnty Spllng Chmp; Stanford U; Physician.

RAPACON, KAREN B; Saint Joseph HS; Cerritos, CA; (2); Church Yth Grp; Drama Clb; Spanish Clb; SADD; Variety Show; Hon Roll; Peer Cnslng; Cmmnctns.

RAPACON, MARGARITA C; Vallejo SR HS; Vallejo, CA; (3); Cmnty Wkr; Drama Clb; Model UN; SADD; Teachers Aide; Ed Nwsp; Yrbk; Off Frsh Cls; Pom Pon; Hon Roll; Say No To Drugs Essay 3rd Pl; Valley City USD Savings Bond; San Francisco ST U; Jrnlsm.

RAPALLO, RICK R; La Sierra HS; Riverside, CA; (2); Church Yth Grp; JV Ftbl; Wt Lftg; High Hon Roll; Hon Roll; CSF; Aerosp Engrng.

RAPHAEL, LOUIS; Lycee Francais Laperouse HS; Berkeley, CA; (3); 3/14; Cmnty Wkr; Ski Clb; School Musical; Stage Crew; Yrbk; Sec Frsh Cls; Tennis; Hon Roll; Music; Drama Awd; U CA Berkeley; Engrng.

RAPKA, STEFANI; Nevada Union HS; Grass Valley, CA; (3); Bus Profs of Am; Cmnty Wkr; Computer Clb; Girl Scts; Office Aide; SADD; Teachers Aide; Drill Tm; Powder Puff Ftbl; Trk; Sierra; Comp.

RAPP, CAROL A; Lincoln HS; Stockton, CA; (3); 140/538; Church Yth Grp; Cmnty Wkr; 4-H; French Clb; Office Aide; Teachers Aide; Church Choir; 4-H Awd; Hon Roll; Cngrssnl Yth Ldrshp Cncl; Cnty Frgn Lang Fair; Awds For Outstndng Frnch Stu.

RAPP, JENNIFER; Chula Vista HS; Imperial Beach, CA; (1); Church Yth Grp; SADD; Off Frsh Cls; Jr Statesman Of Amer; Educ.

RAPP, PATRICIA A; La Reina HS; Agoura Hills, CA; (3); 19/67; Church Yth Grp; Cmnty Wkr; GAA; Letterman Clb; Pres SADD; Variety Show; JV Capt Bsktbl; Crs Cntry; Cit Awd; Hon Roll; Bus.

RAPP, TANNA K; Atascadero HS; Creston, CA; (2); SADD; Hon Roll; CSF.

RARALIO, MELISSA; Gahr HS; Norwalk, CA; (4); 28/445; Dance Clb; Nwsp; Yrbk; Treas Soph Cls; Rep Stu Cncl; JV Capt Cheerldng; High Hon Roll; NHS; Pres Acad Fit Awd; CA ST U Long Bch; Mtrls Engr.

RASASNSKI, PRITIKA; Washington HS; Fremont, CA; (3); Drama Clb; GAA; Intnl Clb; Spanish Clb; Nwsp; Swmmng; Tennis; UC Santa Barbara; Sci Med.

RASBERRY, JACKIE E; C K Mc Clatchy HS; Sacramento, CA; (4); 30/470; Art Clb; Debate Tm; French Clb; Key Clb; Math Clb; Science Clb; Varsity Clb; Stu Cncl; Var Capt Bsktbl; JV Crs Cntry; Berkeley U; Criminal Justice.

RASIAH, PRASANNA; Oak Grove Schl; Ojai, CA; (4); Drama Clb; School Play; Phtg Ed Yrbk; JV Co-Capt Bsktbl; Var Co-Capt Socr; Precussion Grp Prfrmd Africian & Latin Rythyms; Wesleyan U.

RASIC, ANTHONY M; Mater Dei HS; Huntington Bch, CA; (2); Church Yth Grp; SADD; JV Socr; Var Tennis; High Hon Roll; Hon Roll; Jr NHS; NHS; Srfng Club; CSF; Skng; Bsbl; Bsktbl; UCLA; Med.

RASMUSSAN, CHRISTINE M; Irvine HS; Irvine, CA; (2); Church Yth Grp; Hosp Aide; JA; VP Ski Clb; Nwsp; Stat Socr; Hon Roll; Co Treas Of APA; Writer.

RASMUSSEN, AMY C; Apple Valley HS; Apple Valley, CA; (2); High Hon Roll; Hon Roll; Sprt Clb; Dsgn Advrtsmnt.

RASMUSSEN, CLAY L; Foothill HS; Bakersfield, CA; (3); Boy Scts; Church Yth Grp; Drama Clb; FFA; School Play; Var Wrstlng; Hon Roll; CSF; BYU; Chiroprctr.

RASMUSSEN, DEE DEE A; Victory Christian Schl; Sacramento, CA; (4); Church Yth Grp; Office Aide; Pep Clb; Yrbk; Sec Jr Cls; VP Stu Cncl; Var Cheerldng; Var Sftbl; High Hon Roll; NHS; Phys Thrpy.

RASMUSSEN, ERICA; San Marin HS; Novato, CA; (4); German Clb; Latin Clb; High Hon Roll; Ntl Merit Ltr; Pres Acad Fit Awd; CA Schlrshp Fed Life Membershp; Soc Of Women Engrs Awd; Natl Latin Exam Maxima Cum Laude; UC Davis.

RASMUSSEN, JENNIFER; Pacifica HS; Garden Grove, CA; (3); Church Yth Grp; Girl Scts; Ski Clb; Drill Tm; Yrbk; San Diego ST; Inter Dsgn.

RASMUSSEN, LA RONDA M; Fortuna Union HS; Hydesville, CA; (4); Library Aide; Off Yrbk; High Hon Roll; Hon Roll; Kiwanis Awd; Prfct Atten Awd; Pres Acad Fit Awd; Raise Money Cls Prom & Safe & Sober Grad Nite; Hlp Constrct Floats Hmcmng Parades; Brooks Coll; Fash Merc.

RASMUSSEN, RYAN P; Caruthers Union HS; Fresno, CA; (1); Church Yth Grp; Cmnty Wkr; Letterman Clb; Band; Mrchg Band; Variety Show; JV Ftbl; JV Tennis; JV Wrstlng; MVP JV Tennis Team 89-90.

RASOR, MATT; San Clemente HS; Capistrano Bch, CA; (1); Church Yth Grp; JV Bsbl.

RASSAVONG, SOUTSADA L; Kearny SR HS; San Diego, CA; (3); French Clb; Intnl Clb; JCL; Office Aide; Teachers Aide; Rep Jr Cls; Hon Roll; USD; Acctng.

RASTAGAR, SULIMAN; Mission Viejo HS; Mission Viejo, CA; (2); 23/500; Key Clb; CSF; Golden ST Exams Hgh Hnrs In Algbra 1989; U Of CA Irvine; Bio Chem.

RATANASADUDI, APRIL; Whitney HS; Lakewood, CA; (3); French Clb; Hosp Aide; JA; Key Clb; Flag Corp; Yrbk; Off Frsh Cls; Off Soph Cls; Socr; JV Swmmng.

RATCLIFF, AMANDA E; Oakland HS; Oakland, CA; (3); German Clb; Service Clb; Teachers Aide; Band; Flag Corp; Jazz Band; Cit Awd; Hon Roll; UC Davis; Elem Schl Tchr.

RATCLIFF, KRISTEN L; Portola JR/Sr HS; Portola, CA; (1); 2/63; Church Yth Grp; Band; Swing Chorus; Rep Frsh Cls; Sec Stu Cncl; Bsktbl; Trk; Vllybl; Pres Acad Fit Awd; Pres 4-H; Yth To Yth; Phys Thrpy.

RATCLIFFE, MONICA M; South San Francisco HS; South San Francis, CA; (3); Boy Scts; Cmnty Wkr; Drama Clb; Stage Crew; Gym; Pom Pon; Cmmty Svc Awd; Natl Champ Pompon Squad; Skyline Coll; Ed.

RATFIELD, SUNSHINE S; Sonora HS; Sonora, CA; (3); 75/400; Office Aide; Science Clb; Ski Clb; Teachers Aide; Stat Var Bsktbl; Stat Var Ftbl; Var JV Score Keeper; L Var Sftbl; Hon Roll; Vrsty Ftbl Trnr; Vrsty Sftbl; Fast Rnnr Awd; Hnr Rl; Grl Scts; Law.

RATHEL, JEFFREY F; Bishop Montgomery HS; Hawthorne, CA; (3); Ski Clb; Varsity Clb; Bsbl; Socr; Hon Roll; CA Schlrshp Fed; Car Club.

RATHGEBER, TOBY; San Clemente HS; San Clemente, CA; (3); Chrmn FBLA; Office Aide; Capt Flag Corp; Corp Law.

RATKOVIC, MICHAEL P; Loyola HS; Los Angeles, CA; (1); Boy Scts; Math Clb; Math Tm; Spanish Clb; Intrml Ftbl; Wt Lftg; Hon Roll; UCLA; Mgmt.

RATLIFF, LAURA; Marina HS; Westminster, CA; (3); Church Yth Grp; Service Clb; Drill Tm; Ed Lit Mag; JV Trk; High Hon Roll; GSA Silver Awd; Athl Against Substance Abuse; Hardest Wrkr Drill Team; CA ST; Lib Arts.

RATLIFF, TIFFANY D; Oak Ridge HS; Cameron Park, CA; (3); Church Yth Grp; French Clb; SADD; Var Cheerldng; Mascot; Stephen E Austin; Intr Dsgn.

RATLIFF, VERONICA R; Oak Ridge HS; El Dorado Hills, CA; (3); Church Yth Grp; Cmnty Wkr; Hon Roll; Golden St Awd Math; Biola; Psych.

RATSYTHONG, BOUANIT L; MUHSD Merced HS; Merced, CA; (4); Bus Profs of Am; FTA; Hon Roll; Merced Coll; Bus.

RATTAN, JENNIFER D; Elsinore HS; Lake Elsinore, CA; (2); 1/600; FBLA; Hon Roll; CSF; Med.

RATTRAY, KIM; Chula Vista HS; Chula Vista, CA; (3); Church Yth Grp; Pep Clb; JV Capt Cheerldng; JV Vllybl; Black Stu Union; Bio.

RATZLAFF, MELODY A; Turlock HS; Turlock, CA; (1); 9/550; AFS; Church Yth Grp; Pres VP FBLA; Key Clb; Rep Band; Mrchg Band; Orch; NHS; Sal; Bank Of Amer Achvt Awd Fnlst, Fine Arts; CA St Voc Olympics Mktg Math 3rd Pl; Supt Svc Awd; Westmont Coll; Intl Bus.

RAU, CATHERINE; Gahr HS; Cerritos, CA; (2); L Var Sftbl; JV Waterpolo; Coaches Awd; Blue & Gold Awd Engl; Forensic Psych.

RAUB, JOSHUA D; Sutter Union HS; Sutter, CA; (2); Boy Scts; FBLA; FFA; JV Trk; Hon Roll; Prfct Atten Awd; Frstry.

RAUCH, HAROLD; Hueneme HS; Port Hueneme, CA; (1); Church Yth Grp; Wrstlng; Spcl Olympcs Vlntr; Aviation.

RAUCH, PATRICIA A; North Salinas HS; Salinas, CA; (3); FBLA; Girl Scts; Pep Clb; Science Clb; Cheerldng; Gym; Pom Pon; Swmmng; Wt Lftg; Cit Awd; Attended Coop Work Experience Class; Coop Education; U Of Sf; Marine Biology.

RAUCH-LEIBA, JOSEPH; Edison HS; Stockton, CA; (2); Computer Clb; French Clb; Rptr Yrbk; Rep Jr Cls; JV Bsktbl; JV Ftbl; Var Swmmng; High Hon Roll; NHS; Pres Acad Fit Awd; Photo; Water Polo; Eastern Trvl; Cal; Civil Engrng.

RAUCKHORST, LISA H; Torrey Pines HS; Encinitas, CA; (1); Var Swmmng; USD; Med.

RAUDMAN, TAD C; Enterprise HS; Palo Cedro, CA; (3); 47/428; Math Clb; Model UN; Mu Alpha Theta; Hon Roll; Golden ST Exam Hnrs Gemtry; Outstndng Stu; Congrsnl Schlr Natl Yng Ldrs Conf 90.

RAUGHTON, STACI L; Bolsa Grande HS; Garden Grove, CA; (4); Church Yth Grp; Drama Clb; Math Clb; Pep Clb; Speech Tm; Teachers Aide; Prfct Atten Awd; Scndry Ed.

RAUGUST, JAMES E; Whittier Christian HS; Fullerton, CA; (1); Church Yth Grp; Yrbk; Var L Trk; Hon Roll; NHS; CSF; Arts.

RAUZON, R RYAN; Irvine HS; Irvine, CA; (1); Boy Scts; Letterman Clb; Temple Yth Grp; Crs Cntry; Trk; Wrstlng.

RAVAIOLI, GINA; Moorpark HS; Moorpark, CA; (4); 5/206; Church Yth Grp; FHA; Key Clb; Chorus; Var Cheerldng; JV Sftbl; High Hon Roll; Jr NHS; CSF Hist; Psych.

RAVAL, PAUL J; Clovis HS; Clovis, CA; (2); Tennis; High Hon Roll; Hon Roll; CSF; Intl TAG; Block C Club Acadc; Odyssy Mind; Sci.

RAVANO, SUZANNE M; Notre Dame HS; San Carlos, CA; (2); Church Yth Grp; School Play; Mgr Jr Cls; Socr; Hon Roll; NHS; CSF; CA Yth Soccer Assn; Acctng.

RAVELO, BEATRIZ; Santa Ana HS; Santa Ana, CA; (2); Hon Roll; Prfct Atten Awd; Stu Of Mnth; Achvt; Rancho Santiago Coll; Comp.

RAVENKAMP, SCOTT; Ontario HS; Ontario, CA; (4); Debate Tm; VP Letterman Clb; Office Aide; Pres Quiz Bowl; Teachers Aide; Band; Mrchg Band; JV Capt Bsbl; Var Capt Bsktbl; Capt Var Trk; All ST Schltc Bsktbl Team; All Vlyt Bsktbl; Chaffey Coll; Bus.

RAVET, JENNIFER A; Saint Joseph Notre Dame HS; Alameda, CA; (3); 5/100; Church Yth Grp; Cmnty Wkr; Computer Clb; High Hon Roll; Hon Roll; NHS; CA Schlrshp Fed; Socl Jstc Cmmtte; Lions Awd Svc; Poltcl Sci.

RAVINDRA, RITA; Irvine HS; Irvine, CA; (2); Cmnty Wkr; Hosp Aide; Key Clb; VP Temple Yth Grp; Hon Roll; Pres Acad Fit Awd; Engl Heritage Awd; Goldn St Exam Geom & Alg Hnrs; Corp Law.

RAVNIK, TATJANA M; Bishop O'dowd HS; Oakland, CA; (3); 36/240; Cmnty Wkr; Debate Tm; GAA; Ski Clb; Band; Jazz Band; Rptr Nwsp; JV Var Sftbl; JV Vllybl; High Hon Roll; Bio.

RAWAL, SANJAY D; San Leandro HS; San Leandro, CA; (2); 1/365; Boy Scts; Computer Clb; Rep Intnl Clb; Band; Jazz Band; Rep Frsh Cls; Rep Soph Cls; Var L Crs Cntry; Var L Socr; Var L Trk; Exc USSR 1989-90; Harvard; Intl Rel.

RAWLINGS, BARBRANN M; El Camino HS; Oceanside, CA; (4); Office Aide; ROTC; Wt Lftg; Psych.

RAWLINGS, KATHRYN T; Irvington HS; Fremont, CA; (2); Key Clb; Rep Stu Cncl; JV Var Crs Cntry; JV Swmmng; Hon Roll; Kiwanis Awd; Dixie Coll; Nurse.

RAWLINS, KIMBERLY; Brethren SR HS; Long Beach, CA; (1); Church Yth Grp; Chorus; Cheerldng; Hon Roll; Biola U; Intr Dsgn.

RAWLINS, PRINCE A; San Fernando CIP HS; Los Angeles, CA; (2); Ftbl; Wt Lftg; High Hon Roll; Hon Roll; Stanford; Obstrcn.

RAWLINSON, JILL; Orange HS; Orange, CA; (3); Intnl Clb; Key Clb; Office Aide; Pep Clb; Rptr Yrbk; Rep Stu Cncl; Stat Wrstlng; Cit Awd; Hon Roll; UCLA; Commnctns.

RAWLS, ADELE L; Bloomington Christian HS; Bloomington, CA; (2); Church Yth Grp; Computer Clb; Sec Stu Cncl; Var Capt Cheerldng; Hon Roll; Sprts Med.

RAWLS, MATIKA; Rancho Cordova SR HS; Rancho Cordova, CA; (2); Church Yth Grp; Girl Scts; Model UN; Pep Clb; Varsity Clb; Drill Tm; Cheerldng; Pom Pon; Jr NHS; Opt Clb Awd; Harvard U; Med.

RAWORTH, JENNIFER M; Villa Park HS; Orange, CA; (3); Drama Clb; Key Clb; SADD; Treas Jr Cls; Var L Sftbl; Cit Awd; Hon Roll; Pres Acad Fit Awd; Church Yth Grp; Red Cross Aide; Sftbl All Leag; Sftbl All CIF; All Southern CA; San Luis Obispo U.

RAWSON, STEVEN J; Central Valley HS; Central Valley, CA; (3); 43/273; Scholastic Bowl; Hon Roll; Rgnl Chmp Sci Olympc Tm; US Naval Acad; Ncl Engr.

RAY, ALLISON M; Laguna Hills HS; Laguna Hills, CA; (2); Church Yth Grp; Church Choir; Intrml Trk; Darma Awd; Stu Govt; BYU; Teacher.

RAY, AMY L; Modoc HS; Alturas, CA; (3); 12/71; 4-H; Letterman Clb; Rptr Nwsp; JV Var Powder Puff Ftbl; Var L Sftbl; JV Var Vllybl; Cit Awd; High Hon Roll; Hon Roll; Prfct Atten Awd; Oceangrphy.

RAY, ANTHONY C; Skyline HS; Oakland, CA; (3); Band; Jazz Band; Var Bsbl; JV Socr; Hon Roll; Pres Acad Fit Awd; MESA; UC Berkeley; Geology.

RAY, CHRISTOPHER K; Bonita HS; La Verne, CA; (2); 295/360; Church Yth Grp; FCA; Letterman Clb; VP Soph Cls; VP Stu Cncl; Var Crs Cntry; Var Trk; Hon Roll; MVP Crss Cntry 88 & 89; U AZ; Pre-Med.

RAY, HEATHER E; Whittier Christian HS; Yorba Linda, CA; (3); Church Yth Grp; Speech Tm; Cheerldng; CA Schlrshp Fed; Bus.

RAY, JAMES R; Troy HS; Fullerton, CA; (2); Boy Scts; Computer Clb; Hon Roll; Orange Cnty Acad Dcthln 2nd Pl Lit, 5th Pl Math; Comp Sci.

RAY, JENNIFER O; St Anthony HS; Lakewood, CA; (3); Cmnty Wkr; Dance Clb; Drama Clb; Natl Beta Clb; Office Aide; Spanish Clb; Teachers Aide; Band; School Play; Stage Crew; Pepperdine; Bus.

RAY, JOHN J; Troy HS; Yorba Linda, CA; (1); Church Yth Grp; Drama Clb; JV Swmmng; JV Wrstlng; High Hon Roll; Schlr Ath Awd 89-90; Hnrs At Entrance Merit Awd; UC Santa Barbara.

RAY, JOLENE M; Analy HS; Sebastopol, CA; (2); 7/256; Church Yth Grp; Dance Clb; French Clb; Model UN; Acpl Chr; Band; Jazz Band; Mrchg Band; Pep Band; School Musical; Aviation Club; Pilot.

RAY, JOVONNE R; Analy HS; Sebastopol, CA; (3); 2/243; Church Yth Grp; Dance Clb; French Clb; Model UN; Band; Chorus; Jazz Band; Mrchg Band; Pep Band; School Musical; CA St Smmr Schl Arts 90; Stu Mnth; Music.

RAY, MALANCHA; Arcadia HS; Arcadia, CA; (3); 35/643; Church Yth Grp; Cmnty Wkr; French Clb; Hosp Aide; Office Aide; Red Cross Aide; Hon Roll; NHS; Prfct Atten Awd; Pres Acad Fit Awd; Amnsty Intl; YDAT; Engl.

RAY, MARCUS R; Turlock HS; Turlock, CA; (2); AFS; Boy Scts; Church Yth Grp; NFL; Am Leg Boys St; Ftbl; Tennis; Wrstlng; CA Schlrshp Fed; Electrnc Engr.

RAY, MICHAEL; Capistrano Valley Christian HS; Laguna Beach, CA; (2); 7/52; Church Yth Grp; Drama Clb; Ski Clb; Varsity Clb; Chorus; School Play; Ftbl; Socr; Vllybl; Hon Roll; Mst Likely To Succeed; Bst Drssd.

RAY, NATALIE; Enterprise HS; Palo Cedro, CA; (3); 31/448; Church Yth Grp; Intnl Clb; Mu Alpha Theta; Drill Tm; Pom Pon; Swmmng; High Hon Roll; All Amer Pom Pon Girl 89; Natl Dance Team Champs 90; CA U; Intl Bus.

RAY, TAHIRAH ONI; Baldwin Park HS; Baldwin Park, CA; (3); Treas JA; Office Aide; Pep Clb; Science Clb; Teachers Aide; Chorus; Drill Tm; School Musical; Rep Frsh Cls; Treas Jr Cls; Christn Childrns Sponsor; Pasadena City Coll; Clincl Psyc.

RAYA, ANNA LISA; Ramona Convent Secondary Schl; Los Angeles, CA; (3); 16/96; Treas GAA; Model UN; Phtg Yrbk; JV Bsktbl; Var Trk; NHS; Pres Acad Fit Awd; CA Schlrshp Commtte VP; Prom Cmmtte Brd; Comm.

RAYA, AURORA; Wasco Union HS; Wasco, CA; (4); 26/153; Church Yth Grp; Latin Clb; Teachers Aide; Church Choir; Nwsp; Yrbk; High Hon Roll; Pres Acad Fit Awd; Migrant Clb-Pres; Hispanic Excllnc Schlrshp; CA ST U-Bakersfield; Math.

RAYA, SILVIA; Palo Verde HS; Blythe, CA; (2); Secy.

RAYAS, PEDRO; Norco HS; Corona, CA; (3); Latin Clb; Socr; Cit Awd.

RAYBORN, SEAN; West Covina HS; West Covina, CA; (3); French Clb; SADD; Teachers Aide; Varsity Clb; Tennis; Cal Poly Pomona; Bus Admin.

RAYES, NATHALIE; St Monica Catholic HS; Marina Del Rey, CA; (2); Cmnty Wkr; Sec Rep Frsh Cls; Sec Treas Soph Cls; Rep Jr Cls; High Hon Roll; Hon Roll; Amer Druze Soc; Heal The Bay Mem; Cmp Cnslr; USC; Lawyer.

RAYFORD, WAYNE L; Apple Valley HS; Apple Valley, CA; (4); Church Yth Grp; Cmnty Wkr; Teachers Aide; Varsity Clb; JV Bsbl; Var L Bsktbl; Intrml Ftbl; Hon Roll; Ntl Merit Ltr; People To People Yth Sci Exchng Pgm; CA ST U Fullerton; Engrng.

RAYGOZA, JESUS; Willows HS; Willows, CA; (3); 4/90; Letterman Clb; Var Bsktbl; Var Ftbl; Hon Roll; U Of S CA.

RAYLS, HEIDI B; Woodland HS; Woodland, CA; (3); Drill Tm; Mrchg Band; Pep Band; Jr NHS; Crmnl Lwyr.

RAYMOND, CATHY S; John Burroughs HS; Burbank, CA; (3); Dance Clb; Service Clb; Temple Yth Grp; Chorus; School Musical; Nwsp; Yrbk; Score Keeper; Vllybl; Cit Awd; U Of Santa Barbara; Child Psych.

RAYMOND JR, DONALD L; Andrew P Hill HS; San Jose, CA; (3); Drama Clb; Q&S; School Play; Lit Mag; Hon Roll; Bio.

RAYMOND, HEIDI; Oakridge HS; Cameron Park, CA; (1); Church Yth Grp; High Hon Roll.

RAYMOND, JIMMY A; Etiwanda HS; Cucamonga, CA; (2); Welding.

RAYMOND, SINTIA Y; Mar Vista HS; San Diego, CA; (1); ROTC.

RAYMOND, STEPHANIE; Monache HS; Springville, CA; (4); 1/290; Pres 4-H; Band; Rep Frsh Cls; Pres Soph Cls; Rep Jr Cls; Rep Sr Cls; Var Capt Swmmng; Var L Vllybl; Cit Awd; Lion Awd; Tulare Cnty Tailwaggers Raise Guide Dogs Blnd; Migrant Educ Swm Instrctr; UC Santa Barbara; Biolgcl Sci.

RAYMOND, ZINZI A; John Muir HS; La Canada Flintri, CA; (3); Debate Tm; Drama Clb; FBLA; Key Clb; Latin Clb; Math Clb; Speech Tm; Jazz Band; Orch; Ed Nwsp; Acad Decathln; JV Badminton Team; Med.

RAYNER, SHAUNA L; Alhambra HS; Martinez, CA; (4); 6/196; Church Yth Grp; Cmnty Wkr; Math Clb; School Play; Ed Nwsp; Stu Cncl; High Hon Roll; Ntl Merit Ltr; Pres Acad Fit Awd; Treas AFS; Camp Cnslr; Envrnmntl Grp; CA Poly Sn Luis Obispo; Soclgy.

RAYO, JUAN C; San Leandre HS; San Leandro, CA; (3); #40 In Class; Boy Scts; Teachers Aide; High Hon Roll; Opt Clb Awd; Prfct Atten Awd; Schl Recog For Tkng/Pssng Golden St Geomtry Tst; Cal ST Hayward; Bus Admin.

RAYOS, ANGELA H; Mt Whitney HS; Goshen, CA; (3); Church Yth Grp; FBLA; Library Aide; Coll Of Sequoias; Crt Reptr.

RAYSHEL, ERICA; Ramona HS; Riverside, CA; (4); 1/276; Sec Church Yth Grp; Drama Clb; Chorus; Church Choir; School Musical; School Play; Stage Crew; Sec Soph Cls; VP Jr Cls; Off Sr Cls; CA Schlrshp Fed Life Mem; CA All St Hnr Chrs; Panhellenic Assoc Schlrshp & Rohr Indstrs Schlrshp; U Of CA Riverside; Engl.

RAZI, MARJAN; Hamilton HS; Los Angeles, CA; (3); Phtg Ed Yrbk; High Hon Roll; Hon Roll; NHS; Pres Acad Fit Awd; Prin Awd; Phy.

RAZO, CLAUDIA B; Manual Arts HS; Los Angeles, CA; (3); Var Tennis; Rep Frsh Cls; Cmmnty Work Trophy; U CA-SANTA Barbara; Med.

RAZO, GLORIA; Eisenhower HS; Rialto, CA; (2); Teachers Aide; Bsktbl; Mgr(s); High Hon Roll; Hon Roll; Sci Dept Awd 89-90; Ldrshp Cls As Campus Cnrvnmnt Cmmssnr; Med.

RAZO, RAUL; Sweetwater HS; National City, CA; (2).

RAZO, RENEE; Arlington HS; Riverside, CA; (2); Chorus; Color Guard; Rep Stu Cncl; Hon Roll; Crmnl Law.

RAZZANI, MICHELE; Perris HS; Nuevo, CA; (4); 10/400; JA; Teachers Aide; Cheerldng; Capt Socr; Capt Swmmng; High Hon Roll; Hon Roll; Europe Clb VP; Jr Hnr Grd; Cal ST Long Beach; Med.

READ, ADAM J; Coast Joint Union HS; Cambria, CA; (3); AFS; Am Leg Boys St; Church Yth Grp; Math Clb; Pep Clb; Science Clb; Pres SADD; Church Choir; Var Tennis; High Hon Roll; Cmmty Yth Grp Orgnzr; Missionary.

READ, ALICIA; Santa Catalina Schl; Pebble Beach, CA; (4); Cmnty Wkr; Sec Spanish Clb; Speech Tm; Chorus; Nwsp; Yrbk; Var Cheerldng; Sftbl; Capt Var Tennis; U AZ; Spanish.

READ, AUDREY L; Fountain Valley HS; Fountain Valley, CA; (1); Church Yth Grp; Off Frsh Cls; Var L Crs Cntry; JV Swmmng; High Hon Roll; Pres Acad Fit Awd; PAL Clb.

READ, CHRISTINE A; Anderson Union HS; Anderson, CA; (4); FCA; Office Aide; Spanish Clb; SADD; Rptr Yrbk; Crs Cntry; JV Swmmng; Hon Roll; Jobs Dghtrs; Shasta Coll; Engr.

READ, CICELY C; Tulare Western HS; Tulare, CA; (3); Var JV Cheerldng; Hon Roll; Outstndng Acad Excllnc Frgn Lang; Tlr Wstrn Hspnc Yth Ldrshp; SNAP Tutor Acad Awd; U Of San Francisco; Nrsng.

READ, MATT; Yosemite Union HS; Ahwahnee, CA; (3); Drama Clb; French Clb; School Play; Treas Soph Cls; Var Crs Cntry; JV Trk; Hon Roll; Intl Studies Assn Schlrshp; Fndr/Pres Role Playing Game Clb; UC Santa Cruz; Marine Bio.

READ, STEPHANIE M; Carlmont HS; Belmont, CA; (3); Am Leg Aux Girls St; Church Yth Grp; Key Clb; Church Choir; School Musical; San Diego ST; Cmmnctns.

READ, SUSANNE; Hawthorne HS; Hawthorne, CA; (3); Pres Church Yth Grp; Drama Clb; Chorus; Church Choir; Drill Tm; School Musical; School Play; Variety Show; Hon Roll; CSF; Brigham Young U; Elem Educ.

READ, TISA; Palm Desert HS; Palm Desert, CA; (4); 38/300; Sec Sr Cls; Var Capt Bsktbl; Var Trk; Var Vllybl; Stu Yr; 88; Athlete Yr 90; Pitzer Coll.

READ, WENDY D; Liberty Union HS; Byron, CA; (1); Dance Clb; Jazz Band; Odessey Of Mind-St Cmptn; Optometry.

READE, MICHELLE; Valley HS; Sacramento, CA; (4); 60/480; Church Yth Grp; German Clb; Girl Scts; Letterman Clb; ROTC; Var Gym; Hon Roll; NHS; Schl Mines & Tech SD; Engr.

READER, ANGELA; Harbor HS; Santa Cruz, CA; (3); JV Capt Cheerldng; Var Capt Pom Pon; Var Trk; Key Clb; Rep Stu Cncl; SADD; Church Yth Grp; USA Europe Tour 88; Eagle Aloha Bowl Tour 89; Barbizon Modeling Schl Grad 89; Cabrillo Coll; Psych.

READY, DREW W; Arcadia HS; Temple City, CA; (3); Aud/Vis; School Play; Var Socr; Pres Acad Fit Awd; Apache News Asst Dir, Audio Spclzng Edtng; Prescot AZ; Eclgy Fld.

REAGER, AMY L; Lowell HS; San Francisco, CA; (3); Boy Scts; VP French Clb; Chorus; Orch; Stage Crew; Nwsp; Rep Frsh Cls; JV Socr; Ntl Merit Ltr; Gldn St Awds Alg High Hnrs, Geom Hnrs; Psych.

REAGLE, LEANNA; North HS; Bakersfield, CA; (1); Church Yth Grp; Drama Clb; French Clb; Chorus; Stage Crew; Nwsp; Cheerldng; Gym; Socr; Hon Roll; Miss CA Natl Teen 90; Cmmnctns.

REAL, MICHELLE D; Escondido HS; Escondido, CA; (2); Drama Clb; Pep Clb; School Play; Hon Roll; 2 Drama Awds Bst & Spprtng Actrs; UCLA; Prfrmng Arts.

REAL, WILLIAM F; Alahambra HS; Martinez, CA; (3); Var Crs Cntry; Var JV Socr; Var Trk; Mst Imprvd Crss Cntry Athl 87; Diablo Valley Coll; Coaching.

REARDEN-HAMLY, JULIA F; Torrey Pines HS; Rancho Santa Fe, CA; (3); Rep Church Yth Grp; Cmnty Wkr; VP French Clb; Hosp Aide; Sec Key Clb; Speech Tm; SADD; Chorus; School Play; Rep Frsh Cls; Engl.

REARDON, JENNA; Canyon HS; Canyon Country, CA; (2); Church Yth Grp; Pep Clb; Chorus; JV Cheerldng; Var L Swmmng; Hon Roll; CA Schlrshp Fed; UCLA; Med.

REARDON, KERRI; Burbank HS; Burbank, CA; (2); Church Yth Grp; Cmnty Wkr; French Clb; Hosp Aide; Office Aide; Pep Clb; Red Cross Aide; Drill Tm; Pres Jr Cls; Rep Stu Cncl; Natl Charity League Burbank Chapter; Intl Order Jobs Daughters Queen; U CA; Med.

REAVES, ANGEL; Arlington HS; Roanoke Rapids, NC; (4); Boy Scts; Church Yth Grp; Cmnty Wkr; ROTC; Teachers Aide; Chorus; Flag Corp; School Musical; Hon Roll; VFW Auxlry Weighs/Means Asst Chrmn; Amer Vtrns Natl Awd; 90 Spcl Olympcs Vlntr; Halifac CC.

REAVES, MATTHEW B; Edison HS; Fresno, CA; (1); Cmnty Wkr; Hon Roll; IRS Vlntr; CA U; Astronomy.

REBEIRO, TRINA M; Diamond Bar HS; Walnut, CA; (3); 126/518; FBLA; Spanish Clb; Hon Roll; CSF; Wrkd Lcl Radio Sta; Cmmnctns.

REBELES, FIDEL C; Golden West HS; Visalia, CA; (2); Math Clb; Math Tm; Science Clb; Orch; JV Tennis; Cit Awd; High Hon Roll; Jr NHS; Prfct Atten Awd; Pres Acad Fit Awd; Sci Olympiad; CSF; 2nd Pl Kings & Tulare Cntys Math Cmptn; Stanford; Elec Engrng.

REBER, KLAUS-THOMAS; North Salinas HS; Salinas, CA; (4); Boy Scts; Computer Clb; Dance Clb; Latin Clb; Rep Stu Cncl; Var Capt Swmmng; Hon Roll; Rotary Awd; Rifle Clb; Intl Clb; Explorer Scts; Sheriffs Dept; Photo Clb; Sci.

REBER, MARRIETTA R; Foothill HS; Santa Ana, CA; (4); Church Yth Grp; Cmnty Wkr; Teachers Aide; Acpl Chr; Chorus; School Musical; Cit Awd; High Hon Roll; Hon Roll; Kiwanis Awd; Acadmc Scholar BYU; Lead In Schl Play; Disneyland Creatvty Chllnge Awd; Madrigals; Knight Singers; BYU; HS Engl Teacher.

REBLANDO, JANET; Rowland HS; Pacoima, CA; (4); Dance Clb; Math Tm; Pres Frsh Cls; Pres Soph Cls; VP Jr Cls; Vllybl; High Hon Roll; CA ST U Northridge; Chem.

REBMAN, ALICIA C; Etiwanda HS; Alta Loma, CA; (2); Computer Clb; JA; Model UN; Ski Clb; Hon Roll; Pres Acad Fit Awd; Advncd Dance Pgm; U CA; Fine Arts.

REBMAN, BRIDGETT A; Chino HS; Ontario, CA; (2); FHA; Var Swmmng; High Hon Roll; Spirit Club.

REBOLLINI, MICHAEL; South San Francisco HS; South San Francis, CA; (2); Bsbl; Bsktbl; 3 Acad Awds; SFSU; Bus.

RECAIDO, LESLIE S; Samuel F B Morse HS; San Diego, CA; (2); 131/764; Intnl Clb; Flag Corp; Mrchg Band; Hon Roll; NHS; 3rd Pl SHARP Drl Dwn; Grad John Casablancas Mdlng Ctr; 3rd Zoology Div Sci Fr; Miss San Marcelino; USC; Pharmacy.

RECALDE, FRANCES; Warren HS; Downey, CA; (4); 53/408; FBLA; Mu Alpha Theta; Ed Yrbk; Sec Frsh Cls; Rep Stu Cncl; Powder Puff Ftbl; Var Tennis; Cit Awd; NHS; Spanish NHS; Loyola Marymount U; Bus.

RECENDEZ, PRIMITIVO; Lincoln HS; Sheridan, CA; (3); Socr.

RECH, TRACY K; Ramona HS; Riverside, CA; (2); 2/450; Science Clb; Spanish Clb; Varsity Clb; Stu Cncl; Socr; Swmmng; High Hon Roll; NHS; Pres Acad Fit Awd; CSF; Acad Dcthln; UC Riverside; Psych.

RECHS, MATTHEW AARON; Bear River HS; Grass Valley, CA; (2); Church Yth Grp; Cmnty Wkr; SADD; JV Capt Ftbl; JV Trk; Cit Awd; High Hon Roll; Hon Roll; CSF; Feed Hungry Prog.

RECINOS, ELIZABETH; Valencia HS; Placentia, CA; (3); Am Leg Aux Girls St; Science Clb; Spanish Clb; Flag Corp; Yrbk; High Hon Roll; NHS; Prfct Atten Awd; Pres Acad Fit Awd; Participatn Sthrn CA Citiz Smnr Pepperdime U; MESA-MATH,Engl,Sci Achvt-Trsr SR Yr; Claremont Mc Kenna Coll; Psych.

RECK, LESLIE M; Monte Vista HS; Spring Valley, CA; (2); 39/422; Church Yth Grp; Off Pep Clb; Rep Soph Cls; Var Diving; Var Swmmng; Hon Roll; ASB Commissioner Of Judicial Affairs; Coll; Marine Bio.

RECLUSADO, TRACY A; South Tahoe HS; South Lake Tahoe, CA; (3); Key Clb; SADD; Pres Band; Pep Band; ROP Computerized Accntng Cert; UC San Bernardino; Paralegal.

RECORD, CARMEN R; Enterprise HS; Palo Cedro, CA; (3); Church Yth Grp; Intnl Clb; Mu Alpha Theta; Band; School Musical; Hon Roll; BYU; Music Ed.

RECORD, JUSTIN J; Enterprise HS; Palo Cedro, CA; (4); Aud/Vis; Boy Scts; Mu Alpha Theta; Science Clb; High Hon Roll; Hon Roll; Pres Acad Fit Awd; CSF; Eagle Sct; Acad Ltr; Physics Engrng.

RECOTTA, DAMON E; Pioneer HS; San Jose, CA; (3); Key Clb; JV Var Bsktbl; JV Ftbl; JV Var Tennis; San Diego ST; Mrktg.

RECTOR, JAMIE; Rubidoux HS; Mira Loma, CA; (3); 19/627; Cmnty Wkr; Office Aide; Pep Clb; Varsity Clb; Church Choir; Yrbk; Rep Frsh Cls; VP Soph Cls; Rep Jr Cls; Var Cheerldng; Yth Ctznshp Seminar, Yth To Yth Drug Free Seminar Pepperdine U; Accntng.

RECTOR, TAMMY M; North HS; Bakersfield, CA; (3); Church Yth Grp; Teachers Aide; Chorus; Hon Roll; English Teacher.

RED, GINGERIE; Etiwanda HS; Rancho Cuccamonga, CA; (3); Art Clb; Church Yth Grp; Cmnty Wkr; High Hon Roll; NHS; CA Schlrshp Fed; Physics Bowl Super Achvt Awd; Art Cont 2nd Prz Wnnr; Hnr Guard; GATE Stu; UCLA; Med.

RED, JENNIFER; Ontario HS; Ontario, CA; (2); Church Yth Grp; School Play; Swmmng; Prfct Atten Awd; Jobs Daughters; Peperdine; Ct Reporter.

REDDEN, DAVE J; Wasco Union HS; Wasco, CA; (3); Church Yth Grp; FCA; Math Clb; Math Tm; Band; Church Choir; Jazz Band; Mrchg Band; Pep Band; School Musical; Masters Coll Of Newhall; Music.

REDDI, SRIDHAR; Irvine HS; Irvine, CA; (3); 6/506; Treas Chess Clb; Hosp Aide; JV Trk; High Hon Roll; NHS; Pres Acad Fit Awd; ACS Tm 89; CSF; Scrtry Indian Clb; 3rd Pl Chem Orange Cnty Sci & Engrng Fr 90; Med.

REDDIG, DANIEL E; Winters HS; Vacaville, CA; (2); Aud/Vis; Boy Scts; Var JV Ftbl; JV Trk; Hon Roll; Aeronautics.

REDDIN, JASON D I; Apple Valley SR HS; Apple Valley, CA; (3); Teachers Aide; Band; Jazz Band; Orch; Pep Band; High Hon Roll; USC; Music.

REDDY, KITTY K; James Logan HS; Union City, CA; (3); Intnl Clb; Ed Nwsp; Rptr Yrbk; Hon Roll; Treas World Evnts Clb; Outing Clb; Chabot Coll; Jrnlsm.

REDDY, KURUGANTI; Bishop Amat HS; Covina, CA; (4); 40/400; Cmnty Wkr; Computer Clb; Hosp Aide; Speech Tm; JV Var Tennis; High Hon Roll; Hon Roll; NHS; Comp Pgm, Bldg.

REDDY, RIMA S; River City HS; W Sacramento, CA; (3); Cmnty Wkr; French Clb; SADD; Band; Jazz Band; Mrchg Band; Pep Band; Ed Yrbk; Sftbl; Tennis; Sacramento Dixieland Jubilee; Sacramento ST; Med.

REDDY, SWAPNA V; Notre Dame HS; Salinas, CA; (2); 2/80; Cmnty Wkr; Hosp Aide; Treas Science Clb; Speech Tm; School Play; Var L Tennis; Var Trk; High Hon Roll; NHS; CSF; Med.

REDFIELD, KEIRI M; Rio Lindo Acad; Woodland, CA; (4); Ski Clb; Spanish Clb; Band; Chorus; Orch; Stage Crew; High Hon Roll; Pres Acad Fit Awd; Sftbl; Vllybl; Acad Awds; Walla Walla Adventist; Psych.

REDFORD, MARY; Armijo HS; Suisun City, CA; (1); GAA; Key Clb; Band; Jazz Band; Mrchg Band; Pep Band; Stu Cncl; Crs Cntry; Swmmng; Trk; ASU; Science.

REDIGER, DAREN R; Village Christian Schls; Glendale, CA; (3); 29/123; Computer Clb; Drama Clb; English Clb; Math Clb; Mu Alpha Theta; Spanish Clb; Bsktbl; Crs Cntry; Golf; Tennis; Cal Poly; Arch.

REDING, CHRISTINA L; Paramount HS; Paramount, CA; (2); 155/599; SADD; Teachers Aide; Band; Jazz Band; Mrchg Band; Pep Band; Sftbl; Hon Roll; Honr Orch; Irvine U; Chld Ed.

REDJAI, ALI; Newport Harbor HS; Newport Beach, CA; (2); JV Socr; JV Tennis; Math Gldn St Tst; Imprvmnt Awd; UCI; Cmptr Engnr.

REDLIN, HEATHER R; Victor Valley HS; Victorville, CA; (3); Teachers Aide; Var L Vllybl; Hon Roll; Fencing; Bus.

REDLIN, WILLIAM P; Victor Valley HS; Victorville, CA; (2); Boy Scts; Varsity Clb; Band; School Play; JV Bsbl; Ftbl; Wt Lftg; High Hon Roll; Hon Roll; IA U; Bus.

REDMON, JOHN PAUL; Golden Gate Acad; Oakland, CA; (1); Church Yth Grp; Drama Clb; Teachers Aide; Church Choir; School Musical; School Play; Pres Frsh Cls; Sftbl; Swmmng; Hon Roll; Music Awds; Oakwood Coll; Bus Admin.

REDMON, MARY E; Golden Gate Acad; Oakland, CA; (3); Church Yth Grp; Drama Clb; Teachers Aide; Chorus; Church Choir; Drill Tm; School Play; Yrbk; Pres Frsh Cls; VP Soph Cls; Schl Of Med ; Med Doctor.

REDONDO, JEFFREY J; Fontana HS; Fontana, CA; (2); Church Yth Grp; Drama Clb; Acpl Chr; Swing Chorus; Hon Roll; Active Cmnty Theater; Psych.

REDONDO, LORI L; Grossmont HS; La Mesa, CA; (3); 69/390; SADD; Var Bsktbl; Var Trk; Var Vllybl; All Leag Bsktbl; Daisy Chain; U Of AZ; Engrng.

REECE, CHRISTINA L; Vander HS; Travis A F B, CA; (4); 62/151; Cmnty Wkr; Drama Clb; SADD; School Play; Lit Mag; Stu Cncl; Office Aide; Spanish Clb; Color Guard; Stage Crew; 3rd Pl Wnnr Aloma St Pgnt; Graphic Desgn.

REECE, MATTHEW P; El Cajon Valley HS; El Cajon, CA; (3); 51/393; Church Yth Grp; Drama Clb; Var Swmmng; Hon Roll; Waterpolo Coachs Awd 88-90; Most Sprtnl Player Awd 89-90; Cert Outstndg Achvt 90; Hnrs Clses 87-90; Biola.

REECE, MISTY; Hesperia HS; Hesperia, CA; (2); 16/720; Church Yth Grp; Pep Clb; Drill Tm; Yrbk; JV Var Cheerldng; JV Var Pom Pon; High Hon Roll; Prfct Atten Awd; Hon Roll; Pep Assmbly Cmmttee; ASB Rep; Pepperdine; Elem Educ.

REED, ADAM; Miramonte HS; Orinda, CA; (4); 8/274; Boy Scts; Letterman Clb; NFL; Spanish Clb; Speech Tm; Band; Jazz Band; Mrchg Band; School Musical; Rep Sr Cls; Mock Trial Atty; U CA Berkeley.

REED, ALISHA; Palmdale HS; Agua Dulce, CA; (4); 15/620; GAA; Math Clb; Math Tm; Var Swmmng; Var Tennis; Pres Acad Fit Awd; UC Santa Barbara; Microbio.

REED, BETH A; Elk Grove HS; Sacramento, CA; (4); Pres Church Yth Grp; Dance Clb; French Clb; Office Aide; Spanish Clb; Chorus; Church Choir; Drill Tm; Mgr(s); Mgr Wrstlng; Show Choir; Camp Cnslr; Rgnl Occptnl Pgm; CA ST U Sacramento; Lbrl Stds.

REED, BRYAN C; Claremont HS; Claremont, CA; (1); Teachers Aide; Bsbl; Ftbl; Golf; Nortre Dame; Real Estate.

REED, CHAD B; Fontana HS; Fontana, CA; (2); 10/1000; Varsity Clb; Band; JV Bsbl; Var Ftbl; High Hon Roll; Engrng.

REED, CHRISTOPHER A; South Pasadena HS; S Pasadena, CA; (3); Boy Scts; Church Yth Grp; Latin Clb; SADD; Lbrn Band; Jazz Band; Lbrn Mrchg Band; Pep Band; School Musical; Dir Awd For Jazz Band 2 Yrs; Geology.

REED, DOUG T; Pasadena HS; Pasadena, CA; (3); Boy Scts; Church Yth Grp; French Clb; Teachers Aide; Acpl Chr; Band; Mrchg Band; Orch; Pep Band; School Musical; Arch.

REED, HEATHER; San Juan HS; Citrus Heights, CA; (2); 64/250; GAA; Pep Clb; Teachers Aide; Varsity Clb; School Play; Cheerldng; Sftbl; Child Psych.

REED, JAY; Mc Kinleyville HS; Mc Kinleyville, CA; (4); 1/130; Church Yth Grp; Cmnty Wkr; German Clb; Key Clb; Letterman Clb; Math Tm; Scholastic Bowl; SADD; Varsity Clb; JV Bsktbl; CSF; Hmbldt Cnty Sci Fair 3rd Pl; Cornell U; German.

REED, JENNIFER C; Carlsbad HS; Carlsbad, CA; (1); Church Yth Grp; Hon Roll; Rotary Awd; Interact Clb Co-VP; Hstry Club Co-Pres; Acctng.

REED, JOAN E; Burlingame HS; Burlingame, CA; (3); Church Yth Grp; Var Socr; Var Sftbl; Engl Teacher.

REED, JODAH B; Oakmont HS; Roseville, CA; (2); 1/440; Church Yth Grp; German Clb; Math Tm; JV Ftbl; High Hon Roll; Anl Roseville Math Day; CSF; Geolgy.

REED, JULIE A; Mesa Verde HS; Citrus Heights, CA; (3); 30/227; Drama Clb; School Play; Variety Show; Vllybl; Wt Lftg; Hon Roll.

REED, LORI L; Clovis HS; Fresno, CA; (4); 83/536; Church Yth Grp; Cmnty Wkr; Dance Clb; Drama Clb; Office Aide; Stage Crew; Variety Show; Hon Roll; Bnk America Cert Wnnr Prfrmng Arts; Friday Night Live; Phillips JC; Comp Acctng.

REED, MARCELLA L; Oak Park HS; Agoura Hills, CA; (3); 5/85; GAA; Teachers Aide; Ed Nwsp; Co-Ed Yrbk; VP Sr Cls; Var Capt Bsktbl; Var Capt Sftbl; Cit Awd; High Hon Roll; Hon Roll; Jrnlsm.

REED, MARY E; Davis SR HS; Davis, CA; (2); Church Yth Grp; Teachers Aide; Chorus; Church Choir; School Musical; Pres Acad Fit Awd; CSF; Biological Sci.

REED, MATT; Mc Kinleyville HS; Trinidad, CA; (3); 8/135; Church Yth Grp; School Play; Ftbl; Wrstlng; Hon Roll; CSF.

REED JR, RICHARD LEON; Living Way Christian Acad; Duarte, CA; (4); Boy Scts; Church Yth Grp; Teachers Aide; School Musical; Mgr Stage Crew; Rptr Nwsp; Rptr Yrbk; JV Var Bsktbl; JV Var Ftbl; Var Sftbl; Distingshd Chrstn Stu 88-89; Acad Excllnc Awd 87-89; U CA Davis; Vet.

REED, ROBERT M; Laguna Hills HS; Laguna Hills, CA; (1); Model UN; Intrml Crs Cntry; Intrml Socr; Intrml Trk; Hon Roll; Bus.

REED, RUBEN D; Downey HS; Downey, CA; (2); Church Yth Grp; JV L Ftbl; JV Trk; Piano; Cyclng; MIT; Comp Prgmr.

REED, SARAH; Apple Valley HS; Lucerne Valley, CA; (2); FFA; High Hon Roll; Hon Roll; Equestrian Trials Intl Clb; Child Psych.

REED, SHEILA R; Rim Of The World HS; Running Springs, CA; (2); Pep Clb; Phtg Nwsp; Phtg Yrbk; Stu Cncl; JV Cheerldng; High Hon Roll; Prfct Atten Awd; Ballet; Skng; Acadc Ltr; Pres AFS Intl Club.

REED, STEPHANIE; Cabrillo HS; Lompoc, CA; (4); 87/200; Teachers Aide; Drill Tm; Var Cheerldng; Mgr(s); JV Swmmng; Hon Roll; Interact Club; Shadow Pgm; Alan Hancock; Bus Admin.

REED, STEPHANIE L; Yucaipa HS; Yucaipa, CA; (3); #12 In Class; Am Leg Aux Girls St; Church Yth Grp; Spanish Clb; Rep Jr Cls; Stu Cncl; Stat Bsbl; Capt Powder Puff Ftbl; JV Sftbl; High Hon Roll; Hon Roll; CA Schltc Fed; Interact Club Cmnty Svc Club; Congressional Schlr; Bus Admin.

REED, STEPHANIE M; Novato HS; Novato, CA; (1); Spanish Clb; Band; U CA Davis; Vet.

REED, STEVE E; Redlands HS; Redlands, CA; (2); Drama Clb; Stage Crew; Wrstlng; San Diego ST; Mrn Bio.

REED, TAMASHA; Lincoln Prep HS; San Diego, CA; (4); 5/220; Church Yth Grp; Dance Clb; Pres Letterman Clb; Church Choir; Rep Jr Cls; Var L Sftbl; Var L Vllybl; High Hon Roll; Hon Roll; Prfct Atten Awd; Sci Achvt Awd; Art Wrtng Cont Wnnr; Baker U; Elec Engrng.

REED, TAWILI M; San Leandro HS; San Leandro, CA; (3); Church Yth Grp; Cmnty Wkr; Dance Clb; Letterman Clb; Office Aide; Service Clb; Teachers Aide; Church Choir; Rptr Nwsp; Hon Roll; Hampton Coll; Med.

REED, TIFFANY L; Centennial HS; Corona, CA; (3); 86/720; Church Yth Grp; Spanish Clb; Band; School Musical; School Play; Stage Crew; High Hon Roll; Hon Roll; Street Dance & Wrkout; CA HS Prfcncy Exam Hghst Rcrd; RN.

REED, TRENT A W; Edison HS; Warwick, RI; (1); Church Yth Grp; Model UN; Capt Socr; Vllybl; Bus.

REED, WENDY M; Laguna Hills HS; Laguna Hills, CA; (4); French Clb; Key Clb; Office Aide; SADD; Ed Yrbk; Trk; Kiwanis Awd; Pres Acad Fit Awd; Mck Trl; UCSB; Poltcl Sci.

REED, YAEKO; Alhambra HS; Alhambra, CA; (4); 220/690; Dance Clb; Pep Clb; Red Cross Aide; Spanish Clb; Ed Phtg Yrbk; Hon Roll; NHS; Ntl Merit Ltr; Lavlea Tri-Hi-Y Clb Histrn, Sgt At Arms; Amnesty Action, Amnesty Intl; Stu Reltns Cmmtte; CA ST U Los Angeles; Engl.

REEDY, JAMIE; Palmdale HS; Acton, CA; (2); 116/900; FFA; Ski Clb; JV Bsbl; Pres Acad Fit Awd; Engr.

REEK, NICOLE; Oakmont HS; Danville, CA; (1); Drama Clb; Trk; San Francisco ST; Jrnlsm.

REEL, KIN-MING; Claremont HS; Claremont, CA; (2); Drill Tm; Variety Show; Occidental Coll.

REEM, ADENA M; El Dorado HS; Placerville, CA; (2); JV Tennis; Hon Roll; CSF; Molecular Bio.

REEN, AMIKJIT S; Mission San Hose HS; Fremont, CA; (3); Cmnty Wkr; Math Clb; Science Clb; Spanish Clb; Tennis; Hon Roll; Hnrs In Chemathon; Med.

REEP, RICHARD W; Apple Valley HS; Apple Valley, CA; (1); 46/435; Drama Clb; Thesps; Band; Mrchg Band; Orch; Pep Band; Stage Crew; Hon Roll; Ed.

REES, JENNIE; Foothill HS; Pleasanton, CA; (3); 45/292; Teachers Aide; Var Socr; Var Tennis; Santa Barbara; Commnctns.

REES-PARKER, TANISHA M; Moreau HS; Fremont, CA; (4); Church Yth Grp; SADD; Rep Frsh Cls; Pres Soph Cls; Rep Jr Cls; Rep Sr Cls; L Stu Cncl; High Hon Roll; NHS; Pres Acad Fit Awd; Black Hstry Month Yth Awd 88-89; Princpls Awd 90; Stu Govt Svc Awd 87 & 90; San Francisco ST U; Mech Engrn.

REESE, CHRIS M; John Wesley North HS; Riverside, CA; (4); Cmnty Wkr; Teachers Aide; School Play; Stage Crew; Wt Lftg; Hon Roll; RCC.

REESE, JENNIFER L; Oxnard HS; Oxnard, CA; (2); #14 In Class; Church Yth Grp; Cmnty Wkr; Hon Roll; California Scholarship Federation; After School Job; Church Activist; CA Poly Tech U; Elem Schl Tchr.

REESE, JERALYN; Polytechnic HS; Pasadena, CA; (1); Band; Chorus; Orch; High Hon Roll; Pres Acad Fit Awd.

REESE, JOHN G; Irvine HS; Irvine, CA; (2); Ski Clb; Var JV Ftbl; Vllybl; Var Wt Lftg; UC Santa Barbara; Liberal Arts.

REESE, KRISTI; Kingsburg HS; Kingsburg, CA; (2); FFA; Hon Roll; Fresno ST U; Doctor.

REESE, MARK A; Dos Palos HS; Dos Palos, CA; (2); AFS; Boy Scts; Letterman Clb; Teachers Aide; Varsity Clb; Band; Jazz Band; Mrchg Band; Pep Band; Var Bsbl; U Of SC; Lwyr.

REESE, MARY JANE; Lemoore HS; Nas Lemoore, CA; (2); FHA; JV Crs Cntry; Cit Awd; Hon Roll; UCLA; Bus.

REESE, MICHAEL; South San Francisco HS; South San Francis, CA; (3); French Clb; Band; Var Bsbl; Var JV Bsktbl; Var Ftbl; San Jose ST; Bus Admin.

REESE, ROGER D; Selma HS; Selma, CA; (4); 5/194; Computer Clb; FTA; Teachers Aide; Sec Lit Mag; High Hon Roll; Prfct Atten Awd; Outstndng Awd 87-88; Gldn St Exm Geom Hnrs 88; CSF 87-90; CSU Fresno; Comp Sci.

REESE, STACEY L; Fairfax HS; Hollywood, CA; (3); NFL; Speech Tm; VP Lit Mag; Hon Roll; Acad Decthln Tm 90; UC Santa Cruz.

REESE, WILLIAM T; Fontana HS; Fontana, CA; (3); 37/1026; Am Leg Boys St; Church Yth Grp; Stu Cncl; Var Bsbl; Var Ftbl; Wrstlng; High Hon Roll; NHS; Ntl Merit Ltr; Pres Acad Fit Awd; Naval Arch.

REEVE, JOY; Yosemite Union HS; Oakhurst, CA; (2); Church Yth Grp; Service Clb; Rptr Yrbk; Hon Roll; PRIDE; MAUI; UCLA; Jrnlst.

REEVE, SARA J; James Lick HS; San Jose, CA; (1); Drama Clb; School Play; Hon Roll; Jobs Dghtrs Mscnc Grls Grp; Ballet, Tap & Jzz Dnc; Teach Ballt; UCLA; Actrss.

REEVES, ANTAUNE T; St Anthonys HS; Long Beach, CA; (2); Church Yth Grp; Cmnty Wkr; SADD; JV Bsbl; Var Bsktbl; Wt Lftg.

REEVES, CHRISTY N; Turlock HS; Turlock, CA; (1); Church Yth Grp; Hon Roll; CA ST U Stanislaus; Vet.

REEVES, JEREMY; Escalon HS; Escalon, CA; (3); 9/123; German Clb; Key Clb; Treas Frsh Cls; Capt Bsktbl; Ftbl; Powder Puff Ftbl; Trk; Hon Roll; CA Schlstc Fed VP; Schlr Athl Awd 3 Yrs; Comp Engrng.

REEVES, KIMBERLY; North Salinas HS; Salinas, CA; (3); Art Clb; Drama Clb; Pres French Clb; SADD; Thesps; School Play; Var Trk; Cit Awd; High Hon Roll; Hon Roll; Top 100 Stu; Lwyr.

REEVES, KRISTIE B; Oak Ridge HS; El Dorado Hills, CA; (1); Dance Clb; Drill Tm; JV Cheerldng; Cit Awd; Davis; Bio.

REEVES, MALINDA; East Union HS; Manteca, CA; (2); Sec Church Yth Grp; French Clb; Pep Clb; SADD; Band; Church Choir; Mrchg Band; Pep Band; Treas Band Cncl; Fresno ST U; Music.

REEVES, MARI K; Chaminade HS; Simi Valley, CA; (4); Drama Clb; Letterman Clb; Varsity Clb; School Musical; Stage Crew; Yrbk; Lit Mag; Off Jr Cls; Off Sr Cls; Stat Bsktbl; CSF Gold Seal Bearer; U CA Berkeley Ulumni Schlrshp; US Insti Peace Essy Cntst; U CA Berkeley; Poli Ecnmy.

REEVES, STACY; Lindsay HS; Lindsay, CA; (3); GAA; Teachers Aide; JV Vllybl; Hon Roll; Prfct Atten Awd; Golden ST Bus Coll; Crt Rptr.

REGALA, JAY J; Diamond Bar HS; Diamond Bar, CA; (1); Acpl Chr; Chorus; Jazz Band; School Musical; Cit Awd; Hon Roll; GATE Stu; Law.

REGALADO, GUILLERMO; Alisal HS; Salinas, CA; (2); Computer Clb; Drama Clb; Latin Clb; Math Clb; Bsktbl; Swmmng; Tennis; Vllybl; Hon Roll; Hartnell Coll; Arch.

REGALADO JR, MANUEL; Damien HS; Ontario, CA; (4); 57/188; Church Yth Grp; SADD; Hon Roll; Pres Acad Fit Awd; Medcl.

REGAN, ALAN; Garceo Memorial HS; Bakersfield, CA; (4); 7/118; Sec Treas Computer Clb; JA; Science Clb; Ed Lit Mag; High Hon Roll; Hon Roll; Chldrn Of Amer Rvltn; Spc Adac; Trvl Clb; Bus.

REGAN, LAURIE A; Glendora HS; Glendora, CA; (4); 5/375; Church Yth Grp; Color Guard; Yrbk; Bsktbl; L Crs Cntry; Trk; Hon Roll; Am Legion Honrble Mentn; Acdmic Decathlon; Lions Cl Spch Cntst Winner; U C Santa Barbara; Engls Major.

REGAN, SEAN P; Foothill HS; Santa Ana, CA; (2); Church Yth Grp; Chorus; Var Ftbl; Var Wt Lftg; High Hon Roll; Order Of Night Awd; Perfct Attndnc; Hnr Roll.

REGE, ANJALI A; Irvine HS; Irvine, CA; (2); Orange Cty Acadmc Dcthln; Stu For Scl Respnsblty Club; Med.

REGELE, DANIELA M; Del Campo HS; Carmichael, CA; (3); Church Yth Grp; JA; Office Aide; Ski Clb; SADD; Chorus; Cheerldng; Swmmng; UC Davis; Equine Genetics.

REGIS, MARY; Fontana HS; Fontana, CA; (2); Aud/Vis; Color Guard; Ed School Musical; Hon Roll; Pres Acad Fit Awd; Achvt Awd 89-90; Trphy Outstndg Alg 88-89; Scripps Inst Of Oceanography.

REGISTER, JENNIFER C; Lowell HS; San Francisco, CA; (3); Treas SADD; Chorus; School Musical; Rep Stu Cncl; Yth Ambssdr-Exchng Pgm Israel; Israeli Cltr Clb; U Of CA; Intl Bus.

REGISTER, KIMBERLY J; Del Campo HS; Fair Oaks, CA; (3); Church Yth Grp; French Clb; Treas Soph Cls; Treas Sr Cls; CSF; MESA; Jack & Jill Of Amer; Bus.

REGLER, DEBRA S; Shafter HS; Shafter, CA; (3); 1/220; VP Church Yth Grp; Cmnty Wkr; Treas FHA; Library Aide; Math Clb; Pres VP SADD; Church Choir; Tennis; Bausch & Lomb Sci Awd; High Hon Roll; Bible Clb Teacher; Peer Cnslg; Biola U; Med.

REGLI, DUANE; Poway HS; Poway, CA; (3); ROTC; Tennis; Cit Awd; High Hon Roll; Hon Roll; Med.

REGNANI, CHRISTINA R; Trinity HS; Weaverville, CA; (2); Drama Clb; Ski Clb; Yrbk; Pres Frsh Cls; VP Jr Cls; VP Stu Cncl; Var JV Cheerldng; JV Sftbl; Hon Roll; Shasta Coll; Arch Dsgn.

REGO, LAURA M; Riverdale HS; Riverdale, CA; (3); 4-H; FFA; Ski Clb; Spanish Clb; SADD; Teachers Aide; Off Yrbk; Var Score Keeper; High Hon Roll; EMT Explorer; Kings River CC; Horticltr.

REGOLI, NATALIE L; Atascadero HS; Atascadero, CA; (2); Cmnty Wkr; Key Clb; Sec SADD; Flag Corp; Mrchg Band; School Play; Score Keeper; JV Socr; Var Swmmng; High Hon Roll; Set Schl Swmmng Rcrd 200 Medley Relay 88-89; CA Mathmtcs Leag 89; Berkley; Med.

REGONAY, ROWENA; Notre Dame HS; Salinas, CA; (4); Church Yth Grp; Computer Clb; Drama Clb; Spanish Clb; Speech Tm; SADD; Church Choir; School Musical; Yrbk; High Hon Roll; Bank Of Amer Cert Of Achvt In Soc Stds; CSF; Engl, Hstry & Sci Hnrs; St Marys Coll; Commnctns.

REHANA, MICKIE; Turlock HS; Turlock, CA; (3); 193/700; Church Yth Grp; Cmnty Wkr; Teachers Aide; Church Choir; Sun Schl Tchr; Teen Line Vlntr; Elem Ed.

REHN, RANDY C; North Salinas HS; Salinas, CA; (2); High Hon Roll; Rotary Awd.

REICH, ASHLEY J; Camarillo HS; Camarillo, CA; (4); Drama Clb; Lit Mag; Stu Cncl; Cit Awd; Hon Roll; Sonoma ST U; Commnctns.

REICHENBACH, ANDREA J; Las Plumas HS; Oroville, CA; (2); #22 In Class; Church Yth Grp; French Clb; Hon Roll; Pres Acad Fit Awd; Pres Schlr; Spcl Schl Handicappd Chldrn Vlntr; UC Berkeley; Phys Thrpy.

REICHERT, JEANELL C; Hemet HS; Idyllwild, CA; (2); Church Yth Grp; 4-H; Sftbl; Cit Awd; 4-H Awd; Teacher.

REID, CAMERON A; Garces Memorial HS; Bakersfield, CA; (3); Cmnty Wkr; Letterman Clb; SADD; Var Bsktbl; JV Trk; Hon Roll; Peer Cnslng; Campus Mnstry; Bus.

REID, CRYSTAL M; Mira Costa HS; Manhattan Beach, CA; (3); Intnl Clb; Quiz Bowl; Service Clb; Stu Cncl; Hon Roll; Word Proc Degr Comp Oper 88; Oscar Awds; Excllnc Phys Educ; Loyola Marymount U; TV Prdctn.

REID, ERIN; Paradise HS; Magalia, CA; (2); Thesps; School Musical; School Play; Stage Crew; Theatre.

REID, GLEN; Yosemite HS; Oakhurst, CA; (3); Church Yth Grp; Letterman Clb; Ski Clb; Varsity Clb; Nwsp; JV Var Bsbl; JV Var Ftbl; UCSB; CPA.

REID, GWENDENECE; Hamilton HS; Los Angeles, CA; (4); Church Yth Grp; Cmnty Wkr; Service Clb; Spanish Clb; Church Choir; Kiwanis Awd; Yng Black Schlr; Northridge; Psych.

REID, HEATHER; Silver Valley HS; Newberry Spgs, CA; (4); 2/74; Church Yth Grp; Key Clb; Letterman Clb; Office Aide; SADD; Teachers Aide; Yrbk; Var Cheerldng; Powder Puff Ftbl; High Hon Roll; Wtrski Clb; Acad All Armcn Schlr; NE LA U; Bus Mngmnt.

REID, KATHRYN; San Marcos HS; San Marcos, CA; (3); JCL; Key Clb; Scholastic Bowl; Yrbk; Socr; High Hon Roll; NHS.

REID, KRISTIE; Serrano HS; Pinon Hills, CA; (1); FBLA; Drill Tm; Hon Roll; Santa Clara; Phys Thrpy.

REID, MALIA A; Skyline HS; Oakland, CA; (2); Church Yth Grp; Office Aide; SADD; High Hon Roll; Hon Roll; NHS; Comp Intro Awd Of Excl; CA Jr Schlstc Fed; U HI; Zoology.

REID, MARLETT R; Luther Burbank HS; Sacramento, CA; (2); Band; Church Choir; Mrchg Band; Pep Band; Stage Crew; JV Trk; UC Davis; Tchr.

REID, MATTHEW J; El Camino HS; Sacramento, CA; (3); 34/366; Church Yth Grp; Ski Clb; School Musical; Var Trk; High Hon Roll; Piano; Actvts.

REID, NATHANAEL DAVID; Lindsay HS; Lindsay, CA; (2); Church Yth Grp; Cmnty Wkr; FCA; SADD; Church Choir; JV Var Bsbl; JV Var Bsktbl; High Hon Roll; Amer Lgn Essay Awd; HOBY; All-Star Bsbl Team; Stanford; Sprts Med.

REID, ZEVIT S; Montclair HS; Montclair, CA; (2); Teachers Aide; Band; Mrchg Band; Pep Band; School Play; Stat Bsktbl; Stat Ftbl; JV L Sftbl; Sports Law.

REIDER, SCOTT A; Lassen Union HS; Susanville, CA; (3); 14/228; Bausch & Lomb Sci Awd; High Hon Roll; Hon Roll; CSF; U Of CA Berkely; Acctg.

REILLY, CHRISTINE M; St Joseph HS; Cerritos, CA; (2); 9/200; Cmnty Wkr; GAA; Var Bsktbl; Hon Roll; CSF Stu; 1st Pl & 2nd Pl Schl Awd For Natl Math League In Alg & Geom; Long Beach ST U; Sci.

REILLY, JEANNE; St Patrick-St Vincent HS; Benicia, CA; (4); 3/148; Science Clb; SADD; Teachers Aide; JV Bsktbl; Var Socr; Var Tennis; High Hon Roll; Math Tutor; Co-MVP Vsty Tnns 89; 1st Pl Wmns Sngls Tnns; Santa Clara U; Cvl Engrng.

REILLY, MICHELLE A; California HS; Whittier, CA; (3); Church Yth Grp; Cmnty Wkr; Letterman Clb; SADD; Teachers Aide; Varsity Clb; School Musical; Rep Soph Cls; Rep Jr Cls; Rep Sr Cls; Blue & Gold Hons Soc 2 Yrs; Hons Alg & Geo Golden St Exam; Bus.

REILLY, SONYA C; Santa Clara HS; Camarillo, CA; (2); Church Yth Grp; Swmmng; Hon Roll; Bus.

REIMANN, JANINE A; Imperial HS; Arcadia, CA; (2); Church Yth Grp; Speech Tm; Chorus; Church Choir; School Musical; Trk; Hon Roll; Chrch Actvts; Cosmetology.

REIMER, PAUL N; Fresno Christian HS; Fresno, CA; (2); Church Yth Grp; Letterman Clb; Acpl Chr; Var L Bsbl; JV Bsktbl; JV Ftbl; Var L Socr; Var L Tennis; Cit Awd; High Hon Roll.

REINA, INGRID C; California HS; Whittier, CA; (4); French Clb; Latin Clb; Red Cross Aide; Spanish Clb; Cit Awd; Pres Acad Fit Awd; Spanish NHS; Bank Of Amer Achvt Awd; Fullerton Coll; Law.

REINDEL, ANDY; A A Stagg HS; Stockton, CA; (2); Ski Clb; Bsbl; Cheerldng; Ftbl; Wt Lftg; Wrstlng; Delta; Pro Golfer.

REINECKER, JAMES G; Northview HS; Covina, CA; (3); Church Yth Grp; Treas Soph Cls; Var Bsbl; Intrml Bsktbl; Var Ftbl; Hon Roll; Karate; Sccr Recrtnl; Criminal Justice.

REINER, ALISAHN G; Carson HS; Carson, CA; (2); Latin Clb; Teachers Aide; Drill Tm; Capt Flag Corp; Stu Cncl; Var Crs Cntry; Var Trk; Med.

REINER, NANCY; Ernest Righetti HS; Santa Maria, CA; (3); 10/450; Treas Church Yth Grp; Cmnty Wkr; Band; Mrchg Band; Var Socr; High Hon Roll; Deans List; CSF; Interact Clb; Cal Poly SLO; CPA.

REINER, ROBERT J; Grossmont Union HS; El Cajon, CA; (1); Church Yth Grp; Band; Mrchg Band; Orch; Pep Band; Hon Roll; Acctng.

REINESTO, DENA B; San Marcos HS; Santa Barbara, CA; (2); Key Clb; Drill Tm; JV Sftbl; High Hon Roll; NHS; Acctng.

REINHARDT, DANIELLE C; Enterprise HS; Redding, CA; (3); 162/450; Rptr Yrbk; Score Keeper; JV Vllybl; Pres Acad Fit Awd; Sacramento ST Coll; Psych.

REINHARDT, TED A; North Tahoe HS; Tahoe City, CA; (1); 11/114; JV Var Bsbl; JV Bsktbl; JV Ftbl; Hon Roll; Phys Thrpy.

REINHEIMER, BETSY L; Tunipero Serra HS; San Diego, CA; (2); 36/460; Church Yth Grp; Pep Clb; Ski Clb; Drill Tm; Off Stu Cncl; Var Cheerldng; Hon Roll; Piano; Dance; Awd Outstanding Achievement In English; Law.

REINING, MATTHEW T; Loyola HS; Northridge, CA; (1); Boy Scts; Church Yth Grp; Computer Clb; L Trk; High Hon Roll; Soccer Team Club; Fantasy Role Plyng Club; Piano Recitals.

REINKE, ALLEN J; Enterprise HS; Palo Cedro, CA; (3); 106/427; FFA; Math Clb; Mu Alpha Theta; Acpl Chr; Chorus; JV Bsbl; Intrml Bsktbl; Intrml JV Ftbl; Var Trk; Intrml JV Wt Lftg; NAL All Star Ftbl Tm; Choir VP; Law Enfrcmnt.

REINYS, EMILY; Poway HS; Poway, CA; (3); 23/763; Church Yth Grp; VP Key Clb; Varsity Clb; Rep Stu Cncl; Var L Crs Cntry; Var L Trk; High Hon Roll; NHS; Peer Cnslng, Shclr-Athlt Awd, Acad Tm; Fndrsng Chrmn Amnsty Intl; CA Schlrshp Fed All-Cif 1st Tm Crs; Biochem.

REIS, KRISTINA M; Westmoor HS; Pacifica, CA; (3); Church Yth Grp; Debate Tm; Office Aide; Service Clb; Teachers Aide; Stage Crew; Vllybl; Hon Roll; U CA Davis; Psych.

REIS, TERESA; Quartz Hill HS; Lancaster, CA; (3); 34/664; Key Clb; SADD; Capt Flag Corp; Nwsp; Yrbk; Hon Roll; CSF; Outstndng Flag 87-88; U Of The Pacific; Phys Thrpy.

REISEN, PHILLIP B; East Bakersfield HS; Bakersfield, CA; (1); Band; Mrchg Band; Pep Band; JV Bsbl; JV Socr; Hon Roll; Altar Svc; Drumline Bugle Corp.

REISING, KIMBERLY ANN; Sequoia HS; Redwood City, CA; (3); Church Yth Grp; Drama Clb; Girl Scts; Office Aide; SADD; Teachers Aide; Thesps; Stage Crew; Hon Roll; Sign Lang Clb; Chrch Plays, Musicals; Theater; Canada Coll; Psych.

REISINGER, KAREN A; Clayton Valley HS; Concord, CA; (2); Office Aide; Chorus; School Musical; Stage Crew; Hon Roll; CSF.

REISNER, MARK S; La Sierra HS; Riverside, CA; (3); Boy Scts; FCA; FFA; Ski Clb; Teachers Aide; Varsity Clb; VICA; Yrbk; Var Socr; Var Tennis; AZ ST U.

REIST, PHILLIP C; Fontana HS; Bloomington, CA; (2); Boy Scts; Computer Clb; Math Tm; SADD; Chorus; Wt Lftg; Wrstlng; Hon Roll; Blue Blt Martl Arts; AZ ST; Comp.

REITER, NATALIE; El Camino Real HS; West Hills, CA; (3); Church Yth Grp; Library Aide; Chorus; Rptr Yrbk; Sec Jr Cls; L Crs Cntry; Intrml Powder Puff Ftbl; JV L Vllybl; Cit Awd; Chrstn Ministry Outreach Peer Cnslng; Mexico Outreach; Young Grils Church Vllybl Coach; Psych.

REITH, SUSANNA D; Live Oak HS; Morgan Hill, CA; (3); VP French Clb; SADD; Orch; Ed Yrbk; High Hon Roll; Bllt; CSF; Physcs 1st Prz & Grnd Prz Altrnt Santa Clara Vlly Sci & Engrng Fr.

REITZ, GREG A; Huntington Beach HS; Huntington Beach, CA; (2); Ftbl; JV Vllybl; Wrstlng; Hon Roll; Cartooning; UCLA; Med.

RELUCIO, MICHAEL; Sweetwater HS; National City, CA; (3); Var Ftbl; Var Trk; SDSU; Phys Thrpst.

REMICK, CORY A; San Marcos HS; Goleta, CA; (3); Church Yth Grp; School Play; CA Poly; Elec Engrng.

REMICK, MELISSA R; Oakmont HS; Roseville, CA; (3); 24/398; Dance Clb; JV Swmmng; High Hon Roll; CSF; FNL VP/Pres; Media Outstndng Achvt Awd 89-90; Acad Mrt Awd; Cmmnctns.

REMLEY, CRAIG C; Valley View HS; Moreno Valley, CA; (2); Letterman Clb; Varsity Clb; Ftbl; Hon Roll; Karate Purple Belt; Vrsty Offensive Coaches Awd.

REMPFER, KIMBERLY K; Lodi HS; Lodi, CA; (2); 17/595; Church Yth Grp; Key Clb; Chorus; Church Choir; High Hon Roll; Hon Roll; Prfct Atten Awd; CSF; CA Music Edctrs Assn Hn R Choir; Friday Night Live Chptr; UC Santa Barbara; Chld Psych.

REMSON, MICHAEL B; Hayward HS; Hayward, CA; (3); Letterman Clb; Varsity Clb; Lit Mag; Var Ftbl; Hon Roll; UC Berkeley Partnrshp Pgm & Pre-Coll Acad; UC San Francisco Smmr Residncy; Med.

REMULLA, MELISSA A; St Bonaventure HS; Moorpark, CA; (3); Rptr Nwsp; Hist Stu Cncl; NHS; CA Schlrshp Fed; Jr Statesmen Of America; Vlntr Work.

REN, HU PING; Abraham Lincoln HS; San Francisco, CA; (3); Computer Clb; Math Clb; Science Clb; Church Choir; Vllybl; CSF; Golden St Exm Hgh Hnr Alg & Geom; U Of CA Berkeley; Med Lab Tech.

REN, HUPING; Abraham Lincoln HS; San Francisco, CA; (3); Computer Clb; Math Clb; Church Choir; CSF; High Hnr Alg Gldn St Exam 88; High Hnr Geom Gldn St Exam 89; U Of CA Berkeley; Medical Lab.

RENARD, JEFF; Notre Dame HS; Chico, CA; (1); Boy Scts; Church Yth Grp; Cmnty Wkr; Teachers Aide; Chorus; Church Choir; School Play; Pres Stu Cncl; Bsktbl; Score Keeper; Harvard U; Math.

RENDON, DALIA D; James Lick HS; San Jose, CA; (2); Sftbl; Vllybl.

RENDON, MICHAEL; St Francis HS; Arcadia, CA; (4); 9/121; Church Yth Grp; Hosp Aide; Letterman Clb; Math Clb; Math Tm; Mu Alpha Theta; Var Bsbl; Var Capt Socr; Hon Roll; NHS; UCLA; Medcl.

RENEAU, ANDRE G; East Bakersfield HS; Bakersfield, CA; (3); JV Ftbl; JV Trk; Intrml Wt Lftg; JV Wrstlng; Hon Roll; Pres Acad Fit Awd; CA ST; Law.

RENFRO, JENNIFER L; Winters HS; Winters, CA; (3); AFS; Church Yth Grp; Pep Clb; SADD; Chorus; Stat Var Trk; Hon Roll; Friday Night Live Publicity Head; AHSME Schl Winner; CA Schlrshp Fdrtn.

RENFROW, JOSHUA E; Patterson HS; Patterson, CA; (3); Church Yth Grp; Cmnty Wkr; Rptr FFA; VICA; Golf; Hon Roll; Archry Clb.

RENNER, KAREN M; Estancia HS; Costa Mesa, CA; (3); Am Leg Aux Girls St; Church Yth Grp; Key Clb; Pep Clb; Treas Sr Cls; Stu Cncl; Cheerldng; Tennis; Hon Roll; Pepperdine Yth Ctznshp Smnr; Pepperdine; Bus.

RENNICK, CHRISTY; Williams HS; Williams, CA; (2); 1/60; Church Yth Grp; Drama Clb; Spanish Clb; SADD; Band; Rep Stu Cncl; JV Bsktbl; Var Sftbl; JV Vllybl; High Hon Roll.

RENSHAW, MATT T; Santa Barbara HS; Santa Barbara, CA; (2); Church Yth Grp; Cmnty Wkr; Vllybl; Gldn St Alg Awd; All Amer Vllybl Jr Olympcs.

RENSLOW, MONIQUE; Liberty Union HS; Byron, CA; (2); 37/400; Church Yth Grp; Church Choir; Pres Soph Cls; Var Diving; Var Swmmng; Hon Roll; Brigham Young U.

RENTERIA, ADRIANA; John F Kennedy HS; Richmond, CA; (4); Latin Clb; Office Aide; Spanish Clb; Hon Roll; CA ST Hayward; Pediatrics.

RENTERIA, CYNTHIA; Saint Genevieve HS; North Hollywood, CA; (3); Chorus; Drill Tm; Yng Mens Inst Cert Achvt; CA ST U Northridge; Educ.

RENTERIA, HAYDEE; Holy Family HS; Los Angeles, CA; (2); Church Yth Grp; Drama Clb; Library Aide; School Play; Trk; Cert Of Apprctn For Library Aide; Cert In Achvt Engl; Optometrist.

RENTERIA, HENRY C; Dos Palos HS; Dos Palos, CA; (2); FFA; Ind Arts.

RENTERIA, HUMBERTO; Fontana HS; Fontana, CA; (2); Latin Clb; Spanish Clb; School Play; Off Soph Cls; Bsbl; Socr; Arch.

RENTERIA, JOHN H; Brawley Union HS; Brawley, CA; (1); Band; Drm Mjr(t); Orch; Pep Band; Crs Cntry; Trk; Prfct Atten Awd; Asstn Sound, Light Techn; Imperial Vally Coll; Elec Tech.

RENTERIA, LUI C; Alisal HS; Salinas, CA; (2); Yrbk; Off Frsh Cls; Hon Roll; Dr.

RENTERIA, MARIA E; Santiago HS; Garden Grove, CA; (2); French Clb; Cit Awd; Hon Roll; Vlntr For 1989-90 Cmpgn; EOPS Clb; UCLA; Bio.

RENTERIA, VALENTINE; Mc Farland HS; Mc Farland, CA; (3); FFA; SADD; Teachers Aide; VICA; Score Keeper; Tennis; Hon Roll; Photo Club; CA ST U; Bus.

RENTORIA, DAVID C; Southwest HS; San Diego, CA; (3); Church Yth Grp; Cmnty Wkr; Computer Clb; Teachers Aide; Yrbk; JV Ftbl; Nature Intrprtv Ctr Vlntr; US Cmndg Naval Air Pacific Air Trng Smmr Clrcl; SDC-JEA 1st Pl Yrbk Copy.

REORDAN, RICHRD L; Will C Wood HS; Vacaville, CA; (3); Church Yth Grp; FBLA; Bsktbl; Intrml Socr; Hon Roll; Jr NHS; NHS; Ntl Merit Schol; Sci Proj Comp; Chrstn Ldrshp Inst Yth Grp; Spts Thrgh Cmmty; Bus.

REOUNG, SANY; Hoover HS; Fresno, CA; (3); Art Clb; Bus Profs of Am; Cmnty Wkr; Computer Clb; French Clb; FTA; Library Aide; Math Clb; Teachers Aide; Hon Roll; Fshn Dsgnr.

REPOLA, SHANNON; Mira Costa HS; Manhattan Beach, CA; (2); Key Clb; Pep Clb; Drill Tm; JV Capt Cheerldng; Cit Awd; Hon Roll; Prfct Atten Awd; Hnrs Golden St Math Exam; UCSB.

REQUIRO, NOREEN; Morro Bay HS; Morro Bay, CA; (3); Art Clb; Dance Clb; FHA; Key Clb; Sftbl; High Hon Roll; Interested In Tailoring; Homemaking; Interior Design; Fashinon Merchandise And Realstate; Woodbury U; Fashion Merchandise.

RESCH, LORI E; Red Bluff Union HS; Paynes Creek, CA; (3); Hosp Aide; SADD; Rptr Nwsp; Hon Roll; Pres Schlr; Steerng Cmmtte; Nwsp Jnrlsm Awd 1st Pl Sprts Wrtng; Humboldt St U Awd 1st Pl On-Spt Sprts Wrtng; Santa Rosa JC; X-Ray Technlgst.

RESCHKE, RACHAEL L; Etiwanda HS; Alta Loma, CA; (1); Teachers Aide.

RESENDEZ, ADRIAN; Mc Farland HS; Mc Farland, CA; (3); FBLA; Stu Cncl; Var Bsktbl; JV Ftbl; Var Trk; JV Wt Lftg; Cmptr Elec.

RESENDEZ, CYNTHIA I; Fred C Beyer HS; Modesto, CA; (1); Hon Roll; Pres Acad Fit Awd; CA ST Hayward; Dermotology.

RESH, KERI; Patrick Henry HS; San Diego, CA; (2); Cmnty Wkr; Model UN; Temple Yth Grp; Nwsp; Yrbk; Treas Stu Cncl; JV Capt Cheerldng; Var Mgr(s); Cit Awd; High Hon Roll; Sci Fair 1st Pl; Sweepstakes Wnnr Talent Dance Cmptn; Ldrshp Camp.

RESHA, CHRIS D; Chino HS; Chino, CA; (2); Hon Roll; Slvr Spur Awd; JV Bdmntn; Achvt In Sci; Corp Law.

RESPICIO, EVANGELINE D; East Union HS; Lathrop, CA; (3); Teachers Aide; Hon Roll; Prfct Atten Awd; UC Davis; Radlgy.

RESSLER, JEFF; Tustin HS; Tustin, CA; (2); 1/489; Church Yth Grp; Quiz Bowl; VP Science Clb; Ed Rep Nwsp; Off Soph Cls; JV Bsktbl; High Hon Roll; NEDT Awd; St Schlr; Acad Decathlon Team Capt; Golden St Exam Awd Wnnr; Bus.

RESTO JR, JOSUE; Madera HS; Madera, CA; (2); Art Clb; Dance Clb; Office Aide; Santa Barbara; Elec Engrng.

RESTREPO, LUIS FELIPE; Will C Wood HS; Vacaville, CA; (1); Cmnty Wkr; Science Clb; Teachers Aide; Var JV Socr; High Hon Roll; Hon Roll; Teams USA; Chess Sci & Coach Yth Sccr; Med.

RESURRECCION, JOMIL P; Sunset HS; Hayward, CA; (2); Bsktbl; JV Var Tennis; Hon Roll; Sci.

RETAMOSA, MARCELLO E; Pius X HS; South Gate, CA; (3); Var Capt Ftbl; Wt Lftg; Hon Roll; Hghst GPA; Cal ST Long Beach; Comm.

RETELSDORF, ROBIN J; Colfax HS; Meadow Vista, CA; (3); 3/160; Church Yth Grp; Teachers Aide; Flag Corp; JV Cheerldng; High Hon Roll; Rgnl Occptnl Pgm Bnkng & Finance; Bus.

RETH, KHAN; Franklin HS; Stockton, CA; (4); 2/384; Cmnty Wkr; 4-H; Hosp Aide; Math Clb; Math Tm; Quiz Bowl; Science Clb; Teachers Aide; Var Socr; Var Vllybl; Pres Franklin Asian Club; UC Davis; Bio Sci.

RETH, LEAKHENA; Grace M Davis HS; Modesto, CA; (3); Art Clb; French Clb; Intnl Clb; Red Cross Aide; Rep Sr Cls; Bsktbl; Tennis; CA Schlr Fed; UC Davis; Bio.

RETHUAL, MARIO G; Lincoln Medical Magnet HS; Los Angeles, CA; (3); Math Tm; Scholastic Bowl; Science Clb; Rptr Nwsp; Phtg Yrbk; Rep Lit Mag; Sec Jr Cls; Tennis; Cit Awd; High Hon Roll; Pre-Med.

RETTIG, SCOTT A; Mission San Jose HS; Fremont, CA; (3); Boy Scts; Church Yth Grp; Letterman Clb; Science Clb; Var Swmmng; High Hnrs Golden St Math Exam Geom; UCLA; Engrng.

REUANGTHONGSAI, THAI; Herbert Hoover HS; San Diego, CA; (2); Church Yth Grp; Off Soph Cls; Cit Awd; Hon Roll; Christian Heritage Coll; Doc.

REUEL, JONATHAN G; San Marcos HS; Redding, CA; (3); Boy Scts; Church Yth Grp; Computer Clb; Band; Church Choir; Mrchg Band; Stage Crew; Rep Stu Cncl; Hon Roll; Achieved The Eagle Scout Award In Boy Scouts; BYU; Computers.

REULBACH, CARRIE H; El Camino Real HS; Woodland Hills, CA; (2); Var L Sftbl; Hon Roll; Law.

REUSCH, MARY C; Notre Dame HS; Hemet, CA; (1); Rptr Phtg Yrbk; Mgr(s); Stat Vllybl; High Hon Roll; CSF; U Of Notre Dame.

REUSCHEL, SUZETTE; Saint Francis HS; Saratoga, CA; (2); Debate Tm; Drama Clb; SADD; Chorus; Capt Color Guard; School Play; High Hon Roll; Hon Roll; Jr NHS; JSA; CSF; Amnesty Intl; Envrnmnt Clb; Peer Cnslng; Shakespeare Clb; Santa Clara U; Envrnmntl Law.

REUSS IV, WILLIAM M; West Valley HS; Cottonwood, CA; (4); 4/152; Church Yth Grp; Var Bsbl; Var Bsktbl; Var Ftbl; Var Trk; Var Wt Lftg; NHS; Pres Acad Fit Awd; Rcrd Srchlght Schlr Athlt Of The Yr; CA Lgsltv Sprts Awd For Outstndng Athlt; US Army Rsrv Schlr/Ath; U Of CA; Pre-Med.

REUTERSKIOLD, DAVID R; Cabrillo HS; Lompoc, CA; (3); 4/215; Am Leg Boys St; Boy Scts; Key Clb; Drm Mjr(t); Var Ftbl; Var Socr; Var Trk; SADD; Band; Jazz Band; Allan Hancock Coll Jazz Band; Natl Assn Of Jazz Edctrs Awd; CA Schlrshp Fed; CA Polytech St U; Arspc Engrng.

REVEL, CURTISE L; Chathsworth HS; Canoga Park, CA; (2); Chess Clb; Church Yth Grp; Debate Tm; SADD; Band; Mrchg Band; Cit Awd.

REVELES, DIANA E; Hueneme HS; Oxnard, CA; (1); Ventura Coll.

REVELES, ROSEMARY D; Channel Islands HS; Oxnard, CA; (2); JV Bsktbl; Var Sftbl; Hon Roll; Schlr Athlt; Chld Dvlpmnt.

REVELES, SAM; Saint Anthony HS; Wilmington, CA; (2); Spanish Clb; JV Trk; CSF; Loyola Marymount U; Comp Sci.

REVILLA, GABRIELLA F; Trabuco HS; Mission Viejo, CA; (2); Church Yth Grp; Dance Clb; Color Guard; Orch; Rptr Nwsp; Wnnr-Dance Cls; Orange Coast Jr Coll For A Day; USC; Jrnlsm.

REVILLA, KRISTINE; Montebello HS; Alhambra, CA; (3); Church Yth Grp; Drama Clb; French Clb; SADD; Band; Sec Sr Cls; Var Capt Cheerldng; Cit Awd; High Hon Roll; Prfct Atten Awd; Corp Law.

REVILLA, REX; Southwest HS; San Diego, CA; (3); 24/493; Key Clb; Band; Off Soph Cls; Off Jr Cls; JV Trk; Pan-Asian Clb; Assoc Stu Body; Awd Hgh Hnrs Gldn St Exam.

REX, KYLE T; Antelope Valley Union HS; Lancaster, CA; (4); Boy Scts; Church Yth Grp; FFA; Vllybl; Hon Roll; Pres Acad Fit Awd; Bnk Amer Achvt Awd; Cert Achvt Ag Hnr Awd; Eagle Sct; Ricks Coll; Engrng.

REX, RYAN G; Edison HS; Huntington Bch, CA; (4); 122/513; Ftbl; Trk; Pres Acad Fit Awd; Art Medallion & Plaque Wnnr; Trk/Field Events Of Yr; Visual Star Advanced Cert; Arts Schlrshp; Art Center Pasadena CA; Dsgn.

REXINGER, DOUG; Colton HS; Colton, CA; (2); VICA; Ftbl; Wrstlng; Hon Roll; NHS; Math.

REXROTH, JILL C; North HS; Bakersfield, CA; (2); Ski Clb; Varsity Clb; Pres Soph Cls; Pres Jr Cls; Vllybl; Hon Roll; NHS.

REY, VERNIETA; Glendora HS; Fontana, CA; (4); Church Yth Grp; Teachers Aide; Chorus; Church Choir; School Play; Ed Yrbk; VP Frsh Cls; VP Soph Cls; Var JV Vllybl; Hon Roll; TAMS; Vrsty Badmntn; Loma Linda U; Bus Mgmt.

REYBURN, ELIZABETH B; Merced Union HS; Merced, CA; (2); Church Yth Grp; Drama Clb; SADD; Band; Mrchg Band; Pep Band; School Musical; School Play; Stage Crew; Hon Roll; Speech Pathology.

REYBURN, ROBERT M; St Bongrenture HS; Thousand Oaks, CA; (3); 10/120; Ftbl; Golf; 1st Pl Physics Cnty Sci Fair; 2nd Team All League Golf; Engr.

REYELTS, MINDI L; Ramona HS; Ramona, CA; (3); Dance Clb; Drill Tm; Stu Of Mnth Engl & Hstry; Psych.

REYERSON, MARK K; Bellarmine HS; San Jose, CA; (3); Church Yth Grp; Intrml Mgr Bsktbl; Var L Ftbl; Intrml Mgr Sftbl; Var L Trk; Var L Wrstlng; Little Leag Bsbl Coach; Phrmcy.

REYES, ADRIANA L; Glendale HS; Glendale, CA; (2); Art Clb; Chorus; High Hon Roll; Hon Roll; NHS; Bio.

REYES, ANDREA F; Kerman HS; Kerman, CA; (2); 35/165; Church Yth Grp; Girl Scts; Band; JV Bsktbl; Var Swmmng; JV Vllybl; Fresno ST.

REYES, ANDREA M; Valley View HS; Moreno Valley, CA; (1); Church Yth Grp; Color Guard; Rptr Yrbk; JV Pom Pon; Songldr 90-91; U CA-SAN Diego; Atty.

REYES, ANGELA; Willits HS; Willits, CA; (1); Pep Clb; SADD; Nwsp; Cheerldng; Hon Roll; Frgn Exchng Stu-Australia 91; U CA Santa Barbara; Elem Tchr.

REYES, ANGELICA; Garfield HS; Los Angeles, CA; (3); French Clb; Stage Crew; Cit Awd; Prfct Atten Awd; Rotary Awd; Golklorico; CSF; Knights & Ladies; Bus Admin.

REYES, ARMANDO G; John C Fremont HS; Oakland, CA; (4); 1/357; AFS; Math Clb; Math Tm; ROTC; Color Guard; Ed Nwsp; High Hon Roll; Val; Close-Up; Marcus Foster Scholar Award; Home Savings Of American Scholarship Award; U C Davis; Chemistry.

REYES, BELINDA; Nogales HS; W Covina, CA; (2); Science Clb; Rptr Yrbk; Var Tennis; Hon Roll; Prfct Atten Awd; JV Badminton; NISA; Peer Hlpng; CSF.

REYES, DANA-MARIE; Immaculate Heart HS; Los Angeles, CA; (4); Math Clb; Mu Alpha Theta; Science Clb; High Hon Roll; Hon Roll; NEDT Awd; Bnk Amer Frgn Lang Cert; CSF Sealbearer; U Irvine; Biological Sci.

REYES, DAVID; John Glenn HS; Norwalk, CA; (3); Math Clb; Prfct Atten Awd; UCLA; Comp Pgmng.

REYES, DENISE P; St Patricks-St Vincents HS; Vallejo, CA; (1); JV Co-Capt Cheerldng; High Hon Roll; Stat Wrstlng; Rnkd 5th Chptr Lvl Natl Frnch Test; CSF; Spirit Clb.

REYES, DIANA Q; Amos Alonzo Stagg HS; Stockton, CA; (1); Band; Jazz Band; Mrchg Band; Pep Band; Musician.

REYES, ELISA E; Lynwood HS; Lynwood, CA; (3); 40/800; Math Clb; Lit Mag; Cit Awd; Frnch Cls Rcgntn; St Francis Medcl Resrce Ctr Vlntr; UCLA; Psych.

REYES, ELODIA M; Porterville HS; Porterville, CA; (3); Church Yth Grp; Spanish Clb; Var Socr; JV Sftbl; Hon Roll; Outstndg Vol Svc Cert Of Appreciation; CAP 7entor Leader; Missionary To Jamaica; Intnl Rltns.

REYES, FAVIOLA; North Hollywood HS; North Hollywood, CA; (3); Hosp Aide; US Marines; Law Enfrcmnt.

REYES, GABRIEL A; Bishop Amat HS; S El Monte, CA; (1); Hon Roll; S El Monte Bsbl; Schl Slvr Scrn Clb; Bus.

REYES, ILIANA; Bonita Vista HS; National City, CA; (4); Church Yth Grp; Cmnty Wkr; Drama Clb; Intnl Clb; Latin Clb; Office Aide; Teachers Aide; Variety Show; High Hon Roll; Hon Roll; Modeling Clb; UCSD; Commnctns.

REYES, IVANA; Montebello HS; Pico Rivera, CA; (1); Chorus; Prfct Atten Awd; UCLA.

REYES, JENNIFER G; Pinole Valley HS; Hercules, CA; (3); Yrbk; Hon Roll; Dancing Jazz; San Francisco ST; Nrsng.

REYES, KRIS J; Santa Cruz HS; Santa Cruz, CA; (2); Ski Clb; Band; Mrchg Band; Orch; Pep Band; JV Socr; JV Vllybl; Hon Roll; CA Schlrshp Fed; Cntrl Coast Sec Hnr Band; Phys Thrpy.

REYES, LUCINDA M; Lakewood HS; Long Beach, CA; (3); Cmnty Wkr; Debate Tm; Office Aide; Spanish Clb; Speech Tm; Teachers Aide; Var Capt Crs Cntry; Var Capt Trk; Cit Awd; DAR Awd; Outstndng Stu Writer CSULB & Kaleidoscope 89; CA Lgsltv Sprts Awd Lakewood Hall Of Fame Cross Cntry; Scndry Ed.

REYES, LUIS A; Fountain Valley HS; Fountain Valley, CA; (2); Sec Boy Scts; Pres JA; Band; Jazz Band; Mrchg Band; Pep Band; School Musical; Hmnts Orgnztn; European Hist Trp Europe; UCLA; Bus.

REYES, MANUEL; Ernest Righetti HS; Guadalupe, CA; (1); CA Poly.

REYES, MANUEL A; John F Kennedy HS; La Palma, CA; (1); UCLA; Comp Engrng.

REYES, MARGARET T; Sacred Heart Of Jesus HS; Los Angeles, CA; (3); Library Aide; Service Clb; School Play; Trk; High Hon Roll; NHS; Swm Tm; Med.

REYES, MARIA; Sweetwater HS; National City, CA; (2); 117/481; San Diego Cty Coll; Psych.

REYES, MARIA V; Duncan Poly Tech; Fresno, CA; (1); Nwsp; Off Frsh Cls; Bsbl; Bsktbl; Socr; Sftbl; Trk; Cit Awd; Hon Roll; Pres Acad Fit Awd; Psych.

REYES, MARIA V; Indio HS; Bermuda Dunes, CA; (2); 17/551; Outsndng Phy Ed; Acad Excllnc; CA Schlrshp Fed Actvty; Early Outreach Actvt; Riverside U; Doctor.

REYES, MELANIE F; Pinole Valley HS; Pinole, CA; (1); Spanish Clb; School Musical; School Play; CSF.

REYES, MEREDITH A; James Logan HS; Union City, CA; (3); Art Clb; Church Yth Grp; Cmnty Wkr; Powder Puff Ftbl; Mount St Marys; Nrsng.

REYES, MICHELE; Palm Springs HS; Palm Springs, CA; (3); Drama Clb; French Clb; Phtg Yrbk; Natl Frnch Exm; Awds Mrt; U Of CA San Diego; Psych.

REYES, MICHELLE; Montgomery HS; San Diego, CA; (3); 4/498; Church Yth Grp; English Clb; Intnl Clb; Pep Clb; Science Clb; Flag Corp; Rep Frsh Cls; Rep Soph Cls; Rep Jr Cls; Stat Ftbl; Schlrshp Awd; Assoc Stu Body Asst Comssnr To Finance; Letterettes; U San Diego; Bus Admin.

REYES, MICHELLE M; St Genevieve HS; North Hollywood, CA; (2); Dance Clb; Band; Drill Tm; Hon Roll; Children Vlntr Work; UCSD; Pediatrician.

REYES, MIKE; William C Overfelt HS; San Jose, CA; (2); Marines; Law Enforcement.

REYES, NORA G; Oxnard HS; Oxnard, CA; (1); Art Clb; Chorus; Bus.

REYES, OLGA; Garfield HS; Los Angeles, CA; (2); Math Tm; Band; Mrchg Band; Orch; Rep Frsh Cls; Rep Soph Cls; Rep Stu Cncl; JV Gym; Cit Awd; High Hon Roll; Yale U; Law.

REYES, PATRICIA; Montebello & Mark Keppel HS; West Coving, CA; (4); Hosp Aide; Teachers Aide; Chorus; Drill Tm; Vllybl; Cit Awd; Most Imprvd Drill Tm; Mt Sack; Law Enfrcmnt.

REYES, PAUL L; Arlington HS; Riverside, CA; (3); FBLA; Hosp Aide; Var Tennis; Hon Roll; Chapman Coll; Med.

REYES, RITA F; Mercy HS; Daly City, CA; (2); School Musical; Rep Stu Cncl; Hon Roll; Prfct Atten Awd; Photo Club Pres; Taught Chldrn Swimming Vol; Med.

REYES, ROSANNE; Hueneme HS; Oxnard, CA; (1); 115/622; Var L Crs Cntry; JV Trk; Future Ldrs Of Amer; Most Dedicated Runnr JV Track; U Of CA Santa Barbara; Jrnlsm.

REYES, SERGIO; El Dorado HS; Placentia, CA; (1); Band; Swmmng; Hon Roll; Prfct Atten Awd.

REYES, SHERRY A; Lincoln HS; Lincoln, CA; (1); Pep Clb; Drill Tm; Yrbk; Air Force.

REYES, STEPHANIE; El Dorado HS; Placentia, CA; (3); Intnl Clb; Pep Clb; Spanish Clb; Varsity Clb; Cheerldng; Pom Pon; Sftbl; Ecology Club.

REYES, STEPHANIE CHRISTINE L; Immaculate Heart HS; Los Angeles, CA; (3); 36/112; Ed Yrbk; Rep Soph Cls; Rep Jr Cls; Hon Roll; CSF; Outstndng Achvt Engl; Grls Athltc Assoc; Loyola Marymount U; Law.

REYES, SUSAN M; Hamilton HS; Los Angeles, CA; (2); Rep Soph Cls; Phy.

REYES, VERONICA; Chula Vista HS; San Ysidro, CA; (3); Spanish Clb.

REYES, VILCIA N; Woodside HS; Redwood City, CA; (2); Drama Clb; Teachers Aide; Mrchg Band; School Play; Variety Show; Cit Awd; High Hon Roll; Hon Roll; Prfct Atten Awd; Pres Acad Fit Awd; Wellesley Coll; News Brdcstng.

REYES RODRIGUEZ, FRANCISCO A; Fresno HS; Fresno, CA; (2); JV Crs Cntry; JV Trk; Bwlng Lg; Fresno ST; Marine Bio.

REYNA, KAREN JEAN; Archbishop Mitty HS; San Jose, CA; (3); 98/250; Church Yth Grp; Cmnty Wkr; VP SADD; JV Fld Hcky; Stat Socr; High Hon Roll; Hon Roll; Excllnc In Relgn & Art I & II; Adv.

REYNAGA, CARLOS E; Oakland Technical HS; Oakland, CA; (1); Capt Var Crs Cntry; Var Wrstlng; Hon Roll; Capt Crss Cntry Tm; Sports; Med.

REYNAGA, MARCUS; Bishop Montgomery HS; Torrance, CA; (2); Drama Clb; Thesps; School Play; Variety Show; Rptr Nwsp; Socr; Cit Awd; French Hon Soc; Hon Roll; Hispanic Cultrl Clb VP; UCLA; Prfrmng Arts.

REYNAGA, REBECCA L; Elk Grove HS; Elk Grove, CA; (3); Art Clb; Band; School Play; Trk; Envrnmnt; Ecology.

REYNANTE, JOCELYN O; Channel Islands HS; Oxnard, CA; (3); FBLA; Intnl Clb; Teachers Aide; Yrbk; Hon Roll; Prfct Atten Awd; CA Schlrshp Fed; Art; Nrsng Phy Asst.

REYNICK, KIMBERLY A; Woodside HS; Redwood City, CA; (2); Cmnty Wkr; GAA; Letterman Clb; Off Frsh Cls; Treas Jr Cls; Var Capt Socr; Var Sftbl; JV Vllybl; High Hon Roll; CSF; Outstndng Acad Achvt Frgn Lang Spansh; Schlr Athl Awds; Prfct Atten; Distngshd Stu Soc.

REYNO, GAREY; Bishop Montgomery HS; Carson, CA; (1); Intrml Bsktbl; JV Ftbl; Piano; UCLA; Bus Admin.

REYNOLDS, AMBER D; Thomas Downey HS; Modesto, CA; (1); Pep Clb; Speech Tm; Orch; Cheerldng; Pom Pon; Hon Roll; Law.

REYNOLDS, ANGELA D; Beaumont HS; Cherry Valley, CA; (3); Church Yth Grp; Teachers Aide; Stu Cncl; Prfct Atten Awd; 2nd Pl Rbbn Wnnr Dist Sci Fair; FIDM.

REYNOLDS, ASHAKI; Campbell Hall HS; Van Nuys, CA; (3); French Clb; Girl Scts; SADD; VP Jr Cls; Rep Stu Cncl; Capt Stat Bsktbl; Var Pom Pon; JV Tennis; High Hon Roll; Hon Roll; CSF; Highlanders Svc Clb; Spellman U; Med.

REYNOLDS, BONNIE J; Venice HS; Los Angeles, CA; (3); Church Yth Grp; Church Choir; Ed Nwsp; Phtg Yrbk; Rep Stu Cncl; JV Crs Cntry; Tennis; JV Trk; Prfct Atten Awd; Peace Clb; Brigham Young U; Bus.

REYNOLDS, BRIAN S; William Howard Taft HS; Woodland Hills, CA; (3); Office Aide; Ski Clb; Rep Frsh Cls; Rep Soph Cls; Hon Roll.

REYNOLDS, DANIEL J; Hesperia HS; Hesperia, CA; (3); Spanish Clb; Hon Roll; Art; Span; Graphic Art.

REYNOLDS, DARVA; Hayward HS; Hayward, CA; (3); 39/237; Church Yth Grp; Spanish Clb; Church Choir; Hon Roll; Black Stu Union Clb; Partnrshp Prog; Spellman U; Comp Engr.

REYNOLDS, DAVID S; North HS; Bakersfield, CA; (3); 19/346; Church Yth Grp; Letterman Clb; Spanish Clb; Chorus; Church Choir; School Musical; Ftbl; Trk; Hon Roll; NHS; Star Awd 2 Times; Engrng.

REYNOLDS, DEANNA J; Morningside HS; Inglewood, CA; (1); Band; JV Bsktbl; Cit Awd; Hon Roll; Surgeon.

REYNOLDS, DEANNE E; Kerman HS; Fresno, CA; (3); German Clb; Teachers Aide; Chorus; Yrbk; Var JV Cheerldng; Hon Roll; CSF; Fresno ST; Med.

REYNOLDS, DEBRA J; Redwood Christian HS; Castro Valley, CA; (3); Drama Clb; Spanish Clb; Speech Tm; Teachers Aide; School Musical; School Play; Yrbk; VP Frsh Cls; High Hon Roll; Ntl Merit Ltr; CSF; ACSI Spch Meet 2nd Pl Upper Div 90; Vet.

REYNOLDS, EVELYN; Southbay Christian HS; Mountain View, CA; (2); Church Yth Grp; Spanish Clb; VP Frsh Cls; Rep Soph Cls; Rep Stu Cncl; Var Bsktbl; Cit Awd.

REYNOLDS, HEATHER E; River City HS; W Sacramento, CA; (1); Church Yth Grp; Drama Clb; Thesps; Stage Crew; Pres Frsh Cls; Pres Soph Cls; Cheerldng; Sftbl; Vllybl; Hon Roll; Friday Night Live Clb; Mock Trial Clb; Jobs Dghtrs; Stanford U; Crmnl Jstce.

REYNOLDS, J JANETTE; Patrick Henry HS; San Diego, CA; (3); Church Yth Grp; Band; Jazz Band; Mrchg Band; Orch; Pep Band; School Musical; Hon Roll; Med.

REYNOLDS, JAMES; North HS; Bakersfield, CA; (2); Spanish Clb; Teachers Aide; JV Ftbl; JV Trk; JV Wrstlng; Hon Roll; JV Ftbl Star, Coachs & Bst Schlr Awds; CA Polytechnic ST U; Engrng.

REYNOLDS, JAMES; South Tahoe HS; South Lake Tahoe, CA; (3); Boy Scts; Math Clb; Orch; Hon Roll; Friday Night Live; Acad Decathalon; Naval Acad Annapolis; Pilot.

REYNOLDS, JIM C; Irvine HS; Irvine, CA; (3); 8/500; Cmnty Wkr; Key Clb; Band; School Musical; School Play; VP Stu Cncl; Wrstlng; High Hon Roll; Kiwanis Awd; Ntl Merit SF; Law.

REYNOLDS, JOHN CHRISTOPHER; Arroyo Grande HS; Nipomo, CA; (2); Cit Awd; High Hon Roll; Hon Roll; Stu Rcgnt Awd Soc Stud.

REYNOLDS, KEITH P; Edison HS; Huntington Beach, CA; (3); Boy Scts; German Clb; Model UN; Teachers Aide; Stage Crew; U Of CA; Engrng.

REYNOLDS, KENNETH; Rosamond HS; Rosamond, CA; (1); Church Yth Grp; Math Tm; Band; Church Choir; Mrchg Band; Pep Band; Bsbl; Ftbl; Cit Awd; Hon Roll; Royal Rangers; Arch.

REYNOLDS, KEVIN; St Francis HS; La Canada, CA; (2); 1/180; Cmnty Wkr; Math Clb; Math Tm; Pep Clb; Spanish Clb; Tennis; High Hon Roll; NHS; Knight Life; Hall Of Fame; LMU; Elec Engr.

REYNOLDS, KRISTA; Orange Glen HS; Escondido, CA; (2); Dance Clb; JV Socr; Cosmetology.

REYNOLDS, KRISTIN M; Oak Ridge HS; Cameron Park, CA; (1); Art Clb; Church Yth Grp; Cmnty Wkr; Hosp Aide; Red Cross Aide; SADD; Church Choir; Hon Roll; FNL; Envrnmnt Club.

REYNOLDS, MADS; San Gorgonio HS; Highland, CA; (3); Boy Scts; Church Yth Grp; Computer Clb; French Clb; Band; Church Choir; Jazz Band; Mrchg Band; Brigham Young U; Elctrncl Engnr.

REYNOLDS, MIKE L; Hanford HS; Hanford, CA; (3); 17/500; Church Yth Grp; Drama Clb; High Hon Roll; Peer Counselor; CSF; Math Tutor; Interact Club; Bio.

REYNOLDS, ROBERT G; Rosamond HS; Rosamond, CA; (4); JV Bsbl; Var L Ftbl; Hon Roll; Adv.

REYNOLDS, SAMANTHA; La Sierra HS; Corona, CA; (1); Drill Tm; Pepperdine Coll; Lawyer.

REYNOLDS, SHARON L; San Lorenzo HS; San Lorenzo, CA; (2); JV Var Cheerldng; Hon Roll; Chobot Coll; Sci.

REYNOSO, ARNULFO; St John Bosco HS; Long Beach, CA; (2); Church Yth Grp; Computer Clb; High Hon Roll; Hon Roll; Jr NHS; Engrng.

REYNOSO, CHRISTINE; West Covina Seventh-Day Advnst HS; West Covina, CA; (2); Chorus; Church Choir; VP Frsh Cls; Hon Roll; HS Tchr.

REYNOSO, GUSTAVO S; Sweetwater HS; National City, CA; (3); Office Aide; Cit Awd; Prfct Atten Awd; Crftsmnshp; Arch.

REYNOSO, MARIBEL V; Anaheim HS; Anaheim, CA; (3); Office Aide; Spanish Clb; Band; Mrchg Band; Pep Band; Intrml Cheerldng; NHS; Yale U; Criminal Law.

REYNOSO, NORAH; Mater Dei HS; Irvine, CA; (4); Church Yth Grp; Cmnty Wkr; GAA; Office Aide; Spanish Clb; Hon Roll; NHS; Rep Frsh Cls; Rep Soph Cls; Rep Jr Cls; Parish Cncl Stu Of St Elizabeth Anne Seton Church; Italian Cath Federation Schlrshp Awd Wnnr; CA Coll Of Court Reporting.

REYNOSO, RONDY C; Galt Union HS; Herald, CA; (3); Church Yth Grp; Debate Tm; FFA; Speech Tm; Church Choir; Var L Bsktbl; High Hon Roll; Hon Roll; Pltcl Sci.

REYNOSO, YVETTE S; Saint Monica Catholic HS; Santa Monica, CA; (4); 9/128; Church Yth Grp; Hosp Aide; Ski Clb; Spanish Clb; Rep Soph Cls; Pres Jr Cls; Pres Stu Cncl; Cit Awd; Elks Awd; Hon Roll; CSF; Hmcmng Qun; Cmps Mnstry; Prncpls Ldrshp Awd; U Of CA Los Angeles; Pre-Med.

REZA, LAURA L; St Joseph HS; Lakewood, CA; (3); GAA; Letterman Clb; Varsity Clb; Var Powder Puff Ftbl; Var Vllybl; Jr NHS; Hon Roll; Math Awd Frshmn & Sphmr Yr.

REZAEI, KATHLEEN; Carlsbad HS; Oceanside, CA; (2); Drama Clb; SADD; Teachers Aide; Thesps; School Play; Stage Crew; Hon Roll; Soccer; Speak Persia; U Of MD; Spc Sci.

REZAI, JASMINE; Schurr HS; Monterey Park, CA; (3); Church Yth Grp; French Clb; Spanish Clb; SADD; Hon Roll; Opt Clb Awd; Intl Stds.

REZAIE, KAMBIZ; Taft HS; Tarzana, CA; (2); Spanish Clb; Bio.

REZINAS, RICHARD M; Oakdale HS; Oakdale, CA; (3); 10/300; Pres Chess Clb; Drama Clb; Math Tm; Quiz Bowl; Scholastic Bowl; Science Clb; Pres Ski Clb; School Play; Yrbk; VP Soph Cls; High Hnrs Golden St Exam Alge, Geom.

REZNIK, ANNA; Skyline HS; Oakland, CA; (3); Intnl Clb; SADD; Tennis; Hon Roll; Amnsty Intl; Math.

REZVANI, SHABAHANG; Wilson HS; Long Beach, CA; (3); French Clb; VP JA; Office Aide; Teachers Aide; Stu Cncl; JV Tennis; Hon Roll; NHS; CA Schltc Fed; USC; Med.

RHAY, RICHARD A; Riverside Polytechnic HS; Riverside, CA; (2); Boy Scts; Church Yth Grp; Drama Clb; Letterman Clb; Church Choir; JV Ftbl; Var Trk; Wt Lftg; Hon Roll; Med.

RHEA, ERIC K; Encina HS; Sacramento, CA; (3); 41/250; Pres Computer Clb; Drama Clb; Teachers Aide; Stage Crew; Mgr Nwsp; Lit Mag; Hon Roll; Lit Mag Tech Ed & Mgr.

RHEA, TRACY L; La Sierra HS; Riverside, CA; (2); Cit Awd; High Hon Roll; Hon Roll; Acadc Ltr; CA Schlrshp Fndtn; Schl Rcgntn Gldn ST Alg Exm; Law.

RHEE, ELLEN S; Homestead HS; Los Altos, CA; (1); Stage Crew; CSF; Octagon Clb; Medcl.

RHEE, HYON P; Eureka HS; Eureka, CA; (1); Ski Clb; Intrml Mgr Bsktbl; JV Ftbl; Var Tennis; NHS; Pres Acad Fit Awd; UCLA; Engrng.

RHEE, KYUNGSOOK; Birmingham HS; Los Angeles, CA; (4); Hon Roll.

RHEE, SUMI; Fremont HS; Sunnyvale, CA; (1); Church Yth Grp; Band; Variety Show; Socr; Tennis; Cit Awd; Hon Roll; Mst Improved Tennis Trophy; Art Projects In De Anzas Art Museum.

RHEIN, ELLEN; Edison HS; Huntington Bch, CA; (4); 31/500; Dance Clb; German Clb; Pep Clb; Cheerldng; Pom Pon; High Hon Roll; Pres Acad Fit Awd; Golden W JC.

RHEINBOLT, JOHN R; Foothill HS; Santa Ana, CA; (3); Drama Clb; JV Swmmng; Hon Roll; Water Polo Jv; Film Clb; CO ST.

RHEINECKER, JODI; Etiwanda HS; Ontario, CA; (2); Church Yth Grp; Dance Clb; Vllybl; Lawyer Model.

RHEINSCHMIDT, STEFAN M; Mc Kinleyville HS; Trinidad, CA; (3); French Clb; FFA; Var Crs Cntry; Var Wrstlng; Engrng.

RHO, HYONSIN K; Mountain View Acad; Los Altos, CA; (4); 1/25; Ski Clb; Band; Chorus; Church Choir; Rptr Nwsp; Rptr Rep Yrbk; Pres Frsh Cls; Sec Soph Cls; Hist Sr Cls; Sec VP Stu Cncl; Pacific Union Coll; Pre Med.

RHOADS, GRADY D; Clovis West HS; Clovis, CA; (4); Band; Mrchg Band; Orch; High Hon Roll; Hon Roll; Fresno ST; Aernutcl Engr.

RHOADS, ROGER W; Trona HS; Trona, CA; (2); FFA; German Clb; UCLA; Comp Pgm.

RHODES, CHRISTOPHER E; Junipero Serra HS; San Mateo, CA; (2); 11/225; Aud/Vis; Computer Clb; Crs Cntry; Mgr(s); High Hon Roll; Hon Roll; U C Berkeley; Engr.

RHODES, DAVID S; Eureka HS; Eureka, CA; (2); Church Yth Grp; SADD; JV Trk; Hon Roll; UC Davis; Engrng.

RHODES, JOSEPH E; El Toro HS; El Toro, CA; (1); Bsktbl; Ftbl; Vllybl; Wt Lftg; Hon Roll; Sci.

RHODES, SARA; Palisades HS; Pacific Palisades, CA; (3); Church Yth Grp; Dance Clb; JA; Chorus; Stu Cncl; Crs Cntry; Trk; DAR Awd; Hon Roll; Pres Acad Fit Awd; Heal Bay Rep; Surfing.

RHODES, STEPHANIE A; Etiwanda HS; Etiwanda, CA; (2); Chorus; School Musical; Bsktbl; Hon Roll; Med.

RHYNE JR, IVIN RAY; Oroville HS; Oroville, CA; (3); 12/193; Band; Mrchg Band; Orch; Pep Band; Nwsp; Hon Roll; Prfct Atten Awd; Peer Tutor; Writing.

RHYNE, PEGEEN; Mission Viejo HS; Mission Viejo, CA; (4); 8/480; Drama Clb; French Clb; Model UN; SADD; Thesps; School Musical; School Play; High Hon Roll; NHS; Ntl Merit SF; U Of San Diego Trustee Schlrshp; U Of San Diego; Intl Rltns.

RIAHI, RAMTIN; Mira Mesa HS; San Diego, CA; (4); UCLA; Bio.

RIAHNAVSKY, PAUL A; Acalanes HS; Lafayette, CA; (1); Church Yth Grp; FCA; 4-H; Spanish Clb; SADD; Teachers Aide; Bsbl; Bsktbl; Crs Cntry; Wt Lftg; Elec Clb; U Of Cal At Berkely; Elec Engr.

RIBADENEIRA, MYLENE; Rio Americano HS; Carmichael, CA; (3); JA; Science Clb; Spanish Clb; Nwsp; Cit Awd; DAR Awd; High Hon Roll; Hon Roll; Writing Awds; Hstry Day Awd 2nd Pl; Acad Achvt Awd; Tutor Stu 12 10 17 Yrs Of Age; U Of CA Davis; Psych.

RIBBLE, ERIC D; Nevada Union HS; Nevada City, CA; (3); Chorus; School Musical; Stu Cncl; Cit Awd; U S CA; Med.

RIBEIRA, MIKE; Bret Harte HS; Copperopolis, CA; (2); Spanish Clb; Wt Lftg; Wrstlng; Hon Roll; Race BMX 3 Yrs; Karate.

RIBEIRO, MICHELLE K; Laguna Hills HS; Laguna Hills, CA; (2); 24/343; French Clb; JA; Key Clb; JV Swmmng; Hon Roll; Photo; CSF; U Santa Cruz; Ed.

RIBERA, RITA M; Indio HS; Grand Terrace, CA; (3); Drama Clb; French Clb; Thesps; School Play; Var Tennis; High Hon Roll; Hon Roll; Jnr Statesmn Amer; CSF; Advertising.

RICAFRENTE, ARSENIO D; Pittsburg HS; Pittsburg, CA; (2); FBLA; Pep Clb; Varsity Clb; Wrstlng; Hon Roll; Fil-Am Clb Ofcr; Med.

RICAFRENTE, JONATHAN D; Vintage HS; Vallejo, CA; (2); Church Choir; Wt Lftg; Prfct Atten Awd; 25th Ag Awd Napa Cnty Fr.

RICARD, KAREN; St Monica HS; Santa Monica, CA; (4); 13/118; SADD; Thesps; Chorus; Flag Corp; School Musical; Stage Crew; JV Cheerldng; Intrml Tennis; Hon Roll; NHS; Bnk Amer Achvt Awd Fine Arts; Acad Decathlon Slvr Mdl 90; Santa Monica Gems Orgnztn Schlrshp; UC Berkeley; Criminal Law.

RICARDO, CECIL; St Genevieve HS; Panorama, CA; (3); Drama Clb; Thesps; School Play; High Hon Roll; Hon Roll.

RICARTE, ALMA D; Sacred Heart Of Jesus HS; Los Angeles, CA; (4); GAA; JA; Spanish Clb; Phtg Yrbk; Pres Jr Cls; VP Stu Cncl; Mgr(s); Hon Roll; NHS; U Of CA Los Angeles; Jrnlsm.

RICASA, MONTI; Bonita Vista HS; Chula Vista, CA; (3); #178 In Class; Church Yth Grp; Phtg Yrbk; Hon Roll; UCLA; Poltcl Sci.

RICCOBUANO, J EREK; Antioch HS; Antioch, CA; (4); Boy Scts; Church Yth Grp; Ski Clb; Trk; Cit Awd; Hon Roll; Eagle Scout Awd 91; BYU; Tchng.

RICCOMINI, CATHERINE; Garces Memorial HS; Buttonwillow, CA; (2); Church Yth Grp; Cmnty Wkr; Key Clb; Pep Clb; Service Clb; Speech Tm; Sec SADD; Var Capt Swmmng; High Hon Roll; U CA Davis; Vet.

RICCOMINI, JULIE A; Mojave HS; Mojave, CA; (3); 11/115; Drama Clb; Thesps; Band; VP Chorus; Church Choir; Mrchg Band; Pep Band; School Musical; School Play; VP Jr Cls; Best Actress Awd Drama 89; Elem Ed.

RICE, ANN F; San Rafael HS; San Rafael, CA; (2); 23/280; French Clb; Variety Show; JV Var Cheerldng; JV Var Pom Pon; High Hon Roll; Most Dedicated Chrldr Awd; Dancing Tap And Jazz; CSF.

RICE, ARLYN T; Livermore HS; Livermore, CA; (3); 113/363; Boy Scts; SADD; Phtg Yrbk; Intrml Swmmng; Intrml Wrstlng; Hon Roll; 1st Pl Tech Drafting Alameda Cnty Fair; Engr.

RICE, BRIAN; North Salinas HS; Salinas, CA; (4); Boy Scts; Letterman Clb; Science Clb; Teachers Aide; Varsity Clb; Var Socr; Var Capt Tennis; High Hon Roll; Prfct Atten Awd; Natl Hispanic Schlr; Ashland Clb; Pickle Ball Champ; Political Sci.

RICE, CHRIS; Bullard HS; Fresno, CA; (4); 34/454; French Clb; Intnl Clb; Key Clb; SADD; Var Crs Cntry; Var Trk; Hon Roll; Astronomy Club Pres; Pepsi Cola Board Awd 89-90; Air Force Acad; Aerospace.

RICE, CHRISTINE A; Santa Teresa HS; San Jose, CA; (3); Office Aide; Pep Clb; Science Clb; Teachers Aide; JV Pom Pon; JV Vllybl; Hon Roll; Ecology Club; San Diego; Business.

RICE, DAWN L; El Toro HS; El Toro, CA; (3); Drill Tm; BYU; Law.

RICE, JENNIFER M; Oakland Tech; Oakland, CA; (2); Drama Clb; School Play; Sec Soph Cls; JV Capt Vllybl; Hon Roll.

RICE, KACEE L; Paradise HS; Magalia, CA; (1); Bsktbl; JV Sftbl; JV Vllybl; Law.

RICE, KALI K; St Patrick St Vincent HS; Vallejo, CA; (1); Stat Bsktbl; JV Cheerldng; Trk; Hon Roll; Pre Law.

RICE, KELLY E; Santa Margarita HS; San Clemente, CA; (3); 79/227; Church Yth Grp; Drama Clb; Model UN; School Play; Stage Crew; Bsktbl.

RICE, KEVIN M; East Nicolaus HS; Pleasant Grove, CA; (3); 8/56; Drama Clb; Ski Clb; Nwsp; Phtg Yrbk; High Hon Roll; Hon Roll; Cert Prfcncy Word Prcssng; Sacramento ST U; Med.

RICE, KRISTEN R; Clovis West HS; Fresno, CA; (4); Church Yth Grp; Cmnty Wkr; FCA; Intnl Clb; Key Clb; Rptr Yrbk; Treas Sr Cls; Hon Roll; Pres Acad Fit Awd; Sthrn Nazarene U; Pre Med.

RICE, LARA M; A V HS; Lancaster, CA; (3); Church Yth Grp; Hosp Aide; Off Frsh Cls; Off Soph Cls; Off Jr Cls; High Hon Roll; Hon Roll; Hgh Hnrs Gldn St Exm; Tchr.

RICE, MICHELLE M; Bishop Amat Memorial HS; Covina, CA; (3); Drama Clb; School Musical; School Play; Stage Crew; Hon Roll; Lacidem Clb; RN.

RICE, NATALIE; St Lucys Priory HS; Covina, CA; (4); 5/111; Church Yth Grp; Drama Clb; NHS; Ntl Merit Ltr; Prfct Atten Awd; Natl Hspnc Schlr Awds Pgm Schlrshp; CSF; Telluride Assn Fnlst; U Of CA San Diego; Chld Psych.

RICE II, ROBERT E; Mt Pleasant HS; San Jose, CA; (1); VP Church Yth Grp; Letterman Clb; Band; Treas Church Choir; Bsbl; Var Bsktbl; L Trk; Hon Roll; Prfct Atten Awd; UC Berkeley; Law.

RICE, SUZANNE R; Fontana HS; Fontana, CA; (4); 2/825; GAA; Treas Frsh Cls; Var Bsktbl; Stat Ftbl; Var Socr; Var Capt Sftbl; Var Capt Vllybl; High Hon Roll; Hon Roll; Lion Awd; Legisltv Cncl; Citrus Belt Area Pepsis Girl Athlete Yr 90; CA Schlrshp Fed; Pepperdine U; Sprts Med.

RICE, TERRY A; Milpitas HS; Milpitas, CA; (4); 33/340; Treas French Clb; JV Crs Cntry; JV Tennis; High Hon Roll; NHS; Pres Acad Fit Awd; CSF Treas; Elec Engrng.

RICH, DAVID; Los Alamitos HS; Los Alamitos, CA; (4); Science Clb; Band; Jazz Band; Mrchg Band; Pep Band; Yrbk; Rep Stu Cncl; JV Golf; Socr; High Hon Roll; UCLA; Chmstry.

RICH, HEATHER A; Agoura HS; Agoura Hills, CA; (2); 11/469; Pep Clb; Spanish Clb; JV Cheerldng; Hon Roll; Backpack Ecology Clb.

RICH, JAMIE S; Quartz Hill HS; Quartz Hill, CA; (4); Drama Clb; NFL; Speech Tm; Thesps; School Play; Ed Nwsp; Ed Lit Mag; JV Trk; High Hon Roll; Pres Acad Fit Awd; Mst Outstndng Engl Stu Awd 90; Outstndng Creative Wrtng Stu 90; CSU Long Beach; Writer.

RICH, MELANIE SUSANNE; Hillsdale HS; San Mateo, CA; (4); 14/296; Art Clb; Church Yth Grp; Treas Orch; School Musical; Tennis; High Hon Roll; Hon Roll; Ntl Merit SF; Badmntn Tm; CA Schlrshp Fdrtn; Aerontcl Engrng.

RICH, SHANNON; Antioch HS; Antioch, CA; (3); 21/623; Art Clb; Church Yth Grp; Drama Clb; Letterman Clb; Office Aide; Spanish Clb; Var Cheerldng; High Hon Roll; Pres Acad Fit Awd; Hnr Grd; Brigham Young U; Med.

RICH, SHANNON; Mesa Verde HS; Citrus Heights, CA; (4); 23/175; Am Leg Aux Girls St; Art Clb; Cmnty Wkr; Debate Tm; Office Aide; Pep Clb; SADD; Teachers Aide; Sec Treas Frsh Cls; Pres Soph Cls; Kops-N-Kids Cnslr 3 Yrs; Safety Pals Cnslr; Schl Site Cncl Mem; American River; Crimnl Law.

RICH, TATUM M; Merced HS; Merced, CA; (3); Church Yth Grp; Key Clb; Band; Color Guard; Mrchg Band; Hon Roll; Hi-Debs Gottschalks Dept Store Mem; Merced Cnty Chamber Of Commerce Ambassador Goodwill Awd.

RICHARD, DIANE E; Villanova Prep; Ojai, CA; (3); 3/55; Church Yth Grp; Cmnty Wkr; Debate Tm; Hosp Aide; Model UN; Var Tennis; JV Vllybl; Gov Hon Prg Awd; High Hon Roll; Ojai Valley Cmnty Tnns Tm; Law.

RICHARD, KARI M; Portola HS; Portola, CA; (2); SADD; Band; Mrchg Band; Stage Crew; Trk; Chico ST; Marine Bio.

RICHARD, KIM M; North HS; Bakersfield, CA; (3); Church Yth Grp; Cmnty Wkr; FCA; Letterman Clb; Office Aide; Spanish Clb; SADD; Teachers Aide; Varsity Clb; Rep Stu Cncl; DARE Offcr; Active Teens Agnst Cmnty Crime; Sports Med.

RICHARD, MICHELLE L; Simi HS; Simi Valley, CA; (2); JV Score Keeper; Var L Tennis; Hon Roll; NHS; Pepperdine U; Bus.

RICHARDS, CHRISTINA L; East Union HS; Manteca, CA; (2); Band; Mrchg Band; Hon Roll.

RICHARDS, CLARK; Lincoln HS; Stockton, CA; (3); 60/538; FBLA; Mu Alpha Theta; High Hon Roll; Hon Roll; CSF; Ducks Unlimited; Wildlife Bio.

RICHARDS, CYNTHIA E; Bullard HS; Fresno, CA; (1); Amer Legn Cert 89; UCLA; Psych.

RICHARDS, DANA; U S Grant HS; Sherman Oaks, CA; (4); 183/692; Church Yth Grp; Rptr Phtg Nwsp; Yrbk; Ed Lit Mag; Golden St Exam-Geom Hnrs; Hnrs Grad; U Of CO-BOULDER.

RICHARDS, DOUGLAS K; Bullard HS; Fresno, CA; (3); 154/500; Boy Scts; Church Yth Grp; SADD; JETS Awd; Mech & Slsmn; UC-SANTA Barbara; Law.

RICHARDS, GWENDOLYN A; Colfax HS; Applegate, CA; (3); Church Yth Grp; 4-H; Teachers Aide; Chorus; 4-H Awd; Hon Roll; Hnrs Engl; Alpha-Omega Pgm; CA ST Coll; Bio Engr.

RICHARDS, JEFFREY H; Las Lomas HS; Walnut Creek, CA; (1); 86/269; SADD; JV Bsbl; Pop Warner Ftbl; Walnut Creek Little Lge All Star; Creative Writing; UC Berkeley; Jrnlsm.

RICHARDS, JOSH; Fall Rivers JR SR HS; Fall River Mills, CA; (4); 8/57; Church Yth Grp; VP Pres FFA; Church Choir; Orch; School Play; Yrbk; Ftbl; NHS; FFA ST Wng Novice Parlmntry Prod Team Stu; Humboldt ST U; Theatre Arts.

RICHARDS, M RAMI; Piedmont HS; Piedmont, CA; (2); Boy Scts; Spanish Clb; SADD; Acpl Chr; VP Soph Cls; JV Ftbl; JV Var Socr; Var Swmmng; Most Outstndng Scout Awd; St Patrol Ldr 90-91; 1st Prz Piedmont High Birdcalling Cont 90.

RICHARDS, MAUREEN J; Los Amigos HS; Santa Ana, CA; (3); Church Yth Grp; Teachers Aide; Chorus; Variety Show; Hon Roll; Kutztown U; Math.

RICHARDS, RYAN; Lincoln HS; Stockton, CA; (4); 50/520; Teachers Aide; JV Bsbl; L Var Ftbl; Var Wt Lftg; Hon Roll; UC Davis; Bio Sci.

RICHARDS, SHANNON L; Whitney HS; Cerritos, CA; (3); VP Dance Clb; Drama Clb; Key Clb; Library Aide; Spanish Clb; Stage Crew; Ed Lit Mag; Hon Roll; Masonic Awd; Intl Ordr Jobs Dghtrs Hnrd Qn; Phys Thrpy.

RICHARDS, STACY; Central Union HS; El Centro, CA; (3); 34/543; Am Leg Aux Girls St; Drama Clb; Teachers Aide; Drill Tm; School Play; Pres Soph Cls; Capt Cheerldng; Gym; Hon Roll; Superstar Invtd Perfrm HI & Ireland; Phys Sci.

RICHARDS, TERI L; Lodi HS; Lodi, CA; (3); Church Yth Grp; Hosp Aide; Office Aide; Acpl Chr; Church Choir; Hon Roll; Prfct Atten Awd; Pres Acad Fit Awd; CSF; Delta Coll; Fashn.

RICHARDS, WALT; Fullerton Union HS; Fullerton, CA; (1); Bsbl; Diving; JV Swmmng; High Hon Roll; Hon Roll; Pres Acad Fit Awd; Water Polo JV; Prof Bsbl Plyr.

RICHARDSON, AMY E; Mesa Verde HS; Citrus Heights, CA; (2); 1/259; English Clb; Math Tm; High Hon Roll; Hon Roll; Prfct Atten Awd; Fri Nght Lv & Safe Rides; UC Santa Barbara; Jrnlsm.

RICHARDSON, CAROL; Washington Prep HS; Los Angeles, CA; (3); Sec Church Yth Grp; Teachers Aide; Chorus; Church Choir; Rptr Nwsp; Cit Awd; Hon Roll; Bank Teller Trng Cert Of Achvt; CA ST Northridge; Jrnlsm.

RICHARDSON, CARRIE M; Redlands SR HS; Pensacola, FL; (2); Art Clb; Church Yth Grp; Hosp Aide; Orch; Cit Awd; Hon Roll; AYSO Sccr; Hrn Orchstra; Harvard; Med.

RICHARDSON, CINDY H; Mount Carmel HS; San Diego, CA; (2); 1/800; Drama Clb; Girl Scts; High Hon Roll; Sign Lang Clb; CSF; 14th Pl Poway Unified Schl Dist Golden St Exm For Geom; Comp.

RICHARDSON, ELIZABETH J; Bishop Montgomery HS; Palos Verdes, CA; (2); Church Yth Grp; Rptr Nwsp; JV Crs Cntry; High Hon Roll; CSF; Greenpeace; Pediatrics.

RICHARDSON, JENNIFER; San Diego HS; San Diego, CA; (4); 32/326; Yrbk; Stu Cncl; Var Co-Capt Cheerldng; Pres Acad Fit Awd; U Of San Diego; Law.

RICHARDSON, JESSE A; Fontana HS; Fontana, CA; (2); Church Yth Grp; Bsbl; Ftbl; Wt Lftg; Wrstlng; Hon Roll; VP Awd & Acad Excllnce Awd; U Of Southern CA; Law.

RICHARDSON, JOSHUA; Tulare Union HS; Tulare, CA; (2); 5/461; Art Clb; Hosp Aide; Math Tm; Mgr Yrbk; JV Tennis; Hon Roll; JV Wrstlng; Golden ST Geom Exam Hnrs; Most Imprvd Plyr JV Tennis 90; Cmptr Prgmg; Pre Med.

RICHARDSON, KANIKA A; Etiwanda HS; Alta Loma, CA; (2); Church Yth Grp; Dance Clb; Color Guard; Hon Roll; Prfct Atten Awd; Jrnlsm.

RICHARDSON, KIMBERLY A; Las Plumas HS; Oroville, CA; (1); Church Yth Grp; French Clb; SADD; Rptr Yrbk; Tennis; Hon Roll; U Of The Pacific; Pharmacy.

RICHARDSON, LATASHA A; Mc Clymonds HS; Oakland, CA; (3); Band; Church Choir; High Hon Roll; Hon Roll; Prfct Atten Awd; Chico ST; Jrnlsm.

RICHARDSON, LOREN G; Central Valley HS; Redding, CA; (3); Am Leg Boys St; Scholastic Bowl; SADD; Hon Roll; 2nd Pl N CA Rgnl Sci Olympiad; Comp Sci.

RICHARDSON, MICHAEL TODD; Fillmore Unified HS; Fillmore, CA; (3); Church Yth Grp; VP Pres FFA; Pres Letterman Clb; SADD; Varsity Clb; Bsbl; Bsktbl; Ftbl; High Hon Roll; Pres Frsh Cls; St Citrus Jdgng Chmpn 90 FFA; St Fnlst Nursy Oper 90 FFA; CA Poly; Ag Bus Mgmt.

RICHARDSON, NICOLE; John F Kennedy HS; La Palma, CA; (1); Boston U; Phy.

RICHARDSON, NINA; Hemet HS; Hemet, CA; (2); Church Yth Grp; Teachers Aide; Hon Roll; Hlth Teacher.

RICHARDSON, PATRICIA MARIE; Pinole Valley HS; Hercules, CA; (2); Church Yth Grp; Band; Drill Tm; Mrchg Band; Var Swmmng; Hon Roll; UC Los Angeles; Pediatrics.

RICHARDSON, REBECCA C; Beaumont HS; Beaumont, CA; (3); 30/140; Math Clb; Science Clb; Teachers Aide; High Hon Roll; Hon Roll; CA Schlstc Fed; UC Irvine; Nrs.

RICHARDSON, REN; Oak Ridge HS; El Dorado Hills, CA; (3); Boy Scts; Church Yth Grp; Letterman Clb; Spanish Clb; JV VP Bsktbl; High Hon Roll; Hon Roll; Brigham Young U; Bus Ec.

RICHARDSON, ROSLYN C; Lynwood HS; Lynwood, CA; (3); 34/840; Math Clb; Ntl Merit Ltr; MESA; AASU; Pres NHS & CSF; Spelman; Psych.

RICHARDSON, SABRINA L; Fontana HS; Fontana, CA; (4); JA; Teachers Aide; High Hon Roll; Hon Roll; ROP Voctnl Pgm; Medcl Sec.

RICHARDSON, SHANONN C; San Juan HS; Citrus Heights, CA; (1); Cit Awd; Hon Roll; Heald Bus; Acctng.

RICHARDSON, SHERRYL D; Mt Eden HS; Hayward, CA; (3); Var Capt Socr; JV Trk; High Hon Roll; Hon Roll; Top Sprinter Trk; UC Davis; Psych.

RICHARDSON, STEPHANIE; Millikan HS; Long Beach, CA; (3); Church Yth Grp; Dance Clb; FCA; Office Aide; Pep Clb; Church Choir; Drill Tm; Var Cheerldng; Var Gym; Var Pom Pon.

RICHARDSON, TYEA NICHELLE; Gardena HS; Gardena, CA; (3); Church Yth Grp; Intnl Clb; Service Clb; Spanish Clb; Church Choir; Drill Tm; Var Cheerldng; High Hon Roll; 4-H; CSF-SGT At Arms; UCLA Fulfillmnt Fund Schlrshp Awd; Law.

RICHARDSON, VALERIE A; Ventura HS; Oak View, CA; (3); 1/430; Am Leg Aux Girls St; Pep Clb; SADD; Rep Jr Cls; VP Stu Cncl; Var L Socr; Var L Trk; High Hon Roll; Ntl Merit Ltr; Olympic Dvlpmnt Dist Slct Sccr Tm; Stanford; Comm.

RICHERT, BEN P; Modoc HS; Alturas, CA; (3); 1/60; Church Yth Grp; Pres Jazz Band; Mrchg Band; Pep Band; Var Bsbl; JV Var Bsktbl; High Hon Roll; Prfct Atten Awd; Acad Decathlon.

RICHERT, KATHARINE V; Modoc HS; Alturas, CA; (2); 1/60; Church Yth Grp; Band; Church Choir; Jazz Band; Mrchg Band; Orch; School Play; Rep Soph Cls; Var Sftbl; JV Vllybl; Aviation Clb; Nrthrn CA HS Hnr Bnd; CSF.

RICHET, BENJAMIN P; Modoc HS; Alturas, CA; (3); 1/60; Church Yth Grp; Pres Jazz Band; Mrchg Band; Pep Band; VP Bsbl; JV VP Bsktbl; VP Trk; High Hon Roll; Prfct Atten Awd; Acad Decthln.

RICHEY, BRIAN P; Huntington Beach HS; Huntington Beach, CA; (2); Church Yth Grp; Spanish Clb; Socr; Intrml Swmmng; Hon Roll; Vrsty Water Polo IM Ltr; UC Berkely; Phys Therapy.

RICHEY, KEITH; Capital Christian HS; Sacramento, CA; (4); Teachers Aide; Rep Stu Cncl; Var Capt Bsktbl; JV Capt Ftbl; Var JV Trk; Wt Lftg; High Hon Roll; CSF; Hghst Acad Schlrshp; CA ST U Sacramento; Engr.

RICHEY, MICHELLE; Atwater HS; Moreno Valley, CA; (2); Church Yth Grp; FCA; JV Var Bsktbl; JV Sftbl; Var Trk; JV Capt Vllybl; High Hon Roll; CSF; CA Cntrl Conf All Leag Acadmcs Bsktbl; Math.

RICHEY, PRISCILLA; Carlmont HS; San Carlos, CA; (2); French Clb; School Musical; Stage Crew; Capt JV Cheerldng; Capt JV Pom Pon; Wt Lftg; Stu For Better Envir Club Secy; Chef.

RICHEY, TABATHA L; Rim Of The World HS; Crestline, CA; (2); Model UN; Rptr Nwsp; Rep Soph Cls; JV Stat Bsktbl; JV Tennis; Var Trk; Jr Statesmn Amer; CSF; Acad Ltr; Psych.

RICHINS, MARGARET A; Cajon HS; San Bernardino, CA; (2); Hosp Aide; Var Trk; Intrml Wt Lftg; Rotary Awd; Writing Poems & Short Stories; Hlpng People Under Priviledge; CO ST Colorado Spgs; CPA.

RICHMOND, DOUGLAS B; Rio Linda SR HS; Rio Linda, CA; (2); French Clb; Var Socr; Hon Roll; Whittman; Architect.

RICHMOND, DYLAN; Pioneer Baptist Christain Schl; Long Beach, CA; (1); Church Yth Grp; Var Bsbl; Cal Tech; Electrncs Tech.

RICHMOND, JAMES; Orange Glen HS; Escondido, CA; (4); Drama Clb; French Clb; German Clb; Band; Church Choir; Jazz Band; Mrchg Band; Pep Band; Nwsp; Hon Roll; AVID Pgm Tutor; OK Baptist U; Teaching.

RICHMOND, KRISTINE D; Mater Dei HS; Huntington Bch, CA; (3); Church Yth Grp; Cmnty Wkr; French Clb; Hosp Aide; Score Keeper; Stat Swmmng; UC Irvine; Psych.

RICHMOND, RHONDA L; John Muir HS; Altadena, CA; (4); Church Yth Grp; Cmnty Wkr; Debate Tm; Girl Scts; Office Aide; Speech Tm; Teachers Aide; Band; Mrchg Band; Nwsp; Yng Black Schlrs Pgm; Tm Chmpn Awd Los Angeles Black Data Processing Assn 89; Comp Prgmmng Cmptn 87; Hampton U; Bus.

RICHMOND, RUSSELL A; San Marcos HS; San Marcos, CA; (3); Art Clb; Church Yth Grp; Cmnty Wkr; JV Var Swmmng; JV Wrstlng; Hon Roll; Prfct Atten Awd; Pres Acad Fit Awd; Water Polo-V; CA Schlrshp Fed; San Marcos City Yth Cncl; Bus Ed.

RICHTER, ASTRID A; Concord HS; Concord, CA; (3); Cmnty Wkr; Pres Math Clb; SADD; Rep Jr Cls; JV Swmmng; JV Vllybl; High Hon Roll; William K Holt Sci Schlrshp Prgm; Mock Trial; Engr.

RICHTER, OWEN; Cabrillo HS; Vandeberg AFB, CA; (4); 18/220; Boy Scts; Treas Chess Clb; Church Yth Grp; Key Clb; JV Tennis; Hon Roll; NHS; Ntl Merit Ltr; Pres Acad Fit Awd; CA Poly; Elec Engrng.

RICHTER, SHELLY L; Ontario HS; Ontario, CA; (2); Church Yth Grp; Drama Clb; Office Aide; Teachers Aide; Thesps; Thesps; Color Guard; Drill Tm; School Musical; School Play; Phys Thrpy.

RICHTER, TIMOTHY B; John F Kennedy HS; Buena Park, CA; (3); Library Aide; Hon Roll; Comp Prgmr.

RICHTMYER, TARA L; Redlands HS; Highland, CA; (2); Science Clb; Ski Clb; Rep Frsh Cls; Socr; Tennis; Cit Awd; High Hon Roll; Hon Roll; Pres Acad Fit Awd; Rotary Awd; Hnrs Geom Gldn St Exam; Ecology Clb; Berkeley.

RICKABAUGH, RICK; Magnolia HS; Anaheim, CA; (1); Intrml Mgr Bsbl; Hon Roll; USC; Math.

RICKARD, APRIL J; San Dieguito HS; La Costa, CA; (2); Church Yth Grp; Varsity Clb; Var Vllybl; Hon Roll; Clb Vllybl; Phys Educ.

RICKARD, CARRIE L; Irvington HS; Fremont, CA; (4); 10/250; Pres Drama Clb; School Musical; Stage Crew; Yrbk; Rep Jr Cls; Off Sr Cls; High Hon Roll; Teachers Aide; CSF Sealbearer; Acad Top Ten; UC Santa Cruz.

RICKARD, JESSICA L; Mesa Verde HS; San Clemente, CA; (2); 12/257; High Hon Roll; Snow & Water Ski; Tnns; Arch.

RICKER, SHANNON MARIE; Mountain View HS; El Monte, CA; (2); GAA; Office Aide; Acpl Chr; Band; Mrchg Band; Pep Band; Stage Crew; Stat Bsktbl; Trk; High Hon Roll; Boston U; Accounting.

RICKETSON, BETH L; Sunny Hills HS; Buena Park, CA; (2); French Clb; Sec FFA; Pep Clb; High Hon Roll; Hon Roll; FFA Parliamentary Procedure Tm Outstndng Sec Southern Rgn Awd; CA Poly Pomona; Vet.

RICKETTS, AMBER L; Oak Park HS; Agoura Hills, CA; (1); Drama Clb; School Musical; Hon Roll; Pres Acad Fit Awd; Dance.

RICKETTS, CARLOS A; Glendale SDA Acad; Los Angeles, CA; (3); Aud/Vis; Church Yth Grp; Acpl Chr; Band; Chorus; Church Choir; Rptr Nwsp; Cit Awd; Hon Roll; Electrcl Estimating; Singing; Write Papers; Santa Monica CC; Jrnlsm.

RICKETTS, HEIDI D; Yucaipa HS; Mentone, CA; (3); Vllybl; Bus.

RICKETTS, WARREN R; Oak Park HS; Agoura Hills, CA; (2); 7/100; Wt Lftg; High Hon Roll; Pres Acad Fit Awd; Bk Clb; Cngrssnl Schlr Yth Ldrshp Cnfrnc; USC; Bus Mgmt.

RICKETTS JR, WILLIAM D; Hilltop HS; Chula Vista, CA; (4); 56/441; Intnl Clb; Letterman Clb; Ed Nwsp; Var Capt Crs Cntry; JV Var Socr; Var Capt Trk; CSF; US Army Rsrve Natl Schlr/Athl Awd; Southwestern JC; Engrng.

RICKMAN, KENNETH A; San Jacinto HS; San Jacinto, CA; (2); Church Yth Grp; Drama Clb; French Clb; Chorus; Mrchg Band; School Play; JV Ftbl; Hon Roll; Prfct Atten Awd; Mt San Jacinto CC; Voice Ed.

RICKS, CHRISTINA M; Canyon SR HS; Newhall, CA; (1); Swmmng; Schl Nwsp; Phi-Delta-Kappa Essay Cont HS Div; UCSB; Writer.

RICO, GEORGE; Don Bosco Technical Inst; Los Angeles, CA; (3); Variety Show; JV Bsktbl; JV Crs Cntry; Trk; Hon Roll; Prfct Atten Awd; People To People.

RICO, GINA R; Woodland HS; Woodland, CA; (3); Sec VP FBLA; Intrml Mgr Bsktbl; JV Var Sftbl; Intrml Mgr Vllybl; Gottschalks Hi Deb Clb 2 Yrs Sec; Powder Puff Sftbl; Mrktng.

RICO, GUADALUPE; Garfield HS; Los Angeles, CA; (2); Prfct Atten Awd; UCLA Mariposa Pgm Cert Of Excllnc; UCLA; Medicine.

RICO, IVONNE; Calexico HS; Calexico, CA; (3); FHA; Teachers Aide; Band; Mrchg Band; Pep Band; Score Keeper; Hon Roll; Jr Statesmen Of Amer; San Diego ST U; Psych.

RIDDELL, PRISCILLA; Cajon HS; San Bernardino, CA; (3); Church Yth Grp; Dance Clb; Office Aide; Chorus; Church Choir; School Play; Swmmng; Vllybl; CA ST U; Law.

RIDDELL, WENDY H; Vacaville HS; Vacaville, CA; (4); 25/562; Service Clb; School Play; Treas Sr Cls; Rep Stu Cncl; High Hon Roll; Hon Roll; Jr NHS; NHS; Ntl Merit Schol; Water Rel Sprts; Mc Kesson Fndtn Schlrshp; Statistician Ftbl, Trk & Wrstlng; CSU Sacramento; Psych.

RIDDELS, PAMELA K; Midway Baptist HS; San Diego, CA; (3); Church Yth Grp; Ed Yrbk; Sec Frsh Cls; Sec Soph Cls; Sec Stu Cncl; Var Bsktbl; Var Sftbl; Var Vllybl; Hon Roll; Seattle Pacific; Tchng.

RIDDIOUGH, ERIC; Righetti HS; Santa Maria, CA; (1); Boy Scts; Church Yth Grp; Band; Mrchg Band; Pep Band; JV Socr; Cit Awd; Prfct Atten Awd; Pres Acad Fit Awd; Engrng.

RIDDIOUGH, TODD; Ernest Righetti HS; Santa Maria, CA; (3); 1/350; Boy Scts; Treas Church Yth Grp; Church Choir; Rep Stu Cncl; Var Capt Socr; High Hon Roll; Hon Roll; Chrch Drama Grp; Engr.

RIDDLE, JOEL T; Redwood HS; Visalia, CA; (3); Chess Clb; German Clb; Letterman Clb; Varsity Clb; Ftbl; Trk; Acad Ltr; Zoology.

RIDDLE, MELINDA M; L A Lutheran HS; Burbank, CA; (3); 2/23; Church Yth Grp; Hosp Aide; Yrbk; Treas Soph Cls; VP Pres Stu Cncl; Var Cheerldng; Var Vllybl; NHS; Ntl Merit SF; Chorus; CSF; Natl Chrty Lgu; Promsng Yng Writer 88; Jr Beta Club; Intl Rltns.

RIDDLE, STEVEN; Davis HS; Modesto, CA; (3); VP VICA; Rep Jr Cls; Crs Cntry; Cit Awd; Hon Roll; VP Emplys Assn & Cmmttes; Black Belt Tammarau Kempo Kuntau.

RIDENOUR, DEBRA J; Wasco Union HS; Shafter, CA; (2); Cit Awd; High Hon Roll; Hon Roll; NHS; Prfct Atten Awd; Breakfast Club Awd For High Degr Of Schltc Profcncy; Music.

RIDENOUR, JENNIFER M; Hemet HS; Hemet, CA; (3); Letterman Clb; Teachers Aide; Band; Mrchg Band; Orch; Stage Crew; Var L Crs Cntry; Var L Trk; Hon Roll; Lion Awd; Art.

RIDENOUR, MONIQUE N; Kennedy HS; La Palma, CA; (3); Cmnty Wkr; Dance Clb; FBLA; Girl Scts; Hosp Aide; Red Cross Aide; Chorus; Drill Tm; Swing Chorus; NHS; Choir Awd & Drll Tm; Outstndng Stdt Engl Clss 2 Yrs; UCR; Ag.

RIDENOUR, SETH; Happy Valley Schl; Ojai, CA; (3); Pres Ski Clb; School Play; Stage Crew; Off Jr Cls; Off Sr Cls; Stu Cncl; Bsbl; Bsktbl; Crs Cntry; Socr; UCSB; Environmental Law.

RIDEOUT, DAVID J; Woodrow Wilson HS; Long Beach, CA; (4); 28/588; Debate Tm; Speech Tm; Teachers Aide; Ftbl; Wt Lftg; Hon Roll; NHS; Prfct Atten Awd; Phi Beta Kappa; CSF; Bank Of Amer Achvmnt Awd; Sonoma ST U; Lib Stud.

RIDER, DAVID S; Watsonville HS; Watsonville, CA; (3); 31/500; 4-H; Science Clb; Lit Mag; 4-H Awd; Hon Roll; Wrkng Twrd Prvt Pilot Licns; Aviation.

RIDER, KIMBERLY; Folsom HS; Folsom, CA; (3); Office Aide; Teachers Aide; Co-Ed Color Guard; Drill Tm; UCLA; Ped.

RIDGE, BRYAN T; Westmoor HS; Colma, CA; (3); Art Clb; Computer Clb; Band; Chorus; Jazz Band; Orch; School Musical; School Play; Variety Show; Intrml Bsbl; 1st Pl CA All St Hnr Band; CSF; U Of CA Berkeley; Elec Engrng.

RIDGE, SHAWNA A; Oak Ridge HS; El Dorado Hills, CA; (1); 34/295; Church Yth Grp; SADD; Gym; High Hon Roll; Gymnastics; Tnns; Chico ST; Choreography.

RIDGLEY, DIANE ELIZABETH; Center HS; Sacramento, CA; (4); 1/145; VP Frsh Cls; Treas Stu Cncl; Var Capt Bsktbl; Var Stat Ftbl; Var L Sftbl; Var L Trk; Capt L Vllybl; NHS; Pres Acad Fit Awd; Val; St Assmbly Sr Yr; Gld Mdlst Schlr/Athltc Cty Nwsp; U Of Southern CA; Elec Engrng.

RIDGWAY, LORI; Del Norte HS; Crescent City, CA; (3); Pres 4-H; VP Frsh Cls; VP Soph Cls; Rep Stu Cncl; JV Var Bsktbl; Powder Puff Ftbl; Var Trk; JV Var Vllybl; Hon Roll; Pres Acad Fit Awd; Hmcmng Princess; Law Enf.

RIDLEY, TAMMY J; Kennedy HS; Buena Park, CA; (3); Church Yth Grp; Chorus; Church Choir; Color Guard; Fullerton CC; Csmtlgy.

RIECK, ALINA K; Redlands HS; Redlands, CA; (3); Church Yth Grp; French Clb; Letterman Clb; Teachers Aide; Yrbk; Off Sr Cls; Capt Swmmng; St Schlr; Kimberly Jrs-Svc Clb-Sec; Gftd/Tlntd Ed-Advsry Stu; Cmmnctns.

RIEDEL, ALLEN; Ernest Righetti HS; Orcutt, CA; (4); 30/365; Church Yth Grp; Cmnty Wkr; JA; School Play; Rptr Frsh Cls; Pres Sr Cls; High Hon Roll; Hon Roll; Calculus Clb Pres; ICC Rep Stu Wanting Envrnmntl Harmony; Engl.

RIEDEL, JOHN C; San Ramon HS; Danville, CA; (2); Church Yth Grp; VP L Ski Clb; Tennis; Hon Roll; Pres Acad Fit Awd; Hunting & Fishing, Wildlife Mgmt; Vrsty Waterpolo & Ski Tm Vrsty Ltrs.

RIEFF, CHRIS; Fountain Valley HS; Fountain Valley, CA; (2); JV Bsktbl; JV Vllybl; Skimbrdng; Arch.

RIEGEL, MARC W; Mount Whitney HS; Visalia, CA; (4); VP Art Clb; Pep Clb; Sec Stu Cncl; Var Swmmng; Hon Roll; NHS; Astronomy Clb; Vrsty Water Polo; UC Santa Barbara; Bio.

RIEGNER-COWLE, LAURA; Del Campo HS; Sacramento, CA; (3); Church Yth Grp; Teachers Aide; Church Choir; Drill Tm; Elem Educ.

RIEGOS, RAQUEL; San Gabriel Mission HS; Los Angeles, CA; (3); 21/156; FBLA; GAA; Girl Scts; Spanish Clb; Chorus; Bsktbl; High Hon Roll; Hon Roll; Pitzer; Elem Ed.

RIELAND, KATHLYNN A; Red Bluff HS; Cottonwood, CA; (2); 10/465; 4-H; Sec French Clb; Mu Alpha Theta; Off Frsh Cls; 4-H Awd; Hon Roll; Jobs Dghtrs; CA Schlrshp Fed; Teenwork 90; U Of CA; Sci.

RIELLY, JENNIFER M; Bishop O'dowd HS; Oakland, CA; (2); Hosp Aide; Chorus; JV Var Sftbl; Hon Roll; Oakland Yth Chorus; UC Riverside; Hosp Admin.

RIES, SEAN M A; Valhalla HS; Lakeside, CA; (2); Hist 4-H; Rep Frsh Cls; High Hon Roll; Hon Roll; Frgn Lang Awd; Cal Tech; Accntnt.

RIESS JR, JOHN K; Bonita Vista HS; Bonita, CA; (3); Teachers Aide; Var L Swmmng; Cit Awd; Hon Roll; CSF; Vrsty Water Polo, 2 Yr Ltr, All-League Hnrb Mntn 89-90; YMCA Camp Lifegrd; Law.

RIETH, DAVID J; Novato HS; Novato, CA; (3); Church Yth Grp; Sec French Clb; Lit Mag; Hon Roll; Val; Pres Harvest Fndrsng Clb; Rlgs/Ed Missions Trip To Mexico; Chiropractics.

RIFKIN, DISA L; California HS; San Ramon, CA; (3); 22/380; Church Yth Grp; Spanish Clb; Teachers Aide; Church Choir; Var Crs Cntry; Var Trk; Hon Roll; Pres Acad Fit Awd; Pres Schlr; BYU; Criminal Justice.

RIGBY, MICHAEL E; Hueneme HS; Port Hueneme, CA; (1); Church Yth Grp; Socr; Hon Roll.

RIGDON, JENNIFER J; Trona HS; Trona, CA; (2); Library Aide; Pep Clb; Spanish Clb; SADD; Nwsp; Yrbk; Bsktbl; Powder Puff Ftbl; Vllybl; Wt Lftg; Antelope Vly JC; Phys Ed Tchr.

RIGG, CYNTHIA L; Quartz Hill HS; Quartz Hill, CA; (4); Office Aide; Hon Roll; Christ Coll Irvine; Law.

RIGGE, SHERRY; Benicia HS; Benicia, CA; (3); Sec Church Yth Grp; Rep Key Clb; Math Clb; Office Aide; SADD; VP Band; Mrchg Band; Stage Crew; Hon Roll; Rnbw Grls; UC-DAVIS; Med.

RIGGINS, SEAN G; Borrego Springs HS; Borrego Springs, CA; (3); VP Frsh Cls; VP Soph Cls; Ftbl; Hon Roll; Prfct Atten Awd; NAU; Elec Engrng.

RIGGIO, ANDY A; Ontario HS; Ontario, CA; (3); 20/350; Art Clb; Key Clb; Spanish Clb; High Hon Roll; Hon Roll; Comp Engrng.

RIGGLE, ANTONIA C; El Camino Fundamental HS; Sacramento, CA; (3); 1/366; French Clb; VP SADD; School Play; Rep Soph Cls; Sec Jr Cls; Var Tennis; High Hon Roll; Hon Roll; NHS; Church Yth Grp; Jr Statesman Of Amer Pres & St Cabinet Officer; Dist Wide Mock Trials Witness; Law.

RIGGS, BRIAN R; El Toro HS; El Toro, CA; (1); Capt Socr; Hon Roll.

RIGGS, DEBBIE S; Serrano HS; Phelan, CA; (4); 28/162; Debate Tm; Pres Rptr FBLA; Chorus; Nwsp; High Hon Roll; Hon Roll; Lion Awd; Voice Dem Awd; Acad All Amer; Vets Frgn Wars Speech Cont; Amer Bus Wmns Assn Awd; CA ST U Bakersfield; Psych.

RIGGS, FLETCHER S; Edison HS; Huntington Beach, CA; (1); Boy Scts; Model UN; Hon Roll; Waterpolo; UC San Diego; Vet.

RIGGS, NICOLE; Oxnard HS; Oxnard, CA; (3); 3/500; Spanish Clb; Teachers Aide; Thesps; Band; Jazz Band; Mrchg Band; High Hon Roll; Prfct Atten Awd; Pres Acad Fit Awd; Engr.

RIGHTNOWAR, MICHAEL D; Rosemead HS; Pasadena, CA; (3); ROTC; Thesps; Color Guard; School Play; Church Yth Grp; Cmnty Wkr; Intnl Clb; SADD; Teachers Aide; Intrml Bsbl; Scl Stds Stu Of Month; Rio Hondo Coll; Meteorology.

RIGLER, ERIN JOSHUA; Ponderosa HS; Shingle Springs, CA; (4); 17/280; French Clb; Ski Clb; Teachers Aide; Hon Roll; Pres Acad Fit Awd; Ski Tm; Northern AZ U; Intl Relations.

RIGNEY, JODI; El Camino HS; Oceanside, CA; (3); 34/364; Dance Clb; SADD; JV Var Cheerldng; Capt Var Gym; Sftbl; Hon Roll; Schlr Athlt 87-88; Stu Of Month Frgn Lang, Spanish; Sec El Caminio League; Bus.

RIHTARSHICH, FRANK R; Casa Grande HS; Petaluma, CA; (3); 74/288; Hon Roll; Pres Acad Fit Awd; Hnr Awd Excllnc In Ag/Forestry; Landscape Engr.

RIISE, MICHAEL; Pinole Valley HS; Pinole, CA; (3); Teachers Aide; JV Bsbl; Var Golf; Hon Roll; Tennis, Golf.

RIKKERS, KRISTIN M; El Camino Fundamental HS; Sacramento, CA; (3); 34/376; Church Yth Grp; VP Latin Clb; Math Tm; Ski Clb; JV Swmmng; Wt Lftg; NHS; Crew; Stu Reaching Out; CA Schlrshp Fed; Marine Bio.

RILES, ELIZABETH L; Berkeley HS; Oakland, CA; (3); Science Clb; Orch; High Hon Roll; Ntl Merit Ltr; Oakland Yth Orch Violinist; CSF; Ballet Arts Perfrmr-San Fran Childrns Civic Light Opera.

RILEY, AMBER R; Livermore HS; Livermore, CA; (1); 24/400; Church Yth Grp; Debate Tm; 4-H; Band; Mrchg Band; Sftbl; 4-H Awd; High Hon Roll; Prfct Atten Awd; Best Frshmn Awd Sftbl; GPA Awd Sftbl; Solo Ensmbl Won Command Prfrmnc; Pediatric Nrs.

RILEY, CHRISTINE; Cornelia Connelly HS; Fullerton, CA; (4); Cmnty Wkr; German Clb; Teachers Aide; Acpl Chr; Yrbk; Lit Mag; Var L Trk; Natl Cncl Tchrs Engl Achvt Wrtg Awd.

RILEY, CORIE; Antelope Valley HS; Lancaster, CA; (2); Hon Roll; Stu Of Wk; Music.

RILEY, DAPHNE E; Mc Kinleyville HS; Mckinleyville, CA; (2); Key Clb; Band; Mrchg Band; Pep Band; Yrbk; Hon Roll; Prfct Atten Awd.

RILEY, ELIZABETH E; Nordhoff HS; Oak View, CA; (4); Teachers Aide; Ed Nwsp; Var Cheerldng; Miss Teen Ojai 2nd Rnnr Up 88 & 89; Faculty Hnrs 89; UCLA; Law.

RILEY, HEATHER; Ontario HS; Ontario, CA; (3); Church Yth Grp; Key Clb; Spanish Clb; Teachers Aide; Church Choir; Hon Roll; Maranatha Clb; CSU San Bernardino; Elem Ed.

RILEY, JENNIFER L; California HS; Whittier, CA; (3); French Clb; FBLA; Key Clb; Office Aide; Drill Tm; CSU Fullerton; Hearng Imprd.

RILEY, JEREMIAH J; San Dieguito HS; Encinitas, CA; (2); Ed Nwsp; L Cheerldng; L Trk; JV Vllybl; Boys & Girls Clb Vlntr; Top Ranked Amateur Cyclist, 1st In Cnty; UCSB; Frgn Bus Admin.

RILEY, JOHN-PAUL; North Monterey Co HS; Salinas, CA; (1); French Clb; SADD; High Hon Roll; U Of Pacific; Teacher.

RILEY, KERRI; Fall River HS; Mc Arthur, CA; (2); Church Yth Grp; FCA; FFA; Letterman Clb; Rptr Yrbk; Sec Frsh Cls; Var Bsktbl; Sftbl; Vllybl.

RILEY, MICHAEL J; Antelope Valley HS; Lancaster, CA; (4); Church Yth Grp; JV Var Crs Cntry; JV Var Trk; Hon Roll; Trk Clb; UC Berkeley; Pre-Med.

RILEY, MIKE; East Union HS; Manteca, CA; (4); 4/264; Key Clb; Pep Clb; Scholastic Bowl; Science Clb; Band; Jazz Band; Mrchg Band; Pep Band; Variety Show; Nwsp; Cnty Hnr Band; HS Mascott; Camp Royal Rtry; Rice U; Music.

RILEY, PATRICK J; Argonaut HS; Ione, CA; (2); JV Bsktbl; Var Tennis; Hon Roll; De Oldy Boys Mosonic Grp Cnslr 89-90; Bus.

RILEY, RAYMOND C; River City HS; W Sacramento, CA; (3); 6/215; SADD; Band; Jazz Band; Mrchg Band; Orch; Pep Band; High Hon Roll; Hon Roll; Prfct Atten Awd; Upward Bound Stu Adv Bd Chmn; MESA; CSF; UC Davis; Engl.

RILEY, ROISILIN; Mt Carmel HS; San Diego, CA; (4); Treas French Clb; FBLA; Office Aide; Treas Q&S; Band; Mrchg Band; Nwsp; Natl Hispanic Schlrshp Semi-Fnlst; Sundevil Stndout Awd; Psychobiology.

RILEY, SHELLY A; Trona HS; Trona, CA; (2); Sec Frsh Cls; JV L Bsktbl; Var L Cheerldng; Acad French II/Math Mdls; Head Majorette-Ftbl; Dead Poets Soc-Engl Clb; Bus.

RILEY-SOREM, ANDREA E.; Concord HS; Concord, CA; (3); Church Yth Grp; Letterman Clb; Band; Flag Corp; Mrchg Band; Pep Band; Rep Stu Cncl; Swing Flag Sqd 90-91; Band Cncl Jr Rep 89-90; Auxlry Rep 90-91; Ed.

RIMMER, M CHRISTA; La Reina HS; Simi Valley, CA; (3); 31/67; Drama Clb; NFL; Speech Tm; VP Jr Cls; Rep Sr Cls; Stu Cncl; Cit Awd; High Hon Roll; Hon Roll; Jr NHS; CSF; Acad Decathlon Team UCAD; Span Hon Society; Bus Adm.

RIMOCAL JR, TOM L; Montgomery HS; San Diego, CA; (2); Boy Scts; Computer Clb; Chorus; JV Ftbl; Cit Awd; Hon Roll; Ntl Merit Schol; CA U San Diego; Mech Engr.

RINCON, LEONARDO; Sherman Oaks C E S HS; Los Angeles, CA; (3); Cmnty Wkr; Office Aide; Teachers Aide; Yng Authr Awd 89-90; CA Poly Pomona; Arch.

RINDAHL, JENNIFER L; Mayfair HS; Lakewood, CA; (1); Church Yth Grp; Cmnty Wkr; English Clb; Church Choir; Jazz Band; Mrchg Band; Pep Band; Var L Sftbl; Var Tennis; High Hon Roll; Golden ST Exam Hnrs Alg; Soroptimist Club Awd Most Outstndng Muscn.

RINDE, ELISA; Andrew Hill HS; San Jose, CA; (2); Church Yth Grp; Dance Clb; Girl Scts; Color Guard; Stu Cncl; JV Cheerldng; Socr; Prfct Atten Awd; Hnr Cert 3.0 GPA; Peer Cnslng Clb; Bio.

RINDELL, MELISSA D; Valley HS; Sacramento, CA; (3); Debate Tm; Drama Clb; Scholastic Bowl; Teachers Aide; School Play; Off Soph Cls; Rep Jr Cls; Stat Bsbl; High Hon Roll; Martin Luther King Jr Writing Awd; Jr Asilomar Delg; Boston U; Poltcl Sci.

RINDONE, DAVID; Castle Park HS; Chula Vista, CA; (4); 3/315; Service Clb; Sec SADD; VP Band; Mrchg Band; Orch; Pep Band; Variety Show; Rep Frsh Cls; Rep Soph Cls; Rep Jr Cls; AZ ST U; Bus.

RINDONE, JACKIE N; Del Campo HS; Fair Oaks, CA; (3); 86/450; Teachers Aide; Stat Bsktbl; Math Tutor.

RINDT, DARCY; Sherman E Burroughs HS; Ridgecrest, CA; (3); 1/420; Varsity Clb; Orch; Var Bsktbl; JV Sftbl; Var Tennis; High Hon Roll; Rensselaer Math, Sci Awd; Prncpls Awd; Xerox Awd For Humns, Soc Sci; MVP Bsktbl; Hnrbl Mntn; Physcis.

RINE, TIM; Damien HS; Upland, CA; (2); 163/269; Ski Clb; Surfing Clb-Vp; CA ST U; Bus.

RING, COLLEEN M; Newbury Park HS; Newbury Park, CA; (4); 23/364; French Clb; Hosp Aide; Key Clb; Library Aide; Spanish Clb; SADD; Teachers Aide; Rep Frsh Cls; Hon Roll; CSF; Loyola U-Chicago; Finance.

RING, LEEANN L; Merced HS; Merced, CA; (3); Spanish Clb; SADD; Hon Roll; Prfct Atten Awd; Court Reprtr.

RING JR, MICHAEL A; Ferndale Union HS; Ferndale, CA; (3); 2/30; Am Leg Boys St; Cmnty Wkr; Drama Clb; Spanish Clb; Phtg Yrbk; Treas Sr Cls; Cit Awd; High Hon Roll; Acad Lttr; CSF; U Of The Pacific; Phrmcy.

RINGGENBERG, KIERAN; Fred C Beyer HS; Modesto, CA; (3); Debate Tm; German Clb; Key Clb; Math Tm; NFL; Science Clb; Speech Tm; SADD; High Hon Roll; CSF.

RINGLAND, RICHARD R; Norco HS; Corona, CA; (3); #7 In Class; Church Yth Grp; FBLA; Model UN; Spanish Clb; Teachers Aide; Cit Awd; High Hon Roll; Hon Roll; Jr NHS; NHS; Cmmncmnt Hnr Ct; Scr Fr 3rd Pl; Little Leag; Karate; Sccr; Frgn Lang Awd Span; Comp Technlgy.

RINGLER, BRANDI T; La Reina HS; Thousand Oaks, CA; (3); 7/90; GAA; Service Clb; Church Choir; Pres Stu Cncl; Capt Tennis; Cit Awd; French Hon Soc; High Hon Roll; Jr NHS; NHS; Alma Mater & Service Schlrshps; Loyola; Ed.

RINGNALDA, KAREN I; Gahr HS; Artesia, CA; (2); 92/500; Church Yth Grp; French Clb; Band; Mrchg Band; Hon Roll; CSULB; Bus Admin.

RINGO, ALEXEA L; Mount Miguel HS; Spring Valley, CA; (4); 26/500; Am Leg Aux Girls St; NFL; Pres Sec Spanish Clb; School Play; Treas Frsh Cls; Treas Soph Cls; VP Jr Cls; Rep Stu Cncl; Lion Awd; Rotary Awd; Most Talented; Accolade; Bank Of Amer Achvt Awd Fine Arts; U Of CA-BERKELEY; Poli Sci.

RINGO, KRISTI; San Gorgonio HS; Highland, CA; (3); 51/400; Cmnty Wkr; Office Aide; Pep Clb; Service Clb; Var Capt Cheerldng; Powder Puff Ftbl; High Hon Roll; NHS; Prfct Atten Awd; Interact Treas; Ca Schlrshp Fed; ACES; Dntstry.

RININGER, TYSON V; Hueneme HS; Port Hueneme, CA; (2); Aud/Vis; Library Aide; Office Aide; Teachers Aide; Swmmng; Prfct Atten Awd; ABEX Speech Cont 2nd Pl; Acad Excllnce Awd; Naval Aviation.

RINKER, NICHOLE; San Bernardino HS; Highland, CA; (4); AFS; Drama Clb; School Play; Cheerldng; Swmmng; Miss Cnty Of San Bernardino; 89-90 Homecoming Qn; Scottsdale Cullnary Inst; Chef.

RINTOUL, NICOLE M; Highlands HS; North Highlands, CA; (1); Girl Scts; Amer River Coll; Inter Dcrtr.

RIOJAS, ANTHONY; Vista HS; Vista, CA; (4); Church Yth Grp; Key Clb; Spanish Clb; Speech Tm; Thesps; Chorus; VP Swing Chorus; JV Swmmng; Wt Lftg; Hon Roll; Schl Fshn & Benefit Shows Model; Loma Linda U; Intl Rltns.

RIOS, AARON J; Hanford HS; Hanford, CA; (1); Church Yth Grp; FBLA; Pres Frsh Cls; Intrml Bsbl; High Hon Roll; Prfct Atten Awd; MESA; CSF; Acad Ltr; Law.

RIOS, ADRIANA M; Gahr HS; Norwalk, CA; (2); Powder Puff Ftbl; Cit Awd; Hon Roll; Prfct Atten Awd; Cerritos Coll; Law.

RIOS, ALEX G; Hanford HS; Hanford, CA; (3); Art Clb; JV Crs Cntry; Var JV Wrstlng; Hon Roll; Pres Acad Fit Awd; Crminiology.

RIOS, COREY; Covina HS; West Covina, CA; (4); Jazz Band; Stage Crew; Nwsp; Yrbk; Stu Cncl; High Hon Roll; Hon Roll; CSF; Devry; Comp Pgmmr.

RIOS, DORIS S; Taft HS; Los Angeles, CA; (3); FIDM; Merch Mktg.

RIOS, ERNESTO F; Simi Valley HS; Simi Valley, CA; (2); ROTC; Bsbl; Waterpolo; Cal Poly Technic; Archaeology.

RIOS, ESTELA; San Fernando HS; San Fernando, CA; (4); 25/530; Office Aide; Science Clb; Spanish Clb; Ed Rptr Lit Mag; High Hon Roll; Kiwanis Awd; Prfct Atten Awd; Pres Acad Fit Awd; Woodbury Schlrshp; 3 Yrs Prfct Atten; U Of Woodbury; Comp Info Systm.

RIOS, FELICIA R; Monte Vista HS; Spring Valley, CA; (2); Debate Tm; Teachers Aide; Bsktbl; Sftbl; Tennis; Trk; Cit Awd; Hon Roll; Prfct Atten Awd; Kick Boxing Course; Ped.

RIOS, FLORENCIO; Rio Linda SR HS; Rio Linda, CA; (2); Boy Scts; Church Yth Grp; Library Aide; Red Cross Aide; Scholastic Bowl; Spanish Clb; Band; Mrchg Band; Ftbl; Socr; UC Davis; Pediatrician.

RIOS, HERMAN; Grossmont HS; El Cajon, CA; (3); Boy Scts; Church Yth Grp; Cartoonist.

RIOS, JEANETTE; Calexico HS; Calexico, CA; (1); Dance Clb; Drama Clb; Drill Tm; Sftbl; Vllybl.

RIOS, JENNY; Bloomington HS; Bloomington, CA; (1); Drama Clb; Tennis; Trk; High Hon Roll; Prfct Atten Awd; CA Schlrshp Fed; Med.

RIOS, JEZEL G; Southwest HS; San Ysidro, CA; (1); San Diego ST U; Cnslr.

RIOS, JOSE D; Montclair HS; Pomona, CA; (3); Church Yth Grp; Latin Clb; Math Clb; Science Clb; Ftbl; Socr; NEDT Awd; Prfct Atten Awd; Natl Latin I Exam Hnrs; Math Hnrs; Electrnc Engr.

RIOS, JOSE L; Indio Rajahs HS; Palm Desert, CA; (2); Band; Jazz Band; Mrchg Band; Pep Band.

RIOS, JOSEPH N; Atwater HS; Atwater, CA; (1); French Clb; FBLA; Hon Roll; Prfct Atten Awd; Interact; Friday Night Live; Falcon Crest Awd; Psych.

RIOS, LAURA A; Hanford HS; Hanford, CA; (1); Church Yth Grp; Chorus; Church Choir; Cit Awd; Hon Roll; NHS; Bilingual Stu; Early Outreach Pgm; Bus.

RIOS, LUIS; South Gate HS; Huntington Park, CA; (2); Key Clb; ROTC; Color Guard; Drill Tm; Var Crs Cntry; Intrml Trk; Hon Roll; Prfct Atten Awd; Marathon Clb; Sons Of Amer Rvltn Awd; Air Force Acad; Aerontcl Engrng.

RIOS, LUPITA; Woodrow Wilson HS; Los Angeles, CA; (3); UCLA; Pre-Med.

RIOS, MARGARITA; Hanford Joint Union HS; Hanford, CA; (3); FBLA; Spanish Clb; Hon Roll; COS Coll; Bus.

RIOS, MARIO; Compton HS; Compton, CA; (3); Boy Scts; Church Yth Grp; Dance Clb; USCLB; Aerospace Engr.

RIOS, MARYULI E; Tustin HS; Tustin, CA; (2); Spanish Clb; Tennis; Vllybl; High Hon Roll; Hon Roll; Mgr Hmn Res.

RIOS, MELISSA; James Lick HS; San Jose, CA; (4); 55/256; Church Yth Grp; Cmnty Wkr; Intnl Clb; Red Cross Aide; Science Clb; Rep Yrbk; Stu Cncl; Sftbl; Hon Roll; Mayo Clb Pres; Just Say No Clb; UC San Diego; Biolgcl Sci.

RIOS, RAQUEL; Somoma Valley HS; Sonoma, CA; (3); Cmnty Wkr; SADD; High Hon Roll; Hon Roll; CA Schlrshp Fed; Soc Sci.

RIOS, SOCORRO; Corcoran HS; Corcoran, CA; (3); JV Bsktbl; Hon Roll; CSF; Fresno ST; Med.

RIOS, SONIA; Strathmon Union HS; Strathmon, CA; (4); 1/74; Am Leg Aux Girls St; Letterman Clb; Service Clb; Off Sr Cls; Stu Cncl; Bsktbl; Crs Cntry; Score Keeper; Trk; Vllybl; Road Relay Tm; Clg Of The Sequoias; Bus Admin.

RIOS, VIRGINIA; Castle Park HS; Chula Vista, CA; (2); French Clb; Necha Clb; Awd Mntng Spprt Systm MECHA Clb; Asstnce Tutr Pgm Elem Schl; UCSD; Psych.

RIOS, YESMI; Sanger HS; Del Rey, CA; (3); Pres Am Leg Aux Girls St; Art Clb; Bus Profs of Am; Computer Clb; Dance Clb; Drama Clb; English Clb; Pres French Clb; FBLA; Math Clb; Math.

RIPA, MICHELE DELLA; St Genevieve HS; Loomis, CA; (4); JA; Pep Clb; Chorus; Pres Jr Cls; Rep Sr Cls; Var Capt Cheerldng; Hon Roll; Hmcmng Prncss 89; Retreat Team; Liturgy & Unity Clbs; Sacramento ST; Engl.

RIPATTI, MAUREEN M; Apple Valley HS; Apple Valley, CA; (3); 20/708; Church Yth Grp; French Clb; Key Clb; Church Choir; Jazz Band; Mrchg Band; Gym; Swmmng; High Hon Roll; Hon Roll; Dance; Vlntr Work; Taught Bible Schl; WA U; Med.

RIPLEY, HEATHER; Thousand Oaks HS; Thousand Oaks, CA; (3); Intnl Clb; SADD; School Play; Rep Jr Cls; Rep Sr Cls; JV Var Cheerldng; Intrml Powder Puff Ftbl; JV Var Swmmng; High Hon Roll; Hon Roll; People To People Grp Russia 90; Chrldng Coach; Miss Natl Teenage Fnlst 88; Intl Rltns.

RIPLEY, MELISSA DIAN; John Glenn HS; Norwalk, CA; (2); French Clb; Band; Mrchg Band; Yrbk; Hon Roll; Interdependence Clb Camp; Brnze Cngrssnl Awd; People/People Stu Ambssdr Pgm 90; Philosophy.

RIPLEY, NICOLE A; Red Bluff HS; Red Bluff, CA; (3); 4-H; GAA; Rptr Nwsp; Treas Jr Cls; Var JV Bsktbl; JV Sftbl; Var JV Vllybl; Hon Roll; Ed.

RIPPE, CHRISTOPHER C; Hueneme HS; Oxnard, CA; (3); 4/450; Church Yth Grp; Computer Clb; German Clb; High Hon Roll; Acad Decathln; Mock Trial; Engr.

RIPPEE, MICHELLE S; Santa Maria HS; Santa Maria, CA; (3); Ski Clb; Hon Roll; Marine Sci.

RIQUE, ARLETTE M; Hilltop HS; Chula Vista, CA; (2); Pres Acad Fit Awd; FLAGS; U CA San Diego; Frgn Lang.

RISDON, SUSAN L; Chaffey Union HS; Ontario, CA; (3); Band; Drm Mjr(t); Mrchg Band; Pep Band; Nwsp; Yrbk; Hon Roll; Prfct Atten Awd; Elem Tchr.

RISENHOOVER JR, ELBA DALE; Clovis HS; Fresno, CA; (2); Dance Clb; Drama Clb; Thesps; Chorus; School Musical; School Play; Stage Crew; Fresno ST U; Actor.

RISHER, CHRISTINE J; Schurr HS; Montebello, CA; (4); Church Yth Grp; Cmnty Wkr; Pres Key Clb; Off Jr Cls; Scrkpr Score Keeper; Vllybl; Wrstlng; YMCA Yth/Govt Pres; Jobs Dghtrs Past Hnr Qn; Miss Mntry Pk Prncss 1st Rnnr-Up; U Of S CA; Cmmnctns.

RISHER, ELISSA; Palmdale HS; Palmdale, CA; (3); 84/600; Church Yth Grp; Dance Clb; Pep Clb; Drill Tm; Cheerldng; Hon Roll; Grmsnstcs Coach; CA ST U; Bus Mgnt.

RISSE, MARCEE M; Moorpark HS; Moorpark, CA; (2); Church Yth Grp; Office Aide; Spanish Clb; High Hon Roll; Alg I Awd; Spnsh Speech & Grammar Awd; Crmnl Law.

RISTUCCIA, KIMBERLY; Bellarmine Jefferson HS; North Hollywood, CA; (1); Letterman Clb; Stage Crew; Off Frsh Cls; Bsktbl; Sftbl; Tennis; Vllybl; High Hon Roll; Jrnlsm.

RITCHEY, DALE D; San Gorgonio HS; San Bernardino, CA; (3); Drama Clb; FFA; Office Aide; Thesps; Stage Crew; Cit Awd; Hon Roll; Stu Of Wk For Acadmcs; Tech Aspcts Of Brdcstg.

RITCHIE, ALISON M; Warren HS; Downey, CA; (1); Church Yth Grp; Acpl Chr; Chorus; School Musical; Swing Chorus; Natl Library Poetry Editrs Choice Awd; CSULA Satrdy Consrvtry Music Awd; Lit.

RITCHIE, ERICK D; Point Arena HS; Manchester, CA; (2); Yrbk; High Hon Roll; Hon Roll.

RITCHIE, JEANA R; Troy HS; Yorba Linda, CA; (1); Church Yth Grp; Cmnty Wkr; High Hon Roll; Spanish NHS; Certified Scuba Diver; CA Poly Pomona; Bus.

RITCHIE, MANDY; Delano HS; Delano, CA; (2); Dance Clb; Letterman Clb; Pep Clb; Var Cheerldng; Hon Roll; NHS; Prfct Atten Awd; Dance Team 1st At I Love Dance Comptn; CSF; UCLA; Engl.

RITCHIE, PHILIP M; Winters Joint Union HS; Winters, CA; (2); Letterman Clb; JV Bsbl; Hon Roll; Police Safety Shows; Med.

RITCHIE, RYAN; Bret Harte HS; Murphys, CA; (2); Church Yth Grp; SADD; JV Bsbl; JV Crs Cntry; High Hon Roll; Fri Nght Live; CA Schlstc Fed; Bear Vly Race Tm 3rd Pl Ski, J2 Men, Granite Chf Clssc; UC Santa Barbara; Phys Thrpy.

RITENOUR, ANDREA; Arlington HS; Riverside, CA; (2); Pep Clb; Sec Soph Cls; JV Cheerldng; Hon Roll; St Schlr; UC Santa Barbara; Publc Rltns.

RITTENHOUSE, SHANNON P; San Deguito HS; Encinitas, CA; (4); 130/522; AFS; Art Clb; SADD; Teachers Aide; Sec Frsh Cls; Amnsty Intl; Miss Encinitas Prtcpnt 90; Outstndng Achvt In Practical Arts 1987; Tv Productions Club; AFS Netherlands; Intl Bus.

RITTER, CARRIE; Western HS; Stanton, CA; (1); Pep Clb; Intrml Cheerldng; Cit Awd; Hon Roll; Acad Achvt Awd; Harvard; Bus Mgmt.

RITTER, DIANA E; Carlmont HS; San Carlos, CA; (3); Teachers Aide; Band; Ed Yrbk; Hon Roll; Psych.

RITTER, JON P; Casa Roble HS; Orangevale, CA; (2); 40/461; Boy Scts; JV Bsktbl; Var Ftbl; JV Socr; JV Trk; Cit Awd; Hon Roll; Prfct Atten Awd; Pres Acad Fit Awd; UC Davis; Med.

RITTER, MICHAEL J; Bellarmine College Prep; San Jose, CA; (3); Letterman Clb; Ski Clb; Varsity Clb; Var Swmmng; JV Wrstlng; Vrsty Water Polo; Hlth.

RITTER, MICHELLE L; Golden West HS; Visalia, CA; (4); Art Clb; Drama Clb; Pep Clb; Spanish Clb; Speech Tm; Thesps; School Musical; School Play; Swmmng; Hon Roll; CA Poly San Luis; Arch.

RITTIERODT, MARC J; California Lutheran HS; Riverside, CA; (2); 7/15; Math Tm; Band; Variety Show; JV Bsktbl; JV Ftbl; Hon Roll; Prfct Atten Awd; Riverside Astronmcl Soc; AYSO Soccer Refree; Knwldge Master Open; Physcs.

RITTTER, ERIC J; Oak Ridge HS; El Dorado Hills, CA; (3); 21/261; Debate Tm; NFL; Speech Tm; Band; Jazz Band; Lit Mag; High Hon Roll; Ntl Merit Ltr; Pres Acad Fit Awd; Jrnlsm.

RITZ, DENISE R; Temecula Valley HS; Temecula, CA; (3); 11/465; Church Yth Grp; Service Clb; Var Bsktbl; Intrml Powder Puff Ftbl; JV Sftbl; High Hon Roll; Bio.

RIVAS, ANDREW R; San Adreas HS; Beaumont, CA; (3); Aut Mechncs; Woodshp; Music; San Bernardino ST Coll; Electr.

RIVAS, ANNETTE M; Dinuba HS; Dinuba, CA; (2); 1/160; Cmnty Wkr; Drama Clb; Math Tm; Service Clb; Rptr Nwsp; Yrbk; Rep Soph Cls; Tennis; Stat Vllybl; High Hon Roll; Mt Holyike; Med.

RIVAS, CARLOS; Daniel Murphy HS; Los Angeles, CA; (2); Debate Tm; Speech Tm; Ftbl; Socr; High Hon Roll; USC; Doctor.

RIVAS, CINDY; Bell Gardens HS; Bell Gardens, CA; (2); Band; Mrchg Band; USC.

RIVAS, DEANNE L; Ernest Righetti HS; Santa Maria, CA; (3); Drama Clb; 4-H; FFA; Teachers Aide; 4-H Awd; Hon Roll.

RIVAS, GINA M; Live Oak HS; Morgan Hill, CA; (3); Church Yth Grp; Spanish Clb; Band; Var Bsktbl; 2nd Pl Wnnr Sci Fair; Davis; Engrng.

RIVAS, JOEY R; Orestimba HS; Newman, CA; (2); JV Bsktbl; High Hon Roll; State Spelling Bee.

RIVAS, JORGE A; Calexico HS; Calexico, CA; (4); 4/465; Math Clb; Math Tm; Spanish Clb; Teachers Aide; Socr; San Diego ST U; Civil Engrng.

RIVAS, KARLA C; Victor Valley SR HS; Victorville, CA; (4); Church Yth Grp; Spanish Clb; 1st Frgn Stu Grad Bgn No Engl Skls; Flght Attndnt.

RIVAS, LAURI A; Sunny Hills HS; Buena Park, CA; (3); Art Clb; Church Yth Grp; Office Aide; Teachers Aide; Cit Awd; High Hon Roll; Hon Roll; Pres Acad Fit Awd; Zenith Soc; GSE 1st Yr Algebra Hnrs; Art.

RIVAS, LIDIA; Woodland HS; Dunnigan, CA; (4); 17/452; Spanish Clb; Teachers Aide; High Hon Roll; Hon Roll; Ntl Merit SF; CSF; MESA; Eaop; UC Davis; Elec Engrng.

RIVAS, MANUEL A; Nathaniel Narbonne HS; Torrance, CA; (2); French Clb; Service Clb; Teachers Aide; Hon Roll; Jr CSF; Gftd/Tlntd Pgm; UCLA.

RIVAS, MARIE M; Arroyo HS; El Monte, CA; (4); 122/425; Key Clb; NFL; Acpl Chr; Rptr Nwsp; Off Frsh Cls; Sec Jr Cls; Capt JV Cheerldng; Ntl Merit SF; Speech Tm; Teachers Aide; Aeolian Choir 2 Yrs, 1 Yr Treas; Arroyos Acadmc Decthln Tm; Psych.

RIVAS, OSCAR E; Birmingham HS; Arleta, CA; (3); Teachers Aide; Wt Lftg; CSUN; Bus.

RIVAS, SALVADOR; Artesia HS; Lakewood, CA; (2); Rep Stu Cncl; Cit Awd; Hon Roll; Upward Bound Prog; Lttrmns Jacket Lttr A.

RIVAS, SOCORRO; Jefferson HS; Daly City, CA; (2); 6/378; Dance Clb; Science Clb; Trk; High Hon Roll; Prfct Atten Awd; CSF; Energy Trnsfrmtn Prsntng Group; GSM; Psychiatrist.

RIVAS, VERONICA S; Roosevelt HS Extension Program; Los Angeles, CA; (3); Nwsp; Yrbk; Swmmng; Hon Roll; U Of CA San Diego; Crmnlgy.

RIVAS, VICTOR; La Jolla HS; San Diego, CA; (4); Model UN; Teachers Aide; Wrstlng; Hon Roll; Boxing Awd; SDSU; Med.

RIVAS, YESENIA; Woodland HS; Yolo, CA; (2); Teachers Aide; Rptr Nwsp; NHS; Jrnlsm.

RIVERA, ALICIA; Deland HS; Delano, CA; (2); Art Clb; English Clb; French Clb; Hosp Aide; Intnl Clb; Key Clb; Math Clb; Science Clb; Speech Tm; French Hon Soc; Exchng Stu Pgm; Bike Rdng Team; Reading Vlntr; UCLA; Med.

RIVERA, ANDREA M; Liberty Union HS; Brentwood, CA; (1); Church Yth Grp; Acpl Chr; Var Cheerldng.

RIVERA, ANNA M; Indio HS; Indio, CA; (2); 4/30; Church Yth Grp; French Clb; GAA; Teachers Aide; Nwsp; Off Soph Cls; Crs Cntry; Trk; Wt Lftg; French Hon Soc; Law.

RIVERA, ARCADIA G; Sunset HS; Hayward, CA; (3); Latin Clb; Tennis; High Hon Roll; Hon Roll; Prfct Atten Awd; Banking Cls; Genetic Engr.

RIVERA, BLANCA E.; Kerman HS; Kerman, CA; (3); Church Yth Grp; Cmnty Wkr; FTA; Hon Roll; Teachers Aide; Chorus; Ed Yrbk; VP Jr Cls; Treas Sr Cls; Var L Cheerldng; Most Vlbl Chrldr 90; Fresno ST; Chld Care.

RIVERA, CAMILO; Modesto HS; Modesto, CA; (2); Intrml Crs Cntry; Intrml Gym; Hon Roll; Arch.

RIVERA, CHRISTINE; San Clemente HS; San Clemente, CA; (2); Hosp Aide; JV Cheerldng; Capt Pom Pon; Hon Roll; Bus.

RIVERA, DAISY H; Hamilton HS; Los Angeles, CA; (4); 46/575; Church Yth Grp; Band; Mrchg Band; Cit Awd; Hon Roll; Val; Sociedad Literaria Ed De Los Angeles 1st Pl; Latin Amer Stu Organ; Wind Ens; CSU; Bio.

RIVERA, DAKEITHA L; Lincoln HS; Stockton, CA; (1); 150/669; Teachers Aide; Spelman; Psych.

RIVERA, DIANA R; Carson HS; Carson, CA; (3); FTA; Latin Clb; Office Aide; Swmmng; Acad Awd Hstry; Super Effort Awd; CA ST U; Elem Ed.

RIVERA, DIEGO E; Central Union HS; El Centro, CA; (3); 130/550; Letterman Clb; Varsity Clb; Var Bsktbl; Var Ftbl; Var Trk; Wt Lftg; Hon Roll; Upwrd Bnd; Sprts Med.

RIVERA, DIGNA R; Bishop Amat HS; West Covina, CA; (3); Church Yth Grp; Spanish Clb; Hon Roll; Fshn Outlk Clb Secy; Peer Mnstr; Friday Nght Live; Mock Trial Juror; Intl Reltns.

RIVERA, DINORAH; Ganesha HS; Pomona, CA; (3); Office Aide; Teachers Aide; Law Enfrcmnt.

RIVERA, DIO; Sacred Heart Of Mary HS; Pico Rivera, CA; (3); GAA; Pep Clb; Chorus; Drill Tm; Variety Show; Off Soph Cls; Var Co-Capt Cheerldng; Yth/Gov 88-89; Wrk Exprnce Pgm 88-90; Kum Laude Scty 89-90; Loyola Marymount U; Poltcl Sci.

RIVERA, EILEEN; Chaffey HS; Ontario, CA; (3); Am Leg Aux Girls St; Church Yth Grp; Cmnty Wkr; Spanish Clb; Band; Mrchg Band; Ed Yrbk; Var Tennis; High Hon Roll.

RIVERA, GABRIEL; Cajon HS; San Bernardino, CA; (2); Sec Soph Cls; JV Socr; Hon Roll.

RIVERA, GILBERT M; Eagle Rock HS; Los Angeles, CA; (3); Art Clb; Church Yth Grp; Prfct Atten Awd; Acad Enrchd & Hnr Classes; U Of S CA; Filmaking.

RIVERA, GRACE; Downey HS; Downey, CA; (3); Church Yth Grp; German Clb; Band; Chorus; School Musical; School Play; Hon Roll; Achvr UIL Solo, Ensmbl; CA ST Fullerton; Sci.

RIVERA, GRACIELA C; Woodside HS; Redwood City, CA; (2); 82/430; Sec Church Yth Grp; Cmnty Wkr; Office Aide; Teachers Aide; Church Choir; Cit Awd; Hon Roll; CSF; Play Vllybl For Church, Sch; Stu Of Yr Sci; UC Berkley; Med.

RIVERA, IBYANG; Grant HS; Sacramento, CA; (3); Cmnty Wkr; Computer Clb; Dance Clb; English Clb; Intnl Clb; Math Clb; Pres Science Clb; Spanish Clb; JV Sftbl; Outstndng Math Engrng Sci Achvt Stu Yr 89 90; Engrng.

RIVERA, JACKIE; Atwater HS; Merced, CA; (1); Church Yth Grp; Cmnty Wkr; Church Choir; Rep Frsh Cls; Rep Stu Cncl; Score Keeper; Hon Roll; Interact Club Secy; Law.

RIVERA, JACQUELINE M; Grant HS; Los Angeles, CA; (2); SADD; Intrml Tennis; Interact Clb; Hand Acrss Campus; Horror F/X; USC; Accntnt.

RIVERA, JALIKA; Warren HS; New York, NY; (3); 91/300; Debate Tm; Drama Clb; SADD; Band; Chorus; School Play; Stage Crew; Rptr Nwsp; Prfct Atten Awd; Pace U; Theatre Arts.

RIVERA, JESSIE B; Santa Maria HS; Santa Maria, CA; (3); Church Yth Grp; JA; Teachers Aide; Varsity Clb; JV Var Bsktbl; Powder Puff Ftbl; Hon Roll; Upward Bnd Smr Pgm.

RIVERA, JO ANN; Wasco HS; Wasco, CA; (2); Church Yth Grp; Chorus; Rep Soph Cls; JV Cheerldng; JV Sftbl; High Hon Roll; NHS.

RIVERA, JOHN; Colton HS; Colton, CA; (3); Stage Crew; UCR; Anthropology.

RIVERA, LAUURICE; Glen A Wilson HS; Hacienda Heights, CA; (3); Band; Flag Corp; Mrchg Band; Pep Band; Variety Show; Trk; Art.

RIVERA, LESBIA; Atwater HS; Atwater, CA; (3); Church Yth Grp; French Clb; Office Aide; Hon Roll; Prfct Atten Awd; Lawyer.

RIVERA, LETICIA M; Sacred Heart Of Jesus HS; Los Angeles, CA; (3); Computer Clb; Debate Tm; FBLA; GAA; Hosp Aide; JA; Office Aide; Chorus; Church Choir; School Musical; Accounting; USC; Accounting & Computer Eng.

RIVERA, LISA M; Pinnicles HS; Soledad, CA; (2); Pres Frsh Cls; JV Cheerldng; Criminal Law.

RIVERA, LOURDES G; Diamond Bar HS; Walnut, CA; (3); Dance Clb; Drama Clb; Spanish Clb; Variety Show; Stat Vllybl; High Hon Roll; Hon Roll; Cuban Cultural Clb; Psych.

RIVERA, LYNN; Southwest HS; San Diego, CA; (3); 34/265; FTA; SADD; Teachers Aide; Cit Awd; Schlrshp Awd; UCSD; Nrsng.

RIVERA, MARIE E; Bullard HS; Fresno, CA; (2); Band; Mrchg Band; Pep Band; Tennis; Jrnlsm.

RIVERA, MARISSA; Bonita Vista HS; Chula Vista, CA; (4); Pep Clb; Nwsp; Yrbk; Var Cheerldng; JV Vllybl; Acctng.

RIVERA, NICOLAS OOKA; Mar Vista HS; Imperial Beach, CA; (4); Church Yth Grp; Capt Var Quiz Bowl; Scholastic Bowl; Stu Cncl; Cit Awd; Hon Roll; Acad Decthln Prtcptn Mdl; Acad Leag MVP; San Diego ST U; Art.

RIVERA, PABLO A; Redwood HS; Visalia, CA; (1); Church Yth Grp.

RIVERA, PATRICIA W D; North Hollywood HS; North Hollywood, CA; (2); Drama Clb; French Clb; Spanish Clb; Chorus; School Play; Hon Roll; Prfct Atten Awd; CSUN Ruture Schlrs; UCLA Partnrshp Pgm; UCLA; Chld Care.

RIVERA, RICARDO A; Hamilton HS; North Hollywood, CA; (3); Band; Jazz Band; Mrchg Band; LA USD All City Band Psdna Rose Prde; Med.

RIVERA, RICARDO J; Bell HS; Cudahy, CA; (3); Church Yth Grp; Rep Frsh Cls; Rep Jr Cls; Hon Roll; Prfct Atten Awd; UCLA; Sprts Med.

RIVERA, ROMANO; Mt Pleasant HS; San Jose, CA; (1); Med.

RIVERA, ROSELLE B; Canyon HS; Anaheim, CA; (3); Chorus; Cit Awd; Hon Roll.

RIVERA, SERGIO A; Novato HS; Novato, CA; (3); San Jose ST; Acctng.

RIVERA, STACY M; Mount Diablo HS; Concord, CA; (1); Cheerldng; UCLA; Fshn Arts.

RIVERA, VIDA; Theodore Roosevelt HS; Los Angeles, CA; (3); Hon Roll.

RIVERO, LORENZA; Acad Of Our Lady Of Peace; Chula Vista, CA; (4); 23/132; Cmnty Wkr; Pres VP French Clb; Sec Key Clb; Service Clb; Teachers Aide; Hon Roll; Kiwanis Awd; Mxcn Amer Hstry, Anthrplgy Smmr Coll Crs; Anthrplgy.

RIVERS, EMMA REBEKAH MARYAM; Sacramento HS; Sacramento, CA; (4); 33/388; Art Clb; Church Yth Grp; Cmnty Wkr; Drama Clb; Teachers Aide; School Play; Ed Nwsp; Reaching Out Group Ldr Stu; Sacramento Mem Schlrshp; St Johns Luth Chrch Schlrshp; Linfield Coll; Eng Ed.

RIVERS, VONETTA J; San Gorgonio HS; Norton, CA; (3); Church Yth Grp; Dance Clb; Teachers Aide; Gym; Tennis; Trk; Vllybl; Cit Awd; Peer Cnslng; Modeling; Valley Coll; Nrsng.

RIVES, TODD M; Lassen Union HS; Susanville, CA; (4).

RIVET, MARY; Elk Grove HS; Elk Grove, CA; (2); Yrbk; JV Bsktbl; JV Vllybl; Hon Roll; Prfct Atten Awd; Pres Acad Fit Awd; UC Davis; Arch.

RIVIELLO, ROBERT; Village Christian HS; Northridge, CA; (3); 1/123; Hosp Aide; Mu Alpha Theta; Jazz Band; Var Capt Crs Cntry; Var Capt Church Yth Grp; Var Trk; Ntl Merit SF; Chem & Algebra II Awds.

RIVIERA, EILEEN; San Fernando Valley Acad; Miami, FL; (2); Art Clb; Intnl Clb; Spanish Clb; Chorus; Drill Tm; School Play; Off Frsh Cls; Bsktbl; Cheerldng; Swmmng; UCLA; Bus.

RIXTER, DAVIDA D; Pleasant Hill JR Acad; Clayton, CA; (2); 1/7; Church Yth Grp; Cmnty Wkr; Drama Clb; Teachers Aide; Band; Chorus; School Musical; School Play; Variety Show; Rptr Yrbk; Stanford; OB/Gyn.

RIZZI, ERICA; Gilroy HS; Gilroy, CA; (3); 51/427; Church Yth Grp; Cmnty Wkr; Office Aide; Teachers Aide; Church Choir; School Musical; School Play; Stage Crew; Variety Show; Var Cheerldng; SAG Prfssnl Actress; Missionary Work In Mexico; Commnty Theater Awds; Commnctns.

RIZZO, MICHELE L; Bishop Montgomery HS; Torrance, CA; (2); Cmnty Wkr; Ski Clb; Crs Cntry; Trk; Hon Roll; Hospital Vlntr; Med.

RIZZO, RHENA K; Saint Joseph HS; La Palma, CA; (3); 59/180; GAA; Var Crs Cntry; JV Sftbl; Hon Roll; Law.

RO, DAVID; Los Amigos HS; Santa Ana, CA; (2); 5/365; Spanish Clb; Bsktbl; JV Capt Vllybl; High Hon Roll; Jr NHS; NHS; Prfct Atten Awd; Tennis; Swimming; Med.

RO, GLORIA; Mt Carmel HS; San Diego, CA; (4); Treas Computer Clb; Rptr FBLA; VP German Clb; Treas VICA; Band; Church Choir; Off Soph Cls; Sec Stu Cncl; Var L Swmmng; San Diego Yth Symphony Viola; Ecology Clb Treas; MA Inst Of Tech; Mech Engr.

RO, JOHN HYUN CHUL; Whitney HS; Cerritos, CA; (3); Cmnty Wkr; Library Aide; Lit Mag; Tennis; Bus.

ROA, MONICA; Notre Dame HS; Riverside, CA; (1); 18/175; Cmnty Wkr; High Hon Roll; CSF; Acctng.

ROACH, CYNTHIA M; Serrano HS; Phelan, CA; (1); Church Yth Grp; Off FBLA; JV Sftbl; JV Vllybl; High Hon Roll.

ROACH, DENISE; Serrano HS; Phelan, CA; (3); 6/213; Church Yth Grp; VP FBLA; Chorus; Drill Tm; Var Trk; High Hon Roll; Pres Acad Fit Awd; CSF; Stu For Stu; Jr Hnr Guard; Scndry Ed.

ROACH, HEATHER M; William C Overfelt HS; San Jose, CA; (1); Church Yth Grp; Science Clb; Band; Jr Stsmn Amer Dir Of Publcty; Camp Fire; Feed The Wrld Club; U CA; Grapho-Analysm.

ROACH, JO ANNE; Gridley Union HS; Gridley, CA; (4); 6/108; Am Leg Aux Girls St; VP Spanish Clb; Ed Yrbk; Sec Frsh Cls; Pres Sr Cls; Var Capt Bsktbl; Pres Acad Fit Awd; Voice Dem Awd; CA Schlrshp Fed; Bnk Amer Achvt Awd Lbrl Arts; Stu Dir Fall Homcmng; CAL Poly; Civil Engrng.

ROACH, KATRINA M; Cajon HS; San Bernardino, CA; (2); 4/34; Hosp Aide; JA; Service Clb; Church Choir; Variety Show; Intrml Tennis; Sec Frsh Cls; Sec Soph Cls; Cit Awd; Gov Hon Prg Awd; Intl Bacc; Black Stu Unifd; Spelman Coll; Medcl.

ROACH, RYAN T; Oakmont HS; Roseville, CA; (1); Drama Clb; Karate; Martial Arts; College; English Novelist.

ROACH, STEVE G; Willits HS; Willits, CA; (3); Church Yth Grp; Teachers Aide; Sprt Ed Nwsp; Socr; Trk; Hon Roll; Sierra HR Coll; Forestry.

ROACHO, ISABEL; Calexico HS; Calexico, CA; (2); AFS; Church Yth Grp; Cmnty Wkr; Dance Clb; FCA; 4-H; GAA; Temple Yth Grp; Band; Chorus; Cities Of Amer Natls; Numerous Awds & Hnrs; U Of CA San Diego; Med.

ROBAINA, LOUISE; Sacred Heart Cthdrl; San Francisco, CA; (3); Chorus; Nwsp; Ed Lit Mag; Cit Awd; Hon Roll; Part Time Job Receptionist; Piano Clsses; Vlntr Parish CCD Clsses; USF.

ROBARDS, CHRIS E; Las Plumas HS; Oroville, CA; (2); Bsbl; Bsktbl; Ftbl; Wt Lftg; Outstndng Defnsv Ftbl Plyr Of Yr Awd; Work Summit Engrs As Survyr; Butte JC; Engrng.

ROBB, KRISTINA; Burroughs HS; Ridgecrest, CA; (2); Church Yth Grp; Dance Clb; Drama Clb; French Clb; FBLA; SADD; Band; Chorus; Church Choir; School Play; Dance Tchr; BYU; Ed.

ROBBINS, AMBER M; Hoopa Valley HS; Willow Creek, CA; (3); Art Clb; Drama Clb; Key Clb; Science Clb; Thesps; School Play; Sec Jr Cls; Var Cheerldng; Hon Roll; Intl Thespian Soc; Tomahawk Clb; Outstndng Artist In Cls; Illustration.

ROBBINS, CARLA W; North Monterey County HS; Watsonville, CA; (3); Church Yth Grp; Cmnty Wkr; SADD; High Hon Roll; Hon Roll; FNL Friday Night Live; Outstndng Hstry, Health Stu Awd 89-90; Hartnell; Vet Med.

ROBBINS, JASON L; Whitney HS; Cerritos, CA; (3); Band; Variety Show; Nwsp; Var Swmmng; Var Water Polo; Fnlst Congress-Bundestag Yth Exchange Schlrshp.

ROBBINS, JENNIFER A; Oakmont HS; Roseville, CA; (2); SADD; Var Socr; High Hon Roll; Hon Roll; NHS; Untd Grls Cmptv Soccer Tm; Cultural Homestay Inst Exchnge Stu To Japan; Advnd Plcmnt Hist; Hnrs Bio; OR ST U; Tchr.

ROBBINS, JENNIFER LEE; Mission Viejo HS; Mission Viejo, CA; (4); 45/443; Pres Drama Clb; Teachers Aide; Pres Thesps; School Musical; Cit Awd; Elks Awd; Hon Roll; NHS; Pres Schlr; Bank Of Amer Achvtmnt Awd Englsh; CSF; Mst Outstndng Actress & Achvtmnt Awd 90; Spirit Of Diablo Awd; Loyola Marymount; TV Prod.

ROBBINS, JULIANNA; Adolfo Camarillo HS; Camarillo, CA; (2); Church Yth Grp; Lit Mag; Swmmng; High Hon Roll; Hon Roll; CSF; Aquarian League; Dist Honor Roll; Brigham Young U; Eng.

ROBBINS, KAREN; Oxnard HS; Oxnard, CA; (2); Art Clb; Church Yth Grp; Cmnty Wkr; Bsktbl; Swmmng; Trk; High Hon Roll; Amercn Soviet Yth Exchng Stu Ambsdr Pgm; Acad Achvt Awds Swmmng & Bsktbl.

ROBBINS, LAURA; Terra Nova HS; Pacifica, CA; (4); Church Yth Grp; Debate Tm; 4-H; Library Aide; Intrml Vllybl; Hon Roll; Var Badmntn; Brigham Young U; Accntnt.

ROBBINS, MICHAEL D; Skyline HS; Oakland, CA; (2); 1/500; Church Yth Grp; SADD; Teachers Aide; Sprt Ed Nwsp; Yrbk; Pres Frsh Cls; Pres Soph Cls; Pres Jr Cls; High Hon Roll; Val; Stanford; Pro Bsbl.

ROBBINS, VALERIE A; Saint Joseph Notre Dame HS; Alameda, CA; (3); Cmnty Wkr; Var Golf; High Hon Roll; Hon Roll; Sonoma ST U; Bio.

ROBBY, AUTUMN; Riverbank HS; Carm, CA; (2); 4/100; Art Clb; Church Yth Grp; Drama Clb; Teachers Aide; Treas Thesps; School Musical; School Play; Stage Crew; Variety Show; Rep Soph Cls; Mock Trial; Wrk With Migrant Chldrn; Julliard; Theatrical Arts.

ROBECK, JASON L; Pasadena HS; Pasadena, CA; (4); Church Yth Grp; Pasadena City Coll.

ROBENALT, ANTHONY; Serra HS; Foster City, CA; (2); 6/200; German Clb; Math Clb; Jazz Band; High Hon Roll; Trivia Clb; CSF; JSA; Hnrs Awd Math 89; Hnrs Awd Grmn 90; UCLA; Movie Prodctn & Dirctn.

ROBERSON, ERIC M; Sonora HS; Soulsbyville, CA; (2); Ski Clb; JV Socr; Hon Roll; 1st Pl CA St Fr Indus & Tech Ed 89 & 90; Golden St Exam 89 Alg I Hnrs; Math.

ROBERSON, KATHLEEN A; El Camino Fundamental HS; Fair Oaks, CA; (3); Cmnty Wkr; Teachers Aide; Hon Roll; Runner Up Design An Ad Cont; 1st Pl Writing Conts; Clg Of Redwoods; Engl.

ROBERSON, KIMBERLY A; Hanford Joint Union HS; Hanford, CA; (3); Art Clb; Treas Rptr FHA; Teachers Aide; Church Choir; Hon Roll; Math, Engrng, Sci Achvt VP CA Schlstc Fed; Spllng Bee, Dist, Cty, St; 1st Pl Trphy St Cmnty Invlmnt; Med.

ROBERSON, KRISTEN D; Notre Dame HS; Salinas, CA; (2); Church Yth Grp; Quiz Bowl; School Musical; Variety Show; Treas Frsh Cls; JV Capt Bsktbl; Var Pom Pon; JV Var Trk; Hon Roll; Prfct Atten Awd; Dance Scholar; Notre Dame Mother/Daughtr Fash Show; Coaches Awd & Mst Imprvd Bsktbl; Track Awds.

ROBERSON, MICHAUNDA; Lincoln HS; Stockton, CA; (3); Church Yth Grp; Church Choir; JV Var Bsktbl; VP Blck Stu Un; Psych.

ROBERSON, OLIVE M; Baldwin Park HS; Baldwin Park, CA; (2); Church Yth Grp; Acpl Chr; Chorus; Church Choir.

ROBERSON, PAMELA M; Victor Valley Union HS; Victorville, CA; (3); Church Yth Grp; Cmnty Wkr; Computer Clb; Dance Clb; Key Clb; Speech Tm; Teachers Aide; Church Choir; Hon Roll; Sal; FL A & M U; Intl Bus.

ROBERSON, VALINE; Washington Preparatory HS; Los Angeles, CA; (4); Cmnty Wkr; Dance Clb; Lit Mag; High Hon Roll; Prfct Atten Awd; Ephebian 90; CSF; Knights/Ladies; U Of AZ; Engl.

ROBERT, MICHELLE C; Fontana HS; Fontana, CA; (3); Office Aide; Hon Roll; Pres Acad Fit Awd; Law.

ROBERTS, ANDREA L; Samuel F B Morse HS; San Diego, CA; (2); Stu Cncl; L Var Socr; Var Sftbl; JV Vllybl; High Hon Roll; NHS; Prfct Atten Awd; CSF.

ROBERTS, ANDREW J; Santa Clara HS; Santa Clara, CA; (4); 9/400; Pres German Clb; Cit Awd; High Hon Roll; Prfct Atten Awd; Pres Acad Fit Awd; Acadmc Achvt Awd; Gldn St Exam Geom High Hnrs; Santa Clara U; Elec Engrng.

ROBERTS, ANGELA C; Thousand Oaks HS; Thousand Oaks, CA; (2); 102/554; Hon Roll; Ambssdrs To Asia Cmptn; U Of Portland; Law.

ROBERTS, BRYAN C; Burlingame HS; Burlingame, CA; (3); Boy Scts; Church Yth Grp; Lit Mag; Bsbl; Mgr(s); Hon Roll; CSF; Eagle Scout; U CA-SAN Diego; Poly Sci.

ROBERTS, CAMERON M; Grossmont HS; El Cajon, CA; (3); 2/400; Church Yth Grp; Girl Scts; Hosp Aide; Intnl Clb; Key Clb; Ski Clb; Var Swmmng; JV Tennis; JV Vllybl; High Hon Roll; Pre-Med.

ROBERTS, CAROL L; Indio HS; Indio, CA; (1); Church Yth Grp; Color Guard; Proj Pursuit.

ROBERTS, CRYSTAL N; Community Educational Services; Riverside, CA; (4); UCR; Biology.

ROBERTS, CYNTHIA A; Victor Valley HS; Victorville, CA; (4); 34/313; Pres Church Yth Grp; Computer Clb; Key Clb; Pep Clb; Church Choir; Color Guard; Yrbk; Sec Stu Cncl; Kiwanis Awd; Soroptimist Yth Ctznshp Awd 1st Pl; Bnk Amer Cert Bus; CA Schlrshp Fed; Victor Valley Coll; Mortry Sci.

ROBERTS, DAWN M; Loyalton HS; Loyalton, CA; (1); Drama Clb; 4-H; Sec FBLA; Spanish Clb; SADD; School Play; Phtg Yrbk; Pres Frsh Cls; 4-H Awd; High Hon Roll; Natl Red Ribbon Wk Actvts Chairman.

ROBERTS, DEBORAH S; South San Francisco HS; So San Francisc, CA; (3); Church Yth Grp; Math Clb; Hist Band; Pep Band; School Musical; Var Stat Tennis; CSF; Hayward ST U; Music.

ROBERTS, DEBRAH M; Corona HS; Corona, CA; (2); 16/475; Band; Stage Crew; Stat Bsbl; Intrml Mgr(s); Intrml Score Keeper; Intrml Sftbl; High Hon Roll; Hon Roll; Pre Of Bnd; Oustndg Achvmnt Band; U Of Calf; Mathematics.

ROBERTS, DONALD ANDREW; Mojave HS; California City, CA; (3); 23/99; Chess Clb; Teachers Aide; School Musical; School Play; Stage Crew; Variety Show; Golf; Cit Awd; Hon Roll; Mock Trial; Repp To Schl Brd Cncrnng JR/Sr Pprom; CA T Bakersfield; Ed.

ROBERTS, DUSTIN J; Ukiah JR Acad; Ukiah, CA; (1); Church Yth Grp; Chorus; Phtg Yrbk; Off Frsh Cls; Pacific Coll; Arch.

ROBERTS, EDWARD J; Westminster HS; Westminster, CA; (2); 3/520; Boy Scts; Tennis; Hon Roll; Rotary Awd; St Schlr; Harvard Med; Gen Prctnr.

ROBERTS, ETOYIA R; San Rafael HS; San Rafael, CA; (2); Cmnty Wkr; Drill Tm; 4-H Awd; Hon Roll; CSF; U CA Berkeley; Acctnt.

ROBERTS, HEATHER; Pleasant Valley SR HS; Chico, CA; (4); 69/250; Church Yth Grp; Service Clb; SADD; Acpl Chr; Mrchg Band; Orch; Lit Mag; Cheerldng; Masters Coll; Early Chldhd Ed.

ROBERTS, JAMES E; Hoover HS; Fresno, CA; (2); Church Yth Grp; Cmnty Wkr; German Clb; Library Aide; Science Clb; Church Choir; Crs Cntry; Trk; Cit Awd; BSU; U CA San Jose; Elec Eng.

ROBERTS, JEFFREY W; Clovis West HS; Fresno, CA; (3); Church Yth Grp; Math Clb; Math Tm; Var Ftbl; Capt Ice Hcky; JV Wrstlng; Pres Acad Fit Awd; U WA; Engrng.

ROBERTS, JENNIFER; Kerman HS; Kerman, CA; (2); Church Yth Grp; Math Tm; Band; Swing Chorus; Sec Soph Cls; Var Swmmng; JV Vllybl; Hon Roll; CSF; Pre-Med.

ROBERTS, JESSE D; Arcata HS; Arcata, CA; (1); French Clb; Bsktbl; L Golf; Var Socr; French Hon Soc; High Hon Roll; Prfct Atten Awd; Math Tutor; Math.

ROBERTS, JOSHUA C; North Tahoe HS; Tahoe City, CA; (2); 26/87; JV L Bsbl; JV L Ftbl; Var L Wrstlng; 1990 Wrestling Most Improved Awardd; A F Acad; Cmmrcl Arlns Pilot.

ROBERTS, KARRI; Cuyama Valley HS; New Cuyama, CA; (3); 2/19; Am Leg Aux Girls St; Church Yth Grp; Church Choir; JV Var Bsktbl; Var Sftbl; JV Var Vllybl; Dnfth Awd; High Hon Roll; Hon Roll; Treas Frsh Cls; MVP Jr Var Vllybl; All Leag Sftbl 2 Yrs; Bus Mgmt.

ROBERTS, KELLY D; El Dorado HS; Placentia, CA; (3); Band; Color Guard; Mrchg Band; Pep Band; School Musical; Hon Roll; Hnr Awd-Gldn St Algebra Exam; Cmptd Equestrian Cmptns-1st Pl; Mscnshp Awd; Cal Poly-Pomona; Cmrcl Art.

ROBERTS, KELLY L; Santa Clara HS; Oxnard, CA; (3); 5/140; Letterman Clb; SADD; Varsity Clb; Sec Treas Sr Cls; Var Socr; JV Sftbl; Hon Roll; NHS; CSF.

ROBERTS, KENNETH BURKE; Clovis West HS; Fresno, CA; (2); Ski Clb; Var Tennis; Law.

ROBERTS, KEVIN P; Willits HS; Willits, CA; (2); Letterman Clb; Library Aide; Model UN; Teachers Aide; Varsity Clb; Rep Stu Cncl; JV Ftbl; Var Tennis; Var Wrstlng; High Hon Roll; Schlr/Athltc; Notre Dame U; Lib Arts.

ROBERTS, LA TONYA D; La Sievra HS; Riverside, CA; (4); Church Yth Grp; Hon Roll; Merit Schol; Prfct Atten Awd; CA ST U; Scndry Ed.

ROBERTS, LISA M; Valley View HS; Moreno Valley, CA; (2); Church Yth Grp; Hosp Aide; Tennis; High Hon Roll; Hon Roll; Interact Clb Hstrn; UCLA; Med.

ROBERTS, MICHELLE C; Monte Vista HS; La Mesa, CA; (4); 13/425; VP Hosp Aide; Key Clb; Ed Nwsp; Var Trk; Hon Roll; Kiwanis Awd; Prfct Atten Awd; Pres Acad Fit Awd; Rotary Awd; Pep Clb; Soc Of Women Engrs Cert Mrt; U CA San Diego; Dentist.

ROBERTS, MICHELLE D; Highlands HS; Rio Linda, CA; (3); Church Yth Grp; Rptr Nwsp; Rep Soph Cls; Rep Jr Cls; Hon Roll; Nwsp Teen Corrspndnt; Yth Cnslr.

ROBERTS, NAKIA L; Dorsey HS; Los Angeles, CA; (2); Drama Clb; SADD; Chorus; School Play; Crs Cntry; Swmmng; Trk; Cit Awd; Hon Roll; Prfct Atten Awd; UCLA Partnrshp Pgm; DARE Pgm; USC; Legal.

ROBERTS, NICOLE R; Canyon Springs HS; Moreno Valley, CA; (2); Intnl Clb; High Hon Roll; CSF; Vlntr Wrk Nursing Hm; Support Goodwill; Yale; Med.

ROBERTS, ROSE M; Imperial HS; Pasadena, CA; (4); Church Yth Grp; FBLA; Speech Tm; Chorus; Church Choir; Hon Roll; Ntl Merit SF; U Southern CA; Psych.

ROBERTS, SALLIE D; Seaside High; Seaside, CA; (4); 30/276; AFS; Am Leg Aux Girls St; Church Yth Grp; Office Aide; ROTC; Spanish Clb; Chorus; Church Choir; Powder Puff Ftbl; Score Keeper; Amer Legion ROTC Schlstc Excel 88-90; Outstndnf Athlt Track 87-89; Dstngshd Athlt Awd 88; USAFA; Dist Atty.

ROBERTS, SARAH; Covenant Christian HS; San Diego, CA; (2); Church Yth Grp; Yrbk; Intrml JV Socr; Intrml JV Sftbl; Intrml JV Vllybl; High Hon Roll; Hon Roll; Pres Acad Fit Awd; Math/Arch.

ROBERTS, SETH I; Bishop Union HS; Bishop, CA; (3); 4-H; Math Tm; Yrbk; JV Bsktbl; Socr; Var L Tennis; High Hon Roll; Pres Acad Fit Awd; Sal Bursey Day Acad Cmptn.

ROBERTS, SHELLEY H; Ponderosa HS; Shingle Springs, CA; (1); Church Yth Grp; Computer Clb; Teachers Aide; Hon Roll; Art Clb; 4-H; Band; Chorus; School Musical; UC Davis; Doctor.

ROBERTS, TAMMY A; Redlands HS; Redlands, CA; (3); Church Yth Grp; Office Aide; Teachers Aide; Band; Mrchg Band; Pep Band; Trk; Cit Awd; Hon Roll; Pres Schlr; CSF; Stanford U; Science.

ROBERTS, THEODORE V; Nevada Union HS; Nevada City, CA; (3); Film.

ROBERTS, TODD A; Atwater HS; Atwater, CA; (4); FCA; Teachers Aide; Hon Roll; Prfct Atten Awd; UC Davis; Aerntcl Engrng.

ROBERTS, TRAVIS M; Nevada Union HS; Grass Valley, CA; (3); 50/535; Chess Clb; Church Yth Grp; Socr; Tennis; Hon Roll; Math.

ROBERTSON, ADAM; Sierra Joint Union HS; Auberry, CA; (4); Boy Scts; Church Yth Grp; Letterman Clb; Orch; Crs Cntry; Socr; Trk; JETS Awd; Sal; CSU Fresno; Engrng.

ROBERTSON, CHANTELLE; Roosevelt HS; Fresno, CA; (1); Pres Church Yth Grp; Chorus; Church Choir; JV Golf; High Hon Roll; Masonic Awd; CA ST U Fresno; Scndry Ed.

ROBERTSON, ELIZABETH; Grossmont HS; El Cajon, CA; (3); 49/389; Chess Clb; Chorus; Church Choir; School Musical; Hon Roll; Hnr Choir; Christmas Pgnt; BYU; Music.

ROBERTSON, HEIDI L; North HS; Bakersfield, CA; (4); Church Yth Grp; FCA; GAA; Letterman Clb; Varsity Clb; Acpl Chr; Chorus; Variety Show; Var L Bsktbl; Var L Sftbl.

ROBERTSON, JAMES W; Monte Vista HS; Spring Valley, CA; (3); 90/379; Boy Scts; Church Yth Grp; Cmnty Wkr; Varsity Clb; Var Diving; Var Swmmng; Wt Lftg; Cit Awd; Pres Acad Fit Awd; BSA Eagle Sct & God/Cntry Awd; TX A&M U; Aerospace Engrng.

ROBERTSON, JEAN; Novato HS; Novato, CA; (2); Church Yth Grp; Cmnty Wkr; Office Aide; Band; Church Choir; Intrml Bsktbl; JV Swmmng; High Hon Roll; Hon Roll; Pres Acad Fit Awd; CA Polytechnc San Luis Obispo.

ROBERTSON, KATHRYN ANNE; Salinas HS; Salinas, CA; (4); 41/350; Church Yth Grp; FBLA; Latin Clb; Library Aide; SADD; Thesps; Acpl Chr; Church Choir; School Musical; Variety Show; Madrigals; Stu For A Better Earth Pres; VA Tech; Commnctns.

ROBERTSON, KELLY R; Desert HS; Edwards, CA; (3); CSF; Mono Lake Cmmttee; U Of NV; Geolgy.

ROBERTSON, KENNAN A; Oakmont HS; Roseville, CA; (3); 1/200; Pres Church Yth Grp; Cmnty Wkr; Dance Clb; Drama Clb; Service Clb; SADD; Church Choir; Drill Tm; School Musical; School Play; Gold Acad Mrt Awd Cumltve 4.0 GPA; BYU; Zoologist.

ROBERTSON, KYLE; Calvary Chapel HS; Huntington Beach, CA; (2); Church Yth Grp; Teachers Aide; Variety Show; Off Soph Cls; Ftbl; Biola; Aerospace.

ROBERTSON, LAURA M; Antioch SR HS; Antioch, CA; (2); Band; Jazz Band; Mrchg Band; Var Sftbl; Hon Roll; Tchng Engl.

ROBERTSON, LINDSAY; Torrey Pines HS; San Diego, CA; (3); 63/422; Church Yth Grp; Cmnty Wkr; Hosp Aide; Key Clb; SADD; Phtg Nwsp; Swmmng; Hon Roll; Var Ltr Swmmng; Pilot Tutorial Pgm Elem Schl Children; Med.

ROBERTSON, MELANIE L; Torrey Pines HS; Solana Beach, CA; (4); AFS; Pep Clb; Teachers Aide; Drill Tm; Cheerldng; Sftbl; Hon Roll; CSF-SEAL Bearer; U Of OR.

ROBERTSON, NAOMI; Valley HS; Sacramento, CA; (1); Church Yth Grp; Church Choir; Capt Cheerldng; Hon Roll; Pres Acad Fit Awd; Blck Stu Union; Friday Nite Live; Harvard U; Lawyr.

ROBERTSON, NATHAN W; Capital Christian Schl; Sacramento, CA; (3); Bsktbl; Ftbl; Hon Roll.

ROBERTSON, SABRINA; St Joseph HS; Arroyo Grande, CA; (3); 22/133; Church Yth Grp; JA; Teachers Aide; Var L Cheerldng; U Of San Diego; Law.

ROBERTSON, SCOTT D; San Gorgonio HS; E Highland, CA; (3); 64/600; Am Leg Boys St; Church Yth Grp; Letterman Clb; Pres Stu Cncl; Var Capt Ftbl; ASB Pres; Ftbl All CBL; 3.50 GPA; Jr Cls Prince Bsktbl Homcmng; Air Force Acad; Aeronctcl Engr.

ROBERTSON, VALEEN; Durham HS; Chico, CA; (2); Spanish Clb; Hon Roll; Interact Grp; UCLA.

ROBERTSON, WILLIAM A; Yucaipa HS; Yucaipa, CA; (1); 71/423; Church Yth Grp; Letterman Clb; VP Soph Cls; Sec Jr Cls; Var L Trk; Hon Roll; Pilot.

ROBEY, MARK R; Chula Vista HS; National City, CA; (3); 9/535; Am Leg Boys St; Boy Scts; Church Yth Grp; Pep Clb; Science Clb; Pres Rep Stu Cncl; Var L Swmmng; Prfct Atten Awd; Pres Acad Fit Awd; Rotary Awd; Waterpolo; ASB Officer,Pres; AF Acad; Engr.

ROBIN, ALYSON G; Aragon HS; San Mateo, CA; (3); Chess Clb; Cmnty Wkr; Debate Tm; SADD; Church Choir; Orch; Rptr Nwsp; Treas Rep Frsh Cls; Rep Jr Cls; Pres Sr Cls; CA Yth Symphny; Union Assoctd Stu Bodies Dist Coordntr; Edctnl Psych.

ROBIN, RCHARD G; John Burroughs HS; Burbank, CA; (3); Am Leg Boys St; Boy Scts; French Clb; JV Tennis; Pres Acad Fit Awd; Outstndng Yth Awd; CA Jr Schlrshp Fed Sealbearer; CA Schlrshp Fed; UC; Engrng.

ROBINETT, ERIN; Willows HS; Willows, CA; (2); High Hon Roll; Frdy Nght Lv; Grdn Angl; Bus.

ROBINETTE, ERINN D; San Gabriel HS; San Gabriel, CA; (3); French Clb; JV Tennis; Hon Roll; Adv Plcmnt Clb; CSF; U Of CO; Cmptr Prgrmmng.

ROBINETTE, TIFFANY A; Hemet HS; Hemet, CA; (3); 113/547; Church Yth Grp; Library Aide; Hon Roll.

ROBINSON, ALONFORD; Bellarmine Prep; San Jose, CA; (4); Cmnty Wkr; JA; Varsity Clb; Nwsp; Yrbk; Off Frsh Cls; Off Soph Cls; Off Jr Cls; Off Sr Cls; Var Capt Ftbl; Coca-Cola Rgnl Schlr 90; Stanford U; Med.

ROBINSON, ALVIN; Fresno HS; Fresno, CA; (1).

ROBINSON, ANNE-MARYE; Mater Dei HS; Orange, CA; (3); Art Clb; Church Yth Grp; Cmnty Wkr; Hosp Aide; Office Aide; Hon Roll; UC Santa Barbara; Jrnlsm.

ROBINSON, ANTHONY; J Eugene Mc Ateer HS; San Francisco, CA; (1); Church Yth Grp; ROTC; Speech Tm; Drill Tm; Wrstlng.

ROBINSON, AYANNA M; Skyline HS; Oakland, CA; (2); Cit Awd; Hon Roll; CSF; Stu Of Mnth; Bus Admin.

ROBINSON, BONNIE J; Summerville Union HS; Sonora, CA; (4); 20/131; Church Yth Grp; Pres Sec 4-H; Quiz Bowl; Acpl Chr; Capt Color Guard; Mrchg Band; Yrbk; Var Cheerldng; 4-H Awd; Hon Roll; Columbia Coll; Gen Studies.

ROBINSON, CASSONJA J; Monterey HS; Seaside, CA; (3); Office Aide; Church Choir; Prfct Atten Awd; Blck Stu Union; Bus Mgmt.

ROBINSON, CHARLOTTE Y; Cordova HS; Mather A F B, CA; (4); ROTC; Teachers Aide; Cit Awd; Hon Roll; ROP; Air Force; Military.

ROBINSON, CINDY L; Junipero Serra HS; San Diego, CA; (4); 16/400; Church Yth Grp; Cmnty Wkr; FHA; Key Clb; SADD; Stage Crew; Rptr Nwsp; Cit Awd; Hon Roll; NHS; CSF; U Of CA San Diego; Psych.

ROBINSON, DONSHA D; Hueneme HS; Port Hueneme, CA; (3); SADD; Teachers Aide; Sftbl; Trk; Prfct Atten Awd; Mc Donalds Future Black Hstry Makers Of Tomorrow; Mock Trial, Pretrial Dfns Atty; BSU VP; Berkeley U; Law.

ROBINSON, HEIDI L; Buena Park HS; Buena Park, CA; (3); 34/369; Drama Clb; Sec Key Clb; Thesps; High Hon Roll; Hon Roll; Aud/Vis; Office Aide; Teachers Aide; School Musical; School Play; Jr Statesmen Amer VP & Secy; Dstngshd Schlr; Hnrs At Entrnc; CSF; Orng Cnty Academc Dcthln; HOBY Alt; Sociology.

ROBINSON, INGA; El Camino HS; Oceanside, CA; (3); 117/364; Dance Clb; JA; Church Choir; Drill Tm; VP Jr Cls; JV Bsktbl; Var Cheerldng; Var Mgr(s); Var Trk; Cit Awd; Assoc Stu Body VP; Comm Activts; Howard U; Physcn.

ROBINSON, JACKIE; Morse HS; San Diego, CA; (3); ROTC; Yrbk; Var Socr; U AR; Elec Engr.

ROBINSON, JENNIFER L; Amos Alonzo Stagg HS; Stockton, CA; (1); Variety Show; JV Sftbl; High Hon Roll; Pres Acad Fit Awd; Sacramento ST U; Atty.

ROBINSON, JENNIFER L; Casa Rable Fundamental HS; Orangevale, CA; (4); 34/345; Dance Clb; Pep Clb; Spanish Clb; SADD; JV Cheerldng; Hon Roll; Ntl Merit Ltr; Pres Schlr; Amer River Coll; Psych.

ROBINSON, JOSH C; Marysville HS; Marysville, CA; (3); 40/120; Var L Ftbl; Hon Roll; Natl Yng Ldrs Conf; San Diego ST; Aerontcl Engrng.

ROBINSON, JULIE A; Colton HS; Colton, CA; (2); Church Yth Grp; Debate Tm; Model UN; NFL; Speech Tm; Church Choir; VP Soph Cls; Hon Roll; Jr NHS; Kiwanis Awd; BYU; Nrsng.

ROBINSON, KELLY L; Mater Dei HS; Santa Ana, CA; (3); Church Yth Grp; Cmnty Wkr; Girl Scts; JCL; Latin Clb; Var L Swmmng; High Hon Roll; NHS; CSF; Girl Sct Gold Awd; People To People Yth Sci Exchnge Pgm USSR 90; Exchnge Stu Ireland 89; Bio.

ROBINSON, KENNETH P; Skyline HS; Oakland, CA; (3); Church Yth Grp; Drama Clb; Thesps; Acpl Chr; Chorus; Church Choir; School Musical; School Play; Swing Chorus; Treas Stu Cncl; Black Stu Union Treas; CSF; Gospel Choir Treas; Stanford U; Fnancl Admin.

ROBINSON, KERRI A; Santa Catalina HS; Oakland, CA; (2); Church Yth Grp; Hosp Aide; Rptr Nwsp; Ed Yrbk; Sec Frsh Cls; Hon Roll; UC Santa Barbara; Engl.

ROBINSON, KIM; Casa Roble HS; Citrus Heights, CA; (3); Hnr Rl; Bus Awd; Comp.

ROBINSON, LESLIE; Atwater HS; Atwater, CA; (1); FCA; Var Socr; JV Sftbl; High Hon Roll; Hon Roll; Rotary Awd; Vrsty Water Polo; Astrnmy.

ROBINSON, LISA A; Birmingham HS; Encino, CA; (3); SADD; Rptr Nwsp; Natl Yth Ldrshp Congress; Brdcst Jrnlsm.

ROBINSON, MANDEE L; Simi Valley HS; Simi Valley, CA; (3); 194/652; French Clb; SADD; Teachers Aide; Bsktbl; Cit Awd; High Hon Roll; Hon Roll; Bowlng,1st Pl Ventura Ct Regnl Trnmnt 90,State Fnls 90; Childcare,Enjoy Watchng & Helpng To Understnd; UCSD; Prosecution Lawyer Teach.

ROBINSON, MICHELLE; Loretto HS; Sacramento, CA; (3); SADD; Rptr Nwsp; Yrbk; Sftbl; Var Capt Vllybl; Hon Roll; Spirit & Sprt Clb VP; CA Berkeley; Psych.

ROBINSON, MOLLY T; El Toro HS; El Toro, CA; (3); Church Yth Grp; Library Aide; Red Cross Aide; Stu Cncl; Hon Roll; Recycling Pgm; Envrnmnt Awareness Pgm; Psych.

ROBINSON, NEFERTIT C; Corona HS; Corona, CA; (4); Service Clb; Drill Tm; Gym; Cit Awd; High Hon Roll; Hon Roll; Clark Atlanta U; Sports Med.

ROBINSON, NICHOLE L; San Bernardino HS; Highland, CA; (3); 21/400; Cmnty Wkr; Model UN; Quiz Bowl; Red Cross Aide; Scholastic Bowl; Stage Crew; Off Jr Cls; High Hon Roll; Hon Roll; NHS; CSF; Academic Decathlon; Prom Comm; Corp Bus Law.

ROBINSON, PARRIN F; Valley HS; Sacramento, CA; (2); 30/500; Church Yth Grp; SADD; Mrchg Band; JV Ftbl; Socr; JV Trk; Cit Awd; Hon Roll; MESA Clb; UCD Outrch Pgm; Aerospc Engrng.

ROBINSON, PETA-GAYE R; James Logan HS; Union City, CA; (3); 121/900; Band; Mrchg Band; Pep Band; Hon Roll; Cal ST Hayward.

ROBINSON, REBECCA; Fontana HS; Fontana, CA; (2); Pep Clb; Psych.

ROBINSON, REBECCA; Santa Barbara HS; Santa Barbara, CA; (4); Art Clb; Dance Clb; Vllybl; Santa Barbara City Coll; Jewlr.

ROBINSON, RHONDA L; John Muir HS; Altadena, CA; (4); 6/375; Church Yth Grp; Science Clb; Sec Jr Cls; Treas Sr Cls; Var Capt Crs Cntry; Var Capt Trk; Hon Roll; Natl Achvt Semi Finalist; Bio.

ROBINSON, SABIYAH C; Pioneer HS; San Jose, CA; (3); 15/392; Church Yth Grp; Teachers Aide; JV Trk; Intrml Wt Lftg; High Hon Roll; Hon Roll; Martial Arts; Foreign Lang; UCLA; Physics.

ROBINSON, SCOTT; North Hollywood HS; North Hollywood, CA; (2); Church Yth Grp; Ed Yrbk; JV Trk; High Hon Roll; CSF; UCLA; Doc.

ROBINSON, SHANN; Ceres HS; Ceres, CA; (4); Church Yth Grp; Dance Clb; French Clb; Pep Clb; Teachers Aide; Yrbk; Cheerldng; Score Keeper; Sftbl; Swmmng; US Davis; Fashion Merch.

ROBINSON, SHANNON L; Monache HS; Porterville, CA; (4); 27/291; Cmnty Wkr; SADD; Teachers Aide; Crs Cntry; Cit Awd; High Hon Roll; Prfct Atten Awd; Pres Acad Fit Awd; Bstr Clb; CSF; Porterville Coll; Scl Sci.

ROBINSON, SHARLA E; St Paul HS; Daly City, CA; (4); 2/36; GAA; SADD; Nwsp; VP Jr Cls; Stat Bsktbl; Var Vllybl; Hon Roll; Sal; CSF; Amnesty Intl; Peace Club Pres; Wellesley Coll; Chem.

ROBINSON, SONYA; Paraclete HS; Lancaster, CA; (3); Drama Clb; Ski Clb; SADD; Cheerldng; Dncng.

ROBINSON, STEVE E; North HS; Bakersfield, CA; (4); Ski Clb; JV Ftbl; Var Trk; Hon Roll; Business Club Member; Kiwanis Club Volunteer; Bakersfield Coll; Bus.

ROBINSON, TAMMY L; Turlock HS; Turlock, CA; (3); 65/603; AFS; Church Yth Grp; Cmnty Wkr; Dance Clb; French Clb; Sec Treas Sr Cls; Mgr(s); CSF; BYU; Psych.

ROBINSON, TAMMY R; Ramona HS; Riverside, CA; (1); 135/582; Chorus; CA ST Santa Barbara.

ROBINSON, TERI C; Fountain Valley HS; Mtn Center, CA; (1); Church Yth Grp; FCA; Gym; Hon Roll; Long Beach ST; Pedtrcn.

ROBINSON, TONYA Y; Washingtonb HS; Los Angeles, CA; (2); Dance Clb; ROTC; Band; Var Trk; WA ST.

ROBISON, KARA D; San Marcos HS; Santa Barbara, CA; (3); 64/370; Church Yth Grp; Teachers Aide; Flag Corp; Yrbk; Hon Roll; Pres Acad Fit Awd; Mem Number 1 Club; Capt Tall Flag Tm; Cal Poly San Luis Obispo; Soc.

ROBITAILLE, ANNETTE T; Torrey Pines HS; San Diego, CA; (3); 135/457; Hosp Aide; SADD; Band; Drm Mjr(t); Mrchg Band; Orch; Pep Band; Hon Roll; Jr NHS; Prfct Atten Awd; CSF; Animal Ctr Volunteer; Sci.

ROBLEDO, LUIS; Orosi HS; Cutler, CA; (3); 12/220; Math Clb; Hon Roll; Rcvd Daughters Am Grad; UCSD; Bio.

ROBLEDO, RENEE T; Santa Barbara HS; Santa Barbara, CA; (3); 144/472; Pep Clb; Teachers Aide; Band; Color Guard; Mrchg Band; Pep Band; Var Cheerldng; Hon Roll; Flamenco Dncng; Biking; UCSB; Law.

ROBLES, ADRIANA R; Gonzales HS; Chualar, CA; (2); FBLA; SADD; High Hon Roll; Readers Theatre; CSF; Gldn St Exam Schl Rcgntn Awd; Bus.

ROBLES, ANA V; Mount Whitney HS; Visalia, CA; (3); Teachers Aide; Orch; Crs Cntry; Trk; Wt Lftg; Hon Roll; NHS; Santa Cruz; Bus Admin.

ROBLES, DAMIAN; Calexico HS; Calexico, CA; (1); Bsbl; Bsktbl; Ftbl; Wt Lftg; Acctnt.

ROBLES, EDNA; Vacaville HS; Vacaville, CA; (3); Church Yth Grp; Spanish Clb; Success Pgm; Fshn Mrchndsng.

ROBLES, ELIZABETH N; Hesperia Christian HS; Hesperia, CA; (3); Church Yth Grp; Teachers Aide; Chorus; Var Cheerldng; Miss Southern CA Natl Teenager 89.

ROBLES, ISRAEL; Banning HS; Banning, CA; (3); Band; Jazz Band; Mrchg Band; Tech Engr.

ROBLES, LILIANA; Castle Park HS; Chula Vista, CA; (4); 23/320; French Clb; Q&S; Teachers Aide; Ed Nwsp; JV Stat Vllybl; Prfct Atten Awd; San Diego ST U; Spnsh HS Tchr.

ROBLES, MARINA; Luther Burbank HS; Sacramento, CA; (3); 42/276; Cmnty Wkr; Sec FTA; Hosp Aide; Office Aide; SADD; Teachers Aide; Cit Awd; Hon Roll; NHS; Hewlett-Packard Awd MESA; UC Berkeley; Jrnlsm.

ROBLES, NANNETTE H; San Gabriel Mission HS; San Gabriel, CA; (3); Church Yth Grp; Drama Clb; French Clb; GAA; Spanish Clb; School Musical; Hon Roll; Merit Awd; Santa Barbara U; Comp Sci.

ROBLES, OSCAR G; John C Fremont HS; Los Angeles, CA; (4); Sec Art Clb; High Hon Roll; Prfct Atten Awd; Cmpng Clb; Bank Of Amer Plaqe Wnnr; CSU; Art.

ROBLES, RICARDO R; Coleville HS; Coleville, CA; (2); Var Bsbl; JV Var Bsktbl; Cit Awd; Hon Roll.

ROBLES, ROBBIE M; Lassen HS; Susanville, CA; (2); 30/190; Boy Scts; Church Yth Grp; Letterman Clb; Ski Clb; Band; Pep Band; Bsbl; Capt Bsktbl; Capt Ftbl; Hon Roll; MVP Bsktbl.

ROBLES, ROMALDO; Gonzales HS; Chualar, CA; (3); Teachers Aide; School Musical; Nwsp; Hon Roll; Newspaper Publication For Playing Guitar At Schl; Healt Coll; Spec Acctg.

ROBLES, ROSE F; Nogales HS; W Covina, CA; (2); Church Yth Grp; Library Aide; Rep Frsh Cls; Stu Cncl; Var Tennis; Hon Roll; JV Badminton; UCLA; Econ.

ROBLES, SILVIA; Merced HS; Snelling, CA; (4); Rep Stu Cncl; High Hon Roll; Hon Roll; Prfct Atten Awd; Pres Acad Fit Awd; Score Clb; CSF; Stanford U; Math.

ROBLES, STACEY; Tokay HS; Stockton, CA; (4); 101/703; Am Leg Aux Girls St; Church Yth Grp; Debate Tm; GAA; NFL; VP Spanish Clb; Pres Speech Tm; SADD; Pres Soph Cls; Pres Sr Cls; CIA; Conflict Mgr; Homcmng Qn; Delta CC; Poltcl Sci.

ROBLES, SYLVIA; Edison HS; Fresno, CA; (1); Church Yth Grp; Cit Awd.

ROBLES-HERNANDEZ, SYLVIA L; Eisenhower HS; Rialto, CA; (4); 16/655; French Clb; Spanish Clb; Phtg Yrbk; High Hon Roll; NHS; Pres Acad Fit Awd; Mock Trial Tm; Acad Decathlon; CA Schlrshp Fed; UC Santa Barbara; Fr.

ROBLETO, DIANA E; Bishop Amat HS; Rancho Cucamonga, CA; (3); Church Yth Grp; Drama Clb; Hosp Aide; Spanish Clb; Phtg Rptr Yrbk; Hon Roll; Jr NHS; NHS; Spanish NHS; Work-Won Employee Of Mnth; Got 5 On A P Exam-Spanish; CA ST; Arts.

ROBSON, ALLISON L; The Bishops Sch; San Diego, CA; (2); AFS; GAA; Var Fld Hcky; Var L Swmmng; Archlgcl Dig Cltrl Exch Greece; Brdcst Jrnlsm.

ROBSON, CHRISTY; Mills HS; Burlingame, CA; (2); Sec Debate Tm; English Clb; Var Tennis; Var Trk; Hon Roll; GATE, CSF Cls Rep; Phlsphy & Interact Club; JR Statsmn Of Amer; Knwldg Masters; Frnds For Anml Rghts.

ROBSON, KATRINA M; Esperanza HS; Yorba Linda, CA; (2); 28/571; Church Yth Grp; Debate Tm; French Clb; Lit Mag; JV Vllybl; High Hon Roll; NHS; Sunday Schl Teacher; Top 25 Stus Awd; Stu Of Mnth; Mock Trial; Engl.

ROCA, LORNA C; Riverbank HS; Riverbank, CA; (2); Church Yth Grp; Office Aide; Teachers Aide; Hon Roll; CA Schlstc Fed; CA ST U Turlock; Tchr.

ROCCHI, JUDITH ROSE; Piedmont Hills HS; San Jose, CA; (4); 87/316; Church Yth Grp; Cmnty Wkr; Math Clb; Red Cross Aide; Science Clb; Service Clb; Spanish Clb; Teachers Aide; Varsity Clb; Band; Exec Cncl Myrs Yth Cnfrnc; ESUHSD YB Cnfrnc; Math Engrng Sci Achv T Clb; U Opprtnts Clb; San Jose ST U; Pre Med.

ROCCO, GINA M; San Pasqua HS; Escondido, CA; (2); Rep Frsh Cls; JV Bsktbl; Var L Swmmng; Cit Awd; Hon Roll.

ROCERO, ORVILLE JAKE P; Rio Lindo SDA Acad; Stockton, CA; (3); Church Yth Grp; Quiz Bowl; Acpl Chr; Band; Variety Show; Rptr Nwsp; VP Frsh Cls; Off Soph Cls; Capt Vllybl; Lived & Studies In E Africa 79-89; Pacific Union Coll; Nrsng.

ROCHA, AMANDA M; Selma HS; Selma, CA; (1); Church Yth Grp; French Clb; Pep Clb; Ski Clb; Cheerldng; Trk; Hon Roll; Kings River CC.

ROCHA, ANNA M; Dos Palos HS; Dos Palos, CA; (4); Spanish Clb; Teachers Aide; CA ST U Stanislous; Bus Admin.

ROCHA, BRANDY R; Golden West HS; Visalia, CA; (2); FHA; JV Crs Cntry; Var Score Keeper; JV Swmmng; Hon Roll; Young Life; Accntng.

ROCHA, CYNTHIA M; John F Kennedy HS; La Mirada, CA; (3); VP FBLA; Color Guard; Hon Roll; Pres Acad Fit Awd; Bus.

ROCHA, JAQUELINE; Linden HS; Stockton, CA; (1); 4/140; Church Yth Grp; Dance Clb; Math Tm; Band; Mrchg Band; Orch; Pep Band; High Hon Roll; Lion Awd; CSF; 5th Pl Annual Math Cmptn; Exclnt Rating CA Music Educ Assn Solo & Ensemble Fstvl; Pediatrician.

ROCHA, JOSE H; Watsonville HS; Freedom, CA; (2); 3/543; Hon Roll; CSF; Goals For Youth; Migrant Sociedad Cultrl Bilngu; San Jose ST; Engr.

ROCHA, KHRISTINE L; Oxnard HS; Oxnard, CA; (3); SADD; Band; Mrchg Band; Orch; Pep Band; Rep Soph Cls; VP Jr Cls; Rep Sr Cls; Pres Stu Cncl; High Hon Roll; Underclassmen Of The Year Awd; Speaker Of The House Of Schls Student Congress; Baylor Coll; Nurse.

ROCHA, MAGALY; Santa Clara HS; Oxnard, CA; (3); 11/150; Chorus; Hon Roll; NHS; Ventura Coll.

ROCHA, SUSAN; Kingsburg Joint Union HS; Kingsburg, CA; (1); SADD; Hon Roll; Acad Blck K.

ROCHA, SYLVIA; Mc Farland HS; Mc Farland, CA; (3); Library Aide; Teachers Aide; Hon Roll; Acad Awds Math, Englsh, Sci & Sewing; Mdlln Awd Englsh; Bakersfield Coll; Bus.

ROCHA, VIRGINIA M; Ontario HS; Ontario, CA; (3); Hon Roll; Prfct Atten Awd; Bus.

ROCHE, BRIAN; Damien HS; Chino Hills, CA; (3); Letterman Clb; Ski Clb; Church Choir; Var JV Bsbl; Bsktbl; Var L Ftbl; Wt Lftg; Hon Roll; Pres Acad Ftnss; Lawyr.

ROCHE, DARDEN P; Orosi HS; Badger, CA; (2); 4-H; Teachers Aide; Bsbl; JV Ftbl; Var Golf; Hon Roll; Fresno ST; Vet.

ROCHE, DEBBIE; Fountain Valley HS; Fountain Valley, CA; (3); Pep Clb; Color Guard; Flag Corp; Hon Roll; Capt Flg Tm; RREC; San Diego ST U; Police.

ROCHE, SARAH; Exeter Union HS; Exeter, CA; (1); Church Yth Grp; Varsity Clb; Diving; Vllybl; Peds.

ROCHELEAU, THOMAS A; Imperial HS; Pasadena, CA; (3); 18/24; Art Clb; Church Yth Grp; French Clb; JA; Math Clb; VICA; Chorus; School Play; Stage Crew; JV Bsktbl; Ambassador Coll; Arch.

ROCHELLE, ERIC; Antioch HS; Antioch, CA; (3); Letterman Clb; Spanish Clb; Teachers Aide; Varsity Clb; Stu Cncl; Intrml Bsktbl; JV Ftbl; Trk; High Hon Roll; Hon Roll.

ROCHESTER, DAWN M; Morning Side HS; Hawthrone, CA; (3); School Musical; Off Jr Cls; UCLA; Doctor.

ROCHLITZER, BRIAN T; Santa Barbara HS; Santa Barbara, CA; (2); Church Yth Grp; German Clb; Land-Speed Rcrd Cars; Wrk 6 Days Per Wk; Engrng.

ROCKENBAUGH, WENDY A; Clayton Valley HS; Concord, CA; (2); Cmnty Wkr; Teachers Aide; Varsity Clb; Var Socr; JV Sftbl; High Hon Roll; Acad Ltr; Outstndng St Home Ed Dept; Outstndng Stu Sci Dept; U Of CA Los Angeles; Astronomy.

ROCKENSTEIN, CATHERINE D; Lower Lake HS; Lower Lake, CA; (3); English Clb; Teachers Aide; Ed Nwsp; Off Jr Cls; VP Sr Cls; Var Capt Sftbl; High Hon Roll; Hon Roll; Sftbl All Leag; 2nd Pl Poetry Cntst 89; 1st Pl Poetry Cntst 90; Chico ST; Atty.

ROCKLEIN, MATTHEW NOEL; Paradise HS; Paradise, CA; (4); 1/240; Art Clb; Church Yth Grp; Scholastic Bowl; Var Golf; Elks Awd; High Hon Roll; Kiwanis Awd; Lion Awd; Val; Lions Clb Exchng Switzerland Smmr; Amer Lgn Yth Envrnmntl Camp; Scaife Fndtn Awd; Santa Clara U; Chem.

ROCKWELL, WENDY R; Westlake HS; Westlake Village, CA; (2); Cmnty Wkr; Var L Sftbl; Var L Vllybl; Phys Thrpy.

ROCZEY, SHAWN; Santa Fe HS; Norwalk, CA; (4); 4/318; FBLA; Speech Tm; Teachers Aide; School Play; Ed Lit Mag; Stu Cncl; Hon Roll; Prfct Atten Awd; MESA Treas; CSF; NY U; Sci.

RODARTE, ALMA D; Winters HS; Winters, CA; (3); Cmnty Wkr; Latin Clb; Teachers Aide; Phtg Yrbk; JV Swmmng; Hon Roll; Amigos Unidos Clb Reporter & Treas; CSF; Educl Opportunity Pgm & Success Pgm; U CA Davis; Psych.

RODARTE, GABRIEL; Torrey Pines HS; Del Mar, CA; (3); 13/422; Science Clb; Ski Clb; Varsity Clb; JV Ftbl; Var Trk; Hon Roll; Ntl Merit SF; Math Tutor; Stanford; Sci.

RODARTE, GABRIELA; Winters HS; Winters, CA; (2); Church Yth Grp; Latin Clb; Spanish Clb; Teachers Aide; Hon Roll; Flight Attendant.

RODARTE, SONIA J; Ramona Convent; Monterey Park, CA; (3); Church Yth Grp; GAA; Girl Scts; Hosp Aide; Letterman Clb; Spanish Clb; Varsity Clb; Variety Show; Var L Sftbl; Hon Roll; Jnr CSF; Fine Arts Clb; Recruitmnt Cmmtte; UC Berkeley; Biochem.

RODARTE, TARA R; Manteca HS; Manteca, CA; (2); 45/420; Key Clb; Band; Mrchg Band; Hon Roll; U Of The Pacific; Psych.

RODAS, CARLA I; Lowell HS; San Francisco, CA; (3); Church Yth Grp; Latin Clb; Spanish Clb; SADD; Band; Hon Roll; Kiwanis Awd; Spanish NHS; Schl Sprt; UC Davis; Med.

RODDY, JANE; Vallejo SR HS; Vallejo, CA; (4); 3/430; Cmnty Wkr; Letterman Clb; Model UN; Red Cross Aide; Science Clb; Band; Jazz Band; Mrchg Band; Pep Band; Swmmng; Acadc Decathlon; U CA Rgnts Schlrshp; Stu Body Rep; U CA Santa Cruz; Engl.

RODE, DAVID C; James Madison HS; San Diego, CA; (3); Church Yth Grp; Latin Clb; NFL; Speech Tm; JV L Golf; Hon Roll; Ntl Merit Ltr; Banking.

RODELA, SIAN; Paraclete HS; Leona Valley, CA; (2); Church Yth Grp; Cmnty Wkr; 4-H; FBLA; Hosp Aide; Office Aide; Teachers Aide; Rep Nwsp; Socr; 4-H Awd; Hosp Aid; High Hnrs Awd; Duke U; Acctng.

RODELL, ANTHONY J; St Bernard HS; Los Angeles, CA; (3); Treas Chess Clb; Church Yth Grp; Cmnty Wkr; Computer Clb; Dance Clb; Debate Tm; Math Clb; Math Tm; Science Clb; SADD; Acting; Dance; Engrng.

RODERICK, MORGAN; Yucca Valley HS; Yucca Valley, CA; (3); Aud/Vis; Drama Clb; Office Aide; SADD; Teachers Aide; Band; Mrchg Band; School Musical; School Play; Stage Crew; Mdcl Assist; UC Santa Barbara; Dr.

RODGERS, ANTHONY C; Tracy HS; Stockton, CA; (2); 4-H; 4-H Awd; Hon Roll.

RODGERS, APRIL R; Francis Polytechnic HS; North Hollywood, CA; (3); Church Yth Grp; Drill Tm; Rptr Nwsp; Yrbk; Sec Stu Cncl; Pom Pon; Hon Roll; Hnr Rl; Home Ec Awd; Outstndng Stu; CSUN.

RODGERS, CAROLINE E; El Camino Fundamental HS; Carmichael, CA; (3); Phtg Rptr Yrbk; Rep Soph Cls; VP Stu Cncl; Var Tennis.

RODGERS, CHRISTINA; Highlands HS; North Highlands, CA; (1); JV Sftbl; Outstndng Achvt Bio; Helpd Grant Spec Ed Chldrn; Wk With Chldrn.

RODGERS, DANIELLE E A; Los Angeles Lutheran HS; Sylmar, CA; (4); Drama Clb; Chorus; School Play; Ed Yrbk; Rep Frsh Cls; Sec Soph Cls; Off Sr Cls; Sec Stu Cncl; Bsbl; Cheerldng.

RODGERS, GENA M; Point Loma HS; San Diego, CA; (1); GAA; Trk; Vllybl; High Hon Roll; Hon Roll; Social Wrkr.

RODGERS, LEANNE MARIE; St Patrick-St Vincent HS; Suisun City, CA; (4); 4/141; Letterman Clb; Chorus; VP Frsh Cls; Var Capt Cheerldng; Var Capt Pom Pon; Var JV Sftbl; Var L Trk; JV Vllybl; High Hon Roll; NHS; Notre Dame U; Math.

RODGERS, MICHELE L; Morro Bay HS; Morro Bay, CA; (3); 4-H; JCL; VP Latin Clb; JV Sftbl; JV Vllybl; Hon Roll; Rockclimbng; Surfing; Real Est.

RODGERS, VALENCIA; Morningside HS; Inglewood, CA; (4); 16/200; Church Yth Grp; Chorus; Church Choir; Cit Awd; Hon Roll; Bnk America Fine Arts Achvt Engrvd Plque; Outstndng Stu Commndtn Engl & Scl Stds Depts; UC Irvine; Bio Sci.

RODIER, RENEE; Mesa Verde HS; Citrus Heights, CA; (2); 15/259; GAA; Off Soph Cls; Capt Mgr Bsktbl; Capt Var Sftbl; Capt Var Vllybl; Wt Lftg; Hon Roll; Coach Orangvale Rec & Park Dist Girls Bsktbl; Hnr All Tourn Player 89; U Santa Barbara; Arch.

RODIGUEZ, PATRICIA E; Rio Mesa HS; Oxnard, CA; (2); Cit Awd; MECHA Mem; Acad Awd Super Spartan; Chiropractor.

RODILLAS, SAGA; Granger JR HS; National City, CA; (1); Cmnty Wkr; Quiz Bowl; Band; Chorus; Church Choir; Intrml Vllybl; Cit Awd; High Hon Roll; Hon Roll; Prfct Atten Awd; Associated Stu Body Rep; Sci Olympiad.

RODRIGUE, JON P; Miraleste HS; Ranchos Palos Ver, CA; (3); 41/150; Boy Scts; Key Clb; Spanish Clb; SADD; Rep Jr Cls; Var Capt Swmmng; Var Water Polo Coaches Awd; Law.

RODRIGUES, ANGELA F; Tulare Union Redskins HS; Tipton, CA; (2); Hon Roll; Portuguese Club.

RODRIGUES, DAWN; Oroville HS; Oroville, CA; (3); 1/200; High Hon Roll; Engl Stu Of Month; CSF; Commnty Achvt Awd 89-90; Early Cldhd Educ.

RODRIGUES, DELIO; Tulare Union HS; Tipton, CA; (4); Color Guard; Off Sr Cls; High Hon Roll; Hon Roll.

RODRIGUES, HOLLY M; Livingston HS; Delhi, CA; (3); Rep Jr Cls; JV Var Bsktbl; Powder Puff Ftbl; JV Var Sftbl; Var Vllybl; High Hon Roll; Hon Roll; MVP Bsktbl; All League, All Area Sun Star Tm Bsktbl; All League Softbl; Athltc Trnr.

RODRIGUES, MICHAEL; Golden West HS; Visalia, CA; (3); Boy Scts; Church Yth Grp; Band; Jazz Band; Pep Band; JV Socr; JV Tennis; Hon Roll; All Americcan Hll Of Fame Band Hnrs; Bus.

RODRIGUEZ, ABRAHAM M; Golden Valley HS; Stockton, CA; (4); Cmnty Wkr; Drama Clb; ROTC; Off Sr Cls; Prfct Atten Awd; Skateboard Club; Delta Coll; Archt.

RODRIGUEZ, ADRIAN; Saint Genevieve HS; Sepulveda, CA; (4); 7/170; Am Leg Boys St; Rep Frsh Cls; Pres Soph Cls; Rep Sr Cls; Stu Cncl; JV Vllybl; NEDT Awd; Church Yth Grp; Drama Clb; Natl Engrng Aptitude Srch St Senators Lttr For Rcgntn Of Outstndng Acad; Stanford U; Micro Bio.

RODRIGUEZ, AILEEN U; Louisville HS; Chatsworth, CA; (1); GAA; Hosp Aide; Chorus; Bsktbl; Score Keeper; Trk; Hon Roll; Yale; Doc.

RODRIGUEZ, ANABEL D; San Gabriel HS; Alhambra, CA; (2); Bus.

RODRIGUEZ, ANALEE; Sweetwater HS; San Diego, CA; (4); Dance Clb; Debate Tm; Girl Scts; Church Choir; Drill Tm; Hon Roll; Prfct Atten Awd; Pres Acad Fit Awd; Job Skills & Sci Awds; San Diego ST U; Nrsng.

RODRIGUEZ, ANN I; Hilltop HS; Chula Vista, CA; (4); 22/444; Art Clb; Hosp Aide; Pres Science Clb; Chorus; JV Crs Cntry; JV Trk; Pres Acad Fit Awd; Co Chrprsn Hmnts Clb; CSF Lifetime Mem; Most Outstndng Stu In Englsh; U Of CA Santz Cruz.

RODRIGUEZ, ANNA K; Will C Crawford HS; San Diego, CA; (2); Church Yth Grp; Key Clb; Mgr Swmmng; Hon Roll; Acad Tm Capt.

RODRIGUEZ, ANTHONY J; Elsinore HS; Lake Elsinore, CA; (3); Cmnty Wkr; ROTC; Band; Mrchg Band; Ftbl; Hon Roll; Riverside Sheriff Explorers; SADD; Law Enforcement.

RODRIGUEZ, BARBARA; Sea Side HS; Ft Ord, CA; (1); Church Yth Grp; Girl Scts; ROTC; Prfct Atten Awd; ROTC.

RODRIGUEZ, BETSY; Eagle Rock HS; Los Angeles, CA; (3); Cmnty Wkr; Dance Clb; Girl Scts; Key Clb; Ski Clb; Spanish Clb; Speech Tm; Chorus; Church Choir; Off Frsh Cls; Real Est Law.

RODRIGUEZ, BRIDGETTE V; Canyon HS; Canyon Country, CA; (1); Girl Scts; Off Soph Cls; Cheerldng; Gym; Socr; Sftbl; Cit Awd; Medcl Doctor.

RODRIGUEZ, CARLOS; King City HS; King City, CA; (3); Cmnty Wkr; Socr; Trk; High Hon Roll; Hon Roll; San Diego ST U.

RODRIGUEZ, CARLOS; Napa HS; Napa, CA; (1); UC Berkeley.

RODRIGUEZ, CARLOS J; Livingston HS; Livingston, CA; (2); JV Bsktbl; JV Ftbl; JV Var Trk; JV Wt Lftg; Hon Roll; Fresno ST; Arch.

RODRIGUEZ, CARLOS R; Coachella Valley HS; Thermal, CA; (2); Red Cross Aide; Ftbl; Hon Roll; Law Enforcement.

RODRIGUEZ, CAROLINA; Garfield HS; Los Angeles, CA; (2); Church Yth Grp; Rptr Nwsp; Hon Roll; Prfct Atten Awd; Hrns Engl; The Butterfly Awd; Bus Admin.

RODRIGUEZ, CAROLINA N; Garfield HS; Arleta, CA; (2); Orch; Prfct Atten Awd; Mck Trl Cmptn LA Cnty Crt Hse 1st Tm Go Qtrs Fnls; Law Clb; Standford U; Crmnl Law.

RODRIGUEZ, CELESTE Y; Alta Loma HS; Alta Loma, CA; (2); Church Yth Grp; Service Clb; SADD; Stat Ftbl; JV Sftbl; Stat Wrstlng; High Hon Roll; Hon Roll; JV Sftbl Team Mst Insprtnl Plyr 90; Bus.

RODRIGUEZ, CESAR; Golden West HS; Ivanhoe, CA; (2); Off Soph Cls; JV Var Bsktbl; Hon Roll; Gldn St Exam Awd Geom; Bsktbl Leag Chmpns; Bio.

RODRIGUEZ, CESAR A; Poway HS; Poway, CA; (1); French Clb; Yrbk; Off Frsh Cls; Bsbl; Swmmng; Wt Lftg; Prfct Atten Awd; Elec Engr.

RODRIGUEZ, CHRISTINA E; Andrew Hill HS; San Jose, CA; (1); Church Yth Grp; Math Clb; Science Clb; Stu Cncl; Vllybl; Wt Lftg; Cit Awd; Prfct Atten Awd; U Of CA Acad Outreach Partnrshp Pgm; MESA Pgm; U Of CA San Francisco; Pedtrcn.

RODRIGUEZ, CHRISTOPHER; Bishop Montgomery HS; Torrance, CA; (3); Church Yth Grp; VP JA; Intrml Bsktbl; JV Golf; Hon Roll; MA Inst Tech; Physics.

RODRIGUEZ, CHRISTOPHER; Downey HS; Pico Rivera, CA; (4); Key Clb; Teachers Aide; Varsity Clb; JV Var Bsbl; Var Capt Socr; Cathlc Relgn Instrctr 3rd-4th Gr Stu; Outstndng Sr Awd Downey Key Clb 90; Coachs Awd Soccr 86; Bus Admin.

RODRIGUEZ, CINDY; Capistrano Valley Christian HS; San Clemente, CA; (4); Church Yth Grp; Yrbk; Sec Frsh Cls; High Hon Roll; Hon Roll; Pres Acad Fit Awd; Smwmng; Missions Clb; Point Loma Nazerene; Psychlgy.

RODRIGUEZ, CINDY A; Nogales HS; La Puente, CA; (3); Swmmng; Med.

RODRIGUEZ, CLAUDIA; Sierra Vista HS; Baldwin Park, CA; (2); FBLA.

RODRIGUEZ, CLAUDIA G; Bell Gardens HS; Bell Gardens, CA; (3); Church Yth Grp; French Clb; Color Guard; Trk; Vllybl; CSF; Girls Lge; Whittier Coll; Bus Adm.

RODRIGUEZ, CLAUDIA M; Notre Dame HS; Hillsborough, CA; (4); 13/85; Spanish Clb; Hon Roll; Acad Achvmt Awds Algb, Spnsh; Santa Clara U; Dentstry.

RODRIGUEZ, CLAUDIA S; Bassett SR HS; La Puente, CA; (2); Spanish Clb; VICA; JV Vllybl; Hon Roll; Jr NHS; NHS; Prfct Atten Awd; Svc Awd Jr Natl Hnr Soc; Achvt Awd; USC; Radio Brdcstng.

RODRIGUEZ, CONSUELO; Pasadena HS; Sierra Madre, CA; (2); Acpl Chr; Church Choir; Flag Corp; Hon Roll; Prfct Atten Awd; Spanish NHS; ROTC Clb; Outstndg Choir Awd; CA ST LA; Lawyer.

RODRIGUEZ, DANIEL; Oxnard HS; Oxnard, CA; (2); 19/604; Key Clb; Spanish Clb; Band; Mrchg Band; High Hon Roll; Hon Roll; Academic Ltr; Stanford U; Math.

RODRIGUEZ, DARIO; Bishop Amat HS; West Covina, CA; (4); Aud/Vis; JV Var Crs Cntry; JV Trk; U Cal Poly Pomona; Bus.

RODRIGUEZ, DAVID; Bishop Amat HS; Bowland Hts, CA; (3); Math Clb; High Hon Roll; NHS; CSF; UCLA; Law.

RODRIGUEZ, DEMETRIUS H; Ventage HS; Napa, CA; (2); Cmnty Wkr; Letterman Clb; Spanish Clb; Chorus; Var Crs Cntry; JV Score Keeper; Var Trk; High Hon Roll; NHS; Spanish NHS; Spec Plympcs Trck/Fld Vol; Sprts Statstcn; Stanford U; Dntstry.

RODRIGUEZ, DIANA ROSEMARY; Hayward HS; Castro Valley, CA; (1); Cmnty Wkr; Latin Clb; Spanish Clb; Teachers Aide; School Musical; Cit Awd; Hon Roll; Spanish NHS; UC Berkeley; Chld Psych.

RODRIGUEZ, EDDIE; Inglewood HS; Inglewood, CA; (2); Boy Scts; Church Yth Grp; ROTC; Color Guard; Stage Crew; Stu Cncl; Bsbl; Ftbl; Socr; Cit Awd; First Aid Awds; Army.

RODRIGUEZ, EDGAR M; Mt Diablo HS; Concord, CA; (3); Spanish Clb; Var Capt Socr; Var Vllybl; High Hon Roll; Spanish NHS; DVC; Engrng.

RODRIGUEZ, ELENA C; Buena HS; Ventura, CA; (3); 1/500; Drama Clb; SADD; Flag Corp; School Musical; Prfct Atten Awd; CSF Acad Lttr; UCSB; Chem Engrng.

RODRIGUEZ, ELSA; Samuel Gompers Secondary Schl; San Diego, CA; (4); French Clb; Office Aide; Spanish Clb; Chorus; Cit Awd; High Hon Roll; Hon Roll; Hnrs Gldn St Geom Exam; Grad Acadc Dstnctn; Wrk Mgr; San Diego ST U; Accntng.

RODRIGUEZ, ERIKA; Sanger HS; Sanger, CA; (2); GAA; Spanish Clb; Varsity Clb; Phtg Nwsp; Phtg Yrbk; Pres Frsh Cls; Pres Soph Cls; Rep Jr Cls; Var Bsktbl; JV Var Sftbl; Soc Wrk.

RODRIGUEZ, GABRIEL; Kerman Union HS; Kerman, CA; (3); 38/206; Band; Chorus; Jazz Band; Mrchg Band; Orch; Pep Band; School Musical; School Play; Variety Show; VP L Bsktbl; Aids Wlk-A-Thn; SHARE Pgm Vlntr; CSU; Music.

RODRIGUEZ, GABRIEL; Mc Ateer HS; San Francisco, CA; (3); Cmnty Wkr; Letterman Clb; Band; Chorus; Jazz Band; Mrchg Band; Orch; Pep Band; School Musical; School Play; Vlnt Latino Aids Prjct; UC Berkeley; Envrnmntl Sci.

RODRIGUEZ, GABRIELLA P; North Hollywood HS; North Hollywood, CA; (2); Rptr Nwsp; JV Cheerldng; CJSF; UCSB; Crmnl Law.

RODRIGUEZ, GINA K; West HS; Bakersfield, CA; (2); Dance Clb; Hon Roll; Bus.

RODRIGUEZ, GONZALO V; Berkeley Hall Schl; Chatsworth, CA; (1); 1/10; Yrbk; Pres Stu Cncl; Capt JV Bsktbl; Capt JV Socr; JV Trk; Cit Awd; High Hon Roll; Opt Clb Awd; Val; L A Cnty Sci & Engl Fair 1st Pl Earth & Spc Catgry; Law.

RODRIGUEZ, HELEN M; Santiago HS; Garden Grove, CA; (2); 156/498; Library Aide; Hon Roll; Teacher.

RODRIGUEZ, IMELDA; Garfield HS; Los Angeles, CA; (2); Cmnty Wkr; Office Aide; Teachers Aide; Stu Cncl; Cit Awd; Hon Roll; Prfct Atten Awd; Pres Acad Fit Awd; Schlrshp & Interact Clubs; Achvt Awd; Sea-Afloat Club; Mech Engrng.

RODRIGUEZ, IRENE; Clovis HS; Clovis, CA; (3); SADD; Bsktbl; Powder Puff Ftbl; Hon Roll; Pres Acad Fit Awd; Cls Rep; Fresno ST; Phys Thrpy.

RODRIGUEZ, IRIS G; Capuchino HS; San Bruno, CA; (3); Church Yth Grp; Teachers Aide; Swmmng; Vllybl; Hon Roll; Badminton; Grafic Desgn.

RODRIGUEZ, ISELA; San Jacinto HS; San Jacinto, CA; (2); French Clb; Sftbl; Tennis.

RODRIGUEZ, ISMAEL; Sweetwater HS; National City, CA; (2); Arch.

RODRIGUEZ, JAIME J; Loyola HS; Los Angeles, CA; (1); Boy Scts; German Clb; JA; Math Tm; Scholastic Bowl; Science Clb; Speech Tm; Stu Cncl; Bsbl; Bsktbl; Stanford; Law.

RODRIGUEZ, JANIE; Madera HS; Madera, CA; (2); Church Yth Grp; Cmnty Wkr; Hon Roll; Fresno ST U; Law.

RODRIGUEZ, JESSE G; Coachella Valley HS; Thermal, CA; (2); Var Golf; Hon Roll; U Of CO; Real Estate.

RODRIGUEZ, JESSE J; Willits HS; Willits, CA; (3); Varsity Clb; Var Socr; JV Wrstlng; High Hon Roll; Skateboard; Snowboarding; Medocino Coll.

RODRIGUEZ, JESSICA L; Norte Vista HS; Riverside, CA; (3); 36/336; Sftbl; Trk; High Hon Roll; Hon Roll; Miss Teen CA Contestant; Cal Poly Pomona; Accounting Law.

RODRIGUEZ, JESUS; Madera HS; Madera, CA; (4); 1/480; Cmnty Wkr; Science Clb; Varsity Clb; Chrmn Mrchg Band; Var Crs Cntry; Var Capt Socr; High Hon Roll; VP NHS; Pres Acad Fit Awd; Val; Exch Clb Schlrshp; Stanford U; Med.

RODRIGUEZ JR, JESUS; Fair Fax HS; Los Angeles, CA; (3); JA; Office Aide; Teachers Aide; School Play; Stage Crew; Swing Chorus; Var Bsbl; Gym; Socr; Sftbl; Law.

RODRIGUEZ, JOEL; Wilson HS; Los Angeles, CA; (3); JV Bsbl; Var Ftbl; MESA Clb; UCLA Partnership; MARIPOSA; Schlr Athl Awds; UCLA; Engrng.

RODRIGUEZ, JORGE A; North Salinas HS; Salinas, CA; (3); 120/400; Rep Stu Cncl; Cit Awd; Hon Roll; US Naval Acad; Elec Engrng.

RODRIGUEZ, JORGE C; Orange HS; Orange, CA; (4); Cmnty Wkr; Key Clb; Math Clb; Sec Science Clb; JV Bsktbl; Var Ftbl; Var Trk; High Hon Roll; Hon Roll; Sec NHS; CA Scholarship Federation Life Member; UCLA; Biology.

RODRIGUEZ, JORGE R; Woodland HS; Woodland, CA; (2); Bsktbl; CA Poly San Luis Obispo; Arch.

RODRIGUEZ, JOSE F; John Muir HS; Pasadena, CA; (2); Prfct Atten; 5th Best Stu Engl Cls; Comp Pgmr.

RODRIGUEZ III, JOSE F; Fairfield HS; Vacaville, CA; (3); Church Yth Grp; Spanish Clb; Teachers Aide; Wrstlng; Hon Roll; NHS; UC Davis; Physician.

RODRIGUEZ, JOSEPH L; Santa Clara HS; Oxnard, CA; (3); 1/145; Intrml Bsktbl; Var Golf; High Hon Roll; NHS; CSF; Med.

RODRIGUEZ, JUAN P; Santa Ana HS; Santa Ana, CA; (3); Var Ftbl; Var Wt Lftg; Bio Med Clb; Aerospace Engr.

RODRIGUEZ, JULIE; Chino HS; Glen Avon, CA; (4); 1/561; Am Leg Aux Girls St; Stu Cncl; Val; CSF; Claremont Mc Kenna; Law.

RODRIGUEZ, KARLA L; Independence HS; San Jose, CA; (3); Teachers Aide; Awds Latinos Good Stus; Advrtsng.

RODRIGUEZ, KIMBERLY; Lindsay SR HS; Lindsay, CA; (3); FBLA; FHA; Letterman Clb; Spanish Clb; Nwsp; Yrbk; Var Cheerldng; Var Pom Pon; Hon Roll; Friday Nght Live; Gottschlks Hi-Deb; U Of CA Snt Brbra; Brdcst Jrnl.

RODRIGUEZ, LARRYSSA; Arlington HS; Riverside, CA; (2); Church Yth Grp; Teachers Aide; Cit Awd; Have An Interest In Softball; Have Interest In Swimming; Medical.

RODRIGUEZ, LAURA; St Paul HS; Pico Rivera, CA; (3); 11/350; Spanish Clb; Rep Frsh Cls; Sec Soph Cls; Sec Jr Cls; High Hon Roll; Hon Roll; NHS; Spanish NHS; CSF; Sante Fe Springs Sr Cities Comm; Med.

RODRIGUEZ, LEE; Modesto HS; Modesto, CA; (2); JV Bsktbl; Cit Awd; Hon Roll; Counselor.

RODRIGUEZ, LETTY; N Monterey C HS; Watsonville, CA; (2); 2/316; French Clb; Chorus; Bus.

RODRIGUEZ, LILIA; Luther Burbank HS; Sacramento, CA; (2); 19/389; Church Yth Grp; Teachers Aide; Hon Roll; Prfct Atten Awd; Accurac Typng Hon Roll; Schlshp Awd; Achvt Awd; Unique Acadmc & Civ Accmplshmnts; Physcl Ftnss; Comp.

RODRIGUEZ, LORELEI; Ramona HS; Ramona, CA; (3); 3/294; Debate Tm; FBLA; Pep Clb; Scholastic Bowl; Spanish Clb; SADD; JV Stat Bsktbl; Cit Awd; Kiwanis Awd; San Diego ST U; Med.

RODRIGUEZ, LORI M; Los Altos HS; Hacienda Hgts, CA; (4); Hon Roll; Painted Mural Of Solor Sys For Art; MT Sal; Commun.

RODRIGUEZ, LOUIS C; Eisenhower HS; Rialto, CA; (3); Church Yth Grp; Cmnty Wkr; SADD; Band; Hon Roll; Bus Law.

RODRIGUEZ, LUIS C; San Fernando HS; San Fernando, CA; (2); Church Yth Grp; Var Bsbl; Hon Roll; Pres Acad Fit Awd; MESA-MATH Engrng Sci Achvt; Rotary Clb Svc Awd; Bsbl/Bsktbl Park Leags; Summer Bsbl Camp-Fresno ST U; AZ ST; Psych.

RODRIGUEZ, LUWANA S; Orosi HS; Orosi, CA; (2); Spanish Clb; SADD; Hnrbl Mntn Poem; Jrnlsm Wrkshp Invtn CSUF; UC Riverside; Jrnlsm.

RODRIGUEZ, MARCEL; Lindsay HS; Lindsay, CA; (3); FFA; Rptr Nwsp; Ftbl; Swmmng; Wt Lftg; Cit Awd; St FFA Degree Top Stu Ag; Outstndng Stu; Star St FFA Ldr; CA Poly; Vet.

RODRIGUEZ, MARCIE R; Ramona HS; Riverside, CA; (2); 114/487; Art Clb; Church Yth Grp; GAA; Science Clb; Spanish Clb; Thesps; School Play; Stage Crew; Variety Show; JV Socr; Riverside CC; Film Work.

RODRIGUEZ, MARGARITA; George Washington HS; Los Angeles, CA; (3); Latin Clb; ROTC; Spanish Clb; School Musical.

RODRIGUEZ, MARIA; Granger JR HS; National City, CA; (1); 31/268; French Clb; Math Tm; Office Aide; Science Clb; Bsktbl; Ftbl; Vllybl; Hon Roll; UCSD; Doctor.

RODRIGUEZ, MARIA; Mount Miguel HS; Spring Valley, CA; (3); 124/370; Spanish Clb; Bus.

RODRIGUEZ, MARIA DEL CARMEN; Orosi HS; Visalia, CA; (4); Latin Clb; Office Aide; Spanish Clb; Chorus; Hon Roll; Coll Of The Sequoias; Librl Art.

RODRIGUEZ, MARIA E; Arvin HS; Lamont, CA; (3).

RODRIGUEZ, MARIA E; Bell Gardens HS; Bell Gardens, CA; (2); Drama Clb; French Clb; Yrbk; UCLA; Comp Tech.

RODRIGUEZ, MARIA J; Coachella Valley HS; Coachella, CA; (4); 2/355; Church Yth Grp; Treas Math Clb; Band; Mrchg Band; Pep Band; Var Soph Cls; Treas Stu Cncl; High Hon Roll; Treas NHS; Claremont Mc Kenna Coll; Bus Ec.

RODRIGUEZ, MARIA J M; Coalinga HS; Coalinga, CA; (4); 9/102; FTA; Teachers Aide; Stu Cncl; Powder Puff Ftbl; Tennis; Vllybl; Elks Awd; High Hon Roll; Treas MASU; Pres Grls Leag; Tutr; St Marys Coll; Educ.

RODRIGUEZ, MARIA L; Montebello HS; Pico Rivera, CA; (2); Church Yth Grp; Sec Chorus; Church Choir; Variety Show; Var Swmmng; Hon Roll; Prfct Atten Awd; UCLA; Commnctns.

RODRIGUEZ, MARIA M; Central Union HS; El Centro, CA; (2); French Clb; Flag Corp; Mrchg Band; Cit Awd; Mexican Amer Clb; Bus Admin.

RODRIGUEZ, MARIAM; Victor Valley HS; Victorville, CA; (1); Legal Sec.

RODRIGUEZ, MARIANA; Santa Cruz HS; Santa Cruz, CA; (1); School Musical; School Play; Yrbk; Hon Roll; 1st & 2nd Pl Spnsh Poetry; SICA Prog; Tchr.

RODRIGUEZ, MARICELA; North Salinas HS; Salinas, CA; (3); Cmnty Wkr; French Clb; Key Clb; Office Aide; Fld Hcky; Med Field.

RODRIGUEZ, MARIO; Hueneme HS; Oxnard, CA; (3); Math Clb; Hon Roll; Math, Engrng & Sci Achvt; Engrng.

RODRIGUEZ, MARTA G; Porterville HS; Porterville, CA; (3); Church Yth Grp; Science Clb; Band; Mrchg Band; Pep Band; Hon Roll; Fresno ST U; Elem Ed.

RODRIGUEZ, MARTIN; Strathmore HS; Strathmore, CA; (4); 20/95; Var Capt Bsbl; Var Capt Ftbl; Var Capt Socr; Var Trk; Hon Roll; Ath & Schlr Awd; Crmnl Justice.

RODRIGUEZ, MARTIN R; Gahr HS; Cerritos, CA; (3); Drama Clb; English Clb; Math Clb; Office Aide; Speech Tm; Varsity Clb; Pep Band; School Musical; School Play; Variety Show; Religious Ed Teacher Asst; Comp.

RODRIGUEZ, MARY A; Mc Farland HS; Mc Farland, CA; (3); 5/25; Drama Clb; FBLA; Library Aide; Math Clb; Office Aide; School Play; Stage Crew; Hon Roll; Prfct Atten Awd; Bio; US Hstry; Engl; Detective.

RODRIGUEZ, MARY ALICE; Lindsay HS; Lindsay, CA; (4); 37/231; Spanish Clb; SADD; Band; Color Guard; 2nd Rnnr Up Mexican Independence Queen; Psych.

RODRIGUEZ, MARY C; Brawley Union HS; Brawley, CA; (1); Church Yth Grp; Drawing, Painting; U Of CA San Diego; Comp.

RODRIGUEZ, MARYLOU; Our Lady Of Loretto HS; Los Angeles, CA; (3); French Clb; FBLA; Intnl Clb; Spanish Clb; Yrbk; Hon Roll; UCLA; Spnsh/Frnch.

RODRIGUEZ, MELISSA; Central Union HS; El Centro, CA; (1); Spanish Clb; Band; Mrchg Band.

RODRIGUEZ, MICHAEL A; Hoover HS; Parlier, CA; (2); Cmnty Wkr; JV Bsktbl; Yth Athl Club-Umpire Cmnty Svc; Regent Gen Altar Boy; John Wooden Pyramid Of Success Awd; Future Engrs; Engr.

RODRIGUEZ, MIGUEL; Righetti HS; Guadalupe, CA; (2); 7/564; Stu Cncl; High Hon Roll; Deans List; CSF; Upward Bound; Stanford; Physcn.

RODRIGUEZ, MIKE; Righetti HS; Guadalupe, CA; (2); 7/546; Stu Cncl; High Hon Roll; Pres Cabinet Upwrd Bnd; Natl Stu Ldrshp Cngrss; Chicano Ltn Yth Ldrsp Conf; Stanford; Med.

RODRIGUEZ, MIRIAM E; Hawthorne HS; Inglewood, CA; (2); Church Yth Grp; Key Clb; Awd Of Merit Dance Perfmnc; Advncd Dance; UCLA; Pedtrcn.

RODRIGUEZ, MONICA; Downey HS; Downey, CA; (2); Church Yth Grp; Girl Scts; Varsity Clb; Church Choir; Score Keeper; Vllybl.

RODRIGUEZ, MONICA CARRIE; Sacred Heart Of Mary HS; Pico Rivera, CA; (2); 23/98; Aud/Vis; Church Yth Grp; Cmnty Wkr; GAA; Pep Clb; School Play; Variety Show; Capt Cheerldng; Mgr(s); HS Acad Schlrshp; Aviation.

RODRIGUEZ, NEFTALI H; Inglewood HS; Inglewood, CA; (1).

RODRIGUEZ, OLIVER; Calistoga HS; Calistoga, CA; (2); Boy Scts; Sec Frsh Cls; JV Bsktbl; Var Socr; Hon Roll; Prfct Atten Awd; Drafting.

RODRIGUEZ, ORPHA RUTH; Dinuba HS; Dinuba, CA; (2); 4/250; FBLA; Hon Roll; Achvt Awd Cert Hstry; Hnr Roll Awd Cert; Acad Excllnc Spnsh II; UCLA; Bio.

RODRIGUEZ, PABLO; Hilmar JR-SR HS; Hilmar, CA; (3); 30/130; Am Leg Boys St; Art Clb; Letterman Clb; SADD; Capt Bsktbl; Intrml JV Ftbl; JV Var Trk; Wt Lftg; Art.

RODRIGUEZ, PATRICIA L; Delano HS; Delano, CA; (4); Church Yth Grp; Cmnty Wkr; Office Aide; Teachers Aide; Color Guard; Capt Drill Tm; Phtg Yrbk; Bsbl; Sftbl; Vllybl; Fresno ST U; Bus Admin.

RODRIGUEZ, PATRICIA M; San Gabriel Mission HS; Duarte, CA; (2); Church Yth Grp; Swmmng; UC-IRVINE; Med.

RODRIGUEZ, PRIMAVERA L; Theodore Roosevelt HS; Fresno, CA; (1); Spanish Clb; JV Cheerldng; Cit Awd; Mexican Amer Clb; Marimba Dance; Stanford; Med.

RODRIGUEZ, RACHEL; Turlock HS; Turlock, CA; (3); 85/575; Church Yth Grp; German Clb; Office Aide; Sec Treas Band; Church Choir; Color Guard; Drm Mjr(t); Mrchg Band; Pep Band; Crs Cntry; Interact; CSF; Poltcl Sci.

RODRIGUEZ, RACHEL A; Merced HS North; Merced, CA; (2); Church Yth Grp; Key Clb; Spanish Clb; JV Var Swmmng; Hon Roll; Prfct Atten Awd; Grls City Sftbll League; Water Polo; Swmmng.

RODRIGUEZ, RAUL; Alisal HS; Salinas, CA; (1); Intrml Ftbl; Hon Roll; Hartnell; Astronomy.

RODRIGUEZ, RAUL R; Sanger HS; Sanger, CA; (2); 4-H; Latin Clb; Science Clb; Ftbl; Wt Lftg; Wrstlng; UCLA; Phy.

RODRIGUEZ, RICARDO C; Hilltop HS; San Diego, CA; (2); Air Force; Aviation.

RODRIGUEZ, RICARDO R; Eagle Rock HS; Los Angeles, CA; (3); Boy Scts; Church Yth Grp; Key Clb; Color Guard; JV Wt Lftg; Hon Roll; Prfct Atten Awd; Nrs Aide; UCLA; Peds.

RODRIGUEZ, RICHARD L; Monte Vista HS; Spring Valley, CA; (2); Prfct Atten Awd; Deans List.

RODRIGUEZ, RICHARD T; Don Bosco Technical Inst; Los Angeles, CA; (3); Bsbl; High Hon Roll; Hon Roll; NHS; Elec Engnrng.

RODRIGUEZ, ROSA ANGELICA; Pittsburg HS; Pittsburg, CA; (1); Hosp Aide; Teachers Aide; Chorus; Vllybl; Cit Awd; Hon Roll; Mildred Stowell Creative Writing Awd; UC Davis; Child Psych.

RODRIGUEZ, ROSA D; King/Drew Medical Magnet HS; Los Angeles, CA; (3); Dance Clb; Hosp Aide; Math Tm; Spanish Clb; Rptr Nwsp; High Hon Roll; Hon Roll; Prfct Atten Awd; Fulfillment Fund Orgnztn; Natl Hispanic Yth Intv Hlth & Plc Dev; NHYI Schlr 90; Multicltrl Clb; UC Irvine; Pre-Med.

RODRIGUEZ, ROSA M; Riverdale Joint Union HS; Riverdale, CA; (3); Sec Intnl Clb; Office Aide; Rep Stu Cncl; Var Bsktbl; Var Trk; Hon Roll; Ntl Merit Ltr; Fresno City Coll; Bus.

RODRIGUEZ, ROY A; Hamilton HS; Los Angeles, CA; (2); Band; Mrchg Band; Stage Crew.

RODRIGUEZ, RUDY; Morse HS; San Diego, CA; (3); Cit Awd; Hon Roll; Bus Admin.

RODRIGUEZ, SAM M; Wasco Union HS; Wasco, CA; (3); Church Yth Grp; Pres FFA; Letterman Clb; Band; Church Choir; Jazz Band; Mrchg Band; School Musical; Pres Frsh Cls; Rep Stu Cncl; St FFA Degree; Gold Tiger Cert; Cal Poly San Luis Obispo; Ag Ed.

RODRIGUEZ, SAMUEL; Schurr HS; Los Angeles, CA; (1); Trk; Prfct Atten Awd; Columbia Squire; Cycling Club; Cal Poly St Obispo.

RODRIGUEZ, SAUL S; Alisal HS; Salinas, CA; (2); Teachers Aide; JV Ftbl; Var Socr; Intrml Hon Roll; UCSC.

RODRIGUEZ, SERGIO; Burbank SR HS; Burbank, CA; (3); Church Yth Grp; Cmnty Wkr; Drama Clb; Red Cross Aide; Spanish Clb; Speech Tm; Church Choir; Orch; Stage Crew; Variety Show; Classical Music & Play Piano & Violin; Aerospace & Build Rockets; UCLA; Economics.

RODRIGUEZ, SHELLY; Rowland HS; Rowland Hts, CA; (4); Church Yth Grp; Office Aide; Teachers Aide; Color Guard; Rifles Sqd; MSAC; Accntng.

RODRIGUEZ, SILVIA; Oxnard HS; Oxnard, CA; (3); Spanish Clb; Comp.

RODRIGUEZ, SYLVIA; Polytechnic HS; Long Beach, CA; (3); Chorus; Latino Clb; Cnslrs Stu Wk Awd; Cal ST U Long Bch; Ed.

RODRIGUEZ, SYLVIO G; Calexico HS; Calexico, CA; (2); Church Yth Grp; Cit Awd; Class Rep; Job Club.

RODRIGUEZ, TAMARA A; La Habra HS; Whittier, CA; (4); 24/320; Dance Clb; Pep Clb; Spanish Clb; SADD; Capt Drill Tm; High Hon Roll; Hon Roll; Prfct Atten Awd; Rotary Awd; CSF; Stu Lgu SR Rep; CA ST U Fullerton; Engl Tchr.

RODRIGUEZ, TAMARA L; Burroughs HS; Ridgecrest, CA; (4); Stat Bsktbl; Intrml Powder Puff Ftbl; Var L Trk; JV Vllybl; Hon Roll; Med.

RODRIGUEZ, TERESA; Caruthers Union HS; Caruthers, CA; (1); Church Yth Grp; Dance Clb; FFA; FHA; Band; Church Choir; Mrchg Band; Pep Band; Var Trk; JV Vllybl; Pilot.

RODRIGUEZ, TERESA U; Woodland HS; Woodland, CA; (2); School Musical; Rptr Nwsp; Yrbk; Off Frsh Cls; Sec Treas Soph Cls; Crs Cntry; Trk; Hon Roll; USVBA; Earth Club; Educ.

RODRIGUEZ, TOMASITA C; Bellermine Jefferson HS; Los Angeles, CA; (3); Church Yth Grp; Dance Clb; Pep Clb; Varsity Clb; Chorus; Drill Tm; School Play; Variety Show; JV Var Cheerldng; Var L Pom Pon; Phys Thrpy.

RODRIGUEZ, TREYA DIANNE; Golden West HS; Visalia, CA; (4); Church Yth Grp; Cmnty Wkr; DECA; Drama Clb; Pres French Clb; Intnl Clb; Pep Clb; Science Clb; School Play; Hon Roll; Envrnmntlst Clb Pres; CA Schlrshp Fndtn; Sci Olympiad Tm; Linfield Coll; Bio.

RODRIGUEZ, VICTOR R; Valley HS; Santa Ana, CA; (3); Treas Art Clb; Computer Clb; Office Aide; JV Bsbl; Intrml Bsktbl; Cit Awd; High Hon Roll; Hon Roll; 1st Pl Art Cntsts; Archtctr.

RODRIGUEZ, VIVIAN; Schurr HS; Montebello, CA; (4); SADD; Rio Hondo CC; Stage Set Dsgnr.

RODRIGUEZ, WILL; Burney JR SR HS; Burney, CA; (4); 15/55; Bsktbl; Var L Ftbl; Var L Trk; Hon Roll; Oregon ST U; Electrical Engrng.

RODRIGUEZ, YOLANDA M; South HS; Bakersfield, CA; (4); 11/320; Cmnty Wkr; Dance Clb; Office Aide; Science Clb; Service Clb; Teachers Aide; Varsity Clb; Treas Jr Cls; Sec Stu Cncl; Sftbl; Pred-Mxcn Amer Rebel Clb Assn; Pblc Rltns Math & Sci Achvt Clb; Bank Of Amer-Achvt N Sci; Cal ST U; Mech Engr.

RODRIGUEZ, YVETTE G; Louisville HS; Chatsworth, CA; (2); GAA; Bsbl; Trk; Hon Roll; USC Loyola.

RODRIGUEZ, YVONNE; Ramona Convent HS; Alhambra, CA; (3); Spanish Clb; School Play; Rptr Nwsp; Yrbk.

RODRIGUEZ, ZOILA C; Valley View HS; Moreno Valley, CA; (1); High Hon Roll; Pres Acad Fit Awd; Outstndng Acad Achvt-Excllnc Cert; Principals List; Sci.

RODRIGUEZ-SANDOVAL, GISELA M; La Cantada HS; La Crescenta, CA; (3); 9/242; Drama Clb; Intnl Clb; Hist Key Clb; Treas Math Clb; Mu Alpha Theta; Sec Science Clb; Stage Crew; Off Jr Cls; Swmmng; Hosp Vlntr.

RODRIQUEZ, ANTHONY P; Helix HS; La Mesa, CA; (3); Boy Scts; Church Yth Grp; Letterman Clb; Teachers Aide; Varsity Clb; Var JV Bsbl; JV Bsktbl; Var JV Ftbl; Var JV Score Keeper; Intrml Wt Lftg; U AZ; Bus.

RODRIQUEZ, CINDY; Kingsburg HS; Kingsburg, CA; (2); FFA; Vet.

RODRIQUEZ, ELIAS; Coachella Valley HS; Indio, CA; (3); Math Clb; Treas Ski Clb; High Hon Roll; Chem Awd; Aerospace Engr.

RODRIQUEZ, GABRIEL; Mt Diablo HS; Concord, CA; (3); JV Trk; JV Wrstlng; Crafts Hnr Pin; Partnership Pgm; Annapolis; Pre-Med.

RODRIQUEZ, JON; Lowell HS; San Francisco, CA; (4); Letterman Clb; Spanish Clb; Chorus; School Musical; Yrbk; JV Bsktbl; Ntl Merit SF; Commnctns.

RODRIQUEZ, MARICELA A; North Salinas HS; Salinas, CA; (3); Cmnty Wkr; French Clb; Key Clb; JV Var Fld Hcky; Trk; High Hon Roll; Rotary Awd; Chmpns Club Awd.

RODRIQUEZ, VICTORIA; John W North HS; Riverside, CA; (2); Drama Clb; Pep Clb; Spanish Clb; School Musical; School Play; JV Cheerldng; Var Pom Pon; Var Swmmng; Hon Roll; Teach Acting & Dancing At Riverside Children Theatre; U CA Riverside; Math.

ROEDER, BRADLEY D; Hilmar HS; Hilmar, CA; (1); Band; Jazz Band; Mrchg Band; Pep Band; Bsbl; Bsktbl; Crs Cntry; High Hon Roll; Stanford; Archengrng.

ROEDER, KELLEY A; King City HS; King City, CA; (3); 10/220; Chorus; JV Var Sftbl; High Hon Roll; Hon Roll; Acad Achvt Awd; Hnr Guard; Hartnell; Pediatrics.

ROEGLER, JESSICA L; John Muir HS; Altadena, CA; (3); Girl Scts; Math Tm; Co-Capt Flag Corp; Orch; Ed Nwsp; JV Swmmng; Cit Awd; High Hon Roll; Acolyte Crucifier Capt; Harvard Outstnd Jr Schlrshp Awd; Girl Scouts Gold Awd; Elem Schl Tchr.

ROELLING, RONALD G; Etiwanda HS; Rancho Cucamonga, CA; (2); 207/768; JV Socr; Hon Roll; Bsbl; Bsktbl; UCLA.

ROEMER, RICHARD A; Bonita Vista HS; Chula Vista, CA; (2); Model UN; Trk; Annapolis; Aerontcs.

ROEN, KRISTIN; Apple Valley HS; Apple Valley, CA; (3); Band; Jazz Band; Mrchg Band; Pep Band; Spirit Chrmn Band 89-91.

ROESCHLAU, CHRISTINE; Fall River JR-SR HS; Cassel, CA; (3); FFA; School Play; Pres Frsh Cls; Var Bsktbl; Var Crs Cntry; Var Trk; Var Vllybl; Hon Roll.

ROESNER, KRIS; Poway HS; San Diego, CA; (4); 2/750; Church Yth Grp; Ski Clb; JV Golf; JV Socr; High Hon Roll; NHS; Pres Acad Fit Awd; Sal; Aid Assn Lutherans Schlrshp; WA U St Louis; Arch.

ROESNER, KRISTEN B; Poway HS; San Diego, CA; (4); 2/750; Church Yth Grp; Mu Alpha Theta; Ski Clb; JV Golf; JV Socr; High Hon Roll; Kiwanis Awd; NHS; Ntl Merit SF; Arch.

ROEST, HERMAN; Hilmar JR/Sr HS; Hilmar, CA; (3); Church Yth Grp; Letterman Clb; Bsbl; Bsktbl; Ftbl; Wt Lftg; High Hon Roll; Hon Roll.

ROFAIL, ELIZABETH A; Saint Monica HS; West Los Angeles, CA; (4); Key Clb; Latin Clb; Pep Clb; Stage Crew; Phtg Mgr Yrbk; Rep Frsh Cls; Var Socr; Var Sftbl; Tennis; Var Capt Vllybl; Head Delg; Stu Ambssdr For Japan Day; Santa Monica Coll; Cinematgrphy.

ROGEL, RAUL; Valley HS; Santa Ana, CA; (3); Cmnty Wkr; Computer Clb; Pres FBLA; Hon Roll; MESA & Coll Partners Clbs; Comp Sci.

ROGENSKI, MARK A; San Rafael HS; San Rafael, CA; (3); Boy Scts; Spanish Clb; Var Socr; Var Trk; Hon Roll; People To People Stu Ambssdr Pgm 89; UCLA; Engrng.

ROGERO, NEWT; Paraclete HS; Lancaster, CA; (4); Debate Tm; JA; VP Sr Cls; Stu Cncl; JV Bsbl; Var Cheerldng; Hon Roll; CA ST Fresno; Bus Admin.

ROGERS, AARON; Mother Lode Christian Schl; Tuolumne, CA; (3); Chess Clb; Church Yth Grp; Cmnty Wkr; Computer Clb; Teachers Aide; Acpl Chr; Band; Chorus; Church Choir; Pep Band; Prof Athl.

ROGERS, ALAN G; Poway HS; Poway, CA; (4); Boy Scts; Varsity Clb; VP Stu Cncl; Var Swmmng; JV Wrstlng; Schlr Athlte; Water Polo; Pr Cnslr; CA ST Poly U; Constrctn Mgmt.

ROGERS, ALEXANDRIA; Abraham Lincoln HS; San Diego, CA; (4); Debate Tm; Drama Clb; FTA; Model UN; Office Aide; Chorus; School Musical; School Play; Variety Show; High Hon Roll; U Of CA Los Angeles; Phy.

ROGERS, ALICIA; San Diego HS; San Diego, CA; (3); Church Yth Grp; Drama Clb; Library Aide; School Play; Stage Crew; Nwsp; Bsktbl; Cit Awd; High Hon Roll; Prfct Atten Awd; Mst Photogenic Awd; Cert Of Appreciation For Elderly Home Aide; UC Irvine; Poltcl Sci.

ROGERS, AMY; Grossmont HS; El Cajon, CA; (4); 14/381; Church Yth Grp; English Clb; Service Clb; SADD; Church Choir; Sec Jr Cls; JV Var Bsktbl; JV Diving; Elks Awd; Hon Roll; Commssnr Grls Actvts; Pres Grls Leg; BYU; Law.

ROGERS, ANDREA D; Mtn Empire JR SR HS; Pine Valley, CA; (2); 30/150; Pep Clb; SADD; Treas Frsh Cls; JV Cheerldng; Var L Sftbl; Var L Vllybl; Cit Awd; Hon Roll; Var Gym; UC Davis; Med.

ROGERS, ANNA M; San Marcos HS; San Marcos, CA; (3); Church Yth Grp; Dance Clb; Key Clb; Pep Clb; School Musical; Var Cheerldng; High Hon Roll; Drama Clb; Stage Crew; CSF; Show Cheer 2nd Pl Tm, CA; Acad Awd 90; Lwyr.

ROGERS, BRIAN K; Bishop O'dowd HS; Berkeley, CA; (3); 28/275; Boy Scts; 4-H; Letterman Clb; Pres Ski Clb; School Play; Stage Crew; Rep Soph Cls; Rep Jr Cls; Pres Stu Cncl; Intrml Bsktbl; Outstndng JR By 1990.

ROGERS, CHAD L; Rio Lindo Acad; Los Angeles, CA; (3); Band; School Play; Variety Show; Nwsp; Yrbk; VP Frsh Cls; Intrml Ftbl; Intrml Sftbl; Intrml Vllybl; Cit Awd; UCLA; Bus.

ROGERS, CHRISTINE D; Rosemead HS; Rosemead, CA; (2); Service Clb; Var L Sftbl; Hon Roll; CSF; Bio.

ROGERS, CHRISTOPHER; Junipero Serra HS; Torrance, CA; (3); Computer Clb; Var Trk; Jr Statesman Fndtn Pgm; Cal ST Long Beach; Comp Sci.

ROGERS, CYNTHIA D; Hesperia HS; Hesperia, CA; (2); 17/700; ROTC; Varsity Clb; Treas Stu Cncl; Var Tennis; High Hon Roll; Bryn Mawr; Poly Sci.

ROGERS, DAVE W; Bishop Montgomery HS; Torrance, CA; (2); JV Bsbl; JV Socr; Wt Lftg; Cit Awd; Hon Roll; Prfct Atten Awd; Pres Acad Fit Awd; UCLA; Med.

ROGERS, DAVID D; Enterprise HS; Shingletown, CA; (3); JV Var Trk; Chrch Athltcs; Smmr Physcs Shasta JC; CA Polytech; Mtrl Engrng.

ROGERS, ERRIN; Woodcrest Christian HS; Riverside, CA; (2); Church Yth Grp; Chorus; Church Choir; CA Baptist Coll; Interior Desg.

ROGERS, GRETA L; Oakmont HS; Rosenville, CA; (1); Airobus; Medical.

ROGERS, JENNIFER D; Sutter Union HS; Sutter, CA; (4); Intnl Clb; Teachers Aide; Hon Roll; Asst Mgr & Mrg Of Food Svc; Yuba Coll; Caterer.

ROGERS, JERMAINE; Banning HS; Banning, CA; (3); Model UN; VICA; Band; Mrchg Band; Pep Band; Var Trk; Off Hon Roll; NHS; Electronics.

ROGERS, JONATHAN; Hesperia Christian HS; Hesperia, CA; (2); 3/42; JV Bsktbl; Var L Crs Cntry; High Hon Roll; CSF-CA Schlrshp Fdrtn; Educ.

ROGERS, JULIE K; Arroyo Grande HS; Nipomo, CA; (1); #167 In Class; Church Yth Grp; Cmnty Wkr; Hosp Aide; NFL; Speech Tm; Sign Lang Activity; Modeling; Writing A Novel; Acting.

ROGERS, KELLIE; Campbell Hall; Van Nuys, CA; (3); Cmnty Wkr; Ski Clb; Drill Tm; Ed Phtg Yrbk; Stat Bsktbl; Var Sftbl; 2nd Pl Cpy Wrtng Yrbk Tech Cmp; Natl Chrty Leag Awd; Hstry.

ROGERS, KELLY A; Acalanes HS; Lafayette, CA; (3); 42/265; Church Yth Grp; SADD; Teachers Aide; Var Sftbl; Hon Roll; Prfct Atten Awd; Sftbl MVP 87-88; Bus.

ROGERS, KRISTINA E; Rio Mesa HS; New Carlisle, OH; (3); Church Yth Grp; Drama Clb; FCA; French Clb; Sec Band; Drill Tm; Jazz Band; Mrchg Band; Pep Band; School Play; Stu Of Mnth; Peer Cnslng Secy; Bethel Coll; Spcl Educ.

ROGERS, LARRY H; Antelope Valley HS; Lancaster, CA; (4); Boy Scts; JV Crs Cntry; Var Socr; JV Trk; Ntl Merit Schol; Tp Sci Stu In SR Clss; Athltc Schlrshp UCSB In Sccr; U Of Santa Barbara; Srgn.

ROGERS, LASONJAY K; Crenshaw HS; Inglewood, CA; (4); 35/400; Church Yth Grp; ROTC; Hon Roll; Pres Acad Fit Awd; Yng Blck Schlrs; HS Imprvmnt Prgrm; Ephbn Soc; AL A&M U; Sclgy.

ROGERS, LASONJIA; Valley HS; Sacramento, CA; (3); FFA; ROTC; Hon Roll; ROP; Chrch Choir; UC Davis; Bus Admin.

ROGERS, LAURA A; Casa Roble HS; Orangevale, CA; (2); 130/461; Drama Clb; Spanish Clb; Thesps; Hon Roll; UC Santa Cruz; Cmmnctns.

ROGERS, LISA M; Fairfield HS; Fairfield, CA; (3); Teachers Aide; Band; Jazz Band; Mrchg Band; Orch; Lit Mag; Sec Ldr Cnty Hnr Band; Sect Ldr Trumpets; Privt Lessns To Yngr Musc Oriented Stu; CA ST U Long Beach; Musc Ed.

ROGERS, MELISSA RUTH; Foothill HS; Sacramento, CA; (3); Church Yth Grp; Drama Clb; Office Aide; SADD; Teachers Aide; Stage Crew; Stat Bsktbl; JV Var Score Keeper; Cit Awd; Stus Agnst Drugs Orange Cnty Shrff Dept Cncl; Help & Cnsl Kids W/Drug Prblms & Kids Agnst Drugs; U Of CA; Vet.

ROGERS, MIKE M; Bishop Amat HS; Temple City, CA; (3); Church Yth Grp; Varsity Clb; Bsbl; Ftbl; Socr; Wt Lftg; CA ST-LONG Beach.

ROGERS, RYAN; Santa Monica HS; Malibu, CA; (4); Cmnty Wkr; FBLA; Office Aide; Ski Clb; Teachers Aide; Stage Crew; Treas Frsh Cls; Stu Cncl; JV Golf; Wt Lftg; CSF Seal Bearer; S CA U Wstsde Almni Schlrshp; S CA U; Bio.

ROGERS, SCHONTEAU R; Pius X HS; Compton, CA; (4); Church Yth Grp; Dance Clb; Pep Clb; Chorus; Church Choir; Sec Jr Cls; Var Cheerldng; Hon Roll; NHS; Miss S CAL Natl Teen-Ager Pageant-Pianist; U CA-IRVINE; Bio Sci.

ROGERS, STANLEY; El Toro HS; El Toro, CA; (3); German Clb; Bus.

ROGERS, STEPHANIE; Lodi Acad; Lodi, CA; (1); Church Yth Grp; Bsktbl; Ftbl; Gym; Sftbl; Vllybl; Lodi Acad.

ROGIN, ALEXANDER M; Piedmont HS; Piedmont, CA; (3); 2/120; Band; Jazz Band; Orch; Pep Band; School Musical; School Play; Var Crs Cntry; Var Socr; Var Trk; Hon Roll; CSF; Music Hnr Soc; Schlr Athlt.

ROGNEBY, CHRISTINE M; Lower Lake HS; Aptos, CA; (4); 17/98; French Clb; Library Aide; Office Aide; High Hon Roll; Hon Roll; Yth Cnsrvtn Club; Friday Night Live; U Santa Cruz; Sci.

ROGNERUD, LAURIE M; Monte Vista HS; Danville, CA; (2); Church Yth Grp; Dance Clb; Stu Cncl; JV Swmmng.

ROGNLEIN, MICHAEL T; Folsom HS; Folsom, CA; (3); Pres Church Yth Grp; Cmnty Wkr; Intnl Clb; Library Aide; Model UN; Spanish Clb; Pres SADD; Ed Nwsp; Yrbk; Rep Stu Cncl; NY U; Music Bus.

ROGSON, TAMIR P; Hamilton HS Academy Of Music; Los Angeles, CA; (2); Chess Clb; Temple Yth Grp; Orch; String Ensmbl; Jewish Stu Union; U CA Irvine; Engrng.

ROHDE, EVAN J; Hamilton Music Acad; Los Angeles, CA; (2); Stage Crew; Matt Marshall Schlrshp; Outstndng Stage Craft Stu 89-90; Stage Mgr & Asst Stage Mgr89-90; Dir Spcl Effects.

ROHDE, JENNIFER; Glen A Wilson HS; Hacienda Heights, CA; (3); SADD; Wt Lftg; Hon Roll.

ROHLAPP, CHRIS L; Casa Grande HS; Petaluma, CA; (2); Chess Clb.

ROHMAN, ANDREA E; Newbury Park HS; Newbury Park, CA; (3); 26/347; German Clb; Hon Roll.

ROHR, REBECCA; Palisades HS; Pacific Palisades, CA; (3); Cmnty Wkr; Hosp Aide; NFL; Pep Clb; Q&S; Ski Clb; SADD; School Play; Ed Nwsp; Sftbl.

ROHRBACH, JOHN W; Bellarmine College Prep; Saratoga, CA; (3); 62/300; Church Yth Grp; Cmnty Wkr; Service Clb; SADD; Yrbk; Intrml Ftbl; Intrml Sftbl; Intrml Vllybl; SIC-TUTRNG Kds, Hlpng Mntlly Hndcpd; U Of Notre Dame; Bus.

ROHRER, BRIDGET M; Paso Robles HS; Templeton, CA; (2); FFA; Q&S; SADD; Teachers Aide; Nwsp; High Hon Roll; Mid St Muscle Cars Secy; U Of La Verne; Auto Photo.

ROHRER, DANIEL C; Clayton Valley HS; Concord, CA; (3); Am Leg Boys St; FBLA; Intnl Clb; Model UN; SADD; Varsity Clb; Lit Mag; Crs Cntry; Trk; UC Davis; Civil Engrng.

ROHWER, JEFFREY T; Clovis HS; Irvine, CA; (4); 9/550; Letterman Clb; Teachers Aide; Var Ftbl; Var Capt Tennis; Wt Lftg; High Hon Roll; Pres Schlr; Life Stu CSF; Hallowell Stu Of Yr; Bk Of Amer Awd Wnnr; U Of CA Irvine; Polit Sci.

ROJAF, CHRISTINE; Fresno HS; Fresno, CA; (4); 78/480; Church Yth Grp; Dance Clb; Thesps; Stu Cncl; Natl Hispnc Schlrshp; San Francisco ST U; Writing.

ROJANALA, ARPITA; James Logan HS; Fremont, CA; (3); Debate Tm; Treas FTA; Math Tm; Science Clb; Spanish Clb; Stu Cncl; Tennis; Hon Roll; Lion Awd; Cmnty Wkr; Travel Clb, Sectry/Treas; Leo Clb, Treas.

ROJAS, ADRIANA; Lynwood HS; Compton, CA; (3); 43/737; Church Yth Grp; Computer Clb; Math Clb; Teachers Aide; NHS; Psych.

ROJAS, ANDREA M; Turlock HS; Turlock, CA; (3); Art Clb; French Clb; Orch; Music.

ROJAS, BLANCA L; Sonoma Valley HS; Glen Ellen, CA; (1); Cmnty Wkr; SADD; Teachers Aide; Trk; Hon Roll; Assist Track; Vlntrd Daycare Ctr; Hlpd Smmr Schl Tchrs; Lawyer.

ROJAS, DAVID L; Moorpark HS; Moorpark, CA; (2); 32/275; Var L Crs Cntry; Var L Trk; High Hon Roll; Tri-Vly Leag Crs Cntry Chmpn CIF Chmpnshps 89; Qlfd CIF Chmpnshp Crs Cntry; Outstndng Awd Vrsty Trck; Math.

ROJAS, DENA M; Savanna HS; Anaheim, CA; (3); FBLA; Pep Clb; Var Crs Cntry; JV Socr; Stat Swmmng; Sec Jr Cls; Sec Sr Cls; SODA; Bus.

ROJAS, DIANA S; Gladstone HS; Azusa, CA; (3); SADD; Capt Drill Tm; Rep Stu Cncl; JV Var Sftbl; High Hon Roll; Hon Roll; Captn Dance Team; CSF; UCLA; Tchr Deaf Chldrn.

ROJAS, ESTELA M; Norco HS; Norco, CA; (3); Model UN; Varsity Clb; Band; Var Socr; Hon Roll; Pres Acad Fit Awd; ST U; Child Psychology.

ROJAS, EVANGELINA; Loretto HS; Sacramento, CA; (4); 15/52; Drama Clb; Chorus; School Musical; Ed Yrbk; Sec Stu Cncl; Elks Awd; Hon Roll; Pres Acad Fit Awd; Cult Pursuits Clb; Peer Mnstry; Mock Trail; CSF Clb; CSF Sealbr; Peace Chld Choir; Yrbk Awd; St Marys Coll.

ROJAS, GUY C; Upland HS; Upland, CA; (2); Speech Tm; Lit Mag; JV Bsbl; Var Bsktbl; OK ST; Commnctns.

ROJAS, LUCRECIA; Marysville HS; Marysville, CA; (2); Hon Roll; Prfct Atten Awd; Friday Night Live.

ROJAS, MARIA A; William Workman HS; Valinda, CA; (3); 26/268; French Clb; Spanish Clb; Rep Stu Cncl; Mgr(s); JV Tennis; Hon Roll; Prfct Atten Awd; Sec Spanish NHS; JV Tnns MVP Dlbls; Psych.

ROJAS, MIKE D; Summerville HS; Twain Harte, CA; (4); 11/135; Quiz Bowl; Ski Clb; Spanish Clb; VP Sr Cls; JV Bsbl; JV Ftbl; Var Socr; High Hon Roll; Pres Acad Fit Awd; Rotary Awd; Bank Of Amer Soc Stud Awd; CSF; Hnr Grd; UC Davis; Engr.

ROJAS, SANDRA M; Notre Dame Acad; Los Angeles, CA; (3); Dance Clb; Hosp Aide; Spanish Clb; Chorus; Church Choir; Cit Awd; Spanish Honors; Music Club Rep; Campus Ministry; Retreat Cove; Science & Math.

ROJO, ANDY M; Etiwanda HS; Etiwanda, CA; (2); Var Capt Bsbl; Hon Roll; Prfsnl Athlt.

ROJO, CORRINE A; Highland HS; Bakersfield, CA; (4); 4/276; Church Yth Grp; Library Aide; Office Aide; Spanish Clb; SADD; Teachers Aide; Sec Sr Cls; Stu Cncl; Socr; Sftbl; E Bakersfield Exch Clb; CA ST Bkrsfld U; Poltcl Sci.

ROJO, VINCENT; James Logan HS; Union City, CA; (3); JV Ftbl; Pltcl Sci.

ROLAND, TERI; Half Moon Bay HS; El Granada, CA; (2); Church Yth Grp; Computer Clb; GAA; Girl Scts; Letterman Clb; Library Aide; SADD; Varsity Clb; Phtg Yrbk; Var L Bsktbl; MVP-BSKTBL/Sftbl; Fresno ST; Phys Ed.

ROLDAN, BRAD; St Ignatius HS; Burlingame, CA; (3); 72/237; Varsity Clb; Ed Yrbk; Var Capt Trk; CSF; Photo Club; Diploma Of Honor From Amer Assn Of Tchrs Of Span & Port; Telecomms.

ROLDAN, EDWARD; Branham HS; San Jose, CA; (2); Boy Scts; Computer Clb; Math Clb; Science Clb; Spanish Clb; Band; Chorus; Bsktbl; Crs Cntry; Socr; Karate, Keyboarding, Comp; Berkeley; Chem.

ROLDAN, JENNIFER; Valley View HS; Moreno Valley, CA; (2); Church Yth Grp; Pres Stu Cncl; Intrml Socr; Capt Var Vllybl; Cit Awd; Hon Roll; Lion Awd.

ROLDAN, VIVIAN L; Wilcox HS; Santa Clara, CA; (1); Cheerldng; Hon Roll; UC Berkeley; CPA.

ROLEFSON, DAVID J; Bishop O'dowd HS; Piedmont, CA; (2); Cmnty Wkr; Debate Tm; Ski Clb; Stage Crew; Stu Cncl; JV Crs Cntry; JV Trk; Var Vllybl; High Hon Roll; Hiking Clb; Bus.

ROLEY, LINDA; University HS; Irvine, CA; (2); JCL; Intrml Crs Cntry; JV Trk; Hon Roll; Pres Acad Fit Awd; Gilf, Swmng, Runng & Readng; CA U Irvine; Med.

ROLFE, KRISTIN; Clovis HS; Clovis, CA; (3); Church Yth Grp; Sec FCA; Varsity Clb; Var Capt Crs Cntry; Var L Trk; High Hon Roll; Hon Roll; Teachers Aide; Acad Sprts Club; MVP X-Cntry, All League NYL; Sec Fellowship Chrstn Athls; Marine Bio.

ROLFE, LISA; Hughson Union HS; Hughson, CA; (1); FFA; Office Aide; SADD; MJC.

ROLL, ALYSHA; San Bernardino HS; San Bernardino, CA; (4); 10/345; Model UN; SADD; School Play; Stu Cncl; Elks Awd; High Hon Roll; NHS; CSF; Acadmc Dcthln; Peer Cnslr.

ROLL, BARBARA A; Modesto HS; Modesto, CA; (1); Off Frsh Cls; Intrml JV Cheerldng; Intrml JV Gym; Hon Roll; Accntnt.

ROLL, JENNIFER S; Arlington HS; Riverside, CA; (3); 111/440; FTA; Teachers Aide; Avid Readr Awd; Cal Poly Pomona; Elem Schl Tchr.

ROLLBERG, ANNIE M; Palmdale HS; Palmdale, CA; (3); 1/640; Girl Scts; Science Clb; Spanish Clb; VICA; Var Trk; High Hon Roll; Jr NHS; NHS; Stu Of Week; Outstndng Acad Achvt Awd 88-89; NASA Sharp Stu; Arch.

ROLLBERG, SUZANNE T; Palmdale HS; Palmdale, CA; (2); Art Clb; 1st Pl Pen & Ink 90 HS Art Show; Fnlst Natl Library Poetry Cont; Art.

ROLLER, JEFF S; Carlmont HS; Belmont, CA; (3); 8/373; Var JV Crs Cntry; Var JV Tennis; Hon Roll; CSF; Nrthrn CA Jr Tnns Leag; Outstndng Achvt Geom Cert Merit 89; U Of CA; Vet Med.

ROLLIN, EVAN A; Edison HS; Fresno, CA; (1); Church Yth Grp; Cmnty Wkr; Computer Clb; French Clb; Tennis; High Hon Roll; Hon Roll; CSF; Envrnmntl Clb; Stanford; Civil Engr.

ROLLIN, SARAH; Oceana HS; San Bruno, CA; (3); 2/175; Chess Clb; English Clb; French Clb; Girl Scts; Red Cross Aide; Science Clb; Stage Crew; High Hon Roll; Hon Roll; NEDT Awd; Gldn St Exm Hgh Hnrs Alg & Geom; CSF.

ROLLINS, JENNIFER J; Bella Vista HS; Citrus Heights, CA; (2); 151/406; JV Sftbl; Forest Conservation; Animal Safety & Wellbeing; Humboldt State U; Forestry Wldl.

ROLLINS, JOEYLYNN JANE; San Juan HS; Citrus Heights, CA; (1); Pres FHA; Girl Scts; School Play; Cit Awd; High Hon Roll; Hon Roll; Pres Acad Fit Awd; FHA St Natls 3rd Pl Plaque & Rgnl Officer Awd; Plastic Surgeon.

ROLLINS, KRISTINA M; Mission Viejo HS; Mission Viejo, CA; (4); 11/560; Church Yth Grp; Cmnty Wkr; Office Aide; Pep Clb; Spanish Clb; Teachers Aide; Lit Mag; High Hon Roll; NHS; Ntl Merit Schol; CA Schlrshp Fed Seal Bearer; Prin Hnr Roll 1987-90; Cert Of Excllnc Math; Champain Coll; Clncl Psych.

ROLLINS, SHANTA N; Victor Valley HS; Victorville, CA; (3); Church Yth Grp; Aud/Vis; Scrkpr JV Crs Cntry; L Var Trk; Hon Roll; Black Stu Union Treas; Modeling; Campus Life; Chld Psych.

ROLSTON, KENNETH G; Irvine HS; Irvine, CA; (1); 38/500; Boy Scts; Drama Clb; Acpl Chr; Chorus; School Musical; School Play; Swing Chorus; Hon Roll; Music.

ROMABILES, NATHANIEL JOSEPH A; Lowell HS; San Francisco, CA; (2); ROTC; Drill Tm; Vllybl; Hon Roll; Jr NHS; Prfct Atten Awd; Lowell Fil-Am Clb; Success Consortium; UC Berkeley; Arch.

ROMAGNOLI, MICHAEL L; Fontana HS; Fontana, CA; (2); Church Yth Grp; Cmnty Wkr; Treas Stu Cncl; Intrml Mgr Bsbl; JV Bsktbl; Intrml Mgr Ftbl; Hon Roll; Pres Acad Fit Awd; Coach Pee Wee Bsktbl, Tee-Ball, Ftbl & Soccer; Scripps Coll; Marine Bio.

ROMAN, FRANCISCA; Caruthers HS; Fresno, CA; (2); 4-H; FHA; Masonic Awd; Prfct Atten Awd; Scottish Scty Of Central CA.

ROMAN, JULIA M; Hilltop HS; Chula Vista, CA; (2); Hon Roll; Ntl Merit Ltr; Pres Acad Fit Awd; U CA Berkeley; Accntng.

ROMAN, LARRY J; Magnolia HS; Stanton, CA; (2); 2/200; Art Clb; Boy Scts; Bus Profs of Am; Church Yth Grp; FBLA; Intnl Clb; Letterman Clb; Red Cross Aide; Service Clb; Varsity Clb; Vlntr Wk Cub Scts; Blood Dnr; West Point Acad; Doctor.

ROMAN, LUIS; Los Amigos HS; Santa Ana, CA; (2); 100/300; Drama Clb; Office Aide; Stage Crew; Bsbl; High Hon Roll; Hon Roll; Prfct Atten Awd; USC; Law.

ROMAN, RENE; Rio Mesa HS; Oxnard, CA; (3); 112/347; Varsity Clb; Bsbl; Ftbl.

ROMANO, MARC D; Esperanza HS; Yorba Linda, CA; (2); Lbrn Cmnty Wkr; Intrml Bsbl; JV Ftbl; Var Wt Lftg; Var L Wrstlng; High Hon Roll; Hon Roll; Oper And Maintn Comp Bulltn Bd; Amnsty Intl, Greenpeace; Engrng.

ROMANO, RACHEL; Arroyo HS; San Lorenzo, CA; (2); Church Yth Grp; GAA; Letterman Clb; Science Clb; Ski Clb; Spanish Clb; Varsity Clb; Var Socr; Var Sftbl; Var Vllybl; Dist Olympc Dvlpmnt Soccer Team 89-90; Northern CA ST Olympc Team 89-90; HAAL All Lgu Soccer 89-90; UC Santa Barbara; Med.

ROMANOV, ANDREW; San Gabriel HS; Rosemead, CA; (3); JA; Church Choir; Jazz Band; Mrchg Band; Orch; Rptr Nwsp; Var Crs Cntry; Var Trk; Cit Awd; Hon Roll; The Natl Deans List 1988-89; JR Athlt Of Yr Achvmnt Awd; Christn Bible Study; Multnomah Schl Of Bible; Mnstry.

ROMANOV, SERGEY; San Gabriel HS; Rosemead, CA; (2); Church Yth Grp; Band; Church Choir; Mrchg Band; Cit Awd; High Hon Roll; Elec Engrng.

ROMANOWSKY, AARON J; Cabrillo HS; Lompoc, CA; (4); 1/220; Pres Key Clb; Math Tm; VP Science Clb; Yrbk; Rep Stu Cncl; JV Trk; Elks Awd; High Hon Roll; Ntl Merit Schol; Acadmc Dcthln Cnty Chmps; UC Berkeley; Physics.

ROMANS, ZACHARY A; Poway HS; Poway, CA; (2); 200/700; Band; Jazz Band; Mrchg Band; Orch; Lcrss; Arch.

ROMASZEWSKI, DIANE; John Burroughs HS; Canoga Park, CA; (2); ROTC; Drill Tm; School Play; CA ST U Northridge; Chld Care.

ROMER, MICHAEL; Montebello HS; Montebello, CA; (2); Boy Scts; Drama Clb; Swmmng; Cit Awd; Hon Roll; USC.

ROMERA, HEIDI D; Boron HS; Boron, CA; (3); 4-H; Office Aide; Ed Yrbk; Mgr(s); Yrbk Photo; Bakersfield Coll; Filmaker.

ROMERIUS, PATRIK V; Caruthers HS; Caruthers, CA; (4); Debate Tm; Letterman Clb; Math Clb; Math Tm; Yrbk; Var L Bsktbl; Var L Ftbl; Var L Trk; Var L Vllybl; Wt Lftg; Bank Of Amer Awd For Math; Cvl Engr.

ROMERO, AMIE C; Tracy Joint Union HS; Tracy, CA; (3); Hon Roll; Heald Bus Coll; Acctng.

ROMERO, ANGELICA A; Etiwanda HS; Rancho Cucamong, CA; (2); French Clb; Color Guard; Mrchg Band; JV Swmmng; Cit Awd; High Hon Roll; Hon Roll; Prfct Atten Awd; Artistic Roller Skating; UC-SAN Diego; Oceanography.

ROMERO, ARACELI D; Baldwin Park HS; Baldwin Park, CA; (3); FBLA; Teachers Aide; Bsktbl; Vllybl; Hon Roll; Keywanettes; Pediatrics.

ROMERO, BARBARA; Central Union HS; El Centro, CA; (3); High Hon Roll; Tall Flags; USC; Law.

ROMERO, BERTHA A; Indio HS; Indio, CA; (2); CSF; Awd Plaq BAC/Mecha Clb Exclnct Wrk; Fash Desgnr.

ROMERO, CARLOS; Don Bosco Technical Inst; West Covina, CA; (1); 55/244; Boy Scts; Chess Clb; Computer Clb; Ski Clb; NEDT Awd; Astronomy Club.

ROMERO, CAROLA; Bonita Vista HS; Bonita, CA; (4); 18/532; Church Yth Grp; Cmnty Wkr; Teachers Aide; Variety Show; Ed Nwsp; Yrbk; JV Vllybl; Cit Awd; DAR Awd; High Hon Roll; Intl Bachlrt Pgm; U Of CA San Diego; Med.

ROMERO, CHRISTOPHER E; Central Union HS; El Centro, CA; (2); Var Trk; Hon Roll; Cycling; Martial Arts; Church; San Diego ST U; Elec Eng.

ROMERO, DANIEL; Hesperia Christian Schl; Hesperia, CA; (3); 3/30; Church Yth Grp; Scholastic Bowl; Chorus; Mrchg Band; School Musical; Pres Jr Cls; Var Bsbl; Var Bsktbl; Var Ftbl; Hon Roll; Biola Coll; Law.

ROMERO, ERIK J; Hemet HS; Hemet, CA; (2); San Diego ST U; Atty.

ROMERO, ERIK M; West HS; Torrance, CA; (2); Church Yth Grp; Spanish Clb; Cit Awd; Hon Roll; Spnsh Achvt Awd; Srgry.

ROMERO, ESTHER; Hathaway HS; Sylmar, CA; (3); Drama Clb; Band; Mrchg Band; Bsktbl; Sftbl; Vllybl; Cit Awd; Secy.

ROMERO, FRANK E; Hesperia HS; Hesperia, CA; (2); Office Aide; Ski Clb; Spanish Clb; JV Bsktbl; Ftbl; JV Socr; Wt Lftg; High Hon Roll.

ROMERO, GABRIELLE; Marina HS; Huntington Beach, CA; (3); Drama Clb; French Clb; School Musical; Hon Roll; Polaris Club; Stu Ldng The Animal Mvmnt; Amnesty Intl; UCLA; Cmmnctns.

ROMERO, JENNIFER L; Notre Dame HS; Belmont, CA; (2); Church Yth Grp; Debate Tm; French Clb; SADD; Pres Frsh Cls; Score Keeper; Hon Roll.

ROMERO, JESSICA M; Hilltop HS; Chula Vista, CA; (2); Intnl Clb; Pep Clb; Spanish Clb; Cit Awd; Hon Roll; Pres Acad Fit Awd; Ayso Soccer; Ucsd; Med.

ROMERO, JOHN S; Ramona HS; Ramona, CA; (2); JV Socr; JV Vllybl; SDSU; Bus.

ROMERO, JOHNNIE R; San Fernando Coll In HS; Sylmar, CA; (2); Church Yth Grp; Pres Band; Drill Tm; Pres Jazz Band; School Musical; Hon Roll; Prfct Atten Awd; Pres Acad Fit Awd; Magnet Pgm; 2 Outstndng Achvt Certs; 2 Cert Of Mrts; UCLA; Med.

ROMERO, JOSE; C K Mc Clatchy SR HS; Sacramento, CA; (2); 1/549; Chess Clb; ROTC; Color Guard; Drill Tm; High Hon Roll; J V Drill Tm ROTC Hnr Scty Outstndng Cadet Awd; Air Force Acad; Pilot.

ROMERO, KATHERYNE; Lowell HS; Pittsburg, CA; (3); GAA; Letterman Clb; Spanish Clb; Teachers Aide; Varsity Clb; School Musical; Gym; Pres Acad Fit Awd; Blood Dr; Law.

ROMERO, LAURA E; Delano Joint Union HS; Pixley, CA; (2); Prfct Atten Awd; CA Achvt Test.

ROMERO, LEONARDO; Servite HS; Lakewood, CA; (3); Socr; NHS; CSF; Off Plyr Of Yr; 2nd Tm All League Soccer; UCI; Med.

ROMERO, LINTON S; Bishop Amat Memorial HS; Los Angeles, CA; (3); Spanish Clb; Bsktbl; Ftbl; Hon Roll; Spanish NHS; U Of Berkeley; Bus Admin.

ROMERO, LIZBETH; Holy Family HS; Los Angeles, CA; (4); Teachers Aide; Chorus; Stat Bsktbl; VP Sec Cheerldng; Glendale CC; Psych.

ROMERO, MABEL; Notre Dame HS; Redwood City, CA; (3); Cmnty Wkr; French Clb; Hosp Aide; Teachers Aide; Chorus; School Musical; Nwsp; Lit Mag; Sec Treas Sr Cls; Rep Stu Cncl.

ROMERO, MARIA ELOISA N; Downey HS; Downey, CA; (2); JV Bsktbl; JV Vllybl; Hon Roll; CSF; UCLA.

ROMERO, MARIA L; Le Grand HS; Planada, CA; (2); Yrbk; Sec Jr Cls; Limosine; Bus.

ROMERO, MARY ANN; Andrew Hill HS; San Jose, CA; (1); Chorus; Hon Roll; Spec Hnrs 9 Awds Prjct 50, Prtnrshp, Mesa; Early Acad Otrch Prtnrshp Pgm U CA; Prjct U Santa Clara; Santa Clara U; Comp.

ROMERO, MELODY; Culver City HS; Culver City, CA; (1); Key Clb; Off Frsh Cls; Tennis; Trk; Cit Awd; High Hon Roll; Hon Roll; Stanford U; Bus.

ROMERO, MONICA; Inglewood HS; Inglewood, CA; (1); Cit Awd; Hon Roll; Atty.

ROMERO, NERY E; Inglewood HS; Inglewood, CA; (2); Hon Roll; Prfct Atten Awd; Cert Of Proficiency, Prfct Attndnce; Atty.

ROMERO, RACHEL E; Will C Crawford HS; San Diego, CA; (2); 1/390; Cit Awd; Hon Roll; Val; CA Bus Ed Assn Cert Rcgntn Outstndng Stu Bus Psych & Automtd Bus; Accntng.

ROMERO, REBECCA A; Mira Mesa HS; San Diego, CA; (2); French Clb; JA; Model UN; Swmmng; Trk; CSF; Jrnlsm.

ROMERO, SARAH; Glen A Wilson HS; Hacienda Heights, CA; (1); Church Yth Grp; Band; Mrchg Band; Civil Engrng.

ROMERO, YESENIA; Thomas Jefferson HS; Los Angeles, CA; (4); 25/400; Church Yth Grp; Cmnty Wkr; Computer Clb; FTA; Hosp Aide; Key Clb; Math Clb; Office Aide; Scholastic Bowl; Science Clb; Gftd Tlntd Stu; Mt St Marys Coll; Liberal Arts.

ROMIG, CHAD; Roseville HS; Rocklin, CA; (2); 9/445; Church Yth Grp; French Clb; SADD; Rptr Yrbk; Lit Mag; Bsktbl; Var JV Socr; Hon Roll; NHS; Fri Night Live.

ROMIG, ERIN; Escondido HS; Escondido, CA; (1); Church Yth Grp; Drama Clb; Tennis; Cit Awd.

ROMITO, ROBERT A; University City HS; San Diego, CA; (4); Church Yth Grp; Ed Nwsp; Var L Trk; Elks Awd; Hon Roll; Pres Acad Fit Awd; Rotary Awd; All City Schltc Trk Team; Schltc Jrnls Yr; Embry Riddle; Aeronautical Sci.

ROMITTI, DARREN K; Summerville Union HS; Tuolumne, CA; (4); Band; Jazz Band; Mrchg Band; Pep Band; Hon Roll; Crtve Wrtng; Archlgy; Guitar-Rock Music; Columbia JR Coll; Poet.

ROMO, ALICIA; Sacred Heart Of Jesus HS; Los Angeles, CA; (3); CA ST; Real Estate.

ROMO, CHRISTINA; St Francis HS; Sacramento, CA; (4); 3/169; Dance Clb; Intnl Clb; Spanish Clb; SADD; Variety Show; Sec Jr Cls; Rep Stu Cncl; JV Capt Cheerldng; High Hon Roll; Hon Roll; Ldrshp Educ & Devlpmnt, Pg&e & Natl Hispanic Schlrshps; Stanford.

ROMO, DANIEL J; Gahr HS; Artesia, CA; (3); JV Bsbl; U C Irvine; Comm.

ROMO, DIANA; Watsonville HS; Watsonville, CA; (2); 80/400; Pep Clb; Cheerldng; Crs Cntry; Trk; Hon Roll; UCLA; Cmmnctns/Dance.

ROMO, ELENA N; Tracy HS; Tracy, CA; (1); 51/565; Karate; Mc George Schl Of Law; Law.

ROMO, GINA M; Walnut HS; Walnut, CA; (4); 7/365; Church Yth Grp; Sec Treas Key Clb; Pep Clb; Teachers Aide; Drill Tm; Ed Nwsp; Stu Cncl; High Hon Roll; Pres Acad Fit Awd; Natl Mrt Fnlst; George Washington U; Poltcl Sci.

ROMO, JAVIER; Bell Gardens HS; Bell, CA; (1); Crs Cntry; Trk; Hon Roll; Pres Acad Fit Awd; Police Explorer; Political Sci.

ROMO, MONICA M; Fontana HS; Fontana, CA; (3); 4/30; FBLA; Office Aide; Teachers Aide; Hon Roll; DARE; Chaffey Coll; Bus.

ROMO, PATRICIA; Sacred Heart Of Jesus HS; Los Angeles, CA; (3); CA ST; Accntnt.

RONAGHI, NADER; University HS; Irvine, CA; (3); Vllybl; Persian Clb Pres; Chmstry.

RONALD, PAUL L; Mesa Verde HS; Citrus Heights, CA; (3); JV Var Bsktbl; Hon Roll; Pilot.

RONCAL, CHRISTINA W; El Camino HS; Daly City, CA; (3); Intnl Clb; Library Aide; Service Clb; Teachers Aide; Varsity Clb; Variety Show; Ed Nwsp; Golden St Exam Recgntn; Badminton Var; Nrsng.

RONDEZ, JENNIFER; North Monterey County HS; Salinas, CA; (4); FBLA; Office Aide; SADD; Sec Soph Cls; Sec Jr Cls; Stu Cncl; Var Co-Capt Cheerldng; Score Keeper; Trk; Hon Roll; Bus.

RONDON, KARINA E; Bellarmine Jefferson HS; Sun Valley, CA; (2); Spanish Clb; High Hon Roll; Hon Roll; U CA Berkeley; Crmnl Law.

RONDONUWU, ANITA; San Gorgonio HS; San Bernardino, CA; (4); 23/418; English Clb; Intnl Clb; Service Clb; Spanish Clb; Teachers Aide; Swmmng; Prfct Atten Awd; UC-SAN Diego; Pharmacy.

RONEY, JODI; Orange HS; Orange, CA; (2); Church Yth Grp; Church Choir; Drill Tm; JV Cheerldng; JV Trk; High Hon Roll; Hon Roll; CSF; UC Davis; Vet.

RONEY, JULIE; Orange HS; Orange, CA; (3); Church Yth Grp; Math Clb; Chorus; Drill Tm; JV Var Cheerldng; JV Var Swmmng; High Hon Roll; Hon Roll; NHS; Chamber Singers.

RONGAVILLA, MARY ANN L; Mark Keppel HS; Alhambra, CA; (4); Teachers Aide; Cit Awd; Hon Roll; Filipino Club; Pasadena; Nrs.

RONK, BENJAMIN J; Seaside HS; Fort Ord, CA; (3); Boy Scts; Church Yth Grp; FTA; Spanish Clb; Teachers Aide; School Musical; Bsbl; Ftbl; Hon Roll; Med.

RONQUILLO, KATHLEEN; Mills HS; Millbrae, CA; (2); Hosp Aide; JV Tennis; Vrsty Badmntn MVP 89-90; Prncpls Awd; Pre-Med.

RONTELLI, GINA M; Hoover HS; Fresno, CA; (2); High Hon Roll.

ROOFIAN, HOOMAN; North Hollywood HS; Studio City, CA; (2); Spanish Clb; Yrbk; Stu Cncl; Ftbl; Wt Lftg; High Hon Roll; Hon Roll; Prfct Atten Awd; Pre-Med.

ROOKE, SUSAN K; Foothill HS; Bakersfield, CA; (2); Church Yth Grp; FCA; Church Choir; Var Socr; JV Capt Sftbl; JV Capt Vllybl; Hon Roll; CSF.

ROOKHUYZEN, ROBERT L; La Sierra HS; Riverside, CA; (1); Boy Scts; Church Yth Grp; FBLA; Hon Roll; Prfct Atten Awd; Friday Nite Live; Brigham Yng U; Law Nfrcmnt.

ROONEY, CHERYL M; Ramona HS; Riverside, CA; (3); 39/403; Varsity Clb; Ed Nwsp; Tennis; Vllybl; High Hon Roll; Hon Roll; Pres Acad Fit Awd; Commnctns.

ROOS, MELINDA S; Downey HS; Downey, CA; (2); Church Yth Grp; Math Clb; Science Clb; Service Clb; Band; Mrchg Band; Yng Envrnmntlsts Clb; Lib Clb; CSF.

ROOSEVELT JR, JAMES M; Bellarmine College Prep; Sunnyvale, CA; (3); 93/300; Church Yth Grp; Cmnty Wkr; Debate Tm; NFL; Service Clb; Speech Tm; Pres SADD; Ed Yrbk; Sec Treas Stu Cncl; Opt Clb Awd; Alumni Of Presdntl Clsrm Yng Amer; Offcr Of Jr Statesman Of Amer; Pres Stu Agnst Drugs & Alchl; Amer U; Poly Sci.

ROOT, DEBORAH; Santa Teresa HS; San Jose, CA; (2); Cmnty Wkr; Model UN; SADD; Med.

ROOT, MARIO D; Marshall Fundamental HS; Pasadena, CA; (4); Key Clb; Spanish Clb; Band; Mrchg Band; Pep Band; Nwsp; Var Bsbl; JV Bsktbl; JV Ftbl; Cit Awd; NAACP; Prm Cmmtte Chm; CA Schlrshp Fed; Baylor U; Accntnt.

ROOT, MICHAEL; Southbay Christian Schl; San Jose, CA; (3); #2 In Class; Letterman Clb; Yrbk; Var Bsbl; Var Bsktbl; Var Socr; Intrml Wt Lftg; Hon Roll; CSF; Eagle Scout; Foreign Exch Stu Spain; Comp Engr.

ROOT, STEPHANIE A; Edison HS; Huntington Beach, CA; (2); Pep Clb; Ski Clb; Spanish Clb; 4V Pepstr; Vrsty Song Pepster, Cptn; CA ST Long Beach; Frgn Reltns.

ROOTSAERT, MICHELLE; Archbishop Mitty HS; San Jose, CA; (4); Church Yth Grp; Cmnty Wkr; GAA; Drama Clb; Ski Clb; Teachers Aide; Variety Show; Pres Soph Cls; Pres Jr Cls; Rep Stu Cncl; Dist, Nor-St, US Rgn IV & Club Sccr Teams; UC Berkeley.

ROPER, MATTHEW M; Village Christian Schls; Burbank, CA; (3); Chess Clb; CSUN; Comp Sci.

ROPER, SHELLEY R; Southern California Christian HS; Anaheim, CA; (3); Church Yth Grp; Acpl Chr; Chorus; Sec Frsh Cls; Hon Roll; Mst Inspirational In Choir; Cal ST Long Beach; Marine Bio.

ROPP, SCOTT; Fountain Valley HS; Laguna Hills, CA; (4); 59/620; Cmnty Wkr; French Clb; Intnl Clb; Ski Clb; Intrml Swmmng; JV Trk; Hon Roll; Grad Distngshd Schlr; Middle Eastern Clb; U AZ; Arch.

ROQUE, GEMMALIN; Bishop Amat Memorial HS; La Puente, CA; (4); 46/400; Church Yth Grp; Cmnty Wkr; Office Aide; Teachers Aide; Hon Roll; CA Schlrshp Fdrtn; CA ST U Of Los Angeles; Nrsng.

ROQUE, TRICIA; Montgomery HS; San Diego, CA; (4); 13/419; Cmnty Wkr; FBLA; Key Clb; Library Aide; Office Aide; Pep Clb; SADD; Teachers Aide; Ed Yrbk; Rptr Lit Mag; Yrbk Soc Sctn Copy Edtr; CSF; Acadmc Leag; UCSB.

ROQUEMORE, COLETTE; John Muir HS; Altadena, CA; (1); Church Yth Grp; Math Clb; Varsity Clb; Church Choir; Drill Tm; JV Bsktbl; Hon Roll; Pasadena Cowgirls Drill Team; Interior Dsgn.

RORABAUGH, DAPHNE B; Chula Vista HS; Chula Vista, CA; (3); 110/500; Art Clb; Dance Clb; Key Clb; Office Aide; Pep Clb; SADD; Drill Tm; Stu Cncl; Cit Awd; Hon Roll; Coa-Cola Svc Awd; Spartan Band Svc Awd; Spartanette Of Yr-Drill Team; Peer Tutor; SDSU; Psych.

ROS, CHAMNAN; California HS; Whittier, CA; (3); 110/369; Art Clb; French Clb; German Clb; Spanish Clb; Stu Cncl; Crs Cntry; Trk; Cit Awd; Prfct Atten Awd; Crss Cntry Medals; CA ST U Fullerton; Physician.

ROS, CHAMNAN; Eisenhower HS; San Bernardino, CA; (2); NHS; Asian Club; Comp Engr.

ROSA, ANTHONY J; Hanford HS; Hanford, CA; (2); JV Bsbl; JV Trk; JV Wt Lftg; MESA Clb; Paramedic.

ROSA, MANUEL; Washington Preparatory HS; Los Angeles, CA; (3); Dance Clb; ROTC; Spanish Clb; Crs Cntry; Socr; Swmmng; Trk; Prfct Atten Awd; Engrng.

ROSA, MARGARET; Mt Miguel HS; San Diego, CA; (4); Church Yth Grp; DECA; Office Aide; Spanish Clb; Fld Hcky; Cit Awd; High Hon Roll; Hon Roll; Lion Awd; Prfct Atten Awd; John F Kennedy Awd 87; U C Davis; Pre-Med.

ROSA, STEPHEN G; Hilmar HS; Hilmar, CA; (3); SADD; Frgn Lang Clb; Jr Statesman; Hstry.

ROSALES, CLAUDIA G; Woodrow Wilson HS; San Francisco, CA; (3); Latin Clb; SADD; Var Jr Cls; Rep Stu Cncl; Peer Cnslr; San Francisco ST U; Scl Workr.

ROSALES, DIANA L; Anaheim HS; Anaheim, CA; (4); FHA; Office Aide; Varsity Clb; Band; Mrchg Band; Pep Band; Var Socr; Var Sftbl; Pres Acad Fit Awd; Fullerton CC; Fshn Dsgn.

ROSALES, ELVIA K; Tranquility Union HS; Mendota, CA; (2); 3/31; SADD; Teachers Aide; Score Keeper; Socr; Trk; Stat Wrstlng; Stanford; Cmmnctns.

ROSALES, GRACE M; Paramount HS; Paramount, CA; (1); Pep Clb; Mrchg Band; Orch; Sftbl; Vllybl; UCLA; Pediatriant.

ROSALES, KRISTIN J; Chino HS; Chino, CA; (2); Church Yth Grp; Pep Clb; ROP Retail Careers; Fash Inst Dsgn Merch; Fash Merc.

ROSALES, LARRY J; Don Antonio Lugo HS; Chino, CA; (2); Church Yth Grp; Var Crs Cntry; Var Trk; Hon Roll; NHS; Prfct Atten Awd; Aviation.

ROSALES, LUCY; Los Banos HS; Los Banos, CA; (3); Treas AFS; Church Yth Grp; Cmnty Wkr; Drama Clb; Hosp Aide; Science Clb; Sec Spanish Clb; Cheerldng; Stat Wrstlng; High Hon Roll; CSF; Bus.

ROSALES, LUISA; Capistrano Valley HS; San Juan Capistra, CA; (3); Church Yth Grp; Med.

ROSALES, RAQUEL C; Ramena Convent Secondary Schl; Hacienda Hts, CA; (3); 13/107; Art Clb; Church Yth Grp; Model UN; Office Aide; Spanish Clb; Stu Cncl; Hon Roll; NHS; CA Schlrshp Fed Sec; Psych.

ROSALES, REINA V; J Eugene Mc Ateer HS; San Francisco, CA; (3); Latin Clb; ROTC; Teachers Aide; Color Guard; Hon Roll; SF ST U; Pres Of Corp.

ROSALES, ROBERTO D; Rio Mesa HS; Oxnard, CA; (4); 41/380; Computer Clb; Hon Roll; Prfct Atten Awd; Pres Acad Fit Awd; Video Clb Treas; Lab Asst; Moorpark Coll; Radio Tv Prod.

ROSANBALM, TAMMY T; California HS; Whittier, CA; (3); 46/369; Church Yth Grp; German Clb; Cit Awd; Girls League Brd Jr Rep; Soc Wrk.

ROSARIO, DON J; Vallejo SR HS; Vallejo, CA; (2); SADD; Rptr Nwsp; Hon Roll; Jr NHS; NHS; Golden St Exam Hnrs Algebra, Geometry; Natl Sci Olympiad Bio Awd; Filipino Cmnty Acad Performance Awd.

ROSARIO, JOANNE; Yerba Buena HS; San Jose, CA; (3); Hosp Aide; Letterman Clb; Math Clb; Chorus; Sec Soph Cls; VP Stu Cncl; JV Tennis; Hon Roll; NHS; CSF VP; Pre Med.

ROSAS, ANEISSA; Bishop Amat HS; La Habra Heights, CA; (2); Church Yth Grp; Dance Clb; Pep Clb; JV Cheerldng; Trk; High Hon Roll; Hon Roll; NHS; Alexandra Ballet Acad; UC Irvine; Med.

ROSAS, CECILIA R; Chino HS; Chino, CA; (2); FFA; Stat Ftbl; Mgr(s); JV Socr; MVP Defense Awd Sccr; AYSO Sccr; Stu Against Animal Cruelty; Mt Sac JC; Ag.

ROSAS, DANEYDA M; Mar Vista HS; San Ysidro, CA; (3); 146/252; Dance Clb; French Clb; Latin Clb; SADD; Teachers Aide; Dance Chrgrphy; Real Estate.

ROSAS, DANNY C; Dos Palos HS; Dos Palos, CA; (3); 33/129; Boy Scts; FFA; SADD; VICA; Band; JV Var Ftbl; JV Var Trk; JV Wrstlng; Hon Roll; Camp Counselor; Fresno Cnty Ldrsh Camp.

ROSAS, DAVID G; James Lick HS; San Jose, CA; (3); Church Yth Grp; Math Tm; Var Bsbl; Var Bsktbl; Var Ftbl; MAYO Club; Bus.

ROSAS, GRACE YAP; Notre Dame HS; Los Angeles, CA; (4); Drama Clb; Intnl Clb; Flag Corp; School Musical; School Play; Variety Show; Powder Puff Ftbl; Tennis; Hon Roll; NEDT Awd; Natl Hspnc Schlrshp; Photo & Art Clb; UC Santa Cruz; Psych.

ROSAS, LAURA; Firebaugh HS; Firebaugh, CA; (1); Spanish Clb; SADD; High Hon Roll; Hon Roll; Fresno ST; Realtor.

ROSAS, LAZARO; Santa Maria HS; Santa Maria, CA; (2); Bsbl; Socr; Cit Awd.

ROSAS, RUBY; Ramona Convent Secondary Schl; Alhambra, CA; (3); 6/98; Cmnty Wkr; Dance Clb; GAA; Math Clb; Model UN; Spanish Clb; Variety Show; Sec Frsh Cls; Pres Soph Cls; Sec Stu Cncl; Spain Trip & Study Of Span; CCD Teacher; Stanford U; Law.

ROSAS, XAVIER; Burbank HS; Burbank, CA; (2); Mrchg Band; Ftbl; Prfct Atten Awd; USC; Bus.

ROSAS, YOLANDA; Livingston HS; Delhi, CA; (2); High Hon Roll; Hon Roll; Merced Coll.

ROSE, ALEASHA N; Palmdale HS; Acton, CA; (3); 78/644; Pres Church Yth Grp; Drama Clb; Hosp Aide; Pres SADD; School Play; Rep Soph Cls; Rep Jr Cls; Cit Awd; Hon Roll; Golden St Ex Rcvd Acdmc Excllnc Awd Geo W/ Hons; Ricks Coll; Elem Ed.

ROSE, ARTESHA M; Castlemont HS; Oakland, CA; (2); Church Yth Grp; JA; Teachers Aide; Chorus; Pres Church Choir; Bsktbl; Cheerldng; Cit Awd; Prfct Atten Awd; Friday Night Live; Clark Coll; Jrnlsm.

ROSE, DAWN; Golden West HS; Visalia, CA; (2); Treas 4-H; Band; Mrchg Band; Pep Band; 4-H Awd; Hon Roll; Outstndng Frshmn Awd-Gldn W Bnd 88-89; Jr All-Amer Hall Of Fame Bnd Hnrs 90; Amer Mscl Fndtn Bnd Hnrs; Fresno CA U; Music.

ROSE, DE ANNA M; Fairfield HS; Suisun City, CA; (2); Church Yth Grp; Chorus; Church Choir; Color Guard; Mrchg Band; Hon Roll; Asst Flag Capt; Flag Capt; Band Rep ASB Ldrshp; Music.

ROSE, DELENA L; Fountain Valley HS; Fountain Valley, CA; (3); Church Yth Grp; Sec French Clb; Church Choir; Chrmn Orch; School Musical; High Hon Roll; Pres Acad Fit Awd; Pres Schlr; CA Schlrshp Fed; U CA Irvine; Lawyer.

ROSE, DENISE; Orestimba HS; Newman, CA; (1); GAA; Pep Clb; Spanish Clb; Color Guard; JV Bsktbl; CSF; Friday Night Live Stu Against Drink & Driving; Bsktbl Homecoming JV Atten.

ROSE, DIONNE M; Arroyo Grande HS; Nipomo, CA; (2); 39/625; Church Yth Grp; FCA; 4-H; SADD; Church Choir; Bsktbl; High Hon Roll; CA Poly; Vet.

ROSE, JENNIFER; Corona Del Mar HS; Newport Beach, CA; (3); Sec Debate Tm; Key Clb; Latin Clb; Chrmn Pep Clb; Sec SADD; SADD; Cheerldng; Pom Pon; Ballet; Piano; Lawyer.

ROSE, JENNIFER A; Arvin HS; Bakersfield, CA; (3); 46/340; Drama Clb; Letterman Clb; Ski Clb; SADD; Teachers Aide; Treas Frsh Cls; Off Sr Cls; Var Bsktbl; Var Score Keeper; Var Sftbl; Phy Thrpy.

ROSE, KENNETH J; Lemoore HS; Lemoore, CA; (3); 2/400; FBLA; Spanish Clb; Teachers Aide; Treas Frsh Cls; Pres Soph Cls; Var Capt Bsbl; Var Ftbl; Var Capt Socr; Cal Berkeley; Accntng.

ROSE, LISA R; Bakersfield HS; Bakersfield, CA; (3); Church Yth Grp; Cmnty Wkr; Drama Clb; JA; Science Clb; VP Thesps; School Musical; School Play; Stage Crew; Variety Show.

ROSE, PAUL; Sonoma Valley HS; Sonoma, CA; (3); Debate Tm; French Clb; Model UN; NFL; Speech Tm; JV Golf; High Hon Roll; Guitar 4 Yrs; UC Davis; Politics.

ROSE, SONIA; San Marcos HS; San Marcos, CA; (4); Church Yth Grp; Dance Clb; Debate Tm; Girl Scts; Office Aide; Speech Tm; Teachers Aide; Drill Tm; Flag Corp; Jazz Band; CSF; Palomar Coll; Hstry.

ROSE, TOM M; South HS; Bakersfield, CA; (3); Teachers Aide; Cit Awd; Hon Roll; NHS; Cal ST Bakersfield; Engrng.

ROSE, XANASHA L; George Washington HS; San Francisco, CA; (3); Church Yth Grp; Cmnty Wkr; Rep Jr Cls; Var Crs Cntry; Stat Ftbl; Mgr(s); Var Trk; Hon Roll; UC Ber Prtnrshp Prog; Photo Club; Genetics.

ROSEN, CHARLOTTE L; Ernest Righetti HS; Orcutt, CA; (4); 14/356; Pres Church Yth Grp; Math Clb; Service Clb; Church Choir; Stu Cncl; High Hon Roll; Hon Roll; NHS; Pres Acad Fit Awd; Ldr In Charge Of Awds, Act, Games, T-Shrts Rgnl Yth Conf; Lcl Wnnr Natl Piano Playing Audtns; Brigham Young U.

ROSEN, NICOLE; Weed HS; Weed, CA; (2); 1/50; Am Leg Aux Girls St; Letterman Clb; Office Aide; Pep Clb; Speech Tm; Sec Soph Cls; Rep Stu Cncl; Stat Bsbl; Var Cheerldng; JV Var Vllybl; Acadmc Dcthln; CSF; 1st Pl Spllng Bee; Humboldt ST U; Envrnmntl Engr.

ROSENBERG, MATTHEW T; Elk Grove HS; Rancho Murieta, CA; (3); 33/609; Cmnty Wkr; Scholastic Bowl; Ed Nwsp; High Hon Roll; Pres Fire Dept Explorer Post; 1st Aid Instructor; Intl Fire Photo Assn; Jrnlsm.

ROSENBERG, RICK; Casa Roble Fundamental HS; Orangevale, CA; (3); 42/400; Church Yth Grp; Spanish Clb; SADD; Band; Mrchg Band; Var Bsktbl; Var Tennis; Hon Roll; Kiwanis Awd; Prfct Atten Awd; Water Polo Jr Var; Phy.

ROSENBERG, SAM; Edison Computech HS; Fresno, CA; (2); Vllybl; Hon Roll; Hnrs Gldn St Exam Geo.

ROSENBERGER, NATASHA; Heritage Christian Schl; Anaheim, CA; (1); 2/13; Church Yth Grp; Math Tm; Speech Tm; Band; Chorus; Cheerldng; Cit Awd; Hon Roll; Pres Acad Fit Awd; Sal; Tchr.

ROSENBLUM, ANDREW E; Palo Alto HS; Palo Alto, CA; (2); Band; Nwsp; Crs Cntry; Trk; Asst Coach Bsbl Tm.

ROSENBLUTH, JULIE M; Dana Hills HS; Laguna Beach, CA; (2); Church Yth Grp; Cmnty Wkr; Hosp Aide; Key Clb; Ski Clb; Spanish Clb; SADD; Temple Yth Grp; Off Soph Cls; Off Jr Cls; Engl Achvt Awd; Tnns Schlr/Athl Awd; UCSD; Med/Orthopdcs.

ROSENFELD, PAUL; Chestnut Ave Baptist Acad; Fresno, CA; (4); Church Yth Grp; Teachers Aide; Band; Chorus; School Musical; School Play; Vllybl; High Hon Roll; Hon Roll; Sn Pstr.

ROSENFELD, TYCHO L; Lowell HS; San Francisco, CA; (3); 1/650; NFL; Sec Pres Q&S; Pres Service Clb; Pres Stu Cncl; Ntl Merit Ltr; Acad Decthln; Jr Statsmn Of Amer; Enterprise Apprentcshp; SFMTA Math Comptn; U Of CA Berkeley; Econ.

ROSENKRANS, KIM A; San Marcos HS; Santa Barbara, CA; (3); 60/420; Key Clb; Ski Clb; Rptr Yrbk; Var Capt Socr; Var Sftbl; JV Vllybl; Pres Acad Fit Awd; Nbr 1 Clb; Acctng.

ROSENQUIST, KRISTINA; Colfax HS; Gold Run, CA; (4); Am Leg Aux Girls St; Pres Sec Church Yth Grp; Girl Scts; Service Clb; SADD; Chorus; Ed Yrbk; Sec Frsh Cls; Sec Soph Cls; Rep Jr Cls; Peer Cnslr; CSU Chico; Psych.

ROSENSTOCK, DAVID H; Torrey Pines HS; La Costa, CA; (3); Cmnty Wkr; Drama Clb; School Play; Variety Show; JV Crs Cntry; Speech Writer; Executive.

ROSENTAL, LUCY; Chadwick HS; Ran. Palos Verdes, CA; (3); Church Yth Grp; Cmnty Wkr; GAA; Chorus; School Musical; Var Cheerldng; Trk; Vllybl; Wt Lftg; Hon Roll; Piano; Bible Study & Church; Cnslr Smmr Camp; Pre-Med.

ROSENTHAL, BLAISE D; Calaveras HS; Mokelumne Hill, CA; (3); Cmnty Wkr; VP Ski Clb; Teachers Aide; Socr; Hon Roll; Tnns; Math Awds; USSF Sccr Refree-Yth Sccr Coach.

ROSENTHAL, CLAUDINE D; Lowell HS; San Francisco, CA; (2); Drama Clb; NFL; Band; School Play; Flnt Frnch, Grmn, Italn; Hnrs Spnsh, Greek; Perfmd Yng Perfmrs Theatre & Chldrns Opera; Vlng Svc Prjcts; United Wrld Coll; Theater.

ROSENTHAL, HAROLD; Heru Schl; Woodland Hills, CA; (1); Boy Scts; Red Cross Aide; Temple Yth Grp; Nwsp; Yrbk; Bsktbl; High Hon Roll; Pres Acad Fit Awd; U Of CO Boulder; Atty.

ROSENTHAL, JAMES JARROD; West Covina HS; West Covina, CA; (2); Church Yth Grp; Bsktbl; JV Trk; Wt Lftg; Friday Night Live; YMI Chrch Usher & Ythldr; Chrch Yth Chmpnshp Vllybl Team; Mt Sac; Sci.

ROSENTHAL, JENNIFER J; Bonita HS; La Verne, CA; (1); GAA; Girl Scts; Letterman Clb; Rptr Nwsp; Ed Yrbk; Var Fld Hcky; JV Tennis; Var Trk; High Hon Roll; Ecology Club; Med.

ROSENTHAL, JILL A; Louisville HS; Woodland Hills, CA; (2); Church Yth Grp; Dance Clb; School Musical; School Play; Off Frsh Cls; Tennis; High Hon Roll; Hon Roll; Prfrmng Arts.

ROSENTHAL, RICHARD A; William Howard Taft HS; Tarzana, CA; (3); Cmnty Wkr; SADD; Teachers Aide; Temple Yth Grp; Rep Frsh Cls; Rep Soph Cls; Rep Jr Cls; Intrml Mgr Bsktbl; JV Var Vllybl; Cit Awd.

ROSENTHAL, SADIE K; North Salinas HS; Salinas, CA; (2); Treas German Clb; Girl Scts; Science Clb; JV Crs Cntry; JV Fld Hcky; JV Swmmng; JV Trk; High Hon Roll; Engrng.

ROSENTHAL, STEVEN S; Coronado HS; Coronado, CA; (3); Art Clb; Drama Clb; Thesps; Stage Crew; Hon Roll.

ROSENWIRTH, CHRISTIE L; Rubidoux HS; Mira Loma, CA; (4); Church Yth Grp; GAA; Church Choir; Var Bsktbl; Var Sftbl; Hon Roll; Pres Acad Fit Awd; Law.

ROSETH, WENDY; Edison HS; Huntington Bch, CA; (2); Dance Clb; High Hon Roll; PALS; Acad Ltr; Acad Booster Clb Awd.

ROSETTE, DOUGLAS V; Calexico HS; Calexico, CA; (3); Spanish Clb; Rptr Nwsp; Var Ftbl; Var Trk; Var Wt Lftg; Hon Roll; All DVL Ftbl Awd; U Of S CA; Elec Engr.

ROSETTE, LIZABETH; Orange HS; Santa Ana, CA; (2); Church Yth Grp; Church Choir; Color Guard; Hon Roll; Key Club; Elementary Schl Teacher.

ROSETTI, ANGELA; Los Alamitos HS; Seal Beach, CA; (3); Church Yth Grp; Cmnty Wkr; SADD; Chorus; School Play; Variety Show; Var Socr; Var Sftbl; Cit Awd; Hon Roll; Med.

ROSETTI, BECKY; Los Alamitos HS; Seal Beach, CA; (1); Church Yth Grp; Cmnty Wkr; Ski Clb; JV Crs Cntry; JV Socr; Var Sftbl; Hon Roll; UCSD; Educ.

ROSIC, ANDREW W; Buena HS; Ventura, CA; (4); 75/530; Church Yth Grp; FCA; FBLA; SADD; Ed Nwsp; Var L Swmmng; Hon Roll; Ntl Merit SF; Pres Acad Fit Awd; Acad Decathlon Awds Wnnr; Water Polo Var Ltr; NWTE; CA Poly; Industrial Engrng.

ROSILES, YOLANDA; Calexico HS; Calexico, CA; (4); Cmnty Wkr; Office Aide; Pep Clb; Teachers Aide; School Musical; Bnkng & Finance Awd; Imperial Vly Coll; Acctng.

ROSIQUE, LISA A; Chino HS; Ontario, CA; (2); Church Yth Grp; SADD; Teachers Aide; Church Choir; Cit Awd; Hon Roll; Loma Linda U; Phy.

ROSKOSKY, ALICIA L; Victor Valley HS; Adelanto, CA; (4); 7/396; English Clb; Acpl Chr; Band; Chorus; Jazz Band; Mrchg Band; School Musical; School Play; Mgr(s); High Hon Roll; Air Force ROTC 3 Yr Schlrshp; The Sun San Bernardino All-Cnty Acad Team; Embry-Riddle U; Aeronautical.

ROSS, AARON E; Santa Monica HS; Santa Monica, CA; (3); Var Ftbl; Golden St Schlr Algebra; Film.

ROSS, AMY; Centennial HS; Corona, CA; (3); Science Clb; Spanish Clb; SADD; Teachers Aide; Chorus; Swm; Dnc; Ed.

ROSS, ANDREW M; Gompers Secondar; San Diego, CA; (2); 1/145; Church Yth Grp; German Clb; Math Clb; Math Tm; High Hon Roll; Acad League Novice Team MVP; Optimist Club Essay Contest 2nd Place; Greater San Diego Sci & Engrng Fr; US Cst Grd Acad; Comp Sci Math.

ROSS, BOBBI K; Hawthorne HS; Hawthorne, CA; (3); Treas Key Clb; Hist Jr Cls; Rep Stu Cncl; Var Capt Socr; Var Vllybl; Hon Roll; 1st Tm All Bay Leag Sccr 89-90; MVP Sccr 89; Bus Admin.

ROSS, BONITA; Sherman Oaks C E S HS; Los Angeles, CA; (4); 15/100; Debate Tm; Drama Clb; Office Aide; Spanish Clb; Speech Tm; Teachers Aide; Chorus; Capt Drill Tm; VP Sr Cls; Rep Stu Cncl; CSF; Young Black Schlrs; Mayors Cert Appctn; CSU Northridge; Bus.

ROSS, BRANDI; Notre Dame Acad; Los Angeles, CA; (4); Cmnty Wkr; Speech Tm; Var Socr; Var Capt Sftbl; Vllybl; NHS; CSF; Sftbl Schlrshp; U HI-HILO; Sci.

ROSS, BRANDON; La Jolla HS; San Diego, CA; (4); 1/315; Cmnty Wkr; Math Tm; Nwsp; Rep Frsh Cls; Var L Bsbl; Crs Cntry; Hon Roll; NHS; Pres Acad Fit Awd; U C Davis; Sci.

ROSS, CARMEL T; Hayward HS; Hayward, CA; (2); French Clb; GAA; SADD; JV Bsktbl; Var Powder Puff Ftbl; Var Score Keeper; Hon Roll; Prfct Atten Awd; BSU; Spelman Clg; Acting.

ROSS, CHRISTINA S; Oak Grove HS; San Jose, CA; (2); Chorus; Color Guard; Hon Roll; Stan Ford; Medicine.

ROSS, CLARA; Inglewood HS; Inglewood, CA; (2); Church Yth Grp; JA; Drill Tm; Phtg Yrbk; Cheerldng; Trk; Cit Awd; Hon Roll; Prfct Atten Awd; UCLA Partnrshp Pgm, Trimntr Pgm & PAL Pgm; Law.

ROSS, COLBY A; Mt Empire HS; Descanso, CA; (2); Cmnty Wkr; Red Cross Aide; Var Socr; Cal Poly; Arch.

ROSS, COLLEEN; Poway HS; Poway, CA; (4); 52/741; Church Yth Grp; Drama Clb; Mu Alpha Theta; SADD; Thesps; Chorus; School Musical; School Play; Rep Stu Cncl; High Hon Roll; PTSA, Outstndng Stu & Drama Schlrshps; U Of CA Los Angeles; Pre-Lw.

ROSS, DENISE; Brentwood Schl; Encino, CA; (4); AFS; SADD; Var Vllybl; Hon Roll; UC Santa Barbara; Commnctns.

ROSS, ELIZABETH ANN; Torrey Pines HS; Del Mar, CA; (3); 104/422; Cmnty Wkr; Variety Show; VP Jr Cls; L Capt Cheerldng; Gym; Socr; DAR Awd; Hon Roll; GSE Math Cmptn Schl Recogntn; Piano; HOBY; Hmcmng Prncs; Valentine Prncs; Vrs Fnd Raisers; Rtry Ldrshp; UCSB; Psych.

ROSS, HEATHER K; Yucaipa HS; Redlands, CA; (1); 4/307; L Drama Clb; FBLA; Pres Thesps; School Play; Variety Show; Yrbk; Crs Cntry; Elks Awd; Bank Of Amer-Fine Arts; CA Arts Schlr-Dance; CSF; U Of Southern CA; Exercise Sci.

ROSS, HOWARD A; Yucaipa HS; Yucaipa, CA; (2); Church Yth Grp; Drama Clb; Hosp Aide; Spanish Clb; Intrml Bsbl; Ftbl; JV Socr; Wt Lftg; JV Var Wrstlng; Loma Linda Med U; Med.

ROSS, JARON D; Red Bluff Union HS; Red Bluff, CA; (2); Boy Scts; Pres Church Yth Grp; Computer Clb; JA; Key Clb; Lit Mag; Var Socr; Cit Awd; High Hon Roll; Hon Roll; Jrnlst For ATV Magz; ATV Racer; Jr Ldrhsp Clb; UC Irvine; Engnrg.

ROSS, JASON L; El Toro HS; El Toro, CA; (3); Church Yth Grp; Key Clb; Varsity Clb; Stage Crew; Mgr Bsktbl; Mgr(s); Trk; Wrstlng; Hon Roll; USC; Law.

ROSS, JENNIFER L; Analy HS; Sebastopol, CA; (3); Art Clb; Band; Ed Nwsp; Crtve Wrtng; Wrtr.

ROSS, JEWERL K; Inglewood HS; Inglewood, CA; (1); Swmmng; Hon Roll; Public Spkng; Photo; Poltcs, Wrld Affairs; Stanford; Bus Admin.

ROSS, JOSEPH J; Clear Lake HS; Lakeport, CA; (4); 1/74; Computer Clb; 4-H; SADD; Band; Jazz Band; Mrchg Band; Pep Band; Pres Jr Cls; Sec Treas Stu Cncl; JV Var Bsktbl; Santa Fe Railway Natl Schlrshp Wnnr; Bnk Of Amer Plaque & Schlrshp Wnnr; U CA Davis Awd Excllnc; Stanford U.

ROSS, KEISHA; Cajon HS; San Bernardino, CA; (3); Hon Roll; NHS; KIDS; Anti Clb.

ROSS, KRISTINA L; Mt Pleasant HS; San Jose, CA; (1); Office Aide; Teachers Aide; Cheerldng; Hon Roll; Santa Clara ST U; Bus Admin.

ROSS, LIZ B; Palm Springs HS; Palm Springs, CA; (3); Cmnty Wkr; Mgr(s); Hon Roll; Prfct Atten Awd; UCSD; Poltcl Sci.

ROSS, LYNETTE; East Bakersfield HS; Bakersfield, CA; (3); 39/445; French Clb; Library Aide; SADD; Nwsp; Treas Frsh Cls; Rep Stu Cncl; JV Cheerldng; High Hon Roll; CA Schlrshp Fed; Mock Trial.

ROSS, MICHELLE K; Clovis HS; Fresno, CA; (1); 36/900; Key Clb; SADD; Band; Jazz Band; Mrchg Band; Orch; Pep Band; School Musical; Cit Awd; High Hon Roll; Frlncrs Drm & Bgl Corp; Fresno ST U; Music Educ.

ROSS, PHILLIP L; Piedmont HS; Piedmont, CA; (4); 14/130; AFS; Cmnty Wkr; French Clb; VP JA; Science Clb; SADD; Teachers Aide; Temple Yth Grp; School Musical; Rptr Phtg Nwsp; Alpha Clan Hnr Scty Mem; CSF Life Mem; Pres Of Schls JR Stsmn Chptr; U Of CO Boulder; Med.

ROSS, RODRICK L; Luther Burbank HS; Sacramento, CA; (3); 100/302; Office Aide; Cit Awd; High Hon Roll; Hon Roll; NHS; Prfct Atten Awd; Eng,Math,Hstry Dept Schlrshp Awds; Bio Chem.

ROSS, SARAH F; Edison HS; Huntington Beach, CA; (1); Teaching.

ROSS, STACY M; Amos Alonzo Stagg HS; Stockton, CA; (3); Art Clb; Key Clb; Pep Clb; SADD; Teachers Aide; Drill Tm; Swmmng; Var L Vllybl; High Hon Roll; Stu In Prevention; CA Schlrshp Fed; Brd Supervisors Awd Stu Of Prevention; Big Brother/Big Sister Pgm; U Of The Pacific; Psych.

ROSS, TANE U; Nevada Union HS; Grass Valley, CA; (3); 53/590; Debate Tm; SADD; Pres Soph Cls; Rep Stu Cncl; Powder Puff Ftbl; Socr; Hon Roll; Masonic Awd; Opt Clb Awd; Jr Olympics Crss Cntry Skiing 90; Arch Drafting Stu Of Yr 89-90; N Amer Ski Games 88-89; Reed U; Arch.

ROSS, TARA T; Western Christian HS; Covina, CA; (3); Church Yth Grp; Cmnty Wkr; Girl Scts; Hosp Aide; Service Clb; Chorus; Church Choir; Yrbk; Sec Stu Cncl; High Hon Roll; Jack & Jill Am Inc; Acteens S Baptists Church; NAACP Yth Chapter; Spleman Coll; Psych.

ROSS, TOSHONNA; International Studies Acad; San Francisco, CA; (4); Cmnty Wkr; Office Aide; Teachers Aide; Acpl Chr; Chorus; Church Choir; Variety Show; Ed Rptr Nwsp; Score Keeper; Bay Area Unitd Way Ambssdr; FIDM; Fashion.

ROSS, ZACHARY M; San Dieguito HS; Encinitas, CA; (2); Boy Scts; Church Yth Grp; Pres Drama Clb; Scholastic Bowl; School Musical; School Play; Var Swmmng; Hon Roll; Actng Awds; Brigham Young U; Bus.

ROSSAL, RODRIGO; John H Francis Polytechnic HS; Sun Valley, CA; (3); Cit Awd; Hon Roll; Electrnc Engr.

ROSSEAU, ANDREW R; Luther Burbank HS; Sacramento, CA; (2); 35/389; FFA; Cit Awd; High Hon Roll; Hon Roll; Film Dir.

ROSSI, LISA; Fred C Beyer HS; Riverbank, CA; (3); Debate Tm; German Clb; NFL; Speech Tm; SADD; Var L Socr; JV Swmmng; Var L Tennis; Hon Roll; Soroptomst Clb; CSF; Broadcast-Jrnlsm.

ROSSI, MEGAN A; Bellarmine Jefferson HS; Burbank, CA; (2); Church Yth Grp; Pep Clb; Spanish Clb; Rep Stu Cncl; JV Capt Cheerldng; Hon Roll; Rep On Spirit Cmmtte; UC Santa Barbara; Hlth Prof.

ROSSI, RUTH S; Eisenhower HS; Rialto, CA; (4); 9/655; Hist Math Clb; Hist Science Clb; Pres Sec Spanish Clb; High Hon Roll; Jr NHS; NHS; Pres Acad Fit Awd; Sobobans Clb; CSF; U Of CA Los Angeles; Med.

ROSSMAN, EMILY F; North Hollywood HS; North Hollywood, CA; (3); Church Yth Grp; Spanish Clb; SADD; DAR Awd; High Hon Roll; Hon Roll; HS Amnsty Intl Clb Treas.

ROSSMAN, LESLEY-ANNE C; Oak Ridge HS; Cameron Park, CA; (4); 72/222; Church Yth Grp; Drama Clb; French Clb; Church Choir; Cit Awd; Hon Roll; Santa Barbara U; Chld Psych.

ROSSMAN, MELISSA; Patrick Henry HS; San Diego, CA; (4); 51/546; Dance Clb; Debate Tm; Office Aide; Varsity Clb; Ed Nwsp; Ed Yrbk; Pres Frsh Cls; Cheerldng; Cit Awd; Hon Roll; Advrtsng.

ROST, PATRICK T; Servite HS; Hacienda Heights, CA; (2); Church Yth Grp; Nwsp; Lit Mag; Var Crs Cntry; Var Trk; CSF; NSH.

ROTH, BRANDON M; Delano HS; Delano, CA; (3); Letterman Clb; Pep Clb; Rep Frsh Cls; Rep Soph Cls; JV Var Bsbl; JV Bsktbl; JV Ftbl; NHS; Campus Life; CSF; GATE Clb; Engnrng.

ROTH, BRIAN J; St Francis HS; Sunnyvale, CA; (1); Church Yth Grp; Intrml Bsktbl; Intrml Ftbl; Hon Roll; AYSO Soccer.

ROTH, DAVID R; Skyline HS; Oakland, CA; (2); Church Yth Grp; Office Aide; Church Choir; Variety Show; Goldn St Exam Excllnce Awd 1st Ur Alg Hnrs; CO Springs; Pre-Med.

ROTH, KATHRYN D; Etiwanda HS; Alta Loma, CA; (4); 29/450; Church Yth Grp; Girl Scts; Red Cross Aide; Ski Clb; Band; Jazz Band; Mrchg Band; Pep Band; High Hon Roll; NHS; Girl Scout Gold Awd; Acad Decathlon; Mock Trail; UC Davis; Bio.

ROTH, KIMBERLY A; Live Oak HS; Morgan Hill, CA; (4); 10/527; Dance Clb; SADD; School Musical; Cheerldng; Var Diving; Var Tennis; Hon Roll; NHS; Var Badminton; Life Time CSF; AZ ST U; Mktg.

ROTH, MELISSA A; Davis SR HS; Davis, CA; (4); Sec 4-H; Pep Clb; Stage Crew; JV Bsktbl; JV VP Powder Puff Ftbl; Hon Roll; Embry-Riddle U; Aerosp Engrng.

ROTH, MICHELE D; San Gorgonio HS; Highland, CA; (3); Pres AFS; Church Yth Grp; Cmnty Wkr; French Clb; German Clb; Key Clb; SADD; Tick Tockers-Natl Charity League; Chiropractor.

ROTH, ROLAND A; San Ramon Valley HS; Alamo, CA; (3); Drama Clb; Teachers Aide; School Play; Stage Crew; Motor Cross-Riding; Street Bike Racing; AZ ST; Bus.

ROTH, RYAN E; Ocean View HS; Huntington Beach, CA; (1); Bsktbl; Trk.

ROTH, SARAH; Claremont HS; Claremont, CA; (4); 1/400; Pres Treas German Clb; Stu Cncl; Stat Bsktbl; Var Capt Crs Cntry; Score Keeper; Var Capt Trk; Hon Roll; Rotary Awd; Stu Rep Clrmnt Unfd Schl Brd; Natl Cnl Tchrs Engl Achvt Awd Wrtng; Bonnie Bell Cir Excllnc Achv; Carleton Coll; Pre-Law.

ROTHENBERGER, SHANE; Marina HS; Huntington Bch, CA; (2); 104/614; Cmnty Wkr; Letterman Clb; Mu Alpha Theta; Ski Clb; Spanish Clb; Chorus; Pres Sr Cls; Var L Ftbl; High Hon Roll; Ntl Merit Schol; Pre-Health Clb Pres; Homcmng Crt; MAA Treas; Psi Beta; Phi Alpha Mu; Alpha Gamma Sigma; UCLA; Pre-Med.

ROTHER, WENDY L; Apple Valley HS; Apple Valley, CA; (3); Band; Drm Mjr(t); Jazz Band; Mrchg Band; Orch; Pep Band; Intrml Swmmng; Hon Roll; Barstow Field Show Trnmt Bst Drum Major Cls A & AA 89; Dodger Battle Bands Chmpns 88 & 90; Music Ed.

ROTHERMEL, ERIN; Saratoga HS; Saratoga, CA; (4); Teachers Aide; Rep Stu Cncl; Var Diving; JV Var Swmmng; JV Var Trk; Guitar 89-90; Chico ST.

ROTHERT, KIP A; Live Oak HS; Morgan Hill, CA; (3); Office Aide; Teachers Aide; Phtg Yrbk; 2nd Pl, 2 Hnrb Mntn Photo Cont; Spcl Effects.

ROTHERY, CHRISTIAN A; Lutheran HS Of Orange County; Orange, CA; (2); Church Yth Grp; Ski Clb; Yrbk; Intrml Bsbl; Intrml Bsktbl; Intrml Ftbl; Intrml Socr; Intrml Sftbl; Intrml Trk; Cal Poly San Luis Obispo; Arch.

ROTHMAN, HEITH; Saddleback HS; Santa Ana, CA; (1); Computer Clb; Debate Tm; Speech Tm; High Hon Roll; Mock Trial; Orange Cnty Acad Decath; Sci Olympd; UCI; Bus.

ROTHMAN, JAKE T; North County Christian Schl; Paso Robles, CA; (1); 2/13; Chess Clb; Church Yth Grp; Math Tm; School Play; Rep Frsh Cls; Stat Bsbl; UCLA; Financial Planning.

ROTHMUND, BRIGITTE N; San Benito HS; Hollister, CA; (3); 1/200; French Clb; GAA; Rep Stu Cncl; Var Swmmng; Var Trk; High Hon Roll; Pres Acad Fit Awd; CSF; Harvard; Finance.

ROTHSCHILD, BLAKE A; El Toro HS; El Toro, CA; (3); Church Yth Grp; Ski Clb; Teachers Aide; Crs Cntry; Socr; Var Trk; Hon Roll; Prfct Atten Awd; Pres Acad Fit Awd; All Cty Jr Cross Country 89; 2nd Team All Cty 89; Most Valuable Runner 89-90; Arch.

ROTHSCHILD, DANA M; Westminster HS; Westminster, CA; (2); Drama Clb; German Clb; Girl Scts; Service Clb; Teachers Aide; Thesps; Drill Tm; School Play; Cert Outstndng Prfrmnce Theatre Arts & Service.

ROTTER, SANDY K; Irvine HS; Irvine, CA; (2); AFS; French Clb; Service Clb; Ski Clb; Intrml Swmmng; High Hon Roll; Hon Roll; Disney Artist.

ROUCH, CHERYL L; Redwood HS; Visalia, CA; (2); German Clb; Q&S; Co-Ed Nwsp; Var Crs Cntry; Var Tennis; Hon Roll; Young Life Club; Eng.

ROUCH, MELISSA L; San Gorgonio HS; Highland, CA; (4); 73/300; GAA; Letterman Clb; Office Aide; Teachers Aide; Var Capt Bsktbl; Capt Powder Puff Ftbl; Hon Roll; CA ST; Bus Admin.

ROUCHLEAU, RACHAEL; Trinity HS; Weaverville, CA; (4); 7/95; VP French Clb; Intnl Clb; Library Aide; Sec Treas Spanish Clb; SADD; Teachers Aide; Chorus; Phtg Yrbk; High Hon Roll; Rotary Awd; Sonoma ST U; French.

ROUDABUSH, GABRIELLE J; Atwater HS; Atwater, CA; (2); AFS; FCA; GAA; Key Clb; Service Clb; L Var Socr; L Var Swmmng; DAR Awd; Hon Roll; Waterpolo Vrsty Ltr; Lfgrd; Comptve Sccr; Hd Coach Boys Under 10 Sccr; Harvard; Bus.

ROUGHAN, STACY; Notre Dame HS; Granada Hills, CA; (2); 10/300; Latin Clb; SADD; Var JV Cheerldng; Hon Roll; NEDT Awd; UCSB; Bus.

ROUND, DOUGLAS A; Lodi HS; Lodi, CA; (2); Church Yth Grp; JV Socr; Var Tennis; High Hon Roll.

ROUNDS, BAHATI; Skyline HS; Oakland, CA; (2); Orch; Ed Nwsp; Yrbk; Hon Roll; Southern; Lw.

ROUNDS, EMILY; Apple Valley HS; Apple Valley, CA; (3); Church Yth Grp; Drama Clb; 4-H; FHA; Chorus; Hon Roll; Rotary Awd; Peer Counseling; Teen Asst & Guide; Nrsng.

ROUNDS, STEPHEN J; Homestead HS; Sunnyvale, CA; (3); SADD; Gldn St Exam Alg & Geom High Hnrs; U Of CA.

ROUNDTREE, JENNA; Adolfo Camarillo HS; Coronado, CA; (2); 7/620; Intnl Clb; Spanish Clb; Var Crs Cntry; Var Trk; High Hon Roll; Pres Acad Fit Awd; CA Schlrshp Fed Sec; Interact; Stanford U; Bus.

ROUNDY, RYAN R; Sweetwater HS; National City, CA; (2); Scholastic Bowl; Ski Clb; Band; Jazz Band; Capt Tennis.

ROUNDY, STEPHANIE; San Lorenzo Valley HS; San Jose, CA; (4); 10/200; Am Leg Aux Girls St; Cmnty Wkr; 4-H; Sec Key Clb; Ski Clb; Spanish Clb; Teachers Aide; Color Guard; Ed Yrbk; High Hon Roll; Scrtry Life Mbr Of CA Schlrshp Fed; Santa Clara U; Bus.

ROUNKE, ROD A; Rim Of The World HS; Blue Jay, CA; (2); 33/352; Church Yth Grp; Spanish Clb; Var L Tennis; Hon Roll; Mexico Orphanage Outreach; U Of IL North Park; Cmmnctns.

ROUSE, JODY L; Mission Viejo HS; Mission Viejo, CA; (2); Church Yth Grp; SADD; Chorus; Church Choir; Sunday Sch Asst; Forensic Sci.

ROUSH, BRANDEN; Bloomington Christian HS; Bloomington, CA; (2); Church Yth Grp; FCA; Rep Soph Cls; Var Bsbl; Var Bsktbl; Var Ftbl; Wt Lftg; High Hon Roll; Prfct Atten Awd; All Leag Ftbl; Bsbl Coachs Awd; Riverside City Coll.

ROUSSELL, JILLIAN L; Grace M Davis HS; Modesto, CA; (3); French Clb; Intnl Clb; Stage Crew; Lit Mag; High Hon Roll; Hon Roll; NHS; Amer Assn U Women Outstndng Schlrshp Awd; Semi-Finlst Telluride Schlrshp; Amnsty Intl Grp Co-Fndr; NY U.

ROUSSELO, GARY S; Buena Park HS; Buena Park, CA; (1); Ski Clb; Bsbl; Hon Roll.

ROUSSEVE, MICHAEL J; Edison HS; Huntington Bch, CA; (2); Church Yth Grp; Lit Mag; Intrml Tennis; 2nd Pl Orange Cty Acdmc Decath; Amateur Radio Tech Cls; U Of CA LA; Biomed Engrng.

ROUSSIN, CHRISTOPHER P; West HS; Torrance, CA; (1); Drama Clb; Chorus; School Play; Acad-Dramtc Arts; Music/Theatre.

ROUTE, SHENIQUE N; Paramount HS; Compton, CA; (3); Letterman Clb; SADD; JV Sftbl; JV Vllybl; Black Schlrs; UCI Ldrshp & Partnrshp Pgms; Tuskegee U; Comp Engrng.

ROUTHIER, JENNIFER E; John F Kennedy HS; Sacramento, CA; (2); 62/525; Dance Clb; French Clb; Ed Yrbk; Rep Frsh Cls; Rep Soph Cls; JV Cheerldng; JV Crs Cntry; Hon Roll; Art Clb; Church Yth Grp; Festa Queen Ital Cltrl Soc; CA Multi-Cltrl Park Fnd Vol; Cal Poly; Arch.

ROUTHIER, MICHELE; Fairfield HS; Suisun City, CA; (4); Science Clb; Church Choir; Tennis; Jr NHS; Millersville U; Oceanography.

ROUVIER, RUTH; Arcata HS; Arcata, CA; (4); 6/165; AFS; VP Treas French Clb; Band; Lit Mag; Cit Awd; VP Sec French Hon Soc; Ntl Merit SF; Spanish Clb; Mrchg Band; Orch; CSF VP; CA Arts Schlr; Cornell U Smmr Pgm; Frgn Lang.

ROVEDA, MICHELLE J; Alameda HS; Alameda, CA; (2); Church Yth Grp; Spanish Clb; Var Bsktbl; Var Tennis; High Hon Roll; UCLA; Law.

ROVIRA, JENNIFER L; Mater Dei HS; Stanton, CA; (3); Church Yth Grp; Cmnty Wkr; Ski Clb; Stu Cncl; JV Trk; JV Capt Vllybl; Stat Wrstlng; Hon Roll; NHS; CSF.

ROWAN, CHRISTOPHER J; Thomas Downey HS; Modesto, CA; (2); Chess Clb; French Clb; SADD; US Naval Acad; Aviation.

ROWAN II, MICHAEL; University City HS; San Diego, CA; (2); Boy Scts; Library Aide; Trk; Hon Roll; Jr NHS; Prfct Atten Awd; U CA-SAN Diego.

ROWAT, STACIE R; Village Christian HS; Sunland, CA; (3); Office Aide; Drill Tm; Cheerldng; Psych.

ROWE, ANGELA; Apple Valley HS; Apple Valley, CA; (1); Spanish Clb; Cit Awd; Hon Roll; Swimming; Skating; Rdng; Bowling; Helping Elderly; Enjoy Animals; WA ST; Phys Thrpy.

ROWE, ELIZABETH A; California Lutheran HS; Carson, CA; (1); Church Yth Grp; Drama Clb; Chorus; School Play; Nwsp; JV Bsktbl; Var Sftbl; Hon Roll; Intr Dec.

ROWE, JENNIFER; Fred C Beyer HS; Modesto, CA; (4); 8/506; Pres VP Church Yth Grp; Cmnty Wkr; Pres Debate Tm; NFL; Pres Speech Tm; Teachers Aide; Church Choir; Rep Voice Dem Awd; Math Clb; CA Schlstc Fdrtn; Educ.

ROWE, KATHERINE; San Ramon Valley HS; Danville, CA; (2); 10/400; German Clb; Intnl Clb; Intrml Bsktbl; Var L Crs Cntry; Var L Socr; Var L Trk; High Hon Roll; Princpls Schlr/Athl Awd; Amnsty Intl Clb; Chem.

ROWE, LISA M; Clayton Valley HS; Concord, CA; (2); Art Clb; SADD; Bsktbl; JV Trk; Hon Roll; Vlntr Wk Little Leag; Interior Desgn.

ROWE, ROBYN; San Dieguito HS; Carlsbad, CA; (4); 23/512; Church Yth Grp; Cmnty Wkr; Hosp Aide; Pres Acad Fit Awd; Biola U; Sprts Physlgy.

ROWE, RUBY I; Burbank HS; Burbank, CA; (3); Cmnty Wkr; Science Clb; VP Treas Frsh Cls; JV Trk; Burbank Amer Red Cross Yth Grp; CSF; Valley Spcl Olympics; NCTE Writing Awd; Pathology.

ROWE, SUSIE; Mills HS; Burlingame, CA; (3); Church Yth Grp; Drama Clb; Chorus; School Musical; School Play; Nwsp; Ed Yrbk; Lit Mag; Var Pom Pon; Hon Roll; CSF; Phlsphy Clb; Cls Up; PALS; Cmmnctns.

ROWEN, JOLENE J; Central Union HS; El Centro, CA; (2); Church Yth Grp; Cmnty Wkr; Girl Scts; Pep Clb; Teachers Aide; Var Bsktbl; Score Keeper; Just Say No Clb; Upward Bnd Smmr Pgm; Bio.

ROWIN, DOUGLAS BOWE; Central Union HS; El Centro, CA; (1); JV Var Crs Cntry; JV Tennis; Hon Roll; UCSD; Comp Engr.

ROWLAND, DIANN; Southwest HS; San Diego, CA; (4); 7/478; Key Clb; Sec SADD; VP Stu Cncl; L Vllybl; Kiwanis Awd; Pres Acad Fit Awd; Math Engr Sci Achvtmnt & Pres & Sec; San Diego Cncl Of Adm Wmn In Ed; Freedoms Fndtn Vally Forge; Math.

ROWLAND, HEATHER; Canyon HS; Anaheim, CA; (1); GAA; Chorus; Stage Crew; Bsktbl; Bright Spot Awd-Drama; UNLV.

ROWLAND, LEANNE S; Chaffey HS; Ontario, CA; (4); Dance Clb; High Hon Roll; Hon Roll; Chaffey Coll; Medcl.

ROWLAND, SHELLY A; Holtville HS; Holtville, CA; (3); Office Aide; Chorus; Hon Roll; Prfct Atten Awd; Spcl Educ Tchr.

ROWLAND, THERESA J; Vallejo SR HS; Vallejo, CA; (3); Church Yth Grp; Cmnty Wkr; Drama Clb; Teachers Aide; Hon Roll; Stu Activity Cncl; Seattle Pacific U; Law.

ROWLAND, TRACY R; Irvington HS; Fremont, CA; (4); 5/253; Church Yth Grp; Teachers Aide; Band; Chorus; Church Choir; Mrchg Band; Variety Show; Sec Soph Cls; Sec Jr Cls; Off Sr Cls; Seal Bearer CA Schlrshp Fed Sec, VP, Pres; Bank Of Amer Awd Socl Stud; Biola U; Mssnry.

ROWLES, ERIC; Redlands HS; Redlands, CA; (4); 137/843; Aud/Vis; Boy Scts; Church Yth Grp; Cmnty Wkr; Var Debate Tm; Var NFL; Rep Service Clb; Pres SADD; Ed Phtg Lit Mag; Intrml JV Bsbl; Schl Cnslrs Awd; CA Spch Semifnlst; Fri Night Live; U Of CA-RIVERSIDE.

ROWLETTE, MIKE; Downey HS; Downey, CA; (4); 22/495; Key Clb; Service Clb; Teachers Aide; Ed Yrbk; High Hon Roll; Pres Acad Fit Awd; Golden ST Exam Hgh Hnrs 87, Hnrs 89; Cal Poly Pomona; Arch.

ROWLEY, JASON; John Muir HS; Pasadena, CA; (2); Drama Clb; Ski Clb; Variety Show; Pres Frsh Cls; Var Bsktbl; Sports Med.

ROWLEY, JEREMY; La Sierra HS; Riverside, CA; (2); Drama Clb; Library Aide; Thesps; School Play; Rotary Awd; CA Arts Schlr.

ROWND, MICHELLE E; Sunset HS; Hayward, CA; (1); Hon Roll; Psych.

ROXAS, REYZA; Bishop Montgomery HS; Carson, CA; (3); Church Yth Grp; Key Clb; SADD; Church Choir; Nwsp; Stu Cncl; Cit Awd; Hon Roll; CSF; Prncpl/Dean Lists; Harvard; Econ.

ROXBERG, TRICIA; Sonoma Valley HS; Sonoma, CA; (3); 69/280; Cmnty Wkr; Model UN; Pep Clb; Ski Clb; SADD; Varsity Clb; Stu Cncl; Cheerldng; Pom Pon; Hon Roll; SRJC; Med.

ROY, ADITI; University HS; Irvine, CA; (2); 30/508; French Clb; Hosp Aide; Band; Mrchg Band; French Hon Soc; Amnsty Intl; Girls Leag Cls Rep; CSF; Northestern; Brdcst Jrnlsm.

ROY, CRAIG; Atascadero HS; Atascadero, CA; (2); Boy Scts; Church Yth Grp; SADD; Var Golf; JV Socr; Hon Roll; Lion Awd; Pres Acad Fit Awd; Phys Thrpy.

ROY, JAN-MICHAEL L; A A Stagg HS; Stockton, CA; (1); Acpl Chr; Ftbl; Hon Roll; Hnrs Show, Jazz Choir.

ROY, JENNIFER; Pacific Grove HS; Pacific Grove, CA; (4); Am Leg Aux Girls St; Key Clb; SADD; VP Sr Cls; JV Var Sftbl; Var Vllybl; Hon Roll; Peer Cnslr; Teen Drug Use Prvntn Confrncs; Santa Barbara City; Commctns.

ROY, JOSHUA J; Fred C Beyer HS; Modesto, CA; (2); Wt Lftg; Wrstlng; NHS; Pres Acad Fit Awd; Roller Hockey; CA Schltc Fed; USA Wrstlng; UCLA; Marine Bio.

ROY, MICHELLE; Crescenta Valley HS; La Crescenta, CA; (3); French Clb; Teachers Aide; Drill Tm; Hon Roll; UC Irvine; Med.

ROY, NEELA; Lincoln HS; San Francisco, CA; (3); Pep Clb; Teachers Aide; Chorus; Cheerldng; Hon Roll; Outdoors Club; U CA Berkeley; Bus Adm.

ROY, SEEMA A; Archbishop Mitty HS; San Jose, CA; (3); Cmnty Wkr; Intnl Clb; JV Fld Hcky; High Hon Roll; Hon Roll; NHS; Cltrcl Actvts; USC; Bus.

ROYBAL, ANTOINETTE; Grossmont HS; El Cajon, CA; (3); French Clb; SADD; Varsity Clb; Band; Mrchg Band; Orch; Pep Band; School Musical; Med.

ROYBAL, VINCENT A; Albany HS; Albany, CA; (2); Drama Clb; Spanish Clb; Acpl Chr; Chorus; School Musical; School Play; JV Ftbl; Drama & Arts.

ROYCE, DEBRA LYNNE; Villa Park HS; Orange, CA; (4); 11/445; Pres Church Yth Grp; Cit Awd; High Hon Roll; Hon Roll; Jr NHS; NHS; Pres Acad Fit Awd; CSF; Home Ec Dept Gold Mdl 90; BYU; Elem Ed.

ROYER, KRISTIN; Tomales HS; Bodega Bay, CA; (3); Hosp Aide; Office Aide; Ski Clb; Spanish Clb; Teachers Aide; Rptr Yrbk; Sec Frsh Cls; Sec Soph Cls; Sec Jr Cls; Bsktbl; U Of CA Davis; Med.

ROYER, NICOLE; Liberty Union HS; Oakley, CA; (2); 7/451; Church Yth Grp; Chorus; Stage Crew; Stat Bsktbl; Ftbl; Hon Roll; Pres Acad Fit Awd; Elem Tutor 2nd Grade; CSF; UC Davis; Law.

ROYZEN, VALERY; George Washington HS; San Francisco, CA; (3); Art Clb; Chess Clb; Library Aide; Math Clb; Swmmng; Hon Roll; Cert Of Achvt Esl Lang; Accntng.

ROZBORIL, DENISE L; Fullerton HS; Fullerton, CA; (1); 33/408; Cheerldng; Spnsh, Engl & Comp Stu Of Month; Engl Stu Of Yr; Cal ST Long Beach; Physiology.

ROZEK, KIM MARIE; Fountain Valley HS; Fountain Valley, CA; (3); Church Yth Grp; Drill Tm; Off Jr Cls; Stu Cncl; Hon Roll; CSF; PALS; Prom Cmmssn; Advrts.

ROZENDAAL, ALEX; Mira Costa HS; Lawndale, CA; (2); Church Yth Grp; Ftbl; Golf; Socr; Tennis; Wt Lftg; Hon Roll; Prfct Atten Awd; U S Air Force; Drug Enfrcmnt Of.

ROZLER, MICHAEL S; Lowell HS; Palo Alto, CA; (2); Pres Chess Clb; VP Math Clb; VP Science Clb; JV Socr; Karate Tae-Kwondo; Ivy Leag Schl; Physics.

ROZO, MONICA G; St Joseph HS; Cerritos, CA; (2); 48/200; Drama Clb; Speech Tm; SADD; High Hon Roll; Hon Roll; NHS; Psych.

ROZOLIS, JENNIFER; Los Alamitos HS; Los Alamitos, CA; (4); 2/600; Cmnty Wkr; JA; Red Cross Aide; Science Clb; Spanish Clb; Jazz Band; School Musical; Off Swing Chorus; High Hon Roll; NHS; Stanford; Vet.

RUACHO, REYNA; San Gabriel Mission HS; Bell Gardens, CA; (2); Drama Clb; GAA; High Hon Roll; Hon Roll; JAM; Loyola Maymount U; Elec Engr.

RUALO, MATESSA THEODORA; Sacred Heart-Cathedral Prep; San Francisco, CA; (4); Church Yth Grp; Variety Show; JV Capt Cheerldng; Pom Pon; Hon Roll; Yng Mns Inst Essy Awd; Frnch Awd; San Francisco ST U; Ed.

RUAN, JOSE DE JESUS; St Bernard HS; Hawthorne, CA; (3); 35/330; French Clb; Latin Clb; Ftbl; Cit Awd; Hon Roll; NHS; CSF; U Of CA Berkeley; Engr.

RUANO, ANGIE; Balboa HS; San Francisco, CA; (3); ROTC; Band; Slvr Seals Stu; San Francisco ST; Bus.

RUANO, MAINOR O; San Marcos HS; Goleta, CA; (3); 74/402; French Clb; Ski Clb; Band; Mrchg Band; Var Crs Cntry; JV Socr; Pres Acad Fit Awd; Gldn ST Exmntn; Acad Exclnc Awd In Geo; Engr.

RUANO, MARITZA; Calexico HS; Calexico, CA; (3); Spanish Clb; Cit Awd; High Hon Roll; Stanford U; Eng Teacher.

RUANO, PATRICIA A; Saratoga HS; Saratoga, CA; (2); Church Yth Grp; Chorus; JV Fld Hcky; Hon Roll; Rainforest Consrvtn Clb; Accntng.

RUBALCAVA, MICHELLE; La Mirada HS; La Mirada, CA; (2); Church Yth Grp; French Clb; Treas Jr Cls; Rep Stu Cncl; Hon Roll; CSF; Chrch Vllybl Tm; Law.

RUBALCAVA, SANDRA R; Thomas Downey HS; Modesto, CA; (4); 23/425; Art Clb; Church Yth Grp; Cmnty Wkr; Debate Tm; JA; Letterman Clb; Q&S; Service Clb; Spanish Clb; SADD; CA ST U Stanislaus; Pre Med.

RUBEL, DAVID J; St Francis HS; Altadena, CA; (2); Art Clb; Chess Clb; Pep Clb; Ski Clb; SADD; JV Bsbl; Hon Roll; 1st Prz Sci Fair; UC Davis; Engrng.

RUBIN, GREG D; Taft HS; Tarzana, CA; (3); Letterman Clb; Teachers Aide; Bsbl; Intrml Bsktbl; High Hon Roll; Hon Roll; Ntl Merit SF; CA Schlrshp Fed; Steering Cmmtte.

RUBIN, JACKIE R; Irvine HS; Irvine, CA; (1); Drama Clb; School Musical; School Play; Stage Crew; Peace Child Tour; Brdcst Jrnlsm.

RUBINGER, TODD S; San Rafael HS; San Rafael, CA; (2); 16/230; Cmnty Wkr; Key Clb; SADD; Temple Yth Grp; Var JV Bsbl; Capt JV Bsktbl; Capt JV Ftbl; High Hon Roll; CSF; Schlr/Athl; MVP Frshmn Ftbl & JV Bsbl; Bstkbl Insprtnl; UCLA; Med.

RUBINO, KIMBERLY; Los Alamitos HS; Surfside, CA; (4); Church Yth Grp; FCA; Spanish Clb; Varsity Clb; Var L Swmmng; High Hon Roll; Hon Roll; NHS; US Swmmng Lng Dstnc All-Amrcn Tm 86, 89; Athlete Mnth 89; 1st Pl Jr Lfgrd Natls 87; GSE Geom Hnrs Awd; Engrng.

RUBINO, STEVE; Central Catholic HS; Tracy, CA; (3); Cmnty Wkr; 4-H; Intnl Clb; Key Clb; Ski Clb; Spanish Clb; SADD; Yrbk; 4-H Awd; Hon Roll; ST Wnr Guide Dogs For Blind Rcrd Bk; ST Wnr Monsanto Ldrshp Cnfrnc WA DC; Comm.

RUBIO, AMELIA; Duncan Polytechnical HS; Fresno, CA; (4); 22/110; Cit Awd; High Hon Roll; Prfct Atten Awd; Fri Night Live; Fresno City Coll; Arch.

RUBIO, FARA J; Bell Gardens HS; Bell Gardens, CA; (2); Drama Clb; French Clb; Acpl Chr; School Musical; School Play; Variety Show; Off Stu Cncl; Var Swmmng; Prfct Atten Awd; Chambers-Advance Choir; Acting.

RUBIO, HEATHER V; San Benito HS; Hollister, CA; (4); 52/250; Art Clb; Girl Scts; Band; Yrbk; Hon Roll; Sonoma ST U; Law.

RUBIO, JENNY E; Gonzales Union HS; Soledad, CA; (2); Church Choir; Sftbl; San Jose ST; Vet.

RUBIO, MARLA; Marian Catholic HS; Chula Vista, CA; (4); 1/85; Drama Clb; Hosp Aide; Pep Clb; Teachers Aide; School Play; VP Soph Cls; VP Pres Stu Cncl; Var Cheerldng; Var Powder Puff Ftbl; Var Socr; Kywntts Pres; UC Berkeley.

RUBIO, ROY M; Mark Keppel HS; Rosemead, CA; (4); Capt Debate Tm; Math Clb; Pres NFL; Q&S; Ed Nwsp; Yrbk; Hon Roll; Opt Clb Awd; Spec Awd Exclnc In Comm; B Of A Achvmnt Awd; Ctf In Comm; Comm.

RUBIO, SANDRA L; Scur HS; Monterey Park, CA; (3); Cmnty Wkr; Parlgl.

RUBIO, TRISHA G; Moorpark HS; Moorpark, CA; (2); Church Yth Grp; Sec Jr Cls; Rep Stu Cncl; JV Bsktbl; JV Sftbl; High Hon Roll; Hon Roll; Marquee Commissioner 90-91; ASB Club 90-91.

RUBIO, WESLEY S; Ponderosa HS; Diamond Springs, CA; (1); Hon Roll; Jr NHS.

RUBIS, JAMES D; Turlock HS; Turlock, CA; (1); 52/700; Sec Chess Clb; Debate Tm; NFL; Speech Tm; Clsscl Lit; Spec Interest Space Exploration & Astronomy; CA Inst Tech; Astrophysicist.

RUBKE, PAUL; Sonoma Valley HS; Sonoma, CA; (1); Golf; Hon Roll; Bikng; Intl Trade.

RUCKER, KARIE J; Red Bluff Union HS; Red Bluff, CA; (3); 54/358; GAA; SADD; Teachers Aide; Intrml Var Bsktbl; Var Crs Cntry; Var Trk; Hon Roll; Amer Lgn Band; Butte Coll; Child Psych.

RUCKS, JEB C; Portola JR/Sr HS; Portola, CA; (3); Ski Clb; Teachers Aide; School Play; Pres Sr Cls; Var Ftbl; Var Golf; MVP Ski Team; OR ST U; Human Rsrcs.

RUDDELL, ANNA M; Wasco Union HS; Wasco, CA; (1); Church Yth Grp; GAA; Band; Mrchg Band; Pep Band; Sftbl; Hon Roll; Pres Acad Fit Awd; CA Poly; Bus.

RUDDICK, CARLA; Liberty Union HS; Brentwood, CA; (2); 44/451; 4-H; 4-H Awd; Hon Roll; Clse Up Fndtn Vstng WA DC Stdyng Govt; Mth Tutor; CA ST U Hayward; Dntstry.

RUDE, ALLY; Turlock HS; Turlock, CA; (2); Church Yth Grp; Pep Clb; SADD; Off Frsh Cls; Capt Cheerldng; Frshmn Cls Rally Commissnr; UC Berkley; Bus.

RUDE, RYAN E; Anaheim HS; Anaheim, CA; (3); Var L Bsbl; L Capt Bsktbl; Varsity Clb; Kiwanis Clb; Cal Poly Pomona; Elec Engr.

RUDERMAN, DANIEL; Fontana HS; Fontana, CA; (4); 4/792; Am Leg Boys St; Boy Scts; FBLA; Ski Clb; Speech Tm; Pres Sr Cls; Var L Swmmng; High Hon Roll; Pres Acad Fit Awd; Waterpolo Vrsty Lttr; Harvard Bk Awd; Spence Reese Schlrshp; Stanford U.

RUDIN, HEIDI A; Etiwanda HS; Alta Loma, CA; (2); Church Yth Grp; Band; JV Crs Cntry; JV Trk; Cit Awd; High Hon Roll; Hon Roll.

RUDNICK, PESHA E; Venice HS; Venice, CA; (2); GAA; Thesps; VP Stu Cncl; Var Gym; Cit Awd; High Hon Roll; Peace Club Pres; Earthday Cmmtte Pres 90; MV Gymnast; Art Awd; Acad Schl Awd; Peer Cnslr; UC Berkeley; Actress.

RUDOMETKIN, JENNIFER; Whittier Christian HS; Whittier, CA; (2); Church Yth Grp; Drama Clb; Speech Tm; School Musical; School Play; Stage Crew; JV Var Vllybl; Hon Roll; Jr Miss Whittier-86; All Leag-89; Dramatic Speech Awd-1st Pl 87; Arch.

RUDOMETKIN, NATE; Sacramento Adventist Acad; Newcastle, CA; (2); 1/45; Drama Clb; Band; Chorus; Stu Cncl; Var Bsktbl; Var Ftbl; Var Vllybl; ASB-SGT Of Arms/Relgn VP/Exec VP; Stanford; Optomlgy.

RUDY, JEFFREY S; Ontario HS; Ontario, CA; (2); Letterman Clb; Spanish Clb; SADD; Varsity Clb; Stage Crew; JV Bsbl; Var Ftbl; Var Wt Lftg; JV Wrstlng; Prfct Atten Awd; U Of NV Reno.

RUDY, JOCELYN C; Bonita Vista HS; Bonita, CA; (2); Church Yth Grp; Dance Clb; Chorus; School Musical; School Play; Cheerldng.

RUDZIEWICZ, LOUIE; Antelope Valley HS; Lancaster, CA; (3); Var L Crs Cntry; JV Socr; Var L Trk; Law.

RUEB, MARK C; Alhambra HS; Martinez, CA; (3); 1/214; Boy Scts; Math Clb; Science Clb; JV Bsktbl; L JV Ftbl; L Var Swmmng; High Hon Roll; Yth Educators; Peer Cnslng; CA Schltc Fed; Stanford; Civil Engrng.

RUEDA, CHARITO SHERRY; Palm Desert HS; Palm Desert, CA; (3); Church Yth Grp; Key Clb; Library Aide; VP Spanish Clb; Crs Cntry; Co-Capt Trk; High Hon Roll; HOBY Ambssdr 89; Coaches Awd Crsscntry Var 88; Top Achvr 87-88; Wrld Cultures; UCLA; Med.

RUEDA, CLAUDIA E; Anaheim HS; Anaheim, CA; (3); Cmnty Wkr; Dance Clb; School Play; Dance; MAES; Emerging Ldrs Of CA ST Fullerton; CA ST Fullerton; Acctng.

RUEDA, MARGARET; Palm Desert HS; Palm Desert, CA; (2); Church Yth Grp; Hosp Aide; Sec Key Clb; Spanish Clb; Pres Frsh Cls; Var Crs Cntry; Powder Puff Ftbl; High Hon Roll; Coachs Awd Vrsty Crss Cntry; Hume Lake Chrstn Camp; Loma Linda U; Med.

RUELAS, BARBARA; Southwest HS; San Diego, CA; (4); Var Bsktbl; SDSU.

RUELAS, ISABEL; Sweetwater Union HS; National City, CA; (2); FTA; Cit Awd; 4-H Awd; Prfct Atten Awd; Pres Acad Fit Awd; Cert Achvt Outstndng P E Stu; Cert Super Perfmnc In Engl.

RUELAS, JOSE J; Carlsbad HS; Oceanside, CA; (2); French Clb; JV Socr; JV Tennis; Cit Awd; Hon Roll; Boys Club Of Amer; Oceanside Swmmng Team 89; Hlth Ftnss Awd; Migrant Educ Pgm; MECHA Club; Gold Card Wnr; UCLA; Srgn.

RUELAS, MANUEL; San Pedro HS; San Pedro, CA; (4); JV Var Bsbl; Var Socr; Hon Roll; Silvr Seal Diploam Maintng Highr 3.0 GPA All 3 Yrs; Harbor Coll; Crmnl Justice.

RUELAS, ROCIO; Hamilton HS; Los Angeles, CA; (3); French Clb; Spanish Clb; Teachers Aide; Drill Tm; Pom Pon; High Hon Roll; Hon Roll; Prfct Atten Awd; Pres Acad Fit Awd; Art Acad Exclinc Awd; Olympn Hnr Soc; Cert Merit Eng, Frnch & Hstry; UCLA; Cmptr Sci.

RUESTMANN, MONIQUE B; Mayfield SR HS; Pasadena, CA; (2); Church Yth Grp; Ski Clb; SADD; Chorus.

RUETER, DAVID L; Valley Christian HS; Bellflower, CA; (2); VP Church Yth Grp; Yrbk; Head Coach Undefeated Boys Vlybl; Acctg.

RUETER, SEAN M; Capostrano Valley HS; Mission Viejo, CA; (3); Boy Scts; Trk; Wrstlng; U Of CA Santa Barbara.

RUEZGA, ALBERT G; Hilmar HS; Delhi, CA; (3); AFS; Art Clb; Church Yth Grp; FFA; Letterman Clb; SADD; Ftbl; Trk; Wt Lftg; Wrstlng; Frgn Lang Clb.

RUFF, MICHELLE; Armona Union Acad; Hanford, CA; (4); 5/10; Church Yth Grp; Drama Clb; Band; Chorus; Ed Nwsp; Ed Yrbk; VP Frsh Cls; Hon Roll; Prfct Atten Awd; Assoc Stu Body Pres; Oakwood Coll; Jrnlsm.

RUFFIN, BETINA L; Eisenhower HS; San Bernardino, CA; (3); Church Yth Grp; FBLA; Science Clb; Teachers Aide; Acpl Chr; Chorus; Church Choir; Swing Chorus; High Hon Roll; Hon Roll; CSU San Bernardino; Music.

RUFFIN, MARSHA D; Notre Dame Acad; Culver City, CA; (3); 47/112; Pep Clb; Spanish Clb; SADD; Rptr Yrbk; Var Cheerldng; Cit Awd; HOPE Clb-Helping Other People Everywhere; Med.

RUFFIN, ZANETA L; Victor Valley HS; Victorville, CA; (3); Church Yth Grp; Cmnty Wkr; SADD; Band; Church Choir; Mrchg Band; Orch; Pep Band; Cit Awd; Gospel Singer.

RUFFINELLI, JOHN W; Crenshaw HS; Los Angeles, CA; (3); Boy Scts; Church Yth Grp; Debate Tm; English Clb; Math Clb; Math Tm; Office Aide; ROTC; Spanish Clb; SADD; Banner & Cert For 3rd Pl; Pepperdine U; Law.

RUFFONI, MICHAEL E; Bullard HS; Fresno, CA; (2); German Clb; School Play; Intrml Tennis; Var Trk; Hon Roll; FSU; Sci.

RUFINO, ERWIN B; Pinole Valley HS; Pinole, CA; (3); Computer Clb; Drama Clb; Intnl Clb; Math Clb; Science Clb; Hon Roll; 1st Pl Scrng High AHSME Alg II; Chrmn Of Yth Chrch; Plyng Chess, Table Tnns; UC Berkeley; Med.

RUGG, JEFF W; Sonara HS; La Habra, CA; (4); Variety Show; Rptr Yrbk; Rptr Lit Mag; Prfssnl BMX Frstyl Bike Ath; CA Poly Pomona; Comp Sci.

RUGG, REBECCA A; The York Schl; Pacific Grove, CA; (4); 2/23; Church Yth Grp; Acpl Chr; Chorus; Church Choir; School Play; Stage Crew; Rep Frsh Cls; VP Soph Cls; Rep Jr Cls; Pres Stu Cncl; Dept Hstry Awd 89; Telluride Assn Schlrshp 89; New Forum Tchr-Stu Soviet Union Exchng Schlrshp 89.

RUGGLES, JEFF R; Live Oak HS; Morgan Hill, CA; (3); Church Yth Grp; Math Clb; Acpl Chr; Band; Swing Chorus; Sec Sr Cls; Pres Stu Cncl; L Swmmng; Tennis; Hon Roll; Mock Trial.

RUGH, SANDRA L; Dana Hills HS; Dana Point, CA; (3); Church Yth Grp; Letterman Clb; Math Clb; Science Clb; Spanish Clb; Acpl Chr; Church Choir; Var Swmmng; Pres Acad Fit Awd; Acad Decathlon; CIF Div 4 Swimming; Water Polo All Amer; CSU Long Bch; Bio Tchr.

RUGNAO, MARY JANE; East Union HS; Manteca, CA; (4); 13/280; French Clb; FBLA; SADD; Teachers Aide; Nwsp; Ed Yrbk; Treas Soph Cls; Pres Jr Cls; VP Stu Cncl; JV Cheerldng; CSF; Rally & Parade Cmmsnr; Stu Rep Manteca Bd Of Ed; Stu Comunist Local Nwsp; U Southern CA; Mrktng Mgmt.

RUHL, GILBERT A; Miramonte HS; Orinda, CA; (1); Boy Scts; Church Yth Grp; Life Sct; CA Schlrshp Fed; CA Maritime Acad; Mrn Trnsprtn.

RUIZ, ADRIANA; Bell Gardens HS; Bell Gardens, CA; (3); Cal ST.

RUIZ, ALMA; Presentation HS; Mountain View, CA; (1); U CA Berkeley Algebra Test Stu Achvt; Doctor.

RUIZ, ANGIE M; North Salinas HS; Salinas, CA; (3); Church Yth Grp; French Clb; FBLA; Girl Scts; Ski Clb; Spanish Clb; SADD; JV Fld Hcky; JV Gym; JV Tennis; Modelng Fash Shws Raisd Money For Drug Rehab Cntrs; Sang At Chrstn Yth Concrts; Bus.

RUIZ, CECILIA; Strathmore HS; Strathmore, CA; (1); Spanish Clb; Wt Lftg; Cit Awd; High Hon Roll; Hon Roll; Teacher.

RUIZ, CHASTIDY I; Indio HS; Indio, CA; (1); JV Cheerldng; Gym; Hon Roll; USC; Commnctns.

RUIZ, CLARIBEL; Oakdale HS; Oakdale, CA; (3); Teachers Aide; Tennis; Vllybl; Fshn Dsgnr.

RUIZ, ELIZABETH; Paraclete HS; Lancaster, CA; (2); Church Yth Grp; Hon Roll; Entertainment Cmmtte; UCSB; Cosmetology.

RUIZ, ERNIE A; Hamilton HS; Sylmar, CA; (4); Band; Jazz Band; Mrchg Band; High Hon Roll; Nevians Hnr Soc; Nmrs Awds Jazz Band; 1st Pl Monterey Jazz Fstvl; U Of SC; Airline Pilot.

RUIZ III, GILBERT P; Serrano HS; Pinon Hills, CA; (1); JV L Bsbl; JV L Bsktbl; High Hon Roll; Stu Mnth Hstry; Top GPA Bsktbl Awd; Aerospc Engrng.

RUIZ, GLENN E; South San Francisco HS; San Bruno, CA; (2); Cmnty Wkr; Math Clb; Sec Frsh Cls; Treas Soph Cls; Tennis; Asian Amer Club; Cal Poly; Aerospc Engr.

RUIZ, GRACIE A; Salinas HS; Salinas, CA; (1); Cmnty Wkr; FBLA; Swmmng; High Hon Roll; NHS; Stanford; Pediatrics.

RUIZ, JAIME; Borrego Springs HS; Borrego Springs, CA; (2); Key Clb.

RUIZ, JANET C; Valhala HS; Jamul, CA; (3); Cit Awd; South Western Coll; CPA.

RUIZ, JAVIER; St Ignatius College Prep; Pacifica, CA; (3); 12/243; Nwsp; Mgr Ftbl; Wt Lftg; High Hon Roll; Hon Roll; CSF; Stanford; Span Lit Tchr.

RUIZ, JESSICA L; San Luis Obispo HS; San Luis Obispo, CA; (2); Church Yth Grp; Spanish Clb; Temple Yth Grp; Acpl Chr; Chorus; Church Choir; Yrbk; Socr; Tennis; Stanford; Med.

RUIZ, JOEL; Fremont HS; Oakland, CA; (2); Bsbl; Wt Lftg; Wrstlng; Civil Engr.

RUIZ, JOSE J; Garfield HS; E Los Angeles, CA; (4); 26/690; VP Chess Clb; ROTC; Teachers Aide; Rep Stu Cncl; Capt Bsktbl; High Hon Roll; Opt Clb Awd; Voice Dem Awd; Ephebian; Mst Likely To Succeed; U Of Southern CA; Aerospc Engr.

RUIZ, JOSE P; Pius X HS; Maywood, CA; (4); Art Clb; Drama Clb; French Clb; School Play; Bsktbl; Ftbl; Powder Puff Ftbl; Socr; French Hon Soc; Hon Roll; UCLA; Med.

RUIZ, JUSTINE M; Santa Barbara HS; Santa Barbara, CA; (2); Boy Scts; Cmnty Wkr; Office Aide; Flag Corp; Mrchg Band; Teen Ldr Girls Clb; Cabin Ldr Cnty Schls; Native Amer Smmr Camp Cnslr; Modeling Labelle Bsc Beauty Crs; UCSB; Acctng.

RUIZ, KAREN; Phillip Burton Academic HS; San Francisco, CA; (4); 11/183; Band; Nwsp; High Hon Roll; Hon Roll; Bio Awd 88; San Francisco ST U; Jrnlsm.

RUIZ, LETICIA; Selma HS; Selma, CA; (3); 66/211; Musical Engrng.

RUIZ, LISA E; Fontana HS; Fontana, CA; (2); Church Yth Grp; Office Aide; Teachers Aide; Cit Awd; Hon Roll; UCLA; Fashn Dsgnr.

RUIZ, LORRAINE C; Pasadena HS; Pasadena, CA; (2); JV Cheerldng; Hon Roll.

RUIZ, MARCELA M; Amos Alonzo Stagg HS; Stockton, CA; (1); Cmnty Wkr; Dance Clb; Intrml Swmmng; JV Capt Vllybl; High Hon Roll; CSF; STAND; Stanford; Med.

RUIZ, MARICEL C; Saint Anthony HS; Carson, CA; (2); French Clb; Hosp Aide; School Musical; Variety Show; VP Soph Cls; Stu Cncl; High Hon Roll; Hon Roll; NHS; HS Mrt Schlrshp; Bus.

RUIZ, MARTA A; Lindsay HS; Lindsay, CA; (1); 48/189; Spanish Clb; Band; Mrchg Band; Pep Band; Ag.

RUIZ, MELANIE B; Tracy Joint Union HS; Tracy, CA; (2); 100/572; Church Yth Grp; Cmnty Wkr; Drama Clb; Office Aide; Spanish Clb; SADD; Teachers Aide; Church Choir; Bsbl; Bsktbl; Singing; Cal Poly; Political Sci.

RUIZ JR, MICHAEL T; Paraclete HS; Lancaster, CA; (2); JA; JV Var Bsbl; JV Ftbl; Hon Roll; Prncpls Awd; West Point; Military.

RUIZ, MICHELLE A; Samuel F B Morse HS; San Diego, CA; (3); 139/641; Church Yth Grp; French Clb; Aud/Vis; Rptr Ed Nwsp; Rep Frsh Cls; French Hon Soc; Hon Roll; Jr NHS; Kiwanis Awd; Pres Acad Fit Awd; SDC/Jea Awd; CA Schlrshp Fed; 3rd Pl Jrnlsm Wrt Offs; Pepperdine U; Cmmnctns.

RUIZ, NANCY; Garfield HS; Los Angeles, CA; (2); Service Clb; Cit Awd; Prfct Atten Awd; Medial Careers Clb; RN.

RUIZ, NOEMI; Moorpark HS; Moorpark, CA; (2); 95/249; Church Yth Grp; Latin Clb; Church Choir; JV Sftbl; Hon Roll; Mecha Club; Cinco De Mayo; Lawyer.

RUIZ, OBISTANO; Roosevelt HS; Los Angeles, CA; (1); Boy Scts; Yrbk; Off Sr Cls; Bsbl; Ftbl; Hon Roll; NHS; Police Officer.

RUIZ, PETE; Rosemead HS; Fontana, CA; (2); FCA; Crs Cntry; Trk; Wrstlng; Cit Awd; Pres Acad Fit Awd; UCSB; Eng.

RUIZ, RAQUEL; North Montery County HS; Salinas, CA; (1); Hon Roll; Acad Achvt Engl; San Diego U ST; Law.

RUIZ, ROBERTO A; Granada Hills HS; Los Angeles, CA; (3); Quiz Bowl; Teachers Aide; Bsktbl; Socr; Wt Lftg; Wrstlng; Cit Awd; Hon Roll; Ntl Merit Ltr; Latino Clb; Cal ST Northridge; Engrng.

RUIZ, ROCIO K; Arlington HS; Riverside, CA; (2); 8/534; Church Yth Grp; Cmnty Wkr; FBLA; FTA; Spanish Clb; Teachers Aide; Vllybl; High Hon Roll; Hon Roll; UC Riverside; Teacher.

RUIZ, ROSALINDA; Pomona Catholic HS; Ontario, CA; (4); 8/95; Treas Church Yth Grp; Cmnty Wkr; Science Clb; Chorus; High Hon Roll; Hon Roll; NHS; Adopt-A-Friend; CA Schlrshp Fed; Vet Med.

RUIZ, SANTIAGO; North Salinas HS; Salinas, CA; (1); Play Major Leaque Sport.

RUIZ, SERGIO; Workman HS; Valinda, CA; (3); JV Bsktbl; Var Ftbl; Var Wt Lftg; Recd 4 Span AP Exam; CA ST U Fullerton; Bus.

RUIZ, SHEILA; Mc Clacthy HS; Sacramento, CA; (4); Drama Clb; FBLA; JA; SADD; Teachers Aide; Thesps; Chorus; Stage Crew; Gym; Swmmng; Bus.

RUIZ, SHERI; Arcadia HS; Arcadia, CA; (4); 321/632; Bsktbl; Cheerldng; Vllybl; Hon Roll; Pres Acad Fit Awd; People/People Ambssdr Russia 89 Smmr; San Diego ST U.

RUIZ, SILVIA C; Tustin HS; Tustin, CA; (1); 25/466; Hon Roll; Wrld Cltrs Awd; Med.

RUIZ, YVETTE; San Benito Joint Union HS; Hollister, CA; (2); Cmnty Wkr; Girl Scts; Hon Roll; Cal Poly San Luis Obispo; Comp.

RULE, JENNIFER; Lemoore HS; Lemoore, CA; (2); 4-H; French Clb; Band; Mrchg Band; Pep Band; JV Tennis; Cit Awd; Hon Roll; Felix Awds; UC Davis; Vet Med.

RULE, MICHELLE; Hilltop High HS; Chula Vista, CA; (3); 15/420; Var Cheerldng; JV Socr; Rptr Nwsp; Ed Yrbk; Intnl Clb; Model UN; Pep Clb; Stu Cncl; Hon Roll; Amer Leag Outstndng Stu; Asscd Stu Body Fin; CSF; CPA.

RULISON, SARA G; San Luis Obispo HS; San Luis Obispo, CA; (2); 4-H; Key Clb; SADD; Band; Mrchg Band; Pep Band; JV Sftbl; 4-H Awd; Hon Roll; CA Polytech U; Vet.

RULL, RUDOLPH P; Chula Vista HS; San Diego, CA; (3); 13/630; Math Tm; Office Aide; Band; Jazz Band; Mrchg Band; Pep Band; Cit Awd; Hon Roll; Pres Acad Fit Awd; CSF; Pan-Asian Amer Fllwshp Soc; Poltcl Sci.

RULLAN, CLARISSA; Southwest HS; San Diego, CA; (3); Church Yth Grp; Treas Key Clb; SADD; Var Tennis; Cit Awd; High Hon Roll; Pres Acad Fit Awd; Music Techlgy Ensmble; CSF; Pan Asian; Comp Sci.

RULZ, JESSICA C; Mesa Verde HS; Citrus Heights, CA; (2); 12/300; Trk; Vllybl; High Hon Roll; Hon Roll; Pres Acad Fit Awd; Pres Schlr; Interior Dsgn.

RUMBAUGH, HEATHER; Rolling Hills HS; Rancho Palos Verd, CA; (2); Church Yth Grp; Drama Clb; Hosp Aide; JA; Pep Clb; Service Clb; Drill Tm; Yrbk; Cit Awd.

RUMIREZ, GEORGINA C; Manuel Arts HS; Los Angeles, CA; (2); Ed Yrbk; Intrml Trk; Math Engrng Sci Achvt MESA 88-90; USC; Draftng.

RUMIS, WINI; Ramona HS; Ramona, CA; (2); Key Clb; JV Var Sftbl; Cit Awd; DAR Awd; Horse Showing; Water Skiing; Var Sftbl Ltr Frosh Yr; Point Loma Coll; Work W Dolphns.

RUMLEAN, IRENE M; Etiwanda HS; Alta Loma, CA; (3); Church Yth Grp; Dance Clb; Chorus; Church Choir; Hon Roll; Gftd & Tlntd Ed Stu; Cert Acad Achvt; Rcgntn Outstndng Achvt Mst Creatv Stu Engl Dept; CSU San Bernardino; Bus.

RUMMEL, JOHN P; North HS; Bakersfield, CA; (3); 18/368; French Clb; Sprt Ed Nwsp; JV Bsktbl; Hon Roll; Jr NHS; Lion Awd; NHS; Explorer; San Jose ST U; Police Sci.

RUMMERY, JENNIFER; Escondido HS; Escondido, CA; (3); Church Yth Grp; Drama Clb; Key Clb; Office Aide; Pep Clb; Science Clb; School Play; Rep Frsh Cls; Rep Chess Clb; Sec Sr Cls; Psych.

RUNDLE, KIMBERLY D; Summerville HS; Tuolumne, CA; (4); 20/150; Church Yth Grp; Cmnty Wkr; English Clb; Office Aide; SADD; Teachers Aide; Band; Jazz Band; Mrchg Band; Orch; Columbia CC; Teacher.

RUNYAN, BECKY; Palm Desert HS; Palm Desert, CA; (4); 1/286; Hist Cmnty Wkr; Pres VP Debate Tm; Pres VP French Clb; Hosp Aide; Model UN; Yrbk; Treas Jr Cls; Treas Stu Cncl; French Hon Soc; High Hon Roll; Teenager Of Yr Palm Desert; Top Adac Achvr Biol Sci Engl; Drug Essay Wnnr Schlrshpfrom Jewish War Vets; Stanford U; Pre-Med.

RUNYAN, ELLIE; Palm Desert HS; Rancho Mirage, CA; (2); Cmnty Wkr; French Clb; Hosp Aide; Science Clb; Treas Soph Cls; High Hon Roll; Hon Roll; Top Achvr Awd Avncd Art II Clss 88-89; Trphy Awd Acrylc Pntng; 1st Pl Mdln Pstr Pblshd Plm Dsrt Cty; UC Santa Barbara; Fine Arts.

RUNYAN, STEVEN G; The Bishops Schl; La Jolla, CA; (3); Boy Scts; Church Yth Grp; Cmnty Wkr; Key Clb; Letterman Clb; Scholastic Bowl; Spanish Clb; Rep Frsh Cls; Rep Soph Cls; Rep Jr Cls; Outstndng Boy Sct Of San Diego 90; Srvc Prgm; Wrld Horizons Carriaceau; Stu Rep Svc Prjct Cmmtte 90-91; Haverford.

RUNYON, JOSHUA R; Orange HS; Orange, CA; (1); Rancho Santiago Coll; Comp Tech.

RUO, BERNICE; Bullard HS; Fresno, CA; (4); 1/454; Hosp Aide; Key Clb; Pres Sec Math Clb; Math Tm; SADD; Lit Mag; Kiwanis Awd; Ntl Merit Ltr; Val; UCSF Biomedl Rsrch Awd; Harvard-Radcliffe U; Med.

RUPLE, WILLIE W; Poway HS; Poway, CA; (1); Temple Yth Grp; Socr; Wt Lftg; Liberal Arts.

RUPLEY, JANINE M; Ponderosa HS; Placerville, CA; (1); Church Yth Grp; Dance Clb; Hon Roll; Jrnlsm.

RUPP, EVA; Lincoln HS; Stockton, CA; (3); Cmnty Wkr; Dance Clb; Chrmn Debate Tm; Sec French Clb; Hosp Aide; Key Clb; Chrmn Speech Tm; SADD; Ed Lit Mag; Hon Roll; Environmntl Clb; Recyclng Clb; Beyond War; Stds Tkng Actn Not Drgs; Proj Be Aware.

RUPP, TERISA; Wallenberg Traditional HS; San Francisco, CA; (2); Drama Clb; French Clb; Chorus; Swmmng; Hon Roll; Pres Acad Fit Awd; Exchng Stu To France; U Of Sthrn CO; Theater.

RUPPERT, CHRISTINA; Aptos HS; Aptos, CA; (2); 54/396; Church Yth Grp; French Clb; Office Aide; Pep Clb; Color Guard; Drill Tm; Nwsp; Yrbk; Powder Puff Ftbl; High Hon Roll; Bus Admin.

RUPRECHT, SUSAN A; Cordova SR HS; Rancho Cordova, CA; (3); Intrml Vllybl; Hon Roll; CSF.

RUSCIGNO, SUSAN; Willow Glen HS; San Jose, CA; (3); Hon Roll; San Jose ST U.

RUSCO, DARREN T; North County Christian HS; Atascadero, CA; (2); Church Yth Grp; Band; Pres Jr Cls; Pres Stu Cncl; Var Bsbl; Var Bsktbl; Hon Roll; Commnctns.

RUSEV, JUDI; Notre Dame HS; Milpitas, CA; (3); Drama Clb; VP Hosp Aide; Intnl Clb; Science Clb; School Play; Rptr Nwsp; Off Sr Cls; Hon Roll; NHS; Rotary Awd; Yth In Govt Awd; San Jose Jr YBA; Commnctns.

RUSH, AMY; Miraleste HS; Rolling Hills Est, CA; (4); Pres Service Clb; Sec Soph Cls; Sec Jr Cls; Sec Stu Cncl; Var JV Cheerldng; Var Trk; NHS; Pres Acad Fit Awd; Homcmng Qn; Natl Assistnce League; UC Los Angeles.

RUSH, DAVID; Las Lomas HS; Walnut Creek, CA; (4); Cmnty Wkr; Letterman Clb; Office Aide; Teachers Aide; Varsity Clb; JV L Bsktbl; Var L Ftbl; Var L Trk; Intrml Mgr Wt Lftg; Jr HS Bsktbl Teams Coach; UC Davis; Phys Thrpy.

RUSH, MARNY L; San Marin HS; Novato, CA; (4); 1/250; Am Leg Aux Girls St; Intnl Clb; Pres Soph Cls; Rep Jr Cls; Pres Sr Cls; Rep Stu Cncl; Stat Ftbl; High Hon Roll; Pres NHS; Ntl Merit SF; Asst Dir Novato Yng Actrs Co; VP, Sr Rep & Kds Dy Fcltr Impct Clb; YMCA Govt Yth.

RUSHING, MARIJANE; Rim Of The World HS; Cedarpines Park, CA; (4); 19/207; Art Clb; Church Yth Grp; Office Aide; Pep Clb; Drill Tm; Hon Roll; Arts Rcgntn & Tlnt Srch 89-90; Bnk Amer Rcgntn Art; Acad Ltr; Inland Empire Envrnmntl Expo Cert; Woodbury U; Dsgn.

RUSHING, MELVIN R; Sweetwater Union HS; National City, CA; (3); 55/429; Teachers Aide; Var Capt Bsktbl; JV Vllybl; Hon Roll; Pres Acad Fit Awd; Ref Elem Stu Ntnl City Bsktbl; AZ ST; Psych.

RUSHMORE, KATHY; College Park HS; Pleasant Hill, CA; (4); 30/300; AFS; Spanish Clb; JV Bsktbl; JV Swmmng; Var Tennis; Yth Educ; Curriculum Assoc; CSF; UC Irvine.

RUSIT, JERIZA MARIE R; James Logan HS; Union City, CA; (3); Art Clb; Math Clb; Spanish Clb; Hon Roll; Medicine.

RUSS, JULIANA; Village HS; Pleasanton, CA; (3); Computer Clb; Office Aide; Teachers Aide; Hon Roll; Prfct Atten Awd; Earthquare Relief Fund; Homeless Family Food Drive; Earth Awareness Prgm; Jrnlsm.

RUSSAKOFF, JENNIFER; Oxnard HS; Oxnard, CA; (1); Cheerldng; Hon Roll; CSF; UCLA; Psych.

RUSSEL, JENIFER; Los Alamitos HS; Seal Beach, CA; (3); Spanish Clb; Ecology Clb; UC San Diego; Marine Bio.

RUSSELL, BONNIE K; El Camino HS; Oceanside, CA; (1); 10/430; Church Yth Grp; Chorus; Variety Show; L Sftbl; JV Tennis; High Hon Roll; Gldn St Exam Geom; CSU Chica; Elem Tchr.

RUSSELL, CARRIE L; Castle Park HS; Chula Vista, CA; (2); 32/625; French Clb; Band; Mrchg Band; Pep Band; Wind Ensmble; Humbolt ST U; Marine Bio.

RUSSELL, CHRISTIE N; Upland HS; Upland, CA; (3); Church Yth Grp; Girl Scts; Office Aide; Teachers Aide; Church Choir; Powder Puff Ftbl; Socr; Hon Roll.

RUSSELL, COLLEEN M; Dos Pueblos HS; Goleta, CA; (3); Office Aide; Pep Clb; Acpl Chr; Orch; Variety Show; JSA; Clsscl Piano Hnrs; Madrigals; U Of CA; Music.

RUSSELL, ERIK; Live Oak HS; Gilroy, CA; (4); Cmnty Wkr; Ski Clb; Speech Tm; SADD; Band; Mrchg Band; Pep Band; JV Bsktbl; Var Golf; Prfct Atten Awd; Fresno ST; Bus Admin.

RUSSELL, GAYLE; Taft HS; Canoga Park, CA; (3); Art Clb; Aud/Vis; Ftbl; Cmnty Wkr; Dance Clb; Girl Scts; Hosp Aide; Intnl Clb; Pep Clb; Ski Clb; Chrch Chld Care; Pedtrcn.

RUSSELL, HEATHER E; Village Christian HS; Glendale, CA; (4); 21/121; Church Yth Grp; Drama Clb; Math Clb; Mu Alpha Theta; Var Bsktbl; Var Sftbl; Cit Awd; High Hon Roll; 2nd Pl Sci Fair Awd; Bsktbl MVP; Columbia Christian; Elem Educ.

RUSSELL, JEREMY; Sonoma Valley HS; Sonoma, CA; (2); 14/252; NFL; Lit Mag; High Hon Roll; Hon Roll; Prfct Atten Awd; CSF; Paleontology.

RUSSELL, JOE M; Etiwanda HS; Alta Loma, CA; (3); Church Yth Grp; Key Clb; Ski Clb; Teachers Aide; JV Bsbl; JV Ftbl; Intrml Socr; Var Tennis; Cit Awd; Hon Roll; Prmdcs.

RUSSELL, JULI; Liberty Union HS; Oakley, CA; (2); Band; Jazz Band; Mrchg Band; Bsktbl; Swmmng; Vllybl; Hon Roll; UOP; Arch.

RUSSELL, JULIE; Redwood HS; Visalia, CA; (4); Am Leg Aux Girls St; Church Yth Grp; Pep Clb; Spanish Clb; SADD; Acpl Chr; Chorus; School Musical; Swing Chorus; Variety Show; Clean Campus Comm; Coll Sequioa; Educ.

RUSSELL, KEVIN; Redwood HS; Visalia, CA; (3); Church Yth Grp; Pres Pep Clb; Spanish Clb; SADD; Mrchg Band; Pep Band; Pres Frsh Cls; Stu Cncl; JV Var Swmmng; JR & Var Waterpolo; Bus.

RUSSELL, KIMBERLY Y; La Quinta HS; Westminster, CA; (3); 5/327; Key Clb; Church Choir; Mrchg Band; Treas Frsh Cls; Sec Soph Cls; Var Capt Crs Cntry; Var Socr; Var Trk; NHS; HOBY Amb; Math.

RUSSELL, LAURA C; El Capitan HS; Lakeside, CA; (2); 23/433; Church Yth Grp; Spanish Clb; SADD; Sec Soph Cls; Var Crs Cntry; Var Trk; Hon Roll; BYU.

RUSSELL, LEAH A; San Diego Acad; El Cajon, CA; (1); Church Yth Grp; Teachers Aide; Yrbk; Off Soph Cls; Hon Roll; 6th Grd Cnslr Pine Springs Rnch; Natl Ftns Standard Awd; Hiking/Cmpng Clb; Med.

RUSSELL, LEE R; Fontana HS; Fontana, CA; (2); Office Aide; Ski Clb; Teachers Aide; Mgr(s); Trk; High Hon Roll; Hon Roll; Prfct Atten Awd; MI U.

RUSSELL, MARK D; Skyline HS; Oakland, CA; (3); Boy Scts; Church Yth Grp; Church Choir; JV Ftbl; Hon Roll; CA Jr Schrlshp Fed; CSF; Ord Arrow Boy Scouts; UCLA.

RUSSELL, MICHAEL D; Lincoln HS; Stockton, CA; (2); Aud/Vis; Ski Clb; Band; Ftbl; Golf; Hon Roll; Guitar; Music Theory, Hstry; Music.

RUSSELL, MIKE L; North HS; Bakersfield, CA; (3); Office Aide; Teachers Aide; Bsbl; Ftbl; Wt Lftg; Hon Roll; MVP-FTBL.

RUSSELL, NICOLE C; Grossmont HS; El Cajon, CA; (2); Hlpng Envrnmnt; U Of CA San Diego; Psych.

RUSSELL, PAM; Calabasas HS; Woodland Hills, CA; (2); Pep Clb; Pep Band; JV Cheerldng; Dance-Jazz; Piano; Law.

RUSSELL, REBECCA; Christian HS; El Cajon, CA; (3); Church Yth Grp; Drama Clb; School Play; Ed Nwsp; Hon Roll; NHS; History.

RUSSELL, RYAN M; Cuyama Valley HS; New Cuyama, CA; (3); 3/15; Am Leg Boys St; Church Yth Grp; Drama Clb; Letterman Clb; School Play; Pres Frsh Cls; VP Soph Cls; Pres Jr Cls; Pres Stu Cncl; Var L Bsbl; 2nd Pl Sci Fair; Westmont Coll; Comm.

RUSSELL, SHARON G; Sklyline HS; Oakland, CA; (2); Church Yth Grp; SADD; Church Choir; High Hon Roll; Hon Roll; Prfct Atten Awd; CA JR Schlrshp Fed; CSF; Gymnstcs; Sports Med.

RUSSELL, SHAWNNA I; Pittsburg HS; Pittsburg, CA; (2); Office Aide; Teachers Aide; High Hon Roll; HS Hnrs Pgm; Acctnt.

RUSSELL, SONIA; Oakland Tech HS; Oakland, CA; (4); Off Church Yth Grp; Pres Dance Clb; Debate Tm; SADD; Capt School Play; Variety Show; Rep Stu Cncl; JV Vllybl; Off Cit Awd; Off Hon Roll; Pres-Mesa; Sut Exchng To USSR; Ftrd On TV As Promising Stu; U C Berkeley; Arch.

RUSSELL, STEVEN P; Seaside HS; Marina, CA; (1); Sec Key Clb; JV Socr; Hon Roll; Artist.

RUSSELL, TODD; Capistrano Valley HS; Sn Jn Capistrano, CA; (4); Drama Clb; Rptr FBLA; Thesps; School Musical; School Play; Ntl Merit SF; Val; Acad Decthln Hnrs; Kiwanis Bwl Tm Cptn; Mock Trl; Stanford U; Intl Rltns.

RUSSELL, VERONICA; Golden West HS; Visalia, CA; (4); Drama Clb; NFL; Pres Speech Tm; SADD; Teachers Aide; Ed Nwsp; Ed Yrbk; Hon Roll; Lion Awd; Assocd Women Pepperdine Schlrshp; HS Jrnlst Yr Awd; Pepperdine U; Jrnlsm.

RUSSLER, AMY K; West HS; Bakersfield, CA; (1); Band; Mrchg Band; Hon Roll; Fresno ST U; Ed.

RUSSO, ANTHONY T; Victor Valley HS; Victorville, CA; (3); Ski Clb; Var Tennis; Hon Roll; Mini Trck Clb; UC Irvine; Arch.

RUSSO, CAROLYN ANN GRACE; La Reina HS; Westlake Villag, CA; (4); 4/84; Cmnty Wkr; VP GAA; Letterman Clb; Teachers Aide; Bsktbl; Sftbl; Capt Vllybl; Cit Awd; High Hon Roll; Kiwanis Awd; 1st Team AU-CIF Sthrn Sctn In Vlybl; CA Schlrshp Fdrtn; MVP Tri-Vly Leag In Vlybl; Loyala Marymount U; Bus.

RUSSO, MAT; South Fork HS; Weott, CA; (3); Bsbl; Bsktbl; Ftbl; Trk; Wrstlng; Auto & Wood Shop.

RUST, TERI L; Thousand Oaks HS; Thousand Oaks, CA; (3); 72/541; Church Yth Grp; Cmnty Wkr; Intnl Clb; Key Clb; High Hon Roll; Jr NHS; NHS; 3rd Pl Wnne Schl Art Fstvl; Cmmssnr Electns; Stu Govt Cls.

RUSTIA, EVANGELINE L; Nogales HS; West Covina, CA; (3); 11/542; Dance Clb; Office Aide; Science Clb; Chorus; Lit Mag; High Hon Roll; Hon Roll; Prfct Atten Awd; Won 2nd Place Martin Luther King Essay Comp; Cert Of Recognition Excellence Soc Std; Nogales HS Amb; UCLA; Medicine.

RUSTIN, CHRISTINA L; Temecula Valley HS; Murrieta, CA; (2); Band; Intrml Bsktbl; JV Intrml Vllybl; UC Santa Barbara; Writer.

RUSTRIAN, NORMA; Belmont HS; Los Angeles, CA; (3); Pep Clb; Bsbl; Cheerldng; Bus Admin.

RUTAN, CRAIG T; Huntington Beach HS; Huntington Beach, CA; (3); Boy Scts; Chess Clb; Cmnty Wkr; Math Clb; Red Cross Aide; Spanish Clb; Teachers Aide; High Hon Roll; Prfct Atten Awd; Tower Awd Histry; GMI; Elec Engr.

RUTE, JENSON; Poway HS; San Diego, CA; (3); Nwsp; Crs Cntry; High Hon Roll; Hon Roll; Cal-Berkeley.

RUTGER, CARMELA; Bishop Amat HS; Walnut, CA; (3); Cmnty Wkr; Drama Clb; Variety Show; Hon Roll; Med.

RUTH, BOBBY D; Oxnard HS; Oxnard, CA; (2); 112/582; Var Swmmng; Prfct Atten Awd; Waterpolo Var Capt; Marine Bio; Horticulture; Pepperdine U; Fireman.

RUTH, MICHAEL W; Mt Whitney HS; Visalia, CA; (4); 8/346; Art Clb; Sec Math Clb; Orch; Var Crs Cntry; Var Trk; Ntl Merit SF; Yth & Govt; CSF Slbr 90; Cst & Pnt Mdl Sldrs; Comp.

RUTHERFORD, JACKSON W; Fairbanks Country Day HS; Escondido, CA; (1); Computer Clb; Letterman Clb; School Musical; School Play; L Socr; L Sftbl; Tennis; L Vllybl; Hon Roll; MIT; Engr.

RUTHERFORD, JIM K; Santa Ynez Valley Union HS; Solvang, CA; (3); 37/156; Pep Clb; Teachers Aide; Rep Stu Cncl; Var Capt Bsktbl; Yth & Govt; Most Imprvd BSKTBL; Best Dfns & Capt JV Bsktbl; Bus Mgmt.

RUTHERFORD, JOSHUA; Lone Pine Unified HS; Lone Pine, CA; (1); Service Clb; Band; Pep Band; Variety Show; Schl Mascot; Delineation/Drafting Apprntc CA Dept Of Transprtn; Drftng/Delineation.

RUTHERFORD, LEA T; John Muir HS; Altadena, CA; (4); 34/360; Church Yth Grp; Acpl Chr; Chorus; Church Choir; School Musical; School Play; Variety Show; Var Trk; Spelman Coll; Bio.

RUTHERFURD, ALY; Analy HS; Sebastopol, CA; (2); French Clb; Yrbk; Cheerldng; Swmmng; Trk; High Hon Roll; Hon Roll; Harvard; Law.

RUTLEDGE, MATTHEW G; Brea-Olinda HS; Brea, CA; (3); French Clb; Letterman Clb; Ed Yrbk; Capt Socr; Cit Awd; High Hon Roll; Hon Roll; Rotary Awd; UC; Mech Engrng.

RUTLEDGE, NOELLA; Hesperia HS; Hesperia, CA; (3); 36/650; Church Yth Grp; Pep Clb; Spanish Clb; Teachers Aide; Drill Tm; VP Sr Cls; Rep Stu Cncl; Capt Cheerldng; Capt Pom Pon; Stat Trk; Dancer Lcl Radio Sta Q-CREW; CA ST Long Beach; Engl Educ.

RUTLEDGE, SARAH; Valley Christian HS; Dublin, CA; (3); Church Yth Grp; Pep Clb; Thesps; Church Choir; Sec Soph Cls; High Hon Roll; NHS; Stat Bsktbl; Var L Sftbl; Natl Young Ldrs Conf 90; Rotary Yth Ldrshp Awd; Chrch Yty Cncl Outreach.

RUTLEDGE, THADDEUS; Fortuna Union HS; Rio Dell, CA; (4); Var Bsbl; Hon Roll; Coll The Redwoods.

RUTTAN, KATHRYN; Armijo HS; Fairfield, CA; (4); 3/375; Church Yth Grp; Church Choir; High Hon Roll; Kiwanis Awd; Lion Awd; NHS; Rotary Awd; Sthrn CA Coll; Math Teacher.

RUTTANASEE, LAPA; Baldwin Park HS; Chino Hills, CA; (2); Band; Mrchg Band; Pep Band; High Hon Roll; Hon Roll; Pres Acad Fit Awd; USD; Premed.

RUTZ, MELENIE; Golden Sierra HS; Garden Valley, CA; (4); 5/89; JA; Letterman Clb; Pep Clb; Varsity Clb; Rep Stu Cncl; Stat Bsbl; Capt Cheerldng; Powder Puff Ftbl; High Hon Roll; Voice Dem Awd; U Pacific; Comp Engrng.

RUVA, NICOLE R; Huntington Beach HS; Huntington Beach, CA; (3); Model UN; Hon Roll; Pres Acad Fit Awd; 5th Pl Wnnr 10th Grade Orange Cty Acad Decathlon 89; Law.

RUVALCABA, ADRIANA; Sanger HS; Sanger, CA; (3); Computer Clb; Spanish Clb; Cit Awd; Hon Roll; NHS; CSF; Dept Stndouts; Schlstc Achvmnt; Acad Achvmnt; CA ST U Fresno; Bus Adm.

RUVALCABA, CAROL; North Monterey County HS; Castroville, CA; (2); Band; Mrchg Band; Pep Band; Rptr Yrbk; Crs Cntry; Trk; UC Davis; Tchr.

RUVALCABA, IRIS; Bishop Manogue HS; West Sacramento, CA; (1); Hon Roll.

RUVALCABA, LUIS J; Irvington HS; Fremont, CA; (3); Cmnty Wkr; Key Clb; Quiz Bowl; Pres Frsh Cls; Rep Soph Cls; Rep Jr Cls; Rep Stu Cncl; Intrml Bsbl; Intrml Bsktbl; Intrml Wt Lftg; Schl Actvts Gld Mdl Wnnr; Pr Cnslr; Lw.

RUVALCABA, SANDRA; Anaheim HS; Anaheim, CA; (4); Church Yth Grp; French Clb; JA; Spanish Clb; Vllybl; Hon Roll; NHS; Friendshp VP; Maes Clb; Intl Bus.

RUVINSKY, EDWARD; Lowell HS; San Francisco, CA; (2); Computer Clb; Teachers Aide; Hon Roll; Goldn St Exam Acad Excllnce Awd; Russian Clb; Stu Involvd In Envrnmnt Clb; Comp Sci.

RUX, NATHAN; Salinas HS; Salinas, CA; (4); Church Yth Grp; Drama Clb; Office Aide; Thesps; Color Guard; School Musical; School Play; Hon Roll; Assn Stu Bdy Salinas HS Mrtrs Svc Awd; Hartnell Coll.

RYALI, SRIKANTH; Sunny Hills HS; Fullerton, CA; (2); High Hon Roll; Stu Of The Month In Frnch & Chem; Silver Mdl In Chem.

RYAN, AARON M; John F Kennedy HS; Buena Park, CA; (1); JA; JV Bsbl; JV Bsktbl; MIP Bsbl; TX; Med.

RYAN, ANA MONICA; San Bernardino HS; San Bernardino, CA; (3); Am Leg Aux Girls St; Model UN; NFL; ROTC; Speech Tm; Var Bsktbl; Var Sftbl; JV Vllybl; High Hon Roll; NHS; MESA; Mock Trail; Acadc Dcthln K; Engl.

RYAN, COREY A; Victory Christian Schl; Orangevale, CA; (3); 3/30; Aud/Vis; Church Yth Grp; Cmnty Wkr; Drama Clb; Pep Clb; Science Clb; Spanish Clb; Teachers Aide; Varsity Clb; School Play; American River JC; Pre-Med.

RYAN, COREY B; Carpinteria HS; Carpinteria, CA; (2); French Clb; Bsktbl; High Hon Roll; Hon Roll; CSF; Math.

RYAN, CORY; Hemet HS; Hemet, CA; (4); Boy Scts; Computer Clb; Debate Tm; Drama Clb; FBLA; Quiz Bowl; Scholastic Bowl; Speech Tm; Teachers Aide; School Play; Comp Tech.

RYAN, EMIKO; El Dorado HS; Placentia, CA; (2); Drama Clb; Stage Crew; JV Bsktbl; JV Trk; High Hon Roll; Hon Roll; Certificate High Hnr & Superior Hnr; Coll; Business Sales Mngr.

RYAN, ERIN; Los Alamitos HS; Los Alamitos, CA; (3); Church Yth Grp; SADD; Sec Stu Cncl; Var Capt Socr; Var L Sftbl; Var L Vllybl; Hon Roll; Natl Charity League; Olympc Devlp Pgm Soccer.

RYAN, KATIE A; Arcadia HS; Arcadia, CA; (3); 183/687; Church Yth Grp; Cmnty Wkr; Ski Clb; Drill Tm; Sftbl; Tennis; Vllybl; Hon Roll; Assisteens Leag Of Arcadia; Job At Robinsons; U C Irvine; Tchng.

RYAN, KEITH A; Argonaut HS; Jackson, CA; (2); Var Bsbl; JV Capt Bsktbl; JV Capt Ftbl; High Hon Roll; UC Davis; Sports Med.

RYAN, KELLY; St Francis HS; Aiea, HI; (2); Cmnty Wkr; 5-7 Hr Old Sccr Coach; Vacation Bible Sch Tchr; Cmmnctns.

RYAN, KURT K; Golden West HS; Visalia, CA; (2); Church Yth Grp; DECA; VP FCA; Var L Bsbl; JV Ftbl; JV Wrstlng; High Hon Roll; Young Life; Golden St Math Schlr.

RYAN, LOUANN A; Monte Vista HS; Kalamazoo, MI; (2); 87/422; Church Yth Grp; Peer Cnslng Clb; Gldn St Exam 1st Yr Alg Hgh Hnrs; Sci.

RYAN, MARIA D L A; San Bernardino HS; San Bernardino, CA; (4); 5/375; Church Yth Grp; Cmnty Wkr; Model UN; NFL; ROTC; Spanish Clb; Sec Speech Tm; Drill Tm; Ed Lit Mag; Cheerldng; U C Berkeley; Math.

RYAN, MYRON J; Washington HS; Los Angeles, CA; (2); JV Bsktbl; Hon Roll.

RYAN, PILAR L; Coast Christian HS; Torrance, CA; (2); 3/28; Church Yth Grp; French Clb; Teachers Aide; Stat Ftbl; Var Sftbl; Hon Roll; Westmont Clg; HS Soc Studs.

RYAN, ROBB; Turlock HS; Turlock, CA; (4); German Clb; ROTC; Science Clb; Ed Yrbk; Hon Roll; Prfct Atten Awd; Acadc Decath Tm Stu 87-88 & 88-89; :lstiniguised Svc Awd TX 88; AFJROTC 88-89; Baylor U; Chem.

RYAN, SHANNON; Poway HS; San Diego, CA; (4); 39/679; Church Yth Grp; DECA; Key Clb; Var Bsktbl; NHS; OK U; Interior Dsgn.

RYAN, STEPHANIE L; Bella Vista HS; Orangevale, CA; (2); 89/406; Church Yth Grp; Cmnty Wkr; FBLA; Spanish Clb; SADD; Fld Hcky; Swmmng; Hon Roll; Jr NHS; Inst Cntry Clb Swm Tm.

RYBICKI, ISABELL; Aptos HS; Freedom, CA; (2); Church Yth Grp; Swmmng; Fluent Spanish Speaker; Took Modeling Classes; Good With Children Of All Ages; San Jose ST U; Veteranian.

RYBINKAR, JENNIFER M; Walnut HS; Walnut, CA; (3); Drama Clb; Key Clb; Speech Tm; Treas Sec Thesps; School Musical; School Play; Variety Show; Hon Roll; Prfct Atten Awd; Engl.

RYDEN, MAX A; Eureka SR HS; Eureka, CA; (3); 27/400; Ski Clb; High Hon Roll; Ca Schl Fed Clb CSF; Pharmacy.

RYE, JENNIFER; El Molino HS; Rio Nido, CA; (4); Am Leg Aux Girls St; Pres Sec FBLA; Letterman Clb; Quiz Bowl; Speech Tm; Sprt Ed Yrbk; Bsktbl; Var Socr; Var Tennis; Cit Awd; Outstndng Girl Athl; Bstkbl Awds; CA ST Hayward; Intl Bus.

RYE, JESSICA; Capital Christian Schl; Rancho Cordova, CA; (1); Church Yth Grp; Drama Clb; Ski Clb; Church Choir; School Musical; School Play; Stage Crew; Var Cheerldng; Cit Awd; High Hon Roll; Intr Dsgn.

RYERSON-CRUZ, GERALDINE Y; Los Angeles County HS For The Arts; Tarzana, CA; (4); Church Yth Grp; Drama Clb; French Clb; Chorus; School Play; Variety Show; Mgr Lit Mag; Rep Stu Cncl; Hon Roll; Ntl Merit SF; Natl Hspnc Soc; Piano Study; Intl Law.

RYKEN, MIKE L; Ventura HS; Ventura, CA; (3); 6/420; Church Yth Grp; Rep Stu Cncl; Var Bsktbl; Gov Hon Prg Awd; High Hon Roll; Hon Roll; Prfct Atten Awd; CA Schlstc Fed; Elec Engrng.

RYKERT, HOLLY; Modesto HS; Modesto, CA; (2); Church Yth Grp; Pep Clb; Chorus; JV Cheerldng; Gym; Hon Roll; Comptng Natl Comp JV Chrldng Sqd Cyprus; Hmcmng Qn 89.

RYKERT, JOSLYN; Modesto HS; Modesto, CA; (2); Church Yth Grp; Pep Clb; Chorus; Variety Show; Cheerldng; Gym; Cit Awd; High Hon Roll.

RYLAND, BECKI D; Lindsay HS; Lindsay, CA; (3); Church Yth Grp; GAA; Key Clb; Letterman Clb; Ski Clb; Teachers Aide; Varsity Clb; Nwsp; Yrbk; Chrmn Stu Cncl; Pepperdine U Girls St; Arch.

RYMAL, STEVE; Coast Union HS; Cambria, CA; (3); Boy Scts; Var JV Bsbl; Var JV Bsktbl; Var Capt Ftbl; CA Maritime Acad; Bus Deck Ofc.

RYNBRANDT, ROBIN A; San Rafael HS; San Rafael, CA; (2); 20/256; Cmnty Wkr; Spanish Clb; SADD; Rep Frsh Cls; Rep Soph Cls; Var Bsktbl; JV Cheerldng; Var Socr; NHS; Pres Acad Fit Awd; Grnd Prz Life Sci Marin Cnty Fair; 2nd Pl SF Bay Area Sci Fair; Hgh Hnrs Gldn St Exam Geom.

RYON, DEBORAH C; Durham HS; Durham, CA; (2); 2/72; Church Yth Grp; FHA; Yrbk; High Hon Roll; Intl Order Of Jobs Daughters; Gold Medal Wnnr Sew & Show; CA Schlrshp Fed; Butte Coll; Seamstress.

RYSSEL, DENNY E; Apple Valley SR HS; Apple Valley, CA; (1); Church Yth Grp; Chorus; Church Choir; Crs Cntry; Cit Awd; Hon Roll; Engr.

RYSSEMUS, FRANS H; Bellarmine College Prep; Santa Clara, CA; (3); Var Socr; Amigos De Las Americas; Med.

RYST, SONJA; Ygnacio Valley HS; Lafayette, CA; (3); 2/400; German Clb; Lit Mag; Tennis; High Hon Roll; Mock Trl; Yth Eductr CA Schlrshp; Acad Decthln Achvmnt Awd.

RYU, EUGENE C; Torrey Pines HS; Carlsbad, CA; (2); 50/503; Church Yth Grp; Spanish Clb; CA Schlrshp Fed; Sci.

RYU, SEUNG Y; Bonita HS; La Verne, CA; (2); Church Yth Grp; Hosp Aide; SADD; Stage Crew; JV Tennis; High Hon Roll; Biology Medicine.

RYZEK, SAMUEL P; Redlands HS; Redlands, CA; (2); Church Yth Grp; ROTC; Intrml L Ftbl; Intrml Wt Lftg; Intrml Wrstlng; U Of CA Irvine; Med.

SAAD, EHAB K; Bellarmine College Prep; Monte Serreno, CA; (4); Computer Clb; English Clb; FBLA; Library Aide; Office Aide; Teachers Aide; VICA; Off Sr Cls; Stu Cncl; Came From N Africa Different Lang Still B Avg; CA U Davis.

SAADAT, ARAZO; Tustin HS; Tustin, CA; (2); Cit Awd; High Hon Roll.

SAAH, DAVID S; Bellarmine College Prep; San Jose, CA; (4); Boy Scts; Church Yth Grp; Letterman Clb; Service Clb; Var Wrstlng; Egl Sct.

SAAVEDRA, CAROLINA; La Serna HS; Whittier, CA; (4); French Clb; Teachers Aide; JV Swmmng; Hon Roll; Prfct Atten Awd; Prncpls List; Long Beach ST; Psych.

SAAVEDRA, ENRIQUE M; Salinas HS; Salinas, CA; (3); Red Cross Aide; High Hon Roll; Engrng.

SAAVEDRA, JUANA; Bell HS; Huntington Park, CA; (3); Service Clb; Spanish Clb; Teachers Aide; Chorus; Tennis; Prfct Atten Awd; UCLA; Tchr.

SAAVEDRA, MELISSA; Encinal HS; Alameda, CA; (2); Church Yth Grp; Key Clb; Hon Roll; NHS; Prfct Atten Awd; CCYM; Cngrssnl Schlr Natl Yng Ldrs Conf; Writing.

SABA, ALEXI M; Edison HS; Huntington Beach, CA; (1); Cheerldng; UCSD; Intr Dsgn.

SABADO, DONNA; North HS; Moreno Valley, CA; (4); Office Aide; Rep Jr Cls; Rep Sr Cls; Cheerldng; Gym; Tennis; Cit Awd; High Hon Roll; Pres Acad Fit Awd; Lib Vlntr; Stu Teacher JA; CSF; U CA Riverside; Biomed Sci.

SABADO, JONATHAN YAO; Don Bosco Technical Inst; Monterey Park, CA; (1); 40/244; Boy Scts; Church Yth Grp; Band; Mrchg Band; Hon Roll; Police Explr Sct; Altar Boy.

SABADO, JOSE P; Alisal HS; Salinas, CA; (3); Red Cross Aide; Mrchg Band; Orch; Pep Band; Var Golf; High Hon Roll; Pres Acad Fit Awd; Acad Decathlon Tm; Spllng Bee Tm; CA Schlrshp Fed; UC Santa Barbara; Comp Engr.

SABAH, BABAK; Chaffey HS; Ontario, CA; (2); Wrstlng; Cit Awd; Hon Roll.

SABAS, CIELOMAE A; Seaside HS; Marina, CA; (3); FBLA; Spanish Clb; Hon Roll; Spartan Schlrs Acad Excllnce Recgntn Awd 2 Yrs; Friday Night Live; Nrsng.

SABATO, STEFAN C; Sacred Heart HS; Atherton, CA; (2); Cmnty Wkr; Sec Treas Jr Cls; JV Capt Socr; Tennis; High Hon Roll; Rotary Awd.

SABAWI, ALA S; Granada Hills HS; Granada Hills, CA; (3); 1/34; Off Jr Cls; Hon Roll; UCLA; Medical Doctor.

SABBE, CHRIS A; Foothill HS; Pleasanton, CA; (3); 11/300; Boy Scts; Debate Tm; FBLA; Math Clb; Scholastic Bowl; Service Clb; Variety Show; Rep Jr Cls; Treas Sr Cls; Rep Stu Cncl; Interact Clb Stu Exchnge Pgm Scotland & England; Typng Awd; UCSB; Engrng.

SABBE, CHRISTOPHER; Foothill HS; Pleasanton, CA; (3); 11/296; Boy Scts; Debate Tm; Sec FBLA; Math Clb; Rep Stu Cncl; Intrml Bsktbl; Intrml Socr; JV Trk; High Hon Roll; Hon Roll; Typing Awd; UCSB; Engrng.

SABEH, NICOLE M; Mira Mesa HS; San Diego, CA; (2); Chorus; Mgr(s); Stat Sftbl; JV Tennis; Prfct Atten Awd; Chrch Cmnty Work; UCSD; Ed.

SABELLA, EMILIO A; Palmdale HS; Palmdale, CA; (3); 46/644; Cmnty Wkr; Office Aide; Swmmng; Tennis; Cit Awd; Hon Roll; Prfct Atten Awd; I Speak Arabic I Was Born In The Country Of Jordan; Ucla; Medicine.

SABET, KAREN; Corona HS; Corona, CA; (2); JV Swmmng; Hon Roll; Phy.

SABHERWAL, SUDHIR; Mills HS; Millbrae, CA; (3); Church Yth Grp; Cmnty Wkr; Letterman Clb; Service Clb; Teachers Aide; Varsity Clb; Ftbl; Trk; Wt Lftg; Bus Mgmnt.

SABILLO, MARICEL; Bishop Amat Memorial HS; Baldwin Park, CA; (3); Math Clb; High Hon Roll; NHS; NEDT Awd; Prfct Atten Awd; Xanadu & Silverscreen Clbs; Nrsng.

SABILLO, ROSARIO; Bishop Amat Memorial HS; Baldwin Park, CA; (2); Math Clb; High Hon Roll; NHS; CSF, Xanadu, Slvr Scrn.

SABIN, LISA M; Atwater HS; Atwater, CA; (2); Band; Jazz Band; Mrchg Band; Stat Bsbl; Score Keeper; Hon Roll; Pr Cnslng Trng Pgm; UC San Diego; Psych.

SABLAN, EILEEN A; Montgomery HS; San Diego, CA; (3); Church Yth Grp; Chorus; Swing Chorus; Cit Awd; Hon Roll.

SABLAN, GEORGINA J; Seaside HS; Marina, CA; (2); Church Yth Grp; Dance Clb; Church Choir; High Hon Roll; U Of San Diego; Pedtrcn.

SABLAN, JOHN J; Fair Field HS; Fairfield, CA; (2); Var Tennis; Hon Roll; Empire Lge Tnns Sngls Fnlst 90, Dbls Chmpn 89; Vrsty MVP/Mst Imprvd Plyr; St Anthonys Dining Hll Vlnt; Stanford U; Pre Med.

SABLAN, MARITA; St Patrick-St Vincent HS; Vallejo, CA; (4); 9/148; Church Yth Grp; Ed Nwsp; Rep Stu Cncl; JV Bsktbl; Var Capt Crs Cntry; Var Capt Trk; Hon Roll; Jr Statesmn Am Sec; 1st Rnnr-Up Vallejo Jr Miss 89; Physcs.

SABLE, KERRY L; Carondelet HS; Danville, CA; (3); Church Yth Grp; Cmnty Wkr; Drama Clb; Pep Clb; Ski Clb; Chorus; School Musical; Rep Frsh Cls; Rep Soph Cls; Rep Jr Cls; Theatre.

SABLOSKY, TERRI; Alisal HS; Salinas, CA; (3); Letterman Clb; Office Aide; Varsity Clb; Capt Cheerldng; Crs Cntry; Powder Puff Ftbl; Tennis; Trk; Cit Awd; High Hon Roll; CSF.

SABO, JOE; B C A Palm Springs Christian HS; Desert Hot Sprngs, CA; (2); Cmnty Wkr; Drama Clb; Letterman Clb; Teachers Aide; Band; Chorus; Drm Mjr(t); Bsbl; Ftbl; Score Keeper; U Of M; Music.

SABO, KRISTIN; Valley Christian HS; Pleasanton, CA; (4); Nwsp; Yrbk; Treas Frsh Cls; Pres Soph Cls; Sec Jr Cls; VP Sr Cls; Rep Stu Cncl; Var Capt Cheerldng; High Hon Roll; NHS; CSU; Home Ecnmcs.

SABOL, HELEN LEE; Yucca Valley HS; Joshua Tree, CA; (2); 1/300; Church Yth Grp; Debate Tm; FBLA; Math Clb; NFL; Speech Tm; School Musical; Treas Soph Cls; Pom Pon; High Hon Roll.

SABORIO, MICHELLE R; Academy Of Our Lady Of Peace; San Diego, CA; (4); Church Yth Grp; GAA; Hosp Aide; SADD; School Musical; Var Sftbl; Hon Roll; Cal Poly; Arch.

SABOW, DEIRDRE E; Mater Dei HS; Santa Ana, CA; (2); Rptr Nwsp; Rep Frsh Cls; Rep Soph Cls; Capt Cheerldng; Spec Olympics Vlntr; Yoma Ballet Thtr; Skir; U Of CA; Marine Bio.

SABSOVICH, IGOR A; Washington HS; San Francisco, CA; (4); Chess Clb; Socr; San Francisco ST U; Cmptr.

SACCONE, ROSA E; El Rancho HS; Pico Rivera, CA; (2); USC; Cmptr Prgmr.

SACCUZZO, JENNIFER A; Poway HS; San Diego, CA; (3); Sec SADD; High Hon Roll; Hon Roll; Spanish NHS; Amnesty Intl; CSF; Leos Club; Advanced Placemtn Civilizations Club; UC San Diego; Med.

SACHS, LORI; Don Antonio Lugo HS; Chino Hills, CA; (2); Am Leg Aux Girls St; Temple Yth Grp; Sec Lit Mag; High Hon Roll; NHS; Pres Schlr; Published Poems; Peer Cnslr; Berkley; Writing.

SACHS, REBECCA L; Encina HS; Sacramento, CA; (3); 37/212; Dance Clb; Drama Clb; SADD; Thesps; Drill Tm; School Play; Stage Crew; Cit Awd; Hon Roll; Drama Clb Pres; Stu Of Mnth-Drama Wnnrs Crcl; OR Inst Of Technology.

SACHS, TODD A; La Jolla Country Day HS; Poway, CA; (2); Cmnty Wkr; Key Clb; Ski Clb; Spanish Clb; SADD; Temple Yth Grp; Chorus; School Musical; School Play; VP Frsh Cls.

SACILIOC, RACHELLE M; Granada Hills HS; Northridge, CA; (3); Cmnty Wkr; Hosp Aide; Service Clb; Hon Roll; UCLA.

SACKS, HANNAH; Los Alamitos HS; Los Alamitos, CA; (3); Teachers Aide; Chorus; Church Choir; Color Guard; Crs Cntry; Trk; Hon Roll; NHS; Natl Chrty Leag; Safe Rides Cmmssnr; Stu Gov Pstn; Law.

SACMAN, CHRISTINE; Saint Francis HS; Santa Clara, CA; (1); 95/388; Church Yth Grp; SADD; Church Choir; High Hon Roll; Recognized Best Overall Performer Easter Musical; Bio Engrng.

SADA, JACOB T; Crawford HS; San Diego, CA; (2); 77/383; Church Yth Grp; Office Aide; JV Ftbl; Var Trk; Var Wrstlng.

SADAC, CHRISTOPHER M; Hanford Joint Union HS; Hanford, CA; (1); Bus Profs of Am; FBLA; JV Bsktbl; Wt Lftg; Med.

SADAC, RANDY M; Hanford HS; Hanford, CA; (4); 64/500; VP Band; Jazz Band; Mrchg Band; Pep Band; JV Tennis; San Diego ST U; Pre-Law.

SADAUSKI, MARK A; Poway HS; Poway, CA; (2); Church Yth Grp; Cmnty Wkr; Spanish Clb; Lcrss; High Hon Roll; Prfct Atten Awd; UCSD; Civil Engrng.

SADDI, ROBERT F; Lemoore HS; Lemoore, CA; (3); Band; Mrchg Band; Orch; Math Awd-Algb; Cert Awd-Outstndng Achvt Spnsh I & Bst In Wrld Hstry Clss; Engr.

SADORRA JR, GRACIANO B; Delano HS; Delano, CA; (4); Computer Clb; Key Clb; Phtg Yrbk; JV Trk; High Hon Roll; Prfct Atten Awd; Press Clb; Bnk Of Amer Achvt Awd; Assoc Stu Body Exemplary Stu Awd; CA Poly ST U; Engrng Tech.

SADRO, STEVEN; La Habra HS; Hacienda Hts, CA; (4); Boy Scts; Science Clb; Stu Cncl; Diving; Swmmng; High Hon Roll; Hon Roll; Pres Acad Fit Awd; Pres Schlr; Pres Film Clb; UC Santa Cruz.

SAE LEE, MUANG; Sacramento HS; Sacramento, CA; (2); 28/500; Hosp Aide; Cit Awd; Med.

SAECHAO, GEN; Shasta HS; Redding, CA; (1); FHA; Just Say No Clb; Stu Helping Stu; Commnctns.

SAECHAO, HUN T; Oroville HS; Oroville, CA; (4); 20/284; Church Yth Grp; Cmnty Wkr; Band; Church Choir; Nwsp; Yrbk; VP Stu Cncl; Socr; Vllybl; Cit Awd; CSU Chico; Math.

SAECHAO, KAO FOU; Enterprise HS; Redding, CA; (2); Hon Roll; Prfct Atten Awd.

SAECHAO, LISA S; Lodi HS; Lodi, CA; (2); 3/32; Chorus.

SAECHAO, MEY S; Richmond HS; San Pablo, CA; (1); Church Yth Grp; Dance Clb; Drama Clb; School Play; Stu Cncl; Tennis; Hon Roll; Most Imprvd Musician; Ed Psychlgst.

SAECHAO, MOUANG K; Richmond HS; Richmond, CA; (2); Hon Roll.

SAECHAO, TAWN T; Sacramento HS; Sacramento, CA; (2); 46/505; Intrml Vllybl; Cit Awd; High Hon Roll; Hon Roll; CSUS; Math.

SAECHAO, TON; Enterprise HS; Redding, CA; (4); FBLA; Cit Awd; Hon Roll; Prfct Atten Awd.

SAEDINIA, ARASH; El Camino Real HS; West Hills, CA; (3); Debate Tm; NFL; Spanish Clb; Crs Cntry; Tennis; Pres Acad Fit Awd; Jnr Statesmn Of Amer; CSF; Harvard; Poly Sci.

SAEFONG, TA NAI S; Richmond HS; San Pablo, CA; (2); Math Clb; Math Tm; JV Tennis; High Hon Roll; Hon Roll; Badmntn Awd; U Of Santa Cruz; Med.

SAELEE, CHAN F; River City HS; West Sacramento, CA; (3); Bsktbl; Ftbl; Wt Lftg; Tech.

SAELEE, ERICKA LIEW; River City SR HS; W Sacramento, CA; (1); Church Yth Grp; Hon Roll; Prfct Atten Awd; Nursing.

SAELEE, FAHM; 6601 Guthrie Way HS; North Highlands, CA; (4); 26/268; Var Socr; Var Tennis; Var Vllybl; Cit Awd; Hon Roll; Prfct Atten Awd; CSF; Heald Coll; Comp Sci.

SAELEE, KAE KOVEI; Richmond HS; Richmond, CA; (4); Intnl Clb; Socr; Tennis; Vllybl; Doctor.

SAELEE, LO C; Merced HS North; Merced, CA; (3); Hon Roll.

SAELEE, MEUI F; Fremont HS; Oakland, CA; (2); Band; Hon Roll; Cngrssnl Schlr; Cert Acad Achvt GPA 3.43; Essy Wnnr; Asian Clb Mem; UC Berkeley; Med.

SAELOR, KEN; Armijo HS; Suisun, CA; (3); Debate Tm; Girl Scts; Band; Chorus; Church Choir; School Musical; Cit Awd; High Hon Roll; Prfct Atten Awd; Secy.

SAEMAN, BRIAN J; Paso Robles HS; Templeton, CA; (2); High Hon Roll; CSF; Princpls Hnr Roll; Med.

SAENZ, GILBERTT A; Santa Teresa HS; San Jose, CA; (2); Var Bsbl; Hon Roll; Pres Acad Fit Awd; U Of A; Elec Engrng.

SAENZ, INGRID D; St Joseph HS; Buena Park, CA; (3); Spanish Clb; Hon Roll; Rptr Yrbk; CSF; U Of CA Irvine; Doctor.

SAENZ, MONICA I; Orange Glen HS; Escondido, CA; (3); Spanish Clb; Band; Mrchg Band; Pep Band; School Musical; Ed Yrbk; Cit Awd; Hon Roll; NHS; Advrtsng.

SAEPHAN, CHAN C; El Cerrito HS; Richmond, CA; (2); Hon Roll; CSF; Fri Nght Live; Psych.

SAEPHAN, DA F; C K Mc Clatchy HS; Sacramento, CA; (4); 109/340; Library Aide; Band; Socr; Vllybl; Wrstlng; Hmong Club; Cal Poly; Architecture.

SAEPHAN, LEWCHOY; Calvin Simmons JR HS; Oakland, CA; (1); Stu Cncl; Cit Awd; Hon Roll; Prfct Atten Awd.

SAEPHARN, MUONG X; Sacramento HS; Sacramento, CA; (2); Church Yth Grp; High Hon Roll; Hon Roll; Pres Acad Fit Awd; Sunday Schl Tchr; Sac ST; Elem Tchr.

SAETERN, SAN S; Oakland HS; Oakland, CA; (3); French Clb; Var Bsbl; Hon Roll; Prfct Atten Awd; UC Berkeley; Bus.

SAETEURN, FAHM LINH; Armijo HS; Suisun City, CA; (2); Cit Awd; High Hon Roll; Hon Roll.

SAETEURN, FEY C; Merced HS; Merced, CA; (2); Hon Roll.

SAETEURN, NAI FINH; Merced High School District; Merced, CA; (3); Hon Roll; Fresno ST Coll; Psychology.

SAETEURN, SAAN; Hiram W Johnson HS; Sacramento, CA; (3); Law.

SAETEURN, TAEN F; Merced Union HS District; Merced, CA; (3); High Hon Roll; Hon Roll; Merced Coll; Bus.

SAETIA, TONG; Arcadia HS; Arcadia, CA; (3); 220/639; Church Yth Grp; Red Cross Aide; Service Clb; Church Choir; Bsktbl; Hon Roll; Prfct Atten Awd; Pres Acad Fit Awd; Schlr Athlt Awd; UC Riverside; Bus Adm.

SAEWUE, AH-LUNG; Mark Keppel HS; Monterey Park, CA; (1); Science Clb; Nwsp; Yrbk; Cit Awd; High Hon Roll; Prfct Atten Awd; Untd For Peace; CSF; Cert Excllnc Frgn Lang; UCLA; Bus.

SAEYANG, KAO F; Live Oak HS; Live Oak, CA; (4); 30/50; Boy Scts; Church Yth Grp; Drama Clb; FHA; Pep Clb; Teachers Aide; Band; Drm Mjr(t); Mrchg Band; Pep Band; John Phillip Sousa Band Awd; Bk Of Amer Awd; Devry Phoenix; Elec Tech.

SAFAEI, SANA; John W North HS; Riverside, CA; (4); Intnl Clb; JA; JCL; Key Clb; Spanish Clb; 4-H Awd; Spanish NHS; Asian Stus Union; Jnr Statmnt Of Amer; CSF; CA ST San Bernardino; Pedtrcn.

SAFARIAN, SHABNAM; Torrey Pines HS; San Diego, CA; (3); 161/457; Intnl Clb; Spanish Clb; Gym; Tennis; Hon Roll; Pres Schlr; Tennis Team Coaches Awd; Spelling Bee Awd; Mesa Coll; Bus.

SAFFORD, DARIN J; Ganesha HS; Diamond Bar, CA; (4); #2 In Class; Church Yth Grp; Math Clb; Teachers Aide; Rptr Nwsp; Ftbl; Var Golf; High Hon Roll; Sal; Golf Schlr-Ath, Var Coaches Awd 90; Hgh Hnrs Gmtry Gldn St Exm 88; CA Poly Pmna; Mktg Mgmt.

SAFFORD, DENISE L; Bishop O'dowd HS; Oakland, CA; (3); Hosp Aide; Chorus; Stage Crew; Rep Stu Cncl; High Hon Roll; Hon Roll; Invlvmnt In Cancer Soc Mny Drvs; Vlntrd Vet Clinic; Assist Tchr Day Care/Pre Schl Cntr; UC Davis; Hmn Dev.

SAFHOLM, STEPHANIE A; Bella Vista HS; Fair Oaks, CA; (3); 70/363; Church Yth Grp; Cmnty Wkr; Spanish Clb; School Musical; CSF; Open Door Stu Exch Poland 90; Sacramento Cty Ofc Of Ed Schl Intl Stud; Intl Stud.

SAFI, AHMAD S; Monterey HS; Monterey, CA; (2); Computer Clb; Intnl Clb; Math Clb; Model UN; Science Clb; Teachers Aide; Cit Awd; High Hon Roll; Hon Roll; Stanford; Med.

SAGE, HEIDI ANNE; Valhalla HS; Jamul, CA; (4); 5/412; Pres Sec 4-H; Ed Nwsp; Ed Lit Mag; Kiwanis Awd; Ntl Merit Schol; Amnesty Intl Sec; Amer Acad Achvt Hnr Stu; Robert C Byrd Hnrs Schlrshp; UCSD.

SAGE, JAMIE; Calvary Baptist HS; Fairfield, CA; (4); Church Yth Grp; Pep Clb; Church Choir; School Play; Yrbk; Sec Soph Cls; Sec Jr Cls; Sec Sr Cls; Var L Bsktbl; Var L Sftbl; Maranatha Baptist Bible Coll.

SAGE, LORA A; Manteca HS; Manteca, CA; (2); 4/420; Cheerldng; Hon Roll; Intl Order Of Rainbow Girls-Worthy Advsr; Fresno ST; Ed.

SAGER, LEAH E; St Joihn Ursuline HS; San Francisco, CA; (4); 11/45; Cmnty Wkr; Debate Tm; Intnl Clb; VP JA; Capt Quiz Bowl; Variety Show; Rptr Nwsp; Ed Lit Mag; Rep Jr Cls; Pres Sr Cls; Bk Of Amer Awd; George Ponti Memrl Awd; CA ST Long Beach; Brdcstng.

SAGHEB, SAM; El Camino Real HS; West Hills, CA; (1); JV Ftbl; JV Trk; JV Wrstlng; High Hon Roll; Hon Roll; CSF; UCLA; Medcl.

SAGOUSPE, JULIE; Los Banos HS; Los Banos, CA; (2); Treas FFA; Pep Clb; Ski Clb; Stu Cncl; Cheerldng; Pom Pon; Hon Roll; CSF; Cal-Poly; Dermtlgst.

SAGOUSPE, SASHA E; Madera HS; Madera, CA; (2); Intrml VP Tennis; Hon Roll; Interact; Horizon.

SAGRADO, EMERY J; Edison HS; Fresno, CA; (3); Letterman Clb; Varsity Clb; Band; Intrml Bsktbl; Var L Crs Cntry; Intrml Tennis; JV Var Vllybl; Hon Roll; Pres Acad Fit Awd; Coach Awd Jr Var Vlybl; Most Imprvd Awd Var Cross Cntry; Most Insprtnl Var Cross Cntry; U CA Davis; Med.

SAGRADO, THERESA M; Edison-Computech HS; Fresno, CA; (2); #1 In Class; Cmnty Wkr; Hosp Aide; JCL; Latin Clb; Service Clb; Orch; JV Bsktbl; JV Vllybl; High Hon Roll; CSF; Natl Jr Clsscl Leag Latin Hnr Soc; Jr Statesmen Amer; Fresno Yth Phlhrmnc Orch; Hnr Orch; Stanford U; Med.

SAGREDO, JOHN-VINCENT P; Brawley Union HS; Brawley, CA; (3); SADD; Rptr Nwsp; Rep Jr Cls; Stat Vllybl; Acad Decathalon; UC Berkeley; Jrnlsm.

SAGUN JR, MICHAEL G; Alisal HS; Salinas, CA; (3); Am Leg Boys St; Art Clb; Church Yth Grp; Drama Clb; Office Aide; Spanish Clb; JV Golf; Cit Awd; High Hon Roll; Prfct Atten Awd; Acad Dcthln; CSF; Close Up; Lawyer.

SAGUYOD, IRA M; Woodside HS; Redwood City, CA; (2); German Clb; Stage Crew; Off Soph Cls; Stu Cncl; Capt Cheerldng; Score Keeper; Var Sftbl; Aviation.

SAH, ALANNA ROBIN; Rio Americano HS; Sacramento, CA; (1); 1/269; Dance Clb; Math Tm; Pep Clb; Service Clb; Rep Frsh Cls; Stu Cncl; Capt Cheerldng; High Hon Roll; NHS; Outstndng Stu Of Yr; CSU Sacramento; Elec Engrng.

SAH, SHERILYN S; Rio Americano HS; Sacramento, CA; (3); 50/250; Debate Tm; Intnl Clb; Latin Clb; Math Tm; Speech Tm; Variety Show; Ed Nwsp; Gym; Hon Roll; CSF; Stu Reaching Out; Sacramento ST U; Med.

SAHAGUN, CLARA M; Santa Maria HS; Santa Maria, CA; (2); 80/527; Color Guard; Flag Corp; Pep Band; Prfct Atten Awd; Lgl Asst.

SAHAI, ANANT; Thousand Oaks HS; Thousand Oaks, CA; (4); 1/540; Math Clb; Math Tm; Science Clb; Bausch & Lomb Sci Awd; High Hon Roll; Ntl Merit SF; Pres Acad Fit Awd; Acad Dcthln Hnrs Div; VP India Cltrl Soc Yth Cmmttee; Elec Engrng.

SAHAI, TRICIA NADIRA; Victor Valley HS; Victorville, CA; (2); 16/602; FBLA; Key Clb; Variety Show; JV Capt Cheerldng; Hon Roll; Stu Mnth Soc Stdys & Frnch; CSF; Air Force Acad; Med Tech.

SAHAKIAN, DEBORAH A; Chaminade College Prep; West Hills, CA; (2); Cmnty Wkr; Computer Clb; Library Aide; Band; Variety Show; Cit Awd; High Hon Roll; Masonic Awd; Pres Acad Fit Awd; Knghts Of Vartan Awd Rcpnt; Ptry Wrtng & Rectng; Perfume Cllctr & Tester; CA ST U Northridge; Bus Admin.

SAHARA, JENNIFER Y; Davis SR HS; El Macero, CA; (4); Church Yth Grp; Key Clb; Model UN; Pep Clb; Spanish Clb; SADD; JV Var Cheerldng; Hon Roll; NHS; Ntl Merit Ltr; Japanese Classical Dncng; U Of CA Davis; Aeronaut Engrng.

SAHBA, SCHAULEH V; Casa Roble Fundamental HS; Orangevale, CA; (3); 33/370; French Clb; Pres Frsh Cls; Pres Soph Cls; Rep Jr Cls; Sec Sr Cls; JV Cheerldng; Var L Tennis; Cit Awd; Hon Roll; Pres Acad Fit Awd; Friday Night Live; Congrsnl Yth Ldrshp Concl.

SAHGAL, TRICIA L; Hawthorne HS; Baldwin Park, CA; (3); Varsity Clb; Crs Cntry; Trk; Cit Awd; Hon Roll; Comp Sci.

SAHIBZADA, MEHNAZ; Taft HS; Woodland Hills, CA; (2); Art Clb; Church Yth Grp; French Clb; German Clb; Intnl Clb; Spanish Clb; Temple Yth Grp; Bsktbl; Swmmng; Tennis; Poetry & Short Literacy Wrks; Sketching & Painting; Psychtry.

SAHL, WENDIE L; John Burroughs SR HS; Burbank, CA; (3); Office Aide; Stage Crew; Capt Var Swmmng; Cit Awd; Hon Roll; Water Polo Tm Jr Var Capt; Clb Gymnastics Tm; Math.

SAHOTA, GURBAX K; Hiram Johnson HS; Sacramento, CA; (2); Rptr FBLA; Band; Drm Mjr(t); Mrchg Band; Hon Roll; Asst Drum Majorette; Math Engrng Sc Achvt Club; Phych.

SAHOTA, NEIL; Servite HS; Seal Beach, CA; (2); NHS; CSF; Srvc Certfct Achvt.

SAIAO, WAYNE; J F Kennedy HS; La Palma, CA; (3); Pres Church Yth Grp; La Palma Celebration Of Arts 2nd & 3rd Pl Awd 89; PTSA Physics Awd; Art.

SAILLE, GERARDO G; Los Banos HS; Los Banos, CA; (3); Hon Roll.

SAINI, SUNITA K; Turlock HS; Turlock, CA; (3); 1/600; Am Leg Aux Girls St; Hosp Aide; Bausch & Lomb Sci Awd; French Hon Soc; High Hon Roll; Pres Acad Fit Awd; AFS; Cmnty Wkr; French Clb; Key Clb; Schlstc Title Young Woman Of Yr 1991; PSTA Awd; Sigma Xi Outstndng Stu Sci Awd 1990; U CA Davis; Med.

SAINZ, ROSAURA; Pasadena HS; Azusa, CA; (2).

SAIS III, EDWARD E; Schurr HS; Monterey Park, CA; (4); 103/580; Key Clb; Teachers Aide; Varsity Clb; Capt Var Golf; Hon Roll; Hspnc Schlr Awds Pgm; Prm Cmmtte Chrmn; Pepperdine U; Telecomm.

SAITO, KELLI; Del Mar HS; San Jose, CA; (4); Am Leg Aux Girls St; Church Yth Grp; Dance Clb; Rep Frsh Cls; Rep Soph Cls; Var Fld Hcky; Cit Awd; Peer Cnslng; Mayors Blue Ribbn Cmmtte; V Badminton; San Diego ST U; Child Psych.

SAITO, MICHAEL J; Miramonte HS; Orinda, CA; (2); JCL; Latin Clb; JV Bsktbl; JV Ftbl; Hon Roll; Magna Cum Laude Natl Latin Exam; Cal U.

SAIZ, LAURENDA J; San Gabriel HS; San Gabriel, CA; (1); Church Yth Grp; Cal Tech; Lwyr.

SAIZ, ORLANDO M; Barstow HS; Barstow, CA; (2); Band; Mrchg Band; JV Bsbl; JV Ftbl; High Hon Roll; Hon Roll; Leag Bsbl 2 Time All Star.

SAJAKUL, NISSA S; Colton HS; Grand Terrace, CA; (3); Key Clb; Pep Clb; SADD; Stu Cncl; Hon Roll; Jr NHS; Psych.

SAJID, MOHAMMED; John F Kennedy HS; Sacramento, CA; (2); SADD; Ftbl; Wt Lftg; Cit Awd; UC At Davis; Med.

SAJOR, TONY; Edison HS; Stockton, CA; (1); Band; Mrchg Band; Pep Band; Ftbl; JV Wrstlng; Hon Roll; Collecting Ftbl Cards; Plyng Bsktbl With My Friends; Lifting Weights; Music Teacher.

SAKAI, CINDY Y; Carmont HS; Foster City, CA; (3); Girl Scts; Pres Temple Yth Grp; Band; Sec Stu Cncl; JV Var Cheerldng; Var Vllybl; CA Schlrshp Fed; Asn-Amer Clb Secy; Rd Rbn Wk Essy Cntst 1st Pl.

SAKAI, EDWARD H; Edison HS; Huntington Bch, CA; (3); Letterman Clb; Varsity Clb; Crs Cntry; Socr; Trk; Cross Cntry 87 & 88; Soccer 87; Track Best Distance Rnr 89; Accntng.

SAKAI, JULIAN M; Edison HS; Huntington Beach, CA; (1); Model UN; Octagon Club Cmnty Svc.

SAKAI, MARIKO; Lowell HS; San Francisco, CA; (3); Cmnty Wkr; Red Cross Aide; SADD; Teachers Aide; Orch; Intrml Bsktbl; Intrml Vllybl; Hrsbck Riding; Equestrian.

SAKAKIHARA, RYAN M; Archbishop Mitty HS; Saratoga, CA; (3); Cmnty Wkr; Crs Cntry; Trk; High Hon Roll; Hon Roll; NHS; Chem, Fine Arts, Frgn Lang Awd; Jack ; Jr Olympics, Tri-City Yth Grp Outstndng Athlete 90.

SAKALDASIS, AMY; Henry M Gunn HS; Palo Alto, CA; (4); Am Leg Aux Girls St; Church Yth Grp; SADD; Teachers Aide; Off Soph Cls; Rep Jr Cls; Rep Sr Cls; Stu Cncl; Var Socr; Piano Playing; Safe Ride; Aerobics; UC Santa Barbara; Bus Econ.

SAKAMOTO, SHERYL H; Montebello HS; Montebello, CA; (2); Acpl Chr; Chorus; Church Choir; School Musical; Variety Show; Hon Roll; Princpls Hon Roll; UC Davis; Animals.

SAKATA, KRISTINE M; Hoover HS; Fresno, CA; (3); 1/550; Am Leg Aux Girls St; Church Yth Grp; Sec Soph Cls; Sec Jr Cls; Pres Stu Cncl; Var Cheerldng; Var Gym; Var Capt Tennis; High Hon Roll; Masonic Awd; Hi-Debs Cmnty Svc For Grls; Camp Royal-Rotary Spnsrd Ldrshp Camp; Stu Body Pres.

SAKATA, ROSS; Lodi Acad; Lodi, CA; (3); 2/21; Ski Clb; Acpl Chr; Band; VP Frsh Cls; Pres Soph Cls; Off Jr Cls; Intrml Var Bsbl; Intrml Bsktbl; Intrml Var Vllybl; High Hon Roll; Pacific Union Coll.

SAKEMI, BRIAN M; Indio HS; Indio, CA; (1); French Clb; Var L Swmmng; Wrstlng.

SAKI, KENICH M; Flintridge Preparatory Schl; Pasadena, CA; (3); Service Clb; Ski Clb; Spanish Clb; Var Swmmng; Water Polo; Eagle Scout.

SAKIOKA, CINDY; Marina HS; Midway City, CA; (4); 86/510; VP Church Yth Grp; Key Clb; Service Clb; Lit Mag; Var Bsktbl; JV Tennis; Peer Asstnc League Clb Secy; Preschl Aide; Educ.

SAKO, AARON; Cerritos HS; Cerritos, CA; (4); 30/554; Boy Scts; Church Yth Grp; Treas Service Clb; Hon Roll; NHS; Opt Clb Awd; Pres Acad Fit Awd; Tae Kwon Do Black Belt; Southeast Yth Orgzntn Bsktbl; UC Irvine; Bio Sci.

SAKODA, KEVIN M; Edison HS; Huntington Beach, CA; (4); 10/483; Boy Scts; Pres Church Yth Grp; Key Clb; Model UN; Off Jr Cls; JV Swmmng; Var L Wrstlng; Ntl Merit SF; Yth Ambssdr To Anjo Japan; CSF; Bus Law.

SAKORN, SOMPHAVONE N; Carson HS; Carson, CA; (3); French Clb; Intnl Clb; Drill Tm; Off Jr Cls; Hon Roll; Prfct Atten Awd; CJSF; CSF; Interact Clb; Poltcl Sci.

SAKOU, KIYOKO; Thomas Downey HS; Modesto, CA; (2); Var Bsbl; Var Bsktbl; MVP Bsbl; Modesto JC; Lang Tchr.

SAKULPONGYUENYONG, DUMRONG; Esperanza HS; Yorba Linda, CA; (4); Variety Show; High Hon Roll; Hon Roll; NHS; UCI; Med.

SAKURAI, TIM M; Marina HS; Huntington Beach, CA; (3); Boy Scts; Cmnty Wkr; Swmmng; Wrstlng; High Hon Roll; Hon Roll; Surfing; Engrng.

SALAHIEH, SHAMS; Covina HS; Covina, CA; (2); French Clb; Band; Mrchg Band; Bsbl; Bsktbl; Crs Cntry; High Hon Roll; Hon Roll; Prfct Atten Awd; Bsbl Fan Clb; USC; Bus.

SALAIS, JOSE L; Calexico HS; Calexico, CA; (3); Math Tm; Var Socr; Var Trk; 4-H Awd; Stu Of Mnth Engl; Var Athl Awd Soccer; Bus Ed Awd Typing; Comm.

SALAKI, SHIRLEY D; Pomona Adventist JR Acad; Fontana, CA; (1); 3/10; Church Yth Grp; Teachers Aide; Band; Ed Yrbk; Sec Frsh Cls; Sec Stu Cncl; Prfct Atten Awd; Excllnce Engl Awd; Excllnce Typng Awd Spd & Accuracy; Nurse.

SALAMANCA, GRACE M; Bishop Amat Memorial HS; Azusa, CA; (3); Hon Roll; Photo Clb; Barkada Clb Filipino Clb; Bus Admin.

SALAMAT, JENNIFER ANN; Sweetwater Union HS; Costa Mesa, CA; (4); Art Clb; Church Yth Grp; Science Clb; SADD; Teachers Aide; Cit Awd; High Hon Roll; JETS Awd; NHS; Filipino Accnts Outstndng Grad Trphy; Outstndng Ecnmc Stu Awd; Sweetwater Almni Schlrshp; Southern CA Coll; Accntng.

SALAO, ALVIN D; Saint Anthony HS; Long Beach, CA; (2); Bsktbl; JV Ftbl; Var Score Keeper; Var Trk; JV Vllybl; Cal ST Long Beach; Bus.

SALAPARE, ROWELA; Don Antonio Lugo HS; Chino, CA; (2); VP Church Yth Grp; German Clb; Off Soph Cls; Cit Awd; High Hon Roll; Pres Acad Fit Awd; CSF; Asian Clb VP; UCLA; Pediatrics.

SALAS, ANNALEE; Narbonne HS; Torrance, CA; (2); Office Aide; Chorus; Hon Roll; Prfct Atten Awd; CA Jnr Schlrshp Fed; Intrior Dsgn.

SALAS, DESIREE L; Escondido HS; Escondido, CA; (4); Letterman Clb; Varsity Clb; Yrbk; Stu Cncl; Var VP Crs Cntry; Powder Puff Ftbl; Var Capt Trk; Wt Lftg; Hon Roll; Pres Acad Fit Awd; Schlr Athlt; MESA; Phys Thrpy.

SALAS, KATHERINE A; Temecula Valley HS; Murrieta, CA; (2); Chorus; Hon Roll; AZ ST; Lwyr.

SALAS, KATHLEEN RENAE; Vintage HS; Vallejo, CA; (3); Church Yth Grp; Cmnty Wkr; Band; Church Choir; Mrchg Band; Pep Band; School Musical; Pres Jr Cls; Key Clb; Pep Clb; Bay Area Chamorro Kids Clb; 101% Awd Chrldng Amrt Awd; Mst Dedctd Woodwind; U Of Pacific; Music.

SALAS, MICKEY R; Hogan SR HS; Vallejo, CA; (2); Hon Roll; Golden St Exam Algebra Hnrs.

SALAS, NANCY C; St Marys Acad; Inglewood, CA; (2); GAA; Service Clb; Stage Crew; Var Bsktbl; Var Capt Vllybl; Hon Roll; Spanish NHS; United Ltn Amer Stus; Spnsh Hnr Soc; Ca Schlrshp Fed.

SALAS, RANDY K; Ramona HS; Riverside, CA; (2); Engr.

SALAS, ROBERT; Righetti HS; Santa Maria, CA; (3); 11/354; Am Leg Boys St; Math Tm; Office Aide; Scholastic Bowl; Water Polo Ltr; HOBY Awd; Yth For Undrstndng Smmr Belgium 90; Sci.

SALAS, SERGIO; Castle Park HS; Chula Vista, CA; (1); 19/200; Art Clb; Ftbl; Tennis; Wt Lftg; Cit Awd; USC; Arch.

SALAS, TARA T; Fairfield HS; Fairfield, CA; (2); Chorus; Jazz Band; Rep Frsh Cls; Hon Roll; U CA Davies; Vet.

SALAS, VICTOR M; Indio HS; La Quinta, CA; (1); Naval Acad; Avtr.

SALAS, WALTER A; Los Angeles HS; Los Angeles, CA; (4); 4/550; Church Yth Grp; Science Clb; Service Clb; Spanish Clb; Teachers Aide; 4-H Awd; High Hon Roll; Hon Roll; Prfct Atten Awd; Best Latn SR; Stu Of Mnth; Prncpl Awd; UC Irvine; Cvl Engrng.

SALAS, YESENIA; Lindsay HS; Lindsay, CA; (4); Drama Clb; Office Aide; Teachers Aide; Band; Color Guard; Mrchg Band; School Play; Friday Nite Live; Natural Helprs; Law.

SALAS-TORRESDEY, BLANCA E; Samuel F B Morse HS; San Diego, CA; (3); Church Yth Grp; FTA; Spanish Clb; Teachers Aide; Church Choir; Sch, Cmnty Svc Awd; Leonard Sheer Attitude Awd; Ldrshp Awd CSF Club; Atty.

SALATA, KATHY E; Bishop Amat Memorial HS; Diamond Bar, CA; (4); Hosp Aide; School Play; Cheerldng; Worked 2 Yrs; Cal Poly Romona; Advertiser.

SALAUN, SHANNON M; Petaluma HS; Petaluma, CA; (4); 79/300; AFS; Church Yth Grp; Pres VP 4-H; Office Aide; Spanish Clb; Rptr Nwsp; Intrml Gym; JV Powder Puff Ftbl; Intrml Swmmng; 4-H Awd; Rep CA Natl Make It Yourself Wool Cont Jr Wnnr; Fashion Instof Desgn; Fashn Dsg.

SALAZAR, ADRIANA M; Workman HS; Valinda, CA; (2); Church Yth Grp; Pres Drama Clb; School Play; Sec Frsh Cls; JV Sftbl; U La Verne; Crmnl Law.

SALAZAR, ALEJANDRO; Ventura HS; Ventura, CA; (3); Church Yth Grp; Model UN; VP Frsh Cls; Intrml Socr; JV Trk; French Hon Soc; Hon Roll; Horse Jmpng Intl Cmptn; Outdoor Occupation Animals.

SALAZAR, ANDREW T; Mt Whitney HS; Visalia, CA; (3); JV Crs Cntry; JV Trk; Hon Roll.

SALAZAR, COCO; San Fernando HS; Pacoima, CA; (4); Dance Clb; Drill Tm; Yrbk; Sec Sr Cls; Pres Stu Cncl; Capt Cheerldng; Powder Puff Ftbl; Cit Awd; Hon Roll; Ephebian; Deservng Stu Awd; Ovrl Excllnc Chrldng Trphy; U Of Southern CA.

SALAZAR, DONA R; Chino HS; Chino, CA; (3); 91/561; Drama Clb; Pres FHA; Science Clb; Teachers Aide; Stu Cncl; Hon Roll; Span & Eng Awds; HS Hme Eco Silver Spur Awd Wnnr; Bus Admin.

SALAZAR, ERIC O; Strathmore Union HS; Strathmore, CA; (3); 25/83; Art Clb; Cmnty Wkr; Computer Clb; English Clb; Letterman Clb; Science Clb; Spanish Clb; Varsity Clb; Hist Awd; HTI Tech Sch; Elec Tech.

SALAZAR, GILBERT P; L B Woodrow Wilson HS; Long Beach, CA; (3); Church Yth Grp; Cmnty Wkr; Band; Mrchg Band; JV Var Crs Cntry; Intrml Var Trk; Hon Roll; MVP Soph Trck 88; Pres Phys Ftns Awd 87; Mst Prmsng Crs Cntry 88; FIDM; Fashn Desgn.

SALAZAR, GINA M; L B Woodrow Wilson HS; Long Beach, CA; (4); Art Clb; Cmnty Wkr; Office Aide; Drill Tm; Off Jr Cls; Off Sr Cls; Hon Roll; NHS; HUG Clb; LBUSD Medalln Awd; Advrtsng Art Cert Achvt Awd; Commrcl Art.

SALAZAR, GLENDA I; Pasadena HS; Pasadena, CA; (1); Spanish Clb; Princpals Hnr Roll; UCLA.

SALAZAR, HENRY; Eisenhower HS; Rialto, CA; (2); Boy Scts; Band; Hnr Rl; UCLA; Lawyer.

SALAZAR, JORGE E; Schurr HS; Los Angeles, CA; (4); 128/620; Pres VP Church Yth Grp; Spanish Clb; VICA; Church Choir; School Musical; Cit Awd; Hon Roll; Prfct Atten Awd; CA ST Polytech U-Pomona; Engr.

SALAZAR, LUCRECIA; Paraclete HS; Bakersfield, CA; (2); Drama Clb; JA; SADD; Hon Roll; Med.

SALAZAR, MANUEL S; John F Kennedy HS; Sacramento, CA; (2); 207/525; JV Ftbl; Pres Acad Fit Awd; Air Force.

SALAZAR, MARIA; Rosary HS; La Habra, CA; (2); French Clb; Pep Clb; Ski Clb; Spanish Clb; High Hon Roll; Hon Roll; Soph Cabinet; CA Schlrshp Fed; JSA Club; UC Irvine; Accntng.

SALAZAR, MARISELA; Mc Farland HS; Mc Farland, CA; (3); Am Leg Aux Girls St; Church Yth Grp; Computer Clb; FCA; Rptr FBLA; VP FTA; Math Clb; Office Aide; SADD; VICA; CA Schlrshp Federation; Student Board Member 89-90; Mock Trial Cmptn 89-90; CSUB; Medicine.

SALAZAR, MONICA; Oceanside HS; Oceanside, CA; (3); 1/287; Acpl Chr; Drill Tm; Var Cheerldng; JV Socr; JV Tennis; Hon Roll; Off Frsh Cls; Rep Soph Cls; Off Jr Cls; CSF; Jnr Vrsty Acad Lgue; Hstry.

SALAZAR, NORMA P; San Gabriel Mission HS; El Monte, CA; (2); 12/139; Drama Clb; French Clb; GAA; Math Clb; Science Clb; Hon Roll; Prfct Atten Awd; Mssn Merit; CA Schlrshp Fed; Psych.

SALAZAR, OSCAR O; Mountain View HS; El Monte, CA; (2); SADD; Club Juvenil; Math.

SALAZAR, RITA M; Escondido HS; Escondido, CA; (3); Letterman Clb; Pep Clb; Science Clb; Varsity Clb; Var Bsktbl; Palomar; Teacher.

SALAZAR, ROMAN C; Banning HS; Banning, CA; (3); Church Yth Grp; Model UN; Spanish Clb; Treas Jr Cls; Capt Var Ftbl; Var Trk; VP Wt Lftg; Hon Roll; NHS; Rotary Awd; Rewrite Schl Cnst; RYLA Rtry Yth Ldrshp Awds; Hnr Guard; Riverside U; Pre Med.

SALAZAR, RONALDO L; Pater Noster HS; Los Angeles, CA; (1); Prfct Atten Awd.

SALAZAR, SUSANA E; John Glenn HS; Norwalk, CA; (4); 32/290; Science Clb; Sec Spanish Clb; High Hon Roll; MESA Day Spllng Chmpn; MESA Club; Intrcctnl Aide; UC Irvine; Bio.

SALAZAR, SUSANA G; Roosevelt HS; Los Angeles, CA; (3); Var Bsbl; Prin Hnr Rl; Hnr Rl; CA ST Los Angeles; Nrsng.

SALAZAR, SUZANNE; Saint Elizabeth HS; Oakland, CA; (4); Church Yth Grp; GAA; Ed Yrbk; Pres Jr Cls; Pres Stu Cncl; Hon Roll; NHS; Pres Acad Fit Awd; Cert Of Life Mbrshp CA Schlrshp Fed; Prin Awd 88-89; Campus Ministry; CA ST U Hayward; Bus Admin.

SALAZAR, TED M; James Logan HS; Union City, CA; (3); JV Bsbl; Var JV Ftbl; High Hon Roll; Hon Roll; Elec Engrng.

SALAZAR, THERESA L; Saint Paul HS; Whittier, CA; (3); Art Clb; Drill Tm; Graphic Art.

SALCEDA, MARIA G; Napa HS; Napa, CA; (2); Church Yth Grp; Intnl Clb; Spanish Clb; Swmmng; Cit Awd; Hon Roll; Supt Schlr; CSF Club; Long Beach ST; Intl Rltns.

SALCEDO, CHRISTINA; Tranquillity HS; Cantua Creek, CA; (3); Church Yth Grp; FTA; Spanish Clb; Hon Roll; Friday Night Live Club; MECHA Club; CA ST U; Ed.

SALCEDO, DANIEL; Serrano HS; Baldy Mesa, CA; (3); 1/213; Am Leg Boys St; Spanish Clb; Cit Awd; High Hon Roll; Pres Acad Fit Awd; Spanish NHS; CSF; Chicano/Latino Yth Ldrshp Conf; Jr Hnr Guard; Victor Valley Coll; Teaching.

SALCEDO, JUDY A; Mountian View HS; El Monte, CA; (4); Church Yth Grp; Pep Clb; Spanish Clb; Teachers Aide; Church Choir; Cit Awd; High Hon Roll; Hon Roll; CSF; Woman Achvt Awd; UCLA; Bio.

SALCEDO, KATHY; La Mirada HS; La Mirada, CA; (4); 48/332; FBLA; Key Clb; Band; Jazz Band; Mrchg Band; Orch; Pep Band; School Play; Cit Awd; Hon Roll; Yth Gvrnmnt; SOS; Ebel, Pta, La Mirada Med Ctr Schlrshps; UCLA; Bio.

SALCEDO, LUMINAIDA D; Sweetwater HS; National City, CA; (3); French Clb; Drill Tm; Cit Awd; Hon Roll; Engr.

SALCEDO, MARIBETH P; Edison HS; Stockton, CA; (3); Latin Clb; Math Clb; Science Clb; Intrml Tennis; Sec NHS; CSF; Meet A Mentor Pgm; CARE Clb; U Of The Pacific; Comp Sci.

SALCEDO, NOE; East Union HS; Lathrop, CA; (2); Intrml Bsktbl; Intrml Ftbl; UOP; Doctor.

SALCIDO, CLAUDIA; Mountain View HS; El Monte, CA; (1); Band; Mrchg Band; Pep Band; Lit Mag; UCLA; Pedtrcns.

SALCIDO, ERIKA; Indio HS; La Quinta, CA; (1); Hon Roll; U CA Santa Barbara; Comm.

SALCIDO, ESMERALDA M; Leuzinger HS; Hawthorne, CA; (3); Church Yth Grp; Cmnty Wkr; Hosp Aide; Spanish Clb; Hon Roll; Prfct Atten Awd; APP I Pgm In Schl; CCD Aide; Ped.

SALCIDO, JESS M; Hueneme HS; Oxnard, CA; (2); 101/503; JV Ftbl; Wt Lftg; Cit Awd; Bus.

SALCIDO, RUDY V; Don Bosco Technical Inst; Montebello, CA; (3); Letterman Clb; Varsity Clb; Band; Mrchg Band; Orch; Hon Roll; NHS; Studying Auto Tech; Outstndng Frosh Band 87-88; 1st Chair Awd Band; Muscnshp Awd 88-90; Cal ST LA; Auto Tech.

SALDANA, ALEX C; Watsonville HS; Watsonville, CA; (2); 200/765; Computer Clb; French Clb; Science Clb; Hon Roll; Prfct Atten Awd; CA Prtnrshp Pgm; UCLA; Med.

SALDANA, ANTOINETTE; Colton HS; Colton, CA; (4); 60/320; Church Yth Grp; Sec DECA; Pep Clb; Teachers Aide; Var L Cheerldng; Var L Pom Pon; Hon Roll; Prfct Atten Awd; Cert Of Achvt Fshn Mrchndsng DECA; Infnt Cntr At Colton HS Schlrshp; San Salvador Chrch Schlrshp; Valley Coll; Nrs.

SALDANA, JANICE M; Chino HS; Chino, CA; (2); VP Soph Cls; Rep Stu Cncl; Stat Ftbl; Mgr(s); JV Cmnty Wkr; Sulver Spur Awd Sci; Advsry Cncl Shrff Dept Drug Use/Life Abuase Pgm; Airline Pilot.

SALDANA, JANINA R; Calexico HS; Spring Valley, CA; (4); Am Leg Aux Girls St; Church Yth Grp; Office Aide; Teachers Aide; Powder Puff Ftbl; El Centro Deanery Rep Diocesan Youth Cncl; Peer Clslng Clb VP; HS Rep Imperial Vly Peer Cnslng Assn; San Diego ST U; Religion.

SALDANA, MAGGIE; Woodlake Union HS; Woodlake, CA; (2); Pep Clb; Hon Roll; Mexican-Amer Yth Assn; Frgn Lang Awd; Stu Nurse Aide; Sequoias Coll; Child Care.

SALDANA, MARIA ISABEL; Saddleback HS; Santa Ana, CA; (3); Drama Clb; FBLA; German Clb; SADD; Hspnc Soc; Grls Leag; Cal ST Fullerton; Lgl Secy.

SALDANA, YOLANDA; Leuzinger HS; Lennox, CA; (3); Flag Corp; Mrchg Band; Rep Yrbk; Rep Soph Cls; Rep Jr Cls; Rep Sr Cls; Sec Stu Cncl; Cheerldng; Prfct Atten Awd; U Of CA Los Angeles; Med.

SALDANHA, MANUEL D; Tracy Joint Union HS; Tracy, CA; (2); Church Yth Grp; Debate Tm; Math Clb; Math Tm; Speech Tm; JV Ftbl; Var Trk; High Hon Roll; Goldn St Math Awd Alg High Hnrs; 1st Prz Wnnr San Joaquin Cnty Essay Cont; Sci Fair Awds; Engrng.

SALDAVIA, APRIL M; East Union HS; Lathrop, CA; (2); 127/431; French Clb; Band; Mrchg Band; Orch; Pep Band; UC Davis; Phy Thrpy.

SALDIVAR, APRIL L; North HS; Bakersfield, CA; (3); Church Yth Grp; Cmnty Wkr; Dance Clb; JA; Ski Clb; Church Choir; Color Guard; Drill Tm; Hon Roll; Biola U; Reg Nrs.

SALDIVAR, CHRISTIAN; King City Joint Union HS; King City, CA; (3); Teachers Aide; Var L Bsbl; L Var Ftbl; Var L Socr; Hon Roll; JV Ftbl MVP; JV Bsbl Team MVP; Phys Ed.

SALDIVAR, JOHNNY; Dinuba HS; Dinuba, CA; (2); French Hon Soc; Hon Roll; Golden St Exam Awd; Industrial Arts Awd.

SALDIVAR, OSCAR L; Fontana HS; Fontana, CA; (3); 172/1035; Var Ftbl; Socr; Trk; Var Wrstlng; Hon Roll; Cal ST Poly U; Aeronautic Tech.

SALDIVAR, STEPHANIE A; Bullard HS; Fresno, CA; (2); FCA; Mrchg Band; Bsktbl; Sftbl; Pepperdine; Med.

SALDIVAR, VICTORIA A; East HS; Bakersfield, CA; (3); SADD; Teachers Aide; Pres Hlth Careers Acad; Interior Desgn.

SALE, ADAM; Mercy HS; Red Bluff, CA; (3); Sec Key Clb; Science Clb; Varsity Clb; Acpl Chr; Chorus; School Musical; Yrbk; Stu Cncl; Var Capt Bsbl; Hon Roll; Friday Nit Live Pres; Rotary Ldrshp Camp Royal; Natl Educl Dev Test; Cal Poly; Engrng.

SALE, JEANIE; Manor Baptist HS; San Leandro, CA; (4); 2/6; Church Yth Grp; Office Aide; Teachers Aide; School Play; Yrbk; Pres Stu Cncl; Var Bsktbl; Var L Cheerldng; Score Keeper; Var Vllybl; Psych.

SALE, ROBERT; Carson HS; Carson, CA; (3); Church Yth Grp; Bsktbl; Ftbl; Wt Lftg; Cit Awd; Bus.

SALEH, LOTF M; Pittsburg HS; Pittsburg, CA; (1); Chorus; Sftbl; Hon Roll; Doctor.

SALEH, NANCY S; Mater Dei HS; Huntington Bch, CA; (3); Treas Church Yth Grp; Cmnty Wkr; Hosp Aide; CSF; Campus Ministry; Partnership Pgm; Frnch Hnrs Pgm; UCI; Pharmacology.

SALEM, ANNEVA ANGELA YANCHA; Tulare Union HS; Tulare, CA; (3); 37/401; Cmnty Wkr; Drama Clb; JA; Pep Clb; Speech Tm; SADD; Pres Frsh Cls; VP Soph Cls; Sec Jr Cls; Rep Stu Cncl; Pres Acadmcs Aawd; Camp Royal Rotary; Cngrssnl Yth Ldrshp Schlr; UCLA; Brdcst Jrnlsm.

SALEM, AUSA ASTERIA YANCHA; Tulare Union HS; Tulare, CA; (4); Church Yth Grp; Hosp Aide; Pep Clb; SADD; School Musical; Pres Frsh Cls; Treas Sr Cls; Stu Cncl; Var Cheerldng; Hon Roll; Miss Philippine Wknd 88; Sngldr Squad Lttr; CA ST U.

SALERNO, SALLYANNE; Los Angeles Baptist HS; Sepulveda, CA; (3); Church Yth Grp; Drill Tm; Sftbl; Hon Roll; Work In Office; Nrsng.

SALERNO, SUZANNE C; Temple City HS; Temple City, CA; (2); Church Yth Grp; Cmnty Wkr; Girl Scts; Key Clb; Hon Roll; NHS; Pres Schlr; Jobs Dtrs Mem; Explorer Scouts BSA; Cngrssnl Schlr CA Rep; Tutor; UCLA; Med.

SALES, FERMINA; East Union HS; Manteca, CA; (4); 12/264; French Clb; Hosp Aide; VP Science Clb; Service Clb; Nwsp; Rep Soph Cls; Treas Jr Cls; Treas Stu Cncl; JV Var Cheerldng; Hon Roll; Asian Clb Treas; Philippine Std Allnce VP; St Anthonys Journy Confirmtn Grp; CCD Facltr; Bus.

SALES, JULIETTE; East Union HS; Manteca, CA; (3); 10/315; Office Aide; Yrbk; Var Cheerldng; Hon Roll; Prfct Atten Awd; U CA; Bus Adm.

SALES, PERRY J; Moreau HS; Hayward, CA; (3); Cmnty Wkr; Rep Frsh Cls; Rep Soph Cls; VP Stu Cncl; Powder Puff Ftbl; Hon Roll.

SALFITI, REEM S; A Lincoln HS; San Francisco, CA; (3); Close Up Pgm; Bowlng League; New Amers Clb; Chico Exchnge Stu Pgm; San Francisco ST U; Comp Engr.

SALGADO, ELIZABETH M; Hamilton Union HS; Orland, CA; (3); Church Yth Grp; FFA; FHA; Spanish Clb; Stu Cncl; Co-Capt Bsktbl; Sftbl; Trk; Vllybl; Wt Lftg; FHA Chap VP & Pres, CA St VP; Chem.

SALGADO, ENRIQUE; Washington Preparatory HS; Los Angeles, CA; (3); Band; Tennis; Hon Roll; Prfct Atten Awd; Engrng.

SALGADO, LILLIAN; Central Union HS; Seely, CA; (2); 107/697; Office Aide; Band; Mrchg Band; Pep Band; Hon Roll; UC Davis; Psych.

SALGADO, MARIA S; Bell HS; Huntington Park, CA; (3); Key Clb; Band; Mrchg Band; Sftbl; Tennis; All-League JV Sftbl; Mount St Marys Coll; Ed.

SALGADO, MICHELLINE C; Franklins JR HS; Vallejo, CA; (1); Math Tm; Hon Roll; Comp Engrng.

SALGADO, MIGUEL; San Diego HS; San Diego, CA; (3); Capt Vllybl; Cit Awd; San Diego ST U; Physics.

SALGADO, NIDIA S; Modesto HS; Modesto, CA; (3); Math Clb; Chrch Grp; MSS; Interior Dcrtr.

SALGADO, REBECCA A; Calexico HS; Calexico, CA; (2); Church Yth Grp; Girl Scts; Pep Clb; Treas Rep SADD; JV Rep Cheerldng; JV Tennis; On City Swim Tm; Teen Work Conf; Soroptomist S Club; Law.

SALIB, MARLENE KAMAL; Holy Family HS; Glendale, CA; (3); Art Clb; Church Yth Grp; Cmnty Wkr; Drama Clb; Library Aide; VP Model UN; Office Aide; School Play; Hon Roll; Prfct Atten Awd; CSF; Med.

SALIM, ALI; Flintridge Prep Schl; Sunland, CA; (4); 1/100; Cmnty Wkr; Debate Tm; Hosp Aide; JCL; Key Clb; Latin Clb; Ed Lit Mag; Cit Awd; High Hon Roll; Hon Roll; Hnr Stu Of Yr 88-89; Runnr Up Hnr Stu 87; NCTE Awd 89; Peer Cnslr 89; Med.

SALIM, CYNTHIA E; Pacifica HS; Garden Grv, CA; (3); 42/240; Dance Clb; Ed Yrbk; JV Socr; Hon Roll; CSF; Ecology Clb Sec; U CA; Humanities.

SALINAS, ADRIANA L; Delano HS; Mc Farland, CA; (3); Church Yth Grp; SADD; Acpl Chr; Drill Tm; Flag Corp; Mrchg Band; Bsktbl; Mgr Ftbl; Score Keeper; Sftbl; MVP Sftbl; Mktng.

SALINAS, BECKY; Orestimba HS; Newman, CA; (1); Church Yth Grp; Cmnty Wkr; GAA; Girl Scts; Spanish Clb; SADD; Var Bsktbl; Var Sftbl; JV Vllybl; Hon Roll; CSF; CA Poly; Teacher.

SALINAS, DAVID; North Hollywood HS; North Hollywood, CA; (4); JV Bsbl; Hon Roll; Eng.

SALINAS, LUIS L; Kingsburg HS; Kingsburg, CA; (3); 23/210; Chess Clb; Church Yth Grp; Computer Clb; FCA; Math Clb; Mu Alpha Theta; Band; Jazz Band; Socr; Hon Roll; Fresno Pacific Coll; Bus.

SALINAS, MARK P; Valhalla HS; El Cajon, CA; (2); 120/800; Church Yth Grp; Cmnty Wkr; Spanish Clb; Church Choir; Wt Lftg; Hon Roll; Prfct Atten Awd; Golden St Exam Algebra Schl Recognition; UC San Diego; Telecmmnctns Eng.

SALINAS, MARTIN; Pater Noster HS; Los Angeles, CA; (2); Cmnty Wkr; Spanish Clb; Crs Cntry; Socr; Vllybl; Hon Roll; Prfct Atten Awd; Comp Engrng.

SALINAS, REBECCA; Orosi HS; Cutler, CA; (3); Spanish Clb; SADD; Nrsng.

SALINAS, STEPHANIE A; Lindsay HS; Lindsay, CA; (1); Church Yth Grp; Pep Clb; Church Choir; JV Bsktbl; JV Cheerldng; JV Powder Puff Ftbl; Pres Frsh Cls; Rep Stu Cncl; Fri Night Live; Dsplnry Cmmtte; Fresno ST U; Psych.

SALINDONG, ANTHONY P; Beyer HS; Modesto, CA; (3); Wt Lftg; Var L Wrstlng; Cit Awd; Hon Roll; Prfct Atten Awd; Friday Night Live SSAD; Tm Capt Vrsty Wrstlng Tm 90-91; Otstndng Athletic Awd Most Imprvd 89-90; MJC; Criminology.

SALISBURY, DAVE W; Bakersfield HS; Bakersfield, CA; (3); 29/600; Church Yth Grp; Key Clb; Science Clb; Varsity Clb; JV Var Bsbl; Var Vllybl; Hon Roll; Ntl Merit Ltr; Art Awd; Surfriders Fnd; Greenpeace Mem; Bus Admin.

SALISBURY, HEATHER E; Lutheran HS; Orange, CA; (2); Church Yth Grp; Band; Pep Band; Var L Crs Cntry; Var L Trk; Runner Up CIF Acad Awds Pgm; Eng.

SALISBURY, LAURA A; Lodi HS; Lodi, CA; (3); 7/531; Art Clb; Key Clb; Letterman Clb; Sec Scholastic Bowl; Spanish Clb; Sec VICA; Stu Cncl; Var Capt Bsktbl; JV Var Sftbl; JV Var Vllybl; League Bsktbl Champ; Girls Allstate Awd; Gold Medal Regions Mech Drftng; Cal Poly; Engrng.

SALISBURY, MICHAELE; West Hills HS; Santee, CA; (2); 6/300; Drill Tm; Ed Nwsp; Off Soph Cls; Stu Cncl; Cit Awd; High Hon Roll; Jrnlst Of Yr San Diego Union-Tribune; Gldn St Exam Hnrs, Geo; Human Rltns Clb; UC Berkeley; Archt.

SALIZZONI, JEREMY; Eureka SR HS; Eureka, CA; (1); Church Yth Grp; Ski Clb; SADD; JV Ftbl; JV Trk; JV Wt Lftg; Poetry; Cmmrcl Art; Humboldt Sst U; Art.

SALLADE, DIONE L; La Mirada HS; La Mirada, CA; (4); 2/333; Key Clb; Drill Tm; Stage Crew; Ed Yrbk; Stu Cncl; JV Tennis; Ntl Merit SF; NEDT Awd; Pres Acad Fit Awd; Sal; CSF Sealbearer; Recog Soc Of Women Engrs; Yth In Govt; Cal Poly-San Luis Obispo; Arch.

SALLADIN, JEFFREY L; Southern CA Christian HS; Buena Park, CA; (2); Church Yth Grp; NFL; Speech Tm; School Play; VP Frsh Cls; Sec Soph Cls; Pres Jr Cls; JV Capt Ftbl; Wrstlng; High Hon Roll; Mst Insprtnl JV Ftbl Plyr; Bible.

SALLEE, CHRIS T; Valley Christian HS; Santa Maria, CA; (4); 3/17; Church Yth Grp; Band; Pep Band; Ed Yrbk; Stu Cncl; Var JV Bsbl; Hon Roll; NEDT Awd; Pres Acad Fit Awd; CA Schlrshp Fed; Pensacola Chrstn Coll; Mech Eng.

SALMAN, DANIEL; Christian Brother HS; Sacramento, CA; (4); 8/126; Am Leg Boys St; French Clb; Math Tm; Rep Jr Cls; Treas Stu Cncl; JV Bsktbl; JV Var Trk; Elks Awd; High Hon Roll; Prfct Atten Awd; Stu Rchng Out.

SALMANS, AMY J; La Reina HS; Westlake Village, CA; (3); 2/72; Church Yth Grp; French Clb; Scholastic Bowl; Service Clb; Rptr Yrbk; Treas Frsh Cls; Rep Jr Cls; French Hon Soc; High Hon Roll; Stu Yr; Knwldg Mstrs Open; Sci Plympd Eng; Med.

SALMON, CADE A; Del Campo HS; Fair Oaks, CA; (3); Boy Scts; Church Yth Grp; Dance Clb; German Clb; Var Trk; JV Vllybl; Cit Awd; Pres Acad Fit Awd; Eagle Scout; Brigham Young U; Orthdntcs.

SALO, PATRICK K; Elk Grove HS; Elk Grove, CA; (1); Science Clb; High Hon Roll; U CA Davis Schlrshp; MESA Hnr; U CA Davis Prfssr Apprntce; Stanford; Elctrncs Engrng.

SALOKANGAS, KATI MARIA; Salinas HS; Finland; (4); AFS; GAA; Intnl Clb; Ski Clb; SADD; Varsity Clb; Treas Chorus; Var Capt Bsktbl; Var Crs Cntry; Var Powder Puff Ftbl; 89-90 Central Coast Sctn Hnr Choir; 89-90 AFS Intl Exchnge Stu Finland; Stanford; Intl Law.

SALOM, BRANDON E; Fremont HS; Sunnyvale, CA; (2); Debate Tm; NFL; Speech Tm; Sec Jr Cls; JV Ftbl; JV Trk; UC.

SALOMON, LINDA; Schurr HS; Montebello, CA; (2); Church Yth Grp; Office Aide; Pep Clb; VP Frsh Cls; Rep Soph Cls; Cheerldng; Pom Pon; Hon Roll; Prom Cmmtte; Stanford; Commnctns.

SALOMON, MICHA N; Berkeley HS; Berkeley, CA; (3); JV Wrstlng; High Hon Roll; Hon Roll; Ntl Merit Ltr; Bd Mem Pltclly Non-Partisan Natl Znst Yth Mvmnt Clb Ldr.

SALOMON, TERESA; Calistoga HS; Calistoga, CA; (2); High Hon Roll; Hon Roll.

SALOMONE, JOHN R; Antioch HS; Antioch, CA; (4); 15/610; Computer Clb; Mu Alpha Theta; Ski Clb; Spanish Clb; Teachers Aide; Band; Gym; High Hon Roll; Pres Acad Fit Awd; UCLA; Comp Engrng.

SALONGA, PAMELA; Gahr HS; Cerritos, CA; (3); Church Yth Grp; Spanish Clb; Color Guard; Flag Corp; Stu Cncl; Blue & Gld Medallion PE 88-89; Most Spirited Colorguard 88-89; Colorguard Top Gun Awd-Rifles 89-90.

SALOUFAKOS, STELLA; Grossmont HS; El Cajon, CA; (1); Church Yth Grp; Key Clb; Red Cross Aide; Church Choir; Crs Cntry; Trk; Cit Awd; Pediatrician.

SALSGIVER, KRISTEN; Alta Loma HS; Alta Loma, CA; (3); 20/550; Art Clb; Church Yth Grp; French Clb; VP FBLA; Red Cross Aide; SADD; Ed Yrbk; JV Swmmng; High Hon Roll; Sierra Srvce Prjct; UC Humboldt; Envrnmntl Sci.

SALTER, LAURA A; Los Altos HS; Mountain View, CA; (3); 17/321; High Hon Roll; Hon Roll; San Jose ST; Bus Mgr.

SALTOS, VICTOR M; Sierra Vista HS; Baldwin Park, CA; (2); Science Clb; SADD; High Hon Roll; Opt Clb Awd; Var Badminton Team; 1st Pl Spch Cont; Elec Engr.

SALTZMAN, TONI M; Tulare Union HS; Tulare, CA; (2); Church Yth Grp; Cmnty Wkr; 4-H; FFA; GAA; Rep Soph Cls; Score Keeper; Sftbl; Vllybl; Hon Roll; Sons Of Italy; COS.

SALUMBIDES, BRENDA; St Genevieve HS; N Hollywood, CA; (2); Drm Mjr(t); Rep Frsh Cls; Hon Roll; Maxima Cum Laude Natl Latin Exam; CSF; Unity Club; Med.

SALUMBIDES, CHRISTINE; Bishop Amat Memorial HS; San Dimas, CA; (4); 8/400; Drama Clb; Math Clb; Office Aide; Chorus; Capt Drill Tm; VP Frsh Cls; Pres Jr Cls; Off Sr Cls; High Hon Roll; Jr NHS; Ldrshp & Svc Awd; 2nd Hnrs Vsl Arts; Med.

SALUMBIDES, TRICIA; St Genevieve HS; N Hollywood, CA; (2); French Clb; SADD; Drm Mjr(t); Rep Frsh Cls; Hon Roll; CSF; The Unity Club.

SALVACION, L ERICH; Estancia HS; Costa Mesa, CA; (4); 2/330; French Clb; German Clb; Chrmn Key Clb; NFL; VP Spanish Clb; Speech Tm; Ed Nwsp; Ed Yrbk; Bsktbl; JV Var Trk; 90 Irvine Co Spectrum Ldr Schlrshp; 90 Bnk America Achvt Awd Math; UC Berkeley; Psych.

SALVADOR, MARIA T; Edison SR HS; Stockton, CA; (4); Church Yth Grp; Cmnty Wkr; Office Aide; Teachers Aide; Church Choir; Prfct Atten Awd; Human Srvcs Agency Vlntr; Delta JC; Bookkeepr.

SALVADOR, NICCOLO M; Montgomery HS; San Diego, CA; (3); Aud/Vis; Band; Jazz Band; Mrchg Band; Orch; Pep Band; Drum Corp; Band Stu Dir; Gen Phys Ftnss; Brdcstng.

SALVAGNO, ANNA; Notre Dame HS; Greenfield, CA; (2); Chorus; High Hon Roll; Hon Roll; Intl Order Of Rainbows/Girls Wrthy Advsr; City Sftbl Leag 6 Yrs; CSF; USAF Acad; Engrng.

SALVATO, KARMA; Santa Monica HS; Malibu, CA; (1); Church Yth Grp; Yrbk; Vllybl.

SALVESON, AMBER L; Canyon Springs HS; Moreno Valley, CA; (2); Art Clb; Ski Clb; JV Vllybl; Cit Awd; High Hon Roll; Hon Roll; Outrch Vlybl Prgm Cal St San Bernardino; Wrkd Canyon Springs Cinema Moreno Vly 9; Gldn St Exam; Cal Poly San Luis; Corp Law.

SALVETTI, A J; Lincoln HS; Stockton, CA; (3); VP Jr Cls; JA; JV Bsktbl; Var Ftbl; Var Golf; Hon Roll; UCLA; Med.

SALVETTI, NICHOLAS D; Lincoln HS; Stockton, CA; (2); 57/568; VP Soph Cls; Off Jr Cls; JV Bsbl; JV Bsktbl; JV Ftbl; Hon Roll; Stckbrkr.

SAM, IRENE T; South HS; Bakersfield, CA; (3); 3/450; Sec Intnl Clb; Pres Key Clb; Var Capt Tennis; JV Vllybl; Hon Roll; NHS; Interact Clb Sec; Girl St; Med Clb.

SAM, JENNIFER M; Mercy HS; Daly City, CA; (4); 7/106; VP Church Yth Grp; French Clb; GAA; Phtg Yrbk; JV Socr; Var Trk; High Hon Roll; NHS; Pres Acad Fit Awd; Spanish NHS; U CA Davis.

SAM, SORITA; Gardena HS; Gardena, CA; (2); Service Clb; Spanish Clb; Teachers Aide; Varsity Clb; Var Bsbl; Var Bsktbl; Score Keeper; Cit Awd; High Hon Roll; Hon Roll; Outstndng Athletic Awds; Schltc Awds; ULCA; Med.

SAM, WINSTON; St Bernard HS; Hawthorne, CA; (3); 33/356; Chess Clb; Hosp Aide; Hon Roll; Sktbrdng; Boydbrdng; USC; Pre-Med.

SAMAGH, DIMPLE T; Glendale Adventist Acad; Glendale, CA; (3); 7/62; Key Clb; Office Aide; Teachers Aide; Nwsp; Treas Stu Cncl; NHS; U Sthrn CA; Neurosrgn.

SAMALA, ELIZABETH; Southwest HS; San Diego, CA; (3); 6/498; Church Yth Grp; VP Key Clb; Color Guard; Church Choir; Yrbk; Treas Jr Cls; Var Tennis; Cit Awd; High Hon Roll; Hon Roll; Pan Asian Sgt At Arms; Acad Leag; ASB Hstrn; UCSD; Med.

SAMANIEGO, CRISTINA; San Pedro HS; San Pedro, CA; (2); Teachers Aide; Drill Tm; School Musical; School Play; Rep Stu Cncl; Hon Roll; Fulfillment Fund Schlrshp; Bus.

SAMANIEGO, FRANCISCO; Dos Palos HS; Dos Palos, CA; (1); Phtg Yrbk; JV Ftbl; Hon Roll; Arch.

SAMANIEGO, YESENIA; Arroyo HS; El Monte, CA; (4); 18/232; Art Clb; Key Clb; Ed Yrbk; Rep Sr Cls; Rep Stu Cncl; Cheerldng; Var Tennis; Var Trk; Hon Roll; UC Santa Barbara; Art.

SAMANO, EVA N; Turlock HS; Turlock, CA; (3); Cheerldng; CSF; Spirit Clb; Family Cnslr.

SAMANTHA, LEE; Cerritos HS; Cerritos, CA; (2); Math Clb; High Hon Roll; Hon Roll; Intnl Clb; Music Teachers Assn Of CA Cert Of Mrt For Piano Study Achvt; Golden St 1st Yr Algebra Exam Schlr 89; UCLA; Bus.

SAMARASINGHE, NADIKA K; Ontario HS; Ontario, CA; (4); Rep German Clb; Key Clb; Letterman Clb; Treas Soph Cls; JV Tennis; Hon Roll; Prfct Atten Awd; Calif Scholarship Fed; Ivy Chain; Volunteer Work At City Library & A Montessori Schl; U Of CA Riverside; Biomedical.

SAMARCO, JAMIE; Clovis HS; Clovis, CA; (4); French Clb; SADD; Teachers Aide; Band; Jazz Band; Mrchg Band; Orch; Pep Band; School Musical; Hon Roll; Manhattan Yth Philharmonic St Hnr Orch; Bank Of Amer Schlrshp Awd For Music; CA ST U Fresno; Attorney.

SAMAWI, ROGER; La Quinta HS; Fountain Valley, CA; (4); 64/329; Intrml Bsbl; Intrml Bsktbl; JV Var Ftbl; Var Intrml Wt Lftg; Hon Roll; Orange Coast Coll; Doc.

SAMAYOA, MONICA; Miraleste HS; San Pedro, CA; (2); Church Yth Grp; Hosp Aide; Office Aide; Service Clb; Spanish Clb; Teachers Aide; Chorus; Church Choir; School Play; Off Frsh Cls; Commodores Awd; San Pedro & Peninsula YMCA 1 Yr Membrshp; Dr.

SAMBORSKY, SANDY; Oak Ridge HS; El Dorado Hills, CA; (1); School Musical; School Play; Bsktbl; Sftbl; Vllybl; UCLA.

SAMENI, GOLNAZ; Le Lycee Francais HS; Beverly Hills, CA; (4); Cmnty Wkr; French Clb; Spanish Clb; Varsity Clb; VP Sr Cls; Hon Roll; Fr Baccaleaureat Diploma; Fr BEPC Diploma; USC; Fr.

SAMI, MONIKA; Carson HS; Torrance, CA; (3); Bus Profs of Am; Cmnty Wkr; Dance Clb; Drama Clb; English Clb; Girl Scts; JA; Library Aide; Drill Tm; Bsktbl; Law.

SAMIA, JENNIFER C; Bishop Montgomery HS; La Mirada, CA; (3); JA; Key Clb; Letterman Clb; NFL; Ski Clb; Speech Tm; Varsity Clb; Yrbk; Off Jr Cls; Off Sr Cls; Now For The Future Clb; Tnns Clb; Concordia; Bus.

SAMIA, KATRINA M; St Joseph HS; Fullerton, CA; (2); 33/196; Spanish Clb; SADD; Acpl Chr; Chorus; Tennis; High Hon Roll; Hon Roll; Martl Arts; CSF; U CA-IRVINE; Bio.

SAMMAH, LAILI; Newark Memorial HS; Fremont, CA; (3); 26/500; French Clb; Var Tennis; JV Trk; Hon Roll; SADD; Sci.

SAMMBRANO, EMILY A; Livermore HS; Livermore, CA; (1); Church Yth Grp; Teachers Aide; Band; Off Frsh Cls; JV Swmmng; Stat Wrstlng; High Hon Roll; Hon Roll; Prfct Atten Awd.

SAMMUT, NATALIE; Immaculate Conception Acad; San Francisco, CA; (4); Rep Frsh Cls; High Hon Roll; Hon Roll; NHS; Bank Of Amer Achvt Math Awd; SFSU; Nursing.

SAMODAL, GRACE T; Bonita Vista HS; Bonita, CA; (3); 15/559; Model UN; Nwsp; Ed Yrbk; Sec Soph Cls; VP Jr Cls; Capt Tennis; DAR Awd; High Hon Roll; Girl Scts; JA; Acad League; ASB Secy; Harvard; Molecular Immnlgst.

SAMOJLOWICZ, MARGARET; Mc Alteer Sota HS; San Francisco, CA; (3); Band; Orch; School Musical; Rep Stu Cncl; Hon Roll; Dance Cmptns; San Francisco ST U; Jrnlsm.

SAMONTE, RICHEL F; Sacred Heart HS; Los Angeles, CA; (3); Church Yth Grp; GAA; Chorus; Church Choir; School Play; Rep Soph Cls; JV Bsktbl; Var Cheerldng; Hon Roll; NHS; Intl Corresponding Schl; Avon Rep 2 Yrs; CA ST Los Angeles; Bus Law.

SAMOUN, ABIGAIL M; Montgomery HS; Kenwood, CA; (2); English Clb; Spanish Clb; Jr NHS; Piano Lssns; Humboldt ST; Psycht.

SAMPANG, MARIA S; J Eugene Mc Ateer HS; San Francisco, CA; (3); Library Aide; Office Aide; Teachers Aide; Hon Roll; CSF; San Francisco ST U.

SAMPANI, FRITZIE P; Fremont HS; Sunnyvale, CA; (3); Sec Church Yth Grp; Intnl Clb; Church Choir; Red & White Awd-Schl Svcs Recogntn-Art; Vrsty Badminton; Am Coll For Applied Arts; Bus.

SAMPANI, MAE P; Fremont HS; Sunnyvale, CA; (2); Church Yth Grp; Debate Tm; NFL; Service Clb; Band; Church Choir; Mrchg Band; JV Badminton; Octagon Clb; Grand Quality Clb; Lawyer.

SAMPLE, FREDERICK J; Mojave HS; California City, CA; (3); Boy Scts; Cmnty Wkr; Letterman Clb; Teachers Aide; Ftbl; Hon Roll; Engr.

SAMPLE, LAUREL; Foothill HS; Santa Ana, CA; (3); Church Yth Grp; Pep Clb; JV Cheerldng; JV Tennis; JV Trk; Hon Roll.

SAMPLE, SPENCER H; Mojave HS; California City, CA; (2); Boy Scts; Cmnty Wkr; Spanish Clb; Chorus; Bsbl; Golf; Hon Roll; Doctor.

SAMPLES, ADAM R; Santa Paula Union HS; Santa Paula, CA; (1); 4/361; Band; Jazz Band; Pep Band; JV Bsktbl; Stat Tennis; High Hon Roll; Hon Roll; CA Schlrshp Fed; UCLA; Arch.

SAMPLES, GERALD R; Trona HS; Trona, CA; (2); Church Yth Grp; Pep Clb; JV Bsktbl; Var Crs Cntry; Tennis; Trk; Fri Night Live Club; Point Loma Nazerene Coll; Vet.

SAMPLES, KELLY L; Etiwanda HS; Alta Loma, CA; (3); 1/606; Pres JCL; Pres Latin Clb; Off Jr Cls; Var Sftbl; Var Tennis; High Hon Roll; NHS; Acad Decathln Tm 3rd Pl; HOBY Fndtn Schl Rep; Amer Chemcl Soc Fnlst; Math.

SAMPSON, BRANDON D; Hiram Johnson HS; Sacramento, CA; (3); 122/398; SADD; Bsbl; Bsktbl; Ftbl; Wt Lftg; Cit Awd; Hon Roll; Prfct Atten Awd; Conponate Acad; Coll; Bus Admin.

SAMPSON, JANET L; Needles HS; Needles, CA; (3); Church Yth Grp; Cmnty Wkr; FHA; Teachers Aide; Acpl Chr; Rep Frsh Cls; Pres Sr Cls; Rep Stu Cncl; Var Bsktbl; Var Sftbl; PHQ Jbs Dghtrs; Umpr Bobby Sox Ftbl; CA ST San Bernardino; Ed.

SAMPSON, JENNIFER L; Woodland HS; Woodland, CA; (2); Church Yth Grp; Band; Chorus; Church Choir; Mrchg Band; Jr NHS; Co-Dir VBS Chrch Grp & Chldrns Musical; Elem Schl Tchr.

SAMPSON, MATT R; Hanford HS; Hanford, CA; (3); Boy Scts; Church Yth Grp; FBLA; Ftbl; Tennis; Wt Lftg; Hon Roll; Intract; Brigham Young U; Med.

SAMPSON, PSHYRA; St Anthony HS; Compton, CA; (2); Drill Tm; Hon Roll; USC; Nrsng.

SAMRA, HARNAK S; Rio Linda HS; Sacramento, CA; (2); Bsbl; Ftbl; Hon Roll; Acctg.

SAMRA, KULWINDER K; Live Oak HS; Live Oak, CA; (3); Office Aide; Spanish Clb; SADD; Teachers Aide; Bsktbl; Trk; Cit Awd; Hon Roll; Butte Coll.

SAMRA, PINDY; Livingston HS; Delhi, CA; (3); Teachers Aide; Hon Roll; Punjabi Club Secy; Merced Coll; Cmptr Sci.

SAMRAN, KIRANDEEP; Livingston HS; Livingston, CA; (2); Math Clb; Cit Awd; Hon Roll; Prfct Atten Awd; Stanislaus ST U; Comp Prgm.

SAMS, CASEY C; Monache HS; Woodville, CA; (3); Church Yth Grp; Letterman Clb; Teachers Aide; Band; Church Choir; Mrchg Band; Pep Band; Var Bsktbl; Var Trk; High Hon Roll; Camp Cnslr; Nazarene Yth Intl Pres; Point Loma Nazarene Coll; Math.

SAMS, JOHN; Forest Lake HS; Auburn, CA; (2); Church Yth Grp; Var Bsbl; JV Bsktbl; Var Socr; Cit Awd; Prfct Atten Awd; TAC Natl Trk Team; U CA Davis.

SAMS, STEPHEN F; Whitney HS; Cerritos, CA; (2); Var L Swmmng; Water Polo Vrsty Team & Vrsty Lttr; Vlntr Asst Lifeguard; Cerritos Aquatic Clb; CA Schltc Fed; Engrng.

SAMSON, ARLENE S; El Cajon Valley HS; El Cajon, CA; (4); 27/314; Service Clb; Ed Yrbk; JV Gym; JV Tennis; Hon Roll.

SAMSON, CATHERINE G; Sunset HS; Hayward, CA; (3); Band; Color Guard; Mrchg Band; Rep Frsh Cls; Pres Soph Cls; Pres Jr Cls; Pres Sr Cls; Var Trk; Hon Roll; Rep Schl HOBY Seminar Soph; Plyd Badminton Soph; UC Davis; Med.

SAMSON, ERIC; Golden West HS; Visalia, CA; (1); French Clb; Band; Mrchg Band; Pep Band; Hon Roll; Percussion Ensemble.

SAMSON, LARS E; Santa Teresa HS; San Jose, CA; (3); Boy Scts; Church Yth Grp; Science Clb; Ski Clb; Spanish Clb; Varsity Clb; Jazz Band; Mrchg Band; Swmmng; CA Poly San Luis Obispo; Arch.

SAMUDIO, JULIE A; Woodrow Wilson HS; Los Angeles, CA; (3); Church Yth Grp; Cmnty Wkr; Hist Key Clb; Chorus; Church Choir; School Musical; High Hon Roll; St Schlr; Fulfillment Fund Schlr; Valley Forge Freedoms Fndtn Schlrshp; UCLA Med Cntrs Minority Rsrsch Prgm; UC Davis; Vet Med.

SAMUEL, ROBERT J; John W North HS; Riverside, CA; (3); 24/435; Boy Scts; Computer Clb; 4-H; Spanish Clb; Var Capt Ftbl; Var Trk; Var Wt Lftg; Var Capt Wrstlng; Cit Awd; Hon Roll; UC Irvine; Sys Analy.

SAMUELSON, ELIZABETH S; Eureka HS; Eureka, CA; (2); Ski Clb; Chorus; High Hon Roll; Stdyng Frnch, Trksh & Mizo Lngs; Plys Piano, Sxophn & Drms; Dncs Bllt & Jzz; Pttry & Crmcs; Stanford U; Mdl.

SAMULEWSKI, PATRICK J; Highlands HS; North Highlands, CA; (2); JV Capt Bsbl; JV Capt Bsktbl; Intrml Capt Ftbl; Hon Roll; 3rd Pl Sacramento Bsktbl; All ST Pitcher Bsbl; UCLA; Accntnt.

SAMWAY, PATRIC J; Skyline HS; Oakland, CA; (1); Cmnty Wkr; Science Clb; Spanish Clb; Bsbl; Bsktbl; Socr; Syracuse; Bio.

SAN, HOEURK; Lincoln HS; Stockton, CA; (4); Dance Clb; 4-H; High Hon Roll.

SAN BUENAVENTURA, MICHAEL; James Logan HS; Union City, CA; (4); Cmnty Wkr; Computer Clb; Hist FBLA; Math Clb; Speech Tm; Teachers Aide; Var Mgr(s); Powder Puff Ftbl; Var Capt Tennis; Hon Roll; Grl Vrsty Tnns Httng Coach; Cal Poly; Elec Engr.

SAN DIEGO, VICTORIA; Immaculate Heart HS; Tujunga, CA; (3); Service Clb; Spanish Clb; Yrbk; Spanish NHS; Archt.

SAN JUAN, ANNE B; Dana Hills HS; Laguna Hills, CA; (1); SADD; JV Gym; SACA; Foto Club Sec; U Of CA Irvine; Obstetrics.

SANABIA, JACOB T; Redlands HS; Redlands, CA; (2); Church Yth Grp; Mrchg Band; Ftbl; Wt Lftg; Cit Awd; Elks Awd; High Hon Roll; Pres Acad Fit Awd; Crtv Wrtng Awd; Mssnry Wrk; UCLA Mth Tst; USAF Acad; Plt.

SANABRIA, KARINA Y; Calexico HS; Calexico, CA; (2); SADD; Hon Roll; Accntnt.

SANABRIA, MARIO; Central Union HS; El Centro, CA; (1); Band; Mrchg Band; Pep Band; Bsbl; Ftbl; Wt Lftg; Wrstlng; Babe Ruth Org, All Star Team 2 Out Of 3 Yrs; Cal Poly; Engr.

SANABRIA, TROY A; Armijo HS; Fairfield, CA; (4); 4/376; Church Yth Grp; ROTC; Ski Clb; Band; Mrchg Band; Var L Socr; Var L Swmmng; High Hon Roll; Hon Roll; Jr NHS; CA Schlrshp Fed Life Mem; Master Of Sprts Awd; Cal Poly San Luis Obispo; Engr.

SANANDAJI, SAM; Birmingham HS; Encino, CA; (1); Letterman Clb; Crs Cntry; Trk; High Hon Roll; Hon Roll; Med.

SANANIEGO, MICHELLE L; Nogales HS; West Covina, CA; (3); 65/700; Boy Scts; Church Yth Grp; Chorus; Hon Roll; Hnr Mdl Humanities Coll Prep Rdng; Psych.

SANASINH, KESONE; Modesto HS; Modesto, CA; (3); Cit Awd; Hon Roll; Prfct Atten Awd; HS Vlly Clb VP; U Of CA Los Angeles; Engrng.

SANBORN, CHERIE A; Mesa Verde HS; Citrus Heights, CA; (2); 37/257; Hon Roll; Prfct Atten Awd; Pres Acad Fit Awd; Inter Desgn.

SANBORN, EZEKIEL W; Berkeley HS; Berkeley, CA; (3); Electronic Engrng.

SANBORN, GENGUS T; Whittier Christian HS; La Habra, CA; (2); Boy Scts; Church Yth Grp; Ski Clb; Church Choir; School Play; Stu Cncl; Bsktbl; Score Keeper; Vllybl; Wt Lftg; Med.

SANBORN, JENNIFER A; Ontario HS; Highland, CA; (3); Church Yth Grp; Pep Clb; Ski Clb; Spanish Clb; Teachers Aide; Cheerldng; Prfct Atten Awd; Outstndng Acvht Frgn Lang; Bst Flyer & Attitude Mdl Vrsty Chr; Bus.

SANBORN, KATHY; Trinity HS; Weaverville, CA; (1); GAA; JV Bsktbl; JV Swmmng; High Hon Roll; Hon Roll; Rgstrd Nrs.

SANCERI, JEFF; Bellflower HS; Bellflower, CA; (3); Cmnty Wkr; Drama Clb; SADD; Thesps; Band; Mrchg Band; Orch; Pep Band; School Musical; School Play; Fencing Clb; Friday Night Live; Peer Cnslr; CA Cncl Of Chldrn & Yth Mentor At Large; Psych.

SANCHEZ, ADAM; Sanger HS; Sanger, CA; (4); 21/350; Cmnty Wkr; Model UN; Spanish Clb; Ntl Merit SF; NEDT Awd; U CA Brkly; Englsh Instrctr.

SANCHEZ, ALBERT; La Sierra Acad; Riverside, CA; (4); Aud/Vis; JA; Ski Clb; Band; School Musical; Rep Frsh Cls; VP Jr Cls; JV Bsktbl; Capt Vllybl; Natl Hispanic Schlrshp Awd Semi-Fnlst; Mech Engrg.

SANCHEZ, ALBERT S; Palm Springs HS; Cathedral, CA; (3); Var Bsbl; Hon Roll; CSF; VICA; Arch.

SANCHEZ, ALICIA; Baldwin Park HS; Baldwin Park, CA; (2); FBLA; Hon Roll; Keywanettes.

SANCHEZ, AMERICA; Arvin HS; Lamont, CA; (4); 15/267; Drama Clb; Ski Clb; SADD; Color Guard; School Play; VP Jr Cls; Score Keeper; Sftbl; Vllybl; Hon Roll; Amer Lgn & Bank Of Amer Achvmnt Awds; CA Poli Sy; Hmn Dev.

SANCHEZ, ANA M; Sacred Heart HS; Los Angeles, CA; (3); Hon Roll; Prfct Atten Awd; Achvt In US Hstry Highest GPA.

SANCHEZ, ANTHONY; La Sierra HS; Stanhope, NJ; (3); Teachers Aide; Prfct Atten Awd; U CA Riverside; Bus Admin.

SANCHEZ, BRISEIDA; Estancia HS; Costa Mesa, CA; (2); Reporter.

SANCHEZ, CARLOS A; Los Altos HS; Hacienda Hgts, CA; (1); Church Yth Grp; FCA; Intrml Capt Ftbl; Intrml Swmmng; JV Vllybl; Cit Awd; Cal Poly; Math.

SANCHEZ, CESAR J; Edison HS; Huntington Beach, CA; (1); Engr.

SANCHEZ, CHRISTINA; Clovis West HS; Fresno, CA; (1); Drama Clb; Intnl Clb; Ski Clb; SADD; Var Cheerldng; Hon Roll; Vlybl & Dance.

SANCHEZ, CLAUDIA; Sierra Vista HS; Baldwin Park, CA; (2); French Clb; Math Clb; Science Clb; Orch; High Hon Roll; Speech Clb; CSF; Genl Practnr.

SANCHEZ, CORINA; Tulare Western HS; Tulare, CA; (3); Bus Awd; Bus.

SANCHEZ, CYNTHIA C; Saint Paul HS; Pico Rivera, CA; (3); Church Yth Grp; Cmnty Wkr; Red Cross Aide; Teachers Aide; Swmmng; High Hon Roll; Hon Roll; NHS; CA Schlrshp Fed; Phys Thrpy.

SANCHEZ, DANIEL J; Pinole Valley HS; Hercules, CA; (2); Band; Mrchg Band; Bowling; Contra Costa Clg; Culinary Arts.

SANCHEZ, DAVID R; Oakmont HS; Roseville, CA; (1); Intrml Bsbl; Intrml Bsktbl; JV Intrml Ftbl; Intrml Gym; Intrml Sftbl; Intrml Swmmng; Intrml Vllybl; Intrml Wt Lftg; Intrml Wrstlng; Cit Awd; Mech Engr.

SANCHEZ, DEANNA D; Canyon HS; Canyon Country, CA; (2); Church Yth Grp; Cmnty Wkr; Pep Clb; SADD; Chorus; VP Soph Cls; Cheerldng; Amnesty Intnl; Warner Drill & Dance Tm; Vol Spec Ed; UCSB; Spec Ed.

SANCHEZ, DENNIS S; Pinole Valley HS; Pinole, CA; (2); Debate Tm; JV Crs Cntry; JV Trk; High Hon Roll; Hon Roll; UC Brkly; Engrg.

SANCHEZ, DIANA; Edison HS; Stockton, CA; (1); Temple Yth Grp; Off Sr Cls; High Hon Roll; Hon Roll; Comp.

SANCHEZ, DONNA; Workman HS; Valinda, CA; (2); Drama Clb; Latin Clb; Swmmng; Trk; Vllybl; Hon Roll; Spanish NHS.

SANCHEZ, EILEEN R; Chaffey HS; Ontario, CA; (4); 38/412; Teachers Aide; Yrbk; Crs Cntry; Powder Puff Ftbl; Score Keeper; Trk; High Hon Roll; Capt X-Cntry Team; Fame Awds Math, Sci & Frgn Lang; Passed Gldn St Exam Geometry; CA ST Polytechnic; Acctg.

SANCHEZ, ELENA L; Herbert Hoover HS; Glendale, CA; (3); Church Yth Grp; Drama Clb; Spanish Clb; Chorus; Drill Tm; Rptr Yrbk; Glendale La Canada Indstry Ed Cncl Awd Home Arts; Psychtry.

SANCHEZ, ELIZABETH; Mater Dei HS; Santa Ana, CA; (3); Church Yth Grp; Cmnty Wkr; Hosp Aide; Spanish Clb; Rep Soph Cls; Rep Jr Cls; Rep Sr Cls; Stu Cncl; Swmmng; Hon Roll; Law.

SANCHEZ, ELIZABETH DE LOURDES; Saint Paul HS; Whittier, CA; (3); Art Clb; Cmnty Wkr; French Clb; German Clb; Spanish Clb; Ed Yrbk; Rep Frsh Cls; Rep Sr Cls; Rep Jr Cls; Rep Sr Cls; Tnns Coach Awd; CSF; Orphnge Vlntr Mexico; Bus Mgmt.

SANCHEZ, ELVIA; El Cajon Valley HS; El Cajon, CA; (2); JV Bsktbl; JV Sftbl; Var Trk; JV Vllybl; Hon Roll; Multi Cultural Club; UCSD; Obstetrichian.

SANCHEZ, EMANUEL; Lynwood HS; Lynwood, CA; (3); 33/830; Boy Scts; Math Clb; Capt ROTC; Drill Tm; VP Stu Cncl; Var L Tennis; Hon Roll; NHS; MESA Mech Engrng Sci Achvt Clb; West Point; Engrng.

SANCHEZ, EMILIO; Brawley Union HS; Brawley, CA; (3); Spanish Clb; Var Socr; Comp.

SANCHEZ, ENEDINA; Riverdale HS; Riverdale, CA; (2); Intnl Clb; Var Trk; Hon Roll; Nrsng.

SANCHEZ, ENRIQUE; Hemet HS; Hemet, CA; (2); Church Yth Grp; JV Ftbl; Var Socr; Var Trk; 2nd Team All Leg Sccr; All Leg Trk Mile Relay & 440 Relay.

SANCHEZ, EVELIA; Sierra Vista HS; Baldwin Park, CA; (2); Church Yth Grp; Debate Tm; Var Pep Clb; Speech Tm; SADD; Variety Show; Rptr Nwsp; JV Cheerldng; Var Trk; Hon Roll; Bus.

SANCHEZ, FAUSTINA; Santa Ana HS; Santa Ana, CA; (3); Cmnty Wkr; Dance Clb; Library Aide; Teachers Aide; Color Guard; Stage Crew; JV Fld Hcky; JV Sftbl; JV Vllybl; Cit Awd; Model Mexican Customs & Prom Dresses Cinco De Mayo Fshn Shw; Stdy Bus Through Project Invest; USC; Anchor Woman.

SANCHEZ, FLOR E; San Fernando HS; Pacoima, CA; (3); Art Clb; French Clb; Drill Tm; Pom Pon; Hon Roll; Bus Admin.

SANCHEZ, FRANK E; Alisal HS; Salinas, CA; (3); Cmnty Wkr; Science Clb; Var Golf; Var Wrstlng; High Hon Roll; Camp Cnslr Monterey County Ofc Of Edu Outdr Sci Schl; Won 1st Pl Hartnells Comm Coll 3rd Annl Elects; Naval Acad; Aerosp Engr.

SANCHEZ, GABRIELA; Saddleback HS; Santa Ana, CA; (3); FBLA; Pep Clb; Spanish Clb; Teachers Aide; Var Cheerldng; Trk; Vllybl; Hon Roll; Mock Trial; Grls Lg; Pltcl Sci.

SANCHEZ, GABRIELA; Warren HS; Downey, CA; (2); School Play; JV Bsktbl; Prfct Atten Awd; Actress.

SANCHEZ, GINA T; John Marshall Fundamental HS; Pasadena, CA; (3); Chess Clb; VP Drama Clb; Ed Nwsp; Rep Stu Cncl; JV Cheerldng; Var Socr; Var Trk; Hon Roll; Chess Tm; Edtr Padadena City Newlttr; Schl Rep Stu Critic Edtrl Brd; CSF; Brandies; Law.

SANCHEZ, GUADALUPE; Gardena HS; Gardena, CA; (2); Aud/Vis; Church Yth Grp; FFA; Chorus; Rep Soph Cls; JV Trk; Hon Roll; Church Lctr; Intnl Sales.

SANCHEZ, HENRY; Bishop Amat HS; Diamond Bar, CA; (4); 7/394; Am Leg Boys St; Church Yth Grp; Cmnty Wkr; Varsity Clb; Var L Crs Cntry; JV Var Trk; Hon Roll; NHS; Acad Decthln Tm Fnls; CSF; Spcl Olympcs; MA Inst Of Tech; Elec Engrng.

SANCHEZ, HILARIO; Baldwin Park HS; Baldwin Pk, CA; (2); 3/31; Boy Scts; Science Clb; SADD; Band; Drm Mjr(t); Jazz Band; Mrchg Band; Orch; Pep Band; JV Bsbl; Friday Night Live Clb; Radiology.

SANCHEZ, HUGO B; Santa Ana HS; Santa Ana, CA; (3); Math Clb; Math Tm; Office Aide; Science Clb; Rptr Yrbk; Intrml Var Ftbl; Cit Awd; High Hon Roll; CA Schlrshp Fed; MESA; Sci.

SANCHEZ, IRMA; Merced HS North; Merced, CA; (3); Score Club; Merced Coll; Comp Prgmr.

SANCHEZ, IRMA N; Sacred Heart HS; Los Angeles, CA; (3); Church Yth Grp; GAA; Letterman Clb; Varsity Clb; Stage Crew; Capt Var Vllybl; Hon Roll; NHS; Prfct Atten Awd; Mt St Marys; Acctng.

SANCHEZ, JAIME A; Hamilton High Music Acad; Los Angeles, CA; (2); Boy Scts; Computer Clb; Mrchg Band; Pep Band; JV Ftbl; JV Powder Puff Ftbl; JV Wt Lftg; USC; Comp Pgmr.

SANCHEZ, JAVIER; St Paul HS; Norwalk, CA; (4); Letterman Clb; Varsity Clb; Bsktbl; Ftbl; Trk; Wt Lftg; Wrstlng; Hon Roll; March For Hunger; Law Enforcement.

SANCHEZ, JENNIFER; Redlands HS; Highland, CA; (3); GAA; Key Clb; Teachers Aide; Varsity Clb; Socr; Hon Roll; NHS; Rotary Awd; UC Davis; Vet.

SANCHEZ, JENNIFER; Wm S Hart HS; Newhall, CA; (3); 56/430; Chorus; Drill Tm; Flag Corp; High Hon Roll; Hon Roll; Pres Acad Fit Awd; CSF; Ghgh Hnrs Alg & Chem Gldn St Exm; Bio Sci.

SANCHEZ, JENNIFER M; Chaffey HS; Ontario, CA; (1); Socr; Hon Roll.

SANCHEZ, JESSE J; San Benito HS; Hollister, CA; (2); Teachers Aide; Wt Lftg; Hon Roll; Real Est Agnt.

SANCHEZ, JILL; Bishop O'dowd HS; San Leandro, CA; (2); Ski Clb; Rep Frsh Cls; Pres Soph Cls; Stu Cncl; JV Bsktbl; JV Sftbl; High Hon Roll; Hon Roll; Outstndng Soph Girl; Latin Amer Clb; CSF.

SANCHEZ, JUANITA; Pioneer HS; San Jose, CA; (3); 98/392; Var Socr; Var Sftbl; JV Tennis; Hon Roll; Hispanic Clb; CA Schlrshp Fed; Asst To Council Mems; Cal Poly U; Arch Engrng.

SANCHEZ, JUANITA S; Abraham Lincoln HS; San Jose, CA; (3); 20/313; Church Yth Grp; Dance Clb; Gym; MESA; Mssntts; Pre-Med.

SANCHEZ, JUDITH I; Notre Dame HS; San Jose, CA; (3); 1/90; Drama Clb; Hosp Aide; Pres Science Clb; Church Choir; School Play; Rptr Nwsp; Rptr Lit Mag; Bausch & Lomb Sci Awd; NHS; Bio/Space Pgm NASA/Ames Rsrch Ctr; Biochem.

SANCHEZ, JULIET; Sacred Heart Of Jesus HS; Los Angeles, CA; (3); Church Choir; Hon Roll; Natl Spnsh Exam Awd.

SANCHEZ, LEONEL A; Lynwood HS; Lynwood, CA; (2); French Clb; Library Aide; Teachers Aide; Cit Awd; Prfct Atten Awd; Sccr; Elec Tech.

SANCHEZ, LORI; King City HS; Greenfield, CA; (2); Drama Clb; Var Chess Clb; JV Sftbl; Hon Roll; Intl Order Rainbow Girls; Psych.

SANCHEZ, LUIS; Alisal HS; Salinas, CA; (4); Cmnty Wkr; French Clb; Var Capt Crs Cntry; Var Trk; High Hon Roll; Rotary Awd; Explrer Scouts Of Amer; Cmp Royal,Spnsrd By Steinbeck Rotary Clb; Cornell U; Law.

SANCHEZ, LUIS A; Downey HS; Downey, CA; (1); Art Clb; Capt Crs Cntry; Capt Trk; Prfct Atten Awd; Arch.

SANCHEZ, LUIS E; Cantwell HS; Los Angeles, CA; (3); Am Leg Boys St; Cmnty Wkr; Dance Clb; Letterman Clb; Math Clb; Science Clb; Spanish Clb; Varsity Clb; Pres Stu Cncl; Var Bsktbl; Ucla.

SANCHEZ, LUIS F; Roosevelt HS; Los Angeles, CA; (2); Key Clb; Hon Roll; NHS.

SANCHEZ, MARCO A; Calexio HS; Calexico, CA; (3); Church Yth Grp; Var Bsbl; Hon Roll; Prfct Atten Awd; Gldn St Exam Alg Rcgntn; Wardbury U; Arch.

SANCHEZ, MARCOS; Dinuba HS; Dinuba, CA; (3); Hon Roll; Excellence In Algebra I & History; Law & Biology; Lawyer.

SANCHEZ, MARITZA; Bonita Vista HS; Chula Vista, CA; (2); Office Aide; Spanish Clb; Rptr Nwsp; JV Trk; Hon Roll; UCSD; Psych.

SANCHEZ, MARJORIE; Mountain View HS; El Monte, CA; (1); Band; Mrchg Band; Hon Roll; UCLA; Psych.

SANCHEZ, MARLO D; Fontana HS; Fontana, CA; (2); Teachers Aide; Cit Awd; High Hon Roll; Hon Roll; Pres Acad Fit Awd; Hghst Avg Sci Awd; Yale; Poltcl Sci.

SANCHEZ, MARTINA; Woodbridge HS; Irvine, CA; (4); 36/360; Church Yth Grp; Cmnty Wkr; Drama Clb; Sec JCL; Service Clb; Mgr School Musical; School Play; Hon Roll; Pres Acad Fit Awd; Pres Ftr Ldrs Of Irvine; Yth Vlntr Coordtr Irvine Tmpry Hsng; Sentinel Mdlln Of Excllnc; Cal ST Fullerton; Blngl Ed.

SANCHEZ, MARVIN N; Venice HS; Los Angeles, CA; (1); Church Yth Grp; Embry Riddle U; Aviation.

SANCHEZ, MELINDA; Hanford HS; Hanford, CA; (2); Math Clb; Office Aide; Science Clb; Spanish Clb; Teachers Aide; Var Crs Cntry; Score Keeper; Var Trk; Hon Roll; CSF Mem; Fresno ST U; Med.

SANCHEZ, MICHAEL A; Pinole Valley HS; Hercules, CA; (4); 14/450; Computer Clb; Math Tm; Ed Nwsp; Ed Yrbk; VP Jr Cls; JV Trk; Yth Eductr 88-90; YMCA Yth & Govt 88-90; Prncpls Advsry Cncl 89-90; UC Berkeley; Civil Engrng.

SANCHEZ, MIKE; San Luis Obispo HS; San Luis Obispo, CA; (4); Rep Stu Cncl; Var Capt Ftbl; Var Capt Wrstlng; Pres Acad Fit Awd; Rotary Awd; Plymouth AAA Troubleshooting Cont; Black & Gold Booster Clb Awd; Cuesta Coll; Engrng.

SANCHEZ, MONIKA; Arroyo HS; San Leandro, CA; (4); 34/237; Teachers Aide; Variety Show; Ed Nwsp; Hon Roll; Prfct Atten Awd; Deans List; Chabot Coll; Law.

SANCHEZ, NEIL JAMES; Katella HS; Anaheim, CA; (4); Church Yth Grp; Varsity Clb; Band; Jazz Band; Mrchg Band; Orch; Pep Band; School Musical; Bsktbl; Hon Roll; Bank Of Amer Achvt Awd Field Music; Semper Fidelis Awd Muscl Exllnce; Caly Poly-Pomona; Mech Engrng.

SANCHEZ, NICK; Bishop Amat Memorial HS; Walnut, CA; (3); JV Socr; Hon Roll; CA Schlrshp Fed; Slvr Screen Clb; UCLA; Med.

SANCHEZ, NICOLE H; Santa Teresa HS; San Jose, CA; (3); 20/480; Boy Scts; French Clb; Sec Treas Sr Cls; Pres Stu Cncl; NHS; Drama Clb; Math Tm; Model UN; Band; Chorus; Acad Decathlon Coach; Amnesty Intl; A M Mickey Moore Awd For Outstndng Stu; Philosophy Club; Georgetown; Intl Relations.

SANCHEZ, NOELIA G; Independence HS; San Jose, CA; (2); Band; Mrchg Band; Cheerldng; Pom Pon.

SANCHEZ, NORMA; Rowland HS; Rowland Hts, CA; (3); Spanish Clb; Powder Puff Ftbl; Hon Roll; Girls Leag; Bus.

SANCHEZ, OSCAR P; Saddleback HS; Santa Ana, CA; (2); Boy Scts; French Clb; Varsity Clb; Band; Mrchg Band; Orch; Var Swmmng; Newport Bch Lfgrd; Water Polo Tm Vrsty; Police Explrr Santa Ana; Berkely U; Med.

SANCHEZ, OSWALDO; Lynwood HS; Lynwood, CA; (2); Church Yth Grp; Arch.

SANCHEZ, PATRICK; St Paul HS; Whittier, CA; (4); 1/280; Debate Tm; Treas French Clb; NFL; Speech Tm; Nwsp; Rep Jr Cls; Treas Stu Cncl; Tennis; NHS; Val; Engrng.

SANCHEZ, PAUL; Eisenhower HS; San Bernardino, CA; (2); Teachers Aide; Cit Awd; Hon Roll; Plyng Sprts For The City; Mltry Marines.

SANCHEZ, RAQUEL; Gardena HS; Gardena, CA; (4); French Clb; Service Clb; Capt Flag Corp; VP Jr Cls; Treas Sr Cls; Treas Stu Cncl; CA Cngrss Of Ptsa Inc Schlr; Ephebian Soc; Math Engrng & Sci Achvt; UC Irvine; Mech Engrng.

SANCHEZ, RAQUEL; John H Francis Polytechnic HS; North Hollywood, CA; (3); Drama Clb; Pep Clb; Red Cross Aide; Service Clb; SADD; Thesps; School Play; Cit Awd; Hon Roll; NCCS Brotherhood Sisterhood Camp; Human Rights Club; Ladies & Squires Knights & Athenians; Boy Scouts; Film Acting Theatre Psychology.

SANCHEZ, RAQUEL R; Fremont HS; Oakland, CA; (3); Church Yth Grp; Cit Awd; Hon Roll; Prfct Atten Awd; MESA; Bus.

SANCHEZ, RENA J; La Reina HS; Simi Valley, CA; (3); GAA; Letterman Clb; Stat Bsktbl; Score Keeper; JV Sftbl; JV Vllybl; Cit Awd; CA Schlshp Federation; Math.

SANCHEZ, RENEE; Huntington Beach HS; Huntington Beach, CA; (3); VP French Clb; Ski Clb; Sftbl.

SANCHEZ, RICARDO S; Palo Verde HS; Blythe, CA; (3); Spanish Clb; Teachers Aide; Band; Phtg Yrbk; Hon Roll.

SANCHEZ, RICHARD; Christian Brothers HS; Sacramento, CA; (3); 5/126; Math Tm; Science Clb; Spanish Clb; SADD; Trk; High Hon Roll; Hon Roll; Prfct Atten Awd; CSF; MESA; Pre-Med.

SANCHEZ, RICHARD; Daniel Murphy HS; Los Angeles, CA; (1); Church Yth Grp; French Clb; Math Tm; JV Vllybl; Hon Roll; UCLA; Engr.

SANCHEZ, RICKY T; Channel Islands HS; Oxnard, CA; (2); 160/640; JV Bsbl; JV Ftbl; Var Wt Lftg; Hon Roll; Fresno ST U; Bus Admin.

SANCHEZ, ROSA; Saint Marys Acad; Inglewood, CA; (4); 1/83; Church Yth Grp; Cmnty Wkr; French Clb; GAA; Hosp Aide; Library Aide; Model UN; Service Clb; VP Frsh Cls; Pres Stu Cncl; Stanford; Biochem.

SANCHEZ, ROSA M; Sanger HS; Sanger, CA; (4); Dance Clb; Teachers Aide; Prfct Atten Awd; ESL Clb; Kings Rvr Cmnty Coll.

SANCHEZ, RUBEN R; Galileo HS; San Francisco, CA; (3); Spanish Clb; Variety Show; Bsbl; Ftbl; Score Keeper; Socr; Wt Lftg; Hon Roll; Biology.

SANCHEZ, SANTIAGO; Gridley Union HS; Gridley, CA; (3); 10/120; Pres Church Yth Grp; Computer Clb; Sec Office Aide; Spanish Clb; VP VICA; Intrml Ftbl; Stat Socr; Cit Awd; High Hon Roll; Hon Roll; VICA Achvt Awd; Auto Mech Awd; His Clb Treas; Frdy Night Live Clb; Chico ST U; Elctrncs Engr.

SANCHEZ, SARAH B; Walnut HS; Walnut, CA; (2); Rptr Nwsp; High Hon Roll; Hon Roll; Prfct Atten Awd; POWER Club; Highest Grade In Geometry Class; 2nd Pl Novice News Category E LA Cnty Jrnlism Write-Off; Aerospace Engineering.

SANCHEZ, SERGIO O; Servite HS; Whittier, CA; (2); Chess Clb; Ski Clb; Bsktbl; Mgr(s); Trk; 3rd Pl Schl Leag High Jmp; Arch.

SANCHEZ, SUZANNE MICHELLE; Walnut HS; Walnut, CA; (3); 19/406; Cmnty Wkr; Sec VP FBLA; Teachers Aide; Off Soph Cls; High Hon Roll; Hon Roll; CSF; Piano; CA ST U; Engl.

SANCHEZ, SYLVIA; Montebello HS; Los Angeles, CA; (2); Key Clb; SADD; Chorus; Var Bsktbl; JV Swmmng; JV Trk; Var L Vllybl; Hon Roll; Hnr Soc.

SANCHEZ, TINA MARIE; Hoover HS; Glendale, CA; (3); JA; Spanish Clb; Band; Drill Tm; Var Cheerldng; Jr Statemen Of Amer; Filipino Club; Pdtrcn.

SANCHEZ, TRACY F; John Glenn HS; Norwalk, CA; (3); Peer Cnslng Grp; Crrtos Coll; Psych.

SANCHEZ, VANESSA M; Sacred Heart Of Jesus HS; Los Angeles, CA; (3); GAA; Variety Show; Yrbk; Lit Mag; Bsktbl; Score Keeper; Trk; Vllybl; Chrstn Action Mvmnt; Liturgical Mnstry; Jr Statesmen; Dominican Coll; Engl Lit.

SANCHEZ, VERONICA; Morningside HS; Inglewood, CA; (3); SADD; High Hon Roll.

SANCHEZ, VERONICA; Reedley HS; Reedley, CA; (3); Church Yth Grp; Computer Clb; French Clb; FTA; Band; Mrchg Band; Pep Band; Sec Jr Cls; VP Sr Cls; Cit Awd; Stanford; Bio Chem.

SANCHEZ, YAQUELINE; Hueneme HS; Oxnard, CA; (3); Var Trk; Var Vllybl; High Hon Roll; Hon Roll; MESA; FLA; Bus.

SANCHEZ ALDANA, MARIANA; Louisville HS; Calabasas, CA; (2); Art Clb; Teachers Aide; Stage Crew; High Hon Roll; Hon Roll; Explrs Club; CSF.

SANCHEZ-ALDANA, GABRIEL; Chula Vista HS; San Diego, CA; (3); 1/535; Treas Computer Clb; Pep Clb; Rep Jr Cls; Stu Cncl; JV Vllybl; Bausch & Lomb Sci Awd; Pres Acad Fit Awd; Asian Fellowshp Organztn-Rep; Greater San Diego Sci/Engrng Fair 1st Pl 89; 2nd Pl St Sci Fair 89; U Of CA; Med.

SANCHEZ-CAZARES, GERARDO; Reedley HS; Reedley, CA; (3); Treas Computer Clb; French Clb; German Clb; Spanish Clb; JV Socr; JETS Club; Waterpolo; UC Berkeley; Engrng.

SANCHEZ-SALAZAR, JENNIFER; San Ramon Valley HS; Danville, CA; (2); VP Church Yth Grp; Drama Clb; Hosp Aide; VP Chorus; Mrchg Band; Sftbl; Swmmng; High Hon Roll; Acad Achvt Awd Frshmn Engl; Princpls Schlr Musician Awd 88-89; 2nd Chair Flutist Symphnc Band; Human Genetics.

SANCIANCO, HAZEL G; Diamond Bar HS; Diamond Bar, CA; (2); Aud/Vis; Church Choir; Pres Jr Cls; Var Trk; 92 Activities Cmmttee.

SANDAGE, KIRSTEN; Point Loma HS; San Diego, CA; (3); Var Cheerldng; Competitive Ice Skating; Flash Theatre Modeling Prod; Gymnastics; Lw.

SANDATE, DARITA; La Sierra HS; Riverside, CA; (1); Church Yth Grp; Spanish Clb; UCLA; Court Reprtr.

SANDBERG, ROBERT; Dana Hills HS; Mission Viejo, CA; (3); Aud/Vis; Church Yth Grp; Cmnty Wkr; Science Clb; Stage Crew; JV Swmmng; JETS Awd; NASA Rsrch Prjcts; Elec Engrng.

SANDBO, ROBERT L; Hesperia HS; Hesperia, CA; (3); 7/605; Am Leg Boys St; Church Yth Grp; Math Tm; Teachers Aide; JV Bsbl; High Hon Roll; Typng Stu Of Yr 87-88; Mst Cnsistnt Spnsh Stu 88-89; Fresh Bsbl Acad Awd 88; Mechnc Engrng.

SANDER, MICHELLE; Santa Clara HS; Oxnard, CA; (2); 42/200; Church Yth Grp; Drama Clb; French Clb; Speech Tm; Dramatic Arts.

SANDERFORD, JASON B; Oakland HS; Oakland, CA; (3); Church Yth Grp; Drama Clb; FCA; Varsity Clb; Church Choir; School Play; Stage Crew; Var Bsbl; Var Ftbl; Var JV Trk; Soph Class Hmcmg King; All City Var Ftbl Player; Church Yth Grp Pres; Comm.

SANDERL, MARK R; La Salle HS; Pasadena, CA; (4); 1/90; Church Yth Grp; Cmnty Wkr; Hosp Aide; Nwsp; Var Bsktbl; High Hon Roll; NHS; CA Schlrshp Fed Sec; HOBY Ldrshp Awd; Stu Senator; St Marys Coll Of CA; Bus Admin.

SANDERS, ALLISON M; Notre Dame Acad; Los Angeles, CA; (3); Spanish Clb; SADD; JV Bsktbl; JV Vllybl.

SANDERS, ANTHONY L; San Fernando HS; San Fernando, CA; (3); ROTC; Teachers Aide; VP Stu Cncl; DAR Awd; Hon Roll; Awds For Success; Adelaide Williams Stu Govt Awd; Amer Lgn All Around Top Stu Awd; Aerontcl Engr.

SANDERS, BAMBIE C; Trinity HS; Weaverville, CA; (2); Church Yth Grp; Spanish Clb; SADD; Stat Swmmng; Hon Roll; St Of CA Art Schlr 90; CSSSA 90.

SANDERS, BETHANY L; Trinity HS; Weaverville, CA; (3); #9 In Class; Art Clb; Church Yth Grp; Church Choir; High Hon Roll; Hon Roll; Nazarene Wrld Mssn Soc Brd.

SANDERS, BRIAN E; Edison HS; Huntington Beach, CA; (3); 43/430; Church Yth Grp; Debate Tm; Model UN; Ski Clb; High Hon Roll; Surfing; Elect Engrng.

SANDERS, DERRICK L; South Bay Junior Acad; Carson, CA; (2); Art Clb; Church Yth Grp; Rep Frsh Cls; JV Bsktbl; Cit Awd; Hon Roll; Morehouse Coll; Law.

SANDERS, DIANE E; Washington Union HS; Fresno, CA; (2); Church Yth Grp; Intnl Clb; Hon Roll; Brdcst Jrnlsm.

SANDERS, ERIC L; Dorsey HS; Los Angeles, CA; (4); Boy Scts; Church Yth Grp; Cmnty Wkr; Computer Clb; Office Aide; Teachers Aide; Church Choir; Ftbl; Trk; Prfct Atten Awd; Upward Bound; CA ST U Northridge; Telcmnctn.

SANDERS, ERIKA; Fresno HS; Fresno, CA; (4); 114/500; Cmnty Wkr; Varsity Clb; Cheerldng; Pom Pon; Fresno City Coll; Psych.

SANDERS, GEOFFREY R; Golden West HS; Visalia, CA; (2); Church Yth Grp; Cmnty Wkr; Band; Mrchg Band; Pep Band; JV Tennis; Cal Poly SLO; Engrng.

SANDERS, HELEN; Calvary Chapel HS; Fountain Valley, CA; (3); Art Clb; Church Yth Grp; Drama Clb; Latin Clb; Pep Clb; Spanish Clb; Chorus; Rep Stu Cncl; Var Cheerldng; Hon Roll; Westmont; Arch.

SANDERS, JENNIFER E; Irvine HS; Irvine, CA; (2); Dance Clb; JV Trk; Hon Roll; Saferides Clb; UCSD; Medcl.

SANDERS, JERRY L; Lassen HS; Susanville, CA; (2); Church Yth Grp; Chorus; Crs Cntry; Trk; Lassen Coll; Comp.

SANDERS, JESSICA B; Edison HS; Fresno, CA; (2); Church Yth Grp; SADD; School Play; Var Swmmng; JV Vllybl; Cit Awd; Photo; Work With Children; Writing Poetry And Music Short Stories; UC; Psych.

SANDERS, JULIA R; School Of The Arts; San Francisco, CA; (2); Orch; School Musical; Russian Tea Clb; Stu For Social Responsibility; Intl Order Of Rainbow For Girls; Music.

SANDERS, JULIE A; Nevada Union HS; Penn Valley, CA; (3); 155/535; Church Yth Grp; Cmnty Wkr; French Clb; Girl Scts; Hosp Aide; Intnl Clb; Pep Clb; Ski Clb; Rep Stu Cncl; Powder Puff Ftbl; Sacremento ST U; Jrnlsm.

SANDERS, MICHELLE C; Central Union HS; El Centro, CA; (2); Church Yth Grp; Cmnty Wkr; Math Tm; Cit Awd; High Hon Roll; Kiwanis Awd; Opt Clb Awd; Pres Acad Fit Awd; Anesthslgy.

SANDERS, NATHAN J; Willow Glen Educational Park HS; San Jose, CA; (1); JV Bsktbl; Parents Clb Achvt Awds-Geom/Genl Sci.

SANDERS, NICHOLE A; Fontana HS; Fontana, CA; (4); 201/794; Art Clb; Drama Clb; Teachers Aide; Hist Acpl Chr; Stage Crew; Mgr(s); Cit Awd; Hon Roll; Slctd Top Artist Art Dept 90; Mst Artstc Sr Cls 90; Bank Amer Awd Art Achvt 90; Desgnd Sets Musical; Chaffey Coll; Art.

SANDERS, PAUL; Arroyo HS; San Lorenzo, CA; (3); Var Trk; High Hon Roll; Hon Roll; UC Davis; Zoology.

SANDERS, REBECCA A; San Pasqual HS; Escondido, CA; (2); 83/420; Church Yth Grp; Cmnty Wkr; Pep Clb; Red Cross Aide; Rep Soph Cls; Treas Jr Cls; Stat Bsbl; JV Crs Cntry; JV Vllybl; Engl.

SANDERS, ROBERT E; Eisenhower HS; Rialto, CA; (2); Prfct Atten Awd; Attitude; CSUB; Army.

SANDERS, SABRINA K; Central Union HS; El Centro, CA; (3); 15/543; Am Leg Aux Girls St; Sec Church Yth Grp; VP 4-H; School Play; Pres Jr Cls; JV Intrml Bsktbl; 4-H Awd; CSF VP; Mock Trial & Speech Tem Best Prosecution Witness; Black Amer Club Secy.

SANDERS, SARA R; Oakland Tech; Oakland, CA; (4); Debate Tm; Teachers Aide; Band; Jazz Band; Cit Awd; High Hon Roll; Aids Pr Edctr; Cnflct Rsltns Clb; UC Santa Cruz; Pre-Med.

SANDERSON, KARL G; Ramona HS; Ramona, CA; (2); 49/345; Hon Roll; Bus.

SANDERSON, SCOTT M; Clayton Valley HS; Concord, CA; (2); 68/374; Letterman Clb; JV Var Bsktbl; Var L Ftbl; Wt Lftg; Hon Roll; Mst Imprvd Plyr Awd Ftbl & Bsktbl.

SANDHU, SHARMILE; El Camino HS; Daly City, CA; (3); Teachers Aide; Bsktbl; Golf; Vllybl; San Mateo; Accntng.

SANDIE, LISA M; Valley Christian HS; Huntington Bch, CA; (3); Church Yth Grp; Office Aide; Speech Tm; Teachers Aide; Rptr Yrbk; Treas Jr Cls; VP Stu Cncl; Stat Bsbl; Var Socr; Var Trk; Psych.

SANDLER, AUBRA; Kennedy HS; Cypress, CA; (2); Dance Clb; Temple Yth Grp; Drill Tm; Nwsp; Cheerldng; Hon Roll; Dance; CSU Humbolt; Child Abuse Cnclr.

SANDLER, LISA; Los Alamitos HS; Seal Beach, CA; (3); Cmnty Wkr; Drama Clb; Pres Temple Yth Grp; Pres Chorus; School Musical; Cit Awd; Hon Roll; Soc Psych.

SANDMAN, JO ANNE; Oakmont HS; Roseville, CA; (3); Church Yth Grp; SADD; Teachers Aide; Mgr(s); Powder Puff Ftbl; Score Keeper; Trk; Vllybl; Wt Lftg; Hon Roll; Sierra JC; Trvl Agnt.

SANDOVAL, AMANDA J; Santa Clara HS; Santa Clara, CA; (2); JV Sftbl; Stat Wrstlng; Hon Roll; Math Tutr; Spnsh Hnrs; Stanford U; Elec Engr.

SANDOVAL, ANGELA R; Apple Valley HS; Apple Valley, CA; (3); Drama Clb; French Clb; Pep Clb; Powder Puff Ftbl; Hon Roll; Mock Trial Tm; Jr Statesman Of Amer; Engl.

SANDOVAL, ANN; Bishop Amat HS; W Covina, CA; (3); Drama Clb; School Musical; School Play; Pres Stu Cncl; Sftbl; Hon Roll; CA Hnr Soc; Business.

SANDOVAL, ARNOLD; Dos Palos HS; Dos Palos, CA; (4); 1/130; Church Yth Grp; Cmnty Wkr; Pres Math Clb; Math Tm; Science Clb; Band; Rep Sr Cls; Capt Var Bsktbl; Spanish NHS; Val; Acad Dcthln; CSF; Stnfrd U; Mech Engrng.

SANDOVAL, CARLOS; Bell Gardens HS; Bell Gardens, CA; (2); Crs Cntry; Trk.

SANDOVAL, CHRISTINE M; Santa Barbara HS; Santa Barbara, CA; (2); Dance Clb; Color Guard; Mrchg Band; CA ST Northridge; Bus Mgmt.

SANDOVAL, CLAUDIA A; Lakewood HS; Long Beach, CA; (2); Latin Clb; Cit Awd; Hon Roll; Coll Bound Partnrshp Pgm.

SANDOVAL, CYBIL; Hanford High West Campus; Hanford, CA; (1); FHA; FTA; Spanish Clb; Teachers Aide; JV Crs Cntry; JV Swmmng; Hon Roll; Dev Disabled Clsrm Dance, Spec Olympic Dances & Firework Booth Chaparon; UC Berkley; Spec Ed.

SANDOVAL JR, DAMIAN; Baldwin Park HS; Baldwin Park, CA; (1); Computer Clb; 4-H; Capt Bsktbl; Capt Vllybl; Hon Roll; Rio Hondo Coll; Elec Engr.

SANDOVAL, DANIEL M; Carson HS; Carson, CA; (2); Prfct Atten Awd; USC; Doctor.

SANDOVAL, DENISE; Santa Monica HS; Santa Monica, CA; (3); Band; Mrchg Band; Pep Band; Anml Rights; UC Davis; Anml Sci.

SANDOVAL, ELIZABETH; La Puente HS; La Puente, CA; (3); Teachers Aide; Teachers Aide; Var Capt Swmmng; Hon Roll; Rio Hondo; Dental Assistant.

SANDOVAL, ELVIA; Sacred Heart Of Jesus HS; Los Angeles, CA; (3); GAA; Crs Cntry; Mgr(s); High Hon Roll; Hon Roll; NHS; Language Arts Awd; Certifcte Awd Chem; Certfct Awd Excellence Algebra II.

SANDOVAL, ESTELA; Santa Paula Union HS; Santa Paula, CA; (1); 6/361; Church Yth Grp; Cmnty Wkr; Hon Roll; CSF; U Partnership Pgm; Secty/Treas; Med.

SANDOVAL, EVITA; Casa Grande HS; Petaluma, CA; (3); 35/288; Church Yth Grp; Spanish Clb; Hon Roll; NHS; Sonoma ST U; Accntng.

SANDOVAL, FRANKIE; Mesa Verde HS; Citrus Heights, CA; (2); 97/290; JV Bsbl; JV Bsktbl; Fire Fghtr.

SANDOVAL, GERARDO; Fillmore HS; Fillmore, CA; (1); Church Yth Grp; Bsbl; Ftbl; CA ST Northridge; Orthodntst.

SANDOVAL, GUILLERMO; Atwater HS; Winton, CA; (4); 350/389; FFA; ROTC; SADD; VICA; Lit Mag; JV Wrstlng; Elks Awd; FFA Team Awds; 5th Pl Overall Indvdl Calcot Cotton St Fnls 89; Merced JC; Ag Bus/Mgmt.

SANDOVAL, HILDA; Sacred Heart Of Jesus HS; Los Angeles, CA; (2); GAA; VP Frsh Cls; Stu Alumnae Rltns Cncl; Lang Arts Awd.

SANDOVAL, IMELDA; Calexico HS; Calexico, CA; (1); Key Clb; Off Frsh Cls; Hon Roll; San Diego ST U; Astrophysics.

SANDOVAL, JACQUELINE; Lynwood HS; Lynwood, CA; (3); 1/500; Math Clb; ROTC; Drill Tm; High Hon Roll; NHS; Prfct Atten Awd; Val; Frnch & Engl Awds; Honor Guard; UCLA; Medicine.

SANDOVAL, JAIME T; East Bakersfield HS; Bakersfield, CA; (2); Church Yth Grp; Teachers Aide; Church Choir; Cit Awd; Hon Roll; San Jose ST U; Drftsmn.

SANDOVAL, JOEL; Carson HS; Carson, CA; (2); Boy Scts; Church Yth Grp; Letterman Clb; Service Clb; School Musical; Lit Mag; JV Bsbl; Score Keeper; Cit Awd; High Hon Roll; CA JR Schlrshp Fed; Long Beach ST ; Aero Engr.

SANDOVAL, JOSE A; Carson HS; Carson, CA; (3); Spanish Clb; Rptr Nwsp; Hon Roll; Jr NHS; NHS; Prfct Atten Awd; Acad Achvt Awds; Ladies & Knights Clb; Loyola Mrymnt U; Bus Admin.

SANDOVAL, JOSE A; George Washington HS; Los Angeles, CA; (3); Latin Clb; Math Tm; Spanish Clb; Socr; Vllybl; Stu Of Yr; Acctng.

SANDOVAL, JOSE G; Chaffey HS; Ontario, CA; (3).

SANDOVAL, JUAN J; Brawley Union HS; Brawley, CA; (1); Boy Scts; Church Yth Grp; 4-H; Intrml Bsbl; Hon Roll; Cal Poly Pomona; Arch.

SANDOVAL, LISA A; Bishop Amat HS; La Puente, CA; (3); Church Yth Grp; Cmnty Wkr; Office Aide; Teachers Aide; Pres Frsh Cls; Stu Cncl; Hon Roll; Delhaven Cmmty Ctr Cert Apprctn; S Gate Police Dept Ride Along Pgm; UCLA; Psych.

SANDOVAL, MICHAEL O; Golden West HS; Visalia, CA; (3); Science Clb; Orch; School Musical; Hon Roll; Violinist Tulare Cty Symphony; Boys ST CA; CA ST Summer Schl For Arts 88.

SANDOVAL, MOISES; Fillmore HS; Fillmore, CA; (1); Art Clb; FCA; Latin Clb; Spanish Clb; Bsbl; Hon Roll; Atty.

SANDOVAL, NICOLAS; American HS; Fremont, CA; (3); 146/310; ROP Industrial Drftg; CADD Cmptr Drftg; Lfgd & Lifesaving Skills Lfgd Prgm; Arch Dsgn; Mech Drftg; Chabot Coll; Arch.

SANDOVAL, NORA L; Manual Arts HS; Lynwood, CA; (4); 30/250; Drama Clb; Math Clb; Math Tm; Spanish Clb; Varsity Clb; Stage Crew; Off Soph Cls; JV Sftbl; JV Var Vllybl; Cit Awd; Pin & Certificate Golden Shawl; Silver Seal Bearer; Honor Society Pin; Volunteer Awds; Citizenship Awds; Mount St Marys Coll; Business.

SANDOVAL, PATRICIA; Bishop Montgomery HS; Torrance, CA; (2); JV Crs Cntry; JV Trk; U Of Santa Barbara; Marine Bio.

SANDOVAL, RICHARD; Antelope Valley HS; Lancaster, CA; (3); 101/631; French Clb; Spanish Clb; Hon Roll; Arch.

SANDOVAL, ROBERTA; La Puente HS; Rialto, CA; (4); Dance Clb; Pep Clb; Red Cross Aide; Teachers Aide; Thesps; Ed Yrbk; Var Cheerldng; Var Pom Pon; Var Score Keeper; Var Swmmng; Girls League; San Bernardino JC; Hlth Care.

SANDOVAL, ROSE; Saint Anthony HS; Long Beach, CA; (3); French Clb; Prfct Atten Awd.

SANDOVAL, SERVANDO; W C Overfelt HS; San Jose, CA; (4); 19/240; Teachers Aide; Band; Jazz Band; Mrchg Band; Lit Mag; VP Frsh Cls; Stu Cncl; Hon Roll; Mesa, G D Forum & WCO Schlrshp; UCLA; Bus Admin.

SANDOVAL, SONIA E; Santa Clara HS; Oxnard, CA; (3); 10/145; Cmnty Wkr; Pep Clb; Off Frsh Cls; VP Soph Cls; Off Jr Cls; Off Sr Cls; NHS; FLOA; Church ECD Teachers Aide; Cal Poly; Bus Law.

SANDOVAL, SOPHIA A; Bellarmine Jefferson HS; Los Angeles, CA; (4); Church Yth Grp; Pep Clb; Chorus; Church Choir; Hon Roll; Bnk Amer Awd Outstndng Achvt In Art; Achvt Awds In Choir, Excllnc In Acads; Hnr Rl; Christ Coll Irvine; Art.

SANDOVAL, THOMAS; Bishop Amat HS; Rowland Hts, CA; (4); 19/400; Service Clb; Rep Stu Cncl; Cit Awd; High Hon Roll; NHS; CA Schlrshp Fed; Spcl Olympics Vlntr; Slvr Screen Clb; Pltcl Sci.

SANDOVAL JR, WILLIAM R; Bakersfield HS; Bakersfield, CA; (2); Office Aide; Treas Frsh Cls; Stu Cncl; JV Ftbl; JV Wrstlng; Hon Roll; CA ST Coll.

SANDQUIST, CATHY A; Pacifica HS; Garden Grove, CA; (3); Church Yth Grp; Science Clb; Chorus; School Musical; Var Swmmng; Var Trk; Stat Wrstlng; Cit Awd; Medcl.

SANDQUIST, THERESE A; Anderson Union HS; Sweden; (4); Acpl Chr; Var Socr; Var Swmmng; Var Tennis; Var Trk; U Of Sweden.

SANDROCK, LORI; William S Hart HS; Valencia, CA; (4); 18/485; Cmnty Wkr; Math Tm; Mu Alpha Theta; Pres Acad Fit Awd; JR Hnr; Actng & Directng Wkshps; CSF; USC; Drama.

SANDS, MONICA; So California Christian HS; Placentia, CA; (3); Band; Pres Chorus; Pep Band; JV Var Cheerldng; Hon Roll; Mst Tlntd Female Vclst 89-90; Mst Insprtnl Vrsty Chrldr 89-90; HS Hnr Grd 88-90; Azusa Pacific U; Music.

SANDS, TODD A; Mission Viejo HS; Mission Viejo, CA; (1); 76/455; Intrml Bsbl; Intrml Ftbl; Intrml Wt Lftg; Prfct Atten Awd; Golf; NE; Med.

SANDVICK, CINDY R; Woodland HS; Woodland, CA; (3); FFA; Girl Scts; Hon Roll; Vlntr; Sftbl; CA Poly; Animal Health Tech.

SANDWELL, KATHLEEN A; Fairfield HS; Fairfield, CA; (2); Church Yth Grp; Band; Mrchg Band; Cit Awd; High Hon Roll; NHS; CA Band Dir Assn St Hnr Band; 1st Chr CMEA Bay Sect Hnr Band; Clarinet Tchr; Pacific U; Music.

SANDY, GISELLA; La Sierra Acad; Riverside, CA; (4); 1/52; Chorus; Orch; Sec Soph Cls; VP Jr Cls; Treas Sr Cls; Var L Crs Cntry; JV Vllybl; NHS; Pres Acad Fit Awd; Val; Loma Linda U; Sci.

SANEZ, ABBY V; Immaculate Heart HS; Los Angeles, CA; (3); 68/112; Cmnty Wkr; Drama Clb; GAA; Yrbk; Off Frsh Cls; Stu Cncl; Hon Roll; Assn To Promote Black Awareness Officer; Film Club Pres.

SANFILIPPO, JOY; Soquel HS; Soquel, CA; (4); 1/300; Church Yth Grp; Ed Yrbk; Pres Frsh Cls; Pres Soph Cls; Stu Cncl; Var Capt Bsktbl; Swmmng; Cit Awd; Ntl Merit Ltr; Val; Young Life; Acadmc Dcthln; U Of CA Davis; Chem Engrng.

SANFORD, COLEENA M; Willow Glen Educational Park HS; San Jose, CA; (1); SADD; JV Swmmng; Wt Lftg; Pres Acad Fit Awd; Engl Schlstc Achvt Awd; Chicgo ST; Ftns.

SANFORD, JANEARE S; Berkeley HS; Berkeley, CA; (3); VP Church Yth Grp; Debate Tm; Band; Church Choir; Pep Band; Sec Soph Cls; Var L Trk; U Of CA Yng Musicns Pgm; MESA; Jnr Statemn Of Amer Bst Debatr Awd; Poly Sci.

SANFORD, JOANNE L; Notre Dame HS; Belmont, CA; (4); Church Yth Grp; Cmnty Wkr; VP Model UN; School Play; Stage Crew; Ed Nwsp; Ed Lit Mag; Trk; Hon Roll; NHS; U Of CA Davis.

SANFORD, KARLA S; Monte Vista HS; Spring Valley, CA; (3); Cmnty Wkr; Pep Clb; Drill Tm; Phtg Yrbk; Sec Jr Cls; Var JV Bsktbl; Cheerldng; Var Trk; Dance Clb; Key Clb; Amer All Star Dance Tm; Dance 22nd Super Bowl; All Leag Trck & Crs Cntry; Teen Workout Video; Health.

SANFORD, LATISHA A; Leuzinger HS; Gardena, CA; (3); Band; Drill Tm; Rep Jr Cls; Rep Stu Cncl; High Hon Roll; Hon Roll; Ebony Nation Club; Law.

SANGHA, BALJINDER K; Livingston HS; Livingston, CA; (3); Cit Awd; Hon Roll; Prfct Atten Awd; CSU; Bus.

SANGHA, SONI; Sunny Hills High; Buena Park, CA; (2); Cmnty Wkr; German Clb; Hosp Aide; Intnl Clb; Key Clb; Model UN; Service Clb; Temple Yth Grp; Rep Stu Cncl; High Hon Roll; Membr And Head Of Publication For Amnesty Intl In The IB Program; U Then Med Schl; Biology & Dr.

SANGSTER, GWENDOLYN A; Dos Pueblos HS; Goleta, CA; (3); 20/338; Church Yth Grp; French Clb; FTA; Sec VP Intnl Clb; Math Clb; Sec Science Clb; Acpl Chr; Band; Mrchg Band; Pep Band; Elem Educ.

SANGSTER, TRACY L; East Bakersfield HS; Bakersfield, CA; (3); 22/441; Church Yth Grp; Pres Drama Clb; Intnl Clb; SADD; Pres Thesps; Chorus; Church Choir; School Musical; School Play; Stage Crew; Video Yrbk Exec Producer; Freedoms Fndtn Vly Forge Trip; Theatre.

SANI, ROYA N; Paso Robles HS; Templeton, CA; (2); #1 In Class; JV Swmmng; Var Tennis; JV Var Trk; Cit Awd; High Hon Roll; CSF; United Nations Club; Hiking/Environmental Club; Golden St Geom Exam Honors; Med.

SANI, SEPEHR; West HS; Torrance, CA; (2); Intnl Clb; ROTC; Teachers Aide; Crs Cntry; Cit Awd; Harvard U; Math.

SANIN, ELIZABETH; Bishop Amat HS; Diamond Bar, CA; (3); Spanish Clb; Hon Roll; Hnrs Spnsh Awd; Bio.

SANITPRACHAKORN, TIM N; Arcadia HS; Arcadia, CA; (3); AFS; Church Yth Grp; Bsktbl; JV Ftbl; Var Vllybl; Cit Awd; High Hon Roll; Hon Roll; NHS; NHS; Gold Seal Grad; Bio.

SANJUAN, MARTHA S; Canyon Springs HS; Moreno Valley, CA; (2); Hon Roll; Dentistry.

SANSON, KAI B; Santa Monica HS; Malibu, CA; (2); Ski Clb; JV Vllybl; Cit Awd; Hon Roll; Pres Acad Fit Awd; Water Polo 2 Yrs; U Of CO Boulder; Real Estate.

SANSONI, JULIE A; Atwater HS; Merced, CA; (3); Church Yth Grp; FCA; Church Choir; High Hon Roll; CA Schlrshp Fed; Making Electv Cnt For Career Achvt; Pre-Med.

SANSOUR, JOHN J; Los Alamitos HS; Los Alamitos, CA; (4); 3/30; Bsktbl; Socr; Vllybl; Bk Amer Achvt Awds; Cmmndtn Awd Eng As 2nd Lang Dept; Long Beach City Coll; Acctg.

SANTA CRUZ, EDUARDO; Downey SR HS; S Gate, CA; (2); Office Aide; Rep Science Clb; Service Clb; Chorus; Cit Awd; Hon Roll; Pres Acad Fit Awd; Rotary Awd; Foreign Lang Awd; CA ST U; Arch.

SANTA CRUZ, REYES; Roseville HS; Rocklin, CA; (1); Varsity Clb; JV Ftbl; JV Wrstlng; AZ ST U; Bus.

SANTA CRUZ, SOFIA; Hesperia HS; Hesperia, CA; (2); VP French Clb; FBLA; Ski Clb; Bus.

SANTACQUA, CARMELA G; San Luis Obispo HS; San Luis Obispo, CA; (3); 18/329; Church Yth Grp; Cmnty Wkr; FFA; High Hon Roll; Prfct Atten Awd; Spcl Olympc Vlntr; Chld Dvlpmnt.

SANTACRUZ, ROCIO R; Sacred Heart Of Mary HS; Los Angeles, CA; (3); Cmnty Wkr; Rep GAA; Church Choir; School Play; VP Stu Cncl; Sftbl; Vllybl; NHS; Cnty Los Angeles Vlntr Awd; Yth Encounter Core Tm; Psych.

SANTAMARIA, JENNIFER B; Colton HS; Grand Terrace, CA; (2); Church Yth Grp; FHA; Key Clb; Cit Awd; Hon Roll; Rep Stu Cncl; JV Bsktbl; Var Trk; JV Vllybl; Aeronautical Engrng.

SANTAMARIA, MALU; Bell HS; Alhambra, CA; (3); Church Yth Grp; Math Clb; Teachers Aide; Chorus; Hon Roll; Memb CSI; Memb Of Latinas Gdg Latinas UCLA; Residncy Desert Stdy Ctr CSU CA; Bioloby Chem Tchr.

SANTAMOOR, DANIELLE M; Winters HS; Winters, CA; (2); Debate Tm; Drama Clb; French Clb; Library Aide; Speech Tm; School Play; Stage Crew; Friday Night Live; CSF; Nrs.

SANTANA, ARACELI; Sacred Heart Of Jesus HS; Los Angeles, CA; (2); Church Yth Grp; Dance Clb; GAA; JV Bsktbl; CA ST Los Angeles; Law Enfrcm.

SANTANA, JIM J; St Ignatius College Prep; San Mateo, CA; (3); Church Yth Grp; Cmnty Wkr; Ski Clb; Varsity Clb; JV Golf; Var Tennis; Hon Roll; CSF; UC Santa Barbara; Law.

SANTANA, JUAN; Montebello HS; Montebello, CA; (4); JV Bsbl; Hon Roll; Cal ST U Los Angeles; Bus Adm.

SANTANA, JUAN M; Fontana HS; Fontana, CA; (3); 25/1275; Teachers Aide; Hon Roll; Prfct Atten Awd; CA Schlrshp Fund; Embry-Riddle Arntcl U; Aviation.

SANTANA, MELISSA D; Grace M Davis HS; Modesto, CA; (2); GAA; Powder Puff Ftbl; Sftbl; Vllybl; Cit Awd; Hon Roll; Doctor.

SANTANA, RAUL M; Don Bosco Technical Inst; El Monte, CA; (3); Church Yth Grp; Cmnty Wkr; JV Bsbl; Cal Poly Pomona; Arch.

SANTANA, SANDRA S; Morningside HS; Inglewood, CA; (2); Church Yth Grp; Hon Roll; Poetry Clb; Drama Clb; Writer.

SANTANA, STEVE Z; Project Outreach HS; Pomona, CA; (3); Wt Lftg; Pomona Coll; Singing Artist.

SANTEE, KELLY; Christian Community Acad; San Jose, CA; (1); School Play; Var Bsktbl; Var Sftbl; Var Vllybl; Hon Roll.

SANTELLI, RENEE ANDREA; S California Christian HS; Anaheim, CA; (1); 9/48; Church Yth Grp; Rptr Nwsp; Var Bsktbl; Hon Roll; Anaheim Sccr Assn; Ed.

SANTHANAM, KUMARAN; Saint Francis HS; Sunnyvale, CA; (2); 3/372; Math Clb; Math Tm; Science Clb; Speech Tm; School Musical; High Hon Roll; Lion Awd; Pres Acad Fit Awd; Piano/Organ; Wstrn-Indian Violin; Carnatic Vocal Music; Cert Of Recog For Acads & Hnrs; Outstndg Achieve; Stanford U; Engrng.

SANTIAGO, BRYAN; Mater Dei HS; Huntington Bch, CA; (2); Cmnty Wkr; German Clb; Band; Mrchg Band; Pep Band; High Hon Roll.

SANTIAGO, HERNAN; Arvin HS; Lamont, CA; (2); Letterman Clb; Teachers Aide; Varsity Clb; Pres Soph Cls; Var Bsbl; Var Bsktbl; Var Ftbl; Var Wt Lftg; Hon Roll; Various Sports Awds; UCLA; Child Dvlpmnt Teacher.

SANTIAGO, HOLLY; Simi Valley HS; Celina, TX; (2); Dance Clb; FHA; School Musical; Variety Show; JV Golf; Child Psych.

SANTIAGO, IRENE; William Howard Taft HS; Encino, CA; (3); Church Yth Grp; Mu Alpha Theta; Band; Color Guard; Mrchg Band; Cit Awd; High Hon Roll; Prfct Atten Awd; Acad Ltr; Recpnt Of Saturday Schlrshp; Ped.

SANTIAGO, JOSE M; Baldwin Park HS; Baldwin Park, CA; (3); Science Clb; Teachers Aide; JV Var Ftbl; JV Wrstlng; Physics.

SANTIAGO, KIMBERLEY A; River City HS; W Sacramento, CA; (3); Chorus; Church Choir; Hon Roll; Mount St Marys Coll; Music.

SANTIAGO, NOELIA; Santa Monica HS; Santa Monica, CA; (1); Cit Awd; Prfct Atten Awd; MECHA Club; Arch.

SANTIAGO, ROBERT; Lincoln Prep HS; San Diego, CA; (3); Cmnty Wkr; Scholastic Bowl; Speech Tm; Mrchg Band; Pep Band; Sec Jr Cls; Rep Stu Cncl; Var Tennis; Hon Roll; Lion Awd; Sci Fair; Med.

SANTILLAN, DOLORES O; Oroville HS; Oroville, CA; (3); Dance Clb; Ski Clb; Band; Mrchg Band; Pep Band; Hon Roll; Prfct Atten Awd; Frshmn Band Mem Yr; Band Block O; Stu Mnth Band; UCLA; Orthdntst.

SANTILLAN, GEORGE; Rio Americano HS; Carmichael, CA; (3); Hon Roll; Comp Oprtr.

SANTILLAN, GRACIELA; Dos Palos Joint Union HS; Dos Palos, CA; (2); Church Yth Grp; Trk; High Hon Roll; Hon Roll; MECHA Pres; CSF; Fshn Dsgn.

SANTILLAN, JESUS; Dos Palos HS; Dos Palos, CA; (2); Math Clb; Spanish Clb; School Play; Crs Cntry; Trk; Wrstlng; Hon Roll; Prfct Atten Awd; Pres Acad Fit Awd; Electrcn.

SANTILLAN, RUMELDA; Dos Palos HS; Dos Palos, CA; (3); Church Yth Grp; Varsity Clb; Chorus; Church Choir; Sftbl; MECHA; Pr Cnslr; Spnsh Clb; Fresno ST; Pfrsnl Sngr.

SANTILLANO, MARIA; Modesto HS; Modesto, CA; (4); 11/277; Teachers Aide; Pres Band; Pres Mrchg Band; Pep Band; Yrbk; Var Crs Cntry; Var Trk; Hon Roll; UC-DAVIS; Med.

SANTINI, CHRISTOPHER D; Lincoln HS; Stockton, CA; (2); 59/568; Band; Mrchg Band; Trk; High Hon Roll; Hon Roll; CSF.

SANTO, RICHARD; Lindhurst HS; Marysville, CA; (2); Band; Mrchg Band; Socr; JV Tennis; Hon Roll; Civil Air Patrl; Aviation.

SANTORA, MAURA K; Carlsbad HS; Carlsbad, CA; (4); 11/350; Pep Clb; Var JV Swmmng; Capt Var Tennis; Cit Awd; High Hon Roll; Pres Acad Fit Awd; UC Santa Barbara; Marine Bio.

SANTOS, ADRIAN; William Workman HS; La Puente, CA; (1); Bsbl; Ftbl; Socr.

SANTOS, ADRIANA; Watsonville HS; Aromas, CA; (2); 74/545; CA U; Bus.

SANTOS, ALEXANDER; John W North HS; Highgrove, CA; (3); Office Aide; Teachers Aide; Ed Nwsp; Cit Awd; Hon Roll; Loma Linda U; Pharmacy.

SANTOS, ARIELLE MISTRAL; Rancho Buena Vista HS; Vista, CA; (4); 31/400; Drama Clb; French Clb; Pep Clb; SADD; School Play; Stu Cncl; Var Capt Cheerldng; Var Capt Gym; Elks Awd; USA Spirit Star Awd; Homcmng Princess; Dance; U CA San Diego; Elem Ed.

SANTOS, BERNIE J; Mt Diablo HS; Concord, CA; (2); Cit Awd; High Hon Roll; Prfct Atten Awd; UC Davis; Comp Engrng.

SANTOS, CONNIE; Venice HS; Los Angeles, CA; (2); Peace Clb; Earth Day Presentations; Screenwriting.

SANTOS, DIANE; Denair HS; Denair, CA; (1); Fresno ST; Nrs.

SANTOS III, DION D; Don Bosed Technical Inst; Monterey Park, CA; (3); Boy Scts; Stat Letterman Clb; Red Cross Aide; Band; Church Choir; Drm Mjr(t); Jazz Band; Mrchg Band; Var Vllybl; High Hon Roll; US Air Force Acad; Mfg Engrng.

SANTOS, DUFFY J; Don Bosco Technical HS; Los Angeles, CA; (3); Church Yth Grp; NHS; CA ST U L A; Art.

SANTOS, DUREZA L; Alverno HS; Glendale, CA; (2); 1/70; VP Church Yth Grp; Sec Intnl Clb; Treas Model UN; Ed Lit Mag; Rep Frsh Cls; Rep Soph Cls; Rep Jr Cls; Var Tennis; French Hon Soc; High Hon Roll; Wrld Hstry; Math Fair Hnrbl Mntn; CA Schlrshp Fed; Editor Ltry Mag; Prnclpls Hnr Roll; Frnch Awd; Stanford U; Sclgy.

SANTOS, ELISABEL; St Paul HS; Whittier, CA; (3); Hon Roll; NHS; Spanish NHS; CSF; Cal ST Fullerton; Tchng.

SANTOS, EVANGELINE G; East Bakersfield HS; Bakersfield, CA; (3); Intnl Clb; Pep Clb; SADD; Cheerldng; Tennis; Hon Roll; Bus.

SANTOS, HAZEL E; Hesperia HS; Hesperia, CA; (3); High Hon Roll.

SANTOS, HEDELITA; Francis Polytechnic HS; N Hollywood, CA; (3); Hon Roll; Apprctn Awd; Prncpls Hnr Roll; Outstndng Stu Awd; CA ST U Northridge; Acctng.

SANTOS, JAVIER; Castle Park HS; Chula Vista, CA; (3); Boy Scts; Church Yth Grp; Chorus; JV Ftbl; Var Socr.

SANTOS, JAYSON EUGENIO; Hesperia HS; Hesperia, CA; (4); 100/500; Sec Chess Clb; Pres Computer Clb; Treas French Clb; Rep Am Leg Aux Girls St; L Swmmng; JV Wrstlng; High Hon Roll; Hon Roll; Comtech Scholarship; Los Doreados Scholarship; Electronics Engineering.

SANTOS, JENNIFER L; Bishop O'dowd HS; San Leandro, CA; (3); Debate Tm; Ed Nwsp; Hon Roll; NEDT Awd; GAPP Exchnge Germany; Jnr Statesmn America; Vet.

SANTOS, JESSICA LYN; Lindhurst HS; Marysville, CA; (1); Church Yth Grp; Sec Frsh Cls; Cheerldng; Pom Pon; Wt Lftg; Hon Roll; Modlng.

SANTOS, JOEY M; Upper Lake Union HS; Upper Lake, CA; (4); 10/56; Am Leg Boys St; Art Clb; Drama Clb; Science Clb; Ski Clb; Spanish Clb; Teachers Aide; Rep Band; School Play; Stage Crew; Mendocino Coll; Law.

SANTOS, JOSE D; Bishop Amat HS; Diamond Bar, CA; (3); Math Clb; Teachers Aide; Comp Lab Asst; Silver Screen Club.

SANTOS, JULIA M; Santa Clara HS; Santa Clara, CA; (1); Church Yth Grp; Chorus; Cit Awd; Hon Roll; Math; Vlybl; Reading; Writing Down Thoughts; Cal Poly; Tech Eng.

SANTOS, KIMBERLY A; Durham HS; Durham, CA; (2); Treas 4-H; GAA; Ski Clb; Rep Frsh Cls; Rep Soph Cls; Off Jr Cls; JV Bsktbl; Var Sftbl; Var Trk; JV Vllybl; CA Schlrshp Fdrtn; Bus Admin.

SANTOS, LORENA ARLENE; Mar Vista HS; San Diego, CA; (3); Art Clb; Drama Clb; Thesps; Variety Show; Rptr Nwsp; Treas Sr Cls; Var Crs Cntry; Hon Roll; Pres Acad Fit Awd; Voice Dem Awd; Mdlng Clb Shws & Tll Tle Cont Fnlst; San Diego ST U.

SANTOS, MARISSA V; Gladstone HS; Azusa, CA; (4); 7/247; German Clb; Science Clb; Nwsp; Yrbk; High Hon Roll; Hon Roll; NHS; JV & V Badminton; Principals Hnr Roll; CSF; Cal-Poly Pomona; Cmptr Info Sys.

SANTOS, MARYLOU; Nogales HS; Walnut, CA; (2); High Hon Roll; Prfct Atten Awd; CSF; UCLA; Med.

SANTOS, MICHELLE B; Whitney HS; Cerritos, CA; (2); Church Yth Grp; Nwsp; Hon Roll; CSF; Filipino Clb; UC Irvine.

SANTOS, MONICA M; Atwater HS; Merced, CA; (2); Church Yth Grp; 4-H; GAA; Var Socr; Hon Roll; Olympc Devlpmnt Soccer.

SANTOS, OLIVER; Piedmont Hills HS; San Jose, CA; (4); 79/319; French Clb; JA; Office Aide; Red Cross Aide; Spanish Clb; Teachers Aide; Mgr(s); Score Keeper; Var JV Tennis; Cmnty Wkr; Assctd Stu Body Publicity Cmmssnr; 10k Race Offcl; U Of CA-SANTA Cruz; Bio.

SANTOS JR, RAUL; William Workman HS; La Puente, CA; (3); 9/294; Letterman Clb; Science Clb; Varsity Clb; VP Stu Cncl; Var Capt Socr; Hon Roll; Prfct Atten Awd; Booster Clb, Soccer Awds; Dist Schlr; Engrng.

SANTOS, RAYMOND; Fremont Christian Schl; Fremont, CA; (1); Church Yth Grp; FCA; VP Frsh Cls; JV Bsktbl; Var Vllybl; Electrnc Engr.

SANTOS, RICARDO J; San Dieguito HS; Encinitas, CA; (4); SADD; Teachers Aide; Var JV Bsbl; Saferide SADD; Mira Costa Coll; Telecommnctns.

SANTOS, ROWENA G; Ramona Convent Secondary HS; El Monte, CA; (3); Pres Art Clb; GAA; Model UN; Office Aide; School Play; Stage Crew; Phtg Yrbk; NHS; Vlntr Homes Devlpmntlly Disable; Tae Kwon Do Self Defns; Pedtrcn.

SANTOS, SELENE; South Gate HS; Downey, CA; (3); Church Yth Grp; Debate Tm; VP Spanish Clb; Hon Roll; Prfct Atten Awd; Psych.

SANTOS, SHEILA; Franklin JR HS; Vallejo, CA; (1); Computer Clb; Drill Tm; Yrbk; Off Frsh Cls; Stu Cncl; Vllybl; High Hon Roll; Hon Roll; Success Club; Hnr Soc; UC Davis; Bus Mgmt.

SANTOS, SUSIE; Castle Park HS; Chula Vista, CA; (4); 21/320; Church Yth Grp; French Clb; German Clb; Service Clb; Sec Lit Mag; Stu Cncl; Hon Roll; Associated Stu Bdy Asst Tribune Of Finance; Banquet Cmmtte Chrprsn; Brigham Young U; Acctng.

SANTOS, TAMMI L; Hanford Joint Union HS; Hanford, CA; (1); Office Aide; Hon Roll; Acad Lttr; JCCA Rodeos; Gymkhana; Law.

SANTOS, VICTOR C; Sanger HS; Sanger, CA; (2); Art Clb; Church Yth Grp; ROTC; Science Clb; Spanish Clb; Cit Awd; High Hon Roll; Hon Roll; Prfct Atten Awd; Berkley; Med.

SANTOYO, GERARDO M; Ontario HS; Ontario, CA; (3); Church Yth Grp; Socr; Hon Roll; Math.

SANTOYO, LORRAINE; Dos Palos HS; Dos Palos, CA; (1); Church Yth Grp; FHA; Spanish Clb; Hon Roll; CAL Poly; Lwyr.

SANTOYO, NANCY; San Joaquin Memorial HS; Firebaugh, CA; (4); Sec Drama Clb; Science Clb; Pres Spanish Clb; Nwsp; VP Sftbl; Hon Roll; ACT Clb; Frdy Nght Live Clb; Peer Cnslr; Acad All-Amer; Fresno ST; Crmnlgy.

SANTUCCI, TRACY L; St Francis HS; Portola Valley, CA; (3); Intnl Clb; Service Clb; SADD; Powder Puff Ftbl; JV Socr; High Hon Roll; Hon Roll; Ed.

SANVICTORES, SHERRY L; John A Rowland HS; Walnut, CA; (3); 57/546; Letterman Clb; Science Clb; Chorus; Swing Chorus; JV Co-Capt Bsktbl; JV Vllybl; High Hon Roll; Hon Roll; NHS; Pres Acad Fit Awd; Med.

SANZONE, LISA; Bonita Vista HS; Bonita, CA; (4); 13/534; Intnl Clb; Sec Service Clb; SADD; Nwsp; Yrbk; Lit Mag; Cit Awd; DAR Awd; High Hon Roll; Pres Acad Fit Awd; Intl Baccalaureite Wrld Cultures Awd; Lwyr.

SAPERSTEIN, ADAM K; Monte Vista HS; Alamo, CA; (2); 11/400; Pres Temple Yth Grp; Acpl Chr; Band; Chorus; Mrchg Band; Orch; JV Bsbl; JV Socr; High Hon Roll; VP NHS; Yth Undrstndg Schlrshp Smmr Aboard Spain 90; St Hnr Choir; Medcl.

SAPIDA, STEVE; Castle Park HS; Chula Vista, CA; (4); 16/360; Pres Art Clb; Church Yth Grp; Pep Clb; Band; Jazz Band; Pep Band; Rep Sr Cls; CSF; MECHA; Aero Engr.

SAPIEN, SHANNON Y; Bonita HS; La Verne, CA; (3); SADD; Teachers Aide; Drill Tm; Hon Roll; Law.

SAPITULA, LESTER L; Don Bosco Technical Inst; Hacienda Hghts, CA; (3); Sec Letterman Clb; Pres Band; Jazz Band; Mrchg Band; Orch; Cit Awd; Hon Roll; Jr NHS; NHS; Pres Acad Fit Awd; Ind Educ Cncl Medallion Awd; Campus Mnstry Grp; Golden Tiger Awd; Stanford; Mech Engrng.

SAPOZNICK, SAM O; Liebe-Wilmerding HS; Daly City, CA; (2); High Hon Roll.

SAPP, ANIESHA I; Bishop O'dowd HS; Oakland, CA; (3); Hon Roll; Hstry Clb; Black Stus Union; Hstry.

SAPP, B BROOK; Clovis West HS; Clovis, CA; (4); Church Yth Grp; Drama Clb; Teachers Aide; Church Choir; Yrbk; Stat Diving; High Hon Roll; Hon Roll; Ed.

SAPPENFIELD, SCOTT B; Clovis West HS; Fresno, CA; (2); Church Yth Grp; Cmnty Wkr; Treas Jr Cls; JV Socr; Hon Roll; CAA Schltc Fed; City Select Soccr Tm; Mrktng Exec.

SAPPINGTON, MARC S; Liberty Union HS; Brentwood, CA; (3); 60/375; Church Yth Grp; FCA; Socr; Tennis; UC Santa Barbara; Accntng.

SAR, SOVANN; Millikan HS; Long Beach, CA; (4); English Clb; FFA; Orch; School Play; Swmmng; JETS Awd; Rgnl Occptnl Prog; LBCC; Auth Mech.

SARAC, LAURA; Arroyo HS; San Leandro, CA; (3); Church Yth Grp; FBLA; Treas SADD; Church Choir; Orch; High Hon Roll; Chldrns Sunday Schl Tchr; CA Schlrshp Foundation Clb; UC Berkeley; Bus.

SARAGUETA, JUSTIN; Hanford Union HS; Hanford, CA; (2); Teachers Aide; JV Bsbl; Rep USA At Wrlds Boys Bsbl Trnmnt Japan; AZ ST; Bus Law.

SARANG, ROBINDER; Anaheim HS; Anaheim, CA; (4); Science Clb; JV Socr; NHS; Prfct Atten Awd; CSU Fullerton; Elec Engrng.

SARANTOPOULOS, PETE; Warren HS; South Gate, CA; (2); Band; Mrchg Band; Pep Band; Cit Awd; Pres Acad Fit Awd; UCLA; Med.

SARAS, JESSICA J; Mission HS; San Gabriel, CA; (3); Dance Clb; Teachers Aide; Variety Show; Capt Var Cheerldng; Hnr Roll; Perfect Attndnc Awd; Choreographic Skills; Loyola Marymount; Prfrmng Arts.

SARASPI, CAROLYN M R; St Joseph Notre Dame HS; Alameda, CA; (3); Cmnty Wkr; Hosp Aide; Church Choir; Phtg Ed Nwsp; Phtg Yrbk; Var Cheerldng; Mgr Socr; High Hon Roll; NHS; Prfct Atten Awd; CSF.

SARASUA, SHERRIE B; Bishop Amat HS; Hacienda Heights, CA; (3); Dance Clb; Drama Clb; Spanish Clb; Trk; Psych.

SARAVIA, JON P; Montebello HS; Montebello, CA; (2); Acpl Chr; JV Vllybl; Prfct Atten Awd; Yth Grp; UCSB; Rel Est.

SARAVIA, MICHAEL; J F Kennedy HS; Buena Park, CA; (3); Debate Tm; Drama Clb; FBLA; Speech Tm; Teachers Aide; Chorus; School Play; Stage Crew; Hon Roll; Goldn ST Geom Hgh Hnrs & Algb I Hnrs; CPA.

SARAZA, VILMA CENA; Delano HS; Delano, CA; (3); Letterman Clb; Varsity Clb; Stat Bsktbl; Capt Var Vllybl; Hon Roll; United Filipino Org; 2nd Rmr Up Miss Phippine Weekend; Most Desire & MVP VLYBL; Comp Sci.

SARDAR, ALEX; Hoover HS; Glendale, CA; (3); German Clb; Nwsp; Off Sr Cls; Germ Hnr Soc; Stu Of Month 89; Outstndng JR Germ 90; Sci.

SARDAR, WINFRED A; Redlands HS; Loma Linda, CA; (2); Boy Scts; Chorus; Bsbl; Hon Roll; Prfct Atten Awd; Doctor.

SARENA, MATTHEW D; Santa Barbara HS; Goleta, CA; (3); Church Yth Grp; Debate Tm; Acpl Chr; Chorus; Bus.

SARFATY, ORIT ALCALAY; John F Kennedy HS; Granada Hills, CA; (2); 1/400; Cmnty Wkr; Hosp Aide; VP Pres Key Clb; Math Clb; Model UN; Temple Yth Grp; Rptr Nwsp; Sec Frsh Cls; Intrml Tennis; JV Vllybl; Black Belt; Pres CA JR Schlrshp Fed; Pres JR Statesmn Of Am; Hugh O Brien Yth Ldrshp Fndtn Ambssdr; Med.

SARFAZ-SATTAR, SHEHRAZ M; Fairfield HS; Fairfield, CA; (1); JV Diving; JV Swmmng; JV Waterpolo.

SARGEANT, STEVE; Los Alamitos HS; Los Alamitos, CA; (4); 3/502; Boy Scts; Church Yth Grp; Science Clb; Service Clb; Var Bsktbl; Var Capt Trk; Hon Roll; NHS; Eagle Scout; Mst Vlbl Ath Trk & Fld 89; CSF; USAF Acad; Arntcl Engrng.

SARGENT, APRIL D; Casa Grande HS; Petaluma, CA; (2); 13/295; Cmnty Wkr; SADD; Cit Awd; Hon Roll; NHS; Pres Acad Fit Awd; CSF; Achvt Awds In Numerous Actvts.

SARGENT, KOJO R; J E Mc Ateer Sota HS; San Francisco, CA; (4); Active Peer Cnslr, Drug Rehab/Suicide Prev; Pharmacists Asst 1 1/2 Yrs; San Francisco ST U; Comp Info.

SARGENT, TODD A; La Quinta HS; Fountain Valley, CA; (4); 63/346; Pres Pep Clb; Pres Chorus; School Musical; Treas Soph Cls; Treas Stu Cncl; JV Cheerldng; Var L Crs Cntry; Elks Awd; Hon Roll; Pres/Founder Boys Leag; Allegheny Coll; Pol Sci.

SARHAD, JON J; Turlock HS; Turlock, CA; (3); 2/500; Church Yth Grp; Debate Tm; Speech Tm; Var Ftbl; JV Swmmng; Var Trk; Var Wt Lftg; High Hon Roll; Hon Roll; Water Polo JV & Vrsty, CCC Chmpn, Ltr; Harvard U; Nuclear Physics.

SARIA, PATRICIA; Tokay HS; Stockton, CA; (3); French Clb; Key Clb; Rep Jr Cls; JV Var Cheerldng; Hon Roll; CSF; UC-DAVIS; Med.

SARIAN, RITA M; Torrance HS; R Cucamonga, CA; (3); 81/398; Teachers Aide; Hon Roll; Awd Frgn Lang Spnsh; Swmmng City Tm.

SARIC, KARIN J; John A Rowland HS; Rowland Hts, CA; (4); 8/548; Church Yth Grp; Spanish Clb; Powder Puff Ftbl; Cit Awd; High Hon Roll; Prfct Atten Awd; Pres Acad Fit Awd; CA Schlstc Fed; Oma Louisa Traylor Memrl Schlrshp; Bk Of Amer Bus Cert; Yth Fndtn Excptnl Schlr; UC Riverside; Bus Admin.

SARIGIANNIDES, JOHN; James Lick HS; San Jose, CA; (2); Church Yth Grp; Dance Clb; Hon Roll; Church Bsktbl; San Jose ST U; Electronics.

SARIO, GOSPEL P; Ramona Convent Secondary Schl; Rosemead, CA; (3); School Play; Off Frsh Cls; VP Soph Cls; Off Jr Cls; Sec Stu Cncl; JV Vllybl.

SARKISIAN, DAWN M; Armenian Mesrobian Schl; Montebello, CA; (3); Church Yth Grp; Library Aide; Office Aide; Teachers Aide; Drill Tm; Rep Frsh Cls; JV Bsktbl; Var JV Cheerldng; Gym; JV Sftbl; Prom Cmmtte; Armenian Yth Fndtn 2 Yrs; CA Poly Pomona; X-Ray Tech.

SARKISSIAN, ANI; Lowell HS; San Francisco, CA; (3); Pres French Clb; SADD; Ed Nwsp; Ntl Merit Ltr; CSF; Scl Sci.

SARKISSIAN, ROSEANI; University City HS; San Diego, CA; (4); Church Yth Grp; Office Aide; Teachers Aide; Mgr(s); Hon Roll; Fri Night Live; San Diego ST U; Bus.

SARMAC, MARK; St Genevieve HS; Sun Valley, CA; (3); Debate Tm; Model UN; Coll; Dentistry.

SARMAK, MARK; St Genevieve HS; Sun Valley, CA; (3); Model UN; Hon Roll; Mock Trl; Med.

SARMENT, JEFF O; Turlock HS; Turlock, CA; (2); Computer Clb; Hon Roll; Modesto JC; Bus.

SARMENTO, SCOTT; San Luis Obispo HS; San Luis Obispo, CA; (3); 99/343; Church Yth Grp; 4-H; FFA; Var L Trk; 4-H Awd; Star Greenhnd, Star Chptr Frmr; FFA VP; 4-H Pres; Cuesta Coll; Soil Sci.

SARMIENTO, AUBREY; St Bonaventure HS; Camarillo, CA; (3); Pep Clb; Variety Show; Cheerldng; Cit Awd; Hon Roll; American Coll Applied Arts.

SARMIENTO, CHERYL ANN T; Lowell HS; San Francisco, CA; (2); Office Aide; Rep Frsh Cls.

SARMIENTO, JOYCE; Holy Family HS; Los Angeles, CA; (2); Art Clb; Church Yth Grp; Cmnty Wkr; Drama Clb; Hosp Aide; Teachers Aide; Church Choir; School Play; Prfct Atten Awd; Schl Nwsp Awd Of Mrt; Schl Campus Mnstry.

SARMIENTO, MARILOU C; William C Overfelt HS; San Jose, CA; (3); 71/484; Girl Scts; Pres Math Clb; Pres Science Clb; Ed Nwsp; Hon Roll; Val; UC Santa Cruz; Aero Engr.

SARMIENTO, RICHARD L; St Francis HS; Sunnyvale, CA; (1); 21/388; Church Yth Grp; Intnl Clb; SADD; Hon Roll; Hnrs Entrance; Engrng.

SARNA, KELLY N; Las Lomas HS; Walnut Creek, CA; (2); 43/256; Hosp Aide; St Equestrian Evnts; Studying Frnch & Spnsh; UC Davis; Lang.

SARNO, DAVID L; Santiago HS; Garden Grove, CA; (2); 96/538; JV Bsbl; Hon Roll; U Of MO; Elec Engrng.

SARNO, ROBIN P; Mira Mesa HS; San Diego, CA; (3); Teachers Aide; Rep Frsh Cls; Stu Cncl; JV Ftbl; Powder Puff Ftbl; Cit Awd; Hon Roll; Pres Acad Fit Awd; Engrng.

SAROCKA, JANNA; Hemet HS; Hemet, CA; (2); Church Yth Grp; SADD; Phtg Yrbk; Intrml Mgr Wt Lftg; Hon Roll; Arch.

SAROSI, LINDA S; Red Bluff Union HS; Red Bluff, CA; (2); Church Yth Grp; Band; Mrchg Band; Hon Roll; Friday Night Live; Rainbow Girls; Humbolt U.

SAROSSY, VERONIKA I; Wilcox HS; Santa Clara, CA; (2); Band; Jazz Band; Mrchg Band; School Musical; Hon Roll; Davis; Vet.

SARPONG, MICHELLE; Ontario HS; Ontario, CA; (2); 26/546; Varsity Clb; VP Soph Cls; Stu Cncl; Var Crs Cntry; JV Socr; JV Trk; Hon Roll; Loma Linda U; Pdtrcn.

SARRAM, LILI; Novato HS; Novato, CA; (1); French Clb; Intnl Clb; SADD; Chorus; Lit Mag; Rep Stu Cncl; Var L Tennis; High Hon Roll; Hon Roll; UC Berkeley; Bus.

SARRIS, VICKIE E; Carlmont HS; Belmont, CA; (3); Church Yth Grp; Cmnty Wkr; FCA; GAA; Varsity Clb; Bsktbl; Trk; Vllybl; WSU; Bus.

SARROCA, ARLENE; Rowland HS; Walnut, CA; (4); 15/550; Letterman Clb; Science Clb; Spanish Clb; Nwsp; Var Co-Capt Vllybl; High Hon Roll; NHS; Pres Acad Fit Awd; Bank Of Amer Awd Hstry; UCLA; Optmtry.

SARS, NICK J; Esperanza HS; Yorba Linda, CA; (2); Boy Scts; German Clb; JV Vllybl; Hon Roll; UC Irvine; Corp Law.

SARTOR, MELISSA; Mt Shasta HS; Mt Shasta, CA; (2); 1/95; Ski Clb; Rptr Nwsp; Swmmng; JV Debate Tm; High Hon Roll; Rotary Awd; Natl Hstry Day Comp 1st Pl Siskiyou Cnty, 2nd Pl ST Lions Clb Speech Cont Club Fnlst; Wildlife Bio.

SARTUCHE, MONICA R; Tulare Western HS; Tulare, CA; (3); Church Yth Grp; FFA; Ski Clb; School Play; Sec Jr Cls; Chrmn Stu Cncl; Var Cheerldng; Var Swmmng; JV Var Vllybl; Hon Roll.

SARUTA, YOSHIKA; Bonita Vista HS; Bonita, CA; (2); Office Aide; Var Cheerldng; Var Gym; Tns; Piano; Fluent In Span & Japanese; UCLA; Lang.

SASAKI, JASON Y; John F Kennedy HS; Sacramento, CA; (2); Church Yth Grp; ROTC; Hon Roll; Fri Night Live.

SASAKI, MONICA; Venice HS; Los Angeles, CA; (3); Church Yth Grp; Teachers Aide; Taiko Drums; Chrch Mrchng Band; Psych.

SASIS, EDNA; Montgomery HS; San Diego, CA; (4); 6/410; Key Clb; Office Aide; Quiz Bowl; Service Clb; Church Choir; Drill Tm; Sprt Ed Nwsp; Rep Jr Cls; Rep Sr Cls; Stat Mgr Tennis; Coca Cola Schl Svc Awd; Bk Of Amer Achvt Awd Lib Arts Field; Delta Kappa Gamma Eta Nu Chptr Schlrshp; UCLA.

SASIS, ELMIRA M; Montgomery HS; San Diego, CA; (2); Aud/Vis; Church Yth Grp; Key Clb; Church Choir; Drill Tm; Yrbk; Cit Awd; Masonic Awd; Prfct Atten Awd; Pres Acad Fit Awd; ASB, Asst Commssnr Finance; 90 Novelty Precision Intl Chmpns Dance Drl Tm.

SASSMAN, DJANGO D; Santa Cruz HS; Santa Cruz, CA; (3); Var Bsktbl; JV Ftbl; Var Capt Swmmng; DAR Awd; High Hon Roll; Pres Acad Fit Awd; Vice Chancellor Of Mens Hnr Scty; Med.

SASSO, LAURA J; Torrey Pines HS; Del Mar, CA; (2); AFS; Drama Clb; Thesps; School Musical; School Play; Stage Crew; Socr; Environmental Club.

SATHONGNHOTH, CHANTHAVEE; Willows HS; Willows, CA; (2); Cal Poly; Graphic Arts.

SATO, AMY T; Santa Teresa HS; San Jose, CA; (1); Church Yth Grp; Church Choir; High Hon Roll; CA Schlrshp Fed Hnry Membrshp; Marine Bio.

SATO, CHRIS M; Carlsbad HS; Carlsbad, CA; (2); JV Ftbl; Var Wrstlng; 88 Wrestlng Coachs Awd; Ftbl MVP Defnsve 2 Yrs; Pro Ftbl.

SATO, GRACE M; Whitney HS; Cypress, CA; (1); Church Yth Grp; French Clb; Key Clb; Band; Mrchg Band; High Hon Roll; Hon Roll; SCSBOA.

SATO, JAMES R; Santa Clara HS; Santa Clara, CA; (3); 16/400; Boy Scts; Chess Clb; 4-H; Spanish Clb; Crs Cntry; Wrstlng; High Hon Roll; Hon Roll; Life Rank In Boy Scts Of Amer; UC Davis; Vet.

SATO, LISA-MARIE; Cordova SR HS; Rancho Cordova, CA; (3); Church Yth Grp; Drama Clb; Key Clb; Thesps; School Musical; School Play; NHS; Opt Clb Awd; Schl Mascot; Alt Stu Rep To Schl Brd; Dramatic Arts.

SATO, TREY K; Adrian C Wilcox HS; Sunnyvale, CA; (4); 9/375; Church Yth Grp; Cmnty Wkr; French Clb; Teachers Aide; Treas Soph Cls; Pres Jr Cls; Capt Var Bsktbl; High Hon Roll; Sci Dept Cert Achvt; All Leag Bsktbl 2 Yrs; Bnk Amer Achvt Awd For Sci; UC Davis; Chemcl Engrng.

SATTER, DAVID R; Whittier Christian HS; Hacienda Hts, CA; (2); Church Yth Grp; Church Choir; JV Bsbl; JV Ftbl; Hon Roll; Pt Loma Nazarene Coll.

SATTERFIELD, KELLY J; Paraclete HS; Palmdale, CA; (2); Hosp Aide; JA; SADD; Psych.

SATTERFIELD, TERRENCE F; Bishop O'dowd HS; Oakland, CA; (2); Aud/Vis; Ski Clb; High Hon Roll; CA Schlrshp Fdrtn; Envrnmntl Engrng.

SATTESON, AMY N; Senior HS; Fresno, CA; (2); 92/300; Church Yth Grp; Hosp Aide; SADD; Yrbk; Gym; Socr; Swmmng; Peer Cnslr; Kiwanis Vlntr; Coast Guard Acad; Plt.

SAUCEDA, AURORA; Gonzales HS; Soledad, CA; (4); 16/165; Church Yth Grp; Cmnty Wkr; SADD; Teachers Aide; Band; Church Choir; Mrchg Band; Pep Band; School Musical; Hon Roll; CSU Fresno; Health Sci.

SAUCEDA, DELIA; Gonzales HS; Soledad, CA; (2); Church Yth Grp; Dance Clb; SADD; Band; Pep Band; High Hon Roll; Prfct Atten Awd; Band Awd; San Jose ST U; Elec Engrng.

SAUCEDO, CAROL M; North Salinas HS; Salinas, CA; (2); Cit Awd; High Hon Roll; Hon Roll; NHS; Ntl Merit Ltr; Pres Acad Fit Awd; Stu Yr; GATE; Top 100 Stu.

SAUCEDO, DALIA; Mountain Em JR-SR HS; Potrero, CA; (2); German Clb; Hon Roll; Law.

SAUCEDO, FERMIN; San Banito HS; Hollister, CA; (2); Ftbl; Hon Roll; MECHA Clb; San Jose ST; Banking.

SAUCEDO, MARIA C; Buena HS; Ventura, CA; (3); Sec Church Yth Grp; SADD; Hon Roll; Mecha Club; Hmnts Club; Redlands; Scndry Educ.

SAUCEDO, MARIA L; San Benito HS; Hollister, CA; (4); 2/250; Art Clb; Church Yth Grp; Church Choir; Cit Awd; High Hon Roll; Hon Roll; Pres Acad Fit Awd; Passed Advanced Placement Test In Economics; Golden State Exam In Geometry; Pacific Union Coll; Nutrition.

SAUCEDO, SAUL; Hawthorne HS; Lennox, CA; (2); Hnrs In Alg II, Span 3, Bio 205.

SAUDE, TIFFINI C; Redwood HS; Visalia, CA; (3); Church Yth Grp; Cmnty Wkr; Pep Clb; Spanish Clb; SADD; Band; Church Choir; Mrchg Band; Pep Band; Score Keeper; CSF; Bus.

SAUER, ANNEMARIE; Immaculate Heart HS; Los Angeles, CA; (3); Pres Church Yth Grp; School Musical; Stage Crew; Rep Frsh Cls; Rep Soph Cls; Rep Jr Cls; VP Sr Cls; High Hon Roll; Hon Roll; Comm.

SAUER, CHRISTINA; St Genevieve HS; Tempe, AZ; (2); Church Yth Grp; English Clb; Pep Clb; SADD; Chorus; Drm Mjr(t); School Play; Hon Roll; Natl Latin Exam Cum Laude Awd 89; CSF; Secy Unity Club; Educ.

SAUER, HEATHER; Fred C Beyer HS; Modesto, CA; (3); Cmnty Wkr; Hosp Aide; Var Swmmng; Hon Roll; NHS; V Waterpolo.

SAUER, KERRY; Cason HS; San Bernardino, CA; (2); Chorus; Var Tennis; Hon Roll; NHS; Rotary Awd; Southern CA SCTA Jr Tennis Plyr; Elem Educ.

SAUER, LISA M; University HS; Irvine, CA; (2); Spanish Clb; SADD; Yrbk; JV Var Fld Hcky; Hon Roll; Laureate Awd Excel Spnsh; Awd Hnrs Gldn ST Exam Geom; STAAND; Envrnmnt Sci.

SAUKKOLA, KERRY L; Villa Park HS; Orange, CA; (3); Church Yth Grp; SADD; Chorus; Off Frsh Cls; JV Bsktbl; JV Cheerldng; Var Pom Pon; Var Swmmng; High Hon Roll.

SAUNDERS, DAWNE; Hilltop HS; Chula Vista, CA; (4); Office Aide; Pep Clb; SADD; Drill Tm; Variety Show; Var Cheerldng; Gym; Hon Roll; Acad All Amer Schl Pgm 87; Variety Show Choreographer; Chrldng Schlrshp; SWC; Engl.

SAUNDERS, ERICA; Clear Lake HS; Lakeport, CA; (4); 19/75; Am Leg Aux Girls St; Church Yth Grp; Cmnty Wkr; Drama Clb; GAA; Girl Scts; Office Aide; Red Cross Aide; Service Clb; Spanish Clb; Stu Yr 90; MD-4 Lions Spch Fnls; HOBY Ambssdr; Peer Cnslng; WA DC Ldrshp Conf; Shasta Coll; Educ.

SAUNDERS, JAMIE N; Granada Hills HS; Northridge, CA; (2); Office Aide; Temple Yth Grp; Rep Frsh Cls; Cheerldng; Sftbl; High Hon Roll; Pres Acad Fit Awd; Jr Stsmn Amer; UC Berkeley; Crmnl Law.

SAUNDERS, LOIS M; La Jolla Country Day HS; Poway, CA; (2); Cmnty Wkr; SADD; Chorus; School Musical; Variety Show; JV Cheerldng; JV Sftbl; Hon Roll; Natl Frnch Exam 4th Pl Lcl 89; Natl Frnch Exam 3rd Pl Lcl, 6th Rgnl 90; V Co-Capt Chrldr Top Scr 90-91; Aviation.

SAUNDERS, MATT; Santa Barbara HS; Santa Barbara, CA; (2); 30/450; Ed Yrbk; Hon Roll; Pres Acad Fit Awd; Drafting.

SAUNDERS, MELA A; San Marcos HS; San Marcos, CA; (3); Dance Clb; Key Clb; Pep Clb; Stage Crew; Cheerldng; Powder Puff Ftbl; Tennis; High Hon Roll; Hon Roll; Pres Acad Fit Awd.

SAUNDERS, PAUL AHANU; Buena HS; Ventura, CA; (1); Church Yth Grp; JV Trk; High Hon Roll; League Coll; Lawyr.

SAUNDERS, SELENA; Saint Bernard Catholic Schl; Los Angeles, CA; (1); Pep Clb; Rep Frsh Cls; Capt Cheerldng; High Hon Roll; Princpals List; Amer Edctnl Travel Stu; CSF; Stanford U; Sprts Med.

SAUNDERS, SHARRIEFF D; Inglewood HS; Inglewood, CA; (1); Teachers Aide.

SAUNDERS, STACEY L; Central Catholic HS; Modesto, CA; (3); Debate Tm; Drama Clb; English Clb; Intnl Clb; Math Clb; Math Tm; Pep Clb; Quiz Bowl; Science Clb; Service Clb; Psych.

SAUNDERS, STEVEN W; St Ignatius College Prep; San Francisco, CA; (3); 140/270; Yrbk; Sec Sr Cls; Bsktbl; Trk; Wt Lftg; Karate; US Naval Acad; Economics.

SAUSER, RODNEY P; Redlands JR Acad; Redlands, CA; (2); 1/19; JA; Ski Clb; Varsity Clb; Chorus; Yrbk; Pres Stu Cncl; Var Bsbl; Var Bsktbl; Var Ftbl; Intrml Sftbl; Vell Choir; Loma Linda Acad.

SAUVAGE, ARNAUD M; El Toro HS; El Toro, CA; (1); 3/30; French Clb; FHA; Math Clb; SADD; Varsity Clb; Orch; Stu Cncl; Var Tennis; French Hon Soc.

SAVA, EMILY M; John F Kennedy HS; Sacramento, CA; (3); 50/422; Teachers Aide; Crs Cntry; Gym; Trk; Hon Roll; Coll.

SAVAGE, BECKY M; Hesperia Scorpion HS; Hesperia, CA; (2); ROTC; VP Spanish Clb; Band; Mrchg Band; Pep Band; Score Keeper; Cmptv Rllr Sktg-Artstc; Elec Engrng.

SAVAGE, JAMES; St Francis HS; Sunnyvale, CA; (2); 169/400; Hon Roll.

SAVAGE, JASON; Avenal HS; Avenal, CA; (3); Pres Letterman Clb; Pres Soph Cls; JV Var Bsbl; JV Var Bsktbl; JV Var Ftbl; JV Var Wt Lftg; Cit Awd; High Hon Roll; Hon Roll; NHS; CSF; Stu Of Mnth Awds; Comm.

SAVAGE, ROBERT S; Beacon Christian HS; Foster City, CA; (4); 2/11; Church Yth Grp; Church Choir; Stu Cncl; Var Bsbl; Var Bsktbl; Var Socr; Elks Awd; Hon Roll; Pres Acad Fit Awd; Sal; Biola U; Pltcl Sci.

SAVAGE, SARAH M; Etiwanda HS; Alta Loma, CA; (3); Church Yth Grp; Key Clb; Cheerldng; High Hon Roll; Hon Roll; Pres Acad Fit Awd; Bus.

SAVAGE, TED; Beacon Christian HS; Foster City, CA; (1); Band; Stage Crew; Variety Show; Yrbk; Socr; Pres Acad Fit Awd; Chabot Coll Steel Drum Band; Ride Off-Road Motorcycles; Play Drums For 5 Years; Engineering/ Music.

SAVAGE, THOMAS WILLIAM; Don Bosco Technical Inst; West Covina, CA; (2); Boy Scts; Cmnty Wkr; Varsity Clb; Var Bsktbl; Hon Roll; Jr NHS; Yth Ldrshp Cnfrnc Mt St Mayrs Coll; Civil Engrng.

SAVAGE, WENDY M; College Park HS; Lafayette, CA; (2); Drama Clb; School Play; Var JV Cheerldng; Chrldg Cmptn 2nd Pl; Coached Pop Warner Team-1st In Cmptn; Actrss.

SAVAIINAEA, JERUSHA A; Granger JR HS; National City, CA; (1); Church Yth Grp; FCA; Chorus; Church Choir; School Musical; Bsktbl; Ftbl; Sftbl; Cit Awd; Hon Roll; Singer.

SAVANT, JULIE; Santa Margarita HS; Anaheim Hills, CA; (1); Church Yth Grp; Computer Clb; French Clb; Pep Clb; Rep Frsh Cls; Cheerldng; Gym; Hon Roll; Bus.

SAVDHARIA, KUNAL; Irvine HS; Irvine, CA; (2); 273/600; Chess Clb; Socr; Musical Intrmnts Awds; Engr.

SAVE, MARIE; Los Alamitos HS; Los Alamitos, CA; (4); Am Leg Aux Girls St; Church Yth Grp; Cmnty Wkr; French Clb; Math Clb; Pep Clb; Service Clb; Spanish Clb; Flag Corp; Stu Cncl; MVP Sccr 87-89; PTSA Prsn Wk 11-89; Cross Cntry Griffin Wek 87-88.

SAVELLA, CHRISTINE L; Garfield Magnet HS; Los Angeles, CA; (4); 18/ 675; Drama Clb; Treas Service Clb; Teachers Aide; Thesps; School Musical; Cit Awd; Hon Roll; Prfct Atten Awd; Rotary Awd; Wellesley Coll; Ed.

SAVKO, YVONNE A; Seaside HS; Seaside, CA; (2); ROTC; Chorus; Drill Tm; Powder Puff Ftbl; Sftbl; Vllybl; Pres Acad Fit Awd; Vet.

SAW, WILLIAM; Palm Desert HS; La Quinta, CA; (3); Boy Scts; Church Yth Grp; High Hon Roll; Hon Roll; Cal Poly; Mech Engrng.

SAWABINI, TASHA R; Grossmont HS; La Mesa, CA; (3); U Of CA San Diego; Photo.

SAWCHUK, HEATHER V J D; Monterey Bay Acad; Pleasant Hill, CA; (4); Var Church Yth Grp; Var German Clb; Office Aide; Band; Chorus; School Musical; Ed Yrbk; Rep Soph Cls; Sftbl; Swmmng; US Acad Dcthln; Pacific Union Coll; Bus.

SAWDON, JENNA M; Monte Vista HS; Diablo, CA; (3); 69/356; Cmnty Wkr; SADD; Teachers Aide; Variety Show; Var Capt Bsktbl; Capt Powder Puff Ftbl; Var Capt Sftbl; JV Capt Vllybl; High Hon Roll; Hon Roll; All Leag Vrsty Sftbl; Hstry Dept Awd; Sftbl & Bsktbl Coaches Awd; Mst Inspirational Plyr Vlybl & Bsktbl; Athltc Trng.

SAWIN, HELENE SHEILA; Los Angeles Baptist HS; Northridge, CA; (3); 18/70; Church Yth Grp; Cmnty Wkr; Pep Clb; Drill Tm; High Hon Roll; Hon Roll; UCLA; Bus.

SAWIRIS, VIOLA; Blair HS; Pasadena, CA; (1); Church Yth Grp; ROTC; Church Choir; Bsbl; Sftbl; Wt Lftg; MESA; JROTC Worker.

SAWITZ, JASON A; Santa Clara HS; Oxnard, CA; (2); 7/191; Letterman Clb; Var L Crs Cntry; Var Trk; High Hon Roll; Var NHS; Prfct Atten Awd; Engl I Awd; Med.

SAWYER, ERIN; St Helena HS; Saint Helena, CA; (3); Key Clb; Ski Clb; Teachers Aide; Capt Cheerldng; Capt Pom Pon; Powder Puff Ftbl; Hon Roll; Educ.

SAWYER, JENNIFER A; Mt Pleasant HS; San Jose, CA; (1); Hnr Soc Pgm; Gold & Brnz Medals Acro Gymnstcs Meets; Stanford U; Vet.

SAWYER, JILL L; Mc Farland HS; Mc Farland, CA; (3); Church Yth Grp; Teachers Aide; Chorus; School Musical; Hon Roll; Outstndng Clss Stu Awd & Medallion Wnnr Clss 89-90; Teaching.

SAWYER, LISA S; Madera HS; Madera, CA; (3); Church Yth Grp; Dance Clb; Drama Clb; Latin Clb; Socr; Sftbl; Swmmng; Fshn Dsgn.

SAWYER, RANDAL L; Lompoc HS; Lompoc, CA; (1); FFA; FFA Parliamentary Procedure Tm; Fishing; Bsktbl.

SAXE, RAYMOND C; Ripon HS; Ripon, CA; (3); Boy Scts; Hon Roll; Comp Sci.

SAXON, DARREN; Cardinal Newman HS; Santa Rosa, CA; (2); 14/99; Church Yth Grp; Service Clb; High Hon Roll; Pres Acad Fit Awd; Frnch I Hghst Hnrs Hstry Hnrs CSF; Stanford; Arntcl Engrng.

SAXON, TIFFANY M; Santa Teresa HS; San Jose, CA; (2); Cmnty Wkr; French Clb; Hosp Aide; Science Clb; JV Crs Cntry; JV Trk; CSF; Sun Schl Tchr; Phlsphy Clb; Stanford; Med.

SAXTON, KATYA; Ramona HS; Ramona, CA; (4); 4/248; Pres Church Yth Grp; Hist 4-H; Pres FBLA; German Clb; VP JA; Cit Awd; 4-H Awd; CSF; Point Loma Nazarene Coll; Scl.

SAY, BRENDA K; El Dorado HS; Placerville, CA; (3); 43/300; SADD; Teachers Aide; JV Var Vllybl; Prfct Atten Awd; Pres Acad Fit Awd; Chef.

SAY, CYNTHIA C; Edison HS; Stockton, CA; (1); Bus Profs of Am; Cit Awd; High Hon Roll; Spanish NHS; Photo Club; UC Berkeley; Bus Admin.

SAY, KOK; King Drew Med Mag HS; Los Angeles, CA; (2); Chess Clb; Computer Clb; Math Tm; Vllybl; High Hon Roll; Most Improved Stu; Harvard; Family Dr.

SAYACHACK, KHAMSOUAY K; Sanger HS; Sanger, CA; (2); ROTC; Chorus; Stage Crew; Cit Awd; Hon Roll; Prfct Atten Awd; Read Books; Drawing; Fresno ST; Bus.

SAYAD, AUDRY; North Hollywood HS; North Hollywood, CA; (3); Hon Roll; Prfct Atten Awd; CSF; Intl Bus.

SAYANI, LAILA; Canyon HS; Canyon Country, CA; (4); Church Yth Grp; French Clb; FBLA; Girl Scts; Intnl Clb; Hon Roll; NHS; CSF; Acad Ltr; U Of CA Santa Barbara; Bio Lab.

SAYASING, KONGCHANH; Luther Burbank HS; Sacramento, CA; (2); 50/300; French Clb; Treas Frsh Cls; Treas Soph Cls; Vllybl; Hon Roll; Prfct Atten Awd; Explr Post; New Commers Clb; Upward Bound Prog; UC-DAVIS.

SAYASY, PHETSAVANE P; Luther Burbank HS; Sacramento, CA; (3); 26/302; Teachers Aide; Drill Tm; Cit Awd; Hon Roll; Prfct Atten Awd; Cert Hnr Art & Englg; Hnr Soc Awd; Schlrshp Awd Sci & Engl; UC Davis; Nurse.

SAYAVONG, PRATHANA; Crawford HS; San Diego, CA; (3); French Clb; Key Clb; Hon Roll; San Diego ST U; Lwyr.

SAYDAK, REBECCA P; Mater Dei HS; Los Alamitos, CA; (3); 1/475; Church Yth Grp; Cmnty Wkr; Model UN; ROTC; Ed Nwsp; Var Swmmng; NHS; Amer Legn Acad Excllnc Mdl; Air Force Assn Mdl; CSF Class Rep; Air Force.

SAYED, ASHRAF; Santa Ana HS; Santa Ana, CA; (4); Chess Clb; Debate Tm; JA; VP Math Clb; Math Tm; Speech Tm; Chorus; Rep Stu Cncl; Cit Awd; Elks Awd; Orange Co Academic Decathlon; 6th Place In Math; Top 90 Student In School District; UCI; Physics.

SAYEGH, RANIA S; Pasadena HS; Pasadena, CA; (3); Cit Awd; High Hon Roll; Hon Roll; Prfct Atten Awd; CA Schlrshp Fed 3 Yrs; GATE; UCLA; Med.

SAYEGH, RICKY; Grossmont HS; El Cajon, CA; (2); JV Ftbl; JV Trk.

SAYER, MATTHEW D; Ferndale HS; Ferndale, CA; (4); 1/35; Am Leg Boys St; Church Yth Grp; Math Tm; Off Frsh Cls; Off Soph Cls; Pres Jr Cls; Pres Sr Cls; Bsktbl; Ftbl; Trk; Azusa Pacific U; Aerontcl Engr.

SAYERS, BETH A; Bastow HS; Barstow, CA; (2); AFS; Church Yth Grp; Color Guard; Nrsng.

SAYFI, ELISA; Hawthorne HS; Hawthorne, CA; (3); Drama Clb; Trk; Cit Awd; Hon Roll; Prfct Atten Awd; UCLA; Med.

SAYLES, ROBERT; Poway HS; Poway, CA; (3); #46 In Class; VP Drama Clb; SADD; School Musical; School Play; Stage Crew; Ed Lit Mag; High Hon Roll; Co Pres Yng Ply Wrgts; Peer Cnslg; Authr Prodcd Ply Cat Socty; Engl.

SAYLOR, TERESSA L; Woodland HS; Woodland, CA; (3); 4-H; Teachers Aide; Humbolt ST; Wildlife Bio.

SAYRE, HEATHER LEE; Upland HS; Upland, CA; (1); Church Yth Grp; Cmnty Wkr; Key Clb; Chorus; Church Choir; Swing Chorus; Variety Show; Rptr Nwsp; Swmmng; Hon Roll; Azusa Pacific; Law.

SAYSANA, SISOUK; Edison HS; Fresno, CA; (1); FBLA; FTA; Library Aide; Spanish Clb; Teachers Aide; Cit Awd; Gov Hon Prg Awd; Hon Roll; Prfct Atten Awd; Pres Acad Fit Awd.

SAYYAH, GOLI; Westlake School For Girls; Los Angeles, CA; (2); Cmnty Wkr; French Clb; French Hon Soc; Prfct Atten Awd; Piano Lessons; Tennis Lssns; Persian Clsses; Hunger Cmmtte Scrtry; Black Amer Culture Club; Columbia Williams.

SBRANTI, TIMOTHY; Dublin HS; Dublin, CA; (1); 6/229; Rptr Nwsp; VP Frsh Cls; Bsktbl; Var Tennis; High Hon Roll; Hon Roll; Pres Acad Fit Awd; Stu Gov; Gldn St Exmntn Acad Excllcne Awd Alg; North Coast Sectn CIF Schlr Athlte; Jrnlsm.

SCADDING, TOMARO M; Fresno Christian HS; Fresno, CA; (4); 1/68; Hosp Aide; Intnl Clb; Chorus; Rptr Nwsp; Treas Lit Mag; High Hon Roll; Pres Acad Fit Awd; Val; Highst Hnrs In Acctng II; CSF Lifetime Mem; CSU; CPA.

SCALES, GLENN; Bullard HS; Fresno, CA; (4); 79/480; Boy Scts; Church Yth Grp; Debate Tm; FCA; French Clb; FBLA; Intnl Clb; NFL; Speech Tm; SADD; Asian Club; Acad Decathlon; CSF Life Mem; UC Santa Barbara; Bus Adm.

SCALISE, SERGIO; Moreau HS; Hayward, CA; (3); Am Leg Boys St; Ski Clb; SADD; Rep Sr Cls; Var Capt Bsbl; Var Ftbl; High Hon Roll; Mst Imprvd Bsbl; Mst Insprtnl Bsbl; Invlvd Japanese For Exchng Pgm; St Marys; Accntng.

SCANNELL, SARAH; Mercy HS; Millbrae, CA; (4); Mgr GAA; Ski Clb; Spanish Clb; Sec Frsh Cls; Pres Jr Cls; Var Capt Bsktbl; Var Sftbl; Var Vllybl; High Hon Roll.

SCARAZZO, KRISTIE; Clovis West HS; Fresno, CA; (3); Church Yth Grp; Intnl Clb; Ski Clb; Spanish Clb; SADD; Rep Soph Cls; Pom Pon; Hon Roll; Miss Drill Team Natls-1st Pl Pep Squad; Cluster III Stu Of Mnth; 1st Pl USA Natl Cmptn; UC Davis; Envrnmntl Law.

SCARLETT, ANGELA M; Fortuna Union HS; Fortuna, CA; (3); Drama Clb; SADD; Stage Crew; Ed Lit Mag; High Hon Roll; VP NHS; Mrt Awds Stu Art Show; Mem CA Schlrshp Fed; Board Mem Of Interact; Mills; Commercial Arts.

SCARMS, DENISE; Palm Springs HS; Palm Springs, CA; (4); Church Yth Grp; Cmnty Wkr; Pres Drama Clb; VP Chorus; School Musical; School Play; Music Clb Pres; Natl Choral Awd; Alex Hammond Memrl Achvt Awd; Bank Of Amer Achvt Awd For Fine Arts; LIFE Bible Coll; Music.

SCATENA, ASHLEY; St Marys HS; Stockton, CA; (3); Key Clb; Drill Tm; Sec Frsh Cls; Treas Soph Cls; Rep Jr Cls; VP Sr Cls; Stu Cncl; JV Socr; Var Trk; Hon Roll; Ree Club Hstrn, Asst Treas & Treas; Lodis Yng Wmn Yr 90; Schl Cabinet.

SCATOLINI, SOCRATES; Mission Bay HS; San Diego, CA; (2); Church Yth Grp; Office Aide; Socr; Tennis; UCSD; Sci.

SCATTINI, HEATHER A; Notre Dame HS; Salinas, CA; (1); 2/90; Church Yth Grp; Cmnty Wkr; 4-H; Letterman Clb; Varsity Clb; Yrbk; Treas Soph Cls; Var Bsktbl; Var Sftbl; JV Vllybl; CSF; Outstndng Achvt Awd Vllybl, Sftbl; Bsktbl Camp; All Star Tm, Best Defnsv Plyr; Bus.

SCATTINI, STEPHANIE L; Notre Dame HS; Salinas, CA; (2); 12/75; Computer Clb; Drama Clb; Pep Clb; Ski Clb; School Play; Pres Frsh Cls; Pres Soph Cls; Cheerldng; Sftbl; 4-H Awd; HS Rodeo; Fair Grand Champ Market Lamb.

SCHAAL, JAMES M; Yosemite HS; Coarsegold, CA; (3); Drama Clb; Spanish Clb; Var Capt Socr; Hon Roll; All Leag Soccr Tm; CA ST Fresno; Bus.

SCHAAL, NANCY J; Marysville HS; Marysville, CA; (1); Church Yth Grp; Spanish Clb; Band; Drm Mjr(t); Mrchg Band; Pep Band; JV Swmmng; High Hon Roll; Hon Roll; Bus Mgmt.

SCHAAN, JENNIFER; Southwest HS; San Diego, CA; (4); 30/564; JA; Key Clb; Model UN; SADD; Rep Frsh Cls; Stu Cncl; Cheerldng; High Hon Roll; Prfct Atten Awd; San Diego ST U; Educ.

SCHAAP, EDWARD JOHN; Mc Farland HS; Mc Farland, CA; (4); 1/110; Am Leg Boys St; Church Yth Grp; Computer Clb; Pres FFA; Letterman Clb; Math Tm; Band; Stu Cncl; Bsktbl; Trk; UC Davis; Vet Med.

SCHACHT, MATT C; Edison HS; Huntington Beach, CA; (3); Boy Scts; Model UN; Var L Swmmng; Water Polo Var Ltr; CSF; Deans List; Acad Ltr; Engrng.

SCHACK, ELIZABETH; San Ramon Valley HS; Danville, CA; (3); Church Yth Grp; Cmnty Wkr; Hosp Aide; SADD; Teachers Aide; Chorus; Church Choir; Treas Jr Cls; High Hon Roll; Sci.

SCHACKER, REBECCA R; Lincoln HS; San Jose, CA; (2); Girl Scts; Latin Clb; Orch; Phtg Yrbk; Var Capt Socr; Var L Swmmng; Var L Trk; Hon Roll.

SCHADT, STEVE J; Monte Vista HS; Danville, CA; (2); 56/440; Church Yth Grp; Drama Clb; Letterman Clb; SADD; Chorus; Stage Crew; Var Swmmng; High Hon Roll; NHS; Pres Acad Fit Awd; USS Swmmng; Altar Served For Church; Saturday Nite Live; Med.

SCHAEFER, AMY L; Upland HS; Upland, CA; (2); Church Yth Grp; GAA; Key Clb; Letterman Clb; Varsity Clb; Bsktbl; Trk; Vllybl; Hon Roll; Pres Acad Fit Awd; 3 HEF Awds; MVP JV Bsktbl Tm 88-89; CO-MVP Vrsty Trck Tm; Physcl Educ.

SCHAEFER, AMY M; Mira Mesa HS; San Diego, CA; (2); Pep Clb; Science Clb; Spanish Clb; Band; Mrchg Band; Pep Band; Intrml Sftbl; Pres Acad Fit Awd; Hnr Band; UCSD; Bio.

SCHAEFER, CAMBRIA; Novato HS; Novato, CA; (2); Cmnty Wkr; School Musical; School Play; Stage Crew; Var Golf; Var Tennis; Hon Roll; Outstndng Stu Drama 89; Tennis Tm Awd 89; Med.

SCHAEFER, CHRISTINA; Rincon Valley Christian Schl; Santa Rosa, CA; (4); 1/15; Pres Church Yth Grp; Model UN; Office Aide; Chorus; Treas Stu Cncl; Capt Cheerldng; High Hon Roll; Val.

SCHAEFER, DAVID M; Valhalla HS; El Cajon, CA; (2); 12/450; German Clb; Key Clb; JV Socr; Var Vllybl; Frgn Lang Awd.

SCHAEFER, LORIN E; Mira Loma HS; Orangevale, CA; (3); Teachers Aide; Hon Roll; Psychiatry.

SCHAEFER, SHAUNA A; Rinion Valley Christian HS; Santa Rosa, CA; (2); 2/30; Sec Church Yth Grp; Teachers Aide; Rep Frsh Cls; Treas Stu Cncl; Var Cheerldng; Var Sftbl; JV Capt Vllybl; High Hon Roll; Pre-Med.

SCHAEFER, TOM C; Mater Dei HS; Fountain Valley, CA; (1); Boy Scts; Church Yth Grp; ROTC; Drill Tm; Intrml Ftbl; A D Altare Dei Medal; Pope Pius XII Medal; Order Of Arrow; USAF Acad; Pilot.

SCHAEFFER, JASON M; Bonita Vista HS; Bonita, CA; (3); 51/450; Sec Frsh Cls; JV Ftbl; JV Capt Socr; Var Vllybl; Hon Roll; Pres Acad Fit Awd; Freedoms Fndtn Valley Forge Participant; Bonitafest Host 90; SOFFA Stu Optimistic For Future Am; Amherst; Law.

SCHAEFFER, KRISTIN N; Ponderosa HS; Placerville, CA; (3); Church Yth Grp; Cmnty Wkr; Hosp Aide; Ed Nwsp; Piano Lessns; Humn Actvts Org; Outlook Nwspr; U Of MO Columbia; Jrnlsm.

SCHAEFFER, MERIDITH L; Troy HS; Yorba Linda, CA; (2); 16/384; FCA; Key Clb; Yrbk; Bsktbl; Trk; Vllybl; Cit Awd; High Hon Roll; Rotary Awd.

SCHAEFFER, STEFANIE; John W North HS; Upland, CA; (2); Hosp Aide; Letterman Clb; Teachers Aide; Acpl Chr; Chorus; Yrbk; Swmmng; Hon Roll; Pres Acad Fit Awd; Environmentlst Clb; Marine Bio.

SCHAER, HEATHER K; Tustin HS; Tustin, CA; (4); 36/400; Chrmn Church Yth Grp; Cmnty Wkr; Teachers Aide; Varsity Clb; Church Choir; Off Sr Cls; JV Var Bsktbl; JV Stat Swmmng; High Hon Roll; Pres Acad Fit Awd; CSF Sealbearer; Vrsty Bsktbl-Mst Imprvd/Mst Inspiratnl Awds; Engl Dept Awd; Point Loma Nazarene Coll; Ed.

SCHAETZL, RANA JOY; Sonora HS; La Habra, CA; (4); 31/293; FBLA; Spanish Clb; Lit Mag; JV Tennis; High Hon Roll; Hon Roll; CSF; Badminton Var; St Capitol Rep 89; Mt San Antonio Coll; Poli Sci.

SCHAFER, LAURENCE M; Laguna Hills HS; Laguna Hills, CA; (4); 69/ 342; Dance Clb; Key Clb; Red Cross Aide; Spanish Clb; SADD; Varsity Clb; Off Soph Cls; Off Jr Cls; JV Var Bsbl; JV Ftbl; Cnty Chmbr Of Commrc J S Penney Schlrshp; USC; Corp Mgmnt.

SCHAFER, SHAWN N; Ceres HS; Ceres, CA; (4); Hist FBLA; Treas GAA; Ski Clb; Var Capt Bsktbl; Var Sftbl; Hon Roll; Modesto JC; Fshn Mdse.

SCHAFF, KARA M; Turlock HS; Turlock, CA; (3); 4/650; AFS; Art Clb; Church Yth Grp; Drama Clb; Key Clb; Letterman Clb; NFL; Pep Clb; Speech Tm; Rep Stu Cncl; U CA San Diego; Chem Engrng.

SCHAFFER, KIMBERLY L; Hemet HS; Hemet, CA; (2); Church Yth Grp; FCA; Varsity Clb; Band; Mrchg Band; Pep Band; Bsktbl; Sftbl; Capt Vllybl; Hon Roll; Cmps Life; Bible Stdy; San Diego ST U; Phy Thrpst.

SCHAFFNER, ALICIA A; Hilltop HS; Bonita, CA; (3); 75/500; Church Yth Grp; Drama Clb; Office Aide; SADD; Teachers Aide; School Musical; School Play; Powder Puff Ftbl; Score Keeper; Vllybl; Work At Least 20 Hrs Week; UC Davis; Prosecuting Attorney.

SCHAIBLE, ULRIKE; Woodcrest Christian Schl; Riverside, CA; (3); Church Yth Grp; Cmnty Wkr; Yrbk; High Hon Roll; Hon Roll; Svc Awd; Art; Chrstn Ldrshp Awd; Teacher.

SCHALCHLIN, CURTIS C; Whittier Christian HS; Whittier, CA; (2); JV Ftbl; Hon Roll; CSF; USC; Entrprnr.

SCHAMP, JANET L; Redondo Union HS; Redondo Beach, CA; (4); 44/415; Church Yth Grp; French Clb; Math Tm; NFL; VP Science Clb; Lit Mag; High Hon Roll; HS Stu Ambssdr Pgm; CSF; Synchrnzs Swmmng Shw Mgr; U Of CA Santa Cruz; Inter Dsgn.

SCHANZ, TRACIE A; C K Mc Clatchy SR HS; Sacramento, CA; (2); Girl Scts; SADD; Yrbk; Sec Soph Cls; Off Jr Cls; Stat Bsktbl; Var JV Cheerldng; Mgr Powder Puff Ftbl; Var Capt Socr; HISP.

SCHAPER, DAVID T; Kennedy HS; Buena Park, CA; (3); Ski Clb; JV Var Ftbl; JV Var Wt Lftg; Hon Roll; Vollswagen Club; GATE.

SCHAPIRO, AARON D; University HS; Irvine, CA; (3); 12/551; Hosp Aide; Treas JCL; Intrml Trk; JV Var Wrstlng; Hon Roll; Ntl Merit Ltr; Sunrise Exchng Club Yth Of Mnth 90; Silvr Mdl Natl Latn Exam 88-90; UC; Law.

SCHAPPER, CAROLYN L; Notre Dame HS; Salinas, CA; (3); 7/60; Science Clb; Chorus; Yrbk; Pres Stu Cncl; Var L Trk; Var Capt Vllybl; High Hon Roll; NHS; CSF; All-League Trk; Girls St; Hartnell JC; Commnctns.

SCHAR, JENNIFER A; Notre Dame HS; Portola Valley, CA; (2); Church Yth Grp; School Play; Stage Crew; Variety Show; Rptr Nwsp; Hon Roll; Drama Clss Awd; Lectoring,Poetry,Wrtng,Sngng,Dirctng,Actng,Jazz Dance; Rosemont; Actress.

SCHARF, DANIELLE R; California HS; Whittier, CA; (2); Church Yth Grp; Service Clb; Band; Jazz Band; Mrchg Band; Pep Band; JV Bsktbl; JV Sftbl; JV Vllybl; Hon Roll; Med.

SCHARF, LISA N; California HS; Whittier, CA; (2); Church Yth Grp; Service Clb; Band; Jazz Band; Mrchg Band; Pep Band; JV Sftbl; JV Vllybl; Hon Roll; Schl Site Cncl Stu Rep; Med.

SCHARFFENBERG, BILL; Lodi Acad; Acampo, CA; (2); Teachers Aide; Band; Off Soph Cls; Cit Awd; High Hon Roll; Prfct Atten Awd; Temple Yth Grp; Chorus; U CA Davis; Bio.

SCHAUER, ANGIE M; Turlock HS; Turlock, CA; (3); 227/650; Church Yth Grp; Cmnty Wkr; Modesto JC.

SCHAUF, AIMEE R; Yreka HS; Hornbrook, CA; (4); 15/130; Church Yth Grp; Ski Clb; Spanish Clb; Rptr Phtg Yrbk; Sec Sr Cls; Rep Stu Cncl; Powder Puff Ftbl; Hon Roll; Pres Acad Fit Awd; Rotary Awd; Heart Federal Savings & Loan Schlrshp; U OR; Intl Rltns.

SCHAUF, SARAH E; Yreka Union HS; Hornbrook, CA; (3); 4/174; Church Yth Grp; Scholastic Bowl; Ski Clb; Spanish Clb; Teachers Aide; Ed Yrbk; Ed Lit Mag; Stu Cncl; Stat Bsktbl; Var Tennis; Tn Mssns Intl To Hngry/Russia; CSF; Intl Bus.

SCHECHTER, DAMON ROSS; La Serna HS; Whittier, CA; (4); 1/343; Boy Scts; Speech Tm; High Hon Roll; Kiwanis Awd; Lion Awd; Pres NHS; Pres Acad Fit Awd; Val; Cmnty Wkr; Pep Clb; Eagle Sct 3 Eagle Palms; Ner Tamid Relgs Awd, Order Of Arrow Chptr Chief; Ldrshp Natl Rcgntn Awd; Stanford U; Med.

SCHECHTER, DAVID A; Atascadero HS; Atascadero, CA; (2); 4-H; Temple Yth Grp; JV Bsbl; High Hon Roll; Acad Exc Awd Golden St Ex 88-89 Geo; Stu Mnth; U C Berkeley.

SCHEELE, PAUL R; Thomas Downey HS; Modesto, CA; (3); Debate Tm; Key Clb; NFL; Spanish Clb; Speech Tm; Var L Bsbl; JV Ftbl; Ntl Merit Ltr; St Schlr; Nor Cal Chmpn Sci Olympiad Tm; U Of CA; Med.

SCHEER, KIMBERLY L; Escondido HS; Escondido, CA; (3); 21/382; Church Yth Grp; Cmnty Wkr; French Clb; German Clb; Key Clb; Pep Clb; Rep Soph Cls; JV Gym; JV Swmmng; JV Tennis; Cmmnctns.

SCHEIBER, TROY M; East Nicolaus HS; Nicolaus, CA; (3); 5/55; Rep Letterman Clb; Ski Clb; SADD; Var Bsbl; JV Bsktbl; Var Capt Ftbl; Var Trk; High Hon Roll; Hon Roll; Pres Schlr; Cal Poly; Engr.

SCHEINER, NATALIE; Los Alamitos HS; Seal Beach, CA; (3); Cmnty Wkr; Dance Clb; Hosp Aide; Pep Clb; Ski Clb; SADD; Temple Yth Grp; Drill Tm; Stat Bsbl; JV Cheerldng; CSF; Intrct Club; Vet.

SCHELL, PAUL F; James Madison HS; San Diego, CA; (4); 77/370; Letterman Clb; Varsity Clb; Nwsp; Ftbl; Powder Puff Ftbl; Wrstlng; Hon Roll; San Diego ST U.

SCHELL, THEODORE L; Rowland HS; Walnut, CA; (2); Varsity Clb; Var L Bsbl; Var L Ftbl; Hon Roll; Vrsty Ftbl All Lg; UCLA.

SCHELLENBERG, MATTHEW; Yosemite HS; Coarsegold, CA; (2); Boy Scts; FFA; Quiz Bowl; Science Clb; Spanish Clb; Hon Roll; FFA Chapter Hghst Awd Swine Shwmnshp, Chptr Farmer Degree, Blue Awd Sectnl Project Cmptn; UC Davis; Zoologist.

SCHELLER, LYDIA A; Bret Harte HS; Murphys, CA; (2); Church Yth Grp; Ski Clb; School Musical; JV Vllybl; Hon Roll; Interact Club; Friday Night Live.

SCHEMEL, JEROME A; Summerville HS; Standard, CA; (3); FFA; ROTC; Hon Roll; UC Davis; Law.

SCHENACH, JOANNE E; Marina HS; Huntington Beach, CA; (2); Drill Tm; JV Cheerldng; U Of CA.

SCHENDEL, TARA-LYNN; Turlock HS; Turlock, CA; (3); VP AFS; Church Yth Grp; Debate Tm; Pres French Clb; Key Clb; NFL; Speech Tm; Hon Roll; Opt Clb Awd; Rotary Awd; PTA Awd; Adv Lacement Coll Pgm CA ST U Stanislaus; Played Piano; Intnl Studies Assn Schlrp; US Intl U; Intl Atty.

SCHEPIS, JULIE A; L A Baptist HS; Granada Hills, CA; (3); 8/100; Church Yth Grp; Treas Thesps; Chorus; Church Choir; School Musical; School Play; Ed Lit Mag; JV Sftbl; Hon Roll; Commnctns.

SCHEPLER, JOHN E; Norco HS; Norco, CA; (3); 5/399; Model UN; Spanish Clb; Teachers Aide; Cit Awd; Prfct Atten Awd; Pres Acad Fit Awd; CA Schlrshp Fed; Phy.

SCHEPMAN, KIM; Monte Vista HS; Diablo, CA; (3); Church Yth Grp; Dance Clb; French Clb; Hosp Aide; Ski Clb; SADD; Teachers Aide; Chorus; Stu Cncl; Powder Puff Ftbl; Yth & Govt Parlimentarian & Assemblywoman; Natl Charity Leag Treas.

SCHERBERT, CHRISTIAN G; Encinal HS; Alameda, CA; (3); 60/246; Key Clb; Teachers Aide; Var L Bsbl; JV Bsktbl; Cit Awd; Hon Roll; Schlr/Athl Awd 88-89; San Diego ST; Arch.

SCHERBERTH, EMILY J; Bonita HS; La Verne, CA; (1); Church Yth Grp; GAA; Hosp Aide; SADD; Acpl Chr; Chorus; School Musical; Variety Show; JV Sftbl; Hon Roll; Music; Wrtng; UCLA Film Schl; Film Editor.

SCHERER, ANNE; Cajon HS; San Bernardino, CA; (4); 1/500; Sec Treas AFS; Chorus; Church Choir; School Musical; Ntl Merit SF; Ballet Prfrmces/Schlrshps, San Bernardino, NYC, San Antonio TX, Mobile, Canada; 1st Pl Wrtng Awds; Engl.

SCHERER, ANTHONY R; Miramonte HS; Orinda, CA; (4); 8/277; Boy Scts; Spanish Clb; Band; Drm Mjr(t); Jazz Band; Mrchg Band; Pep Band; School Musical; Var Vllybl; Hon Roll; Wtr Polo Lttr; Engrng.

SCHERER, CRYSTAL R; Bishop Union HS; Bishop, CA; (3); Dance Clb; 4-H; Math Clb; Ski Clb; Spanish Clb; Teachers Aide; Gym; Sftbl; Vllybl; Hon Roll; Intl Trnsltr.

SCHERER, ERIK A; Desert HS; Rosamond, CA; (3); Letterman Clb; Math Tm; Office Aide; Varsity Clb; Rptr Nwsp; Stu Cncl; JV Var Bsbl; JV Var Bsktbl; JV Var Ftbl; Hon Roll; MVP JV Baseball; JV Football; JV Basketball; School SAT Hall Of Fame; 1140; Radio Tv Broadcasting.

SCHERER, KRISTIN A; Mt Shasta HS; Mt Shasta, CA; (3); Church Yth Grp; Hosp Aide; Band; Chorus; Church Choir; Vllybl; Hon Roll; Sun Schl Tchr; Church Musicals; Coll Of The Sisiyous; Dev Psych.

SCHERER, NICOLE D; Clovis West HS; Clovis, CA; (3); ROTC; Spanish Clb; Chorus; Gov Hon Prg Awd; Hon Roll; U Of WA; Police Sci.

SCHERER, TONY; Miramonte HS; Orinda, CA; (4); 7/277; Boy Scts; German Clb; Spanish Clb; Varsity Clb; Band; Jazz Band; Mrchg Band; School Musical; Var Vllybl; Water Polo V; Engrng.

SCHERLER, TRACI; Hemet HS; Hemet, CA; (4); Teachers Aide; Nwsp; Powder Puff Ftbl; Photography; Mt San Jacinto; Cmptrs.

SCHERMERHORN, JOHN C; Burbank HS; Burbank, CA; (3); Boy Scts; Drama Clb; Teachers Aide; Band; Chorus; Jazz Band; School Play; Hon Roll; 1st Pl Trophys Karate; Plyd Sound Tracks & Actor 11 Yrs; Bu.

SCHERR, BRIAN M; Rim Of The World HS; Crestline, CA; (3); 9/269; Art Clb; Cmnty Wkr; Library Aide; Spanish Clb; Var Socr; High Hon Roll; Hon Roll; Sports Med.

SCHERR, SCOTT A; Rim Of The World HS; Crestline, CA; (2); 19/359; Art Clb; Cmnty Wkr; Letterman Clb; Spanish Clb; Varsity Clb; Stu Cncl; Var Bsbl; High Hon Roll; Hon Roll; Bsbl.

SCHETGEN, SHANNON S; Gilroy HS; Gilroy, CA; (4); 21/331; Cmnty Wkr; Powder Puff Ftbl; Var Socr; Trk; Vllybl; Hon Roll; Off Soph Cls; Off Jr Cls; Off Sr Cls; Litercy Vlntr Amer; USA/Sccr Tm; CA Schlrshp Fed; UC Santa Cruz; Lang.

SCHEVE, NICOLE M; James Logan HS; Union City, CA; (3); FTA; Red Cross Aide; Gym; Cal ST Hayward; Chem.

SCHIANO, MARIA; Victor Valley HS; Spring Valley, CA; (3); Color Guard; Hon Roll; SDSU; Trvl.

SCHIANO, PIETRO G; Sir Francis Drake HS; Fairfax, CA; (2); Intrml JV Ftbl; Intrml JV Wt Lftg; High Hon Roll; Hon Roll; NHS; Olympc Liftng Twice A Day.

SCHIAVONE, ANTHONY M; Servite HS; Anaheim, CA; (2); Hon Roll; NHS; Guitar Clb; CSF; CSU Long Beach; Cmmnctns.

SCHIBIG, MARGRETHE A; St Joseph HS; Long Beach, CA; (2); 66/200; Drama Clb; Drill Tm; Hon Roll; UCLA.

SCHICATANO, ERIN L; Valley Christian HS; Danville, CA; (4); Church Yth Grp; Pep Clb; Spanish Clb; Teachers Aide; Yrbk; Hist Sr Cls; Var Cheerldng; Var Sftbl; Var Vllybl; High Hon Roll; CSF; Biola U; Bus Mgmt.

SCHICK, ALICIA J; Lodi HS; Lodi, CA; (1); Chorus; Cheerldng; Swmmng; Hon Roll; Westmont U; Psych.

SCHICK, JEFF; Edison HS; Stockton, CA; (2); Hon Roll; OH ST U; Stats.

SCHICK, TRAVIS R; Monte Vista HS; Diablo, CA; (3); Church Yth Grp; Computer Clb; French Clb; Chorus; Church Choir; JV Crs Cntry; JV Swmmng; Hon Roll; Prfct Atten Awd; Sci Awd Phys Sci; Bus/Ed Rndtble Awd In Sci & Tech; MIT.

SCHIEFERLE, CHAD J; Redwood HS; Visalia, CA; (3); Boy Scts; Letterman Clb; Math Clb; Math Tm; Spanish Clb; Varsity Clb; VP Sr Cls; Var Ftbl; Var Socr; Var Trk; Med.

SCHIERER, PHILLIP G; Artesia HS; Lakewood, CA; (1); Science Clb; Rep Frsh Cls; Intrml Crs Cntry; Intrml Capt Trk; Hon Roll; Acad Ltr; U Of CA; Astronomy.

SCHIFFMANN, ALYSSA M; Santa Barbara HS; Santa Barbara, CA; (2); Stage Crew; Bsktbl; Var Sftbl; High Hon Roll; Gldn St Exam Acad Excl Awd; Alg Hnr; Astrntcs.

SCHILLER, SUZANNE DANIELLE; Oakwood Secondary Schl; Sherman Oaks, CA; (4); SADD; Ed Lit Mag; Rep Soph Cls; Sec Stu Cncl; Var Capt Vllybl; Ntl Merit SF; Spcl Olympics Vol; Photogrphy Mentoship; Headmaster Awd; Oberlin Coll; Eng.

SCHILLING, JACKIE R; Flintridge Sacred Heart Acad; La Canada-Flint, CA; (4); Church Yth Grp; Cmnty Wkr; Drama Clb; Hosp Aide; Service Clb; Spanish Clb; Variety Show; Off Sr Cls; NHS; CSF; Kairos Ldr Retreat; Boston Coll; Ed.

SCHILLING, JENNIFER; Rosary HS; Orange, CA; (2); French Clb; Spanish Clb; Varsity Clb; Var Crs Cntry; Capt Var Socr; Var Sftbl; High Hon Roll; Pres Acad Fit Awd; Med.

SCHILT, KARIN M; Pomona JR Acad; Alta Loma, CA; (1); 1/10; Church Yth Grp; French Clb; Yrbk; VP Frsh Cls; Pres Stu Cncl; French Hon Soc; High Hon Roll; Loma Linda Acad; Jrnlsm.

SCHIMMER, NICOLE; Moorpark HS; Moorpark, CA; (2); 1/249; Pres VP Church Yth Grp; FBLA; Church Choir; VP Frsh Cls; High Hon Roll; Stu Mnth; Brigham Young U; Med.

SCHIMMER, TONYA; Moorpark HS; Moorpark, CA; (4); Am Leg Aux Girls St; Church Yth Grp; Key Clb; Teachers Aide; Church Choir; Drill Tm; High Hon Roll; Hon Roll; Entrprs Acad Achvt 88-89; Ivy Chain; Chrch Bsktbl Won 2nd Pl Region; Brigham Yng U; Fshn Merch.

SCHINDLER, REBECCA L; San Dieguito HS; Olivenhain, CA; (2); Church Yth Grp; Girl Scts; School Play; Bsktbl; Socr; Cit Awd; Brigham Young U; Math.

SCHINKEL, JEFFREY D; Casa Grande HS; Petaluma, CA; (2); 65/297; Band; Mrchg Band; Pep Band; Hon Roll; Prfct Atten Awd; Achvt Awds In Band, Span & Wdshp; Phrmcst.

SCHIPPER, JAMES M; Valley Christian HS; Lakewood, CA; (2); Chess Clb; Church Yth Grp; Letterman Clb; Varsity Clb; Treas Frsh Cls; Crs Cntry; Tennis; High Hon Roll; NHS.

SCHIPSKE, CHRISTOPHER S; Notre Dame HS; Canyon Lake, CA; (1); Ftbl; Golf; Engrng.

SCHIRLE, JENNIFER L; Live Oak HS; Morgan Hill, CA; (3); 20/530; Church Yth Grp; French Clb; SADD; Ed Yrbk; Lit Mag; Intrml Vllybl; Hon Roll; Pres Acad Fit Awd; Vrsty Bdmntn; CA Jr Schlrshp Fed; Biochem.

SCHIRMER, CHRISTINE; Folsom HS; Folsom, CA; (2); 10/250; Intnl Clb; Model UN; JV Cheerldng; JV Vllybl; High Hon Roll; Opt Clb Awd; Grls Block F; Fri Nite Live; Engl Acad Ltr.

SCHIRNER, TAWNYA; Fountain Valley HS; Fountain Valley, CA; (2); Church Yth Grp; Rep Jr Cls; JV Sftbl; Hon Roll; Wrk Mrs Fields Cookies; Chrch Prjct Vol; Creative Wrtng; Comm.

SCHLACHTA, LILLY V; Castro Valley HS; Castro Valley, CA; (4); 8/336; Acpl Chr; Chorus; Orch; School Musical; School Play; High Hon Roll; Hon Roll; Bank Of Amer Fine Arts Plqe Wnnr; CSF; Piano Perfrmnce.

SCHLAIS, KRISTI A; Pleasant Valley HS; Chico, CA; (3); 61/271; Church Yth Grp; Drama Clb; SADD; Teachers Aide; Varsity Clb; School Play; Lit Mag; Crs Cntry; Socr; Vllybl; Engl Stu Month, Qtr; Most Val Rnr.

SCHLANGEN, CHARLES N W; Montgomery HS; Kenwood, CA; (2); Church Yth Grp; French Clb; Speech Tm; Treas Soph Cls; Rep Stu Cncl; Var Tennis; JV Trk; Cit Awd; Hon Roll; Jr NHS; Shirley Ann Knight Engl Awd; Mst Outstndng Frnch Stu II; 1st Pl N Bay Rgnl Finals Speech Cmptn.

SCHLANGEN, ROBERT P; Rio Mesa HS; Camarillo, CA; (3); 15/367; Trk; High Hon Roll; Hon Roll; Acad Ltr; CSF; Cmptr; UCLA; Engrg.

SCHLATTER, REBECCA A; Ygnacio Valley HS; Walnut Creek, CA; (4); 8/360; Art Clb; Sec FTA; Hosp Aide; Service Clb; Rep Stu Cncl; Var Capt Socr; Var Swmmng; Pres Acad Fit Awd; CSF; Engl Dept Awd; UCLA; Teacher.

SCHLECHT, JOEL A; Los Angeles Baptist HS; Granada Hills, CA; (3); JV Bsbl; JV Var Ftbl; Var Mgr(s); Wt Lftg; Hon Roll; Sierra Clb; UCLA; Med.

SCHLEDORN, REBECCA S; Thousand Oaks HS; Thousand Oaks, CA; (3); Spanish Clb; Teachers Aide; Lit Mag; Powder Puff Ftbl.

SCHLEEDE, JUSTIN B; Dana Hills HS; Laguna Niguel, CA; (2); Tennis; Cit Awd; Sci.

SCHLEHUBER, SHANNON E; Carlsbad HS; Carlsbad, CA; (4); 8/330; AFS; Church Yth Grp; Cmnty Wkr; Hosp Aide; Intnl Clb; Key Clb; Pep Clb; Quiz Bowl; Service Clb; SADD; Traveling; Notre Dame 1; Bus.

SCHLEICHER, SETH; Palmdale HS; Littlerock, CA; (3); 6/644; Church Yth Grp; Cmnty Wkr; VP Sec French Clb; FFA; Intnl Clb; Var L Crs Cntry; Var L Trk; High Hon Roll; Treas Pres NHS; Mexican Folk Danc Trp; Amer Clog Dancg Clb; Spk Frnch, Spnsh & Swahili; Stanford U; Intl Rel.

SCHLEMMER, KAREN M; Bishop O'dowd HS; San Leandro, CA; (2); Service Clb; Band; Church Choir; Orch; JV Sftbl; JV Vllybl; High Hon Roll; Pres Acad Fit Awd; Ed Cert Awd; CSF.

SCHLEMMER, SANDRA A.; Tracy Joint Union HS; Tracy, CA; (2); 57/483; Am Leg Aux Girls St; Church Yth Grp; Spanish Clb; Church Choir; Rep Frsh Cls; Stu Cncl; Capt Cheerldng; CA Schlrshp Fed; Peer Cnslr; CA ST U; Elem Ed.

SCHLENZ, SARAH; San Dimas HS; Colton, CA; (1); Drama Clb; School Play; Stage Crew; Cheerldng; Hon Roll; Make-Up Artst.

SCHLEPP, MARY; St Joseph Notre Dame HS; Alameda, CA; (3); Cmnty Wkr; Nwsp; Phtg Yrbk; Var Pom Pon; Var Tennis; High Hon Roll; Hon Roll; NHS; Prfct Atten Awd; CSF; Vlntr Swmmng Instr; Bus.

SCHLESINGER, JEFFREY N; University HS; Beverly Hills, CA; (3); Boy Scts; Pep Clb; Service Clb; Temple Yth Grp; Varsity Clb; Rep Frsh Cls; JV Var Vllybl; Cit Awd; Hon Roll; Los Angeles Mayors Outstndg Yth Awd; Clean Campus Clb; CSU Northridge.

SCHLESKE, DANA C; Bishop O'dowd HS; Oakland, CA; (3); Church Yth Grp; Cmnty Wkr; Girl Scts; Teachers Aide; Chorus; Church Choir; Rep Frsh Cls; Rep Soph Cls; Var Capt Bsktbl; Stat Score Keeper; Ed.

SCHLEY, ANNE E; Mayfield SR Schl; South Pasadena, CA; (2); Cmnty Wkr; GAA; Library Aide; Ski Clb; SADD; Rptr Nwsp; Phtg Yrbk; Var Bsktbl; Var Trk; High Hon Roll; CSF; Museum Apprntc Rsrch Pgm Monarch Bttrfly Study 89-90; Natl Sci Fndtn Grant; Suba Dvng Certfctn; Duke U; Marine Bio.

SCHLICHT, ROBERTA H; St Anthony HS; Long Beach, CA; (2); Church Yth Grp; Drama Clb; Band; Jazz Band; Mrchg Band; School Musical; School Play; JV Var Trk; High Hon Roll; Hon Roll; CA Schlrshp Fed.

SCHLIENTZ, MARY T; Paraclete HS; Lancaster, CA; (3); Church Yth Grp; Cmnty Wkr; Drama Clb; 4-H; JA; Teachers Aide; Church Choir; Stage Crew; Variety Show; Score Keeper; Bus.

SCHLOBOHM, CHRIS J; St Bonaventure HS; Thousand Oaks, CA; (3); 18/100; Cmnty Wkr; Teachers Aide; Hon Roll; Jr NHS; NHS; CA Schlrshp Fed; UC Santa Barbara; Med.

SCHLOSSER, BEANY E; Sacred Heart Prep; Menlo Park, CA; (2); Var Tennis; Hon Roll; Law.

SCHLOTTHAUER, ERIC; Hoover HS; Fresno, CA; (4); 1/390; Church Yth Grp; VP German Clb; Church Choir; Ed Yrbk; Cit Awd; High Hon Roll; Kiwanis Awd; Prfct Atten Awd; Val; 3 Church Musicals; CA ST U Fresno; Pharm.

SCHLOTZHAVER, JIM; Simi Valley HS; Simi Valley, CA; (4); Teachers Aide; Hon Roll; Video Clb; Earth Day Fstvls; Peer Cnslng; Interior Dsgn.

SCHLUER, STEPHEN S; Modesto Christian HS; Manteca, CA; (3); Church Yth Grp; Rep Sr Cls; Var Bsbl; Var Bsktbl; Var Ftbl; High Hon Roll; Hon Roll; Monteca Police Cadet; Sacramento ST; Law Enfrcmnt.

SCHMALHOFER, KATIE D; Woodcrest Christian HS; Riverside, CA; (2); Church Yth Grp; Model UN; Church Choir; Var Bsktbl; Var Sftbl; Var Vllybl; High Hon Roll.

SCHMEICHEL, KEVIN DAVID; Palos Verdes HS; Palos Vrds Pen, CA; (4); Latin Clb; Swmmng; High Hon Roll; NHS; Ntl Merit Schol; Pres Acad Fit Awd; Natl Hspnc Awds Schlr Fnlst; CSF Gld Searbr; Gldn ST Exm Geom Hghst Hnrs; UCSD.

SCHMELZINGER, DAVID K; Milpitas HS; Milpitas, CA; (3); 159/487; L Var Ftbl; L Var Wrstlng; Cal Poly SLO; Engrng.

SCHMID, KRISTEN M; Woodland HS; Woodland, CA; (3); 3/500; Am Leg Aux Girls St; Sec 4-H; Pres FBLA; Rptr Nwsp; Rptr Yrbk; Rep Sr Cls; JV Bsktbl; Var JV Crs Cntry; JV Var Trk; 4-H Awd; CA St Smr Schl For Arts 90; X Cntry MVP 88; Trck Mst Loyal 89; X Cntry Coachs Awd 7; FBLA St Conf 89; Art Dir.

SCHMID, KRISTY; Royal HS; Simi Valley, CA; (4); 2/500; Church Yth Grp; Key Clb; Ski Clb; Trk; Cit Awd; High Hon Roll; Treas Jr NHS; Sec NHS; Pres Acad Fit Awd; Acad Ltr; Loyola Marymount U; Intl Rltns.

SCHMIDT, ALEXANDRA; Cajon HS; San Bernardino, CA; (3); AFS; Key Clb; Yrbk; Hon Roll; JSA; Intl Bcclrt Stu; Clark U; Adv.

SCHMIDT, AMANDA; Simi Valley HS; Simi Valley, CA; (2); 53/730; Drill Tm; Jr NHS; Pres Acad Fit Awd.

SCHMIDT, BRIAN D; Galt HS; Galt, CA; (2); 1/239; Church Yth Grp; JV Bsktbl; Var L Golf; High Hon Roll; Gldn St Exam Geom Hnrs Cat; MVP Bsktbl; Molecular Bio Stu Yr; Math.

SCHMIDT, DARREN A; Irvine HS; Irvine, CA; (1); 2/575; Church Yth Grp; NHS; Amnesty Intl; CSF; Environmental Preservation Club.

SCHMIDT, ERIKA D; Galt HS; Galt, CA; (2); 1/239; Intnl Clb; Var Tennis; High Hon Roll; Pres Acad Fit Awd; Frgn Lang; Hstry; Writing; Hstry.

SCHMIDT, JENNIFER J; Carlmont HS; Belmont, CA; (3); 30/300; Alg II Awd; CSF; Acad Dcthln Pres; Cal Poly San Luis Obispo; Arch.

SCHMIDT, JENNIFER N; Central HS; Madison, NC; (4); Art Clb; Church Yth Grp; Drama Clb; Spanish Clb; SADD; Band; Church Choir; Color Guard; Mrchg Band; School Play.

SCHMIDT, MARCY DAWN; Pleasant Valley HS; Chico, CA; (4); Church Yth Grp; Intrml JV Bsktbl; Intrml JV Sftbl; Intrml JV Vllybl; Hon Roll; Prfct Atten Awd; Awds Art Work 4 Yrs; Cert Of Cmmndtn Excptnl Achvt Span & Typing; Tennis; Trvlng Soccer Team 2 Yrs; Chico ST U.

SCHMIDT, MATTHEW J; St Ignatius College Prep; San Rafael, CA; (2); 8/308; Cmnty Wkr; Ed Nwsp; Sec Treas Soph Cls; Sec Treas Jr Cls; JV Crs Cntry; JV Vllybl; Hon Roll; HS Sci Fair 2nd P; UC Berkeley; Jrnlsm.

SCHMIDT, MICHAEL B; Shafter HS; Shafter, CA; (3); Church Yth Grp; Treas German Clb; Letterman Clb; Varsity Clb; Var JV Bsbl; JV Bsktbl; High Hon Roll; Hon Roll.

SCHMIDT, MIKE J; Poway HS; San Diego, CA; (1); Boy Scts; German Clb; Band; Jazz Band; Mrchg Band; Hon Roll; UCSB; Sci.

SCHMIDT, PETER; Placer HS; Auburn, CA; (4); Am Leg Boys St; Aud/Vis; 4-H; Cit Awd; High Hon Roll; Hon Roll; Century Clb 88-90; Advncd Plcmnt Engl 89, 90; Photo Achvmt Cert; Govt.

SCHMIDT, ROBERT; Saugus HS; Valencia, CA; (3); 9/460; JV Socr; Var Tennis; NHS; Ntl Merit Ltr; Berkeley; Bus.

SCHMIDT, STEVEN; Cape Valley Christian HS; El Toro, CA; (4); 6/70; Church Yth Grp; FCA; Teachers Aide; Band; Church Choir; Rptr Jr Cls; Var L Crs Cntry; JV Socr; Var L Trk; Hon Roll; Missions Club; Ldrshp Tm Church Yth Grp; Liberty U; Missions.

SCHMIDT, TIFFANY L; Irvine HS; Irvine, CA; (3); 3/540; Church Yth Grp; Hosp Aide; UC Riverside; Med.

SCHMIEDL, DEREK E; Bellarmine College Prep Prep; Gilroy, CA; (3); Church Yth Grp; Cmnty Wkr; JA; Pep Clb; ROTC; Service Clb; Ski Clb; SADD; Teachers Aide; Band; Stanford; Med.

SCHMIERER, JEFFREY A; Edison/Computech HS; Fresno, CA; (2); Church Yth Grp; Hon Roll; CA Schlrshp Fed; Envrnmntl Clb; Mst Imprvd Eng Stu Awd; CA Poly; Arch.

SCHMITT, CHRISTINA M; Monte Vista Christian HS; Scotts Valley, CA; (4); Church Yth Grp; Drama Clb; 4-H; Girl Scts; Teachers Aide; School Play; Stage Crew; Phtg Yrbk; VP Swmmng; 4-H Awd; Southern CA Coll.

SCHMITT, DAVID J; El Dorado HS; Brea, CA; (3); 7/311; Church Yth Grp; Cmnty Wkr; Science Clb; Church Choir; Var Crs Cntry; Var Trk; High Hon Roll; Ntl Merit Ltr; Envrmntl Engr.

SCHMITT, MATTHEW J; Prospect HS; San Jose, CA; (1); Boy Scts; Church Yth Grp; Band; Church Choir; JV Ftbl; UCLA; Cmptr Prgmr.

SCHMITZ, KRISTY A; Calistoga HS; Calistoga, CA; (2); Church Yth Grp; Debate Tm; Teachers Aide; Band; Mrchg Band; Pep Band; VP Frsh Cls; Rep Soph Cls; Cheerldng; Pom Pon; UCSF Med Ctr; Radlgy.

SCHMOE, AMY J; Serrano HS; Wrightwood, CA; (1); Art Clb; Dance Clb; GAA; SADD; Teachers Aide; Chorus; School Play; Swing Chorus; Cit Awd; Hon Roll; Natl Phys Fitness Awd; Meritorius Awd; Beautician.

SCHMOE, ANGIE; Silver Valley HS; Yermo, CA; (2); JV Bsktbl; Var Sftbl; Hon Roll; UNLV.

SCHMUDLACH, MARLIES; Ponderosa HS; Placerville, CA; (4); 14/289; Church Yth Grp; Speech Tm; Band; Rep Jr Cls; Off Sr Cls; Stu Cncl; Var Cheerldng; Var Crs Cntry; Var Trk; Cit Awd; Odd Fllws Rbkhs Untd Ntns 3 Wk Plgrmg NY Spch Tour; WASC Accrdtn Stu 90; Engl Dept Awd; U Of CA Davis; Pltcl Sci.

SCHNEIDER, AMBER; Enterprise HS; Redding, CA; (3); Drama Clb; Spanish Clb; Diving; Wt Lftg.

SCHNEIDER, ANNE; Summerville Union HS; Twain Harte, CA; (3); 5/130; Key Clb; Ski Clb; Sec Spanish Clb; Sec Stu Cncl; JV Golf; CSF Stu Cncl Rep; Acadmc Dcthln; UC Davis; Med.

SCHNEIDER, AUTUMN L; Etiwanda HS; Alta Loma, CA; (2); Girl Scts; SADD; Var Crs Cntry; JV Socr; Var Trk; Hon Roll; Gate Pgm Jr Yr; U CA Davis; Vet.

SCHNEIDER, CLAYTON; Kerman HS; Kerman, CA; (2); 12/130; Letterman Clb; SADD; Teachers Aide; Band; Jazz Band; Mrchg Band; Orch; JV Var Bsbl; JV Capt Ftbl; JV Capt Wrstlng; JV Ftbl Defnsve MVP; JV Wrstlng Otstndng JV Wrstlr Awd; Frstyle Wrstlng Qualified St Trnmnt; Coach.

SCHNEIDER, EDWARD D; Temple Christian Schl; Perris, CA; (2); 1/30; Drama Clb; Letterman Clb; Rep Soph Cls; Var Bsbl; Capt Bsktbl; Hon Roll; NHS; Opt Clb Awd; Yth Ldrshp; Liberty; Missionary.

SCHNEIDER, ELISABETH S; Santa Cruz HS; Santa Cruz, CA; (1); 4-H; Sec Frsh Cls; 4-H Awd; High Hon Roll; Under Grad Awd Wrld Cvlztns & Pin Ldrshp; Outstndng Achvt Pin Phys Educ; Envrnmnt.

SCHNEIDER, KEN S; Clovis HS; Fresno, CA; (2); JV Bsbl; JV Socr.

SCHNEIDER, KURT L; Paraclete HS; Lancaster, CA; (2); Debate Tm; Drama Clb; JA; Math Tm; Scholastic Bowl; Ed Nwsp; Sec Soph Cls; Var Golf; Cit Awd; High Hon Roll; CSF; Math.

SCHNEIDER, LAURIE; Palo Alto HS; Palo Alto, CA; (3); Thesps; Varsity Clb; Var Capt Cheerldng; Var Capt Pom Pon; Rachel H Austin Prize; MENSA.

SCHNEIDER, LEVA A; Ramona HS; Santa Ysabel, CA; (3); 21/294; Dance Clb; Intnl Clb; Cert Outstndng Achvt Coll Rody Whites Prjct; Earth Clb Scty; Anml Rights Clb.

SCHNEIDER, LISA S; Glendale HS; Glendale, CA; (2); Church Yth Grp; Pep Clb; Spanish Clb; Band; Drill Tm; Pom Pon; Hon Roll; Sftbl, Sccr, Vllybl; Phrmcy.

SCHNEIDER, MICHELE M; Cordova HS; Sacramento, CA; (3); Church Yth Grp; Model UN; Office Aide; Teachers Aide; Stat Ftbl; Var JV Sftbl; Cit Awd; Hon Roll; Jr NHS; UC Davis; Psych.

SCHNEIDER, MICHELLE B; Lowell HS; San Francisco, CA; (2); German Clb; Office Aide; Red Cross Aide; Stat Bsktbl; Var Sftbl; Prtcpny Cnstrtn Lowell HS Mural; Vllybl Club.

SCHNEIDER, NICK J; Arlington HS; Riverside, CA; (3); Letterman Clb; Teachers Aide; Stage Crew; Var L Bsbl; Var Mgr(s); Intrml Wt Lftg; Hon Roll; Crmnl Law.

SCHNEIDMILLER, TAMI L; Canyon Springs HS; Moreno Valley, CA; (2); Drama Clb; FBLA; Intnl Clb; Yrbk; Hon Roll.

SCHNELL, CHRISTIANE; Fairfield HS; Suisun, CA; (3); Sec Art Clb; German Clb; Pres Key Clb; Vllybl; Hon Roll; Girls Block F; Davis U; Med.

SCHNELL, JEFFREY L; Whittier Chrisitan HS; Yorba Linda, CA; (2); 1/186; Church Yth Grp; School Play; Stage Crew; JV Trk; High Hon Roll; CA Schlrshp Fdrtn; Ply Piano & Trmpt; Harvard; Law.

SCHNEPP, KRISTIN; San Bernardino HS; San Bernardino, CA; (1); Cmnty Wkr; Dance Clb; GAA; Letterman Clb; Pep Clb; Ski Clb; Speech Tm; Nwsp; Cheerldng; Swmmng; Yth To Yth Prog; CSU-SAN Bernardino; Jrnlsm.

SCHNITTGER, JASON W; Apple Valley HS; Apple Valley, CA; (1); Bsbl; Hon Roll; AZ ST.

SCHNITZER, LEIGH E; Abraham Lincoln HS; San Jose, CA; (3); 27/350; Dance Clb; English Clb; NFL; Scholastic Bowl; Spanish Clb; Var Speech Tm; Temple Yth Grp; School Musical; School Play; Variety Show; Marketing.

SCHNITZER, MIKE; Tomales HS; Dillon Beach, CA; (2); Letterman Clb; SADD; Rep Stu Cncl; JV Bsbl; JV Bsktbl; JV Ftbl; High Hon Roll; Gldn Bell Math Awd; CSF; Acad Awds Bio-Geom-Spnsh; Emery Riddle; Aerosp Tech.

SCHNITZLER, ADRIANE L; Kingsburg HS; Kingsburg, CA; (3); Band; Mrchg Band; School Play; Rptr Nwsp; Rep Sr Cls; Var Bsktbl; Var Vllybl; High Hon Roll; Hon Roll; Rotary Awd; CA Schltc Fed; Block K Awd.

SCHNOCKER, TERRILYN; Polytechnic HS; North Hollywood, CA; (3); Girl Scts; JA; Math Clb; Teachers Aide; School Play; Yrbk; Crs Cntry; Trk; Vllybl; High Hon Roll; Sci.

SCHNORE, SCOTT L; Colton HS; Colton, CA; (2); Var Tennis; Hon Roll; Jr NHS; NHS; Dirt Bikes; Motorcycling; Water Skiing; Snow Skiing; U Of Southern CA; Dntl Hygnst.

SCHNURR, OREN S; Einstein Acad; Los Angeles, CA; (1); US Fencing Assn; Engl Lit.

SCHOEFFIELD, AMY; St Francis HS; Roseville, CA; (2); French Clb; Chorus; School Musical; Off Soph Cls; JV Cheerldng; JV Swmmng; High Hon Roll; NHS; Soph Homecoming Princess & Decorating Comm; Mother Daughter Fashion Show Model; Interior Decorating.

SCHOEFFLER, GINA; Sacramento Country Day Schl; El Dorado Hills, CA; (2); Rptr Yrbk; Var L Bsktbl; High Hon Roll; Math.

SCHOEN, GABRIEL; Buena HS; Ventura, CA; (4); FBLA; German Clb; JA; Letterman Clb; Teachers Aide; Hon Roll; Pres Acad Fit Awd; Gold Seal Bearer CSF; Raquet Intramural; CSU Northridge; Bus Admin.

SCHOENHAUS, SAMANTHA A; Lowell HS; San Francisco, CA; (3); German Clb; Band; Hon Roll; Pre-Med Clb; SADD Publc Reltns Chair; Pre-Med.

SCHOENHERZ, JENNIFER; Alta Loma HS; Alta Loma, CA; (3); Church Yth Grp; French Clb; SADD; Teachers Aide; Band; Rptr Nwsp; Rptr Yrbk; L High Hon Roll; Hon Roll; Hnrs Awd Golden St Math Achvt Test; Campfire; Awd Of Merit Wrld Of Poetry; Elem Ed.

SCHOENWANDT, TONIA H; Cordova SR HS; Mather A F B, CA; (3); Drama Clb; School Play; Nwsp; Yrbk; Lit Mag; Photography; Vol Easter Seal Soc; Photo Jrnlst.

SCHOFIELD, RACHEL E; Mission Bay HS; Hondo, TX; (1); Church Yth Grp; Girl Scts; Hosp Aide; Model UN; Spanish Clb; Drill Tm; Nwsp; Hon Roll; Awd Excllnce Engl; Mst Imprvd Span Stu Awd; Med Resrch.

SCHOFIELD, SHELLY; Bonita Vista HS; Bonita, CA; (4); 20/521; Pres Church Yth Grp; Pep Clb; Service Clb; School Play; Sec Frsh Cls; Stu Cncl; High Hon Roll; CSF; Academic Ltr; Concert Choir; Brigham Young U; Elem Educ.

SCHOLES, BECKY S; Rim Of The World HS; Crestline, CA; (3); Art Clb; Church Yth Grp; Chorus; Hon Roll; Prfct Atten Awd; Acad Ltr; Lake Arrowhead Arts Assn; 3rd Pl Cty-Wide Art Exhbtn 3rd Pl Awd; Child Dev.

SCHOLL, STEPHANIE A; Fairfield HS; Fairfield, CA; (4); Var Tennis; Cit Awd; High Hon Roll; Jr NHS; NHS; Photo CA ST Fr 89; Tnns MVP 89, Mst Insprtnl 90; GSE Hnrs; U Of Pacific; Bus Admin.

SCHOLTZ, MICHELLE ANGELIQUE; Eisenhower HS; Rialto, CA; (4); Teachers Aide; Stat Var Ftbl; L Var Mgr(s); Var L Trk; High Hon Roll; Hon Roll; NHS; Mdlng; Stud Athltc Trnr; Stanford U; Bus.

SCHOMMER, CURT C; Ventura HS; Ventura, CA; (3); 71/431; Pep Clb; Var L Ftbl; JV Trk; Hon Roll; Fresno ST U; Teacher.

SCHONBORN, EDUARDO A; Pius X HS; Huntington Park, CA; (3); 18/195; Science Clb; Var L Trk; High Hon Roll; Hon Roll; UC Irvine; Psych.

SCHOOLAR, J BRIAN; Capistrano Valley Christian Schl; Mission Viejo, CA; (3); 1/47; Aud/Vis; Church Yth Grp; Office Aide; Church Choir; JV Trk; Cit Awd; High Hon Roll; Hon Roll; CSF; Pltcl Sci.

SCHOOLER, JON; Brethren HS; Los Angeles, CA; (4); 9/66; Letterman Clb; Math Tm; Band; Mrchg Band; VP Stu Cncl; Var L Bsktbl; Var Crs Cntry; Var L Tennis; Prfct Atten Awd; Acad Deca; Westmont.

SCHOON, BENJAMIN; Tehachapi HS; Tehachapi, CA; (4); 1/165; Pres Computer Clb; French Clb; Capt Math Tm; Ed Lit Mag; Rep Stu Cncl; High Hon Roll; Hon Roll; Lion Awd; NHS; Val; 1st Intrvw Kern Cnty Acad Dcthln; 1st Indvdl Mathlts; NASA SHARP; MA Inst Technlgy.

SCHORR, CATHI L; Nevada Union HS; Nevada City, CA; (4); 29/477; JV Gym; High Hon Roll; Pres Acad Fit Awd; Interact Clb; CSF; UC Santa Cruz; Astro Physics.

SCHOTT, ERIK P; Moorpark HS; Moorpark, CA; (2); 13/300; Intnl Clb; School Play; Stu Cncl; JV Crs Cntry; Var Trk; High Hon Roll; CSF Secy; Peer Cnslng Club; UCLA; Doc.

SCHOULTEN, MICHAEL W; La Sierra HS; Riverside, CA; (2); Ftbl; Swmmng; Trk; Prfct Atten Awd; Mst Athltc; MVP Ftbl; Riverside City Champ Pole Vault; Engr.

SCHOUTEN, LLOYD J; Riverdale Joint Union HS; Riverdale, CA; (2); SADD; Yrbk; Ftbl; Aerntcs.

SCHOW, SCOTT E; Garden Grove HS; Garden Grove, CA; (1); Ftbl; Hon Roll; Bus.

SCHRAEDER, JULIE A; Miramonte HS; Orinda, CA; (3); Church Yth Grp; Cmnty Wkr; Teachers Aide; Varsity Clb; Mgr Crs Cntry; Var Diving; L Var Socr; Var Trk; JV Vllybl; High Hon Roll.

SCHRAEDER, PETER P; Miramonte HS; Orinda, CA; (2); Boy Scts; Church Yth Grp; JCL; Latin Clb; NFL; Speech Tm; JV Bsbl; Ftbl; Eagle Sct; UCLA; Law.

SCHRAM, LISA L; Notre Dame HS; San Jose, CA; (3); 31/100; Cmnty Wkr; Hon Roll; Social Involvment Corps; Portland ST U; Accntng.

SCHRAMM, BETHANY E; Mission Viejo HS; Mission Viejo, CA; (4); Key Clb; Model UN; Hon Roll; NHS; Pres Acad Fit Awd; CSF Sealbearer; Tutoring Prgm; Intl Baccalaureate Ful Diploma Candidate; Safe Rises; U CA San Diego; Psych.

SCHRAMM, KARLA D; Lodi HS; Woodbridge, CA; (3); 11/518; Church Yth Grp; FCA; Hosp Aide; Letterman Clb; Office Aide; Spanish Clb; Acpl Chr; JV Bsktbl; JV Trk; JV Var Vllybl; CSF; Athlt Of Mnth; Nrsng.

SCHREIBER, ALLEN; Marina HS; Huntington Beach, CA; (2); FBLA; VP JA; Intrml JV Bsktbl; JV Var Tennis; Hon Roll; Pres Acad Fit Awd; Pres Schlr; Attend/Participate Sprtng Events; UCLA; Law.

SCHREIBER, CATHY; Lincoln HS; Stockton, CA; (3); Church Yth Grp; Cmnty Wkr; Math Clb; SADD; Yrbk; Sec Soph Cls; Stu Cncl; JV Socr; JV Var Sftbl; JV Var Vllybl; Asilomar Ldrshp; Asisteens.

SCHREIER, CATHY A; Santa Teresa HS; San Jose, CA; (3); Church Yth Grp; German Clb; Girl Scts; SADD; Band; Jazz Band; School Musical; Rep Stu Cncl; Var Swmmng; NHS; Cnslr-Sci Camp; Vlntr Drvr-Safe Rides; Cmpstn Hnrd At St Cnvtn.

SCHREINER, CHRISTINE; Louisville HS; Woodland Hills, CA; (4); Cmnty Wkr; FHA; GAA; Varsity Clb; Var Swmmng; Hon Roll; Acad Achvt Awd Engl & Algebra; Hearing Hlth Ctr; U Of San Diego.

SCHREINER, JESSE S; Santa Curz HS; Santa Cruz, CA; (1); Band; Mrchg Band; Santa Cruz Yth Symphny; Trdtnl Korean Karate.

SCHREYER, KRISTIN; Redlands HS; Redlands, CA; (2); Drama Clb; Spanish Clb; Chorus; School Play; Cit Awd; Pres Schlr; Certfd CPR/1st Aid/Lifesaving; U CA-SAN Diego; Psych.

SCHRIENER, LORI; Dana Hills HS; Laguna Niguel, CA; (2); Office Aide; Teachers Aide; Bsktbl; Cit Awd; Hon Roll; Jr NHS; Prfct Atten Awd; Vet.

SCHROCK, CHRIS; West Valley HS; Anderson, CA; (3); 20/157; Boy Scts; Cmnty Wkr; Science Clb; Spanish Clb; Rep Frsh Cls; Rep Soph Cls; Rep Jr Cls; Var Crs Cntry; Var Trk; High Hon Roll; Golden ST Schlr; Rtry Yth Ldrshp Awd; CSF; UC Berkeley; Envir Chem.

SCHRODER, TAMARA L; Pasadena HS; Sierra Madre, CA; (4); JA; Q&S; Pres SADD; Mrchg Band; Stage Crew; Rptr Nwsp; Phtg Yrbk; Sftbl; Hon Roll; Sierra Madre Rose Court Prncss 87-88; Acad Decathln Tm; Pasadena City Coll; Law.

SCHRODI, CHRISTINE M; Homestead HS; Sunnyvale, CA; (3); 48/383; JV Var Fld Hcky; Var L Socr; High Hon Roll; Pres Acad Fit Awd; Amnesty Intl; CA Schlrshp Fdrtn.

SCHROEDER, CHRIS D; Mountclair HS; Ontario, CA; (2); Band; Var Swmmng; Hon Roll; Vrsty Water Polo; Music; SDSU; Bus.

SCHROEDER, ERIC E; Lowell HS; San Francisco, CA; (3); Church Yth Grp; Cmnty Wkr; Red Cross Aide; Varsity Clb; Vrsty Pistol & Rifle Teams; Strategic Games Assn Pres; Pltcl Sci.

SCHROEDER, ERIKA; Foothill HS; Bakersfield, CA; (2); Pres German Clb; Key Clb; Library Aide; Band; Sec Frsh Cls; Sec Soph Cls; Off Jr Cls; Var Cheerldng; Var Tennis; High Hon Roll; Outstndng German Stu Awd; Mst Insprtnl Tnns Player; Gifted/Tlntd Pgm; Stanford; Med.

SCHROEDER, JENNIFER; El Camino Fundamental HS; San Rafael, CA; (4); French Clb; Key Clb; SADD; Tennis; Cit Awd; NHS; SADD; Dominican Coll; Ecnmst.

SCHROEDER, JO ANN; Esondido HS; Escondido, CA; (2); Cit Awd.

SCHROEDER, JO ANNA; Highlands HS; Sacramento, CA; (2); Church Yth Grp; Rep SADD; Church Choir; Hon Roll; CSF Pres; U Of CA Davis; Med.

SCHROEDER, KRYSTE L; Rubidoux HS; Riverside, CA; (4); Church Yth Grp; Pep Clb; Varsity Clb; Church Choir; Off Jr Cls; Stat Bsbl; JV Var Cheerldng; Swmmng; Hon Roll; Prfct Atten Awd; New Visions Christian Club; CA Bapotist Coll; Accntng.

SCHROEDER, MATTHEW D; Davis SR HS; Davis, CA; (2); Boy Scts; Church Yth Grp; Rep Frsh Cls; Rep Stu Cncl; JV Var Ftbl; Wt Lftg; Rugby Co-Capt; Explr Scts VP; Engrng.

SCHROEDER, TANYA M; Paradise HS; Paradise, CA; (2); 22/360; Church Yth Grp; Yrbk; Cheerldng; High Hon Roll; Hon Roll; Pres Acad Fit Awd; Jobs Daghtrs; CSF; Ski Tm; Doctor.

SCHROTH, MICHELLE E; Southern Ca Christian HS; Anaheim, CA; (2); Church Yth Grp; Chorus; Bsktbl; Hon Roll; Int Des.

SCHROY, TODD R; Calvary Chapel HS; Irvine, CA; (2); Band; Jazz Band; Pep Band; Drum Corp; Long Beach ST; Music.

SCHRYER, ERIK W; Redwood HS; Visalia, CA; (3); 79/400; German Clb; Office Aide; Band; Mrchg Band; Var Socr; Var Trk; Hon Roll; Rotary Awd; U CA San Diego; Marine Bio.

SCHUBARTH, JULIE; Torrance HS; Torrance, CA; (3); 36/400; Church Yth Grp; JCL; Latin Clb; Letterman Clb; Band; Drm Mjr(t); Mrchg Band; Crs Cntry; Trk; Hon Roll; Outstndg Band Stu; Stu Of Mnth 90; All St Symphnc Band 89 & 90; Music Perf.

SCHUBERT, MAX LOUIS; Hiram West Johnson HS; Sacramento, CA; (2); 63/182; Chess Clb; ROTC; Intrml Bsbl; JV Ftbl; Intrml Score Keeper; Intrml Sftbl; Intrml Vllybl; Hon Roll; NHS; Bsbl Babe Ruth League; Stanford; Law.

SCHUBERTH, LISSETTE A; Mayfield SR HS; La Canada Flintri, CA; (3); 1/50; Cmnty Wkr; Dance Clb; Library Aide; Teachers Aide; Capt Cheerldng; Capt Pom Pon; Hon Roll; Ntl Merit Ltr; Pres Acad Fit Awd; Intl Rltns.

SCHUCHARD, JULIE A; Greenville JR-SR HS; Greenville, CA; (3); Drama Clb; FHA; Office Aide; Chorus; School Play; Variety Show; Rptr Nwsp; Phtg Yrbk; Sec Treas Soph Cls; Sec Treas Sr Cls; Vocal Ensemble; Chico ST; Cmmnctns.

SCHUCKMAN, ANNE; Lincoln HS; Stockton, CA; (3); 11/592; Debate Tm; NFL; Ski Clb; Spanish Clb; Off SADD; JV Var Cheerldng; JV Crs Cntry; Var L Socr; High Hon Roll; NHS; Outstndng-Bio; Stockton Music Tchrs Assoc-Wnnr Piano Cncrto Cmptn 88.

SCHUELLER, JULIE; Bishop Montgomery HS; San Pedro, CA; (4); Church Yth Grp; Key Clb; NFL; Capt Pep Clb; Ski Clb; Speech Tm; SADD; School Play; Rep Sr Cls; Bsktbl; CSF Cls Rep; Chncllrs Awd Of Excel UCSB; CSF Gold Seal Bearer; UCSB.

SCHUELLER, ROBERT S; Bishop Montgomery HS; San Pedro, CA; (3); Church Yth Grp; Cmnty Wkr; JA; Ski Clb; JV Vllybl; Hon Roll; Outstndng Stu Engl; Bus.

SCHUELLER, TERESA J; Santa Clara HS; Newbury Park, CA; (3); 29/155; Am Leg Aux Girls St; Church Yth Grp; Pres French Clb; Pep Clb; Teachers Aide; Ed Yrbk; Off Frsh Cls; Off Soph Cls; JV Bsktbl; Score Keeper; Math Tutor; Loyola Marymount U; Educ.

SCHUERGER, JULIE N; Canoga Park HS; West Hills, CA; (1); Church Yth Grp; Church Choir; Church Handbell Choir; Church Yth Group; Professional Singer.

SCHUETZ, BILL F; Imperial Schls; Pasadena, CA; (4); Chorus; Pres Frsh Cls; Pres Jr Cls; Intrml Mgr Bsktbl; Intrml Mgr Trk; Intrml Mgr Vllybl; Pres Phys Ftnss Awd; Spch Club Pres; Pasadena City Coll; Law.

SCHUGREN, LUKE E; Berkeley HS; Berkeley, CA; (3); Band; Rptr Nwsp; JV Var Lcrss; Statesmn Of Amer; U CA Berkeley.

SCHUH, TRACY; Santa Fe Christian HS; San Diego, CA; (2); Spanish Clb; Phtg Rep Yrbk; Rep Frsh Cls; JV Cheerldng; Trk; Cit Awd; Hon Roll.

SCHUJAHN, DEREK R; Encina HS; Sacramento, CA; (3); 19/212; Cmnty Wkr; Lit Mag; Pres Jr Cls; Pres Stu Cncl; Var Bsbl; Var Ftbl; Hon Roll; Amer Lgn Bsbl Ptchr; Aerospc Engrng.

SCHULBACH, MARK C; Dos Pueblos HS; Santa Barbara, CA; (3); 131/320; Letterman Clb; Pep Clb; Ski Clb; Spanish Clb; SADD; Varsity Clb; Swmmng; Hon Roll; Jr NHS; NHS; Waterpolo V 3rd Team All CIF-2A 90.

SCHULDIES, SHANNON; Santa Teresa HS; San Jose, CA; (2); Var Cheerldng; Treas Crs Cntry; Var Trk; Hon Roll; Fllwshp Clb; Chrldng Advisor; UCLA; Psych.

SCHULE, ALAN E; El Dorado HS; Placentia, CA; (3); 17/362; Intnl Clb; Science Clb; Spanish Clb; Temple Yth Grp; Tennis; Cit Awd; High Hon Roll; NHS; Vet.

SCHULLER, DIANE; Mesa Verde HS; Citrus Heights, CA; (4); 22/175; Church Yth Grp; Spanish Clb; Teachers Aide; Variety Show; Co-Ed Nwsp; Stu Cncl; JV Capt Cheerldng; L Tennis; Hon Roll; Stu Reching Out Pres; Songldr; Friday Night Live; CSU Sacramento; Cmmnctns.

SCHULMAN, JUSTIN H; University HS; Los Angeles, CA; (2); Math Clb; Quiz Bowl; Teachers Aide; L Var Bsbl; Score Keeper; Sftbl; High Hon Roll; Hon Roll; Sec Jr NHS; NHS; Hnrbl Mntn Amer Lgn Awd 88-89; Allen Campbell Awd Hghst Acad Record Of 89 Cls; Schlr Athl 90; Commnctns.

SCHULMAN, SUSANNAH E; Berkeley HS; Berkeley, CA; (4); Drama Clb; Acpl Chr; Chorus; School Musical; School Play; Swing Chorus; Outstndng Stu Awd Prfrmng Arts Dept; Bnk America Awd Excllnce Drama; UC Santa Cruz.

SCHULT, HANNAH R; San Rafael HS; San Rafael, CA; (3); Ski Clb; SADD; Teachers Aide; Pres Acad Fit Awd; Awd For Wrkng With Mentally Handicap; Nrsng.

SCHULTE, DAVEE P; Seaside HS; Marina, CA; (3); French Clb; FBLA; Ftbl; Socr; Bus.

SCHULTE, DEREK E; Upland HS; Upland, CA; (2); 6/700; Boy Scts; German Clb; Band; Jazz Band; Mrchg Band; Orch; School Play; High Hon Roll; Hon Roll; Pres Acad Fit Awd.

SCHULTE, STEPHANIE E; St Joseph HS; Long Beach, CA; (2); 69/200; GAA; Hosp Aide; Vllybl; Hon Roll; UC Santa Barbara; Advertising.

SCHULTZ, ALEX; West Torrance HS; Torrance, CA; (3); Letterman Clb; SADD; Varsity Clb; Bsbl; Ftbl; Socr; Vllybl; Wt Lftg; Hon Roll; All Leag Ftbl & Sccr; USC; Engrng.

SCHULTZ, CARLI L; Archbishop Mitty HS; San Jose, CA; (2); Cmnty Wkr; Math Tm; Treas Soph Cls; Var Socr; JV Vllybl; High Hon Roll; NHS; CSF.

SCHULTZ, CHRIS; Fresno Christian HS; Fresno, CA; (3); 1/50; Letterman Clb; Spanish Clb; Nwsp; Rep Soph Cls; Pres VP Stu Cncl; Var Capt Bsktbl; Var Ftbl; Var Tennis; High Hon Roll; Tennis 3 Time MVP.

SCHULTZ, EMIL F; Bellarmine College Prep; Scotts Valley, CA; (1); Wrstlng; Capitola Jr Lifeguard Pgm-Rgnl Cmptng.

SCHULTZ, JEFF A; Novato HS; Novato, CA; (2); Band; Mrchg Band; Socr; Wrstlng; Hon Roll; Pres Acad Fit Awd; Schl Board Scholar Athlete; Azusa Pacific; Sci.

SCHULTZ, PATRICIA A; Ganesha HS; Diamond Bar, CA; (1); Engr.

SCHULTZ, RUTH E; Delta HS; Courtland, CA; (2); FBLA; Letterman Clb; JV Crs Cntry; JV Sftbl; High Hon Roll; Hon Roll; Fri Night Live; Mc George Schl Of Law; Law.

SCHULTZ, SUSAN M; St Margarets HS; Laguna Beach, CA; (4); Intnl Clb; Chorus; Nwsp; VP Sr Cls; High Hon Roll; Hon Roll; Jr Statesmen Of Amer; Chem Awd; Econ Awd; Pitzer Coll; Econ.

SCHULZ, MEGAN R; Orange Lutheran HS; Orange, CA; (2); Band; Church Choir; Jazz Band; Pep Band; Var Trk; JV Vllybl; Athlt Of Mnth 88; Fresh, JV Vllybl; Valparaiso U; Bio Sci.

SCHULZ, ROBERT A; Mojave HS; California City, CA; (3); Chess Clb; Drama Clb; Teachers Aide; Band; Stage Crew; Variety Show; Var Ftbl; Capt Score Keeper; Wt Lftg; High Hon Roll.

SCHULZE, DANIELLE; Terra Nova HS; Pacifica, CA; (4); Am Leg Aux Girls St; Church Yth Grp; Drama Clb; Rep Frsh Cls; Pres Soph Cls; Pres Jr Cls; Pres Stu Cncl; Stu Mnth; Skyline CC; Elem Schl Tchr.

SCHULZE, TOM M; Alhambra Union HS; Martinez, CA; (3); 12/230; Letterman Clb; Teachers Aide; Varsity Clb; Var L Bsbl; Intrml Bsktbl; Var L Ftbl; Var L Golf; Peer Cnslr; St Marys Moraga; Bus Admin.

SCHUMACHER, JULIE A; Chester JR/Sr HS; Chester, CA; (2); 1/60; Church Yth Grp; Temple Yth Grp; Band; Var L Cheerldng; Var L Gym; Var L Vllybl; High Hon Roll; Yth To Yth; UCLA; Psych.

SCHUMANN, JACOB; Liberty HS; Brentwood, CA; (2); 4-H; Var Bsbl; Ftbl; Intrml Wt Lftg; 4-H Awd; MVP Bsbl; AZ ST; Drafting.

SCHUMANN, TRACY; Oak Ridge HS; Cameron Park, CA; (2); Art Clb; Church Yth Grp; Cmnty Wkr; Hosp Aide; SADD; Hon Roll; Member Environmental Club; Member Of Young Life; Medical Research.

SCHUMER, NICOLE; Santa Ynez HS; Buellton, CA; (2); 84/250; Church Yth Grp; Band; Drm Mjr(t); Mrchg Band; JV Capt Cheerldng; JV Tennis; UCSB; Psych.

SCHUNK, DENISE M; Garden Grove HS; Garden Grove, CA; (1); FHA; SADD; Nwsp; Hon Roll; Bus.

SCHURDELL, NORMAN; San Pasqual HS; Escondido, CA; (2); Church Yth Grp; Var Ftbl; Pro Athl.

SCHURMAN, CARINN M; Santa Barbara HS; Santa Barbara, CA; (2); Hosp Aide; Chorus; Drill Tm; Ed Rptr Nwsp; Cit Awd; Hon Roll; Pres Acad Fit Awd; Own Own Bus; Bio Sci Doctor.

SCHURMAN, LACEY A; Salinas HS; Salinas, CA; (4); 14/357; Key Clb; Var L Bsktbl; Var L Vllybl; Gov Hon Prg Awd; High Hon Roll; NHS; Pres Frsh Cls; VP Soph Cls; VP Jr Cls; VP Stu Cncl; MVP/All Vly/All Leag-Vllybl; Stu Of Month-Jan; Fresno ST; Liberal Studies.

SCHUSTER, AMANDA; Cook JR HS; Santa Rosa, CA; (1); Cheerldng; Ldrshp Cls; UCLA; Advrstng Account Exec.

SCHUSTER, DALE D; Colton HS; Grand Terrace, CA; (2); Church Yth Grp; JV Letterman Clb; Science Clb; JV Ftbl; Tennis; High Hon Roll; Jr NHS; Prfct Atten Awd; Pres Acad Fit Awd; USAF Acad; Pilot.

SCHUTTE, KRISTEN; Turlock HS; Turlock, CA; (2); Hosp Aide; Speech Tm; Var JV Cheerldng; JV Tennis; JV Trk; Medi-Careers Clb; Phy.

SCHUTZ, TIFFANI K; Monte Vista HS; Walnut Creek, CA; (3); 40/423; L Var Bsktbl; JV Sftbl; L Var Vllybl; High Hon Roll; Alla Trnmnt Bsktbl Player Pinole Vly; Attended Stanford Bsktbl Camp.

SCHUTZER, JESSICA; Agoura HS; Agoura Hills, CA; (2); 37/469; Pep Clb; Spanish Clb; Temple Yth Grp; Drill Tm; Mrchg Band; High Hon Roll; Glden St Ex Alg Hnrs; Acctnt.

SCHUYLER, HEATHER; Coachella Valley HS; Thermal, CA; (3); 37/438; Cmnty Wkr; Pep Clb; Ski Clb; Teachers Aide; Varsity Clb; Rep Jr Cls; Stu Cncl; JV Var Cheerldng; Hon Roll; CA ST Long Bch; Aerontcl Engr.

SCHUYLER, SHELLY M; Lompoc SR HS; Lompoc, CA; (3); 6/350; 4-H; FBLA; Intrml Socr; Intrml Tennis; Intrml Vllybl; Stat Wrstlng; High Hon Roll; Prfct Atten Awd; CSF; Engl Achvt Awd; Interact Clb Pres; Cal Poly ST U; Bus Law.

SCHWAB, LAURA; Newbury Park Adventist Acad; Newbury Park, CA; (4); Letterman Clb; Office Aide; Ski Clb; Band; Chorus; Off Jr Cls; Treas Sr Cls; Var L Bsktbl; Var L Vllybl; Varsity Clb; Brooks Coll; Fash Merch.

SCHWAN, NICOLE E; Golden West HS; Visalia, CA; (2); Church Yth Grp; Drama Clb; English Clb; German Clb; Intnl Clb; Speech Tm; Chorus; School Musical; School Play; Stage Crew; Loyla Mrymnt; Corp Law.

SCHWANG, STEPHANIE; Delano HS; Chambersburg, PA; (4); SADD; School Musical; Nwsp; Stu Cncl; Cheerldng; Hon Roll; NHS; Penn ST U; Commnctns.

SCHWARTZ, DEBORAH LYNN; Independence HS; San Jose, CA; (4); 9/850; Service Clb; NHS; Ntl Merit SF; Dnc-Prdctn Grp Asst; Amnsty Intl-Pres; Tutor; Biochem.

SCHWARTZ, ERIC J; Redlands HS; Redlands, CA; (2); Bsbl; Cit Awd; Hon Roll; Pres Acad Fit Awd; Bus.

SCHWARTZ, GREGORY; Rolling Hills HS; Rnch Palos Verde, CA; (4); 62/316; Letterman Clb; Stu Cncl; JV Var Bsbl; JV Bsktbl; JV Var Ftbl; DAR Awd; NHS; Ntl Merit Ltr; Pres Acad Fit Awd; U CA San Diego; Intl Bus.

SCHWARTZ, JENNIFER A; Estancia HS; Costa Mesa, CA; (3); 128/280; Church Yth Grp; Office Aide; Teachers Aide; Prfct Atten Awd; Peer Cnslr; Sewing; HS Engl Tchr.

SCHWARTZ, JENNIFER S; Simi Valley HS; Simi Valley, CA; (2); Dance Clb; Temple Yth Grp; NHS; CA ST U Nrthrdg; Brdcstng.

SCHWARTZ, KELLY; Foothill HS; Bakersfield, CA; (1); Hon Roll; OR ST Coll; Law.

SCHWARTZ, KRISTINE A; Thomas Downey HS; Modesto, CA; (3); Debate Tm; NFL; Speech Tm; Teachers Aide; Lion Awd; Child Dev.

SCHWARTZ, LAURA; Paso Robles HS; Paso Robles, CA; (1); Church Yth Grp; Intrml Cheerldng; JV Swmmng; Hon Roll; 1 Chrldr 89-90; Doctor.

SCHWARTZ, LEAH S; Berkeley HS; Berkeley, CA; (3); Var Swmmng; Hon Roll; Waterpolo Var; Engr.

SCHWARTZ, NOELLE; Whitney HS; Long Beach, CA; (4); Church Yth Grp; Dance Clb; Drama Clb; FTA; GAA; Key Clb; Spanish Clb; Teachers Aide; Varsity Clb; Variety Show.

SCHWARTZ, PATRICIA T; Armijo HS; Fairfield, CA; (2); Drama Clb; Chorus; School Play; High Hon Roll; Hon Roll; Perf Local Plays; Enjoy Creative Wrtg & Rdng; Fine Arts.

SCHWARTZ, RAINBOW; Berkeley HS; Berkeley, CA; (3); Dance Clb; Variety Show; Dance Prodctn Choregrphy & Prfrmnce; Fashion Desgnr.

SCHWARTZ, RYAN A; La Sierra HS; Riverside, CA; (1); JV Bsbl; Hon Roll; Prfct Atten Awd.

SCHWARTZ, SARRAH M; Colfax HS; Alta, CA; (2); 30/170; Pres Church Yth Grp; Cmnty Wkr; Girl Scts; SADD; VP Soph Cls; Sec Treas Jr Cls; Stat Bsbl; JV Cheerldng; Stat Ftbl; JV Trk; Peer Counseling; Pres Of Friday Nite Live; Azusa Pacific U; Marktng Sales.

SCHWARTZ, STEPHANIE M; Foothill HS; Santa Ana, CA; (4); 20/328; Cmnty Wkr; Service Clb; Spanish Clb; JV Tennis; High Hon Roll; Tnwrk; Bd Dirs Drg Us Is Lf Abs; Sf Rds Pres; Northwestern U; Pltcl Sci.

SCHWARTZ, STEVE H; Dos Pueblos HS; Santa Barbara, CA; (3); 46/338; SADD; Treas Temple Yth Grp; Phtg Nwsp; NHS; Opt Clb Awd; Var L Wrstlng; Bsbl Coach; Sunday Schl Teacher; Bus.

SCHWARTZ, TIFFANI M; Tehachapi HS; Tehachapi, CA; (3); 23/188; Drama Clb; Letterman Clb; Office Aide; Varsity Clb; School Play; Cit Awd; Hon Roll; VP Soph Cls; Rep Stu Cncl; JV L Bsktbl; Tehachapis Yng Women Of Yr Pgm 90-91; Miss Teenage CA Pgnt 89-90, 90-91; U Of Pacific; Phys Ther.

SCHWARZ, CHARLEEN K; Tulelake HS; Tulelake, CA; (3); 4/31; Cmnty Wkr; FBLA; Office Aide; Teachers Aide; Treas Soph Cls; JV Bsktbl; Var Cheerldng; Var JV Vllybl; High Hon Roll; Hon Roll; People/People Sci Ambssdr Exchnge 90; Treas Athltc Dept 89-90; FBLA Northern Sctn Conf Typng Cont 89; U Of NV; Nurse.

SCHWARZ, ROBERT A; Santa Teresa HS; San Jose, CA; (3); Science Clb; Teachers Aide; Varsity Clb; Var L Bsbl; Var L Ftbl; Wt Lftg; Swmmg Team 10 Yrs; Bsbl 10 Yrs, Ftbl 4 Yrs; Soccer Team 10 Yrs; Surfing, Cross Cntry 2 Yrs; CA ST; Sports Med.

SCHWEDE, AMY; Forest Lake Christian HS; Chicago Park, CA; (4); Church Yth Grp; Teachers Aide; Pres Frsh Cls; Pres Stu Cncl; Var Bsktbl; Var L Sftbl; Var L Vllybl; Cit Awd; Hon Roll; Masters Coll; Intr Dsgn.

SCHWEDLER, THOMAS G; Whitney HS; Cerritos, CA; (1); Model UN.

SCHWEHR, KURT D; Los Altos HS; Los Altos, CA; (4); 3/330; Aud/Vis; Boy Scts; Computer Clb; Pres French Clb; Math Tm; SADD; Mrchg Band; High Hon Roll; Ntl Merit Ltr; Pres Schlr; Researchr NASA Ames Space Sci Div; Grand Rz Martian Metron Tech Chllng NASA/Fmc; Green Belt Judo; Stanford U; Elem Engr.

SCHWEIGHART, CHRIS M; Torrey Pines HS; Solana Beach, CA; (2); Church Yth Grp; Lit Mag; JV Bsbl; L Socr; Hon Roll; Schlr Athl; Gldn St Exam High Hnrs Alg; JV Bsbl MVP.

SCHWEIKER, HEIDI C; Louisville HS; Tarzana, CA; (1); Church Yth Grp; Dance Clb; School Musical; Variety Show; Cheerldng; High Hon Roll; Subj Awds Phys Sci Adv, Fshn Strategies; Mem CA Schlrshp Fed; Dsgn.

SCHWEININGER, FRANK J; Bellarmine College Prep; San Jose, CA; (3); 66/325; Cmnty Wkr; Letterman Clb; Service Clb; Ski Clb; Teachers Aide; Varsity Clb; Var Crs Cntry; Var Trk; US Air Force; Aeronaut Engrng.

SCHWEIZER, JASON S; Educational Dynamics Inc HS; Escondido, CA; (3); Art Clb; Drama Clb; Model UN; Quiz Bowl; School Play; Rep Frsh Cls; Var Bsbl; JV Ftbl; Var Socr; Hon Roll; Mech Engr.

SCHWENCK, MELANIE M; Madera HS; Madera, CA; (2); AFS; Church Yth Grp; Science Clb; Service Clb; Cit Awd; High Hon Roll; NHS; Prfct Atten Awd; Camp Fire Horizon; Stu Mnth; Campus Life; UCLA; Teacher.

SCHWENKER, ALISON B; Pioneer HS; San Jose, CA; (4); French Clb; Q&S; Teachers Aide; Ed Yrbk; Stu Cncl; JV Capt Bsktbl; Var L Trk; High Hon Roll; NHS; Pres Acad Fit Awd; VP Natl Hnr Scty; CA Schlrshp Fed Sealbearer; UCLA; Bus.

SCHWERIN, CYNTHIA A; Pinole Valley HS; Pinole, CA; (2); Cmnty Wkr; Debate Tm; Spanish Clb; Teachers Aide; Stu Cncl; Hon Roll; Pres Acad Fit Awd; Intl Order Of Rainbow For Girls; 2 Sems CSF; Yth Cmmssn & Cmmssn Liason To City Cncl; Law.

SCHWICHTENBERG, JENNIFER; Serra HS; San Diego, CA; (3); French Clb; Pep Clb; Cheerldng; Cit Awd; Hon Roll; Oceans Club; SADD; Art.

SCIABICA, GIUSEPPE; La Habra HS; La Habra, CA; (3); Chorus; Var Socr; Sccr Bst Scorer Trphy; UCLA; Engnr.

SCIANDRI, RONALD; Serra HS; South San Francis, CA; (4); 18/203; Pres Frsh Cls; Stu Cncl; Intrml Bsktbl; Var L Ftbl; High Hon Roll; Hon Roll; Ntl Merit SF; Rugby Capt Rnkd #2 In Nation; Jr Statemen Of Amer; CA Schlrshp Fed; Duke U; Econ.

SCIANNI, MICHELLE M; California HS; Whittier, CA; (2); Drama Clb; VP German Clb; Varsity Clb; Sec Jr Cls; JV Bsktbl; Capt Crs Cntry; Var Trk; Cit Awd; Hon Roll; Peer Cnslng; Engr.

SCIHI, TOM; Anacapa HS; Santa Barbara, CA; (2); 1/8; English Clb; Rep Soph Cls; High Hon Roll; Srfng Clb; Med.

SCIPIONE, RUTH; Covenant Christian Schl; San Diego, CA; (1); 1/5; Church Yth Grp; Stage Crew; Var Bsktbl; Var Vllybl; Hon Roll; Christian Yth Theatre; Presdntl Phy Ftnss Awd.

SCIUTTO, JAMES B; Clovis HS; Clovis, CA; (3); Cmnty Wkr; Letterman Clb; Red Cross Aide; Ski Clb; Spanish Clb; SADD; Teachers Aide; Varsity Clb; Bsbl; Bsktbl; Waterpolo 4 Yr Var.

SCOFIELD, WALLACE L; Canyon HS; Canyon Country, CA; (3); Mgr Band; Jazz Band; Off Mrchg Band; Pep Band; Variety Show; JV L Socr; Hon Roll; Jr NHS; NHS; Music.

SCOGGINS, CAROL S; Shafter HS; Shafter, CA; (4); 15/165; Church Yth Grp; FHA; Hosp Aide; Key Clb; Pep Clb; Teachers Aide; Hon Roll; Friday Night Live; San Joaquin Vly; Legal Secy.

SCONIERS, MICHELE; Luther Burbank HS; Sacramento, CA; (2); 11/389; Var Bsktbl; Stat Ftbl; JV Tennis; Var Trk; Gov Hon Prg Awd; High Hon Roll; Hon Roll; MESA, Secy; BSU; Soph Cls Rep.

SCOPELITIS, NANCY; St Genevieve HS; Sepulveda, CA; (2); Quiz Bowl; Teachers Aide; High Hon Roll; Hon Roll; Amer Clsscl Leag & Ntl JR Clsscl Leag Latin; Vol Paciomi Elem; UCLA; Bus.

SCOSERIA, IRENE M; Hawthorne HS; Hawthorne, CA; (2); Hon Roll; Diaconians Svc Org Clb; Intl Rainbow For Girls; Key Clb; New Life Clb; Stu Council; Med.

SCOTKIN, STEVE; Raul Walenberg HS; San Francisco, CA; (1); Band; Bus.

SCOTT, ALAN E; Edison HS; Fresno, CA; (1); Band; Jazz Band; Mrchg Band; Intrml Tennis; Cit Awd; Jr Symphony; Music.

SCOTT, ALICIA V; David Starr Jordan HS; Long Beach, CA; (1); Math Clb; Capt Intrml Bsktbl; Coll Assessmnt Test Prep; Young Blk Schlrs; Shlrshp Clb; Lawyer.

SCOTT, ALISON N; Holy Names HS; Vallejo, CA; (4); Drama Clb; Chorus; School Musical; School Play; Yrbk; Hon Roll; St Schlr; Rep Frsh Cls; Sec Sr Cls; Ntl Achvt Schlrshp Pgm-Outstndng Negro Sut; Advncd Plcmnt-Frnch & Engl; Hstry Tchr.

SCOTT, BLOSSOM E S; Bret Harte HS; Angels Camp, CA; (2); Horses 3 Day Trng; Davis; Vet Med.

SCOTT, CAROLYN S; Washington Preparatory HS; Los Angeles, CA; (3); Church Yth Grp; Math Clb; Church Choir; Mrchg Band; Orch; Hon Roll; Prfct Atten Awd; Marthonian Club; Peace Club; Afrikan Stu Alliance; Cal ST Domingez; Bus Admin.

SCOTT, CHRIS P; Granada HS; Livermore, CA; (2); Spanish Clb; Scl Sci.

SCOTT, CORNELIA V; Abraham Lincoln HS; San Francisco, CA; (3); Church Yth Grp; Cmnty Wkr; Dance Clb; Drama Clb; FFA; Hosp Aide; Office Aide; Pep Clb; Teachers Aide; Varsity Clb; Dstngshd Stu; Best Dressed Female; LSU; Court Reporter.

SCOTT, DAMIEN M; Bellarmine-Jefferson HS; Palmdale, CA; (2); Var Bsktbl; Hon Roll; Amer Roundbl Coop Bsktbl Trvlng All-Star Team; Bsktbl Camp Cnslr; Boys Clb Boy Of Mnth; :Unlv; Cmnctns.

SCOTT, DENISE K; Norco HS; Corona, CA; (2); Water Sports Expert; Rare Music Cllctr; Marine Mammal Stud; U Of CA San Diego; Marine Bio.

SCOTT, DONNA J; San Marcos HS; San Marcos, CA; (3); Church Yth Grp; Key Clb; Pep Clb; Band; Mrchg Band; Stu Cncl; JV Var Fld Hcky; Var Swmmng; High Hon Roll; Hon Roll; Stu Of Qrtr Bio,Chem,Spnsh,Hstry & Amer Hstry; CSF; U Of AZ; Aero Engrng.

SCOTT, GINA M; Galt HS; Galt, CA; (2); Church Yth Grp; German Clb; SADD; Band; Jazz Band; Mrchg Band; Orch; VP Soph Cls; Tennis; Hon Roll; Sacramento Yth Symphny; Psych.

SCOTT, JACOB; Chestnut Avenue Baptist Acad; Fresno, CA; (3); Teachers Aide; Chorus; School Musical; School Play; Ftbl; Vllybl; Hon Roll; Work Retirement Home Holiday Gardens; Awds Highest Grd Engl Am Govt 10th Grd; Fresno City; Pilot.

SCOTT, JENNEFER L; Modesto HS; Salida, CA; (4); Church Yth Grp; Dance Clb; French Clb; Color Guard; Flag Corp; School Play; Ricks Coll; Exer Phys.

SCOTT, JENNIFER; Mercy HS; San Bruno, CA; (3); GAA; Girl Scts; Spanish Clb; SADD; Pres Soph Cls; Var JV Bsktbl; Mgr(s); JV Tennis; Var Trk; High Hon Roll; Accepted Hnrs Entrance; Rcvd Genl Schlrshps; Pre-Law.

SCOTT, JENNIFER E; Colfax HS; Colfax, CA; (3); Am Leg Aux Girls St; Service Clb; JV Var Bsktbl; JV Var Trk; High Hon Roll; Alpha Omega Awd; Coach Grsl Bsktbl; Acad Decathlon Team; Stanford U; Pre Med.

SCOTT, JODI; El Modena HS; Orange, CA; (3); Pep Clb; SADD; Teachers Aide; Varsity Clb; Var Cheerldng; JV Sftbl; Cit Awd; High Hon Roll; Hon Roll; Rancho Santiago Coll; Court Rpr.

SCOTT, JOHN F; George Washington Preparatory HS; Los Angeles, CA; (3); Treas Sr Cls; JV Crs Cntry; JV Swmmng; Trk; High Hon Roll; Hon Roll; Jr NHS; Chrch Teacher; Modeling Clb; MESA; Xavier U New Orleans; Arch Engr.

SCOTT, JOHN S; Beyer HS; Modesto, CA; (3); Boy Scts; Church Yth Grp; Church Choir; JV Bsktbl; Var L Trk; Cit Awd; BYU.

SCOTT, JUSTIN; John F Kennedy HS; Granada Hills, CA; (2); High Hon Roll; Hon Roll; Prfct Atten Awd; Publications Clb Local Quill & Scroll; Comp Sci.

SCOTT, KEVIN W; Paraclete HS; Lancaster, CA; (2); Letterman Clb; SADD; Yrbk; JV Var Bsktbl; JV Ftbl; JV Var Trk; High Hon Roll; Hon Roll; Math.

SCOTT, KIM; San Ramon Valley HS; San Ramon, CA; (1); Drama Clb; Office Aide; Band; Chorus; Mrchg Band; School Play; Stage Crew; Var Crs Cntry; Var Trk; Mst Imprvd Fresh Glr Crs Cntry; CO Air Frce Acad; Arntcl Engr.

SCOTT, KRISTEN; Castle Park HS; Chula Vista, CA; (3); 60/555; Dance Clb; Pep Clb; Sftbl; Vllybl; Dance Clb; Acad Achievers; Fashn Desgnr.

SCOTT, LINDA M; Dublin HS; Dublin, CA; (3); Church Yth Grp; Teachers Aide; Color Guard; Stat Bsktbl; Score Keeper; Outstndng Home Ec Stu Ldrshp; U Of NC; Photo.

SCOTT, LORI F; Midway Baptist HS; San Diego, CA; (3); 4/17; Var Church Yth Grp; Drama Clb; Pep Clb; Varsity Clb; Church Choir; School Play; Co-Ed Yrbk; Treas Jr Cls; Var Bsktbl; Var Cheerldng; Invited To Become Congrssnl Schlr & Rep CA In Natl Yng Ldrs Conf Washington DC; Northwood; Bus Admin.

SCOTT, MARIA E; Eisenhower HS; Rialto, CA; (3); Hosp Aide; Library Aide; Intrml Bsktbl; High Hon Roll; Hon Roll; NHS; CSF 88-90; Sobobans Treas 90-91; GSE Geomtry Hnrs 88-89; Bstr Club Awd Outstndng Span II Stu 89-90; CSU Sn Brndno; Ped Nrs.

SCOTT, MARILYN K; Trinity HS; Trinity Center, CA; (3); Church Yth Grp; GAA; Ski Clb; Capt JV Bsktbl; Var Sftbl; Var Trk; Hon Roll; Mst Imprvd Plyr Sftbl Vrsty Tm; Mst Insprtnl Plyr Wolf Gal Bsktbl JV Tm; Cptn Bsktbl Tm JV; BYU.

SCOTT, MARIO K; La Sierra HS; Riverside, CA; (3); FCA; French Clb; JA; Office Aide; Ftbl; Wt Lftg; Wrstlng; Cit Awd; Hon Roll; NYU.

SCOTT, MATT; Bishop Union HS; Bishop, CA; (3); English Clb; 4-H; FFA; Spanish Clb; Teachers Aide; Bsbl; Bsktbl; Ftbl; Socr; Wt Lftg; Phys Thrpy.

SCOTT, MICHELLE M; Amos Alonzo Stagg HS; Stockton, CA; (4); Dance Clb; Teachers Aide; Powder Puff Ftbl; Hon Roll; HOSA; STAND; Most Congenial Dance Awd; San Joaquin Delta Coll; Nrsng.

SCOTT, MICHELLE R; Skyline HS; Oakland, CA; (2); Library Aide; Science Clb; Acpl Chr; Chorus; School Musical; Stage Crew; Swing Chorus; Hon Roll; Prfct Atten Awd; Pres Acad Fit Awd; Oaklnd Yth Chorus; NAACP Act-So Comptn Fnlst 90; Educ.

SCOTT, NATALIE PAIGE; Seoul American HS; Hertford, NC; (2); Band; Pep Band; Var Mgr(s); High Hon Roll; Acad Ltrs; Psych.

SCOTT, NICKY R; Brea-Olinda HS; Brea, CA; (3); 34/300; Dance Clb; Office Aide; SADD; Varsity Clb; Phtg Ed Yrbk; Var L Socr; Var L Trk; Hon Roll; NHS.

SCOTT, OTTO; San Ramon Valley HS; Danville, CA; (4); 4/397; Church Yth Grp; Pres Key Clb; Orch; Stage Crew; Var Swmmng; High Hon Roll; Pres NHS; Water Polo Capt; CSF; Mech Engrng.

SCOTT, PRESTON LEE; Morningside HS; Inglewood, CA; (4); 4/205; FBLA; Library Aide; Math Tm; Office Aide; Science Clb; Teachers Aide; Band; Mrchg Band; Yrbk; Bsktbl; Young Black Schlrs For Outstndng Perfrmnce; CSF; MI U; Acctng.

SCOTT, RACHEL R; Santa Teresa HS; San Jose, CA; (3); Church Yth Grp; German Clb; Fllwshp Clb; Peer Grp Cnslng; Psych.

SCOTT, ROBERT L; Irvine HS; Irvine, CA; (2); 300/330; Aud/Vis; Computer Clb; Drama Clb; Library Aide; Office Aide; Teachers Aide; Stage Crew; Mgr Bsktbl; Mgr Socr; Hon Roll; Tech Crew Awd; U CA Irvine; Elec.

SCOTT, ROGER A; Atwater HS; Atwater, CA; (1); Church Yth Grp; Swmmng; High Hon Roll; CSF; Fri Night Live; Waterpolo; Marine Bio.

SCOTT, SANDRA D; Carson HS; Carson, CA; (3); Hosp Aide; Church Choir; Bsktbl; Var Sftbl; Var Vllybl; Hon Roll; Prfct Atten Awd; 1CLA; Med.

SCOTT, SARAH; Lodi HS; Lodi, CA; (2); Acpl Chr; Chorus; Hon Roll.

SCOTT, SHEREE; Westminster HS; Westminster, CA; (3); Dance Clb; Girl Scts; Hosp Aide; Office Aide; Teachers Aide; Off Frsh Cls; Off Soph Cls; Crs Cntry; Score Keeper; Jr NHS; Girl Scts Slvr Awd; U Of WA; Pre Med.

SCOTT, SILAS; Palm Springs HS; Desert Hot Sprngs, CA; (4); Am Leg Boys St; Boy Scts; Church Yth Grp; Sec Debate Tm; Speech Tm; Teachers Aide; Sec VICA; Bsktbl; Hon Roll; Lion Awd; Henderson City NV Employees Assn Schlrshp; Silver Mdl CA VICA Imprmptu Spch; Acad Dcthln 3 Gold Mdl; Brigham Young U; Physics.

SCOTT, STACEY E; Antioch SR HS; Antioch, CA; (3); Pep Clb; Band; Mrchg Band; Fnlst Yng Authors Wrtng Prjct; Hnr Bk Awd; Phy.

SCOTT, STEPHANIE M; Oroville HS; Oroville, CA; (4); #17 In Class; Co-Ed Nwsp; Off Frsh Cls; Sec Stu Cncl; High Hon Roll; Hon Roll; Dollars For Schlrs Schlrshp; CSF; Christman Frml Chm 88-89; Fshn Show Chm; Rotary Yth Ldrshp Awds; Brooks Coll; Fshn Mrchndsng.

SCOTT, TODD M; Norte Vista HS; Riverside, CA; (3); Library Aide; Teachers Aide; Phtg Yrbk; Wrstlng; Hon Roll; Inter Decorator.

SCOTT, TRINA M; Morningside HS; Inglewood, CA; (3); Church Yth Grp; Office Aide; Rptr Nwsp; Phtg Yrbk; Pres Frsh Cls; Rep Soph Cls; Rep Jr Cls; VP Sr Cls; Rep Stu Cncl; Var Cheerldng; USC; Dentl Asst.

SCOTT, YVETTE N; Bassett HS; La Puente, CA; (3); Drama Clb; Thesps; School Play; Var Cheerldng; Brnze Cngrssnl Awd; Thespians Pres 90-91; UNLV; Theatre Arts.

SCOTT-ROY, ORANDE S; Alhambra HS; Antioch, CA; (3); Teachers Aide; Varsity Clb; Ftbl; Trk; Wrstlng; Hon Roll; Nrsng.

SCOVILL, AARON; Fort Bragg HS; Fort Bragg, CA; (3); Tennis; Culinary.

SCOVILL, WENDY; River City HS; West Sacramento, CA; (2); Pep Clb; JV Cheerldng; Roller Skating Cmptn; UC Davis Medcl Schl; Pediatrcn.

SCOWN, JASON; Moorpark HS; Moorpark, CA; (3); 17/250; Boy Scts; Church Yth Grp; Var L Ftbl; Var Wt Lftg; High Hon Roll; Schlr Athlte Awd; USC; Bus.

SCRIBNER, AMY L; Trinity HS; Lewiston, CA; (1); Ski Clb; Spanish Clb; SADD; Chorus; Bsbl; Bsktbl; 4-H Awd; Bus.

SCRIVEN, WENDY D; Madera HS; Madera, CA; (3); 1/490; Church Yth Grp; Band; Church Choir; Mrchg Band; Pep Band; CA Schrlshp Fed Scribe; Band Mst Vlbl Jr; GSE Geom With Hnrs; Biola U; Elem Ed.

SCROGGIN, NIKKI; Lincoln HS; Stockton, CA; (3); 233/538; French Clb; Chorus; Hon Roll; Swm Instr; Dance.

SCRUGGS, DAWN L; Woodrow Wilson HS; Long Beach, CA; (3); GAA; Varsity Clb; Chorus; Sec Stu Cncl; Var Capt Bsktbl; Trk; Var Capt Vllybl; NHS; Pres Acad Fit Awd; Cngrssnl Schl Nath Yth Ldr Conf; Bio.

SCRUGGS, KOREN G; Castlemont HS; Oakland, CA; (2); Church Yth Grp; Math Clb; Teachers Aide; JV Trk; Cit Awd; Pres Schlr; UC Berkeley; Chem Engr.

SCRUGGS, PAMELA A; Galt Joint Union HS; Galt, CA; (3); 75/209; Church Yth Grp; FFA; Teachers Aide; Chorus; Color Guard; School Musical; Crs Cntry; Score Keeper; Trk; Hon Roll; Friday Night Live Chptr VP, Acting Pres & Outstndng Ldr; Pensacola Chrstn Coll; Elem Edu.

SCUBA, JEFF J; Torrey Pines HS; Rancho Santa Fe, CA; (3); Stage Crew; Ed Yrbk; Bsbl; Ftbl; Trk; Elks Gldn St Exam Geo Hnr.

SCURICH, NATE J; University HS; Irvine, CA; (1); Ftbl; Wrstlng; High Hon Roll; Mrch Of Dimes Dance Prod; Med.

SCURRY, DEREK L; Washington Prep HS; Los Angeles, CA; (3); Cmnty Wkr; Computer Clb; Letterman Clb; Varsity Clb; School Play; Stage Crew; Nwsp; JV Var Bsktbl; JV Tennis; JV Var Trk; Won City Triple Jump 89-90; Mst Imprvd Bsktbl; Long Beach.

SEAGLE, NICOLE R; Walnut HS; Walnut, CA; (2); 69/469; French Clb; Hon Roll; Accomplished Pianist; Adv Plcmnt Stu; Pol Sci.

SEAH, MARVIN; Sunset HS; Hayward, CA; (1); Hon Roll; UC Berkeley; Bus.

SEAH, WILLIAM C K; Sunset HS; Hayward, CA; (2); Cit Awd; High Hon Roll; Hon Roll; UC Berkeley; Bus.

SEALANDER, ANNA K; San Bernardino HS; San Bernardino, CA; (3); Church Yth Grp; Intnl Clb; Spanish Clb; SADD; Interact Clb; RYLA; Commnctns.

SEALE, SHINDALE M; Granada Hills HS; Los Angeles, CA; (2); Church Yth Grp; Sec Church Choir; Young Black Schlrs; Spellman Coll; Adv.

SEALEY, ARIF A; Victor Valley HS; Victorville, CA; (3); JV Wt Lftg; Teachers Aide; UCLA; Accntng.

SEALEY, BRET A; Del Campo HS; Carmichael, CA; (3); Boy Scts; Chess Clb; Cmnty Wkr; ROTC; Teachers Aide; Color Guard; JV Var Swmmng; NHS; Jr Vrsty Water Polo; Amer Leg Gen Mltry Excllnc; Daedalian Achvt Awd; US Naval Acad; Arspc Sci.

SEALS, SONDRA Y; Lindhurst HS; Olivehurst, CA; (3); ROTC; Band; Mrchg Band; Friday Night Live; Blck Stu Union; Intl Bus.

SEAMARK, LAURI A; El Toro HS; El Toro, CA; (4); 23/522; Art Clb; Treas Key Clb; Yrbk; Var Tennis; High Hon Roll; Pres Acad Fit Awd; CSF; Sddlbck Sf Rds Pblcty Cmmssnr; Geom, Engl Hnrs; U Of CA Los Angeles; Art Thrpy.

SEAN, SAMPHORS; Artesia HS; Hawaiian Gardens, CA; (2); Comp Pgmmr.

SEAN, SUE A; Escondido HS; Escondido, CA; (1); Hon Roll.

SEARCY, GERRA; Hanford Joint Union HS; Hanford, CA; (3); VP Cmnty Wkr; 4-H; Sec FFA; FHA; Intnl Clb; Office Aide; Teachers Aide; Cit Awd; 4-H Awd; Hon Roll; Kings Cty Dairy Princess; Jr Grand Natl Mayor Of Cow Town Cncl; Jr Grand Natl Merit Awd; Cal Poly; Dairy Sci.

SEARCY, MICHELLE; La Jolla HS; San Diego, CA; (4); Drama Clb; French Clb; NFL; Pep Clb; Teachers Aide; Thesps; School Musical; School Play; Stage Crew; Rep Soph Cls; Sceta Best Actress Mainstg Prod; San Diego Brnch Engl Spkng Union Fnlst 90; St Forensic Trnmt 89; Theatre.

SEARLS, JAMES G; El Cajon Valley HS; El Cajon, CA; (2); 40/475; Boy Scts; Chess Clb; Church Yth Grp; FCA; Var Swmmng.

SEARS, DEBORAH; James Monroe HS; Northridge, CA; (2); Church Yth Grp; Office Aide; Drm Mjr(t); Mrchg Band; Pep Band; Cit Awd; High Hon Roll; Prfct Atten Awd; Pres Acad Fit Awd; CSF; UC-DAVIS; Zoology.

SEARS, KIMBERLY A; Magnolia HS; Anaheim, CA; (4); Office Aide; Pep Clb; Teachers Aide; Chorus; Grls Lgue; Cal ST Irvine; Bus.

SEARS, KRISTAL R; Victor Valley HS; George AFB, CA; (1); Church Yth Grp; Girl Scts; Chorus; Cit Awd; Hon Roll; Girl Scout Of Yr/Silver Awd; Ed.

SEARS, TERRY L; Santa Teresa HS; San Jose, CA; (2); JA; Letterman Clb; Varsity Clb; Variety Show; Pres Soph Cls; Var Crs Cntry; Var Tennis; Var Trk; Model Macys/Faces Intl/Chrmn ASB Cabinet; Disgretn Cmmtte; Santa Clara U; Law.

SEASHOLS, MATT; Southbay Christian Schl; Belmont, CA; (3); Church Yth Grp; Hon Roll; Pepperdine U; Bus.

SEASTROM, KRISTEN; Rosary HS; Fullerton, CA; (2); Church Yth Grp; Cmnty Wkr; Pep Clb; Rep Frsh Cls; Rep Soph Cls; Hon Roll; Natl Chrty Lg; Nordstrm Fshn Clb; Atty.

SEATON, KATHY A; Brea Olinda HS; Brea, CA; (3); 99/400; Drama Clb; Speech Tm; SADD; Teachers Aide; Varsity Clb; Variety Show; JV Trk; JV Var Vllybl; Hon Roll; Law.

SEATON, SHANNON; Bear River HS; Grass Valley, CA; (2); Church Yth Grp; Pres Debate Tm; Pres Sec 4-H; Sec Treas FFA; Speech Tm; SADD; Sec Jr Cls; Cit Awd; 4-H Awd; Hon Roll; Princpals Ltr; Humboldt ST U; Wildlife Jrnlst.

SEAVER, LORI L; Chula Vista HS; Chula Vista, CA; (2); Rep Church Yth Grp; Girl Scts; Pep Clb; JV Cheerldng; JV Socr; JV Sftbl; Masonic Awd; Amity League; Swrd & Shld Srvc Clb; JSA; Purdue; Pilot.

SEAWELL, PETRA; Beverly Hills Prep Schl; Arcadia, CA; (1); Chorus; Yrbk; Sec Stu Cncl; High Hon Roll; Stu Of Qrtr; Excllnt Atten; Harvard U; Med.

SEBASTIAN, RYAN M; St Joseph HS; Arroyo Grande, CA; (3); Church Yth Grp; Ski Clb; Var L Socr; JV Tennis; JV Trk; Hon Roll; CSF 88-89; JSA; Psych.

SEBEK, STACEY V; Marina HS; Huntington Beach, CA; (4); Am Leg Aux Girls St; Church Yth Grp; French Clb; Office Aide; Ski Clb; Acpl Chr; School Musical; Variety Show; Lit Mag; Var JV Tennis; Fnlst-Dsnylnd Crtvty Chllng; Stanford U; Jrnlsm.

SEBHATU, MEKDEM; Golden Gate Acad; Oakland, CA; (2); Computer Clb; Math Clb; Science Clb; Yrbk; Off Soph Cls; Socr; Swmmng; Tennis; Cit Awd; High Hon Roll; UC Berkeley; Electrnc Engrng.

SEBRA JR, NELSON T; Clovis HS; Clovis, CA; (3); Church Yth Grp; Cmnty Wkr; Hosp Aide; Varsity Clb; Phtg Nwsp; Off Frsh Cls; Off Soph Cls; Var Socr; Var Swmmng; Hon Roll; Water Polo Tm Capt Selected All-Lg, All Vly, All N CA, All Amer Natl Yth Team; Bus Admin.

SEDAM, MIKE; Ferndale HS; Ferndale, CA; (2); #2 In Class; Math Tm; JV Var Ftbl; Var L Trk; Hon Roll; CA Schlsp Fed; Schlr Athlt Awd; USNA; Arntcl Engrng.

SEDANO, YADIRA; El Capitan HS; Lakeside, CA; (3); Chess Clb; German Clb; Spanish Clb; SADD; Teachers Aide; Band; Chorus; Church Choir; Mrchg Band; Rptr Nwsp; FDIM Coll; Fashion.

SEDER, DEREK L; Del Oro HS; Rocklin, CA; (1); Church Yth Grp; Letterman Clb; Varsity Clb; Swmmng; Hon Roll; Vet Med.

SEDIN, DANA L; Del Campo HS; Carmichael, CA; (3); 57/446; JV Ftbl; JV Wrstlng; High Hon Roll; Sports & Outdoor Actvts; CA Poly; Civil Engrng.

SEDLIC, STEVE; Chaminade Coll Preparatory HS; Woodland Hills, CA; (3); Cmnty Wkr; Debate Tm; Model UN; Speech Tm; Pres Sr Cls; Ftbl; Socr; Jr NHS; NHS; CA Schlrshp Fedrtn; Stanford; Law.

SEE, WENDY L; Diamond Bar HS; Diamond Bar, CA; (1); Intnl Clb; Acpl Chr; Hon Roll; Psych Clb, Deans Math & Sci List; Jazz Choir & Hnr Choir.

SEEBOLD, KATIE V; Menlo Schl; Atherton, CA; (4); Capt Socr; Acad All-Amer; Top Ten CIF/Reebok CA Fmle Schlr/Athl; Stanford U; Sprts Med.

SEECK, DAGLEF; Paraclete HS; Palmdale, CA; (1); Asitur Germany; Pilot.

SEED, COLLIN A TIMS; Point Arena HS; Point Arena, CA; (1); Dance Clb; Letterman Clb; Varsity Clb; Var Bsbl; JV Capt Ftbl; Most Imprvd Ftbl Plyr; Bsbl Ltr; USC; Pro Ftbl.

SEELEY, TARA; Dublin HS; Dublin, CA; (1); #1 In Class; Drama Clb; School Play.

SEEMAN, JEANINE L; Mission Bay HS; San Diego, CA; (4); 3/300; Pres Church Yth Grp; Key Clb; Church Choir; Var Capt Bsktbl; JV L Sftbl; Var Capt Vllybl; Bausch & Lomb Sci Awd; High Hon Roll; Rotary Awd; Outstndng Sprtswoman & Schlr; Brigham Young U.

SEEMAN, LAUREN; Cleveland Humanities HS; Van Nuys, CA; (2); Ski Clb; SADD; Drill Tm; Off Soph Cls; Mgr(s); Pom Pon; High Hon Roll; Hon Roll; CSF; Ecology & Envrnmntl Clbs; UCSB; Bus.

SEEMANN, MICHELLE; Laguna Hills HS; Laguna Hills, CA; (4); Church Yth Grp; Cmnty Wkr; Debate Tm; Model UN; Sec Soph Cls; Rep Jr Cls; Sec Sr Cls; Stu Cncl; JV Var Cheerldng; High Hon Roll; St Sci Fair Mst Outstndng Women Engr; Krista Mc Kalluf Fllwshp Pgm; Natl Charity Lgue Pres, VP.

SEERY, TARA E; Louisville HS; Woodland Hills, CA; (2); GAA; Treas Frsh Cls; Rep Soph Cls; Var Capt Crs Cntry; Var Socr; Var Trk; Hon Roll; CSF; High Sierra Club; Acadc Awds; Pre Med.

SEETO, MICHAEL L; Troy HS; Fullerton, CA; (3); Church Yth Grp; French Clb; Math Tm; Natl Beta Clb; Cit Awd; High Hon Roll; Hon Roll; Prfct Atten Awd; CA ST Fullerton.

SEFTON, KATHERINE ANNE; Paso Robles HS; Paso Robles, CA; (3); 34/330; Aud/Vis; Church Yth Grp; Drama Clb; Scholastic Bowl; Science Clb; SADD; Co-Capt Drill Tm; School Play; Stu Cncl; High Hon Roll; 1st Pl St Hstry Day 89; 2nd Pl St 90; Super Perfmnc Natl Lvl Hstry Day 89 90; Mst Spirited 89 90; Ltr 89; Stanford U; Brdcst Jrnlst.

SEGAL, JONATHAN E; Casa Roble HS; Orangevale, CA; (3); 45/370; Spanish Clb; Teachers Aide; Temple Yth Grp; Cit Awd; Hon Roll; Outstndng Effort Awd; Spansh Hnrs; Math/Spanish.

SEGAL, SCOTT; Foothill HS; Santa Ana, CA; (2); 48/327; Art Clb; Cmnty Wkr; Hosp Aide; Key Clb; Latin Clb; Science Clb; Spanish Clb; Temple Yth Grp; Rep Frsh Cls; Rep Soph Cls; Med.

SEGALA, ISABEL; Valley View HS; Moreno Valley, CA; (1); 10/32; High Hon Roll; Delta Coll; Accntng.

SEGARINI, ROCHELLE A; Sonora HS; Sonora, CA; (4); 15/275; Letterman Clb; Varsity Clb; Var Capt Bsktbl; Var Tennis; Prfct Atten Awd; Vlly Oak Leag MVP Bsktbl; Mem All Dist Tm Bkstbl; San Joaquin Delta Coll; Mgmt.

SEGARS, STEPHANIE E; Mira Mesa HS; San Diego, CA; (2); 341/797; Church Yth Grp; Hosp Aide; Flag Corp; JOBS Daughters Honored Queen; Work At Subway And Souplantion.

SEGERSTROM, DANIELE; Pioneer HS; San Jose, CA; (2); Drill Tm; Sec Frsh Cls; Hon Roll; CSF; Interact Clb.

SEGOBIANO, JULIANA T; Mountainview HS; Healdsburg, CA; (4); 1/20; Band; Mrchg Band; Stu Cncl; Sal; Stu Of Yr 1990; Soroptomist Schlrshp; Doyle Schlrshp & Santarosa JC Schlrshp; Snata Rosa JC; Psych.

SEGOVIA, VALERIE; Santa Clara HS; Oxnard, CA; (2); 37/207; Church Yth Grp; Hosp Aide; Hon Roll; Play Clarinet; UCSB; Engr.

SEGURA, ALEXANDRA E; Fontana HS; Fontana, CA; (2); Band; Mrchg Band; High Hon Roll; Hon Roll; Prfct Atten Awd; Bus.

SEGURA, BEN E; Brea Olinda HS; Brea, CA; (3); 22/292; Var Capt Ftbl; Var L Trk; High Hon Roll; CA Schlstc Fdr; Imprl Golf Crs Emply; MA Inst Of Tech; Engrng.

SEGURA, SARAH; Saddleback HS; Santa Ana, CA; (1); Sci Cert Of Achvt; Bus.

SEGURA, VANESSA; Central Union HS; El Centro, CA; (3); Dance Clb; French Clb; Pep Clb; Rptr Nwsp; Yrbk; High Hon Roll; Doctor.

SEH, JACK H; John Burroughs HS; Burbank, CA; (3); 5/37; Boy Scts; Church Yth Grp; FCA; Spanish Clb; Teachers Aide; Band; Drm Mjr(t); Yrbk; Bsktbl; Cit Awd; Chrch Treas; UC Santa Barbara; Chrprctr.

SEIB, CATHERINE J; Estancia HS; Costa Mesa, CA; (1); Church Yth Grp; FCA; Church Choir; School Musical; Lit Mag; Var L Swmmng; Vllybl; High Hon Roll; Vcl Ensmbl; Sci.

SEIBEL, STEPHANIE K; Carlmont HS; Redwood City, CA; (3); Orch; School Play; Var Tennis; Var Badmnttn.

SEID, JACOB; Newport Harbor HS; Costa Mesa, CA; (2); 11/327; Spanish Clb; JV Tennis; CA Schlrshp Fed.

SEIDELL, SEAN T; Central Catholic HS; Modesto, CA; (3); 23/64; VP Pres Art Clb; Cmnty Wkr; Debate Tm; Sec Drama Clb; Intnl Clb; Key Clb; Science Clb; Ski Clb; Speech Tm; Teachers Aide; SEA Clb; Rotary Spch Cont Div Wnnr & 3rd Pl City; Teenwork Conf Schl Rep 90; Modesto Yth Sccr Coach 89; UCSC.

SEIDLER, JEAN; Beyer HS; Modesto, CA; (4); Rep Church Yth Grp; Var Debate Tm; NFL; Red Cross Aide; Ski Clb; VP Spanish Clb; SADD; JV Var Vllybl; High Hon Roll; Library Aide; Mission Clb; CSF; S Clb.

SEIDNER, JILL N; Villa Park HS; Villa Park, CA; (3); Drama Clb; Hist French Clb; Key Clb; Ski Clb; SADD; Stage Crew; Lit Mag; Hon Roll; NHS; Prfct Atten Awd; Frnch Exchng Homestay & Lang Pgm 88; UCLA Media Wrkshp 90; Otis Parsons Pre Coll Pgm Envrnmntl Dsgn; USC; Film.

SEIFEN, MATTHEW; San Gorgonio HS; Highland, CA; (4); 4/418; Am Leg Boys St; Church Yth Grp; Scholastic Bowl; Var Bsbl; Var Capt Crs Cntry; Var Socr; Elks Awd; NHS; Pres Acad Fit Awd; Spanish NHS; Claremont Mc Kenna Coll; Econ.

SEIFERT, JENNIFER R; Hoover HS; Fresno, CA; (3); 101/458; SADD; Varsity Clb; School Musical; Var JV Tennis; Hon Roll; Fresno ST; Med.

SEIFERT, TARA D; San Lorenzo HS; San Leandro, CA; (2); Band; Orch; Sec Frsh Cls; High Hon Roll; Acad Excllnc Awd Eng, Music; UC Berkeley; Music.

SEIGEL, GREGORY A; Clovis West HS; Fresno, CA; (3); Band; Drm Mjr(t); Jazz Band; Orch; Rptr Lit Mag; High Hon Roll; NHS; Opt Clb Awd; Rotary Awd; Spanish NHS; 90 CA All-St Band; Universl Music Apprctn Clb VP; Music.

SEIGFRIED, DANIELLE; Hemet HS; Hemet, CA; (3); Mgr(s); JV Socr; Var Trk; Dentistry.

SEIGLER, LAWRENCE A; Gahr HS; Cerritos, CA; (2); 70/250; Boy Scts; Teachers Aide; JV Bsbl; Hon Roll; Socializing,Drama,Mmovies; Gahr; Engineering.

SEILER, JAMES; Capital Christian HS; Sacramento, CA; (1); Church Yth Grp; FCA; FBLA; Math Tm; Ski Clb; Teachers Aide; Band; Chorus; Jazz Band; Orch; Stanford; Sports Med.

SEILER, JANETTE L; Bellarmine-Jefferson HS; Burbank, CA; (2); Church Yth Grp; Cmnty Wkr; Spanish Clb; Tennis; Hon Roll; UC Irvine; Surgeon.

SEINO, SHIRLEY M; Esperanza HS; Yorba Linda, CA; (3); 62/562; Var Capt Swmmng; High Hon Roll; CA ST Fullerton.

SEISAY, NORA; Amos Alonzo Stagg HS; Stockton, CA; (2); French Clb; High Hon Roll; Hon Roll; Med.

SEITZ, GREG J; Escondido HS; Escondido, CA; (2); Church Yth Grp; German Clb; Science Clb; Var Swmmng; UCSD; Nuclr Engrng.

SEITZ, JASON M; University HS; Irvine, CA; (3); Debate Tm; JCL; Latin Clb; Wt Lftg; JV Wrstlng; High Hon Roll; NHS; Ntl Merit Ltr; Slvr Mdl Natl Latin Exam; 2nd Sea View Leag Wrstlng; 1st, 2nd St Latin Conv 88 89; U Of CA Los Angeles.

SEKANDARI, PARISA; Redlands HS; Redlands, CA; (2); Treas Art Clb; Sec Chess Clb; FBLA; German Clb; Letterman Clb; JV Crs Cntry; Var Trk; Cit Awd; High Hon Roll; Hon Roll; CSF; Ecology Clb; Acad Excel Awd Geo; Sci.

SEKHON, ANUDEEP; James Logan HS; Union City, CA; (4); Office Aide; Teachers Aide; Powder Puff Ftbl; Cit Awd; High Hon Roll; Achvt, Ctznshp Awds; Cal ST Hayward; Psych.

SEKHON, NIREJ; Edison HS; Huntington Beach, CA; (3); Debate Tm; French Clb; JA; Treas Key Clb; Model UN; NFL; Rep Stu Cncl; JV Crs Cntry; JV Trk; Rotary Awd; Orange Cnty Acad Decathalon; Ec.

SEKHON, SHAMIE K; San Ramon Valley HS; Danville, CA; (2); 84/400; Spanish Clb; High Hon Roll; Hon Roll.

SEKI, SHARON K; San Gabriel Acad; Rosemead, CA; (3); Teachers Aide; VP Jr Cls; Sec Stu Cncl; Stat Intrml Bsktbl; Stat Fld Hcky; Intrml Socr; Capt Sftbl; Capt Vllybl; Loma Linda U; Phy.

SEKIKAWA, TAMI E; C K Mc Clatchy SR HS; Sacramento, CA; (2); 33/487; French Clb; SADD; Rep Soph Cls; Sec Treas Jr Cls; JV Bsktbl; Powder Puff Ftbl; CA Schlrshp Fed; Asian Stu Union; Intl Stds.

SEKOL, REBECCA M; San Diegoito HS; Carlsbad, CA; (4); Teachers Aide; Rptr Nwsp; Yrbk; Hon Roll; San Diego ST U.

SELAN, JENIFER A; Mater Dei HS; Garden Grove, CA; (3); Cmnty Wkr; Sec French Clb; Acpl Chr; Chorus; School Musical; NHS.

SELAYA, MATTHEW P; Bellarmine College Prep; Redwood City, CA; (3); Church Yth Grp; Cmnty Wkr; Office Aide; Pep Clb; Service Clb; SADD; Teachers Aide; Intrml Bsktbl; Intrml Vllybl; JV Wrstlng; Eng Tutor; ESL Prgm For Vietnamese Adults; Irish Club; Sci Fiction Club; Grphc Art.

SELBERIS, CHRISTINA; San Gorgonio HS; Highland, CA; (4); 10/418; AFS; Pres Church Yth Grp; Drama Clb; German Clb; SADD; Church Choir; Powder Puff Ftbl; Mgr Vllybl; High Hon Roll; NHS; CSF; Maids Of Athena Pres; Tandy Technlgy Schlrs Awd; U Of CA Riverside; Bus Admin.

SELBY, SHARON; Serrano HS; Pinon Hills, CA; (1); Letterman Clb; Drill Tm; Flag Corp; Hon Roll; Art Schlr; Law.

SELECKY, CHRIS; Marina HS; Huntington Bch, CA; (4); Church Yth Grp; Key Clb; VP Pres Spanish Clb; SADD; Varsity Clb; Off Jr Cls; VP Stu Cncl; Swmmng; Cit Awd; Hon Roll; Wtr Polo- Qtr Fnlst In CIF Jr Yr; Spent 1 Wk W/Severe Hndcppd Prsns, Care 24 Hrs A Day; Bus.

SELF, CHRISTY; Southern California Christian Schl; Anaheim Hills, CA; (3); Church Yth Grp; Dance Clb; Teachers Aide; Chorus; VP Soph Cls; JV Cheerldng; Stat Ftbl; High Hon Roll; Oral Roberts U; Psychlgy.

SELF, TANIA A; El Comino Fundemental HS; Carmichael, CA; (3); Church Yth Grp; Dance Clb; Drama Clb; Latin Clb; SADD; Thesps; School Play; Stage Crew; Variety Show; Drama Cmptns Super Awds; Dance.

SELFRIDGE, TIA; Monterey HS; Monterey, CA; (1); Var Cheerldng; Hon Roll; UCLA.

SELFRIDGE, TRAVIS W; Monterey HS; Monterey, CA; (3); Cmnty Wkr; FCA; Red Cross Aide; Ed Nwsp; JV Var Ftbl; Var Capt Trk; Var Capt Wrstlng; Hon Roll; Prfct Atten Awd.

SELGA, CATHERINE; St Genevieve HS; Northridge, CA; (3); Dance Clb; French Clb; Pep Clb; Drill Tm; JV Vllybl; Hon Roll; St Schlr; Lettergirl Clb.

SELIKOV, LORI E; Mission Viejo HS; Laguna Hills, CA; (2); 91/500; GAA; Model UN; SADD; Treas Jr Cls; Var Socr; Var Trk; Pres Acad Fit Awd; Psych.

SELINGER, ILAN R; Bishop O Dowd HS; Oakland, CA; (3); Ski Clb; Var Swmmng; U Of CA San Diego; Marine Bio.

SELLERS, KEITH L; Los Angeles Baptist HS; Northridge, CA; (3); Art Clb; Computer Clb; Yrbk; Lit Mag; Hon Roll; Arch.

SELLERS, ROBIN; Desert Christian HS; Lancaster, CA; (1); Church Yth Grp; Mgr Drama Clb; FCA; Band; Chorus; Church Choir; School Play; JV Crs Cntry; Cit Awd; Hon Roll; ACSI Festvl Awd; Choir Band Hndbell Pins; Cross Cty Rnng Trophy; TN Temple U; Ed.

SELLERS, SABRINA; West HS; Bakersfield, CA; (4); 95/439; Dance Clb; Key Clb; Ski Clb; Cheerldng; Hon Roll; Chico ST U; Animal Sci.

SELLITTI, PAULO A; Bellarmine College Prep; Gilroy, CA; (3); Cmnty Wkr; Service Clb; Rptr Nwsp; Rep Frsh Cls; Rep Soph Cls; Rep Jr Cls; JV Var Diving; JV Var Wrstlng; High Hon Roll; John Hopkins U; Biomedcl Sci.

SELLMAN, ANDREW T; Bishop O'dowd HS; Oakland, CA; (3); Score Keeper; Rugby Clb; Chico ST U.

SELNA, BLAKE W; Edison HS; Huntington Beach, CA; (1); Capt Swmmng; Wtr Polo Tm; Jr Lfegrds; Set New Rcrd-100 Yd Freestyle Swmmg.

SELPH, DAVID V; Lowell HS; San Francisco, CA; (2); Boy Scts; Church Yth Grp; German Clb; JV Bsktbl; JV Crs Cntry; Pacific Rowing Clb; Tae-Kwon-Do Red Blt; Electrl Engr.

SELTENRICH-JIMENEZ, BRANDON; Saint Ignatius College Prep; San Francisco, CA; (3); Art Clb; Chrmn Debate Tm; Drama Clb; Pres Model UN; NFL; Chrmn Speech Tm; School Musical; Crew; U Of San Francisco; Engl.

SELTZER, CATHERINE A; San Marcos HS; Santa Barbara, CA; (2); Church Yth Grp; Cmnty Wkr; Service Clb; Royal Pages Clb.

SELTZER, JENNIFER; Chatsworth HS; Northridge, CA; (3); SADD; Thesps; Rptr Nwsp; Treas Jr Cls; Cheerldng; High Hon Roll; Hon Roll; Jr NHS; NHS; Pres Acad Fit Awd; Theater.

SELTZER, LEILANI M; Carmel HS; Pebble Beach, CA; (2); Var Sftbl; Var Vllybl; High Hon Roll; Rotary Awd; Athltc Trnr; Sonoma ST; Phys Thrpy.

SELVA, UMAHARAN; Harvard Schl; Sherman Oaks, CA; (4); 20/138; Debate Tm; Model UN; NFL; Quiz Bowl; Service Clb; Speech Tm; Ed Yrbk; Ed Lit Mag; French Hon Soc; Hon Roll; Jr Statesmen Amer; Stanford U; Econ.

SEM, SOPHAL R; Galileo HS; San Francisco, CA; (3); French Clb; Ftbl; Trk; Hon Roll; Sanoma ST U; Bus Mgmt.

SEMANSKY, ANNA C; Bishop O'doud HS; Berkeley, CA; (3); Church Yth Grp; Cmnty Wkr; Hosp Aide; Ski Clb; Stage Crew; Yrbk; Var Vllybl; CSF; Congrssnl Yth Ldrshp; N Coast Sctn Schlr Athl Awd Vllybl.

SEMBAUER, JENNIFER A; Louisville HS; Chatsworth, CA; (3); Church Yth Grp; Cmnty Wkr; FHA; GAA; Service Clb; Crs Cntry; Trk; High Hon Roll; Awd-Outstndng Wrk Algb I & II Geom Engl I & II Spnsh & Bio; Stu Of Mnth; CSUN; Bus Mgmnt.

SEMIEN, NATASHA; St Marys Acad; Carson, CA; (3); 5/90; Bus Profs of Am; Church Yth Grp; Cmnty Wkr; Dance Clb; Debate Tm; GAA; JA; Latin Clb; Pep Clb; Spanish Clb; Loma Linda; Obstetrcs.

SEMIEN, SHANELL; Canyon Springs HS; Moreno Valley, CA; (3); Pep Clb; SADD; Var Cheerldng; Var Pom Pon; Cit Awd; High Hon Roll; Hon Roll; UCLA; Med.

SEMINARIO, NICOLE A; Westlake HS; Glendale, CA; (2); French Clb; JA; Math Tm; Model UN; Red Cross Aide; Spanish Clb; Dance Grp; Prntmkng.

SEMINOFF, JEREMY P; San Benito HS; Hollister, CA; (4); 5/252; Church Yth Grp; Pep Clb; Red Cross Aide; Pres Science Clb; Variety Show; Off Jr Cls; Treas Stu Cncl; High Hon Roll; Ntl Merit SF; Rotary Awd; Stu Advsry Bd Ed Rgn Dir; Med.

SEMINOFF, TRISHA L; La Habra HS; La Habra, CA; (3); Am Leg Aux Girls St; Church Yth Grp; Cmnty Wkr; German Clb; Q&S; Ed Yrbk; Stu Cncl; JV Bsktbl; Var L Socr; Var L Sftbl; People To People Stu Ambssdr Soviet Union; St Brd; Stu Advsry Cncl Chrprsn; Intl Rltns.

SEMPER, JULIE; Samuel F B Morse HS; San Diego, CA; (4); 4/525; Hosp Aide; Scholastic Bowl; Sec SADD; School Play; Ed Nwsp; Var Capt Tennis; Elks Awd; High Hon Roll; Jr NHS; Natl Grls & Women Sprts Day Awd; Outstndng Stu Frgn Lang & Indpndnt Stds; CSF Sealbearer; UC San Diego; Pediatrics.

SEN, KAUSHIK; El Camino Real HS; West Hills, CA; (3); Sec Math Tm; NFL; Service Clb; Speech Tm; Lit Mag; JV Tennis; Hon Roll; JETS Awd; 2nd Pl Rockwell/LAUSD Comp Sci Cmptn; 1st Caramellos Creat A Tune Cont; Outstndng Achvt Awd; MIT; Aerospc Engrng.

SEN, SOMAN; Leffingwell Christian HS; Picorivera, CA; (3); 1/60; Cmnty Wkr; Var Wrstlng; High Hon Roll; Hon Roll; Psysician.

SENA, DAVID S; Alta Loma HS; Alta Loma, CA; (2); Yrbk; High Hon Roll; Hon Roll; Prfct Atten Awd; Pres Acad Fit Awd; CSF; Friday Night Live Orgnztn.

SENECAL, JANELLE S; Bullard HS; Fresno, CA; (2); 58/566; Church Yth Grp; Intnl Clb; Key Clb; SADD; Acpl Chr; Chorus; Variety Show; JV Swmmng; Cit Awd; High Hon Roll; CSF Brd; Jr LARCS Treas; US Air Force Acad; Sci.

SENEGAL, AUDREY D; Mc Clymonds HS; Oakland, CA; (3); Church Yth Grp; Chorus; Church Choir; Nwsp; Yrbk; Off Soph Cls; Rookie Of Yr; Plyr Of Yr; Engr.

SENERIS, CATHERINE; Patten Academy Of Christian Ed; Oakland, CA; (3); 1/6; Church Choir; Orch; Off Soph Cls; Sec Jr Cls; Sec Stu Cncl; UCSF; Med.

SENETHACHITH, AE; Sweetwater HS; San Diego, CA; (4); 8/396; DECA; FBLA; Science Clb; Teachers Aide; Cit Awd; Prfct Atten Awd; CSF; Schltc All Amer; SDSU; RN.

SENG, HUOR; Grace Davis HS; Modesto, CA; (4); 52/500; French Clb; FBLA; Intnl Clb; Hon Roll; Pres Acad Fit Awd; US Hstry Awd; CSF; UC Davis; Gnrl Mgmt.

SENG, WUTHEA; Beyer HS; Modesto, CA; (3); Cit Awd; Hon Roll; Prfct Atten Awd.

SENGCHANTHALANGSY, BOUALOY; Escondido HS; Escondido, CA; (1); French Clb; FBLA; German Clb; Key Clb; Pep Clb; Science Clb; Ski Clb; Score Keeper; JV Swmmng; Cit Awd; Concert Choir; Cls Pres; Outstndng Single; Berkeley; Frgn Lang.

SENGCHANTHALANGSY, PHOKHAM; Escondido HS; Escondido, CA; (3); Am Leg Aux Girls St; Pres French Clb; Rptr FBLA; Pres German Clb; Sec Key Clb; Pep Clb; Science Clb; Cit Awd; Hon Roll; NHS; CADA Smmr 90; Prom Cmmtte; Daisy Chain; Yale U; Med.

SENGCHAREUNE, KHAMSAY; Grant Union HS; Sacramento, CA; (2); Intnl Clb; Acpl Chr; Loma Linda U; Dr.

SENGER, CHRISTINE J; Yucca Valley HS; Joshua Tree, CA; (3); Hist Rptr FTA; Office Aide; Teachers Aide; Ed Lit Mag; Hon Roll; Anml Wlfr Inst; Green Peace; Vlntrs Of Amerca; Puget Sound; Psych.

SENGPASEUTH, VIENGKHAM; Crawford HS; San Diego, CA; (2); Var Tennis.

SENNIKOFF, SHELLY; Brea Olinda HS; Brea, CA; (4); 83/300; Speech Tm; Teachers Aide; Drill Tm; Nwsp; Yrbk; Fullerton CC; Liberal Stds.

SENTIANIN, CHRISTIANE; Palm Desert HS; Palm Desert, CA; (3); Key Clb; Teachers Aide; Var Cheerldng; JV Sftbl; High Hon Roll; CSF; Prom Cmmtt.

SEO, WOO YOUNG; Gardena HS; Gardena, CA; (3); Church Yth Grp; Dance Clb; Drama Clb; Office Aide; Spanish Clb; Teachers Aide; School Play; Stage Crew; Variety Show; Rptr Nwsp; UCLA.

SEOW, DARREN; Glendale HS; Glendale, CA; (2); Church Yth Grp; JV Tennis; Prfct Atten Awd; Pres Acad Fit Awd; Hnrs Awds Algebra, Geom Golden St Exams; 1st Pl Fremont Park Tennis Tournmnt 90; Engrng.

SEPAHER, IRENA; Mills HS; Millbrae, CA; (3); Church Yth Grp; Intnl Clb; JA; Red Cross Aide; High Hon Roll; Hon Roll; Lion Awd; Badmington Var.

SEPAHPOUR, FRANCINE F; San Rafael HS; Novato, CA; (3); 4/208; Debate Tm; Key Clb; SADD; Drill Tm; Ed Nwsp; Pres Jr Cls; JV Cheerldng; Tennis; High Hon Roll; Hon Roll; Spcl Interest Piano; Intership Local Marin Independent Jrnl Nwspaper; Berkeley CA U; Med.

SEPANLOU, SHERI S; Los Altos HS; Hacienda Hgts, CA; (4); Church Yth Grp; Drama Clb; Acpl Chr; Chorus; School Play; Hon Roll; Ind Poetry Prz; CAL ST Los Angeles; Drama.

SEPAROVICH, DAVID R; Christian Brothers HS; Sacramento, CA; (3); JV Var Ftbl; High Hon Roll; Hon Roll; NHS.

SEPEDA, LESLIE; Strathmore HS; Strathmore, CA; (3); 5/83; Am Leg Aux Girls St; Drama Clb; Pep Clb; SADD; Sec Frsh Cls; VP Soph Cls; Rep Jr Cls; Var Cheerldng; Cit Awd; High Hon Roll; Peer Cnslng; Mock Trial; CSF; Bus.

SEPH, TANYA; John Glenn HS; Norwalk, CA; (4); 1/285; Am Leg Aux Girls St; Cmnty Wkr; Key Clb; Band; Sec Stu Cncl; Elks Awd; Kiwanis Awd; Pres Acad Fit Awd; Val; CA ST U Fullerton; Teacher.

SEPLAK, MICHELE A; Foothill HS; Santa Ana, CA; (2); Pres Church Yth Grp; Hosp Aide; Pep Clb; Spanish Clb; JV Cheerldng; Stat Crs Cntry; JV Diving; Var L Gym; Safe Rides; U CA-DAVIS; Vet Med.

SEPP, ARVO; Apple Valley HS; Apple Valley, CA; (2); Chess Clb; JV Score Keeper; JV Tennis; High Hon Roll; Rotary Awd; CSF; Cvl Air Ptrl; U S Air Force Acad; Pilot.

SEPPAMAKI, SHERRY I; Vallejo SR HS; Vallejo, CA; (2); Letterman Clb; Teachers Aide; Vllybl; Hon Roll; NHS; Pres Acad Fit Awd; Badminton Tm; Hnrs Goldn St Exm Agl I & Geom; Acad Ltr.

SEPPI, WILLIAM; Cardinal Newman HS; Healdsburg, CA; (1); 12/114; Boy Scts; Church Yth Grp; Spanish Clb; Rptr Nwsp; Yrbk; Swmmng; High Hon Roll; Golf; Stanford; Accntng.

SEPULVEDA, ANGELA M; Lincoln HS; Roseville, CA; (2); 22/186; SADD; Chorus; School Musical; Variety Show; Rep Stu Cncl; VP Trk; Hon Roll; Pres Acad Fit Awd; Stu Rep Western Placer Schl Brd; Pr Cnslr; Sierra JC; Scl Svc.

SEPULVEDA, DIANA; Sacred Heart Of Jesus HS; Los Angeles, CA; (2); 2/115; Hosp Aide; Variety Show; Rptr Nwsp; Lit Mag; High Hon Roll; NHS; Prfct Atten Awd; CSF; LA Cty USC Med Ctr Womens Hosp Volunteer Of Yr; HS Folklorico Dance Grp; UCLA; Obstetrics.

SEPULVEDA, EILEEN; Dana Hills HS; Dana Point, CA; (3); Teachers Aide; JV Bsktbl; JV Sftbl; Frgn Lang/Spansh.

SEPULVEDA, MARION L; Colton HS; Colton, CA; (3); Ed Yrbk; VP Stu Cncl; JV Var Bsktbl; Var Capt Crs Cntry; JV Powder Puff Ftbl; Var Capt Trk; Hon Roll; NHS; Prfct Atten Awd; No Truancies Awd; Outstndng Stu Track; Coaches Awd; Fnlst Thlet Mnth; Arch.

SEPULVEDA, NANCY; Notre Dame Acad; Los Angeles, CA; (1); Church Yth Grp; Cmnty Wkr; Teachers Aide; Cit Awd; Scl Wrk.

SEQUEIRA, DENISE A; Christian Brothers HS; Sacramento, CA; (3); French Clb; Hosp Aide; Ski Clb; Drill Tm; School Play; Nwsp; Rep Soph Cls; Rep Jr Cls; Swmmng; Cit Awd; Portuguese Representative; Employed; San Fransisca ST; Intrntnl Mkt.

SEQUEIRA, JOHN J; Orestimba HS; Newman, CA; (4); JV Bsbl; JV Bsktbl; JV Var Ftbl; Hon Roll; Gustine Police Dept Explorer; Modesto JC; Law Enfrcmnt.

SEQUEIRA, SARABENET; Tamalpais HS; Mill Valley, CA; (4); Drama Clb; Latin Clb; Band; Chorus; School Play; Stage Crew; Yrbk; High Hon Roll; Ntl Merit SF; Peer Tutoring; Stanford; Psych.

SEQUEIRA, TONIA L; Los Banos HS; Los Banos, CA; (1); Stu Cncl; High Hon Roll; CA Schlrshp Fed; Wntr Ball Cmmtte; Frshmn Float Cmmtte.

SERAFIN, LILIANA; Sierra Vista HS; Baldwin Park, CA; (1); Bsktbl; Hon Roll; Psych.

SERAFINE, KIRSTI J; Mira Mesa HS; San Diego, CA; (2); Drill Tm; School Play; Stage Crew; Variety Show; Rep Frsh Cls; Rep Soph Cls; Mgr Vllybl; Hon Roll; U CA-SAN Diego; Marine Bio.

SERBER, TAMARA N; Cajon HS; San Bernardino, CA; (3); Key Clb; Letterman Clb; Office Aide; Pep Clb; Teachers Aide; Ed Yrbk; Rep Frsh Cls; Cit Awd; Hon Roll; Intl Baccalaureate Eng Class; San Luis Obispo Cal Poly; Psych.

SEREMI, JEANNINE M; Davis SR HS; Davis, CA; (3); Church Yth Grp; Cmnty Wkr; Office Aide; Band; Mrchg Band; Rep Soph Cls; Rep Jr Cls; Rep Sr Cls; Stu Cncl; Bsktbl; Capitol Focus Pgm; Job Outrch Pgm; Grievence Cmmtte Chrprsn; Hum Rltns Vice Chr; Wasc Stu Cmmtte; UC Davis; Intl Rltns.

SERGI, LISA; John A Rowland HS; Rowland Hts, CA; (3); Church Yth Grp; Pres Treas Drama Clb; Hosp Aide; Pres Speech Tm; Hist Thesps; VP Capt Socr; Lion Awd; NHS; Rotary Awd; Letterman Clb.

SERINO, NICOLE; Mount Carmel HS; San Diego, CA; (2); Dance Clb; Var Cheerldng; Pres Acad Fit Awd; Golden ST Esam Acad Awd In Geometry; Mktg.

SERIO, STACY L; Bishop Montgomery HS; Hawthorne, CA; (2); Drama Clb; Key Clb; JV Socr; Law.

SERIO, THOMAS G; Cordova SR HS; Rancho Cordova, CA; (4); 17/450; Chess Clb; Computer Clb; German Clb; Model UN; Jr NHS; UC Davis; Elec Engrng.

SERIOSA, RHODA S; Andrew Hill HS; San Jose, CA; (4); 12/246; DECA; Hon Roll; Pres Acad Fit Awd; CSF; Supt Honor Roll; Span Awd; San Jose ST U; Nrsng.

SERNA, ANA I; Palo Verde HS; Blythe, CA; (3); Drama Clb; Spanish Clb; Teachers Aide; Stage Crew; Vllybl; Palo Verde Coll; Medcl.

SERNA, ANTOINETTE M; Hanford HS; Hanford, CA; (2); Dance Clb; Fresno ST; Bus.

SERNA, EDGAR; Calipatria HS; Calipatria, CA; (3); Computer Clb; English Clb; Key Clb; Math Tm; SADD; Yrbk; JV Tennis; Cit Awd; High Hon Roll; Hon Roll; CSF; Psych.

SERNA, ROSE M; Duarte HS; Duarte, CA; (3); 20/264; Am Leg Aux Girls St; Church Yth Grp; VP Stu Cncl; JV Bsktbl; JV Swmmng; JV Vllybl; Outstndng Stu Yr Offc Occptns; Schltc Hnrs Alg 2; CSF; USC; Arch.

SEROICE, SHANNON; Palm Valley HS; Palm Springs, CA; (1); Chorus; School Play; Yrbk; Var Socr; Var Sftbl; Lion Awd; Greenpeace; Spnsr Chldrn Wrld Vision; Oxford; Jrnlsm.

SEROPIAN, SETTA O; Holy Martyrs HS; Encino, CA; (3); Hon Roll; Pedtrcn.

SERPA, CHRISTINE; Turlock HS; Turlock, CA; (2); 33/675; Church Yth Grp; Dance Clb; FFA; Pep Clb; Speech Tm; JV Cheerldng; CSF; Interact; UC Santa Barbara; Advrtsng.

SERPEKIAN, SONIA NICHOLE; Torrey Pines HS; San Diego, CA; (3); 164/465; Boy Scts; Girl Scts; Service Clb; Chorus; Church Choir; Phtg Yrbk; Intrml Sftbl; Stnt Sen Rep; Brnch Hnrs Mus Fest; Certf Merit; Vlbl Tm Capt; Navasartian Gms Armnn Olymp CA; San Diego ST U.

SERRAN, CECILIA M; Herbert Hoover HS; Glendale, CA; (3); Teachers Aide; Nwsp; Stu Cncl; Bsktbl; Cit Awd; Hon Roll; Jr NHS; Pres Acad Fit Awd; Filipino Club Pres; UCLA; Acctng.

SERRANO, CECILIA R; El Camino HS; Oceanside, CA; (2); Church Yth Grp; SADD; Var JV Tennis; Cit Awd; Hon Roll; CSF Awd & Pin; Cmpus Life; UCSD; Psych.

SERRANO, CLAUDIA; Pasadena HS; Pasadena, CA; (3); Hon Roll; UCLA; Bus Adm.

SERRANO, DELIA; Arlington HS; Moreno Valley, CA; (2); Church Yth Grp; FCA; Bus.

SERRANO, GERALDINE FALMOS; San Ramon Valley HS; Danville, CA; (2); Church Choir; High Hon Roll; Pres Acad Fit Awd; Soccer, Dance & Piano; Schlstc Achvt Rcgntn Awd 1988; CSF; UCLA; Crprt Lwyr.

SERRANO, IRMA V; Anaheim HS; Anaheim, CA; (3); Cmnty Wkr; Spanish Clb; Hon Roll; Univ Preperation Pgm; CA ST Fullerton Emerging Ldrs Clb; CA ST Fullerton; Paralegal.

SERRANO, JOHN A; Silver Valley HS; Yermo, CA; (2); FFA; Hon Roll.

SERRANO, KARINA; Granger JR HS; National City, CA; (1); Church Yth Grp; Office Aide; Teachers Aide; Variety Show; VP Frsh Cls; High Hon Roll; Hon Roll; Prfct Atten Awd; Future Ldrs Amer; MECHA; Sci Olympn; UCSD; Elec Engr.

SERRANO, LISBETH; Morningside HS; Inglewood, CA; (4); 7/165; JA; Rptr Nwsp; Phtg Yrbk; Stu Cncl; Cheerldng; Cit Awd; High Hon Roll; Latino Clb; Pr Cnclr; CA ST Long Beach; Bus.

SERRANO, MEGHAN R; Cajon HS; San Bernardino, CA; (1); 32/516; Rep Soph Cls; JV Cheerldng; Var Swmmng; Intl Baccalaureate Pgm; Future Ldrs Amer Pgm; Stanford.

SERRANO, PATTY; Etiwanda HS; Alta Loma, CA; (2); Dance Clb; Drama Clb; French Clb; JA; Hon Roll; Prfct Atten Awd; Bus.

SERRANO, RALPH A; El Rancho HS; Pico Rivera, CA; (2); JV Ftbl; Cit Awd; High Hon Roll; Awd Sci Prjct Sci Fr; Atten Awds; Bsktbl; Law.

SERRANO JR, REY T; Tulare Union HS; Tulare, CA; (4); Computer Clb; Letterman Clb; Teachers Aide; Var Bsbl; Bsktbl; Var Ftbl; Rcgnt PE Stu Mnth; Bus Mgmt.

SERRANO, SALVADORA ELISA A; Winters HS; Winters, CA; (2); Cmnty Wkr; Pep Clb; SADD; Teachers Aide; Score Keeper; Stat Vllybl; Hon Roll; Vet Clinic Vlntr Wrkr; Actv Hypertntn Cncl Stu; Zlgst.

SERRANO, SANDRA T; Pasadena HS; Pasadena, CA; (2); High Hon Roll; Hon Roll; UCLA; Tchr.

SERRANO, SONIA A; Washington HS; Fremont, CA; (3); 17/306; VP DECA; Teachers Aide; Powder Puff Ftbl; CSF; Schl Recgntn Gldn St Exm Alg; Rgnl Occptnl Pgm Stu Mnth; Advrtsng.

SERRANO, YVETTE A; Notre Dame HS; Salinas, CA; (3); Debate Tm; Pres Intnl Clb; VP Science Clb; Yrbk; JV Swmmng; High Hon Roll; Hon Roll; Jr NHS; NHS; Prfct Atten Awd; CSF; UC Berkeley; Bus Admin.

SERRAO, BRANDI A; Vacaville HS; Vacaville, CA; (3); Yrbk; Hon Roll.

SERRATO, KATHY E; Sanger HS; Del Rey, CA; (3); Drama Clb; French Clb; School Play; Achvmnt Awd; Fresno City Coll; Fshn Merch.

SERRATO, PHILLIP; Bellarmine College Prep; San Jose, CA; (4); 24/306; Cmnty Wkr; Math Clb; Science Clb; Service Clb; JV Crs Cntry; JV Trk; Hon Roll; Evergreen Vly Coll Pres List; UCLA; Planetary Sci.

SERRATO, SANTIAGO; Will C Wood HS; Vacaville, CA; (2); Rep Frsh Cls; Rep Stu Cncl; Capt Bsktbl; JV Ftbl; JV Socr; JV Trk; JV Wt Lftg; Hon Roll; Conflict Mgmt; Stu Mnth; Solano CC.

SERRATO, VICTOR; Dos Palos HS; Dos Palos, CA; (1).

SERTIC, LIKA A; El Camino HS; Sacramento, CA; (3); 99/366; Sec Latin Clb; SADD; Teachers Aide; Intrml Crs Cntry; Hon Roll; ASTEKS; UC Santa Cruz; Marine Bio.

SERVANDE, LISA M; Encinal HS; Alameda, CA; (3); 21/233; Key Clb; Library Aide; ROTC; JV Tennis; Hon Roll; Prncpls Awd; Rfl Tm Vrsty; Psych.

SERVANTES, MARCELLA A; Rubidoux HS; Riverside, CA; (4); Office Aide; Riverside CC; Medcl.

SERVEAU, HEATHER; Red Bluff HS; Red Bluff, CA; (4); 18/300; Spanish Clb; Lion Awd; Rotary Awd; Sr Steering Comm; Mc Connell Schlrshp; Shasta Coll; Math.

SERVELLON, IRIS M; Susan Miller Dorsey HS; Los Angeles, CA; (3); French Clb; Office Aide; Cit Awd; Hon Roll; Prfct Atten Awd; Steering Cmmtte; CSUN; Acctng.

SERVICE, MATT W; Montgomery HS; Santa Rosa, CA; (3); Church Yth Grp; French Clb; FBLA; Treas Frsh Cls; Var Tennis; French Hon Soc; High Hon Roll; Jr NHS; Bus.

SERVIN, JOSE; South West HS; San Diego, CA; (2); 27/645; UCSD; Arch.

SERVIN, SANDRA J; Oakdale HS; Oakdale, CA; (2); Latin Clb; Human Physh.

SERVIN, VERONICA L; William Workman HS; Valinda, CA; (3); High Hon Roll; Hon Roll; Comp Prgmr.

SESAR, JOSHUA BRIAN; Birmingham HS; Encino, CA; (4); #7 In Class; VP FBLA; VP JA; Treas Key Clb; Math Tm; NFL; Sec Speech Tm; Var Trk; Opt Clb Awd; Pres Acad Fit Awd; Sal; UC Berkeley.

SESAR, STEVEN J; Birmingham HS; Encino, CA; (2); FBLA; Key Clb; SADD; Temple Yth Grp; Yrbk; JV Crs Cntry; JV L Trk; Hon Roll; Cmfrmtn; Coach Kids Bstkbl Tm; Bus.

SESHER, ANDIE E; Corning Union HS; Corning, CA; (3); GAA; Intnl Clb; Pep Clb; Var Cheerldng; JV Var Sftbl; Var Capt Vllybl; Hon Roll; Bus.

SESLAR, KIMBERLY N; Turlock HS; Turlock, CA; (3); Science Clb; SADD; Band; Chorus; Mrchg Band; Lit Mag; Trk; High Hon Roll; Hon Roll; Douglas Cnty HS Inaugural Band 89; Teacher.

SESOCK, RAELENE C; Madera HS; Madera, CA; (3); 4-H; Varsity Clb; Rep Yrbk; Off Frsh Cls; Treas Jr Cls; Var Socr; Var Sftbl; Var Vllybl; Cit Awd; High Hon Roll; Jrnlsm Awd; Acad Athl Awd; Vllybl & Soccer Coaches Awd.

SESSAREGO, CARRIE E; El Camino Fundamental HS; Sacramento, CA; (3); 74/376; FTA; Hosp Aide; Acpl Chr; Band; Jazz Band; Pep Band; School Musical; Lit Mag; Baccalaureate Candlebearer; Poetry Awds.

SESSER, CHAD I; Westlake HS; Westlake Village, CA; (2); Spanish Clb; VP Temple Yth Grp; Drill Tm; Hon Roll; Math Stu Awd.

SESSION, IDRISSA; De Anza HS; Richmond, CA; (3); Church Yth Grp; Office Aide; Teachers Aide; Hon Roll; Awd Outstndng Achvt Genrl Mrchndsng, Banking Occupations, Accntng; UC Davis; Bus Mngmnt.

SESSION, LATREASE; Balboa HS; San Francisco, CA; (2); Church Yth Grp; Debate Tm; ROTC; Science Clb; Speech Tm; Teachers Aide; Color Guard; Drill Tm; Drm Mjr(t); Nwsp; Sci Ed Prtnrshp Cntst; Acad Decathlon Team; San Francisco ST U; Pediatrcn.

SET, ERIC J; St Francis HS; Mountain View, CA; (1); 22/388; Intnl Clb; SADD; Band; Mrchg Band; Pep Band; Hon Roll; UC San Diego; Comp Engrng.

SETIAN, HOLLY S; John Marshall Fund HS; Altadena, CA; (3); Cmnty Wkr; Key Clb; Service Clb; Treas Rep Stu Cncl; Var Tennis; Hon Roll; Prfct Atten Awd; Pasadena Pet Hosp; U C Davis; Vet Med.

SETIAN, JO L; John Marshall Fund HS; Altadena, CA; (1); Band; Mrchg Band; Orch; Bsktbl; Vllybl; Cit Awd; Alg Golden St Schlr; U CA-DAVIS; Zoology.

SETO, ANNA; John Marshall HS; Los Angeles, CA; (4); 4/667; VP Church Yth Grp; Hosp Aide; Pres Spanish Clb; Var Capt Vllybl; High Hon Roll; NHS; Prfct Atten Awd; Pres Acad Fit Awd; Rep Stu Cncl; Ray Feeman Hubbard Memrl Schlrshp; Ephebian Soc; Harvard Alumni Bk Awd; Dartmouth Coll.

SETO, CAROL; Alameda HS; Alameda, CA; (4); 10/325; Science Clb; Teachers Aide; Sec Soph Cls; JV Capt Bsktbl; Capt Crs Cntry; Var Trk; High Hon Roll; Prfct Atten Awd; Pres Acad Fit Awd; Natl Girls Wtr Ski Chmpn; U CA Santa Barbara; Bus Econ.

SETO, PHILLIP; Abrham Lincoln HS; San Francisco, CA; (4); Teachers Aide; Var Tennis; City Coll San Francisco; Arch.

SETO, STEVEN; Encinal HS; Alameda, CA; (3); 24/233; FBLA; High Hon Roll.

SETOODEH, KATY M; Montgomery HS; Santa Rosa, CA; (2); Cmnty Wkr; French Clb; Science Clb; Phtg Yrbk; JV Swmmng; Cit Awd; Hon Roll; JV NHS; Pres Acad Fit Awd; Church Bsktbl Tm; SORT; French Awd; Deptmntl Hnrs Hstry; Lamp Of Knowledge Awd; GSE With Hnrs; Surgeon.

SETTI, DAVID M; St Francis Of Assisi HS; Burbank, CA; (2); 20/182; Boy Scts; Chess Clb; Church Yth Grp; Cmnty Wkr; Pep Clb; Band; Nwsp; Hon Roll; U Of PA; Accntng.

SETTIMI, JANINE T; Redwood HS; Visalia, CA; (1); German Clb; Math Tm; Band; Mrchg Band; Var Swmmng; High Hon Roll; Jr NHS; Rainbow Girl.

SETTLE, SUZANNE I; Fontana HS; Fontana, CA; (2); 319/1376; Debate Tm; Quiz Bowl; Speech Tm; Co-Capt Flag Corp; Rep Stu Cncl; Hon Roll; Sci Awd; UCLA; Astrntcs.

SETTLES, VICTOR; Taft Union HS; Mc Kittrick, CA; (3); #1 In Class; Debate Tm; Drama Clb; French Clb; Key Clb; Speech Tm; School Play; Stage Crew; JV Ftbl; Var Tennis; JV Trk; Acad Dec; Mock Trl; CSF; Amer Fed Schlrs; Stanford; Med.

SETVANICH, PHANUWAT J; Royal HS; Simi Valley, CA; (3); Computer Clb; DECA; Band; Cit Awd; High Hon Roll; Hon Roll; Prfct Atten Awd; Acad Penthln Mem 86 & 87; UCLA; Comp Prgmr.

SEUS, SCOTT; Tulelake HS; Tulelake, CA; (3); 4/35; Debate Tm; FFA; Pres Soph Cls; Pres Jr Cls; Rep Stu Cncl; JV Bsktbl; Hon Roll; Outstndng Project Awd FFA 89; Shasta Ag Ield Day 1st Pl Farm Records Cmptn; OIT Rgnl Math Cont; CA Poly San Luis Obispo; Ag.

SEVENANS, KRISTY C; Ramona HS; Ramona, CA; (2); Church Yth Grp; Debate Tm; Sec Pep Clb; Mgr Bsktbl; Stat JV Sftbl; Ricks Coll.

SEVERINO, JENEAN M; Salinas HS; Salinas, CA; (3); AFS; Church Yth Grp; Cmnty Wkr; Drama Clb; FBLA; FTA; Math Clb; Science Clb; SADD; Teachers Aide; Hnr Choir 3 Yrs; Stu Bttr Earth; Cong Schlr Rep CA; Chld Ed.

SEVERSON, MATTHEW L; Washington HS; Fremont, CA; (2); Boy Scts; Pres Soph Cls; Stu Cncl; Var Socr; Prfct Atten Awd; Eagle Sct; BYU; Bus.

SEVERT, AMY J; Mountain Empire HS; Descanso, CA; (2); Art Clb; Church Yth Grp; Pep Clb; Spanish Clb; Rptr Nwsp; Sftbl; NHS; Friday Night Live; CSF; WAC.

SEVIDAL, SAMANTHA E; The Academy Of Our Lady Of Peace; Lemon Grove, CA; (1); Hosp Aide; Speech Tm; School Musical; Rep Frsh Cls; Rep Stu Cncl; Hon Roll; Mrktng.

SEVIER JR, ADAM A; South HS; Bakersfield, CA; (3); 35/424; Teachers Aide; Var Ftbl; Var Trk; Wt Lftg; Hon Roll; Prfct Atten Awd; Mobil Oil Excel Clb Stu; Bus Ed.

SEVIER, RODNEY D; Mission Bay HS; San Diego, CA; (3); 98/305; Boy Scts; Church Yth Grp; Letterman Clb; SADD; Varsity Clb; Band; Var Socr; Vllybl; Hon Roll; San Diegans For Pcfl Wld; Cert Mrt; Skirblinst Amer Vls Of Amer Jwsh Comm; Cngrssnlyth Ldrshp Cncl; UC Berkley; Pltcl Sci.

SEVILLANO, JILL L; Mar Vista HS; Imperial Beach, CA; (1); Quiz Bowl; Var Sftbl; Var Vllybl; Cit Awd; Prfct Atten Awd; Stanford; Engnrng.

SEVO, RANDY A; Valley Christian HS; Pleasanton, CA; (2); Cmnty Wkr; Latin Clb; Spanish Clb; Sec Soph Cls; Sec Jr Cls; Stu Cncl; Hon Roll; Real Estate.

SEVY, JAIMIE B; Sonora HS; Mi Wuk Village, CA; (3); Boy Scts; Church Yth Grp; French Clb; Math Clb; Science Clb; Ski Clb; SADD; Band; Chorus; Church Choir; Natl Eagle Sct BSA; Ordr Arrow; Bandsmn Yr; UC David; Ansthslgy.

SEWARD, JASON A; Rim Of The World HS; Crestline, CA; (1); 16/435; German Clb; Library Aide; JV Golf; High Hon Roll; Prfct Atten Awd; Harvard; Vet.

SEWARD, MICHELLE L; Chula Vista HS; Chula Vista, CA; (1); Cmnty Wkr; Pep Clb; Rep Frsh Cls; 3.5 Ctznshp Avrg; San Diego ST U; Poltcl Sci.

SEWELL, SHAE L; Beyer HS; Modesto, CA; (2); Hon Roll; Al-Teen; Cal Poly-Pomona; Arch.

SEXHUS, SANFORD C; Casa Roble Fundamental HS; Orangevale, CA; (3); 1/390; Treas AFS; Church Yth Grp; Pres French Clb; Science Clb; Var L Crs Cntry; High Hon Roll; Jr NHS; NHS; Ntl Merit SF; Best Science Student; Multiple Involvement Award; Best English Student; Politics.

SEXSON, LINDA C; Pacifica HS; Garden Grove, CA; (3); 8/273; Am Leg Aux Girls St; Church Yth Grp; Pres Spanish Clb; Ed Yrbk; Rep Stu Cncl; Ntl Merit SF; Acadmc Dcthln Team Capt; Kiwanis Bowl; Knwldg Mstr Open; Outstndng Engl Stu; Engl.

SEXTON, AMY; St Francis HS; Cameron Park, CA; (2); Church Yth Grp; Debate Tm; Speech Tm; Teachers Aide; JV Sftbl; Var Vllybl; Hon Roll; Latin Hnr Soc; CSF; SRO.

SEXTON, ANGELA A; Victor Valley HS; Victorville, CA; (2); French Clb; Travel Agnt.

SEXTON, ARIANA L; University HS; Irvine, CA; (2); GAA; Rep JCL; JV Capt Bsktbl; Hon Roll; Traveling With Stu Grp Germany, Czechoslovakia, Austria.

SEXTON, GENEVIEVE C; University Of San Diego HS; San Diego, CA; (2); Drama Clb; French Clb; Intnl Clb; SADD; School Play; Stage Crew; Crs Cntry; Hon Roll; CSF; Confetti-San Diego JR Theatre Svc Clb; Amnesty Intl; 2nd Pl Shakespearan Cmptn; UCSC; Engl.

SEXTON, JAKE M; Carlsbad HS; Carlsbad, CA; (1); Pep Clb; JV Trk; High Hon Roll; Hon Roll; Art; CA Schlstc Fed; Stanford; Author.

SEXTON, JENNIFER R; St Francis HS; Cameron Park, CA; (3); Church Yth Grp; Cmnty Wkr; Teachers Aide; Varsity Clb; School Play; Rptr Nwsp; Vllybl; CA Schlrshp Fed; Stus Rchng Out; Edctnl Cnslng.

SEXTON, TRISH; Chaffey HS; Alta Loma, CA; (3); Office Aide; Teachers Aide; Band; Mrchg Band; High Hon Roll; Hon Roll; Pres Acad Fit Awd; Cal Poly; Bus.

SEYBERT, AUDREY F; Brawley Union HS; Brawley, CA; (2); 3/350; AFS; Hist 4-H; SADD; Stu Cncl; Capt JV Cheerldng; 4-H Awd; High Hon Roll; Piano; CSF; Outstndng JV Cheer Trphy; JR Fair Bd; Stanford U; Bus.

SEYFERTH, JULIA L; Dana Hills HS; Laguna Niguel, CA; (1); Drama Clb; Trk; Vllybl; UCLA; Actng.

SEYMORE, DUNYETTE T; Oakland Technical HS; Oakland, CA; (2); ROTC; Church Choir; School Play; Stage Crew; High Hon Roll; Hon Roll; MESA; Columbia U NY; Bio.

SEYMORE, TRAVIS T J; Mt Whitney HS; Visalia, CA; (4); VP FFA; Spanish Clb; Teachers Aide; Rptr Nwsp; Rep Stu Cncl; JV Bsbl; JV Wrstlng; Hon Roll; Tulare Co Farm Bureau Yth Intern; CA Horse Expo JR Team Penning Champ; Ag.

SEYVERTSEN, TARA; Encina HS; Sacramento, CA; (2); Crs Cntry; Trk; Hon Roll.

SHAAR JR, ROGER; Village Christian Schl; Shadow Hills, CA; (4); 4/119; Church Yth Grp; English Clb; Math Clb; Mu Alpha Theta; Spanish Clb; Band; JV Socr; Hon Roll; NHS; UCLA.

SHACK, JENNIFER R; Poway HS; San Diego, CA; (3); Drama Clb; Key Clb; SADD; Pres Temple Yth Grp; Rptr Nwsp; Stat Wrstlng; Hon Roll; Amnesty Intl; Cmmnctns.

SHACKELFOOT, CHENELL S; Pioneer HS; San Jose, CA; (3); Teachers Aide; San Francisco ST; Atty.

SHACKELFORD, BRIAN C; St Bernard HS; Inglewood, CA; (3); Cmnty Wkr; Ski Clb; Pres Frsh Cls; Pres Soph Cls; Rep Stu Cncl; Var Bsbl; Intrml Bsktbl; Cit Awd; Ldrshp Retreat Cnslr; Psych.

SHACKLETON, AARON; Lodi HS; Lodi, CA; (3); Chess Clb; Church Yth Grp; Teachers Aide; Band; Church Choir; Jazz Band; Mrchg Band; Pep Band; School Musical; Golf; Pres Chrch Yth Grp; Chrch Sftbl Tm; Cert Mrt Piano Pgm; Anderson U; Music Minister.

SHADDOX, TROY J; Colton HS; Grand Terrace, CA; (3); FFA; Hon Roll; NHS; Prfct Atten Awd; Riverside U; Comp Pgm.

SHADWICK, DARRIN; Paradise HS; Magalia, CA; (4); 34/235; Am Leg Boys St; Cmnty Wkr; Pep Clb; Teachers Aide; School Play; Pres Frsh Cls; Pres Soph Cls; Rep Jr Cls; Rep Sr Cls; Rep Stu Cncl; Butte; Bus Admin.

SHADWICK, LA TANYA D; Buena Park HS; Buena Park, CA; (3); Church Yth Grp; 4-H; Church Choir; Hon Roll; Prfct Atten Awd; CA ST U-Fullertn; Tech Writer.

SHAEFFER, KIM N; Santa Monica HS; Santa Monica, CA; (2); JA; SADD; Varsity Clb; Stage Crew; Nwsp; Var Tennis; Cit Awd; High Hon Roll; Pres Acad Fit Awd; JR Stsmn Of Amer; Harvard U; Bus.

SHAEVITZ, GEOFF H; La Jolla County Day School; La Jolla, CA; (2); Cmnty Wkr; Service Clb; Chorus; School Musical; French Hon Soc; High Hon Roll; 17 Magzn Natl Cookng Contest Wnnr 88; Featured Chef Sun Up,Chnnl 8,KFMB-TV 89; Stu Smmr Discvry 90; Psychlgy.

SHAFAGHI, MARYAM; Rancho Bernardo HS; San Diego, CA; (2); Math Clb; Teachers Aide; Chorus; Variety Show; Stu Cncl; Swmmng; High Hon Roll; Hon Roll; Pres Acad Fit Awd; Sufing & Swimming; Reading; Engr.

SHAFER, CHERYL; Fremont Christian HS; Fremont, CA; (4); 1/43; Church Yth Grp; Rep Stu Cncl; JV Var Cheerldng; Var Socr; High Hon Roll; NHS; Pres Acad Fit Awd; Val.

SHAFER, DEE; So Tahoe HS; South Lake Tahoe, CA; (3); Cmnty Wkr; Pres Dance Clb; Debate Tm; Pres Key Clb; Speech Tm; Teachers Aide; Varsity Clb; Pres Sr Cls; Cheerldng; Powder Puff Ftbl; Chrmn Spcl Olympcs; Rtry Spch Cntst; USC; Cmmnctns.

SHAFER, J RYAN; Newport Harbor HS; Wheatridge, CO; (3); #20 In Class; JCL; Latin Clb; Crs Cntry; Trk; High Hon Roll; MVP Crs Cntry; Bst Latin Stu; CO U; Arch.

SHAFER, JENIFER E; San Marcos HS; Santa Barbara, CA; (1); Color Guard; Gov Hon Prg Awd; Art.

SHAFER, JIMMY M; Berkeley HS; Berkeley, CA; (3); Chess Clb; Chorus; School Musical; Tennis; Juggling, Circus Arts; Origami Paper Fldng; Piano; Engrng.

SHAFER, STEPHANIE A; Encina HS; Sacramento, CA; (3); 126/212; Church Yth Grp; FBLA; Scholastic Bowl; Spanish Clb; Off Sr Cls; Swmmng; Stus Reaching Out Pres; Law.

SHAFFER, AUBRE C; Bloomington HS; Bloomington, CA; (3); Acpl Chr; Chorus; Drill Tm; Mrchg Band; Rptr Nwsp; Hon Roll; Jr NHS; CSF; Pre Vet Med.

SHAFFER, BRANDON K; Roseville HS; Roseville, CA; (3); Office Aide; Science Clb; Teachers Aide; Var Capt Wrstlng; Vrsty Wrstlr; CVC Lg Champ Wrstlng 89-90; Schl Tchr.

SHAFFER, BRIAN M; Hemet HS; Hemet, CA; (2); Church Yth Grp; Intrml JV Bsktbl; Hon Roll; Bus.

SHAFFER, NEIL; Modesto HS; Modesto, CA; (4); Church Yth Grp; Letterman Clb; Ski Clb; SADD; Ftbl; Score Keeper; Wt Lftg; Wrstlng; High Hon Roll; Hon Roll; CSF; U CO Boulder; Coroner.

SHAFIZADEH, JAHAN; Monte Vista HS; Alamo, CA; (4); French Clb; Yrbk; JV Trk; High Hon Roll; Hon Roll; U Of CA Davis; Chem Engr.

SHAH, AMY K; Trabuco Hills HS; Mission Viejo, CA; (2); 5/415; Cmnty Wkr; Spanish Clb; NHS; Mck Trl; Acad Dcthln.

SHAH, ANEESH S; Brea Olinda HS; Brea, CA; (1); 2/400; Intnl Clb; NFL; Quiz Bowl; Speech Tm; Rep Stu Cncl; JV Tennis; Cit Awd; High Hon Roll; Jr NHS; Prfct Atten Awd; Interact Club; CSF; Stu Exchng To Japan; Stanford; Med.

SHAH, ASHLEY I; San Rafael HS; San Rafael, CA; (2); 34/256; Var Tennis; High Hon Roll; CSF.

SHAH, DEEPA K; Central Union HS; El Centro, CA; (2); 1/692; Debate Tm; NFL; Service Clb; Speech Tm; High Hon Roll; Hon Roll; Lion Awd; Rotary Awd; Interact Clb; Chsn RYLA 90; Photo, Swmmng, Tnns, Fshn; Envrnmntl Clb; Qlfd St Spch Fnls; Attorney Mck Tl; Med.

SHAH, HOWARD H; Mission San Jose HS; Fremont, CA; (3); 50/430; Cmnty Wkr; Ed Nwsp; Phtg Lit Mag; Stu Cncl; JV Swmmng; High Hon Roll; High Hon Roll; French Clb; Math Tm; CASC; REACH Amer; DARE; Boy Scts Carer Explrs; Engrng.

SHAH, MELISSA; Quartz Hill HS; Quartz Hill, CA; (3); 20/725; Hosp Aide; JA; Spanish Clb; Co-Capt Drill Tm; DAR Awd; High Hon Roll; Hon Roll; Jr NHS; Pres Acad Fit Awd; Z-Club; Medicine.

SHAH, MICHAEL; Prospect HS; Campbell, CA; (3); 1/240; Am Leg Boys St; Debate Tm; Pres JA; Rep Jr Cls; VP Stu Cncl; Capt Var Crs Cntry; Var L Trk; High Hon Roll; NHS; Ntl Merit Ltr.

SHAH, MONA N; American HS; Fremont, CA; (2); 57/385; Cmnty Wkr; Var Trk; Cit Awd; Hon Roll; Natl Yth Ldrshp Cert Mrt; Young Explorers Clb; UC Davis; Med.

SHAH, NAJU N; Bonita HS; La Verne, CA; (2); SADD; Cit Awd; High Hon Roll; Hon Roll; CSF; Humants Clb; Med.

SHAH, NEEVAV V; Whitney HS; Cerritos, CA; (3); Cmnty Wkr; 4-H; JA; Letterman Clb; Varsity Clb; Co-Ed Nwsp; Var Capt Bsbl; Bsktbl; High Hon Roll; Pres Acad Fit Awd; UC Berkeley; Engrng.

SHAH, NIHAR N; Whitney HS; Cerritos, CA; (3); Drama Clb; JA; Key Clb; Spanish Clb; Cheerldng; Swmmng; High Hon Roll; Jr NHS; Ntl Merit SF; Water Polo; MIT; Math.

SHAH, PRANAV P; Culver City HS; Culver City, CA; (2); Church Yth Grp; Cit Awd; Hon Roll; U Of CA; Comp Sci.

SHAH, ROOPALI; Whitney HS; Cerritos, CA; (1); Dance Clb; Key Clb; Service Clb; Phtg Yrbk; Envrnmntl Activist PETA SACA IWC; U Of CA; Jrnslm.

SHAH, SANDIP K; Whitney HS; Cerritos, CA; (3); Boy Scts; Church Yth Grp; Key Clb; Library Aide; SADD; Varsity Clb; Ed Nwsp; JV Var Bsbl; High Hon Roll; Hon Roll; GATE; CSF; CJSF; UCI; Comp Sci.

SHAH, SANJEEV; Ganesha HS; Diamond Bar, CA; (3); 1/300; Cmnty Wkr; Computer Clb; Debate Tm; French Clb; Hosp Aide; Math Clb; Speech Tm; Off Soph Cls; Hist Jr Cls; Rep Sr Cls; UCLA; Pre-Med.

SHAH, SHALU; Alder JR HS; Rialto, CA; (2); Drill Tm; Yrbk; JV Cheerldng; Hon Roll; Pres Acad Fit Awd; CA Jnr Schlrshp Assoc; Partnershp Clb; UCS; Chld Psycht.

SHAH, SHAZIA; John F Kennedy HS; Granada Hills, CA; (4); 3/560; Church Yth Grp; Cmnty Wkr; Hosp Aide; Math Clb; Office Aide; Science Clb; Service Clb; Lit Mag; Rep Frsh Cls; JV Vllybl.

SHAH, SMRUTI M; Silver Creek HS; San Jose, CA; (4); 30/450; Sec Hosp Aide; Boy Scts; English Clb; Math Clb; Math Tm; Red Cross Aide; Spanish Clb; Rptr Yrbk; Treas Soph Cls; Stu Cncl; Acad Decath; Bdmntn Tm; CSF; Med.

SHAHA, LAURA J; Saint Joseph HS; Long Beach, CA; (3); Sec VP GAA; Ski Clb; Teachers Aide; Var Bsktbl; Capt Powder Puff Ftbl; JV Sftbl; Real Estate.

SHAHBAZ, SHAROL; Beyer HS; Modesto, CA; (3); Boy Scts; Key Clb; Varsity Clb; Off Ftbl; Off Wt Lftg; Off Hon Roll; Explor Medical Post; Med.

SHAHBAZIAN, ROY A; Foothill HS; Santa Ana, CA; (4); 34/350; Band; Jazz Band; Mrchg Band; Pep Band; School Musical; High Hon Roll; U Of CA Irvine; Math.

SHAHEEN, KELLIE L; Dublin HS; Dublin, CA; (4); 14/150; Cmnty Wkr; Red Cross Aide; VP Jr Cls; VP Sr Cls; Rep Stu Cncl; Var Socr; JV Sftbl; Var Swmmng; Var Tennis; High Hon Roll; Smith Book Awd 89; CSF Lifetime; Site Cncl & Acad Booster Cncl Rep; UC Davis; Physlgy.

SHAHRDAR, PARISSA; Notre Dame HS; Belmont, CA; (2); French Clb; Variety Show; High Hon Roll; Cert Awd Excllnce Frnch.

SHAHRIYARPOUR, SHAHRAM; Granada Hills HS; Northridge, CA; (2); Church Yth Grp; Church Choir; Rep Stu Cncl; Prfct Atten Awd; Pres Acad Fit Awd; Hnr Soc; Karate; UCLA.

SHAIKH, ABDUL; Lowell HS; San Francisco, CA; (3); Bus Mgmt.

SHAIKH, RIDVANA; Hamilton HS; Culver City, CA; (4); 18/500; Sec French Clb; Teachers Aide; High Hon Roll; Pres Acad Fit Awd; CSF Sealbearer; Bank Of Amer Achvt Awd; UC Riverside; Biomed Sci.

SHAIKH, SAHISTHA; Lowell HS; San Francisco, CA; (3); CSF; Regstry Treas; Chemathon; UC Berkeley; Comp Sci.

SHAIKH, SHOEB; Concord HS; Concord, CA; (4); Cmnty Wkr; Computer Clb; Debate Tm; English Clb; JA; Letterman Clb; Model UN; Spanish Clb; Varsity Clb; Yrbk; UC Davis; Engrng.

SHALTOUT, TAREK; Happy Valley Schl; Ojai, CA; (3); Band; Jazz Band; Diving; Swmmng; Wt Lftg; MED.

SHAMASH, UZI; Novato HS; Novato, CA; (2); Intrml Bsktbl; JV Ftbl; JV Socr; Law.

SHAMASUNDER, BHAVNA; Viewpoint Schl; West Hills, CA; (2); Drama Clb; Key Clb; School Musical; Yrbk; Lit Mag; Sec Soph Cls; JV Crs Cntry; Var Swmmng; Hon Roll; Schlr Athl Awd; Vet.

SHAMBOW, OLIVIA E; Coachella Valley HS; Thermal, CA; (2); Cmnty Wkr; JV Sftbl; Cit Awd; Hon Roll; Accntnt.

SHAMESON, ABRAHAM I; Carlmont HS; Belmont, CA; (4); 9/302; Band; Ntl Merit SF.

SHAMIEH, REEM; Diamond Bar HS; Diamond Bar, CA; (3); Pres Treas Church Yth Grp; Debate Tm; French Clb; Intnl Clb; Library Aide; Science Clb; Ed Nwsp; JV Bsktbl; High Hon Roll; Hon Roll; CSF; Engl.

SHAMIK, RYAN SIMS; Wasco Union HS; Wasco, CA; (3); Church Yth Grp; Kiwanis Awd; FHA; Teachers Aide; Varsity Clb; Bsktbl; Ftbl; Trk; Wt Lftg; High Hon Roll; Military Police Officer.

SHAMIYA, ANWAR S; S San Francisco HS; South San Francis, CA; (3); Math Clb; Ed Nwsp; Var Crs Cntry; Hon Roll; Ntl Merit Ltr; CA Schlrshp Fed; Pol Sci.

SHAMLO, MERCEDE; Santa Monica HS; Canoga Park, CA; (3); French Clb; Math Clb; Orch; JV Bsktbl; Jr Statesmen Of Amer; Amer Yth Symphony Orch; Music Awds; All St & All Southern Orch; CSSSA; UCLA; Med.

SHAMS, NAZANIN; Edison-Computech HS; Fresno, CA; (2); Model UN; JV Socr; JV Tennis; JV Vllybl; Mock Trial; Jr Met Clb; Hi-Deb; Bus.

SHAMSIAN, ASHKAN; Taft HS; Encino, CA; (2); Library Aide; Spanish Clb; Hon Roll; Pres Acad Fit Awd; CSF; USC; Med.

SHANAHAN, KEVIN F; Clovis West HS; Fresno, CA; (2); AFS; Ski Clb; Rep Frsh Cls; Rep Soph Cls; JV Bsbl; JV Socr; High Hon Roll; Hon Roll; CSF; Peer Cnslng; Bus.

SHANDIL, RAJAN; Victor Valley SR HS; Victorville, CA; (2); 1/602; AFS; Pres Key Clb; Quiz Bowl; Service Clb; Mrchg Band; Orch; Pep Band; Variety Show; Yrbk; High Hon Roll; CSF; Highest GPA Awd; Stanford U; Medcl.

SHANEFELT, DAWN T; Beaumont HS; Banning, CA; (2); 4-H; FBLA; Girl Scts; Varsity Clb; Sec Frsh Cls; Stu Cncl; Var Cheerldng; Var Score Keeper; JV Sftbl; JV Swmmng; Long Black ST Coll; Chld Psych.

SHANER, CHAD R; Rim Of The World HS; Crestline, CA; (2); Boy Scts; Church Yth Grp; Cmnty Wkr; Computer Clb; Spanish Clb; Band; Jazz Band; Mrchg Band; Pep Band; Hon Roll; Biola U; Physics.

SHANKS, MELISSA C; California HS; San Ramon, CA; (3); Cmnty Wkr; Dance Clb; Debate Tm; French Clb; Hosp Aide; JA; Ski Clb; Teachers Aide; VICA; Band; Rgnl Occptn Prgm Bus Mgnt & Rtl Mrchndsng Degree; UC Santa Barbara; Corp Law.

SHANKS, NAOMI O; Gompers Secondary HS; San Diego, CA; (4); Church Yth Grp; Quiz Bowl; Red Cross Aide; Service Clb; Rptr Nwsp; High Hon Roll; Hon Roll; Ntl Merit SF; Natl Bicntnnl Comptn 3rd Pl; Mock Trial; Banai Chldrns Cls Tchr; Prof Religious Studies.

SHANKS, SUSAN L; San Clemente HS; San Clemente, CA; (1); German Clb; Math Tm; Cit Awd; Hon Roll; CSF Club; Natl Lang Arts Olympiad Wnnr; Tennis; Stanford; Math.

SHANLEY, MATTHEW B; St Ignatius College Prep; San Francisco, CA; (2); Church Yth Grp; Cmnty Wkr; FCA; Intnl Clb; Speech Tm; JV Socr; Wt Lftg; UC Davis; Vet Med.

SHANNON, JENNIFER; Red Bluff Union HS; Red Bluff, CA; (2); Church Yth Grp; Service Clb; Hon Roll; Fri Nigh Tlive Actvts Chrprsn; Cal Poly SLO; Arch.

SHANNON, RICHARD B; Bullard HS; Fresno, CA; (1); Bsbl; Ftbl; Prfct Atten Awd; Enjoy Golf Tennis & Bsktbl; Collects Foreign Money.

SHANNON, WAADE; Pittsburg HS; Pittsburg, CA; (3); Church Yth Grp; Model UN; SADD; Chorus; Church Choir; Color Guard; School Play; Swmmng; Tennis; Bst Stu Schl; U Of MA; Drama.

SHAO, ESTHER S; Henry M Gunn SR HS; Los Altos Hills, CA; (4); 21/275; Church Yth Grp; French Clb; FBLA; Hosp Aide; Orch; School Musical; Rep Stu Cncl; French Hon Soc; Ntl Merit Ltr; Prvt Math Tutor; Math.

SHAPAZIAN, DAVID J; North HS; Bakersfield, CA; (3); 200/550; Church Yth Grp; Bsbl; Ftbl; Socr; Wt Lftg; Bakerfield Fire Dept Explrs; Fire Fighter.

SHAPIRA, SHARON; Birmingham HS; Calabasas, CA; (4); Cmnty Wkr; FBLA; Red Cross Aide; VP Speech Tm; Rep SADD; Chrmn Temple Yth Grp; Pres Stu Cncl; Var JV Cheerldng; Opt Clb Awd; Pres Acad Fit Awd; Vlntr; Comssnr Of Curriculum & Assemblies; Awd Wnnr; CA Yng Woman Of Yr; U CA Santa Barbara; Commnctns.

SHAPIRO, LINDSAY A; Dos Rublos HS; Goleta, CA; (2); 10/300; Church Yth Grp; Pep Clb; SADD; Orch; NHS; Natl JR Woman Power Santa Barbara Bowling Clb; Cngrssnl Schlr Rep CA Natl Yng Ldrs Conf; U Of CA Berkeley; Engl.

SHAPIRO, NATALIA; George Washington HS; San Francisco, CA; (2); Art Clb; Computer Clb; Dance Clb; Math Clb; Red Cross Aide; Speech Tm; Chorus; Vllybl; Hon Roll; Prfct Atten Awd; Cert Achvt Advncd Alg & Career Ed; Berkeley; Comp Prgmr.

SHAPIRO, SEVYA; Martin Luther King HS; Davis, CA; (3); Church Yth Grp; Chorus; Yth Substnc Abuse Comm; Paralgl.

SHAPLAND, AMY M; Modesto Christian HS; Modesto, CA; (4); #2 In Class; Teachers Aide; Var Bsktbl; Pres Acad Fit Awd; Rotary Awd; Val; Bank Of America Acvt Awd Liberal Arts; CA Schlrshp Federation Highest Hnr; Modest Jr Coll; Elem Schl Tchr.

SHARDINE, CATHERINE; El Capitan HS; Lakeside, CA; (4); 3/418; Church Yth Grp; Girl Scts; Var Capt Swmmng; Hon Roll; JV Wtrpolo; San Diego Imprl Cncl Inc Delg Grl Scts; Coach Awd Grls Swm Tm 89; U Of CA Santa Barbara; Hstry.

SHARER, CATHERINE A; Fremont HS; Sunnyvale, CA; (3); 8/408; Debate Tm; NFL; Speech Tm; JV Var Swmmng; Hon Roll; NHS; Ntl Merit Ltr; Stu Excng Trip; Mock Trial; Pre Med.

SHARIF, AZIMA Z; Banning HS; Banning, CA; (3); 4-H; Office Aide; Spanish Clb; Teachers Aide; Band; Chorus; Jazz Band; School Musical; Bsktbl; Powder Puff Ftbl; Black Club; Friday Night Live Club.

SHARIF, IMAH; Upland HS; Upland, CA; (2); Chess Clb; Computer Clb; Hon Roll; CA Schlrshp Found.

SHARIFF, NAJAH J; Whitney HS; Cerritos, CA; (4); Spanish Clb; Ed Yrbk; High Hon Roll; NHS; Val; Wn Publshng Cont CA St Long Beach; Tutor Yth Plus Litrcy Pgm; CSF; Claremont; Intrntl Reltns.

SHARKEY, JASON; Calvary Chaple HS; Santa Ana, CA; (2); Church Yth Grp; Ftbl; Vllybl; Hon Roll; Pres Acad Fit Awd; Yth Missions Trip Africa 89; Pro Ftbl.

SHARKEY, KENNY L; Savanna HS; Anaheim, CA; (3); Bsbl; Ftbl; Hon Roll; UCI; Lawenforcement.

SHARMA, PAWAN; Milpitas HS; Milpitas, CA; (2); 50/536; JV Trk; High Hon Roll; Comp Engr.

SHARMA, SHEETAL; Holy Names HS; Richmond, CA; (3); Church Yth Grp; Drama Clb; Office Aide; Acpl Chr; School Musical; School Play; Variety Show; Rptr Nwsp; Rep Frsh Cls; Rep VP Jr Cls; St Marys HS Productns Leading Roles; Choral Hnr Scty Holy Names; UCLA; Music.

SHARMA, VIVEK V; Los Alamitos HS; Los Alamitos, CA; (3); Boy Scts; Cmnty Wkr; Intnl Clb; Science Clb; Service Clb; Spanish Clb; SADD; Nwsp; JV Crs Cntry; JV Swmmng; JV Waterpolo Art-Drawing Surfing Bodysurfing; Indian Classical Music-Mridangam Musical Instrument.

SHAROU, DIANA S; Etiwanda HS; Alta Loma, CA; (3); Church Yth Grp; French Clb; ROTC; Rptr Yrbk; Hon Roll; Cal Poly Pomona; Arch.

SHARP, BRIANA; Redondo Union HS; Hermosa Bch, CA; (3); 40/400; Debate Tm; French Clb; NFL; Pep Clb; Speech Tm; JV Var Cheerldng; Cit Awd; Hon Roll; Ldr For Day; Cert Recgntn Engl Hnrs, Frnch; Ivy Chain; Graphic Art.

SHARP, CARMEN N; Oroville HS; Oroville, CA; (1); Church Yth Grp; Varsity Clb; Bsktbl; Capt Sftbl; Tennis; Hon Roll.

SHARP, CRYSTAL; Modesto HS; Modesto, CA; (3); Key Clb; Ski Clb; Color Guard; Gym; Trk; Acctnt.

SHARP, ERIC A; Sunny Hills HS; Fullerton, CA; (3); Church Yth Grp; Computer Clb; Intnl Clb; Spanish Clb; Var L Ftbl; Socr; Var L Trk; High Hon Roll; Youth/Govt.

SHARP, KEITH P; Redlands HS; Redlands, CA; (3); Teachers Aide; Var JV Ftbl.

SHARP, KENDRA; Lincoln HS; Stockton, CA; (3); Hon Roll; Cal Poly; Art.

SHARP, MARC D; Torrey Pines HS; Del Mar, CA; (2); 6/503; Treas Church Yth Grp; Cmnty Wkr; Scholastic Bowl; Church Choir; Hon Roll; CSF; Bio.

SHARP, MARNEY D; Sonora HS; Sonora, CA; (2); 35/400; Spanish Clb; High Hon Roll; Prfct Atten Awd.

SHARP, MATTHEW A; James Logan HS; Union City, CA; (2); Band; Jazz Band; Mrchg Band; Hon Roll; Mck Trl Outstndng Pre-Trl Attrny Awd; Close-Up; Outstndng Slst Awd Jazz Band; Stanford; Law.

SHARP, MISTY D; Elliot Education Center; Modesto, CA; (2); Church Yth Grp; Dance Clb; Drama Clb; German Clb; School Play; Stage Crew; Gym; Cit Awd; Orthdnsty.

SHARP, SUZANNE M; Porterville HS; Porterville, CA; (3); Art Clb; Rep Church Yth Grp; FBLA; Intnl Clb; Science Clb; Drill Tm; School Musical; JV Socr; Cit Awd; Hon Roll; 4th Pl Horse Show; Korean Heritage Camp; Good Morning Today Show Interview; CA ST U; Fshn Buyer.

SHARPE, BENJAMIN A; Kingsburg Joint Union HS; Kingsburg, CA; (2); Art Clb; Church Yth Grp; Letterman Clb; Math Clb; Mu Alpha Theta; Varsity Clb; Bsktbl; Ftbl; JV Trk; Wt Lftg; Var Ltrrmn 90; JV Track Capt; Rnnr-Up Soph Of Yr Var Bsktbl; Notre Dame; Psych.

SHARPE, MELISA; Le Lycee Francais HS; Los Angeles, CA; (4); Model UN; Phtg Yrbk; Var Sftbl; Hon Roll; Cal Poly San Luis Obispo; Arch.

SHARPE, SEF A; Oxnard HS; Oxnard, CA; (3); Letterman Clb; Stu Cncl; Var Bsbl; Var Bsktbl; JV Ftbl; Var Trk; Hon Roll; Yth Ldrshp Dev Smnr Pgm; UCLA; Engr.

SHARPLES, SARAH R; Rio Americano HS; Sacramento, CA; (3); Key Clb; Spanish Clb; Teachers Aide; Socr; Hon Roll; Engl Essay Awd; UC Santa Barbara.

SHARPNACK, ANNA; Maranatha HS; Pasadena, CA; (4); 1/100; Church Yth Grp; Cmnty Wkr; English Clb; 4-H; French Clb; German Clb; Sec Treas JCL; Teachers Aide; Varsity Clb; Band; Biola U; French Educ.

SHARRAH, JASON L; Nevada Union HS; Grass Valley, CA; (3); Band; Elks Awd; Hon Roll; Fire Dept & Rescue; Grass Vly Volunteer; CA ST U-Sacramento; Optomtrst.

SHARRAR, KELLY A; Buena Park HS; Brea, CA; (4); 16/350; Debate Tm; Key Clb; NFL; Speech Tm; Treas Jr Cls; Treas Sr Cls; Var Capt Swmmng; High Hon Roll; Kiwanis Awd; Masonic Awd; CA Schlrshp Fed Life & Seal Bearer; CA Yth Ctznshp Sem Pepperdine U; CA All-Star Water Polo Tm; CA Poly Tech U; Biochem.

SHASH, KHALID A; Westchester HS; Los Angeles, CA; (2); Bsktbl; Socr; Cit Awd; High Hon Roll; Prfct Atten Awd; UCLA; Med.

SHASKI, BRANDY; Palm Desert HS; Palm Desert, CA; (2); Cmnty Wkr; Treas French Clb; Var L Swmmng; Interact VP; Mock Trial; CA Schlrshp Fdrtn CSF.

SHATOS, KANDI; Rosamond HS; Rosamond, CA; (2); Church Yth Grp; Library Aide; Math Tm; Office Aide; Teachers Aide; Church Choir; JV Vllybl; Hon Roll; Ministry Workshop & Training; Child Psych.

SHATTUCK, LAURA J; Clovis West HS; Fresno, CA; (3); Drama Clb; French Clb; Hosp Aide; Ski Clb; Speech Tm; JV Bsktbl; Var Swmmng; AZ ST U.

SHAVER, BECKY; Brethren HS; Long Beach, CA; (3); Church Yth Grp; Math Tm; Yrbk; VP Frsh Cls; Stat Bsktbl; Var L Cheerldng; Var L Tennis; High Hon Roll; Pres Acad Fit Awd; CA Schlrshp Fed; Westmont; Bus.

SHAVER, KIMBERLY A; San Pasqual Acad; Loma Linda, CA; (4); 11/45; Church Yth Grp; Cmnty Wkr; Library Aide; Office Aide; Teachers Aide; Chorus; Church Choir; Rptr Yrbk; Publshd Poet Natl Libry Of Poetry; Loma Linda U; Teach Bio.

SHAVER, KRISTLYN; Paradise HS; Paradise, CA; (4); Library Aide; Service Clb; School Play; JV Bsktbl; Var Cheerldng; Powder Puff Ftbl; Var Swmmng; Cit Awd; Hon Roll; Prfct Atten Awd; Mascot 87-88; Norcal Swimming Chmpnshp 89; Swim Instructor 86-89; Butte CC; Child Dvlpmnt.

SHAVIFI, SOHEIL; University HS; Irvine, CA; (2); Hosp Aide; JV Bsktbl; JV Wt Lftg; Cit Awd; High Hon Roll; Hon Roll; Prfct Atten Awd; Bio.

SHAW, CHRISTOPHER D; Rim Of The World HS; Running Springs, CA; (3); Sec Jr Cls; VP Stu Cncl; Var Bsbl; Var Ftbl; Var Wrstlng.

SHAW, CHRISTY A; Alverno HS; South Pasadena, CA; (2); 30/70; Science Clb; Chorus; Off Soph Cls; Bsktbl; Vllybl; Most Dedicated Player Bsktbl; Sci Clb Awd; Chorus Awd; Aeronaut Engr.

SHAW, EUDEAN; Crescenta Valley HS; La Crescenta, CA; (4); 3/360; French Clb; Key Clb; Letterman Clb; Rep Mu Alpha Theta; Pres Science Clb; Teachers Aide; Ed Lit Mag; NHS; Ntl Merit Ltr; Pres Acad Fit Awd; Water Polo; UC Berkeley; Molecular Bio.

SHAW, JAMIE; Ramona HS; Ramona, CA; (2); 24/345; Spanish Clb; Rep Soph Cls; JV Cheerldng; Var Gym; SDSU; Bus.

SHAW, JASON; St Bonaventure HS; Ventura, CA; (3); JV Var Ftbl; Hon Roll; CSF; Gntc Engr.

SHAW, JENNIFER A; Lemoore Union HS; Lemoore, CA; (4); 8/269; Church Yth Grp; Intnl Clb; Spanish Clb; SADD; Rptr Nwsp; Var Gym; Var Swmmng; Rotary Awd; U Of The Pacific; Bus.

SHAW, JENNIFER L; Riverside Christian HS; Riverside, CA; (3); Rptr Nwsp; Yrbk; Vllybl; Hon Roll; Christ Coll Irvine; Tchr.

SHAW, JENNIFER L; Trabuco Hills HS; Rancho Sante Fe, CA; (2); AFS; Cmnty Wkr; Treas French Clb; Temple Yth Grp; Phtg Ed Yrbk; JV Socr; JV Tennis; High Hon Roll; Hon Roll; Pres Acad Fit Awd; Orange Cnty Acad Decthln Tm; 2nd Pl Scl Stds Lit; Orgnzr Music Fstvl/Ltr Wrtng Cmpgn Save Canyon.

SHAW, JUSTIN L; Loyalton HS; Loyalton, CA; (3); 4-H; FBLA; FFA; JA; Letterman Clb; Office Aide; Spanish Clb; SADD; Teachers Aide; Yrbk.

SHAW, KALAZA; Saint Michaels HS; Inglewood, CA; (1); Church Yth Grp; GAA; School Musical; School Play; Var Trk; Hon Roll; Peer Cnslng; Drill Tm; U Of Honolulu; Crmnl Justc.

SHAW, KARI L; Mission Viejo HS; Mission Viejo, CA; (2); Church Yth Grp; Rep Frsh Cls; Cheerldng; Trk; Spanish NHS; Girls Leag Corrspndng Sec; Yth Ending Hunger; UC Santa Barbara; Law.

SHAW, KERRIE A; Lindsay HS; Lindsay, CA; (2); GAA; Varsity Clb; Powder Puff Ftbl; Var Sftbl; JV Vllybl; Wt Lftg; Hon Roll; Ntrl Hlprs; Schl Cnslng.

SHAW, LION; Rim Of The World HS; Crestline, CA; (3); Ftbl; Golf; Trk; Hon Roll.

SHAW, MATTHEW N; Carpinteria HS; Carpinteria, CA; (2); Cmnty Wkr; JV Bsbl; JV Bsktbl; JV Ftbl; CA Poly San Luis; Bus.

SHAW, MAUREEN; South San Francisco HS; South San Francis, CA; (3); Cmnty Wkr; FBLA; Teachers Aide; Cit Awd; Prfct Atten Awd; UC Davis; Pharmacist.

SHAW, MICHELLE L; River City HS; W Sacramento, CA; (1); Church Yth Grp; Hosp Aide; Law.

SHAW, MURIEL; Independence HS; San Jose, CA; (3); 50/750; Church Yth Grp; Cmnty Wkr; Dance Clb; Drama Clb; Science Clb; Church Choir; Mrchg Band; Cheerldng; High Hon Roll; Hon Roll; Black Stu Union; Chrch Yth Ushr; Tuskegee U; Teacher.

SHAW, NICOLE R; Fillmore HS; Fillmore, CA; (3); SADD; Rep Jr Cls; Stat Bsktbl; Var Crs Cntry; Var Trk; Hon Roll; CSF Secy; Young Life.

SHAW, REGINA; Samuel F B Morse HS; San Diego, CA; (1); Church Yth Grp; Dance Clb; Pep Clb; Church Choir; Variety Show; Off Frsh Cls; Court Rprtr.

SHAW, SHARALYN; Brethren HS; Long Beach, CA; (1); 4/95; Church Yth Grp; Chorus; Cit Awd; Hon Roll; Chrch Drama Tm; Teacher.

SHAW, STEPHEN; Capital Christian HS; Sacramento, CA; (4); 1/40; Aud/Vis; Church Yth Grp; Teachers Aide; Stage Crew; Yrbk; JV Intrml Crs Cntry; JV Fld Hcky; Var Ftbl; JV Socr; Hon Roll; Aerontcl Engrng.

SHAW, TANIA M; Santa Barbara HS; Santa Barbara, CA; (2); 1/500; Hosp Aide; Mrchg Band; Var Tennis; Hon Roll; NHS; Music & Art Cnsrvtry Santa Barb Piano; Stu Ambssdr Soviet Union.

SHAY, MASON; Lakewood HS; Lakewood, CA; (1); Ski Clb; Cit Awd; High Hon Roll; Hon Roll; Sci.

SHAYESTEH, ABDI R; San Marcos HS; La Costa, CA; (2); Key Clb; Quiz Bowl; VICA; JV Ftbl; Var Wrstlng; High Hon Roll; Lion Awd; Church Yth Grp; Dance Clb; Debate Tm; Schl Stu Spkrs Cntst Wnnr 90; Spkr CSF Awds 90; Stanford U; Intl Law.

SHAYKEVICH, ALEX; Terra Nova HS; Pacifica, CA; (4); 4/219; Am Leg Boys St; Computer Clb; Co-Ed Yrbk; Tennis; Pres Schlr; Sal; Piano; Saxophone; Vllybl; UC Berkeley; Chem Engr.

SHEA, CARLA R; Arcata HS; Arcata, CA; (1); Band; Mrchg Band; Pep Band; Variety Show; High Hon Roll; Rotary Awd; Active Amer Lgn Aux Jrs Pres; Humboldt ST U; Vet Med.

SHEA, PATRICIA M; San Leandro HS; San Leandro, CA; (3); 5/361; Cmnty Wkr; Varsity Clb; Var Tennis; High Hon Roll; Ntl Merit SF; CA Schlrshp Fed Presaccelerated HS Stus Pgm UC Berkeley.

SHEALY, WILSON T; Novato HS; Novato, CA; (3); Church Yth Grp; Debate Tm; ROTC; Chorus; Drill Tm; Hon Roll; Med.

SHEAN, ERYNN; Ernest Righetti HS; Orcutt, CA; (1); Church Yth Grp; Cheerldng; JV Sftbl; High Hon Roll; Hon Roll; JR Statesmen Of Amer.

SHEAR, ANTHONY; Balboa HS; San Francisco, CA; (4); Pres French Clb; Phtg Yrbk; Var Tennis; High Hon Roll; Vrsty Fencng Team Capt; JR Statesmn Assn; CSF; Peer Cnslr; Yth Ct Attrng; Cmnty Svc Prvntn Child Abuse; Yale U; Law.

SHEARER, DAVID R; Santa Margarita HS; Mission Viejo, CA; (3); Cmnty Wkr; Letterman Clb; Ski Clb; Varsity Clb; Rep Sr Cls; Pres Stu Cncl; Var Capt Bsktbl; Var Capt Ftbl; Var Trk; High Hon Roll; Bkstbl & Ftbl Stu Athl Of Yr 87-89; Outstndng Engl & Hnr Chem Stu; Pre-Med.

SHEARS, MATTHEW W; Saddleback HS; Santa Ana, CA; (3); Capt Var Ftbl; JV Trk; Var Wt Lftg; JV Wrstlng; Acctnt.

SHECTMAN, SARAH; Flintridge Preparatory HS; Altadena, CA; (3); Sec French Clb; Girl Scts; Service Clb; School Musical; School Play; French Hon Soc; Hon Roll; Jr NHS; NHS; Ntl Merit Ltr; GS Yth Advsr Brd Dir Sierra Modres Girl; GS Cncl Gold Awd; Bus.

SHEDRIN, RENA; Branham HS; San Jose, CA; (2); 68/280; SADD; Temple Yth Grp; JV Swmmng; Peer Counsling; English.

SHEEHAN, JENNIFER L; Bella Vista HS; Fair Oaks, CA; (2); 6/412; Church Yth Grp; Cmnty Wkr; Cit Awd; Kiwanis Awd; Prfct Atten Awd; Spanish NHS; Activity Dir Friday Night Live; 1st Pl Cty Typg Cont; Play Piano; CA Polytechnic ST U; Arch.

SHEEHY, TIMOTHY N; Saint Ignatius College Prep; San Francisco, CA; (2); Yrbk; JV Tennis; Hon Roll.

SHEEKS, PAMELA C; Mt Carmel HS; San Diego, CA; (4); 32/730; Aud/Vis; Cmnty Wkr; Intnl Clb; Service Clb; VP Jr Cls; Hist Sr Cls; Var JV Bsktbl; Office Aide; Teachers Aide; Var JV Bsktbl; Eclby Clb; Amnsty Intl; CSF; Acad Leag; U Of CA San Diego; Bio.

SHEEREN, TODD; Bear River HS; Grass Valley, CA; (3); Drama Clb; Ski Clb; Variety Show; High Hon Roll; Ski Team; Super Comptn Actor Awd; Schlr Athl Awd; San Diego ST Coll; Actor.

SHEETS, TINA; Soquel HS; Scotts Valley, CA; (3); 28/400; Drama Clb; Girl Scts; Ski Clb; Rep Soph Cls; Cheerldng; Gym; Trk; Vllybl; Hon Roll; Stanford; Med.

SHEETS, TROY M; Poway HS; San Diego, CA; (3); Pr Cnslng Clb; CARED; Just Say No Clb; Amer Schlrshp Fed; Engrng.

SHEHATA, MICHAEL; Bishop Amat HS; W Covina, CA; (4); 2/400; Drama Clb; Office Aide; Red Cross Aide; Science Clb; Ski Clb; Varsity Clb; School Play; Off Soph Cls; Off Jr Cls; Stu Cncl; 1st Hnrs Comp Sci & Math; UCLA; Aerospc Engrng.

SHEILS, COLLEEN M; Poway HS; San Diego, CA; (1); Church Yth Grp; Socr; JV Cmnty Wkr; High Hon Roll.

SHEIN, KAESIA; Bakersfield HS; Bakersfield, CA; (2); Dance Clb; Hon Roll; Phileo-1st Treas/VP; Gftd/Tlntd Ed; Math.

SHEK, SELINA; Lowell HS; San Francisco, CA; (2); Teachers Aide; Red Cross Clb; Bio Clb; Pre-Med Clb; Chinese Schl Grad; Law.

SHEKLIAN, LISA E; Bullard HS; Fresno, CA; (1); Actress.

SHELDAHL, ANDY A; El Camino HS; Oceanside, CA; (3); 19/364; Church Yth Grp; High Hon Roll; JV L Bsbl; JV L Bsktbl; Frosh Soc Stud Stu Of Yr; Phrmcy.

SHELDON, JULI; Morro Bay HS; Morro Bay, CA; (4); 1/180; AFS; Chess Clb; Key Clb; Treas SADD; High Hon Roll; Kiwanis Awd; Pres Acad Fit Awd; Val; Acad Decthln 1st Pl Intrvws; CA Schlrshp Fed Lf; CA Polytech ST; Comp Engr.

SHELDON, KATHERINE A; Boron HS; North Edwards, CA; (2); Art Clb; FHA; Math Tm; Teachers Aide; Flag Corp; JV Bsktbl; JV Trk; JV Var Vllybl; Hon Roll; Antelope Vly Coll; Med.

SHELLEN, CHRISTINA D; El Camino Real HS; Woodland Hills, CA; (4); 88/575; SADD; Teachers Aide; Thesps; Hist Chorus; School Musical; Rep Frsh Cls; Hon Roll; Pres Acad Fit Awd; Acad Decathlon; U Southern CA; Cinema-TV.

SHELLEY, JASON P; Vallejo SR HS; Vallejo, CA; (2); Office Aide; SADD; Teachers Aide; Var Bsbl; Var Bsktbl; Var Ftbl; Var Trk; Cit Awd; Hon Roll.

SHELLEY, MONICA E; Saint Francis HS; Mountain View, CA; (2); 22/356; Varsity Clb; Var Crs Cntry; Var Trk; High Hon Roll; CSF; Shakespeare Clb Brd Drctrs; Child Care/Dvlpmnt.

SHELLHAMER, JENNIFER S; Mira Mesa HS; San Diego, CA; (2); Church Yth Grp; Model UN; Science Clb; Spanish Clb; Hon Roll; Pres Acad Fit Awd; PLNC; Molecular Bio.

SHELLMAN, ALISON L; Pioneer HS; San Jose, CA; (2); Socr; Swmmng; Trk; Hon Roll; Scr MVP; Scr 1st Tm All Leag; Scr Bst Ofnsv Plyr; Meteorlgy.

SHELTON, AMBER D; Ukiah HS; Ukiah, CA; (2); 324/554; Cmnty Wkr; Teachers Aide; Hon Roll; Intl Ordr Jobs Dghtrs Bethel 106; Dominican Coll; Hstry Teacher.

SHELTON, DANIEL K; Oakdale HS; Oakdale, CA; (3); 63/224; Church Yth Grp; Teachers Aide; Band; Jazz Band; Mrchg Band; Orch; Pep Band; School Play; Swing Chorus; JV Bsktbl; Otstndng Jazz Band 89-90; Modesto Band Of Stanislaus Cnty; Cmmnty Orch Prod Of Handels Messiah; U Of Pacific; Music Teacher.

SHEN, ANDREW H; Chaminade College Prep; Van Nuys, CA; (3); Church Yth Grp; Hosp Aide; Model UN; Science Clb; Cit Awd; High Hon Roll; Pres Acad Fit Awd; 1st & 3rd Pl LA Cnty Sci Fair; 3rd Pl CA St Sci Fair; Best Spkr & Evaluator Toastmstrs Intl; UCLA; Med.

SHEN, ANTHONY W; Miramonte HS; Moraga, CA; (4); 2/280; Cmnty Wkr; Debate Tm; JCL; NFL; Pres Science Clb; Speech Tm; Var Diving; Hon Roll; Ntl Merit SF; Rotary Awd; Stanford U; Science.

SHEN, BEN; Buena Park HS; La Palma, CA; (3); Off Aud/Vis; Chess Clb; Cmnty Wkr; Computer Clb; Dance Clb; 4-H; Pres Key Clb; Math Clb; Red Cross Aide; VP Stu Cncl; Asian Club; Hspnc Intl Club; Electrnc Engrng.

SHEN, CALEB Y; Manteca HS; Manteca, CA; (2); 1/420; Church Yth Grp; VICA; JV Crs Cntry; JV Ftbl; Stat Swmmng; Var Wrstlng; High Hon Roll; CSF; Arch.

SHEN, CHRISTINE; Eagle Rock HS; Los Angeles, CA; (2); Key Clb; Scholastic Bowl; Acpl Chr; Yrbk; Hon Roll; Berkeley; Medcl.

SHEN, DORIS H; Fountain Valley HS; Huntington Beach, CA; (3); Office Aide; Red Cross Aide; Pres Science Clb; Orch; School Musical; Stat JV Swmmng; High Hon Roll; Ntl Merit SF; Co-Fndr/Earth PALS Assoc 89 VP; Rep 87 & 88, 89 Brd Mem CSF; Prjct Litry US Actvts Chrprsn 90; Envrnmntl Engr.

SHEN, FRANKLYN J; Village Christian HS; Los Angeles, CA; (4); Pres Church Yth Grp; Math Clb; Mu Alpha Theta; Spanish Clb; Church Choir; Jazz Band; Mrchg Band; JV Bsktbl; Var Ftbl; Jazz Band Awd; Most Imprvd Bsktbl Player; USC & ACSI Hnr Band; U Southern CA; Bus Admin.

SHEN, I-SU J; Alhambra HS; Alhambra, CA; (3); Computer Clb; Service Clb; Gldn St Exm Hnrs Alg; Gldn St Exm Hgh Hnrs Geom; UCLA; Electronics Engrng.

SHEN, IRENE H; Los Altos HS; Hacienda Hts, CA; (2); Art Clb; Intnl Clb; JV Swmmng; High Hon Roll; PETA; Greenpeace; SAYAR; Dist Schlr; Keywanettes Club; Pomona Coll Claremont; Psycht.

SHEN, JULIE; Gretchen Whitney HS; Cerritos, CA; (4); Art Clb; French Clb; Key Clb; Band; Mrchg Band; Orch; Nwsp; Lit Mag; Pres Acad Fit Awd; CSF Sealbearer; Natl Merit Schlr; Chinese Clb; CA ST Polytech U-Pomona; Arch.

SHEN, LIMING; J E Mc Ateer HS; San Francisco, CA; (3); Red Cross Aide; Teachers Aide; Vllybl; Chinese Clb; Nrsng.

SHEN, MICHAEL; Etiwanda HS; Diamond Bar, CA; (2); French Clb; Wt Lftg; JV Wrstlng; Hon Roll.

SHEN, MOLLY; Esperanza HS; Yorba Linda, CA; (2); Treas Intnl Clb; JV Bsktbl; Var Sftbl; Var Tennis; High Hon Roll; NHS; CSF.

SHEN, PETER H; Sunny Hills HS; Fullerton, CA; (1); Chess Clb; Computer Clb; French Clb; High Hon Roll; Prfct Atten Awd; Rotary Awd.

SHEN, REBECCA; Torrey Pines HS; Solana Beach, CA; (4); 1/430; Church Yth Grp; French Clb; Math Tm; Church Choir; Ed Lit Mag; JV Fld Hcky; Hon Roll; Ntl Merit Schol; Val; JV/V Acad-County Silver Overall; CSF; Harvard; Physics.

SHEN, SHEREE; Whitney HS; Cerritos, CA; (1); Art Clb; Church Yth Grp; Drama Clb; Color Guard; High Hon Roll; Pres Acad Fit Awd; CA Jr Schlrshp Fndtn; SETA.

SHEN, VICKY H; Cerritos HS; Cerritos, CA; (2); JCL; Math Clb; Hon Roll; Bus Admin.

SHENK, SUZANNA L; Orange Glen HS; Escondido, CA; (3); 22/458; Church Yth Grp; Quiz Bowl; Pres Spanish Clb; Church Choir; Frgn Lang Stu Yr; Southern Methodist U; Spanish.

SHENSKY, CYNTHIA; Dana Hills HS; Laguna Niguel, CA; (4); 43/550; Key Clb; Capt Pep Clb; Red Cross Aide; Ski Clb; Spanish Clb; SADD; Drill Tm; Off Sr Cls; Stu Cncl; Capt Var Cheerldng; Keywanettes; Jnr Statesmn America; Pepperdine U; Sprts Med.

SHEPARD, CHAD M; Grossmont HS; La Mesa, CA; (4); Cmnty Wkr; Var Swmmng; Wt Lftg; Pres Acad Fit Awd; St Schlr; Var Water Polo; CSF; Daisy Chain; San Fransisco ST; Acctnt.

SHEPARD, JENNIFER M; Independence HS; San Jose, CA; (3); 38/750; Cmnty Wkr; Math Tm; Pep Clb; Science Clb; Service Clb; Pres Spanish Clb; Speech Tm; SADD; School Musical; High Hon Roll; San Jose Mayors Yth Ldrshp Conf-Rep; CSF-OFCR/Activities Coordntr; Womens Hstry Month Coordntr 90; Psych.

SHEPARD, JEREMY D; James Madison HS; San Diego, CA; (3); Drama Clb; Latin Clb; Math Tm; Pres Soph Cls; Var Bsbl; JV Capt Ftbl; Powder Puff Ftbl; JV Var Wrstlng; Hon Roll; Top Hnrs Golden St Exam Alg & Geom; SHARE; Civil Engrg.

SHEPARD, LAURIE; Harbor HS; Scotts Valley, CA; (4); 8/250; Bus Profs of Am; Cmnty Wkr; GAA; SADD; Varsity Clb; Sec Treas Stu Cncl; Var JV Socr; JV Tennis; Var Trk; High Hon Roll; Bus Deptmntl Hnrs; Bank America 2nd Pl Appld Arts; UC San Diego; Bus.

SHEPARD, SEAN L; Fairfax HS; Los Angeles, CA; (2); Boy Scts; Church Yth Grp; Computer Clb; FCA; Church Choir; Prfct Atten Awd; Natl Sor Of Phi Delta Kappa; Church Chr, Yth Usher Bd; Jr Deacon, Church Bsktbl; Grambling; Bus.

SHEPARD, TA SHAUNA; San Pedro HS; Los Angeles, CA; (2); Drama Clb; Pep Clb; Speech Tm; Church Choir; School Play; JV Bsktbl; JV Sftbl; Var Trk; JV Vllybl; Intrml Wt Lftg; Law.

SHEPERD, MARIANNE; Poway HS; Poway, CA; (2); Cmnty Wkr; Letterman Clb; Varsity Clb; Gym; Swmmng; High Hon Roll; Hon Roll; Jr NHS; Kiwanis Awd; Pres Acad Fit Awd; Phys Thrpy.

SHEPHARD, APRIL; Carlmont HS; Belmont, CA; (4); Drama Clb; French Clb; SADD; Teachers Aide; Chorus; Variety Show; Yrbk; Off Sr Cls; Hon Roll; Pres Acad Fit Awd; Math Awd Excllnc; Smfnlst Teen Mag Grt Mdl Search Cal Grant B; OH U; Fshn Mrchndsng.

SHEPHARD, LATASHA R; Fillmore HS; Fillmore, CA; (1); Bus Profs of Am; Church Yth Grp; FBLA; Science Clb; Spanish Clb; SADD; Teachers Aide; Temple Yth Grp; Cit Awd; Hon Roll; USBC.

SHEPHERD, ALYSON; Poway HS; Poway, CA; (1); Hon Roll; US Pony Club; West Pony Club Chmpnshps 1st Pl Vet & Stable Mgmt Knwldg; UC Davis; Vet.

SHEPHERD, CHRISTOPHER Y; John F Kennedy HS; Sacramento, CA; (3); AFS; Math Clb; Math Tm; Spanish Clb; Speech Tm; Crs Cntry; Trk; Hon Roll; Ntl Merit Ltr; Acad Decathelon; CA Inst Tech SSSSP Pgm.

SHEPHERD, EARL B; Don Bosco Technical Inst; Whittier, CA; (3); Art Clb; Scholastic Bowl; Vllybl; Hon Roll; Ntl Merit Ltr; Vandenberg Art Show 1st & 2nd Pl Wnnr 87; Whittier Tnns Club 90; 1st Pl Rio Hondo Coll Tech DWG Cmptn; Harvard Mudd Coll; Aeronautics.

SHEPHERD, ISAAC N; Anderson Union HS; Redding, CA; (4); Boy Scts; Cmnty Wkr; Library Aide; Math Tm; Teachers Aide; L Mgr Ftbl; L Var Mgr(s); Score Keeper; Swmmng; L Var Trk; Goldn St Exam Geom Hnr 87-88; Ordr Of Arrw; Certfd Scuba Divng, Lifesavng, WSI & CPR 89; Cal Poly; Engrng.

SHEPHERD, JENNIFER D; Hesperia HS; Hesperia, CA; (2); Drill Tm; High Hon Roll; Hon Roll; CA Schlstc Fed; Law.

SHEPHERD, TAMARA L; East Bakersfield HS; Bakersfield, CA; (3); Sec VP Drama Clb; Pres Thesps; Chorus; School Musical; School Play; Stage Crew; Hon Roll; Kiwanis Awd; Kern Kwns Spnsr Yng Wmn Yr Pgnt Ftnss Awd; Thtre.

SHEPHERD, WADE; Los Alamitos HS; Los Alamitos, CA; (3); Boy Scts; Chess Clb; Church Yth Grp; German Clb; Science Clb; Hon Roll; Chem Engrng.

SHER, JENNIFER K; El Toro HS; El Toro, CA; (3); 43/481; GAA; Letterman Clb; Temple Yth Grp; Varsity Clb; Variety Show; JV Socr; Var Tennis; Hon Roll; Earth Sci Excllnc Awd; CSF; Girls Leag; Psych.

SHERBETAJIAN, JACK G; Don Bosco Technical Inst; Alhambra, CA; (3); Tennis; Hon Roll; NHS; Water Polo Tm; Spanish Awd 1st Pl; Awds Of Acad Excel; UCLA.

SHERBETDJIAN, JACK GEORGE; Don Bosco Technical Inst; Alhambra, CA; (3); Tennis; High Hon Roll; Hon Roll; NHS; Water Polo; 1st Pl Span Stu Of Yr; Outstndng Acad Classes Achvt Awds; UCLA; Elect Engrng.

SHEREDY, KIMBERLY A; Bonita Vista HS; Bonita, CA; (1); 16/533; Model UN; Office Aide; Cit Awd; Hon Roll; UCSD.

SHERER, WENDY L; Lompoc HS; Lompoc, CA; (2); Church Yth Grp; 4-H; FBLA; Library Aide; Sec SADD; 4-H Awd; High Hon Roll; Fshn Dsgng; Chld Psych.

SHERGILL, DAVY S; Oakridge HS; El Dorado Hills, CA; (3); 25/275; Art Clb; Variety Show; Lit Mag; High Hon Roll; Hon Roll; Acad Lttr; UC Sacramento; Bus Admin.

SHERGILL, LOVEJIT K; Turlock HS; Turlock, CA; (2); AFS; Church Yth Grp; Cmnty Wkr; FBLA; Hosp Aide; Key Clb; Math Tm; Science Clb; Teachers Aide; Cit Awd; Black Stu Union; Indian Club; Amnsty Intnl; Sacramento ST U; Ed.

SHERIDAN, BHIMA S; Las Lomas HS; Lafayette, CA; (3); Treas Church Yth Grp; Cmnty Wkr; Spanish Clb; SADD; Teachers Aide; High Hon Roll; Hon Roll; Peer Tutoring Math & Span; Vol Eduador Amigos De Las Amer 90; Bwlng Leag; Engr.

SHERIDAN, LORI A; Arcadia HS; Arcadia, CA; (3); 29/639; Office Aide; Teachers Aide; Chorus; Flag Corp; JV Vllybl; High Hon Roll; Hon Roll; Jr NHS; NHS; Pres Acad Fit Awd; BUS.

SHERIDAN, TARA; Cajon HS; San Bernardino, CA; (4); 12/360; Am Leg Aux Girls St; Cmnty Wkr; Service Clb; Spanish Clb; JV Swmmng; JV Var Vllybl; CSA Pres; CA Citizen Bee; Peer Cnslr; Humanities.

SHERIFF, STEVEN; Silver Valley HS; Newberry Spgs, CA; (2); Key Clb; Spanish Clb; Teachers Aide; Band; Hon Roll; Band Awd Prfct Atten & Prfmnce Concerts; NASA.

SHERLOCK, BRYAN J; Los Amigos HS; Fountain Valley, CA; (3); Boy Scts; Service Clb; Spanish Clb; Teachers Aide; Off Sr Cls; Stu Cncl; Vllybl; Wt Lftg; Hon Roll; UCSB; Bus Mgmt.

SHERLOCK, JASON E; Buena HS; Ventura, CA; (1); Boy Scts; Church Yth Grp; Church Choir; Hon Roll; Opt Clb Awd.

SHERMAN, CELESTE; Ramona HS; Riverside, CA; (2); 22/460; Church Yth Grp; French Clb; Pep Clb; Church Choir; Rptr Nwsp; Jr Cls; Cheerldng; Swmmng; Vllybl; CSF; Piano; Brdcst Jrnlsm.

SHERMAN, CORRIE; Bonita Vista HS; Chula Vista, CA; (2); Cit Awd; Yale; Med.

SHERMAN, DARRIS E; Francis Parker HS; San Diego, CA; (4); 1/58; Boy Scts; Cmnty Wkr; Intnl Clb; Science Clb; Spanish Clb; SADD; Ed Nwsp; Rep Stu Cncl; Var Trk; Var Vllybl.

SHERMAN, DOUGLAS RONALD; Lutheran HS; La Mirada, CA; (3); Boy Scts; Band; Chorus; Jazz Band; Pep Band; School Musical; Var L Wrstlng; Hon Roll; Explorer Ldrshp Awd 2 Time Wnnr; Eagle Scout; Bus.

SHERMAN, ERICA; Mercy HS; Red Bluff, CA; (4); 3/28; Church Yth Grp; Sec Key Clb; Model UN; Capt SADD; Band; Church Choir; School Play; Stage Crew; Ed Yrbk; Stu Cncl; St Marys Coll CA; Integral Pgm.

SHERMAN, JENNIFER; Del Oro HS; Loomis, CA; (3); 34/250; Cmnty Wkr; GAA; Office Aide; Pep Clb; Chorus; Yrbk; JV Var Vllybl; Var Cheerldng; Var Sftbl; JV Var Vllybl; Culture Clb; MVP-SFTBL-89 & 90; Bee Prep Of Wk 90; All Metro Team Sacto Bee/Sacto Nion 90; Sftbl Natls; U Of OK; Law Enforcemnt.

SHERMAN, JENNIFER M; Hilmar JR/Sr HS; Hilmar, CA; (3); AFS; 4-H; Ski Clb; SADD; Rptr Nwsp; JV Bsktbl; Var Powder Puff Ftbl; JV Score Keeper; JV Vllybl; Cit Awd; Dancing Lessions; Ag.

SHERMAN, JESSE Z; Yreka HS; Montague, CA; (3); 15/180; Drama Clb; Library Aide; Ski Clb; Spanish Clb; School Musical; School Play; Ed Nwsp; Yrbk; Sec Treas Sr Cls; JV Ftbl; CA St Acad Hnr Soc; Comp Sci.

SHERMAN, KRISTEN E; Serrano HS; Wrightwood, CA; (2); Off FFA; Var Color Guard; Var Drill Tm; Treas Soph Cls; Hon Roll; FFA Awds; Entmlgy Tm; Ldrshp & Dpndability Awd; CA Poly; Zoology.

SHERMAN, KRISTEN P; Kings Christian HS; Riverdale, CA; (2); 3/17; Church Yth Grp; Drama Clb; Band; Chorus; Yrbk; Var Sftbl; High Hon Roll; Hon Roll; CSF; Baylor U; Law.

SHERMAN, METRALANETTE D; Barstow HS; Barstow, CA; (3); French Clb; Office Aide; Chorus; Church Choir; School Musical; Hon Roll; BSU VP; Howard U; Law.

SHERMAN, THOMAS P; Norco SR HS; Corona, CA; (3); 9/400; Am Leg Boys St; Boy Scts; Church Yth Grp; Model UN; Pep Clb; Scholastic Bowl; Band; Jazz Band; Variety Show; Ftbl; Prin Awd; Mock Trial; Law.

SHERMEKA, THOMAS; East Bakersfield HS; Bakersfield, CA; (3); Trk; Hon Roll; Black Stu Unity; Outside Rlgis Invlvmnt; Fresno ST U; Bus.

SHERRATT, JENNIFER L; Alameda HS; Alameda, CA; (2); 5/290; Church Yth Grp; Rep Frsh Cls; Rep Soph Cls; Var Pom Pon; High Hon Roll; Chldrns Hosp Aux Grp; UC Davis; Bus.

SHERRER, MYESHA N; Inglewood HS; Inglewood, CA; (2); Dance Clb; German Clb; Math Clb; Cit Awd; Hon Roll; Marina Sheriffrs Dept Explorer; Accntng.

SHERRILL, JENNY R; Norte Vista HS; Riverside, CA; (2); Cmnty Wkr; Hosp Aide; ROTC; SADD; Wt Lftg; DAR Awd; Hon Roll; Prfct Atten Awd; JROTC Super Cadet, Cadet Challenge; DIA Excllnc; UCLA; Safety Inspection.

SHERRON, MUHAMMAD K; Arlington HS; San Bernardio, CA; (3); Cmnty Wkr; ROTC; Special Olympics; NM Military Inst; Engrng.

SHERRY, CHRISTOPHER J; Mills HS; Millbrae, CA; (4); Boy Scts; Chess Clb; Debate Tm; Drama Clb; Letterman Clb; Teachers Aide; Varsity Clb; School Musical; Stage Crew; Stu Cncl; Religion Clss Tchr; Coach For Sccr & Trck; Asst Scoutmaster & Eagle Scout; Coll Of San Mateo; Arch.

SHERSTINSKY, MARK; Lowell HS; San Francisco, CA; (3).

SHERWIN, JOHN D; Moorpark HS; New Fairfield, CT; (2); Church Yth Grp; Letterman Clb; Varsity Clb; Rptr Nwsp; Pres Frsh Cls; Capt JV Bsbl; JV Bsktbl; Capt JV Ftbl; High Hon Roll; Hon Roll; Campus Life.

SHERWIN, KRISTEN; Moorpark HS; New Fairfield, CT; (2); Debate Tm; Key Clb; Speech Tm; JV Bsktbl; Var Vllybl; High Hon Roll; CSF.

SHERWOOD, DAVID A; Palos Verdes HS; Palos Vrds Pen, CA; (3); Debate Tm; Library Aide; Model UN; Spanish Clb; Var Bsktbl; Var Crs Cntry; Var Trk; High Hon Roll; NHS.

SHERWOOD, PAMELA RENEE; Western HS; Anaheim, CA; (3); Bsktbl; Vllybl; Cit Awd; Hon Roll; NHS; Bus.

SHERWOOD, SHANE E; Trabuco Hills HS; Mission Viejo, CA; (3); Church Yth Grp; FCA; Spanish Clb; Church Choir; Var Bsbl; Var Ftbl; Var Socr; Hon Roll; NHS; U Of CA San Diego; Engrng.

SHETH, MILAN R; Torrance HS; Torrance, CA; (2); French Clb; Hosp Aide; Science Clb; Intrml Crs Cntry; JV Trk; Cit Awd; High Hon Roll; Hon Roll; Child Care; Travel & Explore Cultures; Photo; Singing; Berkley U; Med.

SHETH, SHRUTI; Whitney HS; Cerritos, CA; (3); Hosp Aide; Sec Key Clb; Office Aide; Color Guard; JV Var Tennis; Bausch & Lomb Sci Awd; High Hon Roll; NHS; Ntl Merit Ltr; Indian/Sri Lankan Clb Sec; Jr Hnr Awd; UCLA; Bio Sci.

SHEU, FEIKAI; San Marino HS; San Marino, CA; (4); 7/248; FBLA; Pres Math Clb; Capt Math Tm; Red Cross Aide; Pres Science Clb; JV Bsktbl; Hon Roll; Pres Acad Fit Awd; CSF VP Serv Schlrshp; Envrnmntl Grp; Rensellaer Math And Sci Awd; MIT; Elect Engr.

SHEU, PHILIP; San Marino HS; San Marino, CA; (4); 7/248; FBLA; Pres Math Clb; Capt Math Tm; Red Cross Aide; Pres Science Clb; JV Bsktbl; Hon Roll; Pres Acad Fit Awd; CSF Srvce Schlrshp; Rensselaer Math/Sci Awd; MA Inst Technology; Elec Engr.

SHEVALIER, KRISTINA B; Eisenhower HS; Yucaipa, CA; (4); 11/653; Am Leg Aux Girls St; Model UN; Hist Frsh Cls; Pres Sr Cls; Sec Stu Cncl; Var Capt Socr; Cit Awd; High Hon Roll; Kiwanis Awd; Pres Acad Fit Awd; California Scholarship Federation; Sobobans; Outstanding Senior Award; U Of C Riverside; Foreign Serv.

SHEVLIN, SHAWNA; Pittsburg HS; Pittsburg, CA; (1); VP Church Yth Grp; Hosp Aide; Cheerldng; High Hon Roll.

SHEWMAKE, SPENCER; Poway HS; Poway, CA; (3); 41/761; Letterman Clb; Mu Alpha Theta; Ski Clb; Varsity Clb; L Var Crs Cntry; JV Socr; L Var Trk; High Hon Roll; Hon Roll; NHS; CA Schlstc Fed; Honors Golden St Exam Testing Alg & Geom; Peer Cnslng Pgm Campus.

SHI, FLEMING; Homestead HS; Cupertino, CA; (3); 70/400; Computer Clb; Library Aide; Gldn ST Hnr Algi & High Hnr Geom; UC Santa Barbara; Comp Engr.

SHI, LIN; L A Co H S For The Arts; La Puente, CA; (2); French Clb; Prfct Atten Awd; Performed In A School Music Concert; Play Piano In School; College; Biology.

SHIA, EUGENE; Lowell HS; San Francisco, CA; (2); JV Ftbl; High Hon Roll; Hon Roll; UC Davis.

SHIAO, GRACE; Los Altos HS; Hacienda Hts, CA; (3); Cmnty Wkr; VP Sec Key Clb; Model UN; Speech Tm; Var Capt Bsktbl; Hon Roll; Prfct Atten Awd; Badminton JV, Vrsty, Capt; Jr Hnr Guard; March Fong Eu Re-Elctn Cmpgn Vlntr; Bus.

SHIAU, EVA L; Leuzinger HS; Lawndale, CA; (2); French Clb; Key Clb; Spanish Clb; Sec Frsh Cls; High Hon Roll; Prfct Atten Awd; Earth Envrnmnt Clb; APPI; CSF; MED.

SHIAU, ROSA L; Leuzinger HS; Lawndale, CA; (3); Key Clb; Prfct Atten Awd; APPI; CA ST Long Beach.

SHIBA, DIANA R; Alverno HS; Monrovia, CA; (2); 4/73; Cmnty Wkr; Chorus; Sec Frsh Cls; Sec Soph Cls; Var Bsktbl; High Hon Roll; Hon Roll; CSF; Multi Cultural Club; Engl & Gen Sci Awds 88-89; Spanish II Awd 89-90; Med.

SHIBATA, BRADLEY; John F Kennedy HS; Sacramento, CA; (3); 42/515; Church Yth Grp; Teachers Aide; Hon Roll; Asian Culture Clb.

SHIBATA, JESSICA A; Bonita Vista HS; Chula Vista, CA; (3); Off Church Yth Grp; Key Clb; Stage Crew; Nwsp; Ed Yrbk; Fld Hcky; Cit Awd; Hon Roll.

SHIBATA, KEN; Mira Costa HS; Manhattan Beach, CA; (3); Hosp Aide; Key Clb; Quiz Bowl; Treas Stu Cncl; Var L Ftbl; JV Socr; Cit Awd; High Hon Roll; Kiwanis Awd; Prfct Atten Awd; VP CA Schlrshp Fed; VP Boys Leag; Golden St Exam Geom High Hnrs; Bio.

SHIBATA, TAMIKO A; Righetti HS; Santa Maria, CA; (2); Var Socr; JV Trk; Cert Achvt Acad Educ; Hnr Roll; Awd Mrt Outstndng Achvt; Deans List; San Diego ST.

SHIBLEY, TONJA; Barstow HS; Barstow, CA; (3); Church Yth Grp; Mrchg Band; Sec Soph Cls; Sec Jr Cls; Rep Stu Cncl; Capt Var Cheerldng; Hon Roll; Band; Sec Sr Cls; Stat Bsktbl; Wind Ensemble; Outstndng Stu Musician; U Of NV Las Vegas.

SHICK, TIFFANY; Garces Memorial HS; Mc Farland, CA; (2); 2/175; Church Yth Grp; Lit Mag; Rep Soph Cls; Var Tennis; High Hon Roll; Piano For 9 Yrs; Travel Club; Campus Ministry Club; U CA; Engrg.

SHIE, HANK; University HS; Irvine, CA; (2); 13/508; Chess Clb; Church Yth Grp; Office Aide; Cit Awd; High Hon Roll; Hon Roll; Laureate Awd; Engrng.

SHIEH, CHARLIE; Carlmont HS; Belmont, CA; (3); Var Crs Cntry; Tennis.

SHIEH, SHU-HORNG; Mark Keppel HS; Monterey Park, CA; (3); 1/700; FBLA; Key Clb; Pres Math Clb; VP Science Clb; Yrbk; Cit Awd; High Hon Roll; Opt Clb Awd; Prfct Atten Awd; Pres Acad Fit Awd; Pres Cathay Clb; CSF; Prfct Scr Gldn St Exm Geom; UC Berkeley; Bus Mgmt.

SHIEH, SUN CHIA DORIS; Phillip & Sala Burton Academic HS; San Francisco, CA; (3); Sec French Clb; Math Clb; Jazz Band; Orch; High Hon Roll; Golden St Exam Awd Hgh Hnr Alg I; UC Berkeley; Engrng.

SHIELDS, HEATHER D; Clovis West; Fresno, CA; (3); 26/580; FCA; Intnl Clb; Key Clb; Spanish Clb; SADD; JV Swmmng; High Hon Roll; AP Us Hist Test; Sect Cal Schlrshp Fed; Fresno Young Woman Of The Year Pageant; AP Spanish Lang Test; UCLA; Broadcasting.

SHIELDS, JENNIFER; Livermore HS; Livermore, CA; (4); Aud/Vis; Church Yth Grp; Drama Clb; 4-H; Pep Clb; Ski Clb; Acpl Chr; Band; Chorus; Mgr Mrchg Band; Las Positas Coll; Psych.

SHIELDS, JESSICA; Arroyo HS; San Leandro, CA; (2); Art Clb; Dance Clb; Drama Clb; Chorus; Drill Tm; School Play; JV Cheerldng; JV Pom Pon; JV Trk; Prfct Atten Awd; TX A&M; Vet Med.

SHIELDS, JON A; Indio HS; Indio, CA; (1); 14/650; Tennis; CSF; UCLA.

SHIELDS, TERESA; Ramona HS; Riverside, CA; (3); 43/400; Letterman Clb; Pep Clb; Teachers Aide; Chorus; VP Jr Cls; Cheerldng; Pom Pon; Trk; NHS; Poltcl Sci.

SHIFFERT, JOYCE L; Coast Christian Schls; Torrance, CA; (3); Art Clb; Church Yth Grp; Computer Clb; Pep Clb; Teachers Aide; Rep Frsh Cls; Rep Stu Cncl; Var Vllybl; Cit Awd; High Hon Roll; Sci Hnr Awd; Educ.

SHIFFLER, MIKE A; Rancho Cotate HS; Rohnert Park, CA; (3); Boy Scts; Socr; JA; Sec Stu Cncl; Var Ftbl; Trk; High Hon Roll; CSF; Frgn Exchng Stu To Norway On Hnr Awd.

SHIFLETT, PATRICK R; Bakersfield HS; Bakersfield, CA; (3); 14/718; JA; Science Clb; Nwsp; Yrbk; Lit Mag; JV L Crs Cntry; JV L Swmmng; JV L Trk; Hon Roll; Ntl Merit Ltr; 1st Pl Mail Edtrl Bakersfield Coll Jrnlsm Day; Publshd Short Strs Ikon Magzn & Panorama.

SHIGEMITSU, MELISSA K; California HS; Whittier, CA; (2); Church Yth Grp; Pep Clb; Drill Tm; JV Capt Cheerldng; Hon Roll; Educ.

SHIH, ALAN Y; Los Altos HS; Hacienda Hgts, CA; (2); Var Church Yth Grp; Var Cmnty Wkr; Var Key Clb; Var SADD; Rep Yrbk; Var Cit Awd; Var Hon Roll; Var Pres Acad Fit Awd; Track & Field; Asian Amer Studnts Schlrshp Awd; Studnt Ambssdr To Europe; Med.

SHIH, BEN; Arcadia HS; Arcadia, CA; (3); 1/660; Off Church Yth Grp; FBLA; Math Clb; Math Tm; Scholastic Bowl; VP Science Clb; Ed Yrbk; JETS Awd; NHS; Pres Sr Men Clb; Engrng.

SHIH, CINDY; Mojave HS; Mojave, CA; (3); Sec Soph Cls; Sec Jr Cls; Cit Awd; Hon Roll; Ntl Merit Ltr; Prfct Atten Awd; Span Club; Bus.

SHIH, DAVEY; Orange HS; Orange, CA; (4); 1/400; Key Clb; Library Aide; VP Math Clb; Math Tm; Treas Science Clb; JV Trk; VP NHS; Rotary Awd; Val; KFWB News 98 Schlrshp Awd Wnnr; Rensselaer Polytech Inst Awd Math/Sci; Irvin Co Awd Spectrum Wnnr; MA Inst Tech; Biochem.

SHIH, KAREN A; San Gabriel HS; San Gabriel, CA; (3); Lbrn Cmnty Wkr; FCA; FBLA; Pres Key Clb; Treas Service Clb; Spanish Clb; Yrbk; Rep Jr Cls; Rep Stu Cncl; High Hon Roll; Red Cross Yth Grp Vlntr; CSF; UC Berkeley; Phrmclgy.

SHIH, LINDA; Huntington Beach HS; Huntington Bch, CA; (4); 4/500; Cmnty Wkr; Pres Key Clb; Model UN; Sec Spanish Clb; Sec Speech Tm; Ed Lit Mag; Stu Cncl; JV Trk; Hon Roll; Pres Acad Fit Awd; Pres Chinese Schl Stu Cncl; Stanford U; Bio.

SHIH, MARIA E; James Madison HS; San Diego, CA; (2); 1/359; Church Yth Grp; Latin Clb; Speech Tm; Band; Treas Mrchg Band; Pep Band; School Musical; NFL; Hon Roll; Lion Awd; Acadmc Leag; CSF; Jrnlsm.

SHIH, MORGAN; Whitney HS; Cerritos, CA; (2); Boy Scts; Varsity Clb; Band; Mrchg Band; JV Capt Bsktbl; Var L Trk; UCI; Med.

SHIH, RITA H; Schurr HS; Montebello, CA; (4); 8/580; Hosp Aide; Math Clb; Treas Spanish Clb; Chorus; Phtg Yrbk; JV Bsktbl; JV Tennis; Hon Roll; NHS; CA Schlrshp Fed; UC Berkeley.

SHIH, TONY; South San Francisco HS; South San Francis, CA; (2); 10/35; Church Yth Grp; Computer Clb; FHA; Letterman Clb; Service Clb; SADD; Varsity Clb; Phtg Yrbk; Bsktbl; Trk; 1st Yr Alg With Honors Golden St Exam Acad Excell Awd 87; Stu Of Yr Home Ec 90; Comp Drftng.

SHILL, PETER D; Edison HS; Huntington Beach, CA; (3); JV Bsbl; Var Wt Lftg; Surf Tm 89-90; Yng Hntrs Soc 87-90; U San Diego.

SHILLINGBURG, MONICA E; Apple Valley HS; Apple Valley, CA; (1); Hon Roll; Azusa Pacific U; Law.

SHILTS, MICAL K; Red Bluff Union HS; Red Bluff, CA; (2); 47/443; Church Yth Grp; VP Key Clb; Pep Clb; Treas Spanish Clb; SADD; Drill Tm; Variety Show; Sec Frsh Cls; Off Soph Cls; Stu Cncl; CSF; UC Davis; Sci.

SHIM, JANE H; West HS; Torrance, CA; (1); 1/344; Church Yth Grp; Intnl Clb; Latin Clb; Service Clb; Drill Tm; Mrchg Band; Pres Frsh Cls; Cit Awd; High Hon Roll; Prfct Atten Awd; CSF; U Of CA; Engr.

SHIMA, ALICE M; Garden Grove HS; Garden Grove, CA; (1); Pres Frsh Cls; JV Capt Bsktbl; Girls Lg; Frsh Rep.

SHIMIZU, RENA; Poway HS; Poway, CA; (2); AFS; Art Clb; Computer Clb; Drama Clb; French Clb; Hosp Aide; Math Clb; SADD; Golf; JV Swmmng; Tutor; Art.

SHIMOMURA, MARK A; Woodland HS; Woodland, CA; (3); 31/500; Boy Scts; Church Yth Grp; Key Clb; Ski Clb; JV Bsbl; JV Bsktbl; Hon Roll; NHS; Sthrn CA Yth Ctznshp Smnr Alt; U Of CA; Law.

SHIMSKY, JAYME R; Fremont HS; Sunnyvale, CA; (2); NFL; Speech Tm; Orch; School Musical; School Play; Stage Crew; Cambridge England; Herpetology.

SHIN, BRUCE A; Los Angeles Baptist HS; Encino, CA; (3); Church Yth Grp; French Clb; Varsity Clb; Band; Ftbl; Trk; Vllybl; Hon Roll; Broke Schl Rcrd 100m Track Team; UCLA; Bus.

SHIN, CHRISTOPHER; Arlington HS; Riverside, CA; (2); SADD; Var Swmmng; Dentist.

SHIN, CHRISTY; Glen A Wilson HS; Hacienda Hts, CA; (3); Flag Corp; School Play; Rep Stu Cncl; Prncpl Hnr Rll; Schlstc Schlr; Fine Arts Clb & Med Club; Market.

SHIN, CONNIE E; Sunny Hills HS; Anaheim, CA; (3); 69/430; Church Yth Grp; Intnl Clb; Key Clb; Latin Clb; Spanish Clb; Ntl Merit Ltr; Safe Rides Nvgtr; Span II Bronze Mdl; ROP; U San Diego; Bio.

SHIN, DONG S; Novato HS; Novato, CA; (1); Band; Mrchg Band; Orch; Pep Band; Hon Roll; High Hnrs Alg I Gldn St Exam; Mem Of CA Schlrshp Fed; Med.

SHIN, ED D; Sunny Hills HS; Fullerton, CA; (2); FFA; Spanish Clb; Swmmng; High Hon Roll; Water Polo; UC Davis; Vet Sci.

SHIN, ESTHER; Whitney HS; Cerritos, CA; (2); VP Rep Church Yth Grp; Cmnty Wkr; JA; Key Clb; Color Guard; JV Swmmng; Var Vllybl; Korean Clb; CSF.

SHIN, GENE; Lowell HS; San Francisco, CA; (2); Computer Clb; Intrml Bsktbl; Intrml Sftbl; Bus.

SHIN, HWAIN; Granada Hills HS; Granada Hills, CA; (3); Church Yth Grp; Cmnty Wkr; Hosp Aide; JA; Scholastic Bowl; Acpl Chr; Chorus; Cit Awd; High Hon Roll; Hon Roll; UCLA; Bio.

SHIN, HYE-JI; Yucaipa HS; Downey, CA; (2); Bus Profs of Am; Math Clb; Spanish Clb; Teachers Aide; Cit Awd; CPA.

SHIN, IHN-CHEOL; Cerritos HS; Cerritos, CA; (3); Art Clb; Computer Clb; Math Clb; Science Clb; JV Tennis; Cit Awd; High Hon Roll; Csf Gold Seal Bearer; Medical.

SHIN, JIM; Santa Teresa HS; San Jose, CA; (4); Church Yth Grp; FCA; Spanish Clb; San Jose ST U; Linguistics.

SHIN, JULIE H; La Sierra HS; Riverside, CA; (4); Hosp Aide; Library Aide; Math Clb; Mu Alpha Theta; Orch; Hon Roll; CSU Long Beach.

SHIN, MICHAEL; West Covina HS; West Covina, CA; (3); 1/500; Am Leg Boys St; Church Yth Grp; Cmnty Wkr; Letterman Clb; Science Clb; Spanish Clb; Varsity Clb; Church Choir; Rptr Yrbk; Var L Tennis; Xerox Schlrshp; Harvard Bk Awd; Schl Brd Rep.

SHIN, SUSAN; Mayfield SR Schl; Pasadena, CA; (3); Cmnty Wkr; Hosp Aide; Sec Intnl Clb; Library Aide; Scholastic Bowl; SADD; Teachers Aide; Sec Frsh Cls; Sec Treas Jr Cls; Treas Stu Cncl; Perf Dance; Liberty Bell Choir; US Figure Skating Assn; Pre-Med.

SHINAGAWA, ALANNA M; Live Oak HS; Morgan Hill, CA; (3); 105/530; Cmnty Wkr; GAA; Rep Frsh Cls; Rep Soph Cls; Rep Jr Cls; Var Fld Hcky; Var Sftbl; Cit Awd; High Hon Roll; Hon Roll; San Jose ST; Accntng.

SHINE, STACEY L; Brea-Olinda HS; Brea, CA; (3); Pep Clb; JV Cheerldng; Dnc Prdctn Hghst Prfrmng Dnc Clss; Acad Achvmnt Awd; Supr & Sprt Awds Sqd Frm USA Chr Cmp; Rl Est Agnt.

SHINH, CHANDERDEEP; Magnolia HS; Anaheim, CA; (1); Bsktbl; Tennis; Cit Awd; Doctor.

SHINH, CHARANJEEV B; Magnolia HS; Anaheim, CA; (2); Varsity Clb; Bsktbl; Diving; CSF; Engr.

SHINZATO, ERIKA N; Schurr HS; Montebello, CA; (2); SADD; Vllybl; Hon Roll; CA Schlrshp Fed; UCLA; Economics.

SHIOTA, FREDDIE; Argonaut HS; Ione, CA; (2); Church Yth Grp; English Clb; Letterman Clb; Ski Clb; Treas Frsh Cls; JV Bsbl; JV Ftbl; JV Trk; Hon Roll; Stanford; Phy.

SHIOYA, MARC T; Edison HS; Huntington Beach, CA; (3); Boy Scts; Key Clb; Model UN; Spanish Clb; Var Golf; Acadmc Dec; Kiwanis Bowl; Distngshd Schlr; Bus.

SHIPE, ANTHONY J; Pittsburg HS; Pittsburg, CA; (1); Church Yth Grp; Pep Clb; Thesps; Acpl Chr; Bsktbl; Ftbl; Golf; Sftbl; Wt Lftg; Cit Awd; Jwlry Cnstrctn.

SHIPLEY, DAVID; Twentynine Palms HS; Twentynine Palms, CA; (3); 4/150; Boy Scts; Pres Church Yth Grp; VP Science Clb; Pres Sr Cls; Rep Stu Cncl; JV Bsktbl; JV Crs Cntry; Var Swmmng; Var Trk; Hon Roll; JR Hnr Guard SR Graduating Cls; All League Cross Ntry; Engrng.

SHIPLEY, PATRICK J; Mater Dei HS; Fountain Valley, CA; (3); Ski Clb; Spanish Clb; School Musical; Stu Cncl; Hon Roll; NHS; Prfct Atten Awd; U San Diego; Corp Law.

SHIPMAN, HEATHER; Calvary Christian HS; Ridgecrest, CA; (2); 1/4; Church Yth Grp; Drama Clb; Ski Clb; Chorus; Drill Tm; School Play; Ed Lit Mag; L Bsktbl; Cit Awd; Hon Roll; Pacific Union Coll; Engl.

SHIPMAN, LAURA M; Kingsburg HS; Kingsburg, CA; (3); Church Yth Grp; FTA; Mu Alpha Theta; Office Aide; SADD; Chorus; Church Choir; Tennis; Trk; Hon Roll; Tchrs Of Tomorrow Club VP; Girls Vrsty Trk Team Leag Chmpns; Engl.

SHIPMAN, MATTHEW R; Grace Davis HS; Modesto, CA; (2); Var Socr; JV Trk; Hon Roll.

SHIPP, MONYULETTE D; Southern CA Christian HS; Santa Ana, CA; (2); Church Yth Grp; Cmnty Wkr; GAA; Office Aide; Acpl Chr; Chorus; Church Choir; School Musical; Variety Show; Bsktbl; Spkng Frgn Lngs; Enhnc Pblc Spkng Sklls; Bus Mgmt.

SHIRA, TODD D; Fremont Christian HS; Fremont, CA; (3); Intnl Clb; Letterman Clb; Office Aide; Ski Clb; Var L Bsbl; San Jose ST U.

SHIRAISHI, KURT M; Bellarmine College Prep; San Jose, CA; (1); Church Yth Grp; Intrml Bsbl; Intrml Ftbl; Hon Roll; Black Blt Tae Kwon Do, 88 Jr Olympcs Brnze Mdl.

SHIRALI, ANUSHREE C; Navato HS; Novato, CA; (1); French Clb; CSF; Craft Clb; Stanford; Phy.

SHIRBROUN, JULIE; Yucca Valley HS; Yucca Valley, CA; (4); 4/150; Church Yth Grp; FBLA; Math Clb; Quiz Bowl; Spanish Clb; Church Choir; Sec Soph Cls; Sec Jr Cls; JV Var Cheerldng; JV Var Gym; Girls State; University Club; Point Loma Nazarene Coll; Med.

SHIREY, THOMAS N; Southern Calif Christian HS; Dana Point, CA; (4); 3/96; Dance Clb; Drama Clb; French Clb; Math Tm; Ski Clb; Jazz Band; Swing Chorus; Ed Yrbk; Pres Sr Cls; Vllybl; USC; Admin.

SHIRI, HEZI; Ginstein Acad; Northridge, CA; (1); Quiz Bowl; Teachers Aide; Temple Yth Grp; School Play; Yrbk; Stu Cncl; Bsbl; Bsktbl; Socr; Vllybl; Best Player Bsbl Tm Awd; Capt Bsktbl Tm Awd; Asst Camp Cnslr; UCLA; Dr.

SHIRINIAN, AUDREY; Holy Martyrs HS; Sherman Oaks, CA; (3); 8/34; Drama Clb; Mgr(s); JV Vllybl; Mgr Cheerldng; Begnnrs Band; UCLA; Corp Law.

SHIRLEY, ALICIA L; Fremont HS; Sunnyvale, CA; (2); DECA; Co-Capt Cheerldng; Fld Hcky; Sftbl; Stanford; Med.

SHIRLEY, CHARLES A; Quincy JR SR HS; Quincy, CA; (2); Spanish Clb; VICA; Var Golf; Fencing Clb; Martial Arts Clb; Rgnl Level Gold Medals & 4th Pl St Level Machining Comptn VICA; Cal Poly Sn Luis Obispo; Physcs.

SHIRLEY, KIA E; Robert A Millikan HS; Compton, CA; (4); 96/726; Pres Church Yth Grp; Drill Tm; Rptr Nwsp; Yrbk; Pres Frsh Cls; Off Jr Cls; VP Stu Cncl; JV Var Cheerldng; JV Var Gym; Hon Roll; Frshmn Yr Awd; Yng Gftd & Blck Awd; Yng Blck Schlrs; Stanford U; Jrnlsm.

SHIRLEY, ROBYNE R; Willows HS; Willows, CA; (2); 4/107; Key Clb; Treas Soph Cls; VP Jr Cls; JV Bsktbl; Var JV Cheerldng; JV Vllybl; High Hon Roll; Friday Night Live Sec 89-90, Pres 90-91; CA Schlrshp Fed Mem; Kiwanis Camp Cnslr 89-90; Bus.

SHIRLEY, WILLIAM E; Bullard HS; Fresno, CA; (2); Church Yth Grp; Teachers Aide; Golden St Exam Awd; Comp Pgm.

SHIROISH, MARK; Mark Keppel HS; Monterey Park, CA; (4); 14/540; Cmnty Wkr; FBLA; Hosp Aide; Key Clb; Letterman Clb; Library Aide; Math Clb; Mu Alpha Theta; Science Clb; Var Bsktbl; UCLA; Med.

SHIROMA, MEGAN T; Cerritos HS; Cerritos, CA; (1); Cit Awd; Hon Roll; Pacific Asian Club; Sci.

SHIU, BRIAN K; Ganesha HS; Diamond Bar, CA; (4); 1/250; JA; Letterman Clb; Pres Math Clb; Varsity Clb; Ed Nwsp; Lit Mag; Treas Soph Cls; Stu Cncl; Var L Socr; Capt Var Tennis; UCLA; Aerospc Engrng.

SHIU, MARK L; Sierra Vista HS; Baldwin Park, CA; (1); JV Bsktbl; UCLA; Pediatrics.

SHIUE, CHI-YU; Alhambra HS; Alhambra, CA; (3); Intnl Clb; Service Clb; Teachers Aide; Chorus; Church Choir; Intrml Bsktbl; Yth Ldrshp Trng Wkshp Awd; Acad Excllnc Awd; Medcl Clb Mst Dedicated Awd; Jr Civitans Svc Clb Pres.

SHIVA, NIMA; Agoura HS; Agoura Hills, CA; (4); Debate Tm; JA; Math Clb; NFL; Speech Tm; Off Frsh Cls; Off Soph Cls; Var Ftbl; Var Socr; High Hon Roll; CSF Gold Seal Bearer & Life Mem; Gftd & Tlntd Ed Club Mem; Natl Yng Ldrs Conf Cngrssnl Schlr; U CA San Diego; Bio.

SHIVELY, JOLEEN A; Fairfield HS; Fairfield, CA; (3); Art Clb; DECA; FBLA; Pep Clb; Ski Clb; JV Cheerldng; Hon Roll; Snowskiing Clb; CFA; Law.

SHIVERS, CYNTHIA E; Castlemont HS; Oakland, CA; (2); ROTC; Spanish Clb; Band; Treas Church Choir; Color Guard; Drill Tm; High Hon Roll; Prfct Atten Awd; Pres Acad Fit Awd; ROTC Super Cadet; UC Berkeley; Math.

SHIVERS, KATHLEEN P; St Joseph HS; Long Beach, CA; (2); Hosp Aide; Key Clb; Spanish Clb; Hon Roll; Prfct Atten Awd; Ballet Pointe; Golf; Alg I Awd; Teacher.

SHLAPAK, IRINA; Lowell HS; San Francisco, CA; (2); Intnl Clb; SADD; Teachers Aide; JV Cheerldng; Russian Clb Pres; UC Berkeley; Bus Mgmt.

SHLESMAN, REBECCA J; Fairfax HS; Los Angeles, CA; (3); Cmnty Wkr; Hosp Aide; Temple Yth Grp; Rep Frsh Cls; Rep Soph Cls; Rep Jr Cls; Var Tennis; St Schlr; Peer Cnslng; Smmr Study Pgm In Israel; Engl.

SHNAYER, SERENA; Santa Teresa HS; Palm Bay, FL; (4); Church Yth Grp; Dance Clb; Spanish Clb; School Musical; Variety Show; Jr NHS; NHS; Brevard CC; Jrnlsm.

SHOCKEY, TRINA M; East Union HS; Manteca, CA; (3); Church Yth Grp; Drama Clb; 4-H; Hosp Aide; SADD; Teachers Aide; School Play; JV Sftbl; JV Vllybl; Hon Roll; CSF; San Diego ST U; Crmnl Law.

SHOCKLEY, TIFFINY A; La Jolla Country Day HS; San Diego, CA; (2); Hosp Aide; SADD; Lit Mag; JV Sftbl; JV Vllybl; Jr Vrsty Vlybl Mst Imprvd Plyr Catp Of Team; Jr Vrsty Sftbl Coaches Awd; 4th Pl Cncrs Natl De Francais; Physcn.

SHODHAN, SHOMI K; Mission HS; Fremont, CA; (1); Hosp Aide; Science Clb; Variety Show; Tennis; High Hon Roll; Pres Acad Fit Awd; Dance; Gldn St Exm Awd Hnrs Alg; CSF; Cross Cultural Clbs; Med.

SHOEMAKER, COREEN M; George Washington HS; San Francisco, CA; (3); Dance Clb.

SHOEMAKER, JENNIFER A; Narbonne HS; Carson, CA; (2); Hist Service Clb; Ed Nwsp; JV Tennis; High Hon Roll; Hon Roll; Prfct Atten Awd; Eclgy Clb; Keywanettes; CSF; Engl.

SHOEMAKER, MEGAN R; Sacramento HS; Sacramento, CA; (1); 86/642; Hon Roll; UC Davis; Psych.

SHOFFSTALL, RICK; Paraclete HS; Lancaster, CA; (3); 1/150; VP Key Clb; Letterman Clb; Var Socr; Var Trk; Hon Roll; NHS; CSF; Play Sccr In Europe-For Cal Sth/Under 18 Slct Tm; CIF-QLFYNG Sccr/Trck Tms; Engrng.

SHOFNER, CHARLEEN K; Salinas HS; Salinas, CA; (1); Church Yth Grp; Cmnty Wkr; FBLA; Band; Church Choir; Mrchg Band; Orch; Pep Band; Swmmng; Hon Roll; Dntl Hygnst.

SHOGREN, TRACY L; Redlands HS; Redlands, CA; (3); Church Yth Grp; German Clb; Ski Clb; Teachers Aide; Hon Roll; Jr NHS; Microbio.

SHOJI, KEITH L; Fontana HS; Fontana, CA; (3); Capt Debate Tm; Capt NFL; Capt Speech Tm; Intrml Tennis; Hon Roll; Poli Sci.

SHOLBERG, TRACEY L; Oak Ridge HS; El Dorado Hills, CA; (1); Bsktbl; Sftbl; Vllybl; JV Bstkbl; JV Sftbl MVP; Vrsty Vlybl Tm Frshmn.

SHOMGLIN, KOME; Mater Dei HS; Garden Grove, CA; (1); Library Aide; Spanish Clb; Band; Mrchg Band; Orch; CA Schlstc Fed; Stanford; Engr.

SHONE, WYI K; Tustin HS; Tustin, CA; (2); 11/300; Chess Clb; Church Yth Grp; Latin Clb; Science Clb; Church Choir; Ftbl; High Hon Roll; Hon Roll; Guitar Chrch Band; Tae Kwon Do; US Airforce Acad; Aerospc Engr.

SHOOK, ANDREW J; Fairfield HS; Fairfield, CA; (2); Church Yth Grp; 4-H; Hon Roll; CSF.

SHOOK, BRIAN J; Santa Teresa HS; San Jose, CA; (2); Church Yth Grp; Ski Clb; Bsktbl; Sci.

SHOOK, STACY A; Skyline HS; Oakland, CA; (2); Computer Clb; English Clb; Teachers Aide; School Play; Vllybl; Cit Awd; Hon Roll; Pres Acad Fit Awd; 4.0 Ctznshp 89-90.

SHOOSHANI, BITA; Birmingham HS; Encino, CA; (2); Cmnty Wkr; FBLA; Hosp Aide; Key Clb; NFL; Speech Tm; SADD; UC Santa Cruz; Envrmntlst.

SHOPFNER, JOSH C; Mayfair HS; Lakewood, CA; (1); Church Yth Grp; English Clb; JA; Intrml Bsktbl; Intrml Ftbl; Pres Acad Fit Awd; Jrnlst.

SHORE, CHRIS D; Forest Lake Christian HS; Grass Valley, CA; (2); Letterman Clb; Teachers Aide; Varsity Clb; Var Bsbl; Var Bsktbl; Var Socr; Var Trk.

SHORE, MIRANDA L; Yreka HS; Montague, CA; (3); #6 In Class; German Clb; SADD; Ed Yrbk; Rep Soph Cls; Score Keeper; High Hon Roll; Hon Roll; CSF; Lang Interpreter.

SHORT, AUSTIN L; Marina HS; Huntington Beach, CA; (3); Church Yth Grp; Achvt Cert-Mach Tool Opertns; Star Pgm Recgntn-Indstrl Tech.

SHORT, DAPHNE D; Sonora HS; Turlock, CA; (3); Cmnty Wkr; French Clb; Office Aide; Band; Chorus; Jazz Band; Mrchg Band; Orch; Pep Band; Tennis; Shrt Stry Cntst Grnd Prz Wnnr; Intl Order Of Rainbow Grnd Crss Of Color; CSU Stanislaus; Prmry Tchng.

SHORT, HEATHER; Del Norte HS; Crescent City, CA; (4); 6/250; Church Yth Grp; Debate Tm; Teachers Aide; Varsity Clb; Tennis; 1st & 2nd Pl Work Exper Awd; Santa Monica JC; Nrsng.

SHORT, JONATHAN S; Caruthers HS; Caruthers, CA; (4); Pres Church Yth Grp; FBLA; Math Clb; Rep Band; Jazz Band; Mrchg Band; Orch; Pep Band; Rep Frsh Cls; Outstndng Yng Citizen Of Yr Awd; CA Ambssdrs Of Music To Europe Tour 90; Music.

SHORT, JOY M; Bella Vista HS; Orangevale, CA; (2); 28/406; Pep Clb; Spanish Clb; Var Cheerldng; Var L Swmmng; High Hon Roll; Pres Acad Fit Awd; U Pacific; Orthodntcs.

SHORT, OKIAH; Carson HS; Carson, CA; (2); Chess Clb; Hosp Aide; Stage Crew; Swmmng; Cit Awd; Hon Roll; Prfct Atten Awd; R N.

SHORTLE, REBECCA; Santa Barbara HS; Santa Barbara, CA; (4); 1/460; SADD; Stu Cncl; High Hon Roll; NHS; Ntl Merit Ltr; Eclgy Clb; Vrs Awds Art; Bio.

SHORTS, KENDRA N; Washington Preparatory HS; Los Angeles, CA; (2); Chorus; Tennis; Hon Roll; CA ST Dominguez Coll Readiness Pgm; Berkeley; Law.

SHOSTAK, ELI; Los Alamitos HS; Los Alamitos, CA; (3); Band; Jazz Band; Mrchg Band; Cit Awd; Hon Roll; Svc Awd Jazz Bnd; Ecology Clb.

SHOTT, JAMES T; Bishop Amat HS; West Covina, CA; (2); Church Yth Grp; Teachers Aide; JV Capt Socr; NHS; MVP Soccer; UC San Diego; Marine Bio.

SHOTWELL, BRET; San Clemente HS; San Clemente, CA; (1); Church Yth Grp; Cit Awd; Med.

SHOUP, JENNIFER J; Leland HS; San Jose, CA; (2); 17/442; Church Yth Grp; Hon Roll; FL St Sci Fair; Top 5% Cls.

SHOUP, SHAWNA; Fall River JR/Sr HS; Fall River Mills, CA; (3); Church Yth Grp; Sec Drama Clb; 4-H; FBLA; Letterman Clb; Band; Chorus; School Musical; School Play; JV Bsktbl; CA Assn Stu Cncls Sectry; Med.

SHOWALTER, NICOLE J; Clovis HS; Fresno, CA; (3); Church Yth Grp; Cmnty Wkr; Dance Clb; FCA; Varsity Clb; JV Cheerldng; L Var Diving; L Var Gym; Intrml Powder Puff Ftbl; High Hon Roll; Gym Coach; Phys Thrpst.

SHOWERS, TRACY L; Alta Loma HS; Alta Loma, CA; (3); Church Yth Grp; Teachers Aide; Mgr(s); Score Keeper; Stat Socr; High Hon Roll; Prfct Atten Awd; Principles Hon Roll 3 Yrs; Acadmc Lttr Var; Cal Poly Pomona; Chldhd Dev.

SHRADER, DONALD L; University City HS; San Diego, CA; (4); JA; Library Aide; Wrstlng; Cit Awd; High Hon Roll; Aerospc Engrng.

SHRATER, PAUL J; Thousand Oaks HS; Thousand Oaks, CA; (3); Math Tm; Science Clb; Pres Spanish Clb; JV Crs Cntry; JV Tennis; JV Trk; Hon Roll; Ntl Merit Ltr; Harvard Smmr Schl; CA Schlrshp Fed; Temple Mens Clb.

SHREVE, JENNIFER L; Salinas HS; Salinas, CA; (3); Church Yth Grp; Drama Clb; French Clb; Chorus; Stage Crew; Variety Show; Ed Nwsp; Stu Cncl; High Hon Roll; Wrkd With Yth Mssn Smmr Outrch Fuji Islands; Peer Cnclng; Comms.

SHRIEVE, JEREMY M; Roseville HS; Roseville, CA; (2); 4-H; Quiz Bowl; Spanish Clb; SADD; JV Bsktbl; JV Capt Socr; 4-H Awd; High Hon Roll; Ntl Merit Schol; American Polled Hereford Assoc; CA NV JR Polled Hereford Assoc; Cal Poly; Animal Science.

SHRIVER, PAT; Los Alamitos HS; Los Alamitos, CA; (3); Church Yth Grp; German Clb; Science Clb; Ftbl; Trk; Hon Roll; Boy Scts; Mdl Rocketry; Interact Clb; Astrnaut.

SHRUM, THOMAS K; Casa Roble Fundamental HS; Citrus Heights, CA; (3); 49/450; Var L Swmmng; Intrml Wt Lftg; Hon Roll; Prfct Atten Awd; Air Force; Aeronautics.

SHTEYNBERG, REGINA; Washington HS; San Francisco, CA; (3); Speech Tm.

SHU, STEVE; Casa Grande HS; Petaluma, CA; (4); Chess Clb; Church Yth Grp; Intnl Clb; SADD; Church Choir; Var Tennis; NHS; UC Santa Barbara; Mech Engnrng.

SHU, THEODORE; Whitney HS; Cerritos, CA; (2); Hosp Aide; Key Clb; Spanish Clb; Orch; Trk; High Hon Roll; Hon Roll.

SHU, VICTOR; San Mateo HS; Hillsborough, CA; (3); Church Yth Grp; French Clb; Hosp Aide; Sec Intnl Clb; Model UN; Sec Varsity Clb; Rptr Nwsp; Rep Stu Cncl; JV Var Tennis; High Hon Roll; Chris Lee Memorial Awd; Mc Konville Awd For Engl; Med.

SHUBECK, DEBORAH; Etiwanda HS; Rialto, CA; (3); Church Yth Grp; Dance Clb; Teachers Aide; Co-Capt Drill Tm; Sec Frsh Cls; Rep Stu Cncl; Cit Awd; Hon Roll; Jr NHS; Ldrshp Cls; Teacher.

SHUBHAKAR, POORNIMA; Monache HS; Porterville, CA; (3); Cmnty Wkr; Speech Tm; Color Guard; Rep Soph Cls; Var Capt Tennis; High Hon Roll; Lion Awd; Prfct Atten Awd; Pres Acad Fit Awd; Voice Dem Awd; Schlr Of Wk; Med.

SHUBOV, DIMA; Lowell HS; San Francisco, CA; (3); VP Chess Clb; Math Tm; ROTC; Variety Show; JV Crs Cntry; JV Ftbl; Var Wrstlng; High Hon Roll; Hon Roll; 2nd Pl San Francisco Wrstlng Chmpnshp; 2nd Pl Tm US HS Chess Chmpnshp; CSF; Astrophyscs.

SHUFELT, CHRISANDRA; Woodbridge HS; Irvine, CA; (3); Church Yth Grp; Cmnty Wkr; Hosp Aide; Office Aide; Pep Clb; SADD; Pep Band; Cheerldng; Hon Roll; Grls Lg Clb; CSF.

SHUFF, ROBERT; University HS; Irvine, CA; (3); VP JCL; Pres Latin Clb; Phtg Yrbk; JV Swmmng; Wrk For Cngrssmn T Swyr Smmrs K; Pltcl Sci.

SHUFFELTON, DAVID; Poway HS; San Diego, CA; (3); 32/715; Computer Clb; Treas Math Clb; Mu Alpha Theta; High Hon Roll; Envrnmntl Awarenss Clb; Acadmc Tm; U Of CA Davis; Vet Med.

SHUFFIELD, VERONICA; Western Christian HS; Baldwin Park, CA; (2); Church Yth Grp; Ski Clb; Spanish Clb; JV Cheerldng; Trk; High Hon Roll; CSF; Attorney.

SHUFORD, LIZ L; St Bonaventure HS; Ventura, CA; (3); Hosp Aide; Service Clb; SADD; Teachers Aide; Band; Nwsp; Hist Sr Cls; NHS; Jr Statesman Of Amer; CSF; Med.

SHUI, DAWIY D; Gahr HS; Cerritos, CA; (3); Treas Church Yth Grp; Cmnty Wkr; Computer Clb; JA; Speech Tm; Intrml Bsktbl; Var Trk; JV Vllybl; High Hon Roll; Hon Roll.

SHUIT, NICK; Rio Mesa HS; Camarillo, CA; (3); AFS; Quiz Bowl; School Play; Ed Nwsp; Lit Mag; Hon Roll; U Of CA Los Angeles; Writing.

SHUKLA, VINEET; Kennedy HS; La Palma, CA; (3); Computer Clb; Key Clb; Stat Bsktbl; Trk; High Hon Roll; Hon Roll; Pres Acad Fit Awd; CSF; Kiwanis Bowl; Comp Sci.

SHUKLIAN, ALLISON; Redwood HS; Visalia, CA; (3); Var Bsktbl; Var Sftbl; Var Vllybl; Hon Roll; Acad Ltr; CSF.

SHULER, CHRISTOPHER D; Independence HS; San Jose, CA; (3); Chess Clb; Cmnty Wkr; French Clb; Math Tm; Ldr Of Indpndnt Order Oddfllws Of CA; Linguistics.

SHULL, AMY K; Downey HS; Modesto, CA; (1); Hon Roll; Stanislaus ST U; Nrs.

SHULL, JAMES; Monterey Bay Acad; Lodi, CA; (4); Aud/Vis; Church Yth Grp; Red Cross Aide; Ski Clb; Teachers Aide; Band; School Play; Nwsp; Ed Yrbk; Capt Gym; Pcfc Un Coll; Prf Phtgrphr.

SHULMAN, ILANA R; Oxnard HS; Oxnard, CA; (2); French Clb; Teachers Aide; Stat Trk; High Hon Roll; Hon Roll; Knowldge Master Open; UCLA; Bus.

SHULTZ, CHRISTOPHER S; Woodside HS; Redwood City, CA; (3); Am Leg Boys St; Church Yth Grp; Cmnty Wkr; Speech Tm; Pres Jr Cls; Pres Stu Cncl; JV L Bsbl; Var L Golf; Hon Roll; Trivia Hunt Team-Co Capt; Poly Sci.

SHULTZ, SHELLEY L; North Bak HS; Bakersfield, CA; (3); French Clb; SADD; Bsktbl; Trk; Vllybl; Hon Roll; Pres Acad Fit Awd; FIDM; Fash Des.

SHULTZ, SUSANNE M; Bonita Vista HS; Bonita, CA; (3); 13/557; Intnl Clb; Model UN; Pep Clb; Ntl Merit SF; CA Schlrshp Fed; Amnesty Intl; Equestrian Showjumping; U Of CA San Diego; Envrnmntl.

SHULTZ, THOMAS R; Seaside HS; Marina, CA; (2); French Clb; High Hon Roll; Hon Roll; Jr NHS; Lion Awd; NHS; Voice Dem Awd; Sci Fair Monterey Cty Wnnr 2nd Pl 88-89; Swimming Mst Imprvd Awd; Bsbl Mst Outstndng Awd; Stanford U; Aerospace Engr.

SHULTZ, TIFFANY S; Cordova SR HS; Sacramento, CA; (4); 17/443; Pres Drama Clb; Rep Thesps; Chorus; School Musical; School Play; Stage Crew; Rptr Yrbk; VP Frsh Cls; Rep Jr Cls; Sec Stu Cncl; Mock Trial Tm; Bnk Amer Plaque Wnnr Fine Arts; Humboldt ST U; Commnctns.

SHUM, CONROY W; Diamond Bar HS; Diamond Bar, CA; (2); Boy Scts; Chess Clb; Key Clb; Ski Clb; Spanish Clb; Varsity Clb; Rep Soph Cls; Var Tennis; Hon Roll; Deans Math List; Gldn St Exam Schl Rcgntn; All Leag Team Tnns.

SHUM, KELVIN F; Alameda HS; Alameda, CA; (4); 1/331; Art Clb; Chess Clb; Red Cross Aide; Science Clb; JV Crs Cntry; Tennis; Trk; High Hon Roll; Hon Roll; Val; CA Schlrshp Fdrtn; Oaklands Annl Art Cont 3rd Pl Awd; Alameda Art Cont 1st Pl Awd; UC Berkeley; Cvl Engrng.

SHUM, MEE K; Silver Creek HS; San Jose, CA; (4); 41/415; Computer Clb; GAA; Intnl Clb; Math Clb; Science Clb; Spanish Clb; Varsity Clb; NHS; Badminton; San Jose ST U; Bus Mgmt.

SHUM, MERRILL K; Diamond Bar HS; Diamond Bar, CA; (2); Boy Scts; Chess Clb; Key Clb; Ski Clb; Spanish Clb; Varsity Clb; Off Soph Cls; Var Tennis; Hon Roll; Var Tnns Mst Imprvd Awd; CSF; Stanford; Law.

SHUM, SUSANA; Raoul Wallenberg Traditional HS; San Francisco, CA; (1); Dance Clb; Sec Frsh Cls; 2nd Hnrs.

SHUMAKER, DAVID A; Foothill HS; Bakersfield, CA; (4); 3/350; Key Clb; Ski Clb; Varsity Clb; Intrml Ftbl; Var L Tennis; Intrml Wt Lftg; Var L Wrstlng; High Hon Roll; Pres Acad Fit Awd; Rotary Awd; CSF Gold Seal Bearer; Outstndng Soc Stud Sci Stu 89-90; Comp Sci.

SHUMAN, CYNTHIA F; Enterprise HS; Redding, CA; (3); Math Clb; Mu Alpha Theta; Band; Jazz Band; Mrchg Band; Pep Band; Hon Roll; US Pony Clb; Biochem.

SHUMAN, MINDY L; Yuba City HS; Yuba City, CA; (2); Chorus; Hon Roll; Blood Dr; Chld Psych.

SHUMARD, BRIAN; Arcata HS; Arcata, CA; (4); Am Leg Boys St; Art Clb; Letterman Clb; Office Aide; SADD; Varsity Clb; Var Capt Bsbl; JV Bsktbl; JV Ftbl; Wt Lftg; Humbold T Eagles Amer Legion Bsbl; Hntng, Fshng, Skiing; Cllct Bsbl Crds; Contra Costa JC; Phys Ed.

SHUMATE III, JEROME A; El Cajon Valley HS; El Cajon, CA; (3); 27/370; Boy Scts; Chess Clb; Cmnty Wkr; Treas Key Clb; Science Clb; Treas Sr Cls; JV Crs Cntry; JV Socr; High Hon Roll; Hon Roll; Treas & Future VP Human Rel Clb; Gldn St Schlr W/Rcgntn 88; CA Schlrhsp Fed; Stanford,Arspc Engr.

SHUMATE, LAURA E; Del Campo HS; Citrus Heights, CA; (3); 35/449; Church Yth Grp; German Clb; Teachers Aide; Yrbk; Cit Awd; Hon Roll; Ntl Merit Ltr; 2 Yrs Tchng Presch Chldrn Chrch; Child Psych.

SHUMPERT, VERDELL E; Morningside HS; Inglewood, CA; (2); Church Yth Grp; Office Aide; Chorus; Church Choir; Variety Show; Stu Cncl; Cit Awd; Hon Roll; Comp; Modeling Club Images; USC; Comp Anlyst.

SHUMWAY, NICOLE; Alemany HS; Northridge, CA; (3); Am Leg Aux Girls St; Church Yth Grp; Cmnty Wkr; Pep Clb; Teachers Aide; Off Frsh Cls; Sec Treas Soph Cls; VP Jr Cls; Var Swmmng; High Hon Roll; Close-Up Pgm 90; Pre-Med.

SHUPE, ADAM K; Cordova SR HS; Rancho Cordova, CA; (3); Boy Scts; Pres Church Yth Grp; Model UN; Office Aide; Science Clb; Church Choir; Var L Swmmng; High Hon Roll; NHS; Ntl Merit Ltr; Surfing; UCSB; Elem Ed.

SHUPE, KEVIN N; San Dimas HS; San Dimas, CA; (3); Teachers Aide; Band; Jazz Band; Mrchg Band; Var JV Wrstlng; Hon Roll; JV Tennis; Certfd Deputy Explorer Los Angeles Cnty Sheriffs Dept; Cal ST Long Beach; Law Enfrcmn.

SHUPER, SALLY A; Rio Americano HS; Carmichael, CA; (4); 1/259; Service Clb; Spanish Clb; Sec Soph Cls; Off Tennis; VP Stu Cncl; JV Var Tennis; NHS; Pres Acad Fit Awd; Val; Bk Of Amer Ahvt Awd Frgn Lang; Dstngshd Schlr Awd; Acad Ltr; CSF Awd; Outstndng Stu Spnsh Awd; Stanford U.

SHURTER, ANNA B; Branham HS; San Jose, CA; (1); Church Yth Grp; French Clb; High Hon Roll; Hon Roll; Piano; CSF; Outstndng Perf Awd Frnch; Med.

SHUSTER, AMY L; Ocean View HS; Westminster, CA; (1); Dance Clb; Drama Clb; Model UN; Temple Yth Grp; School Musical; School Play; Cit Awd; Hon Roll; Pres Acad Fit Awd; Pres Schlr; Ballet Perf Grp Natl Fnlst.

SHUSTER, DAVID L; San Rafael HS; San Rafael, CA; (2); 1/256; Boy Scts; Church Yth Grp; FCA; French Clb; Red Cross Aide; SADD; Band; Jazz Band; Hon Roll; Pres Acad Fit Awd.

SIADATAN, KI M; Mills HS; Burlingame, CA; (3); Debate Tm; French Clb; Hosp Aide; Intnl Clb; Letterman Clb; Math Tm; Speech Tm; Rep Frsh Cls; VP Jr Cls; Rep Stu Cncl; Chrmn Redress Brd; Cls Rep Prncpls Schl Site Cncl; Pre-Med.

SIAU, ESTELLA YA-WUN; Sequoia HS; Redwood City, CA; (4); 11/329; Church Yth Grp; FBLA; Spanish Clb; Church Choir; Ed Nwsp; JV Tennis; Spcl Olypc Wrkr; CA Schlrshp Fdrtn; JV Badmntn; U Fo CA Berkeley; Engrng.

SIAZON, GERALD A; Temple City HS; Temple City, CA; (3); Band; Mrchg Band; Kiwanis Awd.

SIBAYAN, LUCRECIA T; Delano HS; Richgrove, CA; (4); VP Art Clb; Church Yth Grp; Letterman Clb; Library Aide; Capt Crs Cntry; JV Trk; Hon Roll; NHS; CSF; Exemplary Stu Awd; GATE Pgm; Cal Poly San Luis Obispo; Engr.

SIBBITT, MICHELLE R; Leland HS; San Jose, CA; (2); Church Yth Grp; Pres Frsh Cls; VP Soph Cls; Pres Jr Cls; Rep Stu Cncl; Var L Socr; Var Trk; Mayor Delg Cmmtte; CASC Ldrshp Camp; Pepperdine; Commnctns.

SIBLEY, JENNIFER R; Thomas Downey HS; Modesto, CA; (2); Church Yth Grp; Service Clb; Church Choir; Orch; High Hon Roll; CA Schlrshp Fed; U CA.

SIBLEY, MATTHEW T; Golden Sierra HS; Cool, CA; (4); Stage Crew; Var Trk; Var Hon Roll; NSTA Duracell Schlrshp Comptn 3rd Pl Natl; 1st Pl Hmcmng Float 89-90; Elect Awd 88-89; Sierra Coll; Mech Engr.

SIBLEY, SARAH P; Mc Ateer J Eugene HS; San Francisco, CA; (3); Drama Clb; Spanish Clb; Teachers Aide; Variety Show; 4-H Awd; Adult CPR; Stan 1st Aid; Team Wrk Awd; Mc Alteer Sch Of Art; Elem Ed.

SIBONA, PHILLIP; North HS; Bakersfield, CA; (1); Comp Graphics.

SIBOUNHEUANG, PHOUANGPHET; Fred C Beyer HS; Modesto, CA; (3); French Clb; FBLA; Pres Sec Intnl Clb; Teachers Aide; Cit Awd; Hon Roll; JCL; CSF Clb; Stgt A Awd; Sn Dgo ST; Nrsg.

SIBOUNHOM, PHAIVANH L; San Pasqual HS; Escondido, CA; (2); 23/416; Sci.

SICARD, LYN A; Prospect HS; San Jose, CA; (1); Color Guard; Drill Tm; Socl Wrk.

SICHAMPANAKHON, PHOUTHONE C; Grant Union HS; Sacramento, CA; (2); French Clb; Intnl Clb; Science Clb; SADD; Tennis; JV Vllybl; Cit Awd; Hon Roll; Hnr Block; Stu Affirmative Action CSUS; UCLA; Hotel Mgt.

SICHAMPANAKHONE, DOUANGMALY L; Grant Union HS; Sacramento, CA; (1); Yrbk; Cheerldng; Hon Roll; Mesa Club; Stu Rchng Out; UC Berkley; Arch.

SICKAFOOSE, JENNIFER L; Arlington HS; Riverside, CA; (3); Art Clb; Treas Church Yth Grp; Drama Clb; ROTC; School Play; Stage Crew; Hon Roll; VP Of Yth To Yth; Riverside CC; Admin Jstc.

SICKAFOOSE, TODD; San Ramon Valley HS; Danville, CA; (2); Boy Scts; Cmnty Wkr; Band; Jazz Band; Mrchg Band; Orch; School Musical; Stage Crew; Vllybl; Hon Roll; Diablo Yth Symphny Orchstra; Amnesty Intl Clb; U Of CA Berkeley; Fine Arts.

SICKLE, SHAWN M; Pioneer HS; San Jose, CA; (2); Church Yth Grp; Score Keeper; Stat Socr; Golden St Exam Acad Excllnc Awd; Elem Educ.

SICKLER, JUDSON; Santiago HS; Garden Grove, CA; (2); German Clb; Varsity Clb; Bsktbl; Tennis; Hon Roll; Jr NHS; NHS; UC Berkeley; Bus Admin.

SICKLICK, JASON K; Whitney HS; Cerritos, CA; (1); Key Clb; Temple Yth Grp; Hon Roll; CJSF; Physcn.

SICKLICK, JEREMY D; Whitney HS; Cerritos, CA; (2); Bus Profs of Am; FBLA; Key Clb; Temple Yth Grp; Radio Contrl Racer; Gynclgst.

SICKS, BUD R; Tulare Union HS; Tulare, CA; (3); FFA; Math Clb; Teachers Aide; High Hon Roll; Hon Roll; Prfct Atten Awd; Golden St Exam; Schl Recogntn Algebra; Golden St Exam; Schl Recgnstn Geometry; Sequoia; Bus.

SIDA, SYLVIA E; Fontana HS; Fontana, CA; (2); L Color Guard; Vllybl; Hon Roll; Prfct Atten Awd; Vlntr Wrk At Elem Schl; Sci.

SIDDEL, RACHEL F; Redlands HS; Redlands, CA; (2); AFS; Library Aide; Ski Clb; Spanish Clb; School Play; Cit Awd; High Hon Roll; Pres Acad Fit Awd; Rotary Awd; CJSF; CSF; Frgn Lang.

SIDDIQUI, IMRAN T; Bella Vista HS; Fair Oaks, CA; (3); 19/363; Var Trk; Hon Roll; NHS; Dept Awds Sci, Drftng, Socl Sci & PE 1987-90; Sci Olympcs; Berkeley; Engr.

SIDDIQUI, KAUSER; Claremont HS; Claremont, CA; (2); Church Yth Grp; Spanish Clb; Hon Roll; Friday Night Live Clb; Am Fld Soc; U CA Davis; Pdtrcn.

SIDDIQUI, RONA; Moore JR HS; Redlands, CA; (1); Church Yth Grp; Pep Clb; Thesps; Pres Band; Mrchg Band; Pep Band; School Play; Stage Crew; Variety Show; Rep Stu Cncl; CJSF; CA Arts Schlr; Mrt Awd In Piano; Music.

SIDDIQUI, SHEREEN; Redlands HS; Redlands, CA; (4); Pres Drama Clb; Hosp Aide; Speech Tm; School Play; Rptr Nwsp; JV Vllybl; Lion Awd; Pres Acad Fit Awd; Academic Decathlon; U Of MO Columbia; Brdcst Jrnls.

SIDHU, HIRDERAJ S; Andrew Hill HS; San Jose, CA; (1); Med Magnet Prgm; Med.

SIDHU, RAMAN K; San Gabriel Mission HS; La Puente, CA; (3); Church Yth Grp; Cmnty Wkr; French Clb; FBLA; GAA; Math Clb; Science Clb; Trk; Vllybl; High Hon Roll; Gold Mdl All Rnd Vlybl Trnmnt; San Gabriel Indstry Cncl Wrk Exprnc Ed Awd; UC Riverside; Dntst.

SIDHU, RAVINDER PAUL; Newark Memorial HS; Newark, CA; (3); Church Yth Grp; Cmnty Wkr; Spanish Clb; Rep SADD; VP Stu Cncl; JV Crs Cntry; Var Trk; High Hon Roll; Prfct Atten Awd; Pres Acad Fit Awd; Biking; Stu Of Month Awd; Outstndng Athl Awd Track & Field; Stanford U; Pre-Med.

SIDHU, RUPINDER; Oxnard HS; Burbank, CA; (1); Cit Awd; Hon Roll; Prfct Atten Awd; CSF; Med.

SIDIME, ODILLA; Mission HS; San Francisco, CA; (4); 18/320; Cmnty Wkr; Teachers Aide; Mrchg Band; VP Frsh Cls; Pres Soph Cls; Trk; High Hon Roll; Jr NHS; HOB Ldrshp Ambssdr; Xavier U; Engl.

SIEBERT, SARAH; Brethren HS; Long Beach, CA; (2); Church Yth Grp; JV Sftbl; Hon Roll; NHS; Pres Acad Fit Awd; Yth For Chrst-Cmps Lf Clb; Biola U; Psych.

SIEGA, THERESA; Castle Park HS; Chula Vista, CA; (4); 40/328; Treas Drama Clb; Treas Pep Clb; Thesps; School Play; Stage Crew; Mgr(s); Var Socr; Schl Mascot; ASB; U Of CA San Diego.

SIEGEL, DAVID E; Birmingham HS; Encino, CA; (2); Bus Profs of Am; Cmnty Wkr; Debate Tm; FBLA; Key Clb; SADD; Temple Yth Grp; Rep Bus Profs of Am; VP Soph Cls; Rep Stu Cncl; UCLA; Bus.

SIEGEL, ERIK T; Clovis HS; Clovis, CA; (2); 4-H; Band; Mrchg Band; JV Vllybl; JV Wrstlng; 4-H Awd; Hon Roll; US Naval Sea Cadet Corps; Odyssey Of The Mind; Naval Acad; Math.

SIEGEL, MELISSA; Palo Verde HS; Blythe, CA; (4); Sec Treas Church Yth Grp; Cmnty Wkr; Drama Clb; Service Clb; SADD; Rptr Yrbk; Hon Roll; NHS; Key Clb; Pep Clb; CSF; Jobs Dghtrs Hnrd Queen; U Rdlnds; Ed.

SIEGER, ERIC; Notre Dame HS; North Hollywood, CA; (2); Church Yth Grp; Latin Clb; Band; Mrchg Band; School Musical; Tennis; Hon Roll; CSF.

SIEGERT, ANJA SIMONE; James Lick HS; West Germany; (4); Church Yth Grp; Dance Clb; Debate Tm; Drama Clb; French Clb; German Clb; Girl Scts; Latin Clb; Science Clb; Ski Clb; Ski Awds; 1st Of Ger Drama Mem Schl; Friedrich Dessauer Gym; Mngmnt.

SIEGFRIED, BETH; Tri-City Christian Schl; Oceanside, CA; (2); Church Yth Grp; Var Cheerldng; JV Pom Pon; Hon Roll; 1st And 2nd Place In Science Fari; Regional And National Pom Pon Winner; UCLA; High School English Tech.

SIEGLE, SAMANTHA GALE; Oakwood HS; Los Angeles, CA; (4); Cmnty Wkr; SADD; Ed Yrbk; Var Capt Sftbl; Var Vllybl; UCLA; Art.

SIEGLER, CARL F; Victory Christian HS; Carmichael, CA; (3); 6/32; Church Yth Grp; Band; School Play; Phtg Yrbk; Rptr Soph Cls; Pres Jr Cls; Var Bsbl; Var JV Bsktbl; Pres NHS; Ntl Merit Schol; Scndry Ed.

SIELING, JESSICA L; Foothill HS; Sacramento, CA; (1); Church Yth Grp; Computer Clb; Church Choir; Flag Corp; Cit Awd; Hon Roll; UC Santa Barbara; Prefrmng Art.

SIENENPIPER, DAN F; Novato HS; Novato, CA; (4); 1/275; Key Clb; JV Golf; High Hon Roll; JETS Awd; Ntl Merit Ltr; Pres Acad Fit Awd; Val; Dodecahedron Club VP; CA Soc Prfssnl Engrs Awd; CSPE Glnd Gate Schrlshp; U Of CA Los Angeles; Elec Engr.

SIEPERDA, JULIE A; Fresno Christian HS; Kerman, CA; (3); Church Yth Grp; Letterman Clb; Chorus; Sec Soph Cls; VP Sr Cls; Var L Bsktbl; Var L Vllybl; High Hon Roll; Engl Hghst Hnrs; Hghst Hnrs 87-89; Sci.

SIERRA, DANICA J; Rancho Alamitos HS; Garden Grove, CA; (2); Church Yth Grp; Orch; Outstndng Soph Orchstr.

SIERRA, HOA; Grace M Davis HS; Modesto, CA; (3); Church Yth Grp; Cmnty Wkr; Treas DECA; Service Clb; Spanish Clb; Cit Awd; Hon Roll; Vlntr Wk; Marketing.

SIERRA, JAY J; Chino HS; Chino, CA; (2); Var Bsbl;.AR; Pro Bsbl.

SIERRA, MICHAEL D; San Lorenzo HS; San Leandro, CA; (2); Boy Scts; Church Yth Grp; Computer Clb; Office Aide; SADD; Proj EDEN; Close Up Pgm; Achvt Cert; Psych.

SIERRA, MICHELLE; Fillmore HS; Fillmore, CA; (4); 46/200; Church Yth Grp; Pres Intnl Clb; SADD; Teachers Aide; Nwsp; Writing Poetry Awds 87-88; Semi Fnlst Natl Hispanic Schlrs Pgm; St Marys Coll CA; Jrnlsm.

SIERRA, ROSEMARY H; East Bakersfield HS; Bakersfield, CA; (2); Office Aide; Band; Mrchg Band; UC Davis; Med.

SIERRA, VIRIDIANA; Bishop Amat HS; W Covina, CA; (3); Spanish Clb; Speech Tm; Hon Roll; Spanish NHS; Amnesty Intl; CSF; Bus Admin.

SIERRAS, ALISA R; Roosevelt School Of The Arts; Fresno, CA; (3); 51/700; Spanish Clb; Band; Orch; Cit Awd; Hon Roll; Orchestra Achievement; Leadership Club; UC Davis; Pediatrician.

SIEVERS, MARGARET E; Foothill HS; Pleasanton, CA; (3); Ski Clb; Ed Nwsp; Hon Roll; Golden ST Exam 1st Yr Alg; CA Polytech SLO; Math Ed.

SIFFERMANN, MAUREEN L; Louisville HS; Westlake Village, CA; (3); GAA; Hosp Aide; Tennis; Hon Roll; NHS; CSF; Alge II Awd; Phys Sci Awd; Bus.

SIFUENTES, DEBBIE; North Salinas HS; Salinas, CA; (3); Girl Scts; Var Swmmng; High Hon Roll; Hon Roll; NHS; Rotary Awd; Girl Scts Silver Awd; Stu Mnth Scl Sci & Phys Ed; Chmpns Club; Salinas Vly Aquatics; Marine Bio.

SIFUENTES, MARCELLA M; James Lick HS; San Jose, CA; (1); Aud/Vis; Dance Clb; Drama Clb; Stage Crew; Variety Show; Swmmng; Law Judge Magnet Pgm.

SIFUENTES, RUBEN; North Monterey County HS; Salinas, CA; (4); Latin Clb; Crs Cntry; Hon Roll; Devry Inst Of Tech; Engrng Med.

SIGAFOOS, JENNIFER A; San Clemente HS; San Clemente, CA; (4); Church Yth Grp; Cmnty Wkr; French Clb; Science Clb; School Musical; Yrbk; Var L Bsktbl; Var L Vllybl; Treas NHS; Pres Acad Fit Awd; VP Jr Statesman Amer; Ofcr South Co Safe Rides & Acad Decathlon; UCLA; Pol Sci.

SIGDESTAD, CAROL A; Colton HS; Grand Terrace, CA; (2); Church Yth Grp; FFA; Hosp Aide; Red Cross Aide; Sec Soph Cls; Swmmng; Trk; Vllybl; Hon Roll; NHS; High Point Var Swim Team; Floriculture Awd In FFA; USC; Accntng.

SIGFORD, KATHLEEN M; Redlands HS; Redlands, CA; (3); Varsity Clb; Var Bsktbl; Var Crs Cntry; Var Trk.

SIGLER, REED A; Chaffey HS; Ontario, CA; (3); 13/850; Am Leg Boys St; Science Clb; Spanish Clb; Yrbk; Hon Roll; Prfct Atten Awd; Acadmc Dcthln; Med.

SIGMON, BROOKE M; Thomas Downey HS; Modesto, CA; (2); Church Yth Grp; Key Clb; Teachers Aide; Var Swmmng; Prfct Atten Awd; Vrsty Waterpolo; CSF; Dance Prod; UC Davis; Math.

SIGNORELLI, CHAD T; Lompoc HS; Lompoc, CA; (3); 1/375; Am Leg Boys St; Cmnty Wkr; Letterman Clb; Yrbk; Var L Tennis; High Hon Roll; CSF Jr Rep Tutoring Chairprsn.

SIGUR, RACHEL L; St Paul HS; Whittier, CA; (3); JCL; Latin Clb; JV Var Bsktbl; Hon Roll; NHS; CSF; U CA-IRVINE; Med.

SIGURDSSON, LEILA; Laguna Hills HS; Laguna Hills, CA; (1); Hon Roll; Algebra I Stu Of Month; Acad Achvt Awd; Acad Schl Pinss; Law.

SIHACHACK, VASANA C; Westminster HS; Westminster, CA; (3); Computer Clb; English Clb; JA; JCL; Library Aide; Math Tm; Model UN; Science Clb; Teachers Aide; Off Sr Cls; UCLA; Law.

SIHARATH, SONEPHET; Arvin HS; Arvin, CA; (4); 1/361; Drama Clb; SADD; Variety Show; Socr; Tennis; High Hon Roll; Hon Roll; Val; Acad Decthln; Mck Trl; CSF; UC Berkeley.

SIINO, TONY F; Hillsdale HS; San Mateo, CA; (3); Auto.

SIK, ROBIN K; Eagle Rock HS; Los Angeles, CA; (3); Hon Roll; Golden St Exam Hgh Hnr; UC Berkeley; Elctrnc Engrng.

SIKES, GARRY D; W C Overfelt HS; San Jose, CA; (1); CSF; Aeronautics Engrng.

SIKES, KELLY L; San Pasqual HS; Escondido, CA; (2); Church Yth Grp; Girl Scts; Treas Soph Cls; JV Fld Hcky; JV Socr; Hon Roll; Intrst Frgn Lang-Cmpltd Span II & Amer Amer Sign Lang II; Silver Awd Girl Scout; CA ST Long Beach; Phys Thrpst.

SILAGHI, TRAVIS W; Highlands HS; North Highlands, CA; (3); Socr.

SILBERFELD, ASHLEY; Heschel Day Schl; Northridge, CA; (1); Teachers Aide; School Musical; School Play; Variety Show; Nwsp; Pres Stu Cncl; Cheerldng; Liberal Arts.

SILBERMAN, ADRIAN E; John F Kennedy HS; La Palma, CA; (1); Rptr Nwsp; Intrml Ftbl; JV Socr; Intrml Wt Lftg; Cit Awd; High Hon Roll; Pres Acad Fit Awd; Eng Undergrad Awd; U Of CA Irvine; Orthdntst.

SILER, HEATHER S; Merced HS; Merced, CA; (3); FHA; Hon Roll; Merced JC; Ed.

SILER, LISA A; Palmdale HS; Sylmar, CA; (4); Band; Chorus; Jazz Band; Mrchg Band; Orch; Pep Band; Treas Soph Cls; Cit Awd; Hon Roll; Kiwanis Awd; Band Cncl, Unfrm Mngr, Sec; Most Outstndng Stu Awds; Humbolt St U; Music Prfsnl.

SILER, SEAN; Bishop Amat HS; Walnut, CA; (4); VP Band; Drm Mjr(t); Pep Band; School Musical; VP Pres Stu Cncl; Hon Roll; NHS; Civil Air Patrol-Squadron Commander; Drum Line-Instr/Capt; Bank Of Am Music Awd; CA ST Polytech U-Pomona; Engr.

SILIEZAR, EDDIE A; Burroughs HS; Burbank, CA; (2); Boy Scts; Chorus; Church Choir; Trk; Writer.

SILL, DOUG W; Esperanza HS; Yorba Linda, CA; (2); 34/571; Bsktbl; NHS; Stu Of Mnth.

SILLETT, DOMENIQUE; Edison HS; Huntington Bch, CA; (4); 146/502; Library Aide; Office Aide; Lit Mag; Art Golden Key 88-89, Medallion 90; Dance 87-88; Huntington Beach Art Leag Schlrshp 90; Pratt Inst; Commnctns Dsgn.

SILLETT, KRISTEN R; Bonita HS; La Verne, CA; (1); Socr; Little League Grls Sftbl.

SILLONA, FREILANI KAY; St Genevieve HS; North Hollywood, CA; (4); 3/150; Drama Clb; Science Clb; SADD; Stage Crew; VP Pres Stu Cncl; JV Var Vllybl; High Hon Roll; NEDT Awd; Opt Clb Awd; CSF.

SILOS, CARLA C; Archbishop Mitty HS; San Jose, CA; (1); 66/388; JV Vllybl; Cinematolgraphy.

SILOS, FRANCESCA L; Skyline HS; Oakland, CA; (2); Science Clb; Band; Hon Roll; Prfct Atten Awd; Amnsty Intnl Club; UC; Bus.

SILVA, ALBERT G; Don Bosco Technical Inst; Los Angeles, CA; (3); Church Yth Grp; Drama Clb; Red Cross Aide; School Musical; Prfct Atten Awd; CA ST Los Angeles; Bus Mgmt.

SILVA, ANDY T; Irvine HS; Irvine, CA; (4); French Clb; Key Clb; Band; Var JV Crs Cntry; JV Ftbl; JV Trk; Wt Lftg; Hon Roll; Pres Acad Fit Awd; UCI; Civil Engrng.

SILVA, CANDY M; Monte Vista HS; Spring Valley, CA; (3); 70/373; Sec Church Yth Grp; Latin Clb; Hon Roll; Cert Of Merit; Cert Of Achvt; Cert Of Apprctn; Diploma Of Merit For Spnch Cls; Ped Med.

SILVA, CECILIA; Baldwin Park HS; Baldwin Park, CA; (4); Spanish Clb; Drill Tm; Stu Cncl; High Hon Roll; Prfct Atten Awd; Acad Ltr; Bus.

SILVA, CHAD; Arroyo Grande HS; Arroyo Grande, CA; (3); 30/531; Church Yth Grp; Pres DECA; FCA; JV Bsktbl; Hon Roll; CA Polytech U; Bus.

SILVA, CYNTHIA M; Fresno Christian HS; Fresno, CA; (3); Church Yth Grp; Chorus; School Play; Var Bsktbl; Var Powder Puff Ftbl; Var Vllybl; High Hon Roll; Hon Roll; Pres Acad Fit Awd; Dance Clb; Bus.

SILVA, DANIELLE A; El Toro HS; Trabuco Canyon, CA; (4); 135/530; Drama Clb; Girl Scts; Teachers Aide; Var Capt Bsktbl; High Hon Roll; Pres Acad Fit Awd.

SILVA, DAVID; Capuchino HS; San Bruno, CA; (2); Letterman Clb; Band; Mrchg Band; Orch; Pep Band; JV Bsbl; JV Bsktbl; Var Mgr(s); JV L Trk; Hon Roll; Cngrssnl Schlr.

SILVA, DEANA; Compton HS; Compton, CA; (2); JV Socr; Hon Roll; U Of CA Riverside; Comp Sci.

SILVA, DENISE L; Rubidoux HS; Mira Loma, CA; (4); 32/750; Art Clb; Church Yth Grp; Cmnty Wkr; Teachers Aide; Nwsp; Powder Puff Ftbl; JV Var Sftbl; Cit Awd; Hon Roll; New Visions Clb Christian Fllwshp; 1st Pl Art Show Indio Date Fstvl; Teach 3-4 Yr Olds Sunday Schl; Art Ctr Dsgn; Graphic Dsgn.

SILVA, EDGAR; Calexico HS; Calexico, CA; (4); Boy Scts; FBLA; Spanish Clb; Bsktbl; Ftbl; Wt Lftg; Cit Awd; 4 Prfct Atten Awds; Accntng & Bkkpng Awd; 3 Cortez Peters Bus Awds; MBA; Live Prosperly.

SILVA, ERNESTO R; Apple Valley HS; Apple Valley, CA; (3); VICA; High Hon Roll; Future Ldrs Of Amer Prgm; Acad Decthln Club; Sign Lang Club; Engr.

SILVA, FABIOLA; Pasadena HS; Pasadena, CA; (2); French Clb; Hon Roll; MESA Hispanic/African Amer; Upwrd Bnd Pgm; USC Stanford; Medcl.

SILVA, GREGORY L; Golden West HS; Visalia, CA; (2); Art Clb; Boy Scts; 4-H; French Clb; Letterman Clb; Varsity Clb; Church Choir; Crs Cntry; Socr; Trk; 1st Pl Wnnr Bynd War Bllbrd Cont; MVP Trk 90; Plvltng Rcrds; Cnty Hstrcl Soc; CA Poly San Luis Obispo; Bus.

SILVA, HILDA V; Santa Ana HS; Santa Ana, CA; (3); UCI; Nurse.

SILVA, JANELLE; Lodi HS; Lodi, CA; (1); Church Yth Grp; GAA; Chorus; Church Choir; High Hon Roll; Hon Roll; Prfct Atten Awd; Med Sci.

SILVA, JAY P; Lincoln HS; San Jose, CA; (3); Wrstlng; Hnrs Wood; Top Wrstlr; Most Imprvd Engl Stu; Outstndng Stu Smmr Schl; Cal Poly; Indstrl Arts.

SILVA, JOE J; Orosi HS; Orosi, CA; (2); Band; Mrchg Band; Ftbl; Golf; Hon Roll; Fresno ST U; Elec Engr.

SILVA, KELLY D; Apple Valley SR HS; Apple Valley, CA; (3); German Clb; Office Aide; Pep Clb; Rep Stu Cncl; JV Ftbl; High Hon Roll; Hon Roll; Teacher.

SILVA, KIM M; Redondo Union HS; Redondo Beach, CA; (4); 41/409; Church Yth Grp; Drama Clb; Key Clb; Quiz Bowl; SADD; Drill Tm; School Musical; School Play; Cheerldng; Cit Awd; Homcmng Princess; Oscar Pgm; Ldr For Day; CSF; Stand Up Original Comedy Strip; Drama Festvl-1st Pl; UCLA; Bus.

SILVA, KRYSTAL A; Atwater HS; Atwater, CA; (4); 12/425; Cmnty Wkr; Key Clb; Teachers Aide; Capt Powder Puff Ftbl; Var Capt Socr; JV Sftbl; High Hon Roll; Pres Acad Fit Awd; Schlr Athl Achvt Awd; Sccr Coach; A P Chem, Bio, Engl; UC Davis; Biochem.

SILVA, LETICIA; Bishop Amat HS; Baldwin Park, CA; (2); Cmnty Wkr; Spanish Clb; High Hon Roll; Spnsh 2nd Hnrs Awd 89; Natl Spnsh Exam Hnr Diploma 3rd Pl 89, 6th Pl 90; USC; Med.

SILVA, MARIA A; Arlington HS; Riverside, CA; (3); 41/151; Dance Clb; Drill Tm; Vllybl; Hon Roll; Dance Schlr; CSF; Home Ec Achvt Awd; Nrsng.

SILVA, MARK; San Pasqual HS; Escondido, CA; (3); 1/300; Church Yth Grp; Cmnty Wkr; Computer Clb; Spanish Clb; Var Crs Cntry; Var Trk; High Hon Roll; Ntl Merit Schol; Prfct Atten Awd; Val; CSF; Amnsty Intl; Stanford; Comp Sci.

SILVA, MARTIN; Firebaugh HS; Firebaugh, CA; (2); 10/70; SADD; Bsbl; Bsktbl; Ftbl; Wt Lftg; Fresno ST U.

SILVA, PATRICIA; Montclair HS; Montclair, CA; (2); French Clb; FHA; Hosp Aide; Key Clb; Red Cross Aide; Med.

SILVA, PATRICIA ANN; Bear River HS; Auburn, CA; (3); Spanish Clb; Cheerldng; High Hon Roll; Hon Roll; Prfct Atten Awd; Marine Bio.

SILVA, PHILIP J; Redwood Christian HS; San Leandro, CA; (3); Computer Clb; Drama Clb; Spanish Clb; School Musical; School Play; Hon Roll; Phys Sci.

SILVA, RAQUEL R; Escondido HS; Escondido, CA; (1); Hon Roll; Coll; Mathematics.

SILVA, REBECCA; Bishop Amat HS; Baldwin Park, CA; (4); 44/395; Spanish Clb; Prfct Atten Awd; Slvr Scrn Clb; Spnsh AP Coll Bd Exm; Ntl Spnsh Tm; 2nd Hnrs Bus; USC; RN.

SILVA, ROMAN; Yosemite HS; Coarsegold, CA; (2); 1/190; FBLA; Math Clb; Science Clb; Band; Hon Roll; U Of CA Santa Barbara Ambssdr Prog 89-90; Stanford U; Microbio.

SILVA, RONALD E; Arroyo Grande HS; Arroyo Grande, CA; (2); 105/625; JV Wrstlng; U Of CA Berkeley; Bus Admin.

SILVA, ROSA M; Lincoln HS; Lincoln, CA; (4); Church Yth Grp; Cmnty Wkr; Office Aide; Pep Clb; Spanish Clb; SADD; Teachers Aide; Chorus; Hon Roll; Friday Night Live Clb; Sierra Coll; Kndgtn Tchr.

SILVA, RUBY A; Delano Joint Union HS; Earlimart, CA; (3); Computer Clb; Spanish Clb; Federicos Beauty Coll; Csmtlgy.

SILVA, STEVE; Nogales HS; La Puente, CA; (2); 131/741; Science Clb; Band; Mrchg Band; Pep Band; JV Wrstlng; Hon Roll; Amnsty Intl; Acad Dcthln; UC Berkeley; Law.

SILVA, SUMMER; Calaveras HS; San Andreas, CA; (1); Band; JV Cheerldng; High Hon Roll; Hon Roll; U Of Santa Clara; Elem Educ.

SILVA, TIFFANY A; San Benito HS; Hollister, CA; (4); 23/229; Church Yth Grp; GAA; Ski Clb; Ed Yrbk; Treas Jr Cls; Sftbl; Capt Vllybl; Elks Awd; Hon Roll; Pres Acad Fit Awd; Homcmng Princess; U Of CA Santa Barbara; Psych.

SILVA, TIMOTHY S; Garden Grove HS; Garden Grove, CA; (3); 35/350; FCA; Rep Stu Cncl; Var Bsbl; Var Capt Ftbl; Var Capt Socr; Hon Roll; Congrssnl Yth Ldrshp Cncl; Engr.

SILVA, WENDY; Lincoln HS; Stockton, CA; (3); Church Yth Grp; Cmnty Wkr; French Clb; SADD; Thesps; Church Choir; School Play; Variety Show; French Hon Soc; High Hon Roll; FOCUS; Piano Performances; UCLA Berkley; Psych.

SILVAS, DIANA; Aquinas HS; Grand Terrace, CA; (4); 24/101; Key Clb; Stat Bsktbl; L Crs Cntry; L Trk; High Hon Roll; Hon Roll; Natl Hspnc Schlr Awd Semifnlst; Friday Night Live; Claremont Mc Kenna Coll; Accntn.

SILVAS, SERENA D; Manteca HS; Manteca, CA; (4); 37/293; Capt Color Guard; Drill Tm; Flag Corp; Mrchg Band; High Hon Roll; Hon Roll; Prin Awd; Solo Twrlr 86-90; Delta Coll; Vet.

SILVEIRA, CAROLINE A; Tulare Union HS; Tulare, CA; (2); 3/461; Church Yth Grp; Drama Clb; Pep Clb; VP Frsh Cls; VP Soph Cls; Var Cheerldng; Var Trk; High Hon Roll; NHS.

SILVEIRA, DANIEL; Bellarmine HS; San Jose, CA; (1); Church Yth Grp; Cmnty Wkr; Office Aide; Intrml Crs Cntry; Intrml Socr; Intrml Trk; USAF Acad; Astronaut.

SILVEIRA, GARY S; Westmont HS; Campbell, CA; (2); Cmnty Wkr; Teachers Aide; Socr; Hon Roll; West Valley; Med.

SILVEIRA, JEFFREY R; Bellarmine College Prep; San Jose, CA; (4); 55/302; Boy Scts; Science Clb; Stage Crew; Ntl Merit Ltr; Pres Acad Fit Awd; Eagle Sct; Santa Clara U; Mech Engrng.

SILVEIRA, LINDA M; Grace Davis HS; Modesto, CA; (2); Church Yth Grp; Teachers Aide; Church Choir; Hon Roll; MYSA Sccr; CSF.

SILVEIRA, TRACI L; Taft Union HS; Fellows, CA; (3); 35/200; Hon Roll; DECA Clb; Taft Coll; Teach.

SILVER, ALISHA; Montgomery HS; Santa Rosa, CA; (2); Art Clb; French Clb; JA; Key Clb; Pep Clb; Science Clb; Teachers Aide; Chorus; Stage Crew; JV Trk; Schl Rcgntn, Hnrs Golden St Exam; Swmmng.

SILVER, ELI A; Napa HS; Napa, CA; (3); 1/400; Am Leg Boys St; Dance Clb; Band; Chorus; Mrchg Band; Pep Band; Sec Treas Frsh Cls; Var Tennis; Cit Awd; High Hon Roll; 1st Pl Public Schls Wk Essay Cont.

SILVER, JOHN C; Lutheran HS; Orange, CA; (3); French Clb; Band; Jazz Band; Pep Band; Australia Club Trip To Australia, New Zealand & Tahiti; Europe Club Trip Tofrance & Italy; CA Inst Of Arts; Film Prod.

SILVER, LAURIE; Campbell Hall HS; Van Nuys, CA; (1); Cmnty Wkr; Letterman Clb; Service Clb; JV Capt Cheerldng.

SILVER, MICHELLE S; Campbell Hall HS; Van Nuys, CA; (4); Chess Clb; Cmnty Wkr; Service Clb; Spanish Clb; Temple Yth Grp; Band; Ed Nwsp; Ed Lit Mag; Sec Frsh Cls; Hon Roll; Vly Asstns Asstnce League Sthrn CA; Hrsbck Rdng; Stu Trvl; Economics.

SILVER, NICOLE C; Don Antonio Lugo HS; Chino, CA; (4); Drama Clb; Key Clb; Treas Service Clb; Chorus; School Musical; School Play; Variety Show; Treas Stu Cncl; Vllybl; Cit Awd; CSF Schlrshp & Pres; Rotary Schlrshp; Cal ST Fullerton; Chiroprctr.

SILVER, SHERI; Redlands HS; Redlands, CA; (4); 560/850; Church Yth Grp; Drama Clb; Teachers Aide; Mrchg Band; School Play; Ntl Merit Ltr; Warner Southern Coll; Bus.

SILVER, STEPHANIE L; Mesa Verde HS; Citrus Heights, CA; (2); 11/257; Church Yth Grp; Girl Scts; Orch; Socr; JV Sftbl; High Hon Roll; Hon Roll; Crtfct Of Excl & Mrt; Acdmc Awds; UC Davis; Ed Tchr.

SILVER, TEENA L; North Hollywood HS; North Hollywood, CA; (2); Cmnty Wkr; Pres Service Clb; Temple Yth Grp; Rep Frsh Cls; Hon Roll; Jr NHS; Pres Acad Fit Awd; Atten Awds Hebrew HS; ULPAN Pgm Isreal Smmr 90.

SILVER, TODD E; Bullard HS; Fresno, CA; (1); Ski Clb; Sec Treas Frsh Cls; JV Golf; Hon Roll; Oddssy Of Mnd; Sci Olympd; UC Berkley; Electrc Engnr.

SILVERBERG, MICHAEL; Hamilton Humanities Magnet HS; Los Angeles, CA; (4); French Clb; Band; L Bsktbl; Var Tennis; US Army Schlr-Ath Awd; UC San Diego.

SILVERIO, CATHY F; Fairfield HS; Fairfield, CA; (2); School Play; Off Jr Cls; JV Crs Cntry; JV Powder Puff Ftbl; JV Trk; Hon Roll; VP NHS; VP CSF; Jr Stsmn Amer; Acad Dcthln; Engr.

SILVERIO, MAE; San Joaquin Memorial HS; Fresno, CA; (3); GAA; Pres Spanish Clb; Ed Nwsp; Pres Jr Cls; Capt Bsktbl; Capt Powder Puff Ftbl; Capt Var Sftbl; Stat Vllybl; Hon Roll; Geom Excllnce Awd 89; Christian Brothers Ldrshp Retreat 90; Rotary Yth Ldrshp Camp 90; Med.

SILVERMAN, EDWARD; Banning HS; Banning, CA; (1); 1/272; Boy Scts; French Clb; Teachers Aide; Temple Yth Grp; High Hon Roll; Eagle Sct; J Hopkins Ctr Tlntd Yth; 1st Pl Wnnr Inlnd Sci & Engrng Fair; MIT; Sci.

SILVERMAN, LAUREL D; Los Alamitos HS; Fountain Valley, CA; (3); Cmnty Wkr; Key Clb; Service Clb; SADD; Temple Yth Grp; Thesps; Chorus; School Musical; School Play; Variety Show; OCHSA; Yng Americans; PRE-COLL Smmr Pgm At Carnegie Mellon U For Performning Arts; Vlntr Of Yr; Musical Theater.

SILVERMAN, LAUREL E; Piedmont HS; Piedmont, CA; (4); 5/145; JA; Pres Spanish Clb; School Musical; Treas Stu Cncl; Cheerldng; Var Capt Tennis; Pres NHS; Pres Acad Fit Awd; Soc Of Wmn Engrs Hnr Merit; Var Pom Pon Girl; LJW Bird Calling Cont-Johnny Carson Tonight Show; Stanford U.

SILVEROSE, CHAD A; Modesto HS; Modesto, CA; (2); SADD; JV Ftbl; Mgr(s); Swmmng; JV Trk; Yng Demcrts; Staniford U; Nuclear Engr.

SILVERSTEIN, MICHELE L; Thousand Oaks HS; Thousand Oaks, CA; (4); Teachers Aide; Sec Sr Cls; Stu Cncl; JV Capt Cheerldng; Bank Tllr-Cert Of Prfcncy; CA ST Northridge; Bus.

SILVERSTEIN, STUART A; Taft HS; Tarzana, CA; (3); Chorus; Jazz Band; Mrchg Band; Rep Jr Cls; Ftbl; Wt Lftg; Hon Roll; U Of Miami; Prfrmnc.

SILVERTON, JULIA; St Marys HS; Stockton, CA; (3); JA; Key Clb; Model UN; SADD; Drill Tm; School Play; Nwsp; Yrbk; Var Swmmng; High Hon Roll; Nwsp Edtr; Chld Abuse Ctr Volntr; Brdcstng.

SILVESTRE, DIANE M; Mt Whitney HS; Visalia, CA; (2); Church Yth Grp; 4-H; FFA; Hon Roll; Bus.

SILVESTRE, FRAULEIN; Balboa HS; San Francisco, CA; (1); Model UN; Chorus; Co-Ed Sec Yrbk; Treas Jr Cls; Treas Sr Cls; Sec Stu Cncl; Cheerldng; Hon Roll; Val; Schlr-Athl Plq 89; Bank Of Amer Achvt Awd Sci & Math 90; Helmsmen Trphy-Svcs In Schl 90; U CA Davis; Genetic Engrng.

SILVESTRI, GINA; Sunny Hills HS; Fullerton, CA; (4); Church Yth Grp; Pep Clb; Ski Clb; Teachers Aide; Sec Varsity Clb; Stu Cncl; Powder Puff Ftbl; Capt Socr; Sftbl; High Hon Roll; Hmcmng Qn; U AZ; Intl Bus.

SILVETTI, NATALIA; Montclaire Prep Schl; Tarzana, CA; (1); French Clb; Teachers Aide; Cheerldng; French Hon Soc; Hon Roll; NHS.

SILVEY, BONITA L; East Bakersfield HS; Bakersfield, CA; (1); Teachers Aide; Chorus; Hon Roll; Teacher.

SILZER, STEPHANIE; Foothill HS; Pleasanton, CA; (3); 10/286; Church Yth Grp; Cmnty Wkr; Drama Clb; FCA; Chorus; Church Choir; School Musical; School Play; Sec Jr Cls; Sec Stu Cncl; Deleg Congrssnl Yth Ldrshp Cncl; CA Schlrshp Fed; Ed.

SIM, ALBERT K; Rio Americano HS; Sacramento, CA; (3); Treas Church Yth Grp; French Clb; Key Clb; Jazz Band; Wrstlng; Hon Roll; Jr Statesmen Amer; Friday Night Live; U CA Los Angeles; Med.

SIM, BRIAN C; Paramount HS; Bellflower, CA; (4); 35/426; Science Clb; Cit Awd; Hon Roll; Prfct Atten Awd; Pres Acad Fit Awd; CSF; U Of CA Irvine; Biolgcl Sci.

SIM, IVAN; Schurr HS; Monterey Park, CA; (3); French Clb; Key Clb; Q&S; Science Clb; Ed Nwsp; Hon Roll; Ntl Merit Ltr; Prfct Atten Awd; JR Statesmen Am VP; Library Vol; CA Schlrshp Fed Sec.

SIM, JENNY; Redlands HS; Loma Linda, CA; (4); Stu Cncl; Sftbl; U Of CA Riverside; Bio-Chem.

SIM, ROSELYNN; Mater Dei HS; Rancho Santa Marg, CA; (3); Rep Frsh Cls; Off Jr Cls; Off Sr Cls; JV Crs Cntry; JV Stat Trk; High Hon Roll; NHS; CSF; Jr Statesman Of Am Sec/Treas; Hnrsawdentrace/Acceptance Mater Dei; Med.

SIM, SARATH; Modesto HS; Modesto, CA; (4); Vllybl; Hlth Educ.

SIM, TIFFANIE; Schurr HS; Monterey Park, CA; (1); Debate Tm; Key Clb; Tennis; JSA; CSF.

SIMAL, JAMIE; Hilmar HS; Hilmar, CA; (3); Letterman Clb; Teachers Aide; Varsity Clb; Var Ftbl; Hon Roll; Stanislaus ST U; Phys Educ.

SIMANDJUNTAK, FREDY S; Pomona Adventist JR Acad; San Dimas, CA; (2); Church Yth Grp; Teachers Aide; Band; Chorus; Church Choir; Orch; Pep Band; Rep Frsh Cls; Sec Soph Cls; Bsbl; Awd Most Imprvd; Awd Dependblty,Respnsblty & Orgnztn; Loma Linda U; Plastic Surgeon.

SIMANDJUNTAK, SYLVIA D; Pomona Adventist Jr Acad; San Dimas, CA; (1); Church Yth Grp; Cmnty Wkr; French Clb; Office Aide; Band; Chorus; Church Choir; Rptr Yrbk; Pres Frsh Cls; Stu Cncl; Awd Excllnc In Eng; Loma Linda U; Pedtrcn.

SIMAR, SHANNON; Newport Harbor HS; Newport Beach, CA; (3); 39/315; GAA; JCL; Key Clb; Latin Clb; Ski Clb; Spanish Clb; Rep Nwsp; JV Capt Tennis; JV Trk.

SIMAS, ROBERT P; Montgomery HS; Santa Rosa, CA; (2); Boy Scts; 4-H; Science Clb; Spanish Clb; 4-H Awd; Hon Roll; Jr NHS; Most Imprvd Span Stu; Stu Mnth; U C Davis; Vet.

SIMEK, ALLISON L; Venice HS; Mar Vista, CA; (2); Church Yth Grp; Cmnty Wkr; Hosp Aide; Stage Crew; Hist Jr Cls; JV Cheerldng; Hon Roll; Athnian; Chtelaines-Schl Svc; Dlphian-Hnr Rl; Law.

SIMEON, ALLAN S; Santa Clara HS; Santa Clara, CA; (3); Var Trk; Cit Awd; Prfct Atten Awd; Pres Acad Fit Awd; Frgn Lang Awd Frnch; Outstndng Athl Awd Jnr Vrsty Trk; Geogrphy Excllnce; Engrng.

SIMEON, KENNETH R; Montclair HS; Montclair, CA; (3); Ed Phtg Yrbk; JV Var Bsktbl; Var Mgr(s); Var Trk; UCLA; Comp Prgmmng.

SIMEON, PAMELA D; James Lick HS; San Jose, CA; (3); Library Aide; Math Tm; High Hon Roll; NHS; CA Schlrshp Fed; Bibliophile Soc Pres; Badminton #3 Girls Doubles Var; San Jose ST U.

SIMEONE, CARRIE A; Ontario HS; Ontario, CA; (2); Art Clb; French Clb; Key Clb; Ski Clb; Socr; Hon Roll; Prfct Atten Awd; Military Pride; U NV Las Vegas; Psycht.

SIMER, JEREMY O; San Luis Obispo HS; San Luis Obispo, CA; (2); AFS; English Clb; Intnl Clb; School Play; VP Frsh Cls; Friends Of The Earth Fndr & Co-Pres; Amnesty Intl Co-Pres; Stu Popltcl Action VP; CSF; U CA Santa Cruz; Engl.

SIMES, LISA G; Pittsburg HS; Pittsburg, CA; (3); 16/375; Pep Clb; SADD; Rptr Nwsp; Rptr Yrbk; Hon Roll; Comp Prgmng.

SIMI, BERNADETTE; St Francis HS; Sacramento, CA; (2); Church Yth Grp; Cmnty Wkr; JV Cheerldng; JV Socr; Var Swmmng; Prfct Atten Awd; Wrtng Poetry; Cls Princess; SFU; Nursing.

SIMKINS, BRAD S; Branham HS; San Jose, CA; (1); Chemcl Engr.

SIMMA, MANIVANH; Hoover HS; San Diego, CA; (3); Yrbk; Cit Awd; Hon Roll; NHS; Top Of The Mark Club, Jr Sci Dept Medal 89-90; Outstndng Chem Stu Cert; Bus.

SIMMONDS, HEATHER D; Central Union HS; El Centro, CA; (2); NFL; Speech Tm; Crs Cntry; High Hon Roll; Opt Clb Awd; Mock Trial; U CA; Telecommnctns.

SIMMONS, AMY C; Sunny Hills HS; Buena Park, CA; (2); 28/443; AFS; Church Yth Grp; Hosp Aide; Ski Clb; Var Sftbl; Intrml Vllybl; High Hon Roll; Prmry Sndy Schl Tchrs; UC Santa Barbara; Grphc Dsgnr.

SIMMONS, AMY D; Fairfax HS; Los Angeles, CA; (3); Rptr Nwsp; Sec Frsh Cls; Pres Soph Cls; Rep Jr Cls; VP L Crs Cntry; JV Gym; JV Socr; JV Sftbl; Pres Acad Fit Awd; Involved With Planned Parenthoods Ed Fairs & Adolescent Alliance Peer Cnslg Grp; Poly Sci.

SIMMONS, BETSY M; Poway HS; San Diego, CA; (3); 150/700; Office Aide; Varsity Clb; Pres Sr Cls; JV Socr; Var Sftbl; JV Tennis; Hon Roll; Schl Imprvmnt Pgm Rep.

SIMMONS, BEVERLY G; Leuzinger HS; Lawndale, CA; (3); Church Yth Grp; Office Aide; Teachers Aide; Off Soph Cls; Stat Bsktbl; Stat Ftbl; Intrml Sftbl; Hon Roll; Pres Acad Fit Awd.

SIMMONS, BRANDON K; Encina HS; Sacramento, CA; (4); Boy Scts; SADD; Band; Ftbl; Wt Lftg; Hon Roll; Church Yth Grp; Sac Cnty Sheriff Explorer 4 Yrs; Fire Dept & Amblnc Srvc Rep Clss 88-90; CSUS; Pilot.

SIMMONS, BRENT E; El Dorado HS; Placentia, CA; (3); 128/317; Church Yth Grp; Drama Clb; Band; Church Choir; Jazz Band; Mrchg Band; Orch; Pep Band; School Musical; Hon Roll; Most Outstndng Boy Musician 88-89; Music.

SIMMONS, DANIEL B; Buena HS; Ventura, CA; (1); Boy Scts; Drama Clb; High Hon Roll; Prfct Atten Awd; UCSD; Bio.

SIMMONS, DENNY M; Tulave Union HS; Tulare, CA; (3); Church Yth Grp; Cmnty Wkr; FFA; Bsbl; JV Bsktbl; JV Var Ftbl; Socr; Hon Roll; COS; Bus.

SIMMONS, EDDIE C; San Rafael HS; San Rafael, CA; (2); Boy Scts; Debate Tm; French Clb; French Clb; SADD; JV Lcrss; Var Capt Socr; 3rd Pl Marin Cnty Sci Fair; Aviation.

SIMMONS, JAIME LYNN; Foothill HS; Bakersfield, CA; (2); Cmnty Wkr; JA; Ski Clb; JV Cheerldng; Socr; Hon Roll; Law.

SIMMONS, JENNIFER E; Nevada Union HS; Grass Valley, CA; (3); 89/551; Church Yth Grp; Girl Scts; Var Socr; Acad Excllnce Awd Alg 1; Arch.

SIMMONS, JODI L; North HS; Bakersfield, CA; (4); Drama Clb; FTA; Spanish Clb; Speech Tm; SADD; Teachers Aide; School Play; Powder Puff Ftbl; Wt Lftg; Hon Roll; Bakersfield Coll; HS Teacher.

SIMMONS, KARA J; El Dorado HS; Fullerton, CA; (3); Church Yth Grp; High Hon Roll; Hon Roll; Ju Jitsu; Orange Coast Coll; Fshn.

SIMMONS, LEVON J; Vallejo SR HS; Vallejo, CA; (3); Hon Roll; Arch.

SIMMONS, LYNETTE L; Montgomery HS; Santa Rosa, CA; (2); Art Clb; French Clb; JA; Hon Roll; UC Davis; Bio.

SIMMONS, REBECCA; Lower Lake HS; Clearlake Oaks, CA; (2); Cmnty Wkr; Band; Sec Soph Cls; Hon Roll; Ceramics; Rstrnt Brgs Etc Wrkd; UCLA; Frgn Pltcs.

SIMMONS, SARAH; Trinity HS; Weaverville, CA; (4); 5/93; French Clb; Intnl Clb; Ski Clb; Rep Frsh Cls; Rep Soph Cls; VP Jr Cls; VP Pres Stu Cncl; Cheerldng; Rotary Awd; JSA Chptr Pres; Davis; Chem Engrng.

SIMMONS, STEPHANIE; Sutter Union HS; Sutter, CA; (2); German Clb; Ed Yrbk; Hon Roll; Psychology Denistry.

SIMMONS, STEVE M; Enterprise HS; Redding, CA; (3); 66/448; Hon Roll; U Of CA Davis; Elec Engr.

SIMMONS, TODD; Whittier Christian HS; Hacienda Heights, CA; (3); 32/120; Church Yth Grp; FCA; German Clb; Band; Church Choir; Mrchg Band; Pep Band; JV Bsbl; CA Schlrshp Fed; Mst Imprvd-Musician 88; Bus.

SIMMS, BRIAN C; Fontana HS; Fontana, CA; (3); Letterman Clb; Teachers Aide; Var L Bsktbl; Hon Roll.

SIMMS, CAPRELL; Vallejo SR HS; Vallejo, CA; (2); SADD; Stu Cncl; Cheerldng; Gym; Hon Roll.

SIMNEGAR, SAMMY; Taft HS; Woodland Hills, CA; (3); 26/676; Cmnty Wkr; Debate Tm; Spanish Clb; Temple Yth Grp; Pres VP Frsh Cls; VP Soph Cls; Pres VP Stu Cncl; Capt L Bsktbl; JV L Vllybl; Cit Awd; Peer Cnslng, Tutrng; Dir Assmbls; Sch Spirit Athltcs; HOBY; Walt Disney Awd; Shalom Clb, Pars Clb, 1st S; Med.

SIMNITT, WILLIAM J; Atascadero HS; Atascadero, CA; (2); Hon Roll; Engrng.

SIMOES, LORI R; James Lick HS; San Jose, CA; (1); JV Capt Cheerldng; Hon Roll; San Jose ST U; Bus.

SIMON, DANNY M; Villa Park HS; Villa Park, CA; (3); Am Leg Boys St; Key Clb; Letterman Clb; Ski Clb; Spanish Clb; Varsity Clb; Ed Nwsp; Var Capt Crs Cntry; Var Capt Trk; Hon Roll; Make-A-Wish Fndtn; Disneys Doers & Drmrs Awd Wnnr; All Orange Cnty Crss Cntry Awd Wnnr; Ucla; Marktng.

SIMON, JEFF; La Canada HS; La Canada Flintri, CA; (3); 35/252; Boy Scts; Computer Clb; Office Aide; VP Spanish Clb; Rep Stu Cncl; Bsktbl; Diving; Capt Socr; Trk; U CA.

SIMON, JEFFREY A; Mt Carmel HS; San Diego, CA; (3); Church Yth Grp; Band; Mrchg Band; Intrml Bsktbl; JV Trk; CSF; People To People Stu Ambssdr Pgm; S CA Drum Line Circuit.

SIMON, JENNIFER E; Los Amigos HS; Fountain Valley, CA; (2); Drill Tm; Score Keeper; Swmmng; Cit Awd; High Hon Roll; Hon Roll; CA U Irving; Med.

SIMON, S PAUL; Christian Brothers HS; Sacramento, CA; (2); Science Clb; AFS; Stage Crew; Intrml Bsktbl; JV Ftbl; Intrml Wt Lftg; High Hon Roll; CSF; UC Davis Early Acadmc Outreach; Chrstn Bros Merit Schlrshp; Jr Statesmn Amer.

SIMON, STEPHANIE; Diamond Bar HS; Diamond Bar, CA; (4); English Clb; Library Aide; Temple Yth Grp; Rptr Nwsp; Lit Mag; Hon Roll; Pres Acad Fit Awd; Mock Trl; CSF; Sci Fiction Lcub Pres; UC San Diego; Jrnlst.

SIMON, STEVEN; Westmoor HS; Daly City, CA; (2); Model UN; Spanish Clb; SADD; VP Temple Yth Grp; Orch; Rep Stu Cncl; JV Bsktbl; Var Score Keeper; JV Swmmng; Hon Roll; Cnslr In Trngn Camp Arazim Smmr 90; Sccr Refree; Hastings Law Schl; Poltcl Sci.

SIMONE, MARY K; Westminster HS; Westminster, CA; (1); Drill Tm; High Hon Roll; Cert Outstndng Stu & Rcgntn Acad; CA Schlrshp Fed; UNLV; Bus Lw.

SIMONELLI, DAWN E; Mt Whitney HS; Visalia, CA; (1); Church Yth Grp; FBLA; Key Clb; Chorus; Cit Awd; High Hon Roll; Prfct Atten Awd; Med Careers Clb; Environmental Club; Spec Interest Music; Med.

SIMONI, DANIELLE M; John A Rowland HS; Rowland Heights, CA; (3); Church Yth Grp; Science Clb; Spanish Clb; Teachers Aide; JV Var Swmmng; Hon Roll; Prfct Atten Awd; Mex/Span Dancing-Cmptn Trophies; Marine Bio.

SIMONIAN, STACY; Sanger HS; Fresno, CA; (2); Cmnty Wkr; Pep Clb; VP Soph Cls; VP Jr Cls; Rep Stu Cncl; Var Cheerldng; JV Swmmng; High Hon Roll; Prncpl Awd-Athl & Acad Achvt; Hi-Deb Modlng & Cmnty Svc; USC; Bus.

SIMONITSCH, ROBERT M; Burroughs HS; Ridgecrest, CA; (3); Cmnty Wkr; Varsity Clb; Var Ftbl; Cit Awd; Hon Roll; Pres Acad Fit Awd; Apprntce Tech Engr Co-Op Pgm; San Luis Obispo; Engrng.

SIMONS, ELESHA C; Torrey Pines HS; San Diego, CA; (4); Cmnty Wkr; Fndr-Pres Cultural Awrnss Clb; Pres Lcl Teen Chptr Jack & Jill Amer; Stu Disc Jockey Pgm; U Of VA; Rhetoric.

SIMONTON, DAVID; Beyer HS; Riverbank, CA; (3); Debate Tm; Key Clb; Letterman Clb; NFL; Speech Tm; Varsity Clb; Var Swmmng; Cit Awd; Hon Roll; Wtr Polo Vrsty; Hmcmng Prnc; Gldn ST Exmntn-Gmtry-Hnrs; UC; Law.

SIMOS, IMELDA G; Delano HS; Delano, CA; (4); Art Clb; Church Yth Grp; FHA; Key Clb; VICA; Acpl Chr; Church Choir; Stu Cncl; Hon Roll; United Filipino Orgnztn-Treas; Miss Phil Wkend Queen 89; Ms Congenialty/Ms Tlnt; Congrssnl Yth Ldrshp; CA ST-LOS Angeles; Med.

SIMPHALY, OUTHAY; Gladstone HS; Azusa, CA; (3); Varsity Clb; Chorus; Var Tennis; Bus Mgmt.

SIMPKINS, TREVOR L; Alta Loma HS; Alta Loma, CA; (2); Church Yth Grp; Cmnty Wkr; Aud/Vis; SADD; Cit Awd; Hon Roll; Pres Acad Fit Awd; Safe Rides; Paramedic.

SIMPSON, APRIL R; Antioch SR HS; Antioch, CA; (2); Drama Clb; Office Aide; School Play; DAR Awd; Hon Roll; Hi Deb Prgrm; San Diego ST U; Fshn Mrchndsng.

SIMPSON, AUDRA L; Grace M Davis HS; Modesto, CA; (2); Church Yth Grp; French Clb; Pep Clb; Science Clb; SADD; Orch; Hon Roll; Bay Sctn Hnr Orch; Stanislaus Hnr Orch; UC Santa Cruz; Marine Bio.

SIMPSON, BEVERLY K; North Hollywood Zoo-Magnet HS; San Fernando, CA; (2); Debate Tm; Math Tm; Office Aide; Teachers Aide; Tennis; Vllybl; Cit Awd; High Hon Roll; Hon Roll; Bus.

SIMPSON, BYRON D; Golden Gate Acad; Pittsburg, CA; (3); Teachers Aide; Rptr Yrbk; VP Soph Cls; VP Jr Cls; VP Stu Cncl; Intrml Bsktbl; High Hon Roll; Pres Acad Fit Awd; Med.

SIMPSON, CATHERINE M; Rim Of The World HS; Running Springs, CA; (1); Church Yth Grp; Office Aide; Stage Crew; Hon Roll; Prfct Atten Awd; Med.

SIMPSON, DAVID; Tustin HS; Tustin, CA; (3); 3/450; Computer Clb; English Clb; Key Clb; Science Clb; Temple Yth Grp; Lit Mag; Var L Tennis; High Hon Roll; Hon Roll; Pres Acad Fit Awd; Law.

SIMPSON, HEATHER M; Carlmont HS; San Carlos, CA; (2); 11/526; Orch; Rep Frsh Cls; Rep Soph Cls; Gym; Cit Awd; High Hon Roll; Hon Roll; Pres Acad Fit Awd; Golden ST Math Awd; CSF.

SIMPSON, KEINARD L; West Covina HS; Valinda, CA; (3); Church Yth Grp; Dance Clb; Band; Chorus; Mrchg Band; Pep Band; Christ Coll Irvine; Music Teach.

SIMPSON, KRISTEN J; Roseville HS; Rocklin, CA; (3); 1/400; French Clb; Key Clb; Science Clb; School Play; VP Jr Cls; Var Chess Clb; Var Tennis; Var Trk; NHS; Sacramento Ballet Co Dancer; Rotary Yth Ldrshp Awd; Cngrssnl Yth Ldrshp Awd; Med.

SIMPSON, LELA D; Antelope Valley HS; Palmdale, CA; (2); 133/804; Dance Clb; Cit Awd; San Diego; Socl Wrkr.

SIMPSON, MICHELLE; Nevada Union HS; Nevada City, CA; (3); 8/535; Pep Clb; SADD; Rep Stu Cncl; Var Socr; High Hon Roll; St Schlr; Pub Rel Ofcr 90; Arch.

SIMPSON, MICHELLE; San Fernando Valley Acad; Sepulveda, CA; (3); 2/18; Church Yth Grp; Ski Clb; Teachers Aide; Chorus; School Play; Off Frsh Cls; Pres Soph Cls; Pres Jr Cls; Pres Stu Cncl; High Hon Roll; La Sierra Coll; Educ.

SIMPSON II, ROBERT C; Fairfield HS; Fairfield, CA; (1); Church Yth Grp; Cmnty Wkr; Computer Clb; Spanish Clb; Intrml Bsbl; JV Ftbl; Intrml Trk; Cit Awd; Hon Roll; Chamber Of Comm Wmns Div; Stanford; Arch.

SIMPSON, RYAN P; Live Oak HS; San Jose, CA; (3); 113/565; Debate Tm; NFL; Rptr Speech Tm; Rptr Nwsp; Lit Mag; Off Soph Cls; Stu Cncl; JV Bsktbl; JV Var Tennis; Hon Roll; Jr Hgh Pnt Champ S Bay Peruvian Horse Breeders Shw; Natl Frnsc Leg Debates & Stu Cngrss; Envrnmntl Bio.

SIMPSON, TARA M; Oakland Technical HS; Oakland, CA; (2); Church Yth Grp; Cmnty Wkr; Teachers Aide; Church Choir; School Play; Hon Roll; Medcl.

SIMPSON, TIMOTHY; University HS; Lake Isabella, CA; (2); Cit Awd; Hon Roll; Comp Prgrm.

SIMPSON, TRACEE M; Washington Prep HS; Los Angeles, CA; (3); Church Yth Grp; Church Choir; JV Sftbl; High Hon Roll; Hon Roll; Acctng.

SIMPSON, TRAVIS J; John F Kennedy HS; Sacramento, CA; (1); Art Clb; Friday Night Live; Yth To Yth Smnrs; Archtr.

SIMPSON, VALERIE; Hoover HS; Fresno, CA; (2); Church Yth Grp; Lit Mag; Cheerldng; Tennis; Hon Roll; Westmont Christian Clg; Advrtsg.

SIMS, AISHA M; Bishop O'dowd HS; Oakland, CA; (2); Band; Cheerldng; Trk; Hon Roll; Black Stu Union; UCLA; Med.

SIMS, AMY E; Valencia HS; Placentia, CA; (3); Church Yth Grp; Dance Clb; FBLA; Drill Tm; Stu Cncl; Var Capt Cheerldng; Hon Roll; Won Poetry Cntstns; UCSB; Entrtnmnt.

SIMS, DAWN; Righetti HS; Santa Maria, CA; (3); 61/336; FFA; Speech Tm; Treas Chorus; Capt Drill Tm; Flag Corp; High Hon Roll; Hon Roll; ASB Dir Activities; Stu Ambassdr For Soviet Union; FFA; Fshn Mrchndsng.

SIMS, GERMAINE M; St Francis HS; Sacramento, CA; (3); Cmnty Wkr; Drama Clb; Hosp Aide; School Musical; School Play; Trk; Paper On Thrs Of Rcsm Crrntly Beng Cnsdrd Publctn; Mayor Barry Yth Ldrshp Inst; Howard U; Med.

SIMS, GIA L; Vacaville SR HS; Vacaville, CA; (4); Church Yth Grp; GAA; Pep Clb; Off Frsh Cls; Off Soph Cls; Capt Jr Cls; Bsktbl; Cheerldng; Powder Puff Ftbl; Tennis; Black Stu Union Sec; Bsktbl MVP; Howard U; Comp Systms Engrng.

SIMS, LATWILA; Lompoc HS; Lompoc, CA; (2); Church Yth Grp; Chorus; Bsktbl; Trk; Athl Of Month; Interior Dsgn.

SIMS, MARC; Compton HS; Compton, CA; (2); Boy Scts; Church Yth Grp; VICA; Band; Church Choir; Yrbk; Bsktbl; Vllybl; JETS Awd; Long Bch ST U; Eng.

SIMS, MINDY; Righetti HS; Santa Maria, CA; (2); Church Yth Grp; Pres Drama Clb; Acpl Chr; Chorus; Church Choir; School Musical; School Play; Hon Roll; Pres Acad Fit Awd; Campus Christian Fllwshp Ldr; Bethel Coll; Music.

SIMS, NEFATERIA ALICIA; Mark Twain HS; San Diego, CA; (3); JA; Pep Clb; ROTC; Band; Chorus; Drill Tm; Nwsp; Off Frsh Cls; Bsktbl; Sftbl; San Diego City Coll; Law.

SIMS, SHELLEY; Los Alamitos HS; Los Alamitos, CA; (4); Sec Church Yth Grp; FBLA; Intnl Clb; Model UN; Service Clb; Ski Clb; Spanish Clb; SADD; Intrml Trk; Hon Roll; Mock Trial Stu; Clerks Hlpr; USC; Law.

SIMS, TAMYKE; San Bernardino HS; San Bernardino, CA; (2); AFS; Church Yth Grp; German Clb; Key Clb; SADD; Drill Tm; Rptr Nwsp; Pres Soph Cls; Hon Roll; Ntl Merit SF; Intl Rltns.

SIMSON KALLAS, ANNA; Monterey HS; Monterey, CA; (1); Lit Mag; Var Diving; Var Fld Hcky; Var Score Keeper; Trk; High Hon Roll; UC Berkley; Envrnmntl Stds.

SIMUNDICH, ANAMARIE X; Homestead HS; Sunnyvale, CA; (1); Drama Clb; French Clb; Stage Crew; Stu Cncl; Fld Hcky; UCLA; Ed.

SIMURO, BRIAN J; Roseville Joint HS; Rocklin, CA; (1); Cmnty Wkr; French Clb; Red Cross Aide; Band; Jazz Band; Ftbl; Hon Roll; Explorer With Foothill Ambulance; Explorer Roseville Police Dept; Snackbar Mngr For Tri-City Lttl Lgue; Sacramento ST; Emrgncy Med.

SIMURO, CHRIS M; Roseville HS; Rocklin, CA; (3); 40/400; Cmnty Wkr; French Clb; SADD; Capt Var Bsktbl; Capt L Tennis; Hon Roll; NHS; Umpire Lttl Lg Bsbll; Ref For Rec Soccer; Sac ST; Bus.

SIN, DENNIS VU; Oakland HS; Oakland, CA; (2); Computer Clb; Tennis; Hon Roll; Cantonese Clb; Bus.

SIN, MI SUK; Warren HS; Downey, CA; (1); Art Clb; FBLA; Intnl Clb; UCLA; Bus.

SIN, STEPHANIE C; Mills HS; Burlingame, CA; (2); Library Aide; Rep Frsh Cls; Red Crss; Bdmntn Tm; Qlfd 1st Aider; Arch.

SIN, VAY; Garey HS; Pomona, CA; (2); Tai Kwon Do Clb.

SIN, VISETH; Edison HS; Fresno, CA; (2); Math Clb; Math Tm; Southeast-Asian Club; Gldn St Awds; Stanford U; Med.

SINA, MICHEL; University HS; Los Angeles, CA; (4); 152/600; Drama Clb; School Play; Bsktbl; Hon Roll; U Of CA-LOS Angeles; Med.

SINAPI, ROSALIE A; Bishop Amat Memorial HS; West Covina, CA; (2); Drama Clb; Service Clb; School Musical; School Play; Hon Roll; Trnr For Spcl Olympc Cmptrs; Pblctn.

SINCLAIR, EMMA; Southbay Christian HS; Sunnyvale, CA; (2); Church Yth Grp; Cmnty Wkr; Church Choir; School Musical; Treas Soph Cls; Cheerldng; Vllybl; CSF; Medcl.

SINCLAIR, MICHELLE A; Enterprise HS; Redding, CA; (3); Church Yth Grp; Deanery Rep Dioc Yth Cncl; Business.

SINCLITICO, MOLLY G; Torrey Pines HS; Solana Beach, CA; (2); 97/500; Church Yth Grp; Cmnty Wkr; Pep Clb; Cheerldng; Gym; Hon Roll; St Schlr; Clairmont Mc Kenna; Med.

SINDICICH, ROBERT L; Pinole Valley HS; Hercules, CA; (3); JV Bsbl; Var Ftbl; Wt Lftg; Hon Roll; Law Enfrcmnt Explr El Cerrito Police Dept; N Coast Section CIF Schlr Ath; Law Enforcmnt.

SINDONI, JESSICA; Canyon HS; Canyon Country, CA; (3); Am Leg Aux Girls St; Church Yth Grp; Debate Tm; Drama Clb; Pep Clb; Treas Frsh Cls; Var Capt Cheerldng; Var JV Trk; High Hon Roll; Hon Roll; CSF Sctry; Amnsty Interntl Clb; Winter Frml Prncs & Qn; Loyola Marymount U; TV Cmmnctn.

SINELAPAKIT, ANEUNE; Aa Stagg HS; Stockton, CA; (3); Am Leg Aux Girls St; Bus Profs of Am; FBLA; Office Aide; Teachers Aide; VICA; Yrbk; Stu Cncl; Vllybl; Hon Roll; Computer Processing.

SINFUEGO, MARYLOU T; Galileo HS; San Francisco, CA; (4); 7/400; Computer Clb; Math Clb; Pres Service Clb; Cit Awd; High Hon Roll; San Francisco ST U; Elec Engr.

SINFUEGO, MARYROSE T; Galileo HS; San Francisco, CA; (4); Service Clb; Cmptr Sci.

SINGER, KIMBERLY; Arcadia HS; Arcadia, CA; (4); Drama Clb; Ski Clb; Thesps; School Musical; School Play; Variety Show; JV Var Mgr(s); Intrml Sftbl; Intrml Vllybl; Hon Roll; CA Schrlshp Fed; 2nd Rnnr Up Miss Natl Teenager/Talent; San Diego ST U; Bus.

SINGER, NONKULULEKO Y; Schl Of Creative & Performing Arts; San Diego, CA; (3); 2/150; Dance Clb; Drama Clb; SADD; Sec Jr Cls; Rep Stu Cncl; High Hon Roll; Pres Acad Fit Awd; Sal; US Congressnl House Page.

SINGER, RENEE L; Hayward HS; Hayward, CA; (4); 29/204; Church Yth Grp; Sec Spanish Clb; Teachers Aide; Band; Mrchg Band; Pep Band; Treas Sr Cls; Hon Roll; San Jose ST U; Comp Sci.

SINGER, SHERYL J; Village Christian Schls; Lake View Terr, CA; (3); 59/130; Church Yth Grp; Drama Clb; Spanish Clb; School Play; Var Trk; CSF; Bible Study Group; Pre-Med.

SINGERMAN, LIORAH; Sacramento HS; Sacramento, CA; (2); 1/505; Dance Clb; Drama Clb; Pep Clb; Chorus; School Musical; School Play; Variety Show; Cheerldng; High Hon Roll; Pres Acad Fit Awd; Soc Stud Dept Cmmndtn; Stu Reaching Out; Peace Child Intl Poland, Bd; Cmmty & Prof Theater; Theater.

SINGH, AJIT K; Live Oak HS; Live Oak, CA; (2); 4/90; FHA; Spanish Clb; High Hon Roll; Hon Roll; Prfct Atten Awd; Gldn St Exam Math Cert.

SINGH, AMRIT P; Etiwanda HS; Alta Loma, CA; (2); 12/700; Chess Clb; Church Yth Grp; Computer Clb; English Clb; FBLA; High Hon Roll; Prfct Atten Awd; Med.

SINGH, BALBIR K; Modesto HS; Modesto, CA; (2).

SINGH, BHUPKAMAL; Caruthers Union HS; Selma, CA; (1); VICA; Yrbk; Off Frsh Cls; Cit Awd; High Hon Roll; Acctnt.

SINGH, GURDEEP; Turlock HS; Turlock, CA; (2); Temple Yth Grp; Wt Lftg; Spcl Intrst Law Enfrcmnt; Modesto JC; Law Enfrcmnt.

SINGH, HAMLESH K; Valley HS; Sacramento, CA; (3); SADD; Teachers Aide; High Hon Roll; Hon Roll; Prfct Atten Awd.

SINGH, HARJIT; Encina HS; Sacramento, CA; (3); Intnl Clb; Wt Lftg; Hon Roll; Prfct Atten Awd; Engl II Stu Mnth; Sacramento City Coll; Engrng.

SINGH, HARVIN; Grant HS; Sacramento, CA; (4); Intnl Clb; Library Aide; Spanish Clb; Socr; Hon Roll; Prfct Atten Awd; CA ST U; Computer Science.

SINGH, HARVINDER; Monroe HS; Panorama City, CA; (4); 6/530; Church Yth Grp; French Clb; Math Clb; Science Clb; Teachers Aide; Band; Gov Hon Prg Awd; Hon Roll; Pres Acad Fit Awd; CSF Hons & Torch Boyer; Golden St Hons Alg & Geo; Most Outstndng Comp Sci; Mccaulffe Schlrshp; Berkeley; Bus.

SINGH, KAMLESH; Turlock HS; Turlock, CA; (4); Art Clb; FBLA; Hosp Aide; Intnl Clb; Library Aide; Office Aide; SADD; Teachers Aide; Band; Rotary Awd; Cal ST; Radiology.

SINGH, KULDEEP; Central Union HS; El Centro, CA; (3).

SINGH, NAVJIT; Turlock HS; Turlock, CA; (1); 120/700; Science Clb; Lit Mag; High Hon Roll; Hon Roll; Rotary Awd; Cal Poly; Chem Engr.

SINGH, PRAVIN; Luther Burbank HS; Sacramento, CA; (3); 150/276; Office Aide; Teachers Aide; Stage Crew; Cit Awd; Hon Roll; Prfct Atten Awd; Schlrshp Awd Math; Jdgd Debate Tm; UCD; Bus Admin.

SINGH, RAVINDERJIT K; Moreno Valley HS; Moreno Valley, CA; (4); 11/477; Cmnty Wkr; Pres VP Intnl Clb; Key Clb; Math Clb; Sec Science Clb; Cit Awd; High Hon Roll; Hon Roll; NHS; 2nd Pl Dist Sci Fari; Outstndng Wk Awd; Acad Excel Cert Merit 88-89; CA Schlrshp Fed Lftm; CA U Riverside; Med.

SINGH, TRISH; Roseville HS; Rocklin, CA; (1); 18/525; Church Yth Grp; JV Cheerldng; JV Socr.

SINGH, VEENITA; La Puente HS; La Puente, CA; (2); 108/413; Church Yth Grp; Drama Clb; Science Clb; Teachers Aide; High Hon Roll; Hon Roll; Grls Leag; U Of Sthrn CA; Arch.

SINGHARATH, BOUNTHAVY A; Pittsburg HS; Pittsburg, CA; (1); Boy Scts; JCL; Teachers Aide; Socr; Swmmng; Trk; Vllybl; Wt Lftg; Wrstlng; Hon Roll; Crpntr.

SINGHARATH, SOMMANO; Mc Laine HS; Fresno, CA; (4); 113/400; Var Socr; CSUF; Mech Engr.

SINGISER, STEVE G; Mira Costa HS; Manhattan Beach, CA; (3); 17/390; Am Leg Boys St; Math Clb; Quiz Bowl; Scholastic Bowl; Ed Nwsp; Var Trk; High Hon Roll; Hon Roll; Johns Hopkins Cty Pgm 86-89; UC Berkeley; Jrnlsm.

SINGLETON, LA TOYA L; San Bernardino HS; San Bernardino, CA; (2); Church Yth Grp; Cmnty Wkr; Drama Clb; ROTC; Chorus; Church Choir; Stage Crew; Bsbl; West Point Military; Comp.

SINGLETON, LARRY; Cabrillo HS; Lompoc, CA; (4); 36/220; Yrbk; Rep Frsh Cls; VP Soph Cls; Pres Jr Cls; Pres Sr Cls; Capt Bsktbl; Var Ftbl; JV Trk; High Hon Roll; Hon Roll; Intrct Clb; CA Schlrshp Fed; Westmont Coll; Pre-Med.

SINGSON, ANA MARIA P; Fairfax HS; Los Angeles, CA; (2); Spcl Awd Drwng Art Cntst In Japan; Comp Pgmr.

SINGSON, DAISY M; Gardena HS; Gardena, CA; (4); 4/404; Intnl Clb; Spanish Clb; Teachers Aide; JV Capt Vllybl; Cit Awd; Pres Acad Fit Awd; Filipino Yth Clb Pres; Cal ST U Long Beach; Comp Sci.

SINGSON, GILIAN L; Gardena HS; Gardena, CA; (3); Service Clb; Teachers Aide; Cit Awd; Ntl Merit Schol; Dominos Pizza Stu Of Mnth; Med.

SINNACO, CHRISTINE F; Notre Dame HS; Salinas, CA; (4); 7/92; Drama Clb; Pres Speech Tm; Church Choir; Yrbk; Kiwanis Awd; NHS; Awd For Service; CA Schlrshp Fed; Campus Ministry; U Of CA Santa Cruz; Bio.

SINNETT, KASANDRA R; San Bernardino HS; San Bernardino, CA; (3); Cmnty Wkr; JV Var Sftbl; JV Vllybl; Prfct Atten Awd; Loma Linda U; Pediatrcs.

SINNOTT, PAULA K; Bishop Amat Memorial HS; El Monte, CA; (2); Church Yth Grp; Cmnty Wkr; NEDT Awd; Psych.

SINTASATH, DAVID; Saint Augustine HS; San Diego, CA; (2); 1/120; Church Yth Grp; Cmnty Wkr; Speech Tm; SADD; Yrbk; Var Trk; Var Vllybl; Cit Awd; High Hon Roll; Hon Roll; Acad Leag; Ira Huffman Awd; Awds In Engl, Math, Sci, Religion, Frgn Lang; Med.

SINTASATH, LOUIS; Blessed Sacrament HS; San Diego, CA; (1); Boy Scts; Church Yth Grp; Var Ftbl; Cit Awd; High Hon Roll; Hon Roll; Pres Acad Fit Awd; Alter Srvr; Engrng.

SINTHAWANARONG, KAMOLTIP; Bellflower HS; Downey, CA; (3); 16/273; FBLA; Math Clb; Mrchg Band; Rep Sr Cls; Csf; U CA; Bio.

SINUTKO, SETH D; Torrey Pines HS; Olivenhain, CA; (3); Phtg Lit Mag; JV Golf; Cit Awd; Prfct Atten Awd; Pres Acad Fit Awd.

SIOSON, MERRYALYNN; Sierra Vista HS; Baldwin Park, CA; (4); Drama Clb; Sec Math Clb; Speech Tm; JV Tennis; High Hon Roll; Lion Awd; Opt Clb Awd; Pres Acad Fit Awd; Val; Ldrshp Smnr Vly Forge PA; Schls Dcthln Olympd Tm; UC Irvine; Med.

SIPES, KENNETH LANDON; Irvine HS; Irvine, CA; (3); Office Aide; JV Vllybl; Natl Jr Olympcs Vllybl 89; Irvine Big Leag Bsbl 90; Orange Coast Coll; Marine Bio.

SIPHONEKHAM, AMANDA; Sweetwater HS; National City, CA; (1); Library Aide; High Hon Roll; Hon Roll; Prfct Atten Awd.

SIPOS, JEFF D; San Lorenzo HS; San Lorenzo, CA; (2); Church Yth Grp; Cmnty Wkr; Ski Clb; Varsity Clb; Band; Jazz Band; Ftbl; Trk; Chrch Grp Yth Ldr; Law Enfrcmnt.

SIPRUT, MICHELLE M; Bullard HS; Fresno, CA; (3); Teachers Aide; Amnesty International Club.

SIQUEIROS, DONNA; Saint Paul HS; Whittier, CA; (3); 52/300; Church Yth Grp; Sec Treas Frsh Cls; Rep Soph Cls; Off Jr Cls; Sec Treas Sr Cls; Hon Roll; Jr NHS; NHS; CA Schlrshp Fed; Cnslrs Aide; Wacs Cmmtte; CA Poly Pomona; Arch.

SIQUES, CLAUDIA T; Paraclete HS; Palmdale, CA; (2); SADD; JV Capt Bsktbl; Var Capt Socr; Hon Roll; Bishop Ryan Schlrshp; Ltr Wmn Clb; UC-BERKELEY U; Med.

SIRA, SANEHPAL S; Turlock HS; Turlock, CA; (2); Treas Chess Clb; Treas Intnl Clb; Treas Science Clb; Pres VICA; Lit Mag; Hon Roll; Lit Club; UCSD; Engrng.

SIRAKAVIT, CRAIG S; Bellflower HS; Bellflower, CA; (2); 175/341; Band; Mrchg Band; Animatn.

SIRICK, MORISSA L; Redlands SR HS; Redlands, CA; (2); Ski Clb; Band; Hon Roll; CJSF; Chld Psych.

SIRINEO, JOSEPHINE V; Montebello HS; Montebello, CA; (3); Rep Dance Clb; Pep Clb; SADD; Pres Chorus; School Musical; Variety Show; Hon Roll; ICC; CA Schlrshp Fed; Prom Cmmtte; U Irvine; Med Tech.

SIRISUK, SHERN; Glen A Wilson HS; Hacienda Hgts, CA; (3); Key Clb; Ski Clb; Band; Mrchg Band; JV Bsbl; Var Golf; Hon Roll.

SIROF, JAKE; Abraham Lincoln HS; San Francisco, CA; (1); Off ROTC; Color Guard; Drill Tm; Job At Video Rental Store; Identical Twin Bro; Excl In Engl; Annapolis; Officer US Marines.

SISAMONT, MANG JEANETTE; Edison HS; Stockton, CA; (2); French Hon Soc; Hon Roll; Prfct Atten Awd; Pres Acad Fit Awd; Med.

SISANA, THONGKHAM; W C Overfelt HS; San Jose, CA; (3); Teachers Aide; Var Wrstlng; Hon Roll; CCS Chmpns Recgntn Day 2 Yrs; Awd Mst Imprvd Wrstler 89-90.

SISAVATH, SOMBOUM; Christian Brother HS; W Sacramento, CA; (3); Art Clb; Ftbl; Trk; High Hon Roll; Hon Roll; St Marys Coll; Med.

SISCO, CARRIE D; Laguna Hills HS; Laguna Hills, CA; (3); 55/368; Church Yth Grp; Cmnty Wkr; Office Aide; SADD; Nwsp; JV Var Tennis; Var Trk; Stat Wrstlng; Hon Roll; Nal Charity Leag; Bus.

SISCO, GINGER S; Ukiah HS; Ukiah, CA; (2); DECA; Office Aide; SADD; Hon Roll; Pres Acad Fit Awd; Mammalgy.

SISCO, SEAN; Hemet HS; Hemet, CA; (4); 34/550; Teachers Aide; JV Bsktbl; Cit Awd; High Hon Roll; Hon Roll; Prfct Atten Awd; UC Santa Cruz; Econ.

SISK, ANGELA M; Sierra Joint Union HS; Auberry, CA; (2); Spanish Clb; Varsity Clb; Chorus; School Play; Var Cheerldng; Var Crs Cntry; Var Trk; Girls League; Super Cities Walk For Multiple Sclerosis; Top Performer On FS Level Cross Country; Vocalist.

SISK, CHERYL L; Carson HS; Carson, CA; (3); Sec Drama Clb; French Clb; School Play; High Hon Roll; Hon Roll; CSF; Acad Achvt Awds 2 Yrs; Loyola Marymount U; Law.

SISK, CORRINA C; Don A Lugo HS; Chino, CA; (2); Church Yth Grp; Phtg Nwsp; Cit Awd; Masonic Awd; Golden Conquest Awd; Chino Cmmnty Theater; SR Princess In Job Daughters; Fullerton Coll; Anchor Woman.

SISK, DESTINY D; Vacaville HS; Vacaville, CA; (3); Church Yth Grp; Cheerldng; Score Keeper; Hon Roll; Teachers Aide; Drill Tm; Seacamp 89.

SISK, MELANIE J; Cajon HS; San Bernardino, CA; (2); Church Yth Grp; Jrnlsm.

SISKEY, JON J; Orange Glen HS; Escondido, CA; (3); Boy Scts; Church Yth Grp; Ftbl; Wt Lftg; Wrstlng; Hon Roll; Accntng.

SISNEROZ, JOHN G; James Logan HS; Union City, CA; (3); JV Wrstlng; Drawing; Bus; Law Enforcement; Law.

SISODIYA, DEEPAK; San Ramon Valley HS; Danville, CA; (3); FBLA; Var Tennis; Prfct Atten Awd; Pres Schlr; Ped.

SISODIYA, SANJAY R; San Ramon Valley HS; Dublin, CA; (3); 48/408; Computer Clb; Sec FBLA; Math Clb; NFL; Speech Tm; Teachers Aide; Socr; Cit Awd; Hon Roll; Prfct Atten Awd; MBA.

SISON, ALLAN DALE R; Independence HS; San Jose, CA; (4); Art Clb; JA; Model UN; Ed Yrbk; Treas Jr Cls; VP Sr Cls; Hon Roll; NHS; Cal Poly San Luis Obispo; Engr.

SISON, ARCHIE M; Edison HS; Stockton, CA; (1); Latin Clb; VP Frsh Cls; Ftbl; Trk; Wt Lftg; Pres Acad Fit Awd; Asian Clb; UCLA; Law.

SISON, LIEZLE A; Southwest HS; San Diego, CA; (2); Key Clb; Cit Awd; Pan-Asian Clb; CSF-CA Schlrshp Fdrtn; Bus.

SISON, MARIFEL C; Hamilton HS; Los Angeles, CA; (1); Church Yth Grp; Phtg Nwsp; Yrbk; JV Var Swmmng; Var Tennis; Pres Acad Fit Awd; Asian Clb; Jr Statesmen Of Amer; UCLA; Bus Adm.

SISON JR, PETE CHIANG; Samuel F B Morse HS; San Diego, CA; (4); 14/525; Computer Clb; Quiz Bowl; High Hon Roll; Hon Roll; Jr NHS; Prfct Atten Awd; Val; CSF Hnr Grad; Sierra Club; Yosemite Assn; U Of CA San Diego; Comp Engrng.

SITHIXAI, PHIMMASEHN; Edison Computech HS; Fresno, CA; (3); 19/200; Computer Clb; Intnl Clb; JA; Golf; Tennis; Cit Awd; Hon Roll; Ntl Merit Ltr; U CA Davis; Engrg.

SITHOLE, RONIKA S; Bakersfield HS; Bakersfield, CA; (2); Church Yth Grp; Dance Clb; Science Clb; Church Choir; High Hon Roll; Math Engrng Sci Achvt; Gftd & Tlntd Educ Pgm; U CA Davis; Engrng.

SITTON, GARY; Mt Whitney HS; Visalia, CA; (3); 1/356; Church Yth Grp; SADD; Yrbk; Capt Ftbl; Capt Socr; High Hon Roll; Hon Roll; Spanish Clb; JV Bsbl; Wt Lftg; Defnsv MVP Ftbl 88-89; Babe Ruth All Stars 88-89; Indr Soccr 88-89; CA St Olmpc 89; CSF; Passng League.

SITTON, GREG B; Mt Whitney HS; Visalia, CA; (2); Church Yth Grp; Spanish Clb; JV Bsbl; Ftbl; JV Golf; JV VP Socr; CYSA N CA Olympic Devt Soccer Tm Regnl Camp Invtnl All Star Tm 89-90.

SITTRE, MARIA H; Chula Vista HS; Chula Vista, CA; (3); Pep Clb; Acpl Chr; Band; Chorus; Co-Capt Color Guard; Mrchg Band; Lit Mag; Mrn Bio.

SITU, JENNY; J E Mc Ateer HS; San Francisco, CA; (3); Office Aide; Red Cross Aide; Teachers Aide; Chinese Club.

SITU, LISA; George Washington HS; San Francisco, CA; (2); Off Soph Cls; Bus Mgr.

SITU, ROSE; George Washington HS; San Francisco, CA; (4); Off Sr Cls; City Coll Of SF; Fshn Dsgnr.

SITZMANN, MIKE J; Tracy HS; Tracy, CA; (2); 37/483; Church Yth Grp; 4-H; Intnl Clb; Ski Clb; SADD; Band; Jazz Band; Mrchg Band; JV Ftbl; JV Socr; CA Schlrshp Fed; Stockton Select Sccr Club; Med.

SIU, CINDY W; Marina HS; Huntington Beach, CA; (2); Church Yth Grp; Key Clb; Hon Roll; Mdcl.

SIU, HELEN; George Washington HS; San Francisco, CA; (4); Chess Clb; Key Clb; Service Clb; Rep Soph Cls; Rep Jr Cls; Rep Sr Cls; Hon Roll; Kiwanis Awd; Achvmt Cert Bio, Ceramics; San Francisco City Coll.

SIU, MACY; Westmoor HS; Daly City, CA; (2); French Clb; GAA; Math Clb; Vllybl; Hon Roll; Newcmrs Clb; COLL Entrc Clb; Gftd & Tlntd Educ; North Peninsula Leag Awd; Med.

SIU, RACHAEL A; College Park HS; Pleasant Hill, CA; (2); AFS; Cmnty Wkr; GAA; Letterman Clb; Spanish Clb; Varsity Clb; Chorus; Var Diving; Var Swmmng; Cit Awd; High Pnt, Coaches Awd Plesant Hill Dolfins Swm Tm; Part Of Friday Nght Live; Berkley; Bus.

SIU, WENDY; Lowell HS; San Francisco, CA; (2); Red Cross Aide; Band; NHS; CSF, CA Invntnl Chemathon 1st Pl; Chinese Club Vp, Public Rltns Officer; Intl Rltns Club Treas; RCC.

SIV, LENA L; Edison HS; Stockton, CA; (3); Drama Clb; Office Aide; Teachers Aide; Off Jr Cls; Hon Roll; Cambodian Clb Treas 88-89; VP Of Cambodian Clb 89-90; Outstndg Acadc Hrs Awds; Delta Coll; Psych.

SIVANTHAPHANITH, ARA; Milpitas HS; Milpitas, CA; (3); Bus.

SIVELL, NICOLE C; Del Campo HS; Fair Oaks, CA; (3); 69/446; Church Yth Grp; VP Sec Drama Clb; SADD; Church Choir; School Play; Stage Crew; Variety Show; Ed Lit Mag; Ntl Merit Ltr; Moot Court Tm; Zoology.

SIVENPIPER, JULIE A; Novato HS; Novato, CA; (1); Church Yth Grp; Spanish Clb; Band; Mrchg Band; Bsktbl; Socr; High Hon Roll; Stanford,Med Doctor.

SIVONGXAY, DARAVANH J; Covina HS; West Covina, CA; (1); French Clb; Crs Cntry; Trk; Cit Awd; Hon Roll; Prfct Atten Awd; Teachers Aide; Yrbk; Stu Cncl; CA Poly Pomona; Bus.

SIXTOS, GUADALUPE; Victor Valley HS; Oro Grande, CA; (1); Hon Roll.

SIZEMORE-HINKLE, MARNI SUZETTE; Trona HS; Trona, CA; (4); 7/45; French Clb; Office Aide; Teachers Aide; Chorus; Bsktbl; Cheerldng; Powder Puff Ftbl; Vllybl; CSF-LIFE Mem Awd; S CA Edison Eductnl Grant Awd; Dead Poets Soc Clb; Cerro Coso CC; French.

SJOBERG, PAUL H; Footh HS; Sacramento, CA; (2); JV Socr; Hon Roll; Cmptr Prgm.

SKAGGS, JULIA P; Arcata HS; Arcata, CA; (1); Church Yth Grp; Cmnty Wkr; 4-H; VP FFA; JV Bsktbl; Var Sftbl; 4-H Awd; Hon Roll; Fair Brd; Livestock Auction.

SKAGGS, KRISTINA; Highlands HS; Elverta, CA; (2); SADD; Band; Flag Corp; Jazz Band; Mrchg Band; Pep Band; Cheerldng; Sftbl; Hon Roll; San Diego ST; Math.

SKAPINOK, EDWARD J; Concord HS; Concord, CA; (3); Am Leg Boys St; Teachers Aide; Rep Sr Cls; Hon Roll; Diablo Vly Coll; Htl Mgmt.

SKARECKY, JULIA G; Moreno Valley HS; Moreno Vly, CA; (4); Teachers Aide; Rptr Nwsp; Yrbk; High Hon Roll; Hon Roll; Riverside CC; Educ.

SKEEHAN, HEATHER A; Mtn View HS; Mountain View, CA; (2); VP Church Yth Grp; German Clb; Acpl Chr; Chorus; Color Guard; Flag Corp; Mrchg Band; Orch; Swing Chorus; Hon Roll; Sec Of Vocal Clb; Brigham Young U; Ed.

SKEEM, HEATHER; Casa Grande HS; Petaluma, CA; (3); 9/290; French Clb; Ski Clb; Treas Frsh Cls; Pres Soph Cls; Pres Jr Cls; Var Bsktbl; Hon Roll; CSF; Assoctd Stu Body Pres.

SKEEN, HEATHER; Moorpark HS; Moorpark, CA; (2); Church Yth Grp; Cmnty Wkr; Pep Clb; Sec Frsh Cls; Stu Cncl; JV Cheerldng; Cit Awd; High Hon Roll; Pres Acad Fit Awd; Semnry Pgm; Bsktbl Awd; BYU; Bio.

SKEEN, JOSEPH D; Luther Burbank HS; Sacramento, CA; (3); Church Yth Grp; Cmnty Wkr; FFA; Temple Yth Grp; Chorus; Church Choir; VP Jr Cls; JV Var Ftbl; JV Var Vllybl; JV Var Wt Lftg; BOAC Awd 90; VP Luther Burbank Chptr Farmer 90-91; MI ST; Lit Tchr.

SKEETERS, LA DAWN; Ganesha HS; Pomona, CA; (1); Church Yth Grp; Church Choir; JV Bsktbl; Lawyer.

SKELTON, JOHN B; Bellarmine C P HS; Palo Alto, CA; (2); NFL; Speech Tm; Crs Cntry; Cit Awd.

SKELTON, KRISTI L; Rancho Cotate HS; Rohnert Park, CA; (2); Church Yth Grp; Drama Clb; German Clb; Key Clb; SADD; Drill Tm; School Play; High Hon Roll; Hon Roll; Cal Poly San Luis Obispo; Arch.

SKELTON, RICHARD A; Seoul American HS; Apo Sf, CA; (4); Art Clb; Teachers Aide; Intrml Bsbl; Hon Roll; Amercn Scub Clb Korea; Photo; Tae Kwon Do; Graphic Desgnr.

SKEMP, SHEILA C; Quincy JR SR HS; Quincy, CA; (4); 8/84; FBLA; Letterman Clb; Model UN; Office Aide; Teachers Aide; Varsity Clb; Band; VP Soph Cls; Stu Cncl; JV Var Bsktbl; CSF; US Army Rsrve Natl Schlr/Athl Awd; Booster Clb Athl Of Yr; Shasta JC; Arch.

SKIBBA, AMY E; Fountain Valley HS; Westminster, CA; (1); Church Yth Grp; Chorus; Church Choir; Stage Crew; Swmmng.

SKIFIC, MATTHEW J; Vista HS; Vista, CA; (3); 3/500; Am Leg Boys St; Church Yth Grp; Cmnty Wkr; Pres German Clb; JV Var Swmmng; High Hon Roll; Rotary Awd; Assoc Stu Body Pres; Waterpolo JV & Var; Ofcr CSF; Engrng.

SKILLMAN, ALEXANDRA J; University HS; Irvine, CA; (4); 180/486; VP Cmnty Wkr; Pres Dance Clb; French Clb; Var Cheerldng; Var Pom Pon; Hon Roll; Acad Decathlon; Comptv Figure Skating; Young Actors Space; U Southern CA; Bus.

SKILLMAN, STEPHANI; Gilroy HS; Gilroy, CA; (4); Church Yth Grp; Cmnty Wkr; Teachers Aide; Rptr Nwsp; Var Bsktbl; Var Fld Hcky; Powder Puff Ftbl; Var Trk; Hon Roll; Lifeguard/Swim Instructor YMCA; CTA & CSEA Schlrshps; Chico ST; Liberal Stds.

SKILTON, ALORA M; Hamilton Acad Of Music; Los Angeles, CA; (3); Band; Chorus; Mrchg Band; School Musical; School Play; VP Frsh Cls; Rep Stu Cncl; Gov Hon Prg Awd; High Hon Roll; Hon Roll; Psych.

SKILTON, ANGELA MARIE; Hamilton HS Academy Of Music; Los Angeles, CA; (4); 12/500; Cmnty Wkr; Service Clb; Spanish Clb; Chorus; School Musical; School Play; High Hon Roll; CSF; World Poetry Goldn Poet Awd 89; CSU Northridge; Spansh.

SKINNER, CARLTON S; Yucca Valley HS; Yucca Valley, CA; (2); Boy Scts; Computer Clb; Math Clb; Chorus; Hon Roll; Golden St Exam Schl Recog; PA ST; Bio Chem.

SKINNER, CASSANDRA D; More HS; San Diego, CA; (3); 324/676; Am Leg Aux Girls St; Church Yth Grp; English Clb; FHA; JA; Science Clb; SADD; Church Choir; Rptr Yrbk; Rep Sr Cls; Rgnl 10 Pres FHA; Jr Class Exec Cncl; Girls ST Mayor 90; San Diego ST U; Psych.

SKINNER, S ANDREW; Fremont HS; Sunnyvale, CA; (1); Boy Scts; Rep Frsh Cls; JV Ftbl; JV Trk; UC Berkely; Math.

SKINNER, SHELLY; Anderson Union HS; Redding, CA; (3); 35/204; Drama Clb; Acpl Chr; Sec Band; Drill Tm; Drm Mjr(t); Mrchg Band; School Play; Capt Cheerldng; Var Trk; Show Pop Singing & Dancing; Theater.

SKINNER, STEPHANIE T; John Glenn HS; Norwalk, CA; (2); Letterman Clb; JV Bsktbl; Var Stat Ftbl; Var Score Keeper; Var Sftbl; Var Vllybl; Cit Awd; Hon Roll; Norwalk Little Miss Sftbl Assoc; ASA Jr Olympcs Sftbl Trvlng Tm; Cerritos Smmr Leag Vllybl; UNLV; Doctor.

SKINNER, STEVE A; Helix HS; La Mesa, CA; (4); 12/375; Letterman Clb; Science Clb; Ski Clb; Rep Stu Cncl; Var Trk; High Hon Roll; Passed AP Spanish And History; UCSD; Engineering.

SKINNER, TROY D; Granite Hills HS; El Cajon, CA; (4); 13/500; Hosp Aide; Ed Nwsp; Var Capt Socr; JV Var Tennis; Cit Awd; Elks Awd; High Hon Roll; Ntl Merit SF; Mst Insprtnl Tnns Plyr; Mst Sccsfl Sccr Plyr; Stanford; Bus.

SKINNER, WENDY J; Newport Harbor HS; Costa Mesa, CA; (4); 17/323; Pep Clb; Teachers Aide; Thesps; Capt Drill Tm; School Musical; Variety Show; High Hon Roll; Pres Acad Fit Awd; Panhellenic Schlrshp Awd; Admin Assoc Schlrshp Awd; OCC Acad Schlrshp; OCC; Liberal Arts.

SKIPPER, SARAH M; Livermore HS; Livermore, CA; (3); 72/468; Pres Church Yth Grp; Dance Clb; Hosp Aide; Latin Clb; Ski Clb; SADD; Church Choir; Rep Soph Cls; Pres VP Stu Cncl; Var Vllybl; Amer Red Crss Lifeguard Cert; Acadmc Achvt Awds; Pre Med.

SKIPTON, BETH-ANN; Apple Valley HS; Apple Valley, CA; (1); Church Yth Grp; Sec SADD; Teachers Aide; Rptr Nwsp; Hon Roll; Pilot.

SKJERLY, NICHOLE E; Cordova SR HS; Grand Forks, ND; (3); 79/412; Rptr Nwsp; Rep Frsh Cls; JV Capt Cheerldng; Capt Pom Pon; Stat Wrstlng; Hon Roll; Jr NHS; Outstndng Hlth Achvmnt & Pres Acad Achvmnt Awds; Physcl Asst.

SKOLTE, CHAD; Coronado HS; Coronado, CA; (3); Spanish Clb; Var L Ftbl.

SKONIECZNY, MOLLY; Sacramento Waldorf HS; Carmichael, CA; (3); 1/30; Church Yth Grp; Cmnty Wkr; Ski Clb; Jazz Band; Orch; School Musical; School Play; Yrbk; VP Jr Cls; Capt L Bsktbl; All Leag Vllybl & Softbl Awds; All Tourny Basktbl.

SKORA, ANNE M; Roseville HS; Rocklin, CA; (2); 45/445; Drama Clb; French Clb; Drill Tm; Nwsp; Hon Roll; Prncpls Advsry Cmmtte; Perfrmng Arts.

SKOREY, VINCE R; Santa Teresa HS; San Jose, CA; (2); Ski Clb; Crs Cntry; Trk; Dntstry.

SKORUPSKI, ELIZABETH M; Mater Dei HS; Westminster, CA; (1); Church Yth Grp; German Clb; Intrml Diving; Gym; Intrml Socr; Intrml Swmmng; Trk; Cit Awd; High Hon Roll; Hghst Acad Schlrshp Awd; CSF; Stanford U; Lwyr.

SKOVMAND, KIMBERLY; Valley Christian HS; San Jose, CA; (2); Church Yth Grp; Dance Clb; Pep Clb; Var JV Cheerldng; JV Pom Pon; Cit Awd; High Hon Roll; CSF; Erthqk Victims Distrbtn Ctr Volunteer; Acting.

SKRACIC, SUZANNE D; San Pedro HS; San Pedro, CA; (3); Boy Scts; Cmnty Wkr; Girl Scts; Hosp Aide; Math Clb; Service Clb; Ski Clb; Band; Var Socr; Girl Scts Slvr Awd; Gldn St Alg Exam Hnrs; All Leag 1st Team Sccr; Sci.

SKRIPKUS, AIDAS T; Torrey Pines HS; Solana Beach, CA; (3); Church Yth Grp; Intnl Clb; Office Aide; Ski Clb; SADD; JV Crs Cntry; JV Trk.

SKRIPKUS, UGNE J; Torrey Pines HS; Solana Beach, CA; (3); 43/457; Church Yth Grp; Cmnty Wkr; SADD; Ed Yrbk; Off Jr Cls; Hon Roll; CSF; Lithuanian Ateitininkai Clb Photo; Lithuanian Schl; Pre-Med.

SKULTETY, CARRIE; Concord HS; Concord, CA; (4); 18/262; Pres Math Clb; SADD; Band; Jazz Band; Mrchg Band; Rep Stu Cncl; Var Capt Bsktbl; Var Sftbl; Jr NHS; Pres Acad Fit Awd; Army Rsrve Natl Schlr/Athl Awd; Los Medanos CC.

SKYHORSE-JOHNSON, BRANDO; Downtown Business Magnet HS; Los Angeles, CA; (3); Computer Clb; Hon Roll; Full Blooded Native Amer, Tribal Aff, Jaiwacawa White Mtn Apache; Enjoy Writing Short Stories Essays; Stanford U; Corp Law.

SLABOSKY, BEVERLY A; Valencia HS; Anaheim, CA; (2); Lit Mag; Spanish NHS; Loyola Marymount; Theatre Arts.

SLACK, DANIEL O; Barstow HS; Barstow, CA; (3); 28/340; Pres VP Church Yth Grp; Cmnty Wkr; FCA; Letterman Clb; Band; Pres Church Choir; VP Mrchg Band; Pep Band; Variety Show; Intrml Bsktbl; Natl Yng Ldrs Conf; Octagon Clb; Arch.

SLACK, NICOLLE; Glen A Wilson HS; Hacienda Hgts, CA; (3); 43/426; Band; Mrchg Band; High Hon Roll; Hon Roll; Fine Arts Clb; Drum Line; CSF.

SLACK, STEVEN M; Bellarmine College Prep; San Jose, CA; (3); 70/315; Red Cross Aide; JV Ftbl; Var Trk; Wt Lftg; Hon Roll; Pres Acad Fit Awd; History Club; Bowling Leag; U Santa Clara; Criminology.

SLADE, CENCALE L; Grant HS; Sacramento, CA; (2); Cmnty Wkr; Computer Clb; English Clb; Science Clb; Spanish Clb; SADD; Band; Bsbl; Ftbl; Wt Lftg; HAWK Prjct; Prtnrshp Pgm; MESA; Comp Tech.

SLAGE, SHARON G; Fountain Valley HS; Fountain Valley, CA; (3); French Clb; German Clb; Science Clb; Spanish Clb; Teachers Aide; High Hon Roll; Prfct Atten Awd; Fnlst Coronet Awd Spnsh-Hghst Awdgvn By Schl.

SLAGLE, MARK D; Will C Wood HS; Vacaville, CA; (1); Church Yth Grp; Cmnty Wkr; Drama Clb; Science Clb; School Play; Stage Crew; Wt Lftg; Lucky Stores Sci Fair Achvt Awd; Vacavill Teen Cmmtte; Church Admin Cncl Yth Rep; Solano CC; Acting.

SLAMA, TINA; Palm Desert HS; La Quinta, CA; (1); Church Yth Grp; Acpl Chr; Chorus; High Hon Roll; Chef.

SLANE, KEARA; Atascadero HS; Atascadero, CA; (1); Church Yth Grp; Girl Scts; Color Guard; BYU; Math.

SLANEY, ANNE M; Redlands HS; Redlands, CA; (2); Cit Awd; High Hon Roll; CSF; Kimberly Jrs; Assistens; Ldrshp.

SLAPE, SUSAN L; Serrano HS; Wrightwood, CA; (2); Drill Tm; Bsbl; Bsktbl; Vllybl; Davis; Vet.

SLAPNO, JAY AQUINO; Mt Eden HS; Hayward, CA; (2); Band; Pep Band; JV Ftbl; JV Trk; Hon Roll; NHS; Prfct Atten Awd; Pres Acad Fit Awd; Amnesty Intl; MI ST; Med.

SLATE, JESSICA; Beyer HS; Modesto, CA; (1); Cheerldng; Pom Pon; Hon Roll; Modern Dance; San Diego ST U; Psych.

SLATE, NICOLE; Le Grand Union HS; Le Grand, CA; (2); FFA; Teachers Aide; Varsity Clb; Bsktbl; Cheerldng; Score Keeper; Sftbl; Vllybl; Hon Roll; Prfct Atten Awd.

SLATER, JENNIFER L; Burroughs HS; Ridgecrest, CA; (3); Drama Clb; Teachers Aide; Drill Tm; Stage Crew; JV Swmmng; Hon Roll; Technel Mentor Prog; Lfgr Instrctr Swim Lessns; Cal Poly; Archtctr.

SLATER, MARIANNE; Saint Bonaventure HS; Ventura, CA; (3); Church Yth Grp; Hosp Aide; Pep Clb; Service Clb; Teachers Aide; Ed Nwsp; JV Var Cheerldng; Hon Roll; NHS; CSF.

SLATON, EDWARD L; Duncan Polytechnical HS; Fresno, CA; (1); Boy Scts; Math Clb; Math Tm; ROTC; Orch; School Musical; Horsebck Rdng & Cmptn; Fresno ST U; Law Enfrcmnt.

SLATON, SERENA; Mc Clymonds HS; Oakland, CA; (1); Teachers Aide; Stu Cncl; Var Bsbl; JV Bsktbl; Score Keeper; Var Sftbl; Tennis; JV Vllybl; Cit Awd; Gov Hon Prg Awd; Kaiser, Summer Job Prgm; Ped.

SLATON, TERESA M; Rio Lindo Acad; Ukiah, CA; (4); 2/96; Church Yth Grp; Band; Chorus; Church Choir; Variety Show; Ed Yrbk; Hon Roll; Prfct Atten Awd; Pres Acad Fit Awd; Work Experience Awds; Lindaires Slct Choir; Pacific Union Coll; Bus.

SLATON, TORRY E; Rio Lindo Adventist Acad; Ukiah, CA; (2); Church Yth Grp; Ski Clb; Band; Chorus; Ed Yrbk; Bsbl; Bsktbl; Ftbl; Socr; Sftbl; Pacific Union Coll; Comp Prog.

SLATTERY, KAREN M; Woodside HS; Redwood City, CA; (2); Girl Scts; Band; Off Frsh Cls; Off Soph Cls; Stu Cncl; Var Cheerldng; Var Sftbl; Hon Roll; Grl Sct Slvr Awd; Peer Cnslr; Bus.

SLATTERY, SCOTT; Los Gatos HS; Los Gatos, CA; (3); Hon Roll; Golden ST Exam High Hnrs Geom; Engrng.

SLAUGH, CYNTHIA MARIE; Wilcox HS; Sunnyvale, CA; (1); French Clb; FHA; Band; Mrchg Band.

SLAUSON, KEITH M; Alameda HS; Alameda, CA; (2); 33/275; Boy Scts; JV Bsbl; JV Bsktbl; High Hon Roll; Hon Roll; Pres Acad Fit Awd; CAL Berkley; Elec Engr.

SLAVEN, DEVIN E; Huntington Beach HS; Huntington Beach, CA; (3); Boy Scts; German Clb; Science Clb; SADD; Band; Mrchg Band; Pep Band; Swmmng; Hon Roll; UCLA; Bus.

SLAVENS, JOE; North Valley Christian HS; Redding, CA; (4); 1/10; Church Yth Grp; Drama Clb; Office Aide; Speech Tm; Chorus; Church Choir; School Play; Stage Crew; Pres Frsh Cls; Pres VP Stu Cncl; Cedarville Coll; Politician.

SLAVENS, JOSEPH CRAIG; North Valley Christian HS; Madras, OR; (4); 1/10; Church Yth Grp; Drama Clb; Math Tm; Office Aide; Speech Tm; Chorus; Church Choir; School Play; Rep Stu Cncl; Var Bsbl; Cedarville Coll; Bus.

SLAVIN, AMY C; Carondelet HS; Concord, CA; (3); 55/185; Cmnty Wkr; Pres Girl Scts; Intnl Clb; Service Clb; Band; Co-Capt Flag Corp; School Musical; Ed Nwsp; Hon Roll; NHS; CSF; Walt Disneys Dreamers & Doers Awd; Yth For Undrstndng Intl Exch.

SLAY, CLAVI; San Bernardino HS; San Bernardino, CA; (3); ROTC; Drill Tm; Futr Blck Ldrs; Amer Lgn Schltc Achvt; USMC Devil Pups; CA ST San Bernardino; Arm Frc.

SLAY, JULIE A; University HS; Irvine, CA; (4); 96/496; Var Capt Bsktbl; Spanish NHS; Laurcate Award In Physics; U Of Calif; Psychology.

SLAYTON, DAVID; Western Christian HS; Azusa, CA; (4); Church Yth Grp; Treas Model UN; Var Crs Cntry; Var L Trk; High Hon Roll; Ntl Merit SF; Stu For Explrtn & Devlpmnt Of Space; CSF; U CA Irvine; Aerospace Engrng.

SLEEPER, JENNIFER L; Santa Monica HS; Santa Monica, CA; (1); Library Aide; Teachers Aide; Ice Hcky; Vet.

SLESSMAN, GEORGE; Mt Whitney HS; Visalia, CA; (2); 1/400; Rep Stu Cncl; JV Ftbl; JV Trk; JV Wt Lftg; High Hon Roll; Jr NHS; Pres Acad Fit Awd; Golden St Exm High Hnrs Wnnr; CSF; Acad Lttr; Engrng.

SLEZAK, MARK S; Salinas HS; Salinas, CA; (3); Boy Scts; Ski Clb; JV Var Swmmng; Cit Awd; High Hon Roll; Hon Roll; NHS; UCSB; Bus Admin.

SLIDER, CHRISTOPHER A; Fontana HS; Fontana, CA; (2); Boy Scts; Teachers Aide; Yrbk; Swmmng; Eagle Sct; Chaffey Coll; Robotics.

SLIDER, THOMAS RICHARD; Fontana HS; Fontana, CA; (4); Stage Crew; Ed Nwsp; Ed Yrbk; Var Swmmng; Water Polo Ltr, Mst Dedctd 88-90, 90; Gldn St Exams Hgh Hnrs 1st Yr Alg 87; Stu Legsltv Cncl; Comp Sci.

SLIGHTOM, TINA M; Durham HS; Durham, CA; (3); Church Yth Grp; FHA; Key Clb; SADD; Rep Frsh Cls; JV Trk; Hon Roll; 2nd Pl Amer Lgn Essay Writng Cont; Bus.

SLINGER, KARINA; Rim Of The World HS; Blue Jay, CA; (3); Drama Clb; Speech Tm; Chorus; Drm Mjr(t); Jazz Band; Mrchg Band; School Play; Var Bsktbl; High Hon Roll; Hon Roll; Outstndng Musician Awd 89-90; Marine Bio Music.

SLININGER, STEVE; Franklin JR HS; Vallejo, CA; (1); Hon Roll; Vallejo; Engrng.

SLINKO JR, LAWRENCE LUKE; El Capitan HS; Lakeside, CA; (4); 27/418; JV Crs Cntry; Var Tennis; Hon Roll; Prfct Atten Awd; Masonic Awd; San Diego ST U; Bio.

SLITER, DENISE; Chowchilla HS; Chowchilla, CA; (4); Dance Clb; FHA; Office Aide; Pep Clb; Teachers Aide; Chorus; Cheerldng; Hon Roll; Kndrgrtn Teacher.

SLIVKOFF, JUBILEE G; Apple Valley HS; Apple Valley, CA; (2); Church Yth Grp; French Clb; Key Clb; Church Choir; Hon Roll; Music; Bus Mgmt.

SLOAN, BETH A; North Salinas HS; Salinas, CA; (2); 2/300; Cmnty Wkr; French Clb; Intnl Clb; Math Tm; Rep Stu Cncl; Cit Awd; High Hon Roll; NHS; Pres Acad Fit Awd; Rotary Awd; Acad Decathln; Stanford; Bus Admin.

SLOAN, DAVID LYLE; Sierra Joint Union HS; Clovis, CA; (4); 29/175; VP Letterman Clb; SADD; Varsity Clb; Stage Crew; Variety Show; Pres Frsh Cls; Stu Cncl; Var Bsktbl; Var Ftbl; Var Trk; Accrdtn Cmmtt 89-90; Fresno City Coll; Bus Mgmt.

SLOAN, JAMES R; Palo Alto HS; Palo Alto, CA; (2); Chess Clb; French Clb; High Hon Roll; Hon Roll; CA Math Cncl & CA ST Dept Math Awd; Cmmnty Svc Piano Perfrmnce Convalescent; Music Prfmnce.

SLOAN, JERAD B; Clovis West HS; Clovis, CA; (2); Computer Clb; Drama Clb; French Clb; Intnl Clb; NFL; School Musical; School Play; Danny Awd Wnnr Best Spprtng Actor; Fresno City Coll; Theatre Arts.

SLOAN, KAREN T; Baptist HS; Canyon Country, CA; (3); 11/100; French Clb; Thesps; School Musical; School Play; Rptr Nwsp; Lit Mag; JV Var Score Keeper; Stat Trk; Stat Vllybl; Hon Roll; JR Statsmen Fdn; Cmptr Sci.

SLOAT, JODI L; Marina HS; Huntington Beach, CA; (4); Treas Church Yth Grp; Drama Clb; Intnl Clb; JA; Spanish Clb; Thesps; Chorus; School Musical; Hon Roll; Opt Clb Awd; Orng Cnty Yth Chr Mem 90; CA Lutheran U; Acctng.

SLOCUM, NIKKI R; Torrey Pines HS; Del Mar, CA; (3); 40/422; Treas Drama Clb; Pres Girl Scts; Thesps; Band; Church Choir; School Play; Rptr Nwsp; Var Swmmng; High Hon Roll; Pres Acad Fit Awd; Envirnmntl Stewrdshp Grp; Yth Ending Hunger Clb; Backpckng/Outdoors Clb-Pres/Foundr; Church Ldrshp Team; Environmntl Sci.

SLOSS, WILLIAM; Tracy Joint Union HS; Tracy, CA; (4); 3/439; Am Leg Boys St; Computer Clb; Key Clb; Math Clb; Math Tm; Service Clb; High Hon Roll; Hon Roll; CSF; Hstry Club Pres; Bank Of Amer Plaque; UCLA; Genetic Engrng.

SLOTA, SANDRA; Rosary HS; Brea, CA; (4); 35/135; Church Yth Grp; Cmnty Wkr; Spanish Clb; Speech Tm; Stage Crew; Yrbk; JV Var Bsktbl; Hon Roll; NHS; Rotary Awd; Rotarian Yth Ambssdr To Italy; Cmps Mnstry Ldrshp Team For Jr & Sr Yr; Membr Of CA Schlrshp Fed; Cal-State U; Pltcl Sci.

SLOVER JR, DOUGLAS; Serrano HS; Phelan, CA; (2); Church Yth Grp; French Clb; Hon Roll; Prfct Atten Awd; Tap & Jazz Dance; Engrng.

SLOVER, JAMEY; Fontana HS; Crestline, CA; (4); 80/847; Hon Roll; Lion Awd; Pres Acad Fit Awd; Princpls Acad Achvt Awd; Sons Italy Schlrshp; Chaffey JC; Radiology.

SLOVER, JASON; Fontana HS; Crestline, CA; (4); 80/847; Hon Roll; Lion Awd; Pres Acad Fit Awd; Sons Of Italy Schlrshp; Principals Acad Achvt Awd; Chaffey JC; Radiology.

SLUSSER, AMBER M; El Cajon Valley HS; El Cajon, CA; (2); 29/469; Church Yth Grp; Letterman Clb; Chorus; School Musical; Variety Show; JV Swmmng; Honor Choir Most Outstndng Soprano 1989-90; Most Dedicated JV Swmmr 1989-90; SDSU; Music.

SLUSSER, FRANK; Edison-Computech HS; Fresno, CA; (3); Boy Scts; Church Yth Grp; Math Tm; Ed Lit Mag; Ftbl; Socr; BSA Eagle Awd; Luth Living Faith Awd; Enrironmental Awareness Club.

SLUSSER, GREG L; Edison-Computech HS; Fresno, CA; (1); Boy Scts; Tennis; Vllybl; High Hon Roll; CA Schlrshp Fed; Elec Engr.

SLUSSER, MICHAEL A; Rim Of The World HS; Crestline, CA; (3); 3/200; Boy Scts; Chess Clb; Sec Drama Clb; Model UN; School Play; Ed Nwsp; Yrbk; Hon Roll; NHS; Rotary Awd; 3 Tm Wrtng Clebrtn Wnnr; 2 Bst Cameo Drama Awds; Design Engrng.

SLUTSKE, JEFFREY L; Thousand Oaks HS; Thousand Oaks, CA; (3); Boy Scts; Cmnty Wkr; Key Clb; Model UN; Office Aide; Ski Clb; SADD; Stu Cncl; JV Var Bsbl; JV Score Keeper; Katate; Business.

SLUTSKY, SONIA; Beverly Hills HS; Beverly Hills, CA; (4); Spanish Clb; DAR Awd; Hon Roll; Advncd Dance Thtr Grp 88-90; Los Angeles Stu Coaltn; Ythl Ldrshp Pgm; Interntl Relations.

SLY, LAURREL M; Del Campo HS; Citrus Heights, CA; (3); 47/446; Church Yth Grp; French Clb; German Clb; Drill Tm; Var Tennis; BYU; Dntl.

SLYKER, BRENDAN J; Montgomery HS; Santa Rosa, CA; (2); Spanish Clb; Var Socr; High Hon Roll; NHS; Vrsty Badminton; Schl Rcgntn Gold St Exams; Span Frgn Lang Awd; Stckbrkr.

SMALL, MATT D; Poway HS; San Diego, CA; (2); VP FBLA; JV Wrstlng; Hon Roll; Pres Acad Fit Awd; Math Stu Of Month.

SMALL, STACEY L; Turlock HS; Keyes, CA; (3); 140/600; Church Yth Grp; Office Aide; Pep Clb; Spirit Club; CA ST U Stanislaus; Adv.

SMALLEY, DAVID; Sonoma Valley HS; Glen Ellen, CA; (2); 8/252; Church Yth Grp; Cmnty Wkr; Bsktbl; Wt Lftg; High Hon Roll; Hon Roll; Prfct Atten Awd; Gldn St Math Exm; Intrct Clb; CSU; Engr.

SMALLEY, MIKE; Hesperia HS; Hesperia, CA; (2); 5/800; Cmnty Wkr; FBLA; Spanish Clb; Hon Roll; Explorer Post 152; San Diego ST U; Jrnlsm.

SMALLEY, STACEY; Sonoma Valley HS; Glen Ellen, CA; (4); 21/285; Church Yth Grp; Var L Bsktbl; Powder Puff Ftbl; JV Sftbl; High Hon Roll; Hon Roll; Pol Sci.

SMALLING, SHANNA; Washington Prep; Los Angeles, CA; (4); 6/540; Dance Clb; Speech Tm; Drill Tm; Stu Cncl; Stat Bsktbl; Cit Awd; High Hon Roll; Prfct Atten Awd; Knights & Ladies Clb; Spelman Coll; Math.

SMALLWOOD, DONNA K; Ocean View HS; Huntington Bch, CA; (4); 46/417; Speech Tm; School Musical; Vrsty Bdmntn Ltr; Vocal Ensemble; Golden West Coll; Vet.

SMALLWOOD, ERIK T; Edison HS; Newport Beach, CA; (2); Cmnty Wkr; Key Clb; Teachers Aide; Private Band; Skateboarding; Orange Coast CC; Small Bus.

SMALLWOOD, JASON A; Fontana HS; Fontana, CA; (2); Boy Scts; Phtg Nwsp; Phtg Yrbk; Intrml Bsbl; JV Wrstlng; High Hon Roll; Hon Roll; Pres Acad Fit Awd; Fri Night Live Pres; US Naval Acad; Psych.

SMART, JOANNA C; Pioneer HS; San Jose, CA; (1); Church Yth Grp; Cmnty Wkr; JV Tennis; Peer Cnslng; U Of CA; Psych.

SMART, JOHN; Kearny HS; San Diego, CA; (4); 55/297; Treas Am Leg Boys St; Aud/Vis; Boy Scts; Drama Clb; Model UN; SADD; School Play; Stage Crew; Rep Jr Cls; Rep Sr Cls; Sons Of Amer Rvltn Brnz Good Ctznshp Medl; Outstndg SR Boy; Outstndg ASB Stu; Bnk Of Amer Achvt Awd; San Diego ST U; Spch Cmmnctns.

SMART, KARA; Elk Grove HS; Elk Grove, CA; (4); 54/250; Church Yth Grp; Cmnty Wkr; Church Choir; Ed Yrbk; Powder Puff Ftbl; High Hon Roll; Jr NHS; NHS; JR & SR Asilomr; CSF; BYU; Acctnt.

SMART, KIM A; Oakdale HS; Oakdale, CA; (2); Nrs.

SMAY, MATT J; Village Christian Schl; Sunland, CA; (3); 24/123; Math Clb; Mu Alpha Theta; Varsity Clb; Var Bsbl; Var Ftbl; Var Wt Lftg; Elect Engrng.

SMEATON, KIM M; Ygnacio Valley HS; Concord, CA; (3); Church Yth Grp; Dance Clb; Pep Clb.

SMELCER, MICHELLE RENEE; Capistrano Valley Christian HS; Laguna Niguel, CA; (2); Church Yth Grp; Cmnty Wkr; JV Bsktbl; Director.

SMETS, JOANNE; Oak Park HS; Agoura Hills, CA; (2); Church Yth Grp; JV Sftbl; High Hon Roll; Oil Pntng, Drwng; Peer Cnclng Group; Art.

SMIAROWSKI, KRISTEN E; John Muir HS; Pasadena, CA; (3); Dance Clb; Service Clb; Orch; School Musical; Pom Pon; Story Prntd Schl Literary Mag; Wrk With Chldrn.

SMICK, BRANDON M; St Francis HS; Sunnyvale, CA; (2); 30/370; JV Bsktbl; JV Golf; Hon Roll; Loyola Marymount; Arch.

SMIGA, CHRIS K; Dublin HS; Dublin, CA; (3); 40/158; Boy Scts; Band; Mrchg Band; Var Swmmng; Hon Roll; Lifeguard; Arch.

SMILEY, CHELON DARICE; Granada HS; Livermore, CA; (4); Teachers Aide; Hon Roll; Prfct Atten Awd; Las Positas; Nrsng.

SMILEY, CHRISTA; Clovis HS; Fresno, CA; (3); Drama Clb; French Clb; School Musical; School Play; Stage Crew; Hon Roll; Liberal Arts.

SMILEY, JAMAL; John F Kennedy HS; Sacramento, CA; (1); Church Yth Grp; German Clb; ROTC; Ftbl; Hon Roll; 5 A Awd; Parents Blck Stu Achvt Awd; Air Force Acad; Chef.

SMILEY, MARTINITA C; Silver Valley HS; Fort Irwin, CA; (2); Church Yth Grp; Band; Church Choir; Drm Mjr(t); Mrchg Band; Pep Band; Off Soph Cls; Stu Cncl; Var Bsktbl; Powder Puff Ftbl; VP Band Cls 89-90; Bst Dancer 89-90; Asst Cndctr Band Cls 88-89; Hnr Band Soc 89-90; Bus Mgmt.

SMITH, AARON C; The Bishops Schl; La Jolla, CA; (3); Off Church Yth Grp; Letterman Clb; Chorus; Varsity Clb; Yrbk; JV Gym; Var Capt Vllybl; Study Abrd Span; AP Photo, Span, Engl; All Leag Hnrbl Mntn Vllybl; Jrnlsm.

SMITH, AARON D; Temecula Valley HS; Murrieta, CA; (2); 114/590; Cmnty Wkr; 4-H; Ski Clb; Teachers Aide; Prfct Atten Awd; Contractor.

SMITH, ADAM C; Coronado HS; Coronado, CA; (3); Letterman Clb; Service Clb; JV Var Bsktbl; Intrml Fld Hcky; Co-Capt Ftbl; Hon Roll; Bus.

SMITH, ADAM M; Santa Clara HS; Oxnard, CA; (3); 16/145; Computer Clb; JV Crs Cntry; JV Trk; High Hon Roll; Hon Roll; NHS; Japanese Pen Pal; Denver U; Aerospc Dsgn.

SMITH, ADAM R; Bishop O'dowd HS; Oakland, CA; (2); Ski Clb; Var Crs Cntry; Var Socr; Var Trk; Hon Roll; NEDT Awd; St Schlr.

SMITH, AIMEE M; Hilmar HS; Stevinson, CA; (3); Teachers Aide; Nwsp; Pres Jr Cls; Pres Stu Cncl; JV Bsktbl; Var JV Sftbl; High Hon Roll; Hon Roll; Friday Night Live; Crt Reporting.

SMITH, ALEXANDER W; Montgomery HS; Santa Rosa, CA; (2); Dance Clb; Spanish Clb; SADD; Varsity Clb; Stage Crew; Sec Frsh Cls; Off Soph Cls; Rep Stu Cncl; Var Bsbl; Var Socr; Gldn St Alg Exam High Hnrs; Princeton; Bus.

SMITH, ALICIA A; Ventura HS; Ventura, CA; (3); Church Yth Grp; SADD; Ed Yrbk; High Hon Roll; Opt Clb Awd.

SMITH, ALISSA K; Burbank HS; Burbank, CA; (2); Pres Church Yth Grp; Pep Clb; Red Cross Aide; Service Clb; Church Choir; Drill Tm; Variety Show; Off Frsh Cls; Rep Stu Cncl; JV Bsktbl; BYU; Bus.

SMITH, ALLISON L; Patrick Henry HS; San Diego, CA; (3); Church Yth Grp; Dance Clb; Drama Clb; School Play; Gym; Trk; Cit Awd; Hon Roll; Pres Acad Fit Awd; Med.

SMITH, AMANDA; Monterey HS; Carmel, CA; (2); Church Yth Grp; Dance Clb; Model UN; Hon Roll; Grphc Arts.

SMITH, AMBER; Saddleback HS; Atlantic, IA; (4); 64/580; Art Clb; Math Clb; Pep Clb; Service Clb; Varsity Clb; Lit Mag; Var Socr; Var Sftbl; Var Vllybl; Prfct Atten Awd; N W MO ST U; Ceramics.

SMITH, AMY M; Sonora HS; Sonora, CA; (3); Ski Clb; Yrbk; Stat Bsbl; Cheerldng; Europe Tour; Intrct; Hmcmng Dcrtng Comm; CSU Chico.

SMITH, AMY P; Desert Chrstian HS; Lancaster, CA; (2); Church Yth Grp; Girl Scts; Rptr Nwsp; Co-Ed Yrbk; Ed Lit Mag; VP Frsh Cls; JV Cheerldng; JV Socr; Hon Roll; Fnlst Teenage Amer Cont; Marine Bio.

SMITH, ANGELA M; Woodland HS; Woodland, CA; (2); Church Yth Grp; School Musical; VP Frsh Cls; Rep Soph Cls; VP Jr Cls; Bsktbl; Tennis; Trk; High Hon Roll; Jr NHS; Chrch Dance Team; Certfd Red Crss; Brigham Young U; Schl Cnslr.

SMITH, ANGELA V; Hesperia HS; Hesperia, CA; (4); 57/442; Church Yth Grp; Ski Clb; Spanish Clb; SADD; Teachers Aide; Chorus; JV Trk; High Hon Roll; Hon Roll; Speed Clb; Victor Valley Coll; Engl.

SMITH, ANGELINA M; Channel Islands HS; Oxnard, CA; (3); Key Clb; Science Clb; Flag Corp; Var Crs Cntry; JV Socr; Hon Roll; CSF; Gftd & Tlntd Educ; Poltcl Sci.

SMITH, ANTHONY D; College Park HS; Pleasant Hill, CA; (3); 95/317; Church Yth Grp; Var Bsbl; Wt Lftg; Hon Roll; Stu Of Month.

SMITH, ARLO; King Drew Medical Magnet; Los Angeles, CA; (2); Pres VP Stu Cncl; Score Keeper; Cit Awd; High Hon Roll; Hon Roll; Prfct Atten Awd; Sal; Multi-Cultural Club; Nrs.

SMITH, BAIBA B; Mc Lane HS; Fresno, CA; (2); Pep Clb; Cheerldng; Pom Pon; Swmmng; Horsebck Rdng; UC Santa Barbara.

SMITH, BARBARELLA A; Ripon HS; Ripon, CA; (3); Girl Scts; Office Aide; Teachers Aide; High Hon Roll; Hon Roll; MJC; Child Psych.

SMITH, BARCLAY R; Moorpark HS; Moorpark, CA; (3); 10/221; Debate Tm; Crs Cntry; Wrstlng; High Hon Roll; Hon Roll; Ntl Merit SF; CA Tech; Engrng.

SMITH, BERNADETTE P; St Genevieve HS; Reseda, CA; (2); Church Yth Grp; Dance Clb; SADD; Drill Tm; Hon Roll; Loyola Marymount U; Med.

SMITH, BOBBY G; Los Banos HS; Los Banos, CA; (2); Drama Clb; Spanish Clb; Band; Mrchg Band; Hon Roll.

SMITH, BRAD; Dana Hills HS; Dana Point, CA; (2); Spanish Clb; Socr; Swmmng; Hon Roll; Pres Acad Fit Awd; UCSC; Envrnmntl Lawyr.

SMITH, BRADLEY S; Clovis West HS; Fresno, CA; (3); Church Yth Grp; German Clb; Varsity Clb; JV Socr; Var L Trk; Hstry.

SMITH, BRANDON C; Antioch HS; Antioch, CA; (2); Aud/Vis; Xmas Decor Cont-1st Pl 89; Econ.

SMITH, BRANDON M; Caruthers HS; Caruthers, CA; (4); Church Yth Grp; Pres FFA; Letterman Clb; Math Clb; Math Tm; Rep Stu Cncl; Var Bsktbl; Var Tennis; Var Capt Vllybl; Hon Roll; CA St Farmer Degree; CA Poly; Ag Engrng.

SMITH, BRANDY; Hueneme HS; Los Angeles, CA; (1); Chorus; UCLA; Nursing Asst.

SMITH, BRIDGET; Cleveland HS; West Hills, CA; (2); Debate Tm; Intnl Clb; Office Aide; Spanish Clb; Var Socr; NHS; Pres Acad Fit Awd; Sccr Team Cultural Exchng Trip Europe 87; UC Berkeley; Anthrplgst.

SMITH, CARRIE; Valley HS; Sacramento, CA; (2); SADD; Teachers Aide; Var Mgr(s); Var Powder Puff Ftbl; JV Score Keeper; JV L Sftbl; Var L Vllybl; High Hon Roll; Hon Roll; Psych.

SMITH, CARRIE L; Riverside Christian HS; Riverside, CA; (2); 2/10; Church Yth Grp; Girl Scts; Teachers Aide; Church Choir; Yrbk; VP Soph Cls; Sec Treas Stu Cncl; Co-Ed Cheerldng; Vllybl; High Hon Roll; Girl Scout Slvr Awd & Slvr & Gold Ldrshp Awds; 2 Poems Pblshd In Girl Scout News Lttr; Pensecola Christian Coll; Tchr.

SMITH, CHAD D; Atwater HS; Atwater, CA; (3); Mchncl Engr.

SMITH III, CHARLES STEWART; Buena HS; Ventura, CA; (4); 17/492; High Hon Roll; Hon Roll; Ntl Merit Schol; Pres Acad Fit Awd; Fencg; Cal Tech; Engrng.

SMITH, CHERYL J; Buena Park HS; Buena Park, CA; (3); Church Yth Grp; Letterman Clb; Church Choir; School Play; Treas Frsh Cls; Sec Soph Cls; Var Capt Swmmng; Hon Roll; Water Polo Statistician; U Of CA Santa Barbara; Jrnlsm.

SMITH, CHERYL R; Skyline HS; Oakland, CA; (3); Church Yth Grp; Cmnty Wkr; Band; Chorus; Church Choir; Jazz Band; Orch; Pep Band; Variety Show; VP Frsh Cls; Black Stu Un; Poltcl Sci.

SMITH, CHRIS T; Caruthers HS; Fresno, CA; (4); 2/70; Pres Letterman Clb; Ed Yrbk; VP Soph Cls; VP Jr Cls; Sr Cls; JV VP Bsbl; VP Capt Bsktbl; VP Capt Ftbl; Hon Roll; Pres Acad Fit Awd; Cal Poly San Luis Obispo; Ag.

SMITH, CHRISTINA M; Eisenhower HS; Fontana, CA; (2); Office Aide; Teachers Aide; High Hon Roll; Hon Roll; NHS; Pres Acad Fit Awd; C Clb; Ltr K Clb; Homework Clb; UCLA; Aerospace Engrng.

SMITH, CHRISTINA N; Encinal HS; Alameda, CA; (1); 130/280; Spanish Clb; Teachers Aide; Band; Color Guard; Mrchg Band; Cit Awd; Hon Roll; Sales Rep.

SMITH, CHRISTINE M; Bella Vista HS; Fair Oaks, CA; (4); 14/370; Church Yth Grp; French Clb; Orch; School Musical; Stu Cncl; French Hon Soc; High Hon Roll; NHS; Friday Night Live; UC Davis; Vet Sci.

SMITH, CHRISTINE V; Palm Springs HS; Palm Springs, CA; (2); High Hon Roll; Kiwanis Awd; Prfct Atten Awd; Schl Silver Sands Awds.

SMITH, CHRISTOPHER B; Escondido HS; Escondido, CA; (1); Bsbl; Socr; Prfct Atten Awd; Lang Achvt Awd; Bus.

SMITH, CHRISTY; Cajon HS; San Bernardino, CA; (2); Church Yth Grp; Drama Clb; Pep Clb; School Musical; School Play; Stage Crew; JV Pom Pon; NHS; Rotary Awd; Intl Baccalaureate; CSF.

SMITH, CLAUDIA; Simi HS; Simi Valley, CA; (2); 567/739; Pep Clb; Rep Frsh Cls; Rep Soph Cls; JV Cheerldng; Gym; JV Pom Pon; JV Var Powder Puff Ftbl; UCSB; RN.

SMITH, CLAYTON Q; California HS; San Ramon, CA; (3); Teachers Aide; JV Bsbl; NCS Schlr/Athl 88-89; Chico ST; Bus Admin.

SMITH, COURTNEY W; Monte Vista HS; Danville, CA; (2); Chorus; Var L Swmmng; Hon Roll.

SMITH, DANIELLE; Upper Lake HS; Winter Springs, CA; (2); Treas Spanish Clb; SADD; Lit Mag; Sec Soph Cls; Var Bsktbl; JV Cheerldng; Hon Roll; Lake Cnty Hstry Day 1st Pl; Bsktbl 1st In Leag; Advertising.

SMITH, DARREN M; South HS; Bakersfield, CA; (3); Boy Scts; Church Yth Grp; Hon Roll; College; Science Field.

SMITH, DAVE; San Ramon HS; Danville, CA; (1); Church Yth Grp; Ftbl; Wt Lftg; Hon Roll; Dermtlgst.

SMITH JR, DAVID E; Bellarmine College Prep; Los Gatos, CA; (3); 30/300; Computer Clb; Teachers Aide; Intrml Bsktbl; Intrml Ftbl; Intrml Sftbl; Aeronautical Engrng.

SMITH, DAVID F; Oxnard HS; Oxnard, CA; (2); Ftbl; UCLA; Real Est.

SMITH, DAVID M; Lutheran HS Of Orange County; Norco, CA; (2); Church Yth Grp; Quiz Bowl; Scholastic Bowl; JV Socr; OCAD; Usad; Comp & Elec; Comp Sci.

SMITH, DENISE E; Oakdale HS; Oakdale, CA; (4); 4/230; Pres Church Yth Grp; Dance Clb; Drama Clb; Church Choir; School Play; Stage Crew; Elks Awd; High Hon Roll; Yth For Christ; Acad Decathlon; CA Schlrshp Fed Sec; Biola U.

SMITH, DESIRA; Antioch SR HS; Antioch, CA; (4); Church Yth Grp; Pep Clb; Spanish Clb; Teachers Aide; Band; Chorus; Church Choir; Mrchg Band; Orch; Pep Band; Christian Life Coll; Missionary.

SMITH, DIANA; Mountain View HS; Mountain View, CA; (3); 117/319; Dance Clb; Teachers Aide; Variety Show; JV Swmmng; Hon Roll; Stu Month Engl Dept 10th Grd; San Jose ST U; Jrnlsm.

SMITH, DOUG D; Mt Whitney HS; Visalia, CA; (4); FFA; Co-Capt Var Wrstlng; Most Outstndng Vrsty Wrstlr; Gov Cmmtte Dsabld Prsns Schlr Hnrbl Mntn; Athlt Awd Teamsters Schlrshp; Fresno ST; Bus.

SMITH, DUNCAN; Los Alamitos HS; Los Alamitos, CA; (4); Model UN; High Hon Roll; NHS; Ntl Merit SF; Acad Dcthln; Princeton U; Elec Engrng.

SMITH, DYLAN D; Mayfair HS; Lakewood, CA; (3); SADD; Golf; High Hon Roll; Hon Roll; Stanford; Engrng.

SMITH, ELEAH M; Foothill HS; Sacramento, CA; (3); Church Yth Grp; Sec VP Drama Clb; School Musical; School Play; Acad Decathln Team 90; Teen Fshn Brd; U Of UT; Ed.

SMITH, ELSIE; Torrance HS; Torrance, CA; (3); 55/414; FHA; Band; Rep Jr Cls; Math Engrng Sci Achvt; CSF; Ywca; Stanford U; Med.

SMITH, EMANUEL Q; Saint Francis HS; Menlo Park, CA; (2); Church Yth Grp; Cmnty Wkr; Drama Clb; English Clb; French Clb; Band; Church Choir; JV Var Bsktbl; JV Ftbl; Mgr(s); De Paul; Bus.

SMITH, EMELDA D; Nogales HS; West Covina, CA; (3); Dance Clb; Teachers Aide; High Hon Roll; Hon Roll; Devry U; Cmptr Prgmr.

SMITH, EQUAAN D; California HS; San Ramon, CA; (4); Church Yth Grp; Cmnty Wkr; Teachers Aide; Band; Mrchg Band; Rep Frsh Cls; VP Soph Cls; Pres Jr Cls; Rep Stu Cncl; Hon Roll; Bicentnnl Honorary Awd & Civics Team; Smith U; Mrktng.

SMITH, ERICA M; College Park HS; Pleasant Hill, CA; (1); Drill Team; Med.

SMITH, ERNESTINE; Perris HS; Chicago, IL; (4); Bus Profs of Am; Church Yth Grp; Drama Clb; 4-H; JA; Acpl Chr; Church Choir; Stage Crew; Rep Yrbk; Trk; Prncpl Schlrs Pgm; Honeywell Pgm; De Vry; Comp Prgmr.

SMITH, ESBEN H; Caruthers HS; Fresno, CA; (3); VP Sec Letterman Clb; Yrbk; Treas Frsh Cls; VP Bsbl; VP Bsktbl; VP Ftbl; Hon Roll.

SMITH, ETHAN; Eureka HS; Eureka, CA; (1); Hon Roll; Schl Roleplny Clb; Art.

SMITH, GABRIELL; Los Gatos HS; Los Gatos, CA; (3); Teachers Aide; High Hon Roll; Hon Roll; Amnesty Intl; Help The Environmnt Live Peacefully; Humbolt; Envirnmntl Chem.

SMITH, GARY P; Hillsdale HS; San Mateo, CA; (3); Boy Scts; Chess Clb; Church Yth Grp; FCA; Letterman Clb; Office Aide; Teachers Aide; Varsity Clb; Church Choir; JV Bsbl; All Leag Bsktbl Plyr; UCLA; Law.

SMITH, GARY R; Apple Valley Sun Devils HS; Apple Valley, CA; (1); Hon Roll.

SMITH, GENA B; Bear River HS; Auburn, CA; (2); 22/232; Church Yth Grp; Science Clb; Spanish Clb; SADD; JV Bsktbl; Var Trk; High Hon Roll; Pepperdine U; Bus.

SMITH, GRANT J; Red Bluff U HS; Red Bluff, CA; (3); 23/450; Cmnty Wkr; Ski Clb; Spanish Clb; SADD; Acpl Chr; Chorus; School Musical; Variety Show; JV Bsktbl; JV Var Ftbl; Vrsty Ski Team; Chico ST U; Bus Mgmt.

SMITH, HEATHER; Abraham Lincoln HS; San Jose, CA; (4); Office Aide; Teachers Aide; Chorus; Var Capt Cheerldng; Hon Roll; Interact Clb; Fresno ST U; Child Dvlpmnt.

SMITH, HEATHER; Tomales HS; Bodega Bay, CA; (3); Cmnty Wkr; Drama Clb; French Clb; GAA; Letterman Clb; Ski Clb; School Play; Nwsp; Pres Frsh Cls; Treas Soph Cls; Hnrs Wmn Engrs Am Awd; Schlr Athl Awds; Mock Trl.

SMITH, HEATHER A; Mira Loma HS; Sacramento, CA; (3); SADD; Drill Tm; Var Cheerldng; American River JC.

SMITH, HEATHER E; La Serna HS; Whittier, CA; (2); Cmnty Wkr; JCL; Latin Clb; Model UN; Var Crs Cntry; JV Trk; Hon Roll; Lancer Leag Treas; Golden St Exam Alg Hgh Hnrs; Acctg.

SMITH, HEATHER L; Ernest Righetti HS; Santa Maria, CA; (4); Church Yth Grp; Cmnty Wkr; Drama Clb; JA; Spanish Clb; School Play; Stat Vllybl; Hon Roll; Pep Clb; Temple Yth Grp; Photp Publshd Photogrphs Forum, Finalst In Cntst 90; Peer Ldrshp, Cnslr Cert Of Achvt; Cal Poly San Luis Obispo; Bus.

SMITH, HEATHER P; South Fork HS; Miranda, CA; (4); Art Clb; SADD; School Play; Nwsp; Ed Yrbk; Vllybl; Hon Roll; Amnsty Intl Club; CA Arts Schlr Arts Rcgntn & Tlnt Srch Pgm 89-90; Humboldt ST U; Art.

SMITH, HEATHER R; Lompoc HS; Lompoc, CA; (3); Letterman Clb; Band; Drill Tm; Flag Corp; Mrchg Band; Rptr Nwsp; Var Cheerldng; JV Swmmng; Associated Stu Body Club; Psych.

SMITH, HEIDI E; Senior HS; Seal Beach, CA; (2); Chorus; Cheerldng; Var Gym; JV Trk; Elite Gymnst Trng Olympcs; Snow Skiing; U Of AZ; Chld Psych.

SMITH, HOPE M; Merced HS; Merced, CA; (3); Hon Roll; Art.

SMITH, JAIMI R; Diamond Bar HS; Diamond Bar, CA; (2); Key Clb; Varsity Clb; Vllybl; Kiwanis Awd; Vlybl MVP; Black Stu Union; Howard U; Arch.

SMITH, JAKE; Garces Memorial HS; Bakersfield, CA; (4); 14/118; JA; Ski Clb; Var Swmmng; Var Tennis; Hon Roll; Club Bllybl; Cal Poly San Luis Obispo; Bus.

SMITH, JAMES; Palo Verde HS; Blythe, CA; (2); Church Yth Grp; Computer Clb; Dance Clb; Drama Clb; FCA; Letterman Clb; Varsity Clb; Off Soph Cls; Stu Cncl; Bsktbl; USC; Actg.

SMITH, JAMES W; Summerville HS; Sonora, CA; (3); Cmnty Wkr; 4-H; Teachers Aide; Intrml Bsktbl; Intrml Socr; Little Lge Umpire; Columbia Coll; Bus Admin.

SMITH, JAMIE; Yosemite Union HS; Raymond, CA; (3); 4/174; Pres Church Yth Grp; FFA; Band; Mrchg Band; High Hon Roll; Fresno ST; RN.

SMITH, JANIS E; Trabuco Hills HS; Mission Viejo, CA; (2); 17/420; Church Yth Grp; Spanish Clb; JV Socr; JV Tennis; JV Trk; High Hon Roll; NHS; Cert Merit Piano Study; Tennis MVP Awd; CSF; U CA; Bus Adm.

SMITH, JASON; Mount Pleasant HS; San Jose, CA; (3); English Clb; FCA; Varsity Clb; Bsbl; Bsktbl; Ftbl; Trk; Wt Lftg; Prfct Atten Awd; BSU; UNLV; Business.

SMITH, JASON E; Hueneme HS; Oxnard, CA; (2); Letterman Clb; Var Swmmng; Water Polo JV; USAF Acad; Math.

SMITH, JASON P; Apple Valley HS; Apple Valley, CA; (2); Church Yth Grp; JV Golf; High Hon Roll; Hon Roll; Civil Air Patrol Cadet Prgm Master Sgt; US Naval Acad; Engrng.

SMITH, JAYSON R; Grossmont HS; El Cajon, CA; (1); Church Yth Grp; Band; Mrchg Band; Orch; High Hon Roll; Hon Roll; Goldn St Exam High Hnrs Alg; Physics.

SMITH, JEFFREY NOAH; Lodi HS; Lodi, CA; (4); 16/425; Boy Scts; Church Yth Grp; FTA; Science Clb; VP Spanish Clb; Speech Tm; SADD; Acpl Chr; Band; Church Choir; CA Stu Cncls Assn; Mock Trial Clb; Order Of Arrow; Stu Advsry Brd; BYU; Aerospace Engr.

SMITH, JENEA A; Armijo HS; Suisun, CA; (2); Pep Clb; Cheerldng; Hon Roll.

SMITH, JENNIFER; Yosemite Union HS; Coarsegold, CA; (2); Drama Clb; French Clb; School Play; Hon Roll; UCLA; Drama.

SMITH, JENNIFER L; Irvine HS; Irvine, CA; (3); French Clb; CA ST; Engl.

SMITH, JENNIFER M; Arcata HS; Bayside, CA; (3); Var Capt Bsktbl; Var L Crs Cntry; Var L Sftbl; Var L Vllybl; Hon Roll; All-Cnty Bsktbl & Sftbl; Phys Thrpy.

SMITH, JENNIFER M; Armijo HS; Fairfield, CA; (1); Church Yth Grp; Hosp Aide; Flag Corp; School Play; Alisa Ann Ruch Burn Fndtn Bridge To Life Courage Awd; U Of CA Davis Med Ctr Burn Vctm Supprt Grp; Hastings Law Schl; Law.

SMITH, JENNIFER M; Hoover HS; Fresno, CA; (2); Church Yth Grp; Spanish Clb; SADD; Band; Mrchg Band; Orch; High Hon Roll; GSE Geom Awd; Fresno-Madero Cnty Hnr Band; CSF; Med.

SMITH, JENNY; Fortuna Union HS; Fortuna, CA; (2); Rptr FHA; SADD; Rptr Yrbk; JV Cheerldng; CSF; HOBY Ambssdr 90; CA Poly; CPA.

SMITH, JEREME N; Nevada Union HS; Nevada City, CA; (3); Church Yth Grp; Var Trk; High Hon Roll; BUS Admin.

SMITH, JEREMY T; California HS; San Ramon, CA; (4); 10/415; English Clb; High Hon Roll; NHS; Prfct Atten Awd; U Of CA Davis; Biolgcl Sci.

SMITH, JERI R; North HS; Bakersfield, CA; (1); Church Yth Grp; FHA; Teachers Aide; Color Guard; Hon Roll; CA ST; Child Psych.

SMITH, JERMOND N; Redwood HS; Visalia, CA; (3); Church Yth Grp; Computer Clb; Debate Tm; Drama Clb; English Clb; FCA; French Clb; FBLA; Letterman Clb; Math Clb; Trk Coachs Awd; Trk Bst Hurdler 90; Law.

SMITH, JESSICA D; Los Amigos HS; Fountain Valley, CA; (2); 17/365; Church Yth Grp; Drama Clb; Sec Thesps; Capt Flag Corp; Mrchg Band; Orch; School Musical; School Play; High Hon Roll; Hon Roll; AZ St; Interior Design.

SMITH, JILENE A; Arcata HS; Fieldbrook, CA; (2); Church Yth Grp; Drama Clb; SADD; Hon Roll.

SMITH, JILL C; Beyer HS; Modesto, CA; (2); Hosp Aide; Ski Clb; Color Guard; Hon Roll; Mdl; Gottchalks Hi Deb Pgm.

SMITH, JONATHAN E; St Ignatious College Prep; San Francisco, CA; (4); Pres Drama Clb; School Musical; School Play; Stage Crew; Variety Show; Stu Cncl; Christian Life Community; Big Brothers; CA Schlrshp Fed; Loyola Marymount U; Theatre Art.

SMITH, JOSH P; Fontana HS; Fontana, CA; (2); High Hon Roll; Hon Roll; Bus.

SMITH, JOSLYN A; Del Campo HS; Austin, TX; (3); 215/525; Church Yth Grp; Cmnty Wkr; Treas French Clb; Sec Jr Cls; Mock Trail Lawyer; Conflict Manager; Stu Rep San Juan USD Bd; U TX Austin; Law.

SMITH, KADINGA S; Mc Clymondo HS; Oakland, CA; (3); Bus Profs of Am; Computer Clb; Varsity Clb; Band; Jazz Band; Stage Crew; VP Frsh Cls; VP Sr Cls; Var Bsbl; JV Bsktbl; Upward Bound Mills Coll; MESA; UC-DAVIS; Civil Engrng.

SMITH, KANDI M; Mission Bay HS; San Diego, CA; (3); 90/350; Am Leg Aux Girls St; Cmnty Wkr; DECA; Teachers Aide; Sec Jr Cls; JV Vllybl; Cit Awd; Hon Roll; Pres Acad Fit Awd; Rotary Awd; Interact; Rotary Yth Ldrshp Awd; Campus Beautiful Chrprsn; U Of Redlands; Bus.

SMITH, KAREN J; Piedmont HS; Piedmont, CA; (4); Cmnty Wkr; German Clb; Girl Scts; Hosp Aide; SADD; Teachers Aide; Stage Crew; Rptr Nwsp; Yrbk; Stat Trk; Var Crew; San Diego ST U; Telecomm.

SMITH, KARI; Temecula Valley HS; Temecula, CA; (3); Church Yth Grp; Pep Clb; SADD; Varsity Clb; Var L Cheerldng; Var Capt Pom Pon; Cit Awd; High Hon Roll; Hon Roll; Prfct Atten Awd; Perf, Attendance, Acad & Ctznshp Hnr Roll; Pep Squad Hist 89-90; U MO Columbia; Acctg.

SMITH, KATHLEEN R; Vacaville HS; Vacaville, CA; (4); German Clb; Service Clb; Stage Crew; Variety Show; Rep Stu Cncl; Hon Roll; NHS; Bus.

SMITH, KATHLEEN V; Homestead HS; Sunnyvale, CA; (3); 80/383; JV Socr; CSF 89; U Of CA Santa Cruz; Sci.

SMITH, KEELY R; Roseville HS; Roseville, CA; (1); German Clb; Flag Corp; Trk; Cit Awd; Hon Roll; NHS.

SMITH, KEISHNA M; Oroville HS; Oroville, CA; (2); 90/221; SADD; Mgr(s); Hon Roll; Bus.

SMITH, KELLI A; West HS; Bakersfield, CA; (2); Band; Hon Roll; U San Francisco; Interior Dcrtr.

SMITH, KENDRA M; Rincon Valley Christian HS; Santa Rosa, CA; (2); Church Yth Grp; Church Choir; Co-Capt Flag Corp; Var Bsktbl; Var Sftbl; Var Vllybl; Cit Awd; High Hon Roll; Pres Acad Fit Awd; Sonoma Cnty Jr Symphny; Arts.

SMITH, KENNETH R; Bishop Amat Memorial HS; West Covina, CA; (4); Golf; Socr; Hon Roll; NYLC; Astrnt.

SMITH, KEVIN; Rincon Valley Christian HS; Santa Rosa, CA; (3); 1/20; Band; Church Choir; Mrchg Band; Orch; Pep Band; Rep Soph Cls; Rep Jr Cls; Var Bsktbl; High Hon Roll.

SMITH, KEVIN; Strathmore HS; Porterville, CA; (4); 1/70; Treas Church Yth Grp; Debate Tm; Letterman Clb; SADD; Ed Nwsp; Capt Var Tennis; Cit Awd; High Hon Roll; NHS; CIF Reebok Schlrshp Valley Runner-Up; U Of The Pacific; Bus.

SMITH, KIMBERLIE D; Gladstone HS; Azusa, CA; (3); Science Clb; SADD; Chorus; Capt Drill Tm; Var Swmmng; Drama Clb; Ed.

SMITH, KIMBERLY; Tustin HS; Tustin, CA; (2); Nwsp; Hon Roll; Phrmcy.

SMITH, KIMBERLY A; Hemet HS; Hemet, CA; (3); 70/535; Church Yth Grp; Cmnty Wkr; Office Aide; Powder Puff Ftbl; Stat Sftbl; JV Vllybl; Hon Roll; Otstndng Bus Awd 87-88; Westmont Christian Coll; Nrsng.

SMITH, KRISTEN M; Pittsburg HS; Pittsburg, CA; (2); Cmnty Wkr; Pep Clb; Band; Flag Corp; Mrchg Band; NEDT Awd; Prfrmng Arts Club; Gldn St Exam Schlr; Psych.

SMITH, KRISTIN A; Westmoor HS; Daly City, CA; (3); 58/395; Boy Scts; Church Yth Grp; Cmnty Wkr; Drama Clb; Service Clb; SADD; Teachers Aide; Band; Chorus; Co-Chm Act Friday Night Live; Carl Vinson Club; Ricks Coll; Early Chdld Ed.

SMITH, KRISTY; Strathmore Union HS; Porterville, CA; (3); 4/90; Am Leg Aux Girls St; Church Yth Grp; VP Frsh Cls; Treas Soph Cls; Rep Jr Cls; JV Var Bsktbl; Var Tennis; Cit Awd; High Hon Roll; SADD; Natl Tnns Rankng Grls; Pre-Law.

SMITH, LATAYNA M; Washington Prep HS; Inglewood, CA; (3); Art Clb; Pep Clb; SADD; Teachers Aide; Chorus; Drill Tm; Trk; Cit Awd; Hon Roll; MESA; Tlnt Srch; 1st Annl Gspl Dptnt; Arch.

SMITH, LATEEFAH M; Pasadena HS; Pasadena, CA; (3); Church Yth Grp; Office Aide; Teachers Aide; Acpl Chr; Chorus; Church Choir; Variety Show; JV Sftbl; JV Vllybl; Hon Roll; Blck Stu Union; After Schl Job; Howard U; Psych.

SMITH, LAURA E; Albany HS; Albany, CA; (2); 17/206; Pres Service Clb; Spanish Clb; Stat Bsktbl; JV Intrml Sftbl; Var JV Vllybl; Hon Roll; Gldn St Exam 1st Yr Algebra Hnrs, Geom Hnrs; Alameda Cnty Real Wmn Wrtng Cont 2nd Pl.

SMITH, LAURA R; James Lick HS; San Jose, CA; (1); Math Tm; Off Frsh Cls; High Hon Roll; CSF; Myrs Blu Rbn Cmmtte; UC Santa Cruz; Mrn Bio.

SMITH, LENARD; Crenshaw HS; Los Angeles, CA; (3); Hon Roll; Northridge Coll; Jrnlsm.

SMITH, LERI N; John Muir HS; Altadena, CA; (2); Crs Cntry; Trk; Cit Awd; Prfct Atten Awd; Modlng-Nordstrom; U Of CA Los Angeles; Med.

SMITH, LINDA M; Pinole Valley HS; Richmond, CA; (3); Hon Roll; Wrld Of Ptry Cntst Hnrbl Mntn; Natl Lbry Of Ptrycntst Semi-Fnlst; Pegasus Press Cntst Semi-Fnlst; Piablo Vly Coll; Educ.

SMITH, LORI J; Live Oak HS; Morgan Hill, CA; (3); Pres Sec 4-H; Rptr FFA; 4-H Awd; Hon Roll; U CA Davis; Vet Med.

SMITH, LYN THARIN; Edison HS; Huntington Beach, CA; (2); Chinese Clb; U CA Davis; Vet.

SMITH, LYNDELL; Mt Carmel HS; San Diego, CA; (3); Church Yth Grp; FTA; Variety Show; Intrml Bsktbl; Var L Cheerldng; Var L Gym; Intrml Sftbl; Intrml Vllybl; Intrml Wt Lftg; Church Congrgtn Yth Ldr; BYU; Tchr.

SMITH, MARCY; Ramona HS; Ramona, CA; (3); 49/294; Church Yth Grp; Dance Clb; Drama Clb; FBLA; Chorus; Church Choir; School Play; Sec Jr Cls; Stu Cncl; JV Socr; Dance Concert; Amnesty Intl; BYU.

SMITH, MARCY L; Ceres HS; Ceres, CA; (4); 7/214; French Clb; FBLA; Intnl Clb; Office Aide; Service Clb; SADD; Teachers Aide; High Hon Roll; Lion Awd; Pres Acad Fit Awd; CA Schlrshp Fed; Bank Of Amer Awd In Engl; Intl Clb Schlrshp; Modesto JC.

SMITH, MARGARET A; Fremont HS; Sunnyvale, CA; (2); 88/421; Church Yth Grp; Debate Tm; Rep Frsh Cls; JV Cheerldng; Var Socr; NSA Fife & Drum Corps; Counselor.

SMITH, MARIAMA B; Far West EBCE HS; Oakland, CA; (4); 5/20; Church Yth Grp; Dance Clb; French Clb; Hosp Aide; Ed Nwsp; Rptr Yrbk; Pres Jr Cls; Pres Jr Cls; Sec Stu Cncl; High Hon Roll; Stanford U; Human Bio.

SMITH, MARILYN L; Desert Christian HS; Indio, CA; (3); 3/8; Church Yth Grp; Teachers Aide; Chorus; Church Choir; Sec Frsh Cls; Sec Soph Cls; VP Stu Cncl; Var Bsktbl; Cit Awd; Hon Roll; Biola U; Scndry Ed/Sci.

SMITH, MARLAN K; Golden West HS; Visalia, CA; (4); Acpl Chr; Band; Drm Mjr(t); Mrchg Band; Pep Band; Hon Roll; Church Yth Grp; Chorus; Teachers Aide; Outstanding Contributions To Band; Jr & Sr All Amer Hall Of Fame Band Honors; Riverside CC; Music.

SMITH, MARLIN B; Elsinore HS; Murrieta, CA; (4); 1/375; Service Clb; Church Choir; School Musical; Pres Sr Cls; L Bsktbl; Hon Roll; Lion Awd; NAACP Lcl Pres Awd; Black Stu Union; C A Teacher Yr Slctn Comm; Harvard U; Envrmntl Geoscience.

SMITH, MARLON L; Seaside HS; Ft Ord, CA; (4); Church Yth Grp; ROTC; Drill Tm; Var L Bsktbl; Var Crs Cntry; Var L Ftbl; Hon Roll; U Of W FL; Law.

SMITH, MARY A; Hueneme HS; Oxnard, CA; (4); Drama Clb; Library Aide; Thesps; Color Guard; School Musical; School Play; Stage Crew; Variety Show; JV Var Socr; Masonic Awd; Kndgtn Tchr.

SMITH, MARY A; Pittsburg HS; Pittsburg, CA; (2); Teachers Aide; Drill Tm; Stat Bsbl; Stat Vllybl; CA ST Hayward U; Med.

SMITH, MARY L; Warren HS; Downey, CA; (3); Debate Tm; German Clb; SADD; Chorus; JV Bsktbl; Var Swmmng; Hnrs Oooooon Golden St Exam Algebra; PTA Awd SADD; Phys Thrpy.

SMITH, MATT G; Mt Whitney HS; Visalia, CA; (3); Church Yth Grp; Cmnty Wkr; Pep Clb; Service Clb; Acpl Chr; Chorus; Church Choir; School Musical; Stage Crew; Stu Cncl; COS; Teacher.

SMITH, MATTHEW F; Sacred Heart Prep; Atherton, CA; (2); Church Yth Grp; Chorus; School Play; Sec Frsh Cls; VP Jr Cls; JV Socr; Var Tennis; Hon Roll; UC Berkeley; Pediatrics.

SMITH, MATTHEW T; La Habra HS; Whittier, CA; (3); 64/325; Pep Clb; Var JV Bsbl; JV Bsktbl; Var JV Ftbl; Hon Roll; Golden St Schlr For Alg; All League Offnsv Lineman; Sprts Med.

SMITH, MAXINE E; Tokay HS; Stockton, CA; (2); Church Yth Grp; Cmnty Wkr; Girl Scts; Model UN; Rptr Nwsp; Hon Roll; Prfct Atten Awd; Tchng.

SMITH, MELANIE; Pacifica HS; Garden Grove, CA; (1); 31/299; Chorus; Drill Tm; Hon Roll; CSF; CA ST; Law Enfrcmnt.

SMITH, MELANIE L; Canyon Springs HS; Moreno Valley, CA; (2); Church Yth Grp; Teachers Aide; High Hon Roll; Music Piano; Ice Skating; UC Santa Barbara; Dental Hygie.

SMITH, MELISSA C; Tulare Union HS; Tulare, CA; (1); Hon Roll; Cal Poly; Dietican.

SMITH, MELISSA MARIE; Silver Creek HS; San Jose, CA; (1); JV Cheerldng; Spnsh I, Engl I, Geom & Sci Achvt Certs; Stanford U; Child Psych.

SMITH, MEREDITH D; Cordova SR HS; Rancho Cordova, CA; (3); Cmnty Wkr; German Clb; Hosp Aide; Teachers Aide; Chorus; Sec Soph Cls; Rep Jr Cls; Var L Diving; High Hon Roll; Hon Roll; Friday Night Live; Phy.

SMITH, MICHAEL; San Luis Obispo SR HS; San Luis Obispo, CA; (2); 19/319; Stu Cncl; High Hon Roll; CSF; Med.

SMITH, MICHAEL C; La Serna HS; Whittier, CA; (1); 68/430; Bsbl; Capt Ftbl; Hon Roll; Exmplry Atten Awd; CSF; U Southern CA; Med.

SMITH, MICHELLE; Atwater HS; Winton, CA; (2); Drama Clb; FFA; Gym; Hon Roll; UC Davis; Bnkr.

SMITH, MICHELLE; Sweetwater Union HS; National City, CA; (2); Cit Awd; Hon Roll; Astronaut.

SMITH, MICHELLE L; Yucca Valley HS; Morongo Valley, CA; (4); 11/139; Dance Clb; High Hon Roll; Kiwanis Awd; Pres Schlr; Congressional Yth Ldrshp Cncl; Wilsonian Awd; Convocators Schlrshp; CA Lutheran U; Pre-Law.

SMITH, MIGUEL A; Downtown Business Magnet HS; Los Angeles, CA; (2); Cmnty Wkr; Computer Clb; Rptr Nwsp; JV Tennis; Hon Roll; Jr NHS; Dsrvng Stu Awd; Civil Air Patrol; CA Cadet Corps Offcr; Bus Admin.

SMITH, MIKE P; St Francis HS; Mountain View, CA; (2); JV Tennis; Hon Roll; Pilot.

SMITH, MILENA; Poway HS; San Diego, CA; (3); 64/276; Church Yth Grp; Cmnty Wkr; Letterman Clb; Varsity Clb; Var L Socr; High Hon Roll; Hon Roll; NHS; Cultrl Rep House Finland; UC; Psych.

SMITH, MOLLY; San Leandro HS; San Leandro, CA; (4); 29/351; Rptr DECA; Pep Clb; Ski Clb; Rep Soph Cls; Rep Jr Cls; Treas Stu Cncl; Var Pom Pon; High Hon Roll; Ballet; U Of CA Irvine; Bio.

SMITH, MONIKA K.; Atascadero HS; Atascadero, CA; (3); Drama Clb; SADD; Drill Tm; School Musical; Variety Show; Cheerldng; Hon Roll; Acad Kids; San Luis Jazz; Grphc Dsgn.

SMITH, NAMAY; Ramona HS; Ramona, CA; (1); Pep Clb; Off Frsh Cls; Cheerldng; Hon Roll; Pres Acad Fit Awd; Stu Of Mnth Englsh & Gymnstcs.

SMITH, NATALIE S; Alta Loma HS; Alta Loma, CA; (2); Church Yth Grp; Cmnty Wkr; Dance Clb; GAA; Girl Scts; Model UN; Office Aide; Pep Clb; Ski Clb; Teachers Aide; AZ ST; Psych.

SMITH, NEVADA S; Liberty Union HS; Oakley, CA; (2); JV Bsbl; JV Socr; Hon Roll; Acad Dcthln Cls & Team; Team USA Yth Soccer Trnmts; Bus Law.

SMITH, NIA; University HS; Newport Beach, CA; (3); Debate Tm; Drama Clb; Hosp Aide; Band; Jazz Band; Mrchg Band; Tennis; Trk; Vllybl; De Paul U; Music.

SMITH, NICHOLE L; Elk Grove HS; Elk Grove, CA; (3); 219/609; SADD; Powder Puff Ftbl; Var Socr; Mdlng Through Sears Dept Store; UC Santa Cruz; Attorney.

SMITH, NICHOLE S; Washington Prep; Los Angeles, CA; (4); 31/550; Church Yth Grp; Church Choir; Rep Sr Cls; Hon Roll; CSF; Empress Servce Clb, Assistnt Pres; San Diego ST U; Nrsng.

SMITH, NICKIE LYNN; Julian Union HS; Julian, CA; (4); 4/47; Am Leg Aux Girls St; Spanish Clb; Chorus; Variety Show; Phtg Yrbk; VP Frsh Cls; Pres Soph Cls; Pres Jr Cls; Pres Stu Cncl; Var Bsktbl; Wnnr Dist, Clb And Zone Lvl Lions Clb Spch Cntst; CA Schlrshp Fed; Dstngshd Ldrshp Awd; Laurls For Ldr; Long Beach ST U; Engl Teacher.

SMITH, NICOLE; Valley HS; Sacramento, CA; (4); 37/449; GAA; Spanish Clb; Teachers Aide; Varsity Clb; Stu Cncl; Cheerldng; Gym; Mgr(s); Powder Puff Ftbl; Tennis; Stu Reaching Out; UCLA; Med.

SMITH, NYSHA N; Western Christian HS; Phillips Ranch, CA; (4); Treas Jr Cls; Rep Stu Cncl; JV Var Cheerldng; Var Gym; Var Trk; High Hon Roll; Hon Roll; Winterball Prncss; Yng Blck Schlr; CSU Northridge; Cmmnctns.

SMITH, PATRICIA; Ernest Righetti HS; Santa Maria, CA; (3); French Clb; Quiz Bowl; Speech Tm; Sec Soph Cls; JV Bsktbl; Score Keeper; High Hon Roll; Hon Roll; ASB Dirctr Of Elections; ASB Sec; CA ST Fullerton; Pre-Med.

SMITH, PATRICK L; Fresno Christian HS; Fresno, CA; (2); Church Yth Grp; Drama Clb; Church Choir; School Play; Rptr Nwsp; Ed Yrbk; Rptr Lit Mag; JV Bsktbl; High Hon Roll; Hon Roll; CSF; Pilot.

SMITH, PATRICK R; Huntington Beach HS; Huntington Beach, CA; (2); Exchng Stu Newport Bch; Commrcl Artist.

SMITH, PAUL WILLIAM; Thomas Downey HS; Modesto, CA; (3); Rptr FFA; JV Bsbl; JV Var Bsktbl; Ftbl.

SMITH, PENELOPE J; Del Campo HS; Fair Oaks, CA; (3); 23/446; Church Yth Grp; Cmnty Wkr; Key Clb; Model UN; Chrmn Spanish Clb; Rptr Nwsp; Yrbk; Off Sr Cls; Intrml Socr; JV L Sftbl; Muscular Dystrphy Assn Vol; Yth Scer Coach, Referee; JR Prom Chrprsn; Bio Sci.

SMITH, PERI L; San Pasqual HS; Escondido, CA; (3); Ed Lit Mag; Amnsty Intl; Interact; Cnty Wide Outstndng Achvt Wrtng Awd; Engl Teacher.

SMITH, PHILLIP; Lassen HS; Susanville, CA; (2); 18/228; Boy Scts; Church Yth Grp; Ski Clb; Band; Mrchg Band; Pep Band; Rep Soph Cls; JV Bsbl; JV Bsktbl; Hon Roll; Bus Mgmt.

SMITH, PIA M; Arlington HS; Riverside, CA; (2); ROTC; Drill Tm; Hon Roll; Outstndng Cadet Awd; Cardiology.

SMITH, RACHELLE; Roseville HS; Rocklin, CA; (2); 26/445; Spanish Clb; Hon Roll; Rrtnl Sftbl; Rcrtnl Dance; Intr Dcrtng.

SMITH, RAMON H; Canyon Springs HS; Moreno Valley, CA; (3); ROTC; Band; Drill Tm; Mrchg Band; Pep Band; Hon Roll; Boy Scts; Chorus; Rep Frsh Cls; Rep Soph Cls; Mech Engr.

SMITH, REBBECCA L; El Dorado HS; Brea, CA; (3); 142/300; Church Yth Grp; Intnl Clb; Chorus; Church Choir; School Musical; School Play; Hon Roll; Pres Acad Fit Awd; Smmr Exchange Stu England 89; Bethel U; Elem Ed.

SMITH, REBECCA; San Marcos HS; San Marcos, CA; (2); Dance Clb; Pep Clb; JV Cheerldng; High Hon Roll; Hon Roll; Psych.

SMITH, REBECCA L; Clovis West HS; Clovis, CA; (2); Church Yth Grp; Drama Clb; FHA; Hosp Aide; Intnl Clb; SADD; Chorus; Church Choir; Swmmng; Hon Roll; CSF; GATE.

SMITH, REISTA; San Luis Obispo HS; San Luis Obispo, CA; (4); AFS; Am Leg Aux Girls St; Intnl Clb; JA; Office Aide; Ski Clb; Pres Jr Cls; Pres Sr Cls; Var JV Powder Puff Ftbl; Var JV Vllybl; Exchange Stu To Spain 90-91; Bus.

SMITH, ROBERT; Mountclair HS; Pomona, CA; (4); Church Yth Grp; Bsbl; Ftbl; Powder Puff Ftbl; Wt Lftg; Wrstlng; Mount Sal; Photo.

SMITH, ROBIN M; Edison HS; Huntington Beach, CA; (2); Model UN; JV Sftbl; JV Vllybl.

SMITH, RYAN; Clovis West HS; Fresno, CA; (3); Church Yth Grp; Debate Tm; VP French Clb; Intnl Clb; Cit Awd; Gov Hon Prg Awd; High Hon Roll; Hon Roll; UC-BERKLEY; Law.

SMITH, RYAN; Moreau HS; Fremont, CA; (4); 13/278; Am Leg Boys St; Boy Scts; Church Yth Grp; JA; Var Crs Cntry; Capt Golf; High Hon Roll; NHS; Pres Acad Fit Awd; US Naval Acad; Aviator.

SMITH, RYAN L; Don Antonio Lugo HS; Chino, CA; (2); 54/745; Boy Scts; Church Yth Grp; Letterman Clb; Band; Jazz Band; Mrchg Band; High Hon Roll; Hon Roll; Perfect Attendance Semnry Class; Comp.

SMITH, RYAN P; Helix HS; La Mesa, CA; (2); 96/780; Spanish Clb; Var JV Bsbl; JV Bsktbl; Var Wt Lftg; Accntng.

SMITH, SABRA D; Foothill HS; Citrus Heights, CA; (4); 2/250; Church Yth Grp; Drama Clb; Pres French Clb; Science Clb; Teachers Aide; Church Choir; School Play; Variety Show; Vllybl; Cit Awd; Chrch Bible Quiz Team Capt; CSF Stu; Chrch Drama Co Star; Point Loma Nazarene Coll Hnr Schlrshp; Point Loma Nazarene; Chld Psych.

SMITH, SAMANTHA A; Arlington HS; Riverside, CA; (3); Church Yth Grp; Chorus; Church Choir; School Musical; JV Vllybl; RCC; Accntng.

SMITH, SANDRA; Morro Bay HS; Los Osos, CA; (4); 18/208; Pep Clb; SADD; Stu Cncl; JV Var Cheerldng; Var Powder Puff Ftbl; Var Socr; Var Swmmng; Var Trk; High Hon Roll; Pres Acad Fit Awd; Presdntl Clssrm; CA St Chrldng Chmpns; UCLA; Law.

SMITH, SCOTT; Tustin HS; Tustin, CA; (2); JA; Science Clb; Rep Soph Cls; Intrml Crs Cntry; Intrml Trk; Hon Roll; Sports Clb; Biochem.

SMITH, SCOTT C; Rowland HS; Rowland Heights, CA; (2); Boy Scts; Rptr FFA; Band; Mrchg Band; Hon Roll; CAL Poly Pomona; Vet.

SMITH, SCOTT C; Woodland HS; Woodland, CA; (3); 45/500; Drama Clb; French Clb; Rep Thesps; School Musical; Variety Show; Sec Frsh Cls; L Var Crs Cntry; L Var Tennis; Jr NHS; NHS; Rotry Ldrshp Camp; Mst Imprvd Boys Tnns Tm 89; HEROES Awd; Film Stds.

SMITH, SCOTT D; Grace M Davis HS; Modesto, CA; (2); 84/575; SADD; Band; Jazz Band; Mrchg Band; Pep Band; Cit Awd; Hon Roll; Cnty Hnr Band; Cnty Band Stanislaus/Modesto; Rtd 92 Pct To 99 Pct Math Natl Schlstc Tests; AF Naval Acad; Math.

SMITH, SCOTT R; El Camino Real HS; Woodland Hills, CA; (3); Church Yth Grp; 4 Wheeling Off Roading; Desert Exploration; Camping; Backpacking; CO Schl Of Mines; Geology.

SMITH, SEAN; Bonita Vista HS; Chula Vista, CA; (4); 58/521; Art Clb; Cmnty Wkr; Intnl Clb; Key Clb; Pep Clb; Pres Service Clb; SADD; Ed Nwsp; Ed Yrbk; Var Capt Swmmng; Water Polo; Bio Awd 87-88; Vice Chrmn Cty Youth Cmmssn; CSF Life Mbr; San Luis Obispo; Enrmntl Bio.

SMITH, SEAN; Colton HS; Grand Terrace, CA; (1); Boy Scts; German Clb; Hon Roll; Skate Boarder 2 Yrs; Science/Astronomy Interest; MIT; Astronomer.

SMITH, SEAN J; Liberty Union HS; Brentwood, CA; (3); 80/350; Band; Jazz Band; Mrchg Band; Pep Band; Var Ftbl; Wrstlng; GSE Alg Knrs; Engrng.

SMITH, SEAN K; Clovis West HS; Fresno, CA; (3); 46/587; German Clb; Rep Stu Cncl; Var L Crs Cntry; JV Socr; Var L Trk; Cit Awd; High Hon Roll; Pres Acad Fit Awd; CSF 87-90; Hall Of Fame 90; Arch.

SMITH, SEAN M; St John Bosco HS; Bellflower, CA; (2); Drama Clb; Pres VP 4-H; Sec Treas French Clb; Var Key Clb; 4-H Awd; Hon Roll; NHS; Arch.

SMITH, SENNA; Valley HS; Sacramento, CA; (2); 11/434; Math Clb; Math Tm; Speech Tm; SADD; Orch; Cheerldng; Gym; High Hon Roll; Hon Roll; CSF; Sacrament Yth Symphony Violin; Pianist; Violinist; Stanford U; Obstetric.

SMITH, SHADRACH A; Bishop Montgomery HS; Lomita, CA; (3); Church Yth Grp; Varsity Clb; Var L Vllybl; Hon Roll; CSF; El Camino JC; Arch.

SMITH, SHANYN L; Barstow HS; Hinkley, CA; (4); Church Yth Grp; Office Aide; SADD; Drill Tm; Stu Cncl; Cheerldng; Pom Pon; Powder Puff Ftbl; Score Keeper; Hon Roll; CA ST San Bernardino; Pblc Ac.

SMITH, SHARLECIA; Crenshaw HS; Los Angeles, CA; (3); Teachers Aide; School Play; JV Sftbl; JV Vllybl; Schlrshp Smmr Pgm CA St L A; CA ST Long Beach; Elem Educ.

SMITH, SHELENA; John F Kennedy HS; Richmond, CA; (3); Co-Ed Nwsp; Rep Jr Cls; Var Sftbl; Var Trk; Bst Rookie Sports Edtr; Jnr Hmcmng Prncss; Prm Qn; Chabot; Jrnlsm.

SMITH, SHELLY R; Golden West HS; Visalia, CA; (1); Band; Hon Roll; Muisc; UCLA; Criminal Law.

SMITH, SHERI D; Mira Loma HS; Sacramento, CA; (3); Art Clb; Church Yth Grp; Cmnty Wkr; Girl Scts; Math Clb; SADD; Church Choir; Tennis; Trk; Hon Roll; Jobs Dghtr; U Of S CA; Mgmt.

SMITH, SHILO W; Casa Roble Fundamental HS; Orangevale, CA; (3); Teachers Aide; Var Capt Bsktbl; Var Capt Ftbl; Wt Lftg; Bsktbl Congrss Intl All Trny Tm; Nmrs All Leag, All Trnmt Tms; CA Bsktbl Preview 90.

SMITH, SIDONIE A; Enterprise HS; Palo Cedro, CA; (3); Am Leg Aux Girls St; 4-H; Rep Frsh Cls; VP Soph Cls; Pres Jr Cls; Stu Cncl; Capt L Bsktbl; Swmmng; 4-H Awd; High Hon Roll; Law.

SMITH, STACIA L; Poway HS; Poway, CA; (2); Church Yth Grp; Band; Jazz Band; Mrchg Band; Cit Awd; High Hon Roll; Hon Roll; Prfct Atten Awd; Pres Acad Fit Awd; Music Ed.

SMITH, STACIE M; Bishop Montgomery HS; Lomita, CA; (3); Church Yth Grp; GAA; VP JA; Key Clb; Sec Letterman Clb; SADD; Ed Yrbk; Rep Stu Cncl; Var Capt Bsktbl; Var Capt Sftbl; CSF; MVP Bsktbl, Sftbl; 1st Team All Angelus Leag Bsktbl, Sftbl; Springfield; Phys Thrpy.

SMITH, STACY J; Canyon HS; Canyon Country, CA; (2); Church Yth Grp; GAA; JV L Vllybl; BYU; Med.

SMITH, STEPHANIE S; Lemoore HS; Stratford, CA; (3); Church Yth Grp; Cmnty Wkr; Treas FHA; SADD; Church Choir; Hon Roll; Prfct Atten Awd; COS; Bus.

SMITH, STEPHEN P; El Dorado HS; Placentia, CA; (3); Cmnty Wkr; FCA; Letterman Clb; Red Cross Aide; Science Clb; SADD; Teachers Aide; Varsity Clb; Var L Bsbl; JV Bsktbl; DARE; BASICS; Hawk Cncl Ftbl Clb; AZ ST U; Phys Thrpy.

SMITH, STEVEN W; Casa Roble Fundamental HS; Orangevale, CA; (3); 49/370; Math Tm; Var Bsktbl; Cit Awd; Hon Roll; Schl Wnnr Amer HS Math Exam; Bst Jr Math Stu.

SMITH, SUNSHINE M; Coleville HS; Coleville, CA; (2); VP 4-H; Rep Soph Cls; JV Var Bsktbl; JV Var Cheerldng; Var Sftbl; JV Var Vllybl; 4-H Awd; Hon Roll; Prfct Atten Awd; Acad Olympc Team; Acad Exclince Hstry & Alg; UC Davis; Vet Med.

SMITH, TABITHA L; Bonita HS; La Verne, CA; (3); 30/426; Church Yth Grp; Drama Clb; GAA; Teachers Aide; JV Var Bsktbl; Cit Awd; High Hon Roll; Hon Roll; Musc Clb Tres; Hum On Campus Clb; Law.

SMITH, TAKEISHA L; King Drew Medical HS; Los Angeles, CA; (3); Church Yth Grp; Hosp Aide; Math Clb; Science Clb; Church Choir; Crs Cntry; Hon Roll; USC; Med.

SMITH, TAMARA L; Aptos HS; Watsonville, CA; (4); Church Yth Grp; SADD; Ed Nwsp; Powder Puff Ftbl; JV Sftbl; JV Vllybl; Pres Acad Fit Awd; Watsonville Brd Realtors Schlrshp; 1st Presbyterian Chrch SC Schlrshp; Jrnlsm Clb VP & Pres; Sonoma ST U; Liberal Arts.

SMITH, TAMIE L; Del Nolte HS; Crescent City, CA; (2); Drill Tm; Stat Sftbl; Hon Roll; Diablo Valley Coll; Police Acad.

SMITH, TANIA D; Cate Sch; Oakland, CA; (4); Church Yth Grp; Cmnty Wkr; GAA; Library Aide; Math Clb; Sec Science Clb; Teachers Aide; Stage Crew; Sec Frsh Cls; Rep Stu Cncl; Minority Stu Union Co-Fndr, Pres; Delta Sigma Theta Schlrshp; Chrch Usher Brd; A Better Chnc Pgm; Yale U; Bio.

SMITH, TANISIA; Barstow HS; Barstow, CA; (3); Church Yth Grp; Drama Clb; FBLA; Chorus; Rptr Yrbk; Rep Frsh Cls; Rep Stu Cncl; Var Cheerldng; Hon Roll; Opt Clb Awd; Best Vocal Methods Stu; Engl/Lit Awds.

SMITH, TARA M; Mission San Jose HS; Fremont, CA; (3); 105/400; Science Clb; Teachers Aide; Drill Tm; Bsktbl; JV Var Cheerldng; Prncpls Plcy Advsry Brd; Ldrshp Cncl; CA Schlrshp Fed.

SMITH, TAWNYA C; L A Lutheran HS; Granada Hills, CA; (4); 5/23; Jazz Band; Yrbk; VP Frsh Cls; VP Soph Cls; Treas Stu Cncl; Capt L Bsktbl; Capt L Vllybl; Dnfth Awd; NHS; Tch Music.

SMITH, TEMETRA J; James Logan HS; Union City, CA; (3); Girl Scts; Chorus; SMU; Accntng.

SMITH, TERA E; Oakland Technical HS; Oakland, CA; (3); ROTC; Band; Mrchg Band; Lit Mag; Hon Roll; Taekwondo; Sftbl Tm; OPC; Acctng.

SMITH, TIFFANY; Tehachapi HS; Tehachapi, CA; (3); 15/219; Am Leg Aux Girls St; Church Yth Grp; Girl Scts; SADD; Mrchg Band; Ed Yrbk; Sec Soph Cls; Stu Cncl; Cheerldng; JV Sftbl; CA Poly Sn Luis Obsp; Jrnlsm.

SMITH, TIFFANY A; Etiwanda HS; R Cucamonga, CA; (2); Computer Clb; Dance Clb; Drama Clb; Chorus; Drill Tm; School Musical; School Play; Pres Stu Cncl; High Hon Roll; Pres Schlr; Blck Stu Union; Acad Pentathln; Princpls Hnr Roll; Spellman; Arospc Engrng.

SMITH, TIMOTHY L; Yucaipa HS; Yucaipa, CA; (2); Church Yth Grp; Letterman Clb; JV Bsbl; Var L Ftbl; Wt Lftg; Schlr Athlt Ftbl, Bsbl; Acadc Ltr; Air Frc Acad.

SMITH, TOBY LEE; Escondido HS; Escondido, CA; (1); Church Yth Grp; JV Wrstlng; Hon Roll; Schlr Athlt Awd Wrstlng 89-90; Med.

SMITH, TRACIE; Palmdale HS; Palmdale, CA; (4); Teachers Aide; Pres Acad Fit Awd; Rotary Awd; Stu Of Mont 90; Antelope Valley Coll.

SMITH, TRACY; Fairfield HS; Fairfield, CA; (4); Dance Clb; Ed Nwsp; Sec Treas Soph Cls; Off Sr Cls; Stu Cncl; Var L Tennis; Trk; French Hon Soc; NHS; Ntl Merit SF; Jrnlsm.

SMITH, TRISHA L; Grossmont HS; El Cajon, CA; (1); Var Bsktbl; Var Sftbl; Spanish NHS; UCLA; Arch.

SMITH, TRISTA; Los Altos HS; Hacienda Hts, CA; (1); Church Yth Grp; Pep Clb; Nwsp; Off Soph Cls; Bsktbl; Cheerldng; Vllybl; Hon Roll; Smmr Cmp Prgm; Hd Chrldr; BUY; Law.

SMITH, TRUDY E; Wm S Hart HS; Valencia, CA; (1); Church Yth Grp; Crs Cntry; BYU; Teacher.

SMITH, TYLER J; Palo Verde HS; Blythe, CA; (2); 15/300; Drama Clb; Ed Nwsp; Var Golf; JV Wrstlng; 4-H Awd; Hon Roll; Pres Acad Fit Awd; U Of AZ; Bus Mgmt.

SMITH, VALERIE; Clovis HS; Clovis, CA; (2); Church Yth Grp; Dance Clb; Hosp Aide; Off Frsh Cls; Off Soph Cls; Bsbl; Vllybl; Hon Roll; Pres Acad Fit Awd; Private Dance Lessons; Fresno ST U; Ped Nrs.

SMITH, WILLIAM A; Irvington HS; Fremont, CA; (3); Rep Stu Cncl; Var Capt Ftbl; Var Capt Trk; JV Wrstlng; BSU; Chabot Clg; Bus Mgt.

SMITH, WILLIAM BOBBY; Lincoln HS; Stockton, CA; (4); 29/543; Am Leg Boys St; Var JV Bsbl; Var JV Ftbl; High Hon Roll; Hon Roll; Amer Legn Bsbl; Awd Exc Span, Alg, Geo, Trig; CA ST U; Engr.

SMITH, WYVON; Eisenhower HS; Rialto, CA; (2); Office Aide; Teachers Aide; VICA; Band; Chorus; School Musical; Variety Show; Intrml Bsktbl; Intrml Mgr(s); Intrml Score Keeper; Riverside Poly; Social Worker.

SMITH, YVONNE C; College Park HS; Pleasant Hill, CA; (3); French Clb; Office Aide; Teachers Aide; Smr Apprntcshp Invstgtn Prgm Univ Of PR; William Holt Schlrshp Lawrence Halls Of Sci; Schl Mrt Awds; Diablo Valley Coll; Sci.

SMITH, ZACHARY M; Bullard HS; Fresno, CA; (1); Boy Scts; Intnl Clb; Math Tm; Ski Clb; Band; Mrchg Band; Off Soph Cls; Sci Olympd Comptn; Odyssy Of Mind Comptn; Intl Comp Pblm Slvng Comptn; MIT; Engrng.

SMITH, ZACK J; Alhambra HS; Martinez, CA; (4); 8/190; Treas Math Clb; Treas Science Clb; Band; Jazz Band; Mrchg Band; Variety Show; Nwsp; Stu Cncl; Var Tennis; Pres Acad Fit Awd; CSF Sealbearer; Amer Lgn Awd; Semper Fidelis Awd For Musical Excllnc; UC Santa Barbara; Bus.

SMITH, ZEKE E; Point Arena HS; Annapolis, CA; (2); Treas Soph Cls; Treas Jr Cls; Var L Bsbl; High Hon Roll; Pres Acad Fit Awd.

SMITH JOHNSON, JOHN E; Skyline HS; Oakland, CA; (4); Church Yth Grp; Computer Clb; Drama Clb; Intnl Clb; SADD; Thesps; Med Explrs; Cal ST Schlr; Gldn ST Hnrs; CSU; Pre-Med Radiology.

SMITHEMAN, TARTA M; Summerville HS; Sonora, CA; (2); Acpl Chr; School Musical; School Play; Rotary Awd; Dance; CA Art Schlr; Columbia Actors Repretory.

SMITHLINE, DANIEL S; Magnolia HS; Anaheim, CA; (3); Varsity Clb; JV Bsktbl; JV Ftbl; Var Capt Tennis; Hon Roll; Engrng.

SMITHSON, KIMBERLY A; Shasta HS; Redding, CA; (4); GAA; Model UN; Science Clb; Ski Clb; Spanish Clb; Varsity Clb; VP Sr Cls; Capt Var Bsktbl; Capt Var Cheerldng; Var Swmmng; Powder Puff Ftbl; U FL; Accntng.

SMITHSON, WM SCOTT; Alma Heights Christian Acad; Pacifica, CA; (4); 2/6; Church Yth Grp; Acpl Chr; School Play; Rep Soph Cls; Rep Jr Cls; Off Sr Cls; Stu Cncl; High Hon Roll; Pres Acad Fit Awd; Sal; Advanced Math Awd; ACSI Distinguished Chrstn HS Stu Awd; Biola U; Bio.

SMITHTRO, ROBIN; Adolfo Camarillo HS; Camarillo, CA; (4); 29/367; Church Yth Grp; Cmnty Wkr; Treas Band; Jazz Band; Pep Band; High Hon Roll; Pres Acad Fit Awd; Willamette U; Ecnmcs.

SMOLENSKI II, RICHARD W; Norco HS; Norco, CA; (2); 13/281; Model UN; JV Tennis; High Hon Roll; Pres Acad Fit Awd.

SMYTH, LANETTA L; Los Banos HS; Los Banos, CA; (3); AFS; Sec Pres Drama Clb; Science Clb; VP Spanish Clb; School Play; Ed Yrbk; Treas Frsh Cls; Stu Cncl; NHS; CSF; UC Santa Barbara; Thtr.

SMYTH, MIRIAM; Marian Catholic HS; Chula Vista, CA; (4); 3/85; Cmnty Wkr; Drama Clb; French Clb; GAA; JA; Key Clb; Letterman Clb; Office Aide; Scholastic Bowl; SADD; Spirit Of Coca Cola Scholarship Award; Walt Disney Dreamers & Doers Award; SADD; Student Council; Coll Of The Holy Cross.

SNAPP, LAWRENCE A; Bellarmine Prep; San Jose, CA; (4); 40/312; Cmnty Wkr; Debate Tm; FBLA; Letterman Clb; NFL; SADD; Teachers Aide; Varsity Clb; Capt Var Swmmng; Cit Awd; Waterpolo Co-Capt; Swm Capt; U Southern CA; Bus.

SNARE, EDWARD A; Willow Glen HS; San Jose, CA; (2); Boy Scts; Cmnty Wkr; FCA; Capt Socr; Police Athltc Lg Scer Tm; Mssnry Wrk England; Athlts Intl; UCLA; Engnrng.

SNAVELY, CHRIS J; Tehachapi HS; Tehachapi, CA; (1); Band; Mrchg Band; School Musical; Hon Roll.

SNEDDEN, CASEY A; Bakersfield HS; Bakersfield, CA; (3); 1/650; Chess Clb; Debate Tm; Math Clb; NFL; Speech Tm; Orch; Var Swmmng; Hon Roll; Ntl Merit Ltr; Stu Of Wrld Cnsrvtn Co Pres; Clsscl Piano; 2nd Leag In Acad Dcthln; Music.

SNEDKER, KAREN A; Tracy HS; Tracy, CA; (2); 12/483; Dance Clb; Drama Clb; School Musical; School Play; Stage Crew; Capt Swmmng; High Hon Roll; Hon Roll; Ldrshp Awds; Hugh O'brian Rep & Asilomar Rep; Water Polo Tm Cap; CA Schlrshp Fed; U Of Santa Clara; Bus.

SNEED, DANIEL J; De La Salle HS; Concord, CA; (3); 30/240; French Clb; Band; Rep Frsh Cls; Rep Soph Cls; Rep Stu Cncl; Vllybl; Wrstlng; French Hon Soc; High Hon Roll; NHS; Wilderness Expdtn Soc; Campus Minstry; Yth Edctr; UC Davis; Engrng.

SNEED, SICELY N; Downtown Business Magnet HS; Los Angeles, CA; (3); Drama Clb; Spanish Clb; School Play; Hon Roll; Ntl Merit Schol; Pres Acad Fit Awd; Acad Of Finance; U San Francisco; Bus Mgmt.

SNELL, CASEY D; Rio Linda SR HS; Sacramento, CA; (2); Church Yth Grp; SADD; JV Ftbl; JV Swmmng; JV Trk; Hon Roll; Outstndng 1st Yr Draftng Stu; Acad Excllnce Awd, Gldn St Exm, 1st Yr Alg Hnrs; Aeronautical Engrng.

SNELL, DANNY G; Branham HS; San Jose, CA; (1); Boy Scts; Church Yth Grp; Library Aide; Var Tennis; Vet.

SNELL, DOUG E; Lemoore HS; Lemoore, CA; (2); 98/342; Treas Drama Clb; Var Speech Tm; L Var Golf; Hon Roll; CSF; His Ed.

SNELL, ROBIN R; Morro Bay HS; Morro Bay, CA; (1); Math Tm; Spanish Clb; SADD; Vllybl; High Hon Roll; USC; Medcl.

SNELLING, SARAH; Hillsdale HS; San Mateo, CA; (4); 40/289; Church Yth Grp; Acpl Chr; Chorus; Church Choir; School Musical; School Play; Hon Roll; Ntl Merit Ltr; Bio-Engrng.

SNIDER, CATTALIYA; San Gorgonio HS; Highland, CA; (4); 7/418; Cmnty Wkr; Capt Cheerldng; Elks Awd; High Hon Roll; NHS; Pres Acad Fit Awd; Spanish NHS; Interact Clb-Pres; CA Schlrshp Fed-Pres; U Southern CA; Brdcst Jrnlsm.

SNIEGOWSKI, MATTHEW G; Paso Robles HS; Paso Robles, CA; (3); Teachers Aide; Wt Lftg; Wrstlng; Hon Roll; Tnns; Golf; Cuesta Coll; Bus Mgmt.

SNIVELY, GILLIAN R; Live Oak HS; Morgan Hill, CA; (3); 6/516; French Clb; Hosp Aide; Math Tm; Jazz Band; Mrchg Band; Diving; Socr; Ntl Merit SF; Pres Acad Fit Awd; CA Schlrshp Fed Pres.

SNODGRASS, CHERIE F; Strathmore HS; Porterville, CA; (3); 17/77; Sec Church Yth Grp; FFA; Teachers Aide; High Hon Roll; Hon Roll; Horse Jdgng Tm; Christian Club Cncl; Chrch Puppet Tm; Wrtrs Club; Cal Poly; Ag.

SNODGRASS, GREGG L; Corcoran HS; Corcoran, CA; (3); 1/150; Am Leg Boys St; Rep FBLA; Science Clb; VP Varsity Clb; JV Var Bsktbl; Ftbl; Var Golf; High Hon Roll; USS Smmng; Pres CA Schlrshp Fdrtn; Cmptr Sci.

SNOW, ABRAHAM D; Beaumont HS; Cherry Valley, CA; (1); Church Yth Grp; Ftbl; Wt Lftg; High Hon Roll; Hon Roll; Boy Scts; Temple Yth Grp; Comm.

SNOW, CHELSEA; East Bakersfield HS; Bakersfield, CA; (1); Am Leg Aux Girls St; Chorus; Swmmng; Pres Acad Fit Awd; OR ST; Engl Educ.

SNOW, CRYSTAL E; Tulare Union HS; Tulare, CA; (1); 114/496; Church Yth Grp; Cmnty Wkr; Chorus; Church Choir; Hon Roll; Portuguese Clb; Tulare Yth Bowlng Assn; Amer Muscl Fndtn Band Hnrs Awd; Police Sci.

SNOW, DONNA J; Christian Brothers HS; Hood, CA; (3); 4-H; FBLA; FHA; Model UN; Spanish Clb; Rep Jr Cls; Trk; 4-H Awd; Hon Roll; NHS; Mock Trial-Outstndng Lawyer And Team Mate; U Of CA-DAVIS; Atty.

SNOW, HOLLIE; Miramonte HS; Orinda, CA; (3); Latin Clb; Spanish Clb; Nwsp; Cheerldng; Pom Pon; Orinda Teen Cncl VP; Amigos De Las Americas Vlntr 90.

SNOW, JAMES E; Mira Mesa HS; San Diego, CA; (3); 168/777; Boy Scts; Cmnty Wkr; Debate Tm; FBLA; NFL; Speech Tm; School Play; Rptr Nwsp; High Hon Roll; Church Yth Grp; Acad Leag; Econ.

SNOW, JUSTIN A; Temecula Valley HS; Temecula, CA; (2); 55/568; Debate Tm; Speech Tm; VICA; Bsktbl; Crs Cntry; GM Inst Of Engrng/Mgmt; Mfg Sy.

SNOW, LISA; Hemet HS; Hemet, CA; (4); Church Yth Grp; SADD; Band; Mrchg Band; Pep Band; Cheerldng; Swmmng; Hon Roll; Lion Awd; Svc Above Self-Coaches Awd-Vrsty Chrldng 89-90; Cerritos Coll; Dental Hygiene.

SNOWDEN, KIMBERLEE M; Morningside HS; Inglewood, CA; (1); Drill Tm; Var Cheerldng; Cit Awd; Hon Roll; Rotary Awd; Cvl Rghts Lwyr.

SNYDAL, JONATHAN S; Bellarmine College Prep; San Jose, CA; (3); 14/300; Band; Drm Mjr(t); Jazz Band; Mrchg Band; Orch; Pep Band; School Musical; Intrml Bsktbl; Intrml Sftbl; Williams Coll Bk Awd; Jane Patorio Meml Schlrshp; Exchng Stu In France; Intl Stds Assn Grant; Urban Dsgnr.

SNYDER, ANNA; Fall River Joint Schl; Fall River Mills, CA; (2); Church Yth Grp; FHA; Math Clb; SADD; Drill Tm; School Musical; School Play; Stat Bsktbl; Score Keeper; Stat Vllybl; Chico; Teacher.

SNYDER, COUPE C; Orestimba HS; Newman, CA; (2); FFA; Bsktbl; Wt Lftg; Hon Roll.

SNYDER, DAVID; Oceana HS; Pacifica, CA; (3); 10/176; Var L Bsktbl; Var L Ftbl; Var L Trk; Wt Lftg; High Hon Roll; Hon Roll; UCLA; Bus Mgmt.

SNYDER, ERIC W; Apple Valley HS; Apple Valley, CA; (3); Ski Clb; JV Tennis; High Hon Roll; Hon Roll; Ski Club Snowboarding; Mini-Truck Clb Cmptns & Events; RC Car Racing Cmptns & Events; UCSD; Mech Engr.

SNYDER, GLENN T; Novato HS; Novato, CA; (3); Boy Scts; Cmnty Wkr; Latin Clb; Spanish Clb; Teachers Aide; Bsbl; Vllybl; Hon Roll; Slvr Mdl Ntl Latin Exam; Schl Rcgntn Golden St Exam Geom & Alg; Advrtsng.

SNYDER, HEIDI; Hart HS; Valencia, CA; (3); 97/575; Church Yth Grp; Cmnty Wkr; Hosp Aide; SADD; Rep Soph Cls; VP Jr Cls; Stu Cncl; L Capt Cheerldng; Gym; Powder Puff Ftbl; 1 Of 5 Fnlst Grls St; Most Outstndng Chrldr HS 90; Chsn By Prs As Jr Bsktbl Hmcmng Prncss; Loyola Marymount; Drams.

SNYDER, JAMES; Tulare Union HS; Tulare, CA; (3); 14/400; Art Clb; FFA; High Hon Roll; Hgh Hnrs 1st Yr Geom Golden St Exam; Futr Farmers Am Nursery Opertns Profcncy Awd; Sec CA Schlstc Fed; Bio.

SNYDER, JANET M; Highlands HS; North Highlands, CA; (3); 1/231; Chorus; Powder Puff Ftbl; Swmmng; Cosmetology.

SNYDER, MARIE O; Bishop O Dowd HS; Oakland, CA; (4); Art Clb; Church Yth Grp; Ski Clb; Hon Roll; Peace Group; Grapic Art.

SNYDER, MEGAN; Twentynine Palms HS; 29 Palms, CA; (2); 2/200; AFS; Church Yth Grp; Quiz Bowl; Science Clb; Treas Spanish Clb; SADD; Rep Stu Cncl; Prfct Atten Awd; Schls Writing Celebration 1st & 2nd Pl Ribbons; Acad Lttr; Teaching.

SNYDER, MEGAN A; Whitney HS; Lakewood, CA; (1); Dance Clb; Model UN; YMCA Indoor Sccr; Dance; Bus.

SNYDER, NICOLE A; John F Kennedy HS; Sacramento, CA; (3); AFS; Pres Church Yth Grp; Dance Clb; French Clb; Teachers Aide; Chorus; Hon Roll; Jobs Daughters Recorder, Musician & Chaplain; Camp Fire Inc Mem 10 Yrs; Golden St Exm Geom Hnrs 89; Teacher For Deaf.

SNYDER, PHIL; Mother Lode Christian HS; Sonora, CA; (2); Boy Scts; Church Yth Grp; School Musical; Bsbl; Bsktbl; Socr; Cnsrvtn Awd; AWANA; Engr.

SNYDER, REBECCA; Moorpark HS; Moorpark, CA; (2); JV Stat Sftbl; High Hon Roll; Hon Roll; Cal Tech; Astronaut.

SNYDER, SHANNON L; North Salinas HS; Aromas, CA; (3); Church Yth Grp; Science Clb; Spanish Clb; SADD; Var Trk; High Hon Roll; Hon Roll; Psych.

SNYDER, SHERI A; Turlock HS; Turlock, CA; (3); 142/600; Church Yth Grp; FFA; Church Choir; Yrbk; Sftbl; Potsdam U; Elem Tchr.

SNYDER, SUSAN M; Winters HS; Winters, CA; (2); FFA; Ski Clb; SADD; Ed Yrbk; Treas Frsh Cls; Bsktbl; Stat Ftbl; Score Keeper; Swmmng; Capt Vllybl; CSF; UCLA; Poltcl Sci.

SNYDER, TRACY; Miramonte HS; Moraga, CA; (3); Church Yth Grp; Cmnty Wkr; Dance Clb; Letterman Clb; NFL; Pep Clb; Speech Tm; Church Choir; Stu Cncl; Var Cheerldng; Pres Of Natl Charity Leag; Dance; U Of AZ; Child Psych.

SO, BONNY; Sanger HS; Sanger, CA; (2); Latin Clb; Science Clb; Chorus; Nwsp; Yrbk; CA Schlrshp Fed; Asian Club.

SO, KIM G; Lowell HS; San Francisco, CA; (3); Cmnty Wkr; Hon Roll; Vlybl Clb Pres & Sctry; Med Explrs; SF ST; Med.

SO, NAEMI I; Lowell HS; San Francisco, CA; (2); Aud/Vis; Teachers Aide; Band; Mrchg Band; Pep Band; High Hon Roll; Hon Roll; VP Jr NHS; Agape Flshp-Flshps Of Chrstn Stu.

SO, WELLINGTON K; West Covina HS; West Covina, CA; (1); 23/350; Computer Clb; French Clb; Science Clb; SADD; JV Tennis; Stat Vllybl; High Hon Roll; Hon Roll; Prfct Atten Awd; UCLA; Pdtrcn.

SO, WENDY S; Fremont Union HS; Sunnyvale, CA; (2); 74/421; Church Yth Grp; Debate Tm; Drama Clb; Speech Tm; Church Choir; Stage Crew; Score Keeper; Var Swmmng; Hon Roll; Pres Acad Fit Awd; Ken Wright Memorial Schlrshp Awd; Octagon Clb; CSF; Pharm.

SO, WINNIE; Abraham Lincoln HS; San Francisco, CA; (1); Hon Roll; UC Berkeley; Bus.

SO AN, ELIZABETH J; James Logan HS; Union City, CA; (2); 148/904; Church Yth Grp; Cheerldng; Pom Pon; DAR Awd; Hon Roll; Gollden State Honors Algebra Awd; Golden State Recognition In Geometry; Leo Club; Education.

SOANE, PULE P; Mission Bay HS; San Diego, CA; (1); Cmnty Wkr; Girl Scts; Pep Clb; Yrbk; Off Frsh Cls; Stanford U; Marine Bio.

SOARES, SANDRA R; American HS; Fremont, CA; (2); 16/385; French Clb; Science Clb; Spanish Clb; SADD; Swmmng; Hon Roll; Stu Recgntn-Gldn St Exam; Chrldr-Fremont Ftbl Leag; :Spirit Week.

SOARES, TERESA L; Tulare Western HS; Tulare, CA; (3); Church Yth Grp; Drama Clb; Chorus; Church Choir; Yrbk; Hon Roll; Sequoias Coll; Jrnlst.

SOBALVARRO, CESAR A; Oak Grove HS; San Jose, CA; (2); St Schlr; UCLA; Phy.

SOBALVARRO, MARTHA A; Abraham Lincoln HS; San Francisco, CA; (3); Yrbk; Bsktbl; Nurse.

SOBAYO, SURULERE M; Cupertino HS; Cupertino, CA; (2); Hon Roll.

SOBRINO, RUBY; Bell-Jeff HS; Sun Valley, CA; (4); French Clb; Math Clb; Pep Clb; Spanish Clb; Rep Jr Cls; High Hon Roll; Sec NHS; Pres Acad Fit Awd; CSF; Thomas More Awd; Sci Club; Cal ST U Northrdg; Bus Adm.

SOCHULAK, LISA; St Joseph HS; Santa Maria, CA; (4); 16/116; JA; Key Clb; Science Clb; Service Clb; SADD; Teachers Aide; Hon Roll; Vclst Of Schl Rock Band Knight Flight; Christian Svc Clb Offcr Of Pblcty; Frgn Lang Clb; Biolgcl Sci.

SODERSTROM, KATARINA A; Gahr HS; Lakewood, CA; (4); 15/440; Drama Clb; Socr; Hon Roll; Blud, Gold Awd Acadmc Excllnc Hlth And St; RN.

SODHA, SAMIR V; Arcadia HS; Arcadia, CA; (2); NHS; Pres Acad Fit Awd; Future Phy Clb Treas; Card Collctrs Clb Histrn; Med.

SOEDA, JARVIS N; Edison HS; Huntington Beach, CA; (2); Model UN; Band; Mrchg Band; Orch; Pep Band; GSE Golden St Exam; Acad Excllnc Awd; Acad Booster Club; Achvt Awd HS; Mdl United Ntns; Cmmndtn Awds; U Of CA.

SOEHENDRA, EMILY; Calvary Baptist HS; Azusa, CA; (4); 1/10; Church Yth Grp; School Musical; Hon Roll; Prfct Atten Awd; Blue Ribbon ACSI Piano Fstvl; Rbbns Frm ACSI Amt Fstvl; LA Cnty Fair Art Fstvl; UCLA; Bus.

SOELLNER, HOLLY C; Modesto Christian HS; Modesto, CA; (3); Church Yth Grp; Pep Clb; Sftbl; Tennis; Vllybl; Hon Roll; CA Schlrshp Fed Mem; Gould Med Fndtn Med Explorer Post 600 Mem; Hi-Debs, Retail Chain Store Modeling; Med.

SOFFEL, NICHOLE; Heritage HS; Buena Park, CA; (2); Pep Clb; Ski Clb; Sftbl; Vllybl; Hon Roll; Law.

SOGAMOSO, DANIEL; Sunny Hills HS; Fullerton, CA; (1); Intrml Ftbl; Intrml Socr; Intrml Trk; Intrml Wt Lftg; DAR Awd; Stu Of Mnth Social Sci 90; USC; Sprts Med.

SOHAEI, ATI; Trabuco Hills HS; Mission Viejo, CA; (4); 23/350; Cmnty Wkr; SADD; JV Crs Cntry; Hon Roll; NHS; Orange Cnty Natl Acad Decthln; CSF Cmmtte; NHS Sealbr; CA U Irvine; Bio Sci.

SOHAL, INDERJIT K; Gridley Union HS; Gridley, CA; (3); 19/100; Drama Clb; FHA; Hosp Aide; Library Aide; Spanish Clb; Teachers Aide; School Play; Rep Frsh Cls; Stu Cncl; Trk; Rtry Spch Cntst; Lions Spch Cntst 1st Pl; Social Studies Club Secy; Spnch Club; CA Schlrshp Fed; CA ST U; Med.

SOHN, BRENT A; Monte Vista HS; Spring Valley, CA; (3); 64/373; Boy Scts; Church Yth Grp; Var Ftbl; Var Wt Lftg; Hon Roll; Machine Tool Operator Rgnl Occupational Pgm; Eagle Sct; Bus Admin.

SOHN, LOUIS K; Whitney HS; Cerritos, CA; (1); Church Yth Grp; Computer Clb; Drama Clb; FBLA; Latin Clb; Model UN; Ed Nwsp; Var Bsbl; Var Score Keeper; High Hon Roll; Bsbl Card Collctr; Stanford; Bus.

SOHNREY, CAROLYN K; Durham HS; Durham, CA; (3); 4-H; FFA; FHA; GAA; SADD; Var JV Sftbl; Var JV Vllybl; 4-H Awd; Butte CC; Phys Thrpst.

SOHOLT, RENNIK P; Arlington HS; Riverside, CA; (3); Church Yth Grp; Var L Socr; Hon Roll; CSF; GATE; Psych.

SOHR, SHAWNA M; Valhalla HS; La Mesa, CA; (2); Church Yth Grp; Dance Clb; Hosp Aide; Key Clb; JV Socr; Var Trk; JSA.

SOJKA, JEFF D; Livermore HS; Livermore, CA; (4); 11/356; Pres Art Clb; Church Yth Grp; Debate Tm; NFL; Jazz Band; Var Capt Swmmng; Rotary Awd; Cngrs-Bundestage Awd Schlrshp; Yth Ctznshp Awd; Harrie M Merrill Schlrshp; UC Santa Barbara; Cmnctns.

SOJOURNER, JENNIFER L; Ramona HS; Ramona, CA; (2); Church Yth Grp; Cmnty Wkr; German Clb; GAA; Pep Clb; SADD; Band; Church Choir; Flag Corp; U San Diego; Law.

SOK, DAVID S; Phillip & Sala Burton Academic HS; San Francisco, CA; (3); Chess Clb; Office Aide; Teachers Aide; Chorus; High Hon Roll; Hon Roll; Comp Club; Golden St Exam Received Honors; San Francisco ST U; Accntng.

SOK, GNEB; San Gabriel HS; Rosemead, CA; (2); Spanish Clb; SADD; JV Tennis; High Hon Roll; Hon Roll; Geolgy Clb; CA Schlrshp Fndtn; UCLA; Pdtrcn.

SOK, SOPHORN; Edison HS; Stockton, CA; (3); Church Yth Grp; Hon Roll; Pres Cambodian Club; Cmptr Prog.

SOK, TOUCH L; Fremont HS; Oakland, CA; (2); Hon Roll; Media Acad; Upwrd Bnd Pgm; Cambodia Clb VP; Secrtrl.

SOKKUN, VANNAK; Crawford HS; San Diego, CA; (4).

SOKOL, DAVID W; Bakersfield HS; Bakersfield, CA; (2); JA; Teachers Aide; Temple Yth Grp; JV Ftbl; Wt Lftg; Marines.

SOKOLOW, DEBORAH A; Davis SR HS; Davis, CA; (2); 127/377; French Clb; Key Clb; Temple Yth Grp; Chorus; Church Choir; Pres Acad Fit Awd; CSF; U Of IL; Arch Dsgn.

SOKOLOWSKI, RYAN; Serrano HS; Wrightwood, CA; (1); Dance Clb; Ski Clb; Stu Cncl; Bsktbl; Crs Cntry; Golf; Socr; Tennis; Cit Awd; High Hon Roll; USD; Sci.

SOLANKI, DEVEN; Gahr HS; Cerritos, CA; (2); JV Bsbl; JV Bsktbl; JV Ftbl; UCLA; Elec.

SOLANKI, JYOTI U; Ramona Convent Secondary Schl; Monterey Park, CA; (3); Dance Clb; Model UN; Chorus; Phtg Yrbk; Off Soph Cls; Rep Jr Cls; Rep Sr Cls; Var Sftbl; JV Tennis; Dance Cmptn Awds; UC Irvine; Bio.

SOLANKI, PRATIMA; Ramona Convent HS; Monterey Park, CA; (3); Model UN; Ed Yrbk; Off Soph Cls; Off Jr Cls; Off Sr Cls; JV Var Tennis; Los Ageles Pediatric Soc Summer Medical Career Pgm, Miss CA Empire Schlrshp Pageant Teen Div 90; UC Irvine; Bio.

SOLANO, CLAUDIA P; Sacred Heart Of Jesus HS; Los Angeles, CA; (3); GAA; Chorus; Lit Mag; Prom Cmmtte Chrprsn; Loyola Marymount; Film.

SOLANO, JASON; Damien HS; Alta Loma, CA; (3); 13/231; Spanish Clb; JV Crs Cntry; Hon Roll; Pres Acad Fit Awd; Outstndng Soph Stdt Wrld Hstry; Mst Vlbl JV Crss Cntry.

SOLANO, KAREN G; International Studies Acad; San Francisco, CA; (4); Drama Clb; VP Science Clb; Service Clb; Spanish Clb; Teachers Aide; School Play; Stage Crew; Hon Roll; San Fran Shakespeare Fstvl 90; Peer Cnslng; Bus Admin.

SOLAREWICZ, KONRAD S; Del Campo HS; Fair Oaks, CA; (4); 30/446; Chess Clb; Math Tm; SADD; Intrml JV Crs Cntry; Sci Olympd.

SOLAREWICZ, KRZYSIA SYLVIA; Del Campo HS; Fair Oaks, CA; (2); Church Yth Grp; Cmnty Wkr; Dance Clb; VP FBLA; Red Cross Aide; School Musical; Hon Roll; CA Multi-Cultrl Park Fndtn Vlntr; Bus.

SOLDATI, ADAM; Sonoma Valley HS; Sonoma, CA; (2); Ski Clb; Var JV Bsbl; Var JV Bsktbl; Var JV Ftbl; Swmmng; High Hon Roll.

SOLDMANN, CHRISTINE; John W North HS; Riverside, CA; (2); 14/520; Drill Tm; Mrchg Band; School Musical; High Hon Roll; Novelty Tm 88-89; Dance Tm 89-90; Intl Bcclrt Pgm 88-90; GATE Pgm 88-90; Math.

SOLEYMANI, NAVID; University HS; Los Angeles, CA; (2); Debate Tm; VP Temple Yth Grp; Rep Jr Cls; High Hon Roll; Hon Roll; CSF; Jr Statesmn Amer; Human Relatns Pres; Attrny.

SOLEYMANI, SHIRLEY; Hamilton Music Acad; Los Angeles, CA; (1); Art Clb; Dance Clb; Drama Clb; Drill Tm; School Musical; School Play; Swing Chorus; Variety Show; High Hon Roll; UCLA.

SOLHEIM, JEFFREY; Apple Valley HS; Apple Valley, CA; (4); Church Yth Grp; Debate Tm; Spanish Clb; Teachers Aide; School Play; Cit Awd; Hon Roll; NHS; Pres Acad Fit Awd; Concordia Clg; Minister.

SOLIDUM, MELISSA A; Sacred Heart Cathedral Prep; San Bruno, CA; (1).

SOLIMAN, MADETTE A; Louisville HS; West Hills, CA; (1); Church Yth Grp; JV Bsktbl; Var Sftbl; Vllybl; High Hon Roll.

SOLIMAN, TAMMER M; Clovis West HS; Fresno, CA; (2); High Hon Roll; Hon Roll; Asstnt Dist Mgr Mens Clthng Stores; Fresno ST; Bus Adm.

SOLIS, ADAM M; Don Bosco Technical Inst; Temple City, CA; (3); 64/164; Church Yth Grp; Computer Clb; Letterman Clb; Bsbl; Bsktbl; Var L Trk.

SOLIS, ADRIAN H; Lindsay HS; Lindsay, CA; (1); JV Bsktbl; JV Ftbl; JV Trk; Hon Roll; Fishing Club; U Notre Dame; Acctng.

SOLIS, ALEXIA; La Serna HS; Whittier, CA; (1); SADD; Rptr Nwsp; Jessamy West Young Wrtrs Conf 1st Pl Short Fctn; Whittier Union HS Dist Jrnlsm Cont 5th Pl Nws Wrtng; U C Berkley; Pol Sci.

SOLIS, ALMA; Live Oak HS; Morgan Hill, CA; (4); Church Yth Grp; Spanish Clb; SADD; Teachers Aide; Mgr Mc Donalds In Morgan Hill 88; Tutroing Smll Chldrn; San Jose ST U; Chld Spychlgst.

SOLIS, ANDREA; Ramona HS; Ramona, CA; (3); Church Yth Grp; Cmnty Wkr; Office Aide; Pep Clb; Teachers Aide; Rep Frsh Cls; JV Var Cheerldng; Cit Awd; Opt Clb Awd; UCSD; Bilingual Tchr.

SOLIS, ANGELICA; St Anthony HS; Wilmington, CA; (2); NHS; CSF; Arch.

SOLIS, CLAUDIA; Lynwood HS; Lynwood, CA; (1); Math Clb; ROTC; Color Guard; Hon Roll; NHS; MESA Clb; MECHA Clb; IOF; CSULB; Engrng.

SOLIS, DAPHNE; Clayton Valley HS; Concord, CA; (2); JA; Office Aide; Red Cross Aide; Ski Clb; Cit Awd; High Hon Roll; Hon Roll; CSF; Friday Night Live; UC Davis; Med.

SOLIS, GRETHEL; Birmingham HS; Los Angeles, CA; (4); Latin Clb; Drill Tm; Var Jr Cls; Var Sr Cls; Stu Mnth Art & Spnsh 89 & 90; Lw Enfrcmnt.

SOLIS, JIMMY S; Arroyo Grande HS; Grover City, CA; (2); 227/580; JV Bsbl; JV Ftbl; JV Var Socr; Notre Dame; Tchr.

SOLIS, LAURIE; Canyon HS; Canyon Country, CA; (3); Church Yth Grp; FBLA; Intnl Clb; Flag Corp; Hon Roll; Stu Of Sem Phys Sci; GPA Acad Lttr; William S Hart Schlrshp Awd; UCLA Drtmouth; Archlgy.

SOLIS, MARIA DE JESUS; Burbank HS; Burbank, CA; (2); Teachers Aide; Chorus; Bsktbl; Hon Roll; Prfct Atten Awd; Med.

SOLIS, MAXIMILIANO; Johm Glenn HS; Norwalk, CA; (2); Band; Mrchg Band; Pep Band; Socr; Hon Roll; Arch.

SOLIS, MICHAEL A; Arroyo Grande HS; Grover City, CA; (1); Church Yth Grp; Hon Roll; U MI Ann Arbor; Elect Engrg.

SOLIS, MIRELLA A; Pittsburg HS; Pittsburg, CA; (1); La Rassa Clb; Comp Sci.

SOLIS, OSCAR M; Fillmore HS; Mexico; (4); Spanish Clb; ITESM; Engrng.

SOLIS, ROBERTO; Don Bosco Technical Inst; Los Angeles, CA; (3); Church Yth Grp; Letterman Clb; L Var Crs Cntry; Fld Hcky; L Var Trk; High Hon Roll; NHS; Campus Ministry; Newmen Club; Bib Bro Program; U Of Southern CA; Biomed Engr.

SOLIS, THERESA T; Louisville HS; Winnetka, CA; (3); Art Clb; Church Yth Grp; Cmnty Wkr; Drama Clb; FHA; GAA; Service Clb; Thesps; Chorus; School Musical; Hunger Proj; Greenpeace; Anti-Apartheid Mvmt; Prfssnl Theatr.

SOLIZ, ANNA MARIE; Gladstone HS; Azusa, CA; (3); 51/267; Boy Scts; Pres Sec Church Yth Grp; Sec Drama Clb; Hosp Aide; SADD; Chorus; Church Choir; Drill Tm; School Musical; School Play; U Of S CA; RN.

SOLIZ, DENISE R; Eisenhower HS; Rialto, CA; (3); Church Yth Grp; Band; Mrchg Band; Hon Roll; Spcl Educ Tchr.

SOLIZ, MICHELLE Y; Western Christian HS; Azusa, CA; (4); Church Yth Grp; Teachers Aide; Chorus; JV Trk; Wt Lftg; High Hon Roll; Hon Roll; CSF 3 Yrs; Westmont; Acctng.

SOLIZA, JOAQUIN REYES; Channel Islands HS; Oxnard, CA; (2).

SOLL, JASON; Santa Monica HS; Santa Monica, CA; (4); 1/800; Pres Dance Clb; Band; Mrchg Band; Orch; Rep Jr Cls; Intrml Socr; JV Swmmng; Kiwanis Awd; Ntl Merit SF; UCLA Schlr.

SOLL, LIANA V; Santa Monica HS; Santa Monica, CA; (3); French Clb; Acpl Chr; Church Choir; High Hon Roll; Pres Frnch Clb; Malcolm Kerr HS Schlr To Tunisia.

SOLOKI, LESLIE P; Bellarmine-Jefferson HS; Burbank, CA; (2); 18/158; Math Clb; Science Clb; Spanish Clb; JV Capt Bsktbl; Var Score Keeper; JV Sftbl; High Hon Roll; NHS; CA Schlrshp Fed; Guard Pride Rcgntn Awd; UCLA; Phys Thrpy.

SOLOMON, BRIAN C; Bishop Montgomery HS; Gardena, CA; (3); Aud/Vis; Church Yth Grp; Speech Tm; Ftbl; Trk; Hon Roll; Young Tlntd Achvrs Acad Schlrshp Pgnt-King 88-89; People To People Intl Caravan-USSR Ambssdr; Blk Clb; Stanford; Comp Info Sci.

SOLOMON, JACOB W; Berkeley HS; Richmond, CA; (4); High Hon Roll; Hon Roll; Eastern Stu Union Pres; Elctd Vtng Postn BSEP; Flying; Brandeis U.

SOLOMON, KRISTIE L; Victor Valley HS; Victorville, CA; (3); 13/424; Cmnty Wkr; Computer Clb; Sec Key Clb; Church Choir; High Hon Roll; Hon Roll; Prfct Atten Awd; Blck Stu Union Sctry; CA Schlstc Fdr; Dprtmntl Cmmndtn Spnsh; GA Inst Of Tech; Elec Engnr.

SOLOMON, MICHAEL A; Bishop Amat Memorial HS; Walnut, CA; (3); Wrstlng; Hon Roll; Prfct Atten Awd; Barkada Clb; Sci.

SOLOMON, SHOSHANNA; Brea-Olinda HS; Brea, CA; (2); 55/344; Dance Clb; French Clb; Variety Show; Hon Roll; Hi Hnrs Golden St Exam Alg & Geom; Bus Acctg.

SOLORIO, BERTA M; Lemoore HS; Lemoore, CA; (3); 25/323; FHA; Spanish Clb; Teachers Aide; Hon Roll; CSF; Fresno ST U; Psych.

SOLORIO, JOSE; Gonzales HS; Gonzales, CA; (2); FBLA; JV Bsktbl; Hon Roll; ORALE; CSF; Interact Clb; Whole Erth Soc; FBLA Treas; Prncpls Hnr Roll; Cal Poly; Cnstrctrl Engr.

SOLORIO, JUANA M; Los Banos HS; Los Banos, CA; (3); Latin Clb; Office Aide; Science Clb; Spanish Clb; Teachers Aide; Acpl Chr; Color Guard; Stat Bsbl; Stat Sftbl; Stat Vllybl; Interact Clb; Educ.

SOLORIO, MARTHA E; San Dieguito HS; Encinitas, CA; (3); Church Yth Grp; Intnl Clb; Teachers Aide; Hon Roll; Azteca Clb; U CA-IRVINE; Cnslng.

SOLORIO, RAQUEL Y; Montebello HS; Los Angeles, CA; (1); 1/40; Debate Tm; Teachers Aide; Chorus; Mgr Drill Tm; JV Tennis; Cit Awd; Hon Roll; Solost; UCLA; Law.

SOLORIO JR, RICHARD J; Orestinba HS; Newman, CA; (2); JV Bsbl; JV Ftbl; U AZ; Engr.

SOLORZANO JR, CARLOS M; Sweetwater HS; National City, CA; (2); Boy Scts; Church Yth Grp; Latin Clb; JV Ftbl; JV Capt Socr; Cit Awd; Hon Roll; Prfct Atten Awd; Pres Acad Fit Awd; Ftr Ldrs Amer; UCSD; Mdcn.

SOLTERO, ROSIE; Bassett HS; La Puente, CA; (2); NHS; CA ST Polytech U Step-To-Coll Pgm; Stanford U; Psych.

SOLTESZ, WENDY K; San Juan HS; Citrus Heights, CA; (4); Cmnty Wkr; Key Clb; Capt Math Tm; Science Clb; Service Clb; Spanish Clb; High Hon Roll; NHS; Pres Acad Fit Awd; CSF; U Of CA Davis; Med.

SOLTYSIK, NATASHA; Dos Pueblos HS; Goleta, CA; (4); 3/364; Debate Tm; Varsity Clb; Bsktbl; Sftbl; Vllybl; NHS; Ntl Merit Ltr; 1st Tm All Amercn Vlybl; Vlybl Schlrshp; Mck Trl Tm 3rd St Cmptn 90; U Of The Pacific; Comp Engrng.

SOM, SITHA; Santa Rosa HS; Fulton, CA; (4); Teachers Aide; Acpl Chr; Cit Awd; High Hon Roll; Masonic Awd; Prfct Atten Awd; Hon Roll; Pres Acad Fit Awd; CSF; Sonoma ST; Bio.

SOMBOUN, SOMBAT; Edison HS; Stockton, CA; (3); Sec Boy Scts; French Clb; Socr; High Hon Roll; Hon Roll; NHS; Electrncs.

SOMERHALDER, JENNI L; Liberty Union HS; Knightsen, CA; (1); Band; Mrchg Band; Fri Night Live.

SOMERS, AURORA L; Rim Of The World HS; Crestline, CA; (2); 19/352; Church Yth Grp; Intrml Sftbl; Intrml Vllybl; High Hon Roll; Lion Awd.

SOMKAMSAENG, TONY; John Muir HS; Pasadena, CA; (2); Prfct Atten Awd; Electrnc Engrng.

SOMMER, JODI L; Ramona HS; Ramona, CA; (2); Church Yth Grp; Temple Yth Grp; Ricks Coll; Tchr.

SOMMER, KARIN V; Willow Glen Ed Park HS; San Jose, CA; (1); JV Var Cheerldng; Hon Roll; Prncpls Stu Advsry Cncl; U CA Berkeley; Law.

SOMMERLAD, DEIRDRE M; Del Mar HS; San Jose, CA; (3); Key Clb; ROTC; Teachers Aide; Chorus; Color Guard; Drill Tm; School Musical; Numerous Schl Awds; Mock Trial; San Jose ST; Law.

SOMMERS, BENJAMIN; Paraclete HS; Lancaster, CA; (4); 13/129; Debate Tm; Letterman Clb; Var Ftbl; Var Golf; Mgr(s); High Hon Roll; CSF; Sci Apprntcshp Edwards AFB; Law.

SOMMERS, KAREN D; Atascadero HS; Atascadero, CA; (1); Church Yth Grp; Chorus; Church Choir; Stage Crew; Variety Show; Gymnstcs Comptn Team; San Luis Opispo Cnty Shrt Stry Cntst 1st Pl; Show Choir; Elem Schl Tchr.

SOMOGYI, MICHELLE A; San Dieguito HS; Encinitas, CA; (2); Key Clb; School Play; Stage Crew; Coast Kids Mscl Theatre; Tech Theatre.

SOMOGYI, ZOLTAN; Santa Monica HS; Santa Monica, CA; (2); Chess Clb; Math Tm; Teachers Aide; Hon Roll; Amer HS Math Exam 90 Hnr Roll; UCLA; Sci.

SOMRETH, SOPHAL; Buena HS; Ventura, CA; (2); JV Crs Cntry; JV Trk; Golden St Exam Geom Hnrs; Elec Engrng.

SOMSAK, CHRIS J; Westminster HS; Westminster, CA; (2); Band; Mrchg Band; Orch; Pep Band; Hon Roll; Acad Booster Clb Ltr; Comp Pgmr.

SON, ANITA K; Warren HS; Downey, CA; (3); Sec Art Clb; Hosp Aide; Treas Letterman Clb; Spanish Clb; SADD; Teachers Aide; Rep Frsh Cls; Intrml Cheerldng; Var Crs Cntry; Intrml Gym; Dntstry.

SON, PETER C; Pinole Valley HS; Pinole, CA; (3); Church Yth Grp; FCA; Math Clb; Math Tm; Church Choir; Ftbl; Socr; Vllybl; High Hon Roll; UCB; Engrng.

SON, SUSAN; Westlake Schl; Los Angeles, CA; (4); Art Clb; Math Tm; Capt L Swmmng; Capt L Vllybl; High Hon Roll; Piano.

SONG, AMY; South San Francisco HS; South San Francis, CA; (3); 2/300; Cmnty Wkr; Computer Clb; Library Aide; Math Clb; Science Clb; Speech Tm; High Hon Roll; Opt Clb Awd; Sal; Soc Women Engrs Hghst Hnrs; Principals Awd; CSF; Aerosp Engr.

SONG, ANNA; Bishop Amat HS; Walnut, CA; (4); 13/400; Church Yth Grp; Cmnty Wkr; Chorus; Rep Stu Cncl; High Hon Roll; NHS; Silver Screen Clb; CSF Sec; Amnesty Intl; Pomona Coll; Pltcl Sci.

SONG, ANNA; Garces Memorial HS; Bakersfield, CA; (4); 5/121; Sec Church Yth Grp; VP French Clb; Pres Math Clb; Scholastic Bowl; Science Clb; Chorus; School Musical; Sec Treas Frsh Cls; Sec Jr Cls; Sec Sr Cls; 1st Pl Sci Fair 89; Bank Of Amer Plaque Wnnr; UCLA.

SONG, BONNIE; San Gabriel Acad; San Gabriel, CA; (2); Teachers Aide; Band; Chorus; Church Choir; Orch; School Play; Ftbl; Tennis; Vllybl; Fld Hcky; Med.

SONG, CLARA; North Hollywood HS; Studio City, CA; (4); Debate Tm; Hosp Aide; JA; Chorus; Var Capt Cheerldng; Cit Awd; High Hon Roll; Prfct Atten Awd; CSF Seal Bearer; Ephebians; Acad Decathlon Tm; UC San Diego; Bio-Med.

SONG, CLARA; Santa Margarita HS; Irvine, CA; (3); 1/250; Dance Clb; Drama Clb; Pep Clb; Chorus; Church Choir; School Musical; School Play; Variety Show; Stu Cncl; Cheerldng; Sunday Schl Tchr; Smmr Camp Cnslr; Scl Activites & Dir Chrch Yth Grp.

SONG, DAVID; John F Kennedy HS; Buena Park, CA; (1); JV Ftbl; JV Wt Lftg; UCLA; Med.

SONG, ELLEN Y; Warren SR HS; Downey, CA; (2); VP Church Yth Grp; Debate Tm; Teachers Aide; Band; Mrchg Band; Sec Frsh Cls; JV Vllybl; High Hon Roll; Prfct Atten Awd; Pres Acad Fit Awd; VP Chrch Yth Grp 89-90; All Cnty Band 88-89; Hghst Hnrs In NY St Music Assn Lvl 6; Harvard; Poltcl Sci.

SONG, ERWIN; San Gabriel Acad; Fullerton, CA; (3); Church Yth Grp; Teachers Aide; JV Ftbl; Capt Socr; JV Vllybl; UC San Francisco; Pharmcy.

SONG, GRACE; San Gabriel Acad; San Gabriel, CA; (4); 1/37; Office Aide; Chorus; Sec Jr Cls; Sec Sr Cls; Rep Stu Cncl; Intrml Ftbl; Intrml Vllybl; NHS; Bk Of Amer Achvmnt Awd In Lab Sci; Hon Mntn LA Cnty Sci & Engr Fair; Marie Curie Chem Awd; Microbiology.

SONG, JAMES Y; Sunny Hills HS; Fullerton, CA; (2); 75/463; Chess Clb; Church Yth Grp; Chorus; School Play; JV Vllybl; High Hon Roll; Hon Roll; Jr NHS; Prfct Atten Awd; Drama Awd; Med.

SONG, JUDY; Los Altos HS; Hacienda Heights, CA; (3); Church Yth Grp; 4-H; Teachers Aide; Varsity Clb; Tennis; Trk; Hon Roll; Acad Bstr Clb; Bell Choir; Mt Sac U; Nrsg.

SONG, MISTI; Monterey Bay Acad; Glendora, CA; (4); Church Yth Grp; Red Cross Aide; Acpl Chr; Ed Yrbk; VP Stu Cncl; Vllybl; Cit Awd; High Hon Roll; Prfct Atten Awd; Val; Ply Piano; Rdng; Exrcsng; Stanford U; Med.

SONG, NATASHA; El Camino Real HS; Woodland Hills, CA; (4); 19/575; Am Leg Aux Girls St; Church Yth Grp; Teachers Aide; Drill Tm; Rptr Yrbk; Off Frsh Cls; Sec Soph Cls; Off Jr Cls; High Hon Roll; NHS; Acad Dcthln Tm-Cty Chmps; CA Yth Ctznshp Smnr; Grls Leag Pblcty Dir, Elctd Pres; Columbia U; Pre-Law.

SONG, PHOENG; Hoover HS; Fresno, CA; (2); High Hon Roll; Fresno ST; Ed.

SONG, SALLY H; Warren HS; Downey, CA; (3); Treas Art Clb; Treas Church Yth Grp; French Clb; FBLA; Intnl Clb; Key Clb; Mu Alpha Theta; Science Clb; Service Clb; Spanish Clb; CSF Clb.

SONG, SARAH; Palisades HS; Los Angeles, CA; (3); Am Leg Aux Girls St; Cmnty Wkr; Library Aide; Math Clb; Service Clb; Teachers Aide; Varsity Clb; Pres Frsh Cls; Pres Stu Cncl; Var JV Bsktbl; Fashn Dsgn.

SONG, SUSAN; William S Hart HS; Newhall, CA; (4); 3/480; Church Yth Grp; Hosp Aide; Mu Alpha Theta; Church Choir; Sec Soph Cls; Stu Cncl; JV Trk; High Hon Roll; NHS; Opt Clb Awd; Chamber Of Commerce Schlrshp; Stanford U.

SONG, SUSANNA; Glen A Wilson HS; Hacienda Hgts, CA; (4); Dance Clb; Pres German Clb; Key Clb; Red Cross Aide; Ski Clb; Band; Flag Corp; Ed Nwsp; JV Vllybl; High Hon Roll; Jr Statesman Of Amer Secy; School Schlr; Boston U; Med.

SONG, TAC S; Oakland HS; Oakland, CA; (2); Computer Clb; Cit Awd; Hon Roll; Med.

SONGCO, LOUISE S; Immaculate Heart HS; Los Angeles, CA; (3); 17/112; Cmnty Wkr; GAA; Hosp Aide; Sec Math Clb; Spanish Clb; Yrbk; Sec Of Asian Clb; CSF VP; Med.

SONGCO, MELVIN J; Saint Francis HS; San Carlos, CA; (3); 43/289; Church Yth Grp; Cmnty Wkr; Math Clb; Science Clb; Mgr(s); High Hon Roll; Hon Roll; Radio Clb; Art Awd; Tnns; Stanford; Engrng.

SONGER, TODD E; Grossmont HS; El Cajon, CA; (3); 10/400; Cmnty Wkr; Key Clb; Teachers Aide; Lit Mag; Var L Trk; Ntl Merit SF; CSF.

SONI, RUPAM; Hawthorne HS; Hawthorne, CA; (4); 4/500; Cmnty Wkr; Hosp Aide; Math Tm; Temple Yth Grp; Ed Yrbk; VP Jr Cls; Stu Cncl; Pres Acad Fit Awd; CSF; Amer Lgn Sch Awd; R C Byrd Hnrs Schlrshp; UCLA; Elec Engr.

SONICO, JOHN; Independence HS; San Jose, CA; (2); UCO Hnr Rl; Electrnc Engr.

SONICO, PEARLA S; Saint Francis HS; Mountain View, CA; (3); 52/289; Service Clb; Ed Nwsp; Ed Yrbk; High Hon Roll; NHS; CA Schlrshp Fed; Hstry.

SONKE, DANIEL J; Ripon Christian HS; Manteca, CA; (4); 3/48; Treas Church Yth Grp; Acpl Chr; Band; Pep Band; School Play; Treas Jr Cls; Hon Roll; Ntl Merit Ltr; Pres Acad Fit Awd; Sal; Dordt Coll; Comm.

SONNENBERG, KEVIN M; Modesto HS; Modesto, CA; (3); Aud/Vis; Spanish Clb; Teachers Aide; JV Bsbl; Intrml Bsktbl; Var Tennis; Cit Awd; Hon Roll; Prfct Atten Awd; Aeronaut Engrng.

SONNENBURG, APRIL S; Gridley HS; Gridley, CA; (4); French Clb; FFA; FHA; SADD; Teachers Aide; Chorus; Variety Show; Ed Nwsp; Var Cheerldng; Stat Socr; Site Cncl; Schl Pride Awd; Woodleaf Cnslr; Peer Cnslng; Chico ST U; Jrnlsm.

SONNIKSEN, MELISSA; King City Joint Union HS; King City, CA; (4); Cmnty Wkr; Pep Clb; Service Clb; SADD; Sec Frsh Cls; Stu Cncl; VP Capt Cheerldng; Pom Pon; JV Sftbl; Hon Roll; CSU, Fresno; Lib Studies.

SONODA, IRENE; Fallbrook Union HS; Fallbrook, CA; (4); 80/370; AFS; Church Yth Grp; French Clb; FHA; Teachers Aide; Rptr Yrbk; Stat Bsktbl; Hon Roll; Golden St Exmntn Hnrs Alg; Warrior Heads Top 10% Snr Cls Ldrshp; U Of NV Las Vegas; Accntng.

SONTRA, SUSAN RENE; Elk Grove HS; Elk Grove, CA; (2); Church Yth Grp; Debate Tm; Drama Clb; Model UN; JV Gym; Semi-Fnlst Congrss-Buntestag Exchnge Stu Schlrshp; Stu Reachng Out; UC Los Angeles; Theatr Arts.

SOO HOO, LORI NICOLE; Bell HS; Cudahy, CA; (3); Debate Tm; French Clb; Math Clb; Pep Clb; School Play; Variety Show; Off Jr Cls; Stu Cncl; Pom Pon; Cit Awd; Bell At Harbor Pgm 87-88; Math Clb-MESA; Jr Statesmn Of Amer/Attnded Close-Up; UCLA; Arch.

SOOHOO, DAVID; Lincoln HS; San Francisco, CA; (1); JV Bsktbl; Hon Roll.

SOON, ANNE; Williams HS; Williams, CA; (2); Yng Life.

SOON, WENDY V; Washington HS; San Francisco, CA; (3); Pres Key Clb; Service Clb; High Hon Roll; Hon Roll; Hnrs Golden St Examd Algebra, Geom; Mem CA Schlrshp Fed; Mem Chinese-Amer Club; Engrng.

SOONG, STEVEN M; Bellarmine College Prep; San Jose, CA; (3); 2/300; Hosp Aide; Letterman Clb; Service Clb; Intrml Ftbl; Var Mgr(s); JV Trk; Tutorial Society; Church Vlntr; Med.

SOONTHORNSAWAD, AMORNTAT JOE; Chaminade Coll Prep; Simi Valley, CA; (3); Boy Scts; Intnl Clb; Service Clb; JV Swmmng; JV Tennis; San Diego ST U.

SOPER, SARA N; Grace M Davis HS; Modesto, CA; (1); French Clb; CSF; Vet.

SORA, MICHELLE; Sunny Hills HS; Fullerton, CA; (2); Church Yth Grp; Sec Debate Tm; Sec FFA; Cit Awd; Hon Roll; Parli Pro Outstanding Sec At Section & Region; Dairy Production Award; Cal Poly; Veterinarian.

SORACCO, JERALD A; Mira Loma HS; Carmichael, CA; (3); 20/300; Boy Scts; Church Yth Grp; Math Clb; Band; Jazz Band; Pep Band; Stu Cncl; Socr; Wt Lftg; Hon Roll; UCD; Econ.

SORAVILLA, ANDREW; California HS; San Ramon, CA; (4); Church Yth Grp; Teachers Aide; Church Choir; Ed Yrbk; Work 20 Hrs Wk; USC; Bus.

SORBEL, SHAYNA R; Troy HS; Yorba Linda, CA; (1); Church Yth Grp; Cmnty Wkr; Key Clb; Socr; Tennis; Wt Lftg; Cit Awd; Gov Hon Prg Awd; High Hon Roll; Outstndng Stu Awd; Soccer Schltc Achvt Awd; UCLA; Bus.

SORBER, JULIE M; Lincoln HS; Lincoln, CA; (4); 52/139; Debate Tm; Drama Clb; JA; Office Aide; Scholastic Bowl; Varsity Clb; Chorus; School Play; Hon Roll; Lion Awd; Bofa Awrd; Joe Vargas Schlrshp; Brdcstr.

SORENSEN, ALAN T; Acalanes HS; Lafayette, CA; (4); 8/290; Boy Scts; Drama Clb; SADD; Ed Yrbk; Var Capt Bsbl; Var Bsktbl; Ftbl; Ntl Merit SF; 1st Team All Leg Bsbl; Church; BYU; Strctrl Engrng.

SORENSEN, AUSTIN; Palo Verde Valley HS; Blythe, CA; (2); 1/185; Boy Scts; Church Yth Grp; Sec Letterman Clb; SADD; Band; JV Bsktbl; Var Crs Cntry; Var Trk; High Hon Roll; NHS; Eagle Scout Awd; CSF.

SORENSEN, CHRISTIAN C; Santa Ynez Valley Union HS; Buellton, CA; (3); 11/162; Am Leg Boys St; Boy Scts; Church Yth Grp; Drama Clb; Rptr FBLA; Math Tm; School Musical; School Play; Stage Crew; Elks Awd; Order Arrow.

SORENSEN, DAWN CHARMANE; Glendora HS; Glendora, CA; (3); Church Yth Grp; Drama Clb; Service Clb; Thesps; Pep Clb; Mgr Stage Crew; JV Var Fld Hcky; Hon Roll; Tchng.

SORENSEN, KIRSTIN; Hanford Joint Union HS; Hanford, CA; (1); Church Yth Grp; Band; Jazz Band; Mrchg Band; Pep Band; School Musical; Tennis; High Hon Roll; Jr NHS; NHS; Interact Clb; Frgn Exchnge Clb; Brigham Yng U; Accntnt.

SORENSEN, MELISSA; Coalinga HS; Coalinga, CA; (3); 3/105; Pres Church Yth Grp; Pres SADD; Band; Mrchg Band; Var L Bsktbl; Intrml Diving; Art Assn Schlrshp; Assoc Frgn Stus Co Chairperson; 2nd Girl Schlr; Edinburg U; Arch.

SORENSEN, MICHELLE; Bolsa Grande HS; Garden Grove, CA; (1); Church Yth Grp; German Clb; Var Cheerldng.

SORENSON, ANNE B; La Canada HS; La Canada, CA; (4); 6/260; Spanish Clb; Nwsp; Sec Jr Cls; Stu Cncl; Var Tennis; Hon Roll; Ntl Merit SF; Principal Policy Advisory Brd Sec; UCLA; Commnctns.

SORENSON, MAT; Los Alamitos HS; Los Alamitos, CA; (2); Var Cit Awd; Bus Mgmt.

SORENSON, MELISSA; Dos Palos HS; Dos Palos, CA; (2); AFS; Band; Drm Mjr(t); Mrchg Band; Stat Bsbl; Var Tennis; Hon Roll; Intr Dsgn.

SORENSSON, BOEL; Viewpoint HS; Calabassas, CA; (2); Art Clb; Girl Scts; Library Aide; Chorus; Rep Frsh Cls; Sec Soph Cls; JV Vllybl; Wt Lftg; High Hon Roll; Hon Roll; Art Center; Art.

SORG, WINDY L; Vacaville HS; Vacaville, CA; (3); Girl Scts; Teachers Aide; Hon Roll; Jr NHS; NHS; Girl Scouts Cmnty Svc.

SORGATZ, BRIAN; Buena HS; Ventura, CA; (4); Chorus; Ntl Merit SF; Interact Clb; Dir Intl Undstndg; Ventura CC.

SORHEIM, CAREY L; Ernest Righetti HS; Santa Maria, CA; (4); 34/347; Pres Church Yth Grp; Office Aide; Teachers Aide; Church Choir; Stu Cncl; High Hon Roll; Hon Roll; Golden Warrior Awd; Hancock ASB Schlrshp; Prom Cmmttee-Chairperson; Hancock Coll; Elem Ed.

SORIA, LETICIA T; Holy Family HS; Los Angeles, CA; (2); Art Clb; Church Yth Grp; Church Choir; Vllybl; Hon Roll; Prfct Atten Awd; Hnr Stu; Engr.

SORIA, MARIA E; Fontana HS; Fontana, CA; (2); High Hon Roll; Prfct Atten Awd; UCLA; Accountant.

SORIA, MICHAEL; Robertson HS; Fremont, CA; (3); 75/138.

SORIANO, DONATO H; Azusa HS; Azusa, CA; (3); 17/275; Boy Scts; Band; Mrchg Band; Pep Band; Var Tennis; High Hon Roll; NHS; CSF; Band Pres; UCLA; Pre-Med.

SORIANO, GIRLIE SAMEDRA; William C Overfelt HS; San Jose, CA; (3); 2/365; Art Clb; Cmnty Wkr; Math Clb; Math Tm; Science Clb; Ed Yrbk; Lit Mag; High Hon Roll; Pres NHS; Sal; Filipino Amer Mvmnt Educ Schlrshp Awd; Hmntrn Yr Awd; Tandry Tech Schlr Top 2% Awd; U Of CA Davis; Envrnmntl Engr.

SORIANO, JANNIS G; Mt Eden HS; Hayward, CA; (3); Church Yth Grp; Dance Clb; Office Aide; SADD; Wt Lftg; Fullerton Coll; Bus Mgmt.

SORIANO, JIM C; San Gorgonio HS; San Bernardino, CA; (3); Computer Clb; French Clb; Vllybl; CSF; CA ST Polytech Pomona; Engrng.

SORIANO, JONARD D; St Anthony HS; Lakewood, CA; (3); Art Clb; JV Bsktbl; Hon Roll; Art.

SORIANO, JUAN G; Chula Vista HS; San Diego, CA; (2); 199/558; Var Swmmng; JV Vllybl; Var Water Polo; UCSD; Med.

SORIANO, KAREN E; Fremont Christian HS; Fremont, CA; (1); Hon Roll; CA Schlrshp Fed; Outstndng Achvt Engl.

SORIANO, LAURA A; Chaffey HS; Ontario, CA; (3); Church Yth Grp; French Clb; Spanish Clb; Band; Mrchg Band; Pep Band; Variety Show; Cit Awd; French Hon Soc; High Hon Roll; Golden St Exam Awd Algebra; Schl Ivy Chain; Frnch Merit Awd; Azuza Pacific U; Accntnt.

SORIANO, LISA M; Baldwin Park HS; Baldwin Park, CA; (3); Church Yth Grp; Teachers Aide; Var Swmmng; Hon Roll; VMP JV Girls Swim Team; CA ST; Midwife.

SORIANO, RAQUEL S; W C Overfelt HS; San Jose, CA; (1); Science Clb; Hon Roll; CSF Secy.

SORIANO, ROCEL; Whitney HS; Cypress, CA; (3); Cmnty Wkr; Dance Clb; VP Key Clb; Variety Show; Rptr Nwsp; Clb Kaibigan Pilipino Dance Troup; CA Schlrshp Fed.

SORIANO, VILMA A; Washington Prep; Van Nuys, CA; (2); JV Cheerldng; Hon Roll; Peer Cnslr; Fulfillment Fund; UCLA Prtnrshp Pgm; UCLA Law Schl; Crmnl Law.

SORIBEN, BERNADETTE F; Mercy San Francisco HS; San Francisco, CA; (2); Pres Church Yth Grp; GAA; Pres Frsh Cls; Off Soph Cls; Stu Cncl; JV Bsktbl; Asian Clb; Dance; Singing & Acting; U Of CA Santa Cruz; Bio.

SORICH, JASON; Cardinal Newman HS; Rohnert Park, CA; (3); 8/85; Church Yth Grp; Cmnty Wkr; Spanish Clb; Bsktbl; High Hon Roll; Hon Roll; Altr Boy 8 Yrs; CSF; Cmnctns.

SORICH, MARISA A; Mountain View HS; Los Altos, CA; (4); Pres Dance Clb; Drama Clb; Teachers Aide; School Musical; School Play; Var L Cheerldng; Var L Pom Pon; Hon Roll; Comm Theatre; Dance, Tap, Jazz, Ballet.

SORIENTE, ENGELBERT F; Turlock HS; Turlock, CA; (3); Boy Scouts Of Philippines 86-88; Aviation.

SORISHO, CARMEN; Turlock HS; Turlock, CA; (2); AFS; Science Clb; Orch; High Hon Roll; Prfct Atten Awd; Law.

SORKIN, ELY J; Einstein Acad; Los Angeles, CA; (1); 1/15; Chess Clb; Math Clb; Science Clb; Yrbk; Stephen S Wise; Med Sci.

SORRELL, GEORGIA; Huntington Park HS; Huntington Park, CA; (3); Cmnty Wkr; Sec Dance Clb; Key Clb; Teachers Aide; Hon Roll; CSF; Amnsty Intl; Yth Cmnty Service; Psych.

SORRELL, JOSEPH A; Crawford HS; San Diego, CA; (3); 60/332; Dance Clb; Pres French Clb; Letterman Clb; Church Choir; School Musical; School Play; Stage Crew; Variety Show; Var Bsbl; Var Ftbl; San Diego Tribune All Acadmc Team Bsbl; AZ ST U; Bus Admin.

SORRENSEN, NADINE C; Poway HS; New Zealand; (4); AFS; Hon Roll; New Zealand Exchng Stu.

SORRENTINO, FELIX; San Lorenzo Valley HS; Ben Lomond, CA; (4); 17/200; Science Clb; Ski Clb; Spanish Clb; JV Socr; Hon Roll; Art Awd Achvt In Ceramics; 3rd Pl Sci Fair; 2nd Sci Club Ecological Action For Prsrvtn Of Envrnmnt; U Of CA Santa Cruz.

SOSA, CHRISTOPHER M; Chino HS; Chino, CA; (2); Letterman Clb; SADD; Teachers Aide; Varsity Clb; Rptr Lit Mag; Var Trk; Cit Awd; High Hon Roll; Hon Roll; Prfct Atten Awd; Natl Cont For Plywrt; USC; Law Enfrcr.

SOSA, JUAN J; Ontario HS; Ontario, CA; (2); Pep Clb; JV Tennis; Cit Awd; Prfct Atten Awd; Ftnss Test Most Situps Trphy.

SOSA, KAIN; Calexico HS; Calexico, CA; (2); Church Yth Grp; Upward Bound Club; Gldn St Exam Hgh Hnrs; UC Berkeley; Elec Engr.

SOSA, MARIVEL; Abraham Lincoln HS; San Jose, CA; (3); 1/250; Church Yth Grp; Treas Latin Clb; Bausch & Lomb Sci Awd; Hon Roll; Prfct Atten Awd; MESA VP; MAYO Sectry; CSF; Accntng.

SOSA, MELANIE S; Bonita Vista HS; Chula Vista, CA; (3); Chorus; Sec Jr Cls; Var Fld Hcky; High Hon Roll; Amnesty Intl; John Hopkins U; Envrnmntl Engrn.

SOSA, RAY A; Cantwell HS; Los Angeles, CA; (3); 5/50; Letterman Clb; Spanish Clb; Varsity Clb; Sec Stu Cncl; Capt Bsktbl; Capt Ftbl; Intrml Mgr Vllybl; Intrml Mgr Wt Lftg; High Hon Roll; Hon Roll; Schltc Achvt Awd; Engrng.

SOSA, ROBERTO M; Upper Lake HS; Lucerne, CA; (3); CSUS; Engrng.

SOSMENA, HANNAH KRISHNA; Mater Dei HS; Tustin, CA; (3); Art Clb; Cmnty Wkr; Computer Clb; Hosp Aide; Intnl Clb; JA; Spanish Clb; JV Sftbl; Hon Roll; Cal ST Long Bch; Nrsng.

SOTA, ANDREA; Bishop Amat HS; Ontario, CA; (4); 48/425; Hon Roll; Cal Poly Pomona; Lbrl Stds.

SOTELLO, TAMI L; La Sierra HS; Riverside, CA; (3); SADD; JV Swmmng; Hon Roll; CA Schrlshp Fed; La Verne U; Accntnt.

SOTELO, ANGELA M; Covina HS; West Covina, CA; (3); Drama Clb; Hon Roll; Vol Amer Cancer Soc; Poltcl Sci.

SOTELO, JUSTIN; Williams HS; Williams, CA; (4); 3/30; Am Leg Boys St; Treas FFA; SADD; Treas Sr Cls; Pres Stu Cncl; JV Var Bsktbl; JV Var Ftbl; JV Var Trk; High Hon Roll; Hon Roll; Bio Sci.

SOTELO, RAFAEL A; Mark Keppel HS; Monterey Park, CA; (3); Varsity Clb; Wrstlng.

SOTELO, RENEE; Williams HS; Williams, CA; (1); 4/50; FFA; Band; Rep Frsh Cls; JV Bsktbl; JV Vllybl; Hon Roll.

SOTELO, ROSARIO A; Calipatria HS; Calipatria, CA; (3); FBLA; Library Aide; Pep Clb; Yrbk; Stu Cncl; Cit Awd; Hon Roll; Lion Awd; Hnrb Mntn Assay On Fut Of Amer; Co-Host Spring Talent Show 90; Camp Cnslr.

SOTHISOM, BOPHA P; Los Alamitos HS; Long Beach, CA; (3); Art Clb; Church Yth Grp; Teachers Aide; JV Crs Cntry; JV Trk; Cit Awd; OCHSA; Most Imprvd Artist Awd; Best Artist Of Yr; Med.

SOTO, AUDRA M; Ernest Righetti HS; Santa Maria, CA; (1); Church Yth Grp; JV Sftbl; Hon Roll; Got Most Improved For JV Softball; Goint To Australia Jan 91 Through AISE Student Exchange; Physical Therapy.

SOTO, CRISTINA; Irvine HS; Irvine, CA; (4); AFS; VP JA; Key Clb; Spanish Clb; Teachers Aide; Band; Vllybl; Latin Amer Leag Secy; Bus.

SOTO, DAVID D; Sanger HS; Sanger, CA; (3); FCA; Band; Jazz Band; Mrchg Band; Pep Band; Var Ftbl; Var Trk; Var Wrstlng; Fresno ST; Medcl Doctor.

SOTO, ERMELINDA; William Workman HS; La Puente, CA; (2); Cmnty Wkr; Tennis; Cit Awd; Hon Roll; USC; Psych.

SOTO, GABRIELLA; Bonita Vista HS; Bonita, CA; (3); Art Clb; Cmnty Wkr; Hosp Aide; Latin Clb; Office Aide; Pep Clb; SADD; Teachers Aide; JV Co-Capt Vllybl; Hon Roll; Merit Rec Optmstc Intnl; Muscular Dstry Vol; U CA Los Angeles; Med.

SOTO, JOSE DE JESUS; San Clemente HS; Capistrano Beach, CA; (2); Boy Scts; Church Yth Grp; Bsbl; Socr; Cit Awd; Prfct Atten Awd; San Diego ST; Carpentry.

SOTO, JOSEPH L; Ramona HS; Riverside, CA; (3); 27/408; Church Yth Grp; Teachers Aide; Stu Cncl; Var Bsktbl; Var Cheerldng; Var Capt Ftbl; Var Trk; Var Wt Lftg; Hon Roll; Jr NHS; Med.

SOTO, JUAN DONALD O; Brawley Union HS; Brawley, CA; (1); Church Yth Grp; Pep Clb; High Hon Roll; CSF; SDSU; Doc.

SOTO, MAGDA A; Saddleback HS; Santa Ana, CA; (1); French Clb; Color Guard; Prfct Atten Awd; UCI Prtnrs-Outrch Prmg; STEP Clb; MESA.

SOTO, MARIO A; Garfield HS; S Gate, CA; (3); Computer Clb; Scholastic Bowl; SADD; High Hon Roll; Ntl Merit Ltr; Gettysburgh; Med.

SOTO, MARK A; Barstow HS; Barstow, CA; (1); JV L Bsbl; JV L Socr; Hon Roll; Bus.

SOTO, RAQUEL L; St Anthony HS; Carson, CA; (4); 8/184; Pres French Clb; SADD; Stu Cncl; DAR Awd; High Hon Roll; Kiwanis Awd; Opt Clb Awd; Xerox Awd; Soc Women Engrs; Biomedcl Engrng.

SOTO, ROBERT A; Monache HS; Porterville, CA; (3); Church Yth Grp; Bsktbl; Ftbl; Wt Lftg; USC; Engrng.

SOTO, ROBERTO; Sierra Vista HS; Baldwin Park, CA; (1); Church Yth Grp; Math Clb; Church Choir; Rep Frsh Cls; Rep Stu Cncl; Intrml Bsbl; Intrml Ftbl; Hon Roll; Pres Acad Fit Awd; USC.

SOTO, VERONICA; Alexander Hamilton HS; Los Angeles, CA; (4); 56/556; Library Aide; Office Aide; Teachers Aide; Oranized Black Hist Mnth Assy/Cert Awd; Outstndng Accmplshmntcomp/Cert Awd; Pan Am U TX; Occu Ther.

SOTO, VERONICA; Atwater HS; Winton, CA; (3); Church Yth Grp; High Hon Roll; Hon Roll; CSU; Pst Pres, Secy Score Clb; History Teacher.

SOTO, VICTOR; Orosi HS; Orosi, CA; (3); Ftbl; Hon Roll; Nvl Acad; USMC Offcr.

SOTO, VICTOR O; Orange Glen HS; Valley Center, CA; (4); Bsbl; Bsktbl; Hon Roll; Rotary Awd; U Of CA San Diego; Elec Engrng.

SOUBLET, ERIKA; Skyline HS; Oakland, CA; (4); 67/542; Latin Clb; Teachers Aide; School Musical; Stage Crew; Ed Nwsp; Lit Mag; Hon Roll; Pres Acad Fit Awd; CSF; Lake Merrit Rowing Club; Jr Schlrshp Fdrtn Outstndng Stu 87; Gonzaga U; Broadcast Jrnlsm.

SOUCIE, DENISE; Desert Christian HS; Palmdale, CA; (1); Drama Clb; Variety Show; Hon Roll; Editrs Choice Awd Poem; Obstetrcs.

SOUDAH, MIKE; Herbert Hoover HS; Glendale, CA; (2); Church Yth Grp; JA; Science Clb; Band; Yrbk; Off Soph Cls; Bsktbl; Prfct Atten Awd; Cert Athltc Achvmt; AYSO Soccer Champ; USC; Eng.

SOUDANT, LISETTE R; Mater Dei HS; Villa Park, CA; (1); Church Yth Grp; Cmnty Wkr; Church Choir; JV Color Guard; Flag Corp; Jr NHS; Flag Corp Frshmn Of Yr Awd; 2 Acad Exclnc Commndtns Relgn & Algbr I; USD; Psych.

SOUDERS, JEREMY M; Grossmont HS; El Cajon, CA; (1); 45/475; Hon Roll; Doc.

SOUDERS, JULIE A; Oroville HS; Oroville, CA; (2); FFA; Spanish Clb; Hon Roll; Prfct Atten Awd; Cmnty Achvt Awd Schlstc Exclnc; Natl FFA Rcgnzng Achvt Frt Tree Prod; Bk Amer Prjct Cmptn Slvr Awd; Cal Poly; Arch.

SOUGHAYER, JOSEPH S; College Park HS; Martinez, CA; (2); Church Yth Grp; Model UN; Var Bsktbl; Var Ftbl; Var Wt Lftg; High Hon Roll; Golden St Exam Geom & Alg I High Hnrs; Med.

SOUKSAMLANE, KHAMLANOY; Mark Keppel HS; Rosemead, CA; (1); Drama Clb; Key Clb; Prfct Atten Awd; CSF; UCLA.

SOUKSAMLANE, TOU; Arlington HS; Riverside, CA; (2); Var Swmmng; Hon Roll; CSF; Dentstry.

SOUKSAVANE, BOONY; Bakersfield HS; Bakersfield, CA; (2); Orch; Hon Roll; Teacher.

SOUKSAVONG, BOURLIEN; Bullard HS; Fresno, CA; (4); 32/455; Pres Church Yth Grp; VP FBLA; Intnl Clb; Teachers Aide; Hon Roll; Spanish NHS; U CA Davis; Civil Engrng.

SOULAGES, GAIL L; San Gorgino HS; San Bernardino, CA; (3); VP Band; Mrchg Band; Orch; Pep Band; Mrchng Band Sq Of Yr 87-89; Band Mst Imprvd 88 & 90; CA ST Long Beach; Music.

SOULE, GEOFF H; San Diego HS; San Diego, CA; (3); Boy Scts; Jazz Band; Pres Acad Fit Awd; Golden St Exam Acad Excllnce Awd Geom.

SOULE, JASON P; Liberty Unido HS; Byron, CA; (3); 33/450; School Play; Variety Show; Tennis; Wrstlng; High Hon Roll; Hon Roll; Editor-In-Chief Of Schl Nwspapr; Edtrl Edtr; USC-CAL Poly; Jrnlsm.

SOUN, VISITH; Santiago HS; Garden Grove, CA; (2); French Clb; Model UN; Bsktbl; Trk; Cit Awd; Hon Roll; NHS; Prfct Atten Awd; CSF Clb; UCI; Pilot.

SOUPHOMMAVONG, XAYXANA; Banning HS; Banning, CA; (2); Chess Clb; Spanish Clb; Jazz Band; Tennis; Hon Roll; Prfct Atten Awd; Asian-Amer Club; Acad Exclinc; Schlr Athlete; CA Schlrshp Fed Mem; UCLA; Mrktng.

SOURIYANYONG, PHOSAI; Fresno HS; Fresno, CA; (4); Bsktbl; Socr; Swmmng.

SOURMELIS, CHRIS A; Brea Olinda HS; Brea, CA; (3); Art Clb; Church Yth Grp; French Clb; Pep Clb; Speech Tm; Church Choir; Wt Lftg; Hon Roll; Disneyland Art Awd; 4 Speech Trphys; Modeling Awd.

SOUS, MALY C; Warren HS; South Gate, CA; (3); Art Clb; GAA; Math Clb; Mu Alpha Theta; JV Capt Vllybl; Photo Clb; Les Amies; LB ST; Law.

SOUSA, ASHLEE L; Arroyo Grande HS; Arroyo Grande, CA; (2); Teachers Aide; Hon Roll; Child Care.

SOUSA, DARLENE; Dos Palos HS; Dos Palos, CA; (3); 20/250; AFS; Church Yth Grp; Cmnty Wkr; FCA; FFA; GAA; Hosp Aide; Letterman Clb; Pep Clb; SADD; CSF; Pres SAD; VP Pep/Spirit; Merced Symphny & Orch; UOP; Music.

SOUSA, GARY J; Dos Palos HS; Dos Palos, CA; (2); FFA; Letterman Clb; SADD; Varsity Clb; Var Ftbl; Var Trk; Var Wt Lftg; Ag Engr.

SOUSA, ISOLDA M; Hilmar Unified School District; Hilmar, CA; (3); Teachers Aide; Hon Roll; Spanish NHS; Modesto JC; HS Eng Tchr.

SOUSA, JULIE; Dos Palos HS; Dos Palos, CA; (2); Church Yth Grp; FFA; Color Guard; Vllybl; Hon Roll; FFA Prfcncy Awd; Grnhnd; Tlnt Shw 2nd Pl; CA Poly.

SOUSA, MANUEL R; Los Banos HS; Gustine, CA; (3); Am Leg Boys St; FFA; JV Bsbl; Var Capt Bsktbl; High Hon Roll; NHS; CSF-TREAS; Intl Camp Royal; Am Fratrnl Fed-St Trustee/St Treas/St VP; Aeronautical Engrng.

SOUSA, NATALIE M; Tulare Western HS; Tulare, CA; (3); FFA; Temple Yth Grp; Var Socr; Var Swmmng; Hon Roll; Rotary Awd; CSF; Awd Frng Lang; CA Poly; Ag Bus.

SOUSA, PAUL B; Turlock HS; Turlock, CA; (3); Church Yth Grp; FFA.

SOUTHE, CHARLES W; Arlington HS; Riverside, CA; (2); Cmnty Wkr; ROTC; Military.

SOUTHER, SHELBY L; Orange Glen HS; Valley Center, CA; (3); 17/450; Spanish Clb; Rptr Nwsp; Capt Cheerldng; Hon Roll; NHS; CA Schlstc Fed Sec & VP; Dance; Elem Ed.

SOUTHERN, ELIZABETH L; Petaluma HS; Petaluma, CA; (2); Church Yth Grp; Cmnty Wkr; FCA; Sftbl; Cit Awd; DAR Awd; Hon Roll; USC; Pediatrician.

SOUTHWELL, HEATHER; Archbishop Mitty HS; San Jose, CA; (3); Art Clb; Sec Church Yth Grp; 4-H; Math Tm; SADD; Chorus; High Hon Roll; NHS; Vrsty Badminton; Amnesty Intl; CSF; Educ.

SOUTHWELL, JENNIFER C; Point Loma HS; San Diego, CA; (4); 36/420; Pres Key Clb; School Musical; Capt JV Cheerldng; Var Crs Cntry; Capt Var Socr; High Hon Roll; NHS; Pres Acad Fit Awd; Interact Club; Freedoms Foundation Schlrshp; Deputy Sheriffs Assn Schlrshp; UCLA.

SOUTHWICK, ALICE; Willits HS; Willits, CA; (1); Church Yth Grp; SADD; Var Cheerldng; Var Pom Pon; Boston U; Animals.

SOUTHWICK, TINA; Atwater HS; Atwater, CA; (2); French Clb; SADD; Capt Color Guard; Mrchg Band; JV Bsktbl; High Hon Roll; Pres Acad Fit Awd; CSF; BSU; Fresno ST; Nrsng.

SOUTHWORTH, REBECCA A; Ontario HS; Ontario, CA; (3); Church Yth Grp; Drama Clb; Thesps; School Musical; School Play; Stage Crew; Brigham Young U; Drama Arts.

SOUZA, BRANDON O; Atwater HS; Winton, CA; (1); FFA; Bsbl; Bsktbl; Ftbl; Hon Roll.

SOUZA, JOSEPH B; Oakdale HS; Oakdale, CA; (3); Pres Frsh Cls; Var JV Bsbl; JV Bsktbl; Var JV Ftbl; Hon Roll; Stu Body Rally Commsioner; Pedriatrics.

SOUZA, LESLEY R; Turlock HS; Turlock, CA; (3); 22/500; AFS; Art Clb; Dance Clb; French Clb; Key Clb; Science Clb; Var Trk; High Hon Roll; Hon Roll.

SOUZA, RICH A; Calistoga JR/Sr HS; Calistoga, CA; (3); SADD; Band; Jazz Band; Pep Band; School Musical; JV Var Bsbl; JV Bsktbl; JV Var Ftbl; Hon Roll; AZ Tech Inst.

SOUZA, STACY; Cupertino HS; Santa Clara, CA; (2); Church Yth Grp; GAA; Letterman Clb; Teachers Aide; Varsity Clb; Pres Nwsp; Off Soph Cls; Var Gym; Co-Capt JV Pom Pon; JV Vllybl; Schlr Athl 89-90; Activity Awd 89-90; U AZ; Nrsng.

SOUZA, TANYA M; Victory Christian Schl; Sacramento, CA; (2); Church Yth Grp; High Hon Roll; Hon Roll; Natl Wildlife Assn; Bio.

SOV, CHAY; Jurupa Valley HS; Riverside, CA; (2); Chess Clb; Spanish Clb; Yrbk; Treas Soph Cls; Treas Stu Cncl; Mgr Bsktbl; Capt Tennis; Cit Awd; High Hon Roll; Hnrs In Golden St Exm Geom; Grant For Air Pollution Prjct; Stu Achvt Riverside CC; Engrng.

SOVAN, CHANMACH M; Andrew Hill HS; San Jose, CA; (1); Cmnty Wkr; Hosp Aide; Intnl Clb; Cit Awd; Hon Roll; Prfct Atten Awd; HS Med Magnet Pgm; Med/Health Prof Magnet Sch; Med Magnet Stu; GATE; Stanford; Med.

SOVANMONY, MAO; Lakewood HS; Long Beach, CA; (4); Aud/Vis; Computer Clb; Office Aide; Socr; Wt Lftg; Petroleum Tech.

SOVEY, SHANNON ELYCE; Louisville HS; Chatsworth, CA; (1); Hosp Aide; Chorus; Hon Roll; Prfct Atten Awd.

SOWAR, KATHLEEN; Monte Vista HS; Walnut Creek, CA; (3); 47/356; Church Yth Grp; Dance Clb; Cheerldng; High Hon Roll; Hon Roll; NHS; CSF.

SOWARD II, WARREN E; South Hills HS; Covina, CA; (3); 56/223; Science Clb; Teachers Aide; L Band; Jazz Band; Mrchg Band; School Musical; School Play; Outstndng Frshmn Musician 88, Soph 89; Aad Olympiad Club Sec; Gftd/Tlntd Ed Seminar.

SOWDERS, CORRIE A; Coleville HS; Coleville, CA; (2); 3/15; SADD; Treas Soph Cls; Var L Bsktbl; Var L Sftbl; Var Vllybl; Hon Roll; Coaches Awd Sftbl; Sierra JC; Vet.

SOWELL, BILL L; Downey HS; Modesto, CA; (3); Band; Jazz Band; Mrchg Band; School Play; Bsbl; Ftbl; Tennis; Wrstlng; Modesto JC; Acctng.

SOWER, SCOTT R; Imperial HS; Sylmar, CA; (3); 6/23; Church Yth Grp; Office Aide; Teachers Aide; Band; Rptr Nwsp; Yrbk; L Var Bsktbl; L Trk; L Var Vllybl; Wt Lftg; Chrch Yth Outstndng Athl Awd 89; Chrch Yth Actvty Prtcptn Awd 88-90; Pres Phys Ftnss Awd; Mens Spch Clb.

SOYINTHISANE, VANH; Edison Computech HS; Fresno, CA; (3); 92/190; High Hon Roll; Hon Roll; Fresno ST U; Engrng.

SPACKMAN, KATE; Woodbridge HS; Irvine, CA; (3); Church Yth Grp; French Clb; Pep Clb; Chorus; Church Choir; Rep Frsh Cls; Rep Stu Cncl; JV Var Cheerldng; Hon Roll; BYU; Prfssnl Singer.

SPAETH, TIM A; Servite HS; La Mirada, CA; (2); JV Socr; NHS; NEDT Awd; Jr Statesmn Amer JSA; CSF; Bus.

SPAGNA, JOSEPH C; Ramona HS; Riverside, CA; (3); 2/300; Quiz Bowl; School Musical; L Ftbl; L Trk; Intrml Wt Lftg; Capt Wrstlng.

SPAMPINATO, JUAN PIER; Albany HS; Albany, CA; (3); Boy Scts; Ski Clb; JV Var Trk; Hon Roll; Gldn St Exam Alg Hnrs & Geo Hnrs; Karate Club; UCLA; Arspc Engrng.

SPANGENBERG, MIA M; Brea-Olinda HS; Brea, CA; (2); 10/335; Ed Nwsp; High Hon Roll; Jr NHS; Pres Acad Fit Awd; CSF; Strt Envrnmnt Clb Prtctng Air; Envrnmntl Stds.

SPANGLER, CHARITY A; Helix HS; Lemon Grove, CA; (3); Pres Church Yth Grp; Pep Clb; Chorus; Church Choir; Variety Show; Audtnd & Prfrmd San Francisco Ballet Nutcracker 87-88; Hghst Vocal Awd 90; San Diego ST U.

SPANGLER, JOSH M; Lincoln HS; Stockton, CA; (2); 260/570; Office Aide; Teachers Aide; Socr; Sports Admin.

SPANGLER, SARILEE F; Helix HS; Lemon Grove, CA; (3); Church Yth Grp; Pep Clb; Chorus; Church Choir; Variety Show; Audtnd & Prfrmnd San Francisco Ballet Nutcracker 87-88; Hghst Vocal Awd; San Diego ST U.

SPANN, BYRON D; Bellflower HS; Bellflower, CA; (2); Boy Scts; Band; Rep Soph Cls; JV Bsktbl; Var Ftbl; Score Keeper; Socr; Wt Lftg; High Hon Roll; Hon Roll; CO.

SPANNE, AUTUMN; Lompoc HS; Lompoc, CA; (2); Nwsp; Rep Soph Cls; Hon Roll; CA Schlrshp Fed.

SPAR, DARCIE L; C K Mc Clatchy HS; Sacramento, CA; (3); 1/418; Girl Scts; Key Clb; Math Clb; Spanish Clb; Stage Crew; Friday Night Live Secy; Odyssey Of Mind 1st Pl Rgn & 3rd Pl St 90; Intl Relations.

SPARKMAN, JEFFREY B; Tracy Joint Union HS; Tracy, CA; (2); 112/580; Rptr Yrbk; Lit Mag; Hon Roll; Leo Clb; Goldn St Exam 1st Alg Schl Recgntn; Art/Writng.

SPARKS, CHRIS R; Redlands HS; Redlands, CA; (2); Drama Clb; JA; School Play; Stage Crew; Rptr Nwsp; Phtg Yrbk; JV Trk; Hon Roll; Prfct Atten Awd; Outdoor Clb; Spcl Recog Sci.

SPARKS, DANIEL E; Fremont Christian HS; Fremont, CA; (3); Var Tennis; Hon Roll; USAF Acad; Aeronaut Engrng.

SPARKS, DEBBIE; Leland HS; San Jose, CA; (3); Church Yth Grp; Girl Scts; Girl Sct Gold Awd; Wstrn Rgnl Athl Cmmssnr US Twrlng Assn; Spirit Squad Twrlr; Bus.

SPARKS, GNELL M; Tulare Union HS; Tulare, CA; (4); #31 In Class; Church Yth Grp; GAA; Teachers Aide; Var JV Sftbl; Capt Var Vllybl; Hon Roll; Sftbl Schlrshp-CA ST-BAKERSFIELD; 1st Team EYL-SFTBL; All Area Ctr Fielder-Sftbl; CA ST-BAKERSFIELD; Nrsng.

SPARKS, MAI J; Fontana HS; Fontana, CA; (3); Drama Clb; Ski Clb; Chorus; Drill Tm; Stu Cncl; UCLA; Psych.

SPARTA, JASON M; University Of San Diego HS; La Mesa, CA; (2).

SPATES, TANYA N; Westminster HS; Huntington Beach, CA; (3); Dance Clb; Drama Clb; Hosp Aide; Office Aide; Pep Clb; Ski Clb; Spanish Clb; Teachers Aide; Drill Tm; School Play; Nrsg.

SPATH, KRISTIN L; Mt Carmel HS; San Diego, CA; (4); Teachers Aide; VP Band; Mrchg Band; Yrbk; Stu Cncl; Cit Awd; Hon Roll; Kiwanis Awd; Pres Acad Fit Awd; All-Sthrn CA Hnr Musician; Russia US Sci Ambsdr; 1990 Yrbk Stff Membr Yr; 90 Dirctr Awd Band; San Diego ST U; Bio/Vet Med.

SPAYDE, ERIK; Thousand Oaks HS; Westlake Village, CA; (3); 1/523; Math Tm; NFL; Science Clb; Spanish Clb; Var Crs Cntry; Var Trk; Bausch & Lomb Sci Awd; High Hon Roll; Ntl Merit Ltr; St Wnnr Natl Piano Playing Auditions; Hgh Hnrs Golden St Geom Test; Mst Vlbl Var Crss Cntry Rnnr 89; Med.

SPEAR, ALANA R; Vacaville HS; Vacaville, CA; (4); Church Yth Grp; Library Aide; Quiz Bowl; Teachers Aide; Church Choir; Trk; Vllybl; Stage Manager/Director Brdwy Production Musical; Jr High Counselor; S CA Coll; Child Psychology.

SPEARE, MARISHA A; Notre Dame HS; San Bernardino, CA; (3); 20/140; FHA; Ski Clb; Spanish Clb; Var Trk; High Hon Roll; NHS; Treas Spanish NHS; CA Schlst Fed; Psych.

SPEARS, DAVID; Livermore HS; Livermore, CA; (2); Acpl Chr; Church Choir; Jazz Band; Mst Prmsng Musician Awd 90.

SPEARS, GINA M; San Lorenzo HS; San Leandro, CA; (4); DECA; Ski Clb; Var JV Cheerldng; Competed Deca St & Dist Confrncs 2 Yrs; Competed CA Chrldng Champnshps 90; Cal ST; Bus Adm.

SPEARS, PHILLIP R; Portola JR SR HS; Portola, CA; (2); Cmnty Wkr; Letterman Clb; Band; Chorus; Swing Chorus; Rep Frsh Cls; Pres Soph Cls; Pres Stu Cncl; JV Var Bsktbl; JV Ftbl; Yth To Yth West Coast Conf; UC Davis.

SPEASE, JASON V; Luther Burbank HS; Sacramento, CA; (3); 28/276; FFA; Cit Awd; FCA; Prfct Atten Awd; Star Chptr Frmr, Grnhnd Degree, Chptr FFA Degree; BOAC Achvt Awd Engl; Hnr Soc Awd; Woods Schlrshp; Sacramento City Coll; Bus Admin.

SPECK, JAMIE J; Del Oro HS; Loomis, CA; (2); 1/267; Var Crs Cntry; Var Swmmng; NHS; KMPG Peat Marwick Press Awds Essy Cntst; Awdrd Cum Laude Acad Distnctn Awd; UCD; Mrn Bio.

SPEER, STEVEN E; Montclair HS; Montclair, CA; (1); Church Yth Grp; Letterman Clb; Rep Bsktbl; Rep Stu Cncl; Hon Roll; Pres Acad Fit Awd; Cert Of Excll Drftng; Mech Engr.

SPEER, WILLIAM F; Los Amigos HS; Fountain Valley, CA; (3); Boy Scts; Ski Clb; Stu Cncl; Var Bsbl; JV Bsktbl; Hon Roll; NHS; Bsktbl Awd-Most Insprtnl; Bsbl Awd-Coachs Awd; Cal Poly San Luis Coll; Engrng.

SPEICHER, MICHELLE; Santa Rosa HS; Santa Rosa, CA; (4); 120/550; JA; Pep Clb; Spanish Clb; Chorus; School Play; Nwsp; Yrbk; Vllybl; Cit Awd; High Hon Roll; Pepperdine.

SPENCE, COLIN R; Saint Paul HS; La Mirada, CA; (3); Boy Scts; Treas Latin Clb; Bsktbl; Var Tennis; Hon Roll; NHS; NEDT Awd; US Air Force Acad; Engrng.

SPENCE, JUSTIN S; Homestead HS; Sunnyvale, CA; (1); Boy Scts; Church Yth Grp; Band; Church Choir; Mrchg Band; Orch; Pep Band; Hon Roll; Lttl Lg Bsbl; JW Vlybl; BYU; Vet.

SPENCE, KATHLEEN GALE; Kern Valley HS; Lake Isabella, CA; (2); Letterman Clb; VP Frsh Cls; JV VP Bsktbl; VP Sftbl; VP Trk; VP Vllybl; Hon Roll; Pres Acad Fit Awd; Mst Otstndng Achvr Phys Ed 89-90; MIP Grls JV Bsktbl 89; Otstndng Acad Excllnc Awd 89; Cal Poly; Law Enfrcmnt.

SPENCER, CRESENCIA S; Summerville HS; Sonora, CA; (3); 10/145; AFS; French Clb; Quiz Bowl; VP Spanish Clb; Band; Jazz Band; High Hon Roll; Academic Decathlon; Cmnty Orch; CSF; Brown U; Elem Schl Admin.

SPENCER, DAVID; Turlock HS; Turlock, CA; (3); 7/600; Boy Scts; Key Clb; Swing Chorus; Variety Show; Vllybl; High Hon Roll; NHS; Sal; Outstndng JR Sci Stu & PTSA Physcl Ed Awds; BYU; Pre Med.

SPENCER, HEIDI E; Valhalla HS; El Cajon, CA; (2); 110/435; Dance Clb; Drama Clb; GAA; Ski Clb; Variety Show; Off Jr Cls; Cheerldng; Gym; Socr; Teach Acrobatics; Achvd Numerous Awd Dance Conts; Commnctns.

SPENCER, JAMIE; Western Chr HS; Ontario, CA; (3); 1/88; Church Yth Grp; Service Clb; Spanish Clb; Teachers Aide; Ed Yrbk; Treas Jr Cls; Golf; High Hon Roll; NHS; Rotary Awd.

SPENCER, JEANETTE D; Ponderosa HS; Plymouth, CA; (1); Church Yth Grp; Intrml Bsktbl; Intrml Sftbl; Intrml Vllybl; Hon Roll; Cooking; Tutoring Sci; Brigham Young U; Educ.

SPENCER, JENNIFER M; Rancho Buena Vista HS; Oceanside, CA; (4); Church Yth Grp; JA; Pep Clb; Var Capt Crs Cntry; Var Capt Trk; Ltrmns Cert Awd; Seminary Grad; UCSB; Educ.

SPENCER, JESSICA; Desert Christian HS; Lancaster, CA; (1); Church Yth Grp; Chorus; VP Stu Cncl; JV Tennis; Cit Awd; High Hon Roll; Piano; LIFE Bible Coll; Bible.

SPENCER, JESSICA L; Santa Clara HS; Oxnard, CA; (2); 24/191; Cmnty Wkr; High Hon Roll; Hon Roll; NHS; Chrch Smr Pgm Tchr; Spec Educ.

SPENCER, JIM; Las Plumas HS; Oroville, CA; (2); French Clb; JV Bsbl; JV Bsktbl; JV Ftbl; JV Wt Lftg; San Diego ST U; Sports Med.

SPENCER, JOI; Downtown Business Magnet HS; Moreno Valley, CA; (4); 3/170; Office Aide; Variety Show; Ed Nwsp; Pres Frsh Cls; Rep Soph Cls; Pres Jr Cls; Pres Stu Cncl; Cit Awd; High Hon Roll; Ephebian Hnr Soc; CSF Life Time; Yng Blck Schlr Grad; Acad Of Fin Rcpnt; Bnk Of Amer Plq Awd; Stanford U.

SPENCER, KATHERINE D; Grace M Davis HS; Modesto, CA; (4); French Clb; FBLA; Key Clb; Hon Roll; NHS; Pres Acad Fit Awd; Acad Decthln; UC Santa Barbara; Bus.

SPENCER, MARIANNE E; Marysville HS; Marysville, CA; (2); Church Yth Grp; 4-H; Acpl Chr; Vllybl; 4-H Awd; Hon Roll; Humboldt ST Coll; Elem Ed.

SPENCER, MATTHEW B; C K Mc Clatchy HS; Sacramento, CA; (2); 91/442; JV Bsktbl; Prfct Atten Awd; MESA; Early Outreach Program; Outstndng MESA & Early Outreach Awd For Gpa.

SPENCER, MICHAEL C; El Camino HS; Carmichael, CA; (3); 34/366; School Play; NHS; Prfct Atten Awd; Cal Poly Sn Luis Obispo; Engr.

SPENCER, MICHELLE L; Middletown HS; Middletown, CA; (3); FBLA; SADD; Teachers Aide; Sec Frsh Cls; Cheerldng; Var Tennis; Var Trk; Hon Roll; Empire Bus Coll; Bus.

SPENCER, ROWYNN E; King-Drew Medical Magnet HS; Los Angeles, CA; (3); Church Yth Grp; Math Clb; Rep Frsh Cls; VP Jr Cls; Rep Stu Cncl; Score Keeper; Vllybl; Hon Roll; Acadmc Dcthln; Tall Flag Team; Outstndng Atten; UCLA; Med.

SPENCER, SEAN L; Arroyo Grande HS; Oceano, CA; (1); SMART Clb; Yale; Orthdntst.

SPENCER, TAMARA; Galt HS; Acampo, CA; (2); 34/239; Intnl Clb; Pep Clb; Stage Crew; JV Cheerldng; DAR Awd; Hon Roll; Accntng.

SPENCER, TONI; Elk Grove HS; Elk Grove, CA; (4); Dance Clb; FFA; SADD; Teachers Aide; Band; Co-Capt Color Guard; Variety Show; Hon Roll; Bus Awd; Booster Clb-Treas; Homcmng Cmmttee.

SPENDLOVE, SHAWN PRESTWICH; Santa Paula Union HS; Santa Paula, CA; (3); Boy Scts; Church Yth Grp; Letterman Clb; Varsity Clb; Var Socr; High Hon Roll; Hon Roll; Eagl Sct; CSF; Brigham Young U; Math.

SPENSER, KARYN E; Foothill SR HS; Sacramento, CA; (2); Church Yth Grp; BYU; Inter Dsgn.

SPENST, RENEE O; Santa Rosa HS; Santa Rosa, CA; (3); SADD; Gym; Var Stat Wrstlng; Hon Roll; Ntl Merit Ltr; Peer Cnslng.

SPICER, KRISTINIA M; Walnut HS; Walnut, CA; (2); 65/495; French Clb; Hosp Aide; Ed Nwsp; JV Crs Cntry; High Hon Roll; Hon Roll; Cngrssmn Yth Vlntr Awd; Chld Psychlgy.

SPICER, KRISTY M; Thousand Oaks HS; Thousand Oaks, CA; (3); Church Yth Grp; SADD; Chorus; Lit Mag; Stat Bsktbl; Yth To Yth; Pepperdine; Law.

SPICER, TAMMIE; Mt Whitney HS; Visalia, CA; (4); 73/373; French Clb; Color Guard; Rptr Nwsp; High Hon Roll; Hon Roll; Lifetime Member California Scholarship Federation-Seal Bearer; Academic Varsity Letter; Coll Of The Sequoias; Cvl Attny.

SPICKLER, JASON A; Foothill HS; Bakersfield, CA; (3); Computer Clb; German Clb; Teachers Aide; Excelled In Comp Sci; Know 4 Comps Langs; Bakersfield Coll; Comp Prgrmmr.

SPIECKERMAN, DAMIAN C D; Lick-Wilmerding HS; San Francisco, CA; (2); Church Yth Grp; Drama Clb; Phtg Yrbk; Lit Mag; Hon Roll; Pres Acad Fit Awd; Intern UCSF 90; Lab Asst; Phillips Exeter Acad 89; Awd For Achvt Chinese Lang, Wrld Civilztns.

SPIEGEL, TRACY L; Western HS; Buena Park, CA; (3); Color Guard; Trk; Hon Roll; NHS; Intl Order Of Rainbo For Girls; Commercial Arts.

SPIELDENNER, ANDREW R; Novato HS; Petaluma, CA; (4); French Clb; SADD; School Musical; Ed Yrbk; Off Soph Cls; VP Jr Cls; Rep Sr Cls; Swmmng; Creative Wrtng Prose Awd; UC Berkeley; Writer.

SPIER, KARYN M; Glendale Adventist Acad; Glendale, CA; (2); Hosp Aide; Acpl Chr; Band; Chorus; Church Choir; Rptr Nwsp; Sec Jr Cls; SCSBOA Indiv Local & Rgnl Superior Rtngs; SYMF 1st Pl 1988; Pacific Union Coll; Bus Admin.

SPIESS III, RAYMOND E; Chaffey HS; Ontario, CA; (1); German Clb; Spanish Clb; Sec Soph Cls; JV Tennis; Coed Sftbl; Role Playing Games Club; Air Force.

SPIKER, LUONNE E; Branham HS; San Jose, CA; (2); 16/277; Church Yth Grp; SADD; JV Bsktbl; JV Tennis; Hon Roll; Var Badminton; CSF.

SPILLANE, ADAM P; Lowell HS; San Francisco, CA; (3); Red Cross Aide; Speech Tm; Teachers Aide; Intrml Bsktbl; Var L Golf; Pres Acad Fit Awd; Elect Engrng.

SPILLANE, CHARITY; Orange Glen HS; Escondido, CA; (3); 58/458; Drama Clb; Thesps; Acpl Chr; Chorus; School Musical; School Play; Variety Show; Treas Yrbk; Off Soph Cls; Hon Roll; Tri-M Mdrn Music Mstrs Sec; Cmmnty Theatre; Yng Wmn Chrch Jesus Christ Latter Day Sts Pres; SDSU; Prfrmng Arts.

SPILLANE, DANIEL J; Bellarmine College Prep; Belmont, CA; (3); 28/300; Cmnty Wkr; Debate Tm; NFL; Service Clb; Speech Tm; Variety Show; Rptr Nwsp; Mgr Yrbk; High Hon Roll; Ntl Merit SF; Engl.

SPILLER, GREG S; Oakdale HS; Oakdale, CA; (1); 117/340; 4-H; FFA; Science Clb; Ftbl; Wt Lftg; Wrstlng.

SPILLER, LON; Dinuba Joint Union HS; Dinuba, CA; (4); JV Swmmng; Var Trk; Elks Awd; Ornamental Horticulture Club; Kings River Coll; Landscape Mgt.

SPILLER, SHERRON; Dorothy Vena Johnson HS; Los Angeles, CA; (4); Band; Chorus; Nwsp; Off Sr Cls; Trk; Cit Awd; Hon Roll; Prfct Atten Awd; Serv Awd; Merit Awd; Prncpl And Deans List; Teacher.

SPILLERS, CHRIS S; Mission Viejo HS; Mission Viejo, CA; (3); 86/417; Library Aide; Office Aide; Ski Clb; Teachers Aide; Wt Lftg; Pres Acad Fit Awd; Pres Schlr; U CA-SAN Diego.

SPILLMAN, TROY G; Valley Christian HS; Livermore, CA; (2); Church Yth Grp; Ski Clb; Spanish Clb; Hist Frsh Cls; Treas Soph Cls; Treas Jr Cls; Var Bsbl; High Hon Roll; Hon Roll; NHS; Piano; CSF; U Of CA; Law.

SPINDEL, DEBBIE L; Silver Creek HS; San Jose, CA; (1); Church Yth Grp; Color Guard; Hon Roll; Liberty U; Business Music.

SPINDLER, BRIAN M; Los Angeles Baptist HS; Mission Hills, CA; (4); 10/90; Aud/Vis; Church Yth Grp; Teachers Aide; Stage Crew; JV Bsktbl; Intrml Socr; Cit Awd; High Hon Roll; Hon Roll; NHS; Sprtl Life Slflssnss Awd; CA ST U; Bus Admin Acctng.

SPINDLER, NIKKI M; Simi Valley HS; Simi Valley, CA; (2); Church Yth Grp; JV Capt Bsktbl; JV Socr; JV Trk; Pres Acad Fit Awd; Bsktbl 2 All Trnmnt Trophys/MVP Awd; Scr 2 All Trnmnt Tphys/Best Dfndr/Coaches Awd; Loyola; Teacher.

SPINELLA, ALISE; Los Gatos HS; Los Gatos, CA; (4); Art Clb; Drama Clb; Spanish Clb; Var Diving; Powder Puff Ftbl; Hon Roll; Natl Hispanic Schlr Semi Fnlst; Santa Clara Intl Swim/Dive Clb; Amnesty Intl Clb; UCLA; Physics.

SPINELLI, TONY T; Bellarmine College Prep; Mount View, CA; (1); Debate Tm; NFL; Speech Tm; Prfct Atten Awd; Pres Acad Fit Awd; Sprts.

SPINKS, KIMBERLY M; Ramona HS; Ramona, CA; (2); 31/345; Dance Clb; Debate Tm; FBLA; SADD; Eqstrn Events 89 Ramona Rodeo Partcpnt; Anti-Drg Essy Cont 1st Pl; Swmmng; Wrtng; U Of CA San Deigo; Marine Bio.

SPINKS, TRICIA K; Mt Carmel HS; San Diego, CA; (4); Band; Mrchg Band; Orch; Pep Band; Semper Fidelis Awd Musicl Excllnc US Mrns; John Philip Sousa Musicl Excllnc Awd; UC Berkeley; Cvl Engrng.

SPINOZZI, JOE S; North HS; Bakersfield, CA; (2); Church Yth Grp; Drama Clb; French Clb; Math Tm; School Musical; School Play; Golf; High Hon Roll; NHS; Chrch Yth Ldrshp Cncl; MIT; Aerspc Engrng.

SPIRITO, ROBERT T; Carlsbad HS; Oceanside, CA; (4); 138/338; AFS; Key Clb; Letterman Clb; Pep Clb; SADD; Varsity Clb; Off Yrbk; JV Bsktbl; JV Tennis; JV Girl Scts; Stu Athltc Trnr; Booster Clb Schlr Athlt Awrd; Coll; Physcl Ed Med Schl.

SPIRLING, TAMIKA; El Camino Fundamental HS; Sacramento, CA; (3); Church Yth Grp; Cmnty Wkr; Band; Pep Band; Bsktbl; Trk; Hon Roll; Pres Acad Fit Awd; Frdy Nght Live; Blck Stu Union; Early Acadmc Outrch UC Davis; Spelman Coll; Polit Sci.

SPITLER, JASON S; Yucaipa HS; Yucaipa, CA; (1); Boy Scts; Cmnty Wkr; Debate Tm; Spanish Clb; JV Crs Cntry; JV Trk; High Hon Roll; Hon Roll; NHS; Pres Acad Fit Awd; UCLA; Envrnmntl Arch Dsgn.

SPITZER, DEBBIE L; San Ramon Valley HS; Danville, CA; (3); 189/420; Teachers Aide; Band; Stained Gls; Bowling.

SPITZER, MARC G; Eureka HS; Eureka, CA; (4); 30/303; FBLA; VP JA; Band; Orch; High Hon Roll; Common Trash; Sr Cls Night Sound; Dracula Tech Dir; CA Poly Sn Luis Obispo; Engr.

SPIVACK, DANIEL E; Torrey Pines HS; San Diego, CA; (2); Key Clb; Spanish Clb; Swmmng; Cit Awd; High Hon Roll; Hon Roll; Pres Acad Fit Awd; Cmnty Yth Grp VP; Medcl.

SPIVEY, SANDRA L; Eisenhower HS; Rialto, CA; (3); Church Yth Grp; Cmnty Wkr; Teachers Aide; Acpl Chr; Chorus; Church Choir; Swing Chorus; Hon Roll; St CA Assmbly Schltc Achvt Awd; Psych.

SPLAVEC, LEAH N; Poway HS; Poway, CA; (3); 3/750; Letterman Clb; Varsity Clb; Var L Tennis; High Hon Roll; NHS; CSF; Peer Cnslng; All Palomar Tennis Lgu; Bus.

SPLINGAERD, TAMARA E; J Eugene Mc Ateer Schl Of The Arts; San Francisco, CA; (3); Church Yth Grp; Debate Tm; Drama Clb; Office Aide; Thesps; School Play; Stage Crew; JV Fld Hcky; Var Vllybl; High Hon Roll; Girls Sccr City.

SPOELSTRA, ANDREW J; East Union HS; Manteca, CA; (1); 36/490; Key Clb; Ftbl; JV Socr; Var Swmmng; Hon Roll; Prfct Atten Awd; Manteca City Swim Team; Lfgrd & Swim Lssns Tchr.

SPOELSTRA, NOELLE D; Amos Alonzo Stagg HS; Stockton, CA; (2); SADD; JV Cheerldng; Var Socr; Fnlst Poetry Cont; Vlntr Spcl Olympcs; Hghst Hnr Rll; Sci Cmp Cnslr; Louis & Clark; Ed.

SPONKO, YARIV; Calabasas HS; Woodland Hills, CA; (3); Debate Tm; Speech Tm; USC; Film Prodctn.

SPOONER, TRAY-C; Willows HS; Willows, CA; (4); Key Clb; Yrbk; Var L Tennis; Grphc Dsgn.

SPOOR, JASON P; Sierra Vista HS; Baldwin Park, CA; (2); Pres Chess Clb; Science Clb; Chorus; Yrbk; Intrml Ftbl; Var Trk; JV Wrstlng.

SPOOR, MELISSA; Righetti HS; Los Alamos, CA; (4); 56/457; Capt Church Yth Grp; School Play; Ed Nwsp; Rep Frsh Cls; Rep Soph Cls; Rep Jr Cls; Var L Cheerldng; Var L Pom Pon; Var Swmmng; High Hon Roll; Interact Pres; Telecommnctns.

SPORER, KEN F; North HS; Bakersfield, CA; (3); 72/370; Letterman Clb; Office Aide; Ski Clb; Var Ftbl; JV Trk; Var Wt Lftg; NHS; Accntng.

SPRADLEY, SEAN E; Mt Whitney HS; Visalia, CA; (2); Trk; Wt Lftg; Wrstlng; High Hon Roll; Pres Acad Fit Awd; Chsn Cnfrnc Tn Srvl Tns Agnst Drgs; CA Poly San Luis Obispo; Engrg.

SPRADLING, AMY D; Placer HS; Auburn, CA; (3); FHA; GAA; Stu Cncl; Cheerldng; Capt Socr; Vllybl; Hon Roll; Crtfd Phlebotomistm, Wrkng In Hosp; RN.

SPRADLING, TYCHO B; Cajon HS; Riverside, CA; (3); Church Yth Grp; Treas Key Clb; Spanish Clb; Nwsp; Var JV Crs Cntry; Var JV Trk; JV Wrstlng; Acad Decthln; Engrng.

SPRAGG, CYNTHIA; Earnest Righetti HS; Santa Maria, CA; (4); 4-H; Rptr Pres FFA; Rptr Nwsp; JV Sftbl; JV Vllybl; Hon Roll; Fresno ST U CA; Ag Bus Mgmnt.

SPRAGGINS, AMBER; Tracy Joint Union HS; Tracy, CA; (2); 73/483; Pep Clb; SADD; School Musical; School Play; Stu Cncl; Cheerldng; Swmmng; Hon Roll; Pres Acad Fit Awd; Peer Cnslng; Stu League Cmmtte; Swimming Ltr; Dance.

SPRAGUE, MYRA J; John Burroughs HS; Burbank, CA; (2); Church Yth Grp; Chorus; Stage Crew; Variety Show; Co-Ed Nwsp; Ed Yrbk; VP Frsh Cls; Cit Awd; NHS; Pres Acad Fit Awd; Boston U.

SPRAGUE, NATHAN C; Casa Roble Fundamental HS; Orangevale, CA; (2); Church Yth Grp; French Clb; Band; JV Bsbl; JV Bsktbl; High Hon Roll; Prfct Atten Awd.

SPRANKLE, SAGE M; Capistrano Valley HS; Mission Viejo, CA; (4); Dance Clb; Speech Tm; Drill Tm; VP Soph Cls; Sec Stu Cncl; JV Sftbl; Pres Acad Fit Awd; Rotary Awd; Fresh Homcmng Prncs; Rep Bus Womns Schlrshp; Grad Spkr; UC San Diego.

SPRATT, JOANNA T; San Dieguito HS; La Costa, CA; (2); 1/530; Pres Debate Tm; Letterman Clb; NFL; Quiz Bowl; Scholastic Bowl; Service Clb; Pres Speech Tm; French Hon Soc; High Hon Roll; Prfct Atten Awd; Flute Plyr 7 Yrs 1st Pl Sr Div; UCSD; Med.

SPRAY, JAMES W; Antelope Valley HS; Lancaster, CA; (3); 80/670; AFS; Am Leg Boys St; Debate Tm; German Clb; Model UN; ROTC; Service Clb; School Play; VP Frsh Cls; Pres Soph Cls; Civil Air Patrol Mitchell Awd; CSF; JV Fencing & JV Waterpolo; USC; Pltcl Sci.

SPREKELMEYER, MICHELLE K; Casa Roble Fundamental HS; Folsom, CA; (2); 31/461; Church Yth Grp; French Clb; Church Choir; Ed Yrbk; Hon Roll; Pres Acad Fit Awd; Friday Night Live; Engl.

SPRING, CHRISTIAN B; O'farrel Schl Creatv & Perform Arts; San Diego, CA; (1); 1/230; Boy Scts; Church Yth Grp; School Musical; School Play; Hon Roll; Pres Schlr.

SPRING, KEVIN R; Carlsbad HS; Carlsbad, CA; (3); Teachers Aide; Ftbl; Wt Lftg; Wrstlng; Pres Acad Fit Awd; Athl Mnth; Sales.

SPRINGBORN, HOLLY; Atwater HS; Atwater, CA; (3); Church Yth Grp; FCA; JA; High Hon Roll; Hon Roll; Advertisement Bus.

SPRINGER, DAVID L; Arcadia HS; Temple City, CA; (2); Boy Scts; Office Aide; Teachers Aide; Hon Roll; Pres Acad Fit Awd; Hnrs Gldn St Exams-Geom & Algb; Mtrlgy.

SPRINGER, KYLE J; Dana Hills HS; Laguna Niguel, CA; (4); 15/650; Math Tm; Science Clb; Spanish Clb; Var L Vllybl; Hon Roll; Ntl Merit SF; Val; JR Statesmn Of Amer; SAVE & OCAD; USCD.

SPRINGER, MARQUIS D; John Muir HS; Altadena, CA; (2); Church Yth Grp; Drama Clb; Church Choir; Rep Soph Cls; JV Bsbl; JV Ftbl; Hon Roll; Prfct Atten Awd; Black Stu Un Rep; AR ST U; Bus Mgmt.

SPRINGER, SHAD M; Esperanza HS; Yorba Linda, CA; (3); 57/500; Church Yth Grp; French Clb; Nwsp; Lit Mag; Crs Cntry; Trk; High Hon Roll; NHS; Northwestern; Jrnlsm.

SPRINGMAN, TWYLA M; North HS; Oildale, CA; (3); 64/306; Color Guard; Bsktbl; JV Powder Puff Ftbl; Var Sftbl; Vllybl; Hon Roll; Coaches Awd Sftbl; Mst Imprvd Sftbl; Bowling 1st, 2nd; Tchr.

SPRINKLE, MELISSA L; Serrano HS; Phelan, CA; (2); Dance Clb; Spanish Clb; Drill Tm; High Hon Roll; Hon Roll; U HI; Med.

SPRIVEY, NELSON R; Sunset HS; Castro Valley, CA; (4); 36/264; Church Yth Grp; Band; Jazz Band; Mrchg Band; Orch; Pep Band; Wrstlng; High Hon Roll; Hon Roll; Waukesha WI Bible Schl; Mssnry.

SPROUSE, JESSICA P; John F Kennedy HS; Fullerton, CA; (3); Girl Scts; Teachers Aide; Sftbl; Chld Psych.

SPROWL, DANIEL W; Hemet HS; Hemet, CA; (2); Church Yth Grp; Wt Lftg; Cit Awd; Hon Roll; Chiropractor.

SPRUCE, CRAIG M; The Bishops Schl; La Jolla, CA; (3); Church Yth Grp; Scholastic Bowl; Spanish Clb; Teachers Aide; Var L Crs Cntry; Var L Trk; 2nd Pl Santa Barbara Exam Bio 89-90; Dartmouth Book Awd 89-90; Otstndng Spnsh Stu 89-90; Natl Sp Exam; Law.

SPURLOCK, CAMERON W; Kingsburg HS; Kingsburg, CA; (2); Art Clb; Church Yth Grp; SADD; Art.

SQUARE, LA KEISHA; Banning HS; Los Angeles, CA; (2); Church Yth Grp; Girl Scts; Band; Mrchg Band; Treas Soph Cls; High Hon Roll; Jr NHS; Prfct Atten Awd; U Southern CA; Arch.

SQUELLATI, DAVID A; St Francis HS; Sunnyvale, CA; (3); 16/350; Church Yth Grp; Drama Clb; Letterman Clb; Office Aide; SADD; School Musical; School Play; JV Bsbl; JV Bsktbl; Var JV Ftbl.

SQUIRE, ERICA B; Granada Hills HS; Granada Hills, CA; (3); SADD; Teachers Aide; Lit Mag; Teach.

SQUIRE, JEANETTE L; Calistoga HS; Calistoga, CA; (3); 1/40; Am Leg Aux Girls St; Sec 4-H; School Play; Rep Frsh Cls; Treas Stu Cncl; Var Bsktbl; JV Cheerldng; JV Tennis; JV Var Vllybl; High Hon Roll; Chmbr Cmmrc Yng Ctzn Yr 89; Educ.

SQUIRE, RYAN C; Arcadia HS; Arcadia, CA; (3); 269/639; Church Yth Grp; Cmnty Wkr; Debate Tm; French Clb; Speech Tm; Band; Color Guard; Mrchg Band; Orch; Pres Acad Fit Awd; Principals Recognitn Roll; Golden St Ex Awd Geo; Cal St Fullrtn Awd Ex Debate; Engl.

SQUIRES, HEATHER M; Garces Memorial HS; Bakersfield, CA; (3); Church Yth Grp; Cmnty Wkr; French Clb; JA; Key Clb; Letterman Clb; Science Clb; Varsity Clb; Yrbk; Tennis; CA Schlrshp Fed; Mdcl.

SQUIRES, JENNIFER; Del Oro HS; Loomis, CA; (3); Pres Church Yth Grp; Pep Clb; Ski Clb; Spanish Clb; Varsity Clb; Drill Tm; Rep Jr Cls; VP Stu Cncl; Bsktbl; Cheerldng; BYU HI.

SREEKAKULA, RAVI K; John W North HS; Riverside, CA; (4); Debate Tm; Intnl Clb; Key Clb; Model UN; Scholastic Bowl; SADD; Nwsp; Lit Mag; Bsktbl; High Hon Roll; Jr Statesmen Of Amer Pres; U Of CA Santa Cruz.

SRI JAERAJAH, KRISHANI; Paraclete HS; Palmdale, CA; (3); 4/138; Cmnty Wkr; Drama Clb; Hosp Aide; Key Clb; Stage Crew; High Hon Roll; NHS; Piano Branch & Fstvl Hnrs; Violin Branch Hnrs; Dance Tamils Of CA Hnrs; Pre-Med.

SRIDHAR, ANGIE N; Canyon HS; Anaheim, CA; (1); Computer Clb; Drama Clb; GAA; Spanish Clb; Varsity Clb; Tennis; Trk; Cit Awd; High Hon Roll; Hon Roll; Med.

SRIJAERAJAH, KRISHANI; Paraclete HS; Quartz Hill, CA; (3); 1/150; Cmnty Wkr; Drama Clb; Hosp Aide; Key Clb; Stage Crew; High Hon Roll; Hon Roll; NHS; Suzuki Music-Violin, Piano; Hnrs Awd; Tchr Merit Awd; Fnd Raiser Tamil Assn Amer; Hnrs Dance; Harvard; Pre-Med.

SRIJEMAC, ROBERT; Mission San Jose HS; Fremont, CA; (1); 93/466; Science Clb; Stu Cncl; Intrml Bsktbl; Intrml Crs Cntry; High Hon Roll; Hon Roll; Pres Acad Fit Awd; Ldrshp Cncl; Schl Rcgntn Golden ST Exam Algbr I; John Hopkins U; Gntc Engr.

SRINIVASAN, RAMYA; Corona SR HS; Corona, CA; (3); Drama Clb; French Clb; Rptr Nwsp; High Hon Roll; Ntl Merit Ltr; Pres Acad Fit Awd; Dcthln; CSF Mem; Corono Cmmty Hosp Vlntr; Gntcs.

SRIPIPATANA, ALEX A; Woodrow Wilson HS; Long Beach, CA; (3); Orch; Var Ftbl; High Hon Roll; Berkeley; Bus Law.

SRISAMANG, RICHARD E; Whitney HS; Cerritos, CA; (3); JA; Key Clb; Off Jr Cls; JV Tennis; Hon Roll; Waterpolo JV; Engrng.

ST CHARLES, LELAND S; Apple Valley HS; Apple Valley, CA; (2); Spanish Clb; Key Clb; JV Tennis; Hon Roll; Schl Diablos Del Sol Span Clb; Hnrs Engl 89 & 90; 1st Pl Victor Vly Tnns Tourn.

ST CLAIR, AMY L; Brea-Olinda HS; Brea, CA; (1); Pres Frsh Cls; Stu Cncl; JV Gym; JV Tennis; High Hon Roll; Jr NHS; U Of CA Santa Barbara; Med.

ST CLAIR, TRISHA M; Mira Loma HS; Sacramento, CA; (4); 2/300; Ed Lit Mag; High Hon Roll; Lion Awd; NHS; Ntl Merit Ltr; Sec Art Clb; Cmnty Wkr; Sec French Clb; Math Clb; Science Clb; Ntl Cncl Tchrs Engl Awd; Prncpls Awd; Acadmc Decath Tm; Sci Olympc Tm; Stu Of Mnth Vars Subjcts; Occidental; Liberal Arts.

ST JOHN, CINDY K; Loyalton HS; Calpine, CA; (3); Dance Clb; Drama Clb; VP FBLA; Ed Nwsp; Ed Yrbk; Rep Stu Cncl; JV L Cheerldng; Var L Sftbl; Var L Vllybl; High Hon Roll; 3rd Pl Entrprnrshp Sctn FBLA Cmptn; Outstndng Spnsh Stu.

ST JOHN, SHANE K; Chaffey HS; Ontario, CA; (2); Church Yth Grp; Teachers Aide; Varsity Clb; JV Capt Bsktbl; JV Ftbl; Hon Roll; Prfct Atten Awd; UNLV; Bus.

ST JOHN, TIFFANY E; Manteca HS; Manteca, CA; (3); 117/336; Church Yth Grp; FBLA; Key Clb; Church Choir; Hon Roll; Vlntr Wrk Mickey Grove Zoo; Delta Coll; Animal Trainer.

ST JOVITE, TOM A; Casa Grande HS; Petaluma, CA; (2); Drama Clb; High Hon Roll; Hon Roll; Jr NHS; U Of San Francisco; Pharm.

ST LOUIS, CAROL D; Bullard HS; Fresno, CA; (4); 1/525; Capt Debate Tm; German Clb; Intnl Clb; Math Tm; Model UN; Pres NFL; Speech Tm; Rep Soph Cls; JETS Awd; Ntl Merit SF; Natl Cncl Tchrs Engl Cmmndtn; UC Coll Crative Stud 2nd Pl Bio; Cal Poly Frnscs Invit 1st Pl Tm Dbte; UCLA; Economics.

STAATS, ANGELA M; Palmdale HS; Agua Dulce, CA; (3); 45/642; Capt Dance Clb; Sec Treas Drama Clb; Key Clb; VP SADD; Capt Drill Tm; Ed Yrbk; Hon Roll; CSF; Hmcmng Prncss; Miss Agua Dulce; Cmnty Qn; CA ST U Northridge; Fine Arts.

STAATS, LAURA L; Paraclete HS; Palmdale, CA; (3); GAA; Spanish Clb; SADD; Varsity Clb; Variety Show; Var Sftbl; Pres Acad Fit Awd; All CIF Southern CA 88-89, 89-90; All-League 87-88, 88-89, 89-90; All-Valley 89-90; Commnctns.

STABE, JUSTIN M; Oakmont HS; Roseville, CA; (1); Church Yth Grp; Band.

STABEN, GRACIELA E; Terra Nova HS; Pacifica, CA; (2); Hon Roll; San Francisco ST U; Accntng.

STABER, SHANNON M; San Pedro HS; San Pedro, CA; (2); Church Yth Grp; GAA; Office Aide; Bsktbl; Sftbl; Hon Roll; Princpls Hnr Roll 3.0; Nrsng.

STABIO, MICHELLE; Bonita HS; La Verne, CA; (1); French Clb; Hon Roll; Envrnmntl Clb SAVE; UC Davis; Sci Vet.

STACHELEK, ELLEN J; University City HS; San Diego, CA; (3); Church Yth Grp; Pres Pep Clb; SADD; Phtg Yrbk; Crs Cntry; Mgr(s); Powder Puff Ftbl; JV Sftbl; JV Vllybl; High Hon Roll; CSF-SEC/Histrn; Art Dept Awd; Young Art 90; Intl Exhibition-Japan; Design.

STACK, NICOLE L; El Toro HS; El Toro, CA; (3); 50/510; French Clb; Band; Drm Mjr(t); Jazz Band; Mrchg Band; Orch; School Musical; High Hon Roll; Mck Trl; CSF; Yng Astrnts Amer Inst; Santa Clara; Sci.

STACKER, SHARON; St Michaels HS; Los Angeles, CA; (3); Church Yth Grp; Cmnty Wkr; Hosp Aide; School Play; Yrbk; Hon Roll; Xavier U; Bus Admin.

STACKS, DEVRA; Lindhurst HS; Olivehurst, CA; (4); 6/173; Am Leg Aux Girls St; Sec Frsh Cls; Sec Soph Cls; Sec Jr Cls; Sec Stu Cncl; Var Capt Bsktbl; Var Capt Sftbl; Var Capt Vllybl; DAR Awd; Prfct Atten Awd; MVP, All Lge, All Area; CA ST U Sacramento; Comp Sci.

STACKS, GEOFFREY LAYNE; Lompoc HS; Lompoc, CA; (4); 4/300; Am Leg Boys St; Church Yth Grp; SADD; Band; Church Choir; Jazz Band; Pres Treas Mrchg Band; Orch; Pep Band; School Musical; Bank Amer Awd Music; Natl J P Sousa Music Awd; CA Baptist Coll.

STACY, LISA M; Lemoore HS; Lemoore, CA; (2); FFA; FHA; Girl Scts; Spanish Clb; Elks Awd; High Hon Roll; Clss Prncss 88-89; CSF; Coll Of Sequoias; Landscpg Arch.

STACY, SANDRA D; Liberty Union HS; Oakley, CA; (4); 4-H; FFA; Ski Clb; Teachers Aide; Chorus; Orch; 4-H Awd; Hon Roll; FFA Awd; Los Medanos Jr Coll; Accntnt.

STACY, STEPHANIE; Valley Christian HS; San Jose, CA; (2); Cheerldng.

STACY, TINA L; Redlands HS; Redlands, CA; (3); Drama Clb; Pep Clb; Thesps; School Play; Stage Crew; Co-Ed Yrbk; Cal ST Fullerton; Art.

STADLER, BRYAN J; Don Antonio Lugo HS; Chino, CA; (2); Boy Scts; Band; Jazz Band; Mrchg Band; Pep Band; High Hon Roll; NHS; Prfct Atten Awd; CSF; Geom Golden St Exam Hnrs; Arch.

STADLER, MIKE D; El Cajon Valley HS; El Cajon, CA; (2); 2/496; Church Yth Grp; Letterman Clb; Var Bsbl; Var Bsktbl; JV Ftbl; Wt Lftg; Hon Roll; Masonic Awd.

STADLER, TAO A; Santa Cruz HS; Santa Cruz, CA; (2); Letterman Clb; Tennis; Hon Roll; UC Davis; Arch.

STADLER, TINA M; Livermore HS; Livermore, CA; (3); Treas Sec 4-H; Office Aide; Pep Clb; Rep Jr Cls; Var L Socr; Var Trk; 4-H Awd; High Hon Roll; Prfct Atten Awd; CSF; Goldn St Exam Alg & Geom Hnrs.

STADNYK, GEOFF G; Carlsbad HS; Carlsbad, CA; (3); Boy Scts; Acpl Chr; Chorus; Stu Cncl; Bsbl; Socr.

STAFFORD, BILLY J; Casa Grande HS; Petaluma, CA; (2); Rptr Nwsp; Hon Roll; Svc Awd Vlntr Wrk Hamilton AFB; CA Intl Air Show; Jrnlsm.

STAFFORD, CHRISTIAN G; Gossmont HS; La Mesa, CA; (3); 98/435; Debate Tm; Key Clb; NFL; Ski Clb; Speech Tm; Varsity Clb; Rep Stu Cncl; Var L Socr; Var L Tennis; Hon Roll; CSF; ASB Commissoner Sales; UCSB; Adv.

STAFFORD, DAVID; Monte Vista Christian HS; Folsom, CA; (4); 5/88; Church Yth Grp; Teachers Aide; Chorus; Hon Roll; CA Schlrshp Fed; Amer River JC; Comp.

STAFFORD, JAMES M; St Francis HS; Sunnyvale, CA; (4); 6/326; Intnl Clb; Letterman Clb; Math Clb; Pep Clb; Science Clb; Service Clb; Pres SADD; JV Var Bsbl; High Hon Roll; NHS; UC Los Angeles; Elec Engrng.

STAFFORD, JENNIFER E; Novato HS; Novato, CA; (1); ROTC; Band; Color Guard; Drill Tm; Flag Corp; Mrchg Band; JV Socr; Hon Roll; Dghtrs Of Fndrs/Patrons America; Astronaut.

STAFFORD, MI KEESHA; Mc Clymonds HS; Oakland, CA; (3); 2/140; Cmnty Wkr; Dance Clb; GAA; Math Clb; Spanish Clb; Varsity Clb; Band; Chorus; Jazz Band; Pep Band; Mills Coll; Psych.

STAFFORD, MOLLY L; Montgomery HS; Kenwood, CA; (3); Cmnty Wkr; VP Sec Spanish Clb; Pres Band; VP Sec Jazz Band; Ed Nwsp; Ed Yrbk; Crs Cntry; Socr; JV Trk; Wt Lftg; Mst Imprvd Ply Vrsty Sccr; N Coast Schlr Athlte Vrsty Sccr; Psych.

STAFFORD, SHELLEY A; Tri-City Christian HS; Oceanside, CA; (2); Church Yth Grp; Church Choir; Rep Frsh Cls; Rep Soph Cls; Stat Bsktbl; Tennis; Var Vllybl; Hon Roll; Christian Heritage Coll; Mssnry.

STAFNE, ERIKA J; Redwood Christian HS; San Leandro, CA; (4); 4/34; Church Yth Grp; Off Sr Cls; Var L Cheerldng; Var L Crs Cntry; Var L Socr; Var L Trk; High Hon Roll; Ntl Merit SF; Parable; Med Dr.

STAGG, DANIELLE; St Genevieve HS; Reseda, CA; (3); 4/160; Church Yth Grp; Drama Clb; French Clb; SADD; School Play; Var Socr; High Hon Roll; NEDT Awd; Mck Trial Cmptn Sponsored By Constitutional Rights Fndtn; Outstndg Achvt In Frnch 2 & 3; Child Services.

STAGG, SEANINE; St Genevieve HS; Reseda, CA; (3); 7/165; Church Yth Grp; Drama Clb; SADD; Ed Nwsp; Yrbk; High Hon Roll; Hon Roll; NEDT Awd; Opt Clb Awd; CSF.

STAGGERS, LA RHONDA; Inglewood HS; Inglewood, CA; (2); Church Yth Grp; JA; Cit Awd; Hon Roll; Prfct Atten Awd; Essay & Spch Cntsts; Prep SAT Clses; UC Brkly; Crmnl Law.

STAHL, DENNIS; Bonita HS; La Verne, CA; (2); French Clb; Bsbl; Wrstlng; Pres Acad Fit Awd; MVP Awd JV Bsbl; Mst Imprvd Var Wrstlr; CA ST Fullerton.

STAHL, SARAH; University HS; Irvine, CA; (2); Cmnty Wkr; Hosp Aide; JCL; Latin Clb; Teachers Aide; Swmmng; JV Vllybl; Natl Charity Leag.

STAHLMAN, PATTY; Notre Dame HS; San Mateo, CA; (2); Church Yth Grp; Cmnty Wkr; Debate Tm; 4-H; Hosp Aide; Model UN; Chorus; Church Choir; School Musical; School Play; UCLA; Actress.

STAINES, AARON A; La Sierra HS; Riverside, CA; (3); Teachers Aide; DAR Awd; Prfct Atten Awd; Wrtng; Writer.

STAJKOWSKI, MICHELE; King City Joint Union HS; San Ardo, CA; (2); 4-H; SADD; Cheerldng; Crs Cntry; Pom Pon; Trk; 4-H Awd; Prfct Atten Awd; Pres Acad Fit Awd; Friday Night Live Clb; Safe Rides; Interact; MI ST Coll; Nurse.

STALCUP, MEG M; Skyline HS; Oakland, CA; (3); Cmnty Wkr; Debate Tm; Red Cross Aide; Score Keeper; High Hon Roll; NHS; Pres Acad Fit Awd; Rotary Awd; Chorus; Yrbk; Golden ST Exam Geom & US Hstry; EARO; Amnesty Intl.

STALCUP, THEODORE D; Skyline HS; Oakland, CA; (4); 170/590; Hosp Aide; Letterman Clb; SADD; Varsity Clb; Capt Crs Cntry; Var Trk; Hon Roll; Ntl Merit SF; Sccr Coach-Jnr Leag; U Of CA Berkeley; Law.

STALDER, ANDREA K; Nordhoff HS; Ojai, CA; (4); 11/160; Science Clb; Sec Chorus; Church Choir; Tennis; High Hon Roll; Jr NHS; NHS; Pres Acad Fit Awd; CA Poly Pomona; Anml Sci.

STALDER, ANNE; Mission College Preparatory HS; San Luis Obispo, CA; (3); Key Clb; Service Clb; Teachers Aide; Chorus; Yrbk; JV Crs Cntry; Var Trk; High Hon Roll; Hon Roll; Co Fndr & Co Pres Envrnmntl Clb; Campus Mnstry.

STALEY, BECKY; Desert Christian HS; Lancaster, CA; (2); Church Yth Grp; Drama Clb; Hosp Aide; Yrbk; High Hon Roll; CA Baptist Coll.

STALLINGS, LORREY M; Helix HS; La Mesa, CA; (2); 32/449; Drama Clb; SADD; Pres Band; Score Keeper; Orch; Pep Band; School Play; Hgh Hnrs-Alg & Geo; Outstndg Stu Band; 1st Chair Tuba Band & Orch; UCLA; Actrss.

STALLINGS, MELISSA R; Bakersfield HS; Bakersfield, CA; (3); 83/691; Church Yth Grp; Cmnty Wkr; Band; Mrchg Band; Hon Roll; Tae-Kwon-Do Prpl Blt; Emrgncy Anml Clnc Vlntr; Abilene Chrstn U; Vet.

STALLINGS, SHARON; Foothill HS; Pleasanton, CA; (2); Church Yth Grp; Pep Clb; SADD; High Hon Roll; JV Cheerldng; JV Pom Pon; Var Swmmng.

STALLWORTH, LA TONYA M; Pittsburg HS; Pittsburg, CA; (4); 44/277; Cmnty Wkr; Dance Clb; Treas Science Clb; VP Ski Clb; School Play; Sec Sr Cls; Stu Cncl; Stat Bsktbl; Var VP Vllybl; Hon Roll; Homecoming Queen 89-90; Anthony S Belleci Perp Mem Schlrshp 89-90; Rainbow Ben Soc Schlrshp 89-90; FL A&M U; Bus Admin.

STALLWORTH III, LAWRENCE; Grant Union HS; North Highlands, CA; (4); Art Clb; Ftbl; Powder Puff Ftbl; Hon Roll; Schlrshp Awd Art; Schlrshp Awd Acad, Athltcs Omega Psi Phi Frat; NE Lincoln U; Bio Sci.

STALLWORTH, NICOLE D; Gardena HS; Compton, CA; (4); Sec Church Yth Grp; Debate Tm; Drama Clb; JA; NFL; Spanish Clb; Speech Tm; Band; Color Guard; Drill Tm; Yng Blck Schlrs; 1st Pl All City Speech Chmpnshp Frnsc Team; Johnson C Smith; Crmnl Jstc.

STALLWORTH, REIMONT A; Luther Burbank HS; Sacramento, CA; (3); Boy Scts; Church Yth Grp; Church Choir; Bsktbl; Ftbl; Vllybl; Cit Awd; Prof Bsktbl; CA ST.

STALTERI, JENNIFER; Village Christian HS; Sylmar, CA; (4); Cmnty Wkr; Office Aide; Teachers Aide; Chorus; Stage Crew; Variety Show; Pom Pon; Prfct Atten Awd; Woodbury U; Interior Dsgn.

STAMBAUGH, KELLY; Campbell Hall HS; Sherman Oaks, CA; (1); Ski Clb; Var Cheerldng; Var Sftbl; Hon Roll; USC; Pediatrics.

STAMBOULIAN, ARLETTE B; Holy Martyrs HS; Northridge, CA; (2); Sec Stu Cncl; Cheerldng; Hon Roll; AYF; Univ Of CA Irvine; Law.

STAMER, PAUL L; Fontana HS; Fontana, CA; (3); 49/1051; Am Leg Boys St; Church Yth Grp; VP Frsh Cls; Var L Ftbl; High Hon Roll; Hon Roll; Pres Acad Fit Awd.

STAMIROWSKI, SUSAN; Notre Dame HS; Belmont, CA; (2); Chorus; Church Choir; JV Bsktbl; JV Swmmng; Hon Roll; Crmnl Lawyer.

STAMP, LISA M; Mater Dei HS; Irvine, CA; (3); Ski Clb; SADD; Stu Cncl; Crs Cntry; Hon Roll; Dance Ballet Tap & Jazz; Marine.

STAMPER, CRYSTAL N; Coalinga HS; Coalinga, CA; (2); Stat Bsktbl; Stat Crs Cntry; Score Keeper; Stat Trk; Elks Awd; High Hon Roll; Hon Roll; Jr NHS; Pres Acad Fit Awd; US Santa Cruz; Marine Bio.

STAMPER, HARLEN L; Turlock HS; Turlock, CA; (3); Science Clb; Ftbl; Tennis; Medi-Careers Clb; Modesto JC; Law Enfrcmnt.

STAMPLEY, THOMASINA; Crenshaw HS; Los Angeles, CA; (2); Church Yth Grp; Dance Clb; GAA; SADD; Band; Church Choir; Drm Mjr(t); Jazz Band; Mrchg Band; Nwsp; UC Santa Barbara; Bus.

STANARD, JONATHON E; Eureka HS; Eureka, CA; (2); Boy Scts; Key Clb; Brigham Young U; Archtctr.

STANARD, TRICIA; La Sierra HS; Riverside, CA; (1); Church Yth Grp; Girl Scts; Pep Clb; SADD; Teachers Aide; Varsity Clb; JV Cheerldng; Var Swmmng; Hon Roll; Most Val Var Swimmer.

STANBRIDGE, HELENA; Corona Del Mar HS; Corona Del Mar, CA; (3); AFS; Debate Tm; Drama Clb; VP English Clb; Speech Tm; Thesps; School Play; Stage Crew; Masonic Awd; Ntl Merit Ltr; Vrsty Badmntn.

STANCIL, DENNIS S; Nevada Union HS; Grass Valley, CA; (3); 126/551; Socr; Hon Roll; Sierra Coll; Wrtng.

STANCIL, JENNIFER; Saint Ignatius College Prep; Daly City, CA; (1); Cmnty Wkr; Debate Tm; Model UN; Speech Tm; Variety Show; Rptr Nwsp; Sec Frsh Cls; High Hon Roll; Hon Roll; NHS; CSF; Jr Stsmn Of Am; Itln Cath Fed Schlrshp; Stnfrd U; Pltcl Law.

STANCIL, VALERIE; Bonita Vista HS; Bonita, CA; (3); Cmnty Wkr; Dance Clb; Girl Scts; Office Aide; Pep Clb; SADD; Teachers Aide; Church Choir; Variety Show; Cheerldng; NANBPW Cotillion Deb; Law.

STANDART, JENNIFER L; Modesto HS; Modesto, CA; (1); Prfct Atten Awd; Bowling; Stu Curriculum Cmmttee; CA Schlstc Fed; Modesto JC; Tchng.

STANDLEE, PAMELA L; Hueneme HS; Port Hueneme, CA; (3); 165/302; Dance Clb; Drama Clb; Latin Clb; Pep Clb; SADD; Thesps; Drill Tm; School Musical; Off Jr Cls; JV Trk; Harvard; Law.

STANESCU, OANA; Redondo Union HS; Redondo Beach, CA; (4); 25/400; Math Clb; Math Tm; Science Clb; Lit Mag; High Hon Roll; Pres Acad Fit Awd; Synchrnzd Swim Team; Stu For Scl & Envrnmntl Awrnss; UC Irvine Admssn With Dstnctn; UCLA; Math.

STANEVICIUS, ANDREW R; Torrey Pines HS; Rancho Santa Fe, CA; (2); Var Wrstlng; UCLA; Mech Engr.

STANFORD, ERIKA L; Compton HS; Compton, CA; (2); Dance Clb; Pep Clb; Church Choir; Cheerldng; Hon Roll; Stanford; Pediatrics.

STANFORD, LAURIE; Sunny Hills HS; Fullerton, CA; (1); Church Yth Grp; Cmnty Wkr; Hosp Aide; Pep Clb; Spanish Clb; Teachers Aide; Acpl Chr; Cheerldng; Gym; Score Keeper; Natl Chrty Leag; Soph Yr Stu Govt; UC; Law.

STANFORD, SCOTT; Hesperia Christian Schl; Hesperia, CA; (1); Church Yth Grp; Band; JV Ftbl; Hon Roll; Prfct Atten Awd; Arch.

STANFORD, SCOTT M; Nevada Union HS; Chicago Park, CA; (3); Church Yth Grp; Var Socr; Hon Roll.

STANFORD, WENDY E; Foothill HS; Santa Ana, CA; (3); 11/316; Cmnty Wkr; VP Dance Clb; Drama Clb; Service Clb; Sec Treas Spanish Clb; Flag Corp; School Musical; School Play; Cit Awd; High Hon Roll; Keywanettes VP; PTO Outstndng Spnsh Stu; Law.

STANGER, DANIEL LEE; Orange Glen HS; Escondido, CA; (4); Art Clb; Drama Clb; Science Clb; Church Choir; School Musical; School Play; Stage Crew; Variety Show; Phtg Yrbk; Intrml Bsktbl; UCLA; Filmaker.

STANGLAND, MIYONG L; 29 Palms SR HS; Twentynine Palms, CA; (3); Library Aide; Teachers Aide; Hon Roll; Prfct Atten Awd; Stu Store Cert; Sls & Mrchndsng Clss Cert; Nrsg.

STANIER, KRISTINA; Bella Vista HS; Fair Oaks, CA; (2); 2/420; Math Tm; Pep Clb; Cheerldng; Spanish NHS; SRO; Girls Senate; Spec Awds Economics, Span, Math.

STANIMIROVICH, JESSE; Sweetwater Union HS; National City, CA; (2); 42/589; Church Yth Grp; Computer Clb; Library Aide; Math Tm; Office Aide; Scholastic Bowl; Stage Crew; Cit Awd; Hon Roll; Prfct Atten Awd; Lgl Atty.

STANIOTES, ANTHONY M; St Ignatius College Prep; San Francisco, CA; (3); 20/244; Cmnty Wkr; Teachers Aide; Hon Roll; U Of San Francisco; Medical.

STANKA, MICHAEL S; Victor Valley HS; Victorville, CA; (2); Computer Clb; Spanish Clb; ROP Awd; Stu Voc Olympics; Comp Prgmng.

STANKO, SCOTT A; University HS; Irvine, CA; (3); 148/551; Church Yth Grp; AYSO Yth Coach; Aerospace.

STANKOVICH, ALEXANDRA M; Notre Dame HS; San Jose, CA; (3); Library Aide; Office Aide; Teachers Aide; Thesps; Stage Crew; Hon Roll; Milpts Rnbw Theatr-Outstndng Prsn Of Yr & Yth Dir Intrnshp; HS Outstndng Achvt-Crmcs & Art; San Jose ST; Art.

STANLEY, BUMPER S; Tehachapi HS; Tehachapi, CA; (2); JV Ftbl; Wt Lftg; Capt Var Wrstlng; MIP Vsty Wrstlng; Desert-Inyo League Outstndng Wrstlr; Tchr.

STANLEY, CAWANDE D; Canyon Springs HS; Moreno Valley, CA; (3); Letterman Clb; Pep Clb; SADD; Varsity Clb; Var Capt Bsktbl; Hon Roll; Pres Acad Fit Awd; CSF; Bus.

STANLEY, JAMES; University HS; Irvine, CA; (2); 40/550; Intrml Mgr Bsktbl; High Hon Roll; Hon Roll; Engl Laureate Awd 90.

STANLEY, JENENE E; St Paul HS; Whittier, CA; (3); Church Yth Grp; Girl Scts; Church Choir; School Musical; School Play; Native Dghtrs Gldn West; US Postal Svc Spcl Achvt Awd; Mount St Marys; Phys Thrpy.

STANLEY, JENET N; Narbonne HS; Harbor City, CA; (3); Church Yth Grp; Teachers Aide; School Play; Hon Roll; Outstndng Stu; Amer Stds Dept Awd; CA ST Long Bch; Doctor.

STANLEY, KATRINA; Dixon HS; Dixon, CA; (1); Cmnty Wkr; Pep Clb; SADD; School Musical; Variety Show; Pres Frsh Cls; JV Cheerldng; Var Tennis; Lions Clb Spch Cont Rnnr Up; UC Davis; Ob/Gyn.

STANLEY, TAMMIE L; Sequoia HS; Redwood City, CA; (3); 12/487; Teachers Aide; Sftbl; Vllybl; CA Schlrshp Fed; Young Life; Sacramento ST; Psych.

STANMAN, DEYA; Palisades HS; Topanga, CA; (4); Cmnty Wkr; Hosp Aide; JA; Ski Clb; SADD; Chorus; Stu Cncl; JV Vllybl; Hon Roll; Close Up Prog; Namaste Pres; Promising Yng Wrtrs Awd; Anthro.

STANNARD, DENISE M; South Pasadena HS; South Pasadena, CA; (4); Drama Clb; Science Clb; Spanish Clb; Chorus; Orch; School Musical; Ed Lit Mag; USGF Cmptr Lvl 9 Gymnstcs; Ballet; Piano; Sngng.

STANSBURY, DONNA M; Hayward HS; Modesto, CA; (1); Spanish Clb; School Musical; Filam Soc; Med.

STANSFIELD, ALLISON; Del Campo HS; Carmichael, CA; (3); 25/460; Church Yth Grp; Cmnty Wkr; Pep Clb; Capt Drill Tm; Socr; Swmmng; Tennis; High Hon Roll; NHS; Spnsh Exchng Pgm; CSF.

STANTON, LISL S; Torrey Pines HS; Del Mar, CA; (2); Teachers Aide; Peer Cnslng; NAU Flagstaff.

STANTON, RA NAE M; Los Amigos HS; Fountain Valley, CA; (3); 2/301; Church Yth Grp; Dance Clb; Treas German Clb; Hosp Aide; Key Clb; Science Clb; Chorus; Church Choir; High Hon Roll; Orange Cty Acad Decathlon; UC Riverside; Physician.

STANTON, SUSAN S; Butte Valley HS; Dorris, CA; (2); 3/24; FHA; Yrbk; High Hon Roll; CSF 89-90; Yng Wrtrs Cmp 88 & 89; Job Dghtrs Qun, St Membrshp Trphy 90; Job Dghtrs Grnd Rep WI 89-90; Linfield Coll; Cmnctns.

STANWOOD, SHELLEY; Palmdale HS; Palmdale, CA; (2); 47/850; VP JA; Sec Temple Yth Grp; CSF; UCSB.

STAPCHUK, KIM; Saddleback HS; Santa Ana, CA; (3); Church Yth Grp; Band; Mrchg Band; Pep Band; Rep Stu Cncl; JV Bsktbl; Var Tennis; Trk; High Hon Roll; CA Schlrshp Fdrtn; Mst Outstndng Band; Med.

STAPLES, WAYNE H; Downtown Business Magnet HS; Los Angeles, CA; (3); Library Aide; Jazz Band; Orch; Var Sftbl.

STAPLETON, KRISTIE A; North HS; Bakersfield, CA; (3); Church Yth Grp; Drama Clb; English Clb; Pep Clb; Spanish Clb; Teachers Aide; School Musical; School Play; Stage Crew; Var Socr; Intrct Clb; U Of CA Santa Barbara; Engl.

STAPLETON, REBEKAH R; Seaside HS; Marina, CA; (2); Hon Roll; Mst Outstndng Stu PE Unit.

STAR, SHADEE; Lynbrook HS; San Jose, CA; (3); French Clb; Hosp Aide; Pep Clb; Service Clb; Acpl Chr; Rep Stu Cncl; Var Capt Cheerldng; Hon Roll; NHS; Golden St Exam Algebra Hnrs Recogntn; Dentistry.

STARK, ANN MARIE; Mission Viejo HS; Mission Viejo, CA; (4); 20/450; Band; Mrchg Band; Orch; Pep Band; School Musical; JV Tennis; Var Trk; Grls Leag Pblcty Chrmn; Cert Mrt Piano, Hnrbl Mntn Bach, Fstvl; U Of CA Los Angeles.

STARKEY, ADAM; Arcata HS; Arcata, CA; (1); Yrbk; Off Frsh Cls; Soph Cls; Stu Cncl; Ftbl; Cit Awd; Top 10 Fresh Cls; Spcl Recognition For Publshng Schl Accntblty Card 89-90; UCLA; Engrng.

STARKEY, DON W; Cardova SR HS; Rancho Cordova, CA; (3); 7/550; FBLA; Model UN; Speech Tm; Rep Soph Cls; Sec Treas Jr Cls; Stu Cncl; High Hon Roll; Lion Awd; Masonic Awd; NHS; Folsom-Cordova USD Schl Bd; Working In Wells Fargo Bank As Teller; On Dist SAB & CAC; Stanford U; Pre-Law.

STARKEY, KELLYN M; Poway HS; Poway, CA; (3); Drama Clb; Girl Scts; Band; Mrchg Band; Orch; Pep Band; School Musical; Stage Crew; Powder Puff Ftbl; Cit Awd; UCLA; Marine Bio.

STARKEY, KEVIN K; Will C Wood HS; Vacaville, CA; (2); Teachers Aide; JV Capt Bsktbl; Hon Roll; NC; Med.

STARKOVICH, MICHAEL W; Davis SR HS; Davis, CA; (2); Band; Pep Band; Swmmng; Cal Poly San Luis Obispo; Engr.

STARKS, KATRINA M; Valley HS; Sacramento, CA; (4); 76/485; Dance Clb; Math Tm; Teachers Aide; School Play; Rep Stu Cncl; Hon Roll; Prfct Atten Awd; MESA & CSF; African Amer Stu Assoc; News Brdcstr.

STARKS, MAXWELL E; Ventura HS; Fresno, CA; (2); Band; Jazz Band; Mrchg Band; Orch; Pep Band; Fresno ST; Psych.

STARN, KATHERINE; Fred C Beyer HS; Modesto, CA; (4); 51/501; Cmnty Wkr; Pres Sec 4-H; Teachers Aide; Rep Capt Color Guard; Cit Awd; 4-H Awd; Hon Roll; CA Bus Wk Delg 89; Patriot Awd Mdl Wnnr Bus; GATE Stu; CSF; U Pacific; Bus.

STASSUN, KEIVAN; Sherman Oaks CES HS; Encino, CA; (4); 2/100; Boy Scts; VP Debate Tm; NFL; Q&S; VP Speech Tm; School Play; Ed Nwsp; Var L Vllybl; Ntl Merit SF; Sal; US Naval Acad; Astronautics.

STATEN, PHILIP M; San Marcos HS; Santa Barbara, CA; (3); French Clb; Key Clb; Ed Nwsp; Var Bsktbl; Var Tennis; CSF; Bus.

STATHEM, MICHAEL E; Del Campo HS; Fair Oaks, CA; (2); 10/460; SADD; VP Frsh Cls; Treas Soph Cls; Chrmn Jr Cls; JV Capt Bsktbl; JV Capt Ftbl; High Hon Roll; 4 X Recipient Of Cougar AAA Awd; Hnrs Awd Geom Golden St Awd 89; Math.

STATTON, DAVID C; Miramonte HS; Lafayette, CA; (2); Latin Clb; JV Ftbl; JV Trk; High Hon Roll; CSF; Engrng.

STAUB, WENDY D; Independence HS; San Jose, CA; (3); Cmnty Wkr; Service Clb; Var Swmmng; Environmental Protection Club; Outstndng Woman Recgntn Frm Independence; U Of Santa Barbara; Marine Bio.

STAUB, YVONNE V; Clovis West HS; Clovis, CA; (3); Chorus; Color Guard; Hon Roll; Dnc.

STAUBER, DEBORAH J; Santa Monica HS; Malibu, CA; (3); Band; Orch; Hon Roll; Equestrian Competitions; Interscholastic Equestrian League; Junion Statesman Of America; Equestrian Science.

STAUBER, ERIK O; Mountain View HS; Los Altos, CA; (3); 34/319; Band; Jazz Band; Mrchg Band; Orch; Pep Band; School Musical; Avid Cyclist; UC Santa Cruz; Physics.

STAUFENBEIL, TIMOTHY B; Valhalla HS; Jamul, CA; (2); Ski Clb; Spanish Clb; Teachers Aide; Wt Lftg; Cit Awd; Hon Roll; San Diego ST U.

STAUSS, JADE; Fairfield HS; Fairfield, CA; (4); Church Yth Grp; Cmnty Wkr; SADD; Teachers Aide; School Play; Stage Crew; Variety Show; Bsktbl; High Hon Roll; Hon Roll; Westmont Coll; Law.

STAVELEY, SARA E; Irvine HS; Irvine, CA; (3); 120/575; AFS; Dance Clb; Pep Clb; Ski Clb; Spanish Clb; Band; Mrchg Band; Variety Show; Vllybl; Hon Roll; UC; Langs.

STAVERS, JASON B; Crystal Springs Uplands HS; San Mateo, CA; (4); 3/65; Church Yth Grp; FFA; Hosp Aide; Temple Yth Grp; Drill Tm; Ed Nwsp; Capt Pom Pon; Var Vllybl; High Hon Roll; Ntl Merit SF; Fnded Chrstns For Satan Chptr At Schl; Oral Roberts U; Satanism.

STAVROULAKIS, CHRIS; Victor Valley HS; Victorville, CA; (2); Aud/Vis; Boy Scts; Drama Clb; Sec French Clb; JA; Rep Key Clb; Office Aide; SADD; Treas Jr Cls; Rep Stu Cncl; HOBY 90; Odessy Television Prod; UCLA; Television Exec.

STEADMAN, TAMMY; Mt Carmel HS; San Diego, CA; (4); Boy Scts; Pres Church Yth Grp; FBLA; Key Clb; Church Choir; Jr NHS; NHS; Prfct Atten Awd; Pres Acad Fit Awd; Fed-Mart Schlrshp; Natl Young Leaders Conf 90; BYU; Home Ec Ed.

STEANS, JASON B; Foothill HS; Sacramento, CA; (1); 7/425; JV Bsktbl; JV Ftbl; Socr; High Hon Roll; Hon Roll; Pres Acad Fit Awd.

STEARNS, CHARLIE I; Modoc HS; Alturas, CA; (2); 7/60; Band; Mrchg Band; Pep Band; Stage Crew; JV Trk; Hon Roll; Aviation Clb; Bicycling Clb; CA Schlrshp Fed; Comp Sci.

STEARNS, MICHELLE L; Atwater HS; Atwater, CA; (2); Treas Church Yth Grp; French Clb; FBLA; Key Clb; Church Choir; Mrchg Band; High Hon Roll; Acctng.

STECK, KIMBERLY R; Ramona HS; Ramona, CA; (3); 63/294; Church Yth Grp; Dance Clb; FBLA; SADD; Teachers Aide; Var Mgr(s); JV Trk; JV Vllybl; Athl Trainer; Dance Concert; Amnesty Intl; San Diego ST U; Phys Thrpy.

STECK, SHAWN R; Thomas Downey HS; Modesto, CA; (1); Science Clb; Var L Socr; Comps; Boston Coll; Bus.

STECKEL, EILEEN M; Alta Loma HS; Rancho Cucamonga, CA; (2); Church Yth Grp; Powder Puff Ftbl; Hon Roll; Prfct Atten Awd; Stu Store Bus Mgmt; Med.

STECKER, THERESA N; Rancho Alamitos HS; Garden Grove, CA; (3); Dance Clb; Drill Tm; Ed Yrbk; Sec Stu Cncl; Stat Bsktbl; Var Cheerldng; Score Keeper; Swmmng; Hon Roll; NHS; Presndtl Clssrm; 4 Yr Lttr-Coaches Awd Swmmng; UC San Diego; Marine Bio.

STECKLER, JODY R; Point Arena HS; Pt Arena, CA; (4); Art Clb; Cmnty Wkr; JV Vllybl; Cit Awd; High Hon Roll; Bk Of Amer Achvt Awd In Soc Sci; Imprvmnt Awds In Engl, US Hstry & Civics; 1 Yr In Mexico Frgn Stu; Santa Barbara CA U; Grphc Arts.

STECKMEST, JULIA L.; Leland HS; San Jose, CA; (2); Church Yth Grp; Cmnty Wkr; Dance Clb; Key Clb; SADD; Drill Tm; Pom Pon; NHS; Yth Commsnr For City; Dance Fnlst 2nd Pl In Nation; Duke U; Poltcl Sci.

STEDDICK, JENNIFER A; College Park HS; Martinez, CA; (3); 47/350; Letterman Clb; Spanish Clb; Teachers Aide; Varsity Clb; Var L Crs Cntry; Var L Socr; Var L Trk; Hon Roll.

STEDMAN, TERESA; Coast Union HS; Cayucos, CA; (3); 1/64; AFS; Cmnty Wkr; FBLA; FFA; Spanish Clb; SADD; Teachers Aide; Nwsp; Treas Jr Cls; Var L Bsktbl; Natl Yng Ldrs Conf; CSF; US Air Force Acad; Comp Engrng.

STEEB, CHRISTOPHER G; Coast Union HS; Cambria, CA; (4); 10/68; Computer Clb; FBLA; FHA; Speech Tm; SADD; Teachers Aide; Varsity Clb; Yrbk; Rep Stu Cncl; Bsbl; MVP Bsktbl & Tennis; CSF; Best Athl 90; Cuesta Coll; Bus.

STEEL, JASON M; Fillmore HS; Fillmore, CA; (4); Church Yth Grp; FCA; Treas FFA; Teachers Aide; Jazz Band; Mrchg Band; School Play; Wrstlng; Cit Awd; Hon Roll; Ventura Cnty Jr Fair Brd Treas; Grnd Champn Heifer Calf & Veal Calf 89-90; St Shwmnshp 89-90; Ventura Coll; Fireman.

STEEL, PAMELA; Fillmore HS; Fillmore, CA; (2); Church Yth Grp; Cmnty Wkr; Dance Clb; FCA; JV Capt Pep Clb; Science Clb; SADD; Drill Tm; Treas Soph Cls; JV Capt Cheerldng; Bus.

STEELE, AMBER N; Colfax HS; Applegate, CA; (2); French Clb; Var Bsktbl.

STEELE, DIANE M; Montgomery HS; Santa Rosa, CA; (2); Church Yth Grp; Band; Mrchg Band; Var JV Vllybl; High Hon Roll; Hon Roll; Pres Acad Fit Awd; Outstndng Wld Hstry Achvt; Eng.

STEELE, ERIC; Westlake HS; Westlake Village, CA; (2); Church Yth Grp; Cmnty Wkr; Var L Crs Cntry; JV Socr; Var L Trk; Hon Roll; Prfct Atten Awd; Pres Acad Fit Awd; Gldn ST Awd Math.

STEELE, SUZANNA M; Tehachapi HS; Tehachapi, CA; (3); Church Yth Grp; Sec FHA; Chorus; Treas Color Guard; Off Jr Cls; Var Sftbl; JV Art Clb; Hon Roll; Jr Miss Contstnt 90; CA Miss Teen Pgnt 90; CA ST U Bakersfield; Music.

STEELE-IDEISHI, KELLI M; Moorpark HS; Moorpark, CA; (3); 13/225; Am Leg Aux Girls St; Key Clb; Teachers Aide; Stu Cncl; Stat Bsktbl; VP Sftbl; JV Vllybl; High Hon Roll; CYLC; Long Beach ST; Chld Psych.

STEELMAN, JILL; Los Angeles Baptist HS; Sunland, CA; (3); 5/102; Pres Church Yth Grp; French Clb; Thesps; Co-Capt Drill Tm; Lit Mag; Pres Jr Cls; JV Trk; Vllybl; Hon Roll; HOBY Ldrshp Smnr Ambssdr 1989.

STEENBERGEN, MELISSA; Santiago HS; Garden Grove, CA; (2); Church Yth Grp; Pep Clb; SADD; Rep Soph Cls; Rep Stu Cncl; Cheerldng; JV Swmmng; Hon Roll; Pres & Previously Treas Girls League; ORE; Bio.

STEENWERTH, KERRI L; Torrey Pines HS; Del Mar, CA; (3); 26/500; Church Yth Grp; Spanish Clb; Varsity Clb; Var Capt Jazz Band; JV Var Socr; High Hon Roll; CSF; Trvlng Sccr Tm 5 Yrs.

STEEVES, KELLY A; Bonita Vista HS; Chula Vista, CA; (1); Church Yth Grp; Rep Stu Cncl; JV Crs Cntry; JV Trk; Cit Awd; Schlrshp Awd; Hnrs On Alg Gldn ST Exam; U CA; Med.

STEFANAC, SUSAN M; Lincoln HS; Stockton, CA; (2); 3/568; Church Yth Grp; French Clb; Math Tm; SADD; Color Guard; JV Crs Cntry; Tennis; JV Trk; High Hon Roll; Jr NHS; CISV Norway Interchnge 89; Georgetown; Engl.

STEFANCIC, BENJAMIN L; George Washington HS; San Francisco, CA; (4); High Hon Roll; San Francisco ST U; Econ.

STEFFAN, HEATHER D; Arvin HS; Arvin, CA; (2); Church Yth Grp; Ski Clb; SADD; Chorus; Church Choir; Color Guard; Trk; Hon Roll; GATE.

STEFFANUS, KATHY J; Montclair HS; Ontario, CA; (2); Church Yth Grp; Pres FHA; Friends Are Important; Studying Hard; Trying My Best; Flight Attendant.

STEFFEN, AUDREY L; Kerman HS; Kerman, CA; (2); Letterman Clb; Varsity Clb; JV Var Bsktbl; Var Capt Swmmng; JV Var Vllybl; Hon Roll; CPA.

STEFFEY IV, LOTT C; Newbury Park HS; Newbury Park, CA; (4); 52/380; Crs Cntry; Trk; Wrstlng; CA Polytech U; Landscape Arch.

STEFFEY, MICHELE A; Davis SR HS; Davis, CA; (4); VP 4-H; Hist Key Clb; Yrbk; Var JV Bsktbl; 4-H Awd; Ntl Merit Schol; Pres Acad Fit Awd; AFS; Pep Clb; Spanish Clb; CSF; UCD Alumni Schlrshp; UCD Chancellors Awd; U CA Davis; Bio Sci.

STEFFY, JANELLE K; John W North HS; Riverside, CA; (3); Pres Church Yth Grp; Drama Clb; German Clb; Band; Chorus; Color Guard; Jazz Band; Mrchg Band; Pep Band; Hon Roll; BYU; Music.

STEGMAIER, LAURA M; Canyon Springs HS; Moreno Valley, CA; (1); Church Yth Grp; Pep Clb; JV Cheerldng; High Hon Roll; Hon Roll; Supts High Hnrs List; UCSD; Educ.

STEHLING, TIMOTHY J; Redlands HS; Redlands, CA; (3); 106/1000; School Musical; School Play; L Bsbl; L Bsktbl; Var JV Ftbl; Socr; Wt Lftg; Hon Roll; Pres Acad Fit Awd; Otstndng Schlrshp Ctznshp Dept Awds In Bus, Soc Stds & Health; Coachs Trnmnt Bsktbl Awfs & MVP Bsbl; Bus Mngmt.

STEIBER, HEIDI; Garces HS; Bakersfield, CA; (3); Cmnty Wkr; GAA; Office Aide; Service Clb; SADD; Var Tennis; High Hon Roll; Highly Ranked Natl Tennis Player; Pre-Law.

STEIDEL, MARIA C; Woodside HS; Redwood City, CA; (1); 19/278; Church Yth Grp; VP FBLA; Band; Church Choir; Nwsp; Off Frsh Cls; Off Soph Cls; Stu Cncl; Var Swmmng; Elks Awd; U CA Davis; Music.

STEIMLE, WES E; San Dieguito HS; Encinitas, CA; (2); 97/600.

STEIN, CANDICE L; Emerson HS; Anaheim, CA; (3); Yrbk; Chld Psych.

STEIN, CHAD D; California HS; San Ramon, CA; (4); Church Yth Grp; Teachers Aide; JV Bsbl; JV Capt Ftbl; Var Capt Socr; High Hon Roll; Hon Roll; CA Poly; Sci.

STEIN, COREY S; El Cajon Valley HS; El Cajon, CA; (4); 99/300; VP Dance Clb; Pres FTA; Intnl Clb; Office Aide; Teachers Aide; Variety Show; Stu Cncl; JV Var Cheerldng; Mgr(s); Wt Lftg; Head Mat Maid Wrstlng; Grossmont JC; Atty.

STEIN, JAKE J; Chaffey HS; Upland, CA; (3); Boy Scts; Band; Mrchg Band; Pep Band; Stage Crew; Tennis; High Hon Roll; Cal Poly Pomona; Eng.

STEIN, KEREN S; Einstein Acad; South Pasadena, CA; (1); Cmnty Wkr; JV Sftbl; Israel Scts Org.

STEIN, RYAN M; Bloomington HS; Riverside, CA; (3); Art Clb; Hon Roll; UCI; Commrcl Art.

STEIN, SHANNON; Lincoln HS; Stockton, CA; (3); Pres Church Yth Grp; VP Cmnty Wkr; Debate Tm; VP Key Clb; NFL; Ski Clb; Spanish Clb; Speech Tm; SADD; Pres Temple Yth Grp; Cntrl Westrn Area Fed Of Temple Yth Soc Action VP; Poltics.

STEINBACH, REBECCA H; Miramonte HS; Orinda, CA; (1); Drama Clb; NFL; Ski Clb; Speech Tm; School Play; Stage Crew; Bsktbl; Trk; High Hon Roll; Wrk Frncs Flrst.

STEINBACHER, KIMBERLY ANNE; St Bernard HS; Los Angeles, CA; (4); 1/239; Nwsp; Phtg Yrbk; Capt Var Sftbl; High Hon Roll; NHS; Ntl Merit Schol; NEDT Awd; Pres Acad Fit Awd; Val; UCLA Schlr, Regents Schlr; CA Schlrshp Fed CA Shclrshp Fed Vp Pres,Treas, Life Mem; UC Berkeley; Arch.

STEINBECK, ANDREA N; Paso Robles Joint Union HS; Paso Robles, CA; (2); 32/378; Church Yth Grp; Stage Crew; Rep Frsh Cls; Var Swmmng; High Hon Roll; Prfct Atten Awd; San Diego ST; Marine Bio.

STEINBECK, MELISSA L; Paso Robles HS; Paso Robles, CA; (4); 27/207; Church Yth Grp; Cmnty Wkr; Office Aide; SADD; Teachers Aide; Stage Crew; Stu Cncl; Cit Awd; High Hon Roll; Prfct Atten Awd; Ldrshp, Bus & Home Ec Stu Of Yr; Cresta Cmnty; Bus.

STEINBERG, CARRIE A; Lowell HS; San Francisco, CA; (3); Band; Amnesty Intl; Ballet Dance Class; Genetic Research.

STEINBERG, JOHANNA B; Valhalla HS; El Cajon, CA; (2); Cmnty Wkr; Key Clb; Pep Clb; Ski Clb; SADD; Temple Yth Grp; Sec Soph Cls; High Hon Roll; Humn Reltns Clb; Greenpeace; Yale; Envrnmntl Law.

STEINER, SCOTT A; Villa Park HS; Orange, CA; (2); Chess Clb; Rep Soph Cls; Cit Awd; High Hon Roll; Hon Roll; Orange County Academic Decathlon; Chapman College; Political Sci.

STEINHAUER, STEVEN; Colfax HS; Auburn, CA; (4); 6/158; Science Clb; Service Clb; Variety Show; Ed Yrbk; JV Tennis; High Hon Roll; Lion Awd; Ntl Merit SF; Rotary Awd; Jnr Statesmn America Pres; Cal Poly San Luis Obispo; Engr.

STEINHOFF, JAIME; Willows HS; Willows, CA; (2); Off Soph Cls; JV Cheerldng; JV Golf; Hon Roll; FNL; CYO; Navy.

STEINKE, JENNIFER; Palm Desert HS; Palm Desert, CA; (3); Church Yth Grp; Teachers Aide; Pres Frsh Cls; Stat Bsbl; Stat Bsktbl; Stat Ftbl; L Trk; High Hon Roll; Youth For Christ; Med.

STELLY, CHRISTIE J; Westlake HS; Thousand Oaks, CA; (2); Lit Mag; High Hon Roll; Golden Poet Awd 89; Editors Choice Awd 89; CA Schlrshp Fed; Interact Clb; Silver Poet 90.

STEM, JACOB; Chula Vista HS; Chula Vista, CA; (1).

STEMLER, CODY L; Bret Harte HS; Angels Camp, CA; (2); Cmnty Wkr; 4-H; FFA; Letterman Clb; Pep Clb; Bsktbl; Ftbl; Wt Lftg; 4-H Awd; Hon Roll; Wildlife.

STEMPINSKI, MERIDITH J; Don A Lugo HS; Chino, CA; (2); Drama Clb; Teachers Aide; Thesps; School Play; Stage Crew; Invlvd In Cmnty Theater; Actress.

STENDER, KATHLEEN L PRESSBURG; Levzinger HS; Hawthorne, CA; (4); 39/350; Hist AFS; VP Church Yth Grp; VP French Clb; VP Treas Key Clb; Science Clb; Teachers Aide; Chorus; Church Choir; Off Sr Cls; Var Crs Cntry; Directors Awd Select Chorale; Rookie Of The YR Select Chorale; Bd Membr Of The YR Key Club; El Camino; Cybernetics Comp Sci.

STENGER, DANIEL J; Poway HS; Poway, CA; (3); AFS; Science Clb; Spanish Clb; SADD; Hon Roll; Surf Club; SDSU; Psych.

STENGER, DEBORAH J; Poway HS; Poway, CA; (1); Church Yth Grp; Cmnty Wkr; Girl Scts; High Hon Roll; U CA; Sci.

STENNECKE, KENDRA L; Torrey Pines HS; Del Mar, CA; (4); Drama Clb; Intrml Golf; Intrml Sftbl; High Hon Roll; Hon Roll; Gldn St Awds-Alg Exam, Geom Exam 88, 90; Jnr Golf Assn; U Of CA San Diego; Frgn Svc.

STENNER, JONATHAN; Fortuna HS; Fortuna, CA; (1); Church Yth Grp; JV Trk; Var Wrstlng; Hon Roll; Graphic Arts.

STENNIS, TAMIKA; Edison HS; Fresno, CA; (1); Rep Frsh Cls; JV Bsktbl; Var Trk; Vllybl; Masonic Awd; Blck Stu Union; UCLA; Biochem.

STENZEL, NICHOLAS J; Granada Hills HS; Northridge, CA; (2); Boy Scts; Teachers Aide; School Play; JV L Bsbl; High Hon Roll; Hon Roll; Prfct Atten Awd; Rdng Of Clssc Lit; Cllctng, Plyng & Wtchng Bsbl.

STEPAN, RHONDA; Presentation HS; El Sobrante, CA; (3); 10/82; Aud/Vis; Church Yth Grp; Cmnty Wkr; French Clb; Hosp Aide; Library Aide; Quiz Bowl; Red Cross Aide; Service Clb; Acpl Chr; CSF; Conflct Mgmt; Eqstrn Clb; TX A&M; Vet Med.

STEPANIAN, JEFFREY M; Kingsburg HS; Selma, CA; (2); Computer Clb; Mu Alpha Theta; Ski Clb; Mgr Nwsp; JV Tennis; Armenian Chrth Yth Orgnztn Corrspndng Secy; Odyssey Of Mind Comptn; Most Imprvd Tennis Team.

STEPANOVICH, DAVID R; Davis HS; Modesto, CA; (2); Var Socr; Cit Awd; Cmmnty Svc; Ajax Soccer Trvlng Tm; MJC; Elect Engr.

STEPHAN, AUDREY; La Jolla HS; La Jolla, CA; (4); Church Yth Grp; Math Tm; Science Clb; Sec Service Clb; Spanish Clb; VP SADD; Off Frsh Cls; Var Swmmng; High Hon Roll; NHS; Cum Laude Socty; CSF Life-Time; Acad Excllnc Awd-Gldn St Exam Geom; U Of CA Berkeley; Med.

STEPHAN, BETSY J; Casa Roble Fundamental HS; Orangevale, CA; (4); 19/390; Spanish Clb; SADD; Hon Roll; NHS; Pres Acad Fit Awd; CA Coll Of Arts/Crafts; Arts.

STEPHANIE, LOGAN; Mt Whitney HS; Visalia, CA; (2); Hosp Aide; Band; Mrchg Band; JV Tennis; Hon Roll; CA Schlrshp Fdr; Acad Lttr; Engnrng.

STEPHEN, JEFFREY S; St Anthony HS; Long Beach, CA; (3); Var Ftbl; Var Vllybl; Wt Lftg; Hon Roll; Bus.

STEPHENS, ANTHONY A; Tulare Western HS; Tulare, CA; (3); Letterman Clb; Teachers Aide; JV Var Bsbl; JV Var Ftbl; Wt Lftg; Hon Roll; Golden State Exam Top 1% In State; Pharmacist.

STEPHENS, CAMELLA; Yuba City HS; Yuba City, CA; (3); 1/475; Treas German Clb; Letterman Clb; Pep Clb; SADD; JV Var Bsktbl; JV Var Cheerldng; Var Gym; Var Trk; High Hon Roll; Pres Acad Fit Awd; Delta League Champ Track & Field 90; Awd Golden St Ex Geo; Med.

STEPHENS, CHRIS J; Grossmont HS; La Mesa, CA; (2); 32/430; Boy Scts; Church Yth Grp; Cmnty Wkr; Acpl Chr; Chorus; Church Choir; School Musical; School Play; CA Lutheran; Music.

STEPHENS, CHRISTIN E; Redlands HS; Redlands, CA; (2); Church Yth Grp; Church Choir; Cit Awd; Hon Roll; Flrl Dsgnr.

STEPHENS, DAVINA J; Fremont HS; Oakland, CA; (2); Hon Roll; Georgeton; Comp Prog.

STEPHENS, EDITH; Yosemite HS; Coarsegold, CA; (4); 15/155; Church Yth Grp; SADD; Chorus; Church Choir; Color Guard; Mrchg Band; Rptr Nwsp; Var Crs Cntry; Hon Roll; Pres Acad Fit Awd; Mock Trial; Chrchs Prts; Amnesty Intl; Brigham Young U; Engl.

STEPHENS, EMID R; St Francis HS; Altadena, CA; (2); Pep Clb; Var Capt Bsktbl; Hon Roll; NHS; Pres Acad Fit Awd; Little Leag Bsbl Coach-YMCA; Stanford; Law.

STEPHENS, ERIN R; Van Nuys HS; Sunland, CA; (2); Church Yth Grp; Service Clb; Band; Mrchg Band; Orch; Phtg Yrbk; DAR Awd; FYSL Sccr All Star; Crtfd Lifeguard; UC Davis; RNOB.

STEPHENS, GREG B; De Lano HS; Delano, CA; (2); Church Yth Grp; 4-H; Bsbl; Ftbl; Wrstlng; Hon Roll; 89 Resrve Grand Chmpn Hog; Bus.

STEPHENS, HEATHER L; Colfax HS; Colfax, CA; (3); 16/152; Church Yth Grp; GAA; Teachers Aide; Yrbk; JV Var Bsktbl; Trk; Hon Roll; Physcl Thrpy.

STEPHENS, HEATHER M; Highlands HS; North Highlands, CA; (1); SADD; Color Guard; Prfct Atten Awd; MESA; Outreach; Stus Reaching Out.

STEPHENS, JASON A; Carmel HS; Carmel, CA; (4); 9/174; Var L Ftbl; Var L Socr; Var L Trk; High Hon Roll; CSF; Cal Poly San Luis Obispo; Engr.

STEPHENS, JESSICA; Fortuna HS; Fortuna, CA; (2); SADD; Acpl Chr; Band; Mrchg Band; Variety Show; Cheerldng.

STEPHENS, KARA L; Lutheran High Of Orange; Norco, CA; (2); Chorus; Church Choir; Var L Bsktbl; Var L Trk; JV Vllybl; Training Riding Horses; CIF Prelims Finals; Coaches Award Vllybl; Team Thrwr Awardtrack; Bsktbl Trnm Tm; Cal Poly; Veterinarian.

STEPHENS, MARCHETTA D; Washington HS; Los Angeles, CA; (2); Teachers Aide; School Play.

STEPHENS, MOLLY R; Mt Whitney HS; Visalia, CA; (1); Church Yth Grp; Church Choir; Var Socr; JV Sftbl; High Hon Roll; Kiwanis Awd; CSF; Kywntts.

STEPHENS, SHARNETTE R; Washington Prep HS; Los Angeles, CA; (3); Church Yth Grp; Dance Clb; Drama Clb; Pep Clb; Chorus; Color Guard; Drill Tm; School Musical; Variety Show; Stu Cncl; Martin Luther King Symposium Hostess; Achi Acad Achvt Awd 89-90; Bus.

STEPHENS, SONYA L; Tehachapi HS; Tehachapi, CA; (3); Co-Capt Dance Clb; FFA; Ski Clb; Teachers Aide; Band; Mrchg Band; CSUN; Bus Mgmt.

STEPHENS, YVETTE; El Rancho HS; Pico Rivera, CA; (4); Rio Hondo Coll.

STEPHENSON, JENNIFER R; Bolsa Grande HS; Garden Grove, CA; (1); Boy Scts; Church Yth Grp; VP Frsh Cls; JV Capt Bsktbl; Stat Swmmng; JV Vllybl; Var Hon Roll; Karate; Parttime Job-Retail Sales And Office; Biology.

STEPHENSON, JONATHAN L; Calvery Baptist Schls; Pomona, CA; (3); 1/10; Boy Scts; Drama Clb; Chorus; School Musical; Var L Bsbl; Var L Bsktbl; Score Keeper; Var L Vllybl; Hon Roll; UT Austin; Aerospace Engrng.

STEPHENSON, REBECCA; Calvary Baptist HS; Pomona, CA; (2); 1/10; Boy Scts; Girl Scts; Chorus; Church Choir; School Musical; Var Capt Bsktbl; Var Capt Cheerldng; Var L Sftbl; Var L Vllybl; High Hon Roll; Harvard; Law.

STEPHENSON, TIMOTHY; Etiwanda HS; Rancho Cucamonga, CA; (2); Church Yth Grp; Cmnty Wkr; FHA; Intrml Bsktbl; Var L Socr; Hon Roll; Mst Hnrb Mntn Hacienta Leag Vrsty Sccr; Bus.

STEPIEN, BETTY; Corona HS; Corona, CA; (2); 2/492; GAA; Hosp Aide; SADD; Rptr Nwsp; Yrbk; Lit Mag; Rep Stu Cncl; JV Vllybl; Pres Acad Fit Awd; Val; CSF; GATE PAC Stu Yr; Pre-Med.

STEPP, TARA A; Sanger HS; Fresno, CA; (2); Church Yth Grp; Chorus; Bsktbl; Swmmng; Tennis; Vllybl; High Hon Roll; NHS; V Bsktbl.

STERCK, STEPHANIE L; El Dorado HS; Placentia, CA; (3); 63/317; Intnl Clb; Teachers Aide; Varsity Clb; JV VP Tennis; Cit Awd; High Hon Roll; Hon Roll; Pres Acad Fit Awd; Psych.

STERK, JENNIFER; Mount Diablo HS; Concord, CA; (1); 35/270; Rptr Nwsp; High Hon Roll; Writer.

STERLING, ANTHONY J; San Gorgonio HS; San Bernardino, CA; (3); 35/600; German Clb; Var Crs Cntry; Var Trk; CSF; Advanced Curriculum Exploration Soc; Elect Engrng.

STERLING, CORY C; Point Arena HS; Gualala, CA; (2); Cmnty Wkr; VP Jr Cls; JV Bsktbl; Wt Lftg; High Hon Roll.

STERLING, JOSH; Irvine HS; Irvine, CA; (2); Ski Clb; Rep Frsh Cls; Rep Soph Cls; JV Crs Cntry; Ftbl; Var L Socr; JV Trk; Intrml Wt Lftg; Hon Roll; SDSU; Bus.

STERLING, MARC; Oxnard HS; Oxnard, CA; (4); 43/400; French Clb; Office Aide; SADD; Stu Cncl; Capt Var Sftbl; Hon Roll; Pres Acad Fit Awd; San Diego ST U; History Tchr.

STERN, DAVID J; Chula Vista HS; Chula Vista, CA; (3); 100/650; Boy Scts; Varsity Clb; Band; Jazz Band; Mrchg Band; Var Ftbl; Var Wrstlng.

STERN, ILISSA; Agoura HS; Agoura Hills, CA; (2); 57/469; Key Clb; Var Sftbl; Hon Roll; CIF Chmpnshp Sthrn Sect Sftbl Wnnr 89 & 90; Engl.

STERN, JASON S; Foothill HS; Santa Ana, CA; (3); Am Leg Boys St; Chrmn FBLA; SADD; Temple Yth Grp; Ed Nwsp; Off Sr Cls; Capt Var Tennis; Hon Roll; 6th Pl Sports Wrtng; Climbed Mt Rainier 89; Bus.

STERN, KEITH L; Whitney HS; Cerritos, CA; (2); JA; Rptr Nwsp; JV Bsktbl; Var Trk.

STERN, TSAFRIR; Beverly Hills HS; Beverly Hills, CA; (4); Cmnty Wkr; Computer Clb; Math Clb; Math Tm; Science Clb; JV Crs Cntry; Intrml Trk; Intrml Wt Lftg; High Hon Roll; Hon Roll; Comp Engrng.

STERNS, KASY; San Diego HS; San Diego, CA; (3); Thesps; Drama Clb; Speech Tm; School Play; Rptr Nwsp; Sec Frsh Cls; Rep Stu Cncl; Bsktbl; Cheerldng; Essay Cont 1st Pl Wnnr-Trp To Vly Forge; Military Ordr Of Wrld Wars; Wnnr Coll Ready Essy; Educ.

STERNSHEIN, SANFORD M; Los Alamitos HS; Los Alamitos, CA; (3); Temple Yth Grp; Var Ftbl; Pre Schl Teacher; Youth Center; Coll; Film Maker.

STERRETT, CAROLE A; Lower Lake HS; Clearlake Park, CA; (3); 22/160; Cmnty Wkr; Drama Clb; FBLA; Girl Scts; Letterman Clb; Pep Clb; Teachers Aide; Score Keeper; Hon Roll; Masonic Awd; Past Wrthy Advisor Intl Order Rainbow For Girls; Charter Pres Friday Night Live; Yuba; Ed.

STERTON, CARA; Fountain Valley HS; Fountain Valley, CA; (3); Church Yth Grp; Drama Clb; Thesps; Lbrn Chorus; Church Choir; School Musical; School Play; Stage Crew; Film.

STETLER, GRETCHEN K; Mountain Empire JR/Sr HS; Pine Valley, CA; (3); Var L Trk; Hon Roll; Golden ST Hstry Exam; Cyclng Clb.

STETSON, AMBER L; Red Bluff Union HS; Los Molinos, CA; (2); Art Clb; Church Yth Grp; French Clb; Library Aide; Church Choir; Trk; High Hon Roll; Hon Roll; Prfct Atten Awd; Friday Night Live Clb; Bible Clb; Point Loma Coll; Arch.

STETSON, STEPHANIE D; Capistrano Valley HS; Mission Viejo, CA; (3); German Clb; Band; Mrchg Band; Lit Mag; Hstry Day Achvt; Wrld Hstry Excllnc; UC Santa Cruz; Cmmnctn.

STETTER, MARY; Southwest HS; San Diego, CA; (2); Church Yth Grp; Drama Clb; SADD; Chorus; Rep Stu Cncl; Mgr(s); Cit Awd; Hon Roll; Pres Acad Fit Awd; Office Aide; ASB; UCSD; Ed.

STEVE, LY; George Washington HS; San Francisco, CA; (3); Ftbl; Wt Lftg; Cit Awd; Hon Roll; Hotel Mgmt.

STEVENS, ALAN K; Sherman E Burroughs HS; Ridgecrest, CA; (3); Boy Scts; Pres Church Yth Grp; Sec FBLA; Intrml Ftbl; Var L Wrstlng; Hon Roll; Brigham Young U; Engr.

STEVENS, CHRIS; Hesperia HS; Jamestown, CA; (2); Ski Clb; Bsktbl; Ftbl; Wt Lftg.

STEVENS, CHRISTOPHER L; Rio Americano HS; Fair Oaks, CA; (4); Art Clb; Debate Tm; Key Clb; Ski Clb; Speech Tm; SADD; Varsity Clb; Stage Crew; Treas Jr Cls; JV Bsbl; Water Polo St Chmpnshp Tm; Bus.

STEVENS, COLLEEN E; College Park HS; Lafayette, CA; (1); Sec 4-H; Hon Roll.

STEVENS, DULON J; Hogan HS; Vallejo, CA; (2); Church Yth Grp; Cmnty Wkr; Dance Clb; FCA; SADD; Teachers Aide; Var Bsbl; Var JV Ftbl; Var Wt Lftg; Var Cit Awd; All-Tourney Awd Baseball; Best Dress Awd; Law.

STEVENS, ERICA; Alemany HS; Panorama, CA; (3); Chorus; School Musical; Variety Show; Cheerldng; Hon Roll; NHS; Graphic.

STEVENS, GARY P; Thomas Downey HS; Modesto, CA; (4); Pres Band; Chorus; Pres Jazz Band; Pres Mrchg Band; Orch; Pres Pep Band; School Play; Louis Armstrong Jazz Awd; Most Imprvd Plyr & Marcher 87; CA ST U Stanislaus; Physician.

STEVENS, JOHN C; Saddleback HS; Costa Mesa, CA; (2); Church Yth Grp; Cmnty Wkr; Math Clb; Science Clb; Teachers Aide; Acpl Chr; Chorus; Church Choir; Variety Show; High Hon Roll; Karate Clb-Green Belt; UCI Partners Clb; Math/Engrng/Sci Assn; CSF; Algebra/Geometry Golden St Awds; Princeton; Math.

STEVENS, JULIANNA; Downey HS; Downey, CA; (3); VP French Clb; Math Clb; Science Clb; Service Clb; SADD; High Hon Roll; CSF.

STEVENS, KATHY V; La Canada HS; La Canada Flintri, CA; (3); Church Yth Grp; Girl Scts; Hon Roll; Psych.

STEVENS, KRISTIN; Santa Rosa HS; Santa Rosa, CA; (4); 15/525; Dance Clb; Pep Clb; Acpl Chr; Chorus; Cheerldng; L Var Swmmng; High Hon Roll; Pres Acad Fit Awd; CSF; Sonoma Co Jnr Miss 1st Rnnr Up & Poise/Appearnce Schlrhsps; UC Davis; Intl Rltns.

STEVENS, LAURA; West HS; Bakersfield, CA; (3); Church Yth Grp; School Play; Variety Show; Treas Jr Cls; JV Cheerldng; JV Powder Puff Ftbl; Hon Roll; NHS; CSF; Interact-Rotary Serv Clb; Prom Decorations Chrmn; Brigham Young U.

STEVENS, MICHELLE ELAINE; Lowell HS; San Francisco, CA; (2); Church Yth Grp; Dance Clb; Debate Tm; French Clb; Church Choir; Orch; Hon Roll; Math Engrng Sci Achvt; Pres Lowell Chptr Jr Statesmn Amer; St James Epscpl Acolytes Pres; Bus.

STEVENS, NAOMI J; Costa Mesa HS; Costa Mesa, CA; (3); Church Yth Grp; Cmnty Wkr; German Clb; Acpl Chr; Chorus; Church Choir; School Musical; School Play; Hon Roll; Bundestag Schlshp SR Yr Germany 91; Rotary Club Singer Of Yr 89; CA ST Fullerton; Psych.

STEVENS, NATHAN; Mt Whitney HS; Visalia, CA; (4); VP Art Clb; Swmmng; Hon Roll; UCSB.

STEVENS, TERI; Ygnacio Valley HS; Concord, CA; (3); Treas 4-H; Orch; School Musical; 4-H Awd; 4-H Allstar; UC Davis; Vet.

STEVENS, TODD; Cajon HS; San Bernardino, CA; (2); Hon Roll; CSF; Vanerbilt U; Med.

STEVENSON, CARRIE L; Capistrano Valley HS; Mission Viejo, CA; (3); Band; Church Choir; Mrchg Band; Orch; Pep Band; Ed.

STEVENSON, DANIELLE A; Pasadena HS; Alhambra, CA; (3); Church Yth Grp; JA; Band; Chorus; School Musical; Rptr Yrbk; Rep Stu Cncl; JV Capt Bsktbl; Var Capt Cheerldng; Var Capt Pom Pon; ROP Medcl Asst; MESA; BSU; Xavier U; Med.

STEVENSON, DAWN; Willows HS; Willows, CA; (4); 2/105; Am Leg Aux Girls St; Var Trk; High Hon Roll; Sal; Bllt Lssns; CSF Stu & Pres; Acad Dcthln Stu-Mdl In Intrvw & Spr Qz Hnrb Mntn; Mth.

STEVENSON, JOHN F; Willow Glen HS; San Jose, CA; (1); Church Yth Grp; JV Bsktbl; JV Crs Cntry; Hon Roll; Mst Imprvd Bsktbl Awd.

STEVENSON, KATHRYN A; Lassen HS; Susanville, CA; (3); 8/219; Church Yth Grp; Cmnty Wkr; Pres VP 4-H; FHA; Hosp Aide; Pep Clb; Ski Clb; Band; Stu Cncl; Var Cheerldng; Azuza Pacific U; Nurse.

STEVENSON, SARA; Douglass JR HS; Woodland, CA; (1); Dance Clb; Drill Tm; Cheerldng; Gym; Pom Pon; Hon Roll; Jr NHS; UCLA.

STEVENSON, SHELLY; Foothill HS; Bakersfield, CA; (3); Church Yth Grp; 4-H; JA; Teachers Aide; JV Cheerldng; JV Tennis; Hon Roll; Fshn Merch.

STEVES, THOMAS A; Lincoln HS; Stockton, CA; (3); Drama Clb; Chorus; School Musical; School Play; Stage Crew; Swing Chorus; Variety Show; Hon Roll; Stage Make-Up; Schl Drama Proj Extra Crrclr Work; San Joaqun Delta Coll; Artist.

STEWARD, NICOLE M; Modoc HS; Alturas, CA; (2); 23/63; JV Bsktbl; Var L Sftbl.

STEWART, ALEXANDER M; College Park HS; Concord, CA; (4); Treas AFS; Chess Clb; Computer Clb; French Clb; Math Clb; Math Tm; Model UN; Ntl Merit SF; Opt Clb Awd; Slvr Mdl Acad Decthln; Pres, Fndr Acad Decathln Clb; Comp Sci.

STEWART, ALISON; Argonaut HS; Ione, CA; (2); Church Yth Grp; 4-H; FBLA; FHA; Key Clb; Science Clb; Spanish Clb; Stat Bsbl; Stat Bsktbl; Cit Awd; Med.

STEWART, ANDREW; Rio Mesa HS; Camarillo, CA; (3); Aud/Vis; Cmnty Wkr; FCA; Letterman Clb; Scholastic Bowl; Varsity Clb; Variety Show; Stu Cncl; JV L Ftbl; Var Socr; Mck Trl Lead Defnse Attny; Bus.

STEWART, ANDREW DOUGLAS; Newport Harbor HS; Newport Beach, CA; (4); Boy Scts; JCL; Latin Clb; Hon Roll; Pres Schlr; Egl Sct; U Of Redlands; Bio.

STEWART, DANA E; Chaminade College Prep; Northridge, CA; (3); Chorus; Drill Tm; Rep Frsh Cls; JV Sftbl; High Hon Roll; NHS; Pres Acad Fit Awd; Chrldng-Vly Conf; Tennis Tourney At Priv Club; Asian-Am Friendship Club; UCLA; Med.

STEWART, DEBBIE E; Lassen HS; Janesville, CA; (3); FHA; School Play; Fld Hcky; Hon Roll; Wkd In Computer Str; Parade In 58 Ford; Horses; WA ST.

STEWART, GREG R; San Dieguito HS; Cardiff By The Se, CA; (2); Church Yth Grp; Cmnty Wkr; 4-H; Bsbl; JV Bsktbl; 4-H Awd; Prfct Atten Awd; Cal Poly Pomona; Arch.

STEWART, HEATHER J; Mission Viejo HS; Mission Viejo, CA; (4); 18/431; Church Yth Grp; Model UN; Pep Clb; Rep Spanish Clb; SADD; JV Cheerldng; Var Pom Pon; High Hon Roll; NHS; Pres Acad Fit Awd; CA Schlrshp Fed; Girls League; Pepperdine U; Intl Comm.

STEWART, JASON; Hanford Joint Union HS; Hanford, CA; (2); Church Yth Grp; Cmnty Wkr; 4-H; FFA; Intnl Clb; Speech Tm; Varsity Clb; Ftbl; Wt Lftg; 4-H Awd; CA Schlrshp Fed; FFA Pres, St Chmpn Agronomy Tm, Hgh Indvdl; Mc Donalds Acad Awd; Med.

STEWART, JEFF H; Grossmont HS; El Cajon, CA; (3); 19/385; FBLA; Intnl Clb; Key Clb; Math Clb; Math Tm; SADD; Varsity Clb; JV Socr; Var L Swmmng; Kiwanis Awd; Water Polo Jv V; CA Scholstic Fed Life Membr; 3.5 GPA.

STEWART, JENNIFER M; Mission Viejo HS; Mission Viejo, CA; (4); 2/430; Church Yth Grp; French Clb; Model UN; SADD; DAR Awd; High Hon Roll; NHS; Ntl Merit Ltr; Pres Acad Fit Awd; Sal; Horse Showing Lcl & Ntl Lvls; Georgetown U; Intl Rel.

STEWART, JENNY; St Francis HS; Sacramento, CA; (2); JV Cheerldng; Crs Cntry; Swmmng; Hon Roll; Prfct Atten Awd; Biking.

STEWART, JOHN S; Upland HS; Upland, CA; (2); JV Bsbl; JV Socr; Hon Roll; Highlander Educl Fnd Awd Eng 90; Golden St Exam High Hnrs Algebra I; Syracuse; Comm.

STEWART, JULIA D; Mira Mesa HS; San Diego, CA; (2); 1/797; Pres Church Yth Grp; Church Choir; Yrbk; Off Soph Cls; Hon Roll; San Diego City Yth Advsry Cncl; CJSF; CSF; Arch.

STEWART, KAREN; Will C Wood HS; Vacaville, CA; (2); Intnl Clb; Pep Clb; Yrbk; Cheerldng; Gym; High Hon Roll; Hon Roll; NHS; Harvard; Lawyer.

STEWART, KAREN E; Patterson HS; Patterson, CA; (3); Rep Art Clb; Drama Clb; Spanish Clb; Teachers Aide; Chorus; Church Choir; School Play; High Hon Roll; Jr NHS; NHS; JR Statesmean Of Amer PR Ofcr; CSF; CCD Teacher; Acad Decathlon 88-90; San Francisco U; Radio Brdcstng.

STEWART, KATHRINE A; Mira Mesa HS; San Diego, CA; (3); Pres Church Yth Grp; Church Choir; Ed Yrbk; Cit Awd; Hon Roll; NHS; Pres Acad Fit Awd; CSF; U Of CA Sad Diego; Math.

STEWART, KELLY; Hogan SR HS; Vallejo, CA; (3); Church Yth Grp; Teachers Aide; Church Choir; Bethany Bible Coll; Childhd Ed.

STEWART, KELLY SHANNON; Santa Monica HS; Los Angeles, CA; (2); Var Bsktbl; Var Trk; Outstndg Yth Awrd Mayor Of L A; Hnrbl Mntn Am Legion; Captn Drill Team.

STEWART, KRISTEN; Nevada Union HS; Nevada City, CA; (3); 8/551; Sec Girl Scts; Teachers Aide; Variety Show; Var Socr; Var Tennis; Cit Awd; High Hon Roll; Hon Roll; Prfct Atten Awd; Girl Sct Gold & Silver Awds; Most Imprvd Tnns Plyr Awd 88; Arch.

STEWART, LA TASHA; Oceanside HS; Oceanside, CA; (1); SADD; Hon Roll; Engl.

STEWART, LASHONTA MARCEL; Alhambra HS; Martinez, CA; (2); VP Church Yth Grp; Pres Frsh Cls; Rep Soph Cls; Off Jr Cls; Var Capt Ftbl; Var JV Trk; Wt Lftg; High Hon Roll; Hon Roll; IM-JV Schlr Athlt; Blck Stu Spprt Grp; Cmmssnr Stu Rghts; Stu Rep Brd Of Ed; U Of CA Berkeley; Law.

STEWART, LYNETTE M; Carson HS; Carson, CA; (2); Office Aide; School Play; JV Bsbl; Black Heritage Club.

STEWART, MALIKA C; Eisenhower HS; Rialto, CA; (3); Hon Roll; NHS; Comp Sci.

STEWART, MARTINA; Edison-Computech HS; Fresno, CA; (4); 1/218; Cmnty Wkr; Model UN; Teachers Aide; Band; Mrchg Band; Pep Band; Rptr Lit Mag; High Hon Roll; Kiwanis Awd; Masonic Awd; Mock Trial Tm; Natl Achvt Schlrshp Recipnt; Natl Bicentl Of Constitn CA ST; Yale U; Atty.

STEWART, MAUREEN; Loretto HS; Sacramento, CA; (4); 6/55; Chorus; Ed Lit Mag; Sec Stu Cncl; JV Vllybl; High Hon Roll; Hon Roll; NHS; Pres Acad Fit Awd; Bank Of Amer Achvt Awd; Punctuality Awd; Magna Cum Laude; CSU Sacramento; Comm.

STEWART, MELANIE; Calvary Christian Acad; Vallejo, CA; (3); Church Yth Grp; Drama Clb; Spanish Clb; Teachers Aide; Nwsp; Ed Yrbk; JV Var Trk; Cit Awd; High Hon Roll; Hon Roll; Schlstc Achvt Hghst GPA 87-90; MVP Trck; Stanford; Orthdntcs.

STEWART, MICHAEL; San Marcos HS; San Marcos, CA; (2); Hon Roll; U CA San Marcos; Bus.

STEWART, NANCY L; Ocean View HS; Westminster, CA; (3); Library Aide; Band; Jazz Band; Mrchg Band; Pep Band; Medcl Explrs; Coastline ROP.

STEWART, NICOLE M; Pinole Valley HS; Pinole, CA; (1); Office Aide; Vllybl; Hon Roll; X-Ray Tech.

STEWART, RUBY C; Hueneme HS; Oxnard, CA; (3); 59/378; NY U; Journalism.

STEWART, SARAH; Christian Life HS; Corte Madera, CA; (1); Drama Clb; ROTC; Drill Tm; Airln Pilot.

STEWART, SEAN; San Leandro HS; San Leandro, CA; (2); Key Clb; Ed Yrbk; JV Crs Cntry; Hon Roll; Strctrl Engr.

STEWART, STEPHANIE A; Gridley Union HS; Gridley, CA; (3); 2/120; Dance Clb; Red Cross Aide; Ski Clb; School Play; Variety Show; Yrbk; Cheerldng; Powder Puff Ftbl; Hon Roll; Rotary Awd; Brigham Young U.

STEWART, TAVIS A; Newark Memorial HS; S Laguna, CA; (1); French Clb; Science Clb; Teachers Aide; French Stu Star Awd; Hnr Soc; Jrnlsm.

STEWART, TIFFANY MIA; Louisville HS; Thousand Oaks, CA; (1); Church Yth Grp; Drama Clb; GAA; School Play; Sec Frsh Cls; JV Sftbl; High Hon Roll; Pres Acad Fit Awd; St Schlr; CSF; Young Miss Ventura Cty; Harvard U; Stock Broker.

STEWART, WENDY C; Flintridge Sacred Heart HS; Altadena, CA; (4); Church Yth Grp; Drama Clb; Pres Intnl Clb; Math Clb; Thesps; School Play; Stage Crew; Sec Frsh Cls; Stu Cncl; Suzuki Methd; Yng Blck Schlrs; Astronomcl Engrng.

STEWART JR, WILLIAM R; Selma HS; Selma, CA; (3); 2/183; Am Leg Boys St; Church Yth Grp; Drama Clb; Letterman Clb; SADD; Off Soph Cls; VP Jr Cls; Chrmn Sr Cls; Rep Stu Cncl; Var L Bsbl; CSF; USAF Acad Smmr Scntfc Smnr; US Mltry Acad; Ofcr.

STEWART, YONDONDO D; David Starr Jordan HS; Long Beach, CA; (3); JV Bsbl; JV Var Bsktbl; Bsktbl Freshman MVP, Jr Bst Offensive Player; Comp.

STICKELS, KRISTIN; University City HS; San Diego, CA; (4); Model UN; Yrbk; JV Bsktbl; Var Sftbl; JV Vllybl; High Hon Roll; Pres Acad Fit Awd; Golden St Math Exam Hnrs; CA Schlstc Fed 100% Lifetime; UCLA.

STIDGER, AMBER; Oakmont HS; Roseville, CA; (4); Hon Roll; Prfct Atten Awd; Pres Acad Fit Awd; Photo Clb; Acadmc Merit Awd 2; UC Davis; Vet Med.

STIDHAM, CHRIS L; West Mc Kinley Christian HS; Fresno, CA; (3); Church Yth Grp; Var Bsktbl; Capt Ftbl; High Hon Roll; United Serve Washington DC Yth Cnsl; Law.

STIEBER, CARYN E; Oakmont HS; Roseville, CA; (3); Cmnty Wkr; GAA; Hosp Aide; Letterman Clb; Office Aide; Service Clb; Ski Clb; Thesps; Temple Yth Grp; Varsity Clb; CA Youth Cncl; Ray A Krok Youth Achvt Awd.

STIEH, CASSANDRA; Notre Dame HS; Nuevo, CA; (2); 35/170; VP Church Yth Grp; Rptr Nwsp; JV Capt Cheerldng; Gym; JV Capt Pom Pon; Hon Roll; Royal Acad Dance Ballet Pgm Hnr Stu; Scripps Coll; Marine Bio.

STIER, TED G; Ramona HS; Ramona, CA; (2); Intrml Bsbl; Intrml Socr; Hon Roll; Comp; UCSD; Sci.

STIERS, HILARY; Ceres HS; Modesto, CA; (3); 32/405; GAA; Scholastic Bowl; Stat Bsbl; Stat Bsktbl; Stat Swmmng; Var Tennis; Var Trk; Var Vllybl; Stat Wrstlng; High Hon Roll; People To People Yth Sci Exch; Early Grad; Cal ST Stanislaus; Plstc Srgn.

STILES, DEREK J; Poway HS; Poway, CA; (4); 66/750; AFS; Band; Mrchg Band; School Play; Swing Chorus; Hon Roll; NHS; Pres Acad Fit Awd; CA Schrlshp Fed; 5th Pl Rgnl Concours Natl De Francais; UC San Diego; Lngstcs.

STILES, KEVIN; Madrea HS; Madera, CA; (4); 65/455; Church Yth Grp; Science Clb; Hon Roll; Sic Olympiad 2nd Pl Qualitative Analysis; Top 14 Pct Of Grad Clss; Fresno ST U; Elect Engnrng.

STILL, BUFFY; Coleville HS; Coleville, CA; (3); 2/17; English Clb; 4-H; FFA; Girl Scts; JA; Math Clb; Office Aide; Teachers Aide; Varsity Clb; VICA; CSF Treas; NV HS Rodeo Assn; Silver St Gymkahna Clb; U NV Reno; Equestrian Sci.

STILL, CHRISTIE L; Fontana HS; Fontana, CA; (2); Church Yth Grp; FCA; Band; Church Choir; Mrchg Band; Orch; Yrbk; Off Frsh Cls; Rep Stu Cncl; L Bsktbl; Kare Yth Lgue; Mission Mexico Aid Earthquake Vctms 88; Music Schlrshp Smmr Stdy; Astrnt Trng Cmp 90; Spce Tech.

STILLINGS, TONY LEE; Los Altos HS; Hacienda Hts, CA; (2); Church Yth Grp; Computer Clb; Letterman Clb; Varsity Clb; Var L Swmmng; High Hon Roll; Hon Roll; Prfct Atten Awd; Pres Acad Fit Awd; Civil Air Patrol; Var Water Polo; FAA Stu Plt Cert; USAF Acad; Aviator.

STILLMAN, TAMMY R; Thousand Oaks HS; Thousand Oaks, CA; (3); Art Clb; Church Yth Grp; Dance Clb; Pep Clb; Church Choir; Hon Roll; Brdcstng.

STILLSON, MELANIE J; Cordova SR HS; Rancho Cordova, CA; (3); Church Yth Grp; Hosp Aide; Key Clb; Model UN; Band; Jazz Band; Orch; Yrbk; Bsktbl; Score Keeper; CA Schlrshp Fed; Amer River; Pre-Med.

STILLWELL, KATHERINE; University Of San Diego HS; San Diego, CA; (2); Church Yth Grp; Ski Clb; Chorus; JV Var Cheerldng; Gym; Var Trk; Hon Roll; Bible Study; CA Schlrshp Fed; Outdoor Wilderness Experience; Arch.

STILLWELL, KIMBERLYN; West HS; Bakersfield, CA; (1); Debate Tm; NFL; Hon Roll.

STILLWELL, MICHELLE L; Oroville HS; Oroville, CA; (3); Sec Intnl Clb; SADD; Yrbk; Powder Puff Ftbl; Socr; Hon Roll; CSF; Friday Night Live; Stu Ldrshp; Bus Mgmt.

STILLWELL, TONYA M; Rio Mesa HS; Oxnard, CA; (3); Church Yth Grp; Key Clb; Speech Tm; Teachers Aide; Ed Nwsp; Rep Soph Cls; Var Diving; JV Var Swmmng; Opt Clb Awd; Rep Drama Clb; Peer Counselor; NYU; Law.

STIMAC, VANESSA R; Villa Park HS; Orange, CA; (3); GAA; Key Clb; Spanish Clb; SADD; Yrbk; Off Jr Cls; JV Bsktbl; JV Vllybl; Hon Roll; Prin GPA Hnr Roll; Cmmnctns.

STIMLEY, MATTHEW R; Millikan HS; Long Beach, CA; (3); German Clb; JV Var Ftbl; Hon Roll; UC San Diego; Marine Bio.

STIMMEL, ROBERT E; John Wesley North HS; Riverside, CA; (2); 66/520; Boy Scts; Church Yth Grp; Band; Jazz Band; Mrchg Band; Pep Band; Hon Roll; Pres Acad Fit Awd; Arch.

STINE, BARBARA; Victor Valley Christian HS; Apple Valley, CA; (3); Church Yth Grp; Drama Clb; Spanish Clb; Teachers Aide; School Musical; Yrbk; Pres Soph Cls; High Hon Roll; Hon Roll; Rotary Youth Ldrshp Awd 90; Youth Group Ldr; Psych.

STINEBAUGH-HARWOOD, JENNIFER; Monte Vista HS; Danville, CA; (2); Church Yth Grp; Color Guard; Flag Corp; Off Soph Cls; Off Jr Cls; Stu Cncl; JV Swmmng; Med.

STINNETT, TERA-LEE; Clovis HS; Fresno, CA; (3); Aud/Vis; Church Yth Grp; Office Aide; SADD; Stage Crew; Cheerldng; Crs Cntry; Cit Awd; High Hon Roll; Hon Roll.

STINSON, JEREMY M; San Rafael HS; San Rafael, CA; (3); 24/224; Boy Scts; French Clb; Band; Jazz Band; Orch; Pep Band; School Musical; School Play; Stage Crew; JV Bsktbl; Sci Fr Marin Cnty 1st Pl.

STINSON, LORI; Vacaville HS; Vacaville, CA; (3); Hosp Aide; Service Clb; Band; Mrchg Band; Pep Band; Hon Roll; Stu Coach Bowlng; Sacramento ST.

STINSON, NICOLE A; Valley View HS; Moreno Valley, CA; (1); Ed Yrbk; Var JV Cheerldng; Prin List; San Diego ST; Psych.

STIRLING, PATRICIA LYNN; Foothill HS; Santa Ana, CA; (2); Church Yth Grp; Spanish Clb; Chorus; Church Choir; School Musical; Var L Trk; Police Explr-Corporal; Acad Decthln Team; Lawyer.

STIRRAT, JUSTIN J; East Union HS; Manteca, CA; (2); SADD; Band; JV Bsktbl; High Hon Roll; Hon Roll; Prfct Atten Awd; Technel Engr.

STITS, MICHAEL C; Valley View HS; Moreno Valley, CA; (1); VICA; Bsktbl; Hon Roll; Rvrside Cnty Indstrl Educ Expo 2nd Pl 90; UCLA; Arch.

STITT, DARYL; Montclair HS; Ontario, CA; (2); Computer Clb; Ski Clb; Teachers Aide; JV Ftbl; JV Socr; Wt Lftg; Hon Roll; Comp Pgmng.

STITT, KATHERINE; San Dimas HS; San Dimas, CA; (3); Girl Scts; Library Aide; Capt Pep Clb; SADD; Teachers Aide; Rep Soph Cls; Sec Stu Cncl; Capt Var Cheerldng; Capt Pom Pon; Cit Awd; Amercn Hrtg Pres; Clubs Comm ASB; Vrsty Badmttn; Teach.

STITZ, MELISSA; S California Christian Schl; Orange, CA; (2); Var JV Cheerldng; Var Sftbl; Church Yth Grp; Office Aide; Score Keeper; High Hon Roll.

STIVERS, SARAH; Summerville HS; Long Barn, CA; (4); Church Yth Grp; Scholastic Bowl; Spanish Clb; SADD; Teachers Aide; Church Choir; Yrbk; Cheerldng; Cit Awd; Sonoma ST U; Teacher.

STOBER, SHELLY L; Paso Robles HS; Paso Robles, CA; (3); 4-H; FFA; 4-H Awd; Hon Roll; Teacher.

STOCK, SARAH A; Ganesha HS; Diamond Bar, CA; (3); Church Yth Grp; Sec French Clb; Hosp Aide; Sec Math Clb; Teachers Aide; Rep Stu Cncl; Socr; Tennis; High Hon Roll; Prfct Atten Awd; CA ST Polytech U; Hosp Admin.

STOCKDALE, BECKY L; Fresno Christian HS; Fresno, CA; (3); Color Guard; Var L Tennis; JV Vllybl; Cit Awd; High Hon Roll; Hon Roll; Pres Acad Fit Awd; Fresno Pacific; Int Dcrtng.

STOCKTON, RYAN C; Hemet HS; Hemet, CA; (2); Bsbl; Wt Lftg; Hon Roll.

STOCKTON, TODD A; Edison HS; Stockton, CA; (4); Church Yth Grp; Drama Clb; Teachers Aide; School Musical; School Play; Stage Crew; Var Capt Bsbl; Capt L Ftbl; High Hon Roll; Hon Roll; Sacramento ST U; Marketing.

STOCKWELL, SARAH R; Gompers Secondary Schl; San Diego, CA; (4); 26/100; Scholastic Bowl; Pres Science Clb; Ski Clb; Pres Spanish Clb; Teachers Aide; Lit Mag; Sec Soph Cls; Ntl Merit SF; Opt Clb Awd; Sal; Cnty Sci Fair; Altrnt Swpstks; Sci Olympiad Pres & Tm Cptn; Swarthmore Coll; Physcs.

STODDARD, CATHERINE; Oakmont HS; Roseville, CA; (3); Church Yth Grp; Drama Clb; Office Aide; Drill Tm; School Play; Variety Show; Stat Trk; Hon Roll; Prfct Atten Awd; Modeling Schlrshp From Mannican Mnr; Friday Night Live Membr; Sac ST; Engl.

STOESSEL, JENNIFER L; Del Oro HS; Loomis, CA; (2); 16/267; Church Yth Grp; JV Vllybl; Cit Awd; High Hon Roll; Stu Of Mnth In Span; UC Davis; Psych.

STOEVER, JENNIFER L; Ramona HS; Riverside, CA; (2); 1/447; French Clb; JA; Band; Color Guard; Nwsp; High Hon Roll; Jr NHS; 1st Pl Schl, Dist & Inland Empire Sci Frs; Golden St Exam Rcgntn Awd Alg I; Hnrbl Mntn Wrtng Cont; Engl Ed.

STOFER, ANNABEL L; Bella Vista HS; Fair Oaks, CA; (2); 93/412; Church Yth Grp; Band; Mrchg Band; Pep Band; Prfct Atten Awd; Humboldt ST; Marine Bio.

STOFFEL, JEFFREY A; Carlsbad HS; Carlsbad, CA; (2); JV Trk; Hon Roll; California Scholarship Federation.

STOFFELS, BRYANT P; San Dieguito HS; Encinitas, CA; (3); 96/570; German Clb; Ski Clb; Var L Swmmng; Hon Roll; Pres Acad Fit Awd; Pres Schlr; CSF; CA Interschltc Fed; Bus.

STOH, DEBBIE; Hemet HS; Hemet, CA; (2); Church Yth Grp; Band; Church Choir; Mrchg Band; Pep Band; Sftbl; Band.

STOHL, LAURIE L; Dinuba HS; Dinuba, CA; (2); 12/200; Church Yth Grp; Drama Clb; Math Tm; Ski Clb; School Play; Tennis; Hon Roll; Keywanettes Historian; Interact; Berkeley; Archeology.

STOKER, RANDY; Bonita Vista HS; National City, CA; (4); 6/521; Cmnty Wkr; Computer Clb; Key Clb; Pres Frsh Cls; VP Stu Cncl; Var Bsktbl; High Hon Roll; Prog Dir SOFFA; Freedoms Foundtn Vly Forge Ldrshp Conf; Links Inc Achvr Prog; Engrng.

STOKES, FRANCES; Vanden HS; Vacaville, CA; (4); 17/143; Church Yth Grp; Sec Spanish Clb; Band; Church Choir; Lit Mag; Sec Soph Cls; High Hon Roll; Jr NHS; NHS; Pres Acad Fit Awd; Outstndng Bus Stu, Music Stu; Cert Of Excellence; Solano CC; Comp Prgmg.

STOKES, HILARY A; Lakewood HS; Long Beach, CA; (4); Orch; Var Capt Gym; Jr NHS; NHS; High Hon Roll; CSF; Faculty Awd; Camp Fire Mdlln; LBCC.

STOKES, JULIE E; Sanger HS; Sanger, CA; (2); Church Yth Grp; FCA; Sec Model UN; ROTC; Science Clb; Ski Clb; Var L Swmmng; Hon Roll; Water Polo Statscn; Aquatics Clb; CA Schlstc Fed; Intl Law.

STOKES, KAHLIL G; Hamilton HS; Los Angeles, CA; (2); Prfct Atten Awd; Directed 2 Student Films & Filmed A 3 Hr Musical 89-90; USC; Photography.

STOKES, SHAUNA R; Los Alamitos HS; Los Alamitos, CA; (3); Church Yth Grp; Cmnty Wkr; FBLA; Hosp Aide; Teachers Aide; Orch; Goal Setting Pgm; Brigham Young U; Math Ed.

STOKES, TASHA L; Lassen Union HS; Susanville, CA; (2); FHA; Hon Roll; Lassen CC; Jrnlsm.

STOKOLS, SHULA I; Irvine HS; Irvine, CA; (2); Cmnty Wkr; JA; Key Clb; Intrml Swmmng; Hon Roll; Womans Advsry Brd; Jr Vlntr Hosp; Engrng.

STOLEE, KARA L; Grossmont HS; La Mesa, CA; (3); 22/500; Acpl Chr; Chorus; Church Choir; Orch; School Musical; Variety Show; L Var Gym; Var Trk; High Hon Roll; Pres Acad Fit Awd; Gnld St Exam Awd Hghst Hnrs; Point Loma Nazarene; Physics.

STOLOW, KAREN L; Torray Pines HS; San Diego, CA; (2); 94/500; Ed Yrbk; Pres Frsh Cls; Treas Stu Cncl; JV Gym; Greater San Diego Sci, Engr Fair 89; Achvt Awd Overall Schltc 89.

STOLPE, DAWN; Antioch HS; Antioch, CA; (3); AFS; Debate Tm; French Clb; NFL; Pep Clb; Scholastic Bowl; Spanish Clb; Rep Soph Cls; JV Var Cheerldng; Gym; Natls Chrldng; St Qlfr Lincoln Douglass Debate; UCSD; Lingstcs.

STOLTE, NICOLE; California HS; San Ramon, CA; (3); Service Clb; Spanish Clb; High Hon Roll; CSF; San Diego ST U; Finance.

STOLWORTHY, LORRAINE; South HS; Bakersfield, CA; (3); 7/458; Hon Roll; CA Schlrshp Fndtn; Santa Barbara U; Elec Engr.

STOMMEL, KRISTIN M; Hoover HS; Fresno, CA; (2); Cmnty Wkr; Hosp Aide; Hon Roll; Fresno ST U; Civil Engr.

STONE, ADAM; Damien HS; San Dimas, CA; (3); Boy Scts; Cmnty Wkr; Rptr Yrbk; Hon Roll; Var Swmmng; Vrsty Water Polo; UCLA; Ecnmcs.

STONE, ADRIENNE M; Santa Barbara HS; Santa Barbara, CA; (2); 50/500; Cmnty Wkr; FTA; Hosp Aide; VP Soph Cls; Tennis; Hon Roll; Pres Acad Fit Awd; Prfrmng Ballet Dance Troop; Dartmouth; Bus.

STONE, AMIE L; Lemoore HS; Lemoore, CA; (2); 4-H; FFA; Girl Scts; Ski Clb; SADD; Church Choir; Rep Soph Cls; JV Bsktbl; Powder Puff Ftbl; JV Sftbl; CSF.

STONE, ANDRIA T; Fort Bragg HS; Fort Bragg, CA; (2); 4/125; Cmnty Wkr; Chorus; Hon Roll; NHS; Pres Acad Fit Awd; Redwood Writing Awd; Peer Cnslng; CSF; Clinical Psych.

STONE, CLAUDIA; Bullard HS; Fresno, CA; (2); School Musical; CSF; Amer Horse Show Assn Mdl Fnlst 3 Yrs; Publc Brdcstng Systms Vlntr; UC Santa Barbara; Bus Econ.

STONE, DORI R; Oak Ridge HS; El Dorado Hills, CA; (3); Church Yth Grp; Intnl Clb; SADD; Rep Stu Cncl; Var JV Cheerldng; JV Vllybl; High Hon Roll; Jr NHS; NHS; Rotary Awd; CA Assn Stu Cncls Rgn 2 Publc Rltns Dirctr 88-89; Bus Commnctns.

STONE, DOUG; Mt View HS; Burney, CA; (1); Dsl Mechnc.

STONE, EMILY; Sonoma Valley HS; Sonoma, CA; (3); 17/300; Capt Dance Clb; Model UN; Sec Service Clb; Stu Cncl; Stat Bsktbl; JV Sftbl; JV Vllybl; High Hon Roll; Peer Counslr; Office Job Marys Pizza Shack; Marktng.

STONE, EMILY; Thomas Downey HS; Modesto, CA; (3); Key Clb; NFL; Ski Clb; Spanish Clb; Orch; Sec Sr Cls; JV Cheerldng; Var Swmmng; Var Tennis; Lion Awd; Best Lkng Awd 89-90; Brigham Young U; Muscl Entrtnr.

STONE, ERICA T; Bullard HS; Fresno, CA; (3); 1/500; German Clb; Key Clb; SADD; School Play; Ed Nwsp; Rep Stu Cncl; Swmmng; CSF; Schlr Engl Awd; Schlr/Athl Awd; Golden St Exam Awd Geom & Algebra I; Swimming Coaches Awd; Jrnlsm.

STONE, ERIK D; Rio Americano HS; Sacramento, CA; (3); 70/300; Art Clb; FBLA; Quiz Bowl; Ski Clb; Ed Lit Mag; JV Bsbl; Var Capt Socr; Var Capt Vllybl; Hon Roll; Falming Varmnt Jugglng; Achvt A P Bio; Acad Ltr; UCLA; Commnctns.

STONE, JEFF; Encinal HS; Alameda, CA; (4); Boy Scts; Church Yth Grp; Math Tm; Teachers Aide; School Play; Tennis; High Hon Roll; Goldn St Exm Hnrs; Asian Clb; Physicist.

STONE, JENNIFER; Redwood HS; Visalia, CA; (4); 11/300; Math Clb; Math Tm; Science Clb; SADD; Varsity Clb; Ed Yrbk; Var Capt Bsktbl; Var Trk; Hon Roll; NHS; U C Davis.

STONE, JENNIFER R; Chino HS; Chino, CA; (3); 8/538; Intnl Clb; Treas Pep Clb; Ski Clb; JV VP Tennis; High Hon Roll; Prfct Atten Awd; JV Bdmntn; CSF 87-90; Mdlln Schlr 87-90; Slvr Spur Awd Cmptrs 90,Nom Span & Physcs 90; Gldn St Exm 88; UCR; Med.

STONE, JESSICA M; Loretto HS; Loomis, CA; (1); Nwsp; Norte Dame; Bus.

STONE, JILL; Oroville HS; Oroville, CA; (1); 4/295; Church Yth Grp; Band; Flag Corp; Mrchg Band; Pep Band; Lit Mag; High Hon Roll; Lawyer.

STONE, JOHN; Palo Verde HS; Blythe, CA; (3); 12/350; Drama Clb; FFA; School Play; Variety Show; Hon Roll; NHS; Boys St Rep Fnlst; U AZ; Phrmcy.

STONE, JON C; Nevada Union HS; Grass Valley, CA; (3); Boy Scts; SADD; Ftbl; UCLA; Comp Prgm.

STONE, JONATHAN; Palo Alto HS; Palo Alto, CA; (2); Boy Scts; Church Yth Grp; Cmnty Wkr; Service Clb; Nwsp; Off Frsh Cls; Off Soph Cls; Var L Tennis; High Hon Roll; Hon Roll; Golden St Math Awd Hnr Algebra; Palo Alto HS Boys Tnns Tm High Acad; PA Mecl Explorers; Pre-Med.

STONE, JULIA L; Santa Barbara HS; Santa Barbara, CA; (3); Hon Roll; Pres Schlr; Modeling; Liberal Arts.

STONE, KRISTOPHER R; Channel Islands HS; Oxnard, CA; (4); 35/480; Church Yth Grp; Science Clb; Teachers Aide; JV Crs Cntry; JV Trk; Var L Wrstlng; Hon Roll; Pres Acad Fit Awd; Gldn St Schlr Hnr Rcgnt Geom; Outstndng Athlte Yr; Venura Cnty Sports Hall Fame; CS ST U; FBI.

STONE, LAURA L; Mission HS; San Francisco, CA; (4); Learning Through Servng Vlntr; Fashion Dsgn.

STONE, LESLIE; Capistrano Valley HS; Mission Viejo, CA; (2); Church Yth Grp; Pep Clb; JV Cheerldng; High Hon Roll; CSF; Saddleback Sci Fair Hnbr Mntn; Orange Cty Sci Fair.

STONE, LINDA M; Monterey HS; Monterey, CA; (2); Service Clb; Band; Mrchg Band; Rep Stu Cncl; JV Fld Hcky; Hon Roll; Pres Acad Fit Awd; BYU; Spec Edu.

STONE, LISA C; Ygnacio Valley HS; Concord, CA; (2); Church Yth Grp; Hosp Aide; Key Clb; Model UN; Spanish Clb; High Hon Roll; Lion Awd; Humnts Fstvl Speeck Cont Made Semi-Fnls; UC U; Med.

STONE, MATTHEW; Palo Alto HS; Palo Alto, CA; (3); Debate Tm; Ski Clb; Spanish Clb; Temple Yth Grp; Nwsp; Swmmng; Hon Roll; Ntl Merit SF; Smmr Intrnshp Dist Cngrssnl Offc; Ski Tm Stu Tahoe; Schl Mck Trl Tm; Law.

STONE, REBECCA C; De Anza HS; El Sobrante, CA; (4); 25/240; Church Yth Grp; French Clb; Teachers Aide; Acpl Chr; Chorus; Church Choir; School Musical; Ed Nwsp; Lit Mag; Hon Roll; Blck Stu Union De Anza; Friday Night Live Chptr De Anza; Excllnc Awd Crtv Wrtng 89; San Francisco ST U; Jrnlsm.

STONE, SUZANNE; Tracy Joint Union HS; Tracy, CA; (3); Cmnty Wkr; Teachers Aide; Stat Bsbl; Var Cheerldng; Stat Wrstlng; Hon Roll; Jr Mis Physcl Ftns Awd, Schlrshp; Stu Legue; Crmnlgy.

STONE, TAMARA L; Ventura HS; Ventura, CA; (2); Church Yth Grp; Drama Clb; School Play; JV Socr; JV Swmmng; Hon Roll; Nrsng.

STONEHOCKER, JODY L; Manteca HS; Manteca, CA; (2); 5/420; Church Yth Grp; Cmnty Wkr; Hosp Aide; Pep Clb; SADD; VP Frsh Cls; Treas Jr Cls; JV Vllybl; High Hon Roll; Hon Roll; CA Schlrshp Fed Treas, Pres.

STONEKING, DENNA M; San Gorgonio HS; San Bernardino, CA; (3); Sec FBLA; Sec Sr Cls; Cnslg.

STONER, CARLA A; Hoover HS; Fresno, CA; (2); Church Yth Grp; Dance Clb; Spanish Clb; SADD; Hon Roll; Awd For Being Top 5% In Cls Academically 2 Yrs; Scl Services.

STONER, MICHELLE R; Sweetwater HS; Imperial Beach, CA; (4); Church Yth Grp; Dance Clb; Teachers Aide; Socr; Swmmng; Tennis; Vllybl; Hon Roll; San Diego ST U; Phy Ed.

STONG, CANDICE R; Fullerton Union HS; Fullerton, CA; (4); 22/400; Cmnty Wkr; Off Dance Clb; Teachers Aide; Cheerldng; Capt Pom Pon; High Hon Roll; Rotary Awd; Outstndng Cmnty Invlvmt City Fullerton; Svc Awd; Cal ST Fullerton; Bus.

STOOPS, TRINA L; Temecula Valley HS; Murrieta, CA; (3); Tennis; Cit Awd; Hon Roll; SDSU; Law.

STOPANI, RACHAEL M; Bonita Vista HS; Bonita, CA; (2); Office Aide; Teachers Aide; Var Crs Cntry; Var Trk; Var Cross-Cntry & Trck; Child Psych.

STOPHER, MARK A; Ocean View HS; Fountain Valley, CA; (1); Bsktbl; Tennis; UCLA.

STOPPA, SHELLY M; Northview HS; Covina, CA; (2); GAA; Spanish Clb; Chorus; Treas Soph Cls; Var Crs Cntry; Var Trk; High Hon Roll; Hon Roll; Pres Acad Fit Awd; CSF; Trk Coaches Awd; Glnd St Exam Alg Hnrs; Educ.

STOPPENHAGEN, ERIC P; Mission Viejo HS; Mission Viejo, CA; (2); 12/450; Church Yth Grp; Bsktbl; Tennis; High Hon Roll; Delphi; Intl Baccalaureate Pgm; Water Polo.

STOPPENHAGEN, TODD; Warren HS; Downey, CA; (1); Boy Scts; Church Yth Grp; Drama Clb; FBLA; SADD; Thesps; Var Gym; Bus Admin.

STORDAHL, STEPHENIE D; El Toro HS; El Toro, CA; (3); 84/474; Church Yth Grp; Cmnty Wkr; Drama Clb; Capt Drill Tm; School Musical; School Play; Hon Roll; Girls Leag Cmmsnr, VP; Church Camp Cnslr; Summit Ministries; Elem Ed.

STOREY, WENDY H; Willits HS; Willits, CA; (2); Office Aide; Nwsp; Cheerldng; Jrnlsm.

STORK, GREGORY H; San Luis Obispo SR HS; San Luis Obispo, CA; (2); Cmnty Wkr; Math Tm; JV Bsbl; L Crs Cntry; Hon Roll; Stanford; Math.

STORK, RICHARD TAYLOR; Bonita Vista HS; Chula Vista, CA; (3); Cmnty Wkr; Key Clb; Variety Show; Rptr Nwsp; Yrbk; JV Bsktbl; Var Ftbl; Hon Roll; ASB Cmmssnr; Bus Marktng.

STORLIE, KRISTIN; Independence HS; Crescent City, CA; (2); 1/900; Drama Clb; GAA; Letterman Clb; Varsity Clb; Var L Crs Cntry; Var L Trk; High Hon Roll; NHS; Pres Acad Fit Awd; Stanford; Writer.

STORM, ILENE TRACEY; Beverly Hills HS; Beverly Hills, CA; (3); Art Clb; Office Aide; Science Clb; Ski Clb; Temple Yth Grp; Hon Roll; Bus.

STORM, RYAN J; Marysville HS; Marysville, CA; (1); Church Yth Grp; Ski Clb; JV Socr; Var Swmmng; High Hon Roll; Prfct Atten Awd; Rotary Awd; CA Schlrshp Fed; Frgn Lang Clb; Phy.

STORMS, CATHERINE; Madera HS; Madera, CA; (3); Bus Profs of Am; Church Yth Grp; Sec Pres FBLA; Office Aide; Teachers Aide; Band; Mrchg Band; Cit Awd; Hon Roll; Prfct Atten Awd; Catholic Class Teacher; Madera High School Business Dept; Fresno State; Teacher.

STORRS, SUZETTE C; Valhalla HS; El Cajon, CA; (3); 30/423; Pres Church Yth Grp; French Clb; Pep Clb; SADD; Chorus; Stu Cncl; Var Capt Bsktbl; Var Trk; Var Capt Vllybl; Pres Acad Fit Awd; Human Relations Club; Bsktbl & Vllybl MVP; BYU.

STORTROEN, TRACIE L; Oxnard HS; Oxnard, CA; (2); 73/602; Band; JV Vllybl; Cit Awd; High Hon Roll; Prfct Atten Awd; Mck Trl; Pre-Law.

STORY, GLEN A; Valley HS; Sacramento, CA; (3); 27/600; Boy Scts; Church Yth Grp; Rptr Nwsp; JV Socr; Hon Roll; CA Schlrshp Fdrtn-Treas; MESA-VP; Gate Clb Membr.

STORY, JODY; Maxwell Unified HS; Maxwell, CA; (2); Teachers Aide; Band; Jazz Band; Mrchg Band; Treas Soph Cls; Var Bsbl; JV Bsktbl; Var Ftbl; Hon Roll; FBLA-FTR Bus Ldrs Of Amer; Bio.

STOUDER, JANET M; Mission Viejo HS; Mission Viejo, CA; (3); Church Yth Grp; Ed Nwsp; JV Swmmng; Saddleback Comm Coll; Jrnslt.

STOUGHTON, MICHELLE K; Manteca HS; Manteca, CA; (2); 3/420; Church Yth Grp; Key Clb; Letterman Clb; Band; Sec Frsh Cls; Stu Cncl; Swmmng; Tennis; High Hon Roll; Ntl Merit Ltr; Mst Imprvd Tnns & Swmmng & Lttrd; CA Schlrshp Fed Clb; Miss Teen CA Pgnt; Stanford; Med.

STOUT, COURTNAY B; Castle Park HS; Chula Vista, CA; (2); Cmnty Wkr; Drama Clb; English Clb; Model UN; School Play; Ed Nwsp; Ed Lit Mag; High Hon Roll; Hon Roll; NHS; HOBY Fdtn Ambssdr; Engl Outstndng Achvt Awd; West Point U; Spnsh.

STOUT JR, JAMES T; Newport Harbor HS; Costa Mesa, CA; (2); Boy Scts; Church Yth Grp; Church Choir; Ftbl; Trk; Wrstlng; Natl Ski Patrl; Smmr Mssn Trip Dominican Repblc 89; Medcl Mssnry.

STOUT, JESSICA L; Etiwanda HS; Alta Loma, CA; (2); Church Yth Grp; Girl Scts; Scholastic Bowl; Chorus; Nwsp; Yrbk; Bsktbl; Sftbl; Vllybl; High Hon Roll; MVP & Hnrbl Mntn Bsktbl; San Diego ST; Marine Bio.

STOUT, KATIE; Lindsay HS; Lindsay, CA; (3); 3/160; Church Yth Grp; Treas GAA; Ed Nwsp; Ed Yrbk; Pres Frsh Cls; Treas Soph Cls; Pres Jr Cls; Pres Sr Cls; VP Stu Cncl; Var Capt Bsktbl; Camp Royal 90; Exchng Stu Japan; Cngrssnl Yth Ldrshp Cncl 90; Jrnlsm.

STOUT, ROBERT; Arvin HS; Lamont, CA; (1); Letterman Clb; Teachers Aide; Varsity Clb; Ed Nwsp; JV Bsbl; Intrml Ftbl; Var Socr; High Hon Roll; Hon Roll; Pres Acad Fit Awd; CA Poly; Aeronautical Engr.

STOVALL, ERICA L; Wheatland HS; Yuba City, CA; (4); 3/103; Am Leg Aux Girls St; Church Yth Grp; Service Clb; Ed Yrbk; Rep Stu Cncl; Var L Trk; Lion Awd; Rotary Yth Ldrshp Awd; Spelman Coll.

STOVALL, KRISTINE; Dinuba HS; Dinuba, CA; (4); 3/169; Am Leg Aux Girls St; Church Yth Grp; Service Clb; Ski Clb; Band; Chorus; Church Choir; Color Guard; Pep Band; VP Soph Cls; CSF; Natrl Hlprs Pr Cnslr; Chrstn Yth Clb; Cnty Hnr Choir; Intl Music Fstvl Canada; CA ST U; Math.

STOVALL, ROSHELLE; Clovis West HS; Fresno, CA; (2); Church Yth Grp; Cmnty Wkr; SADD; Church Choir; Bsktbl; Trk; Hon Roll; Mem BSU Nxt Yr Pres; Mem MESA; Howard U; Orthopedist.

STOVER, MICHELLE; Cabrillo HS; Vafb, CA; (3); Cmnty Wkr; Dance Clb; Spanish Clb; Variety Show; Capt Chess Clb; Capt Pom Pon; Sftbl; Gov Hon Prg Awd; High Hon Roll; Hon Roll; CSF; U HI; Psycht.

STOWE, APRIL M; Woodland SR HS; Woodland, CA; (3); Church Yth Grp; Treas FBLA; FFA; Var Sftbl; JV Vllybl; High Hon Roll; Jr NHS; Pres Acad Fit Awd; Pres Schlr; Point Loma Nazarene Coll; Bus.

STOWELL, JENNIFER T; Montclair HS; Chino, CA; (2); Church Yth Grp; Key Clb; SADD; Var Socr; Var JV Vllybl; 1st Tm All Leag Var Bllybl Plyr; Hnrbl Mntn All Leag Soccr Plyr; Var Hnrs GATE; UCSD Pepperdine; Vet.

STOWELL, LISA M; Roseville HS; Rocklin, CA; (3); 24/411; French Clb; German Clb; Science Clb; Ed Nwsp; High Hon Roll; NHS; CSF; Badminton Vrsty Team; Golden St Exam Acad Excllnc Awds/Hnrs-88 & 89; Jrnlsm.

STOWELL, NOELLE; Los Alamitos HS; Seal Beach, CA; (3); GAA; Office Aide; JV Var Socr; Hon Roll; San Jose ST.

STOWERS, MELISSA; Cajon HS; San Bernardino, CA; (2); Key Clb; SADD; Stanford; Bus.

STRACHAN, DANDRINE; South Gate HS; South Gate, CA; (4); Church Yth Grp; Key Clb; Pep Clb; Service Clb; Teachers Aide; Bsktbl; Crs Cntry; Trk; Cit Awd; Hon Roll; Track & Crscntry Awds; YBS Schlrshp & Achvt Awd; U Of CA; Psych.

STRACHAN, JOHN E; Eureka SR HS; Eureka, CA; (4); FFA; JA; ROTC; Hon Roll.

STRADER, BRETT K; Victory Christian HS; Sacramento, CA; (2); 1/35; Aud/Vis; Church Yth Grp; Science Clb; Church Choir; School Play; VP Frsh Cls; Pres Soph Cls; JV Bsktbl; Hon Roll; Pres Acad Fit Awd; Sacramento Yth Symph 1st Chair Oboe; Pianist & Accompanist; Mexico Mission Outreach Span Translator; Physics.

STRADER, CHARITY S; Contra Costa Christian HS; Concord, CA; (1); Art Clb; French Clb; JV Vllybl; Hon Roll; Yth Mission; Psych.

STRADLING, JANET L; Point Loma HS; San Diego, CA; (3); Church Yth Grp; Cmnty Wkr; Girl Scts; Hosp Aide; Letterman Clb; Church Choir; JV Cheerldng; Socr; JV Sftbl; Cngrssnl Yth Ldrshp Cncl; CA ST U; Chld Dvlpmnt.

STRAHL, CHRISTY A; Atascadero HS; Atascadero, CA; (1); Church Yth Grp; Chorus; Drill Tm; School Play; High Hon Roll; 1st Pl Drl Dwn USA Drl Cmp 1990; UCSB; Vet Sci.

STRAHL, PHILIP J; Atascadero HS; Atascadero, CA; (4); Cmnty Wkr; Science Clb; Ed Yrbk; JV Crs Cntry; Var L Trk; High Hon Roll; Pres Acad Fit Awd; Tandy Technlgy Schlrs Awd; Recrd Hldr 400 M Relay Track 89-90; CA Polytech ST U; Comp Sci.

STRAIN, KIRSTEN; Casa Grande HS; Petaluma, CA; (2); French Clb; JV Sftbl; Hon Roll.

STRAIT, MONIQUE D; Andrew Hill HS; San Jose, CA; (3); SADD; Hist VICA; Hist Chorus; Swing Chorus; Cheerldng; Swmmng; Trk; OICA Cmptn; Stanford; Fshn.

STRAIT, REBECCA; Archbishop Mitty HS; Sunnyvale, CA; (4); 12/215; Cmnty Wkr; Math Tm; Red Cross Aide; Band; Chorus; Orch; Lit Mag; High Hon Roll; NHS; Ntl Merit SF; Tutoring In Math, Sci & Eng; Regents Schlrshp To UCSD; UCSD; Bio.

STRAITS, NANCY A; Magnolia HS; Anaheim, CA; (2); Cmnty Wkr; Color Guard; Off Frsh Cls; High Hon Roll; Hon Roll; NHS; Prfct Atten Awd; Princpls Hnr Roll; CSF & Frnch Awds; Voluntr At Anaheim Gen Hosp; CA ST U; Tchr.

STRALOW, SANDRA J; Vacaville HS; Vacaville, CA; (4); 137/500; Church Yth Grp; French Clb; German Clb; Teachers Aide; JV Var Diving; High Hon Roll; Hon Roll; NHS; High Hnrs On Alg CA Achvt Tsts; Solano Coll; Sociology.

STRANG, JEREMY; Oroville HS; Oroville, CA; (3); 48/229; Art Clb; Intnl Clb; Key Clb; Spanish Clb; SADD; Band; JV Ftbl; JV Var Trk; Hon Roll; U Houston TX; Optometry.

STRANGMAN, ALEXIS; Santa Ynez Valley Union HS; Santa Ynez, CA; (3); Church Yth Grp; FBLA; Pres Hosp Aide; Pep Clb; Drill Tm; Sprt Ed Yrbk; JV Swmmng; Campus Chrstn Fllwshp; Mascot; Network Drug Free Yth; Attorney.

STRANSKE, TIMOTHY R; Whittier Christian HS; Whittier, CA; (2); Church Yth Grp; Band; Mrchg Band; Pep Band; Bsktbl; Vllybl; Air Force Acad; Lawyer.

STRASBURG, ANNA; Quartz Hill HS; Palmdale, CA; (3); 9/740; Am Leg Aux Girls St; FBLA; SADD; Pres Soph Cls; Pres Jr Cls; Pres Stu Cncl; JV Var Cheerldng; Powder Puff Ftbl; Var Swmmng; High Hon Roll; Natl Hnr Scty; Z-Clb; CA Poly; Pblc Rltns.

STRASKULIC, ROBYN Q; Sacred Heart Prep; Redwood City, CA; (3); Drama Clb; GAA; Model UN; Speech Tm; School Play; Bsktbl; Crs Cntry; Fld Hcky; Hon Roll; Boston U; Spnsh.

STRASSER, STEPHANIE N; Academy Of Our Lady Of Peace; Chula Vista, CA; (1); Church Yth Grp; Church Choir; Var L Trk; Hon Roll.

STRASSNER, DONTRELL M; Grant Union HS; Sacramento, CA; (2); Church Yth Grp; English Clb; Math Tm; Science Clb; Speech Tm; Acpl Chr; Church Choir; Jazz Band; Orch; Pep Band; Engrng.

STRAUB, ALLEN; Sunny Hills HS; Buena Park, CA; (2); Boy Scts; Church Yth Grp; Cmnty Wkr; FBLA; Intrml Swmmng; Honors Entrance 88; Golden St Exam 90; Boys Clb Of Amer; Military Acad; Pilot.

STRAUB, DONALD A; Woodrow Wilson HS; Long Beach, CA; (3); 78/763; Drama Clb; School Play; Golf; Hon Roll; NHS; CSULB; Fil Director.

STRAUB, ERIN R; La Sierra HS; Riverside, CA; (1); Band; Mrchg Band; Pep Band; Hon Roll.

STRAUB, RICHARD E; Paraclete HS; Lancaster, CA; (2); Church Yth Grp; JV Bsbl; JV Ftbl; Hon Roll; Chapman Coll Orange CA; Lwyr.

STRAUCH, GRETCHEN; Liberty Union HS; Byron, CA; (3); 1/400; Pres VP Church Yth Grp; Drama Clb; French Clb; Thesps; Acpl Chr; Band; Jazz Band; Mrchg Band; Pep Band; School Play; Golden St Exam High Hnrs Alge I, Geom; Mock Trial Tm; Johns Hopkins U Talnt Srch St Awd.

STRAUCH, HILARY S; Liberty Union HS; Byron, CA; (1); 1/400; 4-H; Acpl Chr; Band; Mrchg Band; JV Bsktbl; JV Sftbl; JV Trk; JV Vllybl; High Hon Roll; NHS; Math.

STRAUSE, TIFFANY; Acalanes HS; Lafayette, CA; (1); Spanish Clb; Temple Yth Grp; Chorus; JV Swmmng; Hon Roll; Pres Acad Fit Awd; Boalt Hall; Lawyer.

STRAUSS, ADAM B; Brea Olinda HS; Brea, CA; (1); 1/400; Cmnty Wkr; Intnl Clb; NFL; Speech Tm; Temple Yth Grp; Tennis; High Hon Roll; Jr NHS; Hgh Hnrs Gldn ST Exm Algbra; Intrct & Kiwanis Clb; Elec Engr.

STRAUSS, MARTIN C; Atwater HS; Atwater, CA; (3); FFA; JV Ftbl; Mgr(s); Wt Lftg; Hon Roll; Outstndng Woodworking Awd Merced Cty Fair Exhib FFA; Merced Coll.

STRAZZO, MICHAEL; Cordova HS; Sacramento, CA; (3); Church Yth Grp; Office Aide; JV Var Bsbl; JV Ftbl; Var Socr; High Hon Roll; Hon Roll; Natural Hlpr; Psych.

STREET, DAVID R; Thomas Downey HS; Modesto, CA; (3); Church Yth Grp; Band; Mrchg Band; Pep Band; Cit Awd; Hon Roll; CSF Mem; Acad Excl Awd; Aero Eng.

STREET, JULIE L; Glendora HS; Glendora, CA; (4); 6/150; Church Yth Grp; Key Clb; Math Clb; Office Aide; Service Clb; Teachers Aide; Sec Band; Church Choir; Color Guard; Mrchg Band; CSF; Delta Kappa Gamma Coll Schlrshp; Point Loma Nazarene Coll; Ed.

STREET, KIMBERLY; Silver Valley HS; Ft Irwin, CA; (3); Sec Church Yth Grp; SADD; Band; Church Choir; Mrchg Band; Powder Puff Ftbl; Hon Roll; Prfct Atten Awd; U Of AL Birmingham; Dntstry.

STREET, SHAUNIELLE L; O'farrell SCPA; San Diego, CA; (3); Dance Clb; Office Aide; Hon Roll; CA Schlrshp Fed; Outstndng Achvt Hstry, Eng, Typng 87-88; Treas Dance Club; Pre-Med.

STREFF, KRISTINA M; Village Christian Schl; Northridge, CA; (3); 77/123; Church Yth Grp; English Clb; Math Clb; Spanish Clb; Crs Cntry; Mgr(s); Powder Puff Ftbl; Sftbl; Coll Of The Canyons; Intl Bus.

STREICHER, JENNIFER L; Bear River HS; Grass Valley, CA; (2); Cit Awd; Hon Roll; Vrsty Snow Ski Team Racng; Fashn Mrchndsng.

STREIFEL, MAGDALENA O; Chaffey HS; Ontario, CA; (1); German Clb; Hon Roll; Prfct Atten Awd; CSF; Vet.

STRETCH, BILL; Madera HS; Madera, CA; (2); Treas 4-H; Letterman Clb; Rep Stu Cncl; JV Bsktbl; JV Ftbl; Trk; 4-H Awd; Hon Roll; Teachers Aide; Slvr Mdl Natl Jr Olympcs; Acad Athltc Awd; UCLA; Engr.

STRIBLEN, JOSHUA L; Oarnge Glen HS; Escondido, CA; (1); Church Yth Grp; German Clb; Math Tm; Quiz Bowl; Scholastic Bowl; Ftbl; Socr; Tennis; High Hon Roll; Hon Roll; N Cnty Acad League; Arch.

STRIBLEN, JUSTIN M; Orange Glen HS; Escondido, CA; (3); 1/450; Church Yth Grp; Spanish Clb; Band; Jazz Band; Mrchg Band; Pep Band; School Musical; JV Swmmng; NHS; CSF; N Cnty Acad League; Doctor.

STRICKER, W BEN; Bella Vista HS; Orangevale, CA; (3); AFS; Church Yth Grp; Cmnty Wkr; Ed Nwsp; JV Bsbl; Var L Ftbl; JV Var Wt Lftg; Housed AFS Exch Stu From Finland; Most Outstndng Mem Chrch Yth Grp; Bus.

STRICKLAND, JOCELYN D; Fairfield HS; Fairfield, CA; (1); French Clb; FHA; Black Stu Un; Boston U; Lwyr.

STRICKLAND, ROB W; Miramonte HS; Orinda, CA; (3); Church Yth Grp; Debate Tm; Drama Clb; Letterman Clb; NFL; Speech Tm; SADD; Band; Sec Phtg Yrbk; Stu Cncl.

STRICKLER, SONYA L; Pioneer HS; San Jose, CA; (1); Church Yth Grp; German Clb; JV Capt Socr; JV Sftbl; JV Vllybl; High Hon Roll; MVP Soccer.

STRIEBY, JOSH; Springs Of Living Water Acad; Modesto, CA; (1); Orch; Bsktbl; High Hon Roll; Hon Roll; Comp Wrk; TV Wrk; Music.

STRINGER, ANDREW P; Victory Christian HS; Sacramento, CA; (2); 3/35; Chess Clb; JV Stat Bsktbl; High Hon Roll; NHS; Hghst Sci Avg Awd; 1st Pl Rbbn SCCS Chess Trnmt.

STRINGER, CRYSTAL R; Lowell HS; San Francisco, CA; (3); Cmnty Wkr; Yth Aide St CA.

STRINGER, JOSHUA A; Fontana HS; Fontana, CA; (3); 5/1026; Am Leg Boys St; Ski Clb; Band; Var Crs Cntry; Intrml Ftbl; Capt L Socr; L Var Tennis; Capt L Trk; High Hon Roll; Prfct Atten Awd; Acad Decathlon; Forestry.

STRINGER, MATTHEW J; Del Campo HS; Fair Oaks, CA; (3); 159/446; Church Yth Grp; Office Aide; ROTC; Teachers Aide; Ftbl; Acad Decathln-Bronze In Math; ROTC C/Sg Chf Admin,Drl Team,Clr Grd-1st In Rgnl Cmptn,XO Rgnl Encmpm; OR ST U; Military Law.

STRINGFELLOW, BRITTANY; Brethren HS; Lakewood, CA; (1); Church Yth Grp; Pep Clb; JV Var Cheerldng; Hon Roll; USC; Psychlgy.

STRINGFELLOW, JENNIFER L; Grossmont HS; La Mesa, CA; (1); Church Yth Grp; Cmnty Wkr; Jr Camp Cnslr; Church Grp Ldr; U TX; Bus Mgmt.

STRINGFIELD, CHRIS; San Pasqual HS; Escondido, CA; (3); Teachers Aide; Phtg Yrbk; High Hon Roll; Certfd Underwater Scuba Diver 88-90; UC San Diego; Marine Bio.

STROBER, ZACK M; San Rafael HS; San Rafael, CA; (2); 13/256; SADD; JV Ftbl; Hon Roll; Golden St Exam Acad Excllnc Awd; Hnrs Engl.

STROBL, STACI E; Granite Hills HS; El Cajon, CA; (3); Church Yth Grp; Cmnty Wkr; Intnl Clb; JV JV Chorus; Church Choir; Ed Nwsp; Ed Lit Mag; Stu Cncl; Crs Cntry; Diving; CA Art Schlr Creatv Wrtng 90; Enrvnmntl Spplmnt Nwsp Editor; Jrnlsm.

STROH, JENNIFER; Dana Hills HS; Dana Point, CA; (1); Science Clb; Stage Crew; Off Frsh Cls; Hon Roll; Athltc Awds Cllgrphy; Acad Achvmnt Awd For Sci; UC Davis; Vet.

STROH, VALERIE A; Carpinteria HS; Carpinteria, CA; (3); 21/176; French Clb; Science Clb; SADD; Band; Mrchg Band; Powder Puff Ftbl; JV Sftbl; Cit Awd; High Hon Roll; NHS; UC Santa Barbara; Oceanogrphy.

STROHL, JONATHAN G; Willows HS; Willows, CA; (2); Church Yth Grp; JV Bsbl; Var JV Ftbl; JV Mgr(s); JV Trk; Hon Roll; Friday Night Live; Sacramento ST; Accntng.

STROHMAN, JACKIE; Oakmont HS; Roseville, CA; (1); Church Yth Grp; GAA; Intrml Bsktbl; JV Sftbl; JV Vllybl; Hon Roll; Sftbl Coachs Awd, All-Trnmt Awd JV; UCLA; Child Psych.

STROM, ADAM; Valhalla HS; El Cajon, CA; (3); Cmnty Wkr; Key Clb; Library Aide; Ed Nwsp; Stu Cncl; Ftbl; Outstndng Video Work Awd Ftbl Team Cameramn; Human Rltns Clb; USD; Poltcl Sci.

STROM, ERIN M; Vacaville HS; Vacaville, CA; (3); Church Yth Grp; JV Bsktbl; Stat Score Keeper; Var L Vllybl; Hon Roll; Phys Educ.

STROMLE, CHERI L; Milpitas HS; Milpitas, CA; (3); 67/487; Pep Clb; Spanish Clb; Hon Roll; Astrnmy Clb; Engrng.

STROMSNESS, RUNE D; Dunsmuir HS; Dunsmuir, CA; (4); 1/28; Boy Scts; Band; Orch; Ed Yrbk; Pres Jr Cls; Pres Sr Cls; Stu Cncl; Stat Bsktbl; Pres NHS; Ntl Merit SF; TV Prdctn; Elec Engrng.

STROMSOE, CHRIS B; Bonita HS; La Verne, CA; (2); French Clb; Hon Roll; Physics.

STRONG, CHRIS M; North Bakersfield HS; Oildale, CA; (2); Office Aide; Spanish Clb; Teachers Aide; Hon Roll; Spanish NHS; Explorer; Camp Cnslr; CA ST U; Police Officer.

STRONG, CORTLAND B; Millikan HS; Long Beach, CA; (4); Math Clb; Dnfth Awd; High Hon Roll; Prfct Atten Awd; Pres Acad Fit Awd; Blck & Frtd Honorm; Mdl Of Mrt; Medlln Awd; DARE Spksprsn; Peer Cnslr; R C Clb; Acad Excllnc Awd; U Of CA Irvine; Engrng.

STRONG, COURTNEY; Capo Valley HS; Mission Viejo, CA; (2); Church Yth Grp; JV Cheerldng; Work; BYU; Teaching.

STRONG, DEREK S; Mission San Jose HS; Fremont, CA; (4); Var Swmmng; Duke; Bus.

STRONG, KANITRA M; Alverno HS; Altadena, CA; (2); Intnl Clb; Model UN; Science Clb; Service Clb; Teachers Aide; Chorus; Variety Show; Off Soph Cls; Bsktbl; Tennis; St U Smmr Coll Prgm; Schlrshp College Prep HS ; Edtrl Cmmnts Pblshd; Vassar; Law.

STRONG, SUZETTE J; Cloverdale HS; Cloverdale, CA; (3); 5/75; Church Yth Grp; FHA; Teachers Aide; Pres Soph Cls; Sec Sr Cls; JV Bsktbl; High Hon Roll; Hon Roll; CSF Mem; U CA Davis; Animal Sci.

STROUP, JULIE; Tracy HS; Tracy, CA; (3); 29/501; Am Leg Aux Girls St; Cmnty Wkr; Dance Clb; Debate Tm; 4-H; NFL; Pep Clb; Speech Tm; SADD; Teachers Aide; Stu League VP; Dance Cheer Swim Instr; Young Woman Of Yr; UCLA; Engl.

STROUP, LESLIE; Bakersfield HS; Bakersfield, CA; (3); 8/718; Church Yth Grp; FHA; Science Clb; Church Choir; High Hon Roll; Hon Roll; CA Schlrshp Fed; Teacher.

STROUPE, ERIC; Bishop Amat Memorial HS; Diamond Bar, CA; (4); 30/398; Cmnty Wkr; Jazz Band; Pres Stu Cncl; High Hon Roll; CSF; Natl Scl Stds Olympiad; Frst Aid/CPR St Cmptn Gold Medal; Politcal Sci.

STROUPE, KIRK V; Bishop Amat Memorial HS; Diamond Bar, CA; (3); Church Yth Grp; Cmnty Wkr; FCA; Letterman Clb; Service Clb; Varsity Clb; VICA; School Play; Stage Crew; Wt Lftg; Loyola Marymount U; Ed.

STROUSE, GREGG H; Santa Monica HS; Malibu, CA; (3); Teachers Aide; Rep Stu Cncl; JV Ftbl; Hon Roll; Mck Trl Clb Dfns Atty; Tutr 7th Grd Stu.

STROUSE, MINDY; Western HS; Anaheim, CA; (4); Treas Church Yth Grp; Cmnty Wkr; VP DECA; Treas Pep Clb; Varsity Clb; VP Soph Cls; Rep Stu Cncl; Var Cheerldng; Hon Roll; NHS; CA Schlrshp Fed Sec; Los Angls Trd Tech Clb; Design.

STRUB, CARLA; Banning HS; Banning, CA; (4); 6/142; Spanish Clb; Capt Color Guard; Treas Sr Cls; JV Bsktbl; Var Capt Sftbl; Hon Roll; Hs Of Rep; Schl Site Cnsl; CSF; The Bryman Schl; Radiology.

STRUBBE, ELIZABETH; Brethren HS; Redondo Beach, CA; (2); Church Yth Grp; Acpl Chr; School Musical; Var Socr; JV Vllybl; High Hon Roll.

STRUBLE, IAN K; Palos Verdes HS; Palos Vrds Pen, CA; (3); Boy Scts; German Clb; Model UN; JV Crs Cntry; Var Trk; Hon Roll; NHS; CAP.

STRUEBING, SCOTT; San Jacinto HS; Hemet, CA; (3); Chess Clb; English Clb; FFA; Letterman Clb; Varsity Clb; JV Var Bsbl; JV Ftbl; Hon Roll; San Bernardino U; Bus.

STRUTTON, CATINA M; Anderson Union HS; Anderson, CA; (4); Office Aide; Teachers Aide; Acpl Chr; Hlth Sci.

STRUTZ, ADRIAN A; Las Lomas HS; Walnut Creek, CA; (3); 25/275; SADD; High Hon Roll; Achvt Awd Engl 88-89; Aviation.

STRWART, ANDY H; La Sierra HS; Riverside, CA; (1); Boy Scts; Pres FFA; Band; Mrchg Band; Trk; Police Explorers; Citizen Band Radio Operator; REACT; Riverside CC; Police Officer.

STRYBING, KRISTIN; Marysville HS; Brownsville, CA; (4); 1/150; Debate Tm; Key Clb; NFL; Speech Tm; VP SADD; Varsity Clb; Rep Stu Cncl; Var Swmmng; JV Tennis; Pres Acad Fit Awd; U Of CA Santa Barbara; Psych.

STUART, ERIK A; Rio Americano HS; Carmichael, CA; (4); 1/275; Boy Scts; Math Tm; Band; Jazz Band; Pep Band; JV Bsbl; Capt Var Bsktbl; L Var Trk; Ntl Merit SF; HOBY Ambassador N Cal Smnr 88; Acadc Decathlon Coach 87-89; Wstrn US Tlnt Srch 1st Cty 86.

STUART, HEATHER; Westmont HS; Campbell, CA; (4); 10/240; Church Yth Grp; Treas French Clb; Chorus; Church Choir; Capt Drill Tm; School Musical; Treas Sr Cls; French Hon Soc; High Hon Roll; Pres Acad Fit Awd; CSF; Hmcmng Qn; UC Santa Barbara.

STUART, JENNIFER R; Oak Park HS; Agoura Hills, CA; (1); Church Yth Grp; School Musical; School Play; Stat JV Bsktbl; Stat Vllybl; High Hon Roll; Pres Acad Fit Awd; Stanford; Engl.

STUART, SARAH A; Arcata HS; Arcata, CA; (1); Cmnty Wkr; High Hon Roll; Prfct Atten Awd; Camp Fire Yth Schlrshp; Marine Bio.

STUART, TERRI L; Hoopa HS; Orleans, CA; (3); Drama Clb; SADD; School Play; Rptr Nwsp; Pres Frsh Cls; Treas Stu Cncl; Var JV Bsktbl; Var JV Sftbl; Var JV Vllybl; Stat Wrstlng; Stu Cncl Secy & Treas; All Star Team Sftbl; UC Davis; Vet.

STUART, VICKI; Western HS; Buena Park, CA; (4); Band; Chorus; Jazz Band; Pep Band; Natl Hnrs Soc; All St Hnr Band.

STUBBLEFIELD, ANTHONY; Sonoma Valley HS; Sonoma, CA; (4); 18/290; Var Bsbl; Var Ftbl; High Hon Roll; San Luis Obispo ST U; Arntcl.

STUBBLES, JASON; North Monterey County HS; Castroville, CA; (2); SADD; Ftbl; High Hon Roll; Hon Roll; Cmmnty Gathering Walkathon For Disabled; Arch.

STUCKEY, AMY E; Pasadena HS; Pasadena, CA; (3); 1/400; Church Yth Grp; Key Clb; Q&S; Service Clb; Mgr Yrbk; Sec Frsh Cls; Sec Stu Cncl; JV Swmmng; JV Var Vllybl; Hon Roll.

STUDER, KELLY L; Monte Vista HS; Danville, CA; (3); 46/356; Church Yth Grp; Cmnty Wkr; Dance Clb; School Play; Cheerldng; Capt Pom Pon; Hon Roll; Pres Acad Fit Awd; Ntl Chrty League; Nrdstrm Fash Brd 90; Trvlng Cmptv Jazz Dance Team; UCLA; Bus.

STUDER, MELISSA J; Argonaut HS; Ione, CA; (2); Cmnty Wkr; French Clb; Library Aide; Tennis; High Hon Roll; Hon Roll; CSF; Miss Teen CA St Fnls; Math Hnr Roll; Pepperdine U; Astrophysics.

STUDT, CHARLES; San Ramon Valley HS; Danville, CA; (4); 11/400; Aud/Vis; Treas Church Yth Grp; Key Clb; Band; Mrchg Band; Orch; Pep Band; High Hon Roll; NHS; Ntl Merit SF; CSF; US Air Force Acad Smmr Scntfc Smnr; Acad Deca Team; Bus.

STUERTZ, JUSTIN G; Montgomery HS; San Diego, CA; (3); Church Yth Grp; Cmnty Wkr; Letterman Clb; Pep Clb; Ski Clb; Spanish Clb; SADD; Varsity Clb; Stage Crew; JV Bsktbl; San Diego ST U; Psych.

STUEVE, JONATHAN GUY; Oakdale HS; Oakdale, CA; (2); Chess Clb; Church Yth Grp; Cmnty Wkr; Drama Clb; 4-H; FFA; Office Aide; Ski Clb; SADD; Varsity Clb; Point Loma.

STUHLER, RANDALL E; Monterey HS; Monterey, CA; (2); Letterman Clb; Model UN; Ski Clb; Ftbl; Wt Lftg; Outstndng Stu Berkeley MUN Cnfrnc; Mst Outstndng Plyr Yr; Art.

STULL, JESSICA; Banning HS; Whitewater, CA; (2); Chess Clb; French Clb; Letterman Clb; Model UN; Office Aide; Pep Clb; Varsity Clb; Rep Soph Cls; Var L Cheerldng; Cit Awd; CSF Awd 1990; Acad Lttr 1990; Stu Of Mnth 1990; Englsh Acad & Frnch Acad Awds 1990; UCLA; Pre Med.

STULL, TISHA; Hemet HS; Hemet, CA; (2); Math Clb; Science Clb; Band; Mrchg Band; Pep Band; Hon Roll; Conservation Club; Sheriffs Explorer Scouts Pres; Outstndng Musical Achvts Awd; UCLA; Law.

STULLER, NICOLE S; Point Loma HS; San Diego, CA; (2); Swmmng; Won A Mathematics Award For Outstanding Effort; Penn ST; Psychologist.

STULTS, BRANDY L; Antelope Valley HS; Lancaster, CA; (2); Church Yth Grp; Cmnty Wkr; Intnl Clb; Pep Clb; Teachers Aide; Sccr Clb; Mdcl Fld.

STUMP, NATHAN J; Enterprise HS; Millville, CA; (3); 4/430; Math Clb; Math Tm; Mu Alpha Theta; Quiz Bowl; Scholastic Bowl; High Hon Roll; Hon Roll; Sierra Mtn Ecology; Cal Poly San Luis Obispo; Engr.

STUPI, LAURA K; Casa Grande HS; Petaluma, CA; (2); 18/295; French Clb; JV Bsktbl; JV Sftbl; Var Vllybl; High Hon Roll; NHS; Prfct Atten Awd; CA Schlrshp Fed; Awd Of Excl Girls PE.

STUPIN, GABRIEL A; Huntington Beach HS; Huntington Beach, CA; (3); Var L Ftbl; Intrml Capt Vllybl; Ftbl Best Deffnsv Plyr, Offensv Lineman, MVP; Bus.

STURDIVANT, KIMBERLY N; Rancho Cotate HS; Rohnert Park, CA; (2); Cmnty Wkr; FTA; JA; Teachers Aide; Chorus; Bsktbl; Crs Cntry; Trk; Cit Awd; Hon Roll; Santa Rosa JC; Tchng.

STURGEON, AMANDA; Los Banos HS; Los Banos, CA; (2); Church Yth Grp; Drama Clb; Girl Scts; Spanish Clb; Chorus; Stage Crew; High Hon Roll; NHS; CA Schlrshp Fed; Coll Play; Air Force.

STURGEON, DANIEL W; Palmdale HS; Palmdale, CA; (2); Boy Scts; Band; Jazz Band; Mrchg Band; Pep Band; CA ST U Northridge; Music.

STURGEON, JULIE D; Modoc HS; Alturas, CA; (3); 4/70; Am Leg Aux Girls St; Church Yth Grp; Cmnty Wkr; Pres Sec 4-H; Band; Church Choir; Mrchg Band; Pep Band; Sec Jr Cls; Stat Bsbl; Sci.

STURGEON, TRACY S; Fresno HS; Fresno, CA; (3); 62/500; FTA; Sec Key Clb; SADD; Rptr Yrbk; Sec Frsh Cls; Sec Soph Cls; Sec Jr Cls; VP Stu Cncl; Var L Socr; Var L Tennis; Bus.

STURGES, JEFF A; Hamilton HS; Woodland Hills, CA; (2); Debate Tm; Band; Mrchg Band; Hon Roll; Pres Schlr; St Schlr; Acad Of Music; Cal Tech; Engrng.

STURGILL, NICOLE L; Hillcrest Christian Schl; Moorpark, CA; (3); 1/11; Church Yth Grp; JA; Mgr Yrbk; Rep Jr Cls; Sftbl; Vllybl; Cit Awd; High Hon Roll; NHS; Mst Vlble Plyr Sftbl; US Army Rsrve Natl Schlr/Athlte Awd.

STURTEVANT, CHRISTY L; Buena HS; Ventura, CA; (4); Church Yth Grp; Pres VP Girl Scts; SADD; Stage Crew; JV Swmmng; Pres Acad Fit Awd; Germany Exchng Stu; Emory U; History.

STUTZ, KRISTOPHER J; Fontana HS; Fontana, CA; (4); Library Aide; Teachers Aide; Rep Stu Cncl; Journalism.

SU, ANNIE; Mark Keppel HS; Monterey Park, CA; (4); 2/637; Key Clb; Math Clb; Office Aide; Science Clb; Service Clb; Bausch & Lomb Sci Awd; DAR Awd; High Hon Roll; Kiwanis Awd; Pres Acad Fit Awd; Crown & Sceptre; Leos Clb; Excllnce Frgn Lang; UCLA; Biochem.

SU, ELEANOR W; Workman HS; Valinda, CA; (1); Intnl Clb; Science Clb; Hon Roll; Prfct Atten Awd; UC Berkeley; Arch.

SU, LAC; Alhambra HS; Alhambra, CA; (2); Art Clb; Key Clb; Library Aide; Office Aide; Teachers Aide; JV Swmmng; JV Wtr Polo; Gldn Exm; Alhambra Scl Sci Dept Awd; Hlth.

SU, LEON; Monta Vista HS; Cupertino, CA; (4); 1/378; Cmnty Wkr; Pres Science Clb; Service Clb; Mrchg Band; Ed Rptr Nwsp; Stu Cncl; Tennis; NHS; Pres Acad Fit Awd; Val; Thomas J Watson Sr Meml Schlrshp; Tandy Tech Schlrs; CSF; U CA Berkeley; Biochem.

SU, STACEY; Bullard HS; Fresno, CA; (3); 1/500; French Clb; VP Intnl Clb; Key Clb; Math Clb; Spanish Clb; SADD; Orch; High Hon Roll; Hon Roll; Ynt Keybd Artist Assn Intl Cmptn 1st Pl Piano Concerto Div 89; Pepsi Cola-San Fran Symph 2nd Pl 90; Med.

SU, TERRY; Mills HS; Millbrae, CA; (3); Math Tm; Hon Roll; Pres Acad Fit Awd; Med.

SU, THOMAS; Rosemead HS; Rosemead, CA; (2); Cmnty Wkr; FBLA; Treas Intnl Clb; Key Clb; Math Clb; Lit Mag; Off Frsh Cls; Var L Tennis; High Hon Roll; Prfct Atten Awd; Acad Decthln Tm & Clb Treas; Outstndng Stu Of Mnth 1990; El Monte Easter Tnns 2nd Pl; U CA Berkeley; Gentcs.

SUANGPO, WISHA; Artesia HS; Cerritos, CA; (2); Bsbl; Bsktbl; U Of CA Los Angeles; Elec Engr.

SUAREZ, EDDIE M; Sunset HS; Hayward, CA; (1); 46/180; Hispanic Ccmmnty Affrs Cncl Awd 90; Cobat Coll.

SUAREZ, GEORGINA; St Monica HS; Los Angeles, CA; (4); 14/135; Church Yth Grp; Ski Clb; School Play; Swing Chorus; VP Soph Cls; Rep Jr Cls; Sec Stu Cncl; Var Vllybl; Elks Awd; Hon Roll; U Of CA; Biochemistry.

SUAREZ, KARLA L; Calexico Mission Acad; Calexico, CA; (2); Teachers Aide; Chorus; Hon Roll; Readng & Piano Playing; Loma Linda U; Med.

SUAREZ, NANCY; Channel Islands HS; Oxnard, CA; (3); Girl Scts; Latin Clb; Spanish Clb; JV Sftbl; JV Swmmng; Treas Span Club; Crmnl Lwyr.

SUAREZ, SANTIAGO; Eagle Rock HS; Los Angeles, CA; (3); Art Clb; Drama Clb; Tennis; High Hon Roll; Hon Roll; Prfct Atten Awd; Cert Achvmnt & Merit Bus Ed; USC; Avtn.

SUAREZ, VICTOR A; Mater Dei HS; Fountain Valley, CA; (3); 1/450; ROTC; Ski Clb; Rep Frsh Cls; Rep Sr Cls; Rep Stu Cncl; Var JV Golf; Hon Roll; NHS; UCLA; Bio.

SUAREZ, YANEL; Dos Palos HS; Dos Palos, CA; (3); Church Yth Grp; FTA; JV Bsktbl; JV Crs Cntry; JV Sftbl; Var Trk; Var Vllybl; MECHA Club; Merced Coll; Fshn Dsgn.

SUAREZ GOLDBERG, DAVID F; Cel Campo HS; Fair Oaks, CA; (2); 6/460; Tennis; High Hon Roll; Pres Acad Fit Awd; Triple A Awd; U CA Davis; Pre Law.

SUAZO, GUILLERMINA; John F Kennedy HS; Buena Park, CA; (4); Teachers Aide; Var Bsktbl; Var Score Keeper; Hon Roll; Kiwanis Awd; Pres Acad Fit Awd; Arch.

SUBER, DONIELLE; Pinole Valley HS; Pinole, CA; (1); Bsktbl.

SUBUDHAYANGKUL, SARUNTORN; San Marcos HS; Santa Barbara, CA; (2); Church Yth Grp; Chorus; High Hon Roll; Hon Roll; CA Schlrshp Fed; U Of CA; Med.

SUCATRE, HILARY E; Montgomery HS; Santa Rosa, CA; (3); Church Yth Grp; Spanish Clb; Band; Church Choir; Jazz Band; Mrchg Band; Pep Band; Yrbk; Var Tennis; High Hon Roll; Yth Mnstry Mexicali 2 Yrs; Span Camp; Clean Teens; Forgn Lang.

SUCGANG, JOANNE; Franklin JR HS; Vallejo, CA; (1); Co-Capt Drill Tm; Rptr Nwsp; Yrbk; Pres Frsh Cls; Hon Roll; Stu Actvty Cncl; Band & Spirit Cncls; Bus.

SUCGANG, LOWELLEN; Franklin JR HS; Vallejo, CA; (1); Church Yth Grp; Drama Clb; Office Aide; VP Thesps; School Play; Stage Crew; High Hon Roll; Hon Roll; YMCA Gymnstcs Pgm; GVRD Sports; Sci.

SUCHARD, MARC A; Edison HS; Huntington Beach, CA; (3); Cmnty Wkr; French Clb; Treas German Clb; Model UN; Quiz Bowl; JV Crs Cntry; Bausch & Lomb Sci Awd; Ntl Merit Ltr; Excng Stu W Berlin; Fncng Team; City Stff Vlntr; Biochem.

SUCHKA, SUSAN S; Arlington HS; Riverside, CA; (3); Church Yth Grp; Band; Chorus; Church Choir; Co-Ed Yrbk; VP Jr Cls; Var Cheerldng; Hon Roll; Bus Mgt.

SUCHOSKI, VENETIA T; Washington HS; Fremont, CA; (3); 1/330; Ski Clb; Yrbk; Treas Jr Cls; VP Sr Cls; Powder Puff Ftbl; JV Swmmng; Var Trk; High Hon Roll; Lion Awd; Mem CSF; Harvard U; Law.

SUCHY, MELISSA A; Bullard HS; Fresno, CA; (1); Cmnty Wkr; Debate Tm; French Clb; Key Clb; NFL; Ski Clb; SADD; VP Teen Chartr Philanthrpc Clb.

SUDA, KEIKO E; Elk Grove HS; Elk Grove, CA; (1); 1/700; Sec Hosp Aide; SADD; Band; Mrchg Band; Lit Mag; JV Socr; Hon Roll.

SUDANAGUNTA, SHARMILA; Castilleja HS; Los Banos, CA; (3); Cmnty Wkr; Hosp Aide; Ed Yrbk; Sec Frsh Cls; Sec Soph Cls; Sec Jr Cls; Socr; Vllybl; High Hon Roll; French Clb; Badminton; Smith Coll Bk Awd; Frnch Concours Awd; OB/Gyn.

SUDDUTH, KRISTINA M; Adolph Leuzinger HS; Lawndale, CA; (3); 56/328; Church Yth Grp; Cmnty Wkr; Science Clb; Church Choir; Capt Flag Corp; Rep Stu Cncl; Hon Roll; CSF Stu; Outstndg Tall Flag Awd By HS Band; APPI For Coll Bound Stus; UCLA; Educ.

SUDDUTH, MELVIN; Washington Prep HS; Los Angeles, CA; (4); 37/500; Boy Scts; Cmnty Wkr; FBLA; Spanish Clb; Teachers Aide; JV Bsktbl; Hon Roll; San Diego ST U; Bus.

SUDDUTH, TERI DENISE; Hoover HS; Fresno, CA; (3); Drama Clb; Ftbl; Trk; Arch.

SUE, VERA; Oakland HS; Oakland, CA; (3); Spanish Clb; Chorus; School Play; Swmmng; Dance; Swmmng; Bus.

SUEDAS, ANNETTE; St Lucys Priory HS; San Dimas, CA; (2); Capt Cheerldng; Hon Roll; Modeling; Schlrshp Awd To St Lucys; Chrldng Capt; Grp Ldr St Lucys; Bus.

SUEKUT, PAULA J; Galt Joint HS; Herald, CA; (2); Church Yth Grp; Drama Clb; 4-H; German Clb; Intnl Clb; JA; 4-H Awd; High Hon Roll; Hon Roll; Jr NHS; Sacramento ST; Pre-Law.

SUEMNICK, BOYD A; Redwood HS; Visalia, CA; (2); 15/398; Chess Clb; Church Yth Grp; FBLA; JV Ftbl; JV Golf; JV Socr; High Hon Roll; Jr NHS.

SUEN, ANDREW; Garces Memorial HS; Bakersfield, CA; (2); 1/160; Cmnty Wkr; Key Clb; Letterman Clb; Ski Clb; JV Socr; JV Trk; High Hon Roll; Trk Coaches Awd 2 Yrs; Top Ranking 2 Yrs; Stanford; Med.

SUEN, SAM C; Hillsdale HS; Foster City, CA; (3); Math Tm; Science Clb; Teachers Aide; Rptr Yrbk; JV Ftbl; JV Wt Lftg; Asian Clb; Math Hnr; UC Davis; Real Estate.

SUEN, SHIRLEY W; Rosemead HS; Rosemead, CA; (3); Cmnty Wkr; Intnl Clb; Hon Roll; Futurist Clb Secy.

SUGAHARA, KENJI B; Workman HS; Valinda, CA; (2); Intnl Clb; Pres Frsh Cls; JV Ftbl; Var Capt Wrstlng; Hon Roll; Prfct Atten Awd; Spirit Clb; Algebra Golden St Exam Recognition; Wrstlng Most Imprvd Awd; UCLA; Arch.

SUGIHARA, JO ANN R; Cupertino HS; Cupertino, CA; (3); Debate Tm; Pres FBLA; Hosp Aide; Pres Speech Tm; Phtg Nwsp; Off Frsh Cls; Stu Cncl; High Hon Roll; Hon Roll; Jr Statesman Summer Schls, Pres & Rgnl Officer; Mills Coll; Intl Relations.

SUGIMOTO, KRISTINA; Lynbrook HS; Saratoga, CA; (4); Sec Key Clb; Pep Clb; Teachers Aide; Mgr Nwsp; JV Var Cheerldng; NHS; CSF.

SUGITA, JILL T; Walnut HS; Walnut, CA; (2); 26/450; FBLA; Key Clb; Spanish Clb; Yrbk; Var Trk; Top Spnsh I Stu; U CA; Math Tchr.

SUGUI, AURORA G; Edison HS; Stockton, CA; (1); Church Yth Grp; Cmnty Wkr; Computer Clb; Science Clb; Acpl Chr; Church Choir; School Play; Hon Roll; UCLA; Med.

SUGUITAN, ARLENE A; South San Francisco HS; S San Francisco, CA; (2); French Clb; FBLA; Spanish Clb; Cheerldng; Asian Club; Real Est Agent.

SUH, JAE WON; Tokay HS; Lodi, CA; (2); Key Clb; JV Cheerldng; Hon Roll; CSF; Asian Clb; 90 San Joaquin Cnty Intl Fest Korean Qn.

SUH, JOON; Mc Ateer HS; San Francisco, CA; (3); Hon Roll; Close Up Prgm New Americans; Korean Clb.

SUH, JOSHUA H; Redlands HS; Redlands, CA; (3); Boy Scts; Treas Chess Clb; Treas German Clb; Band; Mrchg Band; Pep Band; Acad Decathlon; Engrng.

SUH, KAREN; Whitney HS; Lakewood, CA; (1); Church Yth Grp; Pep Clb; Spanish Clb; Stage Crew; Nwsp; Rep Stu Cncl; Bsktbl; Capt Cheerldng; Gym; Cit Awd; Cls 93 Dir Spec Evnts & Comm Dances; Clb Kaibigan Sgt Arms; Mock Trl Lawyer; Stanford; Pharmacist.

SUH, SCOTT; Dublin HS; Dublin, CA; (2); 9/224; Church Yth Grp; VP Soph Cls; Intrml Bsktbl; JV Crs Cntry; Var L Trk; Hon Roll; Interact Clb; Peer Cnslng; Jr Toastmasters; Arch.

SUH, SHELLEY J; Villa Park HS; Villa Park, CA; (3); 30/500; GAA; Key Clb; Spanish Clb; Orch; VP Frsh Cls; Pres Soph Cls; Rep Jr Cls; Pres Sr Cls; JV Bsktbl; Trk; Pal Peer Cnslng; Amnesty Intl.

SUH, STEPHEN; Irvine HS; Santa Ana, CA; (3); 75/510; Boy Scts; Pres Church Yth Grp; Ed Yrbk; Orch; JV Golf; Hon Roll; Eagle Scout; Pred Medicine.

SUING, TIMOTHY; Fairfax HS; Los Angeles, CA; (3); Boy Scts; Drama Clb; JV Bsbl; Mck Trl Tm; Bggst Beatle Fan; Law.

SUITER, WAYNE D; Hilltop HS; Chula Vista, CA; (2); French Clb; U Of CA Santa Barbara; Hstry.

SUKPRASERT, OKLA-ANNE; San Fernando CIP Magnet HS; North Hollywood, CA; (3); Art Clb; Computer Clb; Pres FBLA; Girl Scts; Science Clb; SADD; Band; School Musical; Ed Nwsp; Ed Yrbk; Keywanettes Lt Govr; Pediatrician.

SULENTOR, MARY K; Bishop Montgomery HS; Rancho Palos Vrds, CA; (3); Church Yth Grp; Letterman Clb; Pres Ski Clb; Var L Tennis; JV Trk; CSF.

SULIAFU, UNGA L; Chaffey HS; Ontario, CA; (2); French Clb; Hosp Aide; Rep Soph Cls; JV Crs Cntry; JV Tennis; French Hon Soc; Hon Roll; Pre-Med.

SULLANO, MARK J; Chula Vista HS; San Diego, CA; (1); 6/203; Service Clb; Var Crs Cntry; JV Trk; CSF; Asian Fellowship Clb.

SULLIVAN, AMY; Foothill HS; Clovis, CA; (2); Church Yth Grp; English Clb; Office Aide; Science Clb; Church Choir; Lit Mag; JV Capt Bsktbl; JV Swmmng; JV Vllybl; Cit Awd; Lfguard; Wrtng Awds; Most Insprtnl Vllybl & JV Bsktbl; Lit.

SULLIVAN, CHRISTEN A; Palm Springs HS; Palm Springs, CA; (3); 9/550; Church Yth Grp; Drama Clb; French Clb; School Play; Stage Crew; High Hon Roll; Hon Roll; JSA; CSF; Silver Sands Awds; Golden St Exam Algebra Hnrs; Psych.

SULLIVAN, CORRINN; Poway HS; San Diego, CA; (3); 61/650; Cmnty Wkr; FBLA; Letterman Clb; Red Cross Aide; SADD; Varsity Clb; Acpl Chr; Chorus; Stat Bsktbl; Ftbl; Pres Saferides Cmnty Svc Drvng Stu; Med Athltc Trnr.

SULLIVAN, DAN C; Lone Pine HS; Lone Pine, CA; (3); Letterman Clb; Varsity Clb; Pres Frsh Cls; Treas Sr Cls; Rep Stu Cncl; Bsbl; Var JV Bsktbl; Var JV Ftbl; Law.

SULLIVAN, DAVID A; Hamilton Union HS; Orland, CA; (3); 3/45; Church Yth Grp; FFA; Letterman Clb; Band; Sec Frsh Cls; Bsktbl; JV Capt Ftbl; Trk; Wt Lftg; Hon Roll; Advncd Drftng & Excllnc In Art Outstndng Achvt; Civil Engr.

SULLIVAN, ERIN; St Rose Acad; San Francisco, CA; (4); Am Leg Aux Girls St; Church Yth Grp; Rep JCL; Pres Latin Clb; Service Clb; VP Pres Sr Cls; Hon Roll; NHS; Pres Acad Fit Awd; Voice Dem Awd; UC Davis; Bio.

SULLIVAN, JANETTE Y; James Lick HS; San Jose, CA; (2); Church Yth Grp; Pep Clb; Treas Soph Cls; Cheerldng; Golden St Exam Hnr; Vrsty Badminton.

SULLIVAN, JENNIFER; Ontario HS; Ontario, CA; (4); 12/400; Church Yth Grp; French Clb; Thesps; Band; Mrchg Band; School Musical; Cheerldng; Elks Awd; High Hon Roll; Pres Acad Fit Awd; U Of Southern CA; Amer Stud.

SULLIVAN, KATHLEEN M; Mater Dei HS; Santa Ana, CA; (3); Church Yth Grp; Drama Clb; French Clb; Sec Band; Sec Mrchg Band; Pep Band; School Musical; School Play; Stage Crew; CSF; Child Psych.

SULLIVAN, KEARY; Washington HS; San Francisco, CA; (2); Math Clb; VP Science Clb; Spanish Clb; Golf; Trk; Elks Awd; Jr NHS; Pres Acad Fit Awd.

SULLIVAN, KELLI J; Central Union HS; El Centro, CA; (2); Church Yth Grp; Treas German Clb; Band; Church Choir; Drill Tm; JV Tennis; Play Piano & Keybd; Dancr Ballet & Jazz; Danc Recitals & Musicals; Music.

SULLIVAN, KERRY M; Marysville HS; Marysville, CA; (3); 14/202; Church Yth Grp; Debate Tm; German Clb; Key Clb; Sec Soph Cls; Sec Jr Cls; Sec Stu Cncl; Var Swmmng; Hon Roll; Lion Awd; Cls Homcmng Atten; GATE Stu Senate; WASC Stu Cmmtte; CSF; Yuba Coll Hnrs Luncheon; Frgn Lang Stu Month; Psych.

SULLIVAN, LANA R.; Troy HS; Fullerton, CA; (3); 11/316; FCA; Ski Clb; Phtg Ed Yrbk; JV Capt Cheerldng; Var L Crs Cntry; Var L Socr; Var L Swmmng; Var L Trk; High Hon Roll; Rotary Awd; Cal ST Fullerton; Bio.

SULLIVAN, MICHELLE E; Southern CA Christian HS; Yorba Linda, CA; (3); Church Yth Grp; Teachers Aide; VP Soph Cls; Stat Bsktbl; Hon Roll.

SULLIVAN, MIYA V; Santa Teresa HS; San Jose, CA; (2); Church Yth Grp; Dance Clb; Girl Scts; Spanish Clb; Teachers Aide; Church Choir; JV Capt Bsktbl; Var Crs Cntry; Var Trk; Prfct Atten Awd; MVP-JV Bsktbl Team; JV All Tournament Awd-Bsktbl; U; Phys Ed.

SULLIVAN, PATRICIA; Claremont HS; Claremont, CA; (3); Cmnty Wkr; Girl Scts; Teachers Aide; ROP Cert; WISE&MEP Cert; Vlntr Memrl Park Day Care; Aerospc Engrng.

SULLIVAN, SARAH B; Modesto Christian HS; Modesto, CA; (3); Church Yth Grp; Variety Show; Pres Jr Cls; Pres Sr Cls; Stu Cncl; JV Vllybl; Hon Roll; Modestos Yng Wmn Of Yr; CSF; Concerned Wmn Of Amer; Psych.

SULLIVAN, TODD C; Capistrano Valley HS; Mission Viejo, CA; (3); Am Leg Boys St; Church Yth Grp; Debate Tm; Drama Clb; School Play; Lit Mag; Stu Cncl; Crs Cntry; Trk; Pres Acad Fit Awd; Science Fair; U Of Calif; Film.

SULLIVAN, TUNORA; Antelope Valley HS; Lancaster, CA; (1); Pres Church Yth Grp; Dance Clb; Math Tm; Spanish Clb; Church Choir; Orch; School Musical; School Play; Intrml Bsktbl; Intrml Sftbl; Howard; Comp Engrng.

SULLIVAN, YVETTE; Live Oak HS; Morgan Hill, CA; (4); 41/508; Church Yth Grp; Cmnty Wkr; FBLA; JA; Sec Science Clb; Pres Spanish Clb; Varsity Clb; Church Choir; Rptr Lit Mag; Sec Sr Cls; Wtr Polo; Mercury News HS Hnr Roll; Santa Clara U; Bio Sci.

SULTAN, NAOMI J; Mc Ateer HS; San Francisco, CA; (3); School Play; Rep Jr Cls; High Hon Roll; Hon Roll; Smith Coll Bk Awd; Russian Tea Clb; USSR-USA Mnth Long Exchnge; Mc Ateer Coll Scty; CSF; Actor.

SULTANY, STEPHANIE; Escondido HS; Escondido, CA; (3); Church Yth Grp; Key Clb; Rep Stu Cncl; Var Capt Bsktbl; Capt Powder Puff Ftbl; Var Vllybl; Hon Roll; NHS; Athltc Schltc Awd; U Of CA.

SULTANYAN, ELIZABETH; Pasadena HS; Pasadena, CA; (4); 21/433; Church Yth Grp; Drama Clb; JA; Science Clb; Sec Spanish Clb; Capt Swmmng; Hon Roll; CSF Sec; William C Miller Schlrshp, Pasadena City Coll; Armenian Clb Treas; Pasadena City Coll; Med.

SULZMAN, GARRETT A; Bellflower HS; Bellflower, CA; (3); 36/265; Church Yth Grp; Drama Clb; Quiz Bowl; Teachers Aide; Treas Thesps; Acpl Chr; Church Choir; School Play; Swing Chorus; High Hon Roll; Vrsty E-Clss Fencing; Long Beach City CC; Music.

SUM, DAVID C; Leuzinger HS; Lawndale, CA; (4); JA; Color Guard; JV Ftbl; Tennis; JV Vllybl; Wt Lftg; Hon Roll; Opt Clb Awd; Pres Acad Fit Awd; MBPD Police Explorer Lt; CA ST U Long Bch; Elec Eng.

SUM, TONY K; Leuzinger HS; Lawndale, CA; (2); Key Clb; Treas Soph Cls; Stu Cncl; JV Ftbl; JV Vllybl; High Hon Roll; Hon Roll; Prfct Atten Awd; CSF; Vlybl Club.

SUMAMPONG, LORETA; Amos Stagg HS; Stockton, CA; (2); Hon Roll.

SUMAN, SAUNJA; Saddleback HS; Santa Ana, CA; (4); 22/524; Chrmn Church Yth Grp; English Clb; Girl Scts; Chorus; Church Choir; Mrchg Band; Variety Show; Sec Treas Jr Cls; Var JV Cheerldng; Pres Acad Fit Awd; Brigham Young U; Accntng.

SUMBLIN, VERNIDA FAYE; Live Oak HS; San Martin, CA; (3); Dance Clb; Drama Clb; FHA; GAA; Model UN; ROTC; Chorus; School Play; Nwsp; Yrbk; Mr & Mrs Live Oak Body Bldg Cont; Gavilan Coll; Nrs.

SUMMERALL, JENNI J; Ramona HS; Ramona, CA; (2); 35/345; Co-Capt Drill Tm; Capt Flag Corp; Otis-Parson; Art.

SUMMERS, AMY J; Palo Verde HS; Blythe, CA; (3); 4/212; Drama Clb; Teachers Aide; School Play; Var Capt Cheerldng; JV Vllybl; Bausch & Lomb Sci Awd; High Hon Roll; Hon Roll; NHS; CA Schlrshp Fed; Mock Trial; UCSD; Med.

SUMMERS, JULIE A; Barstow HS; Barstow, CA; (1); Yrbk; Bsbl; Bsktbl; Score Keeper; Sftbl; Vllybl.

SUMNER, BRENDA; Saddleback HS; Santa Ana, CA; (4); #17 In Class; Art Clb; Church Yth Grp; English Clb; FBLA; Sec Treas Pep Clb; SADD; Ed Yrbk; Biola U; Bus Admin.

SUMNER, STEPHANIE; Mission Viejo HS; Mission Viejo, CA; (3); Church Yth Grp; Cmnty Wkr; Girl Scts; Hosp Aide; Key Clb; SADD; Ed Nwsp; Stat Bsktbl; NHS; Grls Leag Rep On Cncl.

SUMNER, TORIE M; Louisville HS; Malibu, CA; (3); VP FHA; GAA; Nwsp; Yrbk; Var Capt Vllybl; Hon Roll; Opt Clb Awd; Bus.

SUMPTER, GREG G; Pasadena HS; Altadena, CA; (3); Church Yth Grp; Cmnty Wkr; JA; Var Bsktbl; Hon Roll; Gamma Lambda Pres; MESA Clb; Commnctns.

SUMWALT, TODD W; Golden Westi HS; Visalia, CA; (2); Church Yth Grp; FBLA; Chess Clb; Off Soph Cls; Var L Swmmng; High Hon Roll; Pres Acad Fit Awd; Water Polo JV MVP.

SUN, DEBORAH A; Irvington HS; Fremont, CA; (4); Pres SADD; Rptr Yrbk; High Hon Roll; Hon Roll; Jr NHS; NHS; Pres Acad Fit Awd; Cmptv Swmmr 9 Yrs; SADD Pres 3 Yrs; Arch.

SUN, HUI H; Edison HS; Stockton, CA; (3); FTA; Hon Roll; U CA Davis; Elem Ed.

SUN, JENNIFER P; Notre Dame HS; Hillsborough, CA; (3); 3/95; Nwsp; Rep Soph Cls; Off Jr Cls; Rep Sr Cls; Rep Stu Cncl; Var Crs Cntry; JV Swmmng; Var Vllybl; NHS; Prfct Atten Awd.

SUN, KAI Y; George Washington HS; San Francisco, CA; (3); Hon Roll; Golden Gate Exam Hnr; UC Davis; Bus.

SUN, NANCY; Westlake HS; Agoura, CA; (3); Pres Key Clb; Sec Frsh Cls; Sec Jr Cls; Sec Sr Cls; Rep Stu Cncl; Swmmng; High Hon Roll; Prfct Atten Awd; Pres Acad Fit Awd; CSF; Jnr Bach Fest Fnlst.

SUN, NICK H; North Hollywood HS; North Hollywood, CA; (2); Chess Clb; Hosp Aide; Natl Beta Clb; Service Clb; Teachers Aide; Cit Awd; High Hon Roll; Hon Roll; CJSF; CSF; Med.

SUN, PETER CHAO-KANG; Mills HS; Daly City, CA; (3); Church Yth Grp; Church Choir; Lit Mag; Crs Cntry; Hon Roll; Pres Acad Fit Awd; Boys Clb Fine Arts; Tkn All Avlble AP & Hnr Clses; Wrk; Creative Arts.

SUN, RITHY; Novato HS; Novato, CA; (3); French Clb; Teachers Aide; Var Tennis; Var Vllybl; 4-H Awd; Hon Roll; Prfct Atten Awd; Pres Acad Fit Awd; Fr Awd; U Of CA; Psych.

SUN, SERENA; Aragon HS; San Mateo, CA; (3); Cmnty Wkr; Girl Scts; Ski Clb; Yrbk; Off Jr Cls; Swmmng; Hon Roll; Adidas Tnns Camp; Wrk Parents Corp; UC Santa Barbara; Intl Bus.

SUN, SIVOURN; Edison HS; Stockton, CA; (4); 2/32; Church Yth Grp; Yrbk; Off Sr Cls; Bsktbl; Ftbl; Hon Roll; Hearld Coll; Typing.

SUN, VIVIAN; Monta Vista HS; Cupertino, CA; (2); 146/340; Drama Clb; FBLA; Math Tm; Service Clb; Chorus; Cheerldng; Score Keeper; Swmmng; Trk; Amnesty Intl Clb; Grls Waterpolo; CSF Awd; Chinese Schl; Chinese Olympics Swmng Gold Mdl; Med.

SUN, WEI-LUNG; Orange Glen HS; Escondido, CA; (2); 1/572; High Hon Roll.

SUNAMORO, RANA M; Hoover HS; Fresno, CA; (3); Stu Cncl; JV Var Socr; Hon Roll; Principal Awd; Hmcmng Princess; Prom Princess; Fresno ST; Psych.

SUNDE, ERIC A; Chaminade College Prep; Northridge, CA; (3); Boy Scts; Cmnty Wkr; Drama Clb; Intnl Clb; Key Clb; Model UN; School Play; Stage Crew; Rptr Nwsp; JV Crs Cntry; L A Cnty & CA St Sci Fair.

SUNDEEN, JOHNNA M; Fontana HS; Fontana, CA; (3); Pres Church Yth Grp; Teachers Aide; Chorus; Drill Tm; Swing Chorus; High Hon Roll; Hon Roll; Med.

SUNDEEN, MEGAN; Pasadena HS; Pasadena, CA; (3); Var Sftbl; JV Tennis; Hon Roll; Ntl Merit Schol; PHS Greenpeace Clb Orgnzr/Chrtr; Vet Hospt Vlntr; UCSB; Vet.

SUNDGREN, NATHAN; Hesperia Christian Schl; Hesperia, CA; (2); 1/42; Quiz Bowl; Scholastic Bowl; JV Ftbl; Wt Lftg; High Hon Roll; Hon Roll; CSF; UCLA; Med.

SUNDSTEDT, MATT M; El Camino HS; Oceanside, CA; (1); 25/450; Church Yth Grp; School Musical; Treas Frsh Cls; High Hon Roll; Bsktbl; Guitar; Piano; Berklee Sch Music; Guitarist.

SUNG, ALAN W; Foothill HS; Santa Ana, CA; (2); Key Clb; Spanish Clb; JV Vllybl; High Hon Roll; Hon Roll; MIP JV Sq; Best Defense Awd; UC San Diego; Bus.

SUNG, CAROLIN T; Lowell HS; San Francisco, CA; (2); German Clb; Vietnames Clb; Korean Clb; Orient Exprss Clb; UC Berkeley; Arch.

SUNG, DEREK H; Granada Hills HS; Northridge, CA; (3); Cmnty Wkr; Hosp Aide; Spanish Clb; SADD; Teachers Aide; JV Bsktbl; Var Capt Swmmng; High Hon Roll; Hon Roll; NHS; CSF; Jr Stateman Of Amer; JV Waterpolo; LA City Swim Chmpn Vars Awds; Arch.

SUNG, DERRICK; Piedmont HS; Piedmont, CA; (4); 1/120; Band; Jazz Band; Orch; School Musical; Crs Cntry; Trk; L Vllybl; Ntl Merit SF; Pres Acad Fit Awd; Val; Stanford U.

SUNG, JEFF D; La Serna HS; Whittier, CA; (4); 1/350; Pres Soph Cls; VP Jr Cls; Rep Stu Cncl; Var Capt Socr; Var JV Tennis; NHS; Pres Acad Fit Awd; Val; Southern CA Edison Schlrshp; UC Santa Barbara; Bio.

SUNG, KI-EUN; Birmingham HS; Encino, CA; (4); Math Tm; Speech Tm; Off Jr Cls; Off Sr Cls; Intrml Vllybl; High Hon Roll; Sec Jr NHS; Pres Acad Fit Awd; Sal; Math & Sci Awd By Wmn In Engrng; UC Berkeley.

SUNG, PETER; Lincoln HS; Stockton, CA; (3); 48/592; Church Yth Grp; Mu Alpha Theta; JV Bsktbl; JV Trk; High Hon Roll; Pres Acad Fit Awd; CSF; Asn Clb; MA Inst Of Tech; Aerosp Engr.

SUNG, SANDY; Mt Carmel HS; Layton, UT; (4); German Clb; Intnl Clb; Math Tm; Band; Mrchg Band; Pep Band; High Hon Roll; NHS; Pres Acad Fit Awd; UC Riverside; Biomedcl.

SUNG, WEI-LING; Bishop O'dowd HS; San Leandro, CA; (2); Church Yth Grp; Chorus; Variety Show; Hon Roll; CSF.

SUNG, YEN-LING; Lowell HS; San Francisco, CA; (2); Church Yth Grp; Hosp Aide; Chorus; Church Choir; School Musical; Mgr Stat Ftbl; Mgr(s); Mgr Swmmng; Hon Roll; Cndctr Chrch Chldrns Choir & Pianist; Tour Asia W/Prof Choir; Teach Sunday Schl For Kids; Wrk Tour Co; UC Sys; Oncology.

SUNGA, IRENE Y; Hogan SR HS; Vallejo, CA; (3); VP Dance Clb; Science Clb; Spanish Clb; Drill Tm; Variety Show; Yrbk; Hon Roll; Badmiton; Hnr Scty; Med.

SUNICO, DENNIS; Bellarmine Jefferson HS; Sunland, CA; (3); Var Crs Cntry; Var Trk; Hon Roll; NHS.

SUNWOO, STEPHANIE; Oxnard HS; Oxnard, CA; (2); 1/600; Art Clb; Debate Tm; Pres Speech Tm; Lion Awd; Photo Clb VP; Undergrnd Shakespeare Scty; CSF; Photogrphy.

SUNWOO, STEVE; Oxnard HS; Oxnard, CA; (1); 2/700; Boy Scts; Computer Clb; Tennis; UCLA; Arch.

SUO, SHANNON T; Casa Roble Fundenmental HS; Orangevale, CA; (4); 6/374; Treas French Clb; SADD; Intrml Cheerldng; Var L Trk; High Hon Roll; NHS; Ntl Merit SF; Acad Decathlon 1st Pl Speech, Highest Score Speech; Best Effort Soph Clss; Most Inspirational Track; UC Davis; Pediatrician.

SUPNET, ERIK P; Woodland HS; Woodland, CA; (2); FFA; Var Capt Crs Cntry; JV Capt Trk; Jr NHS; Pres Acad Fit Awd; IV/Delta League Champ Crss Cntry; IV League Champ Trk; Deans List; HEROS Awd; Lawyer.

SUPRAI, GURDISH K; Sutter Union HS; Yuba City, CA; (2); 4/95; FBLA; FHA; Rptr Nwsp; Hon Roll; CSF; FNL; San Jose ST U; Advrtsng.

SURA, EDWIN; San Rafael HS; San Rafael, CA; (2); School Play; JV Bsbl; JV Crs Cntry; JV Ftbl; Var Socr; JV Trk; Indian Valley Coll; Bus.

SURATOS, ROMMEL Q; Vacaville HS; Vacaville, CA; (3); 8/670; Quiz Bowl; Band; Jazz Band; Mrchg Band; Pep Band; School Musical; JV Trk; Intrml Wt Lftg; JV Wrstlng; High Hon Roll; Mst Imprvd Plyr Ftbl; Quz Bwl Chmps; Hgh Hnrs Gldn St Gmtry Exm; Engnrng.

SURENDRANATH, RICHARD; Venice HS; Los Angeles, CA; (2); Science Clb; Service Clb; Teachers Aide; Intrml Ftbl; Intrml Trk; Intrml Vllybl; Cit Awd; High Hon Roll; Prfct Atten Awd; CSF; U CA-BERKELEY; Engrng.

SURFACE, JENNIFER L; Pacifica HS; Stanton, CA; (2); #4 In Class; Var Bsktbl; Var Sftbl; Hon Roll; CSF; Bus.

SURFAS, DAMON R; Foothill HS; Santa Ana, CA; (3); VP Temple Yth Grp; Hon Roll; Intrml Crs Cntry; JV Trk; Scuba Diving; Kung Fu; Arch.

SURH, MATILDA C; Skyline HS; Oakland, CA; (2); Cmnty Wkr; Key Clb; Variety Show; Mgr Yrbk; Hon Roll.

SURMENIAN, ANNY; Alverno HS; Pasadena, CA; (3); 5/67; Model UN; Ed Lit Mag; Sec Soph Cls; Rep Jr Cls; Hon Roll; CSF; Campus Life; Frnch III Awd; Engl Ii Hnrs Awd; Law.

SURO, MARITA A; Pacific Grove HS; Pacific Grove, CA; (3); Teachers Aide; School Musical; Rptr Pom Pon; Pres Soph Cls; Var Bsktbl; Var Swmmng; Hon Roll; Ntl Merit Ltr; Hnrs Golden St Exam In Geom; Pediatrician.

SURWILL, ROB M; Quartz Hill HS; Palm Dale, CA; (2); Church Yth Grp; Spanish Clb; Drill Tm; Stat Vllybl; High Hon Roll; Pres Schlr; Sea Cadets; Friday Night Live Clb; Crmnlgy.

SUSENO, AUDREY D; Huntington Beach HS; Huntington Beach, CA; (2); Pres Key Clb; Red Cross Aide; Spanish Clb; JV Var Trk; High Hon Roll; Jr NHS; VP Tn Clb; Orgnc Chem.

SUSILASATE, WILBUR; Whitney HS; Cerritos, CA; (3); Key Clb; Hon Roll; Jr Hnr Guard; CSF; Mech Engrng.

SUSON, JOSEPH D; Clovis HS; Clovis, CA; (2); Hon Roll; Fresno City Coll; Crpntr.

SUSSOEV, NATASHA J; Los Altos HS; Hacienda Hts, CA; (3); 15/370; Church Yth Grp; GAA; Capt Varsity Clb; Var Capt Bsktbl; Cit Awd; High Hon Roll; Var Vllybl; Southern CA U; Comp Sci.

SUSTAITA, JUANITA; Tulare Union HS; Tulare, CA; (4); Am Leg Aux Girls St; Art Clb; Cmnty Wkr; Hosp Aide; Office Aide; Speech Tm; SADD; Teachers Aide; Varsity Clb; Rep Frsh Cls; COS; Public Relations.

SUSTERSIC, JOY L; Irvine HS; Irvine, CA; (1); Church Yth Grp; JV Co-Capt Tennis; Hon Roll; Miami U; Bus.

SUSTICH, HOLLY A; Hogan SR HS; Vallejo, CA; (2); High Hon Roll; Hon Roll; UC Davis; Vet.

SUSZKO, KATHY J; Poway HS; Poway, CA; (4); Office Aide; Varsity Clb; Stat Bsktbl; Intrml JV Sftbl; JV Vllybl; San Diego Tribunes All Acad Tm; MVP Frshmn & Jr Vrsty Sftbl; Coachs Awd Vrsty Sftbl; San Diego ST U; Tele Commnctns.

SUTCLIFFE, LESLIE B; Fort Bragg HS; Fort Bragg, CA; (2); 5/150; Bsktbl; Hon Roll; NHS; Sacramento ST; Pediatrcn.

SUTER, STEFANY N; Loretto HS; Elk Grove, CA; (2); Girl Scts; Library Aide; SADD; Teachers Aide; Varsity Clb; Rptr Nwsp; Var Socr; Raise Black Labs; Chico ST; Psych.

SUTHAR, ANJALI M; Santa Teresa HS; San Jose, CA; (1); Cmnty Wkr; Rptr 4-H; Model UN; Spanish Clb; SADD; JV Tennis; 4-H Awd; High Hon Roll; Amnesty Intl; Supreme Crt Cabinet; Stanford.

SUTHERLAND, APRIL M; Inglewood HS; Inglewood, CA; (1); Bus Profs of Am; Computer Clb; English Clb; FBLA; Office Aide; ROTC; Speech Tm; Off Soph Cls; Var Bsktbl; Gym; Marines; Law.

SUTHERLAND, KERRI M; Fort Bragg HS; Fort Bragg, CA; (3); 4/126; Church Yth Grp; Cmnty Wkr; GAA; Intnl Clb; Letterman Clb; Spanish Clb; SADD; Teachers Aide; Varsity Clb; Yrbk; Eng Achvt, Hstry Awds; CA Schltc Fed; Rotary Ldrshp Assembly; Soroptimist Youth Forum Girls St Rnnr Up; Psych.

SUTHERLAND, MICHELLE A; Turlock HS; Turlock, CA; (3); Church Yth Grp; Cmnty Wkr; Teachers Aide; Chorus; Church Choir; Teen Line; MJC; Tchng.

SUTHERLAND, TARA; North Salinas HS; Salinas, CA; (2); Drama Clb.

SUTLIFF, MATTHEW E; Chaffey HS; Ontario, CA; (2); Boy Scts; Church Yth Grp; Pres German Clb; Model UN; Office Aide; Teachers Aide; DAR Awd; Hon Roll.

SUTRO, DEREK S; Live Oak HS; Live Oak, CA; (2); 14/105; Computer Clb; Ftbl; Tennis; Hon Roll; Electrncs; Heald Inst Of Technlgy; Elctrnc.

SUTTON, CATHY A; Yucca Valley HS; Yucca Valley, CA; (4); Church Yth Grp; FBLA; Quiz Bowl; Speech Tm; Teachers Aide; Rptr Yrbk; Sec Frsh Cls; Rep Stu Cncl; Capt Var Cheerldng; Var L Gym; Christ Coll Irvine; Lib Arts.

SUTTON, COLEMAN E; Bullard HS; Fresno, CA; (3); JV Bsktbl; Var L Tennis; CSF; Hnrs GSE Geom.

SUTTON, DANIEL; Clovis HS; Clovis, CA; (1); 4-H; SADD; Band; Jazz Band; Mrchg Band; Pep Band; Yrbk; Tennis; 4-H Awd; High Hon Roll; CSF; Medicine.

SUTTON, JESSICA P; California HS; San Ramon, CA; (3); 25/368; Church Yth Grp; Teachers Aide; Varsity Clb; Rep Soph Cls; Var L Bsktbl; High Hon Roll; Hon Roll; NHS; Pres Acad Fit Awd; CSF; Chrch Acolyte; Acad Ltr 3 Semesters; Sonoma ST U; Psych.

SUTTON, KELLI A.; Brea-Olinda HS; Brea, CA; (3); 5/300; Church Yth Grp; Capt Flag Corp; High Hon Roll; CSF VP.

SUTTON, NIKKI; North HS; Redondo Beach, CA; (4); 34/466; Pep Clb; Capt Pom Pon; Cit Awd; Hon Roll; Pres Acad Fit Awd; 2 Yr Participant Annual Dance Prod; 2 Yr Membr CA Scholarship Fed Gold Tassel; Treas Flying Club; UCSB; Bus & Spanish.

SUTTON, PHILIP MATTHEW; Don Bosco Technical Inst; San Gabriel, CA; (1); 1/244; Boy Scts; Band; Church Choir; Drm Mjr(t); Jazz Band; Mrchg Band; Engrng.

SUTTON, SCOTT D; Indio HS; Indio, CA; (1); Boy Scts; Church Yth Grp; John Hopkins U; MD.

SUZUKI, RYAN T; North Tahoe HS; Kings Beach, CA; (3); 3/60; Cmnty Wkr; Teachers Aide; Var Socr; Var Wrstlng; High Hon Roll; NHS; Opt Clb Awd; Var Wrstlg Coach Awd; Golden St Exam Hnrs Alg 87 Geo 88; Judges Awd Arts For Schls 88; Bus.

SUZUKI, SCOTT D S; Los Altos HS; Hacienda Hgts, CA; (3); Var Bsktbl; Cit Awd; Hon Roll; Prfct Atten Awd.

SUZUKI, SHIHO KAREN; Westminster HS; Westminster, CA; (3); Intnl Clb; Spanish Clb; Ed Nwsp; Fld Hcky; Japanese; Odori Japanese Dance, Koto Japanese Intrmnt; Nurse.

SVARCZKOPF, KEVIN S; Norte Vista HS; Riverside, CA; (2); 21/554; JA; Var Crs Cntry; JV Trk; Hon Roll; Arch.

SVARVARI, WARD; Arcata HS; Bayside, CA; (1); Boy Scts; French Clb; JV Crs Cntry; Score Keeper; JV Wrstlng; Hon Roll; Stu Exprssng Common Sns; Bsbl; Bus Admin.

SVENDSEN, INGER; Santa Fe Christian HS; Carlsbad, CA; (4); 3/41; Church Yth Grp; Cmnty Wkr; Drama Clb; French Clb; Band; School Play; Stage Crew; Yrbk; Pres Jr Cls; L Crs Cntry; Repblcn Wmns Schlrshp Awd; Liberty U; History Educ.

SVENDSGAARD, DUDLEY; Alameda HS; Alameda, CA; (2); Art Clb; Spanish Clb; JV Crs Cntry; Var Trk; UC Berkley; Graphic Ats.

SVIEN, BRANDI; Hanford Joint Union HS; Hanford, CA; (3); Acpl Chr; Chorus; Madrigal Singers; Fresno ST; Zoology.

SWAGER, KRISTA A; Pinole Valley HS; Hercules, CA; (2); Drama Clb; Service Clb; Thesps; Drm Mjr(t); School Musical; School Play; Stage Crew; Intrml Gym; Hon Roll; CSF; GSE Algebra Test High Hnr Awd Wnnr.

SWAIM, KELLIE L; Southern California Christian Schl; Orange, CA; (1); High Hon Roll.

SWAIM, KENDRA K; Woodcrest Christian HS; Riverside, CA; (2); Church Yth Grp; Stat Bsbl; JV Bsktbl; Stat Sftbl; JV Vllybl; Phy.

SWAN, BENJAMIN G; Templeton HS; Templeton, CA; (2); 4-H; FFA; Letterman Clb; Off Jr Cls; JV Bsbl; JV Bsktbl; JV Var Ftbl; Wt Lftg; 2nd Team League Ftbl; Cal Poly; Engr.

SWAN, LILIA M; Valley Christian HS; Campbell, CA; (3); Church Yth Grp; Teachers Aide; Band; Tennis; Trk; Hon Roll; Grap Clb; Chem.

SWAN, MCIHELLE R; Will C Wood HS; Vacaville, CA; (1); Church Yth Grp; Sftbl.

SWAN, STEPHANIE F; Vacaville HS; Vacaville, CA; (4); Church Yth Grp; Teachers Aide; Band; School Musical; Mgr(s); Score Keeper; High Hon Roll; Hon Roll; Pres Acad Fit Awd; Badmitten Team; Longs Educ Grant; CA ST Coll Nrthrdg; Bus.

SWANGER, TIFFANY A; Eureka SR HS; Eureka, CA; (3); 151/352; Church Yth Grp; Drama Clb; FCA; Key Clb; NFL; Acpl Chr; Lion Awd; Ntl Merit Ltr; Pres Acad Fit Awd; Voice Dem Awd; Biochem.

SWANK, NEAL K; St Francis HS; Los Altos, CA; (3); Church Yth Grp; Letterman Clb; SADD; Var L Bsktbl; Var L Ftbl; Hon Roll; USA Bsktbl Tms Russia, Denmark, Sweden; Specl Olympcs Pre-Schlrs Vlntr; Bus.

SWANLAND, ALEXANDRA J; Point Loma HS; San Diego, CA; (1); 119/499; Frshmn To Watch Yrbk Cmmtte; The Ballet Cnsrvtry Prfrmnce Grp; Frnch; Russion.

SWANN, DAWN J; Long Beach David Starr Jordan HS; Long Beach, CA; (3); English Clb; GAA; Varsity Clb; Band; Orch; Pres Soph Cls; Rep Jr Cls; Var Sftbl; Hon Roll; Pres Acad Fit Awd; Hnr Guard; Homcmng Prncss; U NV-LAS Vegas; Cmmnctns.

SWANSON, AMY; Benicia HS; Benicia, CA; (3); Church Yth Grp; Key Clb; Pep Clb; Ski Clb; Rep SADD; Stu Cncl; Var Capt Cheerldng; Powder Puff Ftbl; Hon Roll.

SWANSON, CARRIE A; El Cajon Valley HS; El Cajon, CA; (3); 99/370; VP Pres Church Yth Grp; Letterman Clb; Varsity Clb; Var Mgr(s); Trk; Leos Club Treas; UCSD; News Brdcstr.

SWANSON, CHRISTOPHER D; Grossmont HS; Santee, CA; (4); Church Yth Grp; Church Choir; Cit Awd; Hon Roll; Rotary Awd; Gldn St Exm Algbr, Geomtry High Hnrs; Natl Bicentennial Comptn Constn & Bill Rights; SDSU; Zoolgst.

SWANSON, ERIC A; El Toro HS; El Toro, CA; (3); Aud/Vis; Rep Key Clb; JV Tennis; High Hon Roll; Pres Acad Fit Awd; CSF.

SWANSON, JEFFREY J; Dublin HS; Dublin, CA; (3); JV Ftbl; Var Capt Wrstlng; St Schlr.

SWANSON, JENNIFER; Capo Valley Christian HS; Dana Point, CA; (3); Church Yth Grp; Color Guard; Drill Tm; DAR Awd; Rdng Club Pres; UC Davis; Vet Med.

SWANSON, JEVON C; Redwood HS; Visalia, CA; (2); Cmnty Wkr; VP German Clb; Teachers Aide; Rep Stu Cncl; Hon Roll; NEDT Awd; Yth-Govt Visalia Dlgtn; CSF; Acad Ltr Awd.

SWANSON, LYNN; Monta Vista HS; Cupertino, CA; (2); 126/342; Church Yth Grp; French Clb; Office Aide; Drill Tm; UC Santa Barbara; Child Psych.

SWANSON, MICHELLE; Esperanza HS; Yorba Linda, CA; (2); 47/530; Dance Clb; Drill Tm; High Hon Roll; Hon Roll; NHS; Pres Acad Fit Awd; CSF,CA Schlrshp Fed; UCLA; Child Psychology.

SWANSON, NICOLE A; James Logan HS; Union City, CA; (3); 62/972; Color Guard; Mrchg Band; Hon Roll; Pediatric Nursing.

SWANSON, REBECCA B; Brea-Olinda HS; Brea, CA; (3); French Clb; Girl Scts; Model UN; SADD; Orch; School Musical; Swmmng; High Hon Roll; Hon Roll; Ntl Merit SF; Won 5th In IN Frnch Tst Cntst; CA Schlrshp Fdr; UC ST Cruz; Eng Mjr.

SWANSON, ROBERT T; San Benito HS; Hollister, CA; (4); Church Yth Grp; Letterman Clb; Pep Clb; Ski Clb; Teachers Aide; Variety Show; Phtg Rptr Nwsp; Yrbk; Off Sr Cls; Stu Cncl; CA Assn Of Stu Cncls; CSF; U Of CA-DAVIS.

SWANSON, SEASON E; Clovis HS; Clovis, CA; (2); Church Yth Grp; Dance Clb; German Clb; Hosp Aide; Pep Clb; SADD; Varsity Clb; Rep Soph Cls; Off Jr Cls; Pom Pon; Block C; 4 Pt GPA 1st Sem; Harvard; Corp Lawyer.

SWANSON, SHANE; Western HS; Anaheim, CA; (4); 3/330; Boy Scts; Church Yth Grp; Service Clb; Band; Mrchg Band; Yrbk; NHS; CSF Gold Seal Awd; Kiwanis Bowl; Yth Govt.

SWANSON, SHAUNDRA R; Grossmont HS; Pine Valley, CA; (3); German Clb; Model UN; Office Aide; Ski Clb; SADD; Mgr(s); Swmmng; Wt Lftg; 4-H Awd; Hon Roll; Vol 286 Hrs Grossmont Hosp; CA Hwy Patrol.

SWANSON, SUZANNE; Lincoln HS; Stockton, CA; (3); 1/550; Church Yth Grp; French Clb; GAA; Hosp Aide; Mu Alpha Theta; Service Clb; SADD; Rptr Nwsp; Stu Cncl; Var Tennis; CSF; Med.

SWANSON, THOMAS; Williams HS; Williams, CA; (2); Church Yth Grp; Band; Mrchg Band; Pep Band; Rptr Nwsp; Rptr Yrbk.

SWAROOP, ASHA; Corona Del Mar HS; Providence, RI; (4); Cmnty Wkr; Hosp Aide; Key Clb; SADD; Orch; Stu Cncl; Tennis; Ntl Merit SF; Pres Acad Fit Awd; Peer Asstnc Leag; Brown U; Med.

SWART, JENNIFER L; Montgomery HS; Santa Rosa, CA; (2); Cmnty Wkr; Girl Scts; JA; Key Clb; Pep Clb; Spanish Clb; Bsktbl; Sftbl; Vllybl; High Hon Roll; Acctng.

SWARTH, BRIAN D; Culver City HS; Culver City, CA; (2); Temple Yth Grp; Band; Mrchg Band; Orch; School Musical; Var JV Ftbl; Hon Roll; Bnai Brith Yth Org AZA; USCB; Psych.

SWARTS, ERIC D; North HS; Bakersfield, CA; (2); Teachers Aide; Ftbl; Trk; Wt Lftg; Cit Awd; Hon Roll; Law Enfcrmnt.

SWARTS, JENNIFER; Sierra Union HS; N Fork, CA; (2); SADD; Yrbk; Girls Leag; Fri Night Live.

SWARTZ, KAREN M; Novato HS; Novato, CA; (1); Church Yth Grp; Girl Scts; ROTC; Service Clb; Band; Church Choir; Drill Tm; Mrchg Band; Hon Roll; Excllnt Rtng-CMEA Solo & Ensmbl Fstvl; Stanford; Pedtrcn.

SWARTZ, LAUREL K; Irvine HS; Irvine, CA; (3); Church Yth Grp; Cmnty Wkr; Dance Clb; French Clb; German Clb; Sec Key Clb; Pep Clb; Treas Service Clb; Varsity Clb; Variety Show; Hertge Awd; Goldn St Exm Geom Hgh Hnrs; Wn Mdls Debate; USC; Lawyer.

SWATZKE, JENNIFER; Mt Whitney HS; Visalia, CA; (3); AFS; Spanish Clb; JV Bsktbl; Var Sftbl; Var Vllybl; SAS; Crafts Clb; UCSD; Mar Bio.

SWEANEY, TALITHA; Riverside Christian HS; Riverside, CA; (2); 1/11; Art Clb; Dance Clb; School Play; Yrbk; Sec Soph Cls; Var Cheerldng; Var Vllybl; High Hon Roll; Hon Roll; Val; UC Irvine; Psych.

SWEANEY, TALITHA I; Riverside Christian HS; Riverside, CA; (2); 1/11; Art Clb; Dance Clb; School Play; Yrbk; Sec Soph Cls; Cheerldng; Vllybl; High Hon Roll; Hon Roll; Val; Spllng Bee; Girl Scouts; Bsktbl; Irvine UC; Psych.

SWEARINGEN, JENNIFER D; Hoover HS; Fresno, CA; (4); 9/398; Church Yth Grp; Teachers Aide; Chorus; Church Choir; High Hon Roll; Jazz Choir; Church Organist; Dir Music Awd; Brigham Young U; Scndry Music.

SWEAT, ANNA C; Montgomery HS; Santa Rosa, CA; (2); Drama Clb; Pep Clb; Spanish Clb; Drill Tm; Phtg Yrbk; Cheerldng; Hon Roll; Pres Acad Fit Awd; Prncpls Awd; Clean Operating Rooms Santa Rosa Surgery Ctr; Asst Allergists Office.

SWEDBLOM, VICTOR G; North HS; Bakersfield, CA; (3); 21/368; Teachers Aide; Rep Stu Cncl; Hon Roll; Certified Brake Tech; Universal Tech Inst; Auto Tech.

SWEENEY, COLLEEN M; Mills HS; San Bruno, CA; (3); VP Intnl Clb; Service Clb; VP Spanish Clb; Ed Yrbk; Stage Crew; Bdmntn Tm-Var; CA Schlrshp Fed; Amnsty Intl; Adv.

SWEENEY, HEATHER N; Arroyo Grande HS; Nipomo, CA; (2); Church Yth Grp; SADD; Chorus; JV Capt Cheerldng; Var Vllybl; High Hon Roll; Hon Roll; Pres Acad Fit Awd; Northern Leag Vrsty Vlybl HS; JR Olmpcs NM Tm; Elem Schl Tchr.

SWEENEY, MARK R; San Marcos HS; Santa Barbara, CA; (2); Cmnty Wkr; Dance Clb; Drama Clb; Chorus; School Musical; School Play; Hon Roll; Cmnty Theatre; Acting.

SWEENY, ROBIN D; Oakdale HS; Oakdale, CA; (3); 40/350; Dance Clb; Science Clb; Spanish Clb; Cheerldng; Powder Puff Ftbl; J Clb; Occptnl Olympics; Martin Bio.

SWEENY, SCOTT P; Mission College Prep; San Luis Obispo, CA; (3); Boy Scts; Cmnty Wkr; Service Clb; Teachers Aide; JV Var Bsbl; JV Var Bsktbl; Var Capt Ftbl; Intrml Vllybl; Hon Roll; Edi-Peli-Amer-Japanese Exchng Pgm; Teacher.

SWEET, AMANDA J; Notre Dame HS; Salinas, CA; (1); Cmnty Wkr; JV Capt Cheerldng; High Hon Roll; CSF; Natl Edcntl Dvlpmnt Test Awd; Recrtn League Sftbl All-Star Team.

SWEET, JOE; North HS; Bakersfield, CA; (2); Ski Clb; Teachers Aide; JV Bsbl; Hon Roll; NHS; Engr.

SWEET, PATRICIA K; Lincoln HS; San Francisco, CA; (2); Chorus; Enterainment.

SWEET, SHARONDA; Edison HS; Stockton, CA; (2); Church Yth Grp; GAA; Hosp Aide; Speech Tm; Church Choir; Stage Crew; VP Soph Cls; Bsbl; Bsktbl; Trk; Outstndng Grls Bsktbl Awd; UCLA; Law.

SWEETEN, NIKKI; Turlock HS; Turlock, CA; (2); Church Yth Grp; Drama Clb; JV Tennis; Hrsbck Riding & Showng; Wrtng; U Of CA Davis; Law.

SWEGLES, MELISSA J; Fred C Beyer HS; Modesto, CA; (1); Pilot.

SWEIGARD, JOHN; Livingston HS; Winton, CA; (4); 6/225; Church Yth Grp; FFA; Stu Cncl; Var L Ftbl; Var Capt Trk; Hon Roll; Bk Am Applied Arts Awd Plq Wnnr; Cal Poly SLO; Ag Engrng.

SWEITZER, ROBERT; Yucaipa HS; Yucaipa, CA; (2); Boy Scts; Computer Clb; Spanish Clb; Color Guard; Crs Cntry; Trk; Hon Roll; Prfct Atten Awd; Pres Acad Fit Awd; Stanford; Invstmnt Banking.

SWENDIMAN, CHELSEY; Shasta HS; Redding, CA; (2); 95/442; Church Yth Grp; Chorus; School Musical; Stu Cncl; JV Cheerldng; JV Pom Pon; Score Keeper; Sftbl; Hon Roll; U WA; Teaching.

SWENDSEID, NICOLE; Mission Viejo HS; Mission Viejo, CA; (3); Church Yth Grp; Cmnty Wkr; Debate Tm; Model UN; Pep Clb; Spanish Clb; JV Intrml Cheerldng; Capt Var Pom Pon; Saddleback Coll; Inter Dsgn.

SWENSEN, MICHAEL D; Antelope Valley HS; Lancaster, CA; (3); Boy Scts; Red Cross Aide; Crs Cntry; Socr; Swmmng; Trk; Hon Roll; Paramedic.

SWENSEN, MICHELE; Thousand Oaks HS; Thousand Oaks, CA; (2); Art Clb; Church Yth Grp; Cmnty Wkr; Teachers Aide; Church Choir; Orch; School Play; Bsktbl; Mgr(s); Cit Awd; BYU; Phys Thrpy.

SWENSON, ROBIN; Ontario HS; Ontario, CA; (3); 30/525; French Clb; Co-Capt Flag Corp; Hon Roll.

SWENSON, RONNY; Ontario HS; Ontario, CA; (2); 25/550; Boy Scts; French Clb; Letterman Clb; Ski Clb; Varsity Clb; Rep Stu Cncl; Tennis; Co-Capt Wrstlng; Hon Roll; Mem CSF; Hnrs Golden ST Exam.

SWENSON, SHEA LYNN; Atascadero HS; Atascadero, CA; (2); Church Yth Grp; FFA; Pep Clb; SADD; Drill Tm; Stat Swmmng; Hon Roll; Envrnml Clb; Ricks JC; Med.

SWERDLOFF, RYAN J; John Muir HS; Altadena, CA; (2); Intnl Clb; Ski Clb; High Hon Roll; Hon Roll; USC; Arch.

SWERDLOFF, TANYA; Claremont HS; Yucaipa, CA; (2); 1/15; French Clb; Math Clb; Spanish Clb; Stu Cncl; Var Bsktbl; Var Cheerldng; Var Sftbl; Var Vllybl; Hnrbl Mntn All Express League Vllybl; 1st Tm All Express League Sftbl; Otstndng Frgn Lang Stu; Whittier Coll; Frgn Svc.

SWETT, THOMAS M; Argonaut HS; Jackson, CA; (4); 3/100; VP 4-H; Pres Key Clb; Letterman Clb; Pres Science Clb; Ski Clb; Drm Mjr(t); Mrchg Band; Yrbk; Pres Sr Cls; Ftbl; HOBY; U NV Reno; Wildlife Bio.

SWIERK, JASON S; Wm S Hart HS; Valencia, CA; (4); 4/488; Math Clb; Math Tm; Mu Alpha Theta; Science Clb; Ed Nwsp; Lit Mag; Rep Stu Cncl; L Crs Cntry; L Socr; JV Trk; Stanford; Mech Engrng.

SWIFT, JENNIFER E; San Dieguito HS; Encinitas, CA; (2); Drill Tm; Flag Corp; School Play; Cit Awd; Hon Roll; Bio.

SWIFT, JENNIFER J; Lowell HS; San Francisco, CA; (3); Cmnty Wkr; Hosp Aide; Letterman Clb; Red Cross Aide; Teachers Aide; Sec Band; Rep Frsh Cls; Rep Soph Cls; Rep Jr Cls; Crs Cntry; Shield & Scroll Hon Soc; CSF; Cncl For Stu Affairs; Pre-Med.

SWIFT, KIMBERLEY M; Alverno HS; Sierra Madre, CA; (2); 17/72; Church Yth Grp; Girl Scts; Intnl Clb; Service Clb; CSF; OR ST U; Med.

SWIFT, LAUREL M; Highland HS; Bakersfield, CA; (4); Art Clb; FHA; Teachers Aide; Yrbk; UCLA; Med.

SWIFT, LISA; East Union HS; Manteca, CA; (1); 32/320; Cheerldng; Vllybl; Hon Roll.

SWIFT, RAIMEE; Bonita Vista HS; Bonita, CA; (4); 49/521; Church Yth Grp; Pep Clb; SADD; VP Jr Cls; Hon Roll; Pres Acad Fit Awd; ASB Cmmsnr Of Actvts; San Diego St U; Elem Educ.

SWIFT, WINDIGO M; El Dorado HS; Somerset, CA; (3); 16/368; Co-Capt Debate Tm; JA; School Play; Lit Mag; Bsktbl; High Hon Roll; Hon Roll; NHS; Horses; CSF; UC Davis; Research Sci.

SWINDLE, JASON; La Sierra Acad; Riverside, CA; (3); Church Yth Grp; Model UN; Ski Clb; Color Guard; Drill Tm; JV Bsktbl; High Hon Roll; NHS; VP Cyclng Clb; Engrng.

SWINDLER, EMILY; El Capitan HS; Lakeside, CA; (4); 1/418; Spanish Clb; SADD; Band; Mrchg Band; Orch; Var L Tennis; Elks Awd; Gov Hon Prg Awd; High Hon Roll; Masonic Awd; Acad Decathalon; Sci Olympiad Team; Coordinating Invnt Amer; Hnrb Mntn Sci/Engrng Fair; U CA San Diego; Biomedcl Engr.

SWINEA, JOSEPH; Monte Vista HS; La Mesa, CA; (2); 46/461; Church Yth Grp; JV Tennis; Cit Awd; Pres Acad Fit Awd; GATE; CA ST U Math Diagnostics Testing Project Score Of 49 Out Of 50; Arch.

SWINNEY, JEFF D; Dos Palos HS; Dos Palos, CA; (3); AFS; FCA; Pres Letterman Clb; Pres Frsh Cls; Var Bsktbl; Var Ftbl; High Hon Roll; Hon Roll; Bus.

SWINSCOE, HEIDI C; Orange Glen HS; Escondido, CA; (3); 20/450; Capt Scholastic Bowl; Spanish Clb; Chorus; Church Choir; Hon Roll; NHS; Rotary Awd; Cmnty Yth Soccer League Coach & Ref; Westmont Coll; Engl Tchr.

SWITKES, JENNIFER M; Acalanes HS; Lafayette, CA; (4); 14/290; Service Clb; Var Diving; Ntl Merit SF; Art; Peer Tutrng; Harvey Mudd Coll; Mthmtcs.

SWITLIK, JENNIFER J; Glendora HS; La Verne, CA; (4); German Clb; Rptr Nwsp; Kiwanis Awd; Outstndng Work Experience Stu; Chrus JC; Bus.

SWITZER, WILLIAM D; San Pasqual HS; Escondido, CA; (2); Intrml Bsktbl; JV Ftbl; Golden St Exam Alg I Hgh Hnrs; U Of CA; Elec Engrng.

SWITZKY, JOSHUA E; William Howard Taft HS; Encino, CA; (2); Off Soph Cls; CSF; UC Berkeley; Econ.

SWORD, ERIC R; Redwood HS; Visalia, CA; (4); 1/318; Pres Chess Clb; Pres FBLA; Pres Speech Tm; Var Swmmng; Lion Awd; Ntl Merit SF; Opt Clb Awd; Var Water Polo; YMCA Yth & Govt St Pgm Cmmttee; Mock Trial; Stanford; Astrophyscs.

SWORDS, DARCY H; Arroyo Grande HS; Nipomo, CA; (3); 29/540; AFS; VP Art Clb; Church Yth Grp; Pres Rptr 4-H; NFL; Speech Tm; SADD; Capt Cheerldng; JV Diving; High Hon Roll; CSF; Stanford U; Law.

SWORDS II, MICHAEL; Arcata HS; Arcata, CA; (1); Band; Ftbl; Wt Lftg.

SY, JOHANNA; Hogan HS; Vallejo, CA; (3); Chess Clb; Spanish Clb; Drill Tm; Nwsp; Sftbl; Vllybl; Sacramento ST; Medcl.

SY, SUSAN A; Notre Dame HS; Hillsborough, CA; (3); 1/90; Intnl Clb; Nwsp; Lit Mag; Pres Soph Cls; Pres Stu Cncl; JV Vllybl; NHS; CA Schlrshp Fed; Xerox Awd Hum, Socl Sci; Soc Wmn Engrns Cert Of Merit Math & Sci.

SYDOW, VICKI L; California Lutheran HS; Anaheim, CA; (1); Church Yth Grp; Chorus; School Play; Cheerldng; Vllybl; Hon Roll.

SYED, SAQI; Rowland HS; Rowland Hts, CA; (2); Cmnty Wkr; Trk; Cit Awd; Hon Roll; Law.

SYHANATH, SOUKHALINE; Lincoln Prep; San Diego, CA; (3); San Diego City Coll; Nrsng.

SYJUCO, STEPHANIE S; Lowell HS; San Francisco, CA; (3); Cmnty Wkr; Chorus; Variety Show; Ntl Merit SF; St Schlr; Cncl Stu Affrs; Amnsty Intl VP, Publcty Mgr; Fine Art.

SYKES, CARI M; Alisal HS; Salinas, CA; (3); Hon Roll; Prfct Atten Awd; Outstndng Acad Achvmnt Cmptr Prgm; U Southern CA; Elec Engr.

SYKES, MAYA E; Skyline HS; Oakland, CA; (3); Dance Clb; Hon Roll; SF ST; Bus.

SYLVA, JOSE J; Ramona HS; Riverside, CA; (2); Teachers Aide; Chorus; Bsbl; Bsktbl; Prfct Atten Awd; UCR; Engrng.

SYLVESTER, CASSANDRA D; Washington Prep; Los Angeles, CA; (4); Church Yth Grp; Dance Clb; Office Aide; Spanish Clb; Sftbl; Hon Roll; Bus & Financial Mgrs Assn; Sonoma ST U; Commnctn Stds.

SYLVESTER, JENNIFER; Half Moon Bay HS; Half Moon Bay, CA; (4); 23/177; 4-H; Hosp Aide; Spanish Clb; SADD; Chorus; Stu Cncl; Hon Roll; Big Sister Little Sister; Humbold & ST U; Pharmacist.

SYME, KARY R; Chino HS; Ontario, CA; (2); Church Yth Grp; Pep Clb; VP Frsh Cls; JV Var Cheerldng; JV Socr; Hon Roll; Bus Admin.

SYMEOU, KLEA; Rawland HS; Walnut, CA; (2); Sftbl; UCLA; Pediatrics.

SYMES, HELEN E; Bear River HS; Grass Valley, CA; (2); SADD; Band; School Play; JV Swmmng; Cit Awd; High Hon Roll; Hon Roll; Pres Acad Fit Awd; Oustndng Musicianship; Artis.

SYNDERGAARD, JASON C; Pasadena HS; Pasadena, CA; (2); Teachers Aide; Hon Roll; Sports; Sci Fictn Novls, Movies; UC Berkeley; Electrns Tech.

SYNNES, AMANDA K; Santa Clara HS; Oxnard, CA; (2); 3/191; Church Yth Grp; Capt Debate Tm; Sec French Clb; Capt NFL; Capt Speech Tm; High Hon Roll; Hon Roll; Lion Awd; Pres NHS; Opt Clb Awd; CSF; Early Acad Outrch.

SYQUIA, CHRISTINE M; St Joseph HS; Cerritos, CA; (3); Church Yth Grp; Debate Tm; French Clb; JV Crs Cntry; Hon Roll; Acad Dcthln; Fshn Mrchndsng.

SYRENGELAS, DEAN V; Huntington Beach HS; Huntington Beach, CA; (3); Intrml Crs Cntry; Var Capt Socr; Intrml Trk; Intrml Vllybl; Hon Roll.

SYRETT, MONICA; San Gorgonio HS; San Bernardino, CA; (3); Cmnty Wkr; SADD; Teachers Aide; Pres Acad Fit Awd; Miami FL Instl Fine Arts Coll.

SYVERTSEN, SHANNA L; Bullard HS; Fresno, CA; (2); 58/510; Church Yth Grp; Church Choir; Var Crs Cntry; Jnr Lares Sec; Azusa Pacific U; Math.

SZABO, DEBORAH A; Trabuco Hills HS; Mission Viejo, CA; (2); Pep Clb; Spanish Clb; SADD; Color Guard; San Luis Obispo; Anml Trng.

SZABO, ZITA M; Villa Park HS; Orange, CA; (4); 32/433; Key Clb; Gym; Trk; Cit Awd; High Hon Roll; Hon Roll; NHS; U CA Irvine; Hmnts.

SZADY, BRIAN D; Fremont HS; Sunnyvale, CA; (3); 30/496; Church Yth Grp; Debate Tm; Pres JA; Key Clb; Ski Clb; Speech Tm; SADD; Varsity Clb; Band; Jazz Band; Notre Dame; Poltcl Sci.

SZALAY, GRANT; Redwood Christian HS; Oakland, CA; (4); 1/34; Am Leg Boys St; Drama Clb; School Musical; School Play; Yrbk; Bsktbl; Var Tennis; Capt Vllybl; NHS; Val; Sierra Acad; Aeronautics.

SZAREJKO, KATHLEEN M; Apple Valley HS; Apple Valley, CA; (3); Stat Ftbl; Stat Socr; High Hon Roll; Hon Roll; Pres Acad Fit Awd; Obstetrcs.

SZEKERES, DAVID L; Villa Park HS; Villa Park, CA; (2); Key Clb; Treas Jr Cls; Var Socr; Var Trk; Hon Roll; NHS; CSL Soccer; UCLA; Law.

SZELENYI, PATRICIA M; Valhalla HS; El Cajon, CA; (1); Church Yth Grp; Capt Flag Corp; Spnsh Comptn; Bus.

SZENDREY, MARNI; Captial Christian HS; Citrus Heights, CA; (4); 1/48; Church Yth Grp; Cmnty Wkr; Intnl Clb; Service Clb; School Musical; High Hon Roll; Hon Roll; CA ST U Sacramento; Psych.

SZETO, CHAPMAN; Mission HS; San Francisco, CA; (3); Bus Profs of Am; FBLA; VICA; Cit Awd; Gov Hon Prg Awd; Pres Acad Fit Awd; Pres Schlr; Asian Hnr Scty; Standford; Bus.

SZETO, DON J; C M Mc Clatchy SR HS; Sacramento, CA; (1); 15/588; Chess Clb; JV Swmmng; Asian Stu Union; Berkeley; Engrng.

SZETO, JENNY; Phillip Burton HS; San Francisco, CA; (2); Church Yth Grp.

SZETO, MELISSA; Mira Mesa HS; San Diego, CA; (2); French Clb; Intnl Clb; Teachers Aide; Prfct Atten Awd; U Of CA; Govt.

SZETO, NANCY; Arroyo HS; San Leandro, CA; (4); 11/268; Church Yth Grp; Cmnty Wkr; VP FBLA; Library Aide; Teachers Aide; Var Capt Tennis; JV Vllybl; High Hon Roll; Hon Roll; Prfct Atten Awd; Badminton Co-Ed Tm Capt, All League & Girls Doubles 1st HAAL & NCS 90; Army Rsrv Natl Schlr Hnr; U Of CA Santa Cruz; Comp.

SZETO, TZE CHING; College Park HS; Pleasant Hill, CA; (4); 11/295; Treas French Clb; JA; Model UN; Treas Spanish Clb; SADD; Teachers Aide; JV Vllybl; Hon Roll; Prfct Atten Awd; Pres Acad Fit Awd; Distngshd Stud Awd Math Sci; CA Schlrshp Fed; Hghst Hnr Schlrshp Cert Awd & Lfe Mbrshp; Gldn St Exm; U Of CA; Accnt.

SZEW, LEONARDO; Palisades HS; Los Angeles, CA; (4); 1/450; Office Aide; Teachers Aide; Varsity Clb; Rep Frsh Cls; Var Socr; Hon Roll; Pres Acad Fit Awd; Gldn St Exam Hgh Hnr Awds Geom; Distngshd Schlr Rand-Revere Cmptn 2nd Prz; UCLA; Engrng.

SZURA, MATTHEW; Will C Wood HS; Vacaville, CA; (1); Boy Scts; Church Yth Grp; Cmnty Wkr; Drama Clb; Science Clb; Ski Clb; SADD; Teachers Aide; Chorus; School Play; Monticello Cyclng Clb; Teen Cmmtte; City Wide Sci Fair 2nd Pl; Pacific Gas & Elect Engrng Awd; USC; Mktg.

SZWARCSZTEJN, ERIKA; Bonita Vista HS; Chula Vista, CA; (3); French Clb; Model UN; Pep Clb; SADD; Temple Yth Grp; Variety Show; Ed Yrbk; Lit Mag; Off Jr Cls; JV Capt Fld Hcky; San Francisco ST U; Engl.

SZYTEL, LISA M; Orange Glen HS; Valley Center, CA; (3); 14/458; Am Leg Aux Girls St; Church Yth Grp; Spanish Clb; Cit Awd; Hon Roll; Pres NHS; Opt Clb Awd; Frgn Lang Stu 87-88; Career Awrns Stu 88-89; Scl Sci Stu 89-90; CSF; Gld Mdl Freestyle Ice Skt; Math.

TA, DUC-TRUNG; George Washington HS; San Francisco, CA; (2); Office Aide; Hon Roll.

TA, DUVAN; James Monroe HS; Panorama City, CA; (4); 65/500; Computer Clb; Intnl Clb; Math Clb; Science Clb; Service Clb; Off Jr Cls; Tennis; Cit Awd; High Hon Roll; Hon Roll; Svc Schlrshp; CSF Torch Bearer & Gold Seal; UCI.

TA, HANH M; Narbonne HS; Carson, CA; (3); School Play; JV Bsktbl; Var Trk; Hon Roll; Pre-Med.

TA, JONATHAN H; University HS; Irvine, CA; (3); 32/552; Debate Tm; Key Clb; Hon Roll; Pres Acad Fit Awd; Spanish NHS; CSF; Golden St Exam Geom Hnrs; Natl Mrt Commended Schlr; Aerospace Engrng.

TA, KHOI; Chaffey HS; Fontana, CA; (2); 2/735; Prfct Atten Awd; CSF; UCSB; Bio.

TA, MINHDUNG; Bonita HS; La Verne, CA; (4); 3/336; Church Yth Grp; FCA; Pres GAA; Varsity Clb; Stu Cncl; Var Capt Fld Hcky; Var Capt Sftbl; Var Capt Tennis; High Hon Roll; Pres Acad Fit Awd; CSF Pres, VP, Treas & Sctry; John Seymour Memrl Schlrshp; CIF Schlr/Athlt; U Of CA Berkeley.

TA, MYDUC; Poway HS; Poway, CA; (3); 35/761; Cit Awd; High Hon Roll; NHS; CSF; Anmsty Intl; Sci.

TA, NGA; Skyline HS; Oakland, CA; (2); English Clb; French Clb; Math Clb; Off Soph Cls; Bsbl; Sftbl; Tennis; Vllybl.

TA, NGHI CHI-VU; Chaffey HS; Fontana, CA; (3); Science Clb; Spanish Clb; Hon Roll; Prfct Atten Awd; Yng Schl Pgm; Rotary Yth Ldrshp Awd; Cmmnty Interact Svc Club; Pre Med.

TA, NGHIA T; Santa Clara HS; Santa Clara, CA; (4); Socr; Hon Roll; San Jose ST U; Engr.

TA, NHI; Mira Mesa HS; San Diego, CA; (2); French Clb; Science Clb; Cit Awd; 4-H Awd; Hon Roll; Wrld Relief Clb; CSF; UCSD; Reg Nurse.

TA, PHUONG; Basett HS; La Puente, CA; (2); Cit Awd; Hon Roll; Real Estate Agent.

TA, TRANG; Mater Dei HS; Westminster, CA; (1); Church Yth Grp; French Clb; JV Trk; Cit Awd; High Hon Roll; Hon Roll; Prfct Atten Awd; Psych.

TA, VAN; Cerritos HS; Cerritos, CA; (1); Church Yth Grp; Model UN; JV Bsktbl; Hon Roll; Pres Acad Fit Awd; UCLA; Bus Mgmt.

TA, YEN; Millikan JHS; Los Angeles, CA; (1); Church Yth Grp; Cmnty Wkr; Pres Computer Clb; Intnl Clb; Teachers Aide; Bsktbl; Trk; Hon Roll; CA JR Schlrshp Fdrtn; Bys Athltc Clb-BAC.

TABADA, MARITA; Oroville HS; Oroville, CA; (4); Art Clb; Church Yth Grp; SADD; Powder Puff Ftbl; Score Keeper; Trk; Hon Roll; Art & Phy Ed Stu Of Month; Natl Art Hnr Soc Awd; 1st Pl Awd Native Daughtrs Of Golden West; Butte Coll.

TABARANGO, JAMES R; Highlands HS; N Highlands, CA; (2); 25/300; Boy Scts; Church Yth Grp; JV Bsktbl; JV Ftbl; Powder Puff Ftbl; Var Wt Lftg; Hon Roll; Pres Acad Fit Awd; Vrsty Kckbxng; UCD Outrch; UC Berkeley; Arch.

TABARYAEI, BITA; University HS; Los Angeles, CA; (3); Cmnty Wkr; Hosp Aide; Office Aide; Teachers Aide; Rep Frsh Cls; Tennis; Hon Roll; Prfct Atten Awd; Spanish NHS; Piano; Speak 3 Langs; UCLA; Bio.

TABAYOYONG, MICHAEL A; Whitney HS; Cerritos, CA; (3); VP JA; Key Clb; Ed Nwsp; Pres Stu Cncl; Vllybl; High Hon Roll; Hon Roll; Kaibigan Clb Filipino Clb, VP & Treas; Bramiks Mial Prcssng Co, VP; UCLA; Bus.

TABB, KAYLIN; St Elizabeth HS; Oakland, CA; (1); 6/150; Intrml Bsktbl; JV Var Ftbl; High Hon Roll; Xclnc In Math; Comp Opers; Comp Pgmg.

TABB, KIM; Nogales HS; W Covina, CA; (2); Color Guard; JV Bsktbl; Hon Roll; Awd Advncd Engl; MVP JV Bsktbl; UNLV; Comp Prgmr.

TABBUT, SHELLEY; Banning HS; Banning, CA; (3); 4/200; Church Yth Grp; Treas French Clb; Intnl Clb; Model UN; Stat Socr; Var Sftbl; Var Capt Vllybl; High Hon Roll; Sec NHS; Prom Cmmtte; CSF; Schlr Athlt.

TABELIN, EVANGELINA C; Paso Robles HS; Paso Robles, CA; (4); Dance Clb; Teachers Aide; Color Guard; Drill Tm; Rep Frsh Cls; JV Var Pom Pon; Hon Roll; Cuesta CC; Nrsng.

TABER, BARBARA J; Pt Loma HS; San Diego, CA; (3); 43/431; Church Yth Grp; Intnl Clb; SADD; Varsity Clb; Off Jr Cls; Off Sr Cls; JV Crs Cntry; Cit Awd; High Hon Roll; Hon Roll; Williams Coll Bk Awd; Sivler Schlr; Gld Mrt Outstndng Acad Achvt; Occidental Coll; Span.

TABER, STEPHENIE; Davis SR HS; Davis, CA; (3); AFS; Church Yth Grp; Key Clb; Pep Clb; Spanish Clb; Gym; Yth Ldrshp Awd Cngrsnl Yth Ldrshp Cncl; CSF; Golden St Exam With Honors; AFS Smmr In Spain 90.

TABIN, JANET M; Lompoc HS; Lompoc, CA; (3); 10/284; Cmnty Wkr; Teachers Aide; Vllybl; Cit Awd; High Hon Roll; Hon Roll; Prfct Atten Awd; Sci Awd 88-89; Prin Lst 88-89; USCD; Psych.

TABLANTE, JOEL; Skyline HS; Oakland, CA; (3); 3/35; Boy Scts; Chorus; Hon Roll; CA Schlrshp Fed; Holocaust Docent Pgm; Bechtel Jr Engrng Corps; UC Berkeley; Mech Engr.

TABLER, AMIE M; Lower Lake HS; Lower Lake, CA; (4); Church Yth Grp; Spanish Clb; Stu Cncl; VP Jr Cls; Var Capt Bsktbl; JV Trk; Var Capt Vllybl; Hon Roll; Bnk Of Amer Achvt Awd Frgn Lang; Intl Frgn Lang Assn Awd; CSF.

TABLIT, GERALDINE D; Hogan HS; Vallejo, CA; (2); Yrbk; Pres Acad Fit Awd.

TABON, TANYA; North Torrance HS; Torrance, CA; (3); 100/437; Church Yth Grp; French Clb; Service Clb; Drill Tm; UCSD; Attorney.

TABOR, ANGELA L; La Sierra HS; Riverside, CA; (3); Math Clb; SADD; Lbrn Hist Band; Jazz Band; Mrchg Band; Orch; Pep Band; School Musical; Hon Roll; Band; CSU Long Beach; Music.

TABORA, CONNIE; Brea-Olinda HS; Brea, CA; (3); 70/300; Cmnty Wkr; VP Pres GAA; NFL; Var Speech Tm; Teachers Aide; Phtg Yrbk; Mgr(s); JV Sftbl; JV Var Vllybl; Hon Roll; CA Hstry Day Comptr; Bus.

TABOT, SCOTT; Brethren HS; Lakewood, CA; (1); Off Church Yth Grp; Capt Bsbl; Cit Awd; Hon Roll; NEDT Awd; Prfct Atten Awd; L Bsktbl; CA JR Schlrshp Fdrtn; Assoc Chrstn Schls Intl Spllng; Reuben E Ekenberry Schlrshp Otstndng Acad; Naval Acad; Pilot.

TABRIZCHI, ALI; Las Lomas HS; Walnut Creek, CA; (3); Cmnty Wkr; Library Aide; Math Tm; Chorus; Stu Cncl; Capt Var Ftbl; Var Trk; French Hon Soc; High Hon Roll; Pres Acad Fit Awd; Pre Med.

TACAN, RON P; Edison HS; Stockton, CA; (3); Variety Show; Hon Roll; Spanish NHS; 1st Pl Talent Show-Piano Solo.

TACAZON, ANDREW; Hesperia Christian Schl; Hesperia, CA; (2); Band; High Hon Roll; CSF; Med.

TACBAS, JEREMY; Mt Shasta HS; Dunsmuir, CA; (3); Ski Clb; Band; Jazz Band; Mrchg Band; Orch; Pep Band; Stage Crew; Rep Frsh Cls; Rep Stu Cncl; Hon Roll; John Phillip Sousa Awd; Work Round Table; Enjoy Fly Fishing; Psych.

TACEY, ALEX D; Wilcox HS; Santa Clara, CA; (1); Acpl Chr; Band; Jazz Band; Mrchg Band; Pep Band; School Musical; Crs Cntry; Score Keeper; Wrstlng; Hon Roll; NAR; Excllnc In Engl & Span; Band Awd; USC; Air Force.

TACHIBANA, JENNIFER E; Aragon HS; San Mateo, CA; (2); Church Yth Grp; Debate Tm; JV Socr; Var Swmmng; Var Trk; Hon Roll; Med.

TACHIQUIN, MARCO A; Don Bogco Technical Inst; Montebello, CA; (3); Art Clb; Chess Clb; Computer Clb; Drama Clb; English Clb; German Clb; Latin Clb; Letterman Clb; Math Clb; Spanish Clb; Cal Poly SLO; Chemical Engrng.

TACKETT, CHRISTIAN B; Ramona HS; Ramona, CA; (2); 21/345; Socr; Hon Roll; Stu Of Mnth-Phys Sci; Soroptimist Intl-Recog For Contrbtns To Yth Smnr; Law.

TACORDA, JOSLYN; Carlmont HS; Redwood City, CA; (3); Church Yth Grp; Key Clb; Service Clb; School Musical; Rep Nwsp; Sec Soph Cls; Pres Jr Cls; Rep Stu Cncl; Var Cheerldng; Var Pom Pon; Mock Trial Team; Publc Rltns Cmssnr.

TACUJAN, JENNIFER C; Canyon Springs HS; Moreno Valley, CA; (4); 10/575; Cmnty Wkr; Dance Clb; VP FBLA; Treas Pres Intnl Clb; NFL; Speech Tm; Stu Cncl; High Hon Roll; Sec NHS; Pres Acad Fit Awd; Cert Awd Engl; Schlrshps Cougar Booster Clb, Panhellenic; Jack In Box Photo/Essay Cont Hnrbl Mntn; UC Riverside; Pre-Bus.

TADDIE, JENNIE; Branham HS; San Jose, CA; (3); Church Yth Grp; Cmnty Wkr; Intnl Clb; Teachers Aide; VICA; Acpl Chr; School Musical; VP Frsh Cls; Sec Rep Soph Cls; Pres Jr Cls; Schlrshp Ldrshp Camp Rotary Yth Awd; Svc Mnstry Trin; Cosmo.

TADROS, NIVEEN S; University HS; Irvine, CA; (3); Church Yth Grp; French Clb; FBLA; Church Choir; Stu Cncl; Fld Hcky; Gym; Trk; French Hon Soc; High Hon Roll; CSF Stu 2 Yrs; Lavreatte Medallion In Bus; Law.

TAEOTUI, IOELU; Woodrow Wilson HS; San Francisco, CA; (4); Band; Rep Frsh Cls; Rep Soph Cls; Var Ftbl; Intrml Wt Lftg; Hon Roll; USF Upwrd Bnd; UC Santa Barbara.

TAFF, ALISHA; Morro Bay HS; Los Osos, CA; (4); 23/180; Cmnty Wkr; 4-H; FFA; Yrbk; Powder Puff Ftbl; Swmmng; 4-H Awd; High Hon Roll; Hon Roll; Ntl Merit Ltr; 1st Pl US Judo Fed Natl 87; Cal Poly San Luis Obispo; Ag.

TAFOLLA, MARIA LUISA; Lemoore HS; Armona, CA; (4); 51/290; Drama Clb; FBLA; Spanish Clb; Teachers Aide; Varsity Clb; Stat Crs Cntry; Gym; Mgr(s); Capt Var Tennis; High Hon Roll; Var Tennis Team MVP, Capt; UC Davis; Med.

TAFOYA, CARLOS; Coachella Valley HS; Coachella, CA; (3); 17/450; Art Clb; Hon Roll; Prfct Atten Awd; Marine Ftns Tm; Art.

TAFOYA, CONSUELO; Sweetwater HS; National City, CA; (2); 2/30; Mdcn.

TAFOYA, GABBY J; Mc Farland HS; Mc Farland, CA; (3); FTA; Spanish Clb; Teachers Aide; Pres Frsh Cls; Pres Stu Cncl; Capt Var Bsktbl; Var Capt Powder Puff Ftbl; Var Capt Trk; Var Capt Vllybl; Schl, Sci, Geom & Engl Awds; Smmr League Bsktbl; San Diego ST; Astronmy.

TAFOYA, LIZA; Rio Linda SR HS; Elverta, CA; (4); Pres English Clb; Science Clb; Speech Tm; Rep Stu Cncl; Var Socr; Swmmng; CSF Sealbearer; UC Davis Partnership Pgm; Physics Clb; Law Tm; Micro-Bio Research Bl; UC Davis; Anesthesiology.

TAFOYA, SCOTT J; Clovis HS; Clovis, CA; (1); Bsbl; Capt Bsktbl; Capt Ftbl; Intrml Wt Lftg; Hon Roll; Pres Acad Fit Awd; Babe Ruth Bsbl MVP; Babe Ruth All Stars; Notre Dame; Sports Med.

TAGABAN, MONICA; Calexico HS; Calexico, CA; (3); Key Clb; Off Sr Cls; Migrant Clb; Prom Cmmtte; UCSD Smmr 89 Early Acad Outreach Pgm; Med.

TAGANAS, CHRISTINA; Alisal HS; Salinas, CA; (3); English Clb; Variety Show; JV Var Bsktbl; JV Var Vllybl; Hon Roll; Pres Acad Fit Awd; Mst Imprvd & Ltr Bsktbl; UC Santa Barbara; Math.

TAGAY, EDGAR R; Fremont HS; Sunnyvale, CA; (3); 103/400; Spcl Interests Bsbl Card Collecting; Stanford U; Telecommunications.

TAGGARD, STEPHEN; Hoover HS; Fresno, CA; (3); Boy Scts; German Clb; JV Wt Lftg; High Hon Roll; Pres Acad Fit Awd; Rl Est.

TAGGART, ADAM; Burroughs HS; Ridgecrest, CA; (3); Cmnty Wkr; Drama Clb; French Clb; JCL; Thesps; Chorus; Rep Stu Cncl; Cit Awd; Hon Roll; Clsscl League Cert Merit Cum Laude; U ID Moscow; Aerosp Engr.

TAGLE, TRACY; J Eugene Mc Ateer HS; San Francisco, CA; (2); Church Yth Grp; Office Aide; Church Choir; Hon Roll.

TAGORE, KULDEEP S; Edison/Computech HS; Fresno, CA; (2); Debate Tm; Latin Clb; NFL; Var Tennis; Hon Roll; Envrnmntl Clb; 4th Pl Humerous Intrprtn Forensics; Wrtng Home Movies; UC San Diego; Med.

TAGUCHI, KARA K; Whitney HS; Cerritos, CA; (2); JA; Key Clb; Service Clb; Spanish Clb; Teachers Aide; Varsity Clb; Ed Nwsp; Rptr Yrbk; Off Frsh Cls; Sftbl; Span.

TAGUE, MATTHEW; Carlsbad HS; Carlsbad, CA; (3); 94/250; Church Yth Grp; FCA; Letterman Clb; Varsity Clb; Church Choir; School Play; Phtg Yrbk; Pres Frsh Cls; Sprt Ed Var Bsktbl; Hon Roll; Holy Cross; Bus.

TAGUINES, JENNY C; John Marshall HS; Los Angeles, CA; (3); Library Aide; Wrld Hstry Mst Outstndng Stu; Prfct Attndnc Awd; Filipino Clb; Humanities Clb; Bord Of Reps; CSF.

TAHA, DARIAN R; Beacon Christian HS; San Carlos, CA; (4); Aud/Vis; Church Yth Grp; Drama Clb; School Play; Stage Crew; Rptr Phtg Yrbk; Rep Soph Cls; VP Sr Cls; VP Stu Cncl; Golf; Menlo Coll; Comp Info Systms.

TAHAJIAN, BRENT LEE; Bullard HS; Fresno, CA; (2); Intnl Clb; Spanish Clb; SADD; Cit Awd; High Hon Roll; Prfct Atten Awd; Pres Acad Fit Awd; Pres Schlr; Cngrssnl Schlr Of Cngrssnl Yth Ldrshp Cncl; CSF Life Stu; CA Golden St Exam High Schlr Math.

TAHARA, WENDY K; San Clemente HS; San Clemente, CA; (2); Cmnty Wkr; Pres German Clb; Hosp Aide; Letterman Clb; Orch; Hon Roll; Bach Fstvl Piano Semifnlst 89; Mst Imprvd Otch 89 & 90; Romantic Music Grmn/Astrn Cmpsrs Cmptn; Piano.

TAHILRAMANI, MAYA E; Southwest HS; San Diego, CA; (3); 4/493; Church Yth Grp; Cmnty Wkr; Science Clb; SADD; Teachers Aide; Yrbk; Off Jr Cls; Cit Awd; Hon Roll; Prfct Atten Awd; Comm ASB; Peace Club; CSF; Acctng.

TAHIRI, ABDULLAH; Magnolia HS; Anaheim, CA; (2); Church Yth Grp; Teachers Aide; Nwsp; Bus Mgmt.

TAHIRI, YOUSUF; Magnolia HS; Anaheim, CA; (3); Nwsp; Engrng.

TAHMASSIAN, AYOUT Y; Herbert Hoover HS; Glendale, CA; (3); Girl Scts; Teachers Aide; Acpl Chr; Church Choir; School Play; Gldn St Exam Algebra Hnrs; Cert Awd For Otstndng Schlrshp Spnsh; Otstndng Stu Of Mnth; CA ST; Accntng.

TAI, ANN W; Cypress HS; Cypress, CA; (2); Chess Clb; Cmnty Wkr; Intnl Clb; Key Clb; Service Clb; Spanish Clb; JV Trk; Prfct Atten Awd; JV Badmntn; Bus Admin.

TAI, BILLY CHIH-HENG; Thousand Oaks HS; Thousand Oaks, CA; (3); Church Yth Grp; Hosp Aide; Intnl Clb; Math Clb; Math Tm.

TAI, CHRISTINE A; San Gabriel HS; San Gabriel, CA; (2); Church Yth Grp; Debate Tm; French Clb; JA; NFL; School Musical; JV Swmmng; High Hon Roll; Hon Roll; Jr NHS; Pasadena Branch Hnrs Fest; S CA Jr Bach Fest; Bus Mgt.

TAI, GLORIA; Woodbridge HS; Irvine, CA; (4); 28/375; Sec French Clb; Sec JA; Sec VP SADD; Drill Tm; Ed Nwsp; Yrbk; Off Frsh Cls; Hon Roll; Pres Acad Fit Awd; Safe Rides; UC Berkeley; Bus.

TAI, JENNY Y; Arcadia HS; Arcadia, CA; (3); 68/639; Church Yth Grp; Color Guard; Drill Tm; High Hon Roll; Hon Roll; Prfct Atten Awd; Pres Acad Fit Awd; Sthrn CA Jr Bach Fstvl; Pre Med.

TAIBY, MOHAMMED J; Sunset HS; Hayward, CA; (2); High Hon Roll; Hon Roll; Cmptr Sci.

TAIN, NICHOLAS C; Jefferson HS; Daly City, CA; (4); 9/250; Computer Clb; Library Aide; Science Clb; Spanish Clb; Bsktbl; Tennis; Trk; High Hon Roll; Hon Roll; CA Math League Awd; Bank Of Amer Achvt Awd Bus; Home Savings Career Awareness Prgm Awd; San Jose ST U; Elect Engr.

TAING, KIM G; Amos Alonzo Stagg HS; Stockton, CA; (3); Teachers Aide; High Hon Roll; Hon Roll; Badmtn; 222 Health Acad; HOSA Hlth Occup Stu Am Sec Trs; Delta; Hlth.

TAING, PEK TRY; Schurr HS; Monterey Park, CA; (4); 112/600; Letterman Clb; Varsity Clb; Variety Show; JV Bsktbl; Var Capt Crs Cntry; Var Capt Trk; Cit Awd; Hon Roll; Opt Clb Awd; Prfct Atten Awd; CA ST U Los Angeles; Psych.

TAING, PHILIP K; San Gabriel HS; San Gabriel, CA; (2); Crs Cntry; Trk; Hon Roll; Dr.

TAING, PO PO LINDA; Mark Keppel HS; Monterey Park, CA; (3); Office Aide; Teachers Aide; Rptr Nwsp; Ed Phtg Yrbk; Cit Awd; Hon Roll; Prfct Atten Awd; Sunshine Girl Kiowa Clb; John Alexander Jrnlsm Awd; Comp.

TAINO, GERALDINE B; Sierra Vista HS; Baldwin Park, CA; (3); Chrmn Church Yth Grp; Cmnty Wkr; Dance Clb; Math Clb; SADD; Teachers Aide; Capt Color Guard; Rep Stu Cncl; High Hon Roll; CSF; UC Riverside; Bus Admin.

TAIRA, NICOLE M; Lowell HS; San Francisco, CA; (3); CSF; Big Brothers, Big Sisters.

TAJERIAN, HOVAN; Ferrahian HS; Van Nuys, CA; (2); Boy Scts; Quiz Bowl; Acpl Chr; Band; Church Choir; Mrchg Band; Hon Roll; Los Angeles Music/Art Schls Dir Awd; Music.

TAJIBOY, MARIA ROSMERY; Bell HS; Maywood, CA; (4); French Clb; Var Crs Cntry; Var Trk; Cit Awd; Ephebian; CSF Sealbearer; Sci Dept Awd; UC Santa Barbara; Bio.

TAKADA, ERIKA; Sacramento HS; Sacramento, CA; (3); 15/424; Sec AFS; Orch; Rep Frsh Cls; Pres Soph Cls; Sec Jr Cls; Rep Stu Cncl; Jr Intrm EKG UCD Mdel Ctr; Concert Mstrss Yth Symphony; Violinist San Francisco Symphony Yth Orch; Pre-Med.

TAKAGI, JONATHAN M; Escondido HS; Escondido, CA; (2); Church Yth Grp; Hosp Aide; Science Clb; Stat Bsktbl; JV Tennis; High Hon Roll; Hon Roll; Prfct Atten Awd; Cert Outstndng Achvt In Coll Ready Wrtng Project; Stu Of Semester Awd; U CA Riverside; Biomedcl Sci.

TAKAGI, YUTAKA; Sunny Hills HS; Fullerton, CA; (3); 40/430; Treas Computer Clb; French Clb; Intnl Clb; Key Clb; Treas Sr Cls; Trk; High Hon Roll; Ntl Merit Ltr; Prfct Atten Awd; Jr Statesmn Of Amer Chaptr VP; Intl Bus.

TAKAHASH, MARLA S; San Marino HS; Tucson, AZ; (4); AFS; Letterman Clb; Varsity Clb; Rep Stu Cncl; JV L Bsktbl; Var L Gym; Stat Mgr(s); Var L Socr; Prfct Atten Awd; CARE Ldr Mentor Prgm; SAB; Self Esteem Goals; U AZ; Psych.

TAKASAKI, LAURA H; Cerritos HS; Cerritos, CA; (2); JV Swmmng; JV Tennis; Hon Roll; Sci.

TAKASAKI, TODD T; Gretchen Whitney HS; Cerritos, CA; (3); Art Clb; Rep Jr Cls; Var Cheerldng; Var Crs Cntry; Hon Roll; CSF; Dentistry.

TAKATA, KELLEY A; San Fernando HS; Arleta, CA; (2); Band; Jazz Band; Mrchg Band; Yrbk; Treas Frsh Cls; Cit Awd; High Hon Roll; NHS; Pres Acad Fit Awd; Schlrshp Awd; UC Santa Barbara; Comp Engr.

TAKAYAMA, YUNO; John Burroughs HS; Santa Monica, CA; (3); French Clb; Library Aide; Hon Roll; Elec Engr.

TAKECHI, DAVID A; Edison Computech HS; Fresno, CA; (2); 101/315; JV Tennis; Cit Awd; Hon Roll; CSF; Edison Env Awareness Clb; Statesmen Of Am; CA Poly ST U; Arch.

TAKEDA, DEREK Y; Los Altos HS; Hacienda Hts, CA; (3); Letterman Clb; Science Clb; Teachers Aide; Varsity Clb; Band; Mrchg Band; Pep Band; Var Capt Wrstlng; Prfct Atten Awd; Judo 2nd Deg Brwn Blt; Cal ST Long Beach; Law.

TAKEDA, TINA; Elk Grove HS; Elk Grove, CA; (2); Church Yth Grp; SADD; Hon Roll; Judo St Chmpnshps 3rd; USJF Natl Jr & Yth Judo Chmpnshp 3rd Pl 89; Hokka Achvt Awd 89; Aeronautcl Engr.

TAKEDA, TYLER A; Sanger HS; Sanger, CA; (3); Ed Nwsp; Sprt Ed Yrbk; Stu Cncl; Mgr Bsbl; JV Ftbl; Prfct Atten Awd; CSF; Jrnlsm Clb VP; Asian Clb; CA ST U Fresno; Jrnlsm.

TAKEI, MAGGIE K; Sondra HS; Fullerton, CA; (4); Sec French Clb; Rep GAA; Math Clb; Rep Frsh Cls; Rep Soph Cls; Rep Soph Cls; Rep Sr Cls; Stu Cncl; Var Bsktbl; Capt Var Socr; CSF Pres; Pepperdine U Sthrn CA Yth Ctznshp Smnr; US Army Rsrv Natl Schlr Athl Awd; US Coast Grd Acad; Mgmt.

TAKEI, YUMI J; Sonora HS; Fullerton, CA; (2); Church Yth Grp; French Clb; GAA; Science Clb; Ski Clb; Var Socr; Var Swmmng; Var Tennis; High Hon Roll; Grls League; CA St Fullerton-Emerging Ldrs Pgm; CA Schlrshp Fed.

TAKENAGA, KEVIN; Arlington HS; Riverside, CA; (3); 1/400; Boy Scts; Chess Clb; Quiz Bowl; Scholastic Bowl; JV Crs Cntry; High Hon Roll; Stu Of Mnth Awd; Golden St Exam Hi Hnrs Alg; Geomtry Hnrs; CSF; Engrng.

TAKETA, KYLE H; Santa Teresa HS; San Jose, CA; (3); Boy Scts; Church Yth Grp; SADD; Yrbk; Ftbl; Eagle Scout Awd 90; Outstndng Jr Of Yr Photog; VP Church Youth Grp; Buddhist Chrch Yth Exch Pgm 90; Phys Therapy.

TAKEUCHI, JOEL Y; Armijo HS; Fairfield, CA; (2); Boy Scts; Church Yth Grp; Ski Clb; Swmmng; Mst Vlbl JR Vrsty Water Polo.

TAKEUCHI, PAMELA; Palisades HS; Pacific Palisades, CA; (3); Cmnty Wkr; Math Clb; Math Tm; Ski Clb; Varsity Clb; Yrbk; JV Var Bsktbl; JV Sftbl; Hon Roll; Pali Outrch; U CA Davis; Vet Med.

TAKEUCHI, RYAN; Edison HS; Huntington Beach, CA; (1); Hosp Aide; Key Clb; Model UN; Scholastic Bowl; JV Tennis; Japanese Sch; Peer Assist League; Cardiac Surgeon.

TAKHAR, CASANDRA M; Amos Alonzo Stagg HS; Stockton, CA; (3); Church Yth Grp; Cmnty Wkr; Dance Clb; GAA; Office Aide; Ski Clb; Teachers Aide; Variety Show; Nwsp; Var Cheerldng; Treas Leos Clb; Vol For 1st Easter Seal Telethon Hispanic; Youth Grp; S J Delta; Sociology.

TAKHAR, PAULINE; Amos Alonzo Stagg HS; Stockton, CA; (1); Church Yth Grp; Cmnty Wkr; Dance Clb; GAA; VP Frsh Cls; VP Soph Cls; Cheerldng; Sftbl; Hon Roll; Marine Bio.

TAKKEN, MARC G; Mission College Prep; Atascadero, CA; (3); Letterman Clb; Teachers Aide; Varsity Clb; Ed Yrbk; Treas Stu Cncl; Crs Cntry; Socr; High Hon Roll; Hon Roll; St Schlr.

TAL, MARTHA; Los Alamitos HS; Seal Beach, CA; (3); Cmnty Wkr; Speech Tm; JV Trk; Yth Dvlpmnt Prjct.

TALALELE, SHARLENE; W C Overfelt HS; San Jose, CA; (2); Church Yth Grp; Cmnty Wkr; Church Choir.

TALAMANTES, OLIVIA; Canyon HS; Canyon Country, CA; (2); Crs Cntry; High Hon Roll; Hon Roll; Spanish NHS; UCLA; Bus.

TALAMAYAN, JOANNE J; Montgomery HS; San Diego, CA; (3); 23/455; Church Yth Grp; JA; Pep Clb; Service Clb; Ed Yrbk; Rep Soph Cls; Rep Jr Cls; Rep Sr Cls; JV Bsktbl; Hon Roll; ASB Vp; Asst Commissioner Art & Pblcty; CSF; Pacific Asian Club Commissioner Of Act; U CA San Diego; Premed.

TALAPATRA, SUNIT K; Servite HS; Fullerton, CA; (3); 2/166; Math Tm; Science Clb; Ed Nwsp; Ed Lit Mag; Var Trk; Hon Roll; Pres NHS; Debate Tm; Quiz Bowl; Stage Crew; CSF Pres; Acad Decathlon Tm; Schl Spelling Bee Fnlst; Stanford U; Health.

TALARICO, NICOLE; Laguna Beach HS; Laguna Beach, CA; (1); Band; Mrchg Band; Swmmng; Hon Roll; Chrldr; Disneyland Creativity Chllnge.

TALBOT, TAMARA P; Loma Linda Acad; Loma Linda, CA; (3); Church Yth Grp; Chorus; Rptr Nwsp; Yrbk; Off Soph Cls; High Hon Roll; NHS; Pres Acad Fit Awd; Dermatology.

TALIANI, CHRISTEN L; Arlington HS; Riverside, CA; (2); Church Yth Grp; Chorus; Drill Tm; UCLA; Bus.

TALIFER, JOHN E; Westlake HS; Westlake Vlg, CA; (2); Chorus; Golf; A Class Act; Select Vocal Group; Ymca Camp Colunteer; Mens Ensemble.

TALKINGTON, CORINA A; Rio Lindo Acad; Redding, CA; (4); 18/120; Church Yth Grp; Hosp Aide; Red Cross Aide; Ski Clb; Spanish Clb; Acpl Chr; Variety Show; Off Soph Cls; Gym; Pres Acad Fit Awd; Yuba City Coll; Legal Secy.

TALLENT, JONATHAN J; Casa Grande HS; Petaluma, CA; (2); 53/295; Church Yth Grp; Cmnty Wkr; JV Socr; JV Trk; JV Capt Wrstlng; Hon Roll; Stu Of Mnth Ind Arts; Volntr Spcl Olympcs; Soccr Referee; PE.

TALLENT, SHONA; Escalon HS; Oakdale, CA; (2); 55/131; English Clb; Key Clb; SADD; Hon Roll; Golden ST Exam Awd; CSF; MJC Coll; Comp Prgmg.

TALLERICO, JULIE; Shasta HS; Redding, CA; (2); 44/442; Dance Clb; SADD; Acpl Chr; School Musical; School Play; Rep Soph Cls; Rep Jr Cls; JV Cheerldng; Waterski, Snowski, Modern Dance; Ldrshp Day; Math Teacher.

TALLEY, WAYMOND M; Wilson HS; Los Angeles, CA; (3).

TALLMAN, ERIN E; Mission San Jose HS; Fremont, CA; (2); GAA; Socr; Sftbl; Trk; HOBY Ldrshp Awd; Arch.

TALLMAN, MIKE; Napa HS; Napa, CA; (1); Cit Awd; High Hon Roll; Prncpls Awd; UCLA.

TALVI, SONJA L ALLER; Fairfax HS; Los Angeles, CA; (3); Hosp Aide; Speech Tm; SADD; School Musical; Rptr Nwsp; Gym; Wellesley Bk Awd Recipient 90; Princeton Poetry Cont Hnrb Mntn 89-90; Mills Coll; Med.

TALWAR, NIKHIL; Hoover HS; Fresno, CA; (3); 54/500; Spanish Clb; Davis U; Comp Engr.

TALWAR, RAJESH K; Anaheim HS; Anaheim, CA; (3); Ftbl; Law.

TAM, ALBERT; Abraham Lincoln HS; San Francisco, CA; (3); Bus Profs of Am; Debate Tm; FBLA; Office Aide; Trk; Hon Roll; Hgh Hnrs In Math; Cert In Alg & Geom; Spec Cls Bus & Hstry; UC Davis; Math.

TAM, AMY; Independence HS; San Jose, CA; (4); 145/728; Art Clb; FBLA; GAA; JA; Science Clb; Teachers Aide; Var Crs Cntry; Hon Roll; Pres Acad Fit Awd; Chinese & Photo Clbs; Vrsty Badmntn; Hayward ST U; Finance.

TAM, AMY MAN-YING; C K Mc Clatchy SR HS; Sacramento, CA; (2); French Clb; Key Clb; Math Clb; Math Tm; Teachers Aide; Orch; Rep Frsh Cls; JV Bsktbl; Powder Puff Ftbl; JV Var Tennis; Med.

TAM, ANNIE C; Mills HS; Millbrae, CA; (3); Orch; Mgr(s); Hon Roll.

TAM, BESSIE B; Galileo HS; San Francisco, CA; (2); Church Yth Grp; Pep Clb; Speech Tm; Variety Show; Hist Frsh Cls; Chrmn Soph Cls; JV Tennis; Hon Roll; Golden St Exam Schl Hnr Alg; Stu Of Mnth; Outstndng Achvt In Acad; UC Berkeley; Bus.

TAM, CHRISTINE; Ochurr HS; Monterey Park, CA; (4); 45/580; Church Yth Grp; Hosp Aide; NFL; Church Choir; Yrbk; Cit Awd; High Hon Roll; NHS; Prfct Atten Awd; Pres Acad Fit Awd; CSF; UCLA; Bus Econ.

TAM, DAVID K L; Phillip Burton HS; San Francisco, CA; (3); Chess Clb; Computer Clb; High Hon Roll; Acad Excllnc Awd; Elec Engrng.

TAM, DEBBIE Y; Lowell HS; San Francisco, CA; (3); Hosp Aide; Teachers Aide; San Francisco ST U; Bus.

TAM, EVA; Eagle Rock HS; Los Angeles, CA; (3); Key Clb; Yrbk; Off Jr Cls; Crs Cntry; Swmmng; High Hon Roll; Hon Roll; Prfct Atten Awd; Rope Bearer; USC; Acctg.

TAM, JOANNA W; John O'connell HS; San Francisco, CA; (4); Cit Awd; Hon Roll; Badminton; Drafting Trade Cert; San Jose ST U; Civil Engrg.

TAM, JUDY; Westmoor HS; Daly City, CA; (3); Sec German Clb; Hosp Aide; Service Clb; High Hon Roll; Hon Roll; CSF; St Marys Moraga; Hlth Svc Adm.

TAM, KATRYNA; Lowell HS; San Francisco, CA; (2); Church Yth Grp; Cmnty Wkr; Library Aide; SADD; Sftbl Clb; Music Apprctn Soc.

TAM, MABEL Y; Brawley Union HS; Brawley, CA; (3); 5/360; Am Leg Aux Girls St; Sec SADD; Teachers Aide; Varsity Clb; Off Jr Cls; Stu Cncl; Powder Puff Ftbl; JV Var Vllybl; High Hon Roll; Hon Roll; Most Insrptnl Vrsty Vllybl 89; U Of Los Angeles; Cmmnctns.

TAM, MANDA; Lincoln HS; Stockton, CA; (3); Key Clb; Mu Alpha Theta; Spanish Clb; Teachers Aide; Hon Roll; Pltcl Clb; Vp Close Up; CSF; Delta Coll; CPA.

TAM, PETER H; Verdugo Hills HS; South Gate, CA; (4); Am Leg Boys St; Boy Scts; Treas French Clb; Math Clb; Scholastic Bowl; Capt Tennis; Hon Roll; Opt Clb Awd; Pres Acad Fit Awd; UC Irvine; Bus Admin.

TAM, RAYMOND; Milpitas HS; Milpitas, CA; (1); Spanish Clb; Hon Roll; Chinese Clb; Med.

TAM, RENEE; Wallenberg HS; San Francisco, CA; (1); Tennis; Hon Roll; Bus.

TAM, STELLA; Lowell HS; San Francisco, CA; (2); Cmnty Wkr; SADD; Hon Roll; Chinese, Tenns & Bio Clbs; U C Berkeley; Bus.

TAM, SUSAN T S; George Washington HS; San Francisco, CA; (3); Cmnty Wkr; Key Clb; Math Clb; Science Clb; Service Clb; High Hon Roll; Golden St Exam Geom Hnrs 88-89; Anti-Litter Cont 2nd Pl; Hong Kong Intl Club Secy; Calpoly; Arch Dsgn.

TAM, SYLVIA S; Milpitas HS; Milpitas, CA; (3); 52/487; Hosp Aide; Pep Clb; Pres Spanish Clb; Ed Nwsp; Sec Jr Cls; Rep Stu Cncl; JV Var Trk; High Hon Roll; NHS; 87-88 Outstndng Span Stu; Clinical Psych.

TAM, WINNIE P; Galileo HS; San Francisco, CA; (4); Cmnty Wkr; JA; Model UN; Pep Clb; Teachers Aide; Varsity Clb; School Play; Off Jr Cls; Off Sr Cls; Stu Cncl; Golden St Exam Math Schlr Awd; Japanese Clb Pres; San Francisco ST U; Intl Bus.

TAMAI, SARAH; Los Gatos HS; Los Gatos, CA; (4); 23/375; French Clb; Pep Clb; JV Var Cheerldng; High Hon Roll; Hon Roll; Rotary Awd; CSF; UCLA.

TAMALII, SABRINA; Los Alamitos HS; Carson, CA; (3); Math Tm; Spanish Clb; Teachers Aide; JV Var Vllybl; Cit Awd; Hon Roll; Golden ST Gmtry Hnr Roll; Los Almts Vlybl Clb BYU Schlrshp Hl; Hnr Roll Drill Tm Clb; CA ST U; Bus Mgmt.

TAMANAHA, LISA L; Drew Medical Magnet HS; Gardena, CA; (3); Debate Tm; English Clb; Hosp Aide; Math Tm; Yrbk; Lit Mag; Treas Sr Cls; High Hon Roll; Skirball Isnt Amer Values Awd; Tsts Engr Aptitude; Math & Sci Tm; Med.

TAMASHIRO, WESLEY S; Warren HS; Downey, CA; (2); Church Yth Grp; German Clb; Science Clb; Ski Clb; Rptr Nwsp; JV Bsktbl; JV Vllybl; Hon Roll; USC; Law Enforcement.

TAMAYO, EVANGELINA; Montebello HS; Pico Rivera, CA; (2); SADD; Acpl Chr; Chorus; Stu Cncl; Stat Bsktbl; Hon Roll; Stu Of Mnth Math.

TAMAYO, MARTHA E; Compton HS; Compton, CA; (3); Chess Clb; Church Yth Grp; Computer Clb; Drama Clb; Spanish Clb; School Play; Rep Jr Cls; JV Tennis; Var Vllybl; Hon Roll; Upwrd Bnd Prgm UCLA; UCLA & Irvine Prtnrshp Prgm; UCLA; Ed.

TAMAYO, RUBEN; Pater Noster HS; Los Angeles, CA; (2); 18/57; Drama Clb; Quiz Bowl; Service Clb; Church Choir; Phtg Nwsp; Ed Yrbk; Pres Soph Cls; Pres Jr Cls; JV Trk; Cit Awd; Outstndng Acad Achvt Hnrs Engl; Loyola Marymount U; Graphic Art.

TAMEEZ, HAMEDA; Etiwanda HS; Alta Loma, CA; (2); Spanish Clb; SADD; Teachers Aide; Band; Stage Crew; Crs Cntry; Cit Awd; Hon Roll; Dntl Asst.

TAMEZ, MICHAEL; Clovis HS; Clovis, CA; (3); Church Yth Grp; Office Aide; Spanish Clb; Varsity Clb; Var Capt Wrstlng; Cit Awd; Hon Roll; Pres Acad Fit Awd; Fresno ST; Engrng.

TAMM, JASON R; Fullerton Union HS; Fullerton, CA; (4); ROTC; Teachers Aide; Band; Drm Mjr(t); Jazz Band; Phtg Yrbk; L Bsktbl; L Crs Cntry; Var Trk; Hon Roll; Norwich U VT; Commnctns.

TAMPAN, ORFA J; Hawthorne HS; Hawthorne, CA; (3); Treas Soph Cls; Treas Jr Cls; Var Cheerldng; Cit Awd; Hon Roll; Pres Acad Fit Awd; AFS Stu Exchng Prog; Hrns Alg II; UC San Diego; Bus.

TAMPI, JINKIE DAHL A; Glendale Adventist Acad; Los Angeles, CA; (3); 19/65; Girl Scts; Office Aide; Varsity Clb; Church Choir; Treas Frsh Cls; Sec Soph Cls; Score Keeper; Vllybl; Loma Linda; Orthodontist.

TAMRAZI, ANOBEL; Leland HS; San Jose, CA; (2); 2/30; Chess Clb; Church Yth Grp; Computer Clb; French Clb; German Clb; Math Clb; Band; Yrbk; Bsktbl; Socr; Assyrian Clb; Berkley; Med.

TAN, ALISON; Mark Keppel HS; Monterey Park, CA; (3); Hist Pres French Clb; Hosp Aide; Service Clb; Rptr Nwsp; VP Sr Cls; Stu Cncl; JV Tennis; High Hon Roll; Hon Roll; CA Schlrshp Fed.

TAN, AUDREY C; Mater Dei HS; Cypress, CA; (3); Church Yth Grp; French Clb; Hosp Aide; Spanish Clb; VP Speech Tm; Rep Jr Cls; Off Sr Cls; High Hon Roll; NHS; SOS/Styng Alive; 4.0 Brkfst-Mass Awd; Hnrs Entrnc HS; UCLA.

TAN, BON; Westminster HS; Westminster, CA; (3); 100/416; Pres French Clb; VP Key Clb; Service Clb; Speech Tm; Chorus; VP Sr Cls; Score Keeper; Westminster Boys & Grls Clb Yth Of Yr; Orange Cnty Boys Clb Yth Of Yr; Leo Awd Vcl; Pepperdine; Bus.

TAN, BUN H; Marina HS; Huntington Beach, CA; (4); 160/500; French Clb; Yrbk; Hon Roll; 2 Golden Shield Awds; Golden St Exam Hnr; Golden West JC; Arch.

TAN, CLARICE R; Canyon HS; Anaheim, CA; (2); Spanish Clb; Tennis; Arch.

TAN, ELEANOR; Skyline HS; Oakland, CA; (3); Pep Clb; Red Cross Aide; Rep Frsh Cls; JV Cheerldng; Hon Roll; LITA Pgm; Art Hstry.

TAN, EMMELINE S; Mt Carmel HS; San Diego, CA; (2); Key Clb; Prfct Atten Awd; Acad League 88-89; CA Hnrs Gldn ST Exam Geom; CA Schlrshp Fed; Races United Club 89; UC Berkely; Bus.

TAN, JACK H; Abraham Lincoln HS; San Francisco, CA; (2); Office Aide; Orch; Hon Roll; Stu Lesson Plan Cntst 1st Pl 90; CSF; Soph Club; INCAR; UC Berkeley; Doc.

TAN, JANIS R; Milpitas HS; Milpitas, CA; (1); Cmnty Wkr; Hosp Aide; ROTC; Drill Tm; High Hon Roll; Hon Roll; Amer Leg Schlstc Excl Awd.

TAN, JENNY; Franklin HS; Los Angeles, CA; (4); 37/650; Cmnty Wkr; Hosp Aide; Library Aide; VP Math Clb; Science Clb; Treas Service Clb; Sec Jr Cls; Off Stu Cncl; Cit Awd; Hon Roll; UC Riverside; Business.

TAN, JOHN T; St Francis HS; El Monte, CA; (2); 1/175; Debate Tm; Treas Mu Alpha Theta; Pep Clb; Ed Yrbk; Treas Soph Cls; Treas Stu Cncl; Var Crs Cntry; Var Trk; Treas NHS; Spanish NHS; Cngrssnl Schlr Rep CA Natl Yng Ldrs Conf; Arthur J Schwartz Schlrshp St Francis; Cycling; Stanford U; Aerospace Engrng.

TAN, JORGE L; St Ignatius College Prep; Daly City, CA; (2); 1/308; Cmnty Wkr; Drama Clb; Church Choir; School Musical; Phtg Yrbk; Intrml Vllybl; High Hon Roll; 8th Grade Vldctrn.

TAN, KATHRINE; Fairfield HS; Fairfield, CA; (3); German Clb; Key Clb; Service Clb; Drill Tm; Rep Nwsp; Rep Soph Cls; Stu Cncl; Cit Awd; High Hon Roll; NHS; UC Davis; Phy.

TAN, LAURENCE A; Chula Vista HS; Chula Vista, CA; (2); Hosp Aide; JV Socr; Var Tennis; Cit Awd; Masonic Awd; Prfct Atten Awd; Pres Schlr; Draw; CSF; Pan Asian; Asbs Sword & Shield; Harvard; Elec Engr.

TAN, LEONARD M; Valley Christian HS; Anaheim, CA; (2); Church Yth Grp; VP Band; Jazz Band; Mrchg Band; Pep Band; School Musical; JV Crs Cntry; JV Socr; JV Trk; Hon Roll; UCI; Sci.

TAN, M CARMELA; Bishop Amat HS; Rowland Hts, CA; (4); Teachers Aide; Ed Nwsp; Rep Frsh Cls; Treas Soph Cls; Stu Cncl; Hon Roll; NHS; Ntl Merit Ltr; Pres Acad Fit Awd; UCLA; Law.

TAN, MAI; Rosemead HS; Rosemead, CA; (2); Wt Lftg; Cit Awd; Hon Roll.

TAN, MARIA; South San Francisco HS; Pinole, CA; (3); Cmnty Wkr; FBLA; Cit Awd; Hon Roll; Typewriting Proficiency Cert; Drug Free Promotion Recogntn Cert; Ldrshp Wrkshp Awd Cert; Advrtsng.

TAN, MARIA CARMELA; Bishop Amat HS; Rowland Hts, CA; (4); 8/400; Cmnty Wkr; Service Clb; Ed Nwsp; Rep Frsh Cls; Treas Soph Cls; Hon Roll; NHS; Ntl Merit Ltr; UCLA; Soclgy.

TAN, MELANIE C; Lowell HS; San Francisco, CA; (2); Library Aide; Office Aide; Teachers Aide; Variety Show; Gldn St Alg Exn Hgh Hnrs; Stu Advcts Global Awrns; Cncl Stu Affairs.

TAN, MELISSA M; Acad Of Our Lady Of Peace; San Diego, CA; (3); Church Yth Grp; Off Key Clb; Treas Service Clb; Chorus; Church Choir; School Play; Yrbk; Sec Jr Cls; Var Cheerldng; Trk; Maria Clara De Philipinas Sorority 89; Vlntr Rancho Penasquitos Pblc Library; Keywanette Div; Soc Sci.

TAN, MICHELLE C; Holy Family HS; Glendale, CA; (2); Art Clb; Church Yth Grp; Library Aide; Church Choir; Hon Roll; CA Schlrshp Fdrtn; U Of CA Los Angeles; Nrsng.

TAN, NADYA; Milpitas HS; Milpitas, CA; (1); Band; Jazz Band; Mrchg Band; Stu Cncl; High Hon Roll; Amnesty Intl; Ldrshp Awd; UC Coll; Engl.

TAN, ROANNE; Southwest HS; San Diego, CA; (3); 34/603; Key Clb; Office Aide; Teachers Aide; Flag Corp; Rptr Nwsp; Ed Yrbk; Pres Frsh Cls; Rep Soph Cls; Rep Jr Cls; Bsktbl; 2nd Pl Wnr Sci Fair; CA Schlrshp Fdrtn; Pan Asian; Bus Mgmt.

TAN, ROXANNE; Southwest HS; San Diego, CA; (4); 17/478; Cmnty Wkr; JA; SADD; Flag Corp; Rep Sr Cls; Hon Roll; Pres Acad Fit Awd; CSF Secy; Pan Asian; Assctd Stdt Body Cmmssnr Actvts & Fndrsg; Pre-Med.

TAN, SUSAN; Galileo HS; San Francisco, CA; (4); Church Yth Grp; Office Aide; Red Cross Aide; VP Soph Cls; Bus.

TAN, THOMAS; Pindle Valley HS; Pinole, CA; (2); Intrml Bsktbl; Var Capt Socr; JV Trk; High Hon Roll; Hon Roll; Golden ST Exam; CSF; Geom League; U CA Berkeley; Doctor.

TAN, TONY H; El Cajon Vally HS; El Cajon, CA; (2); Var Crs Cntry; Var Trk; Var Wrstlng; UCSD; Doctor.

TAN, YUE L; A Lincoln HS; San Francisco, CA; (4); 30/800; Computer Clb; U CA Davis; Comp Pgmr.

TANAKA, ALLISON; South HS; Torrance, CA; (2); 49/372; Drill Tm; Off Frsh Cls; VP Soph Cls; Pres Jr Cls; Hon Roll; NCA Drill Tm Superstr Girl; Natl Champ Dance Am Comp; Membr Ca Schlrshp Fed.

TANAKA, DOUGLAS S; El Camino HS; Carmichael, CA; (3); Boy Scts; Cmnty Wkr; Key Clb; Red Cross Aide; Var Crs Cntry; Var Trk; Var Wrstlng; Cit Awd; Hon Roll; Prfct Atten Awd; Eagle Sct; Mst Insprtnl Athl Crss Cntry Tm; U Of OR; Sports Thrpst.

TANAKA, IAN K; Fairfield HS; Fairfield, CA; (2); Teachers Aide; Band; High Hon Roll; Hon Roll; UC Berkeley; Math.

TANAKA, KARLYN K; Bonita Vista HS; Bonita, CA; (2); Rptr Nwsp; Ed Yrbk; JV Tennis; Cit Awd; Prfct Atten Awd; Imprvmnt In Ctznshp & Schlrshps Awd; U Of Boulder CO; Law.

TANAKA, MASAHIKO; El Cajon Valley HS; San Diego, CA; (2); Aud/Vis; Bus Profs of Am; Computer Clb; French Clb; Ski Clb; Jazz Band; Vllybl; Wt Lftg; Horse Riding; Bowling; Japanese Language; UCSD; Scientist-Engr.

TANAKA, RYAN T; Servite HS; Hacienda Hghts, CA; (2); Math Tm; Rptr Nwsp; Treas Soph Cls; Treas Jr Cls; Intrml Bsktbl; High Hon Roll; NHS; CSF Actvty & Stu Tutoring Awd; Acad Decathlon; JR Statesmen Of Amer; Stanford; Econ.

TANAKA, STEPHANIE; Bonita Vista HS; Bonita, CA; (4); 5/523; Art Clb; Cmnty Wkr; Off Frsh Cls; Off Soph Cls; Off Jr Cls; Off Sr Cls; Var Tennis; Cit Awd; High Hon Roll; Hon Roll.

TANAKA, TAKUYA; Gardena HS; Gardena, CA; (4); Service Clb; Ski Clb; Spanish Clb; Rep Frsh Cls; Bsktbl; Hon Roll; Prfct Atten Awd.

TANAKA, TRENT K; James Lick HS; San Jose, CA; (2); Aud/Vis; Boy Scts; Math Tm; Nwsp; JV Bsbl; JV Bsktbl; Mgr(s); Hon Roll; Prfct Atten Awd; CSF; Stu Wk; Frank Burrows Math Fld Day Rcgntn; MIT; Elec Engrng.

TANAP, LARRY D; Hueneme HS; Port Hueneme, CA; (2); Ftbl; Wt Lftg; Hon Roll; FL ST U; Prfssnl Ftbl Player.

TANAQUIN, JOSEPH S; Carson HS; Carson, CA; (3); JV Tennis; USC; Math.

TANCHOCO, JAMES A; Bishop Amat Memorial HS; Rowland Heights, CA; (2); Bsbl; JV Ftbl; Wt Lftg; Hon Roll; NHS.

TANCIOCO, FERNANDO R; John F Kennedy HS; Sacramento, CA; (2); 33/525; High Hon Roll; Hon Roll; Prfct Atten Awd; Golden St Exm Awd 1st Yr Alg W/Hgh Hnrs; UC Berkeley; Cmptr Engr.

TANDBERG, SKY W; Torrey Pines HS; San Diego, CA; (2); Spanish Clb; Hon Roll.

TANDE, TAINA; Simi Valley HS; Simi Valley, CA; (2); 37/753; Church Yth Grp; Rep Frsh Cls; Rep Soph Cls; Stu Cncl; Var Socr; Var Sftbl; Var Vllybl; Cit Awd; High Hon Roll; Hon Roll; CSF.

TANDOC, THOMAS; El Cerrito HS; El Cerrito, CA; (4); Church Yth Grp; Cmnty Wkr; VP Model UN; SADD; Teachers Aide; Church Choir; Ed Nwsp; Hon Roll; Pres Acad Fit Awd; Vol UC Berkeleys Erthqk Engrng Resrch Ctr; Sci Proj Intl Sci & Engrng Fair; U CA Davis.

TANDON, RITU; Chaminade College Prep; Chatsworth, CA; (2); Key Clb; Sec SADD; High Hon Roll; Pres Acad Fit Awd; CA Schlrshp Fed; Cert Of Merit In Study Of Piano; Advncd Snow Skier/Tnns Player; Lawyer.

TANG, ALLEN; Schurr HS; Montebello, CA; (4); 58/582; Treas Church Yth Grp; Computer Clb; VP Spanish Clb; Treas SADD; Rptr Nwsp; Yrbk; JV Trk; High Hon Roll; Prfct Atten Awd; UCLA.

TANG, ALVIN YUE MAN; International Studies Acad; San Francisco, CA; (4); Computer Clb; Math Tm; Science Clb; Lit Mag; Hon Roll; Japanese Clb; CA Schlrshp Fdrtn; UCSF; Pharm.

TANG, AMY H; Alhambra High; Alhambra, CA; (3); Debate Tm; French Clb; Ed Nwsp; Hist Stu Cncl; Hon Roll; Pres Acad Fit Awd; CA Schltc Fed; Geom Schl Recognition; 2nd Pl Expository Speech; Loyola Marymount; Law.

TANG, ANTHONY K; Lowell HS; San Francisco, CA; (3); Latin Clb; Orch; Contrct Bridge Clb; Comp Engrng.

TANG, ANTHONY S; Abraham Lincoln HS; San Francisco, CA; (3); Math Clb; High Hon Roll; Gldn St Exam Alg High Hnr; VSF; UCLA; Engrng.

TANG, BEVERLY; El Monte HS; Baldwin Park, CA; (2); French Clb; Key Clb; Science Clb; Acpl Chr; Chorus; School Musical; Variety Show; Off Frsh Cls; Sec Treas Soph Cls; Sec Jr Cls; CA Poly ST U; Comp Sci.

TANG, CALVIN H; Lowell HS; San Francisco, CA; (3); Computer Clb; Library Aide; Sci Ed Prtnrshp 2nd Pl; Gldn St Exm High Hnrs Geomtry & Rec Alg; Cmptr Sci.

TANG, CHARLIE; Montgomery HS; San Ysidro, CA; (3); Church Yth Grp; Drama Clb; Key Clb; Letterman Clb; Office Aide; Science Clb; Ski Clb; Teachers Aide; Thesps; Church Choir; Campaign Mgr Frosh & Jr; SDSU; Bus Mgt.

TANG, CHI K; Blair HS; Pasadena, CA; (4); 1/170; Chess Clb; Church Yth Grp; Scholastic Bowl; Science Clb; Chorus; School Musical; Variety Show; Off Frsh Cls; Tennis; Vllybl; Amer Assn Of Physics Teachers 5th Pl 89; Southern CA United Nations Essay Cont 2nd Pl 88; UCLA; Math.

TANG, CHI-HONG; Albany HS; Albany, CA; (3); 50/250; Chess Clb; Math Clb; Math Tm; Spanish Clb; Orch; High Hon Roll; Hon Roll; Asian Stu Un Secy; Bike Clb; UC Berkeley; Bus.

TANG, CHI-HUI; Pinole Valley HS; Hercules, CA; (3); Debate Tm; French Clb; NFL; Treas Science Clb; SADD; Acpl Chr; Stage Crew; Nwsp; Crs Cntry; Trk; CSF; Amnsty Intl; U C; Pre-Med.

TANG, CHRISTINE P; Lowell HS; San Francisco, CA; (3); Sec Red Cross Aide; Teachers Aide; Orch; Ntl Merit Ltr; CSF Treas; Bio Clb Pres, Treas; Wellesley Bk Awd; Shield & L Hnr Soc Sec.

TANG, CHUNG MAN; International Studies Acad; San Francisco, CA; (4); Math Tm; Teachers Aide; High Hon Roll; Hon Roll; Rotary Awd; CA Schlrshp Fed; Marines Resrv Enlstd; Acad Of Finance; UCLA; Biochem.

TANG, COURTNEY; Abraham Lincoln HS; San Francisco, CA; (4); Art Clb; Library Aide; CA Schlrshp Fed; Chinese Clb; UC Berkeley; Bus Admin.

TANG, DAVID; Garfield HS; Los Angeles, CA; (2); Var Tennis; Prfct Attend; Upwrd Bnd; CSF.

TANG, ENGSING; Baldwin Park HS; Baldwin Park, CA; (2); Hon Roll; Var Badminton, MVP.

TANG, ERIC; George Washington HS; San Francisco, CA; (3); Cmnty Wkr; Hon Roll; Engineering.

TANG, HELEN; Torrey Pines HS; San Diego, CA; (2); Rptr VICA; Rptr Nwsp; Hon Roll; Interact VP; CSF; Bio.

TANG, HOI PING LINDSEY; Sacramento HS; Sacramento, CA; (1); 13/388; Computer Clb; Science Clb; Teachers Aide; High Hon Roll; Prfct Atten Awd; Outstndng Prfmnce US Govt; CSF Clb; Outstndng Alg; U CA-DAVIS; Comp Sci.

TANG, JIMMY H; Abraham Lincoln HS; San Francisco, CA; (2); ROTC; Scholastic Bowl; Temple Yth Grp; Color Guard; Hon Roll; Prfct Atten Awd; Drill Platoon; Marines.

TANG, KAREN DUC; Kennedy HS; Los Angeles, CA; (2); VP Debate Tm; Key Clb; Math Clb; Ed Lit Mag; High Hon Roll; Hon Roll; Jr NHS; NHS; Ntl Merit Schol; Opt Clb Awd; Golden St Exam Algebra I, Rcvd Sch L Rcgntn Awd; Rcvd Awd Cmptr Literacy; UCLA; Cmptr Systems Analyst.

TANG, KIEN; Mark Keppel HS; Rosemead, CA; (3); Key Clb; Math Clb; Mrchg Band; Var Bsktbl; Trk; Var Vllybl; Hon Roll; Tchr.

TANG, LAM T; Westminster HS; Westminster, CA; (2); Intnl Clb; Acad Booster Clb; CA Schlstc Fed; UCLA; Bio.

TANG, LISA W; C K Mc Clatchy HS; Sacramento, CA; (3); Church Yth Grp; VP Key Clb; Spanish Clb; SADD; Teachers Aide; Church Choir; Var Trk; Hon Roll; Friday Night Live, Treas.

TANG, NICOLE; Mark Keppel HS; Monterey Park, CA; (1); Hon Roll; Prft Atten; UCLA; Bus.

TANG, OU; John Marshall HS; Los Angeles, CA; (4); Chess Clb; French Clb; Key Clb; Teachers Aide; Bsktbl; Cit Awd; CA ST-LOS Angeles; Bus Mgmt.

TANG, PATRICIA; Holy Family HS; Los Angeles, CA; (3); 1/99; Art Clb; Church Yth Grp; Cmnty Wkr; Drama Clb; VP Model UN; Red Cross Aide; Chorus; Church Choir; Stu Cncl; High Hon Roll; Lecturer Mass; Public Spkng; Cabrini Lit Guild 3rd Pl Non-Fctn; Civil Engrng.

TANG, PHUNG; Mark Keppel HS; Monterey Park, CA; (2); Cmnty Wkr; 4-H; Math Clb; Mu Alpha Theta; Stage Crew; Lit Mag; Cit Awd; Hon Roll; Prfct Atten Awd; Math Acadmc Excllnc Awd; Schl Libr Vlntr; Stanford; Psych.

TANG, PHUNG KIM; Lincoln Prep HS; San Diego, CA; (3); 1/26; FTA; SADD; Nwsp; Rep Frsh Cls; Rep Soph Cls; Var Crs Cntry; Var Trk; Hon Roll; Prfct Atten Awd; Voice Dem Awd; CFS Pres; U Of San Diego; Med.

TANG, QUYEN V; Leuzinger HS; Hawthorne, CA; (3); AFS; Computer Clb; Math Clb; Science Clb; Spanish Clb; Teachers Aide; Rptr Nwsp; Crs Cntry; Trk; Cit Awd; Chinese Clb Pres; Peer Tutor; UCLA; Medcl Doctor.

TANG, RANDY K; Buena HS; Ventura, CA; (4); 32/520; FBLA; Lit Mag; Pres Acad Fit Awd; CSF Gold Barrier; UC Irvine; Civil Engrng.

TANG, RAYMOND C; Arroyo HS; San Lorenzo, CA; (4); 17/268; Pres Church Yth Grp; High Hon Roll; Opt Clb Awd; Badmitton Var, Capt N Coast Sec Mens Doubles Champ 89-90; CA ST U; Bus Admin.

TANG, SANG; San Gabriel HS; Rosemead, CA; (3); 2/10; Bsktbl; Swmmng; Tennis; Wt Lftg; High Hon Roll; Prfct Atten Awd; Elctrnc Engrng.

TANG, SEAKHAY; David Starr Jordan HS; Long Beach, CA; (3); French Clb; Var Bsktbl; Var Ftbl; Trk; Var Wrstlng; High Hon Roll; Hon Roll; Prfct Atten Awd; Pres Acad Fit Awd; JV Badminton; Asian Clb; Bus.

TANG, SENGDEUANE; Schurr HS; Monterey Park, CA; (1); Church Yth Grp; JV L Trk; Hon Roll; Psych.

TANG, STEPHANIE M; Aragon HS; San Mateo, CA; (3); Cmnty Wkr; SADD; Yrbk; VP Treas Frsh Cls; Off Soph Cls; Off Sr Cls; JV Var Sftbl; JV Trk; JV Var Vllybl; High Hon Roll; CSF Awd; Actcts Cmmssn; Intract Clb; U Of CA; Med.

TANG, STEVE; Nogales HS; W Covina, CA; (4); 38/560; Computer Clb; Hon Roll; Prfct Atten Awd; Gldn St Exam Algbr Ernd Hnrs; Covina HS Bdmntn Trnmn 1s Pl Bys Dbls; CA Poly; Elctrcl Engrng.

TANG, TUE; Mission San Jose HS; Fremont, CA; (2); 122/428; Debate Tm; Drama Clb; Intnl Clb; Science Clb; Service Clb; Ski Clb; Score Keeper; Vllybl; Golden St Alg Exam Awd; Sci.

TANG, VANESSA R; Hayward HS; Hayward, CA; (2); 1/200; Band; Mrchg Band; Hon Roll; V Badminton; CSF.

TANG, VENUS N; Abraham Lincoln HS; San Francisco, CA; (3); ROTC; Pres Soph Cls; Cit Awd; Hon Roll; Prfct Atten Awd; UC Berkeley; Dentstry.

TANG, VINCENT K; Lowell HS; San Francisco, CA; (3); Boy Scts; Church Yth Grp; Sec VP Chorus; Church Choir; School Musical; Off Sr Cls; Rep Stu Cncl; JV Var Crs Cntry; JV Var Trk; Intrml Vllybl; Scroll & L Hnr Soc; Var Fencing; CSF; Eng.

TANG, VINNARY; Downey HS; Downey, CA; (2); Mrchg Band; Stanford U; CPA.

TANG, WENDY H; John F Kennedy HS; Buena Park, CA; (4); Computer Clb; FBLA; Key Clb; Ed Yrbk; Hon Roll; Pres Acad Fit Awd; U Of CA Los Angeles; Bio-Chem.

TANGEMAN, SARA E; Edison HS; Huntington Beach, CA; (3); Church Yth Grp; French Clb; Ski Clb; Teachers Aide; Var Swmmng; N AZ U; Hotel Mgt.

TANGPRASERTH, MANIVONE; Bassett HS; La Puente, CA; (2); Intnl Clb; Mrchg Band; Hon Roll; Pres Jr NHS; VP NHS; Golden St Exam Alg I Schl Rcgntn.

TANIGUCHI, NICOLE T; Del Campo HS; Carmichael, CA; (4); 39/429; Pres Church Yth Grp; Treas FBLA; JA; Co-Ed Yrbk; Var L Sftbl; Var L Trk; Lion Awd; NHS; Pres Acad Fit Awd; Hosp Phys Thrpy Dept Vlntr; UC Davis; Bio Sci.

TANIKAWA, LARRY M; Blackford HS; San Jose, CA; (2); 54/254; Church Yth Grp; VP Computer Clb; Pres Library Aide; Lit Mag; Comp Cnsltnt; Oxford; Surgeon.

TANINGCO, JULIE H; Seoul American HS; Apo Sf, CA; (4); 55/138; Office Aide; Teachers Aide; Stat Mgr(s); Var Socr; Stat Vllybl; Hon Roll; Achvt & Recgntn In Batik Shows & Exhibitions; Works Pblshd In Art Publications; Art.

TANNAHILL, HEATHER; Pioneer Baptist HS; Norwalk, CA; (1); Church Yth Grp; Pep Clb; Teachers Aide; Bsbl; Bsktbl; Sftbl; Vllybl; Hon Roll.

TANNAHILL, MIKE; Baena HS; Ventura, CA; (1); Prfct Atten Awd; AYSO Soccer Rgn 39; Cal Tech; Aerospace Engrng.

TANNER, DYLAN P; Clovis HS; Clovis, CA; (2); Boy Scts; Debate Tm; NFL; Science Clb; Speech Tm; Hon Roll; Pres Acad Fit Awd; Mock Trial Team; Student Congress; BYU; Lawyer.

TANNER, JENNIFER M; East Bakersfield HS; Bakersfield, CA; (4); 11/435; Hon Roll; CA ST Bakersfield; Tchr.

TANNER, JOE; Rives City SR HS; W Sacramento, CA; (2); 4-H; SADD; Thesps; School Musical; School Play; JV Bsktbl; Var L Ftbl; JV Trk; Hon Roll; JV Bsktbl MVP; Schlstc Ltr Geom.

TANNER, NICOLE R; Chaffey HS; Ontario, CA; (1); Advrtsmnt.

TANNER, PAULA M; Enterprise HS; Shingletown, CA; (3); Church Yth Grp; High Hon Roll; Pres Acad Fit Awd; CSF; Awd For Pre Algebra; Accntng.

TANNONE, JEANNE M; Bonita Vista HS; Bonita, CA; (1); Church Yth Grp; Letterman Clb; Office Aide; Var Crs Cntry; Var Diving; Gym; JV Socr; Cit Awd; Pres Acad Fit Awd; Surf Clb; Pilot.

TANOUS, MICAH V; El Toro HS; El Toro, CA; (3); Boy Scts; Ski Clb; SADD; Variety Show; Lit Mag; Prfct Atten Awd; Arts.

TANTILLA, DANIEL J; Thomas Downey HS; Modesto, CA; (2); Bus Profs of Am; FBLA; FFA; Teachers Aide; Gov Hon Prg Awd; Hon Roll; Jr NHS; NHS; Law Enfrcmnt.

TANTILLO, JAMES W; El Toro HS; Mission Viejo, CA; (3); Church Yth Grp; Band; Jazz Band; Treas Mrchg Band; Orch; School Musical; Hon Roll; Outstndnt Stu Jzz Muscn & Soloist; AZ ST U; Music.

TANTOD, ANJLI; Moorpark HS; Moorpark, CA; (3); 7/240; Intnl Clb; Key Clb; Hon Roll; CA Schlrshp Fedrtn.

TANYAG, HAZEL N; Lowell HS; San Francisco, CA; (2); ROTC; Color Guard; Sec Frsh Cls; Sec Soph Cls; Drill Pltn; Bio-Chem.

TAO, DANNY S; Homestead HS; Sunnyvale, CA; (3); 1/387; Pres Art Clb; Church Yth Grp; NFL; Mrchg Band; School Play; Ed Yrbk; Sec Jr Cls; Sec Stu Cncl; Var Wrstlng; NHS; U Of CA; Engrng.

TAO, KATHRYN C; Torrey Pines HS; Rancho Santa Fe, CA; (2); 13/503; Hosp Aide; SADD; Ed Nwsp; High Hon Roll; Hon Roll; CSF; Golden St Exam High Hnrs Math; Level 6 Cert Mrt Piano; Bach To Rock Clb; Pre-Med.

TAO, KENNY T; Richard Gahr HS; Norwalk, CA; (2); Computer Clb; Pres FBLA; Teachers Aide; Hon Roll; CSF; U CA Irvine; Med.

TAO, LESLIE P; Edison HS; Huntington Beach, CA; (4); 4/511; VP Intnl Clb; Sec Key Clb; Model UN; Pres Spanish Clb; Capt Drill Tm; Stu Cncl; Spanish NHS; Orange Cnty Acad Dcthln-Mth 1st Pl-Essy 5th Pl; US Ldrshp Merit Awd; Schlstc All-Amer; Biochem.

TAO, MIMI T; Dublin HS; Dublin, CA; (3); Church Yth Grp; Dublin Beauty Coll Natl Art Cont Awd; Fashion Dsgn.

TAO, RODNEY T; Watsonville HS; Watsonville, CA; (2); Ski Clb; Var Wrstlng; Hon Roll; CSF; Stu Athl Wrstlng; Cal Poly; Comp Sci.

TAPADO, LIZ; Saint Joseph Notre Dame HS; Alameda, CA; (4); Cmnty Wkr; Office Aide; Ski Clb; School Play; Var Cheerldng; Var Pom Pon; High Hon Roll; NHS; Pres Acad Fit Awd; Bank Of Am Hstry Cert; CSF-LIFE Mem; U CA Berkeley Acclerated HS Stus Pgm; U CA-BERKELEY.

TAPIA, BRENDA A; San Jacinto HS; San Jacinto, CA; (2); Pres French Clb; FBLA; Cit Awd; Prfct Atten Awd; San Diego Cal ST; Law.

TAPIA, CANDIDA; Bishop Amat HS; La Puente, CA; (4); 53/400; Cmnty Wkr; Dance Clb; Color Guard; High Hon Roll; Hon Roll.

TAPIA, LINDA S; San Gabriel Mission HS; San Marino, CA; (2); French Clb; Hon Roll; Encore; JAM; UC Berkeley; Psych.

TAPIA, MANUEL G; Saint Genevieve HS; Panorama City, CA; (2); Church Yth Grp; Hon Roll; Teen Short Story Cont Wnnr; CSUN; Arch.

TAPIA, VANESSA; Campbell Hall HS; Reseda, CA; (4); VP French Clb; Sec GAA; Treas Girl Scts; Treas Science Clb; SADD; Pres Frsh Cls; Mgr(s); Var L Tennis; High Hon Roll; NHS; Stanford; Intl Rel.

TAPPER, JESSICA J; Huntington Beach HS; Huntington Bch, CA; (4); 23/480; Sec Hosp Aide; Model UN; High Hon Roll; Pres Acad Fit Awd; CAHHS Schlrshp Fnlst; Hoag Memrl Hosp Presbyterian Auxiliary Schlrshp; UC Davis; Obstetrics.

TAPSCOTT, VICTORIA R; De Anza HS; Richmond, CA; (3); French Clb; Science Clb; SADD; Teachers Aide; Var Bsktbl; JV Stat Ftbl; Capt Pom Pon; High Hon Roll; Hon Roll; Mst Dedicated Songleader; USC; Historian.

TARAN, YANA; California HS; San Ramon, CA; (3); Chorus; Orch; Hon Roll; 90 Bus Ed Roundtable Cmptn Cert; Music Awd; Bio.

TARANTINO, CARLO D; Serra HS; South San Francis, CA; (2); Math Tm; Office Aide; School Musical; Stage Crew; Bsbl; High Hon Roll; S San Francisco Sister City Yth Grp; Scholars HS Entrance; UC Davis; Pre-Med.

TARAYA, ROBERT W; Pinole Valley HS; Hercules, CA; (2); Cmnty Wkr; Acpl Chr; Band; Mrchg Band; Pep Band; Var L Bsktbl; Var L Ftbl; Var L Trk; Hon Roll; PMA Vocal Group; Civil Engrng.

TARGOWSKI, ERIC B; Tracy Joint Union HS; Tracy, CA; (2); 11/538; 4-H; Science Clb; SADD; Band; Mrchg Band; Pep Band; NHS; Golden St Exam Geom Hgh Hnrs; Drum Line; Stanford; Genetics.

TARIGAN, EDGAR A; Chaffey HS; Ontario, CA; (3); Church Yth Grp; Teachers Aide; Church Choir; High Hon Roll; Hon Roll; Spanish NHS; LMU; Engr.

TARIN, LUCY M; Sierra Vista HS; Baldwin Park, CA; (3); Math Clb; Science Clb; Band; Color Guard; Flag Corp; Ed Yrbk; Pres Stu Cncl; Var Sftbl; Var Trk; High Hon Roll; Gldn St Exm Hnrs Geom 88; Acac Penthln 2nd Fine Arts & 3rd Sci 88; All Leag Hnrb Mntn Sftbl 90; Trinity U; Bio Sci.

TARIN, MARIA L; Sierra Vista HS; Baldwin Park, CA; (3); Math Clb; Science Clb; Band; Color Guard; Flag Corp; Ed Yrbk; Var Sftbl; Var Trk; High Hon Roll; Golden St Exam Hnrs Geom 88; All Lg Hnrb Mntn Sftbl 90; Pepperdine U; Biolgcl Sci.

TARK, EUNICE K; Irvine HS; Irvine, CA; (3); Pres Church Yth Grp; Cmnty Wkr; Key Clb; Chorus; Ed Yrbk; Hon Roll; CSF Schlrshp Cmmtte Chrprsn; Stu Forum Advsmnt Rep; Korean Clb Jnr Cls Rep; Phrmcy.

TARK, IRENE; University HS; Irvine, CA; (1); Church Yth Grp; Hosp Aide; Spanish Clb; Church Choir; Orch; Hon Roll.

TARM, FRANCO A; St Ignatius College Prep; Daly City, CA; (3); Rptr Nwsp; Var Trk; Hon Roll; CSF; Chrch Day Camp Vlntr; UC Los Angeles; Bio.

TAROIAN, HARMICK; Taft HS; Tarzana, CA; (2); High Hon Roll; Hon Roll; Mrt Cert Piano Prfrmncs; Aerntc Engrng.

TARPLEY, MARCELLA; Montgomery HS; San Diego, CA; (4); 25/401; JA; Pep Clb; Phtg Nwsp; Ed Yrbk; Ed Lit Mag; Cit Awd; Prfct Atten Awd; Pres Acad Fit Awd; CA Schlrshp Fed; S W Coll; Mgmt.

TARPLEY, SENA M; Paso Robles HS; Paso Robles, CA; (1); Church Yth Grp; JV Bsktbl; High Hon Roll; Hon Roll.

TARRANT, CHRISTI A; El Toro HS; El Toro, CA; (3); Hon Roll; Chico ST; Bus.

TARRANTS, LESLIE D; Ramona HS; Santa Ysabel, CA; (3); 75/294; Pres Sec 4-H; Varsity Clb; Var Sftbl; 4-H Awd; Hon Roll; Sftbl; Train, Exercise & Show Morgan Horses; Bus Engr.

TARRER, THOMAS; South HS; Bakersfield, CA; (3); 1/463; Am Leg Boys St; JA; Mrchg Band; Crs Cntry; Golf; Socr; Trk; Hon Roll; NHS; Pres Acad Fit Awd; CSF; Hnr Band; Interact Clb Pres; Engrng.

TARVER, TANESHA R; St Michaels HS; Los Angeles, CA; (4); Church Yth Grp; Cmnty Wkr; Pres FBLA; GAA; Hosp Aide; Office Aide; Pep Clb; Church Choir; Variety Show; Phtg Rptr Yrbk; Clark Atlanta; Neurosrgn.

TARVIN IV, JOHN C; Live Oak HS; Morgan Hill, CA; (3); 49/530; Boy Scts; Church Yth Grp; French Clb; FBLA; Nwsp; Ntl Merit SF; Pres Acad Fit Awd.

TARWATER, RICHARD D; Coachella Valley HS; Mecca, CA; (3); 1/350; Boy Scts; Pres Church Yth Grp; Pres Math Clb; Varsity Clb; Band; School Musical; Sec Frsh Cls; Treas Stu Cncl; Var Capt Cheerldng; High Hon Roll; Auto Dsgn Engrng.

TARWATER, SHAWNA MARIE; Coachella Valley HS; Mecca, CA; (2); Church Yth Grp; Cmnty Wkr; GAA; Church Choir; JV Bsktbl; JV Vllybl; Hon Roll; Masonic Awd; Opt Clb Awd; Ricks Coll.

TARZI, HORIA; Laguna Hills HS; Laguna Hls, CA; (3); Dance Clb; French Clb; GAA; Key Clb; Variety Show; Diving; Swmmng; Cit Awd; Hon Roll; Advanced Mrchndsng Cooperative Cls; Creative Fashion; Modeling; U Of CA; Law.

TASH, DEENA L; Vacaville HS; Vacaville, CA; (3); Quiz Bowl; Stage Crew; Yrbk; Cit Awd; High Hon Roll; Hon Roll; 1st Plc Cty Wide Splng Bee HS Div, 1st Plc Swng Cty Voc Sklls Olmpcs 90; Bible Ed Wrk.

TASHIRO, JOANNE; Palisades HS; Los Angeles, CA; (4); Hist Church Yth Grp; Girl Scts; Hosp Aide; JA; Service Clb; Band; Drill Tm; Orch; School Musical; Ed Nwsp; Schlr-Athl Awd; Japanese-Amer Ctzns Leag Schlrshp; Outstndg Achvt Sftbl Awd; U Of CA; Jrnlsm.

TASHJIAN, HEGHNAR; Mountain View HS; Mountain View, CA; (2); Church Yth Grp; Amer Yth Fed.

TASINI, PAEA; Antioch HS; Pittsburg, CA; (1); Boy Scts; Church Yth Grp; JV Ftbl; Wt Lftg; Brigham Young U; Bus.

TASSELL, CLAR; Galt HS; Galt, CA; (3); Church Yth Grp; Pep Clb; Cheerldng; Pom Pon; Trk; Hon Roll; Teacher.

TASSISTRO, EAON ASHLEY; St Margarets HS; Laguna Niguel, CA; (4); 9/28; Letterman Clb; Science Clb; SADD; Yrbk; Var Bsbl; Var Bsktbl; Capt Var Ftbl; High Hon Roll; Hon Roll; Spnsh III Awd; All League Athlt Awd 87-88; All CIF Athlt Awd 89; CIF Ftbl Champs 89; U Of San Diego.

TASTO, NICHOLAS R; St Francis HS; Sunnyvale, CA; (3); 64/289; Church Yth Grp; Var L Golf; Var L Wrstlng; High Hon Roll; Hon Roll; Intern; Radio Clb; Law.

TASTOR, BRIAN W; Oakmont HS; Roseville, CA; (3); Teachers Aide; Varsity Clb; Sprt Ed Nwsp; Intrml JV Bsktbl; High Hon Roll; Hon Roll; Prfct Atten Awd; Oakmont Pride Awd; Math Team; Most Dedicated Bsktbl; Defensive Awd Bsktbl.

TAT, TINA U; Rosemead HS; Rosemead, CA; (2); Spanish Clb; JV L Crs Cntry; Hon Roll; CSF; UC Berkeley; Bus.

TATE, AGOSTIMA TYNESIA; Southbay Christian HS; Fremont, CA; (4); 10/25; Band; Rep Jr Cls; Pres Stu Cncl; Bsktbl; Cheerldng; Vllybl; Cit Awd; High Hon Roll; Jr NHS; CSF; Miss Teenage CA Cont 89; UCLA; Psych.

TATE, CHRISTOPHER J; Los Angeles Baptist HS; Los Angeles, CA; (3); Church Yth Grp; Cmnty Wkr; School Play; Stage Crew; Ed Nwsp; Var L Bsbl; JV L Ftbl; Capt Tennis; Hon Roll; Los Angeles Cnty Jr Lifeguards; Tnns Clb; UCLA; Cmnctns.

TATE, FELICIA D; Washington Prep; Los Angeles, CA; (2); Var Crs Cntry; Var Trk; Prfct Atten Awd; Marine Bio.

TATE, JASON R; Artesia HS; Lakewood, CA; (3); JV Bsktbl; Var L Ftbl; Var L Vllybl; Surf Club; Spec Olympcs; Vlybl Club; Sprts Med.

TATE, RANDALL S; Gunderson HS; San Jose, CA; (4); 71/500; Boy Scts; Church Yth Grp; Variety Show; Tennis; San Jose ST U; Engrng.

TATEOSSIAN, JILL M; Monroe HS; Sepulveda, CA; (2); Band; Mrchg Band; Phtg Yrbk; NHS; Prfct Atten Awd; Prncpls Schl Svc Awd; Harvard; Law.

TATMAN, JENNIFER A; Clayton Valley HS; Concord, CA; (2); Church Yth Grp; GAA; Letterman Clb; Varsity Clb; Var Diving; Stat Score Keeper.

TATSUTA, BLAKE T; Buena Park HS; La Palma, CA; (3); Pres Chess Clb; Computer Clb; Math Tm; Science Clb; Ski Clb; Prfct Atten Awd; Jr Var Badminton; Golden St Exam Hgh Hnr In Geom; Aerospc Engrng.

TATTON, HEATHER; Lincoln HS; Stockton, CA; (3); 13/520; French Clb; Key Clb; French Hon Soc; High Hon Roll; NHS; Deans Schlrshp Amer U; Amer U; Intl Bus.

TATUM, JEREMY J; Turlock HS; Turlock, CA; (3); 35/550; Church Yth Grp; Key Clb; Band; Mrchg Band; Rptr Nwsp; Var Tennis; High Hon Roll; Hon Roll; Voice Dem Awd; King, Mr Camper At Church Camp 90; Interact Club, Key Club; CSF.

TATUM, LORENZO C; Milpitas HS; Milpitas, CA; (2); Bsbl; Ftbl; Hon Roll; Masonic Awd; USC; Engr.

TATZEL, YVONNE T; San Marcos HS; Santa Barbara, CA; (2); Church Yth Grp; Chorus; School Musical; Variety Show; Var Socr; NHS; Pres Acad Fit Awd; USGF Gymnastics.

TAUBMAN, DAVID M; Grossmont HS; La Mesa, CA; (2); AFS; Aud/Vis; Boy Scts; Temple Yth Grp; Band; Mrchg Band; Pep Band; Pres Acad Fit Awd; Job Omars Steak & Burgers; UCLA; Srgn.

TAUGNER, TIA-L; Downey HS; Downey, CA; (3); Hosp Aide; Teachers Aide; Chorus; Swing Chorus; Vllybl; Teach.

TAULA, FIAALUAE L; Armijo HS; Suisun, CA; (1); Chorus; Hon Roll; Lawyer.

TAUMOEPEAU, ANNA HEU; Mills HS; S San Francisco, CA; (3); Church Yth Grp; GAA; Varsity Clb; Band; Pep Band; Bsktbl; Vllybl; Acad Achvt Awd; V Vllybl & Bsktbl Ltr Awd; Golden St Algebra Regntn Awd; Bus Admin.

TAUR, ALAN S; Homestead HS; Los Altos, CA; (4); 1/367; French Clb; Sec FBLA; NFL; Service Clb; Jazz Band; Orch; Ed Nwsp; Rep Stu Cncl; French Hon Soc; High Hon Roll; Prncpl Bassist-Palo Alto Chmbr Orch; FBLA ST Conf-5th Pl Comp Appl; Music Awd; All-St Jazz Band/Orch; Engrng.

TAUSCHER, TODD C; Woodside HS; Redwood City, CA; (3).

TAUTFEST, KRISTY R; Downey HS; Downey, CA; (3); Church Yth Grp; Cmnty Wkr; Spanish Clb; SADD; Pres Frsh Cls; Rep Soph Cls; Cheerldng; Tennis; Hon Roll.

TAVAGLIONE, DAWN M; Arlington HS; Riverside, CA; (3); JV Var Sftbl; Hon Roll; Accntng.

TAVALLAI, OMID R; Fremont HS; Sunnyvale, CA; (2); 45/440; Debate Tm; DECA; FBLA; JA; Math Tm; NFL; Speech Tm; Rptr Phtg Yrbk; Tennis; Cit Awd; Gftd & Tlntd Ed; Hnrs In Gldn St Math; CA U; Bus Proprietortship.

TAVANLAR, KATRINA D; Bishop Amat HS; West Covina, CA; (2); Church Yth Grp; Cmnty Wkr; Spanish Clb; Drill Tm; JV Cheerldng; High Hon Roll; Hon Roll; NHS; NEDT Awd; Prfct Atten Awd.

TAVARES, TAMARA L; Academy Of Our Lady Peace; Poway, CA; (4); 2/130; Art Clb; Cmnty Wkr; Drama Clb; Letterman Clb; Varsity Clb; School Musical; School Play; Rptr Nwsp; Phtg Yrbk; Stu Cncl; MVP Bstkbl; Natl Hnr Soc Schlrshp Cert Mrt; Jack In Box Hnrb Mntn Photo, Essay Schlrshp; Prncpls Awd; St Marys Coll Of CA; Cmmnctns.

TAVAREZ, RICHARD L; Fresno HS; Fresno, CA; (1); FBLA; Hon Roll; Bus.

TAVEGGIA, FRANCESCA; Las Lomas HS; Walnut Creek, CA; (3); Church Yth Grp; German Clb; Office Aide; Ski Clb; SADD; Drill Tm; Flag Corp; Powder Puff Ftbl; Var Sftbl; Chico U; Engl.

TAVERNIER, AARON M; Orange HS; Orange, CA; (1); Bsktbl; Ftbl; Trk; Hon Roll; Pony Leag Bsbl, All Stars, HI Bound Frndshp Trnmnt Tm.

TAVITIAN, JOELLE A; Taft HS; Woodland Hills, CA; (2); Swmmng; Fluent Armenian, French, Eng, Learning Span; Dentist.

TAWIL, PHILIP; Capistrano Valley HS; Mission Viejo, CA; (3); Sec German Clb; VP Science Clb; Sec Orch; School Musical; Hon Roll; Hmn Rghts Clb; CSF; Envrnmntl Clb; U Of CA-SAN Diego.

TAYAG, ALMIRA D; Immaculate Conception Acad; San Francisco, CA; (2); Church Yth Grp; French Clb; Variety Show; Intrml Vllybl; Hon Roll; NHS.

TAYCHACHAIWONGSE, UKRIT ERIC; Rio Lindo Adventist Acad; Healdsburg, CA; (2); VP Frsh Cls; Elec Engr.

TAYCO, PHILIP C; Bishop O'dowd HS; Oakland, CA; (3); Chess Clb; Math Clb; High Hon Roll; Intelligent Systs Tech Apprntc-NASA Ames Rsrch Ctr Summer 90; CA-POLY-SN Luis Obis; Comp Sci.

TAYLOR, ANDREW R; Maranatha HS; Sierra Madre, CA; (4); 11/102; Church Yth Grp; Chorus; Rep Sr Cls; JV Bsktbl; High Hon Roll; Bnk America Achvt Awd Hstry; Pasadena City Coll.

TAYLOR, ANTHONY C; El Camino HS; Oceanside, CA; (2); 10/429; Church Yth Grp; French Clb; Band; Mrchg Band; Pep Band; Hon Roll; Opt Clb Awd; N Cty Hnr Band; Band Cncl; Cornish Coll Arts; Music.

TAYLOR, APRIL D; North HS; Bakersfield, CA; (1); Chorus; Hon Roll; Prfct Atten Awd; Psych.

TAYLOR, ASPEN M; Bella Vista HS; Fair Oaks, CA; (1); 1/418; AFS; Church Yth Grp; Pep Clb; Spanish Clb; School Play; JV Cheerldng; Pedtrcn.

TAYLOR, BETH C; Mission College Prep; Pismo Beach, CA; (3); Cmnty Wkr; SADD; Teachers Aide; JV Bsktbl; Var Trk; HOPES & Soup Kitchen Clbs; Gwynedd Mercy; Nrsng.

TAYLOR, BILLY; Calvary Chapel HS; Orange, CA; (1); Teachers Aide; L Wrstlng; High Hon Roll.

TAYLOR, BRIAN M; Madera HS; Madera, CA; (4); 136/487; Science Clb; Upward Bound Stu Cncl Treas; CA ST U Fresno.

TAYLOR, BRIDGET; Ontario HS; Ontario, CA; (1); Color Guard; Flag Corp; Bus Mgmt.

TAYLOR, BROOKE A; Oakmont HS; Roseville, CA; (1); Church Yth Grp; Ski Clb; Spanish Clb; Bsktbl; Piano; Jazz Dance; Teacher.

TAYLOR, CATHY; North HS; Bakersfield, CA; (4); 5/408; Hosp Aide; Math Tm; Sec Service Clb; Sec Spanish Clb; Band; Drm Mjr(t); Jazz Band; Mrchg Band; Orch; Pep Band; UC Santa Cruz; Psych.

TAYLOR, CHARLENE S; Redwood Christian HS; San Leandro, CA; (4); 4/34; Church Yth Grp; Teachers Aide; School Play; Yrbk; Sec Jr Cls; Stu Cncl; Var Crs Cntry; Var Trk; High Hon Roll; Bnk America Achvt Awd Religious Stds 90; 2nd Pl ACSI Sci Fair 88; Rotary Clb Speech Cmptn Fnlst 89; Simpson Coll; Elem Ed.

TAYLOR, CHRISTINA MARIE; North HS; Bakersfield, CA; (2); 1/550; Church Yth Grp; Spanish Clb; Rep VP Band; Mrchg Band; Pep Band; Hon Roll; NHS; GATE Clb; CSF; Acad Decathln; Jrnlsm.

TAYLOR, CINDY A; Kingsburg HS; Kingsburg, CA; (2); Church Yth Grp; Pep Clb; Treas Soph Cls; Var Cheerldng; Var Diving; Var Pom Pon; Hon Roll; Bus.

TAYLOR, COREY; Santa Ana HS; Santa Ana, CA; (3); Band; Drm Mjr(t); Jazz Band; Mrchg Band; Orch; Pep Band; Rep Stu Cncl; JV Tennis; Hon Roll; John Phillip Sousa Band Awd; Bst Wnng Percntge JV Tnns Tm; Mst Imprvd JV Tnns Plyr; Music.

TAYLOR, COREY A; Oak Ridge HS; Shingle Springs, CA; (2); JV Ftbl; High Hon Roll; Hon Roll; Japanese Clb; Japanese Interpreter.

TAYLOR, DANIEL A; Morningside HS; Inglewood, CA; (4); 8/180; Church Yth Grp; Cmnty Wkr; Teachers Aide; Varsity Clb; Intrml JV Bsktbl; JV Var Crs Cntry; Cit Awd; Hon Roll; Yng Black Schlr; Voted Most Talkative & Nicest; Co-Stu Athl Awd; Tuskegee; Bus Mktg.

TAYLOR, DESIREE J; Washington Prep HS; Los Angeles, CA; (3); GAA; Library Aide; Office Aide; Varsity Clb; Drill Tm; Rep Stu Cncl; Var Bsktbl; Var Sftbl; Var Trk; Var Vllybl; Crmnl Jstc.

TAYLOR, DONALD C; Calistoga St Unified HS; Calistoga, CA; (3); Cmnty Wkr; Letterman Clb; Office Aide; Ski Clb; Pres Soph Cls; Off Jr Cls; Pres Sr Cls; Var L Bsbl; Var L Bsktbl; Var L Ftbl; Bsbl Batting Awd.

TAYLOR, DONYE J; St John Bosco HS; Lynwood, CA; (2); 21/256; Church Yth Grp; JV Ftbl; JV Trk; High Hon Roll; Hon Roll; NHS; Jr Kappa Alpha Psi Membr; Aviator.

TAYLOR, ELIZABETH; San Joaquin Memorial HS; Selma, CA; (3); 9/125; Church Yth Grp; French Clb; GAA; VP Science Clb; VP Service Clb; Rep Jr Cls; Var Tennis; Var Vllybl; High Hon Roll; Optometry.

TAYLOR, ELWIN; West Covina HS; El Monte, CA; (1); Yrbk; Off Frsh Cls; JV Bsktbl; Acctng.

TAYLOR, GORDON E; Huntington Beach HS; Huntington Beach, CA; (2); Church Yth Grp; JV Crs Cntry; JV Trk; Chem.

TAYLOR, GWENDOLYN C; John F Kennedy HS; Sacramento, CA; (3); Church Yth Grp; Cmnty Wkr; Math Clb; Math Tm; SADD; Teachers Aide; Yrbk; Hon Roll; Prfct Atten Awd; MESA; SRO; Humbolt; Comp Sci.

TAYLOR, HAROLD; Turlock HS; Turlock, CA; (3); 60/500; AFS; Church Yth Grp; Cmnty Wkr; Drama Clb; Key Clb; Pep Clb; Ski Clb; Varsity Clb; JV Bsbl; JV Bsktbl; Chico ST.

TAYLOR, HEIDI J; Roseville HS; Rocklin, CA; (2); 103/445; Friday Nite Live; Bus.

TAYLOR, JAMES L; Borrego Springs HS; Borrego Springs, CA; (2); Hon Roll; San Dieto ST U; Comp Prgmr.

TAYLOR, JANE C; Rio Americano HS; Sacramento, CA; (3); 22/290; Aud/Vis; Church Yth Grp; Service Clb; Ski Clb; Spanish Clb; SADD; Drill Tm; Var L Sftbl; Var L Vllybl; High Hon Roll; Acad Achvmt Awd; Athlt Achvmt Awd; Econs.

TAYLOR, JASON A; Oakland HS; Oakland, CA; (3); Church Yth Grp; Stage Crew; High Hon Roll; Phtg Nwsp; Phtg Yrbk; Capt Swmmng; U Of CA Santa Cruz; Marine Bio.

TAYLOR, JENNIFER A; Capistrano Valley HS; Mission Viejo, CA; (3); Art Clb; Hon Roll; CSF.

TAYLOR, JENNIFER E; Ygnacio Valley HS; Concord, CA; (2); Key Clb; Spanish Clb; Color Guard; Flag Corp; Mrchg Band; Lit Mag; High Hon Roll; NHS.

TAYLOR, JEREMY; Willows HS; Willows, CA; (2); 1/100; Church Yth Grp; Pres Key Clb; Letterman Clb; Yrbk; Pres Frsh Cls; Pres Soph Cls; Var Bsktbl; JV Ftbl; Var Tennis; JV Trk; Kiwanis Camp Underprvlgd Chldrn Cnslr; CSF; Hydrojets Swim Tm.

TAYLOR, JEVON L; Colton HS; Colton, CA; (2); Boy Scts; Spanish Clb; Teachers Aide; Varsity Clb; Chorus; School Play; Variety Show; Off Soph Cls; Bsktbl; Swmmng; UCLA; Engrng.

TAYLOR, KATHERINE; Foothill HS; Pleasanton, CA; (3); Church Yth Grp; Debate Tm; French Clb; Q&S; Church Choir; Ed Lit Mag; Var Vllybl; High Hon Roll; CSF Mbr.

TAYLOR, KHRYSTEN; Madera HS; Madera, CA; (2); Drama Clb; NFL; Drill Tm; School Play; JV Cheerldng; Hon Roll; CA Schlrshp Fed; UCLA; Drama.

TAYLOR, KIMBERLY; Sonora HS; Reno, NV; (2); 27/306; French Clb; Science Clb; Ski Clb; Orch; High Hon Roll; Masonic Awd; Pres Acad Fit Awd; Debate Tm; Quiz Bowl; Teachers Aide; Drumline; JR Stsmn Of Amer; CSF; UC Davis; Med.

TAYLOR, KRISTI L; Hemet HS; Hemet, CA; (2); Church Yth Grp; Dance Clb; Drama Clb; Key Clb; Pep Clb; Drill Tm; Flag Corp; School Play; Rep Frsh Cls; Rep Stu Cncl; Bank Of Hemet Awd; Elem Ed.

TAYLOR, KRISTINA L; Trinity HS; Salyer, CA; (3); Drama Clb; Math Tm; Jazz Band; Pep Band; Swing Chorus; Rptr Nwsp; Rep Stu Cncl; Stat Ftbl; High Hon Roll; Hon Roll; Rainbow Girls; Peer Cnslr & Tutor; Rotry Ldrshp Camp; U Of The Pacific; Music Thrpy.

TAYLOR, LISA; Taft Union HS; Taft, CA; (1); French Clb; Var Swmmng; JV Vllybl; Hon Roll; Prfct Atten Awd; Pres Acad Fit Awd; Swim Club; AFS Assn; Frgn Affrs.

TAYLOR, MARK L; Alta Loma HS; Alta Loma, CA; (4); 2/500; Church Yth Grp; Capt Crs Cntry; Capt Trk; High Hon Roll; Pres Acad Fit Awd; Brigham Young U.

TAYLOR, MATTHEW; Capistrano Valley Christian HS; Mission Viejo, CA; (1); Church Yth Grp; JV Bsbl; JV Socr; JV Trk; Hon Roll; Pres Acad Fit Awd; Missions Club-Mexico Outreach Comm Svcs; Church Softball Tm.

TAYLOR, MICHELLE M; South Bay JR Acad; Compton, CA; (2); Drama Clb; Office Aide; Acpl Chr; Chorus; School Musical; Ed Yrbk; Pres Frsh Cls; Rep Stu Cncl; Intrml Vllybl; Cit Awd; Awd Of Merit 90; Playing Piano, Clarinet; Stu Aide At Long Beach SDA Pre-Sch; Pine Forge Acad; Eng.

TAYLOR, MICHELLE N; Yuba City HS; Yuma, AZ; (4); 6/450; Variety Show; Var Socr; Hon Roll; Pres Acad Fit Awd; Pep Clb; Off Frsh Cls; Sftbl; Prsdntl Clsrm Wk WA DC 89; Lftm CSF; Acad Ltr 88 & 90; Nrthrn AZ; Acctng.

TAYLOR, NICOLE; Washington Prep; Los Angeles, CA; (3); Hon Roll; Pharmacy.

TAYLOR, NICOLE M; San Marcos HS; Santa Barbara, CA; (4); CSF 89; Royal Regntn Art Awd 90; Royals Outsndng Acadmc Achvt Awd; Santa Barbara City; Fine Arts.

TAYLOR, PATRICIA D; Silver Valley HS; Barstow, CA; (3); FFA; Hon Roll.

TAYLOR, RANDY S; North County Christian HS; Creston, CA; (2); Chorus; Var Bsbl; Var JV Bsktbl; Cal Poly.

TAYLOR, RICK L; Hesperia HS; Hesperia, CA; (3); Art Clb; Ski Clb; Acad All Amer; Mech Drafter.

TAYLOR, ROBYN C; Bella Vista HS; Fair Oaks, CA; (2); 141/406; Teachers Aide; Physcn.

TAYLOR III, RONALD F; Gladstone HS; Azusa, CA; (3); FCA; Science Clb; Teachers Aide; Band; Chorus; School Play; Ftbl; Trk; Wt Lftg; Prfct Atten Awd; Bus.

TAYLOR, RUTH A; Fall River JR SR HS; Hat Creek, CA; (3); 4-H; Rptr FFA; Letterman Clb; SADD; Teachers Aide; Sec Frsh Cls; Sec Jr Cls; JV Var Vllybl; CA St FFA Chmpns Parlimntry Procedres; CA ST Poly U; Bus.

TAYLOR, SARAH L; Claremont HS; Claremont, CA; (2); JV Sftbl; UC Davis; Vet.

TAYLOR, SHANNON; Bella Vista HS; Orangevale, CA; (2); 91/406; Cmnty Wkr; Dance Clb; Hosp Aide; Drill Tm; Nurse.

TAYLOR, SHAUN Z; Edison HS; Fountain Valley, CA; (2); Band; Jazz Band; Mrchg Band; Orch; Pep Band; Bus Mgr Kiwanis PALS OCAD; Music.

TAYLOR, SHAWN; Sonoma Valley HS; Sonoma, CA; (2); 23/252; Hon Roll; Pres Acad Fit Awd; MIT; Physcs Tchr.

TAYLOR, SHEILA; Vintage HS; Napa, CA; (2); 49/100; Chorus; Cheerldng; Pom Pon; Powder Puff Ftbl; Score Keeper; Day Care.

TAYLOR, TABITHA; Hemet HS; Hemet, CA; (3); 15/547; Church Yth Grp; Drama Clb; Thesps; Acpl Chr; Chorus; Church Choir; School Musical; School Play; Stage Crew; Hon Roll; Thspn Trp 4015 Secy 89-90; CSF; Brigham Young U; Theatrcl Arts.

TAYLOR, TAMRA L; Lower Lake HS; Clearlake, CA; (1); SADD; Band; Jazz Band; Pep Band; Elks Awd; High Hon Roll; Hon Roll; Lion Awd; Yale Coll; Bus.

TAYLOR, TRACEY S; Santa Barbara HS; Santa Barbara, CA; (2); 30/476; Acpl Chr; Church Choir; JV Var Sftbl; Hon Roll; Endowment For Yths Cmmttees Top Female Schlr Awd & Top Female Schlr Of Yr Awd; CA St Senate Cert; UC Berkeley; Medicine.

TAYLOR, TRENT L; Paraclete HS; Lancaster, CA; (3); 25/125; Boy Scts; Key Clb; Letterman Clb; SADD; Crs Cntry; Trk; DAR Awd; Hon Roll; Pres Acad Fit Awd; Eagle Sct; Pres List; Naval Aviation.

TAYLOR III, WALTER; Narbonne HS; Harbor City, CA; (3).

TAYLOR, WILLIAM LESLIE; Lasser Union HS; Susanville, CA; (3); 27/200; Boy Scts; Church Yth Grp; Dance Clb; Red Cross Aide; ROTC; Band; Mrchg Band; Orch; Ftbl; Wt Lftg; Wounded Warrior Awd; Aviation.

TAYLOR, YVETTE C; Serrano HS; Victorville, CA; (3); 59/213; Church Yth Grp; Drama Clb; VP French Clb; Sec Intnl Clb; Sec Stu Cncl; Cheerldng; Hon Roll; Miss Teen CA Cont; High Steppers Dance Studio Annual Production Soloist; Child Psych.

TAYLOR, ZOE E; Sacramento HS; Sacramento, CA; (1); 65/500; Stage Crew; Nwsp; Engl.

TCHANG, HIEN LISA; C K Mc Clatchy HS; Sacramento, CA; (2); 1/550; French Clb; Math Clb; Teachers Aide; Hon Roll; Prfct Atten Awd; CSF; GSE Awd; UC Davis; Arch.

TCHENG, DENISE J; Tustin HS; Tustin, CA; (2); Church Yth Grp; Cmnty Wkr; Stu Cncl; JV Cheerldng; Var L Trk; JV Capt Vllybl; Hon Roll; Pres Acad Fit Awd; Orange Cnty Acad Dcthln Team; Clb Vllybl; Trck Relay Team 1st Pl; Octagon Optimist Clb-Cmnty Svc; Pepperdine U; Bus.

TCHING, VANESSA; Hemet HS; Hemet, CA; (3); Cmnty Wkr; French Clb; Hosp Aide; Key Clb; Letterman Clb; JV Var Tennis; Var Trk; High Hon Roll; CSF; Bio.

TE SELLE, JENNIFER L; Santa Monica HS; Santa Monica, CA; (3); Sec Church Yth Grp; SADD; Church Choir; Stage Crew; Variety Show; Rep Nwsp; Phtg Yrbk; Sec Frsh Cls; Hon Roll; Ntl Merit Ltr; Pssd Gldn St Exam-Hnrs; Voted Most Likely To Succeed; Accntng.

TE VELDE, KIMBERLY A; Baptist Christian HS; San Jacinto, CA; (3); Church Yth Grp; Dance Clb; Drama Clb; FCA; Office Aide; Teachers Aide; Varsity Clb; Church Choir; School Musical; School Play.

TEA, HONG; San Gabriel HS; Alhambra, CA; (2); Debate Tm; Spanish Clb; Vllybl; Cit Awd; Hon Roll; Pres Acad Fit Awd; UC.

TEAFORD, DAWN A; Arlington HS; Riverside, CA; (2); Teachers Aide; Drill Tm; Hon Roll; Rn.

TEAGLE-HERNANDEZ, MICHAEL B; Buena HS; Ventura, CA; (4); 10/499; Band; Mrchg Band; School Musical; School Play; JV Crs Cntry; JV Trk; High Hon Roll; Hon Roll; Pres Acad Fit Awd; Bank Of Amer Achvt Awd Music; CA Schlrshp Fed Gold Seal Bearer; Buena HS SR Hnr Guard; U Of Southern CA; Accntng.

TEAGUE, CASEY A; Lowell HS; San Francisco, CA; (2); Varsity Clb; Rep Frsh Cls; JV Bsbl; Var Bsktbl; Intrml Vllybl; Catholic Yth Organization Bsbl Games Umpire; Golden St Algebra High Hnrs; Geog.

TEAGUE, JUSTIN F; Paso Robles HS; Paso Robles, CA; (2); Church Yth Grp; Letterman Clb; Teachers Aide; Bsktbl; Swmmng; Wt Lftg; High Hon Roll; CSF; Gldn St Exam Outstndng Prfrmnc; UCLA; Med.

TEAGUE, MATTHEW B; Gridley HS; Gridley, CA; (4); 7/109; Am Leg Boys St; Letterman Clb; Pres Spanish Clb; Variety Show; Yrbk; JV Var Bsbl; JV Bsktbl; JV Var Ftbl; JV Var Trk; Wt Lftg; Army Rserve Schlr/Athlete; Amateur Athletic Union Mars Milky Way All-Amer Awd; CA Schlrshp Fdrtn; CA ST U; Mech Engrng.

TEAL, KELLIE A; Elk Grove HS; Elk Grove, CA; (2); SADD; Chorus; Jazz Band; Envrnmntl Prtctn; Prtctn Agnst Anml Crlty.

TEAL, KEN R; Antioch HS; Antioch, CA; (3); Hon Roll; Vet.

TEAL, PATRICIA L; Mt Carmel HS; San Diego, CA; (2); Band; Mrchg Band; Prfct Atten Awd; Golden ST Exam Awd In Algbra; CSF; Tchr.

TEALE, SHERI A; Berkeley HS; Berkeley, CA; (3); Hosp Aide; Key Clb; Crs Cntry; Swmmng; Outstndng Prfrmnce Vlngr Svc/Excllnce Yth Awd; Spec Recgntn Geom Gldn St Exm; YMCA Ldrshp Trng; Pre-Med.

TECLAW, JENNIFER D; Fairfield HS; Fairfield, CA; (3); German Clb; Chorus; Cit Awd; High Hon Roll; Hon Roll; NHS; CMEA Solo-Emsemble Fsvtl.

TECLAW, JODY M; Fairfield HS; Fairfield, CA; (1); Chorus; School Musical; School Play; Hon Roll; Coll.

TECLEAB, YAKOB K; Fremont HS; Oakland, CA; (3); Library Aide; Office Aide; Var Crs Cntry; Var Capt Trk; Hon Roll; Prfct Atten Awd; Cert Of Awd Drug & Hlth Ed Cmmnty Svc Prgm; Cert Of Cmptn Summer Yth Emplymnt & Trnng Prgm; UC Berkeley; Teacher.

TECSON, ARCHIBALD V; Polytechnic HS; Long Beach, CA; (3); French Clb; Science Clb; Spanish Clb; Cit Awd; Rop Trnsprtnl Ocpptn Prgrm; Engrn Inspctr Aide; Cvl Engrn; Cvl Engnr.

TEDBALL, JOANN D; Fresno HS; Fresno, CA; (2); JCL; Latin Clb; SADD; Chorus; Var Trk; Hon Roll; Prfct Atten Awd; Cal Poly; Sound Tech.

TEDESCO, MICHAEL F; Rio Americano HS; Carmichael, CA; (3); 49/290; Cmnty Wkr; Office Aide; Teachers Aide; Var Swmmng; High Hon Roll; Hon Roll; Friday Night Live Club; Var Water Polo Tm Goalie; Cngrssnl Schlr-Natl Yng Ldrs Conf 90; USC; Bus.

TEEL II, DONOVAN; Mother Lode Christian HS; Sonora, CA; (2); 1/16; Ski Clb; Band; VP Soph Cls; Var Bsbl; JV Bsktbl; Stat Vllybl; Hon Roll; Snow Skiing; Water Skiing; Model Power Planes; Monterey Bay Acad; Medical.

TEELE, ANEMONE B; Casa Roble HS; Fair Oaks, CA; (3); French Clb; Pep Clb; Ski Clb; School Play; Var Bsktbl; Capt Cheerldng; High Hon Roll; Hon Roll; SFS U; Communications Bdcstng.

TEEPLE, ANNA MARIAH; South Gate HS; South Gate, CA; (4); Church Yth Grp; Key Clb; Math Tm; Scholastic Bowl; Speech Tm; Acpl Chr; Church Choir; AFS; Chess Clb; Acad Dcthn Tm Highest Raning 89; MESA; Preliminary For Natl Hispanic Schlrshp Awd; Psych.

TEETERS, CHARLA D; Brawley Union HS; Brawley, CA; (3); Church Yth Grp; Key Clb; Science Clb; Spanish Clb; Band; Chorus; Sec Stu Cncl; Sftbl; Prfct Atten Awd; Rotary Awd; 3 Schlrshp Vcl Achvt Olmsted Falls Music Assn; Biolgcl Sci.

TEHRANI, SHARONA; Santa Monica HS; Santa Monica, CA; (3); FBLA; Pep Clb; SADD; Chorus; School Musical; VP Pres Soph Cls; Cheerldng; Socr; Trk; Hon Roll; Chrldng Liason In ASB; UCLA; Doctor.

TEITSWORTH, KAREN L; Bellflower HS; Bellflower, CA; (4); 9/226; Church Yth Grp; Key Clb; Chorus; Var Swmmng; High Hon Roll; Kiwanis Awd; Pres Acad Fit Awd; CSF Pres & VP; Swim Club Secy; San Jose ST U; Graphic Art.

TEITSWORTH, SHARON D; Bellflower HS; Bellflower, CA; (4); 6/223; Church Yth Grp; Key Clb; Quiz Bowl; JV Bsktbl; Var Capt Swmmng; High Hon Roll; Kiwanis Awd; Pres Acad Fit Awd; CA Schlstc Fed Sec & Schlrshp; Bellflower Ed Assn Schlrshp; Indus Arts Awd; San Jose ST U; Phys Ed.

TEIXEIRA, DEREK A; Santa Teresa HS; San Jose, CA; (2); Hon Roll; Surfing; Bass Guitar Band; U CA-SAN Diego; Bio.

TEIXEIRA, FRANK M; Dos Palos HS; Dos Palos, CA; (3); 30/136; AFS; SADD; Rptr Nwsp; Phtg Yrbk; Off Soph Cls; Jr Cls; Stu Cncl; Tennis; Mem ACLU; Tetralingual Spks Eng, Portuguese, Span, Ger; Frgn Lang Interpreter.

TEIXEIRA, MILLIE M; Red Bluff Union HS; Red Bluff, CA; (3); 7/350; Teachers Aide; Varsity Clb; Var L Bsktbl; High Hon Roll; Kiwanis Awd; People To People Yth Sci Exchange To USSR; Friday Night Live; Ed.

TEIXEIRA, MOSES F; Hayward HS; Hayward, CA; (2); Socr; Wt Lftg; Hon Roll; Psych.

TEIXEIRA, POLLY M; Hanford Joint Union HS; Hanford, CA; (1); Church Yth Grp; FHA; Stage Crew; Hon Roll.

TEIXERIA, RICK; Orestimba HS; Newman, CA; (3); Church Yth Grp; Pres Frsh Cls; Pres Soph Cls; Var Bsbl; JV Bsktbl; Var Ftbl; Hon Roll; Optometry.

TEJADA, CLAUDIA; Mountain View HS; S El Monte, CA; (2); GAA; Rptr Nwsp; Tennis; Write For Yth Nwspr; Sprts Edtr Jrnlsm; USC; Jrnlsm.

TEJADA, RYANDER; San Marcos HS; Santa Barbara, CA; (4); 23/300; Drama Clb; French Clb; German Clb; Hon Roll; Rep Stu Cncl; Co-Founder & VP Of Philosophy & Psych Clb; Intl Relations.

TEJADA, SHARON J; Ulysses S Grant HS; Los Angeles, CA; (4); 66/692; Cmnty Wkr; Treas Latin Clb; Hon Roll; Pres Acad Fit Awd; Stu Leag Sec; CA Schlrshp Fed; Assn Of Mexican Amer Educators Schlrshp; UCLA; Pre-Econ.

TEJWANI, SAPNA B; El Toro HS; El Toro, CA; (1); 20/500; High Hon Roll; Law.

TEK, SINOEUN; Modesto HS; Modesto, CA; (2); Speech Tm; Hon Roll; Physcn.

TEKESTE, ZEGHAI; El Camino Real HS; Woodland Hills, CA; (4); 82/575; Cmnty Wkr; Red Cross Aide; Variety Show; Intrml Bsktbl; JV Vllybl; High Hon Roll; Hon Roll; U Of MI; Aerospace Engr.

TELA, STACY; Orosi HS; Orosi, CA; (2); Church Yth Grp; FFA; Quiz Bowl; Speech Tm; SADD; Mrchg Band; VP Soph Cls; Cheerldng; Hon Roll; Lion Awd; Mock Trial, Prosctn Lawyr; Harvard; Envrnmntl Law.

TELEGIN, AMY M; Mt Shasta HS; Mount Shasta, CA; (2); Hon Roll; Secy CSF; Humbolt ST U.

TELFORD, DORIS; Lincoln HS; Stockton, CA; (1); 109/666; Church Yth Grp; Chorus; Stage Crew; Cheerldng; Hon Roll; CA All St HS Hnr Choir; Area Honor Choir; Div Honor Choir; Brigham Young U; Music.

TELFORD, SARAH J; Cornelia Connelly HS; Huntington Beach, CA; (3); GAA; Chrmn Hosp Aide; Intnl Clb; Varsity Clb; Ed Yrbk; Lit Mag; Sec Treas Sr Cls; Var Bsbl; Var Bsktbl; Var Socr; Vlntr For Spec Olympics; Class Play Comm For Prgm; JR Olympics Club Vllybl; Pre Med.

TELKIKAR, GAURI V; Ontario HS; Ontario, CA; (3); Key Clb; Spanish Clb; Treas Soph Cls; Tennis; Hon Roll; Prfct Atten Awd; Tutor.

TELLE, CARIN M; Liberty Union HS; Byron, CA; (4); Church Yth Grp; Drama Clb; FCA; Hist Acpl Chr; School Musical; Cheerldng; Swmmng; Bnk Amer Cert Drama; William Shakespeare Awd Schlrshp Drama; Friday Night Live; Diablo Valley JC; Drama.

TELLER, DAVID D; Irvington HS; Fremont, CA; (3); 51/352; Chess Clb; Church Yth Grp; Computer Clb; Spanish Clb; Varsity Clb; JV Var Trk; JV Var Wrstlng; High Hon Roll; Hon Roll; Gldn St Exm 87-88 Alg Schl Recgntn; Gldn St Exmn 88-89 Geom Hnrs; JV Wrstlng Awd; Bus.

TELLES, MARTIN; Barstow HS; Barstow, CA; (4); Library Aide; Teachers Aide; Bsbl; Bsktbl; Ftbl; Trk; Hon Roll; Engr.

TELLEZ, ERIKA; Baldwin Park HS; Baldwin Park, CA; (2); Church Yth Grp; Intrml Bsktbl; Var Trk; Hon Roll; Friday Night Live; Stewardess.

TELLEZ, JASON A; East Union HS; Manteca, CA; (2); 21/400; Band; Jazz Band; JV Socr; Hon Roll; Golden St Exam Geo High Hnrs; Air Force Acad; Arntcl Engrng.

TELLEZ, KIM; Marina HS; Huntington, CA; (1); High Hon Roll; Hon Roll; Police Ofcr.

TELLEZ, PEDRO I; San Dieguito HS; Encinitas, CA; (3); Boy Scts; Hon Roll; UCSD; Comp Engrng.

TEMBLADOR, DAVID P; Cypress HS; Cypress, CA; (4); Band; Drm Mjr(t); Jazz Band; Mrchg Band; Pep Band; Mgr Stage Crew; Jan Neisou Meml Schlsp 89; Drum Major Class Instr; Cal ST Fullerton; His.

TEMORES, ESMERALDA; Bishop Amat Memorial HS; La Puente, CA; (1); Church Yth Grp; Bsktbl; Hon Roll; Sports Fan Addict Clb; UCLA; Detective.

TEMORES, MARTHA ALICIA; Independence HS; San Jose, CA; (3); Church Yth Grp; Off Sr Cls; Co-Capt Cheerldng; Pom Pon; San Jose ST; Aerontcl Engr.

TEMPLE, BLAKE; Bullard HS; Fresno, CA; (1); Intrml Bsktbl; L Var Tennis; All League & All City Tennis; Nrthn CA Tennis Assn; Dntst.

TEMPLE, CATHIE; Capistrano Valley Christian HS; Mission Viejo, CA; (3); Church Yth Grp; Dance Clb; Drama Clb; Chorus; School Musical; School Play; JV Stat Sftbl; Hon Roll; Pres Acad Fit Awd; Csmtlgy.

TEMPLE, MEGAN R; Davis SR HS; Davis, CA; (3); 1/405; Church Yth Grp; Key Clb; Spanish Clb; Crs Cntry; Var L Tennis; High Hon Roll; NHS; Pres Acad Fit Awd; Goldn St Exam Acad Excllnce Awd 88; Princpls Awd Excllnce; All-League Team Vrsty Tnns 88.

TEMPLETON, CARA L; Tustin HS; Tustin, CA; (1); Church Yth Grp; German Clb; Band; School Play; Hnrs Clss; Ocngrphr.

TEMPLETON, DEBBIE; South Fork HS; Redway, CA; (4); 1/60; Am Leg Aux Girls St; Pres Soph Cls; VP Jr Cls; Pres Stu Cncl; Var L Bsktbl; Var Capt Trk; Capt Var Vllybl; DAR Awd; Rotary Awd; Val; All Cnty Vllybl; All Cnty Track; Stanford.

TEMPLETON, LISA M; Tustin HS; Tustin, CA; (4); 144/398; German Clb; School Play; Stage Crew; Var Socr; Var Trk; Hon Roll; Art Mnth; 1st Pl Drama Atchrs Assn S CA Dsgn Cont; Art.

TEN BERGE, YVETTE J; Ramona HS; Ramona, CA; (2); Church Yth Grp; Dance Clb; Debate Tm; Intnl Clb; Letterman Clb; Cheerldng; Crs Cntry; Cit Awd; High Hon Roll; Hon Roll; Medcl.

TENA, RICHARD L; Tulare Western HS; Tulare, CA; (3); Spanish Clb; Teachers Aide; JV Ftbl; Intrml Wt Lftg; Cit Awd; Hon Roll; Prfct Atten Awd; Cycling Clb; Fresno ST U; Juvenile Law.

TENAGLIA, GIULIANA M; St Joseph HS; Cerritos, CA; (3); Key Clb; High Hon Roll; Hon Roll; CSF; Acad Decathlon.

TENG, ALLEN B; San Dieguito HS; Encinitas, CA; (2); Nwsp; Intrml Bsbl; Intrml Ftbl; Intrml Vllybl; Intrml Wt Lftg; Hon Roll; Prfct Atten Awd; U Of CA San Diego; Bus.

TENG, CYRUS; Bella Vista HS; Fair Oaks, CA; (4); 5/341; VP JA; Math Tm; Science Clb; Chorus; JV Trk; High Hon Roll; Hon Roll; NHS; JV Badminton; U CA Berkeley.

TENGAN, AUDREY M; Fountain Valley HS; Fountain Valley, CA; (3); Church Yth Grp; JA; Sec Band; Church Choir; Jazz Band; Mrchg Band; Orch; Pep Band; School Musical; High Hon Roll; MVP-WIND Ensemble; Golden St Exam-Geom High Hnrs; CSF; Music.

TENHAGEN, JENNIFER; San Gorgonio HS; Sacramento, CA; (4); AFS; English Clb; German Clb; Chorus; Off Jr Cls; Hon Roll; Cal ST U; Elem Ed.

TENHAGEN, KIMBERLY A; Fontana HS; Fontana, CA; (2); Drama Clb; Color Guard; School Play; Stage Crew; Tennis; High Hon Roll; Hon Roll; Prfct Atten Awd; Author Awd; Consumer Sci Awd; Amer Acad Applied Arts; Dsgn.

TENNANT, CARRIE LYNN; Edison HS; Huntington Beach, CA; (4); Church Yth Grp; Teachers Aide; Trk; Dntstry.

TENNANT, JOSH J; Mission Viejo HS; Mission Viejo, CA; (1); 20/500; Swmmng; Hon Roll; Kiwanis Awd; Pres Acad Fit Awd; U Of Chicago; Bus Mgmt.

TENNISON, KATIE; Senior HS; Vallejo, CA; (1); Drama Clb; Teachers Aide; Flag Corp; Mrchg Band; Stage Crew; Hon Roll; Mst Improved; CA ST; Music.

TENO, JASON M; Trabuco Hills HS; Mission Viejo, CA; (2); JV Bsbl; Intrml Bsktbl; L Var Ftbl; USC; Arch.

TENORIO, GINA; Bundy Canyon Christian HS; Canyon Lake, CA; (4); Office Aide; Nwsp; VP Sr Cls; VP Stu Cncl; L Capt Bsktbl; L Capt Sftbl; L Var Vllybl; Cit Awd; High Hon Roll; Stu Ambassador To Soviet Union; Nursing.

TENORIO, MELISSA; Fred C Beyer HS; Modesto, CA; (1); Color Guard; Hon Roll; Fresno ST U.

TEO, SITUTUILA; John Glenn HS; Norwalk, CA; (2); Church Yth Grp; GAA; Letterman Clb; Varsity Clb; Church Choir; Off Soph Cls; JV Bsktbl; Var Score Keeper; Var Capt Sftbl; Var Vllybl; Hand-N-Hand Treas; BYU; Lawyer.

TEP, SARITH; A A Stagg HS; Stockton, CA; (2); Bsktbl; Cambodian Clb; U Of Pacific; Med.

TEPFER, GITA; Santa Barbara HS; Santa Barbara, CA; (3); 240/700; Drama Clb; Acpl Chr; School Play; Madrigal Singers; Art; Theater Arts; UC Davis.

TEPFER, JANELLE; Christian HS; El Cajon, CA; (3); Church Yth Grp; Drama Clb; 4-H; Key Clb; Office Aide; SADD; Teachers Aide; Thesps; School Play; Stage Crew; Vaulting-Brnz & Slvr Medlst; Elem Educ.

TERAN, CLAUDIA; Saratoga HS; Saratoga, CA; (4); Pres Intnl Clb; Pres Spanish Clb; Pres SADD; Chorus; Ed Lit Mag; Rep Stu Cncl; Hon Roll; Ntl Merit Ltr; UC Berkeley; Intl Law.

TERAN, DAVID V; El Cajon Valley HS; El Cajon, CA; (1); Church Yth Grp; Debate Tm; FFA; High Hon Roll; Hon Roll; Coll Prep Cls; Hnrs Cls; Harvard U; Law.

TERASAWA, YUKO; Westmont HS; Campbell, CA; (4); 1/225; Cmnty Wkr; Spanish Clb; Kiwanis Awd; NHS; Pres Acad Fit Awd; Rotary Awd; Bus Dept Accntng Awd; Bank Of Amer Cert; Santa Clara U Acelertd Math 89-90; Badminton; CA U Davis; Bio Chem.

TERBUSH, WILLIAM; Faith Christian HS; Yuba City, CA; (2); Boy Scts; Var JV Letterman Clb; Var Bsbl; JV Capt Bsktbl; Var Socr; Presdntl Phys Ftnss Awd; Bsktbl Coaches Awd; US Air Frc Acad; Astronomy.

TERENKIAN, NAYIRI; Santa Monica HS; Santa Monica, CA; (3); Art Clb; Cmnty Wkr; French Clb; Var Cheerldng; All Acadmc Areas Sch Serv; Intrsts Ballet, Piano; UCSB; Intr Dsgn.

TEREZON, HAROLD O; San Fernando HS; Pacoima, CA; (3); Art Clb; Key Clb; Math Clb; Spanish Clb; Orch; High Hon Roll; Hon Roll; CA Gldn St Awd Geom Hnrs; Hnr Soc; MA Inst Tech; Engrng.

TERHUNE, CYNTHIA M; Mater Dei HS; Huntington Bch, CA; (2); Dance Clb; French Clb; Girl Scts; High Hon Roll.

TERMECHI, NAZANIN; William Howard Taft HS; Woodland Hills, CA; (3); Band; Chorus; Variety Show; High Hon Roll; Tutrng; Vlntr Cmp Cnslr; UCLA; Math Tchr.

TERPSTRA, MICHELLE; Canyon Springs HS; Moreno Valley, CA; (3); Drama Clb; Var Mgr(s); Var Swmmng; Civil Law.

TERRAZAS, CATALINA R M; Escondido HS; Escondido, CA; (2); Girl Scts; Key Clb; Ski Clb; Spanish Clb.

TERRAZAS, NIVIA; Ganesha HS; Pomona, CA; (1); Office Aide; Drill Tm; Stage Crew; Off Frsh Cls; Cheerldng; Wt Lftg; Prfct Atten Awd; Boston U; Priv Det.

TERRELL, ANDREA S; Hoover HS; Glendale, CA; (3); Church Yth Grp; Office Aide; Teachers Aide; Yrbk; Wrkng W/Deaf Vlntr; UC; Cmmnctns.

TERRELL, TRACY A; Etiwanda HS; Fontana, CA; (2); Church Yth Grp; Drama Clb; French Clb; Thesps; Hon Roll; Elem Ed.

TERRIQUEZ, JESUS; La Puente HS; La Puente, CA; (4); 14/282; Science Clb; Band; Drm Mjr(t); Mrchg Band; Pep Band; Hon Roll; Engrng & Rdng Clb; Valle Vista Five Awd; Sigma Svc Awd 89-90; Drctrs & SR Awd; CA ST Plytchnc U; Arch.

TERRONES, CARLOS C; Roosevelt HS; Los Angeles, CA; (2); Computer Clb; School Musical; Wt Lftg; Arch.

TERRY, AIMEE; Mercy HS; Burlingame, CA; (3); Church Yth Grp; VP GAA; Rep Intnl Clb; Treas Spanish Clb; Yrbk; JV Bsktbl; Var Sftbl; JV Var Swmmng; High Hon Roll; Hon Roll; Pres SAAS; Jr Sttsmn Amer Rep; Chrch Lctr; Liberal Stu.

TERRY, ALEXANDER LEE; Overfelt HS; San Jose, CA; (2); Chess Clb; Ftbl; VA Poly Tech; Engr.

TERRY, AMY; Jurupa Valley HS; Riverside, CA; (2); Church Yth Grp; Cmnty Wkr; French Clb; FFA; Office Aide; SADD; Teachers Aide; Sec Band; Jazz Band; Mrchg Band; REACH Pgm; Fri Nght Lv; Wlkathns; Elem Tchr.

TERRY, BEN P; Edison HS; Huntington Beach, CA; (2); Model UN; Var Ftbl; Wt Lftg; Var Wrstlng; Acctng.

TERRY, BRANDI M; James Monroe HS; Panorama City, CA; (2); Art Clb; Hosp Aide; Office Aide; Science Clb; Teachers Aide; Drill Tm; Orch; Vllybl; Pepperdine; Marine Bio.

TERRY, BRIAN; Willits HS; Willits, CA; (2); Pres Computer Clb; JV Socr; High Hon Roll; Pr Cnslng; AZ ST U CAP Pgm Stu Yr 88 & 89; Comp Sci.

TERRY, DANIEL BRADLEY; Lincoln HS; Stockton, CA; (3); 88/592; Boy Scts; Mu Alpha Theta; Ski Clb; Acpl Chr; Rep Band; Jazz Band; Mrchg Band; School Musical; Lit Mag; Hon Roll; County Hnr Band; Beyond War/Glbl Awarenss; 1st Pl Congrssnl Art Cntst 89; Graphc Dsgn.

TERRY, DENISE L; Selma HS; Selma, CA; (4); 3/186; AFS; Church Yth Grp; Drama Clb; English Clb; Pres VP Intnl Clb; VP Letterman Clb; Pres VP Service Clb; Ski Clb; Pres VP SADD; VP Varsity Clb; CSF Ofcr; Cmp Ryl-Rtry Intl; Stanford Mdcl Schl; Phys Thrpy.

TERRY, JACOB J; Kingsbury HS; Kingsburg, CA; (2); MIT; Engrng.

TERRY, KEVIN J; Mc Clyomds HS; Oakland, CA; (3); Cmnty Wkr; Var JV Bsbl; Var JV Bsktbl; Var Ftbl; JV Trk; JV Wrstlng.

TERRY, MARQUITA D; John F Kennedy HS; Granada Hills, CA; (3); Church Yth Grp; Drama Clb; Natl Beta Clb; Pep Clb; Band; School Play; Trk; High Hon Roll; Hon Roll; Prfct Atten Awd; Schlr Athlt Awd 89 & 90; Grad John Casablancas Modeling Schl; UCLA; Cmmnctns.

TERUI, GEN; Carmel HS; Carmel, CA; (3); Teachers Aide; Varsity Clb; Var JV Ftbl; Var JV Wrstlng; High Hon Roll; Hon Roll; Wilderness Clb; SMART; MPC; Bus Econ.

TERUYA, JENNIFER M; Sacramento Adventist Acad; Sacramento, CA; (2); 1/48; Office Aide; Ski Clb; Band; High Hon Roll; Hon Roll; Prfct Atten Awd; Bio Awd; Most Outstndng Dnstry Rltd Exhibit CA Cntrl Vly Sci/Engrng Fair; Med.

TESHERA, JANEL; Yosemite Union HS; Coarsegold, CA; (2); Church Yth Grp; Cmnty Wkr; Sec Service Clb; Drill Tm; Stat Vllybl; Cit Awd; Hon Roll; PRIDE Of CA; Pepperdine; Forensc Pathlgy.

TESHERA, JANEL; Yosemite Union HS; Oakhurst, CA; (2); Church Yth Grp; Cmnty Wkr; Service Clb; Flag Corp; Var Tennis; Hon Roll; PRIDE CA.

TESHIROGI, TAKAHIDE; Mission San Jose HS; Fremont, CA; (3); Church Yth Grp; Cmnty Wkr; Debate Tm; Math Clb; Science Clb; Jazz Band; High Hnr Golden State Exam Algebra, Geom; Schlrshp Awd Study Of German Lang, WEA San Francisco; Earth Cnsrvtn.

TESILLO, OLGA; J Garfield HS; Los Angeles, CA; (3); Church Yth Grp; Color Guard; Mrchg Band; Cheerldng; Gym; High Hon Roll; Hon Roll; Medcl Careers Clb; Mst Outstndng ESC Stu Mdl; UC Santa Cruz; Pediatrics.

TESORO, VICTORIA A; Mayfield SR Schl; San Dimas, CA; (3); Library Aide; Spanish Clb; SADD; Teachers Aide; Chorus; Hon Roll; Chrstn Action Movement; CSF; Sci.

TESS, JENNIFER; Pinole Valley HS; San Pablo, CA; (2); Dance Clb; Debate Tm; NFL; Cheerldng; CA Poly SLO; Phys Thrpy.

TESTA, MICHAEL D; Desert SR HS; Edwards, CA; (2); Drill Tm; Yrbk; Intrml Bsbl; Intrml Ftbl; Cvl Air Patrol, Billy Mitchell Awd; Appntd Cadet Cmmndr Sqdrn, 1st Lt; Electronics.

TETER, AMY; Hanford HS; Hanford, CA; (1); FBLA; FHA; Frgn Exch Club; CSF; Med.

TETER, REBECCA; Canyon HS; Canyon Country, CA; (2); FBLA; Sec Treas Soph Cls; Intrml Bsktbl; Var Socr; JV Vllybl; Hon Roll; Amnsty Intl; HOPE; CSF; Boston U; Pre-Med.

TETER, SETH W; Golden West HS; Visalia, CA; (4); 17/330; Church Yth Grp; Drama Clb; Scholastic Bowl; Thesps; Acpl Chr; Chorus; Church Choir; School Musical; School Play; Nwsp; Stu Rep Visalia Unfd Schl Brd; HOBY Ldrshp Ambssdr; All St Hnr Chr; Wagner Coll; Theatre Arts.

TETREAULT, JILL A; El Camino Fundamental HS; Sacramento, CA; (3); 112/382; Church Yth Grp; French Clb; FTA; SADD; Varsity Clb; Nwsp; JV Diving; JV Sftbl; JV Var Swmmng; JV Wt Lftg; Tri For Fun 1st & 2nd Pl Var Water Polo 1990; Swim Team MVP 1990 & MIP 1988-89; CSUS; Dntl Hygnst.

TEVES, LADY SHAILINI S; Glendale Adventist Acad; Glendale, CA; (1); 1/64; Sec Frsh Cls; Var Gym; High Hon Roll; Acad Hnr Awd; Pacific Union Coll; Med.

TEVES, TANIA I; Bishop Amat HS; West Covina, CA; (2); Stat Bsktbl; JV Tennis; NHS; Barkada Club; Christain Svc Adopt A Grandparent; CA Schlrshp Fed; Psych.

TEVET, NATAN D; El Camino Real HS; Woodland Hills, CA; (2); Art Clb; Adv Scuba Diving; S E Asian Martial Arts; Genl Surgeon.

TEXEIRA, THOMAS JOSEPH; Amos Alonzo Stagg HS; Stockton, CA; (3); JV Bsktbl; JV Var Ftbl; High Hon Roll; Hon Roll; Pres Acad Fit Awd; Pres Schlr; High Hnrs Golden St Exam Geometry; Most Inspirational Jr Var Ftbl; Coach Awd Var Ftbl; Bio Sci.

THACH, HA; Oakland HS; Oakland, CA; (3); French Clb; Intnl Clb; Office Aide; Band; School Musical; Variety Show; Lit Mag; Cit Awd; Hon Roll; Prfct Atten Awd; Schlstc All Amer; Marcus A Foster Educational Inst; Med.

THACH, TAI; Mt Pleasant HS; San Jose, CA; (2); Math Clb; JV Tennis; Hon Roll.

THACHER, SCOTT O; Atascadero HS; Atascadero, CA; (2); JV Bsbl; JV Ftbl; Hon Roll; CSF; JV Bsbl Most Insprtnl; Bus.

THADANI, RESHMA; Northgate HS; Walnut Creek, CA; (4); 11/284; AFS; Hosp Aide; JA; Math Clb; Mu Alpha Theta; Pres Spanish Clb; High Hon Roll; NHS; Pres Acad Fit Awd; 1st Pl Essay Cntst; 300 Hr Awd Cndystrpng; Tufts U; Pediatrician.

THAI, HA L; Pioneer HS; San Jose, CA; (1); German Clb; Socr; Interact Club; Sccr Awd; San Jose ST U; Interior Dsgn.

THAI, HOA M; Mark Keppel HS; Monterey Park, CA; (1); French Clb; Key Clb; Math Clb; Mu Alpha Theta; Treas Frsh Cls; High Hon Roll; Jr NHS; CSF; Math.

THAI, HOA T; San Gabriel HS; Alhambra, CA; (3); French Clb; Library Aide; Service Clb; Tennis; Vllybl; Cit Awd; Hon Roll; UCI; Bus Mrktng.

THAI, HUE JEANETTE; Los Altos HS; Hacienda Hts, CA; (3); FBLA; Keywanettes; USC; Accntng.

THAI, HUNG S; Fremont Union HS; Sunnyvale, CA; (4); 78/389; French Clb; Intnl Clb; Teachers Aide; Bsktbl; Socr; Swmmng; Tennis; Vllybl; SJSU; Dentst.

THAI, KENNETH KHOA; George Washington HS; San Francisco, CA; (2); Cmnty Wkr; JV Bsbl; High Hon Roll; Hon Roll; UC Berkeley; Comp.

THAI, LAM; San Gabriel HS; Alhambra, CA; (2); Band; Trk; Hon Roll.

THAI, MINH; Oakland Tech HS; Oakland, CA; (2); Chess Clb; Computer Clb; Band; Orch; Crs Cntry; Swmmng; Vllybl; Cit Awd; Hon Roll; UCLA; Accntng.

THAI, NGA M; Mark Keppel HS; Monterey Park, CA; (2); French Clb; Key Clb; Treas Math Clb; Treas Mu Alpha Theta; High Hon Roll; Jr NHS; CA Schlrshp Fed; PEER Tutoring; Outstndg Acad Awr.

THAI, PHILIP; Katella HS; Anaheim, CA; (3); Church Yth Grp; Intrml Bsktbl; Intrml Ftbl; Var Trk; CA ST Fullerton; Ed.

THAI, PHUC; San Gabriel HS; Alhambra, CA; (3); Treas Computer Clb; FBLA; Hon Roll; Geolgy Clb.

THAI, SANG; Valley HS; Sacramento, CA; (4); 6/430; Boy Scts; Pres Church Yth Grp; Key Clb; Math Clb; Math Tm; SADD; Teachers Aide; Hon Roll; Rotary Awd; S E Asian Clb Pres; 100% Clb; CSF; U CA Davis; Pre-Med.

THAI, THANH D; San Rafael HS; San Rafael, CA; (1); Teachers Aide; Cit Awd; Elks Awd; Hon Roll; Pres Acad Fit Awd; UC Berkeley; Acctng.

THAI, THUAN C; Washington HS; San Francisco, CA; (4); 109/587; Key Clb; Service Clb; Teachers Aide; Cit Awd; High Hon Roll; Hon Roll; CSF; Gen Srvce Soc; Intramural Bowlng League; UC Santa Cruz.

THAI, THUY T; Atwater HS; Winton, CA; (3); FBLA; Yrbk; Treas Soph Cls; High Hon Roll; CSF 88-90; Mrt Cert 87-90; Advncd Placemnt-Am Hstry/Chem; U CA; Med.

THAI, THY H D; Tustin HS; Santa Ana, CA; (2); 4/300; Am Leg Aux Girls St; French Clb; Girl Scts; Library Aide; Math Tm; Science Clb; Temple Yth Grp; Cit Awd; High Hon Roll; Hon Roll; Gldn St Exam Awd Geo & Alg; Prncpls Hnr Roll; Acad Achvt Awd; UCI; Med.

THAI, VICKY QUAN; International Studies Acad; San Francisco, CA; (3); Computer Clb; Drama Clb; Yrbk; Rep Frsh Cls; High Hon Roll; Hon Roll; Financial Bus Ink; Video Club; CSF; UC Davis; Med.

THAI VAN DAT, JOHANNA; Moreau HS; Hayward, CA; (3); 17/293; Church Yth Grp; Key Clb; Math Clb; Service Clb; SADD; JV Crs Cntry; JV Swmmng; High Hon Roll; NHS; Span Schlrshp 88; Frnch Schlrshp, Swmmng N Cst Sctn Stu Athlt Awd 89; Frgn Lang Awd 90, Theology 87-89; Med.

THAM, YIN D; C K Mc Clatchy HS; Sacramento, CA; (1); 33/588; Prfct Atten Awd; Sec.

THAMMAVONG, KHAMKEO; Clovis HS; Fresno, CA; (2); Block C; Asian Clb Secry 89-90; Phys Thrpy.

THAMMAVONGSA, SIVIXAY; Don Antonio Lugo HS; Chino, CA; (3); Model UN; Office Aide; Teachers Aide; Ed Yrbk; Rep Jr Cls; Cit Awd; Hon Roll.

THAN, PENDLETON; Ocean View HS; Huntington Beach, CA; (1); UCI; Engr.

THAO, BAO; Clovis West HS; Pinedale, CA; (2); Church Yth Grp; Intnl Clb; Fresno ST; Tchr.

THAO, BEE; Fresno HS; Fresno, CA; (3); Bsbl; Socr; Pres Acad Fit Awd; Fresno City Coll.

THAO, CHIA; Modesto HS; Modesto, CA; (3); Treas German Clb; VP Key Clb; Math Clb; Office Aide; SADD; Cit Awd; Hon Roll; Prfct Atten Awd; Engl & Math Tutor; Ed.

THAO, GER; Duncan Polytechnic HS; Fresno, CA; (2); 1/350; Intnl Clb; Science Clb; Band; JV Socr; Vllybl; High Hon Roll; Pharm.

THAO, KOU; Foothill HS; North Highlands, CA; (2); Church Yth Grp; Science Clb; Band; Hon Roll.

THAO, KOUA; Edison HS; Fresno, CA; (2); Yrbk; Bsbl; Score Keeper; Vllybl; Prfct Atten Awd; Fresno ST.

THAO, LENG; Amos Alonzo Stagg HS; Stockton, CA; (2); High Hon Roll; Pres Acad Fit Awd; UC Davis; Med.

THAO, LY; Hoover HS; Fresno, CA; (2); Orch; Asian Club.

THAO, NENG; Redwood HS; Visalia, CA; (3); French Clb; FBLA; Math Clb; Science Clb; High Hon Roll; Hon Roll; CSF Club; Asian Lge Vllybl, Soccer Outside Of Schl; Law.

THAO, SEE; Las Plumas HS; Oroville, CA; (3); Intnl Clb; Key Clb; Math Clb; SADD; Nwsp; Tennis; Cit Awd; Hon Roll; Prfct Atten Awd; Photogrphy Clb; CSU Chico; Cnslng.

THAO, SHO; Tokay HS; Stockton, CA; (2); Teachers Aide; Hon Roll.

THAO, SIPHA; Millikan HS; Long Beach, CA; (3); Teachers Aide; Lit Mag; Off Sr Cls; Sftbl; Swmmng; Trk; Vllybl; Cit Awd; Prfct Atten Awd; Banking.

THAO, SOUK CHAY; Redwood HS; Visalia, CA; (2); Computer Clb; FBLA; Crs Cntry; Piano Synthesizer Currently In Band; Auto Engr.

THAO, TENG; Redwood HS; Visalia, CA; (3); Spanish Clb; Var Socr; Hon Roll; Sec/Treas S E Asian Clb; Engrng.

THAO, VANG; Mission Bay HS; San Diego, CA; (2); 43/380; JA; Library Aide; Model UN; Cit Awd; Hon Roll; Lion Awd; San Diego ST U; Comp Pgmr.

THAO, XEE SAMUEL; Edison-Computech HS; Fresno, CA; (2); 30/300; Sec French Clb; FBLA; Math Tm; High Hon Roll; Hon Roll; Hmong Clb VP; U Of CA; Engrng.

THAO, YE; Edison Computech HS; Fresno, CA; (2); 11/30; Fresno ST; Cmptr Prgrmer.

THAO, YEE; Clovis West HS; Clovis, CA; (3); Fresno ST U; Arch.

THARP, CHRISTINE L; Eureka HS; Eureka, CA; (1); Church Yth Grp; Cit Awd; High Hon Roll; Hon Roll; Prfct Atten Awd; All Star Stu Awd; Eng Lit Comp.

THARPE, RENEE; Palm Springs Christian HS; Dsrt Ht Sprg, CA; (2); Stu Cncl; JV Bsktbl; JV Cheerldng; Gym; Sftbl; Trk; Vllybl; Cit Awd; Hon Roll; Spcl Intrst-Dncng & Trk; Bys & Grls Clb Hnrs; Long Beach Coll; Mrn Bio.

THATCHER, FATIMA L; Summerville HS; Tuolumne, CA; (3); FHA; Office Aide; Ski Clb; SADD; Teachers Aide; Hon Roll; Super Stu Awd; CO JC; Nurse.

THATCHER, JENNIFER; Western Christian HS; Covina, CA; (1); Church Yth Grp; Cmnty Wkr; Office Aide; Spanish Clb; Cheerldng; Hon Roll; OH ST U; Elem Educ.

THAVISACK, BONASY; A A Stagg HS; Stockton, CA; (3); FHA; Teachers Aide; Rptr Lit Mag; Powder Puff Ftbl; Tennis; Hon Roll; Vrsty Bdmntn Tm Mst Vlbl Plyr; Med.

THAYER, DISA; San Marcos HS; Goleta, CA; (2); Art Clb; Key Clb; Cheerldng; High Hon Roll; CA Schlstc Fed; Parsons Schl Of Fine Arts; Dsgn.

THAYER, GINGER M; Lemoore HS; Lemoore, CA; (4); 19/300; Office Aide; SADD; Teachers Aide; Var Capt Bsktbl; Var Mgr(s); Var Sftbl; Var Vllybl; High Hon Roll; Outstndng Girl Of Yr 87-88; Natl Yth Congrssnl Ldr 90; Acad Ltr Awd 88-89; Fresno ST U; Phys Thrpy.

THAYER, LEAH; Los Alamitos HS; Huntington Bch, CA; (3); Sec Treas Drama Clb; French Clb; Teachers Aide; Chorus; Hon Roll; Interact Exec Bd; Safe Rides Exec Bd; Clss Comm; Bus.

THAYER, RAYMOND M; Liberty Union HS; Oakley, CA; (1); Yrbk; Wt Lftg; Hon Roll; UC Berkley.

THAYER, STEVEN R; Orange Glen HS; Escondido, CA; (2); 1/543; Math Tm; Bsktbl; Wt Lftg; Cit Awd; High Hon Roll; NHS; Pres Acad Fit Awd; N Cnty Acad League; CSF; High Hnrs Golden St Exam In Geom; Engr.

THAYER, TELI S; San Marcos HS; Goleta, CA; (4); French Clb; Co-Capt Color Guard; Lit Mag; Sec Sr Cls; Stu Cncl; JV Swmmng; Lion Awd; Pres Acad Fit Awd; Jr Statesman Of Amer; Amnesty Intl; CA Schlrshp Fed Sealbearer; U CA San Diego.

THEILE, KENDRA; California HS; San Ramon, CA; (2); Dance Clb; Model UN; Ski Clb; Spanish Clb; Teachers Aide; JV Cheerldng; Var Swmmng; High Hon Roll; Hon Roll; Pres Acad Fit Awd; CSF; CA ST U Hayward; Psycht.

THELIN, JOSHUA A; Nevada Union HS; Nevada City, CA; (1); Drama Clb; Thesps; Chorus; School Musical; School Play; JV Golf; Pres Acad Fit Awd; Physcst.

THEPBOUPHA, DOUANGPAT; Edison HS; Stockton, CA; (3); High Hon Roll; Seattle Pacific U; Bus.

THERAUBE, YAN B; Los Altos HS; Hacienda Hts, CA; (3); Pres Intnl Clb; Science Clb; Vlntr Year Book Staff; Photography Club; Computer Club; Robotics Classes; Aviation Career.

THERGOOD, DAVID; Valencia HS; Anaheim, CA; (3); Church Yth Grp; FBLA; Mrchg Band; Orch; Pep Band; School Musical; Stage Crew; Pres Acad Fit Awd; JSA; UC Los Angeles; Bus.

THERIAULT, CORESSA L; Nevada Union HS; Nevada City, CA; (3); Chorus; Stage Crew; High Hon Roll; Hon Roll; Masonic Awd; Intl Order Of Rainbow For Girls; Child Psych.

THERIOT, JEAN PAUL; San Dimas HS; San Dimas, CA; (3); Church Yth Grp; Letterman Clb; Rep Frsh Cls; Treas Soph Cls; Var Bsktbl; Var Crs Cntry; JV Trk; Hon Roll.

THERMINY, CAROL J; Etiwanda HS; Alta Loma, CA; (2); Drama Clb; JV Sftbl; U Of AZ Tucson; Law.

THERRIAULT, JESSIE; San Ramon Valley HS; Danville, CA; (3); Dance Clb; Intnl Clb; Var Capt Crs Cntry; Var Trk; High Hon Roll.

THEULE, MATTHEW O; Canyon HS; Santa Clarita, CA; (3); 18/501; Church Yth Grp; Debate Tm; Drama Clb; FBLA; Teachers Aide; Church Choir; JV Tennis; Cit Awd; High Hon Roll; Pres NHS; Brainstormers Champ; Knowledge Masters; Acadc Decathalon.

THIARD, BALRAJ K; Live Oak HS; Live Oak, CA; (4); Chess Clb; Church Yth Grp; Drama Clb; FFA; VP FHA; Letterman Clb; Pep Clb; Spanish Clb; Speech Tm; SADD; Lion Clb Spch Cntst Lcl Wnnr; Acadc Schlrshp Awd From CSUC; CLOSE Schlrshp; Stu Govt Schlrshp; CA ST U Chico; Secondary Tchr.

THIBAULT, JENNIFER; Mt Carmel HS; San Diego, CA; (3); 23/732; Drama Clb; FTA; Service Clb; School Play; Stu Cncl; JV Cheerldng; Kiwanis Awd; CSF; Peer Cnclr; Ready Writers Write-Off Cmptn Wnnr; UCLA; Sci.

THIBAULT, MARK A; Palmdale HS; Little Rock, CA; (2); 56/450; Church Yth Grp; 4-H; FFA; Letterman Clb; Ski Clb; Spanish Clb; JV Ftbl; Var L Swmmng; Cit Awd; 4-H Awd; CIF Prtcpnt; Jr Olumpcs Swmmrs; CO Springs AF Acad; Pilot.

THIBEAULT, JASON N; La Quinta HS; Westminster, CA; (4); 11/375; French Clb; Science Clb; Ski Clb; JV Tennis; Roller Hcky Leag; Wrote A Bk; VCI; Sci.

THIBODEAUX, RON P; Downey HS; Downey, CA; (3); Church Yth Grp; Cmnty Wkr; Key Clb; Spanish Clb; Rep Stu Cncl; Var Capt Bsbl; Var Ftbl; Var Capt Socr; Cit Awd; Hon Roll; Ed.

THIEL, ALEXIS; S Tahoe HS; S Lake Tahoe, CA; (3); Band; School Musical; Score Keeper; Hon Roll; Piano Lssns Since Age 10; Humbolt ST; Sound Engr.

THIEL, BECKY L; Fremont Christian HS; Fremont, CA; (2); Church Yth Grp; Letterman Clb; Service Clb; Teachers Aide; Chorus; Rep Soph Cls; JV Var Bsktbl; Var Trk; Var Vllybl; Bsktbl MVP, Coachs Awd, Ldrshp Awd; Soph Hmcmng Princess; Stanford; Med.

THIEL, JEANNETTE M; Manteca HS; Manteca, CA; (2); 26/420; Church Yth Grp; Cmnty Wkr; FCA; French Clb; Intnl Clb; SADD; Acpl Chr; Band; Chorus; Church Choir; Gymnstcs; Church Musical Tour; Outstndng Alto Choir Awd; Piano & Songwriting; Azusa Pacific U; Music.

THIEL, KATIE; Concord HS; Concord, CA; (3); Pep Clb; Teachers Aide; Varsity Clb; JV Var Cheerldng; Capt Cheerldng; Hon Roll; Nrsng.

THIELBAR-BIRCH, KIRSTEN L; Athenian HS; Oakland, CA; (3); Dance Clb; School Musical; School Play; Stage Crew; Lit Mag; Swmmng; Ntl Merit Ltr.

THIELE, MICHAEL; Oxnard HS; Oxnard, CA; (4); Computer Clb; Drama Clb; Spanish Clb; Teachers Aide; Ed Nwsp; Treas Soph Cls; Stu Cncl; Hon Roll; U CA Santa Cruz; Jrnlsm.

THIELEN, JENNIFER; Roseville HS; Rocklin, CA; (2); 82/420; Dance Clb; French Clb; Science Clb; Spanish Clb; Drill Tm; Hon Roll; Math.

THIENPHETH, LOCKKEO L; Weed HS; Weed, CA; (4); Teachers Aide; Off Sr Cls; High Hon Roll; Hon Roll; Nrsng Aide Schlrsp; Fshn Dsgn; Model; Chico ST; Nrs Fshn Design.

THIERSTEIN, SANDRA E; Nogales HS; W Covina, CA; (2); 29/762; Swmmng; Hon Roll; CSF; UC Irvine; Optometrist.

THIESEN, DIANNE E; Kingsburg HS; Kingsburg, CA; (3); 1/140; Am Leg Aux Girls St; Drama Clb; Math Clb; Mu Alpha Theta; Science Clb; Teachers Aide; Band; Chorus; Church Choir; Boy Scts; Acad Blck K Awd 4.0 GPA; Fresno Pacific Coll; Bio.

THIEU, SHARON; Dos Pueblos SR HS; Santa Barbara, CA; (2); 15/296; Math Clb; Math Tm; Acpl Chr; Flag Corp; Tennis; NHS.

THILL, JODY ANNE; Poway HS; Poway, CA; (4); 55/679; Church Yth Grp; Acpl Chr; Chorus; Cit Awd; Hon Roll; NHS; Prayer Grp; Stu Venture; Christian Heritage Coll; Educ.

THILL, JULIE ANNE; Poway HS; Poway, CA; (4); 11/679; Church Yth Grp; Acpl Chr; Chorus; High Hon Roll; NHS; Stu Venture; Mst Outstndng Frshmn; Achvr Mnth In Frgn Lang; The Masters Coll; Music Educ.

THIND, PAM K; Pinole Valley HS; Hercules, CA; (2); Debate Tm; Spanish Clb; High Hon Roll; Hon Roll; CSF; U CA Berkeley; Math.

THIPHAVONG, JULIE D; Bolsa Grande HS; Garden Grove, CA; (3); Library Aide; Teachers Aide; Orch; Off Frsh Cls; Off Soph Cls; Cit Awd; Hon Roll; CA ST Long Bch; Bus.

THIPSOUVANH, SOUMONTHA A; San Luis Obispo SR HS; San Luis Obispo, CA; (2); 73/319; Church Yth Grp; Key Clb; SADD; Chorus; Church Choir; JV Swmmng; JV Tennis; Hon Roll; Space Shuttle Project; Friends Of Earth; Sci.

THIRAKOMEN, KHANUNGNIJ; Clovis West HS; Fresno, CA; (3); Church Yth Grp; Intnl Clb; Chorus; Church Choir; Color Guard; Orch; Var Tennis; FCA; Piano Cmptn Semifnlst Intl Cont; Var Tnns; Hnr Choir; UC Santa Barbara; Marine Bio.

THIRAKUL, CHITH-ALY T; De Anza HS; San Pablo, CA; (3); French Clb; Science Clb; Teachers Aide; Hon Roll; U Of CA Davies; Pdtrcn.

THO, TRAN T; Galileo HS; San Francisco, CA; (3); Dance Clb; Hosp Aide; Library Aide; Office Aide; Ski Clb; Swing Chorus; Mgr(s); Tennis; Cit Awd.

THOEMMES, HEATHER; Glen A Wilson HS; Hacienda Heights, CA; (3); Dance Clb; English Clb; FTA; Library Aide; Drill Tm; High Hon Roll; Hon Roll; Prfct Atten Awd; Drill Team Awds Mst Outstndng Jnr, Superstar Yr; Cal Poly; Elem Tchr.

THOENE, JACOB BROCK; North HS; Glennville, CA; (2); Cmnty Wkr; FFA; JV Ftbl; Wt Lftg; JV Wrstlng; Hon Roll; Mst Inspirational Wrestler Awd; Recgntn By Natl Sci Teacher Of Yr; Elec Engr.

THOENE, JESSICA RACHEL; North HS; Glennville, CA; (4); 75/400; Church Yth Grp; Debate Tm; FFA; Ski Clb; Speech Tm; Rep Stu Cncl; Dekalb Outstndng Sr Awd; Golden St Farmer Deg; FFA Rgnl & Sctnl Offcr; CA Poly; Ag Educ.

THOLEN, TRACY L; Royal HS; Simi Valley, CA; (3); SADD; Teachers Aide; Ed Nwsp; Cit Awd; Hon Roll; Peer Cnslr; BYU HI; Jrnlsm.

THOLLANDER, JOEL LANCE; Mira Loma HS; Sacramento, CA; (4); 1/257; Drama Clb; JA; Math Clb; Acpl Chr; Chorus; School Musical; School Play; Stage Crew; Var L Bsktbl; Var L Socr; Stanford U; Math.

THOM, BECKI; Grossmont HS; El Cajon, CA; (2); JV Var Cheerldng; JV Var Gym; Theater Dance; SDSU.

THOMAS, ADAM M; Servite HS; Villa Park, CA; (3); Church Yth Grp; Cmnty Wkr; Sec Frsh Cls; Sec Jr Cls; Stu Cncl; JV Ftbl; JV Socr; ASB VP; Jr Statesmn Amer; Bus.

THOMAS, ADELAIDE; St Bernard HS; Los Angeles, CA; (3); AFS; Chess Clb; Church Yth Grp; Cmnty Wkr; Debate Tm; Drama Clb; English Clb; Intnl Clb; JA; Model UN; Yth Awds Spkr 3 Yrs; Spoke Glbl Prsbytrn Rally; Yth & Gvrnmnt; U Rockchester; Pol Sci.

THOMAS, ANDY C; Redwood HS; Visalia, CA; (4); FBLA; Jazz Band; Orch; Hon Roll; NAJE Awd; Mid Vlly Jazz Fstvl Awd; Grove Schl Of Music; Music.

THOMAS, ANGELA M; Bishop Amat HS; Chino, CA; (2); French Clb; Hon Roll; NEDT Awd; CSF; UCLA; Law.

THOMAS, ARIC VINCENT; Riverside Poly HS; Riverside, CA; (4); 36/395; Cmnty Wkr; Letterman Clb; Office Aide; Teachers Aide; VP Frsh Cls; JV Var Bsbl; JV Var Bsktbl; Var Capt Ftbl; High Hon Roll; CIF/Reebok Male Athlt Of Yr; Chancellors Awd; Cabrillo & Uppec Awds; Natl Cngrssnl Yth Ldrsph Cncl; UCR; Bus Law.

THOMAS, ARTHUR R; Compton HS; Compton, CA; (2); Bus Profs of Am; JV Bsktbl; JV Ftbl; JV Swmmng; Hon Roll; Techncl Electronics.

THOMAS, AUTUMN; Biggs HS; Biggs, CA; (1); 2/55; GAA; Band; Bsbl; Bsktbl; Vllybl; High Hon Roll; Hon Roll; UCLA; Med.

THOMAS, BLAINE C; Palma HS; Hollister, CA; (3); 6/80; Cmnty Wkr; Spanish Clb; Yrbk; VP Stu Cncl; Var Bsbl; Var Socr; Hon Roll; NHS.

THOMAS, BRIAN A; Eisenhower HS; Rialto, CA; (2); Hon Roll.

THOMAS, CHRIS M; Golden West HS; Visalia, CA; (2); Boy Scts; Debate Tm; DECA; Drama Clb; FCA; Intnl Clb; Speech Tm; School Musical; School Play; Swing Chorus; VP Peer Hlprs; Spkr DARE Pgm; UC Davis; Bus.

THOMAS, CHRISTINE; Cornelia Connelly HS; Huntington Beach, CA; (3); Church Yth Grp; Cmnty Wkr; GAA; School Play; Yrbk; Treas Lit Mag; VP Soph Cls; Pres Stu Cncl; Var Bsktbl; JV Vllybl.

THOMAS, CLIFF; Fairbanks Country Day HS; Rancho Santa Fe, CA; (1); Band; Hon Roll; Radio Contrlld Mdls; Horsebck Rdng.

THOMAS, COLETTE M; Pacifica HS; Garden Grove, CA; (1); Pep Clb; Drill Tm; U CA; Sci.

THOMAS, CYNTHIA M; Chino HS; Chino, CA; (2); Drama Clb; Pres 4-H; Spanish Clb; Thesps; School Play; Lit Mag; Ftbl; Mgr(s); 4-H Awd; Hon Roll; 4-H; Grl Scts; Writer.

THOMAS, DALLAS D; Dixon HS; Vacaville, CA; (1); Church Yth Grp; Pep Clb; Cheerldng; Pom Pon; Sftbl; Vllybl; Cit Awd; Hon Roll; Pres Schlr; Sacramento ST.

THOMAS, DAMION L; St Bernards HS; Los Angeles, CA; (2); Var Ftbl; L Vllybl; Hon Roll; NHS; Most Improved Player Vllybl 89; Southern CA U; Bus.

THOMAS, DAVID J; Pittsburg HS; Pittsburg, CA; (2); Boy Scts; Hon Roll; Pres Acad Fit Awd; Military.

THOMAS, ERIK C; Narbonne HS; Torrance, CA; (2); Key Clb; Speech Tm; Nwsp; Rep Frsh Cls; Rep Soph Cls; Crs Cntry; Trk; Hon Roll; Pres Acad Fit Awd; Am Legn Awd; Eclgy Clb; Hotl Mgmt.

THOMAS, GEORGE C; Woodland HS; Woodland, CA; (2); Math.

THOMAS, GLORIA; Calvary Baptist HS; Highland, CA; (2); Church Yth Grp; SADD; Church Choir; Yrbk; Azusa Pacific U; Med.

THOMAS, JAMIE A; Coalinga HS; Coalinga, CA; (4); 23/105; Drama Clb; Capt Color Guard; Rep Stu Cncl; Stat Bsktbl; Var Cheerldng; JV Sftbl; Stat Wrstlng; Hon Roll; Sftbl Ch; Santa Rosa JC; Elem Tchr.

THOMAS, JANNA A; Marshall Fund HS; Pasadena, CA; (3); Pres Church Yth Grp; Key Clb; Spanish Clb; Speech Tm; Temple Yth Grp; Church Choir; Variety Show; Var Capt Socr; Var Sftbl; Var Vllybl; MVP Sccr 1st & 2nd Tm All-League; Church Svc & Activities; BYU; Chld Psych.

THOMAS, JASON; Golden West HS; Visalia, CA; (3); Church Yth Grp; Band; Church Choir; Jazz Band; Mrchg Band; Pep Band; Swan Rec Swm Lg; Gldn Wst Wntr Crct Prcssn; Coll Of Sequoias Sci Acad; Sci.

THOMAS, JAY C; Lemoore HS; Lemoore, CA; (3); Var Socr; Hon Roll; Fresno ST; Acctng.

THOMAS, JEFFREY BRIAN; Portola HS; Portola, CA; (3); 3/58; Cmnty Wkr; Ski Clb; Teachers Aide; Phtg Yrbk; Pres Frsh Cls; Rep Soph Cls; Rep Sr Cls; Treas Stu Cncl; JV Bsktbl; JV Var Ftbl; Bst Dfnsv Plyr Awd JV Bsktbl; MVP, Bst Offnsv Bck Awds, All Leag Ftbl 89; Trk Tm Of Chmpns Slctn 90; Math.

THOMAS, JENNIFER; Enterprise HS; Redding, CA; (3); Drama Clb; Key Clb; School Play; Stage Crew; Hon Roll; CA Schlrshp Fed; Linguistcs.

THOMAS, JENNIFER M; Escondido HS; Escondido, CA; (1); JV Bsktbl; Hon Roll; Schl Dance Cls; REACH Achvt Awd; Stu Of Qrtr 90; U Of CA Los Angeles; Psycht.

THOMAS, JERRY S; Seaside HS; Ft Ord, CA; (4); Am Leg Boys St; Jazz Band; Rptr Nwsp; Hon Roll.

THOMAS, JOHN W; Sweet Water Union HS; National City, CA; (3); 64/372; Boy Scts; Church Yth Grp; Debate Tm; 4-H; FBLA; Office Aide; Quiz Bowl; Ski Clb; Teachers Aide; Varsity Clb; Hnrs Engl; CIF Bsktbl Champs Lead Mgr 1990-91; Red Devils Ftbl Team Lead Mgr 1990-91; SDSU; Phys Ed Tchr.

THOMAS, JUSTIN M; El Toro HS; El Toro, CA; (4); Boy Scts; Band; JV Swmmng; Waterpolo; Hnr Hstry Class; Ap Exam; CA ST U Fullerton; Hstry.

THOMAS, KAMRON; Argonaut HS; Ione, CA; (2); 4-H; Letterman Clb; Ftbl; Trk; Hon Roll; POA Circuit; Comp Engrng.

THOMAS, KARLY M; Dana Hills HS; Laguna Beach, CA; (2); SADD; Stat Score Keeper; Swmmng; Wtrng Shrt Stories; Dance; Statstcn Water Polo; Phys Thrpy.

THOMAS, KIMBERLY D; Pinole Valley HS; Hercules, CA; (1); Church Yth Grp; Red Cross Aide; JV Vllybl; High Hon Roll; Conflict Mgmt Tm; U CA Berkeley; Pre-Med.

THOMAS, KRISTIN E; John A Rowland HS; Rowland Heights, CA; (2); Cit Awd; Hon Roll; Prfct Atten Awd; Piano 4 Yrs; Broadway Musicals; CA ST U Fullerton; Comp Sci.

THOMAS, LA TASHA; St Michaels HS; Los Angeles, CA; (3); Hosp Aide; Spanish Clb; JV Vllybl; Hon Roll; US Hstry Achvt Awd; U Of Southern CA; Comp Sys.

THOMAS, LA TONIA; San Rafael HS; San Rafael, CA; (2); 4-H; Girl Scts; Library Aide; Office Aide; Teachers Aide; Stu Cncl; Bsktbl; Trk; High Hon Roll; Hon Roll; Comp Sci.

THOMAS, LATASHA M; St Michaels HS; Los Angeles, CA; (3); Hosp Aide; Spanish Clb; JV Vllybl; Hon Roll; U Southern CA; Comp Sci.

THOMAS, LISA E; Alta Loma HS; Rancho Cucamonga, CA; (2); GAA; Letterman Clb; Varsity Clb; VP Frsh Cls; Cheerldng; Socr; High Hon Roll; Hon Roll; Law.

THOMAS, MARA; Healdsburg HS; Healdsburg, CA; (3); 15/270; Church Yth Grp; GAA; Varsity Clb; Sec Treas Sr Cls; Vllybl; High Hon Roll; Hon Roll; Schlr Athlete Awd; Wkly Athletic T-Bone Awd For Outstndngn Plyng; Mrktng.

THOMAS, MARIE E; Hoover HS; San Diego, CA; (4); 25/304; GAA; Varsity Clb; Var L Bsktbl; Intrml Powder Puff Ftbl; Var L Sftbl; Var Capt Vllybl; Hon Roll; Mst Outstndng Stu Drivers Educ; Grossmont JC; Comp Engr.

THOMAS, MARK E; Redlands HS; Redlands, CA; (3); Boy Scts; Chess Clb; JA; Band; Hon Roll; Role Playing Games; Soph PSAT Scores Verbal 53 & Math 59; Med.

THOMAS, MARLO CATHERINE; Redlands HS; Redlands, CA; (4); Hosp Aide; Var Vllybl; Kimberly Jrs 87-90.

THOMAS, MICHAEL S; Saint Francis HS; Pasadena, CA; (2); Church Yth Grp; Pep Clb; Ski Clb; Ed Yrbk; JV Socr; Var Trk; Hon Roll; Spanish NHS; CSF.

THOMAS, MICHELLE I; Fountain Valley HS; Fountain Valley, CA; (4); 1/630; Cmnty Wkr; Key Clb; Red Cross Aide; VP Science Clb; Spanish Clb; Ed Yrbk; Stu Cncl; High Hon Roll; Ntl Merit Schol; Val; Earth Pals Assoctd Co-Fndr, Pres; Yale U.

THOMAS, MISTY N; Kennedy HS; Buena Park, CA; (2); Church Yth Grp; Band; Chorus; Church Choir; Mrchg Band; Orch; Pep Band; Undrclsmn Achvt Awd Art; Botany.

THOMAS, MONICA L; Modoc HS; Alturas, CA; (2); Church Yth Grp; Teachers Aide; Church Choir; Ed Phtg Yrbk; Powder Puff Ftbl; Cit Awd; GPA Imprvmnt.

THOMAS, NICOLE M; Pacifica HS; Garden Grove, CA; (3); 57/274; German Clb; Science Clb; SADD; Capt Drill Tm; Dance.

THOMAS, PRESTON C; San Penito HS; Hollister, CA; (4); 8/250; Church Yth Grp; Debate Tm; Pep Clb; Red Cross Aide; Science Clb; Ski Clb; Variety Show; Chrmn Stu Cncl; JV Var Bsktbl; JV Var Tennis; UC Davis; Bio Sci.

THOMAS, RAINA M; Del Oro HS; Loomis, CA; (3); 23/259; Am Leg Aux Girls St; Church Yth Grp; Cmnty Wkr; Office Aide; SADD; Varsity Clb; Var Tennis; High Hon Roll; NHS; CSF; Sch Rcgntn On Golden ST Math Exam; Del Oro Chem Hall Of Fame.

THOMAS, RHEDIS E; Torrey Pines HS; Del Mar, CA; (3); 32/422; AFS; Pres Girl Scts; Hosp Aide; Pres Service Clb; Color Guard; JV Sftbl; Hon Roll; W U S Archery Chmpn 89-90; CSF.

THOMAS, SCOTT; La Habra HS; La Habra Hts, CA; (3); Church Yth Grp; Teachers Aide; Band; Jazz Band; Mrchg Band; Pep Band; School Musical; Stage Crew; High Hon Roll; Hon Roll.

THOMAS, SCOTT E; St Margarets Episcopal Schl; San Juan Capistra, CA; (3); Church Yth Grp; Science Clb; Service Clb; JV Bsktbl; JV Crs Cntry; Intrml Ftbl; Pres Acad Fit Awd; Pat Rileys Bsktbl Game Awd 89; Duke U; Video Grphcs.

THOMAS, SHANNON; San Luis HS; San Luis Obispo, CA; (2); 3/300; Church Yth Grp; SADD; Rptr Yrbk; Var Cheerldng; JV Trk; High Hon Roll; Pres Acad Fit Awd; Play Piano; Gymnstcs; Brghm Yng U.

THOMAS, SHANNON L; Armijo HS; Suisun, CA; (2); AFS; Hosp Aide; Key Clb; Cit Awd; High Hon Roll; NHS; CSF; Boston U; Phys Thrpy.

THOMAS, SHARISMA; George Washington Prep; Los Angeles, CA; (2); Church Yth Grp; Dance Clb; English Clb; Math Tm; Pep Clb; Speech Tm; Teachers Aide; Band; Color Guard; Drill Tm; Engl, Prfct Atten & Marching Band Awds; U Southern CA; Musician.

THOMAS, SHAVOUDA D; Cordova SR HS; Rancho Cordova, CA; (2); Church Yth Grp; FCA; ROTC; Acpl Chr; Band; Church Choir; Mrchg Band; Pep Band; Pres Acad Fit Awd; Notre Dame; Corp Law.

THOMAS, STACEY E; Serrano HS; Phelan, CA; (1); Church Yth Grp; Drama Clb; Drill Tm; JV Sftbl; Hon Roll; UC San Diego; Ocngrphy.

THOMAS, STEPHANIE; Gahr HS; Moreno Valley, CA; (4); 49/446; Church Yth Grp; Spanish Clb; Co-Capt Color Guard; Cit Awd; High Hon Roll; Cal St Dominguez Hills Black Schlrs Awd; BAPAC Awd & Schlrshp; UC Irvine; Bio.

THOMAS, TABITHA; Pomona HS; Pomona, CA; (3); Cit Awd; Hon Roll; Comp Sci.

THOMAS, TARA J; Selma HS; Selma, CA; (3); 48/211; Library Aide; Office Aide; Teachers Aide; Var Sftbl; Hon Roll; Kings Rvr CC; Help The Blind.

THOMAS, TERESA; Mira Loma HS; Carmichael, CA; (3); 9/284; Church Yth Grp; Dance Clb; Ski Clb; Chorus; School Play; Stage Crew; Socr; Trk; Cit Awd; High Hon Roll; UC, Davis; Orthodontics.

THOMAS, TINA M; University City HS; San Diego, CA; (4); 42/331; Office Aide; Pep Clb; Teachers Aide; Varsity Clb; Capt Drill Tm; Cit Awd; Hon Roll; Outstndng ROP Stu Awd; Outstndng Bus Awds; Acad Achvt Awds; San Diego ST U; Acctng.

THOMAS, TRISTIN; Laguna Beach HS; Laguna Beach, CA; (3); Cmnty Wkr; Ed Yrbk; Cheerldng; Pom Pon; Powder Puff Ftbl; Sftbl; Hon Roll.

THOMAS, WALTER; Lompoc HS; Lompoc, CA; (4); 22/300; Am Leg Boys St; FBLA; Letterman Clb; Yrbk; Var L Ftbl; Var L Swmmng; Pres Acad Fit Awd; Mck Trl; UC Davis; Biochem.

THOMAS, WARREN A; Crenshaw HS; Los Angeles, CA; (3); Bsktbl; High Hon Roll; Hon Roll; Geom Tutor; Congrssnl Yth Ldrshp Cncl Wshngtn DC; Accntng.

THOMAS, WAYNE; Vacaville HS; Vacaville, CA; (3); Library Aide; Teachers Aide; Stu Cncl; Yth Cngrs Ldrshp Grp; Embry-Riddle Arntcl U; Aviation.

THOMAS, YVONNE M; Portola JR SR HS; Portola, CA; (3); Office Aide; Spanish Clb; Teachers Aide; Var Bsktbl; Var Sftbl; JV Vllybl; Hon Roll; All Leag Team & MVP Sftbl 90; Lawyer.

THOMASON, JENNIFER A; Burney HS; Burney, CA; (2); Teachers Aide; Band; JV Capt Bsktbl; JV Powder Puff Ftbl; JV Trk; JV Vllybl; Hon Roll; St Schlr; Social Services.

THOMASON, KEVIN M; Dinuba HS; Dinuba, CA; (4); Treas Key Clb; Band; Chorus; Mrchg Band; Nwsp; Yrbk; VP Frsh Cls; Kiwanis Awd; Pres Acad Fit Awd; Bank Of Amer Achvt Awd Fine Arts; CA Schlrshp Fed; Coll Of The Sequoias; Theatre.

THOMASSIAN, TOM; Fowler HS; Fowler, CA; (3); 13/120; Church Yth Grp; Drama Clb; FFA; Spanish Clb; Cit Awd; Hon Roll; Bio Awd; U CA Davis; Lawyer.

THOMASSON, NADINE I; Boron JR-SR HS; Boron, CA; (3); Library Aide; Chorus; Hon Roll; NHS; CA Schlsp Fed; Eng.

THOMAZIN, BRETT A; Hesperia HS; Hesperia, CA; (4); Am Leg Boys St; Speech Tm; Teachers Aide; Chorus; Swing Chorus; Rep Soph Cls; Var JV Bsktbl; Hon Roll; HOBY Rep; Acadmc Ltr; U Of NE Lincoln; Brdcst Jrnlsm.

THOME, DARRIN M; Village Christian HS; Glendale, CA; (3); 2/170; Church Yth Grp; English Clb; Math Clb; Mrchg Band; Wt Lftg; High Hon Roll; Hon Roll; NHS; Cal Poly; Ecology.

THOMISON, CHRISTINA; Montgomery HS; San Diego, CA; (3); Library Aide; Pep Clb; SADD; JV Mgr Bsbl; Cheerldng; Cit Awd; Hon Roll; Pres Acad Fit Awd; UC San Diego; Plastic Surgeon.

THOMPSON, AMANDA; Mira Mesa HS; San Diego, CA; (3); Debate Tm; FBLA; Girl Scts; Office Aide; Speech Tm; Teachers Aide; School Musical; School Play; Pres Acad Fit Awd; Myrs Yth Smmt Fcltr 1990; Atty.

THOMPSON, AMY; Encinal HS; Alameda, CA; (3); 9/248; Church Yth Grp; VP Drama Clb; Key Clb; Pep Clb; Ski Clb; School Musical; JV Cheerldng; Var JV Socr; Hon Roll; Engrng.

THOMPSON, ANDREW; Woodland HS; Woodland, CA; (3); Band; JV Capt Bsktbl; Var Golf; Hon Roll; Jr NHS; NHS; Pres Acad Fit Awd; CA Schlrshp Fdr.

THOMPSON, ANDREW P; Silver Valley HS; Ft Irwin, CA; (2); Boy Scts; Church Yth Grp; Hon Roll.

THOMPSON, ANGELA L; Cloverdale HS; Cloverdale, CA; (4); 13/62; Cmnty Wkr; FHA; SADD; Teachers Aide; Band; Jazz Band; Mrchg Band; Pep Band; Cit Awd; Hon Roll; CA Schlrshp Fndtn; Gldn St Geo Exam Hnrs; Amer Lgn Auxiliary Jrs; Berkeley Schl; Music.

THOMPSON, ANNA E; River City SR HS; W Sacramento, CA; (1); JV Bsktbl; JV Trk; 95% Attndnc Awd; Outstndng Achvmt French; Outstng Achvmt Sci; UCLA; Advrtsng Agent.

THOMPSON, BETH A; Modesto HS; Modesto, CA; (3); Church Yth Grp; NFL; Spanish Clb; Var L Crs Cntry; Hon Roll; CSF; Mock Trial; Acad Dcthln; Azusa Pacific U; Bus.

THOMPSON, BETHANY D; Apple Valley HS; Apple Valley, CA; (1); Band; Mrchg Band; High Hon Roll; Hon Roll; History.

THOMPSON, BRANDON D; Willows HS; Willows, CA; (3); 21/93; FFA; JV Golf; High Hon Roll; Hon Roll; Pres Acad Fit Awd; Acadmc Dcthln 1st In Cnty Math, Hstry & Oral Intervw; UC Davis; Intl Rltns.

THOMPSON, CAROL LYNN; Napa HS; Napa, CA; (4); 13/375; French Clb; Key Clb; SADD; Band; Drm Mjr(t); Bsktbl; Swmmng; High Hon Roll; Pres Schlr; CSF; Supt Schl Schlr; U S Collegte Wind Band Europn Tour 90; UC Davis; Phys Ed.

THOMPSON, CAROLL L; Amos Alozo Stagg HS; Stockton, CA; (3); Church Yth Grp; Church Choir; Bsbl; Bsktbl; Ftbl; Trk; Ftbl MVP; Bsktbl Jr Olympic Athl; Black Stu Union.

THOMPSON, CHAD; Colfax HS; Meadow Vista, CA; (3); 4-H; FBLA; Ski Clb; Ftbl; Elks Awd; Hon Roll; Stock Invstr.

THOMPSON, CHRIS W; Dos Pueblos HS; Santa Barbara, CA; (2); 27/296; Var L Tennis; NHS; CSF.

THOMPSON, DANIELLE; Pittsburg HS; Pittsburg, CA; (3); Cmnty Wkr; Hosp Aide; Elks Awd; Tuskegee U; Bus Mgmt.

THOMPSON, DARREN M; Lompoc HS; Lompoc, CA; (3); Hon Roll; Allan Hancock Coll; TV Cmramn.

THOMPSON, DEBORAH A; Prospect HS; San Jose, CA; (4); 1/205; VP Intnl Clb; Sec Key Clb; NFL; School Musical; Yrbk; Sec Stu Cncl; Var L Tennis; High Hon Roll; Opt Clb Awd; United Ntns Plgrmg Yth; Jazz Dance; Ntl Cncl Tchrs Engl Wrtng Awd; Law.

THOMPSON, DIANA M; El Capitan HS; Lakeside, CA; (2); 6/433; Hon Roll; CA Scholshp Fed Membr; USC; Business.

THOMPSON, DION A; San Gorgonio HS; Highland, CA; (4); Cmnty Wkr; Office Aide; L Ftbl; Powder Puff Ftbl; Trk; All CIF Div I Ftbl Tm; Los Angeles Times Inland Empire All Star Tm; Athl Schlrshp; U NM; Engrng.

THOMPSON, DIONA; Clovis HS; Fresno, CA; (2); Church Yth Grp; SADD; Fresno ST U; Chld Care.

THOMPSON, DYLAN R; North Salinas HS; Salinas, CA; (2); Art Clb; Spanish Clb; Band; Mrchg Band; Nwsp.

THOMPSON, ELICIA N; C K Mc Clatchy SR HS; Sacramento, CA; (2); Rep Frsh Cls; Sec Soph Cls; Sec Jr Cls; Cmmnty Of Caring; U CA-BERKELEY; Med.

THOMPSON, ERICK; Pittsburg HS; Pittsburg, CA; (3); Am Leg Boys St; Boy Scts; Cmnty Wkr; FBLA; Intnl Clb; Office Aide; Red Cross Aide; Teachers Aide; VICA; Bsktbl.

THOMPSON, GORDON M; DOS Pueblos HS; Goleta, CA; (3); 140/324; Church Yth Grp; Ski Clb; Stu Cncl; L Bsbl; L Bsktbl; L Ftbl; U AZ; Med.

THOMPSON, HEIDI MARIA; San Gorgonio HS; Highland, CA; (3); Am Leg Aux Girls St; Cmnty Wkr; German Clb; Letterman Clb; Pres Pep Clb; Pres Science Clb; Pres Frsh Cls; Pres Soph Cls; Pres Sr Cls; Rep Stu Cncl; Cngrssnl Yth Ldrshp Cncl; Amer Legn Aux Girls Nation Alt; Spcl Olympics Vlntr; Schl Cmmtte Chrprsn; UCLA; Microbio.

THOMPSON, IAN; Crescenta Valley HS; La Crescenta, CA; (4); Church Yth Grp; Mu Alpha Theta; Teachers Aide; Ntl Merit SF; Prfct Atten Awd; Pres Acad Fit Awd; CSF; Forestry.

THOMPSON, JANETTE I; Fairfield HS; Fairfield, CA; (3); Church Yth Grp; Chorus; High Hon Roll; Hon Roll; Voc Child Care.

THOMPSON, JASON; Highlands HS; North Highlands, CA; (2); French Clb; Ski Clb; Socr; Cit Awd; High Hon Roll; Hon Roll; Prfct Atten Awd; CSF; Stanford U; Bus.

THOMPSON, JAVONDA L; Hueneme HS; Oxnard, CA; (3); Dance Clb; Office Aide; SADD; Var Bsktbl; Var Sftbl; Var L Trk; Cit Awd; Pres Acad Fit Awd; Early Acad Outreach Pgm; Miss Natl Teenager Pgnt; Law.

THOMPSON, JEFF V; Royal HS; Simi Valley, CA; (3); 41/620; Var Trk; Hon Roll; Pres Acad Fit Awd; Bus.

THOMPSON, JENNIFER J; Colton HS; Colton, CA; (2); Church Yth Grp; Cmnty Wkr; Girl Scts; Key Clb; School Musical; Yrbk; Ftbl; JV Score Keeper; Cal St; Wrtng.

THOMPSON, JENNIFER L; San Ramon Valley HS; Danville, CA; (3); #8 In Class; Church Yth Grp; Key Clb; SADD; Chorus; JV Capt Socr; Var Swmmng; Pres Acad Fit Awd; High Hon Roll; CSF; Schlr Athl Awd; Hlth.

THOMPSON, JULIE; Woodcrest Christian Schl; Riverside, CA; (4); 1/28; Church Yth Grp; Drama Clb; Quiz Bowl; Var Capt Bsktbl; Var Sftbl; Var Capt Vllybl; Opt Clb Awd; Pres Acad Fit Awd; Val; CA Interschltc Fdrtn Schl Athl Yr; U Of Riverside Press Entrprs Acadmc Schlr; The Masters Coll.

THOMPSON, KAREN M; Irvine HS; Irvine, CA; (4); 100/529; AFS; Pres Cmnty Wkr; Pres JA; Key Clb; Sprt Ed Yrbk; VP Capt Swmmng; Hon Roll; Natl Charity Leag Pres; OR ST U; Intl Bus.

THOMPSON, KATHI R; Poway HS; Poway, CA; (4); Cmnty Wkr; Service Clb; Ski Clb; SADD; Nwsp; Lit Mag; VP Frsh Cls; Rep Soph Cls; Rep Jr Cls; Rep Sr Cls; Cmnty Swim Team; Traveling Soccer Tm; Long Beach ST CA; Arch Engr.

THOMPSON, KATHLEEN; Arlington HS; Riverside, CA; (4); 31/338; FBLA; Scholastic Bowl; Teachers Aide; Hon Roll; Cert Of Achvt Bus Dept 89; Awd Of Achvt From Bnk Of Amer For Bus Educ 90; Religion.

THOMPSON, KATRINA E; Grand Union HS; Sacramento, CA; (2).

THOMPSON, KEITH A; Atwater HS; Merced, CA; (3); Band; Mrchg Band; Ftbl; Socr; Wt Lftg; Hon Roll; Elem Schl Camp Cnslr; Law.

THOMPSON, KIMBERLY A; Foothill Farms HS; Sacramento, CA; (1); FTA; Hon Roll; Mock Trial; Hstry Prfssr.

THOMPSON, KIMBERLY S; Westminster HS; Westminster, CA; (2); Latin Clb; Stat Bsktbl; JV Vllybl; Hon Roll; Jr NHS; NHS; Pres Acad Fit Awd; Acadmcs Ltr.

THOMPSON, KIRBY J; Woodcrst Christian Schl; Riverside, CA; (1); Church Yth Grp; Mgr(s); Tennis; Vllybl; High Hon Roll; Hon Roll.

THOMPSON, LARA; Los Alamitos HS; Los Alamitos, CA; (3); Science Clb; Color Guard; Interact Clb; CA Schlrshp Red; Ecology Clg; Saferides.

THOMPSON, LAURIE A; Fairfield HS; Fairfield, CA; (4); 18/500; Drama Clb; French Clb; Teachers Aide; French Hon Soc; Hon Roll; Jr NHS; NHS; Stu For Peace Clb; Acad Dcthln; UC Berkeley; Film.

THOMPSON, LAVONDA G; King City HS; King City, CA; (3); 4-H; FFA; Rep Soph Cls; JV Vllybl; 4-H Awd; Hon Roll; Commrcl, Bus Clb; Hartnell; Nrsng.

THOMPSON, MARGARET N; Victor Valley HS; Victorville, CA; (3); 7/424; FHA; Ed Nwsp; Trk; Hon Roll; Jr NHS; Prfct Atten Awd; Trustees Schlrshp Awd 87-89; Natl Frnch Exam Cert Hnr; U Of TX Austin; Pre Law.

THOMPSON, MELINDA D; Escondido HS; Escondido, CA; (1); Pep Clb; Varsity Clb; Stat Bsktbl; Score Keeper; Var Trk; Hon Roll; Pres Acad Fit Awd; Frosh Of Yr For Trk & Field 89-90; Harvard; Law.

THOMPSON, MELONIE CHRISTINE; Diamond Bar HS; Walnut, CA; (3); Church Yth Grp; Debate Tm; Letterman Clb; Ski Clb; Spanish Clb; Varsity Clb; Color Guard; Cit Awd; High Hon Roll; Outstndng Schlrshp Awd; Schl For Span Cert Of Achvt; CSF; UC; Bus Law.

THOMPSON, MICHELLE J; Rancho Bernardo HS; San Diego, CA; (2); Math Clb; Stu Cncl; Stu Body Cmmssnr; USD; Tv Advrtsng.

THOMPSON, NAOMI E; Hawthorne HS; Lawndale, CA; (3); Pres Church Yth Grp; Teachers Aide; Church Choir; Cit Awd; Pres Acad Fit Awd; Trvld Arnd Northern Italy For 10 Days; Help Clean Up Oakland & San Francisco From Earthquake; Helicopter Pilot.

THOMPSON, NATALIE M; Skyline HS; Oakland, CA; (2); SADD; Swmmng; Tennis; Vllybl; Bus.

THOMPSON, NECO; Abraham Lincoln Prep HS; San Diego, CA; (3); Church Yth Grp; Hosp Aide; JV Vllybl; Hon Roll; Opt Clb Awd; Gst San Diego Links Achvr Pgm; Sci/Engrng Smr Naval Acad; Chosen Wrk SDSU Drg/Alchl Trtmnt Stdy; Spelman Coll; Psych.

THOMPSON, NICOLE; Santa Maria HS; Santa Maria, CA; (4); 59/467; Church Yth Grp; Pep Clb; Teachers Aide; Chorus; Church Choir; Rep Stu Cncl; JV Capt Cheerldng; Vrsty Spiritleading; Chrldng 3 Yrs; Yth Grp Worship Tm; Drama; Brag Board Awd; Pol Sci.

THOMPSON, PATRICK W; North Hollywood HS; Van Nuys, CA; (3); Am Leg Boys St; Church Yth Grp; Office Aide; Teachers Aide; Band; Church Choir; Jazz Band; Var Bsktbl; Bus Admin.

THOMPSON, ROBERT; Clovis HS; Clovis, CA; (4); Church Yth Grp; Prfct Atten Awd; FFA; Library Aide; Teachers Aide; 4-H Awd; 4-H; CA ST U Fresno; Tchr.

THOMPSON, RYAN J; California HS; Whittier, CA; (3); #2 In Class; Intrml Var Bsbl; Hon Roll; Sprts Med.

THOMPSON, SARA E; Lodi HS; Lodi, CA; (2); Acpl Chr; Chorus; Church Choir; Var Cheerldng; Var Trk; Hon Roll; Lodi Sitr Sngrs Advncd Choir 1990-91; CSF; Sacrmaneto T; Elem Tchr.

THOMPSON, SARA H; Hesperia HS; Victorville, CA; (4); 9/450; French Clb; German Clb; Key Clb; Pep Clb; Ski Clb; SADD; High Hon Roll; Hon Roll; Pres Acad Fit Awd; CSF Pres; Dcthln Team; Accptd With Pres Hnrs At Humboldt; UC Santa Barbara; Pltcl Sci.

THOMPSON, SEANNA; Academy Of Our Lady Of Peace; El Cajon, CA; (1); Church Yth Grp; Rptr Nwsp; Rep Pres Frsh Cls; High Hon Roll; Acad Leag; CSF; Med.

THOMPSON, SHANNON; Vallejo SR HS; Vallejo, CA; (2); Drama Clb; SADD; Color Guard; School Play; Cheerldng; Hon Roll; Honor Soc VP; Diablo Valley JC.

THOMPSON, SHARAINE; John F Kennedy HS; Granada Hills, CA; (4); Stage Crew; Rep Frsh Cls; Rep Jr Cls; Rep Stu Cncl; Cheerldng; Hon Roll; CA ST U Northridge; Dermatlgy.

THOMPSON, SHERI; Seaside HS; APO New York, NY; (3); Church Yth Grp; FBLA; Var Crs Cntry; Powder Puff Ftbl; Mgr Trk; High Hon Roll; Hon Roll; Intl Bkng.

THOMPSON, SHERI L; Westminster HS; Westminster, CA; (1); Latin Clb; Vllybl; Psycht.

THOMPSON, STACEY; Yosemite HS; Coarsegold, CA; (3); 1/200; Church Yth Grp; Spanish Clb; Teachers Aide; Flag Corp; Rptr Yrbk; Vllybl; Cit Awd; High Hon Roll.

THOMPSON, STEPHEN MATT; Mesa Verde HS; Citrus Heights, CA; (2); 8/250; Scholastic Bowl; JV Bsbl; Intrml Wt Lftg; High Hon Roll; Prfct Atten Awd; Stanford U.

THOMPSON, TIFFANY; Simi Valley HS; Simi Valley, CA; (2); 28/756; Key Clb; SADD; Teachers Aide; Drill Tm; Ed Nwsp; Jr NHS; Prfct Atten Awd; Pres Acad Fit Awd; CSF; Gldn St Exms Hnrs Geom, Alg I; Med.

THOMPSON, TISHA J; Bonita HS; La Verne, CA; (3); Chorus; High Hon Roll; Hon Roll; Ntl Merit Schol; JV Score Keeper; JV Var Vllybl; Cty Fair Art Exhibition Hnrb Mntn; Azusa Pacific U; Art.

THOMPSON, TRACI; Central Catholic HS; Westley, CA; (3); Pres Treas 4-H; Service Clb; Ski Clb; SADD; JV Var Bsktbl; Var Capt Cheerldng; Powder Puff Ftbl; Prfct Atten Awd; Tutor; San Luis Obispo; Arch.

THOMPSON, TRACI; St Lawrence Acad; San Jose, CA; (3); Science Clb; Stage Crew; Variety Show; JV Gym; Var Tennis; Rotary Awd; Amnstr Intl; Sci & Fctn Clb; Hmcmng Cmmttee; U CA Santa Cruz; Math.

THOMPSON, YVONNE M; Apple Valley SR HS; Apple Valley, CA; (3); 31/720; Sec Church Yth Grp; Cmnty Wkr; Drama Clb; Spanish Clb; SADD; Sec JV Bsbl; JV Mgr(s); Powder Puff Ftbl; Sec Var Wrstlng; Hon Roll; CO ST U; Mrktng.

THOMSEN, REBECCA A; Notre Dame HS; San Carlos, CA; (2); Church Yth Grp; School Musical; School Play; Stage Crew; Rep Frsh Cls; Hon Roll; Member Junior Statesman Of America; College; Engineering.

THOMSON, DANIEL R; Capistrano Valley HS; Mission Viejo, CA; (3); Scholastic Bowl; Var Ftbl; Var Wt Lftg; Ntl Merit SF; Golden St Exam Geom High Hnrs; Acad Dcthln 3rd Pl Orange Cnty Imprmptu Speech; Hnrb Mntn All-Lgue Ftbl.

THOMSON, JAMI K; Montgomery HS; Santa Rosa, CA; (2); Spanish Clb; Teachers Aide; High Hon Roll; Hon Roll; Jr NHS; NHS; Lamp Of Knowledge, Hnrs Club, CSF Club; Excl Span Awd, Schl Stu Of Mnth & Wk; U CA Santa Barbara; Math.

THOMSON, KAREN M; Bakersfield HS; Bakersfield, CA; (3); Cmnty Wkr; Dance Clb; Debate Tm; JA; NFL; Ski Clb; Teachers Aide; School Musical; JV Swmmng; JV Vllybl; UC Santa Barbara; Bus.

THOMSON, KIM D; El Toro HS; El Toro, CA; (4); 159/545; Church Yth Grp; GAA; Girl Scts; Pep Clb; Ski Clb; Teachers Aide; Varsity Clb; Stat Bsbl; Var Score Keeper; Var Capt Socr; Girls League; Class Rep; ASU Tempe AZ; Bus.

THOMSON, SCOTT A; Eisenhower HS; Rialto, CA; (2); Yrbk; Bsbl; JV Crs Cntry; High Hon Roll; Hon Roll; Pres Acad Fit Awd; AZ ST; Accntng.

THONG, MICHAEL; George Washington HS; San Francisco, CA; (2); High Hon Roll; Hon Roll.

THONGNOPNUER, VICTOR; Lowell HS; San Francisco, CA; (3); Cmnty Wkr; Dance Clb; JA; Office Aide; Red Cross Aide; Teachers Aide; Jr NHS; Pres Acad Fit Awd; CSF Mem; U CA Davis; Bus Adm.

THONGSY, PHENGSY; A A Stagg HS; Stockton, CA; (3); Teachers Aide; Hon Roll; NHS; Vlntr Big Bros/Bir Sistrs; Delta Coll; Secy.

THONGTHIPVORAVONG, VIENGNGEUN; Fresno HS; Fresno, CA; (3); #10 In Class; Hon Roll; South East Asia Clb; Culture Dance; Engl Awd; Nurse.

THONN, SEIREYRITH; Saddleback HS; Santa Ana, CA; (3); Church Yth Grp; Cmnty Wkr; Teachers Aide; Swmmng; Wt Lftg; Cit Awd; JETS Awd; Prfct Atten Awd; Water Polo; Cambodian Club; Life Guard; UC San Diego.

THOR, JOHN C; Foothill HS; N Highlands, CA; (4); 14/270; Computer Clb; Debate Tm; Treas German Clb; Chess Clb; Key Clb; Math Tm; Science Clb; Teachers Aide; VICA; High Hon Roll; Friday Night Live; Bank Of America Award; Tandy Outstanding Student Award; Math; Comp Science; Science; U Of CA; Biological Sci Phys.

THOR, SHONG P; Sacramento HS; Sacramento, CA; (2); 84/500; AFS; Computer Clb; Science Clb; SADD; Cit Awd; Hon Roll; Prfct Atten Awd; U Of Pacific; Pharmcy.

THORELL, ALANA J; La Quinta HS; Fountain Valley, CA; (3); 88/333; Chess Clb; Teachers Aide; Hon Roll; Natl Lib Poetry Edtrs Choice Awd 90; Love To Read Fntsy Bks; Art.

THORESEN, STEFANIE C; Hemet HS; Hemet, CA; (2); 73/420; Hosp Aide; SADD; High Hon Roll; Hon Roll; Prfct Atten Awd; Vllybl & Sftbl; UCLA; Pharmacist.

THORESON, HEATHER M; Sacramento Adventist Acad; Citrus Heights, CA; (2); Church Yth Grp; Teachers Aide; Band; Variety Show; Treas Soph Cls; Hon Roll; Prfct Atten Awd; Pacific Union Clg; Bus.

THORESON, MATTHEW T; El Camino Fundamental HS; Sacramento, CA; (3); VP Church Yth Grp; Math Clb; Spanish Clb; Var Bsktbl; JV Swmmng; Hon Roll.

THORNBURG, CYNTHIA M; Marysville HS; Browns Valley, CA; (1); Cmnty Wkr; Dance Clb; Pep Clb; Powder Puff Ftbl; Sftbl.

THORNBURG, JILL; Fairfield HS; Fairfield, CA; (3); Sec Treas German Clb; Rep Soph Cls; Rep Jr Cls; High Hon Roll; Hon Roll; NHS; CSF; Elem Ed.

THORNBURG, TAMARA D; Calaveras HS; Wallace, CA; (2); Church Yth Grp; Cmnty Wkr; German Clb; Letterman Clb; Capt Bsktbl; Var Sftbl; High Hon Roll; Hon Roll; Fri Nght Lv; CSF; ROP; Work W/Chldrn.

THORNBURGH, CHARLES; Lowell HS; Key West, FL; (3); Cmnty Wkr; French Clb; Q&S; Band; Mrchg Band; Pep Band; Var Tennis; Jr NHS; Ntl Merit SF; Vrsty All Cty Tnns; Red Belt Tae Kwon Do; Marine Bio/Snorklng; Stanford; Ecnmc.

THORNE, GREGORY M; Atwater HS; Atwater, CA; (4); 13/250; Church Yth Grp; Cmnty Wkr; Debate Tm; FCA; Letterman Clb; Speech Tm; SADD; Church Choir; High Hon Roll; Pres Acad Fit Awd; Dir Chrch Hndbll Chrs; CA Schlrshp Fed Life Mem; Passed 3 AP Tsts; Anderson U; Thlgy.

THORNHILL, KRISTIL E; Marysville HS; Marysville, CA; (1); Church Yth Grp; Spanish Clb; Drill Tm; Advtsg.

THORNHILL, LEE E; Serrano HS; Wrightwood, CA; (2); L Var Ftbl; Trk; Wt Lftg; High Hon Roll; Hon Roll; Machining.

THORNHILL, PATRICIA; Merced HS; Merced, CA; (2); Flag Corp; High Hon Roll; Hon Roll; Gldn St Exam Alg & Geom Hgh Hnrs; Astrnmy.

THORNQUIST, ERIK S; Portola HS; Portola, CA; (3); Am Leg Boys St; Letterman Clb; Teachers Aide; Varsity Clb; Ed Rptr Nwsp; Yrbk; Var Bsbl; Var Bsktbl; JV Mgr(s); JV Var Score Keeper; Otstndng Hstry Stu; Bus.

THORNTON, ANGELA; Sierra Joint Union HS; Tollhouse, CA; (4); Art Clb; Pres VP 4-H; FFA; Intnl Clb; Ski Clb; SADD; Teachers Aide; Tennis; 4-H Awd.

THORNTON, DE SHAWNE T; Cordova SR HS; Rancho Cordova, CA; (2); School Musical; Variety Show; Bsktbl; Dentistry.

THORNTON, ELIZABETH; Newport Christian HS; Corona Del Mar, CA; (1); Ski Clb; School Play; JV Cheerldng; High Hon Roll; Hon Roll; Psych.

THORNTON, GEOFFREY J; Irvine HS; Irvine, CA; (1); 2/591; Boy Scts; Ski Clb; Band; Jazz Band; Mrchg Band; High Hon Roll; Glnd St Exam 1st Yr Alg Hnrs; Med.

THORNTON, MATT A; Santa Cruz HS; Santa Cruz, CA; (1); Hon Roll; U Pacific.

THORNTON, MICHAEL; Emery HS; Emeryville, CA; (3); Teachers Aide; Varsity Clb; Band; Var Bsktbl; Var Ftbl; Var Mgr(s); Hon Roll.

THORNTON, ROBERT J; Fremont HS; Sunnyvale, CA; (3); 164/380; Library Aide; Teachers Aide; Westpoint; Aviation.

THORPE, LOIS K; Livermore HS; Livermore, CA; (3); Church Yth Grp; Cmnty Wkr; Spanish Clb; High Hon Roll; Hon Roll; CSF; Biola U; Elem Ed.

THORSNESS, JEREMY F; Granada HS; Livermore, CA; (2); JV Trk; Nuclr Engr.

THORSON, JAMES; El Dorado HS; Diamond Springs, CA; (3); 45/400; Church Yth Grp; Band; Chorus; Jazz Band; Var Crs Cntry; Var Trk; Hon Roll; Natl HS Math Exam Hghst Score; Most Insprtnl Awd Trk Team; Most Outstndng Chorus; Engrng.

THRAILKILL, HEATHER L; Los Angeles Baptist HS; West Hills, CA; (3); 14/101; Church Yth Grp; Hon Roll; Pres Acad Fit Awd; Span Awd 87 & 89; Camp Cnslr; Piano Cert Of Merit Level VII CSUN; Envrmntl Sci.

THREADGILL, JENNIFER S; Hanford HS; Hanford, CA; (2); Teachers Aide; Sequoias Coll; Dntl Assist.

THREADGILL, MARCHELL L; Tulare Union HS; Tulare, CA; (1); Teachers Aide; Stu Cncl; Score Keeper; Sftbl; Trk; Hon Roll; Blck Stu Union Sec; Mid-Term Grad; Made Deans List At Coll Of Sequotas; Schlrshp From Mt Sinai Grnd Cnc; Coll Of The Sequoias; Crim Just.

THREEWITT, TANYA A; Independence HS; San Jose, CA; (4); 17/850; Cmnty Wkr; German Clb; GAA; Library Aide; Math Clb; Red Cross Aide; Varsity Clb; Socr; High Hon Roll; Hon Roll; Natl Sci Olympiad Awd Chem; UC Davis; Psycht.

THROCKMORTON, D; SR HS; Menlo Park, CA; (1); AFS; Church Yth Grp; Debate Tm; Science Clb; Speech Tm; High Hon Roll; Lang Studies Spnsh & Russian; Socio-Pltcl Studies Eastern Europe; Archaeology Estrn Med Ckassical; Ameri U; Pltcl Sci.

THROOP, LISA; Patrick Henry HS; San Diego, CA; (2); 42/530; Church Yth Grp; Model UN; Church Choir; Variety Show; Cheerldng; Jr NHS.

THU, LONG; Paramount HS; Downey, CA; (3); French Clb; Var Tennis; Prfct Atten Awd.

THU, VYLA; Paramount HS; Downey, CA; (2); 8/666; Pres French Clb; Letterman Clb; SADD; Sec Soph Cls; JV Swmmng; JV Vllybl; Cit Awd; French Hon Soc; High Hon Roll; CSF; Prncpls Achvmnt List; Asian Club.

THUC, LE T; Washington HS; San Francisco, CA; (2); JV Var Gym; Hon Roll; Pres Acad Fit Awd; Child Psych.

THUMA-FURLONG, JENNIFER R; Crescenta Valley HS; La Crescenta, CA; (3); Cmnty Wkr; Sec French Clb; Mu Alpha Theta; Capt Drill Tm; Ed Yrbk; NHS; Dance Clb; Debate Tm; Drama Clb; 4-H; Geom Golden St Exam Hnrs; Poetry Jrnl Secy & Edtr; Peer Cnclr/Tutor; CSF VP; Bus.

THUNG, PETER C; Trabuco Hills HS; Mission Viejo, CA; (2); 11/413; Chess Clb; Spanish Clb; JV Tennis; Comp Sci.

THUONG, NHUT; San Gorgonio HS; San Bernardino, CA; (3); 89/364; Cit Awd; Prfct Atten Awd; U CA-R; Bus Admin.

THUR, STEVEN M; Hayward HS; Hayward, CA; (1).

THURBER, JILL R; Loma Linda Acad; Riverside, CA; (2); Hnr Roll Stu; LLU; Phys Thrpy.

THURBER, SHANA M; El Cajon Valley HS; El Cajon, CA; (2); 1/450; Church Yth Grp; Key Clb; SADD; Teachers Aide; Yrbk; Stat Mgr(s); Cit Awd; High Hon Roll; Hon Roll; Pres Acad Fit Awd; Young Life; Leo Club; Stanford; Tchr.

THURM, JESSICA C; San Luis Obispo SR HS; San Luis Obispo, CA; (2); Church Yth Grp; School Play; Stage Crew; Gym; JV Socr; JV Trk; Hon Roll; Pres Acad Fit Awd; Outdrs Cln; Rdng; U CA Davis; Vet.

THURMAN, AMY; North HS; Torrance, CA; (3); 187/397; Church Yth Grp; Teachers Aide; Sec Band; Mrchg Band; Pep Band; Cit Awd; Oscar Citiznshp Awd; Sunday Schl Tchr; Hand Bell Chr; Azusa Pacific U; Educ.

THURMAN, FRED W; Oroville HS; Oroville, CA; (2); Intnl Clb; Hon Roll; St Schlr; Tres Of Collectors Club.

THURMAN, LESLIE KAY; Woodland HS; Woodland, CA; (2); Church Yth Grp; French Clb; SADD; School Musical; Ed Nwsp; Ed Yrbk; Off Frsh Cls; Off Soph Cls; Hon Roll; Jr NHS; BYU; Hstry.

THURMAN, LOIS S; Monte Vista HS; Spring Valley, CA; (2); Church Yth Grp; Band; Mrchg Band; Pep Band; Berkley; Law.

THURMAN, MARFA; Marina HS; Huntington Bch, CA; (2); Red Cross Aide; Band; Mrchg Band; Orch; Pep Band; School Musical; Peer Asst League Pres; NODS; Govt Affrs Clb; Hstry.

THURMAN, MARIA; Maranatha HS; Pasadena, CA; (4); 16/103; Teachers Aide; Varsity Clb; Stu Cncl; Socr; Sftbl; Vllybl; NHS; Phys Thrpy.

THURMAN, MARK; Le Grand HS; Le Grand, CA; (2); FFA; Stage Crew; FFA Outstndng Soph & Str Chptr Frmr; Agmchncs Tm Wnng Awds; Cal Poly; Auto Engr.

THURN, JASON A; Nevada Union HS; Grass Valley, CA; (3); Letterman Clb; Teachers Aide; Varsity Clb; Bsktbl; Ftbl; Trk; Wt Lftg; Hon Roll; Stu Of Mnth 89; Stu Of Yr 88-89; ATV Rcng Chmp; NV St Chmpn 85-86 & 88; Stck Car Rcng 89-90; Chico ST U.

THURSTON, CHRISTINA; La Vista HS; Citrus Heights, CA; (4); Pesnl Grwth Cnslng Cls; Rock Clmbng; Friday Night Live; Comp.

THURSTON, MACI L; Manteca HS; Manteca, CA; (2); 54/400; Church Yth Grp; Hosp Aide; SADD; Teachers Aide; Band; Color Guard; Drill Tm; Flag Corp; Jazz Band; Mrchg Band; MVP Band, On Band Cncl; Delta Coll; Sci.

THWEATT, DEBORAH L; Orange Glen HS; Valley Center, CA; (4); 4-H; FFA; Library Aide; Teachers Aide; Yrbk; Lit Mag; Var Score Keeper; Intrml Var Socr; 4-H Awd; High Hon Roll; U CA Riverside; Hist.

THYMES, DEONZA; Downtown Busines Mag HS; Palmdale, CA; (2); Teachers Aide; Drill Tm; School Play; Off Soph Cls; Tennis; Tlnt Shw 90; Renaissance Fair & Aided Yrbk; Dance & Track; Purdue; Engr.

TIAFFAY, GEORGE; Oreotimba HS; Newman, CA; (4); 5/60; Am Leg Boys St; Letterman Clb; Math Tm; Pep Clb; Quiz Bowl; Science Clb; SADD; Off Soph Cls; Stu Cncl; Ftbl; 20-30 Hrs Wk Work; CSF; Engrng.

TIAMZON, KATHLEEN; Rosary HS; Anaheim, CA; (3); French Clb; Variety Show; Off Jr Cls; Hon Roll; CSF; Archt.

TIBAYAN, LIZA S; Valley HS; Hayward, CA; (3); 10/650; Cmnty Wkr; Math Tm; Office Aide; Spanish Clb; Teachers Aide; Drill Tm; Sec Frsh Cls; JV Var Cheerldng; High Hon Roll; NHS; Sanford; Biochemistry.

TIBBELS, CYNTHIA D; Bloomington HS; Bloomington, CA; (3); Drill Tm; Ed Nwsp; Yrbk; Mgr(s); Hon Roll; Dance Tm; CA ST San Bernardino; Elem Ed.

TIBBITS, RACHEL; Oak Grove HS; Ojai, CA; (4); Cmnty Wkr; Drama Clb; German Clb; Chorus; School Play; Yrbk; Pres Frsh Cls; Var JV Socr; Tennis; Var Trk; Congress-Bundestag Yth Exhcng Stu Full Schlrshp To Germany 88-89; Lewis & Clark; Intnl Affrs.

TIBBLES, BARBRA M; Foothill HS; Santa Ana, CA; (3); 5/328; Dance Clb; Drama Clb; Service Clb; Thesps; Chorus; School Musical; Variety Show; High Hon Roll; Hon Roll; Ed Doyle Music Awd Vcl Wnr 90; Disneyland Crtvty Chllng Mdl Wnnr 90; Nmrs Cmmnty Theatre Prod.

TIBBS, SUZANNE M; Ontario HS; Ontario, CA; (3); 1/375; Math Clb; Spanish Clb; Teachers Aide; High Hon Roll; Hon Roll; Prfct Atten Awd; CSF; Gate Clb; UC Riverside; Bus Mgmt.

TICA, JENNIFER; Burlingame HS; Hillsborough, CA; (3); Hosp Aide; Spanish Clb; Var Tennis; JV Trk; Hon Roll; San Mateo Cnty Srch & Rescue Team; San Mateo Cnty Hlth Dept Peer Resrc Prjct; CSF; Annapolis; Hlth.

TICKENOFF, JOHSUA P; Calvary Chapel HS; Santa Ana, CA; (2); Church Yth Grp; Ski Clb; Vllybl; Hon Roll; Pres Acad Fit Awd; CA Poly San Luis Obispo; Arch.

TICKLER, KRISTINA; Ygnacio Valley HS; Concord, CA; (4); 14/363; Church Yth Grp; Debate Tm; Drama Clb; French Clb; Letterman Clb; Pep Clb; Spanish Clb; SADD; Thesps; Varsity Clb; San Diego ST U; Pol Sci.

TICOULET, VINCE L; Mtn View HS; Mountain View, CA; (3); 74/400; French Clb; Var Bsbl; High Hon Roll; Hon Roll; St Schlr; US Air Force Acad; Aviation.

TIDD, MARIE A; Chaffey HS; Rancho Cucamonga, CA; (3); 23/518; Treas French Clb; Teachers Aide; Rptr Nwsp; JV Swmmng; JV Vllybl; High Hon Roll; Pres Acad Fit Awd; VP Keywanettes Club; CSF.

TIDRICK, STEVEN G; The Head-Royce Schl; Oakland, CA; (4); Pres Debate Tm; JCL; Pres Latin Clb; NFL; Rep Stu Cncl; High Hon Roll; Ntl Merit SF; Princeton Bk Awd Acad Exclince; Amer Chem Scty HS Chem Awd; 3rd Pl CA ST Debate Champs 89.

TIDWELL, ALAN J; Santa Teresa HS; San Jose, CA; (3); Boy Scts; Church Yth Grp; JA; Spanish Clb; Ed Yrbk; High Hon Roll; Hon Roll; BYU; Bus Admin.

TIEDTKE, KRISTA M; Savanna HS; Anaheim, CA; (3); 4/315; Am Leg Aux Girls St; Treas Service Clb; Rep Soph Cls; Rep Jr Cls; Rep Stu Cncl; Stat Bsktbl; JV Stat Gym; JV Vllybl; CSF Secty & VP.

TIEN, MY; Canoga Park HS; Canoga Park, CA; (1); Dr.

TIEN, TRAM; Western HS; Anaheim, CA; (3); JV Swmmng; JV Tennis; Var Trk; Hon Roll; NHS; Acad Deca; MV Swmng 88; Most Imprvd Tenns 8-89; UCI; Med.

TIENKEN, BRANDI L; Lindsay HS; Lindsay, CA; (1); Church Yth Grp; Cmnty Wkr; Ski Clb; Spanish Clb; Rep Frsh Cls; Off Soph Cls; JV Bsktbl; Mgr(s); Powder Puff Ftbl; Var Swmmng; Vly CIF Swm Chmpnshps Medley Relay Teem 5th Pl; Educ Of Handicappd Chldrn.

TIENKEN, CHAD J; Lindsay HS; Lindsay, CA; (3); 3/140; Am Leg Boys St; Church Yth Grp; Cmnty Wkr; Letterman Clb; Pres Ski Clb; Spanish Clb; Sec Sr Cls; JV Bsktbl; JV Var Ftbl; Var Swmmng; Camp Royal Rotary Yth & Ldrshp Awd; Goldn St Hnrs Geom; Dist Spellng Bee Chmpn; Chem/Ag Engrng.

TIEP, NGUYEN V; Clairemont HS; San Diego, CA; (3); Dance Clb; Hon Roll; Gldn St Exam Awd Acad Exclince; San Diego ST; Mechncl.

TIET, EDDIE; Schurr HS; West Covina, CA; (4); 118/580; Key Clb; Teachers Aide; Band; Ftbl; Capt Wrstlng; Hon Roll; Pres Acad Fit Awd; Core Leader For Church Yth Grp; Top 6th Wrstlr Southern CA; Mst Vlb Ftbl; Spcl Tm Awd Ftbl; UC Irvine.

TIET, HAO; Whitney HS; Lakewood, CA; (3); Church Yth Grp; Intnl Clb; JV Bsktbl; Crs Cntry; VP Trk; High Hon Roll; Acad Decathlon; Pre Med.

TIET, PHUONG; Alisal HS; Salinas, CA; (2); Powder Puff Ftbl; Tennis; Cit Awd; High Hon Roll; Math Awds; Keyboarding Awd; U CA Davis; Dentist.

TIETJEN, AMANDA S; Riverbank HS; Riverbank, CA; (3); Church Yth Grp; SADD; Yrbk; Hon Roll; CSF; Modesto JC; Med.

TIETJEN, TIM J; Riverbank HS; Riverbank, CA; (2); Church Yth Grp; Hosp Aide; SADD; Church Choir; Wt Lftg; Cit Awd; Med.

TIETTMEYER, ERIC J; Loyola HS; Santa Monica, CA; (1); 75/320; Boy Scts; Bus Profs of Am; Church Yth Grp; Cmnty Wkr; FBLA; School Play; Stage Crew; JV Bsbl; OR ST Wash; Bus Owner.

TIETZ, RYAN M; Paradise HS; Paradise, CA; (2); 38/250; Spanish Clb; Bsktbl; Socr; Tennis; Hon Roll; Chico ST U.

TIEU, CATHERINE; Rosemead HS; El Monte, CA; (2); Spanish Clb; JV Crs Cntry; Hon Roll; Prfct Atten Awd; Golden ST Exam 1st Yr Algbr Hnrs; CSF; UC Berkeley; Accntng.

TIEU, HIEU; Strathmore HS; Strathmore, CA; (3); 1/83; FFA; Letterman Clb; Math Clb; Math Tm; Science Clb; SADD; Bsktbl; Tennis; Cit Awd; High Hon Roll; Bus.

TIEU, KHAI T; Westminster HS; Westminster, CA; (2); Cmnty Wkr; Spanish Clb; High Hon Roll; Rotary Awd; Acad Decathlon; CA Schlrshp Fed; Amer Chem Soc Orange Cnty Cmptn; Stanford U; Med.

TIEU, LAN K; Alhambra HS; Alhambra, CA; (3); Treas Service Clb; Spanish Clb; Acad Excllnce Awd Gldn St Exm; Schl Recgntn Goldn St Exm; Stu Reltns Cmmtte; CPA.

TIEU, LE O; Alhambra HS; San Gabriel, CA; (3); Cmnty Wkr; Debate Tm; French Clb; Math Clb; Model UN; Service Clb; Ed Nwsp; Cit Awd; Hon Roll; Brdcstng.

TIEU, LIEN; Rosemead HS; San Gabriel, CA; (2); High Hon Roll; Hon Roll.

TIEU, QUYEN K; Anaheim HS; Anaheim, CA; (3); Key Clb; Math Clb; Science Clb; High Hon Roll; NHS; Prfct Atten Awd; UCLA; Optometrist.

TIEU, THANG V; Abraham Lincoln HS; San Francisco, CA; (2); 4-H; Band; Crs Cntry; Ftbl; Socr; Trk; Wt Lftg; Wrstlng; 4-H Awd; Pres Acad Fit Awd; All Cty Track, Fld Chmp; Bus.

TIEU, VAN; Saddleback HS; Santa Ana, CA; (4); 16/510; Chess Clb; Math Clb; Mu Alpha Theta; Science Clb; JV Tennis; High Hon Roll; Hon Roll; Brdg Club; UCI Prtnrshp Club; Comp Engrg.

TIGER, JEFFREY; San Bernardino HS; San Bernardino, CA; (2); 1/400; Key Clb; School Play; Pres Frsh Cls; Chrmn Soph Cls; Var L Swmmng; High Hon Roll; Hon Roll; Rotary Awd; Church Yth Grp; Drama Clb; CSF; Vrsty Waterpolo Ltr; UC Berkeley; Aviation.

TIGERT, JAMES T; Ygnacio HS; Concord, CA; (3); 51/371; Boy Scts; Var Ftbl; Var Vllybl; Hon Roll; Spevandle Club; St Marys Coll CA.

TIGERT, VERONICA A; Riverbank HS; Riverbank, CA; (3); Church Yth Grp; Pres Jr Cls; Pres Stu Cncl; Var Bsktbl; Var Powder Puff Ftbl; Var Tennis; Var Trk; Var JV Vllybl; High Hon Roll; 3 Tms Schlr Athlte; CSF; Mst Insprtngl Plyr Bsktbl & Tnns; CA Poly; Arch.

TIGHE, DEVIN K; University City HS; San Diego, CA; (3); Computer Clb; Key Clb; Teachers Aide; Rptr Lit Mag; Hon Roll; NHS; Acadc Dcthln; Culture Club; Close Up; U CA San Diego; Med.

TIGHE, KEN R; Atascadero HS; Atascadero, CA; (2); Church Yth Grp; Rptr Nwsp; Lit Mag; Bsbl; Swmmng; Tennis; Wrstlng; Hon Roll; Campus Life; Newspaper Reprtr.

TIGNER, WILLIAM E; Riverbank HS; Riverbank, CA; (4); Band; Jazz Band; Mrchg Band; Pep Band; Tennis; Trk; Wrstlng; Hon Roll; Church Yth Grp; Library Aide; John Philip Souza Band Awd; Mrn Corp Dstngshd Muscn; Modesto JR Coll; Music.

TIKARAM, SAGAR S; Monterey HS; Seaside, CA; (4); 9/252; Computer Clb; Library Aide; Math Tm; Rep Stu Cncl; Stat Socr; Stat Tennis; Stat Trk; High Hon Roll; Hon Roll; Tae Kwon Do Brown Belt; Australian Math Cmptn Rnkd 4th, 4th, & 6th Out Of Approx 12,000; UC, Santa Cruz; Aviation.

TILBURY, STACIE N; Torrey Pines HS; Rancho Santa Fe, CA; (3); Church Yth Grp; Cmnty Wkr; Dance Clb; Sec Service Clb; Church Choir; Hon Roll; People To People Schl Std Ambssdr; Chrch Yth Grp Ldrshp; Educ.

TILCOCK, WAYNE T; Fairfield HS; Suisun City, CA; (1); Boy Scts; Hon Roll; U Sacramento Of CA.

TILDEN, CHARLES H; Pinole Valley HS; Richmond, CA; (2); Church Yth Grp; Cmnty Wkr; NFL; SADD; Band; Jazz Band; Mrchg Band; Orch; Pep Band; School Musical; Clnry Arts.

TILGHMAN, JENNA; Bakersfield HS; Northport, AL; (2); Debate Tm; Stu Cncl; High Hon Roll; Hon Roll.

TILL, SALLY M; Casa Grande HS; Petaluma, CA; (3); 26/288; French Clb; SADD; Chorus; School Musical; School Play; Variety Show; Hon Roll; NHS; Pres Concert Choir; Pre-Med.

TILLERY, ROBERT E; Porterville HS; Porterville, CA; (3); Cmnty Wkr; Drama Clb; Teachers Aide; School Play; Stage Crew; Stu Cncl; Bsktbl; Ftbl; Golf; Trk; Ftbl Hnrs-All Leag Team, Hrdst Httr Awd; Scored 12 Of 17 Touchdowns San Diego St Pasing Tourn; San Diego ST; Bus.

TILLMAN, DANNIELLE J; Helix HS; Lemon Grove, CA; (2); Debate Tm; English Clb; French Clb; Girl Scts; Speech Tm; Nwsp; Yrbk; Powder Puff Ftbl; Sftbl; Wt Lftg; Stu Connection; Engl.

TILLMAN, DONALD J; Enerprise HS; Shingletown, CA; (3); 16/480; Church Yth Grp; Var JV Bsktbl; JV Trk; High Hon Roll; Hon Roll; Pres Acad Fit Awd; US Naval Sea Cadet Corps; Snowbrdng; Record Srchlght Eng Wrtng Awd; Engrng.

TILLMAN, DORLISA I; Pasadena HS; Pasadena, CA; (1); Church Yth Grp; Library Aide; Office Aide; Church Choir; MESA Grad; USC; Med.

TILLMAN, KAREN L; John Muir HS; Pasadena, CA; (2); Band; Mrchg Band; Pep Band; JV Swmmng; Ntl Merit Ltr; Bsktbl; Drill Tm; Bsktbl; Sftbl; Trk; Music; K Robert Neeley Memrl Schlrshp Fndtn; Music.

TILLMAN, SUHA; Palm Springs HS; Thousand Palms, CA; (2); Cmnty Wkr; Tennis; High Hon Roll; Hon Roll; Rotary Awd; Amnsty Intl; UC San Diego.

TILLNER, LAUREN L; Lodi HS; Woodbridge, CA; (2); 16/587; Sec Church Yth Grp; Dance Clb; Debate Tm; French Clb; NFL; Speech Tm; Church Choir; School Musical; VP Jr Cls; Trk; CA Arts Schlr; NASA Space Tomato Seed Proj; Ginger De Bow Awd.

TILLSON, REBECCA; Del Norte HS; Crescent City, CA; (2); Dance Clb; Band; Mrchg Band; JV Capt Cheerldng; High Hon Roll; Hon Roll; Math Fnls-1st Pl Alg; Mst Dedicated Dance Awd; CSF; Santa Rosa JC; Zoology.

TILMAN, PATRICK A; Montclair HS; Montclair, CA; (2); Var Wrstlng.

TILSON, JULIE KRISTIN; El Dorado HS; Placerville, CA; (4); 1/350; Pres 4-H; Speech Tm; 4-H Awd; High Hon Roll; Lion Awd; NHS; Pres Acad Fit Awd; Voice Dem Awd; 90 Scl Sci Stu Yr; UC Davis; Phys Thrpy.

TILTON, BEN K; Marina HS; Huntington Beach, CA; (2); Crs Cntry; Socr; Trk; Cit Awd; Bsbl Card Clb; Law.

TIMBANG, ROCHELLE C; Mira Mesa HS; San Diego, CA; (3); Cmnty Wkr; Teachers Aide; Sec Soph Cls; Sec Jr Cls; Sec Sr Cls; Off Stu Cncl; Powder Puff Ftbl; Pre-Med.

TIMBERMAN, AARON M; Armijo HS; Suisun, CA; (4); Letterman Clb; Office Aide; ROTC; SADD; Teachers Aide; Varsity Clb; VICA; Ftbl; Trk; Wt Lftg; Offns Defnsv Ftbl Camp; Sac ST; Bus Mgnt.

TIMM, AMY; Palmdale HS; Pearblossom, CA; (2); 55/600; Church Yth Grp; Hosp Aide; JA; Key Clb; Ski Clb; Var JV Cheerldng; Hon Roll; San Diego ST; Englsh.

TIMM, DEREK; Lincoln HS; Stockton, CA; (4); 53/600; Sec Art Clb; Boy Scts; Sec Debate Tm; Pres French Clb; Pres Key Clb; Mu Alpha Theta; NFL; School Play; Yrbk; Trk; Secretary Of State Art Award & Scholarship; Berkeley Law School; Law.

TIMM, MIKE A; Modoc HS; Alturas, CA; (2); 10/63; Var Bsbl; JV Bsktbl; JV Wt Lftg; Cit Awd; JV Hon Roll; JV Prfct Atten Awd; JV Pres Acad Fit Awd.

TIMMERMAN II, TIMOTHY L; Hesperia HS; Hesperia, CA; (2); 30/706; Spanish Clb; High Hon Roll; Water Skiing; Trapshtng; Drftng; Civil Engr.

TIMMINGS, MINDY J; Bullard HS; Fresno, CA; (2); SADD; Socr; Hon Roll; Bio Mtr Awd; UCSD; Marine Bio.

TIMMONS, CASANDRA E; El Cajon Valley HS; El Cajon, CA; (3); 31/370; School Play; Hon Roll; I Like To Swim; I Like To Travel; I Also Enjoy Working With Children; Humanities.

TIMONE, ANGELA M; San Luis Obispo HS; San Luis Obispo, CA; (2); Key Clb; Chorus; Yrbk; Swmmng; Hon Roll; Pres Schlr; Law.

TIMONY, JAMES; Christian Center Acad; Colton, CA; (4); Art Clb; Church Yth Grp; Teachers Aide; Nwsp; Ed Yrbk; Rep Stu Cncl; JV Bsktbl; JV Ftbl; Hon Roll; Prfct Atten Awd; Toastmasters Intl Awd; FIDM; Bus Mgmt.

TIMPLE, SHERYL; Paraclete HS; Lancaster, CA; (4); 5/128; Drama Clb; Key Clb; Var L Crs Cntry; Var L Trk; High Hon Roll; NHS; NEDT Awd; NASA Shrp Stu 89; CSF; Prncpls Lst; Plq Wnnr Lbrl Arts; Span, Rel, Alg, Bio, Chem & Trck Awds; Aerontcl Engrng.

TIMS III, FRANK L; El Capitan HS; Lakeside, CA; (2); 14/433; Church Yth Grp; Var Ftbl; Cit Awd; High Hon Roll; Math.

TIN, ANTHONY P; Bridgemont HS; San Francisco, CA; (3); 6/30; Church Yth Grp; Church Choir; Rptr Yrbk; Intrml Bsbl; Var Trk; Var Vllybl; Hon Roll; Relgn; Pacific Luthern U; Med.

TIN, DAISY; Schurr HS; S San Gabriel, CA; (3); Hosp Aide; Sec Key Clb; Spanish Clb; SADD; Ed Nwsp; Hon Roll; Prfct Atten Awd; Rotary Awd; Jr Statesmn Amer Treas; CSF Jr Rep; Rep Montebello Rotary Ldrshp Conf; Psych.

TIN, SAMMY S; Lowell HS; San Francisco, CA; (2); Church Yth Grp; Red Cross Aide; Science Clb; Church Choir; Intrml Bsbl; Intrml Bsktbl; Gov Hon Prg Awd; High Hon Roll; Stanford; Elect Engr.

TIN, SOK THEA; River City HS; W Sacramento, CA; (2); French Clb; Math Clb.

TINAJERO, ANGELICA; Delano HS; Delano, CA; (3); Church Yth Grp; Dance Clb; Latin Clb; Socr; Cit Awd; NEDT Awd; Exemplry Stu Awd; Discipline Awd-Vrsty Sccr; Bakersfield Coll; Bus Admin.

TINAJERO, BLANCA E; John F Kennedy HS; Buena Park, CA; (3); GAA; JV Capt Bsktbl; JV Swmmng; JV Vllybl; Doctor.

TINAJERO, MONICA A; St Joseph HS; Norwalk, CA; (2); Church Yth Grp; Drama Clb; Key Clb; Spanish Clb; SADD; School Play; Stage Crew; Hon Roll; U Southern CA; Theatr Arts.

TINCHER, BRENT; Christian Brothers HS; Sacramento, CA; (2); Spanish Clb; High Hon Roll; CA Schlrshp Fdrtn; Erly Outrch Pgm; UC Coll; Scntfc Fld.

TINCKNELL, TRACEY A; Mira Mesa HS; San Diego, CA; (3); 32/777; Church Yth Grp; Drama Clb; FBLA; Teachers Aide; School Play; Work; USIU; Accounting/Law.

TINDALL, JOSHUA J; Roseville HS; Rocklin, CA; (3); Drama Clb; English Clb; German Clb; Key Clb; Letterman Clb; Science Clb; Teachers Aide; Varsity Clb; School Play; Rptr Nwsp; HOBY Smnr Rep; Engl.

TINDERHOLT, ERIC R; Lompoc HS; Lompoc, CA; (3); Band; Jazz Band; Mrchg Band; Orch; Pep Band; Hon Roll; Prfct Atten Awd; Instrmntlst Mag Musicnshp Awd; GSE Acad Excllnc Awd; Eng Achvt Awd.

TING, JAMES H; Palos Verdes HS; Palos Verdes Est, CA; (3); Service Clb; Spanish Clb; Orch; Treas Jr Cls; VP Sr Cls; L Intrml Bsktbl; Var L Trk; Hon Roll; Treas NHS; Ntl Merit Ltr; Bay Leag Trpl Jump Chmpn, Rcrd Hldr Track 89.

TING, OLIVIA; Lowell HS; San Francisco, CA; (4); Q&S; Teachers Aide; Band; Orch; Var L Tennis; Hon Roll; Ntl Merit Ltr.

TING, PEITE; Beacon Christian HS; San Mateo, CA; (2); Sec Church Yth Grp; Chorus; School Musical; Pres Soph Cls; Rep Stu Cncl; Var Bsktbl; Var Cheerldng; Var Sftbl; Var Vllybl; Hon Roll; Vllybl & Sftbl All League Awds.

TING, SUZANNE; Abraham Lincoln HS; San Francisco, CA; (2); Chinese Clb; Pediatrics.

TINGLE, BRIAN C; Rubidoux HS; Riverside, CA; (4); 24/570; Computer Clb; Debate Tm; FBLA; Model UN; NFL; Quiz Bowl; Science Clb; Speech Tm; Yrbk; Bausch & Lomb Sci Awd; Acad Dcthln; Mock Trl; CLR; Envrnmntl Sci.

TINKLER, MELISSA; Whitney HS; Cerritos, CA; (3); Dance Clb; Drama Clb; Intnl Clb; Pep Clb; Thesps; School Musical; School Play; Off Frsh Cls; Hon Roll; NHS; Pioneer Elec Schlrshp 88; Ecology Clb Pres; Dance Awd 89; Mst Inspirational Perfrmr 90; Marlboro; Intl Stds.

TINNEY, NNIKA D; Lincoln HS; Stockton, CA; (4); 103/540; Church Yth Grp; Trk; Hon Roll; Chrch Choir; UC Davis; Bus Econ.

TINNIN, CAMERON B; Etiwanda HS; Rancho Cucamonga, CA; (2); Church Yth Grp; Dance Clb; Drama Clb; FHA; JA; Letterman Clb; Variety Show; Bsktbl; Trk; Hon Roll.

TINOCO, ALFREDO; Clairemont HS; San Diego, CA; (2); 38/254; Church Yth Grp; Var Bsbl; JV Ftbl; Cit Awd; Hon Roll; Prfct Atten Awd; Sci Proj Selected Cnty Sci Fair; Notre Dame; Engl.

TINOCO, EDWARD; Norte Vista HS; Riverside, CA; (1); Wt Lftg; Hon Roll; Engr.

TINOCO, NEIL A; Bishop Montgomery HS; Lomita, CA; (2); L Var Bsbl; L Var Ftbl; Certified Scubadiver; Backpacking & Camping; Marine Bio.

TINTARY, LEE H; West Covina HS; W Covina, CA; (4); 1/440; Am Leg Boys St; Boy Scts; Trk; Elks Awd; Lion Awd; Pres Acad Fit Awd; Val; Eagle Sct Awd; CA Schlstc Fed VP & Sec; Interact Clb Pres; Brandeis U; Archaelogy.

TINTOCALIS, MELISA J; Paraclete HS; Palmdale, CA; (2); Church Yth Grp; 4-H; Hosp Aide; JA; Key Clb; Red Cross Aide; Var Socr; Var Trk; 4-H Awd; Hon Roll; Tch Kids Swim; Law.

TIONG, MELANIE J; University City HS; San Diego, CA; (3); Am Leg Aux Girls St; Intnl Clb; Service Clb; Spanish Clb; SADD; Rptr Yrbk; Rep Stu Cncl; High Hon Roll; Jr NHS; NHS; Cal-Poly San Luis Obispo; Elec.

TIPKANOK, TARRA; Richard Gahr HS; Cerritos, CA; (3); Spanish Clb; Hon Roll; Prfct Atten Awd; Century 2000 Club; CSULB; Medical Nurse Anastheti.

TIPPETTS, RENDAL L; Etiwanda HS; Alta Loma, CA; (2); Boy Scts; Church Yth Grp; High Hon Roll; Hon Roll; Ntl Merit Schol; Pres Acad Fit Awd.

TIPPIT, ROBERT D; Palo Verde HS; Blythe, CA; (2); Church Yth Grp; Drama Clb; SADD; School Musical; Var Crs Cntry; JV Trk; JV Wrstlng; Hon Roll; Prfct Atten Awd.

TIPTON, ALISA M; Santa Teresa HS; San Jose, CA; (3); 4-H; German Clb; Girl Scts; Letterman Clb; Library Aide; ROTC; Varsity Clb; Band; JV Bsktbl; Powder Puff Ftbl; MVP Vllybl; AR ST U; Phys Thrpst.

TIPTON, HEATHER L; Alameda HS; Alameda, CA; (2); 29/290; Church Yth Grp; Office Aide; School Play; Stage Crew; Off Soph Cls; Var Bsktbl; Var Trk; Var Vllybl; High Hon Roll; Hon Roll; Poetry & Ltrtr; Uth Endng Hngr.

TIPTON, MIA L; Apple Valley SR HS; Victorville, CA; (3); Dance Clb; Girl Scts; JA; Key Clb; Pep Clb; Spanish Clb; Chorus; Drill Tm; Cheerldng; Pom Pon; Pharmacist.

TIPTON, MICHELLE; Franklin HS; Stockton, CA; (2); Cheerldng; Pom Pon; Hon Roll; 4 Yr Coll; Business Admin.

TIRONA, ANGELA B; Phillip & Sala Burton Academic HS; San Francisco, CA; (4); Dance Clb; Rptr Nwsp; Rep Frsh Cls; Rep Soph Cls; Rep Jr Cls; Vllybl; Hon Roll.

TISCARENO, JAVIER; Bell Gardens HS; Bell Gardens, CA; (1); Am Leg Boys St; FCA; Ftbl; Wt Lftg; Electrncs Cmptrs.

TISCARENO, PATRICIA; Bell Gardens HS; Bell Gardens, CA; (2); Chess Clb; Bsktbl; Sftbl; Vllybl; Prfct Atten Awd; Vrsty Bsktbl Schlr/Athl Awd; Vrsty Vlybl & JV Bsktbl MVP.

TISCHER, RACHEL A; Clovis West HS; Fresno, CA; (3); Church Yth Grp; Cmnty Wkr; French Clb; Hosp Aide; NFL; SADD; Stage Crew; Rep Stu Cncl; JV Crs Cntry; JV Swmmng; U CA Santa Cruz; Bio.

TISDALL, ROBYN E; Fontana HS; Fontana, CA; (1); Hon Roll; Indian Cultural Clb; UC Davis; Vet.

TISDEL, BECKY M; Shasta HS; Redding, CA; (2); JV Var Cheerldng; JV Var Swmmng; Psych.

TISON, MICHELLE; Arvin HS; Bakersfield, CA; (4); 48/263; Computer Clb; Drama Clb; Letterman Clb; Ski Clb; SADD; Varsity Clb; School Play; Variety Show; VP Stu Cncl; Var Bsktbl; 1st Pl Constitution Cmptn Fundamental Rights; Freedoms Fndtn Valley Forge; MVP Sftbl Pitcher; Bakersfield Coll; Educ.

TISSIER, TRICIA; Burlingame HS; Millbrae, CA; (3); Am Leg Aux Girls St; Church Yth Grp; Cmnty Wkr; Treas Debate Tm; Girl Scts; Band; Drm Mjr(t); Mrchg Band; Orch; Pep Band; Umpire/Coach Yng Grls Sftbl; Refree/Coach AYO Sccr; US Military.

TITCOMB, CELESTE; San Pasqual HS; Escondido, CA; (4); 36/400; Church Yth Grp; Pep Clb; Off Sr Cls; JV Gym; JV Swmmng; Elks Awd; Hon Roll; Pres Acad Fit Awd; Capt Drill Tm; Rep Frsh Cls; Student Venture; Palomar JR Coll; Political Sci.

TITH, CHENDA; Woodrow Wilson HS; Long Beach, CA; (3); Church Yth Grp; Intnl Clb; Teachers Aide; Church Choir; Intrml Bsktbl; Intrml Sftbl; Var Tennis; JV Vllybl; Cit Awd; Prfct Atten Awd; Badminton Team; Vice Pres Of Badminton Club; Award For MVP In JV Volleyball.

TITSWORTH, MELISSA C; Hueneme HS; Port Hueneme, CA; (3); Church Yth Grp; Co-Capt Drill Tm; Mrchg Band; High Hon Roll; Dance Team; UCSB; HS Tchr.

TITTRINGTON, SCOTT R; Poway HS; Poway, CA; (2); Church Yth Grp; Letterman Clb; Varsity Clb; Var Bsbl; JV Ftbl; Hon Roll; Prfct Atten Awd; Hnrbl Mntn, All Palomar Leag Bsbl Ptchr; Brigham Young U; Pro Bsbl.

TITUS, CHEKESHA; Arlington HS; Riverside, CA; (1); Church Yth Grp; Pep Clb; Chorus; School Musical; VP Frsh Cls; JV Cheerldng; Stat Sftbl; Cit Awd; Hon Roll; Class VP; Pediatrician.

TITUS, EUGENE; Arlington HS; Riverside, CA; (3); 61/465; Church Yth Grp; VP Frsh Cls; VP Sr Cls; Var L Bsktbl; Var JV Bsktbl; L Var Ftbl; Var L Trk; Hon Roll; Outstndng Ldrshp Awd; Associated Stu Body Dir Of Spcl Events; Black Stu Union Clb; Prfct Atten Awd; Sports Med.

TITUS, GRETCHEN; Tomales HS; Valley Ford, CA; (2); Sec French Clb; Letterman Clb; Library Aide; Yrbk; Ed Lit Mag; Var L Tennis; French Hon Soc; Hon Roll; Sprts Columnst; Jrnlsm.

TITUS, RODRICK; Pius X HS; Cerritos, CA; (4); 30/200; Drama Clb; Bsktbl; Crs Cntry; Trk; Hon Roll; NHS; Acad All-Amer Schlr; Schlr-Alth Awd; UC Santa Barbara U; Commnctn.

TIU, CHRISTINE; Dublin HS; Dublin, CA; (2); AFS; Band; Mrchg Band; Pep Band; Med.

TIYAAMORNWONG, KEVIN; Bullard HS; Fresno, CA; (2); #80 In Class; Spanish Clb; Hon Roll; GSE Hgh Hnrs Alg; Geom Hnrs; Mdcl Fld.

TJHEN, HARY; Magnolia HS; Anaheim, CA; (2); Hon Roll; NHS; CA ST Fulerton; Bus.

TJOE, IVAN; Granada Hills HS; Northridge, CA; (2); Ftbl; Pres Acad Fit Awd; UCLA; Lawyer.

TJOE, MICHELLE; St Genevieve HS; Panorama City, CA; (4); 1/153; Pep Clb; Sec Science Clb; SADD; Chorus; Drill Tm; Ed Yrbk; JV Vllybl; High Hon Roll; NEDT Awd; Pres CSF; Peer Facltng Prog Cnslr; Hnrb Mntn Skirball Inst; UCLA; Pharmacy.

TKACH, JON P; Mater Dei HS; Tustin, CA; (3); Pres Ski Clb; Spanish Clb; Rptr Nwsp; Natl Yth Ldrshp Cncl; Hstry.

TLEEL, GINA; Louisville HS; Reseda, CA; (2); Art Clb; Church Yth Grp; Science Clb; School Play; Variety Show; Nwsp; Var Crs Cntry; Var Trk; Hon Roll; CSF; GAA; U Of Southern CA; Bus.

TM, TERRY; Bullard HS; Fresno, CA; (1); German Clb; Intnl Clb; Science Clb; OM; Engr.

TN, HIEN T; Westminster HS; Midway, CA; (3); Vietnamese Club; UCI; Drftng.

TO, AMANDA; Pasadena HS; Pasadena, CA; (3); Hon Roll; Prfct Atten Awd; Creative Awd; Asian Club; Bus.

TO, DENISE; Schurr HS; Monterey Park, CA; (3); Key Clb; Varsity Clb; Nwsp; Off Jr Cls; JV Capt Bsktbl; Var Trk; Var Vllybl; Hon Roll; Prfct Atten Awd; UCSD; Bio Sci.

TO, GIAI T; Pasadena HS; Pasadena, CA; (4); High Hon Roll; Prfct Atten Awd; Meric Awd; Cert Of Recog.

TO, KY; Pasadena HS; Pasadena, CA; (3); Hon Roll; Cert Of Regntn.

TO, LARRY; International Studies Acad; San Francisco, CA; (2); Philanthrpy Clb Co-Pres; Amnsty Intl; Stanford U; Doctor.

TO, MARYANN; Garces Memorial HS; Bakersfield, CA; (4); 3/115; VP JA; Math Clb; Math Tm; Pres Science Clb; Lit Mag; Var Bsktbl; JV Vllybl; High Hon Roll; Rep HOBY Ldrshp Sem; Schl Acad Decathlon Tm Mem; Notre Dame U; Chem.

TO, THANH N; Mark Keppel HS; Rosemead, CA; (4); FBLA; Key Clb; Library Aide; Teachers Aide; Cit Awd; Hon Roll; Opt Clb Awd; Prfct Atten Awd; CSF; Optimst 3rd Pl Awd 89; Prfct Atten 86-89; Frndshp Clb Rep; Girls League; Cal ST Los Angeles; Comp Info.

TO, UON; Oakland HS; Oakland, CA; (2); Girl Scts; Spanish Clb; Hon Roll; UC Davis; Nrs.

TO, WILLIAM H; Saddleback HS; Santa Ana, CA; (2); Boy Scts; Computer Clb; Quiz Bowl; Science Clb; Spanish Clb; Lisa Essy Wnnr 3rd Pl; Sci Fr Wnnr 3rd Pl; U Of CA Berkeley; Pre-Med.

TOAILOA, LOTOALOFA; Richmond HS; Richmond, CA; (2); GAA; Office Aide; Score Keeper; Var Sftbl; Humbolt; Eng Lit.

TOBAR, ANDRES; L A Lutheran HS; Glendale, CA; (2); Church Yth Grp; Jazz Band; School Musical; Socr; Swmmng; Art Center; Layout Artist.

TOBEY, NICOLE K; Rio Americano HS; Sacramento, CA; (3); Church Yth Grp; French Clb; Swmmng; Tennis; Hon Roll; Pres Acad Fit Awd; Ed Yrbk; Friday Night Live; Jr Statesmen Amer Pblcty; Biola; Bus.

TOBIANO, PHOEBE STEPHANIE C; San Marino HS; San Marino, CA; (4); Math Clb; Q&S; Red Cross Aide; Science Clb; Band; Mrchg Band; Phtg Yrbk; Hon Roll; Outstndng Spansh Stu; UCLA; Doctor.

TOBIAS, ABIGAIL; The Bishops Schl; Encinitas, CA; (4); AFS; Church Yth Grp; Cmnty Wkr; Acpl Chr; Chorus; Orch; School Musical; Ed Lit Mag; Rep Soph Cls; Rep Jr Cls; Tri-M Music Hnr Soc Hstrsn 89, Treas 90; Blood Drive Coord 90; Antioch Coll; Educ.

TOBIAS, JOSUE E; Magnolia HS; Stanton, CA; (3); Army.

TOBIAS, MICHELLE L; Pinole Valley HS; Vellejo, CA; (1); French Clb; Hon Roll; UC Berkeley.

TOBIN, BO G; Lassen Union HS; Susanville, CA; (2); 8/235; Letterman Clb; Spanish Clb; Var Bsbl; JV Bsktbl; JV Ftbl; High Hon Roll; CSF; Presdntl Phys Ftnss Awd; Bio, Engl & US Hstry Hnrs; Med.

TOBOL, LAURANNA S; Ygnacio Valley HS; Concord, CA; (2); Var L Socr; Var L Trk; Var L Vllybl; Scl Svc.

TOBON, ELIZABETH; Savanna HS; Anaheim, CA; (2); Tennis; Cit Awd; Prfct Atten Awd; Intr Dsgn.

TOBY, BRANDII; Don Antonio Lugo HS; Chino, CA; (1); Cheerldng; Hon Roll; Dance; Performing Arts Cls; Stanford; Sci.

TOCCO, LINDA N; Fontana HS; Fontana, CA; (3).

TOCI, CAROLYN KAY; Grossmont HS; El Cajon, CA; (4); 31/350; Varsity Clb; Variety Show; Var Crs Cntry; Var Trk; Intrml Wt Lftg; Hon Roll; Pres Acad Fit Awd; CSF; SD Tribunes All Acad Team; Outstndng Achvt Span; UC-DAVIS; Cmmnty Nutrtn.

TOCK, A RYANN; Sonoma Valley HS; Sonoma, CA; (3); Church Yth Grp; Girl Scts; Acpl Chr; Band; Chorus; Stage Crew; Hon Roll; Engl.

TODD, DANA C; Kerman HS; Kerman, CA; (2); 15/225; Church Yth Grp; FFA; Band; Chorus; Jazz Band; Mrchg Band; JV Bsktbl; Hon Roll; Pres Acad Fit Awd; Jazz Chorus; Fresno State U; Business Mgmnt.

TODD, DELILAH A; Arlington HS; Moreno Valley, CA; (3); Teachers Aide; Chorus; ; Acctng.

TODD III, JOHN B; East Bakersfield HS; Bakersfield, CA; (1); Band; Mrchg Band; Tennis; Wrstlng; Cit Awd; Elks Awd; Hon Roll; Prfct Atten Awd; GATE Prgm; Perfect Attendance; Received Var Sport Letter; Aero Engrng.

TODD, MATT; Redwood HS; Visalia, CA; (3); JV L Bsktbl; Var L Golf; High Hon Roll; Prof Glfr.

TODD, MICHELLE D; Enterprise HS; Redding, CA; (4); 2/325; Pres Church Yth Grp; Cmnty Wkr; Sec FBLA; Hosp Aide; Mu Alpha Theta; Church Choir; School Play; JV Bsktbl; Var Swmmng; Cit Awd; BYU; Elem Educ.

TODD, REGAN; Point Loma HS; San Diego, CA; (3); 57/476; Key Clb; Ski Clb; Acpl Chr; Cheerldng; Jrnlsm.

TODD, RYAN N; Los Gatos HS; Los Gatos, CA; (2); Debate Tm; Nwsp; Swmmng; Hon Roll; Vrsty Swm; UCSB; Mrn Bio.

TODD, SARAH C; Dos Palos HS; Dos Palos, CA; (3); 4-H; Pep Clb; Spanish Clb; Hon Roll; Pres Acad Fit Awd; Stat Bsktbl; Var Capt Cheerldng; Var Trk; JV Var Vllybl; Mst Valbl Trk Seasons 89-90.

TODD, STACEY; Fairfax HS; Los Angeles, CA; (4); Church Yth Grp; Hosp Aide; Speech Tm; Rep Jr Cls; Rep Sr Cls; Capt Cheerldng; Hon Roll; Bank Amer Achvt Awd; Barbizon Modeling Schl Grad; Howard U; Acctng.

TODD, STEVEN R; Oakdale HS; Oakdale, CA; (1); Drama Clb; Ski Clb; JV Bsktbl; JV Ftbl; JV Wt Lftg; Modesto JC; Vet.

TOEDTEMEIER, JENNIFER M; Nevada Union HS; Chicago Park, CA; (4); 71/448; Intnl Clb; Thesps; High Hon Roll; Hon Roll; Fshn Inst Dsgn & Merch; Buyer.

TOEPFER, CARA L; Paraclete HS; Lancaster, CA; (2); Church Yth Grp; GAA; Letterman Clb; Varsity Clb; Var Sftbl; JV Capt Vllybl; High Hon Roll; Hon Roll; Span Awds; Pepprdn.

TOERPER, ROBIN E; Serrano HS; Wrightwood, CA; (4); 3/140; High Hon Roll; Sal; CSF Sealbearer; Engrng.

TOFANELLI, SAGE; Chico SR HS; Chico, CA; (2); Church Yth Grp; Cmnty Wkr; JA; SADD; Church Choir; School Play; Stage Crew; Yrbk; Cheerldng; Pom Pon; Bus.

TOKESHI, STEVE; Fountain Valley HS; Fountain Valley, CA; (3); VP Latin Clb; Off Frsh Cls; VP Soph Cls; VP Jr Cls; Ftbl; Trk; High Hon Roll; CSF; Baron Acad Sci; Jpnse Clb.

TOKIYAMA, STEFANIE; Long Beach Polytechnic HS; Lakewood, CA; (4); 1/700; Cmnty Wkr; Computer Clb; German Clb; Pres Intnl Clb; Key Clb; Science Clb; Service Clb; Varsity Clb; VP Sr Cls; Stu Cncl; Intrntl Amb For Poly High; Pursuit Of Exc Acad Awards From Poly HS; Private Music Lessons Piano; U CA.

TOKUMOTO, CAREY A; Hanford HS; Hanford, CA; (3); 17/380; FBLA; VP Treas Science Clb; Off Soph Cls; Mrchg Band; Pep Band; Var Tennis; Hon Roll; Member Of CA Schlrshp Fed; Member Of Interact Club; Tresurer Of The Exchange Club; Computer Engineer/Comp Sci.

TOKUTAKE, HIROSHI; San Fernando Valley Acad; Reseda, CA; (2); 2/20; Teachers Aide; Rep Soph Cls; Prfct Atten Awd; Photography Clb; Associated Stu Body Secy; Acctnt.

TOKUYOSHI, SONIA K; Rio Vista HS; Walnut Grove, CA; (3); VP FHA; Letterman Clb; Science Clb; Spanish Clb; Treas Soph Cls; Pres Sr Cls; Var JV Bsktbl; Var JV Sftbl; Var JV Vllybl; Hon Roll; Hnrbl Mntn All Lg Vrsty Sftbl; CA ST U Fresno; Bus.

TOLANEY, MICHAEL M; Arcadia HS; Arcadia, CA; (3); 73/639; Var Tennis; Hon Roll; NHS; Prfct Atten Awd.

TOLBERT, TABITHA R; Rio Linda SR HS; Rio Linda, CA; (2); Church Yth Grp; Office Aide; Hon Roll.

TOLBERT, TINA; Venice HS; Venice, CA; (2); Church Yth Grp; JV Tennis; Med.

TOLBY, BRYAN A; Central Catholic HS; Modesto, CA; (3); 21/52; Art Clb; Science Clb; Service Clb; Spanish Clb; JV Socr; Cit Awd; Hon Roll; NHS; Art Clb Treas; Santa Clara U; CPA.

TOLCHIN, STACY E; Pasadena HS; Sierra Madre, CA; (2); JV GAA; Pres Jr Cls; JV Tennis; High Hon Roll; Hon Roll; Amnsty Intrnl; Green Peace; CSF.

TOLEDO, CLAUDIA M; North Hollywood HS; North Hollywood, CA; (2); Drama Clb; Hosp Aide; Natl Beta Clb; Service Clb; Variety Show; Ed Lit Mag; Stu Cncl; Var L Crs Cntry; Var L Trk; High Hon Roll; CA Schlrshp Fed; Pre-Med Clb Pres, Secy; Cngrssnl Yth Ldrshp Schlr; Pre-Med.

TOLEDO, GLADYS E; Hamilton Music Acad; Sylmar, CA; (3); Church Yth Grp; Dance Clb; Hosp Aide; Latin Clb; Library Aide; Spanish Clb; Band; Mrchg Band; Variety Show; Gym; UCLA; Ped.

TOLEDO, LUIS A; W C Overfelt HS; San Jose, CA; (3); Church Yth Grp; Cmnty Wkr; Spanish Clb; Teachers Aide.

TOLEDO, MICHELLE; St Joseph HS; Downey, CA; (4); Math Tm; Chorus; Hon Roll; Cal ST Pomona; Pre-Vet Med.

TOLENTINO, AARON; Aragon HS; Honolulu, HI; (2); Teachers Aide; Var Ftbl; Var Wt Lftg; JV Wrstlng; Pres Acad Fit Awd; U Of HI.

TOLENTINO, GRACE H; Deland Joint Union HS; Earlimart, CA; (3); Key Clb; Band; Mrchg Band; Orch; Cit Awd; High Hon Roll; Hon Roll; Ethnic Grp United Filipino Orgnz; Band Awd; San Jose ST; Acctnt.

TOLENTINO, JOSE M; Sweetwater HS; National City, CA; (2); 31/543; Church Yth Grp; Engr.

TOLENTINO, MARSHA L; Etiwanda HS; Alta Loma, CA; (2); Chess Clb; JA; High Hon Roll; Prfct Atten Awd; CSF; Medicine.

TOLENTINO, RUDY; El Camino HS; Daly City, CA; (3); Cmnty Wkr; JV Bsktbl; Comp Sci.

TOLFO, MICHAEL; Poway HS; San Diego, CA; (2); School Play; Yrbk; Tennis; Trk; Hon Roll; Peer Cnslg; CSF; Interact.

TOLKIN, STACY; Cypress HS; Cypress, CA; (4); Cmnty Wkr; Letterman Clb; Pep Clb; Science Clb; Service Clb; Temple Yth Grp; Varsity Clb; Var L Cheerldng; Var L Cheerldng; JV Gym; Bronze-Congrssnl Mdl Hnr 90; Cypress CC; Child Psych.

TOLLEFSON, JULIE; Del Campo HS; Fair Oaks, CA; (2); 3/465; Church Yth Grp; Pep Clb; Drill Tm; Yrbk; Cheerldng; High Hon Roll; Hon Roll; NHS; CA Schlrshp Fed; Crockett Ballet Co; United Spirit Assn Camp/Drill Team Superior Awds; UCD; Comp Tech.

TOLLERTON, ELENA M; Sacramento Adventist Acad; Sacramento, CA; (4); Chorus; Church Choir; Ntl Merit Ltr; Pres Acad Fit Awd; UC Davis; Interior Dsgn.

TOLLEY, DANIELLE R; Leuzinger HS; Lawndale, CA; (2); Office Aide; JV Vllybl; Cit Awd; Hon Roll; Wrtng; USC; Jrnlsm.

TOLNAY, TIMERI; Burbank HS; Burbank, CA; (4); 40/429; Church Yth Grp; Cmnty Wkr; English Clb; Pep Clb; Science Clb; Service Clb; Speech Tm; SADD; Teachers Aide; Chorus; Madrigal Membr; Pres, Sect Natl Charity League; Santa Clara U; English.

TOLNER, KIM; Ramona HS; Ramona, CA; (2); Pres 4-H; Ski Clb; Gym; 4-H Awd; Hon Roll; President Of Ramona 4-H Rancheros; Cival Air Patrol Buck Sergent Flight Commander; Air Force Acad; Aerospace.

TOLONE, BARBARA; Santa Ana Valley HS; Santa Ana, CA; (2); 1/60; Art Clb; Church Yth Grp; Cmnty Wkr; Quiz Bowl; Cit Awd; Gov Hon Prg Awd; High Hon Roll; Kiwanis Awd; CSF; Acad Awds; Dist Sci Fr Brnz Mdl; Gld Mdl Excllnce Over All & Wrd Prcssng; U Of CA Irvine; Med.

TOLOSA, DENNIS J; Don Boslo Technical Inst; Los Angeles, CA; (3); Hon Roll; NHS; Pres Acad Fit Awd; Vrsty Waterpolo Tm Capt; U CA; Bus.

TOLSON, ELINOR Y; La Quinta HS; Fountain Valley, CA; (2); Var Trk; Hon Roll; UCLA.

TOLSON, LEIGH A; Lowell HS; San Francisco, CA; (2); School Play; Trk; Capt Pacific Rowing Clb Novice Wmns Crew; St Chmpnshp Novice Wmns 4 Crew; Placed In All City Shot-Put.

TOM, AIMEE L; Bishop O'dowd HS; Oakland, CA; (3); Cmnty Wkr; Dance Clb; Drama Clb; Chorus; Church Choir; High Hon Roll; CSF.

TOM, ALLEN K; Edison HS; Stockton, CA; (3); Church Yth Grp; Computer Clb; Latin Clb; NFL; Scholastic Bowl; Pres Science Clb; JV Socr; Var Swmmng; High Hon Roll; Hon Roll; UC Davis; Med.

TOM, ALLEN L; Saint Ignatius College Prep; San Francisco, CA; (4); 50/298; Art Clb; Computer Clb; French Clb; Model UN; Science Clb; Teachers Aide; Intrml Bsbl; Intrml Ftbl; Intrml Sftbl; High Hon Roll; CSF Life; U CA Berkeley; Bus Admin.

TOM, BRANDON; Lowell HS; San Francisco, CA; (2); Rep Frsh Cls; Rep Soph Cls; JV Bsktbl; JV Capt Ftbl; Hon Roll; Goldn St Exam Alg Hnrs; UC Berkeley; Med.

TOM, DAVID; Gretchen Whitney HS; Cerritos, CA; (3); Art Clb; Cmnty Wkr; Drama Clb; French Clb; Hosp Aide; Sec JA; Key Clb; Latin Clb; Spanish Clb; Capt Var Socr; Var Water Polo Tm; West Point; Bio.

TOM, JENNIFER L; Nogales HS; W Covina, CA; (2); 18/650; Science Clb; Chorus; Rptr Yrbk; JV Tennis; High Hon Roll; Peer Hlpr; CA Schlrshp Fed; NISA; Bus.

TOM, LISA; University HS; Los Angeles, CA; (2); JV Sftbl; JV Vllybl; Cit Awd; Hon Roll; Prfct Atten Awd; U S Jewish War Vetrns Outstndng Srvce Awd; 1st Pl Prz Sunshine Games Vlybl; UC Davis; Vet Me D.

TOM, LUCRECE G; Abraham Lincoln HS; San Francisco, CA; (2); Lbrn Library Aide; CSF; Golden St Awd Alb, Hnrs; U CA-SAN Francisco; Phrmcy.

TOM, MICHAEL R; Milpitas HS; Milpitas, CA; (1); Math Tm; Hon Roll; Chinese Clb; Jr Statesmen Of Amer; Elec Engrng.

TOM, SABRINA M; Lowell HS; San Francisco, CA; (3); Hosp Aide; VP Intnl Clb; NFL; Office Aide; Treas Science Clb; Ntl Merit Ltr; St Schlr; Med Explr Post 496 Photo; Chinese Clb Pblcty Mgr; Shield & L Hnr Soc.

TOM, SUSAN K; Skyline HS; Oakland, CA; (2); Hosp Aide; Intnl Clb; JA; Library Aide; Math Clb; Math Tm; Office Aide; Vllybl; Cit Awd; Hon Roll; Asian Stu Union; Princeton U; Med.

TOM, TRAVIS J; Ramona HS; Riverside, CA; (3); 46/410; Boy Scts; Church Yth Grp; French Clb; Tennis; Hon Roll; Dentistry.

TOM, WYNNYEE; Lowell HS; San Francisco, CA; (2); Church Yth Grp; Cmnty Wkr; FCA; GAA; SADD; Bsktbl; Cit Awd; High Hon Roll; Pres Acad Fit Awd; St Moritz Ice Sktng Clb Inc; Stanford; Graphic Arts.

TOMAS, MAYRA E; Liuzinger HS; Hawthorne, CA; (3); VP Spanish Clb; Cit Awd; Prfct Atten Awd; Dominquez Hills; Dental.

TOMASELLI, MIKAL R; Burlingame HS; Sa Mateo, CA; (3); Cmnty Wkr; Drama Clb; Office Aide; School Play; Stage Crew; Socr; Theater Tech Dir; Stagecrft Awd Excllnc; Film.

TOMASJ, ANDREW B; Redlands HS; Loma Linda, CA; (2); Ski Clb.

TOMASZEWSKI, MISHELLE L; William S Hart HS; Newhall, CA; (3); Church Yth Grp; Girl Scts; BYU HI; Marine Bio.

TOMCZYK, CHRISTINA M; St Josephs HS; Lakewood, CA; (2); Church Yth Grp; Drama Clb; GAA; Girl Scts; Ski Clb; JV Bsktbl; Hon Roll; Cmnty Svc; CCD Tchrs Aid; Plsh Flk Dnc Grp-Trng Europe; U Of Irvine; Mdcl Fld.

TOMCZYK, JILL C; Santa Teresa HS; San Jose, CA; (3); Pres Church Yth Grp; GAA; Pep Clb; Spanish Clb; Var Crs Cntry; Var Socr; Var Trk; JV Vllybl; Hon Roll; Jr NHS; CSF; CA Poly San Luis Obispo; Arch.

TOMEI, SCOTT J; Arroyo Grande HS; Arroyo Grande, CA; (4); Letterman Clb; Varsity Clb; Var L Bsbl; L Ftbl; JV Wrstlng; High Hon Roll; Hon Roll; Pres Acad Fit Awd; Ofcr Yth Gvrnmnt Day 89-90; Soc Stdy Hnr 87-88; Weight Lftng; UCSB; Bus Eco.

TOMEO, ADAM; Saint Paul HS; Brea, CA; (3); 11/300; Hosp Aide; NFL; Speech Tm; Ed Nwsp; Var L Ftbl; Var L Trk; Var Wt Lftg; High Hon Roll; NHS; Ntl Merit Ltr; CSF; 1st Tm All Angeles Leag Shotput; Med.

TOMEY, HEATHER M; Mayfair HS; Bellflower, CA; (1); Church Yth Grp; JV Sftbl; JV Vllybl; Hon Roll.

TOMICH, JENNIFER; Durham HS; Chico, CA; (4); 5/68; Drama Clb; Key Clb; Spanish Clb; SADD; Band; School Play; Stage Crew; Rptr Yrbk; Rep Sr Cls; JV Trk; Hrsbck Rdng; Amer Lgn Axlry Schlrshp; GATE; UC Davis; Life Sci.

TOMIDY, MARK; Bishop Amat HS; Baldwin Park, CA; (4); 36/400; Cmnty Wkr; Treas Intnl Clb; Office Aide; Speech Tm; Treas Sr Cls; Hon Roll; CA Schlrshp Fed; Adopt-A-Grandparent Vlntr; Special Olympics Vlntr; Loyola Marymount U; Psych.

TOMINNA, TIMMOTHY; Valhalla HS; El Cajon, CA; (4); 13/435; Church Yth Grp; Drama Clb; Quiz Bowl; Scholastic Bowl; SADD; Thesps; School Play; Trk; High Hon Roll; Pres Acad Fit Awd; Amnesty Intl Pres; Little League Coach; UCSD; Pre Med.

TOMITA, EDDIE K; Glendale Adventist Acad; West Covina, CA; (3); Church Yth Grp; Chorus; Orch; NHS.

TOMKIEL, KIMBERLI L; Bolsa Grande HS; Garden Grove, CA; (1); Drama Clb; Drill Tm; Cit Awd.

TOMMERAASON, JILL; Woodland HS; Woodland, CA; (4); 3/400; Am Leg Aux Girls St; Sec Treas Soph Cls; Sec Treas Jr Cls; Rep Stu Cncl; JV Var Bsktbl; JV Capt Vllybl; Pres NHS; Pres Acad Fit Awd; CSF Lf, Secy; Robt C Byrd Hnrs Schlr St CA; U Of CA San Diego.

TOMOOKA, BRIAN; Ernest Righetti HS; Santa Maria, CA; (3); 14/370; Var Bsbl; Var Golf; Cit Awd; Hon Roll; CSF.

TOMOOKA, CHRISTIAN; Bishop Amat Mem HS; Alta Loma, CA; (4); 25/400; VP Frsh Cls; VP Soph Cls; Var Capt Socr; Var Trk; High Hon Roll; Black Belt Karate; Bio Engrg.

TOMOOKA, JULIE; Ernest Righetti HS; Santa Maria, CA; (2); 7/500; JV Golf; JV Tennis; Cit Awd; Hon Roll; Prfct Atten Awd; CSF.

TOMPKINS, MIKE R; Mira Mesa HS; San Diego, CA; (3); Cmnty Wkr; Variety Show; Pres Jr Cls; Ftbl; Trk; Hmecmng Chrmn; Head Coach Pwdr Puff Ftbl; Airband Chrmn; CO ST U.

TOMPKINS, STEPHEN P; Torrey Pines HS; Solana Bch, CA; (2); Boy Scts; Chess Clb; Church Yth Grp; Cmnty Wkr; Mgr Bsktbl; Mgr(s); Yth Sccr Tm Asstnt Coach; Nvy Plt.

TOMPKINS, YEVETTE; Los Angeles Ctr For Enriched Studies; Los Angeles, CA; (3); Teachers Aide; School Musical; School Play; Cit Awd; Hon Roll; CSF; Young Black Schlrs; Acctng.

TOMSIK, KATHRYN; J H Francis Polytechnic HS; North Hollywood, CA; (3); Am Leg Aux Girls St; GAA; SADD; Band; Church Choir; Sec Stu Cncl; JV Bsktbl; Var Trk; JV Capt Vllybl; Hon Roll; Piano; Elem Educ.

TON, ALLAN K L; Phillip And Sala Burton Acadmc HS; San Francisco, CA; (2); Band; High Hon Roll; Mandarin Clb; Wrld Of Finance Pgm; Art; Fshn Dsgn.

TON, CHANTHAN; Hoover HS; Fresno, CA; (3); #275 In Class; Debate Tm; Church Choir; School Musical; Nwsp; Cit Awd; Hon Roll; Ntl Merit Ltr; Prfct Atten Awd; Top 5 Pct Awd; BSU Clb; CSU Fresno; ESL Tchr.

TON, QUY X; Bolsa Grande HS; Fullerton, CA; (3); Chess Clb; Spanish Clb; Off Frsh Cls; Off Soph Cls; Rep Jr Cls; Var JV Bsktbl; Var JV Vllybl; Hon Roll; JV & Vrsty Badminton; Frshmn, Soph, & Jr Cncl; Cal Long Beach; Physcn.

TON, SAMMY; Galleo HS; San Francisco, CA; (4); Dance Clb; French Clb; Quiz Bowl; Off Frsh Cls; Off Soph Cls; Off Jr Cls; Off Sr Cls; Hotl Mgmt.

TON, TIEN; Westminster HS; Orange, CA; (4); 7/400; Treas French Clb; Key Clb; Off Frsh Cls; Off Soph Cls; Off Jr Cls; Off Sr Cls; Tennis; High Hon Roll; Hon Roll; NHS; Bank Amer Math Cert Wnnr; Stu Mnth Dec 89; Athlte Mnth Oct 89; UC Irvine.

TON, TUAN N; Cordova SR HS; Rancho Cordova, CA; (3); 20/478; Key Clb; Model UN; Spanish Clb; Tennis; Cit Awd; High Hon Roll; Jr NHS; Top Wrld Cultrs Std; U Of CA Davis; Med.

TON, VAN; Hoover HS; San Diego, CA; (2); Office Aide; Cit Awd; High Hon Roll; Hon Roll; NHS; Cert Mrt; Cert Recgntn; Outstndng Schlstc Achvt Awd; Art.

TONASUT, ANDREA V; San Fernando Valley Acad; Woodland Hills, CA; (2); 1/23; Office Aide; Teachers Aide; Acpl Chr; School Musical; Treas Frsh Cls; Rep Soph Cls; High Hon Roll; Hon Roll; Prfct Atten Awd; UCLA; Med.

TONEGATO, BRIAN J; Mills HS; Burlingame, CA; (3); High Hon Roll; Hon Roll; Elect.

TONER, HEATHER C; Oak Ridge HS; El Dorado Hills, CA; (1); Var L Swmmng; Hon Roll; Jr NHS; Pres Acad Fit Awd.

TONER, MATTHEW C; Rim Of The World HS; Crestline, CA; (1); Boy Scts; Debate Tm; Spanish Clb; Bsktbl; Ftbl; Hon Roll; High Hnrs Goldn St Exam.

TONEY, JUSTIN D; St Ignatius College Prep; San Rafael, CA; (2); Service Clb; JV Bsktbl; JV Crs Cntry; JV Swmmng; Hon Roll; Pres Acad Fit Awd; CA Schlrshp Fed; Bus.

TONEY, TRENA L; Vallejo HS; Vallejo, CA; (4); 19/450; Church Yth Grp; French Clb; SADD; Church Choir; School Play; Off Frsh Cls; Hon Roll; Ed Yrbk; Gspl Choir; BSU; CSF; Sacramento ST U; Bus Admin.

TONEY, TRISHA J; Enterprise HS; Redding, CA; (4); 2/350; Mu Alpha Theta; Ski Clb; Chorus; Var L Diving; Gym; High Hon Roll; Pres Acad Fit Awd; Pres Schlr; Sal; Chrch Yth Grp; Tandy Technlgy Schlr; CSF; US Air Force Math/Sci Awd; U Of CA Davis; Elec Engrng.

TONG, DIEM; Norte Vista HS; Riverside, CA; (3); Computer Clb; FBLA; JA; Math Tm; Science Clb; Swmmng; Tennis; Hon Roll; NHS; Prfct Atten Awd; RCC; Comp Pgmr.

TONG, EUGENE Y; Milpitas HS; Milpitas, CA; (1); Hon Roll; Chinese Club; Sci Fiction Club VP.

TONG, HUY T; San Jose High Acad; San Jose, CA; (4); Spanish Clb; Hon Roll; JETS Awd; Lion Awd; San Jose ST U; Elec Engr.

TONG, KHANH; La Quinta HS; Westminster, CA; (1); 2/344; Key Clb; Pep Clb; Tennis; Hon Roll; NHS; Ntl Merit Schol; Prfct Atten Awd; Rotary Awd; Stanford; Med.

TONG, LI-LI; Santa Monica HS; Santa Monica, CA; (2); Treas Art Clb; French Clb; Math Clb; Math Tm; High Hon Roll; Hon Roll; UCLA; Biolgcl Sci.

TONG, MINH T; Valley HS; Santa Ana, CA; (3); High Hon Roll; CSF; Partnrs Clb; UC Irvine.

TONG, NGAN W; George Washington HS; San Francisco, CA; (3); High Hon Roll; Hon Roll; Accntng.

TONG, PHONG HUY; Richard Gahr HS; Cerritos, CA; (2); Teachers Aide; Bsktbl; Crs Cntry; Socr; Swmmng; Trk; Cit Awd; Aerospace Engr.

TONG, THUY; Saddle Back HS; Santa Ana, CA; (4); 51/520; Drama Clb; English Clb; French Clb; Band; Mrchg Band; School Play; VP Frsh Cls; Treas Soph Cls; Treas Jr Cls; Var JV Tennis; Lib Stds.

TONG, TOBY M Y; Fairfax HS; Fresno, CA; (3); Church Yth Grp; Chorus; Church Choir; Chld Psych.

TONG, TRACY M; Dublin HS; Dublin, CA; (3); 19/158; Teachers Aide; Color Guard; Rptr Yrbk; Hon Roll; Discpline Cmmtte; Acad Boosters Cnsl; CSF; Film Stds.

TONG, TRICIA S; South San Francisco HS; South San Francis, CA; (3); 2/300; Church Yth Grp; Treas Stu Cncl; Mgr(s); Var Tennis; High Hon Roll; Sal; Var Badmntn; Society Of Wmn Engr; Prncpls Awd.

TONG, TUNG; Carlsbad HS; Carlsbad, CA; (3); Socr; Vllybl; Hon Roll; Math Clb,Math Tm; Sci Clb; Engr.

TONG, WINNIE; Tennyson HS; Hayward, CA; (2); 24/250; Debate Tm; French Clb; VP Frsh Cls; Var Pom Pon; Hon Roll; Var Badminton; Golden St Exam Alg Hnrs; Asian Clb; Peer Cnslng; CA Schlrshp Fed; Close-Up; UC Santa Barbara; Sci.

TONINI, TIMOTHY D; Golden West HS; Visalia, CA; (2); 1/420; Church Yth Grp; German Clb; VP Intnl Clb; Math Clb; Math Tm; Off Science Clb; Nwsp; Pres Soph Cls; JV Swmmng; High Hon Roll; JR Vrsty Water Polo; Peer Hlprs; CSF; Stanford; Pre Med.

TONNU, DANH C; San Gorgonio HS; Highland, CA; (3); #1 In Class; French Clb; Intnl Clb; Key Clb; Powder Puff Ftbl; JV Tennis; Cit Awd; NHS; CA Schltc Fed; Advncd Curr Explrtn; U CA Los Angeles; Bus.

TONSETH, CHRISTINA; Silver Valley HS; Newberry Spgs, CA; (3); Chorus; School Play; Yrbk; High Hon Roll; Hon Roll; Botany, Imunology, Genetics.

TONSICH, JO ANN M; St Joseph HS; Cerritos, CA; (3); 45/180; Church Yth Grp; SADD; Phtg Rptr Nwsp; Hon Roll; Speech Thrpy.

TOOLE, DIERDRE A; Gompers Secondary HS; San Diego, CA; (2); 26/150; Girl Scts; Drill Tm; Vllybl; Hon Roll; CSF; Oceanography Club; Mock Trial; UC Berkeley.

TOOLE, JASON C; South San Francisco HS; South San Francis, CA; (2); Drama Clb; Band; School Musical; School Play; MESA Club; Italian Club; CSF; UC Davis; Vet Med.

TOOLEY, CHRISTINA M; Upper Lake Union HS; Nice, CA; (3); French Clb; Office Aide; Spanish Clb; Teachers Aide; Bsktbl; Vllybl; Hon Roll; Native Amer Clb Secy Publicist 88-90; Psych.

TOOMEY, CHRISTINE M; Immaculate Heart HS; Altadena, CA; (3); 8/112; GAA; Pres Service Clb; Pres Stu Cncl; JV Var Vllybl; High Hon Roll; NEDT Awd; CSF; Harvard Alumni Assn Bk Awd; Stanford; Psych.

TOOMEY, HEATHER E; University HS; Irvine, CA; (2); Cmnty Wkr; GAA; Girl Scts; Var Bsbl; Natl Chrty Leag.

TOOMMALY, POHN; El Cerrito HS; Richmond, CA; (4); Acpl Chr; Var Socr; UC Davis; Music.

TOON, MALCOLM M; Arcata HS; Arcata, CA; (1); Computer Clb; Wt Lftg; Ply Gtr; Comp Prgrmmr; Comp Prgrmng.

TOORANI, BEHZAD; Milpitas HS; El Toro, CA; (4); VP Pres JA; Ice Hcky; Socr; Swmmng; High Hon Roll; Hon Roll; Prfct Atten Awd; U Of Calif Irvine; Med School.

TOOVEY, KELLY L; Mt Whitney HS; Visalia, CA; (2); Var L Bsktbl; Var L Sftbl; JV Capt Vllybl; Hon Roll.

TOPACIO, PAMELA C; Saint Joseph HS; Cerritos, CA; (3); Cmnty Wkr; Hosp Aide; Pep Clb; Spanish Clb; SADD; Teachers Aide; Drill Tm; High Hon Roll; Hon Roll; St Finalist Natl Teenage Pageant; CA St Finalist Amer Coed Pageants; 1st Pl Runne88, 89, 90 Piano Rec.

TOPALIAN, JEANNINE; Ferrahian HS; Van Nuys, CA; (2); Sec Frsh Cls; Treas Stu Cncl; U CA-SANTA Barbara; Lawyer.

TOPALIAN, TALINE; Ribet Acad; Tujunga, CA; (2); 2/23; Aud/Vis; Cmnty Wkr; Drama Clb; Hosp Aide; Office Aide; Teachers Aide; School Play; Cheerldng; Sftbl; Cit Awd; UCLA; Psycht.

TOPALOFF, JINELL; Granada Hills HS; Northridge, CA; (3); Chorus; Drill Tm; Prfct Atten Awd; CA ST U Northridge.

TOPDJIAN, KEVORK; Holy Martyrs HS; Canoga Park, CA; (2); Boy Scts; Band; School Play; Cit Awd; Hon Roll; Pres Schlr; Ntl Leadership & Sci Awds; Chiropractic Med.

TOPETE, CYNTHIA E; Sacred Heart Of Mary HS; Los Angeles, CA; (3); 8/80; Aud/Vis; GAA; Library Aide; Teachers Aide; School Musical; Stage Crew; Cit Awd; High Hon Roll; Hon Roll; NHS; Cum Laude Assoc & Buther Butler Soc; Natl Lang Clb; Litrgcl Clb; UC Riverside; Bus Admin.

TOPETE, LUIS; Alisal HS; Salinas, CA; (4); French Clb; Sec Science Clb; Var Tennis; High Hon Roll; Hon Roll; Pres Acad Fit Awd; MECHA-VP; CSF; U CA-LOS Angeles; Aerosp Engr.

TOPETE, MARIA; Skyline HS; Oakland, CA; (2); Ed Nwsp; Hon Roll; Latino Clb; Engr.

TOPETE, ROSALBA; El Rancho HS; Pico Rivera, CA; (2); FTA; Library Aide; Chorus; Crs Cntry; Trk; Hon Roll; Prfct Atten Awd.

TOPETE, VERONICA Y; St Joseph HS; Cypress, CA; (3); Church Yth Grp; Cmnty Wkr; Spanish Clb; SADD; Powder Puff Ftbl; Hon Roll; Prfct Atten Awd; College.

TOPETE, VICTOR J; Foothill SR HS; Sacramento, CA; (2); Hon Roll; Engl Mrt Awd 89; UC San Diego; Elec Engrng.

TORBATI, SHABNAM; El Camino Real HS; Woodland Hills, CA; (3); Math Clb; SADD; Temple Yth Grp; High Hon Roll; Hon Roll; Hands Across Campus Club; ESL Club; JSA Club; Essay Awd Kings Wks Fstvl; Gldn St Exam Hnr Lvl; UCLA; Med.

TORCHIA, SAMUEL G; West HS; Bakersfield, CA; (2); Debate Tm; NFL; Ski Clb; Spanish Clb; Band; Mrchg Band; School Musical; JV Crs Cntry; Intrml Mgr Ftbl; JV Socr; Hnrs Gldn St Exm; Engrng.

TORGESON, JOHN E; Granada Hills HS; Northridge, CA; (2); Church Yth Grp; JV Bsbl; JV Ftbl.

TORIBIO, BRENDA LYNN Q; Coachella Valley HS; Thermal, CA; (3); #1 In Class; VP FBLA; Sec FHA; Varsity Clb; Var Tennis; Var Trk; Cit Awd; High Hon Roll; Pursuit Of Awrnss Through Coll Exprnc Pres; Stu Yr Acctng, US Hstry, Spnsh,Chem & Engl; Sci Fair 2nd; Intl Bus.

TORIGIANI, BREE M.; Shafter HS; Buttonwillow, CA; (4); Church Yth Grp; 4-H; Key Clb; Pep Clb; Ski Clb; Teachers Aide; Sec Stu Cncl; Cheerldng; 4-H Awd; Hon Roll; Bakersfield JC; Psych.

TORINO, JASMIN P; Santa Clara HS; Santa Clara, CA; (2); Cmnty Wkr; Spanish Clb; Spanish NHS; CSF Clb; UCLA; Pedtrcn.

TORIO, CELESTE MARIE; Lowell HS; San Francisco, CA; (3); Intnl Clb; Math Clb; Office Aide; Science Clb; SADD; Teachers Aide; School Play; Sec Soph Cls; Sec Jr Cls; High Hon Roll; Spellng Bee Gld Mdl MESA; Advnce Plcmnt Cls; UC Berkeley.

TORIO, SUSAN FABIA; Mt Carmel HS; San Diego, CA; (2); Church Yth Grp; VP Frsh Cls; Rep Stu Cncl; Cit Awd; Hon Roll; Prfct Atten Awd; Pres Acad Fit Awd; Hnrs Geomtry Gldn St Exm; UCLA; Engrng.

TORIZ, ROCIO D; Sweetwater HS; National City, CA; (3); 21/481; Band; Yrbk; Var JV Bsktbl; Var JV Dnfth Awd; High Hon Roll; Hon Roll; Prfct Atten Awd; Church Yth Grp; FTA; ASB Atty General; Future Leaders Amer; Law.

TORNBERG, TINA NICOLE; Central Union HS; El Centro, CA; (4); 16/380; Library Aide; Office Aide; Flag Corp; Mrchg Band; High Hon Roll; Grad Top 20; Imperial Valley Coll; Bus.

TORNEROS, GRACE; Valhalla HS; El Cajon, CA; (3); 86/450; Band; Drm Mjr(t); Flag Corp; Mrchg Band; Outstndng Mem Awd Band; Calpoly San Luis Obispo; Arch.

TORNOW, CHRIS A; Lutheran HS Of Orange County; Santa Ana, CA; (3); Scholastic Bowl; Band; Church Choir; Pep Band; Rep Sr Cls; Var Tennis; Hon Roll; U S Acad Decathln; Politics.

TORO, MICHELLE M; River City HS; W Sacramento, CA; (3); 54/204; Rep Soph Cls; Hist Stu Cncl; Capt Var Bsktbl; JV Sftbl; Var Tennis; Hon Roll; MESA; PEER; Civil Engrng.

TOROS, YEZEG H; Saint Joseph HS; Santa Maria, CA; (3); Aud/Vis; Capt Church Yth Grp; Letterman Clb; SADD; Varsity Clb; Nwsp; Yrbk; JV Bsbl; Var L Tennis; Cal Poly; Bus.

TOROSS, NANCY; Mission Viejo HS; Mission Viejo, CA; (3); Dance Clb; Sec French Clb; Key Clb; Pep Clb; Capt Color Guard; Orch; Var Trk; Pres Acad Fit Awd; Girls League Clb, Jr Cls Rep, Pblcty Chrmn; Outstnd French Stu Of Yr 88-89; Music Awd; Advrtsng.

TOROSYAN, ANDRANIK A; Herbert Hoover HS; Glendale, CA; (3); Key Clb; Spanish Clb; Var Bsktbl; Pres Acad Fit Awd; Verdugo Bus Wk; Hstry Awd 88; Accntng.

TORRE, JOSETTA R; North Salinas HS; Salinas, CA; (2); Spanish Clb; Teachers Aide; Var Cheerldng; JV Trk; Hon Roll; Prfct Atten Awd; Stu Of Yr 90; Dnc & Twirl Team Stu Of Yr 90; Navy Cadet Pgm 88-89; U Of Santa Barbara; Jrnlsm.

TORRE, MONICA M; San Gabriel Mission HS; Covina, CA; (3); 1/125; Am Leg Aux Girls St; Church Yth Grp; FBLA; Spanish Clb; Var Cheerldng; High Hon Roll; Jr NHS; NHS; Prfct Atten Awd; Medallion Plq Wnnr Scl Sci 90; 1st Prz Am Assoc Tchrs Spnsh, Portuguese 88; 3rd Skirball Essay Cont 89; USC; Law.

TORREBLANCA, ESMERALDA; Orosi HS; Orosi, CA; (3); 49/177; Quiz Bowl; Spanish Clb; Teachers Aide; Yrbk; Hon Roll; Prfct Atten Awd; COS.

TORREBLANCA, JOSE; Downey HS; Downey, CA; (1); Key Clb; Var Tennis; Kiwanis Awd; CSF Awd; Med.

TORRENCE, ANGIE MAY; Mira Mesa HS; San Diego, CA; (4); 191/748; Church Yth Grp; Hosp Aide; Teachers Aide; Church Choir; Yrbk; Var JV Mgr(s); Mgr Var Sftbl; Mgr JV Vllybl; Hon Roll; Pres Acad Fit Awd; Past Hnrd Queen PHQ; Past Sweetheart, San Diego Chptr Order Of De Molay; Vp Church Yth Cncl; UCSD; Med.

TORRENCE, LATEEFAH M; Presentation HS; San Jose, CA; (4); Off Drama Clb; NFL; Spanish Clb; Chorus; Rep Soph Cls; Hon Roll; Opt Clb Awd; Peer Mnstry; Natl Achvt Smi-Fnlst; Cmnctns.

TORRENTE, JOTHELYN R; Phillip & Sala Burton Academic HS; San Francisco, CA; (2); Teachers Aide; Chorus; Cit Awd; High Hon Roll; Law.

TORRENTE, MARIA C; Pittsburg HS; Pittsburg, CA; (2); Church Yth Grp; SADD; Italian Clb.

TORRES, ABRAHAM; Kingsburg HS; Kingsburg, CA; (3); Socr; Fresno City; Arch.

TORRES, ANITA; Independence HS; San Jose, CA; (3); Cmnty Wkr; German Clb; Rptr Nwsp; Lit Mag; Stu Cncl; JV Bsktbl; JV Sftbl; Var Tennis; Reed Coll; Engl.

TORRES, ANNA M; East Union HS; Lathrop, CA; (3); Office Aide; SADD; Teachers Aide; Prfct Atten Awd; Educ.

TORRES, BERNADETTE M; King-Drew Medical Magnet HS; Carson, CA; (2); Rep Cmnty Wkr; Drama Clb; Sec FTA; Pep Clb; VP Science Clb; SADD; Teachers Aide; Chorus; Co-Capt Drill Tm; Stage Crew; Help With Cmnty & The Homeless; Principals Awd; LMU; Pre-Med.

TORRES, BETTIE; Eisenhower HS; Rialto, CA; (3); Office Aide; Flag Corp; Cheerldng; Var Swmmng; Hon Roll; Chrldng Sprt Awd; Ofc Oprtns Awd; Frnch II & Athtc Schlr Awds; Bus Mgmt.

TORRES, BOBBY; Sanger HS; Sanger, CA; (2); JV Var Bsbl; JV Capt Ftbl; Socr; Wt Lftg; Wrstlng; Fresno ST; Bus.

TORRES, BRITA M; John Marshall Fundamental HS; Pasadena, CA; (3); Church Yth Grp; Cmnty Wkr; Key Clb; Office Aide; Teachers Aide; Rptr Nwsp; Stu Cncl; JV Var Tennis; High Hon Roll; Hon Roll; Engl Lit.

TORRES, CARLOTTA R; San Benito HS; Hollister, CA; (2); Teachers Aide; Hon Roll; Part-Time Job; Spare Time Wrk On Needle Pt, Crochet; Partnership Pgm; Stanford; Pre-Med.

TORRES, CATRINA; Temple City HS; Temple City, CA; (3); Church Yth Grp; Dance Clb; Pep Clb; Spanish Clb; Chorus; Church Choir; School Musical; School Play; Variety Show; Select Singing Grp; Engl.

TORRES, CESAR; Roosevelt HS; Los Angeles, CA; (4); Hnr Stu E Aurora HS; E Los Angeles Coll; Archtct.

TORRES, CHARLIE M; Buena Park HS; Fullerton, CA; (1); 120/458; Intrml Tennis; Hon Roll; Prfct Atten Awd; Dir.

TORRES, CHRIS R; Santa Cruz HS; Santa Cruz, CA; (3); Hon Roll; Med Sci.

TORRES, CONNIE M; Riverside Poly HS; Riverside, CA; (2); Church Yth Grp; Church Choir.

TORRES, DANIEL; James Lick HS; San Jose, CA; (3); Intnl Clb; Library Aide; Math Clb; Math Tm; Tennis; Trk; Hon Roll; School Site Councel; Summer HS Apprenticeship Res Prgrm For NASA; V-P Of Bibliophile Society; Stanford; Business.

TORRES, DAVID; Orangewood A Acad; Fountain Valley, CA; (2); Church Yth Grp; Computer Clb; Drama Clb; Chorus; Variety Show; Treas Frsh Cls; Off Soph Cls; Off Jr Cls; Stu Cncl; NHS; Walla Walla Coll; Mech Engrng.

TORRES, EDWARD; North Monterey County HS; Salinas, CA; (1); Boy Scts; Chess Clb; Church Yth Grp; Dance Clb; Hosp Aide; ROTC; SADD; Bsktbl; Fld Hcky; Ftbl; Plc Offcr.

TORRES, ELIZABETH; Ramona Convent HS; Alhambra, CA; (3); GAA; JV Bsktbl; Hispanic Soc Club; Fine Arts Club; UCLA; Bus Admin.

TORRES, ELIZABETH A; Mountain View HS; Mountain View, CA; (4); Church Yth Grp; Treas Cmnty Wkr; Dance Clb; Office Aide; Variety Show; Treas Sr Cls; Hon Roll; CSF; Cal Poly San Luis Obspo; Bus Ad.

TORRES, ERICA; Valley View HS; Moreno Valley, CA; (1); Off Frsh Cls; Bsktbl; Sftbl; CIF Awd Sftbl; Hnr Rl; Law Enfrcmnt.

TORRES, ERICA ARAIZA; Rosemead HS; San Gabriel, CA; (2); JV Tennis; Hon Roll; U Of CA; Bus.

TORRES, FREDERICK C; Tustin HS; Tustin, CA; (2); Varsity Clb; Ftbl; Wt Lftg; Wrstlng; High Hon Roll; Hon Roll; CA Schlrshp Fed Member; Top 25 Stus Of Class; Congrsnl Yth Ldrshp Cncl; San Diego St U; Bus.

TORRES, GABRIEL; Chaffey HS; Ontario, CA; (3); Spanish Clb; Teachers Aide; Ftbl; Powder Puff Ftbl; Hon Roll; Wrkng Part Time Brunswick Upland Bowl; Scratch Bwlng League Avrg 176.

TORRES, GENEVIEVE A; St Patrick/St Vincent HS; Vallejo, CA; (1); Bsktbl; Hon Roll.

TORRES, IGNACIO; Don Bosco Technical Inst; Alhambra, CA; (3); JV Crs Cntry; Var Trk; Hon Roll; NHS; Prfct Atten Awd; Cngrssnl Yth Ldrshp Cncl; People To People Yth Sci Exchng; CA Plytechncl U; Elect Engr.

TORRES, IMELDA; Chula Vista HS; Chula Vista, CA; (1); Church Yth Grp; Sec Chorus; Church Choir; Treas Cheerldng; Mgr Ftbl; Mgr(s); Mgr Socr; Mgr Trk; JV Vllybl; UCSD Upward Bound Pgm; UC San Diego; Marine Bio.

TORRES, IRENE ELIZABETH; Independence HS; San Jose, CA; (2); 179/934; Cmnty Wkr; Office Aide; Teachers Aide; Orch; Var Swmmng; Var Trk; Intrml Wt Lftg; Hon Roll; Latin Stu Acad Achvt Awd; U Of CA Davis; Vet Med.

TORRES, ISRAEL A; Tustin HS; Tustin, CA; (2); Chess Clb; Band; Jazz Band; Mrchg Band; Orch; Pep Band; Trk; Sci.

TORRES, JACQUELYNE; St Joseph HS; South Gate, CA; (4); 1/173; Cmnty Wkr; Drama Clb; Spanish Clb; Ed Yrbk; High Hon Roll; NHS; NEDT Awd; Pres Acad Fit Awd; Val; Robert C Byrd Hnrs Scholar; Latin Bus Fndtn Scholar; Georgetown U; Lawyer.

TORRES, JAZMIN; Arcadia HS; Arcadia, CA; (3); Church Yth Grp; Cmnty Wkr; Dance Clb; Pep Clb; Ski Clb; Spanish Clb; Variety Show; Bsktbl; Cheerldng; Gym; U CA San Diego; Law.

TORRES, JESUS; Milor HS; Rialto, CA; (2); 11/200; Prfct Atten Awd; Cnslng.

TORRES, JESUS; Rio Mesa HS; Oxnard, CA; (3); Yrbk; JV Bsbl; Intrml Ftbl; Cal ST Northridge; Engr.

TORRES, JESUS A; Sierra Vista HS; Baldwin Park, CA; (3); Band; Mst Imprvd Plyr Band 88-89.

TORRES, KIM; Francis Polytechnical HS; Arleta, CA; (4); Computer Clb; Sec FFA; Service Clb; Teachers Aide; Band; Chorus; Orch; JV Bsktbl; JV Var Sftbl; JV Vllybl; CSUN; Psych.

TORRES, KRIS MICELLE; Pasadena HS; Pasadena, CA; (2); Var Cheerldng; Hon Roll; Asian Amer Club; Csf; Med.

TORRES, LENNARD F; Lowell HS; San Francisco, CA; (2); 4-H; Science Clb; High Hon Roll; Natl JR Tennis League Trnmnts; USC; RN.

TORRES, LILIA; Sunset HS; Hayward, CA; (1); Hon Roll; Migrant Ed Pgm; Smmr Inst Ldrshp & Comp Awakeness Stanford U; Yth Conf Sacramento ST U; San Diego ST; Jrnlsm.

TORRES, MARCILENA C; Coalinga HS; Huron, CA; (4); Teachers Aide; Band; Mrchg Band; Pep Band; Hon Roll; Bk Amer Achvt Awd-Music; CA ST U Fresno; Tchr.

TORRES JR, MARCOS; Lompoc HS; Lompoc, CA; (2); L Var Crs Cntry; L Var Trk; Cal Poly San Luis Obispo; Arch.

TORRES, MARCY V; St Marys HS; Stockton, CA; (2); Socr; Vllybl; Hon Roll; Grls Cabint.

TORRES, MARIA; Indio HS; Indio, CA; (3); 49/446; Church Yth Grp; Cmnty Wkr; NFL; Spanish Clb; Speech Tm; JV Cheerldng; Var Gym; Rotary Awd; JSA Clb; Early Outreach Prgm; Cal-St San Bernardino Study Prgm; UC Riverside; Bus Admin.

TORRES, MARTHA; Tracy Joint Union HS; Tracy, CA; (2); 42/483; SADD; High Hon Roll; Hon Roll; Teaching.

TORRES, MARY GRACE T; Bonita HS; La Verne, CA; (2); Church Yth Grp; GAA; SADD; Score Keeper; JV Var Vllybl; Cit Awd; Hon Roll; Pres Acad Fit Awd; Badminton; Humanities On Campus; UC Riverside; Psych.

TORRES, MATEO M; Independence HS; San Jose, CA; (2); Church Yth Grp; Teachers Aide; Intrml Vllybl; Cit Awd; High Hon Roll; Hon Roll; U & Coll Opprtnty Soph Of Yr; Sci.

TORRES, MIA; Kelseyville HS; Petaluma, CA; (4); Cmnty Wkr; 4-H; German Clb; JA; Office Aide; SADD; Sec Frsh Cls; Rep Sr Cls; Rep Stu Cncl; Bsktbl; Stu Exchng/Austria; CA ST U-Chico; Bio.

TORRES, MONICA; South Tahoe HS; South Lake Tahoe, CA; (3); Dance Clb; Latin Clb; Science Clb; Spanish Clb; Nwsp; High Hon Roll; Comp.

TORRES, NATALIE C; John Glenn HS; Norwalk, CA; (3); 50/400; Am Leg Aux Girls St; German Clb; Q&S; Ed Nwsp; Cit Awd; High Hon Roll; NEDT Awd; CCNMA Journ Wkshp CSUN; LA Cty Outdr Sci Schls Sci Camp Cabin Ldr; U S CA; Ed.

TORRES, PATRICIA; Bishop Amat HS; West Covina, CA; (4); 5/398; Cmnty Wkr; Debate Tm; NFL; Speech Tm; School Play; Stu Cncl; High Hon Roll; NHS; Ntl Merit Ltr; Hnrs Soc, CA Schlrshp Pres; Harvard Bk Awd; Stu Senate; Lawyer.

TORRES, RACHEL R; Center HS; North Highlands, CA; (2); Red Cross Aide; High Hon Roll; Hon Roll.

TORRES, RAUL; John H Francis Polytechnic HS; North Hollywood, CA; (3); Aud/Vis; Office Aide; Teachers Aide; Bsbl; Bsktbl; Ftbl.

TORRES, ROBERT E; Downey HS; Downey, CA; (4); Cmnty Wkr; Key Clb; Teachers Aide; School Play; JV Bsbl; Var Bsbl; L Bsbl; Var Cheerldng; Capt Cheerldng; JV Socr; CA ST U Fullerton; Law.

TORRES, RUTH; Woodrow Wilson HS; Los Angeles, CA; (3); Church Yth Grp; Hosp Aide; Math Tm; Church Choir; Stage Crew; Hon Roll; Nrsng Schlrshp; Hosp Occptns Achvt Awd; Spcl Rcgntn Awd Stu Rcgntn Day; Lesley Coll; Pre-Med.

TORRES, SONIA; Morningside HS; Inglewood, CA; (1); Hon Roll; Prfct Atten Awd.

TORRES, VALERIE A; Mc Ateer School Of The Arts HS; San Francisco, CA; (3); Dance Clb; Variety Show; Intrml Crs Cntry; Hon Roll; Danceline Lttr; Schl Of Arts Dance Prgrm; Profsnl Ballet; Piano; Julliard; Profsnl Ballet.

TORRES, VERONICA; Garfield HS; Long Beach, CA; (4); French Clb; Flag Corp; Rep Sr Cls; Var Swmmng; Hon Roll; Pres Acad Fit Awd; Most Dedicated 89; MVP 90; Hi Point Swmmg 90; Hnr Stu Of Mnth 87; CA ST U LA; Nrsg.

TORRES, VICENTE; Colton HS; San Bernadino, CA; (4); Teachers Aide; Sprt Ed Yrbk; JV Bsktbl; Pres Acad Fit Awd; San Bernardino Vly Coll; P Ed.

TORRES, VICTOR J; Westmoor HS; Daly City, CA; (2); Bsktbl; L Crs Cntry; Hon Roll; Frgn Exc Stu France; Harvard U; Corp Law.

TORRES, VINCENT; San Gabriel HS; Alhambra, CA; (2); Debate Tm; JA; Stage Crew; JV Socr; NAJAC Summer 89; Cinematgrphy.

TORRES, VIVIAN C; Baldwin Park HS; Baldwin Park, CA; (2); FBLA; Var Sftbl; Hon Roll; Dntl Asst.

TORRES, YAZMIN R; Calexico HS; Calexico, CA; (2); Drama Clb; FHA; Pep Clb; School Play; JV Bsktbl; Math Fest 1st Pl; Golden St Exam; SDSU; Chem Engr.

TORRES P, ALMA DELIA; Roseville HS; Roseville, CA; (3); Off Sr Cls; Hon Roll; Cosmetology.

TORRES-MC DONALD, FABIOLA F; Orangewood Acad; Santa Ana, CA; (4); Teachers Aide; Chorus; Church Choir; Rptr Nwsp; Wt Lftg; High Hon Roll; Jrnlsm Awd; Mst Imprvd Phy Ed Stu; Orange Cty Anti-Drug Newsletter; Acad Achvt Awd; CA U Fullerton; CPA.

TORRESDAL, CANDICE A; Woodside HS; Redwood City, CA; (3); Church Yth Grp; Drama Clb; Sec VP 4-H; Stage Crew; Sec Stu Cncl; JV Var Socr; Var Capt Trk; JV Var Vllybl; Jr Ath Of Yr; Cntrl Coast Vlybl Clb; Peninsula Attackers CYSA Sccr; Pre-Med.

TORRESLUNA, MONTSERRAT; Corona SR HS; Corona, CA; (3); Pres SADD; Cit Awd; FNL; San Diego ST; Marine Bio.

TORREY, BILL W; Cupertino HS; Santa Clara, CA; (2); 1/280; Sec FBLA; Treas Spanish Clb; Ed Nwsp; Rep Frsh Cls; Rep Soph Cls; Rep Stu Cncl; High Hon Roll; Hon Roll; Spanish NHS.

TORREY, LISE; East Union HS; Manteca, CA; (3); 50/400; French Clb; Pres SADD; Thesps; School Play; Stage Crew; Hon Roll; SADD Pres; Partners In Prvntn; Natl Yng Ldrs Cnvntn; Psych.

TORREZ, ANDRE; Delano HS; Delano, CA; (4); 14/300; Church Yth Grp; Phtg Yrbk; Golf; High Hon Roll; CSF; Athenian Hnr Scty; Exemplary Stu; U CA-BERKELEY; Comp Sci.

TORREZ, KATHY L; Rosamond HS; Rosamond, CA; (3); Yrbk; Pres Frsh Cls; Pres Soph Cls; Pres Jr Cls; Var Capt Cheerldng; DAR Awd; Hon Roll; Kiwanis Awd; Masonic Awd; Supt Hnr Roll; Bus Mgmt.

TORREZ, NICHOLAS D; Delano Joint Union HS; Delano, CA; (2); Church Yth Grp; Pep Clb; Teachers Aide; Bsbl; Bsktbl; Ftbl; Score Keeper; Tennis; Hon Roll; Prfct Atten Awd; Vlntr Coach For Parks & Rec Bsbl & T-Ball; Bakersfield JC; Bus Mgmt.

TORREZ, ROBERT R; Madera HS; Madera, CA; (4); Wrstlng; Mex/Am Clb; Homcmng King; Fresno ST U; Phys Thrpst.

TORRICO, MARCOS; Mountain View HS; El Monte, CA; (2); Boy Scts; Intrml Ftbl; Police Officer.

TORRICO, MARIA G; Carlsbad HS; Carlsbad, CA; (3); Hon Roll; Penn ST; Lawyer.

TORRIJOS, ALFREDO; St Genevieve HS; N Hollywood, CA; (2); JV Bsktbl; Var L Crs Cntry; Natl Ltn Hnr Awd; Eglsh Hnrs; Geo Hnrs; Wrld Hstry Hnrs.

TORTONA, JOHN P; Carson HS; Carson, CA; (2); Church Yth Grp; Intnl Clb; Rptr Nwsp; Rep Frsh Cls; Mgr(s); Tennis; Cit Awd; Hon Roll; Prfct Atten Awd; Math Awd; Jrnlsm Awd; Schlrshp Awd; Gftd & Tlntd Prgm; Joining Acad Decathlon Tm; USAF Acad; Doctor.

TOSIO, JILL T; San Ramon Valley HS; Danville, CA; (3); 156/420; Church Yth Grp; Teachers Aide; Chorus; School Play; Ed Nwsp; Stu Cncl; Var Co-Capt Cheerldng; Hon Roll; Pres Acad Fit Awd; Pepperdine U; Jrnlsm.

TOSTADO, RAMON; Mc Lane HS; Fresno, CA; (4); #324 In Class; Elect Engr.

TOSTE, ANGELA M; Lemoore Union HS; Lemoore, CA; (2); 17/342; GAA; Spanish Clb; Swmmng; Trk; Hon Roll; Fresno ST U; Law.

TOSTE, DEBBIE F; Arcata HS; Arcata, CA; (1); French Clb; Church Choir; Rptr Nwsp; Sec Soph Cls; JV Bsktbl; L Var Crs Cntry; Powder Puff Ftbl; L Var Trk; French Hon Soc; High Hon Roll; Schl Awds; Law.

TOSTI, AREND M; Del Campo HS; Fair Oaks, CA; (2); 79/460; Boy Scts; ROTC; Intrml Golf; Intrml Socr; Pilot.

TOTTEN, TRACY S; Coachella Valley HS; Thermal, CA; (2); Var Sftbl; Hon Roll; Sftbl Coaches Awd; Acad Excllnc For Algebra II; HI Pacific Coll.

TOUCH, ARUN; Norwalk HS; Norwalk, CA; (2); French Clb; Library Aide; Math Clb; Office Aide; Hon Roll; UCLA; Pharm.

TOUCH, CHHOUR; Millillan HS; Long Beach, CA; (3); AFS; Key Clb; Lit Mag; Off Jr Cls; French Hon Soc; Club & Amiable Student Social Club/V Pres; CA St U; Engineer & Welder.

TOUCHATT, KIMBERLY A; Fred C Beyer HS; Modesto, CA; (1); Hon Roll; Cecchetti Cncl Amer Dance Exam Awd Ballet; Aerobics & Gymnstcs Awds Aim For As; Ballet Tap Jazz 8 Yrs; Dance.

TOUFFER, DEBBIE; Fairfax HS; Los Angeles, CA; (3); French Clb; Spanish Clb; Off Frsh Cls; JV Bsktbl; Score Keeper; JV Tennis; Cit Awd; Hon Roll; U CA; Math.

TOUGAW, CHRISTINE A; Oak Ridge HS; Cameron Park, CA; (3); 24/250; Cmnty Wkr; FBLA; Key Clb; SADD; VP Sr Cls; Intrml Bsktbl; Var Cheerldng; Hon Roll; Pres Acad Fit Awd; HOBY; Sierra Srvce Prjct.

TOUNEH, VU H; Independence HS; San Jose, CA; (4); Art Clb; Cmnty Wkr; Spanish Clb; Teachers Aide; Varsity Clb; Band; Jazz Band; Mrchg Band; Orch; Pep Band; Entrepreneur Club; Akido; Karate; San Diego ST U; Bus Admin.

TOUPONCE, CHRISTOPHER M; Encina HS; Sacramento, CA; (3); Boy Scts; Air Force.

TOURNEY, DAVID A; Bakersfield HS; Bakersfield, CA; (3); 18/800; Church Yth Grp; German Clb; Key Clb; Science Clb; Service Clb; Ski Clb; Teachers Aide; Band; Jazz Band; Mrchg Band; Enterprise Coll; Bus.

TOURVILLE, ZACHARY; Palisades HS; Topanga, CA; (3); Boy Scts; Math Clb; Math Tm; Var Crs Cntry; Var Golf; Var Trk; Hon Roll; Engrng.

TOUSSAINT, REBECCA L; Hayward HS; Hayward, CA; (1); Cmnty Wkr; Spanish Clb; Treas Frsh Cls; Bsktbl; Vllybl; Hon Roll; 89 Vlntr Yr HARD; Naval Acad; Marine Bio.

TOVAR, ALBERTO S; Bellarmine-Jefferson HS; Glendale, CA; (1); 2/144; Bsktbl; High Hon Roll; NHS; CA Schlrshp Fdrtn; Yng Mens Chrstn Assn.

TOVAR, CELIA; Anaheim HS; Anaheim, CA; (3); Color Guard; Drill Tm; Flag Corp; Mrchg Band; Cheerldng; Pom Pon; UC Irvine; Bio.

TOVAR, CYNTHIA Z; Fountain Valley HS; Fountain Valley, CA; (4); Church Yth Grp; French Clb; Red Cross Aide; Science Clb; Spanish Clb; Color Guard; Flag Corp; High Hon Roll; Hon Roll; U Of CA; Comm.

TOVAR, ELIZABETH; North Salinas HS; Salinas, CA; (3); French Clb; Hosp Aide; Key Clb; Var Crs Cntry; JV Fld Hcky; Var Trk; Hon Roll; NHS; U Of San Francisco; Com Pgrm.

TOVAR, OSWALDO; Bellflower HS; Bellflower, CA; (3).

TOVAR, PRISCILLA; Hoover HS; Fresno, CA; (2); Church Yth Grp; Chorus; JV Swmmng; Cit Awd; Hon Roll; Fresno ST U; Engr.

TOVAR, VERONICA; Hemet HS; Perris, CA; (3); 19/475; Church Yth Grp; French Clb; Key Clb; Cit Awd; High Hon Roll; CSF; Med.

TOVES, CHAD; Channell Islands HS; Oxnard, CA; (2); 71/750; Church Yth Grp; Treas French Clb; Mgr Bsktbl; JV Ftbl; Hon Roll; Interact Clb.

TOWE, ODLE D; Hilmar HS; Hilmar, CA; (1); Church Yth Grp; Cmnty Wkr; VICA; Trk; Wrstlng; Hon Roll; Acad Excllnc Mech Drwng; VICA Cmptn Intro Drftng; Yth Sccr Team; CA Poly San Luis Obispo; Art.

TOWER, STACIA; Brookside Christian HS; Wasco, IL; (1); School Play; Var Bsktbl; JV Var Crs Cntry; Var Socr; Var Vllybl; Shw Hunter Jumper Horses; Sccr; UC Davis; Vet.

TOWERY, CHERYL; Coastal Christian Schl; Grover City, CA; (3); Church Yth Grp; Pres Frsh Cls; Pres Soph Cls; Sec Jr Cls; Var Bsktbl; Var Capt Cheerldng; Var Sftbl; Var Vllybl; Masters Coll; Law.

TOWEY, JAMIE; Cardinal Newman HS; Rohnert Park, CA; (2); 1/90; High Hon Roll.

TOWFIGH, ABDULA; Santa Monica HS; Santa Monica, CA; (3); Cmnty Wkr; French Clb; JA; Stu Cncl; Public Relations Clb; Norineo Sportsmens Clb; Heal The Bay Clb; Japan Karate Assn; UCLA Internship; UCLA.

TOWFIGH, ALI A; Santa Monica HS; Santa Monica, CA; (3); Boy Scts; Math Tm; Teachers Aide; Bsktbl; High Hon Roll; Hon Roll; Hnrs Golden St Exam Geom; UCLA; Med.

TOWFIQ, MANDY; Dana Hills HS; San Juan Capistra, CA; (1); Socr; Trk; SAVE-STUS Against A Vanishing Envrnmnt; Dolpin Of Month-Span II; Berkeley; Forest Ranger.

TOWLE, JASON L; York Schl; Salinas, CA; (4); Boy Scts; Cmnty Wkr; Debate Tm; JA; Key Clb; Math Tm; Science Clb; Ski Clb; Var L Crs Cntry; Var L Socr; Stu Of Mnth Awd; Math Calculus 4th Pl; The Herald Selected Schlr Awd; CA Poly Tech U; Engr.

TOWLE, REBEKAH L; Troy HS; Fullerton, CA; (2); 39/334; Church Yth Grp; Cmnty Wkr; Key Clb; Pres Spanish Clb; High Hon Roll; Hon Roll; Jr NHS; Peer Asstnt Lgu Treas; CSF; UCLA; Elem Tchr.

TOWLE, STEPHANIE L; Salinas HS; Salinas, CA; (1); Church Yth Grp; Band; Church Choir; Mrchg Band; School Musical; Hon Roll; Intl Order Of Jobs Daughters Jr Princess; Fresno ST; Bus Admin.

TOWLES, NYLA; Pasadena HS; Pasadena, CA; (3); Dance Clb; Black Stu Union Clb; Cal ST Long Beach; Bus.

TOWNE, LESLIE; Corning Union HS; Corning, CA; (4); Yrbk; Cit Awd; High Hon Roll; Prom Cmmtte; Butte Coll; Engl.

TOWNS, RAHSAANA; Santiago HS; Santa Ana, CA; (2); Drama Clb; Pep Clb; SADD; Drill Tm; School Play; Variety Show; Sec Stu Cncl; Cheerldng; Pom Pon; UCLA; Psych.

TOWNSEND, GWEN; Rosamond HS; Rosamond, CA; (4); Office Aide; Teachers Aide; Rptr Nwsp; Yrbk; VP Frsh Cls; VP Soph Cls; Var Capt Cheerldng; Hon Roll; Prfct Atten Awd; Frosh Winterrail Queen; Hmcmng Queen; PAL Club; AV Antelope Vly Coll; Teacher.

TOWNSEND, KAREN; Cajon HS; San Bernardino, CA; (2); Church Yth Grp; Lit Mag; NHS; New Life Clb; Clown For Chldrn & Retrmnt Hms.

TOWNSEND, RONALD P; Ocean View HS; Huntington Beach, CA; (2); Band; Jazz Band; Mrchg Band; Orch; Outstndng Jazz Slst 89-90; CA U Irvn; Music Dir.

TOWNSEND, VIANNE C; Southern California Christian HS; Yorba Linda, CA; (1); School Play; Treas Frsh Cls; U BC Vancouver Canada; Thrpst.

TOWNSON, DONALD R; Montclair HS; Montclair, CA; (2); Boy Scts; Church Yth Grp; Drama Clb; School Play; JV Crs Cntry; JV Swmmng; Bible Club Secy; Envrnmntl Mgmt.

TOY, AMY; Cajon HS; San Bernardino, CA; (2); Cmnty Wkr; GAA; Varsity Clb; Var Socr; Var Swmmng; Hon Roll; NHS; CA Schlrshp Fed; Nation Charity Leag; Soccer AYSO Referee.

TOY, MARGIE; Whitney HS; Cerritos, CA; (4); 1/169; Church Yth Grp; Pres FBLA; Key Clb; Ed Nwsp; Ed Yrbk; L Var Crs Cntry; Cmnty Wkr; Teachers Aide; Variety Show; Lit Mag; CA St Brd Ed CNAC Rep; Ambssdr To Orient; Prin Advisory Brd; U PA; Intl Relations.

TOY, SHARON; Castro Valley HS; Castro Valley, CA; (3); Cmnty Wkr; Acpl Chr; Chorus; School Musical; Variety Show; Stu Cncl; Mgr(s); Interact Club, A Comm Svc Club; 3 Yrs As Rally Song Girls; An Employee At Ross Dept Store 1 Yr; Piano; UCLA; Bus Adm.

TOY, WILSON W; Abraham Lincoln HS; San Francisco, CA; (2); Cit Awd; High Hon Roll; Math & Chinese Schl Schlrshp Awds; UC Berkeley; Mech Engr.

TOYAMA, KYLE S; Casa Roble Fundamental HS; Citrus Heights, CA; (2); Spanish Clb; Var Tennis; Var Wrstlng; Fri Night Live; UCLA; Orthpdc Srgn.

TRAC, LANDI; Lowell HS; San Francisco, CA; (2); Library Aide; Office Aide; Teachers Aide; Var Crs Cntry; Mgr Gym; NHS; Mem BBSO; Mem CSF; Golden Sst Exam Algrbra; Med.

TRACHTA, ADREINNE; El Cajon Valley HS; El Cajon, CA; (2); 15/469; Letterman Clb; JV Cheerldng; Var Swmmng; Hon Roll; Dance Co; CSF; UCSD; Psych.

TRACHTA, MICHELLE; El Cajon Valley HS; El Cajon, CA; (3); 11/370; Girl Scts; Stu Cncl; Capt JV Cheerldng; JV Swmmng; High Hon Roll; Rotary Awd; Dance Co VP; CSF VP; U Of San Diego; Bus.

TRACY, CHERYL L; Ramona HS; Ramona, CA; (3); Church Yth Grp; French Clb; Teachers Aide; Church Choir; Rep Stu Cncl; Hon Roll; Ntl Merit Ltr; Puppet Team; Chrstn Music Mnstry; CO Chrstn U; Music Prfrmnc.

TRACY, MATT J; Ventura HS; Ventura, CA; (3); 36/550; Hosp Aide; Var L Bsbl; JV L Bsktbl; High Hon Roll; Acad Ltr 3 Yrs; Cert Of Mrt Piano 3 Yrs; Pilot.

TRAEGER, JIM A; Dinuba HS; Dinuba, CA; (2); Church Yth Grp; JV Bsbl; L Var Bsktbl; JV Ftbl; Stanford.

TRAHAN, TIMOTHY C; Junipero Serra HS; Compton, CA; (3); JA; Letterman Clb; Red Cross Aide; Varsity Clb; Yrbk; Hon Roll; Spanish Clb; Pres Frsh Cls; Pres Jr Cls; Rep Sr Cls; Bus.

TRAHERN, ROBIN L; Nevada Union HS; Nevada City, CA; (1); 132/589; Chorus; High Hon Roll; Hon Roll; Vcl Prfrmnc; Plyng Piano & Sax; Chld Psychlgst.

TRAISTER, SAARA R; The Athenian Schl; Danville, CA; (3); Cmnty Wkr; French Clb; Ski Clb; SADD; Bsktbl; Trk; Vllybl; Hon Roll; UC-SANTA Cruz; Mar Bio.

TRAM, KHOI; Bolsa Grande HS; Garden Grove, CA; (1); Band; Drill Tm; Jazz Band; Mrchg Band; Pep Band; School Musical; Cit Awd; Hon Roll; Prfct Atten Awd; Sci Awd; USC; Math.

TRAM, QUYEN M; Alhambra HS; Alhambra, CA; (3); FBLA; Library Aide; Office Aide; Science Clb; Temple Yth Grp; Vietnamese Stu Assn; Advntr Clb; Med Clb; CA ST Northridge; Bus.

TRAM, UYEN; Fountain Valley HS; Fountain Valley, CA; (4); 4/630; Red Cross Aide; Science Clb; High Hon Roll; Pres Acad Fit Awd; CSF; Coronet Sci Awd Fnlst; UC Irvine; Bio Sci.

TRAMEL, ELIZABETH; Patrick Henry HS; San Diego, CA; (4); 18/575; Hosp Aide; Spanish Clb; Off Frsh Cls; Var Socr; JV Var Swmmng; JV Var Vllybl; High Hon Roll; Jr NHS; NHS; Schlr-Athl Awd; Mst Imsprtnl Vllybll 89; City Conf All-Acad Team Vllybll, Sccr & Swmmng; Pepperdine U; Med.

TRAMMELL, TERRY D; O'farell SCPA HS; San Diego, CA; (3); Pres Dance Clb; Office Aide; Stage Crew; Hon Roll.

TRAMMELL, TIM T; La Serna HS; Whittier, CA; (3); 50/250; JV Var Bsbl; Princpals List; Bus.

TRAN, AMY M; Lowell HS; San Francisco, CA; (3); Cmnty Wkr; Red Cross Aide; Service Clb; Hon Roll; Chinese Schl.

TRAN, AN-KHANG V; La Quinta HS; Santa Ana, CA; (1); 2/344; Boy Scts; Science Clb; Physc.

TRAN, ANDY; Edison HS; Huntington Beach, CA; (2); Key Clb; JV Tennis; Hon Roll; High Hnrs Golden ST Exam Geom; U CA Irvine; Bio.

TRAN, ANH; Hawthorne HS; Lawndale, CA; (4); 3/45; Lbrn Cmnty Wkr; Capt JV Vllybl; High Hon Roll; CSF Clb; UCI; Bus.

TRAN, ANH; Mt Carmel HS; San Diego, CA; (3); Church Yth Grp; Cmnty Wkr; Drama Clb; Hosp Aide; Intnl Clb; SADD; Teachers Aide; Rptr Nwsp; Off Frsh Cls; Off Soph Cls; Vietnamese PTSA Acad Achvt; Medcl Care Unit Treas, Actvty Comssnr; UCSD; Bio.

TRAN, ANH; University City HS; La Jolla, CA; (4); Letterman Clb; Office Aide; Science Clb; Teachers Aide; Varsity Clb; Rptr Nwsp; Cit Awd; High Hon Roll; Hon Roll; Badminton Acad Tm, All City Conf; Golden St Exam Math Hnrs; U CA San Diego; Bio.

TRAN, ANH H; Mt Pleasant HS; San Jose, CA; (4); 18/400; Art Clb; Cmnty Wkr; French Clb; High Hon Roll; NHS; Mock Trl Team 88-90; CSF; Violin; Santa Clara U; Bio Sci.

TRAN, ANNA UYEN; Norco SR HS; Corona, CA; (3); 32/399; Teachers Aide; School Musical; Hon Roll; Pres Acad Fit Awd; Dentistry.

TRAN, ANTHONY; Mission Viejo HS; Mission Viejo, CA; (3); Spanish Clb; Yrbk; JV Tennis; U CA; Bus.

TRAN, BADIEP N; Mark Keppel HS; San Gabriel, CA; (4); Math Clb; Science Clb; Orch; Cit Awd; High Hon Roll; Prfct Atten Awd; Pres Acad Fit Awd; Wmn Clb Schlrshp; Sci Awd; UC Riverside; Bio-Med.

TRAN, BAN; Saddleback HS; Santa Ana, CA; (4); 27/527; AFS; Cmnty Wkr; Drama Clb; English Clb; French Clb; German Clb; Model UN; School Play; Off Sr Cls; High Hon Roll; UCI; Math Tchr.

TRAN, BAO; Poly HS; Riverside, CA; (4); Art Awd.

TRAN, BAO LOC; George Washington HS; San Francisco, CA; (2); Girl Scts; Hon Roll; Hnr In Algebra GSE; CSF 89-90; Berkley; Med.

TRAN, BECKY N; Ontario HS; Ontario, CA; (2); Rep Math Clb; Hon Roll; Prfct Atten Awd; UCI; Pedtrcn.

TRAN, BECKY N; San Gabriel HS; Rosemead, CA; (1); Debate Tm; Pep Clb; Spanish Clb; Variety Show; High Hon Roll; Pres Acad Fit Awd; SADD; Glgy Clb; UCLA; Phrmclgy.

TRAN, BENJAMIN B; Westminster HS; Westminster, CA; (2); School Play; Stage Crew; Wt Lftg; Acad Decathln 88-89 89-90; Vendor; Biolgcl Sci.

TRAN, BICH CHAU BETTY; Galileo HS; San Francisco, CA; (2); French Clb; Temple Yth Grp; Cit Awd; High Hon Roll; Hon Roll; Prfct Atten Awd; Chinese Culture Club Clb; WA DC Close Up Foundtn Prgm; Cert Of Prgm Awd; San Francisco ST U; Arch Engr.

TRAN, BICH THI-NGOC; Valley HS; Sacramento, CA; (3); 4-H; Office Aide; Red Cross Aide; SADD; Teachers Aide; Band; Nwsp; Cit Awd; High Hon Roll; Hon Roll; Sacramento ST; Nrs.

TRAN, BINH; Westminster HS; Westminster, CA; (3); Art Clb; Church Yth Grp; Drama Clb; Acpl Chr; Nwsp; Lit Mag; Off Jr Cls; Bsbl; Bsktbl; Sftbl; Fshn Dsgnr.

TRAN, BINH N; Damien HS; Cucamonga, CA; (4); 51/200; Art Clb; Science Clb; Ski Clb; Teachers Aide; Varsity Clb; Intrml Tennis; Intrml Vllybl; Hon Roll; NHS; CSF; Tennis & Vllybl Clbs; U CA Irvine.

TRAN, CHANNING; Lowell HS; San Francisco, CA; (2); Science Clb; Golden St Exam Hnr Awd; UC Davis; Engr.

TRAN, CHRISTINE D; Artesia HS; Cerritos, CA; (3); French Clb; Intnl Clb; Science Clb; Teachers Aide; Chorus; Rep Jr Cls; JV Cheerldng; Hon Roll; Cal ST Long Beach; Bus Admin.

TRAN, CHRISTINE T; Mira Mesa HS; San Diego, CA; (3); Intnl Clb; Key Clb; Science Clb; High Hon Roll; Hon Roll; NHS; CSF; Top 100 HS; Acad League; Bus Admin.

TRAN, CINDY; Del Mar HS; San Jose, CA; (2); Library Aide; Teachers Aide; Bsktbl; Tennis; Vllybl; UC Berkeley; Engrng.

TRAN, CINDY N; George Washington HS; San Francisco, CA; (2); U Of CA; Bus.

TRAN, COY W; Lakewood SR HS; Lakewood, CA; (3); Office Aide; Intrml Bsktbl; JV Vllybl; Prfct Atten Awd; Best Soph Eng; CSF Mem; Hnrs GSE Geom; UCLA; Eng.

TRAN, CUONG; Andrew Hill HS; San Jose, CA; (2); Math Tm; Socr; Bus.

TRAN, CUONG; Encinel HS; Alameda, CA; (4); 34/222; Math Tm; Office Aide; Teachers Aide; Rep Frsh Cls; Cit Awd; High Hon Roll; Hon Roll; Pres Acad Fit Awd; Fosters Achvt Awd; Med.

TRAN, CUONG D; Leuzinger HS; Hawthorne, CA; (3); Computer Clb; Science Clb; Tennis; Trk; Hon Roll; Prfct Atten Awd; CSF; CSU Pomona; Engrng.

TRAN, CUONG D; Los Amigos HS; Santa Ana, CA; (3); 2/331; Sci Olympics; CA Schlrshp Fed; All A's; Mech Engrng.

TRAN, CUONG D; San Gabriel HS; San Gabriel, CA; (4); 62/737; French Clb; Key Clb; Office Aide; Spanish Clb; Teachers Aide; Tennis; Cit Awd; High Hon Roll; Prfct Atten Awd; Cal Poly Pomona; Arch.

TRAN, DANH L; John F Kennedy HS; Mission Hills, CA; (2); Orch; Bsktbl; Hon Roll; Prfct Atten Awd; Pres Acad Fit Awd; Dental.

TRAN, DAO; Ventura HS; Ventura, CA; (2); Hon Roll; Prfct Atten Awd; UCSB; Nurse.

TRAN, DAT T; San Gabriel HS; Rosemead, CA; (2); FBLA; Key Clb; Spanish Clb; SADD; Teachers Aide; JV Bsktbl; JV Vllybl; Cit Awd; High Hon Roll; Hon Roll; Asst Coach Bsktbl Tm; USC; Pre-Med.

TRAN, DENNIS D; George Washington HS; San Francisco, CA; (3); Cmnty Wkr; Tennis; High Hon Roll; Hon Roll; Golden St Exam Algebra Schl Recognition, Geom High Hnr; Economy.

TRAN, DINH H; San Gabriel HS; Monterey Park, CA; (3); Red Cross Aide; Teachers Aide; Phtg Yrbk; JV Tennis; High Hon Roll; Hon Roll; Courtesy Cmmtte; Grls Leag-Sec; Riverside U; Economics.

TRAN, DO T; Ventura HS; Ventura, CA; (3); 20/431; Hon Roll; Prfct Atten Awd; CSF Club.

TRAN, DOMINIC D; Huntington Beach HS; Huntington Beach, CA; (4); 3/500; Boy Scts; Chess Clb; Church Yth Grp; Key Clb; Math Clb; Math Tm; Model UN; Lit Mag; Trk; Gov Hon Prg Awd; Mltry Exlprs; Sci Fctn Clb; AYSO Asstnt Coach; U CA Irvine; Phrmclgy.

TRAN, DUC; Fremont HS; Sunnyvale, CA; (1); Church Yth Grp; Computer Clb; FHA; German Clb; JA; School Play; JV Var Ftbl; JV Var Wrstlng; High Hon Roll; Hon Roll; Karate Awds For Cmptns; Grphc Arts; Karate For Demos In Schls; UCLA; Bus.

TRAN, DUC T; Antelope Valley HS; Lancaster, CA; (3); 14/631; JA; Teachers Aide; Bsbl; Bsktbl; Cheerldng; Crs Cntry; Diving; Ftbl; Golf; Socr; Engr.

TRAN, DUNG; Workman HS; La Puente, CA; (2); Art Clb; Computer Clb; Math Clb; Science Clb; Spanish Clb; School Musical; Socr; Tennis; JETS Awd; Opt Clb Awd; Med.

TRAN, DUNG T; Fremont HS; Sunnyvale, CA; (3); 151/408; Var Trk; Vietnamese Clb; Bus.

TRAN, DUONG; Montclair HS; Montclair, CA; (4); 18/500; Cit Awd; High Hon Roll; Hon Roll; Prfct Atten Awd; CA Schlrshp Fdr; Cal ST Pomona; Math Teacher.

TRAN, DUYENHAI; Norte Vista HS; Riverside, CA; (1); 1/492; High Hon Roll; Hon Roll; Prfct Atten Awd; UCR; Dntst.

TRAN, EILEEN; Palm Desert HS; Palm Desert, CA; (4); 34/330; Cmnty Wkr; Dance Clb; Hosp Aide; Key Clb; Model UN; Pep Clb; Service Clb; Mrchg Band; Cheerldng; Pom Pon; UC Irvine; Pre-Med.

TRAN, ELIZABETH T; Pospect HS; Saratoga, CA; (1); Art Clb; Chess Clb; Dance Clb; FBLA; Key Clb; Science Clb; Bus.

TRAN, FRED X; Moorpark HS; Moorpark, CA; (3); 3/230; Var L Ftbl; Var L Trk; Rotary Awd; Pepperdine Coll.

TRAN, GEE; Phillip & Sala Burton Academic HS; San Francisco, CA; (2); Chess Clb; Band; High Hon Roll; Hon Roll.

TRAN, GIAO; Pioneer HS; San Jose, CA; (1); Cmnty Wkr; Debate Tm; Spanish Clb; Interact Clb; Vietnamese Clb; Stanford; Model.

TRAN, HA N; Gardena HS; Gardena, CA; (2); Intnl Clb; Library Aide; Spanish Clb; Ed Yrbk; VP Stu Cncl; Tennis; Fshn Dsgn.

TRAN, HAI; Abraham Lincoln HS; San Jose, CA; (4); Vietnamese, Chinese Club; Catonsville JC; Elect Engrg.

TRAN, HAI; Edison HS; Stockton, CA; (2); Temple Yth Grp; School Musical; Hon Roll; CSU.

TRAN, HAN D; Mark Keppel HS; Monterey Park, CA; (3); French Clb; Key Clb; Pres Math Clb; Mu Alpha Theta; Science Clb; Tennis; High Hon Roll; Prfct Atten Awd; CSF; Amnesty Intl; CA U Los Angelos; Aerospace.

TRAN, HANG; Santa Teresa HS; San Jose, CA; (3); 13/30; Church Yth Grp; Cmnty Wkr; Typing Compitition; Teach Holy Cross & Being Treasurers; Vietnames Club; Teach Dancing; San Jose ST U; Nurse.

TRAN, HANH T; Leuzinger HS; Hawthorne, CA; (3); Church Yth Grp; Computer Clb; Science Clb; Church Choir; Off Jr Cls; Stu Cncl; Cit Awd; Hon Roll; Prfct Atten Awd; Pr Tutor; CSF; UCLA; Biochem.

TRAN, HEN; James Lick HS; San Jose, CA; (1); 2/30; NCAA Hnrs; Vrsty Badminton Tm; UC Prtnrshp; UC Berkeley; Doctor.

TRAN, HIEN; Valley HS; Sacramento, CA; (4); Teachers Aide; Hon Roll; CSF; Bnk America Achvt Awd.

TRAN, HIEN N; California HS; Whittier, CA; (2); German Clb; Trk; USC; Comp Sci.

TRAN, HOA; Baldwin Park HS; Baldwin Pk, CA; (2); French Clb; Hon Roll.

TRAN, HOA; Hawthorne HS; Hawthorne, CA; (2); Key Clb; Sec Science Clb; High Hon Roll; Hon Roll; CSF; AFS; UCLA; Bus.

TRAN, HOA K; Skyline HS; Oakland, CA; (3); Spanish Clb; Cit Awd; Hon Roll; CSF.

TRAN, HOA T; The Bishops Schl; San Diego, CA; (3); Sec Spanish Clb; Speech Tm; Sec Sr Cls; Fnlst Santa Barbar Sci Cntst; Hnr Rll 1 Sem; Psych.

TRAN, HOI N; Los Amigos HS; Santa Ana, CA; (2); Natl Beta Clb; NHS; U Of S CA; Mech Engr.

TRAN, HONG T; Moreno Valley HS; Moreno Vly, CA; (4); Church Yth Grp; Teachers Aide; Hon Roll; Sn Joaquin Delta Coll; Comp Prg.

TRAN, HONG-NHI P; Westminster HS; Westminster, CA; (1); Model UN; Hon Roll; Vietnamese Club; Phrmcy.

TRAN, HUE KRISTINE; Alhambra HS; Alhambra, CA; (2); Church Yth Grp; Var Capt Bsktbl; Cheerldng; Var Var Crs Cntry; Stat Wrstlng; Tri-Hi-Y Club; UCLA.

TRAN, HUE MY; Lincoln HS; Stockton, CA; (3); 22/592; Spanish Clb; High Hon Roll; Hon Roll; CSF; Bdmntn Tm.

TRAN, HUNG; Irvine HS; Irvine, CA; (2); Key Clb; Lcrss; Hon Roll; MVP Of 89 Irvine Lacrosse Clb; U Of Irvine CA; Bio-Med.

TRAN, HUNG; Pittsburg HS; Pittsburg, CA; (4); Var Tennis; Govt, Hstry, Math; Diablo Valley Coll; Math.

TRAN, HUNG Y; San Gabriel HS; Rosemead, CA; (1); Key Clb; Hon Roll; CSF; Geolgy; UCLA.

TRAN, HUONG; Hoover HS; San Diego, CA; (2); Key Clb; School Play; Variety Show; Mgr(s); Var Tennis; Cit Awd; High Hon Roll; Jr NHS; NHS; Pharmacy.

TRAN, HUONG; Skyline HS; Oakland, CA; (3); Cit Awd; Hon Roll; Hayward ST U; Financl Accntng.

TRAN, HUY H; Sacred Heart Cathedral Prep; San Francisco, CA; (1); Ski Clb; High Hon Roll; Doctor.

TRAN, JENNIFER; La Quinta HS; Westminster, CA; (2); 25/362; Key Clb; Pep Clb; SADD; Intrml Crs Cntry; Intrml Tennis; Intrml Vllybl; Hon Roll; UCI; Ophthalmology.

TRAN, JOHN; Abraham Lincoln HS; San Francisco, CA; (4); Computer Clb; Math Clb; Teachers Aide; Chorus; Phtg Yrbk; Rep Sr Cls; JV Bsbl; Var Vllybl; Pres Acad Fit Awd; Pres Schlr; UC Davis; Comp Info Systems.

TRAN, KENNETH; Buena Park HS; Fullerton, CA; (3); Chess Clb; Speech Tm; Band; Jazz Band; Mrchg Band; Pep Band; Tennis; High Hon Roll; Rep Dare To Say No; CSF; Ca Poly; Engr.

TRAN, KHANH; Encina HS; Carmichael, CA; (3); #7 In Class; Computer Clb; Debate Tm; Sec Intnl Clb; Spanish Clb; SADD; Treas Co-Capt Temple Yth Grp; Variety Show; Ed Frsh Cls; Lit Mag; Off Sr Cls; Spnsh Club; CSF; UCD Outreach Pgm; U Of Pacific; Phrmcy.

TRAN, KHOA N; Glendale Adventist Acad; Glendale, CA; (2); Hon Roll; NHS; Mech Engr.

TRAN, KHOI; Candea Park HS; Reseda, CA; (2); 8/35; Computer Clb; Dance Clb; FBLA; Library Aide; Math Tm; Office Aide; Science Clb; Spanish Clb; SADD; Teachers Aide; Archt.

TRAN, KIM A; La Quinta HS; Fountain Valley, CA; (4); Key Clb; Math Clb; Pep Clb; Spanish Clb; Teachers Aide; Band; JV Tennis; Hon Roll; NHS; Vietnamese Clb Pres; Ldrshp Awd; CSULB; Nrsng.

TRAN, KIM-OANH T; Santiago HS; Santa Ana, CA; (2); Church Yth Grp; French Clb; Church Choir; Hon Roll; CSF Fed; UCI; Med.

TRAN, KIMPHUONG T; Mt Pleasant HS; San Jose, CA; (3); Math Clb; Teachers Aide; Hon Roll; Vietnamese Clb; Cloth Dsgnr.

TRAN, KYM L; La Quinta HS; Westminster, CA; (4); Teachers Aide; Pres Acpl Chr; Chorus; Orch; Hon Roll; CSF; Med.

TRAN, LAN T; San Gabriel HS; San Gabriel, CA; (3); 15/736; FBLA; Red Cross Aide; Hon Roll; Acad Decathlon Clb Pres; CSF; Acad Achvt Awd; Med.

TRAN, LAWRENCE THANH; Sonora HS; Fullerton, CA; (2); 1/316; Math Clb; Math Tm; Spanish Clb; JV Tennis; High Hon Roll; Orange Cnty Acad Decathlon; Statsman Of America; Amer Chem Soc; UCLA; Law.

TRAN, LE; La Quinta HS; Garden Grove, CA; (3); Dance Clb; Key Clb; Pep Clb; Science Clb; Teachers Aide; Cit Awd; High Hon Roll; NHS; Badmntn; Med.

TRAN, LIEM; Norwalk HS; Norwalk, CA; (3); French Clb; Math Clb; Math Tm; Science Clb; Badminton; U Of Southern CA; Comp Bus.

TRAN, LIEN MY; Saddleback HS; Santa Ana, CA; (4); Drama Clb; French Clb; Girl Scts; Chorus; Yrbk; Var Capt Tennis; NHS; Prfct Atten Awd; Badminton Var; Vietnamese Club Sec; Chinese Club; Cal ST U Pomona; Elec Engrng.

TRAN, LILA; Andrew P Hill HS; San Jose, CA; (2); Rep Stu Cncl; Var Tennis; Psych.

TRAN, LINH; San Gabriel HS; Alhambra, CA; (3); Computer Clb; Mgr JA; Red Cross Aide; Science Clb; Service Clb; Spanish Clb; Cit Awd; High Hon Roll; Schltc Awd; Nrsng.

TRAN, LINH; Skyline HS; Oakland, CA; (3).

TRAN, LINH M; Armijo HS; Suisun, CA; (3); AFS; VICA; Cit Awd; Hon Roll; Prfct Atten Awd; Asian/Amer & Mexican Clbs; San Jose ST; Elem Tchr.

TRAN, LINH M; C K Mcclately HS; Sacramento, CA; (4); Church Yth Grp; Office Aide; Church Choir; Orch; Hon Roll; Treasurer Of Church Youth Group; Work Experience; Special Interest Tennis & Football; U C Davis; Psychiatry.

TRAN, LINH U; University HS; Irvine, CA; (1); Debate Tm; Spanish Clb; JV Trk; Candy Striping Hosp; Medical Clb; Girls League; UCLA; Med.

TRAN, LOAN K; Norte-Vista HS; Riverside, CA; (1); High Hon Roll; ARCH.

TRAN, LOAN T; Montclair HS; Montclair, CA; (3); 46/420; French Clb; Orch; Hon Roll; Natl Ltn Exm Awd; U CA Davis; Med.

TRAN, LONG; San Gabriel HS; San Gabriel, CA; (3); Cmnty Wkr; FBLA; Library Aide; Teachers Aide; Cit Awd; Hon Roll; Prfct Atten Awd; CSF 87-88; Prjct Apprctn; Won 5th Plc Name Tag Dsgn FBLA Gold Coast Sctn Cnfrnc.

TRAN, LONG H; Hawthorne HS; Lawndale, CA; (2); Yrbk; Bsbl; Bsktbl; Vllybl; Cit Awd; Prfct Atten Awd; Pres Acad Fit Awd; OH ST U; Bus Mgmt.

TRAN, LONG Q; Skyline HS; Oakland, CA; (2); Chess Clb; Math Clb; CA Schlrshp Fed; Bio.

TRAN, MAI N; Silver Creek HS; San Jose, CA; (3); Computer Clb; Math Clb; Hon Roll; Interact Club; Photo Club, Fut Med Wrkr Club; Awd Of Merit & Achvt; Optometry.

TRAN, MANDY; Saddleback HS; Santa Ana, CA; (2); Orch; STEP & VCU Partners Clb; CSF; Hnr Orchestra Awd; Berkeley; Math.

TRAN, MARTINA P; Laguna Hills HS; Laguna Hills, CA; (2); 11/343; Church Yth Grp; Cmnty Wkr; English Clb; French Clb; Hosp Aide; Intnl Clb; Key Clb; Math Clb; Model UN; SADD; Stanford U; Pre-Med.

TRAN, MARY L; Tustin HS; Tustin, CA; (2); Hosp Aide; Key Clb; Hon Roll; U Of Irvine.

TRAN, MELISSA; Independence HS; San Jose, CA; (3); Art Clb; Debate Tm; Math Clb; Science Clb; Spanish Clb; Teachers Aide; Cit Awd; Gov Hon Prg Awd; High Hon Roll; Santa Clara; Bus.

TRAN, MIKE; Damien HS; Chino, CA; (2); 69/269; Letterman Clb; Varsity Clb; Nwsp; JV Ftbl; Var Socr; Var Trk; Wt Lftg; Cit Awd; Hon Roll; Pres Acad Fit Awd; Sccr Clb; Santa Clara; Psych.

TRAN, MIKE P; Huntington Beach HS; Huntington Beach, CA; (2); Boy Scts; Church Yth Grp; Cmnty Wkr; Model UN; Color Guard; JV L Trk; High Hon Roll; Hon Roll; Military Explorers; Med.

TRAN, MILTON; Lowell HS; San Francisco, CA; (2); Church Yth Grp; Cmnty Wkr; Pres Acad Fit Awd; Earth Day Envrnmntl Bch Clean Up; UC Davis; Arch.

TRAN, MINHDUC D; Abraham Lincoln HS; San Francisco, CA; (3); Temple Yth Grp; UC Berkeley; Aerospace Engrng.

TRAN, MUOI HONG LAM; Mt Pleasant HS; San Jose, CA; (1); Math Clb; High Hon Roll; Vietnamese Club; Uc BERKELEY; Psych.

TRAN, MY DUYEN; Andrew Hill HS; San Jose, CA; (3); Dance Clb; French Clb; Math Tm; Swmmng; Tennis; Vllybl; Hon Roll.

TRAN, MY LINH; Baldwin Park HS; Baldwin Park, CA; (2); Hosp Aide; VP Math Clb; JV Swmmng; Var Tennis; JV Vllybl; High Hon Roll; Hon Roll; Stanford; Bus Mgmt.

TRAN, MYLINH; Baldwin Park HS; Baldwin Park, CA; (2); VP Math Clb; JV Swmmng; Var Tennis; JV Vllybl; Hon Roll.

TRAN, NAM; Galileo HS; San Francisco, CA; (4); Computer Clb; French Clb; Math Clb; Science Clb; Teachers Aide; San Francisco ST U; Acctng.

TRAN, NANCY N; Montclair HS; Montclair, CA; (1); Temple Yth Grp; Variety Show; JV Tennis; Hon Roll; Prfct Atten Awd; Gate Club; UCLA; Bus Mgmt.

TRAN, NGHI H; Buena Park HS; Anaheim, CA; (3); 34/400; Church Yth Grp; French Clb; Key Clb; Science Clb; Varsity Clb; VP Jr Cls; Var Crs Cntry; Var Socr; High Hon Roll; NHS; Asian Clb; Stu Of Mnth.

TRAN, NGOC M; San Gabriel HS; Rosemead, CA; (2); Teachers Aide; Chorus; Tennis; Cit Awd; Hon Roll; CA ST; Fshn Dsgnr.

TRAN, NGOCLAN T; Santiago HS; Garden Grove, CA; (2); Math Clb; Band; Orch; Hon Roll; UCI; Med.

TRAN, NGUYEN; Leuzinger HS; Hawthorne, CA; (1); Cit Awd; High Hon Roll; CSF; Yale; Astronomy.

TRAN, NGUYET M; Mission Viejo HS; El Toro, CA; (3); Church Yth Grp; French Clb; Key Clb; Var Tennis; Cit Awd; Hon Roll; CSF; Med.

TRAN, NGUYET T; Bolsa Grande HS; Garden Grove, CA; (1); Tennis; Mdl Mst Imprvd Track; Awd CIF Qlfr Track; Rsprty Thrpst.

TRAN, NHAN; San Bernardino HS; San Bernardino, CA; (3); Art Clb; Cmnty Wkr; Math Clb; Var Tennis; High Hon Roll; Hon Roll; Asian Club; Hunger Buster Club; Hnrbl Mntn & 3rd Pl My Amer Art Cntst; Cal Poly Pomona; Engrng.

TRAN, NHAN C; Poly HS; Long Beach, CA; (2); 1/700; Cmnty Wkr; Hosp Aide; Intnl Clb; Math Clb; Scholastic Bowl; Speech Tm; L Orch; JV Tennis; High Hon Roll; L NHS; Acad, Athl & Art Lttrs; Acad Challenge Bowl; Stanford; Medicine.

TRAN, NHAN L; John F Kennedy HS; Mission Hills, CA; (3); Library Aide; Service Clb; Bsktbl; Prfct Atten Awd; Pres Acad Fit Awd; CSUN; Chld Psych.

TRAN, NHU-Y; Senior HS; Stockton, CA; (4); Yrbk.

TRAN, NHUAN; Troy HS; Fullerton, CA; (2); Key Clb; Math Clb; Spanish Clb; Vllybl; Wt Lftg; High Hon Roll; Medical.

TRAN, NINH; Learny HS; San Diego, CA; (2); Boy Scts; Off Jr Cls; Wt Lftg; Hon Roll; Mgr.

TRAN, OANH T; Garden Grove HS; Garden Grove, CA; (3); Intnl Clb; CSF; Cal Poly Pomona; Comp Sci.

TRAN, OLIVIER; Alhambra HS; Alhambra, CA; (3); Spanish Clb; CSF; 5 On French AP Lang Exam; UCLA; Dentistry.

TRAN, PAUL V; Oakland HS; Oakland, CA; (3); Pres German Clb; Key Clb; Color Guard; Drill Tm; Hon Roll; San Jose ST; Comp Engr.

TRAN, PETER T; Richard Gahr HS; Artesia, CA; (3); Boy Scts; French Clb; JA; Teachers Aide; Phtg Yrbk; Tennis Club; Blue & Gold Awd; Sea Scouts; Knowledge Master; Bus.

TRAN, PHONG V; Workman HS; Valinda, CA; (3); Varsity Clb; High Hon Roll; Hon Roll; Prfct Atten Awd; Vrsty Bdmntn; UCLA; Comp Prog.

TRAN, PHUNG MY; Gompers SR Schl; San Diego, CA; (2); 8/145; Spanish Clb; Hon Roll; Jr NHS; NHS; Pan-Asian Club; California Scholarship Federation; Job As Orthodontic Assist; Mock Trail; Letter Excllnc; English.

TRAN, PHUONG B; Independence HS; San Jose, CA; (4); FBLA; Science Clb; The Young Astronauts Club; San Jose ST U; Business Manage.

TRAN, PHUONG D; El Toro HS; El Toro, CA; (2); 8/557; German Clb; Key Clb; Intrml Bsktbl; Intrml Crs Cntry; Intrml Trk; Cit Awd; Hon Roll; Physician.

TRAN, PHUONG JESSICA; San Gabriel HS; Alhambra, CA; (1); Hon Roll; NHS; Prfct Atten Awd; Stretcher Crew; U Of CA Riverside; Phrmcst.

TRAN, PHUONG K; Andrew Hill HS; San Jose, CA; (3); French Clb; Math Clb; Math Tm; High Hon Roll; Hon Roll; Anti-Graffiti; CSF.

TRAN, PHUONG K; Ramona HS; Riverside, CA; (3); Chess Clb; FBLA; Intnl Clb; High Hon Roll; Pres Acad Fit Awd; Medicine.

TRAN, PHUONG MARY; Valley HS; Sacramento, CA; (4); 10/412; Teachers Aide; Elks Awd; High Hon Roll; Hon Roll; Prfct Atten Awd; CSF; SE Asian Clb; Cls Of 90 Top Ten Awd; CA ST U; Teachng.

TRAN, PHUONG N; Alhambra HS; Alhambra, CA; (3); Computer Clb; Spanish NHS; Math & Sci Hnr Society; Engrng.

TRAN, PHUONG PRISCILLA M; Skyline HS; Oakland, CA; (2); Rep French Clb; Science Clb; SADD; Teachers Aide; Cit Awd; High Hon Roll; Hon Roll; JSF; CSF; Int Decorator.

TRAN, PHUONG T; Wilson HS; Long Beach, CA; (3); Hosp Aide; Math Tm; Orch; Tennis; Vllybl; NHS; Prfct Atten Awd.

TRAN, PHUONG THAO; Saddleback HS; Santa Ana, CA; (3); Art Clb; Chess Clb; FBLA; Mu Alpha Theta; Science Clb; Acad Lttr; Gldn St Exm Awd.

TRAN, PHYLLIS; Abraham Lincoln HS; San Francisco, CA; (1); Hon Roll; Chinese Clb.

TRAN, QUAN L; Oakland Technical HS; Oakland, CA; (2); French Clb; JV Bsktbl; Vietnamese Stu Assn; Phys Thrpy.

TRAN, QUANG; Oxnard HS; Oxnard, CA; (1); JV Socr; Hon Roll; Aviation Clb; UCLA; Medcl.

TRAN, QUANG M; Leuzinger HS; Hawthorne, CA; (3); Pres Computer Clb; Science Clb; JV Crs Cntry; JV Trk; Cit Awd; Hon Roll; Engr.

TRAN, QUANG N; Crawford HS; San Diego, CA; (1); Latin Clb; SADD; Band; Tennis; High Hon Roll; Hon Roll; NHS; Prfct Atten Awd; Pres Acad Fit Awd.

TRAN, QUE-TRAN; Westminster HS; Westminster, CA; (3); JCL; Key Clb; Latin Clb; Letterman Clb; Service Clb; Teachers Aide; Varsity Clb; Fld Hcky; Tennis; Vllybl; Bdmntn Jr Natl Team Rgn; Jr Natl CSF; CA Schlrshp Fed; AP Advnc Plcmnt Clb; ASU; Ed.

TRAN, QUY N; John F Kennedy HS; Sacramento, CA; (1); 1/564; Boy Scts; High Hon Roll; Hon Roll; Prfct Atten Awd; Math.

TRAN, QUYEN; Hoover HS; Fresno, CA; (1); High Hon Roll; Hon Roll; Prfct Atten Awd; Pres Acad Fit Awd; Frshmn Tp 5% Aws; Govrnrs Acad Achvmnt Awds; Princpls Awd Acad Excllnc; Elec Engr.

TRAN, QUYNH D; Hawthorne HS; Hawthorne, CA; (3); Cmnty Wkr; Hosp Aide; Key Clb; Math Clb; Hon Roll; CSF; Long Beach ST; Nrsg.

TRAN, REBECCA; Oakland HS; Oakland, CA; (3); French Clb; German Clb; Key Clb; Yrbk; Sec VP Soph Cls; VP Jr Cls; Cit Awd; High Hon Roll; Real Estate.

TRAN, RICHARD CHAN; Marina HS; Huntington Bch, CA; (4); 105/484; JA; Key Clb; Spanish Clb; Hon Roll; Vietnamese Clb Treas, Pres & VP; Advncd Cert Archtrl Drftng; Survey Cert Bus; U Of AZ; Arch.

TRAN, RICKY H; Buena Park HS; Buena Park, CA; (3); Acad Awds Pgrm; Vrsty Badmntn & Won CIF Sctn 4-A Champ; Drwng & Radio Cntrl; Cal Poly Pomona.

TRAN, SAM N; Oakland HS; Oakland, CA; (2); Math Tm; School Musical; Stu Cncl; Hon Roll; UC; Bus.

TRAN, SANG; Montebello HS; Montebello, CA; (2); Hon Roll; Prfct Atten Awd; Engr.

TRAN, SANG E; John F Kennedy HS; Los Angeles, CA; (3); Cmnty Wkr; Key Clb; Math Clb; Teachers Aide; Cit Awd; High Hon Roll; Prfct Atten Awd; JFK Math Hon Soc Outstndng Tutor 89.

TRAN, SHARON H; Gardena HS; Gardena, CA; (3); Intnl Clb; Service Clb; Spanish Clb; Rptr Nwsp; Ed Yrbk; JV Vllybl; Pres Acad Fit Awd; Pres Schlr; Squires; Oscar Awd.

TRAN, SON V; Edison HS; Stockton, CA; (2); French Clb; Var Tennis; UCO Clb; CA Poly; Engr Auto Desgn.

TRAN, STEPHANIE V; Hayward HS; Hayward, CA; (3); Church Yth Grp; German Clb; Pep Clb; Science Clb; Band; Color Guard; Mrchg Band; Rep Soph Cls; Var Cheerldng; Var Pom Pon; Sci.

TRAN, STEVEN; Schurr HS; Montebello, CA; (2); Cmnty Wkr; Drama Clb; Intnl Clb; Stage Crew; Hon Roll; Prfct Atten Awd; NY U; Med.

TRAN, STEVEN M; Skyline HS; Oakland, CA; (3); Chess Clb; Hon Roll; Aisan Stu Union; U CA-BERKELEY; Bus.

TRAN, SUSAN; San Gabriel HS; San Gabriel, CA; (1); VP Debate Tm; NFL; Spanish Clb; Speech Tm; Rep Frsh Cls; Var Trk; Vllybl; Hon Roll; YMCA Svc Club; Stu Govt/Ldrshp Exec Brd; Govt Ldrshp Awd; UC Berkeley; Law.

TRAN, SUSAN H; Live Oak HS; Morgan Hill, CA; (3); 2/530; French Clb; Hosp Aide; Treas Key Clb; Service Clb; Mrchg Band; Rep Stu Cncl; JV Fld Hcky; High Hon Roll; Ntl Merit SF; Pres Acad Fit Awd; PLUS; Peer Tutr 88-90; Smmr Anlytcl Chem Fllwshp; And & Color Grd Soviet Union Tour 90.

TRAN, TAI; Independence HS; San Jose, CA; (3); 45/963; Chess Clb; Church Yth Grp; French Clb; Math Tm; Science Clb; Service Clb; VP Soph Cls; Intrml Tennis; Intrml Vllybl; U CA Davis; Bio-Chem.

TRAN, TALSON H; La Sierra HS; Corona, CA; (1); Var L Tennis; Cit Awd; Gov Hon Prg Awd; High Hon Roll; Opt Clb Awd; Prfct Atten Awd; Pres Acad Fit Awd; Harvard U; Phy.

TRAN, TAM C; Hart HS; Newhall, CA; (2); High Hon Roll; Prfct Atten Awd; Pres Acad Fit Awd; UCLA; Comp Tech.

TRAN, TARYN H; San Gabriel HS; Rosemead, CA; (2); French Clb; FBLA; Office Aide; Service Clb; SADD; JV Tennis; Hon Roll; Cal Poly Pomona; CIS.

TRAN, THAI; Workman HS; Valinda, CA; (3); Varsity Clb; High Hon Roll; Hon Roll; Prfct Atten Awd; Vrsty Bdmntn; UCLA; Math.

TRAN, THAITO; California HS; Norwalk, CA; (3); 32/328; Church Yth Grp; French Clb; German Clb; Library Aide; Math Clb; Teachers Aide; Church Choir; JV Crs Cntry; JV Tennis; Hon Roll; Stu Of Mnth Rcgntn Of Soc Sci; CSF; Acad Decathlon.

TRAN, THANH; Crawford HS; San Diego, CA; (3); French Clb; Cit Awd; High Hon Roll; Hon Roll; NHS; Pres Acad Fit Awd; Rgnl Occptnl Pgm Cert; Accuracy Typing Hnr Rl; Golden St Exam Awd Acad Excllnc.

TRAN, THANH; Luther Burbank HS; Sacramento, CA; (3); 12/276; Cit Awd; Hon Roll; Sec Newcomers Clb; Chem Awd; U Of Pacific; Phrmcst.

TRAN, THANH; Orange HS; Westminster, CA; (4); 7/400; Cmnty Wkr; Math Clb; Math Tm; Mu Alpha Theta; Science Clb; JV Var Crs Cntry; Var L Tennis; Cit Awd; High Hon Roll; Hon Roll; Alt CIF Crss Cntry 89; Cal Poly-Pomona; Mech Engrng.

TRAN, THANH B; John F Kennedy HS; Fremont, CA; (2); Church Yth Grp; French Clb; Science Clb; Spanish Clb; SADD; Intrml Ftbl; JV Tennis; High Hon Roll; Hon Roll; Prfct Atten Awd; N Coast Section CIF Scholar Athl; CSF; UC Santa Barbara; Cmptr Sci.

TRAN, THANH C; Chaffey HS; Ontario, CA; (3); 28/250; Library Aide; Treas Science Clb; Spanish Clb; Teachers Aide; Hon Roll; Prfct Atten Awd; CSF; Spllng Be Chmpn; CA ST Pomona; Astrnmy.

TRAN, THANH C; Etiwanda HS; Cucamonga, CA; (3); JV Socr; Hon Roll; Prfct Atten Awd; Pres Acad Fit Awd; CA ST Polytechnic U Pomona.

TRAN, THANH C; Taft HS; Canoga Park, CA; (2); Service Clb; Pres Acad Fit Awd; CSF; Gldn St Exam-Hnr Geom Awd; Dr.

TRAN, THANH V; Westminster HS; Westminster, CA; (2); Church Yth Grp; Cmnty Wkr; JV Bsktbl; Score Keeper; UCLA; Engrng.

TRAN, THAO; Live Oak HS; San Jose, CA; (3); 11/530; FBLA; SADD; JV Tennis; Hon Roll; Prfct Atten Awd; CSF; Vlntr Tutoring Pgm.

TRAN, THAO D; Mt Pleasant HS; San Jose, CA; (4); NHS; CSF; Vietnamese Club; San Jose ST U; Bus.

TRAN, THAO H; Anaheim HS; Anaheim, CA; (4); Variety Show; Asian Clb; Vietnm Mrtl Arts Clb; Intl Bus.

TRAN, THAO H; Saddleback HS; Santa Ana, CA; (4); 41/508; French Clb; Prfct Atten Awd; GSE Hnr; ESL Outstndng Cert; UCI Prtnrs; Bio Sci.

TRAN, THAO NGOC; Lakewood SR HS; Long Beach, CA; (3); 25/788; Debate Tm; VP French Clb; Lit Mag; Rep Frsh Cls; Rep Soph Cls; Intrml Vllybl; High Hon Roll; Hon Roll; NHS; Drwng & Painting; Grls League; Med.

TRAN, THAO P; River City HS; W Sacramento, CA; (2); Church Yth Grp; French Clb; Bsktbl; Upward Bound Pgm; UC Davis; Med.

TRAN, THAO T; Pasadena HS; Pasadena, CA; (2); Debate Tm; Q&S; Speech Tm; Pres Nwsp; Pres Lit Mag; Hon Roll; Rotary Awd; CA Schlrshp Fed; Psych.

TRAN, THAO T; Westminster HS; Westminster, CA; (3); Dance Clb; Girl Scts; Latin Clb; Spanish Clb; SADD; Teachers Aide; Temple Yth Grp; Pres Acad Fit Awd; Mst Athltc Female; Southern CA Coll Optometry.

TRAN, THERESA; Marian HS; Huntington Bch, CA; (4); 75/500; Church Yth Grp; JA; Key Clb; Spanish Clb; SADD; Color Guard; Lit Mag; Hon Roll; Yale; Lawyer.

TRAN, THIEM QUOC; Hoover SR HS; San Diego, CA; (2); Var Tennis; High Hon Roll; Hon Roll; NHS; Vietnamese Amer PTA Rcgntn Of Acadmc Excllnc; UCSD; Mech Engr.

TRAN, THIEN; Madison HS; San Diego, CA; (3); 2/349; Am Leg Aux Girls St; Latin Clb; Treas Frsh Cls; Stu Cncl; Var L Tennis; High Hon Roll; NHS; Prfct Atten Awd; All Cntrl Leag Girls Tennis Tm Champn 89-90; Natl Young Leaders Congrssnl Schlr; Law.

TRAN, THIEN Q; Leuzinger HS; Hawthorne, CA; (1); Church Yth Grp; School Play; UCLA.

TRAN, THIEN Q; Rosemead HS; Rosemead, CA; (3); Computer Clb; Key Clb; Math Clb; Science Clb; Spanish Clb; Teachers Aide; High Hon Roll; Hon Roll; Prfct Atten Awd; CSF; Key Clb Awd; Cal Poly U; Electronics.

TRAN, THO T; Westminster HS; Westminster, CA; (3); Church Yth Grp; French Clb; FFA; Key Clb; JV Bsktbl; JV Tennis; JV Vllybl; Cit Awd; High Hon Roll; Lion Awd; 90 Orange Cnty Fr Advertising Graphics Awd; UCLA; Art.

TRAN, THUY; Cleveland HS; Northridge, CA; (4); FFA; Hosp Aide; Service Clb; Teachers Aide; Hon Roll; CSUN; Bus.

TRAN, THUY; Rosemead HS; Rosemead, CA; (3); 3/35; High Hon Roll; Hon Roll; Prfct Atten Awd; CSF; Cal Poly Pomona; Engr.

TRAN, THUY T; Anaheim HS; Anaheim, CA; (3); Math Clb; Science Clb; Cal ST Fullerton; Acctg.

TRAN, THUY T; Tustin HS; Tustin, CA; (2); Church Yth Grp; UCI; Elec Engrng.

TRAN, THY N; Buena Park HS; Buena Park, CA; (3); 3/260; Hosp Aide; Intnl Clb; Sec JA; Sec Key Clb; Red Cross Aide; Science Clb; JV Bsktbl; JV Var Tennis; High Hon Roll; NHS; Asian Club Pres; JSA Secy; Badminton Tm CIF 4-A Div; UCLA; Med.

TRAN, TIET; Kearny HS; San Diego, CA; (3); Boy Scts; Hon Roll; USTTA; Air Trffc Cntrllr.

TRAN, TRACY T; San Gabriel HS; Alhambra, CA; (2); Dance Clb; FBLA; Hon Roll; JETS Awd; Chinese,Vietnmes Clb; Hnrbl Ment Sci; CA ST; Tchr.

TRAN, TRAM B; Garfield Computer Magnet HS; Los Angeles, CA; (3); Computer Clb; Math Clb; Q&S; Science Clb; Variety Show; Rptr Nwsp; Rptr Lit Mag; Rep Stu Cncl; JV Tennis; Hon Roll; UC Riverside; Bus.

TRAN, TRAM N; Crawford HS; San Diego, CA; (1); Church Yth Grp; Girl Scts; Intnl Clb; Spanish Clb; Nwsp; High Hon Roll; CSF; Bus.

TRAN, TRANG T; Edison HS; Huntington Beach, CA; (3); 4/425; Church Yth Grp; Dance Clb; Hosp Aide; Spanish Clb; SADD; High Hon Roll; 1Cl Awd Top Girl Stu Sci & Math; Golden Key Awd; Chroprctr 3rd Pl Essay Wnnr; UCLA; Pre Med.

TRAN, TRANG THI DOAN; Westminster HS; Westminster, CA; (4); 121/420; Chess Clb; French Clb; Key Clb; Service Clb; Teachers Aide; Church Choir; Book Club ; Library Club; Ap Club; Sign-Language Club; UCI; Psychology.

TRAN, TRANGNGOC THI; Valley HS; Sacramento, CA; (4); Teachers Aide; Hon Roll; CSF; Bnk America Achvt Awd; CSU Hayward; Intl Rltns.

TRAN, TRINH; Thomas Downey HS; Modesto, CA; (4); 58/436; Key Clb; Service Clb; Spanish Clb; Chorus; Cit Awd; Hon Roll; Prfct Atten Awd; CSF; Bank Of Amer Awd For Bus; Accntng Clb; San Jose ST U; Bus.

TRAN, TRINH K; Encina HS; Carmichael, CA; (2); #1 In Class; Treas Computer Clb; French Clb; VP Intnl Clb; Spanish Clb; Temple Yth Grp; Mgr Nwsp; Lit Mag; VP Soph Cls; Socr; Vllybl.

TRAN, TRINH N; Saddleback HS; Santa Ana, CA; (2); Science Clb; Cit Awd; High Hon Roll; Tutrng Mth,Eng, Sci, AP & GATE Clss; Cmptr Awd; CA Schlstc Fed; Hughes Smmr Sci Acad; U Of CA Irvine; Bio.

TRAN, TRINH Y; Bolsa Grande HS; Garden Grove, CA; (1); Cit Awd; Hon Roll; UC Irvine; Bus.

TRAN, TRUNG T; Montclair HS; Montclair, CA; (2); FBLA; Hon Roll; 9th Annual Writing Celebration Author; Cert Excllnc Cmptrs; Acad Achvt Awd Eng I Hnrs; :Cmptr Sci.

TRAN, TU; Andrew Hill HS; San Jose, CA; (3); Bus Profs of Am; English Clb; French Clb; FBLA; Math Clb; Math Tm; Speech Tm; Drm Mjr(t); School Musical; School Play.

TRAN, TU; Mira Mesa HS; San Diego, CA; (2); French Clb; Science Clb; Mgr(s); Cit Awd; Hon Roll; NHS; Prfct Atten Awd; Pres Schlr; 3rd Pl Sci Fair; World Relief Clb; CSF; Ucsd; Phrmst.

TRAN, TUAN; Anaheim HS; Anaheim, CA; (3); Art Clb; Computer Clb; Math Clb; Science Clb; Temple Yth Grp; Off Sr Cls; Socr; Math Hnr; UC Irvine; Med.

TRAN, TUAN A; Milpitas HS; Milpitas, CA; (1); 100/548; Library Aide; High Hon Roll; Hon Roll; Frnds Of Milpitas Cmmty Libr; Philatelist Columbia Squires; Tae Kwon Do; CA ST U; Electrnc Engrng.

TRAN, TUMAI D; Orange HS; Orange, CA; (3); GAA; Pres Key Clb; Math Clb; Model UN; Pres Science Clb; Rptr Nwsp; L Tennis; High Hon Roll; Jr NHS; NHS; Decathlon; Mock Trial; Cultures In Action; UCI; Med.

TRAN, TUONG C; Hiram Johnson HS; Sacramento, CA; (1); 44/190; UC Davis; Elec Engr.

TRAN, TUYEN; Herbert Hoover HS; Glendale, CA; (4); Bus Profs of Am; Nwsp; Off Sr Cls; Sftbl; Tennis; Vllybl; Hon Roll; Prf Oprtr; Data Entry; CA ST Los Angeles; Bus Accntn.

TRAN, TUYET T; Troy HS; Fullerton, CA; (2); 39/330; Spanish Clb; High Hon Roll; Law.

TRAN, UY T; Mountain View HS; El Monte, CA; (1); 2/30; English Clb; Math Clb; Science Clb; Hon Roll; Prfct Atten Awd.

TRAN, VICTORIA; Ocean View HS; Huntington Bch, CA; (4); Cmnty Wkr; FBLA; Red Cross Aide; JV Tennis; Prfct Atten Awd; Vietnamese Clb VP; Loma Linda U; Drmtlgy.

TRAN, VINH D; San Gabriel HS; Rosemead, CA; (2); Computer Clb; SADD; JV Bsktbl; Intrml Crs Cntry; Hon Roll; Pharm.

TRAN, VINH T; Independence HS; San Jose, CA; (2); San Jose ST U; Mech Engr.

TRAN, VU; La Puente HS; La Puente, CA; (3); Chess Clb; Science Clb; Hon Roll.

TRAN, VU; San Gorgonio HS; San Bernardino, CA; (3); 19/400; Boy Scts; Church Yth Grp; SADD; High Hon Roll; Prfct Atten Awd; Golden St Ex Hnrs Alb,Geo; Cal Poly Pomona; Arch.

TRAN, VY H; Foothill HS; Pleasanton, CA; (3); Sec Debate Tm; FBLA; Hosp Aide; Var Swmmng; Hon Roll; CSF; Piano; Extra Commnctn Courses Jr Coll; Santa Clara U; Pre-Law.

TRAN, WILLIAM; Magnolia HS; Anaheim, CA; (1); Tennis; Cit Awd; Hon Roll; NHS.

TRAN, XUAN H; Kearny HS; San Diego, CA; (2); 10/378; Chess Clb; Math Clb; Model UN; Phtg Yrbk; High Hon Roll; Lion Awd; Pres Acad Fit Awd; Sal; Monty Awd; Acadmc Excllnc Vietnamese Amer PTA 86-90; Math Stu Of Yr Awd 88-89; UCSD; Comp Pgmr.

TRAN, YEN; Andrew Hill HS; San Jose, CA; (3); Church Yth Grp; Cmnty Wkr; Variety Show; Score Keeper; Hon Roll; UC Davis; Med.

TRAN, YEN; Los Amigos HS; Santa Ana, CA; (2); 12/412; French Clb; Treas Key Clb; Scholastic Bowl; Tennis; High Hon Roll; CSF; UCLABUS.

TRAN, YEN; Rancho Alamitos HS; Garden Grove, CA; (4); Computer Clb; Science Clb; Spanish Clb; Teachers Aide; High Hon Roll; Hon Roll; NHS; Prfct Atten Awd; CA Poly U-Pomona; Comp Sci.

TRAN, YEN N; Mira Mesa HS; San Diego, CA; (2); Hon Roll; Bus Admin.

TRAN, YENTRAN; Dos Pueblos HS; Goleta, CA; (3); 22/320; Pep Clb; Science Clb; Teachers Aide; Ed Nwsp; Ed Yrbk; Score Keeper; Jr NHS; NHS; Prfct Atten Awd; Marine Bio Club; CSF.

TRAN, YNHU T; Mission Viejo HS; El Toro, CA; (1); 1/250; Church Yth Grp; Band; Mrchg Band; Hon Roll; Top 25 Cls Frshmn #1; Hgh Hnrs Awd GSE Math; Stanford; Pedtrcn.

TRANCHI, THAO H; Kennedy HS; Granada Hills, CA; (3); Boy Scts; Yrbk; Bsktbl; Vllybl; Hon Roll; Prfct Atten Awd; Med.

TRANG, MAI N; Oakland HS; Oakland, CA; (3); French Clb; Library Aide; Service Clb; SADD; Teachers Aide; Yrbk; Cit Awd; Hon Roll; Close-Up Club; Keywanettes Club Co-Secy.

TRAPP, JENNIFER; Righetti HS; Santa Maria, CA; (3); 4/350; Stu Cncl; High Hon Roll; St Schlr; JSA Vc & Rgnl Assmbly Dir; Acad Dcthln Tm; Claremont Mc Kenna Coll; Govt.

TRAUB, CLIFFORD G; Modesta Christian HS; Modesto, CA; (3); Church Yth Grp; Letterman Clb; Office Aide; Scholastic Bowl; Varsity Clb; Band; Chorus; Church Choir; Pep Band; School Musical; Mission To Mexico; Azusa Coll; Business.

TRAUGOTT, KATHLEEN D; Etiwanda HS; Rancho Cucamonga, CA; (2); Church Yth Grp; Math Tm; Band; Mrchg Band; Pep Band; High Hon Roll; Jr NHS; Prfct Atten Awd; Animal Rights Clb; Acctng.

TRAVER, DAN R; Poway HS; San Diego, CA; (4); Computer Clb; Math Clb; Varsity Clb; CA Scholastic Federation; Head Student Athletic Trainer For Football And Womens Soccer; San Diego St U; Athltc Trainer.

TRAVERS, DEVON C; El Toro HS; El Toro, CA; (3); 25/550; Sec Bsktbl; JV Var Cheerldng; JV Vllybl; High Hon Roll; St Schlr; Frgn Lang Stu Of Mnth; Excllnc Awds-Engl & U S Hstry; U Of CA San Diego.

TRAVERS, SHAUN RANDALL; La Quinta HS; Westminster, CA; (4); 35/338; Church Yth Grp; Drama Clb; Thesps; Band; Church Choir; Drm Mjr(t); Mrchg Band; School Play; Yrbk; NHS; Clss Schlr Yr; Fn Arts Schlr Yr; CA Lutheran U.

TRAVERSO, THOMAS E; Montgomery HS; Santa Rosa, CA; (2); Church Yth Grp; French Clb; Letterman Clb; Tennis; High Hon Roll; Hon Roll; Jr NHS; Opt Clb Awd; Prfct Atten Awd; Pres Acad Fit Awd; Tennis Clb.

TRAWICK, MICHELLE D; Tehachapi HS; Tehachapi, CA; (1); Teachers Aide; Flag Corp; Cheerldng.

TRAYLOR, LAKISHA C; George Washington Prep HS; Los Angeles, CA; (2); Church Yth Grp; Girl Scts; Math Clb; ROTC; SADD; Teachers Aide; Church Choir; School Play; Nwsp; Yrbk; Harvard; Lawyer.

TRAYNOR, ERIN; Palmdale HS; Palmdale, CA; (1); 172/583; Aud/Vis; Church Yth Grp; GATE Pgm 89-90; Recd 2 Hnrb Mntn HS Art Show 90; Psycht.

TRAZO, ROBERT; Narbonne Math/Science Magnet HS; Carson, CA; (4); Key Clb; Math Tm; Band; Drm Mjr(t); Trk; Cit Awd; Hon Roll; Church Yth Grp; Debate Tm; Pep Band; Congressnl Awd Recipient; Schlr Athlete Awd 87-90; Key Club Pres, Sec, Jr Rep; UCLA; Mech Engrng.

TREADWAY, LARA D; Clairemont HS; San Diego, CA; (3); 2/212; Hosp Aide; Teachers Aide; Band; Mrchg Band; Rptr Nwsp; Treas Sr Cls; Crs Cntry; JV L Swmmng; Var L Tennis; CSF; Math & Sci Awd-Rensselaer Medl.

TREADWELL, MARGARET L; Berkeley HS; Berkeley, CA; (3); Teachers Aide; High Hon Roll; Gldn St Exm Geomtry Hnrs Awd; JSA; Csf; Physics.

TREAGUS, CHRIS M; Santa Rosa HS; Santa Rosa, CA; (2); School Play; Writers Clb; Author.

TREE, MEADOW; Santa Clara HS; Santa Clara, CA; (3); 99/420; Church Yth Grp; Capt Debate Tm; French Clb; JA; Pep Clb; Teachers Aide; Chorus; Church Choir; Variety Show; Score Keeper; Wildrnss Adventrs Clb, Natrl Issues Comm; Rep Assembly; Voice.

TREER, TANISIA; Woodrow Wilson HS; San Francisco, CA; (4); Rep Sr Cls; Sec Stu Cncl; Rep Frsh Cls; Rep Soph Cls; Rep Jr Cls; Starquest Clb Sci Fctn Pres & Fndr; Sonoma ST U; Englsh.

TREIBER, JAMES A; Foothill HS; Santa Ana, CA; (3); Boy Scts; Church Yth Grp; Var L Crs Cntry; Var Trk; Boy Sct LDS Duty To God Awd; Order Of Knight; Combat Fghtr Pilot.

TREICHLER, DENISE E; River City HS; W Sacramento, CA; (1); 7/304; High Hon Roll; PEER; CSF; FNL; Stanford; Med.

TREICHLER, JOY C; River City HS; W Sacramento, CA; (1); Church Yth Grp; SADD; Thesps; Church Choir; Mrchg Band; School Play; Cheerldng; Hon Roll; Drama Clb; Drm Mjr(t); Galena Street East Sacramentos Prfrmng Ambssdrs; Dance.

TREICHLER, MATTHEW R; Poway HS; San Diego, CA; (4); 25/728; Letterman Clb; Varsity Clb; Treas Stu Cncl; L Var Swmmng; Wrstlng; Hon Roll; NHS; Water Polo Tm Cptn Vrsty Tm; UC Davis; Cvl Engr.

TREICK, RACHEL; Community Christian HS; Bakersfield, CA; (3); 1/20; Computer Clb; Office Aide; Teachers Aide; Chorus; Church Choir; Sec Frsh Cls; Pres Soph Cls; Pres Jr Cls; Var Cheerldng; Var Powder Puff Ftbl; Commnctn.

TREJO, AMADO A; Norte Vista HS; Riverside, CA; (4); Art Clb; Church Yth Grp; Computer Clb; Latin Clb; Spanish Clb; Ftbl; Sftbl; Wt Lftg; Wrstlng; Hon Roll; Natl Educ Center; Bus Tech.

TREJO, DEVIN T; Buena HS; Ventura, CA; (4); French Clb; FBLA; SADD; JV Crs Cntry; JV Golf; JV Tennis; High Hon Roll; Hon Roll; Pres Acad Fit Awd; Natl Fed Music Piano Wnnr 3 Yrs; CA Poly San Luis Obispo; Med.

TREJO, GABRIEL; Theodore Roosevelt HS; Los Angeles, CA; (4); Church Yth Grp; Var Bsktbl; Var Vllybl; Hon Roll; UCLA; Math.

TREJO, IRMA G; Fountain Valley HS; Fountain Valley, CA; (4); Latin Clb; Ski Clb; Spanish Clb; Off Frsh Cls; Off Soph Cls; Off Jr Cls; Long Beach ST; Cmptr Sci.

TREJO, JACKIE; San Gabriel Mission HS; Pico Rivera, CA; (2); Church Yth Grp; GAA; Teachers Aide; Ped.

TREJO, MARIA I; Calistoga JR/Sr HS; Calistoga, CA; (3); Hosp Aide; Office Aide; Spanish Clb; Cit Awd; High Hon Roll; Hon Roll; Santa Rosa JR Coll; Bus Admin.

TREJO, ROBERTO C; Inglewood HS; Inglewood, CA; (3); Church Yth Grp; Church Choir; Cit Awd; Hon Roll; Med.

TREJO, SILVIA R; Pasadena HS; Pasadena, CA; (3); Chess Clb; Church Yth Grp; Cmnty Wkr; French Clb; Key Clb; Red Cross Aide; Service Clb; Spanish Clb; SADD; Church Choir; Vlntr Wrk At Childrens Crippled Society & Eisenhower Convalescent Hosp; Organizer Church Choir Mexico; U Of Gualajura; Accntng.

TREJO, TANYA; Palo Verde HS; Blythe, CA; (4); Drama Clb; School Musical; School Play; Stage Crew; Nwsp; Hon Roll; NHS; Mock Trial; CA Schlrshp Fed; Natl Hispanic Schlrshp Fnlst.

TREJOS, NORMA; Manor Baptist HS; Hayward, CA; (4); Church Yth Grp; Band; Church Choir; Yrbk; Capt Bsktbl; Cheerldng; Sftbl; Vllybl; Hon Roll; Speech Tm; CA ST U Hayward; Bus Admin.

TRELSTAD, ANN M; St Josephs HS; Santa Maria, CA; (3); Church Yth Grp; Ski Clb; Spanish Clb; Trk; Vllybl; High Hon Roll; Hon Roll; Schlr Athlte Awd.

TREMAIN, NICOLE; Los Gatos HS; Los Gatos, CA; (4); 24/380; Art Clb; Cmnty Wkr; Spanish Clb; Var Capt Socr; Var Swmmng; Var Trk; High Hon Roll; Hon Roll; Pres Acad Fit Awd; Camp Cnslr Sci Camp; Sccr Invlvmnt N CA ST Team; Gldn St Geom Hnrs; Stanford U; Pre-Med.

TREMBA, JOE K; Leland HS; San Jose, CA; (2); Church Yth Grp; Stu Cncl; JV Var Bsktbl; Hmcmng Prince.

TREMOUREUX, EMILY S; Nevada Union HS; Nevada City, CA; (1); 1/550; Chorus; High Hon Roll; Pres Acad Fit Awd; Theater; Piano; SAFE.

TREMP, PATRICIA A; Mater Dei HS; Huntington Beach, CA; (1); 1st, 2nd Hnrs; Natl Scl Stds Olympiad Awd, Mdl.

TREMPE, JENNIFER L; Academy Of Our Lady Of Peace; San Diego, CA; (3); Church Yth Grp; Cmnty Wkr; Spanish Clb; School Musical; Var Cheerldng; Var Trk; High Hon Roll; Spanish NHS; Natl Bicentnnl Cmptn-Constitution & Bil Of Rights St Fnlst; Acad Leag; Acad Decthln; Scndry Tchr.

TRENDA, BEN; Chino HS; Ontario, CA; (3); Art Clb; Math Tm; Band; Gov Hon Prg Awd; High Hon Roll; Hon Roll; Pres Acad Fit Awd; Schlrshp Awds; Art.

TRENERY, SCOTT D; Albany HS; Albany, CA; (2); Band; Jazz Band; Pep Band; Var JV Bsbl; JV Ftbl; Intrml Sftbl; Intrml Vllybl; Intrml Wt Lftg; High Hon Roll; Hon Roll.

TRENKLE, JEFF; Fountain Valley HS; Fountain Valley, CA; (2); Bsktbl; Ftbl.

TRENNER, MATTHEW K; Sherman E Burroughs HS; Ridgecrest, CA; (3); Boy Scts; Teachers Aide; Hon Roll; UC Riverside; Bus Admin.

TRENT, JESSICA R; Tranquillity Union HS; Tranquillity, CA; (2); Church Yth Grp; Drama Clb; Ski Clb; Var Stat Tennis; High Hon Roll; Hon Roll; Enrichment Clb; Bus Hnr Soc; CSF; San Diego ST; Marine Bio.

TRENT, JOHN W; Modoc HS; Alturas, CA; (2); 3/70; Boy Scts; Letterman Clb; L Bsktbl; L Ftbl; Hon Roll; NHS; Prfct Atten Awd; Pres Acad Fit Awd.

TRENT, KATHERINE M; Modoc HS; Alturas, CA; (3); Treas Spanish Clb; Hon Roll; Intl Order Rainbow PWA; Decthln; Math Tchr.

TRENT, LINDA; Bret Harte HS; Hathaway Pines, CA; (1); Math Tm; Band; Pep Band; Hon Roll; Sec Frsh Cls.

TRENT, TRACY L; Bret Harte HS; Hathaway Pines, CA; (2); AFS; Math Tm; Band; Mrchg Band; Pep Band; Stat Vllybl; Hon Roll; U Of Pacific CA; Music.

TRENTZ, TANYA A; Placer HS; Auburn, CA; (2); French Clb; Chorus; Yrbk; Photo; Horses; Water Skiing; Photo.

TRESENRIDER JR, DENNIS J; Esperanza HS; Yorba Linda, CA; (2); 227/500; Bsbl; Bsktbl; Ftbl; Vllybl; ITT; Comp Tech.

TRESIERRAS, ARTHUR; Crespi HS; Granada Hills, CA; (3); Church Yth Grp; Letterman Clb; Ski Clb; SADD; Varsity Clb; Ftbl; Trk; Wt Lftg; Wrstlng; CPA.

TRETERA, JERRY R; Ramona HS; Ramona, CA; (2); Church Yth Grp; Var Ftbl; Var Wt Lftg; Zoology.

TRETHEWAY, JASON L; Bellarmine College Prep; San Jose, CA; (4); Cmnty Wkr; Hosp Aide; Speech Tm; Teachers Aide; JV Wrstlng; Scl Invlvmnt Corps 88-90; Peer Cnslng 89-90; Jazz Dance 87-89; San Jose ST U; Psych.

TRETO, AMELIA; Alverno HS; Pasadena, CA; (2); Church Yth Grp; Service Clb; Off Soph Cls; Cit Awd; High Hon Roll; Hon Roll; Spanish NHS; Athltcs Clb; CSF; Psych.

TREVELLICK, TONI; Clear Lake HS; Lakeport, CA; (3); Drama Clb; Pep Clb; Drill Tm; Cheerldng; Gym; Pom Pon; High Hon Roll; Hon Roll; CSF; San Diego State; Marine Bio.

TREVETHAN, MICHELLE H; Victor Valley HS; Victorville, CA; (3); 20/423; SADD; Teachers Aide; Sec Jr Cls; Hon Roll; CSF; U Of Santa Barbara; Bus Admin.

TREVEZAS, PATTY; Downey HS; Downey, CA; (3); Pres French Clb; Intnl Clb; Math Clb; Science Clb; Teachers Aide; High Hon Roll; Keywntts Svc Clb Cmmttc Ldr; CA Schlrshp Fed; Envrnmntlsts Clb Hstrn; Engrng.

TREVINO, EDDIE; Orosi HS; Orosi, CA; (2); SADD; Yrbk; Bsbl; Bsktbl; Wt Lftg; Hon Roll.

TREVINO, ELIZABETH; San Jose High Acad; San Jose, CA; (2); Tennis; Hon Roll; ST U St Jose.

TREVINO, JASON R; Brethren HS; Pico Rivera, CA; (1); Church Yth Grp; JV Bsbl; Bsktbl; Hon Roll.

TREVINO, SEPTEMBER N; Hiram Johnson HS; Sacramento, CA; (2); 1/220; FBLA; School Play; Rptr Nwsp; Rep Stu Cncl; High Hon Roll; NHS; Friday Night Live; Safe Rides; Commnctns.

TREVISANUT, ANN M; Mesa Verde HS; Citrus Heights, CA; (2); 6/257; English Clb; Math Clb; Math Tm; Spanish Clb; Orch; Rptr Nwsp; High Hon Roll; Hon Roll; FNL; CA Schltc Fed; Brigham Young U.

TREVIZU, ERIC P; Gahr HS; Artesia, CA; (2); Boy Scts; Church Yth Grp; JA; Varsity Clb; Variety Show; Var Golf; JV Trk; High Hon Roll; Hon Roll; Pres Acad Fit Awd; UCI; Business.

TRIARSI, ALLISON M; Flintridge Preparatory Schl; Covina, CA; (3); Cmnty Wkr; French Clb; Nwsp; Off Soph Cls; Off Jr Cls; Bsktbl; Cit Awd; French Hon Soc; Hon Roll; NHS; Flintridge Press; CSF Bronz Medal; Senate News; MVP Bsktbl; Tm Capt Jr Var Bsktbl; Equestrian Tm; U CA San Diego; Med.

TRIAS, MICHELLE P; Whitney HS; Cerritos, CA; (2); Dance Clb; Key Clb; Band; Church Choir; Mrchg Band; Hon Roll; UC Irvine; Biochem.

TRIBBY, COLLEEN MARIE; Bear River HS; Auburn, CA; (2); 10/294; School Play; Stage Crew; Sec Soph Cls; Var Capt Bsktbl; Var Sftbl; JV Vllybl; Cit Awd; High Hon Roll; Hon Roll; Jazz Choir 88-90; Bsktbl 7 Gr Coach 89-90; Gonzaga U Spokane.

TRIBE, LESLIE A; Yucaipa HS; Yucaipa, CA; (3); Spanish Clb; Teachers Aide; Ped Nrs.

TRIBUZIO, KRISTI M; Manteca HS; Manteca, CA; (3); 27/450; Church Yth Grp; SADD; Sftbl; Vllybl; Hon Roll; Pres Schlr; UC Santa Barbara; Spec Ed Tchr.

TRICE, RICK; Big Pine HS; Long Beach, CA; (3); 3/15; Cmnty Wkr; SADD; Pres Jr Cls; Var L Bsbl; Var L Bsktbl; Var L Ftbl; Gov Hon Prg Awd; Hon Roll; Ski Clb; Spanish Clb; Gov Mdl For St Service; Yth In Yth; UCLA; Pre-Med.

TRIEBWASSER, JENNIFER H; Laguna Beach HS; Laguna Beach, CA; (4); 4/180; Cmnty Wkr; Math Tm; Model UN; Service Clb; School Play; Swmmng; Cit Awd; High Hon Roll; NHS; Rotary Awd; Stanford; Interpretr.

TRIEU, BAO G; Mark Keppel HS; Alhambra, CA; (3); FBLA; Key Clb; Frndshp Clb; Grls League; Bdmntn; U CA Irving; Bus.

TRIEU, CHAU H; San Bernardino HS; San Bernardino, CA; (4); 20/360; Hon Roll; Sec Asian Club 88-89; Prft Atten Cls 87-88; CSU; Acctng.

TRIEU, HUNG C; Mark Keppel HS; Alhambra, CA; (3); Key Clb; Service Clb; Teachers Aide; High Hon Roll; Hon Roll; Prfct Atten Awd; Pres Acad Fit Awd; Friendship Clb; NCCJ Camp; Brotherhood/Sisterhood Clb.

TRIEU, LINH M; Ocean View HS; Huntington Beach, CA; (1); Drill Tm; JV Tennis; Cit Awd; Keywanettes Clb.

TRIEU, LINH T; Mark Keppel HS; Alhambra, CA; (1); FBLA; Service Clb; High Hon Roll; Prfct Atten Awd.

TRIEU, NGUYEN H; Independence HS; San Jose, CA; (3); Science Clb; Se Anza CC; Technique Engr.

TRIEU, STEVE T; Mira Mesa HS; San Diego, CA; (2); Chess Clb; French Clb; Intnl Clb; Key Clb; Math Clb; Intrml Trk; Cit Awd; Prfct Atten Awd; Acad Hnr Awd; Cert Of Appreciation & Accomplishment; UCSD; Engr.

TRIEU, THAO; Mira Mesa HS; San Diego, CA; (2); French Clb; Key Clb; Math Clb; NHS; Prfct Atten Awd; U CA San Diego; Calculus.

TRIEU, THUAN; Mira Mesa HS; San Diego, CA; (3); Key Clb; Library Aide; Vllybl; NHS; Prfct Atten Awd; CA Schlrshp Fed; U CA San Diego; Calculus.

TRIEU, TUNG V; Mark Keppel HS; Monterey Park, CA; (3); Mu Alpha Theta; Office Aide; Science Clb; High Hon Roll.

TRIEU, UYEN; Mark Keppel HS; Monterey Park, CA; (2); JV Vllybl; Frndshp Club Secy; Peer Cnslng; Cal ST; Pedtrcn.

TRIEVEL, COURTNEY L; University HS; Santa Ana, CA; (2); Pres Church Yth Grp; Dance Clb; Drama Clb; FCA; 4-H; German Clb; Church Choir; Lit Mag; Rep Soph Cls; Cit Awd.

TRIFFO, ROGER W; Walnut HS; Walnut, CA; (4); FBLA; Pres Frsh Cls; Pres Soph Cls; Pres Jr Cls; Pres Sr Cls; Rep Stu Cncl; Cit Awd; DAR Awd; High Hon Roll; Kiwanis Awd; CSF Life Mem; Jr Statesmen Of America; 1st Pl Soroptimist Yth Ctznshp Awd; U CA Riverside; Bus Adm.

TRIGG, LAURA; Loyalton HS; Loyalton, CA; (4); 7/32; Am Leg Aux Girls St; Church Yth Grp; Dance Clb; Pres VP 4-H; Treas FBLA; Ski Clb; Varsity Clb; Church Choir; School Play; Ed Nwsp; Sonoma ST U; Bus.

TRIGLER, JACOB; St Joseph HS; Santa Maria, CA; (4); 4/117; Am Leg Boys St; Pres Key Clb; Ski Clb; VP Stu Cncl; Var L Ftbl; Var Capt Socr; High Hon Roll; VP NHS; CSF Pres; USAFA; Pilot.

TRILLANES, MYRA; Bishop Montgomery HS; Carson, CA; (2); SADD; High Hon Roll; Hon Roll; CSF; Outstndng Spanish Awd, Spanish II; U Of CA; Nrsng.

TRIMBLE, JACQUELINE R; Hanford HS; Hanford, CA; (3); Church Yth Grp; Dance Clb; Teachers Aide; Rep Jr Cls; JV Swmmng; Hon Roll; Scorekpr Bsktbl; Hnrs Eng 89-91; Athletic Trnr; U Of CA; Psych.

TRIMBLE, PEGGY; Cloverdale HS; Cloverdale, CA; (3); 4/68; FHA; Band; Jazz Band; Mrchg Band; Pep Band; Rep Frsh Cls; Rep Jr Cls; High Hon Roll; Spanish NHS; CSF; U CA Davis; Psych.

TRIMBLE, WENDY ANN; Bullard HS; Fresno, CA; (4); 145/477; Church Yth Grp; Hosp Aide; Model UN; NFL; SADD; School Play; Stage Crew; CSF; Pepperdine U.

TRIMILLOS, RIC L; Don Antonio Lugo HS; Chino, CA; (3); 24/608; Am Leg Boys St; Boy Scts; Church Yth Grp; Pres Science Clb; Chrmn Jr Cls; Mgr Stu Cncl; JV Socr; JV Var Tennis; High Hon Roll; Opt Clb Awd; CSF Treas.

TRINH, ANNA; George Washington HS; San Francisco, CA; (2); Computer Clb; High Hon Roll; California Scholarship Federation Club; Provisional General Service Society; Mandarin Sppech Contest; Business Skills.

TRINH, BINH N; Villa Park HS; Orange, CA; (2); French Clb; Science Clb; JV Socr; JV Vllybl; High Hon Roll; Hon Roll; NHS; CSF; Sci Olympd; Harvard; Med.

TRINH, CHUNG Q; Irvine HS; Santa Ana, CA; (2); Chess Clb; Key Clb; Tennis; UCLA; Elect Engrng.

TRINH, DAT; Saddleback HS; Santa Ana, CA; (2); Mu Alpha Theta; Natl Beta Clb; Science Clb; Bsktbl; Score Keeper; Schlr Ath Awd & Mst Insprtn Bdmntn; Dept Awd Frgn Lang Span & Bio; Elec Engr.

TRINH, DIEN Q; Saddleback HS; Santa Ana, CA; (4); French Clb; FBLA; Mu Alpha Theta; Science Clb; Acad Exc Awd In Gmtry W/Hnr Gldn ST Exam; Acad Exc Awd 1st Yr Algebra W/Hnr Glnd ST Exam; Comp Sci.

TRINH, ERIC Q; George Washington HS; San Francisco, CA; (2); Service Clb; Off Frsh Cls; Hon Roll; Uc Berkeley; Engrng.

TRINH, HUIU; Abraham Lincoln HS; San Francisco, CA; (3); Church Yth Grp; Library Aide; Office Aide; Science Clb; Band; Church Choir; School Play; Bsbl; Bsktbl; San Francisco ST U; EE.

TRINH, HUY D; Mark Keppel HS; Monterey Park, CA; (2); Badminton; CA ST LA; Acctng.

TRINH, JIM H; Bellarmine College Prep; San Jose, CA; (3); Computer Clb; Trk; Martl Arts; Cmmnty Svc; UC Berkeley; Engrng.

TRINH, KIEN C; Mission HS; San Francisco, CA; (3); San Francisco ST U; Comp Sci.

TRINH, KIEN L; C K Mc Clatchy HS; Sacramento, CA; (1); 63/588.

TRINH, KIM; Magnolia HS; Anaheim, CA; (3); Tennis; Vllybl; Hon Roll; NHS; CSF; Phrmcy.

TRINH, LAN N; Westsminster HS; Westminster, CA; (2); Jr NHS; Interact Clb; Vietnamese Clb; Psych.

TRINH, LE A; Mira Mesa HS; San Diego, CA; (2); 1/830; Yrbk; 36th Annl Grtr San Diego Sci & Engrng Fair, 3rd Pl Sr Div; Sci Fair 1st Pl.

TRINH, LE G; Bolsa Grande HS; Garden Grove, CA; (2); #1 In Class; Chess Clb; Math Clb; Science Clb; Spanish Clb; Bsktbl; Cit Awd; High Hon Roll; Hon Roll; NHS; Pres Acad Fit Awd.

TRINH, LIEN N; Santiago HS; Santa Ana, CA; (2); 10/498; Computer Clb; Math Clb; Hon Roll; CA Schlrshp Fed; Bio.

TRINH, LINH N; Bolsa Grande HS; Garden Grove, CA; (3); Spanish Clb; Cit Awd; Hon Roll; Prfct Atten Awd; Badminton Jr Var & Var; Vietnamese Clb; CSF; Chinese Clb; UCI; Pharmacy.

TRINH, LINH T; Madison HS; San Diego, CA; (4); 1/387; Debate Tm; Hosp Aide; Mu Alpha Theta; NFL; Scholastic Bowl; Speech Tm; Ed Nwsp; NHS; Ntl Merit SF; Acdmc Dcthln Tm Capt.

TRINH, LOC H; Kearny HS; San Diego, CA; (3); 1/300; Am Leg Boys St; Debate Tm; Speech Tm; Variety Show; Tennis; High Hon Roll; Hon Roll; UCSD; Medcl.

TRINH, LOI; Westmoor HS; Daly City, CA; (2); French Clb; Service Clb; Spanish Clb; Vllybl; High Hon Roll; Hon Roll; Coll Entrnc Clb; CSF; Frdy Night Tme Clb; U CA Davis.

TRINH, MAI N; Mt Pleasant HS; San Jose, CA; (1); Math Clb; Hon Roll; Vietnamese & Asian Clubs; CSF; High Hnrs Engl & Spnsh Awds; Nrsng.

TRINH, MINH VY; Orange HS; Garden Grove, CA; (3); Hosp Aide; JA; Teachers Aide; Tennis; Rancho Santiago Coll; Electrnc.

TRINH, MUOI; C K Mc Clatchy HS; Sacramento, CA; (2); 34/487; High Hon Roll; Hon Roll; UC Davis; Cmptr Prog.

TRINH, NGOC-OIEM; Lincoln HS; Stockton, CA; (3); Girl Scts; Key Clb; Math Clb; Mu Alpha Theta; Temple Yth Grp; NHS; Prfct Atten Awd; USC; Dentstry.

TRINH, NHU; Galileo HS; San Francisco, CA; (2); Hon Roll; Tchr.

TRINH, NICK H; Irvine HS; Irvine, CA; (3); Chess Clb; Church Yth Grp; French Clb; Key Clb; Speech Tm; Orch; Bsktbl; Ftbl; Tennis; Wt Lftg; Woodbury; Bus Admin.

TRINH, OAI B; San Gabriel HS; Rosemead, CA; (3); Debate Tm; FBLA; Key Clb; NFL; Speech Tm; Nwsp; Hon Roll; CSF; Southern CA Chaur Jon Assoc; Explr Post 270; CA Poly Tech; Bus.

TRINH, PHIO D; Lowell HS; San Francisco, CA; (2); Hosp Aide; Office Aide; Red Cross Aide; Science Clb; Teachers Aide; Rep Soph Cls; St Schlr; Bch Clean Up Vlntr; Stu Advocates For Global Awrnss; Vllybl Club.

TRINH, PHONG P; Costa Mesa HS; Santa Ana, CA; (3); ROTC; Spanish Clb; Wt Lftg; Vietnamese Clb; Mechanic.

TRINH, QUYEN C; William Workman HS; La Puente, CA; (4); Church Yth Grp; Intnl Clb; Library Aide; Red Cross Aide; Treas Science Clb; Spanish Clb; Church Choir; Rep Stu Cncl; High Hon Roll; Hon Roll; JV/Vrsty Badminton; Schl Schlr; Bank Of Am Achvt; CA ST Poly U-Pomona; Arch.

TRINH, SAMANTHA; Cleveland HS; Canoga Park, CA; (2); Church Yth Grp; Latin Clb; Library Aide; Chorus; Off Soph Cls; Diving; Gym; Score Keeper; Swmmng; Trk; Merit Outstndng Schlstc Achvmnt; CSF CA Schlrshp; Read-A-Thon For March Of Dimes; Chinese Clb; Nrthwstrn IL; Doctor.

TRINH, SISSY; John A Rowland HS; Rowland Heights, CA; (2); French Clb; Key Clb; Science Clb; Gov Hon Prg Awd; CSF; Creatv Wrtng Clb; Photo; Music.

TRINH, TAI V; Mark Keppel HS; Rosemead, CA; (4); Chess Clb; Spanish Clb; Tennis; Cit Awd; Hon Roll; CA ST Los Angeles; Bus Admin.

TRINH, THANG T; Independence HS; San Jose, CA; (3); San Jose ST U; Comp.

TRINH, THUY N; Mt Pleasant HS; San Jose, CA; (3); 1/440; Math Clb; High Hon Roll; Hon Roll; NHS; CSF; Badmngt; Vietnamese Clb; U Of Davis; Biochem.

TRINH, VIEN; San Gabriel HS; Rosemead, CA; (3); Off Sr Cls; Hon Roll; Vietnamese Clb.

TRINH, VINH T; Lowell HS; San Francisco, CA; (2); Boy Scts; Hosp Aide; Var Ftbl; Gov Hon Prg Awd; Hon Roll; Pre Med Clb; Sftbl Clb; Movie Clb; Adventurers Clb; CSF Stu; Berkeley; Sci.

TRINIDAD, CECILIA R; Sweetwater Union HS; National City, CA; (4); NFL; Science Clb; Speech Tm; Yrbk; Off Soph Cls; Off Jr Cls; Off Sr Cls; Tennis; Trk; Hon Roll; Associated Stu Body; Asian Intl Assn; Acctng.

TRINIDAD, ERMA R J; Bellarmine Jefferson HS; Los Angeles, CA; (2); Cmnty Wkr; French Clb; Library Aide; JV Sftbl; High Hon Roll; Hon Roll; CSF Chpr No 451 SC; PSAT Soph Yr 1 Of 15; UCLA; Aero Engrng.

TRINIDAD, HAZEL E; Gompers Secondary HS; San Diego, CA; (2); 41/145; Church Yth Grp; Cmnty Wkr; Key Clb; Science Clb; Sec Spanish Clb; Church Choir; Sec Frsh Cls; Hon Roll; Jr NHS; Gftd & Tlntd Ed Pgm; Golden St Exam Recog 89; CSF 89-90.

TRINIDAD, MARY ANN L; St Anthony HS; Corona, CA; (3); 16/163; Dance Clb; Drill Tm; Hon Roll; Prfct Atten Awd; CA All Star Drll Tm; Pharmacy.

TRINIDAD, RHODORA; South West HS; San Diego, CA; (3); Church Yth Grp; SADD; Teachers Aide; Var Crs Cntry; Var Tennis; Var Trk; Hon Roll; Pan-Asian Kaibagan-Filipino Group; USCD; Med Doctor.

TRINIDAD, ROSANNA M; Notre Dame HS; Chino Hills, CA; (2); 9/164; GAA; Spanish Clb; JV Bsktbl; Var Tennis; Var Trk; High Hon Roll; Spanish NHS; CSF; Multi Cultural Clb; Marine Bio.

TRINNAMAN, JAY G; San Marino HS; San Marino, CA; (4); AFS; Boy Scts; French Clb; FBLA; Math Clb; Science Clb; Var Trk; Pres Acad Fit Awd; AFS Stu To New Zealand 89; Vanderbilt U; Econ.

TRIPLETT, DAWN; Bellflower HS; Norwalk, CA; (3); Drama Clb; Office Aide; Chorus; Yrbk; Hon Roll; Peer Cnslr; Interior Dsgn.

TRIPLETT, TRICIA; Canyon Springs HS; Moreno Valley, CA; (3); Church Yth Grp; Science Clb; SADD; Thesps; School Musical; Yrbk; JV Var Cheerldng; Var Pom Pon; Hon Roll; Rotary Awd.

TRIPOLI, CURTIS D; Simi Valley HS; Simi Valley, CA; (4); 30/800; Spanish Clb; SADD; Cit Awd; Prfct Atten Awd; Spanish NHS; CSUN; Bus.

TRIPOLI, EMERSON; Lindsay HS; Lindsay, CA; (2); Key Clb; Hon Roll; Hnrs GBE.

TRIPPET, JASON; Newport Christian HS; Huntington Beach, CA; (1); Var Bsktbl; Var Vllybl; High Hon Roll; Schlrs Bowl; Computers; UC Berkeley; Mech Engnrng.

TRITASAVIT, STEWART S; Lowell HS; San Francisco, CA; (3); Letterman Clb; Varsity Clb; Var Capt Bsbl; U Of CA; Med.

TRIVEDI, NEIL N; Servite HS; Fountain Valley, CA; (2); 2/155; Cmnty Wkr; Math Tm; Yrbk; Lit Mag; High Hon Roll; NHS; Jr Statesmen Of America; Coll Schlrshp Fed Treas; The Stand Cmnty Service; Med.

TRIVEDI, RAAJ; John F Kennedy HS; Cypress, CA; (3); Teachers Aide; Varsity Clb; Var JV Ftbl; Var JV Trk; Wt Lftg; JV Stat Wrstlng; Sci.

TRIVEDI, SANJANA; Cajon HS; San Bernardino, CA; (3); 29/535; Cmnty Wkr; Drama Clb; Library Aide; Temple Yth Grp; School Musical; Lit Mag; Hon Roll; NHS; AFS; CSF; UCLA; Pdtrcn.

TRIVEDI, SHEELA P; John F Kennedy HS; Cypress, CA; (1); Indian Cult Dance; Sci.

TRIVINO, MARLON; Nogales HS; West Covina, CA; (3); Tennis; Hon Roll; Prfct Atten Awd; Val; Tnns MVP Awd; Commendation Awd Best Presssure Player & Best Backhand; Cal Poly; Engrng.

TROBEE, SARAH J; Del Campo HS; Citrus Heights, CA; (1); 10/461; Church Yth Grp; ROTC; Bsktbl; Sftbl, Vllybl, Golf; Engrng.

TROLLMAN, HEIDI; Henry M Gunn SR HS; Los Altos Hills, CA; (4); Church Yth Grp; Cmnty Wkr; Debate Tm; Intnl Clb; Church Choir; Rptr Nwsp; Var Cheerldng; JV Tennis; Natl Honor Roll; Medcl Soc Pres; Santa Clara U.

TROMBA, DANTE P S; Willow Park HS; Apple Valley, CA; (4); Boy Scts; Chess Clb; Band; Mrchg Band; Intrml Ftbl; Socr; Capt Sftbl; Wt Lftg; Cit Awd; Hon Roll; Sgt Hi Desert Marines; Army; Military Sci.

TROMBELLA, MARCUS J; Escalon HS; Farmington, CA; (4); 4/100; Church Yth Grp; 4-H; German Clb; Quiz Bowl; ROTC; Teachers Aide; Band; Mrchg Band; Pep Band; School Musical; CA Schlrshp Fed Rep; Bnk Amer Achvt In Sci; UC Davis; Comp Sci.

TROPEA, SUZANNE; Silver Valley HS; Fort Irwin, CA; (2); Church Yth Grp; Var Cheerldng; Powder Puff Ftbl; JV Sftbl; Var Vllybl; Cit Awd; High Hon Roll; Hon Roll; Prm Dcrtng Comm; U GA; Bus.

TROSTLE, ROBERT H; Etiwanda HS; Etiwanda, CA; (4); Church Yth Grp; Cmnty Wkr; Latin Clb; Teachers Aide; Variety Show; Sprt Ed Yrbk; Pres Frsh Cls; VP Pres Stu Cncl; Var L Cheerldng; Capt Var Ftbl; Ldrshp Ltr Awd; Ldrshp Awd Cmnty Svc From Ontario Pop Warner Ftbl; People To People Stu Ambssdr Pgm; Cntrl Coll Pella; Pltcl Sci.

TROTH, CHRISTINE; Sacramento HS; Sacramento, CA; (3); Cmnty Wkr; GAA; Pep Clb; Variety Show; Rep Jr Cls; Var Capt Cheerldng; Var Capt Pom Pon; Hon Roll; WA ST; Psych.

TROTTER, ESTHER M; I'sot HS; Canby, CA; (2); Church Yth Grp; 4-H; Church Choir; School Play; 4-H Awd; Comp Sci.

TROTTER, HENRY M; Rio Mesa HS; Camarillo, CA; (3); Am Leg Boys St; Boy Scts; Church Yth Grp; FCA; Pres FTA; Var Ftbl; Hon Roll; Prfct Atten Awd; CSF; Peer Cnslng; Hstry.

TROTTER, JONATHAN; Sanger HS; Fresno, CA; (2); FCA; ROTC; SADD; Var Bsbl; Var Bsktbl; Var Ftbl; Wt Lftg; High Hon Roll; NEDT Awd; Rotary Awd; Hgh Hnrs Gldn St Math Exm; Stu Of Mnth; Prin Awd Acadmcs; CA Plytech; Elec Engr.

TROTTER, NICOLE A; Antioch HS; Antioch, CA; (2); Band; Chorus; Church Choir; Nwsp; Sec Frsh Cls; Hon Roll; Pilot.

TROTTER, TIMOTHY J; Servite HS; Hacienda Heights, CA; (3); Church Yth Grp; Cmnty Wkr; SADD; JV Swmmng; Hon Roll; NHS; NEDT Awd; Water Polo; Archery; Surfing; UC San Diego; Bus Admin.

TROTTMAN, DAVID M; Burroughs HS; Ridgecrest, CA; (3); 64/416; Church Yth Grp; Science Clb; Teachers Aide; Church Choir; Wt Lftg; Hon Roll; Prcs Acad Fit Awd; Memrl Day Essay Cont Cash Awd; Wrtng Awds; Stu Of Month; US Naval Acad.

TROUPE, MATTHEW E; Palmdale HS; Palmdale, CA; (3); 6/642; Am Leg Boys St; Boy Scts; Church Yth Grp; Math Tm; Quiz Bowl; SADD; Teachers Aide; Church Choir; Variety Show; Pres Soph Cls; Warner Pac Bible Clg; Theology.

TROUT, ALLISON C; Lodi Acad; Galt, CA; (4); Church Yth Grp; Letterman Clb; Office Aide; Treas Ski Clb; VP Spanish Clb; Capt Varsity Clb; Off Soph Cls; Treas Jr Cls; Off Sr Cls; Intrml Var Bsktbl; Work Awd; Pacific Union Coll; Med.

TROUT, AMY L; Etiwanda HS; Alta Loma, CA; (2); Church Yth Grp; JA; Cit Awd; Hon Roll; Pres Acad Fit Awd.

TROUT, KENYON M; Sonora HS; Sonora, CA; (4); 8/264; Am Leg Boys St; Letterman Clb; Spanish Clb; Rep Sr Cls; JV Var Bsbl; JV Var Bsktbl; JV Var Ftbl; High Hon Roll; Kiwanis Awd; Prfct Atten Awd; CA Schlrshp Fed; Radio Clb Sports Drctr; Bank Of Amer Cert Wnnr Scl Sci; Sonoma ST; Commnctns.

TROUTMAN, APRIL; Atascadero HS; Atascadero, CA; (2); Church Yth Grp; Cmnty Wkr; Drama Clb; 4-H; NFL; Pep Clb; Speech Tm; SADD; School Musical; School Play; CSF VP; Reach Out For Christ As King; Modlng; Arch.

TROVATO, TIFFANY D; Mt Diablo HS; Pittsburg, CA; (1); Var Trk; Var Vllybl; Prncpls Awd Grades & Sports; Mdlng.

TROWBRIDGE, ANDREW; Hesperia Christian HS; Hesperia, CA; (1); 1/43; Church Yth Grp; Scholastic Bowl; Var Crs Cntry; High Hon Roll; CFS.

TROWBRIDGE, DAVID; Rancho Cotate HS; Rohnert Park, CA; (3); 4/400; Drama Clb; NFL; ROTC; Ski Clb; Speech Tm; School Play; Var L Crs Cntry; Var L Trk; JV L Wrstlng; US Air Force Acad; Engrng.

TROWEL, OREN L; San Bernardino HS; San Bernardino, CA; (2); Prfct Atten Awd.

TROWER, KATE S; Ferndale HS; Garberville, CA; (3); Am Leg Aux Girls St; Art Clb; Drama Clb; Pep Clb; SADD; Teachers Aide; Acpl Chr; Band; Bsktbl; Capt Powder Puff Ftbl; Sftbl MVP 89; Ms Hstle Vllybl 89; Chico ST; Vet Med.

TROXEL, ANDY P; Marantha HS; Azusa, CA; (2); Art Clb; Church Yth Grp; French Clb; Acpl Chr; JV Socr; Hon Roll; Yrbk; Azusa Pacific U.

TROXEL, EVAN W; Alta Loma HS; Alta Loma, CA; (2); Boy Scts; Church Yth Grp; JV Tennis; High Hon Roll; Hon Roll; Outstndng Draftr Draftng I & Arch I; Arch.

TROXEL, RACHAEL J; Las Lomas HS; Walnut Creek, CA; (3); Art Clb; Church Yth Grp; Varsity Clb; Stu Cncl; JV Bsktbl; Powder Puff Ftbl; Trk; Span Awd; Ftbl Athltc Trnr; BYU; Bus Adm.

TROXELL, KRISTINA; Antelope Valley HS; Lancaster, CA; (3); 76/547; Spanish Clb; Antelope Valley JC; Bus.

TROY, ERIC G; Turlock HS; Turlock, CA; (3); Chess Clb; Red Cross Aide; Teachers Aide; Bsbl; Bsktbl; Crs Cntry; Ftbl; Socr; Trk; Vllybl; MJC; Arch Draftng.

TROYAN, KYRA; Carlmont HS; Belmont, CA; (3); Ntl Merit Ltr; Rssn Schl/Holy Prtctn Schl; St George Pathfienders Yth Sct Orgnztn; Job; CA U; Psych.

TRUAX, MIKE; Garden Grove HS; Garden Grove, CA; (1); Computer Clb; UCI; Cmptrs.

TRUCHAN, ALYSON C; Patrick Henry HS; San Diego, CA; (2); Girl Scts; Quiz Bowl; SADD; Church Choir; NHS; Pres Schlr; San Diego ST U; Math.

TRUCKENBROD, MELANIE L; Fairfield HS; Fairfield, CA; (1); Church Yth Grp; Church Choir; Hndbl Choir; Vol Church; Dgstng & Babystng Svc; Museum Curtr.

TRUDELL, SARAH C; Acad Of Our Lady Of Peace; Lakeside, CA; (2); 12/140; Church Yth Grp; Cmnty Wkr; Teachers Aide; School Play; Nwsp; Yrbk; Lit Mag; Hon Roll; NEDT Awd; Pres Acad Fit Awd; Engl II & Geomtry Awd; JRNLSM.

TRUDO, RACHEL L; Fontana HS; Fontana, CA; (4); 87/728; Office Aide; Teachers Aide; High Hon Roll; Gold Acad Achvt Medal 90; Princpls Hnr Roll 88-90; Child Carep ROP Cert; Child Psych.

TRUESDALE, TERRY S; Wilcox HS; Sunnyvale, CA; (1); 15/413; Pres Frsh Cls; Rep Stu Cncl; JV Bsbl; JV Bsktbl.

TRUEX, CHRISTY L; Oroville HS; Oroville, CA; (1); 11/240; 4-H; SADD; Off Frsh Cls; Score Keeper; Cit Awd; High Hon Roll; Hon Roll; Top Ten; Stu Mnth Engl & Math.

TRUEX, JULIE S; Oroville HS; Oroville, CA; (3); 18/172; Intnl Clb; Office Aide; Pep Clb; SADD; Teachers Aide; Stu Cncl; Stat Bsbl; Cheerldng; Pom Pon; Score Keeper; Butte Coll; Travel.

TRUJILLO, ALVARO; Santa Barbara HS; Santa Barbara, CA; (3); 50/373; Teachers Aide; JV Bsbl; Hon Roll; MESA-MATH/Engrng/Sci Achvt; Link Pgm; U Of CA; Law.

TRUJILLO, CHRISTINA M; California HS; Whittier, CA; (3); Drama Clb; Hosp Aide; School Musical; Attnd Plays; Drawing Cartoon Charactrs; Work With People, Help Out; CA ST Fullerton; Advtsmnt.

TRUJILLO, DEBBIE; St Francis HS; Sacramento, CA; (4); 61/145; Church Yth Grp; Drama Clb; French Clb; Hosp Aide; Intnl Clb; Spanish Clb; SADD; School Musical; JV Crs Cntry; Var Trk; Socl Actn Clb; CA ST U; Trsm.

TRUJILLO, GINA P; Thomas Downey HS; Modesto, CA; (1); FFA; Hon Roll; FFA Bst Infrmd Greenhnd Cont 10th Pl; UC Berkeley; Teacher.

TRUJILLO, JASON R; Eureka SR HS; Eureka, CA; (2); Intnl Clb; Key Clb; Band; Orch; Pep Band; Var Crs Cntry; High Hon Roll; CSF; Stanford U; Chem Engrng.

TRUJILLO, JENNIFER N; Fullerton HS; Fullerton, CA; (2); 119/425; Chorus; School Musical; Dance; Tm 2000/Acad Achvt Pgm; Fshn Dsgnr.

TRUJILLO, JORGE; Atwater HS; Winton, CA; (4); French Clb; Office Aide; Hon Roll; Bus.

TRUJILLO, LYDIA; Estancia HS; Costa Mesa, CA; (3); Church Yth Grp; FCA; Church Choir; Flght Atten.

TRUJILLO, MARGARET L; Los Angeles County HS For The Arts; Baldwin Park, CA; (4); 77/148; School Play; Stage Crew; Treas Sr Cls; Hon Roll; Shakespeare Soc Sec; Stu Envirnmntl Awareness Sec; LOS Angeles Stu Coalition; NYU; Actress.

TRUJILLO, MARIA A; St Joseph HS; Bellflower, CA; (2); Church Yth Grp; Cmnty Wkr; Drama Clb; French Clb; Spanish Clb; SADD; Church Choir; Stage Crew; High Hon Roll; Keywanettes VP; Psych.

TRUJILLO, MARIBEL; Garfield HS; Los Angeles, CA; (2); Office Aide; Teachers Aide; Bus.

TRUJILLO, MARLO; South HS; Bakersfield, CA; (4); 14/399; Sec Church Yth Grp; FCA; Key Clb; Sec Band; Mrchg Band; Sec Stu Cncl; Var L Cheerldng; Var L Crs Cntry; JV L Swmmng; Hon Roll; CSUB; Ministry.

TRUJILLO, MIGUEL ANGEL; Rosemead HS; La Puente, CA; (4); Key Clb; Band; Mrchg Band; Pep Band; Var Crs Cntry; Var JV Trk; Hon Roll; Prfct Atten Awd; CSF Gld Seal Bearer; UCLA; Arspc Engrng.

TRUJILLO, PAUL A; Palm Desert HS; La Quinta, CA; (4); FFA; Hon Roll; Phys Ed Sr Athl Of Yr; Landscape Mgmt/Maintnc Cert Of Trng; Coll Of Desert.

TRUJILLO, SHAMMARIE J; Chaffey HS; Ontario, CA; (3); Art Clb; Church Yth Grp; FHA; Office Aide; Spanish Clb; FIDM; Interior Design.

TRUJILLO, TIMOTHY T; Escondido Adventist Acad; Escondido, CA; (3); 2/20; Cmnty Wkr; Ski Clb; Phtg Nwsp; Ed Yrbk; VP Frsh Cls; VP Soph Cls; Capt Gym; Var Vllybl; Church Yth Grp; Office Aide; Stu Assoc, VP; Stu Assoc Relgs, VP; Pacific Union Coll; Aerntcl Eng.

TRUMAN, PETER; Saddleback HS; Santa Ana, CA; (2); Chess Clb; Computer Clb; Treas Science Clb; Tennis; Prfct Atten Awd; Bridge Clb; Acad Lttr; CA Schlrshp Fed; Berkeley; Arspc Engrn.

TRUMBLY, ROBYN E; El Camino Fundamental HS; Sacramento, CA; (3); 80/366; Church Yth Grp; Stage Crew; JV Socr; JV Vllybl; Palmer Clg Of Chiro; Chiroprctc.

TRUNNELL, SERENA; Nova HS; Redding, CA; (1); Church Yth Grp; Hon Roll; Miss CA Coed St Fnlst; U Of CA Berkley; Phys Thrpst.

TRUONG, AIMY N; Stagg HS; Stockton, CA; (3); UC Davis; Elec Engrng.

TRUONG, AMY H; Milpitas HS; Milpitas, CA; (2); Intnl Clb; Hon Roll; Bus.

TRUONG, BRUCE; Chinese Christian Schls; Oakland, CA; (2); Church Yth Grp; Color Guard; Drill Tm; Arch.

TRUONG, BU; A A Stagg HS; Stockton, CA; (4); 3/26; 4-H; FTA; Intnl Clb; SADD; Teachers Aide; Varsity Clb; Jazz Band; Lit Mag; Ftbl; Socr; Delta; Civil Engr.

TRUONG, CHAU N; San Gabriel HS; Rosemead, CA; (3); French Clb; FBLA; VP Math Clb; VP Science Clb; Hon Roll; Chrprsn Fundraisng Cmmtte Interact Clb; CSF; Pedtrcn.

TRUONG, CHAU Q; Leuzinger HS; Hawthorne, CA; (3); Key Clb; JV Var Crs Cntry; JV Var Trk; Cit Awd; High Hon Roll; Hgh Hnrs GSE; CSF; Chinese Club; UCLA; Engr.

TRUONG, DAVID Q; Milpitas HS; Milpitas, CA; (1); French Clb; Hon Roll; Vietnms Clb; Elec.

TRUONG, DINH; Magnolia HS; Anaheim, CA; (3); Intnl Clb; Rep Service Clb; JV Tennis; High Hon Roll; Sec NHS; CSF Sec; Badminton Var; Ldrshp Acad; Med.

TRUONG, DUC; Saddleback HS; Santa Ana, CA; (2); Intrml Tennis; CSF; Salesmn.

TRUONG, DUC N; San Gabriel HS; Alhambra, CA; (2); Intnl Clb; Math Clb; Office Aide; Science Clb; Teachers Aide; Chinese Clb; CA Poly; Comp Sci.

TRUONG, DUNG YUNG; Moorpark HS; Moorpark, CA; (3); 9/250; French Clb; Sec Intnl Clb; Key Clb; Library Aide; Office Aide; Teachers Aide; Bsktbl; High Hon Roll; Hon Roll; Prfct Atten Awd; CSF; Hmcmng Cmmttee; UCLA; Pharm.

TRUONG, DUONG; Calvin Simmon JR HS; Oakland, CA; (1); Band; Orch; Stu Cncl; Cit Awd; High Hon Roll; Hon Roll; Prfct Atten Awd; Doctor.

TRUONG, HIEP D; Thomas Downey HS; Modesto, CA; (4); Nwsp; Tennis; Hon Roll; SOSP; Cnty Spllng Bee Chmpn 88 & 89 & 90; CSF Sealbearer; Santa Cruz.

TRUONG, HOA T; Davis HS; Modesto, CA; (2); Art Clb; French Clb; Intnl Clb; Red Cross Aide; SADD; Cit Awd; Hon Roll; Prfct Atten Awd; Phrmcst.

TRUONG, HUN; Grace Davis HS; Modesto, CA; (2); Art Clb; French Clb; Intnl Clb; Humbolt; Airline Stewardist.

TRUONG, HUNG V; Eagle Rock HS; Los Angeles, CA; (2); Varsity Clb; Off Soph Cls; Bsktbl; Tennis; High Hon Roll; Hon Roll; Prfct Atten Awd; Rotary Awd; UCSB; Elctrncl Engr.

TRUONG, HUONG; Calvin Simmons JR HS; Oakland, CA; (1); Cit Awd; Hon Roll; Prfct Atten Awd; Nurse.

TRUONG, HUY N; San Gorgonio HS; San Bernardino, CA; (3); 11/450; Church Yth Grp; 4-H; French Clb; Key Clb; JV Tennis; Cit Awd; French Hon Soc; 4-H Awd; High Hon Roll; Hon Roll; Russian Clb VP; Vietnamese Clb VP; Harvard; Pre-Med.

TRUONG, JASON; Westminster HS; Westminster, CA; (3); English Clb; Office Aide; ROTC; Spanish Clb; Bsktbl; Socr; Wt Lftg; Cit Awd; Hon Roll; Pres Acad Fit Awd; Vietnamese Clb; Cal ST U; Bus Mgt.

TRUONG, KIET; Independence HS; San Jose, CA; (3); Art Clb; Dance Clb; Math Tm; Ed Lit Mag; Hon Roll; Skate Wrlds Dance/Fgrs Clb 5 1st Pls; 1st Prz Villa Montavo Yng Wrtr Cont; Bst Schl/Shw Dist Art Shw; Berkeley; Dentistry.

TRUONG, KIET; Mark Keppel HS; Rosemead, CA; (3); Hon Roll; Prfct Atten Awd; 1st Yr Alb Gldn St Exm Hnr Rl; Pasadena City Coll; Auto Mechnc.

TRUONG, KIEU T; Hueneme HS; Pt Hueneme, CA; (3); FBLA; Sec SADD; High Hon Roll; Prfct Atten Awd; Acctng.

TRUONG, KIM NGOC T; Sunny Hills HS; Fullerton, CA; (4); Pep Clb; Spanish Clb; Teachers Aide; Off Yrbk; High Hon Roll; Sugar N Spice Girls Club Hstrn; Bus Silver & Gold Medals; ASB Convtn Delg 90; CA ST Fullerton.

TRUONG, LAN; Oakland HS; Oakland, CA; (4); 1/30; Cmnty Wkr; French Clb; Hosp Aide; Intnl Clb; Math Clb; Science Clb; School Play; Cit Awd; High Hon Roll; Hon Roll; Vietnamese Clb Treas/Secty; Trophy Vietnmese Outstndng Stu; San Francisco ST U; Nurse.

TRUONG, LAN T; San Gabriel HS; San Gabriel, CA; (2); FBLA; High Hon Roll; Prfct Atten Awd; CSF; Chinese Clb.

TRUONG, MICHAEL; James Lick HS; San Jose, CA; (1); Math Tm; JV Bsktbl; Var Tennis; High Hon Roll; CSF; Superntdnts Hnr Roll; AUC Coll; Communtn.

TRUONG, MICHAEL; Leuzinger HS; Hawthorne, CA; (3); El Camino; Math.

TRUONG, MINH A; Santiago HS; Garden Grove, CA; (1); French Clb; Off Soph Cls; Cit Awd; High Hon Roll; Hon Roll; NHS; Bus.

TRUONG, NGOC BICH P; Norte Vista HS; Riverside, CA; (3); 1/400; Cit Awd; High Hon Roll; Hon Roll; Pres Acad Fit Awd; Doctor.

TRUONG, NGOC C; Mira Mesa HS; San Diego, CA; (2); 227/797; Church Yth Grp; French Clb; FBLA; Intnl Clb; Off Frsh Cls; Off Soph Cls; Off Jr Cls; Stu Cncl; Cit Awd; Prfct Atten Awd; ASB VP; UCSD; Dentist.

TRUONG, NHUT; San Gorgonio HS; San Bernardino, CA; (3); Vrsty Badminton Team; UCR; Bus Admin.

TRUONG, PHUOC T; Sierra Vista HS; Baldwin Park, CA; (1); Math Clb; Intrml Bsktbl; Hon Roll.

TRUONG, PHUONG M; Artesia HS; Lakewood, CA; (4); Cmnty Wkr; French Clb; Intnl Clb; Science Clb; Var Tennis; Cit Awd; Hon Roll; Prfct Atten Awd; CSF; Smmr Yth Pgm; CA ST Polytechnic U; Arch.

TRUONG, SARA T; Lowell HS; San Francisco, CA; (3); Chess Clb; Red Cross Aide; Service Clb; SADD; High Hon Roll; Goldn St Exam High Hnrs Geom, Hnrs Alg; Brd Schl & Cmnty Srvcs Rep; Dentstry.

TRUONG, TAI U; Oakland Technical HS; Oakland, CA; (2); Math Clb; High Hon Roll; Peer Tutorng; Genetic Engrng.

TRUONG, TEDDY H; Fremont HS; Sunnyvale, CA; (2); 42/420; Cmnty Wkr; Debate Tm; Drama Clb; NFL; Speech Tm; School Musical; Yrbk; Elks Awd; High Hon Roll; Waterpolo, Badmntn; Most Imprvd, Inspirtnl Badmnt; Envrnmntl Clb; UCLA; Bus.

TRUONG, TERRY; Skyline HS; Oakland, CA; (3); Computer Clb; Intnl Clb; Cit Awd; Hon Roll; Vietnamese Stu Union Clb; U C Berkely; Acctng.

TRUONG, THU-THAO T; Colton HS; San Bernardino, CA; (4); 3/320; FBLA; Science Clb; Hon Roll; NHS; Prfct Atten Awd; Pres Acad Fit Awd; Hnrs Geom Goldn St Exm; Redlands Chmbr Cmmrce Essy Wnnr; Life & 100% Mem CSF; CA ST U; Accntng.

TRUONG, THUYEN T; Mark Keppel HS; Monterey Park, CA; (3); Church Yth Grp; Cmnty Wkr; Computer Clb; Dance Clb; English Clb; French Clb; Library Aide; Math Clb; Math Tm; Science Clb; UCLA; Comp Sci Engr.

TRUONG, THUYHANH N; La Quinta HS; Westminster, CA; (4); 5/319; French Clb; Math Clb; Spanish Clb; Orch; Cit Awd; High Hon Roll; NHS; Val; CSF; Golden Aztec Hnr Roll; Prncpl Mdl; UCLA; Bus.

TRUONG, TOM Q; Los Amigos HS; Santa Ana, CA; (2); 25/365; Hon Roll; Elec Engr.

TRUONG, TON H; Warren HS; Downey, CA; (3); Computer Clb; Office Aide; Off Sr Cls; Var Tennis; UC Irvine; Comp Tech.

TRUONG, TRINH T; William Workman HS; Valinda, CA; (4); Computer Clb; French Clb; Intnl Clb; Key Clb; Science Clb; Ski Clb; Hon Roll; Badminton; Schl & Dist Schlrs Awds; CA ST-FULLERTON; Bio Sci.

TRUONG, TU; Herbert Hoover HS; San Diego, CA; (2); Intnl Clb; Key Clb; JV Sftbl; Hon Roll; NHS; SDSU; Engr.

TRUONG, TUAN- ANH; Sunny Hills HS; Fullerton, CA; (2); 27/464; Spanish Clb; High Hon Roll; Rotary Awd; Acad Letter; Acad Engl Achvt Awd; Portuguese Clb.

TRUONG, TUONG; Saddleback HS; Santa Ana, CA; (2); Chess Clb; Math Clb; Mu Alpha Theta; Quiz Bowl; Science Clb; Nwsp; Tennis; Kiwanis Awd; Pres Acad Fit Awd; Aerosp Engr.

TRUONG, TUYEN; Thomas Downey HS; Modesto, CA; (4); Computer Clb; French Clb; Latin Clb; Socr; Vllybl; Wt Lftg; Cit Awd; Hon Roll; Prfct Atten Awd; Arch Engrng.

TRUONG, XUAN; Armijo HS; Suisun City, CA; (2); French Clb; SADD; Cit Awd; High Hon Roll; Hon Roll; Acad Ltr; UC Davis.

TRUONG, YUNG N; Moorpark HS; Moorpark, CA; (3); 7/255; Computer Clb; English Clb; French Clb; Intnl Clb; JA; Key Clb; Library Aide; Math Tm; Office Aide; Teachers Aide; UCLA; Phrmcy.

TRUSCHEL, AMY; St Paul HS; La Mirada, CA; (3); Church Yth Grp; Teachers Aide; Var Bsktbl; High Hon Roll; NHS; Spanish NHS; U Of San Diego.

TRUSCOTT, DAVID; Manor Baptist HS; Castro Valley, CA; (4); 5/7; Aud/Vis; Church Yth Grp; Office Aide; School Musical; School Play; Stage Crew; Yrbk; Var Bsktbl; Score Keeper; Var Socr; Mst Imprvd Schlstc Wrk Awd; Tchrs Aide; Betheny Bible Coll; Pastor.

TRUSCOTT, JAMES R; San Lorenzo HS; Hayward, CA; (4); Hon Roll; UC Berkeley.

TRUSHET, DENEKE; Anaheim HS; Anaheim, CA; (4); French Clb; Math Clb; Office Aide; Bsktbl; Socr.

TRUTNA, DENNIS M; Bonita Vista HS; Bonita, CA; (3); 20/550; Boy Scts; Cmnty Wkr; Yrbk; Off Sr Cls; Var Crs Cntry; Var Trk; Cit Awd; DAR Awd; High Hon Roll; Acad Leag & Decathlon; Golden St Hgh Hnrs Math 2 Yrs & Hstry; Schlstc Ltrmn; U Of CA.

TRUTNA, KIMBERLY D; Hoover HS; Fresno, CA; (3); 23/450; Church Yth Grp; French Clb; Swmmng; Vrsty Swmmng Coaches Awd; Top 5% Cls; Health.

TRUTTMAN, TRACEY; Tomalas HS; Pt Reyes Sta, CA; (1); 4-H; Ski Clb; Spanish Clb; Vllybl; 4-H Awd; High Hon Roll; JR Coll; Prsctng Lawyer.

TRYK, KRISTY; Santa Paula Union HS; Santa Paula, CA; (3); Drama Clb; French Clb; Key Clb; Color Guard; Flag Corp; Yrbk; Hon Roll.

TRYTHALL, DANIEL M; Oakmont HS; Roseville, CA; (3); 25/400; Boy Scts; Church Yth Grp; Letterman Clb; Rep Frsh Cls; JV Var Bsbl; JV Var Bsktbl; High Hon Roll; Prfct Atten Awd; Pres Acad Fit Awd; Rotary Awd; Brigham Young U; Political Sci.

TSAI, BRIAN; University HS; Orange, CA; (2); Intnl Clb; Intrml Ftbl; JV Trk; Chinese Cltrl Awrnss Clb; Orntl Clb; Bus.

TSAI, CHANTHANA; Baldwin Park HS; Baldwin Park, CA; (3); Drill Tm; Yrbk; High Hon Roll; Hon Roll; Associated Stu Body Secy; Hnr Soc Club; Gldn St Exam Awd Alg I Hnrs.

TSAI, CHI WEI; Gahr HS; Norwalk, CA; (2); Church Yth Grp; Intnl Clb; Chinese Clb.

TSAI, CHRISTINE; Lynbrook HS; San Jose, CA; (3); Church Yth Grp; French Clb; JA; Rep NFL; Red Cross Aide; Speech Tm; Band; Chorus; Mrchg Band; Tennis; Share The Dream Essay Cont-Fnlst; Asian Am Clb-VP; Pediatrcs.

TSAI, CINDY; Walnut HS; Walnut, CA; (2); 26/480; Key Clb; Rep Soph Cls; Var Trk; Hon Roll; Sci Fctn & GATE Clb; Art.

TSAI, DIANA; Mills HS; Millbrae, CA; (3); French Clb; Math Clb; Math Tm; Vrsty Badmntn; Golden St Exam Geom High Hnrs; Principals Awd 88-89; Berkeley; Engrng.

TSAI, DINO T; Milpitas HS; Milpitas, CA; (3); 193/487; Pres Intnl Clb; Off ROTC; Pres Science Clb; Drill Tm; Stu Cncl; U Southern CA; Med.

TSAI, EUNICE; Gahr HS; Norwalk, CA; (2); Church Yth Grp; FCA; Chinese Club.

TSAI, HENRY C; University HS; Irvine, CA; (2); 16/508; Boy Scts; Intnl Clb; Band; Intrml Crs Cntry; Intrml Ftbl; Intrml Trk; Intrml Wt Lftg; Intrml Wrstlng; High Hon Roll; Hon Roll; MIT; Engr.

TSAI, JAMES J; San Marino HS; San Marino, CA; (3); JCL; Latin Clb; Math Clb; Science Clb; Band; Mrchg Band; Orch; Pep Band; Bsktbl; Southwestern Yth Music Fstvl 1st Pl Viola Solo; SCSBDA All Sthrn Hnr Orch; Trnmt Roses Hnr Band; Engrng.

TSAI, JENNY; Palo Verde HS; Blythe, CA; (4); 1/153; Drama Clb; Girl Scts; VP Key Clb; Treas Pep Clb; School Play; Yrbk; Stu Cncl; JV Sftbl; High Hon Roll; Lion Awd; UCLA; Poli Sci.

TSAI, JONATHAN C; University HS; Irvine, CA; (1); Intnl Clb; Med Club; Med.

TSAI, LARRY S; Santa Clara HS; Santa Clara, CA; (1); Aud/Vis; JV Crs Cntry; Hon Roll; CA Schlrshp Fed; Soroptomist Clb; PTSA Reflections Cont Awd; Berkeley U; Creative Dsgn.

TSAI, MARK; John F Kennedy HS; Buena Park, CA; (4); Boy Scts; Cmnty Wkr; Computer Clb; FBLA; Key Clb; Chorus; Intrml Crs Cntry; Intrml Trk; Intrml Wrstlng; Cit Awd; Bicycling; Body Building; UCI; Bio.

TSAI, PATRICIA S; Arcadia HS; Arcadia, CA; (3); 2/640; Am Leg Aux Girls St; Treas French Clb; Treas Math Tm; Treas Red Cross Aide; Pres Science Clb; Mrchg Band; JETS Awd; NHS; Opt Clb Awd; Biochem.

TSAI, PATRICIA Y; John F Kennedy HS; Sacramento, CA; (2); Treas Church Yth Grp; Hosp Aide; Math Clb; Spanish Clb; Hon Roll; CSF; Stu Reaching Out; Goldn St Exm Awds Alg & Geom; Med.

TSAI, PETER; John F Kennedy HS; Buena Park, CA; (1); Bsktbl; Ftbl; Wt Lftg; Hon Roll; UCI; Bio.

TSAI, PO-HUNG; Pasadena HS; San Marino, CA; (2); Chess Clb; Library Aide; Math Clb; Math Tm; Science Clb; Mathmatic.

TSAI, SANDRA L; Mountain View HS; Los Altos, CA; (3); Sec Service Clb; Pres Sr Cls; Powder Puff Ftbl; Var L Socr; JV Tennis; Var L Trk; High Hon Roll; Hon Roll.

TSAI, TA-MING; San Gabriel HS; Alhambra, CA; (3); Debate Tm; German Clb; Sec Key Clb; NFL; Treas Science Clb; High Hon Roll; Lion Awd; CSF; Bio.

TSAI, TERRY; Mills HS; Millbrae, CA; (3); Bsktbl; Crs Cntry; Trk; San Francisco ST; Bus.

TSAI, WILLY C; Whitney HS; Norwalk, CA; (2); FBLA; Intnl Clb; JA; JV Bsktbl; JV Tennis; High Hon Roll; Prfct Atten Awd; Pres Acad Fit Awd; Mecl & Chinese Clbs; Pre-Med.

TSAI, YUEH H; Artesia HS; Cerritos, CA; (3); Pres Chess Clb; Treas Pres Church Yth Grp; Intnl Clb; Math Tm; Science Clb; Church Choir; High Hon Roll; Fluent Span Speaker; High Achvt Comp Prgrmng; Play Classical Guitar; CA Inst Of Tech; Bio.

TSAN, JENNY Q; John F Kennedy HS; Los Angeles, CA; (2); Key Clb; Nwsp; Cit Awd; Hon Roll; Prfct Atten Awd; Math Awd; Pepperdine; Psych.

TSANG, BECKY; Lowell HS; San Francisco, CA; (2); Red Cross Aide; Big Broths/Sistrs Orgnztn; Physics.

TSANG, CATHERINE S; George Washington HS; San Francisco, CA; (4); Art Clb; Key Clb; Office Aide; Red Cross Aide; Service Clb; School Play; Swmmng; Vllybl; High Hon Roll; Senators Of White House Painting Awd; Schl Of Bus & Cmmrc Cert; City Art Cntst Awd; Adv Dsgn.

TSANG, ELIZABETH T; Clovis West HS; Fresno, CA; (2); Drama Clb; Intnl Clb; Ski Clb; Rep Soph Cls; JV L Crs Cntry; JV Tennis; Trk; High Hon Roll; Teen Inst; Intl Law.

TSANG, HILLARY; Chinese Christian Schls; Hercules, CA; (2); Sec Church Yth Grp; Hon Roll; Drm & Bll Corp; Chinese Chrstn HS Ladies Ensmbl; Chrch Yng Adlt Chr; Grphc Dsgn.

TSANG, JIM WEI-CHIEN; Troy HS; Fullerton, CA; (2); 10/330; Chess Clb; Computer Clb; Teachers Aide; High Hon Roll; Rotary Awd; Sci Olympiad; Chinese Sch; Ped.

TSANG, JO ANN C; Cupertino HS; Cupertino, CA; (3); Drama Clb; FBLA; Pres Spanish Clb; Speech Tm; Acpl Chr; Chorus; School Play; JV Var Fld Hcky; High Hon Roll; Ntl Merit Ltr; Psych.

TSANG, JULIE S; George Washington HS; San Francisco, CA; (2); Boy Scts; Hosp Aide; Treas Soph Cls; High Hon Roll; Hon Roll; Hong Kong Intl Clb; Chinese Amer Clb; UCSF Nrsng Explorer Scts Sec, Biotechnlgy Explorer Scts; Med.

TSANG, MARIA S; Mark Keppel HS; Monterey Park, CA; (4); 16/600; Dance Clb; Debate Tm; Math Clb; Cit Awd; Hon Roll; Pres Acad Fit Awd; ExclInce & Suprtry Spkng Awds; CA ST; Poltcl Sci.

TSANG, RELIANG; John Swett HS; Rodeo, CA; (4); 20/80; Computer Clb; Drama Clb; Pep Clb; Science Clb; SADD; Chorus; Mrchg Band; School Play; Lit Mag; Pres Soph Cls; Art Shw Exhbtr; Poem Pblshd; Fnlst CA ST Smmr Schl For Arts; U Of CA Santa Cruz; Educ.

TSANG, SHUN-LING; Los Altos HS; Hacienda Hgts, CA; (2); 11/400; Church Yth Grp; Cmnty Wkr; Intnl Clb; Drill Tm; Stat Bsktbl; Hon Roll; Prfct Atten Awd; Keywanettes Pres 90-91; Calif Scholastic Fed Member 2 Yrs; Friend To Friend; Principles Award; Pre Med.

TSANG, SIMON; Luther Burbank HS; Elk Grove, CA; (4); 2/240; Drama Clb; VP Math Clb; Quiz Bowl; School Play; Rep Stu Cncl; JV Trk; High Hon Roll; Ntl Merit SF; Pres Acad Fit Awd; Dsgn Ad Cntst 2-Tm Wnr; Stu Acad Math, Sci, Engrng; U Of CA San Diego; Mlclr Bio.

TSAO, ALISON L; Lowell HS; San Francisco, CA; (3); Debate Tm; NFL; Red Cross Aide; Speech Tm; Teachers Aide; Band; CSF; Shield Block L Hnr Soc; Golden St Exams Alge, Geom High Hnrs; Law.

TSAO, BENNY P; Katella HS; Anaheim, CA; (4); Hon Roll; Cal Poly Pomona; Engr.

TSAO, DAVID C; Glen A Wilson HS; Hacienda Hts, CA; (4); 7/361; Church Yth Grp; Red Cross Aide; Science Clb; JV Tennis; High Hon Roll; Pres Acad Fit Awd; Hacienda La Puente Unfd Schl Dist Schlr; Hgh Hnrs Alg I, Geom Gldn ST Exm CA; U Of CA Los Angeles; Biochem.

TSAO, HELEN; Oxnard HS; Oxnard, CA; (2); 2/640; Church Yth Grp; Math Tm; Science Clb; Chorus; Ed Yrbk; Rep Stu Cncl; Intrml Trk; DAR Awd; Jr NHS; Engrng.

TSAO, MEG; John A Rowland HS; Rowland Hts, CA; (4); Church Yth Grp; French Clb; Red Cross Aide; Treas Science Clb; Varsity Clb; Hon Roll; Var Badminton; Red Cross Blood Dr; Bus.

TSCHINKEL, HEATHER M; Alverno HS; San Gabriel, CA; (3); 30/67; Science Clb; Rep Soph Cls; Rep Jr Cls; JV Bsbl; 3rd Pl Math Fair Math Game Dsgn; Top A Stu Art Cls; Pumpkin Carvng Cntst Wnnr; Bus.

TSCHUDY, JENNIFER L; La Canada HS; La Canada Flintri, CA; (3); 21/250; Hosp Aide; Key Clb; Math Clb; Mu Alpha Theta; Science Clb; Color Guard; NHS; CA Schlrshp Fed; Aerospc Engr.

TSE, DOROTHY; Skyline HS; Oakland, CA; (3); Cit Awd; Arch.

TSE, EMILY K; Notre Dame Acad; Los Angeles, CA; (3); 3/112; Cmnty Wkr; English Clb; Service Clb; Teachers Aide; Rep Frsh Cls; VP Soph Cls; Pres Jr Cls; VP Stu Cncl; Cit Awd; High Hon Roll; HOBY Ldrshp Smnr Ambssdr & JR Cnslr 89-90; Sthrn CA Yth Ctznshp Smnr Ambssdr; JR Statesmen Pgm; Math.

TSE, MEI YEE; Lowell HS; San Francisco, CA; (2); Hosp Aide; Rep Stu Cncl; Bsktbl; JV Crs Cntry; Var Trk; Gldn St Exam 1st Yr Alg Hnrs; Adv.

TSE, TOM; Skyline HS; Oakland, CA; (2); Bsbl; Bsktbl; Swmmng; Vllybl; Cit Awd; Hon Roll; Stu Mnth; Mechanic.

TSE, WAIYI; Valley HS; Santa Ana, CA; (1); 2/1159; Key Clb; Band; Mrchg Band; High Hon Roll; Orange Cty Acad Decathln; Princeton; Jrnlsm.

TSEN, HSIANG-I; Kennedy HS; La Palma, CA; (4); 1/410; Computer Clb; Pres VP FBLA; Key Clb; Sec Speech Tm; Temple Yth Grp; Varsity Clb; Band; Var Crs Cntry; Var Tennis; Ntl Merit SF; CSF Treas; Natl Merit Fnlst; Outstndng Chem Stu; Harvard; Economics.

TSENG, HENRY; Arcadia HS; Arcadia, CA; (4); 4/632; Red Cross Aide; Service Clb; Temple Yth Grp; Orch; Var Trk; Cit Awd; High Hon Roll; NHS; Ntl Merit Ltr; Amer Yng Buddhist Assn; Intl Buddhist Prgrs Soc; Stanford U; Med.

TSENG, JEFF C; Mills HS; Millbrae, CA; (2); Math Clb; Math Tm; Band; Orch; Tennis; Piano; Swmmng; Med.

TSENG, JOHN; Monta Vista HS; Cupertino, CA; (3); 57/384; Cmnty Wkr; Computer Clb; JA; Band; Jazz Band; Mrchg Band; Orch; Pep Band; School Musical; High Hon Roll; ALOT Voluntr; Comp Awd; Hgh Hnrs GSE; Elec Engr.

TSENG, JOHN H; Palmdale HS; Palmdale, CA; (2); JV Tennis; Hon Roll; Pres Asian Pacific Clb; Boys Tennis Clb; Psychtry.

TSENG, LILI; Clovis West HS; Fresno, CA; (3); Debate Tm; English Clb; French Clb; GAA; JA; Key Clb; Math Clb; Math Tm; NFL; Scholastic Bowl; CA Jnr Statesmn America Pres; Wall Fame.

TSENG, MICHAEL H; Los Altos HS; Hacienda Hgts, CA; (1); Prfct Atten Awd.

TSENG, SAM; Thousand Oaks HS; Thousand Oaks, CA; (3); 19/573; Church Yth Grp; Cmnty Wkr; Intnl Clb; Math Tm; High Hon Roll; Sci.

TSENG, STEVE; Palos Verdes HS; Palos Verdes Est, CA; (3); Chess Clb; Cmnty Wkr; JCL; Hist Latin Clb; Library Aide; Service Clb; Teachers Aide; NHS; JV Trk; Natl Latin Hnr Soc; CA St Latin Convntn Roman Hstry Cmptn 1st Pl 88-90; Med.

TSENG, VIVIAN; Hoover HS; Fresno, CA; (3); French Clb; Hosp Aide; Mu Alpha Theta; VP Science Clb; Sec SADD; French Hon Soc; Acad Dcthln Tm; Sci Olympd Tm.

TSENG, WANRU; San Gabriel HS; Alhambra, CA; (1); Debate Tm; Drama Clb; French Clb; School Musical; School Play; Stage Crew; Sftbl; Tennis; Cit Awd; High Hon Roll; Fleet Rsrve Assn Essay Cont 2nd Pl; Hnr Clb & Acad Field Day Chrprsn.

TSENG, WILLIAM F; Artesia HS; Cerritos, CA; (2); Science Clb; Rep Soph Cls; JV Tennis; Hon Roll; All Amer HS Math Exm; Scrd 8th Natl Math Leag; 1st Pl Wnnr Northrop U Sci Cmptn; UCLA; Comp Prgmr.

TSENG, YIN; Burlingame HS; San Mateo, CA; (2); Art Clb; Intnl Clb; Hon Roll; Asian Clb-Treas/VP; Med.

TSIAGKAS, NICK; St Ignatius College Prep; Daly City, CA; (2); JV Ftbl; Trk; Hon Roll; CSF; Chrstn Life Cmmnty.

TSO, CHRISTINE C; American HS; Fremont, CA; (3); Rep French Clb; Spanish Clb; SADD; Sec Frsh Cls; Pres Soph Cls; Rep Stu Cncl; JV Var Tennis; Stat Trk; French Hon Soc; High Hon Roll; Gldn Globe Chmpn Tm Ldr; CA Schlrshp Fed; Arthtctr.

TSOI, DOUG T; Saratoga HS; Saratoga, CA; (4); Treas Debate Tm; Drama Clb; School Play; Nwsp; Ed Yrbk; Rep Stu Cncl; Hon Roll; Ntl Merit SF; UC Davis.

TSOU, ELDA E; La Canada HS; La Canada-Flint, CA; (3); English Clb; Teachers Aide; Ed Nwsp; Lit Mag; JV Swmmng; NHS; CSF; Harvard Prz Bk Awd; Chrch Pianst; Surgeon.

TSOU, ESTHER; Alhambra HS; Alhambra, CA; (2); Church Yth Grp; Lit Mag; JV Vllybl; CA St Sci Fair Wnnr; Peer Tutor.

TSOU, LYNNA M; Notre Dame HS; Foster City, CA; (3); Hosp Aide; Sec Treas SADD; Ed Nwsp; Sec Treas Jr Cls; Sec Stu Cncl; High Hon Roll; NHS; Intrn Cngrssmn; Wnnr Jr Bach Fstvl 90; CA Schlrshp Fed.

TSOULOS, JENNY M; The Bishops Schl; Escondido, CA; (3); Cmnty Wkr; Intnl Clb; Ski Clb; Teachers Aide; Sec Frsh Cls; Sec Soph Cls; VP Jr Cls; L Var Fld Hcky; Mgr(s); L Var Socr; Nacel Pgm France.

TSU, NAOMI R; Acalanes HS; Lafayette, CA; (4); 1/290; VP French Clb; Model UN; SADD; Teachers Aide; Chorus; Crew Vrsty; Amnsty Intl; CA Fdrtn Schlstc; Intl Rltns.

TSUCHIYA, NATHAN S; San Leandro HS; San Leandro, CA; (3); 14/300; Boy Scts; Off Soph Cls; Off Jr Cls; Off Sr Cls; JV Tennis; High Hon Roll; Ntl Merit Ltr; CA Schlrshp Fed.

TSUDA, DIANE M; Mills HS; San Bruno, CA; (3); GAA; Intnl Clb; Teachers Aide; School Play; Stage Crew; Outstndng Effor ROP Vet Asstng Pgm; Outstndng Voc Stu Awd; San Diego ST U; Marine Bio.

TSUEI, JUDY; Abraham Lincoln HS; San Francisco, CA; (2); Teachers Aide; Orch; Hon Roll; San Francisco ST U; Vocl Music.

TSUI, FRANKIE; Wallenberg HS; San Francisco, CA; (4); 1/108; Cmnty Wkr; Intnl Clb; Service Clb; Orch; Stu Cncl; Var Vllybl; High Hon Roll; Hon Roll; Pres Schlr; Student In Pre-College Academy; Participant Of Academic Decathlon; Recipient Of Harvard Book; Occidental Coll; Medicine Or Ed.

TSUJI, CARLOS Y; Downey HS; Downey, CA; (3); French Clb; Hosp Aide; JA; Key Clb; Pres Library Aide; Spanish Clb; VP SADD; Hon Roll; Prfct Atten Awd; PTA Stu Recognition; Alg I & Geom Awds; Law.

TSUJI, GEORGE; Downey HS; Downey, CA; (1); Key Clb; Math Clb; Ftbl; Vllybl; Won Rtry Club Essy Cmptn; USC; Law.

TSUJI, YUKIKO; Chatsworth HS; Canoga Park, CA; (4); CSUN; Accntng.

TSUKAMOTO, JEANIFER; Cupertino HS; Cupertino, CA; (2); Church Yth Grp; JV Bsktbl; JV Fld Hcky; Hon Roll; De Anza Athl Leag All Leag Awd; UC Davis.

TSUKUDA, JOHN; James Lick HS; San Jose, CA; (4); JA; Math Tm; Nwsp; Yrbk; High Hon Roll; Hon Roll; Suprntndts Hnr Rl; Stu Wk; Evergreen; Comp Sci.

TSUNG, MICHAEL S; Los Alamitas HS; La Palma, CA; (3); Hosp Aide; Science Clb; Spanish Clb; Tennis; Trk; Doctor.

TSUNG, QUEENIE; Western HS; Stanton, CA; (4); 5/307; Computer Clb; Teachers Aide; JV Tennis; Hon Roll; NHS; SOWE Cert Of Merit; CS Fullerton; Accntnt.

TSUNODA, MIHO; San Pedro HS; Rancho Palos Vrds, CA; (2).

TSURUDA, DIANA; Center HS; North Highlands, CA; (1); 4/243; French Clb; VP Frsh Cls; Cheerldng; High Hon Roll; CSF; MESA.

TSUTAGAWA, MICHELE M; El Camino HS; Oceanside, CA; (3); Church Yth Grp; Debate Tm; Speech Tm; Teachers Aide; JV Capt Cheerldng; Opt Clb Awd; Pop Warner Chrldng Team Coach 90-91; Long Beach ST U; Lingstcs.

TSUTAOKA, NEIL; Lodi HS; Lodi, CA; (4); 18/408; Pres VICA; Var Trk; High Hon Roll; CSF; Cal Poly Sn Luis Obispo; Engr.

TSUTSUI, NAO; Fountain Valley HS; Fountain Valley, CA; (2); Stu Achvt Awd; U Of CA.

TU, ALICE E; William C Overfelt HS; Cupertino, CA; (2); Church Yth Grp; Chorus; Color Guard; Hon Roll; CSF; Engrng.

TU, BILLY Y; Los Alamitos HS; Seal Beach, CA; (2); Church Yth Grp; Hosp Aide; Model UN; Bsbl; Bsktbl; Hon Roll; UC Berkeley; Pre Med.

TU, BINH T; Seaside HS; Seaside, CA; (2); French Clb; FBLA; Math Tm; Spanish Clb; SADD; Cit Awd; High Hon Roll; NHS; Pres Acad Fit Awd; Close Up Clb; Nurse.

TU, CHAU T; Andrew Hill HS; San Jose, CA; (2); French Clb; High Hon Roll; Prfct Atten Awd; Pres Acad Fit Awd; CA Schlrshp Fed; Vietnamese Stu Assn; Santa Clara U.

TU, LE T; Galileo HS; San Francisco, CA; (4); Nrs.

TU, PHAT T; Westminster HS; Midway City, CA; (4); 25/415; Computer Clb; English Clb; French Clb; Key Clb; Science Clb; Bsktbl; French Hon Soc; High Hon Roll; Opt Clb Awd; CA Schlrshp Fed; Ap Club; Vietnamese Club; UCLA; Bio Sci.

TU, QUAN KARINA; Balboa HS; San Francisco, CA; (3); Library Aide; ROTC; Teachers Aide; Hon Roll; St Schlr; San Jose ST U; Bus Mgt.

TU, ROGER; Galileo HS; San Francisco, CA; (3); French Clb; JV Var Bsbl; High Hon Roll; Hon Roll; Civil Engrng.

TU, THANH B; Garden Grove HS; Garden Grove, CA; (2); Cit Awd; High Hon Roll.

TU, TRAN; Saddleback HS; Santa Ana, CA; (1); Stage Crew.

TUAN, JO ANN C; Washington HS; Fremont, CA; (4); 12/280; VP French Clb; Service Clb; Pres Spanish Clb; Teachers Aide; Phtg Yrbk; Var Mgr(s); High Hon Roll; Pres Acad Fit Awd; UCLA; Comp Sci.

TUASON, REINA V; St Joseph HS; Cypress, CA; (4); 39/173; SADD; High Hon Roll; Hon Roll; Prfct Atten Awd; Pres Acad Fit Awd; CA Schlrshp Fed Schlr/Seal Bearer; Congressional Yth Ldrshp Cncl Schlr; Outstndng Acad Achvt Alg II; Marymount Coll; Bus.

TUAZON, DIANNE M; Burbank S HS; Burbank, CA; (2); Teachers Aide; Band; Stage Crew; Co-Ed Nwsp; Rep Stu Cncl; Hon Roll; Pres Acad Fit Awd; Acad Games; Jrnlsm Clb; UCLA; Med.

TUAZON, GERALINE D; Don Antonio Lugo HS; Chino, CA; (2); Dance Clb; School Musical; Variety Show; Hon Roll; Choreographer/Co-Capt Dance Team; Don Lugo Honor Stu Awd; Nrsng.

TUAZON, NANCY D; J Eugene Mc Ateer HS; San Francisco, CA; (3); Teachers Aide; Hon Roll; Fil-Am Clb; Vlntr; U Of San Francisco; Nrsg.

TUBAL, HEATHER; Bishop Amat Memorial HS; Baldwin Park, CA; (4); GAA; NFL; Rep Stu Cncl; Var JV Vllybl; Hon Roll; NHS; Ntl Merit SF; CSF; Amnsty Intl; UC Berkeley; Engl.

TUBBS, BRETT A; Hoover HS; Fresno, CA; (4); 78/417; Cmnty Wkr; Science Clb; Ski Clb; Swmmng; Wrstlng; Wtr Polo Jr LARCS; Gldn St Geomtry Awd; Cal Poly San Luis Obispo; Mech.

TUBBS, CODY ANDREW; Nevada Union HS; Nevada City, CA; (3); Ed Nwsp; Stu Cncl; Var Tennis; Cit Awd; High Hon Roll; Hon Roll; Dist Brd Of Trustees Stu; CSF; Congrsnl Yth Ldrshp Schlr; Pol Sci.

TUBBS, KATIE; Santa Rosa HS; Santa Rosa, CA; (3); 10/540; Church Yth Grp; Teachers Aide; School Play; Cheerldng; Cit Awd; Hon Roll; Peer Cnslr; Outstndng Yng Wrtrs Awd; Jessie R Smith Hnr Awd 88; Chapman Coll; Thtr Arts.

TUCKER, ADAM; Redwood HS; Visalia, CA; (3); Church Yth Grp; Cmnty Wkr; German Clb; Varsity Clb; Church Choir; Rptr Nwsp; Capt JV Bsbl; Var Ftbl; Wt Lftg; San Joaquin Valley Schlstc Pres Assn; CA Press Women HS Jrnlsm Awd; Bsbl Coaches Awd & Mst Imprvd; Fresno ST; Sports Med.

TUCKER, AIMEE J; Homestead HS; Sunnyvale, CA; (4); 37/359; Drama Clb; Pep Clb; Teachers Aide; Color Guard; Flag Corp; Stu Cncl; Pres Acad Fit Awd; CSF; Gldn St Exam Alg Hgh Hnrs & Geom Hnrs; Cls Grad Spkr; U Of CA Davis; Psych.

TUCKER, ANDREW; Greenville JR/Sr HS; Greenville, CA; (4); 2/30; Drama Clb; Service Clb; Teachers Aide; Varsity Clb; Band; Jazz Band; Pep Band; Ed Nwsp; Pres Sr Cls; JV L Bsktbl; Schl Board Stu; Vlntr Fire Dept; Bst Of Show Plumas Cnty Sci Fair; Berkeley CA U; Physics.

TUCKER, BETHANY J; Apple Valley HS; Apple Valley, CA; (3); 12/780; Church Yth Grp; Cmnty Wkr; French Clb; Hosp Aide; Key Clb; Red Cross Aide; Ski Clb; Church Choir; JV Vllybl; High Hon Roll; CSF; Stanford; Neuro Sci.

TUCKER, CARLA J; Orange Glen HS; Escondido, CA; (4); Math Tm; Band; Pres Frsh Cls; Rep Stu Cncl; Var Powder Puff Ftbl; NHS; Pres Acad Fit Awd; UC Berkeley; Bio.

TUCKER, CARRIE L; Mayfair HS; Lakewood, CA; (4); Jazz Band; VP Pres Mrchg Band; Pep Band; Hon Roll; Pres Acad Fit Awd; Music Dept & Directrs Awds; Long Beach City Coll.

TUCKER, CHRISTINA; Whittier Christian HS; Whittier, CA; (2); Art Clb; Church Yth Grp; Drill Tm; JV Capt Cheerldng; Hon Roll; Art.

TUCKER, JENNIFER; Maranatha HS; Arcadia, CA; (4); Church Yth Grp; Band; Stage Crew; VP Frsh Cls; JV Var Cheerldng; Swmmng; Elks Awd; Hon Roll; Pres Acad Fit Awd; Biola U; Accntng.

TUCKER, LESLEY A; Lowell HS; San Francisco, CA; (3); Drama Clb; Sec French Clb; SADD; Band; Orch; School Play; Stage Crew; Gym; Socr; Shiel & L Soc Hnr Soc; Adventurers Alliance; Lang.

TUCKER, MELISSA L; Victor Valley HS; Victorville, CA; (3); Aud/Vis; Key Clb; Spanish Clb; Pepperdine U; MBA.

TUCKER, MICHAEL G; Monterey Bay Acad; Angwin, CA; (2); Church Yth Grp; Cmnty Wkr.

TUCKER, TANJI; El Camino Real HS; Woodland Hills, CA; (4); 38/530; Church Yth Grp; Ski Clb; Church Choir; Ed Lit Mag; Off Sr Cls; Hon Roll; Yng Black Schlrs; Grad Coord; Ephebian Soc; FL A&M; Bus Adm.

TUCKER, TRISTEN O; Arcata HS; Bridgeville, CA; (2); Drama Clb; SADD; Chorus; Stage Crew; Lit Mag; Hon Roll; Pres Acad Fit Awd; Val; CA Schltc Fndtn; Law.

TUCKER, VERONICA R; El Cerrito HS; San Pablo, CA; (4); SADD; Frnch.

TUCKEY, KEVIN; Crescenta Valley HS; Glendale, CA; (3); German Clb; Math Clb; Mu Alpha Theta; Science Clb; NHS; Econ.

TUDELA, INGRID; David Star Jordan HS; Long Beach, CA; (1); Drill Tm; School Play; Fshn Mdse.

TUDOR, REED M; Monte Vista HS; Danville, CA; (3); Acpl Chr; Chorus; Crs Cntry; Socr; Trk; Yth & Govt; U Of OR; Tchng.

TUER, SHANNON L; Monterey HS; Fort Ord, CA; (2); Church Yth Grp; Cmnty Wkr; Model UN; School Play; JV Fld Hcky; JV Swmmng; Hon Roll; Leag Sftbl; Fine Arts Day Hartnell Coll; Art.

TUFT, JACOB R; George Washington HS; San Francisco, CA; (3); JV Tennis; High Hon Roll; Hon Roll; San Francisco-Osaka Sistr Cty Schlrshp; Mech Engrng.

TUFT, MACI; Piner HS; Santa Rosa, CA; (4); 29/400; JA; Office Aide; SADD; Teachers Aide; Temple Yth Grp; Yrbk; Off Jr Cls; Off Sr Cls; Stu Cncl; Cheerldng; Chico ST U; Bus.

TUFTS, BRYAN R; North Mont Co HS; Salinas, CA; (2); Hon Roll.

TUFTS, CHRISTOPHER M; Sanger HS; Sanger, CA; (2); Church Yth Grp; Science Clb; Bsktbl; Fresno ST; US Hstry Ed.

TUGADE, EMY G; Delano HS; Delano, CA; (3); Drama Clb; French Clb; Hosp Aide; Band; Chorus; Church Choir; Color Guard; Drill Tm; Mrchg Band; Pep Band; Unitd Filipino Orgnztn VP; Bus Law.

TUGADE, MICHELE; Westmoor HS; Daly City, CA; (3); 1/500; Pres Frsh Cls; Rep Soph Cls; VP Stu Cncl; Capt Var Cheerldng; High Hon Roll; Cmnty Wkr; French Clb; Model UN; SADD; Chorus; CADA Ldrshp; Renaissance Stu Coordntr; Harvard U; Bus Mrktng.

TUGADE, RUBY; Westmoor HS; Daly City, CA; (3); 1/500; Cmnty Wkr; Model UN; SADD; Band; VP Frsh Cls; VP Soph Cls; Cheerldng; High Hon Roll; N CA Ambssdr HOBY Intl Ldrshp Smnr; GATE Stu; Jefferson Union HS Dist Planningcmmtte Mem; Harvard U; Bus Mrktng.

TUGGLE, ARIANA M; Skyline HS; Oakland, CA; (2); Art Clb; Varsity Clb; Orch; Lit Mag; Var Socr; Var Trk; JV Vllybl; Hon Roll; NHS; Pres Acad Fit Awd; CSF; UC-BERKLEY; Vet.

TUGGLE, KORI; Diamond Bar HS; Diamond Bar, CA; (3); Pres Pep Clb; Ski Clb; Spanish Clb; Varsity Clb; Variety Show; Sec Sr Cls; Stu Cncl; Capt Var Cheerldng; JV Tennis; Hon Roll; Santa Barbara; Bus.

TUGMAN, DAVID R; Edison Computech HS; Fresno, CA; (3); Teachers Aide; Hon Roll; Teens Education At Rick Children; Excell In Reading Skills; African American Presentation Team; College; Teacher.

TUGMAN, RAY; Edison HS; Fresno, CA; (3); 24/240; Hon Roll; Fresno City Coll; Chemist.

TUHOLSKI, STANISLAUS JOHN; De La Salle HS; Concord, CA; (4); 1/218; Boy Scts; Church Yth Grp; Debate Tm; Speech Tm; JV Bsbl; Var Trk; Elks Awd; High Hon Roll; NHS; Pres Acad Fit Awd; Order Of The Arrow; U Of Notre Dame; Chmcl Engr.

TUI, TAO A; Abraham Lincoln HS; San Francisco, CA; (2); Chess Clb; Math Clb; ROTC; Teachers Aide; Acpl Chr; High Hon Roll; Hon Roll; CSF Clb; Madarin Clb; Stu Of Month; U CA; Comp Engrng.

TUITA, KATHY; Pioneer HS; San Jose, CA; (1); Church Yth Grp; Cmnty Wkr; Debate Tm; Spanish Clb; JV Var Sftbl; JV Vllybl; Hon Roll; Interact Clb; Sftbl JV & Vrsty Cntrl Coast Sctn Trnmnt; BYU; Nurse.

TULAO, NICOLETTE JOY; Bonita Vista HS; Bonita, CA; (4); Pep Clb; SADD; Flag Corp; Variety Show; Rep Frsh Cls; JV Co-Capt Cheerldng; Hon Roll; NHS; Acad Excllnc-Alg II; CSF; Asian Culture Clb.

TULIO, JON J; Monterey Bay Acad; Los Angeles, CA; (1); Church Yth Grp; Ski Clb; Band; Intrml Bsktbl; Intrml Ftbl; Intrml Vllybl; U Of CA Los Angeles; Bio.

TULK, WENDY LYNN; Baker Valley Unified HS; Apple Valley, CA; (4); 2/6; Drama Clb; Office Aide; Pres Stu Cncl; Cheerldng; Vllybl; High Hon Roll; Victor Valley Coll; Psychlgy.

TULL, JEFFREY J; St Anthony HS; Garden Grove, CA; (2); Boy Scts; Chess Clb; Church Yth Grp; Crs Cntry; Trk; High Hon Roll; CSF; HOBY; Cal Poly San Luis Obispo; Comp.

TULL, JONATHAN D; Hesperia HS; Hesperia, CA; (4); 2/450; Science Clb; Mrchg Band; Ed Yrbk; Intrml Wrstlng; High Hon Roll; Pres Acad Fit Awd; Sal; Sci Project At St Sci Fr; U CA Riverside; Engrng.

TULLIS, WENDY; Arroyo Grande HS; Arroyo Grande, CA; (2); School Play; Crs Cntry; Trk; Hon Roll; Fshn Mdlng; Mrktng.

TULLOS, SHAWN L; Beyer HS; Modesto, CA; (3); Pep Clb; Ski Clb; SADD; Nwsp; Swmmng; Hon Roll; Coach Spcl Olympics Swmmng; Coll.

TULLY III, JOHN F; Bullard HS; Fresno, CA; (1); SADD; Rep Stu Cncl; Intrml Ftbl; Mgr(s); Score Keeper; Intrml Socr; Wt Lftg; Prfct Atten Awd; CA U; Lawyer.

TULLY, MONICA J; Birmingham HS; Van Nuys, CA; (3); Church Yth Grp; GAA; Service Clb; Varsity Clb; Church Choir; Bsktbl; Score Keeper; High Hon Roll; JETS Awd; Vlybl JV Bst Dfnsv Plyr; Vlybl Var Mst Insprtnl; UCLA; Biochem.

TUMA, GABRIELIA; Mira Costa HS; Hermosa Beach, CA; (2); Church Yth Grp; French Clb; JV Tennis; JV Trk; Cit Awd; High Hon Roll; Hon Roll; Schlr Athl; UCLA; Design.

TUMANUVAO, DIANA; Fremont HS; Oakland, CA; (3); Church Yth Grp; Chorus; Church Choir; Bsktbl; Sftbl; Vllybl; Cit Awd; Hon Roll; Vllybl Trophys; BYU HI.

TUMASIAN, STEPHANIE R; Carondelet HS; Danville, CA; (3); 24/162; Church Yth Grp; Hosp Aide; Spanish Clb; Rep Frsh Cls; Off Sr Cls; JV Crs Cntry; JV Trk; High Hon Roll; Hon Roll; NHS; Svc Awd; Mem CA Schlrshp Fed; Pres Span Hnr Society; Psych.

TUMBOKON, RADIEL F; St John Bosco HS; Norwalk, CA; (2); #17 In Class; Computer Clb; Cit Awd; High Hon Roll; Hon Roll; Prfct Atten Awd; Achvmnt In Geo, Bio & Spanish II; Cal Poly; Engnrng.

TUMILTY, MICHAEL C; St Helena HS; St Helena, CA; (4); Drama Clb; Ski Clb; Band; Jazz Band; Pep Band; School Musical; Hon Roll; Pres Acad Fit Awd; Cert Of Mrt Awds In Piano, Theory; Natl Guild Awd Piano Perfrmnc; Bnk Amer Awd Achvt In Music; U Of CA Santa Cruz.

TUMINIA, CHRISTY E; Willow Glen HS; San Jose, CA; (4); 23/295; Church Yth Grp; Science Clb; SADD; Stat Bsktbl; Mgr(s); Mgr Swmmng; Var Trk; High Hon Roll; Hon Roll; Pres Acad Fit Awd; 2nd Pl Cnty Sci Fr; Amnsty Intl; VP Prsnl Jr Achvt Corp; West Valley Coll; Bus Mgmt.

TUN, SARAH PHEAP; Modesto HS; Modesto, CA; (3); Intnl Clb; Teachers Aide; Sec Jr Cls; Cit Awd; Hon Roll.

TUNG, CHI HO; Monte Vista Christian HS; Canada; (4); 8/90; Intnl Clb; Chorus; Crs Cntry; Tennis; High Hon Roll; CSF; Santa Cruz Cnty Math Cntst 3rd Pl 88; Columbia U; Comp Sci.

TUNG, GRACE Y; South Pasadena HS; South Pasadena, CA; (3); 100/300; Computer Clb; Intnl Clb; School Musical; Physics Hnr; Calculas; Bus Mgmt.

TUNG, KAREN WOON YIU; International Studies Acad; San Francisco, CA; (3); Science Clb; Speech Tm; Teachers Aide; High Hon Roll; Close Up Pgm; Gldn St Exam Alg Hnrs; Chinese Club; Comp Sci.

TUNG, LINDA F; Galileo HS; San Francisco, CA; (4); JA; Spanish Clb; Hon Roll; Prfct Atten Awd; Bk Of Amer Achvt Awd; San Francisco ST U; Accntng.

TUNG, MONICA K; Don Antonio Lugo HS; Chino Hills, CA; (3); Cmnty Wkr; SADD; Nwsp; Gldn Conquest Awds Bio, 11th Hnrs Engl; AYSO Soccer; Psychtry.

TUNG, ROGER; La Mirada HS; La Mirada, CA; (2); Art Clb; Church Yth Grp; Math Clb; Spanish Clb; Tennis; Trk; Bausch & Lomb Sci Awd; Hon Roll; Prfct Atten Awd; CSF; UCI; Archtctr.

TUNG, YEN C; Clovis West HS; Fresno, CA; (2); Chess Clb; Debate Tm; Math Clb; Math Tm; NFL; High Hon Roll; Opt Clb Awd; CSF; Sci Olympd.

TUNNELL, MARY; San Mateo HS; Foster City, CA; (3); 1/350; Rep Am Leg Aux Girls St; Church Yth Grp; Latin Clb; Rptr Nwsp; Sec Soph Cls; Off Jr Cls; Stu Cncl; JV Capt Cheerldng; Var L Swmmng; High Hon Roll.

TUNSON, SHAWN P; George Washington HS; San Francisco, CA; (3); Boy Scts; Church Yth Grp; Band; Church Choir; Bsktbl; Ftbl; Trk; Cit Awd; Hon Roll; Bus.

TUOMALA, HEATHER M; Lutheran HS; Mission Viejo, CA; (2); Church Yth Grp; Girl Scts; Trk; Poem Publshd Great Poems Of Westrn Wrld; Achvd Slvr Awd Girls Scts; Jrnlsm.

TUONG, HOA M; Wilson HS; Long Beach, CA; (3); CA Schlrshp Soc; An-Nam Clb.

TUPAHAN, VIVIAN; John F Kennedy HS; Buena Park, CA; (2); Computer Clb; Key Clb; CSF; Plain Wrap Club; UCLA; Doc.

TUPASI, NYREE D; South San Francisco HS; South San Francis, CA; (2); Cit Awd; Hon Roll; Prfct Atten Awd; CSF; Italian Clb; Close-Up; Medcl.

TUPHAN, YVETTE Y; John F Kennedy HS; Buena Park, CA; (3); FBLA; Key Clb; Chorus; Rep Frsh Cls; Rep Soph Cls; Rep Stu Cncl; PTSA Rep; Diati Clb; Plainwrp Clb; CSF Clb; UCI.

TUPUA, DEMI P; El Camino HS; Daly City, CA; (3); Math Tm; Band; Jazz Band; Orch; School Musical; High Hon Roll; CSF; U CA Berkeley; Arch.

TURANGE, VERONICA; El Camino HS; Sacramento, CA; (4); 61/341; Drama Clb; NHS; Music.

TURAY, SCOTT C; Valley View HS; Moreno Valley, CA; (2); L Socr; Hon Roll; UCSD; Med.

TURBEVILLE, ASHLEY B; California HS; San Ramon, CA; (3); 25/450; Pres Church Yth Grp; Cmnty Wkr; French Clb; Off Jr Cls; Sec Stu Cncl; Var Capt Cheerldng; JV Var Tennis; Var Trk; High Hon Roll; NHS; Mem Macys Teen Brd; Sctry CSF; Acad Ltgtr Schlstc Achvmnt; U Of CA; Mrktng.

TURBEVILLE, MARSHALL; Geyserville HS; Geyserville, CA; (2); AFS; Boy Scts; Science Clb; Teachers Aide; Band; VP Soph Cls; Var Bsbl; JV Bsktbl; Var Socr; Hon Roll; 1st Pl Best Of Show Sci Fair 89; 1st Pl Sci Fair 90; CA Poly San Luis Obsp; Engrng.

TURELL, DANA M; Foothill HS; Tustin, CA; (3); Church Yth Grp; Drama Clb; Teachers Aide; Thesps; Varsity Clb; Chorus; Church Choir; School Musical; School Play; Stage Crew; New Life Clb Pres; Safe Rides.

TURK, SHANNON M; Hart HS; Valencia, CA; (2); Church Yth Grp; Cmnty Wkr; Mu Alpha Theta; JV Var Bsktbl; JV Sftbl; High Hon Roll; Hon Roll; Clb Sccr Tm 2 Yrs; Asst Coach 7-9 Yr Olds Gls Sftbl; Asst Coach 10 Yr Olds Bsktbl & Sccr Tm; Refre Sccr; Phys Thrpy.

TURLEY, JOSHUA A; Valley View HS; Moreno Valley, CA; (2); 33/500; Pres Church Yth Grp; Treas Stu Cncl; Var L Bsktbl; Cit Awd; Hon Roll; U Of AZ; Poli Sci.

TURNBAUGH, JIM F; Apple Valley HS; Apple Valley, CA; (2); Church Yth Grp; Band; Jazz Band; Mrchg Band; Var Crs Cntry; Var Swmmng; San Diego ST; Music.

TURNBULL, MATTHEW S; Mission Viejo HS; Mission Viejo, CA; (2); Var Swmmng; High Hon Roll; CSF; Advncd Plcmnt & Intl Baccalaureate; Prncpls Hnr Roll; UCLA; Intl Mrktng.

TURNER, ALICE M; Lowell HS; San Francisco, CA; (4); 6/626; Hosp Aide; Model UN; Band; Pep Band; Stage Crew; Ntl Merit SF; CSF; Vlntr In Ecuador 89; High Hnrs Geo Gldn St Exam; U Of Chicago; Bio.

TURNER, ALLEN S; California HS; San Ramon, CA; (3); Church Yth Grp; Debate Tm; FCA; Hosp Aide; Spanish Clb; Chorus; Church Choir; Ftbl; Trk; Aud/Vis; Natl Choir Dirctr Of Yr Gospel; Howard; Law.

TURNER, ATHA R; Morse HS; San Diego, CA; (3); Sec Spanish Clb; Band; Phtg Yrbk; Rep Stu Cncl; Var Bsktbl; JV Var Sftbl; Lawyer.

TURNER, CHRIS L; San Bernardino HS; San Bernardino, CA; (2); #278 In Class; Church Yth Grp; Debate Tm; Speech Tm; Hon Roll; Chrch Bsktbl & Vlybl; Comp.

TURNER, CHRISTIAN R; Colton HS; Colton, CA; (2); High Hon Roll; Hon Roll; Prfct Atten Awd; Math.

TURNER, CRYSTAL M; Downtown Business Magnet HS; Los Angeles, CA; (2); Service Clb; Chorus; JV Bsktbl; Hon Roll; Rep Stu Cncl; Word Procssng.

TURNER, DASH E; River City HS; W Sacramento, CA; (1); Cmnty Wkr; JV Crs Cntry; Var Swmmng; High Hon Roll; Hon Roll; Elect Engrng.

TURNER, DAVID C; Vahalla HS; El Cajon, CA; (4); Yrbk; Crs Cntry; Trk.

TURNER, DEBORAH KAYE; Thousand Oaks HS; Thousand Oaks, CA; (4); 23/530; Ski Clb; Ed Nwsp; Var L Crs Cntry; Powder Puff Ftbl; Var L Trk; High Hon Roll; NHS; Opt Clb Awd; Pres Acad Fit Awd; CSF Golden Seal Bearer; U Of NM; Acct.

TURNER, EDDIE F; San Benito HS; Hollister, CA; (2); Rptr FFA; Bsbl; Ftbl; Wt Lftg; Hon Roll; Cattle Mgnt.

TURNER, GILLIAN A; Los Amigos HS; Fountain Valley, CA; (2); 17/365; VP 4-H; Pep Clb; Spanish Clb; Yrbk; JV Bsktbl; JV Sftbl; 4-H Awd; High Hon Roll; Masonic Awd; 4 H Awds; St Book Wnnr; Bk Amer Schlrshp; Tchr.

TURNER, JANEE; Dos Pueblos HS; Goleta, CA; (3); Church Yth Grp; Latin Clb; Math Clb; Science Clb; Acpl Chr; Co-Capt Color Guard; Flag Corp; NHS; Dance.

TURNER, JASON; Bear River HS; Auburn, CA; (4); 19/150; AFS; Letterman Clb; SADD; Var Bsktbl; Var Capt Golf; High Hon Roll; Hon Roll; Chico ST; Bus.

TURNER, JASON MICHAEL; Clayton Valley HS; Concord, CA; (2); Boy Scts; Letterman Clb; SADD; Teachers Aide; Hon Roll; Eagle Prjct Scouts; Acadc Lttr.

TURNER, JENNIE; Crescenta Valley HS; Glendale, CA; (1); Church Yth Grp; Drill Tm; Gym; San Luis Obispo; Nrs.

TURNER, JERMAINE; Poly HS; Riverside, CA; (3); Lcrss; JV Bsktbl; JV Mgr(s); Wt Lftg; Hnr Mention; Engrng.

TURNER, JULIE K; Newbury Park HS; Newbury Park, CA; (3); Church Yth Grp; Socr; Swmmng; Tennis; Hon Roll; Golden St Geom Exam Hnrs; Early Chldhd Dev.

TURNER, JULIETTE E; Sacramento HS; Sacramento, CA; (2); 115/500; Orch; School Musical; Hon Roll; Sacramento Area Yth Chorale; Camellia Symphny; Sacramento Yth Symphny; CSU Sacramento; Music Tchr.

TURNER, KATHLEEN; Arroyo Grande HS; Arroyo Grande, CA; (3); Hon Roll; Jrnlsm.

TURNER, KATIE; Livermore HS; Livermore, CA; (1); Cheerldng; High Hon Roll; Med.

TURNER, LIESA M; Lincoln HS; Lincoln, CA; (3); 27/157; Church Yth Grp; Cmnty Wkr; FBLA; GAA; Office Aide; Pep Clb; SADD; Rptr Yrbk; Sec Stu Cncl; Cheerldng; Prom Cmmtte; Christmas Dance Cmmtte; 89 Eagle Aloha Bowl Halftime Show HI Chrstms Day; Travel West Acad; Travel.

TURNER, LOREE S; Warren HS; Downey, CA; (2); Pres SADD; Air Force.

TURNER, MATTHEW G; Poway HS; Poway, CA; (1); Boy Scts; SADD; Var Bsbl; JV Ftbl; Hon Roll; Pres Acad Fit Awd; Sci.

TURNER, MELISSA A; El Camino HS; Brisbane, CA; (3); Teachers Aide; Variety Show; Var Pom Pon; Prfct Atten Awd; Frgn Lang Stu Mnth Spnsh; Indstrl Tech Stu Mnth; Acadmc Achvt Spnsh For Yr.

TURNER, MIKE; St Lawrence Acad; Campbell, CA; (2); Church Yth Grp; Office Aide; Var Capt Bsktbl; Score Keeper; Var Socr; Jr NHS; Sprts Trnr.

TURNER, MONICA L; Brawley Union HS; Imperial, CA; (4); 2/290; Am Leg Aux Girls St; Church Yth Grp; Math Tm; Rep Band; VP Stu Cncl; Var L Crs Cntry; Var L Socr; Var L Trk; Pres Acad Fit Awd; Sal; Christ Coll Irvine; Pre-Med.

TURNER, NICK B; Torrance HS; Torrance, CA; (2); 109/441; Church Yth Grp; Chorus; Mem Acad Excllc Awd; New Life Clb; Most Imprvd Concert Choir; Most Irprvd Drummer; USC; Lawyer.

TURNER, ONNA L; Marysville HS; Marysville, CA; (2); Church Yth Grp; Letterman Clb; SADD; Varsity Clb; Band; Mrchg Band; Bsktbl; Trk; Hon Roll; Hnr Band; JV Bsktbl Capt; Law.

TURNER, RACHELLE T; El Camino HS; Oceanside, CA; (3); 13/365; Sec Debate Tm; French Clb; NFL; Quiz Bowl; Sec Speech Tm; Teachers Aide; Rptr Nwsp; JV Socr; Hon Roll; CSF; Soroptmst Intl Yth Forum Wnnr; Cmssnr Ecology Trhu Schl Cncl; Biochem.

TURNER, REIKA Y; Ygnacio Valley HS; Concord, CA; (2); Church Yth Grp; Key Clb; Math Clb; Model UN; Spanish Clb; High Hon Roll; Acad Ltr; Med.

TURNER, ROQUEL L; West Covina HS; West Covina, CA; (1); Treas Chorus; Capt Bsktbl; Score Keeper; Sftbl; U S CA; Pediatrician.

TURNER, SHANNA A; Mojave HS; California City, CA; (1); Church Yth Grp; Letterman Clb; SADD; Flag Corp; Var Sftbl; USC; Tchr.

TURNER, SHANNON R; James Logan HS; Union City, CA; (1); Dance Clb; Color Guard; Mrchg Band; Hon Roll; Cal Berkeley; Law.

TURNER, SHAYLEEN A; Edison SR HS; Stockton, CA; (3); Math Clb; Math Tm; Acpl Chr; Chorus; School Play; Rep Stu Cncl; Hon Roll; Golden St Exam Alg High Hnrs/3rd Pl Alg I 88; Bus.

TURNER, SHELLEY A; Victor Valley HS; Victorville, CA; (2); 8/608; FBLA; Girl Scts; JA; Key Clb; Quiz Bowl; Orch; Golf; Trk; Hon Roll; Pres Acad Fit Awd; Ed.

TURNER, THANDEKA D; South Bay Lutheran HS; Los Angeles, CA; (1); Church Yth Grp; Girl Scts; Hosp Aide; Office Aide; Church Choir; School Play; Off Frsh Cls; Stu Cncl; Sftbl; Cit Awd; Ped.

TURNER, THOMAS L; Santa Teresa HS; San Jose, CA; (3); Letterman Clb; Science Clb; Varsity Clb; Bsbl; San Jose ST U.

TURPIN, KELLI R; Downey HS; Bellflower, CA; (4); Drama Clb; Library Aide; Office Aide; School Musical; Yrbk; High Hon Roll; Pres Acad Fit Awd; Vanderbilt U; Spcl Educ Tchr.

TURSE, JOSH E; Carlsbad HS; Carlsbad, CA; (1); Church Yth Grp; Pres Science Clb; Orch; Pep Band; Swmmng; Gov Hon Prg Awd; High Hon Roll; Pres Of Ecology Clb; Mem Of Civic Yth Orch Palomar Coll; Punahou; Doctorate.

TURSKEY, JULIE; Mercy HS; Cottonwood, CA; (4); 1/30; Am Leg Aux Girls St; VP Key Clb; Sec Model UN; Pres Science Clb; Pres SADD; Orch; VP Stu Cncl; Capt Cheerldng; Var Trk; Val; Tandy Math/Sci Schlr Awd; Homcmng Qn 90; Rotary Clb Freedom Yth Ldrshp Conf Delg; St Marys Coll; Accntng.

TURTURICI, GINA; Soquel HS; Scotts Valley, CA; (2); German Clb; Hosp Aide; Tennis; CA Schlrshp Fdrtn-Sec; Hnr Clb; Hgh Hnrs In Sci; Bus Admin.

TUSANT, JILL S; Arcadia HS; Arcadia, CA; (2); 90/599; Church Yth Grp; Drama Clb; Thesps; Chorus; Church Choir; Drill Tm; School Play; High Hon Roll; Hon Roll; Pres Acad Fit Awd; Hmecmng Queen 89; Gold Seal Grad 89.

TUSHLA, TODD D; St Bonaventrue HS; Santa Paula, CA; (3); 10/122; Cmnty Wkr; Quiz Bowl; JV Var Bsbl; Var Capt Bsktbl; High Hon Roll; NHS; Ntl Merit Ltr; Boy Scts; Letterman Clb; Intrml Golf; DARE; CSF; Med.

TUSTIN, JENNIFER N; Culver City HS; Culver City, CA; (2); Church Yth Grp; Off Frsh Cls; Off Soph Cls; Pres Jr Cls; French Hon Soc; High Hon Roll; Pres Acad Fit Awd; High Hnrs Golden ST Exam Geom; Boston U; Spch Ther.

TUTOR, LYNDA J; Westminster HS; Westminster, CA; (1); Drama Clb; Teachers Aide; School Play; Wght Lftng; Sgn Lang; Arts.

TUTTLE, ERIC B; Holtville HS; Holtville, CA; (3); AFS; FBLA; NFL; Pep Clb; Chorus; Stage Crew; Phtg Yrbk; Lit Mag; VP Jr Cls; Stu Cncl; Physics.

TUTTLE, JOHN T; Chatsworth HS; West Hills, CA; (3); Varsity Clb; Var Ftbl; JV Trk; Var Vllybl; Hon Roll; U CA Santa Barbara; Bus.

TUTTLE, MIKE A; San Marcos HS; Santa Barbara, CA; (2); Church Yth Grp; Cmnty Wkr; ROTC; Band; Jazz Band; Mrchg Band; Pep Band; Rep Stu Cncl; JV Tennis; High Hon Roll; Civil Air Patrol; Auxiliary Of USAF; Flying; AF Acad; AF Fighter Pilot.

TUTTLE JR, RICHARD O; Sutter Union HS; Sutter, CA; (3); 3/85; Am Leg Boys St; Church Yth Grp; Drama Clb; Sec Intnl Clb; Library Aide; School Play; VP Jr Cls; JV Bsktbl; Hon Roll; Lion Awd; Church Sftbl; CSF 89-90; Yuba Clg; Math.

TUTULUGDZIJA, ANICA; Cypress HS; Cypress, CA; (1); Cheerldng; Hon Roll; French/Engl Stu Of Month Awd; Stanford; Law.

TUXEN, BRIGIT LYN; Amos Alonzo Stagg HS; Stockton, CA; (1); Cmnty Wkr; Drama Clb; Key Clb; Thesps; School Musical; Stage Crew; Stu Cncl; JV L Socr; L Swmmng; L Tennis; Earth Day Celebration Chrmn 90; Stu Take Action Not Drugs; AAA Natl Schl Trffc Sfty Poster Pgm 1st Pl.

TUYEN, NGUYEN; Andrew Hill HS; San Jose, CA; (3).

TUYNMAN, JOSHUA P; Troy HS; Yorba Linda, CA; (4); Drama Clb; French Clb; Ski Clb; School Play; Var Capt Swmmng; High Hon Roll; Ntl Merit SF; U Southern CA.

TVEDT, VALERIE MARIA; Barstow HS; Barstow, CA; (3); AFS; Am Leg Aux Girls St; Girl Scts; Band; Mrchg Band; Pep Band; High Hon Roll; 3rd Pl Fictn Desert Heritage Writng Cont; San Bernardino Cnty Hnr Band; Engl Teacher.

TVEIT, JASON C; Tulare Union HS; Tulare, CA; (2); 33/500; Pres Boy Scts; Cmnty Wkr; Speech Tm; Rep Frsh Cls; Rep Soph Cls; FCA; Lion Awd; Tutor; Natl Boy Sct Jamboree 89; St Johns Seminary; Theology.

TWADDELL, STACI; Folson HS; Folsom, CA; (2); JA; Teachers Aide; JV Socr; Cit Awd; Hon Roll; NHS; CA Poly; Bus.

TWEEDIE, NATHAN T; Grace M Davis HS; Modesto, CA; (2); JV Bsktbl; Cit Awd; High Hon Roll; Hon Roll; St Schlr; Comp.

TWEEDY, PAMELA C.; Chaffey HS; Ontario, CA; (3); 2/600; Church Yth Grp; Drill Tm; JV Cheerldng; Score Keeper; High Hon Roll; Ntl Merit Ltr; Math Dprtmnt Awd; Englsh Dprtmnt Awd; Ivy Chain Prtcpnt; Acctng/Bus.

TWER, CANYON T; Oakdale HS; Oakdale, CA; (3); Chess Clb; Scholastic Bowl; Science Clb; Var Crs Cntry; Var Trk; Hon Roll; NHS; St Schlr; Wghtlftng Qualifier For St; Acctng II & Rtl Math Cmptn; Sci Bowl; Cal Poly, San Luis Obispo.

TWISSELMANN, ERIC; Victory Christian Schl; Rocklin, CA; (2); 1/35; VP Science Clb; Pep Band; School Musical; Nwsp; Rep Frsh Cls; Treas Soph Cls; Rep Stu Cncl; JV Bsktbl; High Hon Roll; NHS; Mst Insprtnl Plyr Jr Vrsty Bsktbl 89-90; Boys Phys Ed Dept Awd 88-89; Trig During Smmr Sierra JC; Teaching.

TWIST, DAMON L; Victor Valley HS; Victorville, CA; (4); 11/390; Am Leg Boys St; English Clb; Pep Clb; Speech Tm; Jazz Band; Swing Chorus; Pres Stu Cncl; Elks Awd; Kiwanis Awd; Mock Trial Tm; UCLA; Pol Sci.

TWU, CONNIE C; Brea HS; Brea, CA; (1); Intnl Clb; Key Clb; Hon Roll; Piano Cmptn; UCLA.

TYAN, TONY; Northview HS; Covina, CA; (4); Science Clb; Hon Roll; Pres Acad Fit Awd; Covina Lions Brkfst Clb Yng Man Of Mnth Awd 90; Bank Of Amer Plq Awd Math & Sci; U Of CA Irvine.

TYE, KAREN; Hayward HS; Castro Valley, CA; (2); Dance Clb; Pep Clb; Ski Clb; Spanish Clb; Chorus; Variety Show; Pres Jr Cls; Pom Pon; Sftbl; Hon Roll; CSF Tutr & Actv; Intrst Sgn Lng; Santa Barbara; Cmmnctns.

TYGENHOF, HEATHER T; Tustin HS; Tustin, CA; (1); Church Yth Grp; Bsktbl; Stu Athltc Trnr Sprts Med; Law.

TYLER, DONNA; Woodlake Union HS; Woodlake, CA; (4); 9/125; Church Yth Grp; FHA; Ed Yrbk; JV Bsktbl; Hon Roll; Congrssnl Yth Ldrshp Cncl 90; Coll Fo Sequioa; Elem Educ.

TYLER, JENNIPER AUTUMN; Moorpark HS; Moorpark, CA; (2); FBLA; Color Guard; Trk; High Hon Roll; Hon Roll; Opt Clb Awd; USC; Biology.

TYLER, KATIE L; Kern Valley HS; Lake Isabella, CA; (1); FFA; JV Bsktbl; Powder Puff Ftbl; Var Trk; Hon Roll; Prfct Atten Awd; Acad Awd Vrsty Grls Trck 90; Schlrshp Awd FFA.

TYLER, RODELL J; Turlock HS; Turlock, CA; (2); 327/500; Church Yth Grp; VP Church Choir; JV Bsktbl; Devry; Comp Tech.

TYLER, TYKESHA Q; Palisades HS; Los Angeles, CA; (2); Church Yth Grp; Teachers Aide; Church Choir; JV Bsktbl; Prfct Atten Awd; Howard U; Pediatrician.

TYRRELL, STEVEN M; Clayton Valley HS; Concord, CA; (3); Cmnty Wkr; JA; JV Swmmng; JV Wrstlng; Cit Awd; Pres Acad Fit Awd; Comptd In CA JR Wrtng; CA ST U; Bus.

TYSOR, JEFF J; Indio HS; Indio, CA; (1); French Clb; L Swmmng; Prfct Atten Awd; CA Schlrshp Fed; Jr Var Water Polo; Bus.

TYSOR, JEREMY B; Indio HS; Indio, CA; (3); 1/400; JV Var Bsbl; High Hon Roll; Prfct Atten Awd; Jr Statesmn Amer; Waterpolo Vrsty; CSF; Optime; Bch Vllybl Clb, VP; Golden St Exm Geom Schl Recgntn.

TYSZLER, HENRY P; Hamilton HS Academy Of Music; Los Angeles, CA; (2); Orch; School Musical; Hon Roll; Prfct Atten Awd; Music.

TYZZER, LAURA K; El Capitan HS; Lakeside, CA; (2); 18/433; Church Yth Grp; Cmnty Wkr; SADD; Church Choir; Drill Tm; Variety Show; Mgr(s); Hon Roll; Flying Magzn Natl Cont Wnnr; Aerospace Engrng.

TZADOK, SHIRA; Covina HS; W Covina, CA; (4); 33/262; Temple Yth Grp; Ed Yrbk; Trk; Hon Roll; Cal ST Long Bch; Educ.

TZE, STEVEN W; University HS; Irvine, CA; (3); 69/551; Cmnty Wkr; Hosp Aide; Science Clb; Teachers Aide; Varsity Clb; Var Crs Cntry; Var Capt Tennis; High Hon Roll; Hon Roll; Pres Acad Fit Awd; Acad Decthln; St Exmn Math Cmmnded Hnrs; CSF; Bio.

TZENG, DAVID; Schurr HS; Montebello, CA; (2); Boy Scts; Chess Clb; Math Clb; JV Tennis; Engrng.

UBALDO, GLO ANNE G; Abraham Lincoln HS; San Francisco, CA; (1); Cheerldng; Swmmng; Tennis; Trk; Vllybl; Hon Roll; Ntl Merit Ltr; Delg Div Sci Cmptn Philippines; Delg Div Eng & Spelling Quiz Bee Philippines; Hnr Pupil; San Francisco ST U; Nrsg.

UBER, REGINA L; Modesto HS; Modesto, CA; (2); Var Socr; Hon Roll; Greenpeace Clb; CSF; Modesto Yth Sccr Assoc; Marine Bio.

UBERT, CYNTHIA; Rosary HS; Whittier, CA; (3); Hosp Aide; Science Clb; Rptr Nwsp; Lit Mag; JV Vllybl; High Hon Roll; CSF Vice Pres; Loyola Marymount; Bus.

UBONGEN, MARY L; Skyline HS; Oakland, CA; (2); Rep Yrbk; Cit Awd; Hon Roll; Student Of The Month; Magna Cum Laude-National Latin Exam.

UCEDA, ROSA M; Mayfair HS; Long Beach, CA; (2); Aud/Vis; Church Yth Grp; Cmnty Wkr; GAA; Teachers Aide; Chorus; Church Choir; School Musical; School Play; Nwsp; Air Line Stewardist.

UCHIDA, HILARY; Davis SR HS; Davis, CA; (3); Cmnty Wkr; Key Clb; Pep Clb; Spanish Clb; Teachers Aide; Vllybl; Hon Roll; Kiwanis Awd; Careers With Chldrn-Help Elem Cls; Rainbw Summu Camp For Kids; Yth Entrtnmnt Brd-HS Yth Grp.

UCHIDA, MARIKO; Mira Costa HS; Manhattan Bch, CA; (3); Key Clb; Pep Clb; Flag Corp; Cheerldng; Pom Pon; Prfct Atten Awd; UC Davis; Bio Chem.

UCHIDA, RICHARD N; John Burroughs HS; Burbank, CA; (3); Band; Chorus; Stage Crew; U Of Santa Barbara.

UCHIDA, TRACIE K; Glen A Wilson HS; Hacienda Hgts, CA; (4); 49/372; Ski Clb; Ed Yrbk; Powder Puff Ftbl; JV Var Socr; Stat Swmmng; Hon Roll; Pres Acad Fit Awd; Schl Schlr 3 Yrs; U Of AZ.

UCHINO, YUTAKA K; Rancho Alamitos HS; Stanton, CA; (3); Church Yth Grp; Debate Tm; Science Clb; Service Clb; Ski Clb; Spanish Clb; Stu Cncl; Var JV Bsktbl; Hon Roll; Sci Fair 2nd Pl; CSF; Yth In Govt Econ Developer; U CA; Surgeon.

UCHISHIBA, MARI; James Lick HS; San Jose, CA; (3); 6/276; Sec Church Yth Grp; Intnl Clb; Orch; Rptr Nwsp; Var Tennis; High Hon Roll; Hon Roll; VP NHS; CA Schlrshp Fed 87-90; Underclassman Deptmntl Sci Awd 89; Stu Of Mnth 90.

UDOJI, ROBIN N; Santa Clara HS; Oxnard, CA; (3); 29/170; Church Yth Grp; Computer Clb; Hosp Aide; Phtg Yrbk; Hon Roll; NHS; Vet Med.

UEDA, KARA K; Lincoln HS; Stockton, CA; (2); Church Yth Grp; Cmnty Wkr; Debate Tm; JCL; Latin Clb; NFL; Speech Tm; Hon Roll; Natl Piano Gld Wnr; Vlntr Piano Plyr Lcl Nrsng Hm; Phrmcy.

UEHA, MISAE; Irvine HS; Irvine, CA; (2); JA; Key Clb; SADD; Drill Tm; Orch; Capt Socr; Hon Roll; CSF; Med.

UEHARA, JUAN O; South Pasadena HS; S Pasadena, CA; (3); Chess Clb; Cmnty Wkr; Computer Clb; JV Bsktbl; Prfct Atten Awd; Oberlin Coll; Astrnmy.

UFFELMAN, KORI; Huntington Beach HS; Huntington Beach, CA; (3); Drill Tm; Hon Roll; Baton Twirler; Tower Award; ASU; Business.

UGALE, DAVID P; Castle Park HS; San Diego, CA; (2); 1/473; French Clb; JV Bsbl; JV Ftbl; Cit Awd; High Hon Roll; Pres Acad Fit Awd; Val; USC; Physics.

UGARTE, JOSE L; Point Loma HS; San Diego, CA; (4); 219/402; Boy Scts; Church Yth Grp; Spanish Clb; JV Var Ftbl; San Diego ST U; Comp Engrng.

UGOT, ARTHEMIUS JEFF; Galileo HS; San Francisco, CA; (2); Sci.

UH, JINNA; Irvine HS; Irvine, CA; (2); German Clb; JV Tennis; High Hon Roll; Korean Clb; U CA Irvine; Law Enfrcmnt.

UHAS, GARY P; John A Rowland HS; Rowland Hts, CA; (1); Art Clb; Church Yth Grp; Dance Clb; Office Aide; Band; School Musical; Stage Crew; Yrbk; Ftbl; Cit Awd; Law Enf.

UHM, ALEX K; University HS; Irvine, CA; (2); Church Yth Grp; Rep JCL; Church Choir; JV Bsktbl; High Hon Roll; Hon Roll; Pres Acad Fit Awd; Laureate Awd AP US Hstry; 99 Pct PSAT; Hgh Hnrs Gldn ST Exm Alg I, Geom; Med.

UITZ-MEDINA, BLANCA; Hillsdale HS; Foster City, CA; (3); Spanish Clb; Teachers Aide; Clg Of San Mateo.

UKANWA, ALEXANDER; Santa Teresa HS; Hollister, CA; (4); 28/504; Library Aide; Science Clb; Spanish Clb; Teachers Aide; High Hon Roll; Hon Roll; Ntl Merit Ltr; MESA Pres 89-90; MESA VP 88-89; Stanford U; Elec Engrng.

UKKERD, KIMBERLEY L; Roseville HS; Rocklin, CA; (3); Debate Tm; Spanish Clb; Speech Tm; Var Trk; Lion Awd; Wn 4 Lvls Spch Cmptn; Dist Lvl Wn Schlrshp; CA ST; Bus Mgmt.

ULANDAY, MELISSA M; Glendale Adventist Acad; Eagle Rock, CA; (3); 8/65; Teachers Aide; Band; Church Choir; Sec Frsh Cls; Off Soph Cls; Hon Roll; Intraumurals Badminton; Eta Pi Mu Tau Mu; La Sierra; Medical Field.

ULATE, RAFAEL; Homestead HS; Sunnyvale, CA; (4); 24/361; FBLA; Spanish Clb; Bsktbl; High Hon Roll; NHS; Pres Acad Fit Awd; Spanish NHS; Bank Amer Schlr; Natl Cncl Tchrs Span & Portuguese 2nd Pl Natnlly; Stanford U; Bio Sci.

ULBERG, AMY N; Paraclete HS; Lancaster, CA; (3); Teachers Aide; Varsity Clb; Var L Sftbl; Hon Roll; Pres Acad Fit Awd; Nrsng.

ULBERG, THERESA; Grant HS; Sacramento, CA; (3); Sec Intnl Clb; Teachers Aide; Band; Cit Awd; Hon Roll; Prfct Atten Awd; Stanford U; Pediatrics.

ULITSKAYA, JULIA; Lowell HS; San Francisco, CA; (2); French Clb; VP Model UN; Teachers Aide; Lit Mag; French Hon Soc; High Hon Roll; JR Stsmn Of America Fnd; Phlnthpy Clb; Outstndng Wrtr Of Engl Awd; Berkley; Pltcl.

ULLOA, PHILLIP; Colton HS; Colton, CA; (3); Teachers Aide; JV Bsbl; High Hon Roll; Hon Roll; JC San Bernardino Vly; Pol Sci.

ULMER, MELISSA; Ramona HS; Ramona, CA; (3); 13/294; Dance Clb; Spanish Clb; Var Trk; JV Capt Vllybl; Cit Awd; Hon Roll; Gymnstcs; Physcl Therpy.

ULRICH, ERRYN; Los Alamitos HS; Los Alamitos, CA; (4); 13/502; Church Yth Grp; Cmnty Wkr; Pep Clb; Science Clb; Ski Clb; Spanish Clb; High Hon Roll; Hon Roll; NHS; Safe Rides; Interact; UCSB.

ULRICH, KRISTIN; Adolfo Camarillo HS; Camarillo, CA; (1); 66/556; French Clb; SADD; Sec Chorus; Church Choir; Co-Capt Cheerldng; High Hon Roll; Music.

ULRICH, MIKE V; Edison HS; Huntington Beach, CA; (3); FBLA; German Clb; JA; Ski Clb; Teachers Aide.

ULRICH, TAMBRIA B; North Salinas HS; Salinas, CA; (2); Pres German Clb; Yrbk; JV Fld Hcky; Var Swmmng; High Hon Roll; NHS; Rotary Awd; UC Santa Barbara; Marine Bio.

UMALI, MINETTE; Glendale HS; Glendale, CA; (3); Hosp Aide; Intnl Clb; Hon Roll; NHS; Excllnc Math Trophy; Bell Choir; CSF; Med.

UMALL, WILLIAM B; Glendale HS; Glendale, CA; (2); Spanish Clb; Hon Roll; Prfct Atten Awd; Gldn St Exm Awd 1st Yr Alg Hnrs; Pilot.

UMANA, LEONEL; George Washington Prep HS; Los Angeles, CA; (4); 99/525; Chess Clb; Math Clb; Math Tm; Speech Tm; Var Intrml Crs Cntry; Var JV Trk; Decthln Tm Wnnr Gold Math/Slvr Sci, Hist, Brz Econ, Plaq Hghst Score Conf; UCLA; Elec Engrng.

UMEZU, TINA M; Fairview JR Acad; San Bernardino, CA; (2); Church Yth Grp; Ski Clb; Teachers Aide; Band; Chorus; School Play; VP Frsh Cls; VP Soph Cls; Var Bsbl; Cit Awd; Bell Choir; Biology Achievement Award; Backpacking Club; Oncologist.

UMHOFER, BRYN E; Mission College Prep; San Luis Obispo, CA; (3); AFS; Cmnty Wkr; Drama Clb; Chorus; School Play; Ed Yrbk; VP Frsh Cls; Var Crs Cntry; Hon Roll; Nursing.

UMLAUF, KIMBERLY M; Glendale Adventist Acad; Glendale, CA; (1); Model UN; Ski Clb; Speech Tm; Band; Chorus; Ed Yrbk; Sftbl; Swmmng; Pres Acad Fit Awd; Glendale Adventist Acad; Law.

UMPHREY, SHAWNEE A; Hiram Johnson West Campus HS; Sacramento, CA; (3); Church Yth Grp; Cmnty Wkr; Pres Intnl Clb; Red Cross Aide; ROTC; Teachers Aide; Color Guard; School Play; Rep Soph Cls; Pres Jr Cls; Friday Night Live; Safe Rds Pgm; Law.

UMSTATTD, RYAN; James Lick HS; San Jose, CA; (4); 1/257; Church Yth Grp; Intnl Clb; Treas Jr Cls; VP Sr Cls; Var Trk; High Hon Roll; Treas NHS; Ntl Merit SF; Val; WASC Accrdtn Stu Rep On Prcss Cmmtte; Stanford U; Astrphyscs.

UNDERBERG, NATALIE M; Poway HS; Poway, CA; (1); Church Yth Grp; Cmnty Wkr; Spanish Clb; Cit Awd; High Hon Roll; UCSD; Psych.

UNDERELL, ASHLEY E; Torrey Pines HS; Del Mar, CA; (2); Rptr Nwsp; Var Gym; Hon Roll; 2 Consecutive Yrs Var Optional Gymnstc; Most Imprvd Gymnstc 90; William & Mary; Law.

UNDERHILL, JENNIFER; Irvine HS; Irvine, CA; (1); 45/580; Pep Clb; Band; Mrchg Band; Pep Band; Sng Sqd.

UNDERHILL, MIKE D; Poway HS; San Diego, CA; (2); Cmnty Wkr; Service Clb; JV Bsbl; Wt Lftg; Cit Awd; High Hon Roll; Hon Roll; Interact Club; AZ ST; Med.

UNDERWOOD, BLAKE G; Gompers Secondary HS; San Diego, CA; (1); Speech Tm; Band; Orch; High Hon Roll; Opt Clb Awd; Outstndng Stu Achvr; Spcl Recgntn In Engl, Physics, Band & Advanced Math; Creative Comp Pgrmng Cont; Comp.

UNDERWOOD, CELINE; Tomales HS; Inverness, CA; (1); 4-H; Pres Frsh Cls; Stat Bsktbl; Score Keeper; JV Sftbl; JV Vllybl; 4-H Awd; High Hon Roll; Stats For J V Boys Bsktbl; Anthrplgst.

UNDERWOOD, KIM; Buena Park HS; Buena Park, CA; (4); Church Yth Grp; German Clb; Red Cross Aide; Cit Awd; High Hon Roll; Hon Roll; Stu Of Mo; Hghst GPA Grmn 1-3 Awds; FJC; Pharm.

UNDERWOOD, LESLIE; Taft Union HS; Taft, CA; (2); #10 In Class; Church Yth Grp; Drama Clb; Key Clb; Pres Frsh Cls; Pres Soph Cls; Stu Cncl; Var Cheerldng; Var Pom Pon; High Hon Roll; Hon Roll; USVB Vlybll Clb; Interact Clb; Campus Life Clb; Cal Poly San Luis; Arch.

UNDERWOOD, MICHELLE R; Antioch HS; Antioch, CA; (2); Church Yth Grp; Drama Clb; Pep Clb; Teachers Aide; Chorus; School Play; Trk; Hon Roll; Chld Psych.

UNDERWOOD, SUZANNAH; Rio Mesa HS; Camarillo, CA; (3); 32/369; Sec AFS; Cmnty Wkr; Dance Clb; Drama Clb; FCA; Letterman Clb; Pep Clb; Varsity Clb; School Play; Jr Cls; Super Sprtn Awd; Peer Counseling; Song Ldr 5th Natl Comptn; Engl.

UNG, LONG N; Woodrow Wilson HS; Long Beach, CA; (4); Library Aide; Math Tm; Var Bsktbl; Var Trk; High Hon Roll; Hon Roll; CAIA Awds; Stu Of Yr Indus Art; Outstndng Achvt Awds; CSU Long Beach; Mech Engr.

UNG, PEARL; Wallenberg HS; San Francisco, CA; (1); Bsktbl; Crs Cntry; Swmmng; Tennis; Vllybl; Prfct Atten Awd; Many Awds For Athltc Actvts; UC Berkeley; Interior Dsgnr.

UNGLES, MARK B; Atla Loma HS; Alta Loma, CA; (4); 9/540; Pres Acad Fit Awd; Cum Laude Soc; US Army Reserve Schlr/Athl Awd; Bnk Of Amer Achvt Awd In Engl; UC Davis; Engrng.

UNHERSMA, STEPAHNIE J; Bishop Union HS; Bishop, CA; (3); Drama Clb; Ed Yrbk; Stu Cncl; Bsktbl; Powder Puff Ftbl; Tennis; Hon Roll; Communications.

UNION, NICKIE M; Foothill HS; Pleasanton, CA; (3); Church Yth Grp; Sec Jr Cls; Stu Cncl; Var Capt Bsktbl; Var Sftbl; Var Trk; Hon Roll; Pres Acad Fit Awd; T V Brdcstng.

UNLAND, WENDY M; Pioneer HS; San Jose, CA; (1); Cmnty Wkr; Red Cross Aide; Service Clb; JV Socr; Presdntl Acad Ftnss Awd 89-90; Commcntns.

UNSER, LYNN; Anaheim HS; Anaheim, CA; (1); French Clb; Hosp Aide; Key Clb; Pep Clb; Chorus; Capt Cheerldng; Cit Awd; Hon Roll; Jr NHS; Pres Acad Fit Awd; USC; Dental Med.

UNSWORTH, JUSTIN R; Costa Mesa HS; Costa Mesa, CA; (3); French Clb; Band; Jazz Band; Mrchg Band; Orch; School Musical; Var Wrstlng; Vrsty Shotput; CA ST-FULLERTON; Music.

UNTALAN, CHERYL A; Arroyo Grande HS; Grover City, CA; (4); 35/374; Church Yth Grp; Key Clb; Treas Sr Cls; Hon Roll; Pres Acad Fit Awd; Filipino Yth Club VP; Tutor; CA Polytech ST U; Bio.

UNTALAN, CYRILLE MAE S; St Joseph HS; Long Beach, CA; (2); Church Yth Grp; Cmnty Wkr; Key Clb; SADD; Teachers Aide; Hon Roll; TASC; Piano & Accordian Awds; CCD Stu Aide; Child Phych.

UNTALAN, TAMARA; Marina HS; Huntington Bch, CA; (4); Spanish Clb; Teachers Aide; Off Jr Cls; JV Bsktbl; Stat Ftbl; Powder Puff Ftbl; Tennis; Trk; Vllybl; Wt Lftg; Associated Stu Body Secy; Active Marina Inspiration Pres; CA ST Long Beach; Phys Ther.

UNTER, MARIJANE E; Los Angeles Baptist JR/Sr HS; Northridge, CA; (3); 1/100; Church Yth Grp; French Clb; Teachers Aide; Yrbk; Sec Treas Soph Cls; Sec Treas Sr Cls; Var Capt Bsktbl; Var Crs Cntry; Var Trk; Vllybl; Accntng.

UNTIEDT, HOPE; Western HS; Anaheim, CA; (4); Drama Clb; Girl Scts; Speech Tm; Teachers Aide; School Play; Nwsp; Yrbk; Tennis; NHS; Ed.

UNZUETA, MARTHA; Ramona HS; Riverside, CA; (1); 167/587; Law.

UNZUETA, MIGUEL; Capital Christian Schl; Sacramento, CA; (3); 1/65; Church Yth Grp; Computer Clb; FCA; Ski Clb; Rptr Yrbk; Pres Frsh Cls; Pres Soph Cls; Pres Jr Cls; Treas Stu Cncl; JV Bsktbl; Outstndng Stdnt Engl; Stanford; Bus.

UNZUETA, PEDRO; Compton HS; Compton, CA; (2); Swmmng; Tennis; Hon Roll; Law.

UPACHAK, VENG; Orestimba HS; Newman, CA; (3); Trk; Hon Roll; MSC.

UPCHURCH, COREY; Oxnard HS; Oxnard, CA; (2); Church Yth Grp; Cmnty Wkr; French Clb; Stu Cncl; JV Bsktbl; Trk; Wt Lftg; Cit Awd; French Hon Soc; High Hon Roll; Chrch Jr Usher Board Pres; Acadc Awd; Vac Bible Schl Awd; Stanford U; Engrng.

UPCHURCH, TAMEKA R; Valley HS; Sacramento, CA; (2); 76/446; JV Cheerldng; Var Powder Puff Ftbl; Hon Roll; Prfct Atten Awd; Jr Asilomar; Black Stu Union Secy; MESA; Spelman; Eng.

UPPAL, ROHIT; Lanen HS; Susanville, CA; (3); Cmnty Wkr; Computer Clb; Math Clb; Math Tm; Red Cross Aide; Ski Clb; Spanish Clb; Cit Awd; High Hon Roll; Hon Roll; UNR; Phy.

URANE, DOREEN; Hueneme HS; Oxnard, CA; (2); Church Yth Grp; Cheerldng; Swmmng; Trk; Peperdine; Nrs.

URANGA, JOSHUA S; Arcadia HS; Arcadia, CA; (3); Am Leg Boys St; Church Yth Grp; Pres Drama Clb; Thesps; School Musical; School Play; Off Frsh Cls; Off Soph Cls; Pres Jr Cls; Pres Stu Cncl; Psych.

URANGO, MONICA C; Oxnard Union HS; Oxnard, CA; (3); 146/400; Church Yth Grp; Cmnty Wkr; GAA; Teachers Aide; Var L Bsktbl; JV Stat Score Keeper; UCSB; Math & Sci.

URANWALA, LEENA; Amador HS; Pleasanton, CA; (3); Band; Mrchg Band; Orch; Swmmng; Hon Roll; Dnc.

URATA, RYOHEI; Homestead HS; Sunnyvale, CA; (1); JV Ftbl; JV Wt Lftg; Japanese Lang Schl; Palo Alto Chmbr Orch; Cello.

URBAN, NICHOLE M; Fontana HS; Fontana, CA; (3); 79/1100; Pep Clb; Varsity Clb; Variety Show; Rep Frsh Cls; Rep Stu Cncl; Cheerldng; Pom Pon; High Hon Roll; Hon Roll; CA Schlrshp Fnd; RCC; Dntl Hygnst.

URBAN, TIM; Monte Vista Christian HS; Aptos, CA; (4); Am Leg Boys St; Pres Soph Cls; Pres Jr Cls; Pres Sr Cls; Var Bsbl; Capt JV Bsktbl; Var JV Socr; Capt Vllybl; High Hon Roll; NHS; Mock Trial 88-90; HOBY 88; CSF; US Naval Acad; Naval Aviation.

URBANY, BROOK; Santa Clara HS; Santa Clara, CA; (3); French Clb; GAA; Service Clb; Variety Show; Stu Cncl; Var Bsktbl; Var Vllybl; Cit Awd; Hon Roll; Nrsg.

URBIEN, AIMEE; Bishop Amat HS; Walnut, CA; (3); JV Vllybl; Hon Roll; Mst Insprtnl Vlybl Tm 2nd Honors Latin II 89; 8 Years Of Piano Lessons; Med.

URBIEN, MICHELLE A; Bishop Amat Memorial HS; Walnut, CA; (3); Rptr Yrbk; Var Vllybl; Hon Roll; Prfct Atten Awd; Coachs Awd Vlybl.

URBINA, CYNTHIA; San Benito Union HS; Hollister, CA; (3); French Clb; Color Guard; Drill Tm; Flag Corp; Yrbk; Sec Stu Cncl; Hon Roll; San Benito Cty LULAC; UC Berkeley; Engrng.

URBINA, YVETTE M; San Gabriel Mission HS; Alhambra, CA; (2); 4/120; VP Drama Clb; FBLA; GAA; Math Clb; Science Clb; Chorus; School Musical; Stage Crew; Sec Soph Cls; Treas Jr Cls; Choir, Prfrmd W/Kenny Loggins At Benefit; Stanford U; Aerospc Engr.

URENA, JAVIER; Modesto HS; Modesto, CA; (2); Math Clb; Math Spr Bwl; Sci Olympd 2nd/5th Cnty St; Berkeley; Engrng.

URENA, RICARDO; Modesto HS; Modesto, CA; (2); Math Clb; Science Clb; Hon Roll; Stanford U; Engr.

URENIA, RAMON C; Analy HS; Sebastopol, CA; (2).

URENO, ANA E; Chula Vista HS; San Diego, CA; (2); Aud/Vis; Orch; Stage Crew; Stu Cncl; Vllybl; Tae Kwon Do Red Belt Blck Tip; Sword & Shld Club Offcr Tckts & Hstrn; Video Photo.

URES, STEPHEN A; Flintridge Preparatory Schl; Toluca Lake, CA; (2); Drama Clb; French Clb; Ski Clb; Spanish Clb; Band; Pep Band; School Musical; School Play; Stage Crew; Pres Frsh Cls; Yale U; Bus.

URESTE, LYNETTE C; Manteca HS; Manteca, CA; (3); Church Yth Grp; English Clb; Key Clb; Stanford; Sr Engr.

URETA, WILMA LIZA SANTOS; St Joseph HS; Cerritos, CA; (3); Cmnty Wkr; Intnl Clb; Spanish Clb; School Musical; Hon Roll; Prfct Atten Awd; Acad Decathlon; Peer Counselor.

URIBE, CARLA; Bonita Vista HS; Chula Vista, CA; (4); English Clb; Girl Scts; Cit Awd; San Diego ST U; Comp Sci.

URIBE, CARMEN; San Jose HS Acad; San Jose, CA; (3); Teachers Aide; Phtg Yrbk; VP Sr Cls; JV Capt Bsktbl; Trk; Hon Roll; Photo Clb; San Jose ST U.

URIBE, CLAUDIA I; Calexico HS; Calexico, CA; (4); Church Yth Grp; Library Aide; Teachers Aide; Church Choir; Chldrns Choir Dir At Church; Imperial Vly Coll; Lgl Secy.

URIBE, ELIA; Garfield HS; Los Angeles, CA; (2); Hon Roll; Prfct Atten Awd; CA Schlrshp Fed; Mariposa Prgrm Cert Excllnc; Bus Awd-Typg; UCLA; Med.

URIBE, MARIANA; Lemoore HS; Stratford, CA; (3); Spanish Clb; Teachers Aide; Hon Roll; Tchr.

URIBE, OSCAR S; Santa Ana Valley HS; Santa Ana, CA; (3); JV Bsktbl; UCI Prtnrshp Pgm; Mech Engrng.

URIBE, PABLO J; Saint Ignatius HS; San Francisco, CA; (4); Cmnty Wkr; Spanish Clb; City Coll San Fran; Elctrncs.

URIBE, ROSANNA I; Bishop Montgomery HS; Hawthorne, CA; (2); Cmnty Wkr; Key Clb; Letterman Clb; SADD; Teachers Aide; Var Socr; Hon Roll; CSF.

URIBE, SILVINA; Washington Union HS; Fresno, CA; (2); Pres French Clb; FTA; Band; Mrchg Band; Pep Band; Cheerldng; Hon Roll; Work Carls Jr Restaurant; Fresno ST U; Prof.

URIBE, SONIA G; La Puente HS; La Puente, CA; (3); Science Clb; Service Clb; Band; Mrchg Band; Co-Ed Yrbk; Off Jr Cls; Hon Roll; CA Schlrshp Fed; Grls Lg; U CAZ San Diego; Ped.

URIBES, BECKY L; Yucaipa HS; Yucaipa, CA; (3); 11/356; Pres Church Yth Grp; French Clb; Letterman Clb; Pep Clb; Varsity Clb; Socr; Trk; Hon Roll; Prfct Atten Awd; Pres Acad Fit Awd; Cal Poly San Luis Obispo; Bus.

URICK, SAMANTHA A; Hemet HS; Hemet, CA; (3); Church Yth Grp; Dance Clb; Service Clb; SADD; Teachers Aide; Drill Tm; Flag Corp; Cmnty Wkr; FIDM; Cosmtlgy.

URIE, BREE; San Mateo HS; Foster City, CA; (4); 16/315; Church Yth Grp; Debate Tm; Pep Clb; Rep Soph Cls; Rep Jr Cls; Rep Sr Cls; JV Cheerldng; JV L Gym; Pom Pon; Powder Puff Ftbl; CSF; Bank Amer Frgn Lang Awd; Explorer Search & Rescue; Lewis & Clark Coll; Intl Econ.

URITZ, JOLIE B; Los Alamitos HS; Los Alamitos, CA; (3); Off Drama Clb; Ski Clb; VP Temple Yth Grp; Pres Chorus; Hon Roll; NHS; Eclgy Clb; Amnsty Intl.

URLING, AMY; Carlmont HS; Belmont, CA; (3); 16/373; Church Yth Grp; Cmnty Wkr; Dance Clb; Pep Clb; Church Choir; School Musical; Cheerldng; Pom Pon; Trk; Hon Roll; Math, Comp Sci & Analytic Geom Outstndng Achvt Awds 90; UC Santa Barbara.

URQUHART, BRAD D; Lindsay HS; Lindsay, CA; (2); Church Yth Grp; Debate Tm; Key Clb; SADD; Nwsp; Yrbk; Sec Jr Cls; Wt Lftg; Hon Roll; Fresno ST U; Teacher.

URQUICO, RAXAJACK; Carson HS; Torrance, CA; (4); Chess Clb; Church Yth Grp; Cmnty Wkr; Computer Clb; Science Clb; Service Clb; Bsktbl; Hon Roll; Pres Acad Fit Awd; Stephen M White Jr HS Typing Champ; Bus & Bio Awds; UC Irvine; Pharmacy.

URREA, ANGELA; Grant HS; Sacramento, CA; (3); Science Clb; Spanish Clb; Phtg Yrbk; Rep Frsh Cls; Cit Awd; Elks Awd; Hon Roll; Lion Awd; Pres CSF; Stu Reaching Out.

URREA, CECILIA M; Los Banos HS; Los Banos, CA; (3); Cmnty Wkr; Drama Clb; Latin Clb; Science Clb; Spanish Clb; Teachers Aide; Band; Stage Crew; Rep Soph Cls; Rep Jr Cls; Bus Wk Stanislause; Davis; Med.

URRETE, JOCYLIN B; Sierra Vista HS; Baldwin Park, CA; (4); 2/260; VP Math Clb; Science Clb; Speech Tm; SADD; JV Tennis; High Hon Roll; Opt Clb Awd; Sal; Won Sevl Essay Contests Spnsrd By Optimist Club; U Of CA Irvine; Biological Maj.

URRIQUIA, JOHN A M; Wagner HS; Cincinnati, OH; (4); 21/130; Church Yth Grp; Cmnty Wkr; FBLA; Office Aide; Red Cross Aide; Scholastic Bowl; School Play; Rep Yrbk; JV Trk; JV Vllybl; Announcer Schl Talent Show; 1st Pl FBLA Cmptn Bus Eng; Cert Recog From Dir Ambulatory Svcs Red Cross; U Cincinnati; Psych.

URRUTIA, AURA M; Rubidoux HS; Mira Loma, CA; (4); 57/518; French Clb; FBLA; Girl Scts; Powder Puff Ftbl; Score Keeper; Sftbl; Hon Roll; Prfct Atten Awd; U CA Riverside; Bus Admin.

URRUTIA, JOSE; Rubidoux HS; Mira Loma, CA; (4); FBLA; Hon Roll; Prfct Atten Awd; Long Beach ST; Intr Commnctns.

URSEM, PERRY JOHN; Simi Valley HS; Simi Valley, CA; (3); 55/666; SADD; Pres Thesps; Acpl Chr; School Play; JV Crs Cntry; JV Trk; Jr NHS; Pres Acad Fit Awd; Best Mnlg; Dir Awd 89-90; Simi Vlly HS Chrl Music; CA ST U Northridge; Bus Admin.

URSUA, ROXANNA L; Moreau HS; Castro Valley, CA; (4); Varsity Clb; Powder Puff Ftbl; JV Var Vllybl; Hon Roll; Pres Acad Fit Awd; Vllybl; Piano & Flute; Awd Maintng 3.6 Drgn Vllybl Seasn; Grad Cum Laude; UC Davis; Pre-Med.

URSULO, ARTHUR; Sierra Vista HS; Baldwin Park, CA; (3); Var Capt Crs Cntry; Var Capt Trk; Hon Roll; Pres Acad Fit Awd; L A Marathn 2 Yrs Came In Top 4 Amng HS Stu; Azusa Pacific U; Pilot.

USHIGOME, KIM K; Gardena HS; Gardena, CA; (4); 36/404; Intnl Clb; JCL; Latin Clb; Red Cross Aide; VP Service Clb; Teachers Aide; Hon Roll; Pres Acad Fit Awd; JV Capt Vllybl; Vars Art Acknwldgmnts; U Of CA Los Angeles; Philosphy.

USHIGOME, ROZ K; Gardena HS; Gardena, CA; (4); 22/404; JA; JCL; Latin Clb; Hist Service Clb; Band; Ed Nwsp; Vllybl; High Hon Roll; Hon Roll; Pres Acad Fit Awd; UCLA; Bio.

USHIJIMA, LORI Y; Whitney HS; Cerritos, CA; (4); Sec Key Clb; Var Capt Bsktbl; JV Var Tennis; High Hon Roll; Hon Roll; NHS; CSF; UCLA; Business.

USHIZAKI, AKIRA; Mills HS; Burlingame, CA; (4); Intnl Clb; Math Tm; Var Bsbl; Var Socr; JV Tennis.

USMAN, AYAZ; Mira Mesa HS; San Diego, CA; (2); Church Yth Grp; Science Clb; Ed Nwsp; Cit Awd; High Hon Roll; Hon Roll; MD Inst Of Tech; Arontcl Engr.

USONG, ANNE M; Presentation HS; San Jose, CA; (4); 1/137; Cmnty Wkr; Math Clb; NFL; Chorus; Orch; Var Tennis; Ntl Merit Ltr; Band; Variety Show; Hon Roll; Pres Asian Clb; Offcr Peer Tutoring; Tandy Tech Schlrs Outstndng Stu Awd; Stanford U; Corp Law.

USREY, TRINA K; San Marcos HS; Vista, CA; (4); 32/499; Yrbk; High Hon Roll; Hon Roll; NM ST U.

USSERY, JASON D; Norwalk HS; Norwalk, CA; (2); Boy Scts; JV Var Bsktbl; Hon Roll; Prfct Atten Awd; CA ST U-Long Bch; Ed.

USSHER, JEREMY D; St Michaels Prep; Brea, CA; (1); Art Clb; Nwsp; Yrbk; Pres Frsh Cls; Stu Cncl; Rm Ldr; Dntstry.

USTACH, CAROLYN; Fred C Beyer HS; Modesto, CA; (4); 18/506; Debate Tm; German Clb; NFL; Speech Tm; JV Swmmng; High Hon Roll; Hon Roll; Ntl Merit Ltr; Stu Exchng Ukraine; Water Polo Statstcn; Advocady 89; HS Teach.

UTER, NATHAN T; Torrey Pines HS; Del Mar, CA; (3); Var L Bsbl; JV Socr; Hon Roll; Pres Acad Fit Awd; Golden St Exam High Hnrs Algebra & Geom; Schlt Athl Awd; CSF.

UTICK, BETH A; Mater Dei HS; Westminster, CA; (3); Church Yth Grp; Dance Clb; Drama Clb; Hosp Aide; Latin Clb; Acpl Chr; Chorus; School Musical; Variety Show; Hon Roll; Southwestern Music Fstvl 3rd Pl Baroque 4th Qlfd; Cert Mrt Lvl 3; Music.

UTTER, DORA V; Lompoc HS; Lompoc, CA; (4); Drama Clb; FBLA; SADD; Thesps; Chorus; Church Choir; Rep Frsh Cls; Rep Sr Cls; L Mgr(s); Hon Roll; 2 Choir Lttrs In Cncrt Choir & Wmns Choir; Pres Of Wmns Choir; Allan Hancock Coll; Comp Tech.

UTTER, KRISTINE A; Serrano HS; Phelan, CA; (3); 5/213; Sec Drama Clb; Sec 4-H; Quiz Bowl; High Hon Roll; Jr Hnr Grd; Wrtng Clbrtn Dist Wnnr 2 Yrs; CSF; Writer.

UVALLE, YOLANDA; Santa Maria HS; Santa Maria, CA; (3); 68/467; 4-H; Office Aide; Chorus; Hon Roll; Allan Hancock Clg; Bus Admn.

UY, HAZEL; Glendale HS; Glendale, CA; (3); Church Yth Grp; Key Clb; Latin Clb; Spanish Clb; Stat Tennis; High Hon Roll; NHS; CA Schlrshp Fed; Hnrs Geom Gldn St Exam; Intl Bus.

UY, KARLYLLE; Irvine HS; Irvine, CA; (2); Hosp Aide; Key Clb; High Hon Roll; Hon Roll; Ethnc Advsry Forum; CA Schlrshp Fdrtn; U CA; Law Englsh.

UY, KIMHOU; Artesia HS; Lakewood, CA; (3); Intnl Clb; Science Clb; Spanish Clb; CSF; UCI; Aerospace Engr.

UY, LAWRENCE; Victor Valley Christian Schl; Victorville, CA; (3); School Musical; Stage Crew; Rptr Yrbk; Var Bsbl; JV Ftbl; High Hon Roll; Chapel Planning Cmmtte; Hnr Soc; Harvard; Lawyer.

UY, MELVIN O; El Toro HS; El Toro, CA; (4); 98/526; Art Clb; Sec Chess Clb; Pres Computer Clb; Debate Tm; French Clb; Teachers Aide; Mrchg Band; Tennis; High Hon Roll; Hon Roll; CSF Seal Bearer; CSU Fullerton; Comp Sci.

UY, SAMANTHA; Silver Creek HS; Milpitas, CA; (2); Score Keeper; Hon Roll; Mrt Awd Cert Engl; San Jose St Coll; Sci.

UY-BARRETA, DON-JOSEPH P; So San Francisco HS; S San Francisco, CA; (2); French Clb; Hon Roll; Bdmnt Team; Asian Amer Clb; Santa Cruz Coll; Chef.

UYCHOCDE, ROWENA C; Nogales HS; Walnut, CA; (3); Hon Roll; Prfct Atten Awd; CSF; Medcl Tech.

UYEDA, KENNETH; Bishop Montgomery HS; Gardena, CA; (3); JA; Service Clb; JV Trk; Cit Awd; Hon Roll; Engrng.

UYEDA, LAUREN; Homestead HS; Los Altos, CA; (3); 44/330; Hosp Aide; Teachers Aide; Stu Cncl; Var Swmmng; NHS; Ntl Merit Ltr; Spanish NHS; Cmnty Soccer; Work Doctors Office; Actuarial Sci.

UYEDA, SHELLEY M; Homestead HS; Los Altos, CA; (4); 40/359; Spanish Clb; Teachers Aide; JV Socr; Var Swmmng; High Hon Roll; Pres Acad Fit Awd; Spanish NHS; CSF; Natl Hnr Roll; Outstndng Achvt Frgn Lang Awd 90; UC Davis; Exploratory.

UYEDA, SHERRILL; Troy HS; Fullerton, CA; (4); Art Clb; Dance Clb; French Clb; Pep Clb; Drill Tm; Yrbk; Cheerldng; Pom Pon; Powder Puff Ftbl; Hon Roll; Les Amis Des Femmas Charity Leag; USC; Bus.

UYEHARA, TODD K; Fremont HS; Sunnyvale, CA; (2); Boy Scts; Temple Yth Grp; Band; Mrchg Band; JV Bsktbl; CSF.

UYEHRAA, KAREN T; Homestead HS; Sunnyvale, CA; (4); Sec Church Yth Grp; French Clb; Band; Mrchg Band; Orch; Var JV Bsktbl; NHS; Pres Acad Fit Awd; CSF Life Mem; U CA San Diego; Comm.

UYEMATSU, CRYSTAL; Watsonville HS; Watsonville, CA; (1); 16/762; Pep Clb; Ski Clb; Temple Yth Grp; Rep Stu Cncl; Cheerldng; High Hon Roll; Hon Roll; CA Schlrshp Fed.

UYEMATSU, KAREN; Watsonville HS; Watsonville, CA; (1); 1/762; Pep Clb; Ski Clb; Temple Yth Grp; Cheerldng; High Hon Roll; Prfct Atten Awd; CSF.

UYEMURA, ROBERT; Sanger HS; Fresno, CA; (4); 11/349; Church Yth Grp; Model UN; ROTC; Science Clb; Treas Sr Cls; Stu Cncl; Var Crs Cntry; Var Trk; Wt Lftg; Var Wrstlng; Kendo; Collct Bsbl Cards; Cal ST U Fresno; Elec Engr.

UYEN, TRINH; Tokay HS; Stockton, CA; (4); Church Yth Grp; French Clb; Spanish Clb; Church Choir; Cit Awd; High Hon Roll; Hon Roll; Prfct Atten Awd; Pres Acad Fit Awd; Photo Clb Secy; CSU Chico; Dntstry.

UYENO, LORI; Cypress HS; Cypress, CA; (4); 3/364; Am Leg Aux Girls St; Debate Tm; Key Clb; NFL; Speech Tm; Drill Tm; Var Cheerldng; JV Tennis; High Hon Roll; Pres Acad Fit Awd; Mock Trial Orange Cnty Champs; CSF; Yth Commission; Northwestern U; Surgeon.

UYENO, TRACY; Holy Family HS; Los Angeles, CA; (3); Art Clb; Library Aide; Office Aide; Rep Sr Cls; Var JV Cheerldng; Engl Hnrs Cls 3 Yrs; Med.

UYTINGCO, RIMINI; Bishop Amat HS; Diamond Bar, CA; (3); Church Yth Grp; Hosp Aide; Var Tennis; NHS; VP Jr Cls; U CA San Diego; Pre-Med.

VA, VITH DARA; Modesto HS; Modesto, CA; (3); JV Socr; Math Super Bowl; Sci Olympd Tm; CSF Club; Math.

VACA, CARL D; Artesia HS; Hawaiian Gardens, CA; (2); Rep Frsh Cls; Rep Stu Cncl; CA Jr Schltc Fed; Acad Let; Phys Ftnss Awd Medallion; UCI; Med.

VACA, LIZA M; Riverbank HS; Escalon, CA; (2); Hon Roll; Hlpng People; Babysttng; Med.

VACA, MICHAEL M; Redwood HS; Visalia, CA; (2); JV Bsktbl; High Hon Roll; Acad Letterman.

VACCAREZZA, ALDO D; Bellarmine College Prep; San Jose, CA; (3); 42/300; Chess Clb; Cmnty Wkr; Letterman Clb; Library Aide; Service Clb; Varsity Clb; Pres Stu Cncl; L Var Wrstlng; High Hon Roll; Pres Acad Fit Awd; Natl Yng Ldr Amer-Cngrsnl Schlr; Stu Ambssdr; Rtrt-Orntatn Ldr; Law.

VACHANI, STEVEN; Irvine HS; Irvine, CA; (2); AFS; Chess Clb; Computer Clb; French Clb; Key Clb; Band; Jazz Band; Mrchg Band; High Hon Roll; UC Berkeley; MBA.

VAGADORI, LISA; Beyer HS; Modesto, CA; (3); Debate Tm; NFL; Service Clb; Speech Tm; SADD; Ed Nwsp; Rep Soph Cls; Rep Stu Cncl; JV Score Keeper; Var Tennis; CSF Treas; Grn Prty Envrnmntl Clb; Rl Est.

VAGT, KATHLEEN C; Redwood HS; Visalia, CA; (3); Church Yth Grp; Spanish Clb; SADD; Varsity Clb; Acpl Chr; Chorus; Color Guard; School Musical; Var L Swmmng; NHS; U San Diego; Ed.

VAHALIK, TAMARA M; El Cajon Valley HS; El Cajon, CA; (2); 43/469; Teachers Aide; Yrbk; JV Diving; Score Keeper; JV Swmmng; Stat Wrstlng; Hon Roll; Acctnt.

VAID, JENNIFER H; Mt Pleasant HS; San Jose, CA; (1); Pres Acad Fit Awd.

VAIL, CRISPIN T; Mountain Empire JR SR HS; Campo, CA; (3); Church Yth Grp; Letterman Clb; Spanish Clb; SADD; Teachers Aide; Varsity Clb; JV Var Bsbl; JV Bsktbl; Var Capt Ftbl; Var Socr; Fishing & Hunting; Paint Ball/Paint War; Tchr.

VAIL, MARK; Village Christian HS; Tujunga, CA; (3); Church Yth Grp; Letterman Clb; Spanish Clb; Acpl Chr; Chorus; Pres Sr Cls; Stu Cncl; Bsbl; Bsktbl; JV Var Ftbl; 1st Team Lge Ftbl Var; Lge Bsbl Var; MVP Var Ftbl; MVP Soccer; UCLA.

VAILLANCOURT, MICHELLE D; Chino HS; Chino, CA; (2); Teachers Aide; Band; Chorus; Color Guard; Cit Awd; Hon Roll; San Diego ST; Tchr.

VAIS, KATHERINE T; San Benito HS; Hollister, CA; (3); Church Yth Grp; Cmnty Wkr; Varsity Clb; Yrbk; Tennis; Hon Roll; Portugens Queen SDES 89-90; Cthlc Cnfrmtn Fcltatr; Vlntr Tnns Tchr; Jrnlsm.

VAITAI, SIOSELINE; Chaffey HS; Alta Loma, CA; (3); Church Yth Grp; Teachers Aide; High Hon Roll; Hon Roll; Bus.

VAKSBERG, SVETLANA; Fairfax HS; Los Angeles, CA; (4); 64/650; Pep Clb; VP Stu Cncl; JV Crs Cntry; DAR Awd; Mock Trial Tm; Stus Social Rspnsblty; Jewish Stu Union; UCLA; Hstry.

VALADAO, ELIZABETH S; Arcata HS; Arcata, CA; (2); High Hon Roll; Prfct Atten Awd; CSF; Ed.

VALADAO, MICHAEL J; Burlingame HS; Burlingame, CA; (3); Church Yth Grp; Teachers Aide; Chorus; JV Bsktbl; Hon Roll; LUSO Portuguese-Amer Fed; Santo Cristo Soc; Navy.

VALADEZ, IRMA; Winters HS; Winters, CA; (3); Church Yth Grp; Cmnty Wkr; Dance Clb; Pep Clb; Spanish Clb; SADD; Teachers Aide; Church Choir; Trk; High Hon Roll; Phy.

VALADEZ, JUSTIN M; Winters HS; Vacaville, CA; (2); Church Yth Grp; Debate Tm; Teachers Aide; Wrstlng; Cit Awd; High Hon Roll; Hon Roll; Prfct Atten Awd; Golden ST Exam Awd; MI; Math.

VALADEZ, KENNY; Manteca HS; Manteca, CA; (3); 42/410; Boy Scts; Church Yth Grp; Cmnty Wkr; SADD; Band; Drm Mjr(t); Jazz Band; Mrchg Band; Pep Band; Tennis; Band Cncl Pres; BACH VP; Peer Mnstry Cnslr; Sci Camp Cnslr; Stanford; Comp Sci.

VALADEZ, PATRICIA; Mar Vista HS; Imperial Beach, CA; (3); 22/264; Scholastic Bowl; SADD; Socr; Cit Awd; Hon Roll; Prfct Atten Awd; SDSU; Psych.

VALADEZ, SOFIA; San Gabriel Mission HS; Pasadena, CA; (2); Church Yth Grp; Drama Clb; GAA; Girl Scts; Pep Clb; Chorus; Cit Awd; Hon Roll; NHS; Silver Awd Girl Scts; Med.

VALADEZ, TINA; Hesperia Christian HS; Apple Valley, CA; (3); 2/32; Scholastic Bowl; Teachers Aide; Band; Chorus; Rep Jr Cls; Var Cheerldng; Var Crs Cntry; Var Trk; High Hon Roll; CA Schlrshp Fed; Air Force Acad; Med.

VALCARCE, CARLOS; Damien HS; Ontario, CA; (2); Cmnty Wkr; Ski Clb; JV Bsktbl; Intrml Ftbl; Hon Roll; Current Affrs Clb; U Of CO; Law.

VALDERRAMA, JASON; Moor Park HS; Moorpark, CA; (2); 6/288; Band; Jazz Band; Mrchg Band; Pep Band; Bsktbl; Var L Crs Cntry; High Hon Roll; Prfct Atten Awd; Pres Acad Fit Awd; Olympc Traing Ctr Field Hockey; Olympc Fest Mens Field Hockey, Brnz Medl Wnnr; Cal Poly; Physcs.

VALDERRAMA, JOSE L; Buena Park HS; Fullerton, CA; (3); Intnl Clb; Latin Clb; Spanish Clb; Varsity Clb; Band; Var Socr; JV Trk; Cit Awd; High Hon Roll; Hon Roll; UCLA; Arch.

VALDERRAMA, JOSIE; Sherman Oaks CES HS; Los Angeles, CA; (3); Church Yth Grp; Debate Tm; Hosp Aide; Sec NFL; Spanish Clb; Speech Tm; Rptr Yrbk; Cheerldng; Hon Roll; Ntl Merit Ltr; Jrnlsm.

VALDES, CHRISTINE M; Apple Valley HS; Apple Valley, CA; (2); High Hon Roll; Hon Roll; Yng Marines.

VALDES, ESTHER R; Chula Vista HS; San Diego, CA; (3); 69/580; Church Yth Grp; Debate Tm; JA; Pep Clb; Church Choir; Ed Nwsp; Tennis; Pres Acad Fit Awd; MECHA; UCSD; Poltcl Sci.

VALDEZ, AGUSTIN F; Arvin HS; Lamont, CA; (3); Cmnty Wkr; Variety Show; Ftbl; Hon Roll; Explorer Post 611; Law Enforcement.

VALDEZ, ALLISON D; Livingston HS; Livingston, CA; (2); GAA; Pep Clb; Chorus; Rep Frsh Cls; Pres Soph Cls; Pres Jr Cls; Stu Cncl; JV Capt Cheerldng; Stat Score Keeper; Sftbl; Var Chrldng Capt; Mst Inspirational Sftbl Tm 2 Yrs; Music.

VALDEZ, BRENDA; Orosi HS; Orosi, CA; (3); Spanish Clb; SADD; Teachers Aide; Band; Chorus; Mrchg Band; Hon Roll; Galen Coll; Bus Admin.

VALDEZ, DANIELLE R; Wasco Union HS; Wasco, CA; (4); Library Aide; Teachers Aide; Socr; Hon Roll; Cert Clrk Typsts, Gnrl Ofc Clrk; Santa Barbara Bus Coll; Acctng.

VALDEZ, ELISEA C; Orosi HS; Orosi, CA; (3); 10/177; VP FHA; VP Spanish Clb; VP SADD; Chorus; VP Frsh Cls; Pres Soph Cls; VP Jr Cls; Pres Sr Cls; Rep Stu Cncl; Capt Powder Puff Ftbl; CA Schlrshp Fndtn Mem; HI-Y Stu Exchng Pgm Mem; Fresno ST; Health Sci.

VALDEZ, FERNANDO; Bell Gardens HS; Commerce, CA; (1); Cit Awd; Studying Fghtr Jts.

VALDEZ, FIEL L; Westmoor HS; Daly City, CA; (3); Treas German Clb; Math Clb; Model UN; Band; Jazz Band; Nwsp; Hon Roll; Drama Clb; Pep Band; Stage Crew; GATE; People To People Yth Sci Exch To Soviet Union; Society Of Women Eng Awd; U Of CA Berkeley; Physics.

VALDEZ, GEORGE; Santa Ana HS; Santa Ana, CA; (3); Air Force; Engrng.

VALDEZ, JEFF D; Rio Hondo Prep; San Gabriel, CA; (3); Chorus; School Play; Bsbl; Bsktbl; Ftbl.

VALDEZ, JEREMY D; Hueneme HS; Oxnard, CA; (2); Math Clb; Math Tm; Office Aide; Teachers Aide; Varsity Clb; Off Jr Cls; Stu Cncl; JV Var Bsbl; JV Bsktbl; JV Ftbl; CASC Ldrshp; Cal Poly; Arch Engr.

VALDEZ, JOSE C; Huntington Park HS; Huntington Park, CA; (2); Band; Jazz Band; Mrchg Band; Orch; Pep Band.

VALDEZ, JOSE M; Chula Vista HS; Chula Vista, CA; (3); Teachers Aide; JV Ftbl; Wt Lftg; JV Var Wrstlng; Bsktbl & Bsbl Clb; UCSD; Math.

VALDEZ, JULIE A; Mt Pleasant HS; San Jose, CA; (2); Debate Tm; Latin Clb; School Play; Socr; Cmnty Helpng Hands; Pre-Med.

VALDEZ, KRISTIN D; Orange Lutheran HS; Corona, CA; (2); Hosp Aide; Pep Clb; Rep Jr Cls; Cheerldng; Vlntr Hosp; Long Beach ST; Reg Nrs.

VALDEZ, LUPE M; Orosi HS; Orosi, CA; (3); 14/177; Office Aide; Spanish Clb; SADD; Chorus; Flag Corp; Variety Show; Off Jr Cls; Off Sr Cls; Stu Cncl; Powder Puff Ftbl; CSF; Ldrshp Cls; Fresno ST; Engr.

VALDEZ, MARCELA; Oxnard HS; Oxnard, CA; (3); Uxmal Clb; Comp Engr.

VALDEZ, MARIA J; Tulare Union HS; Tulare, CA; (3); Hon Roll; MAPA Cert Acad Excllnce; Law.

VALDEZ, MATHEW M; Nevada Union HS; Grass Valley, CA; (3); Treas FFA; SADD; Hon Roll; FFA Ag Mechanics Team; WY Tech Inst; Diesel Mech.

VALDEZ, MENDY R; Mt Whitney HS; Visalia, CA; (4); Drama Clb; FFA; Hist FHA; School Play; Hon Roll; CSF; Early Opportunity Pgm-Pres; FHA 3rd Pl Manual Chaptr Div Exhibit; UOP; Pharmcy.

VALDEZ, OLIVIA G; North Salinas HS; Salinas, CA; (4); Church Yth Grp; Cmnty Wkr; Drama Clb; Thesps; Church Choir; School Play; Stage Crew; Ed Yrbk; Elks Awd; High Hon Roll; Hartnell JC; HS Engl Tchr.

VALDEZ, PETER G; Etiwanda HS; Etiwanda, CA; (2); Church Yth Grp; Cmnty Wkr; Band; JV Socr; Hon Roll; Prfct Atten Awd; Childrens Doctor.

VALDEZ, ROSEMARY; Fillmore HS; Fillmore, CA; (1); #4 In Class; Church Yth Grp; Dance Clb; Pep Clb; Cheerldng; Pom Pon; Socr; Sftbl; Prfct Atten Awd; Comp.

VALDEZ, SANDRA; San Pedro HS; Wilmington, CA; (3); Science Clb; Crs Cntry; Trk; Emrgncy Servce Clb.

VALDEZ, SHANE M; Savanna HS; Anaheim, CA; (4); Church Yth Grp; JA; Teachers Aide; Mrchg Band; Ed Yrbk; Rep Frsh Cls; Rep Sr Cls; Bsktbl; JV Ftbl; Trk; Fullerton JC; Cmmnctns.

VALDEZ, STEPHANIE M; David Star Jordan HS; Long Beach, CA; (3); Am Leg Aux Girls St; Key Clb; Pep Clb; Flag Corp; Rep Soph Cls; Pres Jr Cls; Pres Stu Cncl; Var Co-Capt Cheerldng; Sftbl; Pblc Health.

VALDEZ, VICKIE; Woodlake HS; Woodlake, CA; (4); Church Yth Grp; Cmnty Wkr; Drama Clb; FFA; Office Aide; Pep Clb; Teachers Aide; Pep Band; Stage Crew; Yrbk; Awd Excel; Green Hand Awd 86-87; Multlth Oprtr; Coll Sequoias; Tech.

VALDIVIA, DIANA; San Benito HS; Hollister, CA; (3); Church Yth Grp; Latin Clb; Band; Mrchg Band; Hon Roll; Fresno ST; Acctng.

VALDIVIA, MELISSA E; Fohi HS; Fontana, CA; (2); Sec FBLA; Var Tennis; Hon Roll; CJSF; MECCA; Bus.

VALDIVIA, RICARDO; St John Bosco HS; La Palma, CA; (4); Boy Scts; Letterman Clb; Spanish Clb; Varsity Clb; Ed Yrbk; Swmmng; Wrstlng; Hon Roll; VP Vrsty Club; CIF Qlfr Wrstlng; Fnlst Ntl Hspnc Schlrshp Prgm; USC; Bus Admin.

VALDIVIA, SONIA; North Monterey County HS; Salinas, CA; (2); Teachers Aide; Score Keeper; Var Trk; Var Vllybl; Wt Lftg; Hon Roll; Lawyer.

VALDIVIEZ, FORREST R; Mt Whitney HS; Visalia, CA; (2); Crmnlgst.

VALDMAN, JONATHAN; Taft HS; Woodland Hills, CA; (3); Boy Scts; Pres Temple Yth Grp; Swmmng; Spcl Hnrs Ctgry Law & Pltcs In LA Hstry Essy Cntst; Jwsh Teen Ldrshp Smnrs.

VALDORIA, ANA M; St Joseph HS; Long Beach, CA; (4); Art Clb; SADD; Drill Tm; Cit Awd; Hon Roll; Prfct Atten Awd; Pres Acad Fit Awd; Cal ST Fullerton; Pre Med.

VALDOVINOS, CARLOS J; Santa Paula Union HS; Santa Paula, CA; (1); 38/300; Church Yth Grp; UCSB; Dentist.

VALE, CHRIS C; Coalinga HS; Coalinga, CA; (2); Church Yth Grp; Treas Debate Tm; SADD; Band; Jazz Band; Orch; Wrstlng; Hon Roll; Pres Acad Fit Awd; U Of CA-REDLANDS; Musician.

VALE CRUZ, IAN MARTIN; Southwest HS; San Diego, CA; (2); 38/673; Church Yth Grp; Band; Jazz Band; School Play; Intrml Stat Vllybl; Cit Awd; High Hon Roll; Hon Roll; Pres Acad Fit Awd.

VALEAU, DWAYNE E; Bishop O'dowd HS; Hayward, CA; (4); 63/241; Church Yth Grp; Cmnty Wkr; Band; School Musical; Nwsp; Ftbl; High Hon Roll; Ntl Merit Ltr; Rotary Awd; Letterman Clb; Cmps Mnstry Tm; Retrt Tm; Bsktbl Announcer; Bio.

VALENCIA, ANDREA F; Hamilton HS; Los Angeles, CA; (3); Cmnty Wkr; Service Clb; Teachers Aide; Yrbk; Sec Frsh Cls; Var Co-Capt Tennis; High Hon Roll; Hon Roll; Pres Acad Fit Awd; Nevians-CA Schlrshp Clb; Pre-Med.

VALENCIA, CHARMINA; David Starr Jordan HS; Long Beach, CA; (3); Sec Church Yth Grp; Pep Clb; Service Clb; Band; Church Choir; Flag Corp; Orch; Variety Show; Ed Nwsp; VP Frsh Cls; CA ST U; Commnctns.

VALENCIA, CYNTHIA; Palmdale HS; Palmdale, CA; (3); 34/644; Spanish Clb; Teachers Aide; Cit Awd; Hon Roll; CSF; World Hstry & Spnsh Spcl Achvt Awds; Ob/Gyn.

VALENCIA, ENRIQUE; Edison SR HS; Stockton, CA; (1); Berkeley; Elect Engr.

VALENCIA, FLORA I; Roosevelt HS; Los Angeles, CA; (4); Hosp Aide; Pres Intnl Clb; JA; SADD; Hon Roll; USC; Bus.

VALENCIA, GLADYS; Fremont Christian HS; Newark, CA; (1); Church Yth Grp; Drama Clb; School Play; Stage Crew; Yrbk; JV Bsktbl; Var Socr; JV Sftbl; JV Vllybl; Cit Awd; Standford; Arch.

VALENCIA, KIMBERLY A; Rowland HS; Rowland Hts, CA; (3); Teachers Aide; Powder Puff Ftbl; JV Var Sftbl; JV Var Vllybl; Hon Roll; Achvt Awd Child Care; Athltc Awd Sierra Leag Sftbl 88-89; Preschl Tchr.

VALENCIA, LAURA; Bell HS; Bell, CA; (4); 22/649; Cmnty Wkr; French Clb; Key Clb; Math Tm; Pep Clb; Off Frsh Cls; Rep Sr Cls; Stu Cncl; Tennis; Hon Roll; Goldn Eagl Prtnshp Prgm; Natl Hispnc Schlrshp Fndtn; U CA Irvine; Bio Sci.

VALENCIA, MA ESMERALDA A; North Hollywood HS; Mission Hills, CA; (2); Hosp Aide; Natl Beta Clb; Science Clb; Service Clb; Spanish Clb; Teachers Aide; JV Vllybl; High Hon Roll; CSF; Pre-Med Club; Congrssnl Yth Ldrshp Cncl; Med.

VALENCIA, MONICA; Alverno HS; Sierra Madre, CA; (3); 9/65; Cmnty Wkr; Science Clb; Lit Mag; Off Soph Cls; Off Jr Cls; Stu Cncl; High Hon Roll; Hon Roll; NHS; St Schlr; Peer Cnslr; Rose Float Club; Stu Action Corps For Animals; People For Ethical Treatment Of Animals; Engrg.

VALENCIA, NANCY V; Mission HS; San Francisco, CA; (4); Chorus; Church Choir; Sec Jr Cls; VP Stu Cncl; Intrml Bsktbl; Var Tennis; Hon Roll; Intrml Bsbl; Intrml Sftbl; Intrml Vllybl; CSF; Prjct Openhand Vlntr; UC Davis; Hlth Sci.

VALENCIA, RAFAEL; South Gate HS; South Gate, CA; (4); 15/612; Am Leg Boys St; VP Pres Key Clb; Scholastic Bowl; Sec Sr Cls; Stu Cncl; Capt Tennis; Elks Awd; Hon Roll; Kiwanis Awd; Rotary Awd; Hosp Vlntr; Cornell U; Pre Med.

VALENCIA, RUTH; Sierra Vista HS; Baldwin Park, CA; (4); Church Yth Grp; Cmnty Wkr; Math Clb; Speech Tm; Teachers Aide; Church Choir; Hon Roll; Ntl Merit SF; Opt Clb Awd; 3rd Yr Peer Cnslr; Child Psych.

VALENCIA, VERONICA L; Manual Arts HS; Los Angeles, CA; (3); Drama Clb; Office Aide; Varsity Clb; Var Sftbl; JV Vllybl; Cit Awd; Hon Roll; Prfct Atten Awd; Peer Cnslng; DARE; Cnflct Mgmt Prog.

VALENCIA, YVETTE; Sacred Heart HS; Los Angeles, CA; (2); Teachers Aide; Bsktbl; Trk; High Hon Roll; Hon Roll; NHS; CCD Tchr; Loyolal; Law.

VALENCIANA, ALMA; Garey HS; Pomona, CA; (2); CA Poly Pomona; Arch.

VALENT, ROYCE O; Canyon HS; Anaheim Hills, CA; (1); Church Yth Grp; Bsbl; Hon Roll; Tribal Council; AZ ST U; Orthopedic Surgeon.

VALENTE, MADELINE L; Granada HS; Livermore, CA; (4); 1/297; Cmnty Wkr; Pres Service Clb; High Hon Roll; Pres Acad Fit Awd; Val; CA Schlrshp Fed Treas; Jazz/Mdrn Dnce; Tndy Schlr; U Of CA Davis; Med.

VALENTIN, MARIA VIRGINIA; St Genevieve HS; N Hollywood, CA; (2); Hon Roll; Rcvd Hnr Awd For Outstndng Achvt In Life Sci; USC; Prdntstry.

VALENTINE, AMY L; Huntington Beach HS; Huntington Beach, CA; (2); Pres Church Yth Grp; Girl Scts; Hosp Aide; Model UN; Red Cross Aide; Spanish Clb; Yrbk; JV Swmmng; High Hon Roll; Algebra Tower Awd & Golden St Exam Hnrs; UC Santa Barbara; Med.

VALENTINE, KRISTI L; Valley Christian HS; Norwalk, CA; (1); GAA; Band; Mrchg Band; Intrml Bsktbl; Var Sftbl; Intrml Vllybl; AZ ST U; Arch Drftng.

VALENTINEZ, ANGELINA P; James Logan HS; Newark, CA; (4); 69/690; Computer Clb; FTA; GAA; Intnl Clb; Science Clb; Band; Crs Cntry; Fld Hcky; Ice Hcky; Socr; Creative Wrtng; Music; Stu Against Abuse Of Animals; UC Santa Cruz; Marine Bio.

VALENZUELA, AILEEN T; Burbank HS; Burbank, CA; (4); 1/421; Church Yth Grp; Cmnty Wkr; French Clb; Service Clb; Co-Ed Yrbk; Co-Ed Lit Mag; Mgr(s); JV Tennis; Cit Awd; Opt Clb Awd; People To People Sci Ambssdr To USSR; Berkeley; Opthmlgy.

VALENZUELA, ANTHONY R; St John Bosco HS; Montebello, CA; (3); Letterman Clb; Varsity Clb; Trk; Wt Lftg; Embry Riddle Aerontcl U; Plt.

VALENZUELA, APRIL; Antioch JR HS; Antioch, CA; (1); Pep Clb; Band; Cheerldng; Pom Pon; Hon Roll; Marine Bio.

VALENZUELA, CYNTHIA; Castle Park HS; Chula Vista, CA; (3); 40/422; French Clb; CSF; Engr Arch.

VALENZUELA, JOSE B; Kingsburg Joint Union HS; Mesa, AZ; (2); Cmmnty Coll; Elctr Tech.

VALENZUELA, KATHY; Central Union HS; El Centro, CA; (2); Band; Mrchg Band; Pep Band; Hon Roll.

VALENZUELA, LISA; Selma HS; Selma, CA; (3); 47/211; Church Yth Grp; Dance Clb; GAA; Office Aide; Varsity Clb; Flag Corp; Off Sr Cls; JV Var Bsktbl; Var Sftbl; JV Var Vllybl; UCLA; Law.

VALENZUELA, MONIKA A; Bishop Amat Memorial HS; Hacienda Heights, CA; (2); Church Yth Grp; Drill Tm; Hon Roll; NHS; UCSD; Med.

VALENZUELA, OSCAR A; Saddleback HS; Santa Ana, CA; (2); Var Swmmng; Capt Of Jr Vrsty Water Polo Team; Engr.

VALENZUELA, PABLO M CASTILLON; Santa Teresa HS; San Jose, CA; (2); Var JV Wrstlng; Ltl Lg Bsbl Won 2 Yrs Champs; 5 Yrs Oak Grove Pop Warner Yth Ftbl; Plyf Vctrs; 2 Chmpnshps Ftbl; San Jose St; Drama Actng.

VALENZUELA, RON N; Central Union HS; El Centro, CA; (1); JV Bsktbl; JV Ftbl; JV Wt Lftg; High Hon Roll; Santa Barbara U; Engrng.

VALENZUELA, SARA; Nordhoff HS; Ojai, CA; (3); Church Yth Grp; Cmnty Wkr; Library Aide; Office Aide; Chorus; Stu Cncl; JV Var Bsktbl; Var Powder Puff Ftbl; Var Sftbl; Var Wt Lftg; Teacher.

VALENZUELA, SIRENIA; Los Amigos HS; Santa Ana, CA; (2); Var Sftbl; Hon Roll; San Diego Coll; Marine Bio.

VALENZUELA JR, SYLVANO; Fontana HS; Fontana, CA; (3); Church Yth Grp.

VALENZUELA, TANYA; Holy Family HS; Glendale, CA; (1); NEDT Awd; U CA-LOS Angeles.

VALENZUELA, VERONICA; Palo Verde HS; Blythe, CA; (3); Church Yth Grp; Drama Clb; Key Clb; Office Aide; Pep Clb; Spanish Clb; SADD; Stu Cncl; Vllybl; Hon Roll; Fshn Dsgnr.

VALENZUELA, VERONICA; Patrick Henry HS; San Diego, CA; (2); Cmnty Wkr; Drama Clb; Girl Scts; Chorus; Church Choir; School Musical; School Play; Variety Show; Prfct Atten Awd; Vlntrng Peer Cnslr Trbld Teens; Tutr; Radio Brdcstng.

VALENZUELA, VICKY; Beaumont HS; Beaumont, CA; (3); 12/167; Cit Awd; High Hon Roll; Hon Roll; NHS; Prfct Atten Awd; CSF; Pediatrics.

VALENZUELA, VICTORIA L; Villa Park HS; Orange, CA; (3); Cmnty Wkr; Key Clb; Pres Service Clb; SADD; Church Choir; Off Sr Cls; Var L Sftbl; JV Mgr Vllybl; Hon Roll; NHS; PAL; PUSH; CSF; Bus Admin.

VALERIO, ALFRED; Granada Hills HS; Granada Hills, CA; (3); Cmnty Wkr; FBLA; ROTC; Science Clb; Lit Mag; Var Swmmng; High Hon Roll; Hon Roll; Outstndng Acad Achvt; Presdntl Acad Ftnss Awds Pgm; U Of CA Berkley; Ec.

VALERIO, CINDY C; Watsonville HS; Watsonville, CA; (2); Church Yth Grp; Teachers Aide; Band; Stage Crew; Socr; High Hon Roll; CA Schlrshp Fed; Nomntd ST Schlr; USC; Aerospace Engrng.

VALERIO, CLAUDIA M; Valencia HS; Placentia, CA; (3); Science Clb; Spanish Clb; Yrbk; Cit Awd; High Hon Roll; Pres Acad Fit Awd; Spanish Awards; Distinguished Scholar Award.

VALERIO, KRISTINE JOYCE; Nogales HS; Walnut, CA; (2); Dance Clb; Pep Clb; Spanish Clb; Pep Band; Cheerldng; Hon Roll; Optometry.

VALERIO, MELESIA V S; Fullerton HS; Roswell, NM; (3); Church Yth Grp; NFL; Speech Tm; Hon Roll; Engl Awd; Intl Baccalaureate Pgm; Peer Cnslr; U Norther CO; Writer.

VALERO, ARCELIA; Orosi HS; Cutler, CA; (2); Mrchg Band; Hon Roll; Prfct Atten Awd; Southern CA U; Med.

VALERO, ELSA; Orosi HS; Cutler, CA; (2); Band; Mrchg Band.

VALERO, PHILLIP A; Woodlake Union HS; Woodlake, CA; (2); FFA.

VALERO, SHEA J; Bonita Vista HS; Bonita, CA; (2); Off Frsh Cls; Var Swmmng; Cit Awd; High Hon Roll; Hon Roll; Pres Acad Fit Awd; CA Poly San Luis Obispo; Arch.

VALES, BRENDA C; Mills HS; Millbrae, CA; (3); GAA; Intnl Clb; Latin Clb; Spanish Clb; Mgr(s); Socr; Vllybl; Prfct Atten Awd; Rotary Awd; Sec Rotary Clb; Pres Latin Clb; Heald Business Coll; Acctg.

VALES, RESIE; Mira Mesa HS; San Diego, CA; (3); 121/777; Acpl Chr; Drill Tm; Powder Puff Ftbl; Pres Acad Fit Awd; President Of The Space Club; Member Of The California Junior Scholastic Federation-Vp; Medicine.

VALFER, RACHEL; Berkeley HS; Berkeley, CA; (2); Drama Clb; Latin Clb; Temple Yth Grp; Orch; Lit Mag; High Hon Roll; Hon Roll.

VALINE, LAWRENCE J; Elk Grove HS; Rancho Murieta, CA; (3); 100/620; SADD; Rep Stu Cncl; Pres Acad Fit Awd; UC Santa Cruz; HS Tchr.

VALLE, ANTHONY C; Lowell HS; San Francisco, CA; (3); CSF; Golden ST Exam Hnrs Alg & Geom; Law.

VALLE, BEATRIZ A; Exeter Union HS; Farmersville, CA; (1); Church Yth Grp; Fresno ST; Pediatrics.

VALLE, CARLOS R; El Camino Real HS; Los Angeles, CA; (3); Var L Ftbl.

VALLE, GABRIELA; Inglewood HS; Inglewood, CA; (2); Hon Roll; Pedtrcn.

VALLE, LISA M; Santa Margarita Catholic HS; El Toro, CA; (3); 88/227; Aud/Vis; Church Yth Grp; Cmnty Wkr; Key Clb; Pep Clb; Ed Nwsp; Yrbk; Stu Cncl; Hon Roll; Acts Ltr In Stu Cncl.

VALLE, MARCO E; La Canada HS; La Canada-Flint, CA; (3); Key Clb; Math Clb; ASB VP; U Of Pacific NW; Psych.

VALLE, MARIE A; Carson HS; Carson, CA; (2); Latin Clb; Color Guard; Phtg Nwsp; Loyola Marymount U; Chem.

VALLE, MARISOL; Bell HS; Cudahy, CA; (3); Hon Roll; NHS; California Scholarship Federation; U Of Miami.

VALLE, MARUBENIA; El Rancho HS; Pico Rivera, CA; (4); Teachers Aide; Rptr Nwsp; JV Var Bsktbl; Score Keeper; High Hon Roll; Hon Roll; Rio Hondo Coll; Psych.

VALLE, WILFREDO; Roosevelt HS; Los Angeles, CA; (2); VP Soph Cls; Prfct Atten Awd; Pro Bsbl.

VALLECILLA, ANDRES A; Glendale HS; Glendale, CA; (3); 100/690; Letterman Clb; Crs Cntry; Trk; Hon Roll; JV Crss Cntry MVP Awd; Norba Natl Uphll Mntn Bkng 1st Pl; Cngrssnl Yth Ldrshp Cncl; UC Santa Barbara.

VALLEJO, ANA M; Inglewood HS; Inglewood, CA; (2); Church Yth Grp; Hosp Aide; JV Sftbl; Cit Awd; Hon Roll; 3rd Pl GSE; Comp Sci.

VALLEJO, OSCAR; Lindsay HS; Porterville, CA; (3); Art Clb; Spanish Clb; SADD; Ftbl; Trk; Wrstlng; OK ST; Art.

VALLEJO, PATRICIA; Paramount HS; Paramount, CA; (3); SADD; JV Bsktbl; Var Trk; Hnrs Pgm AP Courses; Criminology.

VALLELY, AMY; San Ramon Valley HS; Danville, CA; (2); GAA; Intnl Clb; Teachers Aide; Band; High Hon Roll; CA Schlrshp Fdrtn; Aerospc Engr.

VALLES, COLLEEN M; Santa Teresa HS; San Jose, CA; (2); French Clb; Hosp Aide; Science Clb; Var Crs Cntry; Var Trk; CSF; Math/Engrng & Sci Achvt; Acad Decathln Team; UCLA; Med.

VALLES, DAVID J; Santa Teresa HS; San Jose, CA; (3); Science Clb; Spanish Clb; Var Crs Cntry; Var Trk; CSF; Math/Engrng/Sci Achvt; CA Poly San Luis Obispo; Engr.

VALLESER, ANNA C; Bishop Montgomery HS; Bellflower, CA; (2); Art Clb; Computer Clb; Drama Clb; SADD; Thesps; Band; Jazz Band; Mrchg Band; School Musical; Stage Crew; Peopl To Peopl Stu Ambssdr Prgrm; UCLA; Art.

VALLIER, LEANA M; Armijo HS; Fairfield, CA; (2); Band; Drm Mjr(t); Flag Corp; Jazz Band; Mrchg Band; Orch; High Hon Roll; UC Davis; Elem Teacher.

VALLIERE, CHRISTOPHER J; Westwood HS; Westwood, CA; (3); Drama Clb; VP Letterman Clb; Spanish Clb; Pres VP Varsity Clb; Stage Crew; Rptr Nwsp; Yrbk; Var L Bsbl; Var L Bsktbl; Var Capt Ftbl.

VALLIEU, DENISE M; Armijo HS; Fairfield, CA; (2); Girl Scts; Band; Mrchg Band; Orch; Pep Band; Frnch Hrn Sec Ldr; Tchr.

VALLNER, JASON J; Southbay Christian HS; Los Altos, CA; (3); Art Clb; Church Yth Grp; Letterman Clb; Natl Beta Clb; Chorus; VP Frsh Cls; VP Soph Cls; Capt Bsktbl; Capt Socr; Capt Tennis.

VALLO, ANITA; Barstow HS; Barstow, CA; (1); Off Soph Cls; Var Swmmng; Hon Roll; US & Southern CA Swmmng; Western Zone Team 3x Medal 1500, 800, 400 Free Style & 200 Fly; Stanford; Comp Tech.

VALMEO, ROMEL V; Carson HS; Carson, CA; (4); Office Aide; Rptr Nwsp; Bsbl; Bsktbl; Crs Cntry; Vllybl; High Hon Roll; Hon Roll; Acad Decathlon; U CA Riverside; Bus Admin.

VALMONTE, KENNETH L; Duarte HS; La Verne, CA; (4); 10/235; Key Clb; Science Clb; SADD; Teachers Aide; Yrbk; Lit Mag; Rep Stu Cncl; JV Var Bsktbl; Var JV Tennis; Pres Acad Fit Awd; CSF; Schl Site Cncl; Strng Cmmttee; UC-RIVERSIDE; Biomed.

VALOIS, TAMMY L; Homestead HS; Sunnyvale, CA; (3); Debate Tm; NFL; Speech Tm; Ed Nwsp; Var L Trk; NHS; Ntl Merit Schol; Cornell Summr Coll Std; Goldn St Examn Hnrs Geom; Valley Journl Wrtr.

VALOT, DAVID R; Bishop Montgomery HS; Torrance, CA; (2); Service Clb; High Hon Roll; Hon Roll; Prfct Atten Awd; Acad Cert Of Awd; CSF Awd For Service Hrs.

VALOT, SUSAN M; Bishop Montgomery HS; Lomita, CA; (2); Drama Clb; Girl Scts; Hon Roll; CA Schlrshp Fdrtn; Grl Scout Slvr Awd.

VALSTAD, ANDREA; Pinole Valley HS; Hercules, CA; (1); Spanish Clb; Chorus; Hon Roll; Real Est Agt.

VALTERZA, STACIA A; C K Mcclatchy HS; Sacramento, CA; (2); Church Yth Grp; French Clb; Off Frsh Cls; VP Jr Cls; Capt Powder Puff Ftbl; Tennis; Vlntr Lcl Soup Ktchn; UC Davis; Bio.

VALVERDE, LOUIS G; Edison HS; Stockton, CA; (3); #12 In Class; Church Yth Grp; Phtg Yrbk; JV Bsbl; JV Bsktbl; Var Socr; Hon Roll; Elec Engr.

VALVERDE, MARCELLINA; Santa Paula Union HS; Santa Paula, CA; (4); 11/240; Library Aide; Office Aide; Treas Stu Cncl; Vllybl; Hon Roll; CA Schlrshp Fed; Pres Clssrm Yng Amercns.

VAN, DAI V; San Gabriel HS; Rosemead, CA; (2); Nwsp; Cit Awd; Engrng.

VAN, DANH; Andrew Hill HS; San Jose, CA; (3).

VAN, HONG T; Sunny Hills HS; Buena Park, CA; (4); Rptr FBLA; Key Clb; Spanish Clb; Teachers Aide; Yrbk; High Hon Roll; Rotary Awd; Bank Of Am Bus Awd; U CA-IRVINE; Bio.

VAN, NGHIA H; Pacifica HS; Garden Grove, CA; (3); Intrml Bsktbl; Hon Roll; UCI; Bus Admin.

VAN, PHUONG; Mc Clymonds HS; Oakland, CA; (1); 1/200; Rptr Nwsp; Rptr Yrbk; Cit Awd; High Hon Roll; Hon Roll; Prfct Atten Awd; Multi Cultural Clb; Achvt Awd For E W Conf 90; UC Davis; Med.

VAN, SOPHIA; South HS; Bakersfield, CA; (3); 22/482; Hist French Clb; Pres Math Tm; Natl Beta Clb; Capt Speech Tm; Cit Awd; High Hon Roll; NHS; Pres Acad Fit Awd; Placed 5th Overall Natl Acad Olympics; 35th Natl Global Challenge 88; 6th La St French Rally 89; U Of CO; Sports Medicine.

VAN, THIEN H; San Gabriel HS; San Gabriel, CA; (2); Debate Tm; FBLA; JA; NFL; Service Clb; Swmmng; Tennis; Hon Roll; NHS; Pres Acad Fit Awd; Elderly Indo-Chinese Assn Schlrshp; Hstry Day Los Angeles 1st Pl Wnnr; UCLA; Chem.

VAN, TO LINH; George Washington HS; San Francisco, CA; (4); Computer Clb; Library Aide; Teachers Aide; School Play; Nwsp; Yrbk; Off Sr Cls; Bsktbl; Vllybl; High Hon Roll; Merit Awd; City Coll; Pharm.

VAN, TOMMY S; San Lorenzo HS; San Lorenzo, CA; (2); Boy Scts; Ski Clb; JV Capt Bsktbl; Ftbl; Tennis; Hon Roll; Schl Recgntn Golden St Math Exam; UC Davis; Engrng.

VAN ANDEL, HEIDI M; Hanford HS; Hanford, CA; (1); FHA; Letterman Clb; Ski Clb; Spanish Clb; Teachers Aide; Off Frsh Cls; Off Soph Cls; Swmmng; High Hon Roll; NHS; CSF; Lawyer.

VAN ATTA, ROBERT J; Lowell HS; San Francisco, CA; (2); Boy Scts; Chorus; School Musical; Crs Cntry; Trk; Crew Of Pacific Rowing Clb; Bus.

VAN BEVEREN, LIESEL J; Warren HS; Downey, CA; (3); Art Clb; Sec Church Yth Grp; Service Clb; SADD; Church Choir; Greenpeace Head Envrnmntlst; U Of CA Santa Barbara; Acctg.

VAN BRASCH, JENNIFER G; Castro Valley HS; Castro Valley, CA; (3); French Clb; Treas SADD; Teachers Aide; Acpl Chr; Variety Show; Hon Roll; Interact Club Treas; Friday Night Live; Peer Counseling; Cal St Hayward; Teacher.

VAN BUREN, LUCIANA; Woodrow Wilson HS; San Francisco, CA; (1); Church Yth Grp; Library Aide; Math Clb; Spanish Clb; SADD; Teachers Aide; Church Choir; Sec Frsh Cls; High Hon Roll; Spanish NHS; Pediatrician.

VAN CAMP, BRANDON; Ukiah HS; Ukiah, CA; (2); Church Yth Grp; Cmnty Wkr; FCA; Bsbl; Ftbl; Wt Lftg; Rotary Awd; Theology.

VAN CAMP, GREG J; Westminster HS; Westminster, CA; (1); JCL; Treas Latin Clb; Intrml Bsktbl; JV Tennis; Hon Roll; VP Jr NHS; Frshmn Schlr Athl Bsktbl; UCSD; Pre-Dental.

VAN CAMPEN, SUSAN; Mira Mesa HS; San Diego, CA; (2); French Clb; Science Clb; Acpl Chr; Stu Cncl; JV Socr; NHS; Acadmc Leag; St Lvl Comptv Leag Socr; Acadmc Ltr; Sci.

VAN CASTER, LORRIE M; Petaluma HS; Petaluma, CA; (4); Treas Art Clb; Hist Sec 4-H; Spanish Clb; SADD; 4-H Awd; Hon Roll; Interact; JV Badminton; Pork Producer Princss 89; Santa Rosa JC; Vet Med.

VAN DAM, DEVON L; Alverno HS; Monrovia, CA; (3); GAA; Office Aide; Science Clb; Teachers Aide; Rep Soph Cls; Off Jr Cls; Off Sr Cls; JV Var Swmmng; DAR Awd; Mst Imprvd Swmmr 88; Mst Dedctd Swmmr 89; Zoology.

VAN DE HOEVEN, VINCENT G; Filmore Unified HS; Fillmore, CA; (4); Rptr Yrbk; JV Crs Cntry; JV Var Trk; Pres Acad Fit Awd; CSF Lifetime Mbr; Cal Poly San Luis Obispo; Engr.

VAN DE WATER, REBECCA L; San Marino HS; San Marino, CA; (3); 172/258; FBLA; Crs Cntry; Trk; Los Angeles Unifd Sch Dist; Var Ltr Cross Cntry; San Diego ST U; Child Dev.

VAN DEN BRINK, TINA; John A Rowland HS; Rowland Heights, CA; (3); Band; Drill Tm; Flag Corp; Mrchg Band; JV Sftbl; High Hon Roll; Hon Roll; Sci Outstndng Stu Yr 89; San Diego; Marine Bio.

VAN DER STAP, LENA D; Patrick Henry HS; San Diego, CA; (3); 30/528; Church Yth Grp; Key Clb; Spanish Clb; Chorus; Hon Roll; Jr NHS; Pres Acad Fit Awd; UC San Diego; Arch.

VAN DEVANTER, KRYSTAL D; Cajon HS; San Bernardino, CA; (3); Boy Scts; VP Church Yth Grp; Sec Key Clb; Band; Capt Flag Corp; Mrchg Band; Schlrshp Band; Mst Outstndng Explr Sct; Mst Outstndng Clarinet; Alg II Schlrshp Norton AFB; Math.

VAN DIEST, JULIE; Fresno Christian HS; Fresno, CA; (3); Church Yth Grp; Hosp Aide; Varsity Clb; Chorus; Rep Frsh Cls; Var Sftbl; JV Var Vllybl; High Hon Roll; Hon Roll; Pres Acad Fit Awd.

VAN DILLEN, ALEX P; Torrey Pines HS; Del Mar, CA; (2); 250/500; Church Yth Grp; JV Crs Cntry; JV Tennis; JV Trk; Pres Acad Fit Awd; Water Skiing; U CO Boulder; Bus.

VAN DOREN, ZACHARY; San Dieguito HS; Encinitas, CA; (2); JV Bsktbl; L Golf; Cit Awd; Hon Roll; Pres Acad Fit Awd; Radio Club; U Of Pacific; Bus.

VAN DRIEL, KARINA; Culver City HS; Culver City, CA; (3); Service Clb; Off Frsh Cls; Off Soph Cls; Off Jr Cls; Hon Roll; CSF.

VAN DUSEN-MC LEOD, AIMEE; Enterprise HS; Redding, CA; (3); Teachers Aide; Sec Ed Yrbk; Hon Roll; Law.

VAN DYKE, ALICE R; Temple Christian HS; Canyon Lake, CA; (2); Church Yth Grp; Speech Tm; Band; Church Choir; Variety Show; VP Soph Cls; Treas Jr Cls; Score Keeper; L Sftbl; L Vllybl; Yth Wrkr; Cnslng.

VAN DYKE, BILL D; Buchanan HS; Running Springs, CA; (3); Teachers Aide; Acpl Chr; Band; Chorus; JV Bsbl; JV Trk; Var Wrstlng; Hon Roll; Hollywood Boys Club Camp Cnslr; Teacher.

VAN DYKE, FRANKLIN ALEXANDER; Luther Burbank HS; Sacramento, CA; (2); 81/389; Boy Scts; Church Yth Grp; SADD; Bsktbl; Ftbl; Trk; Cit Awd; Hon Roll; MVP & Mst Outstndng Offnsve Plyr Ftbl 89 & Athlt Track 90; Scntl Champ 400 Meter 90; CSUS Testng; Bus Mgmt.

VAN DYKE, GEOFF T; Las Lomas HS; Walnut Creek, CA; (2); 1/266; Band; JV Bsktbl; Var Capt Socr; High Hon Roll; Rudgear Meadows Swim Team; Engl.

VAN DYKE, JESSICA S; Barstow HS; Barstow, CA; (1); Attorney.

VAN DYKE, ROBERT D; East Nicolaus HS; Pleasant Grove, CA; (2); 7/45; Church Yth Grp; Letterman Clb; Ski Clb; Varsity Clb; Band; Pep Band; Hon Roll; Rptr Yrbk; Rep Frsh Cls; Rep Pres Soph Cls; Friday Night Live; Golden ST Schlr; Engrng.

VAN DYKE, TERRA; Clovis HS; Clovis, CA; (2); Church Yth Grp; Drama Clb; Band; School Musical; Hon Roll; Law.

VAN EERDE, MATTHEW D; Dos Pueblos HS; Goleta, CA; (1); VP Church Yth Grp; Math Clb; Quiz Bowl; Band; Mrchg Band; Orch; Pep Band; NHS; Chess; CA Poly San Luis Obispo; Music.

VAN EERDE, MILO D; Dos Pueblos HS; Goleta, CA; (1); VP Church Yth Grp; Math Clb; Quiz Bowl; Band; Mrchg Band; Orch; Pep Band; NHS; Chess; CA Poly San Luis Obispo; Music.

VAN EIZENGA, JENNIFER R; Edison HS; Huntington Beach, CA; (1); Church Yth Grp; German Clb; Girl Scts; Band; Church Choir; Mrchg Band; BYU; Med.

VAN ERP, JOHN W; Folsom HS; Folsom, CA; (3); 9/200; Math Tm; Model UN; Tennis; High Hon Roll; Jr NHS; Ntl Merit Ltr; Opt Clb Awd; Explorer Scout; Cal Poly San Luis Obispo; Engr.

VAN ERT, KERRY; Chico HS; Chico, CA; (2); Office Aide; Pep Clb; Teachers Aide; Cheerldng; Diving; Tennis; UC Irvine; Marine Bio.

VAN GELDER, NATALIE; Ocalanes HS; Lafayette, CA; (1); JV Capt Cheerldng; Powder Puff Ftbl; Var L Swmmng; Swm Chmpnshps 90; DFAL Fnlst Swmmnr; Stnfrd; Mech Engrg.

VAN GINKEL, CARRIE L; Ripon Christian HS; Ripon, CA; (4); Church Yth Grp; Teachers Aide; Sec Soph Cls; VP Sr Cls; Var JV Bsktbl; Var JV Sftbl; Var Capt Vllybl; High Hon Roll; Hon Roll; Kiwanis Awd; Modesto JC; Nrsng.

VAN HALA, KRISTEN M; Canyon Springs HS; Moreno Valley, CA; (2); Thesps; Band; School Musical; School Play; Stage Crew; Hon Roll; Show Choir; Chamber Singers; Music.

VAN HEERDE, JASON E; Eisenhower HS; Rialto, CA; (3); Church Yth Grp; Cmnty Wkr; Key Clb; Letterman Clb; Off Frsh Cls; Stu Cncl; Bsbl; High Hon Roll; Hon Roll; Jr NHS; Umpre For Lttle Leag Bsebl; Ebgr.

VAN HERK, TRACY R; John F Kennedy HS; La Palma, CA; (4); Church Yth Grp; Cmnty Wkr; Key Clb; Varsity Clb; VP Capt Socr; Hon Roll; NHS; Azusa Pacific U; Math.

VAN HEST, JASON R; Mission Bay SR HS; San Diego, CA; (1); Aud/Vis; Band; Chorus; Jazz Band; Pep Band; School Musical; Stage Crew; Swing Chorus; Variety Show; AZ ST U; Architecture.

VAN HORN, VANESSA L; Live Oak HS; Morgan Hill, CA; (4); 4-H; Ed Nwsp; Lit Mag; 4-H Awd; Evergreen; Writer.

VAN HULZEN, ERIKA; Apple Valley Christian Schl; Apple Valley, CA; (2); 1/21; Church Yth Grp; Office Aide; School Musical; School Play; VP Frsh Cls; VP Soph Cls; Stat Bsbl; Stat Bsktbl; Var Vllybl; High Hon Roll; Outstndng Achvmnts Engl, Spnsh & Bio; Yng Mthmtcn; Stff Cmp Cherith; Med.

VAN HYFTE, SHANEEN; Ontario HS; Ontario, CA; (2); 9/620; Church Yth Grp; Key Clb; Ski Clb; Spanish Clb; SADD; Varsity Clb; School Musical; Rptr Nwsp; Pres Jr Cls; Capt Cheerldng; HOBY Ambsdr 89-90; Jr Statesman Of Amer Yth Fndtn; UCLA; Corp Lwyr.

VAN INGEN, LISA M; Herbert Hoover HS; Fresno, CA; (3); 1/453; Church Yth Grp; French Clb; JV Gym; Var L Swmmng; High Hon Roll; Hon Roll; Ntl Merit Ltr; Pres Schlr; Jr LARCS Club; Amnesty Intnl; U Southern CA; Bus Admin.

VAN KINKLE, BLOSSON M; Novato HS; Novato, CA; (1); Mrchg Band; Orch; Hon Roll; UC Davis; Arch.

VAN KIRK, KELLY L; Rim Of The World HS; Running Springs, CA; (1); Church Yth Grp; Drama Clb; Church Choir; Stu Cncl; JV Socr; JV Sftbl; Hon Roll; Dntl Hygnst.

VAN KIRK, KRISTA L; Rim Of The World HS; Running Springs, CA; (1); Church Yth Grp; Cmnty Wkr; Drama Clb; Office Aide; Spanish Clb; Church Choir; Sec Frsh Cls; Stu Cncl; JV Socr; Hon Roll; Peer-Cnslng Pres; VBS; Clwns For Cmnty Fair; Hstry Tchr.

VAN KONYNENBURG, MATT D; Modesto Christian HS; Modesto, CA; (2); Art Clb; Drama Clb; German Clb; Intnl Clb; Ski Clb; Rep Frsh Cls; Script Wrtr Chrch Drama Grp; Fshn Mrktng.

VAN KOOTEN, ANNELIES; Yucaipa HS; Yucaipa, CA; (4); Sec Church Yth Grp; High Hon Roll; Hon Roll; Prfct Atten Awd; CSF; Sectry Ambssdrs; Loma Linda U; Engl.

VAN LANDUYT, CHRISTINE Y; Imperial HS; Pasadena, CA; (4); Church Yth Grp; JA; Library Aide; Chorus; Rptr Nwsp; Hon Roll; 1st Pl Fiction Awd; 4th Pl Art Awd.

VAN LEER, GREGORY R; Richard Gahr HS; Cerritos, CA; (1); VP Church Yth Grp; Letterman Clb; Band; Jazz Band; Off Frsh Cls; Stu Cncl; Intrml Bsktbl; Intrml Capt Ftbl; Intrml Var Trk; Hon Roll; CO U; Accntnt.

VAN LOBEN SELS, JEFF E; C K Mc Clatchy HS; Sacramento, CA; (2); Boy Scts; Socr; Tennis; CA Arts Schlr; Yrbk Art; Photo & Video; UC Davis; Art.

VAN LOON, TRACIE E; Madera HS; Madera, CA; (2); Letterman Clb; Varsity Clb; Yrbk; Var Socr; JV Swmmng; Var Vllybl; UC; Chld Psych.

VAN METER, STEPHANIE J; Palmdale HS; Palmdale, CA; (4); 39/586; Stu Cncl; Ntl Merit SF; SHARP 89; Physcs.

VAN METRE, JENNIFER M; Edison HS; Huntington Beach, CA; (1); Pres Girl Scts; Service Clb; Teacher.

VAN MIDDLESWORTH, JUDI E; Santa Teresa HS; San Jose, CA; (1); Spanish Clb; Yng Amer Bwlng Allnce Yth Bowlger; Shepherd Coll; Teacher.

VAN NEST, JENNIFER A; Central Valley HS; Redding, CA; (4); Dance Clb; FBLA; Acpl Chr; School Musical; Ed Yrbk; Ed Lit Mag; Stu Cncl; Swmmng; Trk; Vllybl; UC Riverside; Biochem.

VAN OS, ADRIANA; Mater Dei HS; Anaheim, CA; (1); Church Yth Grp; Cmnty Wkr; Drama Clb; Hosp Aide; SADD; Stu Cncl; Stat Ftbl; Swmmng; Stat Wrstlng; Fashion Mrchndsng.

VAN PATTEN, CARLEE R; Los Amigos HS; Santa Ana, CA; (2); Spanish Clb; Drill Tm; Hon Roll.

VAN PROYEN, JOEL D; Patrick Henry HS; San Diego, CA; (3); 166/528; Church Yth Grp; Var Capt Swmmng; Vrsty Water Polo Cptn; Air Force Acad; Officer.

VAN RHEENEN, MICHELE; Thousand Oaks HS; Thousand Oaks, CA; (3); Church Yth Grp; Spanish Clb; Teachers Aide; High Hon Roll; NHS; Yth To Yth Drug Free Org; Ed.

VAN SANTEN, TONYA T; Lodi HS; Lodi, CA; (3); Church Yth Grp; Spanish Clb; Band; Mrchg Band; Pep Band; High Hon Roll; Lib Band Cncl; CSF; Bio.

VAN SICKLE, RAQUEL; Woodland HS; Woodland, CA; (3); Church Yth Grp; FBLA; Girl Scts; Library Aide; Cheerldng; Gym; Tennis; Vllybl; Hon Roll; Med.

VAN STOCKUM, IRENE K; Notre Dame HS; Riverside, CA; (3); 19/140; Art Clb; Spanish Clb; Stage Crew; High Hon Roll; CSF; Friday Night Live; UCR Scrips Inst; Botany.

VAN TIFFLIN, TRACY A; Pacifica HS; Garden Grove, CA; (3); Church Yth Grp; Hosp Aide; JA; Math Tm; Ski Clb; Spanish Clb; SADD; Variety Show; Var Powder Puff Ftbl; Var Sftbl; Nmntd Miss Teenage Amer 90; Chrch Actvts; Rep St Plycmp Schl Splng Cntst Diocese; Cnslr Psychlgy.

VAN TONGEREN, ERIN; Cornelia Connelly HS; Anaheim, CA; (1); Debate Tm; Chorus; JV Sftbl; Hon Roll; Sci.

VAN VALKENBURG, TONI B; Central Union HS; El Centro, CA; (4); 34/387; Church Yth Grp; Drama Clb; French Clb; Speech Tm; SADD; Ed Lit Mag; Swmmng; Academic Decathlon; 3rd In State Eng; Super Quiz; UCR; Eng Pre-Law.

VAN VEEN, JENNIFER M; Point Home HS; San Diego, CA; (2); Var Swmmng.

VAN VIEGEN, MARCO A; Chino HS; Chino, CA; (2); Boy Scts; Ski Clb; JV Socr; JV Trk; Civl Air Patrl Aux Of US Air Force; Genl Billy Mitchell Awd Civl Air Patrl; Amelia Earhart Awd; Avtn.

VAN VOOREN, CHELSEA; Central Catholic HS; Hughson, CA; (3); AFS; Hosp Aide; Ski Clb; Spanish Clb; SADD; Teachers Aide; JV Cheerldng; Socr; Var Trk; Var Vllybl.

VAN WINKLE, MICHAEL CHAD; Fillmore HS; Fillmore, CA; (4); 34/200; Church Yth Grp; Letterman Clb; Office Aide; SADD; Teachers Aide; L Capt Bsbl; L Capt Bsktbl; L Capt Ftbl; Hon Roll; Bsbl All Cnty, All Leag, All CIF 2 Yrs; Ftbl All Leag, All Cnty All CIF 2 Yrs; DARE; ASB Cnvtn Day; Pilot.

VAN ZANDT, JUSTIN S; Ramona HS; Ramona, CA; (2); 30/400; Chess Clb; JV Vllybl; Peer Cnsclr.

VAN ZANTEN, ANGI N; St Joseph HS; Long Beach, CA; (2); Church Yth Grp; Cmnty Wkr; Debate Tm; English Clb; GAA; Intnl Clb; Letterman Clb; Ski Clb; SADD; Rep Frsh Cls; San Diego ST; Jrnlsm.

VAN ZWALUWENBURG, BRENT A; Ripon Christian HS; Manteca, CA; (4); Am Leg Boys St; Church Yth Grp; Acpl Chr; Band; Pep Band; School Play; Rep Soph Cls; Hon Roll; Kiwanis Awd; Pres Acad Fit Awd; Calvin Coll; Poltcl Sci.

VANALEK, DAVID T; Rancho Cotate HS; Rohnert Park, CA; (4); 2/280; Am Leg Boys St; Pres Drama Clb; NFL; Pres Speech Tm; Var Tennis; High Hon Roll; NHS; Sal; Cmnty Wkr; Hosp Aide; Acad Dcthln; UCLA; Law.

VANCE, DWAYNE; Norco HS; Norco, CA; (3); 150/450; Pres Art Clb; Church Yth Grp; FCA; Teachers Aide; Stu Cncl; JV Wrstlng; Cit Awd; Hon Roll; Work CA Disneyland; Outstndng Art Stu Frosh; Cal ST Schl; Grphc Illus.

VANCE, JACOB S; St John Bosco HS; South Gate, CA; (2); French Clb; SADD; JV Socr; JV Intrml Trk; Hon Roll; Med Doc.

VANCE, KRISTI A; Sanger HS; Sanger, CA; (3); Church Yth Grp; Computer Clb; Teachers Aide; Flag Corp; Mgr(s); Powder Puff Ftbl; Score Keeper; Hon Roll; Intl Ordr Rainbow Girls Worthy Advsr; Sti Athltc Trnr; Fresno City Coll; Elem Ed.

VANCE, TERRI L; Silver Creek HS; San Jose, CA; (3); Church Yth Grp; FCA; GAA; Teachers Aide; Church Choir; Drill Tm; Variety Show; Rep Frsh Cls; Stat Bsktbl; Stat Score Keeper; Delete; Acteens; Howard; Psych.

VANDAM, MARK R; St Margarets HS; San Clemente, CA; (3); Ski Clb; Teachers Aide; Rptr Nwsp; Yrbk; Var L Crs Cntry; Var Socr; Hon Roll; Coaches Aide.

VANDE HEI, DANA M; David SR HS; Davis, CA; (3); Church Yth Grp; Computer Clb; Office Aide; Ski Clb; JV Bsktbl; JV Mgr(s); Cal Poly; Bus.

VANDE MERGHEL, LAURA M; Los Amigos HS; Fountain Valley, CA; (2); Church Yth Grp; Key Clb; Science Clb; Chorus; Flag Corp; Variety Show; JV Swmmng; Hon Roll; UC Irvine; Med.

VANDEN BERG, DENISE; La Reina HS; Simi Valley, CA; (4); 8/88; Church Choir; Rptr Nwsp; Yrbk; Cit Awd; High Hon Roll; Pres Acad Fit Awd; Spanish NHS; Amnesty Intl; CA Lutheran U; Engl Lit.

VANDENBERG, TIMOTHY S; Los Angeles Baptist HS; Sepulveda, CA; (4); 2/90; Church Yth Grp; Thesps; School Play; Off Stu Cncl; Var JV Crs Cntry; Var JV Trk; Cit Awd; High Hon Roll; NHS; Pres Acad Fit Awd; AWANA Citation Awd; Bank Of American Achvt Awd/Religious Studies; Alpha Chi Sigma Recipient; UCLA; Youth Pastor.

VANDER FEER, CHRISTY L; Tulare Union HS; Tulare, CA; (3); 106/397; FFA; Hon Roll; Merchant Banker.

VANDER LINDEN, TRAVIS T; Point Loma HS; San Diego, CA; (2); Art Clb; Church Yth Grp; Latin Clb; Nwsp; Crs Cntry; Wt Lftg; Hon Roll; Pres Acad Fit Awd; Med.

VANDER MADEN, TASHA; Casa Roble Fundamental HS; Orangevale, CA; (4); AFS; Church Yth Grp; Spanish Clb; Teachers Aide; Trk; Cit Awd; High Hon Roll; Hon Roll; Blue Crew Spirit Crowd Sec; Outstndng Acads Schlrshp Awd; CA ST U; Rcrdg Engr.

VANDER VIS, MARYANN; Valley Christian HS; Cerritos, CA; (4); Church Yth Grp; Cmnty Wkr; GAA; Varsity Clb; Band; Mrchg Band; Orch; School Musical; Powder Puff Ftbl; Score Keeper; Tnns Hi Acad; Bnk Of Amer Engl Cert; UCLA; Civil Engrng.

VANDER WAL, DIANE; Fred C Beyer HS; Modesto, CA; (3); Church Yth Grp; Service Clb; Church Choir; Hon Roll; Prfct Atten Awd; Outstndng Ctznshp Awd; CSF; Biola; Mssns.

VANDER WAL, JEFFREY A; Huntington Beach HS; Huntington Beach, CA; (2); Model UN; Spanish Clb; Varsity Clb; Var Bsktbl; Var Vllybl; Wt Lftg; Cit Awd; High Hon Roll; Prfct Atten Awd; MUN Accmdtns; Pepperdine; Oceangrphr.

VANDER WERF, SARAH; Novato HS; San Rafael, CA; (4); Church Yth Grp; Cmnty Wkr; VP JA; Model UN; Office Aide; SADD; Teachers Aide; Var Swmmng; Cit Awd; High Hon Roll; Acad Schlrshp; Mission-Cmnty Svc Tm Capt; Santa Rosa JC; Law.

VANDER YACHT, JEFFREY R; La Quinta HS; Santa Ana, CA; (2); 4/362; Drama Clb; School Play; Variety Show; Hon Roll; Schlr Of Yr; Impvstn Show Drama; Psych.

VANDERBUNDT, KARA; Norte Vista HS; Riverside, CA; (3); 6/472; Drama Clb; Math Tm; Sec Speech Tm; Band; School Musical; School Play; Rep Stu Cncl; Var Cheerldng; High Hon Roll; Bst Ovrall Thspn-Drama 90; Comm.

VANDERBYL, KIMBERLY ANNE; Del Mar HS; San Jose, CA; (4); 21/222; Pep Clb; SADD; Teachers Aide; L Var Bsktbl; Var L Sftbl; Var L Tennis; Hon Roll; NHS; Pres Acad Fit Awd; CSF; West Valley SCSU; Animal Sci.

VANDERGAST, AMY; Los Alamitos HS; Seal Beach, CA; (3); Church Yth Grp; Chorus; School Musical; Swing Chorus; High Hon Roll; Hon Roll; Orange Cnty HS Prfmng Arts Muscl Theatre; CSF Hnr Prog; GATE Prog; NYU; Drama.

VANDERHOOF, JENNIFER; San Pedro HS; San Pedro, CA; (3); Aud/Vis; JA; Teachers Aide; School Musical; School Play; Stage Crew; Score Keeper; Math.

VANDERSCHALIE, ANNE; Poway HS; San Diego, CA; (3); 3/761; Church Yth Grp; Sec German Clb; Library Aide; Ed Yrbk; NHS; CA Schlrshp Fdr; German.

VANDERSLOOT, DEREK J; San Ramon Valley HS; Danville, CA; (3); 40/415; Var Ftbl; Wt Lftg; High Hon Roll; Hon Roll; Orthopedic Srgn.

VANDERWALL, GREG S; Yucaipa HS; Yucaipa, CA; (2); Drama Clb; FCA; Capt JV Bsbl; Intrml Bsktbl; Intrml Socr; Hon Roll; Engrng.

VANDEVEN, JOANNA H; Mater Dei HS; Santa Ana, CA; (3); Church Yth Grp; Cmnty Wkr; French Clb; Hosp Aide; Ski Clb; Stat Bsktbl; JV Socr; Var Trk; Hon Roll; NHS; CA Schlrshp Federation.

VANDIVER, ROBYN; Valley HS; Sacramento, CA; (4); 8/450; Chess Clb; Debate Tm; Hist Drama Clb; English Clb; FTA; German Clb; JA; Service Clb; SADD; Thesps; CSF Sealbearer; Life Mem; Voted Most Likely To Become Hippie 90; Ensmbl Actg Awd; Lenaea Reg Thtr Fest; U CA Davis; Eng Ed.

VANG, AILEEN; Granada Hills HS; Los Angeles, CA; (2); FIDM; Interior Dsgn.

VANG, BLIA LE ANNE; Luther Burbank HS; Sacramento, CA; (2); School Musical; School Play; JV Swmmng; JV Vllybl; Hon Roll; Opt Clb Awd; Newcomers Clb; UC Santa Cruz.

VANG, BOUPHA LINDA; Duncan Polytechnical HS; Fresno, CA; (1); Church Yth Grp; DECA; FBLA; FFA; Girl Scts; Hosp Aide; Girl Scts; Library Aide; Math Clb; Math Tm; Fresno ST; Nrsng.

VANG, CHENG; Mc Lane HS; Fresno, CA; (4); 15/420; CSF; Southeast Asian Club; Fresno City Coll; Elec Engr.

VANG, CHER; Clovis HS; Fresno, CA; (1); Orch; Ballet & Typng; ABC; Orch.

VANG, CHIA; Edison HS; Fresno, CA; (1); Church Yth Grp; FTA; Intnl Clb; Hon Roll; CA Golden ST Exam Algebra I Rcgntn; UC Davis; Intr Dcrtr.

VANG, CHING; Luther Burbank HS; Sacramento, CA; (3); ROTC; Drill Tm; Var Wrstlng; High Hon Roll; Hon Roll; Asian Clb.

VANG, CHINOK; Edison HS; Fresno, CA; (3); Church Yth Grp; Intnl Clb; Socr; Tennis; Hon Roll; Finance.

VANG, CHONG; Mc Lane HS; Fresno, CA; (3); 37/460; French Clb; School Musical; Vllybl; Fresno ST CA; General Ed.

VANG, CHORNENG; River City HS; West Sacramento, CA; (3); 1/300; French Clb; Key Clb; Socr; Hon Roll; CSF; MESA; Multi Cult Club; Fri Night Club; Hmong Stu Assn Of Sacto; Hmong Pheng Com Org; SCC; Dntst.

VANG, CHOU; Edison HS; Fresno, CA; (1); Asian Clb; Arch.

VANG, DANG D; Duncan Polytechnical HS; Fresno, CA; (1); Pres Acad Fit Awd; Engl Exclince Mdl; World Cultres Exclince Cert; UC Davis; Doctor.

VANG, DAO V; Clovis HS; Clovis, CA; (2); 88/660; Intnl Clb; Vllybl; High Hon Roll; Hon Roll; Sect Asian Club; Human Relation Cncl; Engr Women; U Of CA San Francisco; Med.

VANG, FOUNG V; Edison-Computech HS; Fresno, CA; (2); 10/30; Church Yth Grp; JV Vllybl; Asian Club; Hmong Club; Art; UCLA.

VANG, FUA; Edison HS; Stockton, CA; (1); English Clb; Science Clb; JV Socr; Hon Roll; NHS; Spanish NHS; UC Davis; Phy.

VANG, GNIA; Merced HS; Merced, CA; (3); Intrml Socr; Hon Roll; Prfct Atten Awd; Yth Culture Clb; UTI; Electronics.

VANG, HUE; Clovis HS; Clovis, CA; (1); French Clb.

VANG, KAO N; Mc Lane HS; Fresno, CA; (4); 12/546; Pres Intnl Clb; Science Clb; Jazz Band; Mrchg Band; Cit Awd; High Hon Roll; Prfct Atten Awd; Mc Lder Schlrshp; CSF; Alpha & MESA; Fresno ST; Dentstry.

VANG, KONA; Hiram Johnson West Campus HS; Sacramento, CA; (3); 19/220; Rptr Nwsp; Cit Awd; Hon Roll; NHS; Culture Clb; Berkeley; Psych.

VANG, LO; Herbert Hoover HS; San Diego, CA; (1); French Clb; Prfct Atten Awd; UCSD; Med.

VANG, MAIZOUA; Grace M Davis HS; Modesto, CA; (2).

VANG, MAO; Banning HS; Fresno, CA; (2); Chess Clb; Spanish Clb; Var Socr; Var Tennis; Hon Roll; Asian-Amer Clb; CA Schlstc Fed; Bio.

VANG, MAY KIA; Foothill HS; North Highlands, CA; (1); Sec French Clb; Pres Frsh Cls; Pres Soph Cls; JV Cheerldng; Socr; High Hon Roll; Hon Roll; Opt Clb Awd; Schlsp Athlt Awd; Outstndng Achvmts Eng Awd Of Merit; Outstndng Stu Fr I Awd Of Merit; U CA Santa Barbara; Eng.

VANG, MENG S; Redwood HS; Visalia, CA; (2); French Clb; Science Clb; Rptr Nwsp; Hon Roll; Quill & Scroll Ntl Awd; CA Press Women Hs Jrnlsm Awd; CSF; Stanford; Med.

VANG, NA LEE; Edison HS; Stockton, CA; (2); Church Yth Grp; FTA; Science Clb; Service Clb; Hon Roll; U & Coll Opportunity; Alpine Clb; Tchrs Of Tomorrow; U Of The Pacific; Ped.

VANG, NENG; A A Stagg HS; Stockton, CA; (1); JV Socr; Hon Roll.

VANG, NHIA; Fountain Valley HS; Fountain Valley, CA; (3); Spanish Clb; Band; UCI; Med.

VANG, PAO; Edison HS; Fresno, CA; (4); Hosp Aide; High Hon Roll; Hon Roll; Asian Clb-Pres; U Of Davis; Psych.

VANG, PHONG; Atwater HS; Winton, CA; (1); High Hon Roll; CSF; Falcon Crest Awds; GSE Hnrs Alg; UC Berkeley.

VANG, PO; Oroville HS; Oroville, CA; (3); Var Socr; Chico ST; Doctor.

VANG, SEE; Grant Union HS; West Sacramento, CA; (2); Church Yth Grp; Cmnty Wkr; Debate Tm; Temple Yth Grp; Church Choir; Stu Cncl; Hon Roll; Prfct Atten Awd; English Clb; French Clb; HOBY Fnd Ldrshp Seminar; Upward Bound Pgm; Healds Coll; Missionary.

VANG, SO; Edison HS; Stockton, CA; (3); Boy Scts; Pres French Clb; VP Science Clb; SADD; Stu Cncl; Hon Roll; NHS; Badmintn Champ 90; Edison Sci Olympia Tm; Alpine Clb, Explorers Post; MIT; Electrnc Engrng.

VANG, SU B; Grant Union HS; Sacramento, CA; (4); Debate Tm; Intnl Clb; Speech Tm; Stu Cncl; Tennis; High Hon Roll; Hon Roll; Opt Clb Awd; Prfct Atten Awd; Stu Reaching Out; U Of Pacific; Intl Rltns.

VANG, THAI; Mc Lane HS; Fresno, CA; (3); FTA; SADD; Teachers Aide; School Musical; Lit Mag; Off Sr Cls; Vllybl; Hon Roll; Electrncs.

VANG, TOU C; Clovis HS; Fresno, CA; (3); Cit Awd; High Hon Roll; CSF; Asian Clb; Prncpls Hnr Rl Awd; Block C Awd; U Of Pacific; Doctor.

VANG, TOY M; San Diego HS; San Diego, CA; (3); 18/533; Cmnty Wkr; Crs Cntry; Cit Awd; Prfct Atten Awd; Schl Hnr PE; Hstry Club; CSF Club; UCSD; Bus.

VANG, VANG MAI; Roosevelt HS; Fresno, CA; (3); Church Yth Grp; Library Aide; Chorus; Church Choir; JV Vllybl; Cit Awd; Hon Roll; Prfct Atten Awd; Tchrs Tmrrow Clb Cmmssnr Actvts; Bus.

VANG, WA; Edison HS; Fresno, CA; (1); Med.

VANG, XENG; Roosevelt HS; Fresno, CA; (4); 13/600; Art Clb; Science Clb; Hon Roll; Yng Writers Conf; Writing Cont, Won William Saroyan Awd; U Fresno; Med.

VANG, YEE; Fresno HS; Fresno, CA; (1); Hon Roll; Prfct Atten Awd; SEA Club; CSU Fresno.

VANGANI, AKASH V; Irvine HS; Irvine, CA; (2); French Clb; High Hon Roll; Hon Roll; Hnrs On Golden St Alg Exam; Arntcl Engr.

VANHOORN, PETER; Lincoln HS; Stockton, CA; (3); 100/600; Spanish Clb; Bio Sci.

VANIER, ANDRE D; Gompers Secondary HS; San Diego, CA; (1); 1/280; Church Yth Grp; Math Tm; Scholastic Bowl; Science Clb; Treas Frsh Cls; Jr NHS; Opt Clb Awd; Sci Olympiad.

VANLOO, STEPHANIE L; Culver City HS; Culver City, CA; (1); Church Yth Grp; Hon Roll; Gldn St Exmntn Schlr Hnrs Alg; Psych.

VANN, PISITH P; San Pedro HS; San Pedro, CA; (3); Chess Clb; Office Aide; Hist Teachers Aide; Cit Awd; Hon Roll; Prfct Atten Awd; Pres Acad Fit Awd; Harbor Coll; Med.

VANNAVONG, SAENG; Patrick Henry HS; San Diego, CA; (3); FTA; Spanish Clb; Yrbk; Cit Awd; Hon Roll; NHS; Prfct Atten Awd; Pres Acad Fit Awd; Mbr Friday Nght Live Clb; Tchr.

VANNI, HEATHER N; Mt Shasta HS; Mount Shasta, CA; (2); Teachers Aide; Phtg Yrbk; Var Intrml Sftbl; High Hon Roll; CSF VP; Hnrs CA Gldn ST Exam; Ski Tm; Bus.

VANNORSDALL, ROSE M; Golden West HS; Ivanhoe, CA; (2); Debate Tm; French Clb; Intnl Clb; Math Clb; NFL; Var Trk; CSF; Athltc Congrss; Friday Night Live; Cal Poly San Luis Obispo; Arch.

VANSCOY, GENIE; Rio Mesa HS; Oxnard, CA; (1); Church Yth Grp; SADD; Capt Cheerldng; L Var Trk; Commnctns.

VANSON, LINDA N; Bolsa Grande HS; Garden Grove, CA; (2); 2/380; Math Clb; Science Clb; Sec Spanish Clb; Off Soph Cls; Rep Stu Cncl; JV Tennis; High Hon Roll; Jr NHS; U CA Berkeley; Law.

VANTA, LESLIE S; Montgomery HS; San Diego, CA; (3); 30/480; Cmnty Wkr; Hosp Aide; Band; Church Choir; Mrchg Band; Cit Awd; Hon Roll; Prfct Atten Awd; CSF; Golden St Exam Awd; U CA-SAN Diego; Med.

VANUS, GEORGE M; Montclair HS; Montclair, CA; (2); JV Bsbl; Hon Roll; AZ St; Bus Owner.

VAPLON, SARA M; Apple Valley HS; Apple Valley, CA; (3); 7/900; Church Yth Grp; Chorus; Off Frsh Cls; JV Bsktbl; Stat Ftbl; Powder Puff Ftbl; Capt L Sftbl; High Hon Roll; Acad Decathlon Tm; Stu Of Mnth; Bio.

VAR, RATHNA; Edison HS; Stockton, CA; (4); Chess Clb; Computer Clb; Teachers Aide; 4-H Awd; High Hon Roll; Hon Roll; 2 Yrs Cert Accmplshmnt.

VARADARAJAN, RANJANI; Torrey Pines HS; Solana Beach, CA; (3); Art Clb; Chess Clb; Church Yth Grp; Debate Tm; Intnl Clb; Key Clb; NFL; Speech Tm; Hon Roll; Opt Clb Awd; Animal Env Rights Act Clb; Yth Rep; Indian Classcl Music.

VARALLA, KYLEE B; Rim Of The World HS; Running Springs, CA; (1); 16/435; Debate Tm; JV Tennis; Hon Roll; Sch Rcgntn Algebra Golden St Exam; CJSF; Stanford U; Math.

VARCA, BRIAN E; Trabuco Hills HS; Mission Viejo, CA; (1); Bsbl; Socr; Hon Roll; NHS.

VAREAS, NELSON D; Baldwin Park HS; Baldwin Park, CA; (3); Var Ftbl; Var Trk; Wt Lftg; Hon Roll; Prfct Atten Awd.

VARELA, BRYAN; Palmdale HS; Agua Dulce, CA; (3); 4/650; FFA; Math Tm; VICA; JV Var Ftbl; JV Var Wt Lftg; JV Var Wrstlng; High Hon Roll; Hon Roll; Pres Acad Fit Awd; CSF; San Diego ST U; Grphc Arts.

VARELA, CARA M; Hueneme HS; Oxnard, CA; (2); Church Yth Grp; Drill Tm; Socr; Hon Roll; Tchng.

VARELA, RUTH; Cajon HS; San Bernardino, CA; (3); Church Yth Grp; School Play; Ed Yrbk; Treas Jr Cls; Sec Sr Cls; Kids Agnst Crime Yth Brd Of Dirs Secy; U San Diego; Intl Relations.

VARELA, YOLANDA; Eagle Rock HS; Los Angeles, CA; (2); Cmnty Wkr; Hosp Aide; Key Clb; Office Aide; JV Crs Cntry; JV Trk; Cit Awd; High Hon Roll; Hon Roll; Prfct Atten Awd; Hnr Stu; Stanford; OB/Gyn Doc.

VARELA, YVONNE T; Sunshine HS; San Francisco, CA; (3); Girl Scts; School Play; Stage Crew; Treas VP Jr Cls; Stu Cncl; Hon Roll; Prfct Atten Awd; Sec Soph Cls; Berkely Coll; Phys Thrpy.

VARGA, BARBARA K; Rancho Bernardo HS; San Diego, CA; (2); German Clb; U Of Southern CA; Langs.

VARGA, BRANDON L; Burbank HS; Burbank, CA; (3); Teachers Aide; Hon Roll; Stu Of Week Awd; Let Of Cmmndtn Phys Sci I Highst Grade; Burbank Mayors Cmmndtn Aux Fire Dept Ctzn Prg; Glendale CC; Math.

VARGAS, ALEJANDRA; Ontario HS; Ontario, CA; (3); 18/600; English Clb; French Clb; Key Clb; Math Clb; Varsity Clb; Chorus; Socr; Tennis; Trk; High Hon Roll; Ivy Chain; Civil Engr.

VARGAS, ANA B; East Nicolaus HS; Olivehurst, CA; (2); 12/42; Church Yth Grp; Cmnty Wkr; GAA; Letterman Clb; Pep Clb; Ski Clb; SADD; Varsity Clb; Yrbk; Hon Roll; MVP Track; Sac ST; Bus.

VARGAS, ANTONIO T; Tulare Western HS; Tulare, CA; (4); Var Bsbl; Capt Socr; Prfct Atten Awd; Bus Mrktng.

VARGAS, BARBARA L; Liberty Union HS; Oakley, CA; (2); 33/500; Hon Roll; Lawyer.

VARGAS, BERNADETTE M; Mater Dei HS; Anaheim, CA; (1); Church Yth Grp; JV Bsktbl; Stat Ftbl; JV Sftbl; Hon Roll; CSF; 2nd Pl ASA Natl Tourn; Notre Dame; Hstrn.

VARGAS, BRETT; Apple Valley HS; Apple Valley, CA; (3); Key Clb; Trk; Hon Roll; Loyola Maramount U; Psych.

VARGAS, CARLA L; El Dorado HS; Placentia, CA; (2); Drama Clb; Intnl Clb; Band; Mrchg Band; Pep Band; Off Frsh Cls; JV Stat Bsktbl; Stat Score Keeper; High Hon Roll; Hon Roll; Acad Decathln 1st Pl Lit; DARE Prgm; Csf; Soccer; UCLA; Psychlgy.

VARGAS, CINDY; Pomona Catholic HS; Baldwin Park, CA; (2); Church Yth Grp; GAA; Hosp Aide; Pep Clb; Cheerldng; Hon Roll; U Santa Barbara; Dermatology.

VARGAS, EDUARDO; J W North HS; Riverside, CA; (3); Med.

VARGAS, ERNESTO; Calexico HS; Calexico, CA; (3); Spanish Clb; Ftbl; Gldn St Exam Schl Rcgntn; Archt.

VARGAS, GEORGE M; Bonita Vista HS; Chula Vista, CA; (2); Model UN; Cit Awd; CSF 90; Wrld Tang Soo Do Karate Assn Green Blt; Engl As 2nd Lang Stu Aide Smmr Schl; U Of CA San Diego; Engrng.

VARGAS, GLADYS; Castle Park HS; Chula Vista, CA; (3); French Clb; Psych.

VARGAS, IRMA; Benjamin Franklin HS; Los Angeles, CA; (4); Church Yth Grp; Computer Clb; FTA; Chorus; Church Choir; Awd Tchrs Of Tomrrw Clb; Human Rights Clb; Yth Cmmnty Srvc; CSU; Comp Sci.

VARGAS, IVAN O; Bell Gardens HS; Bell Gardens, CA; (4); 17/530; Science Clb; Varsity Clb; Var L Bsktbl; Var L Ftbl; Hon Roll; Bnk Amer Awd; Ralph Whitey White Awd; U Of NV Las Vegas.

VARGAS, JASON; Bishop Amat Memorial HS; Upland, CA; (4); 25/425; Band; Jazz Band; Mrchg Band; Orch; Pep Band; High Hon Roll; Harvey Mudd Coll; Chem Engr.

VARGAS, JEFFREY R; St John Bosco HS; Los Alamitos, CA; (2); 50/230; Church Yth Grp; Ftbl; Var Socr; Hon Roll; Pro Sccr Plyr.

VARGAS, JUAN; Live Oak HS; Live Oak, CA; (3); 5/100; Teachers Aide; VP Jr Cls; Var L Bsbl; Var JV Ftbl; JV L Wrstlng; High Hon Roll; Hon Roll; Juvenile Just Cmmssnr; CSF; Engrng.

VARGAS, LISA; Del Oro HS; Newcastle, CA; (4); 13/250; Cmnty Wkr; GAA; Service Clb; Stu Cncl; JV Bsbl; Stat Ftbl; Var L Socr; Var L Tennis; High Hon Roll; Hon Roll.

VARGAS, M XIMENA; Glendale Adventist Acad; Glendale, CA; (2); 1/57; Hosp Aide; Office Aide; Teachers Aide; Rptr Nwsp; VP Frsh Cls; Sec Soph Cls; Var Bsktbl; JV Vllybl; NHS; UCLA; Medcl Phy.

VARGAS, MANUEL; East Bakersfield HS; Bakersfield, CA; (3); 11/441; Church Yth Grp; Capt Debate Tm; NFL; Speech Tm; Orch; Ed Nwsp; High Hon Roll; Hon Roll; Ntl Merit Ltr; CSF; MESA; St Stu Congrss Fnlst; Natl Forensics League Triple Ruby.

VARGAS, MARCELA F; Montebello HS; Montebello, CA; (1); Chorus; Swmmng; Hon Roll; Wtr Polo; Swm Tm; Lfgrd; JSA Lgsltv Offcr; Biolgst.

VARGAS, MARIA J; East Nicolaus HS; Rio Oso, CA; (3); 7/47; Church Yth Grp; FFA; Pep Clb; SADD; VP Frsh Cls; High Hon Roll; Prfct Atten Awd; 2nd Pl FFA Creed Cont; Word Prcssr.

VARGAS, MARK S; Kingsburg HS; Kingsburg, CA; (2); 1/170; Letterman Clb; Ski Clb; JV Bsktbl; Var Capt Crs Cntry; Var Trk; High Hon Roll; Rotary Awd; Hikng/Camping; Piano.

VARGAS, MARTHA E; Theodore Roosevelt HS; Los Angeles, CA; (3); French Clb; Key Clb; Pres Jr Cls; Pres Stu Cncl; Capt Cheerldng; Cit Awd; High Hon Roll; Rotary Awd; Media.

VARGAS, MOISES; Saint John Bosco HS; San Dimas, CA; (2); Letterman Clb; Library Aide; Office Aide; Varsity Clb; Var Trk; Var Wt Lftg; Hon Roll; The Outdoors Men Club; Med.

VARGAS, NATALIA; Watsonville HS; Watsonville, CA; (2); Cmnty Wkr; Hon Roll; Comp.

VARGAS, NELSON D; Baldwin Park HS; Baldwin Park, CA; (3); Var Ftbl; Var Trk; Wt Lftg; Hon Roll; Prfct Atten Awd.

VARGAS, PETER J; Oxnard HS; Oxnard, CA; (3); Var Bsbl; Var Ftbl; Var Swmmng; USC; Bus.

VARGAS, PHILLIP; Palm Desert HS; Palm Desert, CA; (4); Art Clb; Boy Scts; Church Yth Grp; Cmnty Wkr; English Clb; Teachers Aide; Band; Jazz Band; Mrchg Band; Golf; CA Arts; Animation.

VARGAS, REBECCA; Selma HS; Selma, CA; (3); 23/211; Math Clb; Science Clb; SADD; Color Guard; Hon Roll; Civil Engr.

VARGAS, REYNALDA; East Nicolaus HS; Olivehurst, CA; (4); 15/42; Drama Clb; Pep Clb; SADD; School Play; Nwsp; Yrbk; Sec Stu Cncl; Var Capt Bsktbl; Trk; Vllybl; All Leag Bsktbl; Yth Grp 4 Yrs; CSU; Civil Engrng.

VARGAS, RICARDO A; Bishop Montgomery HS; Torrance, CA; (4); Treas Jr Cls; Stu Cncl; Var L Crs Cntry; Var Trk; Hon Roll; Torrance Cty Yth Cncl; Natl Hspnc Merit Smfnlst; CA Schlstc Fdrtn; Tulane; Arch.

VARGAS JR, RICHARD; Montebello HS; Montebello, CA; (2); Boy Scts; VICA; JV Ftbl; JV Vllybl; Hon Roll; USC; Pharm.

VARGAS, RICK E; Baldwin Park HS; Baldwin Park, CA; (4); Bsktbl; Ftbl; Trk; Wt Lftg; Hon Roll; Prfct Atten Awd; Chrprctr.

VARGAS, RIGOBERTO; Alisal HS; Salinas, CA; (3); French Clb; FBLA; Varsity Clb; Var Crs Cntry; Var Socr; Var Trk; JV Wrstlng; Hon Roll; Prfct Atten Awd; MECHA; GATE Bilingual; Arch.

VARGAS, RUBEN; San Fernando HS; Pacoima, CA; (3); ROTC; Teachers Aide.

VARGAS, RUBY; Sierra Vista HS; El Monte, CA; (2); Church Yth Grp; Band; Color Guard; Rep Frsh Cls; High Hon Roll; Second Place School Academic Pentathalon In Science; Special Interest In Working With Children; U Of CA L A; Psychology.

VARGAS, SELENA; William Howard Taft HS; Los Angeles, CA; (3); Library Aide; Office Aide; Service Clb; Spanish Clb; Teachers Aide; UCLA; Psych.

VARGAS, STACEY K; Apple Valley HS; Apple Valley, CA; (1); Library Aide; School Play; Bsktbl; Vllybl; Cit Awd; High Hon Roll; Hon Roll; Drama.

VARGAS, TONIA I; Serra HS; San Diego, CA; (2); Church Yth Grp; Cmnty Wkr; Science Clb; Acpl Chr; Church Choir; School Musical; Rep Frsh Cls; JV Bsktbl; High Hon Roll; Hon Roll; Pres Acad Fit Awd; Miss OH Yth Conf 89; Miss Amer Coed Pageant St Fnlst; Criminal Law.

VARGAS, VERONICA; Ben Gardens HS; Commerce, CA; (3); Dance Clb; FCA; GAA; Pres Frsh Cls; Rep Stu Cncl; Powder Puff Ftbl; Score Keeper; Sftbl; Trk; Vllybl; ASB Asst Treas, Treas & Chief Of Justice.

VARGAS, XOCHITL TANYA; Bell Gardens HS; Bell, CA; (4); 18/528; Dance Clb; Pep Clb; Lit Mag; Rep Sr Cls; Stu Cncl; Var Cheerldng; Intrml Powder Puff Ftbl; Var Trk; JV Vllybl; Hon Roll; Supreme Ct; Gldn St Exm Geom; Ceramic Crfts; UCLA.

VARGUS, TERRI; Orestimba HS; Newman, CA; (4); 4/64; Church Yth Grp; VP Letterman Clb; VP SADD; Pres Band; Drm Mjr(t); Jazz Band; VP Sr Cls; Rep Stu Cncl; Var Capt Bsktbl; Var Capt Sftbl; John Philips Souza Music Awd; Semper Fidelis Awd; Humbolt ST U; Frstry.

VARIAS, EDWARD N; Bellflower HS; Bellflower, CA; (2); 19/341; Hist Drama Clb; Hist Thesps; Pres Chorus; School Musical; School Play; Stage Crew; Pres High Hon Roll; Hon Roll; 33rd Dist PTA Scndry Conf 90; CSF; US Fncng Assn; CAL Long Bch.

VARNEDOE, KRISTEN; Concord HS; Concord, CA; (2); Church Yth Grp; Pep Clb; SADD; Chorus; Var Cheerldng; Cit Awd; Hon Roll; Cal Poly; Teaching.

VARNER, CHERI; Huntingfton Beach HS; Huntington Beach, CA; (1); Astronomer.

VARNER, DONNA J; Bishop Amat Memorial HS; Glendora, CA; (2); Church Yth Grp; Cmnty Wkr; Dance Clb; French Clb; Office Aide; Drill Tm; High Hon Roll; Hon Roll; HOBY Smnr 90.

VARNER, WILLY K; Gladstone HS; Azusa, CA; (3); Am Leg Boys St; Boy Scts; SADD; Chorus; VP Stu Cncl; JV Var Ftbl; JV Var Vllybl; Wt Lftg; Hon Roll; JR Statesman Of Amer; Brighan Young U; Comm Artist.

VARNEY, SHANNON L; Miramonte HS; Moraga, CA; (3); Church Yth Grp; Drama Clb; JCL; Latin Clb; NFL; Speech Tm; School Play; Vllybl; Hon Roll; Jr NHS; Mock Trial Club; Boston U; Commnctns.

VAROS, KIM RENEE; Schurr HS; Monterey Park, CA; (2); Church Yth Grp; Girl Scts; Art Clb; JV Trk; JV Vllybl; Hon Roll; Yale; Pedtrcn.

VARTANIAN, ARIANE S; Apple Valley SR HS; Apple Valley, CA; (3); FFA; Trk; Cit Awd; Hon Roll; Comp Engrng.

VARTANIAN, ERIK; Cupertino HS; San Jose, CA; (2); Church Yth Grp; Art Clb; Beginning Chem Algb II Trig & Pre-Calculus; UC Berkeley; Med DR.

VARTANIAN, JOSEPH; Saint Francis HS; Sierra Madre, CA; (2); Math Clb; Nwsp; JV Bsktbl; JV Trk; Hon Roll; Spanish NHS; CSF; 1st Pl Microbio Schl Sci Fair & Pasadena Area Fair; Stanford U; Med Doc.

VARUGHESE, BINDHU; Rio Mesa HS; Camarillo, CA; (3); 15/369; Church Yth Grp; FCA; Key Clb; Varsity Clb; Bsktbl; Tennis; Trk; Hon Roll.

VASCONCELLOS, MICHAEL J; American HS; Fremont, CA; (2); 100/385; Quiz Bowl; Science Clb; Hon Roll; Prfct Atten Awd; Explorers Engrng Grp; U Of CA Davis; Physicist.

VASCONEZ, VANESSA MARIA; Saint Genevieve HS; N Hollywood, CA; (4); Teachers Aide; Drill Tm; Hon Roll; U Southern CA; Engrng.

VASH, KIMBERLY; Saddleback HS; Santa Ana, CA; (1); English Clb; SADD; Hon Roll; Prncpls Awd; CA ST Long Beach; Psych.

VASQUEZ, ADRIAN; Coachella Valley HS; Mecca, CA; (3); JV Var Socr; Prfct Atten Awd; St Marys; Comp Engr.

VASQUEZ, ADRIANA; San Benito HS; Hollister, CA; (1); Church Yth Grp; Color Guard; Astronomy.

VASQUEZ, ALEJANDRO; Garfield Computer Sci Magnet HS; Los Angeles, CA; (2); Chess Clb; School Play; L Trk; UCLA; Bus.

VASQUEZ, ANA; El Camino Real HS; Los Angeles, CA; (3); Art; Wrtng; Bus Admin.

VASQUEZ, ANA B; Bell HS; Maywood, CA; (3); Latin Clb; Pep Clb; Drill Tm; Hon Roll; U CA LA; Sociologist.

VASQUEZ, ANDRE J; Fillmore HS; Fillmore, CA; (1); Church Yth Grp; FCA; Science Clb; JV Bsktbl; JV Ftbl; Wt Lftg; Cit Awd; Hon Roll; Prfct Atten Awd; Pres Acad Fit Awd; Bst Defensive Plyr Bsktbl; CSUC.

VASQUEZ, ANDREA; Washington Union HS; Fresno, CA; (3); 9/170; Am Leg Aux Girls St; FBLA; Intnl Clb; Treas Band; Mrchg Band; Pep Band; Treas Soph Cls; Stu Cncl; Mgr(s); Score Keeper; U Of CA Davis; Law.

VASQUEZ, ANN MARIE; Hueneme HS; Port Hueneme, CA; (2); Hon Roll; Hnr Circle; Engr.

VASQUEZ, CHRISTINE; Bishop Amat HS; Azusa, CA; (4); Drama Clb; Varsity Clb; School Play; Stage Crew; Yrbk; Sftbl; Cmmnctns.

VASQUEZ, CLAUDIA M; Los Banos HS; Los Banos, CA; (3); AFS; FBLA; Stu Cncl; JV Trk; Hon Roll; Bst Bus Drssd, Mst Cnfdnce Awd Bsc Occptnl Bus Skll Cls; UC Davis; Bus.

VASQUEZ, DANIELA; Bell Gardens HS; Bell Gardens, CA; (2); Drill Tm; Prfct Atten Awd; Cal ST Long Beach; Bus.

VASQUEZ, EDWARD R; Willits HS; Willits, CA; (2); Socr; Swmmng; Wrstlng; Pr Cnslng; UCLA; Bus.

VASQUEZ, IVAN; Bellarmine College Prep; San Jose, CA; (3); 74/300; Cmnty Wkr; Debate Tm; Elem Tutor; Natl Hispnc Schlr Awd Pgm Sem Fnlst; Engrng.

VASQUEZ, JASON M; Santa Maria HS; Santa Maria, CA; (4); 2/385; Teachers Aide; JV Socr; Hon Roll; Sal; Tp 10 Stu Awd 1987-89; CSF 1987-88; CA Poly U; Mech Engr.

VASQUEZ, JERICO M; North Hollywood HS; North Hollywood, CA; (3); Acpl Chr; Chorus; Cit Awd; High Hon Roll; Hon Roll; Sthrn CA Piano Schlrshp 89; 31st Dist PTSA Piano Schlrshp 89-91; Musical Amer Madrigals Accmpnst; U CA Santa Barbara; Music.

VASQUEZ, JOSE M; San Pedro HS; San Pedro, CA; (3); Art Clb; Letterman Clb; Spanish Clb; Varsity Clb; Off Sr Cls; JV Bsbl; JV Var Ftbl; Wt Lftg; Commodr/Svc Clb Stu Gd Ctznshp, Acad Grds; Acad Al-Str; UCLA; Frfghtr.

VASQUEZ, JOSEPH D; Rosemead HS; Rosemead, CA; (2); JV Wrstlng; US Congrssnl Page 90; US Naval Acad; Poltcl Sci.

VASQUEZ, LILIA; Castle Park HS; Chula Vista, CA; (4); 33/320; Office Aide; Pres SADD; Yrbk; Rep Sr Cls; Hon Roll; Trojan Knght VP; San Diego ST U; Pltcl Sci.

VASQUEZ, LILY J; Antelope Valley HS; Lancaster, CA; (4); Cit Awd; Hon Roll; Prfct Atten Awd; Stu Of Wk; Arch.

VASQUEZ, LISA; Mountain View HS; Mountain View, CA; (4); 91/260; Dance Clb; Pep Clb; Teachers Aide; Rep Stu Cncl; JV Cheerldng; Var Gym; Hon Roll; Santa Clara U; Cmbnd Sci.

VASQUEZ, MARIA E; Fontana HS; Fontana, CA; (3); Band; Treas Mrchg Band; JV Bsktbl; Var L Crs Cntry; Var Trk; JV Vllybl; Hon Roll; Prfct Atten Awd; Achvt Awd 1st & 2nd Smstr Gold Mdl, Daisy Chain 89-90; U Of CA Riverdale; Biomed Engr.

VASQUEZ, MARLINA R; Vista West North HS; Bakersfield, CA; (3); Church Yth Grp; GAA; Library Aide; Model UN; Office Aide; Spanish Clb; Teachers Aide; Band; Chorus; Bsktbl; Psych.

VASQUEZ, MARYANN M; Brawley Union HS; Brawley, CA; (2); Church Yth Grp; Pep Clb; Band; Mrchg Band; High Hon Roll; Hon Roll; Friday Night Live; Imperial Valley Cmnty Band; Phy.

VASQUEZ, MICHAEL A; Baldwin Park HS; Baldwin Pk, CA; (1); Mrchg Band; Pep Band; Hon Roll; 1st Pl Fine Arts, 2nd Pl Engl Schl Vlvl Acad Penthln; Symphnc Band; Yale U; Law.

VASQUEZ, MIKE E; Mater Dei HS; Santa Ana, CA; (2); Ski Clb; JV Ftbl; Intrml Socr; Var Wt Lftg; JV Wrstlng; High Hon Roll; UC Santa Cruz; Commnctns.

VASQUEZ, OLIVER J; Granada Hills HS; Northridge, CA; (2); Yrbk; Stat Bsktbl; Stat Tennis; Hon Roll.

VASQUEZ, PATRICK; Richard Gahr HS; Cerritos, CA; (1); Intnl Clb; Spanish Clb; Band; Jazz Band; JV Bsbl; JV Crs Cntry; Var Socr; Var Tennis; Cit Awd; High Hon Roll; Stock Market Awds; U NV Las Vegas; Math.

VASQUEZ, PEDRO JAMES; Escondido HS; Escondido, CA; (4); 27/330; Church Yth Grp; Dance Clb; Pres Drama Clb; School Play; Rep Frsh Cls; Rep Soph Cls; Rep Jr Cls; Treas Sr Cls; Crs Cntry; High Hon Roll; CSF Life Stu; Harold/Mimi Steinberg Schlrshp-Juilliard Schl; Yth Ldrshp Camp Cnslr; Juilliard Schl; Dramatic Arts.

VASQUEZ, RAUL; Arroyo Grande HS; Oceano, CA; (2); 217/625; Cal Poly San Luis Obispo Upwrd Bnd Pgm; San Francisco ST U; Brdcstng.

VASQUEZ, RAUL; Tulare Western HS; Tulare, CA; (4); Church Yth Grp; Debate Tm; Rep Sr Cls; Rep Stu Cncl; Ftbl; Socr; Sequoias Coll; Comp Prgmr.

VASQUEZ, ROBERT E; Hanford Joint Union HS; Hanford, CA; (2); 74/350; Art Clb; Bus Profs of Am; FBLA; Science Clb; Band; Jazz Band; Mrchg Band; Tennis; U CA Davis; Bus.

VASQUEZ, ROSARIO; Western HS; Tulare, CA; (2); Color Guard; Flag Corp; Hon Roll; UCSB; Sci.

VASQUEZ, RUBEN J; North Salinas HS; Salinas, CA; (2); Church Yth Grp; Spanish Clb; Bsbl; Bsktbl; Ftbl; Hon Roll; MVP Bsbl 90 Tm; Mst Imprvd Bsktbl Plyr; AZ ST U; Law.

VASQUEZ, SULY J; Antelope Valley HS; Lancaster, CA; (4); Cit Awd; Hon Roll; Opt Clb Awd; Pres Acad Fit Awd; Stu Wk; Med.

VASQUEZ, TIMOTHY; Yucca Valley HS; Yucca Valley, CA; (3); Math Clb; Teachers Aide; Drill Tm; CA Cadet Corps; Cadet Brigade Commander; Intl Clb; Helicopter Pilot.

VASQUEZ, VIRGINIA; Baldwin Park HS; Baldwin Park, CA; (3); Rep Jr Cls; Var JV Cheerldng; Var Capt Pom Pon; Hon Roll; Rep; Lgl Scrtry.

VASQUEZ, ZAIDA M; Venice HS; Venice, CA; (3); Teachers Aide; Chorus; Flag Corp; VP Sr Cls; Cit Awd; Athenians-Ctznshp Schlrshp & Svc To Schl; Pblc/Bus Rltns.

VASS, CHRISTOPHER D; Pioneer HS; San Jose, CA; (2); JV Ftbl; Var Tennis; Ftbl Pioneer Pride Awd, Most Imprvd.

VASTINE, JACOB A; Piedmont HS; Piedmont, CA; (3); Band; Jazz Band; Pep Band; School Musical; Var Swmmng; Hon Roll; Ski Tm; Engrng.

VATASESCU, ROXANE; Newport Christian HS; Laguna Beach, CA; (2); 1/20; Rep Soph Cls; Stu Cncl; Stat Var Bsktbl; Var Vllybl; High Hon Roll; 1st Pl Sci Fair Chem.

VATER, KRISTENA; Lincoln HS; Stockton, CA; (3); Church Yth Grp; Ski Clb; SADD; Sec Band; Church Choir; Jazz Band; Mrchg Band; Orch; Socr; High Hon Roll; Cntry Hnr Band; JR Musician; Outstndng Intr Dsgn Stu; UC San Diego; Bus.

VATH, THAVARO; Modesto HS; Salida, CA; (2); Phtg Yrbk; JV Bsktbl; JV Ftbl; JV Var Trk; Hon Roll; Prfct Atten Awd; MVP Bsktbl; Mst Outstndng Track Awd; Fresno ST; Engr.

VATTANATHAM, PITUCK; Pilgrim Schl; Walnut, CA; (3); Cmnty Wkr; Library Aide; Model UN; Yrbk; Sec Frsh Cls; Sec Soph Cls; Sec Jr Cls; Var Bsbl; Var Ftbl; Cit Awd; Art Awd 90; Pilgrim Acad Soc; Arch.

VAUGHAN, AIMEE L; Tehachapi HS; Tehachapi, CA; (1); FBLA; Piano; CA ST U Bakersfield; Accntng.

VAUGHAN, DYLAN J; San Dieguito HS; Encinitas, CA; (2); 103/650; JV Bsbl; Piano 10 Yrs; Sccr; Aviation.

VAUGHAN, KELLI L; Oakridge HS; El Dorado Hills, CA; (2); 59/250; Teachers Aide; Pres Acad Fit Awd; UC Davis; Med.

VAUGHN, JASON L; Chaffey HS; Ontario, CA; (3); Bsktbl; Hon Roll; CSF.

VAUGHN, JENNY A; School Of Creative & Perfrming Arts; San Diego, CA; (2); Church Yth Grp; Cmnty Wkr; Dance Clb; Letterman Clb; Spanish Clb; SADD; Chorus; Church Choir; School Musical; Hon Roll.

VAUGHN, KARI L; Atwater HS; Atwater, CA; (3); Church Yth Grp; Var Cheerldng; High Hon Roll; Ofcr Friday Night Live; Pres, VP & Treas CSF; Pediatrician.

VAUGHN, STEVE R; Yosemite Union HS; Oakhurst, CA; (2); Church Yth Grp; Varsity Clb; Bsbl; Ftbl; Cuesta; Forestry.

VAUGHN, STEVEN M; Will C Wood HS; Vacaville, CA; (2); Boy Scts; Science Clb; Teachers Aide; Mgr Stage Crew; Crs Cntry; Hon Roll; Lion Awd; NHS; Schlstc All Amer Schlr Dir 88; UC Davis; Med.

VAUGHN, TASHA; Palm Springs HS; Palm Springs, CA; (2); Office Aide; SADD; Temple Yth Grp; School Play; Rep Frsh Cls; Rep Stu Cncl; JV Bsktbl; Hon Roll; BTY; Socialogist.

VAUGHT, JOHN M; University HS; Irvine, CA; (3); Spanish Clb; Bsbl; CA ST San Luis Obispo; Arch.

VAZ, ALICIA N; Louisville HS; Westlake Village, CA; (1); Science Clb; Chorus; Cheerldng; High Hon Roll; Prfct Atten Awd; In The California Scholarship Federation Club Recieved First Place Scholarship Of 100000; Ucla; Pediatrician.

VAZQUEZ, ALMA L; Bloomington HS; Bloomington, CA; (3); Cmnty Wkr; Teachers Aide; Yrbk; Powder Puff Ftbl; Blood Dr; Toys For Tots; Ldrshp; San Bernadino CC; Bookkeeper.

VAZQUEZ, CHRISTINA NOEL; Bishop Amat HS; Rowland Hts, CA; (3); Spanish Clb; Color Guard; Flag Corp; High Hon Roll; Hon Roll; NHS; CSF; Creatve Wrtng Clb.

VAZQUEZ, DARIO; Corona SR HS; Corona, CA; (1); Bsbl; Hon Roll; USC; Comm Engr.

VAZQUEZ, EDITH; Garfield HS; Los Angeles, CA; (3); Math Clb; Ntl Merit Ltr; Prfct Atten Awd; A P Hstry; Hnrs Engl; Scalentes Pgm; Chld Psych.

VAZQUEZ, FEDERICO; San Dieguito HS; Cardiff, CA; (3); Spanish Clb; Band; School Play; Mira Costa Coll; Electronic.

VAZQUEZ, LILA E; Rubidoux HS; Mira Loma, CA; (4); AFS; German Clb; Spanish Clb; School Play; Stage Crew; Variety Show; Sftbl; Hon Roll; Model Cngrs; Mck Trl; Rvrsd CC; Pre-Med.

VAZQUEZ, LUCERO G; Benjamin Franklin HS; Los Angeles, CA; (3); Cit Awd; Cert Adm Regn Fstvl; CA ST; Lib Arts.

VAZQUEZ, MARIA T; Bell Gardens HS; Bell Gardens, CA; (3); Art Clb; Church Yth Grp; Cmnty Wkr; Teachers Aide; Church Choir; Prfct Atten Awd; UCSB; Art Teacher.

VAZQUEZ, MONICA A; St Joseph HS; Cypress, CA; (3); Cmnty Wkr; Spanish Clb; Church Choir; Hon Roll.

VAZQUEZ, RAFAEL E; Glen A Wilson HS; Hacienda Hts, CA; (3); Art Clb; Boy Scts; Teachers Aide; Band; Jazz Band; Mrchg Band; Orch; Pep Band; Gov Hon Prg Awd.

VAZQUEZ, VIRNA; Roosevelt HS; Los Angeles, CA; (4); 19/800; Hon Roll; Bank Of Amer Achvt Awd; Hstry Day L A Cert Of Achvt; Board Of Ed Achvt Awd; Cal ST Los Angeles; Med.

VBARRA JR, FRANCISCO; Riverdale Jt Union HS; Riverdale, CA; (4); 5/78; Cmnty Wkr; FHA; Treas Intnl Clb; Office Aide; SADD; Rep Yrbk; VP Sr Cls; Rep Stu Cncl; High Hon Roll; Hon Roll; CA ST U Fresno; Pre-Med.

VEAL, CARRIE K; Gardena HS; Los Angeles, CA; (2); Church Yth Grp; Latin Clb; JV Bsktbl; JV Trk; MESA; Comp Engr.

VEAL, JIM; Tomales HS; Inverness, CA; (3); High Hon Roll; Hon Roll; JV Var Bsbl; Cert Of Hnr, Outstndng Achvt,Most Inproved/Best Defense-Jr.baseball.

VEALE, KIM L; Nevada Union HS; Nevada City, CA; (2); Cmnty Wkr; 4-H; GAA; SADD; Chorus; School Play; Stu Cncl; Bsktbl; Mgr(s); Score Keeper; Friday Nite Live County Rep; Engl Teacher.

VEEDER, SCOTT R; La Habra HS; La Habra, CA; (3); Science Clb; Var L Bsbl; JV Var Bsktbl; Vrsty Bsbl Freeway Leag Coachs-All Leag Tm & Coachs Awd 89-90; Pitchd 2 Shut Outs; CA ST Fullerton; Game Warden.

VEENSTRA, JENNIFER R; Fresno Christian HS; Fresno, CA; (3); Church Yth Grp; Drama Clb; Office Aide; Pep Clb; Chorus; Stu Cncl; JV Bsktbl; Capt Var Powder Puff Ftbl; JV Var Vllybl; Hon Roll; Extensivly Involved Crch Actvs Bible Schl Teacher/Nrs; Cnclng JR High Stu; Fresno ST U; Ind Tech & Arts.

VEERKAMP, WENDY L; El Dorado HS; Placerville, CA; (3); Church Yth Grp; Teachers Aide; Church Choir; High Hon Roll; Pres Acad Fit Awd; Sacramento City Coll; Dentist.

VEGA, BENJAMIN A; Workman HS; La Puente, CA; (3); 2/264; Intnl Clb; Letterman Clb; Science Clb; Spanish Clb; Ed Nwsp; Pres Frsh Cls; Pres Soph Cls; Pres Stu Cncl; Pom Pon; Var L Swmmng; Vrsty Ltr Polo 2nd Team All Lgu; Hugh O'brian Yth Ldrshp Schlrshp; Stanford U; Law.

VEGA, CARISSA E; Louisville HS; Calabasas, CA; (1); Church Yth Grp; High Hon Roll.

VEGA, EVA; Rio Mesa HS; Oxnard, CA; (3); Church Yth Grp; FTA; Office Aide; Spanish Clb; JV Swmmng; Cit Awd; Peer Helprs Pgm; Peer Hlprs Pgm Advsr; Cal Lutheran U; Schl Cnslr.

VEGA, FRANK; Capistrano Valley HS; San Juan Capistra, CA; (3); Am Leg Boys St; FBLA; JV Bsbl; Bus Adm.

VEGA, GABRIEL; Schurr HS; Monterey Park, CA; (1); Church Yth Grp; Teachers Aide; Crs Cntry; Trk; Pepperdine; Arch.

VEGA, GABRIELA K; Bolsa Grande HS; Garden Grove, CA; (2); 123/377; Spanish Clb; Yrbk; Hon Roll; Acadmc Achvt; U CA Irvine; Lawyer.

VEGA, JORGE L; Live Oak HS; Live Oak, CA; (3); FFA; Spanish Clb; Bsktbl; Tennis; Sacramento ST; Phys Thrpst.

VEGA, JOSE L; Dos Palos HS; Dos Palos, CA; (3); Crs Cntry; Trk; Wrstlng; Hon Roll; Bus Mgmt.

VEGA, MARIO A; St Francis HS; Redwood City, CA; (1); 155/388; Temple Yth Grp; Ftbl; Wt Lftg; Wrstlng; UC Berkeley; Bus.

VEGA, MICHAEL A; Herbert Hoover HS; Fresno, CA; (3); Hosp Aide; Latin Clb; Letterman Clb; Spanish Clb; Varsity Clb; Intrml Bsbl; Var L Bsktbl; JV Ftbl; Intrml Socr; Intrml Sftbl; Mecha Club VP 88-89; CSF 89-91; Stnfrd Med Yth Sci Pgm 90; Stanford U; Elec Engr.

VEGA, OLGA; Calexico HS; El Centro, CA; (1); Off Frsh Cls; Hon Roll; Camarena Clb; Cmptr Sci.

VEGA, OMAR; Bloomington HS; Bloomington, CA; (2); High Hon Roll; NHS; MECHA; Friday Nite Live; Comm.

VEGA, RISHELLINE; Upland HS; Upland, CA; (3); Cmnty Wkr; Dance Clb; GAA; Girl Scts; Model UN; JV Tennis; CSF; Ldrshp Cmmtte; Comp Engr.

VEGA-FOSTER, JEFFREY A; Fred C Beyer HS; Modesto, CA; (3); JV Ftbl; JV Wrstlng; HS Patriot Awd Span; Cal Poly San Luis Obispo; Arch.

VEI, LIN C; Balsa Grande HS; Garden Grove, CA; (3); 24/350; Cmnty Wkr; Math Clb; Science Clb; Spanish Clb; Speech Tm; Var Trk; Hon Roll; CSF; UC San Diego; Dntl.

VEITZMAN, ANNA; San Marcos HS; San Marcos, CA; (3); 47/399; Art Clb; French Clb; Intnl Clb; Library Aide; Temple Yth Grp; High Hon Roll; Acadmc Excellence Awd; Hnr 1st Yr Algebra 89; Cert Of Recog Outstndng Stu Art 89; Acadmc Awd CSF 90; UCSD.

VEIZAGA, CHRISTOPHER R; Crawford HS; San Diego, CA; (2); Church Yth Grp; Key Clb; Doctor.

VEJAR, CARLOS J; Tulare Union HS; Tulare, CA; (3); 26/401; Church Yth Grp; Spanish Clb; SADD; Stage Crew; Variety Show; Rep Soph Cls; JV Bsbl; Capt Bsktbl; Hon Roll; Prfct Atten Awd; MECHA Clb VP; CSF; Friday Night Live; Chicano Latin Yth Ldrshp Conf Delg; Teenwork 90 Conf; Notre Dame U; Aerospace Engr.

VEJAR, OLGA L; Notre Vista HS; Riverside, CA; (1); Hon Roll; Tchr.

VELA, CHRISTINA M; John H Francis Polytechincal HS; Sun Valley, CA; (3); Teachers Aide; Co-Ed Yrbk; U CA Santa Barb; Child Psych.

VELA, GIOVANNI F; Pinole HS; Pinole, CA; (2); Socr; Law.

VELA, LOURDES L; Abraham Lincoln HS; Los Angeles, CA; (3); Drama Clb; Hon Roll; Psych.

VELA, MAYRA; Victor Valley HS; Victorville, CA; (3); Church Choir; Stwrtst.

VELA, VANESSA; Ernest Righetti HS; Santa Maria, CA; (4); 1/356; Pres VP Church Yth Grp; Pres VP 4-H; Math Clb; Ski Clb; Church Choir; JV Trk; Elks Awd; 4-H Awd; Hon Roll; ASB Dir Pettns; Jazz/Ballet; LIFE CSF; UC Davis; Humn Dev.

VELA, VERONICA D; Simi Valley HS; Simi Valley, CA; (2); 202/753; Drama Clb; Spanish Clb; Thesps; Drill Tm; School Musical; Variety Show; Co-Ed Nwsp; Amnsty Intl; Bilingual.

VELARDE, THOMAS G; Montclair HS; Ontario, CA; (2); 40/358; Chess Clb; Var Stat Bsktbl; Var Stat Sftbl; GATE Club; Environmental Club; Aerospace Engr.

VELASCO, JAVIER; Schurr HS; Los Angeles, CA; (1); Ftbl; Wt Lftg; Photography Class 4 Honorable Mentions; Field In Photography.

VELASCO JR, JESUS; Leuzinger HS; Inglewood, CA; (3); Police Officer.

VELASCO, JOSE J; Senior HS; Mc Farland, CA; (3); English Clb; Teachers Aide; Yrbk; Cit Awd; High Hon Roll; Hon Roll; Most Outstndng Advncd Wdshp Stu; Bakersfield Coll; Comp Prgrmmr.

VELASCO, LEO; Montclair HS; Ontario, CA; (1); Bsbl; Bsktbl; Ftbl; Wt Lftg; Prfct Atten Awd; Outstndng Stu Awd; UCLA.

VELASCO, LILIBETH J; Lowell HS; San Francisco, CA; (2); Red Cross Aide; SADD; Vllybl Clb; CA Schlrshp Fed; Acad Excllnc Awd Hnrs; Accntng.

VELASCO, MANUEL R; Chino HS; Chino, CA; (1); Band; Color Guard; Mrchg Band; Pep Band; Cit Awd; Hon Roll; Ntl Merit Ltr; Prfct Atten Awd; Pres Schlr; Gymnastics; Study Hstry Olympic Games; U CA Berkeley; Soc Sci.

VELASCO, MARIA J; James A Garfield HS; Los Angeles, CA; (3); French Clb; Teachers Aide; Actress-Futures Series; Interact; Pepperdine U; Bus Admin.

VELASCO, MARICELA; Mc Farland HS; Mc Farland, CA; (3); English Clb; FHA; Math Clb; Teachers Aide; Rptr Yrbk; Cit Awd; Hon Roll; Pres Schlr; CSF.

VELASCO, MARILYN A; Lowell HS; San Francisco, CA; (2); SADD.

VELASQUEZ, DELILAH T; Alta Loma HS; Alta Loma, CA; (2); Church Yth Grp; Spanish Clb; SADD; Stat Ftbl; Stat Wrstlng; Hon Roll; Prfct Atten Awd; Loma Linda U; Ped.

VELASQUEZ, EDWIN; Calvin Simmons HS; Oakland, CA; (3); Latin Clb; Math Clb; Spanish Clb; Yrbk; Stu Cncl; Bsktbl; Vllybl; Cit Awd; High Hon Roll; Hon Roll.

VELASQUEZ, GLORIA G; Mission HS; San Francisco, CA; (2); Girl Scts; Office Aide; ROTC; Teachers Aide; Chorus; Drill Tm; Yrbk; High Hon Roll; Bus.

VELASQUEZ, HAZEL C; John A Rowland HS; Rowland Hts, CA; (4); Hosp Aide; Science Clb; Spanish Clb; Vlntr-Red Cross; Yth Vlntr; Irvine CA U; Bio-Sci.

VELASQUEZ, JENNIFER; John F Kennedy HS; La Palma, CA; (4); Am Leg Aux Girls St; Church Yth Grp; Cmnty Wkr; Office Aide; Teachers Aide; Church Choir; Pres Jr Cls; High Hon Roll; Val; Goldn St Math Exam Awd, Geom; U Irvine; Pediatrics.

VELASQUEZ, JESSE M; Glendale Adventist Acad; Los Angeles, CA; (3); 20/57; Off Soph Cls; Arch.

VELASQUEZ JR, JOHN; Bellarmine Jefferson HS; Burbank, CA; (1); Hon Roll; Burbank City Soccer; Stu Of Mnth Awd; UCLA; Engr.

VELASQUEZ, LAURA Y; Pittsburg HS; Pittsburg, CA; (2); Office Aide; SADD; Teachers Aide; L Sftbl; L Wt Lftg; Cit Awd; Lawyer.

VELASQUEZ, LILIANA; Highland HS; Dixon, CA; (1); Drama Clb; ROTC; Yrbk; Swmmng; Cit Awd; Drama.

VELASQUEZ, MARIA E; Sacred Heart Of Jesus HS; Los Angeles, CA; (2); Hon Roll; NHS; Prfrm Folklorico Dance Dance; Specl Intrst Drawing & Sketching; UCLA; Bus.

VELASQUEZ, MARIA J; Leuzinger HS; Hawthorne, CA; (3); Spanish Clb; Teachers Aide; Prfct Atten Awd.

VELASQUEZ, MARIA J; Sacred Heart Of Jesus HS; Los Angeles, CA; (2); Office Aide; Hon Roll; UCLA; Psych.

VELASQUEZ, OSWALDO A; Downtown Business Magnet; Los Angeles, CA; (2); Church Yth Grp; Crs Cntry; Sftbl; Cert Of Excllnce Comp; YMCA Teen Ftnss Pgm; UCLA.

VELASQUEZ, RHODORA O; James Logan HS; Union City, CA; (4); Church Yth Grp; SADD; Sec Band; Mrchg Band; Variety Show; Stu Cncl; Cheerldng; Pom Pon; High Hon Roll; Pres Acad Fit Awd; Ldrshp Clss; Seone James Most Outstnd Stu; DARE Pgm; U Of CA San Diego; Surgeon.

VELASQUEZ, VERONICA; King City HS; Greenfield, CA; (2); 4-H; Cit Awd; High Hon Roll; Hon Roll; Pres Acad Fit Awd; UC Davis; Sci/Math.

VELAZQUEZ, ELIA I; Sierra Vista HS; Baldwin Park, CA; (3); Math Clb; Band; Mrchg Band; Swmmng; Trk; Hon Roll; Cal Poly.

VELAZQUEZ, FLAVIO J; Sierra Vista HS; Baldwin Park, CA; (4); High Hon Roll; Hon Roll; CA Poly; Engrng.

VELAZQUEZ, LETICIA; Mar Vista HS; San Ysidro, CA; (1); Dance Clb; Debate Tm; Quiz Bowl; Band; Jazz Band; Mrchg Band; Pep Band; Swmmng; Cit Awd; Hon Roll; UCSD; Gynclgst.

VELAZQUEZ, MARIA ELENA; Santa Ynez Valley Union HS; Solvang, CA; (3); Church Yth Grp; Drama Clb; Spanish Clb; Band; Chorus; Sec Mrchg Band; School Musical; Jazz Choir; Coord Cncl Scl Stds Awd 88-89; Network For Drug Free Yth; Yth To Yth; U Of CA; Span Ed.

VELENCIA, FRANK; San Pedro HS; Los Angeles, CA; (4); Cmnty Wkr; Rep Frsh Cls; Bsktbl; Hon Roll; Stevenson Jnr HS Gftd Magnt; Hs Marine Sci Magnet; El Camino Coll; Chldhd Ed.

VELEZ, JOSE M; Amistad HS; Indio, CA; (2); Air Force.

VELEZ, ROSEANNE; Vintage HS; Napa, CA; (4); Church Yth Grp; French Clb; Chorus; Church Choir; Nwsp; Hon Roll; Sacramento ST; Liberal Arts.

VELIE, KIMBERLY N; Oak Park HS; Agoura Hills, CA; (1); Hosp Aide; Key Clb; Latin Clb; Temple Yth Grp; School Play; JV Bsktbl; JV Sftbl; JV Tennis; Pres Acad Fit Awd; UCSB; Med.

VELIZ, EDWIN O; Ingelwood HS; Los Angeles, CA; (2); French Clb; JA; Office Aide; ROTC; Color Guard; Drill Tm; Stu Cncl; Cit Awd; Hon Roll; Actor.

VELIZ, MARGARET NAOMIE; Notre Dame HS; Salinas, CA; (3); Church Yth Grp; Capt Var Bsktbl; Capt Var Vllybl; Hon Roll; JV Sftbl; Sacramento U; Engrng.

VELLENO, HARRY A; George Washington HS; San Francisco, CA; (2); Boy Scts; Church Yth Grp; Trk; Bsbl; Hon Roll; Hgh Hnrs Alg Golden St Exam; Eagle Sct; UC Davis; Cvl Engr.

VELLES, STEPHANIE; California HS; San Ramon, CA; (2); Hon Roll; Real Estate.

VELLONE, RHEA E; Ramona HS; Ramona, CA; (3); Church Yth Grp; Cmnty Wkr; 4-H; VP German Clb; Girl Scts; SADD; Sec Band; Mrchg Band; Pep Band; School Musical; SDC-CMEA All Cnty Hnr Band; Dir Awd Band; Educ.

VELO, JOY; Bonita Vista HS; Chula Vista, CA; (4); Art Clb; Church Yth Grp; Dance Clb; Math Clb; Office Aide; Pep Clb; SADD; Varsity Clb; Chorus; Mgr Var Bsbl; U CA San Diego; Bio Sci.

VELORIA, GWENDOLYN T; East Union HS; Manteca, CA; (1); Rptr Nwsp; Treas Frsh Cls; JV Bsktbl; Var Trk; Vllybl; High Hon Roll; STAND; Law.

VELOZ, ANDREA C; Woodside HS; Redwood City, CA; (2); Band; Jazz Band; Mrchg Band; Pep Band; Var Socr; JV Var Vllybl; Stanford; Psych.

VELOZA, TAMMY I; Hayward HS; Hayward, CA; (4); 16/209; Pres Drama Clb; Acpl Chr; School Musical; School Play; Stage Crew; Variety Show; High Hon Roll; Choral Aires; Stu Dir; Cal ST Hayward; Music.

VELTHOEN, BRENT; Fred C Beyer HS; Modesto, CA; (3); Church Yth Grp; Debate Tm; German Clb; Key Clb; NFL; Speech Tm; Var Swmmng; High Hon Roll; Cmnty Wkr; Letterman Clb; Asilomar Slctd Ldrshp Clb; CSF; UCSD; Bus.

VELTMAN, LAURA J; Valley Christian HS; Duarte, CA; (2); Church Yth Grp; Band; Mrchg Band; Variety Show; Sftbl; Vllybl; Hon Roll; NHS; Calvin Coll.

VELVES, VALERIE; St Genevieves HS; Van Nuys, CA; (2); Dance Clb; Pep Clb; Drill Tm; Hon Roll; Prfct Atten Awd; Mdcn.

VENDL, DAVID J; Millikan HS; Long Beach, CA; (3); German Clb; Pres JA; Key Clb; ROTC; Drill Tm; JV Crs Cntry; Kiwanis Awd; Lion Awd; Boy Scts; Church Yth Grp; Stunt Man; Super Cadet Awd ROTC; Cambodian Stu Assn; CSULB; Entrepreneur.

VENEGAS, CAROLINA T; Sweetwater Union HS; National City, CA; (4); Latin Clb; Math Clb; Office Aide; Science Clb; Spanish Clb; Speech Tm; Teachers Aide; Off Soph Cls; Off Sr Cls; Off Stu Cncl; San Diego ST U.

VENEGAS, CHRISTINE A; San Gorgonid HS; San Bernardino, CA; (3); Intrml Wt Lftg; Mstrd Prfcncy Tests In 2 Dist; Chld Psych.

VENEGAS, GILBERT N; Central Union HS; Heber, CA; (2); Boy Scts; Color Guard; Pres Acad Fit Awd; San Diego ST U; Crmnl Jstc Adm.

VENEGAS, JOSE A; Gonzales HS; Soledad, CA; (1); JV Ftbl; UCLA; Comp.

VENEGAS, JUANITA; Bishop Amat Memorial HS; La Puente, CA; (3); Treas Debate Tm; Treas Speech Tm; Co-Capt Color Guard; Original Oratory Awd Of Excllnc; Thomas Aquinas Coll; Lbrl Arts.

VENEGAS, YVONNE; Sierra Vista HS; Baldwin Park, CA; (1); UCLA.

VENERACION, CAROL G; Holy Family Girls HS; Los Angeles, CA; (2); Chorus; DAR Awd; Hon Roll; Prfct Atten Awd; CA Schlrshp Fed Club; St Dominics Church Jr Legion Of Mary; UCLA; Med.

VENG, TAING; El Cajon Valley HS; El Cajon, CA; (4); 76/300; Pres Chess Clb; Church Yth Grp; Cmnty Wkr; Socr; L Var Trk; L Var Vllybl; L Var Wrstlng; San Diego ST U; Math.

VENHUIZEN, RYAN M; Lodi HS; Woodbridge, CA; (3); FFA; Teachers Aide; Band; Jazz Band; Hon Roll; San Joaquin County Delta; Music.

VENIDA-HELLER, ADOLFO JOHN; Lemoore Union HS; Lemoore, CA; (2); Art Clb; Cmnty Wkr; DECA; FCA; French Clb; Science Clb; SADD; Intrml Ftbl; JV Socr; JV Trk; CSF; Photo Clb; Bst Photo II Stu; CA Poly; Phys Sci.

VENIEGAS, CINDY; Southwest HS; San Diego, CA; (2); Key Clb; Model UN; Drill Tm; Off Frsh Cls; Off Soph Cls; Hon Roll; Pan Asian; Sword & Shield; U Of CA San Diego; Med.

VENIEGAS JR, ROMEO; Southwest HS; San Diego, CA; (2); JV Ftbl; Hon Roll; Pres Acad Fit Awd; CSF; Pan Asian; ASB Swrd/Shld; UCSD; Med.

VENKATARAMAN, KALYAN G; Flintridge Prep; South Pasadena, CA; (3); Church Yth Grp; JCL; Latin Clb; High Hon Roll; Smmr League Bsktbl Pgm & Flintridge Bsktbl Camp; Med.

VENKATESWARAN, SWAPNA G; Leland HS; San Jose, CA; (2); Key Clb; Hon Roll; Amnesty Intl; UCLA; Lawyr.

VENKUS, LARA; Tokay HS; Stockton, CA; (4); 88/614; FCA; Spanish Clb; Teachers Aide; Var L Crs Cntry; Var L Socr; Var L Trk; JV Var Vllybl; Hon Roll; Pres Acad Fit Awd; Schl Track Record Holder; Natl Hnr Roll MBR; San Diego ST U; Spanish.

VENN, CINDY L; Oak Park HS; Agoura Hills, CA; (3); 9/84; Church Yth Grp; Cmnty Wkr; Letterman Clb; SADD; Teachers Aide; Varsity Clb; Pres Soph Cls; Rep Jr Cls; Sec Sr Cls; Var L Bsktbl; Peer Cnslng; Rep Oak Park HS At Annl Yth Ctzndhsp Smnr Pepperdine U; Med.

VENTI, JOEL PATRICK; Escondido HS; Escondido, CA; (4); Art Clb; Ski Clb; SADD; Nwsp; Yrbk; Rep Frsh Cls; Treas Soph Cls; Pres Jr Cls; Pres Stu Cncl; Var Cheerldng; Laurels For Ldrs Awd; Vrsty Water Polo; CSU Long Beach; Art.

VENTO, GRACIELA; Yokota HS; APO San Francisc, CA; (3); Mu Alpha Theta; Quiz Bowl; Band; Nwsp; Pres Sr Cls; Cit Awd; High Hon Roll; NHS; Harvard Club Of Boston Awd; Bio.

VENTRESS, JESSICA A; Serrano HS; Apple Valley, CA; (3); Church Yth Grp; Drama Clb; Intnl Clb; Letterman Clb; Teachers Aide; Varsity Clb; Bsktbl; Trk; Hon Roll.

VENTROLA, FAITH; Southern Calif Christian HS; Anaheim, CA; (4); Church Yth Grp; French Clb; Office Aide; Teachers Aide; Cheerldng; Score Keeper; Vllybl; Hon Roll; Westmont Coll; Engl.

VENTRONI, DAVID A; Fontana HS; Bloomington, CA; (3); Boy Scts; JA; Var JV Swmmng; Hon Roll; Prfct Atten Awd; Eagle Sct 88; Acad Schlstc Mdl; CA Poly Pomona; Aerospace Engr.

VENTRY, CHRISTOPHER J; Bellarmine College Prep; Santa Cruz, CA; (4); 3/302; Service Clb; Ed Yrbk; Pres Sr Cls; Stu Cncl; Var Trk; Pres Acad Fit Awd; St Schlr; Cmnty Wkr; Ski Clb; VP SADD; Wnnr Bellamine Sprt Awd Grad; Duke U; Intl Bus.

VENTURA, DIANE; Archbishop Mitty HS; Santa Clara, CA; (4); Art Clb; Cmnty Wkr; Hosp Aide; Intnl Clb; Spanish Clb; SADD; Rep Frsh Cls; Rep Soph Cls; Hon Roll; Cmp Vlntr; W Valley Coll.

VENTURA JR, ELPIDIO A; Homestead HS; Sunnyvale, CA; (3); Art Clb; Spanish Clb; Band; Mrchg Band; Stat Tennis; Hon Roll; NHS; 1st Yr Alg Hnrs; Geom Hnrs; Engrng.

VENTURA, XOCHITL; Mc Farland HS; Mc Farland, CA; (3); FTA; Teachers Aide; Varsity Clb; Sec Frsh Cls; Treas Sr Cls; Var Sftbl; JV Var Vllybl; Hon Roll; Lion Awd; Sal; Acad Decathln; Prom Cmmttee; Cuesta Coll; Ed.

VENTURI, JANAY; Mills HS; Millbrae, CA; (2); Church Yth Grp; English Clb; Band; Pep Band; Off Frsh Cls; Rep Soph Cls; Var Mgr(s); JV Swmmng; High Hon Roll; Ped.

VENTURINI, CATHERINE C; Loretto HS; Rocklin, CA; (3); 3/62; Girl Scts; Intnl Clb; Science Clb; Service Clb; Stage Crew; Ed Yrbk; JV Var Swmmng; Var Tennis; JV Vllybl; Bausch & Lomb Sci Awd; Sci Olympd; Mck Trl.

VERA, BLANCA L; Oxnard HS; Oxnard, CA; (3); Drama Clb; Hon Roll; Treas Clb UXMAL; Bilingual Teacher.

VERA, CHRISTOPHER S; St Ignatius College Prep; San Francisco, CA; (3); #72 In Class; Church Yth Grp; SADD; Trk; CSF; Sr Uturgy Grp 90-91; Big Bros; UC Davis; Doc.

VERA, DEBORAH D; East HS; Bakersfield, CA; (2); Trk; High Hon Roll; Hon Roll; Math Teacher.

VERA, EVONNE S; Nogales HS; W Covina, CA; (2); Chorus; School Play; Variety Show; Lit Mag; Vllybl; Hon Roll; Choir Letter; Jrnlsm.

VERA, GERALD; Fontana HS; Fontana, CA; (2); U Of Redlands; Arch.

VERA, JENNIFER L; Antioch HS; Antioch, CA; (2); French Clb; Spanish Clb; Hon Roll; Pres Schlr; Outstndng Frnch I Stu; Outstndng Mlti-Lgst.

VERA, KRISTINE A; Mater Dei HS; Santa Ana, CA; (3); Hosp Aide; Rptr Phtg Yrbk; Hon Roll; NHS; CSF; Cmps Mnstry; UC Berkeley; Engrng.

VERA, YVETTE A; Hawthorne HS; Hawthorne, CA; (3); Dance Clb; Nwsp; Prfct Atten Awd; CA ST Los Angeles; Comp.

VERAN, MELANI; Saint Joseph HS; Norwalk, CA; (2); 31/200; Drama Clb; Key Clb; Spanish Clb; Drill Tm; Hon Roll; SADD Club; CA Schlshp Fed; U C Irvine; Med.

VERARDO, TRACI A; Adolfo Camarillo HS; Camarillo, CA; (2); 15/500; Cmnty Wkr; Hist Stu Cncl; JV Socr; JV Tennis; High Hon Roll; Opt Clb Awd; Prfct Atten Awd; CSF 89-90; Gftd, Tlnd Educ 89-90; Peer Helpers 89-90.

VERASTEGOI, ALBERT P; Tolare Joint Union HS; Pixley, CA; (4); Spanish Clb; Ftbl; Coll Of Sequoias.

VERBANSKY, PAUL; Chaffey HS; Ontario, CA; (2); 3/783; Drama Clb; School Play; High Hon Roll; Rotary Awd; CSF; Stu Of Month Engl & Frgn Lang.

VERBARG, AARON C; San Francisco Christan Schl; San Francisco, CA; (2); Var Bsbl; Var Bsktbl; Var Socr; Hon Roll; Cntrl Cst Sctn Schlstc Achvt Tm; SFC Acad Achvt Awd; Al-Leag Bsktbl, Bsbl; Mdcl Fld.

VERBRUGGE, GREG L; Fontana HS; Fontana, CA; (2); Stu Cncl; Bsbl; Ftbl; Wt Lftg; Wrstlng; Hon Roll.

VERCRUYSSE, KIRSTIE L; Fred C Beyer HS; Modesto, CA; (2); Church Yth Grp; Pep Clb; Ski Clb; Church Choir; Mrchg Band; Gym; Cit Awd; Hon Roll; Green Party Clb.

VERDEJA, RODOLFO; San Luis Obispo HS; San Luis Obispo, CA; (3); Band; Jazz Band; School Musical; Nwsp; Yrbk; Off Jr Cls; Bsbl; Bsktbl; Ftbl; Socr.

VERDIN, DAVID B; Valley View HS; Moreno Valley, CA; (2); Chess Clb; Band; Jazz Band; Mrchg Band; Orch; Pep Band; Stage Crew; Variety Show; Hon Roll; Sthrn CA Schl Band Of Amer Fstvl Excllnt Rtng; USC; Med.

VERDIN, JOHN M; Dinuba HS; Dinuba, CA; (3); Acpl Chr; Chorus; Jazz Band; Mrchg Band; Hon Roll; Gld & Slvr Mdls Magrigals; Outstndng Wrk Engl & Excel German Awds; GATE; Music.

VERDIN, MIRIAM; Sweetwater HS; National City, CA; (2); Library Aide; Office Aide; Scholastic Bowl; Teachers Aide; Hon Roll; Pres Acad Fit Awd; Hnrs Clb Treas:Pr Tutr; San Diego ST U; Bus.

VERDUN, PAMELA R; Serra HS; San Diego, CA; (3); Office Aide; ROTC; Drill Tm; Nwsp; Stu Cncl; Cheerldng; Cit Awd; Hon Roll; Prfct Atten Awd; Pres Acad Fit Awd; Outstndng Scientist Trphy; Commnctns.

VERGARA, PATRICIA; Lincoln HS; Lincoln, CA; (4); GAA; Pep Clb; Spanish Clb; SADD; Rep Stu Cncl; Cheerldng; Sftbl; Ldrshp Class; Sierra Coll; Med.

VERGARA, RUSSELL B; Independence HS; San Jose, CA; (3); Art Clb; Cmnty Wkr; Red Cross Aide; Science Clb; Variety Show; Lit Mag; High Hon Roll; NHS; Pres Acad Fit Awd; Rotary Awd; San Jose Medcl Port VP; Poetry Excllnce Cert; 2 1sr Pl Awds Santa Clara Cnty Yth Expo Prntmkng; Davis; Med.

VERGEER, MICHAEL P; Escondido HS; Escondido, CA; (2); Church Yth Grp; Cmnty Wkr; Science Clb; JV Socr; JV Vllybl; Hon Roll; Opt Clb Awd; Cyclng; CA; Arch.

VERGEL DE DIOS, JOSEPH M R; Inglewood HS; Inglewood, CA; (2); 3/29; Spanish Clb; Teachers Aide; Nwsp; Yrbk; Bsbl; Ftbl; Cit Awd; Hon Roll; Talented Graphic & Cartoon Artist; Major Sports Fan; USC; Journ.

VERGOWVEN, LISA M; El Camino Real HS; Placentia, CA; (2); Hon Roll; Writing Songs Poetry & Short Stories; Training Musician; Enjoy Learning & Teaching; Mi; Music.

VERHAEGH, MARCUS J; Mission College Prep; Cambria, CA; (4); 2/35; Science Clb; Teachers Aide; Ed Nwsp; Ed Yrbk; Var Crs Cntry; Hon Roll; Ntl Merit SF; NEDT Awd; Cal Poly Sp Systs; Cgntv Sci.

VERHAGEN, JULIANN M; Corona HS; Corona, CA; (3); 44/402; Church Yth Grp; Library Aide; School Play; Var L Wrstlng; Hon Roll; CA Poly Pomona; Engrng.

VERHOEVEN, JODI L; Mcfarland HS; Mc Farland, CA; (3); Church Yth Grp; FBLA; Treas FHA; Letterman Clb; Teachers Aide; Chorus; Church Choir; VP Frsh Cls; VP Soph Cls; VP Jr Cls; School Award For Freshman Class; 2 Honors In History World & U S; Fri Night Stu Agnst Drugs Driv Drunk; Business.

VERITY, MICHAEL R; Sunny Hills HS; Fullerton, CA; (3); 30/430; Boy Scts; Church Yth Grp; Letterman Clb; Quiz Bowl; JV Capt Crs Cntry; Var Trk; High Hon Roll; Kiwanis Awd; NHS; Rotary Awd; Piano Study; Eagle Scout; People-People Stu Ambassador 90; Law.

VERMA, KAMNI; Livingston HS; Livingston, CA; (1); CA Schlrshp Fed Clb; UC Berkeley; Med.

VERMA, MUNISH; Livingston HS; Livingston, CA; (3); Bsktbl; Var Tennis; Cit Awd; High Hon Roll; Hon Roll; CSF; Acadmc Dcthln; U Of CA Davis; Hlth.

VERMA, POONAM; Livingston HS; Livingston, CA; (2); Modesto JC; RN.

VERMA, SHARAD; Gunn HS; Los Altos Hills, CA; (3); Boy Scts; Office Aide; Hon Roll; Scoutng Awd 1989; UCLA; Poli Sci.

VERMA, VIJAYENDRA K; Sunny Hills HS; Placentia, CA; (4); 25/450; Stu Cncl; Masonic Awd; NHS; Tennis; Var Capt Socr; Var L Wrstlng; Varsity Clb; FBLA; Rep Jr Cls; Treas Sr Cls; Johns Hopkins Acad Achvmnt Awd; CSF; Yth Govt Awd; U Of CA Riverside; Bio-Med.

VERMETTE, MICHELLE M; Pinole Valley HS; Pinole, CA; (1); Sftbl; Hon Roll; Davis U; Pediatrician.

VERMILION, TIMOTHY J; Community Christian HS; Bakersfield, CA; (4); 2/29; Boy Scts; Church Yth Grp; Letterman Clb; Scholastic Bowl; Yrbk; VP Frsh Cls; VP Soph Cls; VP Sr Cls; Treas Stu Cncl; Var Ftbl; Eagle Scout 3 Palms; Gold Seal Bearer CSF; Distinguished Chrstn HS Stu; Acad Dcthln; Embry-Riddle Aero U; Aerosp Eng.

VERMILLION, JEFF D; Marysville Jt Un Schl Dist; Brownsville, CA; (1); JV Bsbl; JV Ftbl; Wt Lftg; Rotary Awd; 3rd Annual Western States Yth To Yth Conf.

VERMILYA, DAVID J; Laguna Beach HS; Laguna Beach, CA; (2); Hon Roll; Pres Acad Fit Awd; Prncpls Awd Excllnce Phys Educ & Sci; Surf Tm; Bus Admin.

VERNACI, JOSEPH H; Apple Valley SR HS; Apple Valley, CA; (1); Band; Mrchg Band; Hon Roll; Astronaut.

VERNERS, KRISPEN; Kingsburg HS; Kingsburg, CA; (1); Band; Mrchg Band; Socr; High Hon Roll.

VERNEUIL, CHRISTINA L; Sunny Hills HS; Fullerton, CA; (2); 11/440; Rep Church Yth Grp; Intnl Clb; High Hon Roll; Rotary Awd; JV Swmmng; Bio.

VERNON, GREGORY E; University HS; Los Angeles, CA; (4); Boy Scts; Office Aide; School Musical; School Play; Capt Bsktbl; Hon Roll; Mc Donalds All Amer, All Leag, All City, All Westside 1st Tm, All CIF; CA ST U Fullerton; Bus Admin.

VERNON, TIFANI R; Novato HS; Novato, CA; (2); Church Yth Grp; Cmnty Wkr; Band; Mrchg Band; Rep Stu Cncl; JV Cheerldng; Hon Roll.

VERONICA, ALMA V; Mount Pleasant HS; San Jose, CA; (2); Bus Profs of Am; Church Yth Grp; Cmnty Wkr; FBLA; Latin Clb; Spanish Clb; SADD; High Hon Roll; Hon Roll; CSF; Stanford U; Lwyr.

VERRETT, BRIAN; Lynwood Adv Acad; Los Angeles, CA; (1); Boy Scts; FBLA; FHA; Quiz Bowl; JV Bsktbl; Cit Awd; High Hon Roll; Hon Roll; Pres Acad Fit Awd; Val; Bible Bowl Cptn; USC; Ob/Gyn.

VERRETT, LORNELL; North Hills Christian HS; Mare Island, CA; (2); Church Yth Grp; Teachers Aide; Chorus; School Musical; School Play; Hiking Clb; U Of KY; Psych.

VERSTEEG, BOBBI L; Oxnard HS; Oxnard, CA; (2); 11/604; Church Yth Grp; French Clb; Teachers Aide; School Play; Stage Crew; High Hon Roll; Hon Roll; Pres Schlr; Undergrnd Shakespr Soc; Horse Shwng; CSF; Phrmcy.

VERSTEEG, RYAN; John F Kennedy HS; La Palma, CA; (3); Boy Scts; Church Yth Grp; Chorus; Church Choir; Var Swmmng; Hon Roll; Pres Acad Fit Awd; Vrsty Wtrpl Ltrmn; Eagle Scout; Engr.

VERTICAN, GINGER L; Rim Of The World HS; Crestline, CA; (3); Church Yth Grp; Drama Clb; Model UN; Church Choir; Variety Show; Yrbk; Bsktbl; Sftbl; Hon Roll; Lion Awd; House Of Reps; Missions.

VERTICAN, KRISTI; Valencia HS; Placentia, CA; (2); Gym; CA ST Fullerton; Child Care.

VERZOSA, PEARL M; Mira Mesa HS; San Diego, CA; (2); Model UN; Off Soph Cls; JV Bsktbl; Var Trk; JV Vllybl; Acadmc Hnr Awd; Offcl Rep Says Peer Cnslng; GATE; US Naval Acad; Engr.

VESEY, JANNA; Lemoore HS; Lemoore, CA; (3); Drama Clb; Key Clb; Office Aide; SADD; School Play; Treas Frsh Cls; Treas Soph Cls; Stat Trk; LEAF Lemoore Envrnmntl Awrnss Fndtn; FLAL Frgn Lagn Apprctn Clb; UC Berkeley; Comp Engr.

VESHTAJ, RUDOLF; Beaumont HS; Beaumont, CA; (1); Band; Jazz Band; Mrchg Band; Lit Mag; Rcvd Cert Of Excllnc In Physcl Sci; Rcvd Numerous Awds In Different Clss For High Achvt; John Hopkins; Physics.

VESPUCCI, RAFFAELLA; Santa Clara HS; Santa Clara, CA; (4); Intnl Clb; Service Clb; Italn Cath Fed Schlrshp; West Vlly Coll Schlrshp; Certfd Peer Tutor; West Valley Coll; Bio.

VESTER JR, RICHARD L; Encinal HS; Alameda, CA; (1); Church Yth Grp; ROTC; JV Bsktbl; JV Ftbl; JV Trk; Intrml Wt Lftg; Hon Roll; Notre Dame; Phys Ed Instr.

VESTER-DAVIS, JESSICA; Shasta HS; Sacramento, CA; (2); Aud/Vis; French Clb; Teachers Aide; Orch; Rep Frsh Cls; Zoological Soc Vlntr; CSUS.

VETCHER, CANDI J; Bonita Vista HS; Bonita, CA; (3); Church Yth Grp; Cmnty Wkr; Intnl Clb; Office Aide; Pep Clb; SADD; Chorus; Variety Show; Cit Awd; High Hon Roll; Outstndng Stu Awd ASB; CSF; Schlrshp Awds Pr Cnclr; Sccr; Amnsty Intl; Tutr; Comssnr Actvts; UCSD; Psych.

VETICA, STEPHEN M; John F Kennedy HS; La Palma, CA; (1); Church Yth Grp; Bsbl; Bsktbl; Ftbl; Score Keeper; High Hon Roll; Gldn St Math Awd Merit.

VETTER, DAN B; Del Campo HS; Fair Oaks, CA; (3); 40/446; Var L Bsbl; Intrml Bsktbl; Var L Ftbl; JV Socr; Intrml Swmmng; Intrml Wt Lftg; Triple A Awd Bsbl 2 Yrs Row Var & JR Var; CA Schlrshp Fed Mem; Rotary Yth Ldrshp Awd.

VEVIK, MICHAEL; Chula Vista HS; San Diego, CA; (4); 20/600; Chess Clb; JA; Math Tm; Science Clb; JV Ftbl; Var Vllybl; Pres Acad Fit Awd; CA Schlrshp Soc; U Southern CA; Astronomy.

VIA, ANDREA; Montgomery HS; Santa Rosa, CA; (4); Church Yth Grp; JA; Science Clb; Spanish Clb; SADD; Teachers Aide; High Hon Roll; Jr NHS; NHS; Pres Acad Fit Awd; Life Stu CA Schrlshp Fed; Horseback Rdng; Cnslr Faith Lutheran Camp Big Oak; Chem Engr.

VIALPANDO, J STEPHEN; Alhambra HS; Martinez, CA; (4); Am Leg Boys St; Teachers Aide; JV Bsbl; JV L Bsktbl; Var L Trk; Hon Roll; Pres Acad Fit Awd; Amer Assoc Women Cert Merit; Diablo Valley Coll; Orthdntst.

VIAN, CHRISTINE; Mission Viejo HS; El Toro, CA; (3); 29/500; Cmnty Wkr; Intnl Clb; Spanish Clb; SADD; Hon Roll; Jr NHS; NHS; Pres Acad Fit Awd; Piano Trphs; Pdtrcn.

VIAN, DORIS; Mission Viejo HS; El Toro, CA; (2); Cmnty Wkr; Key Clb; Tennis; Hon Roll; Off Frsh Cls; Off Soph Cls; 3rd Pl Symphony Piano Cmptn; UCLA.

VIAYRA JR, RAYMOND M; Bishop Montgomery HS; Harbor City, CA; (3); 21/389; VP JA; Service Clb; JV Crs Cntry; JV Trk; High Hon Roll; Ntl Merit Ltr; Intl Trade Clb Speech Cont Wnnr 89; Exchng Stu To Spain Schlrshp; Outstndng Male Undergrad; Offcr Of Yr; US Naval Acad; Engrng.

VIBE, KAREN D; North High Bkrsfld; Bakersfield, CA; (2); Church Yth Grp; Band; Chorus; Jazz Band; Mrchg Band; Pep Band; Sec Soph Cls; Var Bsktbl; Var Powder Puff Ftbl; Var Powder Puff Ftbl; All Sthrn Hnr Orch, CA; CA Band Dir Assn; All St Hnr Band, Symph; Musician.

VICARIO, CHRISTOPHER R; Ontario HS; Ontario, CA; (3); 126/550; Church Yth Grp; Key Clb; Teachers Aide; Band; Jazz Band; Mrchg Band; Pep Band; Hon Roll; Prfct Atten Awd; Hispanic Yth Ldrshp Conf; Outstndng Jr Musician 89; U Of CA L A.

VICE, ERIKA C; North HS; Bakersfield, CA; (3); Computer Clb; Chorus; Powder Puff Ftbl; Hon Roll; Wn 1st Pl Hstry Paper The Wonders Of Test Tube Babies; CA ST Bakersfield.

VICEDO, MARIVIC; Edison HS; Stockton, CA; (2); Cit Awd; Hon Roll; Prfct Atten Awd; Pres Acad Fit Awd; Spanish NHS; Presdntl Phys Ftnss Awd; Schlrshp Awd.

VICENTE, CORAL; Bell Gardens HS; Bell Gardens, CA; (2); Cit Awd; Hon Roll; Prfct Atten Awd; UCLA; Comp.

VICENTE, JOHN M; Oxnard HS; Oxnard, CA; (3); Crs Cntry; JETS Awd; Cal Poly U; Arch.

VICK, CHRISTINA A; Vallejo SR HS; Vallejo, CA; (2); SADD; Pres Acad Fit Awd; San Diego ST; Bus.

VICKERS, AMY L; Irvine HS; Irvine, CA; (3); 207/512; AFS; Church Yth Grp; Cmnty Wkr; Ski Clb; Orch; Hon Roll; Inter Dsgn.

VICKERS, MELINDA; Livermore HS; Livermore, CA; (3); Pres Church Yth Grp; Cmnty Wkr; Library Aide; Q&S; Pres Spanish Clb; Chorus; Crs Cntry; Trk; Hon Roll; Brigham Young U.

VICKERY, JENNIFER; Oxnard HS; Oxnard, CA; (2); 9/604; Band; Mrchg Band; Orch; Var L Crs Cntry; Var L Trk; High Hon Roll; Acadmc Achvt Awds 88-90; AYSO Sccr; Educ.

VICKROY, ROBERT; De Anza HS; Richmond, CA; (3); Science Clb; Teachers Aide; Varsity Clb; Acpl Chr; JV Bsbl; JV Ftbl; Var Tennis; Hon Roll; Advncd Plcmnt Classes; Bowling; UC Davis; Mech Engrng.

VICTOR, DAMION E; Kearny HS; San Diego, CA; (2); JV Var Bsktbl; JV Ftbl; Var L Trk; Hon Roll; Prfct Atten Awd; Outstndng Soph Boy Of Yr 89; Jr Var Bsktbl MVP & Tm Capt; Yth Bsktbl Assn Tm Capt; UCLA; NBA Player.

VICTORIA, ANNALIZA T; Downtown Business Magnet HS; Los Angeles, CA; (3); Art Clb; Computer Clb; CSF; Nrsng.

VICTORIA, MARIANDREA; Downey HS; Downey, CA; (2); Cerritos Coll; Inger Decrtn.

VICTORIA, REGINALD C; Chula Vista HS; San Diego, CA; (2); 29/605; Off Service Clb; Band; Variety Show; JV Ftbl; JV Trk; Cit Awd; Prfct Atten Awd; Piano/Keybrd Lssns; CSF; Panasian Clb; Dist Tlnt Shows; Aerospc Engrng.

VICUNA, SANTOS M; Leuzinger HS; Hawthorne, CA; (3); Computer Clb; Off Jr Cls; Cit Awd; Hon Roll; Cal ST Long Beach; Bus Admin.

VIDAL, ALEJANDRO C; Lowell HS; San Francisco, CA; (3); Teachers Aide; Church Choir; UC Berkeley; Pltcl Sci.

VIDAL, ANGEL; Baldwin Park HS; Baldwin Park, CA; (2); Church Yth Grp; Science Clb; Band; Mrchg Band; Pep Band; Rep Soph Cls; Rep Stu Cncl; Var Crs Cntry; Swmmng; JV Trk; Drafting Clb Offcr; Water Polo Tm; Aero Engr.

VIDAL, JERRED W; Arroyo Grande HS; Nipomo, CA; (1); 24/580; Debate Tm; 4-H; Letterman Clb; Speech Tm; Varsity Clb; Var Swmmng; 4-H Awd; Hon Roll; Stanford; Bio.

VIDAL, STACEY L; Milpitas HS; Milpitas, CA; (2); 25/500; Church Yth Grp; Pep Clb; Rep Frsh Cls; Rep Soph Cls; VP Jr Cls; Cheerldng; Pom Pon; High Hon Roll; Advrtsng.

VIDALES, ANGEL C; Luther Burbank HS; Sacramento, CA; (3); Dance Clb; Drama Clb; Latin Clb; Bsbl; Cit Awd; Pres Acad Fit Awd; St Schlr; Military; Bus.

VIDALI, AMY; Grossmont HS; La Mesa, CA; (1); Church Yth Grp; Drama Clb; SADD; School Play; JV Vllybl; High Hon Roll; Top Dance; Gymnastics; Engl.

VIDAURE, VALERIE; St Genevieve HS; Chatsworth, CA; (4); 22/156; Cmnty Wkr; SADD; Chorus; Ed Nwsp; Yrbk; High Hon Roll; Peace Clb; CA ST U Northridge; Bus Mgr.

VIDUCIC, NANCY; Capuchino HS; San Bruno, CA; (2); Church Yth Grp; GAA; Hosp Aide; Intnl Clb; Socr; Tennis; Cit Awd; San Francisco ST; Law.

VIEBACH, ERIC J; Canyon Springs HS; Moreno Valley, CA; (2); Boy Scts; ROTC; Drill Tm; Ftbl; Pr Ldrshp Cnslr; Ordr Arrow Hgh Hnr BSA; Air Force.

VIEGAS, SAMANTHA L; St Bernards HS; Eureka, CA; (2); Cmnty Wkr; Service Clb; Sec Frsh Cls; Sec Soph Cls; JV Bsktbl; Stat Ftbl; Var L Sftbl; JV Vllybl; Hon Roll; 3 NCS Schlr Athl Awds; Cert Awd Phys Educ; Humbolt ST U; Psych.

VIEIRA, ALI N; Nevada Union HS; Nevada City, CA; (2); SADD; Rep Stu Cncl; JV Bsktbl; Var Swmmng; JV Tennis; Cit Awd; High Hon Roll; Hon Roll; Prfct Atten Awd; Pres Acad Fit Awd; UCSB; Marine Bio.

VIEIRA, DAVID P; Dixon HS; Dixon, CA; (4); 8/127; Cmnty Wkr; FBLA; Scholastic Bowl; Varsity Clb; Yrbk; Rep Stu Cncl; JV Var Bsktbl; JV Ftbl; High Hon Roll; Lion Awd; Dixon Pks & Recrtn Cmmssnr; CSF; Andrn Elem Outdr Educ Camp Cnslr 90; U Of CA Davis; Elec Engrng.

VIEIRA, WENDY; Tulare Union HS; Tulare, CA; (2); 19/461; Church Yth Grp; Drama Clb; Rptr Nwsp; Off Soph Cls; High Hon Roll; Mock Trl; Schl Rcgntn Gldn ST Algbra Exm; Cmps Scene-Tulare Advncd Rgstr Town Nwspr; SF; U Of CA; Speech Thrpy.

VIELE, ANNA C; Ventura HS; Ventura, CA; (3); Debate Tm; Pres Am Leg Boys St; Letterman Clb; Model UN; Pep Clb; Service Clb; SADD; Nwsp; Ed Lit Mag; Sec Stu Cncl; 1st Pl Light Essay, Hnrbl Mntn Serious Verse Schl Creatv Wrtng Cntst.

VIELE, PORTIA R; J E Mc Ateer HS; San Francisco, CA; (3); Ski Clb; School Musical; School Play; Pres Frsh Cls; Rep Soph Cls; VP Jr Cls; VP Sr Cls; Socr; Hon Roll; Mc Ateer Coll Soc; Fshn Dsgn.

VIELMA, ISAAC; San Fernando Valley Acad; Pacoima, CA; (3); 4/16; Varsity Clb; Band; Chorus; School Musical; Off Soph Cls; VP Jr Cls; Var Vllybl; High Hon Roll; Stu Cncl Secy Of Publicity, Srgnt At Arms & Pres; Med.

VIERBOOM, ALBERTO J; Bonita Vista HS; Bonita, CA; (2); Cmnty Wkr; Surf Club; SDSU; Bus.

VIERECK, MICHELE K; Clairemont HS; El Cajon, CA; (4); Church Yth Grp; FHA; Girl Scts; Library Aide; SADD; JV Trk; Hon Roll; Prfct Atten Awd; Stu Mnth Awd 87; Equestrian Clb.

VIERNES, MELISSA M; Moreau HS; Hayward, CA; (3); Church Yth Grp; French Clb; Red Cross Aide; Powder Puff Ftbl; Vllybl; Cit Awd; NHS; Prfct Atten Awd; Svc Clb; Multi-Cultural Clb; San Francisco ST U; Jrnlsm.

VIERRA, DANA; Amador Valley HS; Pleasanton, CA; (2); 13/350; Cheerldng; High Hon Roll; Golden St Hnrs Geo; Davis Stanford; Med.

VIERRA, REBECCA A; River City HS; W Sacramento, CA; (2); 2/270; Hosp Aide; SADD; Swmmng; High Hon Roll; Hon Roll; AAU Swimmer; Swmmng-All Stars-MVP/Jr Olympcs; 1st W Civilztn Test-Lttr Wnnr; CSF; Med.

VIERTEL, ANDREW; Eagle Rock HS; Los Angeles, CA; (3); Rep Church Yth Grp; Treas Key Clb; Pres SADD; Acpl Chr; Chorus; Ed Nwsp; Stu Cncl; JV L Swmmng; Pres Acad Fit Awd; Fndng Capt ERHS Star Trek Clb; Close Up; Photo Clb; Occidental Coll; Eclgy.

VIEYRA, DAVID Y; High Desert HS; Adelanto, CA; (3); Prfct Atten Awd; AZ ST; Law.

VIGIL, KRISTI; Thousand Oaks HS; Thousand Oaks, CA; (3); 44/541; Church Yth Grp; Cmnty Wkr; Library Aide; JV Var Bsktbl; High Hon Roll; Hon Roll; Ntl Merit Ltr; Prfct Atten Awd; Envrnmntl Stds.

VIGIL, LALENA M; Orange HS; Orange, CA; (3); Church Yth Grp; Drama Clb; School Play; Stage Crew; Rptr Nwsp; Hon Roll; NHS; Mock Trls; Intract Clb Treas; Top 30; Law.

VIGIL, MARCUS H; Bridgemont HS; San Francisco, CA; (2); Sec Treas Frsh Cls; High Hon Roll; Hon Roll; CSF 90.

VIGIL, MARIA E; Chula Vista HS; Chula Vista, CA; (3); ROTC; Acpl Chr; School Musical; Off Soph Cls; Off Jr Cls; Cheerldng; Sec SADD.

VIGNA, DANIEL J; Monte Vista Christian HS; Seaside, CA; (4); Church Yth Grp; Math Clb; Hon Roll; Acad Decathelon; Vol Work; CSF; Aero Engr.

VIGNA, NICOLE J; Poway HS; Poway, CA; (2); 48/827; Church Yth Grp; Key Clb; High Hon Roll; Amer Ballet Ensemble; Med.

VIGO, EMILEE; Carson HS; Carson, CA; (4); Boy Scts; FTA; Church Choir; Hon Roll; Bank Of Amer Awd Fine Art; Peace Corps Vol Global Awareness; CA ST Coll.

VIHANEXAI, KHAMEVAY C; Redwood HS; Visalia, CA; (3); 44/400; Sec FBLA; Math Clb; Spanish Clb; Hon Roll; Prfct Atten Awd; UC Davis; Bus Prof.

VIK, JEREMIAH; Holtville Christian Acad; Holtville, CA; (4); 1/30; Church Yth Grp; School Musical; School Play; Var L Bsktbl; Var L Ftbl; Var L Sftbl; High Hon Roll; Val; CEF Stu; Hghst GPA Awd; Bob Jones U; Evnglsm.

VILAYSANE, KETSANA; Escondido HS; Escondido, CA; (3); Cit Awd; High Hon Roll; Hon Roll; UCSD.

VILAYSOUK, PHOUTHONE; John F Kennedy HS; Sacramento, CA; (3); Hon Roll; Bsktbl; Swmmng; Dance; Sac ST; Banking.

VILCHEZ, ANNA; Mills HS; Millbrae, CA; (3); Latin Clb; Socr; Gldn St Exam; Med.

VILHAUER, CLOVER L; Franklin HS; Stockton, CA; (4); 14/304; Drama Clb; JA; Pep Clb; Mgr Yrbk; JV Cheerldng; Var Sftbl; High Hon Roll; Principals List; Silver Seal Wnnr; Delta Coll; Bus.

VILITCHAI, SOMBATH B; Sa Diego HS; San Diego, CA; (3); 45/415; Art Clb; Church Yth Grp; Latin Clb; Spanish Clb; Tennis; Prfct Atten Awd; San Diego ST U; Bus.

VILLA, ANNA M; Clovis HS; Clovis, CA; (3); Dance Clb; Intnl Clb; High Hon Roll; Hon Roll; :Ucla; Lawyer.

VILLA, BETH A; Mount Pleasant HS; San Jose, CA; (3); Cmnty Wkr; Teachers Aide; Var Diving; Var Socr; Var Swmmng.

VILLA, BRENDA L; Argonaut HS; Ione, CA; (4); 12/85; FBLA; Key Clb; Ski Clb; Teachers Aide; JV Var Sftbl; Stat Wrstlng; Hon Roll; Pr Cnslr; Cuesta CC; Psych.

VILLA, CASHELL; Atascadero HS; Santa Margarita, CA; (2); Gym; Hon Roll; CA Poly San Luis Obispo; Archi.

VILLA, CLAUDIA JANETH; Montgomery HS; Chula Vista, CA; (3); FBLA; Latin Clb; Office Aide; Spanish Clb; Nwsp; Cit Awd; Os Awd Intl Fair; Geometry Pin; Awd In Lang; 2 Yr Coll.

VILLA, ESTHER; Eagle Rock HS; Los Angeles, CA; (3); Band; Jazz Band; Orch; Cit Awd; Hon Roll; Perfct Atten; Law.

VILLA, FRANZ; Oxnard HS; Oxnard, CA; (1); Boy Scts; Computer Clb; Intrml Mgr Bsktbl; Hon Roll; CSF; Asian Amer Clb; UCLA; Comp Sci.

VILLA, JAIME; Bell HS; Maywood, CA; (3); Capt Var Swmmng; Hon Roll; NHS; MESA; CSF Ca Scholarship Federation; GMI; Electrics Engineering.

VILLA, JENNIFER B; Holy Family HS; Glendale, CA; (2); Church Yth Grp; GAA; Chorus; School Play; Stu Cncl; Var Capt Bsktbl; Var Sftbl; Var Trk; Var Vllybl; Hon Roll; CSF VP; Campus Ministry; Stanford; Bus.

VILLA, JOSEPHINE; Carlmont HS; Redwood City, CA; (2); Church Yth Grp; Var Tennis; High Hon Roll; Hon Roll; CSF; Stu Brd; Amnesty Clb; Math Hnrs Awd; Var Badminton Pal Chmpn, Jr Leag Chmpn 89; U Of CA; Sports Med.

VILLA, MARIA; Calexico HS; Calexico, CA; (3); Spanish Clb; Sftbl; Vllybl; Hon Roll; 1st Plc Vlly Scrbbl Scrmbl HS Div; U Of CA Irvine; Elem.

VILLA, NORA H; Salinas HS; Salinas, CA; (4); Spanish Clb; Temple Yth Grp; Church Choir; High Hon Roll.

VILLA, VALERIE; San Marcos HS; Santa Barbara, CA; (3); 66/380; 4-H; Ed Nwsp; Yrbk; Stat Bsktbl; Var L Trk; French Hon Soc; Conservation Clb; Amnesty Intl Clb; Trk Leag Fnls; Vet.

VILLA, VERONICA C; Eagle Rock HS; Los Angeles, CA; (3); Cmnty Wkr; Hosp Aide; Office Aide; Sec Orch; Yrbk; Bausch & Lomb Sci Awd; Cit Awd; High Hon Roll; Hon Roll; Prfct Atten Awd; Med.

VILLA, ZINDAINE; William Workman HS; Valinda, CA; (1); Church Yth Grp; Chorus; Score Keeper; JV Swmmng; High Hon Roll; Hon Roll; Prfct Atten Awd; Water Polo Ststcn; Harvard Med Sch; Pdtrcn.

VILLA, ZULMA G; Wasco Union HS; Lost Hills, CA; (3); Church Yth Grp; Latin Clb; Socr; Vllybl; Cit Awd; High Hon Roll; Hwy Patrol Ofcr.

VILLAGOMEZ, NANCY; Baldwin Park HS; Baldwin Park, CA; (2); Science Clb; Spanish Clb; Band; Mrchg Band; Pep Band; High Hon Roll; Key Wanette Clb; Acad Ltr; Loyola Marimont; Pedtrcn.

VILLAGRAN, MIKE A; West HS; Bakersfield, CA; (3); Intrml JV Bsktbl; Intrml Ftbl; JV Trk; Eyl 2nd Plc Frsh & Jv Bstkbl; 2nd Plc Sci Physcs Bakersfield Coll; Fresno ST; RN.

VILLAJIN, JOSE RAMON P; Cathedral HS; Monterey Park, CA; (3); Church Yth Grp; Computer Clb; Dance Clb; Math Clb; Science Clb; High Hon Roll; NHS; CA Poly San Luis Obispo; Engr.

VILLALBA, MARGARITA; Corning Union HS; Corning, CA; (3); 30/142; FHA; Science Clb; Spanish Clb; Fld Hcky; Score Keeper; Hon Roll; MECHA Clb; Rainbow Grls Clb; Shasta Coll; Teacher.

VILLALOBOS, ALICIA; Brawley Union HS; Brawley, CA; (3); FTA; Hon Roll; Prfct Atten Awd; Psych.

VILLALOBOS, ANTONIA; Santa Monica HS; Santa Monica, CA; (1); Chorus; Ed Yrbk; Hon Roll; UCLA; Accntnt.

VILLALOBOS, ARMIDA; North Salinas HS; Salinas, CA; (1); French Clb; Santa Barbara.

VILLALOBOS, IVETTE S; Notre Dame Acad; Los Angeles, CA; (3); Cmnty Wkr; Library Aide; Office Aide; Teachers Aide; Chorus; Church Choir; Cit Awd; High Hon Roll; Hon Roll; UCLA; Bio Sci.

VILLALOBOS, JENNIFER; Schurr HS; Montebello, CA; (4); 21/580; Am Leg Aux Girls St; Drama Clb; Key Clb; Capt Drill Tm; Mrchg Band; VP Stu Cncl; Cit Awd; High Hon Roll; NHS; Prfct Atten Awd; Dance Clb; Chrch Yth Grp; Grls Leag Sr Rep; U Of South CA; Arch.

VILLALOBOS, MARCO; Schurr HS; Los Angeles, CA; (3); Boy Scts; Chess Clb; Nwsp; Hon Roll; 1st Yr Jrnslm; 18th Of 100 In Novice News E Los Angeles On The Spot Wrtng Cntst.

VILLALOBOS, OSCAR; Lynwood HS; Lynwood, CA; (3); Mrchg Band; Pep Band; Cit Awd; Hon Roll; Photo; Elec; CA ST Long Beach; Bus.

VILLALOBOS, PETER; Schurr HS; Los Angeles, CA; (1); Hon Roll; Prfct Atten Awd.

VILLALOBOS, TINA; Sonora HS; Soulsbyville, CA; (4); 3/280; Church Yth Grp; Jazz Band; Mrchg Band; Off Sr Cls; Bsktbl; Trk; JA; Science Clb; Ski Clb; Band; St Hnr Band; PG&E Schlrshp/Awd; Stanford U.

VILLALOVOS, MATTHEW F; Don Bosco Technical Insti; Pico Rivera, CA; (3); Drama Clb; School Play; JV Crs Cntry; NHS; Medallion Awd Speech/ Drama; Cal ST San Francisco; Cmmnctns.

VILLALPANDO, BEATRIZ; James Lick HS; San Jose, CA; (4); Latin Clb; High Hon Roll; Prfct Atten Awd; Evergreen Coll; Pre-Schl Tchr.

VILLALPANDO, BETTY; California HS; Whittier, CA; (2); Computer Clb; GAA; Off Frsh Cls; Bsktbl; Mgr(s); Score Keeper; Tennis; Vllybl; Law.

VILLALPANDO, CIRA; Galt HS; Galt, CA; (3); 21/209; Pres AFS; Sec Church Yth Grp; French Clb; Sec FHA; Science Clb; SADD; Pres Frsh Cls; Rep Soph Cls; Hon Roll; Acad Decathlon Tm; Awd Most Outstndng Stu Smmr Engrng Pgm; Bus Law.

VILLALPANDO, GILBERT C; Banning HS; Banning, CA; (3); Math Clb; Spanish Clb; Band; Jazz Band; Mrchg Band; Pep Band; JV Bsbl; JV Bsktbl; Cit Awd; Hon Roll; Med.

VILLALUZ, DESIREE A; Bassett HS; La Puente, CA; (3); FBLA; Treas Stu Cncl; Var Vllybl; Cit Awd; Hon Roll; Jr NHS; NHS; Prfct Atten Awd; Badminton; Secy Of Hnr Soc, ASB Treas 90-91; MIT; Comp Sci.

VILLALVAZO, TINA M; Mater Dei HS; Orange, CA; (3); Church Yth Grp; Drama Clb; Hosp Aide; Office Aide; Spanish Clb; Stat Socr; Stat Wrstlng; High Hon Roll; Hon Roll; Pro-Life Grp; Pre Med.

VILLAMIL, PAUL R; Servite HS; La Mirada, CA; (3); Church Yth Grp; Cmnty Wkr; Debate Tm; Red Cross Aide; SADD; Varsity Clb; School Musical; Nwsp; Off Sr Cls; Swmmng; Wtrpolo; Jr Stsmn Of Amer; Gilde; UCSD; Psych.

VILLAMOR, CHRISTINA; Cerritos HS; Cerritos, CA; (2); Model UN; Spanish Clb; Drill Tm; Ed Nwsp; Treas Jr Cls; Treas Sr Cls; Var Cheerldng; Hon Roll; NHS; Academic Letter; FL Natl High Schl Cheerleading Championship Competition; Honor Guard; UCLA; Obstetrician.

VILLAND, LUZ E; Clairemont HS; San Diego, CA; (2); SADD; Drill Tm; Yrbk; CSF; Berkley U; Nrs.

VILLANUEVA, ALVIN O; Village Christian HS; Sun Valley, CA; (3); 13/125; Church Yth Grp; Band; Var JV Bsktbl; Var L Crs Cntry; USSR People To People Frndshp Caravan Ambsdr; Engr.

VILLANUEVA, CHARIFE P; Bolsa Grande HS; Garden Grove, CA; (2); Hosp Aide; Band; Church Choir; Mrchg Band; Pep Band; Rep Frsh Cls; Rep Stu Cncl; Var Trk; OB.

VILLANUEVA, CHRIS R; Montgomery HS; San Diego, CA; (3); 109/419; Pep Clb; Teachers Aide; Stage Crew; Stu Cncl; Hon Roll; Prfct Atten Awd; Pacific Asian Clb; San Diego ST U; Engrng.

VILLANUEVA, DESILU M; Hogan SR HS; Vallejo, CA; (2); Chess Clb; Church Yth Grp; Debate Tm; French Clb; Science Clb; SADD; Church Choir; Rptr Nwsp; Hon Roll; Val; UC Davis.

VILLANUEVA, DIANA; Hamilton Humanities Magnet HS; Los Angeles, CA; (2); Cmnty Wkr; Drama Clb; School Musical; School Play; Rep Frsh Cls; Rep Soph Cls; Var Vllybl; Cit Awd; High Hon Roll; Hon Roll; JR Stsmn Of Amer; CSF; Yth Cmmnty Svc; Prt Tm Job; Georgetown U; Corp Law.

VILLANUEVA, EDWARD E; Central Union HS; El Centro, CA; (2); 4-H; Ftbl; Var Wrstlng; Hon Roll; AZ ST U.

VILLANUEVA, ERIKA G; Beyer HS; Empire, CA; (1); Latin Clb; Spanish Clb; Hon Roll; Advrtsng.

VILLANUEVA, JULISSA; Manteca HS; Manteca, CA; (1); High Hon Roll; Hon Roll; Travel Agent.

VILLANUEVA, MICHAEL; Badwin Park HS; Baldwin Park, CA; (4); 1/350; Math Tm; Scholastic Bowl; Mrchg Band; Orch; Pep Band; Yrbk; Val; Stu Outreach Bible Stu; Bradels U; Comp Sci Math.

VILLANUEVA, ROY A; Diamond Bar HS; Diamond Bar, CA; (3); 25/430; Boy Scts; Chess Clb; French Clb; Band; Mrchg Band; Tennis; Hon Roll; UC Riverside; Psych.

VILLANUEVA, RUTH S; Gladstone HS; Azusa, CA; (3); Church Yth Grp; SADD; Church Choir; Drill Tm; Rptr Nwsp; Hon Roll; Dance Tm; Sweepstakes Wnr Azusa Dist Gate Sci Fair; JR Civitans; Ec.

VILLANVEVA, IRMA; John F Kennedy HS; Granada Hills, CA; (2); Phtg Yrbk; Cit Awd; Hon Roll; Photography Club Treas; UC Davis; Vet.

VILLAR, CECILIA; Dublin HS; Dublin, CA; (4); 4/178; French Clb; Church Choir; Nwsp; VP Frsh Cls; Pres Jr Cls; Stu Cncl; Stat Bsktbl; Co-Capt Cheerldng; Var Co-Capt Pom Pon; French Hon Soc; Hnrs Gldn St Exam-Algb; Hgh Hnrs Gldn St Exam-Geom; UC Santa Barbara; Bio Sci.

VILLAR, KATHERINE E; Louisville HS; Northridge, CA; (3); Art Clb; Church Yth Grp; Cmnty Wkr; GAA; Chorus; School Play; Pres Frsh Cls; Stu Cncl; Var Cheerldng; Var Score Keeper; Excllnc Awd Chld Dvlpmnt; Walk For Charity-200 Mi Frm Woodland Hls To Tijuana; Loyola Marymount; Bus.

VILLARAMA, RACHEL I; Ramona Convent Secondary Schl; Alhambra, CA; (3); Art Clb; Church Yth Grp; GAA; Hosp Aide; Model UN; Lit Mag; Swmmng; Hon Roll; NHS.

VILLARASA, NIKKI A; Palm Spring HS; Palm Springs, CA; (3); Drama Clb; Spanish Clb; Thesps; School Musical; School Play; Stage Crew; JV Sftbl; Hon Roll; Kiwanis Awd; Rotary Awd; Piano; Sec-MAYA Clb; Acted In Schl Plays; U CA Los Angeles; Pre-Med.

VILLARAZA, VALERIE B; Morse SR HS; San Diego, CA; (3); 59/641; DECA; School Play; Yrbk; JV Vllybl; High Hon Roll; Hon Roll; Pres Acad Fit Awd; Indpndnt Studies Seminar; Hnrs Seminar; UCLA; Cmmnctns.

VILLAREAL, RUTH P; Richard Gahr HS; Norwalk, CA; (3); JA; Band; Mrchg Band; Cit Awd; High Hon Roll; Dist Hnr Band; Excl Reg Fest; SCSBOA; Letter Of Merit Band; Blue & Gold Awd; Military.

VILLARREAL, CARLOS; Orosi HS; Orosi, CA; (3); Church Yth Grp; Math Clb; Spanish Clb; Rep Stu Cncl; JV Bsbl; Hon Roll; CSF; Fresno ST U; Elec Engr.

VILLARREAL, CHRISTOPHER R; Prospect HS; San Jose, CA; (1); 32/251; JV Bsbl; JV Ftbl; Hon Roll; FL ST; Geology.

VILLARREAL, GRISELDA; Oxnard HS; Oxnard, CA; (2); MESA Club; Ventura Coll; Comp Pgmr.

VILLARREAL, GRISELDA; Sacred Heart Of Jesus HS; Los Angeles, CA; (2); School Play; Lit Mag; Pres Jr Cls; Hon Roll; NHS; Prfct Atten Awd; Christian Action Movmnt; Span Awd; Folklorico Grp; CA ST U; Bus Admin.

VILLARREAL, LUIS; Orosi HS; Cutler, CA; (2); FFA; Spanish Clb; SADD; Bsbl; Bsktbl; Mgr(s); Sftbl; COS; Arch.

VILLARREAL, MARIA D; San Dimas HS; San Dimas, CA; (2); JV Bsktbl; Var Trk; Hon Roll; ROSES Awd Rcgntn Of Stu Excllnc; Math.

VILLASENOR, ALEJANDRO; South San Francisco HS; South San Francis, CA; (3); Univ; Law.

VILLASENOR, ERIC; Baldwin Park HS; Baldwin Park, CA; (3); Intrml Ftbl; Intrml Trk; Var Wrstlng; Hao Kido Karate Black Belt.

VILLASENOR, JUAN; Armijo HS; Fairfield, CA; (1); Boy Scts; Acad Sci & Technlgy; Loyola Marymount; Pediatrics.

VILLASENOR, LISA; Saint Anthony HS; Long Beach, CA; (2); Hosp Aide; Spanish Clb; Band; Mrchg Band; Rptr Nwsp; JV Bsktbl; Mgr(s); Var Trk.

VILLASENOR, MARIBEL; Tracy Joint Union HS; Tracy, CA; (2); 59/483; Church Yth Grp; FFA; Office Aide; Spanish Clb; Cit Awd; Hon Roll; UC Berkeley; Bus Mgmt.

VILLASENOR, YASMIN T; Alverno HS; Los Angeles, CA; (2); Chorus; Church Choir; Sec Frsh Cls; Sec Soph Cls; Off Jr Cls; Hon Roll; Spnsh I Awd; CA Schlrshp Fed; Advncd Plcmnt Bio Cert; 2nd Pl Annual Math Showcase.

VILLASOR, ANDREA G; St Genevieve HS; Pacoima, CA; (3); Drill Tm.

VILLATORO, KARLA J; Azusa HS; Azusa, CA; (4); Church Yth Grp; FBLA; SADD; Teachers Aide; Chorus; JV Vllybl; Rotary Club Voctnl Schlrshp; Citrus U; Interior Dsgnr.

VILLAVERDE, ANA; El Segundo HS; El Segundo, CA; (4); 3/160; Treas AFS; VP Hist Key Clb; Science Clb; Sec Hist Spanish Clb; Chorus; Stu Cncl; JV Var Swmmng; JV Var Vllybl; High Hon Roll; Hon Roll; Grls ST 89; Natl Hspnc Schlr; Cngrssnl Schlr-Natl Yng Ldrs Cnfrnc 90; Dartmouth Coll; Med.

VILLAVICENCIO, MARIA; Santiago HS; Garden Grove, CA; (2); Spanish Clb; JV Bsktbl; NHS; Doc.

VILLEDA, CLARY O; Fairview JR Acad; Fontana, CA; (2); Church Yth Grp; Office Aide; Teachers Aide; Band; Chorus; Church Choir; School Musical; School Play; Rptr Yrbk; Cit Awd; UCLA; Rgstrd Nrsng.

VILLEGAS, CYNTHIA; Mountain View HS; El Monte, CA; (2); Computer Clb; GAA; Science Clb; Cit Awd; High Hon Roll; CSF; Badminton; Rcvd Demerte Clb Awd 2nd Pl Spch Cntst; USC; Med.

VILLEGAS, DAVID; Rancho Alamitos HS; Garden Grove, CA; (1); Drama Clb; School Play; Music.

VILLEGAS, EMA; Narbonne HS; Harbor City, CA; (3); Art Clb; Teachers Aide; Chorus; School Musical; School Play; Swing Chorus; Wt Lftg; Humanitas Pgm; Commnctns.

VILLEGAS, GENEVIEVE; Pacific Christian HS; Alhambra, CA; (3); 1/20; Capt Pep Clb; Speech Tm; Temple Yth Grp; Church Choir; School Play; Sec Frsh Cls; Pres Soph Cls; Rep Jr Cls; Vllybl; High Hon Roll; Pasadena City Coll; Bus Mgmt.

VILLEGAS, JOSE; Sequoia HS; Menlo Park, CA; (3); 14/260; Bus.

VILLEGAS, JULIO A; Pater Noster HS; Los Angeles, CA; (3); Art Clb; Boy Scts; Chess Clb; Church Yth Grp; Computer Clb; Debate Tm; Math Clb; Science Clb; Spanish Clb; Acpl Chr; CA ST U; Bus Adm.

VILLEGAS, LINDA; Clairemont HS; San Diego, CA; (4); 15/210; Church Yth Grp; French Clb; FTA; Office Aide; Service Clb; Spanish Clb; SADD; Teachers Aide; Trk; High Hon Roll; UC San Diego; Bio.

VILLEGAS, LUPE M; Lindsay HS; Lindsay, CA; (4); French Clb; Treas FHA; Ltr Girl; Friday Night Live Club; Lawyer.

VILLEGAS, MARIA A; San Gorgonio HS; San Bernardino, CA; (3); JV Sftbl; JV Vllybl; Z Clb VP; Latin-Hispanis Clb; Cert High Achvt Alg I Golden St Exam; CA ST U San Bernardino.

VILLEGAS, MARISOL; Notre Dame HS; Van Nuys, CA; (1); Cheerldng.

VILLEGAS, RICHARD P E; Alhambra HS; Alhambra, CA; (2); L Bsktbl; L Trk; Piano Lessons,Church Schl; Aero Engr.

VILLEGAS, ROBERT; Roosevelt HS; Los Angeles, CA; (3); JV Bsktbl; Var Tennis; High Hon Roll; Hon Roll; All Leag Tnns Plyr.

VILLEGAS, ROGELIO; East Bakersfield HS; Bakersfield, CA; (2); Art Clb; Cit Awd; Hon Roll; Prfct Atten Awd; Art Exhbt Awd; 1st Pl Adv Drwng; Bkrsfld Coll; Art.

VILLEGAS, VERONICA; Compton SR HS; Compton, CA; (2); Church Yth Grp; Spanish Clb; Var Socr; Hon Roll; Jr NHS; NHS; GATE; ITT Tchncl; Comp Tchncn.

VILLEGAS, ZULEMA; Victor Valley HS; Victorville, CA; (2).

VILLENA JR, APOLONIO; Savanna HS; Anaheim, CA; (3); JV Bsktbl; Cert Of Achvt Eng As 2nd Lang 89-90; Outstndng Stu Awd Wrld Cultrs Savanna 89-90; Engrng.

VILLICANA, RAFAEL; Bishop Amat HS; Hacienda Hts, CA; (3); Cmnty Wkr; Var Socr; Natl Scl Stds Olympiad.

VILLICANO, DANIEL; Mater Dei HS; Anaheim, CA; (1); Spanish Clb; Jazz Band; JV Wrstlng; Notre Dame; Music.

VILLINES, JOHN W; Manteca HS; Manteca, CA; (4); 13/293; Church Yth Grp; Key Clb; SADD; Church Choir; Stage Crew; Ed Nwsp; JV Socr; Var Tennis; High Hon Roll; Hon Roll; Anti Drug Musical; Lifetime Stu & Sealbearer CSF; Acad Ltr Club; Modesto JC; Eng.

VILLON, CARMELA E; St Anthony HS; Long Beach, CA; (2); Art Clb; Treas Soph Cls; Treas Jr Cls; Cheerldng; Gym; Powder Puff Ftbl; Hon Roll; Fishng Clb; Reg Nrs.

VILLOSIS, RICHARD; Loyola HS; Glendale, CA; (2); Stage Crew; Rptr Nwsp; Hon Roll; NEDT Awd; CSF; Geology/Paleontology Soc; Chrstn Life Cmmttc; UCLA; Med.

VINCELLI, MAUREEN D; Monroe HS; Panorama City, CA; (4); 91/450; Service Clb; School Musical; School Play; Treas Soph Cls; Treas Jr Cls; Stu Cncl; L Var Sftbl; L Var Vllybl; Dance Clb; Office Aide; Ephebian; CSU Northridge; Theatre Arts.

VINCENT, BRADLEY JAY; Del Campo HS; Citrus Heights, CA; (4); 12/429; Boy Scts; Scholastic Bowl; Spanish Clb; SADD; Band; Mrchg Band; High Hon Roll; Hon Roll; Pres Acad Fit Awd; Jazz & Dixieland Jazz Band; CSF Hghst Hnr; Acad Dcthln Tm; UC Brkly; Elec Engrg.

VINCENT, BRADY J; Marina HS; Huntington Beach, CA; (3); Boy Scts; Band; Mrchg Band; Pep Band; Vet.

VINCENT, DENE; Lemoore Union HS; Lemoore, CA; (3); Church Yth Grp; Cmnty Wkr; Drama Clb; Intnl Clb; Pep Clb; Chorus; Church Choir; Cheerldng; Pom Pon; Hon Roll; Chrmn Chrch Yth Grp; Chldrns Chrch Choir Dir; 1st Pl Solo, Duet Kngs Cnty Chrstn Tlnt Srch; Sthrn CA Coll; Kndrgrtn Tchr.

VINCENT, LUKE; Hanford HS; Clovis, CA; (3); Pep Clb; Rep Frsh Cls; Rep Soph Cls; Rep Stu Cncl; CSF; Natl Assn Stu Cncls Natl Cnvtn; SIMULATORS; Biochem.

VINCENT, MIGNONNE V; Upland HS; Upland, CA; (2); Church Yth Grp; Office Aide; Teachers Aide; Band; Mrchg Band; Hon Roll; Wrtng Celebraion Awd; Achvr Awds For Alg & Engl I; Davis U; Vet.

VINCENT, STEPHEN L; Escondido HS; Escondido, CA; (1); San Diego ST U; Med.

VINCENT, THOMAS T; Red Bluff Union HS; Manton, CA; (2); Art Clb; 4-H; Fri Nght Live Club; Dr Who Fan Club Of Amer; Chem.

VINCIGUERRA, ANTOINETTE; Arcadia HS; Arcadia, CA; (3); 260/639; Ski Clb; Band; Mrchg Band; Orch; Hon Roll; Prfct Atten Awd; Pres Acad Fit Awd; Reach A Club; Cmptr Sci.

VINCZE, CLARE A; St Genevieve HS; Reseda, CA; (4); JA; Pep Clb; Chorus; Nwsp; Ed Yrbk; Catherine Coll Schlrshp; Hrdst Wrkr Awd Yrbk; Hnr Rl; Catherine Coll Bus; Travl Agnt.

VINCZE, SUZIE; St Genevieve HS; Reseda, CA; (2); Hungarian Schl 15 Yrs; Catherine Coll; Trvl & Tourism.

VINE, CHRISTOPHER C; Walnut HS; Walnut, CA; (3); Chess Clb; Var L Ftbl; Wt Lftg; Summa Cum Laude; Deans List.

VINER, EUGENE; George Washington HS; San Francisco, CA; (3); Math Tm; Rsn Clb; Comp.

VINEYARD, JENNIFER; Los Alamitos HS; Seal Beach, CA; (4); Art Clb; Treas Debate Tm; Pres German Clb; NFL; Treas Speech Tm; Ed Nwsp; Ntl Merit SF; Natl Frnscs Leag Dgree Of Dist; Lttrd In Spch & Dbte; Attrny On Mck Trl Tm.

VINGO, JAMES S; Livermore HS; Livermore, CA; (3); 48/500; Church Yth Grp; Ski Clb; Var L Bsbl; Var L Socr; High Hon Roll; Hon Roll; Prfct Atten Awd; N Coast Sctn Schlr Athlte Awd; Outstndng Acad Prfrmnc Awd Golden ST Exam 1989; Acad Achvmnt Awd; Aerontcl Engr.

VINH, LE; Edison HS; Stockton, CA; (2); Computer Clb; French Clb; Math Clb; Math Tm; Science Clb; Bsktbl; Socr; Swmmng; Hon Roll; U C Berkerly; Cnstrctn.

VINH, TONY; Tustin HS; Tustin, CA; (1); Boy Scts; Hon Roll; Tech Ed Mdl; Piano.

VINING, ANGELA D; Pioneer HS; Elk Grove, CA; (3); Ed Nwsp; Pres Stu Cncl; Stat Bsktbl; Hon Roll; Prfct Atten Awd.

VINING, DAVID W; Santa Barbara HS; Santa Barbara, CA; (2); 36/650; Drama Clb; German Clb; Acpl Chr; School Play; Stage Crew; Sec Jr Cls; Stu Cncl; JV Swmmng; Hon Roll; JV Water Polo; Jr Statesmen Amer VP & Rgnl Cabinet; Madrigal Singers; Theater Arts.

VINLUAN, RONALD; Southwest HS; San Diego, CA; (3); 30/500; Cmnty Wkr; JA; Key Clb; Pep Clb; Science Clb; Service Clb; SADD; Off Jr Cls; Stu Cncl; Var Ftbl; Pan-Asian Comm Of Sports; SDSU; Aerontcl Engrng.

VINSON, DANIEL J; Paso Robles HS; Paso Robles, CA; (2); Var Swmmng; High Hon Roll; Vrsty Water Polo Tm; CSF.

VINSON, JEFFREY B; Brea-Olinda HS; Brea, CA; (3); Key Clb; Letterman Clb; Varsity Clb; Mgr Nwsp; Treas Soph Cls; Treas VP Stu Cncl; Var Socr; Wt Lftg; Hon Roll; NHS; Golden St Exam-Hnrs; Safe Rides; Interact Clb; Bus.

VINSON, TRAVIS; Silver Valley HS; Barstow, CA; (4); 2/50; FCA; Sec Letterman Clb; Sec Sr Cls; JV Capt Bsbl; JV Bsktbl; Var L Ftbl; JV Tennis; Wt Lftg; Sal; U Of CA Riversd; Biomedcl Sci.

VINSON, WESLEY W; Barstow HS; Barstow, CA; (1); AFS; Golf; Hon Roll; Wrstlng; Acad Awd Imprvmnt; Most Imprvd JV Wrslr; Math.

VINTHER, AMY; Foothill HS; Pleasanton, CA; (2); Church Yth Grp; Cmnty Wkr; Dance Clb; FBLA; Spanish Clb; Rep Frsh Cls; Rep Soph Cls; JV Cheerldng; High Hon Roll; NHS; Geom Awd; Stanford; Phy.

VINYARD, KERRI J; A A Stagg HS; Stockton, CA; (1); Church Yth Grp; Drama Clb; Thesps; Acpl Chr; School Musical; School Play; Stage Crew; High Hon Roll; Music & Drama Ltrs; UC Santa Cruz; Russian Stds.

VINZANT, ELIZABETH; Christian HS; National City, CA; (4); 13/99; Key Clb; Office Aide; Band; Mrchg Band; Yrbk; Hon Roll; St Schlr; Azusa Pacific U.

VIOLA, SUSAN L; Clovis West HS; Clovis, CA; (3); Teachers Aide; High Hon Roll; Jr Statesman Assn, JSA Club; CSF Club; Playing Piano 10 Yrs; Pharm.

VIOLANDA, ROSARIO M; Balboa HS; San Francisco, CA; (2); ROTC; Off Jr Cls; Cheerldng; Hon Roll; Prfct Atten Awd; CSF; Hmrm VP; S F ST U; Accntng.

VIOLETTE, KALI; Chico SR HS; Chico, CA; (2); Drill Tm; Cheerldng; Pom Pon; CA ST U; Lbrl Arts.

VIOLETTI, WENDY M; Red Bluff Union HS; Cottonwood, CA; (2); 1/243; Church Yth Grp; FCA; Hosp Aide; Key Clb; Spanish Clb; SADD; Band; Mrchg Band; JV Bsktbl; JV Cheerldng; CSF; Medcl.

VIRAMONTES, NATALIA; St Joseph HS; Huntington Park, CA; (2); 30/200; Cmnty Wkr; Drama Clb; Library Aide; Spanish Clb; SADD; Chorus; Hon Roll; Private HS Schlrshp; USC; Civil Engr.

VIRAMONTES, PATRICIA; Montebello HS; Montebello, CA; (2); Dance Clb; Teachers Aide; Acpl Chr; Treas Chorus; Cit Awd; Hon Roll; ITT; Comp Engrng.

VIRAMONTES, SANDRA; Ceres HS; Ceres, CA; (4); Var Cheerldng; Var Tennis; Var Trk; Hon Roll; Ceres Supvs Schlrshp; MVP Tennis; San Jose ST U; Advrtsng.

VIRAMONTES, SUZANA; Chino HS; Chino, CA; (2); Law.

VIRANI, SULAIMAN S; Santa Monica HS; Santa Monica, CA; (2); Cmnty Wkr; Var Trk; Hon Roll; UCLA; Engrng.

VIRASIN, PRISNA; Granada Hills HS; Northridge, CA; (2); Drama Clb; Service Clb; Teachers Aide; Phtg Yrbk; Treas Frsh Cls; Hon Roll; Englsh Awd; Commnctns.

VIRGADAMO, EDITH M; El Cajon Valley HS; El Cajon, CA; (4); 31/297; GAA; Letterman Clb; Office Aide; Varsity Clb; Chorus; Church Choir; Var L Socr; Var L Sftbl; Capt Var Tennis; Var Trk; Bst Dfnc Otfldrs Sftbl; 2nd Plc Trphy Sftbl Season; Made CIF All Star Tm Sftbll Cntrfld; Grossmont Coll; Bkkpng.

VIRK, HARKIRANDEEP SINGH; Simi Valley HS; Simi Valley, CA; (3); Bsbl; Bsktbl; Sftbl; Swmmng; Gldn St Exam Geom; UCLA; Math.

VIRNIG, ERIC; Cardinal Newman HS; Santa Rosa, CA; (3); 2/85; Spanish Clb; Var L Socr.

VIRTICH, BRUNO; El Camino HS; Oceanside, CA; (3); Cit Awd; Hon Roll; Prfct Atten Awd; Surf Club.

VISAGGIO, ALEXANDRA J; Clairemont HS; San Diego, CA; (3); Church Yth Grp; Lit Mag; Hon Roll; Plyd Piano 4 Yrs; UCSD; Writer.

VISAYA, JEFF; Channel Island HS; Oxnard, CA; (4); 36/476; French Clb; FBLA; Science Clb; Hon Roll; Prfct Atten Awd; Asian Amer Clb; CA Poly Tech ST U; Elec Engr.

VISCONTE, MICAH P; Mission Viejo HS; Mission Viejo, CA; (3); Church Yth Grp; Hon Roll; Drafting Clb; Cnty Acad Decathalon Tm; Automotive Engr.

VISICH, NATASHA; Vallejo HS; Vallejo, CA; (3); Library Aide; Teachers Aide; Band; Chorus; Color Guard; Drill Tm; Co-Capt Drm Mjr(t); VP Frsh Cls; Trk; Hon Roll; Royalty Miss Princess, Best Prsnlty & Photo Wnnr; Miss Teen Sacro Fnlst; HI Tropic Pgnt 1st Rnnr Up; UCLA; Chld Psych.

VISMANTAS, ERIC L; Los Alamitos HS; Garden Grove, CA; (3); Science Clb; Band; Jazz Band; Mrchg Band; Orch; Pep Band; High Hon Roll; Hon Roll; All Southern CA Hnr Band 89 & 90; 3rd Pl Fine Arts Orange Cty Acad Decathlon 89; CSF; Surgeon.

VISTA, ERWIN N; Mira Mesa HS; San Diego, CA; (2); 71/797; Boy Scts; Science Clb; Band; Orch; Crs Cntry; Mgr(s); Trk; Prfct Atten Awd; Pres Acad Fit Awd; Arch.

VISTA, RETCHEL A; St Anthony HS; Carson, CA; (2); Art Clb; Spanish Clb; Rep Jr Cls; High Hon Roll; NHS; Prfct Atten Awd; CSF; Ldrshp Essay 3rd Place; UC Irvine; Ped; Lawyer.

VITA, CYNTHIA A S; Alverno HS; Pasadena, CA; (2); 2/70; Church Yth Grp; Chorus; Variety Show; Off Frsh Cls; Off Soph Cls; JV Vllybl; High Hon Roll; NHS; CSF; Play Organ Church Svcs; U C Coll; Bus.

VITAL, CESAR C; Gladstone HS; Azusa, CA; (3); 10/300; Boy Scts; Bus Profs of Am; Church Yth Grp; FBLA; Ski Clb; SADD; Var Ftbl; Cit Awd; Hon Roll; Prfct Atten Awd; U Of Notre Dame; Law.

VITELA, CHRISTINE E; Watsonvillle HS; Watsonville, CA; (2); 201/545; SADD; Hon Roll; Private Caretaker For Grandmother; San Diego ST; Bus Mjr.

VITORIA, MARIA CHRISTINA; Downey SR HS; Downey, CA; (3); JV Capt Bsktbl; Psych.

VITT, JENNIE R; Redlands HS; Redlands, CA; (2); Church Yth Grp; Teachers Aide; Rptr Nwsp; JV Socr; Var Trk; Var Vllybl; Hon Roll; Phy-Ed.

VITTORIA, CHRISTINE MARIE; San Marcos HS; Santa Barbara, CA; (3); 3/400; Cmnty Wkr; Treas 4-H; VP French Clb; Hosp Aide; Key Clb; Chrmn SADD; Rptr Nwsp; Sec Stu Cncl; Var Socr; JV Swmmng; Flst-CA St Brd Of Ed; Cngrss Bundestag Schlrshp; Rtry Yth Ldrshp Awd-Wnnr; Intl Rltns.

VIVAR, HILDA; North Hollywood HS; North Hollywood, CA; (3); French Clb; Tennis; UCLA; Law.

VIVERITO, KERI ANN; Nogales HS; West Covina, CA; (3); Pep Band; Cheerldng; Hon Roll; CA ST-LONG Beach; Vet.

VIVEROS, GEORGE; Fontana HS; Fontana, CA; (2); Debate Tm; French Clb; Library Aide; Teachers Aide; Wt Lftg; Cit Awd; High Hon Roll; Pres Acad Fit Awd; Engrng.

VIVIAN, JONATHAN R; Hoover HS; Fresno, CA; (1); Church Yth Grp; JV Bsktbl; Var L Trk; JV Water Polo; Phys Thrpst.

VIVIAN, KEITH A; Clovis HS; Clovis, CA; (3); 29/631; ROTC; Band; Mrchg Band; Pep Band; High Hon Roll; Hon Roll; USAF Aux; Cadet Advisory Cncl; USAFA; Pilot.

VIZCARRA, CARLOS H; Nogales HS; La Puente, CA; (3); 26/650; Crs Cntry; Trk; High Hon Roll; Hon Roll; U Of CA-LOS Angeles; Ed.

VIZCARRA, JESUS D; Carson HS; Carson, CA; (2); Library Aide; Hon Roll; Pres Acad Fit Awd; Outstndng Achvmnt In Comp Prog; CSF; Outstndng Achvmnt Math; Math/Comp.

VIZCARRA, LETICIA S; Firebaugh HS; Firebaugh, CA; (3) 8/76; Art Clb; FHA; Office Aide; Teachers Aide; Sec Jr Cls; Var Trk; High Hon Roll; Hon Roll; Fresno ST U; Med.

VIZZO, BRIDGET; Silver Valley HS; Newberry Springs, CA; (2); Drama Clb; Letterman Clb; Spanish Clb; Pres Soph Cls; Stat Bsktbl; JV Cheerldng; Var Sftbl; Hon Roll; HOBY Awd; Mock Trial; San Diego ST U; Newsbroadcastr.

VLAD, ANDREEA S; Warren HS; Downey, CA; (1); Church Yth Grp; FHA; Church Choir; Bsktbl; Liberal Arts.

VLASACHE, ALEX; Benicia HS; Benicia, CA; (2); Hon Roll; UC Davis; Elec Engrng.

VLASIC, MARK V; Thousand Oaks HS; Thousand Oaks, CA; (2); 87/554; ROTC; JV Swmmng; Hon Roll; HS Ambssdr; Bus Mgmt.

VLK, JENNIFER L; Victor Valley HS; George Afb, CA; (3); Church Yth Grp; Teachers Aide; Church Choir; Pres Frsh Cls; High Hon Roll; Hon Roll; NHS; Pres Acad Fit Awd; Eastern WA U; Elem Tchr.

VO, BANG; Western HS; Stanton, CA; (4); Boy Scts; French Clb; High Hon Roll; Hon Roll; Jr NHS; NHS; CSF; NHS; CSU Pomona; Arch Engrng.

VO, CAM LINH H; Gardena HS; Gardena, CA; (3); Debate Tm; JCL; Latin Clb; NFL; Speech Tm; Yrbk; Rep Frsh Cls; Lion Awd; Prfct Atten Awd; HS Task Force; Long Beach ST; Brdcst Jrnlst.

VO, CONG T; Gardena HS; Gardena, CA; (2); Chess Clb; French Clb; Teachers Aide; Var Tennis; Elks Awd; Hon Roll; CSF.

VO, DANNY H; University HS; Irvine, CA; (3); French Clb; Socr; Med.

VO, ELIZABETH T; Riverside Polytechnic HS; Riverside, CA; (2); Dance Clb; Drama Clb; GAA; Intnl Clb; Office Aide; SADD; Teachers Aide; Drill Tm; Hon Roll; Prfct Atten Awd; U CO; Law.

VO, HIEP B; Independence HS; San Jose, CA; (2); Intrml Bsktbl; Intrml Ftbl; Stanford; Med.

VO, HONG THI; San Gabriel HS; Rosemead, CA; (3); Bus Profs of Am; FBLA; Nwsp; Yrbk; Off Jr Cls; Bsktbl; Hon Roll; Vietnamese Club; Acctng.

VO, HUONG T; Culver City HS; Culver City, CA; (1); Tennis; Cit Awd; High Hon Roll; Hon Roll; Pres Acad Fit Awd; Vietnamese Trdtnl Music & Operas Awd 87; Hollywood Bowl Museum Exhbt 89-90; Med.

VO, KHANH H; Bolsa Grande HS; Garden Grove, CA; (3); 9/338; Intnl Clb; Latin Clb; Science Clb; Spanish Clb; Sec Frsh Cls; Treas Soph Cls; Stu Cncl; Cit Awd; Hon Roll; NHS; 3rd Cnty Sci Fair; Soc Of Wmn Engrs Awd; Aftrschl Tutor; U CA Irvine; Biochem.

VO, KIM P; Bolsa Grande HS; Westminister, CA; (2); Temple Yth Grp; Hon Roll; Vietnam/Chinese Clb; CA ST Fullerton.

VO, LUA; Rancho Alamitos HS; Anaheim, CA; (3); Hon Roll; Comp Pgmr.

VO, MINH THANH T; Oakland HS; Oakland, CA; (3); Math Clb; Math Tm; Science Clb; Spanish Clb; SADD; Teachers Aide; School Play; Stage Crew; JV Vllybl; Cit Awd; U Of Los Angeles; Psych.

VO, THAO; Independence HS; San Jose, CA; (3); French Clb.

VO, THIEN N; Fremont HS; Sunnyvale, CA; (2); Sec FBLA; Math Clb; NFL; JV Socr; Hon Roll; Pres Acad Fit Awd; CSF; Golden St Exm Alg Hgh Hnrs; UC Davis.

VO, THOMAS T; San Pasqual HS; Escondido, CA; (3); 50/440; Rep Stu Cncl; JV Intrml Bsbl; JV Intrml Ftbl; Cit Awd; Hon Roll; Prfct Atten Awd; Pres Acad Fit Awd; Acad Leag Tm; UCSD; Elec Engr.

VO, THUY T; Santa Teresa HS; San Jose, CA; (1); French Clb; UCLA; Advrtsng.

VO, THUY T; Santiago HS; Garden Grove, CA; (2); Art Clb; Var L Bsktbl; Hon Roll; Jr NHS; USC.

VO, TIN T; Leuzinger HS; Hawthorne, CA; (3); Off Jr Cls; Crs Cntry; Trk; Prfct Atten Awd; Vietnamese Clb; Mdl Airplaine Clb; CA ST Long Beach; Real Est.

VO, TONY P; Lowell HS; San Francisco, CA; (2); Orch; JV Ftbl; Golden St Exam Acad Excllnc Awd; CSF 90; Med.

VO, TRAN-HOANG H; Bolsa Grande HS; Garden Grove, CA; (4); 21/296; Var Socr; Hon Roll; Yth Vietnamese Sccr Tm; Hnr Grad Seal Bearer; Acad Schlrshp; Orange Coast Coll; Arch.

VO, TRANG M; Grace M Davis HS; Modesto, CA; (1); Intnl Clb.

VO, TRANG M; Workman HS; Valinda, CA; (2); 1/30; Intnl Clb; Science Clb; Off Jr Cls; Tennis; High Hon Roll; Prfct Atten Awd; Pres Acad Fit Awd; Sport Badminton; CSF; Literarus; CA ST Fulerton; Bus.

VO, TUAN N-A; Westminster HS; Garden Grove, CA; (1); English Clb; Chorus; High Hon Roll; Golden West Coll; Comp Prgmmng.

VO, VAN NHI T; Don Antonio Lugo HS; Chino Hills, CA; (3); 2/600; Cmnty Wkr; German Clb; Hosp Aide; Tennis; Cit Awd; High Hon Roll; NHS; Prfct Atten Awd; Conquistador, Golden St Awds; U Irvine; Pre-Med.

VO, VIET; Huntington Beach HS; Huntington Beach, CA; (3); Teachers Aide; Cit Awd; Vietnamese Clb; Tower Awd; CA ST-LONG Beach; Intl Bus.

VODDEN, AMBER; Placer HS; Meadow Vista, CA; (2); Drama Clb; French Clb; Key Clb; Science Clb; School Musical; School Play; Stage Crew; High Hon Roll; Hon Roll; Century Club; French Club Vp; Film.

VODDEN, JAMES A J; Argonaut HS; Sutter Creek, CA; (4); 2/100; Boy Scts; Church Yth Grp; Science Clb; Ski Clb; Band; Mrchg Band; Var Capt Socr; JV Trk; JV Wrstlng; High Hon Roll; CSF Pres; Principals Ldrshp Awd; Hwy Patrol Schlrshp; USC; Engrng.

VODICKA, DEVIN F; Nevada Union HS; Grass Valley, CA; (2); 14/550; Drama Clb; VP Frsh Cls; Pres Soph Cls; Rep Stu Cncl; JV Stat Bsktbl; Score Keeper; High Hon Roll.

VOET, DAWN M; Burney JR/Sr HS; Burney, CA; (2); Church Yth Grp; Cmnty Wkr; 4-H; Ski Clb; Teachers Aide; Band; School Musical; Crs Cntry; Powder Puff Ftbl; Socr; U Of Sthrn CA; Arch.

VOGEL, KAREN; Pacifica HS; Garden Grove, CA; (3); 30/400; Spanish Clb; SADD; Teachers Aide; Sec Frsh Cls; Sec Jr Cls; Treas Sr Cls; Sec Stu Cncl; Hon Roll; Eclgy Clb Pres & Pblcty Chrmn; CSF 90.

VOGEL, NIKKI C; Oak Park HS; Agoura Hills, CA; (1); Church Yth Grp; Teachers Aide; Church Choir; Yrbk; Desert Is Dream; Westmont Coll; Elem Educ.

VOGEL, ROBERT M; Tracy Joint Union HS; Tracy, CA; (4); 50/355; Church Yth Grp; Cmnty Wkr; Pres Letterman Clb; Chorus; School Play; Rep Stu Cncl; Var Capt Bsbl; Var L Bsktbl; JV Var Ftbl; Var Capt Socr; Athlete Of Yr Awd 86-87; Coaches Awd Outstnding Ldrshp 87-88; Cert Of Outstnding Achvt Math 88-89; US Naval Acad; Engrng.

VOGEL, SHANNON L; Davis SR HS; Davis, CA; (3); 126/411; Office Aide; Teachers Aide; Rep Stu Cncl; Capt Pom Pon; Var JV Vllybl; Bus.

VOGELSANG, MARYANN S; Palm Springs HS; Cathedral City, CA; (3); Debate Tm; Spanish Clb; Varsity Clb; Var Bsktbl; High Hon Roll; Hon Roll; Kiwanis Awd; Prfct Atten Awd; Vsty Bdmntn; Outstndng Ovrll Acad Achvt Awd; Envrnmntl Engrng.

VOGL, SHAWNDRA K; Red Bluff Union HS; Red Bluff, CA; (2); 40/444; Aud/Vis; Church Yth Grp; Mu Alpha Theta; Rptr Nwsp; Phtg Yrbk; High Hon Roll; Hon Roll; CSF; Alg I Golden St Exam-Hnrs; Acctng.

VOGT, ELIZABETH S; Galt Joint Union HS; Galt, CA; (3); Drama Clb; Office Aide; Pep Clb; Speech Tm; Thesps; School Musical; School Play; Cheerldng; Pom Pon; JV Vllybl; Spcl Olympcs Hostess; Teen Model Of Sc Pageant; U CA-SAN Diego; Bus Law.

VOGT, KIMBERLY; Monterey Bay Acad; Glendale, CA; (4); 1/115; Drama Clb; Ski Clb; Chorus; Church Choir; VP Sr Cls; Bsktbl; Vllybl; Hon Roll; Religious Discussion Ldr; Pacific Union Coll; Pre-Med.

VOGT, LARA L; Orange Glen HS; Escondido, CA; (4); Key Clb; Teachers Aide; CA Schlrshp Fed; Natl Hnr Soc Teas, Sec; UC Davis; Engr.

VOILES, DEMIAN; Victory Christian Schl; Folsom, CA; (2); Var Socr; Var Tennis; Hon Roll; NHS; Prfct Atten Awd; Pres Acad Fit Awd; Cls Ex Bd Mem; Sci.

VOILES, SHERYL; Cajon HS; San Bernardino, CA; (2); GAA; Swmmng; Intl Bacclrt; U CA Riverside; Med.

VOISEY, JILL D; Clovis West HS; Fresno, CA; (3); Church Yth Grp; Spanish Clb.

VOIT, ANDREW; Righetti HS; Santa Maria, CA; (2); 5/250; JV Swmmng; JR Statesman Legislative Invlvmnt Offcr; CSF; CA Mock Trial Cmptn Prosecutor 89; Corporate Law.

VOJTECH, MARCIA A; Pacifica HS; Garden Grove, CA; (2); 2/298; JV Socr; JV Vllybl; High Hon Roll; Hon Roll; CSF Co-Tutor Dir; AYSO Player 2nd Div & Gold Badge Ref; UC; Marine Bio.

VOLEK, HEATHER L; Clovis West HS; Clovis, CA; (3); Varsity Clb; Pres Frsh Cls; Var L Bsktbl; Tennis; Var L Trk; JV Vllybl; Hon Roll; Var Bsktbl Bst Defensive Plyr, Mst Inspirational; Fresno ST; Bus.

VOLKER, JIM; Pinole Valley HS; San Pablo, CA; (1); Spanish Clb; Band; Orch; Lit Mag; Hon Roll; 3rd Pl HS Spllng Bee 1990; U Of CA Los Angeles; Bio.

VOLL, MICHELLE NATALIE; San Dieguito HS; Carlsbad, CA; (4); Church Yth Grp; Orch; Ed Nwsp; Elks Awd; High Hon Roll; CA Schlrshp Fed; Cls Rep; Seallbearer; San Diego Union-Tribune Schlstc Jrnlst Awd; Bk Amer Engl Awwwd; U Of CA San Diego; Cmnctns.

VOLLMANN, JAMILLA M; Mira Loma HS; Sacramento, CA; (3); 20/284; Cmnty Wkr; Sec Math Clb; Teachers Aide; Mgr(s); Var Vllybl; High Hon Roll; Trnd Peer Cnslr; U Of CA Santa Cruz; Envrnmntl.

VOLLMER, KATHRYN R; Casa Grande HS; Petaluma, CA; (1); Cmnty Wkr; Girl Scts; Red Cross Aide; SADD; JV Bsktbl; JV Socr; JV Swmmng; Hon Roll; Pres Acad Fit Awd; Pres Schlr; AZ ST U; Psych.

VOLLOR, TAMMIE L; Hawthorne HS; Lawndale, CA; (3); Cmnty Wkr; Girl Scts; Spanish Clb; SADD; Teachers Aide; Flag Corp; Cit Awd; El Camino; Bus Admin.

VOLMER, ANGELA L; Del Campo HS; Carmichael, CA; (3); 136/446; Church Yth Grp; German Clb; Teachers Aide; Chorus; Church Choir; Hon Roll; Bus.

VOLMER, STEPHEN L; Antelope Valley HS; Lancaster, CA; (3); Boy Scts; German Clb; Ski Clb; Nwsp; Phtg Yrbk; Eagle Scout; Graphic Arts Club; Avid Sufer Snowboarder & Rockclimber; BYU-HAWAII; Psych.

VOLOCK, KELLY; Taft Union HS; Taft, CA; (2); 1/180; Church Yth Grp; Drama Clb; Pres Key Clb; Letterman Clb; Pep Clb; SADD; Varsity Clb; School Musical; School Play; Cheerldng; Soroptimist Girl Of Achvt; U Of Southern CA; Med.

VOLTA, AMANDA K; Marina HS; Huntington Beach, CA; (3); Drama Clb; Speech Tm; Chorus; School Musical; School Play; Stage Crew; Lit Mag; Hon Roll; Crisis Ecology; Golden West Coll Prfmng Arts; UCI; Perfrmng Arts.

VOLTIN, JULIE L; Trabuco Hills HS; Mission Viejo, CA; (4); 17/350; Spanish Clb; SADD; Var Socr; High Hon Roll; Hon Roll; Jr NHS; NHS; Pres Acad Fit Awd; CSF Sealbearer; Peer Asst Ldrshp; Var Sccr Hnrbl Mntn; UC Santa Barbara; Vet Med.

VOLZ, JEFF T; San Dieguito HS; Encinitas, CA; (2); French Clb; Var Tennis; Surfing & Sccr; SDSU; Bus.

VOLZ, STEPHEN J; Woodrow Wilson HS; Long Beach, CA; (4); 23/800; VP Key Clb; Science Clb; Off Jr Cls; Off Sr Cls; Stu Cncl; High Hon Roll; NHS; Pres Acad Fit Awd; DANCE VP; Martin Rogovin American History Award 1989; President Senior Mens Council; USC; Business.

VON ASPERN, JASON P; Alhambra HS; Martinez, CA; (3); 42/224; Church Yth Grp; Letterman Clb; Ski Clb; Spanish Clb; Teachers Aide; Varsity Clb; Rep Jr Cls; Bsbl; Capt Ftbl; Wt Lftg; N Coast Schlr Athl; Bsbll Coaches Awd; Cogswell; Firefighter.

VON BEHREN, JEFFREY; Francis W Parker Schl; El Cajon, CA; (4); 1/57; Ed Nwsp; Pres Frsh Cls; Var Capt Bsktbl; Var Ftbl; Var Trk; DAR Awd; Val; Porterfield Schlr; Cum Laude Soc Pres; Pomona Coll; Law.

VON BUELOW, JEREMY W; Chaminade College Prep; Northridge, CA; (3); Church Yth Grp; Cmnty Wkr; Letterman Clb; Varsity Clb; Var Crs Cntry; Var Trk; High Hon Roll; NHS; Biathlete; Rcvd Outstndg Achvt Awds Alg II,Trig,US Hist,Chem & Sci; Weight Lift.

VON DOEREN, RENEE M; Santa Clara HS; Oxnard, CA; (2); Pep Clb; Hon Roll; NHS; Chrch Vllybl; UC Santa Barbara; Phys Thrpy.

VON DOHLEN, KAREN L; Grace Davis HS; Modesto, CA; (1); AFS; Quiz Bowl; Band; Mrchg Band; Pep Band; Hon Roll; Cecchetti Exams Grad; Interact; Sci.

VON GLAHN, STACEY; Piner HS; Santa Rosa, CA; (2); Church Yth Grp; French Clb; Off Soph Cls; JV Capt Pom Pon; High Hon Roll; Special Recgntn Awd; Ldrsh; USA Chrldng Natls.

VON HELF, DARRIN B; Cajon HS; San Bernardino, CA; (2); Church Yth Grp; JV Tennis; Cit Awd; Pres Acad Fit Awd; Arch.

VON HOERL, SHERVYN; St Ignatius Preparatory Schl; Novato, CA; (2); Wt Lftg; High Hon Roll; CSF; Harvard U; Poltcl Sci.

VON LATTA, CARIN L; Modesto HS; Modesto, CA; (3); AFS; Cmnty Wkr; Hosp Aide; Pep Clb; Teachers Aide; Sec Soph Cls; Sec Jr Cls; VP Stu Cncl; Psych.

VON LOSSBERG, SCOTT A; Crescenta Valley HS; La Canada, CA; (3); Am Leg Boys St; Church Yth Grp; VP Key Clb; Letterman Clb; Mu Alpha Theta; Science Clb; Yrbk; JV Bsbl; Capt Bsktbl; NHS; CSF; Stanford U; Engr.

VON NAGY, DANIELLE; Douglass JR HS; Woodland, CA; (1); Pep Clb; Cheerldng; Hon Roll; Jr NHS; Prfct Atten Awd; Psych.

VONDRA, JAMES; Bethel Christian HS; Lancaster, CA; (2); Church Yth Grp; Varsity Clb; Church Choir; Rep Soph Cls; Var Bsbl; Var Bsktbl; Var Ftbl; Hon Roll; PE Tchr.

VONDRAK, JENNIFER; Menlo Atherton HS; Menlo Park, CA; (3); Off Jr Cls; JV Crs Cntry; Pom Pon; Var Socr; JV Tennis; Hon Roll; Bio.

VONER, JEFFREY T; Whittier Christian HS; Whittier, CA; (3); Boy Scts; Treas Frsh Cls; VP Soph Cls; VP Jr Cls; Var Crs Cntry; Var Socr; Cit Awd; High Hon Roll; Lion Awd; Stanford.

VONG, AN; John F Kennedy HS; Los Angeles, CA; (2); Key Clb; Math Clb; Teachers Aide; JV Tennis; Hon Roll; Prfct Atten Awd; Golden St Exam Geom Hnrs; Schl Math Meet 4th Pl Geom; CSF.

VONG, DAT Q; Independence HS; San Jose, CA; (2); Science Clb.

VONG, HING; Millikan HS; Long Beach, CA; (3); Art Clb; Office Aide; Teachers Aide; Cit Awd; Hon Roll; Prfct Atten Awd; Pres Acad Fit Awd; ROP; CSF; Lafayette Limelighter; LBCC.

VONG, KOSAL; Lincoln HS; Stockton, CA; (2); #92 In Class; French Hon Soc; High Hon Roll; Hon Roll; San Joaquin Delta Coll; Engr.

VONG, MINH K; Arlington HS; Riverside, CA; (3); FBLA; Cit Awd; Hon Roll; Pres Acad Fit Awd; U Of Riverside; Bus Admin.

VONG, ON; Thomas A Edison HS; Fresno, CA; (4); 1/225; Math Tm; Science Clb; JV Tennis; High Hon Roll; JETS Awd; Kiwanis Awd; Ntl Merit Ltr; Val; Odyssey Of Mind; Sci Olympiad; Harvard; Physics.

VONG, STEPHEN; Lowell HS; San Francisco, CA; (3); Aud/Vis; Computer Clb; Office Aide; Red Cross Aide; Co-Capt Swmmng; Civil Air Patrol; San Francisco Cadet Squadron 86; Aerospace.

VONG, TAMMY A; Hoover HS; Fresno, CA; (3); French Clb; FBLA; Science Clb; SADD; Ed Nwsp.

VONGCHANTHA, KHAMSAY; Hoover HS; Fresno, CA; (3); Letterman Clb; Office Aide; Spanish Clb; VP JV Ftbl; Trk; Var Art Clb; Wt Lftg; JV Wrstlng; Cit Awd; Hon Roll; Jv Ftbl Mst Outstndng Offnsv Plyr; 2nd Pl Turlock Wrstlng Trnnt; CSU Fresno; Elctrcn.

VONGKHAMCHANH, CHANHDENG; Edison HS; Fresno, CA; (1); 3/50; Spanish Clb; Rep Stu Cncl; Cit Awd; Hon Roll; Se Asian Clb; Stu Body Pres; U Fresno ST; Scndry Tchr.

VONGPHACHANH, KHAMKO; Edison HS; Fresno, CA; (3); 52/234; Photog Clb; Fresno ST U; Comp Sci.

VONGSA, STACEY; River City HS; W Sacramento, CA; (2); French Clb; Key Clb; SADD; Hon Roll; Prfct Atten Awd; Stu Caring About Stu Club; Cmptr Prgmg.

VONGSENA, PHONSANITH; Modesto HS; Modesto, CA; (3); Cit Awd; Hon Roll; CSF; Bus.

VONGTHONPHANH, LANE; Bellflower HS; Bellflower, CA; (2); 33/341; Spanish Clb; Tennis; High Hon Roll; USC; Bus.

VONGVILAY, BOODSADI; El Camino Real HS; Los Angeles, CA; (3); Boy Scts; Cmnty Wkr; Office Aide; Service Clb; Stage Crew; Swing Chorus; Yrbk; Stu Cncl; Bsktbl; CSUN; Bus.

VONHEEDER, JOSEPH H; Dublin HS; Dublin, CA; (4); 22/145; Boy Scts; Cmnty Wkr; Drama Clb; Teachers Aide; Band; Drm Mjr(t); Jazz Band; Mrchg Band; Orch; Pep Band; USA Drum Major Camp Ldrshp Awd 88; USA Drum Major Camp Supr Awd 88; Golden St Exam Alg Hnrs; San Jose ST; Music.

VOO, IRENE; Marina HS; Huntington Bch, CA; (3); AFS; Church Yth Grp; VP Key Clb; Spanish Clb; Lit Mag; Hon Roll; Prfct Atten Awd; Mock Trl; Chinese Clb Sec.

VOONG, KHI JASON S; Downtown Business HS; Los Angeles, CA; (2); Library Aide; ROTC; Science Clb; Teachers Aide; School Musical; Rep Frsh Cls; Rep Soph Cls; Bsbl; Hon Roll; U CA Snt Brbr; Bus Ecnmcs.

VOONG, KIN S; C K Mc Clatchy HS; Sacramento, CA; (4); Library Aide; Office Aide; Nwsp; Off Sr Cls; Bsbl; Bsktbl; Ftbl; Sftbl; Swmmng; Tennis.

VOONG, LAN K; Montclair HS; Pomona, CA; (3); 13/513; Key Clb; Treas Library Aide; Science Clb; Spanish Clb; Rptr Nwsp; High Hon Roll; Hon Roll; NHS; Prfct Atten Awd; CSF; Envrnmntl Club & GATE Club; Rcgntn Span III, Bio, US Hist, Geom, Span II; Stu Of Mnth 89; UCLA; Intl Bus.

VOORHEES, ERIC V; Venice HS; Marina Del Rey, CA; (3); Church Yth Grp; Cmnty Wkr; FHA; Office Aide; Teachers Aide; Socr; Wt Lftg; High Hon Roll; Hon Roll; Bus.

VOORHEES, STEPHENIE; Mariposa County HS; Midpines, CA; (2); Drama Clb; Office Aide; Spanish Clb; Thesps; Band; Pep Band; School Play; Stage Crew; Hon Roll; Camp CIT; Thtre.

VOORTING, CRAIG; Los Alamitos HS; Los Alamitos, CA; (3); Var Bsbl; JV Capt Bsktbl; Hon Roll; Cmpng; Drt Bk Rcng; Wtrsking; Jet Sking; U Of AZ; Engrng.

VORA, SHEETAL; Archbishop Mitty HS; San Jose, CA; (3); Hosp Aide; Red Cross Aide; Speech Tm; Temple Yth Grp; Yrbk; Stu Cncl; JV Fld Hcky; Treas NHS; HOBY Schlrshp; Etchnic Yth Club Pres; UC Berkeley; Pre Med.

VORAC, FABIOLA B; Mount Miguel HS; Lemon Grove, CA; (4); 23/370; Drama Clb; French Clb; Speech Tm; Stage Crew; Variety Show; Ed Yrbk; Score Keeper; High Hon Roll; Hon Roll; MESA VP; UCSD.

VORALIK, JOHN; San Lorenzo Valley HS; Boulder Creek, CA; (4); 8/219; Am Leg Boys St; Church Yth Grp; Key Clb; Science Clb; Service Clb; Spanish Clb; Chorus; Church Choir; School Musical; School Play; Part-Time Job; Friday Night Live; Scuba Ocean Action Club; JV Bsktbl Coaches Awd; Var Bskt Schlr Athl; UCLA; Arch.

VORCE, GREGORY D; Castle Park HS; Chula Vista, CA; (3); 27/422; Church Yth Grp; Var L Socr; Acad Ltr; CSF; Bus.

VOSBURG, SHANTEL; Chowchilla HS; Henry, IL; (2); Pep Clb; JV Cheerldng; Hon Roll; Head Chrldr; Home Rm Rep; Excllnt Attndc 1989-90; N Western U; Jrnlsm.

VOSBURGH, ERIC; Rowland HS; Rowland Hts, CA; (4); Debate Tm; Letterman Clb; Varsity Clb; Intrml Bsbl; Var Swmmng; JV Wrstlng; Hon Roll; Ntl Merit Schol; Pres Acad Fit Awd; Commendation For Sierra 1st Leag & Schlrshp & Acad Excllnc; Citrus Coll; Guidance.

VOSKUIL, LISA M; Clovis HS; Clovis, CA; (3); Dance Clb; Science Clb; SADD; Color Guard; Mrchg Band; Var JV Swmmng; High Hon Roll; Colorguard Capt 2 Yrs; Ecology Club; Hiking Club; CSF; Psych.

VOSS, JENNIFER L; Richard Gahr HS; Norwalk, CA; (1); Band; Mrchg Band; Pep Band; Hon Roll; Green Peace.

VOSSLER, MEGAN E; Ventura HS; Ventura, CA; (3); Cmnty Wkr; SADD; Teachers Aide; JV Trk; High Hon Roll; Hon Roll; Ntl Merit Ltr; Greenpeace; Amnesty Intl; Ventura Clg Ed Olympcs 2nd Pl Engl 90; Smmr Humanities Inst UC Davis 90; Intl Rltns.

VOSTI, GINA M; Notre Dame HS; Gonzales, CA; (4); 5/92; Church Yth Grp; Cmnty Wkr; 4-H; 4-H Awd; Hon Roll; NHS; Pres Acad Fit Awd; Poltcl Worker; U CA Davis; Ag.

VOSTRY, VONNIE J; Clovis West HS; Fresno, CA; (4); 50/535; Cmnty Wkr; Drama Clb; English Clb; GAA; Hosp Aide; Intnl Clb; Key Clb; Letterman Clb; Library Aide; Service Clb; Dept Store Yth Rep; Daisy Chain; CSF; Fresno City Coll; Advrtsng.

VOTAW, DARLA S; Orange Glen HS; Escondido, CA; (3); Church Yth Grp; Spanish Clb; Band; Var JV Swmmng; Hon Roll; BYU; Psych.

VOTAW, SHANA; Alisal HS; Salinas, CA; (3); Church Yth Grp; Office Aide; Yrbk; Intrml Capt Cheerldng; Var Pom Pon; JV Var Sftbl; High Hon Roll; Hon Roll; Sonoma ST; Sec Educ.

VOUDOURIS, MICHAEL P; Del Campo HS; Fair Oaks, CA; (3); JV Var Ftbl; Var Swmmng; Var Trk; Var Wt Lftg; Master Cnclr Of Sacramento Demolay; American River; History.

VOYLES, ROBERT L; North HS; Bakersfield, CA; (2); ROTC; Teachers Aide; Co-Ed Yrbk; Cit Awd; High Hon Roll; Hon Roll; ROTC Drll Tm; Vltr Toys Tots Drv; Advcd Plcmnt & Hnr Cls; US Military.

VRANES, KEVIN; Woodside HS; Redwood City, CA; (2); Band; Jazz Band; Mrchg Band; Pep Band; U CA Santa Cruz; Astrnmy.

VRANESH, ANNE M; Carondelet HS; Lafayette, CA; (3); Ski Clb; Varsity Clb; Swmmng; DAR Awd; Campfire Girls & Boys Brd Member, Ldr, Yth; Pool Clb Brd Member; Bus.

VREELAND, SHARON M; Edison HS; Huntington Beach, CA; (2); Teachers Aide; Orange Cnty Acad Cmptn; Stu Achvt Awd; Law.

VROBEL, ARIK; Trabuco Hills HS; Mission Viejo, CA; (3); French Clb; Model UN; VP Temple Yth Grp; Ed Nwsp; Intrml Bsbl; Intrml Bsktbl; Intrml Ftbl; Intrml Socr; Intrml Swmmng; Intrml Tennis; Jewish Yth Grps Betar, BBYO Cnclr; Premed.

VROLYKS, NICOLE J; Chaffey HS; Ontario, CA; (1); Cmnty Wkr; High Hon Roll; NHS; Marine Bio.

VROOM, JASON F; University City HS; San Diego, CA; (3); 74/400; Church Yth Grp; Teachers Aide; Ftbl; Trk; Wt Lftg; Wrstlng; Hon Roll; Prfct Atten Awd; Scl Sci Awd 89-90; San Diego Trib Schlr Athl Awd 89-90; UCLA; Engrng.

VROOMAN, JOY; Mar Vista HS; Imperial Beach, CA; (2); 35/435; Dance Clb; Church Yth Grp; Pep Clb; Scholastic Bowl; SADD; Variety Show; Var Cheerldng; Hon Roll; Prfct Atten Awd; Dance Chorecography 2 Yr Dancer; UC Santa Barbara; Engl Tchr.

VROOMAN, STEVEN S; Buena Park HS; Buena Park, CA; (3); 1/380; Am Leg Boys St; Capt Chess Clb; Pres Church Yth Grp; Pres Debate Tm; Drama Clb; Key Clb; NFL; Science Clb; Pres Speech Tm; School Play; Associated Stu Body Pres Elect 90-91; CSF Exec Cabinet Mem & Pres; HOBY Ldrshp Smnr.

VU, ALAN D; El Toro HS; El Toro, CA; (4); 12/514; French Clb; High Hon Roll; Pres Acad Fit Awd; St Schlr; Charger Excllnc Awd Physcs And Alg I; Goldn ST Exam Hnrs Algе I And Geom; Excllnc Awd Eng I & Hnrs Ma; U CA Irvine; Comp Engrng.

VU, ANH; Baldwin Park HS; Baldwin Park, CA; (1); SADD; USC; Obstetrician.

VU, ANH T; Rancho Alamitos HS; Stanton, CA; (3); 24/270; French Clb; Science Clb; Hon Roll; NHS; Vietnamese Clb; CA ST Long Beach; Engrng.

VU, ANHNGOC T; San Gabriel Mission HS; Rosemead, CA; (2); 46/125; Church Yth Grp; Drama Clb; GAA; Pep Clb; Cit Awd; Prfct Atten Awd; Mission Mrt Awd; JAM Club; UCLA; Bus Pediatrician.

VU, BICH NGOC N; Venice HS; Culver City, CA; (1); Tennis; Cit Awd; Hon Roll; Prfct Atten Awd; Intl Vietnamese Club; Tae Kwon Do Black Stripe; UCLA; Med.

VU, CUONG V; Mountain View HS; Santa Ana, CA; (3); Boy Scts; Church Yth Grp; French Clb; Hon Roll; UCLA; Machinist.

VU, DUC H; Gardena HS; Gardena, CA; (3); UCLA; Physcn.

VU, DUNG; Valley HS; Sacramento, CA; (4); Library Aide; Teachers Aide; Socr; Wt Lftg; High Hon Roll; Prfct Atten Awd; U C Davis; Elect Engr.

VU, DUNG M; Laguna Hills HS; Laguna Hills, CA; (4); 2/342; Church Yth Grp; French Clb; Key Clb; Math Clb; Science Clb; L Var Trk; High Hon Roll; Pres Acad Fit Awd; Sal; Orange Cnty Sci & Engrng Fair, Sweepstkes Awd; Christa Mc Auliffe Fllwshp Pgm; UC Berkeley; Pre-Med.

VU, GIANG T; Saint Ignatius College Prep; Daly City, CA; (3); CA Schlrshp Fed; Asian Stu Coalition; Phy.

VU, HA THI; Santiago HS; Garden Grove, CA; (1); French Clb; GAA; Math Clb; Science Clb; Bsktbl; Trk; Vllybl; Cit Awd; Hon Roll; Med.

VU, HUNG; East Union HS; Manteca, CA; (4); 3/269; Key Clb; Science Clb; Band; Jazz Band; Yrbk; Stu Cncl; Crs Cntry; Tennis; Hon Roll; GATE Pgm-Gftd & Tlntd Educ; UCLA; Pdtrcs.

VU, KONG P; Clovis West HS; Pinedale, CA; (2); Intrml Crs Cntry; Positive Attitude Month; Guitar; UCLA.

VU, LE-MINH; Hawthorne HS; Hawthorne, CA; (4); Math Tm; Off Jr Cls; Tennis; Vllybl; Cit Awd; Vietnamese Clb; Sumemr Job SYETP; El Camino Coll; Bus.

VU, LONG V; Santiago HS; Santa Ana, CA; (2).

VU, MARTIN; Valley HS; Santa Ana, CA; (1); CA Jr Schlrshp Fed; DAR Awd; Presdntl Acad Ftnss Awd; UC Davis; Elec Engrng.

VU, MARY; Irvine HS; Irvine, CA; (4); Am Leg Aux Girls St; Hosp Aide; Key Clb; Service Clb; Ed Yrbk; Lit Mag; Cit Awd; High Hon Roll; NHS; Pres Acad Fit Awd; UCI Essay Cont 1st Pl Orange Cnty; Bk Of America Awd Wnnr Achvt Lbrl Arts; Excllnc Awd Natl Jrnlsm; UC Los Angeles; Poli Sci.

VU, MINH T; Leuzinger HS; Lawndale, CA; (3); Computer Clb; Peer Tutor; Hgh Hnr Golden St Exam Geom; Math & Comp; Elec.

VU, MYCHAU; Monte Vista HS; Danville, CA; (2); Math Clb; Outstndng Schlrshp & Cooprtn Engl; UCLA; Bnkr.

VU, PHUOC H; Mount Pleasant HS; San Jose, CA; (3); Math Clb; Tennis; Hon Roll; NHS; U Of CA Berkeley; Law.

VU, PHUONG ANH X; Valley HS; Santa Ana, CA; (3); Art Clb; Church Yth Grp; French Clb; Girl Scts; Key Clb; Office Aide; Church Choir; School Musical; Tennis; Hon Roll; Badminton Vrsty; Cngrssnl Yth Ldrshp Cncl; Music; UCI; Fshn Dsgn.

VU, SCOTT; St Michaels Preparatory HS; Santa Ana, CA; (1); Art Clb; Boy Scts; Church Yth Grp; Var Bsbl; Var Bsktbl; Hon Roll; Jr NHS.

VU, TAN B; Montclair HS; Ontario, CA; (3); 7/400; Chess Clb; Math Clb; Science Clb; Spanish Clb; Swmmng; Wt Lftg; High Hon Roll; Prfct Atten Awd; Pres Acad Fit Awd; Water Polo; GATE; CSF; U Of CA Riverside; Chiroprctcs.

VU, TAY T; Pinole Valley HS; Pinole, CA; (2); French Clb; Tennis; CSF; Goldn St Exam Geom High Hnrs; Biomedcl Engrng.

VU, THANH H; Fremont HS; Oakland, CA; (3); 2/500; Cmnty Wkr; Math Tm; Teachers Aide; Church Choir; Stage Crew; Ed Nwsp; Yrbk; Rptr Lit Mag; VP Jr Cls; Rep Stu Cncl; Xchng Stu Pgm; Moot Ct Cmptn Clb; Prjct Turnaround Tutor.

VU, THOA K; Saddleback HS; Santa Ana, CA; (3); Chess Clb; French Clb; Mu Alpha Theta; Science Clb; Chorus; Church Choir; High Hon Roll; UCI.

VU, THU-HANG T; Westmoor HS; Daly City, CA; (4); French Clb; GAA; Teachers Aide; Band; Rep Frsh Cls; JV Mgr(s); JV Vllybl; Hon Roll; San Francisco ST U; Bus Mrktng.

VU, TIEN K; Westminster HS; Westminster, CA; (2); Bio.

VU, TIEN T; Santa Teresa HS; San Jose, CA; (2); French Clb; Hosp Aide; Tennis; Vietnamese Club; 1st & 2(d Pl Dist Art Fair; CSF.

VU, TRANG A; Marina HS; Huntington Beach, CA; (2); Church Yth Grp; Hon Roll; Prfct Atten Awd; Var Badminton; Cstmtlgy.

VU, TULAM T; Morse SR HS; San Diego, CA; (3); French Clb; FTA; Science Clb; SADD; Band; Orch; French Hon Soc; Jr NHS; Prfct Atten Awd; U City San Diego; Med.

VU, TUNG T; Milpitas HS; Milpitas, CA; (3); Chess Clb; JV Ftbl; High Hon Roll; Chinese & Vietnamese Clb; Santa Clara U; Pre Med.

VU, VAN; Stagg HS; Stockton, CA; (3); French Clb; Girl Scts; Hon Roll; Delta Coll; Nrsng.

VU, VINH; Los Amigos HS; Fountain Valley, CA; (3); French Clb; Hon Roll; Desgnr.

VU, VU JOEY; Los Amigos HS; Santa Ana, CA; (2); 56/365; JV Bsktbl; High Hon Roll; NHS; Vienamese Clb; U CA Irvine; Med Psysician.

VU, XUAN THI; Saddleback HS; Santa Ana, CA; (3); French Clb; Chorus; Prfct Atten Awd; Pres Acad Fit Awd; CSF; Peers In Contact Club, Helping Poor Attendance Stu; History.

VU, YEN; Highlands HS; Sacramento, CA; (2); Hon Roll; U Of CA Davis Erly Acad Outrch Pgm; UC Davis; Law.

VUCELICH, RUDY J; Vallejo SR HS; Vallejo, CA; (2); Spanish Clb; SADD; Yrbk; Illustrator.

VUE, HOUA STACEY; Tulare Union HS; Tulare, CA; (1); Variety Show; Hon Roll; U CA Davis; Med.

VUE, KO; Hoover HS; Fresno, CA; (3); Teachers Aide; Hon Roll; Outstndng Acadmc Excllnc Frnch II; Outstndng Schlrshp Sci; Prncpls Acadmc Excllnc Awd; H U Club Treas; Med.

VUE, LEE P; River City HS; W Sacramento, CA; (1); Socr; Tennis; Vllybl; Hon Roll; Vlybl Club; Multi-Culture Club.

VUE, MAY; River City HS; W Sacramento, CA; (1); 3/30; SADD; Teachers Aide; Cit Awd; French Hon Soc; High Hon Roll; Hon Roll; UC Berkley; Nrs.

VUE, MEE; Merced HS; Merced, CA; (3); Spanish Clb; Hon Roll.

VUE, PHENG; River City HS; West Sacramento, CA; (1).

VUE, PHONG; River City HS; Sacramento, CA; (2).

VUE, SA; Luther Burbank HS; Sacramento, CA; (3); JV Var Socr; Intrml Wt Lftg; Hon Roll; Prfct Atten Awd; Grant Union HS; Cmptr Sci.

VUE, SHAENG; Redwood HS; Visalia, CA; (2); Pres Dance Clb; German Clb; GAA; Intnl Clb; Library Aide; JV Vllybl; Wt Lftg; Hon Roll; FIDM; Fshn Merchandising.

VUE, TOU; Lindhurst HS; Marysville, CA; (3); Var Socr; Cit Awd; Hon Roll; CSF; Dentistry.

VUE, YOUA; Hoover HS; Fresno, CA; (2); Intnl Clb; Library Aide; Chorus; Hon Roll.

VUE, YOUA; Luther Burbank HS; Sacramento, CA; (2); 13/389; Cit Awd; Hon Roll; Prfct Atten Awd; UC Davis; Med.

VUICA, VONYA A; Willow Glen HS; San Jose, CA; (2); Fld Hcky; Socr; Sftbl; Mst Imprvd Plyr Vrsty Fld Hockey 89; MVP JV Sftbl 90.

VUONG, ANN; Venice Magnet HS; Los Angeles, CA; (3); Science Clb; Teachers Aide; Chorus; Hon Roll; Chinese Schl; UC San Diego; Cmmnctns.

VUONG, DARNELL K; Abraham Lincoln HS; San Francisco, CA; (3); Business.

VUONG, HUE MY; Ganesha HS; Pomona, CA; (1); Cit Awd; Hon Roll; Law.

VUONG, HUNG; Luther Burbank HS; Sacramento, CA; (3); Cmnty Wkr; Computer Clb; Debate Tm; French Clb; Library Aide; Math Clb; Math Tm; ROTC; Science Clb; Service Clb; UC Davis; Bus.

VUONG, HUNG T; Oakland HS; Oakland, CA; (3); German Clb; Key Clb; JV Bsbl; JV Sftbl; JV Swmmng; JV Vllybl; Hayward ST; Bus.

VUONG, HUY C; Saugus HS; Valencia, CA; (3); Art Clb; French Clb; Math Clb; Science Clb; Spanish Clb; Ping-Pong Capt; Electronic Clb; Sci.

VUONG, KHANH; Woodrow Wilson HS; Oakland, CA; (4); German Clb; Key Clb; SADD; Teachers Aide; JV Crs Cntry; JV Trk; Sec NHS; Hnrs Golden St Exam Algebra; Mock Trial Tm; ASC Testing U Of Southern CA; CA ST U Hayward.

VUONG, LAM V; Rosemead HS; Rosemead, CA; (3); Computer Clb; FBLA; Intnl Clb; Key Clb; Math Clb; Spanish Clb; Var Bsktbl; Var Trk; High Hon Roll; Prfct Atten Awd; USC; Med.

VUONG, LINH K; Warren HS; Downey, CA; (2); Key Clb; Hon Roll; Word Processing Of Business Honors Day At Centos College; Playing Piano & Swimming; Johns Hopkins; Medical Doctor.

VUONG, LIONG T; Lincoln HS; San Francisco, CA; (3); French Clb; Tennis; Hon Roll; Japanese, Fncng, Chinese Clbs; San Jose ST U; Optcn.

VUONG, PHUNG; Mark Keppel HS; Alhambra, CA; (3); FBLA; Library Aide; Math Clb; Off Science Clb; Teachers Aide; School Musical; Variety Show; Lit Mag; Hon Roll; Prfct Atten Awd; CSF; Alhambra Schl Dist Vlntr Scv Awd; Southrn CA Chaur Jou Assoc; UCLA; Bio.

VUONG, QUYNH-VAN THI; San Clemente HS; San Clemente, CA; (4); Hosp Aide; Math Tm; Spanish Clb; Yrbk; Cit Awd; Elks Awd; High Hon Roll; Pres Acad Fit Awd; Rotary Awd; Val; Highst Achvt Awd Schl Sci Fair; UCI; Chem Physcn.

VUONG, RICK; Orange Glen HS; Escondido, CA; (3); 3/458; German Clb; Math Tm; JV Var Tennis; N Co Acad Leag; CSF.

VUONG, THANH M; Bassett HS; La Puente, CA; (3); FBLA; Teachers Aide; School Play; JV Sftbl; JV Vllybl; NHS; Loud & Proud Clb Pres; Cal Poly Pomona; Engrng.

VUONG, TINH-UYEN C; Adolph Leuzinger HS; Lawndale, CA; (3); Pres AFS; Computer Clb; French Clb; Science Clb; Teachers Aide; Chorus; Ed Rptr Nwsp; Cit Awd; High Hon Roll; Hon Roll; Peer Tutor; Scrtry Of Peer Tutng Pgm; Stu To Belgium 1990; Acad Dcthln; Scrtry Of Chinese Clb; Surgn.

VUTAM, ANDY; Mt Pleasant HS; San Jose, CA; (2); Art Clb; French Clb; School Play; Pres Jr Cls; Hon Roll; Co Fndr Offcr MPHH; CADD & SADD; Stanford U; Med.

VUTIKULLIRD, ARUNYA A; St Joseph HS; Cerritos, CA; (3); 14/188; Science Clb; Hon Roll; CSF; Outstndng Achvt Awd Alg I & U S Hstry; Vlntr Swmmng Instrctr Asstnt; Dentstry.

VUTTHY, VADDANA; Tokay HS; Stockton, CA; (2); Church Yth Grp; Church Choir; Khemrae Club Treas; Cambodian Club; UC Berkeley; Med Doc.

VY, TAI; San Gabriel HS; San Gabriel, CA; (3); Bus Profs of Am; Computer Clb; English Clb; Math Clb; Science Clb; School Play; Lit Mag; Bsktbl; Mgr(s); Wt Lftg; Cal Poly U; Cnstrctn Engrng.

VYAS, DEVESH B; Culver City HS; Culver City, CA; (3); Stage Crew; L Bsktbl; High Hon Roll; AP Prgm & Honor System; Blue & Silver Honor Roll; Harvard; Surgeon.

WAALKES, JOHN C; Canyon Springs HS; Moreno Valley, CA; (3); Band; Jazz Band; Mrchg Band; Pep Band; Phtg Nwsp; Rep Jr Cls; High Hon Roll; Hon Roll; Photographer.

WAANDERS, JASON M; The Bishops Schl; Olivenhain, CA; (3); Scholastic Bowl; Spanish Clb; Jazz Band; JV Swmmng; Bausch & Lomb Sci Awd; Hon Roll; Ntl Merit SF; Pres Acad Fit Awd.

WAASDORP, MIKE S; Portola JR-SR HS; Blairsden, CA; (2); Letterman Clb; Band; Swing Chorus; Variety Show; Bsbl; Bsktbl; Ftbl; Wrstlng; Hon Roll; Prfct Atten Awd; Reach Out Amer; USC; Fed Bureau Invstgtr.

WABS, MICHAEL D; Redlands HS; Redlands, CA; (3); 6/1000; Am Leg Boys St; Boy Scts; FBLA; Math Tm; Scholastic Bowl; Band; Mrchg Band; Pep Band; JV Trk; NHS; 1st Pl St Of CA Wrtng Cont; Vice Chf Order Of Arrow Ldg; 1st Pl Dist Spllng Cont; 3rd Pl Dist Sci Fair; Engrng.

WACHOB, BRANDY L; North HS; Bakersfield, CA; (2); Teachers Aide; Hon Roll; Stu Tutor; Spec Olympcs Hlpr; Fgn Exch Stu Host; Tchr.

WACHTER, MICHELLE; Abraham Lincoln HS; San Jose, CA; (3); 60/370; Computer Clb; Ski Clb; Spanish Clb; JV Var Pom Pon; Var Trk; Hon Roll; Rotary Awd; Natl Chrldng Assoc All Amer; Cngrssnl Yth Ldrshp Cncl Cngrssnl Schlr; Loyola Marymount; Dance.

WADA, NIKOLAS I; Novato HS; Novato, CA; (3); Am Leg Boys St; Drama Clb; School Play; Variety Show; Nwsp; Lit Mag; Var Bsbl; JV Bsktbl; High Hon Roll; Hon Roll; Geom GSE Awds; Drama Awd; Outstndng Engl Stu.

WADDEL, CANDY L; Atwater HS; Atwater, CA; (1); French Clb; CSF; Interior Decrtng.

WADDELL, ANDY J; Red Bluff Union HS; Proberta, CA; (2); FFA; Hon Roll; Ftnss Instrctr.

WADDELL, KARLA; Lodi Acad; Lodi, CA; (4); Church Yth Grp; Chorus; Ed Yrbk; Sec Frsh Cls; Sec Soph Cls; Sec Jr Cls; Treas Sr Cls; Sec Stu Cncl; Ftbl; Vllybl; Pacific Union Coll; Nursing.

WADDELL, MARVIN S; Sacramento Country Day HS; Sacramento, CA; (3); Church Yth Grp; Cmnty Wkr; Debate Tm; FBLA; Spanish Clb; Speech Tm; High Hon Roll; Hon Roll; Jr NHS; NHS; Morehouse; Bus.

WADDLE, MEGAN; Palm Springs Christian HS; Desert Hot Spring, CA; (1); Intrml Bsktbl; Cheerldng; Intrml Sftbl; Intrml Vllybl; Hon Roll; Church Yth Grp; Hosp Aide; Sign Lang Clb; UCLA; Med.

WADE, JENNIFER L; Newbury Park HS; Newbury Park, CA; (1); Church Yth Grp; GAA; Hosp Aide; Key Clb; SADD; School Musical; School Play; Rep Frsh Cls; Rep Stu Cncl; Bsktbl; Communications.

WADE, KIM L; Skyline HS; Oakland, CA; (3); Church Yth Grp; Cmnty Wkr; Girl Scts; Office Aide; Pep Band; Yrbk; Sec Stu Cncl; Cheerldng; Cit Awd; High Hon Roll; Hon Roll; Mills College Upward Bound; Med Expl, Kaiser Hosp; UC Davis; Optomistrist.

WADE, LAUNIE; Burney JR SR HS; Burney, CA; (1); JV Ftbl; Hon Roll; Coll; Computer Programming.

WADE, LISA; Independence HS; San Jose, CA; (2); Dance Clb; VP Debate Tm; Drama Clb; Thesps; School Musical; Stage Crew; Variety Show; Rep Frsh Cls; Rep Soph Cls; JV Var Cheerldng; Drama; Debate Club; Dance; GATE.

WADE, NICOLE C; Morningside HS; Inglewood, CA; (2); Hosp Aide; Teachers Aide; Play Piano; USC; Chld Dvlpmnt.

WADE, RANDY J; Liberty Christian HS; Huntington Beach, CA; (3); Teachers Aide; Bsbl; Bsktbl; Ftbl; Ice Hcky; CA ST Fullerton; Bus Admin.

WADE, REBECCA A; Terra Linda HS; San Rafael, CA; (3); Church Yth Grp; Rptr Nwsp; Yrbk; Lit Mag; Spanish NHS; CSF; VP Stu Soc Respnsblty; Psych.

WADE, ROCHELLE; Turlock HS; Turlock, CA; (3); 37/300; Orch; High Hon Roll; Voice Dem Awd; Natl Schl Orch Awd 89; Hnr Orch/Conf 89; Stanislaus Co Hnr Orch 88-90; CA ST U-Stanislaus; Music.

WADE, SUSAUN J; Westchester HS; Los Angeles, CA; (2); Church Yth Grp; Library Aide; Office Aide; Church Choir; Drill Tm; Cit Awd; Prfct Atten Awd; APBA; PTA; UCLA; Ped.

WADE, TOBY J; Clovis West HS; Fresno, CA; (4); Chess Clb; Intrml Ftbl; San Luis Obispo; Electrncs.

WADE, WINSTON E; Paraclete HS; Quartz Hill, CA; (3); 6/120; Key Clb; Letterman Clb; JV Var Bsktbl; JV Crs Cntry; Var Trk; High Hon Roll; Hon Roll; NHS; Ntl Merit SF; Invtnl Acad Wrkshp & Sci & Engrng Smnr; Chem.

WADESON, CHERYL ANN; North HS; Torrance, CA; (4); Cmnty Wkr; Q&S; VP SADD; Ed Nwsp; Ed Lit Mag; Rep Jr Cls; Capt Sftbl; JV Vllybl; Pres Acad Fit Awd; CSF; Disc Jockey Radio Sta KNHS; Prncpls Hnr Roll; USC; Jrnlsm.

WADIAEFF, VIVIAN N; Taft HS; Woodland Hills, CA; (2); Hist Service Clb; Spanish Clb; Teachers Aide; JV Tennis; Cit Awd; High Hon Roll; Outstndng Spnsh Clb Mem; Cert Outstndng Achvt Piano; Peer Turor; UCLA; Med.

WADLEGGER, SUZANNE; Point Loma HS; San Diego, CA; (3); 11/431; Church Yth Grp; Teachers Aide; Mgr(s); High Hon Roll; Hon Roll; Ldrshp Group; Law.

WADLEY, BRIAN D; Rio Americano HS; Sacramento, CA; (4); #14 In Class; Church Yth Grp; Cmnty Wkr; Key Clb; Band; Church Choir; Jazz Band; High Hon Roll; NHS; Pres Acad Fit Awd; Bank Of Amer Cert In Sci; Point Loma Nazarene Coll; Med.

WADLEY, LEVEN M; Willow Glen Educational Park HS; San Jose, CA; (2); 1/450; Math Clb; Math Tm; Tennis; High Hon Roll; Chemathon 2nd Pl Awd 90; 5th Pl Hnrb Mntn Math Cont; MIT; Physicist.

WADSACK, NATHAN; Fountain Valley HS; Fountain Valley, CA; (2); Church Yth Grp; JV Wrstlng; Hon Roll; Prfct Atten Awd; Cllct Comic Bks; Lstn To Hvy Mtl; UCLA; Bus Ec.

WADY, CAMILLE DIONE; Nogales HS; West Covina, CA; (2); 93/880; Drill Tm; Mrchg Band; Hon Roll; Kiwanis Awd; Honor Foreign Lang Achvt Span I; Soph Yr B Average Adv Span II; Enrolled In Honors Spanish III; Long Bch St/UC San Diego; Bus.

WAGAR, CHRIS; Chino HS; Chino, CA; (2).

WAGELE, JOSEPH; Cardinal Newman HS; Rohnert Park, CA; (2); Church Yth Grp; Cmnty Wkr; JV Ftbl; JV Trk; Wt Lftg; High Hon Roll; Hon Roll; Altar Srvr; N Coast Sect CIF Schlr Athlete; Acadc Achvt Awd.

WAGENER, AMY; Bella Vista HS; Orangevale, CA; (3); 1/363; Church Yth Grp; French Clb; SADD; Band; Mrchg Band; Pep Band; JV Swmmng; French Hon Soc; Hon Roll; NHS; Arch.

WAGENLEITNER, ALLYSON; Fresno Christian HS; Fresno, CA; (1); Church Yth Grp; Var Bsktbl; Var Sftbl; Capt Vllybl; High Hon Roll; Hon Roll; Child Care Vlntr; Day Camps Yth Cnslr.

WAGENLEITNER, JOHN M; Fresno Adventist Acad; Fresno, CA; (3); 4/20; Church Yth Grp; Rep Soph Cls; Intrml Bsktbl; Intrml Ftbl; Intrml Socr; Intrml Cmnty Wkr; Intrml Vllybl; Hon Roll; Fresno ST U.

WAGENVELD, JULIA C; Village Christian HS; Sun Valley, CA; (3); 43/123; Church Yth Grp; Cmnty Wkr; Drama Clb; Math Clb; Spanish Clb; Varsity Clb; Church Choir; Mgr(s); Trk; Hon Roll; UC Davis; Zoology.

WAGGONER, BRYAN K; Glendora HS; Glendora, CA; (4); 2/400; Church Yth Grp; Phtg Nwsp; Var Co-Capt Swmmng; Hon Roll; Photo; Bass Guitar; ASU; Bus.

WAGGONER, LAURA; Chaminade College Prep; Northridge, CA; (3); Hosp Aide; Model UN; Chorus; School Musical; Ed Nwsp; Sec Sr Cls; JV Var Cheerldng; High Hon Roll; Jr NHS; NHS; Scuba Diving; Dance; Duke U; Bio.

WAGNER, AMY; Fred C Beyer HS; Modesto, CA; (4); 1/506; Debate Tm; Hosp Aide; NFL; Service Clb; Speech Tm; Bsktbl; Sftbl; Vllybl; Cit Awd; High Hon Roll; Teenage Republicans Soc; Pres CSF; UC Davis; Psych.

WAGNER, AUDRA K; Oak Ridge HS; Cameron Park, CA; (1); Church Yth Grp; NHS; CSF; Gymnstcs St Lvl; Outstndng Achvt Awd Bio 90; Stanford; Sprts Osteopth.

WAGNER, CARRY; Mc Lane HS; Fresno, CA; (1); Church Yth Grp; Pep Clb; Sec Frsh Cls; Nwsp; OBGYN Dr.

WAGNER, CHRISTIE NICHOL; Etiwanda HS; Rancho Cucamonga, CA; (3); GAA; Ski Clb; SADD; Band; Mrchg Band; Orch; Pep Band; School Musical; High Hon Roll; Hon Roll; Music.

WAGNER, JARRAD R; Hesperia HS; Hesperia, CA; (3); 29/613; Drama Clb; Ski Clb; Spanish Clb; School Play; Stage Crew; JV Ftbl; Var Tennis; High Hon Roll; Span IV Outstndng Stu Of Yr; Schlr/Athlete Awd; CA Schlrshp Fed; Engrng.

WAGNER, JENNIFER L; Rio Mesa HS; Somis, CA; (3); 6/369; Church Yth Grp; French Clb; Chorus; School Musical; Co-Ed Yrbk; Off Jr Cls; Pres Sr Cls; Var Stat Bsktbl; French Hon Soc; NHS; Vrsty Badminton; FLANC Poster Cont Wnnr; Courtside Inter-Clb Tnns Tm; Pomona; Intl Relations.

WAGNER, JENNIFER M; Mt Shasta HS; Weed, CA; (3); 4/86; GAA; Letterman Clb; Varsity Clb; Yrbk; Var Bsktbl; Var Capt Sftbl; High Hon Roll; Hon Roll; Bio.

WAGNER, MELISSA L; Torry Pines HS; Del Mar, CA; (3); Key Clb; Hist Stu Cncl; Pres Acad Fit Awd; Bus Law.

WAGNER, MICHELLE N; American HS; Fremont, CA; (3); Spanish Clb; SADD; Teachers Aide; VP Frsh Cls; Treas Soph Cls; Rep Jr Cls; Pres Sr Cls; Rep Stu Cncl; Var Score Keeper; Var Socr; All MVAL Girls Soccr 1st Tm, 2nd Tm; Outstndng Achvt Awd.

WAGNER, NINA D; California HS; Whittier, CA; (3); Art Clb; FBLA; Pep Clb; SADD; Teachers Aide; Varsity Clb; Rep Frsh Cls; JV Var Cheerldng; Hon Roll; Law.

WAGNER, PHILIP; Hughson HS; Denair, CA; (3); Church Yth Grp; 4-H; FFA; Intnl Clb; Letterman Clb; Ski Clb; Teachers Aide; Rep Jr Cls; JV Bsktbl; Var Capt Socr; FFA Star Grnhand; FFA St Pltry Prdctn Awd; HS Super Stu Awd; UCLA; Agri-Bus.

WAGNER, STEVE D; Beaumont HS; Cherry Valley, CA; (3); Varsity Clb; JV Var Bsbl; High Hon Roll; UC Riverside; Orthopdc Srgn.

WAGNER, TAHLIA; Corona Del Mar HS; Newport Beach, CA; (3); 70/320; GAA; Letterman Clb; Varsity Clb; Capt Var Bsktbl; Var Vllybl; Hon Roll; Pres Acad Fit Awd; All CIF 1st, All Leag Vllybl; All Leag, MVP Bsktbl; Schlr/Athl; Arch.

WAGNER, TAMBRIE; Justin Siena HS; Napa, CA; (3); 5/97; Am Leg Aux Girls St; Key Clb; Service Clb; Chorus; Rep Soph Cls; Rep Jr Cls; Var Cheerldng; High Hon Roll; Rotary Yth Ldrshp Awds & Schlrshp Ldrshp Camp; Loyalty Awds; UC Santa Barbara; Bus Ecnmcs.

WAGNER, TODD R; De Anza HS; El Sobrante, CA; (3); Church Yth Grp; Rep Stu Cncl; JV Socr; Var Swmmng; High Hon Roll; Hon Roll; Close Up Inaugeration 89; Bio Olympiad 88; Civic Air Patrol Aux US Air Force 88-89; US Air Force Acad; Military; Pi.

WAGNER III, WILLIAM; Los Alamitos HS; Los Alamitos, CA; (3); Intnl Clb; SADD; Teachers Aide; Rep Frsh Cls; Rep Soph Cls; Rep Jr Cls; Var JV Bsbl; Gilfted & Talented; Biathlons & Triathlons; Sci.

WAGSTAFF, ROBERT; Canyon HS; Canyon Country, CA; (3); Yrbk; Var JV Bsbl; High Hon Roll; Hon Roll; NHS; CSF; Math.

WAHJUDI, RIA; Saint Monica Catholic HS; Los Angeles, CA; (3); 3/140; Church Yth Grp; Hon Roll; St Schlr; KKIA Yth Activity Dir; UCLA; Bus.

WAHLEITHNER, JAY P; Casa Raoble Fundamental HS; Orangevale, CA; (4); 1/325; Am Leg Boys St; VP Rep Soph Cls; Pres Jr Cls; VP Pres Stu Cncl; Var Socr; Var Tennis; DAR Awd; Elks Awd; High Hon Roll; NHS; Stanford U; Mechanical Engrng.

WAHLMAN, HEIDI R; Bret Harte HS; Altaville, CA; (3); AFS; Church Yth Grp; Cmnty Wkr; FHA; Ski Clb; SADD; Nwsp; L Var Sftbl; L Var Tennis; L Capt Vllybl; Schlr Athl; Advanced Ensemble; CSF; Embry Riddle.

WAHLMEIER, DANIELLE; Poway HS; Poway, CA; (3); JV Socr; High Hon Roll; Hon Roll; NHS; CSF; Peer Cnslng Prgm; Clb Soccer; Med.

WAHLSTROM, JON MARK; Pine Hills JR Acad; Grass Valley, CA; (1); Chorus; School Play; Stu Cncl; Intrml Vllybl.

WAI, JUNE; Lowell HS; San Francisco, CA; (2); German Clb; Intnl Clb; Teachers Aide; Rptr Nwsp; Rep Frsh Cls; Golden St Exam Alg Schl Rcgntn Awd; Japanese & Recyclng Clbs; Psych.

WAI, MARCUS H; San Leandro HS; San Leandro, CA; (3); 63/361; Church Yth Grp; Var L Wrstlng.

WAI, STEPHANIE; Santa Teresa HS; San Jose, CA; (3); Hosp Aide; Science Clb; Phtg Yrbk; CSF; Food Mgmt.

WAIER, JENNIFER L; Brea-Olinda HS; Brea, CA; (3); Dance Clb; Key Clb; Speech Tm; School Musical; Ed Nwsp; Pres Jr Cls; Stu Cncl; Var Socr; Hon Roll; Pres Acad Fit Awd; Girls Lgu Pblcty Comm; Advncd Dance; Dare Prgm; Jrnlsm.

WAIR, ABIGAIL ANNE; Lowell HS; San Francisco, CA; (3); Church Yth Grp; German Clb; Cult Film Clb; U OR; Psych.

WAITE, ALEX; Apple Valley HS; Apple Valley, CA; (2); FBLA; Var L Wrstlng; Bus.

WAITE, CHRIS; Hoover HS; Fresno, CA; (3); #1 In Class; High Hon Roll; Hon Roll; Acad Decathln; 90 Sci Fair Awd; CSF; Physics.

WAITE, CHUCK; Hoover HS; Fresno, CA; (3); #1 In Class; High Hon Roll; Hon Roll; Acad Decathln; CSF; Sci.

WAITE, VENESSA L; Bret Harte HS; Angels Camp, CA; (2); AFS; Drama Clb; FHA; SADD; School Play; Cheerldng; Hon Roll; FFA; Model UN; Ski Clb; Outstndng Achvt Acad Awd; Friday Night Live; Pr Cnslng; Oceanography.

WAITS, WILLIAM W; Skyline HS; Oakland, CA; (3); Boy Scts; Church Yth Grp; Cmnty Wkr; Letterman Clb; Office Aide; Ski Clb; JV Wrstlng; Hon Roll; Ski Team-Vrsty Letter; San Fran/Oakland Rotary Clbs Camp Enterprise; Boy Scouts-Ldrshp Staff.

WAITZ, PAUL A; Westlake HS; Thousand Oaks, CA; (4); Outstndng Peer Cnslr; Peer Cnslng; UCSD; Arch.

WAJDOWICZ, BRIAN P; Newark Memorial HS; Newark, CA; (3); 35/355; French Clb; SADD; Stage Crew; JV Ftbl; Stat Swmmng; JV Trk; French Hon Soc; Hon Roll; Prfct Atten Awd; Cal ST Humboldt; Frstry.

WAKABAYASHI, MARY H; Villa Park HS; Villa Park, CA; (2); French Clb; Key Clb; VP Science Clb; Acpl Chr; Var Swmmng; Hon Roll; US Acad Decathln; Sci Olympiad; Mock Trial; Jr Statesmen Amer; CSF; Med.

WAKAMATSU, KEN K; Fountain Valley HS; Fountain Valley, CA; (2); Debate Tm; Model UN; Bsktbl; High Hon Roll; CSF; Soph Cmmssn; Octagon Optmst Clb Hstrn; Harvard; Med.

WAKE, PAMELA; Compton HS; Compton, CA; (4); Art Clb; Church Yth Grp; Dance Clb; Hosp Aide; Model UN; ROTC; Church Choir; Trk; Hon Roll; Voice Dem Awd; S Coast Constrm Hnrs; Resrve Offcrs Assoc Lds Clbs US; Compton Coll; Pedtrcn.

WAKEFIELD, DANIEL M; Portola HS; Portola, CA; (3); 12/48; Varsity Clb; Band; Var JV Ftbl; Var Trk; Wt Lftg; Wrstlng; High Hon Roll; Hon Roll; Drftng.

WAKEHAM, DEAN R; Irvine HS; Irvine, CA; (3); 44/512; AFS; Boy Scts; Church Yth Grp; Cmnty Wkr; Letterman Clb; Math Tm; Varsity Clb; Stu Cncl; Bsbl; Var L Ftbl; Intl Relations.

WAKEMAN, ALICIA M; Grace M Davis HS; Modesto, CA; (3); 1/580; Pres Drama Clb; German Clb; SADD; Thesps; School Play; Co-Ed Yrbk; High Hon Roll; CSF; Intl Ordr Rainbow Grls Pres; U Of CA Santa Cruz; Psych.

WAKEMAN, REBECCA L; Mesa Verde HS; Citrus Heights, CA; (2); 37/259; Girl Scts; Spanish Clb; Yrbk; Lit Mag; Golf; Sftbl; Hon Roll; Marine Bio.

WAKIM, SALENA A; Mayfair HS; Bellflower, CA; (3); 13/250; AFS; JA; Hist Key Clb; Science Clb; Rptr Lit Mag; Cit Awd; High Hon Roll; Hon Roll; Pres Acad Fit Awd; Acad Decathlon; Astronomy.

WAKIYAMA, TAKAKO; James Logan HS; Union City, CA; (3); 7/900; GAA; Intnl Clb; JV Vllybl; High Hon Roll; Hon Roll; Hnrs Coll Math A; Travel & Asian Clb; Comp Sci.

WAKLEY, ANJELICA L; Del Oro HS; Newcastle, CA; (4); Art Clb; Church Yth Grp; GAA; Library Aide; Office Aide; Service Clb; Teachers Aide; Chorus; Mgr(s); Var L Tennis; Sierra Coll; Real Est.

WALBY, BRIAN C; Diamond Bar HS; Diamond Bar, CA; (4); 200/600; Rptr Nwsp; VP Frsh Cls; JV Var Ftbl; Wt Lftg; Cal Poly S L Obispo; Spts Med.

WALCHUK, NICK P; Oakmont HS; Roseville, CA; (2); 8/435; JV L Bsktbl; JV L Socr; High Hon Roll; Arch.

WALCUTT, PATRICIA; Central Union HS; Heber, CA; (4); SADD; Chorus; Flag Corp; Mrchg Band; Sec Sr Cls; JV Trk; Var JV Vllybl; High Hon Roll; Hon Roll; Ntl Merit Ltr; Part Time Job JC Penny Co Inc; Imperial Vly Coll; Engl.

WALDEN, JESSICA F; C K Mc Clatchy HS; Sacramento, CA; (3); Spanish Clb; School Play; Var JV Diving; Hon Roll; Pres Acad Fit Awd; Mst Vlble Divr Awd 90; Intl Stds.

WALDEN, KRISTINA M; Dublin HS; Dublin, CA; (3); Teachers Aide; Stat Bsbl; Var Socr; Hon Roll; Bus.

WALDEN, MELINDA M; San Gabriel Acad; Altadena, CA; (3); Church Yth Grp; Teachers Aide; Church Choir; Bsktbl; Score Keeper; Sftbl; Vllybl; Pharmacy.

WALDER, LISA; North HS; Torrance, CA; (1); 1/406; French Clb; Color Guard; High Hon Roll; Ctznshp Awd; UCLA; Engl.

WALDON, DARVINA E; Saint Anthony HS; Carson, CA; (2); 35/180; Church Yth Grp; Band; Mrchg Band; Stu Cncl; Cit Awd; Hon Roll; Jr NHS; Fshn Inst Of Dsgn/Mrchndsng.

WALDORF, AMY; Bullard HS; Fresno, CA; (3); 22/550; FCA; Key Clb; Pep Clb; Spanish Clb; SADD; School Musical; Rptr Nwsp; Hist Sr Cls; Capt Cheerldng; High Hon Roll; Jazz & Tap Dance; Leadership; Intl Business Or Communication.

WALDORF, KRIS; Gahr HS; Artesia, CA; (2); Capt Var Bsktbl; Var Powder Puff Ftbl; Hon Roll; Med.

WALDRON, KRISTI L; Valley Christian HS; Norwalk, CA; (3); 16/112; Church Yth Grp; Teachers Aide; Acpl Chr; Church Choir; Rep Soph Cls; Rep Jr Cls; Rep Sr Cls; Stu Cncl; Powder Puff Ftbl; Score Keeper.

WALDRON, MICHAEL J; Oakmont HS; Roseville, CA; (1); SADD; Hon Roll; Bus.

WALEA, JASMINA NAPUAKAHIKINA; Oxnard HS; Oxnard, CA; (2); 123/654; Church Yth Grp; Dance Clb; Drama Clb; French Clb; Science Clb; Thesps; Chorus; School Musical; School Play; Stage Crew; Dorothy Chandler Pavillion Music Ctr Spotlight Awd Smi Fnlst; CASC Rgn VP; AYSO Area Lge Chmpn; Med.

WALEHWA, JOSHUA M; Bolsa Grande HS; Garden Grove, CA; (1); Rptr Nwsp; Var JV Trk; Wt Lftg; Var JV Wrstlng; Law.

WALES, KATIE K; Montgomery HS; Santa Rosa, CA; (2); Church Yth Grp; Cmnty Wkr; GAA; Intnl Clb; Pep Clb; Science Clb; Spanish Clb; Varsity Clb; Ed Yrbk; VP Frsh Cls; Vrsty Badminton Vtd Plyrs As Most Insprtnl Girl; Otstndng Frst Yr Spnsh Stu Awd.

WALES, MELINDA; Dos Pueblos HS; Goleta, CA; (3); 4/338; Am Leg Aux Girls St; Church Yth Grp; Intnl Clb; Science Clb; Off Soph Cls; Rep Jr Cls; Socr; High Hon Roll; NHS; Schl Site Cncl; Educ.

WALGENBACH, ASHLEY J; Mt Shasta HS; Mount Shasta, CA; (2); Church Yth Grp; French Clb; Spanish Clb; Hon Roll; Skiing,Achvt Awd Frnch; UC; Creative Wrtng.

WALI, MASSE S; Helix HS; La Mesa, CA; (2); 115/449; JV Socr; Opt Clb Awd; Most Improved Soccer Player; Ucsd; Heart Surgeon.

WALIA, HARPREET SINGH; Modesto HS; Modesto, CA; (3); Math Clb; Office Aide; VICA; Cit Awd; Hon Roll; Prfct Atten Awd; Badmntn; Elctrncs.

WALKE, LEAH S; Edison Computech HS; Fresno, CA; (2); Ski Clb; Band; Mrchg Band; Socr; Tennis; Vllybl; Hon Roll; Sci.

WALKER, ADAM L; Arlington HS; Riverside, CA; (3); Service Clb.

WALKER, AMY R; Nevada Union HS; Grass Valley, CA; (2); 19/580; Tennis; Trk; High Hon Roll; Hon Roll; Law.

WALKER, AMY S; Eureka HS; Eureka, CA; (3); Church Yth Grp; Cmnty Wkr; FCA; Key Clb; Orch; Rptr Nwsp; Rptr Yrbk; Pres Acad Fit Awd; OR ST U.

WALKER, AMYLYNN; Etiwanda HS; Alta Loma, CA; (3); Church Yth Grp; Key Clb; Ski Clb; SADD; Church Choir; Hon Roll; Prfct Atten Awd; JV Badminton 2 Yrs; Hons Prog 3 Yrs; Stu Model Congrss Debate; Span Pronunctn Cont; 1st Schl Sci Fair; UCSD; Intl Bus.

WALKER, ANNISE S; San Gorgonio HS; San Bernardino, CA; (3); Library Aide; Office Aide; Cit Awd; Hon Roll; Karate 2 Yrs, 5 Trphys; Law.

WALKER, BERNARD N; John A Rowland HS; Rowland Heights, CA; (3); Intnl Clb; Spanish Clb; Rep Jr Cls; Var L Bsktbl; Trk; Hon Roll; Boys Bsktbl MVP 88; JV Boys Bskbl MVP 89; V Boys Bsktbl Coaches Awd 90; UNLV; Engl.

WALKER, BRIAN J; Escondido HS; Escondido, CA; (2); JV Socr; JV Tennis; Prfct Atten Awd; Sccr MVP; JV Tennis Mst Imprvd Player.

WALKER, BRYAN D; Rim Of The World HS; Blue Jay, CA; (3); 170/352; Drama Clb; Ski Clb; Spanish Clb; Stu Cncl; JV Bsktbl; JV Ftbl; Var Golf; Var Tennis; Wt Lftg; Hon Roll; Var Skiing; Soph Stu Cncl; Freshman Cncl; CO Coll; Bus Mgmt.

WALKER, CHARITY A; Fortuna Union HS; Loleta, CA; (3); GAA; JA; Rptr Nwsp; JV Var Bsktbl; Capt Powder Puff Ftbl; Var Capt Sftbl; Var L Vllybl; Hon Roll; Miss Sftbl MVP; All Cnty Sftbl; 4th Pl Fire Poster Cntst For Dept Of Forestry Out Of 1,100 Entries 89.

WALKER, CHRISTINA M; Roosevelt Sch Of The Arts; Fresno, CA; (1); Church Yth Grp; Stage Crew; Hon Roll; HOPE Clb; People To People Stu Ambssdr To USSR 90; CA ST U Fresno; Teacher.

WALKER, CHRISTOPHER; Foothill HS; Pleasanton, CA; (4); 18/325; Church Yth Grp; Cmnty Wkr; Crs Cntry; Tennis; Trk; Cit Awd; High Hon Roll; Hon Roll; Pres Acad Fit Awd; Karate; Awana Yth Cnslr-Chrch; USC; Aerontcl Engrng.

WALKER, DAMON L; San Clemente HS; San Clemente, CA; (2); Drama Clb; Thesps; School Musical; School Play; Stage Crew; Trk; Art Therapist.

WALKER, DAVID C; Hueneme HS; Port Hueneme, CA; (3); Tennis; AZ ST U; Math.

WALKER, DAWN K; Surprise Valley HS; Cedarville, CA; (4); 1/13; VP FBLA; Teachers Aide; Nwsp; Treas Frsh Cls; Pres Soph Cls; Rep Jr Cls; Co-Capt Cheerldng; Var Capt Vllybl; Hon Roll; CSF; Sierra JC; Bus.

WALKER, EDDIE; Eisenhower HS; Colton, CA; (2); FBLA; Chorus; Church Choir; School Play; Ftbl; Wt Lftg; U Of AL; Orthodontist.

WALKER, HEIDI; Western Christian HS; Pomona, CA; (4); Church Yth Grp; Drama Clb; German Clb; Office Aide; Teachers Aide; High Hon Roll; CSF; Marketing Mgmt.

WALKER, JACKIE; Red Bluff Union HS; Red Bluff, CA; (2); Church Yth Grp; Cmnty Wkr; FFA; Variety Show; Cheerldng; Gym; Hon Roll; St & Wstrn Regnl Gymnstcs Qualifier 88-89; Ldrshp Cnfrnc 89-90; UCLA; Phys Ed.

WALKER, JILL; Placer HS; Auburn, CA; (3); Service Clb; Spanish Clb; Var Swmmng; Chico ST; Bus Adm.

WALKER JR, JOHN M; Luther Burbank HS; Sacramento, CA; (2); 112/389; Church Yth Grp; ROTC; IL; Comp Bus.

WALKER, JOSHUA D; Coalinga HS; Coalinga, CA; (3); Am Leg Boys St; Church Yth Grp; Teachers Aide; Sec Sr Cls; Bsktbl; Tennis; Dnfth Awd; UC Berkeley Acad Tlnt Dvlpmnt Pgm.

WALKER, JULIUS; Arlington HS; Riverside, CA; (3); Church Yth Grp; Cmnty Wkr; ROTC; Treas Sr Cls; Sec Stu Cncl; JV Bsktbl; DAR Awd; Hon Roll; ROTC Military Drill Tm Dep Cmmndr 89-90; Spcl Olympc Vlntr; Orgnzd Adopt A Grandparetn Pgm; US Air Force Acad; Aerntcl Eng.

WALKER, KEELY L; Bonita Vista JR HS; Spring Valley, CA; (1); 1/450; Teachers Aide; Hon Roll; Masonic Awd; Citizenship, Schlrshp, Outstndng Stu Awds; Stanford; Vet.

WALKER, KELLEY N; Valley HS; Sacramento, CA; (3); 103/650; FTA; SADD; Teachers Aide; Stat Bsktbl; Mgr(s); Intrml Powder Puff Ftbl; Score Keeper; JV Var Sftbl; Hon Roll; CA U Davis Early Outreach Pgm; Mont Engr Sci A Pgm; JR Prom Royalty Royal Ct & Chrprsn 90; CA ST U; Ed.

WALKER, KIKI; San Jose High Acad; San Jose, CA; (1); 4-H; Stu Cncl; JV Capt Cheerldng; 4-H Awd; Hon Roll; Stanford; Pedtrcn.

WALKER, KIM; Highlands HS; North Highlands, CA; (1); Co-Capt JV Bsktbl; Powder Puff Ftbl; Vllybl; Hon Roll; U Of Davis Early Outreach Pgm; MESA; 93% Clb; Jrnlsm.

WALKER, KIMBERLEE R; Valley HS; Sacramento, CA; (3); 160/650; Office Aide; Off Sr Cls; Stat Bsktbl; Var JV Mgr(s); Intrml Powder Puff Ftbl; Var JV Score Keeper; JV Sftbl; Hon Roll; MESA Pgm; UCD Outreach U C A Davis; Congrssnl Yth Ldrshp Cncl; UC San Diego.

WALKER, KIMBERLY A; Pasadena HS; San Gabriel, CA; (3); Cit Awd; Hon Roll; Prfct Atten Awd; Pasadena Art Center Coll Of Dsgn; BSU; Landscape Arch.

WALKER, KIMBERLY C; North Tahoe HS; Tahoe City, CA; (3); Art Clb; Church Yth Grp; GAA; Letterman Clb; Ski Clb; Spanish Clb; Teachers Aide; Band; Church Choir; School Musical; Vrsty Mst Vlble Rnnr Trck/Crs Cntry; X-Cntry Sking Jnr Olympcs; Cuesta Coll; Interior Desgn.

WALKER, KINEON A; Palos Verdes HS; Palos Vrds Pen, CA; (3); Church Yth Grp; JCL; Key Clb; Math Clb; Service Clb; Rep Frsh Cls; Rep Soph Cls; Rep Jr Cls; Rep Sr Cls; Rep Stu Cncl; Pres Boys League; Sailing; Dartmouth; Bus Law.

WALKER, M SCOTT; Ochenside HS; Oceanside, CA; (4); 2/260; Church Yth Grp; Band; Rptr Nwsp; Lit Mag; Sec Treas Stu Cncl; Var Bsbl; Var Bsktbl; Capt Var Ftbl; Ntl Merit Schol; Sal; Stanford U; Jrnlsm.

WALKER, MARGI E; Petaluma HS; Penngrove, CA; (4); FBLA; Spanish Clb; Teachers Aide; High Hon Roll; Pres Acad Fit Awd; Equestrn Sports; Sons Italy Schlrshp; John Ferina Mem Schlrshp; U CA Davis; Intl Rel.

WALKER, MELISSA; San Gorgonio HS; Highland, CA; (4); #8 In Class; AFS; German Clb; JV Vllybl; Wrstlng; High Hon Roll; NHS; Prfct Atten Awd; CA Schrlrshp Fed; Adv Curriculum Explrtn Soc; Physics Clb; Civil Engrng.

WALKER, MELISSA L; Nevada Union HS; Nevada City, CA; (3); Service Clb; Temple Yth Grp; Acpl Chr; Stage Crew; High Hon Roll; St Schlr; Wrthy Advsr Intl Ordr Rnbw Grls; Grnd Choir Grnd Assmbly CA 90; UC Davis; Vet Med.

WALKER, MICHELE L; Galileo HS; San Francisco, CA; (4); Pres JA; Library Aide; VP Spanish Clb; Band; Prjct Close Up DC; Blck Stu Union; Spec Hnrs Scl Stds; San Francisco ST U.

WALKER, MICHELLE L; Trona HS; Trona, CA; (2); Dance Clb; French Clb; Math Tm; Speech Tm; Rptr Nwsp; Sec Soph Cls; JV Bsktbl; Var Cheerldng; Var Sftbl; Var Trk; Teenwork 90 Conf; Friday Night Live; Homcmng Princess; Santa Barbara ST U; Arch.

WALKER, NATHANIEL; Lincoln HS; Stockton, CA; (2); 5/550; Drama Clb; French Clb; Teachers Aide; Thesps; Acpl Chr; Chorus; Church Choir; School Musical; School Play; Stage Crew; Spk Fluent Frnch; Al-St ACDA Hnr Choir; Stanford U; Mdcn.

WALKER, NICHOLE; Walnut HS; Walnut, CA; (4); Chrmn FBLA; Pep Clb; Stu Cncl; Stat Bsbl; JV Cheerldng; Stat Trk; JV Var Vllybl; Elks Awd; Hon Roll; Prfct Atten Awd; Mt San Antonio Coll; Law.

WALKER, PATRICIA; Coachella Valley HS; Thermal, CA; (4); 45/355; NFL; Ski Clb; Speech Tm; Varsity Clb; Cheerldng; Hon Roll; San Diego ST U; Psych.

WALKER, PRISCILLA K; Arlington HS; Riverside, CA; (3); Aud/Vis; Teachers Aide; Acpl Chr; Band; Chorus; Mrchg Band; Pep Band; School Musical; Lit Mag; Off Frsh Cls; Natl Library Poetry Cont Editors Choice Wnnr; CAL ST San Bernardino; Engl.

WALKER, RACHELLE Y; John A Rowland HS; Rowland Hts, CA; (4); Spanish Clb; Sprt Ed Yrbk; Rptr Lit Mag; Var Stat Bsktbl; Var Trk; JV Vllybl; High Hon Roll; Hon Roll; NHS; Pres Acad Fit Awd; 89 Girls Vrsty Trk MVP; 90 Miss TEEN Los Angeles Cnty Speech Wnnr; Howard U; Sprts Med.

WALKER, RAMONA C; Salinas HS; Salinas, CA; (3); Cmnty Wkr; Sec FBLA; VP SADD; Band; Chorus; Mrchg Band; Rep Stu Cncl; Var Capt Trk; JV Capt Vllybl; Hon Roll; UC Davis.

WALKER, RICHIE T; Cordova SR HS; Rancho Cordova, CA; (3); Key Clb; ROTC; JV Bsktbl; JV Trk; Wt Lftg; Fri Night Live Cls Rep; Safe Rides.

WALKER, ROBERT DAVID; Moorpark HS; Moorpark, CA; (2); 11/250; Boy Scts; Pres Sec Church Yth Grp; Jazz Band; Mrchg Band; Orch; Variety Show; JV Bsbl; JV Bsktbl; Var L Crs Cntry; High Hon Roll; Brigham Young U; Bus.

WALKER, SHELBY A; Hanford HS; Hanford, CA; (3); Church Yth Grp; Cmnty Wkr; 4-H; Hosp Aide; Office Aide; Ski Clb; Teachers Aide; 4-H Awd; Hon Roll; Kings Cnty 4-H Treas; Flight Attendant.

WALKER, SHELLY L; Bullard HS; Fresno, CA; (4); 91/493; Church Yth Grp; Powder Puff Ftbl; Score Keeper; Easter Seals Vlntr.

WALKER, STACEY; California Lutheran HS; Fallbrook, CA; (2); 3/16; Church Yth Grp; Church Choir; Variety Show; Treas Frsh Cls; Rep Soph Cls; Rep Stu Cncl; Var Capt Bsktbl; Var L Sftbl; Var L Vllybl; High Hon Roll; Acad League Bsktbl MVP 90; Dr Martin Luthern Coll; Educ.

WALKER, TODD G; Modesto HS; Modesto, CA; (1); Boy Scts; Chess Clb; Var Swmmng; JV Wrstlng; High Hon Roll; Hon Roll; V Water Polo Tm; V MVP Swmmng; U Of Pacific; Sports Med.

WALKER, TRACY; Apple Valley HS; Apple Valley, CA; (2); Var Capt Socr; Var Sftbl; High Hon Roll; Hon Roll; CSF; Cert Oa Acad Achvt John R Kirk Hnrs Inst; Comp Fld.

WALKER, VALERIE L; Rim Of The World HS; Crestline, CA; (2); Church Yth Grp; Cmnty Wkr; Band; Mrchg Band; Hon Roll; Teacher.

WALKER, WIKIMA D; Abraham Lincoln HS; San Francisco, CA; (2); Dance Clb; Sftbl; Tennis; Trk; Vllybl; Hon Roll; Bus.

WALKER, YOUNG BIO; John C Fremont HS; Los Angeles, CA; (2); Girl Scts; Speech Tm; Church Choir; Drill Tm; School Play; Stage Crew; Pres Sec Frsh Cls; Cit Awd; Hon Roll; Prfct Atten Awd; Achvts In Speech Dlvrs, Essay & Art Cont; Poetry Wrtng Hnrs; Harvard U; Optometrist.

WALKLEY, TRUDI L; Paradise HS; Paradise, CA; (4); Church Yth Grp; Speech Tm; Chorus; Jazz Band; Mrchg Band; Orch; Elks Awd; Hon Roll; Voice Dem Awd; CA Al St Hnr Band 89-90; U UT; Anthroplgy.

WALL, AARON S; Rim Of The World HS; Crestline, CA; (2); Letterman Clb; Var Crs Cntry; Var Socr; JV Trk; Cit Awd; Hon Roll; Pres Acad Fit Awd; AYSO Sccr Team Capt; Humbolt U; Range Mgr.

WALL, EMILY; Beyer HS; Modesto, CA; (1); Church Yth Grp; Hosp Aide; Cit Awd; Hon Roll; CSF; 120 Mile Bike Treck Amer Lung Assoc; Acolyte; Psych.

WALL, ERIC; California HS; San Ramon, CA; (3); Teachers Aide; Rep Jr Cls; Var Diving; Var Swmmng; Var Wrstlng.

WALL, TERESA L; Montgomery HS; Santa Rosa, CA; (2); Art Clb; Drama Clb; Letterman Clb; Pep Clb; Spanish Clb; Drill Tm; JV Cheerldng; Var Diving; Var Swmmng; Hon Roll; Ballet; Jazz Dance; Gymnastics; Sccr; UC Santa Barbara.

WALL, THERESE-MARIE; Fontana HS; Fontana, CA; (2); Drama Clb; Thesps; School Play; Stage Crew; Var Mgr(s); Var Score Keeper; Hon Roll; Sm Fnlst Miss Jr CA 1 Of 15; Friday Night Live; USC; Theater.

WALL, WILLIAM S; Mira Costa HS; Hawthorne, CA; (2); Chess Clb; Church Yth Grp; JV Bsbl; Cit Awd; Hon Roll; ASU; Drftsmn.

WALLA-MURPHY, MEGHAN A; Westlake Schl For Girls; Woodland Hills, CA; (2); Cmnty Wkr; Hosp Aide; Rptr Nwsp; Swmmng; Pres Acad Fit Awd; Photo; Tnns; Sci.

WALLACE, AUSTIN V; Sherman E Burroughs HS; Ridgecrest, CA; (3); Rep Jr Cls; Hon Roll; CA U Berkeley; Chem.

WALLACE, BRIAN E; Orange Glen HS; Escondido, CA; (2); Church Yth Grp; Hon Roll; NHS; NCAL; CSF.

WALLACE, CANDY; Los Amigos HS; Santa Ana, CA; (3); Bsktbl; Sftbl; Wt Lftg; Hon Roll; Golden West CC; Law Enfrcmnt.

WALLACE, CHARITY; Valley Christian HS; San Jose, CA; (1); Church Yth Grp; Cmnty Wkr; Dance Clb; Chorus; Church Choir; School Musical; Sec Frsh Cls; Stu Cncl; Cheerldng; Pom Pon; Miss Amer Teen Pageant 2nd Rnnr Up; Chrch Productions; Acting.

WALLACE, CHRISTIE; Elk Grove HS; Elk Grove, CA; (4); 5/588; Teachers Aide; Ed Yrbk; Var L Crs Cntry; Var L Swmmng; Hon Roll; Golden St Alg Awd; UC Davis; Scl Sci.

WALLACE, CHRISTOPHER J; Bellarmine College Prep; Gilroy, CA; (3); Boy Scts; SADD; Teachers Aide; UC Santa Barbara; Teacher.

WALLACE, DON S; Nevada Union HS; Nevada City, CA; (2); 25/535; SADD; School Play; Ftbl; Var L Vllybl; English Clb; Golden St Exam For Algebra High Hnrs; Ski Team; UCLA; Bus.

WALLACE, ERIC; Los Alamitos HS; Los Alamitos, CA; (3); Pres Church Yth Grp; Cmnty Wkr; Model UN; Jazz Band; Orch; Rep Stu Cncl; Var Ftbl; Var Socr; High Hon Roll; Prfct Atten Awd; Ld Gtrst-Band; Lthrn Yth Cnfrnc Rep; 1st Tm All Leag Kckr; Med.

WALLACE, ERIK; San Ramon Valley HS; Danville, CA; (2); Cmnty Wkr; Teachers Aide; JV Bsbl; Hon Roll; Prin Scholar Athl Awd; Acad Lttr.

WALLACE, FIA; Victor Valley HS; Victorville, CA; (3); Church Yth Grp; Science Clb; Band; Mrchg Band; Var Swmmng; Air Force.

WALLACE, GREG; Lassen Union HS; Susanville, CA; (3); Church Yth Grp; 4-H; Teachers Aide; VICA; Ftbl; Wrstlng; Hon Roll; Gld Mdl VICA Skll Olympcs ST Cmptn; Outstndng Advncd Automotive Stu; Universal Tech Inst; Auto.

WALLACE, JEREMY E; Chaffey HS; Ontario, CA; (2); Church Yth Grp; Cmnty Wkr; Church Choir; School Play; JV Wrstlng; High Hon Roll; Hon Roll; Martial Arts; Race Bycl; Play Guitar; Church Evnts & Mssns; U Of Southern CA.

WALLACE, JESSICA L; Rim Of The World HS; Crestline, CA; (2); 89/213; Church Yth Grp; Var Trk; JV Var Vllybl; Hon Roll; U Of San Diego; Marine Bio.

WALLACE, JOHN J; Corona HS; Corona, CA; (2); Church Yth Grp; Office Aide; Science Clb; Ski Clb; Bsktbl; Var L Crs Cntry; Ftbl; JV Var Socr; Var L Trk; Hon Roll; Honor Gurad; Coaches Awd Crss Cntry; MVP Dfns JV Sccr; Acadmc Ltr; Athltc Schlr Awd Crss Cntry & Trk; Bus.

WALLACE, KATHLEEN; St Francis HS; Cupertino, CA; (2); Art Clb; Flag Corp; Trk; SADD; Vet.

WALLACE, KERI K.; Upland HS; Upland, CA; (3); L Capt Dance Clb; Pep Clb; Chorus; JV Bsktbl; JV Var Cheerldng; Var Pom Pon; Vllybl; Multiple Dance Awds HS Dance Team & Priv; Lt Dance Team 89-90; Capt 90-91; Dance.

WALLACE, LISA; Chula Vista HS; Chula Vista, CA; (1); Pep Clb; Intrml Gym; Capt Socr; Cit Awd; Hon Roll; Pres Acad Fit Awd; Pres Schlr; Acad Pgm Beyond The Basics; Spcl Interest Spkng; Harvard; Attrny.

WALLACE, LYDIA A; Westmoor HS; Daly City, CA; (4); Teachers Aide; Chorus; Swmmng; Masonic Awd; Pres Acad Fit Awd; Bank Of Amer Cert Awd Engl; San Diego ST U; Dvlpmntl Psych.

WALLACE, MALINDA L; Ramona HS; Riverside, CA; (1); 46/587; Church Yth Grp; Treas Frsh Cls; JV Sftbl; Crimnlgy.

WALLACE, MICHAEL D; University City HS; San Diego, CA; (3); 49/373; Cmnty Wkr; Service Clb; Teachers Aide; Ed Nwsp; Sec Stu Cncl; JV L Bsbl; Var L Crs Cntry; Var Trk; Hon Roll; Prfct Atten Awd; CSF; Cngrssnl Schlr Rep CA Natl Yng Ldrs Conf; Close-Up Pgm.

WALLACE, NANCY; Los Amigos HS; Santa Ana, CA; (3); 60/301; Hon Roll; CSF; Orange Cty YABA; HS Chllng Yth Dvsn Bwlng; Psych.

WALLACE, TARA; Silver Valley HS; Ft Irwin, CA; (4); 3/73; Church Yth Grp; SADD; Rep Frsh Cls; Sec Soph Cls; Var Capt Cheerldng; Powder Puff Ftbl; Var Socr; Var Vllybl; High Hon Roll; Jr NHS; Grmn Natl Hnr Soc.

WALLACE, THOMAS J; Bakersfield HS; Bakersfield, CA; (3); 25/725; Cmnty Wkr; Debate Tm; JA; NFL; Speech Tm; Teachers Aide; School Musical; School Play; Stage Crew; Lion Awd; Stu Wlrd Cnsrvtn Actvst Envrnmntl Soc; 5th VP Mrktng Cmptn NAJAC; SAT 1440; Ecnmcs.

WALLE, ANGIE; Santa Ana HS; Santa Ana, CA; (2); Key Clb; Off Soph Cls; JV Diving; Var Trk; Natl Spnsh Exam 3rd Pl; Engl Tchr.

WALLERSTEIN, ADINA T; Montgomery HS; Santa Rosa, CA; (3); Hosp Aide; Math Tm; Science Clb; Treas Spanish Clb; Speech Tm; VP Band; VP Jazz Band; Mrchg Band; Orch; Pep Band; Music Video Cls; Poltcl Sci.

WALLEY, CAREN JOANNE; Corona Del Mar HS; Newport Beach, CA; (4); 60/316; Cmnty Wkr; Hosp Aide; Yrbk; Pres Sr Cls; Rep Stu Cncl; Var Capt Trk; JV Vllybl; Zonta Grl Mnth Feb 90; Candystriper Hoag Memrl Hosp; Yth/Govt, Treas & VP; U Of Southern CA; Pre-Bus.

WALLIN, JACOB; Liberty Union HS; Oakley, CA; (1); 23/444; Ftbl; Hon Roll.

WALLING, JULI R; Summerville Union HS; Mi Wuk Village, CA; (1); Church Yth Grp; Chorus; Church Choir; High Hon Roll; Hon Roll; Rotary Awd; Exec Secretary.

WALLIS, ANGELA C; Banning HS; Banning, CA; (2); Church Yth Grp; Model UN; Band; Mrchg Band; Pep Band; Var Cheerldng; Var Sftbl; Hon Roll; UC San Diego; Medcl.

WALLIS, LEONARD; Atwater HS; Atwater, CA; (3); High Hon Roll; Hon Roll; Aerosp.

WALLOCK, MIKE P; Servite HS; Irvine, CA; (3); Letterman Clb; Ski Clb; Var L Ftbl; NHS; Pres Acad Fit Awd; Schlr Awd; JSA; CSF; 2nd Team All Angeles Leag.

WALLS, JEFF A; Westminster HS; Westminster, CA; (3); Pres Church Yth Grp; Spanish Clb; Church Choir; Stage Crew; Variety Show; Var Ftbl; Golf; Var Wt Lftg; Christian Theatre Grp; Indstrl Tech Awd; Golden West Coll; Arch.

WALLS, JENNY; West Covina HS; West Covina, CA; (2); Teachers Aide; Drill Tm; JV Swmmng; Drill Team Strutter Of Mnth 89 & 90. Hnr Awd 89, Most Dedicated 90; Chrldng Coach Jr All Am Tm 88/89; OR ST; Csmtlgy.

WALLS, JULI; Grossmont HS; La Mesa, CA; (3); 49/385; Hosp Aide; Treas Intnl Clb; Sec Key Clb; Quiz Bowl; Nwsp; Var L Crs Cntry; Var L Diving; Hon Roll; Leag Divng Champ 89-90; Hnrbl Mntn Skirbl Essy Cntst 90; 2nd Pl Cnty Divng 90; Commctns.

WALSH, AMY M; Trabuco Hills HS; Mission Viejo, CA; (3); Church Yth Grp; Pep Clb; Spanish Clb; SADD; Var L Bsktbl; Hon Roll; NHS; CSF; Advrtsng.

WALSH, APRIL L; Salinas HS; Salinas, CA; (3); French Clb; High Hon Roll; CSF; Frgn Exchng Club; Prom Cmmtte; Golden St Exam Awd Of Recognition & Acad Excllnc Awd.

WALSH, CURTIS; Lincoln HS; Stockton, CA; (3); 33/633; Church Yth Grp; Cmnty Wkr; Math Clb; Mu Alpha Theta; Ski Clb; Band; Jazz Band; Mrchg Band; JV Fld Hcky; JV Trk.

WALSH, JENNIFER C; Diamond Bar HS; Diamond Bar, CA; (3); French Clb; FBLA; Letterman Clb; Varsity Clb; Rep Jr Cls; JV Var Socr; Var Trk; Hon Roll; Girls Leag; CSF.

WALSH, JOEL G; Del Campo HS; Sacramento, CA; (2); 17/461; Cmnty Wkr; FCA; ROTC; Scholastic Bowl; Color Guard; Drill Tm; Trk; Hon Roll; Vllybl; Outstndng Cadet JROTC; Amer Vet WWII Korea Vietnm JROTC Natl Awd; Super Perfmnc Awd; USAF Military Acad; Offcr.

WALSH, KAREN M; Irvine HS; Irvine, CA; (2); AFS; Drama Clb; Var Flag Corp; School Play; Hon Roll; Pres Acad Fit Awd; Jobs Daughters; Mock Trl Club; St Fnlst Miss Amer Teen Pgnt; Cmmnctns.

WALSH, PATRICK M; Paraclete HS; Palmdale, CA; (3); Key Clb; Letterman Clb; SADD; Crs Cntry; Trk; High Hon Roll; Hon Roll; Opt Clb Awd; Acctng.

WALSTON, GREGORY S; Miramonte HS; Orinda, CA; (3); Cmnty Wkr; Hon Roll; Schlr Mdvl His; His.

WALSWORTH, AMY; Willows HS; Willows, CA; (3); Church Yth Grp; Cmnty Wkr; 4-H; Key Clb; Treas Soph Cls; Var Tennis; High Hon Roll; Pres Acad Fit Awd; VP Friday Night Live FNL; CSF; Work With Chldrn.

WALTER, DANI C; Dublin HS; Pleasanton, CA; (3); 21/166; Cmnty Wkr; French Clb; FBLA; Office Aide; Teachers Aide; Capt Color Guard; Flag Corp; High Hon Roll; Hon Roll; Crmnl Jstce.

WALTER, ERICA; Palm Desert HS; Palm Desert, CA; (4); Teachers Aide; Off Jr Cls; Tennis; Hon Roll; UC Santa Barbara.

WALTER, JUDI L; Galt HS; Galt, CA; (3); VP Jr Cls; Pres Sr Cls; Stu Cncl; JV Var Bsktbl; High Hon Roll; Hon Roll; CSF; Acad Dcthln; BYU.

WALTER, ROBBY; Grace Davis HS; Modesto, CA; (2); School Musical; School Play; Stage Crew; JV Crs Cntry; Var Trk; Hon Roll; 2nd City Champion, 4th Modesto City Champ; Slvr Medalsit City Comp Var Track.

WALTER, SALAS; Los Angeles HS; Los Angeles, CA; (4); 4/550; Church Yth Grp; Cmnty Wkr; Science Clb; Service Clb; Spanish Clb; Socr; High Hon Roll; Hon Roll; Prfct Atten Awd; Peer Cnslr; Tutor; USC; Civil Engrng.

WALTERS, AARON F; Canyon HS; Canyon Country, CA; (3); Church Yth Grp; Math Clb; Pep Clb; SADD; Teachers Aide; Nwsp; Off Soph Cls; Off Jr Cls; Off Sr Cls; Bsktbl; Bus.

WALTERS, AMANDA; Modesto HS; Modesto, CA; (2); Church Yth Grp; FFA; NFL; Speech Tm; Church Choir; Sec Frsh Cls; Rep Soph Cls; JV Cheerldng; Gym; High Hon Roll; Harvard; Law.

WALTERS, BILLY E; Montclair HS; Montclair, CA; (3); JV Intrml Bsbl; JV Wrstlng; Hon Roll; Jr Leag Div Chmpns; All Star Bsbl Team 87; Math.

WALTERS, JUANITA V; Roseville HS; Roseville, CA; (2); French Clb; Science Clb; Psych.

WALTERS, KELLI R; Kerman HS; Kerman, CA; (3); Church Yth Grp; Nwsp; Yrbk; Var Cheerldng; Hon Roll; Fresno ST U; Elem Educ.

WALTERS, KEVIN C; Woodcrest Christian Schl; Riverside, CA; (1); Church Yth Grp; Church Choir; Var L Tennis; Hon Roll; Med.

WALTERS, KIM C; El Dorado HS; Placentia, CA; (3); 34/317; Band; Drm Mjr(t); Jazz Band; Mrchg Band; School Musical; High Hon Roll; NHS; CSF Secy & Hospitality; Med.

WALTERS, MARIE S; Live Oak HS; Morgan Hill, CA; (3); 83/530; Dance Clb; GAA; Band; Chorus; School Musical; Bsktbl; Fld Hcky; Score Keeper; Hon Roll; Srf Clb; Bus.

WALTERS, MARISSA G; Washington Prep; Los Angeles, CA; (3); Church Yth Grp; Office Aide; Band; Church Choir; Yrbk; Hon Roll; Prfct Atten Awd; UCLA; Social Wrk.

WALTERS, MATTHEW D; Arlington HS; Riverside, CA; (3); Church Yth Grp; Letterman Clb; Varsity Clb; Var Capt Bsktbl; Var Crs Cntry; Var Tennis; Hon Roll; Pres Acad Fit Awd; Scuba Divng; Ceramics; Bus.

WALTERS, MICHAEL; San Luis Obispo SR HS; Paso Robles, CA; (2); Bsbl; Ftbl; Professional Athlete.

WALTERS, NATHAN P; Burroughs HS; Ridgecrest, CA; (2); Boy Scts; Church Yth Grp; Band; JV Socr; Hon Roll; Pres Acad Fit Awd; CSF; Naturalist Clb.

WALTERS, ROBERT S; San Luis Obispo HS; San Luis Obispo, CA; (2); 98/300; VP 4-H; Chorus; Rep Stu Cncl; Var Bsbl; JV Bsktbl; 4-H Awd; Soph Hmcmng Prnc; CIF 4-A Div Chmpnshp Bsbl Tm; Frosh Bsbl Coaches Awd; Cal Poly; Bio.

WALTERS, SUZIE E; Apple Valley SR HS; Apple Valley, CA; (1); 25/778; JV Crs Cntry; Var L Trk; Hon Roll; Swim Tm; Marine Bio.

WALTMAN, DANIEL B; Madison HS; San Diego, CA; (3); Computer Clb; Latin Clb; Crs Cntry; Trk; San Diego ST U; Electrncs.

WALTON, ANDREA D; Dinuba HS; Dinuba, CA; (3); Church Yth Grp; Chorus; Church Choir; VP Sr Cls; VP Trk; Hon Roll; Spnsh & Algbr II Awds; Med.

WALTON, JENNIFER L; Santa Cruz HS; Santa Cruz, CA; (1); Church Yth Grp; Sec Soph Cls; JV L Sftbl; UCLA; State Dept.

WALTON, KILIAH R; Santa Ana Valley HS; Santa Ana, CA; (3); Teachers Aide; Cit Awd; High Hon Roll; Hon Roll; Prfct Atten Awd; Rotary Awd; Secretary.

WALTON, LESLIE A; Sacred Heart Prep; Los Altos, CA; (2); 1/60; Chorus; School Musical; School Play; JV Bsktbl; JV Vllybl; High Hon Roll; NHS; Rotary Awd.

WALTON, RHODES L; Davis SR HS; Davis, CA; (2); Chess Clb; Key Clb; Crs Cntry; Trk; Wrstlng; High Hon Roll; Hon Roll; Pres Acad Fit Awd; UCLA; Bus.

WALTON, RICK; John F Kennedy SR HS; Sacramento, CA; (3); Aud/Vis; Church Yth Grp; Drama Clb; School Play; Wt Lftg; Hon Roll; Psych.

WALTON, ROBERT; Sacred Heart Prep HS; Los Altos, CA; (4); Model UN; School Musical; School Play; Sprt Ed Nwsp; Ed Lit Mag; Var Bsktbl; Var Crs Cntry; NHS; Rotary Awd; St Schlr; Invest In Amer Essay Cont 3rd Pl; Claremont-Mc Kenna; Econ.

WALTON, SHANNON; Washington Union HS; Fresno, CA; (2); FBLA; FTA; Treas Soph Cls; Treas Jr Cls; Stu Cncl; Hon Roll; CSF; FNL; Cal Poly; Acctnt.

WALTON, SHER RE C; Helix HS; San Diego, CA; (2); 113/474; Church Yth Grp; Cmnty Wkr; Drama Clb; FTA; Intnl Clb; Letterman Clb; Red Cross Aide; Scholastic Bowl; Spanish Clb; SADD; Spelman; Psych.

WALTON, SIMONE L; Washington Union HS; Fresno, CA; (3); Library Aide; Office Aide; Chorus; Hon Roll; Achvt Awd; CSF; FNL; U Of CA; Med.

WALTON, YOLANDA Y; Coyon HS; San Bernardino, CA; (3); Church Yth Grp; Drill Tm; Rep Stu Cncl; Var Bsktbl; Var Trk; Law.

WALVOORD, MARLEY; John A Rowland HS; Rowlands Hts, CA; (3); Church Yth Grp; Cmnty Wkr; GAA; Varsity Clb; Off Frsh Cls; Stu Cncl; Powder Puff Ftbl; Socr; Hon Roll; Pres Acad Fit Awd; UC Riverside; Elem Schl Tchr.

WALWORTH, JEFFREY S; Shafter HS; Shafter, CA; (3); 7/250; Rptr Am Leg Boys St; Jazz Band; Mrchg Band; Pep Band; Ed Nwsp; Yrbk; Var L Bsktbl; Var L Ftbl; Var L Golf; High Hon Roll; CSF; Gldn Empr Suns Yth Band; Hnrs Prgm; Arontcl Engr.

WAMBOLD, MIKE A; Rancho Cotate HS; Rohnert Park, CA; (1); JV Bsbl; JV Ftbl; Intrml Wt Lftg; Hon Roll; Babe Ruth Bsbl; Joe Dimgo Bsbl.

WAMPLER, BRENT H; Modesto Adventist Acad; Ceres, CA; (4); 10/25; Church Yth Grp; FCA; Ski Clb; Spanish Clb; Varsity Clb; Band; School Play; Treas Frsh Cls; Off Soph Cls; Treas Jr Cls; Stanislaus ST U.

WAN, HANG-KIT KITTY; Mark Keppel HS; West Covina, CA; (4); 99/550; Treas FBLA; Hist Key Clb; Sec Math Clb; Hon Roll; CA ST U Los Angeles; Acctng.

WAN, JULIA LAI MEI; Phillip Burton Academic HS; San Francisco, CA; (3); Computer Clb; Math Clb; Science Clb; High Hon Roll; Calculas Ap; Japanese Clb; MA Inst Of Tech; Comp Sci.

WAN, MAUREEN M; Eagle Rock HS; Los Angeles, CA; (3); Cmnty Wkr; Treas JA; Rep Key Clb; Treas SADD; Chorus; Hon Roll; Pres Acad Fit Awd; Yale Bk Clb Awd.

WANAMBWA, LILLIAN L; Pasadena HS; Altadena, CA; (3); Office Aide; Pep Clb; Teachers Aide; Yrbk; Stu Cncl; Stat Bsbl; Capt JV Bsktbl; Stat Ftbl; Capt Pom Pon; Stat Sftbl; Most Vlybl Plyr & Grls Bsktbl 88-89; Grls Bsktbl 88-89; UCSD; Fashn Coord.

WANG, ALEXANDER N; Santa Monica HS; Santa Monica, CA; (2); Math Clb; Math Tm; Jr Statesmen Of Amer; Aca Dcthln Tm; Elec Engrng.

WANG, AMY; Warren HS; Downey, CA; (3); Pres Art Clb; Church Yth Grp; Cmnty Wkr; French Clb; German Clb; Sec GAA; Math Tm; Mu Alpha Theta; VP Science Clb; Church Choir; 1st Pl SYMF Piano Cmptn 89; 1st Pl Math Field Day; 1st Pl Regnl & St Sci Olympiad Pentathlon Team 90.

WANG, AMY Y; Sanger HS; Sanger, CA; (2); Debate Tm; Latin Clb; NFL; ROTC; Science Clb; Speech Tm; Drill Tm; Rptr Nwsp; Yrbk; Stu Cncl; UCLA.

WANG, ANDREW; Cerritos HS; Cerritos, CA; (2); Math Clb; Chorus; Prfct Atten Awd; GSE 1st Yr Alg Hgh Hnrs.

WANG, ANGIE; Sanger HS; Sanger, CA; (4); 6/360; Cmnty Wkr; Computer Clb; Var Debate Tm; NFL; Science Clb; Var Speech Tm; Ed Nwsp; Ed Yrbk; Ed Lit Mag; Hon Roll; UC Berkeley; Sci.

WANG, ARTHUR H; Ganesha HS; Diamond Bar, CA; (3); Intnl Clb; Math Clb; Math Tm; Mu Alpha Theta; Science Clb; High Hon Roll; Gldn St Exm Hnr Geom; Doctor.

WANG, BEN S; Cupertino HS; Cupertino, CA; (4); 20/251; Teachers Aide; NHS; Pres Acad Fit Awd; Spanish NHS.

WANG, BROOKE; De Anza HS; Richmond, CA; (3); Intnl Clb; Math Clb; Science Clb; Hon Roll; Pres Acad Fit Awd; Acad Excllnce Awd; Acad Tlnt Srch Smmr Schl Pgm; UC Berkley; Envrnmtl Sci.

WANG, CATHY; Gunn HS; Los Altos Hills, CA; (4); 11/275; Sec FBLA; Hosp Aide; Service Clb; Teachers Aide; Var Cheerldng; JV Crs Cntry; JV Gym; High Hon Roll; Ntl Merit Ltr; Thomas Watson Mem Schlrshp; Pltcl Cmpgn; Asian Stdtns Assn; UC Berlekey.

WANG, CHI-CHI; San Ramon Valley HS; Danville, CA; (1); 2/400; FBLA; Intnl Clb; Math Clb; Ntl Merit Ltr; Pres Acad Fit Awd; Sal; CSF; Volntr Martinez Vets Hosp; Eng, Sci & Math Awds; Robert C Byrd Schlrshp Awd; UC Berkeley.

WANG, CHIH-KUO; Montclair HS; Upland, CA; (4); 1/320; Art Clb; Sec Science Clb; Teachers Aide; Tennis; High Hon Roll; Prfct Atten Awd; Val; Academic Decathlon; Mock Trial; UC Berkley; Engnr.

WANG, CHRISTINA Y; Lowell HS; San Francisco, CA; (2); Church Yth Grp; Cmnty Wkr; Hosp Aide; NFL; SADD; Church Choir; Treas Frsh Cls; Treas Soph Cls; Var Vllybl; Golden St Exam Acad Excllnc Awd 1st Yr Alg Hnrs; Chrch Actvts; Pre-Med.

WANG, CHRISTINE C; St Francis HS; Sunnyvale, CA; (4).

WANG, CINDY Y; C K Mc Clatchy HS; Sacramento, CA; (3); Church Yth Grp; French Clb; Rptr Nwsp; Tennis; Cit Awd; ASU Clb; 3rd Pl Voc Ed Fair; Humanities & Intl Studies Pgm.

WANG, CRAIG C; Etiwanda HS; Alta Loma, CA; (3); Chess Clb; Computer Clb; Math Tm; SADD; High Hon Roll; Computer Bulletin Board Operator; UCLA; Computer Science.

WANG, DAVID I; Los Altos HS; Hacienda Hts, CA; (3); Cmnty Wkr; Letterman Clb; Science Clb; SADD; Band; Off Soph Cls; Off Jr Cls; Treas Stu Cncl; Ftbl; Mgr(s); UC San Diego; Arch.

WANG, EDWARD H; Hoover HS; Fresno, CA; (2); Ski Clb; Spanish Clb; SADD; Top 5%; UCLA; Medcl.

WANG, EDWARD Y; Alhambra HS; Alhambra, CA; (3); Chess Clb; French Clb; Tennis; Cit Awd; Hon Roll; Prfct Atten Awd.

WANG, FEN; Irvine HS; Taiwan; (4); 15/520; Drama Clb; JCL; Latin Clb; School Play; Stage Crew; Ed Yrbk; Rep Frsh Cls; High Hon Roll; JETS Awd; Ntl Merit Ltr; MIT.

WANG, FONG Y; Abraham Lincoln HS; San Francisco, CA; (3); Var Swmmng; Acad Of Finance; Grand Prz Wnnr Invest-In-Amer Ec Essay Cntst; Vol Swmmng Inst.

WANG, FRANK; El Cerrito HS; Richmond, CA; (4); Teachers Aide; Varsity Clb; Treas Stu Cncl; JV Chess Clb; Var Tennis; Hon Roll; Golden St Exam Seal; Chinese Stu Assn-VP; Longs Drug Stores Eductnl Grant 90; U CA-SANTA Barbara; Econ.

WANG, GIA-CHUAN; Woodrow Wilson HS; San Francisco, CA; (4); Band; Jazz Band; Orch; School Musical; San Frncsco Consrvtry; Music.

WANG, HELEN; Westminster HS; Fountain Valley, CA; (3); French Clb; German Clb; Temple Yth Grp; Hon Roll; NHS; Ntl Merit Schol; Pres Acad Fit Awd; UCI; Accntnt.

WANG, HISAO-HENG; Glen A Wilson HS; Hacienda Heights, CA; (3); Art Clb; Dance Clb; German Clb; Science Clb; Teachers Aide; JV Sftbl; JV Vllybl; High Hon Roll; Hon Roll; Prfct Atten Awd; Jr Var Bdmntn; Mgmt.

WANG, INGRID Y; Capistrano Valley HS; Mission Viejo, CA; (3); Pres FBLA; German Clb; Hosp Aide; Math Tm; Orch; Rptr Yrbk; High Hon Roll; Mck Trl; Orange Cnty Yth Symphny; CSF; UCLA; Surgeon.

WANG, JACK; Norwalk HS; Norwalk, CA; (2); Art Clb; Cmnty Wkr; Computer Clb; Hosp Aide; JA; Science Clb; Cit Awd; High Hon Roll; Hon Roll; Prfct Atten Awd; Sci Fair-Bst Of Show 88; Art Expo 87; Maranatha Clb 89-90; UCLA; Aerospace Engrng.

WANG, JACK H; Los Altos HS; Hacienda Hts, CA; (2); Prfct Atten Awd; Elec Engrng.

WARREN, CHRISTINA R; Shafter HS; Bakersfield, CA; (2); Church Yth Grp; Pep Clb; Band; Mrchg Band; Yrbk; Var Vllybl; Hon Roll; Friend To Friend; Psycht.

WARREN, DALE; Ernest Righetti HS; Santa Maria, CA; (2); Ski Clb; Trk; Wrstlng; High Hon Roll; Hon Roll; Jr Statesmen Of Amer; Interact Clb; CSF; Univ Of Southern CA; Corp Mgt.

WARREN, DANA D; Hemer HS; Hemet, CA; (3); 120/523; Church Yth Grp; Wt Lftg; Geom Golden St Exam; Straight A Hnr Roll; U CA San Diego.

WARREN, DAVID B; Palo Alto HS; Palo Alto, CA; (3); 24/270; Am Leg Boys St; Boy Scts; Church Yth Grp; Ed Nwsp; Rep Frsh Cls; Pres Soph Cls; Pres Jr Cls; Socr; Rotary Awd; Ecology Club; Journalism.

WARREN, DERON T; Junipero Serra HS; Millbrae, CA; (2); 25/200; Debate Tm; German Clb; Intnl Clb; Math Clb; Ski Clb; Pres Soph Cls; JV Capt Bsktbl; JV Trk; Hon Roll; Plyd JV Wtr Plo & Rcvd 2nd Tm All League & Most Imrvd; Rcvd Schlr/Athlt & Outstndng Sci Awds; Sprts Med.

WARREN, DIANNA D; Arcadia HS; Temple City, CA; (2); Church Yth Grp; Drama Clb; School Play; Off Soph Cls; Stu Cncl; Var Cheerldng; Hon Roll.

WARREN, JOY D; Escondido HS; Escondido, CA; (3); Treas Key Clb; Science Clb; SADD; School Play; Pres Sr Cls; Swmmng; Elks Awd; NHS; Drama Clb; GAA; JV Water Polo; Schlrshp To Pepperdine Yth Ctznshp Seminar; Pepperdine U; Brdcst Jrnlsm.

WARREN, JULIE A; Monte Vista HS; Spring Valley, CA; (3); 43/373; Key Clb; Var L Socr; Var L Tennis; Var L Trk; Hon Roll.

WARREN, LOUISE; Palo Alto HS; Palo Alto, CA; (2); Church Yth Grp; Drama Clb; Ed Nwsp; Rep Frsh Cls; Pres Soph Cls; Rep Jr Cls; JV Socr; Var Swmmng; Ecology Club.

WARREN, TELANI A; Mt Diablo HS; Pittsburg, CA; (4); 14/222; French Clb; FBLA; Teachers Aide; Chorus; School Musical; Lit Mag; Hon Roll; Most Outstndng Fr Stu Schlsp; Bank Of America Achvmt Awd Eng; 1st Pl Schl Splling Bee; Wrtr.

WARREN, URSULA DENISE; Poway HS; San Diego, CA; (4); 199/799; Flag Corp; Hon Roll; 1st Stu Govt Day Offce Persnnl Mgr; U Of San Diego; Bus Admin.

WARRICK, CHRISTOPHER; Ukiah HS; Ukiah, CA; (3); 188/439; Letterman Clb; ROTC; Ftbl; Wt Lftg; Law Enfrcment.

WARRICK, JENNIFER L; Rim Of The World HS; Crestline, CA; (2); Church Yth Grp; Cmnty Wkr; Drama Clb; FCA; Spanish Clb; Nwsp; Off Frsh Cls; Off Soph Cls; Socr; Cit Awd; Christian Smmr Camp Cnslr; Missnry.

WARSAW, RYAN C; Abraham Lincoln HS; San Francisco, CA; (2); Math Clb; JV Bsbl; JV Ftbl; Hon Roll; Mit; Engr.

WARTANIAN, HOURI A; Arroyo Grande HS; Arroyo Grande, CA; (1); 1/597; Hon Roll; Armenian Heritage; Arroyo Grande HS Acad Achvt Awd; Cal Poly.

WARTHAN, DAWN; Calvary Baptist HS; Suisun City, CA; (2); 3/10; Pep Clb; Church Choir; School Play; L Bsktbl; L Cheerldng; L Sftbl; Swmmng; Tennis; L Vllybl; Hon Roll; Archery; Pianist; Child Care; Pensacola Christian Coll; Nrsng.

WASCHBUSCH, TESSA L; Lemoore Union HS; Lemoore, CA; (2); 1/342; Spanish Clb; Yrbk; Var Bsktbl; Var Trk; High Hon Roll; Lion Awd; CSF; Engrng.

WASHBURN, KRISTY L; Whittier Christian HS; Whittier, CA; (2); Church Yth Grp; Powder Puff Ftbl; Sftbl; Hon Roll; Law.

WASHBURN, SCOTT B; Redlands HS; Redlands, CA; (2); Boy Scts; Church Yth Grp; German Clb; Perfct Atten 3 Yrs; Dept Awd In 6 Subjects; Mst Imprvd Badminton Tm Trphy; Pilot.

WASHINGTON, ANDRE M; Holland HS; Palmdale, CA; (2); Church Yth Grp; Chorus; Church Choir; Off Frsh Cls; Bsktbl; Review Cmmtte; Amer Bys Choir; NAACP Spec Awd Singing.

WASHINGTON, AVIS C; Eisenhower HS; Rialto, CA; (3); Drama Clb; Thesps; Cit Awd; Hon Roll; NHS; Booster Achvt Awd; Comp.

WASHINGTON, CORY D; Lincoln Prep HS; FPO Seattle, WA; (2); Boy Scts; JV Ftbl; Score Keeper; Socr; YMCA Vol; Ed.

WASHINGTON, DARCY; Leuzinger HS; Hawthorne, CA; (3); Band; JV Var Bsktbl; Var L Trk; APPl; Ebony Nation; U NV Las Vegas; Law.

WASHINGTON, JACQUELINE R; Arcadia HS; Arcadia, CA; (4); VP Church Yth Grp; Cmnty Wkr; Sec Debate Tm; Sec Drama Clb; NFL; Spanish Clb; Sec Speech Tm; JV Trk; High Hon Roll; NHS; Stanford U; Lawyer.

WASHINGTON, JAMAL B; Tulare Union HS; Pixley, CA; (4); Church Yth Grp; Drama Clb; 4-H; Office Aide; SADD; Teachers Aide; School Play; Stage Crew; Bsktbl; Sequias; Soc Wrkr.

WASHINGTON, JOHN D; Strathmore HS; Strathmore, CA; (3); 13/77; Math Tm; Teachers Aide; Mrchg Band; Cit Awd; High Hon Roll; Prfct Atten Awd; Math.

WASHINGTON, LEWIS E; John F Kennedy HS; La Palma, CA; (3); Bsktbl; Cit Awd; High Hon Roll; Hon Roll; UCLA.

WASHINGTON, SHERYL M; Oak Ridge HS; Cameron Park, CA; (3); 16/261; Church Yth Grp; FBLA; Hosp Aide; SADD; Teachers Aide; JV Socr; JV Swmmng; Hon Roll; CSF; AP Span 4; 88 Golden St Exam 1st Yr Algebra-Schl Rcgntn; Intl Bus.

WASHINGTON, TAMI R; John Muir HS; Altadena, CA; (3); Yrbk; Stu Cncl; Cit Awd; Black Stu Union; Clark; Bus Mgmt.

WASHINGTON, TAMMIACKA F; Santa Barbara HS; Santa Barbara, CA; (2); 108/450; Church Yth Grp; Pep Clb; JV Bsktbl; JV Cheerldng; JV Trk; Hon Roll; Endwmnt For Yth Cmmtte Outstndng Acad Achvt Awd; Math, Engrng & Sci Achvt Clb; Stanford; Law.

WASHKO, NADINE; Casa Grande HS; Petaluma, CA; (4); Church Yth Grp; Varsity Clb; Chorus; Intrml Bsktbl; Intrml Sftbl; Var Trk; Intrml Vllybl; High Hon Roll; Hon Roll; NHS; CSF; UC Davis; Pre Med.

WASIM, MARY-ANN U; Tennyson HS; Hayward, CA; (4); 9/250; Sec Computer Clb; Pres VP French Clb; Ed Nwsp; VP Jr Cls; Hon Roll; Prfct Atten Awd; Bnk American Cert Frgn Lang; CSF; U CA Berkeley; Doctor.

WASS, LAURA J; San Pasqual HS; Escondido, CA; (3); 10/369; Church Yth Grp; French Clb; German Clb; Pep Clb; Church Choir; Var Trk; Intrml Vllybl; Cit Awd; Hon Roll; CSF; Mst Insprtnl Trck Athlt Awd; UCSD; Mar Bio.

WASSEL, ZIANAB J; Foothill HS; Pleasanton, CA; (3); Church Yth Grp; Drama Clb; FBLA; SADD; Church Choir; School Musical; School Play; Congrssnl Schlr; Bethany Bible Coll; Engl.

WASSERMAN, MICHAEL A; Borroughs HS; Ridgecrest, CA; (4); Boy Scts; Ski Clb; Varsity Clb; Ed Nwsp; Yrbk; Lit Mag; Var JV Ftbl; JV Tennis; High Hon Roll; Hon Roll; US Army Reserve Natl Schlr/Athl Awd; CA Poly; Elec Engrng.

WASSERMAN, RAECHELLE T; Tracy Joint Union HS; Tracy, CA; (4); 37/360; Capt Debate Tm; Drama Clb; NFL; School Musical; School Play; Ed Nwsp; Yrbk; ./Nk Of Am Fine Arts Plaque Awd; Peer Cnslr; Poly Sci.

WASSIELY, MOURAD F; Westminster HS; Westminster, CA; (3); Church Yth Grp; FCA; Hon Roll; CSF; CA ST Fullerton; Engrng.

WASSON, DANIEL L; Carlmont HS; Belmont, CA; (3); 10/280; Cmnty Wkr; Pres Key Clb; Stage Crew; Yrbk; JV Var Tennis; Gov Hon Prg Awd; High Hon Roll; CSF; AYSO Ref; Johns Hopkins U Cty Hnrs Pgm Stu; Poem Pub Amer Peotry Anthology; Genetic Engnrng.

WATANABE, GREGORY W; St Paul HS; Brea, CA; (3); Boy Scts; Letterman Clb; Varsity Clb; Intrml Bsktbl; Var Crs Cntry; Var Ftbl; Var Socr; Intrml Sftbl; Var Trk; Intrml Wt Lftg; Sea Explorers; Comp Sci Awd; 1 Yr Schlrshp; Cal Poly Pomona; Aerospc Engrng.

WATANABE, JEFF K; Daniel Murphy HS; Los Angeles, CA; (3); 14/79; Church Yth Grp; Quiz Bowl; Service Clb; Spanish Clb; Rptr Nwsp; Ed Yrbk; Rep Frsh Cls; Rep Jr Cls; Pres Sr Cls; JV Bsbl; CSF 1989; Tutrl Pgm Englsh 1989-90; Congrssnl Yth Ldrshp Cncl 1990.

WATANABE, KAREN M; Notre Dame Acad; Los Angeles, CA; (3); Cmnty Wkr; Math Tm; Hon Roll; UCSD; Med.

WATANARE, KEITH H; Schurr HS; Rosemead, CA; (4); 12/530; Boy Scts; Church Yth Grp; Variety Show; Phtg Lit Mag; Var Wrstlng; Hon Roll; Ntl Merit SF; Pres Acad Fit Awd; CSF; Eagle Sct; Long Beach; Bus.

WATERBURY, JULIE E; Foothill HS; Tustin, CA; (2); Girl Scts; Pep Clb; Red Cross Aide; Cheerldng; Diving; Var Gym; High Hon Roll; Hon Roll; St Fnlst Miss Amer Teen 90; Med.

WATERMAN, APRIL; Kings Christian HS; Lemoore, CA; (3); 2/16; Cmnty Wkr; Office Aide; Nwsp; Yrbk; Pres Frsh Cls; Sec VP Stu Cncl; Bsktbl; Score Keeper; Sftbl; Vllybl.

WATERMAN, EVONNE H; Claremont HS; Claremont, CA; (4); 35/417; Debate Tm; French Clb; Latin Clb; NFL; Red Cross Aide; Var Fld Hcky; JV Stat Swmmng; Ntl Merit SF; Summa Cum Laude Natl Ltn Exam; High Hnrs Gldn St Exm Geo; CSF; Bio.

WATERS, JASON A; Barstow HS; Barstow, CA; (1); Cal Poly Pomona; Zoolgy.

WATERS, JENNIFER C; Warren HS; Downey, CA; (3); Dance Clb; Key Clb; Pep Clb; SADD; JV Var Cheerldng; Var Capt Pom Pon; High Hon Roll; Hon Roll; NHS; NEDT Awd; Star Search 90 Talent Pgm; UCLA; Engl Educ.

WATERS, MICHELLE; Capistrono Valley HS; Mission Viejo, CA; (4); Hon Roll; Engl Acad Achvt; UC Santa Barbara; Poltcl Sci.

WATERS, PAULA L; Shafter HS; Shafter, CA; (3); 72/105; Church Yth Grp; SADD; Teachers Aide; Hon Roll; BC; Law.

WATERS, ROCKWELL; James Madison HS; San Diego, CA; (3); 75/350; Church Yth Grp; Latin Clb; Band; Chorus; Drm Mjr(t); Mrchg Band; Pep Band; School Musical; Hon Roll; U Of CA; Engrng.

WATKE, PAULA; Rio Americano HS; Sacramento, CA; (4); 7/265; Key Clb; Math Tm; Ski Clb; Treas Spanish Clb; Stage Crew; Yrbk; Var JV Crs Cntry; JV Sftbl; High Hon Roll; Wght Lftng; UCLA; Span.

WATKIN, JENNIFER T; Savanna HS; Alta Loma, CA; (4); Church Yth Grp; Service Clb; Acpl Chr; Church Choir; Mrchg Band; Sec Soph Cls; VP Jr Cls; Stu Cncl; High Hon Roll; Hon Roll; CSF Seal Bearer; Stu Cncl Co-Cmmssnr Of Comm; Acad Hnrs-Gradtn; Pt Loma Nazarene Coll; Bio Tchr.

WATKINS, BRIAN T; Atascadero HS; Atascadero, CA; (4); 18/263; Am Leg Boys St; Boy Scts; Scholastic Bowl; Pres Stu Cncl; JV Var Socr; JV Var Trk; High Hon Roll; Kiwanis Awd; Rotary Awd; Scholastic Bowl; Most Outstndng Sr 90; UC Berkeley; Bus.

WATKINS, DERRICK; Chino HS; Ontario, CA; (1); SADD; Band; Jazz Band; Mrchg Band; Pep Band; JV L Bsbl; JV L Bsktbl; JV L Ftbl; JV L Trk; Cit Awd; Favorite Subject His; UNLV; Doctor.

WATKINS, JENNIFER; San Clemente HS; San Juan Capis, CA; (2); Church Yth Grp; Cmnty Wkr; Flag Corp; Mrchg Band; I Care Pr Spprt Grp; Safe Rides; Outstndng Engl Sut Mnth; U S CA; Engl Spch.

WATKINS, LA KESHA DANYELLE; Bishop O'dowd HS; Oakland, CA; (2); Cmnty Wkr; Chorus; JV Sftbl; High Hon Roll; Hon Roll; UNC Chapel Hill; Poltcl Sci.

WATKINS, MICHAEL L; Arvin HS; Arvin, CA; (2); Ftbl; Trk; CA ST U Bakersfield; CPA.

WATKINS, MICHELE; Golden Sierra HS; Cool, CA; (4); 3/86; Debate Tm; Pep Clb; Thesps; School Play; VP Treas Soph Cls; Treas Stu Cncl; Var Cheerldng; Var Socr; High Hon Roll; Pres Acad Fit Awd; CSF Pres, VP & Treas; 1st Pl CA St Fair; Bank Of Amer Plaque Wnnr; CA Poly ST U; Civil Engrng.

WATKINS, SHAWNNA L; Mojave HS; Mojave, CA; (2); Flag Corp; Boston U; Pediatrics.

WATKINS, TRACEE M; Patterson HS; Patterson, CA; (3); Drama Clb; San Diego ST U; Bus.

WATROUS, RYAN K; Mission Viejo HS; Mission Viejo, CA; (1); Ski Clb; Intrml Ftbl; Intrml Trk; Intrml Wt Lftg; Intl Baccalaureate Pgm; 90 TAC Natl Chmpnshp Cptn-6th Pl 400 M Hurdles.

WATSON, ADAM J; Madera HS; Madera, CA; (1); Science Clb; Ski Clb; Band; Jazz Band; Mrchg Band; Pep Band; High Hon Roll; Sci Dept Awd For Bio; Physician.

WATSON, AIMEE J; Escondido HS; Escondido, CA; (1); Church Yth Grp; Band; Mrchg Band; Pep Band; JV Socr; Hon Roll; Exclnt Rating SCSBOA SW Coll; Supr Rating SCSBOA John Muir JR HS; Exclnt Rating SCSBOA Regnls; Palomar Coll; X-Ray Tech.

WATSON, BECCA D; Canyon HS; Canyon Country, CA; (3); Church Yth Grp; Debate Tm; GAA; Letterman Clb; Ski Clb; SADD; Bsktbl; JV Capt Sftbl; Vllybl; Pres Acad Fit Awd; Pre-Law.

WATSON, BILLY J; Santa Maria HS; Santa Maria, CA; (4); Var JV Crs Cntry; JV Trk; Hon Roll; Pres Acad Fit Awd; 3.0 Cert Of Acad Achvt; Bank Of Amer Cert For Acad Excllnc Hstry; CIF Cert Cross Cntry; San Diego ST U; Chem.

WATSON, BRETT; Rubidoux HS; Riverside, CA; (4); 9/518; JA; Spanish Clb; High Hon Roll; Sut Of Wk May 89; CA ST U; Bus Mgmt.

WATSON, BRIAN J; Indio HS; Indio, CA; (2); 20/550; JV Ftbl; Wt Lftg; St Schlr; St Recog Gldn St Geo Exam; Def Plyr Of Yr; Life Guard; U Of CA-BERKELY; Acctng.

WATSON, CHRISTOPHER M; Poly HS; Riverside, CA; (2); Boy Scts; Key Clb; Letterman Clb; Varsity Clb; Var L Crs Cntry; Var L Trk; High Hon Roll; Hon Roll; Pres Acad Fit Awd; Intl Bus.

WATSON, DAVID R; Hiram Johnson HS; Sacramento, CA; (2); 47/182; Var Wt Lftg; Var Wrstlng; Hon Roll; UC Davis; Law.

WATSON, DEBBIE; Redwood HS; Visalia, CA; (4); 1/320; Am Leg Aux Girls St; Pres Math Clb; Spanish Clb; Jazz Band; Sec Stu Cncl; Var Swmmng; Var Capt Vllybl; DAR Awd; NHS; Opt Clb Awd; Intl Rel.

WATSON, DONJAHLI A; Duarte HS; Duarte, CA; (3); Aud/Vis; Church Yth Grp; Pep Clb; Ed Nwsp; Ed Yrbk; Sec Sr Cls; Cheerldng; Powder Puff Ftbl; Cal ST Long Beach; Intr Dcrtr.

WATSON, HEATHER ANN; Liberty Union HS; Oakley, CA; (4); Teachers Aide; Sec Treas Band; Color Guard; Drill Tm; Jazz Band; Mrchg Band; Pep Band; Rptr Nwsp; Rep Stu Cncl; Swmmng; Paralegal.

WATSON, HOLLY A; C K Mc Clatchy HS; Sacramento, CA; (2); Aud/Vis; Drama Clb; French Clb; Speech Tm; Lit Mag; High Hon Roll; Hon Roll; Academic Decathlon; Ballet; Reed U; Journ.

WATSON, JEANNIE; Coast Christian HS; Hawthorne, CA; (4); 1/22; Church Yth Grp; Drama Clb; Pep Clb; School Musical; School Play; Rep Jr Cls; Pres Stu Cncl; Capt Cheerldng; Sftbl; Val; Homcmng Queen 89; Distngshd Chrstn Stu 90; Stu Athlete Of Yr 90; CA ST Dominguez; Music.

WATSON, KARLI; Foothill HS; Santa Ana, CA; (2); 18/350; AFS; VP Key Clb; Rptr Nwsp; JV Crs Cntry; Hon Roll; CSF; Jrnlsm Deptmntl Awd; Top Schlr Awd; JR Statesmen Of Amer; Bio.

WATSON, KATIE J; Davis SR HS; Davis, CA; (3); 126/480; Band; Mrchg Band; Pep Band; Powder Puff Ftbl; Socr; Hon Roll; Marine Bio.

WATSON, KELLY D; Westlake HS; Thousand Oaks, CA; (2); 133/431; Dance Clb; SADD; Hon Roll.

WATSON, KIMBERLY L; Crenshaw Gifted Magnet HS; Los Angeles, CA; (3); Church Yth Grp; Hosp Aide; Spanish Clb; Church Choir; Drill Tm; Var Cheerldng; Var Trk; Hon Roll; Bus.

WATSON, LEAH D; Pius X HS; Compton, CA; (3); Math Clb; SADD; Chorus; Treas Sr Cls; English Clb; Hon Roll; NHS; Rotary Awd; Alpha Kappa Alpha Yng Gftd Blck Schlr 90; Math Tutor; Christ Coll; Bus Mgmt.

WATSON, LISA; Armona Union Acad; Armona, CA; (1); Drama Clb; Chorus; Church Choir; Sec Frsh Cls; Bsktbl; Vllybl; High Hon Roll; Prfct Atten Awd; Piano.

WATSON, MICHELLE M; Channel Islands HS; Oxnard, CA; (4); 55/475; Church Yth Grp; Science Clb; Rep Soph Cls; High Hon Roll; Hon Roll; Prfct Atten Awd; Outstndng Bus Awd 87; Cngrsnl Schlr 90; CA ST U Northridge; Crmnl Soc.

WATSON, NEELY; Alhambra HS; Martinez, CA; (2); Art Clb; Cmnty Wkr; Dance Clb; Drama Clb; French Clb; Hosp Aide; Pep Clb; SADD; Teachers Aide; Rptr Yrbk; UC Santa Barbara; Modeling.

WATSON, PAMELA L; Village Christian Schl; Glendale, CA; (3); 14/122; Church Yth Grp; Drama Clb; Mu Alpha Theta; Spanish Clb; Var Trk; CSF; Masters Coll; Bus.

WATSON, RACHEL S; Chico SR HS; Durham, CA; (2); Band; Mrchg Band; Nwsp; Hon Roll; Schl Spelling Bee; Stu Magazine Edtr; GATE Pgm; U CA Berkeley; Jrnlst.

WATSON, REBECCA; Valley Christian HS; San Jose, CA; (3); Church Yth Grp; Chorus; School Musical; Sec Jr Cls; Stu Cncl; Sftbl; Vllybl; Hon Roll; Kiwanis Awd; Hmcmng Prncss; San Jose Mayors Yth Conf Delg; S CA Yth Ctznshp Smnr 90; HS PE Tchr.

WATSON, ROBBIE O; Downey HS; Modesto, CA; (1); Church Yth Grp; JV Swmmng; Hon Roll; Water Polo JV Tm; CSF; Harvard U.

WATSON, SARA; St Patrick-St Vincent HS; Vallejo, CA; (3); 3/150; Treas French Clb; Ed Yrbk; JV Swmmng; Hon Roll; Yth Cnsrvtry; CFS; Cal Poly San Luis Obispo; Arch.

WATSON, SHANTRELL; Lowell HS; San Francisco, CA; (2); Pres Church Yth Grp; Cmnty Wkr; ROTC; Pres Church Choir; Drill Tm; Rep Frsh Cls; Rep Stu Cncl; Gov Hon Prg Awd; African Meth Episcopal Wmns Mssnry Soc Coll Schlrshp; Howard U; Arch Engr.

WATSON, SHARON I; Castle Park HS; Chula Vista, CA; (2); 43/591; Cmnty Wkr; JV Crs Cntry; Var Socr; Acdmc Achvt; SDSU; Bus Admin.

WATSON, SHELLY K; Mission Viejo HS; Mission Viejo, CA; (1); 54/455; Hon Roll; Saddleback; Acctnt.

WATSON, STEVEN; Modoc HS; Alturas, CA; (3); 3/75; Boy Scts; French Clb; JA; Letterman Clb; ROTC; SADD; Teachers Aide; Varsity Clb; Var JV Bsbl; Var JV Ftbl; Aviation.

WATSON, STEVEN; Norco HS; Norco, CA; (4); 1/467; Am Leg Boys St; Boy Scts; Model UN; SADD; Acpl Chr; Var L Ftbl; Var L Swmmng; NHS; Pres Acad Fit Awd; Mock Trial; Hnrs Grad; USAF Acad; Pilot.

WATSON, TERENCE A; Hogan HS; Vallejo, CA; (2); JV Trk; High Hon Roll; Hon Roll; Bio.

WATSON, TERRI L; Middletown HS; Cobb, CA; (4); 1/62; Drama Clb; Model UN; Band; Chorus; School Musical; Ed Yrbk; Pres Stu Cncl; High Hon Roll; Val; Fri Night Live Chrprsn; Brigham Young U; Elem Educ.

WATSON, TIMOTHY J; Bellarmine College Prep; Burlingame, CA; (3); 13/300; Boy Scts; Church Yth Grp; Debate Tm; Letterman Clb; NFL; Pep Clb; Service Clb; Varsity Clb; Stu Cncl; Var Crs Cntry; Eagle Sct.

WATSON, WENDY A; San Marcos HS; San Marcos, CA; (3); Church Yth Grp; Teachers Aide; Co-Capt Sftbl; Hon Roll; Team Spirit Awd Sftbl; Princpls Hnr Roll; Pre Schl Teacher.

WATT, APRIL A; Clovis West HS; Clovis, CA; (3); Office Aide; Teachers Aide; Gym; Hon Roll; Cmptd Engl Ridng Eqstrn Evnts; Engl Jumpers & Team Jumpers; Bus.

WATTANA, RONNIE; Etiwanda HS; Alta Loma, CA; (3); High Hon Roll; Hon Roll; CA Schrlshp Fed; Comp Actvts; Cycling, Table Tnns; Engrng.

WATTERS, JOHN H; Livingston HS; Livingston, CA; (3); SADD; Var JV Ftbl; Hon Roll.

WATTERS, JULIE; Homestead HS; Sunnyvale, CA; (1); Church Yth Grp; JV Bsktbl; JV Tennis; CSF; Mst Vlbl Plyr Tnns; 2nd Team All Ealg Plyr Awd Bsktbl; Stanford; Chiropractor.

WATTERS, MELISSA E; Pioneer HS; San Jose, CA; (3); FHA; Teachers Aide; Mgr Socr; Hon Roll; NHS; Dance Clb; SADD; Booster Club; ROP; Phys Thrpy.

WATTERSON, JOHN G; Redlands HS; Redlands, CA; (2); 231/992; Pep Clb; Science Clb; Teachers Aide; Band; Mrchg Band; Pep Band; Stage Crew; Mgr(s); Score Keeper; Cit Awd; Tuba HS Wind Ensmbl Sydney Opera House; Fstvl Slct Band Tuba 90.

WATTERSTON, CAROL A; Santa Barbara HS; Santa Barbara, CA; (3); Thesps; School Play; Stage Crew; Variety Show; Nwsp; Cinematography.

WATTLES, SHAWN; San Ramon Valley HS; Alamo, CA; (3); 41/420; Church Yth Grp; FCA; Pres Key Clb; Math Clb; Math Tm; ROTC; JV Bsktbl; Var Capt Crs Cntry; Var Capt Trk; Hon Roll; Hon Roll; JR Olympic Tac/Age Grp Natl Soometer Champ 90; Pilots License; Engrng.

WATTREE JR, ERIC; Northview HS; Covina, CA; (2); Var Bsktbl; Mesa Achvt; All Leag Bstkbl; All CIF; All Trnmnt Svrl Bsktbl Trnmnts; Commnctns.

WATTREE, KAIUMEKA S; Northview HS; Covina, CA; (3); Teachers Aide; VP Sr Cls; Var Bsktbl; Var Score Keeper; Hon Roll; Mesa Achvt; All Leag Bsktbl; Vkng Yr Bsktbl; Hghst Clsrm Achvt Awd; Mst Insprtnl Bsktbl; Schlr/Athlte Awd; Law.

WATTS, CHAD R; Analy HS; Sebgastopol, CA; (3); 30/234; High Hon Roll; Hon Roll; CSF; Bus.

WATTS, DEHNI; St Bernard HS; Los Angeles, CA; (4); Church Yth Grp; Dance Clb; Drama Clb; Girl Scts; Pep Clb; Spanish Clb; Church Choir; Drill Tm; Lit Mag; Hampton U; Comm.

WATTS, JACKIE; La Puente HS; La Puente, CA; (2); Drama Clb; NFL; Teachers Aide; Chorus; School Play; Trk; Friend To Friend; Greenpeace VP; Intl Order Of Jobs Daughters Hnrd Qn; IN U; Phys.

WATTS, KATHERINE; Dublin HS; Dublin, CA; (1); 1/229; Stat Socr; Var L Vllybl; High Hon Roll; Vrsty Vlybl Mst Imprvd; Crmnlgy.

WATTS, KELLEY; St Francis HS; West Sacramento, CA; (2); Church Yth Grp; Hon Roll; YMCA Yth & Govt Delgtn Pres, Assmblywmn, Bill Authr Spnsr & Alt Cmmtte Chr; Natl Latin Hnr Soc; UCD; Law.

WATTS, LAURA L; Aragon HS; Belmont, CA; (4); Am Leg Aux Girls St; Letterman Clb; Library Aide; Chorus; Bsktbl; Trk; Vllybl; High Hon Roll; NHS.

WATTS, SHELLY M; La Sierra HS; Riverside, CA; (1); Church Yth Grp; Hon Roll.

WAUGH, HEATHER ELISE; Modoc HS; Alturas, CA; (3); 15/70; SADD; Band; Jazz Band; Mrchg Band; Pep Band; Off Sr Cls; JV Capt Bsktbl; Capt Powder Puff Ftbl; Sftbl; Vllybl; Cycling Clb; Fresno ST U; Sprts Med.

WAUGH, MICHELLE; Oroville HS; Oroville, CA; (4); 1/184; Church Yth Grp; SADD; Yrbk; Off Frsh Cls; Off Soph Cls; Off Jr Cls; Stu Cncl; High Hon Roll; Val; Grl Mtn Soroptmst Interntl; CS ST U Chico; Poltcl Sci.

WAUGH, MICHELLE M; Trabuco Hills HS; Mission Viejo, CA; (2); 29/409; Church Yth Grp; Key Clb; Spanish Clb; Intrml Stat Bsktbl; Var L Swmmng; Hon Roll; NHS; Schlr Athlt Awd.

WAY, HOLLY A; Vallejo SR HS; Vallejo, CA; (3); Church Yth Grp; Band; Drm Mjr(t); Mrchg Band; Hon Roll; Psych.

WAY, KARAJANE; St Francis HS; Saratoga, CA; (3); Church Yth Grp; Cmnty Wkr; Service Clb; SADD; Powder Puff Ftbl; JV Sftbl; Intrml JV Vllybl; High Hon Roll; Hon Roll; Natl Chrty Lg.

WAY, SHELLEY M; Quincy HS; Quincy, CA; (4); 1/88; Band; Var Crs Cntry; Var Trk; High Hon Roll; Pres Acad Fit Awd; Val; Vrsty Ski Team-MVP/All Leag/St Fnlst; Girls St Alt; Union Pacific RR Awd/Schlrshp; CA ST U-Chico; Bio.

WAYFER, ANGELA; Holy Names HS; El Cerrito, CA; (2); Church Yth Grp; Cmnty Wkr; Service Clb; Chorus; Trk; Hon Roll; 49 Cmbntn Svc, Soc, Cltrl, Ed Orgnztn-Pstn Corr Sec; U Ed Grp; Drama Play Summr JR Coll; Xavierf U; Child Psych.

WAYMAN, COLETTE; Yosemite HS; Coarsegold, CA; (2); Church Yth Grp; Service Clb; Band; Church Choir; Drm Mjr(t); Jazz Band; Mrchg Band; Vllybl; Hon Roll; Natl Ski Patrol; Military Aviation.

WAYMIRE, PHILIP W; Thomas Downey HS; Modesto, CA; (1).

WAYNE, LIU H; Gardena HS; Gardena, CA; (2); Computer Clb; Vllybl; Cit Awd; Hon Roll; Prfct Atten Awd; 89 Goldn St Exm Geom Hnrs; Cert Mrt Arch Drftng; Cert Mrt Amer Lgn Awd.

WAZIRI, MICHELLE; Homestead HS; Sunnyvale, CA; (1); Drama Clb; Red Cross Aide; Band; Mrchg Band; Pep Band; Stage Crew; Crs Cntry; High Hon Roll; CSF; Golden St Exam High Hnrs; German Awd; Stanford U; Med.

WEAKLEY, CHRIS J; Clovis West HS; Fresno, CA; (2); FCA; French Clb; Intnl Clb; NFL; Ski Clb; Speech Tm; SADD; Var Diving; JV Swmmng; Tennis; Peak Race Team-Ski Team; Buckingham Modeling Agncy-Model; U CA SB; Marine Bio.

WEAN, SHY; Chaminade College Prep; Acton, CA; (3); Church Yth Grp; Drama Clb; 4-H; Band; Church Choir; Variety Show; VP Jr Cls; Stu Cncl; JV Var Cheerldng; JV Var Swmmng; Life 90; Hotel Mgmt.

WEAR, CHRISTINE M; Fontana HS; Fontana, CA; (2); Fontana Grls Sftbl; Peperdine; Med.

WEAR, WENDY D; Fontana HS; Fontana, CA; (3); 4-H; Hosp Aide; Var Tennis; Hon Roll; U Of Irvine; Nrsng.

WEARE, KATE; Lick-Wilmerding HS; Oakland, CA; (4); Dance Clb; Acpl Chr; Ed Lit Mag; Hstry & Spnsh Acadmc Achvt Awds; CSF; Vars Dance Cos; CA Inst Of Arts; Choreogrphr.

WEATHERFORD, DANE; Los Altos SR HS; Hacienda Hts, CA; (3); Teachers Aide; Lbrn Band; Jazz Band; Pep Band; Ed Nwsp; Var Trk; Rotary Awd; CSF; Riverside CC Cmnty Band; Mock Trial Pgm; Psych.

WEATHERFORD, NICHELE D; Compton SR HS; Compton, CA; (2); JV Bsktbl; Hon Roll; Northrop U; Elect Engrng.

WEATHERS, MARIE D; C K Mc Clatchy HS; Sacramento, CA; (4); Score Keeper; Consumnes River Coll; Bus.

WEATHERS, MATT P; Atascadero HS; Atascadero, CA; (4); 1/300; Treas Drama Clb; SADD; Thesps; School Musical; School Play; Lit Mag; Sec Jr Cls; Stu Cncl; Var L Crs Cntry; High Hon Roll; UCLA; Bus.

WEATHERWAX, CAMERON M; Palmdale HS; Littlerock, CA; (2); Hon Roll; UCLA; Financial Consultant.

WEAVER, BRENDA; Barstow HS; Barstow, CA; (2); Socr; Dance Clb; Capt Drill Tm; Capt Flag Corp; JV Mgr(s); Hon Roll; Adv Dance Class At Schl; Dancer For Desert Rose Dance Co; De Vry Inst Tech; Comp Tech.

WEAVER, DARREL L; Edison HS; Huntington Beach, CA; (3); Church Yth Grp; Bsbl.

WEAVER, ELIZABETH L; Morro Bay HS; Los Osos, CA; (4); 18/164; Teachers Aide; Chorus; JV Var Bsktbl; Intrml Powder Puff Ftbl; JV Var Sftbl; JV Var Vllybl; High Hon Roll; Hon Roll; Pres Acad Fit Awd; U Of CO Boulder.

WEAVER, ERIKA J; Grace M Davis HS; Modesto, CA; (3); Church Yth Grp; Dance Clb; Drama Clb; FCA; Pres Pep Clb; Teachers Aide; Chorus; School Musical; Bsbl; Bus.

WEAVER, GREGORY B; Aragon HS; San Mateo, CA; (3); Church Yth Grp; Cmnty Wkr; Intnl Clb; Varsity Clb; Golf; Swmmng; NHS; Prfct Atten Awd; Water Polo Team; Chrch Plnng Cmmtte Prgm; UCSB; Engrng.

WEAVER, JAMES; Antelope Valley HS; Lancaster, CA; (3); 1/631; Math Clb; Math Tm; Teachers Aide; Pres Sr Cls; Wrstlng; High Hon Roll; Ntl Merit SF; Prfct Atten Awd; Val; Gldn St Hgh Hnrs Alg I, Geom; Stu Yr; Hnrs Engl, Bio, Spnsh I, Geom, Alg II; Stanford U; Bus.

WEAVER, JASON M; Beyer HS; Modesto, CA; (1); JV L Swmmng; Cit Awd; Hon Roll; JV Water Polo; Beyer Sci Awd; Chem.

WEAVER, JASON M; Huntinton Beach HS; Huntington Beach, CA; (2); Socr; Tennis; Golf; Law.

WEAVER, JODY L; Rio Lindo Adventist Acad; Lomita, CA; (3); French Clb; Spanish Clb; Girls Club Sec; ASB Pastor; Law.

WEAVER, KELLY; Edison HS; Huntington Beach, CA; (4); Church Yth Grp; Acpl Chr; Chorus; Capt Drill Tm; Rep Frsh Cls; Yng Rpblcn Cptn Rep; Star Grad; Hsty.

WEAVER, KELLY; Moorpark HS; Moorpark, CA; (3); 3/300; Letterman Clb; SADD; Varsity Clb; School Musical; Rep Soph Cls; Rep Jr Cls; Var Socr; JV Vllybl; Hon Roll; Med.

WEAVER, MAWIYAH A; John C Fremont HS; Oakland, CA; (2); Stu Cncl; Jrnlsm; Sls Rep.

WEAVER, MELISSA; Grossmont HS; El Cajon, CA; (1); Hon Roll.

WEAVER, MONA L; Banning HS; Banning, CA; (3); 16/175; Church Yth Grp; Dance Clb; French Clb; Intnl Clb; Teachers Aide; Color Guard; Rptr Nwsp; Powder Puff Ftbl; Hon Roll; CA Schlrshp Fed; Jrnlsm.

WEAVER, NICK; Edison HS; Huntington Bch, CA; (3); Debate Tm; German Clb; Math Tm; Model UN; NFL; Ntl Merit Ltr; Physics.

WEAVER, STEFANI; Elk Grove HS; Elk Grove, CA; (1); Church Yth Grp; FFA; Sec Frsh Cls; Sec Soph Cls; Cheerldng; JV Capt Pom Pon; Hon Roll; FFA Outstndng Frshmn,Bst Infrmd Grnhd.

WEAVER, TYRONE J; Dos Palos HS; South Dos Palos, CA; (3); Church Yth Grp; FHA; Letterman Clb; Office Aide; Band; Church Choir; Mrchg Band; School Play; Var Stu Cncl; Var Bsbl; Rally Cmssnr; Bronco Of Mnth.

WEAVER, WAYNE D; Artesia HS; Cerritos, CA; (3); JA; Letterman Clb; Varsity Clb; Variety Show; Var Ftbl; Var Socr; Var Swmmng; Var Wt Lftg; Cit Awd; UC Santa Barbara; Bus Admin.

WEBB, ANGELA; Grace Davis HS; Modesto, CA; (1); Church Yth Grp; GAA; JV Sftbl; Cit Awd; Hon Roll; Cmptv Sftbl; Gate Cls; Fresno ST Coll; Ed.

WEBB, APRIL E; The Academy Of Our Lady Of Peace; San Diego, CA; (3); Art Clb; Church Yth Grp; Cmnty Wkr; School Play; Sec Frsh Cls; Cheerldng; Cit Awd; Hon Roll; Countywide Spelling Bee 87-88; Miss CA Teen Pageant; Law.

WEBB, CHRISTOPHER G; Trabuco Hills HS; Mission Viejo, CA; (2); Math Tm; Quiz Bowl; Spanish Clb; Lcrss; High Hon Roll; Hon Roll; NHS; Rdng & Wrtng Ptry; UCSB; Engr.

WEBB, DEENA M; Mother Lode Christian HS; Sonora, CA; (2); Church Yth Grp; Pep Clb; Teachers Aide; Chorus; Yrbk; Bsktbl; Cheerldng; Vet Asst; Vet.

WEBB, ELIZABETH LEIGH; Culver City HS; Los Angeles, CA; (4); 13/330; Pres Dance Clb; French Clb; Pres NFL; School Play; Sec Sr Cls; Var Gym; Pres Acad Fit Awd; Stus Leag-Sec/Treas/VP; CSF Sealbearer/Pres; 90 Royal Mdlln Debutante; U Of CA-LOS Angeles; Med.

WEBB, JAMIE H; Corona HS; Corona, CA; (3); Boy Scts; Church Yth Grp; Science Clb; Church Choir; Ftbl; JV Socr; Hon Roll; Prfct Atten Awd; Pres Acad Fit Awd; BYU; Music.

WEBB, KAREN J; Casa Roble Fundamental HS; Orangevale, CA; (4); 8/344; Church Yth Grp; Spanish Clb; Teachers Aide; Church Choir; High Hon Roll; NHS; Pres Acad Fit Awd; CA Cnfrnc Missns Bd Yth Rep; Greenville Coll; Elem Ed Tchr.

WEBB, KERI R; Alta Loma HS; Alta Loma, CA; (4); 18/540; Church Yth Grp; SADD; Teachers Aide; Rep Stu Cncl; DAR Awd; High Hon Roll; Hon Roll; Prfct Atten Awd; Pres Acad Fit Awd.

WEBB, LETICIA I; Las Plumas HS; Oroville, CA; (2); Rptr 4-H; French Clb; Ed Yrbk; JV Socr; 4-H Awd; Hon Roll; Pres Acad Fit Awd; CS; Butte Cnty Media Fstvl Grand Chmpn; U Of Columbia; Jrnlsm.

WEBB, MAXIA K; Highland HS; Palmdale, CA; (1); Key Clb; Math Tm; Band; Mrchg Band; Pep Band; Sec Treas Frsh Cls; Off Soph Cls; Sec Stu Cncl; Hon Roll; CSF; Med.

WEBB, MELISSA L; Watsonville HS; Watsonville, CA; (3); 43/502; Church Yth Grp; Pep Clb; Cheerldng; Pom Pon; Trk; Hon Roll; CSF; Bus.

WEBB, MIKE J; Palm Desert HS; La Quinta, CA; (3); Hon Roll.

WEBB, REBECCA; North HS; Bakersfield, CA; (2); Church Yth Grp; Dance Clb; Teachers Aide; Chorus; Church Choir; Hon Roll; Puppetry Chrch; Tchr Chrch Yngr Chldrn; Yth Ldr Chrch; Bakersfield Coll; Teach.

WEBB, RICHARD ASHLEY; Santa Fe Christian HS; Encinitas, CA; (4); 12/42; Cmnty Wkr; Office Aide; Spanish Clb; Teachers Aide; Bsktbl; Crs Cntry; Ice Hcky; High Hon Roll; Hon Roll; Ntl Merit Ltr; Fnlst For Air Force ROTC 4-Yr Schlrshp; Tutor Algebra & Geom Stus; Cal Poly San Luis Obispo; Engr.

WEBB, SHERRY C; Trabuco Hills HS; El Toro, CA; (3); Boy Scts; Church Yth Grp; Teachers Aide; Varsity Clb; Trk; Vllybl; Hon Roll; Clmbng; Cmpng; Hkng; Auto Mech.

WEBB, WENDY E; Victor Valley HS; Victorville, CA; (2); Capt Dance Clb; Hosp Aide; Sec Key Clb; Ski Clb; Capt Drill Tm; Hon Roll; Sch Hnrs Goldn ST Exam Alge I; Workng Ast Nurse Asst; Sch Hnr Roll; RN.

WEBBER, GABRIELLE; Forest Lake Christian HS; Grass Valley, CA; (3); Church Yth Grp; Yrbk; Rep Jr Cls; Var L Bsktbl; Capt L Sftbl; Var L Vllybl; Cit Awd; Hon Roll; CA Schlrshp Fed.

WEBBER, JENNIFER L; Cajon HS; San Bernardino, CA; (2); Church Yth Grp; Cmnty Wkr; Letterman Clb; Varsity Clb; Stat Swmmng; Var Vllybl; High Hon Roll; NHS; CA Schlrshp Fdrtn; Psych.

WEBBER, MATTHEW B; Justin Siena HS; Sonoma, CA; (4); 20/136; Pres Debate Tm; Ski Clb; Rep Sr Cls; Rep Stu Cncl; JV Crs Cntry; Var Capt Socr; JV Var Trk; Hon Roll; Ntl Merit SF.

WEBBER, TRACEY; St Bonaventure HS; Camarillo, CA; (2); Church Yth Grp; Letterman Clb; JV Var Cheerldng; Var Socr; All Tri-Valley Leag 1st Tm Sccr, Venture Cnty MVP.

WEBBERLEY, GEOFFREY G; Canyon HS; Canyon Country, CA; (3); Church Yth Grp; FCA; Teachers Aide; Church Choir; School Musical; Pres Soph Cls; JV Capt Bsktbl; CA ST U; Elec Engrng.

WEBER, CAROLINE E; Santa Clara HS; Oxnard, CA; (2); Church Yth Grp; Pres Girl Scts; Pep Clb; JV Swmmng; UC Berkeley; Hotel Mgmt.

WEBER, CHANDA M; Fremont Christian HS; Milpitas, CA; (3); Church Yth Grp; Band; Church Choir; Hon Roll; Dale Carnegie Z Awds; Bus.

WEBER, CRAIG J; Bonita Vista HS; Chula Vista, CA; (3); 1/525; Boy Scts; Church Yth Grp; Computer Clb; Intnl Clb; Key Clb; SADD; Church Choir; JV Vllybl; Cit Awd; High Hon Roll; Church Spon Sports/Vllybl/Bsktbl/Sftbl; Tribune 90 Copley Schlrshp; 1st Pl Sch Honors Geom; Brigham Young U; Psych.

WEBER, ELISSA L; Colfax HS; Meadow Vista, CA; (2); 2/208; Treas Service Clb; School Play; High Hon Roll; Wrtng.

WEBER, GREG R; Edison HS; Stockton, CA; (2); Church Yth Grp; Computer Clb; Band; School Musical; Mgr(s); Mgr Vllybl; Hon Roll; Prfct Atten Awd; St Schlr; Smmr Camp Cnslr; U CA; Engrng.

WEBER, JAMES M; Abraham Lincoln HS; San Francisco, CA; (3); JV Swmmng; Var Wrstlng; U IL; Commrcl Art.

WEBER, SHANE Y; Bonita Vista HS; Chula Vista, CA; (2); 1/560; Boy Scts; Church Yth Grp; Drama Clb; SADD; Church Choir; School Play; JV Crs Cntry; JV Trk; JV Vllybl; Hon Roll; Hnrd Golden St Ex Geo; Best Character Actor; Typng Profcncy; Brigham Young U.

WEBER, THEODORE J; Paso Robles HS; Paso Robles, CA; (2); Rep Frsh Cls; Var Capt Swmmng; High Hon Roll; Vrsty Watr Polo; Sch Swmmng Rcrd; MIT; Engr.

WEBSTER, BRION L; Edison HS; Davis, CA; (4); 7/250; Boy Scts; JCL; Latin Clb; Math Tm; Science Clb; High Hon Roll; JETS Awd; Ntl Merit Schol; UC Davis; Bio.

WEBSTER, BRION L; Edison HS; Fresno, CA; (4); 4/219; Boy Scts; JCL; Latin Clb; Math Clb; Math Tm; Science Clb; High Hon Roll; Ntl Merit SF; Pres Schlr; USC; Bio Sci.

WEBSTER, COREY E; Richard Gahr HS; Cerritos, CA; (2); JV Bsktbl; Hon Roll; Bus.

WEBSTER, DANIEL P; Enterprise HS; Redding, CA; (3); Church Yth Grp; Computer Clb; High Hon Roll; Sci Olympd-Comp Prblm Slvng; Sci.

WEBSTER, DEBORAH D; Moorpark HS; Moorpark, CA; (3); Drama Clb; Band; Mrchg Band; Orch; Pep Band; School Musical; School Play; Variety Show; Rep Soph Cls; Stu Cncl; Band Lttrwmn Band Sectnldr; CSF; Band Board Publcty; Moorpark Coll; Drama Acting.

WEBSTER, JOHANNA L; Etna HS; Etna, CA; (3); 2/80; Church Yth Grp; Pres Drama Clb; Band; Rep Frsh Cls; Stu Cncl; L Var Bsktbl; L Var Trk; L Capt Vllybl; Bausch & Lomb Sci Awd; Elks Awd; All-Shasta Cascade Lgue Hnrs Trk & Vlybl; Westmont Coll; Ahtltc Trng.

WEBSTER, MICHELLE; Los Alamitos HS; Seal Beach, CA; (4); Church Yth Grp; Cmnty Wkr; Dance Clb; FCA; French Clb; Hon Roll; Prfct Atten Awd; Guitar Playng; Ballet; Vlntr Wrk Childrns Homes; Christn Educ.

WEBSTER II, RONALD L; Seaside HS; Ft Ord, CA; (3); Am Leg Boys St; ROTC; Color Guard; Drill Tm; Hon Roll; Prfct Atten Awd; Rotary Awd; SAI Ledrshp JROTC; Acad Excllnce JROTC; Law Enfrcmnt.

WEBSTER, SHANNON M; Cal HS; Whittier, CA; (2); Teachers Aide; Stat Bsbl; Stat Bsktbl; Score Keeper; Hon Roll; Fullerton; Psych.

WEDDE, TRACE; Atwater HS; Atwater, CA; (1); Church Yth Grp; High Hon Roll; Hon Roll; Pres Acad Fit Awd.

WEDDLE, JENNIFER A; Gladstone HS; Glendora, CA; (3); Science Clb; Ski Clb; SADD; Var Crs Cntry; JV Sftbl; Hon Roll; Prfct Atten Awd.

WEDEMEYER, KUNIKO; Fremont Christian HS; San Jose, CA; (1); Treas Frsh Cls; JV Bsktbl; JV Vllybl; High Hon Roll.

WEDGE, JOHN; Live Oak HS; Morgan Hill, CA; (4); JV Var Bsbl; Hon Roll; Prfct Atten Awd; SADD; Chess Clb; Church Yth Grp; Pep Clb; JV Bsktbl; Art Clb; Math Clb; SHARP-NASA/Ames Pgm; MVP Bsbl; Sn Luis Obispo Poly; Mech Engr.

WEDIN, ERIN D; Brea-Olinda HS; Brea, CA; (3); 16/300; Pres Church Yth Grp; Cmnty Wkr; Church Choir; School Musical; Ed Yrbk; Score Keeper; Hon Roll; NHS; Jobs Dghtrs Hnrd Qn.

WEED, KORI L; El Cajon Valley HS; El Cajon, CA; (2); 21/469; Church Yth Grp; Dance Clb; Letterman Clb; Cheerldng; Diving; Golf; Hon Roll; Campus Life Yth For Christ; Dance.

WEEDEN, MATTHEW L; Turlock HS; Delhi, CA; (3); 80/800; Art Clb; Pres Church Yth Grp; Key Clb; VP Letterman Clb; Ski Clb; Varsity Clb; VP L Swmmng; Voice Dem Awd; Water Polo-Vrsty Letterman; Interact-Brd Ofc; Stu Of Month; U Of CA-SANTA Barbara; Phys Ed.

WEEKES, JASON; Whittier Christian HS; Whittier, CA; (3); Church Yth Grp; Church Choir; JV Bsbl; JV Socr.

WEEKS, CASSIE L; Valhalla HS; El Cajon, CA; (3); 36/423; Pres Sec Church Yth Grp; Spanish Clb; SADD; Teachers Aide; Chorus; Church Choir; Variety Show; Var Crs Cntry; Cit Awd; Hon Roll; Mixed Ensemble, Toured San Fran, Boston, New York; Church Pianist; Spanish Comp 87 & 88 1st Pl; BYU; Cmmnctns.

WEEKS, DEBORAH D; Central Union HS; El Centro, CA; (2); Band; Pep Band; Var Swmmng; Hon Roll; Stu Of Futurist Orgnztn At Schl Cenviromentalist; BYU; Bio.

WEEKS, MICHELLE L; Santa Clara HS; Oxnard, CA; (2); Church Yth Grp; Cmnty Wkr; Drama Clb; French Clb; Pep Clb; Swmmng; Hon Roll; Pres Acad Fit Awd; Miss Teen Port Hrne Prncss; Miss Teen Ventura Cnty Prncs; Ventura Cntys Model Yr; Ventura Coll; Beauty Consultant.

WEEKS, SHIRLEY M; Fontana HS; Fontana, CA; (3); Hon Roll; Prfct Atten Awd; Friday Night Live Pres; Air Force; Data Entry.

WEERASINGHE, SEAN A; Burbank HS; Burbank, CA; (2); Teachers Aide; VP Frsh Cls; VP Soph Cls; Rep Stu Cncl; L Trk; Pres Acad Fit Awd; Hnrs Prog; Schl Rcgntn Golden St Exam 1st Yr Alg; Chem Eng.

WEESE, MELANIE M; Willits HS; Willits, CA; (3); Church Yth Grp; Office Aide; SADD; Teachers Aide; Band; Chorus; Jazz Band; High Hon Roll; Hon Roll; UC Davis Med Schl; Physcn.

WEESE, MELISSA M; Willits HS; Willits, CA; (3); Church Yth Grp; Office Aide; SADD; Teachers Aide; Band; Chorus; Mrchg Band; High Hon Roll; Gldn St Exam Algeb; Nrsg.

WEGENER, AMY F; Cloverdale HS; Cloverdale, CA; (4); 5/66; Am Leg Aux Girls St; Church Yth Grp; School Play; VP Frsh Cls; VP Soph Cls; VP Jr Cls; JV Var Bsktbl; Stat Ftbl; High Hon Roll; Pres Acad Fit Awd; Elem Lvl Tutoring & Cnslrng; Stu Rep Prin Intrvw & Slctn Cmmtte; UC Santa Cruz.

WEGENER, KATHRYN E; Patrick Henry HS; San Diego, CA; (3); Church Yth Grp; Cmnty Wkr; Sec DECA; Pres FTA; Rptr Nwsp; Yrbk; Jr NHS; Elem Schl Teacher.

WEGIS, GENA E; Cuyama Valley HS; Maricopa, CA; (3); Drama Clb; 4-H; Pep Clb; School Play; Treas Soph Cls; Cheerldng; Vllybl; Hon Roll.

WEGNER, JUDITH E; Banning HS; Banning, CA; (3); Church Yth Grp; Cmnty Wkr; Ed Yrbk; Sec Sr Cls; Hon Roll; Daisy Chain 90; Med.

WEGRZYN, JENNIFER L; John Burroughs HS; Burbank, CA; (4); Cmnty Wkr; Hosp Aide; Teachers Aide; Rep Frsh Cls; Rep Stu Cncl; Mgr(s); Sftbl; High Hon Roll; Pres Acad Fit Awd; Toluca Lake Art Assoc Jr Awrd 89-90; CO U; Interior Design.

WEHAGE, JENNY; Warren HS; Downey, CA; (1); Church Yth Grp; Pep Clb; Cheerldng; Arch.

WEHE, KIMBERLY ANNETTE; San Leandro HS; San Leandro, CA; (4); 13/322; DECA; Key Clb; Office Aide; Teachers Aide; Chorus; School Musical; Swing Chorus; Stat Bsktbl; High Hon Roll; Pres Acad Fit Awd.

WEHLING, MICHELLE; Fountain Valley HS; Fountain Valley, CA; (3); Rep Church Yth Grp; Sec German Clb; Rep Pep Clb; Rep Service Clb; Pres Stu Cncl; Var JV Cheerldng; Hon Roll; Pres Acad Fit Awd; Rep Frsh Cls; Rep Soph Cls; Miss Teen Orange Cnty 88; Pepperdine U Sthrn CA Yth Ctznshp Smnr 90; UCLA; Bus Admin.

WEHNER, AMY M; Woodland HS; Woodland, CA; (3); FFA; Bsktbl; Sftbl; Swmmng; Tennis; Vllybl; 4-H Awd; High Hon Roll; Jr NHS; Pres Acad Fit Awd; UCLA; Accntng.

WEHRLY, BRANDON M; Bishop O'dowd HS; San Leandro, CA; (2); Drama Clb; School Play; Ftbl; JV Golf; Hon Roll; Hiking Clb.

WEI, BEN; Arcadia HS; Arcadia, CA; (3); 58/640; AFS; Art Clb; Church Yth Grp; Service Clb; Bsktbl; NHS; CSF; Principals Rcgntn Roll; Sr Men Club Of Arcadia; UC Berkeley; Bus Economics.

WEI, CHRIS; Wilcox HS; Sunnyvale, CA; (2); French Clb; Hon Roll; Asian Clb.

WEI, JULIA M; Mills HS; Belmont, CA; (2); Art Clb; Debate Tm; Pep Clb; Ed Nwsp; Ed Lit Mag; JV Bsktbl; JV Cheerldng; Var Mgr(s); Hon Roll; GATE.

WEI, KENNY K; Herbert Hoover HS; Glendale, CA; (3); JCL; Key Clb; Latin Clb; Letterman Clb; Math Tm; Varsity Clb; Var Tennis; High Hon Roll; Ntl Merit SF; CSF; Med.

WEI, LIVIA Y; John F Kennedy HS; Buena Park, CA; (3); FBLA; Key Clb; Band; Mrchg Band; Pep Band; JV Vllybl; High Hon Roll; Vrsty Bdmntn; Emeral Urain Top 10 Prcnt In Schl; Band; UCLA; Math.

WEICHELT, ERIK A; Grossmont HS; El Cajon, CA; (4); 102/400; Letterman Clb; Teachers Aide; Varsity Clb; Variety Show; Off Soph Cls; Stu Cncl; JV Capt Bsbl; Var Capt Ftbl; Var Wrstlng; Brethard Awd; Union/Trbn All Acad Awd; MVP Ftbl; AZ ST U; Bus Admin.

WEICHERS, LOGAN E; Willows HS; Willows, CA; (3); JV Var Bsktbl; JV Var Trk; Intrml Wt Lftg; High Hon Roll; Hon Roll; Cngrssnl Schlr WA DC; BYU; Dntstry.

WEICK, WENDY A; Valhalla HS; El Cajon, CA; (3); 105/408; Cit Awd; Spnsh Oral Prtcptn Awd; Hnrs Spnsh Cls Awd; SDSU; Elem Educ.

WEIDERT, JOEL C; Bellarmine College Prep; San Jose, CA; (3); Boy Scts; Church Yth Grp; Cmnty Wkr; Ski Clb; Socr; Wt Lftg; Wrstlng; U Of CA; Med.

WEIGAND, JAMES J; Central Valley HS; Redding, CA; (3); Computer Clb; Math Clb; Math Tm; High Hon Roll; Hon Roll; NHS; Brain Drain Cmptn; Sci Olympiad; Aerospace Engrng.

WEIGEL, BRENDA B; Alameda HS; Alameda, CA; (3); 12/276; Var Crs Cntry; Var Swmmng; Hon Roll; JV Wtrpolo; Ntl Level Piano; N Coast Qulfr Swmmng; UC San Diego; Phy Thrpy.

WEIGHTMAN, DAVID J; Las Lomas HS; Walnut Creek, CA; (3); 20/290; SADD; Band; VP Tennis; High Hon Roll; Bus.

WEIGHTMAN, HEATHER L; Grossmont HS; La Mesa, CA; (1); Drama Clb; School Play; Hon Roll; SDSU.

WEIGLE, CHAD; Beaumont HS; Cherry Valley, CA; (4); Office Aide; Teachers Aide; Varsity Clb; Band; Jazz Band; Mrchg Band; Orch; Pep Band; Ftbl; Wt Lftg; CA ST San Bernardino; Fnc.

WEILAND, CARRIE L; Villa Park HS; Orange, CA; (4); 39/400; Sec VP 4-H; German Clb; Teachers Aide; Yrbk; Hon Roll; NHS; CSF Seal Bearer; U Of CA San Diego; Teach.

WEILAND, JAY; Villa Park HS; Orange, CA; (2); Key Clb; Science Clb; Spanish Clb; Cit Awd; High Hon Roll; Sci Olympd.

WEINBERG, LAURA; Fairfield HS; Fairfield, CA; (2); Pep Clb; Rep Soph Cls; Cheerldng; Sftbl; Hon Roll.

WEINBERGER, DANA; Ulysses S Grant HS; Sherman Oaks, CA; (3); Capt Math Tm; Speech Tm; VP Sec Temple Yth Grp; Var Crs Cntry; Var Trk; High Hon Roll; Ntl Merit Ltr; Debate Tm; JA; Kiwanis Awd; Edgar M Bronfman Yth Fellowship In Israel 90; Amnesty Intl; CA Acad Decathlon 90; Sci.

WEINDORT, ANNETTE M; California Lutheran HS; Sylmar, CA; (2); Sec Church Yth Grp; Chorus; Church Choir; Variety Show; Var Cheerldng; L Mgr(s); Sftbl; Hon Roll; UCLA; Engr.

WEINER, MICHELLE; Capistrano Valley HS; Mission Viejo, CA; (4); Mgr Dance Clb; Drama Clb; Teachers Aide; School Musical; School Play; Rptr Yrbk; Cit Awd; High Hon Roll; Hon Roll; Humboldt ST; Elem Ed.

WEINGOLD, CHRISTOPHER C; Mc Kinleyville HS; Mckinleyville, CA; (1); 27/70; Letterman Clb; Chorus; Bsktbl; JV Ftbl; L Golf; Tennis; Surf; Acoustic & Electric Guitar; U CA LA; Bus.

WEINHEIMER, AMY E; San Benito HS; Hollister, CA; (3); GAA; Pep Clb; Science Clb; Varsity Clb; Sec Ed Nwsp; Off Frsh Cls; Off Soph Cls; Off Jr Cls; Crs Cntry; Powder Puff Ftbl; CA Schlrshp Fed VP; MVP Track; League & Rgnl Champ 100m & 200m Track; Sprts Psych.

WEINHEIMER, LARA C; San Benito HS; Hollister, CA; (4); 2/265; Art Clb; GAA; Math Clb; Sec Science Clb; Varsity Clb; Var L Swmmng; Capt Var Trk; Wt Lftg; Elks Awd; Sal; People To People Yth Sci Exchng Soviet Union; CA Schlrshp Fed; U Of CA Davis.

WEINMAN, CHRISTINE; San Dimas HS; San Dimas, CA; (4); 46/275; Library Aide; Chorus; Swing Chorus; Var Trk; Hon Roll; Bus.

WEINSTEIN, KAREN E; Livermore HS; Livermore, CA; (1); German Clb; Band; Mrchg Band; Orch; L Swmmng; High Hon Roll; CSF; Schlr Athl; Yth Orchestra Southern Alameda Cnty.

WEINSTEIN, MATTHEW I; El Comino Real HS; West Hills, CA; (3); Treas Debate Tm; NFL; Treas Speech Tm; Temple Yth Grp; Off Frsh Cls; Off Soph Cls; Var Crs Cntry; Var Trk; High Hon Roll; Hon Roll; Natl Bible Cont Champ; Intl Bible Cont Fnlst Jerusalem; NCTE Wrtng Cont Schl Champ.

WEINTHAL, TEVYA A; University City HS; San Diego, CA; (3); 49/373; SADD; JV L Ftbl; JV L Socr; JV L Tennis; Var Capt Vllybl; High Hon Roll; Hon Roll; Pres Acad Fit Awd; CA Schlrshp Fed; San Diego Tribunes All-Acdmc 1st Tm Bys Vllybl; CA Intrschlstc Fed 1st Tm By Vllybl; U Of CA Santa Barbara.

WEIR, MICHELLE N; Casa Grande HS; Petaluma, CA; (2); GAA; Letterman Clb; Ski Clb; Varsity Clb; Band; Chorus; Var Frsh Cls; Stu Cncl; Socr; Hon Roll; Sonoma St Coll Bound Pgm; Vrs Cls Achvt Awds; UCLA.

WEIRICK, SHANE T; Roseville HS; Rocklin, CA; (2); German Clb; JV Bsbl; JV Ftbl; Hon Roll; Cmptrs; Work Jolly Super Mkt; Study Bus Mgt; Arch.

WEIRUM, SCOTT J; Cuyama Valley HS; New Cuyama, CA; (2); Drama Clb; FFA; Pep Clb; Rep Frsh Cls; Rep Soph Cls; JV Bsktbl; Var Ftbl; Pres Acad Fit Awd.

WEISS, BRIAN T; Rim Of The World HS; Rimforest, CA; (1); Letterman Clb; Band; Mrchg Band; Pep Band; School Musical; Wrstlng; U Of MN; Vet.

WEISS, CANDACE M; Ganesha HS; Diamond Bar, CA; (2); Treas Church Yth Grp; Red Cross Aide; Church Choir; Intrml Wt Lftg; High Hon Roll; Hon Roll; Christ Coll Irvine; Engl Lit.

WEISS, CHRISTINA M; Casa Grande HS; Petaluma, CA; (3); 101/283; Teachers Aide; School Play; Variety Show; Hon Roll; Prfct Atten Awd; Cousteau Soc; World Wildlife Fund; UCSC; Marine Bio.

WEISS, ELI S; St Ignatius HS; San Francisco, CA; (3); Hon Roll; Pres Acad Fit Awd; CSF; Arch.

WEISS, ELIZABETH; George Wahington HS; San Francisco, CA; (2); Teachers Aide; Stu Cncl; High Hon Roll; Hon Roll; Natl Jr Hnr Soc; Vlntr Spcl Arts Fstvl; Vlntr CA Acad Sci; U CA Davis; Zoology.

WEISS, ILENE S; Prospect HS; Calabasas, CA; (2); 68/268; Intnl Clb; Temple Yth Grp; Score Keeper; Prfct Atten Awd; Stght A Avg Spnsh 2 88-89; Lang.

WEISS, KARA E; Orange Glen HS; Valley Center, CA; (4); German Clb; Pep Clb; Band; Chorus; Flag Corp; Mrchg Band; Pep Band; School Play; Stage Crew; Swing Chorus; CA Schlstc Fed; UC Santa Barbara; Marine Bio.

WEISS, LISA; University HS; Irvine, CA; (3); AFS; Yrbk; VP Frsh Cls; Off Jr Cls; Off Sr Cls; Cheerldng; JV Swmmng; French Hon Soc; Hon Roll; Church Yth Group; Ed.

WEISS, MARK; El Camino Real HS; Woodland Hills, CA; (4); Computer Clb; Debate Tm; Math Clb; Math Tm; SADD; Ed Sec Lit Mag; Rep Soph Cls; Rep Sr Cls; Var Capt Trk; Cit Awd; Acad & Schlt Athl Awds; UC San Diego; Genetic Engrng.

WEISS, MICHAEL J; North HS; Turlock, CA; (2); French Clb; Science Clb; Band; Orch; Rep Frsh Cls; JV Ftbl; JV Wrstlng; Hon Roll; Envrnmntlst; Photo; Music; MI ST U; Bio Genetic Engrng.

WEISS, SANDRA; La Canada HS; La Canada-Flint, CA; (3); 29/250; NHS; Co-Capt Equestrian Tm, Hgh Point Rider 88-89; UC Davis; Vet.

WEISS, SCOTT; El Camino HS; Daly City, CA; (4); Church Yth Grp; VP Rep Frsh Cls; Treas Soph Cls; Rep Jr Cls; Rep Sr Cls; Rep Stu Cncl; Intrml Capt Bsbl; JV Capt Bsktbl; Mgr(s); Intrml Socr; Close Up Pgm; San Jose St U; Bus.

WEISS, STEPHANIE P; La Jolla Country Day Schl; Poway, CA; (2); French Clb; Girl Scts; Math Tm; Acpl Chr; Chorus; School Musical; French Hon Soc; High Hon Roll; Piano Cert Mrt; Bio.

WEISS, STEVE I; Prospect HS; San Jose, CA; (1); 32/250; Church Yth Grp; NHS; Smmr Mssn Trp Navajos AZ 90; Outstndng Phys Ed Awd 89-90.

WEISSER, MIKE J; Hanford Joint Union HS; Hanford, CA; (3); Drama Clb; JA; Varsity Clb; School Musical; School Play; Rep Soph Cls; Rep Jr Cls; Ftbl; Wt Lftg; Wrstlng; Brd Trustees HS; DARE; Peer Cnslng; St Marys; Poltcl Sci.

WEITZEIL, KEVIN S; Argonaut HS; Ione, CA; (2); Spanish Clb; Bsktbl; Var L Socr; High Hon Roll; Bowling VP; Acad Talent Srch 89; Mother Lode Yth Sccr Assn; Grphc Art.

WEITZEL, SHAWN R; Fontana HS; Fontana, CA; (2); Math Tm; Pres Science Clb; Jazz Band; Mrchg Band; Hon Roll; Physicist.

WELARATNA, RUWAN; Los Altos HS; Los Altos, CA; (4); Thesps; School Play; Rptr Nwsp; Rep Jr Cls; Treas Sr Cls; Ntl Merit Schol; Pres Acad Fit Awd; Voice Dem Awd; Harvey Mudd Coll; Physics.

WELCH, AUSTIN C; Chino HS; Chino, CA; (2).

WELCH, BARBARA ELIZABETH; Rancho Buena Vista HS; Vista, CA; (4); Drama Clb; French Clb; Mu Alpha Theta; SADD; Cit Awd; Hon Roll; Pres Acad Fit Awd; Lttl League Coach; CA Poly; Ind Engrng.

WELCH, BEN J; Orange Glen HS; Valley Center, CA; (1); 1/647; Ftbl; Wt Lftg; High Hon Roll; Hon Roll; UCLA; Phys Thrpy.

WELCH, BILLY J; Orange Glen HS; Valley Center, CA; (3); 5/458; Band; Mrchg Band; Pep Band; Stu Cncl; High Hon Roll; Hon Roll; NHS; CSF; UCLA; Engrng.

WELCH, BRANDI M; East Union HS; Manteca, CA; (1); 9/339; Church Yth Grp; Hon Roll; Prfct Atten Awd; STAND; CSF; Wrtng Poetry; Ply Clrnt, Kybrd; Fine Arts.

WELCH, CHRIS D; Ramona HS; Ramona, CA; (3); 5/294; Am Leg Boys St; Church Yth Grp; Spanish Clb; Varsity Clb; Var L Ftbl; Var L Socr; Cit Awd; High Hon Roll; Hon Roll; Kiwanis Awd; San Diego Tribunes All Acad Tm; U CA Berkeley; Engr.

WELCH, CHRISTINE; Ganesha HS; Diamond Bar, CA; (4); 20/250; Church Yth Grp; Pep Clb; Stu Cncl; Pom Pon; Cit Awd; High Hon Roll; Hon Roll; Pres Acad Fit Awd; Cornet; Math & Engrng Assn; Yng Schlr Pgm; U Of CA Riverside; Bus.

WELCH, CINDY; Oakland Technical HS; Oakland, CA; (2); Drama Clb; German Clb; Model UN; Intrml Crs Cntry; High Hon Roll; Hon Roll; Prfct Atten Awd; Phy.

WELCH, JACKIE L; Fontana HS; Fontana, CA; (1); Hon Roll; Chaffey JC; Vet.

WELCH II, JAMES W; Central Union HS; El Centro, CA; (2); 1/692; Church Yth Grp; Treas Computer Clb; Math Tm; L Speech Tm; High Hon Roll; Lion Awd; Ntl Merit Ltr; Intrml Wrstlng; CA Schlstc Fed; Fr Dept Hnrs; Lttrd In Acad, Speech; Treas Comp Club; Stu Mnth 89; French Hnrs; Stanford; Bio-Chem.

WELCH, JEFFREY; Modesto HS; Modesto, CA; (4); 65/480; Church Yth Grp; Computer Clb; Ed Yrbk; Hon Roll; CSF; Yng Rpblcns Clb; Electrnc Engrng.

WELCH, JOHANNA W; Woodland HS; Esparto, CA; (4); Drama Clb; Pres French Clb; Pres Thesps; School Musical; School Play; Variety Show; Trk; Hon Roll; Jr NHS; NHS; Theatre.

WELCH, JOSETTE; St Michaels HS; Los Angeles, CA; (3); Sec Church Yth Grp; Spanish Clb; Church Choir; Pres Acad Fit Awd; Speech Tm; Pdtrcn.

WELCH, KAREN E; Troy HS; Fullerton, CA; (2); Off Church Yth Grp; French Clb; Church Choir; Var Tennis; Var Trk; Wt Lftg; High Hon Roll; Hon Roll; Awd Exclinc-Wght Trng; Frnch Art & Hlth; Hlth.

WELCH, LORI M; Santa Cruz HS; Santa Cruz, CA; (3); GAA; Library Aide; Phtg Yrbk; Var Powder Puff Ftbl; JV Var Sftbl; JV Var Vllybl; High Hon Roll; Traveling Sftbl Tm; CS Fresno; Bus.

WELCH, MOIRA; Bellarmine Jefferson HS; Tujunga, CA; (2); Sftbl; Vllybl; Hon Roll; Pres Acad Fit Awd.

WELCH, SEAN P; Sequoia HS; San Carlos, CA; (2); Debate Tm; Letterman Clb; Rep Soph Cls; Rep Stu Cncl; Var Swmmng; High Hon Roll; Ntl Merit Schol; Pres Acad Fit Awd; Natl Yth Congressional Awd; Outstndng Moderators Awd 89-90; VP Jr Statesman Of Amer; UC; Genetics.

WELCH, TODD; Etiwanda HS; Alta Loma, CA; (3); 11/630; Boy Scts; Church Yth Grp; JV Var Bsktbl; Hon Roll; NHS; CSF; Hnr Guard; Gldn St Exam Alg Hnrs; Med.

WELDON, MIKE; Strathmore HS; Strathmore, CA; (3); 1/80; Am Leg Boys St; Computer Clb; Pres Science Clb; Tennis; Cit Awd; High Hon Roll; Friday Night Live; Mock Trial Tm; Comp Engrng.

WELDON, RYAN W; Watsonville HS; Watsonville, CA; (2); Church Yth Grp; Science Clb; SADD; Tennis; Hon Roll.

WELDON, TRACY A; Capuchino HS; San Bruno, CA; (3); Cmnty Wkr; Ed Lit Mag; Off Frsh Cls; Sec Soph Cls; Sec Stu Cncl; High Hon Roll; CSF; Friday Nght Live; U WA; Lgl Secy.

WELKER, DENISE L; Hilltop HS; Chula Vista, CA; (2); Art Clb; Quiz Bowl; Science Clb; Spanish Clb; JV Capt Vllybl; Cit Awd; Amer Legion Schl Awd; Outstndng Stu; Prfct Score LSD Scripture Chase; Birgham Young U; Comp Sci.

WELLAND, RUTH A; Capital Christian HS; Sacramento, CA; (3); Art Clb; Church Yth Grp; Spanish Clb; Teachers Aide; Church Choir; Off Jr Cls; High Hon Roll; Hon Roll; Music Awds; Checker Awd; Chrch Vlntr; Trophy Memrztn Bible; Pediatric Nurse.

WELLCOME, JEFF; David Starr Jordan HS; Long Beach, CA; (3); Golf; Comp.

WELLENDORF, JANET; St Francis HS; Sacramento, CA; (3); Church Yth Grp; Dance Clb; Debate Tm; French Clb; SADD; Rep Soph Cls; Intrml JV Cheerldng; Var Swmmng; Hon Roll; Dentistry.

WELLERT, ELIZABETH; Springs Of Living Water Acad; Chico, CA; (3); Church Yth Grp; Spanish Clb; Pres Soph Cls; VP Jr Cls; Pres Acad Fit Awd; Scripture Awd; Butte Coll; Nrsg.

WELLES, JEANETTE H; Alexander Hamilton HS; Los Angeles, CA; (2); Stage Crew; Hon Roll.

WELLINGTON, KELLEY L; Esperanza HS; Anaheim, CA; (2); 87/571; Treas Intnl Clb; JV Bsktbl; L Var Trk; JV Vllybl; High Hon Roll; Gldn St Exm Awds, Alg Hgh Hnrs, Gen Hnrs; CSF; Top 25 Awd Yr; Stu Mnth Span; U Of CA Irvine; Pre-Med.

WELLMAN, ALEX; Mojave HS; California City, CA; (2); Letterman Clb; Math Clb; Math Tm; Spanish Clb; Golf; High Hon Roll; CAP Mitchell Awd; CA Schlrshp Fed; USAFA; Aeronautics.

WELLMAN, ALLISON; Southbay Christian HS; Sunnyvale, CA; (1); 1/50; Chorus; Sec Frsh Cls; High Hon Roll; Drama & Music; Piano Lssns.

WELLMAN, JADON; Sir Francis Drake HS; Fairfax, CA; (2); Variety Show; JV Bsktbl; L Var Golf; L Co-Capt Swmmng; High Hon Roll; Hon Roll; CSF; Maxima Cum Laude Natl Latin Exam; Goldn St Exam Geom High Hnrs 88-89.

WELLMAN, NANCIE M; Arroyo Grande HS; Arroyo Grande, CA; (2); 13/600; Letterman Clb; Varsity Clb; Band; Drm Mjr(t); Mrchg Band; Var L Swmmng; High Hon Roll; Hon Roll; Pres Acad Fit Awd; CSF; Swimming CA Interschlstc Fed; UCSB; Arch.

WELLMAN, ROBERT; Palo Verde HS; Blythe, CA; (2); Drama Clb; Treas 4-H; School Musical; School Play; Intrml Swmmng; JV Wrstlng; 4-H Awd; High Hon Roll; Pres Acad Fit Awd; Gym; Columbia U; Pre-Med.

WELLS, AMY E; Hesperia HS; Hesperia, CA; (2); Science Clb; Spanish Clb; Phtg Yrbk; Stat Score Keeper; JV Sftbl; Hon Roll; Ed.

WELLS, ERIN C; Bishop Montgomery HS; Manhattan Beach, CA; (2); Var L Vllybl; South Bay Vlybl Club; Piano; Public Relations.

WELLS, JASON; Monterey Bay Acad; Redlands, CA; (4); 12/115; Church Yth Grp; Cmnty Wkr; Drama Clb; Ski Clb; Teachers Aide; Band; Orch; Pep Band; School Musical; Yrbk; Stu Bdy Pres; Yrbk Editor; Principal Trumpet In Elite Wind/Percussion Ensemble; Pacific Union Coll; Public Rltn.

WELLS, JOEY W; Clovis West HS; Clovis, CA; (2); Boy Scts; Church Yth Grp; SADD; Varsity Clb; JV Bsbl; Var Bsktbl; JV Ftbl; High Hon Roll; U Of AZ; Prfsnl Bsktbl Plyr.

WELLS, JUSTIN O; St Ignatius College Prep; San Anselmo, CA; (3); 1/240; Am Leg Boys St; Debate Tm; Service Clb; School Musical; School Play; Ed Nwsp; VP Frsh Cls; Socr; Hon Roll; Eng.

WELLS, KATHRYN; Vacaville HS; Vacaville, CA; (4); 1/560; Pres Church Yth Grp; Key Clb; Band; Church Choir; Sec Stu Cncl; JV Bsktbl; Capt Powder Puff Ftbl; High Hon Roll; Sec NHS; Val; Prin Ldrshp Awd; Tandy Tech Schlr; Bank Of Amer Top Stu Of Engl; Brigham Yng U; Pltcl Sci.

WELLS, KELLY; Maxwell HS; Maxwell, CA; (3); 2/27; Church Yth Grp; Cmnty Wkr; Debate Tm; FFA; Pep Clb; Spanish Clb; SADD; Varsity Clb; Band; Jazz Band; Theater.

WELLS, LESLIE A; Westlake HS; Thousand Oaks, CA; (2); 1/430; Church Yth Grp; Speech Tm; High Hon Roll; Explorers Secy; AYSO Asst Coach.

WELLS, LORI L; Valley Christian HS; Long Beach, CA; (4); Church Yth Grp; Pep Clb; Acpl Chr; Band; School Musical; Rptr Nwsp; Rptr Yrbk; JV Cheerldng; Var Socr; Madrigal Choir; LBCC; Elem Ed.

WELLS, MARY E; Clovis HS; Clovis, CA; (3); 32/675; Art Clb; Dance Clb; Letterman Clb; SADD; Varsity Clb; Yrbk; Cheerldng; Pom Pon; Tennis; Hon Roll; 4th Pl Natl Chrldng Cmptn; 2nd Pl Natl Pompon Chmpnshp Dallas TX; Coaches Awd; U Of AZ; Fshn Merch.

WELLS, MICHAEL; Highlands HS; North Highlands, CA; (3); Aud/Vis; Church Yth Grp; Ski Clb; Band; Chorus; Bsktbl; Cit Awd; Hon Roll; Opt Clb Awd; Pres Acad Fit Awd; Engrng.

WELLS, NICOLE; Madison HS; San Diego, CA; (3); JV Bsktbl; Var L Cheerldng; Chrldng Squad Came In 13th Pl Natl Cmptn; AZ ST U; Psych.

WELLS, QUINTA D; Tokay HS; Lodi, CA; (4); German Clb; Teachers Aide; Varsity Clb; Band; Jazz Band; Mrchg Band; Gym; High Hon Roll; Hon Roll; CA Sch Emplys Assn; Sacramento ST; Frng Lang Tchr.

WELLS, RANDEL E; Sutter Union HS; Yuba City, CA; (4); 1/75; Am Leg Boys St; Pres Science Clb; Pres Sr Cls; Val; JV Bsktbl; Pres Church Yth Grp; School Play; Pres Acad Fit Awd; Chorus; Church Choir; Acad Deca 89-90; Robert C Byrd Schrlshp Wnnr; CSF; U Munster; Bio.

WELLS, REBECCA; Buena HS; Ventura, CA; (4); 58/492; Am Leg Aux Girls St; Church Yth Grp; Cmnty Wkr; FCA; SADD; School Play; Pres Frsh Cls; Pres Soph Cls; Sec Stu Cncl; Var Bsktbl; HOBY Ambssdr; Las Patronas Debutante 90; Hall Of Fame; CA Poly Tech SLO; Soil Sci.

WELLS, REBEKAH M; Oroville HS; Oroville, CA; (4); 44/155; Church Yth Grp; SADD; Varsity Clb; Var Socr; Var Vllybl; Hon Roll; Vlntry Wrk Chrstn Camp; Butte Coll; Bus.

WELLS, STACEY L; Alta Loma HS; Rancho Cucamonga, CA; (1); Church Yth Grp; Stu Cncl; Hon Roll; Azusa Pacific U; Ministry.

WELSCH, ALISA K; Mission College Prep; San Luis Obispo, CA; (3); Church Yth Grp; Cmnty Wkr; Hosp Aide; Rptr Nwsp; Phtg Yrbk; Hon Roll; Piano; Wrtng; UCSB; Psych.

WELSCH, NICOLE C; Diamond Bar HS; Diamond Bar, CA; (1); Church Yth Grp; Hosp Aide; Chorus; Perf Arts Drama; UCLA; Med.

WELSCH, ROSALVA; Trinity HS; Lewiston, CA; (4); 1/93; Am Leg Aux Girls St; Pres Intnl Clb; Pres Spanish Clb; Pres SADD; Var Bsktbl; JV Capt Trk; High Hon Roll; Prfct Atten Awd; Rotary Awd; Val; CA St Smmr Schl Arts; CA Yth Cncl; Yale; Bio.

WELSHONS, PATTY E; Oxnard HS; Oxnard, CA; (3); Cmnty Wkr; Teachers Aide; Chorus; Sftbl; Cit Awd; High Hon Roll; Hon Roll; Prfct Atten Awd; Schl Achvt Awd Top Stu Cls; Awd Comp Wiz, Math Wiz & Spellng Wiz; Boston U; Law.

WELT, NISSA N; John Muir HS; Pasadena, CA; (2); Spcl Recgntn Prtcptn "expressing Feeling Thrgh Art" Exhbt Prjct; CA ST U LA; Reg Nrs.

WELTER, TIMOTHY; Cardinal Newman HS; Santa Rosa, CA; (1); 1/120; Boy Scts; Color Guard; Off Frsh Cls; Ftbl; Trk; Wt Lftg; Cit Awd; DAR Awd; High Hon Roll; Hon Roll; US Air Force Aux Civil Air Patrol; US A Frc Acad; Astrnmncl Engr.

WEMMER, ADAM RICHARD; Fountain Valley HS; Fountain Valley, CA; (3); JA; JV Var Bsbl; Bsktbl; Wt Lftg; High Hon Roll; Pres Acad Fit Awd; CSF; UC San Diego.

WEN, ANGELA; Skyline HS; Oakland, CA; (3); Church Yth Grp; Key Clb; Service Clb; Band; Sec Jr Cls; JV Capt Vllybl; High Hon Roll; CSF; Explorers Law Post; Asian Stu Union; UC Berkeley; Law.

WEN, KI MING; C K Mc Clatchy HS; Sacramento, CA; (2); Chess Clb; French Clb; Tennis; Hon Roll.

WEN, LOUISE S; Fremont HS; Sunnyvale, CA; (3); 10/408; Cmnty Wkr; Debate Tm; Pres Intnl Clb; NFL; Pres Treas Service Clb; Speech Tm; Teachers Aide; Rptr Yrbk; Lit Mag; NHS; High Hnrs CA Golden St Exam Geom; Chem Awd; Success Essay Cont; Brown.

WENDELL, AMY E; Pinole Valley HS; San Pablo, CA; (2); Office Aide; Acpl Chr; Cheerldng; Hon Roll.

WENDELL, DESIREE A; La Mirada HS; La Mirada, CA; (4); Church Yth Grp; Powder Puff Ftbl; Tennis; Hon Roll; Erly Grad 90; Pepperdine U; Bus Mgmt.

WENDLING, LEIGH A; College Park HS; Pleasant Hill, CA; (4); French Clb; SADD; Teachers Aide; Yrbk; Socr; Sftbl; Swmmng; Tennis; French Hon Soc; High Hon Roll; Diablo Valley Clg.

WENDROFF, JOSH L; Las Lomas HS; Walnut Creek, CA; (3); Co-Ed Nwsp; NHS; Art; Skiing; UCLA; Adv.

WENDT, SARA; San Marin HS; Novato, CA; (3); SADD; Rep Soph Cls; Rep Jr Cls; Sec Stu Cncl; JV Bsktbl; JV Cheerldng; JV Var Sftbl; Hon Roll; YMCA Yth Govt Pgm 2 Yrs Cmmtte Chrprsn; CSF; Stu/Schl Brd Cmmnctn Cmmtte.

WENG, PEGGY; Los Altos HS; Hacienda Hgts, CA; (4); Key Clb; Library Aide; Office Aide; Service Clb; Teachers Aide; Stat Vllybl; Hon Roll; Pres Acad Fit Awd; Frgn Lang Dept Awd; UC Riverside; Law.

WENG, RENEE R; John F Kennedy HS; La Palma, CA; (2); Art Clb; Key Clb; Spanish Clb; Chorus; Bsktbl; Socr; Tennis; Hon Roll; Prfct Atten Awd; UCLA; Med.

WENG, WENDY T; San Gabriel HS; San Gabriel, CA; (4); Computer Clb; Red Cross Aide; Spanish Clb; Teachers Aide; School Play; Cit Awd; High Hon Roll; Hon Roll; UCLA; Bus Econ.

WENGER, CHRISTINA M; Clovis West HS; Clovis, CA; (2); Church Yth Grp; Debate Tm; Drama Clb; French Clb; Intnl Clb; NFL; Speech Tm; School Play; Variety Show; High Hon Roll; Training & Breeding Horses; Cambridge; Anthrplgy.

WENGER, KYLE W; Ramona HS; Ramona, CA; (3); Boy Scts; Church Yth Grp; Pres Key Clb; L Var Ftbl; L Var Tennis; L Var Wrstlng; Order Of The Arrow-Scouts 90; San Diego ST U; Bus Admin.

WENNER, TANYA C; Seaside HS; Marina, CA; (4); Office Aide; Yrbk; JV Capt Bsktbl; Powder Puff Ftbl; Score Keeper; Hon Roll; Prfct Atten Awd; Psych.

WENNING, JOSHUA O; Hilltop HS; Chula Vista, CA; (4); 35/460; Church Yth Grp; FCA; French Clb; Intnl Clb; Letterman Clb; NFL; Ski Clb; Speech Tm; Teachers Aide; Chorus; Jorge Herrera Akers Mem Awd Insprtn Hilltop Trnmnt; San Diego Tribune Acad Awds Ftbl,Bstkb & Trck; Grossmont Coll; Physcl Ed.

WENRICH, JENNIFER E; Elsinore HS; Sinking Spring, PA; (3); 23/550; Dance Clb; ROTC; Drill Tm; Rep Stu Cncl; High Hon Roll; Cass Memorial Awd; AFSROTC-LETTER Drill Team/Natl Sojourners Awd; Sons Of Am Revolutn Awd; Math Ed.

WENRICK, JASON; Bishop Amat HS; Duarte, CA; (3); Church Yth Grp; Letterman Clb; Varsity Clb; JV Var Ftbl; High Hon Roll; Hon Roll; Gftd & Tlntd Prog; U Of La Verne; Engrng.

WENSLEY, KEVIN M; St Bernard HS; Playa Del Rey, CA; (3); Am Leg Boys St; Var L Bsbl; Var L Ftbl; Bausch & Lomb Sci Awd; Cit Awd; High Hon Roll; CSF; Religious & Sci Studs Awd; Schlr Athlete Awd; St Marys Coll; Engr.

WENSTRAND, SARAH C; Turlock HS; Turlock, CA; (4); 30/600; AFS; Art Clb; Treas VP FBLA; German Clb; Teachers Aide; Phtg Nwsp; Stat Bsktbl; Stat Trk; Var L Vllybl; Turlock Jrnl Athlete Week; CSU Stanislaus; Art.

WENTWORTH, HEATHER K; Lincoln HS; Stockton, CA; (2); 40/568; Rotary Awd; French Clb; Key Clb; NFL; Speech Tm; Lion Awd; Masonic Awd; Cmmnty Theatre; Jobs Daughters; Intl Exchng Stu Norway & Japan; Intl Rltns.

WENTWORTH, MELISSA R; Pinole Valley HS; San Pablo, CA; (1); AFS; Hon Roll; CSF; Math/Ed.

WENZEL, GINA L; Hesperia HS; Hesperia, CA; (2); 1/767; ROTC; High Hon Roll; AFJROTC Drill Tm Letter; CSF; Univ Club; Teach.

WERDER, CARRIE J; Canyon HS; Canyon Country, CA; (2); Church Yth Grp; Spanish Clb; SADD; Phtg Yrbk; Var Swmmng; UCLA; Pedtrcn.

WERGELAND, PETER L; Bonita Vista HS; Bonita, CA; (3); 83/559; Key Clb; Teachers Aide; JV Var Tennis; Cit Awd; Hon Roll; Phlsphy Clb; U CA Coll; Crmnl Law.

WERKHOVEN, EDWARD R; Victor Valley HS; Helendale, CA; (4); 6/398; Debate Tm; English Clb; High Hon Roll; Kiwanis Awd; NHS; Val; Peer Cnslng; CSF; Sheriff Stu Advisory Cncl; UC Santa Barbara; Corp Law.

WERKMEISTER, JENNIFER R; El Camino HS; Oceanside, CA; (1); 116/430; Cit Awd; Hon Roll; Engnrng.

WERLICH, MICHELLE K; La Reina HS; Westlake Village, CA; (3); 1/60; Debate Tm; Rep Drama Clb; NFL; Pres Speech Tm; Rptr Nwsp; Stu Cncl; French Hon Soc; Jr NHS; NHS; Ntl Merit Ltr; Acad Decthln; Mock Trial Cmptn; Natl Yth Ldrshp Conf DC; Claremont Mc Kenna Coll; Lawyr.

WERLIN, JAMES P; College Park HS; Pleasant Hill, CA; (3); Concord Polc Explorer Capt; Polc Offcr.

WERNECKE, BRENDA; Bethel Christian Acad; Quartz Hill, CA; (1); Art Clb; Cit Awd; High Hon Roll; Prfct Atten Awd.

WERNER, AARON S; Live Oak HS; Live Oak, CA; (2); 9/100; Church Yth Grp; Varsity Clb; JV Bsbl; JV Ftbl; High Hon Roll; Hon Roll; Prfct Atten Awd; CSF; Stanford U; Comp Sci.

WERO, JEFFREY; James Lick HS; San Jose, CA; (2); Boy Scts; Golf; Hon Roll; MESA Clb; Santa Clara; Elect Tech.

WERTZ, JOSHUA R; Montgomery HS; Santa Rosa, CA; (2); Science Clb; Spanish Clb; High Hon Roll; Jr NHS; Pres Acad Fit Awd; Goldn St Exam Algbra & Geom Hnrs; Math.

WERTZ JR, SCOTT L; Imperial Schls; Pasadena, CA; (2); Church Yth Grp; Computer Clb; Chorus; Church Choir; VP Soph Cls; Bsktbl; Vllybl; Hon Roll; Boys Speech Club; Bus.

WERVE, ALEXANDRA A; Santa Margarita HS; Laguna Niguel, CA; (3); Church Yth Grp; Pep Clb; Treas Frsh Cls; Treas Soph Cls; Treas Jr Cls; Treas Sr Cls; Rep Stu Cncl; Var Capt Socr; Var Capt Vllybl; Cit Awd; Hmcmng Prncss 89; Vllybl Club; CSF 89-90; Sports Doc.

WERVE, SHAWN; Oxnard HS; Oxnard, CA; (2); #6 In Class; Letterman Clb; Var Crs Cntry; JV Socr; Var Trk; High Hon Roll; Hon Roll; Prfct Atten Awd; Crmnl Law.

WERZYN, CHRISTINE E; Don Antonio Lugo HS; Chino, CA; (2); Church Yth Grp; French Clb; SADD; Band; Mrchg Band; Pep Band; Stat Diving; Stat Swmmng; Hon Roll; Mount St Marys Coll; Aviation.

WESCH, BECKY L; Gompers Secondary Schl; San Diego, CA; (2); Var Vllybl; Hon Roll; CSF.

WESIR, DINA M; Delano HS; Delano, CA; (2); Church Yth Grp; Drama Clb; Hosp Aide; Teachers Aide; Church Choir; Psych.

WESLEY, ERIC C; San Fernando HS; Northridge, CA; (3); Art Clb; VP Key Clb; Science Clb; Teachers Aide; Band; Nwsp; Golf; DARE Poster Cntst 1st Pl; Natl Cncl Alchl & Drug Dpndncy Poster Cntst 2nd Pl; Earch Wk Poster Cntst; U Of CA Los Angeles; Art.

WESLEY, SARAH T; Point Arena HS; Gualala, CA; (2); Girl Scts; School Play; Yrbk; Stat Bsktbl; JV Stat Vllybl; High Hon Roll; Sivler Awd; U Of CA; Law.

WESSELING, GERRIT R; Oakmont HS; Roseville, CA; (1); Ski Clb; Ftbl; JV Trk; High Hon Roll; Press Tribune Paper Rt; Engel Constrction; Diploma De Merito-Spnsh Awd; UCLA; Lwyr.

WESSELMAN, TODD T; St Paul HS; Pico Rivera, CA; (3); Capt Varsity Clb; Intrml Bsktbl; JV Swmmng; Var Capt Vllybl; NHS; Pres Acad Fit Awd; CA St-Fullerton.

WESSELS, AARON M; Roseville HS; Roseville, CA; (2); 56/445; Church Yth Grp; Spanish Clb; JV Swmmng; Hon Roll; Acad Merit HS Awd; U Of Santa Barbara; Arch.

WESSELS, AMBER; Luther Burbank HS; Sacramento, CA; (3); 7/276; AFS; Church Yth Grp; ROTC; Color Guard; Rptr Yrbk; Treas Soph Cls; Rep Stu Cncl; High Hon Roll; Ntl Merit Ltr; Frgn Exchng Stu AFS Netherlands; TAG; Intl Bus Mgmnt.

WESSELY, JENNY; La Reina HS; Moorpark, CA; (2); 35/90; Drama Clb; GAA; Hosp Aide; Stage Crew; Yrbk; Cheerldng; Gym; Cit Awd; Hon Roll; Piano & Dance; News Chronicle Awd; USC; Pre Law.

WESSMAN, CHELSEA; Alhambra HS; Martinez, CA; (2); Art Clb; Dance Clb; SADD; Nwsp; Cit Awd; Hon Roll; Peer Cnslr; UC Santa Cruz; Marine Bio.

WEST, CATHERINE C; Whittier Christian HS; Anaheim, CA; (2); Church Yth Grp; Dance Clb; Speech Tm; Chorus; Drill Tm; Var JV Cheerldng; Gym; High Hon Roll; Hon Roll; Chrldng Short Flags; Point Loma Coll; Math.

WEST, CHALITA L; Mc Clymonds HS; Oakland, CA; (2); Art Clb; Church Yth Grp; Dance Clb; Chorus; Bsktbl; High Hon Roll; Hon Roll; Dare To Imagine Club; Stanford U; Nrs.

WEST, COURTNEY D; Valhalla HS; El Cajon, CA; (2); 11/455; Pep Clb; Ski Clb; SADD; Thesps; Variety Show; Rep Soph Cls; JV Capt Cheerldng; Exec Brd Human Relations; Mrktng.

WEST, ELAINE M; Rio Lindo Adventist Acad; Rio Linda, CA; (3); Drama Clb; Acpl Chr; Rptr Nwsp; Var Vllybl; Stu Church Ofcr; Tchr.

WEST, ELIZABETH M; Arroyo Grande HS; Shell Bch, CA; (4); 31/420; French Clb; Yrbk; Hon Roll; UCSB.

WEST, JASON D; Junipero Serra HS; San Diego, CA; (2); FTA; SADD; Var Swmmng; Hon Roll; CA Newspaper Carrier Fndtn Inc Schlrshp; Bus Dept Awd Of Excllnc; U CA San Diego; Bus.

WEST, JOHN JASON; College Park HS; Martinez, CA; (3); 4/340; Am Leg Boys St; Cmnty Wkr; Letterman Clb; Spanish Clb; Jazz Band; Mrchg Band; Off Frsh Cls; Sec Soph Cls; Off Jr Cls; Stu Cncl; Outstndng Fresh Boy; Advncd Plcmnt HS SR Attd UC Berkeley 1/2 Day; Broke Schl Trk Record 800m; Ivy Leage Coll; Bio Chem.

WEST, KRYSTAL; Brethren HS; La Palma, CA; (4); 6/67; Church Yth Grp; French Clb; GAA; Acpl Chr; Nwsp; Sec Jr Cls; Capt Cheerldng; Trk; Hon Roll; Pres Acad Fit Awd.

WEST, LA SHONDA; Washington HS; Los Angeles, CA; (3); Church Yth Grp; Church Choir; Hon Roll; Comp.

WEST, MATTHEW; Chaffey HS; Ontario, CA; (3); 17/500; Church Yth Grp; Cmnty Wkr; German Clb; Band; Drill Tm; Drm Mjr(t); Flag Corp; Jazz Band; Mrchg Band; Orch; Culinary Arts.

WEST, NOEL; Oak Ridge HS; Cameron Park, CA; (2); 14/289; Letterman Clb; Spanish Clb; SADD; Teachers Aide; Rep Stu Cncl; Capt Bsktbl; Capt Sftbl; Capt Vllybl; Cit Awd; High Hon Roll; Law.

WEST, ROBERT E; San Gorgonio HS; Highland, CA; (3); English Clb; Comp Pgmng.

WEST, STACEY L; Ramona HS; Ramona, CA; (3); FHA; Teachers Aide; Cit Awd; Chld Dev.

WEST, STEVEN T; Huntington Beach HS; Huntington Beach, CA; (3); L Swmmng; All-Amer Swmmng; CA Intrschltc Fed Champ Swmmng 100 Yd Brst Stroke.

WEST, TAMARI L; Sacrament Adventist Acad; Auburn, CA; (3); Church Yth Grp; Pres Drama Clb; Spanish Clb; Speech Tm; Teachers Aide; Acpl Chr; School Play; Teach.

WEST, TANYA L; Sacramento Adventist Acad; Auburn, CA; (2); 3/47; Church Yth Grp; Intrml Trk; Hon Roll.

WEST, TED; N Monterey County HS; San Jose, CA; (4); 8/250; Chess Clb; FBLA; SADD; High Hon Roll; NHS; Ntl Merit Ltr; Prfct Atten Awd; CSF; Close-Up; Environmental Club; UC Berkeley; Bus Admin.

WEST, TRAVIS R; Ferndale Union HS; Ferndale, CA; (3); 1/40; Am Leg Boys St; Math Tm; Scholastic Bowl; Rptr Nwsp; Yrbk; VP Jr Cls; Bsbl; Bsktbl; Ftbl; Hon Roll; CA Schltc Fed; Golden St Exam Acad Excl Awd Geometry High Hnrs; USA Reserve Distinguished Schlr Awd; Chem Engrng.

WEST, VINCENT J; James Lick HS; San Jose, CA; (2); Boy Scts; Intnl Clb; Library Aide; Diving; Hon Roll; Treas Bibliophile Soc; Earth Day Clb; Outstndng Reader Of Yr Awd; Herpetlgst.

WESTALL, AMY M; Etiwanda HS; Alta Loma, CA; (2); Band; Color Guard; Mrchg Band; CA U; Librn.

WESTBROOK, RUTH E; Tulare Western HS; Tulare, CA; (3); 14/250; Church Yth Grp; Sec JA; Letterman Clb; Var Crs Cntry; Var Socr; JV Tennis; Hon Roll; Vet Med, Sci; U Of CA Davis; Vet.

WESTBROOK, TAMMY J; Oxnard HS; Oxnard, CA; (3); Church Yth Grp; Drama Clb; French Clb; Pep Clb; SADD; Var Socr; JV Trk; JV Vllybl; Cit Awd; High Hon Roll; Peer Hlpr; CSF; Mardi Gras Empress 90; LAW.

WESTBROOK, TOM W; Red Bluff HS; Red Bluff, CA; (1); Boy Scts; Church Yth Grp; Church Choir; Bsktbl; Ftbl; Wt Lftg; Hon Roll; Shasta Coll.

WESTBY, ADRIANA A; Dorsey HS; Los Angeles, CA; (3); Church Yth Grp; Spanish Clb; School Play; Variety Show; Rptr Nwsp; Sftbl; Vllybl; Hon Roll; West Adams Foresquare Church Yth Usher; Jr Scndry Belize CA Christian Cncl VP; UC San Diego; Med.

WESTCOTT, JENNIFER; Lincoln HS; Stockton, CA; (3); 78/592; French Clb; Swmmng; Hon Roll; Rec Clb.

WESTERGAARD, CHAD C; Turlock HS; Turlock, CA; (2); Church Yth Grp; Band; Chorus; Mrchg Band; Pep Band; Stanislaus ST U; Bus.

WESTERHOLD, TAMMY S; Fremont HS; Sunnyvale, CA; (3); Band; Mrchg Band; Pep Band; Capt Var Bsktbl; Score Keeper; Capt Var Swmmng; Var Trk; Majorette; Phys Thrpy.

WESTERHOUT, RENEE; El Capitan HS; Lakeside, CA; (2); Pep Clb; JV Tennis; Var Trk; Girls Ten Most Improved Plyr Awd 89-90; Pamona ST U; Hotel Mgmt.

WESTERLING, LAURA N; Kingsburg HS; Kingsburg, CA; (1); Church Yth Grp; Band; Mrchg Band; Pep Band; JV Score Keeper; JV Swmmng; High Hon Roll; Hon Roll; Mem Envrnmntl Club; Played Piano 9 Yrs; Avid Reader.

WESTERLING, RICHARD L; Kingsburg HS; Kingsburg, CA; (3); Hon Roll; Police Explorer; Fresno City Clg; Law Enfrcmnt.

WESTERMEYER, KYNAN; Encinal HS; Alameda, CA; (4); 11/222; ROTC; Creighton U; Engr.

WESTHAFER, LISA M; Gahr HS; Cerritos, CA; (3); 55/460; Church Yth Grp; Cmnty Wkr; Rptr Yrbk; Hist Jr Cls; Stu Cncl; Var Mgr(s); Powder Puff Ftbl; Hon Roll; Blue & Gold Awd; Spec Olynpcs Vlntr; K-Pin Knts Brry Frm; Bus.

WESTIN, TOM S; Irvine HS; Irvine, CA; (1); German Clb; Math Tm; Ftbl; Hon Roll; Amature Skateboarder; Engl.

WESTLUND, ANDREW R; Pacifica HS; Garden Grove, CA; (3); JV Bsbl; Var Ftbl; Wt Lftg; Mariners Who Care-Anti Drunk Driving Clb; CA ST-FULLERTON; Bsbl Coach.

WESTMORELAND, JULIE; East Union HS; Manteca, CA; (2); 4/400; Pres Church Yth Grp; Key Clb; Teachers Aide; JV Capt Cheerldng; Stat Score Keeper; Swmmng; High Hon Roll; Lncr Of Mnth-Chsn By Soc Sci Dept-Cnslng Dept; GATE Pgm; CSF-CA Schlstc Schlrshp Fdrtn; Brigham Young U; Elem Educ.

WESTON, JUDITH; Desert HS; Edwards, CA; (1); Cheerldng; Pom Pon; UF; Drama.

WESTON, LAUREL M; Grace Davis HS; Modesto, CA; (3); Church Yth Grp; Drama Clb; Key Clb; Pep Clb; Ski Clb; Speech Tm; School Play; Cheerldng; Swmmng; Hon Roll; Yearly Drama Awards Best Actress; Speech Tournaments 3rd Place; Psychology.

WESTON, PATRICK T; Serra HS; Redwood City, CA; (2); 1/220; Boy Scts; Church Yth Grp; Computer Clb; Ski Clb; School Play; High Hon Roll; Dept Hnr Awds-Math, Sci, Engl, Social Stud & Frgn Lang.

WESTON, WILLIAM B; Lassen Union HS; Milford, CA; (2); 1/251; FFA; Ftbl; High Hon Roll; 2nd Pl Lassen Cnty Weldng Cont, St Fr Cmptn Fnls; CPA.

WESTOVER, BRANDON; Claremont HS; Claremont, CA; (3); Boy Scts; Computer Clb; Debate Tm; Math Clb; Science Clb; Thesps; Varsity Clb; Lit Mag; Pres Frsh Cls; Ftbl; Fncng Club Pres & Fndr; BYU; Nrlgy.

WESTPHAL, ZACKORY M; Mission Bay HS; San Diego, CA; (2); 87/400; Boy Scts; Bus Profs of Am; Church Yth Grp; DECA; Variety Show; Hon Roll; Attend LOS Smnry; Brigham Young U; Bus.

WESTRA, CAROL; Modesto Christian HS; Modesto, CA; (4); 5/45; Church Yth Grp; Drama Clb; Service Clb; Sec Jr Cls; Sec Stu Cncl; Var Bsktbl; Var Stat Trk; Var Capt Vllybl; High Hon Roll; Modesto JC.

WESTREICHER, STACIE L; Serrano HS; Phelan, CA; (1); 4-H; Hon Roll; Law.

WETNER, CLINT L; San Bernardino HS; San Bernardino, CA; (3); German Clb; NHS; Natl German Hnr Soc; Palentology.

WETTELAND, TERRI M; San Ramon Valley HS; Danville, CA; (4); 80/402; Stat Bsktbl; Intrml Socr; JV Var Swmmng; Hon Roll; Torchiana Awd; Waterpolo Stats; U AZ; Poltcl Sci.

WETTER, VICKIE L; Mesa Verde HS; Citrus Heights, CA; (2); 74/257; Church Yth Grp; Teachers Aide; Phtg Yrbk; Gym; Hon Roll; Med.

WETZEL, ANDREW PAUL; Alemany HS; Chatsworth, CA; (2); Church Yth Grp; Cmnty Wkr; French Clb; Band; Rptr Nwsp; Var Swmmng; Hon Roll; NHS; Pres Acad Fit Awd; Bicyclng Clb.

WETZEL, CHRISTINE S; Sherman E Burroughs HS; Inyokern, CA; (3); 53/400; Chorus; School Play; Rptr Nwsp; Hon Roll; Prfct Atten Awd; Tech Mentor; Engl.

WEVERS, CHRIS A; North Hollywood HS; North Hollywood, CA; (2); French Clb; Office Aide; Science Clb; Teachers Aide; High Hon Roll; Hon Roll; Jr NHS; Prfct Atten Awd; Ecology Clb; Med.

WEXLER, JENNIFER L; Clovis West HS; Fresno, CA; (4); 60/600; Rep Frsh Cls; JV Var Tennis; Hon Roll; Pres Acad Fit Awd; U Of CA Irvine; Jrnlsm.

WEY, JANE; Huntington Beach HS; Huntington Beach, CA; (4); 1/457; Girl Scts; Sec Key Clb; Math Tm; VP Speech Tm; Ed Nwsp; Ed Lit Mag; Ntl Merit SF; Badmintn Awd; CSF; Red Cross Club; Bio Sci.

WEY, MELISSA A; Fountain Valley HS; Fountain Valley, CA; (2); Church Yth Grp; Red Cross Aide; Band; Church Choir; Mrchg Band; Pep Band; School Musical; School Play; Off Soph Cls; High Hon Roll; UC Santa Barbara; Music.

WEYER, KIMBERLY; St Bernard HS; Los Angeles, CA; (3); Am Leg Aux Girls St; Church Yth Grp; French Clb; Girl Scts; Hosp Aide; Stu Cncl; JV Bsktbl; Mgr(s); Intrml Vllybl; Hon Roll; Jr Blck Blt Karate; Pre-Med.

WEYH, LISAMARIE; Los Angeles County HS For The Arts; Redondo Beach, CA; (3); Church Yth Grp; Cmnty Wkr; Dance Clb; Key Clb; Pep Clb; Spanish Clb; Teachers Aide; School Musical; Cheerldng; Cit Awd; Hmcmng Ct Rnnr-Up; Winter Ct Prncss; Stu Dir Dance Prods; UCLA; Dance.

WHALEN, LORI A; Alverno HS; San Gabriel, CA; (2); 20/70; Chorus; Nwsp; Swmmng; Chorus Awd; Review Wrtng Cmmndtn; Bst Artwork Plaque; Music Ed.

WHALEY, BONNIE; William S Hart HS; Valencia, CA; (4); Cmnty Wkr; SADD; Off Jr Cls; Off Sr Cls; JV Cheerldng; Hon Roll; Pres Acad Fit Awd; People To People Stu Ambassador; Vrsty Songleader; Baha I Awd; George Washington U; Intl Affrs.

WHALEY, CHRIS L; Crescenta Valley HS; Glendale, CA; (3); Key Clb; Math Clb; Mu Alpha Theta; Spanish Clb; Ed Yrbk; Var Swmmng; NHS; Vrsty Water Polo; CSF; Bus Exec Club; Cmmnctns.

WHALEY, ERIC; Palo Alto HS; Palo Alto, CA; (2); Cmnty Wkr; Service Clb; Spanish Clb; Teachers Aide; Rptr Nwsp; Rep Frsh Cls; VP Soph Cls; Rep Stu Cncl; Var Tennis; Tnns; CA Schlstc Fdrtn-Sec; Acadc Excllnce Awd-Math Gldn St Exam.

WHALEY, JANICE A; Yucca Valley HS; Joshua Tree, CA; (1); Band; Jazz Band; Mrchg Band; Pep Band; Hon Roll; Sunday Schl Tchr; Most Promising Yng Musician 90; Awd Wnng Jazz Combo; Music.

WHALEY, PABLO S; Lowell HS; San Francisco, CA; (2); Band; Sccr & Skiing.

WHALING, CHRIS; Canyon HS; Santa Clanita, CA; (4); 23/548; Rep Am Leg Boys St; VP Debate Tm; Pres Drama Clb; VP FBLA; Pep Clb; Scholastic Bowl; Spanish Clb; Stu Cncl; Var Socr; JV Tennis; CSF; LA Acad Decathln Gold, Silver & Bronze Mdls Wnnr; UC Berkeley; Medcl.

WHANG, ARTHUR Y; Sunny Hills HS; Walnut, CA; (3); Chess Clb; Church Yth Grp; Debate Tm; French Clb; JA; NFL; Quiz Bowl; Speech Tm; High Hon Roll; Hon Roll; UC Riverside; Law.

WHANG, KATHERINE H; Sunny Hills HS; Fullerton, CA; (3); Key Clb; Pres Band; Jazz Band; Mrchg Band; Orch; Pep Band; High Hon Roll; Hon Roll; CSF; Jeff Briggs Memrl Awd; Outstndng Band Stu 88-90; Spirit America Mrchng Band Tour Europe 89; Intl Rltns.

WHARTON, BRANDON; Carson HS; Carson, CA; (2); Bsktbl; Ftbl; Trk; Cit Awd; Prfct Atten Awd; Martial Arts; U CA Santa Barbara; Elec Engr.

WHATLEY, CARRIE; Foothill HS; Bakersfield, CA; (2); Drama Clb; Hosp Aide; JA; Pep Clb; Ski Clb; School Musical; School Play; Var Capt Cheerldng; Hon Roll; CSUB; Englsh.

WHEATER, ROBYN R; Whittier Christian HS; Norwalk, CA; (2); Church Yth Grp; Chorus; Church Choir; Color Guard; Outstndng Choir Stu; CSF.

WHEATLEY, JENNIFER M; Lodi HS; Lodi, CA; (3); Key Clb; Varsity Clb; Mgr Drill Tm; Rep Soph Cls; Pres Jr Cls; Pres Sr Cls; Var Capt Socr; Swmmng; Var Capt Trk; JV Capt Vllybl; Schl Recrd Triple Jump; Jr Womans Clb Sec; Cal Poly; Bus.

WHEELER, AIMEE M; Burbank HS; Burbank, CA; (3); Debate Tm; Speech Tm; Teachers Aide; Drill Tm; Sec Frsh Cls; Off Sr Cls; Var Mgr(s); Var Trk; High Hon Roll; Jr NHS; UCLA; Bus.

WHEELER, BRIAN L; Saint John Bosco HS; Cerritos, CA; (2); High Hon Roll; Outdrsmn Clb; Engrg.

WHEELER, BRIAN W; Placer HS; Auburn, CA; (2); Science Clb; Var Tennis; Hon Roll; Hnrs Golden St Exm Alg; Sci.

WHEELER, CAROL E; Etiwanda HS; Rancho Cucamonga, CA; (3); Dance Clb; French Clb; Chorus; Gym; Tennis; Hon Roll; NHS; Frnch Exchange Stu To Paris; Mrktng.

WHEELER, CHRISTEL A; Vanden HS; Travis A F B, CA; (3); #8 In Class; Church Yth Grp; French Clb; SADD; Band; Drm Mjr(t); Jazz Band; Mrchg Band; Pep Band; Lit Mag; High Hon Roll; Outstndng Engl Stu 89; John Philip Sousa Awd, Outstndng US Hstry Stu 90.

WHEELER, CHRYSTAL; Cajon HS; San Bernardino, CA; (2); Key Clb; SADD; Hon Roll; NHS; CSF; OB.

WHEELER, CRYSTAL S; Quincy HS; Twain, CA; (3); FFA; Library Aide; Office Aide; Chorus; Phtg Yrbk; Hon Roll.

WHEELER, DENISE A; Mt Whitney HS; Visalia, CA; (1); 30/350; Hosp Aide; Band; Mrchg Band; Pep Band; VP Swmmng; Church Bell Choir & Choir; Spch Pthlgy.

WHEELER, GARRETT V; Taft HS; Woodland Hills, CA; (3); Boy Scts; Chess Clb; Eagle Sct; CSUN.

WHEELER, JEFF M; Enterprise HS; Redding, CA; (2); 145/480; Church Yth Grp; Swmmng; Wrstlng; UCLA; Engrng.

WHEELER, JENNIE; Sonora HS; Sonora, CA; (4); 9/276; AFS; French Clb; Ski Clb; Band; Color Guard; Jazz Band; Mrchg Band; Pep Band; School Musical; Elks Awd; Gldn State Exam Geomtry Hnrs; Santa Clara U; Engrng.

WHEELER, JOSHUA P; Qunicy JR/Sr HS; Quincy, CA; (1); FFA; Sacramento ST; Drafting.

WHEELER, JULIE A; College Park HS; Pleasant Hill, CA; (3); Church Yth Grp; Teachers Aide; Sftbl; Hon Roll; Office Aide Ltr Of Rec; Diablo Vly Coll.

WHEELER, LOUIE J; Paso Robles HS; Paso Robles, CA; (3); Bsbl; Ftbl; Fresno ST; Welding.

WHEELER, MEREDITH LEIGH; Buena HS; Ventura, CA; (2); Band; Chorus; Drm Mjr(t); Mrchg Band; Pep Band; Band Cncl; Surgical Nrs.

WHEELER, TIMOTHY E; Oakdale HS; Oakdale, CA; (3); Church Yth Grp; Science Clb; Teachers Aide; Church Choir; Variety Show; Var L Ftbl; Var Wt Lftg; Model & Genrl Aviation; Arospc Engrng.

WHEELOCK, DARREN; Silver Valley HS; Barstow, CA; (4); 11/70; Church Yth Grp; Key Clb; Letterman Clb; Pep Clb; Capt Scholastic Bowl; Sec Jr Cls; Capt Bsbl; Wt Lftg; Wrstlng; Cit Awd; Assoc Stu Bdy Stu Rep Brd Trusts; Mck Trl Cptn; Outstndng Achvt Awd; USC; Corp Law.

WHELTON, KAMA M; Presentation HS; Sunnyvale, CA; (4); 18/126; Art Clb; Church Yth Grp; Cmnty Wkr; VP Pres 4-H; Chorus; School Play; Variety Show; Ed Lit Mag; High Hon Roll; NHS; Peer Mnstry Awd; Relgn Dept Awd; Jesuit Cmmnty Schlrshp Loyola Marymount; Loyola Marymount U; Cmmnctns.

WHETNIGHT, SHELLEY K; La Sierra HS; Riverside, CA; (4); Hon Roll; CA ST Fullerton; Bus Ad Acctg.

WHIAT, ANDREW K; San Clemente HS; San Juan Capis, CA; (3); 25/500; Am Leg Boys St; Debate Tm; English Clb; German Clb; Science Clb; Service Clb; Speech Tm; Off Jr Cls; Bsktbl; Vllybl; Junior Statesmen Of America; Attorney At Mock Trial; Summer Scientific Seminar At USAFA; USAF Acad; Aeronautical Enginr.

WHIDDON, CHRISTY R; Mission Viejo HS; Mission Viejo, CA; (2); Church Yth Grp; Drama Clb; Model UN; Spanish Clb; Thesps; Chorus; Church Choir; School Musical; High Hon Roll; Acad Decathalon; Pol Sci.

WHIPKEY, ELIZABETH; Ukiah HS; Willits, CA; (4); 32/306; Church Yth Grp; Drama Clb; Teachers Aide; Band; Mrchg Band; School Play; Stage Crew; Nwsp; Var Trk; Hon Roll; Physt Thrpy.

WHIPPLE, KIRSTIN LUNDEN; Lassen HS; Susanville, CA; (3); Cmnty Wkr; Drama Clb; Ski Clb; Teachers Aide; School Play; Cit Awd; Hon Roll; NHS; Ed Nwsp; Aerobics.

WHIPPLE, MICHELLE D; San Rafael HS; San Rafael, CA; (1); Church Yth Grp; High Hon Roll; Music Piano And Voice.

WHISENANT, SUNDANCE; Mt Empire JR-SR HS; Jacumba, CA; (3); 2/125; Am Leg Aux Girls St; Pep Clb; VP Spanish Clb; Ed Yrbk; Capt Cheerldng; Vllybl; High Hon Roll; VP NHS; Pres Acad Fit Awd; Rep Frsh Cls; High Hnr Roll; Bus.

WHISENANT, TRAVIS W; Damien HS; Upland, CA; (4); 55/210; Church Yth Grp; Cmnty Wkr; English Clb; FCA; Letterman Clb; Office Aide; Ski Clb; SADD; Teachers Aide; Varsity Clb; All Baseline Leag Lnbckr 88-90; Tm Capt Vrsty Ftbl 86 & 89, Dfnsv MVP 86 & 87; Natl Ftbl Lnbckr Awd; U Of CA Santa Barbara; Law.

WHISNER, REBECCA; St Joseph HS; Long Beach, CA; (2); Church Yth Grp; GAA; Church Choir; Off Soph Cls; JV Bsktbl; High Hon Roll; Hon Roll; Jr NHS; Intl Childrens Choir Stu; Vlntr Camp Cnslr; UCSD; Tch Elem Schl.

WHITACRE, LESTER C; Victor Valley HS; Victorville, CA; (4); 5/330; Computer Clb; English Clb; Teachers Aide; JV Var Socr; High Hon Roll; Kiwanis Awd; Fncng Sgt At Arms; CA ST Poly Pomona.

WHITACRE, MARY L; Victor Valley HS; Victorville, CA; (3); 12/400; English Clb; Drill Tm; Off Sr Cls; High Hon Roll; Fencing-Took 3rd Place In San Bernardino Dvsn 89-90; Qulfd To Enter Natl Chmpshps; CA Schlshp Fed 3yr.

WHITAKER, ANNE M; Rio Americano HS; Carmichael, CA; (3); 1/290; VP Spanish Clb; Teachers Aide; Ed Nwsp; Capt Var Bsktbl; Var L Sftbl; High Hon Roll; CSF.

WHITAKER, JENNIFER; Fall River JR SR HS; Fall River Mills, CA; (3); 4-H; Treas FBLA; Teachers Aide; Chorus; Hon Roll; Bus Admin.

WHITAKER, KARLA KAY; Rio Mesa HS; Camarillo, CA; (3); Cmnty Wkr; Drama Clb; Service Clb; Pres Speech Tm; School Play; Stage Crew; Cit Awd; High Hon Roll; Opt Clb Awd; Prfct Atten Awd; Drama & Acad Vrsty Ltrs; Renaissance Pgm; U CA.

WHITAKER, KAYCEE S; Sacramento Country Day Schl; Sacramento, CA; (3); Art Clb; Cmnty Wkr; Dance Clb; Hosp Aide; Quiz Bowl; Ski Clb; Chorus; School Musical; Ed Nwsp; Sec Frsh Cls; USC; Brdcst Jrnlsm.

WHITAKER, STACEY J; Washington Preparatory HS; Los Angeles, CA; (3); Church Yth Grp; ROTC; Color Guard; Drill Tm; High Hon Roll; Prfct Atten Awd; CSF; Acad Dcthln Tm Mem; Top 10 Pct Vandenberg AFB Ldrshp Schl.

WHITAKER, TERRENCE; South Bay Lutheran HS; Los Angeles, CA; (3); Church Yth Grp; Church Choir; High Hon Roll.

WHITCOMB, IAN D; Victor Valley HS; Victorville, CA; (2); Air Force Acad; Pilot.

WHITE, AMY R; Mission San Jose HS; Fremont, CA; (1); Drama Clb; Peer Cnslng; Pncpl Policy Advsry Brd; Ldrchp Cncl; Cal Berkeley; Educ.

WHITE, ANDREW M; Valley View HS; Moreno Valley, CA; (2); Capt Quiz Bowl; Ed Lit Mag; High Hon Roll; NHS; Pres Acad Fit Awd; Rotary Awd; Interact Clb VP; Comp Sci.

WHITE, ANDREW S; Westmont HS; San Jose, CA; (4); Church Yth Grp; Sec French Clb; Teachers Aide; Varsity Clb; School Musical; Variety Show; Rep Stu Cncl; Stat Diving; Golf; Powder Puff Ftbl; Coustau Soc; Greenpeace; Smithsonian; De Anza Coll; Marine Bio.

WHITE, ARROWA; Inglewood HS; Los Angeles, CA; (2); Dance Clb; Drama Clb; 4-H; Key Clb; El Camino; Law.

WHITE, BARBARA A; Monte Vista HS; Spring Valley, CA; (3); 118/373; Church Yth Grp; French Clb; Chorus; School Musical; School Play; Dance; U Of CA; Bus Admin.

WHITE, BECKY; Elk Grove HS; Elk Grove, CA; (4); Cmnty Wkr; Teachers Aide; Yrbk; JV Bsktbl; Var Sftbl; Cit Awd; Hon Roll; Vlntr Sftbl Coach-Girls; Sacramento City Coll; Sprts Med.

WHITE, BRANDY R; Red Bluff Union HS; Red Bluff, CA; (2); Vllybl; Hon Roll; Kiwanis Awd; Prfct Atten Awd; Pres Acad Fit Awd; Triton Swm Clb; Lwyr.

WHITE, CEDRIC G; Dorsey HS; Los Angeles, CA; (2); Var Bsktbl; Var Ftbl; Var Trk; Hon Roll; Bus Admin.

WHITE, CHRIS D; Mira Vista HS; Redondo Beach, CA; (2); Quiz Bowl; Science Clb; JV Bsktbl; JV Tennis; Cit Awd; Tnns Awd; Bus.

WHITE, CHRISTINE H; Novato HS; Novato, CA; (2); French Clb; VP Key Clb; Spanish Clb; Piano; San Jose ST U; Public Rltns.

WHITE, CHRISTOPHER A; Fairfield HS; Fairfield, CA; (2); Boy Scts; Ski Clb; Ftbl; Hon Roll; Several Stu Rcgntn Awds; Hnrs Engl & Sci; MBA.

WHITE, CHRISTY F; Fontana HS; Fontana, CA; (4); 63/792; JV Var Tennis; Hon Roll; Pres Acad Fit Awd; Bowling; Z Clb 2 Yrs; CSF 2 Yrs; U CA Riverside; Hstry Ed.

WHITE, CLAY; Paso Robles HS; Shandon, CA; (3); FFA; Spanish Clb; Varsity Clb; Var Bsbl; Var Bsktbl; Hon Roll; Lion Awd; HS Rodeo; CA Polytech U; Ag Bus.

WHITE, CORINNE N; La Reina HS; Thousand Oaks, CA; (3); Pres Drama Clb; Hosp Aide; Thesps; Chorus; School Musical; School Play; Variety Show; Stu Cncl; Hon Roll; Ntl Merit Ltr; CA ST Northridge; Commnctn.

WHITE, CRISTOPHER J; Fremont HS; Sunnyvale, CA; (2); Church Yth Grp; Debate Tm; Drama Clb; JA; NFL; Speech Tm; Swmmng; Trk; CA Schltc Soc, Golden St Geom Awd; Antique Arms, Armor Collectr; Fossil Collectr, Dealer; Hstry.

WHITE, DANIELLE A; Vacaville HS; Vacaville, CA; (3); Cmnty Wkr; SADD; Teachers Aide; Varsity Clb; Chorus; Rep Soph Cls; L Capt Bsktbl; L Capt Sftbl; L Capt Vllybl; Cit Awd; TX Tech U; Sprts Med.

WHITE, DARRYL T; Hesperia HS; Hesperia, CA; (3); French Clb; Var Bsktbl; Hon Roll; Pres Acad Fit Awd; UNLV; Acctng.

WHITE, DAWN; Artesia HS; Cerritos, CA; (3); 7/360; Church Yth Grp; Treas Drama Clb; Letterman Clb; Science Clb; Teachers Aide; Thesps; Pres Chorus; School Musical; School Play; Stage Crew; Best Actress HS 90; Most Insprtnl Player Track, Field; Engrng.

WHITE, DOUGLAS L; Los Banos HS; Los Banos, CA; (3); AFS; Cmnty Wkr; Drama Clb; FBLA; Letterman Clb; Teachers Aide; Band; Mrchg Band; Pep Band; School Musical; Rotary Yth Exchnge Germany; Cal Poly; Intl Bus Mgmt.

WHITE, ELIZABETH L; Antelope Valley HS; Lancaster, CA; (4); 7/360; Science Clb; Teachers Aide; Gym; Cit Awd; Gov Hon Prg Awd; High Hon Roll; NHS; Pres Acad Fit Awd; Pres Schlr; Gymnstcs Comptn Levl Class I; Coachng Gym; Painting Awds; U C Davis; Bio.

WHITE, EMILY K; Mayfield SR Schl; San Gabriel, CA; (3); Sec Church Yth Grp; Cmnty Wkr; Pres Girl Scts; Library Aide; Scholastic Bowl; Spanish Clb; Church Choir; Phtg Yrbk; Tennis; Hon Roll; CSF; Wrtng Clb.

WHITE, HEATHER M; North County Christian Schl; Paso Robles, CA; (1); Church Yth Grp; Drama Clb; 4-H; Office Aide; School Play; Bsktbl; Vllybl; Cit Awd.

WHITE, JANE E; Maricopa HS; Lebec, CA; (4); 3/37; Cmnty Wkr; Drama Clb; GAA; School Play; Sec Treas Sr Cls; Hon Roll; CSF; Acad Decthln; Bank Of Amer Achvt Awd Bus; CA ST Bakersfield; Bus Admin.

WHITE, JASON P; Sanger HS; Clovis, CA; (2); Church Yth Grp; Drama Clb; Model UN; ROTC; Chorus; School Musical; Stage Crew.

WHITE, JEFFREY S; Tehachapi HS; Tehachapi, CA; (4); Church Yth Grp; FFA; FHA; Key Clb; Speech Tm; Teachers Aide; Jazz Band; Mrchg Band; Wt Lftg; Rcvd Awds & Won Trphys In TAE-KWON-DO Tourn; OH ST U; Radiologist.

WHITE, JENNIFER L; Torrance HS; Torrance, CA; (3); Art Clb; Church Yth Grp; Cmnty Wkr; French Clb; Sec Teachers Aide; Sec Acpl Chr; Treas Chorus; Variety Show; JV Sftbl; Cal ST Northridge; Accntng.

WHITE, JEROME M; Clayton Valley HS; Bound Brook, NJ; (3); Drama Clb; Orch; School Musical; School Play; Rptr Nwsp; Var Trk; Hon Roll; Rnnr Up Stu Yr; Awd Outstndng Sci Stu Jr Cls; Yth Eductrs; Ldrshp Conf Hayward St U; CSF; Pre-Med.

WHITE, JILL S; Antioch HS; Antioch, CA; (4); 17/605; Church Yth Grp; Letterman Clb; Teachers Aide; Hon Roll; Hnr Guard; Acad Dcthln; Cal ST Los Angeles; Jrnlsm.

WHITE, JODI L; Armijo HS; Fairfield, CA; (1); Church Yth Grp; Cmnty Wkr; Chorus; Rep Frsh Cls; Pres Soph Cls; Biloa.

WHITE, JOHN C; Brea Olinda HS; Brea, CA; (3); 2/190; Debate Tm; Pres Letterman Clb; NFL; VP Speech Tm; Rptr Yrbk; L Var Swmmng; High Hon Roll; Hon Roll; NHS; Sptlght On Yth Awd; Engrng.

WHITE, JON C; Sacramento Waldorf HS; Auburn, CA; (3); Chorus; Var Bsbl; Var Bsktbl; Var Socr.

WHITE, JOSHUA L; Modoc HS; Alturas, CA; (2); 13/59; Rptr FFA; FHA; Drill Tm; Bsktbl; Ftbl; Swmmng; Wt Lftg; Prfct Atten Awd; U NC; Cmmnctns.

WHITE, JUANITA L; University HS; Los Angeles, CA; (2); Church Yth Grp; Girl Scts; Office Aide; Teachers Aide; Band; Chorus; Off Soph Cls; Stu Cncl; Cheerldng; Mgr(s); CSF; MESA; Peace Clb; Howard; Law.

WHITE, JUSTIN C; Irvine HS; Irvine, CA; (2); Church Yth Grp; Var Golf; Club Hockey, Alt Capt; Golden St Exam High Hnrs Rcvr; Ethnic Panel To Twaianese Stus; NM ST; Arch.

WHITE, KATHERINE R; Vintage HS; Napa, CA; (4); Cmnty Wkr; Office Aide; Var Capt Bsktbl; Capt Powder Puff Ftbl; Trk; Wt Lftg; Cit Awd; Hon Roll; Peer Cnslr Jr/R; Sacramento ST; Elem Ed.

WHITE, KEISHA; Edison HS; Stockton, CA; (1); Chorus; School Play; Bsktbl; Ftbl; Mgr(s); Trk; Prfrmng Arts.

WHITE, KENNETH J; North County Christian HS; Paso Robles, CA; (2); Rep Soph Cls; Rep Stu Cncl; JV Bsktbl; Comp.

WHITE, KIM; Santa Rosa HS; Santa Rosa, CA; (2); Church Yth Grp; Pep Clb; Teachers Aide; Church Choir; Rep Frsh Cls; Rep Stu Cncl; Capt JV Cheerldng; High Hon Roll; Hon Roll; Pres Acad Fit Awd; Babysitting; Cnslr Chrstn & Missnry Alliance Cmp; Teach Piano Lssns; Westmont; Scndry Ed Engl.

WHITE, KRISTINE N; Valencia HS; Fullerton, CA; (3); Drama Clb; FBLA; School Play; Stage Crew; Outstndng Spanish Stu Awd; UCSB; Bus.

WHITE, KRISTOPHOR; Redwood HS; Visalia, CA; (3); Teachers Aide; Band; Jazz Band; Mrchg Band; Pep Band; JV Var Bsktbl; Ftbl; High Hon Roll; Hon Roll; Jr NHS; COS; Law.

WHITE, LAURA A; Pierce HS; Arbuckle, CA; (2); GAA; JV Sftbl; Hon Roll; Airline Stewardess.

WHITE, LIBRA; Washington HS; Los Angeles, CA; (3); Pep Clb; Ed Nwsp; High Hon Roll; Hon Roll; Prfct Atten Awd; Athenians Hnr Soc; CSF; U CA Berkeley; Law.

WHITE, MARINDA; Garces Memorial HS; Bakersfield, CA; (1); 2/167; High Hon Roll; Dance Tap, Ballt.

WHITE, MARLENE D; Norco SR HS; Corona, CA; (2); Sec Church Yth Grp; Church Choir; JV Bsktbl; Vllybl; Frshmn Vllybl Team Best Offense; Howard; Corporate Law.

WHITE, MEGAN H; Moorpark HS; Moorpark, CA; (2); Sec FHA; Teachers Aide; Chorus; Stu Cncl; JV Bsktbl; Cit Awd; High Hon Roll; Hon Roll; Sec NHS; Stanford.

WHITE, MELANIE D; Victor Valley HS; Oro Grande, CA; (3); Church Yth Grp; Office Aide; Band; Mrchg Band; Pep Band; Stat Var Crs Cntry; Stat Score Keeper; Stat Trk; Cit Awd; Hon Roll; Black Stu Union; Fishers Of Men Sec; U Of PA; Law.

WHITE, MELANIE E; Leuzinger HS; Hawthorne, CA; (1); French Clb; Key Clb; Spanish Clb; Mgr Stu Cncl; CSF; Save The Earth Club.

WHITE, MICHAEL J; Foothill HS; Sacramento, CA; (1); German Clb; Ski Clb; Band; Pep Band; JV Mgr(s); JV Score Keeper; Hon Roll; Pres Acad Fit Awd; CSF; Med.

WHITE, MICHELLE L; San Leandro HS; San Leandro, CA; (3); JV Sftbl; Hon Roll; Acctnt.

WHITE, MICHELLE M; Escondido HS; Escondido, CA; (1); Church Yth Grp; Cmnty Wkr; Drama Clb; FCA; GAA; Key Clb; Letterman Clb; SADD; Teachers Aide; Band; USC; Ped.

WHITE, MICHELLE M; Foothill HS; Santa Ana, CA; (2); Red Cross Aide; Spanish Clb; Chorus; Flag Corp; School Musical; High Hon Roll; NEDT Awd; Hnry CA Gdwll Ambssdr; Hgh Schl Stu Ambssdr Orient; CA Schlrshp Fed Mem; Bus Mngmnt.

WHITE, NATHANAEL; Western HS; Buena Park, CA; (4); Church Yth Grp; French Clb; VICA; High Hon Roll; Hon Roll; NHS; 1st Arch Drwngs CA St Fair; 89 Disneylnd Crtvty Cntst; Orange Co Chptr Am Inst Arch 1st/Bst Mdl; Cal Poly San Luis Osisbp; Arch.

WHITE, PAUL H; La Habra HS; La Habra Hts, CA; (4); 18/390; Boy Scts; Band; Jazz Band; Mrchg Band; Pep Band; Variety Show; Stu Cncl; JV Socr; Great Books/Film Clb VP; Economics.

WHITE, PEARL G; Sweetwater HS; San Diego, CA; (4); 4/374; Treas Science Clb; Ed Nwsp; Yrbk; Rep Stu Cncl; L Socr; Cit Awd; DAR Awd; High Hon Roll; Hon Roll; Prfct Atten Awd; Assocd Stu Bdy Comssnr 87 89 90; Sci Olympiad Rep, Medlst 88; CSF Sealbearer 87-90; U Of CA San Diego; Med.

WHITE, RAGAN M; Fairfield HS; Fairfield, CA; (2); Church Yth Grp; Cmnty Wkr; Computer Clb; Drama Clb; 4-H; French Clb; Hosp Aide; Church Choir; School Play; Stage Crew; UC Davis; Med.

WHITE, RAMEY L; Santa Cruz HS; Santa Cruz, CA; (1); Church Yth Grp; JV Socr; JV Swmmng; Hon Roll; JV Waterpolo Team.

WHITE, RAYFORD A; Argonaut HS; Sacramento, CA; (4); Cmnty Wkr; Drama Clb; FHA; ROTC; Speech Tm; SADD; Teachers Aide; Church Choir; Stu Cncl; Hon Roll; Chld Abuse Prvntn; FBL Amer; Bus Prof Amer; Military; Bus.

WHITE, RAYNETTE; Sacramento HS; Sacramento, CA; (2); Church Yth Grp; GAA; SADD; Church Choir; Drill Tm; Bsktbl; Sftbl; Vllybl; Wt Lftg; Hon Roll; Georgetown; Med.

WHITE, RICHARD H; Notre Dame HS; Riverside, CA; (1); Crs Cntry; Wrstlng; High Hon Roll; U Of AK; Comp Sci.

WHITE, RONDA E; Newark Memorial HS; Newark, CA; (4); 30/346; Church Yth Grp; Church Choir; Var Bsktbl; JV Sftbl; Var Trk; Var Vllybl; Hon Roll; Outstndng Athltc Achvt; Afro-Am Schlrshp Wnnr; U CA-BERKELEY; Comp Engrng.

WHITE, RUSSELL W; Montclair HS; Ontario, CA; (1); Boy Scts; Swmmng; Wrstlng; Water Polo; Accntng.

WHITE, RYAN J; Adolfo Camarillo HS; Camarillo, CA; (4); Church Yth Grp; Drama Clb; Spanish Clb; Var Crs Cntry; Surfing As My Favorite Sport; SKA As The Best Music In The World; Thrift Shopping Club; Ventura Coll; English.

WHITE, RYAN M; Huntington Beach HS; Huntington Beach, CA; (3); Var Diving; UCSB; Engr.

WHITE, SCOTT E; Rosemead HS; Rosemead, CA; (2); Church Yth Grp; Band; Church Choir; Mrchg Band; Orch; Pep Band; Intrml JV Ftbl; Intrml JV Wrstlng; Marine Bio.

WHITE, SETH T; Bellarmine Coll Prep; Monte Sereno, CA; (1); Debate Tm; NFL; Speech Tm; Opt Clb Awd; San Jose St U Awd Expstry Spkng; Wrter Bellarmine Strtgc Games; Comp Ind.

WHITE, SHANNON D; Vallejo SR HS; Vallejo, CA; (2); Church Yth Grp; Dance Clb; Science Clb; Ski Clb; SADD; Band; Church Choir; Mrchg Band; Hon Roll; NHS; Phrmcy.

WHITE, SHIRLEY A; Palo Verde HS; Blythe, CA; (3); Drama Clb; Teachers Aide; School Musical; School Play; Ed Yrbk; Hon Roll; Jobs Daughters Hnrd Qn; Palo Verde Coll.

WHITE, SIANE; Los Angeles Ctr For Enriched Stds; Los Angeles, CA; (4); Debate Tm; Math Clb; Science Clb; Ed Nwsp; Off Jr Cls; Chrmn Sr Cls; Chrmn Stu Cncl; Gym; Cit Awd; Hon Roll; 2nd Purple Blt Tae Kwon Do; Swm Tm; Ephebian Soc; Jr Statesmn Amer; CSF; Chrmn Intl Rltn Cmmtte; MESA; U Of CA Los Angeles; Med.

WHITE, STEPHANIE; Clovis HS; Clovis, CA; (3); VP Intnl Clb; NFL; Speech Tm; SADD; Teachers Aide; Var Swmmng; Hon Roll.

WHITE, STEPHANIE D; Kingsburg HS; Kingsburg, CA; (2); Drama Clb; Letterman Clb; SADD; Orch; School Play; Stage Crew; Trk; Hon Roll; 4-H; FFA; Engl.

WHITE, SUSAN L; San Gorgonio HS; San Bernardino, CA; (3); English Clb; FBLA; Key Clb; Teachers Aide; Color Guard; Flag Corp; Mrchg Band; Var Cheerldng; Prfct Atten Awd; ACES; U Redlands; Chem Engrng.

WHITE, THERESA L; Calico HS; Yermo, CA; (3); ROTC; Chorus; Comp Prog.

WHITE, TIFFANY M; El Toro HS; El Toro, CA; (4); Debate Tm; Pep Clb; Ski Clb; Teachers Aide; Rptr Nwsp; Var Cheerldng; Mgr(s); JV Sftbl; High Hon Roll; Hon Roll; Grad Spkr; Most Enthusiastic Spkr Awd Forensics; Keywanettes; UCSB; Brdcst Jrnlsm.

WHITE, TIMOTHY R; Paso Robles HS; Paso Robles, CA; (2); FFA; JV Var Tennis; High Hon Roll.

WHITE, TINA L; Escondido HS; Escondido, CA; (1); Church Yth Grp; Letterman Clb; Band; Drm Mjr(t); Jazz Band; Mrchg Band; Orch; Pep Band; Powder Puff Ftbl; Sftbl; Amer Musical Fndtn Band Hnrs; Outstndng Band Stu 90; USC; Child Psych.

WHITE, VENUS A; Linden HS; Linden, CA; (2); Dance Clb; Teachers Aide; Drill Tm; Flag Corp; School Musical; School Play; UC Davis.

WHITE JR, WILBUR B; Eisenhower HS; Rialto, CA; (2); JV Ftbl; Wt Lftg; Cit Awd.

WHITE, WILLIE B; South Bay Lutheran HS; Los Angeles, CA; (3); Church Yth Grp; Dance Clb; Office Aide; Varsity Clb; Var Bsktbl; Var Crs Cntry; Var Ftbl; Cit Awd.

WHITE, ZUBERI J; John F Kennedy HS; Richmond, CA; (1); Computer Clb; Hon Roll; U NV-LAS Vegas; Comp Prog.

WHITED, JULIE; Whitney HS; Lakewood, CA; (4); Church Yth Grp; Dance Clb; Thesps; Color Guard; School Play; Hon Roll; Jr Statesmen Of Amer-Chptr Treas; Natl Hispanic Schlr-Semi Flnst; UCLA; Envrnmntl Sci.

WHITEFORD, JEFF L; Antelope Valley HS; Palmdale, CA; (3); Am Leg Boys St; Teachers Aide; Varsity Clb; Var L Bsbl; JV Ftbl; Home Run Clb; Psych.

WHITEHEAD, KENIA L; Gompers Secondary HS; San Diego, CA; (2); 10/208; Capt Dance Clb; Science Clb; Band; Capt Drill Tm; Stu Cncl; Co-Capt Cheerldng; Hon Roll; Ntl Merit Ltr; Opt Clb Awd; Prfct Atten Awd; Schl, City & St Level Sci Fair 1st Pl; Natl Sci Olympd; Howard Hughes Fllwshp Pgm; Mrn Photobio.

WHITEHEAD, KEVIN L; San Dieguito HS; Encinitas, CA; (2); 5/30; Church Yth Grp; Office Aide; Pep Clb; Jazz Band; Yrbk; Sec Stu Cncl; Bsktbl; Mgr(s); Tennis; Cit Awd; Bio.

WHITEHEAD, LAURA J; Edison HS; Huntington Beach, CA; (1); Band; Mrchg Band; Orch; Pep Band; Hon Roll; USC; Musical.

WHITEHEAD, NANCY L; Garden Grove HS; Garden Grove, CA; (3); Church Yth Grp; Cmnty Wkr; Pep Clb; SADD; Church Choir; Stu Cncl; Var Crs Cntry; Var Socr; JV Swmmng; Var Trk; Azusa Pacific U; Nrsng.

WHITELEY, LEE M; Clovis HS; Clovis, CA; (2); Cmnty Wkr; Dance Clb; Drama Clb; SADD; Chorus; Church Choir; Stage Crew; Cit Awd; Fresno ST U; Bus.

WHITELEY, RACHEL A; O'farrell Schl/Creatv & Perfrm Arts; San Diego, CA; (1); 1/219; Church Yth Grp; Hon Roll; Jr Thtre Grp; Med.

WHITELEY, REBECCA A; Redwood HS; Visalia, CA; (2); Church Yth Grp; 4-H; Church Choir; Color Guard; 4-H Awd; Hon Roll; Coll Of The Sequoias; Elem Ed.

WHITEMAN, ANGELINA; Foothill HS; Bakersfield, CA; (3); 13/378; Am Leg Aux Girls St; Church Yth Grp; Letterman Clb; Chorus; School Musical; Var Cheerldng; JV Crs Cntry; L High Hon Roll; Chrch Yth Rcgntn Awd; Brigham Young U.

WHITEMAN, ERICA L; Apple Valley HS; Apple Valley, CA; (3); Teachers Aide; Crs Cntry; Mgr(s); Hon Roll; Frgn Lang.

WHITEMAN, JACQUELINE L; Esperanza HS; Yorba Linda, CA; (2); 16/500; Church Yth Grp; Chorus; Var Trk; NHS; Stu Mnth Bio; Math.

WHITESIDE, DOUG C; Apple Valley HS; Apple Valley, CA; (1); Band; Mrchg Band; Hon Roll; Air Force.

WHITESIDE, KIM E; Tulare Union HS; Tulare, CA; (3); Church Yth Grp; 4-H; JV Bsktbl; Var Crs Cntry; Var JV Swmmng; Var Trk; Hon Roll; Portuguese Clb; Pol Sci.

WHITFIELD, ARTHUR; Mc Lane HS; Fresno, CA; (1); Chorus; Trk.

WHITFIELD, BARTON; Dorsey HS; Los Angeles, CA; (4); Bsktbl; Engrng.

WHITFIELD III, WILLIE B; Calvary Baptist HS; Pomona, CA; (3); Drama Clb; Office Aide; Teachers Aide; Chorus; School Play; UCLA; Bus Mgmt.

WHITING, JAMIE J; Nevada Union HS; Grass Valley, CA; (3); Am Leg Aux Girls St; Church Yth Grp; Red Cross Aide; SADD; Church Choir; School Musical; Lit Mag; Rep Stu Cncl; Hon Roll; CPR Instrctr; Brigham Young U; Elem Educ.

WHITING, TERESA; Poway HS; Poway, CA; (3); 27/760; FBLA; SADD; Varsity Clb; Var L Gym; Powder Puff Ftbl; High Hon Roll; Hon Roll; NHS; CA Schlrshp Fed; Socr Tm Coach; Bus.

WHITING, TRAVIS W; Palmdale HS; Palmdale, CA; (3); Church Yth Grp; FFA; Hon Roll; Air Force; Aircrft.

WHITLATCH JR, LYMAN; Redwood HS; Visalia, CA; (4); 8/302; Church Yth Grp; Cmnty Wkr; Pres Science Clb; Spanish Clb; Band; Jazz Band; Ed Nwsp; Stu Cncl; Var Swmmng; Pres Acad Fit Awd; U Notre Dame; Med.

WHITLEY, CHARLIE M; Portola JR SR HS; Portola, CA; (1); Ski Clb; Spanish Clb; JV Bsbl; JV Bsktbl; Hon Roll; Yth To Yth; Sr Leag Bsbl All Stars; Bus.

WHITLOCK, BRAD; Oak Ridge HS; Rescue, CA; (1); JV Crs Cntry; JV Trk; High Hon Roll; Jr NHS; Acad Tlnt Srch CSUS Engrng Cls.

WHITLOCK, ROB P; Salinas HS; Salinas, CA; (3); Church Yth Grp; Ski Clb; Thesps; School Play; Stu Cncl; JV Bsbl; Var Bsktbl; High Hon Roll; NHS; CSF; Schlr/Athl; UCSB; Chem.

WHITMAN, JEREMY R; Desert HS; Edwards, CA; (3); Church Yth Grp; Drama Clb; Band; Chorus; Var Intrml Bsktbl; Intrml Bsktbl; L Var Ftbl; L Var Socr; L Var Wrstlng; Hon Roll; Crmnlgy.

WHITMAN, STEPHANIE; San Ramon Valley HS; Alamo, CA; (3); 19/420; Key Clb; Orch; Swmmng; DAR Awd; Hon Roll; CSF.

WHITMAN, TRACIE; Woodbridge HS; Irvine, CA; (1); 35/472; Hosp Aide; VP JCL; Rep Soph Cls; High Hon Roll; Jobs Daughters-Hon Queen; Piano Cert O Fmerit Level 3 ST Of CA; CSF; Girls Lge.

WHITMARSH, MATTHEW L; Ukiah HS; Ukiah, CA; (4); Math Clb; Math Tm; SADD; Varsity Clb; Band; Nwsp; Stu Cncl; Ftbl; Tennis; Pres Acad Fit Awd; 1st Pl VA St Poetry Wrtng Cnse; U Of CA San Diego; Math.

WHITMARSH, SANDRA N; So Calif Christian HS; Brea, CA; (3); Yrbk; Sftbl; Vllybl; Hon Roll; Nursing.

WHITMER, KEITH P; Mira Costa HS; Redondo Beach, CA; (2); Key Clb; Quiz Bowl; Scholastic Bowl; JV Socr; Hnrs Engl, Hstry; US Amateur Surfing Chmnshp & NSSA Natl.

WHITMER, LISA JOY; Palo Alto HS; Palo Alto, CA; (3); 8/300; Drama Clb; Teachers Aide; School Play; Rptr Nwsp; Gym; High Hon Roll; Rachel Austin Awd Engl; Sci & Math Dept Awds; Hstry Dept Awd; Williams Coll; Educ.

WHITMEYER, CLINTON; Castlemont HS; Oakland, CA; (3); Aud/Vis; JA; Band; Stage Crew; Off Jr Cls; Stu Cncl; Cit Awd; Hon Roll; Prfct Atten Awd; Carpentry.

WHITMIRE, CHRISTA; Wm S Hart HS; Newhall, CA; (4); 50/450; Rep Church Yth Grp; Capt Red Cross Aide; Sec Service Clb; VP Treas Chorus; Church Choir; Capt Color Guard; School Musical; Mgr Stage Crew; High Hon Roll; Pres Acad Fit Awd; CSF Pres 89-90; Sound Vibrations Show Choir Secy Hist 87-90; 1M Ldr VP; Rep Church Yth Grp; Drama Clb; UC Riverside; Liberal Studies.

WHITMIRE, JENIFER; Davis SR HS; Davis, CA; (2); JV Bsktbl; JV Gym; JV Capt Vllybl; Gldn St Exam Acad Excllnc Awd 1st Yr Alg Hrns; CSF; Bus.

WHITMIRE, STACEY M; Santa Monica HS; Santa Monica, CA; (2); Swmmng; Tennis; Hon Roll; Jr NHS; NHS; Pres Acad Fit Awd.

WHITNACK, ZACHARY E; Del Campo HS; Citrus Heights, CA; (3); Church Yth Grp; Stu Cncl; JV Trk; Var Capt Vllybl; Prdcr Video Yrbk; Compose Music; Write Drct Prdc Films Music Videos; UCLA; Film Prdctn.

WHITNEY, HEATHER M; St Joseph HS; Lakewood, CA; (2); Church Yth Grp; French Clb; Key Clb; Hon Roll; CA Schlrshp Fdr; Cert Ntbl Accmplsmnt Rlgn II; Psychlgy.

WHITNEY, JENNIFER; Somoma Valley HS; Sonoma, CA; (2); Cmnty Wkr; Stu Cncl; Var Swmmng; Var Tennis; Hon Roll; Peer Counseling.

WHITNEY, JENNIFER A; Saint Monicas HS; Los Angeles, CA; (2); Art Clb; Key Clb; Ed Nwsp; High Hon Roll; CSF; Readng Clb VP; Marine Bio.

WHITNEY, KRISTEN M; Ernest Righetti HS; Santa Maria, CA; (4); Hist 4-H; Varsity Clb; L Var Swmmng; High Hon Roll; Hon Roll; NHS; Pres Acad Fit Awd; Photo Clb Treas; Hancock CC; Human Dev Ed.

WHITNEY, LAURA J; Atwater HS; Atwater, CA; (3); Church Yth Grp; FCA; Girl Scts; Band; Mrchg Band; Pep Band; Rep Frsh Cls; Rep Stu Cncl; Var Swmmng; Hon Roll; Grl Scout Slvr Awd; Mem CA Schlrshp Fed; Tufts U; Med.

WHITNEY, MARK; Covina HS; Covina, CA; (4); Cmnty Wkr; Model UN; Science Clb; SADD; Hon Roll; Rotary Awd; CSF 87-90; CA U Brkly.

WHITNEY, MATTHEW R; Dublin HS; Dublin, CA; (3); 12/180; Var Vllybl; High Hon Roll; Hon Roll; Jr NHS; NHS; Pres Acad Fit Awd; USGF Cmptv Gym; Pres Inter-Act; Cmmnty Svc Org; Coach Girls Vllybl Tm; Air Force Acad; Aero Engr.

WHITNEY, MINDY; St Francis HS; Saratoga, CA; (1); Church Yth Grp; Debate Tm; English Clb; NFL; Pep Clb; Speech Tm; SADD; Hon Roll; Duke; Intl Bus.

WHITNEY, PATRICIA L; Roosevelt HS; Fresno, CA; (2); Dance Clb; Cit Awd; Hon Roll; Prfct Atten Awd; Prfssnl Dance.

WHITNEY, ROBERT M; Shafter HS; Shafter, CA; (3); 4/215; Debate Tm; Phtg Yrbk; JV Var Trk; Hon Roll; Mck Trl; Acad Decthln; Santa Cruz; Psych.

WHITNEY, SARAH; Rim Of The World; Running Springs, CA; (3); 10/259; Church Yth Grp; Band; Nwsp; Hon Roll; NHS; Med.

WHITSITT, CHRISTINE; Yucaipa HS; Yucaipa, CA; (3); Church Yth Grp; Spanish Clb; Band; Orch; Var Trk; Hon Roll; San Diego; Psych.

WHITT, STACY; East Bakersfield HS; Bakersfield, CA; (2); Church Yth Grp; Cmnty Wkr; Dance Clb; Chorus; School Musical; Hon Roll; Amer Leg Aux Jr Mem; Teachers Aid; NW MO St Univ; Physcl Thrpst.

WHITTAKER, JARED W; Canyon Springs HS; Moreno Valley, CA; (3); Boy Scts; Church Yth Grp; JV Tennis; JV Trk; High Hon Roll; Hon Roll; Gldn ST Exm Hnrs Alg; Gldn ST Exm Schl Rcgntn Geom; Egl Sct Awd; Brigham Young U; Mdcl.

WHITTAKER, KEVIN; Summerville Union HS; Tuolumne, CA; (3); 4/146; Am Leg Boys St; Church Yth Grp; ROTC; Pres Spanish Clb; Jazz Band; Rep Stu Cncl; JV Var Bsktbl; Var Socr; Tennis; High Hon Roll; Coast Grd Acad AIM Prog; Air Force Acad S3 Prog; Air Force Acad; Engr.

WHITTAKER, ROBYN; Los Baptist HS; Los Angeles, CA; (3); Church Yth Grp; Acpl Chr; Capt Jazz Band; Off Soph Cls; Var Co-Capt Cheerldng; Trk; Hon Roll; Big Sis; Marine Bio.

WHITTED, TRAVIS A; Monterey HS; Salinas, CA; (2); Boy Scts; High Hon Roll; Rifle Clb-2nd; CSF.

WHITTEN, DAVID L; Burlingame HS; Burlingame, CA; (2); Boy Scts; Tennis; CA Golden St Exam Alg Hons; CA Golden St Exam Geo Hons; Eagle Sct; Order Of Arrow; UC Davis; Civ Engr.

WHITTENBURGE, ADINA; O'farrell SCPA HS; San Diego, CA; (1); Church Yth Grp; Drama Clb; Acpl Chr; Swing Chorus; Cit Awd; High Hon Roll; Hon Roll; Pres Schlr; Gldn St Exam Awd; O Farrell SCPA; Vet.

WHITTICOM, JAMES E; Bishop O'dowd HS; Oakland, CA; (2); Ftbl; Lcrss; Socr; High Hon Roll; Pres Acad Fit Awd.

WHITTIER, BRANDY L; San Pedro HS; San Pedro, CA; (3); Hosp Aide; Service Clb; Rep Frsh Cls; Sec Pres Stu Cncl; Var Crs Cntry; Var L Socr; Hon Roll; Prfct Atten Awd; CSF; Chld Dvlpmnt.

WHITTINGTON, PORCHE N; Washington Prep; Los Angeles, CA; (2); Cmnty Wkr; Girl Scts; Office Aide; Bsktbl; Empress Clb; Cert GS; Police Offcr.

WHITTINGTON, ROBYN; Etna HS; Fort Jones, CA; (3); FFA; VICA; Yrbk; Var Cheerldng; Hon Roll; U CA-DAVIS; Engl.

WHOLLEY, JENNIFER L; Arlington HS; Riverside, CA; (2); Hon Roll; 4th Grd Teacher.

WHYMAN, PAMELA J; Madera HS; Madera, CA; (2); Intrml Tennis; Spirit Clb.

WHYTE, MARCIA; Vivian Webb HS; Upland, CA; (2); Church Yth Grp; Cmnty Wkr; Hosp Aide; Service Clb; Ski Clb; Yrbk; Vllybl; Natl Charity League; Engl.

WHYTE, WILLIAM S; Loyola HS; Manhattan Beach, CA; (2); 1/315; Hosp Aide; Varsity Clb; Rptr Nwsp; Co-Ed Lit Mag; Var Tennis; High Hon Roll; Spanish NHS; Outstndng Soph; CSF; Pol Soc.

WIBBERLEY, DEIDRE N; Mira Costa HS; Manhattan Beach, CA; (1); JV Vllybl; Hon Roll; Pres Acad Fit Awd; MVP Vllybl Tm; Schlr Athl Awd.

WICHMAN, MICHAEL J; Tracy HS; Tracy, CA; (2); 10/525; Boy Scts; Church Yth Grp; Intnl Clb; JV Bsktbl; Var L Tennis; High Hon Roll; Hon Roll; Ashimar; Hnrs On GSE; Schl Rcgntn On GSE.

WICHMANN, JEFF A; Orange Lutheran HS; Anaheim, CA; (2); 6/135; Church Yth Grp; Var Bsbl; Intrml Bsktbl; High Hon Roll.

WICKER, KATHRYN T; Bishop Montgomery HS; Manhattan Beach, CA; (2).

WICKLINE, AMY S; Bakersfield HS; Bakersfield, CA; (2); Church Yth Grp; Girl Scts; Ski Clb; Teachers Aide; JV Swmmng; Hon Roll; Prfct Atten Awd; Assisteens/Teen Grp Of Asstnc League.

WICKLUND, JENNIFER G; American Christian Acad; Citrus Heights, CA; (2); Church Yth Grp; Band; JV Cheerldng; JV Vllybl; High Hon Roll; Sacramento ST U; Tchr.

WICKMAN, MELISSA; Mira Mesa HS; San Diego, CA; (2); 1/797; GAA; Science Clb; Spanish Clb; Varsity Clb; Stu Cncl; JV Bsktbl; Var Trk; Var Vllybl; Pres Acad Fit Awd; Chrldr & Recd Rgnl Schlr Awd From Pop Warner; Coaches Awd For Vrsty Vlybl; Outstndng Field Event; U Of HI; Bio.

WICKSTROM, BRIAN; Woodland HS; Woodland, CA; (3); Boy Scts; FBLA; Ski Clb; Bsbl; Stat Bsktbl; JV Ftbl; Hon Roll; Sch Rcgntn Golden St Exam Geom; Bus Adm.

WICKSTROM, HEATHER; Grace Christian Schl; Sacramento, CA; (1); 2/6; Church Yth Grp; Teachers Aide; Nwsp; Intrml Bsktbl; Intrml Sftbl; Intrml Vllybl; Cit Awd; Hon Roll; Guatemala Missnry; Creative Wrtng; Oral Robers U; Jrnlsm.

WICKWARE, LISA D; Venice HS; Los Angeles, CA; (4); Pres Thesps; Gym; High Hon Roll; Peer Cnslng; San Diego ST U; Drama.

WIDDIFIELD, SHANNON; Rolling Hills HS; Rnch Palos Verd, CA; (4); Spanish Clb; SADD; Sec Treas Jr Cls; Off Sr Cls; Rep Stu Cncl; Stat Ftbl; JV Var Trk; Pres Acad Fit Awd; Sr Ctzns Movabl Feast Hostess; Golden St Xm Geomtry Hi Hnrs; CSF; U Of CA; Pltcl Sci.

WIDELSKI, AMY; Moorpark HS; Plymouth, MN; (2); 8/260; Var Bsktbl; JV Vllybl; Engl Lit.

WIDENHAM, TIM T; Chowchilla Union HS; Chowchilla, CA; (4); Teachers Aide; Varsity Clb; VICA; Intrml Bsbl; Var Bsktbl; Var Tennis; High Hon Roll; Prfct Atten Awd; Voice Dem Awd; Merced JC; Educ.

WIDGA, MELISSA; Barstow HS; Barstow, CA; (3); Drama Clb; Library Aide; School Play; Stage Crew; Rep Nwsp; Int Decorator.

WIDLE, CHARLIE D; Ernest Righetti HS; Santa Maria, CA; (3); Letterman Clb; Ski Clb; SADD; Varsity Clb; Intrml JV Bsbl; Intrml Bsktbl; Intrml JV Ftbl; Wt Lftg; Hon Roll; Pres Acad Fit Awd; OBC; Rnng Wild Assoc; U Of CA; Phys Thrpy.

WIDMAR, ERIC W; Irvington HS; Fremont, CA; (2); 8/365; Boy Scts; Church Yth Grp; Letterman Clb; Scholastic Bowl; Pres Soph Cls; Pres Jr Cls; JV Capt Ftbl; Var Trk; Var Capt Wrstlng; High Hon Roll; MVP JV Ftbl; Eagle Scout; Stu Of Mnth; USC; Pltcl Sci.

WIDNER, JOLEE D; Hesperia Christian Schl; Hesperia, CA; (3); Church Yth Grp; FCA; Library Aide; School Musical; Nwsp; Yrbk; Bsktbl; Vllybl; Hon Roll.

WIDNER, MELODY E; Holtville HS; Mustang, OK; (3); 29/379; Art Clb; Church Yth Grp; Cmnty Wkr; Drama Clb; FHA; Library Aide; Office Aide; School Musical; Swing Chorus; Lit Mag; CSF; OCU; Law.

WIDYAWATI, GABRIELLE G; Cornelia Connelly HS; Garden Grove, CA; (3); Cmnty Wkr; Hosp Aide; Library Aide; Sec Science Clb; VP Chorus; Trk; Hon Roll; NHS; Ntl Merit Schol; School Play; Sci Fair-3rd Pl-Chem; Engrng Fair-Hnrbl Mention-Med & Hlth; Rest Hm Volunteer; Med.

WIEBE, LISA; Capital Christian HS; Folsom, CA; (1); 3/90; Art Clb; Church Yth Grp; Band; Church Choir; Orch; School Play; High Hon Roll; Hnr Band; Biola U; Bus Mgmt.

WIEBE, SHARON; Capital Christian HS; Folsom, CA; (4); 2/47; Art Clb; Ed Yrbk; Pres Stu Cncl; High Hon Roll; CA Schlrshp Fed; Outstndng Stu Yr; Supts Awd; Biola U; Graph Arts.

WIEBE, SHERILYN M; Whittier Christian HS; La Mirada, CA; (4); 19/179; Church Yth Grp; Drill Tm; Rep Stu Cncl; Capt Cheerldng; Azusa Pacific U; Bus.

WIEBERG, KIMBERLY M; Twentynine Palms HS; Twentynine Palms, CA; (2); Church Yth Grp; Cmnty Wkr; Teachers Aide; Varsity Clb; Var Bsktbl; Var Sftbl; JV Vllybl; High Hon Roll; Hon Roll; Prfct Atten Awd; Coaches Awd; Sportsmanship Awd; CSF; Writing Celebration Awd; UNLV; Orthopedic Surgeon.

WIEBORG, SCOTT; Palm Desert HS; Palm Desert, CA; (4); 12/319; Model UN; Band; Mrchg Band; Var Crs Cntry; JV Trk; Hon Roll; Band Cncl Pres; Aero Engrg.

WIEDEL, CARI A; Notre Dame Catholic HS; Riverside, CA; (1); Chorus; School Musical; Stage Crew; Hon Roll; UCLA; Med.

WIEDENFELD, DAWN G; Grossmont HS; El Cajon, CA; (2); 83/429; Hosp Aide; JV Sftbl; JV Vllybl; Hon Roll; Schl Recog Gldn St Alg Exam 89; UCSD; Med.

WIEDERHOLD, MICHAEL D; Oakmont HS; Granite Bay, CA; (2); Boy Scts; Pres Church Yth Grp; Spanish Clb; Church Choir; Rptr Nwsp; Sec Soph Cls; Hon Roll; CSF; Advncd Placement Cls; Lifeguard; BYU; Engr.

WIEGNER, JULIE; St Vincent HS; Petaluma, CA; (4); 10/53; French Clb; Letterman Clb; Pep Clb; Ski Clb; Ed Yrbk; Var Stat Bsbl; JV Var Cheerldng; Powder Puff Ftbl; Var Sftbl; Hon Roll; CSF; Peer Cnslng; SADD Friday Night Live Rep; U Southern CA; Bus.

WIEKAMP, JOHANNA L; Ontario HS; Ontario, CA; (3); Art Clb; Church Yth Grp; French Clb; Key Clb; Phtg Rptr Yrbk; Hon Roll; Mexico Missn Outreach 3 Yrs; Point Loma Nazarene Coll; Art.

WIELAND, AMY L; Carlsbad HS; Carlsbad, CA; (1); SADD; Sftbl; JV Vllybl; Athl Of Mnth Sftbl; Hlth Ftnss Awd.

WIELAND, JEFFREY L; Aptos HS; Aptos, CA; (1); 1/450; Rep Stu Cncl; Bsktbl; JV Vllybl; Bus Clb; Site Cncl; U PA; Bus.

WIELANDT, MELISSA A; Foothill HS; Santa Ana, CA; (2); Bsktbl; Sftbl; High Hon Roll; Hon Roll; All Century Leag 1st Team; Fresno ST; Police Detective.

WIELANDT, NATHAN; Covina HS; W. Covina, CA; (4); French Clb; Teachers Aide; Band; Drm Mjr(t); Mrchg Band; Orch; Pep Band; Lion Awd; Band Booster Schlrshp; Sharp All-Amer Camps Instrctr; Cntrl CA Drum Major Chmpn; Citrus Coll.

WIELENGA, HEATHER; Laguna Hills HS; Laguna Hills, CA; (2); 48/350; Church Yth Grp; Cmnty Wkr; Drama Clb; Math Clb; SADD; Hon Roll; NHS; Pres Schlr; Mck Trl; Cmp Cmslr Absd Kids Cmp; Psych.

WIELENGA, LAURIE B; El Dorado HS; Placentia, CA; (3); Church Yth Grp; Drama Clb; Pres VP Girl Scts; Band; Mrchg Band; School Play; Rptr Nwsp; High Hon Roll; Hon Roll; NHS; Cngrssnl Yth Ldr; Cmp Cnslr; Crtv Wrtng; U Of Santa Barbara; Comm.

WIENECKE, JENNIFER; Marina HS; Huntington Bch, CA; (1); German Clb; Ed Yrbk; Hon Roll; Wrtg Poetry & Short Stories; Organic Gardening; Chapman Coll; Wrtr.

WIENS, ERIKA J; Clovis HS; Clovis, CA; (3); Church Yth Grp; French Clb; SADD; Church Choir; Hon Roll; Singing; Piano; Music.

WIERENGA, AUNA T; Paraclete HS; Palmdale, CA; (3); Church Yth Grp; Varsity Clb; Pres Frsh Cls; Off Soph Cls; Stu Cncl; JV Bsktbl; Var L Crs Cntry; JV Var Vllybl; Hon Roll; NHS; CSF; San Diego ST; Comm.

WIERSCHEM, NATALIE; Morro Bay HS; Los Osos, CA; (2); 31/225; Math Tm; Band; Rep Frsh Cls; Pres Soph Cls; JV Bsktbl; Var Crs Cntry; Var Swmmng; Var Vllybl; Hon Roll; NHS; Math Tm; Jr Natl Soc.

WIERSCHEM, NATALIE I; Morro Bay HS; Morro Bay, CA; (2); Church Yth Grp; Girl Scts; Math Tm; Band; Rep Frsh Cls; Pres Soph Cls; JV Bsktbl; Var Crs Cntry; Var Swmmng; Var Vllybl; Egyptology.

WIERSEMA, JEAN M; Turlock HS; Turlock, CA; (2); 83/600; Drama Clb; Speech Tm; JV Tennis; Hnrs Engl.

WIERTZEMA, ELIZABETH; Culver City HS; Culver City, CA; (3); Chess Clb; VP Cmnty Wkr; Pep Clb; Teachers Aide; Drill Tm; Off Soph Cls; Off Jr Cls; Off Sr Cls; JV Cheerldng; JV Pom Pon; S-Clb VP, Pres; SMC; Med.

WIESE, PAMELA M; Mater Dei HS; Garden Grove, CA; (3); Chorus; School Musical; School Play; Variety Show; High Hon Roll; NHS; UC Irvine; Medicine.

WIGER, MATTHEW; Damien HS; Covina, CA; (2); JV Ftbl; JV Wrstlng.

WIGGINS, CHRISTINA M; Oroville HS; Chico, CA; (4); Hosp Aide; Vlntr; Miss Teen USA Schlstc Pageant; CA Culinary Acad; Chef.

WIGGINS, LISA G; Canyon HS; Canyon Country, CA; (3); FBLA; SADD; School Play; Pres Frsh Cls; Pres Soph Cls; Var L Swmmng; High Hon Roll; YMCA Yth & Govt; CSF; Frgn Rels.

WIGGINS, TIA; San Fernando HS; Lakeview Terrace, CA; (4); Church Yth Grp; Dance Clb; FBLA; Girl Scts; Pep Clb; SADD; Chorus; Ed Nwsp; Sec Soph Cls; Ftbl; Future Schlrs; CA ST U; Hotel Motel Mgmt.

WIJESEKERA, SHIRVINDA; Los Alamitos HS; Los Alamitos, CA; (3); 15/510; Cmnty Wkr; Hosp Aide; Math Tm; SADD; Var Swmmng; Cit Awd; High Hon Roll; Hon Roll; Vrsty Wtrpolo; Eclgy Clb Ofcr, Bd; Intract Clb; Mdcl Dr.

WIKSTROM, DANIELLE; Capital Christian HS; Sacramento, CA; (4); 37/48; Pres Art Clb; Church Yth Grp; High Hon Roll; NHS; Outstndng Stu In Govt & Econ, Bio; Piano; CA Poly San Luis Obispo; Arch.

WIKSTROM, DANIELLE C; Capital Christian HS; Sacramento, CA; (4); 2/48; Pres Art Clb; High Hon Roll; Outstndng Stu Ec Gov; Karate; CSF; CA Poly San Luis Obispo; Arch.

WILBERT, TESSA; John F Kennedy HS; Richmond, CA; (4); 3/236; Sec Treas Sr Cls; Stat Bsbl; Stat Bsktbl; Stat Ftbl; Mgr Nwsp; Pres Frsh Cls; VP Soph Cls; Stat Sftbl; CSF Sealbearer Hnr Grad; Bnk Of Amer Achvt Math; Ldrshp; MESA Pres; U Of CA Davis; Comp Engrng.

WILBOURN, LESLIE D; Tulare Union HS; Tulare, CA; (2); Church Yth Grp; 4-H; FFA; Flag Corp; Mrchg Band; 4-H Awd; FFA Hnr Hrse Jdgng Tm.

WILBUR, KAESA; Durham HS; Chico, CA; (4); 11/70; Am Leg Aux Girls St; Church Yth Grp; Pres 4-H; Band; Ed Yrbk; Pres Sec Stu Cncl; DAR Awd; 4-H Awd; Hon Roll; Fine Arts Plaue Wnnr; CSU Chico; Educ.

WILBUR, KELLEY A; Tulare Western HS; Tulare, CA; (3); 7/300; Church Yth Grp; 4-H; JA; Letterman Clb; Ski Clb; Band; Church Choir; Sec Soph Cls; Treas Jr Cls; Pres Stu Cncl; Goldn St Awd High Hnrs; CA Delg Natl Assn Stu Cncls Conf; Psych.

WILBUR, WILLIAM J; Durham HS; Chico, CA; (2); 4-H; Letterman Clb; Ski Clb; Rep Frsh Cls; Rep Soph Cls; JV L Bsktbl; JV L Crs Cntry; JV L Trk; 4-H Awd; Hon Roll; CSF.

WILCH, KEVIN A; Whittier Christian HS; La Habra Hts, CA; (4); Church Yth Grp; German Clb; Capt Bsktbl; Ftbl; Trk; Vllybl; High Hon Roll; Evangelist.

WILCHER, MYISHA T; University HS; Los Angeles, CA; (2); Church Yth Grp; Capt Drill Tm; Phtg Yrbk; Rep Frsh Cls; Rep Soph Cls; Cit Awd; Hon Roll; JV Sngldr; Spkr 9th Gr Grad; Spelman; Comm.

WILCOX, AIMEE; C K Mc Clatchy HS; Sacramento, CA; (2); 1/500; Drama Clb; French Clb; High Hon Roll; Gldn St Awd Hnrs Math; Frnch Clb Pres; UC San Diego; Pre-Med.

WILCOX, BRIAN M; Castro Valley HS; Castro Valley, CA; (4); 17/366; Church Yth Grp; French Clb; School Musical; School Play; Lit Mag; Rep Stu Cncl; High Hon Roll; Ntl Merit SF; Prt Tm Job As Sls Cnslr; Awds For Piano; Vlntr Wrk At Lcl Chrch; Mthmtcs.

WILCOX, JEANNE M; Dixon HS; Dixon, CA; (2); AFS; Intnl Clb; Office Aide; Cit Awd; Hon Roll; Fri Night Live; CSF; Gldn St Exam Schl Rcgntn; Substnc Abuse Tsk Frc Dist Cmmtte; Exchng Stu Germany.

WILCOX, JENNIFER A; Antioch HS; Antioch, CA; (4); 287/583; Church Yth Grp; Cmnty Wkr; Hosp Aide; Library Aide; Teachers Aide; Chorus; Stat Var Bsktbl; Hon Roll; Prfct Atten Awd; Elite San Francisco Mdlng Schl Cert; Med Scl Wrkr.

WILCOX, ROBERT J; Ukiah HS; Ukiah, CA; (3); 85/439; JV Trk; Job; Bike Rdng; Sci.

WILCOX, SHAUNTEL; Susan Miller Dorsey HS; Los Angeles, CA; (3); Church Yth Grp; Dance Clb; Drama Clb; Varsity Clb; School Play; Rep Jr Cls; VP Stu Cncl; Var Cheerldng; Stat Trk; Cit Awd; Grambling U; Psych.

WILCOX, SHELBY L; Clovis West HS; Clovis, CA; (2); FCA; Varsity Clb; Var Socr; Var Sftbl; Var Vllybl; High Hon Roll; CA Schltc Fed; Mst Imprvd Vllybl; CO-MVP Sccr; Criminology.

WILCZEWSKI, LISA M; Palmdale HS; Palmdale, CA; (3); 40/650; French Clb; SADD; Teachers Aide; Off Jr Cls; Bsbl; Mgr(s); Powder Puff Ftbl; Score Keeper; Hon Roll; Scl Sci Clb; Peer Hlpr; Keywanettes; CSUN; Phys Thrpy.

WILDE, AMY; Rio Mesa HS; Ventura, CA; (3); Dance Clb; Ventura Coll; RN.

WILDE, DAVID F; Sunny Hills HS; Fullerton, CA; (3); 157/421; Letterman Clb; Varsity Clb; JV Var Bsktbl; JV Var Ftbl; Var Wt Lftg; Hon Roll; Stu Coalition; James Madison U; Hstry.

WILDE, FRANK S; Mission San Jose HS; Fremont, CA; (3); Boy Scts; Ski Clb; Hon Roll; Bsbll; U Of CO-BOULDER; Bus.

WILDE, MEIRA; Canyon HS; Canyon Country, CA; (4); 27/431; Cmnty Wkr; French Clb; Hosp Aide; Capt Drill Tm; Lit Mag; Hon Roll; Masonic Awd; NHS; Hnrd Queen Of Intl Jobs Dghtrs; Safe Riders; Satying Alive; U Of CA Campus; Marine Bio.

WILDE, SEAN J; Etiwanda HS; Alta Loma, CA; (2); Boy Scts; Church Yth Grp; French Clb; Ski Clb; Bsbl; Ftbl; Capt Socr; Wt Lftg; Cit Awd; Hon Roll; Pres Church Yth Group; Wrtng Poetry & Lit; BYU; Kinesiology.

WILDER, MARCIA R; San Leandro HS; San Leandro, CA; (3); 11/361; Hosp Aide; Rep Jr Cls; Stat Bsktbl; Stat Socr; Stat Vllybl; Cit Awd; High Hon Roll; Hon Roll; NHS; Opt Clb Awd; CSF.

WILDER, RICHARD; Valhalla HS; El Cajon, CA; (4); 2/450; Church Yth Grp; Key Clb; SADD; Swmmng; High Hon Roll; Prfct Atten Awd; Sal; Amnsty Intl; Water Polo; Harvrd Bk Clb Awd; Stanford U; Biolgcl Sci.

WILDEY, JENNIFER L; Mc Kinleyville HS; Arcata, CA; (3); Church Yth Grp; 4-H; Office Aide; Band; Mrchg Band; Pep Band; 4-H Awd; Hon Roll; UC Davis; Vet.

WILDHABER, ALISSA J; Rim Of The World HS; Blue Jay, CA; (2); Church Yth Grp; VP Spanish Clb; Band; Tennis; Hon Roll; Tennsi Tm Slvr Mdl; Bus Adm.

WILDS, SHAWNA L; Savanna HS; Anaheim, CA; (3); Office Aide; Color Guard; Flag Corp; Variety Show; Rep Jr Cls; Achvt Poem Published; Fullerton JR Coll; Sec.

WILES, DENNIS; Ribet Acad; Los Angeles, CA; (1); Church Yth Grp; Var Bsbl; JV Bsktbl; Hon Roll.

WILEY, BELINDA; Atascadero HS; Atascadero, CA; (3); Capt Flag Corp; High Hon Roll; Capt Flg Tm; Schl Sprt Prmtr; Bus.

WILEY, HEATHER ANN; Ramona HS; Riverside, CA; (1); 16/582; Church Yth Grp; Chorus; Church Choir; Orch; School Musical; Pres Acad Fit Awd; Redlands U; HS Engl Tchr.

WILEY, JAMES J; Cerritos HS; Cerritos, CA; (4); 75/565; Teachers Aide; Var Socr; Hon Roll; Ntl Merit SF; Young Black Schlrs; MESA VP; United Togthr Clb; Engr.

WILEY, JANET L; Antioch HS; Antioch, CA; (4); 70/590; Drama Clb; Office Aide; Teachers Aide; Cit Awd; Hon Roll; Prfct Atten Awd; Los Medanos Coll; Child Dev.

WILEY, KAREN J; Valhalla HS; El Cajon, CA; (3); 11/408; Church Yth Grp; Cmnty Wkr; Rep Hosp Aide; Key Clb; Scholastic Bowl; Ski Clb; SADD; JV Swmmng; March Dimes Internshp Awd; Amnsty Intl; UCSD; Bio.

WILEY, RANEE BRENDA; Madera HS; Madera, CA; (3); French Clb; JA; Teachers Aide; Tennis; Hon Roll; CA Schltc Fed; San Jose ST; Psych.

WILHELM, CHRIS J; San Rafael HS; San Rafael, CA; (2); 4-H; Rep Key Clb; Var Bsbl; Var Bsktbl; Var Ftbl; Hon Roll; Hnrbl Mntn Vrsty Ftbl.

WILHELM, CHRISTINE; Carlsbad HS; Carlsbad, CA; (3); 92/320; French Clb; Pep Clb; Nwsp; Hon Roll; 11th Pl Editorial Writing, San Diego Cty JEA Write-Offs 90; Cert Of Rcgntn Lancer Exp Sch Nwsppr; Oberlin; Engl.

WILHELM, KEVIN T; Pioneer HS; San Jose, CA; (4); Boy Scts; Q&S; Ed Nwsp; Var Golf; JV Socr; Hon Roll; NHS; Pres Acad Fit Awd; Bank Of America Cert Wnnr Comm; Acad Dcthln; Comm Dept Awd; CSU Sacramento; Grphc Dsgn.

WILHELM, SHARON A; Ramona HS; Riverside, CA; (3); 47/300; Chess Clb; Vllybl; Hon Roll; Jr NHS.

WILHELM, SHELLEY A; Pioneer HS; San Jose, CA; (1); Spanish Clb; JV Bsktbl; L Var Trk; Hon Roll; CSF; Interact Clb; CIF Schlstc Achvt Awd.

WILHITE, CHRISTOPHER T; North HS; Bakersfield, CA; (3); 15/500; Var JV Ftbl; Golf; Wt Lftg; Hon Roll; U Of SC; Engrng.

WILHITE, PETE E; Calaveras HS; San Andreas, CA; (3); 14/190; JV Capt Bsbl; JV L Bsktbl; Var L Socr; Hon Roll; Archery; Riflery; Mntnrng; Us Army Helicopter Pilot.

WILK, STACEY L; Clairemont HS; San Diego, CA; (2); 66/356.

WILKE, JON C; Loarg HS; Anaheim, CA; (4); Band; High Hon Roll; NHS; CSF; Dept Awd Industrial Arts; Orange Cnty Yth Expo Gold Awd Wood Wrkng; Fullerton Coll.

WILKEN, GREG A; West HS; Bakersfield, CA; (2); Church Yth Grp.

WILKEN, MARK R; Monte Vista HS; La Mesa, CA; (4); 6/450; Church Yth Grp; Ski Clb; High Hon Roll; Hon Roll; Ntl Merit SF; Pres Acad Fit Awd; St Schlr; JV Bsktbl; Var Ftbl; CSF; Jr Hnr Aisle; Stu Congress; UC Santa Barbara; Mech Engrng.

WILKENS, CHRISTOPHER S; Ventura HS; Santa Paula, CA; (4); Drama Clb; Thesps; School Play; Stage Crew; Ftbl; Hon Roll; JETS Awd; Kent ST U.

WILKERSON, MATT; Hesperia Christian HS; Hesperia, CA; (2); 1/45; Church Yth Grp; Scholastic Bowl; Band; Mrchg Band; Var L Bsbl; JV Bsktbl; JV Ftbl; Wt Lftg; High Hon Roll; CSF.

WILKERSON, RENTHENIA; South Bay Lutheran HS; Los Angeles, CA; (3); Church Yth Grp; Cmnty Wkr; Church Choir; Stu Cncl; Var Bsktbl; Var Sftbl; Trk; High Hon Roll; Hon Roll; USC; Law.

WILKERSON, TIFFANY M; Washington High Prep; Los Angeles, CA; (3); Cmnty Wkr; Math Tm; Drill Tm; School Play; Yrbk; Off Stu Cncl; Trk; Cit Awd; Hon Roll; Talent Search; UCLA Upward Bound; Engineer.

WILKES, ASHLEY B; Grossmont HS; La Mesa, CA; (3); 33/385; Pep Clb; Teachers Aide; Score Keeper; Var Socr; Var Sftbl; Var Vllybl; Hon Roll; Psych.

WILKES, BRIAN; Bret Harte Union HS; Arnold, CA; (2); Library Aide; Ski Clb; Yrbk; Bsbl; Hon Roll; Columbia JC; Fire Sci.

WILKES, TIMOTHY D; El Toro HS; El Toro, CA; (4); 80/550; Boy Scts; Math Tm; Quiz Bowl; VP Band; Jazz Band; Mrchg Band; Orch; Pep Band; High Hon Roll; Hon Roll; Winston Churchill Essay Cont Wnnr 89; 3rd Pl CA Hstry Day 89; Acad Decthln; Hstry.

WILKINS, ERIC A; Pioneer HS; San Jose, CA; (2); Boy Scts; Church Yth Grp; Temple Yth Grp; L Crs Cntry; L Trk.

WILKINS, MICHELLE L; San Clemente HS; San Clemente, CA; (2); Church Yth Grp; Spanish Clb; Varsity Clb; Intrml Vllybl; Mem Of Vrsty Surf Tm 1988-90.

WILKINS, NYLA B; Saint Anthony HS; Long Beach, CA; (2); Drama Clb; Hosp Aide; Letterman Clb; School Musical; School Play; Var Trk; JV Vllybl; Hon Roll; NHS; Smi Fnlst Natl Lbry Ptry Cntst; UCLA; Law.

WILKINS, STEPHANIE; Vacaville HS; Vacaville, CA; (4); 12/536; French Clb; German Clb; Hosp Aide; Quiz Bowl; Service Clb; Teachers Aide; JV Cheerldng; High Hon Roll; NHS; Prfct Atten Awd; USC; Bus.

WILKINS, YOLANDA Y; Granada Hills HS; Los Angeles, CA; (2); Computer Clb; GAA; Service Clb; Spanish Clb; Thesps; Yrbk; JV Bsktbl; JV Vllybl; Cit Awd; Harvard; Chem.

WILKINSON, CONSTANCE; King City HS; Soledad, CA; (4); 1/180; Am Leg Aux Girls St; Library Aide; Teachers Aide; Pres Stu Cncl; Var Bsktbl; Var Crs Cntry; Var Trk; Cit Awd; High Hon Roll; Val; All-League Bsktbl; All Salinas Valley; Track All-League; Acad Block; Otstndng SR Athlete 90; Hartnell CC.

WILKINSON, KEELY D; River City HS; W Sacramento, CA; (1); Church Yth Grp; Band; Mrchg Band; Pep Band; Hon Roll; River Cty Rowing Clb; Jrs Prgm; BYU; Sci.

WILKINSON, MICHELE N; San Pasqual HS; Escondido, CA; (3); 43/369; Church Yth Grp; Debate Tm; Speech Tm; Vllybl; Hon Roll; Vllybl Clb; Bus.

WILKINSON, SINCLAIR; Aptos HS; Aptos, CA; (4); 79/273; German Clb; Ski Clb; Band; Var Crs Cntry; JV Ftbl; Hon Roll; CSF; Peer Tutor Chem; Soc Sci Outstndng Stu; Cabillo Coll; Marine Bio.

WILKOV, DAVID M; Bellarmine College Prep; San Jose, CA; (3); 25/308; Aud/Vis; Church Yth Grp; Model UN; NFL; Speech Tm; Band; Drm Mjr(t); Mrchg Band; Pep Band; School Musical; 3rd Pl CA H S Speech Tournament; Outstanding Student/Temple Emanu El Religious School.

WILL, KIMBERLY ANN; Savanna HS; Anaheim, CA; (4); Church Yth Grp; Cmnty Wkr; GAA; Hosp Aide; JA; Letterman Clb; Pep Clb; Teachers Aide; Acpl Chr; Chorus; CA ST Fullerton; Bus.

WILLAIMS, KIMBERLY; Ramona HS; Riverside, CA; (2); Girl Scts; Office Aide; Orch; Rptr Nwsp; JV Bsktbl; Cit Awd; Hon Roll; Prfct Atten Awd; Bdmttn; US Govt Studies; Law Study.

WILLAIMS, ZACHARY D; Irvine HS; Irvine, CA; (1); Orch; Var Diving; Hon Roll; Pres Acad Fit Awd; Stanford U; Sprts Med.

WILLARD, ALLEN W; Hanford Union Joint HS; Hanford, CA; (1); High Hon Roll; Hon Roll; Davis; Med.

WILLARD, DEANA M; Westminster HS; Westminster, CA; (3); Bus.

WILLARD, KILEY H; Lincoln HS; Stockton, CA; (2); Band; Jazz Band; Mrchg Band; Pep Band; School Musical; Pres Acad Fit Awd; UC Santa Cruz; Music.

WILLARD, MOLLIE A; North HS; Bakersfield, CA; (3); French Clb; JA; Office Aide; Hon Roll; Bakersfield Coll; Dental Hygnst.

WILLARD, NICHOLE; North Salinas HS; Salinas, CA; (4); 55/350; Am Leg Aux Girls St; Church Yth Grp; Pep Clb; Red Cross Aide; Church Choir; Treas Stu Cncl; Var Capt Bsktbl; Var Capt Vllybl; High Hon Roll; Kiwanis Awd; All-Salinas Vly Bsktbl, Vllybl; All-Leque Vllybl, Bsktbl; MVP Vllybl, Bsktbl & Vllybl; CA Baptist Coll; Chem.

WILLCOCKSON, JOSEPH D; Santa Monica HS; Santa Monica, CA; (2); Church Yth Grp; Latin Clb; Chorus; Var Socr; Hon Roll; Kiwanis Awd; Engl.

WILLDEN, JOY A; Lompoc HS; Lompoc, CA; (3); Church Yth Grp; FBLA; FHA; SADD; Chorus; Church Choir; Wrstlng; Brave Of The Month; Air Force; Real Est.

WILLEFORD, SEAN; Redwood HS; Visalia, CA; (4); Church Yth Grp; SADD; Rep Yrbk; Pres Soph Cls; Var Bsbl; Var Ftbl; High Hon Roll; Hon Roll; Linfield Coll; Bio.

WILLETT, DUSTIN A; Antioch HS; Antioch, CA; (2); 211/738; Church Yth Grp; Letterman Clb; Model UN; Acpl Chr; Band; Chorus; Intrml Ftbl; Var Trk; Pres Acad Fit Awd; Natl Jr HS Hnr Choir; UC-BERKLEY; Audio Elec Engr.

WILLEY, TIFFANY R; Village Christian Schls; North Hollywood, CA; (3); 36/123; Church Yth Grp; Drama Clb; Spanish Clb; Teachers Aide; Chorus; School Musical; Stage Crew; Rep Frsh Cls; Intrml JV Sftbl; Hon Roll; Doctor.

WILLHALM, HEATHER L; Saint Francis HS; Sunnyvale, CA; (3); 38/289; Church Yth Grp; Cmnty Wkr; SADD; Ed Yrbk; Capt Var Swmmng; High Hon Roll; Hon Roll; Jr NHS; NHS; Pres Acad Fit Awd; Synchrnzd Swim Coach; U Of SAN Diego; Orthdntst.

WILLIAMS, AARON; Hanford HS; Hanford, CA; (2); Radio Contrl Racing; Certf Awd Outstndng Sci.

WILLIAMS, AARON; Lindhurst HS; Olivehurst, CA; (4); 4/180; Boy Scts; Pres Science Clb; Mrchg Band; Pep Band; Var Socr; High Hon Roll; Pres Acad Fit Awd; Eagle Scout; U Of CA Berkeley; Chmcl Engrng.

WILLIAMS, ABENA; Bellarmine Jefferson HS; Burbank, CA; (2); Church Yth Grp; Pep Clb; School Musical; School Play; Rep Frsh Cls; Var Bsktbl; Var Cheerldng; Trk; Var Vllybl; Hon Roll.

WILLIAMS, ABIKE Y; Cerritos HS; Los Angeles, CA; (4); Spanish Clb; Teachers Aide; Mrchg Band; Ed Yrbk; Trk; Hon Roll; Deb Alpha Kappa Alphs Sority 89; Young Black Schlrs; Howard U; Chem.

WILLIAMS, ADRIAN L; River City HS; W Sacramento, CA; (1); Church Yth Grp; Cmnty Wkr; Church Choir; Jazz Band; Ftbl; Trk; Hon Roll; Engrng.

WILLIAMS, ALYSON C; Tehachapi HS; Tehachapi, CA; (3); Church Yth Grp; Computer Clb; FCA; FFA; FHA; Teachers Aide; Church Choir; Stage Crew; Bsktbl; Sftbl; Phys Ed Tchr.

WILLIAMS, AMY; Saint Bonaventure HS; Ventura, CA; (2); Cmnty Wkr; GAA; Teachers Aide; Var Bsktbl; Var Vllybl; Hon Roll; Prfct Atten Awd; UCSB; Engr.

WILLIAMS, AMY M; Victory Christian HS; W Sacramento, CA; (4); 2/26; Teachers Aide; Rep Soph Cls; Treas Sr Cls; Sec Stu Cncl; Capt JV Cheerldng; Hon Roll; Sal; Schlr/Athl Awd; Engl Awd; CA ST U Sacramento; Jrnlsm.

WILLIAMS, ANDREA M; South HS; Bakersfield, CA; (3); Drama Clb; JA; Teachers Aide; Church Choir; Psych.

WILLIAMS, ANGELA J; Chula Vista HS; Chula Vista, CA; (2); Debate Tm; Drama Clb; Pep Clb; Treas SADD; School Musical; School Play; Cit Awd; Peer Contact; Mst Spirited Awd; SPEAK; UCLA; Drama.

WILLIAMS, ANTONETTI; Stagg HS; Stockton, CA; (2); Church Yth Grp; Office Aide; SADD; Church Choir; JV Sftbl; JV Vllybl; U C Davis; Doctor.

WILLIAMS, APRIL; Poway HS; Poway, CA; (3); 220/750; Dance Clb; FBLA; Letterman Clb; Library Aide; Pep Clb; Ski Clb; SADD; Varsity Clb; Rep Stu Cncl; Co-Capt Cheerldng; Fri Night Live-Activities Cmmssnr; Am Lit Mrt Cert; Interact Clb; Surf Clb-Treas; UCLA; Telecmmnctns.

WILLIAMS, APRIL M; Venice HS; Los Angeles, CA; (3); Church Yth Grp; Service Clb; Orch; Treas Frsh Cls; Pres Jr Cls; JV Var Sftbl; Prfct Atten Awd; CSF.

WILLIAMS, ARLANA DEBORAH; Pius X HS; Compton, CA; (4); 7/185; Cmnty Wkr; Science Clb; Var Pom Pon; Hon Roll; NHS; Actvts Clb; Yng Blck Schlrs; Magna Cum Laude Plaq; CSF; USC; Accntng.

WILLIAMS, BARRY L; Etiwanda HS; Etiwanda, CA; (2); Boy Scts; Badminton; Loma Linda U; Pre-Med.

WILLIAMS, BECKY; Bethel Baptist HS; Garden Grove, CA; (4); Church Yth Grp; Drama Clb; School Play; Yrbk; Pres Sr Cls; Pres Stu Cncl; Var L Bsktbl; Var L Vllybl; High Hon Roll; Ntl Merit Ltr; Curt Pringles Yth Advsry Cmmtte; Pacific Coast Bapt Bible Coll.

WILLIAMS, BERNARDETTE; George Washington HS; Daly City, CA; (4); Church Yth Grp; Drama Clb; Hosp Aide; Office Aide; Pep Clb; Teachers Aide; JV Bsktbl; JV Cheerldng; Var Mgr(s); Hon Roll; Homcmng Prncss 2 Yrs; San Franciso ST U; Comp Engr.

WILLIAMS, BRANDI D; San Gorgonio HS; Highland, CA; (3); Cmnty Wkr; Hosp Aide; Pres Q&S; Teachers Aide; CSF; Peer Cnslr; VP Russian Club; Fine Arts.

WILLIAMS, BRENT C; West HS; Bakersfield, CA; (3); Boy Scts; Pres Church Yth Grp; FCA; FFA; Hon Roll; CA ST U; Bus Admin.

WILLIAMS, BRIAN; Imperial HS; Imperial, CA; (4); 1/85; Am Leg Boys St; FFA; Math Tm; VP Pres Frsh Cls; VP Pres Jr Cls; Var Bsbl; Var Capt Bsktbl; Var Ftbl; Val; Cal Poly Pomona; Comp Engrng.

WILLIAMS, BRIAN D; Fresno Christian HS; Fresno, CA; (3); Church Yth Grp; FCA; Science Clb; Spanish Clb; SADD; Teachers Aide; Band; Jazz Band; Mrchg Band; Pep Band; Point Loma Nazareen Coll.

WILLIAMS, BRICE A; Monterey HS; Del Rey Oaks, CA; (3); Band; Mrchg Band; Gym; Hon Roll; Golden St Awd For Algebra; Adv Art Stu; Amer Coll Applied Arts Ldn; Art.

WILLIAMS, BRYCE M; Mission Viejo HS; Mission Viejo, CA; (4); Model UN; Teachers Aide; Var Capt Bsktbl; Var L Ftbl; Capt Var Trk; Hon Roll; Bsktbll MVP Soph & Jr Yr; All League & All Cnty Ftbll Teams; Asst Mgr Edwards Theatre; Saddleback; Engr.

WILLIAMS, CHANNON C; Skyline HS; Oakland, CA; (3); Church Yth Grp; Chorus; School Play; Rptr Nwsp; JV Bsktbl; Var Trk; Hon Roll; Prfct Atten Awd; Law.

WILLIAMS, CHARLA E; Arvin HS; Lamont, CA; (1); Hon Roll; Prjct 2000; GATE; CSF.

WILLIAMS, CHARNETTE P; Pittsburg HS; Pittsburg, CA; (1); Aud/Vis; Trk; Hon Roll; Prfct Atten Awd; Acad Achvt Awd; Math.

WILLIAMS, CHERI; Bloomington HS; Bloomington, CA; (3); Band; Jazz Band; Mrchg Band; Orch; Crs Cntry; Hon Roll; Sci.

WILLIAMS, CHRISTIAN J; Capital Christian HS; Rancho Cordova, CA; (3); Aud/Vis; Church Yth Grp; Drama Clb; Library Aide; Acpl Chr; Chorus; Church Choir; School Play; Stage Crew; Ed Nwsp; ASCI Mscl Cmmnd Perfmnc Fnlst 89 90; Natl Fine Arts Fstvl Fnlst 89; Yth Choir, Bass Sctn Ldr; Azusa Pacific U; Music.

WILLIAMS, CHRISTINA; Yuba City HS; Penn Valley, CA; (3); 176/450; Church Yth Grp; Fld Hcky; Mgr(s); Powder Puff Ftbl; Score Keeper; Hon Roll; Friday Night Live; Yng Life; Phrmcy.

WILLIAMS, CHRISTOPHER R; Seaside HS; Ft Ord, CA; (4); 25/256; Lit Mag; High Hon Roll; Hon Roll; NHS; Pres Acad Fit Awd; James L Rucker Acad Achvt Awd 89 & 90; Bnk Of Amer Achvt Awd, Trde & Indstry 90; Penn ST U; Archt.

WILLIAMS, CHRISTOPHER T; Junipero Serra HS; Compton, CA; (3); JV Bsbl; Var Trk; Cit Awd.

WILLIAMS, CHRYSTAL; Palo Verde HS; Blythe, CA; (4); Church Yth Grp; Drama Clb; Key Clb; SADD; Flag Corp; JV Sftbl; Var Trk; Hon Roll; Prfct Atten Awd; Recvd Awd Schlrshp NAACP; Awd Schlrshp Blackwomen In Action; Awd Schlrshp St Pauls Missionary Society; Seattle U; District Attorney.

WILLIAMS, CINDY L; Orange Glen HS; Escondido, CA; (3); 90/458; Church Yth Grp; Hosp Aide; Key Clb; Pep Clb; Spanish Clb; Chorus; Cit Awd; Hon Roll; Pres Acad Fit Awd; Rotary Awd; San Diego ST U; Erly Chldhd.

WILLIAMS, CORA; Compton HS; Compton, CA; (1); Church Yth Grp; English Clb; Math Clb; Hon Roll; Prfct Atten Awd; Hstry Day; Mock Trl; CSULB 2nd Pl MESA; CSULB; Engr.

WILLIAMS, DACIA CRISTINE; Durham HS; Durham, CA; (2); Church Yth Grp; Cmnty Wkr; FHA; SADD; Phtg Rptr Yrbk; Ntl Merit Ltr; GATE; The Art Center; Law.

WILLIAMS, DAN P; Whittier Christian HS; Whittier, CA; (2); Church Yth Grp; Band; Mrchg Band; JV Vllybl; CSF; Arch.

WILLIAMS, DANA R; Montgomery HS; Santa Rosa, CA; (2); Hosp Aide; SADD; Cheerldng; Water Sports; Snow Skiing; Horsebck Rdng; Marine Bio.

WILLIAMS, DANELLE L; Alta Loma HS; Alta Loma, CA; (2); Dance Clb; Drama Clb; Pep Clb; Spanish Clb; SADD; Acpl Chr; School Musical; Vllybl; High Hon Roll; Hon Roll; Performing Arts.

WILLIAMS, DANIEL A; St Anthony HS; Long Beach, CA; (3); Var Bsbl; Hon Roll; Camino Real League All League Bsbl 2nd Tm; UC Davis; Atmospherel Sci.

WILLIAMS, DANTE L; Ganesha HS; Bloomington, CA; (3); Sec Sr Cls; JV Bsktbl; Var Ftbl; Hon Roll; Pres Acad Fit Awd; Bus.

WILLIAMS, DAVID; Coronado HS; Coronado, CA; (3); Ski Clb; Var Lcrss; Hon Roll; Round Table Debate Clb Pres; NAV; Poly Sci.

WILLIAMS, DAVID; River City SR HS; W Sacramento, CA; (1); JV Bsbl; JV Var Bsktbl; JV Ftbl; JV Trk; Hon Roll; Outstndng JV Ftbl Player; U NV-LAS Vegas; Am Hstry Ed.

WILLIAMS, DAWN M; Etiwanda HS; Etiwanda, CA; (2); Ski Clb; Phtg Yrbk; Var Socr; High Hon Roll; St Schlr; Animal Rights Clb; UC Davis; Bio.

WILLIAMS, DE ANNA; Monterey HS; Monterey, CA; (2); High Hon Roll; Hon Roll; Comp Sci.

WILLIAMS, DENISE K; Rio Linco Adventist Acad; Healdsburg, CA; (3); Church Yth Grp; Hosp Aide; Red Cross Aide; Spanish Clb; Off Soph Cls; 1st Aid & CPR Cert; Grls Club Pres; 1st Loma Linda U Intro To Med Schl Smmr 89; Loma Linda U; Nrs Prctnr.

WILLIAMS, DOYLE; James Logan HS; Union City, CA; (3); Cmnty Wkr; JA; Red Cross Aide; Rep Stu Cncl; Ftbl; Hon Roll; Berkeley Partnership Prgm U; CA Polytech ST U; Elec Engrng.

WILLIAMS, DREA L; Santa Clara HS; Santa Clara, CA; (3); Church Yth Grp; Library Aide; Chrldng PAL Yth Leag; Santa Clara U; Corp Law.

WILLIAMS, ELLA J; Bassett HS; Baldwin Park, CA; (2); 5/53; Cmnty Wkr; Math Tm; Co-Ed Q&S; SADD; Teachers Aide; Varsity Clb; Chorus; Ed Nwsp; Co-Ed Yrbk; JV Var Bsktbl; Vlntrd Aboretum; JTPA Awd; Data Proc.

WILLIAMS, EMILY J; Monte Vista HS; Alamo, CA; (2); Church Yth Grp; Dance Clb; Chorus; Var Diving; Var Socr; Sccr Team 2nd Western Rgnls 90; Teacher.

WILLIAMS, ERIC; Hesperia HS; Hesperia, CA; (3); Boy Scts; Computer Clb; 4-H; Hon Roll; Eagle Scout Awd; Cal ST San Bernardino.

WILLIAMS, EVANGELA L; Lynwood HS; Lynwood, CA; (3); 150/600; Pres Church Yth Grp; Teachers Aide; Pres Church Choir; Yrbk; UC Berkeley; Corp Law.

WILLIAMS, FANNIE R; Pittsburg SR HS; Pittsburg, CA; (2); Church Yth Grp; Trk; Hon Roll; Pres Acad Fit Awd; Healds Bus Sch; Accntng.

WILLIAMS, GARY; Far West HS; Oakland, CA; (3); 2/15; Cmnty Wkr; Computer Clb; Teachers Aide; VICA; Hon Roll; Schlrshp UC Berkeley Smr Prgm; CA ST Hayward; Comp Sci.

WILLIAMS, GOLDEN D; Calvary Chapel HS; Newport Beach, CA; (2); Church Yth Grp; Cmnty Wkr; Chorus; Church Choir; Gym; Mssnry Cmnty Svc Phlpns 90.

WILLIAMS, HEATHER; Mira Mesa HS; San Diego, CA; (2); Church Yth Grp; Key Clb; Quiz Bowl; SADD; Chorus; School Musical; Stage Crew; Off Soph Cls; Rep Stu Cncl; Hnr Chr; San Diego ST U; Arch.

WILLIAMS, HEATHER P; El Camino Fundamental HS; Sacramento, CA; (3); 131/366; Rptr French Clb; Hosp Aide; Teachers Aide; Rep Soph Cls; VP Jr Cls; VP Sr Cls; JV Bsktbl; Var Cheerldng; JV Var Swmmng; JV Vllybl; Fri Night Live; Jr Statesman Of Am; Med.

WILLIAMS, HOPE D; Mc Clymonds HS; Oakland, CA; (1); JV Var Cheerldng; Pom Pon; Cit Awd; High Hon Roll; Hon Roll; Spelman; Pediatrician.

WILLIAMS, IRA; Silver Valley HS; Ft Irwin, CA; (3); Aud/Vis; Varsity Clb; High Hon Roll; Hon Roll; Jr NHS; NHS; Pres Acad Fit Awd; Var Bsktbl; JV Ftbl; JV Var Socr; Comp Sci.

WILLIAMS, JACKIE C; Bishop Amat HS; Claremont, CA; (1); French Clb; Hosp Aide; Hon Roll; Natl Chrity Leag; Loma Linda U; Dentist.

WILLIAMS, JANAYA L; Hart HS; Santa Monica, CA; (2); Church Yth Grp; Intnl Clb; Math,Engrng,Sci Achvt Clb; Wrtrs Clb; Psych.

WILLIAMS, JANNA C; Mojave HS; Mojave, CA; (4); 18/96; Church Yth Grp; FHA; Pep Clb; SADD; Rep Frsh Cls; Rep Soph Cls; Pres Stu Cncl; Bsktbl; Vllybl; Hon Roll; Safe Rides; Chrmn Pep Rllies; Bsktbl Mst Insprtnl; Jr Cls Wntr Ball Prncss; Sr Prm Prncss; Bst Sense Hmr; Cuesta CC; Psych.

WILLIAMS, JASON L; Woodcrest Christian Schl; Riverside, CA; (2); Church Yth Grp; Office Aide; Scholastic Bowl; Church Choir; Sec Stu Cncl; Golf; High Hon Roll; Hon Roll; Obstetrcn.

WILLIAMS, JASSON D; Fremont HS; Sunnyvale, CA; (2); Church Yth Grp; Cmnty Wkr; Computer Clb; Drama Clb; Office Aide; ROTC; Chorus; School Play; Yrbk; Bsbl; Rsrch Dev.

WILLIAMS, JAY A; Chino HS; Chino, CA; (2); 2/631; Church Yth Grp; Science Clb; Stage Crew; JV Bsktbl; JV Ftbl; Var Swmmng; Cit Awd; High Hon Roll; CSF; Chino Childrns Theatr.

WILLIAMS, JEANNETTE K; Apple Valley HS; Apple Valley, CA; (4); 111/500; Drama Clb; Pres VP Girl Scts; Key Clb; Pep Clb; Spanish Clb; Flag Corp; Hon Roll; Emplyd Costco Whlsl; Hmbldt ST Coll; Math Tchr.

WILLIAMS, JEANNINE; Monte Vista HS; Spring Valley, CA; (3); 51/373; Am Leg Aux Girls St; Dance Clb; Pep Clb; School Musical; VP Jr Cls; Off Sr Cls; JV Var Bsktbl; Var Socr; JV Var Sftbl; Var Capt Vllybl; 1st Tm All Leag Vllybl & 3rd Tm All CIF; 2nd Tm All Leag Sftbl; Hnrbl Mntn Vllybl.

WILLIAMS, JEFF; Faith Baptist HS; West Hills, CA; (4); 2/39; Church Yth Grp; Drama Clb; Teachers Aide; School Play; Stage Crew; L Var Trk; High Hon Roll; Sal; CSF; Elec Engr.

WILLIAMS, JEFFREY J; Kennedy HS; La Palma, CA; (4); Church Yth Grp; Cmnty Wkr; Drama Clb; Pep Clb; Red Cross Aide; Teachers Aide; Chorus; School Play; Variety Show; Rep Soph Cls; Water Polo All League MVP; All CIF-SS 1st Tm; Princpls Hnr Rl; WASC; USC; US Senate.

WILLIAMS, JENNIFER ANNE; Atwater HS; Winton, CA; (2); SADD; Ed Yrbk; Rep Soph Cls; Stat Wrstlng; Hon Roll; Russian Lang; CSU Fresno; Law.

WILLIAMS, JENNY; Escalon HS; Escalon, CA; (1); 69/150; German Clb; Yrbk; JV Golf; Art; Helpng Elderly People; Saving Envrnmnt/Wrld; Stanford Med Schl; Medcl.

WILLIAMS, JERMEL; Bellflower HS; Long Beach, CA; (3); Computer Clb; Varsity Clb; School Play; Var Capt Bsktbl; Cit Awd; Georgetown; Comp.

WILLIAMS, JILL C; Clovis West HS; Clovis, CA; (1); Church Yth Grp; Chorus; Church Choir; Hon Roll.

WILLIAMS, JOY D; Clovis West HS; Clovis, CA; (3); Church Yth Grp; FCA; Hosp Aide; Capt Powder Puff Ftbl; Cit Awd; High Hon Roll; Wall Of Fame; Biola U; Child Psych.

WILLIAMS, JUANITA R; Dr James Hogan SR HS; Vallejo, CA; (3); Church Yth Grp; Office Aide; Church Choir; Hon Roll; Jr NHS; NHS; Hogan Gospel Choir; Acad Achvt Awd; ESRP Engrng Summer Prgm; Arch.

WILLIAMS, KAMILI; Sacred Heart Prep; Atlanta, GA; (4); 15/58; Am Leg Aux Girls St; Nwsp; Yrbk; Lit Mag; Pres Sr Cls; Rep Stu Cncl; JV Bsktbl; Cheerldng; Var Sftbl; DAR Awd; Cmmttee For Undrstndg; Campus Mnstry; Peer Cnslng; Spelman Coll; Pol Sci.

WILLIAMS, KAREN A; Los Angeles HS; Los Angeles, CA; (4); 23/400; Science Clb; Teachers Aide; Hon Roll; Prfct Atten Awd; Acad Finance 2 Yr Bus Prgm W/Hnrs; Riordan Prgm Bus UCLA Cmpltn; 3rd Pl Mdl Spnsh Poetry Cont; CA ST U Northridge; Bus Admin.

WILLIAMS, KAREN L; Bonita Vista HS; San Diego, CA; (3); Chorus; Church Choir; Off Jr Cls; Hon Roll; Prfct Atten Awd; ASB Srvc Awd; Alfa Kappa Alfa Debutant 90; PTA Trophy Talent Shw Soloist 88; Artwrk Dsply Bnk America; Law.

WILLIAMS, KELLEY J; San Marcos HS; Santa Barbara, CA; (2); Church Yth Grp; Key Clb; Pep Clb; SADD; Teachers Aide; Sec Jr Cls; Cheerldng; CA Schlrshp Fed; #1 Clb; Biola U; Ed.

WILLIAMS, KELLY E; Yreka Union HS; Montague, CA; (3); 12/173; Church Yth Grp; Pres 4-H; Drama Clb; Pres Spanish Clb; Teachers Aide; Sec Treas Soph Cls; Powder Puff Ftbl; 4-H Awd; Cngrssnl Schlr Natl Yng Ldrs Conf; CA Schltc Fed; Siskiyou Cnty Top 100 Prgm; CSU Chico; Frng Lang.

WILLIAMS, KENDRA L; El Cerrito HS; Richmond, CA; (2); Cmnty Wkr; Dance Clb; Red Cross Aide; Teachers Aide; Exclrtd Tutorial Cls; Acadc Hnrs Clses; San Francisco; Law.

WILLIAMS, KEVIN J; Oak Ridge HS; Shingle Springs, CA; (2); SADD; JV Bsbl; JV Socr; Hon Roll; Lwyr.

WILLIAMS, KIM; Valley HS; Sacramento, CA; (3); Sec Dance Clb; Cheerldng; Gym; Hon Roll; Early Outreach Pgm; Spelman Coll; Commnctns.

WILLIAMS, KIMBERLY A; Channel Islands HS; Oxnard, CA; (1); Band; Flag Corp; Jazz Band; Mrchg Band; Pep Band; Hon Roll; Acad Excllnc Engl Awd 9th Grade; Space Pgm.

WILLIAMS, KIMBERLY S; Merced HS; Merced, CA; (3); Church Choir; Hon Roll; Prfct Atten Awd; Fresno ST; Bus.

WILLIAMS, KRYSTAL; Fairfax HS; Los Angeles, CA; (2); Cmnty Wkr; Computer Clb; Office Aide; Ski Clb; Yrbk; Sftbl; Vllybl; Cit Awd; Hon Roll; Prfct Atten Awd; Med.

WILLIAMS, LANCE TYLER; Woodlake Union HS; Woodlake, CA; (4); 1/132; Key Clb; Science Clb; Rptr Nwsp; Pres Stu Cncl; JV Bsktbl; Var L Swmmng; Elks Awd; Pres Acad Fit Awd; Val; CSF Hghst Hnrs; U Of CA Santa Barbara; Ec.

WILLIAMS, LATRICIA Y; Castro Valley Adult Schl; Castro Valley, CA; (3); FHA.

WILLIAMS, LAURA K; Thousand Oaks HS; Thousand Oaks, CA; (3); Church Yth Grp; Cmnty Wkr; Key Clb; SADD; Nwsp; Pres Soph Cls; Pres Stu Cncl; Cit Awd; HOBY Ambsdr; Future Fnd Yth Cong; Top 10 Finalist Miss Teenage CA Schlrshp; U CO-BOULDER; Pol Sci.

WILLIAMS, LETICIA S; Castle Park HS; Chula Vista, CA; (2); German Clb; Hosp Aide; SADD; Teachers Aide; Ed Lit Mag; Tutor-Family Life, Tender Loving Zoo Vol; Theatre Dance; Greenpeace & Natl Forest Supporter; Wellesley Coll; Obstrn.

WILLIAMS, LEVESTER P; Morningside HS; Inglewood, CA; (2); Church Yth Grp; Cmnty Wkr; Crs Cntry; Trk; Prfct Atten Awd; UCLA; Med.

WILLIAMS, LIBBY L; Antioch HS; Antioch, CA; (4); 30/590; Dance Clb; French Clb; Letterman Clb; Pep Clb; Ski Clb; Teachers Aide; Drill Tm; Score Keeper; High Hon Roll; Hon Roll; 88-89 Grad Hnr Guard; Acad A Clb; Acad Awd; Outstndng Svc Trophy-Marching Band; 87-88 Dance Capt; CA Poly-San Luis Obispo; Vet.

WILLIAMS, LISA R; Skyline HS; Oakland, CA; (2); Teachers Aide; Yrbk; Socr; Cit Awd; Hon Roll; Pres Acad Fit Awd; All Lgue Sccr; MVP Sccr 90; Harvard; Psych.

WILLIAMS, LISA S; John F Kennedy HS; La Palma, CA; (3); Church Yth Grp; GAA; Chorus; Church Choir; Swing Chorus; Variety Show; Socr; High Hon Roll; Bdmntn; Music.

WILLIAMS, MANDO R; Live Oak HS; Live Oak, CA; (2); JV Ftbl; JV Tennis; Cal ST U Chico.

WILLIAMS, MARA H; Del Mar HS; San Jose, CA; (2); Girl Scts; Intnl Clb; Key Clb; Chorus; School Musical; Var Swmmng; Svc Awd; Mdrgls; Grl Sct Slvr Awd; Tchr.

WILLIAMS, MARCUS J; John F Kennedy HS; Richmond, CA; (1); Teachers Aide; Faculty Stu Of Yr; Outstndng Frnch Stu; Outstndng Bio Achvt.

WILLIAMS, MARISSA L; Channel Islands HS; Oxnard, CA; (2); Art Clb; Drill Tm; VP Frsh Cls; VP Soph Cls; Hist Stu Cncl; Powder Puff Ftbl; Hon Roll; Prfct Atten Awd; Devry; Acctg.

WILLIAMS, MARK A; Estancia HS; Costa Mesa, CA; (3); Church Yth Grp; Cmnty Wkr; Drama Clb; Ski Clb; Thesps; Acpl Chr; Chorus; Church Choir; School Musical; School Play; Care Kids; Vocal Ensmbl Pres; UC Berkeley; Bus.

WILLIAMS, MATT P; Irvine HS; Irvine, CA; (2); Stu Cncl; JV Bsktbl; High Hon Roll; Pres Acad Fit Awd; CA Schlstc Fed; Golden St Alg Exam Hgh Hnrs; UCLA; Phys Thrpy.

WILLIAMS, MATTHEW K; Hesperia HS; Hesperia, CA; (3); 14/571; Boy Scts; Treas Sec Computer Clb; FBLA; Teachers Aide; High Hon Roll; Hon Roll; Phys.

WILLIAMS, MELANIE B; Mira Mesa HS; San Diego, CA; (3); 32/777; Church Yth Grp; Drama Clb; Office Aide; Band; School Play; Stage Crew; Hon Roll; Pres Acad Fit Awd; Freedoms Foundation Leadership Conference At Valley Forge.

WILLIAMS, MELISSA A; Ventura HS; Ventura, CA; (4); Church Yth Grp; Pep Clb; SADD; Stu Cncl; Cit Awd; Hon Roll; Presdntl Classroom; Intl Stu Ldrshp Pgm; CA Assn Of Stu Cncls.

WILLIAMS, MICHELE Y; Novato HS; Novato, CA; (1); Spanish Clb; Band; Mrchg Band; Hon Roll; Eqstrn Clb; UC Davis; Vet.

WILLIAMS, MICHELLE M; Casa Roble Fundamental HS; Citrus Heights, CA; (3); 107/370; French Clb; VP Jr Cls; Hon Roll; Gymnstcs; Brdcstng.

WILLIAMS, MIKE D; Pt Loma HS; San Diego, CA; (3); 80/431; Var Bsbl; JV Ftbl; JV Wrstlng; Crmnlgy.

WILLIAMS, MIKELL; Folsom HS; Folsom, CA; (3); Church Yth Grp; GAA; Pep Clb; Var Cheerldng; Var Trk; Var Vllybl; High Hon Roll; Pres Acad Fit Awd; Sec Stu Cncl; U CA Riverside; Bus.

WILLIAMS, MONICA; San Pedro HS; Los Angeles, CA; (3); FBLA; Drill Tm; School Musical; Modern Dance; Bus Admin.

WILLIAMS, MONIK; Santa Cruz HS; Santa Cruz, CA; (2); GAA; Flag Corp; Mrchg Band; Yrbk; Bsktbl; Trk; Hon Roll; Black Stu United Union VP; Georgetown.

WILLIAMS, MYEISHA C; Woodrow Wilson HS; San Francisco, CA; (3); GAA; Ski Clb; Scl Workr.

WILLIAMS, NATALIE M; Apple Valley HS; Apple Valley, CA; (2); Church Yth Grp; Cmnty Wkr; Hosp Aide; High Hon Roll; Hon Roll; Chld Psych.

WILLIAMS, NATALIE R; Hawthorne HS; Hawthorne, CA; (1); Church Yth Grp; Math Clb; Pep Clb; JV Cheerldng; Cit Awd; Advncd Prfrmng Dance; APPI; Actng & Modlng John Casablancas Coll; UCLA; Pedtrcn.

WILLIAMS, NATOSHA; Vallejo SR HS; Vallejo, CA; (2); ROTC; SADD; Band; Color Guard; Flag Corp; Mrchg Band; Cheerldng; Hon Roll; San Francisco ST; Crmnl Jstce.

WILLIAMS, NIA B; Hogan HS; Vallejo, CA; (2); JA; Office Aide; Pep Clb; SADD; Teachers Aide; Rptr Nwsp; VP Frsh Cls; VP Stu Cncl; Gov Hon Prg Awd; Hon Roll; U CA Berkeley; Law.

WILLIAMS, NICOLE; O'farrell SCPA HS; San Diego, CA; (2); 1/180; Church Yth Grp; Dance Clb; JA; Spanish Clb; School Play; Stage Crew; Sec Frsh Cls; Sec Soph Cls; Hon Roll; SADD & CJSF Clbs; UCLA; Med.

WILLIAMS, NICOLE A; Loara HS; Anaheim, CA; (4); Office Aide; Q&S; Drill Tm; Ed Nwsp; Yrbk; Engl Biography Achvt Cert; CA ST-FULLERTON; Engl.

WILLIAMS, NIKKI; Thomas Downey HS; Modesto, CA; (2); Rptr FFA; Teachers Aide; Chorus; School Musical; Rptr Nwsp; Intrml Trk; Englsh Achvt Awd; Ag Awd Soil & Wtr Mngmnt; Fresno St; Ag.

WILLIAMS, OLEVIA J; Hogan SR HS; Vallejo, CA; (2); Church Yth Grp; Office Aide; Chorus; Church Choir; Rptr Yrbk; Hon Roll; Play Piano; Bd Usher; Schl Choir Dir; Court Rprtr.

WILLIAMS, OLYMPIA C; Independence HS; San Jose, CA; (2); Dance Clb; Intnl Clb; Band; Color Guard; Mrchg Band; Pep Band; High Hon Roll; Hon Roll; Spcl Achvt Awd Outstndng Prfrmnc; Spcl Awd Outstndng Prsvrnc; Corp Law.

WILLIAMS, PAUL; Poway HS; Poway, CA; (3); Church Yth Grp; Key Clb; Science Clb; Spanish Clb; Tennis; DAR Awd; High Hon Roll; NHS; U Of CA; Biolgl Sci.

WILLIAMS, PAULETTE; Washington HS; Los Angeles, CA; (4); 30/500; Church Yth Grp; Band; Drill Tm; High Hon Roll; Yng Clbk Schlrs; Long Beach ST; Nurse.

WILLIAMS, PRINCE R; Morningside HS; Inglewood, CA; (2); VP Frsh Cls; VP Soph Cls; Bsktbl; JV Vllybl; Hon Roll; Comp Engr.

WILLIAMS, RACHEL J; Woodcrest Christian HS; Riverside, CA; (3); Office Aide; School Play; Var Cheerldng; Var Powder Puff Ftbl; JV Sftbl; JV Vllybl; Hon Roll; Comp Engrng.

WILLIAMS, RACHEL S; Bella Vista HS; Fair Oaks, CA; (3); 38/363; JA; Letterman Clb; SADD; Teachers Aide; Varsity Clb; Var Bsktbl; Var Sftbl; Var Capt Vllybl; Cit Awd; Hon Roll; Omaha Woodmen Life Ins Society Outstndng Prfcncy Amer Hstry Awd; All Leag Vlybl, Bsktbl & Sftbl 90; Criminal Justice.

WILLIAMS, RAINA D; The Head-Royce Schl; Oakland, CA; (4); VP Church Yth Grp; Cmnty Wkr; Key Clb; Hon Roll; Wellesley Bk Awd; Cmmnd Natl Outstndng Negro Stdt; Piano; Law.

WILLIAMS, RASHIDA M; St Michaels HS; Inglewood, CA; (3); Church Yth Grp; Drill Tm; School Musical; Hon Roll; UCLA; Psych.

WILLIAMS, REBECCA L; Brookside Christian HS; Stockton, CA; (3); 1/33; Church Yth Grp; Teachers Aide; Rep Frsh Cls; Sec Sr Cls; Stu Cncl; Var Capt Bsktbl; Var L Sftbl; Var Capt Vllybl; High Hon Roll; Hon Roll; MVP Bsktbl Vly Sftbl; Golden Knight Awd Foru Outstndng Academics & Athletics; Missionary Work Mexico; Phys Ed.

WILLIAMS, REGINA; Skyline HS; Oakland, CA; (2); Church Yth Grp; GAA; Hosp Aide; Teachers Aide; Chorus; Church Choir; Orch; School Musical; Nwsp; Trk; Cit Awd; Overall Chmpnshp-Athltcs; U CA-DAVIS; Med Sci.

WILLIAMS, RICHARD L; Seaside HS; Seaside, CA; (3); Church Yth Grp; VP Soph Cls; VP Jr Cls; Pres Stu Cncl; Var JV Ftbl; Powder Puff Ftbl; Score Keeper; Wt Lftg; High Hon Roll; Bus.

WILLIAMS, SARAH K; Yosemite Union HS; Coarsegold, CA; (3); Church Yth Grp; GAA; Spanish Clb; Varsity Clb; Band; Jazz Band; Pep Band; Bsktbl; Sftbl; Hon Roll; Jobs Daughters.

WILLIAMS, SARAH L; Twenty-Nine Palms HS; Twentynine Palms, CA; (3); 10/200; Pres Church Yth Grp; Drama Clb; Spanish Clb; Band; Church Choir; Mrchg Band; School Musical; School Play; Stu Cncl; Prfct Atten Awd; Missions Liberty U; Chrstn Cnsr.

WILLIAMS, SCOTT A; Southern California Christian HS; Anaheim, CA; (2); Chess Clb; Var L Bsbl; Var L Bsktbl; Cheerldng; JV Ftbl; Cit Awd; Hon Roll; Mst Insprtnl Bsktbl; 2 Yrs All Leag Crs Cntgry & MVP; 2nd Tm All Leag Bsbl; Comp Sci.

WILLIAMS, SETH; Manteca HS; Manteca, CA; (1); 15/457; Church Yth Grp; FFA; JV Bsbl; JV Ftbl; JV Wrstlng; High Hon Roll; Hon Roll; Babe Ruth Smmr Bsbl & All Star Tm; U Of TN.

WILLIAMS, SETH K; Turlock HS; Turlock, CA; (3); 16/525; AFS; Treas Key Clb; Ski Clb; Orch; Intrml Bsbl; Var L Swmmng; High Hon Roll; Pres Acad Fit Awd; Interact Club Treas; Water Polo Var Ltr; Block T Club Treas; Ortho Surgeon.

WILLIAMS, SHAELER A; Junipero Serra HS; San Diego, CA; (3); Church Yth Grp; Letterman Clb; Ski Clb; Lcrss; Hon Roll; Pres Schlr; Humbolt ST; Bus.

WILLIAMS, SHANNON B; Fontana HS; Rialto, CA; (3); Bsktbl; Wt Lftg; UCLA; Hstry.

WILLIAMS, SHEILA; Bassett HS; La Puente, CA; (2); Computer Clb; French Clb; Girl Scts; Office Aide; Nwsp; Powder Puff Ftbl; Bassett; Real Estate.

WILLIAMS, SHENAY R; Hogan SR HS; Vallejo, CA; (2); Church Yth Grp; Chorus; Church Choir; Var Trk; Var Vllybl; Hon Roll; Reading; Gospel Music; Tuskegece; OB/Gyn.

WILLIAMS IV, SHERMAN A; Redwood Christian HS; Castro Valley, CA; (3); Am Leg Boys St; Aud/Vis; Church Yth Grp; Debate Tm; Drama Clb; Letterman Clb; Speech Tm; Acpl Chr; Chorus; Church Choir; TV Production; UCLA; Film.

WILLIAMS, STACI A; Huntington Beach HS; Huntington Beach, CA; (3); Church Yth Grp; Hosp Aide; Drill Tm; Intrml Cheerldng; Medcl.

WILLIAMS, STACY N; Ganesha HS; Pomona, CA; (3); Office Aide; VP Sr Cls; Rep Stu Cncl; JV Stat Bsktbl; Hon Roll.

WILLIAMS, STEFANIE L; Oakdale HS; Oakdale, CA; (3); FFA; Spanish Clb; Speech Tm; SADD; Stu Cncl; JV Bsktbl; Var Powder Puff Ftbl; Var Score Keeper; JV Sftbl; JV Var Vllybl; Reprtr For FFA; Bus Schlrshp To Stanislaus St Bus Wk; Peer Tutrng And Cnclng; Fresno ST; Ag Mktg.

WILLIAMS, STEPHEN; Arlington HS; Riverside, CA; (3); 27/450; Pres Frsh Cls; Stu Cncl; JV Var Ftbl; Var L Tennis; Hon Roll; Rnnr Up Boys St; Pepperdine Yth Ldrshp Smnr Smmr Schlrshp; 1 Yr Mem CSF; UCR; Bio.

WILLIAMS, TAIJUANA K; West HS; Bakersfield, CA; (4); 57/389; Church Yth Grp; Letterman Clb; Bsktbl; Intrml Powder Puff Ftbl; Var Trk; JV Vllybl; Hon Roll; MESA; CA ST U; Civil Engrng.

WILLIAMS, TAMIKA; A Lincoln HS; San Francisco, CA; (4); 30/444; Drama Clb; FTA; Teachers Aide; Acpl Chr; Phtg Yrbk; JV Bsktbl; JV Crs Cntry; JV Trk; Hon Roll; NHS; San Francisco ST U; Radio.

WILLIAMS, TAMMY; Novato HS; San Rafael, CA; (3); Church Yth Grp; Cmnty Wkr; Drama Clb; Teachers Aide; School Play; Pres Soph Cls; Stu Cncl; Bsktbl; Swmmng; High Hon Roll; Pres Yth Alive; UCLA; Finance.

WILLIAMS, TANISHA G; St Pope Pius X HS; Lynwood, CA; (3); Math Clb; Band; High Hon Roll; Dentistry.

WILLIAMS, TAWNDRA S; San Benito HS; San Juan Bautista, CA; (1); 20/468; Cheerldng; Hon Roll; Stanford U; Art.

WILLIAMS, TEDRA S.; Manteca HS; Manteca, CA; (2); 19/420; Cmnty Wkr; Pep Clb; Variety Show; Pres Frsh Cls; Pres Soph Cls; Capt JV Cheerldng; Hon Roll; CSF; Engl Dept Awd; Phys Ed Dept Awd; Fresno ST; Engl.

WILLIAMS, TERA J; Highlands HS; North Highlands, CA; (2); Teachers Aide; Cit Awd; High Hon Roll; Hon Roll; Pres Schlr; Outstndng Engl Stu Certs; Jrnlst.

WILLIAMS, TERESA R; Tracy Joint Union HS; Tracy, CA; (3); 99/496; Church Yth Grp; Debate Tm; French Clb; FFA; NFL; Speech Tm; School Play; Lit Mag; Trk; Hon Roll; Fresno ST Coll; Phys Thrpy.

WILLIAMS, THOMAS C; Menlo-Atherton HS; Menlo Park, CA; (4); 71/356; German Clb; Latin Clb; Band; Jazz Band; Off Jr Cls; Bsktbl; Socr; Tennis; Hstry.

WILLIAMS, TONI; Valley View HS; Moreno Valley, CA; (2); High Hon Roll; Hon Roll; Voice Dem Awd; UCR-RCC; Elem Tchr.

WILLIAMS, TRICIA RAQUEL; Yucca Valley HS; Yucca Valley, CA; (4); 2/150; Church Yth Grp; FBLA; Bsktbl; Swmmng; High Hon Roll; Pres Acad Fit Awd; Sal; Dance Tm Capt; CSF; Univ Club; CA Lutheran U; Commnctns.

WILLIAMS, TRINA D; Woodland HS; Woodland, CA; (3); 4-H; French Clb; Ed Yrbk; Stat Wrstlng; Humbolt ST; Jrnlsm.

WILLIAMS, VAUGHN M; Washington Prep; Los Angeles, CA; (2); Church Yth Grp; Drama Clb; Office Aide; Acpl Chr; Chorus; Church Choir; School Musical; School Play; Stage Crew; Nwsp; Most Imprvd Stu All Arnd Awd; UCLA; Telecmmnctns.

WILLIAMS, WAYNE E; Clovis HS; Clovis, CA; (2); Crs Cntry; Trk; Wt Lftg; Hon Roll; Notre Dame.

WILLIAMS, YORANNA D; Skyline HS; Oakland, CA; (2); Pres Church Yth Grp; Dance Clb; Hosp Aide; Pres Church Choir; Pres Frsh Cls; Trk; Cit Awd; Hon Roll; Pres Acad Fit Awd; Pediatrics.

WILLIAMS, YVONNE; Seaside HS; Fort Ord, CA; (3); FBLA; JCL; Sec Chorus; Rptr Nwsp; Phtg Yrbk; Var Trk; High Hon Roll; Sec Jr NHS; Pres Acad Fit Awd.

WILLIAMS-LA FOUNTAIN, DENISE; Rio Linda Adventist Acad; Marysville, CA; (3); Church Yth Grp; Cmnty Wkr; Varsity Clb; Spanish Clb; Variety Show; Off Soph Cls; Dorm Pres 90; Loma Linda U 1st Medcl Stu Outlook Pgm Smmr 89; La Sierra-Loma Linda U; Pre-Med.

WILLIAMSON, CARLIN R; Campolindo HS; Moraga, CA; (4); 39/236; Church Yth Grp; Intnl Clb; SADD; Acpl Chr; School Musical; Variety Show; Rep Jr Cls; JV Cheerldng; Hon Roll; Life Time Stu CA Schlrshp Fed; Prfrmng Theater Arts.

WILLIAMSON, CHRISTIE M; Woodside HS; Woodside, CA; (2); Library Aide; JV Tennis; Hon Roll; Rep Soph Cls; Woodside Pony Club; UC Davis; Vet Med.

WILLIAMSON, DALE; York Schl; Salinas, CA; (4); German Clb; Latin Clb; Math Clb; Math Tm; Science Clb; Yrbk; Var Crs Cntry; Var Golf; Var Trk; Hon Roll; Gmi; Elec Engrng.

WILLIAMSON, ELIZABETAH A; Redwood Christian HS; Hayward, CA; (2); 5/65; Church Yth Grp; Chorus; School Play; Sec Soph Cls; JV Bsktbl; Hon Roll; Piano.

WILLIAMSON, JOANNA; El Camino Real HS; West Hills, CA; (2); Church Yth Grp; Hon Roll; Poetry Club; Frgn Exchng To Frnc; Camp Cnslr; UCSD; Engl Lang.

WILLIAMSON, JULIETTE A; El Toro HS; El Toro, CA; (3); German Clb; Drill Tm; Hon Roll; Excllnc Awd German; 1st Deg Black Belt Tae Kwon Do; 2nd Deg Black Kenpo Karate; Teach Karate.

WILLIAMSON, LAURENCE D; Kennedy HS; Granada Hills, CA; (2); Boy Scts; Cmnty Wkr; JA; Band; Tennis; Camp Cnslr; Cal ST; Writer.

WILLIAMSON, MENDI; Capital Christian HS; Orangevale, CA; (2); Church Yth Grp; FCA; Office Aide; Pep Clb; Church Choir; Treas Soph Cls; Var L Bsktbl; JV Vllybl; High Hon Roll; Hon Roll; CSF; Stanford; Med.

WILLIAMSON, NATHAN E; Fort Bragg HS; Ft Bragg, CA; (4); 30/121; SADD; Sequoia Inst; Mech.

WILLIAMSON, PHILLIP D; North Monterey County HS; Salinas, CA; (2); Chess Clb; Church Yth Grp; German Clb; Hon Roll; Law.

WILLIAMSON, STACY R; Cypress HS; Cypress, CA; (2); Cmnty Wkr; Drama Clb; Library Aide; Office Aide; Office Aide; Band; Mrchg Band; Pep Band; Hon Roll; U Of Southern CA; Music.

WILLIAMSON, TRACY L; Turlock HS; Turlock, CA; (3); 120/544; Pres 4-H; Mgr(s); Var JV Sftbl; 4-H Awd; CA Cngrssnl Awd; 4-H Stanislaus Cnty All Star.

WILLIE, KRISTEN C; Santa Clara HS; Santa Clara, CA; (3); 15/369; Cmnty Wkr; Hosp Aide; Spanish Clb; Teachers Aide; Yrbk; Elem Ed.

WILLIE, KRISTEN R; Whittier Christian HS; La Habra, CA; (4); 8/179; VP Church Yth Grp; French Clb; Church Choir; School Musical; Crs Cntry; High Hon Roll; Ballet Cls & Prfrmncs; Cert Of Mert Tstng For Flute & Piano; Elem Tchr.

WILLINGHAM, MELISA D; Paraclete HS; Lancaster, CA; (3); Church Yth Grp; Key Clb; Church Choir; School Play; Yrbk; Stu Cncl; Var Sftbl; High Hon Roll; GATE; Educ.

WILLIS, DAVID A; John F Kennedy HS; Buena Park, CA; (3); Drama Clb; Teachers Aide; Chorus; School Play; Citizen Bee; U CA; Comp Sci.

WILLIS, DONALD K; Cabrillo HS; Lompoc, CA; (3); 68/213; Am Leg Boys St; Church Yth Grp; FCA; Letterman Clb; Off Sr Cls; Stu Cncl; Stat Bsktbl; Var Capt Ftbl; Var Trk; Hon Roll; 3rd Natl Jr Olympics Discus 89; Camp MVP All Star; U Of WA; Aerontcl Engrng.

WILLIS, FLOYD J; Washington Prep HS; Los Angeles, CA; (3); Letterman Clb; Teachers Aide; Stage Crew; Ftbl; Trk; Wt Lftg; Hon Roll.

WILLIS, GREG J; Leland HS; San Jose, CA; (2); Boy Scts; Red Cross Aide; JV Golf; Hon Roll; Var Water Polo; Aerontcl Engrng.

WILLIS, HEATHER M; Don Antonio Lugo HS; Chino, CA; (3); French Clb; Teachers Aide; Chorus; Stage Crew; Hon Roll; Boston U; Interpretr.

WILLIS, JAMES; Montclair HS; Montclair, CA; (3); Var Capt Bsktbl; High Hon Roll; Notre Dame; Poltcl Sci.

WILLIS, MARY JANE B; St Marys Acad; Los Angeles, CA; (4); Church Yth Grp; Cmnty Wkr; JA; SADD; Varsity Clb; Church Choir; School Play; Stage Crew; Variety Show; Yrbk; UC Santa Barbara; Visual Arts.

WILLIS, OLIVIA P; Edison HS; Stockton, CA; (3); French Clb; GAA; Temple Yth Grp; Off Sr Cls; Socr; Swmmng; French Hon Soc; Hon Roll; NHS; Prfct Atten Awd; UC Davis; Veterinarian.

WILLIS, STARLA L; Marshall Fundamental HS; Altadena, CA; (1); Cmnty Wkr; Variety Show; Pres Acad Fit Awd; UCLA; Law.

WILLMARTH, JOEL C; Modesto HS; Modesto, CA; (2); Drama Clb; 4-H; Var L Swmmng; 4-H Awd; JV Waterpolo; 4-H Exchng Pgm; US Pony Club; Stanford; Bus.

WILLMON, LEE; Sonora HS; Groveland, CA; (3); 19/309; 4-H; German Clb; Letterman Clb; Var Bsbl; Var Bsktbl; 4-H Awd; High Hon Roll; Sprts Med.

WILLOUGHBY, CRAIG; Berkeley Hall Schl; Reseda, CA; (1); Church Yth Grp; Stage Crew; Yrbk; Treas Stu Cncl; Bsktbl; Schlrshp Awd 1st Semstr Frshmn; Airpln Pilot.

WILLOUGHBY, GEOFF M; Del Campo HS; Citrus Heights, CA; (2); 44/460; Ski Clb; SADD; Varsity Clb; Band; Mrchg Band; JV Crs Cntry; Var L Trk; Hon Roll; Vrsty Lttr; Med.

WILLS, RONALD H; Rim Of The World HS; Running Springs, CA; (3); 1/435; Church Yth Grp; Rep Band; L Orch; High Hon Roll; Otstndng Frshm Mscn.

WILLSON, BRYAN; Moreno Valley HS; Moreno Valley, CA; (4); 13/400; Math Clb; Ed Nwsp; Stu Cncl; Hon Roll; Ntl Merit Ltr; Pres Acad Fit Awd; CA Schlrshp Federation; United States Academmic Decathlong; Bank Of Americ A Awd-History; U Of CA San Diego; Engineering.

WILLSON, LISA; Sonora HS; Sonora, CA; (4); 6/297; Church Yth Grp; Hosp Aide; Treas Spanish Clb; Speech Tm; Acpl Chr; JV Bsktbl; High Hon Roll; Kiwanis Awd; Pres Acad Fit Awd; AWANA Leader; Cal Poly San Luis Obispo; Med.

WILLWEBER, STEPHEN; Los Angeles Lutheran HS; Granada Hills, CA; (4); 1/23; Church Yth Grp; Letterman Clb; Off Jr Cls; Rep Sr Cls; Var Capt Bsktbl; Var Crs Cntry; Var Socr; Var Trk; High Hon Roll; NHS; Chrch Acolyte & Usher; CA Poly; Civil Engrng.

WILLWERTH, JULI M; Walnut HS; Walnut, CA; (2); 81/479; GAA; Key Clb; Letterman Clb; Varsity Clb; Rptr Nwsp; Stu Cncl; Var L Crs Cntry; Var L Socr; Var L Trk; Hon Roll; Pres Phys Ftnss Awd; GATE; Envrnmntl Club POWER; Jrnlsm.

WILMETH, STEPHANIE; Kingsburg HS; Kingsburg, CA; (2); 10/268; Church Yth Grp; FFA; GAA; Off Soph Cls; Capt Bsktbl; Trk; Cit Awd; Hon Roll; Lion Awd; ST Bus Chmpnshp Tm-Frm Bus; Mst Insprtnl Bsktbl Awd; Cmmnty Bsktbl Coach; Cal Poly San Luis; Agribus.

WILMOTH, JOSHUA C; Clovis HS; Clovis, CA; (1); Drama Clb; School Play; Hon Roll; Cal Poly San Luis Obispo; Archc.

WILNAI, IRIS; Homestead HS; Sunnyvale, CA; (2); Pres Temple Yth Grp; Piano; Flk Dncng-Israeli; Israeli Scouts; Psych.

WILSON, AARON R; Bishop O'dowd HS; Oakland, CA; (2); Boy Scts; Ski Clb; Stage Crew; JV Ftbl; JV Trk; Hon Roll; Black Stu Union; Jack & Jill Of Am; UCLA; Law.

WILSON, ALICIA D; Hogan SR HS; Vallejo, CA; (3); Church Yth Grp; Drama Clb; Spanish Clb; SADD; Teachers Aide; Nwsp; JV Sftbl; Hon Roll; NHS; Prfct Atten Awd; Essay Comptn Awds; Psycht.

WILSON, ALISON W; Live Oak HS; San Jose, CA; (4); French Clb; SADD; Teachers Aide; School Play; Rep Stu Cncl; High Hon Roll; Hon Roll; Peer Tutoring Pgm; U Of NM.

WILSON, AMANDA; Brethren Christian HS; Long Beach, CA; (3); Church Yth Grp; GAA; Letterman Clb; Pep Clb; Teachers Aide; Varsity Clb; Acpl Chr; Chorus; Church Choir; School Musical; Biola; Law.

WILSON, AMBER F; North Salinas HS; Salinas, CA; (4); 76/380; Dance Clb; Office Aide; Stu Cncl; Score Keeper; Cit Awd; High Hon Roll; Hon Roll; Hartnell Schlrshp; Hartnell JC; Psych.

WILSON, AMY; Santa Rosa HS; Santa Rosa, CA; (4); 64/530; Church Yth Grp; Debate Tm; 4-H; FFA; JA; Speech Tm; Cit Awd; 4-H Awd; High Hon Roll; St Schlr; St Champn Farm Records Team FFA; FFA Spcl Srvc Awd; CSF; UC Davis; Intl Ag.

WILSON, ANGELA T; Crawford HS; San Diego, CA; (2); Church Yth Grp; Off Soph Cls; Mgr(s); Hon Roll; SDSU; Bus Adm.

WILSON, ANJEANETTE; Yucaipa HS; Canada, CA; (1); Church Yth Grp; Spanish Clb; Drill Tm; Hon Roll; High Hon Roll.

WILSON, ANN; Alta Loma HS; Cucamonga, CA; (3); Hon Roll; Chaffey Coll; Nurse.

WILSON, BARRY D; Dorsey HS; Los Angeles, CA; (3); ROTC; Mrchg Band; Ftbl; Wt Lftg; Cmptr.

WILSON, BRADFORD W; Mt Whitney HS; Visalia, CA; (3); Church Yth Grp; French Clb; FBLA; Office Aide; Band; JV Trk; Fresno ST U; Physcics.

WILSON, BRANDI M; Torrey Pines HS; San Diego, CA; (3); AFS; Cmnty Wkr; Intnl Clb; Office Aide; Ski Clb; SADD; Flag Corp; Stage Crew; Mgr(s); Swmmng; New Commrs Clb; Yth Endng Hngr; Actvst Clb; San Diego ST U; Sci.

WILSON, BRETT; Antelope Valley HS; Lancaster, CA; (3); 122/631; Boy Scts; Church Yth Grp; 4-H; Letterman Clb; SADD; JV Bsbl; Capt VP Wrstlng; Job As Busboy; UCLA; Engr.

WILSON, CARI L; Manteca HS; Manteca, CA; (1); 40/411; Band; Mrchg Band; Hon Roll; Coach Yth Ftbl & Chrldng Orgnztn.

WILSON, CINDY M; Arlington HS; Riverside, CA; (3); Church Yth Grp; Cmnty Wkr; Girl Scts; Hosp Aide; Teachers Aide; Chorus; Church Choir; Hon Roll; Travel Agency.

WILSON, COLLEEN J; San Dieguito HS; Encinitas, CA; (2); Drama Clb; German Clb; School Play; Stage Crew; JV Fld Hcky; Hon Roll; People To People Ambssdr Pgm; Bethlehem Luth Teens Chrch Yth Grp; CSF; Frgn Svc.

WILSON, CRYSTAL; Bloomington HS; Colton, CA; (2); 6/330; Chess Clb; Church Yth Grp; Cmnty Wkr; Dance Clb; Debate Tm; Drama Clb; English Clb; FTA; GAA; Girl Scts; Pgnt Wnng; Friday Night Live; Grls Leag Clb; San Diego ST; Elem Educ.

WILSON, DAVID C; Moorpark HS; Moorpark, CA; (3); 16/243; Drama Clb; Pres Key Clb; School Musical; High Hon Roll; NHS; Ntl Merit Ltr; CSF.

WILSON, DEBRA; Acalanes HS; Martinez, CA; (4); 60/300; Sec AFS; Church Yth Grp; Drama Clb; SADD; School Play; Treas Jr Cls; Treas Sr Cls; Sftbl; Cit Awd; DAR Awd; Srptmst Ctznshp Awd; UC Davis; Physlgy.

WILSON, DENETTE M; Brawley Union HS; Brawley, CA; (3); 15/340; 4-H; SADD; Teachers Aide; Varsity Clb; Yrbk; VP Jr Cls; VP Sr Cls; Bsktbl; Powder Puff Ftbl; Tennis; Jr Fair Board; AFS Exchange To Finland; Pediatrics.

WILSON, DENISE A; Warren HS; Downey, CA; (3); Church Yth Grp; Key Clb; VP Frsh Cls; JV L Bsktbl; JV Score Keeper; Var L Tennis; Hon Roll; USTA Rnked 47 88-89, Rnked 74 90-91; San Gabriel Vly Lg Ten Chmpnshps Wnnr; Stu Month; UCSD; Ortho Srgn.

WILSON, DOUGLAS F; Banning HS; Cabazon, CA; (4); 84/193; Chess Clb; Church Yth Grp; Cmnty Wkr; Computer Clb; Chorus; Church Choir; Southern CA Coll; Law.

WILSON, DUSTY L; Woodland HS; Woodland, CA; (3); Office Aide; Teachers Aide; Bsktbl; JV Crs Cntry; JV Sftbl; JV Vllybl; High Hon Roll; Hon Roll; Pres Acad Fit Awd; CSF; Young Republicans; HERO; UC Irvine; Aeronautical Engr.

WILSON, EDWARD L; Montgomery HS; Santa Rosa, CA; (2); Boy Scts; Church Yth Grp; Spanish Clb; JV Ftbl; JV Trk; Hon Roll; Pres Acad Fit Awd; Outstndng 9ty Grdr Awd; Excllnt Span Stu Awd; BYU.

WILSON, ELIZABETH E; Tracy Joint Union HS; Tracy, CA; (2); 110/486; FHA; Band; Mrchg Band; Socr; Tennis; Hon Roll; Friends Of Spcl Olympcs; Purdue; Interior Dsgn.

WILSON, ERIC M; Oakdale HS; Oakdale, CA; (2); FBLA; Hon Roll; Miami U In FL; Law.

WILSON, ERIN K; Napa HS; Napa, CA; (3); 5/350; Cmnty Wkr; Hosp Aide; Key Clb; Band; Tennis; Hon Roll; JR Girls ST; Gldn ST Exam Geom Hnrs; CSF; Cal Poly; Math.

WILSON, FRANCHON; Lincoln Prep HS; San Diego, CA; (3); FTA; Spanish Clb; School Play; Rep Soph Cls; Rep Stu Cncl; JV Var Cheerldng; Hon Roll; Yng Life; Girard Hnr Pgm; Psych.

WILSON, FREDRICK A; Corona SR HS; Corona, CA; (3); Boy Scts; Church Yth Grp; Var L Swmmng; Cit Awd; Hon Roll; Prfct Atten Awd; Pres Acad Fit Awd; BYU; Engrng.

WILSON, GREG; Yucaipa HS; Yucaipa, CA; (3); 2/350; Church Yth Grp; Debate Tm; Key Clb; Math Clb; NFL; Spanish Clb; Speech Tm; Sec Band; Jazz Band; Mrchg Band; Sci Smnr US Air For Acad; Biola U.

WILSON, GRETCHEN Y; Calaveras HS; San Andreas, CA; (3); 7/174; Church Yth Grp; SADD; Chorus; Church Choir; JV Vllybl; Stat Wrstlng; Cit Awd; High Hon Roll; Hon Roll; RCP Med Trng.

WILSON, HEATHER D; Elk Grove HS; Elk Grove, CA; (4); 179/484; Chorus; Swing Chorus; Score Keeper; Var Socr; Prfct Atten Awd; All Delta Leag Hnrbl Mntn Sccr; USA Sccr Team To Europe; UC Davis; Med.

WILSON, HELEN R; El Toro HS; El Toro, CA; (3); Debate Tm; Sec Chrmn French Clb; VP German Clb; Speech Tm; Var L Socr; Var Sftbl; High Hon Roll; Ftbl Athl Trnr; Keywanettes; Orange Cnty Stu Advsry Cncl; USC; Law.

WILSON, HENRY L; Fontana HS; Fontana, CA; (3); Cmnty Wkr; Office Aide; Variety Show; Var Bsktbl; Var Trk; Var Ltr 89-90; Bstkbl & Trk Certs 89-90; Intl Bus.

WILSON, HOLLY; Ramona HS; Ramona, CA; (3); 4/280; FBLA; Pep Clb; Spanish Clb; SADD; Treas Soph Cls; VP Stu Cncl; Var Cheerldng; Var Sftbl; High Hon Roll; Earth Clb; Stu Ambssdr; Bus Admin.

WILSON, IAN C; Nogales HS; Walnut, CA; (3); Letterman Clb; Varsity Clb; Capt L Bsktbl; High Hon Roll; Pres Acad Fit Awd; Law.

WILSON, JAMES; Exeter Union HS; Exeter, CA; (3); 8/217; Am Leg Boys St; VP Pres Key Clb; Letterman Clb; Pres Band; Drm Mjr(t); Jazz Band; Pres Mrchg Band; Pep Band; Var Bsktbl; Var Diving; V Water Polo; Life CSF; 2nd Pl Grand Natls For Drum Major; USC; Bus.

WILSON, JAMES T; Silver Valley HS; Fort Irwin, CA; (3); Drama Clb; Spanish Clb; School Play; Var Capt Ftbl; Var Socr; Var Swmmng; Hon Roll.

WILSON, JASON; Moreno Valley HS; Lake Elsinore, CA; (4); Rptr Nwsp; JV Wrstlng; Hon Roll; Riverside CC; Comp.

WILSON, JASON B; Montgomery HS; Santa Rosa, CA; (2); Cmnty Wkr; JA; Spanish Clb; Band; Jazz Band; Mrchg Band; Pep Band; Hon Roll; Med.

WILSON, JEFF; Salinas HS; Salinas, CA; (4); 50/350; FFA; Ftbl; High Hon Roll; Hon Roll; Ag; Engrng; CA Poly; Ag.

WILSON, JEFF M; Mission Bay HS; San Diego, CA; (1); 155/413; Bsktbl; Ftbl; Hon Roll; Cmmrcl Artst.

WILSON, JENNIFER; Clovis West HS; Fresno, CA; (4); 10/540; Treas FBLA; Treas Intnl Clb; Math Clb; Var Cheerldng; Ntl Merit Ltr; Pres Acad Fit Awd; CSF Life Mem; Tandy Tech Scholar; 4th Pl Job Interview CA St FBLA Conf; U CA Los Angeles; Bus Econ.

WILSON, JENNIFER; Fairfield HS; Suisun, CA; (3); Key Clb; Pres Band; Pres Mrchg Band; Orch; Off Jr Cls; Hist Sr Cls; Sec Treas French Hon Soc; Gov Hon Prg Awd; High Hon Roll; Hon Roll; Soc For Humnties; USA Jr Statesmn Of Amer.

WILSON, JENNIFER D; Apple Valley HS; Apple Valley, CA; (1); French Clb; Pep Clb; Hon Roll; Fresno ST U; Chld Psych.

WILSON, JENNIFER J; San Marcos HS; San Marcos, CA; (3); Pep Clb; Teachers Aide; Variety Show; JV Var Cheerldng; Var Gym; Var Pom Pon; Socr; Hon Roll; Pres Acad Fit Awd; KY ST; Bio.

WILSON, JENNIFER L; Mater Dei HS; Cypress, CA; (2); Church Yth Grp; Cmnty Wkr; Drama Clb; Cypress Pop Warner Ftbl Chrldng Coach; Snorkeling; Penn ST U; Child Pysch.

WILSON, JENNIFER L; Ukiah HS; Redwood Valley, CA; (2); Church Yth Grp; French Clb; Band; Jazz Band; Mrchg Band; Pep Band; U C Davis.

WILSON, JERRY; Nevada Union HS; Penn Valley, CA; (4); High Hon Roll; Hon Roll; Prfct Atten Awd; Pres Acad Fit Awd; Bass Guitar; Sierra Coll; Elec Engrng.

WILSON, JOANNA E; Arlington HS; Riverside, CA; (3); ROTC; Chorus; Drill Tm; Nrsng.

WILSON, JOSHUA G; Shafter HS; Shafter, CA; (2); Treas Church Yth Grp; Var Golf; Wt Lftg; Hon Roll; Prfct Atten Awd; CSF; HS Radio Clb Pres & Fndr; Farmer.

WILSON, JOSHUA L; El Camino HS; Oceanside, CA; (3); Treas French Clb; JV Tennis; High Hon Roll; Gldn St Exam Geom High Hnrs; Math Stu Yr; JV Acadmc Leag 88-90; Elec Engrng.

WILSON, JULIE; Dublin HS; Dublin, CA; (3); 4/200; Cmnty Wkr; FBLA; Service Clb; Sec Jr Cls; Stu Cncl; Cheerldng; Trk; High Hon Roll; Hon Roll; CSF 3 Yrs; Golden St Exam Awd Alegbra, Geom; Acad Block; NS Cathletic Acad; Mock Trial 89-90; Animal Behavior.

WILSON, JULIE M; Bishop Union HS; Bishop, CA; (3); 4-H; FFA; Ski Clb; Teachers Aide; Bsbl; Gym; Vllybl; Wt Lftg; Hon Roll; PE Awds; Chrch Yth Grp; HS Rodeo Comptn Dist 9; U Of Reno; Physcl Thrpy.

WILSON, KATHERINE A; Mira Mesa HS; San Diego, CA; (2); 100/900; Church Yth Grp; Girl Scts; Library Aide; Spanish Clb; Teachers Aide; Chorus; School Play; Yrbk; JV Crs Cntry; JV Trk; Psych.

WILSON, KEITH; C K Mc Clatchy HS; Sacramento, CA; (3); 14/418; SADD; Ftbl; Golf; High Hon Roll; CA Poly; Arch.

WILSON, KIIA C; Moreno Valley HS; Moreno Vly, CA; (4); Church Yth Grp; FHA; Math Clb; Office Aide; Pep Clb; Speech Tm; Teachers Aide; Band; Church Choir; Mrchg Band; RCC; Bus Admin.

WILSON, KIMBERLY; Elk Grove HS; Elk Grove, CA; (4); Church Yth Grp; Cmnty Wkr; FHA; SADD; Teachers Aide; Acpl Chr; Co-Capt Cheerldng; Stus Reaching Out; All Amer Chrldr Awd; Reading; U C Davis; Bio.

WILSON, KIMBERLY M; Inglewood HS; Hawthorne, CA; (4); 4/500; Aud/Vis; Teachers Aide; Yrbk; Capt Cheerldng; High Hon Roll; Hon Roll; Ntl Merit Schol; Pres Schlr; Vlntr Cmp Cnslr Sci; Yng Blck Schlrs; Stanford; Math.

WILSON, LEVI D; Sonora HS; Sonora, CA; (2); Cmnty Wkr; SADD; Chorus; Music.

WILSON, LORNA S; Glendale HS; Glendale, CA; (2); Sec Church Yth Grp; Mgr(s); JV Swmmng; Theology.

WILSON, MARK A; Pater Noster HS; Los Angeles, CA; (2); #12 In Class; Nwsp; Yrbk; Bsktbl; JV Crs Cntry; Var Socr; JV Trk; Hon Roll; NEDT Awd; USC.

WILSON, MELISSA A; Torrey Pines HS; Del Mar, CA; (3); 121/422; Teachers Aide; JV Var Gym; JV Var Socr.

WILSON, MELISSA M; Presentation HS; San Jose, CA; (4); 1/135; Rep Church Yth Grp; Cmnty Wkr; Debate Tm; Drama Clb; Pres NFL; Service Clb; SADD; School Musical; School Play; Nwsp; Juvenile Justice Cmsnr; Dir Of Chldrns Mscls; Stanford U.

WILSON, MIASA SY; John F Kennedy HS; Richmond, CA; (3); Art Clb; Chorus; Diving; Rcrdng Artist.

WILSON, MICHAEL KEITH; Bear River HS; Grass Valley, CA; (2); Ski Clb; Var Tennis; Cit Awd; High Hon Roll; Pres Acad Fit Awd; V Ski Team.

WILSON, MICHELLE S; Ramona HS; Ramona, CA; (2); 10/350; Var Socr; Cit Awd; Hon Roll; Stanford.

WILSON, MITCHEL D; Shafter HS; Shafter, CA; (3); Ski Clb; Band; Jazz Band; Mrchg Band; Pep Band; School Play; Ed Yrbk; Socr; Tennis; High Hon Roll; Gldn Empr Suns Yth Band Astrla, Cnda 88 & 89; Hnrs Hstry Al-Cnty Cnstitutn Cmptn 5th Pl; Cal Poly San Luis Obispo; Engr.

WILSON, NATHAN H; Lindsay HS; Lindsay, CA; (3); 7/190; Am Leg Boys St; Letterman Clb; Ski Clb; Spanish Clb; Rep Sr Cls; Capt Bsktbl; Capt Ftbl; Capt Trk; Hon Roll; Geom Golden St Exam Hnrs; UCSB; Financial Advsr.

WILSON, NICOLE; Mayfield SR HS; Pasadena, CA; (3); Church Yth Grp; Cmnty Wkr; GAA; Ski Clb; Varsity Clb; Bsktbl; Swmmng; Tennis; Trk; Hon Roll; USC; Law.

WILSON, ODESSA F; Lincoln HS; Stockton, CA; (2); Church Yth Grp; FCA; SADD; Band; Jazz Band; Mrchg Band; Pep Band; Trk; Hon Roll; Sacramento ST; Music.

WILSON, PAMELA M; Whitney HS; Lakewood, CA; (2); Church Yth Grp; Cmnty Wkr; Key Clb; Spanish Clb; Band; Church Choir; Mrchg Band; Orch; Lit Mag; Hstry Day LA Sr Div Cty Fnlst; CA ST U Long Beach; Med Sci.

WILSON, PAUL A; Las Plumas HS; Oroville, CA; (4); 32/213; Cmnty Wkr; VP Pres French Clb; VP Pres Letterman Clb; Ski Clb; Pres Soph Cls; VP Pres Jr Cls; Capt Var Bsktbl; JV Ftbl; Capt Var Golf; Hon Roll; BUTTE JC; Arch.

WILSON, PEGGY; Arroyo HS; San Leandro, CA; (2); Drama Clb; School Play; Cheerldng; Pom Pon; Baton Twrlng Cmptve; CSUH; Actress.

WILSON, RAE L; Lemoore Union HS; Hanford, CA; (3); 24/323; Spanish Clb; Photo Clb VP; CSF; West Hill JC.

WILSON, REBECCA; International Studies Acad; San Francisco, CA; (2); GAA; Hosp Aide; VICA; High Hon Roll; Pres Acad Fit Awd; Intl Summit NM Essay & Interview Wnnr; Med.

WILSON, RICK K; Red Bluff Union HS; Red Bluff, CA; (3); 68/472; Computer Clb; FFA; Math Clb; Ski Clb; Stu Cncl; Wt Lftg; Ski Tm; US Coast Guard; Elec Tech.

WILSON, RUTH D; Trinity HS; Lewiston, CA; (2); AFS; Sec Church Yth Grp; Cmnty Wkr; German Clb; Pres Intnl Clb; Service Clb; Ski Clb; SADD; Chorus; Stu Cncl; Yth To Yth & Teen Work; Bicyclng, Back Pckng.

WILSON, RYAN J; Mira Mesa HS; San Diego, CA; (2); Aud/Vis; Rep Frsh Cls; Var Crs Cntry; Var Trk; Cit Awd; Hon Roll; Jr NHS; Prfct Atten Awd; Pres Acad Fit Awd; UCSD; Sanitation Engr.

WILSON, SCOTT LLORENS; Leffingwell Christian HS; La Palma, CA; (4); 2/50; Church Yth Grp; Drama Clb; Letterman Clb; Varsity Clb; L Var Ftbl; Tennis; Vllybl; Wt Lftg; High Hon Roll; Sal; Skating Club 86-87; Loyola Marymount U; Bus.

WILSON, SEAN E; Carson HS; Carson, CA; (2); Bsktbl; Hon Roll; Morehouse Coll; Seriffs Deputy.

WILSON, SHANNON M; Del Campo HS; Fair Oaks, CA; (3); 188/446; French Clb; Tennis; OR ST; Liberal Arts.

WILSON, SHARI L; Livermore Union HS; Livermore, CA; (2); Church Yth Grp; Church Choir; High Hon Roll; Hon Roll; Church Musicals/Drama.

WILSON, SHEKA; Leuzinger HS; Los Angeles, CA; (4); Cmnty Wkr; Pep Clb; Off Frsh Cls; Off Soph Cls; Off Jr Cls; Rep Sr Cls; Rep Stu Cncl; JV Var Cheerldng; Var Trk; Kiwanis Awd; El Camino; Nurse.

WILSON, SHERRI D; Chino HS; Chino, CA; (2); Church Yth Grp; FFA; Science Clb; Spanish Clb; Teachers Aide; JV Mgr(s); High Hon Roll; FFA Awd; CSF; Vet.

WILSON, SHONDELLE; Hogan SR HS; Vallejo, CA; (2); Model UN; SADD; Flag Corp; Rptr Yrbk; Hon Roll; Standford; Med.

WILSON, SONYA L; Lassen HS; Susanville, CA; (2); 22/200; Church Yth Grp; Drama Clb; Sec 4-H; VP FHA; VP Spanish Clb; Sec SADD; Church Choir; School Musical; Stage Crew; CSF; BYU.

WILSON, STEVEN; Los Alamitos HS; Los Alamitos, CA; (4); Boy Scts; Church Yth Grp; Cmnty Wkr; Intnl Clb; Science Clb; Service Clb; Chorus; School Musical; Hon Roll; NHS; Eagle Scout; Engrng.

WILSON, TERESSA C; Notre Dame HS; Mira Loma, CA; (1); 8/120; Church Yth Grp; Stat Bsktbl; Score Keeper; High Hon Roll; Hon Roll.

WILSON, TERI D; Brawley Union HS; Brawley, CA; (3); 12/400; Cmnty Wkr; Service Clb; VP Treas SADD; Variety Show; Sec Soph Cls; Stu Cncl; Capt Var Cheerldng; Hon Roll; CA Schlrshp Fed; Gymnstcs Clb Coach; Gymnstcs Clb Mem.

WILSON, TIMOTHY P; Antelope Valley HS; Lancaster, CA; (2); Church Yth Grp; JA; Hon Roll.

WILSON, TINEKA N; Monte Vista HS; Spring Valley, CA; (2); 82/461; Hosp Aide; Hon Roll; Mrt Cert Spnsh Cls; Los Amigos Clb; Harvard; Pediatrics.

WILSON, TITUS; South Bay Lutheran HS; Los Angeles, CA; (1); 4/32.

WILSON, TRAVIS; Gompers Secondary HS; San Diego, CA; (4); Debate Tm; Key Clb; Math Tm; Quiz Bowl; Teachers Aide; School Play; Mgr Nwsp; Rep Sr Cls; Stu Cncl; Var L Crs Cntry; UC Berkeley; Engrng.

WILSON, TROY SCOTT; Mar Vista HS; Imperial Beach, CA; (2); 3/613; SADD; JV Bsbl; JV Bsktbl; JV Ftbl; Cit Awd; Hon Roll; Prfct Atten Awd; UC Davis; Pre-Med.

WILSON, TYLER J; Savanna HS; Anaheim, CA; (3); Intnl Clb; Science Clb; Nwsp; Trk; Ldrshp Acad; 1 Yr Track Lgue Chmps; Acad Dcthln; UCSB Jr Smmr Sessns Prgm; UC Davis; Math.

WILSON, VANESSA BROOKE; Red Bluff HS; Red Bluff, CA; (2); 27/443; Chrmn Church Yth Grp; Dance Clb; Key Clb; Sec Letterman Clb; Pep Clb; Sec Spanish Clb; SADD; Sec Soph Cls; Sec Stu Cncl; Hon Roll; United Spirit Assn; Spec Perfmnc Awd; Crss Cntry St Qlfr Div 2; UCLA; Commnctns.

WILSON, WENDY M; El Camino Fundamental HS; Carmichael, CA; (3); Church Yth Grp; SADD; Hist Stu Cncl; Socr; Swmmng; U Of CA Santa Barbara; Engl.

WILSON, WILLIAM; Savanna HS; Anaheim, CA; (2); Church Yth Grp; Cmnty Wkr; Office Aide; Teachers Aide; Off Frsh Cls; Swmmng; Pres Acad Fit Awd; Pres Schlr; St Schlr; Waterpolo; Archtct; Engr.

WILSON-BEVINS, CHRISTEL; Bel-Air Prep Schl; Los Angeles, CA; (3); Dance Clb; Hon Roll; Ntl Merit Ltr; Outstndng Scl Sci & Lang Arts; Jrnlsm.

WILSTERMAN, SONYA; Walnut HS; Walnut, CA; (3); Key Clb; Spanish Clb; Hon Roll; Ice Hcky; U Of TX Arlngtn; Philsophy.

WILT, MICHELLE; Trabuco Hills HS; Mission Viejo, CA; (4); Office Aide; Teachers Aide; Varsity Clb; JV Var Socr; CA ST Fullerton; Acctng.

WILVANG, GINA LAREE; Hawthorne HS; Hawthorne, CA; (4); 8/520; Am Leg Aux Girls St; Cmnty Wkr; Dance Clb; Sec Drama Clb; Hosp Aide; Math Clb; Quiz Bowl; Treas Service Clb; Ski Clb; School Musical; CSF-VP/Seal Bearer; Soroptomist Awd-Hawthrne/Inglewd; Princpls Svc Awd; Gate Achvt Awd-Gftd/Tlntd Pgm; U CA-DAVIS; Biochem.

WILWANT, MICHELLE R; Rim HS; Crestline, CA; (3); Church Yth Grp; Cmnty Wkr; Church Choir; Miss Crestline Pageant; RYSL Sftbl Team; Music.

WIMBERLY, NATAUSHA R; North HS; Bakersfield, CA; (2); Church Yth Grp; Library Aide; Chorus; Church Choir; Hon Roll; Prin Schlstc Hnrs Awd For Outstndng Schlrshp; Acctng.

WIMP, JEFF B; Redwood HS; Visalia, CA; (3); Letterman Clb; Q&S; Varsity Clb; Band; Jazz Band; Mrchg Band; Pep Band; School Musical; Stage Crew; Co-Ed Nwsp; 2nd Pl Cntrl Dist CA Wmns Press Assn Sprtswrtng; Jrnlst.

WINANS, KYLE; El Cajon Valley HS; El Cajon, CA; (2); 37/431; Prin Hnr Roll; SDSU; Sci.

WINANT, CELESTE D; Torrey Pines HS; Solana Beach, CA; (3); 8/457; Lit Mag; Var Swmmng; High Hon Roll; Hon Roll; Ntl Merit Ltr; CSF; CA Arts Schlr; Scripps Charter Soc Schlrshp; Physics.

WINCH, KIM J; Cabrillo HS; Lompoc, CA; (2); Spanish Clb; SADD; Yrbk; JV Var Vllybl; Hon Roll; Teacher.

WINCHELL, DAWN MICHELLE; Elsinore HS; Lake Elsinore, CA; (4); Church Yth Grp; Cmnty Wkr; Dance Clb; Drama Clb; Teachers Aide; Thesps; Acpl Chr; Chorus; Church Choir; School Musical; Chmbr Singers; Ldrshp & Cmmnty Awds Music; CA Lutheran U; Liberal Arts.

WINCKLER, LORI M; Pioneer HS; San Jose, CA; (3); 19/392; Cmnty Wkr; Ski Clb; Phtg Yrbk; JV Var Cheerldng; JV Tennis; Hon Roll; Interact Clb; Engrng.

WINDETT, LARA; Mountain View HS; Mountain View, CA; (4); 28/275; Letterman Clb; Teachers Aide; Ed Nwsp; JV Cheerldng; Var Capt Swmmng; JV Var Trk; High Hon Roll; Hon Roll; U CA Davis; Art Hist.

WINDHAUSER, BRAD T; William Howard Taft HS; Reseda, CA; (2); Spanish Clb; Rep Soph Cls; JV Var Crs Cntry; JV Var Trk; Pres Acad Fit Awd; Bus.

WINDHORST, KIMBERLY M; Westlake HS; Westlake Vlg, CA; (2); Church Yth Grp; Hosp Aide; JV Cheerldng; Gym; Var Swmmng; CSF; Interact Clb.

WINDOM, LYNETTE P; St Bernard HS; Los Angeles, CA; (3); Church Yth Grp; Cmnty Wkr; Drama Clb; VP Thesps; Chorus; Church Choir; School Musical; School Play; Yrbk; Bst Feml Voclst 89-90; Actrss Of Yr 89-90; U Of CA San Diego; Comm.

WINDSOR, AMANDA; Mc Kinleyville HS; Eureka, CA; (4); Debate Tm; German Clb; Rep Soph Cls; DAR Awd; High Hon Roll; Pres Acad Fit Awd; Congress Bundestag Exchnge Schlrshp.

WINDSOR, JESSICA D; Poway HS; Poway, CA; (2); Church Yth Grp; Varsity Clb; Color Guard; Flag Corp; Mrchg Band; Var Cheerldng; Hon Roll; UC Santa Barbara; Bus.

WINE, RANDY A; Norte Vista HS; Riverside, CA; (3); ROTC; JV Trk; Hon Roll; JROTC Super Cadet Medals & Patrick Henry Awd; Bus Mgmt.

WINEINGER, BRIAN S; Norco HS; Corona, CA; (3); 34/399; FBLA; Model UN; Science Clb; Dist Sci Fair Hnrb Mntn; Sci Teacher Awd; Marine Bio.

WINFREY, DONNA M; El Camino Real HS; West Hills, CA; (4); 11/550; Teachers Aide; High Hon Roll; U NV Las Vegas; Htl Mgmnt.

WING, BRAD R; Eureka HS; Eureka, CA; (1); Pres Acad Fit Awd; Bcyclng; Crmnl Invstgtn.

WING, JESSICA R; Manteca HS; Manteca, CA; (4); 10/256; Key Clb; High Hon Roll; CSF; ST Wnnr Fed Wnms Clb Essay Cntst; Schlstc Letter Clb; Case Western Rsrv U; Nrs.

WINGARD, ELIZABETH; Grace Christian HS; San Diego, CA; (3); Church Yth Grp; Teachers Aide; Chorus; Church Choir; Rep Frsh Cls; Rep Stu Cncl; High Hon Roll; Hon Roll; Pres Acad Fit Awd; Rhema Bible Training Ctr.

WINGE, HEATHER; Notre Dame HS; Salinas, CA; (1); Hon Roll; Art.

WINGET, LISA D; Redlands HS; Redlands, CA; (4); Drama Clb; JA; SADD; Thesps; Chorus; School Play; Stage Crew; Cit Awd; Pres Acad Fit Awd; UC Riverside; Psych.

WINGO, JOHN E; Leuzinger HS; Hawthorne, CA; (3); 3/700; Pres Church Yth Grp; Cmnty Wkr; VP Key Clb; SADD; Chorus; Church Choir; JV Bsbl; JV Crs Cntry; Intrml Tennis; Cit Awd; NSF Young Schlrs Pgm Fnlst; Hawthorne Outstndng Vlntr; U CA Riverside; Biochem.

WINIARSKI, CATHERINE E; Palos Verdes HS; Rolling Hills, CA; (2); 1/300; Dance Clb; JCL; Treas Latin Clb; Math Clb; Service Clb; Variety Show; High Hon Roll; Prfct Score Natl Latin Exam; Actv Jr Statesmen Of Amer; Physcn.

WININGHAM, EMMA; Chino HS; Chino, CA; (2); Drama Clb; Chorus; Intrml Golf; Intrml Tennis; Hnrs Engl; UCLA; Law.

WINK, BRIAN C; Valley Christian HS; Cerritos, CA; (3); Church Yth Grp; JV Tennis; NHS; Eng.

WINKELMAN, MARK; Ambassador Baptist HS; Rialto, CA; (2); Church Yth Grp; Church Choir; Rptr Nwsp; Rep Stu Cncl; Capt L Bsbl; Capt L Bsktbl; Var Ftbl; High Hon Roll; Prfct Atten Awd; All Leag Vrsty Bsbl & Bsktbl; Engrng.

WINKLER, LAURIE A; Village Christian HS; Sunland, CA; (4); 15/121; Church Yth Grp; Drama Clb; English Clb; Mu Alpha Theta; Spanish Clb; Teachers Aide; VP Pres Band; Mrchg Band; Orch; CSF; Nature Clb Treas; Pensacola Christian Coll; El Ed.

WINKLER, MICHELLE Y; Poly HS; Lakewood, CA; (2); Ed Nwsp; Ed Yrbk; Lit Mag; Hon Roll; Jr NHS; Faculty Awd; Gldn St Exam Geom Hnrs; Outstndng Jrnlsm Yrbk Stu; PACE Pgm; Pltcl Sci.

WINN, BENJAMIN; Manor Baptist Christian Schl; Oakland, CA; (4); 3/6; Church Yth Grp; FCA; Speech Tm; Church Choir; School Musical; School Play; Nwsp; Stu Cncl; Bsktbl; Cit Awd; Prncpls Awd; Bus Adm.

WINN, DWIGHT R; San Ramon Valley HS; Danville, CA; (2); Church Yth Grp; Cmnty Wkr; Teachers Aide; School Play; JV Bsbl; Var Bsktbl; JV Ftbl; Hon Roll; Jck & Jll Of Amer Mem; Wrt Artcls Hmtwn Sprts Nwspr; Bus.

WINN, GENTRY; Arlington HS; Riverside, CA; (3); Boy Scts; Church Yth Grp; Teachers Aide; JV Socr; Hon Roll; Psych.

WINN, LESLIE; Edison/Computech HS; Sonora, CA; (1); 20/225; Letterman Clb; Treas SADD; Band; Co-Capt Color Guard; Treas Soph Cls; Treas Jr Cls; Treas Stu Cncl; Mgr(s); Var Swmmng; High Hon Roll; Child Psych.

WINN, MICHAEL D; St Joseph HS; Santa Maria, CA; (3); Boy Scts; Science Clb; SADD; Swmmng; UC Davis; Med.

WINN, ROB D GILLESPIE; Trabuco Hills HS; Mission Viejo, CA; (2); Doctor.

WINN JR, ROBERT J; Bakersfield HS; Bakersfield, CA; (2); Wrstlng; Hon Roll; Mst Imprvd Wrstlng.

WINSHIP, JANELLE; Yuba HS; Yuba City, CA; (4); Church Yth Grp; Variety Show; Cheerldng; Powder Puff Ftbl; Sftbl; Trk; Rotary Awd; Aerobics Instr; Amer River Coll; Intl Ntwk Assn.

WINSLOW, BRETT R; Rio Mesa HS; Oxanrd, CA; (3); Varsity Clb; VP Stu Cncl; Var Crs Cntry; Var Trk; JV Wrstlng; Hon Roll; CSF; AFS.

WINSLOW, CHERYL M; Valhalla HS; Jamul, CA; (3); Church Yth Grp; Cmnty Wkr; VP Intnl Clb; Spanish Clb; SADD; Lit Mag; Cit Awd; Hon Roll; Kiwanis Awd; Prfct Atten Awd; Miss Teen CA Majestic 1990; Miss Lovely Teen 1990; Quest Qualty Stu Yr; San Diego ST U; Tchr.

WINSLOW, CHRISTI M; Mater Dei HS; Huntington Beach, CA; (1); Church Yth Grp; Swmmng.

WINSLOW, CODIE; Chula Vista HS; Chula Vista, CA; (3); Church Yth Grp; Hosp Aide; Key Clb; Office Aide; Pep Clb; School Play; Nwsp; Phtg Yrbk; Hist Frsh Cls; Var Socr; Comm.

WINSLOW, ROSEMARY L; Branham HS; San Jose, CA; (2); Cmnty Wkr; Hosp Aide; Off SADD; Co-Ed Yrbk; Hon Roll; CSF Hnr Society; Part Time Job; Vlntr At Mission Skilled Nrsng Facility Actvty Dept; U Of CA; Med.

WINSTEAD JR, JAMES R; San Benito HS; Hollister, CA; (4); Jazz Band; Phtg Ed Nwsp; Phtg Ed Yrbk; Elks Awd; Hon Roll; Close-Up Pres; Peer Ldrshp-Treas; Santa Clara U; Lawyer.

WINSTON, AARON M; Westchester HS; Los Angeles, CA; (2); Tennis; Moto Crss Racing 3rd Pl Smmr Series 89; Vrs Trophies In Motorcycle Racing.

WINSTON, JACKIE; Middletown HS; Middletown, CA; (4); 21/58; Dance Clb; Office Aide; Teachers Aide; Color Guard; Drill Tm; Flag Corp; Var Cheerldng; Var Pom Pon; Hon Roll; UCSB CA; Preschl Tchr.

WINTER, JOEL; Lincoln HS; Stockton, CA; (4); 76/520; Latin Clb; Mu Alpha Theta; Yrbk; Var Capt Ftbl; Var L Trk; Wt Lftg; High Hon Roll; NHS; Pres Acad Fit Awd; UC Davis; Biolgcl Sci.

WINTER, REBECCA; Alexander Hamilton HS; Los Angeles, CA; (4); 5/500; Cmnty Wkr; Debate Tm; School Play; Ed Lit Mag; Swmmng; High Hon Roll; Ntl Merit SF; Jr Statesman Of Amer, Senator; Brthrhd/Sisterhood USA, Yth Ldr; Reed Coll; Anthropology.

WINTER, TIMOTHY W; Fred C Beyer HS; Modesto, CA; (4); Treas Band; Mrchg Band; Orch; Hon Roll; Mancini Schlrhsp; CSU; Music Ed.

WINTERS, JAMES; Summerville HS; Soulsbyville, CA; (4); Church Yth Grp; Drama Clb; 4-H; Quiz Bowl; Ski Clb; Spanish Clb; Jazz Band; Mrchg Band; Pep Band; JV Bsktbl; Columbia JC; Archtct.

WINTERS, JILL M; Fred C Beyer HS; Modesto, CA; (1); Church Yth Grp; Hon Roll; Acctnt.

WINTERS, JOHN; Davis HS; Modesto, CA; (4); Scholastic Bowl; Science Clb; Thesps; School Play; Stage Crew; Hon Roll; Jr NHS; Ntl Merit Ltr; Drama Awd; Antioch Coll; Comp Music Cmpsr.

WINTERS, PATRICK K; Del Oro HS; Loomis, CA; (1); 41/260; Bsbl; Bsktbl.

WINTERS, SCOTT E; Woodland HS; Woodland, CA; (2); Church Yth Grp; Cmnty Wkr; FFA; Ski Clb; SADD; Teachers Aide; JV Bsbl; Ftbl; Score Keeper; Wt Lftg; Wldrnss Clb Dglss Jr HS Pres; Agribusinessman Star Chptr; BOAC Dglss Jr HS; Shasta Coll; Mchncl Engrng.

WINTERS, TIFFANY E; Yucca Valley HS; Yucca Valley, CA; (4); Aud/Vis; Library Aide; Teachers Aide; Yrbk; Swmmng; Cit Awd; Hon Roll; Accntng.

WINTERSTEIN III, MICHAEL J; Washing HS; Fremont, CA; (2); 98/350; Bus Profs of Am; Drama Clb; Band; Drm Mjr(t); Mrchg Band; Stage Crew; Phtg Yrbk; Treas Frsh Cls; Soc For Advncmnt Precocious Stu; Scott T Apel Achvt Awd; Covert Govt Operations.

WINTON, FRANK; Alemany HS; Santa Clarita, CA; (4); Am Leg Boys St; Letterman Clb; Ski Clb; Variety Show; Pres Sr Cls; Capt Var Ftbl; Capt Var Swmmng; JV Var Trk; Wt Lftg; High Hon Roll; Schl Schlr Athlete Yr; Most Outstndng Player Burbank Glendale All-St Ftbl Classic; UC Berkeley; Pre-Med.

WINTRINGER, JEREMY C; Gompers Secondary HS; San Diego, CA; (2); 27/145; Pres Chess Clb; Cmnty Wkr; German Clb; Math Tm; Science Clb; JV Vllybl; High Hon Roll; Hon Roll; Val; Sci Olympiad St Tm 4th Pl Indiv 2nd Tm; Princeton; Econ.

WIPFF, LISA; Moorpark HS; Moorpark, CA; (4); #8 In Class; French Clb; Key Clb; VP Pres Ski Clb; Band; School Musical; School Play; Var Bsktbl; High Hon Roll; Hon Roll; Gldn ST Exm Awd-Alg I; Outstndng Achvt Awd 88-89; Loyola Marymount U; Intl Bus.

WIRA, WENDY J; Grossmont HS; La Mesa, CA; (1); Hon Roll; Hnr Cls; Sports; U CA San Diego; Marine Bio.

WIRCHANSKE, KRISTEN M; Taft HS; Tarzana, CA; (1); Church Yth Grp; Cmnty Wkr; Chorus; Drill Tm; Hon Roll; Write Poetry & Song Lyrics.

WIRKKALA, MICHELLE; Bullard HS; Naselle, WA; (1); FHA; Pep Clb; Spanish Clb; SADD; Band; Pep Band; JV Bsktbl; Trk; Cit Awd; Hon Roll; Spnsh Awd; UCLA.

WISCHNIA, SARAH B; San Luis Obispo SR HS; San Luis Obispo, CA; (2); Intnl Clb; SADD; Temple Yth Grp; Thesps; School Play; Sec Frsh Cls; Sec Stu Cncl; Prfct Atten Awd; Pres Acad Fit Awd; Amnesty Intl Treas; CA Arts Schlr; CA Schlrshp Fed; Ed.

WISDOM, JULIE A; Chino HS; Chino, CA; (3); 7/500; Church Yth Grp; High Hon Roll; Pres Acad Fit Awd; Slvr Spur Awd; Woodmens Awd Amer Hstry; Biola Univ; Psych.

WISE, BRIAN L; Atwater HS; Atwater, CA; (3); FCA; Speech Tm; Phtg Nwsp; Rptr Yrbk; High Hon Roll; Ntl Merit Ltr; Rotary Awd; Schl Tutor; Atwater New Times Jrnlsm Awd 90; U Of CA; Biolgcl Sci.

WISE, JASON; Hawthorne HS; Hawthorne, CA; (2); Math Clb; Quiz Bowl; VP Soph Cls; JV Vllybl; Intrml Wt Lftg; Var Wrstlng; High Hon Roll; Pres Acad Fit Awd; GSE Golden St Ex Alg Hgh Hons; Knights Srvc Orgnztn Hanthorne Schl & Cmmnty; U AZ; Aeronautical Engr.

WISE, JIMMY; Sanger HS; Sanger, CA; (2); JV Bsbl; JV Bsktbl; JV Ftbl; Hon Roll; Prncpls Awd 3.5 GPA; Coach Awd Ftbl & Bsbl; Fresno ST U; Engr.

WISE, LEAH; Fontana HS; Fontana, CA; (2); Band; Mrchg Band; Hon Roll; CA Poly U; Bus Mgr.

WISE, SHANNON M; Mission Viejo HS; Mission Viejo, CA; (3); Church Yth Grp; Cmnty Wkr; Key Clb; Model UN; Quiz Bowl; Scholastic Bowl; Spanish Clb; SADD; Color Guard; Flag Corp; Natl Scer Tm; UCI; Med.

WISECARVER, KRISTINE H; Antioch SR HS; Antioch, CA; (2); 187/723; Drama Clb; GAA; Office Aide; Pep Clb; SADD; Teachers Aide; Thesps; Chorus; School Play; Stage Crew; CJSF; CSF; Bus.

WISEHART, LAURA; 29 Palms HS; Aloha, OR; (2); Church Yth Grp; Drama Clb; Science Clb; Spanish Clb; SADD; School Musical; School Play; DAR Awd; Hon Roll; CSF; Amer Frgn Exchng Stu; Peer Ldr.

WISEMAN, BENJAMIN T; Montgomery HS; Santa Rosa, CA; (2); Boy Scts; Church Yth Grp; Letterman Clb; Spanish Clb; Intrml Bsktbl; Var L Socr; Intrml Trk; Cit Awd; High Hon Roll; Maintain Part Time Job; Lift Wghts; Active LDS Church; Brigham Young U; Arch.

WISEMAN, JENNIFER R; Grossmont HS; El Cajon, CA; (1); Key Clb; Teachers Aide; Temple Yth Grp; Chorus; Var L Tennis; Hon Roll; Georgetown U; Law.

WISENER, ARYN C; Carlsbad HS; Carlsbad, CA; (1); GAA; Ski Clb; Chorus; Intrml Sftbl; Hon Roll; MVP Sftbl & Bst Dfnsv Plyr; Sftbl Plyr Of Mnth; USCB; Tchr.

WISKUS, DIANE; Rosary HS; La Mirada, CA; (3); Science Clb; Varsity Clb; School Play; Treas Soph Cls; Var L Bsktbl; JV Sftbl; Var Vllybl; Hon Roll; NHS; Mst Vlbl Plyr Bsktbl; 1st All Leag Angelus Leag; Stu Of Month; Pediatrics.

WISNIEWSKI, BRENDA; Bishop Amat HS; W Covina, CA; (4); 48/400; Church Yth Grp; GAA; VP Pep Clb; Drill Tm; Var JV Cheerldng; JV Vllybl; Hon Roll; NHS; CSF; CA ST Fullerton; Bus Admin.

WISSLER, KARI; Livermore HS; Livermore, CA; (2); 150/424; Church Yth Grp; Cheerldng; Hon Roll; BYU.

WISSMATH, LISA; Silver Creek HS; San Jose, CA; (1); Off Frsh Cls; JV Cheerldng; Fashion Desgnr.

WITCHER, SAMUEL M; Monache HS; Porterville, CA; (4); 1/305; Pres Service Clb; VP Orch; Rep Stu Cncl; Capt Tennis; High Hon Roll; Lion Awd; Ntl Merit SF; Rotary Awd; Val; Voice Dem Awd; U CA; Bus Admn.

WITHAM, DAVID L; Alhambra HS; Alhambra, CA; (3); Cmnty Wkr; Science Clb; Hist Service Clb; VICA; JV Var Tennis; Hon Roll; Leo Clb; Physcs Clb; TX U Astn; Mech Engr.

WITHERS, THERESA L; Watsonville HS; Watsonville, CA; (2); 113/545; Church Yth Grp; Cmnty Wkr; Color Guard; Mrchg Band; Support Our Stu Grp Peer Cnslr; USC; Cnslng.

WITHERSPOON, NICOLE S; Victor Valley Union HS; Victorville, CA; (2); Church Yth Grp; Church Choir; Bsktbl; Hon Roll; Spelman.

WITHROW, CYNDI; Elk Grove HS; Elk Grove, CA; (3); Church Yth Grp; Pep Clb; SADD; Rep Stu Cncl; JV Var Cheerldng; JV Sftbl; High Hon Roll; Hon Roll; Pre Med.

WITHROW, KIMBERLY; Mt View HS; Burney, CA; (1); 4-H; FFA; Teachers Aide; Chorus; Bsktbl; Cheerldng; Ftbl; 4-H Awd; Shasta Clg; Bus.

WITT, ERIC; Poway HS; Poway, CA; (3); Treas Church Yth Grp; Key Clb; Math Clb; Model UN; Quiz Bowl; Science Clb; Pres Sr Cls; Rep Stu Cncl; Ntl Merit Ltr; Rotary Awd.

WITT, JENNIFER; Oak Ridge HS; Cameron Park, CA; (1); Church Yth Grp; Hon Roll; Brigham Young U; Gen Ed.

WITT, JENNIFER M; Hoover HS; Fresno, CA; (2); Church Yth Grp; French Clb; Library Aide; Ski Clb; Spanish Clb; SADD; Cit Awd; High Hon Roll; Hon Roll; Prncpls Awd Acad Excllnc; Chld Psych.

WITT, MONICA A; Poway HS; Poway, CA; (3); Dance Clb; Model UN; Pep Clb; School Musical; Cit Awd; Cmnty Wkr; Computer Clb; Drama Clb; 4-H; German Clb; Interact Clb; Lit Awd; Doctor.

WITT, RYAN F; Nevada Union HS; Penn Valley, CA; (3); 23/560; Ed Yrbk; Temple Yth Grp; Var Capt Tennis; Hon Roll; Northern CA Jr Tnns Trnmnts; Natl Video Commercial Cmptn Hnrbl Mntn; Commnctns.

WITTE, CINDY B; Porterville HS; Porterville, CA; (3); 3/400; Rep French Clb; GAA; Mu Alpha Theta; Band; Mrchg Band; Orch; Pep Band; School Musical; Mgr Nwsp; Lit Mag; Top Engl Hnrs 89-90; Columbia Christian Coll; Engl.

WITTEN, JAMIE A; Edison HS; Huntington Beach, CA; (3); 28/464; Model UN; Off Jr Cls; Ntl Merit SF; Hlth.

WITTENBERG, DAVID A; Victor Valley HS; Victorville, CA; (2); Boy Scts; Church Yth Grp; Hon Roll.

WITTIG, TERESA; Palm Springs HS; Desert Hot Spring, CA; (3); Debate Tm; Drama Clb; French Clb; JA; School Play; Bsktbl; Powder Puff Ftbl; Hon Roll; Jr Statesmen Of Amer; CSF; Amnesty Intl; Pre Med.

WITTING, JUDY; Trinity HS; Douglas City, CA; (2); SADD; Trk; Hon Roll; Coll Redwoods Upwrd Bnd Prog; HSU; Psych.

WITTLER, JOSHUA D; Nevada Union HS; Camptonville, CA; (3); JV Var Bsbl; JV Var Ftbl; Wt Lftg; Hon Roll; Cal Poly; Arch.

WITTMAN, HEATHER M; Academy Of Our Lady Of Peace; San Diego, CA; (3); 4/210; Key Clb; Library Aide; School Musical; School Play; Variety Show; Ed Yrbk; Sec Frsh Cls; High Hon Roll; NEDT Awd; Pres Acad Fit Awd; Spec Olympics Volunteer; Theater Arts.

WITTNEBEL, LISA M; Cordova SR HS; Rancho Cordova, CA; (2); Church Yth Grp; Model UN; Office Aide; Church Choir; Outstndng Offce Asstnt Awd 2 Yrs; Friday Night Live; UC Davis; Vet Asstnt.

WITUL, JACOB H; Alhambra HS; Martinez, CA; (3); 9/205; Am Leg Boys St; Ed Nwsp; Ed Lit Mag; VP Sr Cls; JV Bsktbl; Var Socr; Intrml Vllybl; High Hon Roll; Ntl Merit Ltr; Xerox Humanities/Scl Sci Awd; Polymer Sci.

WITZTUM, MOSHE A; Patrick Henry HS; San Diego, CA; (3); VP Temple Yth Grp; Yrbk; VP Frsh Cls; Hon Roll; Jr NHS; Pres Acad Fit Awd; First Place CA St Science Fair 87; First Place San Diego County Science Fair 87-88; Medicine.

WIVELL, BRANDI L; Palmdale HS; Agua Dulce, CA; (3); 61/644; School Play; Hon Roll; Bus.

WIZBOWSKI II, RAYMOND V; Fresno Christian HS; Fresno, CA; (4); Boy Scts; Pres Band; Pres Mrchg Band; Pres Frsh Cls; Pres Jr Cls; Pres Sr Cls; Var Bsbl; Var L Ftbl; Cit Awd; Hon Roll; John Philip Sousa Awdfstu Of Mnth; Fresno ST U; Comm.

WLASCHIN, AMY A; Lemoore Union HS; Lemoore, CA; (3); Teachers Aide; Tiger Buddies; Coll Of Sequoias; Teacher.

WOELFEL, ERIKA-AMBER; Lakewood HS; Lakewood, CA; (2); Ed Nwsp; Ed Yrbk; Lit Mag; Off Soph Cls; Hon Roll; Jr NHS; Opt Clb Awd; CA Jr Schlrshp Fed Awd; Schlstc All-Amer Schlr; Pblshd Poet; Jrnlst.

WOELFEL, LOU; La Sierra HS; Riverside, CA; (1); Boy Scts; Intrml Ftbl; Var Capt Trk; Wt Lftg; Cit Awd; High Hon Roll; Prfct Atten Awd; Pres Acad Fit Awd; UCLA; Med Field.

WOESSNER, DAVE A; Orange Glen HS; Escondido, CA; (3); FFA; Office Aide; SADD; VICA; Sec Stu Cncl; Var Ftbl; Capt Golf; JV Trk; Var Wt Lftg; Gov Hon Prg Awd; Outstndng GPA Blue Rbbn Art Instrctn Schl; AZ Automotive Inst; Mech Drftg.

WOEST, JAMES; Edison HS; Huntington Beach, CA; (3); Church Yth Grp; Treas Computer Clb; JA; Library Aide; Model UN; Stage Crew; High Hon Roll; NHS; NEDT Awd; Jim Brown Frshmn Eng Awd; Sci Fctn Club; Yng Repblcns Club; Marine Bio.

WOFFINDEN, ERIN E; Trabuco Hills HS; Trabuco Canyon, CA; (2); Church Yth Grp; French Clb; Socr; Trk; Vllybl; Wt Lftg; Mst Athl Girl.

WOFFORD, CATHY; Contra Costa Christian HS; Danville, CA; (2); AFS; Church Yth Grp; Drama Clb; Chorus; School Play; Pres Frsh Cls; Rep Stu Cncl; Var Cheerldng; Var Socr; Hon Roll; Princeton U.

WOFFORD, DAN M; Lemoore Union HS; Lemoore, CA; (2); Hon Roll; Sci Stu Of Month; Elctrnc Engr.

WOFFORD, ELLEN E; Manteca HS; Manteca, CA; (2); 25/420; Sec Jr Cls; Var Vllybl; High Hon Roll; Hon Roll; Outstndng Achvt Span I Awd 1989; Var Vlby Bst Def Plyr, Mst Outstndng Plyr 1989; Cmmnctns.

WOFSY, KEVIN A; Lowell HS; San Francisco, CA; (3); Drama Clb; NFL; Q&S; Band; Orch; Rep Frsh Cls; Rep Soph Cls; Ntl Merit SF; Mst Crtv Prjct Awd Sci Fair; 1st Pl Awd Chemathon; Cmnd Prfrmnc-Orgn Cmpstn-CA Msc Ed Assn.

WOHLE, ERIC; East Union HS; Manteca, CA; (3); 3/294; Letterman Clb; Science Clb; VICA; JV Ftbl; Capt L Swmmng; High Hon Roll; Prfct Atten Awd; CSF; Engr.

WOHLERS, BRYAN; S Tahoe HS; S Lake Tahoe, CA; (3); 27/211; Church Yth Grp; Drama Clb; Thesps; School Musical; School Play; Stage Crew; Variety Show; JV Ftbl; Var Ftbl; Var Swmmng; Stu Forum Wnnr; Bus.

WOHLFIEL, ALLISON E; Ramona HS; Ramona, CA; (3); 1/294; Key Clb; Quiz Bowl; Spanish Clb; SADD; Ed Mgr Nwsp; Tennis; High Hon Roll; Hon Roll; Harvard Bk Clb Awd; 38th Annl CS Schlstc Press Assoc CA Polyjrnlsm Wkshp; Psych.

WOHLFORD, HOLLY; Irvine HS; Irvine, CA; (2); French Clb; German Clb; Key Clb; Pep Clb; Sec Frsh Cls; Off Soph Cls; Cheerldng; JV Diving; Socr; Hon Roll; Jobs Dghtrs Hnrd Queen; Chrty Clb; Zephyrs; Accntng.

WOICIK, CHRISTOPHER P; Tri City Christian HS; Oceanside, CA; (4); 4/19; Church Yth Grp; JV Var Bsktbl; Var Crs Cntry; Hon Roll; Yth Church Drama Grp; Pol Sci.

WOISH, CYNTHIA J; De Anza HS; Richmond, CA; (4); Drama Clb; Acpl Chr; Band; Chorus; School Musical; School Play; Stage Crew; Gym; Hon Roll; Friday Night Live; San Francisco ST U; Drmtc Arts.

WOJTKOWSKI, KRISTIN M; Monterey HS; Monterey, CA; (2); Church Yth Grp; Key Clb; Ski Clb; Varsity Clb; Nwsp; Yrbk; Fld Hcky; Swmmng; High Hon Roll; Hon Roll; Stanford; Poly Sci.

WOJTKOWSKI, LISA; Prospect HS; San Jose, CA; (4); 11/180; Art Clb; Bus Profs of Am; Church Yth Grp; FBLA; Key Clb; Varsity Clb; Jazz Band; Orch; Ed Yrbk; Treas Frsh Cls; U CA Santa Barbara; Bus.

WOLBACH, KIM; Prospect HS; San Jose, CA; (1); 32/150; JV Diving; JV Sftbl; U WA; Arts.

WOLCOTT, CHAD A; Enterprise HS; Redding, CA; (3); 35/450; Church Yth Grp; Drama Clb; 4-H; Mu Alpha Theta; Thesps; VP Sr Cls; JV Ftbl; 4-H Awd; Hon Roll; CJSF; Bus.

WOLF, AIME; Warren HS; Downey, CA; (2); Church Yth Grp; Drama Clb; Teachers Aide; Thesps; School Play; Stage Crew; Gym; Hon Roll; Masonic Awd; Golden Bear Awd For Drama; CSF Awd; Acting.

WOLF, ANDY; Los Alamitos HS; Seal Beach, CA; (4); Boy Scts; NFL; Quiz Bowl; Service Clb; L Treas Speech Tm; School Musical; School Play; Swing Chorus; NHS; Drama.

WOLF, ELIZABETH R; Miraleste HS; Rancho Palos Verd, CA; (3); 17/190; Church Yth Grp; Girl Scts; Model UN; Spanish Clb; Church Choir; JV Var Bsktbl; High Hon Roll; Hon Roll; NHS; Spanish NHS.

WOLF, GREGORY M; San Rafael HS; San Rafael, CA; (4); 7/222; Cmnty Wkr; Spanish Clb; Jazz Band; Tennis; Elks Awd; Hon Roll; Pres Acad Fit Awd; CA Schlrshp Fedrtn CSF Life Mbr; Nrth Cst Sect CIF Schlr Athl; Elks Natl Fndtn Mst Val Stu Awd 4th; U CA Los Angeles; Cmmnctns.

WOLF, JAIME; San Rafael HS; San Rafael, CA; (3); 1/200; SADD; Chorus; School Musical; School Play; Rep Soph Cls; Pres Jr Cls; Rep Sr Cls; Var Socr; Var Tennis; Ntl Merit SF; Walt Disney Doers & Dreamers Awd; Outstndng Math & Sci Stu Soc Of Women Engrs; UC Brkly Acclrtd Pgm; Stanford U.

WOLF, JESSICA; Half Moon Bay HS; El Granada, CA; (2); Cmnty Wkr; FBLA; Letterman Clb; SADD; VP Soph Cls; Pres Jr Cls; JV Cheerldng; Var Crs Cntry; Var Trk; High Hon Roll; Girls Vrsty Trk MVP 2 Yrs; Friday Night Live Fndr; Yth Gymnstcs Coach; Sprts Med.

WOLF, KIM; Mojave HS; California City, CA; (2); Math Tm; Band; Mrchg Band; Bsktbl; Cheerldng; Sftbl; Vllybl; Cit Awd; High Hon Roll; Pres Acad Fit Awd; Comp Sci.

WOLF, LAURA; Davis SR HS; Davis, CA; (3); SADD; School Play; Variety Show; Bsktbl; Cheerldng; Fld Hcky; Powder Puff Ftbl; Sftbl; Swmmng; Tennis; Water Skiing; Cal Poly; Phy Ed.

WOLF, SEP A; Aptos HS; Aptos, CA; (1); Church Yth Grp; Cmnty Wkr; Teachers Aide; Pres Soph Cls; Var L Socr; High Hon Roll; Prfct Atten Awd; Pres Acad Fit Awd; CA St Select Olympc Dvlpmnt Soccer Team; Clb Soccer Team Top Scorer, Rgnl Chmpn; Santa Clara U.

WOLF, TROY J; Seaside HS; Fort Ord, CA; (3); SADD; JV Bsbl; Intrml Crs Cntry; JV Ftbl; JV Socr; Wt Lftg; Hon Roll; Bst Outstndng Soph Awd; Hlth.

WOLF, WESLEY T; California Lutheran HS; Laguna Hills, CA; (1); Rep Stu Cncl; JV Bsbl; JV Bsktbl; High Hon Roll; Rowing; Bowling.

WOLFE, CHRISTOPHER D; Woodcrest Christian HS; Riverside, CA; (3); 30/110; Church Yth Grp; Var Bsktbl; Var Trk; Var Vllybl; Elks Awd; Hon Roll; Employed 3 Years; S CA Coll; Accountant.

WOLFE, DERON S; Victorvalley SR HS; Victorville, CA; (2); 9/25; Aud/Vis; Drama Clb; School Play; Stage Crew; Variety Show; Victor Valley JC; Acting.

WOLFE, ERIC H; Simi HS; Simi Valley, CA; (3); 113/665; Temple Yth Grp; Hon Roll; Jr NHS; Video Annual; CSUN; Motion Pictures.

WOLFE, GINA C; Rubidoux HS; Riverside, CA; (4); 5/580; Church Yth Grp; Cmnty Wkr; Teachers Aide; High Hon Roll; NHS; Prfct Atten Awd; New Vision Chrstn Clb Sctry; Stu Wk; Dept Awds Englsh Cmpstn & Scl Sci.

WOLFE, JULIE F; Piedmont HS; Piedmont, CA; (3); Church Yth Grp; Sec German Clb; Intnl Clb; Stu Cncl; Var Capt Bsktbl; Var Capt Crs Cntry; Var Capt Sftbl; NHS; St Schlr; Sunday Schl Teacher; Smith Book Awd.

WOLFE, JUSTIN PAUL; San Luis Obispo HS; San Luis Obispo, CA; (2); Key Clb; VP Soph Cls; Var Crs Cntry; JV Socr; Var Tennis; High Hon Roll; Hon Roll; Coaches Awd MVP Sccr 89, Mst Imprvd Var Tnns 90; Golden Tiger Acad Comp Sci & Scl Sci; Engrng.

WOLFE, KELLY D; Artesia HS; Lakewood, CA; (3); 8/371; Rep Jr Cls; Sec Stu Cncl; Var Sftbl; Var JV Vllybl; Pet Assistance Leag; CA Schlstc Fed; Acad Ltr 5 Semesters; Bus.

WOLFE, WENDY A; Clayton Valley HS; Concord, CA; (4); 1/422; Church Yth Grp; Math Clb; Treas Service Clb; Var L Socr; Var L Swmmng; Ntl Merit Schol; Pres Acad Fit Awd; Val; CA Schltc Fed Pres; Stanford U; Math.

WOLFENBARGER, JENIFER; Hesperia HS; Hesperia, CA; (2); Church Yth Grp; Key Clb; Library Aide; Flag Corp; Rptr Nwsp; Stat Bsktbl; Var Vllybl; High Hon Roll; Hon Roll; Vllybl Capt; CA ST U San Diego; Marine Bio.

WOLFERSBERGER, MARK A; Bakersfield HS; Bakersfield, CA; (3); Boy Scts; Church Yth Grp; German Clb; Band; Church Choir; Jazz Band; Mrchg Band; Orch; Crs Cntry; Socr; 1st Chr Percssnst CA St Hnr Cncrt Band; Super Rtng Marimba Solos; Cmnd Perfmnc Snare Drum Solo; Brigham Young U; Music.

WOLFF, LENA; Idyllwild Schl Of Music And The Arts; Idyllwild, CA; (4); School Musical; School Play; Hon Roll; Photo; Oil Pantng; Drawng; Studio Art.

WOLFF, NEAL M; Pasadena HS; Sierra Madre, CA; (3); Boy Scts; Band; Mrchg Band; Orch; Pep Band; School Musical; R G Canning Yth Achvt Awd; Comp Sci.

WOLFF, SHANNON T; Mater Dei HS; Westminster, CA; (3); Art Clb; Red Cross Aide; Spanish Clb; Nwsp; Stu Cncl; Stat Bsktbl; High Hon Roll; NHS; Cmnty Wkr; Hosp Aide; CA Schlrshp Activities Coord; Youth Volunteer Of Yr March Of Dimes; Outstndng Art Achvmnt Awd; Graphic Arts.

WOLFF, TARA M; North Tahoe HS; Carnelian Bay, CA; (3); 1/59; Letterman Clb; Ski Clb; Variety Show; High Hon Roll; Opt Clb Awd; Sec Treas Soph Cls; Pres Jr Cls; Stu Cncl; JV Var Bsktbl; Var Capt Powder Puff Ftbl; Vrsty Vlybl MVP/1st Tm All St & Leag; Femle Athl Yr 89-90; Rudy Suwara Vlybl Cmp MVP; CSF; Engrng.

WOLFGRAMM, MARLENA M; Skyline HS; Oakland, CA; (3); Church Yth Grp; GAA; Speech Tm; Varsity Clb; Acpl Chr; Chorus; Church Choir; Off Frsh Cls; Rep Soph Cls; Rep Stu Cncl; UCLA; Teacher Soc Sci.

WOLFSON, THERESA A; Bishop Amat Memorial HS; El Monte, CA; (3); Church Yth Grp; JA; Pep Clb; Varsity Clb; Var Bsktbl; Var Cheerldng; Powder Puff Ftbl; Var Vllybl; Hon Roll; NHS; CSF; UCLA; Bus Admin.

WOLLARD, GARILYNN; Adolfo Camarillo HS; Camarillo, CA; (2); 45/506; Church Yth Grp; Cmnty Wkr; Drama Clb; Rep Stu Cncl; Var JV Cheerldng; JV Swmmng; High Hon Roll; Hon Roll; Pres Of Interact Clb; Stanford U; Corp Lawyer.

WOLLIN, WADE A; Ygnacio Valley HS; Concord, CA; (4); Chess Clb; Church Yth Grp; Spanish Clb; Church Choir; Rep Soph Cls; Var L Ftbl; Var Pom Pon; Var Powder Puff Ftbl; Var Wt Lftg; Herald Christ; Wheaton Coll; Commnctns.

WOLSCHLAGER, MICHELLE L; Mira Mesa HS; San Diego, CA; (2); Science Clb; Yrbk; Ed Lit Mag; Rep Soph Cls; Pres Acad Fit Awd; CSF.

WOLSKE, JAMES S; College Park HS; Martinez, CA; (3); Boy Scts; Chorus; Church Choir; School Musical; L JV Crs Cntry; L Var Trk; Hon Roll; Pres Acad Fit Awd; Athltc Awd; CSU San Francisco; Bus Mgmt.

WOMACK, CYNTHIA L; Monterey HS; Seaside, CA; (3); Cmnty Wkr; Pres Drama Clb; Pres Thesps; School Musical; School Play; Stage Crew; Variety Show; Ed Lit Mag; Hon Roll; Thspn Trpe; Vlntr Lcl Art Msm; Italn Clb; NYU Film/Drama Schl; Dir Stg.

WOMACK, JASON W; Arroyo Grande HS; Oceano, CA; (3); Dance Clb; Yrbk; Hon Roll; Dance Kldscpe; CPA.

WON, ARLENE J; Westmoor HS; Daly City, CA; (2); French Clb; Spanish Clb; Rep Frsh Cls; Rep Soph Cls; CEC; Communications.

WON, LISA; Lincoln HS; San Francisco, CA; (4); 204/444; Cmnty Wkr; Office Aide; Service Clb; Teachers Aide; Rep Frsh Cls; VP Soph Cls; Rep Jr Cls; Pres Sr Cls; Rep Stu Cncl; Var Score Keeper; Acad Finance; Cmnty Stds & Service Clss; U San Francisco; Poltcl Sci.

WON, SUSAN; Beaumont HS; Beaumont, CA; (3); 1/400; Pres Church Yth Grp; Cmnty Wkr; Sec FCA; VP French Clb; FBLA; Hosp Aide; Math Clb; Model UN; Capt Pep Clb; Quiz Bowl.

WONACOTT, DOUG W; Paradise HS; Paradise, CA; (2); Golf; Socr; Hon Roll; USAF.

WONDERLEY, EMILY C; Magnolia HS; Anaheim, CA; (4); JV Tennis.

WONDERS, JACOB L; Noro HS; Norco, CA; (2); Var Crs Cntry; Hon Roll; Prfct Atten Awd; Landscape Architecture.

WONG, ABIEL; Lincoln HS; Stockton, CA; (3); Cmnty Wkr; Mu Alpha Theta; Science Clb; Spanish Clb; Variety Show; Intrml Mgr Bsktbl; High Hon Roll; Golden St Ex Geo Hgh Hons; Jr Clss Rep CIA; Awd Wnnr Stcktn Music Tchrs Asso CA Violin; Biological Sci.

WONG, ALAN; Gardena HS; Gardena, CA; (3); Art Clb; Bsktbl; Vllybl; Hon Roll; Harbor Gateway Logo Cntst 2nd Pl 90; Get Out & Vote Pstr Cntst Hnrbl Mntn 90; Art Exhib USC Fnlst 88; Arch.

WONG, ALAN; Raoul Wallenberg Traditional HS; San Francisco, CA; (2); Church Yth Grp; Band; Bsbl; High Hon Roll; Hon Roll.

WONG, ALEXIS D; El Camino HS; Sacramento, CA; (3); Pres Chess Clb; Debate Tm; Nwsp; Pres Sr Cls; Sec Stu Cncl; Var Ftbl; High Hon Roll; Hon Roll; NHS; People To People Intl; Stu Ambssdrs Soviet Union; Yo-Yoing.

WONG, ALLAN C; South San Francisco HS; S San Francisco, CA; (3); VP FBLA; Math Clb; Math Tm; Teachers Aide; JV Bsktbl; Cit Awd; Prfct Atten Awd; Imprvmnt Task Force; Stu Store Mgr; Bus.

WONG, ALLEN; Abraham Lincoln HS; San Francisco, CA; (2); Church Choir; Cit Awd; Hon Roll; Prfct Atten Awd; Gifted Pgm; Stanford; Med.

WONG, ALTON; Sacred Heart Cathedral Prep; San Francisco, CA; (1); Ski Clb; Hon Roll.

WONG, AMY; Mt Whitney HS; Visalia, CA; (3); 8/300; AFS; Am Leg Aux Girls St; Art Clb; Spanish Clb; Hon Roll; Rotary Awd; Stu Agnst Substance Abuse; Sci Olympiad; Best Chem Stu Awd; Arch.

WONG, ANDREW W; Norte Vista HS; Riverside, CA; (1); Boy Scts; JV Tennis; Hist DAR Awd; High Hon Roll; NASA Scientist.

WONG, ANDY K; Lowell HS; San Francisco, CA; (2); CSF; U Of CA; Arch.

WONG, ANGELA D; Westmoor HS; Daly City, CA; (2); French Clb; GAA; Chorus; Intrml Gym; Hon Roll; Chinese Club; Straight A Soph; U CA Berkley; Bus.

WONG, AUDREY S; Holy Family HS; Los Angeles, CA; (2); Chorus; Var Trk; L Var Vllybl; High Hon Roll; Hon Roll; NEDT Awd; Prfct Atten Awd; CSF Treas; Med.

WONG, AURELIA K; Claremont HS; Walnut, CA; (4); Hosp Aide; VP Pep Clb; Stage Crew; JV Cheerldng; Var Pom Pon; Powder Puff Ftbl; High Hon Roll; Hon Roll; Lion Awd; Ntl Merit SF; Advrtsng.

WONG, BERNARD Y; Lowell HS; San Francisco, CA; (3); Aud/Vis; Q&S; Ntl Merit Ltr; Goldn St Exam High Hnrs; Hnrb Mntn Chem Trnmt; UC Berkeley.

WONG, BOBBY; George Washington HS; San Francisco, CA; (2); UC Davis; Engr.

WONG, BONNIE; Eagle Rock JR/Sr HS; Los Angeles, CA; (3); Library Aide; Orch; Phtg Yrbk; Sec Frsh Cls; Cit Awd; Hon Roll; Prfct Atten Awd; Chem Clb; Hosp Vlntr; Executive Cncl Stu Body Sec; Engrng.

WONG, BRIAN ALAN-MINGWAY; Palo Alto SR HS; Palo Alto, CA; (2); Debate Tm; JCL; NFL; Orch; Ed Nwsp; Pres Frsh Cls; Pres Soph Cls; Rep Jr Cls; Sec Stu Cncl; JV Socr; Palo Alto Chmbr Orch 5 Yrs; 1st Wnnr W Valley Coll Short Story Cntst 88-89; 3rd Pl HS Cntst 88-89; Stanford U.

WONG, CALVIN; Downtown Business Magnet HS; Los Angeles, CA; (2); Computer Clb; Tennis; Cal Tech; Elec Engrng.

WONG, CATHERINE J; Lowell HS; San Francisco, CA; (3); Yth Govt Jrnlst; Scl Work.

WONG, CATHY; El Cerrito HS; El Cerrito, CA; (4); French Clb; SADD; Teachers Aide; Variety Show; Pres Acad Fit Awd; CSF; FIDM; Fshn Dsgn.

WONG, CHERYL N; Abraham Lincoln HS; San Francisco, CA; (2); DAR Awd; Hon Roll; CA Schlrshp Fed; City Coll; Hotel Mgmt.

WONG, CHRISTOPHER T; A Lincoln HS; San Francisco, CA; (1); Rep Frsh Cls; Hon Roll; Golden St Exam Prtcpnt Algebra; PSAT Prtcpnt; UC Berkeley.

WONG, CHUNG Y; Laguna Hills HS; Laguna Hills, CA; (2); French Clb; Swmmng; UCLA; Radiology.

WONG, CINDY; South San Francisco HS; South San Francis, CA; (3); Computer Clb; French Clb; Math Clb; JV Tennis; Mrtkng Analyst.

WONG, CINDY S; San Gabriel HS; Alhambra, CA; (1); Pep Clb; Cit Awd; Hon Roll.

WONG, CINDY Y; San Leandro HS; San Leandro, CA; (2); 1/399; Cmnty Wkr; Intnl Clb; Key Clb; VP Frsh Cls; Treas Soph Cls; Var Trk; JV Vllybl; High Hon Roll; Hon Roll; Opt Clb Awd; 90 Alameda Cnty Soviet Exchnge Stds Soviet Union.

WONG, CLIFFORD; Lowell HS; San Francisco, CA; (2); Debate Tm; NFL; Speech Tm; SADD; Variety Show; Sec Frsh Cls; Rep Soph Cls; Stu Cncl; Var Swmmng; Gold St Exm Alg Hnrs; Civil Engrng.

WONG, CONNIE; Eagle Rock JR/Sr HS; Los Angeles, CA; (3); Rptr Yrbk; Sec Frsh Cls; High Hon Roll; Hon Roll; CSF 89-90; Kabanokas-Schl Svc Clb 89-90; Med.

WONG, CONNIE L; Lincoln HS; Stockton, CA; (2); 168/568; Key Clb; Spanish Clb; Yrbk; Hon Roll; Sci.

WONG, CYNTHIA; Mission HS; San Francisco, CA; (2); VP Soph Cls; Pres Jr Cls; Tennis; High Hon Roll; Outstndng Frshmn Yr Trphy; CSF; Acad Excllnce Awd Bio; Berkeley; Law.

WONG, DANNY Y; San Gabriel HS; Rosemead, CA; (1); Key Clb; School Play; Hon Roll; Karate; Med.

WONG, DARRYL Y; Saint Ignatius College Prep; San Francisco, CA; (4); 110/299; Pres Chess Clb; Cmnty Wkr; Model UN; Office Aide; Red Cross Aide; VP Science Clb; SADD; Ed Nwsp; Co-Ed Yrbk; Hon Roll; Sci Awd 88; U Of CA Davis; Sociology.

WONG, DAVID H; Alameda HS; Alameda, CA; (3); Chess Clb; Computer Clb; Cit Awd; Hon Roll; Pres Acad Fit Awd; CSF; Comp Sci.

WONG, DAVID S; San Gabriel HS; Rosemead, CA; (2); Chess Clb; Tennis; High Hon Roll; UC-IRVINE; Bus Admin.

WONG, DAVID T; San Gabriel HS; Alhambra, CA; (1); Intrml Tennis; Hon Roll; Berkeley; Engrng.

WONG, DIANA; Lowell HS; San Francisco, CA; (2); Hosp Aide; Office Aide; Chorus; Mgr(s); CSF; U CA-DAVIS.

WONG, DIANE Q; Lowell HS; San Francisco, CA; (2); Dance Clb; Rep Soph Cls; CA Schlrshp Fed; Big Brother & Sister Org; UC Berkely; Dentistry.

WONG, DINA N; South San Francisco HS; S San Francisco, CA; (4); 47/298; French Clb; Sec FBLA; JA; Outstndng Bus Stu Of 90; Bank Of Amerca Plaque Wnnr; Hnrs At Grad; San Francisco St Univ; Bus.

WONG, DONNA LEE; Glen A Wilson HS; Hacienda Heights, CA; (1); Drill Tm; Hon Roll; USC; Med.

WONG, DONNY; Lowell HS; San Francisco, CA; (3); Chess Clb; Service Clb; Orch; Var L Tennis; Ntl Merit SF; Natl Spansh Exam 5th Pl Natly; 1st Pl San Francisco Math Cmptn; 1st Pl Hnrs/A P Lvl Bay Area Chemathon; Engrng.

WONG, DORA W; Mt Diablo HS; Concord, CA; (1); Band; Jazz Band; Mrchg Band; Pep Band; Hon Roll; UCLA; Math.

WONG, EILEEN; Wallenberg HS; San Francisco, CA; (2); Mgr(s); High Hon Roll; Intnl Clb; Bdmntn.

WONG, ELIZABETH; C K Mc Clatchy HS; Sacramento, CA; (4); 11/443; Intnl Clb; Key Clb; Treas Stu Cncl; High Hon Roll; Hon Roll; Prfct Atten Awd; JV Var Cheerldng; Intrml Powder Puff Ftbl; JV Var Tennis; JV Var Trk; UC Berkely; Intl Bus.

WONG, FRANCIS P; Edison HS; Fresno, CA; (3); 7/250; JCL; Latin Clb; Letterman Clb; Science Clb; Lit Mag; VP Jr Cls; Pres Stu Cncl; Var L Ftbl; Var L Wrstlng; High Hon Roll; Ecology Club Pres; U Of CA 90 Bio-Med Research Awd; Stanford; Biological Sci.

WONG, FRANCIS S; Abraham Lincoln HS; San Francisco, CA; (3); Bausch & Lomb Sci Awd; CSF; Why Graffiti Isnt Cool Poster Cont Awd Schlrshp; Japanese Clb Pres; U Pacific; Dentstry.

WONG, GARY C; John Glenn HS; Norwalk, CA; (2); Band; Mrchg Band; Ed Nwsp; High Hon Roll; Prfct Atten Awd; CSF; Astrophysic Engrng.

WONG, GARY W; Gilroy HS; Gilroy, CA; (1); Bsbl; High Hon Roll; CA Schlrshp Fed; UC Berkley; Accntnt.

WONG, GLENN D; Bishop O'dowd HS; Alameda, CA; (3); Aud/Vis; Church Yth Grp; Ski Clb; Varsity Clb; JV Lcrss; Var Tennis; High Hon Roll; Hon Roll; UCLA; Vet.

WONG, GORDON K; Galileo HS; San Francisco, CA; (2); ROTC; High Hon Roll; Hon Roll; Prfct Atten Awd; ROTC Drum Corps; Advrtsng.

WONG, GRACE T; Skyline HS; Oakland, CA; (2); Intnl Clb; Yrbk; Cit Awd; Hon Roll; Prfct Atten Awd; Keywanettes Club; Asian Stu Union; Vietnamese Stu Union; Art.

WONG, GREGORY P; James Madison HS; San Diego, CA; (3); 1/420; Latin Clb; VP Soph Cls; Off Jr Cls; Off Sr Cls; JV Var Bsktbl; High Hon Roll; Ntl Merit Ltr; UCSD Erly Admissns Hnrs Pgm; Natl Endwmnt Humanities 89-90 Yng Schlr; Cngrssnl Schlr Natl Yng Ldrs Cn.

WONG, HANSEN L; Bellarmine College Prep; Morgan Hill, CA; (3); 4/300; Church Yth Grp; Cmnty Wkr; Varsity Clb; Stat Mgr Bsktbl; Asst Coach Girls Vllybl Tm; Med.

WONG, HECTOR; Orange HS; Orange, CA; (4); Computer Clb; Key Clb; Pres Math Clb; Math Tm; Mu Alpha Theta; Teachers Aide; Hon Roll; NHS; Rotary Awd; Awd Of Excllnc Math & Frgn Lang; UCLA; Math.

WONG, HELEN; Granada Hills HS; Los Angeles, CA; (2); Tennis; Var Vllybl; NEDT Awd; Prfct Atten Awd.

WONG, HENRY Y; Lowell HS; Daly City, CA; (4); 105/626; VP Chess Clb; Orch; Rep Frsh Cls; Rep Soph Cls; Rep Jr Cls; Rep Sr Cls; Rep Stu Cncl; Var Ftbl; Intrml Sftbl; U CA Alumni Schlrshp; Nor Cal Champ & Natl Rnnr-Up Chess Team; CSF Life; U CA; Mech Engrng.

WONG JR, HUMBERTO; Calexico Mission Acad; Calexico, CA; (2); 1/25; Church Yth Grp; Teachers Aide; Church Choir; High Hon Roll; Won Table Tnns Schl Tourn; Piano; Spk Spnsh.

WONG, IVAN; Washington HS; San Francisco, CA; (2); Hon Roll; Arch.

WONG, JACK; Schurr HS; Rosemead, CA; (4); 21/589; Church Yth Grp; Cmnty Wkr; Math Tm; Chorus; Church Choir; Yrbk; High Hon Roll; NHS; Pres Schlr; St Schlr; CSF Life Mbr; Tutor Engl Math & Bio; U CA Los Angeles; Bio.

WONG, JAMES G; Laguna Hills HS; Laguna Hills, CA; (1); 4/350; Math Clb; Band; Mrchg Band; Pep Band; High Hon Roll.

WONG, JANET E; San Gabriel Mission HS; Alhambra, CA; (2); 11/124; Drama Clb; French Clb; FBLA; Phtg Yrbk; CSF; Math Sci Clb Treas; Sci.

WONG, JASON J; Abraham Lincoln HS; San Francisco, CA; (3); Cmnty Wkr; Teachers Aide; High Hon Roll; St Schlr; Congrssnl Schlr; Lincoln Recyclng Ctr & Clb Pres; Big Bro/Big Sis & Earth Day Vlntr.

WONG, JASON J; Pilgrim Schl; Upland, CA; (3); Model UN; Yrbk; Rep Soph Cls; Var Bsbl; JV Bsktbl; Var Ftbl.

WONG, JASON R; Mark Keppel HS; Monterey Park, CA; (3); Drama Clb; Service Clb; Stu Cncl; JV Bsbl; Var Trk; Prfct Atten Awd; Film.

WONG, JAY K; Savanna HS; Buena Park, CA; (4); Band; Jazz Band; Mrchg Band; Trk; High Hon Roll; NHS; Prfct Atten Awd; Pres Acad Fit Awd; Bank Amer Achvt Fine Arts; Gldn ST Exam Awd Algbr I; CSF; UC Irvine.

WONG, JEAN S; Edison HS; Fresno, CA; (2); Church Yth Grp; JV Vllybl; Cit Awd; High Hon Roll; Hon Roll; CSF; Env Awrnss Clb; Art Awds.

WONG, JEANIE S M; Phillip & Sala Burton Academic HS; San Francisco, CA; (4); 4/177; Ski Clb; Acad Fncne; Acad Dcthln; Jnr Engr Tchncl Scty.

WONG, JEFFREY; Sacramento HS; Sacramento, CA; (3); Teachers Aide; JV Crs Cntry; Var Trk; Var Vllybl; Intrml Wt Lftg.

WONG, JEFFREY R; Amos Alonzo Stagg HS; Stockton, CA; (3); 1/475; Treas Am Leg Boys St; JA; VP Spanish Clb; Speech Tm; Sprt Ed Yrbk; Treas Stu Cncl; Var Swmmng; Pres NHS; Acad Dcthln; Vrsty Water Polo; Bus.

WONG, JEFFREY W; Abraham Lincoln HS; San Francisco, CA; (2); Swmmng; Tennis; Comp Sci; Drwng Awd; High Potnl Swmmng & Tnns; Standford U; Med.

WONG, JEFFREY Y; Thomas Edison HS; Stockton, CA; (2); Science Clb; Hon Roll; Prncpls Lst; U Of CA Berkeley; Elec Engr.

WONG, JENNIFER; Rosemead HS; Rosemead, CA; (2); Science Clb; Spanish Clb; JV Tennis; JV Trk; High Hon Roll; Prfct Atten Awd; CSF; Goldn St Exam Schl Rcgntn Geom; Med.

WONG, JENNIFER D; South San Francisco HS; S San Francisco, CA; (3); FBLA; Math Clb; Science Clb; JV Trk; Pres & Treas Student Social Sciences Club; History Day 2nd Place Co Compete; FBLA 2nd School Compete.

WONG, JENNIFER J; Mills HS; Burlingame, CA; (3); Church Yth Grp; Intnl Clb; Ed Lit Mag; High Hon Roll; Orch.

WONG, JENNIFER L; Corona SR HS; Corona, CA; (3); 4/473; Cmnty Wkr; Band; Jazz Band; Rptr Nwsp; Ed Yrbk; Treas Stu Cncl; Bsktbl; Pres Acad Fit Awd; Val; CSF; Educ.

WONG, JENNY; George Washington HS; San Francisco, CA; (3); Teachers Aide; Chorus; Church Choir; Hon Roll; CSF; Red Cross Club.

WONG, JESSICA; Crawford HS; San Diego, CA; (2); French Clb; Hon Roll; Jr NHS; Prfct Atten Awd; CSF; Engrng.

WONG, JIMMY K H; Lowell HS; San Francisco, CA; (4); 10/642; Rep Fld Hcky; Bsbl; Rep Science Clb; Service Clb; NHS; Ntl Merit SF; Bay Area Sci Fair 89 4th Pl; NSTA SSIP Mars Cont Hrbl Mntn; GSE High Hnrs & Perfect; Aero Engrng.

WONG, JOANNA W; Skyline HS; Oakland, CA; (3); Cmnty Wkr; Yrbk; Rep Stu Cncl; Hon Roll; Envrnmntl & Animal Rghts Org Pres; CSF; Natl Frat Stu Musicians.

WONG, JOHN F; Patterson HS; Patterson, CA; (3); Drama Clb; Yrbk; Off Soph Cls; Var Bsbl; Var Bsktbl; Hon Roll.

WONG, JONATHAN J; Encinal HS; Alameda, CA; (1); 19/279; Chess Clb; Trk; U Of CA.

WONG, JONATHAN T; Burlingame HS; Hillsborough, CA; (3); Math Clb; JV Bsktbl; Var Golf; Hon Roll; Bus.

WONG, JOSHUA; George Washington HS; San Francisco, CA; (2); Chess Clb; Computer Clb; Band; JV Bsbl; JV Var Tennis; Hon Roll; Chinese Amer Club; Backgammon Club; Stanford; Eng.

WONG, JOYCE P; A A Stagg HS; Stockton, CA; (3); Debate Tm; NFL; Science Clb; Spanish Clb; Speech Tm; Thesps; Orch; Socr; High Hon Roll; NHS; Encore Show Choir; Acad Decatln Team; Sams Jazz Show Choir.

WONG, JOYCE Y; St Joseph Notre Dame HS; Alameda, CA; (3); 2/101; Art Clb; Drama Clb; Math Clb; Science Clb; Rep Service Clb; Bausch & Lomb Sci Awd; Zonta Z Clb; Scl Jstc Cmmtte; Piano; UC Berkeley; Elec Engrng.

WONG, KAREN; John F Kennedy HS; La Palma, CA; (4); Treas Church Yth Grp; Cmnty Wkr; Computer Clb; 4-H; Hosp Aide; Key Clb; Sec Service Clb; Hon Roll; NHS; Pres Acad Fit Awd; Acad Hnrs Grad; Smmr Ldrshp Acad 89; U Southern CA; Phrmcy.

WONG, KAREN K; Galileo HS; San Francisco, CA; (4); 30/400; GAA; JA; Nwsp; Capt Vllybl; Hon Roll; UC Santa Cruz.

WONG, KEITH H; Mount Pleasant HS; San Jose, CA; (1); Hon Roll; Prfct Atten Awd; Fish; Gardening; Comp; Engrng.

WONG, KENNETH; Bishop O'dowd HS; Oakland, CA; (2); Art Clb; Cmnty Wkr; Hosp Aide; Math Clb; Math Tm; Ed Nwsp; Ed Yrbk; High Hon Roll; CSF Orgnzng Cmmtte.

WONG, KENNETH; Pinole Valley HS; Hercules, CA; (2).

WONG, KENNY; Atwater HS; Atwater, CA; (2); Hon Roll; UC Davis; Optimistic.

WONG, KENRIC S; Mission San Jose HS; Fremont, CA; (4); Cmnty Wkr; French Clb; Science Clb; Ski Clb; Spanish Clb; Var Bsktbl; Var JV Ftbl; NHS; Prfct Atten Awd; Leo Club; Crss Cultural Club; Badminton Vrsty Tm Capt; UC Santa Cruz; Biomed Sci.

WONG, KEVIN; Skyline HS; Oakland, CA; (2); CSF; U CA Berkeley.

WONG, KEVIN J; Rosemead HS; Rosemead, CA; (2); Hon Roll; Prfct Atten Awd; UCI; Engrg.

WONG, KRISTINE A; Carlmont HS; Belmont, CA; (3); 10/253; Ed Nwsp; Pres Frsh Cls; Stu Cncl; JV Tennis; CSF Pres & Hnrs Soc; Tnns MVP; Hnrs Math Stu; Cert Mrt Hnrs Piano Stu; Mock Trial Team.

WONG, KWOK Y; Elk Grove HS; Sacramento, CA; (4); 13/500; Library Aide; Math Clb; Teachers Aide; High Hon Roll; Prfct Atten Awd; Academic Letter; U Of CA Davis; Civil Eng.

WONG, LAWRENCE Y; Lowell HS; San Francisco, CA; (3); Church Yth Grp; Math Clb; Science Clb; Teachers Aide; High Hon Roll; Ntl Merit Ltr; Pres Acad Fit Awd; Golden St Exam In Algebra & Geom; Engr Club; UC Berkeley; Elect Engr.

WONG, LAWSON L; Lowell HS; San Francisco, CA; (3); JA; Science Clb; Service Clb; Variety Show; Intrml Vllybl; Cit Awd; NHS; Gldn St Exams-Alg-Hgh Hnrs; Gldn St Exams-Geom-Hnrs; Berkeley U; Bus.

WONG, LEANNE M; Eagle Rock HS; Los Angeles, CA; (2); Girl Scts; Key Clb; Teachers Aide; Yrbk; Off Soph Cls; Var Golf; Hon Roll; Pres Acad Fit Awd; 2 Time Wnnr Optimist Jr World Chmpnshp Golf 86 & 88; UCLA; Professional Golf.

WONG, LEE; Garfield HS Magnet; Huntington Park, CA; (2); Yrbk; High Hon Roll; Hist NHS; Prfct Atten Awd; Pres Acad Fit Awd; Gldn St Exms Hgh Hnrs; CSF.

WONG, LEE A; Beaumont HS; Beaumont, CA; (1); Drama Clb; JV Vllybl; Cit Awd; CSF Mem.

WONG, LEO; Abraham Lincoln HS; San Francisco, CA; (1); Cmnty Study & Service Cls; U Of CA; Bus Admin.

WONG, LEO Y; El Toro HS; El Toro, CA; (2); Art Clb; Boy Scts; Chess Clb; Computer Clb; German Clb; High Hon Roll; Hon Roll; Jr NHS; NHS; Cinematgrphy; Sailing; Cinematgrphy.

WONG, LEONA; Patterson HS; Patterson, CA; (3); Cmnty Wkr; Chorus; Rptr Nwsp; Yrbk; Sec VP Stu Cncl; Hon Roll; Girls Ledrshp; Acad Deca; Job As Chasier; U C Davis; Lawyer.

WONG, LESLIE; Liberty Christian Schl; Huntington Bch, CA; (3); 1/16; Teachers Aide; Chorus; Ed Yrbk; Pres Frsh Cls; Pres Soph Cls; Pres Jr Cls; Treas Stu Cncl; Capt Cheerldng; Cit Awd; High Hon Roll.

WONG, LIANA; Richard Gahr HS; Cerritos, CA; (2); 12/375; Cmnty Wkr; Debate Tm; Speech Tm; Off Soph Cls; JV Cheerldng; Hon Roll; CA Schlrshp Fed; Prom Cmmtte; Comm.

WONG, LIANE N; Skyline HS; Oakland, CA; (2); German Clb; Hon Roll; Wrld Culture Stu Of Mnth; CJSF; Cal ST Hayward; Accntng.

WONG, LILY; Hemet HS; Hemet, CA; (2); Library Aide; Cit Awd; Hon Roll; Prfct Atten Awd; Conservation Clb; Marine Bio.

WONG, LILY H; Canyon HS; Newhall, CA; (1); Hon Roll; CSF; UCLA; Bus Mgr.

WONG, LINDA; Downtown Business Magnet HS; Los Angeles, CA; (4); Art Clb; French Clb; Key Clb; Office Aide; Yrbk; Cit Awd; High Hon Roll; Prfct Atten Awd; High Hnrs GSE Geomtry; Close Up Prog-Wash DC; Elec Engr.

WONG, LINDA; International Studies Acad; San Francisco, CA; (2); Math Clb; Science Clb; High Hon Roll; NHS; Pres Acad Fit Awd; CSF; Peer Cnslng; Stanford U; Bus Mgmt.

WONG, LISA; Pinole Valley HS; Pinole, CA; (2); NHS; Prfct Atten Awd; UC Berkeley.

WONG, LUTZ; Wallenberg HS; San Francisco, CA; (1); Office Aide; Hon Roll; Peer Tutoring; Award For Outstanding Work In Keyboarding; Boston Coll; Journalism.

WONG, MADELINE; International Studies Acad HS; San Francisco, CA; (3); Cit Awd; High Hon Roll; Hon Roll; Prfct Atten Awd; CA Leg Assmbly Cert Of Apprctn; Humanities.

WONG, MANDA R; South San Francisco HS; South San Francis, CA; (2); Church Yth Grp; French Clb; Math Clb; Math Tm; Red Cross Aide; Church Choir; Musical Instrument Piano; Schls Acadc Awd; Int Designer.

WONG, MARIO A; Calexico HS; Calexico, CA; (3); Am Leg Boys St; Var JV Ftbl; Wrstlng; JV Ftbl MVP; Acad Awds-Spnsh & Geom; Awd Recgntn Boys St; Astrnmy.

WONG, MARK J; Glendale Adventist Acad; Glendale, CA; (3); 5/57; Church Yth Grp; Teachers Aide; Varsity Clb; Acpl Chr; Band; Phtg Yrbk; Off Jr Cls; Ftbl; Vllybl; NHS; Pacific Union Coll; Sci.

WONG, MARY; Garfield HS; Huntington Park, CA; (3); Math Tm; Treas SADD; Co-Ed Nwsp; Lit Mag; Treas NHS; Ntl Merit Ltr; Pres Acad Fit Awd; VP Rtry Intract; CSF; Rtry Yth Ldrshp Awds Conf; Harvard Bk Awd.

WONG, MAUREEN; George Washington HS; San Francisco, CA; (3); JA; Key Clb; Red Cross Aide; Service Clb; Speech Tm; Stage Crew; Var Gym; JV Swmmng; Hon Roll; Ntl Merit Ltr.

WONG, MAY; El Cerrito HS; El Cerrito, CA; (4); Dance Clb; Debate Tm; French Clb; NFL; Office Aide; Speech Tm; Teachers Aide; Var Trk; High Hon Roll; NHS; UC Berkeley; Law.

WONG, MAY M Y; Westmoor HS; Daly City, CA; (4); 13/325; French Clb; German Clb; Model UN; Service Clb; Band; Treas Soph Cls; VP Jr Cls; Var JV Crs Cntry; Var Mgr(s); JV Tennis; Badmntn; CSF VP & Pres; Coll Entrance Clb Pres & Treas; UC Davis.

WONG, MELINDA; Abraham Lincoln HS; San Francisco, CA; (3); Office Aide; ROTC; Yrbk; Hist Stu Cncl; Mgr(s); Mgr Swmmng; Cit Awd; High Hon Roll; Jr Statesmn Amer.

WONG, MELISSA M; Immaculate Heart HS; Los Angeles, CA; (3); 20/127; GAA; Math Clb; Mu Alpha Theta; Spanish Clb; Rptr Nwsp; Rep Sr Cls; Hon Roll; CA Schlrshp Fed; 40/40 Service Clb; Span Hnr Soc; UCLA; Arch.

WONG, MICHAEL L; Calexico HS; Calexico, CA; (2); Church Yth Grp; Cmnty Wkr; 4-H; Intrml JV Bsbl; Var Score Keeper; Cit Awd; 4-H Awd; High Hon Roll; Hon Roll; CSF; GSE; Erly Outreach Prgm.

WONG, MICHAEL M; Central Union HS; El Centro, CA; (2); 1/692; Church Yth Grp; Math Clb; Math Tm; Band; Mrchg Band; Pep Band; Var Bsbl; VP Frsh Cls; VP Soph Cls; VP Jr Cls; Chrch Vllybl Team.

WONG, MILTON D; Lowell HS; San Francisco, CA; (2); Cmnty Wkr; Office Aide; Hon Roll; CA Invtnl Chemathon 2nd Prz 90; Gldn St Exam Alb High Hnrs 89; CSF; CSF Tutor; Yth Bsbl Leag; CA Polytech Inst Tech; Automtv.

WONG, MONICA L; Abraham Lincoln HS; San Francisco, CA; (3); CSF; CA ST Coll; Sci.

WONG, NAOMI C; Ramona Convent Secondary Schl; Los Angeles, CA; (3); Off Church Yth Grp; French Clb; Model UN; Chorus; Church Choir; Mgr(s); Hon Roll; NHS; CSF; Philomatheon Hon Soc; Ecology Club Vp; CA ST U; Ind Dsgn.

WONG, NORTON; Abraham Lincoln HS; San Francisco, CA; (1); Church Yth Grp; Church Choir; JV Bsbl; St Schlr; Chrch Sftbl Tm, Outreach Pgm; Cls Of 92 Clb; San Jose ST U; Engr.

WONG, OLIVER D; Livermore HS; Livermore, CA; (3); Boy Scts; Letterman Clb; Ski Clb; Spanish Clb; Off Jr Cls; JV Crs Cntry; Var Socr; Var Trk; High Hon Roll; Hon Roll; Stu Actvts Cmssn.

WONG, PAUL; Chula Vista HS; Chula Vista, CA; (3); Church Yth Grp; Cmnty Wkr; Dance Clb; Varsity Clb; Chorus; Nwsp; Off Jr Cls; Vllybl; SDSU; Engr.

WONG, PAULA; Mills HS; Millbrae, CA; (3); Var Mgr(s).

WONG, PAULA M; Rio Linda SR HS; Sacramento, CA; (2); Spanish Clb; Hon Roll; CSF; Goldn St Exam Schl Recgntn Awd Geom 89; Smmr Acad Intl Stds Sacramento 90.

WONG, POLLY P; Los Altos HS; Hacienda Hgts, CA; (3); Church Choir; JV Tennis; Hon Roll; CA ST U Fullerton; Acctng.

WONG, RANDY; Mark Keppel HS; Monterey Park, CA; (2); High Hon Roll; CSF; Goldn St Exam Hnrs 1st Yr Alg; Outstndng Achvt Geom; UCLA.

WONG, RICHARD C; Lowell HS; San Francisco, CA; (3); Science Clb; Shield/Scrll Hnr Soc; Earth Day Ocean Bach Clean Up; 5th Pl Ovrl CA Invtnl Chemathon 1st Pl Trphy; UC Berkeley; Engrng.

WONG, ROGER; St Ignatius College Prep; San Francisco, CA; (3); Aud/Vis; Church Yth Grp; Cmnty Wkr; Ed Nwsp; 89-91 Florence Heaffy Schlrshps; Grphc Arts.

WONG, ROSAMOND; Immaculate Heart HS; Los Angeles, CA; (4); French Clb; Math Clb; Mu Alpha Theta; Science Clb; Service Clb; Yrbk; Hon Roll; NHS; NEDT Awd; Soc Womens Engr Awd; Bk Amer Plaque Math/Sci; 1st Pl Harvard Schl Intl Write On; UCLA; Elec Engrng.

WONG, ROSELINA S; Rosemead HS; Rosemead, CA; (3); JV Bsktbl; Hon Roll; Secy, VP SAGATHS; #1 Grls Dbls, #3 Mx Dbls JV Badmntn; CSF; Art Stu Mnth June; 2nd Pl Slgn/Logo Cont; Art History.

WONG, RUSSELL W H; Don Bosco Technical Inst; San Gabriel, CA; (4); Cmnty Wkr; Computer Clb; Debate Tm; Math Tm; Teachers Aide; Nwsp; Yrbk; Bsktbl; Stat Vllybl; High Hon Roll; Bnk America Achvt Awd Comp; Medlln Awd Math; Rio Hondo Coll Awd Mrt 1st Pl Electrncs; UC Berkeley; Elec Engrng.

WONG, SALLY KIM; James Logan HS; Union City, CA; (4); Sec Cmnty Wkr; Hosp Aide; Pres Acad Fit Awd; 1st Pl Bhvrl Sci/Sci Fair; USMC Awd For Sci Prjct; CSF Awd; Sci, Scl Sci & Englsh Awds; U CA Los Angeles; Psych.

WONG, SHING; Reedley HS; Dinuba, CA; (3); 1/310; Pres Computer Clb; French Clb; FBLA; Science Clb; VP VICA; Gov Hon Prg Awd; High Hon Roll; Hon Roll; Prfct Atten Awd; California Scholarship Federation; Academic Decathlon; Junior Engineering Technical Society.

WONG, SHIRLEY; Bishop Amat HS; Rowland Heights, CA; (2); Cmnty Wkr; Hon Roll; NHS; NEDT Awd; Prfct Atten Awd; CA Schlrshp Fed.

WONG, SINCERE; George Washington HS; Daly City, CA; (2); Intnl Clb; Office Aide; High Hon Roll; Close-Up Pgm; U Of CA.

WONG, STACIE; Alhambra HS; Monterey Park, CA; (4); 8/690; Church Yth Grp; NFL; Pres Pep Clb; Sec Service Clb; Rep VICA; Ed Rptr Nwsp; VP Frsh Cls; Capt Cheerldng; High Hon Roll; Opt Clb Awd; Jostens Fndtn Natl Schlrshp Wnnr; UC Berkeley; Arch.

WONG, STELLA M; El Toro HS; El Toro, CA; (4); 152/452; Church Yth Grp; Cmnty Wkr; Band; Drill Tm; Mrchg Band; Orch; School Musical; Stage Crew; Hon Roll; NHS; Grls Leag Secy, Pres; Baker U; Music.

WONG, STEVEN MAUNG; Phillip And Sala Burton Acad HS; San Francisco, CA; (4); Computer Clb; Math Clb; Math Tm; Science Clb; Ski Clb; Teachers Aide; Band; Orch; Cit Awd; High Hon Roll; Chinese Achvmnts; Acad Decathlon; Jets Club; U CA; Elec Engr.

WONG, SUSAN; John F Kennedy HS; Sacramento, CA; (3); Art Clb; French Clb; FBLA; Vllybl; Work Part Time; Medicine.

WONG, THERESA; Alhambra HS; Monterey Park, CA; (2); German Clb; Pep Clb; Nwsp; Hon Roll; Tri Hi YMCA Club; Delta Epsilon Phi; Elec Engrng.

WONG, VAN; Downtown Business Magnet HS; Los Angeles, CA; (1); Computer Clb; Prfct Atten Awd; Golden St Exam Algebra Hnrs; Outstndng Stu Awd; Mst Imprvd Comp Sci Awd; Cal Tech; Engrng.

WONG, WILLIAM J; Lodi HS; Stockton, CA; (3); 22/518; Cmnty Wkr; Debate Tm; FBLA; NFL; Speech Tm; Hon Roll; Pres Acad Fit Awd; San Joaquin Drug Prevention Program; VC Davis; Comp Sci Major.

WONG, WING K; Mark Keeple HS; Monterey Park, CA; (2); Library Aide; Hon Roll.

WONG, WINNIE M; Lowell HS; San Francisco, CA; (3); Office Aide; Teachers Aide; CSF; Goldn St Exam High Hnrs Alg & Geom; Red Crss Clb; Big Brothr/Big Sistr.

WONG, YEE M; Lowell HS; San Francisco, CA; (3); Cmnty Wkr; Science Clb; Am Inst Of Archt Drftng Cmptn 88 & 89; Chmthn 90; Sci-Fi Clb; Drftng Clb; Ath Clb; UC Brkly; Arch.

WONG, YU HEUNG; Raoul Wallenberg HS; San Francisco, CA; (3); Band; Hon Roll; Dance-Ballet; Peer Tutor.

WONG, YVONNE; Lowell HS; San Francisco, CA; (3); Church Yth Grp; Science Clb; Teachers Aide; Church Choir; Orch; School Musical; Chinese Clb; Vietnamese Clb Sec & Publcty Mgr; UC Davis; Surgeon.

WONG, ZI Y; Escondido HS; Escondido, CA; (1).

WONG-FOY, ANNJOE G; Gompers Secondary Schl; San Diego, CA; (2); 1/150; Math Tm; Science Clb; Lit Mag; Stu Cncl; High Hon Roll; NHS; Opt Clb Awd; French Clb; Math Clb; Jr NHS; Music; Creativity Clb; Mock Trial Tm.

WOO, ALYSSA; Crescenta Valley HS; La Crescenta, CA; (2); Drama Clb; Hosp Aide; Intnl Clb; Key Clb; Math Clb; Mu Alpha Theta; Service Clb; Spanish Clb; Chorus; Nwsp; Peter Meremblum Pathfinder Yth Orch; Dentistry.

WOO, DARRICK J; Chester HS; Chester, CA; (3); VP Sr Cls; Var Ftbl; Hon Roll; Vrsty Ski Tm.

WOO, DERRICK; El Camino HS; Daly City, CA; (4); 5/264; Cmnty Wkr; Math Clb; Service Clb; Var Capt Tennis; Bank Of Amer Cert-Math; U Of CA Berkeley; Mech Engrng.

WOO, ELAINE; Abraham Lincoln HS; San Francisco, CA; (1); Hon Roll; Ntl Merit Ltr; U Berkeley; Dentistry.

WOO, JOAN SUSIE; Crescenta Valley HS; Glendale, CA; (1); Intnl Clb; Key Clb; Math Clb; Mu Alpha Theta; Chorus; Rotary Awd; Edtr Schl Poetry Magzn Ark; Foothl Flute Chr; Meremblum Pionr Yth Orchstr; Piano & Flute.

WOO, JUNG A; Herbert Hoover HS; Glendale, CA; (2); Golden St Exam Geom High Hnr; UC Berkeley; Molecular Bio.

WOO, JUSTIN B; Ernest Righetti HS; Santa Maria, CA; (4); 10/400; Treas French Clb; Treas Math Clb; Stu Cncl; Var JV Ftbl; L Capt Trk; High Hon Roll; Pres Acad Fit Awd; Art Clb; Math Tm; Service Clb; CSF; Goldn St Exam Geom High Hnrs; U Southern CA; Elec Engrng.

WOO, KAROLYN A; Bullard HS; Fresno, CA; (4); 15/455; Dance Clb; French Clb; Key Clb; SADD; Nwsp; Sec Jr Cls; High Hon Roll; Prfct Atten Awd; Pres Acad Fit Awd; Xerox Schlr Schlrshp U Rochester; Marguerite Amlty Bllt Cmptn; St Hstry Fr; UCLA; Econmcs.

WOO, MICHAEL H; Cordova SR HS; Rancho Cordova, CA; (3); 8/460; Key Clb; Model UN; Office Aide; Scholastic Bowl; Teachers Aide; Bsktbl; High Hon Roll; NHS; Engrng.

WOO, NELSON; Chula Vista HS; National City, CA; (2); Math Tm; Hon Roll; UCSD.

WOO, PERRY Y; Indio HS; Indio, CA; (1); Var Swmmng; WY U; Pharmacy.

WOO, SALLY; Abraham Lincoln HS; San Francisco, CA; (4); Church Yth Grp; FTA; Teachers Aide; Stage Crew; Ed Yrbk; Hon Roll; San Francisco ST U.

WOO, SUEMAY; George Washington HS; San Francisco, CA; (4); Teachers Aide; Hon Roll; San Francisco ST U.

WOO, SUSIE; Arcadia HS; Arcadia, CA; (3); VP Dance Clb; Office Aide; Variety Show; Rep Stu Cncl; Var Cheerldng; Var Pom Pon; Hon Roll; NHS; CJSF Hnrs; Dance; U CA.

WOO, SUZANNE; Abraham Lincoln HS; San Francisco, CA; (3); Church Yth Grp; Mgr Church Choir; Mgr Stu Cncl; Sftbl; Hon Roll; Stu Lesson Dsgn Cont 3rd Pl 88; Lincs Hnr Soc; Prom Cmmtte 90.

WOO, VIVIAN J; Lowell HS; San Francisco, CA; (2); Office Aide; Red Cross Aide; School Play; Golden ST Exmntn Awrd; BBSO; UC Davis; Accntng.

WOOARD, ROSILYN C; Pius X HS; Los Angeles, CA; (4); Dance Clb; Drama Clb; GAA; Speech Tm; Varsity Clb; Church Choir; L Capt Socr; L Capt Trk; L Var Vllybl; Hon Roll; Clark Coll; Dentistry.

WOOD, AMY D; Antelope Valley HS; Lancaster, CA; (2); Church Yth Grp; Hosp Aide; Off Frsh Cls; Hon Roll; Stu Of Week; CSF; Brigham Young U.

WOOD, BRIAN; Loyola HS; Pacific Palisades, CA; (2); JV Swmmng; Hon Roll; Amnesty Intl; Chrstn Life Cmmnty; JV Waterpolo; Bus.

WOOD, CHANDALEE; Victor Valley HS; Victorville, CA; (4); 5/26; Church Yth Grp; Speech Tm; Chorus; School Musical; School Play; VP Sec Stu Cncl; Var Capt Bsktbl; Var Capt Vllybl; High Hon Roll; Azusa Pacific U; Music.

WOOD, DANIEL N; Oak Ridge HS; El Dorado Hills, CA; (3); 1/290; Pres Debate Tm; French Clb; Intnl Clb; Math Tm; Speech Tm; High Hon Roll; Hon Roll; Pres Acad Fit Awd; CA Schrlshp Fed; Edtr Of Nwslttr; Envrnmntlst Clb; Acad Dcthln; Stanford U; Bus.

WOOD, DEAN W; Edison HS; Fresno, CA; (2); 1/328; Computer Clb; Hon Roll; Odyssey Of Mind; CA Schlrshp Fed; Envrnmntl & Amateur Radio Clb; CA Poly San Luis Obispo; Comp.

WOOD, EMILY; Lawrence Cook JR HS; Santa Rosa, CA; (1); Church Yth Grp; Drama Clb; Pep Clb; Spanish Clb; School Play; Var Cheerldng; Hon Roll; Hnr Soc Pres; Outstndng Actrs Awd; Crmnl Law.

WOOD, ERIN M; Etiwanda HS; Fontana, CA; (3); 62/642; Key Clb; SADD; JV Bsktbl; Var L Trk; Hon Roll; Peer Cnslr; Red Rbbn Wk; Citizens Against Substance Abuse Cert Of Appreciation; Pediatrician.

WOOD, GREG; Marina HS; Huntington Bch, CA; (1); JCL; Latin Clb; Cit Awd; High Hon Roll; Hon Roll; Stu Pilot; Golf; Jet Skiing; UC Irvine; Anestheslgst.

WOOD, GREGORY R; Escondido HS; Escondido, CA; (4); 1/300; Am Leg Boys St; Boy Scts; Letterman Clb; Quiz Bowl; Science Clb; Varsity Clb; Capt L Crs Cntry; Var L Socr; Var L Trk; Elks Awd; Air Force Acad Smmr Scntfc Smnr 89; CSF; US Air Force; Aerospace Engr.

WOOD, JACK G; Don Antonio Lugo HS; Chino, CA; (2); 50/900; Boy Scts; Church Yth Grp; German Clb; Band; Jazz Band; Mrchg Band; Var Crs Cntry; Var Trk; U CA Irvine.

WOOD, JAMES L; Montgomery HS; Santa Rosa, CA; (3); Boy Scts; Church Yth Grp; Spanish Clb; Enthusiastic Span Lang Use Awd.

WOOD, JENIFFER; North HS; Bakersfield, CA; (2); Church Yth Grp; Cmnty Wkr; Drama Clb; Teachers Aide; Chorus; Church Choir; School Play; Stage Crew; Hon Roll; Theatrcl Arts.

WOOD, JEREMY R; Hemet HS; Idyllwild, CA; (3); Am Leg Boys St; Rep Frsh Cls; Var JV Bsbl; Var JV Bsktbl; JV Intrml Ftbl; Hon Roll; Prfct Atten Awd; Drftng Clb; CSF; CA Poly; Arch Engr.

WOOD, JULIE; S Pasadena HS; South Pasadena, CA; (2); Church Yth Grp; Drama Clb; Ski Clb; SADD; Chorus; Church Choir; School Musical; Mgr(s); JV Tennis; Outstndng Soph Concert Choir; VP Friday Night Live; Ldrshp For Campers Chrstn Fllwshp; UCLA; Med.

WOOD, KAMALA A; Aptos HS; Watsonville, CA; (1); Church Yth Grp; 4-H; Band; Var Trk; High Hon Roll; Hon Roll; Pres Acad Fit Awd; Interact Club; Sci.

WOOD, KARMA L; John H Francis Polytech; Sun Valley, CA; (3); Color Guard; Hon Roll.

WOOD, KATHERINE; Huntington Beach HS; Huntington Beach, CA; (2); Model UN; Red Cross Aide; Treas Jr Cls; JV Trk; Var Vllybl; Hon Roll; Pres Acad Fit Awd; Orange Cnty Vllybl Clb; JR Statesmn Of Am; Law.

WOOD, KEVIN E; Del Oro HS; Newcastle, CA; (3); 7/266; Boy Scts; Chess Clb; Church Yth Grp; Var L Socr; High Hon Roll; Chem Hall Of Fame; Med.

WOOD, LORI E; Carlsbad HS; Carlsbad, CA; (1); Hon Roll; Pres Acad Fit Awd; Straight A Stu Spnsh; Physcl Thrpst.

WOOD, MELANIE K; San Pasqual HS; Escondido, CA; (2); 30/416; Drama Clb; School Play; Stage Crew; Lit Mag.

WOOD, MICHELLE L; St Francis HS; San Jose, CA; (1); Art Clb; Church Yth Grp; Cmnty Wkr; GAA; Hosp Aide; SADD; Stat Bsktbl; JV Score Keeper; Stat Socr; JV Swmmng; Outstdng Fresh Awd; Track; Duke; Ob Gyn.

WOOD, MISHA A; Mira Mesa HS; San Diego, CA; (2); Church Yth Grp; French Clb; Intnl Clb; Cit Awd; Jobs Dghtrs; Amnsty Intl; Politics.

WOOD, PAMELA J; Flintridge Prep; Glendale, CA; (3); French Clb; Hosp Aide; Band; Ed Yrbk; Stu Cncl; Var Swmmng; Hon Roll; NHS; Peer Counseling; CSF; Liberal Arts.

WOOD, STEFANIE D; Hanford Joint Union HS; Hanford, CA; (1); Church Yth Grp; Girl Scts; Library Aide; Office Aide; Teachers Aide; Chorus; School Musical; Swmmng; Pres Acad Fit Awd; Bus.

WOOD, STEVE M; Garden Grove HS; Garden Grove, CA; (1); Chess Clb; German Clb; JV Bsbl; Intrml Ftbl; Hon Roll; Bio.

WOOD, TIMOTHY G; Valhalla HS; El Cajon, CA; (3); 93/430; Drama Clb; Thesps; Band; School Play; Stage Crew; Theater Arts.

WOOD, TRYSHA L; Vacaville HS; Vacaville, CA; (3); SADD; Band; School Musical; Hon Roll; Rotary Frgn Exchng Stu Grmny 90-91; Jr Vlntr Prsdntl Offc; U Of Boston; Music Prdcr.

WOOD, VIRGINIA F; Clovis West HS; Fresno, CA; (2); Aud/Vis; Drama Clb; English Clb; Ski Clb; JV Socr; JV Swmmng; Hon Roll; 1st Pl ST Film Cont CMLEA; CA Schlstc League; Western Riding& Cutting; Film.

WOOD, ZACK J; Hueneme HS; Hueneme, CA; (2); #78 In Class; Pres Acad Fit Awd; Bus.

WOODARD, GREG E; Norco HS; Norco, CA; (3); 1/400; Am Leg Boys St; Debate Tm; Model UN; Speech Tm; JV Bsktbl; JV Golf; JV Socr; VP L Tennis; Intrml Vllybl; High Hon Roll; CA Inst Of Tech; Engrng.

WOODARD, KIMBERLY L; Riverside Poly HS; Riverside, CA; (4); 45/345; Intnl Clb; Cit Awd; Hon Roll; Ntl Merit Ltr; Pres Acad Fit Awd; U Of CA Riverside; Lawyer.

WOODARD, LORETTA A; Dublin HS; Dublin, CA; (3); Cmnty Wkr; Teachers Aide; Hon Roll; Vet.

WOODARD, RAQUEL; Edison HS; Huntington Beach, CA; (2); Ed Yrbk; Span Hnrs Soc; CSF; Keywantettes-Sec; U CA Berkeley; Math.

WOODBRIDGE, MARK L; Chino HS; Chino Hills, CA; (1); Band; JV Crs Cntry; Var Trk; High Hon Roll; CSF; Silver Spur Awds.

WOODBURNE, EMILY M; Rim Of The World HS; Running Springs, CA; (2); French Clb; Intnl Clb; Pep Clb; Phtg Yrbk; Rep Frsh Cls; Rep Soph Cls; VP Jr Cls; Capt Var Cheerldng; Hon Roll; Prfct Atten Awd; U CA; Marine Bio.

WOODBURY, LEAH K; Morro Bay HS; Los Osos, CA; (3); 45/235; Varsity Clb; Var L Bsktbl; Var Powder Puff Ftbl; Var L Vllybl; Bsktbl Var All Leag & All Cnty 89-90; Scndry Ed.

WOODBYRNE, MITCH S; Lompoc SR HS; Lompoc, CA; (1).

WOODCOX, SHELLEY R; Paradise HS; Paradise, CA; (3); French Clb; Pep Clb; Teachers Aide; Acpl Chr; Chorus; Bsktbl; Cheerldng; Sftbl; Vllybl; Hon Roll; U Of Santa Barbara; Psych.

WOODDELL, SUSAN M; Lindhurst HS; Marysville, CA; (3); Red Cross Aide; Teachers Aide; Ski Clb; Flag Corp; Mrchg Band; Gym; U Of Tampa; Accountant.

WOODHOUSE, JACKIE L; Enterprise HS; Redding, CA; (4); Drama Clb; School Play; Stage Crew; Bsktbl; Powder Puff Ftbl; Swmmng; Hon Roll; Bus.

WOODIN, JARED W; Pittsburg HS; Pittsburg, CA; (1); Church Yth Grp; Ed Nwsp; Yrbk; JV Bsbl; JV Bsktbl; JV Wt Lftg; High Hon Roll; Lwilliam A Cadmen Awd; Schlt Athl Awd; Subway Pirate Player Of Week Awd; Stanford.

WOODIN, NICHOLAS D; Palmdale HS; Palmdale, CA; (3); 42/612; Teachers Aide; Var Capt Tennis; Hon Roll; Kiwanis Awd; Pres Acad Fit Awd; Ed.

WOODLAND, BRAD R; Antioch HS; Antioch, CA; (3); Ski Clb; Varsity Clb; Band; JV Crs Cntry; Ftbl; Var Trk; Hon Roll; Pres Acad Fit Awd; Academic Letter Club; Medical.

WOODLEY, CRISTINA A; Cupertino HS; San Jose, CA; (2); Ltr Commendation Frosh Eng; Div Champ Horse Show; Gold Awd For Foods; Trng Hunter.

WOODRING, REBECCA M; Leuzinger HS; Hawthorne, CA; (3); Church Yth Grp; Girl Scts; Pep Clb; VP JV Cheerldng; VP JV Sftbl; Hon Roll; Pres Acad Fit Awd; Ed.

WOODRING, SHANNON; Atwater HS; Winton, CA; (2); Church Yth Grp; Dance Clb; FCA; Pep Clb; Teachers Aide; Cheerldng; Gym; Powder Puff Ftbl; Jr Chrldng Tm Advsr; Dntl Hyg.

WOODRUFF, CYNTHIA L; Serrano HS; Phelan, CA; (1); Church Yth Grp; FFA; Quiz Bowl; Red Cross Aide; Temple Yth Grp; Chorus; Church Choir; Hon Roll; Chrch Sports; BYU; Marine Bio.

WOODRUFF, KEVIN G; Shasta HS; Redding, CA; (4); 1/338; Pres Chess Clb; Computer Clb; Pres Debate Tm; FBLA; Pres Model UN; Science Clb; Band; Mrchg Band; School Musical; Rep Stu Cncl; Comp Clubs; Stnfrd; MBA.

WOODRUFF, MELISSA D; Chaparral HS; Phelan, CA; (4); Church Yth Grp; Debate Tm; French Clb; Rptr Off FFA; JV Crs Cntry; Hon Roll; FFA-ADVSRS Awd/2nd & 3rd Pl Mrkt Sheept Showmnshp/Sentinel.

WOODRUFF, TANYA D; Carlsbad HS; Carlsbad, CA; (2); Church Yth Grp; Drama Clb; Girl Scts; Model UN; Pep Clb; Acting Awd; Presdntl Ftnss Awd.

WOODRUM, KIM; Christian HS; Bonita, CA; (3); Church Yth Grp; Key Clb; Office Aide; Pep Clb; Ski Clb; Teachers Aide; Varsity Clb; School Play; VP Stu Cncl; JV Cheerldng; Westmont.

WOODS, ANNALISA L; Paradise HS; Paradise, CA; (3); Church Yth Grp; Letterman Clb; Varsity Clb; Church Choir; Var Bsktbl; JV Powder Puff Ftbl; Var Trk; Hon Roll; Yng Life Clb; Coll Connection; Envrnmntl Camp Cnslr; Butte Coll; Cnslr.

WOODS, APRIL M; Summerville HS; Sonora, CA; (3); 25/150; Spanish Clb; SADD; Chorus; Color Guard; Drill Tm; Flag Corp; Mrchg Band; School Musical; School Play; Swing Chorus; Ftbl Tm Statscn; Jazz Choir; Dance; Stanislaus ST; Music.

WOODS, BRENDA; La Serna HS; Whittier, CA; (2); Drama Clb; Pep Clb; SADD; Thesps; Stage Crew; Cheerldng; Cit Awd; Hon Roll; Captain Of Varsity Cheer; University; Business.

WOODS, DAVID; San Gabriel HS; San Gabriel, CA; (3); Church Yth Grp; Key Clb; Teachers Aide; Stage Crew; Stu Cncl; Var Ftbl; Var Socr; Hi-Y Clb YMCA; Ecology.

WOODS, DOMENIQUE; Moreau HS; Hayward, CA; (2); Hosp Aide; JV Cheerldng; Var Trk; Hon Roll; CA Polytech ST U; Aeronautics.

WOODS, ELLEN A; Downtown Business Magnet HS; Los Angeles, CA; (2); Computer Clb; JA; Math Tm; Office Aide; Spanish Clb; Teachers Aide; Varsity Clb; Band; Church Choir; Drill Tm; UC Los Angeles; Law.

WOODS, HEATHER A; Tulare Union HS; Tulare, CA; (3); Band; Mrchg Band; Rptr Nwsp; Rep Frsh Cls; VP Soph Cls; Treas Jr Cls; Hon Roll; CA Schlrshp Fed; K-RED Radio; Comm.

WOODS, JEFF; Pioneer HS; San Jose, CA; (4); 6/300; JA; VP Key Clb; Letterman Clb; Varsity Clb; Pres Sr Cls; Capt L Swmmng; High Hon Roll; Hon Roll; Kiwanis Awd; NHS; Water Polo Vrsty Lttr; Cal Poly San Luis Obispo.

WOODS, JEREMY M; University HS; Los Angeles, CA; (3); SADD; Var Bsbl; Hon Roll; Pres Acad Fit Awd; Schlr Athlte Awd; Tutoring; Cmmnty Svc; Hmcmng Prince; Cmmnctns.

WOODS, JORY N; Downtown Business Magnet HS; Los Angeles, CA; (2); Boy Scts; Church Yth Grp; French Clb; Var L Golf; Acad Finance; U Of PA; Bus.

WOODS, KACEY R; Fillmore HS; Fillmore, CA; (4); 18/170; Pres Dance Clb; SADD; Teachers Aide; Hon Roll; Pres Acad Fit Awd; Acad All Amer Jrnlsm; Achvt Acad Ntl Awd; Chico ST U; Eng.

WOODS, KAMI L; Folsom HS; Folsom, CA; (4); Church Yth Grp; FBLA; Intnl Clb; Mrchg Band; Yrbk; Sftbl; Trk; Vllybl; High Hon Roll; Hon Roll; Brigham Young U; Law.

WOODS, KELLEY A; St Joseph HS; Lakewood, CA; (3); GAA; Varsity Clb; Var Powder Puff Ftbl; Var Socr; Hon Roll; Best Defense Awd Soccer; U San Diego; Sports Med.

WOODS, LAURA; Rosemead HS; El Monte, CA; (4); Church Yth Grp; Office Aide; SADD; Teachers Aide; JV Bsktbl; Help Young Sports; UCLA; Lawyer.

WOODS, LEANA; Channel Islands HS; Oxnard, CA; (2); Church Yth Grp; Drama Clb; Key Clb; SADD; Church Choir; Outstndng Trainee Awd Space Acad Lvl 1 Huntsville AL; Aerospc Engr.

WOODS, MICHELE; Cloverdale HS; Cloverdale, CA; (2); 8/59; Church Yth Grp; Cmnty Wkr; Teachers Aide; Church Choir; High Hon Roll; Hon Roll; Prfct Atten Awd; Rep Town Mss Teen Pgnt; UC Santa Cruz; Exec VP.

WOODS, NICOLE; John F Kennedy HS; Buena Park, CA; (1); Church Yth Grp; Pep Band; School Play; Swmmng; Cit Awd; Prfct Atten Awd; Cypress JC; Med.

WOODS, ROBERT; Gompers Secondary Schl; San Diego, CA; (1); 1/267; Teachers Aide; Var Vllybl; High Hon Roll; Prfct Atten Awd; Spec Recgntn Awds Excllnce Basic Prgmr; Outstndng Stu Achvr Awd; Physcs Seminar; Frnch 5-6.

WOODS, SONYA J; Del Campo HS; Citrus Heights, CA; (3); 131/446; Church Yth Grp; VP Sec Drama Clb; ROTC; Chorus; Church Choir; Variety Show; Students Reaching Out Awd; Golden Empire Music Festival Solo & Small Ensemble; Best Of Broadway.

WOODS, STEVEN R; Escondido Adventist Acad; Escondido, CA; (3); Church Yth Grp; Ski Clb; Teachers Aide; Band; Chorus; Phtg Yrbk; Pres Frsh Cls; Off Soph Cls; VP Stu Cncl; Var Bsktbl; Pre Med.

WOODS, TANSY K; Arcata HS; Arcata, CA; (3); SADD; Phtg Yrbk; Var Cheerldng; Var Tennis; Cit Awd; High Hon Roll; CSF; UCSD; Marine Bio.

WOODS, TRINITY L; Washington HS; Fremont, CA; (3); 50/306; Drama Clb; School Play; Stage Crew; Var Socr; Most Spirited Player Var Soccer Soph Yr; Best Character Actress 87-88; Bus.

WOODS, VANESSA E; Gardena HS; Gardena, CA; (3); Capt Drill Tm; Treas Stu Cncl; Bus Educ Awd; Mdrn Dance Awd; San Diego ST; Cmmrcl Art.

WOODS, VERA M; Millikan HS; Long Beach, CA; (3); Drama Clb; Orch; School Musical; School Play; Rptr Nwsp; Yrbk; Rep Frsh Cls; Jr NHS; Ntl Merit SF; Cngrssnl Yth Ldrshp Cncl; Theater.

WOODSHANK, JOANN L; Escondido HS; Escondido, CA; (1); Church Yth Grp; Key Clb; Pep Clb; Stu Cncl; JV Cheerldng; Stat Wrstlng.

WOODSIDE, BRIANNE M; Upland HS; Upland, CA; (2); 38/700; Animal Rights Clb; Stu Recgntn Awds Achvt, Engl, Art; Reg Nrs.

WOODSON, PAUL G; Albany HS; Richmond, CA; (4); 6/205; Chorus; Orch; School Musical; School Play; Variety Show; Ed Nwsp; Lit Mag; Sec Frsh Cls; Off Soph Cls; Off Jr Cls; UCLA; Musical Theater.

WOODSTOCK, ERNESTIENE J; Duarte HS; Duarte, CA; (3); Church Yth Grp; Key Clb; Red Cross Aide; Phtg Yrbk; Hon Roll; CA ST Long Beach; TV Jrnlst.

WOODWARD, AMY; Madera HS; Madera Ranchos, CA; (2); Church Yth Grp; SADD; High Hon Roll; Hon Roll; Friday Night Live; Vol Special Olympics; Lawyer.

WOODWARD, AMY E; Rio Mesa HS; Camarillo, CA; (3); AFS; Varsity Clb; Var Capt Bsktbl; Var JV Tennis; JV Trk; Hon Roll; Prfct Atten Awd.

WOODWARD, JENI; Northview HS; Covina, CA; (2); Sec Frsh Cls; VP Jr Cls; JV Var Cheerldng; JV Sftbl; JV Tennis; Prfct Atten Awd; HOBY; Girls League; GALS; Interior Dsgn.

WOODWARD, MARC D; Chino HS; Chino, CA; (3); 51/561; Letterman Clb; Varsity Clb; Var Bsbl; Hon Roll; 3 Yr All Leag Bsbl; 4 Yr Vrsty Lttrmn; 2 Yr Athltc Acadmc Awd; Physcl Therapy.

WOODWARD, SHAWNA A; Elsinore HS; Canyon Lake, CA; (3); Dance Clb; Dance Productions; Fullerton; Elem Ed.

WOODWORTH, ANDREW; Bellarmine HS; San Jose, CA; (3); Boy Scts; Church Yth Grp; Wrk Study Prog NASA Ames Spc Rsrch Ctr; Aerosp Engrng.

WOODWORTH, TIFFANY S; San Dieguito HS; Carlsbad, CA; (4); Library Aide; Teachers Aide; Rptr Nwsp; High Hon Roll; Pres Acad Fit Awd; CSF; Hnr Ct; CA Schl Of Ct Rprtng; Bus Adm.

WOODWORTH, VALERIE S; James Lick HS; San Jose, CA; (3); Drama Clb; Intnl Clb; Teachers Aide; Var Trk; Cit Awd; Hon Roll; Prfct Atten Awd; Arch.

WOODY, NATHAN R; Oak Grove HS; San Jose, CA; (2); Boy Scts; Church Yth Grp; Computer Clb; ROTC; Church Choir; Var L Socr; League Soccer; Foothill JC; Gemologist.

WOOLAM, K PEARL; Sherman E Burroughs HS; Ridgecrest, CA; (4); Am Leg Aux Girls St; Sec Drama Clb; Pep Clb; Teachers Aide; Sec Thesps; Chorus; School Musical; School Play; JV L Cheerldng; Hon Roll; Dnce Cls; Ballet Soloist; CA St Smmr Sch Arts; Cmmnty Thtre Mscls & Plys; Drama.

WOOLDRIDGE, BONNIE; Barstow HS; Barstow, CA; (2); Hon Roll; Art; Outstndng Awd Needlework; AZ Automotive Inst; Advrtsmnt.

WOOLDRIDGE, NICOLE M; St Bernard HS; Los Angeles, CA; (3); Drama Clb; French Clb; Office Aide; Phtg Yrbk; Var Socr; Var Sftbl; JV Vllybl; Prfct Atten Awd; San Diego ST U; Cmmnctns.

WOOLDRIK, KARA; St Francis HS; Sacramento, CA; (3); Intnl Clb; Office Aide; Spanish Clb; Varsity Clb; Yrbk; Off Jr Cls; Socr; Vllybl; Hon Roll; Xerox Awd Hum & Soc Sci; Jr Statesman Of America Pblcty Offcr.

WOOLEY, VICKI D; Lowell HS; San Francisco, CA; (3); German Clb; Science Clb; Spanish Clb; Speech Tm; Chorus; School Musical; Hon Roll; Voice Dem Awd; Amnesty Intl; Engl.

WOOLHEATER, KERRI E; Casa Grande HS; Petaluma, CA; (2); 18/295; Church Yth Grp; Cmnty Wkr; SADD; Varsity Clb; Band; Var L Bsktbl; Var L Socr; Var L Trk; High Hon Roll; NHS; CSF; MVP Trck-Bsktbl; CS St Track Qulfr 89-90; U Of CO Boulder; Sprts Med.

WOOLINGTON, CHRIS; Lassen HS; Susanville, CA; (3); Band; Chorus; Mrchg Band; Pep Band; Cheerldng; Trk; Lassen CC; HS History Teacher.

WOOLLEY, KATHRYN E; Clovis West HS; Fresno, CA; (3); Pres Church Yth Grp; Dance Clb; French Clb; Intnl Clb; SADD; High Hon Roll; Hon Roll; JR Statesmen Of Amer; Fresno ST; Intl Bus.

WOOLSTENHULME-SMITH, LISSA M; Wm S Hart HS; Newhall, CA; (3); Church Yth Grp; Office Aide; Yth Senate Rep; Intrmrl Ldrshp; Elem Ed.

WOOLWINE, SONJA G; Gardena HS; Gardena, CA; (2); Spanish Clb; Church Choir; Drill Tm; Sftbl; CA Schlrshp Fdr; Ballet 7 Yrs; Brigham Young U; Kndrgrtn Tchr.

WOON, DYLAN C; Westmoor HS; Daly City, CA; (4); 1/330; Chess Clb; Church Yth Grp; Hosp Aide; Crs Cntry; Tennis; Hon Roll; Ntl Merit Schol; Pres Acad Fit Awd; Val; Voice Dem Awd; Mth Tutorng; UC Berkeley; Elctrcl Engrng.

WOORE, MICHAEL; Mater Dei HS; Placentia, CA; (4); 1/526; Church Yth Grp; Pres Computer Clb; VP German Clb; School Musical; Stu Cncl; Var L Trk; NHS; CSF Pres; Disneyland Outdr Vndng Host/Trnr; Orange Cty Centennial Ldr; U San Diego; Bus Admin.

WOOTEN, MICHELLE L; Modoc HS; Alturas, CA; (2); 9/63; Church Yth Grp; Letterman Clb; Band; Mrchg Band; Pep Band; School Play; Pres Soph Cls; JV Bsktbl; Var Cheerldng; Var Trk; HOBY; Nor-Cal Hnr Band; Embry-Riddle U; Aerospace.

WOOTEN, TERRENCE A; Bishop Amat HS; West Covina, CA; (3); Boy Scts; Church Yth Grp; Math Clb; Stu Cncl; High Hon Roll; Hon Roll; NHS; VP Creative Writing Club; Black Scholar Club; Pre-Medicine.

WOOTON, ADRIENNE; Fremont Christian Schl; Fremont, CA; (2); Var Tennis; San Luis Obispo; Tchng.

WOOTTON, ADRIENNE; Fremont Christian Schl; Fremont, CA; (2); Var Tennis; Cal Poly; Tchng.

WORD, DOROTHY Y; Highlands HS; North Highlands, CA; (2); Ski Clb; Spanish Clb; SADD; Varsity Clb; Powder Puff Ftbl; JV Score Keeper; JV Swmmng; JV Capt Vllybl; Hon Roll; Prfct Atten Awd; UC Berkeley; Nuclear Physics.

WORK, BRIAN R; Clovis HS; Clovis, CA; (2); Boy Scts; French Clb; Harvard; Doc.

WORKMAN, CHRISTI L; Norte Vista HS; Riverside, CA; (1); Church Yth Grp; Dance Clb; Drama Clb; GAA; Girl Scts; Math Tm; Office Aide; Pep Clb; Teachers Aide; School Play; Dncd-Awds; Prtcptn Awd For Drama.

WORKMAN, JASON C; Montgomery HS; Santa Rosa, CA; (2); Church Yth Grp; Band; Mrchg Band; Pep Band; Var L Bsbl; Var L Bsktbl; JV Ftbl; Intrml Trk; Army; Mechanic.

WORKMAN, JOHN R; St Francis HS; La Crescenta, CA; (2); 14/160; Ski Clb; JV Var Bsbl; JV Bsktbl; Hon Roll; NEDT Awd; CSF; Fshng Clb.

WORKMAN, WENDI P; Diamond Bar HS; Diamond Bar, CA; (4); Debate Tm; French Clb; Library Aide; Science Clb; High Hon Roll; Hon Roll; NHS; Ntl Merit Ltr; Pres Acad Fit Awd; Golden St Geom Exam Hnrs; Psych Clb; Amnsty Intl; UC San Diego; Animal Physics.

WORLEY, CASSANDRA A; Mira Loma HS; Sacramento, CA; (3); 13/284; Church Yth Grp; Letterman Clb; SADD; Orch; JV Var Fld Hcky; High Hon Roll; Hon Roll; Pres Acad Fit Awd; Cmnty Wkr; GAA; CA Jr Schlrshp Fed Hnr Awd; Peer Cnslng; Lang.

WORLEY, REBECCA L; Bakersfield HS; Bakersfield, CA; (4); 55/669; Am Leg Aux Girls St; Drama Clb; French Clb; Hosp Aide; JA; Science Clb; Teachers Aide; Thesps; Chorus; Stage Crew; Spindt Schlstc Awd; Frdms Fndtn At Vally Forge; BYU; Russian Lang.

WORLEY, WILLIE M; Red Bluff HS; Red Bluff, CA; (2); #21 In Class; FFA; Hon Roll.

WORREL, SHAWNA; Palm Springs HS; Palm Springs, CA; (3); Capt Drill Tm; Cit Awd; DAR Awd; Elks Awd; Hon Roll; Brooks Inst; Fashion Merch.

WORSHAM, ISOLDE FAE; Claremont Private HS; Buena Park, CA; (4); 2/20; Drama Clb; School Play; Rptr Nwsp; Off Yrbk; Off Lit Mag; Pres Sr Cls; Pres Stu Cncl; Var Cheerldng; Cit Awd; Hon Roll; Hmcmng Prncss 89; Pres Of Schl 90; Hmcmng Queen & Prom Queen 90; Cal ST U, OH; Psych.

WORSTER, BRADLEY L; Foothill HS; Sacramento, CA; (3); Cmnty Wkr; Science Clb; Teachers Aide; Hon Roll; CSF; U Of The Pacific; Lawyer.

WORTHAM, MELISSA Y; Chaffey HS; Ontario, CA; (3); Sec Church Yth Grp; FBLA; Spanish Clb; Band; Church Choir; Mrchg Band; High Hon Roll; Hon Roll; NHS; Ntl Merit Ltr; 1st Pl Wnnr Rgnl Acctng Cmptn; Azuza Pacific U; Acctng.

WORTHINGTON, OPEL; Kingsburg Joint Union HS; Kingsburg, CA; (2); Church Yth Grp; Teachers Aide; Band; Mrchg Band; Pep Band; School Play; Tennis; Hon Roll; Phys Thrpst.

WOYSHNER, JEFFREY S; Independence HS; San Jose, CA; (2); Electrn.

WREN, KATHERINE L; Junipero Serra HS; San Diego, CA; (2); 21/460; Key Clb; Pep Clb; Drill Tm; Flag Corp; Nwsp; High Hon Roll; Kiwanis Awd; Psych.

WREN, THOMAS; Serra HS; San Diego, CA; (3); 18/391; Key Clb; Scholastic Bowl; High Hon Roll; Hon Roll; Kiwanis Awd; Pres Acad Fit Awd; UC San Diego.

WRENCH, MELANIE L; Mira Mesa HS; San Diego, CA; (2); 1/800; JV Var Tennis.

WRETA, SHEBA C; Beyer HS; Modesto, CA; (3); Drama Clb; FBLA; Intnl Clb; Pep Clb; Spanish Clb; SADD; Teachers Aide; Sec Treas Chorus; School Musical; School Play; Green Party, Philosphy & S Clbs; CSF; Modesto JC; Comp Acctng.

WRIGHT, AARON J; Madera HS; Madera, CA; (1); Intnl Clb; JV Socr; Gov Hon Prg Awd; Hon Roll; Prfct Atten Awd; CSF; Pilot.

WRIGHT, ADAM M; Arlington HS; Riverside, CA; (2); Intrml Bsbl; Intrml Bsktbl; Intrml Ftbl; Intrml Golf; Intrml Tennis; Intrml Vllybl; Vet Aide; Cert Achvt Comp Sci; UCLA; Adv.

WRIGHT, ALENE J; St Francis HS; Sacramento, CA; (4); 4/145; Art Clb; German Clb; Math Tm; Office Aide; Science Clb; Cit Awd; Elks Awd; High Hon Roll; Jr NHS; NHS; Stu Reaching Out; Cal St Artistic Club; U San Francisco; Med.

WRIGHT, ALISA C; Junipero Serra HS; San Diego, CA; (2); 1/450; Church Yth Grp; Drama Clb; Key Clb; Pep Clb; Ski Clb; SADD; Rep Stu Cncl; Swmmng; Cit Awd; High Hon Roll; Campus Life; UCSB; Law.

WRIGHT, ALLISON L; Villa Park HS; Orange, CA; (3); Band; Mrchg Band; Pep Band; Law.

WRIGHT, ANDREA K; Baptist Christian HS; Hemet, CA; (3); Church Yth Grp; Drama Clb; School Play; Sec Treas Stu Cncl; JV Var Bsktbl; Var L Cheerldng; Var L Sftbl; Var L Vllybl; Hon Roll; CSF-VP; Bus.

WRIGHT, ANDREA L; Saugus HS; Saugus, CA; (4); 8/395; Hist FBLA; Sec SADD; Drill Tm; School Musical; School Play; Nwsp; High Hon Roll; Lion Awd; NHS; Yng Stu Activists VP; Writers Soc Editor In Chief; Bank Of Amer For Drama Cert; Poltcl Sci.

WRIGHT, ANDREW; Palo Verde HS; Blythe, CA; (2); Bsbl; Var L Ftbl; Wt Lftg; High Hon Roll; NHS.

WRIGHT, ANNE E; Oakmont HS; N. Andover, MA; (1); Speech Tm; Nwsp; Hon Roll; Opt Clb Awd; Water Safty & First Aid; Jrnlsm.

WRIGHT, BENJAMIN T; Downtown Business Magnet HS; Canoga Park, CA; (2); Chess Clb; VP Key Clb; Ed Nwsp; Ed Yrbk; Co-Ed Lit Mag; Sec Frsh Cls; Stu Union Co-Fndr; Sushi By The Pool Pblshr.

WRIGHT JR, BERT L; Hesperia HS; Hesperia, CA; (2); ROTC; Spanish Clb; Cit Awd; Ntl Merit Ltr; UCLA Medcl Schl; Med.

WRIGHT, BRANDY E; Kennedy HS; Lapalma, CA; (1); Church Yth Grp; Chorus; Variety Show; Var Swmmng; Hon Roll; CIF Fnlst 100 Yrd Bckstrk 2-A; Cmptv Swmmr Fullerton Aquatics Sprts Tm; Mst Cntrbutng Undrclssmn Awd.

WRIGHT, BROOKE A; Santa Barbara HS; Santa Barbara, CA; (1); Ski Clb; Flag Corp; UCSB; Elem Schl Teacher.

WRIGHT, CARISA; Tokay HS; Stockton, CA; (4); FTA; Teachers Aide; Stu Cncl; Var JV Crs Cntry; Var JV Socr; Var JV Sftbl; JV Vllybl; High Hon Roll; Hon Roll; Pres Acad Fit Awd; Cal Poly San Luis Obispo; Bus.

WRIGHT, CATHLEEN; Bakersfield HS; Frazier Park, CA; (2); Sec Church Yth Grp; Drama Clb; GAA; Sec Spanish Clb; Var Bsktbl; JV Vllybl; Hon Roll; Lion Awd; CA Schlrshp Fed Mem 89-90; Envrnmntl Sci.

WRIGHT, CHARLOTTE; Mercy HS; S San Francisco, CA; (3); GAA; Ski Clb; Rep Jr Cls; Tennis; High Hon Roll; Hon Roll; Jnr Statesmn Amer Schl Rep; CSF; Hostess Clb; Italian Clb.

WRIGHT, CRYSTAL J; Corona SR HS; Corona, CA; (2); Cmnty Wkr; Drama Clb; VP SADD; School Play; JV Swmmng; Pres Acad Fit Awd; Geo, Gldn St Exam, Schl Rcgntn; CSF; U Of CA.

WRIGHT, CURTIS J; Hesperia HS; Hesperia, CA; (2); Boy Scts; Church Yth Grp; ROTC; JV Bsktbl; High Hon Roll; Prfct Atten Awd; BYU.

WRIGHT, DARIN; Patten Acad; Oakland, CA; (1); 1/16; Church Yth Grp; Cmnty Wkr; Math Tm; Band; Chorus; Drm Mjr(t); Orch; Pep Band; Stage Crew; JV Bsktbl; Helped Schl Fund Raisers; Play Percussion Church Orch; Stanford U; Teacher.

WRIGHT, DARREN; Mc Kinleyville HS; Mckinleyville, CA; (2); Art Clb; Hon Roll; Prfct Atten Awd; Mrt Awd Water Color Painting 90; Vrs Ribbons For Artwork 89-90; Hamboldt ST; Art.

WRIGHT, DAVID; Mc Clymonds HS; Oakland, CA; (1); Art Clb; Boy Scts; Computer Clb; Math Tm; Rptr Yrbk; Var Ftbl; Var Trk; Var Wt Lftg; Var Wrstlng; Tech Engrng.

WRIGHT, DAVID A; Concord HS; Concord, CA; (3); Var Crs Cntry; Var Trk; Hon Roll; Sports; Humbolt ST.

WRIGHT, DAWN; Fresno Christian HS; Fresno, CA; (1); Church Yth Grp; Chorus; Pres Frsh Cls; Powder Puff Ftbl; High Hon Roll; Stu Cncl Awd; Ed.

WRIGHT, DIONNE; Fremont Christian HS; Fremont, CA; (1); Drama Clb; School Play; Stage Crew; Cheerldng; Fashion Dsgnr.

WRIGHT, ELIZABETH L; University HS; Irvine, CA; (3); Church Yth Grp; GAA; Church Choir; Orch; Off Sr Cls; Hon Roll; Distingshd Ldrshp-Orch; Outstndng Muscl Perfrmnc 89-90; Yth Symph 87-89; Music.

WRIGHT, ERIC A; Ukiah HS; Ukiah, CA; (2); Teachers Aide; JV Bsbl; JV Bsktbl; JV Ftbl; Sftbll.

WRIGHT, ETHAN C; Arroyo Grande HS; Halcyon, CA; (3); ROP Cert Achvt; Hancock JC; Tax Law.

WRIGHT, GEOFFREY T; Eureka SR HS; Eureka, CA; (3); 100/375; Boy Scts; Cmnty Wkr; ROTC; Teachers Aide; Temple Yth Grp; Color Guard; Drill Tm; Cit Awd; Hon Roll; Prfct Atten Awd; Qtr Mstr-Sea Scnts; Lcnsd Stm Eqpmnt Oprtr; NJROTC Ldrshp; Daedln Mdl Rcpnt Awds; Tm Ldr Awd; Dctr.

WRIGHT, GINNY R; Modoc HS; Alturas, CA; (4); 6/52; Chorus; Ed Nwsp; VP Sr Cls; High Hon Roll; Pres Acad Fit Awd; Outstndng SR Mscn Awd Chrs.

WRIGHT, HEATHER; Independent Study HS; Escondido, CA; (2); Church Yth Grp; ROTC; Chorus; Skatng; Tckl Ftbl; NRC Spprt Grp Teens; UCSD; Beautician Accntnt.

WRIGHT, IAN W; Bloomington HS; Bloomington, CA; (3); 7/550; German Clb; Model UN; Scholastic Bowl; Swmmng; High Hon Roll; Hon Roll; Pres Acad Fit Awd; CSF; Golden St Exam Algebra & Geom Hnrs; UC Riverside; Civil Engrng.

WRIGHT, J R; Grace Davis HS; Modesto, CA; (2); SADD; JV Capt Bsktbl; Hon Roll; Elem Tchr.

WRIGHT, JAMES P; Yuba City HS; Yuba City, CA; (3); Boy Scts; Church Yth Grp; Band; Mrchg Band; Pep Band; Ftbl; Sftbl; Hon Roll; Eagle Sct; Order Of Arrow; Brigham Young U; Pilot.

WRIGHT, JANEL E; Foothill Farms HS; Sacramento, CA; (1); Church Yth Grp; French Clb; Science Clb; Band; Powder Puff Ftbl; Swmmng; Hon Roll; Chrldr 90-91; Schl Wide Recgntn Eng Awd; Engrng.

WRIGHT, JASON A; Vanden HS; Vacaville, CA; (4); 20/144; Boy Scts; Latin Clb; Teachers Aide; JV Var Socr; JV Var Trk; High Hon Roll; Hon Roll; Pres Acad Fit Awd; Eagle Sct; CA Schlrshp Fed; U Of CA Davis; Civil Engrng.

WRIGHT, JENNIFER A; Junipero Serra HS; San Diego, CA; (3); 52/391; Dance Clb; Letterman Clb; Pep Clb; Drill Tm; Hon Roll; Peer Tutoring; Woodbury U; Fshn Dsgn.

WRIGHT, JENNIFER L; Castle Park HS; Cerritos, CA; (1); 27/614; French Clb; Swmmng; Cit Awd; High Hon Roll; Hon Roll; U CA Santa Barbara; Marine Bio.

WRIGHT, JENNIFER M; Del Mar HS; San Jose, CA; (1); Church Yth Grp; Cmnty Wkr; Hosp Aide; Rep Frsh Cls; VP Soph Cls; Stu Cncl; JV Bsktbl; Var L Crs Cntry; Var Trk; Hon Roll; Helped Organize Wk Long Anti-Drug Campaign, Toy Drive For Children Watsonville Earthquake; Cal Poly; Med.

WRIGHT, JESSE V; Valhalla HS; El Cajon, CA; (2); Boy Scts; Amnesty Intl; MIT.

WRIGHT, JOHN A; Flintridge Prep; Pasadena, CA; (3); Computer Clb; French Clb; Math Clb; Variety Show; Rptr Nwsp; Ed Yrbk; JV Ftbl; JV Tennis; French Hon Soc; SPACE-PRES; Fndr-Stu For Explrtn & Dev Of Spc & Natl Exec Brd; Pomona Coll; Mech Engrng.

WRIGHT, JOHNNY L; Los Angeles HS; Los Angeles, CA; (2); Boy Scts; Church Yth Grp; Office Aide; Wt Lftg; Yng Astronauts Pgm; Prncpls Awd; LA CC; Grphc Art.

WRIGHT, JUSTIN; Buena HS; Ventura, CA; (4); 34/470; Church Yth Grp; Bsktbl; Var Golf; High Hon Roll; Pres Acad Fit Awd; Golf MVP; LA Jr Open Golf Trnmnt Wnnr 86; Channel Leag 1st Tm 89 & 90; San Jose ST U; Bus Admin.

WRIGHT, KAREN V; Bethel Christian HS; Lancaster, CA; (2); Drama Clb; Nwsp; Ed Yrbk; Var Cheerldng; Var Mgr(s); Var Score Keeper; Var Sftbl; Hon Roll; Aud/Vis; Teachers Aide; Natl Yng Ldrs Conf Rep; 2nd Pl Sci Fair; Hmcmng Prncss; US Naval Acad; Aviation.

WRIGHT, KATHLEEN N; Mariposa County HS; Catheys Valley, CA; (4); 10/120; Drama Clb; FBLA; Office Aide; Speech Tm; Teachers Aide; School Play; Stage Crew; Variety Show; JV Bsbl; Var Sftbl; Gldn St Exam Alg High Hnrs, Geom Hnrs; Gldn Glove Awd Sftbl 90; CA ST U Fresno; Bus Mktng.

WRIGHT, KEVIN Y; Atascadero HS; Atascadero, CA; (1); Crs Cntry; Wt Lftg; Hon Roll; Big Brother, Big Sister Pgm; Camp Hapitok; Cal Poly; Astronaut.

WRIGHT, KIMBERLY A; Hiram Johnson HS; Sacramento, CA; (3); 22/120; Red Cross Aide; ROTC; JV Bsktbl; Var Sftbl; JV Vllybl; Cit Awd; High Hon Roll; Hon Roll; Outstanding Defnsve Plyr Ftbl 89 & 90; Friday Night Live Dont Drink/Drive; Criminology.

WRIGHT, KRISTEN; St Marys Acad; Los Angeles, CA; (3); Chorus; Church Choir; Pep Band; School Musical; School Play; Stage Crew; Variety Show; Rep Jr Cls; Cit Awd; Hon Roll; Awd-Art Exprnc/Calligrphy; Ctznshp Hnr Roll; Johnson Oconnor Rsrch Fndtn; Spelman Coll; Bus Admin.

WRIGHT, LISA; Helix HS; San Diego, CA; (4); 55/367; Service Clb; Yrbk; Sec Soph Cls; Rep Stu Cncl; JV Var Cheerldng; Wt Lftg; Stat Wrstlng; Hon Roll; NHS; Dance Schlrshp; Gldn St Xm For Math Hnrs; Grossmont JC; Bus Mgmt.

WRIGHT, LISA C; Fresno HS; Fresno, CA; (3); 20/600; Girl Scts; JA; SADD; Color Guard; Yrbk; Stu Cncl; Cit Awd; High Hon Roll; Hon Roll; Prfct Atten Awd; Fresno City.

WRIGHT, LOVELY LADY; Fremont HS; Oakland, CA; (2); Rptr Nwsp; Lit Mag; Cit Awd; Hon Roll; Schl Media Acad; Lwyr.

WRIGHT, MAJADI K; Lynwood HS; Lynwood, CA; (4); Library Aide; Teachers Aide; School Play; Young Blacks Schlr; African-Amer Stu Union; CA ST Northridge; Lib Stud.

WRIGHT, MELANIE A; East Union HS; Manteca, CA; (2); 21/400; Drama Clb; Key Clb; SADD; Thesps; School Play; Stage Crew; Cit Awd; Hon Roll; UCLA; Law.

WRIGHT, MICHELLE L; Dixon HS; Dixon, CA; (2); Church Yth Grp; Intnl Clb; Rep Stu Cncl; High Hon Roll; CSF; Outstndng Stu Awd; Psych.

WRIGHT, MIKE A; North Monterey Co HS; Salinas, CA; (2); JV Socr; Var Trk; Hon Roll; Pres Acad Fit Awd; Phys Ed Schlstc Awd; Block Lttr With Awd; MVP Track.

WRIGHT, NIKOLE L; Westminster HS; Garden Grove, CA; (2); Church Yth Grp; Drama Clb; Ski Clb; School Play; Swmmng; Hon Roll; Pres Acad Fit Awd; Crmnl Law.

WRIGHT, ROBERT W; South Pasadena HS; S Pasadena, CA; (4); 73/292; Treas Band; Jazz Band; Mrchg Band; Treas Jr Cls; Treas Sr Cls; Ftbl; Randall Yth Dvlpmnt Schlrshp; U Of CA Riverside; Bus Admin.

WRIGHT, RONDA L; Irvine HS; Santa Ana, CA; (1); Pep Clb; JV Swmmng; WA ST U; Med.

WRIGHT, SHANE; Christian Brothers HS; Sacramento, CA; (2); Drama Clb; German Clb; School Musical; School Play; Swmmng; High Hon Roll; Hon Roll; Mgt.

WRIGHT, STACEY C; Clear Lake HS; Lakeport, CA; (1); GAA; School Musical; School Play; Variety Show; Rep Soph Cls; JV Bsktbl; JV Vllybl; High Hon Roll; Prfct Atten Awd; Pres Acad Fit Awd; CSF Life Mem; Schlr Athl; Bst Of Show Cty Fair; CA U; Ped.

WRIGHT, STEPHANIE; Prospect HS; San Jose, CA; (4); 17/190; Art Clb; Pres Church Yth Grp; Dance Clb; FBLA; GAA; Key Clb; Pep Clb; High Hon Roll; Opt Clb Awd; Pres Acad Fit Awd; CA Golden St Exam Hnrs; Hmcmng Qn; BYU; Bus.

WRIGHT, STEPHANIE LYNN; Loara HS; Anaheim, CA; (3); 15/380; Drill Tm; JV Capt Sftbl; Var L Sftbl; Hon Roll; Prfct Atten Awd; Var JV Cheerldng; MVP Awd Vrsty Sftbl 90, 1st Tm All Leag 90; MVP Awd JV Bsktbl 90; ASD-USA Sftbl Tm 90; CSF; UCLA; Med.

WRIGHT, STEPHANIE R; Selma HS; Selma, CA; (3); 13/211; Treas French Clb; Q&S; Band; Jazz Band; Mrchg Band; Orch; Pep Band; School Musical; Phtg Nwsp; Hon Roll; Fresno Madera Cnty Hnr Orch 3 Yrs; Hnr Band Fresno Madera Cnty Band 2 Yrs; Cal Poly; Arch.

WRIGHT, SYDNEY; Etna Union HS; Etna, CA; (3); Band; Pres Frsh Cls; Rep Soph Cls; Treas Pres Stu Cncl; JV Bsktbl; Var Cheerldng; Intl Order Of Jobs Daughters; Acad Decathlon; Asst Spec Ed Summer Schl Vol; Med.

WRIGHT, TIMOTHY L; Bloomington Christian Schl; Bloomington, CA; (1); 1/30; Church Yth Grp; Band; Yrbk; Rep Frsh Cls; Var L Ftbl; Var L Wrstlng; Hon Roll.

WRIGHTING, DYANA; Washington Prep; Los Angeles, CA; (4); 68/525; Hon Roll; Prfct Atten Awd; Yng Black Schlrs 4 Yrs; Physics Clb; Outstndng Acad Achvt Engl; CA ST Dominguez Hills; Acctnt.

WRIGLEY, JENNIFER E; Monroe HS; Sepulveda, CA; (2); Teachers Aide; Chorus; Drill Tm; School Play; Co-Ed Yrbk; Rep Frsh Cls; Hist Soph Cls; High Hon Roll; CA Schlrshp Fed; CSUN.

WRIGLEY, ROBERTA C; Eureka SR HS; Eureka, CA; (3); Drama Clb; Intnl Clb; Sec Service Clb; Drill Tm; School Play; Stage Crew; Nwsp; Yrbk; Var Powder Puff Ftbl; Cit Awd; Comm.

WRISTEN, SEAN; Lassen HS; Susanville, CA; (2); 21/276; Cmnty Wkr; Letterman Clb; Spanish Clb; SADD; Varsity Clb; School Play; Stage Crew; Off Jr Cls; Stu Cncl; Ftbl; SAC ST; Bus.

WROBEL, CAREY; Paradise HS; Paradise, CA; (2); 25/30; Church Yth Grp; Pep Clb; Ski Clb; SADD; Bsbl; Bsktbl; Crs Cntry; Golf; Music Piano; UCLA; Youth.

WRUCK, DEAN E; California HS; Whittier, CA; (3); #4 In Class; Am Leg Boys St; JV Var Bsbl; JV Bsktbl; Stat Ftbl; Hon Roll; UCLA; Math.

WU, ALBERT; Mills HS; Burlingame, CA; (3); Aud/Vis; Boy Scts; Church Yth Grp; Math Tm; L Var Crs Cntry; Var Tennis; High Hon Roll; Hon Roll; Elec Engrng.

WU, ALEX; Covina HS; West Covina, CA; (4); 1/266; VP Math Clb; Office Aide; High Hon Roll; Lion Awd; Rotary Awd; Concert Band; Badminton Tm Most Imprvd Plyr; Bank Of Am Awd Math, Sci.

WU, ALICE EI-MANG; Poway HS; Poway, CA; (4); 7/728; VP AFS; Pres FBLA; Orch; Rptr Nwsp; Var L Swmmng; JV Tennis; Kiwanis Awd; Ntl Merit SF; Stu Of Mnth In Englsh 89; Mst Imprvd Swmr 87-88; CA ST Brkly; Engrng.

WU, ANNE Y; Sunset HS; Hayward, CA; (2); 1/273; Drama Clb; Chorus; Mrchg Band; Off Soph Cls; High Hon Roll; Mt Eden; Bus Mgmt.

WU, BENJAMIN Y; Canyon HS; Anaheim, CA; (4); 1/300; Key Clb; Sec Math Clb; Math Tm; Mu Alpha Theta; Quiz Bowl; High Hon Roll; NHS; Ntl Merit SF; Asian Clb Treas; CSF; Physics.

WU, BETTY; Galileo HS; San Francisco, CA; (3); Cmnty Wkr; Speech Tm; Comp.

WU, BLAIR P; Mission HS; San Francisco, CA; (3); Bsbl; Gym; UC Berkeley; Bus.

WU, CHARLES; Lincoln HS; Stockton, CA; (2); Cmnty Wkr; Mu Alpha Theta; Science Clb; Var Tennis; High Hon Roll; Magna Cum Laude Ntl Latin Exam; Vol ST Hosp; Med.

WU, CHARLIE; Arcadia HS; Claremont, CA; (3); Church Yth Grp; FCA; Orch; JV Bsktbl; Ftbl; JV Swmmng; Tennis; JV Vllybl; NHS; Prfct Atten Awd; Acad Excllnc Awd Geom & Alg; Prin Recgntn Awd; Asian Game Clb; Culture Service Clb; Bus.

WU, CHERRY Y; George Washington HS; San Francisco, CA; (2); Dance Clb; Service Clb; Drill Tm; High Hon Roll; Hon Roll; Japanese Clb; Chine Amer Clb; St Marys Chinese Lang Schl Cls Rep; Math.

WU, CHIEN; Washington HS; Fremont, CA; (4); 1/287; Sec French Clb; German Clb; Intnl Clb; VP Pres Spanish Clb; Teachers Aide; Var Crs Cntry; NHS; Vrsty Badmintn; UC Berkeley; Bus Admin.

WU, CHRISTINE C; Mills HS; Millbrae, CA; (2); Math Clb; Mgr(s); Tennis; Hon Roll; Jr NHS; Pres Acad Fit Awd; Earth Clb; Dist Wnnr Natl Piano Plyng Auditns.

WU, CINDY C; Phillip & Sara Burton Academic HS; San Francisco, CA; (3); Hon Roll; Biotech & Nrsng UCSF Explorers Post; UCSF Schl Of Nrsng Smmr Apprntcshp Pgm; UC David; Med.

WU, CONNIE; Escondido HS; Escondido, CA; (1); Cit Awd; Hon Roll; Pres Acad Fit Awd; Brdcstng.

WU, DENNIS H; San Gabriel HS; San Gabriel, CA; (4); 44/737; Key Clb; NFL; Aud/Vis; SADD; Stu Cncl; JV Crs Cntry; Var Swmmng; JV Trk; Ntl Merit SF; Spanish NHS; Engr.

WU, DIANE YAN YING; Galileo HS; San Francisco, CA; (2); Spanish Clb; Off Jr Cls; Nrs.

WU, DONNA; Monta Vista HS; Cupertino, CA; (3); German Clb; Hosp Aide; VP JA; Pep Clb; Chorus; Drill Tm; Mrchg Band; NHS; Spanish NHS; CA Yth Symphny; Peninsula Symph Msc Awd; Company Of Yr Rgnl.

WU, EN LIN; South Hills HS; Covina, CA; (4); Church Yth Grp; Math Tm; Teachers Aide; Church Choir; School Play; Ed Lit Mag; High Hon Roll; Hon Roll; Pres Acad Fit Awd; Gldn St Exam Geom, Gldn St Schlr; CA St Poly Tech U; Lib Stud.

WU, FRANK; Arcadia HS; Arcadia, CA; (4); 46/596; VP Computer Clb; VP FBLA; Treas Service Clb; Speech Tm; Var Bsktbl; Var Crs Cntry; Intrml Ice Hcky; Var Trk; Hon Roll; Prfct Atten Awd; Aikido; Purdue U; Engrng.

WU, HENRY K; Phillip & Sala Burton Academic HS; San Francisco, CA; (4); 11/180; Boy Scts; Computer Clb; Math Clb; Red Cross Aide; Science Clb; Teachers Aide; High Hon Roll; Hon Roll; Elec Engr.

WU, JAMSON; Bellarmine College Prep; San Jose, CA; (3); 8/300; Cmnty Wkr; Computer Clb; Math Clb; Service Clb; SADD; Band; Jazz Band; Pep Band; Crs Cntry.

WU, JANET HUA-YU; Phillip & Sala Burton Academic HS; San Francisco, CA; (3); Art Clb; Chess Clb; Church Yth Grp; Cmnty Wkr; Computer Clb; English Clb; FBLA; JA; JCL; Math Clb; U Of CA Berkeley; Medcl.

WU, JENNIFER; Garden Grove HS; Garden Grove, CA; (1); Chorus; Church Choir; Stanford; Poli.

WU, JENNIFER; San Leandro HS; San Leandro, CA; (2); Church Yth Grp; Math Clb; Spanish Clb; Stu Cncl; JV Bsktbl; Var Sftbl; High Hon Roll; Octagon Club Treas Elect; CSF VP Elect; Gldn St Exam Alg Outstndng Achvt 89; UC Berkeley; Psych.

WU, JIM; San Gabriel HS; San Gabriel, CA; (3); French Clb; Varsity Clb; JV Bsktbl; JV Crs Cntry; JV Var Vllybl; Kirma Es Aei Clb; CA Schlrshp Federation; Engr.

WU, JIN ZHONG; Hemet HS; Hemet, CA; (4).

WU, JOANNE; Cerritos HS; Cerritos, CA; (4); Church Yth Grp; Key Clb; Math Clb; Office Aide; Science Clb; Church Choir; School Musical; Hon Roll; NHS; Sec Of Churhs Fellowship; V-Pres Of Chuches Chior; Math Contest Awards; Cal Poly; Chemical Engineer.

WU, JOHN H; Arcadia HS; Arcadia, CA; (3); 13/639; AFS; Teachers Aide; Band; Chorus; Mrchg Band; Orch; School Musical; School Play; Stage Crew; Pres Stu Cncl; TV News Prdctn Producer & Anchor.

WU, JONATHAN; Arcadia HS; Arcadia, CA; (3); Cmnty Wkr; Hosp Aide; Math Clb; Office Aide; Spanish Clb; Teachers Aide; Cit Awd; High Hon Roll; Hon Roll; Prfct Atten Awd; Goldn ST Exam Acad Excllnc Awd In Algbra & Geo; CSU; Engr.

WU, JOSEPH I C; Los Altos HS; Hacienda Hgts, CA; (2); Science Clb; High Hon Roll; Prfct Atten Awd; CSF; Opthlmlgy.

WU, JUDY HUA-LING; J F Kennedy HS; Granada Hills, CA; (4); Church Yth Grp; Math Clb; Service Clb; Teachers Aide; Tennis; High Hon Roll; Hon Roll; CSF; UC Riverside.

WU, JULIE; El Cerrito HS; El Cerrito, CA; (2); Church Yth Grp; Hist Sec FTA; Math Tm; Mrchg Band; School Musical; Swmmng; Tennis; High Hon Roll; Jr Statesman Of Amer Pres; Fri Night Live Pres, Secy, Hstrn; Med.

WU, KATHERINE; Mission San Jose HS; Fremont, CA; (1); 1/466; Hosp Aide; JA; Orch; CSF; Fleet Rsrve Assn Essay Cont 1st Pl Wnnr; UC Berkeley; Gyn.

WU, KENNY; Lowell HS; San Francisco, CA; (3); Church Yth Grp; Cmnty Wkr; Latin Clb; Service Clb; Band; Orch; Aviation Clb-Co-Founder/VP; 90 Chem-A-Thon-2nd Pl; San Francisco ST.

WU, MENG; Novato HS; Novato, CA; (4); Socr; Tennis; Vllybl; SRJC; Engrng.

WU, MICHELLE; Fountain Valley HS; Fountain Valley, CA; (3); French Clb; Hon Roll; Golden ST Exam Acad Excllnce Awd; Cert PAL Training; Peer Cnslng Club; Arch.

WU, MICHELLE; Galileo HS; San Francisco, CA; (4); Cmptr Sci.

WU, MICHELLE K; Arcadia HS; Arcadia, CA; (3); Art Clb; Church Yth Grp; Pres Cmnty Wkr; Debate Tm; FBLA; Math Tm; NFL; Science Clb; Speech Tm; Band; Octagon Clb Pres; Acad Dcthln Team; Bus.

WU, MIKE; San Ramon Valley HS; Danville, CA; (3); 20/420; Computer Clb; FBLA; Key Clb; Math Clb; NFL; Vlntr Danville Convlcnt Hosp, Wang NMR Pokas Comp; Berkeley; Medcl.

WU, OLIVIA; Los Altos HS; Hacienda Hts, CA; (2); GAA; Chorus; Tennis; Hon Roll; GSE 1st Yr Alge High Hnrs; GSE Geom Hnrs; Singing, Art; Bus.

WU, PAMELA; Lincoln HS; Stockton, CA; (3); Mu Alpha Theta; Science Clb; Treas Spanish Clb; Teachers Aide; Acpl Chr; Hon Roll; JV Badminton Tm; CSF; CA Inst Technology; Bus Econ.

WU, PATRICIA L; Sunset HS; Hayward, CA; (4); 24/218; Cmnty Wkr; Debate Tm; Teachers Aide; Rptr Nwsp; Yrbk; Stat JV Bsktbl; Var Score Keeper; JV Var Vllybl; High Hon Roll; Pres Acad Fit Awd; Eclgy Clb; Chabot Coll; Psych.

WU, PETER; Walnut HS; Walnut, CA; (3); 70/400; Intnl Clb; Trk; High Hon Roll; CSF; Engrng.

WU, PETER W; Alameda HS; Alameda, CA; (3); 7/280; Church Yth Grp; Cmnty Wkr; French Clb; Science Clb; Var Crs Cntry; Var Trk; Vllybl; High Hon Roll; Schlrshp Clb; Cal Berkeley; Civil Engr.

WU, QI TING; Abraham Lincoln HS; Los Angeles, CA; (1); Hon Roll; CSF; Occidental Coll; Bus.

WU, RHODA; San Gorgonio HS; Highland, CA; (4); 29/400; Church Yth Grp; Latin Clb; Office Aide; Band; Orch; JV Trk; NHS; Prfct Atten Awd; CA Schlrshp Fed; SYMF 1st, 2nd, 3rd Pl Awds Music; Chrstn Alive Club; UC Berkeley; Petroleum Engrng.

WU, RONALD; Edison HS; Stockton, CA; (3); Hon Roll; Engrng.

WU, SANDRA; Chaminade HS; Simi Valley, CA; (2); Art Clb; Hosp Aide; JV Var Cheerldng; Hon Roll; Jr NHS; Cert Mrt; Stanford; Pedtrcs.

WU, STANLEY S; Lowell HS; San Francisco, CA; (2); Acad Exclnc Awd Algbr Gldn St Exmntn Hgh Hnrs; CSF; Bsbl, Ftbl, Tnns, Bdmntn, Vllybl, Swmmng & Rdng; UC Berkeley; Accntng.

WU, STEVEN M; Oakland HS; Oakland, CA; (3); French Clb; German Clb; Key Clb; Math Clb; Math Tm; Var L Tennis; Cit Awd; Hon Roll; After Schl Job; Civil Engrng.

WU, SUSAN I; Upland HS; Upland, CA; (4); 62/619; Church Yth Grp; Cmnty Wkr; Hosp Aide; NFL; Sec Spanish Clb; Ed Nwsp; Rep Stu Cncl; Var Fld Hcky; Intrml Tennis; L Var Trk; Jr Statesmn Of Amer; Acad Decthln; Intl Reltns.

WU, SUSAN K; Lowell HS; San Francisco, CA; (2); Red Cross Aide; Science Clb; SADD; Hon Roll; JV Badminton Team; War Against Graffitti 1st Pl; Hnrs GSE Alg; UC Berkeley; Bus Mgt.

WU, THEODORE; South Pasadena HS; Monte Bello, CA; (3); Key Clb; Tennis; Hon Roll; Acad Achvt Awd; Golden St Exam Geom Hnr; UCLA; Phy.

WU, THOMAS S; John F Kennedy HS; Sacramento, CA; (2); 1/530; Bsbl; Socr; Tennis; UC Davis; Elec Engr.

WU, TIFFANY L; Mc Ateer HS; San Francisco, CA; (3); Boy Scts; San Francisco ST U; Bus.

WU, TINA W; Edison HS; Stockton, CA; (2); Hon Roll; Arch.

WU, WANPIN W; Alhambra HS; Alhambra, CA; (2); Spanish Clb; Tennis; High Hon Roll; Zool.

WU, WENDY; Whitney HS; Cerritos, CA; (1); Cmnty Wkr; Dance Clb; Debate Tm; French Clb; Key Clb; Model UN; Varsity Clb; Cheerldng; High Hon Roll; Pres Acad Fit Awd; Under Sec Of Conf Mun Prog; Class Rep Key Clb 93; Hotel Mngmnt.

WU, WINSTON; Whitney HS; Cerritos, CA; (3); Boy Scts; Computer Clb; Treas French Clb; Hosp Aide; JA; Key Clb; Latin Clb; Office Aide; Teachers Aide; Variety Show; Talent Show Wnnrs; SETA; Greenpeace; Berkeley; Bus.

WU, XINYAN; J Eugene Mc Ateer HS; San Francisco, CA; (3); Red Cross Aide; Teachers Aide; Hon Roll; Chinese Clb; UCSF Nrs Trng Prgm; UC Berkeley; Bus.

WU, YVONNE Y; Sunny Hills HS; Fullerton, CA; (2); 24/464; Intnl Clb; Sec Model UN; JV Bsktbl; JV Swmmng; High Hon Roll; Rotary Awd; Jr Statesman Of Amer Treas; Amnesty Intl Conf Coord; Stu Coalition; Bus.

WUCHNER, MARK; Poway HS; San Diego, CA; (3); Letterman Clb; Var Bsbl; Var Bsktbl; NHS.

WUERTZ, TROY D; Woodbridge HS; Irvine, CA; (3); 62/416; Cmnty Wkr; Var Bsbl; JV Crs Cntry; High Hon Roll; CSF; Mock Trials; Intrnshp For Assemblymen Gil Ferguson 89 & 90; U CA; Bus.

WUEST, TOBI A; Fontanta HS; Fontana, CA; (2); Poly Sci.

WUESTE, MICHELLE M; San Marcos HS; Santa Barbara, CA; (3); 12/380; French Clb; Hosp Aide; Chorus; School Musical; Variety Show; Hon Roll; Cnsrvtn Clb; Secret Stuents Pres CA Clb Writes Teachers; Royal Pages Club; Number 1 Club.

WULBERT, KERA EM; Torrey Pines HS; Del Mar, CA; (3); Cmnty Wkr; GAA; Letterman Clb; Ski Clb; SADD; Varsity Clb; Gym; Pres Acad Fit Awd; Psych.

WULFMAN, MICHAEL J; Rim Of The World HS; Twin Peaks, CA; (1); 26/400; Library Aide; Band; Golf; Hon Roll.

WUN, HERRICK; Rolling Hills HS; Rancho Palos Verd, CA; (4); 6/340; Sec Chess Clb; Church Yth Grp; Cmnty Wkr; Computer Clb; Pres Math Clb; Capt Math Tm; Model UN; Pres Science Clb; Orch; School Musical; Continental Math League Natl Calculus Awd; CSF; Natl Mrt Fnlst; Yale U; Molecular Biochem.

WUN, KENNETH; Lowell HS; San Francisco, CA; (3); Science Clb; Teachers Aide; CSF; CA Invtnl Chemathon Superior Achvt 90.

WUNCE, KATIE A; Santa Cruz HS; Santa Cruz, CA; (1); Mrchg Band; Trk; Hon Roll.

WURFFELL, KIRK J; Mission Viejo HS; Mission Viejo, CA; (2); Boy Scts; Church Yth Grp; Computer Clb; Band; Mrchg Band; School Musical; Bsktbl; Hon Roll; Eagle Scout; USC; Engr.

WV, CHUNG H; Downey HS; Downey, CA; (3); French Clb; Math Clb; Science Clb; Service Clb; Spanish Clb; Tennis; High Hon Roll; St Schlr; USC; Harvard; Physcn.

WYANT, JEFFREY T; Magnolia HS; Anaheim, CA; (3); Var Trk; Stu Trnr; Loma Linda; Sprts Med.

WYATT, AMY A; Lincoln HS; Lincoln, CA; (1); 6/170; Pep Clb; Ski Clb; SADD; Pres Frsh Cls; JV Sftbl; JV Vllybl; Hon Roll; CA Berkeley; Arch.

WYATT, BRIAN D; Rio Americano HS; Sacramento, CA; (3); 1/300; Aud/Vis; Church Yth Grp; Debate Tm; Key Clb; School Play; Crs Cntry; High Hon Roll; Ntl Merit Ltr; CA Child Nutrition Cncl; Friday Night Live; Econ.

WYATT, JENNIFER F; La Serna HS; Whittier, CA; (4); 17/351; Church Yth Grp; Pres Cmnty Wkr; Capt Dance Clb; Debate Tm; Hosp Aide; Library Aide; Office Aide; Pep Clb; Ski Clb; Sec Spanish Clb; Natl Charity Leag; Hmcmng Fnlst; CSF; U Of CA Santa Barbara.

WYATT, JOLIE; Hilltop HS; San Diego, CA; (3); Church Yth Grp; Pres 4-H; Pep Clb; Band; Chorus; Sec Soph Cls; Stu Cncl; Var Bsktbl; 4-H Awd; High Hon Roll; Miss Teenage Amer Bty Pageant; Vet.

WYATT, REENA B; University City HS; San Diego, CA; (3); SADD; Rep Jr Cls; JV Bsktbl; Var Cheerldng; Var Crs Cntry; Powder Puff Ftbl; Var Tennis; Var Trk; Hon Roll; Prfct Atten Awd; Bio.

WYATT, TASRA; Lynbrook HS; Santa Clara, CA; (3); 110/284; Church Yth Grp; Cmnty Wkr; Pep Clb; Chorus; Church Choir; Drill Tm; Var Cheerldng; JV Var Tennis; High Hon Roll; Coachs Awd V Tnns; LUCY Ldr; Psych.

WYATT, TRULY M; Central Union HS; El Centro, CA; (2); Imperial Valley Coll; Elem Ed.

WYCHICO, FRANCES A; Victor Valley HS; Victorville, CA; (2); Color Guard.

WYCINSKY, JONATHAN J; Capital Christian HS; Sacramento, CA; (3); Art Clb; Church Yth Grp; Ski Clb; Var Bsbl; Var Bsktbl; Var Ftbl; Var Socr; Pres Acad Fit Awd.

WYCKOFF, STACEY A; Edison HS; Huntington Beach, CA; (3); JA; Model UN; Ski Clb; Rep Frsh Cls; MUN Georgetown Conf Awd; MUN Sanger Conf Rapporteur Wnnr; UCSD; Bus.

WYKOFF, ANGELA CHRISTINE; Fort Bragg HS; Fort Bragg, CA; (3); Sec FBLA; Pep Clb; Teachers Aide; Chorus; Hon Roll; Bio Awd; Santa Rosa JC.

WYLAND, AMBER; John F Kennedy HS; Buena Park, CA; (4); Office Aide; Teachers Aide; Cit Awd; Hon Roll; Prfct Atten Awd; Physcl Erth Sci Excllnce Awd; Irshgrm GPA Recmmndtn Awds; Penn ST; Bus.

WYLIE, AMANDA L; Lowell HS; San Francisco, CA; (4); Drama Clb; Girl Scts; NFL; Speech Tm; Thesps; Acpl Chr; Chorus; School Musical; School Play; CA ST Chmpn-Humorous Intrptn NFL; 9th Pl USA Humorous Intrptn NFL; Best All Arnd Prfmr-Drama Stud; Actrss.

WYLIE, HEATHER; Central Valley HS; Redding, CA; (2); Cmnty Wkr; FHA; Model UN; Band; Sec Soph Cls; Cheerldng; Mgr(s); Powder Puff Ftbl; Swmmng; Gov Hon Prg Awd; Duchess Of Bsktbl Homcmng; Cls Pres; Stu Of Month; Corp Lawyer.

WYLIE, KIMBERLY; Salinas HS; Salinas, CA; (2); Ski Clb; Intrml Cheerldng; Intrml Trk; High Hon Roll; Hon Roll.

WYLIE, TANYSIA L; Silver Creek HS; San Jose, CA; (3); Church Yth Grp; Cmnty Wkr; Dance Clb; Drama Clb; SADD; Teachers Aide; Acpl Chr; Church Choir; Drill Tm; School Musical; Engl, Math & Choir Awds; UC Berkeley; Law.

WYMA, HEATHER; Apple Valley HS; Apple Valley, CA; (2); French Clb; Key Clb; JV Bsktbl; JV Vllybl; CSF; Prncpls Hnr Rl; Sprt Clb; Med.

WYMAN, ANTHONY W; Norco HS; Norco, CA; (4); 15/460; Drama Clb; Letterman Clb; Model UN; Pep Clb; Varsity Clb; Ed Nwsp; Var Capt Trk; High Hon Roll; Pres Acad Fit Awd; CSF; 4 Yr Acadmc Ltrmn; All Mnt View Leag Acadmc Team; CA ST Fullerton; Cmmnctns.

WYMAN, JUSTIN; Santa Fe Christian HS; Encinitas, CA; (4); Boy Scts; Church Yth Grp; FCA; Ski Clb; Spanish Clb; School Play; Stage Crew; Pres Sr Cls; Bsktbl; Crs Cntry; Eagle Scout; Gld Hlmt Awd All Lg Ftbll Plyr; U Of Santa Barbara; Law.

WYNEKEN, J D; Edison HS; Huntington Beach, CA; (3); Church Yth Grp; JV Intrml Bsktbl; Intrml Socr; Hon Roll; Envrnmntl Clb; Hstry Teacher.

WYNEKEN, MARK; Los Alumetos HS; Seal Beach, CA; (3); Letterman Clb; Ski Clb; SADD; Teachers Aide; Var L Swmmng; Hon Roll; Bus Admin.

WYNN, DE SHAWN N; Point Loma HS; San Diego, CA; (3); 124/431; Church Yth Grp; Mgr(s); Vllybl; Avid; Secy Of EOC Umoja Club; Psych.

WYNN, TRACY; Westwood HS; Westwood, CA; (3); 1/28; FHA; Spanish Clb; Band; School Play; Pres Frsh Cls; Pres Jr Cls; Sec Stu Cncl; JV Var Bsktbl; JV Cheerldng; Var JV Trk; Top Stu Grade Awd.

WYNNS, PAUL; Junipero Serra HS; San Diego, CA; (3); 1/391; Am Leg Boys St; Quiz Bowl; High Hon Roll; Ntl Merit Schol; Prfct Atten Awd; Var Tennis; Jr Cngrss 90; Wtrpolo-Var Lttr; Quiz Bowl Lttr-Acad 88-90; IS Naval Acad; Aerospc Engrng.

WYRICK, AIMEE; Lodi Adventist Acad; Acampo, CA; (2); Church Yth Grp; Ski Clb; Rptr Nwsp; Bsbl; Bsktbl; Ftbl; Treas Gym; Vllybl; Hon Roll; Prfct Atten Awd; UC Berkeley; Marine Bio.

WYSZYNSKI, CHARLOTTE L; John F Kennedy HS; Sacramento, CA; (2); Church Yth Grp; Teachers Aide; Yng Life Chrstn Grp.

WYZLIC, MELINDA; Apple Valley HS; Apple Valley, CA; (1); Church Yth Grp; FHA; Hon Roll; Victor Valley CC; Reg Nurse.

XA, TRUNG Q; Santiago HS; Santa Ana, CA; (2); Hon Roll; NHS; CSF; UCI; Med.

XANTHOPOULOS, ERIC P; Bellarmine College Prep; Milpitas, CA; (2); 1/320; Cmnty Wkr; Debate Tm; NFL; Science Clb; Speech Tm; Teachers Aide; JV Crs Cntry; JV Trk; High Hon Roll; Hon Roll; U Of CA Berkeley; Med.

XAVIER, MARTINE M; James Logan HS; Union City, CA; (1); Church Yth Grp; Debate Tm; Girl Scts; SADD; Chorus; School Musical; Swing Chorus; Stu Cncl.

XAYAVONG, SIAMPHONE; Roosevelt HS; Fresno, CA; (3); Girl Scts; Office Aide; Chorus; JV Tennis; Jazz; Piano; Ballet; Bus Mgmt.

XAYAVONG, THIPHAPHONE T; Arlington HS; Riverside, CA; (2); FBLA; Rep Frsh Cls; Socr; Cit Awd.

XAYCHALEUNSOUK, PANY; Modesto HS; Modesto, CA; (2); Intnl Clb; Office Aide; Chorus; MJC; Sec.

XIAO, JING F; George Washington HS; San Francisco, CA; (3); Hon Roll; Honor Roll Certificate; ST U; Cosmetology.

XIE, ANNA; Oakland HS; Oakland, CA; (2); UC Berkeley; Pediatrics.

XIE, LISA; Abraham Lincoln HS; San Francisco, CA; (2); Library Aide; CSF; UC Davis; Bus Mgmt.

XIEU, KING YEE; Millikan JR HS; Los Angeles, CA; (1); GAA; VP Service Clb; Teachers Aide; Rptr Nwsp; Bsktbl; Vllybl; Cit Awd; Hon Roll; Prfct Atten Awd; Pres Acad Fit Awd; CJSF; Optometry.

XIONG, BOUN MA; Merced HS; Merced, CA; (3); Red Cross Aide; VICA; Vllybl; Hon Roll; Ka Tor; Sci Awd; Staniulas; CHP Pilot.

XIONG, CHEE VICKI; Mc Lane HS; Fresno, CA; (3); Church Yth Grp; Cit Awd; Hon Roll; Prfct Atten Awd; Fresno ST; Bus.

XIONG, CHUA; Redwood HS; Visalia, CA; (2); GAA; Math Clb; Spanish Clb; Score Keeper; JV Vllybl; Cit Awd; Hon Roll; Vlybl MVP; Comp.

XIONG, CHUE; Thomas Downey HS; Modesto, CA; (3); French Clb; FBLA; Office Aide; Cit Awd; Hon Roll; Modesto JC; Accntng.

XIONG, CHUE K; Cordova HS; Rancho Cordova, CA; (3); 61/476; Church Yth Grp; Key Clb; Model UN; Spanish Clb; JV Socr; NHS; Ntrl Hlpr; Med.

XIONG, GAONOU; Dos Pueblos HS; Goleta, CA; (3); Library Aide; Pep Clb; Yrbk; NHS; Marine Bio; Span; Econ; Bus.

XIONG, KAO; Bullard HS; Fresno, CA; (3); French Clb; Key Clb; Spanish Clb; Bsbl; Socr; Vllybl; High Hon Roll; Hon Roll; Medical Doctor.

XIONG, KAU; Thomas Edison HS; Stockton, CA; (2); French Clb; Math Clb; Science Clb; Hon Roll; Badminton Team Var; UC Davis; Dr.

XIONG, KHAI; Oroville HS; Oroville, CA; (4); French Clb; FTA; Hosp Aide; Math Tm; Office Aide; Speech Tm; Teachers Aide; VICA; Socr; Vllybl; Butte Coll; Teacher.

XIONG, LIA; Lindhurst HS; Olivehurst, CA; (2); JV Socr.

XIONG, MAY NGUA; Lindhurst HS; Marysville, CA; (2); Pres Church Yth Grp; Drama Clb; Key Clb; Church Choir; JV Tennis; High Hon Roll; Engl Excllnc Awd; Sec CA Schlrshp Fed Clb; Stu Month Awd; Engl Educ.

XIONG, NAYONG N; Clovis West HS; Fresno, CA; (1); Church Yth Grp; Computer Clb; FBLA; Cit Awd; Pres Acad Fit Awd; Asian Club; UC Davis; Comp Prgmmng.

XIONG, NU; Thomas Edison SR HS; Stockton, CA; (2); High Hon Roll.

XIONG, SHOUA; Thomas Edison SR HS; Stockton, CA; (3); Church Yth Grp; Science Clb; Spanish Clb; Socr; Sftbl; Vllybl; Hon Roll; Sci Olympiad Tm; Hmong Clb; UCO Clb; De Vry; Bus Oper.

XIONG, TSONG; Merced High School North; Merced, CA; (2); French Clb; FBLA; Office Aide; Cit Awd; High Hon Roll; Hon Roll; Prfct Atten Awd; California Scholarship Federation; College.

XIONG, XAY; Tulare Western HS; Tulare, CA; (3); Chess Clb; Church Yth Grp; Socr; Wrstlng; Hon Roll; Cmptr Pgmng.

XIONG, YANG; Merced HS; Merced, CA; (3); Boy Scts; 4-H; French Clb; FBLA; Hon Roll; Kiwanis Awd; Key Clb; BYU; Psych.

XIONG, YOUA; Lindhurst HS; Marysville, CA; (2); Church Yth Grp; ROTC; Drill Tm; Hon Roll; CSF.

XU, JIAN; Galileo HS; San Francisco, CA; (1).

XU, WEI XIN; Schurr HS; Rosemead, CA; (4); Aud/Vis; Computer Clb; FBLA; FTA; Intnl Clb; Math Clb; Teachers Aide; Yrbk; Tennis; Vllybl; Nw Lnd Schlrshp; Math.

XU, XIAO KANG; Skyline HS; Oakland, CA; (2); Church Yth Grp; Math Tm; Hon Roll; Prfct Atten Awd; Stu Mnth; Comp Sci; UC Berkeley; Doctor.

XU, XIAO LI; A Lincoln HS; Daly City, CA; (2); ROTC; Teachers Aide; Chorus; Drill Tm; School Musical; High Hon Roll; CSF; U Of CA Berkeley; Bus.

YABU, CHRISTINE; Lowell HS; San Francisco, CA; (3); VP Church Yth Grp; Cmnty Wkr; Teachers Aide; Chorus; Treas Stu Cncl; High Hon Roll; Vlntr SPCA; UC; Cmmnctns.

YABUT, CLARISA D; Lakewood SR HS; Long Beach, CA; (3); VP JA; Teachers Aide; Hon Roll; Peer Cnslr; DARE Pgm; CA Schlrshp Fed.

YABUT, URSULLA; Leuzinger HS; Hawthorne, CA; (3); JV Bsktbl; Var L Trk; Hon Roll; Prfct Atten Awd; Rcrd Hldr Discus 90; Most Outstndng Girls Fld Evnt Athl 89-90; Med.

YABUTA, SILVIA Y; Castle Park HS; Chula Vista, CA; (3); 3/422; French Clb; Latin Clb; Band; Mrchg Band; JV Swmmng; NEDT Awd; Syncronized Swim; Japanese Awd Embassy; Golden St Exam Hnrs Geom; UCSD; Actuarial Sci.

YACAWYCH, JENNIFER J; Garey HS; Pomona, CA; (2); Drama Clb; Hosp Aide; Key Clb; School Play; Chrmn Jr Cls; Var Cheerldng; Schl Gymnstcs Olympcs Gold Medal; Ldrshp Conf Cnslr; UC Davis; CA Assn Stu Cncl.

YACKLEY, JODY D; Antelope Valley HS; Lancaster, CA; (3); Am Leg Aux Girls St; Church Yth Grp; Pep Clb; Teachers Aide; Rep Frsh Cls; Rep Soph Cls; Rep Jr Cls; Score Keeper; Var L Trk; JV Capt Vllybl; Law.

YACOUBIAN, SEVAN; Armenian Mesrobian HS; Pasadena, CA; (3); Girl Scts; Library Aide; Quiz Bowl; Rep Jr Cls; JV Var Bsktbl; Hon Roll; Fshn Dsgn.

YACOVETTA, ELLIE; Gunn HS; Palo Alto, CA; (3); Yrbk; JV Cheerldng; Capt Var Pom Pon; French Hon Soc; Interact Clb; CSF; Saferides; CO U Boulder; Intrntl Bus.

YADA, MICHAEL W; Mount Whitney HS; Visalia, CA; (3); Boy Scts; Church Yth Grp; DECA; VP FBLA; Office Aide; SADD; Ed Nwsp; Rep Stu Cncl; Cheerldng; Life Boy Scout; Teen Tempo Staff Writer Competion; 2nd Place Entreprenewrship Competition; Cal Poly,UC Davis; Mech Engrg.

YAEGER, HEATHER M; Mt Whitney HS; Visalia, CA; (3); Spanish Clb; Crs Cntry; Hon Roll; Astrnmy Clb; Coll Of The Sequias; Psych.

YAGER, ANGELA L; Ramona HS; Ramona, CA; (2); SADD; Band; Jazz Band; Mrchg Band; Pep Band; School Musical; Stage Crew; Stat Bsktbl; Score Keeper; Amnesty Intl; SDSU; Law.

YAGI, BRETT; El Camino Real HS; West Hills, CA; (4); Math Clb; JV Tennis; Cal ST U; Computer Science.

YAKOOB, NADIA H; Brea O'linda HS; Fullerton, CA; (2); Church Yth Grp; Cmnty Wkr; Debate Tm; Drama Clb; French Clb; Hosp Aide; Key Clb; Office Aide; Ski Clb; Speech Tm; Work Wells Fargo Bank Teller; Nordstroms Fshn Bd Fshn Show; Fluent Spkr Eng Urdu Fr & Meymehn; UCLA; News Brdcstr.

YAKUBYAN, NVARD; Sherman Oaks CES; Los Angeles, CA; (1); Computer Clb; Drama Clb; French Clb; Trk; Cit Awd; Harvard; Law.

YALONG, ALLAN T; Bellarmine College Prep; San Jose, CA; (4); 35/305; Chess Clb; Cmnty Wkr; Math Clb; Service Clb; Teachers Aide; Bsktbl; Trk; Pres Acad Fit Awd; Carl J Saxenmeir Schlrshp; CA Polytech St U; Aero Engrng.

YAM, BRIAN D; Lowell HS; San Francisco, CA; (3); Boy Scts; Mrchg Band; High Hon Roll; Med Explorers; U CA Los Angeles; Med.

YAM, BRIAN H; Warren HS; Downey, CA; (2); Computer Clb; CSF; Med.

YAM, BRONWYN; Mills HS; Millbrae, CA; (2); Math Tm; Teachers Aide; Band; Hon Roll; Stanford; Bus.

YAM, CHHOEUY; Lincoln HS; Stockton, CA; (2); 1/500; High Hon Roll; Frnch III Cert & Acad Ltr; UC Davis; Engr.

YAM, PHANNY; Grace M Dvis HS; Modesto, CA; (2); FHA; Spanish Clb; Sftbl; Vllybl; Cit Awd; Teacher.

YAM, VUY L; La Quinta HS; Westminster, CA; (3); Chess Clb; Computer Clb; French Clb; Latin Clb; Tennis; High Hon Roll; Hon Roll; Dentist.

YAM, YOC L; La Quinta HS; Westminster, CA; (3); Chess Clb; French Clb; Science Clb; Tennis; High Hon Roll; Badmntn Sprt; Cal ST Pomona; Engr.

YAMADA, CATHY; Archbishop Mitty HS; San Jose, CA; (2); Dance Clb; SADD; Band; Pep Band; JV Cheerldng; High Hon Roll; NHS; Badminton Vrsty; Campfire Amer; CSF.

YAMADA, DAN; Mt Eden HS; Hayward, CA; (2); Boy Scts; JV Ftbl; Pres Acad Fit Awd; Engrng.

YAMADA, JENNIFER J; Woodbridge HS; Irvine, CA; (3); VP Church Yth Grp; SADD; Var L Bsktbl; Fshn Mrchndsng.

YAMADA, JUN; Corona Del Mar HS; Irvine, CA; (2); Science Clb; Spanish Clb; Trk.

YAMADA, LANCE Y; Vista HS; Vista, CA; (2); 12/487; Var Co-Ed Socr; High Hon Roll; UCSB; Comp Sci.

YAMADA, NANCY R; Bonita Vista HS; Chula Vista, CA; (3); 1/559; Variety Show; Cheerldng; Cit Awd; High Hon Roll; Dartmouth Club Bk Awd; Frnch Awd; Outstndng Schlrshp Awd 90.

YAMADA, RICKY; Dos Pueblos HS; Santa Barbara, CA; (4); 7/303; Boy Scts; Pres Latin Clb; Math Clb; Teachers Aide; Sec Stu Cncl; Var Capt Socr; Var Capt Swmmng; NHS; Opt Clb Awd; Rotary Awd; Waterpolo Team Capt; Athltc Rnd Tbl Schlr Athl; Assctd Stu Body Secy; Santa Clara U; Mech Engrng.

YAMADA, TATSUYA; Gahr HS; Cerritos, CA; (2); Swmmng; Hon Roll; UCLA; Engrng.

YAMAGUCHI, INA A; University HS; Irvine, CA; (2); Var L Swmmng; Hon Roll; Golden St Exam Geom Hnrs.

YAMAGUCHI, MONIQUE MARI; Bishop Amat Memorial HS; Monrovia, CA; (4); 50/400; Drill Tm; Rptr Yrbk; Rep Stu Cncl; Var L Crs Cntry; Var L Trk; High Hon Roll; NHS; Acad Decathlon 89-90; Bnk Amer Achvt Awd 90; Cmmndtn Chrstn Svc Pgm; U Of Southern CA; Pediatrics.

YAMAMORI, AKIKO; Mills HS; Millbrae, CA; (3); Intnl Clb; Math Tm; High Hon Roll.

YAMAMOTO, BLAKE M; Glen A Wilson HS; Hacienda Hgts, CA; (3); Band; Mrchg Band; Hon Roll; Piano Guild Founders Medal; Golden ST Exam 1st Yr Al High Hnrs; Golden ST Exam Geometry Hnrs; UC Riverside; Med.

YAMAMOTO, HENRY H; Mt Carmel HS; San Diego, CA; (2); Just Say No To Drugs; Skatbrdng; UCSD; Phy.

YAMAMOTO, JULIE; Newport Christian Schls; Huntington Bch, CA; (4); 1/13; Am Leg Aux Girls St; Quiz Bowl; Scholastic Bowl; School Play; Ed Yrbk; Ed Stu Cncl; Hon Roll; NEDT Awd; Journ.

YAMAMOTO, KEITH M; Narbonne HS; Torrance, CA; (3); Cmnty Wkr; Band; Mrchg Band; Orch; Hon Roll; Prfct Atten Awd; Band, Bus & Scl Stds Awds 88; UNLV; Bus Mgmt.

YAMAMOTO, KIMI D; Tokay HS; Stockton, CA; (2); 52/694; Var Trk; Jpnese Club; CSF; Bus.

YAMAMOTO, NICOLE; Glen A Wilson HS; Hacienda Heights, CA; (2); Church Yth Grp; Band; Church Choir; Mrchg Band; JV Swmmng; Hon Roll; Piano; UC-SANTA Cruz; Bio.

YAMAMOTO, SUSAN F; Lowell HS; San Francisco, CA; (3); Orch; U Of CA Berkeley; Comp Sci.

YAMAMOTO, TRACY; Archbishop Mitty HS; San Jose, CA; (3); 13/255; Art Clb; Cmnty Wkr; Math Tm; Rep Frsh Cls; Rep Soph Cls; High Hon Roll; NHS; CSF Sec.

YAMAMOTO, YOICHI; William Workman HS; La Puente, CA; (2); Bsbl; Bsktbl; Ftbl.

YAMAMURA, SCOTT; Lincoln HS; Stockton, CA; (3); 17/592; Boy Scts; German Clb; Mu Alpha Theta; Ski Clb; Crs Cntry; High Hon Roll; Asian Clb; CSF; Gldn St Exm Awd Algbra & Geo; Sci.

YAMANAKA, RYAN A; Napa HS; Napa, CA; (1); Boy Scts; Ski Clb; Spanish Clb; Orch; Socr; Pres Acad Fit Awd; Pres Schlr; Ski Team Alpine Meadows Lake Tahoe Ski Team; Jr Olympics 88; Napa Vly JR Symph Orch 86-88; Dartmouth.

YAMANE, CHERIE H; Redondo Union HS; Redondo Beach, CA; (4); 40/400; Teachers Aide; Ed Yrbk; Elks Awd; Hon Roll; Hula Dncng Comptn; Spnsh Cert Merit; Frnds & Parents Rcgtn Awd; Mt St Marys Coll; Educ.

YAMANE, ERNEST T; Walnut HS; Walnut, CA; (3); 56/406; Intnl Clb; Key Clb; Office Aide; High Hon Roll; Gftd & Tlntd Educ Cabinet; CSF; U CA Irvine; Mech Engrng.

YAMANI, ZAIN A; Irvine HS; Irvine, CA; (2); 2/500; Tennis; High Hon Roll; SSR; CA Schlrshp Fed; UCLA; Econ.

YAMANISHI, STACY C; John F Kennedy HS; La Palma, CA; (2); Pres Church Yth Grp; Key Clb; Varsity Clb; JV Var Bsktbl; JV Var Vllybl; Hon Roll; CSF.

YAMASAKI, BRIAN Y; Gardena HS; Gardena, CA; (4); 1/404; Boy Scts; Church Yth Grp; NFL; Teachers Aide; Mrchg Band; Nwsp; Yrbk; Var L Tennis; Jr NHS; Ntl Merit SF; Acad Decathalon Team; 2nd Pl Rgnl Citizen Bee Comp; Xerox Humanities & Social Studies Awd; Med.

YAMASAKI, SHAWN KURT; Poway HS; Poway, CA; (4); AFS; Key Clb; VP Math Clb; VP Mu Alpha Theta; Quiz Bowl; Var Scholastic Bowl; Service Clb; SADD; Swmmng; Cit Awd; Hnrs Gldn ST Exm; Clmn Pblshd Bernardo Nws Jrnl; Amer Chem Soc Exm Rep; Physcs.

YAMASHIROYA, RYAN K; Cerritos HS; Cerritos, CA; (1); Church Yth Grp; JV Bsbl; Pres Acad Fit Awd; Pacific Asian Club; U Of HI; Arch.

YAMASHITA, BRENT A; San Benito HS; Hollister, CA; (3); 12/370; Am Leg Boys St; Cmnty Wkr; Var L Wrstlng; High Hon Roll; Hon Roll; Spec Olympcs Vlntr; Mst Vlbl JV Wrstlr 88-89; Cmmnty Fndrsrs; U Of Southern CA; Phys Thrpy.

YAMASHITA, RICHARD; Aragon HS; San Mateo, CA; (3); Aud/Vis; Church Yth Grp; Computer Clb; VP Math Clb; Math Tm; Phtg Nwsp; High Hon Roll; Hon Roll; Prfct Atten Awd; Japanese Stud Schlrshp; Photography Awd 1990; Tensho-Kotai-Jingu-Kyo; Mech Engrng.

YAMAT, ZARINA Z; Notre Dame HS; Salinas, CA; (1); Hon Roll; CSF; UCLA; Nuclear.

YAMATO, JASON T; Bonita HS; La Verne, CA; (2); Chorus; JV Bsktbl; Hon Roll; Pres Acad Fit Awd.

YAMAUCHI, TETSU; St Francis HS; Los Angeles, CA; (2); Boy Scts; Chess Clb; Cmnty Wkr; French Clb; Ftbl; DAR Awd; French Hon Soc; Hon Roll; NHS; Prfct Atten Awd; CSF; Med.

YAMAURA, TAE; Rolling Hills HS; Rancho Palos Vrd, CA; (4); #13 In Class; Q&S; Service Clb; Mrchg Band; Orch; School Musical; Phtg Yrbk; Hon Roll; NHS; Pres Acad Fit Awd; Bnk Amer Cert Wnnr In Music; SW Yth Symphny Orch Mst Vlbl Musician; Susan B Nelson Awd; U Of CA Berkeley.

YAMRAJ, GANESH N; San Leandro HS; San Leandro, CA; (3); 14/361; Band; Var L Wrstlng; High Hon Roll; Prfct Atten Awd.

YAMSUAN, MA SHEILA; Fontana HS; Fontana, CA; (2); Band; Mrchg Band; Yrbk; Tennis; Hon Roll; Photo; Advertising.

YAN, HEUNG-WAH; J Eugene Mc Ateer HS; San Francisco, CA; (4); 1/400; Church Yth Grp; Cmnty Wkr; JA; Teachers Aide; Chorus; Church Choir; School Musical; Stage Crew; Elks Awd; High Hon Roll; CSF; Bank America Achvt Awd, Sci/Math Plque Wnnr; Acad Dcthln Gold Medalst Math, Brnze Medlst Econ; Stanford U; Comp Sci.

YAN, JENNIFER; Mt Carmel HS; San Diego, CA; (2); Key Clb; Band; Mrchg Band.

YAN, KA M; Skyline HS; Oakland, CA; (2); Asian Clb; UC Berkeley; Arch.

YAN, MICHAEL A; Lowell HS; San Francisco, CA; (3); Computer Clb; ROTC; Science Clb; Teachers Aide; Color Guard; Hon Roll; Spr JR Cadet Awd; SR Army Instrctr Awd; Ord Of Daedallions Awd; Unit Profcncy Awd; Ind Drill Down Awd; Aviation.

YAN, SUSANNA S; Schurr HS; Montebello, CA; (2); Dance Clb; Drill Tm; Mrchg Band; Hon Roll; Arch.

YAN, TAK CHUNG; J E Mc Ateer HS; San Francisco, CA; (3); Tennis; Hon Roll; Close Up Clb; CSF; Acad Dcthln; UC Berkeley; Engr.

YANCEY, BLAIN; Oak Ridge HS; Rescue, CA; (3); 26/261; Var Bsbl; Var Ftbl; Bus.

YANCEY, MICHELLE; Clovis HS; Clovis, CA; (2); Church Yth Grp; FCA; JV Capt Socr; Pres Acad Fit Awd; Socr Club; Chrch Yth Ldrshp; Sunday Schl Tchr; Modeling For Grimme; Biola U; Adv.

YANCY, XELINDA A; Notre Dame Acad; Los Angeles, CA; (3); Church Yth Grp; Spanish Clb; SADD; Stage Crew; Var Trk; Cit Awd; Hon Roll; Prfct Atten Awd; HOPE Club; Campus Mnstry; Drama.

YANDELL, CHRISTY M; Piner HS; Windsor, CA; (2); Church Yth Grp; Stage Crew; Nwsp; Bsbl; Bsktbl; Cheerldng; Trk; Hon Roll; 3rd Degree Green Belt Karate; Law Enfrcmnt.

YANEZ, AVELARDO C; Roseville HS; Rocklin, CA; (3); 10/411; Church Yth Grp; Math Tm; Science Clb; Spanish Clb; Teachers Aide; Var Bsktbl; Var Ftbl; Var Trk; High Hon Roll; NHS; CSF; Capital Valley All Conf Ftbl Tm; People To People Stu Ambassador; Engrng.

YANEZ, DANIEL; Saddleback HS; Santa Ana, CA; (3); FBLA; Cit Awd; Hon Roll; Prfct Atten Awd; Pres Acad Fit Awd; MESA; Hispanic Soc; UCLA; Bus Admin.

YANEZ, ELAINE C; Oxnard HS; Oxnard, CA; (2); 59/604; Church Yth Grp; Drama Clb; Spanish Clb; Hon Roll; Sectry/Treas Mck Trl Tm; Engl.

YANEZ, KIM; Perris HS; Pierris, CA; (2); Computer Clb; SADD; Teachers Aide; Drill Tm; Sftbl; Hon Roll; USC; Comp Tech.

YANEZ, LORENA; Hawthorne HS; Inglewood, CA; (2); Dance Clb; Key Clb; Jrnlst.

YANG, AI; Hoover HS; Fresno, CA; (2); Off Sr Cls; CA St U; Business.

YANG, ARLENE; Foothill HS; Pleasanton, CA; (3); Church Yth Grp; Mrchg Band; French Hon Soc; Hon Roll; NHS.

YANG, BECKY I; Santa Monica HS; Santa Monica, CA; (3); Ski Clb; Teachers Aide; Band; Mrchg Band; Orch; Pep Band; Hon Roll; Semi Fnlst Cngrss Bndstag Yth Exhcng Prgm; Jr Philharmonica Orch; Usc; Hstry.

YANG, BOUN MEE; Edison HS; Fresno, CA; (1); Church Yth Grp; Swmmng; Tennis; Med.

YANG, BRENDA; Homestead HS; Sunnyvale, CA; (1); Math Clb; High Hon Roll; Hon Roll; Prfct Atten Awd; Badmntn; UCLA.

YANG, CAROLYN S; Mountain View HS; Los Altos, CA; (3); 17/319; AFS; Model UN; Spanish Clb; Rptr Nwsp; Treas Jr Cls; JV Bsktbl; Var Crs Cntry; Var Trk; Var Wt Lftg; High Hon Roll; Cie/Usa Outstndng Achvt Awd Schlshps; Schlstc Chmpnshp Tm Crs Cntry 87; CIF Schlstc Achvt Awd; Law.

YANG, CHANG MEE; Roosevelt HS; Fresno, CA; (3); Church Yth Grp; FCA; Chorus; Church Choir; Prfct Atten Awd.

YANG, CHAO; Hoover HS; San Diego, CA; (3); 64/365; Teachers Aide; Cit Awd; ITT; Math.

YANG, CHONG X; Grace M Davis HS; Modesto, CA; (3); Church Yth Grp; FHA; Intnl Clb; SADD; Chorus; Church Choir; Tennis; Cit Awd; Hon Roll; Prfct Atten Awd; Stanislaus CA ST U; Bus Admin.

YANG, CHU; Melane HS; Fresno, CA; (1); High Hon Roll.

YANG, CINDY; Huntington HS; Huntington Beach, CA; (2); Rep Key Clb; Model UN; Capt Flag Corp; Phtg Rptr Yrbk; JV Bsktbl; JV Sftbl; Red Cross Pblcty Ofcr For HS; Chrstian Unity Clb; UC Berkeley; Pre-Med.

YANG, CINDY; Monterey Bay Acad; La Selva Beach, CA; (2); Band; Hon Roll; UC Berkeley; Accntng.

YANG, DAVID; Servite HS; Anaheim, CA; (3); Var Tennis; NHS; Vlntr Wrk UCI Med Hosp; Acad Excllnc Awd; CA Schlrshp Fed; US Tnns Assoc; Jr Stateman Of Amer.

YANG, DER; Cajon HS; San Bernardino, CA; (2); Tennis; Valley Coll; Tech Engr.

YANG, DOROTHY; Mills HS; Millbrae, CA; (2); Church Yth Grp; Band; Church Choir; Orch; Pep Band; Sec Frsh Cls; Treas Soph Cls; Mgr(s); Tennis; High Hon Roll; Stanford.

YANG, EDDIE W; University HS; Irvine, CA; (4); 24/530; Church Yth Grp; Cmnty Wkr; Intnl Clb; Math Tm; Model UN; Tennis; Wrstlng; Hon Roll; Ntl Merit Ltr; Bckd Socr Tm; Berkeley Med Schl; Med.

YANG, GEORGE; North Vista HS; Riverside, CA; (4); ROTC; Science Clb; High Hon Roll; Riverside City Coll; Bus.

YANG, GERALD; Mira Loma HS; Carmichael, CA; (1); 3/280; Math Clb; Math Tm; Science Clb; JV Golf; High Hon Roll; Sci Olympiad Team; CA Music Teachers Assn Cert Of Merit.

YANG, GHAOYOUA ICE; Crawford HS; San Diego, CA; (2); 19/382; Office Aide; Chorus; Drill Tm; Mgr(s); Hon Roll; Bus.

YANG, JANNY C; Lowell HS; San Francisco, CA; (3); Church Yth Grp; ROTC; Chorus; Drill Tm; Gldn St Exm Hgh Hnrs; Fil-Am Clb; Cadet Mnth Awd Jan 90; Stanford U; Bus.

YANG, JE; Cajon HS; San Bernardino, CA; (3); Computer Clb; Dance Clb; Math Clb; Math Tm; Bsbl; Socr; Sftbl; Swmmng; Tennis; Vllybl; Cal ST CA; Comp Sci.

YANG, JEANNIE; Burlingame HS; Hillborough, CA; (4); 6/274; Intnl Clb; VP Math Clb; Capt Math Tm; Office Aide; Service Clb; Teachers Aide; Lit Mag; Stu Cncl; JV Tennis; High Hon Roll; Gldn St Exm Geom Hgh Hnrs; Bank Amercn Achvt Awd Math; US Space Acad Lvl I Wings; U Of CA Berkeley; Vet.

YANG, JENNIFER; Glen A Wilson HS; Hacienda Heights, CA; (2); Library Aide; Capt Drill Tm; Schl Schlr 88-89; Spcl Intrst Ballet Jazz & Dance.

YANG, JIN H; University HS; Los Angeles, CA; (3); Cmnty Wkr; Ftbl; U Of CA Los Angeles; Chrprctc.

YANG, KATHRYN K; Esperanza HS; Yorba Linda, CA; (2); 1/571; German Clb; Hosp Aide; Sec Soph Cls; JV Sftbl; Cit Awd; High Hon Roll; Jr NHS; NHS; Intl Clb; CA Schlrshp Fed; N Orange Cntry Chinese Culture Assn; John Hopkins; Pre Med.

YANG, KEELAN; San Mateo HS; Foster City, CA; (4); 9/340; VP Latin Clb; VP Pres Math Clb; Capt Math Tm; Sec Model UN; Science Clb; Sec Sr Cls; Var L Crs Cntry; Var L Trk; Hon Roll; Ntl Merit Ltr; R*ennselaer Polytech Inst Mdl Math & Sci; PTA Outstndng Stu Awd Sci; Crrclm & Policy Cmmtee Jr Rep; Engr.

YANG, KI S; Seaside HS; Marina, CA; (2); French Clb; Wt Lftg; Hon Roll; Prfct Atten Awd.

YANG, LENG; San Gorgonio HS; San Bernardino, CA; (3); English Clb; CA Schlrshp Fedrtn; 5th Annl Acad Awds Assmbly; CA ST; Cmptr Sci.

YANG, LESTER F; El Dorado HS; Placentia, CA; (2); 1/362; Intnl Clb; Math Clb; Band; Mrchg Band; Pep Band; High Hon Roll; NHS; Orange Cnty Acad Dcthln Tm 1st Lang Art.

YANG, LINH H; San Rafael HS; San Rafael, CA; (4); 15/219; Debate Tm; Sec Drama Clb; VP Pres Intnl Clb; Elks Awd; Pres Acad Fit Awd; Rotary Awd; People For Env Awareness & Cultural Equality; Stu For Union For Stu Of All Colors; CSF Awd; UC Davis.

YANG, LINH N; Montclair HS; Upland, CA; (3); Chess Clb; FBLA; Key Clb; Science Clb; Spanish Clb; Var Tennis; Hon Roll; Prfct Atten Awd; CSF; Gate Clb; Friends Library Clb; Tnns MVP & MIP Awds; Cal ST Fullerton; Teacher.

YANG, LISA; Verdugo Hills HS; Los Angeles, CA; (4); Pep Clb; Rep Soph Cls; Rep Jr Cls; Rep Sr Cls; VP Stu Cncl; Var Capt Tennis; Cit Awd; Hon Roll; Pres Acad Fit Awd; Asian Clb Pres; Stu Leag Pres; CSF; UCLA; Law.

YANG, LO J; Cordova SR HS; Rancho Cordova, CA; (3); Church Yth Grp; Key Clb; Model UN; Spanish Clb; Socr; Hon Roll; NHS; Med.

YANG, LUE; Edison HS; Fresno, CA; (4); 30/93; Cmnty Wkr; French Clb; Hosp Aide; SADD; Off Sr Cls; South East Asia Clb Acts Dir; America Hmong Clb; Bus.

YANG, MARY; Irvine HS; Irvine, CA; (2); Key Clb; Chinese Clb; Stu For Scl Rspnsblty; Schlrshp For Irvine Chinese Schl.

YANG, MAY NOU; Merced HS; Merced, CA; (3); Hon Roll; Prfct Atten Awd; Acctng.

YANG, MEE; Fresno HS; Fresno, CA; (2); #1 In Class; Sftbl; High Hon Roll; Hon Roll; Chlds Care; San Francisco ST U; Ped.

YANG, MEI; San Gabriel HS; San Gabriel, CA; (3); Cit Awd; Hon Roll; Prfct Atten Awd.

YANG, MELINDA T; Edison HS; Huntington Beach, CA; (3); Model UN; Band; Mrchg Band; Keywannettes, Chinese Clb 88-90; U UT; Pharmacy.

YANG, NAI; Lompoc SR HS; Lompoc, CA; (3); 56/200; JV Socr; NHS; UCSB Upward Bound; U CA Santa Barbara; Cmptr Engr.

YANG, NAREEE; Lindhurst HS; Marysville, CA; (2); Church Yth Grp; SADD; Tennis; Culture Clb; CA Schlrshp Fndtn; Peer Cnslng; Friday Night Live; U Of Davis; Sci.

YANG, NENG; Edison HS; Fresno, CA; (1); 5/32; JV Chess Clb; Teachers Aide; Vllybl; Cit Awd; Hon Roll; Prfct Atten Awd; Best Overall Comp Lit II Stu; Asian Clb.

YANG, PA; Clovis HS; Clovis, CA; (2); Church Yth Grp; FTA; Intnl Clb; SADD; Fresno ST U.

YANG, PA; Eureka HS; Eureka, CA; (1); SADD; Cit Awd; Hon Roll; UC Davis; Fashion Dsgnr.

YANG, PANG I; Thomas Downey HS; Modesto, CA; (2); French Clb; Sec FFA; Hon Roll; Fashn Merch.

YANG, PAO S; Thomas Downey HS; Modesto, CA; (2); Spanish Clb; Hon Roll; CA ST U Of Stanislaus.

YANG, PAOKOU; Fountain Valley HS; Fountain Valley, CA; (3); Band; Socr; Hon Roll; NHS; Prfct Atten Awd; Pres Acad Fit Awd; UCI; Phy.

YANG, PHOUA; Beaumont HS; Beaumont, CA; (2); Church Yth Grp; French Clb; Math Clb; Office Aide; Science Clb; Bus.

YANG, PHUONG H; San Rafael HS; San Rafael, CA; (2); 1/256; High Hon Roll; CSF; High Hnrs Golden St Exam Geom 89.

YANG, PUA; Edison HS; Stockton, CA; (1); Speech Tm; Nwsp; Hon Roll; CSF; Engr.

YANG, ROBERT; La Jolla Country Day Schl; Carlsbad, CA; (2); Church Yth Grp; SADD; Var Ftbl; Var Trk; Wt Lftg; Hon Roll; Phys Thrpst.

YANG, SAEWON; Palos Verdes HS; Palos Vrds Pen, CA; (3); German Clb; Hosp Aide; Model UN; Color Guard; Ed Yrbk; JV Trk; High Hon Roll; NHS; Leo Club; Keyettes.

YANG, SETH C; Dana Hills HS; Laguna Beach, CA; (1); Boy Scts; Orch; Orange Cty Yth Symphny Orch & Acad Dcthln; Med.

YANG, SHOUA; Clovis HS; Clovis, CA; (3); Church Yth Grp; French Clb.

YANG, SING TAI; Phillip And Sala Burton HS; San Francisco, CA; (3); Art Clb; Chess Clb; Spanish Clb; Band; Off Sr Cls; Phrmcst.

YANG, SONG; Duncan Polytechical HS; Fresno, CA; (1); Office Aide; Chorus; Prfct Atten Awd; Bus.

YANG, STEVEN; Newport Harbor HS; Newport Beach, CA; (3); 34/302; Intrml Capt Bsktbl; Most Imprvd Plyr, Capt Badmntn; Chinese Club.

YANG, SU; Hoover HS; San Diego, CA; (4); Church Yth Grp; JA; Library Aide; Church Choir; Cit Awd; Hon Roll; U San Diego; Lawyer.

YANG, THOMAS; Lowell HS; San Francisco, CA; (2); Hon Roll; Goldn St Exm Alg Hnr; UC Berkeley; Astrophysicst.

YANG, TINA; Marina HS; Huntington Bch, CA; (1); JV Tennis; JV Trk; Stanford; Law.

YANG, TOU; Downey HS; Modesto, CA; (4); DECA; Cit Awd; Hon Roll; Prfct Atten Awd; San Diego ST U.

YANG, TOU LEE; Saddleback HS; Santa Ana, CA; (3); Spanish Clb; Intrml Ftbl; Var Wrstlng; Cit Awd; Prfct Atten Awd; CSF-CA Schlstc Fdrtn; CSUF; Elec Engrng.

YANG, VANG; Golden West HS; Visalia, CA; (4); Art Clb; French Clb; Science Clb; Intrml Bsktbl; Intrml Ftbl; Intrml Socr; Intrml Swmmng; Intrml Tennis; Intrml Trk; Intrml Vllybl; UC Davis; Aerontcl Engrng.

YANG, XEE DENISE; Roosevelt HS; Fresno, CA; (3); Church Yth Grp; French Clb; JA; Chorus; Bsktbl; Vllybl; Hon Roll.

YANG, YOUA; Beaumont HS; Beaumont, CA; (4); 10/148; Church Yth Grp; French Clb; JA; Office Aide; Church Choir; Cit Awd; Hon Roll; Opt Clb Awd; Prfct Atten Awd; Azusa Pacific U; Acctng.

YANN, THOY V; Savanna HS; Anaheim, CA; (3); Am Leg Aux Girls St; Pres Art Clb; Cmnty Wkr; Intnl Clb; Key Clb; Pep Clb; Red Cross Aide; Service Clb; Capt Varsity Clb; Nwsp; Stu Of Mnth; Athlete Of Wk; Most Enthusiastic Ldrshp Acad; Stanford; Law.

YANNONE, JENNIFER; Loara HS; Anaheim, CA; (2); Church Yth Grp; Dance Clb; Drill Tm; Variety Show; Off Frsh Cls; Rep Stu Cncl; Stat Swmmng; Hon Roll; GATE Clb; Mst Depndble & Helpfl Drill Tema Stu.

YANOS, STEPHANIE E; La Habra HS; Whittier, CA; (2); 11/400; Swmmng; Rotary Awd; Hmcmng Prncss 89-90; Yrbk Stff 90-91; Marine Bio.

YANTIS, TACY R; Shasta HS; Chester, CA; (3); 68/450; Treas Frsh Cls; Rep Soph Cls; Crs Cntry; Powder Puff Ftbl; Socr; Swmmng; Trk; Vllybl; Hon Roll; Pres Acad Fit Awd; Aviation.

YANZ, NICOLE; Ribet Acad; Glendale, CA; (4); 3/28; Church Yth Grp; Cmnty Wkr; Math Clb; Ski Clb; Varsity Clb; Chorus; Church Choir; Yrbk; Off Sr Cls; Stu Cncl; Merci Awd Chrty Leag; Mst Sprtd Chrldr; Loyola Marymount; Pre-Med.

YAO, CHRIS; Bishop Amat HS; Valinda, CA; (1); JV Ftbl; JV Vllybl; JV Wt Lftg; Prfct Atten Awd; UCLA; Bus.

YAO, JULIE; Cerritos HS; Artesia, CA; (1); Science Clb; Spanish Clb; Gym; Hon Roll; Prfct Atten Awd; Bus/Sec.

YAO, NANCY; George Washington HS; San Francisco, CA; (3); Intnl Clb; Key Clb; Math Clb; Office Aide; Red Cross Aide; Science Clb; Teachers Aide; High Hon Roll; Hon Roll; Gen Svc Soc; Achvmt Awds Bio Chinese Typ & Teaching Asst; Chinese Speech Contest; U CA Davis; Chem.

YAO, PETER; Fountain Valley HS; Fountain Valley, CA; (4); 21/627; Church Yth Grp; Pres German Clb; Science Clb; Band; JV Vllybl; High Hon Roll; NHS; Mc Donnell Douglas Schlrshp Fndtn Awd Wnr; Sr Spkr Grad Cmmncmt; City Fountain Vly Tn Ctzn Awd Wnr; U Of CA Irvine; Elec Engrng.

YAO, PO; Covina HS; West Covina, CA; (3); Math Clb; Band; Socr; Tennis; Trk; Vllybl; High Hon Roll; Hon Roll; 2nd Pl El Monte Easter Trnmt; UCLA; Spc Engr.

YAP, NANETTE; Acalanes HS; Lafayette, CA; (4); SADD; Acpl Chr; Band; Church Choir; School Musical; Cheerldng; Var Pom Pon; Hon Roll; Dist Hnr Band; UC Davis; Pre-Med.

YAP, PAUL; La Mirada HS; La Mirada, CA; (2); French Clb; Ftbl; Trk; Vllybl; High Hon Roll; Hon Roll; Comp Sci.

YAP, ROGER; Long Beach Polytechnic HS; Long Beach, CA; (4); Church Yth Grp; Capt ROTC; Drm Mjr(t); Jazz Band; Mrchg Band; Mgr(s); Capt Trk; Rotc Mdls, Awds & Hnrs; NM Military Inst; Engrng.

YAP, SOESIJAWATI; Pasadena HS; Temple City, CA; (4); Boy Scts; Church Yth Grp; Library Aide; Acpl Chr; Lit Mag; Off Sr Cls; PCC; Finance.

YAPJOCO, JOY; Paramount HS; Downey, CA; (2); Drama Clb; Key Clb; School Play; Pres Jr Cls; Hon Roll; UCLA; Show Bus.

YAR-KHAN, ABBAS; El Camino Real HS; Woodland Hills, CA; (3); High Hon Roll; Hon Roll; Golden St Awd Alg High Hnrs; Golden St Awd Geom Hnrs; UCLA; Eng.

YARBER, PANYA L; Washington HS; Fremont, CA; (2); 1/310; German Clb; Pres Pep Clb; Varsity Clb; JV Bsktbl; Var Crs Cntry; Var Trk; High Hon Roll; Opt Clb Awd; Amnesty Intl; CSF.

YARBROUGH, JANE K; Hanford HS; Hanford, CA; (1); Art Clb; Church Yth Grp; Church Choir; Var L Crs Cntry; Var L Trk; CA Baptist Coll.

YARBROUGH, JENNIFER R; Clovis HS; Fresno, CA; (4); Art Clb; Drama Clb; School Musical; School Play; Stage Crew; High Hon Roll; Environmentalist; Animal Rights Supporter; Opthamology.

YARBROUGH, LISA; Cajon HS; San Bernardino, CA; (2); GAA; Socr; Hon Roll; San Diego ST U; Marine Bio.

YARBROUGH-DIAZ, CYNRA; Trona HS; Trona, CA; (3); Cmnty Wkr; Dance Clb; Debate Tm; English Clb; Math Tm; Speech Tm; SADD; Teachers Aide; Co-Ed Nwsp; Phtg Yrbk; Kid Corps; Writing Celebration; Chiropractic.

YARED, ENDRIAS J; Bishop Amat HS; Arcadia, CA; (1); Ftbl; USC; Med.

YARINA, JESSICA ANNE; Los Amigos HS; Fountain Valley, CA; (2); 12/406; Drama Clb; Pep Clb; Speech Tm; Thesps; Stage Crew; Var Cheerldng; Vllybl; High Hon Roll; Hon Roll; French Spkng Camps; Gldn St Exam Algebra & Geom High Hnrs & Hnrs; Mock Trail; Law.

YARISAIED, SHAHAB; Branham HS; San Jose, CA; (4); Art Clb; Cmnty Wkr; Key Clb; Letterman Clb; Teachers Aide; Varsity Clb; JV Bsbl; JV Var Ftbl; Var JV Trk; Wt Lftg; Ftbl Chmps; West Valley Coll; Med Rsrchr.

YAROSLASKI, DAVID P; Paraclete HS; Lancaster, CA; (3); Drama Clb; Pres Letterman Clb; Rep Frsh Cls; Rep Soph Cls; Rep Jr Cls; Rep Stu Cncl; Var Bsbl; Var Ftbl; Var Socr; Hon Roll.

YARRALL, ANGELA J; Western HS; Anaheim, CA; (4); 7/300; Church Yth Grp; Sec Computer Clb; French Clb; Spanish Clb; Teachers Aide; School Musical; Hon Roll; NHS; Pres Acad Fit Awd; Won Orange Cnty HS Cmptr Contest Schl Team; Rcvd Certs Schl For Calculus AP, AP Chem, AP Engl; Biola U; Math.

YARRIS, JONATHAN P; Torrey Pines HS; Solana Beach, CA; (1); Intrml Bsktbl; CA Schltc Assoc.

YARRIS, KRISTIN E; Torrey Pines HS; Solana Beach, CA; (4); 24/455; Church Yth Grp; Rotary Awd; Horseback Riding/Cmptns; Am Horse Shows Assn Schlrshp Wnnr; Pacific Lutheran U; Relgn.

YASHARAL, SHARONA; University HS; Los Angeles, CA; (3); Hosp Aide; JCL; Office Aide; Spanish Clb; Speech Tm; Var Tennis; Hon Roll; Jr NHS; Spanish NHS; UCLA; Law.

YASSINGER, MARC A; Rio Americano HS; Carmichael, CA; (4); 8/259; JA; Spanish Clb; Temple Yth Grp; Yrbk; JV Bsktbl; Ftbl; Var Golf; JV Var Socr; Lion Awd; NHS; UCLA; Econ.

YASUDA, MIDORI L; James Logan HS; Union City, CA; (4); 20/700; Church Yth Grp; Cmnty Wkr; Science Clb; Ski Clb; Band; Mrchg Band; Orch; Pep Band; School Musical; Rep Stu Cncl; Bank Amer Awd Music; Grad Magna Cum Laude CSF Sash/Mdl Durng Grad; Schlrshps Band,Chrch,Japan-Amer Ct; U Of CA Berkeley; Psych.

YATES, DANIEL E; Junipero Serra HS; Los Angeles, CA; (3); Computer Clb; Dance Clb; FCA; JA; Varsity Clb; Stu Cncl; Bsktbl; Cit Awd; Hon Roll; Comp Prgmng.

YATES, JENNIFER; Seaside HS; Marina, CA; (3); AFS; Drama Clb; Teachers Aide; Band; Var Cheerldng; High Hon Roll; Explorers.

YATES, MATT L; Santa Clara HS; Santa Clara, CA; (1); Aud/Vis; Boy Scts; Church Yth Grp; JV Socr; Hon Roll; SCU; Technel Dsgn.

YATES, SAM J; Del Campo HS; Carmichael, CA; (2); 16/465; Church Yth Grp; Pres Frsh Cls; VP Soph Cls; Treas Jr Cls; JV Socr; Var Tennis; JV Vllybl; JV Wrstlng; Pres Acad Fit Awd; CSF; 3 A Awd; Tioga Ski Clb Pres; UCLA; Arch.

YATES, SEAN; Red Bluff HS; Red Bluff, CA; (2); 38/450; Boy Scts; Church Yth Grp; Mu Alpha Theta; Swmmng; Hon Roll; San Luis Obispo; Arch Engr.

YATES, TOM; St Patrick-St Vincent HS; Vallejo, CA; (4); 14/148; Science Clb; Teachers Aide; Var Diving; Var Socr; Var Swmmng; High Hon Roll; Hon Roll; Tutorng; Soccer Champships; Santa Clara U; Math.

YAU, EMILY H; La Sierra HS; Riverside, CA; (1); Var JV Swmmng; High Hon Roll; CSF; Marine Bio.

YAU, KATHERINE; Eagle Rock HS; Los Angeles, CA; (4); Intnl Clb; Science Clb; Service Clb; Jazz Band; Bausch & Lomb Sci Awd; Hon Roll; Prfct Atten Awd; Pres Acad Fit Awd; U Of CA Los Angeles; Chem.

YAU, LAWRENCE; West Covina HS; West Covina, CA; (3); 3/500; Cmnty Wkr; Spanish Clb; SADD; Varsity Clb; Ed Yrbk; Var L Crs Cntry; High Hon Roll; Pres Acad Fit Awd; CA Schltc Fed; Gldn ST Exam Hghst Hnrs Alg & Geo.

YAU, LUCIA; Eagle Rock HS; Los Angeles, CA; (3); Pres VP Intnl Clb; Teachers Aide; Chorus; Cit Awd; Hon Roll; Prfct Atten Awd; CA Schlrshp JR Fed; Tutor; Golden St Exam Acad Excllnc Awd Alg I; Arch.

YAZDANPANAH, HADI M; Clovis West HS; Fresno, CA; (2); Phtg Nwsp; Bsktbl; Ftbl; Trk; Piano; UCLA; Med.

YBARRA, CHRISTINA M; Fresno Christian HS; Fresno, CA; (1); Church Yth Grp; Letterman Clb; Band; Mrchg Band; Pep Band; Var Bsktbl; Var Sftbl; JV Vllybl; Hon Roll; Tchr.

YBARRA JR, FRANCISCO; Riverdale HS; Riverdale, CA; (4); FHA; VP Intnl Clb; Office Aide; SADD; Rptr Yrbk; VP Sr Cls; Rep Stu Cncl; High Hon Roll; Hon Roll; Outstndg Stu Awd Engl & Frgn Lang; Bank Amer Stu Achvt; Fresno ST; Bio.

YBARRA, JOSEPH J; Bishop Amat HS; West Covina, CA; (2); Var Tennis; High Hon Roll; Hon Roll; NEDT Awd; VP Sprts Clb; Awd Otstndng Achvt Natl World Hstry Test; Claremont Mc Kenna Coll; Eco.

YBARRA, NICOLE L; Robert A Millikan HS; Long Beach, CA; (4); Cmnty Wkr; Hosp Aide; SADD; Teachers Aide; Rep Stu Cncl; Cit Awd; Hon Roll; Prfct Atten Awd; Marine Bio Clb; UC Irvine; Humanities.

YBARRA, PATRICIA; La Habra HS; Whittier, CA; (4); 6/350; Sec Drama Clb; VP NFL; Pres Spanish Clb; VP Speech Tm; School Play; Ed Nwsp; High Hon Roll; Pres NHS; Ntl Merit SF; Columbia U; Russian.

YBARRA, RAQUEL V; Mater Dei HS; Santa Ana, CA; (2); Spanish Clb; Hon Roll; Cal ST U Fullerton; Accntng.

YBARRA, RAYMOND; Luther Burbank HS; Sacramento, CA; (2); Boy Scts; Church Yth Grp; Math Clb; ROTC; Off Frsh Cls; Off Soph Cls; Hon Roll; Prfct Atten Awd; Royal Rangers-Jr Cmmndr-Gold Achvt Mdl; Math/Engrng/Sci/Achvt-MESA-PRES; Explorer Scouts-Pres; Comp Engr.

YBARRA, ROBERTO J; La Sierra HS; Riverside, CA; (3); Cit Awd; High Hon Roll; Hon Roll; Prfct Atten Awd; Stanford; Civil Engr.

YBARRA, SONIA; Hueneme HS; Oxnard, CA; (2); Church Yth Grp; Stat Bsktbl; Var L Crs Cntry; Score Keeper; Stat JV Trk; Acctg/Bus.

YEAGER, LESLEE; Canyon HS; Canyon Country, CA; (4); Nwsp; JV Var Mgr(s); Law Enfrcmnt.

YEARGIN, BRENNA M; North Monterey County HS; Watsonville, CA; (3); Amnesty Intl; Cabrillo Coll; Culinary Arts.

YEARRY, RICHARD A; San Clemente HS; San Clemente, CA; (1); Intrml Bsbl; Var Wrstlng; Envrnmntlst.

YEATS, TODD E; American HS; Fremont, CA; (3); 30/310; German Clb; Band; Drm Mjr(t); VP Pres Jr Cls; Pres Stu Cncl; Ftbl; Var Socr; Var Capt Trk; Cit Awd; Rotary Awd; USMC Devil Pups Ctznshp Awd Co Hnrs 89; Lewis E Weyand Meml Awd; Poly Sci.

YEAV, KOURNG SOK; Herbert Hoover HS; San Diego, CA; (3); Intnl Clb; Key Clb; Math Clb; Office Aide; High Hon Roll; Hon Roll; NHS; Pres Acad Fit Awd; UCSD; Bus Mgmt.

YEE, ALANA; John F Kennedy HS; Sacramento, CA; (3); #43 In Class; Art Clb; Cmnty Wkr; Debate Tm; Trk; CSF; UC Davis; Bio.

YEE, ALLAN F; George Washington HS; San Francisco, CA; (2); High Hon Roll; Hon Roll; UC Santa Cruz; Comp Engrng.

YEE, ALLEN K; Lowell HS; San Francisco, CA; (2); Cmnty Wkr; Teachers Aide; Orch; Sec Frsh Cls; CSF; YMCA Weight Trnr; Man Of The Yr East/West Nwspr 88; Yale; Archaeology.

YEE, ANTHONY; John F Kennedy HS; Sacramento, CA; (2); FBLA; German Clb; Latin Clb; Math Clb; Orch; Bus Mgt.

YEE, BRIAN K; Lowell HS; San Francisco, CA; (3); Red Cross Aide; SADD; Band; Var Tennis; All City Doubles Semi-Fnlst Tennis; Exploratorium Vlntr; CSF; U Of CA Berkeley; Arch.

YEE, CHRISTOPHER S; San Marino HS; San Marino, CA; (4); French Clb; FBLA; Letterman Clb; Math Clb; Q&S; Science Clb; Varsity Clb; Ed Nwsp; Socr; Trk; UC Irvine; Bus.

YEE, ERIKA J; Rio Linda SR HS; Sacramento, CA; (4); 9/300; Sec Treas Church Yth Grp; English Clb; Office Aide; Spanish Clb; Teachers Aide; Band; Church Choir; Mrchg Band; Hon Roll; CA Schlrshp Fed Sec; Future Tchrs Of Amer Schlrshp; CA ST U Sacramento; Lbrl Stds.

YEE, GORDON; Washington HS; San Francisco, CA; (2); Hon Roll; San Francisco ST U.

YEE, JONATHAN DAVID; College Park HS; Martinez, CA; (3); 5/325; Church Yth Grp; Spanish Clb; JV Trk; High Hon Roll; CA Schlrshp Fed; Asian/Amer Club; Golden St Acad Excllnc Awd High Hnrs Geom; Natl Math Lg Awd; Engrng.

YEE, JOSEPH D; College Park HS; Martinez, CA; (1); 9/400; Church Yth Grp; JV Trk; High Hon Roll; CSF; Asian Clb.

YEE, JUDY; Lowell HS; San Francisco, CA; (3); French Clb; Hosp Aide; Office Aide; Red Cross Aide; ROTC; Teachers Aide; Cheerldng; Mgr(s); Bio.

YEE, KANDICE; Tustin HS; Tustin, CA; (4); Hosp Aide; JA; Teachers Aide; Crs Cntry; Hon Roll; Voice Dem Awd; Tustin Area Womens Clb Heritage Essay Cont, 1st Pl Awd; UC Irvine; Med.

YEE, KAREN; Abraham Lincoln HS; San Francisco, CA; (3); FTA; Service Clb; Treas Frsh Cls; Treas Soph Cls; Treas Jr Cls; Stu Cncl; High Hon Roll; Fresh, Soph, Jr Class Clubs; Prom Cmmtte.

YEE, KAREN A; John F Kennedy HS; Sacramento, CA; (2); 41/530; Hon Roll.

YEE, KELLY T; Whitney HS; Cerritos, CA; (3); 1/176; Cmnty Wkr; FBLA; Band; Variety Show; Ed Nwsp; Yrbk; NHS; Prncpls Advsry Bd; Pblshd Wrtr CSULB Kleidoscp 90; John Hopkins U Ctr Tlntd Yth Pgm; Jrnlsm.

YEE, KEVIN B; Whitney HS; Cerritos, CA; (2); Sec Computer Clb; FBLA; Intnl Clb; Model UN; Hon Roll; UC Irvine; Bus Mgmt.

YEE, LAUREN S; Washington HS; Fremont, CA; (3); 26/306; Trk; Gymnstcs; CSF; Bus.

YEE, LILI Y; San Marcos HS; Santa Barbara, CA; (2); Lit Mag; Rep Stu Cncl; Hon Roll; Prfct Atten Awd; #1 Clb; Royal Pages Sec/Treas; Bus.

YEE, MA AMY LAI; Wallenberg Traditional HS; San Francisco, CA; (1); Band; Rptr Nwsp; Vllybl; Cit Awd; Hon Roll.

YEE, MELISSA A; Baldwin Park HS; Baldwin Park, CA; (4); Chess Clb; Cmnty Wkr; Computer Clb; Dance Clb; Math Clb; Ed Lit Mag; Stu Cncl; Trk; Hon Roll; Jr NHS; Lawyer.

YEE, MELODY; Baldwin Pk HS; Baldwin Pk, CA; (4); Computer Clb; Dance Clb; Library Aide; Ed Lit Mag; Stu Cncl; Trk; Hon Roll; Jr NHS; NHS; Prfct Atten Awd; Pre-Law.

YEE, NANG; Fairfield HS; Fairfield, CA; (1); Spanish Clb; Yrbk; Hon Roll; Harvard.

YEE, NORMAN; Milpitas HS; Milpitas, CA; (4); Chess Clb; Key Clb; Var Tennis; Var Vllybl; CSU Haywood; Geology.

YEE, PILIALOHA; Wallenberg HS; San Francisco, CA; (2); Church Yth Grp; Intnl Clb; Spanish Clb; Band; High Hon Roll; Hon Roll; Fencing; U Southern CA.

YEE, RICHARD W; Saint Ignatius College Prep; Oakland, CA; (4); 12/287; Chess Clb; Cmnty Wkr; Hosp Aide; Phtg Yrbk; Intrml Ftbl; Intrml Sftbl; JV Trk; Intrml Vllybl; Hon Roll; CSF; High Hnr Grad; UC Davis; Bio Sci.

YEE, SHEREEN P; Lowell HS; San Francisco, CA; (3); Office Aide; Science Clb; Golden ST Exam Geom Hnrs; Chemathon 90; Big Brother/Sister Orgnztn.

YEE JR, TONY S; Clovis HS; Clovis, CA; (3); Debate Tm; FBLA; Math Clb; Math Tm; NFL; Science Clb; Speech Tm; Off Soph Cls; Intrml Tennis; High Hon Roll; Cornell U; Comp Science.

YEE, VINCENT K; Salinas HS; Salinas, CA; (3); Chess Clb; Cmnty Wkr; Science Clb; Ski Clb; Spanish Clb; Teachers Aide; Trk; Wt Lftg; High Hon Roll; Hon Roll; GSE Recgntn; U Of HI; Engrng.

YEE, WINNIE; George Washington HS; San Francisco, CA; (3); Cmnty Wkr; Computer Clb; Intnl Clb; Key Clb; Math Clb; Science Clb; Service Clb; Band; High Hon Roll; Prfct Atten Awd; GATE; Gldn St Exm Geom Hnrs 89; GSE 88 1st Yr Alg W/Hnrs.

YEEND, ERICA; Henrt M Gunn HS; Los Altos, CA; (4); 50/275; Cmnty Wkr; Office Aide; Red Cross Aide; SADD; Off Frsh Cls; Pres Soph Cls; Sec Jr Cls; JV Var Pom Pon; Hon Roll; Friendship Project; U Of CO Boulder; Advertising.

YEEND, KIRSTIN E; Cornelia Connelly HS; Santa Ana, CA; (4); Latin Clb; Model UN; Science Clb; High Hon Roll; NHS; Ntl Merit Schol; Pres Acad Fit Awd; Vlntr Math Tutr; Stage Mgr Tech Crew; Bank Amer Plaq Wnnr Math & Sci; U Of Notre Dame; Math.

YEGANEH, NIOSHA N; Cornelia Connelly HS; Anaheim, CA; (2); Intnl Clb; Yrbk; Hon Roll; UCLA; Psych.

YEGGE IV, FRANK H; Damien HS; Diamond Bar, CA; (4); 33/200; Church Yth Grp; Debate Tm; German Clb; Letterman Clb; NFL; Office Aide; Ski Clb; Speech Tm; SADD; Teachers Aide; Cal Poly Pomona; Mfg Engrg.

YEGVIAN, GASSIA; Arcadia HS; Arcadia, CA; (3); Art Clb; Church Yth Grp; Drama Clb; Ski Clb; Teachers Aide; Thesps; School Play; JV Bsktbl; CSUN; Psych.

YEH, CHRISTOPHER S; Santa Monica HS; Santa Monica, CA; (4); 1/593; Dance Clb; Math Tm; Orch; Ed Lit Mag; Hon Roll; Ntl Merit SF.

YEH, DIANA; Leigh HS; San Jose, CA; (4); 1/210; Boy Scts; French Clb; Hosp Aide; VP Key Clb; Speech Tm; Yrbk; Ed Lit Mag; NHS; Pres Acad Fit Awd; Life Stu CSF; San Jose Exchng Clbs Yth Of Yr Awd; Stu Santa Clara Cnty Yth Hall Of Fame 90; UC San Diego; Pediatrician.

YEH, EMILY; Alhambra HS; San Francisco, CA; (4); French Clb; FBLA; Service Clb; High Hon Roll; Hon Roll; Teem Clb-Treas; Math & Sci Hnr Soc; Physics Clb; Berkeley U.

YEH, JAMES W; Montclair HS; Montclair, CA; (4); 25/350; Pres Sr Cls; Rep Stu Cncl; Var Bsktbl; Cit Awd; High Hon Roll; Hon Roll; Hacienda Leag Awd Of Dist; Stu Govt Ldrshp Awd; Life Membr Of CA Schlrshp Fdrtn; Mt Sac; Hstry.

YEH, JEFF C; J F Kennedy HS; Buena Park, CA; (3); Chess Clb; Church Yth Grp; Cmnty Wkr; Computer Clb; FBLA; Key Clb; Science Clb; Teachers Aide; Chorus; Sec Jr Cls; Bus.

YEH, JEFFREY C; John F Kennedy HS; La Palma, CA; (3); Chess Clb; Cmnty Wkr; Chrmn Computer Clb; FBLA; Key Clb; Teachers Aide; Chorus; Variety Show; JV Bsktbl; JV Swmmng; Most Imprvd In Swim; UCLA; Mktg.

YEH, JIMMY; San Lorenzo HS; San Leandro, CA; (2); Orch; JV Bsbl; JV Bsktbl; JV Ftbl; High Hon Roll; CSF; Civil Air Patrol; MA Inst Of Tech; Airspc Engr.

YEH, JUDY C; San Lorenzo HS; San Leandro, CA; (3); 4/255; Teachers Aide; Orch; Var Tennis; High Hon Roll; Var Badmntn Tm; Close-Up Clb; CSF; UC Berkeley; Med.

YEH, THOMAS Y; University HS; Irvine, CA; (2); German Clb; Hon Roll; Irvine City Orch; CA Inst Of Tech; Elec Engr.

YEH, TOM; George Washington HS; Hayward, CA; (3); Boy Scts; Church Yth Grp; Hosp Aide; Pres Intnl Clb; Key Clb; Pres Math Clb; Red Cross Aide; Pres Science Clb; VP Frsh Cls; Band; UCSF Sci Lssn Cntst 3rd Pl; UC Davis Exchng Pgm-Stu Crdntr; UC; Bio-Chem.

YEH, TSUNG J; William Howard Taft HS; Woodland Hills, CA; (3); Church Yth Grp; Pres Computer Clb; Chorus; Gym; L Trk; Hon Roll; Prfct Atten Awd; CSF; Table Tnns Clb VP; Biochem.

YEH, WEN-HAO; Santa Monica HS; Santa Monica, CA; (1); JV Vllybl; High Hon Roll.

YEH, WENDY H; Mtn View HS; Los Altos, CA; (3); French Clb; Yrbk; High Hon Roll; Badminton; Asian Clb.

YEH WONG, LUCRETIA J; George Washington HS; San Francisco, CA; (2); Key Clb; Math Clb; Red Cross Aide; ROTC; Science Clb; Service Clb; Speech Tm; Teachers Aide; Drill Tm; Drm Mjr(t); Badmtn Team; 7 Cert Of Achvts; CA Schlrshp Fdrtn-Executive Cncl.

YEKENIAN, MARLENE; La Qunita HS; Westminster, CA; (2); Bsktbl; Cheerldng; Swmmng; Cit Awd; Hon Roll; Prfct Atten Awd; Law.

YELIN, JENNIFER; El Camino Real HS; West Hills, CA; (2); Debate Tm; NFL; Thesps; School Play; Trk; Cit Awd; High Hon Roll; Hon Roll; Jr NHS; NHS.

YELOWITZ, JASON A; Fremont HS; Sunnyvale, CA; (4); Spanish Clb; VP Temple Yth Grp; High Hon Roll; Jr NHS; NHS; Ntl Merit SF; CSF.

YELVERTON, SYREETA; Mark Keppel HS; Monterey Park, CA; (1); Orch; Nwsp; Gym; Trk; High Hon Roll; Hon Roll; Prfct Atten Awd; Law.

YEN, ALLISON; Santa Monica HS; Santa Monica, CA; (2); Dance Clb; Intnl Clb; Orch; JV Bsktbl; Hon Roll; Asian Clb; Tnns; Drwng & Painting; Jr Statesmen Of Amer; Fshn Dsgnng; Symphny Orch In Natl Ed Cnvntn; U CA Los Angeles; Psych.

YEN, BRIAN J; Rio Mesa HS; Camarillo, CA; (3); 5/275; Drama Clb; Letterman Clb; Service Clb; Stage Crew; JV Vllybl; Cit Awd; Hon Roll; Opt Clb Awd; Ventura Cnty Chinese Amer Club Youth Group Co-Chm; HS Mock Trial Team; Peer Cnslr; UC San Diego; Biochem.

YEN, JOHN C; Fontana HS; Fontana, CA; (3); 11/1200; Computer Clb; Teachers Aide; High Hon Roll; Comp Sci.

YEN, MAY; El Camino HS; Daly City, CA; (3); Intnl Clb; Math Tm; Service Clb; Teachers Aide; Thesps; School Musical; Rptr Nwsp; Stu Cncl; Hon Roll; Multi Cultural Club Treas; CSF; UC Berkeley; Acctng.

YEN, SAMUEL J; St Ignatius College Prep; San Francisco, CA; (3); 1/244; Letterman Clb; Science Clb; Service Clb; Var Ftbl; JV Socr; Var Vllybl; Ntl Merit Ltr; Aerospc Engrng.

YEN, WENDY; Canyon Springs HS; Moreno Valley, CA; (3); Thesps; Varsity Clb; Band; Chorus; School Musical; Variety Show; Tennis; High Hon Roll; Hon Roll; Loma Linda U; Bio-Med.

YEN, YI-WYN; Whitney HS; Cerritos, CA; (3); Key Clb; Hist Band; Mrchg Band; Ed Nwsp; Score Keeper; L Var Swmmng; JV Tennis; High Hon Roll; Hon Roll; JV Water Polo; Wind Ensemble Band; Cerritos Aquatic Clb; Dist Hnr Band; Sputnik Yth Tour; Jrnlsm.

YEO, ANN M; Carson HS; Torrance, CA; (2); Band; Drill Tm; Flag Corp; Orch; Vllybl; Cit Awd; Hon Roll; Prfct Atten Awd; Lds & Sqrs; CSF; Acad Achvt Awd Eng & Span; UCLA; Fine Arts.

YEO, GILES; St Ignatius College Prep; South San Francis, CA; (4); 14/293; Church Yth Grp; Cmnty Wkr; Service Clb; School Musical; High Hon Roll; Hon Roll; CSF; UC Berkeley; Molecular Bio.

YEOMANS, ELIZABETH M; El Camino HS; Oceanside, CA; (3); 2/360; Capt Debate Tm; French Clb; NFL; Capt Speech Tm; Lit Mag; Var Tennis; High Hon Roll; CIF Tennis Qulfr; Mem All-Avocado Lg Tennis Tm; UC Santa Cruz; Lib Arts.

YEON, CHRISTINE; Riverside Polytechnic HS; Riverside, CA; (4); 4/400; Cmnty Wkr; Hosp Aide; Model UN; Quiz Bowl; Ed Nwsp; Lit Mag; Cit Awd; High Hon Roll; Hon Roll; NHS; NCTE Essay Comp Awd; UCLA; Biochem.

YEPEZ, FREDDY A; Fremont HS; Sunnyvale, CA; (1); JV Ftbl; Hon Roll; Fresno ST; Pro Ftbl.

YEPEZ, JUAN; Morningside HS; Inglewood, CA; (1); Computer Clb; Latin Clb; Math Tm; Bsbl; Bsktbl; Diving; Ftbl; Socr; Hon Roll; Prfct Atten Awd; Camino Coll; Tchr.

YEPIZ, JUANITA; Hanford HS; Lemoore, CA; (2); Art Clb; Spanish Clb; Chorus; Off Frsh Cls; Off Soph Cls; Hon Roll; Fresno ST Coll; Dermatolgy.

YEPIZ, MARIA; Hanford HS; Lemoore, CA; (1); Art Clb; Drama Clb; MESA; Bsh; CA ST U; Microorganism Bio.

YERASI, RAJESH; John A Rowland HS; Rowland Heights, CA; (3); 13/525; Hosp Aide; Science Clb; Service Clb; Spanish Clb; Stu Cncl; Var L Swmmng; High Hon Roll; VP NHS; Ntl Merit SF; Water Polo Vrsty; Safe Rides Pgm; Acad Cmptn Clb.

YERGER, KATHRYN E; Napa HS; Napa, CA; (1); School Play; Variety Show; Cit Awd; Hon Roll; Dance Cls; RENS Wnnr In Engl.

YERMAN, JORDAN M; Novato HS; Novato, CA; (2); Treas Key Clb; Var Swmmng; Water Polo.

YESAYAN, MELDIA; Glendale HS; Glendale, CA; (2); Church Yth Grp; Dance Clb; Drama Clb; Service Clb; Teachers Aide; Drill Tm; School Musical; Yth In Govt; Vlntr Day Camp Cnslr YMCA.

YEUNG, ANNA H; Mission HS; San Francisco, CA; (3); Cmnty Wkr; Sec Service Clb; Teachers Aide; Orch; Sec Frsh Cls; Rep Soph Cls; Intrml Vllybl; Hon Roll; CSF Secy; Cmmnty Girls Sftbl Team Chmpns; UCLA; Tchng.

YEUNG, CHERYL M; Wallenberg Traditional HS; San Francisco, CA; (2); Church Yth Grp; Intnl Clb; Science Clb; Varsity Clb; Band; Treas Jr Cls; Tennis; Hon Roll; CSF; Bdmntn Tm; Ped.

YEUNG, CHI KEN; Skyline HS; Oakland, CA; (2); Library Aide; Cit Awd; Hon Roll; Mech.

YEUNG, CHRISTOPHER W; San Gabriel HS; Rosemead, CA; (4); 96/737; French Clb; Key Clb; Service Clb; SADD; Pres Sr Cls; Stu Cncl; JV Vllybl; Hon Roll; CSF; A P Clb; San Diego ST U; Bus Admin.

YEUNG, ERIC C; James Logan HS; Union City, CA; (3); CA ST-HAYWARD; Electrncs.

YEUNG, GINA; Mission HS; San Francisco, CA; (2); Cmnty Wkr; Intnl Clb; ROTC; Service Clb; Drill Tm; Vllybl; Sftbl & Vlybl Chinese Rcrtn Ctr; CA ST U; Bus.

YEUNG, PETE; Misson San Jose HS; Fremont, CA; (3); 49/397; Spanish Clb; CSF; Goldn St Awd Alg; Medcl.

YEUNG, SIMON T; George Washington HS; San Francisco, CA; (2); Church Yth Grp; Hon Roll; Pres Acad Fit Awd; Gen Srvce Soc; Chinese Amer Clb; Engrng.

YEUNG, THOMAS; San Gabriel HS; San Gabriel, CA; (4); Chess Clb.

YEUNG, WINGSZE; Oakland HS; Oakland, CA; (2); Dance Clb; Girl Scts; Cit Awd; Hon Roll; UC Davis; Med.

YI, CATHY; Downey HS; Downey, CA; (3); French Clb; Key Clb; Math Clb; Science Clb.

YI, CHI U; Gahr HS; Cerritos, CA; (3); 51/462; Church Yth Grp; Spanish Clb; Sec Soph Cls; Stu Cncl; Stat Bsktbl; Stat Ftbl; Var Mgr(s); Stat Swmmng; Gov Hon Prg Awd; Irvine; Med.

YI, DAVID U; Adrian Wilcox HS; Santa Clara, CA; (2); Church Yth Grp; Red Cross Aide; ROTC; JV Capt Ftbl; Wt Lftg; Wrstlng; Hon Roll; Prfct Atten Awd; MVP Ftbl 89-90; All Leag Ftbl 89-90; Cvl Air Patrol Hnr Cadet; USC; Bus.

YI, ELIZABETH K; Glendale HS; Glendale, CA; (4); 112/695; Art Clb; French Clb; Acpl Chr; Nwsp; Hon Roll; Jr NHS; NHS; Prfct Atten Awd; Film.

YI, ERIC; Arcadia HS; El Monte, CA; (2); 95/636; Church Yth Grp; FBLA; Intnl Clb; Service Clb; JV Tennis; Cit Awd; Hon Roll; Prfct Atten Awd; UCLA; Elec Engr.

YI, EUNICE; Marina HS; Huntington Bch, CA; (4); 15/480; Church Yth Grp; JA; JCL; Rep Key Clb; Latin Clb; Office Aide; Ski Clb; SADD; Nwsp; Lit Mag; CA Schlrshp Fed; CSULB Artist Awd; Distinguished Schlr; UC Berkeley; Bus.

YI, HE-TEH; Montclair HS; Montclair, CA; (3); Am Leg Boys St; Ski Clb; Rptr Nwsp; JV Var Tennis; Hon Roll; Envrnmntl Clb; Economics.

YI, HELEN; American HS; Fremont, CA; (4); 7/353; Treas SADD; Yrbk; Off Frsh Cls; Pres Soph Cls; Off Jr Cls; Pres Stu Cncl; Capt Cheerldng; Var Pom Pon; High Hon Roll; Stu Body Electns Cmmssnr; Santa Clara U; Pre-Med.

YI, HETEH K; Montclair HS; Montclair, CA; (3); 1/400; Ski Clb; Nwsp; Var Tennis; Envrnmntl Clb; 53rd Annual CA Gldn Boys St.

YI, JOHN S; Villa Park HS; Orange, CA; (2); Key Clb; Treas Science Clb; Spanish Clb; Ed Yrbk; Ed Lit Mag; JV Capt Vllybl; High Hon Roll; NHS; Natl Sci Olympd; Head Of Pblctns Asian Clb; CA Tech; Comp Engrng.

YI, LISA H; Prospect HS; San Jose, CA; (1); Church Yth Grp; Cmnty Wkr; Spanish Clb; Church Choir; Bsktbl; Powder Puff Ftbl; Vllybl; Hon Roll; Pres Acad Fit Awd; Frgn Lang Clb; Psych.

YI, MEE K; Narbonne Math Science Magnet HS; Carson, CA; (2); Computer Clb; Drama Clb; Hosp Aide; Library Aide; Math Clb; Math Tm; NFL; SADD; Teachers Aide; School Play; PEEC; Awds Of Excllncy & Superiority Speech Comptns; CJSF; Law.

YI, RANDY W; Whitney HS; Cerritos, CA; (2); 91/168; JV Bsbl.

YI, SCOTT R; Villa Park HS; Orange, CA; (4); 53/495; Drama Clb; Key Clb; Latin Clb; SADD; School Musical; Ed Lit Mag; Treas Soph Cls; Church Yth Grp; Debate Tm; Pres Science Clb; CSF Pres; OCAD Sci Olympd; Mock Trial; UC Berkeley; Law.

YI, SUNG-JI; Sunny Hills HS; Fullerton, CA; (3); Pres Church Yth Grp; JCL; Key Clb; Latin Clb; Spanish Clb; Church Choir; Jr Var Badminton; CSF; UC San Francisco; Pharmacy.

YI, TAE S; University HS; Los Angeles, CA; (3); Church Yth Grp; FCA; Math Tm; Natl Beta Clb; Quiz Bowl; Teachers Aide; Hon Roll; Jr NHS; NHS; Prfct Atten Awd.

YI, YONG-A; James Lick HS; San Jose, CA; (2); VP Church Yth Grp; Intnl Clb; Math Tm; Sec Soph Cls; L Cheerldng; Var Tennis; High Hon Roll; Hon Roll; UC Berkeley; Bio.

YIE, YA-LING; Irvington HS; Fremont, CA; (4); 23/300; Church Yth Grp; Cmnty Wkr; Key Clb; FTA; SADD; High Hon Roll; Hon Roll; Church Choir; Acpl Chr; Teachers Aide; Yang Schlrshp; Cal ST Hayward; Liberal Stds.

YILLIK, ANNA C; Diamond Bar HS; San Dimas, CA; (1); Cmnty Wkr; Drama Clb; Key Clb; SADD; Varsity Clb; Rep Stu Cncl; Var Tennis; Stat Wrstlng; Commctns.

YIM, ANDREW W; Fountain Valley HS; Fountain Valley, CA; (2); Bus Profs of Am; Computer Clb; Math Clb; Spanish Clb; Church Choir; Tennis; Wt Lftg; Korean Club; UC-BERKELEY; Bus Admin.

YIM, HYUN S; Monterey HS; Marina, CA; (3); Church Yth Grp; FCA; School Musical; Bsktbl; Var Trk; Wt Lftg; Cit Awd; French Hon Soc; High Hon Roll; Hon Roll; Upward Bound.

YIM, JACK C; George Washington HS; San Francisco, CA; (1).

YIM, JEFFREY J; Los Altos HS; Hacienda Hts, CA; (1); Church Yth Grp; Cmnty Wkr; Band; Church Choir; Mrchg Band; Pep Band; Bsktbl; JV Vllybl; Hon Roll; Pres Acad Fit Awd.

YIM, JESSIE F; Mark Keppel HS; Monterey Park, CA; (4); 20/550; Cmnty Wkr; FBLA; Math Clb; Mu Alpha Theta; Service Clb; Band; Mrchg Band; Pep Band; Yrbk; Sec Stu Cncl; U Of CA Irvine; Social Sci.

YIM, MAN O; Lowell HS; San Francisco, CA; (2); Cmnty Wkr; Library Aide; Band; Rep Frsh Cls; Crs Cntry; Trk; 2nd Pl All City 65 Meter High Hurdles; Bio Clb; UC Berkeley.

YIM, RATT; Stagg HS; Stockton, CA; (3); Orch; Hon Roll; Prfct Atten Awd; Delta Coll; Elect.

YIMLAMAI, DEAN; Orange HS; Orange, CA; (3); Debate Tm; Capt Quiz Bowl; Bausch & Lomb Sci Awd; High Hon Roll; Jr NHS; NHS; Pres Acad Fit Awd; Sec Key Clb; Pres Math Clb; Pres Math Tm; Rennsaeler Sci Awd; Gold Mdl Acad Decthln; LA Museum Of Natrl Hstry Yng Schlrs Pg; Physics.

YIN, ALAN C; Huntington Beach HS; Huntington Bch, CA; (4); 90/460; Debate Tm; Treas French Clb; Rep Key Clb; Model UN; Red Cross Aide; Speech Tm; Var JV Trk; Intrml Wrstlng; Hon Roll; Jr Statesmen Of Am-Pres/Treas; Teen Safe Rides; Acad Decathln; U CA-SANTA Barbara; Intl Rltns.

YIN, TERESA L; Mission San Jose HS; Fremont, CA; (3); 9/420; French Clb; Math Clb; Science Clb; SADD; Ed Yrbk; High Hon Roll; Ntl Merit Ltr; REACH Amer; Peer Cnslng; Badminton; Bus Admin.

YIN, TONY; Independence HS; San Jose, CA; (3); Church Yth Grp; Cmnty Wkr; Intnl Clb; ROTC; SADD; Variety Show; Rep Stu Cncl; JV Crs Cntry; Var Trk; San Jose ST; Bus Admin.

YING, MONA; Whitney HS; Lakewood, CA; (2); 27/168; Cmnty Wkr; FBLA; VP JA; Treas Key Clb; Variety Show; Hon Roll; CA Schlrshp Fed Hstrn; CA Jr Schlrshp Fed Treas; Arch.

YIP, ANNEMARIE; Gilroy HS; Gilroy, CA; (2); 2/450; Church Yth Grp; Letterman Clb; SADD; Band; Mrchg Band; Stat Bsktbl; Score Keeper; Var Tennis; High Hon Roll; Hon Roll; Acad Stu Of Month; 1st Pl Santa Clara Co Sci Fair; Univ Of Pacific; Pharm.

YIP, CONNIE; Thomas Edison SR HS; Stockton, CA; (4); 14/350; SADD; Capt Var Tennis; Cit Awd; High Hon Roll; Hon Roll; Treas NHS; Prfct Atten Awd; CA Schlrshp Fdrtn; Keywanetts; Badminton Vrsty; Cal Poly San Luis Obispo; Engr.

YIP, HELENA T; San Leandro HS; San Leandro, CA; (2); 4/400; French Clb; Math Clb; Sec Service Clb; Speech Tm; Trk; Hon Roll; U C Berkeley; Med.

YIP, MILENE W; San Lorenzo HS; San Leandro, CA; (1); Intnl Clb; Orch; School Musical; Var Tennis; High Hon Roll; Vrsty Badmntn; Schl Dist Solo Comptn Piano Schlrshp; UC Berkeley; Chem Engrng.

YIP, SUN FAI; Schurr HS; Monterey Park, CA; (3); Cmnty Wkr; Computer Clb; Intnl Clb; Science Clb; Cit Awd; High Hon Roll; Hon Roll; Prfct Atten Awd; St Schlr; Young Schlr Pgm; UCLA; Med.

YIP, VICTOR Y; Whitney HS; Cerritos, CA; (1); 1/140; JA; Band; Mrchg Band; JV Bsbl; Cit Awd; High Hon Roll; Jr NHS; Pres Acad Fit Awd; HS Hstry Day Cont 1st Pl; Harvard.

YIU, INGRID; Abraham Lincoln HS; San Francisco, CA; (3); Science Clb; Service Clb; Acpl Chr; Yrbk; St Schlr; Life Mem CSF; U Of CA Los Angeles; Arch.

YLAGAN, NATALIE M; Pinole Valley HS; Hercules, CA; (2); Church Yth Grp; Rep Soph Cls; UCLA; Real Estate.

YNOSTROZA, MAYA; Piedmont HS; Piedmont, CA; (4); Pres Spanish Clb; VP SADD; Band; Orch; Rep Stu Cncl; Var JV Cheerldng; Pom Pon; Var Socr; Var Tennis; High Hon Roll; Chicano & Latino Yth Ldrshp; Rotry Cmp Entrprs; Rotry RYLA; CA Music Ed Assn Awds; Duke U; Law.

YOCKEL, JUSTIN R; Costa Mesa HS; Costa Mesa, CA; (4); 1/230; Boy Scts; Church Yth Grp; VP Spanish Clb; Rptr Nwsp; Pres Jr Cls; Pres Stu Cncl; Var L Bsktbl; Var L Vllybl; High Hon Roll; Val; UC San Diego; Communications.

YOGI, YUKO; Villa Park HS; Orange, CA; (2); Key Clb; Band; Mrchg Band; Pep Band; Ed Nwsp; JV Tennis; Hon Roll; NHS; Intnl Clb; CSF; Los Angeles Rep Jr Smmt Okinawa Jpn 90; Cmntns.

YOHANNES, DAGEMAWI E; Saint Monica HS; Los Angeles, CA; (3); Letterman Clb; Varsity Clb; Bsbl; Bsktbl; Ftbl; Socr; Wt Lftg; Prfct Atten Awd; Berkeley; Engrng.

YOKOI, EMI; Saddleback HS; Santa Ana, CA; (4); 47/500; FBLA; SADD; Chorus; VP Jr Cls; Var Capt Cheerldng; NHS; U Sthrn CA; Pre-Bus.

YOKOMIZO, TARA; Dublin HS; Dublin, CA; (2); 1/224; FBLA; Temple Yth Grp; Var Socr; Var Swmmng; High Hon Roll; Pres Acad Fit Awd; 2nd Pl Northern CA St Gymnstcs Meet Lvl 6; Ply Cert Merit Hnr Recital Piano; Marine Bio.

YOKOTA, DEREK; North HS; Torrance, CA; (4); 1/466; Boy Scts; FBLA; JA; Scholastic Bowl; Service Clb; Ski Clb; JV Golf; Bausch & Lomb Sci Awd; Ntl Merit Ltr; Val; UCLA.

YOKOYAMA, JEAN H; Mark Keppel HS; Monterey Park, CA; (2); Sec Church Yth Grp; Pres Girl Scts; Service Clb; Chorus; Rep Soph Cls; Sec Jr Cls; JV Capt Bsktbl; Var Trk; Hon Roll; Odori & Japanese Dancing.

YOM, JOHN; Troy HS; Placentia, CA; (2); 3/323; Sec Treas Church Yth Grp; High Hon Roll; Church Yth Grp Band; Several Outstndng Achvt Mrt Certs; Fullerton Sunrise Rotary Clubs Awd Of Excllnc.

YON, HUGO; Lowell HS; San Francisco, CA; (3); Church Yth Grp; Letterman Clb; Sec Q&S; Pres Service Clb; Band; Church Choir; Pres Stu Cncl; Gym; Var Tennis; High Hon Roll; Stu Govt-Chrmn Of Bd Cls Ofcrs; Cmnty Svc-Stu & Rep; UC Berkeley; Bus Admin.

YON, HYONOK; Tustin HS; Santa Ana, CA; (2); Cmnty Wkr; Cit Awd; Hon Roll; Korean Clb; Keywante Clb.

YONCE, STACY C; Mayfair HS; Lakewood, CA; (2); Church Yth Grp; Teachers Aide; Chorus; Var Tennis; Hon Roll; Elem Educ.

YONEDA, IKUYO; Alisal HS; Salinas, CA; (4); 7/270; Teachers Aide; Off Soph Cls; Stu Cncl; JV Trk; JV Var Vllybl; High Hon Roll; Hon Roll; Pres Acad Fit Awd; UC Santa Barbara; Tchng.

YONEDA, MARI; Lincoln HS; Stockton, CA; (3); Latin Clb; Office Aide; Yrbk; JV Cheerldng; JV Pom Pon; Hon Roll; Mbr Of Schl Clb,SAVE; Mbr Schl Clb,STAND; Special Intrst,Animal Rghts.

YONEMORI, CINDY L; Edison HS; Huntington Beach, CA; (3); JA; Teachers Aide; Band; Mrchg Band; Pep Band; Off Jr Cls; NHS; Ntl Merit Ltr; Flute, Piccolo 1st Chair, Sctn Ldr; Engrng.

YONG, ALEX P; Irvine HS; Irvine, CA; (3); 48/515; Boy Scts; Chess Clb; Church Yth Grp; Orch; Tennis; Hon Roll; Piano Cert Mrt; UCLA; Bus.

YONG, ANGELA; Edison HS; Huntington Beach, CA; (2); Hist Church Yth Grp; Model UN; JV Capt Bsktbl; Var JV Trk; Hon Roll; CSF; Piano; UCLA; Acctnt.

YONG, BILL L; Santa Cruz HS; Ben Lomond, CA; (2); JV L Bsbl; Hon Roll; Golden St Exam Math; Bsbl; UC Berkeley; Bus Admin.

YONG, DARRYL; Capital Christian Schl; Rancho Cordova, CA; (2); Chess Clb; Math Clb; High Hon Roll; CSF; Math & Typng Awds; Comp Sci.

YONG, YVETTE YEE TENG; San Luis Obispo HS; San Luis Obispo, CA; (1); Science Clb; Chorus; High Hon Roll; Engl.

YOO, AMY; Mission Viejo HS; Mission Viejo, CA; (4); 2/451; Art Clb; Treas Church Yth Grp; Key Clb; Spanish Clb; Treas Soph Cls; Var L Tennis; High Hon Roll; Hon Roll; NHS; Pres Acad Fit Awd; Soc Of Women Engrs Cert Of Mrt; Bnk Of Amer Awd Sci & Math; UCLA; Elec Engrng.

YOO, DALY D; Lowell HS; San Francisco, CA; (3); Computer Clb; Science Clb; AFS; Rptr Nwsp; JV Ftbl; High Hon Roll; Hon Roll; NHS; Congressional Yth Ldrshp Cncl; UCLA; Med.

YOO, HELEN; Rolling Hills HS; Rancho Palos Verd, CA; (3); Art Clb; Church Yth Grp; Cmnty Wkr; 4-H; Intnl Clb; Key Clb; Math Clb; Spanish Clb; SADD; Score Keeper; U Southern CA; Arch.

YOO, HENRY H; John F Kennedy HS; Granada Hills, CA; (3); Church Yth Grp; Key Clb; Yrbk; Health.

YOO, JOHN; Magnolia HS; Garden Grove, CA; (3); Am Leg Boys St; Chess Clb; Drama Clb; Teachers Aide; Intrml Crs Cntry; Intrml Trk; High Hon Roll; NHS; Opt Clb Awd; CSF VP; UC Davis; Bio.

YOO, LAWRENCE G; Alhambra HS; Alhambra, CA; (2); French Clb; Rep Soph Cls; Ftbl; Swmmng; Tri-Hi-Y Clb Chaplain; Boys Fed; HS Legislature; UCLA; Sprts Med.

YOO, RICHARD; Los Alamitos HS; Seal Beach, CA; (3); Cmnty Wkr; JA; Math Clb; Science Clb; Mgr Nwsp; Hon Roll; Ntl Merit SF; Eclgy Clb Pres; Nwsp Achiever Of Yr Awd; Stanford U; Med.

YOO, YOUNG C; Alameda HS; Alameda, CA; (3); 16/287; Church Yth Grp; Rep Stu Cncl; Intrml Bsktbl; JV Crs Cntry; JV Trk; High Hon Roll; Hon Roll; Korean Clb; Goldn ST Exm Awd; Comp Sci.

YOO, YOUNG-CHUL; Alameda HS; Alameda, CA; (3); 18/287; Church Yth Grp; FBLA; Rep Stu Cncl; Intrml Bsktbl; JV Crs Cntry; Var Trk; Intrml Vllybl; High Hon Roll; Ntl Merit Ltr; Chemathon Awd; Sci Fr Awd; Golden St Exm Awd; Comp Engrng.

YOO, YOUNG-SUK Y; Alameda HS; Alameda, CA; (4); Church Yth Grp; Science Clb; Church Choir; Socr; Hon Roll; CA Schlrshp Fdrtn; Pres Korean Clb; Capt Intramural Indr Sccr; U Of CA San Diego; Mech Engrng.

YOON, ALBERT H; Daniel Murphy HS; Los Angeles, CA; (2); 4/100; Chess Clb; Cmnty Wkr; Math Clb; Science Clb; Rptr Nwsp; Rptr Yrbk; JV Bsbl; High Hon Roll; CSF; Campus Ministry; Stanford; Med.

YOON, ANNA A; Sonora HS; Fullerton, CA; (3); Pres Art Clb; Church Yth Grp; Cmnty Wkr; Math Clb; Treas Spanish Clb; Church Choir; Var Cheerldng; Hon Roll; NHS.

YOON, DANIEL T; John F Kennedy HS; La Palma, CA; (3); Church Yth Grp; Band; Jazz Band; Mrchg Band; Orch; Pep Band; JV Capt Vllybl; Jv Vllybll Mvp; Band Mst Imprvd; Band Outstndng Jr.

YOON, HANA; Abraham Lincoln HS; San Francisco, CA; (4); 55/450; Cmnty Wkr; Hosp Aide; VP Service Clb; Pres Mgr Stu Cncl; JV Swmmng; Var Tennis; Opt Clb Awd; St Schlr; Xerox Schlrs Awd; Bank Amer Achvt Awd,Humants; Bryn Mawr Coll; Engl Tchr.

YOON, HYE JEONG; San Marcos HS; Torrance, CA; (3); 16/400; Sec VP Church Yth Grp; French Clb; Intnl Clb; JA; High Hon Roll; Prfct Atten Awd; Jr Hnrgrd; UC; Bus.

YOON, JAMES; Marina HS; Huntington Beach, CA; (2); JCL; Latin Clb; Math Clb; Math Tm; High Hon Roll; Pres Acad Fit Awd; MIT; Engrng.

YOON, KAREN G; Prospect HS; Campbell, CA; (3); FBLA; Key Clb; JV Tennis; High Hon Roll; Key Clb; Forgn Lang Exchng Clb; Long Beach ST; Med.

YOON, NANCY; Palisades HS; Los Angeles, CA; (2); Church Yth Grp; Drama Clb; Church Choir; Orch; School Musical; UCLA; Psych.

YOON, PAUL; Whitney HS; Cerritos, CA; (2); Chess Clb; FBLA; Library Aide; JV Socr; Med.

YOON, SUZIE; Mount Whitney HS; Visalia, CA; (1); Church Yth Grp; Chorus; Church Choir; Orch; Hon Roll; Lcl Music Schlrshp; U IN; Psychlgy Fshn Dsgng.

YOON, SUZIE; Trabuco Hills HS; Mission Viejo, CA; (2); 8/415; French Clb; JV Bsktbl; Var Cheerldng; High Hon Roll; NHS; SAFE; Keywanettes; Mck Trl.

YOON, UNGBIN; Gahr HS; Norwalk, CA; (3); Art Clb; Computer Clb; Intnl Clb; Math Clb; Church Choir; Hon Roll; St Schlr; CSF; Bst Geom Stu Awd; UCB; Engr.

YOON, WON S; Lowell HS; San Francisco, CA; (2); Church Yth Grp; Debate Tm; NFL; Service Clb; Speech Tm; Teachers Aide; Ed Nwsp; Rep Frsh Cls; Rep Soph Cls; JV Bsktbl; CTY Johns Hopkins U Tlnt Srch; CA St Math Exam High Hnrs Awd; Bay Area San Francisco Sci Fair 3rd Pl; Law.

YORK, AARON W; Weed HS; Weed, CA; (3); 3/45; Ski Clb; Teachers Aide; Band; Jazz Band; Mrchg Band; Sec Treas Stu Cncl; JV Var Ftbl; JV Socr; JV Var Trk; Civil Air Patrol Cadet Sgt; Gldn St Exam Alg Hnrs; Air Force Acad; Aeronaut Engrng.

YORK, HELEN; Garden Grove HS; Garden Grove, CA; (3); Office Aide; Pep Clb; Teachers Aide; Capt Cheerldng; Capt Pom Pon; Hon Roll; All Amer Grl NSA Chr Cmp 89; Mst Sprtd; Fnlst Sprt Prncs & Winterfest Qn; U Of Long Beach; Psych.

YORK, KAREN K; Bullard HS; Fresno, CA; (4); Cmnty Wkr; German Clb; Q&S; SADD; Band; Mrchg Band; School Musical; School Play; Stage Crew; Stu Cncl; Slvr Poets Awd 89; Indigo Ptry Cntst 3rd Pl 88; Strybk Shrt Stry Cntst 2nd Pl 90; Fresno City Coll; Thtr Arts.

YORK, KRISTEN R; Rincon Valley Christian HS; Santa Rosa, CA; (2); Church Yth Grp; Teachers Aide; Band; Chorus; Church Choir; Mrchg Band; Pep Band; Stat Bsktbl; JV Var Score Keeper; Var L Sftbl; Chldrns Church Ldr; Relse Time Aide; Hnrbl Mntn Lgue Sftbl; Biola U; Tchr.

YORK, MICHELLE D; Atwater HS; Atwater, CA; (2); VP Drama Clb; Pres German Clb; SADD; School Play; Stage Crew; Rep Stu Cncl; JV Tennis; JV Trk; Hon Roll; Friday Night Live Clb; German.

YOSANOVICH, DENNIS; Los Alamitos HS; Los Alamitos, CA; (4); Cmnty Wkr; Computer Clb; FBLA; Math Clb; Math Tm; Pep Clb; Science Clb; Service Clb; Spanish Clb; SADD.

YOSHIDA, JUDY; Lincoln HS; Stockton, CA; (3); Church Yth Grp; Key Clb; Mu Alpha Theta; Lit Mag; Hon Roll; CSF; STAND; Asian Clb; UCLA; Psych.

YOSHIDA, MICHELLE M; Apple Valley HS; Apple Valley, CA; (3); Drama Clb; VP Pres French Clb; Pep Clb; Varsity Clb; Stat Bsktbl; Powder Puff Ftbl; Var Trk; Var Vllybl; Hon Roll; Pres Acad Fit Awd; UC Riverside.

YOSHIDA, SHINOBU; Pacifica HS; Stanton, CA; (1); 15/300; Spanish Clb; Band; Mrchg Band; JV Tennis; Var Trk; UCI; Frnch Intrprtng.

YOSHIDA, TINA; Buena Park HS; Buena Park, CA; (4); French Clb; Intnl Clb; Key Clb; Math Clb; Band; Mrchg Band; L Crs Cntry; Var Trk; Elks Awd; High Hon Roll; Ldrshp; UCI; Psych.

YOSHIHARA, DEAN DENNIS; Huntington Beach HS; Huntington Bch, CA; (4); 77/479; Art Clb; Teachers Aide; Phtg Yrbk; JV Vllybl; Hon Roll; St Schlr; Tower Nom; U AZ; Fine Arts.

YOSHIKAWA, BRIAN A; Pioneer HS; San Jose, CA; (2); JV Bsbl; JV Capt Bsktbl; Var Ftbl; All Lg Rnng Bck JV Ftbl; Yth Bsktbl All Str; Mst Vlbl Athlt Bsktbl 89-90; San Jose ST U; Sprts Med.

YOSHIKAWA, JILL F; C K Mc Cratchy HS; Sacramento, CA; (3); 27/418; Church Yth Grp; Cmnty Wkr; Intnl Clb; Sec Key Clb; Pep Clb; Sec Treas Soph Cls; Sec Treas Jr Cls; Capt Var Bsktbl; Var JV Vllybl; Hon Roll; Asian Stu Union; Jr Prom Co-Chair; Electn Cmmtte Chrprsn; Intl Rltns.

YOSHIMOTO, JANEL; Morro Bay HS; Los Osos, CA; (2); Church Yth Grp; Latin Clb; Pep Clb; Cheerldng; Powder Puff Ftbl; High Hon Roll; Sports; Marine Bio.

YOSHIMOTO, RYAN K; Morro Bay HS; Los Osos, CA; (3); Church Yth Grp; Band; Jazz Band; Mrchg Band; Ftbl; Golf; Wt Lftg; CA Poly; Aerontcl Engr.

YOSHIMOTO, YOSHIO; Glendale HS; Glendale, CA; (4); Computer Clb; German Clb; Ski Clb; Hon Roll; Pres Schlr; Tae Kwon Do; Weight Trng; Golf; USC; Cmptr Sci.

YOSHIMURA, JEFF KENSHI; John F Kennedy HS; Sacramento, CA; (3); 70/450; Boy Scts; Debate Tm; NFL; Pres Frsh Cls; VP Soph Cls; Pres Jr Cls; Pres Stu Cncl; JV Var Bsktbl; Hon Roll; Stu Advsry Cncl VP; Conflict Mgmt; Bus.

YOSHIMURA, RYAN F; Sonora HS; La Habra, CA; (2); Church Yth Grp; Math Clb; Spanish Clb; Off Jr Cls; JV Bsktbl; Occidental; Med.

YOSHIOKA, GENE T; John F Kennedy HS; La Palma, CA; (3); Chess Clb; Office Aide; Band; Socr; Hon Roll; CSF; Kumon Edctnl Inst; UC Davis; Vet.

YOST, JENNIFER D; Downey HS; Downey, CA; (2); Church Yth Grp; Service Clb; Color Guard; Hon Roll; UC Santa Barbara; Psych.

YOU, CELESTE M; Vanden HS; Travis A F B, CA; (1); #12 In Class; JV Sftbl; High Hon Roll.

YOU, HORT; A A Stagg HS; Stockton, CA; (1); Bankteller.

YOU, VANTHUON; Bell Gardens HS; Bell Gardens, CA; (3); Dance Clb; Library Aide; Office Aide; Teachers Aide; Swmmng; Wt Lftg; French Hon Soc; Prfct Atten Awd; Ofc Occptn Cert Of Achvt; Elec Tech Cert Awd; Outstnndng Imprvmnt Folklorico Dance; Cal Poly Coll; Astronomer.

YOUHANA, RAMONA; Turlock HS; Turlock, CA; (4); AFS; Church Yth Grp; Cmnty Wkr; Debate Tm; Drama Clb; FBLA; Girl Scts; Hosp Aide; JA; Key Clb; CSF; CSUS; Math.

YOUNAN, JOSEPHINE S; St Monica Catholic HS; Los Angeles, CA; (3); VP Key Clb; Socr; High Hon Roll; Hon Roll; Literary Soc Pres.

YOUNG, ALICIA; Ernest Righetti HS; Santa Maria, CA; (1); 2/700; Pres Church Yth Grp; Church Choir; JV Socr; Cit Awd; High Hon Roll; Pres Acad Fit Awd; Sal; CSF; Goldn Warrior Awds; Hnrs Gate Pgm; Cal Poly San Luis Obispo; Engr.

YOUNG, AMY M; Cajon HS; San Bernardino, CA; (1); 1/825; Pres Church Yth Grp; English Clb; Church Choir; Ed Lit Mag; High Hon Roll; Music; Brigham Young U.

YOUNG, BARBARA A; Argonaut HS; Pioneer, CA; (2); FBLA; FHA; Sec Key Clb; Band; Mrchg Band; Ed Yrbk; Trk; Hon Roll; Jobs Dghtrs Past Hnrd Qn 89-90; Gldn St Exam Alg; Fresno ST.

YOUNG, BONNIBEL E; Apple Valley HS; Apple Valley, CA; (2); Cit Awd; High Hon Roll; Hon Roll; Theocratic Mnstry Schl; CSU; City Mgmt.

YOUNG, BRADLEY; Paramount Brethren HS; Downey, CA; (2); JV Bsbl; Cit Awd; Hon Roll; CSF; Poli Sci.

YOUNG, BRENDA; Simi Valley HS; Simi Valley, CA; (3); Church Yth Grp; French Clb; Girl Scts; Chorus; Church Choir; JV Pom Pon; Hon Roll; Jr NHS; NHS; Show Horses; Wrk W/Chldrn; Chld Psych.

YOUNG, BRENT M; Fred C Beyer HS; Modesto, CA; (1); Bsbl; Hon Roll; Sci.

YOUNG, CAROL; William Howard Taft HS; West Hills, CA; (4); Pres Art Clb; Hosp Aide; JA; Ski Clb; Ed Yrbk; Hon Roll; NHS; Ntl Merit Ltr; Pres Acad Fit Awd; Acad Decathlon Tm 89-90; UC Berkeley Alumni Schlr; UC Berkeley; Integrative Bio.

YOUNG, CHICK; Eagle Rock HS; Los Angeles, CA; (2); Art Clb; Computer Clb; Yrbk; High Hon Roll.

YOUNG, CHRISTIE; Nogales HS; West Covina, CA; (3); 27/542; Library Aide; Varsity Clb; Chorus; High Hon Roll; Hon Roll; Gldn St Exam Algebra I, Geometry Hnr Awds; Acad Ambssdrs For Excllnc; Tentative Acad Decathln Team; Math.

YOUNG, CHRISTINA L; Apple Valley HS; Apple Valley, CA; (2); 13/709; Church Yth Grp; Teachers Aide; Band; Mrchg Band; High Hon Roll; Hon Roll; UCLA; Nrsg.

YOUNG, COURTNEY R; Nogales HS; W Covina, CA; (2); Chorus; Rep Stu Cncl; Hon Roll; CSF; Badminton JV Rsrv Mst Dedicated Awd; UCLA; Med.

YOUNG, DAMON K; St Ignatius College Prep; San Francisco, CA; (3); 76/245; Cmnty Wkr; Spanish Clb; Rptr Yrbk; Intrml Bsktbl; Intrml Ftbl; JV Var Socr; Var Vllybl; Hon Roll; Big Brother Pgm; Bus Admin.

YOUNG, DANIEL C; St Margarets Episcopal Schl; Mission Viejo, CA; (2); JV Ftbl; Var Socr; Hon Roll; Cert Of Mrt Natl Frnch; Georgetown U; Pltcl Sci.

YOUNG, DEVONA J; David Starr Jordan HS; Long Beach, CA; (3); 78/594; Teachers Aide; Yrbk; ESSENCE Treas; Young Black Schlrs; Wilberforce U; Child Ther.

YOUNG, DOMINIQUE A; Wallenberg HS; San Francisco, CA; (1); Dance Clb; Variety Show; High Hon Roll; Dance Ldg Role Clara In Nutcracker W/San Francsc Bllt; Tchr Catechism; Stds Ballet Joffrey Royal Bllt; Pro Ballet Dncr.

YOUNG, DONALD L; Pasadena HS; Pasadena, CA; (2); Pres Frsh Cls; Rep Soph Cls; JV Bsktbl; JV Var Ftbl; Fri Night Live; Actvts Cmmssn; 600 Lb Club.

YOUNG, EDITH S; Hueneme HS; Oxnard, CA; (4); 29/270; GAA; Office Aide; SADD; Teachers Aide; Varsity Clb; Bsktbl; Crs Cntry; Trk; Vllybl; Cit Awd; Ventura Coll; Vet.

YOUNG, ERIC; Bishop Amat HS; Covina, CA; (3); Bsbl; JV Wrstlng; High Hon Roll; CA Schltc Fed; Silver Screen Clb; Acctng.

YOUNG, ERIC C; George Washington HS; San Francisco, CA; (1); Chess Clb; Computer Clb; Math Clb; Bsbl; Bsktbl; Ftbl; Trk; Hon Roll; UC Berkeley; Bus.

YOUNG, GINGER A; San Ramon Valley HS; Danville, CA; (2); Rep Treas Church Yth Grp; SADD; Chorus; Rptr Nwsp; JV Bsktbl; L Var Trk; Intrml Wt Lftg; Hon Roll; Pacfc Cntrl Dist Yng Relgs Unitarn Treas; Mustang Soccr Leag; Travl 5 Continents.

YOUNG, GLENDA; Oakland HS; Oakland, CA; (4); SADD; Hon Roll; GATE; San Francisco ST; Psych.

YOUNG, HARLAN; Abraham Lincoln HS; San Francisco, CA; (2); ROTC; UC; Psych.

YOUNG, HEATHER; Bishop Union HS; Bishop, CA; (4); 4-H; Cheerldng; 4-H Awd; High Hon Roll; CA ST U Sacramento; Lbrl Stud.

YOUNG, HEATHER S; Bella Vista HS; Fair Oaks, CA; (3); 1/368; AFS; VP FBLA; Math Tm; Spanish Clb; Stage Crew; Cit Awd; High Hon Roll; Hon Roll; Lion Awd; NHS; CA Schlrshp Fed; Treas Chem Club; Treas Friday Night Live; Bio Med Engrng.

YOUNG, JENNIFER I; Redlands HS; Redlands, CA; (3); 70/1300; Sec Church Yth Grp; French Clb; VP Pep Clb; SADD; Teachers Aide; Color Guard; Capt Flag Corp; Orch; Off Frsh Cls; Off Sr Cls; Sci Prjct Awds; UC Irvine; Psych.

YOUNG, JIM S; Monta Vista HS; Cupertino, CA; (4); 17/390; Math Clb; Science Clb; Treas Sec Service Clb; Stage Crew; Ed Nwsp; NHS; Ntl Merit SF; CSF Pblcty Chrmn & Treas.

YOUNG, JOEY A; Del Norte HS; Crescent City, CA; (2); VP 4-H; Band; Mrchg Band; Pep Band; School Musical; Var Cheerldng; 4-H Awd; Hon Roll; Del Notre Cnty Hstrcl Soc Vlntr; Music Educ.

YOUNG, JOHN M; Corona HS; Corona, CA; (4); 117/487; Letterman Clb; Ftbl; U MS; Mech Engrng.

YOUNG, JUDY A; Raoul Wallenberg HS; San Francisco, CA; (2); Band; Hon Roll; Peer Resource Smmr Pgm; United Yth Club Secy; Pltcl Sci.

YOUNG, JULIE A; Hoover HS; Fresno, CA; (4); 67/339; Church Yth Grp; French Clb; FHA; SADD; Teachers Aide; JV Gym; High Hon Roll; Hon Roll; Fresno City Coll.

YOUNG, JULIE A; Red Bluff HS; Gerber, CA; (3); Church Yth Grp; Dance Clb; 4-H; FFA; 4-H Awd; Hon Roll; Grand Natl Cow Palace Showing Sheep 88-89; FFA & Co Ldrshp Conf; Showing Sheep Co Fair; Bus.

YOUNG, KECIA; Hoover HS; Fresno, CA; (3); 146/895; Hosp Aide; Var Vllybl; SADD; Fresno City Coll; Psychlgy.

YOUNG, KELLEY ANNE; Amos Alonzo Stagg HS; Stockton, CA; (1); Cmnty Wkr; Library Aide; Teachers Aide; Treas Soph Cls; High Hon Roll; Pres Acad Fit Awd; CSF; Jr Brd Stcktn Fgr Sktng Clb; U S Fgr Sktng Assn.

YOUNG, KELLY A; Groosmont HS; La Mesa, CA; (3); 14/392; Hosp Aide; Intnl Clb; Key Clb; Var Capt Crs Cntry; Var Trk; High Hon Roll; Pres Acad Fit Awd; Photo Hnrs; CA Schltc Fed; Marine Bio.

YOUNG, KENNETH L; Del Campo HS; Fair Oaks, CA; (3); 90/500; Boy Scts; Church Yth Grp; ROTC; Rep Frsh Cls; JV Bsktbl; L Var Golf; L Var Socr; Hon Roll; NHS; Military.

YOUNG, KENNETH S; Templeton HS; Templeton, CA; (2); 4-H; Treas Soph Cls; JV Ftbl; Var Socr; Engr.

YOUNG, KEVIN M; California HS; San Ramon, CA; (4); 7/415; German Clb; Ski Clb; Off Soph Cls; JV Socr; JV Trk; High Hon Roll; NHS; Ntl Merit SF.

YOUNG, KIM; Whitney HS; Lakewood, CA; (2); 62/165; Mrchg Band; JV Bsktbl; CSF; MIT; Engrng.

YOUNG, KIMBERLY; Apple Valley HS; Apple Valley, CA; (1); Drama Clb; Ski Clb; Boston Coll.

YOUNG, KIMBERLY M; Coalinga HS; Coalinga, CA; (4); 5/102; SADD; Teachers Aide; Band; Mrchg Band; Swmmng; Vllybl; Elks Awd; High Hon Roll; NHS; Pres Acad Fit Awd; U Of CA Riverside; Teacher.

YOUNG, KRISTEN E; Foothill HS; Bakersfield, CA; (4); JA; SADD; Band; Chorus; Drm Mjr(t); Mrchg Band; Orch; Var Swmmng; Pres Schlr; CA Ambassadors Music Mem/Europe Tour 90; Bakersfield Coll; Psych.

YOUNG, KRISTEN H; Santa Clara HS; Oxnard, CA; (3); Cmnty Wkr; Letterman Clb; Pep Clb; Varsity Clb; JV Var Bsktbl; JV Var Trk; JV Var Vllybl; NHS; CSF; UCSD; Pre-Med.

YOUNG, KRISTINA I; Modesto HS; Modesto, CA; (3); Sec FBLA; SADD; Yrbk; Hon Roll; Physcl Thrpy.

YOUNG, LARRY N; Loyola HS; Monterey Park, CA; (2); Computer Clb; Nwsp; Hon Roll; CSF; Christian Life Comm; Geology Palentlgy Soc; CA Inst Of Tech; Elec Engr.

YOUNG, LAURIE L; Mt Whitney HS; Visalia, CA; (3); 49/322; Church Yth Grp; SADD; Hon Roll; Ntl Merit Ltr; Pres Acad Fit Awd; Law.

YOUNG, LISA A; Gilroy HS; Gilroy, CA; (4); 17/400; Church Yth Grp; Drama Clb; Band; Chorus; Church Choir; Drm Mjr(t); Mrchg Band; School Musical; School Play; Nwsp; CSF Sealbearer; Bank Of Amer Awd Fine Arts; Westmont Coll; Cmmnctns.

YOUNG, LISA C; Oakmont HS; Roseville, CA; (1); Trk; Hon Roll; Law.

YOUNG, LORA L; Galt HS; Galt, CA; (2); Boy Scts; Model UN; SADD; Hon Roll; Jr NHS; Princpls Awd; Certs Apprctn; Psych.

YOUNG, LOVETTE; Garces HS; Bakersfield, CA; (1); 3/170; Key Clb; Ed Lit Mag; Bsktbl; Vllybl; Hon Roll; Hnrs In Math, Eng & Hist; Loyola Marymount; Acctng.

YOUNG, MANDY B; Los Angeles County HS For The Arts; Pasadena, CA; (2); Church Yth Grp; Dance Clb; German Clb; Hon Roll.

YOUNG, MAQUEDA J; Esperanza HS; Anaheim, CA; (3); 162/562; GAA; Teachers Aide; Rptr Nwsp; Var Socr; Var Trk; Wt Lftg; Cit Awd; Hon Roll; Mc Donalds Black Hstry Makers Tomorrow Semi-Fnlst; Black Stu Union Treas; Public Rltns.

YOUNG, MARY-LOUISE J; Saratoga HS; Saratoga, CA; (4); 4/300; Church Yth Grp; Teachers Aide; JV Socr; Var Trk; Stat Wt Lftg; High Hon Roll; Ntl Merit Schol; Pres Acad Fit Awd; Foothill Amer Heritage Awd; Episcopalian Happening Prgm; UC Davis; Bio.

YOUNG, MICHAEL C; Shafter HS; Buttonwillow, CA; (3); 15/168; Am Leg Boys St; Church Yth Grp; Key Clb; Ski Clb; Varsity Clb; VP Stu Cncl; Var Ftbl; Var Golf; High Hon Roll; Mock Trl; CSF.

YOUNG, MICHELLE; Herbert Hoover HS; Glendale, CA; (2); French Clb; FBLA; Hon Roll; Bus.

YOUNG, MIKE H; Lowell HS; San Francisco, CA; (3); Latin Clb; Letterman Clb; Socr; High Hon Roll; Hon Roll; Ntl Merit Ltr; Pres Acad Fit Awd; Yth Educator, Drug Educ; Ivy League; Med.

YOUNG, NORVEL; Thomas Downey HS; Modesto, CA; (2); Bsbl; Bsktbl; Ftbl.

YOUNG, PAMELA A; Susan Miller Dorsey HS; Los Angeles, CA; (4); Church Yth Grp; French Clb; GAA; Letterman Clb; Office Aide; Teachers Aide; Varsity Clb; L Capt Bsktbl; L Capt Sftbl; L Capt Swmmng; Young Black Schlrs 90; Vrsty Bsktbl All Leag 2nd Tm; Schlr Athl; UNLV; Bus Admin.

YOUNG, PATRICK L; Servite HS; La Habra, CA; (3); JV Tennis; Hon Roll; NHS; CSF; Jr Statesmn America.

YOUNG, PAULA M; Oakdale HS; Waterford, CA; (2); Church Yth Grp; Dance Clb; Hon Roll; Chrch Camp Cnslr; Law.

YOUNG, REBECCA M; Valhalla HS; El Cajon, CA; (4); Dance Clb; English Clb; Girl Scts; SADD; Teachers Aide; Church Choir; School Musical; Ed Lit Mag; High Hon Roll; Tchr Prep Pgm Lcl Elem Schl; Elem Schl Tchr.

YOUNG, REBEKAH; Capital Christian Schl; Sacramento, CA; (1); Church Yth Grp; Pep Clb; Tennis; Vllybl; Hon Roll; CSF.

YOUNG, ROBERT T; Edison HS; Huntington Bch, CA; (3); Church Yth Grp; English Clb; JA; Lit Mag; JV Trk; Prfct Atten Awd; Bus.

YOUNG, ROWENA ARANGCON; Woodrow Wilson HS; San Francisco, CA; (3); Debate Tm; Drama Clb; FBLA; VP Frsh Cls; VP Soph Cls; Pres Jr Cls; Treas Stu Cncl; Trk; Vllybl; Hon Roll.

YOUNG, RYAN M; North HS; Bakersfield, CA; (1); Church Yth Grp; Ski Clb; Intrml L Ftbl; Var L Golf; JV L Socr; Hon Roll; Pres Acad Fit Awd; Star Awd Frosh-Soph Ftbl.

YOUNG, SARAH J; Clovis West HS; Clovis, CA; (3); Church Yth Grp; Debate Tm; German Clb; Lit Mag; Ntl Merit SF; Masters Coll.

YOUNG, SARAH J; Torrey Pines HS; Solana Beach, CA; (2); School Play; Variety Show; JV Crs Cntry; JV Trk; Hon Roll; CSF; Public Commnctns.

YOUNG, SAWAR C; Arcata HS; Arcata, CA; (2); German Clb; SADD; Variety Show; Pres Frsh Cls; Pres Soph Cls; Stu Cncl; Capt Var Cheerldng; Capt Var Vllybl; High Hon Roll; Church Yth Grp; Humboldt-Del Norte Interschltc Affrs; Stanford; Medcl.

YOUNG, SHARON M; Homestead HS; Santa Clara, CA; (3); Cmnty Wkr; Debate Tm; French Clb; Hosp Aide; NFL; Speech Tm; Orch; Nwsp; French Hon Soc; NHS.

YOUNG, SHAWHEEN P; Alameda HS; Alameda, CA; (1); 8/299; Church Yth Grp; JV Bsktbl; Jack In The Box Schlr Athlete; Golden St Exam-Acad Excllnc Awd; 1st Yr Alg Hnrs; U CA-BERKELEY; Engrng.

YOUNG, SOPHIA L; Washington Preparatory HS; Los Angeles, CA; (2); JV Crs Cntry; Var Trk; Cit Awd; High Hon Roll; Hon Roll; :Ucla; Htl Mgmt.

YOUNG, STACY D; Salinas HS; Salinas, CA; (3); AFS; Church Yth Grp; Cmnty Wkr; Pres Treas Key Clb; Treas Spanish Clb; Rptr Ed Nwsp; Rptr Lit Mag; Cit Awd; High Hon Roll; NHS; Vlntr Comm KHDC; Vlntr Dark Star Prod; Bus Media Profsn.

YOUNG, STEPHANIE J; Etiwanda HS; Etiwanda, CA; (2); Color Guard; High Hon Roll; Bus.

YOUNG, THERESA; Clayton Valley HS; Clayton, CA; (4); 25/444; Church Yth Grp; FBLA; Capt Bsktbl; Var Capt Vllybl; Pres Acad Fit Awd; Mock Trial; Pres/Sr Women Svc Org; CSF Sealbearer; Clayton Vly Black Women; BVAL Scholar Athl Awd; U Of La Verne; Comm.

YOUNG, TIFFANY N; Liberty Union HS; Oakley, CA; (2); Church Yth Grp; Drama Clb; Hosp Aide; SADD; Swmmng; Vllybl; Cit Awd; Hon Roll; Hearld Bus Coll; Travel.

YOUNG, TIFFINY R; Lindhurst HS; Marysville, CA; (3); Teachers Aide; Capt Flag Corp; High Hon Roll; Hon Roll; Yuba Coll Teacher Recruitment Pgm; ROP Early Childhd Ed; Yuba Coll; Elem Educ.

YOUNG, TIMOTHY H; The Bishops Schl; La Jolla, CA; (3); Church Yth Grp; Cmnty Wkr; Spanish Clb; Varsity Clb; Var Diving; JV Lcrss; JV Socr; Var Swmmng; Hon Roll; Var Water Polo.

YOUNG, TRACEY N; Silver Valley HS; Daggett, CA; (2); Church Yth Grp; Yrbk; JV Stat Bsktbl; Stat Ftbl; Var L Mgr(s); JV Var Score Keeper; JV Sftbl; Law Enfrcmnt.

YOUNG, VIVIAN; Flintridge Prep; Los Angeles, CA; (3); Nwsp; Phtg Yrbk; Var Tennis; Hon Roll; NHS; CSF Brnze Mdl; Piano; People/People Stu Ambssdr.

YOUNG, WENDY; Roseville HS; Roseville, CA; (2); Cmnty Wkr; Drama Clb; Jazz Band; VP Mrchg Band; Variety Show; Sec Treas Frsh Cls; Capt Var Cheerldng; Socr; Galena St E; Cmnty Theater; Musical Theater.

YOUNG, WING Y N; George Washington HS; San Francisco, CA; (2); Key Clb; Service Clb; Teachers Aide; Tennis; High Hon Roll; Engrng.

YOUNG FAULKNER, AMARA D; Carson HS; Los Angeles, CA; (2); Var Bsktbl; Lawyer.

YOUNGBLOOD, ANGIE L; Red Bluff Union HS; Red Bluff, CA; (1); Key Clb; SADD; Cheerldng; Cit Awd; Elks Awd; Hon Roll; Frosh Prgm; Public Rel.

YOUNGCLAUS, SHANDON; San Joaquin Memorial HS; Fresno, CA; (3); 3/200; Debate Tm; Drama Clb; NFL; Chorus; Pres Frsh Cls; High Hon Roll; NHS; Pres Acad Fit Awd; Musical Theatre Co; CA Dancing Raisin; Tech Theatre.

YOUNGER, KELLY; Bishop Amat HS; West Covina, CA; (4); 45/398; Pres Sec Drama Clb; Band; School Musical; School Play; Variety Show; Stu Cncl; High Hon Roll; Hon Roll; Loyola; Engl.

YOUNGKER, JAHROME M; Coleville HS; Spokane, WA; (3); Church Yth Grp; School Play; Var Bsbl; JV Var Bsktbl; JV Socr; Hon Roll; Acad Olympics Team; Engrng.

YOUNGKIN, MARIAH; Poway HS; Poway, CA; (3); 3/700; Church Yth Grp; Spanish Clb; SADD; Treas Jr Cls; Rep Stu Cncl; JV Bsktbl; Sftbl; High Hon Roll; NHS; Diabetes Research Pgm; Santa Clara U; Nutrition.

YOUNGREN, DEANNA M; New Life Christian Acad; Cherry Valley, CA; (4); 1/12; Church Yth Grp; Sec Chorus; Var L Cheerldng; Var L Sftbl; Var L Vllybl; NHS; Val; Pres Acad Fit Awd; High Hon Roll; Yrbk; Natl Yng Ldrs Conf-Yth Ldrshp Awd; Dstgshd Chrstn HS Stu; CIF Athlete; S CA Coll; Poly Sci.

YOUNGS, CHAD A; Sonora HS; Davis, CA; (3); 32/276; Boy Scts; Pres Church Yth Grp; Ski Clb; Teachers Aide; Band; Drm Mjr(t); High Hon Roll; Hon Roll; Prfct Atten Awd; Eagle Sct; Duty To God Awd; On My Honor Awd; BYU; Intl Rltns.

YOUNT, SAMUEL R; Fall River HS; Mc Arthur, CA; (1); Cmnty Wkr; Computer Clb; Off Frsh Cls; Ftbl; Wrstlng; Hon Roll; Just Say No Clb; Comp Prgrmr.

YOUSHAEI, NAHEED; Taft HS; Woodland Hills, CA; (2); Art Clb; Debate Tm; Pres VP Spanish Clb; Speech Tm; Rep Stu Cncl; High Hon Roll; NHS; Persion Club Pres & Founder; UCLA; Bus.

YOUSIF, MARTIN; Thomas Downey HS; Modesto, CA; (2); Bsktbl; Hon Roll; Standiford; Engrng.

YOUSO, MICHELLE; Montgomery HS; San Diego, CA; (4); Pep Clb; SADD; Teachers Aide; Yrbk; Rep Soph Cls; Rep Jr Cls; Rep Sr Cls; Stat Bsktbl; JV Var Sftbl; Most Hnrbl Mnt All Leag Sftbl; SW Cmnty JC; Zlgy.

YOUSSEF, HANI; Daniel Murphy HS; Granada Hills, CA; (4); Letterman Clb; Quiz Bowl; Var Capt Bsbl; Var Capt Ftbl; Var Socr; Hon Roll; St John Vianney Awd; All Leag Ftbl/Bsbl Teams; Homcmng & Prom Ct-Rnnr Ups; CA ST U-Northridge; Ed.

YOUSSEF, LOBNA H; Westlake HS; Thousand Oaks, CA; (2); 23/431; SADD; High Hon Roll; CA Schlrshp Fed; Stu Month; Poems Pblshd Sch Lit Magz; UCLA.

YOUTSEY, ERIC J; San Dieguito HS; Encinitas, CA; (2); Church Yth Grp; Band; Pep Band; JV Bsktbl; Hon Roll; CA Schlstc Federation Mem.

YOUTSEY, SEAN J; San Dieguito HS; Encinitas, CA; (2); Church Yth Grp; Band; Pep Band; Hon Roll; CSF; Engr.

YOW, MAY; George Washington HS; San Francisco, CA; (2); Hon Roll; CSF; Gldn St Exam Hgh Hnrs Alg; Cert Of Achvt; U Of CA; Med.

YRA, CHRIS P; Moreau HS; Union City, CA; (4); Cmnty Wkr; JV Trk; High Hon Roll; NHS; Pres Acad Fit Awd; Latin Schlrshp; CA Schltc Fed; Grad Magna Cum Laude; De Anza Coll; Engrng.

YSLAS, BRONZON D; Fairfield HS; Fairfield, CA; (1); Wrstlng; Conservation Clb; Arch Drafting.

YU, ALLEN; Sacred Heart Cathedral Prep; San Francisco, CA; (1); Hon Roll; Bowling Club; Bowling Trphy; Bus.

YU, AMY; Abraham Lincoln HS; San Francisco, CA; (2); Band; Orch; Trk; Soph Clb; FIDM.

YU, ANNA; Helix HS; La Mesa, CA; (1); Library Aide; Office Aide; Rep Stu Cncl; Cit Awd; Hon Roll; Prfct Atten Awd; Stu Cncl; Harvard; Law.

YU, ANNA YUANPING; George Washington HS; San Francisco, CA; (3); Intnl Clb; High Hon Roll; Hon Roll; Hgh Hnrs In Gldn ST Exm; George Washington HS Cert Of Achvmnt In Englsh & Math; Acctng.

YU, BEN; Bellarmine College Prep; San Jose, CA; (1); JV Tennis.

YU, BENJAMIN; Woodbridge HS; Irvine, CA; (2); Chess Clb; Hosp Aide; Service Clb; Spanish Clb; Band; High Hon Roll; Rotary Awd; Orange Cty Acad Team; CS St Sci Fair Fnlst 89; U CA Irvine Neurobio Rsrch; Phy.

YU, BRADY; Alameda HS; Alameda, CA; (3); 22/276; Art Clb; Table Tenns; UCLA; Engrng.

YU, CALVIN; Skyline HS; Oakland, CA; (2); Art Clb; Chess Clb; Computer Clb; Dance Clb; Drama Clb; English Clb; French Clb; Intnl Clb; JA; Math Clb; Table Tennis Champ; U Of CA; Elec Engr.

YU, CATHERINE K; San Marino HS; San Marino, CA; (4); 16/243; Math Clb; Q&S; Red Cross Aide; Science Clb; Service Clb; Capt Color Guard; Mrchg Band; Orch; Yrbk; Hon Roll; Winter Guard; Herbert Mc Cormick Awd; Promethean; U CA-BERKELEY; Bus Admin.

YU, CHARLES; Lowell HS; San Francisco, CA; (3); Office Aide; Science Clb; CA Schlrshp Fed; 5th Annl CA Invtnl Chemathon 4th Pl; Bio Club; Med.

YU, CHENG-EN; Woodrow Wilson HS; San Francisco, CA; (4); Vllybl; Hon Roll; Chinese Clb; San Francisco ST U; Bus.

YU, CINDY SHU QIONG; Phillip Burton Academic HS; San Francisco, CA; (2); Chess Clb; Red Cross Aide; Chorus; High Hon Roll; Rd Crss Clb Awd; Engrng.

YU, DAPHNE; George Washington HS; San Francisco, CA; (4); 1/583; Chess Clb; Pres Key Clb; Math Clb; Pres Service Clb; Acpl Chr; Rep Frsh Cls; Rep Soph Cls; Rep Jr Cls; Rep Sr Cls; Vllybl; Acad Decthln Tm Spch Brnz Mdl; Bio Technlgy Sympsm 1st Pl; Sci Educ Cont 2nd & 3rd Pl; UCLA; Bio Chem.

YU, DAVID; Sierra Vista HS; Baldwin Park, CA; (2); Hon Roll; Photo.

YU, DAVID Y; Torrey Pines HS; Del Mar, CA; (2); Chess Clb; Church Yth Grp; Hon Roll; Sci.

YU, DIANA D; San Gabriel HS; San Gabriel, CA; (3); Hon Roll; Prfct Atten Awd; Bus Ed Cert Of Achvt 90; GSE Acad Excllnc Awd Geometry Hnrs 89; 1st Yr Algebra Hgh Hnrs 88; Bus Admin.

YU, DONALD; San Gabriel HS; Alhambra, CA; (1); Debate Tm; Mrchg Band; Tennis; Hon Roll; Acad Achvt Awd; Electrncs.

YU, GEORGE; Oak Ridge HS; Cameron Park, CA; (1); Art Clb; Hon Roll; UC-BERKLEY; Med.

YU, GEORGE S; Schurr HS; Monterey Pk, CA; (4); Key Clb; Off Sr Cls; Var Wrstlng; Hon Roll; CSF; Cal ST Long Beach; Bus.

YU, GERALDINE F; St Anthony HS; Long Beach, CA; (2); Teachers Aide; Hon Roll; NHS; CA Schlrshp Fed.

YU, JEANNIE C; Lowell HS; San Francisco, CA; (2); Orch; CA Golden St Exam High Hon 1st Yr Algebra 89; CA Invtnl Chemathon 1st Pl Wnnr 90.

YU, JERRY; Thousand Oaks HS; Thousand Oaks, CA; (3); Church Yth Grp; Math Tm; Var Tennis; Hon Roll; Tm Marmonte Leag Chmpns; 1st Tm Marmonte Leag Sngls; Bus.

YU, JERRY; Whitney HS; Cerritos, CA; (1); Computer Clb; FBLA; Model UN; Bsktbl; High Hon Roll; Astronomy Clb Spcl Events Dir.

YU, JERRY J; Leland HS; San Jose, CA; (4); 1/393; Cmnty Wkr; Debate Tm; Math Clb; NFL; Spanish Clb; Speech Tm; Teachers Aide; Chorus; Orch; Stage Crew.

YU, JUDY N; Lowell HS; San Francisco, CA; (3); Orch; CA Schlrshp Fdrtn; Rgstry Rep; Red Cross Clb; Cmnty Studies & Svcs Stu & Vlntr; Soc Sci.

YU, KAREN W; San Diego HS; San Diego, CA; (4); Cmnty Wkr; Intnl Clb; Sec Key Clb; L Var Socr; Jr NHS; NHS; Pres Acad Fit Awd; Grad With Acad Distinction; Deans List 87-88; San Diego ST U; Marketing.

YU, KATHY; Notre Dame Acad; Manhattan Bch, CA; (4); 3/100; Debate Tm; French Clb; NFL; Sec Speech Tm; Ed Lit Mag; Cheerldng; Hon Roll; NHS; Pres Acad Fit Awd; HOPE Sec; U Of Notre Dame; Pre-Professnl.

YU, KELLY; Mission HS; San Francisco, CA; (3); Orch; English Award; Junior Class Club; Coll; Business/Design.

YU, LARRY T; Saratoga HS; Saratoga, CA; (3); Intnl Clb; Spanish Clb; Intrml Var Trk; High Hon Roll; CSF; Comp Sci.

YU, LAURA; A Lincoln HS; San Francisco, CA; (3); Special Interest In Design; Drawing; Table Tennis; Coll; Design.

YU, LAURENCE W; Gunn HS; Los Altos, CA; (4); Drama Clb; Pres Latin Clb; Variety Show; Fenced Jr Olympcs; U CO Boulder; Advrtsng.

YU, MICHAEL; Abraham Lincoln HS; San Francisco, CA; (2); Hon Roll; CSF; Merit Awd; UCSF; Engrng.

YU, MICHAEL C; Carlmont HS; Belmont, CA; (3); Fnlst San Mateo Cnty Spllng Bee; Alg II Math Awd.

YU, NAM; Edison HS; Huntington Bch, CA; (2); Church Yth Grp; Key Clb; Math Tm; Model UN; Intrml Bsktbl; Intrml Tennis; High Hon Roll; Orange Co Acad Decathlon.

YU, NANCY; George Washington HS; San Francisco, CA; (3); Dance Clb; Red Cross Aide; Science Clb; Teachers Aide; Vllybl; High Hon Roll; Hon Roll; CSF; Chinese-Amer Club; Dance Perf In Schl; UC Berkeley; Bus.

YU, PATRICK; Westmoor HS; Daly City, CA; (1); Hon Roll; Prfct Atten Awd.

YU, PAULINE; George Washington HS; San Francisco, CA; (2); Pep Clb; School Musical; Rep Frsh Cls; L Cheerldng; Mgr(s); Hon Roll; Chinese Amer Club; Liberal Arts.

YU, QIANG; Fremont HS; Oakland, CA; (1); Rptr Nwsp; Ed Yrbk; Hon Roll.

YU, REBECCA; Sierra Vista HS; Seal Beach, CA; (4); 21/295; Dance Clb; Science Clb; Spanish Clb; Teachers Aide; Lit Mag; Stu Cncl; Swmmng; High Hon Roll; Hon Roll; Prfct Atten Awd; 1st Pl Natl Bilingual Creative Essay Cont; Natl Assembly Awd; Bnk Amer Recgntn Awd; Badminton Tm; U CA Berkeley; Bus.

YU, RENO; San Marino HS; Pasadena, CA; (3); Church Yth Grp; FBLA; Stat Bsktbl; United Nations Assn; Law.

YU, ROSALYN Q; Oakland Technical HS; Richmond, CA; (4); 2/363; Intnl Clb; Math Clb; Math Tm; High Hon Roll; Hon Roll; Sal; VP Chinese Stu Union; Prfct Score GSE Geom 88; 3rd Pl-Spcl Awd San Francisco Sci Fair; UC Berkeley; Cvl Engrng.

YU, SHELDON S; Torrance HS; Torrance, CA; (1); Trk; Hon Roll; Awd Hnrs By Golden ST Exam In Alg I.

YU, SIMON; Mills HS; Burlingame, CA; (3); Var JV Letterman Clb; Var Swmmng; Var Wt Lftg; Judo, Jujitsu Top Cls Martial Arts; Water Polo Coaches Awd; Dntl.

YU, SUSANNA W; Venice Magnet HS; Los Angeles, CA; (3); Treas Church Yth Grp; Computer Clb; Debate Tm; Intnl Clb; Hist Science Clb; Service Clb; Church Choir; Stu Cncl; Ntl Merit Ltr; Bible Drill Wnnr, Assn & Rgnl; Ladies Hnr Soc; Intl Bus.

YU, TOM H; Oakland HS; Oakland, CA; (4); German Clb; VP JA; VP Math Clb; Math Tm; Treas Science Clb; Bausch & Lomb Sci Awd; High Hon Roll; Kiwanis Awd; Pres Acad Fit Awd; Golden St Exam Awd; UCLA; Materials Engr.

YU, VICTOR; Alameda HS; Alameda, CA; (4); 30/325; Art Clb; Chess Clb; Science Clb; Table Tennis; UCLA; Pre Med.

YU-POSHAN, ANNE; James Lick HS; San Jose, CA; (4); 8/250; Art Clb; Cmnty Wkr; Computer Clb; Dance Clb; Intnl Clb; Math Tm; Service Clb; Church Choir; High Hon Roll; Bus.

YUDISTIRA, LEONARD; Milpitas HS; Milpitas, CA; (2); Hon Roll; Berkeley; Engr.

YUE, FEE L; Lowell HS; San Francisco, CA; (2); Cmnty Wkr; Teachers Aide; Phtg Ed Yrbk; JV Crs Cntry; JV Trk; Pres Acad Fit Awd; Golden ST Hgh Hnr Alg & Geom Awds; Berkeley; Bus Mgmt.

YUE, IRENE C; San Gabriel HS; San Gabriel, CA; (3); French Clb; Library Aide; Math Clb; Red Cross Aide; Science Clb; Service Clb; High Hon Roll; U Of CA Los Angeles; Med.

YUE, LUCY S; Fountain Valley HS; Fountain Valley, CA; (2); Church Yth Grp; Red Cross Aide; Science Clb; Spanish Clb; Chorus; Amer Chem Soc; Peer Asst Ldrshp; CSF; Public Library & Veteran Hospital Vlntr; U CA; Child Psych.

YUEN, CHRISTINE; Westminster HS; Huntington Beach, CA; (2); Teachers Aide; Cit Awd; Hon Roll; Outstndng Stu Cert; Badminton Team; CSF; Court Reporter.

YUEN, DANIEL; Marina HS; Huntington Bch, CA; (3); Key Clb; Math Clb; Math Tm; Var L Tennis; High Hon Roll; Math/Sci Stu Yr; Math Golden Shld Clsrm Excllnce; Chem Stu Yr; Mck Trl.

YUEN, GARY K; Lowell HS; San Francisco, CA; (3); JV Crs Cntry; JV Trk; Wt Lftg; Var Wrstlng; 1st Place AAA Cross Cntry 87-88; 3rd AAA Varsity Wrstlng 89-90; Most Promising Wrstlng Best 1st Year; Architectural Engineering.

YUEN, JENNIFER; Aragon HS; San Mateo, CA; (4); 35/312; Cmnty Wkr; JA; Teachers Aide; Yrbk; Tennis; Trk; High Hon Roll; Pres Acad Fit Awd; CSF; Asian Amer Club Treas; U Of CA Davis.

YUEN, LESLEY L; Vanden HS; Vacaville, CA; (3); 13/150; Art Clb; Church Yth Grp; Treas French Clb; SADD; Teachers Aide; JV Var Vllybl; DAR Awd; High Hon Roll; Jr NHS; NHS; 1st Pl Lit Mag; Davis Engrng Smmr Rsdncy Pgm; Elec Engrng.

YUEN, MARIA; Phillip & Sala Burton HS; San Francisco, CA; (2); Drama Clb; Color Guard; Orch; High Hon Roll; Jack Sen Benevolent Assn Schlrshp Awd; UC Berkeley; Law.

YUEN, PATRICIA; Lowell HS; San Francisco, CA; (3); GAA; Q&S; Service Clb; Sftbl; Sftbl All City Hnrb Mntn; Schl Bwlng Leag Hgh Avg; Quill & Scroll Soc; Prjct Star Volntr; U Of CA Los Angeles; Med.

YUEN, SPENCER; Bishop Amat Memorial HS; Rowland Hts, CA; (3); Math Clb; Hon Roll; NHS; Fontasci Clb; CSF; Slvr Scrn Clb.

YUEN, STAN; Lowell HS; San Francisco, CA; (3); Boy Scts; Rep Latin Clb; ROTC; Rep, VP Brdge Clb.

YUH, GRACE E; Pacific Union College Prep Schl; Angwin, CA; (2); Church Yth Grp; Band; Church Choir; Musicisti-String Quartet; Woodwind Quintet; Pacific Union Coll.

YUH, JENNIFER I; Lakewood HS; Lakewood, CA; (4); 1/750; Am Leg Aux Girls St; Pres Art Clb; Cmnty Wkr; English Clb; VP FTA; Pres Intnl Clb; Treas SADD; Ed Yrbk; Ntl Merit SF; Sci & Math Rnsslr Mdln; Hrvrd Bk Awd; Outstndng Achvt Awd; UCLA; Vsl Arts.

YUH, JIA-ANN; Western HS; Anaheim, CA; (3); Spanish Clb; Teachers Aide; Lit Mag; Stat Trk; Hon Roll; CSF; Girls League; SOS; U CA Irvine; Bio Sci.

YUHAN, HEENA K; Laguna Hills HS; Laguna Hills, CA; (3); 4/326; Rep Church Yth Grp; French Clb; Hosp Aide; Key Clb; Math Clb; Model UN; Orch; Vllybl; High Hon Roll; Pres Acad Fit Awd; Hstry Day 2nd Rgnls, 1st Cnty & Schlrshp In St; Acadmc Dcthln Team; UPHSS U Of CA Irvine; Med.

YUHAS, RICHARD J; Sunset HS; San Larenzo, CA; (3); High Hon Roll; Hon Roll; Carpentry.

YUK, MICHAEL M; Lowell HS; San Francisco, CA; (2); Bsktbl; UC Berkeley; Cmptr Sci.

YULIP, ANNIE LIZA I; Colton HS; Colton, CA; (3); Girl Scts; JA; ROTC; Teachers Aide; Band; Church Choir; Sec Nwsp; Sec Frsh Cls; Sec Soph Cls; Sec Jr Cls; Nrsng.

YUN, DAVID C; Hogan SR HS; Vallejo, CA; (3); Chess Clb; Computer Clb; Spanish Clb; Band; Mrchg Band; Rptr Nwsp; Rep Jr Cls; High Hon Roll; Uc Berkeley; Bus.

YUN, HEA-SOON; Gardena HS; Gardena, CA; (2); Church Yth Grp; FCA; Intnl Clb; Spanish Clb; Church Choir; Sftbl; Vllybl; Cit Awd; UCLA; Nrsng.

YUN, HO; Glen A Wilson HS; Hacienda Heights, CA; (1); VP Church Yth Grp; Band; Mrchg Band; Harvey Mudd; Comp Sci.

YUN, HYON UK; William H Taft HS; Woodland Hills, CA; (2); Gov Hon Prg Awd; High Hon Roll; CA Schlstc Fed.

YUN, OK K; Saddleback HS; Santa Ana, CA; (1); 1/900; Church Yth Grp; French Clb; Church Choir; Prfct Atten Awd; UCI Partners; Tae Kwon Do Black Belt; Stanford; Pediatrics.

YUN, SUNG H; Kennedy HS; Granada Hills, CA; (3); Church Yth Grp; Key Clb; Office Aide; Teachers Aide; Church Choir; Bsktbl; High Hon Roll; Hon Roll; Med.

YUN, SUNNY; Whitney HS; Cerritos, CA; (4); FBLA; Hosp Aide; Key Clb; Church Choir; Phtg Nwsp; Phtg Yrbk; Ed Lit Mag; JV Swmmng; High Hon Roll; UCLA; Econ.

YUNG, DEREK N; Cupertino HS; Cupertino, CA; (3); 1/300; Church Yth Grp; Ed Yrbk; VP Frsh Cls; Pres Soph Cls; VP Stu Cncl; Capt Socr; Var Trk; RYLA; HOBY; CASC; Stanford U; Bus.

YUNG, DOMINIC; James Logan HS; Brentwood, CA; (4); 1/651; Cmnty Wkr; Computer Clb; French Clb; FBLA; German Clb; Treas Math Clb; Science Clb; Ski Clb; High Hon Roll; NHS; Badmington Var Capt; Asian Clb; Advance Plcmnt Club; U CA-LOS Angeles; Intl Bus.

YUNG, GRACE; University HS; Irvine, CA; (2); 48/508; French Clb; Latin Clb; JV Bsktbl; Hon Roll.

YUNG, TIFFANY Y; Alhambra HS; Alhambra, CA; (3); Church Yth Grp; Teachers Aide; Church Choir; JV Vllybl; Lavlea Soc YMCA Afflt Clb; Vllbl League For Church; CSF Frshmn Yr; Med Pediatrician.

YUNKA, STEFANY J; Dos Pueblos HS; Goleta, CA; (1); Church Yth Grp; JA; SADD; Acpl Chr; Band; Chorus; Church Choir; Mrchg Band; Pep Band; Stu Cncl; Outstnd Vocalist 89; Timothy Awd, 6 Yrs Chrstn Clb AWANA; Wnnr 3 Spllng Cont, Greendale Spllng Fnlst; Biola U; Engl.

YUNKER, JENNIFER; Tokay HS; Stockton, CA; (4); 54/480; FHA; Office Aide; Spanish Clb; Drill Tm; Variety Show; Socr; High Hon Roll; Hon Roll; Pres Acad Fit Awd; Fresno St.

YUO, MEAGO; Kennedy HS; Buena Park, CA; (2); JV Bsktbl; Var Trk; Coach Awd Trk 90; MIP Bsktbl 88-89; X-Cntry; Mdcn.

YUTANCO, BEVERLY A; Nogales HS; La Puente, CA; (4); Dance Clb; Intnl Clb; Office Aide; Science Clb; Teachers Aide; Chorus; Cit Awd; High Hon Roll; Hon Roll; Prfct Atten Awd; CA ST U Long Beach; Nrsng.

YUTANCO, JOSEPH A; Bishop Amat HS; La Puente, CA; (2); French Clb; Var Trk; JV Wrstlng; Brain Surgeon.

YUTUC, ROSEMARIE L; Mercy HS; Daly City, CA; (4); 25/104; Speech Tm; Chorus; Co-Ed Yrbk; High Hon Roll; Hon Roll; NHS; Bank Of Amer Achvt Awd Bus; Excllnce Calligraphy; 1st Pl Orgnl Oratory Speech Meet; San Francisco ST U; Nrsng.

YZAGUIRRE, RICHARD A; Arroyo Grande HS; Oceano, CA; (3); Church Yth Grp; FCA; Teachers Aide; Bsbl; Ftbl; Trk; Wt Lftg; Wrstlng; Most Val Wrestler; PE.

ZABALA, JENNIFER; College Park HS; Pacheco, CA; (3); Hosp Aide; Spanish Clb; Teachers Aide; Church Choir; Vllybl; Hon Roll; Clb Vllybl; San Francisco ST U; Arch.

ZABALA, LORI M; Whitney HS; Cerritos, CA; (3); Sec VP Church Yth Grp; Jr NHS; Red Cross Aide; Rep Soph Cls; Var Sftbl; High Hon Roll; Opt Clb Awd; Pilipino Clb Dance Troupe & Secy; Peer Cnslr; Church Orgnst; Med.

ZABATTA, ANNAMARIA A; Providence HS; Glendale, CA; (2); Santa Barbara; Law Enfrncmnt.

ZABAYLE, DENISE N; Sacred Heart Of Mary HS; Montebello, CA; (3); Computer Clb; French Clb; Stage Crew; VP Soph Cls; NHS; Hnrs CA Schlrshp Fed, Cum Laude Soc, Mother Butler Soc; Chrstn Action Clb; Hostess Clb; U Of CA Los Angenes; Med.

ZABEL, JEFFREY; Brethren HS; Lakewood, CA; (2); Church Yth Grp; FCA; Acpl Chr; Church Choir; Off Frsh Cls; JV Bsbl; JV Ftbl; Wt Lftg; Hon Roll; Aviation.

ZABEN, JOSEPH SHAE; West HS; Bakersfield, CA; (1); Church Yth Grp; JV Socr; JV Trk; Hon Roll; USC; Fincl Mgr.

ZACARIAS, JEANNE SARA; Chatsworth HS; Northridge, CA; (2); Drama Clb; Thesps; Stage Crew; VP Stu Cncl; Cheerldng; Hon Roll; Nobel Hnr Orgnztn VP; Steering Cmmtte; CSF; Yale; Law.

ZACARIAS, RAMON; Watsonville HS; Watsonville, CA; (2); JV Crs Cntry; JV Trk; Var Wrstlng; Hon Roll; Prfct Atten Awd; UCSC.

ZACKULA, JOHN L; Rio Hondo Prep; Duarte, CA; (2); Aud/Vis; Church Yth Grp; Drama Clb; FCA; Band; Chorus; Mrchg Band; Pep Band; School Musical; School Play; PCC; Elec Engr.

ZACKULA, TRACY M; Rio Hondo Prep; Duarte, CA; (1); Church Yth Grp; FCA; Acpl Chr; Band; Chorus; Pep Band; School Musical; School Play; Bsktbl; Cheerldng; Assistant Coach To Girls 6-8 In Softball Volleyball Basketball & Drill Team; PCC; Math.

ZADOURIAN, ZHANNA; Fowler HS; Fowler, CA; (3); 1/90; Church Yth Grp; Cmnty Wkr; Math Tm; Sec SADD; L Band; Chorus; Church Choir; School Play; Stage Crew; Rptr Nwsp; Fwlr Fall Fstvl Qun 89-90; Piano Yng Mscns Concerto Cmptn-1st Pl; Cngrssnl Schlr & Natl Yng Ldrs 90; Law.

ZAENGLE, CARRIE L; Lassen HS; Susanville, CA; (3); Church Yth Grp; Cmnty Wkr; Drama Clb; Girl Scts; School Musical; School Play; Variety Show; Yrbk; Stu Cncl; Bsktbl; Int Dcrtng.

ZAFRA, BERNADETTE E; Rowland HS; Rowland Heights, CA; (2); Acpl Chr; Chorus; School Musical; Bsktbl; Score Keeper; Vllybl; ROP; Animation; Teachers Aid; Engl.

ZAGHA, AARON M; El Camino Real HS; Woodland Hills, CA; (2); Ski Clb; Teachers Aide; Capt Bsktbl; JV Vllybl; High Hon Roll; Hon Roll; Pres Acad Fit Awd; JR Statsmn Of Amer; Steering Commty; Schlr Athlt Awd; PA U; Bus.

ZAGHI, TANYA; Henry M Gunn HS; Los Altos, CA; (1); Debate Tm; Key Clb; SADD; Temple Yth Grp; JV Cheerldng; Intrct Clb Scrtry; Atty.

ZAHAROPOULOS, KIKI; Cajon HS; San Bernardino, CA; (2); Letterman Clb; Var Socr; High Hon Roll; Hon Roll; Vtrnry Med.

ZAHEED, MURSHED; La Sierra HS; Riverside, CA; (3); 1/420; Letterman Clb; Math Clb; Spanish Clb; Var Capt Crs Cntry; JV Tennis; High Hon Roll; Prfct Atten Awd; CA Schlrshp Fed; All Acad Crss Cntry Tm; Mst Imprvd Coaches Awd; UCLA; Pre-Med.

ZAHORCHAK, JENNIFER; Fountain Valley HS; Fountain Valley, CA; (2); Church Yth Grp; School Musical; Crs Cntry; Trk.

ZAHRADNICEK, JIRINA; Sonoma Valley HS; Sonoma, CA; (3); 35/278; French Clb; Model UN; Crs Cntry; Hon Roll; Vlntr Tn Sfrd; Intl Bus.

ZAIDES, ILYA; University HS; Irvine, CA; (3); 53/557; Cmnty Wkr; JCL; JV Trk; Var Wrstlng; High Hon Roll; Pres Acad Fit Awd; Brown U; Intl Rltns.

ZAIDI, SHAHAB; Etiwanda HS; Alta Loma, CA; (2).

ZAIDI, SHAHID; El Dorado HS; Placentia, CA; (4); 1/344; Intnl Clb; Pres Math Tm; ROTC; Var JV Bsktbl; High Hon Roll; NHS; Pres Acad Fit Awd; Val; CSF Pres; Golden Hawk Awd; Bank Of Amer Awd; Stanford U; Pre-Med.

ZAIDMAN, YASMINA J; Santa Cruz HS; Santa Cruz, CA; (3); Drama Clb; JA; Thesps; Chorus; School Musical; School Play; Stage Crew; Lit Mag; High Hon Roll; Hon Roll; Theatre Arts.

ZAIED, ZOHAR A O; Willits HS; Willits, CA; (3); Teachers Aide; Socr; Trk; Hon Roll; Pr Cnslng Spec Awd; Music.

ZAKAR, CANDICE; Moorpark HS; Moorpark, CA; (4); 38/180; Office Aide; Teachers Aide; Chorus; Color Guard; Drill Tm; Hon Roll; UCLA; Bus.

ZAKARIA, JOSEPH; Hawthorne HS; Lawndale, CA; (3); Ftbl; Trk; Wt Lftg; Cit Awd; Pilot.

ZAKRZEWSKI, EVA M C; Mater Dei HS; Mission Viejo, CA; (4); 1/524; Ski Clb; Rep Spanish Clb; Rep Sr Cls; Stu Cncl; Capt Swmmng; High Hon Roll; Hon Roll; NHS; Pres Acad Fit Awd; All-Amer Swmmng; Jr Natl Qulfr Swmmng; Rough Water Swmmng Champ; Yale; Bio.

ZALDIVAR, DAISY; Leuzinger HS; Hawthorne, CA; (3); Church Yth Grp; Treas Spanish Clb; Church Choir; Ed Nwsp; Hon Roll; APPI Recog Awds; Pres Yth Grp; Hnr, AP Classes; Ed.

ZALDIVAR, VERONICA L; Hawthorne HS; Lennox, CA; (2); Dance Clb; Spanish Clb; Law.

ZALETEL, MARY C; Dos Pueblos HS; Goleta, CA; (3); GAA; Bsktbl; Vllybl; Hon Roll; NHS; Bus.

ZAMARO, STEPHANIE R; Mater Dei HS; Garden Grove, CA; (4); 220/524; Sec Hosp Aide; Red Cross Aide; SADD; Stat Score Keeper; High Hon Roll; Hon Roll; NHS; CSF; Ldrshp In Ed & Dev Minorities Schlrshp; Photo Club; U San Diego; Bus.

ZAMBETTI, DEBRA; Santa Clara HS; Los Gatos, CA; (4); Church Yth Grp; French Clb; VP Science Clb; VP Sec Service Clb; Teachers Aide; Church Choir; Rep Frsh Cls; Rep Soph Cls; Pres Sr Cls; JV Vllybl; Rudy Gatti Ctznshp/Svc/Excllnc Awd; Mary Ellen George Svc Awd-Continuing Ed; Amnesty Intl; U Of CA Davis; Intl Relations.

ZAMBRANO, GILDA; Workman HS; Valinda, CA; (2); Church Yth Grp; Chorus; School Musical; Swing Chorus; Variety Show; Cit Awd; Hon Roll; Mst Dedctd Choir Plaque Awd; Cal ST Fullerton; Bus Adm.

ZAMBRANO, LAURA V; Pioneer HS; Whittier, CA; (2); Hon Roll; Rio Hondo Coll; Acctng.

ZAMBRANO, MARIA R; Roosevelt HS; Los Angeles, CA; (2); Church Yth Grp; Office Aide; Drill Tm; Off Frsh Cls; Cit Awd; Hon Roll; Prfct Atten Awd; USSB; Comp Prgmr.

ZAMBRANO, RAY E; Chaffey HS; Ontario, CA; (3); Var Bsbl; Var Ftbl; Hon Roll; Econ.

ZAMBRANO-RUNCIMAN, SUSY; Midland HS; Ojai, CA; (4); 2/16; School Play; Pres Sr Cls; VP Stu Cncl; Var Socr; Var Sftbl; JV Vllybl; Cit Awd; High Hon Roll; Hon Roll; Ldrshp Awd; Mills Coll.

ZAMORA, BENJAMIN A; Golden West HS; Visalia, CA; (2); Math Clb; Math Tm; Science Clb; Orch; Off Soph Cls; Tennis; High Hon Roll; Prfct Atten Awd; Pres Acad Fit Awd; Congrssnl Schlr-Natl Young Ldrs Conf; Stanford U; Comp Sci.

ZAMORA, ELIZABETH; Notre Dame Acad; Culver City, CA; (3); Church Yth Grp; LAUSD; Aids Project; DOVES Pgm; Middlebury Coll; Intl Bus.

ZAMORA, HAROLD; Huntington Beach HS; Huntington Beach, CA; (3); FCA; Library Aide; Teachers Aide; Vrsty Bsbl; Archit.

ZAMORA, JULIEN R; Don Bosco Technical Inst; Alhambra, CA; (2); 8/250; Aud/Vis; Boy Scts; Cmnty Wkr; Computer Clb; Drama Clb; Science Clb; Spanish Clb; Orch; School Play; Stage Crew; Yale U; Matl Sci Engrng.

ZAMORA, MARGARITA M; Bell Gardens HS; Bell Gardens, CA; (3); French Clb; Orch; Swmmng; Hon Roll; UC Berkley; Med.

ZAMORA, MARK A; Merced HS North; Merced, CA; (2); Church Yth Grp; JV Bsktbl; Cit Awd; High Hon Roll; Hon Roll; UCLA.

ZAMORA, PATRICIA; Pius X HS; South Gate, CA; (4); 40/182; Aud/Vis; Pres Math Clb; Mu Alpha Theta; Office Aide; Stage Crew; Powder Puff Ftbl; Hon Roll; JR Bowling League Coach; Chem.

ZAMORA, RUBY; Sweetwater HS; National City, CA; (2); 6/589; Scholastic Bowl; Spanish Clb; Teachers Aide; Cit Awd; Hon Roll; Prfct Atten Awd; Pres Acad Fit Awd; UCSD; Med.

ZAMORA, VALERIE; Mark Keppel HS; Rosemead, CA; (1); Drama Clb; Latin Clb; School Play; Cit Awd; Hon Roll; Comp.

ZAMORA, VALGALAHAD R; Milpitas HS; Milpitas, CA; (2); 150/536; Church Yth Grp; JV Ftbl; JV Trk; Wt Lftg; Hon Roll; Outrggr Canoe Pddlng; AF Acad; Fghtr Pilot.

ZAMORA, VERONICA; Pius X HS; Downey, CA; (4); 9/180; GAA; Sec Spanish Clb; Co-Capt Socr; Hon Roll; NHS; Bio-Med Club; Magna Cum Laude Plaq; Travel Club Treas; CSF; UCI; Law.

ZAMPA, JULIE M; Schl Of Creative & Performing Arts; San Diego, CA; (2); 1/187; French Clb; SADD; Chorus; School Musical; Variety Show; High Hon Roll; Jr NHS; Amer Sign Lang; CA St Smmr Schlr For Arts Smmr 88 & 89.

ZAMUDIO, DORA MARIE; San Jacinto HS; San Jacinto, CA; (2); Church Yth Grp; Spanish Clb; Inter Dcrtr.

ZAMUDIO, ELISA T; Bullard HS; Fresno, CA; (1); Law.

ZAMUDIO, FRANCES; Castle Park HS; Chula Vista, CA; (3); Dance Clb; ASB Cabinet-Tribune Of Svc; Outstndng Svc Trojan Knights; Paralegal Sec.

ZANDER, TODD; Los Gatos HS; Los Gatos, CA; (2); Debate Tm; Key Clb; Ski Clb; Speech Tm; Teachers Aide; Temple Yth Grp; Tennis; Hon Roll; Pepperdine U; Finance.

ZANDER, VIRGINIA; Southbay Christian Schl; Los Altos, CA; (1); Church Yth Grp; Cmnty Wkr; Girl Scts; Church Choir; Vllybl; High Hon Roll; Hon Roll; Swmmng, Sailing, Gymnastics, Sccr, Comp, Camping, Volunteering.

ZANDONATTI, KAISSA; Ventura HS; Ventura, CA; (2); 42/500; Sec Church Yth Grp; GAA; Girl Scts; SADD; Variety Show; Mgr(s); Score Keeper; JV Socr; JV Sftbl; Cit Awd; Acctnt.

ZANG, JIHONG; University HS; Irvine, CA; (3); 9/558; Math Clb; Math Tm; Science Clb; French Hon Soc; High Hon Roll; Hon Roll; Sci Fair-Outstndng Proj Awd-Dist; CSF.

ZANGARI, BERTA; Poway HS; Poway, CA; (4); Drama Clb; Thesps; Color Guard; Flag Corp; School Musical; School Play; Stage Crew; JV Crs Cntry; JV Trk; Amnesty Intl; Stu Non Violent Soc; ACLU Cnota; San Diego ST; Sociology.

ZANGARI, CHRIS B; Clairemont HS; San Diego, CA; (3); 15/212; Tennis; Var Trk; UCSD; Engrng.

ZANIEWSKI, BRIAN; Huntington Beach HS; Huntington Beach, CA; (2); Drama Clb; Stage Crew; Hon Roll; Pres Acad Fit Awd; Young Explorers; MESA; Cal Tech; Research.

ZANNI, ADAM J; Mt Shasta HS; Mount Shasta, CA; (3); Chorus; Var Bsbl; JV Bsktbl; JV Var Ftbl; Powder Puff Ftbl; Hon Roll; All Lgue Ftbl; Law.

ZANOTELLI, DANIELLE R; Alhambra HS; Martinez, CA; (2); 13/220; Treas Stu Cncl; Var Socr; Var Trk; Pres Acad Fit Awd; Medicine.

ZANOTTO, CHRISTINA; Livermore HS; Livermore, CA; (2); Church Yth Grp; Drama Clb; Pres Frsh Cls; JV Var Cheerldng; High Hon Roll; Hon Roll; UCSB; Pre Law.

ZAPANTA, ERNALYN C; Independence HS; San Jose, CA; (2); Cmnty Wkr; San Jose ST; Chld Psych.

ZAPATA, ALICE Y; Baldwin Park HS; Baldwin Park, CA; (3); Church Yth Grp; SADD; Band; Mrchg Band; Pep Band; Ed Yrbk; Cit Awd; Hon Roll; Med.

ZAPATA, LILA; Alder JR HS; Fontana, CA; (1); Cheerldng; CSF; UCLA; Doctor.

ZAPATA, MICHAEL A; Granada Hills HS; Los Angeles, CA; (2); Boy Scts; Office Aide; Spanish Clb; SADD; Teachers Aide; Latino Clb; Law Enfrcmnt.

ZAPATA, VERONICA X; Garden Grove HS; Garden Grove, CA; (3); 25/352; Church Yth Grp; Hon Roll; Schlrshp Cont 3rd Pl; Econ.

ZARAGOZA, AMELIA; Merced HS; Merced, CA; (3); Spanish Clb; Church Choir; Off Sr Cls; Sftbl; Hon Roll.

ZARAGOZA, ELVIRA; Le Grand Union HS; Le Grand, CA; (2); Drill Tm; Pom Pon; Archtct.

ZARAGOZA, JAIME; Calexico HS; Calexico, CA; (3); FBLA; FFA; FHA; VP Intnl Clb; Math Tm; VICA; Var Tennis; Hon Roll; St Schlr; Schls Jr Statesmen Of Amer Clb VP; CYLC Natl Yth Ldrshp Awd; 4th Pl Region Natl Fren Cont.

ZARAGOZA, VICENTE; Coachella Valley HS; Thermal, CA; (2); Boy Scts; English Clb; FFA; Hosp Aide; Library Aide; Office Aide; Spanish Clb; SADD; Teachers Aide; Varsity Clb; Soccer Player.

ZARATE, ANALIZA M; Holy Family HS; Los Angeles, CA; (2); Cmnty Wkr; High Hon Roll; Hon Roll; CSF; UCLA; Accntnt.

ZARATE, ARTHUR S; Bishop Amat HS; Diamond Bar, CA; (3); Church Yth Grp; JV Socr; Hon Roll; CA ST U; Electrical Engineer.

ZARATE, ERIK; Lynwood HS; Lynwood, CA; (3); 91/671; Letterman Clb; ROTC; Varsity Clb; Drill Tm; Yrbk; Stu Cncl; Var Bsbl; Var Ftbl; Prfct Atten Awd; Long Beach City COLL; Pilot.

ZARATE, JUAN C; Don Bosco Technical Inst; Maywood, CA; (3); JV Bsbl; Cal ST Los Angeles.

ZARATE, VICTORIA; Palo Verde HS; Blythe, CA; (4); Letterman Clb; Teachers Aide; Varsity Clb; JV Var Bsktbl; JV Var Sftbl; Var Vllybl; Hon Roll; Acctng.

ZARAZUA, MARIA L; Alisal HS; Salinas, CA; (1); Office Aide; Santa Cruz U.

ZARBAFIAN, PARISA; University HS; Irvine, CA; (4); 24/468; French Clb; Orch; Capt Bsktbl; French Hon Soc; High Hon Roll; Sal; CSF; Grad Top 10% Schl; U Of CA Irvine; Bio Sci.

ZARBO, CARLA N; Chula Vista HS; San Diego, CA; (3); 65/535; Church Yth Grp; Sec English Clb; Girl Scts; VP Pep Clb; Sec Science Clb; Church Choir; Pres Frsh Cls; Var Mgr(s); JV Socr; Var Swmmng; ASB Co-Commssnr Of Pep; CASC Rgn 18 Sec; Pres Of Asian Fllwshp Clb; Physcl Thrpy.

ZARCO, ESMERALDA; Indio HS; Indio, CA; (1); 1/656; Art Clb; Church Yth Grp; Dance Clb; French Clb; FBLA; Cit Awd; High Hon Roll; Prfct Atten Awd; UC Riverside; Medcl.

ZAREK, BETH A; Morro Bay HS; Los Osos, CA; (2); 2/279; Church Yth Grp; French Clb; FFA; Math Tm; Yrbk; High Hon Roll; St Schlr; Envrnmntl Orgnztns; Med.

ZAREK, DEBBI T; Morro Bay HS; Los Osos, CA; (3); 4/238; Church Yth Grp; French Clb; Teachers Aide; Sec Frsh Cls; JV Var Cheerldng; JV Vllybl; High Hon Roll; St Schlr; Peer Commnctns; Geom Golden St Exam High Hnrs, Algebra Hnrs; Bus.

ZARGANIS, LYDIA; El Camino HS; S. San Francisco, CA; (1); Cheerldng; Cit Awd; Hon Roll; Stanford.

ZARICK, RYAN; Valley HS; Sacramento, CA; (3); 85/600; Dance Clb; Office Aide; Teachers Aide; Rep Frsh Cls; Rep Soph Cls; Rep Jr Cls; Rep Stu Cncl; JV Bsbl; Var JV Ftbl; Var JV Wt Lftg; Golden St Exam High Hnrs Alg & Geom; UCLA; Math.

ZARUBIN, NADYA; Southbay Christian Schl; Milpitas, CA; (4); 3/27; Church Yth Grp; Teachers Aide; Cit Awd; French Hon Soc; Hon Roll; NHS; CSF 1st Sem Pres; Natl Yth Cngrssnl Ldrshp Schlr; Fresno Pacific Coll; Comp Sci.

ZARZA, BEATRIZ; Castle Park HS; Chula Vista, CA; (2); 10/473; French Clb; JV Bsktbl; Var Tennis; Prfct Atten Awd; Acad Achvrs Clb; Atty.

ZARZA, DAVID; Castle Park HS; Chula Vista, CA; (1); 88/614; Church Yth Grp; Debate Tm; French Clb; Speech Tm; SADD; Tennis; Cit Awd; Notre Dame; Doc.

ZASKE, ANNA J; Mount Migel HS; Lemon Grove, CA; (4); 65/370; San Diego ST U; Acctng.

ZASTOUPIL, LYNN A; La Habra HS; Whittier, CA; (3); Church Yth Grp; Treas Drama Clb; FBLA; Office Aide; SADD; School Play; Stage Crew; Lit Mag; Stu Cncl; Cit Awd; Stu Advsry Cncl Agnst Substnc Abuse; Jobs Dghtrs Past Hnrd Qn; CA ST Fullerton; Law.

ZASTROUPIL, LYNN; La Habra HS; Whittier, CA; (3); Church Yth Grp; Drama Clb; FBLA; SADD; School Play; Stage Crew; Lit Mag; Stu Cncl; Cit Awd; High Hon Roll; Jobs Dghts Past Hnrd Qn; Stu Advsry Cncl Agnst Substnc Abuse; CA ST Fullerton; Law.

ZATARAIN, IRMA L; Warren HS; Bell, CA; (2); 51/543; Dance Clb; Office Aide; Band; Jazz Band; Mrchg Band; Pep Band; JV Crs Cntry; Var Trk; Hon Roll; Pres Acad Fit Awd; UC Berkeley.

ZATARAIN, MARLENE; Schurr HS; Monterey Park, CA; (2); Hon Roll; CSF; UC Berkeley; Psych.

ZAVADIVKER, ALLISON B; California HS; San Ramon, CA; (4); 53/384; Cmnty Wkr; Debate Tm; French Clb; Office Aide; Service Clb; Speech Tm; Ed Rptr Nwsp; JV Var Tennis; Hon Roll; Cmpltn Of Inst Of Chldrns Lit; Bus Intrn Contra Coasta Times; Piano Cmpent & Rctls; CA Poly; Intl Bus.

ZAVALA, ADRIAN J; Pomona HS; Pomona, CA; (3); Church Yth Grp; CA Poly Pomona Step-To-Coll Prgrm; MECHA; Physcs Clb; CA Poly Pomona; Engl.

ZAVALA, ARLETTE; Fontana HS; Fontana, CA; (2); Drama Clb; Stage Crew; Hon Roll; Law.

ZAVALA, ART R; Fontana HS; Fontana, CA; (3); JV Crs Cntry; Vrsty Badminton; UCSD; Elect Engr.

ZAVALA, CRISTINA; Charter Oak HS; Glendora, CA; (4); 26/388; Cmnty Wkr; Drama Clb; Letterman Clb; Office Aide; Spanish Clb; SADD; Varsity Clb; School Musical; School Play; Off Sr Cls; UC Irvine; Psych.

ZAVALA, EDNA; Herver Hoover HS; San Diego, CA; (4); 18/304; Church Yth Grp; Cmnty Wkr; Sec FTA; Sec Latin Clb; Teachers Aide; Var Crs Cntry; Var Socr; Var Trk; Var Vllybl; Cit Awd; Ecivres; Top Stu Englsh Cls; 2 1st Mdls Bst Stu; San Diego City Coll; Comp Pgmmr.

ZAVALA, GERSON A; Jefferson HS; Los Angeles, CA; (2); Hon Roll; USC Med Cor Pgm; U Of SC; Engr.

ZAVALA, LAURA A; Castle Park HS; Chula Vista, CA; (2); SADD; Cit Awd; Prfct Atten Awd; Law.

ZAVALA, MARGARITA; Indio HS; Indio, CA; (1); Interior Dsgn.

ZAVALA, MATT A; Notre Dame HS; Riverside, CA; (1); High Hon Roll; Hon Roll; NHS; Pres Schlr.

ZAVALA, MICHELLE; Azusa HS; Azusa, CA; (4); Letterman Clb; Pep Clb; SADD; Teachers Aide; Band; Pom Pon; High Hon Roll; Cerritos; Acctng.

ZAVALA, OSCAR; Santa Clara HS; Oxnard, CA; (2); JV Bsbl; JV Ftbl; Mgr(s); Cit Awd; Naval Aviator/Pilot.

ZAVALA, RENE; Castle Park HS; Chula Vista, CA; (2); 50/473; Jazz Band; Mrchg Band; Cit Awd; Hon Roll; Pres Schlr; Val.

ZAVALA, VICTORIA; Notre Dame HS; E Palo Alto, CA; (3); Latin Clb; Chorus; Hon Roll; CSF; Culture Awrnss; Med.

ZAVALA, YVETTE I; Hoover HS; Fresno, CA; (3); #65 In Class; Band; Mrchg Band; Orch; CSF; CA ST U-Fresno.

ZAVODSKY, STORMY L; Thomas Downey HS; Modesto, CA; (4); Teachers Aide; Chorus; School Musical; Var Sftbl; JV Vllybl; Knights Achvt Awd; Modesto JC.

ZAWAIDEH, LIMA W; Mercy HS; San Francisco, CA; (4); GAA; Spanish Clb; Teachers Aide; Hon Roll; Prfct Atten Awd; Dance Ensemble; Dance Achvt Awd; ST U Of SF; Corp Law.

ZAWALICK, DAVID C; Valley HS; Sacramento, CA; (3); 12/600; Science Clb; SADD; Intrml Ftbl; High Hon Roll; Hon Roll; NHS; Ntl Merit SF; Nuclear.

ZAWATSKI, MARK N; Sonora HS; Fullerton, CA; (4); Art Clb; Boy Scts; FBLA; Latin Clb; Ski Clb; SADD; Stu Cncl; JV Socr; L Var Swmmng; Hon Roll; Vrsty Swmmng Mst Inspirational 90; U Southern CA; Arch.

ZAYAS, BEATRIZ O; Calexico HS; Calexico, CA; (2); Church Yth Grp; FHA; Pep Clb; SADD; Band; Flag Corp; Mrchg Band; S Clb; Span A P Clb; Music Awd.

ZAZUETA, JEFF M; Trabuco Hills HS; Rancho Santa Marg, CA; (2); Chess Clb; Quiz Bowl; Scholastic Bowl; Science Clb; Intrml Golf; Var Lcrss; Hon Roll; Prfct Atten Awd; Art; USAFA; Aerospace Engr.

ZAZUETA, MARIBEL; Central Union HS; El Centro, CA; (2); Math Tm; Drill Tm; High Hon Roll; Hon Roll; Psych.

ZAZUETA, PEGGY; Maranatha HS; Temple City, CA; (4); 19/101; Church Yth Grp; Pres Soph Cls; Pres Sec Stu Cncl; Var L Sftbl; Pasadena Trnmnt Roses Ryl Ct Princess 90; Miss Temple City 2nd Rnnr Up 90; CAF; UCLA; Pol Sci.

ZAZUETA, ZAIDA I; Rowland HS; Rowland Heights, CA; (2); Medicine.

ZDRAVECKY, LARA C; San Ramon Valley HS; Danville, CA; (3); 16/429; Dance Clb; Drama Clb; Teachers Aide; School Play; Variety Show; Var Diving; JV Vllybl; Hon Roll; Poems Pub Sch Lit Mag; U C Irvine; Lwyr.

ZEBOTT, SARAH L; College Park HS; Pleasant Hill, CA; (3); Teachers Aide; High Hon Roll; Hon Roll; Atten Cngrssnl Yth Ldrshp Conf Washington DC 90; Diablo Valley Coll; Bus.

ZEE, ALAN C; Bullard HS; Fresno, CA; (2); French Clb; School Play; Swmmng; U CA-BERKLEY; Arch.

ZEE, PATRICK; Woodside Priory Schl; San Carlos, CA; (4); 2/19; Boy Scts; Computer Clb; Math Clb; Ski Clb; Var Bsktbl; Var Crs Cntry; Var Swmmng; Hon Roll; Rotary Awd; Deans Awd; Invest In Amer Essy Cntst 1st Pl; UCLA.

ZEFF, AIMEE M; Woodside HS; Woodside, CA; (2); Letterman Clb; Rep Frsh Cls; Rep Stu Cncl; JV Socr; JV Tennis; U CA; Mrktng.

ZEGHBIB, DANIELLE T; San Dieguito HS; Encinitas, CA; (2); Church Yth Grp; French Clb; Intnl Clb; Science Clb; Orch; Cit Awd; French Hon Soc; Hon Roll; U CA.

ZEGLEN, CARRIE C; San Marcos HS; San Marcos, CA; (3); High Hon Roll; Hon Roll; UC San Diego; Ed.

ZEHRUNG, LISA D; Berean Christian HS; San Pablo, CA; (4); Church Yth Grp; Teachers Aide; Chorus; Church Choir; School Musical; School Play; Hon Roll; Cedarville Coll; Elem Ed.

ZEIDERS, JARED S; North HS; Bakersfield, CA; (2); JA; SADD; Trk; Hon Roll; Ducks Unlimited; CA Poly; Ag.

ZEIDMAN, MICHELLE S; North Hollywood HS; North Hollywood, CA; (3); Church Yth Grp; Teachers Aide; Hon Roll; CSUN; Fashn Desgn.

ZEIGER, KEVIN J; Bonita HS; La Verne, CA; (1); Art Clb; Teachers Aide; Temple Yth Grp; VP Bsktbl; VP Capt Crs Cntry; Var Capt Trk; U Of La Verne; Bus.

ZEIGLER, HEATHER; Carlsbad HS; Carlsbad, CA; (3); Cmnty Wkr; Debate Tm; Hosp Aide; Key Clb; Speech Tm; Stage Crew; Nwsp; Hon Roll; RYLA; US Hstry Kilroy Awd; Psych.

ZEIGLER, JEFFREY S; Mission San Jose HS; Fremont, CA; (3); 81/397; Orch; School Musical; Var Trk; Tri-Cities Awd Phlhrmnc Cmptn; Leah Carlender Awd; Prncpl Cllst San Jose & Oakland Yth Orch; Music Performance.

ZEIGLER, KRISTINE A; El Capitan HS; Lakeside, CA; (2); 9/433; French Clb; Science Clb; School Play; Pres Frsh Cls; JV L Swmmng; Hon Roll; Honors Seminars Of San Diego Rep; JV Girls Swim MVP 89 & 90; 1st Pl San Diego Cty Hstry Fair; Stanford; Engrng.

ZEINEH, MICHAEL M; Servite HS; Fullerton, CA; (3); 2/160; Debate Tm; Math Tm; Quiz Bowl; Lit Mag; Var Tennis; Hon Roll; NHS; Ntl Merit SF; Rennsealer Sci Awd Best Sci/Math Stu; UC Irvine; Med.

ZEISLER, GREG; San Ramon Valley HS; Danville, CA; (1); Band; Mgr Tennis; High Hon Roll; CSF.

ZEITZ, ZACK; Berkeley HS; Berkeley, CA; (3); Ski Clb; Var Bsktbl; Var Ftbl; Var Wrstlng; Rugby Club.

ZELAYA, JANET M; El Cajon Valley HS; El Cajon, CA; (2); 46/549; Church Yth Grp; Dance Clb; Key Clb; Variety Show; Spch Clb; SDSU; Cmnctns.

ZELENKA, KERRI M; Lemoore Union HS; Lemoore, CA; (2); 82/250; Spanish Clb; SADD; Teachers Aide; JV Capt Gym; Capt Powder Puff Ftbl; Cit Awd; Hon Roll; Pres Acad Fit Awd; Photo Club; Gymnastic Club; Fresno City Coll; Nrsng.

ZELENKA JR, THOMAS; Hanford HS; Hanford, CA; (1); Spanish Clb; JV Capt Bsbl; JV Capt Bsktbl; JV Capt Ftbl; Cit Awd; Arch.

ZELIDON-ZEPEDA, JOSE A; Lowell HS; San Francisco, CA; (2); Soc.

ZELL, KENNY; Fillmore HS; Fillmore, CA; (4); 1/160; Am Leg Boys St; Church Yth Grp; Letterman Clb; SADD; Off Jr Cls; Pres Stu Cncl; JV Var Bsktbl; JV Var Ftbl; JV Var Trk; Bausch & Lomb Sci Awd; Occidental Coll; Med.

ZELLER, CHRISTOPHER MICHAEL; Bear River HS; Grass Valley, CA; (2); Drama Clb; 4-H; Intnl Clb; Science Clb; School Play; Stage Crew; 4-H Awd; High Hon Roll; Hon Roll; Lion Awd; Principals Lttr Awd; Sci Distance Awd; MIT; Nuclear Engrng.

ZELLER, NICOLE M; Sir Francis Drake HS; San Anselmo, CA; (4); 10/145; Church Yth Grp; Spanish Clb; Teachers Aide; School Musical; School Play; Variety Show; Rptr Nwsp; Ed Lit Mag; Score Keeper; Hon Roll; Cert In Drama; CSF; Humboldt ST.

ZELLERS, ADRIAN; Cabrillo HS; Lompoc, CA; (4); 4-H; Library Aide; SADD; Teachers Aide; Chorus; Off Sr Cls; Cheerldng; Ftbl; Tennis; Trk; Prfmng Arts.

ZEMAITIS, MICHAEL J; Paso Robles HS; Paso Robles, CA; (2); FFA; Teachers Aide; Bsbl; High Hon Roll; Hon Roll; Pres Acad Fit Awd; Fresno ST U; Bus.

ZEMAN, KRISTIE L; Mira Costa HS; Manhattan Beach, CA; (1); French Clb; Service Clb; Hon Roll; Sea Explorers; Marine Bio.

ZEMAN, ZACHARY J; Arroyo Grande HS; Arroyo Grande, CA; (4); 18/500; Am Leg Boys St; Band; Var Trk; Elks Awd; Hon Roll; Ntl Merit Ltr; Pres Acad Fit Awd; Rotary Awd; CA Band Dir Assn 4 Yrs; All St Hnr Band; 1st Pl CA St Hstry Day Grp Proj 1988-89; U CA Berkeley.

ZEMANOVIC, JASON R; Cabrillo HS; Lompoc, CA; (4); 1/200; Jazz Band; VP Sr Cls; Var L Socr; Var L Trk; Cit Awd; Elks Awd; Kiwanis Awd; NHS; Ntl Merit Ltr; Pres Acad Fit Awd; Bank Am Achvt Awd; John Philip Sousa Music Awd; Robert C Byrd Hnrs Schlr; UCLA; Bio.

ZEMELLA, MICHAEL A; San Marcos HS; Santa Barbara, CA; (3); 37/401; Church Yth Grp; Cmnty Wkr; Spanish Clb; Church Choir; Yrbk; JV Golf; JV Capt Socr; JV Var Tennis; Hon Roll; Pre-Med.

ZEMNY, ALISON C; Aptos HS; Corralitos, CA; (2); 4-H; German Clb; Cheerldng; Crs Cntry; Trk; 4-H Awd; Hon Roll; 4-H VP 89-90; Cal Poly SLO; Grphc Art.

ZEMPO, MIZUHO C; Norte Vista HS; Ontario, CA; (3); Hosp Aide; Treas Science Clb; Spanish Clb; VP Pres Band; Mrchg Band; Pep Band; High Hon Roll; CSF 1988-90; GATE; Hnr Ct; U CA Davis; Vet.

ZENDEJAS, DAVID; Edison HS; Stockton, CA; (4); 16/400; Am Leg Boys St; VP Chess Clb; Dance Clb; Teachers Aide; Golf; High Hon Roll; UC Davis; Elect Engr.

ZENDEJAS, DIEGO C; Calipatria HS; Niland, CA; (3); FFA; Office Aide; JV Bsktbl; Yth Consrvtn Corps Ldr; Comp Prg.

ZENDEJAS, MARIA; Elsinore HS; Lake Elsinore, CA; (1); Church Yth Grp; Dance Clb; French Clb; Teachers Aide; Chorus; Cit Awd; High Hon Roll; Hon Roll; Prfct Atten Awd; Law.

ZENDEJAS, MARIO P; Jefferson HS; Daly City, CA; (2); Band; Jazz Band; JV Swmmng; Hon Roll; Music Awd; Hnrs Engl, Hstry; Stanford; Astrnmy.

ZENDEJAS, SERGIO A; Sequoia HS; Redwood City, CA; (3); Chess Clb; Math Clb; JV Bsktbl; Var JV Tennis; Hon Roll; Math Engrng Sci Achvt-Won 3 Mdls 90; U Of CA; Bio.

ZENG, JASON Q; George Washington HS; San Francisco, CA; (3); Letterman Clb; Var JV Ftbl; Var JV Trk; Var Wrstlng; High Hon Roll; Hon Roll; Pre Med.

ZENG, JIANAN; Galileo HS; San Francisco, CA; (4); Bus Profs of Am; Debate Tm; English Clb; Intnl Clb; Math Clb; Math Tm; Quiz Bowl; Science Clb; Teachers Aide; VICA; Sn Jse ST U; Cvl Engrg.

ZENG, TINA; Galileo HS; San Francisco, CA; (3); French Clb; ROTC; Science Clb; Service Clb; Drill Tm; Hon Roll; Intl Bus.

ZENG, XIAO Y; Pasadena HS; Pasadena, CA; (4); JA; High Hon Roll; NHS; Prfct Atten Awd; NASA Spce Expmnt Dsgn Comptn Regnl Wnr; Caltec Specl Audtng Prgm; USC Hnrs Prgm 89; Pres Acadmc Ftns; MIT; Elect Engrng.

ZENIALI, POUNEH; Canyon HS; Canyon Country, CA; (4); 45/484; Treas FBLA; Intnl Clb; Hon Roll; NHS; Prfct Atten Awd; Spanish NHS; CSF Treas; Red Cross Volunteer; CA ST U; Pre-Bus.

ZENT, NICOLE S; Live Oak HS; Morgan Hill, CA; (3); 50/550; Church Yth Grp; Cmnty Wkr; FBLA; Key Clb; Pres Spanish Clb; Teachers Aide; Lit Mag; Tennis; Trk; Hon Roll; Italian Club; Badminton; Piano Lessons; Tae Kwon Do Lessons; Volunteer Counseling Center; Work Part Time; Santa Clara U; Aviation.

ZENTGRAF, MICHELLE R; St Anthony HS; Long Beach, CA; (3); Boy Scts; Church Yth Grp; Drama Clb; GAA; JA; Ski Clb; SADD; School Play; Stage Crew; Nwsp; Socr; UC Santa Cruz; Marine Bio.

ZEPEDA, ALMA Y; John H Francis Polytechnic HS; Pacoima, CA; (3); Office Aide; Teachers Aide; NHS; 1st Pl Spllng Bee.

ZEPEDA, BERTOLDO; St Ignatius College Prep; San Francisco, CA; (3); 146/251; Cmnty Wkr; Latin Clb; Pilot.

ZEPEDA, DEANNA L; John Burroughs HS; Burbank, CA; (4); Cmnty Wkr; Office Aide; Teachers Aide; Color Guard; Nwsp; High Hon Roll; Hon Roll; Los Angeles Valley Coll; Psych.

ZEPEDA, LUCIA; Broadway HS; San Jose, CA; (4); Library Aide; Teachers Aide; Cit Awd; Hon Roll; Santa Clara U; Court Reprtng.

ZEPP, MARK S; Palm Valley HS; Rancho Mirage, CA; (3); Church Yth Grp; German Clb; School Play; Rptr Nwsp; Ed Yrbk; Treas Frsh Cls; VP Capt Bsktbl; VP Capt Socr; Stat Sftbl; High Hon Roll; 1st Prefect Jr Yr Stu Gov; Latin,Engl & Bio Awrds Socer Schl MVP; 1st Team All Lea (Intrnl Lea).

ZERBE, BARBARA M; Casa Roble HS; Citrus Heights, CA; (2); 27/500; French Clb; Red Cross Aide; Drill Tm; Sec Frsh Cls; Sec Soph Cls; Var Cheerldng; JV Var Swmmng; High Hon Roll; Studs Rechng Out; CSF; Psych.

ZERBIB, ANDRE A; Abraham Lincoln HS; San Francisco, CA; (3); Bsbl; Bsktbl; Ftbl; Socr; Swmmng; Trk; Wt Lftg; Wrstlng; MVP Socr 88 89; All Cty Wnnr Socr 88 89; Bst Offnsv Plyr Socr 89; Dntl.

ZERILLI, LISA M; Mira Loma HS; Carmichael, CA; (3); 43/284; Cmnty Wkr; Office Aide; Pep Clb; SADD; Sec Soph Cls; Off Jr Cls; Stu Cncl; Var Socr; Hon Roll; Treas Rotary Awd; Cls Homcmng Princess; Socr; Bus.

ZEROSKI, STACEY M; Downey HS; Downey, CA; (2); Church Yth Grp; Color Guard; Hon Roll; Keywnttes; Acad Exclinc Awd-1st Yr Alg/Hnrs.

ZERTUCHE, PETER; Lincoln HS; Los Angeles, CA; (3); Pres Jr Cls; UCLA; Alg Teacher.

ZERWER, STACY L; Edison HS; Huntington Beach, CA; (2); Church Yth Grp; Girl Scts; Spanish Clb; Hon Roll; Prfct Atten Awd; Pres Acad Fit Awd; U CA; Inter Dsgn.

ZETLMAIER, NICHOLAS J; San Gabriel HS; San Gabriel, CA; (2); Church Yth Grp; Cmnty Wkr; Service Clb; Spanish Clb; Yrbk; Intrml Bsktbl; JV Vllybl; Hon Roll; Pres Acad Fit Awd; Gldn St Exam Algebra-High Hnrs; Saturday High Art Clsses; GATE Stu; Film Dir.

ZETOUNA, NICOLE; Monte Vista HS; Spring Valley, CA; (4); 25/436; Cmnty Wkr; Computer Clb; Library Aide; Office Aide; Teachers Aide; Varsity Clb; Orch; Rptr Nwsp; Sec Frsh Cls; Rep Stu Cncl; U Of San Diego.

ZETTERBERG, JAMIE A; Moreau HS; Fremont, CA; (3); Church Yth Grp; Cmnty Wkr; Computer Clb; Hosp Aide; Key Clb; Science Clb; SADD; JV Sftbl; JV Trk; JV Vllybl; YMCA Smr Cnslr; Soup Ktchn Vlntr; Harvard; Intl Bus.

ZGRABIK, KRISSY; Louisville HS; Van Nuys, CA; (3); Church Yth Grp; FHA; GAA; Girl Scts; Office Aide; Gym; Hon Roll.

ZHAN, LI F; Milpitas HS; Milpitas, CA; (2); High Hon Roll; Astrnmy & Chinese Clbs; UC Santa Barbara; Mech Engrng.

ZHANG, ALICE; Abraham Lincoln HS; San Francisco, CA; (2); Church Yth Grp; The Close Up Pgm; San Francisco ST U.

ZHANG, ALLEN; Schurr HS; S San Gabriel, CA; (1); Crs Cntry; Trk; UCLA; Bio.

ZHANG, DAVID Y; Abraham Lincoln HS; San Francisco, CA; (3); Computer Clb; Intnl Clb; UC Davis; Bus.

ZHANG, ELLIOT G; George Washington HS; San Francisco, CA; (4); Church Yth Grp; Swmmng; Tennis; High Hon Roll; Hon Roll; City Coll Of San Fran; Acctng.

ZHANG, GENG-HUA HARRY; San Marcos HS; Santa Barbara, CA; (2); Hon Roll; UC Berkeley.

ZHANG, HUI; El Toro HS; El Toro, CA; (3); Intnl Clb; Math Clb; Math Tm; High Hon Roll; Soc Wmn Engrng Awd; Continental Math Leag Math Cntst Wnnr; Engrng.

ZHANG, JIAN; Saddleback HS; Santa Ana, CA; (2); Chess Clb; French Clb; VP Sec Mu Alpha Theta; NFL; Pres Science Clb; Spanish Clb; Speech Tm; Tennis; Acadmc Dcthln; CSF Hstrn; Bridge Club; Comp Sci.

ZHANG, JUNE; George Washington HS; San Francisco, CA; (2); High Hon Roll; Hon Roll; Nrsng.

ZHANG, KEVIN; International Studies Acad; San Francisco, CA; (2); High Hon Roll; UC Berkeley; Math.

ZHANG, LILY; George Washington HS; San Francisco, CA; (2); Church Yth Grp; School Musical; Swmmng; Tennis; High Hon Roll; Hon Roll; ST U Of CA; Nrsng.

ZHANG, PATRICK; Encinal HS; Alameda, CA; (3); 27/233; Golden St Exam; Badminton/Table Tnns; Clltng Stamps/Wrtng; U CA Davis; Chem Engr.

ZHANG, XIN; Phillip & Sala Burton Academic HS; San Francisco, CA; (4); 1/180; German Clb; Math Clb; Science Clb; Teachers Aide; Lit Mag; Hon Roll; Ntl Honor Roll; 1st Pl Shirt Dsgn Forgn Lang Wk; Biol.

ZHAO, MARK; George Washington HS; San Francisco, CA; (2); Math Clb; Math Tm; ROTC; Socr; Cllct Stamps; Berkeley U; Engr.

ZHAO, STELLA; Galileo HS; San Francisco, CA; (2); Pep Clb; Service Clb; Hon Roll; Dsgn.

ZHENG, AMY; South Pasadena HS; San Gabriel, CA; (4); Intnl Clb; Library Aide; Science Clb; Service Clb; Spanish Clb; Prfct Atten Awd; CA Schlrshp Fdrtn; Hnr Awd For 1st Yr Algebra-Gldn St Exam; Los Angeles U; Pre-Bio.

ZHENG, YIXIAN; Galileo HS; San Francisco, CA; (2); Hon Roll; Stanford; Law.

ZHONG, TIMOTHY HU; James Lick HS; San Jose, CA; (1); Church Yth Grp; Intnl Clb; Church Choir; Off Frsh Cls; Var Tennis; High Hon Roll; Prfct Atten Awd; Bibliophile Society, Asian Clb; CSF.

ZHOU, LAURA; Oakland HS; Oakland, CA; (3); French Clb; Math Clb; Service Clb; Cit Awd; Hon Roll; Hosp Vlntr; Keywntts Clb; UC Berkeley; Intl Bus Mgmt.

ZHU, JIM YIN X; Blair HS; Pasadena, CA; (3); Art Clb; Chess Clb; Computer Clb; Library Aide; Office Aide; Red Cross Aide; ROTC; Teachers Aide; Color Guard; Drill Tm; Rsrv Ofcrs Assn Of US; Amer Lgn For Schlstc Excl.

ZHUANG, GRACE; California HS; San Ramon, CA; (3); Debate Tm; French Clb; Hosp Aide; Model UN; NFL; Speech Tm; Lit Mag; Hon Roll; Jr NHS; NHS; CSF; Outstndng Frnch Achvt Awd; Med.

ZHUANG, JANIE; Oakland HS; Oakland, CA; (3); Cit Awd; Hon Roll; Bus Mgmnt.

ZIA, ADEMIR N; Mark Keppel HS; Monterey Park, CA; (3); FCA; Varsity Clb; Var Capt Ftbl; Var Socr; Var Trk; High Hon Roll; Kiwanis Awd; Var Ftbl Mssn Vlly Lg 2nd Tm D B; Ftbl Sw Vlly Tm 89; Schlrshp Kaiwani FCA Ftbl Cmp; Air Force Acad; Aero Sci.

ZIAKAS, CHRISTINA M; American HS; Fremont, CA; (2); 24/385; French Clb; French Hon Soc; High Hon Roll; San Jose ST U; Prfrmng Arts.

ZIALCITA, GERALD W; Fairfield HS; Suisun City, CA; (1); Church Yth Grp; Rep Frsh Cls; Bsktbl; Score Keeper; Hon Roll; UCLA; Engrng.

ZICARELLI, SHANAN D; Rim Of The World HS; Crestline, CA; (2); #2 In Class; Church Yth Grp; FCA; Scholastic Bowl; Spanish Clb; Nwsp; Yrbk; Rep Frsh Cls; Hist Soph Cls; Var Socr; High Hon Roll; Photo.

ZIEGENBUSCH, JEFF; Kennedy J F HS; La Palma, CA; (1); Church Yth Grp; Band; Mrchg Band; Bsbl; USC; Pro Athl.

ZIEGLER, DAVID J; Barstow HS; Barstow, CA; (4); 11/250; AFS; Scholastic Bowl; Chorus; Hon Roll; Pres Acad Fit Awd; Pres CSF 89-90; Mck Trl Acad Decthln 89-90; U Of NV Las Vegas; Bus Admin.

ZIEGLER, ELIZABETH; Silver Valley HS; Ft Irwin, CA; (3); 1/87; Church Yth Grp; French Clb; Ski Clb; Treas Jr Cls; Rep Stu Cncl; Var Cheerldng; Mgr(s); JV Vllybl; High Hon Roll; Teachers Aide; Mck Trl; Wrtng Clbrtn; Notre Dame; Bus.

ZIEGLER, RUSSELL M; College Park HS; Martinez, CA; (3); Letterman Clb; Var Crs Cntry; Var Trk; Chem.

ZIELINSKI, MICHELLE A; Apple Valley HS; Apple Valley, CA; (4); High Hon Roll; Hon Roll; NHS; Pres Acad Fit Awd; CA U San Diego; Qntttv Ecs.

ZIERDT, BRIAN T; San Jose HS Acad; San Jose, CA; (2); 24/231; JV Var Trk; Hon Roll.

ZILLGES, SHAWNA RENEE; Mt Whitney HS; Visalia, CA; (4); 9/355; Math Clb; Spanish Clb; Band; Phtg Yrbk; Pres Soph Cls; Stu Cncl; Trk; NHS; Keywanettes Pres; Astrnmy Club; U Of CA Santa Barbara; Phys Sc.

ZIMMER, LORI; Poway HS; San Diego, CA; (3); Church Yth Grp; SADD; High Hon Roll; NHS; Nwsp; Cmnty Svc Clb Interact; Piano Stu Enrolled In Cert Of Mrt Pgm.

ZIMMER, SEAN D; Los Amigos HS; Santa Ana, CA; (2); Hon Roll.

ZIMMERMAN, ERIC D; Mission Viejo HS; Mission Viejo, CA; (4); Key Clb; Spanish Clb; SADD; Pres Jr Cls; Var Bsbl; JV Bsktbl; Var Ftbl; High Hon Roll; NHS; Pres Acad Fit Awd; Gold Seal Bearer CSF; Prncpls Hnr Rl; U Of CA Santa Barbara; Envrmnt.

ZIMMERMAN, JASON; Moorpark HS; Moorpark, CA; (2); Church Yth Grp; Ski Clb; JV Bsktbl; JV Ftbl; Var Trk; High Hon Roll; Hon Roll; Loyola Marymount U; Lawyr.

ZIMMERMAN, LESLIE; Cupertino HS; Santa Clara, CA; (2); Church Yth Grp; German Clb; Rep Soph Cls; Stu Cncl; JV Trk; Var Vllybl; Prfct Atten Awd; UC San Diego; Commnctns.

ZIMMERMAN, SUSAN A; Westlake HS; Westlake Vlg, CA; (2); 1/432; Church Yth Grp; Hosp Aide; Letterman Clb; Math Clb; Math Tm; Science Clb; Spanish Clb; Varsity Clb; Var L Crs Cntry; JV Trk; Winner Ventura Cty Sci Fair & 5 Spcl Awds; Best Defense Witness On Mock Trial Team For County; Stanford; Medicine.

ZIMMERMANN, AMELIA D; Sonoma Valley HS; Sonoma, CA; (3); 1/300; Church Yth Grp; Cmnty Wkr; Debate Tm; Intnl Clb; Model UN; NFL; Pep Clb; Sec Spanish Clb; Speech Tm; School Musical; CSF Treas; Golden St Exam High Hnrs Algebra & Geom; Math.

ZIMMERMANN, CHRISTINE; Brethren HS; Long Beach, CA; (1); 15/93; Church Yth Grp; Band; Chorus; Drm Mjr(t); Mrchg Band; Vllybl; Hon Roll; CA Schlstc Fed.

ZIMMERMANN, SCOTT A; Clayton Valley HS; Concord, CA; (3); 1/400; German Clb; Math Clb; Math Tm; Var Swmmng; V Water Polo; CA Schlrshp Fed; Yth Educators; Engrng.

ZIMNAVODA, AVIGAIL F; Thousand Oaks HS; Thousand Oaks, CA; (2); 123/570; Cmnty Wkr; Temple Yth Grp; Hon Roll; Journ.

ZINDA, CHRISTY; Apple Valley HS; Apple Valley, CA; (2); Drama Clb; German Clb; Hon Roll; Jobs Dghtrs, Pst Hnrd Queen; Bus Law.

ZINK, TARA L; Brea Olinda HS; Brea, CA; (2); 26/344; Dance Clb; GAA; Cheerldng; Socr; Tennis; High Hon Roll; Hon Roll; CSF; Ltr Schlr; Head Jr Var Chrldr; Commnctns.

ZINSER, MELANIE; San Dieguito HS; Cardiff By The Se, CA; (2); Church Yth Grp; School Play; Lit Mag; Rep Frsh Cls; Wt Lftg; High Hon Roll; Hon Roll; Prfct Atten Awd; Pres Acad Fit Awd; Hgh Hnrs Geom/Alg-Golden St Exam; Stu Outreach-Mexico 90; Camp Cnslr 87-90; Advrtsng.

ZINSSER JR, WILLIAM A; Victor Valley HS; Victorville, CA; (3); 5/375; Church Yth Grp; JV Trk; Church Cncl Yth Chrmn; Engrng.

ZINZA, JASON E; Washington HS; Fremont, CA; (2); Cmnty Wkr; French Clb; Intnl Clb; Quiz Bowl; Scholastic Bowl; Temple Yth Grp; Socr; High Hon Roll; Hon Roll; Amnsty Intl; Greenpeace; Berkeley; Ed.

ZINZUN, ARMANDO; Edison HS; Fresno, CA; (1); Fresno ST; Arch.

ZIRKLE, REBECCA S; La Canada HS; La Canada Flintri, CA; (3); Piano, Art, Rlgn; Mnstry.

ZIROVICH, MILENA D; Arcadia HS; Arcadia, CA; (3); 130/639; Church Yth Grp; Hist Service Clb; School Play; Sec Jr Cls; Pres Sr Cls; JV Bsktbl; Var Trk; Hon Roll; NHS; U S CA Bk Awd; CSF; Jr Statesmen Of America.

ZIRPOLI III, BOB M; Henry M Gunn HS; Palo Alto, CA; (4); German Clb; Pres Key Clb; Var L Crs Cntry; Var L Trk; Ballroom Dancing; Physics Clb-VP; Harvey Mudd Coll; Engrng.

ZIVELIN, NADAV; University City HS; San Diego, CA; (3); 22/400; Rop; UCSD.

ZIYAD, KARIM J; Inglewood HS; Inglewood, CA; (2); Capt Bsktbl; Swmmng; Chiropractor.

ZLOTNICK, BRANDON M; Mountain View HS; Mountain View, CA; (3); 1/325; Debate Tm; Sec French Clb; NFL; Speech Tm; Mrchg Band; Ed Nwsp; JV Crs Cntry; JV Tennis; High Hon Roll; Harvard U Bk Awd.

ZLOTNICK, KATHRYN B; Junipero Serra HS; San Diego, CA; (3); 52/391; Church Yth Grp; Drama Clb; Ed Nwsp; Mgr(s); Var L Swmmng; Hon Roll; San Diego Tribunes All Acad Team; Swim Club; San Diego ST; Journlsm.

ZLOTNIK, ANDREW; Francis Parker HS; El Cajon, CA; (1); Drama Clb; Temple Yth Grp; School Musical; School Play; Stage Crew; Variety Show; JV Ftbl; Var Tennis; Cmptv Tennis San Diego Rnkd No 22 San Diego County; USC Film Schl; Film Dir.

ZMARZLY, ERIC; Cardinal Newman HS; Santa Rosa, CA; (3); 10/100; Cmnty Wkr; JA; Letterman Clb; Rptr Nwsp; VP Soph Cls; Hist Stu Cncl; Socr; Var Tennis; High Hon Roll; NHS; Pres Schlr Ath; Vrsty Wtrpolo; Ldrshp Awd; Robotics.

ZODA, PAUL M; Santa Clara HS; Santa Clara, CA; (2); 4/400; Spanish Clb; Speech Tm; Band; Drill Tm; Mrchg Band; Orch; Pep Band; Diving; Swmmng; Wrstlng; Santa Clara U; Law.

ZOFCIN, CHRISTA M; Loretto HS; Roseville, CA; (1); Church Yth Grp; VP Frsh Cls; VP Soph Cls; Var Tennis; High Hon Roll; Hon Roll; NEDT Awd; Frdy Nght Live Clb; On Site Recruitment; Young Repblcns; Stanford U; Law.

ZOGG, SAMANTHA; University San Diego HS; San Diego, CA; (2); Church Yth Grp; Cmnty Wkr; Drama Clb; Hosp Aide; Ski Clb; SADD; Thesps; School Play; VP Soph Cls; Rep Stu Cncl; HOBY; Diary Of Anne Frank San Diego Jr Theatre; Schlrshp Old Globe; Sci.

ZOLFAGARI, RAMIN; Taft HS; Woodland Hills, CA; (2); VP Chess Clb; German Clb; High Hon Roll; Hon Roll; Prfct Atten Awd; Spanish NHS; UCLA; Dental.

ZOLLER, ANGIE; Colusa HS; Colusa, CA; (3); 11/100; Art Clb; Church Yth Grp; 4-H; Letterman Clb; Pep Clb; Red Cross Aide; Band; Jazz Band; Mrchg Band; Orch; Amer Cancer Soc Plaque; Amer Air Resources Bd Awd For Sci Project; Amer Lung Assn Awd For Sci Project; Chico ST; Comm Art.

ZOLLER, TIMOTHY L; Elsinore HS; Lake Elsinore, CA; (3); 25/500; Church Yth Grp; Var Crs Cntry; JV Trk; Hon Roll; Music.

ZOMETA, EVELYN; St Michaels HS; Los Angeles, CA; (2); French Clb; Math Tm; Spanish Clb; SADD; Flag Corp; Bsktbl; Vllybl; Hon Roll; SCROC Banking; Los Angeles City Coll; Accntng.

ZOMISKY, RAMIE; Hoover HS; San Diego, CA; (4); 34/304; JCL; Key Clb; Sec NFL; Scholastic Bowl; Treas Service Clb; High Hon Roll; Hon Roll; NHS; San Diego Jr Miss First Rnnr-Up 90; Rotary Yth Ldrshp Awd 89; Auburn U; Aerospace Engrng.

ZONCA, SARAH R; Mira Loma HS; Sacramento, CA; (3); 59/280; Cmnty Wkr; Dance Clb; Drama Clb; GAA; Intnl Clb; Spanish Clb; Chorus; Rep Frsh Cls; Rep Soph Cls; Sec Jr Cls; UC Santa Cruz.

ZOOK, ANGELA C; Simi Valley HS; Simi Valley, CA; (3); 57/665; Art Clb; Teachers Aide; NHS; Bus Admin.

ZOQUE, KAREEM; Don Bosco Technical Inst; Walnut, CA; (3); JV Var Bsbl; Bsbl Most Imprvd Plyr; Golden Tiger Awd; Princ List 87-90; Ed.

ZORDILA, EMIL M; William Workman HS; La Puente, CA; (3); 5/260; Band; Drm Mjr(t); Mrchg Band; VP Soph Cls; Tennis; Hon Roll; Prfct Atten Awd; Pres Acad Fit Awd; Philosophy.

ZORDILLA, EMIL; William Workman HS; La Puente, CA; (3); 6/250; Ski Clb; Spanish Clb; Band; Drm Mjr(t); Mrchg Band; VP Frsh Cls; VP Soph Cls; Tennis; Hon Roll; Prfct Atten Awd; Psych.

ZORNOW, JENNIFER L; Clairemont HS; San Diego, CA; (3); 11/270; Pres Model UN; School Play; Co-Ed Nwsp; Lit Mag; High Hon Roll; Pres Acad Fit Awd; Rotary Awd; Sem Acad Pgm Pres; CSF; Amnesty Intl; Jrnlsm.

ZOROGHLIAN, ANITA; La Canada HS; La Canada, CA; (3); English Clb; Key Clb; Math Clb; Mu Alpha Theta; Science Clb; Chorus; Pres Jr Cls; Swmmng; NHS; California Scholarship Federation Memer; Ice Skating; College; Medicine.

ZORYAN, KEVORK; Notre Dame HS; Tarzana, CA; (4); 14/248; Church Yth Grp; Letterman Clb; Varsity Clb; Band; Drm Mjr(t); Mrchg Band; Lit Mag; Stu Cncl; JV Var Swmmng; High Hon Roll; Piano; Natl Hnr Roll & St Fnlst; Water Polo JV, Vrsty; Avid Bsbl Card Collector; U S CA; Bus Mngmnt.

ZOUNAIOTIS, TINA; Whittier Christian HS; La Habra, CA; (2); Church Yth Grp; Drama Clb; VP Soph Cls; JV Bsktbl; JV Vllybl; Hon Roll.

ZOUNATIOTIS, JIMMY; Whittier Christian HS; La Habra, CA; (2); Church Yth Grp; Hon Roll; JV Vllybl; Arch.

ZUBER, JILL M; Rio Mesa HS; Camarillo, CA; (3); 6/369; Pres FCA; Hosp Aide; Varsity Clb; Var Bsktbl; JV Crs Cntry; Hon Roll; Opt Clb Awd; CSF; Civil Air Patrl, Mitchill & Earhart Awds; Point Loma CA; Comp Sci.

ZUBKO, KATE C; Rim Of The World HS; Cedar Glen, CA; (1); 1/473; Church Yth Grp; Cmnty Wkr; Debate Tm; Model UN; Spanish Clb; Off Frsh Cls; VP Soph Cls; DAR Awd; Hon Roll; NHS; CSF; Prof Dancer.

ZUBRICKY, SUSANNA E; Etna Union HS; Etna, CA; (1); Church Yth Grp; FFA; Letterman Clb; School Play; Sec Treas Frsh Cls; Rep Stu Cncl; Hon Roll; Pres Acad Fit Awd; Local & CA St Spelling Cmptns; Writers Clb; Pediatric Med.

ZUCCARELLI, CARA N; Monterey Bay Acad; Grand Terrace, CA; (4); Cmnty Wkr; Drama Clb; Ski Clb; Teachers Aide; Chorus; School Play; Nwsp; Gym; Hon Roll; Pres Acad Fit Awd; Pacific Union Coll; Engl.

ZUK, CARY E; Canyon HS; Canyon Country, CA; (1); Acpl Chr; Hon Roll; U Of CA Los Angeles; Phy.

ZUKERMAN, VICTORIA; Brea Olinda HS; Brea, CA; (1); 2/360; Intnl Clb; Key Clb; Speech Tm; Hist Temple Yth Grp; Chorus; School Musical; High Hon Roll; Jr NHS; Dance; Intrct Clb; Tutoring.

ZUL, JOSE; Santa Ana HS; Santa Ana, CA; (3); Latin Clb; Office Aide; Santiago Coll.

ZULIM, BECKY D; Clovis HS; Clovis, CA; (2); Church Yth Grp; SADD; Hon Roll; Vet.

ZULIM, MICHELLE; Mc Lane HS; Clovis, CA; (1); JV Debate Tm; VP Frsh Cls; Var Cheerldng; JV Swmmng; Harvard; Pre-Law.

ZULUAGA, ANGELA M; Burlingame HS; Millbrae, CA; (3); Computer Clb; Drama Clb; Math Clb; Spanish Clb; School Play; Stage Crew; Crs Cntry; USF; Brdcstng Arts.

ZULUETA, LISA; Capistrano Valley Christian HS; Mission Viejo, CA; (2); 8/62; Church Yth Grp; Stat Socr; JV Vllybl; Hon Roll; CA Schlrshp Fdrtn; UC Davis.

ZULVETA, VERONICA; Azusa HS; Azusa, CA; (3); 4/275; Drama Clb; Teachers Aide; Swing Chorus; Fld Hcky; High Hon Roll; NHS; Pres Acad Fit Awd.

ZUMWALT, MICHELLE; Hesperia HS; Hesperia, CA; (1); Church Yth Grp; JV Tennis; Cit Awd; High Hon Roll; Hon Roll.

ZUNDEL, MICHELLE I; La Sierra HS; Riverside, CA; (2); Church Yth Grp; FBLA; Teachers Aide; JV Tennis; Hon Roll; FBLA Sec; Chrch Yth Grp Sec & Pres; Sftbl; Brigham Young U; Ed.

ZUNG, JONATHAN; Mills HS; Millbrae, CA; (2); Cmnty Wkr; Band; Jazz Band; Pep Band; Rep Frsh Cls; Capt Swmmng; High Hon Roll; Hon Roll; Pres Acad Fit Awd; Aeronautics Club; Arch.

ZUNIGA, ANDREA G; Roosevelt HS Magnet; Los Angeles, CA; (2); Cmnty Wkr; Pep Clb; Pres Frsh Cls; Cit Awd; Hon Roll; Prfct Atten Awd; Schlrshp Awd; Ctznshp Hnr Roll; Conf Cmmtte Clb; T V Brdcstng.

ZUNIGA, JENNIFER; Mira Mesa HS; San Diego, CA; (2); Church Yth Grp; Spanish Clb; School Play; JV Bsktbl; JV Sftbl; JV Var Vllybl; Cit Awd; High Hon Roll; Hispanic Intl Pride Clb Treas; CA Schlstc Fed; Prin 4.0 Clb.

ZUNIGA, JENNIFER L; Hiram Johnson West Campus HS; Sacramento, CA; (2); 5/182; Math Tm; Hon Roll; NHS; Cert Hnr Span,Sci,Geo,Eng; Phys Sci.

ZUNIGA, JOANNE; San Benito HS; Hollister, CA; (4); 35/229; Cmnty Wkr; Pep Clb; Treas Ski Clb; Teachers Aide; Stu Cncl; Capt Cheerldng; Hon Roll; Yth Ftbl Chrldrs Coach; Ftbl Hmcmng Qn; UC Santa Barbara; Pblc Admin.

ZUNIGA, JULIO C; Coachella Valley HS; Coachella, CA; (3); Church Yth Grp; FBLA; Teachers Aide; Chorus; Church Choir; School Play; Swmmng; Vllybl.

ZUNIGA, LAURA; Lompoc SR HS; Lompoc, CA; (3); SADD; Teachers Aide; Drill Tm; Cheerldng; Annl Chicano Latino Yth Ldrshp Conf 89; Upward Bnd; Az ST U; Law.

ZUNIGA, LUZ E; Sweetwater HS; National City, CA; (2); Scholastic Bowl; Band; Jazz Band; Mrchg Band; JV Sftbl; Cit Awd; Hon Roll; Prfct Atten Awd; Pres Acad Fit Awd; Hnrs Clb Pres; San Diego ST U; Educ.

ZUNIGA, MACEDONIO M; Mt Pleasant HS; San Jose, CA; (1); Hon Roll; Pilot.

ZUNIGA, RODOLFO F; Inglewood HS; Inglewood, CA; (4); Fld Hcky; Ftbl; Wt Lftg; Hon Roll; Print Shope; Sherrifs Explore Acad; Santa Monica JC; Ntrlst.

ZUNIGA, TERI; San Marcos HS; Santa Barbara, CA; (3); 56/412; Key Clb; Service Clb; Ski Clb; SADD; VP Frsh Cls; Rep Soph Cls; Rep Jr Cls; Var Cheerldng; Var Sftbl; JV Vllybl; Cmmssnr Orgnztns ASB HS; Female Athlt Yr Sftbl Grtr Santa Barbara Area; Schlr Athlt Girls Sftbl 90; Law.

ZUNO, ADOLFO; Caliexico HS; Calexico, CA; (3); Intrml Bsktbl; Var Ftbl; Var Trk; U Of CA San Diego; Auto Mech.

ZUNO, GABRIELA; Calexico HS; Calexico, CA; (2); Church Yth Grp; Rep Soph Cls; French Hon Soc; GATE Pgm; U Of CA San Diego; Dntst.

ZURABYAN, SUZANNA; Glendale HS; Glendale, CA; (3); Art Clb; School Musical; Var Tennis; Hon Roll; Honor Cert In Recognition Of Super Achvt; Attorney.

ZUVELA, JANET B; St Anthonys HS; Long Beach, CA; (3); Cmnty Wkr; Girl Scts; Letterman Clb; Band; Mrchg Band; Orch; Pep Band; Comp Sci.

ZVINAKIS, JENNIFER; Encinal HS; Alameda, CA; (4); 22/222; Teachers Aide; School Musical; Swmmng; Hon Roll; CSF; Vol Wrkr Vet Hosp; UC Davis; Vet Med.

ZWANZIGER, SARA; Fairfield HS; Fairfield, CA; (1); Rep Frsh Cls; High Hon Roll; Hon Roll; CA ST U Sacramento; Spec Ed.

ZWEBER, ANDREW; Warren HS; Downey, CA; (3); Church Yth Grp; FBLA; Letterman Clb; Mu Alpha Theta; Teachers Aide; Varsity Clb; VP Frsh Cls; Pres Soph Cls; Off Sr Cls; Stu Cncl; Stu Of Month.

ZWIBEL, DAWN E; Grossmont HS; El Cajon, CA; (1); Church Yth Grp; Dance Clb; Drama Clb; JA; High Hon Roll; Hon Roll; School Play; Schl Of Performing Arts.

ZWICK, HEIDI; Lodi Acad; Lodi, CA; (3); Church Yth Grp; Ski Clb; Spanish Clb; Band; Chorus; Off Jr Cls; Prfct Atten Awd; Temperance Spch Oration 2nd Pl; PUC Invtnl Band Fstvl; Pacific Union Coll; Home Ec.

ZYLSTRA, CHRISTOPHER J; Cabrillo HS; Indian Harbour Bc, FL; (2); Church Yth Grp; Band; Pep Band; Rptr Nwsp; Rptr Yrbk; Var JV Swmmng; Surfing & Wrtng; FL Inst Tech; Marine Bio Teach.

ZYROMSKI, LAURA R; Analy HS; Sebastopol, CA; (2); 12/246; Church Yth Grp; Letterman Clb; Service Clb; Acpl Chr; Lit Mag; Var Bsktbl; Capt JV Vllybl; High Hon Roll; Piano; Schlr Athlt Awds For Vllybll & Bsktbll.

ZYROMSKI, MICHELLE VALERIE; Analy HS; Sebastopol, CA; (4); 8/215; Church Yth Grp; Cmnty Wkr; Letterman Clb; Ed Yrbk; Stu Cncl; Var JV Bsktbl; JV Var Vllybl; Pres Acad Fit Awd; N Coast Section Schlr-Athl; Piano; U Of San Diego.

ZYSKOWSKI, PAUL J; Redwood Christian HS; San Leandro, CA; (3); 5/45; Am Leg Boys St; Church Yth Grp; Treas Sr Cls; Var Tennis; High Hon Roll; Hon Roll; JETS Awd; CSF; U 71; Cmptr Engr.

GUAM/AMERICAN SAMOA

ABIADOR, STEVE; John F Kennedy HS; Tamuning, GU; (2); Math Tm; Band; JV Vllybl; High Hon Roll; Jr NHS; CVC 89-90; Top 10 Awd 89; CA ST U Berkeley.

ACOSTA, DAHLIA B; John F Kennedy HS; Agana, GU; (4); Church Yth Grp; Math Clb; Treas VP Science Clb; Off Frsh Cls; Var Crs Cntry; Var Tennis; Var Trk; NHS; MVP Trck & Flds 89; Athlt Mnth; Mst Insprtnl Plyr Tnns; Filipino Clb; Crs Cntry Clb; Tnns Clb; U Of HI Manoa; Bus Admin.

ADAMOS, DEBORAH R; John F Kennedy HS; Agana, GU; (3); Church Yth Grp; Spanish Clb; Rep Stu Cncl; Var Bsktbl; JV Vllybl; Hon Roll; Jr NHS; Vllybl Clb VP.

AGUON, THERESE D J; George Washington HS; Sinajana, GU; (3); Church Yth Grp; FBLA; JA; Office Aide; Teachers Aide; Church Choir; Stu Cncl; Hon Roll; Jr NHS; U Of Guam; Nurse.

ALBRIGHT, SHANNON; John F Kenendy HS; FPO San Francisc, CA; (4); Stage Crew; Cit Awd; Hon Roll; Naturlst Clb; Schl Recogntn Golden St Exam For Geom; Attnd Sr Cls Mtngs & Projects; U Of CA San Diego; Marine Ag.

ALFELOR, KAREN; John F Kennedy HS; Dededo, GU; (3); Treas Church Yth Grp; JA; Treas Science Clb; Spanish Clb; Band; Trk; Hon Roll.

ALVARADO, KATHERINE; Simon Sanchez HS; A A F B Yigo, GU; (3); Ed Nwsp; Lit Mag; Ftbl; Hon Roll; Poetry Publshd Isl Wide Publctn Slctd Pieces Poetry; U Of Guam; Jrnlsm.

ANDRADA, FELY; John F Kennedy HS; Dededo, GU; (2); Drama Clb; Math Clb; Band; Pep Band; Bus Mgmt.

APILADO, VERA V; John F Kennedy HS; Dededo, GU; (2); Church Yth Grp; Pediatric Nrs.

AQUINO, DANIEL; John F Kennedy HS; Tamuning, GU; (3); Math Clb; ROTC; JV Crs Cntry; Var Trk; Hon Roll; Rnng Clb; Mech Engr.

AQUINO, MADELEINE; John F Kennedy HS; Dededo, GU; (3); Cmnty Wkr; Hosp Aide; JA; Band; Pep Band; Jpns Clb; Bus.

AQUINO, MARIA DOROTHY A; John F Kennedy HS; Tamuning, GU; (4); Drama Clb; Hosp Aide; Office Aide; Chorus; Tennis; U Of CA; Med Tech.

ARANAS, JOEL C; John F Kennedy HS; Tamuning, GU; (4); Boy Scts; Math Clb; Science Clb; Church Choir; Off Sr Cls; Bsktbl; U Of Guam; Arch.

ASAHAN, JOAN LESLIE J; John F Kennedy HS; Dededo, GU; (4); 36/320; Office Aide; Spanish Clb; SADD; Teachers Aide; Band; Chorus; Treas Yrbk; Hon Roll; Sr Coronation Royal Ct Co-Chairperson; Spnsh Prom Royal Ct Co-Chairperson; Duty Free Shoppers Ltd; U GU; Educ.

BAGALAWIS, UNICHELLE; John F Kennedy HS; Dededo, GU; (3); DECA; Var Tennis; Marquette U; Civil Engrng.

BALAGTAS, PRUDENCIO S; John F Kennedy HS; Dededo, GU; (3); 11/400; Cmnty Wkr; Computer Clb; Hosp Aide; JA; Scholastic Bowl; Spanish Clb; Band; Jazz Band; Mrchg Band; Pep Band; UC San Diego; Med.

BALDEVARONA, JANE F; John F Kennedy HS; Dededo, GU; (2); Pres Church Yth Grp; Church Choir; Sec Frsh Cls; Sec Soph Cls; Rep Stu Cncl; Hnrs Wrld Hist 89-90; Island Ldrshp 88-89; Bus Mgmt.

BALDWIN, CYRUS A; Tinian HS; Tinian Island M P, GU; (3); 2/13; FBLA; FFA; Natl Beta Clb; Science Clb; Rep Jr Cls; Rep Stu Cncl; Var Crs Cntry; Var Bausch & Lomb Sci Awd; Marianas Isl Sci Fair Chem 1st Pl; 30 Km Bike A Thon Wnnr; Aviation.

BENAVENTE, LIANA; Simon Sanchez HS; Tamuning, GU; (3); Church Yth Grp; French Clb; Rep Jr Cls; Hon Roll; Drug Free Club Treas; Chamorro Club.

BENITEZ, LOUVILLE; Simon A Sanchez HS; Dededo, GU; (4); 13/232; Rep Sr Cls; Treas Stu Cncl; JV Bsktbl; Var Pom Pon; Cit Awd; High Hon Roll; NHS; Prfct Atten Awd; Filipino Clb UFSA; Schlstc Achvt Awds; U Of GU; Polit Sci.

BLAS, PETER; John F Kennedy HS; Piti, GU; (4); ROTC; Var Capt Bsbl; Intrml Bsktbl; Score Keeper; Wt Lftg; High Hon Roll; Hon Roll; Creative Artwrk; Cal ST U; Comm Graphics.

BONTO, ARNEL; John F Kennedy HS; Tamuning, GU; (2); Var Tennis; Hon Roll; Elec Engrng.

CALMA, RICHARD; Simon Sanchez HS; Tamuning, GU; (4); 9/232; Church Yth Grp; Letterman Clb; Band; Yrbk; Rep Frsh Cls; Sec Soph Cls; Rep Jr Cls; Sec Sr Cls; Mgr(s); Var Capt Socr; All Island Soccer Team Defense; Univ Of Guam Merit Schlrshp; Simon Sanchez HS Overall Sci Fair Wnnr; Cal ST Long Beach; Cvl Engr.

CARINA, JAY A; Simon A Sanchez HS; Barrigada, GU; (3); 4-H; Band; Jazz Band; School Play; Var Socr; High Hon Roll; Hist Jr NHS; Close Up Clb; Guam Territrl Band & Jazz Band; Spcl Olympe Vlntr; Arch.

CARLOS, GLENN; Harvest Christian Acad; Tamuning, GU; (1); 2/24; Church Yth Grp; Dance Clb; Drama Clb; Natl Beta Clb; School Play; Variety Show; Hon Roll; Pres Acad Fit Awd; JV Var Ftbl; JV Vllybl; Duke U; Med.

CARREON, SALLY; John F Kennedy SR HS; Agana, GU; (4); Church Yth Grp; Chorus; Church Choir; Treas Rep Frsh Cls; Pres Stu Cncl; JV Bsktbl; Vllybl; NHS; High Hon Roll; Jr NHS; Bwlng Clb; Top 10 Awd; Mock Trl Team.

CASTANO, SUZANNE; John F Kennedy HS; Tamuning, GU; (1); Library Aide; Office Aide; Rptr Nwsp; Hon Roll; NHS; Prfct Atten Awd; Pres Acad Fit Awd; Philippine Assoc Clb; Frgn Clb; Doc Of Med.

CASTILLO, ARLENE MARQUEZ; John Fitzgerlad Kennedy HS; Kaiser Dededo, GU; (4); Teachers Aide; Prfct Atten Awd; International Bus Coll; Acctg.

CASTRO, ROSEANNA T G; John F Kennedy HS; Dededo, GU; (3); JA; Sec Jr Cls; High Hon Roll; Hon Roll; Jr NHS; NHS; Pres Acad Fit Awd; Pres Schlr; Church Yth Grp; Cmnty Wkr; Close Up Prtcpnt Washignton DC 90; Mt St Marys Schlrshp; U Of CA Berkeley; Pre-Law.

CEPEDA, FRANZMARIE R M; Notre Dame HS; Sinajana, GU; (4); 3/74; Yrbk; Pres Frsh Cls; Var Socr; Var Trk; High Hon Roll; Jr NHS; NHS; Pres Acad Fit Awd; Spanish NHS; Socl Cmmtte Treas; Regis Coll; Med.

CERALDE, RAY M; Simon A Sanchez HS; Tamuning, GU; (4); 3/280; Capt Quiz Bowl; ROTC; Capt Scholastic Bowl; Spanish Clb; Drill Tm; Rep Stu Cncl; High Hon Roll; NHS; Pres Acad Fit Awd; Voice Dem Awd; Natl Army ROTC Schlrshp; Soc Of Amer Military Engrs Schlrshp; 1st Pl Best Ofcr HSROTC Guam; U Of WA; Cvl Engrng.

CHANG, EASY P; John F Kennedy HS; Tamuning, GU; (3); Cmnty Wkr; 4-H; Scholastic Bowl; Rptr Nwsp; Var Tennis; JV Trk; JV Vllybl; Intrml Wt Lftg; Hon Roll; 4-H Arch Tech Clb; Guam Meml Hosp Vol Pgm; Surfing; CA ST San Diego; Bus.

CHARGUALAF, EDWARD B; John F Kennedy HS; Tamuning, GU; (3); Mrchg Band; Orch; Pep Band; School Musical; Gov Hon Prg Awd; High Hon Roll; U CO Boulder; Arch.

CHENG, WENDY; Harvest Christian Acad; Agana, GU; (1); 1/24; Natl Beta Clb; Chorus; Capt Socr; Intrml Vllybl; Hon Roll; Music Clb; Harvard; Law.

CHOU, CINDY H; John F Kennedy HS; Tamuning, GU; (2); JA; Red Cross Aide; Science Clb; Spanish Clb; Off Soph Cls; Off Jr Cls; Trk; Hon Roll; NHS; U CA; Med Tech.

CHOU, JULIE HUANG; John F Kennedy HS; Tamuning, GU; (4); 2/220; JA; Pres VP Science Clb; Trk; NHS; Japanese Clb Treas; Top 10 Awd; Chinese Clb; Accntng.

CHOU, PAN; John F Kennedy HS; Tamuning, GU; (4); 4-H; JA; Red Cross Aide; Pres Science Clb; Ed Nwsp; Var Trk; Var Vllybl; Treas NHS; Nrthest All Star Bsbl Team; Elec Engr.

CHOU, STEVE; John F Kennedy HS; Tamuning, GU; (4); 16/342; Cmnty Wkr; Debate Tm; Hosp Aide; JA; Quiz Bowl; Red Cross Aide; Scholastic Bowl; Science Clb; Chorus; Nwsp; Guam Yth Congrs; Japan Clb; Holiday Hotline; U Of WA Seattle.

CRUZ, JUDITH T; John F Kennedy HS; Tamuning, GU; (1); Teachers Aide.

DE JESUS, LUCELE; John F Kennedy HS; Dededo, GU; (3); JV Crs Cntry; JV Socr; JV Trk; Acctng.

DELIQUINA, GERALDINE; John F Kennedy HS; Dededo, GU; (4); English Clb; French Clb; Chorus; Rep Frsh Cls; Rep Soph Cls; Rep Jr Cls; Rep Sr Cls; Mgr(s); Mgr Wrstlng; Hon Roll; U Guam; Elem Tchr.

DIGMA, JULIUS; Harvest Christian Acad; Barrigada Hgts, GU; (4); 1/7; Church Yth Grp; Math Clb; Pres Natl Beta Clb; Chorus; Church Choir; Ed Nwsp; Yrbk; Intrml Bsktbl; Intrml Ftbl; Intrml Vllybl; A Clb Awd; Outstndng Stu Awd; Bob Jones U; Accntng.

DIMARUCUT, ALICIA; John F Kennedy SR HS; Tamuning, GU; (4); Church Yth Grp; Cmnty Wkr; JA; Office Aide; Science Clb; Ed Nwsp; VP Soph Cls; Stu Cncl; Jr NHS; NHS; Wrstlng Team Mgr; Wrstlng Club Treas; Dance Group Prfssnl; U CA Irvine; Engrng.

DIZON, ALVIN G; Simon A Sanchez HS; Dededo, GU; (4); 20/246; VP JA; Rptr Nwsp; Rptr Lit Mag; Sec Jr Cls; Rep Stu Cncl; Mgr(s); Var Socr; High Hon Roll; NHS; Yth Cngrs 89-90; Close Up VP; Mst Imprvd Plyr Sccr 88-89; Psych.

DULOS MORTERA, CYNTHIA MARIE; John F Kennedy HS; Tamuning, GU; (4); Aud/Vis; Office Aide; Chorus; Rep Frsh Cls; Rep Jr Cls; Rep Sr Cls; Rep Stu Cncl; Hon Roll; Tourism Clb; Intl Business Coll; Bus Mgmt.

EDQUILANE, DON ANTONIO ADA; Guam CC HS; GMF Barrigada, GU; (3); Church Yth Grp; FBLA; Off Soph Cls; Hon Roll; Top Of Shop Awd Mrktng Edctn 88-89; Bio Awd 88-89; Bus.

ELOMINA, EDISON VICENTE; John F Kennedy HS; Dededo, GU; (4); Crs Cntry; Socr; Trk; JFK Running Clb; HI U Manoa; Elec Engr.

EMRALINO, SIMONETE; John F Kennedy HS; GMF, GU; (4); 8/330; Science Clb; Spanish Clb; SADD; Ed Yrbk; High Hon Roll; Hon Roll; Jr NHS; NHS; Filipino Stu Assn; Oakland U MI; Med/Lab.

ENDO, MIE; John F Kennedy HS; Tamuning, GU; (2); GAA; JV Var Mgr(s); Var Sftbl; JV Intrml Vllybl; CVC.

FORTES, DON; John F Kennedy HS; Dededo, GU; (4); 35/334; Church Yth Grp; Office Aide; Spanish Clb; Varsity Clb; Wrstlng; Electronics.

FRANQUEZ, JENNY B; John F Kennedy HS; Mangilao, GU; (1); Church Yth Grp; JV Cheerldng; Fshn Dsgnr.

GARCIA, ERNIE; John F Kennedy HS; Sinajana, GU; (3); JA; Science Clb; School Play; Treas Lit Mag; Var Tennis; Cit Awd; Jr NHS; Prfct Atten Awd; Japenese Clb; Tnns Clb Treas; Creative Wrtng Treas; Bus.

GARRIDO, JOSHUA; John F Kennedy HS; Dededo, GU; (2); Church Yth Grp; Band; Mrchg Band; Pep Band; Ftbl; Hon Roll.

GATMEN, DAISY; John F Kennedy HS; Dededo, GU; (2); Sec Drama Clb; JA; Rep SADD; Chorus; School Play; Rptr Nwsp; Sec Stu Cncl; Sftbl; Tennis; Jr NHS; Seattle U; Jrnlsm.

GAULT, DIANA CHRISTINE; John F Kennedy HS; Agana, GU; (4); Cmnty Wkr; GAA; Varsity Clb; Chorus; Bsktbl; Crs Cntry; Mgr(s); Socr; Csmetic Srgn.

GOLEZ, MANUELITO BAGAS; John F Kennedy HS; Agana, GU; (4); 9/335; ROTC; Scholastic Bowl; Science Clb; Spanish Clb; SADD; Band; Church Choir; Treas Jr Cls; Stu Cncl; Trk; Filipino Stu Assn Pres; Mock Trial; Close Up; Cvl Engrng.

GOMEZ, MILAGROS ARLENE D; John F Kennedy HS; Dededo, GU; (4); Letterman Clb; Spanish Clb; SADD; Chorus; Ed Nwsp; JV Var Crs Cntry; JV Var Trk; Cit Awd; Hon Roll; Prfct Atten Awd; John F Kennedy Running Clb Treas; Running Clb Races Volunteer; Engl Awd; Medcl.

GRIFFIN, LYDA; John F Kennedy HS; Dededo, GU; (2); Church Yth Grp; Cmnty Wkr; Drama Clb; Church Choir; Mock Trial 89-90; Peer Counselor; Criminal Justice.

GUERRERO, JENNIFER M T; John F Kennedy HS; Dededo, GU; (4); 26/320; Church Yth Grp; Pres SADD; Band; Pep Band; Pres Frsh Cls; JV Cheerldng; Engl Awd 87; Excell Awd 87; Cert Appreciation Spec Olympics Vol 88; Marquette U; Engrng.

GUTIERREZ, ELLYN C; John F Kennedy HS; Tamuning, GU; (3); Vllybl; Civil Engrng.

HARPEL, JOHN C; John F Kennedy HS; Silverdale, WA; (2); Church Yth Grp; Band; Pep Band; High Hon Roll.

HERNANDEZ, JOJUANA MARIE; John F Kennedy HS; Dedeo, GU; (1); Church Yth Grp; 4-H; Red Cross Aide; SADD; Band; Church Choir; Mrchg Band; 4-H Awd; High Hon Roll; Jr NHS; Chamorro Clb; U GU; Music Tchr.

HERRERA, EUGENE; Oceanview HS; Tamuning, GU; (4); 11/146; Bsktbl; Ftbl; High Hon Roll; Hon Roll; NHS; Pres Schlr; Otis Parsons; Commercial Dsgn.

HIDALGO, ROMUALDO Z; Simon Sanchez HS; Dededo, GU; (3); 8/283; Letterman Clb; Band; School Play; Var Crs Cntry; Var Socr; Var Trk; Var JV Vllybl; High Hon Roll; Hon Roll; NHS; Rookie Of Yr 87-88; 1st Pl Overall Schl Sci Fair 89-90; Goucher Coll; Comp Sci.

HUANG, JIMMY K; John F Kennedy HS; Tamuning, GU; (3); Debate Tm; 4-H; Math Clb; Science Clb; Tennis; MA Inst Tech; Elec Engrng.

IRISH, TOTSUMA; Guam Adventist Acad; Yona, GU; (4); Church Yth Grp; 4-H; Teachers Aide; Rptr Nwsp; Pres Jr Cls; Treas Stu Cncl; Socr; Ntl Merit SF; Walla Walla Ccoll; Engr.

IZUMIHARA, RYAN; Harvest Christian Acad; FPO Sn Francisco, CA; (3); 2/12; Chess Clb; Church Yth Grp; Treas Natl Beta Clb; School Play; Pres Soph Cls; Rep Stu Cncl; Capt Ftbl; Vllybl; High Hon Roll; Prfct Atten Awd; Sthrn CA U; Engrng.

JARA, JANE; John F Kennedy HS; Dededo, GU; (2); Drama Clb; Math Clb; Sec Band; Pep Band; Variety Show; High Hon Roll; Hon Roll; Islandwide Hnr Band 90; Commnctns.

JENSEN, CHRISTY; John F Kennedy HS; Murray, UT; (4); 9/435; Pres Sec Church Yth Grp; French Clb; Pres Rep Frsh Cls; Var L Crs Cntry; Var Trk; High Hon Roll; NHS; Pres Acad Fit Awd; Freedom Fndtns Yth Ldrshp Conf-Vly Forge; Mock Trial-Witness/Lawyer; BYU.

JOCSON, ANGELITA MADRILEJOS; Simon Sanchez HS; Dededo, GU; (3); 6/283; Band; Jazz Band; Mrchg Band; Pep Band; Yrbk; High Hon Roll; Hon Roll; Jr NHS; Hnr Band 88-89; United Filipino Stu Assn 87-90; Engrng.

JONES-RONQUILLO, CINDY; John F Kennedy HS; Tamuning, GU; (1); Jr NHS; U Of HI; Pedtrcn.

JOSE, CAROLINE B; John F Kennedy HS; Tamuning, GU; (4); Church Yth Grp; Drama Clb; Office Aide; Spanish Clb; SADD; Chorus; The A Club; Intl Bus Coll Guam; Acctng.

JOSE, ROSALINDA; John F Kennedy HS; Tamuning, GU; (2); Church Yth Grp; Achvrs Club.

JUNIO, DWIGHT F; John F Kennedy HS; Dededo, GU; (3); 5/420; Boy Scts; ROTC; Var Crs Cntry; Capt Var Trk; Capt Var Vllybl; High Hon Roll; Hon Roll; Jr NHS; NHS; Eagle Sct Awd; Outstndng Cadet Of Yr Air Force JROTC; US Air Force Acad; Engrng.

KAZUMA, EMERLEEN D; John F Kennedy HS; Tamuning, GU; (1); Band; NHS; U Of HI.

KIM, ANDREW; Harvest Christian Acad; Agana, GU; (2); 2/24; Chess Clb; Natl Beta Clb; School Play; Rep Frsh Cls; Var Stat Ftbl; Var Vllybl; High Hon Roll; Hon Roll; Prfct Atten Awd.

KIO, DAI DIM P; Simon Sanchez HS; Yigo, GU; (3); 14/250; Church Yth Grp; Cmnty Wkr; Spanish Clb; Pres Varsity Clb; Rep Frsh Cls; Rep Soph Cls; Rep Jr Cls; JV Bsktbl; Var Capt Crs Cntry; Var Capt Tennis; U NC; Med.

KONG, MIN KI; John F Kennedy HS; Tamuning, GU; (3); Rptr Nwsp; Korean Teen Clb.

KOSH, MARGARET A; John F Kennedy HS; Agat, GU; (4); 33/500; Chorus; Socr; Var Capt Sftbl; Trk; Var Capt Vllybl; NHS; Sftbl All Island Pitcher 88-89; Track & Fld 1st Pl Triple Jmp 88-89; Vllybl All Island Plyr 89-90; Bus.

KRELL, TIFFANY RENEE; John F Kennedy HS; Agana, GU; (3); Cmnty Wkr; Drama Clb; French Clb; German Clb; Girl Scts; School Play; Score Keeper; Vllybl; Cit Awd; High Hon Roll; Stanford; Bus Admin.

KUO, YEA ZONG; John F Kennedy HS; Agana, GU; (2); Drama Clb; French Clb; Math Clb; Service Clb; Chorus; High Hon Roll; Jr NHS; Chns Clb; Aerontcs Engrng.

LAU, ANGEL; Harvest Christian Acad; Tamuning, GU; (2); 3/24; Drama Clb; Hosp Aide; Natl Beta Clb; School Play; High Hon Roll; Hon Roll; Prfct Atten Awd.

LAU, KUEN CHINE; John F Kennedy HS; Agana, GU; (3); 4-H; Hosp Aide; JA; Science Clb; JV Crs Cntry; Var Tennis; JV Trk; High Hon Roll; NHS; WA U; Acctng.

LAYGO, AGNES T; John F Kennedy HS; Agana, GU; (2); Nrsng.

LAYGO, MARIAM; John F Kennedy HS; Agana, GU; (4); 70/337; U Of Guam; Nursing.

LEE, FRANCES T; John F Kennedy HS; Dededo, GU; (4); 1/355; Drama Clb; FBLA; Hosp Aide; Pres Spanish Clb; Treas SADD; Off Frsh Cls; Off Soph Cls; Off Jr Cls; Off Sr Cls; High Hon Roll; Spanish Awd; Acctng Awd; U Of WA; Arch.

LEGASPI, MARLON V; John F Kennedy HS; Dededo, GU; (3); ROTC; Vllybl; Comp Pgrmmr.

LEYBLE-LUBAS, MARIBELLE ROSE; John F Kennedy HS; Dededo, GU; (2); Church Yth Grp; Dance Clb; Drama Clb; Math Clb; Variety Show; Off Frsh Cls; Off Soph Cls; Hon Roll; Jr NHS; Prfct Atten Awd; Acteens; Stu Mscl Tlnt Assoc-Japanese Cltrl Exchng; Dely MO Trip Korea; U WA; Microbio.

LIMTIACO, ANGELA; John F Kennedy HS; Agana, GU; (4); Church Yth Grp; Cmnty Wkr; Hon Roll.

LIMTIACO, STEPHANIE; John F Kennedy HS; Agana, GU; (3); Church Yth Grp; Cmnty Wkr; Teachers Aide; Hon Roll.

LIN, CHIA YU; John F Kennedy HS; Tamuning, GU; (2); 4-H; Hosp Aide; Math Clb; Red Cross Aide; Spanish Clb; Church Choir; Tennis; Gov Hon Prg Awd; Hon Roll; Pres Acad Fit Awd; Vldctrn Chinese Schl Gu; Gov Math Clb; Engineering.

LIN, YI-CHENG; Tinian HS; Tinian, GU; (2); 2/30; Science Clb; Nwsp; Yrbk; Hon Roll; Prfct Atten Awd; Sec Logo Cont 2nd Pl; Mietetsu Art Cont; Japanese Clb Stu Exchng; U CA; Fashion Dsgn.

LIQUETE, EMILIO; John F Kennedy HS; Dededo, GU; (3); Band; Tennis; Hon Roll; Cert Of Achvt Awd; U UT Salt Lake City; Law.

LIWAG, JOSEPH L; John F Kennedy HS; Dededo, GU; (1); 1/27; Band; MIT; Doctor.

LIZAMA, ELONA; John F Kennedy HS; Dededo, GU; (3); Church Yth Grp; JA; Science Clb; Spanish Clb; High Hon Roll; Hon Roll; Law.

LOPEZ, CHRISTINA; John F Kennedy HS; Dededo, GU; (1); Math Clb; Var L Crs Cntry; Var Socr; Hon Roll; 12th Pl Var Japan Kanto Plains Cross Cntry Champs 89-90; Harvard; Law.

LUSA, JESSICA A; Rota HS; Rota MP, GU; (3); 1/32; Cmnty Wkr; Office Aide; Rptr Nwsp; Treas Jr Cls; Cit Awd; High Hon Roll; Prfct Atten Awd; Brdcst Jrnlsm.

MANANSALA, ELADIO; John F Kennedy HS; Dededo, GU; (4); Teachers Aide; School Play; Var Crs Cntry; Var Capt Socr; Var Trk; Running Clb; Engrng.

MANGLONA, EVELYN; Tinian HS; Tinian, GU; (2); 4-H; Girl Scts; Science Clb; Rptr Nwsp; Yrbk; VP Sec Stu Cncl; Sftbl; Trk; Vllybl; Hon Roll; Lawyer.

MANGLONA, LOU CONNIE B; Tinian HS; Tinian Tt, GU; (3); Girl Scts; Science Clb; Rptr Nwsp; Yrbk; Sftbl; Vllybl; High Hon Roll; Hon Roll; Prfct Atten Awd; Drug Tsk Frce; Close-Up Fndtn; Gov Awd; Nurse.

MANTE, JENNIFER R; John F Kennedy HS; Agana, GU; (2); Rep Stu Cncl; Stat Mgr(s); JV Vllybl; High Hon Roll.

MANUEL, ELEANOR; John F Kennedy HS; Dededo, GU; (2); JA; Church Choir; Off Frsh Cls; VP Soph Cls; Hon Roll; Islnd Ldrshp Day-Yth Mnth; Cntrprt-Lt Neese; Wpns Offer NAS; Over All Co-Chrprsn; Swthrts Ball 90; News Brdcstr.

MATEO, SHIRLEY; John F Kennedy HS; Tamuning, GU; (3); JA; Red Cross Aide; Spanish Clb; Teachers Aide; VP Soph Cls; VP Sr Cls; Jr NHS; Island Ldrshp Rep Guam Cmnty Coll 89, Bureau Budgt/Mgmt Resources 90; U HI; Accntng.

MENDIOLA, ROSALIND; John F Kennedy HS; Dededo, GU; (2); Church Yth Grp; Hon Roll; Drug-Free Orgnztn.

MENO, FRANK S; Simon Sanchez HS; Dededo, GU; (3); Cmnty Wkr; Letterman Clb; Varsity Clb; Stage Crew; Var Crs Cntry; Var Vllybl; Hon Roll; Jr NHS; Prfct Atten Awd; Pres Acad Fit Awd; Syracuse U; Arch.

MOLINOS, CATHERINE H; John F Kennedy HS; Dededo, GU; (4); 51/346; Sec Church Yth Grp; Library Aide; Teachers Aide; Lit Mag; Mgr Jr NHS; Law.

MONTANO, MARILOU; John F Kennedy HS; Dededo, GU; (2); Cmnty Wkr; Drama Clb; SADD; Band; School Play; Bsktbl; Prfct Atten Awd.

MONZON, PAULINE; John F Kennedy HS; Dededo, GU; (3); Church Yth Grp; JA; Quiz Bowl; Science Clb; Spanish Clb; Off Jr Cls; Hon Roll; NHS; U CA San Diego; Sci.

MONZON, PHELIA; John F Kennedy HS; Dededo, GU; (2); Church Yth Grp; Math Clb; Quiz Bowl; Church Choir; Mgr Soph Cls; Hon Roll; Arts.

NABUA, MARYVILLE R; John F Kennedy HS; Tamuning, GU; (4); 77/399; Teachers Aide; Chorus; Yrbk; Hon Roll; Prfct Atten Awd; Nrsng.

NG, EDNA; John F Kennedy HS; Temple City, CA; (2); Sec Drama Clb; Math Clb; Band; Jazz Band; Pep Band.

NG, FANNY C; John F Kennedy HS; Agana, GU; (4); 102/334; 4-H; Spanish Clb; SADD; Chorus; Rptr Nwsp; Rep Stu Cncl; Mgr(s); Hon Roll; Mock Trial; U HI; Bus Mgmt.

NGUYEN, NHUNG THI; John F Kennedy HS; Dededo, GU; (1).

OLNAGAN, LEILANNIE C; John F Kennedy HS; G M F Barrigada, GU; (4); Hosp Aide; JA; Spanish Clb; SADD; Band; Sec Stu Cncl; Mck Trl; Spec Olympcs Vlntr.

OLNAGAN, LEO C; John F Kennedy HS; G M F Barrigada, GU; (1); Band; Chorus.

OPLE ORDEN, SHEILA ANITA; John F Kennedy HS; Dededo, GU; (4); Hosp Aide; Sec Spanish Clb; Sec SADD; Church Choir; Rep Jr Cls; JV Var Vllybl; High Hon Roll; Jr NHS; Pres NHS; Top Ten Awd; Christmas Ball Royal Princess 88-89; Jr Prom Royal Princess 88-89; Nrsg.

ORDEN, SHEILA ANITA; John F Kennedy HS; Dededo, GU; (4); #6 In Class; Hosp Aide; Sec Spanish Clb; Sec SADD; Church Choir; JV Var Vllybl; High Hon Roll; Jr NHS; Pres NHS; Pres Acad Fit Awd; St Francis Coll Nrsng Schlrshp; U Of Gaum Mrt Schlrshp Repnt; Sr Prom Baroness; Nurse.

ORDEN, VENUS J; John F Kennedy HS; Dededo, GU; (2); Church Choir; VP Frsh Cls; Stu Cncl; Var Vllybl; High Hon Roll; Hon Roll; Chamorro Vllybl Clb.

ORTEGA, AILEEN; John F Kennedy HS; Agana, GU; (2); Drama Clb; JA; Off Math Clb; Mgr Trk; Close Up Clb; Acad Challenge Bowl Team.

ORTEGA, DONNA V S; Simon Sanchez HS; Dededo, GU; (4); 1/260; Cmnty Wkr; Pres VP JA; Capt Scholastic Bowl; Lit Mag; Var Mgr(s); Var L Socr; High Hon Roll; Pres NHS; Ntl Merit SF; Val; Schl Advsry Cncl Stu Rep; Accreditation Team Process Cmmtte; Natl Trnmt Acadmc Exclnc Team Guam 88-90; Georgetown U; Med.

PARK, YOUNG KYUNG; John F Kennedy HS; Agana, GU; (4); VP Sec Church Yth Grp; Hosp Aide; Spanish Clb; Band; Church Choir; Hon Roll; Bus.

PEDRO, MARY C; John F Kennedy HS; Dededo, GU; (3); Hosp Aide; JA; Science Clb; Spanish Clb; SADD; Church Choir; School Play; Tennis; Jr NHS; Island Ldrshp Yth Day; Cmmtte Chrprsn Jr Prom 90; Commnctns.

PEREZ, MARIDEL R; John F Kennedy HS; Dededo, GU; (1); Educ.

PEREZ, MICHAEL R; John F Kennedy HS; Dededo, GU; (4); 19/355; Science Clb; Spanish Clb; Chorus; JV Crs Cntry; Var Capt Wrstlng; NHS; Wrstlng All Island Meet 1st Pl, 2nd Pl & 3rd Pl 87-89; Mst Likely Succeed 87-89; Columbia U; Elect Engrng.

QUERIMIT, RACHELLE MAE; John F Kennedy HS; Tamuning, GU; (2); U Of HI; Bus Mgmt.

QUEZADA, LYNN B; John F Kennedy HS; Dededo, GU; (4); JA; Science Clb; VP Spanish Clb; Pres Soph Cls; Rep Stu Cncl; Hist NHS; Close Up; Top Ten; Guam Ballet Arts Thtre; Lwyr.

QUINTANILLA, LADISA D; John F Kennedy HS; Dededo Guam, CA; (2); JA; Red Cross Aide; Science Clb; Band; Hon Roll; Comm.

QUINTANILLA, LEIA D; John F Kennedy HS; Dededo Guam, CA; (4); 3/330; JA; Red Cross Aide; Science Clb; Spanish Clb; Hon Roll; Jr NHS; JA VP Prsnnl & Corp Scrtry; A-Club Awd; E OR ST Coll; Bio.

RANOLA, HAZEL BABASA; John F Kennedy HS; Tamuning, GU; (2); Math Clb; Church Choir; Tennis; Hon Roll; NHS; Close Up Rep 90; Med.

READ, TANYA; Harvest Christian Acad; APO San Francisc, CA; (3); 1/10; Church Yth Grp; Natl Beta Clb; Chorus; Church Choir; School Play; Intrml Vllybl; High Hon Roll; Prfct Atten Awd; Guams Yth Cong; A-Clb; Bob Jones U; Crml Law.

REYES, JOSIE; John F Kennedy HS; Dededo, GU; (2); Church Yth Grp; Cmnty Wkr; Drama Clb; School Play; Mgr(s); Score Keeper; Socr; Prfct Atten Awd; Nrsng.

RIVO, DORALIA; John F Kennedy HS; Tamuning, GU; (3); GAA; SADD; Band; Drm Mjr(t); Rep Frsh Cls; Crs Cntry; Trk; Hon Roll; Prfct Atten Awd; Bowling; U Of HI.

ROGESS, KRISTINE; John F Kennedy HS; Agana, GU; (3); Church Yth Grp; Computer Clb; FBLA; Hosp Aide; JA; Chorus; Rep Frsh Cls; Rep Soph Cls; Stat Bsktbl; Mgr(s); Johns Hopkins U; Pdtrcs.

SABLAN, RAYMOND B; Tinian HS; Tinian, GU; (3); Boy Scts; Office Aide; Science Clb; Rptr Nwsp; Treas Stu Cncl; Cit Awd; Hon Roll; Prfct Atten Awd; Pres Acad Fit Awd; Prncpls Awd; Cls-Up Fndtn; Drg Tsk Frc; Bus Admin.

SAGUN, MARY ANN O; John F Kennedy HS; Dededo, GU; (4); Science Clb; Spanish Clb; SADD; Band; Treas Stu Cncl; Mock Trial; U Of GU; Accntnt.

SALVADOR, XENIE; John F Kennedy HS; Tamuning, GU; (1); Church Yth Grp; Sec Frsh Cls; Rep Stu Cncl; U GU; Accntnt.

SAN NICOLAS, MARTIN V; George Washington HS; Agana, GU; (2); Art Clb; Church Yth Grp; SADD; JV Bsktbl; Wt Lftg; Wrstlng; Hon Roll; U Of WA; Art.

SANTAYANA II, ALFREDO C; John F Kennedy HS; Gmf, GU; (2); Cmnty Wkr; Debate Tm; Drama Clb; VP Math Clb; Quiz Bowl; Scholastic Bowl; Teachers Aide; Band; Mrchg Band; Pep Band; Med.

SANTOS, ARLEEN MARIE SABLAN; John F Kennedy HS; Tamuning, GU; (1); Hon Roll; Jr NHS; Law.

SAPALARAN, ALAN; John F Kennedy HS; Dededo, GU; (4); 44/364; Drama Clb; Chorus; School Play; Ed Nwsp; Cit Awd; Hon Roll; Pres Acad Fit Awd; 3rd Annual Western Sts Yhth Trng Cmpltn; U Of Guam; Psych.

SHINOHARA, SAMUEL V; John F Kennedy HS; Dededo, GU; (2); Chorus; Off Soph Cls; JV Crs Cntry; JV Vllybl; CVC; CA Coll; Educ.

SOTIC, MARY JOY; John F Kennedy HS; Dededo, GU; (2); Church Yth Grp; Debate Tm; Treas Drama Clb; Sec Math Clb; Off Soph Cls; High Hon Roll; Top Ten Frshmn Yr; Bus Mgmnt.

TAI, YIN FEN CYNDI; John F Kennedy HS; G M F, GU; (4); 3/325; Capt Debate Tm; Drama Clb; Pres JA; Quiz Bowl; Rep Frsh Cls; Rep Soph Cls; Stu Cncl; Trk; Vllybl; High Hon Roll; Mock Trial; Denver U; Pre-Med.

TAITANO, MELISSA G; John F Kennedy HS; Tamuning, GU; (4); 3/2000; Church Yth Grp; Latin Clb; Pres Spanish Clb; Pres Treas Varsity Clb; Church Choir; VP Jr Cls; L Var Bsktbl; Var Crs Cntry; Var L Socr; Trk; Hnry Ambssdr At Large; Congression Hearing; Georgetown U; Intl Reltns.

TAITANO, RANDEL J C; John F Kennedy HS; Yigo, GU; (3); Church Yth Grp; Cmnty Wkr; 4-H; JA; SADD; Rep Stu Cncl; Var L Bsktbl; Var L Socr; Var L Vllybl; NHS; CU Boulder; Arch Engr.

TAITINGFONG-PAULINO, JOANN M; John F Kennedy HS; Agana, GU; (4); Church Yth Grp; Cmnty Wkr; Drama Clb; Hosp Aide; Band; Church Choir; Homeroom Rep & Alt; Schl Fashion Show.

TALLADA, CHERRYLYN R; John F Kennedy HS; Tamuning, GU; (3); School Play; U GU; Tourism.

TANGCO, ELVIRA; John F Kennedy HS; Barrigada, GU; (3); Acctng.

TEMENGIL, SUSANNE; John F Kennedy HS; Barrigada, GU; (3); JA; Pres Frsh Cls; High Hon Roll; Hon Roll; Close Up Clb; Soc Fld, Med.

TINIO, ANA MELANIE; John F Kennedy HS; Tamuning, GU; (4); JA; Spanish Clb; Filipino Stu Assoc, VP; Jr Prom Tckts/Prgms Cmmtte Co-Chrprsn; Sci Fr; U Of Santo Tomas; Med Tech.

TSOU, JACK; Harvest Christian Acad; Tamuning, GU; (2); 1/24; Chess Clb; Natl Beta Clb; Var Intrml Ftbl; Intrml Vllybl; High Hon Roll; Hon Roll; Prfct Atten Awd.

TUZON, ARLENE; John F Kennedy HS; Agana, GU; (1); Church Yth Grp; Nurse.

TUZON, JANE DECANO; John F Kennedy HS; Dededo, GU; (4); 24/335; Treas Spanish Clb; SADD; Chorus; Hon Roll; Jr NHS; U Of CA-BERKELEY; Acctng.

TUZON, MARILYN; John F Kennedy HS; Dededo, GU; (1); Church Yth Grp; Off Frsh Cls; High Hon Roll; Hon Roll; Jr NHS; Pres Acad Fit Awd; Japanese Clss 6th Pl; UDH; Pediatrician.

VALENCIA, JENNIFER REYES; John F Kennedy HS; Dededo, GU; (4); Office Aide; Teachers Aide; Chorus; Rep Stu Cncl; Jr NHS; Bus Mgmt.

VILLAFLORES III, DOMINGO I; John F Kennedy HS; Dededo, GU; (1); Church Yth Grp; Cmnty Wkr; Church Choir; Variety Show; Jr NHS; Chem.

VILLAFLORES, MELLANIE; John F Kennedy HS; Dededo, GU; (2); Sec Church Yth Grp; Cmnty Wkr; Drama Clb; JA; Church Choir; Stage Crew; Off Frsh Cls; Off Soph Cls; High Hon Roll; Jr NHS; Co-Chrprsn For 88-89 Homcmng Float Cmmtte; Elec Engrng.

WANG, ETHEL I; John F Kennedy HS; Tamuning, GU; (4); 38/325; Computer Clb; Science Clb; Spanish Clb; Yrbk; Japnese Clb Treas.

WANG, PHILIP; John F Kennedy HS; Tamuning, GU; (3); Intnl Clb; Math Clb; Off Stu Cncl; Chinese Clb Pres; Scty Distngshde Amercns.

WENDLAND, MARI; Harvest Christian Acad; Agana, GU; (2); VP Natl Beta Clb; Chorus; Stat Ftbl; Intrml Vllybl; Hon Roll; Ntl Merit Ltr; Prfct Atten Awd; Japanese Schl Vladtrn; Med.

WONG, EVON; Simon Sanchez HS; Yigo, GU; (3); Var Tennis; Hon Roll; Tnns Clb; Yrbk Stff 90-91; Jpns Clb Secy, Hstrn 90-91; 1st Plc SSHS Sci Fair 89; Spec Olmpcs 90; UH; Med.

WONG, THERESA; John F Kennedy HS; Dededo, GU; (4); 36/345; Office Aide; Sec Science Clb; Church Choir; Medcl.

WOO, EVELYN; John F Kennedy HS; Tamuning, GU; (3); Hosp Aide; JA; Spanish Clb; Hon Roll.

WOO, RENEE RUH NI; John F Kennedy HS; Tamuning, GU; (4); 16/332; JA; SADD; Pres Cls; VP Sr Cls; Var Vllybl; Hon Roll; NHS; Drama Clb; FBLA; Pep Clb; Spcl Olympcs & Hosp Vlntr; U Of CA Santa Cruz.

WU, JOHNNY JEANG JONG; John F Kennedy HS; Tamuning, GU; (4); ROTC; Science Clb; Spanish Clb; Color Guard; Drill Tm; Chinese & Japanese Clbs; Cadet Capt AFJROTC; U HI Manoa; Bus Sci.

YANZA, EUGENE; Simon Sanchez HS; Agana, GU; (4); #2 In Class; Pep Clb; Spanish Clb; Tennis; Vllybl; NHS; Sal; Wnnr 88-89 Schl Sci Fr; Awd Achvng 4.0 GPA Bttr; U Of Southern CA; Aerospc Engr.

YEH, SHEVE-CHING; John F Kennedy HS; Agana, GU; (4); 10/341; JA; High Hon Roll; Hon Roll; Jr NHS; NHS; Miss Hemisphere 1st Rnnr-Up 90; NSF Young Schlrs Summer Pgm 88; U Guam; Bus Admin.

YEN, ANGELA; John F Kennedy HS; Agana, GU; (4); Dance Clb; Math Clb; VP Frsh Cls; Bsktbl; Mgr(s); Score Keeper; Vllybl; Chem.

YOUNG, BRIAN T; John F Kennedy HS; Dededo, GU; (2); ROTC; Mltry Ordr Of Wrld Wars Mdl ROTC; Chf Oper ROTC; Bwlng Clb; Plt.

HAWAII

ABAD, GRACHELA T; Leilehua HS; Mililani Town, HI; (2); 8/392; 4-H; Tennis; High Hon Roll; Hon Roll; Interact Rndrsng Chrprsn & Pres 90-91; Tnns Mgr; U Of CA Northridge; Bus.

ABAOAG, NORMA; Waimea HS; Kekaha, HI; (2); Church Yth Grp; Hon Roll; Hopsitalty Cmtt; Clss Ring; Hmcmng Cmtt; Recrdng Engr.

ABE, BRIAN T; Mililani HS; Mililani, HI; (2); 15/509; Church Yth Grp; Teachers Aide; Mrchg Band; Var Tennis; Hon Roll; Jr NHS; Pres Acad Fit Awd; Stu Exchng Pgm; Optometry.

ABEJON, MICHELLE K; Kailua HS; Waimanalo, HI; (2); 31/301; Hosp Aide; Hon Roll; Nalt Libry Ptrys Editors Choice Awd 89; U HI; Bus.

ABELLA, OLIVER G; James Campbell HS; Ewa Beach, HI; (2); Rep Stu Cncl; JV Ftbl; JV Var Trk; High Hon Roll; Hon Roll; Prfct Atten Awd; Lt JPO.

ABENES, RAYBURN K; Honoka'a HS; Kamuela, HI; (3); 4/149; FHA; High Hon Roll; Hon Roll; U Of HI Manoa; Bus.

ABERO, KIMI M; Waipahu HS; Waipahu, HI; (1); 55/513; Library Aide; Office Aide; Chorus; Stat Cheerldng; Sci.

ABRAHAM, TEDLINA; James Campbell HS; Waipahu, HI; (4); Teachers Aide; Chorus; Leeward CC; Hawaiian.

ABREU, JOHNETTE M; St Francis HS; Waipahu, HI; (2); 22/80; Library Aide; Pep Clb; Pysch.

ABUBO, MAILE L; Waialua HS; Waialua, HI; (3); Aud/Vis; Girl Scts; Letterman Clb; Chorus; Var L Socr; Var L Vllybl; Hon Roll; Soph Homcmng Princess; San Diego ST U; Psych.

ABUT, NORMALYN; Lahainaluna HS; Lahaina Maui, HI; (3); Prfct Atten Awd; Maui CC; Accntng.

ACCETTA, JULIANN; Radford HS; Honolulu, HI; (3); 30/394; Cmnty Wkr; Spanish Clb; Chorus; Stu Cncl; High Hon Roll; Hon Roll; Selected As Miss Sonkan 88-Thailand; Harvard U; Lawyr.

ACOBA, MICAH A; Iolani Schl; Honolulu, HI; (4); Chess Clb; Key Clb; Quiz Bowl; Lit Mag; Stu Cncl; JV Bsbl; Var Bsktbl; Trk; Var Vllybl; High Hon Roll; Cum Laude Soc; US Chess Fed HI Chess Fed Ranked Player; Harvard U.

ACOBA, ROWENA R; Waipahu HS; Waipahu, HI; (1); 132/513; Band; Mrchg Band; U Of HI Manoa; Nurse.

ACOHIDO, MARK A; St Louis HS; Aiea, HI; (2); 39/151; Bsktbl; Ftbl; Trk; Hon Roll.

ACOPAN, JEFFREY T; Mid-Pacific Inst; Honolulu, HI; (2); 1/225; Cmnty Wkr; Math Tm; JV Tennis; Hon Roll; Jr NHS; NHS; Pres Schlr; Jnr Natl Hnr Soc Pres; Straub Hosp Volntr; GA Tech; Actuary.

ACORDA, TITA V; H P Baldwin HS; Wailuku, HI; (2); 1/395; FTA; Band; High Hon Roll; Prfct Atten Awd; Play Flute & Bsbl; Hnr Band; U HI Manoa; Bus.

ACOSTA, LAURA K; Radford HS; El Paso, TX; (1); 79/466; Flag Corp; JV Bsktbl; U TX El Paso; Lawyer.

ACOSTA, SHARON G; Pearl City HS; Pearl City, HI; (2); 8/511; Church Yth Grp; Key Clb; Treas Frsh Cls; Treas Soph Cls; Stat Bsktbl; Hon Roll; NHS; 1st Pl Leeward Dist Math Bowl 89; Bus.

ADACHI, BROOKE M; Aiea HS; Aiea, HI; (2); 44/347; Band; Stat Bsbl; Score Keeper; High Hon Roll; Hon Roll; Interact Clb; Pharmacy.

ADAME, LAVON M; Kalani HS; Honolulu, HI; (1); 23/246; Hon Roll; Sci Fr Awd; Vet Med.

ADAMS, ANGEL; Redemption Acad; Waianae, HI; (4); Pres Church Yth Grp; Debate Tm; Drama Clb; Speech Tm; Chorus; Church Choir; School Musical; School Play; Stage Crew; Yrbk; Outstndng Choral Mem; Church Yth Pres & Secy; Choral Singing Youth Ldr; Hotel Mgmt.

ADAMS, ANGELA D; Radford HS; Honolulu, HI; (3); 43/394; SADD; Chorus; Rep Frsh Cls; Stu Cncl; Cheerldng; Trk; Hon Roll; Museum Of Fine Arts; Art.

ADERINTO, PHILLIP A; Ka'u HS; Pahala, HI; (4); 12/58; Pres Letterman Clb; Math Tm; Band; Chorus; Pres Soph Cls; VP Jr Cls; Var L Bsktbl; Var L Trk; Var L Vllybl; Elks Awd; Honolulu Advertsr HI All Star Ath 88-90; US Army Res Schlr Ath 90; BIIF 300 M Intermed Champ 90; De Vry Inst Of Tech; Elec Tech.

ADRIC, MAUREEN K; Waianae HS; Waianae, HI; (2); 130/455; Var Bsktbl; Var Vllybl; PAAC; Prncpls List; Drug Free Pgm; U Of HI; Newscstr.

AFRICA, JOSALYN; Waipahu HS; Waipahu, HI; (3); 75/409; Office Aide; Spanish Clb; SADD; Teachers Aide; Ed Yrbk; Stu Cncl; Filipino-Amer Yth Clb; Leeward CC.

AGAPAY, ROBERT A; Lahainaluna HS; Lahaina, HI; (3); VP Jr Cls; VP Sr Cls; JV Bsktbl; Var Ftbl; Hon Roll; NHS; Prfct Atten Awd; Aloha Clb; Elec Engrng.

AGARPAO, RONEL R; Waipahu HS; Waipahu, HI; (2); 14/440; High Hon Roll; Hon Roll; Cert Mrt Geometry; Gftd/Tlntd Conf 90; Close Up Fndtn Pgm; Cert Awd Driver & Traffic Safety Ed; Phy.

AGBAYANI, JULIUS A; Farrington HS; Honolulu, HI; (3); 73/600; JV Var Bsktbl; Var Ftbl; Var Vllybl; Hon Roll; Prfct Atten Awd; Phys Educ Instrctr.

AGCAOILI III, AMANCIO-ANTHONY; Damien Memorial HS; Waipahu, HI; (4); #41 In Class; Debate Tm; FBLA; Math Tm; ROTC; Speech Tm; Drill Tm; Bsbl; Ftbl; Trk; Wt Lftg; Most Outstndng Athl; Hnr Roll; All St & All Star Wide Rcvr Ftbl; 2nd Pl Trk; 1st Pl Spch Comptn; U Of Portland; Tchr.

AGENA, STACIE F; Waimea HS; Kekaha, HI; (2); 4/200; Church Yth Grp; Girl Scts; Key Clb; Math Tm; School Play; Ed Nwsp; Treas Frsh Cls; Sec Jr Cls; Var Cheerldng; NHS; Med.

AGNES, RICHARD S; Roosevelt HS; Honolulu, HI; (3); 1/360; Intnl Clb; Math Clb; Math Tm; Science Clb; Hon Roll; NHS; Med.

AGONOY, ESTEBAN G; Farrington HS; Honolulu, HI; (3); 75/633; French Clb; Key Clb; Cit Awd; Hon Roll; Prfct Atten Awd; Outstndng Achvt Frnch I, II; Close-Up Pgm; Yth Helping Yth; U Sydney Australia; Med.

AGOO, VALERIE M; Waiakea HS; Waialua, HI; (2); Science Clb; Hon Roll; U Of HI.

AGOOT, YUKI M; Konawaena HS; Captain Cook, HI; (3); 13/294; Church Yth Grp; French Clb; Rep Jr Cls; Rep Stu Cncl; Var Bsktbl; Hon Roll; NHS; YMCA Yth Legsltr Outstndng Rep Awd; Lets Get Togthr Exchng Pgm; Pre-Law.

AGPALZA, ROCHELLE; Pahoa HS; Pahoa, HI; (1); Pres Frsh Cls; High Hon Roll; U Of HI Manoa; Lwyr.

AGPAWA, RAELYNNE L; Waiakea HS; Hilo, HI; (3); JA; JV Var Cheerldng; Elem Ed.

AGRIGADO, ALMA C; Waipahu HS; Waipahu, HI; (2); GAA; JV Bsktbl; Sftbl; High Hon Roll; Hon Roll; Accntnt.

AGSALUD, EVELYN U; Lahainaluna HS; Lahaina, HI; (4); 11/136; Letterman Clb; Math Tm; Science Clb; Service Clb; Yrbk; Treas Soph Cls; Treas Sr Cls; Capt Cheerldng; Hon Roll; Prfct Atten Awd; Stu Staying Straight Clb; Aloha Clb; Maui CC; Nrsg.

AGTAGUEM, JEANETTE; Maui HS; Pukalani, HI; (2); 8/388; Science Clb; Band; Mrchg Band; High Hon Roll; Hon Roll; Jr NHS; Prfct Atten Awd; Rutgers U; Acctng.

AGUADA, JEROME G; St Louis HS; Honolulu, HI; (3); 7/150; Cmnty Wkr; Intnl Clb; Quiz Bowl; Spanish Clb; Crs Cntry; NHS; Arch.

AGUDA, RUTH MAE; Hawaii Baptist Acad; Honolulu, HI; (3); 18/86; Church Yth Grp; Cmnty Wkr; Drama Clb; Hosp Aide; JA; Spanish Clb; Thesps; Chorus; School Musical; School Play; Ldrshp Cncl; Pres Aloha Cncl; U WA; Pre Med.

AGUINALDO, HARRY; Baldwin HS; Kahului, HI; (1); Key Clb; Htl Mgmt.

AGUINALDO, RAYMANETTE L; Henry Perrine Baldwin HS; Kahului, HI; (2); 38/395; Church Yth Grp; SADD; Church Choir; Yrbk; Hon Roll; Aloha Clb; Service Awd; Phy.

AGUNAT, WAYNE S; Farrington HS; Honolulu, HI; (4); 42/549; Art Clb; Chorus; Stage Crew; Hon Roll; State High School Champion Bowling; Farrington High School Athlete Of The Year; Electrical Engineer.

AGUNOY, KEALOHALANI K; Waipahu HS; Waipahu, HI; (4); DECA; FHA; Pep Clb; Teachers Aide; Leeward CC; Bus.

AGUSTIN, CYNTHIA; Henry Perrine Baldwin HS; Kahului, HI; (3); 50/385; Rep Soph Cls; Treas Jr Cls; Hon Roll; Jr Promenade Prncs; Bus.

AGUSTIN, LISA M; Sacred Hearts Acad; Waipahu, HI; (1); Pep Clb; Color Guard; Mrchg Band; Pep Band; Rept Damien HS For Boys Hmcmng Princess; Prtcptd Health Wlk A Thon Cmmnty Svc Prjcts; Bus Mngmnt.

AGUSTIN JR, ROBERT; Kauai HS; Lihue, HI; (3); 7/231; French Clb; Key Clb; Library Aide; Math Tm; Science Clb; Treas Sr Cls; High Hon Roll; Hon Roll; NHS; Leo Clb; 3rd Pl St Frnch I Oral & Wrttn Test; Pacific & Asian Affs Cncl VP; Comp Sci.

AH CHOY, VANESSA R L; Radford HS; Honolulu, HI; (2); 29/411; Rep Frsh Cls; Rep Soph Cls; Rep Stu Cncl; Cit Awd; High Hon Roll; Hon Roll; Prfct Atten Awd; Hawaiian Club VP; Inner Schl Clun Cncl Rep; Prof Hula Dancer; Hotel Mgmt.

AH MOO SANG, SAMSON; Roosevelt HS; Honolulu, HI; (2); Teachers Aide; JV Ftbl; High Hon Roll; Hon Roll; Dnc Clb; Univ Of HI; Gynclgst.

AH YOLI, DONOVAN E K; Leilehua HS; Wahiawa, HI; (2); 37/392; Band; Bsktbl; Ftbl; Trk; Vllybl; Wt Lftg; Hon Roll; U Of HI.

AHMED, SEEMA S; University Laboratory Schl; Honolulu, HI; (4); VP Thesps; Band; Chorus; Jazz Band; Pep Band; School Musical; School Play; Stage Crew; Mgr JV Swmmng; JV Trk; Wellesley Bk Awd; Yth Vlntr Cncl; Wnnr Century III Ldrs Schlrshp; Intl Studies.

AIONA, MELANIE A K; Kohala HS; Kapaau, HI; (3); 3/65; Teachers Aide; Mgr Bsktbl; Var Sftbl; JV Vllybl; High Hon Roll; Hon Roll; Prom Prncss; Most Insprtnl Sftbl Plyr; Hotel Mgmt.

AIPOALANI, CHERYL; Nanakuli HS; Waianae, HI; (2); Church Yth Grp; Cmnty Wkr; Office Aide; Pep Clb; Teachers Aide; Flag Corp; Rep Frsh Cls; Sec Soph Cls; Var Cheerldng; Var Pom Pon; U Of HI; Lwyr.

AIWOHI, KANOELANI K; Baldwin HS; Wailuku, HI; (2); Church Yth Grp; Cmnty Wkr; Dance Clb; Girl Scts; Letterman Clb; Pep Clb; Service Clb; SADD; Temple Yth Grp; Varsity Clb.

AKAGI, CATHY K; Leilehua HS; Wahiawa, HI; (2); 78/392; JV Trk; Hon Roll; HI Beauty Coll; Cosmtlgst.

AKAMINE, JENNIFER Y; Waiakea HS; Hilo, HI; (1); 26/478; JA; Service Clb; Band; Mrchg Band; Pep Band; Hon Roll; Hilo Jr Bowler; Mock Trial Tm; Photojrnlst.

AKANA, ELTON H; Kohala HS; Kapaau, HI; (2); 5/65; VP VICA; JV Wrstlng; Cwby Of Yr Awd 88-89; 3rd Pl VICA Cnst Cont; Crpntr.

AKASHI, SHARI ANN REIKO; Iolani HS; Mililani Town, HI; (4); 24/217; Sec Debate Tm; 4-H; Key Clb; NFL; Q&S; Sec Speech Tm; Band; Mrchg Band; Ed Nwsp; Cit Awd; Ray A Kroc Yth Achvt Awd; Cum Laude Soc; Sr Bazaar Co-Chairperson; U CA San Diego; Med.

AKEMOTO, DANIEL K; Kalani HS; Honolulu, HI; (3); Math Tm; Sec Band; Drm Mjr(t); Jazz Band; Mrchg Band; Orch; Var Bsbl; Var Tennis; Music.

AKIMOTO, CAMY M; Leilehua HS; Wahiawa, HI; (4); 1/320; Debate Tm; Drama Clb; Library Aide; Math Tm; NFL; VP Pres Speech Tm; School Play; Stage Crew; Ed Nwsp; Ed Yrbk; Lang Arts Shwcs Wnnr Shrt Stry & Drmtc Scrpt; Tutrg Math & Sci; Physcs.

AKINA, MICHELLE I; James Campbell HS; Ewa Beach, HI; (4); 78/347; Office Aide; Teachers Aide; Treas Sr Cls; Dnfth Awd; Hawaaian Clb; Yth Endng Hngr; Chld Psych.

AKIONA, NICHOLAS P K; Mililani HS; Mililani, HI; (3); 81/507; Aud/Vis; Service Clb; Band; Mrchg Band; Pep Band; Rep Frsh Cls; Rep Soph Cls; Hon Roll; Band Solo Ensmbl Red Mdlst Trumpet; Piano; U HI; Poly Sci.

AKONA, HENRY; Mid Pacific Inst; Kailua-Kona, HI; (3); Aud/Vis; Dance Clb; Drama Clb; French Clb; NFL; Speech Tm; Thesps; Chorus; School Musical; School Play; Piano Stu; Compuser Of Orginl Shows; NYU; Admin Of Arts.

AKUNA, JENERY; Henry Perrine Baldwin HS; Wailuku, HI; (4); Debate Tm; Pres Treas FTA; Sec Hist SADD; Sec Stu Cncl; Hon Roll; Sec NHS; Rotary Awd; Baldwin Aloha Clb; Maui Cnty Yth Rcgntn Awd Ltry Arts 1st Pl; Crrclm Enrchmnt Clb; Pre Med.

ALAIMO, MICHAEL V; Kohala HS; Hawi, HI; (1); 3/61; Math Tm; Band; Jazz Band; Pres Frsh Cls; Wrstlng.

ALBANO, DANIELLE; Theodore Roosevelt HS; Honolulu, HI; (3); Hist French Clb; Rptr Nwsp; Pres Soph Cls; Crs Cntry; Trk; Acctnt.

ALBOLERO, RAENETTE V; Maui HS; Pukalani, HI; (2); 25/388; Church Yth Grp; Math Clb; Science Clb; Hon Roll; Arch.

ALBRIGHT, CASEY R; H P Baldwin HS; Kihei, HI; (1); 20/466; Boy Scts; Band; JV Bsktbl; Hon Roll.

ALCAIDE, GERI A; Waialua HS & Intermed; Waialua, HI; (3); French Clb; Science Clb; Speech Tm; Rep Frsh Cls; Rep Soph Cls; Rep Jr Cls; Stat Bsktbl; Stat Ftbl; Var Tennis; JV Var Vllybl; Drug Buster; Alona Civic; Hula Dancer; :Mdcl Fld.

ALDOVER, DONARCO Q; Admiral Arthur W Radford HS; Honolulu, HI; (2); 20/411; Band; Jazz Band; Mrchg Band; Pep Band; JV Capt Ftbl; JV L Trk; L Wt Lftg; High Hon Roll; Prin Achvt Awd 90; Central Dist HS Hnr Band 89 & 90; All Hawaiian Hula Bowl Marching Band 89 & 90; U Of HI Manoa; Ed.

ALEJANDRO, JORDAN; Kohala High And Elem; Kapaau, HI; (2); 5/61; VICA; Band; Pep Band; Hon Roll.

ALEJO, LYNETTE; Sacred Hearts Acad; Ewa Beach, HI; (4); Cmnty Wkr; Pep Clb; Science Clb; Spanish Clb; Stat Var Ftbl; L Var Swmmng; Schltc Art Awd; Physics Olympcs; Ballet Awds; Western ST Coll; Sprts Thrpy.

ALFEREZ JR, PAUL A; Waianae HS; Waianae, HI; (2); 45/449; JV Capt Ftbl; JV Wt Lftg; Hon Roll; Electrncs.

ALFONSO, RONETTE L; Honokaa HS; Honokaa, HI; (4); 14/136; Church Yth Grp; Dance Clb; DECA; 4-H; Girl Scts; Library Aide; Office Aide; Band; School Musical; Rep Soph Cls; Jay Teens; Inter Rels; 2 Awds Engl, Acctg; Hilo U; Legl Sec.

ALI, ROSE T; Sacred Hearts Acad; Waipahu, HI; (4); 15/108; Spanish Clb; Band; Chorus; Color Guard; Stu Cncl; High Hon Roll; NHS; Math Clb; Pep Clb; Quiz Bowl; Close-Up Prgm 89; Retreat Ldr, SHA Merit Awd 89-90; Brown Bags To Stardom 87-88, 3rd Prz 89-90; U Of HI; Med.

ALIPIO, JOHN; St Louis HS; Honolulu, HI; (2); 35/151; Bsktbl; Ftbl; Georgetown U; Frgn Svcs.

ALIPIO, MARY JANE P; Waialua HS; Waialua, HI; (3); 11/170; Intnl Clb; Letterman Clb; Science Clb; Spanish Clb; Var Capt Bsktbl; Var Sftbl; Var Vllybl; High Hon Roll; Hon Roll; Prfct Atten Awd; Bus Admin.

ALLEN, DARNISHA M; Radjord HS; Honolulu, HI; (2); 157/448; Church Yth Grp; Letterman Clb; ROTC; SADD; Church Choir; Rep Frsh Cls; Sec Soph Cls; Var Capt Trk; Close Up; Black Amer Clb; Coll Syracuse; Cmmnctns Sprtcst.

ALLEN, DAWN R; Kaiser HS; Honolulu, HI; (3); Drama Clb; School Play; Var Socr; Var Vllybl; All St Sccr Goalie; Amnstry Intrntl Clb; U Of HI; Psych.

ALLEN, FREDRICK D; Kalani HS; Honolulu, HI; (3); Art Clb; Aud/Vis; Stage Crew; Rep Stu Cncl; Interior Dsgn.

ALLEN, MARKELA J; Leilehua HS; Schofield Bks, HI; (2); Church Yth Grp; Hon Roll; Zonta Clb; Merit Hnr Roll; Chld Cr; Cmmrcl Art.

ALLEN, TERILYN Y; Lanai HS; Lanai City, HI; (4); 11/47; Hosp Aide; Letterman Clb; Rep Nwsp; Ed Yrbk; Ed Lit Mag; Var Cheerldng; Stat Score Keeper; High Hon Roll; Hon Roll; U S Army Rsrv Natl Schlr Athlt Awd; Pblc Reltns Chrprsn; Cls Wk Chrprsn; U Of HI Manoa; Lbrl Arts.

ALOANG, ELVIRA S; St Francis HS; Honolulu, HI; (3); Art Clb; Pres Aud/Vis; Cmnty Wkr; Library Aide; Mu Alpha Theta; Speech Tm; Hon Roll; U Of HI-MANOA; Audio Engr.

ALONZO, ERLINE MARY; Radford HS; Kaaawa, HI; (4); 38/351; Cmnty Wkr; VP Spanish Clb; Teachers Aide; Rptr Nwsp; Yrbk; Rep Stu Cncl; Mgr(s); Hon Roll; Amnesty Intl; Close Up Prog Sec; Sterling Schlr Frgn Lang; U HI; Brdcst Jrnlsm.

ALONZO, MICHELLE A; Teilehna HS; Wahiawa, HI; (2); Church Yth Grp; Sec 4-H; Hosp Aide; Spanish Clb; Church Choir; Hon Roll; Intl Frgn Lang Awd 88-89; HI U; Ped.

ALONZO, STACEY; Kalaheo HS; Kailua, HI; (4); Church Yth Grp; Cmnty Wkr; Hon Roll; Mediation; Windward CC; Elem Ed.

ALTOMARE, JOHN K; Waimea HS; Waimea, HI; (3); 18/198; Var Ftbl; Var Socr; NHS; Violin 8 Yrs; Ocean Sports; Math.

ALVIAR, SHARLENE N; Honokaa HS; Kamuela, HI; (3); 42/437; English Clb; Hon Roll; Bus Mgmt.

AMARAL, CRAIG J; Maui HS; Pukalani, HI; (3); 16/354; Treas SADD; Hon Roll; Prfct Atten Awd; Aquarium/Terraium Clb-Sec; Civil Air Patrol-Sgt.

AMARAL, TAMMIE A; Waiakea HS; Mt View, HI; (3); 13/368; Rep Church Yth Grp; Treas FHA; FTA; Sec JA; Service Clb; Rep Jr Cls; High Hon Roll; NHS; Schlstc Hnrs 88-90; Outstndng Service Awd 89; Elem Ed.

AMBROCIO, MARITESS P; Farrington HS; Honolulu, HI; (3); 196/759; Service Clb; Band; Variety Show; Rep Stu Cncl; Nakia Aina Clb; Radiology.

AMBROSIO, EDGAR M; Leilehua HS; Wahiawa, HI; (2); 47/392; Church Yth Grp; Hon Roll.

AMIAN, MICHELLE M M; Farrington HS; Honolulu, HI; (4); Church Yth Grp; Pres French Clb; Hikng Clb; Kokua Ainas; Sci Proj Awd 88; Kapiolani Scc; Nrsng.

AMINA, CHRISTINE K; Kaimuki HS; Honolulu, HI; (3); Library Aide; Teachers Aide; Off Jr Cls; Vllybl; Hon Roll; Mediator Vlybl Tm Conf Champs; Mediator May Day Ct; Jr Prom Ct Princess & Selected To Chair Sr Yr Luau; KCC; Math.

AMORIN, KATHERINA M; Saint Francis HS; Waipahu, HI; (2); 53/80; Drama Clb; 4-H; GAA; Letterman Clb; Pep Clb; Chorus; Drm Mjr(t); School Musical; Off Frsh Cls; Stu Cncl; U Of HI; Ed.

AMSTRONG, ANDRE D; Mililani HS; Mililani Town, HI; (2); 41/509; Rptr Nwsp; Var Diving; Var Swmmng; Hon Roll; NHS; Pres Acad Fit Awd; Currently Training To Compete As A Triathelete; Aquaculture.

ANAYA, DANELLE R; Mililani HS; Mililani, HI; (3); Computer Clb; Teachers Aide; Band; Pep Band; Voice Dem Awd.

ANCHETA JR, BENJAMIN; Kamehameha Schls; Waipahu, HI; (4); 4/420; Spanish Clb; SADD; Capt Var Socr; Carleton Coll; Poltcl Sci.

ANCHETA, FELGRACE; Pahoa HS; Pahoa, HI; (3); Computer Clb; FBLA; FTA; Spanish Clb; Rptr Nwsp; Yrbk; Sec Jr Cls; Hon Roll; NHS; Upward Bnd; Photo Clb Pres; U Of WA; Ed.

ANCHETA, JEANNIE C; Kauai HS; Lihue, HI; (4); FHA; Bsktbl; Socr; Outstndng Typing Achvt; Leo Clb; U Of HI-MONCA; Engrng.

ANCHETA, NOEL; Moanalua HS; Honolulu, HI; (2); 9/500; Church Yth Grp; Pres FTA; VP Spanish Clb; Rep Stu Cncl; High Hon Roll; Hon Roll; NHS; Pres Acad Fit Awd; Hmne Soc Vol; Toys For Tots Chrmn; Aftrsch Tutor.

ANCOG, MARK; Kaimuki HS; Honolulu, HI; (3); Var Bsktbl; Vlntr Boys And Girls Clb.

ANDERSON, AUBREY; Laupahoehoe HS; Ookala, HI; (3); Math Tm; Pep Clb; Science Clb; Rptr Nwsp; Sec Frsh Cls; Sec Soph Cls; Bsktbl; Tennis; Hon Roll; Upward Bound Prog; Gifted & Talented Class.

ANDERSON, LAURA M; Lutheran HS; Kaneohe, HI; (1); 1/38; Rep Frsh Cls; Var Bsktbl; High Hon Roll; Prfct Atten Awd; Law.

ANDERSON, TRESA K; Leilehua HS; Mililani, HI; (3); 5/305; Church Yth Grp; VP French Clb; Red Cross Aide; Sec SADD; Rep Stu Cncl; Var Capt Diving; Var Swmmng; High Hon Roll; NHS; Pres Acad Fit Awd; OIA West Diving Champ; Drug Coalition Team; Prncpls List; OR ST U; Bio.

ANDRADA, JULIE M; Farrington HS; Honolulu, HI; (3); 13/600; JA; Ed Phtg Nwsp; Ed Yrbk; Lit Mag; Hon Roll; Leo Club; YMCA Vlntr; U Of CA San Diego; Math.

ANDRASICK, CHRISTOPHER J; Iolani Schl; Honolulu, HI; (4); Intnl Clb; JA; Model UN; Rep Sr Cls; High Hon Roll; Hon Roll; Ntl Merit SF; JV Watrpolo; Amnesty Intl Ofcr; Aerosp Engr.

ANDRES, JOHN ERIC; James Campbell HS; Ewa Beach, HI; (2); 7/348; Church Yth Grp; Science Clb; High Hon Roll; Hon Roll; Blue Wtr Marine Lab Smmr Ocean Stds Stu U Of HI 90; U Of HI; Med.

ANDRES, MARITA; Farrington HS; Ewa Beach, HI; (3); 26/600; Drama Clb; ROTC; School Play; Hon Roll; Prfct Atten Awd; US Army Awd; Write Shrt Novels; U HI; Comp Pgmr.

ANDRES, PAMLA A P; Kau HS; Pahala, HI; (4); 9/58; Church Yth Grp; Hosp Aide; Letterman Clb; Band; Chorus; Treas Frsh Cls; VP Stu Cncl; Golf; Socr; Hon Roll; Peer Cnslr; U NV Las Vegas; Bus Mktg.

ANDREWS, MARK; Iolani Schl; Aiea, HI; (4); 10/220; Church Yth Grp; Debate Tm; JA; Model UN; Chorus; Ed Lit Mag; High Hon Roll; Ntl Merit SF; Japanese Snt Schlrsp; Cum Laude Soc; Outstndng Filipino SR; Georgetown; Intl Rel.

ANGAY, LORETTA L; Pahoa HS; Pahoa, HI; (3); 7/98; FHA; U Hilo; Comp.

ANGELES, DANNIS R; Mc Kinley HS; Honolulu, HI; (2); 38/545; Computer Clb; English Clb; Math Tm; Science Clb; Spanish Clb; Swmmng; Trk; Vllybl; NHS; Sal; UCLA.

ANIYA, VALERIE; Mid-Pacific Inst; Wahiawa, HI; (4); 14/171; Office Aide; SADD; School Play; Sec Stu Cncl; JV Vllybl; High Hon Roll; NHS; NEDT Awd; Judge Chuck Mao Schlrshp Awd; Lewis & Clark Coll; Law.

ANMAY, LAM; Kailua HS; Kailua, HI; (4); 1/280; Church Yth Grp; Debate Tm; Drama Clb; Math Clb; Math Tm; Model UN; Science Clb; Service Clb; Spanish Clb; Speech Tm; Hovatio Alger Schlrshp Rcpnt; Juvenille Justice Advsry Grp Yth Rep; HI St Yth Ambssdr; NY U; Law.

ANSEL, AMY I; Leilehua HS; Schofield Bks, HI; (3); 3/339; Church Yth Grp; GAA; SADD; Var Capt Bsktbl; Var Capt Vllybl; High Hon Roll; Hon Roll; NHS; Pres Acad Fit Awd; Ldrshp Cls; Vrsty Vllybl Plaque; Schlr Athl 89-90 Plaque; Fresh Acad Stu 1st Six Weeks; CO ST U; Pre-Law.

ANSELMO, ANGELA M; Radford HS; Honolulu, HI; (2); 42/420; Art Clb; FCA; Pres SADD; JV Cheerldng; Mgr(s); Stat Wrstlng; Hon Roll; Jr NHS; U TX; Art.

ANTOLIN, LYNN; Konawaena HS; Kailua Kona, HI; (1); 84/371; Pep Clb; Temple Yth Grp; Band; Mrchg Band; Pep Band; JV Cheerldng; BYU; Bus.

ANTONIO, DONNA B; Farrington HS; Honolulu, HI; (4); 19/549; Sec Key Clb; Spanish Clb; Tennis; Hon Roll; Luch Club; Kokua Ainas; U Of HI; RN.

ANTONIO, RHONETTE A; Waipahu HS; Ewa Beach, HI; (1); Teachers Aide; Band; Mrchg Band; Occupational Physician.

ANTONIO JR, SALVADOR C; Saint Louis HS; Honolulu, HI; (3); School Play; Intrml Vllybl; Hon Roll; U Of HI Manoa; Med.

APANA, JOSHUA; Kapaa HS & Intermed; Kapaa, HI; (2); Dance Clb; Math Clb; Band; Rep Frsh Cls; JV Bsktbl; JV Trk; JV Wrstlng; High Hon Roll; Hon Roll; Prfct Atten Awd; Excllntship Graphic Arts; Speak Japanese.

APLACA, JARED; Kahuku HS; Laie, HI; (4); 19/233; Boy Scts; Church Yth Grp; Var Capt Socr; Hon Roll; NHS; Pres Acad Fit Awd; Most Insprtnl Player Awd Soccer; Brigham Young U-HI; Aero Engr.

APO, ANNA MARIE L; Kamehameha Schl; Kahului, HI; (1); 155/451; JA; Dorm Cncl; Medicine.

AQUI, JASON T; Kapaa HS & Intermed; Kapaa, HI; (3); Church Yth Grp; Cmnty Wkr; Church Choir; Var Trk; Var Vllybl; Hon Roll; NHS; Chrch-Knghts Of Altar-Pres; Electrncs Engrng.

AQUINO, AILEEN G; Radford HS; Honolulu, HI; (3); 17/394; Sec Church Yth Grp; Hon Roll; NHS; Statistician Yr Round Sports; Class Cncl; Japanese Clb 87-90; Vrsty Athletics Awd; UCLA; Bus/Comp Sci.

AQUINO, RANDAL H; Kaimuki HS; Kaneohe, HI; (3); 112/387; Letterman Clb; JV Crs Cntry; JV Var Ftbl; JV Var Trk; JV Wrstlng; U HI; Bus Mgmnt.

AQUINO, VALERIE A; Kauai HS; Lihue, HI; (1); 17/254; JV Bsktbl; Var Trk; Var Vllybl; Hon Roll; LDS Chrch Yng Wmn Beehive & Mia Maid Cls Pres; Law.

ARAGON, JODI H; Kailua HS; Waimanalo, HI; (2); 41/360; Church Yth Grp; Cmnty Wkr; Teachers Aide; Score Keeper; Gov Hon Prg Awd; Hon Roll; Physcl Ed Pgm Excptnl Learner; Physcl Thrpst.

ARAKAKI, ANNE F; Waiakea HS; Hilo, HI; (4); 37/412; 4-H; Pres Service Clb; Color Guard; Variety Show; Rep Frsh Cls; Chrmn Rep Soph Cls; Rep Sr Cls; Var Crs Cntry; Var Trk; 4-H Awd; CO ST U; Intr Dsgn.

ARAKAKI, ANTHONY T; Baldwin HS; Wailuku, HI; (3); 82/385; Cmnty Wkr; Drama Clb; Stage Crew; Hon Roll; Elec Club; Stu Staying Straight; Chrstn Man Hnr; Maui Cmmty Thtr Sound Tech; Stevens Inst Of Tech; Engrg.

ARAKAKI, LESLIE E; Moanalua HS; Honolulu, HI; (1); 26/545; Math Clb; Rep Stu Cncl; Var Tennis; Hon Roll; Jr NHS; Okinawau Dncng; Gftd & Tlntd Pgm; Pacific Asian & Affrs Cncl Pres; Math.

ARAKAKI, PEARL; Hilo HS; Hakalau, HI; (3); 8/367; Math Tm; Band; Mrchg Band; Rep Soph Cls; Rep Jr Cls; Stat Bsktbl; JV Var Crs Cntry; Var L Tennis; Hon Roll; NHS; Keywanettes.

ARAKAWA, JENNIFER S; Honokaa HS; Paauilo, HI; (3); Aud/Vis; Science Clb; Ed Nwsp; Yrbk; Socr; Hon Roll; OR ST U.

ARAKI, DENISE K Y; James Campbell HS; Ewa Beach, HI; (2); 4/348; Girl Scts; Science Clb; High Hon Roll; Hon Roll.

ARAKI, JOHN T; Baldwin HS; Wailuku, HI; (2); 9/392; Key Clb; Math Tm; Pres Service Clb; Hon Roll; St Essay Cont On Energy-1st Pl; HI Eductnl Assn Essay Cont-3rd Hnrbl Mention.

ARAKI, KATHERINE; Pahoa HS; Pahoa, HI; (4); 1/103; Sec Service Clb; Band; Stu Cncl; Var Tennis; Hon Roll; Pres NHS; Leo Clb Pres; Intl Yth Camp; U HI At Manoa; Pre-Nursing.

ARAMAKI, KARI J; Hawaii Baptist HS; Honolulu, HI; (3); 26/87; Church Yth Grp; FCA; Office Aide; Teachers Aide; Chorus; Church Choir; JV Bsktbl; JV Var Swmmng; Hon Roll; U Of HI Manoa; Ed.

ARAUJO, TAMMY L; Waiakea HS; Hilo, HI; (3); Church Yth Grp; Service Clb; Teachers Aide; Nwsp; Cit Wk Am Lung Assoc & Easter Seals; Upward Bound; U Of HI Manoa; Occptnl Thrpst.

ARES, JANELLE; The Kamehameha Schls; Kailua, HI; (1); 5/461; SADD; Chorus; Rep Frsh Cls; Hon Roll.

ARESTA, ERIK W; Mc Kinley HS; Honolulu, HI; (2); Boy Scts; Dance Clb; Speech Tm; Band; Jazz Band; Mrchg Band; School Play; Mdlng; Friendly Hnrs; Yale; Bus.

ARIAS, ARNEL; Laupahoehoe HS; Papaaloa, HI; (3); Science Clb; SADD; Band; Yrbk; Rep Frsh Cls; Rep Soph Cls; Treas Jr Cls; Var Bsbl; JV Var Bsktbl; Vllybl.

ARIAS, RICHARD P; Waiakea HS; Hilo, HI; (3); 23/400; Key Clb; Band; VP Jr Cls; VP Stu Cncl; Var Crs Cntry; Var Trk; Hon Roll; NHS; Pr Tutor Awd; Svc Awd; Cert Mrt; Pre-Med.

ARINAGA, JENNIFER A; Hawaii Baptist Acad; Pearl City, HI; (1); Math Tm; Band; Hon Roll; Jr NHS; Engr.

ARISUMI, MELANIE E; H P Baldwin HS; Kahului, HI; (4); 52/356; Science Clb; Service Clb; High Hon Roll; Hon Roll; Keywanettes Club; Japanese Clb Co-Historian & Co Treas; Cum Laude Grad; U HI Manoa; Bus.

ARTUS, RAYMUND GERARD D; Mililani HS; Mililani, HI; (2); 1/509; Bsktbl; Wt Lftg; Hon Roll.

ASAKURA, KERI ANN; Aiea HS; Aiea, HI; (4); 9/366; Key Clb; Math Clb; Teachers Aide; Band; High Hon Roll; NHS; Pres Acad Fit Awd; Interact Japanese & Leo Clubs; Cntrl Dist Gifted & Talented Band; U Of Southern CA.

ASATO, NATALIE A; Mid-Pacific Inst; Honolulu, HI; (3); Var Cheerldng; Hon Roll; Japanese Club VP & Pres; Prom Cmmtte; Elem Educ.

ASATO, TAMMY; Iolani HS; Honolulu, HI; (3); 67/250; JA; Key Clb; Speech Tm; Stage Crew; Var Cheerldng; Intrml Sftbl; JV Tennis; High Hon Roll; Stu Cncl Chrmn Of Winterball; Co Chrmn Of Homcmng Ct Cmmtte; Peer Counselor; U Of CA LA; Arch.

ASATO, TAMMY F; Leilehua HS; Wahiawa, HI; (3); 77/322; Hon Roll; Photogrphr.

ASATO, VICKI M; Waipahu HS; Waipahu, HI; (4); 18/418; Math Clb; Q&S; Band; Ed Nwsp; Lit Mag; High Hon Roll; Hon Roll; NHS; Natl Hnr Rl; Nwspr Most Vlbl Stffr; U HI Jrnlsm Day-2nd Pl Sprtswrtg Div; AZ ST U; Jrnlsm.

ASUNCION, NOEL F; Lahainaluna HS; Lahaina, HI; (1); 10/223; Pacific Asian Affairs Cncl; Top 10 In Cls; Stu Staying Straight.

ASUNCION, RANDY T; Kauai HS; Koloa, HI; (3); Band; Jazz Band; Mrchg Band; Pep Band; Yrbk; Crs Cntry; Socr; Trk; Boogie Boarding; Surf Club; Dance.

ASUNCION, ROSELYN L; Wallace Rider Farrington HS; Honolulu, HI; (3); GAA; Variety Show; Rptr Nwsp; Ed Yrbk; Ed Lit Mag; Off Frsh Cls; Off Soph Cls; Off Jr Cls; JV Bsktbl; JV Vllybl; Bus Mgmt.

AU, ALLISON; Leilehna HS; Wahiawa, HI; (1); 27/497; Church Yth Grp; Cmnty Wkr; Hosp Aide; School Play; Rep Frsh Cls; Rep Stu Cncl; Hon Roll; U HI.

AU, CHI YEE; Mc Kinley HS; Honolulu, HI; (3); 6/545; Cmnty Wkr; Girl Scts; Pres Math Clb; Math Tm; Stage Crew; Capt Jr Cls; Capt Stu Cncl; Gov Hon Prg Awd; Jr NHS; Prfct Atten Awd; Phrmcy.

AU, KAM LAN E; Mc Kinley HS; Honolulu, HI; (2); 49/588; School Play; Stage Crew; Off Soph Cls; Hon Roll; Winterball Crt; Schl Spirit Cmmtte; Chinese Club; Med.

AU, ROBIN K; Leilehua HS; Wahiawa, HI; (4); 32/304; Pres Band; Jazz Band; Pres Mrchg Band; Pres Orch; Pres Pep Band; Hon Roll; NHS; Schltc All Amer; HI Ambssdrs Of Music; U Of HI; Engrng.

AU, RODDY K; Waialua HS & Intermed; Kahuku, HI; (2); Boy Scts; Hon Roll; Body Boarding; Skateboarding; Hiking.

AUKER, CASSANDRA L; Punahou Schl; Kailua, HI; (4); Art Clb; Cmnty Wkr; GAA; Varsity Clb; Band; School Musical; Variety Show; Trk; Amnesty Intl Clb; Various Art Awds; Boston U; Art.

AUTELE, TABITHA T; Mililani HS; Mililani, HI; (2); 38/509; Letterman Clb; Service Clb; Varsity Clb; Band; Mrchg Band; Pep Band; Rptr Yrbk; Var Sftbl; Hon Roll; St HI House Of Rep Awd Of Yr Interact Clb; U OR; Ed.

AVILA, KIMBERLY; Radford HS; Kahului, HI; (3); Pres Jr Cls; Prncpls Achvt Awd Indstrl Art 88-89; Most Outstndng Jr Awd; Jrnlsm.

AWBER, RONA M; Roosevelt HS; Honolulu, HI; (2); Band; Mrchg Band; Hon Roll; Body Brdng; Vlntr Wrkr Amer Cancer Soc; U HI; Bus.

AYRES, LORINDA M; Admiral Arthur W Radford HS; Honolulu, HI; (3); 12/426; Church Yth Grp; Band; Pres Mrchg Band; Pep Band; Chrmn Stu Cncl; Socr; High Hon Roll; NHS; Masonic Org Jobs Dghtrs; Spec Educ.

AYUDAN, KIMBERLY S; Waimea HS; Kekaha, HI; (2); 30/186; Rep Frsh Cls; Rep Stu Cncl; Hon Roll; U Of HI Hilo; Elem Schl Tchr.

AZEKA, FAYE M; Kapaa HS; Hanalei, HI; (3); Church Yth Grp; Debate Tm; French Clb; Tennis; High Hon Roll; Hon Roll; Jr NHS; NHS; Art Awds; Art Center Of Pasadena; Advrtsn.

BABAS, FERDINAND G; Kau HS; Pahala, HI; (4); 3/56; Chess Clb; Church Yth Grp; Math Clb; Pep Clb; Band; Chorus; VP Soph Cls; Treas Sr Cls; Bsktbl; Vllybl; U ID; Resource Management.

BACANI, RAPHAEL C; James Campbell HS; Ewa Beach, HI; (2); 38/348; Church Choir; Lit Mag; U Of HI; Grphc Art.

BACCAM, SAKHONE; Waialua HS & Intermed; Haleiwa, HI; (3); 12/167; French Clb; FTA; Science Clb; Speech Tm; SADD; Yrbk; Capt Bsktbl; Trk; French Hon Soc; Hon Roll; Bayanihan Club; Publicity Cmmtte; U Of HI; Ed.

BACCAM, SOMNUCK; Waialua High Int; Haleiwa, HI; (2); Drama Clb; French Clb; Speech Tm; Chorus; Color Guard; Pres Frsh Cls; JV Swmmng; Hon Roll; Youth Helping Youth; Coalition For A Drug Free Hawaii; Drug Busters; A School Drug Free Program; Judo.

BACHILLER, MICHELLE; Waipahu HS; Waipahu, HI; (3); 18/409; DECA; FTA; Spanish Clb; Chorus; Variety Show; Lit Mag; High Hon Roll; Hon Roll; NHS; Pres Acad Fit Awd; Assmbly & Spirit Cmmttes; Spelling Bee; U Of HI; Psycht.

BACKLUND, BILLY V; Leilehua HS; Schofield Brks, HI; (3); Boy Scts; SADD; Ftbl; Trk; Eagle Sct; Army Yth Actvts Bsbl Team 87-90.

BACKUS, GERALD K; Radford HS; Honolulu, HI; (2); Church Yth Grp; Hon Roll; Admrls Awd; Gftd & Tlntd Prgrm; Arch.

BACSA, SHERYL S; Waipahu HS; Waipahu, HI; (3); 70/409; VP Hist FHA; Drill Tm; Stu Cncl; Hon Roll; Dance; HI Bus Coll; Accntnt.

BADOYEN, KRISTI L; H P Baldwin HS; Kula, HI; (1); 15/470; Debate Tm; Key Clb; Math Tm; NFL; SADD; Band; Cheerldng; Hon Roll; Dancing; Mdlng; Writing; UC Beeley; Jrnslm.

BADUA, DELLIA R; Farrington HS; Honolulu, HI; (4); Cmnty Wkr; Math Clb; Math Tm; Spanish Clb; Variety Show; Chrmn Stu Cncl; Hon Roll; Prfct Atten Awd; HI Tlnt Srchrs Clb; Toastmaster Intl Spch Craft; Leo Clb Corrspndng Secy; U Of HI Manoa; Nurse.

BADUA, EDISON LONGBOY; Kohala HS; Kapaau, HI; (1); VICA; Band; Rep Frsh Cls; High Hon Roll; U Of OR; Doc.

BADUA, KATHERINE P; James Campbell HS; Ewa Beach, HI; (4); 21/300; Key Clb; Library Aide; Science Clb; Treas Spanish Clb; Rep Frsh Cls; Hon Roll; Mock Trial Team; Cum Laude; UH Manoa; Civil Engrng.

BADUA, VIDA L; Waimea HS; Waimea, HI; (3); 7/206; FHA; Key Clb; SADD; Stu Cncl; Var Tennis; Var Trk; High Hon Roll; Hon Roll; Treas NHS; Pride Clb; U Of HI.

BAGALAYOS, MYRNA C; Mililani HS; Mililani, HI; (2); 44/509; Office Aide; Service Clb; Spanish Clb; Band; Chrmn Frsh Cls; Chrmn Soph Cls; Hon Roll; HOBY HI Ldrshp Seminar Stu Ambassador 90; Phys Thrpy.

BAILEY, TROY C; St Louis HS; Mililani, HI; (3); Var Ftbl; Var Socr.

BALAIS, ALFIE; Radford HS; Honolulu, HI; (2); 58/411; Hon Roll; Prfct Atten Awd; Amnsty Intl; PAAC; HI U.

BALDWIN, JENNIFER E; Radford HS; Honolulu, HI; (2); Church Yth Grp; Letterman Clb; Socr; Yth For Christ Trnmnt 1st Pl B Div; Bus.

BALILA JR, JUAN; Mc Kinley HS; Honolulu, HI; (3); Drama Clb; School Musical; School Play; Stage Crew; Intrml Bsktbl; Var Tennis; Var Trk; Hon Roll; Japanese Club; Hum Perf Arts Ctr; Best Supporting Actor Awd Schl Film Fstvl; Brdcst Jrnlst.

BALISACAN, LORELEI T; Waimea HS; Kekaha, HI; (2); Dance Clb; Pep Clb; Variety Show; Rep Frsh Cls; Rep Stu Cncl; Hon Roll; Homecoming Clb; Hula Dncng; Business.

BALLES, SHEREEN P; Roosevelt HS; Honolulu, HI; (3); Cmnty Wkr; Drama Clb; Sec Spanish Clb; School Musical; School Play; Stage Crew; Hon Roll; Prfct Atten Awd; Mst Hard Wrkr Awd Spansh Clb 90; Natl Spnsh Exam 3rd Yr Spnsh 1st Lvl 2nd Pl Wnnr; U HI; Frgn Lang.

BANASAN, MARY JANE B; Waiakea HS; Keaau, HI; (1); JV Bsktbl; Pres Acad Fit Awd; U HI Manoa; Bus Admin.

BANASIHAN, MARK J; Waimea HS; Eleele, HI; (3); Church Yth Grp; Pep Clb; SADD; Var Tennis; Hon Roll; Wrld Awrns Club; Cngrssnl Schlr Rep HI Natl Yng Ldrs Conf; U HI Manoa; Trvl Mgr.

BANTOLINA, GLORINA B; Farrington HS; Honolulu, HI; (3); Church Yth Grp; Cmnty Wkr; FCA; Band; Church Choir; Fine Arts Fstvl; Bus.

BAPTISTA, JULIET L; Lanai High & Elem Schl; Lanai City, HI; (1); Band; VP Frsh Cls; VP Stu Cncl; High Hon Roll; Outstndng Achvt-Math; Mst Outstndng-Lang Arts; Rnnr-Up Ruth M Tabrah Crtv Wrtng Cntst; Cannons BC; Bus.

BARAQUIO, BERNADETTE P; Moanalua HS; Honolulu, HI; (3); 37/462; Q&S; Church Choir; Rptr Nwsp; Phtg Yrbk; Rep Frsh Cls; Rep Soph Cls; Var Capt Bsktbl; Var Crs Cntry; High Hon Roll; Hon Roll; Presdntl Phys Ftnss Awd; Jrnlsm.

BARAQUIO, THERESE P; Moanalua HS; Honolulu, HI; (3); 23/462; Church Yth Grp; Q&S; Church Choir; Ed Nwsp; Phtg Yrbk; VP Frsh Cls; Rep Soph Cls; Var Capt Bsktbl; Var Capt Crs Cntry; High Hon Roll; Bus Admin.

BARAYUGA, ELLEN B; Moanalua HS; Honolulu, HI; (2); 46/488; Hosp Aide; Key Clb; Band; Mrchg Band; Pep Band; Rep Soph Cls; High Hon Roll.

BARCARSE, TANYA M; Waiakea HS; Hilo, HI; (1); Church Yth Grp; Pep Clb; Service Clb; Spanish Clb; Temple Yth Grp; Color Guard; Hon Roll; BYU; Child Psych.

BARCINA, PETER; Waialua HS & Intermed; Haleiwa, HI; (2); Art Clb; Church Yth Grp; Science Clb; JV Bsktbl; Intrml Socr; Hon Roll; Prfct Atten Awd; Pres Acad Fit Awd; Elec Engr.

BARROGA, CAROLYN; Waipahu HS; Waipahu, HI; (1); 80/513; Church Yth Grp; Band; Med Tech.

BARROS, JODI; Hanalani Schls; Miliani, HI; (2); Church Yth Grp; Letterman Clb; Band; Bsktbl; Cheerldng; Socr; Vllybl; Hon Roll; Pres Acad Fit Awd; Pres Schlr.

BARSHAW, JEREMY S; Kailua HS; Kailua, HI; (3); 42/347; Church Yth Grp; Office Aide; ROTC; SADD; Teachers Aide; Var Crs Cntry; Var Socr; AYSO Sccr Coach; Phys Thrpy.

BARTOLOME, MARTY C; Waipahu HS; Waipahu, HI; (1); #47 In Class; Church Yth Grp; Band; Jazz Band; Pep Band; Off Frsh Cls; Wrstlng; Hon Roll; Frnkln Awd Soc Stds; U Of Sthrn CA.

BARTOLOME, MARYLOU T; Pahoa HS; Pahoa, HI; (4); 13/109; Treas Pres Church Yth Grp; French Clb; FFA; Stat Bsktbl; Socr; Hon Roll; NHS; Ptry Prntd Litry Clb Bk; FL Memrl Coll; Arwy Comp Sci.

BARTON, AMY M; Leilehua HS; Wahiawa, HI; (4); 46/304; Rep Church Yth Grp; Pres Girl Scts; Treas SADD; Chorus; Hon Roll; Bus Admin.

BARUEL, LISA; Hilo HS; Papaikou, HI; (4); 23/308; Church Yth Grp; 4-H; Hosp Aide; Ed Yrbk; Rep Soph Cls; Rep Sr Cls; Rep Stu Cncl; Dnfth Awd; Elks Awd; Hon Roll; Keywanettes Clb; Rep For Drug Free Amer Coalition; Kapiolani CC; Radiology.

BARUT, LISA M; Mc Kinley HS; Honolulu, HI; (2); 53/588; Church Yth Grp; Band; Jazz Band; Hon Roll; Jr NHS; Prfct Atten Awd; Mgmt.

BATALON, ERIC B; James Campbell HS; Ewa Beach, HI; (2); 28/348; DECA; Band; Mrchg Band; Pep Band; Lit Mag; Canons Business Coll; Bus Admin.

BATTUNG, NICOLE R; Farrington HS; Honolulu, HI; (2); Chrmn Variety Show; Ed Nwsp; Chrmn Stu Cncl; JV Bsktbl; Mgr(s); Score Keeper; JV Vllybl; Pres Acad Fit Awd; Jr Class Sec 90-91; U Of HI; Mech Engr.

BAUER, BENJAMIN S; Kaimuki HS; Honolulu, HI; (2); 57/325; JV Bsktbl; Hon Roll; Ctzn Bee St Of HI; Hstry.

BAUTISTA, DENNIS R; James Campbell HS; Ewa Beach, HI; (3); 4/386; Aud/Vis; Key Clb; Band; Ed Nwsp; Pres Soph Cls; Pres Jr Cls; Stu Cncl; Intrml Mgr Bsktbl; NHS; Chaminade U; Cmmnctns.

BAUTISTA, MARY ANN P; Mc Kinley HS; Honolulu, HI; (3); 40/537; Treas Art Clb; Spanish Clb; Rptr Nwsp; Pres Frsh Cls; Hon Roll; Amer Lgn Schl Awd; U HI; Psych.

BAUTISTA, TRACY M; Baldwin HS; Wailuku, HI; (4); Treas Art Clb; FTA; Library Aide; Spanish Clb; Hist SADD; Teachers Aide; Band; Yrbk; Sec Sr Cls; Hon Roll; U HI; Fshn Mrchndsng.

BAYANG, HAROLD; Campbell HS; Ewa Beach, HI; (4); Chrmn Aud/Vis; FBLA; Pres Key Clb; Mrchg Band; JV Bsktbl; JV Ftbl; Capt Var Tennis; Bwlng Capt Var; U Of HI-MANOA; Comm.

BAYSA, LOVISA H P; Kamehameha Schls; Hilo, HI; (4); JA; Letterman Clb; Office Aide; Spanish Clb; Varsity Clb; Rep Frsh Cls; Rep Jr Cls; JV Var Bsktbl; Stat Ftbl; Mgr(s); U Of HI Hilo; Acctg.

BAZ, SANANDA; St Anthony JR-SR HS; Kahului, HI; (4); Computer Clb; Math Clb; Math Tm; Service Clb; Spanish Clb; Teachers Aide; Hon Roll; Excllnc-Tech & Religious Studies; Cntl Math League; UH At Manoa; Engrng.

BEACH, ERICA; Kalaheo HS; Kailua, HI; (2); Drama Clb; Thesps; School Play; Hon Roll; Masonic Awd; Treas Of Thespian; Air Force Acad.

BEALS, KENYAN K; Waiakea HS; Hilo, HI; (3); 94/368; CO ST U; Wildlife Bio.

BEAMER, MICHELLE N; James Campbell HS; Ewa Beach, HI; (3); Church Yth Grp; Drama Clb; Key Clb; Speech Tm; Church Choir; School Play; 2nd Pl Accntng Cmptn Awd; Accntng.

BEARD, CARLA D; Mililani HS; Wahiawa, HI; (3); 115/490; Cmnty Wkr; Library Aide; ROTC; Color Guard; Drill Tm; Flag Corp; School Play; Hon Roll; Prfct Atten Awd; Law.

BEARIS, MICHAEL C; James Campbell HS; Ewa Beach, HI; (3); 32/371; Aud/Vis; Church Yth Grp; JA; Pep Clb; Chorus; Church Choir; Intrml Bsktbl; JV Ftbl; Powder Puff Ftbl; Hon Roll; U Of HI; Elec Engr.

BECKER, JENNIFER L; James Campbell HS; Ewa Beach, HI; (3); Church Yth Grp; Drama Clb; FCA; Teachers Aide; School Musical; School Play; High Hon Roll; Yth Chrst Vllybl Trnmnt; U Of HI; Sci Teacher.

BECKER, JESSICA J; Kalani HS; Honolulu, HI; (3); Art Clb; Drama Clb; French Clb; Latin Clb; Science Clb; Teachers Aide; School Play; Nwsp; Yrbk; Hon Roll; HI Regnl Schltc Art Exhib 89-90; Prof Model; Santa Cruz; Liberal Art.

BEE, LUCADIA L; Saint Francis HS; Pearl City, HI; (2); 48/80; Cmnty Wkr; Library Aide; Office Aide; Chorus; Care Bears; St Louis Pep Clb; U Of HI Manoa; Elem Tchr.

BELL, CYNTHIA D; Radford HS; Honolulu, HI; (4); 46/466; Excllnc In Spnsh; Marine Bio.

BELL, RAYNEE; Kamehameha HS; Hilo, HI; (2); 50/443; Church Yth Grp; Spanish Clb; Temple Yth Grp; Chorus; Church Choir; Stat Var Bsktbl; JV Score Keeper; JV Vllybl; Hon Roll; Vet.

BELLO, DAVID M; Waipahu HS; Waipahu, HI; (4); 400/1200; Var Wrstlng; 1st HI Industrial Arts Fair; Hnrd For Industrial Achvts; Universal Tech Inst; Techncn.

BELLO, REGGIE K; Kohala HS; Kapaau, HI; (2); 5/71; Letterman Clb; VP Pres SADD; VP Pres Stu Cncl; JV Capt Bsktbl; Var Capt Trk; Var Vllybl; Hon Roll; Intnl Clb; VP Pres Spanish Clb; Yrbk; Mock Trl; Close Up; BIASC; Hmrm Rep; Grls Bsktbl Stats; Outstng Frgn Lang Achvt; San Francisco ST U; Sports Med.

BELTRAME, LEHUALANI; Kapaa HS; Anahola, HI; (3); Cmnty Wkr; Dance Clb; Drama Clb; Pres Chorus; School Musical; Rep Frsh Cls; VP Soph Cls; Pres Jr Cls; Capt Sr Cls; Stu Cncl; Hula Dancing.

BELTRAN, ARMI; Lanakila Baptist HS; Waipahu, HI; (1); Spanish Clb; Stu Cncl; Bus.

BELTRAN, MICHAEL A; Waipahu HS; Waipahu, HI; (1); 79/513; Rep Frsh Cls; JV Bsktbl; JV Ftbl; High Hon Roll; U Of HI; Bus.

BENEVIDES, JENNIFER L; Maui HS; Pukalani, HI; (2); 60/388; Band; Chorus; Mrchg Band; Pep Band; Stat Bsktbl; Var Sftbl; Hon Roll; Prfct Atten Awd; U HI Hilo; Psych.

BENITEZ, MARISSA L; Baldwin HS; Wailuku, HI; (2); FHA; Pep Clb; Cheerldng; Socr; Sftbl; Trk; Hon Roll; Notice Of Cmmndtn; UH Manoa; Acctnt.

BENJAMIN, SHELLIE; Waipaha HS; Waipahu, HI; (3); Var Bsktbl; Var Capt Ftbl; Var Capt Trk; High Hon Roll; Hon Roll; Psych.

BENNETT, HOLLY; Kalaheo HS; Kailua, HI; (2); Aud/Vis; Teachers Aide; Off Frsh Cls; Sec Stu Cncl; JV Bsktbl; High Hon Roll; Hon Roll; Cert Achvt Kalaneo Cmmnctns Arts Lrng Ctr; AATF Natl Frnch Tst; Windward Dist Stu Cncl Rep; Nurse.

BENNETT, STEPHANIE A; H P Baldwin HS; Wailuku, HI; (3); Teachers Aide; Music Ed.

BERG, JENNIFER L; Mililani HS; Mililani, HI; (3); 7/490; Church Yth Grp; Drama Clb; Girl Scts; Hosp Aide; Red Cross Aide; Spanish Clb; Thesps; Band; School Musical; School Play; Make Up Cmmtte-Chairperson; Cmmnctns.

BERMUDEZ, CELIA A; W R Farrington HS; Honolulu, HI; (3); 23/600; Key Clb; Band; Off Frsh Cls; Off Soph Cls; Off Jr Cls; Hon Roll; Mst Imprvd Concert Band; Leo Clb; Gov Athl Assn Clb Treas 90-91; Japanese Clb; Yth Of Ambssdrs.

BERRY, ECSTASY L; Roosevelt HS; Honolulu, HI; (2); Church Yth Grp; Trk; Vllybl; Own Dance Grp; BYU; Sociology.

BERTELMANN, SOMMER K; Lahainaluna HS; Captain Cook, HI; (1); Chorus; Socr; Tchr.

BIGNO, KIRSTIE K; Kauai HS; Lihue, HI; (1); 87/254; Band; Mrchg Band; Var Tennis; Hon Roll; Arch.

BIRN, BRANDIE S; Kaiser HS; Honolulu, HI; (1); 1/255; Pep Clb; JV Cheerldng; High Hon Roll; Hon Roll; Interact Clb; Med.

BISARRA, CAROLYN P; Waimea HS; Kekaha, HI; (4); 54/200; Pacific Asian Affair Cncl; Loyola Marymount U; Elec Engrng.

BISQUERA, MICHAEL N; Baldwin HS; Kahului, HI; (3); Hon Roll; Elec Engrng.

BISQUERA, MILDA V; Leilehua HS; Wahiawa, HI; (3); Girl Scts; Math Clb; Teachers Aide; Hon Roll; Kaisahan Clb; Kapiolani CC; Accntnt.

BITANGA, EMELITA P; Waipahu HS; Waipahu, HI; (3); Sec Aud/Vis; DECA; Science Clb; Var Crs Cntry; Hon Roll; Prfct Atten Awd; Interact Club Pres; Prjct Healthstart Pgm; Into To Basic Patient Care Trng Cert Cmpltn; Kapiolani CC; Rgstrd Nrs.

BLAND, MONICA M; Moanalua HS; Honolulu, HI; (3); 123/576; Aud/Vis; Letterman Clb; Spanish Clb; Rep Stu Cncl; L JV Bsktbl; L Capt Socr; L Var Trk; Hon Roll; Pres Acad Fit Awd; Sccr All Star; MVP Sccr, Trck 89-90; U Of TX Austin; Brdcst Jrnlsm.

BLANDO, DANNY; Baldwin HS; Kahului, HI; (2); Hosp Aide; Key Clb; Stage Crew; JV Ftbl; Nrsng.

BLUMER-BUELL, NALIN H; Hana HS; Hana Maui, HI; (1); Girl Scts; Library Aide; Hon Roll; Girl Sct Slvr Awd.

BOAZ, RANDY; Moanalua HS; Honolulu, HI; (4); 41/416; Letterman Clb; Teachers Aide; VP Soph Cls; Bsktbl; Ftbl; Hon Roll; HI Yth For Christ; HE Pacifi U; Bus.

BOBBITT, LISA C; Hawaii School For Girls; Dallas, TX; (3); Cmnty Wkr; French Clb; German Clb; Pres Library Aide; Pep Clb; Spanish Clb; Thesps; Acpl Chr; Chorus; School Musical; Erly Grad; SMU; Cmmnctns.

BOGGS, MALIA K; Mid-Pacific Inst; Honolulu, HI; (3); Cmnty Wkr; Dance Clb; Hosp Aide; Service Clb; SADD; Nwsp; High Hon Roll; Hon Roll; Jr NHS; NHS; Amnesty Intl Clb; Japanese Clb; Holomua Hnr Soc.

BOHLIN, SAMUEL M; Henry Perrine Baldwin HS; Haiku, HI; (3); Lbrn Debate Tm; VP NFL; Science Clb; Speech Tm; Band; Mrchg Band; Pep Band; Hon Roll; U Of HI Manoa; Law.

BOLLHORST, LISA E; Baldwin HS; Pukalani, HI; (2); 56/400; Wt Lftg; Pep Clb; SADD; Band; Mrchg Band; Orch; Pep Band; Mock Trial Team, Full Time Summer Job, Maui Pineapple Co; Japanese Club; Interact Club; HI Cncrt Orch; Harvard; Law Career.

BOLOSAN, SHANE D; Damien Memorial HS; Haleiwa, HI; (3); 24/117; Var Ftbl; Var Trk; Hon Roll; NHS; Filipino Cthlc Club Schrshp; Engrng.

BONDOC, GRICHEL A; Kailua HS; Waimanalo, HI; (3); 6/339; Spanish Clb; Hon Roll; Project Hltst Prgm; All Amer Scholars; Cngrssnl Scholar; CA ST Fullerton; Accntng.

BONGOLAN JR, SILVESTRE D; Waipahu HS; Waipahu, HI; (2); 21/440; High Hon Roll; Hon Roll; Pres Acad Fit Awd; Canons Bus Coll; Comp Operator.

BONIFACIO, JENNIFER T; James Campbell HS; Makakilo, HI; (2); 12/348; Key Clb; Science Clb; Treas Soph Cls; Mgr(s); High Hon Roll; Hon Roll; Mgr Bsktbl.

BONILLA, FERN T; Farrington HS; Honolulu, HI; (2); 87/696; French Clb; Library Aide; Office Aide; Tennis; Hon Roll; Jr NHS; Santa Clara U.

BONNELL JR, ROBERT S; W R Farrington HS; Aiea, HI; (3); 64/600; JA; Key Clb; Office Aide; Chorus; Rptr Nwsp; Lit Mag; Stu Cncl; Voice Dem Awd; Commnctns.

BOQUER, MARIE M; Moanalua HS; Honolulu, HI; (1); Girl Scts; Band; Trk; Hon Roll; Comp Tech.

BORCE, JOEL; Farrington HS; Honolulu, HI; (1); U Of HI; Arch.

BORELLO, NATALIE A; Leilehua HS; Wahiawa, HI; (4); 18/304; Sec Pres Service Clb; Teachers Aide; Ed Yrbk; Rep Chrmn Frsh Cls; Rep Soph Cls; Rep Jr Cls; Rep Sr Cls; Rep Pres Stu Cncl; L Socr; High Hon Roll; HOBY Rep; Mghty Mule; Rep HI Natl Yng Ldrs Cnfrnc; Educ.

BORLING, NORA C; Maui HS; Makawao, HI; (2); 43/452; Hon Roll; Prfct Atten Awd; Bowling & Typing; Sec.

BORSTING, ESBEN A; Waiakea HS; Hilo, HI; (3); 96/368; JA; Math Clb; Band; Jazz Band; Mrchg Band; Orch; Pep Band; Prfct Atten Awd; U HI Manoa; Music Educ.

BOTELHO, SHERRY A; Waiakea HS; Hilo, HI; (1); Drama Clb; Rep Frsh Cls; Rep Stu Cncl; U Of HI Manoa; Fshn Mrchndsng.

BOWDEN, CAROLINE; Saint Joseph HS; Hilo, HI; (2); Pres Soph Cls; Hon Roll; Bus Mgmt.

BRADFORD, AMANDA P; Lahainaluna HS; Lahaina, HI; (4); 4/169; DECA; Math Tm; VP Science Clb; Sec Service Clb; Rep Frsh Cls; Rep Soph Cls; Rep Sr Cls; Rep Stu Cncl; Var L Cheerldng; JV Crs Cntry; Mock Trial Tm; Natl Hnr Rl; All-Amer Schlr.

BRADFORD, TIA L; Campbell HS; Ewa Beach, HI; (3); 7/371; Cmnty Wkr; Key Clb; Library Aide; Quiz Bowl; SADD; Ed Nwsp; Stu Cncl; High Hon Roll; Hon Roll; NHS; Yth Ending Wrld Hunger; U WA; Jrnlst.

BRADSHAW, JONATHAN L; Kahuku HS; Laie, HI; (3); 52/272; Boy Scts; Church Yth Grp; Cmnty Wkr; Computer Clb; Dance Clb; Letterman Clb; Temple Yth Grp; Varsity Clb; Rptr Lit Mag; Bsktbl; Eagle Sct.

BRANCO, JENNIFER; St Joseph HS; Hilo, HI; (4); 1/36; Cmnty Wkr; NFL; Red Cross Aide; Pres Speech Tm; Chorus; Variety Show; Pres Soph Cls; Dnfth Awd; High Hon Roll; NHS; YWCA Brd Of Dir, Vlntr Of Yr Awd 87; HOBY Fndtn Ldrshp Smnr Ambssdr; U HI; Speech Commnctn.

BRANDL, JESSE R; Mid-Pacific Inst; Honolulu, HI; (2); Boy Scts; Civil Air Patrl; Big Brothrs/Big Sistrs HI; Vrsty Water Polo; Civil Engr.

BRAS, GARETT A; Maui HS; Haiku, HI; (2); #40 In Class; Aud/Vis; Church Yth Grp; Cmnty Wkr; Key Clb; Math Tm; Science Clb; SADD; Variety Show; Var L Tennis; Wt Lftg; Hall Fame Most Spirited; Close Up 90; Japanese Club; U Sthrn CA; Arch.

BRAS, RAENELLE M; Maui HS; Haiku, HI; (4); 7/303; Rep Church Yth Grp; VP Computer Clb; Treas Math Tm; Quiz Bowl; Rptr Nwsp; Treas Sr Cls; High Hon Roll; Jr NHS; NHS; Strlng Schlr Soc Sci; Smmr Prgm Enhncmnt Of Basic Ed Chinese Stu Ctr; Close Up 90; Summa Cum Laude Grad; U Of HI Manoa; Pre-Med.

BRAUN, BROOKS; Kapaa HS; Kapaa, HI; (3); Church Yth Grp; Bsbl; Bsktbl; Hon Roll; NHS; Aviation.

BRINLEY, CHANDRA; Pahoa HS; Keaau, HI; (4); Computer Clb; FTA; Library Aide; Science Clb; Teachers Aide; High Hon Roll; NHS; Awd Marine Scr Fr; U Of HI Hilo.

BRINTON-JAMES, KRISTINA M; Mid-Pacific Inst; Honolulu, HI; (2); 4/150; Cmnty Wkr; Drama Clb; NFL; Q&S; Spanish Clb; Speech Tm; School Musical; School Play; Stage Crew; Rep Soph Cls; Hld 5 Wrk Schlrshp Pstns; Ed.

BRITOS, DEAN; St Louis Schl; Honolulu, HI; (2); 2/152; Math Clb; Math Tm; Rptr Nwsp; Treas Frsh Cls; Treas Soph Cls; Rep Stu Cncl; Crs Cntry; Socr; High Hon Roll; Prfct Atten Awd; Smmr Fun Pgm Jr Ldr 2 Yrs; UCLA; Pediatrics.

BROCK, STEPHANIE G; Hawaii Baptist Acad; Wahiawa, HI; (2); Church Yth Grp; Drama Clb; Library Aide; Office Aide; Thesps; Drill Tm; School Musical; School Play; Stage Crew; Hon Roll; Deans List; Intl Thespians Awd; U Of HI; Law.

BROCKMAN, MICAH J; Leilehua HS; Wahiawa, HI; (2); 197/392; Church Yth Grp; Cmnty Wkr; VP Drama Clb; Speech Tm; Thesps; Church Choir; School Play; Stage Crew; Sftbl; Wt Lftg; Dept Ed Cert PRAISE; AZ ST U; Bus.

BRODERICK, KRISTINA; Kalaheo HS; Kailua, HI; (2); 5/287; Off Soph Cls; JV Var Bsktbl; Var Socr; Var Tennis; Var Vllybl; High Hon Roll; St John Lutheran; Serteens Clb; Cert Achvt Kalaheos Cmmntn Arts Lrng Ctr.

BRODERICK, SCOTT A; Radford HS; Syracuse, NY; (3); 114/394; Boy Scts; ROTC; Intrml Socr; Eagle Scout; Order Of The Arrow; JROTC Rifle Team; Engrng.

BRODEUR, BUFFY L; Moanalua HS; Oak Harbor, WA; (4); VP Church Yth Grp; FHA; Teachers Aide; Variety Show; Ntl Merit Ltr; Skagit Valley Coll.

BRODY, YANAH MALIA; Kalaheo HS; Kailua, HI; (3); 54/240; Church Yth Grp; Cmnty Wkr; Drama Clb; Thesps; Church Choir; School Musical; School Play; Stage Crew; Swing Chorus; Socr; Engl.

BROOKS, JEREMY P; Moanalua HS; Honolulu, HI; (2); Church Yth Grp; Computer Clb; JV Bsbl; U Of TX; Law.

BROOKS, NATALIE N; Leilehua HS; Scholfield Bks, HI; (2); 150/392; Girl Scts; Red Cross Aide; Band; Mrchg Band; Pep Band; Trk; Teen Cncl Secy; Embry-Riddle; Elec Engr.

BROOME, LUKA; Konaweana HS; Kailua Kona, HI; (2); 64/380; Chess Clb; Church Yth Grp; Drama Clb; Spanish Clb; Church Choir; School Play; Swmmng; Hon Roll; Flight Attendant.

BROTHERS, SHANNON M; Mililani HS; Wahiawa, HI; (3); 221/490; Church Yth Grp; Cmnty Wkr; Band; Drill Tm; Bsktbl; Phys Thrpst.

BROWN, BRANDY; Kalani HS; Honolulu, HI; (1); 57/246; Church Yth Grp; Cmnty Wkr; Girl Scts; Band; Mrchg Band.

BROWN, CUTTER R; Hawaii Preparatory Acad; Princeville, HI; (2); Chorus; Variety Show; Nwsp; Rep Soph Cls; Rep Stu Cncl; Var L Crs Cntry; Var L Socr; Var L Trk; Hon Roll; Built Solar Car Race Cmtpns; Dsgn & Build Car Undr 16000.

BROWN, DEANNA; Kalaheo HS; Kailua, HI; (1); Tennis; Hon Roll; Law Clb; Georgetown U; Law.

BROWN, GULLIVER; Waiakea HS; Pahoa, HI; (2); Art Clb; Drama Clb; English Clb; Speech Tm; Band; Mrchg Band; School Play; Stage Crew; Var Socr; Cit Awd; Skate Boarding; UCLA; Artist.

BROWN, JEFF; Radford HS; Pensacola, FL; (3); ROTC; Socr; Police Ofcr.

BROWN, ROSE; James Campbell HS; Ewa Beach, HI; (2); High Hon Roll; NHS; Ntl Merit Ltr; Pres Acad Fit Awd; Law Or Science.

BROWNING, MONICA D; Leilehua HS; Wahiawa, HI; (2); 110/392; JV Trk; U Of FL; Law.

BRUTON, MAE M; Mililani HS; Mililani Town, HI; (3); 106/490; Church Yth Grp; Office Aide; Teachers Aide; Pres Frsh Cls; Var Tennis; Micronesian Olympcs, Chuuk St Tm,Saipan-Nmi Tnns; Photo Jrnlsm; Debate; Baylor U; Intl Law.

BRYANT, DONNA A; Mililani HS; Mililani, HI; (2); 71/516.

BUCK, KAREN E; Punahou Schl; Honolulu, HI; (4); Art Clb; Church Yth Grp; Mgr Varsity Clb; Socr; Art Awd; Hiking; Envrnmntl Artist.

BUCO, IRENE B; Waipahu HS; Waipahu, HI; (1); 18/513; Rep Frsh Cls; JV Trk; High Hon Roll; Hon Roll; Interact Clb Elected Brd Of Dir; U Of HI; Engl.

BUENCONSEJO, KELLI L; Leilehua HS; Mililani, HI; (4); 14/304; Church Yth Grp; Treas Spanish Clb; Chrmn Jr Cls; Chrmn Sr Cls; Chrmn Stu Cncl; Score Keeper; Stat Trk; NHS; Rotary Awd; HI Rep Attnd Wrld Affrs Smnr; Sci Fr Wnnr; Lt Gov Interact Dist 500; U Of HI; Social Work.

BUENO, DWAYNE; Waipahu HS; Waipahu, HI; (4); 19/418; Sec Band; Drm Mjr(t); Jazz Band; Mrchg Band; Pep Band; Co-Ed Lit Mag; Off Frsh Cls; Chrmn Soph Cls; Chrmn Jr Cls; Sec VP Sr Cls; Older Bros/Older Sis Helping-Chairperson; Excllnc Cert-Scl Stds/Typing/Acctng; Close Up Pgm 89; U Of La Verne; Law.

BUGARIN JR, RODOLFO M; W R Farrington HS; Kailua, HI; (2); 15/700; Church Yth Grp; Math Tm; Service Clb; SADD; Ed Nwsp; Chrmn Soph Cls; Var L Tennis; High Hon Roll; Pres Jr NHS; Sarteens Intl; Hnrbl Mention-Natl Schlstc Writing Awds-Poetry; 90 HI St Stu Conf Delg; Sports Med.

BUILLARD, LEILANI; Saint Francis HS; Pearl City, HI; (2); 18/80; Cmnty Wkr; Library Aide; Pep Clb; Hon Roll; Care-Bear; Notre Dame; Archit.

BUKOSKI, DAVID L; Kauai HS; Koloa, HI; (4); Pep Clb; ROTC; SADD; Varsity Clb; Chorus; Drill Tm; Off Frsh Cls; Rep Soph Cls; Capt Var Bsbl; Var Bsktbl; UH Hilo.

BULOSAN, DONAH M; Roosevelt HS; Honolulu, HI; (2); 14/360; Church Yth Grp; FTA; Sec Key Clb; Spanish Clb; Teachers Aide; Mrchg Band; Nwsp; Tennis; NHS; Biomed Resrch Prgm U HI Internshp 90; U HI Manoa; Medcn.

BULUSAN, CARMEL; Henry Perrine Baldwin HS; Wailuku, HI; (4); 60/360; Pres Church Yth Grp; DECA; FTA; Service Clb; SADD; Band; Mrchg Band; Pep Band; Treas Sr Cls; High Hon Roll; Brigham Young U; Arch Engrng.

BUNAO, ROSSANO C; Kaimuki HS; Honolulu, HI; (3); Var JV Bsktbl; JV Ftbl; Var JV Trk.

BUNGHANOY, GRACE P; Leilehua HS; Wahiawa, HI; (2); 4-H; Band; Interact Clb; Psych.

BUNGHANOY, WILLY-GRACE; Leilehua HS; Wahiawa, HI; (2); 25/406; 4-H; Band; Pep Band; Intract Clb; Psych.

BURCENA, DANA; Pahoa HS & Elem; Keaau, HI; (2); FFA; Letterman Clb; VP Frsh Cls; Bsbl; Cheerldng; Mgr(s); Prfct Atten Awd; 2nd Prncss Jr Ms Sampaguita 89-90; Delg Cmp HOBY; Trvl Indstry Mgmt.

BURGESS, RICHARD K; Kauai HS; Kapaa, HI; (4); Church Yth Grp; FTA; Key Clb; Band; Var JV Bsktbl; Var Capt Crs Cntry; Var Capt Trk; Var Capt Vllybl; NHS; VP Jr Cls; St Chmp In Hurdles; Mst Outstndng Athl Awd; Leag All Star Vllybl & Bsktbl; Biola U; Sports Physiology.

BURKE, BONNIE LORAIN; Saint Francis HS; Ewa Beach, HI; (2); 3/80; Church Yth Grp; Office Aide; Speech Tm; Teachers Aide; School Play; High Hon Roll; Hon Roll; NHS; Georgian Court Coll; Lawyer.

BURKE, MICHAEL T; Hawaii Baptist Acad; Waianae, HI; (2); VP JA; Math Tm; Science Clb; School Musical; Rep Frsh Cls; Treas Soph Cls; Hon Roll; Serteens; IM Bwlng; Chrch Secy; UCLA; Pre-Law.

BURLEY, JENNIFER; Waipahu HS; Waipahu, HI; (2); 50/440; Science Clb; JV Capt Crs Cntry; Yth For Christ Vllybl; Campus Life Clb.

BURNZ, CARLA K; Kauai High & Int Schl; Lihue, HI; (3); 18/231; Q&S; Treas SADD; Band; Co-Ed Yrbk; L Trk; High Hon Roll; Hon Roll; Prfct Atten Awd; Cert Achvt Natl Fed Parents For Drug Free Yth; RADD; OR ST U; Jrnlsm.

BURROWS, LEATRICE W; Lahainaluna HS; Hoolehua, HI; (1); 10/170; VP Church Yth Grp; Chorus; Yrbk; Bsktbl; Sftbl; Hawaiiana Clb; Hana Kupono O Olokai; U HI Manoa; Comp Engr.

BUSBY III, GILBERT L; Radford HS; Honolulu, HI; (3); 1/394; Pres Chess Clb; Debate Tm; VP Math Clb; Math Tm; Mu Alpha Theta; NFL; Rep Frsh Cls; High Hon Roll; NHS; 2ND Pl JV Debate St Fnls; Med.

BUSH, ALISON; Waiakea HS; Volcano, HI; (4); 74/412; Drama Clb; French Clb; Rptr Nwsp; Var Crs Cntry; Var JV Trk; High Hon Roll; Hon Roll; Cum Laude Grad; Elem Teacher.

BUSTAMANTE, JOSE M; Moanalua HS; Makakilo, HI; (2); 15/500; Cmnty Wkr; Service Clb; JV Bsktbl; High Hon Roll; Hon Roll; Lion Awd; Pres Acad Fit Awd; Rutgers U; Bus Adm.

BUTLER, MELINDA Y; Radford HS; Ewa Beach, HI; (3); 60/394; Band; Mrchg Band; Pep Band; Japanese II Cert Awd Excllnce 88-89; OBDA Solo/Ensmble Clarint Duet Silver Mdl Awd 88-89; UH Manoa; Music.

BYRD, ANTONIO D; Moanalua HS; Honolulu, HI; (2); 149/488; Boy Scts; Church Yth Grp; Computer Clb; Band; Mrchg Band; Pep Band; JV Bsktbl; Hon Roll; Aviation.

CABACUNGAN, GRACE; Roosevelt HS; Honolulu, HI; (1); 38/252; Science Clb; Spanish Clb; Cit Awd; Stanford U; Phy.

CABAEL, CRISTINA C; Waipahu HS; Waipahu, HI; (4); 33/418; High Hon Roll; Hon Roll; Grad Cum Laude W/Hnrs; SMILE Prgm Stus Mkng Indvdl Lives Easier; Leeward CC; Bus.

CABAEL, GERALD C; Molokai High & Intermediate Schl; Kaunakakai, HI; (3); 9/94; Cmnty Wkr; JA; Band; Var Bsbl; High Hon Roll; Hnrs Clb; Advncd Placement Pgm; USC.

CABANAYAN, DAVE A; Radford HS; Honolulu, HI; (2); French Clb; Band; Mrchg Band; Pep Band; Hon Roll; Band Partcptn Awd; Piano & Bass Drums; Bus Mgmt.

CABATU, RODNEY C; Lanai HS; Lanai City, HI; (4); Aud/Vis; Church Yth Grp; Letterman Clb; VP VICA; Band; Sec Soph Cls; Intrml Wt Lftg; Var Wrstlng; HI Rotry Yth Fndtn Bus Smnr; Fnlst St Sterling Schlrshp; 2nd Yr Upward Bound; Elec Engrng.

CABBAB, LORYANN A; Sacred Hearts Acad; Honolulu, HI; (4); Cmnty Wkr; French Clb; Math Clb; Service Clb; Rep Sr Cls; French Awd 87; COPE Rep; Sacred Heart Acad Svc Awd 90; Grad Awd; U Of HI Manoa; Arch Engrng.

CABEL, CHRISTOPHER B; Lanaina Luna HS; Lahaina Mani, HI; (2); 103/235; Science Clb; VP Frsh Cls; Bsktbl; Mani CC; Aeronautics.

CABRAL, SANDRA T; Farrington HS; Honolulu, HI; (3); 120/600; Drama Clb; Chorus; Nwsp; Yrbk; Kokua Aina Club; Outstndng Achvmt Awd Japanese; CA Trvlg Sch; Travel Ind.

CABRERA, PETER A L; Damien HS; Honolulu, HI; (3); Intrml Bsktbl; Intrml Ftbl; U HI.

CACAL, DIGNA C; Waipahu HS; Waipahu, HI; (1); Hon Roll.

CACHERO, CATHLEEN J G; Punahou Schl; Honolulu, HI; (4); SADD; Orch; Var JV Bsktbl; Gov Hon Prg Awd; NHS; Ntl Merit SF; Punahou Jr Schl Camp Cnslr; Punahou Carnival Div Head; Biological Basis Of Behavior.

CADELINA, NOEL A; Farrington HS; Honolulu, HI; (2); 115/696; JV Bsbl; JV Bsktbl; Hon Roll; Auto Mechanic.

CADIENTE, JASON J; Waipahu HS; Waipahu, HI; (4); 2/418; Cmnty Wkr; High Hon Roll; Hon Roll; Sal; Hnr Cert Excllnc Geom 88; Excllnc Japanese 90; Outstndg Bus Stu Gen Bus 88; Lee Ward Kenpo Karate Stu; U Of HI Manoa; Gen Bus.

CADIENTE, JINGLE B; W R Farrington HS; Honolulu, HI; (2); Band; Mrchg Band; Orch; Pep Band; Hon Roll; Prfct Atten Awd; U Of HI; RN.

CADIZ, ELIZABETH; Farrington HS; Ewa Beach, HI; (3); Red Cross Aide; Treas Spanish Clb; Hon Roll; Leo Clb; Tlnt Show Cmmtte; Accntng.

CADIZ, ROBERTO C; Farrington HS; Honolulu, HI; (1); Stu Cncl; Cit Awd; Hon Roll; Prfct Atten Awd; Pres Acad Fit Awd; Hnrb Mntn Motor Bldrs; 1st Pl Category At Monologues In Dclmtn Cont; 1st Pl Turkey Trot Meet 2 Yrs.

CAHN, JULIE L; Kaiser HS; Honolulu, HI; (3); Service Clb; JV Var Swmmng; Hon Roll; Pres Acad Fit Awd; Wrk W/Ride Horses; Swmmng Tm; CO ST; Vet.

CAITANO, IAN K; Roosevelt HS; Honolulu, HI; (2); Band; Vlntr; Jrnlsm.

CAJSKI, CATHERINE M; St Francis HS; Kailua, HI; (3); 1/65; Mu Alpha Theta; NFL; VP Speech Tm; VP Soph Cls; Pres Stu Cncl; Var Socr; Var Vllybl; Pres NHS; Campus Ministry; Mother Teresa Co-Wkrs; Med.

CALAMAYAN, FLORDELIZA; Pahoa High & Elementary Schl; Pahoa, HI; (3); 23/116; VP FBLA; FHA; FTA; Office Aide; Quiz Bowl; Teachers Aide; Church Choir; Cit Awd; Hon Roll; NHS; Leo Clb; Photogrphy Clb; Creative Wrtg Clb; UH Coll; Tchr.

CALAMAYAN, GEORGE B; Viaipahu HS; Waipahu, HI; (2); 7/440; Drama Clb; Math Clb; Science Clb; Phtg Nwsp; Yrbk; High Hon Roll; Colmbn Sqrs Knghts Of Col; CAT; Various Bsktbl Tms; U HI Manoa; Elec Engrng.

CALAPINI, ESTHER; Lahainaluna HS; Lahaina, HI; (3); Church Yth Grp; Treas Band; Mrchg Band; Pep Band; Rep Soph Cls; Lahainaluna Soc Stud, Engl Acadmc Awd; U HI Manoa; Poltcl Sci.

CALILAO, PAMELA MAY E; Lanai HS; Lanai City, HI; (4); Church Yth Grp; FHA; Letterman Clb; Spanish Clb; Band; Yrbk; Pres Frsh Cls; Stu Cncl; JV Bsktbl; Gov Hon Prg Awd; Alumni Schlrshp; Justice Benjamin Menor Schlrshp; U Of HI Manoa; Lib Arts.

CALLEJO, RUSSELL D; St Louis HS; Mililani, HI; (2); 4/151; Intrml Bsbl; JV Var Ftbl; JV Trk; High Hon Roll; Hon Roll; Schlr Athl Awd; Pilot.

CALPITO, ROWENA; Waipahu HS; Waipahu, HI; (3); 29/409; Math Clb; Spanish Clb; Hon Roll; Ec Club; Soc Avid Readers; Spelling Bee Contestant; WA ST U; Ped.

CAMACHO, ELIZABETH M; Waiakea HS; Hilo, HI; (3); Church Yth Grp; FCA; Teachers Aide; Chorus; Church Choir; Variety Show; Yrbk; Rep Stu Cncl; Score Keeper; Nominated Alulike Outstndng Summer Yth; Corning CC; Law Enforcement.

CAMACHO, LANAE; Waiakea HS; Hilo, HI; (1); 99/478; JA; Vllybl; Hon Roll; Polynesian Ukelele Band.

CAMACHO, MARISA L; Kailua HS; Kaneohe, HI; (2); 27/301; Sec Jr Cls; Var Cheerldng; Hon Roll.

CAMBE, RICHARD A; Domien Memorial HS; Honolulu, HI; (4); 25/127; Aud/Vis; Dance Clb; Pep Clb; ROTC; Band; Mrchg Band; High Hon Roll; Hon Roll; Ntl Merit Ltr; Ldrshp Awd ROTC; U Of HI; Comp Sci.

CAMPBELL, KAWEHILANI C; Kaimuki HS; Kaneohe, HI; (4); JA; Teachers Aide; Hon Roll; Child Care Svc.

CAMPBELL, SONYA; Mililani HS; Mililani, HI; (3); Church Yth Grp; SADD; Var Trk; Hon Roll; TX A&M U; Civil Engr.

CAMPBELL, TONY L; Mc Kinley HS; Honolulu, HI; (4); Math Tm; Quiz Bowl; Science Clb; School Play; Stage Crew; Variety Show; JV Ftbl; High Hon Roll; Hon Roll; NHS; Robotics; Sci Fiction; Bsktbl; Worcester Poly Inst; Robotics.

CAMPOS, MARY JANE C; Maui HS; Kahului, HI; (2); 34/388; Math Clb; Science Clb; JV Var Cheerldng; Lion Awd.

CANDIDO, MARLA M; St Francis HS; Waipahu, HI; (3); 14/58; Art Clb; Church Yth Grp; Math Clb; Pep Clb; Spanish Clb; Teachers Aide; Ed Yrbk; GPA Achvt Awd; Most Creative & Highest Grade Art; Soc Wrkr.

CANLIS, JP C; St Louis HS; Honolulu, HI; (2); 25/151; Pres Soph Cls; Ftbl; Tennis; Vllybl; Hon Roll.

CAO, QUANG; Waipahu HS; Honolulu, HI; (4); 6/418; High Hon Roll; Hon Roll; Outstndng Trig Awd; Economic Club Pres; GA Tech; Elect Engrng.

CAPA, ROMEO; 660 S Lono Ave HS; Kahului, HI; (2); Ftbl.

CARBONEL, TRICIA; Lanakila Baptist HS; Waipahu, HI; (1); Intrml Vllybl; Hon Roll; NHS; Lab Schl; Med Field.

CARCUEVA, CECILIE M; Waimea HS; Kekaha, HI; (3); 40/186; Church Yth Grp; JV Bsktbl; Sftbl; Trk; Hon Roll; U HI Hilo; Cmptr Sci.

CARDEJON, ARDIS; Waimea HS; Kekaha, HI; (2); 21/186; Pres Chrmn Church Yth Grp; Math Tm; Speech Tm; Var Vllybl; Hon Roll; NHS; Treas Soph Cls; BYU; Elem Ed.

CARDONA, VALERIE B; James Campbell HS; Ewa Beach, HI; (2); 21/348; Church Yth Grp; Library Aide; Sec Band; Church Choir; Mrchg Band; Hon Roll; Acctng.

CAREY, KALAI; Hana HS; Hana, HI; (2); 1/25; Band; Nwsp; VP Frsh Cls; Pres Soph Cls; Rep Stu Cncl; High Hon Roll; Hon Roll; Sec NHS; Bus Mgmt.

CARINO, DAVID F; Saint Louis HS; Mililani, HI; (2); 26/151; Var L Bsbl; JV L Ftbl; Var L Socr; Hon Roll; Prfct Atten Awd; Numerous Awds & Achvt In Sccr, Ftbl, Bsbl 88-90; UCLA.

CARLOS, ALMA C; Moanalua HS; Honolulu, HI; (3); Hosp Aide; Treas Jr Cls; Var Mgr(s); Hon Roll; Med.

CARNATE, MAY B; Moanalua HS; Honolulu, HI; (2); 41/488; VP FTA; Interact Club; U Of HI; Ed.

CARPENTER, DERRICK T; Kaiser HS; Honolulu, HI; (4); 1/291; Pres Church Yth Grp; Key Clb; Math Tm; Lit Mag; Intrml Vllybl; Wrstlng; Hon Roll; JETS Awd; NHS; Ntl Merit SF; Yale Bk Awd; NCTE Achvt Awd For Wrting; Stanford U; Engrng.

CARR, JONATHAN J; Radford HS; Honolulu, HI; (4); Ski Clb; Chorus; School Musical; School Play; Variety Show; Miss NY St Pgnt Troupe 89; Slct Shw Chr 86-89; NY St Schl Music Assn Solo Cmptn A Rtng 89.

CARROLL, LINDA; Hilo HS; Hilo, HI; (3); 17/343; Var L Crs Cntry; Var L Tennis; Hon Roll; Keywanettes Sec; UH Hilo; Nrsng.

CARSON, JARED; Kalaheo HS; Kailua, HI; (1); Boy Scts; Church Yth Grp; Hon Roll; Brigham Young U.

CARTER, GIL D; Radford HS; Honolulu, HI; (3); Church Yth Grp; JA; ROTC; Teachers Aide; Var L Bsbl; Hon Roll; Young Author Awd Wnnr 87; Southwest MO ST U; Mltry Plt.

CARTER, KATINA; Leilehua HS; Wahiawa, HI; (3); Pep Clb; VP Spanish Clb; Rep Frsh Cls; Rep Jr Cls; Rep Stu Cncl; Bsktbl; Pom Pon; Hon Roll; Auburn U; Bus Admin.

CARTER, RAVI HOPE; Roosevelt HS; Honolulu, HI; (3); Cmnty Wkr; Drama Clb; Thesps; Chorus; School Musical; School Play; Stage Crew; Lit Mag; NEDT Awd; Pres Schlr; People To People Stu Ambssdr To Soviet Union 90; Numerous Achvts & Certs In Art Cmptns; Illustration.

CARTWRIGHT, ROBERTA; Kahuku HS; Hauula, HI; (4); Bsktbl; Sftbl; Cit Awd; High Hon Roll; Hon Roll; Carpenter.

CARUMBANA, CARLETTE; Maryknoll HS; Honolulu, HI; (2); Church Yth Grp; Spanish Clb; Band; Color Guard; Mrchg Band; Rptr Lit Mag; Trk; Vllybl; Lang Arts Showcase Wnnr Short Story; Jrnlsm.

CARVALHO, MARY KINAU K; Saint Francis HS; Honolulu, HI; (3); 15/58; Mu Alpha Theta; Band; Chorus; Color Guard; Yrbk; VP Frsh Cls; Hon Roll; Prfct Atten Awd; HI Pacific Coll; Comp Sci.

CASEM, FLOYD C; Leilehua HS; Wahiawa, HI; (3); 45/322; Rep Stu Cncl; Capt Vllybl; Hon Roll; Vllybl All Star; U Of HI; Comp Sci.

CASEN, NARLYN U; Waialua HS; Haleiwa, HI; (2); Dance Clb; Math Clb; Math Tm; Quiz Bowl; Rep Frsh Cls; Sec Soph Cls; Var Socr; High Hon Roll; Hon Roll; Prfct Atten Awd; Social Cmmtte; Englsh Handbk; U Of HI.

CASINO, KATHLEEN G; Kallai HS; Hanamaulu, HI; (1); Band; Mrchg Band; Hon Roll; JV L Bsktbl.

CASPILLO, PAUL HARRIS; Molokai HS; Kaunakakai, HI; (3); 23/94; Var Bsbl; Var Wrstlng; U Of HI Hilo; Carpentry.

CASPILLO, SHAYNEE H; Kapaa HS; Kapaa, HI; (3); 14/179; FHA; Spanish Clb; High Hon Roll; NHS.

CASTILLO, FILEMON C; Waipahu HS; Waipahu, HI; (1); 55/513; Stu Cncl; JV Bsbl; Var Crs Cntry; Prfct Atten Awd; Wntrbll Escrt; Al-Str Bsbl.

CASTILLO, FRIEDA C; Radford HS; Honolulu, HI; (1); 56/466; Kaha Ki'i-An Artistic Discovery Hnr; Gov Awd Congrssnl Art Cmptn 90; Natl Schlstc Art Cont Check Wnnr.

CAWAGAS, LIZA F; Konawaena HS & Intermed; Kailua Kona, HI; (2); 1/357; NFL; Off Frsh Cls; Off Soph Cls; Hon Roll; NHS; Prfct Atten Awd; Cls Up Clb; Clss Spkr Schls Sng Cont; UH Manda; Med.

CAYA, RALLEN A; Kalaheo HS; Kailua, HI; (3); Aud/Vis; Drm Mjr(t); Stat Golf; Stat Tennis; Stat Wt Lftg; ITT Tech Inst.

CAYABAN, DAVID J K; Saint Louis HS; Honolulu, HI; (3); Church Yth Grp; Letterman Clb; Spanish Clb; Varsity Clb; Rep Frsh Cls; Rep Soph Cls; Rep Jr Cls; VP Stu Cncl; Intrml Bsbl; Var L Ftbl; FIRES Yth Cnslr; UC Berkeley; Law-Crmnl Jstce.

CAYABAN, JANICE D; Maui HS; Pukalani, HI; (2); Band; Mrchg Band; Cit Awd; Hon Roll; Pharm.

CAYABYAB, AMPARO V; Kapaa HS; Kapaa, HI; (2); Showlites Modelng Schl Grad; HI Business Coll.

CAYME, MELALYN Y; Pahoa HS; Pahoa, HI; (2); 16/117; FHA; Spanish Clb; Rep Frsh Cls; Rep Soph Cls; Sec Stu Cncl; Cit Awd; Hon Roll; NHS; Prfct Atten Awd; Pres Acad Fit Awd; Peace Club Treasurer; Committe Head Awards; Psychology.

CENAL, TRACI M; St Andrews Priory HS; Pearl City, HI; (3); Key Clb; Service Clb; Spanish Clb; Chorus; Treas Jr Cls; Rep Stu Cncl; JV Vllybl; High Hon Roll; Hon Roll.

CEPEDA, CLINT F; Mounalua HS; Honolulu, HI; (2); Var JV Ftbl; Hon Roll; Prfct Atten Awd; USC; Law.

CEZAR JR, BENJAMIN; Radford HS; Honolulu, HI; (3); 6/394; JV Crs Cntry; High Hon Roll; Hon Roll; Achvt Japanese Level 1 & 2; Bio.

CHALKER, TAE K; Waiakea HS; Hilo, HI; (2); Sec 4-H; VP JA; Flag Corp; Variety Show; Var L Trk; Hon Roll; Mck Trl Pgm; Natl Scl Stds Olympd Cert; Outstndng VP Persnnl/Corp Sectry J A; Pre-Med.

CHAMBERS, JAMES ALAN; Hanalani HS; Milani, HI; (2); 3/11; Church Yth Grp; Sec Frsh Cls; VP Soph Cls; High Hon Roll; All Amer Scholar; Notre Dame; Law.

CHAMBERS, TRACI M; Waipahu HS; Waipahu, HI; (3); Church Yth Grp; Drama Clb; Service Clb; Rep Soph Cls; Stu Cncl; Stat Bsktbl; Hon Roll; SMILE; Leo Clb; Stu Orgnztn Cncl Chrprsn; UH Manoa; Elem Ed.

CHAN, ALICE S; Mc Kinley HS; Honolulu, HI; (1); 17/490; Math Clb.

CHAN, ANTHONY; Damien Memorial HS; Honolulu, HI; (3); 3/115; Debate Tm; Math Clb; Math Tm; NFL; ROTC; VP Speech Tm; Yrbk; Hon Roll; NHS; 1st Hnrs; Jr Vrsty Debate 2nd Pl In St 88; ROTC Medals Outstndng Acadmc Achvt; Rice U; Chem Engrng.

CHAN, DAVID J; St Louis Schl; Honolulu, HI; (3); 17/158; Cmnty Wkr; French Clb; Intnl Clb; Math Tm; ROTC; Science Clb; Rep Frsh Cls; JV Var Tennis; High Hon Roll; JV, Vrsty Rfl Tm; NYU; Bus Admin.

CHAN, JESSICA HUNG MUI; Mc Kinley HS; Honolulu, HI; (2); Math Clb; Science Clb; Tennis; Hon Roll; Sci Fair; UCLA; Sci.

CHAN, JOANIE K Y; Maryknoll HS; Aiea, HI; (4); Sec Frsh Cls; Var Capt Bsktbl; Var Vllybl; High Hon Roll; Schlr/Athl, Japanese & Bio Awds; Boston Coll; Bus/Fshn.

CHAN, JUNE Y; Mc Kinley HS; Honolulu, HI; (4); 47/547; Church Yth Grp; Cmnty Wkr; Hosp Aide; Treas Spanish Clb; Orch; School Musical; Crs Cntry; Trk; Hon Roll; Physic Clb Pres; Brandeis U; Pre-Med.

CHAN, LILLY; President William Mc Kinley HS; Honolulu, HI; (2); 183/588; Rep Chess Clb; Hosp Aide; Phtg Nwsp; Chrmn Soph Cls; Prfct Atten Awd; Bnqt Decor Chmn; Intrmrl Archery Tourn-2nd Prz; Outstndg Schl Svc; Bus.

CHAN, OWEN; Damien Memorial HS; Honolulu, HI; (4); 2/125; Debate Tm; Math Clb; NFL; ROTC; Ed Yrbk; High Hon Roll; NHS; NEDT Awd; Pres Acad Fit Awd; Sal; Brown U.

CHAN, WAI KEE; Kalani HS; Honolulu, HI; (2); 4/213; Key Clb; Math Tm; Service Clb; SADD; Sec Jr Cls; JV Crs Cntry; Var Socr; JV Trk; High Hon Roll; Hon Roll; U HI; Bus.

CHAN, YAT FAI; Kaiser HS; Honolulu, HI; (3); Chess Clb; Church Yth Grp; Computer Clb; Math Tm; Office Aide; Quiz Bowl; Pres Science Clb; Service Clb; Spanish Clb; VP VICA; Asian Clb-VP; Comp Sci.

CHANG, ALLISON S; Iolani Schl; Honolulu, HI; (4); Cmnty Wkr; Orch; Rptr Nwsp; Chrmn Stu Cncl; Var L Bsktbl; High Hon Roll; Hon Roll; Ntl Merit SF; Art Clb; French Clb; Judo St Champ; St Yth Symph; Prncpl Cello Concert Orch; Radiologist.

CHANG, CHRISTINE; Moanalua HS; Honolulu, HI; (1); 32/600; Stu Cncl; Hon Roll; UCLA; Lawyer.

CHANG, DARRIN G; Mc Kinley HS; Honolulu, HI; (3); 123/537; Var L Bsktbl; Var L Vllybl; Comp Sci.

CHANG, ERICA W; Kaimuki HS; Honolulu, HI; (3); 71/360; Hosp Aide; Nrsg.

CHANG, HOPE H M; Mary Knoll HS; Honolulu, HI; (2); JA; Math Tm; Science Clb; Rptr Nwsp; Lit Mag; Pres Soph Cls; Rep Stu Cncl; High Hon Roll; NHS; Amnesty Intl; Animal Rights; Mandarin Club; Recpnt Wo Intl Schlrshp; Cvl Air Patrol Spc Acad Huntsville.

CHANG, JADE H Y; Maryknoll Schls; Honolulu, HI; (4); Library Aide; Math Clb; Math Tm; Mu Alpha Theta; JA; Cv Ar Ptrl; Mandarin Clb; Mt Holyoke Coll; Lbrl Arts.

CHANG, JASON; President William Mc Kinley HS; Honolulu, HI; (2); 70/492; Boy Scts; JV Tennis; Camping, Hiking, Math; Star Sct; Sr Patrol Ldr; MIT; Elec Engr.

CHANG, JODI LYNN; Star Of The Sea HS; Hauula, HI; (4); JA; VP Soph Cls; Rep Jr Cls; Sec Sr Cls; Rep Stu Cncl; Hon Roll; Lion Awd; U Of Hi At Manoa; Business Acct.

CHANG, LON S; Mililani HS; Mililani, HI; (2); Math Tm; Mu Alpha Theta; High Hon Roll; Athlon Awd; Engrng.

CHANG, ROBERT A; Kauai HI & Inter; Lihue, HI; (1); 35/254; Band; Jazz Band; Mrchg Band; High Hon Roll; Comp.

CHAR, KRIS K; President William Mc Kinley HS; Honolulu, HI; (4); 83/547; School Play; Stage Crew; Ed Lit Mag; Off Jr Cls; Stu Cncl; JV Bsktbl; JV Vllybl; All-Amer Schlr; AS-PACC Spectra; Santa Clara U; Finance.

CHATMAN, STACI; Kalaheo HS; Kailua, HI; (3); Office Aide; Chorus; Rptr Nwsp; Rep Jr Cls; Capt Cheerldng; Var Capt Vllybl; Cit Awd; Hon Roll; Law Clb; Close-Up Pgm; Bus.

CHAVES, NICOLE N; Maui HS; Makawao, HI; (2); 108/390; Church Yth Grp; French Hon Soc; Prfct Atten Awd; Modeling; Math; Controller.

CHEN, ARCHIE; Lutheran High School Of Hawaii; Honolulu, HI; (2); Hon Roll; Sci.

CHEN, EDMUND; Saint Louis HS; Honolulu, HI; (3); Aud/Vis; Cmnty Wkr; Intrml Ftbl; Var JV Tennis; Hon Roll; U HI; Hotel Mgmt.

CHEN, GRACE L; Mililani HS; Mililani, HI; (3); 1/512; Treas Church Yth Grp; Sec Math Clb; Math Tm; Mu Alpha Theta; Rep Soph Cls; Hon Roll; Prfct Atten Awd; Yng Mans Christian Assn-Yth Ldrshp Pgm; UC Los Angeles; Sci.

CHEN, JIMMY; Lutheran HS Of Hawaii; Mililani, HI; (1); Computer Clb; Phtg Yrbk; Hon Roll; Comp Prgmr.

CHESSUM, SHARON J; Kailua HS; Kailua, HI; (3); 2/339; Hosp Aide; Red Cross Aide; Pres Spanish Clb; Sec Bsktbl; JV Sftbl; High Hon Roll; Hon Roll; HI St Foreign Lang Fest Gold Medal; Water Sfty Instr; Advncd Lfsvg; 1st Aid & CPR Cert; Bus.

CHEUNG, APRIL; Mc Kinley HS; Honolulu, HI; (3); Sec Spanish Clb; Teachers Aide; Chorus; Leo Clb; Senrtts, Tgrtts Cmmtte Chrprsn; Tchr.

CHEUNG, KIT; Kalani HS; Honolulu, HI; (2); 3/213; Treas German Clb; Hosp Aide; Library Aide; Service Clb; Tennis; High Hon Roll; Hon Roll; NHS; Phrmcy.

CHIN, CHU HUI; Kaimuki HS; Honolulu, HI; (3); Pep Clb; Cheerldng.

CHINEN, BRUCE K; Waipahu HS; Waipahu, HI; (2); 42/450; Letterman Clb; Tennis; High Hon Roll; Tennis MVP 88-90.

CHINEN, CYNTHIA; Kalani HS; Honolulu, HI; (2); 69/213; Pep Clb; Intrml Mgr Trk; Hon Roll; Prfct Atten Awd; Svc Awd; Japanese Club; Interschl Club; U Of HI; Adv.

CHING, CHERYL R; Lutheran HS; Kaneohe, HI; (1); Band; Hon Roll; Japanese Clb.

CHING, DOUGLAS T; Kalani HS; Honolulu, HI; (1); 1/246; Hon Roll; Hawaii State Science Fair; 2nd Pl Science Fair.

CHING, ERIC C; Kohala HS; Kapaau, HI; (3); U HI Hilo; Bus Admin.

CHING, JASON Y C; Roosevelt HS; Honolulu, HI; (1); 1/362; Band; Mrchg Band; HI ST Sci & Engrg Fair Fnlst 90.

CHING, LANCE; Maui HS; Kula, HI; (4); Aud/Vis; Computer Clb; Science Clb; Band; Stage Crew; Hon Roll; Prfct Atten Awd; Japanese Clb 4 Yrs; Leo Clb-Svc Clb; Maui Yth Ambssdr Sec; U Of HI Manoa; Hotel Mgmt.

CHING, MILA S Y; Sacred Hearts Acad; Honolulu, HI; (3); Hosp Aide; Math Clb; Quiz Bowl; High Hon Roll; NHS; Pharmacy.

CHININEA, JASMIN C; Radford HS; Honolulu, HI; (2); 18/411; Debate Tm; Drama Clb; French Clb; Chorus; Var Tennis; High Hon Roll; Chem.

CHO, HAN JIN; Moanalua HS; Honolulu, HI; (3); 8/462; Math Clb; Math Tm; Tennis; Arch.

CHO, HAN-HI M; Roosevelt HS; Honolulu, HI; (3); 13/352; French Clb; Flag Corp; Hon Roll; NHS; Intl Reltns Clb; Outstndng Achvmnt In Japanese I-II Awds; Psych.

CHO, HYON CHU; Mc Kinley HS; Honolulu, HI; (4); 1/600; ROTC; Ed Nwsp; VP Frsh Cls; Rep Jr Cls; Sec Stu Cncl; DAR Awd; High Hon Roll; Hon Roll; Ntl Merit SF; U HI; Ed.

CHO, MICHAEL W; Moanalua HS; Honolulu, HI; (2); 43/488; Var Crs Cntry; JV Trk; Hon Roll; 2nd Pl St Ethics Essay; Bus.

CHOCK, KEVIN J; St Louis HS; Honolulu, HI; (2); Cmnty Wkr; Quiz Bowl; ROTC; Rptr Nwsp; Sec Jr Cls; Intrml JV Bsbl; Intrml JV Vllybl; High Hon Roll; Hon Roll; NHS; YMCA Youth Leadership Program; Air Force Acad; Aviation.

CHOCK, VALERIE Y; Punahou Schl; Honolulu, HI; (4); Cmnty Wkr; Hosp Aide; Pres VP JA; Capt Math Tm; Service Clb; Orch; Lit Mag; Var L Crs Cntry; NHS; Ntl Merit SF; Rensselaer Polytchnc Inst Awd Math & Sci; Amer Chemcl Soc Ex Awd; Invitatn Orchstr Perfrm Carnegie Hll; Chem Engr.

CHOI, DERRICK K Y; Maryknoll HS; Honolulu, HI; (2); NFL; Speech Tm; Color Guard; Orch; High Hon Roll; Mandarin Clb; Cvl Air Patrol; HI Yth Symphny; HSTA Violin Medl 89-90; HI Wing Camp Outstndg Flt Awd.

CHOI, JANE J; Kailua HS; Kailua, HI; (2); 58/301; Hon Roll; Japanese Clb.

CHOI, SOOMI; Mc Kinley HS; Honolulu, HI; (2); 100/600; Art Clb; Cmnty Wkr; French Clb; FBLA; JA; Library Aide; Math Clb; Service Clb; Teachers Aide; Church Choir; Poly Action Club; Decor & Pblcty Chrprsn Soph; Korean Club; U PA; Bus.

CHOI, THOMAS; Mc Kinley HS; Honolulu, HI; (4); 110/540; Science Clb; Spanish Clb; U CA Riverside.

CHOI, YUAHJESSICA; Mid-Pacific Inst; Honolulu, HI; (2); 5/195; VP French Clb; Rep Frsh Cls; Pres Soph Cls; Rep Jr Cls; Cit Awd; NHS; Pres Schlr; Amnesty Intl; Pblctns.

CHONG, AENG CHULY; Mc Kinley HS; Honolulu, HI; (2); 1/588; Cmnty Wkr; NFL; Speech Tm; School Musical; Rep Frsh Cls; Rep Soph Cls; Pres Jr Cls; Poltcl Actn Clb; Fndr And Pres Outstndng Lang Art Stu; Poltcl Sci.

CHONG, BRENDA Y; Moanalua HS; Honolulu, HI; (3); 60/462; Hon Roll; Prfct Atten Awd; VP Bus Clb; Korean Clb; U Of HI Manoa; Bus.

CHONG, CAMILLE N; Hawaii Baptist Acad; Kaneohe, HI; (2); Cmnty Wkr; FTA; Office Aide; Karate; Japanese Club.

CHONG, CHAK H; Mililani HS; Mililani, HI; (3); 37/490; Church Yth Grp; Math Clb; Mu Alpha Theta; Chorus; High Hon Roll; Hon Roll; With Simplcty I Lrnd It & W/O Envy I Commnct It; Enronmntl Study.

CHONG, DE ANNE S; Mid-Pacific Inst; Honolulu, HI; (3); Hon Roll; Prom Cmmtte; Japanese Clb; Elem Educ.

CHONG, REBECCA M; Hawaii Baptist Acad; Honolulu, HI; (2); Church Yth Grp; Drama Clb; Hosp Aide; Varsity Clb; Chorus; Church Choir; Var Cheerldng; Pres Aloha Cncl.

CHONG, SCOTT K; Roosevelt HS; Honolulu, HI; (1); 90/362; Boy Scts; Church Yth Grp; JV Wrstlng; Crmnl Law.

CHONG, YONG; Mililani HS; Mililani, HI; (2); Math Clb; Mu Alpha Theta; High Hon Roll; Hon Roll; Graphic Desgn.

CHOO, JEANNA R T; Pearl City HS; Pearl City, HI; (4); 73/478; DECA; Var Socr; Hon Roll; Aiea/Pearl City Bus Cmnty Schlrshp; Sccr Awds & Hnrs; U HI Hilo; Elem Ed.

CHOU, VINCENT K W; Hawaii Baptist Acad; Honolulu, HI; (2); 6/90; Church Yth Grp; JA; Math Tm; Chorus; Variety Show; JV Tennis; High Hon Roll; Servant Grp; JV Bowling; Outstndng Alg I & II Stu Awd; PTF High Acad Avg Awd; MA Inst Of Tech; Mech Engnrng.

CHOUNRAMANY, LALA; Kaimuki HS; Honolulu, HI; (3); U Of HI; Htl Mgnt.

CHOW, MICHAEL I; St Louis Schl; Honolulu, HI; (2); 4/151; Cmnty Wkr; ROTC; Rptr Nwsp; Sec Frsh Cls; Rep Soph Cls; JV L Bsktbl; Var L Ftbl; High Hon Roll; NHS; Schlr/Athl Awd.

CHOY, JASON S; Saint Louis HS; Kaneohe, HI; (3); 24/150; Cmnty Wkr; Intnl Clb; Hon Roll; LIFE Clb; Psych.

CHOY, JOCELYN M; St Francis HS; Honolulu, HI; (2); 3/80; Aud/Vis; Math Tm; Mu Alpha Theta; Pep Clb; Color Guard; Lit Mag; Jr NHS; NHS; NEDT Awd.

CHU, JASON; Moanalua HS; Honolulu, HI; (2); Chess Clb; Math Clb; Mu Alpha Theta; Quiz Bowl; Treas Science Clb; Hon Roll; Jr NHS.

CHUN, AILEEN M; President Theodore Roosevelt HS; Honolulu, HI; (4); 1/318; Debate Tm; Drama Clb; French Clb; Spanish Clb; Speech Tm; Thesps; School Play; NHS; Val; Shaksprsn Fstvl Rectns Wnnr 89-90; 3rd Pl Wnnr Brown Bags Stardom 90; Music Theory; Willamette U; Theatrical Drama.

CHUN, BRENT N; H P Baldwin HS; Puunene, HI; (3); 9/400; FTA; Key Clb; Math Clb; Off Math Tm; SADD; JV Trk; High Hon Roll; Hon Roll; St Wnnr Lang Arts Showcase; St Qlfr Sci, Engrng Fair; Electrnc, Audio Equip; IL Inst Of Tech; Comp Sci.

CHUN, DIANA KWAI LAN; Kaimuki HS; Honolulu, HI; (2); 17/325; Girl Scts; SADD; Band; Flag Corp; Jazz Band; Mrchg Band; School Musical; JV Vllybl; Hon Roll; Leo Clb; U Of HI Manoa; Educ.

CHUN, ELIZABETH M L; Roosevelt HS; Honolulu, HI; (3); 20/350; Hosp Aide; Key Clb; Pres Frsh Cls; Pres Soph Cls; Pres Jr Cls; Pres Sr Cls; Var Cheerldng; Var Trk; Hon Roll; ST HI World Sprints Of Canoe Rep; Paddling New Zealand.

CHUN, JACOB W; Maryknoll HS; Kaneohe, HI; (2); Lit Mag; High Hon Roll; Hiking Clb.

CHUN, JONATHAN G H; Mid-Pacific Inst; Mililani, HI; (3); Church Yth Grp; Spanish Clb; Capt Var Bsktbl; Capt Var Ftbl; Var JV Trk; Hon Roll; Jr NHS; NHS; Pres Schlr; Honolulu Nwsp Hnrb Mntn Vrsty Ftbl 89; Mid Pacific Inst Mst Spirited Male Athl & MVP Trk 90; Phys Ed.

CHUN, KENDRIC M; St Louis HS; Aiea, HI; (2); 31/151; Riflery.

CHUN, MIKE G Y; Lutheran HS; Honolulu, HI; (2); Band; School Play; Stage Crew; JV Bsktbl; JV Ftbl; Prfct Atten Awd; Japanese Clb; Pilot.

CHUN, NOLAN K; Saint Louis HS; Kailua, HI; (3); 76/150; ROTC; Band; Hon Roll; Mainland Coll; Dentistry.

CHUN, ROSALIE; Molokai HS & Intermed; Kaunakakai, HI; (4); 13/94; Art Clb; ROTC; Church Choir; Rep Sr Cls; Hon Roll; Hnrs Club; Socl Cmmtte; U HI; Comp Sci.

CHUN, TAMMI J; Moanalua HS; Honolulu, HI; (4); 4/469; Treas Aud/Vis; Church Yth Grp; Hosp Aide; Hist Band; Jazz Band; Capt Mrchg Band; VP Frsh Cls; Pres Stu Cncl; Sec NHS; Ntl Merit SF; Mock Trl Tm; Centry III Ldrs Prgrm ST Smi Fnlst; Menehune Of Yr Otstndng Stu Of Yr.

CHUNG, NAHN; Kaiser HS; Honolulu, HI; (3); 1/325; Co-Capt Math Tm; Quiz Bowl; Mgr Mgr(s); Hon Roll; NHS; Prfct Atten Awd; Keywanettes Pres.

CHURCH, MALIA C; Kamehameha HS; Hana, HI; (3); 112/450; Drama Clb; Girl Scts; Pep Clb; Science Clb; SADD; School Play; Rptr Lit Mag; Sec Frsh Cls; Rptr Stu Cncl; Hon Roll; Jrnlsm.

CLARK, SEAN; Moanalua HS; Honolulu, HI; (2); 82/488; Hon Roll; Pres Acad Fit Awd; MIT; Bus Admin.

CLARK, SIMONE; Roosevelt HS; Honolulu, HI; (4); 5/320; Debate Tm; 4-H; French Clb; Model UN; Quiz Bowl; Mrchg Band; Orch; Ed Lit Mag; Sec Soph Cls; Sec Jr Cls; Yng Schlrs Smmr Sssn; Yale Bk Awd; Sterling Schlr Socl Sci Rnnr Up; U Of PA; Hstry.

CLEVELAND, HEATHER; Kalaheo HS; Honolulu, HI; (3); Sec Thesps; School Play; Art Hstry.

COBALLES, REGINALD A; Damien Memorial HS; Honolulu, HI; (4); 19/165; Church Yth Grp; Dance Clb; JA; Quiz Bowl; ROTC; Rptr Nwsp; Crs Cntry; High Hon Roll; Hon Roll; NHS; Canoe Paddling; Christian Svc; Yth Ministry; U HI-MANOA; Cvl Engrng.

COBALLES, VIVIAN A; Sacred Hearts Acad; Honolulu, HI; (3); Math Clb; Pep Clb; Teachers Aide; Nwsp; Rep Frsh Cls; Rep Soph Cls; Rep Jr Cls; Stu Cncl; High Hon Roll; NHS; HI St Sci & Engrng Fair Cert Of Mrt 31st Pl; Exec Womens Intl Outstndng Bus Stu; U HI; Accntng.

COBBS, BETH; Lanakila Baptist HS; Makakilo, HI; (3); 1/19; Girl Scts; Spanish Clb; Teachers Aide; Yrbk; Rep Frsh Cls; VP Soph Cls; L Gym; JV Vllybl; Hon Roll; NHS; Engr.

COFFMAN, CHRISTINA; St Andrews Priory HS; Aiea, HI; (3); 9/60; Pres Church Yth Grp; VP Drama Clb; Thesps; Orch; School Musical; School Play; Rptr Nwsp; High Hon Roll; Hon Roll; Drama.

COGO, HENRY; Hilo HS; Hilo, HI; (4); Chess Clb; Treas French Clb; Math Clb; Math Tm; Science Clb; Speech Tm; School Play; Variety Show; Var L Trk; Hon Roll; Pr Cnslr; Dist & St Sci Fr Fnlst; Vlntr Tutr; Engrng.

COHEN, RACHEL L; Roosevelt HS; Honolulu, HI; (2); 67/364; Intnl Clb; Model UN; School Musical; Rptr Nwsp; JV Socr; Hnr Mntn Cmmrcl Cntst Scott Newman Ctr; Russn Stu Exch Intl Yth Ambssdrs; Malaikahana Cmpng Awd 90; CSU; Flm Indstry.

COLEMON, MARYAH; Kalaheo HS; Kailua, HI; (1); 16/261; Dance Clb; Variety Show; Hon Roll; Dallas Art Inst; Singer.

COLLINS, AMBER; Pahoa HS; Pahoa, HI; (3); 5/98; Drama Clb; Treas Spanish Clb; School Musical; School Play; Stage Crew; Rptr Nwsp; Hon Roll; NHS; Photo Clb VP; Mock Trl; Libry Sci.

COLLMER, VEDA M; Mililani HS; Mililani, HI; (3); 134/490; Girl Scts; Hosp Aide; Library Aide; Band; Mrchg Band; Pep Band; Rptr Nwsp; Lit Mag; Golf; Hon Roll; Jrnlsm.

COLOBONG, JOYCE M; Waipahu HS; Waipahu, HI; (2); 45/513; SADD; Off Frsh Cls; Stu Cncl; JV Stat Bsbl; JV Score Keeper; Campus Life; Bus Mgr.

COLOMA JR, ERNEST A; Waimea HS; Lawai, HI; (2); Aud/Vis; Key Clb; Hist Soph Cls; High Hon Roll; NHS; Drftng Club; U Of HI; Mech Engrng.

COLON, AUGUST BORERO LOPAKA; Molokai High & Interm Schl; Maunaloa, HI; (2); 10/115; Letterman Clb; Band; Drm Mjr(t); Jazz Band; Mrchg Band; Pep Band; Rep Frsh Cls; Rep Soph Cls; Var L Socr; Var L Trk; UH Manor Rainbow Marching Band Clinic; Midsummer Latin Concert; Brownbags To Stardom Talent Cntst; HI U; Elec Engr.

COMER, CARRIE A; Maui HS; Makawao, HI; (3); 47/354; Treas French Clb; Pres Service Clb; Hon Roll; Prfct Atten Awd; SSS Clb; Outstndng Accmplshmnts Awd Food Srvce Clb; Nrsng.

COMER, MELISSA N N; Maui HS; Makawao, HI; (4); 32/303; Church Yth Grp; Pres French Clb; FTA; SADD; Teachers Aide; High Hon Roll; Hon Roll; Prfct Atten Awd; Music & Glee Clb; Mock Trial; Maui CC; Early Chldhd Educ.

COMPOC, COTY L; Kamehameha Schls; Lawai, HI; (3); 140/450; Aud/Vis; Church Yth Grp; Scholastic Bowl; Teachers Aide; Chorus; Church Choir; Stu Cncl; Stat Bsktbl; Mgr Mgr(s); Hon Roll; Concert Glee Club; U Laverne; Broadcasting Jrnlsm.

CONCEPCION, KIMBERLY P; Radford HS; Alea, HI; (2); 10/420; Hosp Aide; Intnl Clb; ROTC; Mgr Band; Off Drill Tm; Mrchg Band; Hon Roll; NHS; Pres Acad Fit Awd; HS Phys Trng Tm; Jr Class Secy 90-91; Med.

CONCEPCION, PATRICK T; St Louis Schl; Mililani, HI; (3); 34/150; Cmnty Wkr; Spanish Clb; Intrml Bsktbl; Intrml Ftbl; Intrml Wt Lftg; High Hon Roll; Hon Roll; Prfct Atten Awd; HI St Lang Fest Span 88; Pacific Asian Affairs Cncl; Hosp Volunteer; U Dayton; Bus.

CONNERS IV, RAYMOND RICHARD; The Parker Schl; Kailua Kona, HI; (4); 1/28; Church Yth Grp; Intnl Clb; Office Aide; Quiz Bowl; Speech Tm; School Play; Treas Frsh Cls; VP Jr Cls; Pres Sr Cls; Sec Stu Cncl; W HI Rep Diocs Honolulu Yth Cncl; 1st Pl Ctzn Bee Prvt HI Schls; Ray Kroc Yth Achvt Awd; U Of Notre Dame.

CONRADT JR, RICHARD T; Hilo HS; Hilo, HI; (2); 139/359; Cmnty Wkr; Key Clb; Rep Soph Cls; Var Socr; Hon Roll; REACH Pgm; Big Brothers Little Brothers; Bus.

COOK, DERREK M; Waialua Hightinter Schl; Waialua, HI; (3); Art Clb; Socr; High Hon Roll; Salvage Diver In Navy.

COOK, JONATHAN K; Punahou Schl; Honolulu, HI; (4); Art Clb; Stu Cncl; JV Swmmng; JV Vllybl; JV Wrstlng; Vrsty Water Polo; Art Awd 88-89; Kung-Fu Aikido Stu; Evergreen ST; Fine Art.

COPSON, TILIN; William Mc Kinley HS; Honolulu, HI; (4); German Clb; Library Aide; Red Cross Aide; Spanish Clb; Variety Show; Nurse.

CORDEIRO, DRENA N; Kamehameha Schls; Pearl City, HI; (3); 89/420; Church Yth Grp; Chorus; JV Var Socr; HI ST Girls Var Scr Champnshp Tm; HI U; Elem Ed.

COROUZ, APRIL; Kauai HS; Lihue, HI; (3); Church Yth Grp; FHA; FTA; SADD; Teachers Aide; Hon Roll; NHS; Leo Clb; U Of HI Manoa; Ed.

CORTEZ, FRANCIS A; Waiakea HS; Hilo, HI; (2); 70/497; Drama Clb; Band; Jazz Band; Mrchg Band; Pep Band; Variety Show; Hon Roll; Elctrncs Tech.

COSIER, BRICILLE L; Waimea HS; Kalaheo, HI; (2); Pep Clb; Pep Band; Off Frsh Cls; Off Soph Cls; Stu Cncl; Stat Mgr(s); Var Score Keeper; Vllybl; Healanis Hula Halau; Merric Monarch Fstvl; U Of HI Hilo; Anatomy.

COTE, ANNETTE J; Kapaa HS; Kapaa, HI; (3); Church Yth Grp; Hon Roll; UCSB; Psych.

COTTEN, MARYA; Hilo HS; Hilo, HI; (3); 2/370; French Clb; JA; Varsity Clb; Var Socr; High Hon Roll; NHS.

COUGHLIN, ERIN M; St Francis HS; Ewa Beach, HI; (2); 11/80; Mu Alpha Theta; JV Bsktbl; Hon Roll; NHS; NEDT Awd; Med.

COX, JOHN P; Kauai HS; Lihue, HI; (3); Band; L Bsbl; L Bsktbl; High Hon Roll; NHS; Math.

COX, LANI V; Mililani HS; Mililani, HI; (3); 204/490; Drama Clb; School Musical; School Play; Stage Crew; Variety Show; Teaching.

CRAFT, TRUDY A; St Francis HS; Honolulu, HI; (2); Cmnty Wkr; Mu Alpha Theta; Hon Roll.

CRAGHEAD, DENISE L; Moanalua HS; Honolulu, HI; (3); 83/462; FCA; Red Cross Aide; Mrchg Band; School Musical; Swing Chorus; Rep Frsh Cls; Sec Soph Cls; Var Socr; Var Vllybl; Hon Roll; Red Crs Awds; Cert Prm Prtcptn Close Up; Dist Band & Chorus Awds; WA ST U; Hotl/Restrng Mgmt.

CRAIG, HOLLI K; Molokai HS; Kualapuu, HI; (2); Church Yth Grp; Math Tm; Pep Clb; Science Clb; Band; Church Choir; Rep Frsh Cls; Pres Soph Cls; Stu Cncl; Var Cheerldng; Japanese Club; Brigham Young U.

CRINER, ROGER D; Leilehua HS; Schofield Bks, HI; (2); 39/406; Church Yth Grp; Drama Clb; Pep Clb; ROTC; Band; Jazz Band; Mrchg Band; Pep Band; Hon Roll; West Point.

CRISOLOGO, JESSICA; Maui HS; Haiku, HI; (2); Church Yth Grp; Cmnty Wkr; Girl Scts; Pep Clb; Science Clb; Var JV Cheerldng; High Hon Roll; Hon Roll; SSS; CO ST U; Astronomy.

CRISTOBAL, JOY JOJI; W R Farrington HS; Honolulu, HI; (1); ROTC; JV Bsbl; Hon Roll; Prfct Atten Awd; Med.

CROOKS, KATRINA W; Radford HS; Honolulu, HI; (3); 138/394; Spanish Clb; Yrbk; Sec Frsh Cls; Stu Cncl; JV Socr; Hon Roll; Campus Beautification Week Slogan Cont 1st Pl Awd; UT El Paso; Engl.

CROOT, DONICA T; Kalani HS; Honolulu, HI; (2); 13/213; Church Yth Grp; Hosp Aide; Service Clb; SADD; Rep Soph Cls; Hon Roll; NHS; Keywanettes-VP; Mock Trial; U Of HI.

CROW, DARCIE; Mililani HS; Mililani, HI; (3); 70/500; Church Yth Grp; English Clb; Key Clb; Spanish Clb; Teachers Aide; Flag Corp; Rptr Yrbk; Score Keeper; Wrstlng; High Hon Roll; Advncd Plcmnt Engl & US Hstry Hnrs; Yrbk Bst Layout/Dsgn 1st Pl.

CUI, STEPHEN M; James Campbell HS; Ewa Beach, HI; (2); Hon Roll; Civil Hnr Guard; Awd Sch Sci Fair; USAF Acad; Avionics.

CULLEN, TROY C; St Louis HS; Waipahu, HI; (3); Boy Scts; Debate Tm; Drama Clb; Color Guard; School Play; JV Var Ftbl; Swmmng; DAR Awd; Hon Roll; Pres Acad Fit Awd; ROTC Outstndng Cadet; Aeronautical.

CUMMINGS, LYLE R; Maui HS; Haliimaile Maui, HI; (3); Church Yth Grp; Treas Key Clb; Letterman Clb; Teachers Aide; Var JV Bsbl; Var JV Ftbl; Wt Lftg; Prfct Atten Awd; Ftbl All Star Guard/Tackle; Lbrl Arts.

CURTIS, THOMAS A; Radford HS; Honolulu, HI; (3); Band; Chorus; Drm Mjr(t); Hon Roll; Law Enfrcmnt.

CUSTODIO, DELDRINE L; Pahoa HS; Pahoa, HI; (3); Computer Clb; FHA; Library Aide; Office Aide; Teachers Aide; Yrbk; Off Jr Cls; Diving; Swmmng; Hon Roll.

CUTTER, KEVIN Y; St Louis HS; Honolulu, HI; (1); 22/175; ROTC; Drill Tm; Hon Roll; Prfcncy Mdl ROTC; Comp Sci.

CZECH, DAVID V; St Louis HS; Kaneohe, HI; (2); 28/150; ROTC; Ftbl; Hon Roll; Bsbl; Pilot.

D OZOUVILLE, AXELLE M; Mid-Pacific Inst; Honolulu, HI; (2); Chess Clb; Drama Clb; GAA; JA; Ski Clb; Swmmng; Tennis; French Hon Soc; Jr NHS; NHS; Rec Sec Of The Organization Of Stud Int; Girls Tennis Player Of The Yr; Language Arts Dept Chinese Awd; Princeton; Intl Correspondance.

DACE, ROSE LYNN; Waipahu HS; Waipahu, HI; (4); 1/418; FHA; Hosp Aide; Lit Mag; Off Frsh Cls; Off Soph Cls; Off Jr Cls; Treas Sr Cls; High Hon Roll; Hon Roll; Lion Awd; Outstndng Filipino HS Sr HI 89; Rep Julie Duldulao Schlsp Awd; 1st Runner Up Oxy 10 Schlsp Contest; Seattle U; Nrsg.

DACOCO, JENNY B; James Campbell HS; Ewa Beach, HI; (3); 21/371; Church Yth Grp; Color Guard; Rep Frsh Cls; Treas Soph Cls; Stu Cncl; Hon Roll; Med Career Clb; Mst Outstndng Soph; Alpha Soc; U Of HI Manoa; Reg Nurse.

DAIMARU, JANET; Hilo HS; Hilo, HI; (4); 18/308; Science Clb; Service Clb; Teachers Aide; Var JV Crs Cntry; Mgr(s); Crss Cntry-Mgr, Jnr Vrsty Mst Insprtnl/Jnr Vrsty Awd 87, 88; Crss Cntry Capt Mst Insprtnl Vrsty Rnnr; U Of HI Manoa; Hlth.

DAIMARU, LISSA; Hilo HS; Hilo, HI; (2); 1/391; Math Tm; Science Clb; Treas Band; Mrchg Band; Pep Band; Crs Cntry; High Hon Roll; Hon Roll; Interact Clb; Top Ten; Frgn Lang Achvt Japanese.

DALIRE, SHANNON; Kamehameha Schls; Kaneohe, HI; (3); 172/419; Dance Clb; Letterman Clb; SADD; Varsity Clb; Rep Jr Cls; JV Var Bsktbl; Var Mgr(s); Var Score Keeper; Intrml Sftbl; HI Lang Stu; U HI Manoa; Bus Mgmnt.

DAMASO, MARJORIE C; Theodore Roosevelt HS; Honolulu, HI; (1); Med.

DAMO, DENISE N; James Campbell HS; Ewa Beach, HI; (3); 44/403; Pres FBLA; Hon Roll; Prncpls List; Cannons Bus Coll; Hotel Tourism.

DANAO, MARCOS T; Moanalua HS; Honolulu, HI; (3); 92/462; Art Clb; Church Yth Grp; Cmnty Wkr; Key Clb; Band; Jazz Band; Mrchg Band; Pep Band; Variety Show; Trumpet Sctn Ldr; Dance; U Of HI Manoa; Med.

DANDO, CHUCK D; Baldwin HS; Wailuku, HI; (2); Bsbl; Wt Lftg.

DANG, HONG T; Mc Kinley HS; Honolulu, HI; (3); Drama Clb; Key Clb; Off Jr Cls; Stu Cncl; Tennis; Hon Roll; NHS; Prfct Atten Awd; Actress.

DANG, HUNG C; Roosevelt HS; Honolulu, HI; (3); Socr; Hon Roll; HI Bus Stu Conf Of Adv Typewriting Was Rcgnzd For Outstndng Achvt; Comp.

DANG, KIMBERLY; Punahou Schl; Honolulu, HI; (4); Teachers Aide; Variety Show; Treas Jr Cls; JV Var Swmmng; JV Var Trk; Hon Roll; Jr NHS; NHS; Ntl Merit Ltr; Yrbk-Sr Section Editor; Georgetown U; Frgn Langs.

DAOG, DARLENE C; Waiakea HS; Keaau, HI; (3); Sec FHA; Ed JA; SADD; Flag Corp; VP Sr Cls; Hmcmng Crt As JR Cls Attndnt; FHA Dist Isl VP; 2nd Rnnr Up HI Miss Teen Of Amer Pageant 89; U HI Manoa; Marine Bio.

DAOG, MICHELE T; Waiakea HS; Hilo, HI; (3); 69/368; Church Yth Grp; Service Clb; Teachers Aide; Band; Drm Mjr(t); Mrchg Band; Pep Band; Variety Show; Mst Outstndng Musician 3 Yrs; Kapiolani CC; X-Ray Tech.

DAQUIP, DESIREE R; Farrington HS; Honolulu, HI; (3); 147/600; Church Yth Grp; Hon Roll; Japanese Clb; Bus.

DATO, DENNIS J; Kapaa HS; Kilauea, HI; (2); 26/179; Var Ftbl; Var L Socr; Var Wt Lftg; Hon Roll; UH Manoa; Pre Law.

DAVID, MARIEL M; James Campbell HS; Ewa Beach, HI; (2); 1/474; Intnl Clb; Teachers Aide; Bowling; Prin Awd; Most Improved Stu Rcgntn Awd; Arch.

DAVIDSON, KYMBERLY LYNELL; Radford HS; Honolulu, HI; (2); Church Yth Grp; Dance Clb; Band; Church Choir; Hon Roll; Peer Mediator; Blck Amer Club; Modeling Courses W/John Robert Powers Agncy & Schl; U Of NC; Psych.

DAVIS, ALISON; Kauai HS; Kalaheo, HI; (4); 7/246; Drama Clb; School Play; Variety Show; Hon Roll; NHS; Kauai CC.

DAVIS, CHRISTIAN; Radford HS; Hickam A F B, HI; (3); 19/487; Band; Mrchg Band; Pep Band; Hon Roll; Jr NHS; NHS; Prfct Atten Awd; Crmnl Law.

DAVIS, HEATHER C; Konawaena HS; Kailua Kona, HI; (2); Drama Clb; French Clb; SADD; Pres Soph Cls; Var Capt Bsktbl; Vllybl; Hon Roll; Humboldt ST U; Ed.

DAWSON, WILLIAM T; Radford HS; Honolulu, HI; (4); 70/350; Letterman Clb; ROTC; JV Ftbl; Socr; Capt Tennis; Hon Roll; Prfct Atten Awd; U Of HI Manoa; Law.

DAY, VIRGINIA K; Hana HS; Haiku, HI; (3); FFA; Band; Rptr Nwsp; Hon Roll.

DE BERRY, ANDREW B; Leilehua HS; Wahiawa, HI; (4); 42/301; Debate Tm; Drama Clb; French Clb; Teachers Aide; Var Crs Cntry; Var Socr; Var Trk; High Hon Roll; NHS; U Of HI Manoa; Bus.

DE BERRY, RACHEAL; Leilehua HS; Wahiawa, HI; (2); 4/406; Var Bsktbl; Hon Roll.

DE BERRY, RACHEAL J; Leilehua HS; Wahiawa, HI; (2); 4/406; Var Bsktbl; Hon Roll.

DE LA CRUZ, RACHEL; James Campbell HS; Ewa Beach, HI; (4); Church Yth Grp; FTA; JA; Key Clb; Science Clb; Teachers Aide; Church Choir; Co-Ed Nwsp; Rep Jr Cls; Hon Roll; All Amer Schlr; Acad Excllnc Alg Awd; U HI Manoa; Scndry Ed.

DE LEON, CHERRY GRACE Z; Farrington HS; Honolulu, HI; (1); 97/360; Art Clb; 4-H; JV Crs Cntry; Cit Awd; 4-H Awd; 3rd Pl St Flower St Wide; Art & Crafts.

DE LEON, MARILYN; Henry Opukahai Schl; Keaau, HI; (2); Church Yth Grp; FCA; Teachers Aide; Church Choir; Off Soph Cls; Bsbl; Bsktbl; Vllybl; Hon Roll; Stewardss.

DE MATTOS, DORIN; Hilo HS; Pepeekeo, HI; (2); Cmnty Wkr; High Hon Roll; Pres Acad Fit Awd.

DE MELLO, CHRISTY; St Joseph HS; Hilo, HI; (2); Church Yth Grp; Chorus; Sec Frsh Cls; Sec Stu Cncl; High Hon Roll; NEDT Awd; U San Fran; Psych.

DE SOTO, BRIAN D; Moanalna HS; Honolulu, HI; (3); 12/470; Chess Clb; Church Yth Grp; Quiz Bowl; Band; Off Jr Cls; Stu Cncl; High Hon Roll; Masonic Awd; Pres NHS; Mock Trial Team St Champs, Lawyer & Wtnss; Poltcl Sci.

DE SOTO, DESIRE A; Pearl City HS; Waianae, HI; (3); Hosp Aide; JV Bsktbl; Var Swmmng; Cande Club; Backstroke St Champn 89-90; Med.

DEAS, SUSANA R; Radford HS; Honolulu, HI; (2); 4/432; Church Yth Grp; Var Trk; High Hon Roll; Hon Roll; Jr NHS; Tutor Elem Chldrn Math; Babysitting; Princeton; Pedtrcn.

DECAMBRA, ESTHER; Hilo HS; Hilo, HI; (2); 2/370; Latin Clb; Rep Soph Cls; Var Crs Cntry; Var L Socr; High Hon Roll; JR Grnpc Svc Clb.

DEL ROSARIO, JUDITH S; Waipahu HS; Waipahu, HI; (2); DECA; Science Clb; Band; Stu Cncl; Hon Roll; Interact Clb Sec; HI Bus Stu Conf Outstndng Achvt Spllng; SMILE; U Of HI; Bus.

DELA CRUZ, NATHALIE JUNE G; W R Farrington HS; Honolulu, HI; (4); 26/549; JA; Pres VICA; Stage Crew; Variety Show; Ed Yrbk; Rep Soph Cls; Chrmn Sr Cls; Stu Cncl; Hon Roll; Lion Awd; Mst Outstndng Sr Awd; Leo Clb Pres, Correspndng Sec & Dist 50 Pres; UH Manoa; Graphic Arts.

DELK, NIKKI A; Radford HS; Honolulu, HI; (2); 1/420; Dance Clb; Church Choir; Sec Soph Cls; Trk; High Hon Roll; Jr NHS; NHS; Radford Black American Club; After School Latin Class; MS Black Teenager Hawaii Pageant; Best Talent; Duke; Business Management.

DEMERLY, HEATHER; Henry Opukahaia Schl; Keaau, HI; (4); 1/13; Church Yth Grp; Teachers Aide; Church Choir; School Play; VP Jr Cls; Pres Sr Cls; Pres Stu Cncl; Vllybl; Cit Awd; High Hon Roll; Bethel; Christian Ministries.

DEMPSEY, STACEY; Leilehua HS; Valrico, FL; (3); 58/347; Church Yth Grp; Dance Clb; Sec 4-H; Spanish Clb; SADD; Thesps; Chorus; Stage Crew; 4-H Awd; Hon Roll; Horseback Riding & Instr; Modeling; Criminal Tech.

DENG, YI LE; Farrington HS; Honolulu, HI; (2); 16/731; Computer Clb; Hon Roll; Prfct Atten Awd; Farrington Sci Fair-2nd Pl Novice Div 90; U Of HI; Engrng.

DENIS, CORINNE; Hilo HS; Hilo, HI; (2); 58/359; English Clb; NFL; Speech Tm; Phtg Nwsp; Conflict Mediatn; Jrnlsm.

DENIS, ETHEL ANN; Konawaena HS; Honaunau, HI; (3); 16/294; Church Yth Grp; French Clb; Church Choir; High Hon Roll; U Of HI Manoa; Erly Chldhd Ed.

DEPP, CATHERINE A; Waiakea HS; Hilo, HI; (1); 161/478; Pres Church Yth Grp; Latin Clb; Church Choir; Brigham Young U Provo; Fine Art.

DERENNE, BROOKE L; Hawaii Baptist Acad; Honolulu, HI; (1); Church Yth Grp; Chorus; JV Bsktbl; Score Keeper; Var Vllybl; Hon Roll; Kamalii Vlybl Clb; Srvnt Grp; Grls Ath Clb.

DEVENNEY, ALICIA D; Theodore Roosevelt HS; Honolulu, HI; (1); 40/363; Library Aide; SADD; Chorus; Hon Roll; Peer Ed; Photo Grp; Ed.

DEVERATURDA, RENEE; Mililani HS; Mililani, HI; (3); 42/490; Band; Mrchg Band; Pep Band; Ed Yrbk; Hon Roll; Clsscl Piano Trng; Lcl Rock Band; Pblcty; U HI; Med.

DEWEY, JEREMIAH; Hawaii Baptist Acad; Haleiwa, HI; (3); 15/100; Church Yth Grp; Drama Clb; 4-H; French Clb; Thesps; School Play; Stage Crew; 4-H Awd; Outstndng Alg Stu; Le Toumeau U; Aviation.

DEZZANI, SUSAN S; Miliani HS; Mililani, HI; (3); Church Yth Grp; SADD; Church Choir; Hon Roll; Advrtsng.

DIAZ, KEOLA K; Radford HS; Honolulu, HI; (2); 26/411; Dance Clb; Intnl Clb; JA; Natl Beta Clb; Variety Show; Ed Nwsp; Chrmn Soph Cls; Vllybl; Cit Awd; Hon Roll; Lawyer.

DIAZ, LEOLANI B; Mid-Pacific Inst; Kapaa, HI; (3); Sec French Clb; Service Clb; Speech Tm; High Hon Roll; NHS; Amnesty Intl; MPI Schlr; Holomua.

DICK, KATRINA E; Leilehua HS; Wahiawa, HI; (2); Math Tm; Model UN; Tennis; High Hon Roll; Hikng Clb; Japanese Clb; Karate; Advertsng Prodctn.

DIMAYA JR, BALDOVINO R; Farrington HS; Honolulu, HI; (3); Weldng.

DIXON, KERSTIN S; Baldwin HS; Kihei, HI; (3); Church Yth Grp; French Clb; Library Aide; Pep Clb; Hon Roll; FIDM; Vsl Prsntn.

DIXON, ZACHARY D; Waiakea HS; Hilo, HI; (2); 64/532; Boy Scts; Science Clb; Var Socr; Hon Roll; USD.

DIZOL, LEANORA P; Waimea HS; Koloa, HI; (3); Church Yth Grp; Cmnty Wkr; Computer Clb; Debate Tm; Intnl Clb; Speech Tm; Nwsp; High Hon Roll; Hon Roll; NHS; St Aha Opio O Oha; Pacific/Asian Affrs Cncl & Frgn Lang Cmptn; Pres/Fndr Wrld Awrns Clb; U Of HI Manoa; Law.

DO, VINH; Kaimuki HS; Honolulu, HI; (3); 23/361; Church Yth Grp; Math Tm; Scholastic Bowl; SADD; Church Choir; Diving; Swmmng; Trk; Wrstlng; Hon Roll; U Of HI; Elec Engr.

DOAN, HANH MY; Mc Kinley HS; Kailua, HI; (2); Speech Tm; Lit Mag; Hon Roll; Ophthamologist.

DOAN, MY-HUONG; Mc Kinley HS; Kailua, HI; (3); 77/537; Speech Tm; Rptr Nwsp; Lit Mag; Pres Acad Fit Awd; Guidance Cmmtte Pblshr; Pediatrician.

DOCHIN, PAULINE; Konawaena HS; Kailua-Kona, HI; (4); 10/296; Pres Key Clb; Rep Frsh Cls; Rep Jr Cls; Rep Sr Cls; Treas Stu Cncl; High Hon Roll; Hon Roll; NHS; HI ST Stu Conf Delg; U Of HI Manoa; Bus.

DODGE, KALIA L; Seabury Hall HS; Kula, HI; (4); 3/31; Sec French Clb; Stu Cncl; Var Capt Bsktbl; Var Capt Socr; Var Vllybl.

DODSON, KAI A; Baldwin HS; Kihei, HI; (1); 13/466; Band; Hon Roll; U Of HI; Bus Admn.

DOI, KIMBERLY K; Pearl City HS; Pearl City, HI; (4); 4/469; Hosp Aide; Model UN; Hon Roll; NHS; Ntl Merit SF; Lgsltv Cmmtte; Wellesley Coll Bk Awd.

DOI, MELANIE T; Kaiser HS; Honolulu, HI; (3); 34/325; Chorus; Color Guard; Flag Corp; Treas Sr Cls; Hon Roll; Pres Acad Fit Awd; Ldrshp Training Crs; U Of HI; Nrsng.

DOI, TALBERT L; Hawaii Baptist Acad; Ewa Beach, HI; (4); Chess Clb; Church Yth Grp; Math Tm; Chorus; VP Church Choir; School Play; Golf; Swmmng; Vllybl; Hon Roll; Bowlng Capt; Wichita ST U; Aernutcl Engr.

DOLLENTE JR, QUINTIN M; Farrington HS; Honolulu, HI; (2); 12/696; Band; Jazz Band; Mrchg Band; Pep Band; Cit Awd; High Hon Roll; HI St Sci & Engrng Fair Fnlst; Mst Outstndng Band III Player; Law.

DOLLY, ERIN E; Kalaheo HS; Kailua, HI; (3); 19/250; Key Clb; Off Frsh Cls; Off Soph Cls; Off Jr Cls; Hon Roll; Chrmn Yr Awd; Group Ldr Childrns Ldrshp Camp; Bus Adm.

DOMINGO, CHAD M; Waipahu HS; Waipahu, HI; (1); 132/513; Pep Clb; VP Frsh Cls; Stu Cncl; Assmbly Cmmtte; Pride Cmmtte; Hmcmng Cmmtte; Hmcmng Escort; U Of HI; Arch.

DOMINGO, CHERYL C; W R Farrington HS; Honolulu, HI; (1); 12/360; Band; Church Choir; Mrchg Band; Rep Frsh Cls; Hon Roll; U Of HI Manoa; Fshn Magzn Edtr.

DOMINGO, EVELYN; Kauai HS; Lihue, HI; (4); DECA; FHA; Capt Var Bsktbl; Hon Roll; NHS; Bus Admin.

DOMINGO, FLORDELISA D; Leilehua HS; Wahiawa, HI; (4); 15/304; Church Yth Grp; FTA; Sec Soph Cls; Chrmn Jr Cls; Chrmn Sr Cls; Rep Stu Cncl; Hon Roll; NHS; Rep Rotary Awd; Kaisahan Clb Pres 88-90 & Sec/Treas 87; HS Crdt Union Pres 89 Treas 90 & Sec 87; UH Manoa; Acctng.

DOMINGO, JENNIFER C; Wallace Rider Farrington HS; Honolulu, HI; (1); 97/360; Band; School Musical; VP Frsh Cls; Leo Clb; Moanaloa CC; Prctcl Nurse.

DOMINGO, MELANIE C; Radford HS; Honolulu, HI; (3); 39/371; Rep Jr Cls; Hon Roll; Pedtrcn.

DOMINGO, MONA E; Baldwin HS; Kahului, HI; (2); Cmnty Wkr; SADD; Pianist; Teach Chldrn Dance; Med.

DOMINGO, NELLIE; Lahainaluna HS; Lahaina, HI; (3); DECA; Science Clb; Spanish Clb; Band; Mrchg Band; Pep Band; Bsktbl; High Hon Roll; Hon Roll; Aloha Clb; Pul Rel; Triple S Clb; U HI Manoa; Comp Prgrmmr.

DOMINGO, NORA; Maui HS; Kahului, HI; (4); 13/303; Treas Computer Clb; Key Clb; Math Clb; Science Clb; High Hon Roll; Lion Awd; Prfct Atten Awd; Video Clb VP; Leo Clb Pres; Spirit Clb; UH Manoa; Dentstry.

DOMINGO, PHILIP S; Henry Perrine Baldwin HS; Kahului, HI; (2); 54/395; Boy Scts; Jazz Band; Mrchg Band; Pep Band; Hon Roll.

DOMINGO, QNY D; Konawaena HS; Captain Cook, HI; (2); 3/338; Church Yth Grp; FTA; Intnl Clb; Spanish Clb; SADD; Church Choir; Hon Roll; Prfct Atten Awd; Intl Yth Clb Kona Pres.

DOMINGO, RAYMOND D; Leilehua HS; Wahiawa, HI; (2); Elec Engr.

DOMINGO, SHAREN D; Waipahu HS; Waipahu, HI; (3); 40/409; Teachers Aide; Drill Tm; Rep Frsh Cls; Rep Soph Cls; Rep Jr Cls; Hon Roll; U Of HI Manoa; Pediatrician.

DOMINGO, SHIRLEY R; Farrington HS; Honolulu, HI; (2); 1/721; Computer Clb; Math Tm; SADD; Chorus; Nwsp; Treas Frsh Cls; Treas Jr Cls; JV Var Crs Cntry; High Hon Roll; Karate; Upward Bound Pgm; Med.

DOMINGSIL, ELSIE V; Farrington HS; Honolulu, HI; (1); 1/362; 4-H; Ed Yrbk; Chrmn Frsh Cls; 4-H Awd; High Hon Roll; Hon Roll; Acting.

DONIN, ANGIE L; Baldwin HS; Wailuku, HI; (1); 13/466; Math Tm; Band; Var Socr; Hon Roll; HI St Sci Fr; UCLA; Interior Desgn.

DOO, SHAWN; Kapaa HS; Kapaa, HI; (3); 18/191; Aud/Vis; Church Yth Grp; Pres Key Clb; Q&S; Ed Yrbk; VP Sr Cls; Rep Stu Cncl; JV Var Bsktbl; Var Ftbl; Var Capt Trk; Kiwanis & John A Burns Schlrshps; Schlr Athl; St Indstrl Arts Fair 3rd Pl; U HI Hilo; Scndry Ed.

DOQUISA, RONALYNN; Leilehua HS; Wahiawa, HI; (3); Hosp Aide; Red Cross Aide; Teachers Aide; Chorus; Hon Roll; Natl Hosp Ldrshp & Svc Awd; Hiking Club; U Of CA; Jrnlsm.

DORAN, MICHAEL C; Pahoa HS; Pahoa, HI; (2); Art Clb; Drama Clb; FFA; Speech Tm; School Play; Stage Crew; Stu Cncl; Socr; UCLA; Bus.

DOTE, BRIAN M; Waipahu HS; Waipahu, HI; (4); 11/450; Letterman Clb; Math Tm; Quiz Bowl; Band; Mrchg Band; Pep Band; JV VP Tennis; Hon Roll; Rotary Awd; Leo Club Pres; Mock Trial; Hui Makaala Sch Recipient; U HI Manoa; Pre-Med.

DOUGHERTY, PETER W; Radford HS; Honolulu, HI; (3); 149/374; Art Clb; Ski Clb; Spanish Clb; Nwsp; Yrbk; John Hopkins U; Pre-Med.

DOWNER, TRISHA D; Lahaina Luna HS; Lahaina, HI; (1); 6/175; Church Yth Grp; Church Choir; Hon Roll.

DRACULAN, LORENA B; Waiakea HS; Hilo, HI; (1); Pep Clb; Band; Bsktbl; Mgr(s); Stat Vllybl; Hon Roll; Prfct Atten Awd; Natl Sci Mrt Awd; UCLA; Astronomy.

DROGE, CLARISSA A; Waiakea HS; Mountain View, HI; (3); 63/368; Church Yth Grp; DECA; Upwrd Bnd; Clinical Psych.

DROSE II, BENJAMIN; Kapaa Intermediate HS; Kapaa, HI; (3); Aud/Vis; Math Tm; Teachers Aide; Band; Mrchg Band; Pep Band; Capt Jr Cls; Capt Stu Cncl; Hon Roll; St Champ Mock Trial Tm 90; Prclmtn From Myr Of Kauai; Rcgntn From HSTAS Praise Pgm.

DROST, NOAH E; Lutheran HS Of Hawaii; Kaneohe, HI; (1); JA; Bsktbl; Hon Roll; Japanese Lang Stud; Aikido; Marine Bio.

DUARTE, ROCHELLE S; Pahoa HS; Pahoa, HI; (3); Band; Psych.

DUARTE III, THOMAS; Saint Louis Schl; Honolulu, HI; (3); Cmnty Wkr; VP Intnl Clb; Math Clb; Math Tm; ROTC; Rep Frsh Cls; Rep Soph Cls; Sec Jr Cls; Rep Stu Cncl; Treas NHS; Rifle Tm Vrsty, JV Tm Cptn; 1st Gilliland Schlr Schl Hstry; Pres Japanese Clb; Envrnmntl Engrng.

DUDOIT, RONDA A; Nolokai High & Inter; Kaunakakai, HI; (3); 11/95; GAA; Sec Stu Cncl; Var Mgr(s); Var Vllybl; Hon Roll; I Was The Scholar Athlete For The B Ball Team In 1989 90; U Of HI At Hilo; Elem Schl Tchr.

DUFRENE, A A; Kaiser HS; Honolulu, HI; (3); Bsktbl; U Of HI; Astronaut.

DULAY, MADELYN D; Maui HS; Kahului, HI; (3); Drama Clb; Science Clb; Flag Corp; Rep Stu Cncl; Hon Roll; Prfct Atten Awd; Cert Rcgntn Ouststndng Achvt Scl Stds; SPEBE Chinese Stds; 1st Pl Mauis Nmbr 1 Mon Essay Cont; U Of HI; Bus.

DUMAG, HELEN L; Molokai HS; Kaunakakai, HI; (2); 1/87; Drama Clb; Quiz Bowl; Teachers Aide; VP Frsh Cls; Hon Roll; Hana Kupono Clb-Pres; Hawaiian Dance Clb; Mock Trial; Friendly Isle United Fund Cmmttee; Stu Of Month.

DUMBRIQUE, JOY L; Kauai HS & Intermed; Lihue, HI; (4); 21/239; Church Yth Grp; FHA; Teachers Aide; High Hon Roll; Hon Roll; NHS; Hula Group; Leo Club; Grad Magna Cum Laude 90.

DUMLAO, DELVER S; Nanakuli HS; Waianae, HI; (2); Math Clb; Math Tm; Quiz Bowl; Band; JV Bsktbl; Capt JV Ftbl; High Hon Roll; Hon Roll; Jr NHS; Universal Tech Inst; Elctrncs.

DUNNO, DAWN M; Moanalua HS; Honolulu, HI; (2); 89/500; Hon Roll; Modeling Classes; Tennis; Law.

DUONG, SANDRA YEN; Mc Kinley HS; Honolulu, HI; (1); 41/492; Hon Roll; Prfct Atten Awd; Chinese Club; U Of HI; Educ.

DURAN, RAY B; Waialua Inter HS; Haleiwa, HI; (3); VICA; Auto Clb; AAI; Auto Mech.

DURAN, RONA C; Mid-Pacific Inst; Lihue, HI; (2); Church Yth Grp; Cmnty Wkr; Intnl Clb; High Hon Roll; Hon Roll; Prfct Atten Awd; 1st Intl Yth Camp-Japan Rep; Am Diabetes Assn Natl Yth Congrss Rep; Intl Medcl Symposium Speaker 89; U Of CO-BOULDER; Med.

EALA, MICHELLE L; Molokai HS; Kualapuu, HI; (3); 10/94; FHA; Hon Roll.

EDAYAN, HARMONY; Leilehua HS; Wahiawa, HI; (2); 98/392; Drama Clb; Girl Scts; Chorus; Rifle Tm Cmptn; Fshn Dsgn.

EDGE, ROBERT C; Mid Pacific Inst; Honolulu, HI; (2); Var Tennis; Landscape Arch.

EDRADA, YOLANDA T; Waialua HS; Waialua, HI; (2); 6/155; Science Clb; Spanish Clb; Lit Mag; Rep Soph Cls; Hon Roll; Prfct Atten Awd; HI Pacific Coll; Pediatrics.

EDRALIN, ATAMANTE; St Louis HS; Waimanalo, HI; (3); Aud/Vis; Cmnty Wkr; Service Clb; Spanish Clb; Church Choir; Stu Cncl; Bsktbl; Ftbl; Hon Roll; Prfct Atten Awd; HPC; Engrng.

EDWARDS, EDRIENNE L; Waimea HS; Kekaha, HI; (3); 14/198; Pres Church Yth Grp; Church Choir; Pres Frsh Cls; Pres Soph Cls; Pres Jr Cls; Pres Stu Cncl; Capt Var Cheerldng; Var Vllybl; Hon Roll; Var NHS; Natl Walter Disneys Dreamers & Doers Awd St Of HI Semifnlst; BYU.

EDWARDS, LEWIS W; Radford HS; Honolulu, HI; (3); 7/394; Math Clb; Capt Math Tm; Mu Alpha Theta; High Hon Roll; Hon Roll; Ntl Merit Ltr; Worchester Polytech Inst; Arspc.

ELAM, TODD B; Lahainaluna HS; Lahaina, HI; (1); 20/260; Math Clb; Science Clb; Wrstlng; Woods Club; Dntst.

ELIES, JOEL S; Lahainaluna HS; Lahaina, HI; (3); 44/225; Math Tm; Quiz Bowl; Band; Mrchg Band; Pep Band; Intrml Bsktbl; Var Socr; NHS; All Amercn Hall Of Fame Band Hnrs; U HI-MANOA; Ed.

ELIKAN, LARRY P; Radford HS; Honolulu, HI; (2); Var Crs Cntry; Var Socr; Var Trk; UTSA; Aerodynamic Eng.

ELLIS, CARRIE; Hawaii Prep Acad; Lihue, HI; (2); JV Bsktbl; JV L Crs Cntry; JV Trk; High Hon Roll.

ELLORIN, DEBORA R; James Campbell HS; Ewa Beach, HI; (3); 53/380; VP SADD; Hon Roll; Part-Time Job; U Of HI; Civil Engr.

ELLS, SHONTELL; Waiakea HS; Keaau, HI; (3); Sec JA; Stu Cncl; High Hon Roll; Hon Roll; Chrprsn Commencement Clean Up; Jr Achvt Awd; Hawaiian Clb; U Of HI Hilo; Trsm Mgmt.

ELM, K LEINANI; Henry J Kaiser HS; Honolulu, HI; (1); Girl Scts; Key Clb; Speech Tm; SADD; Band; Hon Roll; Aloha Girl Scout Ensmbl; Melinda Carroll Singers; Cecelio/Kapono Choir; Hula Halau O Leolani; Silver Awd; Med.

ENGLE, LILA LEHUA; Waiakea HS; Volcano, HI; (1); Latin Clb; Math Clb; Math Tm; Pep Clb; UH Hilo; Pilot.

ENGORING, JON A; Maui HS; Haiku, HI; (2); 118/300; Hon Roll; Stu Styng Strght; U Of HI; Bus Mgmt.

ENOMOTO, HEATHER E; Moanalua HS; Honolulu, HI; (3); 24/462; Q&S; Rptr Nwsp; Yrbk; Hon Roll; Japanese Club.

ENOS, SHANNON K; The Kamehameha Schls; Honolulu, HI; (3); 120/420; VP Dance Clb; SADD; Teachers Aide; Band; Mrchg Band; Pep Band; Hawaiian Clb; Hula; U HI; Ed.

ENRIQUE, JO RINA A; Kapaa HS; Kilauea, HI; (3); 35/185; Church Yth Grp; Cmnty Wkr; Church Choir; Drama Clb; 4-H; Speech Tm; Chorus; Stage Crew; Bsktbl; Vllybl; U CA; Math Teach.

ENRIQUEZ, EDWARD P; St Louis HS; Mililani, HI; (3); Church Yth Grp; High Hon Roll; Hon Roll; Prfct Atten Awd; Park Time Job; Outside Bsktbl; Camping; Bus.

ERECE, MARY JANE P; Kau HS; Pahala, HI; (4); 8/58; FFA; Treas Letterman Clb; Pep Clb; Chorus; Rep Sr Cls; Var Stat Bsktbl; Var Socr; Hon Roll; U HI Hilo; Bus Mgt.

ERQUIZA, SUSAN M; Pearl City HS; Waipahu, HI; (3); 85/527; French Clb; Teachers Aide; Chrmn Jr Cls; Chrmn Sr Cls; Stu Cncl; Var JV Mgr(s); Var JV Score Keeper; Hon Roll; Wrld Of Poetry Hnrb Mntn; Congrssnl Yth Ldrshp Cncl; Bus.

ESCHER, ROBIN P; Mililani HS; Mililani, HI; (3); 47/490; Church Yth Grp; Drama Clb; English Clb; Science Clb; SADD; Teachers Aide; Thesps; Band; Mrchg Band; School Musical; Schl Ledrshp Awd; Mc Donalds Hula Bowl Mrchng Band; Med.

ESERA, CHRISTINE; Kahuku HS; Hauula, HI; (4); 3/240; Sec Church Yth Grp; Capt Color Guard; Drm Mjr(t); Mgr Nwsp; Pres Frsh Cls; Treas Soph Cls; VP Stu Cncl; JV Var Bsktbl; VP NHS; Val; Natl & Dist Elks Awd; Lions Club Awd; Pres Acadmc Ftnss Awd; Boise ST U; Math.

ESGUERRA, VIBENJOHN B; Moanalua HS; Honolulu, HI; (2); 30/488; Church Yth Grp; Math Clb; Science Clb; Ed Yrbk; Rep Soph Cls; Var Vllybl; Hon Roll; Altr Srvr St Philomena Prsh; Annl St Cnfrnc Filipino Yng Adlts Delg; Co-Chrprsn Ed Frm Cmmtte; Loyola Marymount U; Cmmnctns.

ESPANIA, CHARMAINE; Maui HS; Pukalani, HI; (3); Drama Clb; Key Clb; Science Clb; Band; Mrchg Band; Pep Band; Var Swmmng; Var Tennis; Hon Roll; Prfct Atten Awd; Dist Hnr Band; Japanese Clb; Mck Trl; U Of HI Manoa; Prfrmng Arts.

ESPERANZA, BOISSE O; Damien HS; Waipahu, HI; (4); Boy Scts; Church Yth Grp; Computer Clb; ROTC; Church Choir; Bsbl; Bsktbl; Ftbl; Trk; Vllybl; Army Rsrv Natl Guard; U Of HI Manoa; Med.

ESPIAU, ASIA A; Kalaheo HS; Kailua, HI; (3); 20/264; Rep Frsh Cls; Rep Soph Cls; Rep Jr Cls; Treas Sr Cls; Rep Stu Cncl; JV Bsktbl; Var Socr; JV Vllybl; High Hon Roll; Hon Roll; U Of HI; Acctng.

ESPIRITU, ELSIE D; Lanai HS; Lanai City, HI; (3); Church Yth Grp; FHA; FTA; Pep Clb; Service Clb; Speech Tm; Teachers Aide; Off Soph Cls; Cheerldng; Sftbl; Cannon Bus Coll; Offc Clrk.

ESPIRITU, ERWIN C; Damien Memorial HS; Waipahu, HI; (3); 23/130; ROTC; Intrml JV Bsktbl; Intrml JV Ftbl; High Hon Roll; U Of HI; Nrs.

ESTEBAN, MARY ANN; Farrington HS; Honolulu, HI; (3); Q&S; Service Clb; VP Spanish Clb; SADD; Ed Nwsp; Ed Lit Mag; Chrmn Stu Cncl; Tennis; Jr NHS; NHS; Engr.

ESTRADA, MICHAEL E; Kailua HS; Kailua, HI; (3); Boy Scts; Church Yth Grp; Cmnty Wkr; Drama Clb; Hosp Aide; Teachers Aide; Thesps; Chorus; School Musical; School Play; Vocalist Numerous Schl Activities; Perf Art.

ESTRELLA, ALYSON M; Mililani HS; Mililani Town, HI; (3); 38/490; Church Yth Grp; Intnl Clb; Key Clb; Teachers Aide; High Hon Roll; Hon Roll; Clss Cncl Chrprsn; Outstndg Frgn Lang Awd Span; Religious Educ Tchr; Bus.

ESTRELLA, EDWINA LYNN M; Wallace Rider Farrington HS; Honolulu, HI; (3); Library Aide; Q&S; Service Clb; Spanish Clb; VP VICA; Variety Show; Nwsp; Stu Cncl; Var Tennis; Hon Roll; 1st Pl Div Korea Soc Essy Cntst Schlrshp; 1st Pl Nws Div UH Jrnlsm Day Cmptns; Jrnlsm.

EVSLIN, TANYA; Kavai HS; Kapaa, HI; (3); Pres Drama Clb; Pres Q&S; Speech Tm; School Play; Ed Nwsp; L Swmmng; Hon Roll; Pltcl Sci.

EWE, LEILA ANN PUAMELIA; Waialua HS; Haleiwa, HI; (2); 31/161; Church Yth Grp; Hon Roll; Prfct Atten Awd; Peer Mediation; BYU; Elem Ed.

FAAGATA, ALATISE S; Saint Louis HS; Honolulu, HI; (3); 39/152; Church Yth Grp; Cmnty Wkr; Variety Show; Bsktbl; Ftbl; Socr; Trk; Vllybl; Wt Lftg; Hon Roll; Hui O Na Opio Clb; U Notre Dame.

FABAY, MARICAR C; Radford HS; Honolulu, HI; (2); 8/411; Band; Hon Roll; Japanese Frndshp Clb; Frnch I Conversatnl Japanese Cert Awd; U Miami Schl Music; Rcrdng Engr.

FAHEY, ANDREW L; Mc Kinley HS; Honolulu, HI; (4); 1/545; Capt Computer Clb; Office Aide; High Hon Roll; Sal; Chaminade U; Comp Sci.

FAIDIT, JOSHUA; Pahoa HS; Pahoa, HI; (4); 6/125; Socr; Vllybl; Hon Roll; NHS.

FAILANO, JENNIFER F; James Campbell HS; Ewa Beach, HI; (2); 10/400; Teachers Aide; VP Soph Cls; Cit Awd; Hon Roll; NHS; Harvard; Arch.

FANTOLI, JEFFREY J; Henry J Kaiser HS; Jamestown, RI; (1); 52/255; L Var Golf.

FARIAS, MICHAEL NAONE; Hilo HS; Hilo, HI; (4); 27/310; Aud/Vis; Key Clb; Math Clb; Math Tm; Variety Show; Rep Sr Cls; Capt Crs Cntry; Var Swmmng; Hon Roll; Hghst Score Math Assoc Am Exam; Soroptomst Clb Awd; Loyola Marymount U; Elec Engrng.

FARLEY, CHARITYANNE M; Hawaii Baptist Acad; Hilo, HI; (2); 2/92; FTA; JA; Q&S; Ed Nwsp; High Hon Roll; NHS; Vol Spcl Olympics; 1st Pl Statewide Jrnlsm Cont Feature Wrtng; Outstng News Reprtr.

FAUGHT, KIMBERLY; James Campbell HS; Ewa Beach, HI; (2); 25/348; Science Clb; Chorus; Blue-Water Marine Lab Smmr Ocean Stds Pgm; Jrnlsm.

FAVINGER, XANDA K; Maui HS; Haiku, HI; (3); 92/384; Church Yth Grp; Computer Clb; Temple Yth Grp; Var Bsktbl; Prfct Atten Awd; Pres Acad Fit Awd; Pre-Law.

FEITEIRA, WENDY K; Maui HS; Kahului, HI; (2); 32/388; Cmnty Wkr; Letterman Clb; Pep Clb; Band; Var L Trk; Stus Staying Straight; Leo Clb; Ann-Rae Intl Model; U Of HI; Travel Indstry Mgmt.

FELIPE, JUNE G; Maryknoll HS; Honolulu, HI; (4); Church Yth Grp; Sec Spanish Clb; JV Vllybl; High Hon Roll; Hon Roll; Jr Cathlc Clb Pres; Loyola Marymount U; Law.

FELIX, MICHELLE I; James Campbell HS; Ewa Beach, HI; (3); 30/371; Church Yth Grp; Band; Mrchg Band; Sec Stu Cncl; Stat Mgr(s); Hon Roll; Prfct Atten Awd.

FENG, SAIYUAN; Kalani HS; Honolulu, HI; (3); Elec.

FENG, XING CI; Mc Kinley HS; Honolulu, HI; (4); Art Clb; Church Yth Grp; Cmnty Wkr; Dance Clb; Hosp Aide; Library Aide; Math Clb; Office Aide; School Play; Stage Crew; Outstndng Stu Achvt; Tuition Waiver Awd; Wrld Of Poetry Hnrb Mntn Awd Merit Cert; Chinese Yth HI; U HI; Tchng.

FENWICK, ELIZABETH E; Baldwin HS; Madison, WI; (3); 33/393; Dance Clb; Drama Clb; Library Aide; Teachers Aide; Band; School Musical; School Play; Variety Show; Gov Hon Prg Awd; High Hon Roll; Excllnc In Acadmcs Awd; Arch.

FERNANDES, KIRK J; Henry Perrine Baldwin HS; Kahului, HI; (2); 30/395; Key Clb; Math Tm; Band; Hon Roll; Stu Styng Strght Orgnztn; Maui Dist Stu Cncl SAC; HOBY Yth Ldrshp Fndtn Schl Ambsdr; Hnr Band; MA Inst Tech; Comp Sci.

FERNANDEZ, BABELYN A; Maui HS; Paia, HI; (2); 25/388; Hon Roll.

FERNANDEZ, GLENN T; Kalani HS; Honolulu, HI; (2); 45/213; Phtg Aud/Vis; Computer Clb; Var Socr; Hon Roll; Save The Earth Clb; Electronics Clb; Engrng.

FERNANDEZ, LISA F; Waialua HS; Waialua, HI; (2); 13/163; Science Clb; Sec Frsh Cls; Hon Roll; Prfct Atten Awd; Japanese Club; Aloha Civic Club; U Of HI; Bus.

FERNANDEZ III, LOUIS; Maui HS; Haiku, HI; (3); 44/354; Pres Drama Clb; Stage Crew; Nwsp; Close-Up; Engrng.

FERREIRA, TAMMY KEIKO; Sacred Hearts Acad; Honolulu, HI; (4); Damien Hmncng Qn; Natl Hispanic Schl Awds Semi-Fnslt 90; 3rd Pl Essay Catholic Dghtrs Of Amer 89; U Of Southern CA.

FETTE, RACHEL; Leilehua HS; Wahiawa, HI; (3); Band; Pep Band; Ed Nwsp; Hon Roll; OK Southwestern ST; Phrmcy.

FETUI, CATHY; Hawaii Baptist Acad; Honolulu, HI; (2); Church Yth Grp; Cmnty Wkr; Office Aide; Service Clb; Band; Chorus; Pep Band; School Musical; School Play; Intrml Bsktbl; Bus.

FEVELLA, MICHAEL E; James Campbell HS; Ewa Beach, HI; (2); Band; Jazz Band; Mrchg Band; Pep Band; JV Bsbl; Cmmnty Leag Bsktbl; PAL Leag Bsktbl; MI U; Liberal Arts.

FIELD, ERIC C; James Campbell HS; Ewa Beach, HI; (2); 19/360; Church Yth Grp; Cmnty Wkr; Key Clb; Chorus; Stage Crew; Wt Lftg; Gov Hon Prg Awd; Hon Roll; Architect.

FIFER, RICHARD L; Leilehua HS; Schofield Barraks, HI; (2); Boy Scts; Var Socr; Notre Dame Coll IN; Med.

FILLERS, DONALD F; Honokaa HS; Honokaa, HI; (3); Pep Clb; Rep Stu Cncl; Var Socr; Music.

FISHER, SAMUEL V; Honokaa HS; Honokaa, HI; (2); 11/155; JV Capt Ftbl; High Hon Roll; Hon Roll; Spnsh Mastery II Awd.

FITZGERALD, JAMIE A; Kalani HS; Honolulu, HI; (3); Pres French Clb; Nwsp; French Hon Soc; High Hon Roll; NHS; Wellesley Bk Awd; Outstndng Stu Scl Stds 88-89; Theater.

FITZGERALD, MICHAEL; Hwaiian Mission Acad; Honolulu, HI; (3); 7/45; Church Yth Grp; Chorus; Church Choir; Bus Profs of Am; School Play; Stage Crew; Bsktbl; Ftbl; Gym; Vllybl; Yth Ldrshp Cncl; U Of HI; Bus Mgmt.

FITZGERALD, SHANNON M; Waiakea HS; Hilo, HI; (2); 132/497; Cmnty Wkr; 4-H; GAA; JA; Key Clb; Letterman Clb; Service Clb; SADD; Flag Corp; Var Swmmng; Keywnttes Clb; Northern IL U; Bus.

FLEISCHMAN, ARNOLD W; Mc Kinley HS; Honolulu, HI; (3); 36/512; Cmnty Wkr; French Clb; Quiz Bowl; Socr; Tennis; NHS; Bus.

FLEISHER, MICHELE K; Moanalua HS; Honolulu, HI; (3); VP Art Clb; Math Tm; SADD; Pres Frsh Cls; Pres Jr Cls; Treas Stu Cncl; Crs Cntry; Powder Puff Ftbl; Tennis; High Hon Roll; Commnctns.

FLEMING, JENNIFER; Kauai HS & Intermed; Lawai, HI; (1); Rptr Nwsp; High Hon Roll; Hon Roll; Music.

FLORES, BRANDON K; Iolani Schl; Mililani, HI; (4); 37/220; Var L Bsktbl; JV Bausch & Lomb Sci Awd; Var L Trk; Var L Vllybl; High Hon Roll; Hon Roll; Ntl Merit SF; All ILH Hnrbl Mntn Vlybl; Jr Prom Attndt; Law.

FLORES, JENNIFER; Lanakila Baptist HS; Waianae, HI; (4); Teachers Aide; Ed Yrbk; JV Vllybl; Hon Roll; Englsh Hnrs; Kapiolani CC; Nrsng.

FLORINO, STEPHEN; Mililani HS; Mililani, HI; (2); 81/509; Acpl Chr; Band; Mrchg Band; Pep Band; UCLA; Kinesilogy.

FLOYD, WENDY C; Radford HS; Honolulu, HI; (2); Art Clb; French Clb; Teachers Aide; Trk; High Hon Roll; Hon Roll; Psych.

FOGELSANGER, TANIA L; Lutheran HS; Honolulu, HI; (3); Church Yth Grp; Drama Clb; FCA; Chorus; Nwsp; Lit Mag; Rep Frsh Cls; Sec Soph Cls; Sec Jr Cls; VP Stu Cncl; Vlntr Annl Wheelchair Marathon; Secndry Educ.

FOK, DEREK; Kailua HS; Kailua, HI; (3); 6/349; Boy Scts; Math Tm; Quiz Bowl; Spanish Clb; Var Wrstlng; Hon Roll; NHS; Dartmouth Coll; Comp Engrng.

FOLLANTE, LEILANI S; Moanalua HS; Honolulu, HI; (3); 66/462; SADD; Band; Mrchg Band; Variety Show; Sec Stu Cncl; Hon Roll; Sec Jr NHS; Ser Teens Clb HI Secty; Elctns Cmmtte Co-Chrprsn; Close Up Prtcptn; U Of HI Manoa.

FONG, FLORENCE Y W; Mc Kinley HS; Honolulu, HI; (2); Office Aide; Teachers Aide; Kong Tow Society; Lung Kong Phys Culture Club; Chineses Yth Of HI Newsltr; Arch.

FONTES, ELLSWORTH J; Waiakea HS; Keaau, HI; (1); Church Yth Grp; Prfct Atten Awd; Pres Acad Fit Awd; Na Pua Noeau Ctr Gftd, Tlntd Navite Hawaiian Chldrn; Amer Acad Of Dramatic Arts.

FOREMAN, KIMBERLY; Kalaheo HS; Kailua, HI; (3); Pep Clb; SADD; Rep Stu Cncl; Capt Var Cheerldng; Trk; Hon Roll; Bus.

FOREMAN, STEPHEN; Kalaheo HS; Kailua, HI; (1); 32/266; Hon Roll.

FORMOSO, CHARMAINE M; Leilehna HS; Wahiawa, HI; (1); Church Yth Grp; 4-H; Hosp Aide; Church Choir; Mgr(s); Score Keeper; Hon Roll; Medcl Doctor.

FOSTER, CARRIE; St Joseph HS; Hilo, HI; (3); VP French Clb; Pres Math Clb; Yrbk; VP Jr Cls; Var L Sftbl; Var L Vllybl; Hon Roll; NHS; NEDT Awd; Cmptv Swm USS; Grl Scts Amer-Indvdl; Bio.

FOUST, BENJAMIN; Pahoa HS; Keaau, HI; (2); 5/123; French Clb; Var Socr; Hon Roll; NHS; Arspc Engrng.

FOWLER, RYAN L; Baldwin HS; Kihei, HI; (1); 52/466; Boy Scts.

FOX, RONALD L; Radford HS; Honolulu, HI; (2); 46/466; Church Yth Grp; ROTC; Church Choir; Color Guard; Trk; Hon Roll; Cadet Of Yr ROTC; Element Ldr Cvl Air Ptrl; Seasl ROTC; Air Force Acad.

FRANCISCO, FLORENCE R; Radford HS; Honolulu, HI; (2); Church Yth Grp; Hosp Aide; Intnl Clb; Red Cross Aide; Church Choir; U Of HI; Hotel Indstry Mgmt.

FRANK JR, LAWRENCE P; St Louis HS; Honolulu, HI; (2); 51/151; Teachers Aide; Intrml JV Bsktbl; Intrml JV Vllybl; Hon Roll; MVP Awd Intermediate & JV Vllybl 88-89; MVP Awd Intermediate Bsktbl; 2nd Earth Day Essay Cont 90; Airline/Travel.

FRASCARELLI, FRANCES M; Mid-Pacific Inst; Pearl City, HI; (2); Hosp Aide; Math Tm; JV Tennis; High Hon Roll; Hon Roll; Gymnstcs; Piano; Japanese Clb; Bus Admin.

FREITAS, ANDREW C; Kaiser HS; Honolulu, HI; (2); JV Ftbl; JV Trk; U Of HI; Bus Mgmt.

FREITAS, CATHY L; St Francis HS; Honolulu, HI; (2); 14/80; Library Aide; Lit Mag; Pres Soph Cls; Hon Roll; Prfct Atten Awd; Bus Admin.

FRIEDEL, ERICA; Kalaheo HS; Kaneohe, HI; (2); SADD; Vllybl; Hon Roll; Psych.

FRONDA, FRED; Lahaina Luna HS; Lahaina, HI; (2); Church Yth Grp; FFA; Church Choir; JV Bsktbl; Intrml Vllybl; Hon Roll; Prfct Atten Awd.

FUERTE, KY F; Baldwin HS; Wailuku, HI; (2); Band; Mrchg Band; Pep Band; Dist Hnr Band; Santa Clara; Social Sci.

FUJIHARA, ANGEL U; Kailua HS; Kailua, HI; (2); Hon Roll; Bowlng; Hawaiian Clb; Acctnt.

FUJII, ALII-MANA T; William Mc Kinley HS; Waipahu, HI; (2); 35/588; Hon Roll; CA Tech; Cmptr Sci.

FUJII, DENNIS; Moanalua HS; Honolulu, HI; (2); 38/488; Boy Scts; Mrchg Band; Orch; JV Var Ftbl; JV Var Wrstlng; High Hon Roll; Pres Acad Fit Awd; Judo; BYU; Med.

FUJII, ROSS; Lutheran HS; Honolulu, HI; (4); 1/50; Math Tm; Quiz Bowl; Band; Rptr Nwsp; Treas Soph Cls; JV Bsbl; JV Bsktbl; High Hon Roll; NHS; Hnry Navy Offcr For Day 89; HI Sut Sci Training Pgm 89; U Of HI Jrnlsm Day 1st Pl Wnn Sports Wrtng; U Of MI; Engrng.

FUJII, SCOTT; Hilo HS; Hilo, HI; (4); 8/341; Key Clb; Letterman Clb; Science Clb; Varsity Clb; Band; Mrchg Band; Pep Band; Var L Crs Cntry; Var Trk; Var L Wrstlng; Slctd Into Cntys Slct Band Of HS Stus; Sci Dept Awd; CA U Davis; Bio.

FUJIKAWA, DEBRA-ANN K; Moanalua HS; Honolulu, HI; (3); 54/471; Chorus; VP Frsh Cls; Stu Cncl; Japanese Clb Treas; U Of HI Mahoa.

FUJIMURA, KRISTIN A; Mc Kinley HS; Pearl City, HI; (3); Spanish Clb; Var Socr; NHS; Keywanettes.

FUJITA, JENNI M; Lutheran HS; Honolulu, HI; (1); Yuukikai Clb; Outstndng Work In Japanese I; CPA.

FUJIUCHI, LAUREE J; Kapaa HS; Kapaa, HI; (2); Key Clb; Pep Clb; Rep Soph Cls; Hist Stu Cncl; Var Capt Cheerldng; MV Chrldr 89-90; Bus.

FUJIWARA, FLYNN M; Punahou HS; Pearl City, HI; (4); Cmnty Wkr; ROTC; Variety Show; Yrbk; Ntl Merit SF; Japanese Clb; Ranger Clb; U CA Irvine; Cvl Engrng.

FUJIYAMA, IAN I; Waiakea HS; Hilo, HI; (4); 1/412; Sec Key Clb; JV Ftbl; Var Capt Wrstlng; Bausch & Lomb Sci Awd; Pres NHS; St Schlr; Val; Sterling Scholar Sci; Male Scholar Athlete; Exch Club Youth Of Month; U PA; Biochem.

FUKAMI, JONI L; Henry Perrine Baldwin HS; Kahului, HI; (2); 1/395; Church Yth Grp; Math Clb; Math Tm; Science Clb; Service Clb; Band; Mrchg Band; Pep Band; High Hon Roll; Englsh Wrtng Awd Schl, Dist & ST.

FUKUDA, LORI A; Pearl City HS; Pearl City, HI; (4); 49/478; Church Yth Grp; DECA; Hosp Aide; Key Clb; JV Score Keeper; JV Var Sftbl; Gov Hon Prg Awd; High Hon Roll; Hon Roll; U Of HI; Med.

FUKUDA, TRACY K; Mid-Pacific Inst; Honolulu, HI; (2); FCA; Rep Frsh Cls; Vllybl; Hon Roll; Adv.

FUKUI, JAMIE N; Hawaii Baptist Acad; Aiea, HI; (2); 6/94; Hosp Aide; VP JA; Math Tm; Q&S; Ed Nwsp; Intrml Sftbl; High Hon Roll; NHS; Bowling Team; Japanese Clb; Psych.

FUKUMOTO, RALPH; Moanalua HS; Honolulu, HI; (3); 79/462; Band; Hon Roll; Graphc Arts; Advrtsng Arts; Speedsktng; Advrtsng Artist.

FUKUMURA, KELLIE A; Maryknoll HS; Honolulu, HI; (3); Math Tm; Science Clb; Service Clb; School Musical; Lit Mag; Treas Frsh Cls; Treas Soph Cls; Off Jr Cls; High Hon Roll; NHS; Accredtn Cmmtte; Spirit Cmmtte; Retreat Tm; Pedtrcn.

FUKUSHIMA, LAURIE H; Maui HS; Pukalani, HI; (2); Church Yth Grp; Key Clb; Treas Soph Cls; Var Swmmng; Var Trk; Hon Roll.

FUKUSHIMA, LYNN; Roosevelt HS; Honolulu, HI; (3); 74/352; Band; Mrchg Band; Yrbk; Stat Wrstlng; U HI Manoa; Early Ed.

FUKUSHIMA, REID K; Maui HS; Kahului, HI; (2); 50/388; Boy Scts; Church Yth Grp; Key Clb; VP Band; Mrchg Band; Pep Band; JV Ftbl; Var Swmmng; UH Manoa; Tchr.

FUKUSHIMA, RHODA M; Moanalua HS; Honolulu, HI; (2); 13/488; Stat Bsbl; Capt JV Cheerldng; High Hon Roll; Japanese Club; Gftd & Tlntd Art Cls; U HI.

FUKUSHIMA, TRICIA K; Henry Perrine Baldwin HS; Kihei, HI; (3); Church Yth Grp; Band; Hon Roll; Dist Hnr Band; Japanese Clb; Counterpart & Grad Chrprsn Of Awds & Diplomas; U Of HI; Arch.

FUKUYAMA, COLETTE H; Kohala HS; Kapaau, HI; (1); FFA; FHA; FTA; U Portland Linfield.

FUKUYAMA, TAKAMI; Saint Francis HS; Honolulu, HI; (2); 1/80; Mu Alpha Theta; Tennis; NHS; Math Leag.

FULLER, MITCHELL K; Roosevelt HS; Waimanalo, HI; (3); Boy Scts; Church Yth Grp; Var Bsktbl; Var Ftbl; HI All Star Bsktbl Tm To Play Las Vegas Trnmnt 90; N CO; Pro Bsktbl.

FULLERTON, AMY J; Waiakea HS; Hilo, HI; (3); 81/368; JA; Pep Clb; Var Bsktbl; Chrprsn SGA Svc Cmmtte; Interact Club Mem; Tutor Waiakea Elem Schl; Tchr.

FUNG, AIMEE; Hilo HS; Hilo, HI; (3); 5/360; French Clb; JA; Varsity Clb; Var Sftbl; Var Tennis; High Hon Roll; NHS; Pres Acad Fit Awd; Charminade U; Sociology.

FUNK, YONG SUN; Moanalua HS; Honolulu, HI; (3); 28/462; Comp Sci.

FUNTANILLA, WOODLEY P; Moanalua HS; Honolulu, HI; (3); 35/462; JV Ftbl; JV Var Wrstlng; High Hon Roll; Hon Roll; Local Awd In Art; Cngrssnl Art Awd; Sec Art Awd; Arch.

FURUICHI, ERIN E; Waialva HS; Waialua, HI; (3); Drama Clb; Quiz Bowl; Chrmn Service Clb; VP Speech Tm; School Play; Socr; Hon Roll; Prfct Atten Awd; Upward Bound; Anti-Drug Clb; Ed.

FYRBERG, TAI HOKULII; Punahou HS; Honolulu, HI; (3); Church Yth Grp; Dance Clb; Science Clb; Service Clb; Nwsp; Yrbk; Cheerldng; Hon Roll; Jr NHS; NHS; Dancer Of Yr 88-90; Nutcracker Perf 86-89; KDEO Cntry Dancers Of HI Perf; Medcl.

GABAYLO, VERONICA C; Nanakuli HS; Ewa Beach, HI; (3); 9/146; Church Yth Grp; High Hon Roll; Hon Roll; Outstndng Tu Rcrdkpng, Eng, Modern HI Hstry; 1st Pl Choral Rdng; Comp Pgmr.

GABINA, JULIANA R; Maui HS; Wailuku, HI; (4); 90/303; Sec Computer Clb; Science Clb; Service Clb; Hon Roll; Lion Awd; Sterling Schlr Schl Indstrl Arts Wnnr; Outstndng Genl Metals Stu; Yth Ambssdrs Clb-Schl & Intl-Pres; Maui CC; Electrncs.

GABRIEL, HEIDI; Hilo HS; Papaikou, HI; (4); 5/304; Rep Sr Cls; Rep Stu Cncl; Capt Cheerldng; High Hon Roll; Hon Roll; Sec NHS; Outstdng Filipino HS Cls Std; Med.

GABRIEL, JASON; James Campbell HS; Ewa Beach, HI; (2); 57/350; Aud/Vis; Lit Mag; Engr.

GACULA, GILBERT A; Honokaa HS; Paauilo, HI; (4); Church Yth Grp; Math Tm; Science Clb; JV Bsktbl; Capt Wrstlng; Hon Roll; Intl Karate Lg 6 Yrs, 5 Trophies; HI Army Natl Grd Rep Training 3rd Bst Mrksmn; U HI Manoa; Arch.

GALAM, PENNEY; Molokai HS & Intermed; Kaunakakai, HI; (3); Church Yth Grp; Art Clb; Teachers Aide; Church Choir; Yrbk; Bsbl; Sftbl; Vllybl.

GALIMA, APRIL K; Waiakea HS; Pahoa, HI; (1); FHA; Pep Clb; Pep Band; High Hon Roll; Hon Roll; Work UNN Na Pua Noeau; Phy Mentor Or Cosmotologist Mentr; UH Manoa; Psych.

GALIZA, CAROLYN R; Waialua HS; Waialua, HI; (2); 3/160; Hosp Aide; Math Tm; Office Aide; Science Clb; High Hon Roll; Physician.

GALON, STACY L; James Campbell HS; Ewa Beach, HI; (2); JV Capt Bsktbl; JV Score Keeper; JV Var Sftbl; U Of HI; Accntng.

GALZOTE, GLENDA G; Hawaiian Mission Acad; Kailua, HI; (4); 3/36; Church Yth Grp; Computer Clb; 4-H; Hosp Aide; Office Aide; Chorus; Church Choir; School Musical; Nwsp; Treas Soph Cls; Kettering Coll Of Med Arts; Nrs.

GAMATERO, GARY B; Farington HS; Honolulu, HI; (3); 85/350; Hon Roll; Honolulu CC; Elec.

GAMBLE, SONIA N; Pahoa HS; Pahoa, HI; (4); 41/106; Rptr FFA; FHA; Treas Letterman Clb; Pep Clb; Teachers Aide; Yrbk; Pres Frsh Cls; Sec Soph Cls; Rep Jr Cls; Off Sr Cls; Bwlng; Navy; Avtn.

GAMIAO, MELANIE R; Kaimuki HS; Honolulu, HI; (2); 97/325; GAA; Var Vllybl; U Of HI-MANOA.

GAMPONG, ROMEO; University Laboratory Schl; Honolulu, HI; (4); Acpl Chr; Chorus; Church Choir; Pres Soph Cls; High Hon Roll; NHS; Church Yth Grp; Band; Jazz Band; Variety Show; St Art Cmptitn Finlst; Ftbll Leag Alls Tr 2nd Team; U OR; Archtctr.

GANAL, ROWENA C; Waupahu HS; Waipahu, HI; (3); 111/409; Off Frsh Cls; Stu Cncl; Student Govt Hospitality Chairperson; Chosen As One Of The Outstanding Studs Of The Renaissance Prog; U Of Hi; Travel Industry.

GANDIA, LAILA E; Kauai HS; Lihue, HI; (1); Band; Racism Clb, Stu Agnst Tacism.

GANOOT, CHERYL; Sacred Hearts Acad; Waipahu, HI; (2); Pep Clb; Var Cheerldng; Spnsh I Exclnnce; Kapiolani CC; Accntng.

GAPUSAN, SHERRILYN B; Wallace Rider Farrington HS; Honolulu, HI; (3); 37/600; Drama Clb; JA; Acpl Chr; Chorus; School Play; Stage Crew; Nwsp; Lit Mag; Cit Awd; Hon Roll; Hotel Mgmt.

GARCIA, ALWINSON S; Waialua HS; Waialua, HI; (2); Aud/Vis; Cmnty Wkr; Latin Clb; Service Clb; Spanish Clb; Church Choir; JV Bsktbl; JV Tennis; Hon Roll; Bayanihan Clb; Frgn Affairs Clb; 2nd Pl Inter Seminary Table Tnns Trnmnt; U HI; Mathmtcs.

GARCIA, ANGIE M; St Francis HS; Honolulu, HI; (3); 3/58; Mu Alpha Theta; Q&S; Red Cross Aide; Speech Tm; Nwsp; Ed Lit Mag; Rep Soph Cls; Vllybl; High Hon Roll; Hon Roll; HI Humane Scty Vol; RC Vol; TX A&M; Vet Med.

GARCIA, BEVERLY A; Maui HS; Paia, HI; (3); FHA; Yrbk; Hon Roll; Prfct Atten Awd; Stu Art 90 Cert Merit; Maui CC; Clths Dsnr.

GARCIA, DOREEN K; Lahainaluna HS; Lahaina, HI; (1); 45/231.

GARCIA, EVACITA J; Konawaena HS; Kealakekua, HI; (3); 26/294; Church Yth Grp; French Clb; Pep Clb; Quiz Bowl; Hon Roll; NHS; Girl Guards Troop Ldr; Hm Lg Historian; Bus.

GARCIA, GLEN L; Maui HS; Paia, HI; (3); 148/354; Boy Scts; Church Yth Grp; Band; Var Intrml Bsktbl; JV Socr; Harvard Med Schl; Chem.

GARCIA, JANETH T; Farrington HS; Honolulu, HI; (3); Band; Capt Color Guard; Capt Drill Tm; Capt Flag Corp; Jazz Band; Mrchg Band; Rep Stu Cncl; Hon Roll; HCC; Soc Wrkr.

GARCIA, LIZA-ANN L; Waimea HS; Kekeaha, HI; (3); Pres FHA; Key Clb; Red Cross Aide; VP Spanish Clb; Trk; Hon Roll; NHS; Civil Air Patrl; Embry-Riddle; Aeronautical Engr.

GARCIA, MARY JANE T; Waipahu HS; Honolulu, HI; (4); 82/418; Church Yth Grp; Cmnty Wkr; Dance Clb; French Clb; Intnl Clb; Orch; School Play; Rptr Nwsp; Rep Frsh Cls; Rep Jr Cls; Bus.

GARDNER, SUSANNAH; St Andrews Priory HS; Honolulu, HI; (3); #8 In Class; Church Yth Grp; Drama Clb; Intnl Clb; Service Clb; Yrbk; High Hon Roll; NHS; Arts.

GAREN, VANESSA P; Farrington HS; Honolulu, HI; (3); 80/600; Service Clb; Hon Roll; Pre-Med/Business.

GARMA, ATHENA L; Waipahu HS; Waipahu, HI; (2); Var Stat Ftbl; Woodbury U; Fash Merch.

GARO, ROBERT D; Maui HS; Kahului, HI; (3); 81/354; Science Clb; Crs Cntry; Ftbl; Leo Clb; Mayi CC; Auto Mech.

GARO, SHERYL P; Waianae HS; Waianae, HI; (1); 106/449; Art Clb; Rep Frsh Cls; Rep Stu Cncl; Intrml Tennis; Voc Fest 89 Hnrb Mntn 100% Accrcy Advncd Typng; Annl HI Bus Stu Conf Advnd Typng; Achvt Photo Awd; Hotel Mgmt.

GARRETT, BETH E; Kalaheo HS; Kailua, HI; (3); Phtg Yrbk; Off Frsh Cls; JV Bsktbl; High Hon Roll; Hon Roll; Teaming For Tomorrow; Fashion Design.

GASMEN, JOEY-ANN KIMIYO; Sacred Hearts Acad; Mililani, HI; (3); Church Yth Grp; Cmnty Wkr; French Clb; Hosp Aide; Math Clb; Teachers Aide; Chorus; Taking Care Fish; Plntng Flowers, Herbs; Cooking; Mkng Other People Happy; Acctng.

GASPER, LORENZO; Radford HS; Honolulu, HI; (1); ROTC; JV Ftbl.

GAY, SHARI D; Henry O HS; R H E, CA; (3); 1/20; Church Yth Grp; Cmnty Wkr; Library Aide; Teachers Aide; Off Soph Cls; Stu Cncl; High Hon Roll; Hon Roll; Azusa Pacific Coll.

GAZMEN, RYCHELLE C; Henry Perrine Baldwin HS; Kahului, HI; (1); Church Yth Grp; Cmnty Wkr; JA; Library Aide; Pep Clb; Service Clb; Speech Tm; Teachers Aide; Band; School Play; Japanese Club; Kiwanis Club; Acad Achvt; Pediatrician.

GEIER, CHRISTINE; Kalaheo HS; Kailua, HI; (1); 2/600; Cmnty Wkr; Girl Scts; SADD; Hon Roll; Jr NHS; PEOPEL; Sci.

GEMENO, CHAD; Waialua HS; Waialua, HI; (2); 29/160; Art Clb; Aud/Vis; FFA; SADD; Band; Bsbl; Ftbl; Wt Lftg; Hon Roll; Outstndng Vllybl Plry; Surfing Cont 3rd Pl; UCLA; Surfing.

GENG, CLAUDIA M; Maui HS; Kahului, HI; (3); 50/354; Flag Corp; Hon Roll; Leo Club; Close Up We Did Volunteer Serv And Went To Wa To See How Govt Works; Business.

GENG, HONG; Mc Kinley HS; Kaneohe, HI; (4); 1/547; Math Tm; Hon Roll; JETS Awd; Dartmouth SEED Prmg Smmr 89; MIT; Engrng.

GERGIS, DANIEL S; Lutheran HS; Honolulu, HI; (2); 5/47; Drama Clb; Thesps; Orch; School Play; Stage Crew; Rep Soph Cls; High Hon Roll; Hon Roll; Prfct Atten Awd; Japanese Clb; Outstndng Awd In Hstry; Law.

GERONIMO, AILEEN G; Mc Kinley HS; Honolulu, HI; (4); 66/547; Quiz Bowl; Church Choir; Hon Roll; NHS; Mabuhay Clb Pres & VP; Magna Cum Laude; Mckinley Hon Grad 90; U HI Manoa; Bus Mgmt.

GIBBONS, MELINDA; St Andrews Priory HS; Honolulu, HI; (2); 4/60; Hosp Aide; Key Clb; Science Clb; Orch; Yrbk; Sec Soph Cls; JV Tennis; High Hon Roll; NHS; Japanese Clb; Hawaiian Clb; Pre Med.

GIBBS, JEANETTE A; Mililani HS; Baltimore, MD; (2); 120/560; Dance Clb; JV Crs Cntry; JV Var Trk; Photo.

GIBO, JULIANNE H; Mc Kinley HS; Honolulu, HI; (2); 62/588; Band; Jazz Band; Pep Band; Med.

GIBSON, JENNIFER D; Mililani HS; Mililani, HI; (2); Pres Church Yth Grp; Drama Clb; Science Clb; Rep Frsh Cls; Rep Soph Cls; Sec Stu Cncl; Voice Dem Awd; Civil Air Patrol Flight Cmndr; Pilot.

GIDDENS, KAUIOKALEWA K; Kamehameha Schl; Pearl City, HI; (3); 50/419; JA; Teachers Aide; Hon Roll; Bus Admn.

GINOZA, CARRIE; Aiea HS; Aiea, HI; (4); 19/366; VP FTA; JA; Band; Mrchg Band; Rep Sr Cls; Var L Tennis; Hon Roll; Masonic Awd; NHS; Interact Clb Sec; Bowling Tm Var Ltr; Leo Clb; Tri-M Music Hnr Soc Sec, Treas, Outstndng Member; Seattle U.

GINOZA, STANFORD K; Waipahu HS; Waipahu, HI; (3); Var Wrstlng; Judo; SMILE; Frnln Awd; Bus.

GINOZA, STEVEN M; University Laboratory Schl; Honolulu, HI; (4); Science Clb; Band; Chorus; Jazz Band; Capt Var Bsktbl; Capt Var Vllybl; High Hon Roll; Hon Roll; Prfct Atten Awd; Pres Acad Fit Awd; Stu ARTS Matson Navigation Awd 89; Schlstc Art Shw Xhbtn 90; Schl Lit Mag Co-Edtr.

GO, ANNIE MARIE; Moanalua HS; Waipahu, HI; (4); 19/416; SADD; Band; Mrchg Band; Pep Band; Sec Sr Cls; Stu Cncl; Hon Roll; NHS; Jap, Leo Clb; Loyola Marymoutn U; Med.

GODDARD, BRANDON P; Maui HS; Kahului, HI; (3); 33/354; Key Clb; Letterman Clb; Science Clb; Var Ftbl; Var Wrstlng; Oustndng Wrestlr 89-90; MIL Wrestlng 2nd & 3rd Pl Mdl; All Amer Schlr; Aerosp Engrng.

GOLASKI, LORIEN; Iolani Schl; Honolulu, HI; (3); Church Yth Grp; Dance Clb; Drama Clb; Hosp Aide; Pep Clb; School Musical; School Play; Stage Crew; Nwsp; Cheerldng; Cmmnctns.

GOLDBERGER, JUDY H; Mililani HS; Mililani, HI; (3); Church Yth Grp; Cmnty Wkr; Drama Clb; Pep Clb; Red Cross Aide; Scholastic Bowl; School Play; Ed Lit Mag; Rep Soph Cls; Var Cheerldng; Presdntl Phys Ftns Awd; Mdcl Sci.

GOLDEN, MARK A; Maui HS; Kula, HI; (3); 142/354; Hon Roll; Prfct Atten Awd; Cvl Air Patrol; Medtn Clb; FFA; Air Force; Pilot.

GOLIS, ANTOINETTE P; Maui HS; Haiku, HI; (2); Church Yth Grp; SADD; Rep Frsh Cls; Rep Soph Cls; Vrsty Bowling; Culinary Arts.

GOLIS, KIMBERLY K; Maui HS; Haiku, HI; (2); 51/381; Key Clb; Pep Clb; Teachers Aide; Vet.

GOMES, LIANE Y; Maui HS; Pukalani, HI; (3); Key Clb; Science Clb; Band; Mrchg Band; Pep Band; Hon Roll; Prfct Atten Awd.

GOMES, LISA A; Leilehua HS; Wahiawa, HI; (3); 45/322; Church Yth Grp; VP Math Clb; Pres Math Tm; Service Clb; Band; Mrchg Band; Pep Band; JV Mgr(s); Hon Roll; U Of CA Berkeley; Law.

GOMES, MELANIE L; Kaiser HS; Honolulu, HI; (3); 22/325; SADD; Hon Roll; Amnsty Intl; Grad Cmmtte.

GONGORA, CHRISTOPHER; Lanakila Baptist HS; Ewa Beach, HI; (4); 2/18; Spanish Clb; Teachers Aide; VP Sr Cls; VP Stu Cncl; Capt Vllybl; Hon Roll; Jr NHS; VP NHS; Ntl Merit Schol; Prfct Atten Awd; Prncpls Awd; All Amer Schlr; Rotry Yth Ldrshp; U Of HI Manoa; Med.

GONGORA, JENNIFER; Lanakila Baptist HS; Ewa Beach, HI; (2); Yrbk; Sec Frsh Cls; Vllybl; High Hon Roll; Hon Roll; Jr NHS; Prfct Atten Awd; Believrs Bibl Clb; U Of HI.

GONSALVES, MATTHEW K; Kapaa HS; Kapaa, HI; (3); Boy Scts; Pres Church Yth Grp; Cmnty Wkr; SADD; Rep Stu Cncl; Bsbl; Capt Bsktbl; Ftbl; Golf; Trk; Commnctns.

GONSALVES, TINO; Aiea HS; Aiea, HI; (4); 15/361; Math Clb; Spanish Clb; Teachers Aide; JV Trk; High Hon Roll; Ntl Merit SF; Interact Clb; U CA Berkeley; Microbio.

GOO, JUSTIN M W; Mid-Pacific Inst; Honolulu, HI; (2); 1/150; Chess Clb; High Hon Roll; Jr NHS; NHS; Pres Acad Fit Awd; Rep Soph Cls; Treas Stu Cncl; Karate & Tai Chi Black Belt Lvl; Chinese Clb; Hoo Cho Chinese Sch Grad; Bus.

GOODYEAR-KAOPUA, JENNIFER; Kamehameha Schls; Kaneohe, HI; (2); 1/443; Church Yth Grp; SADD; Band; Flag Corp; Stu Cncl; JV Capt Cheerldng; JV Diving; NHS; Duke U Tlnt ID Pgm; Ed.

GORGONIO, MARY-CHARMAINE A; St Francis HS; Honolulu, HI; (3); 7/58; Church Yth Grp; Cmnty Wkr; Math Clb; Mu Alpha Theta; Q&S; Nwsp; High Hon Roll; Hon Roll; NHS; Singing, Piano, Theater & Drama; Muisc Perfmnce.

GOROSPE, LOIDA; Hilo HS; Hilo, HI; (4); 13/304; JA; Pres Multi Cltrl Clb; U Of HI Hilo; Liberal Arts.

GOULD, JENNIFER L; Farrington HS; Honolulu, HI; (3); 18/600; Cmnty Wkr; ROTC; Color Guard; Variety Show; Bsktbl; Vllybl; Hon Roll; Rotary Club Ethics Essay Cont 1st Pl; Supr Jr Cadet Decoration Awd; Close-Up Fndtn.

GOYA, FRED M; Roosevelt HS; Honolulu, HI; (2); 18/360; Mech Engr.

GRABER, JENNIFER; St Joseph HS; Hilo, HI; (3); Church Yth Grp; Drama Clb; French Clb; Girl Scts; NFL; Speech Tm; School Play; Ed Nwsp; Ed Yrbk; Treas Jr Cls; Bowling Tm Cptn; Commnctns.

GREAN, JEFF T; Mililani HS; Mililani, HI; (3); 110/490; Art Clb; Boy Scts; Church Yth Grp; Cmnty Wkr; Letterman Clb; Q&S; Spanish Clb; Ed Nwsp; Var Socr; Var Vllybl; Brotherhood Of Hnr Campers; Graphic Arts Awd; UCLA.

GREEN, AMMABELLE C; Radford HS; Honolulu, HI; (1); 38/468; Dance Clb; Intnl Clb; Latin Clb; Science Clb; Spanish Clb; Band; Chorus; Flag Corp; Yrbk; Cheerldng; Bsktbl Tm Co-Capt; Sci Clb Asst; Flag Corp Tm Ldr; Med.

GREEN, CHRISTINE M; Hawaii Baptist Acad; Honolulu, HI; (1); Church Yth Grp; Cmnty Wkr; Debate Tm; Drama Clb; FCA; Office Aide; Speech Tm; Chorus; Church Choir; School Musical; Won The Crown Of Miss HI Teen Model 89; Fash Show For Takeo, Etro, Eric, Chanel 90; Dance, Ballet; George Mason; Jrnlsm.

GREEN, KALEOLANI ALICE-LYNN; Kailua HS; Kailua, HI; (3); 16/339; Church Yth Grp; Cmnty Wkr; Rptr Nwsp; Ed Yrbk; Rep Soph Cls; Hon Roll; Newspaper Journalist.

GREENWELL, KATHY; Hawaii Preparatory Acad; Holualoa, HI; (2); Church Yth Grp; FFA; Letterman Clb; Pep Clb; Science Clb; Chorus; Ed Nwsp; JV Bsktbl; L Ftbl; L Mgr(s); Stu Pilot; Soil Cnsrvtn; Yth Lgsltve Pgm; US Air Force Acad; Arntcl Engr.

GREER, MICHELE; Kalaheo HS; Kaneohe, HI; (4); 10/272; FBLA; Girl Scts; Key Clb; Pep Clb; Spanish Clb; SADD; Ed Yrbk; High Hon Roll; Hon Roll; Jr NHS; Chem & Spanish Awds; U HI; Med.

GRIFFIN, HIJEE; Moana Lua HS; Honolulu, HI; (2); 26/501; Church Yth Grp; Band; Chorus; Mrchg Band; JV Trk; High Hon Roll; Compete Western Pleasure Horseback Riding; Accntng.

GRIFFIS, DANIEL N; Kaimuki HS; Honolulu, HI; (2); 30/400; ROTC; Color Guard; Drill Tm; JV Ftbl; JV Var Trk; JV Wrstlng; Vlntr Honolulu Boys & Grls Clbs; Part Time Work; U ID; Art.

GRILHO, BOBBIE JEANNE; Mililani HS; Mililani, HI; (2); 120/509; Church Yth Grp; Band; Flag Corp; Yrbk; U Of HI; Trvl Toursm.

GRIMSLEY, HEATHER; Kalaheo HS; Kailua, HI; (2); 2/263; Aud/Vis; Girl Scts; Math Tm; Natl Beta Clb; Red Cross Aide; SADD; High Hon Roll; Yale; Doctor.

GRUNE, JESSE M; Waiakea HS; Keaau, HI; (3); Math Clb; U ID; Recreation Mgmnt.

GUALDARAMA, DELOLA V; Leilehua HS; Wahiawa, HI; (3); 11/322; Stu Cncl; Hon Roll; Engl III Awd; Acad Awd; Wahiawa Terr Yth Assn-VP; Nrsng.

GUERPO, GWENIEVE; Baldwin HS; Kihei, HI; (1); 109/466; Cheerldng; UCLA.

GUERRA, JENICA; Roosevelt HS; Honolulu, HI; (2); Spanish Clb; JV Bsktbl; Var Crs Cntry; Hon Roll; Park Lg Sprts Sftbl, Bsktbl; Int Decorating.

GUERRERO, JONATHAN N; Waialua HS & Intermed; Waialua, HI; (3); Aud/Vis; Bsktbl; Hon Roll; Prfct Atten Awd; Bus Mngmnt.

GUIDRY, STEPHEN L; Admiral Authur Radford HS; Ewa Beach, HI; (4); Art Clb; ROTC; Drill Tm; Nwsp; Yrbk; Ftbl; Aviation.

GUILLERMO, NORMAN; Kalaheo HS; Kailua, HI; (1); Dance Clb; Off Frsh Cls; JV Bsktbl; Hon Roll; U Of HI; Astronomy.

GUILLERMO, ROWENA-NORA; St Francis HS For Girls; Kailua, HI; (3); 21/60; Art Clb; Library Aide; Pep Band; Stage Crew; Variety Show; JV Bsktbl; JV Vllybl; Rep Frsh Cls; Sec Treas Soph Cls; VP Jr Cls; Co-Wrkrs Mthr Theresa Orgnztn; U Of OR; Arch.

GUINN, NATHANIEL; Radford HS; Andrews AFB, DC; (3); VP Church Yth Grp; Cmnty Wkr; Band; Mrchg Band; Pep Band; Hon Roll; Pres Black Amer Clb Schl; Memphis ST U.

GUITTAP, JANE G; Mc Kinley HS; Honolulu, HI; (2); Church Yth Grp; Spanish Clb; Church Choir; JV Tennis; Prfct Atten Awd; Bus Clb; Mabuhay Clb Uni Clb Rep; Christ College Irvine; Bus Mgmt.

GULBRANDSEN, ERIC N; Kalani HS; Honolulu, HI; (3); Orch; Rep Frsh Cls; Stu Cncl; Hon Roll; Co-Capt Swmmng; Honolulu Symphny, IN U String Acad & Maui Philharmnc Soc Schlrshps; Presdntl Phys Ftnss Awd.

GULICK, JENNIFER K; St Francis HS; Kailua, HI; (2); 2/80; Church Yth Grp; Math Tm; Mu Alpha Theta; Quiz Bowl; Speech Tm; School Play; Lit Mag; High Hon Roll; Sec Jr NHS; NHS; Sea Life Pk HI Stu Vlntr; Quizzard Team Mem; Actress.

GUMTANG, JO ANN A; Farrington HS; Honolulu, HI; (3); Drama Clb; Hosp Aide; Math Tm; Q&S; Quiz Bowl; SADD; Variety Show; Nwsp; Var Tennis; Hon Roll; Leo Club; Serteens Club Of HI; Engl Ed.

GUPTILL, MICHELLE; Kalaheo HS; Kailua, HI; (3); Church Yth Grp; DECA; Drama Clb; Girl Scts; Off Rep Jr Cls; VP Sr Cls; Rep Stu Cncl; JV Var Bsktbl; Hon Roll; Bus.

GUSMAN III, GEORGE; Kamehameha HS; Waipahu, HI; (4); 15/415; Cmnty Wkr; Letterman Clb; ROTC; Var Bsbl; Var Ftbl; High Hon Roll; NHS; Ntl Sci Olympd Chem; All Leag, All State Ofnsv Linemn Ftbl; Santa Clara U; Intl Bus.

GUTIERREZ, SHERWIN MANZANO; Lahainaluna HS; Lahaina, HI; (3); Boy Scts; Dance Clb; School Play; Variety Show; Cheerldng; Hon Roll; Bayanihan Clb.

GUYER, LEE R; Mid-Pacific Inst; Mililani, HI; (2); Art Clb; Letterman Clb; Socr; Hon Roll; Vet Med.

GUZMAN, GEOFFREY T; Damien Memorial HS; Honolulu, HI; (3); 37/114; ROTC; Band; Mrchg Band; Intrml JV Trk; Hon Roll; Concert Band; U Of WA; Pre-Med.

GUZMAN, JO JO S; Farrington HS; Honolulu, HI; (2); 54/696; Band; Var Bsbl; Hon Roll; Airline Mechnc.

GWALTNEY, KAREN; Mililani HS; Mililani, HI; (2); 43/509; Church Yth Grp; Red Cross Aide; Church Choir; Var Swmmng; Hon Roll; Wo Intl Schlr; Outstndng Engl Stu; Hnrs Cls Engl, Hstry, Sci.

HA, LINH H; Mc Kinley HS; Honolulu, HI; (2); Debate Tm; Ed Nwsp; Yrbk; Tennis; Ed Lit Mag; Close-Up; Pediatrics.

HAAE, CHRISTOPHER; Kamehameha HS; Waianae, HI; (4); 111/406; Sec Frsh Cls; Hon Roll; Mandarin Cinese Hghst GPA; 1st In Poen Rctntn Cntst; 2nd Annlt St Of Hawaii Lang Fstvl; Japanese 4 Yrs; Leeward CC; Englsh.

HABER, GEMMA C; Baldwin HS; Kahului, HI; (2); 43/395; Art Clb; Bus Profs of Am; Spanish Clb; SADD; Hon Roll; Prfct Atten Awd; Pres Acad Fit Awd; U Of HI Manoa; Acctng.

HADA, RAYNETTE K; Waiakea HS; Hilo, HI; (3); Pres 4-H; Sec JA; Speech Tm; 4-H Awd; Hon Roll; Jr Achvt Awds; SPEBE Pgm 90; Mock Trial; Interact Clb.

HALAMA, LYLLA A; Waianae HS; Waianae, HI; (2); 45/499; Cit Awd; Hon Roll; Receptnst.

HALEAKALA, MALIA; Saint Anthony HS; Makawao, HI; (4); 9/67; Teachers Aide; Yrbk; Rep Sr Cls; Var JV Cheerldng; Sftbl; High Hon Roll; Hon Roll; Jr NHS; NHS; Hawaiian Clb Pres; Excllnc Math Awd; Schlr Athl Awd; U Of HI Manoa Campus; Elem Ed.

HALFMANN, APRIL A; James Campbell HS; Makakilo, HI; (2); 6/348; Church Yth Grp; Band; Orch; Pres Acad Fit Awd; Church Puppet Ministry; Vacation Bible School Aid; Early Childhood Education.

HALFMANN, JOE S; James Campbell HS; Makakilo, HI; (3); 1/400; Church Yth Grp; Quiz Bowl; Rptr Nwsp; High Hon Roll; NHS; Naval Officer For A Day; NSF Young Scholar; Electrical Engineer.

HALL, JENNIFER L; Henry J Kaiser HS; Honolulu, HI; (3); 7/325; Church Yth Grp; NFL; Science Clb; Off Frsh Cls; Rep Soph Cls; High Hon Roll; Prfct Atten Awd; Outstndng Stu Cmmnctn Arts Awd; Bst Flm LCC Flm Fstvl Awd; Cnmtgrphy.

HALL IV, WILLIAM A K; Saint Louis Schl; Mililani, HI; (2); 44/144; Computer Clb; Debate Tm; ROTC; Spanish Clb; Stage Crew; Hon Roll; Good Behavr Awd; Vrsty Bowlng Team; U MI; Aerospace Engr.

HAMADA, KRIS M; Kapaa HS; Kapaa, HI; (4); 7/190; Chess Clb; Math Tm; Hon Roll; NHS; Kapaa Hnr Soc Secy; U HI Manoa; Physics.

HAMADA, WINTER C; Konawaena HS; Captain Cook, HI; (2); 1/349; Pres Sec 4-H; Pres FTA; JV Var Bsktbl; 4-H Awd; High Hon Roll; Hon Roll; Masonic Awd; NHS; U Of HI Manoa; Educ.

HAMAI, STEPHANIE S; Maui HS; Kula, HI; (3); 1/354; VP Church Yth Grp; Treas 4-H; Letterman Clb; VP Math Tm; Treas Science Clb; Treas Sec Band; Chrmn Stu Cncl; Var Tennis; High Hon Roll; VP NHS; Yale Bk Awd; Semifnlst Japan-US Senate Schlrshp; Grls Outstndng Tennis Awd; Bus.

HAMAJI, IRIS A; Roosevelt HS; Honolulu, HI; (2); Church Yth Grp; Girl Scts; Temple Yth Grp; Band; Church Choir; Mrchg Band; Hon Roll; Slvr Awd GSA; Padma Awd; U HI.

HAMAJI, JO ANN S; Mc Kinley HS; Honolulu, HI; (3); Teachers Aide; Hmcmng Cmmtt; Bodyboarding; Keywannetes Clb; U HI; Zoology.

HAMAMOTO, REID S; Punahou Schl; Honolulu, HI; (4); Pres VP 4-H; VP JA; Chorus; JV L Tennis; NHS; Ntl Merit SF; Amnesty Intl; Vlntr Svc Cmt; Pre-Med.

HAMAMOTO, SEAN A; Mililani HS; Mililani, HI; (3); 16/490; Key Clb; JV Bsbl; High Hon Roll; Hon Roll; Elec Engrng.

HAMASAKI, SHELLY; Aiea HS; Aiea, HI; (4); Yrbk; Pres Frsh Cls; VP Soph Cls; Pres Jr Cls; High Hon Roll; Hon Roll; NHS; U Of HI-MANOA.

HAMBERG, CASEY L; Kauai HS; Kauai, HI; (4); 16/239; Aud/Vis; Sec Key Clb; Science Clb; Band; Mrchg Band; Off Soph Cls; Hist Jr Cls; VP Stu Cncl; Var Capt Swmmng; Var Tennis; SPEBE Smmr Biochem Pgm; U Of Rochester; Genetics.

HAMMER, MINNA IRA; Waiakea HS; Hilo, HI; (1); 1/25; Natl PTA Cert; PTSA ST HI All HS Stu; Fshn Dsgn.

HAN, REGINA C; Roosevelt HS; Honolulu, HI; (3); Cmnty Wkr; FTA; Intnl Clb; Key Clb; Math Clb; Math Tm; Tae Kwon Do; Aerosp Engrng.

HAN, SONG I; Mc Kinley HS; Honolulu, HI; (3); 68/537; Latin Clb; Math Clb; Chrmn SADD; Band; Jazz Band; Mrchg Band; Var Capt Swmmng; Hon Roll; Congrssnl Schlr; Chem Clb-Sec; Yale; Bio.

HANAKAHI, ALICIA; Leilehua HS; Wahiawa, HI; (4); 38/304; Service Clb; Bsktbl; Socr; Hon Roll; Chrch Yth Grp; HI U Manoa; Educ.

HANAMOTO, SHELDON; Hilo HS; Hilo, HI; (3); 19/356; Math Clb; Math Tm; NHS; Varsity Bowling; HI U Manoa; Internatl Bus.

HANANO, JANA L; Kamehomeha HS; Hawi, HI; (1); 103/450; Hon Roll; San Diego ST; Bus Mgmt.

HANATO, BAYLEN A; Saint Louis HS; Aiea, HI; (3); Cmnty Wkr; Band; Mrchg Band; Pep Band; Hon Roll; Amnsty Clb; Law.

HANCOCK, FRANK R; Lei Lehua HS; Ft Campbell, KY; (2); 55/450; French Clb; Speech Tm; Mr Soph.

HANDLEY, KALENA R; Radford HS; Honolulu, HI; (3); 182/394; Aud/Vis; Cmnty Wkr; Hon Roll; State Fianlist Int He MS US Teen Hawaii Competition; Notre Dame CA; Interior Design.

HANES, CATHERINE; Kalaheo HS; Kailua, HI; (3); 8/240; Church Yth Grp; Debate Tm; SADD; Chorus; Rptr Lit Mag; Var Vllybl; Cit Awd; Pres Acad Fit Awd; Pres Schlr; Acctnt.

HANG, BINH LE; Mc Kinley HS; Honolulu, HI; (2); Var Tennis; High Hon Roll; Keywanettes Club; Prom Cmmtte; Acctng.

HANKE, KIMBERLY J; Sacred Hearts Acad; Mililani, HI; (3); Teachers Aide; Yrbk; Sunday Schl Tchr; Cnfrmd May 901st Yr Win Prfct Attendnc Awd; Bus.

HANNA, DALIA; University Labratory HS; Kaneohe, HI; (4); Church Yth Grp; Cmnty Wkr; Hosp Aide; Chorus; Orch; Sec Sr Cls; Var Swmmng; JV Trk; Hon Roll; Pres Acad Fit Awd; Greek Dancing Grp; Paddeling Tm; U HI; Med.

HANTKE, CHRISTOPHER S; Mililani HS; Wahiawa, HI; (4); Boy Scts; Mu Alpha Theta; Hon Roll; Schl Achvt Awd Electronics; Engrng.

HANZAWA, AMY A; Hawaii Baptist Acad; Waianae, HI; (2); Lbrn Band; Pres Aloha Cncl; Oahu Band Dir Assoc; Signlang Clb; Vlntr Rehab Hosp; Publc Relations.

HARAGUCHI, DAVE M; Waiakeu HS; Hilo, HI; (2); 15/497; Key Clb; Wrstlng; High Hon Roll; Hon Roll; U HI; Engrng.

HART, ANGELIQUE R; Radford HS; Honolulu, HI; (2); 14/411; Church Yth Grp; Cmnty Wkr; Debate Tm; Math Tm; Mu Alpha Theta; Treas Jr Cls; Cheerldng; JV Trk; Hon Roll; Opt Clb Awd; NE U Las Vegas; Comm.

HARTMAN, AMY L; Hawaii Baptist Acad; Wahiawa, HI; (3); 6/86; Church Yth Grp; Cmnty Wkr; Drama Clb; Service Clb; Thesps; School Play; Stage Crew; Treas Stu Cncl; High Hon Roll; NHS; Aloha Cncl Pres; AZ St U Ctr For Acad Precocity; U AZ; Acctng.

HARVEY, PAMELA; Kahuku HS; Laie, HI; (4); 5/233; Pres Church Yth Grp; Service Clb; Spanish Clb; Band; Church Choir; Mrchg Band; Yrbk; High Hon Roll; Hon Roll; Yng Wmnhd Rcgntn Awd; Bus Club Pres; Brigham Young U; Acctng.

HASBROUCK, KIMBERLY E; Radford HS; Omaha, NE; (2); 1/411; Church Yth Grp; Treas French Clb; VP Girl Scts; Var Swmmng; Hon Roll; HI St Chmpshp Sftbl Team 90; Tch HS Engl.

HASEGAWA, NATALIE H; Mid-Pacific Inst; Mililani Town, HI; (2); Chess Clb; Church Yth Grp; Teachers Aide; Rep Frsh Cls; Rep Soph Cls; High Hon Roll; Hon Roll; Jr NHS; NHS; Perfrmng Arts Japanese Classcl Dncng; Japanese Club; Envrnmntl Club; Law.

HASEGAWA, WENDI S; Mc Kinley HS; Honolulu, HI; (1); Off Soph Cls; High Hon Roll; Hon Roll; Pediatrics.

HASHIMOTO, ERIN M; Henry Perine Baldwin HS; Kula, HI; (1); 1/466; Pres 4-H; Key Clb; Band; Mrchg Band; Pep Band; Pres Frsh Cls; High Hon Roll; Prfct Atten Awd; Stu Delg To Gov 1st Educ Summit; Hnr Band; HI Educ Assn St Wrtng Awd; Law.

HASHIMOTO, HARVEY E; Leilehua HS; Wahiawa, HI; (2).

HASHIMOTO, LISA A; Waiakea HS; Hilo, HI; (2); Hist 4-H; JA; Pep Clb; Science Clb; SADD; Capt Color Guard; Lion Awd; Leo Club Secretary; Architect.

HASHIMOTO, MELISSA E; Maui HS; Kula, HI; (1); 47/451; Church Yth Grp; Sec Band; Orch; Sec Frsh Cls; Var Vllybl; Hon Roll.

HASHIZAKI, KRISTI; Hilo HS; Hilo, HI; (4); 4/304; Cmnty Wkr; Math Tm; Service Clb; Teachers Aide; Varsity Clb; Variety Show; Rep Frsh Cls; Rep Jr Cls; VP Stu Cncl; Var Capt Tennis; St Plnnr Bg Islnd Assn Stu Cncls; Chrprsn Gen Hmcmng Co; St Rep Frdms Vlly Frg; Poli Sci.

HATCH, TERESA T; Pearl City HS; Ft Leavenworth, KS; (3); 127/527; VP French Clb; Teachers Aide; JV Bsktbl; Rotary Awd; PEP; Mck Trl; Lgsltv Cmmtte.

HAUMEA, RACHELLE N; Kamehameha Schls; Kapaa, HI; (3); 10/179; Library Aide; SADD; Band; Hon Roll; Med.

HAWKINSON, CHRISTIAN E; Damien Memorial HS; Flanders, NJ; (4); 23/125; Church Yth Grp; Cmnty Wkr; Office Aide; Pep Clb; ROTC; Rptr Nwsp; Intrml Bsktbl; Mgr(s); Hon Roll; Viriliter Age; Bro Thomas P Rowland Svc Awd; Bradley U.

HAYASHI, RICK; Baldwin HS; Kahului, HI; (3); 12/385; Band; Jazz Band; Mrchg Band; Pep Band; Ftbl; Socr; Trk; High Hon Roll; Hon Roll; Japanese Clb.

HAYASHIBARA, KYLE T; Mc Kinley HS; Honolulu, HI; (3); 7/537; Math Clb; Quiz Bowl; Treas Science Clb; Stage Crew; High Hon Roll; Pres NHS; Schlrshp 1st Wic Focus On Japan Prgm; Outstndng Stu Awd; Grad With Hnrs Ft Gakuen Japanese Lang Schl; Bus.

HAYASHIDA, TAMRA A; Moanalua HS; Honolulu, HI; (2); 42/488; Sec Band; Mrchg Band; Pep Band; Trk; Preschl Vlntr Wrkr; Leo Club; HI Music Edctrs Assn Solo & Ensmbl Comptn Blue Slvr Red Slvr Red Gold; Elem Educ.

HAYDEN, MELANIE A; Hawaii Baptist Acad; Kaneohe, HI; (1); Church Yth Grp; GAA; Office Aide; JV Bsktbl; JV Vllybl.

HAYES, STEPHANIE L; Waiakea HS; Keaau, HI; (1); 40/487; Cmnty Wkr; Drama Clb; GAA; JA; Pep Clb; School Play; Stage Crew; Variety Show; Rep Frsh Cls; Rep Stu Cncl; WA ST U; Law.

HAYWARD-HARTLEY, NAJA; Campbell HS; Ewa Beach, HI; (3); Aud/Vis; Bus Profs of Am; Dance Clb; Drama Clb; French Clb; Girl Scts; Key Clb; Thesps; School Play; Stage Crew; NY U; Film.

HEAFNER, DEREK J; Med Pacific Inst; Honolulu, HI; (2); Chess Clb; Science Clb; JV Var Tennis; Hon Roll; Jr NHS.

HEIM, MICHELLE R; Moanalua HS; Honolulu, HI; (3); 23/462; Chorus; Hon Roll; Pres Acad Fit Awd; Essay Cntst Wnnr; Chorus & Madrigals Pin & Ltr; Bus Mgmt.

HEINER, KELLIE A; Henry Perrine Baldwin HS; Kihei, HI; (3); 29/385; Church Yth Grp; Debate Tm; Speech Tm; SADD; Varsity Clb; Var L Bsktbl; Var L Vllybl; Hon Roll; Pres Acad Fit Awd; Kihei Canoe Clb; MVP Vllybl; Bus.

HELLRIEGEL, KEVIN H; Kapaa HS & Intermed; Kapaa, HI; (4); 9/193; Boy Scts; Church Yth Grp; Math Tm; Varsity Clb; English Clb; Band; Jazz Band; Mrchg Band; Crs Cntry; Capt Swmmng; Pres Hnr Soc; Sterling Schlr; U WA; Arch.

HENDERSON, APRIL K; Roosevelt HS; Honolulu, HI; (3); 12/382; Debate Tm; Intnl Clb; Key Clb; Letterman Clb; Model UN; NFL; Speech Tm; Lit Mag; Sec Treas Soph Cls; VP Jr Cls; Mock Dmcrtc Natl Cnvntn; Telluride Schlrshp Semifnlst; Malaekahana Camping Awd; Anthrplgy.

HERKLOTZ, MICHELLE L; Kauai HS; Koloa, HI; (3); French Clb; SADD; Teachers Aide; Hon Roll; NHS; UC Davis; Vet Med.

HERMES, MYRLIN A; Seabury Hall HS; Kula, HI; (2); Dance Clb; Drama Clb; English Clb; French Clb; Thesps; School Musical; School Play; Stage Crew; High Hon Roll; Hon Roll; Drama.

HERMOSURA, DAVEN T; James Campbell HS; Ewo Beach, HI; (2); 37/348; Am Leg Boys St; Church Yth Grp; Cmnty Wkr; Key Clb; Rptr Lit Mag; Var Capt Bsbl; JV Capt Bsktbl; Var Capt Vllybl; Hon Roll; Math.

HERODIES, LYDELL J; Damien Memorial HS; Pearl City, HI; (4); 62/125; Cmnty Wkr; JV Var Bsbl; JV Var Ftbl; MVP Bsbl 89-90; 1st Hnr In Recognition Of Outstndng Acad Achvt 88-89; Portland U; Bus.

HERVOL, PATRICK D; Radford HS; Honolulu, HI; (2); 4/411; Math Clb; Math Tm; Mu Alpha Theta; Quiz Bowl; High Hon Roll; Hon Roll; NHS; Span Awd Excllnc; MA Inst Of Tech; Aerospc Engr.

HESAPENE, AUDREY M; Waimea HS; Kekaha, HI; (3); 51/200; Church Yth Grp; Sftbl; High Hon Roll; Spanish NHS; Kekaha Pop Warner Chrldr & Stu Adv; U HI Manoa; Acctg.

HESS, TAMMY; Honoka'a HS; Kamuela, HI; (4); Nwsp; Yrbk; Stu Cncl; Powder Puff Ftbl; Hon Roll; Chrprsn Green & Gold Fair; Konakaa HS Exec Cncl & Rep Assmbly; U HI-HILO; Sec Educ.

HEW, CLIFTON Y F; William Mc Kinley HS; Honolulu, HI; (4); 57/547; Chess Clb; Office Aide; Teachers Aide; Ed Nwsp; U Of HI; Engrng.

HEYA, TERI-ANN; Leilehvia HS; Wahiawa, HI; (3); 84/322; Capt Vllybl; Leo Clb Trea 89-90 & Pres 90-91; USVBA Wvlypbl Clb; Arch.

HIGA, KATHY T; Waiakea HS; Hilo, HI; (3); 39/370; Church Yth Grp; Service Clb; Rep Frsh Cls; Rep Soph Cls; Chrmn Stu Cncl; Var Crs Cntry; Var Capt Socr; Var Trk; Hon Roll; Conflct Mediation Mediator; Ctzn Bee; Stu Govt Hndbk Cmmtte Chrprsn.

HIGA, LIGAYA M; St Francis HS; Kaneohe, HI; (2); 10/80; Hon Roll; Pres Acad Fit Awd; Specl Artstc Contrbtns Awd.

HIGA, MARK H; Mililani HS; Mililani, HI; (3); 79/500; FBLA; FHA; Key Clb; Rep Jr Cls; Rep Sr Cls; Rep Stu Cncl; Var L Wrstlng; High Hon Roll; Hon Roll; U Of HI Manoa; Arch.

HIGA, STEPHANIE RAE K; Kalani HS; Honolulu, HI; (4); 96/207; Girl Scts; Teachers Aide; Var Socr; Var Trk; Intrml Vllybl; Gold Awd Rcpnt Girls Scouts 90; Kapidani Cmnty Coll; Elem Ed.

HIGASHI, KATHRYN Y; Iolani HS; Honolulu, HI; (4); 2/218; Key Clb; Mrchg Band; Nwsp; Pres Stu Cncl; Capt Var Crs Cntry; Capt Var Trk; Ntl Merit Ltr; St Schlr; Val; Harvard Bk Awd; Vrsty HI Canoe Paddling; Sr Japanese Club; Harvard U; E Asian Studies.

HIGASHI, WENDY; Pearl City HS; Pearl City, HI; (3); 115/527; Key Clb; U Of HI; Elem Educ.

HIGASHIGUCHI, KRISTA E; Henry Perrine Baldwin HS; Wailuku, HI; (2); 23/395; Key Clb; Pep Clb; Hon Roll; Interact, Japanese Clbs; Hmcmng Cmmttee; Phrmcst.

HIGUCHI, CORI ANNE C; Kaiser HS; Honolulu, HI; (1); 56/255; Church Yth Grp; Service Clb; Band; Mrchg Band; Jr Ldr Kilauea Rcrtn Ctr Smmr Fun Enrchmt Pgm; Bsktbl, Sccr, Bsbl Coach; U Of HI Manoa; Elem Sch Tchr.

HIGUCHI, SHAWN K; Hawaiian Mission Acad; Pearl City, HI; (3); 1/50; Church Yth Grp; Teachers Aide; Chorus; Church Choir; Off Frsh Cls; VP Jr Cls; Bausch & Lomb Sci Awd; Prfct Atten Awd; Surgeon.

HILL, JUDI; Saint Francis HS; Honolulu, HI; (4); 8/64; Church Yth Grp; Pep Clb; JV Cheerldng; JV Vllybl; Cathlc Dghtrs Amer 1st Pl Art Awd; Dsgn.

HILLIARD, LEE; Kalaheo HS; Kailua, HI; (4); Yrbk; Stu Cncl; Var Ftbl; Var Capt Socr; Hon Roll; Fort Lewis Coll.

HILLS, K MICHAEL; Star Of The Sea HS; Honolulu, HI; (3); 2/110; Aud/Vis; Church Yth Grp; Debate Tm; Math Clb; Spanish Clb; SADD; Nwsp; Yrbk; Rep Frsh Cls; Rep Soph Cls; Schltc Ltr; Law.

HILTON, RACHEL; Kalaheo HS; Kailua, HI; (4); German Clb; Nwsp; Yrbk; Rep Frsh Cls; Rep Soph Cls; VP Jr Cls; JV Trk; Hon Roll; HOBY Intl Ldrshp Smnr; U Of OR; Jrnlsm.

HINTACUTAN, ANJANETTE K; Mililani HS; Mililani, HI; (3); GAA; Bsktbl; Powder Puff Ftbl; Marketing; Fashion Clothes.

HIRAI, BRANDIE; Kalani HS; Kaneohe, HI; (2); Teachers Aide; Band; Mrchg Band; Var Bsktbl; Var Mgr(s); Var Sftbl; High Hon Roll; Hnrbl Mntn In HI All Star Sftbl; TX U; Sprts Med.

HIRANO, LANCE K; Leilehua HS; Wahiawa, HI; (3); #2 In Class; Rep Frsh Cls; Rep Soph Cls; VP Jr Cls; JV Var Bsbl; High Hon Roll; NHS; Leo Clb.

HIRAO, DAWN A; Mililani HS; Mililani, HI; (3); 50/490; Mu Alpha Theta; Pres Band; Flag Corp; Jazz Band; Rep Frsh Cls; Rep Soph Cls; NHS; Intract Clb Treas; Engr.

HIRASUNA, MAILE ANN; Kailua HS; Kailua, HI; (4); 10/286; Hosp Aide; Teachers Aide; Rptr Nwsp; Stat Bsbl; Sftbl; Hon Roll; NHS; Tuition Waiver; Hnr Rl 4 Yrs; Nrsng.

HIRATA, DAVID M; Waiakea HS; Keaau, HI; (3); 42/368; Boy Scts; Church Yth Grp; Intnl Clb; VP Speech Tm; Band; Orch; Pep Band; School Play; Hon Roll; US Cngrss-Bundestag Yth Exchnge Pgm Semi-Fnlst; Commnctns.

HIRATA, LANCE K; Baldwin HS; Wailuku, HI; (2); Band; Surfing.

HIRAYAMA, TRACEY; Hilo HS; Hilo, HI; (4); 10/304; Sec JA; Math Tm; Science Clb; Hon Roll; NHS; Intrct Clb; Smmr Prgrm Enhncmnt Bsc Educ 89; U Of HI Manoa; Archt Engnrng.

HIROKAWA, IAN C; Maryknoll HS; Honolulu, HI; (2); High Hon Roll; Hon Roll; Japanese Clb; USC; Bus.

HIROKAWA, LISA C; Moanalua HS; Honolulu, HI; (2); 66/488; Color Guard; Co-Capt Flag Corp; Mrchg Band; Orch; JV Bsktbl; Hon Roll; Interact Clb.

HISAMURA, NATHAN; Waipahu HS; Waipahu, HI; (4); 10/435; Aud/Vis; VP Chess Clb; Pres Math Clb; Capt Math Tm; Science Clb; Service Clb; Speech Tm; Teachers Aide; Lit Mag; Stu Cncl; Scholar Athlete Army Reserve; Inst Of Eng & Elec Student Of The Yr; Ellison Orizuka Outstanding Schola; Purdue U; Aerospace Engineering.

HITZEMAN, LEHUA K; Kamehameha HS; Waianae, HI; (2); 35/451; GAA; Pep Clb; Powder Puff Ftbl; Trk; Hon Roll.

HIVELY, VALENTINA K; Mc Kinley HS; Honolulu, HI; (4); 84/547; Art Clb; Band; Ed Yrbk; Lion Awd; UH Manoa.

HIYAMA, DANIEL T; Radford HS; Honolulu, HI; (3); 140/346; Treas VICA; Rep Jr Cls; Var Bsbl; Var Ftbl; U Of HI.

HO, APRIL A; Moanalua HS; Honolulu, HI; (3); Spanish Clb; Teachers Aide; Color Guard; Rep Jr Cls; Cheerldng; DAR Awd; Hon Roll; Prom Sub-Cmmtte Chrprsn; Hmcmng Cmmtte; U HI Manda; Prfrmng Arts.

HO, CHADWICK A; Damien Memorial HS; Kaneohe, HI; (4); 1/125; ROTC; VP Stu Cncl; Intrml Bsktbl; French Hon Soc; St Schlr; Val; Voice Dem Awd; Church Yth Grp; Debate Tm; Math Tm; Fornsc Natl & ST Chmpns; Natl Semi Fnlst Amer Legn Oratory; Stanford U; Law.

HO, JIN; Hawaii Baptist Acad; Honolulu, HI; (4); Cmnty Wkr; Drama Clb; French Clb; Math Tm; Chorus; Stage Crew; Ed Lit Mag; Rep Stu Cncl; JV Tennis; JV Trk; Natl Sci Fndtns Yng Schlr; Adv Smmr Expstry Wrtng Course; Wellesley Coll.

HO, JOLYN N S; Pahoa HS; Pahoa, HI; (2); FHA; Hawn Lang & Cltre Clb; HI Lang Cls; Lawyer.

HO, JOO; Kaimuki HS; Honolulu, HI; (2); 7/325; Chess Clb; Cmnty Wkr; French Clb; Quiz Bowl; SADD; Cit Awd; French Hon Soc; High Hon Roll; NHS; Ctzn Bee; Med.

HO JR, JOSEPH K; Kamehameha Schls; Ewa Beach, HI; (3); 70/419; ROTC; Spanish Clb; JV Crs Cntry; JV Socr; High Hon Roll; Hon Roll; Pilot.

HO, LAREINA K L; Maryknoll HS; Pearl City, HI; (4); Church Yth Grp; Hosp Aide; Q&S; Treas Spanish Clb; Teachers Aide; Nwsp; Lit Mag; High Hon Roll; NHS; Kapiolani Mdcl Ctr Mst Outstdng Teen Volntr Awd 88 & 89; Carleton Coll; Med.

HO, SKYE K; Mid-Pacific Inst; Waimanalo, HI; (2); 6/200; Variety Show; VP Soph Cls; Cit Awd; High Hon Roll; NHS; Pres Acad Fit Awd; Work Schlrshp; Big Bros/Sisters; Bus Admin.

HOAPILI, VELMA L; Kailua HS; Kailua, HI; (2); 41/301; VP Soph Cls; Stat Bsktbl; JV Cheerldng; JETS Awd.

HOAPILI, VERNA KUULEI KEIKO; Kailua HS; Kailua, HI; (4); 21/275; Teachers Aide; Var Bsktbl; JV Var Vllybl; Hon Roll; Prfct Atten Awd; Pres Schlr; All Amer Schlr; Intl Frgn Lang Awd; Anti Drug Awd; Engl Awd; HI Pacific U; Bus Admin.

HOEPTNER, JENNIFER; Hilo HS; Hilo, HI; (3); 45/388; Church Yth Grp; Cmnty Wkr; Hosp Aide; Key Clb; Pres Latin Clb; Sec Frsh Cls; VP Soph Cls; Chrmn Sr Cls; VP Stu Cncl; L Crs Cntry; Intl Ordr Of Rainbow; Amer Lung Assn Adv Cncl; Close-Up Prog 90; Dist Stu Cncl VP; Med.

HOFF, MAILE A; H P Baldwin HS; Kihei, HI; (1); 90/466; Socr.

HOFFLER, STEPHANIE; Kailna HS; Kailua, HI; (3); Church Yth Grp; Church Choir; Off Jr Cls; Off Sr Cls; Co-Capt Socr; U Of HI.

HOGG, JAMES A; Mid Pacific Inst; Kailua, HI; (2); Hon Roll; UCLA; Pilot.

HOGGE, MARK S; Arthur W Radford HS; Honolulu, HI; (3); 10/394; Art Clb; Rptr Yrbk; Var L Bsbl; High Hon Roll; Hon Roll; 3rd St Mxd Media AK; Sprts; G/T Art & Acad; Sci.

HOKAMA, JASON M; Castle HS; Kaneohe, HI; (4); 3/376; Treas Key Clb; Pres Math Tm; Speech Tm; Band; JV Bsbl; High Hon Roll; Ntl Merit SF; JETS; Lang Arts Shwcs; Amer Invtnl Math Exam; Caltech; Engr.

HOLCK, NOELLE P; Mililani HS; Mililani, HI; (3); 53/490; VP Drama Clb; School Musical; School Play; Hon Roll; Tri-Schl Prod; U Of NV Las Vegas.

HONDA, LORI ANN F; Moanalua HS; Honolulu, HI; (2); 54/488; Church Yth Grp; Hist Service Clb; Band; Mrchg Band; Orch; Pep Band; Stu Cncl; Hon Roll; U Of HI Manoa; Elem Ed.

HONDO, WADE H; H P Baldwin HS; Kahului, HI; (3); VP Pres Art Clb; Pres Boy Scts; Pres Key Clb; Letterman Clb; Science Clb; Var Capt Swmmng; Var Trk; High Hon Roll; Hon Roll; VP NHS; Art Show Best In Show Wnnr.

HONG, EUGENE S; St Louis Schl; Honolulu, HI; (3); Boy Scts; Intnl Clb; ROTC; Color Guard; Off Jr Cls; Hon Roll; Bwlng Jr Var Capt MVP 89-90; Superior Cadet Awd DA; Wrld Cnsrvtn Awd BSA; Med.

HONG, LESLEY A; Hawaii Baptist Acad; Honolulu, HI; (2); Church Yth Grp; FTA; JA; Ed Nwsp; Trk; Hon Roll; Jr Ldr/Vlntr; Japanese Clb; U Of HI; Ed.

HONGYEE, LAURA; James Campbell HS; Ewa Beach, HI; (4); 17/347; Church Yth Grp; Church Choir; Pres Soph Cls; Pres Jr Cls; Pres Sr Cls; High Hon Roll; Hon Roll; NHS; Yth Ambssdr HOBY HI St Smnr 88; John Ii Awd Outstndng Ldrshp; Magna Cum Laude Grad 90; U Of HI Manoa; Bus Admin.

HOOHULI, DORI ANN; Waiakea HS; Hilo, HI; (1); 39/497; Var Vllybl; Hon Roll; Na Opio O HI JR Vlybl Assn; U Of HI Hilo.

HOOKS, TERRI; Mililani HS; Nellis Afb, NV; (3); 127/490; Art Clb; Nwsp; San Jose ST; Intrior Dsgn.

HOOPII, REGINA K; Lahaenaluna HS; Wailuku, HI; (2); 113/230; Sec FFA; Yrbk; Mgr Ftbl; Mgr(s); Hon Roll; Outstndng Chapt Farmer Awd; Maui CC; Bus.

HOOVER, LOUISA; Mc Kinley HS; Honolulu, HI; (2); Art Clb; High Hon Roll; Hon Roll; U Of HI; Bus.

HOPE, DALE; St Joseph HS; Hilo, HI; (2); Math Clb; Math Tm; JV Capt Bsktbl; Hon Roll; Arch Engrng.

HORITA, GERRAINNE M; Kauai HS; Lawai, HI; (2); JV Bsktbl; Var Sftbl; Hon Roll.

HORIUCHI, ANNE T; Mililani HS; Mililani, HI; (3); 9/490; Church Yth Grp; Math Clb; Thesps; School Play; Chrmn Frsh Cls; Chrmn Soph Cls; Chrmn Jr Cls; Rep Stu Cncl; Pres NHS.

HORIUCHI, JESSICA; Iolani HS; Honolulu, HI; (2); Dance Clb; JA; JV Var Cheerldng; Sftbl; High Hon Roll; Japanese Clb; Hawaiian Clb; Hdmstrs Lst.

HORROCKS, TIM S; Radford HS; Honolulu, HI; (2); VICA; JV Bsbl; JV Ftbl; Intrml Wt Lftg; JV Wrstlng; Hon Roll; Outstndng Woods II Stu.

HOSE, KIALANI K; Radford HS; Honolulu, HI; (2); 43/483; Hon Roll; Sftbl; Vlntr; U Of Southern CA; Chem.

HOTEMA, VICKIE S; Hawaii Baptist Acad; Pearl City, HI; (4); FTA; Hosp Aide; Spanish Clb; Teachers Aide; Chorus; Lit Mag.

HOTZ, TROY; Hilo HS; Hilo, HI; (3); Speech Tm; Var Socr; Var Vllybl; Hon Roll; U GI Manoa; Arch.

HOWARTH, DIANELLA G; Moanalua HS; Honolulu, HI; (1); 33/545; Math Clb; Math Tm; SADD; Band; Mrchg Band; Pep Band; Hon Roll; Natl Trampoline Comptn 4th Pl; Clarinet Solo Comptn Red Slvr Medal; Molecular Bio.

HRUBIK, JENNIFER; Leilehua HS; Ft Huachuca, AZ; (3); Church Yth Grp; Red Cross Aide; Sec Speech Tm; SADD; Hon Roll; Frnch Awd; Law Club; Nrthrn AZ U; Env Stdys.

HSIN, HELEN; St Andrews Priory HS; Honolulu, HI; (3); 15/53; Drama Clb; Intnl Clb; Key Clb; Stage Crew; Yrbk; JV Tennis; Hon Roll; Hdmstrs Lst; Srtns Clb HI; Jap Clb.

HSU, MERNA H; Leilehua HS; Mililani, HI; (2); Math Clb; Math Tm; Model UN; ROTC; SADD; High Hon Roll; Hon Roll; Masonic Awd; Prfct Atten Awd; Var Crs Cntry; Frdms Fndtn Valley Forge George Washington Hnr Mdl Yth Excllnc Essy; St HI Cert Achvt Dept Of Ed; US Mltry Acad.

HU, LINDA; Sacred Hearts Acad; Honolulu, HI; (4); 5/110; Cmnty Wkr; French Clb; Quiz Bowl; Red Cross Aide; Service Clb; Church Choir; Nwsp; Hon Roll; Prfct Atten Awd; Sci, Frgn Lang & Hnr Awd Wnnr Grad; UH Manoa; Civil Engrng.

HU, MEI TUCK B; Moanalua HS; Honolulu, HI; (3); 52/462; Science Clb; Teens Helping Teens; Interact Clb Brd Of Dir; Ethnic Day Cmmtte.

HU, YI KANG; Saint Louis HS; Honolulu, HI; (3); 5/150; Math Clb; Math Tm; Hon Roll; NHS; HI Humane Soc Vol; Kaiser Permanente Vol; Sci Awd 90; Physcn.

HUANG, HSIN-YI; Waiakea HS; Hilo, HI; (4); 45/412; Church Yth Grp; FTA; Math Clb; Science Clb; Service Clb; Speech Tm; Teachers Aide; School Musical; Hon Roll; NHS; U HI Manoa; Educ.

HUANG, HUI FANG; Mc Kinley HS; Honolulu, HI; (2); 13/492; Hon Roll; U Of HI Manoa; Bus.

HUANG, XI J; Mc Kinley HS; Honolulu, HI; (3); 28/537; Math Clb; Math Tm; Archt.

HUANG, XIAO FENG; Mc Kinley HS; Honolulu, HI; (3); 30/537; Math Clb; U Of HI; Accntnt.

HUANG, XIOA FENG; Mc Kinley HS; Honolulu, HI; (3); 30/537; Math Clb; U Of HI; Acctnt.

HUCKESTEIN, WILLIAM; Saint Louis HS; Honolulu, HI; (3); Model UN; SADD; Var Tennis; Var Vllybl; Wt Lftg; Hon Roll; NHS; Prfct Atten Awd; Most Outstng Bus Awd,Bi-Lingual; Scuba Dvng Dive Mstr; Rcktbll,Sccr,Spear Fshng; Tnns Schlrshp Mil Acad; Chaminade U; Marine Bio.

HUDDY, NOEL K; James Campbell HS; Ewa Beach, HI; (3); 56/371; Sec Church Yth Grp; GAA; Temple Yth Grp; JV Var Bsktbl; Capt Powder Puff Ftbl; Var L Sftbl; Var Trk; Capt JV Vllybl; High Hon Roll; Hon Roll.

HUDNALL, JESSE A; Radford HS; Honolulu, HI; (3); ROTC; Band; Drill Tm; Jazz Band; Mrchg Band; Pep Band; Var Diving; Intrml Vllybl; Hon Roll; Pres Acad Fit Awd; Prncpls Achvt Awd Ind Arts; Band 1st Chr Coronet, Sctn Ldr; V Ltrmn; Psych.

HUDSON, CHRISTINE R; Kalani HS; Honolulu, HI; (1); 27/246; Band; Pep Band; Hon Roll; U Of HI; Vet.

HUI, JOHN I J; Hawaii Baptist Acad; Honolulu, HI; (1); Math Tm; Rptr Mgr Nwsp; Off Frsh Cls; Hon Roll; Ping Pong Clb; Engrng.

HUI, YAU MEI; Mc Kinley HS; Aiea, HI; (3); 60/544; Pres Stu Cncl; Capt Cheerldng; Capt Pom Pon; Dnfth Awd; Hon Roll; Mst Insprtnl Awd-Chrldng 90; Outstndng Schl Lbry Media Stu 90; Ovrall Chrprsn HS Hmcmng Clbrtn 89; WA ST U; Bus.

HUMME, ALEA N; Waimea HS; Cowallis, OR; (2); 18/190; Church Yth Grp; Band; Mrchg Band; Pep Band; Rptr Nwsp; Stu Cncl; Trk; Hon Roll; NHS; 89 Travld With HI Ambssdrs Of Music Concert Band; Nrsng.

HUNT, SUSANNA; University Laboratory Schl; Honolulu, HI; (4); Teachers Aide; Pres Thesps; Band; Chorus; School Musical; JV Capt Bsktbl; JV L Sftbl; Var L Vllybl; High Hon Roll; Pres Acad Fit Awd; US Army Reserve Natl Schlr/Athl Awd; Coin Clb Co-Fndr & Pres; U HI Manoa; Pre-Med.

HUTCHESON, CHRISTI M; Lutheran HS Of Hawaii; Aiea, HI; (4); Church Yth Grp; Drama Clb; FCA; French Clb; Girl Scts; Teachers Aide; Chorus; Church Choir; School Musical; School Play; Campus Chpl Mnstry Tm; Geneva Coll; Spch Pthlgst.

HUTCHESON, KAREN I; Lutheran HS Of Hawaii; Aiea, HI; (2); 1/50; Church Yth Grp; Drama Clb; Office Aide; School Musical; School Play; Lit Mag; Hon Roll; NHS; Prfct Atten Awd; Frshmn May Day Prncss; Campus Chpl Mnstry Tm; 2nd Plc Statewide Fleet Rsrv Spnsrd Essy Cntst; Brdcst Jrnlsm.

HUTCHINSON-BALLESTEROS, LEBON; Radford HS; Honolulu, HI; (3); Wrstlng; High Hon Roll; Hon Roll; Pres Acad Fit Awd; U Of HI; Arch.

HUYNH, HAI G; Roosevelt HS; Honolulu, HI; (3); 35/350; School Play; Var Capt Crs Cntry; JV Var Trk; Var Wrstlng; Hon Roll; Pres Acad Fit Awd; Outstndng Male Stu Phys Educ 88-89.

HUYNH, MICHELLE; Sacred Hearts Acad; Honolulu, HI; (3); French Clb; Pep Clb; Chorus; Hon Roll; Phys Sci & Algebra I Cert Of Excllnc; Choral Music Cert Of Recognition; Pharmacy.

HWANG, MI SOOK; Roohevelt HS; Honolulu, HI; (3); Church Yth Grp; Cmnty Wkr; Yrbk; Tennis; Hon Roll; YMCA; 400 Running; Med.

IBARRA, CATHERINE A; Waipahu HS; Waipahu, HI; (4); 5/418; Quiz Bowl; Lit Mag; Off Chess Clb; Treas Soph Cls; Treas Jr Cls; Treas Sr Cls; High Hon Roll; Lion Awd; VP NHS; Sterling Schlr Wnnr; Exec Women Intl Schlrshp; Stu Of Yr 88-89; Seattle U; Medicine.

IBERA, ROSIELYN A; Farrington HS; Honolulu, HI; (2); #25 In Class; Hon Roll.

ICHISE, EMILY M; Pearl City HS; Pearl City, HI; (2); 9/511; Church Yth Grp; Flag Corp; Mrchg Band; Off Frsh Cls; Off Soph Cls; Stu Cncl; Hon Roll; NHS; Interact Clb; Schlr.

IDEMOTO, STEVEN; Hilo HS; Hilo, HI; (2); 16/359; JV Bsktbl; High Hon Roll; Hon Roll.

IFUKU, RAELENE K; Kaimuki HS; Honolulu, HI; (3); Office Aide; Band; Flag Corp; Mrchg Band; Phtg Rptr Yrbk; VP Stu Cncl; Hon Roll; Japnse Clb; Intr Dsgn.

IGNACIO, JOANNE L; Waipahu HS; Waipahu, HI; (2); 60/440; FHA; Science Clb; Rep Frsh Cls; Rep Soph Cls; Rep Stu Cncl; Hon Roll; SOAR Bk Clb; Nrsng.

IIDA, CHAD; Hawaii Baptist Acad; Honolulu, HI; (1); Boy Scts; Chess Clb; Math Tm; VP Frsh Cls; VP Stu Cncl; Intrml Bsktbl; Wt Lftg; Hon Roll; MIT; Elec Engr.

IIDA, ROBERT K; Hawaii Baptist Acad; Honolulu, HI; (3); Pres Jr Cls; JV Var Ftbl; High Hon Roll; Hon Roll; Engrng.

IIDA, SHERWOOD K; Kapaa HS; Kapaa, HI; (3); 6/179; Key Clb; Math Tm; L Var Bsbl; L Var Bsktbl; Var Crs Cntry; L Var Vllybl; NHS; Congressional Schlr Natl Yng Ldrs Conf 90; USAFA; Engrng.

IKEDA, CHERIE K; Waiakea HS; Hilo, HI; (4); 18/412; Pres VP 4-H; Lbrn Band; Mrchg Band; Pep Band; Rep Sr Cls; L Var Socr; 4-H Awd; NHS; Pres Acad Fit Awd; Aikido Blck Belt & Asst Instrctr; Chrch Asst Tchr; Music Dept Awd; U Of CO Boulder; Aerospc Engr.

IKEDA, JANICE I; Waiakea HS; Hilo, HI; (2); Church Yth Grp; Pep Clb; JV Cheerldng; Hon Roll.

IKEI, CHRISTINA F; University HS; Pearl City, HI; (4); Math Tm; Teachers Aide; Band; Jazz Band; Orch; Treas Soph Cls; Pres Jr Cls; Treas Sr Cls; Co-Capt Socr; High Hon Roll; Hakubi Kyoto Kimono Schl Schlrshp-Japan; Japan-U S Senate Schlrshp-Semifnlst; Principals Ldrshp Awd; U Of HI-MANOA; Engrng.

IKEMORI, ALLISON M; Waiakea HS; Hilo, HI; (4); 36/412; 4-H; Math Tm; VP Science Clb; Service Clb; Mrchg Band; Diving; Trk; 4-H Awd; High Hon Roll; NHS; U WA; Engrng.

ILAE JR, RONALD P; Waianae HS; Waianae, HI; (2); JV Bsbl; JV Wrstlng; Electronics.

IMAMURA, CANDACE A; Waimea HS; Kekaha, HI; (4); Church Yth Grp; Letterman Clb; Band; Ed Nwsp; Treas Frsh Cls; Treas Jr Cls; Treas Stu Cncl; Var Capt Socr; Var Vllybl; High Hon Roll; Mst Outstndng Japanes Lang Stu 87-88; 1st Dist Brown Bage To Stardom Grp; UH Manoa; Sci Tchr.

IMAMURA, GRANT R; Hawaii Baptist Acad; Kaneohe, HI; (4); 7/96; FCA; 4-H; Math Tm; Treas Jr Cls; VP Var Golf; High Hon Roll; Jr NHS; Natl Schlt Athlte; Hghst GPA Males HI Baptst Acad 88-90; Vrsty Glf Tm MVP 87-90; U Of HI Manoa; Elec Engrng.

INATSUKA, CAROL S; Moanalua HS; Honolulu, HI; (2); Mrchg Band; Orch; Hon Roll; Acctng.

INES, PHILIP J; Honokoa HS; Kamuela, HI; (2); 18/155.

ING, KRISTIN E; Punahou Schl; Honolulu, HI; (4); Cmnty Wkr; Dance Clb; Service Clb; SADD; Chorus; Variety Show; Rep Stu Cncl; Hon Roll; Jr NHS; NHS; Dance Corps Ballet Solist; Dance Awd; Eng Awd.

ING, MARSHA M; Roosevelt HS; Honolulu, HI; (1); Yrbk; JV Vllybl; U HI.

INOUYE, DEE ANN K; Maui HS; Kahului, HI; (4); 8/303; Sec Key Clb; Math Clb; Treas Band; Rep Soph Cls; Rep Jr Cls; Rep Sr Cls; Hon Roll; NHS; Amer Rd Crss Crtfd Wtr Sfty Instrctr, Lfgrd; U Of HI Manoa; Bus.

INOUYE, ERIN R; Mililani HS; Mililani, HI; (2); Dance Clb; Key Clb; Mu Alpha Theta; Band; Mrchg Band; Off Soph Cls; Hon Roll; Hero Clb; Dermtlgy.

INOUYE, LESLIE M; Leilehua HS; Wahiawa, HI; (4); VP Service Clb; Co-Capt Nwsp; Rep Frsh Cls; Rep Soph Cls; Rep Jr Cls; Rep Sr Cls; High Hon Roll; Hon Roll; NHS; All-Amer Schlr; Intl Frgn Lang Awd; U Of HI.

INOUYE, LISA M; Maui HS; Kahului, HI; (4); 16/303; Church Yth Grp; Dance Clb; FTA; Library Aide; Math Clb; Science Clb; Teachers Aide; Hon Roll; NHS; Prfct Atten Awd; MHS Bus Comp Clb Treas, Pres; Keywntts; Leo Clb; U HI; Ed.

INOVEJAS, BRAD; Kalaheo HS; Kailua, HI; (2); JV Bsktbl; JV Crs Cntry; JV Trk; Hon Roll; Body Boarding, Ftbl, Billards, Wght Lftng, Vlyb; Arch.

ISAACS JR, BARNEY KAPONO; Kamehameha Schls; Honolulu, HI; (1); 194/407; Boy Scts; Letterman Clb; ROTC; Varsity Clb; Chorus; Church Choir; Capt Var Bsktbl; Capt Var Ftbl; Capt Var Trk; Deputation Team; U Of UT; Elec Engrng.

ISAACS, CHRISTINE; Kamechameha Schls; Honolulu, HI; (3); 79/443; Dance Clb; VP Pep Clb; Sec SADD; Rptr Phtg Yrbk; Rep Soph Cls; Rep Jr Cls; Stu Cncl; Var JV Cheerldng; Hon Roll; U HI Manoa; Dentistry.

ISAACS, RUBY; Kohala HS; Kapaau, HI; (3); 3/60; Church Yth Grp; FHA; Hosp Aide; Library Aide; SADD; Yrbk; VP Frsh Cls; Var Vllybl; Hon Roll; NHS; Spon Amer Bus Smnr BOE; Cngrssnl Yth Ldrshp Cncl Wshngtn DC; 1st Pl St HI Wrtng Essy Famous Women; Hotel Mgmt.

ISARA, BARRY J; W R Farrington HS; Honolulu, HI; (3); Chorus; Ed Nwsp; Var Crs Cntry; Hon Roll; Prfct Atten Awd; Grad Cmmtte.

ISHII, LORI S; Waimea HS; Eleele, HI; (2); 19/186; Church Yth Grp; High Hon Roll; Hon Roll; U Of HI-MANOA; Elem Ed.

ISHII, SEAN; Mc Kinley HS; Makakilo, HI; (3); 13/537; Math Clb; Math Tm; Band; Jazz Band; Pep Band; Bausch & Lomb Sci Awd; Physics.

ISHIKUNI, MARI; Kauai HS; Lihue, HI; (3); FHA; SADD; Ed Yrbk; Var Cheerldng; Crs Cntry; Socr; Hon Roll; NHS; VP Leo Clb; U Of HI; Frgn Lang.

ISHIZU, CHRISTINE M; Kauai HS; Lihue, HI; (3); 30/235; Church Yth Grp; Drama Clb; FBLA; FHA; FTA; Letterman Clb; Pep Clb; Speech Tm; SADD; Thesps; Japanese Clb; Spec Friends Pgm; Peer Cnslrs; Psych.

ISIDRO, JENNIFER; Mary Knoll HS; Honolulu, HI; (2); Church Yth Grp; Cmnty Wkr; Dance Clb; JA; Library Aide; Office Aide; Pep Clb; Science Clb; Spanish Clb; SADD; Marchng Band, Colorgrd 88-90; Books, Beyong Achvt Awd 87-88; Alge I Awd 88-89; Nrsng.

ISLA, FLOREDICK A; Leilehua HS; Wahiawa, HI; (3); 29/322; ROTC; Teachers Aide; Hon Roll; Jr NHS; HI Bus Stu Conf Gnrl Bus; U Of HI; Med.

ISNEC, MAY ROSE L; Leilehua HS; Wahiana, HI; (2); 44/392; Church Yth Grp; 4-H; Hosp Aide; Off Jr Cls; Hon Roll; Civil Air Ptrl; Interact Clb; U Of CA Los Angeles; Phy.

ITO, CORINNE; Kailua HS; Waimanalo, HI; (3); 3/349; Yrbk; Treas Soph Cls; Treas Jr Cls; High Hon Roll; Sec NHS; Engl Awd; All Amer Schlr; Horatio Alger Smnr Planner.

IWAMURA, JILL K; Kailua Kailua; Kailua, HI; (2); Teachers Aide; Var Socr; Var Tennis; Var Soft Tennis; Japanese Club; Zonta Club; Interact Club; HI Pacific U; Ed.

IWASAKA, RYAN M; H P Baldwin HS; Wailuku, HI; (4); 1/353; Sec Key Clb; Math Tm; VP NFL; Science Clb; Spanish Clb; Rep Sr Cls; Stat Ftbl; VP NHS; Rotary Awd; Val; Westinghouse Sci Tlnt Srch Natl Fnlst; Intl Sci Engrng Fr Fnlst; Prncpls Natl Ldrshp Awd; Claremont Mc Kenna Coll; Law.

IWASAKI, RYAN; Waiakea HS; Hilo, HI; (3); Key Clb; Rep Jr Cls; Rep Stu Cncl; Var Bsktbl; L Bsktbl; Var Trk; L Trk; Hon Roll; NHS; Outstndg Svc Awd.

IZUMI, SAM K; Moanalua HS; Honolulu, HI; (1); 14/545; Letterman Clb; JV Bsbl; Var Socr; High Hon Roll; Hon Roll; U HI Manoa; Arch.

JACINTO, KEVIN; Kauai HS; Lihue, HI; (2); 4/219; Rptr Nwsp; High Hon Roll; Hon Roll; NHS; Dist Sci & Engrng Fair Awd; Comp Sci.

JACINTO, MARGIE R; Waipahu HS; Waipahu, HI; (4); 180/420; Art Clb; Cmnty Wkr; Math Clb; Quiz Bowl; ROTC; Science Clb; Spanish Clb; VICA; Church Choir; Variety Show; Phil-Amer Club; Aloha Close-Up Club; Food/Nutrition Cls Achvt Cert; Leeward CC; Secy.

JADRNICEK, SUNNY; Kalaheo HS; Haymarket, VA; (2); Aud/Vis; JV Cheerldng.

JAKAHI, LAYNE K; Moanalua HS; Honolulu, HI; (3); 85/462; Hon Roll; U Of HI; Electrncl Engr.

JAMORA, YOLETTE N; Waialua HS; Waialua, HI; (3); 20/157; Church Yth Grp; Church Choir; Stat Bsbl; JV Cheerldng; JV Vllybl; Hon Roll; Japanese Clb; Leo Clb; Interact Clb; Vet.

JANG, ELISE Y; Scared Hearts Acad; Honolulu, HI; (3); Sec Math Clb; Quiz Bowl; Science Clb; High Hon Roll; Hon Roll; Prfct Atten Awd; Vet Med.

JARAMILLO, LESLIE U; Lahainaluna HS; Lahaina, HI; (3); FFA; Office Aide; Paddling; Stu Staying Straight; MCC; Bus.

JARDIN, CLARISSA M B; Waimea HS; Kekaha, HI; (2); 17/186; Off Soph Cls; Cheerldng; Crs Cntry; Trk; High Hon Roll; Hon Roll; NHS; Mock Trial; PRAISE; Wrtng Poetry.

JARDINE, KAYCI J H; Waiakea HS; Hilo, HI; (3); Pep Clb; Rep Soph Cls; Waiakea J-Teens; Hi Lo Jr Bwlrs; Waiakea Grls Bwlng Tm Vrsty; UH Manoa; Psych.

JARDINE, SHANEL L; Waiakea HS; Hilo, HI; (3); Pres JA; Var Cheerldng; Chaminade U Honolulu.

JAURIGUE, CANDICE C; Maui HS; Haiku, HI; (2); 29/388; Drama Clb; Science Clb; School Play; Stage Crew; Tennis; Hon Roll; Prfct Atten Awd; Japanese Club.

JAVIER, JANETTE L; Waiakea HS; Hilo, HI; (2); 1/497; Drama Clb; 4-H; JA; Latin Clb; Chorus; Color Guard; Hon Roll; St Ethics Cmmssn Essay Awd 1st Pl; Leo Club; Med.

JEN, TRISHA L; Hawaiian Mission Acad; Honolulu, HI; (4); 2/37; Aud/Vis; Church Yth Grp; Library Aide; Teachers Aide; Chorus; School Musical; School Play; Stage Crew; Variety Show; Pres Frsh Cls; Avtn Clb; HI Missn Acad Almni Schlrshp Awd; Publsh Stud Dircty; Juliette Lau Meml Schlrshp Awd; Loma Linda U; Med.

JENNINGS, KRISTEN S; Punahou Schl; Honolulu, HI; (4); Art Clb; Church Yth Grp; Cmnty Wkr; Drama Clb; Teachers Aide; Chorus; Church Choir; Stage Crew; Variety Show; Stu Cncl; Art Apprctn Awd In Jwlry Dsgn, Skll; Technel Theatre Awd; St Wide Stardom Cmptn 1st Pl Vocals; Mills Coll; Lang.

JENSEN, KELLY A; Waialua HS; Waialua, HI; (3); Dance Clb; Rep Stu Cncl; JV Var Bsktbl; Var Sftbl; JV Trk; JV Vllybl; Hon Roll; Pres Jpnese Clb; Co-Chrmn Hmcmng; Frgn Rltns.

JINBO, JENNIFER T; Leilehua HS; Wahiawa, HI; (4); 10/304; Rep Frsh Cls; Rep Soph Cls; Rep Jr Cls; Off Sr Cls; VP Stu Cncl; Hon Roll; NHS; Intl Frgn Lang Awd.

JINBO, TRICIA A; Lutheran HS; Pearl City, HI; (3); 16/42; FCA; Variety Show; Phtg Yrbk; Rep Frsh Cls; Rep Soph Cls; Pres Jr Cls; Var Cheerldng; Hon Roll; Natl Yng Ldrs Cnfrnc Washington DC 90; Trvl Indstry Mngmnt.

JOCO, JEREMY B J; Damien Memorial HS; Waipahu, HI; (3); Boy Scts; Hosp Aide; Phtg Yrbk; VP Sr Cls; Var Tennis; Var Vllybl; Hon Roll.

JOHNSON, CAROLYN; Aiea HS; Aiea, HI; (4); 37/366; DECA; French Clb; Treas FBLA; Rep Sr Cls; Rep Stu Cncl; JV Var Trk; High Hon Roll; Lion Awd; Rotary Awd; Purdue U; Bus Mgmt.

JOHNSON, CHRISTOPHER; Kalaheo HS; Kailua, HI; (1); Hon Roll.

JOHNSON, JULIAN; Moanalva HS; Honolulu, HI; (3); 103/462; Church Yth Grp; FCA; Band; Jazz Band; Mrchg Band; Pep Band; JV Capt Bsbl; Jazz, Hula Bwl & Hnr Bands; U Of HI; Elec Engr.

JOHNSON, KEISHA S; Parker Schl; Kamuela, HI; (2); Dance Clb; Drama Clb; Spanish Clb; School Musical; Rep Soph Cls; Swmmng; Intrml Mgr Wt Lftg; High Hon Roll; Hon Roll; Dir Choice Awd Bst Actor/Actrss Yr; Jazz Perfrmnce; Stu Cncl Pres; Med.

JOHNSON, RODNEY C; Punahou Schl; Honolulu, HI; (4); JA; Trk; Ntl Merit Ltr; JA Sls Awd; Faces Intl; Chef.

JOHNSTON, WENDY; Lahainaluna HS; Lihue, HI; (1); Am Leg Aux Girls St; Church Yth Grp; FFA; GAA; Girl Scts; Chorus; Rep Frsh Cls; JV Crs Cntry; JV Trk; Hon Roll; Hawaiiana Clb; Jr Aux Amer Lgn; Fashion Dsgn.

JONES, AARON C; Hawaii Baptist Acad; Honolulu, HI; (2); Boy Scts; Church Yth Grp; Math Clb; Math Tm; Band; School Musical; Pres Soph Cls; JV Socr; High Hon Roll; NHS; Engnrng.

JONES, DAWN; Nanakuli HS; Waianae, HI; (4); 10/111; Letterman Clb; Band; Nwsp; Off Soph Cls; Off Jr Cls; Bsktbl; Crs Cntry; High Hon Roll; Hon Roll; Japanese Club; Santa Rosa JR Coll; Hotel Mngm.

JONES, ERIKA M; Mililani HS; Wahiawa, HI; (3); 36/490; French Clb; Model UN; Service Clb; SADD; School Musical; School Play; Stage Crew; Rep Jr Cls; Hon Roll.

JONES, JACQUELIN; Kalaheo HS; Gulf Breeze, FL; (3); Off Soph Cls; Rep Jr Cls; Hon Roll; Jr NHS; Jobs Dghtrs 87-90; Keywanettes 88-90; Civil Air Patrol 88-89; Bus Admin.

JONES, KRISTIN MEDELLE; Henry Opukahaia Schl; Captain Cook, HI; (4); 3/13; Debate Tm; Drama Clb; French Clb; Latin Clb; Church Choir; Yrbk; Off Sr Cls; JV L Bsktbl; Hon Roll; Voice Dem Awd; Chairperson Sr Cls Actvts, Banquet Cmmtte; Co-Coord St Cls Fundraising Cmmtte; Bethel Coll; Anthropology.

JONES, MIMOSA L; Kauai HS; Koloa, HI; (3); 19/246; Debate Tm; French Clb; Key Clb; Math Tm; Pep Clb; Science Clb; Rptr Lit Mag; Pres Frsh Cls; Rep Soph Cls; Pres Sec Stu Cncl; Vlntr; HOBY Fndtn; Bus.

JOOSSE, MARK; Kohala HS; Canada; (2); Church Yth Grp; U Nations; Graphic Dsgn.

JORDAN, JOHN MATTHEW; Baldwin HS; Kihei, HI; (4); Pres Drama Clb; NFL; Speech Tm; Thesps; VP Jr Cls; VP Sr Cls; Hist NHS; 3rd Time St Champ Natl Forensics League; 3rd Time Brd Of Educ Natl Achvt Awd Wnnr; Boston U; Acting.

JOSE, MARIA; St Joseph HS; Paauilo, HI; (3); Cmnty Wkr; Science Clb; VP Frsh Cls; VP Soph Cls; Socr; Trk; Hon Roll; NHS; Pep Clb; NEDT Awd; Asst AYSO Sccr Coach; Intl Karate Leag; Vet Med.

JOSE, VICTOR R; Pahoa HS; Pahoa, HI; (2); Var Bsktbl; U Of HI-HILO; Carpentry.

JUAN, MARSHA A; Baldwin HS; Kihei,Maui, HI; (1); 101/466; Stu Staying Strght Triple S; Japanese Clb; Hote Mgmt.

JUERGENS, PARICHAT; Mililani HS; Mililani, HI; (3); Church Yth Grp; Band; Flag Corp; Mrchg Band; Socr.

JULIAN, GLENISH; Sacred Hearts Acad; Waipahu, HI; (2); GAA; Teachers Aide; Band; Mrchg Band; Yrbk; Off Frsh Cls; Stu Cncl; Vllybl; Hon Roll; Prfct Atten Awd; Nurse.

JUNKMAN, PATRICIA E; Mililani HS; Mililani Town, HI; (3); 68/490; Drama Clb; French Clb; SADD; Thesps; Chorus; School Musical; School Play; Stage Crew; Swing Chorus; Variety Show; Dramatic Arts.

JUSTO, CATHERINE G; Wallace Rider Farrington HS; Honolulu, HI; (4); 49/549; Library Aide; Spanish Clb; Band; Church Choir; Color Guard; Flag Corp; Jazz Band; Mrchg Band; Pep Band; Cit Awd; U San Francisco; Nrsng.

KAAUWAI IV, DANIEL K; Waianae HS; Waianae, HI; (1); 45/608; Cmnty Wkr; Band; Pep Band; JV Bsbl; Pop Warner Ftbl-Midget Div; Pal Bsbl Pony Leag-Colt Div; Jr Ldr; U Of HI; Elect Engrng.

KAAWALOA, AMY; Pahoa HS; Pahoa, HI; (3); 2/115; FHA; Service Clb; Sec Frsh Cls; VP Soph Cls; Rep Jr Cls; JV Var Socr; Var Vllybl; NHS; Civics Clb; Close Up Clb; Publcty Assn Chrprsn; Archaelgy.

KADOOKA, RUSS T; Mc Kinley HS; Honolulu, HI; (3); 95/570; Boy Scts; Science Clb; Var Socr; Var Tennis; Hon Roll; Athlt Of Yr 89-90; Japanese Clb; SPEBE Comp Sci; Engrng.

KAGAWA, SHANNON M; Waiaka HS; Hilo, HI; (2); 27/500; JA; Key Clb; Math Tm; Rep Frsh Cls; Rep Soph Cls; JV Cheerldng; Prfct Atten Awd; Pres Acad Fit Awd; Pre-Law.

KAHALEKULU, AMI K; Radford HS; Wichita Falls, TX; (2); 32/411; Drama Clb; Math Clb; Math Tm; SADD; Variety Show; JV Bsktbl; Arch.

KAHOOKELE, JEANMARY K; Hana HS; Maui, HI; (2); 3/30; Spc Acad Lvl 1; Plasma Physics.

KAI, DEAN; Hawaii Baptist Acad; Mililani, HI; (2); Hon Roll.

KAI, KELSY E; Mid Pacific Inst; Honolulu, HI; (2); Pep Clb; Chorus; Treas Frsh Cls; Rep Stu Cncl; Var Crs Cntry; Var Tennis; Hon Roll; Washington ST U; Animal Med.

KAIO, CHARILYN; Redemption Acad; Waianae, HI; (2); Church Yth Grp; Drama Clb; French Clb; Library Aide; Office Aide; Teachers Aide; Chorus; Vllybl; High Hon Roll; Hon Roll; Acctng.

KAJIWARA, JODI S; Mid Pacific Inst; Mililani, HI; (1); Hon Roll; WA U; Med.

KAKUDA, SUSAN T; Waimea HS; Hanapepe, HI; (3); 1/200; Pres VP Church Yth Grp; VP Hist 4-H; Math Tm; Treas Science Clb; Band; Ed Nwsp; Sec Soph Cls; Bausch & Lomb Sci Awd; High Hon Roll; NHS.

KAKUNI, AMY; Hawaii Baptist Acad; Milalani, HI; (2); 2/100; Hosp Aide; Chorus; Co-Ed Yrbk; Rep Frsh Cls; Rep Soph Cls; Rep Stu Cncl; High Hon Roll; Hon Roll; Jr NHS; NHS; Japanese Clb; Stu Amb USSR; Outstndng Engl Awds; High Scorer Natl Sci Olymp; Calligraphy Clb; U Of HI Manoa; Pharmacy.

KALA, MARY KAUI; Hana HS; Hana Maui, HI; (1); 2/30; Church Yth Grp; Office Aide; Teachers Aide; Temple Yth Grp; Band; Tennis; Trk; High Hon Roll; Hon Roll; All Amer Schlrs Clb; Vlntry Tutoring; U Of HI; Law.

KALAMA IV, CHARLES A; St Louis Schl; Kailua, HI; (2); Intrml JV Ftbl; High Hon Roll; Hon Roll; U HI; Doctor.

KALAOLA JR, VALMORES D; Waipahu HS; Waianae, HI; (4); 40/500; Cmnty Wkr; Debate Tm; Letterman Clb; Varsity Clb; Var Capt Ftbl; JV Var Trk; Var Wt Lftg; Var Wrstlng; Hon Roll; Ntl Bicntnl Comptn Awd; Grad Hnrs Cum Laude; Eastern OR ST Coll; Engr.

KALAWE, JAYMIE U; Pahoa HS; Keaau, HI; (3); 15/135; Church Yth Grp; FHA; Bsktbl; Sftbl; Tennis; Trk; Vllybl; Cannons Bus Schl; Hotel Mgmt.

KALBERG, AMY; Kalaheo HS; Kaneohe, HI; (3); 13/245; Aud/Vis; Church Yth Grp; Teachers Aide; Bsktbl; Sftbl; Jr NHS; BYU; Advertising.

KALBERG, JASON; Kalaheo HS; Kaneohe, HI; (1); Aud/Vis; Boy Scts; Church Yth Grp; Hon Roll; Willamette U; Law.

KALUA, ATHENA; Pahoa HS; Pahoa, HI; (4); FBLA; Quiz Bowl; SADD; Teachers Aide; Hon Roll; NHS; Stu Tchr Of Spnsh-Elem Stus; Bus Mgmt.

KALUA, MONICA P; Hawaiian Mission Acad; Honolulu, HI; (2); Drama Clb; Varsity Clb; School Play; Variety Show; Gym; Powder Puff Ftbl; Sftbl; Vllybl; Most Vlbl Trphy Sftbl; Pacific Union Coll; Bus.

KAM, DAVID Y; Maryknoll HS; Kailua, HI; (2); Aud/Vis; Chess Clb; ROTC; Color Guard; JV Trk; High Hon Roll; Prfct Atten Awd; Intramural Bowling; Hiking Club; Hnrs Algebra III Mrt Cert; Engrng.

KAM JR, JOSEPH K H; Kaimuki HS; Honolulu, HI; (3); JA; Library Aide; Stage Crew; Facentng.

KAM, MITCHELL M K; St Louis Schl; Honolulu, HI; (3); 24/160; Boy Scts; Cmnty Wkr; Ftbl; Wt Lftg; Hon Roll; Eagle Sct; Paramedit.

KAM, STEVEN H; Maryknoll HS; Kailua, HI; (4); 6/124; VP Chess Clb; ROTC; Pres Science Clb; Flag Corp; Var JV Crs Cntry; Var JV Trk; Bausch & Lomb Sci Awd; High Hon Roll; Hon Roll; NHS; Chem Awd; Billy Mitchell Awd CAP; Govt Awd; U HI; Med.

KAMA, JOWENNA; Waiakea HS; Hilo, HI; (4); Church Yth Grp; Cmnty Wkr; Computer Clb; JA; Teachers Aide; School Musical; Stu Cncl; Hon Roll; Prfct Atten Awd; Hawaiian Clb; Hilo Clb JR Jaycees; Hula Halau O Ka Ua Kahi Lehua Dncr; UH Of Hilo; Spch.

KAMAKA, AMBERSTEINA; Waianae HS; Waianae, HI; (2); Church Yth Grp; JV Var Bsktbl; Photo Clb; Csmtlgst.

KAMEMOTO, JANICE A; President T Roosevelt HS; Honolulu, HI; (4); 39/318; Hosp Aide; Pres Sec Math Clb; Math Tm; Teachers Aide; Band; Mrchg Band; Pep Band; Natl Guild Piano Tchrs HS Diplma; Honolulu Symphny Yth Tlnt Pool Wnnr; UH Manoa.

KAMITA, RENE Y; Mc Kinley HS; Honolulu, HI; (4); 5/527; Service Clb; Flag Corp; Lit Mag; Pres Jr Cls; Pres Stu Cncl; Var Mgr Bsbl; Sec Treas NHS; Ntl Merit SF; Miss Mc Kinley; Centry III Ldrs ST Fnlst; Pol Sci.

KAMIYA, JAN J; President William Mc Kinely HS; Waipahu, HI; (2); Band; Jazz Band; Mrchg Band; Orch; Pep Band; School Musical; School Play; Rep Soph Cls; NHS; St Solo/Ensmbl Cmptn Silver/Red Mdls; U Of HI Manoa; Jrnlsm.

KAMIYA, KYLE K; Hawaii Baptist Acad; Aiea, HI; (2); Band; Tennis; Comp Sci.

KAMIYA, LISA L; Roosevelt HS; Kaneohe, HI; (3); Cmnty Wkr; Flag Corp; Bus.

KAN, PETER A; Roosevelt HS; Honolulu, HI; (2); 12/360; Hosp Aide; Math Clb; Math Tm; Quiz Bowl; Science Clb; Var Crs Cntry; Var Tennis; Var Trk; Hon Roll; NHS; Riflery; Crss Cntry Co-Capt; Phy.

KANAE, CHRIS H; Mililani HS; Mililani, HI; (2); Drama Clb; Math Clb; Chrmn Frsh Cls; Chrmn Soph Cls; Chrmn Soph Cls; Rep Stu Cncl; Intrml Bsbl; Intrml Bsktbl; JV Var Ftbl; Hon Roll; Mediation Tm Pres; Aloha & Awds Cmmttes Chrprsn; Interschl Cmmtte; Engr.

KANAELE, JOCELYN N; Maui HS; Haiku, HI; (3); Pres VP FHA; Acad Awd Cert Frnch; Acad Cert Awd Food Service; Stu Of Mnth 2 Times; May Day Pgm 89-90; Food Service.

KANAKAOLE, KAUI; Hana HS; Hana, HI; (1); Treas Frsh Cls; High Hon Roll; Hon Roll; Bus Mgt.

KANEALII, PRIAM K; Kamehameha Schls; Mililani, HI; (3); 103/457; Boy Scts; ROTC; Teachers Aide; Chorus; Swmmng; Waterpolo; Chem.

KANEKO, DAVID; Pearl City HS; Pearl City, HI; (4); 6/478; Cmnty Wkr; Key Clb; Quiz Bowl; Phtg Yrbk; Phtg Lit Mag; High Hon Roll; NHS; Natl Gold Key Schltc Natl Stu Art Exhbtn Photogrphy; Schl Pictures Inc Photgrphy Cont Hnrb Mntn; UH Manoa; Chem Engrng.

KANEKOA, KAMAKA K; Maui HS; Kahului, HI; (3); 15/354; Boy Scts; Church Yth Grp; Science Clb; Band; Church Choir; Mrchg Band; Ftbl; Swmmng; Hon Roll; NHS; Outstndng Seminary Stu; Band Schlr Awd; Brigham Young U.

KANEMORI, GAVEN T; Hawaii Baptist Acad; Kaneohe, HI; (4); 28/93; Q&S; Chorus; Ed Nwsp; Pres Treas Stu Cncl; Var Golf; Cit Awd; Elks Awd; NHS; Pres Acad Fit Awd; JV Bsktbl; HI Most Valuable HS Jrnlst; Grad With Honors; U Of WA; Med.

KANEMOTO, LYNN M; Honokaa HS; Honokaa, HI; (4); 7/130; Band; Ed Yrbk; VP Pres Sr Cls; Mgr(s); L Socr; Hon Roll; NHS; Jayteens Clb Secy; Intrreltns Clb; Green & Gold Fair Cls Chrprsn; U Of HAWAII Manoa.

KANESHIGE JR, MORRIS N; Lanakila Baptist HS; Ewa Beach, HI; (4); 15/18; Boy Scts; Drama Clb; Letterman Clb; Teachers Aide; School Play; Nwsp; Pres Jr Cls; Intrml JV Bsktbl; Intrml JV Vllybl; Hon Roll; Spring Arbor; Psych.

KANESHIRO, CRYSTAL; Hilo HS; Hilo, HI; (2); Rep Soph Cls; Hon Roll; NULA.

KANESHIRO, DAWN M; Lahaina Luna HS; Lahaina, HI; (1); 68/223; GAA; Service Clb; Band; Mrchg Band; Pep Band; Sftbl; Tennis; Hon Roll; JR Golf; U Of HI Manoa; Bus Mgr.

KANESHIRO, DYAN H; Roosevelt HS; Honolulu, HI; (3); Math Tm; Science Clb; Spanish Clb; Nwsp; Hon Roll; JETS Awd; NHS; Frank Gannett Nwsp Carrier Schlrshp; Natl Test Of Engrng Apt Math & Sci Cmptn St Team Mem; St Sci Fair; Oberlin Coll; Pre-Med.

KANESHIRO, JAMES S; Punahou Schl; Honolulu, HI; (4); Pres JA; Off ROTC; Nwsp; Yrbk; Stu Cncl; Hon Roll; Ntl Merit SF; ROTC Ldrshp Awd; Vsty Riflery; JR Schl Camp Cnslr; Finance.

KANG, MIKKI; Moanalua HS; Honolulu, HI; (3); Treas Church Yth Grp; Hosp Aide; Treas Intnl Clb; Playing Classical Piano Music; U Of Hawaii; Accounting.

KANG, SO YOUNG; Baldwin HS; Kahalui, HI; (3); #63 In Class; Pep Clb; Band; Hon Roll; Jayteens; U Of Manoa; Intl Bus.

KANG, WOO SEOK; Moanalna HS; Honolulu, HI; (2); Church Yth Grp; Math Clb; Science Clb; Baseball; U Of Hawaii; Science.

KANIHO, RICHARD K; Honokaa HS; Kamuela, HI; (4); Boy Scts; Church Yth Grp; FCA; 4-H; Letterman Clb; Varsity Clb; Off Sr Cls; Stu Cncl; Bsbl; Ftbl; HI HS Rodeo Assn Bull Riding, Bareback Bronc & Double Mugging; Natl Fnlst FCA Cowboy Cptr 90; ND ST U Bottineau; Forestry.

KANIHO, TERRI K; Honokaa HS; Kamuela, HI; (3); 24/146; Scholastic Bowl; Teachers Aide; Chorus; Rep Frsh Cls; Pres Soph Cls; VP Stu Cncl; Stat Bsbl; Mgr(s); Var Powder Puff Ftbl; Var Sftbl; In Charge Of Hmcmng Act, Assemblies & Dec Cmmtte; Typing & Clerical Kind Of Jobs; Wrk Part-Time; UH Hilo Coll; Bus Mgmt.

KANSANA, MAKALANI T; Molokai HS; Kaunakakai, HI; (3); Office Aide; Yrbk; Hon Roll; UCI; Chiroprctr.

KAO, JOHN I; Kaiser HS; Honolulu, HI; (4); 11/300; Science Clb; Var Swmmng; Var Tennis; Hon Roll; Prfct Atten Awd; Chinese Club Secy; Interact Club; Soft Tnns MVP Awd; UCLA.

KAPOOR, KEN; Kaimuki HS; Honolulu, HI; (2); JA; Hon Roll; Prfct Atten Awd; Close-Up Pgm; YMCA; U HI; Physician.

KAPUA, CRYSTAL K; Waipahu HS; Waipahu, HI; (3); 20/409; Capt Dance Clb; Drama Clb; Capt Drill Tm; Variety Show; Lit Mag; Rep Frsh Cls; Pres Soph Cls; Pres Jr Cls; Pres Sr Cls; Stat Bsbl; Soph Stu Of Yr; Dist Sci Fr Hnrbl Mntn; Smmr Intern; U Of HI; Bus.

KASPER, CHERYL D; Kailua HS; Kailua, HI; (3); Cmnty Wkr; Swmmng; Teacher.

KATANO, JAY; Pearl City HS; Pearl City, HI; (4); 1/478; Computer Clb; Math Tm; Quiz Bowl; VICA; Hon Roll; NHS; Val; U Os HI Manoa; Elec Engrg.

KATJANG, KIMBERLY ANN; James Campbell HS; Ewa Beach, HI; (3); 15/371; Var Cheerldng; Hon Roll; Winterbll Cmmttee; Princpls Awds; NM Military Inst; Arch.

KATO, DEBBIE; Kohala HS; Kapaau, HI; (4); 3/50; Treas Rptr FFA; FHA; SADD; Pres Frsh Cls; Pres Soph Cls; Pres Sr Cls; Treas Stu Cncl; Stat Bsktbl; Sec NHS; Hop Cmmttee; Chrprson Prom Ct; Hmcmng Attndnt; Grad Hnr Grd; Ray A Crok Achvt Awd; May Day Ct Attndnt; U Of Portland; Bus.

KATO, KIBERT; Mililani HS; Mililani, HI; (4); 61/408; Church Yth Grp; Key Clb; Band; Jazz Band; Mrchg Band; Orch; Pep Band; School Musical; VP Frsh Cls; Rep Sr Cls; Outstndng Bandsmn Awd; Judo Tm; HI Rep Natl Yth Ldrshp Conf; U HI Manoa; Pre Optmtry.

KATO, LESLIE K; Kaiser HS; Honolulu, HI; (3); 1/325; Pres Band; Color Guard; Jazz Band; Mrchg Band; Var L Bsktbl; Var L Crs Cntry; Var L Socr; Hon Roll; Sec NHS; Ntl Merit Ltr.

KATSUNO, LAURA L; Mid-Pacific Inst; Kailua, HI; (2); Library Aide; Swmmng; Psych.

KAUAHI, CRYSTAL; Waimea HS; Kekaha, HI; (2); Art Clb; Service Clb; SADD; Bsktbl; Mgr(s); Socr; Hmcmng Cmmtte; Praise; Art.

KAUAHI, DENISE K; Kamemeha Schls; Lawai, HI; (4); 15/426; Aud/Vis; Drama Clb; SADD; Acpl Chr; Stage Crew; JV Capt Bsktbl; JV Vllybl; High Hon Roll; Hon Roll; Loyola Marymount U; Commnctns.

KAUFFMAN, JOSHUA N; Konawaena HS; Kailua Kona, HI; (3); 91/294; Church Yth Grp; Cmnty Wkr; French Clb; Variety Show; Music.

KAUHANE, NOAH; Kamehameha Schls; Kaheohe, HI; (4); 7/415; Math Clb; Mu Alpha Theta; Spanish Clb; JV Ftbl; High Hon Roll; Hon Roll; Duke U Tlnt Id Pgm 88; U HI Haumana Biomed Pgm 89; Princeton; Math.

KAUI, JACQUELINE K; Kapaa High & Inter; Kapaa, HI; (3); Rep Frsh Cls; Pres Soph Cls; Pres Sr Cls; VP Stu Cncl; Var Bsktbl; JV Cheerldng; Var Sftbl; Var Vllybl; Hon Roll; NHS; HI St Stu Conf Plnnr; Tri M Musc Hnr Soc; Outstndng Soph HOBY; Pre Law.

KAULU, JOEY K; Kailua HS; Waimanalo, HI; (3); Off Frsh Cls; Var Vllybl; Hon Roll; HI Teamng For Tomrrw Conf; Bus Mgmt.

KAULULAAU, NATALIE K; Waimea HS; Waimea, HI; (2); 43/186; VP Treas Church Yth Grp; Letterman Clb; Pep Clb; SADD; Band; Jazz Band; Mrchg Band; Pep Band; Stat Bsktbl; Co-Capt Swmmng; Simmng MVP.

KAUPOE, MICHAEL H; Farrington HS; Honolulu, HI; (2); Church Yth Grp; Dance Clb; FCA; Mrchg Band; Pep Band; JV Bsbl; JV Bsktbl; JV Ftbl; JV Trk; JV Wrstlng; OR; Electronics.

KAUPU, KATHERINE M; Molokai HS & Intermed; Kaunakakai, HI; (3); Pres Drama Clb; Letterman Clb; School Play; Stage Crew; Treas Soph Cls; Off Jr Cls; Chrmn Stu Cncl; JV Capt Bsktbl; Var Capt Sftbl; Hon Roll; Maui Intrschlstc Lg Sftbl 1st Tm & All St Hnrb Mntn & Bsktbl 2nd Tm; Flm & Tlvsn.

KAWAAUHAU, MELANIE K; Konawaena HS; Captain Cook, HI; (4); Pres Church Yth Grp; Letterman Clb; Sec Office Aide; Church Choir; Co-Capt Vllybl; Hon Roll; NHS; Nrsng.

KAWACHI, THALASSA K; Kau HS; Pahala, HI; (3); FFA; Letterman Clb; Math Tm; Pep Clb; Rep Jr Cls; Treas Stu Cncl; Var Tennis; Var Vllybl; Hon Roll; Voice Dem Awd; Xerox Awd; Mock Trial Team; Marine Bio.

KAWAHA, WARREN S; Waiakea HS; Hilo, HI; (1); 112/478; School Musical; Intrml Bsktbl; Ftbl.

KAWAHAKUI, NOHEALANI A; The Kamehameha Schls; Waialua, HI; (3); 39/419; Cmnty Wkr; Hosp Aide; Math Clb; SADD; Band; Mrchg Band; Pep Band; High Hon Roll; Hon Roll; NHS; Natl Yng Ldrs Confrnc Jan 90 Wash DC; Schlr Athlt Riflery 89-90; Natl Jr Olympc Riflery Chmpnshps.

KAWAHARA, ALYSSA S; Aiea HS; Aiea, HI; (3); 24/350; Key Clb; Rep Soph Cls; Rep Jr Cls; Rep Stu Cncl; Hon Roll; Outstndng Achvt Scl Stds, Frnch I, Beg Typng, Genrl Bus & Notetakng; St Fnlst NCTE Achvt Awd Wrtng; Nrsng.

KAWAI, MICHELLE E; Kohala HS; Kapaau, HI; (1); 10/60; FHA; FTA; Teachers Aide; Rep Frsh Cls; JV Bsktbl; Vllybl; UH Manda; Bus Mgmt.

KAWAMATA, BYRON K; Kailua HS; Kailua, HI; (2); 21/301; Library Aide; Hon Roll; Kapiolani CC; Culinary Arts.

KAWAMOTO, RYAN C; Waiakea HS; Pahoa, HI; (1); 15/478; Boy Scts; Pres Chess Clb; Math Clb; Band; Jazz Band; Mrchg Band; Pep Band; High Hon Roll; Hon Roll; Field Show.

KAWAMURA, BRYAN T; Baldwin HS; Kahului, HI; (2); 71/395; Key Clb; JV L Ftbl; Hon Roll; Prfct Atten Awd; Stu Staying Straight.

KAWAMURA, CHELSIE H; Kauai HS; Kapaa, HI; (1); 56/251; FHA; Key Clb; Band; Piano.

KAWAMURA, GRANT M; St Louis Schl; Kaneohe, HI; (2); 29/129; Cmnty Wkr; JV Bsbl; Hon Roll; Coach Bsbl; Rep HI Goodwill Bsbl Team; Ring Cmmtte; U Of HI; Sci.

KAWAMURA, LORNA N; Waiakea HS; Hilo, HI; (3); Key Clb; Stat Bsbl; Hon Roll; Yth Against Cancer; Leo Clb; U Of HI Manoa; Civil Engr.

KAWAMURA, REID T; Moanalua HS; Aiea, HI; (2); Var Bsbl; JV Ftbl.

KAWATA, KIMI K; Hawaii Baptist Acad; Honolulu, HI; (2); Cmnty Wkr; VP FTA; JA; Rptr Yrbk; Swmmng; Hon Roll; Jr NHS; Japanese Clb; Bus Econ.

KAWATO, JANALYN L; Roosevelt HS; Honolulu, HI; (2); 22/360; Band; Mrchg Band; Pep Band; Hon Roll; CA Inst Tech; Arch.

KAYA, JOANNE Y; Waiakea HS; Hilo, HI; (1); 40/478; JA; Service Clb; Band; Mrchg Band; Pep Band; Hon Roll; U Of HI Manoa; Bus.

KEALOHA, ELENA; Kauai HS; Kalaheo, HI; (1); Var Bsktbl; Var Sftbl; Var Capt Vllybl; Hon Roll; UH Manoa; Psych.

KEENEN, CHRISTINE M; Moanalua HS; Honolulu, HI; (2); 96/488; Church Yth Grp; Drama Clb; School Play; Hon Roll; HI ST Gymnstcs Chmpn 90; Law.

KEKAULA, ROSE KAHAE; Kamehameha HS; Honolulu, HI; (3); Pres Church Yth Grp; Church Choir; Oahu Hnr Choir; Concert Glee Club; Happy Day Clb VP; BYU UT; Music.

KEPLER, KENNETH B; H P Baldwin HS; Wailuku, HI; (2); VP Drama Clb; Thesps; Church Choir; School Musical; School Play; Stage Crew; Var Crs Cntry; Var Socr; Var Trk; Pres Acad Fit Awd.

KESHISHIAN, CHRISTINA M; Maui HS; Pukalani, HI; (3); Church Yth Grp; Drama Clb; French Clb; Girl Scts; Office Aide; Science Clb; School Play; Stage Crew; Rep Frsh Cls; Var L Swmmng; SSS Clb; Teaming For Tmrrw Schl Wnnr; CO ST U; Pre-Vet.

KESSLER, DEBRA A; Henry J Kaiser HS; Honolulu, HI; (3); 17/328; Pres Church Yth Grp; Cmnty Wkr; Drama Clb; Science Clb; Chrmn Speech Tm; School Play; Rptr Nwsp; Rep Pres Stu Cncl; JV L Swmmng; Hon Roll.

KESSLER, SCOTT B; Moanolua HS; Silver Spring, MD; (2); 5/488; Cmnty Wkr; Math Clb; Science Clb; Temple Yth Grp; Hon Roll; Law Clb; Mock Trl Team; Cntntl Math Leg; Accntng.

KEYHANI, DARIUS; Lahaina Luna HS; Lahaina, HI; (3); 3/224; DECA; Math Clb; Math Tm; Science Clb; Spanish Clb; VP Frsh Cls; Var Capt Wrstlng; High Hon Roll; Hon Roll; John Hopkins U; Med.

KHENMY, LINDA; Mc Kinley HS; Honolulu, HI; (2); Church Yth Grp; Science Clb; Temple Yth Grp; Prfct Atten Awd; Hiking Club; Vietnamese Club; Close Up Pgm; Law.

KIA, ROSALIND K; Kaimuki HS; Honolulu, HI; (3); 45/361; Drama Clb; SADD; Teachers Aide; Variety Show; Rep Stu Cncl; High Hon Roll; Hon Roll; Pres Acad Fit Awd; Mgr.

KIANG, KARMA WEN; H P Baldwin HS; Kihei, HI; (3); 27/420; Cmnty Wkr; Red Cross Aide; Speech Tm; SADD; Band; Jazz Band; Variety Show; Hon Roll; Kihei Canoe Clb Brd Dir; Mst Enthstc 88 & 89; Amer Red Crs Vlntr; Yth Vlntr Yr 90; Russian Clb Offcr; U Northern CO; Teacher.

KIDO, KENDALL H; Hawaii Baptist Acad; Honolulu, HI; (2); Church Yth Grp; Q&S; Ed Nwsp; JV Bsktbl; Hon Roll; Pres Acad Fit Awd; HSK Karate; U Of HI; Arch.

KIESE, MICHELLE M; Pearl City HS; Pearl City, HI; (2); Band; Mrchg Band; Orch; Pep Band; U Of Southern CA.

KIHOI, SCOTT C; Damien Memorial HS; Aiea, HI; (4); 25/125; Debate Tm; French Clb; NFL; Office Aide; Pep Clb; Treas Speech Tm; Teachers Aide; Rptr Nwsp; Rep Jr Cls; Rep Sr Cls; Japanese Club President; Japan Hwaii Foreign Exchange; Sterling Scholar Foreign Language; U Of Calif; Intl Business.

KIKUYAMA, MAILE K; H P Baldwin HS; Kihei, HI; (3); Church Yth Grp; DECA; Band; Mrchg Band; Pep Band; Hon Roll; DECA; Marketing.

KIM, ANGELA P; Mililani HS; Mililani, HI; (3); FHA; Teachers Aide; Chorus; Yrbk; Stat Bsktbl; Mgr(s); Stat Vllybl; Honolulu Police Actvts Leag Statstcn; Mililani Dist Pk Smmr Fun Jr Ldr; U Of HI Manoa; Food Svc.

KIM, DOSIK; Moanalua HS; Honolulu, HI; (2); 82/488; Church Choir; Gym; Hon Roll; ASU; Archtctr.

KIM, DOUGLAS; Roosevelt HS; Honolulu, HI; (2); 15/360; Hon Roll; UCLA; Engr.

KIM, HUI YONG; Leilehua HS; Wahiawa, HI; (2); 6/392; Drama Clb; FTA; Chorus; Zonta Clb-Treas; Stephens Coll; Med.

KIM, HUN HEE; President William Mc Kinley HS; Honolulu, HI; (2); 1/600; Lit Mag; Treas Soph Cls; Sec Stu Cncl; High Hon Roll; Hon Roll; VP NHS; Prfct Atten Awd; Hiking Clb; Harvard; Med.

KIM, JASON; Moanalua HS; Honolulu, HI; (1); Bus Profs of Am; Chess Clb; Math Clb; SADD; Teachers Aide; Band; Jazz Band; Mrchg Band; Pep Band; Stage Crew; Teens Helping Teens; Peer Cnslr; U HI; Eng.

KIM, JAYNE P; Moanalua HS; Honolulu, HI; (2); 11/501; Pres Church Yth Grp; Band; Color Guard; Flag Corp; Mrchg Band; Pep Band; Var Tennis; Rep Soph Cls; Sentr Schl Stu Assoc; Soft Tnns; Leo Clb; Jnr Cls VP 90-91.

KIM, JENNIFER C; Mc Kinley HS; Honolulu, HI; (2); 1/588; Hosp Aide; Lit Mag; Hon Roll; Keywanettes Vp; Poly Action Club Secy; Stanford; Psych.

KIM, JINNY; St Andrews Priory HS; Honolulu, HI; (4); 8/50; Intnl Clb; Key Clb; VP Latin Clb; Science Clb; JV Var Tennis; Hon Roll; Save Erth Clb Secy; Jpns Clb; Cmpns; Bus Adm.

KIM, JOLENE; Henry O'pukahaia HS; Hilo, HI; (1); Church Yth Grp; Teachers Aide; Chorus; Yrbk; Var Bsktbl; JV Vllybl; High Hon Roll; HI U; Lwyr.

KIM, KAY C; Saint Francis HS; Honolulu, HI; (2); 1/80; Aud/Vis; Library Aide; Math Clb; Math Tm; Mu Alpha Theta; NFL; Pep Clb; Quiz Bowl; Speech Tm; Flag Corp; Natl Sci Fndtn Young Schlrs; Natl Math Exam Schl Wnnr; Corp Law.

KIM, MICHELLE G; Mid-Pacific Inst; Honolulu, HI; (1); Math Tm; Band; Treas Frsh Cls; JV Sftbl; NHS; Japanese Club; Natl Jr Hnr Soc Pres; Pres List.

KIM, RISABELLE K; Moanalua HS; Honolulu, HI; (3); Math Clb; Math Tm; Mu Alpha Theta; Science Clb; Orch; Rep Stu Cncl; Yth Tlnt Pool Auditns Hnrb Mntn.

KIM, SALLY; St Andrews Priory HS; Honolulu, HI; (4); Drama Clb; French Clb; Intnl Clb; Treas Speech Tm; Teachers Aide; School Play; Nwsp; Stu Cncl; JV Swmmng; JV Trk; Fndr & Pres Save The Earth Envrnmntl Clb; Evergreen ST Coll; Sci.

KIM, SUE C; Kaiser HS; Ewa Beach, HI; (3); 39/325; Aud/Vis; VP Band; Co-Ed Yrbk; High Hon Roll; Hon Roll; U Of The Pacific; Bio.

KIM, VICKI; Mc Kinley HS; Honolulu, HI; (4); Office Aide; Orch; School Play; Rptr Nwsp; Treas Sr Cls; JV Crs Cntry; Hon Roll; Prfct Atten Awd; Baylor U; Bus.

KIMOTO, JAMES; James Campbell HS; Ewa Beach, HI; (4); 10/450; Key Clb; Quiz Bowl; Band; Jazz Band; Mrchg Band; Orch; Intrml Bsktbl; Var Crs Cntry; Intrml Powder Puff Ftbl; Var Tennis; SPEBE; UH Manoa; Mech Engr.

KINAKA, KRISTINE N Y; Henry Perrine Baldwin HS; Wailuku, HI; (1); 15/466; Debate Tm; Math Tm; NFL; Speech Tm; SADD; Band; Church Choir; Trk; High Hon Roll; Hmcmng Actvts Chrmn; Bishops Awd Japanese Lang Schl; Corp Law.

KING, CHRISTIE; Baldwin HS; Kihei, HI; (3); Rep Church Yth Grp; Chrmn French Clb; Hosp Aide; Pres Math Clb; Math Tm; Science Clb; SADD; Church Choir; Co-Ed Yrbk; Rep Stu Cncl; Exchng Stu To France; SPEBE Biochem Pgm U Of HI Smmr; HI Scndry Lang Cont, Japanese; Pre Med.

KING, JANICE; Radford HS; Roosevelt, NY; (3); Red Cross Aide; Teachers Aide; JV Var Bsktbl; Powder Puff Ftbl; JV Var Trk; High Hon Roll; Hon Roll; Pres Acad Fit Awd; Yth Ending Hunger Org; Atty.

KINJO, KORINNE N; Mililani HS; Waipahu, HI; (3); 41/490; French Clb; Hosp Aide; Sec Key Clb; Band; Color Guard; Flag Corp; Mrchg Band; Pep Band; Hon Roll; Vrsty, Capt, Ltr & Mvp Awd Bowling; Judi Stat.

KINOSHITA, JENNIFER F; H P Baldwin HS; Wailuku, HI; (1); 20/466; Church Yth Grp; Service Clb; Band; High Hon Roll; Triple S; Keywanettes; Japanese Clb; Educ.

KIRK, JASON W; Mid-Pacific Inst; Makakilo, HI; (2); Boy Scts; Computer Clb; Red Cross Aide; Teachers Aide; Yrbk; Cit Awd; Hon Roll; Jap Clb; U Of WA; Dr.

KIRKLAND, JOSE; Pahoa HS; Pahoa, HI; (4); 3/110; Drama Clb; Math Tm; Pres Spanish Clb; Pres Speech Tm; Var Socr; High Hon Roll; NHS; Ntl Merit SF.

KIRKPATRICK, MICHAEL T; Waipahu HS; Azle, TX; (1); 72/513; Tennis; Hon Roll; US Air Force Acad; Math.

KIRN, MICHELLE; Star Of The Sea HS; Honolulu, HI; (2); Treas Soph Cls; JV Vllybl; Hon Roll; Vllybl Ltr.

KISHIDA, KENDALL M; Hawaii Baptist Acad; Honolulu, HI; (2); Tennis; Cit Awd; High Hon Roll; Prfct Atten Awd; Vet.

KITABAYASHI, LORI K; Kapaa HS; Kapaa, HI; (3); 5/360; Church Yth Grp; Cmnty Wkr; French Clb; Key Clb; Library Aide; Math Tm; Red Cross Aide; Spanish Clb; Band; Jazz Band; Flrl Arrngr A Rmntc Rose; U Wash.

KITASHIMA, HEIDI K; Kamehameha Schls; Pearl City, HI; (4); Pres Church Yth Grp; GAA; Chorus; Church Choir; Orch; Vllybl; Hawaiian Clb; BYU; Ed.

KIYOTA, BRENT; St Joseph HS; Hilo, HI; (4); Math Clb; Science Clb; Acpl Chr; VP Frsh Cls; VP Soph Cls; Sec Stu Cncl; Var Capt Bsbl; Var Capt Bsktbl; Hon Roll; Doctor.

KIYUNA, DENISE K; Moanalua HS; Kaneohe, HI; (2); 147/488; Church Yth Grp; Band; Mrchg Band; Pep Band; Rep Frsh Cls; Stat Bsbl; Interact Club; U HI Manosi; Elem Teacher.

KIYUNA, LANCE C; Kalani HS; Honolulu, HI; (3); JV Bsbl; JV Bsktbl; JV Var Ftbl; Tech Engr.

KLEIN, MICHELLE M; Maryknoll HS; Kailua, HI; (2); Church Yth Grp; Cmnty Wkr; NFL; Science Clb; Speech Tm; Lit Mag; JV Bsktbl; JV Socr; High Hon Roll; HI St Sci Engrng Fair St Fnlst Indv Grant.

KLUGE, GEORG; Konawaena High & Inter HS; Kailua-Kona, HI; (4); Hon Roll; Camera Clb & Solar Car Tm; Sci.

KLUTKE, MAXWELL L S; Kapaa HS; Kapaa, HI; (3); Aud/Vis; Debate Tm; Key Clb; Golf; Civil Air Ptrl US Air Force Acad; Yth Leg Rookie Of Yr; Bdy Brd; Cmmrcl Pilot.

KO, HYUN; Mc Kinley HS; Honolulu, HI; (3); 6/565; Treas Debate Tm; Science Clb; Band; Capt Crs Cntry; Tennis; Capt Trk; Hon Roll; Treas Jr NHS; Korean Club Rep; Univ Club Chairperson; Track Most Outstndng; Cross Cntry Most Inspirational; Brown U; Psych.

KOBASHIGAWA, KIRT; Hawaii Baptist Acad; Kaneohe, HI; (3); Church Yth Grp; Cmnty Wkr; Rep Frsh Cls; Intrml Bsktbl; Var Vllybl; Hon Roll; Ldrshp Cncl VP; USC; Engrng.

KOBAYASHI, DIONE; St Joseph HS; Hilo, HI; (2); Church Yth Grp; Sec French Clb; Letterman Clb; Math Clb; Varsity Clb; Mgr Yrbk; Var Sftbl; Hon Roll; Arch.

KOBAYASHI, JANN M; Moanalua HS; Honolulu, HI; (3); 47/462; Cmnty Wkr; Hosp Aide; Band; Mrchg Band; Orch; Pres Sec Stu Cncl; Stat Socr; Freedoms Fndtn Smnr; Leo Clb; Frnsc Sci.

KOBAYASHI, KRISTINE; Pahoa HS; Pahoa, HI; (2); 1/123; Drama Clb; Sec Math Tm; Sec Treas Service Clb; Band; Rep Frsh Cls; Rep Soph Cls; Socr; High Hon Roll; NHS.

KODAMA, JULIE; Iolani HS; Waimanalo, HI; (3); 133/227; Dance Clb; Hosp Aide; JV Var Cheerldng; Mgr(s); Intrml JV Socr; Hon Roll; Japanese, Philosophy & Hawaiian Clubs; Med.

KOENIG, FIASILI P; Saint Francis HS; Honolulu, HI; (2); Chorus; School Play; Lit Mag; Hon Roll.

KOFF, EMILY R; Mid-Pacific Inst; Honolulu, HI; (4); 25/180; Drama Clb; French Clb; Temple Yth Grp; School Play; Variety Show; Yrbk; Gym; Swmmng; High Hon Roll; Hon Roll; Waterpolo; Canoe; Ldrshp Awd Honorary Naval Ofcr; Psychlgy.

KOGASAKA, SHANNON; Maui HS; Kahului, HI; (2); 6/388; Key Clb; Math Clb; Science Clb; Band; JV Score Keeper; Var L Sftbl; Hon Roll; Outstndng Achvtmnt Awd Physcl Sci & Gemtry; Close Up Prgm Wash DC.

KOHATSU, KELLY H; Maui HS; Kahului, HI; (2); 24/388; Church Yth Grp; Cmnty Wkr; Letterman Clb; Service Clb; Var Sftbl; Close-Up Pgm 90.

KOIKE, LINCOLN K; Ajea HS; Aiea, HI; (4); 94/366; Church Yth Grp; JA; Service Clb; Var Bsbl; Var Socr; Leo Clb; U Of HI.

KOJIMA, DORI A; Moanalua HS; Aiea, HI; (1); VP Aud/Vis; Lit Mag; Lang Arts Shwcs Wnnr-Poetry & Shrt Stry 90; Moanaluas Media & Comm Lrng Ctr.

KOLB, KERI L; Mililani HS; Mililani, HI; (3); Capt Dance Clb; Capt Color Guard; Mrchg Band; Variety Show; Ed Yrbk; UT Austin; Commnctns.

KOLLER, ELISHA A; Radford HS; Honolulu, HI; (2); 200/420; French Clb; Office Aide; JV Var Fld Hcky; Var Gym; Var Trk; Var Mgr(s); JV Var Socr; Var Sftbl; VI ST Champ Gymnastics Best All Around 88 Class IV.

KOMATSU, SHELLI; St Andrews Priory HS; Honolulu, HI; (4); 6/51; Church Yth Grp; Girl Scts; Intnl Clb; Latin Clb; Church Choir; Ed Rptr Yrbk; High Hon Roll; Hon Roll; Grl Sctng Gld Awd 89, Slvr Awd 86, Cncl Dlgte Cncl Pacfc 90-91 Trm; Japanese Clb 85-90; USC; Accntng.

KONDO, GAYLE; Mc Kinley HS; Kailua, HI; (3); 22/537; Cmnty Wkr; GAA; JA; Treas Key Clb; Var Capt Vllybl; Hon Roll; Banquet Co-Chairperson; Jr Prom Co-Chairperson; Sr Class Slide Show Co-Chairperson; Hi Bus Stu Conf 90; Bus.

KONG, GEE HYUN CATHY; Iolani Schl; Honolulu, HI; (4); 60/220; Church Yth Grp; French Clb; Pep Clb; Rep Frsh Cls; VP Sr Cls; Var JV Cheerldng; Var JV Tennis; High Hon Roll; Hon Roll; Pres Acad Fit Awd; Hula; Piano; UC Davis; Law.

KONG, JUSTIN; Kalani HS; Honolulu, HI; (3); 24/270; Aud/Vis; Boy Scts; Church Yth Grp; Letterman Clb; Temple Yth Grp; Varsity Clb; Var L Bsbl; Var L Bsktbl; Var Capt Ftbl; Hon Roll; Hawaiian Culture; U Of HI; Sports Brdcstng.

KORT, ATHENA; Laupahoehoe HS; Hilo, HI; (3); Science Clb; Spanish Clb; SADD; VP Jr Cls; Sftbl; Big Island Assn Stu Cncl Rep; Military.

KORT, TRINA K; Laupahoehoe HS; Hilo, HI; (4); Science Clb; Mgr Yrbk; Treas Sr Cls; Cheerldng; Crs Cntry; All Amer Schlr Awd; Handbook Cmmtte Chrprsrn; May Day Cmmtte Chrprsn; U Portland; Psych.

KORZON, JOEY D; Mililani HS; Mililani, HI; (2); 63/213; JV Crs Cntry; Arts Awd; Bus.

KOVACH, KRISSIE; Konawaena HS; Honaunau, HI; (1); Drama Clb; French Clb; Girl Scts; School Play; JV Vllybl; Hon Roll; Pddlng Sit Strkr; U Of HI Mahoa; Marine Bio.

KOYANAGI, LYDIA M; Farrington HS; Honolulu, HI; (1); 41/360; Tennis; Hon Roll; Airline Stewardess.

KOYANAGI, TRICIA N; Kalaheo HS; Kailua, HI; (3); 51/243; Church Yth Grp; Band; JV Bsktbl; JV Vllybl; Hon Roll; MVP JR Vrsty Bsktbl; U Of HI; Psych.

KRETZ, CHERI C; Kaiser HS; Honolulu, HI; (1); Church Yth Grp; Hon Roll; Prfct Atten Awd; Chrldng Sqd; Drl Tm Dance Classes.

KRETZ, NICOLE M; Kaiser HS; Honolulu, HI; (4); 43/289; Church Yth Grp; Cmnty Wkr; Intnl Clb; Hon Roll; Prfct Atten Awd; 1st Rnnr Up FHA Yth Fair 86-87; U Of HI Manoa; Educ.

KU, KEVIN H; Hawaii Baptist Acad; Waipahu, HI; (2); Math Tm; Band; High Hon Roll; Hon Roll; Semi Fnlst Yng Kybrd Artist Assn Intl Piano Cmptn 89; Tlnt Pool Cmptn 90; Yellow Blt Taekwondo; Aerontcl Engrng.

KU, MIN KYUNG; Kaiser HS; Honolulu, HI; (3); 28/325; Pres Key Clb; Science Clb; Speech Tm; Flag Corp; Mrchg Band; Hon Roll; Bowling Captain; College.

KUAHIWINUI, MERVIN; Hilo HS; Hilo, HI; (3); JA; Ftbl.

KUEHL, DIANE E; Mililani HS; Mililani, HI; (3); 200/490; Church Yth Grp; Service Clb; Teachers Aide; Chorus; Church Choir; School Musical; School Play; Trk; Drug Free Clb; Show Choir.

KUHLMANN, DAWN L; Waipahu HS; Ewa Beach, HI; (2); Library Aide; Office Aide; Pep Clb; Variety Show; Vllybl; Acctng.

KUIKEN, SANDRA L; Radford HS; Honolulu, HI; (3); 61/400; Church Yth Grp; Chorus; Color Guard; Phtg Yrbk; Hon Roll; Marine Bio.

KUMAGAI, JUN; Roosevelt HS; Honolulu, HI; (3); Cmnty Wkr; Socr; Hon Roll; Mech Engr.

KUMANO, BERT S; Mc Kinley HS; Honolulu, HI; (2); Wrstlng; Kendo.

KUMARAN, LAXMI; Waialua HS; Waialua, HI; (3); 15/169; Debate Tm; Treas Drama Clb; French Clb; SADD; School Play; Stage Crew; JV Crs Cntry; JV Var Socr; Var Swmmng; Intrml Vllybl; Commnctns.

KUNISHIGE, ALISON H; H P Baldwin HS; Wailuku, HI; (1); 39/466; Church Yth Grp; Band; Hon Roll; Zoology.

KUO, JACQUELINE M; Kaiser HS; Honolulu, HI; (3); 1/300; Church Yth Grp; Cmnty Wkr; Girl Scts; Key Clb; Math Tm; Quiz Bowl; Chorus; Ed Nwsp; High Hon Roll; NHS; Girl Scout Silver Awd; Outstndng Achvt In Engl 89-90; NSF Young Schlrs Pgm 89; SPEBE Biochem 90; Notre Dame; Sci.

KURAOKA, JAN C; Mililani HS; Mililani, HI; (4); 98/411; Key Clb; Band; Co-Capt Flag Corp; Stat Bsbl.

KURATA, JOEY F; Kalaheo HS; Kailua, HI; (3); English Clb; French Clb; FTA; Teachers Aide; Bsktbl; Cit Awd; Hon Roll; U HI; Ed.

KURODA, SHINO; Mc Kinley HS; Honolulu, HI; (3); Church Yth Grp; Band; Church Choir; Jazz Band; Orch; Var Socr; Congress-Bundestag Yth Exch Prgm Semi Fnlst; Speech Thrpy.

KUSHI, NYSSA C; Waiakea HS; Hilo, HI; (2); 14/497; Church Yth Grp; Sec 4-H; Latin Clb; Science Clb; Service Clb; Band; Mrchg Band; Variety Show; JV L Crs Cntry; 4-H Awd; Natl 4-H Cngrss Wnnr.

KUWASAKI, CHRISTIAN M; Saint Louis School HS; Mililani, HI; (3); 3/150; Math Clb; Math Tm; Science Clb; Ed Nwsp; Sec Sr Cls; Bausch & Lomb Sci Awd; High Hon Roll; NHS; Ntl Merit Ltr; NEDT Awd; Engrng.

KWAN, GEORGINA; Mc Kinley HS; Honolulu, HI; (2); 49/590; Stu Cncl; Var Crs Cntry; Var Trk; Northwestern; Law Enfrcmnt.

KWAN, KENT W H; Mc Kinley HS; Honolulu, HI; (2); Rifle Tm; Radio Clb; Elects.

KWOK, EVON; Kaimuki HS; Honolulu, HI; (2); 10/325; French Clb; Teachers Aide; Tennis; Hon Roll; NHS; Hiking Clb; Optometry.

KWOK, STEVE; Kaimuki HS; Honolulu, HI; (3); 7/361; Quiz Bowl; Hon Roll; VP NHS; Electrncs Clb; Arch.

KWOK, TERESA; St Francis HS; Aiea, HI; (3); Aud/Vis; Hosp Aide; Pep Clb; Band; Color Guard; Flag Corp; Mrchg Band; Hon Roll; Natl Span Exam 3 Yrs I III; U Of HI Manoa.

KWOK TAK HING, SHERRY J; Maui HS; Pukalani, HI; (1); 1/451; Band; Mrchg Band; JV Trk; High Hon Roll; Hon Roll; Stu Styng Straight; Stanford U; Bus.

LA, PHU C; Aiea HS; Aiea, HI; (3); 30/350; Church Yth Grp; Var Socr; Wt Lftg; Hon Roll; Commnctn Arts Fest Fnlst.

LA FORTEZA JR, VICTOR M; Farrington HS; Honolulu, HI; (2); Drama Clb; Off Soph Cls; Bsktbl; Drftg.

LAANUI, MAILE C; Kamehameha Secondary Schl; Lahaina, HI; (3); Church Yth Grp; Dance Clb; Rep SADD; Acpl Chr; Band; Church Choir; Pep Band; Variety Show; Mgr(s); Var Trk; Hawaiiana Clb; U Of Hilo; Hawaiian Lang.

LACADEN, SHEREEN L; Kapaa HS & Intermed; Kapaa, HI; (4); 4/193; Cmnty Wkr; Key Clb; Library Aide; Yrbk; High Hon Roll; Hon Roll; Jr NHS; NHS; Aud/Vis; Cannons Bus Coll; Bus Adm.

LACARA, ALICE; Waipahu HS; Waipahu, HI; (4); 12/418; Church Yth Grp; SADD; Sec Stu Cncl; High Hon Roll; Hon Roll; Summa Cum Laude Grad; Hospitality Cmmtte; U HI Manoa; Nutrition.

LACARA, ANNABEL S; Waipahu HS; Waipahu, HI; (1); 11/513; FHA; Band; Mrchg Band; Pep Band; Off Frsh Cls; Hon Roll; Stu Mkng Indvdl Life Easier; Bib Brthrs & Big Sistrs.

LACKEY, RACHEL Y; Radford HS; Honolulu, HI; (3); ROTC; Crs Cntry; Bus.

LACTAOEN, EDDIE I; Waipahu HS; Waipahu, HI; (1); High Hon Roll; Interact Club 89-90; U Of HI Manoa; Electrnc Tech.

LACTAOEN, ELENA I; Waipahu HS; Waipahu, HI; (2); 6/440; High Hon Roll; Hon Roll; Interact Clb 89-90; SOAR Bk Clb 89-90; Stu Hlpr Pearl Cty Rgnl Pblc Lbry; U Of HI Manoa; Teach.

LADAO, CHERYL M; Mililani HS; Mililani, HI; (3); 12/490; 4-H; French Clb; Model UN; Service Clb; SADD; Teachers Aide; School Play; Stage Crew; Rep Sr Cls; Rep Jr Cls; U HI Manoa; Accntng.

LADD, SHANNON; Kamehameha Schls; Honolulu, HI; (4); Debate Tm; Treas Frsh Cls; VP Soph Cls; Pres Jr Cls; Pres Sr Cls; Cheerldng; Cls Ldrshp Awds; CO ST U; Bus.

LAFERRIERE, TRACY E; Waipahu HS; Waipahu, HI; (1); 5/530; Church Yth Grp; Var JV Trk; High Hon Roll; Prfct Atten Awd; Interact Clb; U Of HI; Med.

LAGAT, JOANALYN C; Henry Perrine Baldwin HS; Kihei, HI; (1); 20/466; Art Clb; Service Clb; Spanish Clb; High Hon Roll; Hon Roll; HI Schl Sci & Engnrng Fairs; Keywanettes Clb; SSS; Accntnt.

LAGPACAN, ANITES R; Waialua High & Inter Schl; Waialua, HI; (3); 14/165; Intnl Clb; Treas Spanish Clb; SADD; High Hon Roll; Hon Roll; JETS Awd; Prfct Atten Awd; Bayanihan Clb; Drug Busters Clb; Cannons Bus Coll; Acctnt.

LAGUD, JO-ANN; Waialua HS; Haleiwa, HI; (3); 17/165; Debate Tm; Pres Speech Tm; Church Choir; Rptr Nwsp; Sec Soph Cls; VP Sr Cls; Hon Roll; Prfct Atten Awd; Upward Bound; Drug Busters-Pres; Comm.

LAHIP, EDGAR D; Waipahu HS; Waipahu, HI; (3); JV Bsktbl; Hon Roll; U Of HI Manoa; Engr.

LAI, CREIGHTON K; St Louis Schl; Honolulu, HI; (2); Band; Mrchg Band; Hon Roll; Elec Engr.

LAI, JANICE S; Mililani HS; Mililani, HI; (3); 11/576; English Clb; Math Clb; Service Clb; Thesps; School Musical; School Play; Lit Mag; Rep Soph Cls; Rep Sr Cls; Rep Stu Cncl; Gopher Clb Pres; Pre-Med.

LAI, JENNY H; Mc Kinley HS; Honolulu, HI; (2); 13/588; Math Clb; Hon Roll; Jr NHS; Prfct Atten Awd; Piano,Aikido,Keywantettes Clb.

LAI, RONA; Kamehameha HS; Pearl City, HI; (3); 15/440; Drama Clb; JA; Math Clb; Mu Alpha Theta; SADD; Orch; High Hon Roll; Hon Roll; NHS; Physics Olympiad 3rd Pl; Law.

LAM, AMY; Hawaiian Mission Acad; Honolulu, HI; (2); Art Clb; Band; Chorus; Church Choir; School Musical; School Play; Yrbk; Bsktbl; Socr; Vllybl; Lang Translator.

LAM, GORDEN; Mc Kinley HS; Honolulu, HI; (3); Jazz Band; Tennis; Wrstlng; Hon Roll; Sft Tnns; Judo; Bowlng; Japanese Clb; U Of HI; Arch.

LAM, LISA S S; Saint Francis HS; Honolulu, HI; (2); 14/80; Aud/Vis; Library Aide; Math Tm; Pep Clb; Color Guard; Lit Mag; Hon Roll; Math Ed.

LAM, QUANG; Roosevelt HS; Honolulu, HI; (2); Cmnty Wkr; Model UN; ROTC; Crs Cntry; Trk; Outstndng Cmnty Svc; Amercnsm Essay Cont 2nd Pl; Star & Stripes Forever Awd.

LAM, THANH T; Roosevelt HS; Honolulu, HI; (4); 10/335; French Clb; Intnl Clb; Key Clb; Library Aide; Math Clb; Math Tm; Quiz Bowl; Service Clb; SADD; Crs Cntry; U HI Manoa; Elect Engr.

LAM, YUCONG; Mc Kinley HS; Honolulu, HI; (2); 7/588; Math Clb; Math Tm; High Hon Roll; Schl & HI St Sci Fair; Math Bowl; Eng.

LANCASTER, PAMLYN; Hilo HS; Hilo, HI; (3); 43/343; Church Yth Grp; FHA; Rep Sr Cls; Var Bsktbl; Var Vllybl; All Trny 1st Tm Grls Bsktbl 89-90; 1st Tm Selctn Grls Vlybl 89-90; 2nd Tm Big Island Interschlstc Lgu.

LANDRY, STEVEN M; Kaiser HS; Honolulu, HI; (3); 11/325; Service Clb; VP Stu Cncl; Var Capt Crs Cntry; Var Socr; Var Trk; High Hon Roll; Hon Roll; Congressional Schlr.

LARDIZABAL, ARLENE; Hawaii Baptist Acad; Honolulu, HI; (3); JA; Math Clb; Office Aide; Sec Band; Mrchg Band; School Play; Variety Show; Hon Roll; Pres Acad Fit Awd; Jr Marshall; Miss HI Ms TEEN Semi Fnlst; Fashion Dsgn Club; Northrop; Engrng.

LASMARIAS, VLADIMIR VANCE; Roosevelt HS; Tacoma, WA; (2); 2/350; Church Yth Grp; Cmnty Wkr; Hosp Aide; Model UN; Var Crs Cntry; JV Trk; Hon Roll; Alak'i Malama Likrbnp Club; Surgeon.

LATHAM, CHARLISSIA K; Kamehameha HS; Honolulu, HI; (2); 105/443; Dance Clb; SADD; Band; Color Guard; Mrchg Band; JV Trk; JV Canoe Paddling; Howard U; Bus Law.

LAU, ALICE; Pearl City HS; Waipahu, HI; (4); Church Yth Grp; Cmnty Wkr; Sec Service Clb; SADD; Church Choir; Rptr Nwsp; Stat Bsktbl; Cheerldng; Mgr(s); Score Keeper; Peer Ed Program; Mock Trial; Chaminade Pres Scholarship; Natl Honor Roll; Peer Tutor; Chaminade U; Nursing.

LAU, BONNY C P; Pearl City HS; Waipahu, HI; (4); Church Yth Grp; Cmnty Wkr; Service Clb; Church Choir; Rptr Nwsp; Stat Bsktbl; Cheerldng; Mgr(s); Score Keeper; Hon Roll; Peer Ed Program; Mock Trial; Chaminade Presidential Scholarship; Natl Honor Roll; Peer Tutor; Chaminade U; Education.

LAU, BOULDERSON B; Kaimuki HS; Honolulu, HI; (3); 6/360; French Clb; Math Tm; Quiz Bowl; Rep Stu Cncl; Hon Roll; NHS; U Of CA Berkeley; Marine Bio.

LAU, CLEMENT K; Mc Kinley HS; Honolulu, HI; (2); Band; High Hon Roll; Hon Roll; Jr NHS; Prfct Atten Awd; Pres Acad Fit Awd; Bus.

LAU, CYNTHIA K; Maryknoll HS; Honolulu, HI; (2); Cmnty Wkr; Hon Roll; Theology Awd Excllnc; Japanese Cert Of Recognition; UCLA; Pediatrics.

LAU, EDWARD S; Iolani Schl HS; Mililani, HI; (4); 8/219; Intnl Clb; Math Clb; Co-Capt Math Tm; Model UN; High Hon Roll; Ntl Merit SF; Chinese Clb; Cum Laude Scty; ; Engnrng.

LAU, GRACE Y; Roosevelt HS; Honolulu, HI; (2); 10/360; French Clb; Key Clb; Tennis; Hon Roll; NHS; SPEBE Engrng 90; CA Inst Of Tech; Elect Engr.

LAU, JOHN; Damien Memorial HS; Honolulu, HI; (3); 2/110; Math Tm; NFL; Quiz Bowl; ROTC; Speech Tm; Sprt Ed Nwsp; Rep Frsh Cls; JV Var Tennis; Hon Roll; NHS; Damien Acad Excllnc Awd; Cert Achvt Consumer Ec Ed; ROTC Mdl Schlstc Achvt; Creighton U; Bio.

LAU, LORIANNE; Hawaii Baptist Acad; Aiea, HI; (1); GAA; Band; Chorus; Off Soph Cls; Intrml JV Bsktbl; Intrml Sftbl; Hon Roll; Pres Acad Fit Awd; HS Vrsty Bwlng Tm; Japns Club; Srvnt Group; Sprts Med.

LAU, MARGARET K; Maui HS; Haiku, HI; (4); 1/303; Cmnty Wkr; Math Tm; Quiz Bowl; Science Clb; Church Choir; Var Trk; Var Vllybl; High Hon Roll; Hon Roll; Val; Japanese Clb Secy; U Of HI Manoa; Scndry Educ.

LAU, MARK C; Kaiser HS; Honolulu, HI; (3); 12/325; Treas Stu Cncl; Capt Ftbl; Var Trk; Hon Roll; Ntl Merit Ltr; Bus.

LAU, SHIN Y; Mc Kinley HS; Honolulu, HI; (3); Science Clb; Radio & Hiking Clbs.

LAW, KAR YEE S; Moanalua HS; Honolulu, HI; (3); 1/471; Hon Roll; Ethnc Day Comm; U HI Manoa; Bus.

LAYBON, CAMILLE; Hanalani Schls; Waianae, HI; (1); Hon Roll.

LAZARO, EDIESON; Waimea HS; Eleele, HI; (3); Hon Roll; Prfct Atten Awd; Elctrncs Clb; Elctrnc Engrng.

LE, QUI V; W R Farrington HS; Honolulu, HI; (1); Computer Clb; Med.

LE, TAM V; Kaimuki HS; Honolulu, HI; (1); Art Clb; Computer Clb; Math Tm; Ice Hcky; Mechnc.

LE PENDU, PAEA J; St Louis HS; Honolulu, HI; (2); 1/152; Math Clb; Math Tm; ROTC; Intrml JV Vllybl; High Hon Roll; NHS; Prfct Atten Awd; High Scorer Am Math Exam; Japanese Club; Top Cls Math, Sci, Engl, Soc Sci; Pre-Med.

LEANO, JOHN-GLENN; Damien Memorial HS; Waipahu, HI; (4); 8/324; Church Yth Grp; Dance Clb; JA; Math Clb; Math Tm; ROTC; Band; Jazz Band; Mrchg Band; Pep Band; Loyola Marymount U; Elec Engrng.

LEDWARD, KYRA K; Pahoa HS; Pahoa, HI; (2); 84/117; Church Yth Grp; Cmnty Wkr; FHA; Library Aide; Office Aide; Quiz Bowl; SADD; Teachers Aide; Band; Church Choir; Pres FHA; 1st Pl Wnnr In Drug Poster Contest; U HI Hilo; Comp Srvc Tech.

LEE, ANNA; St Francis HS; Waipahu, HI; (2); 29/82; Girl Scts; Hosp Aide; Pep Clb; Intrml Bsktbl; Intrml JV Cheerldng; Intrml Trk; Intrml Vllybl; Hon Roll; Prfct Atten Awd; Engrng.

LEE, CHAE M; Waipahu HS; Ewa Beach, HI; (1); 37/513; Wrstlng; Hon Roll; Arch.

LEE, CHIA-PEI S; Kaiser HS; Honolulu, HI; (1); 17/255; Math Tm; Hon Roll.

LEE, CORINNE I; Roosevelt HS; Honolulu, HI; (2); 35/360; Hosp Aide; Sec Key Clb; Flag Corp; Rptr Nwsp; Hon Roll; NHS; Med.

LEE, DAVID; Hilo HS; Hilo, HI; (4); 1/300; Math Tm; Service Clb; Varsity Clb; Pres Frsh Cls; VP Soph Cls; VP Jr Cls; Crs Cntry; Trk; NHS.

LEE, DEXTER; Mc Kinley HS; Honolulu, HI; (1); 81/492; U Of HI; Bus.

LEE, DORA Y; Sacred Hearts Acad; Honolulu, HI; (4); 19/110; French Clb; Red Cross Aide; Teachers Aide; Hon Roll; NHS; Prfct Atten Awd; Computer Clb; Math Tm; Quiz Bowl; Senior Homeroom Finance; Service Award; Science Fair Award; U Of Hawaii; Business Admin.

LEE, EDMUND; Konawaena HS & Intermed; Kailua-Kona, HI; (4); 28/291; Math Tm; ROTC; Mrchg Band; Hon Roll; Bowling; Embry-Riddle Aeronautical U.

LEE, FIONA; Mid-Pacific Inst; Honolulu, HI; (3); Intnl Clb; JA; Chorus; School Musical; Piano; HI U; Accntng.

LEE, HIEP H; Kaimuki HS; Honolulu, HI; (3); 15/361; JV Trk; Phy.

LEE, JAMES Y; Mid-Pacific Inst; Aiea, HI; (3); Church Yth Grp; Cmnty Wkr; Math Tm; JV Ftbl; High Hon Roll; Hon Roll; Jr NHS; Pres Acad Fit Awd; Mid-Pacific Schlr; Engrng.

LEE, JANICE S; Mc Kinley HS; Honolulu, HI; (2); 14/588; Church Yth Grp; Cmnty Wkr; Hosp Aide; Spanish Clb; Off Soph Cls; High Hon Roll; Hon Roll; Hikng Clb; Litry Magazne Cmmttee; Schl Svc Awd; Fsci.

LEE, JEANNIE W; Maryknoll HS; Honolulu, HI; (4); 15/125; Cmnty Wkr; Q&S; Ed Yrbk; Sec Soph Cls; Off Jr Cls; VP Stu Cncl; Stat Bsktbl; High Hon Roll; NHS; Peer Cnslng Team; U Of HI-MANOA-PSYCH.

LEE, JENNY JING YI; Mc Kinley HS; Honolulu, HI; (4); 30/547; Math Clb; Service Clb; High Hon Roll; Hon Roll; Outstndng Sci Stu Awd; Summa Cum Laude Hnr Grad & Hnr Mc Kinley Grad; Chinese Club Secy; UH Manoa; Teacher.

LEE, JONATHAN K; Roosevelt HS; Honolulu, HI; (1); Math.

LEE, JULITINA; Mc Kinley HS; Honolulu, HI; (2); Var Tennis; Hon Roll; Prfct Atten Awd; Pres Acad Fit Awd; Ped.

LEE, JUSTIN K; Mid-Pacific Inst; Aiea, HI; (2); Science Clb; Band; Hon Roll; NHS; Pres Schlr; Carnegie-Mellon U; Strctrl Engr.

LEE, KACIE K; Mc Kinley HS; Honolulu, HI; (2); 35/588; School Play; Var Tennis; Tennis Gldn Tiger Athlt.

LEE, KWOK YING; Mc Kinley HS; Honolulu, HI; (2); 25/588; Lit Mag; JV Crs Cntry; JV Trk; Hon Roll; Mandarin Clb; Chnese Yths-HI; Engrng.

LEE, LAURA F; President Theodore Roosevelt HS; Honolulu, HI; (4); 1/318; Cmnty Wkr; Sec French Clb; Hosp Aide; JA; Math Clb; Quiz Bowl; High Hon Roll; Jr NHS; NHS; U Of HI Stu Sci Training Pgm; U Of CA Berkeley.

LEE, MARCIA Y; Mckinley HS; Honolulu, HI; (2); 45/588; Quiz Bowl; Spanish Clb; Rep Frsh Cls; Sec Soph Cls; NHS; All Amer Schlr; U HI Manoa; Psych.

LEE, MATTHEW D; Punahou Schl; Honolulu, HI; (4); Church Yth Grp; Cmnty Wkr; Chorus; Variety Show; Intrml Var Bsktbl; Intrml Vllybl; Hon Roll; Jr NHS; NHS; Vstng Eldrly; Wrkng With Blind Stu & Adlts; Aiding Hmlss; Pacific Luth U.

LEE, MEREDITH J; St Andrews Priory HS; Honolulu, HI; (4); 2/50; Aud/Vis; Pres Intnl Clb; Math Tm; Spanish Clb; Stage Crew; Rep Stu Cncl; Hon Roll; NHS; Ntl Merit Ltr; Pres Acad Fit Awd; Varsity Canoe Paddling; Scripps Coll; Biology Genetics.

LEE, MICHAEL; Pearl City HS; Pearl City, HI; (3); 30/527; Pres Aud/Vis; Church Yth Grp; Computer Clb; Debate Tm; Sec Math Tm; Service Clb; Speech Tm; Off Soph Cls; Off Jr Cls; JETS Awd; Corp Lawyer.

LEE, MINA; Mc Kinley HS; Honolulu, HI; (3); Rep Frsh Cls; Tennis; Soft Tennis; Chinese Club; Japanese Club; U Of HI.

LEE, MYNDA L; Nanakuni HS; Waianae, HI; (3); 28/146; Flag Corp; Hon Roll; Prfct Atten Awd; U HI; Nrse.

LEE, RONNIE W; Kaimuki HS; Honolulu, HI; (2); Math Tm; High Hon Roll; NHS; Calligraphy Classes Chinese; YMCA Clb; Soccer & Ping-Pong; U HI; Physcn.

LEE, SE HYUNG; Mc Kinley HS; Honolulu, HI; (2); 14/588; Church Yth Grp; Hosp Aide; Spanish Clb; Lit Mag; Off Soph Cls; High Hon Roll; Hiking Clb; Svc Awd; Envrnmntl Sci.

LEE, SUNG HWAN; Kaimuki HS; Honolulu, HI; (2); Chess Clb; Drawing; Painting; Classical Guitar; Art.

LEE, TRIMEAKA; Kaleheo HS; Kailua, HI; (1); Cheerldng; Gym; Wt Lftg; Hon Roll; Hal Jackson Tlntd Teens HI Pageant; Psych.

LEE, VARDEN L; Mc Kinley HS; Honolulu, HI; (2); 204/588; JV Bsktbl; Dentist.

LEE, VICTOR; Mc Kinley HS; Honolulu, HI; (3); Band; Yrbk; JV Bsktbl; Var Vllybl; Hon Roll; Japanese Clb.

LEE, YUK WAH; President William Mc Kinley HS; Honolulu, HI; (2); 32/588; Math Clb; Math Tm; Var Tennis; Hon Roll; Prfct Atten Awd; Civil Engr.

LEE SOON, PEPPER T; Moanalua HS; Honolulu, HI; (3); 49/462; Mrchg Band; Orch; School Musical; Rep Jr Cls; Rep Stu Cncl; Vllybl; Hon Roll; CO ST; Ed.

LEIALOHA, STACY; Pahoa HS; Pahoa, HI; (2); 4/123; FFA; JV Bsktbl; Hon Roll; U Of HI Hilo; Marine Bio.

LEIGHNOR, DEREK S; Kamehameha HS; Pearl City, HI; (4); Church Yth Grp; ROTC; Teachers Aide; Acpl Chr; Chorus; Rep Stu Cncl; Leeward Vicariate Rep Diocsn Yth Cncl; Hawaiian Club; U San Francisco; Bus.

LEITE, HEATHER; Waiakea HS; Mount View, HI; (1); 45/493; Rep Stu Cncl; Var Crs Cntry; Var Trk; Hon Roll; Mock Trl; Intrct Clb; Chrstms Ply; YWCA Vlntr Asst Swmmng Instr.

LELEIWI, KAREN L; The Kamehameha Schls; Kailua, HI; (1); 26/450; Church Yth Grp; Intrml Trk; Hon Roll.

LEN, WANDA; Kaiser HS; Honolulu, HI; (3); Rep Jr Cls; Var Bsktbl; Ftbl; Var Sftbl; Hon Roll; Polynesian Dancer; Ntl/St Piano Playrs Auditions; Law.

LENE, SIANA F; Hawaiian Mission Acad; Kailua, HI; (3); Church Yth Grp; Church Choir; Off Frsh Cls; Treas Soph Cls; Bsktbl; Ftbl; Vllybl; Hon Roll; Fml Athlt 89-90.

LENGKEEK, JEFF D; Mililani HS; Mililani, HI; (3); 116/490; Intrml Lcrss; Var Vllybl; U Of HI Manoa; Arch.

LEONARDO, AILEEN J; James Campbell HS; Ewa Beach, HI; (2); 18/348; Color Guard; Mrchg Band; Hon Roll; NHS; Hnrbl Mntn Dist Sci Fair; 2nd Pl Dist Sci Fair; Scl Stds May Fest Booth Cmmtte Chrprsn; Mock Trial; Law.

LEONG, AI-LIN; Mc Kinley HS; Honolulu, HI; (3); #12 In Class; Church Yth Grp; Church Choir; Yrbk; Hon Roll; Comp Sci.

LEONG, GAY; Mc Kinley HS; Honolulu, HI; (2); 10/588; Math Clb; Math Tm; Orch; Tennis; Hon Roll; NHS; Prfct Atten Awd; Bus Clb.

LESIAK, VIVIEN; Mililani HS; Mililani, HI; (4); 28/408; Drama Clb; Spanish Clb; Thesps; Color Guard; School Musical; School Play; Vllybl; High Hon Roll; Hon Roll; Pres Acad Fit Awd; Drama Tuition Schlrshp To U Of HI; U Of HI; Drama.

LEUNG, STEVEN C C; Mc Kinley HS; Honolulu, HI; (2); 1/588; Chess Clb; Science Clb; Pres Nwsp; JV L Crs Cntry; JV L Trk; Hon Roll; Sci Fr; Clbs Chem, Physics, Mandarin; Vlntr; HI-SSTP At Hilo 90; Aerospace Engrng.

LEUNG, WILLIAM C; Farrington HS; Honolulu, HI; (4); 6/560; Math Clb; Math Tm; Ed Nwsp; Yrbk; Lit Mag; Var Bsbl; Var Crs Cntry; High Hon Roll; Hon Roll; Art; Marie Walsh Sharpe Art Schlrshp; Occidental Coll; Cmptr Engrng.

LEUNG, WING SZE; Mc Kinley HS; Honolulu, HI; (4); 11/525; Chess Clb; Treas Math Clb; Co-Capt Math Tm; Swmmng; Tennis; High Hon Roll; Guidance Cmmttee Co Chrprsn; U Of HI; Mech Engr.

LEUNG, YEE-MAN JANET; Mc Kinley HS; Honolulu, HI; (1); Hosp Aide; Orch; Hon Roll; Prfct Atten Awd; U HI; Nurse.

LEYDELMEYER, JULIE K; Konawaena HS; Kailua Kona, HI; (3); 32/294; Girl Scts; Math Tm; Pep Clb; Stage Crew; Variety Show; Off Frsh Cls; Off Stu Cncl; Stat Bsktbl; Score Keeper; Var Tennis; Hugh O Brian Youth Foundation Ambassador; Summer Program For Enrichment Of Basic Education; Business Admin.

LI, MARIE ANN L; Mc Kinley HS; Honolulu, HI; (1); 13/492; Math Clb; Hon Roll.

LI, RI LIAN; Mc Kinley HS; Honolulu, HI; (2); Math Clb; Hon Roll; Drwng; Ply Tnns; U HI.

LI, YAOQI; Mc Kinley HS; Honolulu, HI; (3); French Clb; Science Clb; Crs Cntry; Socr; Trk; Wrstlng; U Of HI; Physics.

LI, ZE JI; Mc Kinley HS; Honolulu, HI; (2); Math Clb; Hon Roll; Prfct Atten Awd; Physics & Chem Clubs; Electrnc Engrng.

LIANA, SHELAINE; Redemption Acad; Waianae, HI; (4); 1/7; Pres Church Yth Grp; Office Aide; Teachers Aide; Church Choir; Ed Yrbk; VP Jr Cls; Pres Sr Cls; Pres Stu Cncl; Var Capt Bsktbl; Var Capt Vllybl; U Denver; Sec Educ.

LIANG, CHUN-CHAN; Mc Kinley HS; Honolulu, HI; (3); ROTC; JV Crs Cntry; JV Trk; U Of HI; Mrsng.

LIANG, MAN DI; Mc Kinley HS; Honolulu, HI; (1); Engrng.

LIBED, AARON K; H P Baldwin HS; Wailuku, HI; (2); Debate Tm; Key Clb; Letterman Clb; Band; Jazz Band; Mrchg Band; Pep Band; Var Socr; Var Tennis; Var Trk; Dist Hnr Band; Mst Outstndng Frosh Band; JV Trck Chmpn; Mst Outstndng Frosh Sccr; Bus.

LICKEY, KRISTINA E; Waialua HS; Waialua, HI; (3); 23/157; Sec Drama Clb; French Clb; School Play; Crs Cntry; Socr; Trk; Hon Roll; Waialua Drig Bustr; Var Jduo; Engrng.

LICOAN, RAE LYNN; Waiakea HS; Hilo, HI; (3); 35/368; Church Yth Grp; Band.

LILO, MERVYN W; Leilehua HS; Wahiawa, HI; (1); Boy Scts; Church Yth Grp; Cmnty Wkr; Var Bsktbl; Var Ftbl; Intrml Vllybl; Var Wt Lftg; High Hon Roll; Hon Roll; Phys Ed Awd; BYU; Lang Arts.

LIM, BRIAN R; Hawaii Baptist Acad; Kailua, HI; (2); 13/100; Church Yth Grp; Pres Band; Sec Chorus; Church Choir; Variety Show; VP Soph Cls; Cit Awd; High Hon Roll; Hon Roll; NHS; W O Intrntl Fllwshp; Focus China; Luke Schlr; Outstndng Engl Stu; Phys Educ Awd; Med Missionary.

LIM, RUDY P; Mc Kinley HS; Honolulu, HI; (2); Bus Comp.

LIMOZ, GINA M; Waianae HS; Waianae, HI; (2); 64/449; Cmnty Wkr; Girl Scts; JA; Teachers Aide; JV Trk; JV Vllybl; High Hon Roll; Hon Roll; Prfct Atten Awd; Pres Acad Fit Awd; Certfd Stu Mediator; Flight Attendnt.

LIN, AN MEI; Mc Kinley HS; Honolulu, HI; (2); 63/588; Church Yth Grp; Hon Roll; Prfct Atten Awd.

LIN, ANMEI; Mc Kinley HS; Honolulu, HI; (2); 63/588; Church Yth Grp; Hon Roll; Prfct Atten Awd.

LIN, JASON C C; J B Castle HS; Kaneohe, HI; (4); 1/375; French Clb; Key Clb; Math Clb; Math Tm; Quiz Bowl; Hon Roll; NHS; Val; Honolulu Advertiser All-State Scholar; Scholastic Award; Annual H S Mathematics Exam Award; Cornell U; Electrical.

LIN, LILLIAN H; Mc Kinny HS; Honolulu, HI; (2); 120/544; Yrbk; Tennis; Cit Awd; Hon Roll; UCLA.

LIN, VIVYAN H; Mc Kinney HS; Tamuning, GU; (3); 9/544; Art Clb; Math Clb; Math Tm; Yrbk; Tennis; Cit Awd; Gov Hon Prg Awd; Hon Roll; NHS; UCLA.

LINDO, ROBILYNN A K; Molokai High & Intermed; Kaunakakai, HI; (3); 19/94; Church Yth Grp; Cmnty Wkr; Dance Clb; JA; Band; Mrchg Band; Pep Band; School Musical; Rep Frsh Cls; VP Soph Cls; HI Sr Career Intern Pgm; WA ST U; Hotel Mgmt.

LINDSAY, JENNIFER M; Honokaa HS; Honokaa, HI; (3); Key Clb; Band; Chorus; High Hon Roll; Hon Roll; Math Achvt Awd 91; Hnrbl Mntn Awd-Dsply Proj-Hybrid Mules Genes; Prncpls List-Hgh Hnrs; U HI Hilo; Vet Sci.

LINEBERG, APRIL M; Miliani HS; Mililani, HI; (1); 27/593; Church Yth Grp; French Clb; School Play; Stage Crew; High Hon Roll.

LITTLE, RACHEL D; Mililani HS; Mililani, HI; (1); 15/600; French Clb; Girl Scts; School Musical; Stage Crew; Hon Roll; Thtre Arts.

LITTLE III, ROBERT B; Radford HS; Franklinton, NC; (2); 219/411; ROTC; UNC.

LIU, KEVIN; Mc Kinley HS; Honolulu, HI; (2); 23/588; Church Yth Grp; ROTC; Science Clb; Color Guard; Lit Mag; Hon Roll; Prfct Atten Awd; Rifle Team; Hnrb Mntn Amer Essay Cont Spon By Ancient & Accepted Scottish Rite Of Freemasonry; Yale; Phy.

LIU, LISA; Star Of The Sea HS; Honolulu, HI; (2); Letterman Clb; Pep Clb; Hon Roll; NHS; Prfct Atten Awd; Acad Ltr & Best Engl II Stu; Best & Outstndng Bio Stu; Excllnc In Acad & Perfct Attndnc; Natl Hnr Scty; Accntng.

LIU, YU PING; Mc Kinley HS; Honolulu, HI; (3); Orch; Var Tennis; U HI; Bus.

LIU, YUHONG; Mc Kinley HS; Honolulu, HI; (1); Orch; Hon Roll.

LIVINGSTON, BONNIE MALIA; St Francis HS; Honolulu, HI; (3); 11/63; Church Yth Grp; Mu Alpha Theta; Q&S; Yrbk; Lit Mag; Pres Jr Cls; JV Vllybl; Hon Roll; NHS; NEDT Awd; Honolulu Diocesan Yth Cncl Co Chm & E Honolulu Yth Rep; People To People Frndshp Crvan Ambssdr; Fransiscan U; Politics Bus.

LLENOS, HEATHER M; Maonalua HS; Mililani, HI; (2); Math Tm; Rptr Nwsp; Ed Yrbk; Rep Soph Cls; Rep Stu Cncl; Psych.

LLOYD, MICHAEL S; Radford HS; Honolulu, HI; (3); German Clb; Red Cross Aide; Band; Orch; Bsktbl; Cit Awd; High Hon Roll; Hon Roll; Jr NHS; Opt Clb Awd; Scuba Dvng; Elec Guitar Frnch Horn; Vlybl; Srgn.

LOESCHER, RICHARD; Kalaheo HS; Landrum, SC; (3); 100/250; JV Wt Lftg; Hon Roll; Frstry.

LOHR, JASON L; Hawaiian Mission Acad; Ewa Beach, HI; (2); 1/43; Chorus; VP Soph Cls; VP Stu Cncl; High Hon Roll; Hon Roll; Prfct Atten Awd; Engr.

LOLOTAI, CHENTELLE S; Kaimuki HS; Honolulu, HI; (3); Church Yth Grp; JA; Band; Mrchg Band; Variety Show; Intrml Cheerldng; JV Var Vllybl; Schlrshp Awd Cannons Bus Coll; Hula Dance Asst Instr; U Of HI; Bus Admin.

LONG, FENG LING; Mc Kinley HS; Honolulu, HI; (2); 51/588; Quiz Bowl; NHS; Prfct Atten Awd; Cert HI Career & Coll Fair; Cert Queens Med Ctr; U HI; Med.

LOO, KIMBERLY S; St Andrews Priory HS; Kaneohe, HI; (3); Intnl Clb; Band; School Play; Stu Cncl; Hon Roll; Lang Arts Showcase Wnnr.

LOO, RENA H; Honokaa HS; Honokaa, HI; (4); Church Yth Grp; Library Aide; Temple Yth Grp; Band; Church Choir; Nwsp; Stu Cncl; Var Cheerldng; High Hon Roll; Sec NHS; Chrldr 7 Yrs; Brigham Yng U Hawaii; Trvl Mgmt.

LOO, SANDRA A; Sacred Hearts Acad; Honolulu, HI; (3); Computer Clb; Drama Clb; Math Clb; NFL; Speech Tm; Stage Crew; Off Frsh Cls; Off Soph Cls; VP Jr Cls; Pres Stu Cncl.

LOOPE, BROOK E; H P Baldwin HS; Makawao, HI; (3); 1/499; Cmnty Wkr; Sec Drama Clb; Teachers Aide; VP Pres Thesps; School Musical; School Play; Stage Crew; Variety Show; Cit Awd; Sec NHS; Plyd Piano Cmpt 5 Natl Guilds.

LOPES, LISA; Nanakuli HS; Waianae, HI; (4); 8/112; Church Yth Grp; Office Aide; High Hon Roll; Hon Roll; Homecoming Attendant; Professional Photo Model.

LOPEZ, MICHELLE C; Maui HS; Pukalani, HI; (4); Church Yth Grp; VP French Clb; FTA; Office Aide; SADD; Teachers Aide; Trk; Hon Roll; Prfct Atten Awd; Mock Trial Team; Music Glee Club; Stus Staying Straight.

LOPEZ, SANDRA; Maui HS; Pukalani, HI; (2); 4/388; Church Yth Grp; Sec French Clb; Var JV Trk; High Hon Roll; Prfct Atten Awd; Stu Styng Strght Tpl S Clb; Frnch I Mst Outstndng Stu Awd 90; MCC; Ed.

LORENZO, JENNIFER L; Mc Kinley HS; Wahiawa, HI; (3); 20/537; French Clb; Band; Var Socr; Hon Roll; Prfct Atten Awd; Hiking Clb Soph VP, JR Uni-Clb Rep; Soccer Athl Awd; Ecology.

LORENZO, JOANN M V; Waimea HS; Eleele, HI; (4); 13/200; Church Yth Grp; Dance Clb; Key Clb; Red Cross Aide; SADD; Varsity Clb; Church Choir; Mgr Nwsp; Sec Sr Cls; High Hon Roll; Outstndng Yth Of Parish; Seattle U.

LORENZO, MELISSA L; Radford HS; Mililani, HI; (2); Cmnty Wkr; ROTC; Drill Tm; Hon Roll; Most Outstndng Soph 1989-90; Soph Bnqt Chrprsn; Pblc Rltns.

LOUIE, LORRAINE; St Andrews Priory HS; Honolulu, HI; (3); Var Swmmng; NHS; Japanese Clb; Hrnbl Mntng Sci Fair.

LOUIS, DARREN K; Kau HS; Pahala, HI; (4); 10/58; Treas FFA; Treas VICA; High Hon Roll; 3rd Pl St Land Apprctn Cont; Various FFA Achvt Awds; Air-Cond Repair.

LOUIS, JACY ANN; Maui HS; Kahului, HI; (2); Teachers Aide.

LOWDER, MARISHA L; Mililani HS; Mililani, HI; (3); 151/490; JA; Band; Mrchg Band; Pep Band; Hon Roll; Bus Admin.

LOYOLA, NICOLE; Konawaena HS; Kailua Kona, HI; (3); 61/294; French Clb; Sec Stu Cncl; JV Capt Bsktbl; Var Mgr(s); Interschl Rltns Cmmtte; 1st Rnnr Up Miss HI Teen USA 91; UH Manoa; Travel Indstry Mgmt.

LU, HAO MIN; Roosevelt HS; Honolulu, HI; (3); 62/350; Yrbk; Prof Photographer.

LU, TRUNG D; Kaimuki HS; Honolulu, HI; (3); Chess Clb; Library Aide; Band; Intrml Bsktbl; Intrml Tennis; Prfct Atten Awd; Table Tennis; Bsnsmn.

LUANGPHINITH, DARA T; President W Mc Kinley HS; Ewa Beach, HI; (1); 54/492; Hosp Aide; Speech Tm; Nwsp; Prfct Atten Awd; U Of HI-MANOA; Med.

LUCAS, LAURA; Saint Joseph HS; Hilo, HI; (2); Church Yth Grp; French Clb; Letterman Clb; Chorus; VP Frsh Cls; Var Bsktbl; Stat Score Keeper; Var Sftbl; Hon Roll; Chaminade U; Elem Schl Tchr.

LUCAS, MAILE M; Kapaa HS; Princeville, HI; (3); Art Clb; French Clb; Girl Scts; Red Cross Aide; SADD; Chorus; Rep Soph Cls; Nwsp; Hon Roll; Kapaa Hnr Soc; Marine Bio.

LUEBKER, JASON C; Lutheran HS; Waipahu, HI; (1); Bsktbl; Crs Cntry; Ftbl; Japanese Clb.

LUFF, CAREY K; Lutheran HS Of Hawaii; Honolulu, HI; (3); Church Yth Grp; Cmnty Wkr; Chorus; Treas Pres Stu Cncl; JV Swmmng; JV Vllybl; Hon Roll; NHS; Pol Sci.

LUIS, ROSIELANI; Pahoa HS; Pahoa, HI; (2); JV Bsktbl; Hon Roll; NHS; Upwrd Bnd; Hui Olelo; Cmptr Sci.

LUIZ, CHRISTIE; St Joseph HS; Pepeekeo, HI; (2); Church Yth Grp; Chorus; Treas Frsh Cls; Treas Soph Cls; Hon Roll; Acad Awd; Cls Awd; U Sthrn CA; Nrsng.

LUKA, KEVIN K; Moanalua HS; Honolulu, HI; (3); Var Crs Cntry; Var Trk; HI U.

LUM, AARON K; Roosevelt HS; Honolulu, HI; (3); 38/350; ROTC; Pres Science Clb; Hon Roll.

LUM, CONNIE; St Andrews Priory HS; Aiea, HI; (3); 5/53; Intnl Clb; Latin Clb; Quiz Bowl; Yrbk; High Hon Roll; NHS; Frgn Svc.

LUM, DAVID; Moanalua HS; Honolulu, HI; (3); 66/462; Computer Clb; Japanese Club; U HI; Elec Engrng.

LUM, EZRA L; Hawaii Baptist Acad; Honolulu, HI; (2); Jr NHS; Outstndng Engl Stu Awd; Bible & Bio Awds; U HI; Engrng.

LUM, IDA; Pearl City HS; Pearl City, HI; (2); 16/527; Sec Key Clb; Color Guard; Rep Frsh Cls; Chrmn Soph Cls; Chrmn Jr Cls; Chrmn Stu Cncl; NHS; Med.

LUM, LIBBY D; Moanalua HS; Honolulu, HI; (2); Church Yth Grp; Cmnty Wkr; Hosp Aide; Band; Church Choir; Mrchg Band; Pep Band; Bsktbl; Hon Roll; Chrmn Stu Actvts; Mock Trial Team & Law Clb; Multiculture Clb; Cardiovascular Surgeon.

LUM, MICHELE C; Farrington HS; Honolulu, HI; (2); 75/696; Computer Clb; GAA; JV Var Crs Cntry; High Hon Roll; Hon Roll; Natural Sci.

LUM KEE, KALIKO C; St Louis Schl; Honolulu, HI; (2); 15/190; Church Yth Grp; Intrml JV Ftbl; Community Sponsored Basketball Leagues; College.

LUN, SHERRY V; Mc Kinley HS; Honolulu, HI; (3); 32/537; Treas Art Clb; Spanish Clb; Rptr Yrbk; High Hon Roll; Hon Roll; All Amer Schlr Awd.

LUU, KIM Y; Kaimuki HS; Honolulu, HI; (2); Cmnty Wkr; Dance Clb; Drama Clb; SADD; Chorus; Stage Crew; Mgr(s); Hon Roll; Hiking Clb; U HI; Dentist.

LUU, TRUNG MINH; Roosevelt HS; Honolulu, HI; (4); 1/320; Math Tm; Spanish Clb; Teachers Aide; Var L Crs Cntry; Var Trk; Hon Roll; Val; Solar Car Prjct; Rensselaer Mdl Achvt Math & Sci; CO Schl Of Mines Mdl; CO Schl Of Mines; Chem Engr.

LUULOA, KEITH H; Molokai Schl; Kaunakakai, HI; (2); 27/115; Letterman Clb; Bsbl; Vllybl; Hon Roll; UH Manoa.

LY, TOAN B; Mc Kinley HS; Honolulu, HI; (3); Art Clb; Bus Profs of Am; Drama Clb; Rep French Clb; Key Clb; School Play; Treas Stu Cncl; 4th Bst Shtr Schl Rifle Team; Judo Team; Asst Hndcppd Stu Vlntr; Elec Engr.

MA, LOU SI; Mc Kinley HS; Honolulu, HI; (1); 13/492; Hon Roll; Prfct Atten Awd; Chinese Clb; Sci Fairs; U Of HI; Bus.

MAAS II, CHARLES; Kalaheo HS; Kailua, HI; (4); 8/300; Church Yth Grp; High Hon Roll; Hon Roll; Medicine.

MAC ARTHUR, ALLEN; Kalaheo HS; Kailua, HI; (3); 25/247; Var Socr; Hon Roll; Windward CC; Firefighter.

MAC GREGOR, KALANI A; Mid Pacific Inst; Honolulu, HI; (4); 6/180; Drama Clb; French Clb; Spanish Clb; Treas SADD; Thesps; Chorus; School Musical; School Play; Stage Crew; Swing Chorus; Yth Lgsltr; Bst Frnch III Stu; Repertry Theatr Co; Vassar; Hstry.

MAC MILLAN, LAURA J; Kailua HS; Kailua, HI; (2); 21/301; Treas Spanish Clb; SADD; Crs Cntry; Tennis; Hon Roll.

MACADAEG, RUSSELL; Waianae HS; Waianae, HI; (2); 8/30; Cit Awd; Hon Roll; Prfct Atten Awd; Cannon; Acctg.

MACEY, DENISE D; Radford HS; Honolulu, HI; (3); 13/394; Math Tm; Mu Alpha Theta; High Hon Roll; Hon Roll; NHS.

MADARAZO, MARIBEL; Kalaheo HS; Kailua, HI; (3); 14/247; Hon Roll; Sec Soph Cls; Sec Jr Cls.

MAEDA, SHELLEA E; Waiakea HS; Hilo, HI; (2); 7/497; Science Clb; Variety Show; Rep Soph Cls; Hon Roll; Leo Club; Schltc Achvmt; Dentist.

MAEDA, SHERI M; Maui HS; Pukalani, HI; (3); 28/385; Treas Math Tm; Science Clb; Service Clb; Varsity Clb; Band; Mrchg Band; Swmmng; Tennis; High Hon Roll; NHS.

MAGSIPOC, SUSAN LUCAS; Farrington HS; Honolulu, HI; (3); 2/607; Church Yth Grp; Dance Clb; Drama Clb; Science Clb; Teachers Aide; Church Choir; Sftbl; Hon Roll; Hnr Rl Stu; Travel.

MAHELONA, RYAN K; Kamehameha HS; Kaneohe, HI; (3); 18/419; Church Yth Grp; Cmnty Wkr; Letterman Clb; ROTC; Varsity Clb; Chorus; Intrml JV Ftbl; Intrml JV Trk; Hon Roll; Engrng.

MAHELONA, SHANNON K; Kau HS; Naalehu, HI; (4); 15/58; Treas Rptr FFA; SADD; Chorus; Ed Yrbk; Pres Frsh Cls; Var JV Bsktbl; Capt Socr; Vllybl; Hon Roll; Hilo CC; Admin Of Just.

MAHER, KIMBERLEY J; Mililani HS; Wahiawa, HI; (3); 17/490; Pres Church Yth Grp; Drama Clb; French Clb; School Play; Rptr Nwsp; Rep Stu Cncl; Var Bsktbl; Capt Var Cheerldng; High Hon Roll; NHS; Brigham Young U; Acctng.

MAILEM, LILIBETH I; Maui HS; Kahului, HI; (1); Math Clb; Science Clb; Spanish Clb; Ed Nwsp; Hon Roll; Prfct Atten Awd; Keywannettes Svc Clb; Japanese Clb; ARI Yng Miss Maui HI Pgnt Miss Photgenic 90; MA Inst Of Tech; Archt Engrng.

MAK, KA LAI; Mc Kinley HS; Honolulu, HI; (2); 35/588; Teachers Aide; Tennis; High Hon Roll; Prfct Atten Awd; Bus Club; Good Qrtr Spec Awd; U Of HI; Htl Mgmt.

MAK, MAHEALANI L; Roosevelt HS; Honolulu, HI; (2); 52/362; Cmnty Wkr; JV Bsktbl; Var Vllybl; Hon Roll.

MAKEKAU, DERRICK N; Baldwin HS; Kahului, HI; (1).

MAKI, DAWN L; Kaimuki HS; Honolulu, HI; (2); 54/325; Ski Clb; Swmmng; Hon Roll; Girl Guides Of Canada; Bi-Lingual Frnch/Engl; Vet.

MALACAS, ETHELENE R; Waialua HS; Waialua, HI; (3); 5/157; Intnl Clb; Sec Spanish Clb; High Hon Roll; Hon Roll; Prfct Atten Awd; Drgbstr Clb; Intrct Clb; Spnsh I II Awds; Sci Fair Awds; Bus.

MALENDRES, CHARLENE; Pahoa HS; Pahoa, HI; (4); 5/104; Church Yth Grp; FHA; Rep Sr Cls; Var Sftbl; Hon Roll; Treas NHS; Upward Bound VP; Coll Opprtnts Pgm; Campus Police Offcr; U Of HI Manoa; Psych.

MALLARI, LEILANI MAC F; Lahainaluna HS; Lahaina, HI; (1); 1/223; Church Yth Grp; Science Clb; VP Frsh Cls; Var Tennis; High Hon Roll.

MALLOY, THERESA; Waimea HS; Kekaha, HI; (2); Church Yth Grp; Socr; Trk; High Hon Roll; UH Hilo; Cnslr.

MALO, ALYSSA; Roosevelt HS; Honolulu, HI; (3); Library Aide; Mdtn Prgm; Hula; Pearl Harbor Civic Clb.

MANDAC, MICHELLE M; Waipahu HS; Waipahu, HI; (1); 22/530; Rep Frsh Cls; Hnr Roll; Floriculture; Clthng Apparel; Bus.

MANDOE, PRANA; Seabury Hall HS; Haiku, HI; (3); Math Clb; NFL; Band; Chorus; Jr NHS; Treas NHS; Pres Acad Fit Awd; Yth Ambssdrs Of Am Pres; Volntr Camp For Handicappd Childrn.

MANEJA, CATHERINE; Hilo HS; Papaikou, HI; (3); VP Computer Clb; French Clb; Sec Math Tm; Sec Treas Science Clb; Rptr Nwsp; Rep Frsh Cls; Rep Soph Cls; High Hon Roll; NHS; VP Finance Serteens; Top Ten In Clss; 1st Pl Lang Fstvl French I.

MANGUBAT JR, FITZGERALD S; Mc Kinley HS; Honolulu, HI; (2); Math Clb; Speech Tm; VP Frsh Cls; Sec Soph Cls; Rep Stu Cncl; Honolulu Dist Stu Cncl Rep; Japanese Clb; Political Action Clb.

MANNER, KEALIIHAUOLI R; The Kamehameha Schls; Nanakuli, HI; (4); 176/406; Church Yth Grp; Office Aide; ROTC; Chorus; Mgr(s); Hon Roll; Natl Yng Ldrs Cnfrnc; U HI Hilo.

MANSFIELD, DAVID E; Mililani HS; Mililani, HI; (3); Chess Clb; Var Capt Bsktbl.

MANUEL, ROGER A; Kohala HS; Kapaau, HI; (1); 1/50; FHA; Math Clb; Math Tm; SADD; Nwsp; Rep Frsh Cls; High Hon Roll; Prfct Atten Awd; Math.

MAPLES, BROOK A; Leilehua HS; Wahiawa, HI; (2); Church Yth Grp; Hosp Aide; Math Tm; Model UN; Rep Soph Cls; JV Capt Cheerldng; Stat Wrstlng; High Hon Roll; Srtns Clb; Cs Up Treas.

MAR, TAMMY A; Waiakea HS; Kurtistown, HI; (3); 105/368; JA; Chorus; Trk; Lion Awd; Bus Mgt.

MARCIEL, KRISTIN K; Maui HS; Pukalani, HI; (3); 8/400; Church Yth Grp; French Clb; Letterman Clb; Math Clb; Science Clb; Church Choir; Var L Trk; High Hon Roll; NHS; Civil Air Patrl, Cadet Awd 89-90; Aerospace Engrng.

MARCIEL, TRICIA; Kalaheo HS; Kailua, HI; (3); 12/240; School Play; Nwsp; Yrbk; Pres Jr Cls; Cheerldng; High Hon Roll; Hon Roll; Rotary Awd; Homcmng Chairperson; Interact Clb; U HI; Dietitian.

MARIANO, JAMES D; Waimea HS; Kekaha, HI; (3); 10/198; Church Yth Grp; Cmnty Wkr; Treas Spanish Clb; Teachers Aide; Rptr Nwsp; Rep Stu Cncl; High Hon Roll; NHS; ST HI Forgn Lang Fstvl; Seattle U; Bus Admin.

MARIANO, JANICE B; Farrington HS; Honolulu, HI; (1); Band; Mrchg Band; Rep Frsh Cls; Hon Roll; Clss Chrprsn; Band Clb; Bnd Librarian; U HI Manoa; Bus Ex.

MARIANO, ZORAH-LEE A; Waipahu HS; Ewa Beach, HI; (4); 37/418; Pres FTA; Math Tm; Teachers Aide; Band; Pep Band; Ed Lit Mag; Rep Frsh Cls; Rep Soph Cls; Rep Sr Cls; Stu Cncl; Teachers Of Tomorrow Schlrshp Pres; 2nd Pl Indus Arts Fr Arch Presentation; U Of HI Manoa; Arch.

MARKHAM, CHRIS M; Konawaena HS; Captain Cook, HI; (3); 3/294; Church Yth Grp; High Hon Roll; Hon Roll; NHS; Prfct Atten Awd; Pres Acad Fit Awd; Sci Fair.

MARKHAM, JESSE; Waiakea HS; Hilo, HI; (2); 51/497; JA; L Var Socr; Var L Trk; Bsbl Card Enthusiast; NC; Sports Brdcstr.

MARKS, JOSEPH R; Leilehua HS; Wahiawa, HI; (3); 73/322; Boy Scts; Pep Clb; Spanish Clb; Teachers Aide; Band; Jazz Band; Mrchg Band; Pep Band; Rep Frsh Cls; Rep Soph Cls; Military; Computer Programmer.

MARSHALL, ERIC B; Leilehua HS; Wahiawa, HI; (2); Church Yth Grp; ROTC; Color Guard; JV Ftbl; Var Trk; Var Vllybl; High Hon Roll; Prfct Atten Awd; Superior Cadet Medal Amer Legion Schlstc Excllnc Mdl; Rifery 1 St Pl Prone Oia Mdl; Vrsty Rifle Tm.

MARTIN, AMY M; Waiakea HS; Hilo, HI; (2); 55/497; 4-H; Key Clb; Color Guard; Flag Corp; L Swmmng; Hon Roll; Soc Stud Olympiad Awd 89; People To People Stu Ambassador USSR 90; Intl Rel.

MARTIN, DEZLIE A S; Waialua HS & Intermed; Waialua, HI; (2); Rep Frsh Cls; Stat Wrstlng; Prfct Atten Awd; U HI; Law.

MARTIN, JASON L; Waiakea HS; Hilo, HI; (2); JV Socr; UH Manoa; Law.

MARTIN, JENNIFER E; H P Baldwin HS; Paia, HI; (2); 52/470; Cmnty Wkr; Band; Crs Cntry; Hon Roll; Kiwanis Awd; YMCA Youth Legis; AIDS Ed Comm; U Of HI Hilo; Law.

MARTINE, KELLY K; Lanakila Baptist HS; El Paso, TX; (4); 4/18; Hosp Aide; Teachers Aide; Ed Yrbk; Treas Jr Cls; Treas Sr Cls; NHS; Rotary Awd; Eckard Coll; Accounting.

MARTINEZ, JOEWE L; Waialua HS & Intermed; Waialua, HI; (2); JV Ftbl; JV Socr; JV Wrstlng; Hon Roll.

MARTINEZ, VERONICA; Hawaiian Mission Acad; Honolulu, HI; (3); Pres Church Yth Grp; Bsktbl; Vllybl; Hon Roll; Engl Awd; Mission Trip To Mrshll Islands.

MARZO, KEHAULANI D; Waiakea HS; Keaau, HI; (2); 124/497; FHA; JA; Key Clb; SADD; School Play; Variety Show; Rep Frsh Cls; Off Soph Cls; Rep Stu Cncl; JV Bsktbl; Serteens VP Pgms; UCLA; Med.

MASAKI, MICHAEL M; Mid-Pacific Inst; Honolulu, HI; (1); Boy Scts; Church Yth Grp; Band; Sec Soph Cls; Hon Roll; Engrng.

MASATSUGU, KRISTIE; Mililani HS; Mililani, HI; (3); 10/490; Church Yth Grp; Key Clb; SADD; Church Choir; Var Socr; JV Var Trk; St Sccr Champs 88; U H Mahow.

MASHIBA, COLLEEN; Hilo HS; Hilo, HI; (3); 30/343; French Clb; SADD; Rep Soph Cls; Rep Jr Cls; Rep Stu Cncl; Stat Bsbl; High Hon Roll; Hon Roll; Hmcmng Rally Chrpsn; Annual St HI Lang Festvl; Cert Frgn Lang Frnch.

MASON, DAMIEN E; Henry Perrine Baldwin HS; Kihei, HI; (2); Drama Clb; Band; School Play; Stage Crew; Variety Show; Var L Socr; JV Vllybl; Wt Lftg; High Hon Roll; Japanese Club.

MASTELLER, KENDRA; Leilehua HS; Santa Ana, CA; (4); Rep Church Yth Grp; Drama Clb; NFL; VP SADD; Church Choir; School Play; Var L Crs Cntry; Var L Trk; Hon Roll; Mock Trial Tm; Wheaton Coll; Premed.

MASUSAKO, SONNIE; Maui HS; Paia, HI; (2); Cmnty Wkr; Pep Clb; Band; Mrchg Band; Orch; Powder Puff Ftbl; Hon Roll; Prfct Atten Awd; Pres Acad Fit Awd; Keywanett Club; Sci.

MATAUTIA, ROY; Roosevelt HS; Honolulu, HI; (2); Church Yth Grp.

MATEO, ESTRELLITA T; Waialua HS; Wahiawa, HI; (3); 3/165; Church Yth Grp; Spanish Clb; Church Choir; Hon Roll; Prfct Atten Awd; Wo Intl Schlrshp; Japanese Clb; Yth Hlpng Yth; U Of HI; Travl Indstry.

MATSUDA, JANNIE S; President Theodore Roosevelt HS; Waipahu, HI; (2); Pres Key Clb; Treas Frsh Cls; Treas Soph Cls; Rflry Team Capt; U Of HI Manoa; Phys Thrpy.

MATSUDA, KRISI K; Kaiser HS; Honolulu, HI; (3); 19/325; Key Clb; Color Guard; Hon Roll; Ntl Merit Ltr; U Of HI.

MATSUDA, YASUO T; Moanalua HS; Honolulu, HI; (3); Boy Scts; Church Yth Grp; Teachers Aide; School Play; VP Pres Stu Cncl; JV Bsbl; JV Capt Bsktbl; Var Capt Golf; BYU; Psych.

MATSUI, CHERI M; Maui HS; Kahului, HI; (3); 72/354; Pres Key Clb; Letterman Clb; Science Clb; Teachers Aide; Off Yrbk; Stat Bsbl; Hon Roll; Jap Clb; U H Manoa; Socl Wrk.

MATSUI, MAILE T; Maui HS; Kahului, HI; (3); 1/400; Church Yth Grp; Key Clb; Science Clb; Varsity Clb; Sec Jr Cls; Sftbl; Trk; High Hon Roll; NHS; Pres Acad Fit Awd; Arch.

MATSUI, STACY T; Baldwin HS; Wailuku, HI; (3); 28/385; Boy Scts; VP Key Clb; Letterman Clb; SADD; School Play; Var Crs Cntry; Var Capt Swmmng; Var Capt Trk; Wt Lftg; High Hon Roll; HI ST Chmpn Swm Evnts; Jr Olympc Qlfr 50 Frestyl Evnt; St Qlfr 200 Mtr Dsh, 400-1600 Rly; Pre-Med.

MATSUMOTO, CAROLE E; Mililani HS; Mililani, HI; (3); 7/490; Sec VP SADD; Thesps; Band; School Musical; School Play; Co-Ed Lit Mag; Hon Roll; VP NHS; Ntl Merit Ltr; Carpe Diem Soc-Pres; Vlntr Anml Hosp; Ctr For Advncd Of Acadmcly Tltntd Yth; Vet.

MATSUMOTO, GRANT S; Hawaii Baptist Acad; Aiea, HI; (2); VP JA; JV Vllybl; High Hon Roll; Hon Roll; Pres Acad Fit Awd; Intramural Bowling; Botanical Trails Club; Servant Group.

MATSUMOTO, KEVIN E; Mililani HS; Mililani, HI; (2); 6/509; Mu Alpha Theta; High Hon Roll; Hon Roll; U Of HI; Elec Engr.

MATSUMOTO, LISA S; Mary Knoll HS; Honolulu, HI; (4); Spanish Clb; High Hon Roll; Hon Roll; Spansh 4 & Physics Achvt Awds; UH Manoa; Engrng.

MATSUMOTO, VAIL; Mid Pacific Inst; Honolulu, HI; (2); FCA; Library Aide; Nwsp; JV Sftbl; JV Vllybl; Hon Roll; Homcmng Ct; UCLA; Jrnlsm.

MATSUMURA, JANELLA T; Waiakea HS; Hilo, HI; (1); 90/478; JA; Band; Mrchg Band; Pep Band; Rep Stu Cncl; Interact Clb; UH Manoa; Bus.

MATSUSHITA, DAVID; Baldwin HS; Kahului, HI; (2); Key Clb; Band; Jazz Band; Mrchg Band; Var L Tennis.

MATSUYAMA, KRISHEN D; Kauai HS; Lihue, HI; (3); Key Clb; Science Clb; Service Clb; SADD; Off Soph Cls; Sec Jr Cls; Hon Roll; NHS; Voice Dem Awd; Elem Schl Tchr.

MATSUYAMA, RACHAEL S; Roosevelt HS; Honolulu, HI; (3); Pres Science Clb; Hist NHS; U Of HI.

MATTHEWS-LAPIN, JASON D; Lutheran HS Of Hawaii; Kailua, HI; (2); 1/50; Church Yth Grp; FCA; Red Cross Aide; Rptr Nwsp; Pres Jr Cls; JV Wrstlng; High Hon Roll; NHS; NEDT Awd; Wght Lftng; Seminary.

MATTOS JR, ALFRED; St Louis HS; Honolulu, HI; (4); 23/155; Aud/Vis; Chess Clb; Cmnty Wkr; Ed Rptr Nwsp; Rep Frsh Cls; Intrml Ftbl; Wt Lftg; High Hon Roll; Kapiolani CC; Bus Admin.

MATTOS, STACEY K; Kaimuki HS; Honolulu, HI; (2); 31/325; JV Capt Bsktbl; Var Sftbl; Hon Roll; U HI; Home Ec.

MATTSON, AULII A; Kamehameha HS; Honolulu, HI; (4); 108/407; Letterman Clb; Library Aide; Pep Clb; SADD; Teachers Aide; Varsity Clb; Ed Yrbk; Rep Frsh Cls; Rep Soph Cls; Rep Jr Cls; Ablty Cmmnct HI Lang; ILH Al-Str Sftbl, Ltrmn; ILH Al-St Chmpnshp Tm Grls Vrsty Sftbl Tm; U Of HI Manoa; HI Hstry.

MATUAUTO, LEILANI J; Leilehua HS; Wahiawa, HI; (2); 72/392; Church Yth Grp; Band; Mrchg Band; Rptr Nwsp; VP Soph Cls; JV Vllybl; Hon Roll.

MAU, MELVILEE ANN U; Maui HS; Haiku, HI; (2); SSS; Bus.

MAU, TANYA K; Kamehameha Schls; Honolulu, HI; (1); 4/451; SADD; High Hon Roll; Hon Roll.

MAYEHARA, SHAWN H; Roosevelt HS; Honolulu, HI; (1); Capt JV Cheerldng; Hula Dancng, Music, Singn, Tennis & Swmng; HI U; Med.

MAYER, ANGELA; Konawaena HS; Kailua-Kona, HI; (4); 50/296; French Clb; Swmmng; Hon Roll; Arch.

MAZUREK, LORI; Saint Francis-School For Girls; Honolulu, HI; (2); 10/80; Church Yth Grp; Cmnty Wkr; Girl Scts; Hosp Aide; Library Aide; Office Aide; Chorus; Variety Show; Cmmrcl Modeling Clss; Jazz Dancing Clss; Tennis Clss; Swimming Tm; U Of HI; Law.

MC CALLISTER, MELISSA A; Mililani HS; Wahiawa, HI; (3); Rep Stu Cncl; Hon Roll; Photo Clb; Foreign Lang Best Stu Awd; Part Time Job; Poly Sci.

MC CANDLESS, BRANDY N; Kaimuki HS; Quebeck, TN; (2); SADD; Teachers Aide; JV Vllybl.

MC CLAIN, BRANDI; Kalaheo HS; Kailua, HI; (2); VP German Clb; Chorus; Orch; Variety Show; VP Soph Cls; High Hon Roll; Opt Clb Awd; Yuma Commnty Orchestra & String Ambssdrs; CO ST U; Pre-Med.

MC CLELLAND, MEGAN M; St Anthony HS; Kihei, HI; (4); 4/65; Spanish Clb; Teachers Aide; Variety Show; Ed Yrbk; Rep Soph Cls; VP Jr Cls; Bausch & Lomb Sci Awd; Cit Awd; High Hon Roll; Jr NHS; Uc Irvine; Child Psych.

MC COLLUM, DAVID; Kalaheo HS; Kaneohe, HI; (1); 22/266; Hon Roll.

MC CORMICK, ABIGAIL; Pahoa HS; Pahoa, HI; (1); Yrbk; Cit Awd; Hon Roll; Vet.

MC COY, JENNIFER L; Mililani HS; Mililani, HI; (2); 26/512; Intnl Clb; Key Clb; Treas Stu Cncl; JV Var Mgr(s); Hon Roll; Homcmng Cmmtte; Mst Spirited Soph Awd; Bus Admin.

MC DAVITT, ANGELIA M; Radford HS; Ewa Beach, HI; (3); Debate Tm; Drama Clb; Letterman Clb; NFL; Speech Tm; Varsity Clb; Socr; Trk; Hon Roll; Natl Flag Day St Rep; ROTC Dstngshd Cadet Of Yr; Naval Sta Pearl Hrbr Hnry Navy Offcr Day; U Of HI; Law.

MC DONALD, CARRIE A; Pearl City HS; Pearl City, HI; (4); 17/478; Drama Clb; Pep Clb; Speech Tm; SADD; Pres Soph Cls; Rep Stu Cncl; High Hon Roll; Interact Clb; Japanese Clb; Recgntn Cmmtte; U Of HI Manoa; Med.

MC DONALD, JOHN A; Pearl City HS; Pearl City, HI; (2).

MC DOWELL, RICHARD P; Leilehua HS; Waipahu, HI; (3); 72/322; JV Var Ftbl; Var Capt Wrstlng; Mighty Mule Awd Wrstlng; 1st Oia W Wrstlng Var 90; 1st Pl Oia Wrstlng JV 89.

MC FARLAND, JON M; Hawaii Baptist Acad; Kaneohe, HI; (3); VP Drama Clb; Off French Clb; Service Clb; Thesps; School Play; Stage Crew; Rep Soph Cls; Var L Swmmng; Hon Roll; Pres Acad Fit Awd; Pres Aloha Cncl; USSI Swimming; Intl Law.

MC GUE, LINDA; Radford HS; Honolulu, HI; (4); Pres Math Tm; Red Cross Aide; Pres Band; Ed Nwsp; Rep Stu Cncl; Socr; NHS; Hosp Aide; Yng Woman Of Yr Schlrshp Pgm; DODOS Pacific-Rgn Hnr Band; Medcl Explorers VP; Miami U; Med.

MC GUIGAN, MARGARETE N; Mid Pacific Inst; Honolulu, HI; (2); Vllybl; Hon Roll; Canoe Paddling; U Of Santa Clara; Law.

MC GUIRE, KALEO; Hawaiian Mission Acad; Honolulu, HI; (3); 10/45; Off Soph Cls; Fld Hcky; Var Gym; Socr; Vllybl; Cit Awd; Hon Roll; Otdr Clb; Flyng Clb.

MC HENRY, ELIZABETH A; St Andrews Priory HS; Honolulu, HI; (2); Debate Tm; French Clb; Speech Tm; Orch; Rptr Nwsp; JV Swmmng; JV Trk; Hon Roll; Vlntr HI Humane Soc; Save The Earth Clb; Nurse.

MC KAY, KACHINA; Mid-Pacific Inst; Honolulu, HI; (4); Drama Clb; Speech Tm; Teachers Aide; School Musical; School Play; Stage Crew; High Hon Roll; Hon Roll; Pres Schlr; Outstndng Prfrmnc Musicl; Mst Insprtl MPI Drama Co; Stg Mgr Asst Dir Fantastics; Bellevue CC; Drma.

MC LAURIN, CHERYL K; Mililani HS; Wahiawa, HI; (3); 23/490; Pres Church Yth Grp; Drama Clb; Natl Beta Clb; Chorus; Church Choir; School Musical; Nwsp; High Hon Roll; Jr NHS; EASE Essay Cont 2nd Pl; Engl.

MC NEILL, TAKISHA; Kalaheo HS; Yuma, AZ; (2); Church Choir; Hon Roll; Syracuse U; Law.

MC QUAID, JENNIFER; Pahoa HS; Pahoa, HI; (1); 5/135; Teachers Aide; Socr; Gov Hon Prg Awd; High Hon Roll; Hon Roll; Prfct Atten Awd; Art Show Awds; Engl.

MC SHANE, EDIE K; Lanakila Baptist HS; Ewa Beach, HI; (4); Drama Clb; Spanish Clb; School Play; Nwsp; Ed Yrbk; Sec Jr Cls; Sec Sr Cls; Treas Stu Cncl; JV Bsktbl; JV Vllybl; Natl Army Rsrvs Schlr, Athlt Awd; Natl Hnr Awd; Natl Schlr Awd; All Star Sports Awd; U HI Manoa; Arch.

MEDEIROS, KRIS; Hilo HS; Hilo, HI; (3); 10/373; French Clb; Key Clb; Letterman Clb; Varsity Clb; Rep Crs Cntry; Socr; Trk; NHS; Bus.

MEDEIROS, LEHUA; Aiea HS; Aiea, HI; (3); Chrmn Soph Cls; Chrmn Jr Cls; Rep Stu Cncl; Hon Roll; Soph Yr 89; Outstnding Achvt Span I & II, Typng II & Scl Stds; U Of HI; Mgmt.

MEDEIROS, LISA M; Konawaena International HS; Kailua Kona, HI; (1); 64/360; Church Yth Grp; VP Frsh Cls; Var Sftbl; Trk; U HI; Nrsg.

MEDEIROS, RAYMOND K; Kohala HS; Kapaau, HI; (3); 14/64; Boy Scts; FFA; Library Aide; Office Aide; Teachers Aide; Church Choir; Variety Show; Bsbl; Ftbl; Vllybl; Close Up Pgm; Upward Bound 3 Yrs; CPO; Homcmng Attendant; Music Cmmtte; WA ST U; Ag.

MEDEIROS, SHELLY ANN; Konawaeua HS; Captain Cook, HI; (3); 16/294; Church Yth Grp; Service Clb; Spanish Clb; Band; Rep Frsh Cls; Hon Roll; NHS; Hikng Club Sec; Close Up; Holmes Bible Coll; Lbr Arts.

MEDEIROS, TERRILYNN LEILANI; Kamehameha Schl; Kaneohe, HI; (3); 91/430; Church Yth Grp; Math Clb; Math Tm; Mu Alpha Theta; Spanish Clb; Varsity Clb; Var Gym; High Hon Roll; Canoe Paddling; Weight Lifting Persnl Interest; Bus Mgmt.

MEDINA, VICTOR; Hilo HS; Clarksville, TN; (2); JA; Band; Mrchg Band; Pep Band; Jr NHS; Pres Acad Fit Awd; Enrchmnt Sci Pgm; CA Inst Of Tech; Med.

MEDRANO, MICHAEL A; Waialua High & Intermediate HS; Waialua, HI; (2); 5/161; Science Clb; VP Frsh Cls; Rep Soph Cls; Hon Roll; Prfct Atten Awd; Storytllng Awd; Acctng.

MELCHOR, MICHAEL; Farrington HS; Honolulu, HI; (2); Math.

MELLON, JENNIFER; Kailua HS; Kailua, HI; (2); 50/301; Band; Mrchg Band; JV Var Cheerldng.

MELTON, JAIME; Radford HS; Aiea, HI; (3); Cmnty Wkr; DECA; Teachers Aide; Chorus; Var L Bsktbl; JV Trk; JV Var Vllybl; High Hon Roll; Jr NHS; Pres Acad Fit Awd; Acad All-Metro Bsktbl Plyr 89; HOBY Awd 88-89; Worked Spec Olympics; Phys Ed.

MELVIN, RACHEL K; Leilehua HS; Wahiawa, HI; (2); 96/392; Travel/Hotel Indstry.

MENCHAVEZ, JOLIE N; St Francis HS; Aiea, HI; (2); Cmnty Wkr; Crmnl Law.

MENDEZ, CHERYL A; Farrington HS; Honolulu, HI; (2); 112/696; Pres Band; Jazz Band; Mrchg Band; Hon Roll; Hula Bowl Bnd; 2 Blue Rbns & 1 Red Rbn Solo & Ensmbl:Wnd Symphny 3rd Pl Dclmtn Cntst; U HI Manoa; Psych.

MENDEZ, NYDIA E; Leilehua HS; Sacramento, CA; (2); 25/406; Hon Roll; Stdt Cncl; Harvard; Lwyr.

MENDONSA, TANYA; Waiaken HS; Hilo, HI; (3); Church Yth Grp; JA; Pep Clb; Stu Cncl; JV Var Bsktbl; Var Vllybl; Congrssnl Ynt Ldrshp Cncl; Med.

MENDOZA, JEFFERSON B; Waialua HS; Waialua, HI; (2); Science Clb; Band; Jazz Band; Mrchg Band; Pep Band; Rep Frsh Cls; Rep Stu Cncl; JV Bsktbl; Hon Roll; Prfct Atten Awd; Japanese Clb.

MENOR, DARLENE Z; Waialua HS; Waialua, HI; (3); 8/157; Art Clb; Debate Tm; Speech Tm; Ed Nwsp; Rep Frsh Cls; Pres Soph Cls; Rep Jr Cls; Pres Sr Cls; JV Vllybl; Hon Roll; Drugbusters Clb VP & Pres; Coalition For Drug Free HI Yth Advisory Brd; Soph Banquet Chairperson; Commnctns.

MENOR, VIRMA C; Moanalua HS; Honolulu, HI; (2); 27/488; Hosp Aide; Law Club; Interact Clb; UCLA; Pediatrician.

MERCADO, MARVINE D; Kau HS; Pahala, HI; (4); 2/56; VP Letterman Clb; Sec Stu Cncl; Stat Bsktbl; DAR Awd; Gov Hon Prg Awd; Hon Roll; Pres Acad Fit Awd; Sal; Camille Chidiac Ed Awd; Prin Ldrshp Awd; Loyola Marymount U; Bus Admin.

MERCADO, SIERRA M; Maui HS; Makawao, HI; (3); 25/350; Church Yth Grp; Drama Clb; Science Clb; Variety Show; Rep Frsh Cls; Rep Jr Cls; Var Socr; Hon Roll; Aquarium Club Sec; Art & Design Cntst; U Of HI Manoa; Arch.

MESSER, TANYA K; Maui HS; Kula, HI; (2); Key Clb; Band; Hon Roll; Psych.

MEYER, JEFFREY; St Joseph HS; Hilo, HI; (3); Science Clb; Chorus; JV Var Bsktbl; High Hon Roll; NHS; Bio.

MICHAEL, JESSICA; Maryknoll HS; Kaneohe, HI; (2); Church Yth Grp; Cmnty Wkr; Hon Roll; Paddling Tm; Hiking Club; Sr Day Cmmtte; Math.

MIKA, CORIANN E; Radford HS; Honolulu, HI; (2); Church Yth Grp; Letterman Clb; Sec Frsh Cls; Rep Stu Cncl; Var Sftbl; Var Trk; Var Vllybl.

MIKI, ELLEN E; Mc Kinley HS; Honolulu, HI; (2); Orch; Prfct Atten Awd; U HI.

MILBY, KYLE W; Radford HS; Ewa Beach, HI; (3); ROTC; Bsbl; Hon Roll; SUNY Albany; Comp Sci.

MILLER, AWSHI J; Kailua HS; Kailua, HI; (2); 6/301; Hon Roll; Jr NHS; Presdntl Acad Ftnss Awd; Outstndng Acad Achvt; Cert Hnr Outstndng Achvt Math; Law.

MILLER, KARIM M; Radford HS; Honolulu, HI; (3); French Clb; Stu Cncl; Var Vllybl; High Hon Roll; Hon Roll; 4th Pl Drivers Ed Precsn Drvng Cmptn Rep Radford; Mdl Hnr Rl; Swmmng Instrctrs Aide.

MILLER, MARY R; Leilehua HS; Wahiawa, HI; (2); Sec Treas Church Yth Grp; Drama Clb; SADD; Temple Yth Grp; Color Guard; Hon Roll; Shrt Stry Cntst Chrstms Cmptn Schl ST Cntst & Schl Cnty; Chld Psychlgst.

MILOVINA, MICHELE A; Seabury Hall HS; Pukalani, HI; (4); 1/31; JA; Pres Spanish Clb; Sec Soph Cls; Pres Jr Cls; Capt Tennis; Capt Vllybl; Hon Roll; St Schlr; Val; U Of CA Santa Barbara; Bio Sci.

MINESHIMA, DALE S; Waipahu HS; Waipahu, HI; (4); 26/418; Hosp Aide; Letterman Clb; Service Clb; Ed Lit Mag; Chrmn Frsh Cls; Chrmn Soph Cls; Chrmn Jr Cls; Chrmn Sr Cls; Var Co-Capt Tennis; High Hon Roll; Santa Clara U; Bio.

MIRANDA, TYLER S; Mililani HS; Wahiawa, HI; (3); Church Yth Grp; SADD; Teachers Aide; Variety Show; Intrml Var Bsktbl; Intrml Ftbl; JV Score Keeper; Intrml Socr; Var Capt Vllybl; Hon Roll; Campus Life; JIKA; :Phys Educ.

MISHIMA, DARIN Y; Maryknoll HS; Aiea, HI; (2); Var Tennis; High Hon Roll; Var Bwlng; Chem, Hnrs Alg II, Hnrs Trig Awds; Bus.

MITCHELL, FAYE A; Kohala HS; Kapaau, HI; (1); Church Yth Grp; FHA; Library Aide; SADD; Socr; Trk; Hon Roll; Gifted & Talented Art; UC Davis; Vet.

MITCHELL, MAILE; Kalaheo HS; Kailua, HI; (2); Art Clb; Aud/Vis; Var Sftbl; Var JV Vllybl; U Of HI; Art.

MITSUDA, BRANDON RAI; Mid Pacific Inst; Honlulu, HI; (1); Boy Scts; Band; Ed Nwsp; Off Frsh Cls; Rep Soph Cls; Cit Awd; Mid Pacific Inst Japanese Club; Mem Grn Belt HI Shotokan Karate Assn; Ed.

MITSUI, DANA-MICHELLE H; Moanalua HS; Mililani, HI; (2); 121/488; Band; Color Guard; Mrchg Band; Pep Band; Hon Roll; Gen Med.

MITSUKA, EVONNE K; Mc Kinley HS; Honolulu, HI; (2); Church Yth Grp; Girl Scts; Prfct Atten Awd; Pres Acad Fit Awd; Jr Ldr Brownie Troop; Princeton; Nurse.

MIURA, CHRISTOPHER; Hilo HS; Hilo, HI; (3); 12/360; Key Clb; Latin Clb; Math Tm; JV Crs Cntry; High Hon Roll; Hon Roll.

MIYAGAWA, RICHIE Y; Waiakea HS; Hilo, HI; (3); 15/368; Chess Clb; Hosp Aide; JA; Latin Clb; Math Tm; Science Clb; Teachers Aide; High Hon Roll; Hon Roll; Ntl Merit Ltr; Engrng.

MIYAGI, JONI M; Waiakea HS; Hilo, HI; (2); Church Yth Grp; 4-H; JA; Latin Clb; Band; Mrchg Band; Pep Band; Variety Show; Rep Frsh Cls; Stat Wrstlng; Servce Awd; Leo Clb; Keywanettes; Phrmcy.

MIYAHIRA, KELCY M; Baldwin HS; Wailuku, HI; (1); 183/466; SADD.

MIYAJI, MICHELLE E; Waiakea HS; Hilo, HI; (3); Hist 4-H; JA; Treas Key Clb; Band; Mrchg Band; Pep Band; UH Manoa; Educ.

MIYAKE, WENDY T; Mid Pacific Inst; Honolulu, HI; (3); 3/200; 4-H; French Clb; Library Aide; Math Tm; Cit Awd; 4-H Awd; High Hon Roll; NHS; Prfct Atten Awd; Mock Trl Tm; Outstndng Frnch II Stu Awd; Dance Concerts; U HI-MANOA; Bus.

MIYAMOTO, COLLIN A; Roosevelt HS; Honolulu, HI; (2); 76/360; Cmnty Wkr; JV Bsbl; L Var Vllybl; YMCA Yth Ldrshp Corps; Dist Sci & Engrng Fair; Med.

MIYAMOTO, LISA K; Mc Kinley HS; Honolulu, HI; (1); Church Yth Grp; Drama Clb; Quiz Bowl; Speech Tm; Band; Church Choir; School Play; Hon Roll; Prfct Atten Awd; U Of HI; Eng.

MIYANAGA, LORI K; Mid Pacific Inst; Honolulu, HI; (1); Chorus; Hon Roll; Law.

MIYASAKI, DONI; Hilo HS; Hilo, HI; (2); JA; Socr; Hon Roll; Engr.

MIYASATO, DANISE H; Maui HS; Wailuku, HI; (3); 9/354; Cmnty Wkr; Key Clb; Math Clb; Math Tm; Teachers Aide; High Hon Roll; Hon Roll; NHS; Enrchd Pgm-Scndry Lang Arts; U Of HI; Engrng.

MIYASHIRO, BRANDIE F; Waipahu HS; Waipahu, HI; (1); 25/513; Rep Frsh Cls; Hon Roll.

MIYASHIRO, CARRIE ANN; Kalaheo HS; Kailua, HI; (3); 7/240; Yrbk; Hon Roll.

MIYASHIRO, GALE M; Kailua HS; Kailua, HI; (2); 1/30; Math Clb; Math Tm; Service Clb; Tennis; High Hon Roll; Hon Roll; NHS; Jap Clb; Zonta Clb; U Of HI; Elem Ed.

MIYATA, KRISTI L; Moanalua HS; Honolulu, HI; (2); 7/488; Church Yth Grp; Treas Band; Mrchg Band; Orch; Pep Band; Stu Cncl; Police Actvts Leag Vllybl; Leo Clb VP.

MIYATAKI, HEATHER E; Hawaii Baptist Acad; Kailua, HI; (2); Church Yth Grp; Treas Drama Clb; Thesps; Chorus; School Musical; School Play; Stage Crew; JV Bsktbl; Presdntl Phys Ftnss Awd 88-90; Young Womans Ekiden Intl Race 89-90; Perf Arts.

MIYATAKI, RYAN K H; Leilehua HS; Wahiawa, HI; (1); 94/497; JV L Bsbl; JV Wrstlng; Hon Roll.

MIYAZAWA, CAROLINE F; Mililani HS; Mililani, HI; (4); 96/408; Church Yth Grp; Math Clb; Science Clb; Hon Roll; Leo Club Rec Secy; Equestrian; Cum Laude Grad; Whittier Coll; Commnctns.

MIYAZONO, LAURIE C; Mid Pacific Inst; Honolulu, HI; (2); Church Yth Grp; Cmnty Wkr; Teachers Aide; Band; Jazz Band; Orch; Hon Roll; Spec Awd Space Camp; Ed.

MIYOSHI, HARLAN J; Waimea HS; Hanapepe, HI; (4); Church Yth Grp; Debate Tm; SADD; Teachers Aide; Phtg Yrbk; Crs Cntry; Tennis; Trk; Hon Roll; Japanese Clb Histrn; U Of HI; Japanese Trnsltr.

MIZUTA, ALLYSON J; Hawaii Baptist Acad; Kaneohe, HI; (1); Chorus; Rptr Yrbk; Hon Roll; Pres Acad Fit Awd; Japanese Club.

MIZUTA, KORI; Kailua HS; Kailua, HI; (3); 20/500; Yrbk; YMCA JR Leader Teen Assistant; Outstanding Legislation Award; Youth Legislature Program; U Of HI.

MOLINA, TAMMY T; Waiakea HS; Hilo, HI; (3); 134/368; DECA; JA; Pep Clb; Service Clb; Rep Jr Cls; Hon Roll; Atletic Svc; Cannons Bus Coll; Bus.

MOLITAU, JOHN K; St Louis HS; Honolulu, HI; (3); 22/151; Bsktbl; Vllybl; Wt Lftg; Hon Roll; NHS; De Vry Schl Of Tech; Elec Engr.

MOMOHARA, BRAD; Laupahoehoe HS; Laupahoehoe, HI; (2); Math Tm; Science Clb; Band; Pres Frsh Cls; VP Soph Cls; Capt Bsktbl; Trk; Vllybl; Hon Roll; U Of HI Manoa.

MOMOSEA, DIANA M; James Campbell HS; Ewa Beach, HI; (4); 22/347; Office Aide; Teachers Aide; Rep Sr Cls; Rep Stu Cncl; Var Powder Puff Ftbl; Var Score Keeper; JV Var Vllybl; Hon Roll; U HI Hilo; Elem Ed.

MONIZ, JEREMY P; Radford HS; Honolulu, HI; (1); 290/466; Boy Scts; Office Aide; Speech Tm; Teachers Aide; Black Belt Karat-Japan Intl; U Of HI; Bus.

MONIZ, TRACI N; Waiakea HS; Hilo, HI; (3); Church Yth Grp; Pep Clb; Hist Rep Stu Cncl; Bus Mgmt.

MONJE, NATHAN; Kaimuki HS; Honolulu, HI; (2); 70/325; Letterman Clb; JV Bsbl; JV Ftbl; Hon Roll; Bus.

MONTERO, ROY J; St Louis HS; Kaneohe, HI; (3); Aud/Vis; Spanish Clb; SADD; Var L Bsktbl; Var L Vllybl; High Hon Roll; Hon Roll; Prfct Atten Awd; US Jr Olympics 90; Aloha St Games Vllybl 90; Engrng.

MONTIBON, AARON B; Kamehameha HS; Waipahu, HI; (4); Boy Scts; Church Yth Grp; Cmnty Wkr; Drama Clb; ROTC; Chorus; School Musical; School Play; Stage Crew; Off Sr Cls; Eagle Sct Awd 89; Wrld War II Awd Mrt 87; Ho O Pa A Mau Schlrshp; Wichita ST U; Aerospace Engr.

MOONS, MICHAEL P; Kailua HS; Kailua, HI; (2); Var L Socr; Vet.

MOORE, JEFFREY B; Radford HS; Honolulu, HI; (3); 28/384; Aud/Vis; Church Yth Grp; Band; Mrchg Band; Pep Band; Crs Cntry; Ftbl; High Hon Roll; Pres Acad Fit Awd; USAF; Pre Med.

MORALA, JOHAN B; Pearl City HS; Aiea, HI; (3); Boy Scts; Variety Show; Hon Roll; Cert Of Profcncy Cntry 21 Typng; U HI.

MORALES, KATHLEEN; Waiakea HS; Hilo, HI; (3); 75/368; Church Yth Grp; Teachers Aide; Hon Roll; Geom & Spansh Tutor; UH Manoa; RN.

MORALES, ROCHELLE; Kapaa HS; Kapaa, HI; (2); Band; Model Of The Year 1990.

MORI, IRIS; St Andrews Priory HS; Honolulu, HI; (2); 6/54; French Clb; Intnl Clb; Yrbk; Hon Roll; Serteens Clb; Sv Earth Clb & Japanese Anmtn Clbs HI; Anmtn.

MORIGUCHI, GREGG TAKEJI; Kauai HS; Lihue, HI; (3); Church Yth Grp; French Clb; FHA; Vllybl; Hon Roll; Prfct Atten Awd; Cvl Air Ptrl; Amer Red Crss Disastr Actn Team-Outstndng Yth Volntr Fnlst St Awd 89-90; Emrgncy Med.

MORIKAWA, JAMIE T; Mid-Pacific Inst; Honolulu, HI; (1); 3/200; Cmnty Wkr; Band; Hon Roll; Japanese Club.

MORIMOTO, SCOTT K; Iovani Schl; Honolulu, HI; (4); 117/220; JA; JV Var Bsbl; High Hon Roll; Hon Roll; Ntl Merit SF; Amnesty Intl; Big Bros; Vlntr Tutor.

MORIOKA, JANET M; Waiakea HS; Hilo, HI; (3); JA; Key Clb; Service Clb; Band; Mrchg Band; Pep Band; Hon Roll; Bus Admin.

MORITA, KERRIE M; Hawaii Baptist Acad; Honolulu, HI; (2); JA; Nwsp; JV Bsktbl; JV Swmmng; High Hon Roll; Hon Roll; Jr NHS; NHS; Choir; YMCA JR Ldr; Bus.

MORREN, ERICA L; Moanalua HS; Leavenworth, KS; (2); Pres Church Yth Grp; Drama Clb; Hosp Aide; JV Cheerldng; Dncng Gymnstcs & Music; CO ST U; Bus Admin.

MORRIS, SEAN M; Mc Kinley HS; Honolulu, HI; (4); 21/537; Chess Clb; Hosp Aide; Key Clb; Math Clb; Quiz Bowl; Science Clb; School Play; Hon Roll; Jr NHS; NHS; Japanese Spch Fstvl Grnd Prz Wnnr; WA Crssng Fndtn Essay Cntst St Fnlst Schlrshp; Natl Spnsh Exam 2nd; U Of HI; Intl Bus.

MORROW, STEPHEN; Radford HS; Annandale, VA; (3); 34/394; Boy Scts; Tnns; Sccr; Comp Tech.

MOSELEY, TERESA M; Leilehua HS; Wahiawa, HI; (2); Math Tm; Model UN; Spanish Clb; Rep Soph Cls; Blck Amer Club Treas; Bus.

MOTOISHI, MICHELLE; Hilo HS; Hilo, HI; (3); 12/360; Service Clb; Drm Mjr(t); Rep Jr Cls; Rep Stu Cncl; Var Mgr(s); High Hon Roll; Hon Roll; NHS; Dance Clb; Band; Outstndng Jap I & Ii Stu 87-89; Kywntts Hstrn 88-89.

MOTOSUE, JULIE K; Roosevelt HS; Honolulu, HI; (4); 23/350; Treas Sec 4-H; Treas Hist French Clb; Intnl Clb; Capt Flag Corp; Ed Nwsp; Yrbk; Treas Sr Cls; Cheerldng; Trk; Hon Roll; HI Delegate WA DC Close Up Pgm; SPEBE; U Of HI; Med.

MOUNSAVATH, PHOUPHET; Farrington HS; Waipahu, HI; (3); 128/600; Key Clb; Library Aide; Off Frsh Cls; Rep Soph Cls; Chrmn Jr Cls; JV Ftbl; Var Socr; Cit Awd; Hon Roll; Lion Awd; Spch Cont 1st Pl; U Of OR; Engr.

MOW, WING YAN; Moanalua HS; Honolulu, HI; (3); 86/462; Art Clb; Church Yth Grp; Red Cross Aide; Hon Roll; Cert Mrt Outstndng Svc Red Crss Cadet Unit 87-88; U Of CA Berkeley; Chemistry.

MOWBRAY, KUMELLA W; Kaiser HS; Boulder, CO; (3); 159/325; Church Yth Grp; Drama Clb; Spanish Clb; SADD; Thesps; School Musical; School Play; Stage Crew; Variety Show; Stu Cncl; CO U Boulder.

MOZIER JR, DANIEL M; Radford HS; Honolulu, HI; (3); 27/420; Band; Mrchg Band; Bsbl; Ftbl; Trk; U CA-USC; Comp Engrng.

MUKAI, RYAN; Baldwin HS; Lahaina, HI; (3); 1/385; Math Tm; High Hon Roll; Ntl Merit Ltr; EISP Cert; HI Dept Of Ed Dist Writing Showcase Cert Of Merit; HI Bronz Medal For Math; Elec/Cmptr Eng.

MULLEN, LUCKIE P; Waialva HS; Haleiwa, HI; (3); 62/220; Art Clb; JV Var Bsbl; JV Var Ftbl; Hon Roll; Prfct Atten Awd; U Of HI; Crpntr.

MUN, HEE-SUN; T Roosevelt HS; Honolulu, HI; (3); Aud/Vis; Cmnty Wkr; Debate Tm; Drama Clb; English Clb; French Clb; FTA; Intnl Clb; JA; Lit Mag; Peer Educ Pgm; Reach-Amer Drug, Alcohol Prevntn Pgm; Brandeis; Psycht.

MURABAYASHI, ALLEN T; Punahou Schl; Honolulu, HI; (4); Model UN; Chorus; Jazz Band; Orch; School Musical; School Play; Variety Show; Nwsp; Rep Frsh Cls; VP Jr Cls; Envrnmntl Clb Fndr, Pres.

MURAKAMI, BRYSON T; Kaiser HS; Honolulu, HI; (3); Teachers Aide; JV Ftbl; Hon Roll; Music; U Of HI Manoa; Law.

MURAKAMI, JOSH J; Hawaii Baptist Acad; Kaneohe, HI; (3); Church Yth Grp; Drama Clb; Science Clb; Band; Church Choir; School Musical; School Play; Rep Frsh Cls; Rep Soph Cls; Socr; Schl Audio Tech.

MURAKAMI, TRACIE K; Leilehua HS; Wahiawa, HI; (3); Speech Tm; JV Var Swmmng; Nakayoshi Kai Clb; U HI; Phys Ther.

MURAOKA, GUY T; Waimea HS; Hanapepe, HI; (3); Key Clb; SADD; Nwsp; Var Crs Cntry; Var Trk; High Hon Roll; Hon Roll; Prfct Atten Awd; Cmptrs; Reading; Engrng.

MURRAY, TAMMIE L; Mililani HS; Mililani, HI; (3); Church Yth Grp; GAA; Service Clb; Band; School Play; Rptr Yrbk; JV Bsktbl; Intrml Vllybl.

MYERS, CHARLES; Kailua HS; Kailua, HI; (4); 5/260; Math Tm; Quiz Bowl; Band; Mrchg Band; Capt Socr; Hon Roll; NHS; Rensselaer Polytechnic Inst Math & Sci Awd; 90 Horatio Alger Yth Smnr; U HI Manoa; Engrng.

NABOA, ZALDY E; Kau HS; Naalehu, HI; (4); 4/56; FTA; Pep Clb; Chorus; Rep Soph Cls; Vllybl; Hon Roll; National Schl Choral Awd; Foreign Languard Awd; Social Studies Awd.

NACINO, SHIRLEY MARIE T; Waipahu HS; Waipahu, HI; (2); Drill Tm; Rep Frsh Cls; Rep Soph Cls; Honolulu CC; Nrsng.

NAEOLE, ANNAMARIE M; Lahainaluna HS; Lahaina, HI; (3); VICA; Hon Roll; Acctnt.

NAGAI, BRIAN; Hawaii Baptist Acad; Honolulu, HI; (2); Church Yth Grp; VP JA; Chorus; School Play; Hon Roll.

NAGAI, DANIEL T; Iolani HS; Aiea, HI; (4); 39/220; Key Clb; Ed Lit Mag; JV Crs Cntry; Ntl Merit SF.

NAGAMINE, TASHA N; Waimea HS; Hanapepe, HI; (2); 5/206; Art Clb; FHA; High Hon Roll; Hon Roll; NHS; Japanese Club; Bionic Menehune; U Of HI Manoa; Bus Mgmt.

NAGAMINE, TIANA; St Anthony HS; Pukalani, HI; (3); Cmnty Wkr; Letterman Clb; Lit Mag; Pres Frsh Cls; Off Soph Cls; VP Stu Cncl; Var Capt Bsktbl; Wt Lftg; Hon Roll; NHS; Japanese Clb; Child Psych.

NAGANO, CHERYL C; Henry Perine Baldwin HS; Kahului, HI; (2); 18/401; Key Clb; Science Clb; Cheerldng; Hon Roll; Japanese Clb; U Of HI Manoa; Med.

NAGANUMA, SHERIANN L; Lahaina Luna HS; Lahaina, HI; (1); Science Clb; JV Crs Cntry; Var Sftbl; Var Tennis; High Hon Roll; Prfct Atten Awd; Pres Acad Fit Awd; PAAC Clb; MIT; Engrng.

NAGATA, SHAWN H; Kaiser HS; Honolulu, HI; (3); 70/325; Aud/Vis; Office Aide; Teachers Aide; VP Frsh Cls; Var Capt Bsktbl; Var Capt Ftbl; Var Capt Trk; Kaiser High Cougar Awd For Schl Svc & Otstndng Ldrshp; Close-Up Program; Ed.

NAGATA, TINA R; Maui HS; Paia, HI; (3); Key Clb; Science Clb; Hon Roll; Spirit Clb; Bus Admin.

NAGATO, GEORGINE M; Pearl City HS; Pearl City, HI; (3); 5/500; Church Yth Grp; Band; Mrchg Band; Capt Tennis; High Hon Roll; Hon Roll; NHS; Yth Against Cancer Club; U Of WA; Nrsng.

NAKADA, MICHAEL M; Mc Kinley HS; Honolulu, HI; (4); Pres Band; Jazz Band; Orch; School Musical; School Play; Stage Crew; Variety Show; Phtg Yrbk; Marine Bio.

NAKAMARU, AMY; Hawaii Preparatory Acad; Kealakekua, HI; (4); Chorus; Ed Nwsp; Yrbk; Var Capt Crs Cntry; Var L Socr; Var L Trk; High Hon Roll; CT Coll.

NAKAMIYO, SUSAN K; Leilehua HS; Wahiawa, HI; (2); 21/406; Band; Jazz Band; Pep Band; Mgr(s); Var JV Swmmng; Hon Roll; Stage Band; Awd Outstndng Proficiency In Eng I; Band Librarian; Elem Educ.

NAKAMOTO, BRYAN M; Baldwin HS; Wailuku, HI; (3); DECA; FBLA; Key Clb; Letterman Clb; Science Clb; Service Clb; SADD; Varsity Clb; Var L Ftbl; Var L Swmmng; Swmmg-All Star; Maui News Tm; Pwrlftng-1st Pl; Bench Press Cntst; Pwrlftng 2nd Pl Brets Gym Pwrlftng; Bus Mgmnt.

NAKAMOTO, JAMES K; Pearl City HS; Pearl City, HI; (4); 43/478; Q&S; Quiz Bowl; Teachers Aide; Rptr Nwsp; Hon Roll; Untd Japanese Soc HI Outstndng Schlr Japanese Lang 89; Bowlng Vrsty, Ltr & Stats; Pacific Asian Affrs; U Of HI; Japanese.

NAKAMURA, CHAD M; Mid-Pacific Inst; Honolulu, HI; (1); Band; Intrml Bsbl; JV Bsktbl; Wt Lftg; Hon Roll; Pres List.

NAKAMURA, DAWN C; Mid-Pacific Institute HS; Honolulu, HI; (3); Pres Chess Clb; High Hon Roll; Hon Roll; Jr NHS; NHS; Japanese Clb; U Of HI.

NAKAMURA, GLEN E; Waipahu HS; Waipahu, HI; (2); 1/400; Math Clb; Science Clb; JV Crs Cntry; High Hon Roll; Hnrb Mntn HI St Sci, Engrng Fair 90; TEAMS 1st Pl Comp Sci; Bst Comp Sci HI St Sci, Engrng Fair 89; Engrng.

NAKAMURA, JASON M; Hawaii Baptist Acad; Waimanalo, HI; (3); 2/86; Boy Scts; Church Yth Grp; Church Choir; Intrml Bsktbl; JV Var Ftbl; JV Var Trk; Intrml Vllybl; Jr NHS; NHS; Pres Acad Fit Awd; Servant Grp; Boys Athltc Clb; PTA Hgh Acad Avg Awd.

NAKAMURA, JODI L; Kauai HS; Lihue, HI; (3); DECA; 4-H; FHA; Library Aide; Service Clb; Band; Crs Cntry; Mgr(s); Score Keeper; Tennis; Teen Mag Rgnl Semi-Fnlst Sprtsgrl Of Yr; Alaha Gms Gld Mdl 4x100 Relay Awd; Bus.

NAKAMURA, KELLY; Mc Kinley HS; Honolulu, HI; (3); 102/537; Hosp Aide; Office Aide; Band; Jazz Band; Pep Band; School Play; Stage Crew; Space Acad & Space Acad II; Embry-Riddle U; Aerospc Engr.

NAKAMURA, LISA F; Kapaa HS; Anahola, HI; (3); FHA; Spanish Clb; U HI; Bus Mgmt.

NAKAMURA, ROSS M; Hawaii Baptist Acad; Honolulu, HI; (3); Church Yth Grp; Hosp Aide; Math Tm; Church Choir; JV Co-Capt Vllybl; High Hon Roll; Hon Roll; Jr NHS; NHS.

NAKANO, JASON; Iolani Schl; Honolulu, HI; (4); Boy Scts; Drama Clb; Intnl Clb; Model UN; School Musical; Stage Crew; High Hon Roll; Outrigger Canoe Paddling; Whittier Coll.

NAKANO, SHERI T; Waiakea HS; Hilo, HI; (4); 23/412; Hosp Aide; Service Clb; Speech Tm; Teachers Aide; Variety Show; Rep Frsh Cls; Off Jr Cls; Off Sr Cls; Swmmng; NHS; UCLA; Corp Law.

NAKANO, TIFFANY Y; Farrington HS; Honolulu, HI; (2); 18/696; Math Tm; Variety Show; Co-Ed Nwsp; Stu Cncl; JV Bsktbl; Hon Roll; Sec Jr NHS; 3rd Pl Schlstc Magzne Poetry Cntst; Gvrnrs Athltc Assn; Artcle Pub Local Nwspr; Aero Engr.

NAKASHIMA, CORY; Mililani HS; Mililani, HI; (2); JV Capt Bsbl; JV Capt Ftbl; U Of Sthrn CA; Bsbl.

NAKASONE, JULIANNE A; Hawaii Baptist Acad; Honolulu, HI; (3); 14/87; Drama Clb; Thesps; Band; School Musical; Stage Crew; Treas Jr Cls; Stu Cncl; Var L Bsktbl; Var Capt Vllybl; Hon Roll; Japanese Clb; Schl Chrch Grp.

NAKASONE, NANCY M; Mid-Pacific Inst; Honolulu, HI; (2); Cmnty Wkr; Var Bsktbl; Var Cheerldng; Miss Teen HI Cntstnt 91; Sofia Coll; Med.

NAKASONE, ROSS M; Iolani Schl; Honolulu, HI; (4); 26/220; Art Clb; VP Dance Clb; Debate Tm; VP JA; Hon Roll; Ntl Merit SF; Aikido.

NAKASONE, VICKY T; Moanalua HS; Honolulu, HI; (2); 24/488; Church Yth Grp; Band; Flag Corp; Hon Roll; Japanese Clb; Untd Okinawan Assnn HI Vlybl Lg.

NAKATA, PAULA S; Sacred Hearts Acad; Honolulu, HI; (3); Math Tm; NFL; Speech Tm; Off Frsh Cls; Off Jr Cls; Stu Cncl; High Hon Roll; NHS; NEDT Awd; Prfct Atten Awd; All Amer Schlr 89; Cmnty Worker; Fleet Reserve Assn 89; Natl Amer Essay Cont Wnnr; Bus Law.

NAKATSU, JASON I; Hawaii Baptist Acad; Kaneohe, HI; (2); Wrstlng; High Hon Roll; Natl Wrstlng Tourn Japan 89-90; Pt Loma Nazarene Coll; Frnc Med.

NAKAYAMA, TRACEY M; Waiakea HS; Hilo, HI; (2); 1/500; 4-H; Math Tm; Science Clb; Service Clb; Crs Cntry; Trk; 4-H Awd; Hon Roll; Mock Trl; Natl Sci Fndtn Yng Schlrs Pgm.

NAKAYAMA, YVETTE M; Pearl City HS; Pearl City, HI; (2); 56/511; Band; Jazz Band; Mrchg Band; Stu Cncl; Interact Club; U Of HI; Med.

NAKAZATO, MICHELLE H; Kalani HS; Honolulu, HI; (2); 19/213; Church Yth Grp; Dance Clb; Hosp Aide; Orch; Rep Soph Cls; JV Crs Cntry; Med.

NAMKUNG, SUN; Roosevelt HS; Honolulu, HI; (2); Intnl Clb; Math Tm; Science Clb; Ed Nwsp; Lit Mag; Hon Roll; NHS; Engrng.

NANEJU, DALEEL; Mid-Pacific Inst; Honolulu, HI; (2); 1/208; Chess Clb; Cmnty Wkr; French Clb; Math Tm; Quiz Bowl; ROTC; Color Guard; Drill Tm; Stage Crew; Yrbk; OSI Pres; Tchncls Schl Plys; CA Tech; Physcs.

NAPOLEON, JEFF S; Moanalua HS; Honolulu, HI; (3); 92/462; Church Yth Grp; Letterman Clb; Teachers Aide; Varsity Clb; Intrml JV Bsbl; Intrml JV Bsktbl; Intrml JV Ftbl; Intrml Wrstlng; Hon Roll; Pres Acad Fit Awd; All Star Ftbll Team 88-89; Danced Merry Monarch Hula Comptn 90; U WA; Bus Mgmt.

NARCISO, JOCELYN; Lanakila Baptist HS; Ewa, HI; (4); 1/18; Ed Nwsp; Yrbk; Pres Jr Cls; Pres Sr Cls; Stu Cncl; JV Bsktbl; Capt Vllybl; High Hon Roll; Pres NHS; U HI Manoa.

NARINE, NICHELLE; Leilehua HS; Wahiawa, HI; (3); Red Cross Aide; ROTC; JV Bsktbl; Intrml Fld Hcky; VFW Awd-Outstndng Achvt & Exceptnl Ldrshp Ability.

NARUSE, TAYA R; Mililani HS; Mililani, HI; (3); Service Clb; Teachers Aide; Band; Color Guard; Flag Corp; Rptr Nwsp; Score Keeper; Stat Wrstlng; Hon Roll; Hnrs & AP Courses.

NASCHKE, HEATHER A; Radford HS; Honolulu, HI; (3); 56/400; Mu Alpha Theta; Varsity Clb; Band; Mrchg Band; Var Tennis; Hon Roll; Fshn Inst Of Tech; Fshn Mrch.

NATER, KRISTY; Maui HS; Makawao, HI; (2); 74/388; Key Clb; JV Cheerldng.

NATIVIDAD, JOSEPH B; Farrington HS; Honolulu, HI; (2); JV Ftbl.

NAVALTA, JENNIFER; Laupahoehoe HS; Laupahoehoe, HI; (4); 1/22; Aud/Vis; Math Tm; Science Clb; Ed Nwsp; Ed Yrbk; VP Soph Cls; Rep Jr Cls; Rep Stu Cncl; Var Tennis; Var JV Trk; Most Insprtnl Tennis Plyr; Outstndg Sr 89-90; Outstndg Young Achvr 89; U Of HI Manoa.

NAVARRO, JENNIFER K; Maryknoll HS; Waipahu, HI; (2); Cmnty Wkr; SADD; Hon Roll; Hui Kokua; Campus Mnstry; Maryknoll Animal Rights Coalition; Hstry.

NAVARRO, JOANNE K; Maryknoll HS; Waipahu, HI; (2); French Clb; SADD; Hon Roll; Amnesty Intl; Campus Mnstry; Animal Rights Coalition; Vet Med.

NAZARENO, JOCELYN G; Wallace Rider Farrington HS; Ewa Beach, HI; (3); 16/600; Sec Service Clb; Chorus; Variety Show; Ed Nwsp; Lit Mag; Pres Frsh Cls; Sec Soph Cls; Sec Jr Cls; Hon Roll; NHS; Amer Legion Schl Awd; HSTA-MST Outstndnt; Lbrl Arts.

NEKOBA, BRYAN O; Waiakea HS; Hilo, HI; (1); 25/480; Chess Clb; JA; Key Clb; Engr.

NEUBECKER, MARCIE D; Parker Schl; Kamuela, HI; (3); 1/24; Church Yth Grp; School Musical; School Play; Stage Crew; Ed Yrbk; Pres Jr Cls; High Hon Roll; NHS; Top Hist Stu 90; Yrbk Awd Ldrshp; Most Spirited; U Washington; Archtctr.

NEWALL, SHANNON C; Waimea HS; Waimea, HI; (2); 13/186; Church Yth Grp; Spanish Clb; SADD; Hon Roll; UH Manoa; Elem Ed.

NEWHOUSE, ANISSA D.; Moanalua HS; Honolulu, HI; (2); 61/488; Debate Tm; Office Aide; Pep Clb; Speech Tm; Band; Drill Tm; Cheerldng; Hon Roll; NHS.

NEWMAN, AMY; Kalaheo HS; Kaneohe, HI; (2); Off Soph Cls; Var Crs Cntry; Var Socr; Var Swmmng; Var Trk; Hon Roll; Oahu Interschlstc Assn Vrsty Chmpn Trk 800 M 1600 M.

NEWTE, MANDY L; Pahoa HS; Pahoa, HI; (3); FHA; Yrbk; Photo Clb, Corrspndnce Sectry; Photo.

NEWTON, VALERIE; Aiea HS; San Jose, CA; (4); Church Yth Grp; Drama Clb; 4-H; FHA; Girl Scts; ROTC; Speech Tm; Teachers Aide; Thesps; School Musical; Trvl Agnt.

NG, ALBERT; Moanalua HS; Honolulu, HI; (3); 6/462; Computer Clb; Quiz Bowl; Pres Science Clb; Hon Roll; Inventions Cmmtt; Engr.

NG, HO LEUNG; Iolani Schl; Honolulu, HI; (4); 2/220; Church Yth Grp; VP Intnl Clb; Math Tm; Model UN; Mrchg Band; Stu Cncl; Var Ftbl; High Hon Roll; NHS; Ntl Merit SF; Stanford; Psych.

NG, JUDY H; William Mc Kinley HS; Honolulu, HI; (3); 17/550; Math Clb; NFL; Speech Tm; School Play; Stage Crew; Lit Mag; JV L Crs Cntry; High Hon Roll; St Sci Fr Fnlst 90; HI Cncl Tchrs Engl Awd; All-Amrcn Schlr; Aerntcl Engnrng.

NG, MICHEL M; Mid-Pacific Inst; Honolulu, HI; (3); 7/200; Cmnty Wkr; Quiz Bowl; JV Tennis; Jr NHS; NHS; NEDT Awd; Pres Schlr; Cmmnty Svc Shriners Hsptl; Psych & Phlsphy & Med; Med.

NGAI, COLIN K; St Louis Schl; Honolulu, HI; (2); Cmnty Wkr; ROTC; JV Vllybl; Hon Roll; U HI.

NGAI, NGA CHING; Mc Kinley HS; Honolulu, HI; (4); Dance Clb; Chinese Club; Chem Club; TEAMS Rep; Cls Rep Handball Hong Kong Chmpns; Yth Mem Red Crss Hong Kong; U Of HI; Liberal Art.

NGO, YEN K SYLVIA; Kaimuki HS; Honolulu, HI; (2); 18/325; Chess Clb; Wrstlng; Wrestling Acad Awd 89-90; U HI Manoa; Bus.

NGUYEN, HOA N; Sacred Hearts Acad; Arlington, TX; (3); Library Aide; Office Aide; Teachers Aide; Stage Crew; Dnfth Awd; Prfct Atten Awd; U Of TX Arlington; Elec Engrng.

NGUYEN, HUY T; Roosevelt HS; Honolulu, HI; (2); 8/360; Model UN; Trk; Hon Roll; Elec Engrng.

NGUYEN, LUCY L; Sacred Hearts Acad; Pearl City, HI; (4); 20/115; Church Yth Grp; Pres French Clb; Library Aide; Pep Clb; SADD; Teachers Aide; Nwsp; Sec Jr Cls; Off Sr Cls; JV Capt Cheerldng; Prom Chrprsn; US Hstry, Engl & Svc Awds; U Of MA Amherst; History.

NGUYEN, THANHTRUC T; Roosevelt HS; Honolulu, HI; (2); 1/360; French Clb; Math Tm; Flag Corp; Mrchg Band; Off Soph Cls; Sec Jr Cls; Stu Cncl; Hon Roll; NHS; Vet.

NGUYEN, TRINH; Mc Kinley HS; Honolulu, HI; (3); 28/545; Math Clb; Hon Roll; Guidance Cmmttee; Intl Bus.

NGUYEN, TRUNG; Waipahu HS; Waipahu, HI; (2); #94 In Class; Church Yth Grp; FCA; Hon Roll; HCC; Carpentry.

NICHOLLS, KALANI L; Maui HS; Lahaina, HI; (3); Letterman Clb; Varsity Clb; Intrml Bsktbl; Var L Wrstlng; Hon Roll; Lahaina Karate Dojo.

NICHOLS, AMBER E; Mililani HS; Mililani, HI; (3); Church Yth Grp; Key Clb; Math Tm; SADD; Nwsp; JV Var Cheerldng; Var Trk; High Hon Roll; Hon Roll; NHS; Physical Therapy.

NICHOLS, JAMES T; Milolani HS; Haleiwa, HI; (3); Hon Roll; Cvl Air Ptrl Cdt Master Sgt Cert Of Apprctn & Accmpshmnt; U Of UT; Frstry.

NIE, JESSICA A; St Francis School For Girls; Honolulu, HI; (2); 40/80; Aud/Vis; Pep Clb; Speech Tm; Cheerldng; Hon Roll; Vlntr; Ed.

NIEZ, MELANIE A; Leilehva HS; Wahiawa, HI; (2); 91/406; Drama Clb; Rep Stu Cncl; Typing IA/Ib And IC/Id; U Of Northn Ky; English.

NIHIPALI, STEPHANY K; Kamehameha HS; Laie, HI; (4); 81/410; Pres Church Yth Grp; Church Choir; Capt Socr; JV Var Trk; Wt Lftg; Hon Roll; Hui Mele; Hawaiaan Club; U Denver; Hotel Mgmt.

NII, DEBORAH; Mililani HS; Mililani, HI; (3); 72/450; Church Yth Grp; Church Choir; Var Socr; Var JV Trk; High Hon Roll; Hon Roll; Pres Acad Fit Awd; MVP JV Track Rnnr; St Champs Sccr 88; U HI Manoa; Med.

NIINO, EMARI; Hawaiian Mission Acad; Honolulu, HI; (3); Church Yth Grp; Acpl Chr; Bsktbl; Diving; Polynesian Clb; Pacific Union Coll; Med.

NIKALDO, NOELLE; Baldwin HS; Kula, HI; (3); Cmnty Wkr; NFL; Red Cross Aide; Socr; Var L Swmmng; Swimmer Of Yr-Mayors Awd For Maui 90; Outstndng Swimmer HI Prep Acad; Yr Round Swimming Cmptns; Jrnlsm.

NIMS, KINAU; Saint Francis HS; Ewa Beach, HI; (3); 8/60; French Clb; Mu Alpha Theta; NFL; Q&S; Speech Tm; Nwsp; Bsktbl; Hon Roll; NHS; Intnl Clb; Catholic Dghtrs Of Amer Edctnl Awd; Advrtsng.

NISHIDA, CARA L; Waiakea HS; Hilo, HI; (3); Church Yth Grp; 4-H; JA; Math Clb; Math Tm; Service Clb; Jazz Band; School Musical; Variety Show; Off Frsh Cls; Interact Clb; Dept Ed Lang Awds Japanese Gld Mdls 1988-; SGA Comm; Optmtry.

NISHIDA, DANIELLE C; Maui HS; Paia, HI; (1); 6/451; Var High Hon Roll; Var Hon Roll; Frosh Top Schlr Awd; MIT; Physicist.

NISHIDA, MARC A; Waiakea HS; Hilo, HI; (2); 4-H; Science Clb; Rep Stu Cncl; Wrstlng; 4-H Awd; Hon Roll; Leo Clb; Parks & Rcrtn Bsbl & Bsktbl; Mock Trial.

NISHIDA, MARIAN M; Hilo HS; Hilo, HI; (2); Band; Mrchg Band; Pep Band; OR ST U; Acctng.

NISHIHAMA, MYLES K; Pearl City HS; Waipahu, HI; (3); 112/527; Computer Clb; Intrml Var Bsktbl; Yth Against Cancer Clb; JV Bsktbl Mst Insprtnl Awd; U Of HI; Comp Sci.

NISHIHIRA, GUY; Hilo HS; Hilo, HI; (4); 10/307; Pres Temple Yth Grp; High Hon Roll; Hon Roll; Jr NHS; NHS; Prfct Atten Awd; Judo 3rd Pl ST Hongwanti Tourny; Japanese Outstndng Stu Cert Merit; Accntng.

NISHIMOTO, RYAN U; Mililani HS; Mililani, HI; (2); 95/565; Capt JV Wrstlng; Hon Roll; Pres Acad Fit Awd; 2 Tim JV Champ OIA; 2 Tim West JV Champ OIA; 4th St JV Var; 2 Tim JV MVP; OR ST U; Law.

NISHIMOTO, SCOTT Y; Mid Pacific Inst; Mililani, HI; (3); JV Bsbl; JV Bsktbl; Var Ftbl; Hon Roll.

NISHIMURA, CARI LEI; H P Baldwin HS; Wailuku, HI; (2); 25/460; VP Boy Scts; Church Yth Grp; FCA; Intnl Clb; Pep Clb; Science Clb; Service Clb; SADD; Band; Church Choir; Rep All St Church Conf; Interact Clb Brd; Japanese Clb; UCLA; Educ.

NISPEROS, MICHAEL D; Pahoa HS; Hilo, HI; (2); 54/117; Church Yth Grp; Basic Elctrncs.

NISPEROS, ROWENA D; Pahoa High HS; Hilo, HI; (3); 25/98; Church Yth Grp; Computer Clb; FBLA; FHA; FTA; Cert Apprctn Awd; Accntng.

NITTA, KEVIN; Lanakila Baptist HS; Waipahu, HI; (2); Rep Soph Cls; High Hon Roll; NHS; NEDT Awd; Prfct Atten Awd; Pres Acad Fit Awd; U Of HI; Sci.

NITTA, MICHELLE N; Moanalua HS; Honolulu, HI; (4); 45/416; Dance Clb; Band; Mrchg Band; Pep Band; School Play; Rptr Yrbk; JV Var Mgr(s); Hon Roll; VP Of Med Explrs Clb; Commndrs Awd F/Schlstc Achvmnt; U Of N CO; Psych.

NIX, DOUGLAS B; Mililani HS; Mililani, HI; (3); 160/490; Aud/Vis; Church Yth Grp; Var Intrml Swmmng; Rdr For Best Bks Yng Adults; Elec Engr.

NOBE, TISHA; Punahou Schl; San Angelo, TX; (4); Church Yth Grp; Cmnty Wkr; Dance Clb; JA; Library Aide; Office Aide; Church Choir; School Play; Variety Show; Tennis; Amnesty Intl; Intl Model; Southern Methodist U.

NOLAN, SHELLEY L; Miluani HS; Aiea, HI; (2); 210/540; Church Yth Grp; SADD; Chorus; School Musical; School Play; Stage Crew; Swing Chorus; Marine Lab; Scripps Inst Of Ocean; Marin Bi.

NORMAN, LISA A; Roosevelt HS; Honolulu, HI; (3); Drama Clb; VP Pres French Clb; Pres Intnl Clb; Mrchg Band; School Musical; Ed Lit Mag; Socr; Trk; High Hon Roll; Pres VP NHS; Coalitn Drug-Free HI Yth Advsry Brd; Engrng.

NORRIS, MAYA M; St Francis HS; Honolulu, HI; (2); Aud/Vis; Intnl Clb; Pep Clb; Color Guard; High Hon Roll; Hon Roll; Jr NHS; NHS; Co-Wrkrs Of Mother Theresa Mem; Vol Hawaiian Humane Soc.

NORTON, JAMES B; Mid-Pacific Inst; Honolulu, HI; (2); Hon Roll; Appeared In Schl Repertory Theater Productions; Australia; Grphc Dsgn.

NOUCHI, ERIC; Baldwin HS; Kahului, HI; (1); 1/466; Key Clb; Band; Jazz Band; Hon Roll; Vrsty Bowlng Team.

NOWLAN, KATHLEEN M; Radford HS; Norfolk, VA; (4); 68/348; Sec Church Yth Grp; Cmnty Wkr; French Clb; German Clb; VP SADD; Treas Frsh Cls; Var Crs Cntry; Var Trk; Hon Roll; Pres Acad Fit Awd; Old Dominion U; Crmnl Justice.

NUUANU, NICOLE J; James Campbell HS; Makakilo, HI; (2); Band; Drill Tm; Pep Band; Hon Roll; Awds Banquet Attendant; Class Ms Congnlty.

O BRIEN, CLAIRE K; Honokaa HS; Honokaa, HI; (3); 18/149; Church Yth Grp; Speech Tm; Yrbk; L Crs Cntry; Socr; Sftbl; Outstndng Achvt Spanish I 88-89 Spanish II 89-90 Engl III 89-90.

O BRIEN, JOSEPH JOHN; Waiakea HS; Hilo, HI; (3); 50/368; Treas Latin Clb; Band; Mrchg Band; Pep Band; Rep Soph Cls; Rep Jr Cls; Rep Stu Cncl; Hon Roll; NHS.

O DELL, KEVIN; Hilo HS; Hilo, HI; (2); 33/367; Key Clb; Latin Clb; JV Bsbl; Var L Socr; Hon Roll; Adopt A Little Brother Pgm; Med.

O DONNELL, LIEF; Pahoa HS & Elem; Pahoa, HI; (2); 4/116; Band; Trk; Hon Roll; NHS; Leo Club.

O HANNIGAN, EVE; Mary Knoll HS; Pearl City, HI; (3); French Clb; ROTC; Band; Mrchg Band; Crs Cntry; Vllybl; Hon Roll; NHS; CAP; Aerospace Sci.

OAMIL, MIRANDA L; Waialua HS & Intermed; Haleiwa, HI; (3); 62/165; Office Aide; Spanish Clb; Teachers Aide; Prfct Atten Awd; Drugbuster Stu Agnst Drgs; Engl Hand Bk; Lions Clb; Cannon Business Coll; Trvl Indu.

OBANIA, JESSE A; Farrington HS; Honolulu, HI; (2); 79/696; Hon Roll; U HI; Mech Engrng.

OBATA, BARON; Mc Kinley HS; Honolulu, HI; (2); Treas Band; Jazz Band; Mrchg Band; Var Golf; Close-Up Fnd Pgm; Learning Ctr For Hum; U HI; Bus.

OCLINARIA, GRACE; Nanakuli HS; Waianae, HI; (2); Pep Clb; ROTC; SADD; Var JV Cheerldng; JV Crs Cntry; Hon Roll; Natl Sojourners Awd; Cadet Physcl Ftnss Chllng Awd; Doctor.

ODA, JULIE M; Hawaii Baptist Acad; Kaneohe, HI; (3); 27/86; Cmnty Wkr; JV Tennis; Boys & Girls Clb Yth Vlntr Awd; 1st Ladys Outstndng Vlntr Awd; Coalitn Drud Free HI; Phrmcy.

ODA, KIMBERLEY K; Waiakea HS; Hilo, HI; (1); 40/478; 4-H; Hon Roll; Prfct Atten Awd; Srvc Awd Top 7 PCT Clss; Interact Club; U Of HI Manoa.

OGATA, BETH N; Konawaena HS; Kealakekua, HI; (2); 13/338; Var Pres Church Yth Grp; Treas 4-H; Service Clb; Lit Mag; Rep Stu Cncl; Hon Roll.

OGATA, KELLY R; Leilehua HS; Wahiawa, HI; (2); Math Tm; Model UN; Treas Band; High Hon Roll; Hon Roll; Jazz Band; Mrchg Band; Pep Band; HI U; Math.

OGAWA, BRENT; Baldwin HS; Wailuku, HI; (2); 30/400; Cmnty Wkr; Intnl Clb; Key Clb; Service Clb; Var Crs Cntry; Var Socr; Var Trk; Hon Roll; Sprts Med.

OGI, RUSSELL K; Waiakea HS; Hilo, HI; (3); 21/368; Variety Show; Rep Jr Cls; NHS.

OH, SANG G; Mc Kinley HS; Honolulu, HI; (3); Chess Clb; Science Clb; Teachers Aide; Var Golf; JV Wt Lftg; U Of HI; Aerospc Engr.

OHTA, CHRIS F; H P Baldwin HS; Wailuku, HI; (2); Boy Scts; Letterman Clb; Rifle Team & Club; CA Tech; Comp Pgmr.

OHTA, LYNN T; Kaimuki HS; Honolulu, HI; (4); 60/340; Church Yth Grp; Cmnty Wkr; Hosp Aide; Crs Cntry; Trk; Hon Roll; Jr Prom Cmmtte; UN Manoa; Elem Ed.

OISHI, TINA M; Pearl City HS; Pearl City, HI; (4); 28/478; Sec Band; Sec Mrchg Band; Rep Soph Cls; Sec Jr Cls; Sec Sr Cls; Capt Stu Cncl; Hon Roll; Leo Club; Alea/Pearl City Bus Assn Schlrshp & Pearl City Comm Assnschlrshp; U HI Manoa; Bus.

OKAHARA, DEE K; Waiakea HS; Hilo, HI; (3); 4-H; Rep Jr Cls; Var Crs Cntry; Var Trk; 4-H Awd; Hon Roll; NHS; Interact Club.

OKAMOTO, LYNN; Waimea HS; Lihue, HI; (4); 1/200; Spanish Clb; SADD; Ed Nwsp; Sec Frsh Cls; Pres Soph Cls; Sec Stu Cncl; Capt Crs Cntry; Capt Trk; Val; Strlng Schlr; Gen Schlrshp; Amer Lgn Sch Awd; 1st Ladys Outstndng Vol Awd; U HI Manoa; Jrnlsm.

OKAMURA, CHRIS T; Saint Louis HS; Aiea, HI; (3); 9/150; Cmnty Wkr; Intrml Bsktbl; Hon Roll.

OKAMURA, WENDY M; Mc Kinley HS; Honolulu, HI; (1); Band; JV Bsktbl; JV Vllybl; Hon Roll; Prfct Atten Awd; 3 Hnrs Classes; Med.

OKIMURA, JUDY T; Roosevelt HS; Honolulu, HI; (3); 4/350; Math Clb; Math Tm; Quiz Bowl; Sec Science Clb; Spanish Clb; Hon Roll; NHS; St Sci Fair; Span II Awd; Hlth Careers Clb; Physcn.

OKINAKA, JEFFREY A; Waiakea HS; Hilo, HI; (1); 49/478; JA; Key Clb; Band; Mrchg Band; Pep Band; Junior Golf; Electrl Engnr.

OKINO, KYLE T; Pres William Mc Kinley HS; Honolulu, HI; (2); 17/588; Math Clb; Quiz Bowl; Band; Jazz Band; VP Soph Cls; Rep Stu Cncl; Hon Roll; NHS; Rep HS Coord Cmmtte Which Discusses Sch Activities & Prob; Competed In HI St Solo & Ensmbl Cmptn; Food Svc.

OKINO, NICOLE R; President William Mc Kinley HS; Honolulu, HI; (3); Score Keeper; JV Var Vllybl; Stat Wrstlng; Hon Roll; Pres Acad Fit Awd; 6 Tms Jr Natl Judo Chmpn 85-90; Vrsty Judo Tm; Schlr Athlte Awd 88 & 90; St Judo Chmpn; 5th Pl HI Vlybl; U Of HI; Trvl Indstry Mgmt.

OKITA, CRAIG M; Henry Perrine Baldwin HS; Kahului, HI; (3); 27/393; Varsity Clb; JV Var Bsbl; High Hon Roll; Hon Roll; U Of HI Manoa; Bus.

OKOJI, MYLES T; James Campbell HS; Ewa Beach, HI; (2); JV Capt Bsbl; Wt Lftg; High Hon Roll; Hon Roll; U Of HI; Bus.

OKUDA, LISA; Lahainaluna HS; Lahaina, HI; (4); Sec Art Clb; FTA; VP Pres Spanish Clb; Band; Drm Mjr(t); Mrchg Band; Pep Band; Rep Soph Cls; Socr; NHS; Pacific Asian Affairs Cncl; Maui CC; Early Chldhd Educ.

OKUDA, SHANA; Waianae HS; Waianae, HI; (4); 3/320; Cmnty Wkr; Debate Tm; Sec Q&S; Sec Spanish Clb; Ed Nwsp; Crs Cntry; Treas NHS; Mnrty HS Stu Rsrch Apprntc Pgm; G/T; Long Island U; Envrnmntl Sci.

OKUNAMI, ROANNE; Hilo HS; Hilo, HI; (2); 12/390; Church Yth Grp; Key Clb; Flag Corp; Rep Soph Cls; Stat Bsktbl; Crs Cntry.

OKUNO, ERIN R; Moanalua HS; Waipahu, HI; (2); Cheerldng; High Hon Roll; Outstndng Frosh; Lawyer.

OKURA, TRICIA; Mid-Pacific Inst; Honolulu, HI; (3); Cmnty Wkr; Band; Mgr Stage Crew; JV Sftbl; JV Vllybl; Cit Awd; High Hon Roll; Hon Roll; Jr NHS; NHS; Japanese Clb 5 Yr Mem & VP 1990-91; Naka Pueo Canoe Clb; Bus Mgmt.

OKUUATA, BRENT K; Hawaii Baptist Acad; Kailua, HI; (2); Church Yth Grp; JA; Math Tm; Hon Roll; Jv, V Bowling; Blackbelt Karate; Dist Sci Fair 89.

OLDAKOWSKI, DANIEL J; Monnalua HS; Honolulu, HI; (2).

OLIVAL, KEVIN; Kalaheo HS; Kailua, HI; (1); 2/261; Tennis; High Hon Roll; Jr NHS; Daunnas Art Studio Schlrshp 90; MI ST U; Vet Sci.

OLIVAL, THERESE M; Mid-Pacific Inst; Kailua, HI; (1); Cmnty Wkr; Hon Roll; Anml Prtctn Inst Of Amer; Prfrmng Arts.

OLSEN, GREGORY B; Mililani HS; Mililani, HI; (3); 21/540; Var L Socr; Var L Trk; Summer 1990 Participant In Chaminade U Bio Chemistry Program On Schlrshp; Winner Of Num Art Award; U Of Wa; Chemical Engineering.

OMALZA, DAWN C; Waimea HS; Lawai, HI; (2); Pep Clb; Band; Mrchg Band; VP Frsh Cls; JV Bsktbl; Hon Roll; Class Chairperson Homecoming Committee; Class Chairperson Spiritweek Committee; Co-Chair For Pep Rally; HI Pacific U; Travel Indstry.

OMELAU, ALEXANDRA K; Waiakea HS; Keaau, HI; (3); GAA; JA; Pep Clb; SADD; Rep Jr Cls; JV Var Bsktbl; Stat Ftbl; Score Keeper; 2nd Pl HI St Lang Fstvl; U HI Mano; Scndry Ed.

OMINE, KATHRYN M; Mc Kinley HS; Honolulu, HI; (2); 64/588; Hosp Aide; Science Clb; Speech Tm; School Play; Stage Crew; Chrmn Soph Cls; Chrmn Jr Cls; Chrmn Stu Cncl; NHS; Spc Acad Lvl II Pgm; Awd Sci Prjct HI St Sci Fair 90.

OMOTO, LISA T; Kavai HS; Lihue, HI; (2); 15/219; FHA; Band; Mrchg Band; Pep Band; Hon Roll; NHS; Keywntts; Accntng.

OMURO, TAKASHI C; Maui HS; Kahului, HI; (3); Key Clb; Science Clb; Rep Frsh Cls; Pres Jr Cls; Bsbl; Hon Roll; Prfct Atten Awd; SPEBE; U Of HI; Engrng.

ONAGA, DANNA L; Mc Kinley HS; Honolulu, HI; (4); 25/576; Church Yth Grp; Treas Frsh Cls; Rep Jr Cls; Rep Sr Cls; Crs Cntry; Trk; High Hon Roll; Hon Roll; NHS; Japanese Club; Leo Club; U Of HI; Pre Med.

ONATO, JUDY; Waipahu HS; Ewa Beach, HI; (1); 37/513; Hon Roll; Renaissance Pgm; Comp Oper.

ONLEY, NERIDA J; Mid Pacific Inst; Honolulu, HI; (2); 9/275; Church Yth Grp; Band; Chorus; High Hon Roll; Hon Roll; Sydney U Australia; Fshn Dsgnr.

ONO, ADELE C; Leilehua HS; Wahiawa, HI; (4); Church Yth Grp; Band; Yrbk; VP Sec Soph Cls; Score Keeper; U Of HI.

ONO, SOLOMON M; Waimea HS; Kalaheo, HI; (3); SADD; Rep Soph Cls; Rep Jr Cls; Pres Sr Cls; Var Bsbl; Var Bsktbl; Var Trk; Var Vllybl; Hon Roll; NHS; Jr Olympic Vllybl Chmpnshp, Asics Vllybl Trnmnt 90; Sports Med.

ONUMA, MICHAEL T; Pearl City HS; Pearl City, HI; (4); 53/500; Computer Clb; Pres JA; Math Tm; Quiz Bowl; Pres VICA; Hon Roll; Close-Up Pres; Ctzn Bee Fnlst; UH Manoa; Mech Engrng.

OOKA, ALLISON M; Hawaii Baptist Acad; Kailua, HI; (2); 1/92; Treas Drama Clb; FTA; Hosp Aide; Thesps; Rep Stu Cncl; Pres Jr NHS; NHS; Servant Group; Asst Coach For Amer Yth Soccer Org Team; Pres Aloha Cncl; Doctor.

ORDONIO, JASMINE R; James Campbell HS; Ewa Beach, HI; (2); Band; Jazz Band; Mrchg Band; U Of HI; Comp Pgmr.

ORIKASA, KRIS; H P Baldwin HS; Wailuku, HI; (1); Key Clb; SADD; Band; Mrchg Band; Pep Band; Japanese Clb; Stu Styng Strght; Maui Jr Golf; Maui Dist Hnr Band.

ORTIZ, CHANTEL H; Maui HS; Makawao, HI; (2); 41/388; Hon Roll; Triple S Stus Staying Strght; Food Srvc Clb Sec; Maui CC; Sec.

ORTIZ, KIM; Redemption Acad; Kaneohe, HI; (2); 1/20; Church Yth Grp; Dance Clb; Intrml Vllybl; Hon Roll; Seattle Pacific U; Med.

OSATO, JODI L; Kaiser HS; Honolulu, HI; (4); Band; Color Guard; Mrchg Band; Hon Roll; U Of HI.

OSATO, MATT S; Mid-Pacific Inst; Pearl City, HI; (3); 9/195; Chess Clb; Teachers Aide; VP Soph Cls; Var Swmmng; High Hon Roll; NHS; Vrsty Wtr Polo Ltr; Jpnese Clb; USS Punahou Aquatcs Swmr 83-90.

OSHIBA, CINDY T; Waiakea HS; Hilo, HI; (1); 129/478; JA; Leo Clb; U Of HI Manoa; Psycht.

OSHIRO, JENNIFER M; Hawaii Baptist Acad; Honolulu, HI; (1); GAA; Hosp Aide; JA; Chorus; Hon Roll; Pres Acad Fit Awd; Japanese Club; Servant Group; Elec Engrng.

OSHIRO, RENEE; Mid-Pacific Inst; Waianae, HI; (3); Church Yth Grp; Hon Roll; Canoe Paddling; Bodyboarding; Hula; U HI.

OSHIRO, TRACIE N; Mid-Pacific Inst; Pearl City, HI; (2); JV Tennis; Cit Awd; Hon Roll; U HI; CPA.

OSHITA, GERI R; Waiakea HS; Hilo, HI; (1); 17/478; Church Yth Grp; Intnl Clb; Service Clb; High Hon Roll; Oral Roberts U; Bus.

OTA, DARREN; Konawaena JR-SR HS; Holualoa, HI; (4); Cmnty Wkr; Letterman Clb; Ed Yrbk; Rep Jr Cls; Rep Sr Cls; Hon Roll; NHS; Bowlng Vrsty HS ST Champ 88-89; 2nd Pl ST Leo Clb Scrapbk Edtr.

OTAKA, RANDY; Mililani HS; Mililani Town, HI; (4); Math Clb; Math Tm; Q&S; Ed Nwsp; Lit Mag; Treas Stu Cncl; JV Crs Cntry; JV Trk; High Hon Roll; Hon Roll; HI Cncl Tchrs Eng Shrt Stry Wnnr; Natl Cncl Tchrs Eng; Swarthmore Coll; Eng.

OTANI, BRYAN T; Maui HS; Pukalani, HI; (3); 46/354; Key Clb; Treas Band; Mrchg Band; Pep Band; Hon Roll.

OTANI, RENEE; Hilo HS; Hilo, HI; (2); 14/390; Treas FHA; Hon Roll; FHA Treas; Trvl Agnt.

OTOMO, LANELL K; Waiakea HS; Hilo, HI; (1); 17/478; Church Yth Grp; Pep Clb; Color Guard; Hon Roll; Interact Club Secy Mem 90; Intl Order Of Rainbow Mem.

OTOMO, LORI ANN N; Mc Kinley HS; Honolulu, HI; (2); JV Tennis; Hon Roll; Prfct Atten Awd; Keywannettes Club; Med.

OTTO, CHRIS A; Kaimuki HS; Honolulu, HI; (2); 88/325; U Of HI; Law Enfrcmnt.

OU, YEN- PING; Kaimuki HS; Honolulu, HI; (3); 12/361; HI Humane Soc 88 Vlntr; Manoa Smmr Fn Vlntr 88; Smmr Pgm Oceanogrphy U Of HI 89.

OU, YEN-PING; Kaimuki HS; Honolulu, HI; (3); 12/361; Hon Roll; Vol HI Humane Soc 88; Vol Jr Ldr Manoa Summer Fun 88; Summer Prgrm Ocngrphy-U Of HI 89.

OUCHI, DEVIN P; Pearl City HS; Waipahu, HI; (2); 67/511; Hon Roll; Little Lg Bsbl; LSU.

OUCHI, MIKEL; Waiakea HS; Hilo, HI; (2); 121/497; Hilo Aikido Clb.

OULAYRACK, TOUNEKEO; Kaimuki HS; Honolulu, HI; (2); 43/325; Hon Roll; U Of HI; Bus Admin.

OULAYRACK, VEOTA; Kaimuki HS; Honolulu, HI; (2); Hon Roll.

OUMI, ARIC H; Hawaii Baptist Acad; Kaneohe, HI; (3); 8/90; Church Yth Grp; Pres Soph Cls; Intrml JV Bsktbl; JV Vllybl; High Hon Roll; Hon Roll; Ldrshp Club; Pres Aloha Cncl; U WA; Engrng.

OWENS, ROBERT B; St Louis HS; Honolulu, HI; (3); 5/152; Cmnty Wkr; Hosp Aide; Quiz Bowl; ROTC; Hon Roll; NHS; Prfct Atten Awd; Princpls List; Arch.

OYAMA, ERIN; Mc Kinley HS; Kailua, HI; (1); 31/492; Orch; School Play; JV L Swmmng; Hon Roll; Prfct Atten Awd; 2nd Pl Sci Fr Dply Div; Video Prjct.

OZAKI, CHANTEL C; Waimea HS; Kalaheo Kauai, HI; (3); Church Yth Grp; Cmnty Wkr; Debate Tm; Key Clb; Math Tm; Science Clb; Speech Tm; SADD; Sec Jr Cls; High Hon Roll; 1st Pl PO Ltr Wrtng Cont; Outstndng Chrch Yth Group Mem; Chrprsn Various Events Hmcmng, Prom; Pre Law.

PAALUHI, FRANCINE K; Nanakuli HS; Waianae, HI; (4); 7/112; Church Yth Grp; Teachers Aide; Rep Soph Cls; Rep Jr Cls; Rep Sr Cls; Treas Stu Cncl; Stat Bsktbl; Mgr(s); Hon Roll; NHS; Prncpls Lst; John Papa Ii Awd; Leeward CC; Trvl Indstry Mgmt.

PABILA, MAILE A; Waiakea HS; Hilo, HI; (3); 7/368; Church Yth Grp; JA; NHS.

PABLO, DARYL JANE R; Farrington HS; Honolulu, HI; (1); Hon Roll; Prfct Atten Awd; 1st Prncs Frshmn Royal Ct; Cls Rep; U Of HI; Reg Nurse.

PABLO, ERNEST T; Kailua HS; Waimanalo, HI; (2); Cmnty Wkr; Ftbl; Wt Lftg; USC; Ftbl.

PABLO, JANE R; Farrington HS; Honolulu, HI; (1); Hon Roll; Prfct Atten Awd; Straigh A Stu; Princee Frshmn Court 89-90; In Class Comm; U HI; RN.

PABRE, GINA; Konawaena HS; Kealakekua, HI; (2); 34/338; Rep Frsh Cls; Rep Soph Cls; Var Sftbl; Var Trk; Hon Roll; Pres Acad Fit Awd; Sprts Med.

PACHECO, CHAD A; Baldwin HS; Wailuku, HI; (3); Church Yth Grp; Letterman Clb; SADD; Varsity Clb; Var L Bsktbl; Wt Lftg.

PACHECO, JOYCELYN L; Pahoa HS; Pahoa, HI; (3); 3/100; Church Yth Grp; Pep Clb; Rptr Nwsp; Pres Soph Cls; VP Stu Cncl; JV Var Bsktbl; Var Cheerldng; Var Crs Cntry; Hon Roll; NHS; Schl Mediator; HOBY Fndtn Ambssdr 89; Willamette U; Med.

PACUBAS, MYRA P; Maui HS; Kahului, HI; (3); 1/374; Science Clb; Stu Cncl; High Hon Roll; Hon Roll; NHS; Engl Awds; Japanese Clb; U Of HI Manoa; Lw.

PAET, LYNETTE S; Maui HS; Wailuku, HI; (3); 41/354; Key Clb; Pep Clb; Hon Roll; Prfct Atten Awd; Triple S; U Of HI Manoa; Comp Sci.

PAGADUAN, RANDY R; Damien Memorial HS; Honolulu, HI; (4); 22/122; Quiz Bowl; JV Var Ftbl; JV Trk; NHS; Bro Thomas B Regan Schlr Athl Awd Wnnr; Longs Drug Stores Ed Grnt Awd Wnnr 90; De Vry Inst Of Tech; Bus Oper.

PAGAT, PRESTON M; Kohala HS; Kapaau, HI; (3); 7/65; Boy Scts; VP FTA; Library Aide; Treas Spanish Clb; Rptr Nwsp; Var L Tennis; Var L Vllybl; Hon Roll; NHS; Hnrbl Mntn Lng Cmpstn HI Lang Arts Shwcs; Sntr Offc HI Affrs Yth Lgsltr; Close Up Prtcpnt WA DC; Elem Ed.

PAGBA, MYRA G; Farrington HS; Honolulu, HI; (2); VP Math Clb; Church Choir; Ed Nwsp; Pres Frsh Cls; Off Soph Cls; Pres Jr Cls; Var Tennis; High Hon Roll; Jr NHS; Outstndng Soph Awd; Pedtrcn.

PAGDILAO, BOBBY C; J Campbell HS; Ewa Beach, HI; (2); JV Ftbl; JV Trk; Hon Roll; U HI; Carpentry.

PAGEL, IRENE R; Kailua HS; Kailua, HI; (3); Spanish Clb; SADD; U Of HI; Psych.

PAGUIRIGAN, GINA B; Radford HS; Honolulu, HI; (3); 15/396; Math Tm; Mu Alpha Theta; Band; Drm Mjr(t); Mrchg Band; Pep Band; Stu Cncl; Stat Mgr(s); High Hon Roll; Sec NHS; HI Amb Of Music To Europe 89; Med.

PAHINAG, GLENN; Kalaheo HS; Kailua, HI; (2); Hon Roll; U Of HI Manoa.

PAI, DAVID; Mc Kinley HS; Honolulu, HI; (3); Spanish Clb; Band; Jazz Band; Pres Frsh Cls; VIPS; Law.

PAI, JIMMY Y; Roosevelt HS; Honolulu, HI; (1); 25/365; Science Clb; Band; Jazz Band; Mrchg Band; Orch; Hon Roll; Sci.

PAI, RUTH; Mililani HS; Mililani, HI; (1); 31/593; Hosp Aide; Band; Mrchg Band; Hon Roll; Arch Engrng.

PAJARILLO, JOCELYN; Waianae HS; Waianae, HI; (4); 12/328; Office Aide; VP Spanish Clb; Teachers Aide; Color Guard; Flag Corp; Sec Soph Cls; Sec Jr Cls; Sec Sr Cls; Stu Cncl; Var Cheerldng; U Of HI; Nursing.

PAJIMOLA, TIMMY J; Kamehameha HS; Captain Cook, HI; (4); AFS; Letterman Clb; Library Aide; Office Aide; Pep Clb; Red Cross Aide; ROTC; SADD; Varsity Clb; JV Bsbl; Skin Scuba Dvr; Dist All Star Wrstlr; U Of HI Hilo; Psych.

PALACAT, TAMI MARIE C; Kalaheo HS; Kailua, HI; (3); 26/294; Bus Profs of Am; Cmnty Wkr; FBLA; JA; SADD; School Play; Stu Cncl; L Var Cheerldng; Hon Roll; Jr NHS; Homcmng Chairprsn; Homcomng Attendent; U Of HI-MANOA; Bus.

PALAKIKO, REIKO H; Kaimuki HS; Honolulu, HI; (3); Art Clb; Hon Roll; Bowling Team; Going To Beach; Kapiolani CC.

PALAMA, SEAN K; Kamehameha HS; Kailua, HI; (4); Cmnty Wkr; Letterman Clb; ROTC; SADD; Var Bsbl; Var Socr; Wt Lftg; Cit Awd; Prfct Atten Awd; Pres Acad Fit Awd; Loyola Marymount U; Bus Admin.

PALMA, FE ETRATA; Farrinton HS; Milpitas, CA; (1); 2/350; Cit Awd; High Hon Roll; Hon Roll; Prfct Atten Awd; San Jose ST; Bus Mgmt.

PALUDIPAN, FRAJOLYN D; Maui HS; Kahului, HI; (2); 7/451.

PAN, JINGXIA; Roosevelt HS; Honolulu, HI; (2); 56/360; Cmnty Wkr; Intnl Clb; Science Clb; Teachers Aide; Tennis; Hon Roll; Kuku Lu Kumuhana; U HI; Pharm.

PANEM, KAYSIE A; St Joseph HS; Pepeekeo, HI; (3); Pep Clb; Science Clb; Chorus; Yrbk; VP Jr Cls; Bsktbl; Cheerldng; Gym; Sftbl; Vllybl; U Of HI Hilo; Travel.

PANG, JODIE; Kalaheo HS; Kaneohe, HI; (1); 2/261; Dance Clb; Teachers Aide; Hon Roll; Child Psych.

PANG, MITCHELL H; St Louis HS; Pearl City, HI; (3); Aud/Vis; Cmnty Wkr; Intrml JV Bsbl; Intrml Ftbl; High Hon Roll; Jap Clb; OUR Clb; AYSO, HYSA; Bus.

PAPPAS, JENNIFER C; Mililani HS; Mililani, HI; (2); 197/515; Church Yth Grp; GAA; Pep Clb; Band; Mrchg Band; Pep Band; JV Bsktbl; Var Mgr(s); Var Score Keeper; Intrml Sftbl.

PAREDES, KYLE T; Pearl City HS; Pearl City, HI; (3); 69/542; Varsity Clb; JV Var Ftbl; Var Trk; Wt Lftg; Wrstlng; Hon Roll; Med.

PARISH, SHAREEN M; Leilehua HS; Wahiawa, HI; (3); 28/322; Church Yth Grp; Pres Spanish Clb; Church Choir; School Play; Ed Nwsp; Phtg Yrbk; Sec Frsh Cls; Var L Trk; Hon Roll; Pres Schlr; Commnctns.

PARK, KUUIPOLANI G; Leilehua HS; Wahiawa, HI; (3); Teachers Aide; Cannons Bus Coll; Bus Admin.

PARK, NEYSA D; Roosevelt HS; Honolulu, HI; (2); Band; Mrchg Band; Pep Band; Harpist; Grad Nvvanv Waikei Gakuen; Med.

PARK, TROY L Y S; Waialua HS; Waialua, HI; (3); 28/157; Var JV Ftbl; Var Trk; Hon Roll; Prfct Atten Awd; Forestry.

PARK, VICTORIA; Pahoa HS; Pahoa, HI; (4); 19/106; FBLA; Pres Service Clb; Phtg Yrbk; Rep Stu Cncl; Hon Roll; NHS; HI Lions Intl Yth Camp; HI ST Stu Cnfrnce; Hugh O'brien Ldrshp Seminar; U Of HI; Trvl Indstry Mngmnt.

PARKER, JUDITH L; Mililani HS; Mililani, HI; (2); 50/509; Hon Roll; Inter Design.

PARKER, ROSEMARIE E; Hawaiian Mission Acad; Waianae, HI; (3); Church Yth Grp; Drama Clb; Hosp Aide; Red Cross Aide; Teachers Aide; Chorus; Church Choir; School Play; Camp Staff; Mission Trp; Med.

PASCUA, ERNALYN Y; Campbell HS; Ewa Beach, HI; (2); Science Clb; Teachers Aide; Hon Roll; Interschool Club; Sophomore Banquet Court; Business.

PASCUA JR, ERNEST; St Joseph HS; Hilo, HI; (3); Church Yth Grp; Cmnty Wkr; Computer Clb; Letterman Clb; Math Tm; Pep Clb; Quiz Bowl; Science Clb; Varsity Clb; Treas Soph Cls; USAF Acad; Space Engrng.

PASCUA, MELISSA A; Mililani HS; Mililani, HI; (4); 110/408; FHA; Key Clb; Band; U Of HI Manoa; Nrsng.

PASION, CHERRY; Pahoa HS; Pahoa, HI; (3); FBLA; FHA; FTA; Spanish Clb; Photo Club; Cert Of Awd Soc Studies; Bus Adm.

PASTOR, DORIS L; Farrington HS; Honolulu, HI; (2); Rep Computer Clb; GAA; Hosp Aide; Key Clb; SADD; Phtg Nwsp; Ed Lit Mag; Rep Frsh Cls; Rep Soph Cls; Var JV Crs Cntry; Upward Bnd; Motor Bldg; Brown; Med.

PATAGUE, REGINO C; Waipahu HS; Waipahu, HI; (1); 80/513; U Southern CA; Bus Mgmt.

PATEL, SONIA G; Molokai High & Intermediate School; Maunaloa, HI; (3); 1/100; VP Drama Clb; Sec Letterman Clb; Math Tm; Science Clb; Sec Soph Cls; Sec Jr Cls; Var L Crs Cntry; Var L Tennis; High Hon Roll; NHS; Harvard Bk Awd; JC Penny Golden Rule Awd; 1st Ladys Outstndng Voluntr Awd; Japan US Senate Schlrshp.

PATRICK, JENNIFER E; Mililani HS; Wahiawa, HI; (2); 73/509; Church Yth Grp; School Musical; School Play; Stage Crew; Variety Show; Off Soph Cls; Stu Cncl; Hon Roll; Voice Dem Awd; Cnslr Chldrns Camp 3 Smmrs; Teach Sndy Schl; Elem Educ.

PATRICK, KIMBERLY S; Mililani HS; Schofield, HI; (3); 23/490; Church Yth Grp; Cmnty Wkr; English Clb; French Clb; Math Clb; Science Clb; SADD; Chorus; Church Choir; School Musical; Fellowship Clb Pres; Camp Cnslr; Wheaton Coll.

PATRICK, STEVE; Henry Opukahaia Schl; Keaau, HI; (3); Church Yth Grp; Quiz Bowl; Ed Yrbk; Sec Soph Cls; Var Capt Bsktbl; Hon Roll; OR ST U.

PAU, LAWRENCE G; W R Farrington HS; Honolulu, HI; (2); 191/696; Computer Clb; Acpl Chr; 1st Pl Wnr Brwn Bags Tlnt Shw; U Of HI; Pdtrcn.

PAULINO, ASHLYNN I; St Francis HS; Ewa Beach, HI; (3); 10/65; Church Yth Grp; Cmnty Wkr; Dance Clb; Hosp Aide; Pep Clb; Spanish Clb; Co-Ed Yrbk; VP Sr Cls; Var Bsktbl; Jr NHS; Prfssnl Polynesian Dance Entertainer; U Of HI; Jrnlsm.

PAUOLE, MATTHEW K; Pahoa HS; Pahoa, HI; (1); Band; Off Soph Cls; Ftbl; Wt Lftg; Hon Roll; Civil Air Patrol; USAF Aviataion.

PAXTON, LISA; Kalaheo HS; Kailua, HI; (2); Off Soph Cls; JV Trk; Hon Roll.

PAZ, EDELYN M; Radford HS; Honolulu, HI; (2); 4/411; Band; Chorus; Mrchg Band; Pep Band; Var Socr; High Hon Roll; Hon Roll; NHS; Mock Trial Tm; Excllnc In Spnsh Awd; Stu Art Exhibition 90; Duke U; Bio-Genetic Engr.

PEA, TRESA P; Waiakea HS; Hilo, HI; (2); Pres Church Yth Grp; DECA; Temple Yth Grp; Band; Pep Band; High Hon Roll; Hon Roll; Cptn Hilo Stake Smnry; 1st Pl Mst Indvdl Points Smnry Bowl; Mst Outstndng Smnry Stu Awd; Med.

PEDERSON, JON D; Radford HS; Hickam Afb, HI; (3); 22/394; Mu Alpha Theta; Rep Stu Cncl; Var Bsbl; JV Var Bsktbl; Var Socr; Hon Roll; NHS; Prfct Atten Awd; Amer Lgn Bsbl.

PEDRO, KILANI M; Kalaheo HS; Las Vegas, NV; (3); 38/240; Off Frsh Cls; Hon Roll; NHS; U Of HI; Arch.

PELEIHOLANI, JULIA; Pahoa HS; Pahoa, HI; (1); FFA; FHA; High Hon Roll; Hon Roll; Prfct Atten Awd; U Of HI; Law.

PELERAS JR, DARRICK J M; Waimea HS; Kekaha, HI; (2); 26/190; JV Var Bsktbl; Var Vllybl; Hon Roll; Electrnc Clb; U Of HI; Electronics.

PELLETIER, MALIA P; Pearl City HS; Pearl City, HI; (3); 103/527; Cmnty Wkr; Dance Clb; FHA; Hon Roll; Cls-Up Trp WA DC 90; Stu Ambssdr Rssa/Peopl-Peopl Frndshp Crvn; Enrchmt Cls; Mdcl Sci.

PELLMAN, ANNA B; James Campbell HS; Honolulu, HI; (3); 5/371; Pres JA; Capt Quiz Bowl; VP Science Clb; School Musical; Rptr Nwsp; Var Bsktbl; JV Vllybl; Bausch & Lomb Sci Awd; High Hon Roll; Hon Roll; 3rd Pl Leeward Dist Sci Fr 90; Tm Cptn Lcl TV Game Shw Qzzrd; Co-Org Renaissance Pgm; Biomed Engrng.

PENARANDA, SUZANNE M; Mililani HS; Mililani, HI; (3); 60/490; Church Yth Grp; Cmnty Wkr; Science Clb; Ed Yrbk; Sec Soph Cls; Rep Stu Cncl; Sccr Referee; Camp Cnslr; Boston U; Orthdntst.

PEPPER, A KIANA; Kalaheo HS; Kailua, HI; (4); German Clb; Key Clb; Crs Cntry; Swmmng; Tennis; Trk; Hon Roll; JVC Swmmr Of Yr; Bus.

PERALTA, TRACY M; St Francis HS; Mililani, HI; (2); Cmnty Wkr; Intrml Var Cheerldng; Intrml Vllybl; Hon Roll.

PEREIRA, SHERI L; Konawaena HS; Kailua Kona, HI; (2); 35/338; JV Bsktbl; Mgr(s); Score Keeper; Smnry Awds; BYU; Bus Comp.

PEREZ, KEVIN A; The Kamehameha Schls; Kamuela, HI; (4); 163/419; Chess Clb; 4-H; JA; Office Aide; Red Cross Aide; ROTC; SADD; Chorus; Church Choir; Color Guard; Rose-Hullman; Aerosp Engr.

PERINI, JEFFERY M; Radford HS; Honolulu, HI; (2); 41/411; Church Yth Grp; Rep Stu Cncl; Var Socr; Close Up Pgm 90; Schl Grievance Cmmtte Chrprsn; Cntrl Dist Stu Cncl 90.

PERKINS, ALLISON; Kalaheo HS; Kailua, HI; (2); Drama Clb; SADD; Thesps; Vllybl; Hon Roll; Jr NHS; Acting.

PERKINS, REBECCA; Lahainaluna HS; Lahaina, HI; (3); Church Yth Grp; DECA; Hon Roll; Jr NHS; SSS; JR Clss Rep; Peer Ed Pgm; Bgng Typng Awd; U Of HI Manoa; Bus Admin.

PERRAS, MICHELLE; Radford HS; Honolulu, HI; (2); 75/411; French Clb; Band; L Trk; Hon Roll.

PERREIRA, CLAUDINE L L; Panoa HS; Pahoa, HI; (3); Bus Profs of Am; Computer Clb; FHA; Library Aide; Pep Clb; Rptr Yrbk; Stu Cncl; Awd Outstng Offcr FHA; Awd Offcr Stu Gov; Recptnst For Airlines.

PERREIRA, DAVID M; Saint Anthony HS; Makawao, HI; (4); 19/65; Library Aide; Spanish Clb; Band; Phtg Yrbk; Rep Jr Cls; Treas Sr Cls; Hon Roll; Sal; Capmus Mnstry; Maui CC; Liberal Arts.

PERREIRA, JODI M; Kaimuki HS; Honolulu, HI; (3); Hon Roll; Bus.

PERREIRA, MICHELLEEN; Milliani HS; Wahiawa, HI; (3); Chorus; Mgr(s); Leo Clb; Loyola Marymount U; Dance.

PERREIRA, TRISHA L; Saint Joseph HS; Honokaa, HI; (3); 4-H; Letterman Clb; Var Bsktbl; Hon Roll; Comp.

PERRY, BRANDON B; Kalaheo HS; Kailua, HI; (3); Office Aide.

PERRY, BRYAN; Hawaiian Mission Acad; Waipahu, HI; (2); Church Yth Grp; Band; Ftbl; Aviation Clb; Outdoor Clb; Walla Walla Coll; Engrng.

PERRY, MARISA M; Moanalua HS; Honolulu, HI; (3); 90/500; Var JV Vllybl; U Of HI Manoa; Bus.

PETERS, KENNETH J; Laupahoehoe HS; Laupahoehoe, HI; (3); Debate Tm; Science Clb; Speech Tm; Band; Rep Frsh Cls; Rep Soph Cls; Rep Jr Cls; Bsbl; Swmmng; Trk; U HI-MANOA; Hotel Mgmt.

PETERS, MARK C; Hilo HS; Hilo, HI; (3); 46/367; Band; U Of HI Hilo.

PHAM, TRACEY D; Maryknoll HS; Kaneohe, HI; (4); 20/125; Cmnty Wkr; GAA; Office Aide; Pres Spanish Clb; Varsity Clb; Capt Tennis; High Hon Roll; Hon Roll; U Of The Pacific; Pharmcst.

PHAN, MAGGIE; Mc Kinley HS; Honolulu, HI; (2); 31/588; Cmnty Wkr; Science Clb; Off Jr Cls; High Hon Roll; Hon Roll; Prfct Atten Awd; Chinese Clb; Bus Clb; Trip To Close Up Prog; Stanford; Bus.

PHAN, MAI CAM; Kaimuki HS; Honolulu, HI; (2); 31/325; SADD; Sec Frsh Cls; Leo Clb; Mock Trial; Chmn Cls Ring Cmmtte; WA U; Pol Sci.

PHAN, PHUONG; Hawaiian Mission Acad; Honolulu, HI; (2); Art Clb; Acpl Chr; School Musical; Socr; Hon Roll; Japanese Lang I Hnr Roll & Schlrshps; Stanford U; Pediatrics.

PHILLIPS III, CHARLES J B; Radford HS; Honolulu, HI; (3); 98/264; ROTC; VP Varsity Clb; VICA; Band; Drill Tm; Var Crs Cntry; Capt Var Ftbl; Capt Var Trk; Var Wt Lftg; Var Wrstlng; Mr Hgh Schl-2 Yrs; Strght OIA; CO ST; Thrpst.

PHILLIPS, SANDRA; Mililani HS; Schofield, HI; (3); 47/490; Key Clb; Library Aide; Speech Tm; Pres VP SADD; Teachers Aide; Stat Ftbl; High Hon Roll; Hon Roll; Jr NHS; Orgnzd Dance & Lunchtime Actvts.

PHOTHISATH, BANGONE; Mililani HS; Mililani, HI; (3); 14/490; Chrmn Stu Cncl; Hon Roll; Chrmn Of Fundrsr & Co Chrmn T-Shrts Awds Cmmttees; Mem Grad, Apprectn, Publcty & Homecmng Cmmttees; U Of HI-MANOA; Med.

PHUONG, LINH KHA; St Andrews Priory HS; Honolulu, HI; (3); 6/53; Intnl Clb; Office Aide; Science Clb; Teachers Aide; NHS; Prfct Atten Awd; CO ST U; Optometry.

PI, LINDA C; Roosevelt HS; Honolulu, HI; (4); 9/343; Debate Tm; Pres French Clb; Intnl Clb; Math Clb; Mrchg Band; Variety Show; Co-Ed Nwsp; Hon Roll; VP Pres NHS; Sal; Yng Wmn Of Yr Schlrshp Pgm; Natl Yng Ldrs Congrssnl Conf; Santa Clara U; Bus Admin.

PICACIO JR, SANTOS G; Radford HS; Honolulu, HI; (3); 50/394; Cmnty Wkr; Spanish Clb; SADD; Jazz Band; School Musical; Stage Crew; 1st Natl Spnsh Exam; Cert By Pres HI Chptr Of Amer Assn Tchrs Spnsh & Portuguese; U Of Pan Am; Army.

PICARD, NICOLE; H P Baldwin HS; Kihei, HI; (2); 43/395; Hon Roll; Amherst Coll; Hotel Mgmt.

PICKELL, GREGORY A; Leilehua HS; Wahiawa, HI; (2); JV Wrstlng; Comp Prgmr.

PICKETT, TIFFANY M; Kalaheo HS; Kailua, HI; (2); 65/271; Hon Roll; Trendsetters Bty Coll; Manicrst.

PIDOT, SHYLA K; Molokai HS; Maunaloa, HI; (3); 17/95; Church Yth Grp; Cmnty Wkr; Dance Clb; School Play; Rep Frsh Cls; Off Soph Cls; Rep Jr Cls; Rep Stu Cncl; Hon Roll; U HI Manoa; Bus Mgmt.

PIERCE, BERNICE; James Campbell HS; Ewa Beach, HI; (2); 69/348; Church Yth Grp; Hosp Aide; Key Clb; Science Clb; JV Trk; High Hon Roll; Hon Roll; U CA-IRVINE; Acctng.

PINDER, MITZI G; Mc Kinley HS; Honolulu, HI; (2); 123/588; JV Var Swmmng; U Of HI St Cmptn Of Jrnlsm-Yngst Reprtr; Cert Of Awd-Acad Prfrmnc Engl II; Jrnlsm.

PINOL, RANDY M; Mc Kinley HS; Honolulu, HI; (3); VP Spanish Clb; School Play; Stu Congress; Psych.

PLADERA, JODELLE P L; Maui HS; Kahului, HI; (2); 11/388; JV Cheerldng; Hon Roll; Awd Excllnce Math; Awd Excllnce Frgn Lang Japanese; San Diego ST; Bus Mgmt.

PLANESI, DERWIN M; Maui HS; Haiku, HI; (3); Letterman Clb; Ftbl; Trk; Wt Lftg; Wrstlng; All Amer Schlr Awd.

PLANESI, KELLY E; Maui HS; Haiku, HI; (2); French Clb; Rptr Nwsp; Hon Roll; Jrnlsm.

PLANK, MARCUS D; Campbell HS; Ewa Beach, HI; (2); 40/348; Computer Clb; School Play; Stage Crew; Yrbk; Var Bsktbl; Var Crs Cntry; High Hon Roll; Hon Roll; Comp Sci.

PLEMER, TRISHA ANN K; Kamehameha Schls; Haleiwa, HI; (1); 105/451; Church Yth Grp; Chorus; Sftbl Slow Pitch Mixed Lge; U Of HI; Elctrncs.

PLONG, KUNTHEA S; Lutheran HS; Honolulu, HI; (3); Church Yth Grp; FCA; Library Aide; Teachers Aide; Chorus; Church Choir; School Musical; Ed Nwsp; Hon Roll; Prfct Atten Awd.

POE JR, SHARLETTE L K; The Kamehameha Schls; Waianae, HI; (4); 154/415; Church Yth Grp; Letterman Clb; Office Aide; Rep Sr Cls; Sftbl; Vllybl; Cncrt Glee Clb; Semi-Fnlst Natl Hspnc Schlr Awd 90; Eastern WA U; Phy Therapist.

POELZING, RENATA P; Mililani HS; Mililani, HI; (2); 188/509; Church Yth Grp; Church Choir; JV Swmmng; Nuclear Med Tech.

POKIPALA, HULALI A; Lanainaluna HS; Lahaina, HI; (1); 100/223; Rep Stu Cncl; Var Cheerldng; U Of HI; Trvl Agency Work.

POMROY, JENNIFER M L; Kauai HS; Lihue, HI; (3); Church Yth Grp; SADD; Chorus; Church Choir; Var L Vllybl; Hon Roll; Prfrmng Arts Acad 87 & 90; Hnr Choir 88; U Of HI; Elem Ed.

PONG, WILLIAM Y; St Louis HS; Honolulu, HI; (2); 11/150; Chess Clb; Hon Roll; NHS; Comp Progrmmng.

PONTTI, JOANNA; Waialua HS; Waialua, HI; (3); 5/157; Math Tm; Quiz Bowl; Rep Frsh Cls; Rep Soph Cls; Sec Jr Cls; Sec Stu Cncl; Var Cheerldng; Stat Ftbl; High Hon Roll; Sec NHS; Japanese Clb Treas; Intrct Clb VP; Cntrl Dist Stu Cncl Rep; Elem Educ.

POQTIS, AMI; Lahaina Luna HS; Kihei, HI; (1); FHA; Science Clb; U Of FL; Scndry Educ.

POTTER, DAVID J; Mililani HS; Mililani, HI; (3); 110/490; Var Tennis; Navy Sci Awd Achvtmnt Cntrl Dist Sci Fair; HI U; Bio Sci.

POTTER, SARA M; Leilehua HS; Wahiawa, HI; (4); 14/300; Church Yth Grp; Cmnty Wkr; Pep Clb; Off Frsh Cls; Off Soph Cls; Off Jr Cls; Off Sr Cls; Rep Stu Cncl; Pom Pon; High Hon Roll; Pepperdine U; Bus Mgmt.

POWELL, MALAEA F; Leilehua HS; Wahiawa, HI; (4); 1/304; Cmnty Wkr; Teachers Aide; Off Frsh Cls; Off Soph Cls; Off Jr Cls; Off Sr Cls; High Hon Roll; NHS; Educ.

POWLES, KIRK R; Komawaena HS; Kailua Kona, HI; (2); 125/300; Band; High Hon Roll; Hon Roll; Kunawaena Solar Car Tm; Brown Bags To Stardm; Srch For Talnt; U HI Manoa.

PRETZ, REBECCA J; Leilehua HS; Wahiawa, HI; (2); 17/402; Church Yth Grp; Drama Clb; Model UN; Sec SADD; School Play; Var Socr; High Hon Roll; Hon Roll; Yale; Advrtsng.

PRIDDY, GLENN S; Radford HS; Honolulu, HI; (3); 20/426; Phtg Yrbk; Var Crs Cntry; Hon Roll; Prfct Atten Awd; Arch.

PRITCHARD, KRISTINA J; Hawaiian Mission Acad; Honolulu, HI; (3); 7/50; Chorus; Ed Yrbk; Fine Arts Club; Bus Educ Awd; Bus.

PRUSE, TAMMY; Maui HS; Makawao, HI; (4); 57/303; Letterman Clb; Pep Clb; Teachers Aide; Varsity Clb; Chorus; Ed Yrbk; Rep Sr Cls; JV Var Cheerldng; Var Socr; Hon Roll; Drawng/Paintng; Wrt Poetry; U Of HI Hilo; Elem Educ.

PU, VANCE; Hana HS; Hana, HI; (2); 1/27; Boy Scts; Band; Rptr Nwsp; Capt Socr; JV Trk; High Hon Roll; Hon Roll; AYSO Div Coach 10 Yr Olds; Plyr Natl AYSO Tourn 2nd Pl; Atty.

PUNG, RAINEE P; Honoka'a High & Elementary Schl; Kamuela, HI; (3); 43/149; Church Yth Grp; FTA; Science Clb; SADD; Teachers Aide; Chorus; Church Choir; U Of HI Hilo; Electrician.

PURDY, PARRISH A; Maui HS; Haliimaile, HI; (3); 138/354; Aud/Vis; Church Yth Grp; Var Bsbl; Var Ftbl; Hon Roll; OK ST U; Phys Thrpst.

PURSE, HEATHER L; Punahou Schl; Kailua, HI; (2); Science Clb; SADD; Var Swmmng; Srvce Clb 88-90; Amnsty Intl 89-90; Law.

PUSTKA, SHANNON DIANE NOELANI; Hawaii Preparatory Acad; Kamuela, HI; (4); 10/64; Quiz Bowl; Teachers Aide; School Play; Nwsp; JV Bsktbl; Var L Cheerldng; Var L Swmmng; JV Vllybl; High Hon Roll; Cum Laude Scty; Coaches Awd Vrsty Smmng; Scuba Dvr; U Of Puget Snd; Bilgcl Sci.

PUU, THERESA; Pahoa HS; Pahoa, HI; (3); FFA; FHA; Pep Clb; Treas Frsh Cls; Rep Soph Cls; VP Jr Cls; Stu Cncl; JV Var Bsktbl; Var Sftbl; Hon Roll; U Of HI Manoa; Comp Sci.

QUELNAN, MARICEL T; Farrington HS; Honolulu, HI; (2); 5/696; High Hon Roll; Hon Roll; Prfct Atten Awd; Homeroom VP; U Of HI; Law.

QUEMADO, JEANIE; Waipahu HS; Waipahu, HI; (1); 11/513; Dance Clb; Band; Mrchg Band; Pep Band; Variety Show; Rep Frsh Cls; Hon Roll; Prfct Atten Awd; U Of Southern CA; Bus.

QUINABO, LU SHANYA W; Henry Perrine Baldwin HS; Wailuku, HI; (2); Dance Clb; Drama Clb; Office Aide; School Play; Prfct Atten Awd; SSS.

QUITEVIS, CHRISTOPHER A; Waialua High & Intermed; Waialua, HI; (3); 27/157; Math Tm; Quiz Bowl; Science Clb; Rep Stu Cncl; JV Var Bsktbl; Var Crs Cntry; JV Var Ftbl; Var Trk; Hon Roll; Prfct Atten Awd; Sgt At Arms Japanese Clb; Partcptn St Sci Fair; Engr.

QUITORIANO, RYAN G; St Louis HS; Pearl City, HI; (3); 51/157; Boy Scts; Band; Drm Mjr(t); Mrchg Band; Pep Band; JV Socr; Hon Roll; JV Rifle Team; U Of HI; Engrng.

RAABE, TRINTJE C; Waiakea HS; Hilo, HI; (3); 11/368; Band; Mrchg Band; Pep Band; Rep Soph Cls; Off Jr Cls; Off Sr Cls; High Hon Roll; NHS; Yth Lgsltr-YMCA; Optmtry.

RABAGO, KATHY J; Waialua HS & Intermed; Waialua, HI; (2); 1/161; FTA; Math Tm; Pres Science Clb; Treas Frsh Cls; Treas Soph Cls; JV Capt Vllybl; High Hon Roll; Hon Roll; Prfct Atten Awd; Japanese Clb; Med.

RABANG, CHRIS J; Maui HS; Makawao, HI; (3); 50/354; Science Clb; Var Bsktbl; Hon Roll; Prfct Atten Awd; Stu Styng Strght Club VP; Santa Clara U; Electrnc Engrng.

RACADIO, DUKIE J; Baldwin HS; Wailuku, HI; (1); Band; Jazz Band; Mrchg Band; Pep Band; Hon Roll; Prfct Atten Awd; Duke U; Med.

RAGOCOS, KIMBERLY A; St Joseph HS; Hilo, HI; (3); Cmnty Wkr; Letterman Clb; Pep Clb; Science Clb; Acpl Chr; Chorus; School Play; Cheerldng; Hon Roll; Cert Achvt Span II & Relgn; Cardinal Singers Prfrmd Oahu; Sang W/Makaha Sons On Niihau Benefit Cncrt; U Of HI Hilo; Bus.

RAGUDOS, GEILA A; St Francis HS; Waipahu, HI; (2); 7/80; Cmnty Wkr; Intnl Clb; Library Aide; NFL; Speech Tm; Lit Mag; Pres Frsh Cls; High Hon Roll; Hon Roll; Jr NHS; Ms Hospitality Hawaii Natl Teenager; 3rd Runner Up Ms Natl Teenager; Co-Worker Of Mother Theresa; USC; Pediatrician.

RAGUINDIN, ARLENE C; Molokai HS; Kaunakakai, HI; (4); 11/94; Aud/Vis; Church Yth Grp; JA; Letterman Clb; Math Tm; Pres Spanish Clb; Rep Frsh Cls; Treas Sr Cls; L Bsktbl; Capt Crs Cntry; U Portland; Nrsg.

RAISER, EUNICE A; Baldwin HS; Kahului, HI; (3); Gov Hon Prg Awd; Hosp Aide; Science Clb; SADD; School Musical; School Play; Stage Crew; San Diego ST; Adv.

RALAR, CHELSEA; Farrington HS; Honolulu, HI; (2); 28/754; Dance Clb; Library Aide; Pep Clb; Chorus; Var Cheerldng; Gym; Score Keeper.

RAMEL, MAE S; Roosevelt HS; Honolulu, HI; (1); 28/362; Band; Mrchg Band; Pep Band; JV Crs Cntry; JV Trk; Hon Roll; Natl Gld Piano Plyng Adtns; 3th Pl HI Indstrl Arts Fr; Bus.

RAMEL, MARION; Roosevelt HS; Honolulu, HI; (2); 39/360; Band; Mrchg Band; Pep Band; Oahu Band Dur Assn Hnrs & Awds F/Solo & Ensmbl 1989; Intr Dsgn.

RAMELB, SHERRI MAE; Waimea HS; Fresno, CA; (3); 2/200; Cmnty Wkr; Hosp Aide; Math Tm; Sec Science Clb; Pres Spanish Clb; Rptr Nwsp; VP Jr Cls; Stu Cncl; High Hon Roll; NHS; Resrchr/Prsntr HA St Marine Sympsm Presntn; Praise 90; CA Poly San Luis Obispo; Arch.

RAMIREZ, LORI A; Pearl City HS; Pearl City, HI; (2); 238/500; Church Yth Grp; Church Choir; U HI.

RAMIREZ, NIMFA; St Francis HS; Honolulu, HI; (4); 13/64; Dance Clb; French Clb; Hosp Aide; Pep Clb; Chorus; Hon Roll; Campus Mnstry Grp-Ldr; Intrst Mdlng; Honolulu Cmnty Coll; Bus Mgmt.

RAMOS, DABIE; Radford HS; Pearl City, HI; (3); Intnl Clb; ROTC; Spanish Clb; Asian & Pacific Affairs PACA; Hunger Proj YEH Club, Yth Ending Hunger; U Of San Diego; Fash Dsgn.

RAMOS, KIMBERLY K; President William Mc Kinley HS; Honolulu, HI; (3); 97/537; JV Stat Bsktbl; Alu Like Native Hawaiian Sr Careere Intern Pgm; Hula; U HI; Bus Mgmt.

RAMOS, LIANA M; Kamehameha Schl; Mililani, HI; (1); Quiz Bowl; JV Bsktbl; Intrml Tennis; Intrml Vllybl; Hon Roll; Pres Acad Fit Awd.

RAMOS III, NORBERTO P; Kamehameha HS; Kailua-Kona, HI; (2); 105/443; ROTC; Chorus; Rep Stu Cncl; JV Bsbl; Intrml Bsktbl; Var Ftbl; JV Wrstlng; Hoike-Boys/Co-Ed Hula Dncng; Boys Glee Clb-Solo/Duet; Chld Psych.

RAMOS, REGAN; Mililani HS; Mililani, HI; (3); Chess Clb; Church Yth Grp; Math Tm; Mu Alpha Theta; Color Guard; Hon Roll; Cvl Air Ptrl Aux; Aerosp Engr.

RAMOS, ROWENA A; Radford HS; Honolulu, HI; (2); Hon Roll; Pediatrics.

RAMOS, SHANE-WESLEY B K; St Louis HS; Mililani Town, HI; (4); Cmnty Wkr; ROTC; Band; Yrbk; Ftbl; U Of HI.

RANCHEZ, ARNOLD G; Waipahu HS; Ewa Beach, HI; (4); 79/418; Cmnty Wkr; Cmmnty Work; Amer Cltrl Club Hstrn 89-90; Art Awd 90; Lang Art Awd; Schlstc Awds Achvt; U HI; Arch.

RAPHAEL, KALANI; St Louis Schl; Aiea, HI; (2); 10/151; Var Bsbl; Vllybl; High Hon Roll; Hon Roll; Phys Educ Awd; Religion Awd; Sports Med.

RAPOZA, TRISH K; Waiakea HS; Hilo, HI; (2); 46/496; JA; Hon Roll; Jayteens; Easter Seals; UH Hilo; Bus.

RAPOZO, LISA; Honokaa High & Elementary Schl; Honokaa, HI; (4); Cmnty Wkr; Dance Clb; Teachers Aide; Hon Roll; Sec Frsh Cls; VP Soph Cls; Sec Stu Cncl; Var Cheerldng; Var Vllybl; Reprsnt Schl Lgsltv Expernc; Stu Chrprsn Cmmttees; Peer Tutr Elem Stu; U HI Hilo; Ed.

RAPOZO, TITUS; Kapaa HS; Anahola, HI; (3); L Ftbl; L Socr; Wt Lftg; Hon Roll; U Of HI; Doc.

RAQUEL, JOSEPH P; Farrington HS; Honolulu, HI; (2); School Musical; Cit Awd.

RAQUEL, RANDALL S; Saint Louis Schl; Kailua, HI; (2); ROTC; Nwsp; Rep Frsh Cls; Sec Soph Cls; High Hon Roll; Hon Roll; HOBY; St Louis Acad Rcgntn Awds Art & Bus; 90 Congrssnl Arts Cmptn; Arch.

RATERMANN, JENNIFER; Moanalua HS; Waipahu, HI; (3); 25/490; Girl Scts; Spanish Clb; SADD; Teachers Aide; Bsktbl; Crs Cntry; High Hon Roll; Church Yth Grp; Drama Clb; Letterman Clb; Close Up; 1st Pl St Art Cmptn Wrld Hlth Day; Teen Helping Teens; Teacher.

RAVER, KATHERINE C; Moanalua HS; Waipahu, HI; (4); 25/450; Drama Clb; FBLA; FHA; Spanish Clb; Teachers Aide; Varsity Clb; School Play; Sec Frsh Cls; Treas Soph Cls; Rep Stu Cncl; U Of CO CO Sprngs; Nrsng.

RAY, KATHERINE A; Iolani Schl; Wayne, PA; (4); 6/220; Treas Rep Drama Clb; French Clb; Math Tm; Office Aide; Stage Crew; Yrbk; Off Stu Cncl; JV Var Crs Cntry; JV Trk; High Hon Roll; Top Stu-Engl 10, Russian Hstry, Frnch 2, Frnch 3 & Russian Lit; Vlntr Stu Tutor; Wellesly Bk Awd; Duke U; Intl Bus.

RAYRAY, GEAN; Lahainaluna HS; Lahaina, HI; (1); #159 In Class; Office Aide; Vllybl; Hon Roll; MCC.

REBAMONTE, JENNIFER B; James Campbell HS; Makakilo, HI; (2); 24/348; Hon Roll; Banquet Cmmtte; Cannons Bus Coll; Trvl Ind Mgmt.

REBUDAL, JOHN B; Henry Perrine Baldwin HS; Wailuku, HI; (3); Var Tennis; U HI Manoa; Elec Engr.

REDFERN, SHAWN T; Radford HS; Honolulu, HI; (3); Boy Scts; JA; Red Cross Aide; Var Crs Cntry; Hon Roll; Air Frc Explr Pst; USN; Comp Sci.

REDFIELD, KRISTY K; Kapaa HS; Princeville, HI; (3); Aud/Vis; Treas French Clb; SADD; Socr; Prom Cmmty; SDSU; Film.

REDMOND, NEIL L; Kalaheo HS; Kailua, HI; (2); 15/280; JV Var Bsbl; Var Crs Cntry; Var Ftbl; Var Socr; Var Tennis; Var Trk; Hon Roll; Sccr All OIA E All Stars, All Sun-Press; Bus.

REGO, MICHELE K; Waialua HS; Waialua, HI; (3); Pep Clb; JV Var Bsktbl; Stat Score Keeper; JV Var Vllybl; Hon Roll; Prfct Atten Awd; Crtfct Achvt HI Schls Ci & Engr Fairs 89; SDSU; Archtctr.

REGO, TEZRA J; Leilehua HS; Wahiawa, HI; (4); 11/304; VP Spanish Clb; High Hon Roll; NHS; Japanese Clb; Interact Clb Sec; U Of HI Manoa; Educ.

REMICK, DAVID; Kalaheo HS; Kailua, HI; (4); 27/232; Boy Scts; Band; Rep Soph Cls; Rep Jr Cls; Rep Sr Cls; Socr; Hon Roll; Stu Ambssdr To Russia; Marine Bio.

REMIGIO, EMMANUEL C; Mid-Pacific Institute HS; Lihue, HI; (2); 10/200; Math Tm; JV Wrstlng; Hon Roll; NHS; Elec Engr.

RESPICIO, MARY JANE V; Maul HS; Kahului, HI; (3); 12/354; Cmnty Wkr; Service Clb; Band; Flag Corp; Mrchg Band; Hon Roll; Lion Awd; Prfct Atten Awd; U HI Manoa; Accntng.

REYES, MARIA VICTORIA; Theodore Roosevelt HS; Waipahu, HI; (3); 66/350; French Clb; Teachers Aide; Ed Yrbk; Var Socr; Co-Chair Jr Prom Cmmtte; Chrprsn Gov Luv; Chrprsn Soph Banquet; Trvl.

REYES, RENEE P; Konawaena HS; Kealakekua, HI; (2); 56/338; Pres Service Clb; Church Yth Grp; Close Up Club.

RICALDE, ELVAVINA A; James Campbell HS; Ewa Beach, HI; (4); 1/350; VP JA; Library Aide; Spanish Clb; SADD; Ed Nwsp; Rep Jr Cls; Gov Hon Prg Awd; High Hon Roll; NHS; Campbell Estate Ldrshp Schlrshp; Amer Soc Of Nwspr Edtrs Awd; Hnry Navy Offcr For A Day Awd; U HI Manoa; Prnt Jrnlsm.

RICE, COURTNEY R; Leilehua HS; Wahiawa, HI; (2); 1/392; Pres French Clb; Model UN; Off Frsh Cls; High Hon Roll; NHS; Fr, Bio, Chem, G/T Hstry Awds; Speech Fstvls; Shakespearean Fstvl; Cvl Rights Wrkshp; EISP; Exch Stu Jpn; Sci.

RICHARDS, NATHANIEL T; H P Baldwin HS; Kihei, HI; (4); 51/356; JV Socr; Hon Roll; NHS; Rotary Awd; 3rd Pl HI St Amateur Skatebd Contest; Cum Laude Grad; U HI Manoa; Arch.

RICHARDSON, BRIE A; Kalaheo HS; Kailua, HI; (3); Rptr Yrbk; Bsktbl; Var Cheerldng; Score Keeper; High Hon Roll; NHS; Stu Mediator; Yth Ambssdrs; Sci Forum.

RICHARDSON, FREDERICK D; Molokai High & Intermid; Maunaloa, HI; (2); 5/124; Science Clb; Band; Trk; Wrstlng; High Hon Roll; Hon Roll; Pres Acad Fit Awd; 1st AJHSME 87; 1st Muni Inv Track Meet 90; Iana U; Math.

RICHTER, KIMBERLY K; Radford HS; Honolulu, HI; (3); 158/394; Girl Scts; Hosp Aide; ROTC; Hon Roll; U Of HI; Nrsng Army Corp.

RIDGLEY, ERIN; Kauai HS; Kapaa, HI; (3); 22/231; Cmnty Wkr; Drama Clb; VP FTA; SADD; School Musical; School Play; VP Rep Stu Cncl; Mgr(s); DAR Awd; Jr NHS; Sci Olympiad Tm; U Of HI; Eng Ed.

RIES, MELISSA A; James Campbell HS; Ewa Beach, HI; (3); 19/371; Church Yth Grp; SADD; High Hon Roll; Hon Roll; Chrprsn SHS; U Of HI.

RIES, VANESSA J; James Campbell HS; Ewa Beach, HI; (3); 19/371; Church Yth Grp; High Hon Roll; Hon Roll.

RINEHART, AMBER M; Radford HS; Honolulu, HI; (3); 237/548; Girl Scts; SADD; Teachers Aide; JV Cheerldng; Hnrb Mntn Awd Congrssnl Art Cont; Commrcl Artist.

RINGLER, MICHELLE O; Kaiser HS; Honolulu, HI; (1); 19/255; High Hon Roll; Prfct Attend; Pdtrcn.

RINGOR, LOIDA B; Mililani HS; Kunia, HI; (3); 54/490; FHA; Service Clb; Church Choir; Hon Roll; U Of HI; Comp Sci.

RIVERA, EMIL L; Mc Kinley HS; Honolulu, HI; (3); Yrbk; Hon Roll; Japanese Clb; U HI; Engrng.

RIVERA, LAILANI R; James Campbell HS; Ewa Beach, HI; (3); 37/371; High Hon Roll; Hon Roll; Stu Assn Cmmnty Rltns Chrprsn; U Of HI; Nrsng.

RIVERA, MARIBEL; Mililani HS; Wahiawa, HI; (3); 226/490; French Clb; Intnl Clb; Spanish Clb; Adopt A Sch; Inter-Amer U; Bus.

RIVERA, SUSAN T; Waipahu HS; Waipahu, HI; (2); Hosp Aide; Library Aide; Math Clb; Math Tm; Office Aide; Quiz Bowl; SADD; Band; Rptr Nwsp; Lit Mag; Whtmn Coll; Spec Ed.

RIVERA, WENDY A; Waipahu HS; Waipahu, HI; (2); 19/440; Science Clb; Stu Cncl; High Hon Roll; Hon Roll.

ROBERTS, SCOTT E; Kaiser HS; Honolulu, HI; (3); Ski Clb; Intrml Socr; JV L Wrstlng; Hon Roll; Real Est.

ROBINOS, LORELEI; Lanahila Baptist Schl; Waipahu, HI; (1); Rep Frsh Cls; High Hon Roll; Jr NHS; Prfct Atten Awd; Med.

ROBINSON, JAIME; Radford HS; Honolulu, HI; (1); Treas SADD; JV Cheerldng; JV Var Mgr(s); JV Var Score Keeper; Stat Wrstlng; Law.

ROBINSON, JON; Waiakea HS; Hilo, HI; (3); Letterman Clb; Treas Frsh Cls; Sec Soph Cls; Pres Jr Cls; Var Bsktbl; JV Crs Cntry; Var Ftbl; Trk; High Hon Roll; Masonic Awd; Mech Engrng.

ROBINSON, RACHEL E; Lahainaluna HS; Lahaina, HI; (3); 61/217; Spanish Clb; Hon Roll; Mem Of Triple S; U HI Mauoa; Ed.

ROBINSON, STUART P; Mililani HS; Fort Ord, CA; (3); Church Yth Grp; Spanish Clb; Stu Cncl; Philosophy Club Mem; EOT & TBS Mem; Soph Outstndng Bio Stu Awd; San Francisco Art Inst; Art.

ROBINSON, WENDY A; Leilehua HS; Wahiawa, HI; (4); 7/304; FTA; Library Aide; NFL; Red Cross Aide; Speech Tm; Teachers Aide; School Play; Stage Crew; Lit Mag; NHS; HI Shakespear Comptn St Semifnlst 88; HI Physics Olympcs Tm; Cntrl Dist Sci Fair Dsply Div Wnnr.

ROCCO, JOE M; Radford HS; Honolulu, HI; (3); Boy Scts; Church Yth Grp; Bsktbl; Score Keeper; Socr; Wrstlng; High Hon Roll; Prfct Atten Awd.

RODRIGUES, CHERYL D; Maui HS; Makawao, HI; (2); 47/392; French Clb; Trk; Hon Roll; Comp.

RODRIGUES, RAYNA L; Konawaena HS; Holualoa, HI; (2); 14/338; VP Jr Cls; Capt Cheerldng; Var Crs Cntry; Var Sftbl; Var Trk; Hon Roll; NHS.

RODRIGUES, SHANE P; Maui HS; Pukalani, HI; (4); 9/303; VP Drama Clb; Band; Stage Crew; Hon Roll; Japanese Club, Video Club Pres, Video Yrbk, Prod, Dir, Ed, Camera; Grad,Jr Prom, Sr Ball Cmmtte; TV Prod.

RODRIGUEZ, SANDRA T; Hawaiian Mission Acad; Honolulu, HI; (3); 2/50; Church Yth Grp; Math Clb; Spanish Clb; Speech Tm; Sec Jr Cls; Intrml Golf; Outstndg Adv Math Awd; Bilingual-Spnsh & Engl; SR Yr Schlrshp; Loma Linda U; Med.

ROMANCHEK, CHRISTIAN KIER; Radford HS; Honolulu, HI; (4); 72/348; Teachers Aide; Var L Tennis; Hon Roll; Cum Laude Grad; U Of S FL; Comp Sci.

ROMERO, LORENA J; Baldwin HS; Kihei, HI; (3); 143/385; Key Clb; Service Clb; SADD; Band; Jazz Band; Mrchg Band; Pep Band; Trk; UH Manoa; Elem Tchr.

RONDON, EMILY L; Maui HS; Haiku, HI; (2); 4/388; FTA; Band; JV Trk; Hon Roll; Aquarium Terrarium Club Secy; Top Schlr Acadmc Awd; Law.

RONEY, MARYANN MILIA; Kailua HS; Kailua, HI; (3); 23/362; Church Yth Grp; 4-H; JA; Spanish Clb; Teachers Aide; Church Choir; Var Bsktbl; Wt Lftg; 4-H Awd; Hon Roll; Prom Cmmtte; Horses; U Of HI; Law.

ROOT, JEROME T; Radford HS; Village Park, HI; (3); ROTC; Color Guard; Drill Tm; Wrstlng; Military.

ROSA, JENNIFER; Saint Francis HS; Kaneohe, HI; (4); 1/64; Mu Alpha Theta; NFL; Q&S; Yrbk; VP Soph Cls; Pres Jr Cls; Pres Stu Cncl; NHS; Val; Kayaking-Sprts; Northwestern U; Ec.

ROSA, MICHELE L; Kauai HS & Intermed; Lihue, HI; (3); 9/231; Church Yth Grp; FTA; SADD; Teachers Aide; Church Choir; Hon Roll; NHS; Early Childhd Ed.

ROSE, KIMBERLY D; Mililani HS; Mililani, HI; (3); 64/490; Art Clb; Church Yth Grp; French Clb; Hosp Aide; Church Choir; Orch; Jr NHS.

ROSE, LISA L; Mililani HS; Mililani, HI; (2); 106/509; Hosp Aide; Science Clb; School Musical; School Play; Stage Crew; Nrsng.

ROSE, STACY K; Farrington HS; Honolulu, HI; (3); Pep Clb; SADD; Yrbk; Cheerldng; Gym; Trk; Law.

ROSEHILL, HEATHER; Kamehameha HS; Hilo, HI; (3); 30/430; Drama Clb; Math Clb; Math Tm; Office Aide; Pep Clb; Science Clb; Spanish Clb; Speech Tm; Band; Mrchg Band; UC Berkeley; Pre-Med.

ROSEHILL, KELLY N; Waiakea HS; Hilo, HI; (1); Var Crs Cntry; JV Trk; Yth Legisltre.

ROSS, BURGESS K; Waipahu HS; Waipahu, HI; (4); 24/418; Lit Mag; Hon Roll; Leo Clb Cmmtte 89-90; Interact Clb Cmmtte; Golden & Silver Poet Awd 89-90; U Of HI; Educ.

ROSS, CHRYSTAL C; Redemption Acad; Waianae, HI; (2); Teachers Aide; Church Choir; Yrbk; Var Vllybl; Hon Roll; Oral Roberts U OK; Arch.

ROSS, GANDHARVA; Molokai HS; Kaunakakai, HI; (3); 6/100; Church Yth Grp; Letterman Clb; Off Soph Cls; Stu Cncl; JV Var Bsbl; Var Capt Crs Cntry; Var Trk; Hon Roll; Forestry.

ROUNTREE, GINGER L; Radford HS; Honolulu, HI; (2); 213/411; Sec Church Yth Grp; Social Work.

ROWE, DUANE K; St Louis HS; Kaneohe, HI; (2); Spanish Clb; JV Bsktbl; JV Ftbl; Var JV Trk; Hon Roll; Loyola Marymount; Psych.

ROXBURGH, HEIDI; Hilo HS; Keaau, HI; (4); 10/307; Church Yth Grp; Cmnty Wkr; 4-H; Science Clb; Service Clb; Chorus; Church Choir; 4-H Awd; High Hon Roll; Prfct Atten Awd; Graceland Coll; Nrsng.

ROYLO, HEATHER E; Mililani HS; Mililani, HI; (2); 85/509; Drama Clb; Hosp Aide; Band; Color Guard; Mrchg Band; School Musical; School Play; Hon Roll; Interschl Cmmtte; U Of HI; Perfmng Arts.

ROZEWSKI, ELIZABETH; Mc Kinley HS; Honolulu, HI; (2); Science Clb; School Play; Var Cheerldng; Hon Roll; Jr NHS; NHS; Tiger Gold Dncr; U Of HI; Acctng.

RUBIO, JOANNA; Mililani HS; Mililani, HI; (3); 98/490; DECA; Office Aide; Teachers Aide; JV Cheerldng; L Var Mgr(s); Hon Roll; UH Manoa; Acctng.

RULONA, ANGIE T; Henry Perrine Baldwin HS; Kahului, HI; (1); 76/466; Band; Mrchg Band; Pep Band; Hon Roll; Bus.

SABADO, LANI J; Lanai HS; Lanai City, HI; (1); Hon Roll.

SABINO, VAUGHN V M; James Campbell HS; Ewa Beach, HI; (3); 12/371; Church Yth Grp; Teachers Aide; High Hon Roll; Hon Roll; NHS; U Of HI; Arch.

SACAYANAN, MARVIN A; Laupahoehoe HS; Papaaloa, HI; (2); Cmnty Wkr; Computer Clb; Dance Clb; Band; Mrchg Band; School Musical; Bsktbl; Crs Cntry; Gym; Swmmng; UHH; Engr.

SADAYASU, CHRIS; Hilo HS; Papaikou, HI; (3); Church Yth Grp; Key Clb; VP Math Clb; Math Tm; Treas Frsh Cls; VP Jr Cls; Tennis; NHS; Sci Awd; Svc Awd; Prnc Hnbl Mntn All Amer For Tennis.

SAFFERY, MERI-BETH; Sacred Hearts Acad; Honolulu, HI; (3); Church Yth Grp; French Clb; Off Jr Cls; Intrml Bsktbl; Intrml Vllybl; Frnch I & II, Religion & Service Awds; Pediatrician.

SAFSTEN, KATHRYN; Kahuku HS; Laie, HI; (3); 7/246; Pres Church Yth Grp; Cmnty Wkr; Pres 4-H; Pres FHA; Nwsp; Stu Cncl; Tennis; High Hon Roll; NHS; Pres Acad Fit Awd; Japanese Clb VP; Outstndng G/T Stu.

SAGARA, BRENDAN M; Leilehua HS; Wahiawa, HI; (3); 13/347; Boy Scts; Band; Mrchg Band; Pep Band; L Var Bsbl; L Var Socr; High Hon Roll; Hon Roll; Enrchmnt Sci Pgm 89.

SAGARA, SHELLEY A; Mc Kinley HS; Waipahu, HI; (2); 66/588; Cmnty Wkr; JV Crs Cntry; JV Trk; YMCA JR Ldr Vlntr; Vlntrs In Pblc Svc To Crts Prgm Vlntr; U Of WA; Law.

SAGAYSAY, ALLAN M; Waialua High & Inter; Waialua, HI; (3); Letterman Clb; Math Tm; Science Clb; Pres Frsh Cls; Rep Soph Cls; VP Jr Cls; JV Var Bsktbl; Var Crs Cntry; JV Var Ftbl; JV Socr; 2nd Pl Dist Sci Fair; Elec Engnr.

SAGUN, DANIELLE; Leilehua HS; Wahiawa, HI; (2); Var Socr; JV Capt Vllybl; UH Manoa; Bus.

SAIFOLOI, LOTOMUA J; Radford HS; Honolulu, HI; (4); 147/348; Church Yth Grp; Off ROTC; Church Choir; Score Keeper; Vllybl; JV Wt Lftg; Prfct Atten Awd; Leeward CC; Comp Sci.

SAIKI, JOY K; Kailua HS; Kailua, HI; (2); 5/301; Service Clb; Band; Mrchg Band; Pep Band; Hon Roll; Intrct & Japanese Clbs; Ophtlmlgy.

SAIKI, TAD; Mc Kinley HS; Honolulu, HI; (3); Math Tm; Band; Co-Ed Yrbk; Var Wrstlng; Mst Inspirational Jr Var Wrestler; Commercial Art.

SAITO, RONALD; St Anthony HS; Pukalani, HI; (3); 5/70; Pres Computer Clb; Letterman Clb; Math Tm; Var JV Trk; High Hon Roll; NHS; Elec Engr.

SAITO, SYUCK; St Louis Schl; Honolulu, HI; (4); Cmnty Wkr; Hosp Aide; Letterman Clb; Math Clb; Math Tm; Quiz Bowl; Science Clb; Spanish Clb; Treas Frsh Cls; Rep Soph Cls; Rflry-Chmpn Var Team-8 Gold Medls; Amnesty Intl; Prncpls List Awd; U Of Chicago; Med.

SAJOR, GRACE B; Radford HS; Honolulu, HI; (3); Church Yth Grp; Chorus; Church Choir; Flag Corp; Gym; Hon Roll; Srgn.

SAKAI, DEAN M; Maui HS; Pukalani, HI; (3); 10/354; Boy Scts; Computer Clb; Science Clb; Art.

SAKAI, NAOMI; Mc Kinley HS; Honolulu, HI; (3); 40/537; French Clb; Band; Jazz Band; Mrchg Band; Hon Roll; Riflery; Japanese Club.

SAKAMOTO, COURTNEE LYNN S; Maui HS; Kahului, HI; (2); 47/388; Church Yth Grp; Key Clb; Letterman Clb; Science Clb; Band; Mrchg Band; Pep Band; Sec Jr Cls; Rep Stu Cncl; VP Tennis; Japanese Clb; Intract; U Of HI Manoa; Art.

SAKAMOTO, KEVIN H; Leilehua HS; Wahiawa, HI; (2); 109/400; Band; Jazz Band; Amateur Radio & Astrnmy; U Of HI; Bus.

SAKAMOTO, SCOTT; Kalaheo HS; Kailua, HI; (2); 25/300; Hon Roll; Jr Bowlers Leag Club.

SAKUMA, LY ANN T F; Mililani HS; Mililani, HI; (3); Church Yth Grp; Cmnty Wkr; Dance Clb; Science Clb; Band; Drill Tm; Flag Corp; Mrchg Band; Stu Cncl; Japanese Clb; UH Manoa; Grphc Arts.

SAKUMOTO, BRIAN M; Hawaii Baptist Acad; Honolulu, HI; (3); Church Yth Grp; Var Golf; Bowling Var; Botanical Trls Club; U HI; Eng.

SAKUOKA, JANELLE M; James Campbell HS; Ewa Beach, HI; (4); FBLA; Key Clb; SADD; Rep Frsh Cls; VP Soph Cls; Rep Jr Cls; Rep Sr Cls; Rep Stu Cncl; Powder Puff Ftbl; Hon Roll; U Of HI; Travl Indstry Mgmt.

SAKURAI, WINSTON; Kalaheo HS; Kaneohe, HI; (3); 10/250; Aud/Vis; Pres Math Clb; Model UN; Mu Alpha Theta; Quiz Bowl; Jazz Band; School Musical; Lit Mag; Off Frsh Cls; Pres VP Stu Cncl; Windward Dist Stu Cncl Rep; HI ST Stu Cncl Rep; Bus Admin.

SAKUTORI, ANNE H; H P Baldwin HS; Wailuku, HI; (2); 4-H; FTA; Art; Drama; U HI; Bus.

SALADINO, CHERYLENE A; Leilehua HS; Wahiawa, HI; (2); Church Yth Grp; Sec Spanish Clb; SADD; Hon Roll; Leo Clb; Lab Tech.

SALANGDRON, MELVIN; Kalaheo HS; Kailua, HI; (3); L JV Ftbl; Var L Tennis; Hon Roll; U HI; Bus.

SALAZAR, BENJAMIN; Leilehua HS; Wahiawa, HI; (2); Treas French Clb; Tennis; Hon Roll; Soft Tennis.

SALCEDO, VICTORIA B; Farrington HS; Honolulu, HI; (3); Art Awds, HI Marine Artist Yth Cmptn; Art Schlrshp; Art.

SALES, ROLANDO R; James Campbell HS; Ewa Beach, HI; (2); 3/348; Var Ftbl; JV Trk; High Hon Roll; Hon Roll; U HI; Arch.

SALUDARES, ROBERT L; St Joseph HS; Hilo, HI; (2); Boy Scts; Church Yth Grp; Treas French Clb; Letterman Clb; Math Clb; Math Tm; Treas Science Clb; Speech Tm; JV Bsktbl; Var Socr; Engrng.

SALUDEZ, LAELEYA S; Waipahu HS; Waipahu, HI; (2); Church Yth Grp; Speech Tm; Church Choir; Capt Jr Cls; High Hon Roll; Stu Mkng Indvdl Lives Easier; Quizzard Cntstnt; Photo Jrnlsm.

SALVADOR, ANNETTE B; Mililani HS; Waipahu, HI; (3); 29/500; Church Yth Grp; FHA; FTA; Hosp Aide; Teachers Aide; Lit Mag; Stu Cncl; High Hon Roll; Hon Roll; Advncd Plcmnt Engl; US Hstry Hnrs; Recognition & Awds For Artistic Excllnc Poster Conts; U OR; Arch Engrng.

SALVADOR, MICHAELJAMES R; Leilehua HS; Wahiawa, HI; (3); 42/322; French Clb; Hiking Club; Filipino Club; Aviation.

SALVATERA, JOSEPH; James Campbell HS; Ewa Beach, HI; (2); 13/348; Var Ftbl; JV Wrstlng; High Hon Roll; Hnrs Engl Cls; U Of HI; Engrng.

SAM FONG, LEE JON; Maui HS; Kahului, HI; (3); 98/354; Boy Scts; Church Yth Grp; Cmnty Wkr; Key Clb; Service Clb; Temple Yth Grp; Varsity Clb; JV Var Bsktbl; JV Var Ftbl; JV Var Trk; UNLV; Bus Mgmt.

SAMPSON, DAYNA L; Lutheran HS; Aiea, HI; (2); FCA; Letterman Clb; Varsity Clb; Band; Yrbk; VP Soph Cls; Sec Stu Cncl; Var Bsktbl; JV Capt Vllybl; Campus Chapel Mnstry Tm; Peer Cnslr; Uth For Christ Vlybl Tm; Vet Med.

SAMSON, CYNTHIA C; Leilehua HS; Wahiawa, HI; (3); 23/347; French Clb; Nrsng.

SANCHEZ, JORY E; Radford HS; Honolulu, HI; (3); 72/523; Treas Band; Jazz Band; Mrchg Band; Pep Band; Ftbl; U Of HI; Business Mngmnt.

SANCHEZ, SHARON R; Waialua High & Intermed; Waialua, HI; (2); Band; Jazz Band; Mrchg Band; Var Sftbl; Hon Roll; Prfct Atten Awd; Otstndng Drgbst 89-90; Drgbstrs VP 90-91; HS Hnr Bnd 88-90; Zoology.

SANDELL, ANDERS; Waiakea HS; Hilo, HI; (1); 1/478; Hon Roll.

SANDELL, JOANNA M; Waiakea HS; Hilo, HI; (4); 16/412; Hon Roll; 1st Pl Dressage HPA Horse Trials 90; Slvr Mdl Frnch 1st Annl St Cmptn 89; U Of Gothenburg; Jrnlst.

SANORIA, LEHUA J; Pahoa HS; Pahoa, HI; (4); Church Yth Grp; Cmnty Wkr; FFA; Letterman Clb; Variety Show; Sec Frsh Cls; VP Soph Cls; Pres Jr Cls; Rep Sr Cls; Stu Cncl; Fnlst Walt Disneys Dreamers & Doers 89; Outstndng Soccer Plyr 88-90; Biif All Star 2nd Soccer Tm Pres; U Of Hawaiiat Hilo; Ag Bus.

SANTIAGO, MARITZA ROSA; Radford HS; Honolulu, HI; (1); 92/466; Band; Jazz Band; Mrchg Band; Pep Band; Hon Roll; Bio.

SANTIAGO, SONNY F; Farrington HS; Honolulu, HI; (1); 14/360.

SANTOS, CHARLOTTE DEE; Waipahu HS; Ewa Beach, HI; (1); Church Yth Grp; Band; Church Choir; Kapiolan CC; Elem Schl Tchr.

SANTOS, JAMES; Maui HS; Kihei, HI; (3); 68/354; High Hon Roll; Hon Roll.

SAREN, MABEL S; Farrington HS; Honolulu, HI; (3); Spanish Clb; Band; Nwsp; Off Jr Cls; JV Tennis; Project Healthstart; U HI; Pediatrician.

SARMIENTO, CHERIE K; Maui HS; Makawao, HI; (2); Cmnty Wkr; GAA; Varsity Clb; Var Sftbl; Var Trk; Hon Roll; Al-St Sftbl Awd 3 Tms; U Of HI; Frgn Lang Trnsltr.

SASAKI, DEBORAH N; Hawaii Baptist Acad; Kaneohe, HI; (2); Teachers Aide; Chorus; School Play; JV Vllybl; High Hon Roll; Pres Acad Fit Awd; Calligraphy Clb; Lawyer.

SATO, DENISE TERESA; Sacred Hearts Acad; Pearl City, HI; (3); Church Yth Grp; Pep Clb; Off Soph Cls; Pres Jr Cls; Var Cheerldng; Hon Roll; Hoby Ambasador; HI ST Stu Cnfrnc 90; Natl Hstrcl Pictorial Map Cntst.

SATO, KEN I; Waipahu HS; Waipahu, HI; (3); 79/438; DECA; JV Trk; Natl Cmptr Distrib Educ Clbs Of Amer; Black Belt Kendo; Bus Admin.

SATO, SHARON M; Waimea HS; Kalaheo, HI; (3); 7/206; Key Clb; SADD; Orch; Ed Nwsp; Rep Jr Cls; Rep Stu Cncl; Var Tennis; Hon Roll; NHS; Prtcptn ST Marine Sympsm; Vrs Cmmtts; US Spc Acad Huntsville AL.

SATOMBA, SHARLA; Waiakea HS; Hilo, HI; (1); JV Trk.

SAVAGE, SHANNON L; Radford HS; Chula Vista, CA; (3); 72/394; Hon Roll; Southwestern CC CA; CPA.

SAVALLNAEA, ELENA K; Kamehameha HS; Honolulu, HI; (1); Dance Clb; School Play; Halau Hula Olana; Canoe Paddler; Song Cntst Asst Dir & Dir; Cmmnctns.

SCHAEFER, TERESA A; Radford HS; Cleveland, OH; (3); Chorus; Drug Free HI Coalition; Peer Counseling; TX Tech; Child Psych.

SCHILLER, AMY M; Leilehua HS; Wahiawa, HI; (3); 3/322; Church Yth Grp; Cmnty Wkr; Varsity Clb; Chorus; Var Tennis; High Hon Roll; Jr NHS; NHS; Natl Hnr Soc Pres 90-91; 1st Pl Dept Dfns Dpndnt Schls Media Fest W Germany; Bus.

SCHMALLE, TRACI L; Mililani HS; Mililani, HI; (2); 39/509; VP Drama Clb; Hosp Aide; Band; Mrchg Band; JV Swmmng; Hon Roll; HI Sci Fair 1st Sch, 3rd Dist; Sci Enrchmnt; Stu Mentor; Orthodntcs.

SCHNEIDER, MICHAEL T; Radford HS; Honolulu, HI; (3); 5/394; Band; Mrchg Band; Pep Band; Ed Nwsp; High Hon Roll; Hon Roll; Jr NHS; NHS; Selected Summer Pgm For The Enhancement Of Basic Ed Center For Modern Media; Video Production; Broadcast/Journalism.

SCHOONOVER, KARIANNE; Waimea HS; Waimea, HI; (3); 7/198; Capt Math Tm; Spanish Clb; Church Choir; Sec Stu Cncl; Trk; Hon Roll; NHS; Amer Lung Assoc-Rep; Cvl Air Patrol-Tech Sgt; Rcrds Cmmttee-Chrprsn; Embry-Riddle U; Intl Pilot.

SCHROCK, JENNIFER C; Leilehau HS; Wahiawa, HI; (4); 1/300; Church Yth Grp; Chorus; Church Choir; Var L Crs Cntry; Var L Socr; Var L Swmmng; Var L Trk; High Hon Roll; VP NHS; Val; Grad Cmmtt; Most Outstngn Frshmn Trck; James Madison U; Pre Med.

SCHROEDER, NICOLE R; Pearl City HS; Waipahu, HI; (3); DECA; Spanish Clb; Stat Wt Lftg; May Day Prgm Hula Dancer; U HI Manoa; Psych.

SCHUBERT, AMANDA J; Radford HS; Honolulu, HI; (3); FTA; Letterman Clb; Varsity Clb; Pres Frsh Cls; Rep Stu Cncl; Var Mgr(s); Score Keeper; JV Trk; Var Vllybl; Hon Roll; Acclrtd Grd; FIDM; Fashn Merch.

SCHWAB, ANDREA T; St Francis HS; Kaneohe, HI; (2); Intnl Clb; Library Aide; Office Aide; Lit Mag; Hon Roll; 2nd Hghst Schl Scr Amer HG Math Exm; Lang Arts Shwcase Wnnr St HI Haiku, Limerick, Hnrb Mntn Poem; UCLA; Pharmacy.

SCHWARZ, LEONARD A; Radford HS; Honolulu, HI; (2); Boy Scts; Church Yth Grp; JA; ROTC; Eagle Scout; Art Ed.

SCZEPANIAK, PATRICIA; Kalaheo HS; Kailua, HI; (1); 16/266; Drama Clb; Girl Scts; Thesps; School Play; Treas Frsh Cls; JV Bsktbl; High Hon Roll.

SEBASTIAN, RODOLFO; Nanakuli HS & Inter; Waianae, HI; (2); 2/173; High Hon Roll; NHS; Cvl Air Patrol; Aerntcl Engr.

SEGISMUNDO, MICHELLE L; Pearl City HS; Pearl City, HI; (4); 86/478; Sec Church Yth Grp; Church Choir; Tennis; Hon Roll; Chrch Ply & Music Band; Seattle Pacific U.

SEKIYA, ALLISON L; Pearl City HS; Pearl City, HI; (2); 42/511; FHA; Key Clb; Hon Roll; Jrnlsm.

SEKIYA, CHAD; Mid-Pacific Inst; Waipahu, HI; (2); Var Bsbl; JV Bsktbl; JV Ftbl; Hon Roll; UCLA.

SEO, JUNGYOON JULIA; Moanalua HS; Aiea, HI; (3); 30/462; Math Clb; Science Clb; Orch; Var Tennis; Hon Roll; Band-Flt; Korean Clb; U Of HI; Intr Dsgnr.

SEQUERRA, RONALD; Lanai HS; Lanai, HI; (3); Marines.

SERIAN, CALVIN M; Waiakea HS; Hilo, HI; (3); 43/300; School Play; Hon Roll; Surf Club; Chorus; Ukulela Band Japan Tour 88.

SERRANO, ZYLDA M; James Campbell HS; Ewa Beach, HI; (2); 34/348; Key Clb; Inter-Schl; Cannons Bus Coll; Accntng.

SERRAO, ROYCE P; St Joseph HS; Hilo, HI; (3); Church Yth Grp; Service Clb; JV Bsktbl; Wt Lftg.

SEUNG, STEPHANIE J; Mililani HS; Mililani, HI; (3); 121/490; Church Yth Grp; Teachers Aide; Band; Chorus; Church Choir; Mrchg Band; Pep Band; School Play; Hawaii State Select Band; Band Directors Awd; Parade Of Young Musicians; Music Education.

SHAKA, ANGELINE M; Walakea HS; Keaau, HI; (3); Dance Clb; Drama Clb; Hon Roll; NHS; PALC; U Of HI Hilo Dance Ensemble; SPEBE; Drama & Theatre Asst Dance Instr 90; Dance.

SHANKLES, GENEVIELI K; Kalani HS; Honolulu, HI; (2); 27/213; Church Yth Grp; JV Bsktbl; Var Score Keeper; JV Vllybl; Aina Haina Smmr Fun Jr Aide Vlntr.

SHANNON, KELLY L; H P Baldwin HS; Pukalani, HI; (2); 13/400; Church Yth Grp; Drama Clb; Church Choir; School Play; Variety Show; Var L Crs Cntry; Var L Trk; High Hon Roll; Jr NHS; Maui CC Pre-Health Sci Nrsng Club; Engl Writing Awds; Lang Arts Showcase; HI Ed Assn Hnrb Mntn; Math.

SHEFFIELD, AMANDA J; Waiakea HS; Hilo, HI; (2); 39/497; High Hon Roll; Hon Roll; Credit Union Clb; Mock Trial Cmptn; UNC Wilmington; Bus.

SHERMAN, CHERIE R; Henry Opukahaia Schl; Kailua Kona, HI; (2); Art Clb; Church Yth Grp; Debate Tm; French Clb; Pep Clb; Yrbk; Hon Roll; U OR Eugene; Psych.

SHERMAN, LII MICHIKO; Kaiser HS; Honolulu, HI; (4); 1/289; Lit Mag; Off Soph Cls; Treas Jr Cls; Hon Roll; NHS; Amnsty Intl-Sec & Pres; Cougar Awd-Ldrshp; Ind Arts Awd-1st Pl Prntng; U HI Maroa 89-90; U CA Santa Cruz; Art.

SHIBAO, LISA A; Kapaa HS & Intermed; Kapaa, HI; (3); Office Aide; Pep Clb; Science Clb; Mgr(s); Score Keeper; Wrstlng; High Hon Roll; Hon Roll; NHS; OR ST U; Hotel Mgmt.

SHIBUYA, ALKO R; Mililani HS; Mililani, HI; (3); Pres Temple Yth Grp; Stu Cncl; Lion Awd; Bus.

SHIBUYA, COLBI M; Henry Perrine Baldwin HS; Kahului, HI; (3); 20/385; Letterman Clb; Var Sftbl; JV Trk; Hon Roll; Electrncs Club; Stus Staying Straight; WA ST U; Arch.

SHIBUYA, TRACI ANN T; Hawaii Baptist Acad; Mililani, HI; (3); 1/90; Church Yth Grp; GAA; Math Tm; Church Choir; Treas Soph Cls; Sec Jr Cls; Var Capt Tennis; Cit Awd; High Hon Roll; NHS; Walt Disneys Dreamers And Doers Hnrbl Mntn Awd; Hugh O Brian Yth Ldrshp Semnr.

SHIGEMATSU, KIMBERLY A; Mid-Pacific Inst; Honolulu, HI; (3); Cmnty Wkr; 4-H; Teachers Aide; Band; Rep Sr Cls; Tennis; 4-H Awd; Hon Roll; U HI Manoa; Psych.

SHIGEMATSU, SHAWN A; Aiea HS; Aiea, HI; (2); Pres Soph Cls; JV Capt Bsbl; Hon Roll; Harvard; Bus Lwyr.

SHIGEOKA, REID M; Waiakea HS; Hilo, HI; (1); Chess Clb; Frgn Lang Fstvl-Japanese Div-1st; San Francisco ST U; Mrktng.

SHIIBA, MICHELLE LEIKO; Hilo HS; Hilo, HI; (4); 26/307; Church Yth Grp; VP JA; Key Clb; Rep Soph Cls; Sec Stu Cncl; L Var Swmmng; High Hon Roll; Hon Roll; MVP Swmmng; Santa Clara U; Intl Bus.

SHIMABUKURO, JAN M; Roosevelt HS; Aiea, HI; (2); Cmnty Wkr; Hosp Aide; Band; Mrchg Band; Pep Band; VP Frsh Cls; Sec Stu Cncl; Var Tennis; JV Vllybl; Stat Wrstlng; Enrchmnt In Sci Prg 89; VET.

SHIMABUKURO, KANDI; Waiakea HS; Hilo, HI; (2); Church Yth Grp; Key Clb; Science Clb; School Play; Var Tennis; Natl Piano Plyng Audtn Guild 90; Med.

SHIMABUKURO, KENDALL K; Henry Perrine Baldwin HS; Kahului, HI; (3); 14/310; Church Yth Grp; Sec Key Clb; Math Tm; SADD; Mgr Band; Jazz Band; Mrchg Band; Pep Band; L Var Tennis; High Hon Roll; Dancing; SPEBE; Maui Philhrmnc Msc Camp 88-90; Engr.

SHIMABUKURO, STACEY M; Mililani HS; Waipahu, HI; (3); U Of HI; Jrnlsm.

SHIMABUKURO, TOMOMI; Farrington HS; Honolulu, HI; (2); 63/721; School Play; Rep Frsh Cls; Rep Stu Cncl; High Hon Roll; Hon Roll; Jr NHS; Bowling; Japanese, Svc Club; Comp Analyst.

SHIMATANI, MIKI; Kaiser HS; Honolulu, HI; (1); 22/255; Service Clb; Band; Jazz Band; Mrchg Band; Pep Band; Ed Lit Mag; Sec Soph Cls; Hon Roll; U HI Manoa; Arch.

SHIMOMURA, WENDY L; Henry Perrine Baldwin HS; Kahului, HI; (3); 79/385; L Debate Tm; Sec NFL; Service Clb; Speech Tm; Treas SADD; Rptr Nwsp; Mck Trl Tm Capt; Natl Cncl Tchrs Engl Awd Wrtng; U Of HI Manoa; Mgzn Jrnlsm.

SHIMONISHI, CHAD; Roosevelt HS; Honolulu, HI; (2); 18/360; Boy Scts; Chess Clb; JV Bsbl; Hon Roll; Pres Acad Fit Awd; Intersch Club Chm; Yth Ldrshp YMCA; U WA; Bus.

SHINAGAWA, JEFFREY S; Waimea HS; Kalaheo, HI; (2); 13/200; Church Yth Grp; Var Capt Bsktbl; Var Vllybl; Hon Roll; NHS; Draftng Clb; Hmcmng & Cls Ring Comm; Teacher.

SHINNO, CHASSIDY C; Kauai HS; Lihue, HI; (3); Church Yth Grp; Cmnty Wkr; Dance Clb; Sec 4-H; French Clb; JA; Key Clb; Pep Clb; SADD; Teachers Aide; Eleson Onizuka 4-H Schlrshp Awd; Poets Soc; SPU; Eng Lit/Prfssr.

SHINSEKI, KYLE K; Kauai HS; Lihue, HI; (3); 1/240; Pres Church Yth Grp; Off Drama Clb; Treas Key Clb; Math Tm; Band; Co-Ed Nwsp; Mgr Stu Cncl; Var L Swmmng; Off NHS; Voice Dem Awd; Kauai Cmnty Plyrs Bd Of Dir; Amer Lunga Ssn Of Hi Kauai Advisory Cncl Stu; Prfmng Arts Ctr; Urban Planning.

SHIOSHITA, RUSSELL; Pahoa High And Elementary Schl; Pahoa, HI; (1); Church Yth Grp; FFA; 4-H Awd; Hon Roll; Prfct Atten Awd; Archery.

SHIRASU, STEWART T; Iolani Schl; Honolulu, HI; (4); 44/220; Debate Tm; Drama Clb; Pres VP JA; Key Clb; Model UN; Orch; Rptr Nwsp; Stu Cncl; High Hon Roll; Ntl Merit SF; Bus.

SHISHIDO, ROBIN K; Maui HS; Pukalani, HI; (1); High Hon Roll; Hun Kag; A&v Riding; Fishing; Northern AZ U; Engrng.

SHODA, CARRIE E T; Roosevelt HS; Honolulu, HI; (1); 7/362; Church Yth Grp; Band; Hon Roll; Teaching.

SHOZUGA, NADINE M; Mid Pacific Inst; Honolulu, HI; (3); Teachers Aide; Band; JV Sftbl; High Hon Roll; Hon Roll; NHS; Reed Coll; Bus.

SHOZUYA, NADINE; Mid Pacific Inst; Honolulu, HI; (3); Band; Pep Band; JV Sftbl; Hon Roll; NHS; Pres Schlr; JV Paddling Crew; Reed Coll.

SHUFFLEBARGER, HEATHER M; Waimea HS; Kekaha, HI; (2); 4-H; Gym; Trk; High Hon Roll; Hon Roll; NHS; Phys Ed Awd.

SIEGEL, BENJAMIN D; Roosevelt HS; Honolulu, HI; (3); 42/225; Art Clb; English Clb; Nwsp; Art; Wrtng; Music; CA; Wrtr.

SIGALA, PAUL A; Henry J Kaiser HS; Honolulu, HI; (2); 1/280; Church Yth Grp; Quiz Bowl; Scholastic Bowl; VP Science Clb; Service Clb; Treas Stu Cncl; JV L Crs Cntry; Var L Socr; High Hon Roll; NHS; TV Quzzard Show Tm; Outstndng Eng Stu Awd; Testifed Before Bd Of Educ & Affected Statewide Policy Chg; Psych.

SIKES, JENNIFER A; Kalani HS; Honolulu, HI; (2); 53/259; Church Yth Grp; Orch; Stu Cncl; Swmmng; Hon Roll; Swmmng Club, Punahow Aquatics; Amer Hstry; Amer Hstry.

SILENCE, CARRIE; Radford HS; Honolulu, HI; (3); 3/394; Mu Alpha Theta; Sec Band; Mrchg Band; Chrmn Stu Cncl; Var Cheerldng; High Hon Roll; NHS; Gymnstcs & ST Meets; Prncpl Achvtmnt Awds 88-80; Spnsh Achvtmnt Awds 89-90; CSU; Engr.

SILETTI, JOSEPH K; Saint Louis Schl; Kailua, HI; (2); Pep Clb; Quiz Bowl; Rptr Nwsp; Rep Frsh Cls; Rep Soph Cls; Intrml JV Bsbl; Intrml Var Bsktbl; Ftbl; Score Keeper; JV Var Vllybl; HI St Jr Olympc Vllybl Team; Hawan St Spllng Bee; Notre Dame; Robotics.

SILVA, BRANDON J; Kamehameha HS; Mililani, HI; (3); 43/419; Letterman Clb; ROTC; Var L Ftbl; High Hon Roll; Hon Roll; Natl Sci Olympd Bio & Chem Awds; Aerospc Engrng.

SILVA, JETTIE W; Farrington HS; Kaneohe, HI; (4); 73/549; ROTC; SADD; Chorus; Off Frsh Cls; JV Vllybl; DAR Awd; Masonic Awd; Pres Acad Fit Awd; Rfl Tm Capt; Canoe Pddlng Tm; Mst Outstndng Crew; U Of HI Manoa.

SILVA, JOLENE N; Waimea HS; Kalaheo, HI; (2); 85/186; Church Yth Grp; Hosp Aide; Church Choir; Hon Roll; Cannons Bus Coll.

SILVA, KATHY; Mary Knoll HS; Kailua, HI; (3); Church Yth Grp; Spanish Clb; Teachers Aide; Yrbk; Rep Frsh Cls; JV Bsktbl; JV Var Socr; Capt Var Sftbl; Var Vllybl; Hon Roll; Prom Clb; Stu Senate Clb; U Of San Diego.

SILVA, MELANIE J; Kalaheo HS; Kailua, HI; (1); Church Yth Grp; Band; Jazz Band; Mrchg Band; Pep Band; School Musical; High Hon Roll; Lanikai Canoe Clb; Berkeley.

SILVERSTEIN, LORISSA W; Seabury Hall HS; Haiku, HI; (3); French Clb; Math Tm; Band; Ed Yrbk; JV Var Bsktbl; JV Capt Sftbl; Var Trk; High Hon Roll; Hon Roll; Ntl Merit SF; Georgetown; Cmmnctns.

SIMBRE, JENNIFER K A; Waialua HS; Waialua, HI; (3); 9/157; FTA; Math Tm; JV Var Bsktbl; Var Socr; Var Swmmng; JV Var Vllybl; High Hon Roll; Hon Roll; Treas NHS; Interact Clb Pres; Leo Clb Treas; Japanese Clb; CO ST U.

SINGLETON, PHILLIP V; St Louis HS; Honolulu, HI; (2); Hon Roll; Naval Acad; Chem Engr.

SINOR, SCOTT P; Lutheran HS Of Hawaii; Honolulu, HI; (3); FCA; Var Bsbl; Var JV Bsktbl; Var Vllybl; Hon Roll; Prfct Atten Awd; VPI; Aerntcl Engrng.

SIOU, YANGHENG; Mc Kinley HS; Honolulu, HI; (3); 70/537; Church Yth Grp; Math Clb; Math Tm; Cmptr Prgm; UHM; Engr.

SIU, KERRI-ANN; Mid Pacific Inst; Pearl City, HI; (1); 2/173; Pres Frsh Cls; JV Sftbl; Hon Roll; Outstndng Frosh 89-90; Mr & Miss MPI Aloha United Way; Mid-Pacific Schlr 89-90; Astrlgy.

SIVERLING, DAWN A; Pres Theodore Roosevelt HS; Honolulu, HI; (3); Church Yth Grp; Drama Clb; Intnl Clb; Model UN; Nwsp; Crs Cntry; Socr; Trk; Worhty Advisor Of Lei Ilima 2fintl Order Of Rainbow Girls; Honoray Coord Of Malaekahan Camping Trip.

SKEELE, MATTHEW; Hilo HS; Hilo, HI; (2); 13/394; Latin Clb; Math Tm; Speech Tm; Chorus; Variety Show; Rep Soph Cls; Tennis; Plyd Ldng Role In Hilo Cmmnty Plyrs Chrstms Prdctn; Strctrl Engrng.

SKELTON, SAM Y; Kohala HS; Kapaau, HI; (1); 4/60; Math Clb; Math Tm; Rep Frsh Cls; Hon Roll; AYSO Soccer; Med.

SLATON, MARK; Kalaheo HS; Kailua, HI; (2); 6/287; Natl Beta Clb; JV Bsktbl; Var Ftbl; Var Trk; Cit Awd; High Hon Roll; Jr NHS; Church Yth Grp; FCA; Math Tm; West Point; Aeronautics.

SLATTERY, DAVID S; Maui HS; Pukalani, HI; (2); 34/388; Boy Scts; Church Yth Grp; Science Clb; Hon Roll; Prfct Atten Awd; Aquarium/Terrarium Clb.

SMART, TERRENCE; Kalaheo HS; Kailua, HI; (2); 12/290; Church Yth Grp; Var Tennis; Hon Roll; Sft Tnns.

SMITH, ALANA; Kalaheo HS; Kaneohe, HI; (3); 1/256; Church Yth Grp; German Clb; Drill Tm; Yrbk; Crs Cntry; Socr; Swmmng; Hon Roll; NHS; Congrss-Bundestag Exchnge Schlrshp 90.

SMITH, CAROL A; Waiakea HS; Hilo, HI; (2); 69/501; Dance Clb; 4-H; French Clb; JA; SADD; Hon Roll; Archery; Strathallen Schl; Bio-Chem.

SMITH, DARRYL; Kalaheo HS; Kailua, HI; (1); Hon Roll; Math.

SMITH, KRISTA JARME; Kalaheo HS; Kaneohe, HI; (4); Cmnty Wkr; Hosp Aide; Red Cross Aide; Drill Tm; Yrbk; Stu Cncl; L Var Crs Cntry; L Var Swmmng; Cit Awd; Hon Roll; All Amer Schlr; Outdoor Rec Tchr.

SMITH, NINA; Mid Pacific Inst; Majuro M H, GU; (2); 2/22; Intnl Clb; JV Sftbl; Hon Roll; Stanford U; Med.

SMITH, SUSAN M; Mililani HS; Wahiawa, HI; (2); 101/509; Chorus; Hon Roll; Wrtng; Psych.

SMITH, TANYA; Kalaheo HS; Kailua, HI; (4); 4/220; Science Clb; Band; Mrchg Band; Ed Lit Mag; Treas Stu Cncl; Tennis; Hon Roll; NHS; Keyettes; Soph Schl; Amercn Schlr; Pre-Law.

SOARES, BRIAN; St Joseph HS; Hilo, HI; (3); Church Yth Grp; Pres Frsh Cls; VP Soph Cls; Trk; High Hon Roll; NHS; Bus Admin.

SOARES, CARITA; Hilo HS; Hilo, HI; (3); Cmnty Wkr; Library Aide; Pep Clb; Off Jr Cls; Hon Roll; Santa Rosa JC CA; Jrnlsm.

SODETANI, CARISA K; Lutheran HS Of Hawaii; Pearl City, HI; (2); Orch; Sec Soph Cls; JV Vllybl; Hon Roll; Prfct Atten Awd; Outstndng Achvt Awd Jpnese I, Bio 89 & 90; Psych.

SOH, JOHN R; Iolani Schl; Kailua, HI; (3); 85/230; Band; Stage Crew; Hon Roll; Aeronautical Engrng.

SOLANO, MARITES D; Farrington HS; Honolulu, HI; (2); 14/362; Rep Frsh Cls; Hon Roll; Prfct Atten Awd; UCLA; Arch.

SOLIVEN, MARK A; Henry Perring Baldwin HS; Kihei, HI; (2); 49/395; Band; Mrchg Band; Pep Band; Hon Roll; UH Manoa; Bus Admin.

SOMERA, CAROLINE R; H P Baldwin HS; Kihei, HI; (3); Band; Jazz Band; Mrchg Band; Orch; Rep Jr Cls; Rep Sr Cls; Rep Stu Cncl; Hon Roll; Hd Various Cmmttes; Sctn Ldr Band; San Barnadino; Bus Admin.

SONG, NINA M; Kaiser HS; Honolulu, HI; (3); Church Yth Grp; Sec Frsh Cls; Pres Soph Cls; VP Pres Stu Cncl; Stat Ftbl; Var Vllybl; Stat English Clb; High Hon Roll; Hon Roll; Med.

SORIA, JULIUS B; Leilehua HS; Wahiawa, HI; (3); High Hon Roll; Educ.

SORIANO, EILEEN; Hanalani HS; Mililani, HI; (2); 1/12; Pres Church Yth Grp; Band; Pres Soph Cls; Var Bsktbl; Var Cheerldng; Var Vllybl; Hon Roll; HOBY; Mecl.

SORIANO, ELAINE M; James Campbell HS; Ewa Beach, HI; (3); FFA; SADD; NHS; Leeward CC; RN.

SORIANO, PAUL L; Leilehua HS; Wahiawa, HI; (3); Church Yth Grp; 4-H; JV Var Bsbl; Socr; Japanese Clb, Leo Clb, Interact Clb; Secndry Educ.

SORIANO, STACI; Hanalani Schl; Wahiawa, HI; (2); Church Yth Grp; Chorus; Stat Bsktbl; Cheerldng; Hon Roll.

SORNEO, JENNIFER C; Waipahu HS; Waipahu, HI; (3); 59/409; Cmnty Wkr; Science Clb; Spanish Clb; SADD; Church Choir; Cit Awd; Hon Roll; Nurse.

SOROTEN, BRENDA U; Leilehua HS; Wahiawa, HI; (3); 11/322; Cmnty Wkr; Hon Roll; HI Pacific U; Reg Nrs.

SOTELO, KRIS J D; Nanakuli HS; Waianae, HI; (4); 4/112; Library Aide; Math Tm; Office Aide; Spanish Clb; VP Jr Cls; Hon Roll; NHS; Outstndng Principals List Awd; Outstndng Physics Stu; Magna Cum Laude Recogntn Diploma; U HI Manoa; Accntng.

SOUKI, JESSE K; Baldwin HS; Wailuku, HI; (2); Boy Scts; Church Yth Grp; Key Clb; Band; Var Ftbl; JV Trk; Wt Lftg; Hon Roll; Prfct Atten Awd; USC; Engrng.

SOUZA, CRAIG L; St Louis Schl; Honolulu, HI; (2); 21/151; JV Bsbl; JV Ftbl; Hon Roll; Sprts Med.

SOUZA, SHANNON C; Saint Joseph HS; Hilo, HI; (3); Church Yth Grp; Letterman Clb; Science Clb; Intrml JV Bsktbl; Mgr(s); Vllybl; High Hon Roll; Hon Roll; Navy; Elec Engrng.

SOWATANANGOON, ANGELA NOI; Lutheran HS Of Hawaii; Honolulu, HI; (4); 3/50; Drama Clb; FCA; FBLA; Teachers Aide; Chorus; School Musical; School Play; Stage Crew; Cheerldng; Crs Cntry; Japanese Clb; Secy Bus Clb; Stu Teacher; Campus Chapel Ministry Tm; HOBY Fndtn St Amb; Whitman Clg; Commnctns.

SPARKS, AMBER; Kalaheo HS; Kailua, HI; (2); Church Yth Grp; Band; Pep Band; School Musical; Sftbl; Var Vllybl; Hon Roll; Jr NHS; Frdms Fdn Valley Frg Hnrbl Mntn Essy; Otstndng Musicians Awd; U Of S FL; Teaching.

SPENCER, DANEKA; Kalaheo HS; Kailua, HI; (2); Var Socr; Hon Roll; U Of WA.

SPENCER, DEVI B; Kapaa HS; Kilauea, HI; (1); 58/220; 4-H; Band; 4-H Awd; Hon Roll; 3rd In St Fnls Horse Show; U Of HI Hilo; Horse Trnr.

SPILLER- REIFF, SASHA M; Molokai HS; Maunaloa, HI; (2); 5/98; Bsbl; Var L Socr; Hon Roll; Jr Body Brd Chmpn; Schl Athlete Awd-Sccr; Marine Bio.

SPINO, VONNA; Kalaheo HS; Kailua, HI; (2); Hosp Aide; Stat Bsbl; Stat Ftbl; Hon Roll; Phy.

SPRINGER, HAKALELEPONI; Honoka'a HS; Kamuela, HI; (3); 78/149; Dance Clb; GAA; Teachers Aide; Band; Chorus; School Musical; Variety Show; Yrbk; VP Jr Cls; Stu Cncl; U Of HI Hilo.

ST ONGE, CELESTE T; Sacred Hearts Acad; Honolulu, HI; (3); Cmnty Wkr; Pep Clb; SADD; Varsity Clb; Off Soph Cls; Stu Cncl; JV Var Cheerldng; Hon Roll; Close-Up; St Of HI Att Gen Offc 90; Nrsng.

STARKEY, SONJA J L; Molokai HS & Intermed; Hoolehua, HI; (3); 4/95; School Play; Hon Roll; U HI Hilo; Bus.

STASZKOW, ZACHARY L; Leilehua HS; Wahiawa, HI; (3); Treas Church Yth Grp; Treas Jr Cls; JV Var Ftbl; JV Var Socr.

STEELE, CARRIE; Radford HS; Honolulu, HI; (1); 1/466; JV Cheerldng; High Hon Roll; Hon Roll; Bus.

STEENSEN, CAROLINE R; Kaimuki HS; Honolulu, HI; (3); Hon Roll; Flght Attendnt.

STEPHEN-HASSARD, C GREG; Hawaii Preparatory Acad; Aiea, HI; (2); L Var Crs Cntry; L Var Swmmng; L Var Trk; High Hon Roll; Hon Roll; Tryng To Form Turtle Snctry On Big Island.

STEPHENSON, AIMEE; Konawaena HS; Kailua-Kona, HI; (4); 10/296; Drama Clb; Band; Chorus; School Musical; Yrbk; Rep Stu Cncl; Bsktbl; Swmmng; Hon Roll; NHS; AZ ST U; Med.

STEPHENSON, TRAVIS; Konawaena HS; Kailua-Kona, HI; (4); 17/296; FHA; Letterman Clb; Pep Clb; Spanish Clb; Var Ftbl; Var Wt Lftg; Capt Wrstlng; Hon Roll; NHS; AZ ST U.

STEWART, TONDA; Lanakila Baptist HS; Ewa, HI; (3); 2/17; Church Yth Grp; Drama Clb; Spanish Clb; Teachers Aide; School Play; Yrbk; Rep Soph Cls; Pres Jr Cls; VP Stu Cncl; Bsktbl.

STOCKSDALE, KAHEA M; Waiakea HS; Hilo, HI; (2); SADD; Vllybl; Htl Mgmt.

STOCKTON, HILARY M; Iolani Schl; Honolulu, HI; (4); 4/220; Dance Clb; Drama Clb; Key Clb; Math Tm; Model UN; Q&S; Orch; School Play; Ntl Merit SF; Rptr Nwsp; HI Yth Symph; Intl Rel.

STONE, ACHARIYA T; Waiakea HS; Hilo, HI; (3); Math Tm; Sec NFL; Sec Speech Tm; Teachers Aide; Ed Nwsp; Hon Roll; Ntl Merit SF; Newspr Most Vlbl Staff; Spch, St Finalst Orignl Oratory; 3 1st Pl Awds Spch Cmptns; Actr U Play; Reed Coll; Engl.

STONE, JEFF M; Radford HS; Honolulu, HI; (3); 72/394; Boy Scts; Church Yth Grp; Var Crs Cntry; Hon Roll.

STONE, JULIE E; Waialua HS; Waialua, HI; (2); JV Bsktbl; Hon Roll; Prfct Atten Awd; U HI.

STONE, PAUL; Saint Anthony HS; Kihel, HI; (3); Church Yth Grp; Drama Clb; Teachers Aide; Speech Tm; Trk; Wt Lftg; High Hon Roll; Jr NHS; Bus Clb VP; U Of HI; Poltcl Sci.

STOREY, TRINA M; Leilehua HS; Wahiawa, HI; (3); 37/347; Church Yth Grp; Band; Pep Band; Hon Roll.

STROM, AMANDA M; Kailua HS; Kailua, HI; (3); 15/349; Church Yth Grp; Flag Corp; Mrchg Band; Pep Band; School Play; Rep Soph Cls; Var Socr; HI Ambssdrs Music.

STUMP, CORY; Pahoa HS; Pahoa, HI; (3); Var Socr; Mst Outstndng Sccr Plyr 88-89; Elec.

STURDIVANT, TIFFANY R; Radford HS; Honolulu, HI; (2); Church Yth Grp; Cmnty Wkr; High Hon Roll; Black Am Clb; Wichita ST; Psych.

STYFFE, CAROLINE A; Moanalua HS; Honolulu, HI; (3); Letterman Clb; Office Aide; Scholastic Bowl; Variety Show; JV Var Bsktbl; Var Sftbl; JV Var Vllybl; Hon Roll; Jr NHS; NHS; MIP Sftbl; Teens Hlpng Teens; Sarah Lawrence Coll; Psych.

SUAAVA, ROXANNE; Waipahu HS; Waipahu, HI; (3); 23/409; Church Yth Grp; Hosp Aide; Church Choir; Bsktbl; Vllybl; Hon Roll; Natl Yth Ldrshp Awd CYLC; Harvard; Pediatrics.

SUDA, TRACIE H; Kaiser HS; Honolulu, HI; (3); Key Clb; Chldhd Ed.

SUEHISA, TINA Y; Henry Perrine Baldwin HS; Kula, HI; (2); 26/400; Math Tm; SADD; Hon Roll; Alhoa, Intract & Japanese Clbs; Ed.

SUENISHI, MICHELLE L; Waiakea HS; Hilo, HI; (3); 4-H; Rep Service Clb; Frndshp Club; Vet Med.

SUEYASU, LAYNIE L; Waimea HS; Hanapepe, HI; (2); SADD; Band; Mrchg Band; Bsktbl; Sftbl; High Hon Roll; Civil Air Patrol; Earned Solo Wings Glider Trng.

SUGA, TRACI; Waiakea HS; Hilo, HI; (2); 55/497; Church Yth Grp; JA; Service Clb; Stat Bsktbl; Hon Roll; Yth Legislature; Elem Ed.

SUGAI, CHERIE-ANN M; Hawaii Baptist Acad; Honolulu, HI; (2); 7/92; Church Yth Grp; VP JA; Math Tm; Office Aide; Q&S; Ed Nwsp; High Hon Roll; Sec Jr NHS; NHS; Vrsty Bowling MVP; Chem.

SUGIBAYASHI, BRENT I; Roosevelt HS; Honolulu, HI; (1); Boy Scts; Spanish Clb; Mrchg Band; JV L Wrstlng; Judo Let Var; Solar Car Racng Tm; Hula Bowl All Star Band; U CA Berkely; Aero Engr.

SUGIHARA, TOD; Hilo HS; Hilo, HI; (3); Pres Key Clb; Math Tm; Pres Frsh Cls; Pres Soph Cls; Pres Jr Cls; Rep Stu Cncl; Capt Swmmng; NHS; HOBY Ambssdr 89; SPEBE-ENGRNG 89; Engrng.

SUGIMOTO, EDWARD D; Kaiser HS; Honolulu, HI; (2); Treas Jr Cls; JV Bsbl; JV Bsktbl; JV Trk; Prfct Atten Awd.

SUGIMOTO, LEE H; Pearl City HS; Pearl City, HI; (1); 28/605; Band; Mrchg Band; Hon Roll; Sci.

SUGIMOTO, LORI M; St Andrews Priory HS; Mililani, HI; (3); 12/53; Key Clb; Science Clb; Band; Stage Crew; Yrbk; Hon Roll; Japanese Lang Club; College.

SULLIBAN, JASON E; St Louis HS; Honolulu, HI; (3); 17/150; Var Letterman Clb; Var Socr; JV Var Vllybl; Hon Roll; Awd For Highest Acad Prfrmnch In Bio; Awds For 3.75 Gpa For 88-9; Schlr Athlt Awd; Vet Med.

SULLIVAN, ERIN L; Leilehua HS; Wahiawa, HI; (2); 97/392; Church Yth Grp; 4-H; French Clb; Chorus; Church Choir; 4-H Awd; CA Dressage Scty; Zoology.

SUMARNAP, KORYN M; Waiakea HS; Hilo, HI; (1); Church Yth Grp; 4-H; JA; Kamehameha Canoe Clb; Hawaiian Lang Speech Cont.

SUMIDA, CARIE K; Waiakea HS; Hilo, HI; (2); Science Clb; Service Clb; Band; Mrchg Band; Pep Band; Lion Awd; Sci.

SUMIDA, KRISTY; Kaimuki HS; Honolulu, HI; (4); 33/334; SADD; Temple Yth Grp; School Play; Stage Crew; Hon Roll; Electrncs Clb Sectry; Sci Dept Awd; St Sci Fr; U Of HI Manoa; Elec Engrng.

SUNADA, JENNIFER M; Waiakea HS; Hilo, HI; (1); 22/478; JA; Band; Mrchg Band; Pep Band; Hon Roll; Leo Club; U Of WA; Phrmcy.

SUNG, JESSICA HYON LA; Roosevelt HS; Honolulu, HI; (3); 11/350; Dance Clb; Quiz Bowl; Teachers Aide; Tennis; High Hon Roll; Hon Roll; Jr NHS; Excllnce Acad Achvt, Cls Spirit & Acad Achvt Japanese I Awds 88; Commercl Artst.

SUNG, STEVEN SE KYONG; Roosevelt HS; Honolulu, HI; (2); 20/360; Golf.

SUNIGA, MARITEL S; Mc Kinley HS; Honolulu, HI; (2); Spanish Clb; Sftbl; Prfct Atten Awd; Bus Club; Mabuhay Club Secy 89-90; U Of Berkeley; Rgstrd Nrs.

SUZUKI, SCOTT M; Maui HS; Kahului, HI; (4); 72/300; Church Yth Grp; Key Clb; Pep Clb; Pres Band; Mrchg Band; Orch; Pep Band; VP Frsh Cls; Japanese Clb; U Of HI Manoa; Arch.

SWENSON, YARROW; Kapaa HS; Hanalei, HI; (1); 19/220; Off Frsh Cls; Stu Cncl; CA ST U; CPA.

SWIER JR, RICHARD M; Lutheran HS; Sarasota, FL; (4); 8/45; FCA; Teachers Aide; Nwsp; Rep Frsh Cls; Rep Soph Cls; Pres Jr Cls; Rep Stu Cncl; Hon Roll; JETS Awd; NHS; Athl Of Yr; Bsktbl Player Of Yr; 1st Tm All St Bsktbl Vrsty; U FL; Engrng.

TABAJUNDA, CHELSEA K; Pahoa HS; Keaau, HI; (3); Girl Scts; Hui Olelo HI O Puna; Pep Squad; Nursing.

TABAREJO, MONICA K; Honokaa HS; Honokaa, HI; (3); 16/150; Pres Church Yth Grp; Cmnty Wkr; Band; Jazz Band; Rptr Nwsp; Ed Lit Mag; JV Capt Bsktbl; Capt Var Socr; High Hon Roll; Hon Roll; All-Amer Schlr Eng; US Bus Ed Awd; Pre-Law.

TABILE, LEILANI E; James Campbell HS; Ewa Beach, HI; (3); French Clb; Science Clb; School Musical; Mgr(s); Powder Puff Ftbl; Medcl.

TABIOLO, ANGELA L; Waipahu HS; Waipahu, HI; (4); 37/418; Chorus; High Hon Roll; U HI; Accntnt.

TABON, NAOMI; Henry Perrine Baldwin HS; Wailuku, HI; (3); 40/385; Letterman Clb; Pep Clb; SADD; Co-Ed Lit Mag; Var Cheerldng; Hon Roll; Spec Olympics & Walk A Thon; Chrldng; Treas 89-90 & Sec 90-91; CO ST U.

TACHERA, MARIA K; Henry J Kaiser HS; Honolulu, HI; (3); Crs Cntry; Trk; Prfct Atten Awd; Pre-Educ; U Of HI; Pre-Educ.

TACLAN, ANDREA B; Baldwin HS; Wailuku, HI; (1); 14/471; Bus.

TADA, MELANIE M; Kauai HS; Lihue, HI; (3); 14/231; Sec 4-H; FHA; JV Stat Bsktbl; Var Crs Cntry; Var Socr; Var Trk; Var Co-Capt Vllybl; Hon Roll; NHS; Keywanettes Treas; Linfield Coll; Acctnt.

TADD, ANDREW R; Mililani HS; Mililani, HI; (2); 21/509; JV Capt Bsktbl; Var Vllybl; High Hon Roll; Hon Roll; TX A&M; Dsgn Engrng.

TAGAWA, HEATHER F; Waiakea HS; Keaau, HI; (4); 11/412; Variety Show; High Hon Roll; NHS; Ballet/Jazz Dance; Summa Cum Laude Grad; U Of HI-HILO; Data Procssng.

TAGUPA, STEVE N; Damien Memorial HS; Honolulu, HI; (4); 22/125; Church Yth Grp; Computer Clb; 4-H; Pep Clb; ROTC; Hon Roll; Cert Educ Dvlpmnt Ntl NEDT; U HI Manoa; Mech Engr.

TAIRA, JAMIE; Baldwinn HS; Kahului, HI; (3); 44/386; Debate Tm; Letterman Clb; Service Clb; Speech Tm; SADD; Sec Jr Cls; Sec Stu Cncl; JV Var Swmmng; Hon Roll; Rotary Awd; Maui Dist Stu Cncl Organization St Planner; HI St Stu Conf Delg; Study Abroad Exchng Pgm; Speech.

TAKAHASHI, AMY; Iolani HS; Kailua, HI; (3); 41/227; Dance Clb; Pres Soph Cls; JV Cheerldng; JV Trk; High Hon Roll; Rotary Awd; Drama Clb; Service Clb; Stage Crew; HOBY; Amnsty Intl Pres; Intl Rltns.

TAKAHASHI, JON; Kaimuki HS; Kaneohe, HI; (3); 73/361; VP JA; Off ROTC; Var L Crs Cntry; Var Ftbl; Var L Wrstlng; Ntl Merit SF; Engrng.

TAKAHASHI, LORI Y; Kaiser HS; Honolulu, HI; (2); 17/260; Band; Drm Mjr(t); Mrchg Band; Hon Roll; Prfct Atten Awd; Ed.

TAKAHASHI, TODD Z; Damien Memorial HS; Waipahu, HI; (3); 18/115; Church Yth Grp; JA; NFL; Speech Tm; Teachers Aide; High Hon Roll; Hon Roll; Japnnese Club Pres; KIPC Head Chairprsn; Poetry Rdng Neighbor Island Sppech Trnmtn 3rd Pl & 6th Pl; Pacific U; Scndry Ed.

TAKAMINE, CRAIG S; Waiakea HS; Hilo, HI; (2); 89/500; Church Yth Grp; Treas 4-H; Sec Band; Sec Mrchg Band; Sec Pep Band; Leo Clb; Bsbl; P&R Bsktbl 88-89; U Of HI Manoa; Bus Admin.

TAKAMORI, KIM E; Maui HS; Kahului, HI; (3); 1/354; Sec Church Yth Grp; Pres 4-H; Sec Letterman Clb; Treas Soph Cls; Var Capt Swmmng; 4-H Awd; High Hon Roll; NHS; Pres Acad Fit Awd; Keywanettes Clb; Optmtry.

TAKAMOTO, WADE K; Mid-Pacific Inst; Honolulu, HI; (2); Boy Scts; Church Yth Grp; Var Socr; High Hon Roll; Hon Roll; Prfct Atten Awd; Pres Acad Fit Awd.

TAKAYAMA, AILEEN P; Waiakea HS; Hilo, HI; (4); 89/412; JA; Ed Yrbk; Hon Roll; UH Hilo; Restaurant Mgmt.

TAKEMORI, DONNA LYN M; Punahou Schl; Aiea, HI; (3); JA; Latin Clb; Spanish Clb; Band; Drill Tm; Mrchg Band; Ed Lit Mag; Var Gym; High Hon Roll; Hon Roll.

TAKEMOTO, ALICIA; Hilo HS; Papaikou, HI; (4); 6/300; Math Clb; Rep Frsh Cls; Rep Soph Cls; Rep Jr Cls; Rep Sr Cls; Rep Stu Cncl; Mgr(s); High Hon Roll; NHS; Keywanettes Club; WA ST U.

TAKEMOTO, TAMI L; Waialua HS; Waialua, HI; (3); Pep Clb; Hon Roll; Prfct Atten Awd; Interact, Leo, Drugbstrs, Japnse Clbs; Hmcmng Prom Comm; Ntl Guild Awd Piano; Spch Lang.

TAKESHITA, DARA M; Kaimuki HS; Honolulu, HI; (3); 31/361; Var L Bsktbl; Var L Sftbl; Hon Roll; Elctrncs.

TAKEUCHI, JOHN KEKOA; Roosevelt HS; Honolulu, HI; (4); Boy Scts; Church Yth Grp; Band; Jazz Band; Mrchg Band; JV Wrstlng; Hon Roll; Outstndng Seminary Stu 87-90; Gold Music Awd 89; HI Ambssdr Music 89; Instrumentalist Magazine Awd.

TAKEUCHI, TRISHA; Farrington HS; Honolulu, HI; (3); 146/600; Band; High Hon Roll; Hon Roll; UCLA; Bio.

TAKIGUCHI, CORINE Y; Hawaii Baptist Acad; Pearl City, HI; (4); 1/95; Church Yth Grp; Capt Math Tm; Ed Yrbk; Sec NHS; Ntl Merit Ltr; Val; Sterling Schlr Fnlst; Rotary Clb Schlrshp Wnnr; Century 3 Ldrs Schlrshp St Fnlst; U Of PA; Bus Admin.

TAKIGUCHI, SHAWN M; Henry Perrine Baldwin HS; Wailuku, HI; (1); 20/466; Sec 4-H; Service Clb; SADD; Band; Mrchg Band; Pep Band; High Hon Roll; Hon Roll; Prfct Atten Awd; Outstndng Stu In Japanses Lang Stud; Baldwin HS Aloha Clb; Wrld Hydrogen Enrgy Cnfrnc 1990; CPA.

TALATALA, MARIA-TERESA B; Moanalua HS; Pearl City, HI; (2); 46/488; Hon Roll; Court Volunteer; NELS 90; Law Club; Hmrm Alt; U Notre Dame; Def Lawyer.

TAM, ANNA; St Andrews Priory HS; Waimanalo, HI; (4); 5/50; Intnl Clb; Key Clb; Latin Clb; Quiz Bowl; Science Clb; Stage Crew; Chrmn Stu Cncl; NHS; Pres Acad Fit Awd; Ray Kroc Yth Achvt Awd 90; Paddling Most Vlbl Athl, All Star Awd, 2nd Team; Japanese Clb Pres; U HI Manoa; Civil Engrng.

TAM, NANCY Y; Mc Kinley HS; Honolulu, HI; (1); 41/492; Treas Frsh Cls; Chinese Clb; Chrprsn Pep Rlly & Bnqt; Med.

TAM, YEUK SAI C; Kaimuki HS; Honolulu, HI; (2); Hon Roll; Music; Sports; Phy.

TAMAI, ALAN Y; St Louis HS; Honolulu, HI; (3); 31/150; Intnl Clb; Band; Mrchg Band; Pep Band; Treas Jr Cls; Hon Roll; Japanese Clb; Interschl Clb.

TAMAKI, TAKUMI; Pahoa HS; Pahoa, HI; (2); FHA; Var Ftbl; Frosh Var Ftbl Hnbl Mntn; Soph Var Ftbl Hnbl Mntn; UH Hilo; Art.

TAMASHIRO, JARED H; Maui HS; Kahului, HI; (2); 66/388; Boy Scts; Key Clb; Math Clb; JV Crs Cntry; JV Trk; Hon Roll; Japanese Club; Triple S Stus Staying Strght.

TAMASHIRO, KRISTEN M; Hawaii Baptist Acad; Honolulu, HI; (4); Treas Soph Cls; Treas Sr Cls; Cit Awd; NHS; Pres Acad Fit Awd; Bowling JV, Var Tm Capt; Ldrshp Cncl Pres; Japanese Club; Loyola Marymount U; Bus Admin.

TAMAYO, DANIEL; Hilo HS; Hilo, HI; (2); 4/367; FHA; Hon Roll; Princpls Awd; U Of HI Manoa; Engrng.

TAMBIO, TRICIA L; Leilehua HS; Mililani, HI; (4); 7/304; Church Yth Grp; Teachers Aide; Hon Roll; NHS; PRAISE Awd; Outstndng Prfcncy Englsh III Awd; Cmmndtn Outstndng 89 Filipno Stu; Bradley U; Engrng.

TAMIMI, MALIK Y; Waiakea HS; Hilo, HI; (4); 42/412; Treas Science Clb; Band; Chorus; Variety Show; Rep Sr Cls; Crs Cntry; Trk; High Hon Roll; Hon Roll; Lion Awd; Bio.

TAMONDONG, KRISTINA M; Leilehua HS; Wahiawa, HI; (4); 6/304; FTA; Spanish Clb; Church Choir; Pres Frsh Cls; Pres Soph Cls; Pres Sr Cls; JV Var Bsktbl; Var Crs Cntry; High Hon Roll; NHS; Outstndng Filipino Snr; HI Yng Woman Yr Schlrshp Pgm; U Of Northern CO; Scndry Educ.

TAMPON, BRANDI; Pahoa HS; Pahoa, HI; (4); 4/10; Aud/Vis; Church Yth Grp; Computer Clb; Pres FFA; Sec FTA; Pres Sr Cls; Capt Bsktbl; Var Cheerldng; Hon Roll; Sec NHS; Natl FFA Wshngtn Conf Pgm Cert; Outstnd Sr Filipino Decent; Outstnd Sprtsmnshp Awd 88-89; U Of HI Hilo; Elem Educ.

TAMURA, JOHN M; Mid-Pacific Inst; Honolulu, HI; (3); Band; Phtg Yrbk; Hon Roll; Jr NHS; Pres Acad Fit Awd; Japanese II Frgn Lang Dept Awd; I B Full Dplma Pgm; Pacific Asian Affrs Cncl; Med.

TAN, BRUCE D; Roosevelt HS; Aiea, HI; (3); 11/352; Intnl Clb; Math Clb; Science Clb; Teachers Aide; Sec Sr Cls; High Hon Roll; Hon Roll; NHS; Outstndng Alg I; Schlstc Hnr; U CA Berkeley; Bio.

TAN, BRUCE D; Roosevelt HS; Honolulu, HI; (3); 11/352; Intnl Clb; Math Clb; Quiz Bowl; Science Clb; Teachers Aide; Sec Sr Cls; High Hon Roll; Hon Roll; NHS; Best Outstndng Algebra I Stu; U CA Berkeley; Bio.

TAN, ERIN; Konawacha HS; Kailua-Kona, HI; (4); 22/291; Dance Clb; French Clb; Ed Yrbk; Sec Soph Cls; Treas Jr Cls; Var Capt Socr; Var Capt Trk; Hon Roll; AYSO Asst Soccer Coach; Big Isl Interschlstc Fed Soccer Team; Outstndng Soccer Athl Awd; U Northern CO; Advrtsmnt.

TANAKA, CECILEE M; Hawaii Baptist Acad; Kaneohe, HI; (2); Church Yth Grp; Cmnty Wkr; Hon Roll; Jr NHS; Serteens; Natl Sci Olympd; Japanese Club; Guitar Club.

TANAKA, CLORINDA N; Hawaiian Mission Acad; Hilo, HI; (2); 2/50; Treas Church Yth Grp; Thesps; Church Choir; School Play; Rep Frsh Cls; Rep Stu Cncl; Hon Roll; Polynesian Clb; Juliette K Lau Mem Schlrshp; Pacific Union Coll; Intl Comm.

TANAKA, DENISE C; Mid Pacific Inst; Honolulu, HI; (3); Bsktbl; High Hon Roll; Hon Roll; Koto Clb; Japanese Clb; Japanese Dance Clb; Law.

TANAKA, LAURIE E; Mc Kinley HS; Honolulu, HI; (2); 1/588; Math Clb; Math Tm; High Hon Roll; Hon Roll; Schltc Achvt Awd; Poltcl Action Clb; Stu Congress; Engrng.

TANAKA, RUTH ANN H; Waiakea HS; Hilo, HI; (3); Sec Pres 4-H; Math Clb; Science Clb; Teachers Aide; Stat Bsktbl; Var Crs Cntry; Hon Roll; Sec NHS; Cls Chrprsn; Outstndng Svc Awd; Med.

TANAKA, TIPSY; Castle HS; Kaneohe, HI; (4); Band; Mrchg Band; Pep Band; Off Sr Cls; Hon Roll; Keywanette Clb Treas; Jap Clb; Stu Of Mnth; U Of HI.

TANAKA, TROY ALAN K; Waiakea HS; Hilo, HI; (3); Boy Scts; Key Clb; Latin Clb; Math Clb; Treas Science Clb; Rep Soph Cls; Rep Jr Cls; Var Crs Cntry; Hon Roll; Outstndng Svc Awd; Engrng.

TANAKA, WENDY A; Maui HS; Kula, HI; (4); 13/305; Church Yth Grp; Drama Clb; Speech Tm; Band; Variety Show; Ed Nwsp; Lit Mag; 4-H Awd; High Hon Roll; Prfct Atten Awd; Chrysthmum Ball; Wn 1st Pl HA Lang Arts Shwcse 3 Yrs; Natl Piano Plyng Auditions; U Of HI Manoa; Vet Sci.

TANG, ANDREW Y K; St Louis HS; Honolulu, HI; (3); 14/150; Intnl Clb; Science Clb; Band; Mrchg Band; Pep Band; Sec Frsh Cls; VP Soph Cls; Pres Jr Cls; Rep Stu Cncl; Intrml Trk; 1st Pl In Homecoming Talent Show 90; Japanese Club; Principals List; Architecture Schl; Ag.

TANG, JOHN C; Roosevelt HS; Honolulu, HI; (3); 31/350; Math Clb; Science Clb; Bsbl; Trk; U Of HI; Engrng.

TANIGUCHI, BERT H; Saint Louis HS; Hauula, HI; (2); ROTC; Ftbl; Trk; Wrstlng; UCLA; Engr.

TANIGUCHI, CHRISTIE; Kamehameha HS; Kaneohe, HI; (2); 153/343; Church Yth Grp; SADD; Rep Soph Cls; JV Cheerldng; JV Sftbl; U WA.

TANIOKA, LARA; Kauai HS; Hanapepe, HI; (3); 10/231; Science Clb; SADD; Off Frsh Cls; Treas Soph Cls; VP Jr Cls; Sec Stu Cncl; Var Vllybl; High Hon Roll; Hon Roll; NHS.

TANIYAMA, JANIS; Maryknoll HS; Aiea, HI; (2); #5 In Class; Church Yth Grp; Hosp Aide; Math Clb; Office Aide; Pep Clb; Cheerldng; High Hon Roll; Engrng.

TANIZAKI, JAMES T; Maui HS; Pukalani, HI; (3); 34/354; Computer Clb; Band; JV Wrstlng; Hon Roll; Prfct Atten Awd; Air Force Acad; Engrng.

TANO, VANCE T; Moanalua HS; Waipahu, HI; (2); 82/488; Band; Color Guard; Drm Mjr(t); Jazz Band; Mrchg Band; Pep Band; U Of HI; Lbrl Arts.

TANOUE, KURT; Laupahoehoe Elem HS; Papaaloa, HI; (3); Math Tm; Science Clb; Band; Mrchg Band; Var Bsbl; JV Var Bsktbl; JV Var Trk; Var Vllybl; Var Wrstlng; USAF Acad; Aerospc.

TANOUYE, NATHAN N; H P Baldwin HS; Wailuku, HI; (2); Band; Jazz Band; Mrchg Band; Pep Band; Music.

TANOUYE, STEFAN; Hilo HS; Hilo, HI; (4); 6/304; Pres Aud/Vis; VP Band; Mrchg Band; Pep Band; JV Bsbl; JV Bsktbl; Cnflct Mdtn; Bus Admin.

TANUVASA, JEANNIE; Mililani HS; Wahiawa, HI; (4); 47/408; Pres Church Yth Grp; Teachers Aide; Chorus; Church Choir; Rep Stu Cncl; Capt Var Bsktbl; Var Sftbl; Var Vllybl; Hon Roll; Wn Gld Mdl Bsktbl HA Aloha St Gms; MVP Bsktbl Tm; Schlrshp Chrch & Bsktbl Camp; U HI Manoa; Bus Mgmt.

TANUVASA, VALERIE F; Mililani HS; Wahiawa, HI; (2); Church Yth Grp; Drama Clb; Church Choir; Var Bsktbl; JV Trk; Gld Mdlst Aloha St Games Bsktbl; U Of HI Manda; Real Estate.

TAO, PHAN T; St Francis HS; Honolulu, HI; (2); Hosp Aide; Intnl Clb; Sec Frsh Cls; Hon Roll; Phrmcy.

TAOSAKA, SHARLA AKIKO; Waiakea HS; Hilo, HI; (4); 77/412; Rep Sr Cls; Hon Roll; Kewyanettes Sr Rep; Konko Mission Hilo Sndy Schl; Jr Ball & Sr Prom Cmmttes; Hmcmng Cmmtte; U Of HI Manoa.

TAPEC, MARITES M; Waialua HS; Waialua, HI; (3); Church Yth Grp; Cmnty Wkr; Math Tm; Science Clb; Var Tennis; Var Vllybl; Ntl Merit Ltr; Japanese Clb; Commnctns.

TASAKA, ALANNE L; Kapaa HS; Hanalei, HI; (2); Pep Clb; Var Socr; Certfd Scuba Diver; Emergency Medcl Tech.

TASHIMA, ROBIN H; Iolani Schl; Honolulu, HI; (4); Drama Clb; 4-H; JA; Key Clb; Stage Crew; Ed Nwsp; High Hon Roll; Hon Roll; Ntl Merit SF; Summa Cum Laude & Magna Cum Laude Awds ; Rspctvly Natl Latin Exam; Cmmnctns.

TATE, LARRY E; Leilehua HS; Wahiawa, HI; (2); 46/392; Band; Mrchg Band; Pep Band; Rep Frsh Cls; Capt Bsbl; JV Capt Bsktbl; Var Capt Ftbl; Trk; Hon Roll; Pres Acad Fit Awd; U Of MN; Math.

TAVARES, SUNRISE K; Mc Kinley HS; Honolulu, HI; (2); 196/588; Art Clb; Church Yth Grp; Science Clb; JV Bsktbl; Prntr Daily Schl Nwsp; Bus Mjr.

TAY, ELROY W; Kauai HS; Lihue, HI; (3); 1/231; Boy Scts; Pres Key Clb; Science Clb; Treas Band; L Crs Cntry; L Trk; Elks Awd; High Hon Roll; NHS; Engrng.

TAYLAN, NANCY P; Kauai HS; Lihue, HI; (4); 24/239; Computer Clb; Speech Tm; Ed Yrbk; Hon Roll; NHS; Leo Clb; Kauai CC; Comp Engr.

TAYLOR, ADAM; Kalaheo HS; Kailua, HI; (1); 5/266; Church Yth Grp; Letterman Clb; Wrstlng; Hon Roll; U FL; Marine Bio.

TAYLOR, CASSANDRA D; Henry Perrine Baldwin HS; Kihei, HI; (2); 1/401; Church Yth Grp; Cmnty Wkr; Service Clb; SADD; Church Choir; School Play; Stage Crew; Rep Soph Cls; High Hon Roll; Stu Staying Straight VP; Engl.

TAYLOR, JEREMY E; Kohala HS; Kapaau, HI; (3); Church Yth Grp; Drama Clb; Numerous Sports; U HI Manoa; Poltcl Sci.

TAYLOR, JULIE L; Hawaii Baptist Acad; Kailua, HI; (2); Drama Clb; Pres VP Chorus; School Musical; School Play; Variety Show; Cit Awd; High Hon Roll; Hon Roll; NHS; Rep Frsh Cls; Stu Aloha Cncl Sec; Whitworth Coll; Music.

TAYLOR, MICHELLE; Kalaheo HS; Kailua, HI; (4); Swmmng; Hon Roll; Pres Acad Fit Awd.

TEFFT, MARIA; Pahoa High And Elem; Pahoa, HI; (3); 1/121; Drama Clb; Math Tm; Sec Spanish Clb; High Hon Roll; NHS; Val.

TEIXEIRA, ANGELA; Kalaheo HS; Kailua, HI; (2); 21/300; French Clb; Library Aide; SADD; Pep Band; Yrbk; Bsktbl; Cheerldng; Cit Awd; French Hon Soc; High Hon Roll; U Of WA; Flight Atten.

TEIXEIRA, RAIN; Waianae HS; Waianae, HI; (2); 87/487; Church Yth Grp; Pep Clb; JV Capt Bsktbl; Hon Roll; Prfct Atten Awd; Outreach To Poor & Homeless; Yth Day Cmmttee For Catholic Dio; Aid For Religious Ed; U HI; Nrsg.

TELLEZ, ARNOLD D; Kailua HS; Kaneohe, HI; (2); Dance Clb; ROTC; Color Guard; Drill Tm; Natl Sjrnrs Mdl; Mltry Ordr Wrld Wars Mdl; Chf Mstr Srgnt USDIJROTC; U Of HI; Sci.

TEMPLE, EVE W; Waiakea HS; Keaau, HI; (3); Church Yth Grp; Hosp Aide; Teachers Aide; Church Choir; School Musical; Variety Show; Var L Trk; High Hon Roll; Hon Roll; BYU.

TEMPLE, RACHEL K; Wiakea HS; Keaau, HI; (1); Drama Clb; Church Choir.

TENGAN, CULLEN; Lutheran HS; Pearl City, HI; (1); Church Yth Grp; FCA; 4-H; Band; Pep Band; JV Bsktbl; Var Vllybl; 4-H Awd; Engr.

TENGAN, JILL M; H P Baldwin HS; Pukalani, HI; (2); 23/395; Art Clb; 4-H; FTA; 4-H Awd; Hon Roll; Cert Scuba Diver; Shooting Sports; Classical Japanese Dance Stu; Marine Bio.

TENGAN, KENNETH; Mc Kinley HS; Honolulu, HI; (1); 68/492; JV Bsktbl; UCLA; Engr.

TENGAN, KIMBERLY LEI; Henry Perrine Baldwin HS; Kahului, HI; (1); 39/466; Church Yth Grp; Cmnty Wkr; Service Clb; SADD; Band; Pep Band; Var L Socr; JV L Trk; Var L Vllybl; Hon Roll; Music Ed.

TENGAN, TY P; The Kamehameha Schls; Wailuku, HI; (1); 26/451; ROTC; Intrml JV Ftbl; JV Capt Wrstlng; Hon Roll; IL; Chem.

TERUYA, ITSUKO; W R Farrington HS; Honolulu, HI; (3); 150/600; Treas Frsh Cls; Rep Soph Cls; Shinwakabakai Clb-Japanese Clb; U Of HI-HONOLULU; Engl.

TEXEIRA, DAWN K; Baldwin HS; Wailuku, HI; (2); Pep Clb; Spanish Clb; Band; Mrchg Band; Pep Band; Hon Roll; Harvard Schl; Law.

THANAVONG, OULAYVANH; Farrington HS; Hauula, HI; (1); 59/301; JV Crs Cntry; Athltc Clb; FDIM; Fshn Dsgn.

THIEU, DANH; Kalmuki HS; Honolulu, HI; (3); U Of HI; Acctng.

THIEU, THULAN T; Kaimuki HS; Honolulu, HI; (2); Dance Clb; Band; School Musical; Stage Crew; Variety Show; High Hon Roll; Hon Roll; Cosmetology.

THOMAS, CHRISTINE; Kalaheo HS; Kailua, HI; (2); Off Soph Cls; Var JV Swmmng; Hon Roll; Pres Acad Fit Awd; Englsh Awd.

THOMAS, HARRY H; Kamehameha HS; Kapaa, HI; (3); Bsbl; Bsktbl; Crs Cntry; Fld Hcky; Gym; JV Socr; Var Trk; Vllybl; Wt Lftg; Wrstlng; Jnr Achvt Awd.

THOMPSON, JOANNE R; Radford HS; Honolulu, HI; (3); Debate Tm; NFL; SADD; Rep Stu Cncl; Hon Roll; Civil Air Patrl; Japanese Clb; Perfmg Arts Clb; Coll; Med.

THOMPSON, KELLY; Kauai HS; Koloa, HI; (2); 1/220; Church Yth Grp; Treas Drama Clb; Treas 4-H; Key Clb; Science Clb; SADD; Ed Nwsp; Pres Frsh Cls; Rep Soph Cls; Rep VP Stu Cncl; U Of CA; Pre-Med.

THOMPSON, LATREASHA D; Moanalua HS; Fort Shafter, HI; (2); 25/488; Treas Pres Spanish Clb; JV Var Vllybl; High Hon Roll; Hon Roll; Jr NHS; NHS; Welcome Cmmttee-Chairperson; Amherst; Med.

THOMPSON, MELISSA R; Radford HS; Honolulu, HI; (3); Church Yth Grp; Letterman Clb; ROTC; SADD; Variety Show; Var L Bsktbl; Var L Sftbl; Rap Dncr; USC; Intr Dsgn.

THOMPSON, SHANNON E; Kauai HS & Intermed; Koloa, HI; (3); Church Yth Grp; Drama Clb; 4-H; Key Clb; Math Tm; Pep Clb; Science Clb; VP SADD; Off Frsh Cls; Off Jr Cls; Vet.

THONGBENJAMAS, THITI; Saint Louis HS; Honolulu, HI; (3); 8/150; Cmnty Wkr; Hosp Aide; Quiz Bowl; ROTC; Color Guard; JV Crs Cntry; JV Ftbl; Var JV Tennis; Hon Roll; NHS; Riflery; Ranger; Princpl List; U Of CA Berkeley; Arch.

TIJAMO, EMMANUEL O; Kaimuki HS; Honolulu, HI; (3); 32/361; Boy Scts; Church Yth Grp; JV Bsktbl; Hon Roll; Hawaiian Elec Mtr Bldng Cont; Electronics.

TING, YI-WEN; Kaiser HS; Honolulu, HI; (1); 88/255; JV Var Bsktbl; JV Var Ftbl; Hon Roll; U HI; Lawyr.

TIPPIT, DEANGELA K; Moanalua HS; Woodbridge, VA; (3); Church Yth Grp; FHA; GAA; Capt Bsktbl; Vllybl; Capt JV Girls Bsktbl Team 87 & 88; Chldrns Chrch Tchr; Ldrshp Trng 89; TX A&M U; Anml Med.

TIUMALU, CHARLENE D; Waipahu HS; Waipahu, HI; (1); 180/513; Church Yth Grp; Church Choir; Vllybl; UC Stanford; Bus.

TOGASNI, ANN M; Waiakea HS; Hilo, HI; (2); 4-H; Math Tm; Service Clb; Variety Show; Rep Stu Cncl; Hon Roll; Leo Spcl Achvt & Outstndng Svc Awds.

TOKAMINE, WADE; Roosevelt HS; Honolulu, HI; (1); Math Tm; Band; Mrchg Band; Pep Band; U Of HI; Author.

TOKI, MAYVIN J; Kapaka HS; Kapaa, HI; (3); Church Yth Grp; FHA; Hist Spanish Clb; JV Cheerldng; Hon Roll; HI Intl Film Fstvl Poster Cntst Grnd Prz; Columbia Coll Chgo; Music Sales.

TOKUDA, SANDY; W R Farrington HS; Honolulu, HI; (3); 4/759; Treas 4-H; Math Clb; Treas Band; Color Guard; Flag Corp; Jazz Band; Mrchg Band; Lit Mag; Rep Frsh Cls; Cit Awd; Sci Tech Fair; Accntng.

TOLBERT, NICOLE A; Radford HS; Honolulu, HI; (3); 69/500; FTA; Intnl Clb; Natl Beta Clb; Ed Yrbk; Var Crs Cntry; JV Sftbl; Var Swmmng; JV Trk; Stu Month 88; FL ST U; Translator.

TOLOUMU, BRENDA; Radford HS; Honolulu, HI; (2); Bus Profs of Am; Church Yth Grp; Cmnty Wkr; Computer Clb; Intnl Clb; JA; Library Aide; Office Aide; Band; Chorus; U Of HI; Nurse.

TOM, KAM DAT; Mc Kinley HS; Honolulu, HI; (4); 22/547; Key Clb; Science Clb; Var Crs Cntry; Var Trk; Hon Roll; Lion Awd; NHS; Prfct Atten Awd; Pres Acad Fit Awd; U Of HI; Engrng.

TOM, PATRICIA-ANNE Y H; Mc Kinley HS; Honolulu, HI; (3); 35/545; French Clb; SADD; Band; Flag Corp; School Musical; Ed Nwsp; Sec Sr Cls; Hon Roll; Rifle Team Vrsty; Jrnlsm.

TOMA, DEIDRE A; Mc Kinley HS; Honolulu, HI; (1); 17/492; Hosp Aide; Math Clb; Orch; Hon Roll; Japanese Clb; U Of HI; Med Technlgy.

TOMA, STEFFANY M; Kalaheo HS; Kailua, HI; (4); 1/235; Math Tm; Mu Alpha Theta; Chrmn Band; Jazz Band; Mrchg Band; School Musical; Lit Mag; Off Jr Cls; Pres Treas NHS; Ntl Merit SF; 2nd Pl Video Natl Stu Media Fstvl; HI Ambssdr Of Music:Chrprsn Of Grdtn Cmmttee; Mi ST U; Pre Med.

TOMACDER, ROMULO J; Farrington HS; Honolulu, HI; (2); Church Yth Grp; Drama Clb; Phtg Yrbk; Cit Awd; High Hon Roll; Hon Roll; Prfct Atten Awd; Film Club; U HI; Electrncs.

TOMITA, LISA A; H P Baldwin HS; Kahului, HI; (3); 31/385; DECA; Hon Roll; Stars Stu Stayng Straight; Acctng.

TOMITA, LORI K; Moanalua HS; Honolulu, HI; (1); 37/545; Service Clb; Band; Mrchg Band; Pep Band; Treas Soph Cls; Mgr Crs Cntry; Var Socr; Hon Roll; Bus Mgmt.

TOMITA, SHELLEY; Hilo HS; Hilo, HI; (4); Treas Key Clb; Math Clb; Math Tm; Rep Soph Cls; Rep Stu Cncl; Hon Roll; NHS; Prfct Atten Awd; Bowling Ltr Co Cptn; Acad Top Ten Awd; Schl Svc Awd; Elect Engr.

TONAKI, DARILYN; Mililani HS; Mililani, HI; (3); Cmnty Wkr; Teachers Aide; Stat Ftbl; Mgr(s); Socr; Stat Mgr Wrstlng; FHA-HERD Clb; Social Cmmtte; U Of HI; Human Devt.

TONG, DORIS W; Moanalua HS; Honolulu, HI; (2); 23/488; Church Yth Grp; FTA; Chorus; Variety Show; Hon Roll; Co-Chrprsn Of Info Booth; Chrprsn Of Winter Bll Bid Sls; Co-Chrprsn Of Cls Rngs Cmmtte; U Of HI; Dentistry.

TONOUCHI, KORY K; Roosevelt HS; Honolulu, HI; (1); 15/373; Boy Scts; Spanish Clb; Hon Roll; Vrsty Rifle Tm; 3rd Pl Ind ST Chmpnshp Rifle Shoot; Aerospc Engr.

TOOTOO, EVENI; Waianae HS; Waianae, HI; (2); Church Yth Grp; Swing Chorus; Ftbl; High Hon Roll; Hon Roll; Prfct Atten Awd; U Of HI; Math.

TORIBIO, MARILYN; Kohala HS; Kapaau, HI; (1); 6/61; VP Pres FHA; Hist VP FTA; VP Rep Frsh Cls; Hon Roll; Lion Awd; U Of Portland; Ed.

TORRES, BRAN-DEE; Kamehameha HS; Kaneohe, HI; (1); 41/451; Church Yth Grp; JA; SADD; Chorus; Intrml JV Sftbl; JV Tennis; Intrml Trk; High Hon Roll; Hon Roll.

TORRICER, WILBERT C; Maui HS; Puunene, HI; (3); 1/354; Church Yth Grp; Science Clb; Church Choir; Mgr(s); Hon Roll; NHS; Prfct Atten Awd; Triple S Club; U HI; Engrng.

TOTH, CATHERINE E; Roosevelt HS; Honolulu, HI; (1); Drama Clb; Model UN; Nwsp; Lit Mag; Score Keeper; JV Vllybl; Hon Roll; Mistletoe Ball Cmmtte; Helpd Stu Cncl, Fresh Class; Cmmtte Chairprsn Fresh Wk; Engl.

TOURVILLE, TRACI; Moanalua HS; Honolulu, HI; (3); 41/462; Cit Awd; Jr NHS; Pres Acad Fit Awd; Race/Human Rltns Awd For Outstnd Svc & Dedication, Integration Pgm; Schlrshp Awd; Peer Cnslng; Nrsng.

TOUW, ERIN C; Leilehua HS; Wahiawa, HI; (2); Church Yth Grp; Cmnty Wkr; Hosp Aide; Model UN; Red Cross Aide; SADD; Church Choir; Socr; Sftbl; High Hon Roll; MI ST U; Sprts Med.

TOYAMA, MALIA M; Waiakea HS; Hilo, HI; (3); 43/368; Key Clb; L Swmmng; Hon Roll; CA ST U Long Bch; Intr Design.

TRAN, JILL C; Moanalua HS; Huntington Beach, CA; (2); SADD; Rep Soph Cls; High Hon Roll; Hon Roll; Pres Acad Fit Awd; SMILE Clb; Yth Helping Yth.

TRAN, LINH N; Mc Kinley HS; Honolulu, HI; (1); U HI.

TRAN, MINH; Mc Kinley HS; Honolulu, HI; (1); 7/541; UCLA; Mech Engr Dsgnr.

TRAN, NGUYEN N; Roosevelt HS; Honolulu, HI; (2); Cmnty Wkr; Math Tm; Crs Cntry; Socr; Trk; Hon Roll; NHS; Prfct Atten Awd; Hospital Vlntr; Engrng.

TRAN, RONALD ONTHIEN; Mc Kinley HS; Honolulu, HI; (2); Bwlng Tm; Grphc Art Clb; Arts.

TRAN, SIEU L; Mc Kinley HS; Honolulu, HI; (1); 41/492; Orch; Swmmng; Hon Roll; UCLA; Psycht.

TRAUTMAN, ERICH M; Mid-Pacific Inst; Honolulu, HI; (2); 5/380; Chess Clb; Computer Clb; Quiz Bowl; Scholastic Bowl; Phtg Yrbk; High Hon Roll; NHS; Spnsh Achvtmnt Test; Natl Merit Schlr Test & PSAT; Natl Hnr Soc; Harvard U; Bus.

TRIEU, VINH C; Kaimuki HS; Honolulu, HI; (1); Hon Roll.

TRINH, BINH L; Kaimuki HS; Honolulu, HI; (2); 38/325; U Of HI.

TRUELOVE, KATHARINA M; Hawaii Baptist Acad; Makakilo, HI; (2); 1/95; Math Clb; Math Tm; Thesps; Rep Church Yth Grp; Rep Soph Cls; Jr NHS; NHS; Pres Acad Fit Awd; Natl Sci Fndtn Yng Schlr Pacific Regn Pgm 1990; Natl Sci Plympd In Bio 1989; Pres Aloha Cncl; Sci.

TRUONG, BAI QUAN; Mc Kinley HS; Honolulu, HI; (2); 28/588; Science Clb; High Hon Roll; Hon Roll; Prfct Atten Awd; Fish Lbbst; Sprt Cmmtte; Mandarin Club; U HI; Vet.

TRUONG, TRANG; Mc Kinley HS; Honolulu, HI; (2).

TSANG, DIANA S; Sacred Hearts Acad; Honolulu, HI; (4); 23/110; French Clb; Pep Clb; Science Clb; Pres Service Clb; Teachers Aide; Treas Soph Cls; Elks Awd; Hon Roll; Campus Ministry; Scl Stds & Bus Awds; U Denver; Liberal Arts.

TSE, AMANDA; Kaimuki HS; Honolulu, HI; (4); 1/330; Sec Treas Church Yth Grp; Treas French Clb; Capt Math Tm; Treas SADD; Church Choir; School Play; Bausch & Lomb Sci Awd; Pres NHS; Ntl Merit Ltr; Val; U HI Regents Schlrshp; HS Hnrs Pgm Material Sci HI Rep; Stravinsky Awds Intl Piano Cmptn Semi Fnlst; U HI; Civil Engrng.

TSE, ELAINE Y; Kaiser HS; Honolulu, HI; (3); 4/328; Key Clb; Math Tm; Hon Roll; VP NHS; Prfct Atten Awd; Pharmacy.

TSUCHIYAMA, DINO M; Leilehua HS; Wahiawa, HI; (4); 70/305; Cit Awd; Hon Roll; Comp Prgmr.

TSUGAWA, ANSON J; Lutheran HS; Honolulu, HI; (3); 1/50; FCA; Letterman Clb; Rep Frsh Cls; Rep Soph Cls; Rep Jr Cls; Intrml Var Ftbl; Intrml JV Trk; Intrml Wrstlng; Hon Roll; NHS; Valparaiso U Awd Excl; Mst Outstndng Bio, Chem Stu; Vet Med.

TSUKAMOTO, VALERIE M; Hawaii Baptist Acad; Aiea, HI; (2); Church Yth Grp; FTA; Hosp Aide; Vllybl; High Hon Roll; Hon Roll; NHS; Pres Acad Fit Awd; Servant Grp; Vol Med Ctr; Outstndng Alg II; Scndry Ed.

TSUKIYAMA, LYNN N; Roosevelt HS; Honolulu, HI; (2); French Clb; Hosp Aide; Hiking Club; Med Career.

TSUNODA, SUSAN S; Pearl City HS; Pearl City, HI; (3); Band; Jazz Band; Mrchg Band; Sec Soph Cls; Sec Jr Cls; Sec Sr Cls; Interact Clb Pres; Educ.

TUAN, PRISCILLA; Punahou HS; Honolulu, HI; (4); Rep Church Yth Grp; Dance Clb; SADD; Church Choir; Orch; Off Soph Cls; Sec Sr Cls; Hon Roll; NHS; Ntl Merit SF; Co Chrmn Punahou Carnvl; Prncpls Awd; Presby Youth Triehhium.

TUI, SHANE; Waianae HS; Waianae, HI; (2); Art Clb; Library Aide; Office Aide; Teachers Aide; Hon Roll; Prfct Atten Awd; Typg; Bus.

TULAFONO, TIMOTEO R; St Louis HS; Honolulu, HI; (2); Art Clb; Church Yth Grp; Dance Clb; Acpl Chr; Rep Frsh Cls; Rep Soph Cls; JV Cheerldng; JV Var Ftbl; Intrml JV Trk; Hon Roll; Park League Vllybl; Prof Dancer Tihati Prod Polynesian Dancing; Southern CA U; Arch.

TUPINIO, CYVETTE N K; Mililani HS; Mililani, HI; (3); Church Yth Grp; Teachers Aide; Var Cheerldng; Stat Wrstlng; Hon Roll; Awd From Japanese C Of C, Achvt In Japanese Lang; Cornish Coll Of Arts; Intr Dsgn.

TUPINO, SANDRA; James Campbell HS; Ewa Beach, HI; (4); 81/347; DECA; Key Clb; Teachers Aide; Band; Color Guard; Flag Corp; Mrchg Band; Rep Soph Cls; Rep Jr Cls; Rep Sr Cls; Travel Indstry Mgmt.

TUPUOLA, JOHNNY; Farrington HS; Honolulu, HI; (2); Boy Scts; Varsity Clb; Band; Church Choir; Mrchg Band; JV Bsbl; JV Bsktbl; JV Ftbl; Var Trk; Var Wt Lftg; Na Kia Aina Clb; Brigham Young U; Real Est.

TWIGGS, QUENTIN; Mc Kinley HS; Honolulu, HI; (1); School Musical; Intrml Bsktbl; Archt.

UEDA, WENDY E; Hawaii Baptist Acad; Honolulu, HI; (1); Church Yth Grp; GAA; Yrbk; Deans Donor Roll.

UEHARA, JENNIFER; H P Baldwin HS; Pukalani, HI; (3); 1/133; Art Clb; FTA; Math Clb; Math Tm; Band; Hon Roll; Hnrble Mntn Cnty Sci Fr; Awd Mrt Cnty Sci Fr; Hnrble Mntn Lahina Ary Scty Art Shw; NSF Yng Schlr; Biolgcl Sci.

UELIGITONE, LEI; Kalaheo HS; Kailua, HI; (3); Teachers Aide; Orch; Hon Roll; Pioneer Schl; Rlgn.

UEMAE, LEIGH K; H P Baldwin HS; Kahului, HI; (3); 35/404; Cmnty Wkr; 4-H; Sec FTA; Hosp Aide; Service Clb; Band; Yrbk; Hon Roll; Hnr Band 2 Yrs; Japanese Clb 2 Yrs; U Of HI Manoa; Psych.

UEMURA, DENBIE; Aiea HS; Aiea, HI; (4); 24/366; VP Sec DECA; Pep Clb; Spanish Clb; Teachers Aide; Rep Stu Cncl; JV Bsktbl; Var L Crs Cntry; Mgr Sftbl; JV Vllybl; High Hon Roll; St Pres & Rep Natl DECA Conf 89-90; Otstndng Stu Bus; Otstndng Stu Mrktng & Distribution; U Of HI Manoa; Bus Mgt.

UEMURA, WISA; Maui HS; Kula, HI; (1); 7/450; Cmnty Wkr; 4-H; VP Frsh Cls; Var Stat Bsktbl; Var Vllybl; 4-H Awd; High Hon Roll; Hon Roll; Prfct Atten Awd; Phys Sci Awd Top Class; Above Club; Dncng Hula; Psych.

UESUGI, STEFANI; Leilehua HS; Wahiawa, HI; (3); Rep Frsh Cls; YMCA Exchange, Pcfc Region Conf, Yth Legislature Pgm & Yth Ldrshp Pgm VP; U HI; Nrsng.

UEZU, SEAN M; Hawaii Baptist Acad; Honolulu, HI; (2); 4/98; Church Yth Grp; JA; Math Tm; Pres Jr Cls; Var Tennis; High Hon Roll; Hon Roll; Pres Acad Fit Awd; Serteens Of HI; Bus Law.

UGANIZA, ANGELA; Farrington HS; Honolulu, HI; (3); Dance Clb; Girl Scts; Model UN; Pep Clb; Band; Jazz Band; Bsbl; Bsktbl; Cheerldng; Ftbl; Cannons Bus Schl; Bus Mgmt.

UIAGALELEI, TYMAN A; Waipahu HS; Waipahu, HI; (1); 45/513; JV L Bsktbl; JV L Ftbl; U HI; Engr.

ULANDEZ, AMY LIEZL; Waianae HS; Waianae, HI; (1); 45/608; Art Clb; Sftbl; Cit Awd; Badminton; Ping Pong; Sci.

ULANGCA JR, NOLAN J; St Louis HS; Wahiawa, HI; (2); 78/157; Bsktbl; Ftbl; Vllybl; Marching Band; UNLV; Phys Ed.

ULEP, GEOFFREY; Waianae HS; Waianae, HI; (4); 2/328; DECA; Treas Spanish Clb; Rep Sr Cls; High Hon Roll; VP NHS; Sal; Outstanding Filipino Hawaii High Schl Student; U Of Hi; Electrical Eng.

ULIT, MICHELLE; Roosevelt HS; Honolulu, HI; (2); Church Yth Grp; Cmnty Wkr; U Of HI; Pediatrician.

ULUAVE, NELLIE; Kahuku HS; Hauula, HI; (3); 23/247; Church Yth Grp; Band; Ed Lit Mag; JV Stat Bsktbl; Hon Roll; Lang Art Shwcs; Togan Soc Acad Awd; Outstndng Smnry Stu; Engrng.

UMAYAM, FLORIEFE R; Waipahu HS; Waipahu, HI; (2); 7/425; Science Clb; High Hon Roll; Cls-Up Clb Histrn; Fil-Am Clb; Cane Tssl Photo; Shksprn Fstvl 90; Cls-Up WA DC; Stu Smmr Intrnshp Pgm 90; Srgcl Dr.

UMBAY, GLORIA F; Waialua HS & Intermed; Waialua, HI; (2); Model UN; SADD; Bsktbl; Hon Roll; Prfct Atten Awd; Med.

UNEMORI, MELISSA A; Henry Perrine Baldwin HS; Wailuku, HI; (4); 1/355; Church Yth Grp; Pres Key Clb; Capt Math Clb; Pres Q&S; Ed Nwsp; Var L Socr; High Hon Roll; NHS; Ntl Merit SF; Val; Nissan Of HI Jrnlsm Hall Of Hnr; Coca Cola Ntl SF; Pres Schlr SF; Cornell U; Comm.

UNO, GARY S; Mc Kinley HS; Honolulu, HI; (2); 93/588; Band; JV Bsbl; Hon Roll; U Of HI.

UNZUETA, SHANNON L; Theodore Roosevelt HS; Honolulu, HI; (2); 35/360; Off Soph Cls; Hon Roll.

UOHARA, MICHAEL R; Kauai High & Intermediate Schl; Lihue, HI; (3); 1/250; Boy Scts; Math Tm; Band; Jazz Band; Rep Soph Cls; Rep Stu Cncl; Tennis; Vllybl; Pres NHS; Keywanettes; Engrng.

UTRERA, NORBENE R; Konawaena HS; Kailua Kona, HI; (4); 171/291; Art Clb; Chess Clb; Computer Clb; Spanish Clb; SADD; Teachers Aide; Stage Crew; Yrbk; Intrml Bsktbl; Score Keeper; UH Manoa; Bus Mgmt.

UY, ANTHONY CHUN; Radford HS; Honolulu, HI; (3); 1/400; Math Tm; VP Mu Alpha Theta; VICA; Crs Cntry; Bausch & Lomb Sci Awd; NHS; Yale Book Awd; Principals Honor Roll; Outstanding Student Council Chairperson.

UYEDA, TODD S; Moanalua HS; Honolulu, HI; (2); Church Yth Grp; JV Bsktbl; Var Swmmng; Cafeteria Help Vlntr; Stanford U; Engr.

UYEMATSU, LISA L; Kauai HS; Lihue, HI; (3); 13/231; Teachers Aide; Var L Bsktbl; Var L Crs Cntry; Var L Sftbl; Var Trk; Capt L Vllybl; High Hon Roll; Hon Roll; Bus.

UYENO, JENNY T; Roosevelt HS; Honolulu, HI; (2); Band; Mrchg Band; Solo/Nsmbl Gld Mdl Awd; Cmnty Svc; Fine Arts.

UYENO, KRISTINE; Waipahu HS; Waipahu, HI; (3); Ed Nwsp; Treas Frsh Cls; Sec Soph Cls; VP Jr Cls; Stu Cncl; Stat Bsbl; Var Cheerldng; High Hon Roll; Spirit Club; Pride Cmmtte; Dist Ctzn Bee Comptn; Jrnlsm.

UYESUGI, BRIAN M; St Louis-Chaminade Education Center; Waialua, HI; (2); 90/151; Var L Ftbl; Hon Roll; Prfct Atten Awd; Pres Acad Fit Awd; JV Ftbl Outstndng Offnsve Back Plyr 89; Civil Engr.

VALASCO, GINA C; Waipahu HS; Waianae, HI; (3); Church Yth Grp; Dance Clb; Drama Clb; FHA; Spanish Clb; Teachers Aide; Drill Tm; School Play; Variety Show; Rep Frsh Cls; HI Pacific U; Trvl Indstry Mgmt.

VALDEZ, EDWARD; Waipahu HS; Waipahu, HI; (4); 4/400; Math Clb; Math Tm; Science Clb; High Hon Roll; U HI Manoa; Elec Engrng.

VALDEZ, JUDY; Waipaha HS; Waipahu, HI; (1); 18/513; Band; Mrchg Band; Pep Band; Off Frsh Cls; Stu Cncl; Tennis; High Hon Roll; Hon Roll; Interact Club; Assmbly Cmmtte; Paralegal.

VALDEZ, SHERYLL T; Waipahu HS; Waipahu, HI; (1); 11/513; Drill Tm; Hon Roll; Stu Govt Rep; Yale; Medcl.

VALENCIA, DELIA S; Kauai HS & Intermed; Koloa, HI; (3); Church Yth Grp; FHA; Girl Scts; Spanish Clb; Flght Attndnt.

VALENCIANO, REYNOLD G; Waimea HS; Kaumakani, HI; (2); Church Choir; JV Bsktbl; Hon Roll; NHS.

VALERA, AILEEN R; Kauai HS; Lihue, HI; (3); 17/231; Aud/Vis; Church Yth Grp; French Clb; FHA; Science Clb; SADD; Chorus; Stage Crew; Vllybl; High Hon Roll; Bus Admin.

VALLEDOR, KELSIE L; Waiakea HS; Hilo, HI; (2); 43/497; Service Clb; Rep Soph Cls; Hon Roll; Kiwanis Awd; Schlstc Awd; Outstndng Keywanettes Awd; Schl Svc Awd; Athl Svc Awd; U Of CO; Clinical Psych.

VAN, GINGGING M; St Andrews Priory HS; Honolulu, HI; (2); French Clb; Treas Intnl Clb; Science Clb; Stage Crew; Yrbk; High Hon Roll; Hon Roll; Accompanist For Schl Choir; USC; Law.

VAN, MAO; Mc Kinley HS; Honolulu, HI; (1); 158/541; Band; Bsktbl; Hon Roll; U HI; Sci.

VAN KEULEN, RENEE; Aiea HS; Aiea, HI; (4); 17/366; Capt Debate Tm; VP French Clb; VP FBLA; Rptr Nwsp; Ed Lit Mag; Rep Frsh Cls; Capt Sftbl; Hon Roll; VP NHS; Voice Dem Awd; Mock Trial; Quizzard; St Senators Schrlshp; U Of MN; Law.

VAN SCOY, TANIA N; Kalaheo HS; Kailua, HI; (2); Church Yth Grp; Dance Clb; Variety Show; Sec Frsh Cls; Sec Soph Cls; Hon Roll; Med.

VANALSTINE, LEAF E; Maui HS; Haiku, HI; (4); 16/208; Science Clb; Crs Cntry; Trk; Hon Roll; Pres Acad Fit Awd; U CO Boulder; Engl.

VARIZE, SHEILA J; Pahoa HS; Pahoa, HI; (3); Art Clb; Church Yth Grp; FBLA; FHA; FTA; Letterman Clb; Spanish Clb; Yrbk; JV Var Bsktbl; Hon Roll; U Of HI Manoa; Secy.

VASQUEZ, ALEXIS A; Waialua HS; Waialua, HI; (2); Speech Tm; Band; Mrchg Band; Pep Band; Pres Soph Cls; Chrmn Stu Cncl; Socr; Trk; Hon Roll; Drugbusters; Polit Sci.

VEA, JENNIFER C; Sacred Hearts Acad; Honolulu, HI; (3); Church Yth Grp; French Clb; Hosp Aide; Pep Clb; Color Guard; Flag Corp; Hon Roll; Acctng.

VEGAS, FRANCHESCA R; Sacred Hearts Acad; Kailua, HI; (3); Church Yth Grp; Cmnty Wkr; Pep Clb; Red Cross Aide; Church Choir; Intrml Mgr Cheerldng; Socr; Trk; Prfct Atten Awd; Cadet Cvl Air Patrol HI; Sci Fr 1st Pl; Blck Blt Karate; BYU; Educ.

VEGAS, RENEE E; James Campbell HS; Ewa Beach, HI; (2); 105/348; FTA; Teachers Aide; Cheerldng; Trk; U Of HI; Preschool Teacher.

VELASCO, RODA L; Waipahu HS; Waipahu, HI; (1); 50/530; FHA; Band; Mrchg Band; SMILE.

VELEZ, JENNI; Kalaheo HS; Kailua, HI; (4); Art Clb; Church Yth Grp; DECA; Drama Clb; Model UN; Pep Clb; SADD; Church Choir; Ed Lit Mag; Socr; Pblctns Awd-Cert Grad; 1st Pl Awds Art-Cert Grad Memphis Prtnrs Inc; Cert Achvt DECA HI St Assoc; U HI; Mrktng.

VENTURA, DAMIEN J; Kapaa HS; Kilauea, HI; (4); 10/191; Spanish Clb; Hon Roll; U Of HI Hilo.

VEROZA, MARGARITA C; Mc Kinley HS; Honolulu, HI; (1); Intnl Clb; ROTC; ROTC Super Ldrshp Awd & Awd Of Mrt; Law.

VICTOR, GINA; Kpnawaena HS; Kealakekua, HI; (3); Spanish Clb; Hon Roll; Dance Cmmtte; Success Strodegies Schlrshp Wnr Summer 90; Outside Schl :Yba Church Grp/Dance Hula; Interior Dsgn.

VIDAD, FELIZON C; Waialua HS; Waialua, HI; (4); 5/156; Treas Jr Cls; Treas Sr Cls; JV Crs Cntry; High Hon Roll; Hon Roll; NHS; Prfct Atten Awd; HI Cncl Tchrs Engl Lang Arts Showcase 1st Pl Short Story; U Redlands.

VIERNES, GARY A; Honokaa HS; Paauilo, HI; (4); 8/133; Boy Scts; Phtg Yrbk; Treas Stu Cncl; JV Var Bsktbl; Capt Crs Cntry; Capt Trk; Hon Roll; Most Outstndng Trk; Hnrs Grad; Harriet Bouslog Union Schlrshp; Hanakua Sugar Schlrshp; U Of HI Manoa; Educ.

VIERNES, NEIL L; Waialua HS; Waialua, HI; (2); 1/168; Math Tm; Science Clb; Band; Jazz Band; Mrchg Band; Pep Band; Rep Frsh Cls; Rep Soph Cls; High Hon Roll; HOBY; Med.

VIERRA, ERIC; St Joseph HS; Hilo, HI; (3); Church Yth Grp; Cmnty Wkr; Letterman Clb; Math Clb; Science Clb; Treas Frsh Cls; Var Bsbl; Var JV Bsktbl; Var JV Trk; Var Vllybl; Vrsty Bwlng; Engr.

VILLA JR, DURANTE H; Farrington HS; Honolulu, HI; (1); 22/360; Ftbl; High Hon Roll; Hon Roll; NHS; Cert Of Merit-Schlstc Art Awds; U HI; Med.

VILLA, HOPE I; Kamihamiha HS; Wahiawa, HI; (4); 180/407; Church Yth Grp; Library Aide; SADD; Trk; Canoe Paddlng Tm; U Of HI Manoa; Travl Ind Mgmt.

VILLALOBOS, ALADIN M; Saint Louis HS; Waipahu, HI; (3); 62/150; Church Yth Grp; Cmnty Wkr; Dance Clb; ROTC; Bsbl; Bsktbl; Ftbl; Tennis; Vllybl; Hon Roll; Bowlng; Elec Engrng.

VILLANUEVA, LEILANI P; Moanalua HS; Honolulu, HI; (2); 66/488; High Hon Roll; Hon Roll.

VILLANUEVA, MELONIE L; Kamehameha Schl; Ewa Beach, HI; (3); 175/419; Church Yth Grp; Cmnty Wkr; Library Aide; Speech Tm; SADD; School Musical; School Play; Powder Puff Ftbl; JV Capt Vllybl; Hon Roll; Recgnzd Gftd/Tlntd Stu; Athltc Trnr Asst; U Of HI Manoa; Athl Trainer.

VILLANUEVA, NIEVES R; Waipahu HS; Waipahu, HI; (4); 15/418; Dance Clb; Quiz Bowl; School Play; Rep Frsh Cls; Cit Awd; High Hon Roll; Hon Roll; Ntl Merit Ltr; Prfct Atten Awd; Shakespearean Fstvl 90; FIL-AM Clb Sec; Aloha Close-Up Clb Treas; Leeward CC; Acctng.

VILLAROZ, NICOLE; Castle HS; Kaneohe, HI; (3); 105/352; Church Yth Grp; Office Aide; Var Socr; JV Swmmng; Intl Relations Clb; Peer Ed Pgm; U Of NV Reno; Jrnlsm.

VILORIA, AUDY V; Farrington HS; Honolulu, HI; (3); 24/600; Key Clb; Tennis; Hon Roll; Engnrng.

VILORIA, ELIZABETH K; Molokdi HS; Hoolehua, HI; (3); Teachers Aide; CO ST; Elect.

VILORIA, IVAN E; Konawaena HS; Kailua Kona, HI; (2); 34/349; Church Yth Grp; JV Capt Ftbl; Tennis; Hon Roll; Tnns Hnrb Mntn Dls.

VOLNER, RICK W; H P Baldwin HS; Wailuku, HI; (2); 35/395; Key Clb; SADD; JV Ftbl; Var Capt Trk; High Hon Roll; Hon Roll; Interact Club VP; Engr.

VON TUNGELN, JOHN; Kalaheo HS; Kailua, HI; (3); Church Yth Grp; Math Tm; Model UN; Quiz Bowl; Band; Rptr Lit Mag; Off Jr Cls; Var L Bsktbl; High Hon Roll; NHS; US Navy Hnry Offcr Day 90; U OK; Aviation.

VUONG, VINH H; Roosevelt HS; Honolulu, HI; (2); French Clb; Band; Off Soph Cls; Stu Cncl; Vllybl; Excllnc Spch; Caring Ldr; Dr.

WADA, DAVID A; Baldwin HS; Wailuku, HI; (3); 29/385; Church Yth Grp; Key Clb; Math Tm; Pres Science Clb; Service Clb; SADD; Golf; High Hon Roll; Maui Cty Dist Wrtng Showcase 88 1st Pl Short Story Category; Amer Essay Cont 89 2nd Pl; Sci Fair 88-89; U HI-MANOA; Bio.

WAGNER, SARAH; Lanakila Baptist HS; Pearl City, HI; (1); VP Church Yth Grp; Church Choir; Rptr Nwsp; Rep Frsh Cls; Rep Stu Cncl; Intrml Vllybl; High Hon Roll; Jr NHS; MD Assn Telethn-Jerrys Kds; Drma.

WAIAU, DORIMALIA; Theodore Roosevelt HS; Honolulu, HI; (2); Cmnty Wkr; Dance Clb; Pres FTA; Hosp Aide; Intnl Clb; Library Aide; Red Cross Aide; Sec Spanish Clb; SADD; Teachers Aide; JR Natl 3rd Pl Water Polo 89; Peer Ed 89-90; Seattle Pacific U; Tchr.

WAIAU, PHYLLIS K; Roosevelt HS; Honolulu, HI; (3); Church Yth Grp; Cmnty Wkr; Library Aide; Office Aide; Q&S; SADD; Co-Ed Yrbk; Off Frsh Cls; Off Soph Cls; Off Jr Cls; Jubilee Literary Awd; Coalition For Drug Free HI; Columbia Schltc Press Assn; US Vllybl Assn Jr Trnmt; HI Pacific U; Adv.

WAKAUMI, KIRK K; Kailua HS; Kailua, HI; (2); Treas Soph Cls; Treas Stu Cncl; Var Crs Cntry; Hon Roll; Hugh O'brien Yth Fndtn 90; Kailua Ldrshp Trng Camp Cmmtte 90; Elem Ldrshp Trng Camp Cnslr 89-90; Standford; Pre Med.

WAKEFIELD, JOEY O; Moanalua HS; Honolulu, HI; (3); 108/462; Church Yth Grp; 4-H; Spanish Clb; Var Sftbl; JV Vllybl; Sci Olympiad No 9; Minot ST U; Acctg.

WAKI, ZUR W; Henry Perrine Baldwin HS; Makawao, HI; (1); 64/466; Boy Scts; Key Clb; Ftbl; Swmmng; Trk; Hon Roll; Eagle Scout; Ueoka-Pohndorf Scholar; Harry Lundeberg Schl Seamanship Scholar.

WAKO, SAYURI; Mc Kinley HS; Waialae, HI; (3); Church Yth Grp; Band; KCC; Accntng.

WALKER, ASIM J; Radford HS; Honolulu, HI; (1); Church Yth Grp; Cmnty Wkr; ROTC; High Hon Roll; Hon Roll; U Of GA.

WALKER, SHINYU P; Kaimuki HS; Honolulu, HI; (2); ROTC; Color Guard; Drill Tm; Rifle Drill Team; Aviation.

WALLACE, TATIANA P; Kahuku HS; Laie, HI; (4); 35/236; Spanish Clb; SADD; Teachers Aide; Band; School Play; Rptr Nwsp; Phtg Yrbk; Rep Frsh Cls; Tennis; High Hon Roll; All Amer Schlr; Miss Frosh; Byu; Law.

WALPOLE, EMILY B; Kapaa HS; Kilauea, HI; (3); 39/179; Tennis; Swimming Instructors Aide Red Cross; Sports Management.

WALSH, BARBARA P; Mc Kinley HS; Honolulu, HI; (3); 71/537; ACE-HI Comp Clb.

WANG, DATONG; Kaiser HS; Honolulu, HI; (3); 28/336; JA; Key Clb; Math Clb; Math Tm; Crs Cntry; Ftbl; Capt Var Trk; Wrstlng; Hon Roll; NHS; Bus.

WANG, SHI-CHING B; Moanalua HS; Honolulu, HI; (2); 36/528; Chess Clb; Hon Roll; Mock Trl Tm; U Of CA, Berkeley; Med.

WARD, LARRY J; Radford HS; Honolulu, HI; (1); 80/466; Church Yth Grp; Computer Clb; FCA; Band; Jazz Band; Mrchg Band; Pep Band; Bsbl; JV Bsktbl; Hon Roll; Law.

WARMAN, KIRK; Kalaheo HS; Kailua, HI; (4); Rep Frsh Cls; Cit Awd; Hon Roll; Hmcmng Cmmtte; Embry Riddle; Aviation.

WARREN, LAURA C; Mililani HS; Mililani, HI; (3); Aud/Vis; Key Clb; Band; Mrchg Band; Rep Stu Cncl; Var L Tennis; Hon Roll; Prfct Atten Awd; Bus Admin.

WASHER, KATHERINE; Saint Francis HS; Wahiawa, HI; (2); 31/80; Boy Scts; Church Yth Grp; Pres Girl Scts; Red Cross Aide; Lit Mag; JV Swmmng; NEDT Awd; Hiking Camp Search & Rescue Explrs; GS Slvr Awd; Natl Ctr West Grl Scout Camp; Troop Camp; UNH; Vet.

WASNER, KATHERINE L; Saint Francis HS; Wahiawa, HI; (2); 31/80; Boy Scts; Church Yth Grp; VP Girl Scts; Library Aide; Red Cross Aide; Lit Mag; JV Swmmng; NEDT Awd; Girl Sct Silver Awd; Search & Rescue Explorers; UNH; Vet.

WASSON, BRADFORD L; Radford HS; Honolulu, HI; (3); SADD; Var Socr; Var Wrstlng; Marine Bio.

WATANABE, CARY M; Honokaa HS; Honokaa, HI; (2); 10/155; JV Ftbl; Var Tennis; Hon Roll; Outstndng Engl Stu; Close-Up Fndtn; St Sci & Engrng Fair Fnlst 90; Astronomy.

WATANABE, DENNIS S; Waipahu HS; Waipahu, HI; (3); U Of HI; Math Tchr.

WATANABE, SHERYL S; Farmington HS; Honolulu, HI; (3); 143/600; 4-H; Q&S; Sprt Ed Nwsp; Leo Clb; HI Upward Bound 2 Yrs; U Of HI; Vet.

WATERS, LELAND R; Lutheran HS Of Hawaii; Honolulu, HI; (1); Rep Frsh Cls; Intrml Bsktbl; Intrml Crs Cntry; Intrml Trk; Debate Tm; Complete Alcatraz Challenge; Complete Cycle To Sun Steepest Bicycle Climb; Hnrd Resolution Cncl Athltc; Bus Exec.

WATERS, TERRA D; Henry Opukahaia Schl; Kailua Kona, HI; (3); Church Yth Grp; Office Aide; Teachers Aide; Yrbk; High Hon Roll; Stu Exchange; Elem Ed.

WATSON, JENNIFER R; Moanalua HS; Makakilo, HI; (2); JV Var Cheerldng; Penn ST; Russian Intrprtr.

WATSON, ROGER K; Saint Louis HS; Kaneohe, HI; (2); Intrml Bsbl; JV Bsktbl; Off Hon Roll.

WATTS, MELISSA; Kalaheo HS; Kailua, HI; (3); 73/246; Band; Drm Mjr(t); Jazz Band; Mrchg Band; Pep Band; School Musical; Photo; CO U; Photo.

WAUKE, ROBYN C; Maui HS; Kahului, HI; (3); Pep Clb; VP Soph Cls; VP Jr Cls; Treas Sr Cls; Hon Roll; Prfct Atten Awd; Japanese Clb; Gen Co-Chrprsn Soph Banqt & Jnr Prom; Puget Sound U; Phys Thrpy.

WEBB, JODI A; Hawaii Baptist Acad; Honolulu, HI; (1); Church Yth Grp; Drama Clb; Varsity Clb; School Play; Yrbk; Vllybl; Hon Roll; Baylor; Corp Law.

WEIDINGER, JO-LEEN K; Hawaiian Mission Acad; Waipahu, HI; (3); Church Yth Grp; Library Aide; Church Choir; School Play; VP Frsh Cls; Sec Soph Cls; Rep Jr Cls; Sec Stu Cncl; Vllybl; Pacific Union Coll; Bus Admin.

WEIS, DAVID K; Maui HS; Pukalani, HI; (3); 76/354; Letterman Clb; Var Crs Cntry; Var Trk; Hon Roll; Prfct Atten Awd; Motocross Rcng; Cycle To The Sun 2nd Pl; Hotel Mgmt.

WELLNITZ, TODD R; Waialua HS; Waialua, HI; (3); VP Letterman Clb; Rep Nwsp; Treas Sr Cls; Var Capt Bsbl; Var Bsktbl; Var Crs Cntry; Var Capt Ftbl; Var Trk; Hon Roll; Prfct Atten Awd; Drug Bstrs.

WELSCH, CYNTHIA C; Mililani HS; Mililani, HI; (3); 28/490; Hon Roll; Bus Mgmt.

WHANG, MICHAEL D; Maryknoll HS; Honolulu, HI; (4); Boy Scts; Spanish Clb; Intrml Crs Cntry; JV Trk; High Hon Roll; Hon Roll; UC Santa Cruz; Ed.

WHITE, DANIELLE; Maui HS; Kula, HI; (3); 120/354; Church Yth Grp; Treas Pep Clb; Capt Crs Cntry; Capt Trk; Stat Wrstlng; Prfct Atten Awd; Stu Styng Strght Cls Rep; Airline Indstry.

WHITE, LYTHA FERN; Kohala HS; Hawi, HI; (1); 4/65; Sec Pres 4-H; JV Chess Clb; Mgr(s); 4-H Awd; Hon Roll; Rodeo Tm Roping/Goat Tying/Pole Bending/Barrels; 1st Pl Cty Art Awd; Arts Cncl Juried Best In Show.

WHITE, MICHELLE A; Leilehua HS; Wahiawa, HI; (4); 20/300; FBLA; NFL; Red Cross Aide; Teachers Aide; Hon Roll; NHS; Cls Senator; U HI Manoa; Med.

WHITEMAN, MATTHEW; Kalaheo HS; Kailua, HI; (1); 10/261; Church Yth Grp; Band; Mrchg Band; Pep Band; JV Bsbl; High Hon Roll; Hon Roll; UC San Diego; Sci.

WHITTLE, NICOLE E; St Francis Of Assisi HS; Honolulu, HI; (2); 10/80; Church Yth Grp; Cmnty Wkr; Variety Show; VP Jr Cls; Hon Roll; Engl Horsebck Rdng; Typing Awd; Animal Sci.

WILBER, MICHELLE; Hilo HS; Keaau, HI; (3); Math Tm; Science Clb; School Musical; Rep Soph Cls; Diving; Hon Roll; Astrophy.

WILEY, HEIDI; St Joseph HS; Hilo, HI; (4); Cmnty Wkr; Drama Clb; Math Tm; Speech Tm; Nwsp; Yrbk; Socr; Vllybl; Sec NHS; Rcd Dgs In AK; 2nd Pl Wrld Pc Poem Stwd; Schl Ply Ld Rl; Nrsng.

WILEY, RACHEL; Waimea HS; Waimea, HI; (2); 3/200; Church Yth Grp; Speech Tm; Ed Nwsp; Var Cheerldng; Var Trk; High Hon Roll; NHS; Mock Trial Team; U Of WA; Educ.

WILHELM, CHERILYN K J; Kamehameha HS; Honolulu, HI; (2); 45/450; Sec Debate Tm; Girl Scts; Office Aide; Sec Speech Tm; SADD; Teachers Aide; Chorus; Hon Roll; Vlntr Wrk, Nrsng Hmes & Schls; Girl Scouts Slvr Awd; Stanford; Pediatrician.

WILKINS, MOLISA; Iolani HS; Honolulu, HI; (2); JA; Pep Clb; Orch; JV Cheerldng; Intrml Vllybl; Japanese Clb; Banquet Cmmtte.

WILLIAMS, DAWN A; Kalaheo HS; Kailua, HI; (2); Dance Clb; Drama Clb; Girl Scts; Pep Clb; Band; Mrchg Band; School Play; Capt Cheerldng; Hon Roll; Homecmng Cmmttee & Float; Hotl Mgr.

WILLIAMS, JOHN; Kailua HS; Waimanalo, HI; (2); Var Ftbl.

WILLIAMS, JONAS S; Kapaa HS; Kapaa, HI; (2); Trk; Phrmcy.

WILLIAMS, MICHELE L; Mililani HS; Mililani, HI; (3); Church Yth Grp; Spanish Clb; Church Choir; School Musical; School Play; Carpe Diem Soc; Direcing.

WILLIAMS, SUSAN M; Kamehameha Schls; Honolulu, HI; (2); 16/450; Var Sftbl; High Hon Roll; Teaching.

WILLIAMS, WENDY; Leilehua HS; Osceola, AR; (2); High Hon Roll; Hon Roll; Law.

WILSON, CYNTHIA ORO; Mililani HS; Honolulu, HI; (2); 45/509; Drama Clb; School Musical; School Play; Stage Crew; Hon Roll.

WINKO, DANIEL J; James Campbell HS; Jacksonville, FL; (3); 7/371; Vllybl; Hon Roll; Pres Acad Fit Awd; Read Books, Skatebd; Comp Sci.

WIRT, FRANK C; Leleihua HS; Wahiawa, HI; (3); VP Soph Cls; Var Bsktbl; Var Ftbl; Var Socr; Var Tennis; Var Vllybl; Hon Roll; V Soft Tennis; HI Pacific Coll; Accntng.

WITECK, LIA T; Mc Kinley HS; Honolulu, HI; (3); 49/537; Treas Spanish Clb; Treas Sr Cls; Hon Roll; Amer Friends Service Cmmtte Brd; Aikido; Piano; Elem Ed.

WITHINGTON, JUSTIN K; Hawaii Preparatory Acad; Hawi, HI; (2); Jazz Band; JV Ftbl; L Swmmng; Var Wrstlng; High Hon Roll; Hon Roll; Yth Legislature Pgm; Reed; Aviation.

WON, GABRIEL K K; Mc Kinley HS; Honolulu, HI; (3); 35/537; Key Clb; Var Tennis; Var Vllybl; Hon Roll; Most Insprtnl Awd Boys Vrsty Sft Tnns; Japanese Club; Sft Tnns Vrsty Team; U Of HI; Arch.

WONG, BRENTON H; Saint Louis Schl; Honolulu, HI; (2); Cmnty Wkr; ROTC; Pres Frsh Cls; Pres Soph Cls; Pres Jr Cls; Intrml Trk; JV Vllybl; Hon Roll; YMCA Yth Grp Volunteer; Lawyer.

WONG, CARISA P; Waiakea HS; Hilo, HI; (3); 74/368; Pres VP 4-H; JA; Service Clb; Church Choir; Mrchg Band; Pep Band; School Play; Variety Show; JV Bsktbl; 4-H Awd; UH Hilo; Bus.

WONG, DARREN L; Kaiser HS; Honolulu, HI; (2); 56/258; JV Bsbl; Accctng.

WONG, DAWN-L A; Kamehameha HS; Aiea, HI; (3); 182/440; Cmnty Wkr; FCA; SADD; Stat Bsktbl; Score Keeper; U Of HI; Psych.

WONG, DERRICK T; Mc Kinley HS; Honolulu, HI; (2); 129/588; JV Bsbl; Mech.

WONG, HERMAN H L; Theodore Roosevelt HS; Honolulu, HI; (2); 90/362; Model UN; Ed Nwsp; Crs Cntry; Hon Roll; Yth Retreat Facilitator; Princeton; Bus.

WONG, LAUREN; Iolani HS; Honolulu, HI; (3); 4/237; Dance Clb; Pep Clb; JV Var Cheerldng; Ntl Merit Ltr; Headmasters List; Acad Excel Awd; Bus.

WONG, LUCY P; Mc Kinley HS; Honolulu, HI; (3); 1/537; Girl Scts; Off Frsh Cls; Stu Cncl; Tennis; Arch.

WONG, MAY YEE; Hawaii Baptist Acad; Honolulu, HI; (3); 3/86; Math Tm; Chorus; School Musical; Variety Show; VP Rep Stu Cncl; Am Leg Boys St; JV Bsktbl; Cit Awd; High Hon Roll; Hon Roll; Accmpanist Schl Musical; 1st Pl Talent Show Dist & Shcl; U Of WA; Psych.

WONG, SANDRA; Kalaheo HS; Kailua, HI; (4); VP Sr Cls; Var JV Bsktbl; Hon Roll; All Amer Schlr; 88 St Chmpn Olympia Natl Schlst Typng Cont; Femle Athlte Yr 88-89; Bus Admin.

WONG, SIMON C; Moanalua HS; Honolulu, HI; (2); Chess Clb; Math Tm; Quiz Bowl; Nwsp; Yrbk; Natl Ctzn Bee Fnlst Top 15 Of 100; Quzzard Tm; HI Bd Edcu Outstndng Achvt 90; Aerospace Engrng.

WONG, SPENCER KALANI; The Kamehameha Schls; Kailua Oahu, HI; (4); 14/415; Mu Alpha Theta; ROTC; Spanish Clb; VP SADD; Capt Mrchg Band; Rep Frsh Cls; Rep Soph Cls; Rep Jr Cls; Rep Sr Cls; Intrml Mgr Bsbl; Babe Ruth HI St & Wrld Srs Chmpnshp Tm Bslb; Grad W/Hnrs 90; Presidential Acad Fitness Awd 89-90; Cornell U; Liberal Arts.

WONG, YEE CENT; Mc Kinley HS; Honolulu, HI; (3); Var L Crs Cntry; Var L Trk; Mc Kinley Golden Tiger Awd; U HI; Physcs.

WONGLEONG, CHRISTYANN P; Sacred Hearts Acad; Honolulu, HI; (3); Church Yth Grp; Sprt Ed Yrbk; Rep Frsh Cls; Treas Soph Cls; Treas Jr Cls; Var Bsktbl; Capt Var Sftbl; NHS; Prfct Atten Awd; Phys Therapist.

WOO, DOUGLAS; Hilo HS; Hilo, HI; (3); 6/310; Boy Scts; Church Yth Grp; Treas Key Clb; Treas Math Tm; Treas Soph Cls; Treas Stu Cncl; Elks Awd; Hon Roll; NHS; Order Of Arrow Bsa; Archery; Hawaii Student Science Training Program 1990 Participant; College; Engineering/History.

WOO, LEHUA L; Sacred Hearts Acad; Makakilo, HI; (3); VP Church Yth Grp; Cmnty Wkr; French Clb; Intnl Clb; Treas Stu Cncl; Hon Roll; NHS; NEDT Awd; Prfct Atten Awd; Ctzn Bee; HI Yth Lgsltr; Ed.

WOODARD, HEATHER R; Radford HS; Honolulu, HI; (3); 71/394; Treas German Clb; Intnl Clb; Teachers Aide; Band; Pep Band; Pcfc Asian Affrs Cncl Pres; Close-Up Clb; MI ST.

WOODARD, JONATHAN; Kailua HS; Kailua, HI; (3); 17/339; Boy Scts; Church Yth Grp; ROTC; Drill Tm; Ed Nwsp; Var L Crs Cntry; Var L Trk; JV Wrstlng; Hon Roll; Cvl Air Ptrl Oprtns Offcr Mitchell Awd; Flyng Gldrs & Pwrd Aircrft; Egl Awd By Scts 90; AERSPC Engrng.

WOODRING, MELISSA Y; Radford HS; Honolulu, HI; (1); 37/466; Nrs.

WORBY, JANET CHRISTINE; Kailua HS; Flowermound, TX; (4); Cmnty Wkr; Co-Ed Nwsp; Co-Ed Yrbk; Stat Bsktbl; North Lake Coll.

WRIGHT, EARLE; James B Castle HS; Kaneohe, HI; (3); 68/399; Cmnty Wkr; Band; Jazz Band; Mrchg Band; Orch; Pep Band; School Musical; Off Jr Cls; JV Bsktbl; NHS; U Of HI; Music.

WRIGHTSMAN, ANNABEL H; Kaimuki HS; Honolulu, HI; (2); Art Clb; Chess Clb; Debate Tm; JA; Teachers Aide; Tennis; Trk; Hon Roll; 1st Pl Scif Air; Freedms Fnd Conf; U CA-BERKELEY; Pre-Law.

WU, ALLAN D C; Hawaii Baptist Acad; Honolulu, HI; (2); 78/92; Chess Clb; JV Tennis; Hon Roll; Chnse Physcl Cltr-Kung Fu; HS Stu Achvt Cncl; Volntr Svcs St Francis Hosp; Chess Tourn/Mtchs; Pedtrcn.

WU, DAVID; Moanalua HS; Honolulu, HI; (3); Chess Clb; Math Clb; Math Tm; Mu Alpha Theta; Quiz Bowl; Hon Roll; NHS; HI St Ctzn Bee Cmptn 3rd 90.

WU, HONG-SHENG; Radford HS; Aiea, HI; (4); 24/348; Intnl Clb; Artistic Discovery Cont Semi-Fnlst; Comp Sci.

WU, WAN YAO; Rossevelt HS; Honolulu, HI; (3); 15/352; Hon Roll; Outstndng Achvt Alg I; U Of HI; Sci.

WUEST, LISA L; Mililani HS; Mililani, HI; (3); 74/490; Sec Key Clb; Lbrn Band; Drm Mjr(t); Flag Corp; Jazz Band; Mrchg Band; Orch; School Musical; Sec Jr Cls; Sec Sr Cls; U Of HI Manoa; Educ.

XIAO, GUAN WEI; Mc Kinley HS; Honolulu, HI; (3); 2/27; Computer Clb; U HI Manoa; Cmptr Prgmr.

XIAO, YANG; Roosevelt HS; Honolulu, HI; (4); 11/340; Crs Cntry; Hon Roll; JETS Awd; Interschlstc Photo; Pwrd Vehicle Cmptn; U HI Manoa; Elec Engr.

YACAPIN, JESEANA; Leilehua HS; Wahiawa, HI; (3); Church Yth Grp; Teachers Aide; JV Var Bsktbl; Var Sftbl; Law Clb; HCC; Crmnl Law.

YAGI, SHERI N; Moanalua HS; Honolulu, HI; (2); 15/488; Cmnty Wkr; Speech Tm; Flag Corp; High Hon Roll; Hon Roll; YMCA Yth Ldrshp Pgm; U HI; Astronomy.

YAGIN, BLAISDELL; Waipahu HS; Waipahu, HI; (1); 167/513; JV Ftbl; JV Wrstlng; Prfct Atten Awd; Electrnc Tech.

YAGIN, LESLIE J; Molokai HS; Kaunakakai, HI; (3); Band; Pep Band; Hon Roll.

YAGO, ADOLPH F; Kauai HS; Lihue, HI; (4); 32/246; Computer Clb; French Clb; FHA; Science Clb; Bsbl; Trk; High Hon Roll; Hon Roll; NHS; Sterling Schlr Visual Arts; Hrn Stu Cum Aude; Arch.

YAGO, ERNEST F; Maui HS; Kahului, HI; (3); 31/354; Church Yth Grp; Cmnty Wkr; Key Clb; Math Clb; Quiz Bowl; Sec Speech Tm; Band; Drm Mjr(t); Mrchg Band; Pep Band; Japanese Clb; Math/Music Teacher.

YAMADA, WENDY Y; Waiakea HS; Hilo, HI; (2); 23/497; Debate Tm; JA; Latin Clb; Math Tm; Speech Tm; Color Guard; Variety Show; Trk; Stat Vllybl; High Hon Roll; Lang Fstvl Awd Latin I, II Brnz Mdls.

YAMADA, WESLEY H; Kaiser HS; Honolulu, HI; (2); Swmmng; Prfct Atten Awd; YMCA Jr Ldrshp Pgm; U Of HI; Elec Engr.

YAMAGATA, DENISE K; Maui HS; Kahului, HI; (4); 1/313; Pres Math Clb; Science Clb; Sec Service Clb; Band; Mrchg Band; Pep Band; Hon Roll; Sec NHS; Ntl Merit SF; Harvard Bk Prize; Natl Sci Fndtn Yng Schlr; Band-Hi Schlr; Aerosp Engrng.

YAMAGUCHI, LAURA M; Kapaa HS; Kilauea, HI; (1); 1/220; Drama Clb; English Clb; Pres Band; Mrchg Band; Pep Band; Socr; High Hon Roll; Engrng.

YAMAGUCHI, SHARI; Maui HS; Pukalani, HI; (3); 7/375; Math Clb; Math Tm; Band; Treas Jr Cls; VP Sr Cls; Hon Roll; NHS; Acad Awd Top Schlr; Awd Acad Achvt; SPEBE Ctr Engrng; Engrng.

YAMAMOTO JR, DANNY K; Waiakea HS; Hilo, HI; (2); 93/497; Boy Scts; Church Yth Grp; Temple Yth Grp; Jazz Band; Variety Show; Jr NHS; 2nd Plc HI Cnty Enrgy Awrnss Cntst Awd; Musician.

YAMAMOTO, JAY A; Kailua HS; Kailua, HI; (3); 24/339; Service Clb; Varsity Clb; JV Var Bsbl; JV Ftbl; Var Socr; Hon Roll; Japanese Clb; Interact Clb; U Of HI.

YAMAMOTO, LISA H; Lutheran HS; Pearl City, HI; (3); FCA; Library Aide; Teachers Aide; VP Jr Cls; Bsktbl; Cheerldng; Hon Roll; Prfct Atten Awd; Chapel Campus Ministry; Newspaper Staff; Yuukikai Clb; Civil Engr.

YAMAMOTO, REID Y; Kaiser HS; Honolulu, HI; (3); 48/392; Am Leg Boys St; Church Yth Grp; FCA; Var Bsbl; Prfct Atten Awd; Body Brdng; U Of HI.

YAMAMOTO, SHARI A; Moanalua HS; Honolulu, HI; (2); 44/488; Art Clb; Hosp Aide; Trk; Leo Club; Interact Club; Bishop Museum Dinosaur Exhibit; Occptnl Thrpy.

YAMAMOTO, SHAWN S; Maui HS; Makawao, HI; (2); Drama Clb; School Play; Var Trk; Hon Roll; Sec Jr NHS; Stu Staying Straight VP; Med.

YAMAMURA, MEGUMI; St Andrews Priory HS; Honolulu, HI; (3); Intnl Clb; Band; Hon Roll; Mnrng Music Clb Schlrshp Awd; Natl Piano Plyng Audtns Superior Pls.

YAMANAKA, LORI A; Kaimuki HS; Honolulu, HI; (2); Stat Wrstlng; Humane Soc Vlntr; Travel Indstry.

YAMANE, GREG Y; Iolani Schl; Aiea, HI; (4); 21/221; Drama Clb; Intnl Clb; Key Clb; Orch; Stage Crew; Rptr Lit Mag; Intrml Bsktbl; High Hon Roll; NHS; Ntl Merit SF; Comp Engnrng.

YAMANE, TRACEY A; Waiakea HS; Hilo, HI; (3); 60/368; Rep Frsh Cls; Rep Soph Cls; Pres Jr Cls; Rep Stu Cncl; JV Trk; Hon Roll; Prfct Atten Awd; Pres Acad Fit Awd; Ldrshp Conf Prjct Prom/Grad 89; HI ST Stu Conf 89; Homcmng Sub Cmmtte Chrprsn 88-89; Grphc Art.

YAMASAKI, BARRY T; Roosevelt HS; Honolulu, HI; (2); JV Capt Bsbl; JV Ftbl; Srfng, Fshng; Washington ST U; Sprts Med.

YAMASAKI, KIMBERLY R; Kauai HS; Lihue, HI; (3); VP Church Yth Grp; Debate Tm; Pres VP 4-H; French Clb; FHA; Library Aide; Q&S; Red Cross Aide; Service Clb; Speech Tm.

YAMASAKI, NATHAN Y; Mc Kinley HS; Kaneohe, HI; (3); Cmnty Wkr; Varsity Clb; Lit Mag; Var Capt Bsktbl; Var Vllybl; Hon Roll; Goldn Tgr Awd; U Of HI; Med.

YAMASHIRO, LISA M; Baldwin HS; Wailuku, HI; (3); 60/390; Pres VP 4-H; Service Clb; SADD; Stu Cncl; Cit Awd; 4-H Awd; Hon Roll; Prfct Atten Awd; VP Stu Staying Strght; 4-H Clthng Awd; U HI; Elem Ed.

YAMASHIRO, LYNNE M; Mc Kinley HS; Kailua, HI; (3); French Clb; Band; Mrchg Band; Keywynettes Clb.

YAMASHIRO, REID N; Baldwin HS; Wailuku, HI; (1); 62/466; Band; Jazz Band; Mrchg Band; Pep Band; JV Trk; HI Engl Assn Short Story Awd; Maui Cnty HS Hnr Band; Phrmcst.

YAMASHITA, BRENT K; Iolani Schl; Honolulu, HI; (4); 12/221; Math Tm; Jazz Band; Pres Frsh Cls; Pres Soph Cls; Pres Jr Cls; Pres Sr Cls; Var Bsbl; High Hon Roll; Ntl Merit SF; Elec Engrng.

YAMASHITA, KARA; Kailua HS; Kailua, HI; (4); 11/275; JA; Pep Clb; Band; Jazz Band; Mrchg Band; Pep Band; Off Frsh Cls; Cheerldng; High Hon Roll; Hon Roll; Santa Clara U.

YAMAUCHI, SARA L; Henry J Kaiser HS; Honolulu, HI; (3); Church Yth Grp; Cmnty Wkr; GAA; Office Aide; Band; Color Guard; Sec Soph Cls; Pres VP Jr Cls; VP Sr Cls; Capt JV Bsktbl; Offcl Fnlst Miss Natl Teenager Pgnt; Jr Prm Atten; Hmcmng Atten; OR ST U; Chld Psych.

YAMAUCHI, SHIRLEY; Pahoa HS; Pahoa, HI; (2); 12/123; Drama Clb; Treas Math Clb; Math Tm; Quiz Bowl; Band; Drm Mjr(t); School Play; Hon Roll; NHS; Leo Clb; Mock Trial; TV Pgms; Med.

YANO, ALANE; Kauai HS; Lihue, HI; (4); 1/240; Rep Stu Cncl; Stat Bsbl; L Crs Cntry; L Swmmng; Bausch & Lomb Sci Awd; High Hon Roll; NHS; Pres Acad Fit Awd; Val; Davis CA U; Optometry.

YANO, JENNIFER FRANCES; St Andrews Priry HS; Honolulu, HI; (3); 13/54; Key Clb; Science Clb; Band; Sec Frsh Cls; Var Sftbl; High Hon Roll; OBDA Mdls; AF Acad; Air Plt.

YANUARIA, JACQUELINE P; Maui HS; Kahului, HI; (4); Computer Clb; Teachers Aide; Hon Roll; Prfct Atten Awd; Leo Clb; Bus Comp Clb, VP & Sectry; Keywanettes Clb; Jr Prm Cmmtte; Sr Ball Cmmtte; U Of HI Manoa; &sych.

YAP, SHARLENE; St Andrews Priory HS; Honolulu, HI; (2); 2/50; Latin Clb; NFL; Science Clb; VP Speech Tm; Capt Drill Tm; High Hon Roll; Hon Roll; NHS; Pres Acad Fit Awd; Magna Cum Laude Ntl Latin Exam; HI ST Yth Vlntr Brd; Cntr For Tlnt Yth; Med.

YAP, WAI LING; Kalani HS; Honolulu, HI; (2); 8/213; Cmnty Wkr; Library Aide; High Hon Roll; Hon Roll; Phone A Friend Pgm; Oahu Facility Nrsng Home Vlntr; 1st Chinese Church Of Christ Preschool Vlntr; U Of HI Manoa; Elem Educ.

YASAY, FLORENILAH L; Wallace Rider Farrington HS; Honolulu, HI; (1); Church Yth Grp; English Clb; Church Choir; Hon Roll; Doc.

YASHIKI, RYLAN; Pearl City HS; Pearl City, HI; (3); Band; Jazz Band; Mrchg Band; Judo Team; Outstndng Ldrshp Awd Band.

YASUDA JR, CARL I; Mililani HS; Mililani, HI; (3); 56/490; Art Clb; FHA; SADD; Vllybl; Hon Roll; HERO Club Cmmtte Chairprsn, Pres; Social Cmmtte; HI Yth For Christ Campus Life Publicity Artist; Civil Engrng.

YASUDA, RYAN S; Iolani Schl; Aiea, HI; (4); Boy Scts; Treas Computer Clb; Orch; School Play; Stu Cncl; Crs Cntry; JV Swmmng; Var Trk; Hon Roll; Ntl Merit SF; Bowling Team,Capt & Co-Capt; Youth Symph; Sr Perfect; Accntng.

YASUDA, TRACIE A; Mid-Pacific Inst; Pearl City, HI; (2); Hosp Aide; Band; Pep Band; Vllybl; Hon Roll; Sci.

YASUI, KARYN Y; Roosevelt HS; Honolulu, HI; (4); 41/318; Teachers Aide; Yrbk; Hon Roll; U Of HI.

YEE, ROLAND; Mc Kinley HS; Honolulu, HI; (4); 6/547; Church Yth Grp; Key Clb; Math Clb; Math Tm; Quiz Bowl; Church Choir; School Play; Stage Crew; Elks Awd; NHS; Campus Life; Harvey Mudd Coll; Biomedcl Engr.

YEE, TAMMY L; Roosevelt HS; Honolulu, HI; (2); 31/360; ROTC; Pres Acad Fit Awd; Supr Jr Cadet Decor Awd JROTC; Let-I; Amer Leg Merit Awd JROTC; Ranger Club; Guidon.

YERE, MICHELLE A; Waimea HS; Waimea Kauai, HI; (3); 2/216; VP FHA; Spanish Clb; Rptr Nwsp; High Hon Roll; NHS; SF N Amer Open Poetry Comp; Miss Phillippines; PAAC; Jrnlsm.

YEUNG, EVA W; Sacred Hearts Acad; Honolulu, HI; (3); Treas Church Yth Grp; Drama Clb; Speech Tm; School Musical; School Play; Stage Crew; Prfct Atten Awd; Concrs Natl De Frncs-1st Pl Cert Hnr; Natl Frnsc Leag 88; Relgn Awd 89.

YI, CYRUS; St Louis HS; Honolulu, HI; (3); 7/157; Aud/Vis; Drama Clb; School Play; Hon Roll; Arch.

YI, JULIA; St Andrews Priory HS; Aiea, HI; (3); 2/60; Church Yth Grp; Drama Clb; Math Tm; Band; Church Choir; School Musical; School Play; Off Jr Cls; Bsktbl; Trk; Fnlst In Alpha Ltr Wrtng Cont 87; Pepperdine U; Bus Ad.

YIM, THOMAS K; Maryknoll HS; Honolulu, HI; (2); JV Crs Cntry; JV Trk; Hon Roll; Hikng Clb; JV Bowlng.

YOKOYAMA, JILL; Waiakea HS; Hilo, HI; (4); 1/400; Sec Church Yth Grp; Service Clb; Sec Soph Cls; Pres Jr Cls; Pres Stu Cncl; Capt Tennis; DAR Awd; NHS; Sal; HOBY Ambssdr; Mock Trial Tm; Santa Clara U; Acctng.

YOKOYAMA, KARI K; Kaiser HS; Honolulu, HI; (3); 26/325; Key Clb; Co-Capt Flag Corp; Stat Wrstlng; Hon Roll; Pres NHS; Outstndng Ldrshp Awd 89-90; Jr Prom Cmmtte/Band Bnqt Cmmtte; Smmr 90 Tutoring Engl In Japan; Law.

YOKOYAMA, KIM Y; Waiakea HS; Hilo, HI; (2); 1/500; Church Yth Grp; 4-H; Math Clb; Science Clb; Service Clb; Treas Frsh Cls; Treas Soph Cls; Pres Jr Cls; Var Tennis; High Hon Roll.

YOSHIDA, KARA L; Waimea HS; Waimea, HI; (3); 4/209; Math Tm; Pep Clb; SADD; Teachers Aide; Ed Nwsp; Treas Soph Cls; Treas Jr Cls; Treas Stu Cncl; Tennis; High Hon Roll; U Of OR; Acctng.

YOSHIDA, KRISTY A; Baldwin HS; Kahului, HI; (2); 42/395; Pep Clb; SADD; Rep Frsh Cls; JV Cheerldng; Hon Roll; Interact Clb; U Of OR; Ed.

YOSHIMORI, DENISE F; Maui HS; Pukalani, HI; (4); Church Yth Grp; Key Clb; Math Clb; Band; Sec Frsh Cls; Treas Soph Cls; Sec Jr Cls; JV Var Cheerldng; Kiwanis Awd; Treas NHS; Homecoming Rep; Jr Prom Ct Princess; Sr Ball Chrprsn; U HI Manoa; Arch.

YOSHIMOTO, GWEN T; Kauai HS; Lihue, HI; (3); 12/231; Treas 4-H; Library Aide; Math Tm; Sec Soph Cls; Sec Sr Cls; L Golf; L Tennis; L Vllybl; 4-H Awd; Hon Roll; Keywanettes Club; Girls Jr Amer Cup/Golf 89; Optimst Jr World Golf Champ; Hotel Mgmt.

YOSHINA, KARA L; Henry Perrine Baldwin HS; Kula, HI; (3); 36/415; Art Clb; Pres 4-H; Key Clb; Letterman Clb; Office Aide; Service Clb; SADD; Teachers Aide; Phtg Yrbk; Capt Socr; Pres Japanese Club; Ntl 4-H Cngrss 89 Rep HI; Bus.

YOSHIOKA, LAURENE H; Kaiser HS; Honolulu, HI; (3); 74/325; JA; SADD; Rep Frsh Cls; Sec Jr Cls; Sec Sr Cls; JV Var Crs Cntry; JV Var Trk; JV Vllybl; Hon Roll.

YOSHIOKA, MICHELLE C; Iolani Schl; Pearl City, HI; (4); 23/220; Drama Clb; 4-H; Key Clb; Q&S; Flag Corp; Nwsp; High Hon Roll; Cum Laude Soc; Kokua Committee; Japanese Clb; Environmental Engrng.

YOSHIOKA, RICHELLE M; Kauai HS; Koloa, HI; (3); 31/233; Pres Church Yth Grp; Sec Key Clb; Sec Q&S; Ed Nwsp; Sec Frsh Cls; Sec Soph Cls; Hon Roll; NHS; Jrnlsm.

YOSHIZUMI, STANLY; Hilo HS; Hilo, HI; (4); 15/304; Key Clb; Latin Clb; Math Tm; Science Clb; Treas Sr Cls; Rep Stu Cncl; Var Crs Cntry; High Hon Roll; Hon Roll; NHS; May Day Ct; Frgn Lang Awd Lat I; SSTP Pgm; U OR; Arch.

YOUN, KRISTI S M; Moanalua HS; Honolulu, HI; (2); 9/501; Cmnty Wkr; Service Clb; Rep Frsh Cls; VP Soph Cls; Stu Cncl; High Hon Roll; Hon Roll; Stu Art Merit Awd 89; Japanese Clb; Spanish Frgn Lang; Pianist & Flutist; Stanford; CPA.

YOUNG, ALLYSON K; St Francis HS; Honolulu, HI; (2); 7/80; VP Intnl Clb; Lit Mag; Hon Roll; Jr NHS; Voice Dem Awd; Nature Conservacy Org & Envrnmntl Dfns Fund; Film Prdcr.

YOUNG, AMY; Hawaii Preparatory Acad; Kailua-Kona, HI; (4); 10/70; Church Yth Grp; NFL; Speech Tm; Church Choir; School Musical; School Play; Trk; Vllybl; Wesleyan U; Molecular Bio.

YOUNG, BRANDON C; St Louis Sch; Honolulu, HI; (4); 15/149; ROTC; Intrml Bsktbl; Intrml JV Vllybl; Hon Roll; NHS; Wrk At A-1 Frgn Exchng & Kamiloiki Schl; U HI; Pharm.

YOUNG, BRIAN S T; St Louis Schl; Honolulu, HI; (4); 16/146; Pres Chess Clb; Computer Clb; ROTC; High Hon Roll; Hon Roll; San Jose ST U; Acctng.

YOUNG, CHRISTINE K L; Roosevelt HS; Honolulu, HI; (4); 10/320; Math Tm; Quiz Bowl; Capt Flag Corp; High Hon Roll; NHS; Mck Trl Tm; Sen Ann Kobayashi Schlrshp; U Of HI; Engrng.

YOUNG, DANA K; Kamehameha HS; Honolulu, HI; (4); 8/406; AFS; Cmnty Wkr; Office Aide; Varsity Clb; JV Crs Cntry; Intrml Var Church Yth Grp; JV Var Trk; Cit Awd; High Hon Roll; Hon Roll; Live On A 45 Ft Sailboat; Award-Midkiff Scholarship; Scholar Athlete Award For Paddling; U Of CO-BOULDER; Business.

YOUNG, HEATHER P; Kalani HS; Honolulu, HI; (2); Key Clb; Orch; Hon Roll; Jr NHS; NHS; Sec Soph Cls; Rep Stu Cncl; HI Yth Symphny Cncrt Orchestra; Vlntr YMCA; St Stu Conf Planning Cmmtte; Psych.

YOUNG, HY GIA; St Andrews Priory HS; Honolulu, HI; (3); 1/53; Hosp Aide; Intnl Clb; Library Aide; Math Clb; Math Tm; Office Aide; Quiz Bowl; Spanish Clb; Band; Pres Frsh Cls; NSF Yng Schlr 89; Sci Fair Wnnr; Solo Ensmbl Medls-Silvr & Brnz; Boston U; Pdtrcn.

YOUNG, KATHLEEN K; Waipahu HS; Waipahu, HI; (1); 51/513; JV Trk; Nrsng.

YOUNG, KENNETH; Kalaheo HS; Kaneohe, HI; (2); 4/287; High Hon Roll; World Hstry Awd 89; Outstndng Schlr Awd 89; IPS Sci Awd 89; Chem.

YOUNG, NICOLE; Roosevelt HS; Honolulu, HI; (1); 10/365; Var Cheerldng; Hon Roll; Art.

YU, HYUNG SUK; Mc Kinley HS; Honolulu, HI; (2); 72/588; Chess Clb; Math Clb; ROTC; Science Clb; JV Crs Cntry; JV Trk; Cit Awd; Prfct Atten Awd; Sons Of Amer Rev Awd; UH; Art.

YU, QIANG; Roosevelt HS; Honolulu, HI; (3); 1/25; Math Tm; Hon Roll; JETS Awd; AHSME Hnr Roll & Awd; Natl Stu Recognition Pgm 90; Math Bowl; Engrng.

YUEN, RENEE M H; Kaimuki HS; Honolulu, HI; (4); 20/334; French Clb; VP Service Clb; Sec SADD; Pres Frsh Cls; Pres Soph Cls; Pres Stu Cncl; JV Crs Cntry; Mock Trial Team Capt; HI St Stu Conf Plannr; Vanderbilt U; Poltcl Sci.

YUKUMOTO, KARA LEE M; Moanalua HS; Honolulu, HI; (1); 26/545; Pres Band; Mrchg Band; Pep Band; HI Yth Symphony Concert Orch; Pharm.

YUM, TAE HO; Mc Kinley HS; Honolulu, HI; (3); 107/550; ROTC; Science Clb; Vrsty Riflery; Geo Washington Hnr Mdl; Comp Sci.

ZACHERLE, NILE; Kalaheo HS; Kailua, HI; (3); 12/247; High Hon Roll; Hon Roll; Art Cmptns; Cmmrcl Art.

ZAMORA, ZINNIA U; Sacred Hearts Acad; Waianae, HI; (4); 18/108; French Clb; Math Tm; Model UN; Quiz Bowl; Chorus; School Play; Off Jr Cls; Off Sr Cls; Hon Roll; NHS; LIFE; SHA Mrt Awd; Schlstc Hnrs Awd; U San Francisco; Pediatrics.

ZANE, JENNIFER; Maui HS; Makawao, HI; (3); Church Yth Grp; Drama Clb; FTA; Girl Scts; Band; Chorus; School Play; Stage Crew; Trk; Triple S; Photo; Project Tops Mediator; Peer Cnslr; U HI Manoa; Ed.

ZEE, NATHAN C; Saint Louis Schl; Honolulu, HI; (4); Quiz Bowl; Science Clb; Spanish Clb; Pres Sr Cls; High Hon Roll; NHS; Santa Clara; Poetry.

ZHANG, WEI; Roosevelt HS; Honolulu, HI; (3); Chess Clb; German Clb; Intnl Clb; Math Tm; Quiz Bowl; Lit Mag; Hon Roll; Treas NHS.

ZHENG, YONG SHEN; Mc Kinley HS; Honolulu, HI; (3); U Of HI.

ZIMMERMAN, MARIE A; Mililani HS; Mililani, HI; (2); 22/509; Church Yth Grp; Math Clb; Math Tm; Treas Science Clb; JV Crs Cntry; High Hon Roll; Hon Roll; Stu Tutor; Outstndng Span, Hstry Stu; Engrng.

ZIPP, TINA J; Moanalua HS; Honolulu, HI; (2); 46/488; Rep Frsh Cls; Sec Soph Cls; Sec Jr Cls; Rep Stu Cncl; JV Var Cheerldng; JV Var Pom Pon; Hon Roll; NHS; Japanese Clb; Cncl Rep; Jrnlsm.

ZURCHER, REBECCA A; Radford HS; Honolulu, HI; (3); Art Clb; Church Yth Grp; German Clb; Pep Clb; Teachers Aide; Varsity Clb; Nwsp; Bsktbl; Cheerldng; Tennis; College; Art Hist/Museum Curatr.

ZWOLENSKY, STEPHEN J; Leilehua HS; Wahiawa, HI; (2); 10/406; French Clb; Trk; High Hon Roll; Air Force Acad; Comp Tech.

CALI-FORNIA

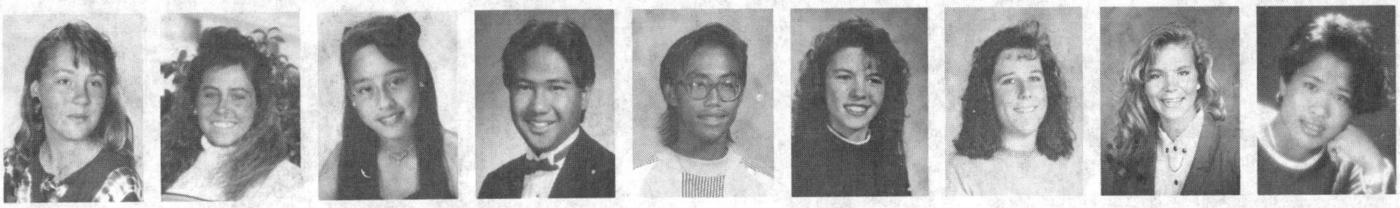

Aarnes, Turi Kenna
Glen A Wilson HS
Hacienda Hts, CA

Aaronson, Brandi
Leland HS
San Jose, CA

Abadajos, Stephanie
Arroyo Grande HS
Grover City, CA

Abakan, Stephen
Santa Monica HS
Santa Monica, CA

Abalos, Jr Melencio
Lemoore Union HS
Lemoore, CA

Abbate, Catherine M
Modoc HS
Likely, CA

Abbott, Heather
Yosemite HS
Oakhurst, CA

Abbott, Susan
Elsinore HS
Lk Elsinore, CA

Abe, Trisha M
Mater Dei HS
Fountain Valley, CA

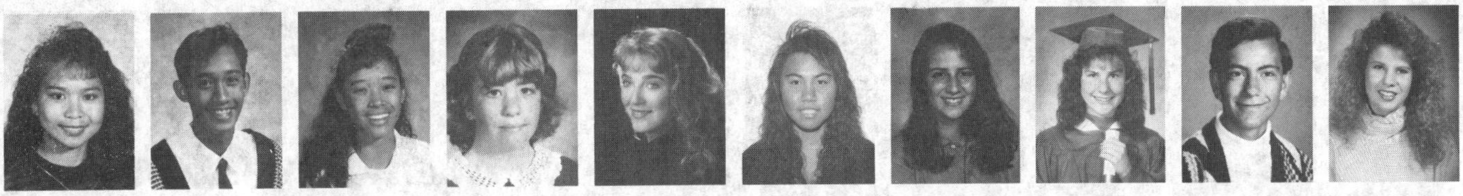

Abella, Claire N
Pasadena HS
Altadena, CA

Abellar, Ronald C
St Joseph Notre Dame HS
Union City, CA

Abello, Lourdes L
Woodside HS
Redwood City, CA

Abels, Kristine L
Dana Hills HS
Laguna Niguel, CA

Abels, Tracy
Dos Pueblos HS
Goleta, CA

Ablog, Elymarie P
Homestead HS
Sunnyvale, CA

Abou Lahoud, Nada
Louisville HS
West Hills, CA

Abracen, Michele
Taft HS
Woodland Hills, CA

Abrahim-Youri, Neboneed
Turlock HS
Turlock, CA

Abrams, Samantha L
Vanden HS
Travis Afb, CA

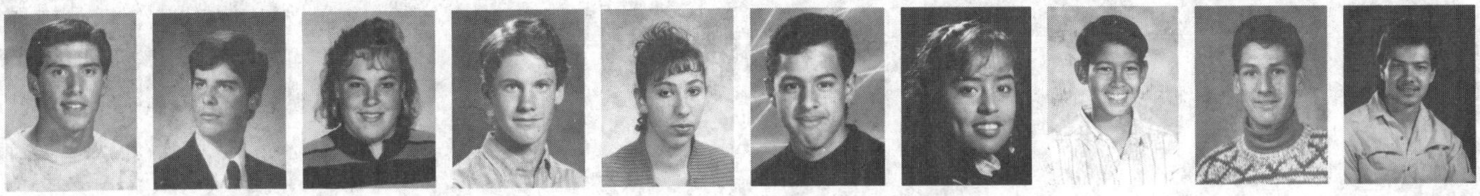

Abril, Frank A
Hemet HS
Hemet, CA

Abronson, Louis S
Beverly Hills HS
Beverly Hills, CA

Absher, Jennifer A
San Benito HS
Hollister, CA

Abshire, Ed D
Village Christian Schls
Los Angeles, CA

Acampora, Tina F
Bishop O'dowd HS
Oakland, CA

Ackenback, Ruben F
East Bakersfield HS
Bakersfield, CA

Acosta, Evelyn
Venice HS
Los Angeles, CA

Acosta, Jr Frank Lugo
Don Bosco Technical Inst
Montebello, CA

Acosta, Joe
Redwood HS
Visalin, CA

Acosta, Luis J
Monache HS
Tulare, CA

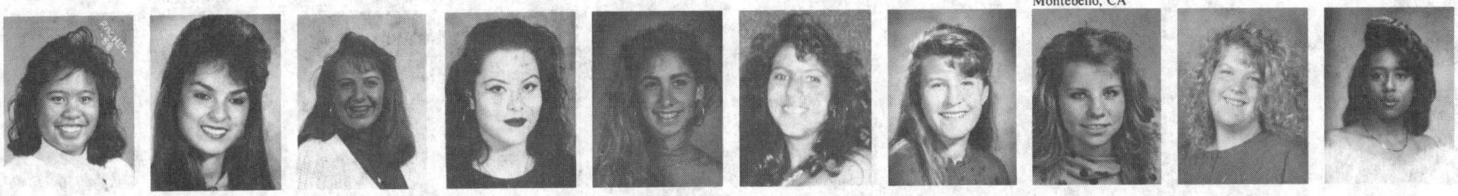

Acosta, Rachel
Alemany HS
Sepulveda, CA

Acosta, Teresa L
Orosi HS
Orosi, CA

Acquistapace, Christina L
Willow Glen HS
San Jose, CA

Acree, Karena J
Alameda HS
Alameda, CA

Acuff, Andrea L
Marysville HS
Marysville, CA

Acuna, Lisa A
Arcadia HS
Arcadia, CA

Adair, Bekki A
Edison HS
Huntington Beach, CA

Adair, Katherine G
Foothill SR HS
Sacramento, CA

Adams, Catherine S
Yucaipa HS
Yucaipa, CA

Adams, Cynthia
Valley HS
Sacramento, CA

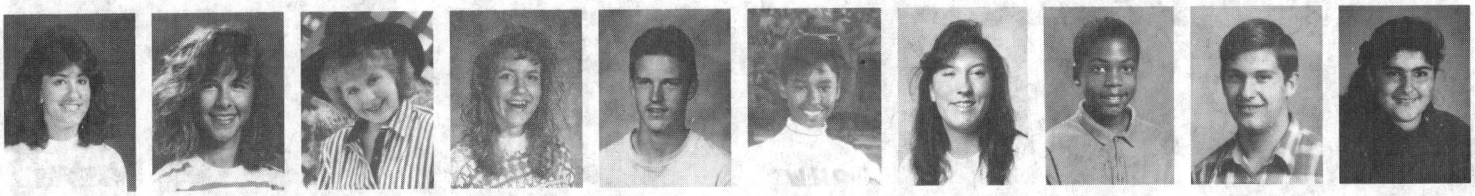

Adams, Janice D
Modesto HS
Modesto, CA

Adams, Kristie
San Marino HS
San Gabriel, CA

Adams, Kristina L
Coalinga Unified HS
Coalinga, CA

Adams, Mary Beth
South Tahoe HS
South Lake Tahoe, CA

Adams, Ryan L
Fairfield HS
Fairfield, CA

Adams, Sabrina
West HS
Bakersfield, CA

Adams, Steffnee D
Buena HS
Ventura, CA

Adams-El, Tariq-Bilal
Mojave HS
California City, CA

Adamson, Dwight
Faith Christian HS
Yuba City, CA

Adamzadeh, Sharlet
Turlock HS
Turlock, CA

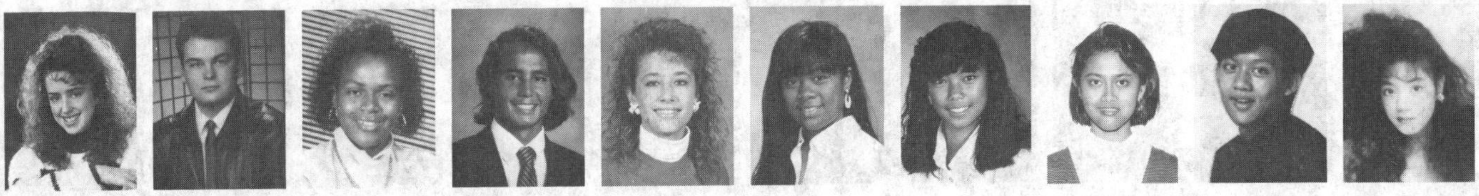

Addis, April
Community Christian
Bakersfield, CA

Adkins, James
El Sereno HS
Citrus Heights, CA

Adkins, Tonisa B
Victor Valley HS
Victorville, CA

Adrian, Donnell
Tusti HS
Tustin, CA

Adrian, Leigh
Banning HS
Banning, CA

Adriano, Janet L
Immaculate Heart
Los Angeles, CA

Adriatico, Elvie R
Monterey HS
Monterey, CA

Adriatico, Mariejoy E
St Joseph HS
Artesia, CA

Adriatico, Ronald
Chaminade College Prep
Bell Canyon, CA

Adrid, Amara A
Serra HS
San Diego, CA

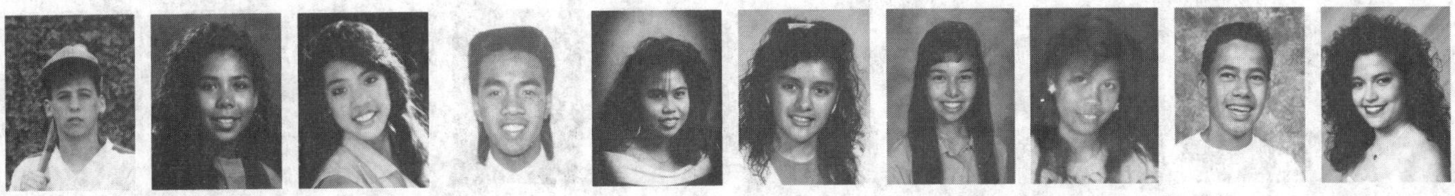

Agamaite, David M
Pacifica HS
Garden Grove, CA

Agepogu, Esther P
Mayfield SR HS
Pasadena, CA

Aglipay, Chleora L
Notre Dame HS
San Jose, CA

Aglipay, Ernest L
Bellarmine HS
San Jose, CA

Agojo, Yvette Marie
Nogales HS
Walnut, CA

Agredano, Yolanda Z
Yerba Buena HS
San Jose, CA

Aguero, Cynthia A
Louisville HS
Simi Valley, CA

Aguilar, Anita
Lemoore HS
Lemoore, CA

Aguilar, Anthony
St Paul HS
Montebello, CA

Aguilar, Deborah
Bishop Amat Memorial HS
West Covina, CA

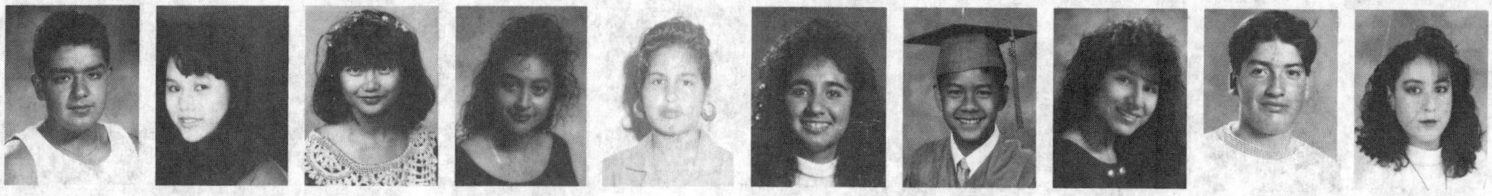

Aguilar, Edward
Philip
Saddleback HS
Santa Ana, CA

Aguilar, Hazel Santos
Peoples HS
Vallejo, CA

Aguilar, Maria
Cecilia
San Diego HS/
WRITING Acad
San Diego, CA

Aguilar, Veronica
Southwest HS
San Diego, CA

Aguilar, Yesenia E
Chula Vista HS
Chula Vista, CA

Aguilera, Sylvia
Lindsay HS
Strathmore, CA

Aguinid, Marcello
John
Providence HS
Burbank, CA

Aguirre, Cynthia
Davis HS
Modesto, CA

Aguirre, Michael C
San Pedro HS
San Pedro, CA

Aguirre, Sonia
Richard Gahr HS
Norwalk, CA

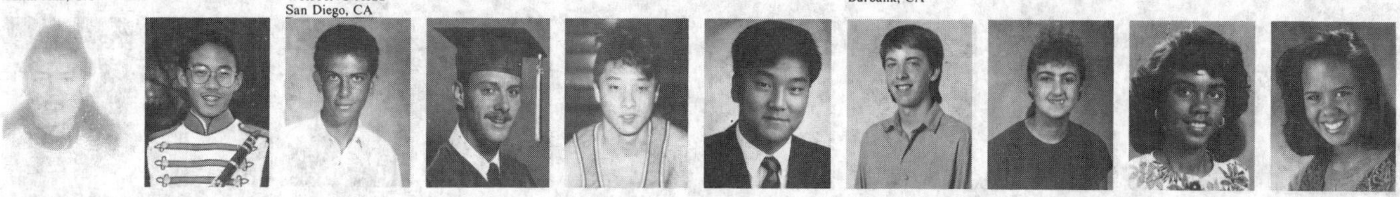

Aguon, Jr Frank S
Silver Valley HS
Fort Irwin, CA

Agustin, Jimmy J
Whitney HS
Cerritos, CA

Aharoni, Ilan
Carlsbad HS
Carlsbad, CA

Ahlefeld, Jimmy C
Hueneme HS
Oxnard, CA

Ahn, Daniel H
West HS
Torrance, CA

Ahn, John Young
Poway HS
Poway, CA

Ahrens, David L
Buena HS
Ventura, CA

Akbar, Maryam
Poly HS
Riverside, CA

Akbar, Saleemah E
Narbonne Math/
Science Magnet HS
Los Angeles, CA

Akers, Michele
Charter Oak HS
Covina, CA

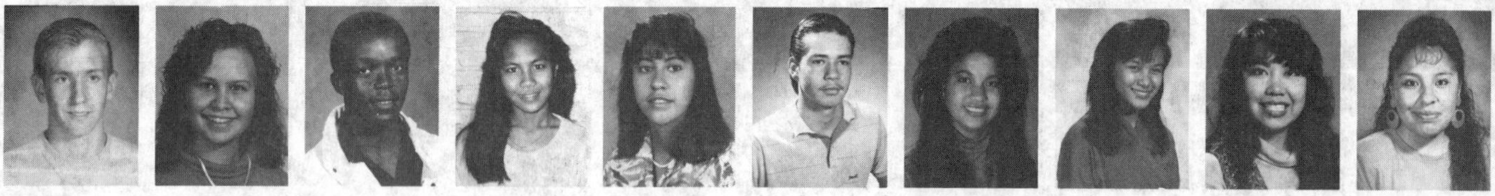

Akins, Eric M
Las Plumas HS
Oroville, CA

Akins, Ruth E
Los Gatos HS
Campbell, CA

Akpan, Enefiok
Solomon
South San Francisco
South San Francis,
CA

Alacar, Gracielle
Gatinga
Louisville HS
Agoura Hills, CA

Alaniz, Rosa
Holtville HS
Holtville, CA

Alarcon, Cris
San Pasqual HS
Yuma, AZ

Alarcon, Maricar
Sacred Heart
Cathedral Prep
Daly City, CA

Alas, Charissa M
Whitney HS
Cerritos, CA

Alba, Cristina G
Baldwin Park HS
Baldwin Park, CA

Alba, Maria H
Santa Ana HS
Tustin, CA

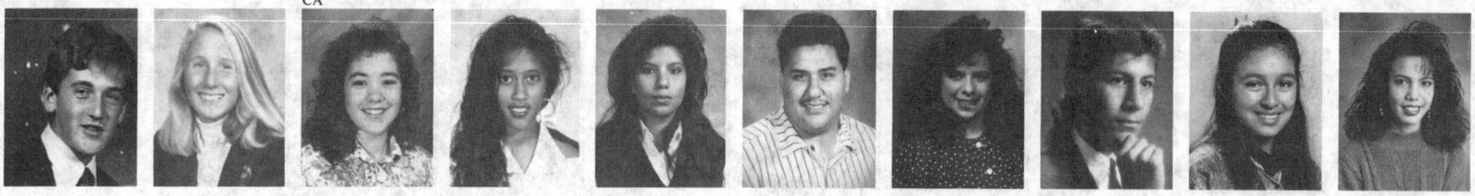

Alban, Blake
Marina HS
Huntington Bch, CA

Albers, Hilary A
St Margarets
Episcopal Schl
San Clemente, CA

Albert, Tammera E
Bishop Amat
Memorial HS
Glendora, CA

Alberto, Gayle Beth
Sacred Heart Of
Mary HS
Montebello, CA

Alcalan, Elita L
St Joseph Notre
Dame HS
Oakland, CA

Alcantar, Randy
John Glenn HS
Norwalk, CA

Aldrete, Alma C
Monte Vista HS
Spring Valley, CA

Aleman, Jr Frank J
Wasco Union HS
Fresno, CA

Aleman, Maritza
Manual Arts HS
Los Angeles, CA

Alemania, Elena T
Fresno Christian HS
Fresno, CA

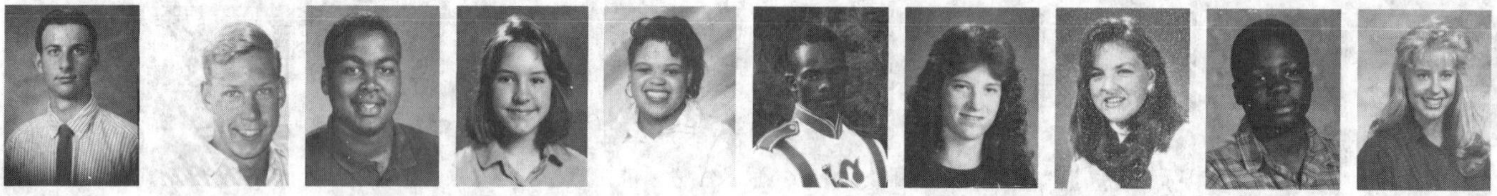

Alexander, Allen
Madera HS
Madera, CA

Alexander, Brandon
Poly HS
Riverside, CA

Alexander, Brian K
Bishop Montgomery
Los Angeles, CA

Alexander, Charlotte
Taft HS
Woodland Hills, CA

Alexander, Chauncey
St Patricks-St
Vincent HS
Vallejo, CA

Alexander, Gregory
Cajon HS
San Bernardino, CA

Alexander, Karen L
Manteca HS
Manteca, CA

Alexander, Krista
Monte Vista HS
Alamo, CA

Alexander, Marquez
George Washington
San Francisco, CA

Alexander, Nicole
Palm Desert HS
Palm Desert, CA

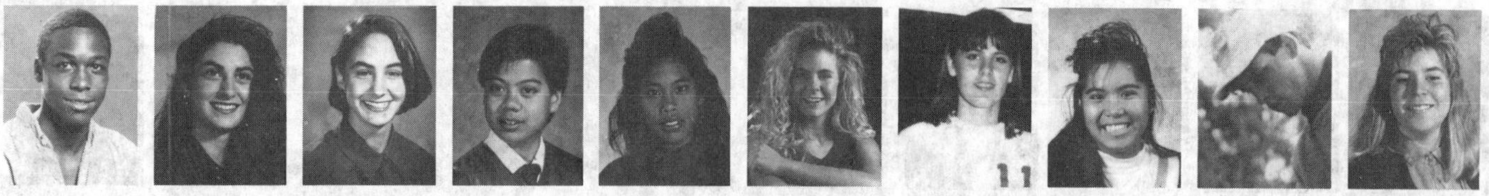

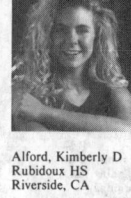

Alexander, Walter L
Arlington HS
Riverside, CA

Alexanian, Julie R
Bullard HS
Fresno, CA

Alfano, Angela M
Huntington Beach
Huntington Beach,
CA

Alfelor, Raymond J
Bellarmine College
Prep
San Jose, CA

Alfiler, Laurie
Santa Clara HS
Santa Clara, CA

Alford, Kimberly D
Rubidoux HS
Riverside, CA

Algarin, Tiffany
Herbert Hoover HS
San Diego, CA

Alger-Alves, Melissa
Valley HS
Sacramento, CA

Algra, Joshua L
Arroyo Grande HS
Arroyo Grande, CA

Alhart, Jennifer L
Lompoc HS
Lompoc, CA

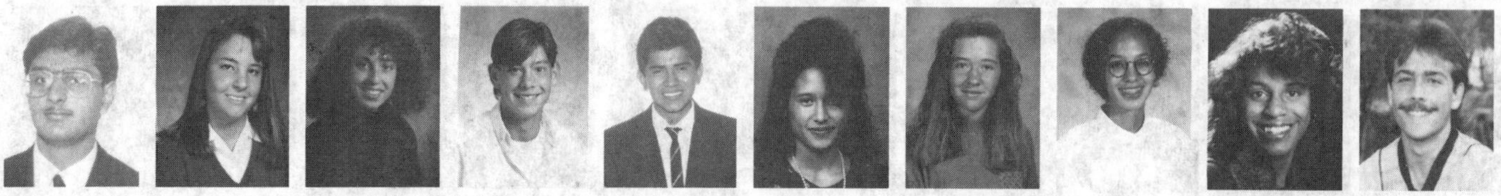

Ali, Irfan B
Santa Monica HS
Santa Monica, CA

Aliberte, Nicole S
La Reina HS
Westlake Village, CA

Alicea, Olga M T
Lincoln HS
Stockton, CA

Alita, Adrian D
Del Mar HS
Campbell, CA

Allavesen, Feliciano
Palomar
John Burroughs HS
Burbank, CA

Allbrooks, Jasmine
O'farrel SCPA HS
San Diego, CA

Alleman, Kellie L
Corona HS
Corona, CA

Allen, Catherine A
Whitney HS
Cerritos, CA

Allen, Erica M
Gardena HS
Gardena, CA

Allen, James
Cerritos HS
Cerritos, CA

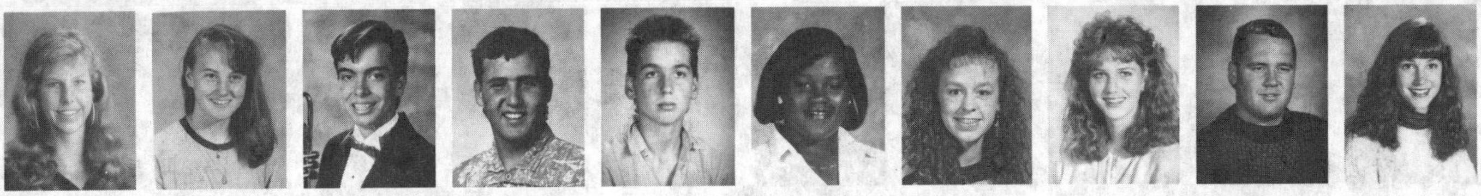

Allen, Jennifer
Capistrano Valley
Christian HS
Dana Point, CA

Allen, Jennifer L
Sacramento Country
Day Schl
Sacramento, CA

Allen, Jeremiah L
Mayfair HS
Bellflower, CA

Allen, John M
Brea-Olinda HS
Brea, CA

Allen, Justin
Livingston HS
Livingston, CA

Allen, Lisha M
Phillip & Sala Burton
San Francisco, CA

Allen, Merideth
Los Alamizos HS
Los Alamitos, CA

Allen, Reagan M
Monterey HS
Monterey, CA

Allenbaugh, Randy B
Foothill HS
Bakersfield, CA

Allendorf, Michelle L
Clear Lake HS
Upper Lake, CA

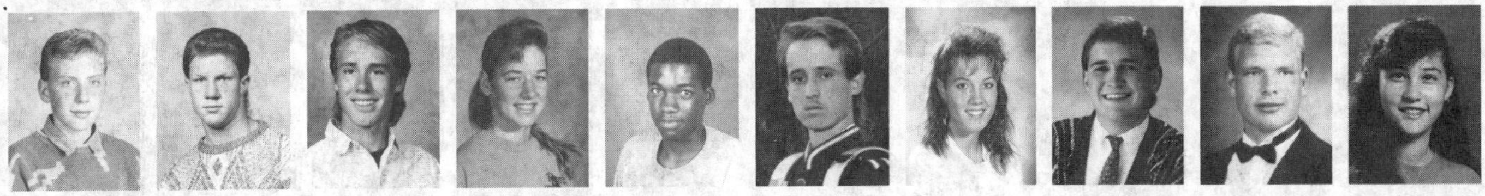

Allensworth, Dave
Sierra HS
Coarsegold, CA

Allett, Brian
Vallejo SR HS
Vallejo, CA

Allingham, William
Grossmont HS
La Mesa, CA

Allis, Katrina
Coastal Christian
Schl
Arroyo Grande, CA

Allison, Eric
Bel-Air Prep HS
Los Angeles, CA

Allor, Jason M
Ramona HS
Riverside, CA

Alloway, Stephanie R
Edison HS
Huntington Beach,
CA

Allred, Michael J
North HS
Bakersfield, CA

Allred, Wade A
Pinole Valley HS
Hercules, CA

Almaguer, Patricia D
Mayfield SR Schl
Pasadena, CA

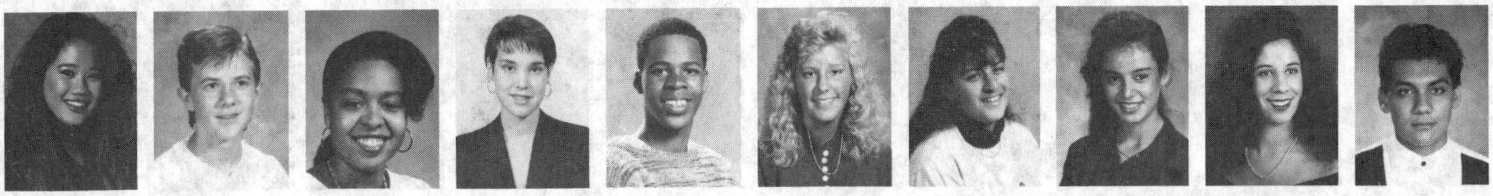

Almalel, Olivia
Hillcrest Christian
Schl
Northridge, CA

Almand, Chris
Pittsburg HS
Pittsburg, CA

Almeda, Genel H
Valley HS
Sacramento, CA

Almer, Marisabel
Immaculate Heart
Los Angeles, CA

Almond, Andre D
Crenshaw HS
Los Angeles, CA

Almquist, Brenda J
El Camino HS
Daly City, CA

Alonso, Amy D
River City HS
W Sacramento, CA

Alonso, Dulce Paloma
South West HS
San Diego, CA

Alonso, Josefina
St Joseph HS
Downey, CA

Alonso, Marcos H
Don Bosco Technical
Inst
Whittier, CA

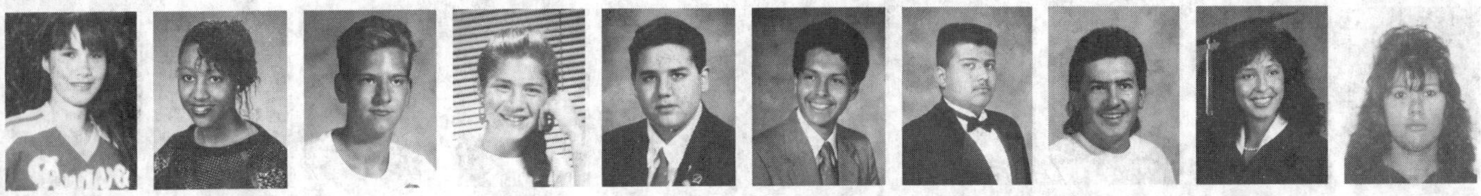

Alquitela, Cynthia B
Baldwin Park HS
Chino Hills, CA

Alston, Ka Shonda M
Mt Diablo HS
W Pittsburg, CA

Alt, Carter
Bullard HS
Fresno, CA

Alvarado, Celeste D
Indio HS
Indio, CA

Alvarado, Daniel
St Michaels Prep
Norwalk, CA

Alvarado, Frank A
John H Glenn HS
Norwalk, CA

Alvarado, Juan
Garey HS
Pomona, CA

Alvarado, Raul Prado
Dinuba Joint Union
Dinuba, CA

Alvarado, Sabrina
Whittier Christian
Pico Rivera, CA

Alvarado, Susana
Coachela Valley HS
Thermal, CA

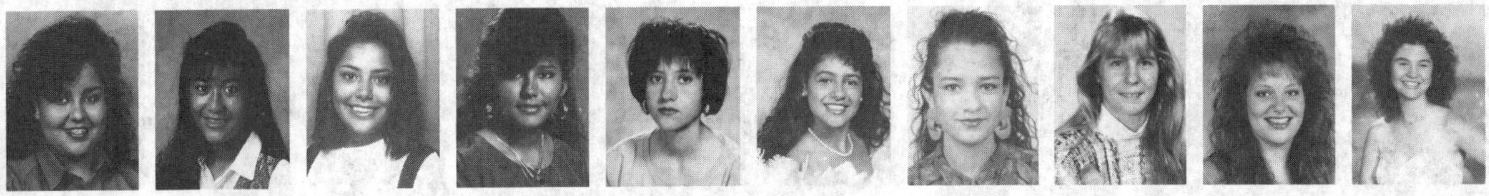

Alvarado, Teresa
Escondido HS
San Marcos, CA

Alvarez, Aileen
Chaminade College
Prep
West Hills, CA

Alvarez, Consuelo
Gardena HS
Gardena, CA

Alvarez, Eva I
Saint Michaels HS
Los Angeles, CA

Alvarez, Fabiola
El Rancho HS
Pico Rivera, CA

Alvarez, Magdalena
Moreau HS
San Leandro, CA

Alvarez, Marina
Calexico HS
Calexico, CA

Alvarez, Vanessa K
Skyline HS
Oakland, CA

Alves, Carrie
Richard Gahr HS
Artesia, CA

Alves, Jeanna M
Atwater HS
Winton, CA

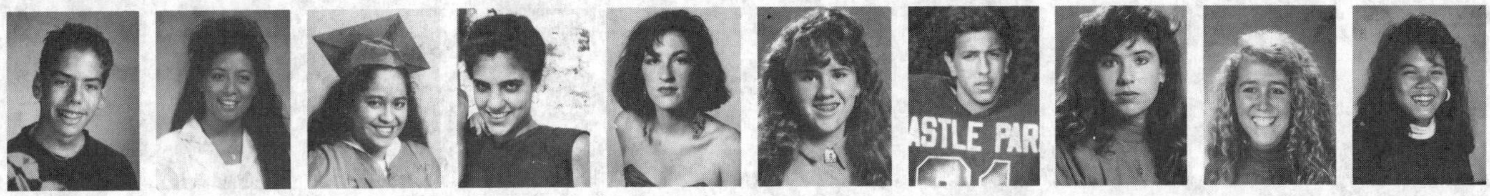

Alves, Lee
Tulare Union HS
Tipton, CA

Alvite, Elaine M
James Logan HS
Union City, CA

Alvizures, Cecilia E
El Rancho HS
Pico Rivera, CA

Amado, Mor
Lowell HS
San Francisco, CA

Amador, Carol A
La Habra HS
La Habra, CA

Amador, Gloria
Maria
Glendale HS
Glendale, CA

Amador, Humberto
Castle Park HS
Chula Vista, CA

Amador, Nelly
Glendale HS
Glendale, CA

Amaro, Kendra
California HS
San Ramon, CA

Amath, Nora K
Andrew Hill HS
San Jose, CA

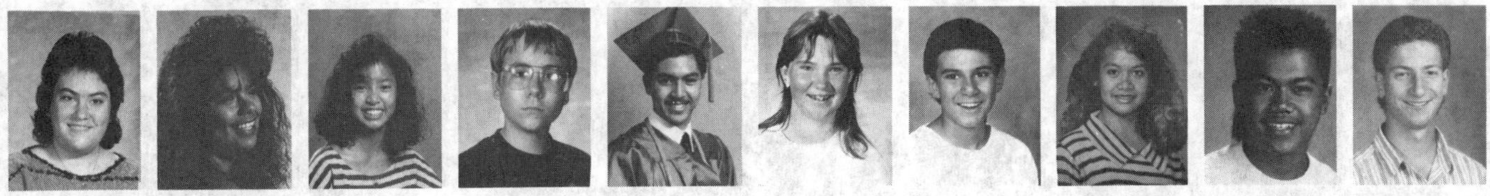

Amato, Donna Denise
San Jose HS Acad
San Jose, CA

Amaya, Diana M
Fred C Beyer HS
Modesto, CA

Ambas, Jennifer
Ontario HS
Ontario, CA

Ambrose, Joseph A
Don Antonio Lugo
Chino, CA

Ambrose, Steve E
Channel Islands HS
Oxnard, CA

Ambuski, Rebecca A
Chino HS
Chino, CA

Amini, Pedram
Grossmont HS
La Mesa, CA

Amiscaray, Rowena
Trabuco Hills HS
Mission Viejo, CA

Amodo, Kenneth S
East Union HS
French Camp, CA

Amos, Bryan
Mt Whitney HS
Visalia, CA

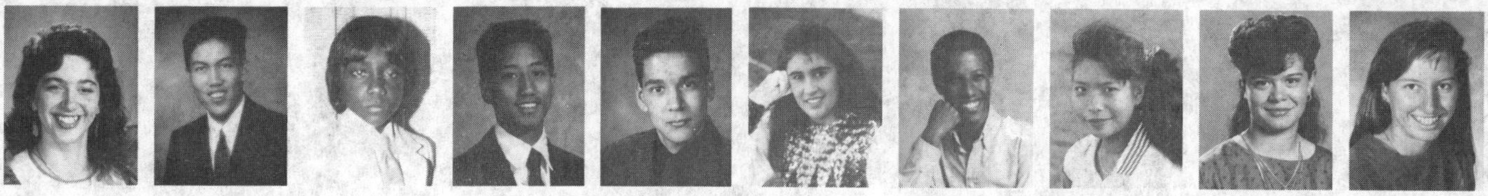

Amro, Tanya L
Clovis HS
Clovis, CA

Anacaya, Calvin
Orangewood
Adventist Acad
Bellflower, CA

Anand, Ronald R
Serra HS
South San Francis,
CA

Ancheta, Andrew I
Saint Ignatius College
Prep
Daly City, CA

Anchondo, Jerry
Imperial HS
Imperial, CA

Andalon, Andrea
Ontario HS
Altaloma, CA

Andargatchew,
Dagmawi
Dublin HS
Dublin, CA

Andaya, Michelle G
Pittsburg HS
Pittsburg, CA

Anderson, Amber
South Bay Lutheran
Los Angeles, CA

Anderson, Carly
Foothill HS
Santa Ana, CA

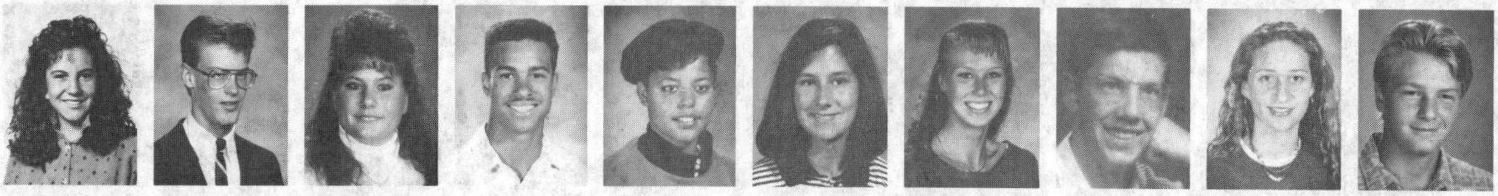

Anderson, Carolyn T
Ontario HS
Ontario, CA

Anderson, David B
Imperial HS
Duarte, CA

Anderson, Dena B
Lincoln HS
Stockton, CA

Anderson, Dennis
Edison HS
Costa Mesa, CA

Anderson, Erica L
Victorvalley HS
Victorville, CA

Anderson, Harlean
College Park HS
Pleasant Hill, CA

Anderson, Heather L
Clovis HS
Clovis, CA

Anderson, James D
Victory Christian
Schls
Carmichael, CA

Anderson, Kate Eden
Sonoma Valley HS
Sonoma, CA

Anderson, Kevin
Kerman HS
Kerman, CA

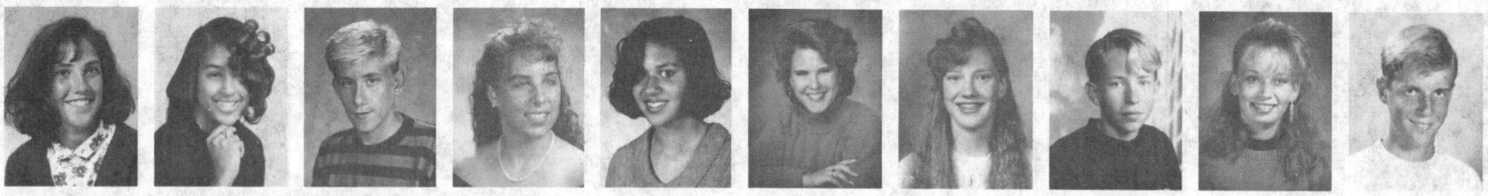

Anderson, Kimberly
Alta Loma HS
Alta Loma, CA

Anderson, Krishna K
Pius X HS
Compton, CA

Anderson, Mark K
Mt Carmel HS
San Diego, CA

Anderson, Maryann
Valley HS
Sacramento, CA

Anderson, Mele
Hilmar JR/SR HS
Hilmar, CA

Anderson, Melissa
Torrey Pines HS
Del Mar, CA

Anderson, Patricia C
O'farrell Schl
San Diego, CA

Anderson, Philip B
King City HS
King City, CA

Anderson, Rae D
Arlington HS
Riverside, CA

Anderson, Sean C
Mira Loma HS
Sacramento, CA

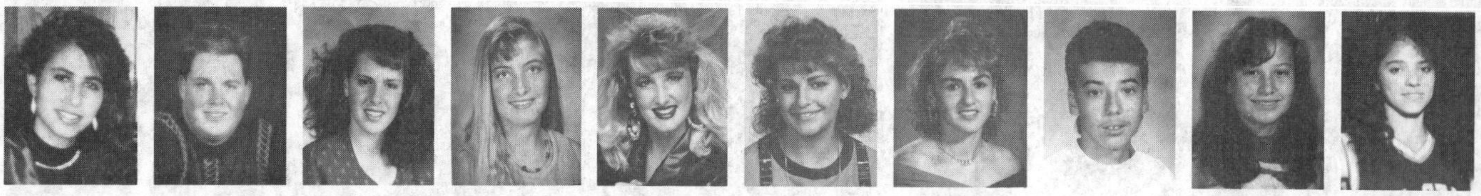

Anderson, Silvia
Bishop Montgomery
Lomita, CA

Anderson, Steven M
Oroville HS
Oroville, CA

Anderson, Tiffany L
Richard Gahr HS
Cerritos, CA

Anderson, Tori R
San Dieguito HS
Encinitas, CA

Anderson, Valerie P
El Toro HS
El Toro, CA

Andolina, Lisa Marie
Foothill HS
Sacramento, CA

Andrade, Alma R
Santiago HS
Santa Ana, CA

Andrade, Anthony C
Independence HS
San Jose, CA

Andrade, Lucia H
Santiago HS
Santa Ana, CA

Andrade, Norma
Amos Alonzo Stagg
Stockton, CA

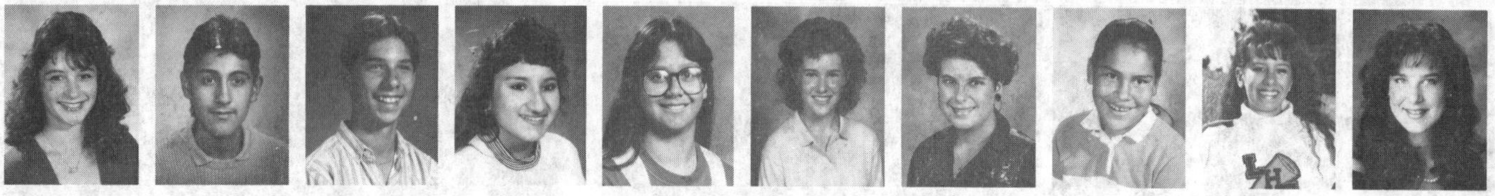

Andrade, Normas A
St Paul HS
Whittier, CA

Andrade, Ruben
Le Grand HS
Le Grand, CA

Andrade, Shawn M
Woodland HS
Woodland, CA

Andrade, Trini M
Brawley Union HS
Brawley, CA

Andraka, Valerie T
Sierra Vista HS
Baldwin Park, CA

Andre, Jennifer C
Louisville HS
Woodland Hills, CA

Andreacchi, Kristen
Ramona HS
Ramona, CA

Andreas, Rebecca
Lee Vining HS
Lee Vining, CA

Andreski, Cindy
Livermore HS
Livermore, CA

Andrews, Alesha
Rio Mesa HS
Camarillo, CA

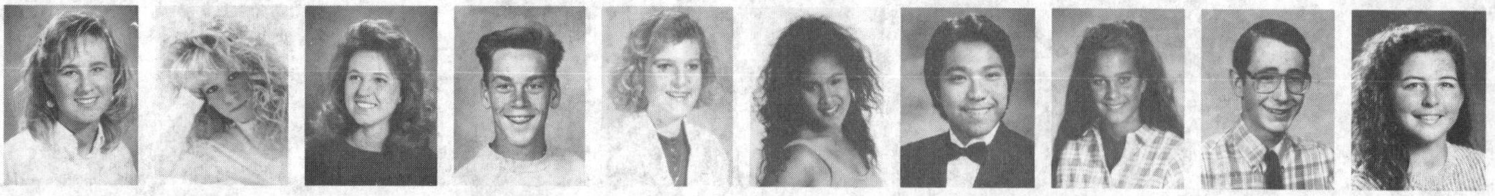

Andrews, Lisa M
Mater Dei HS
Tustin, CA

Andrews, Lisa
Michelle Lauren
San Marcos HS
Santa Barbara, CA

Andrews, Lisa R
Westminster HS
Westminster, CA

Andrus, Jared
Grossmont HS
El Cajon, CA

Andrus, Jennifer L
Lemoore HS
Lemoore, CA

Ang, Venus S
Bonita Vista HS
Coronado, CA

Angelito, Robert S
Pittsburg HS
Pittsburg, CA

Angelopoulos, Crystal
Notre Dame HS
Riverside, CA

Angle, Chris
Calvary Baptist Schl
Suisun, CA

Anglin, Tonya L
Tehachapi HS
Tehachapi, CA

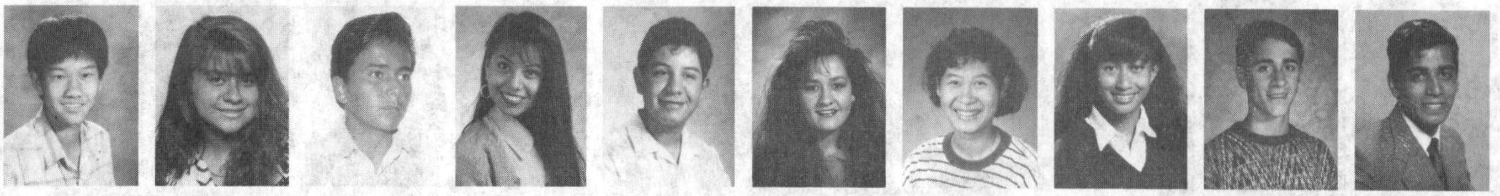

Angsupanich, Kahn
Clear Lake HS
Lakeport, CA

Anguiano, Jennifer
Gladstone HS
Azusa, CA

Angulo, Francisco
Sweetwater HS
National City, CA

Angulo, Janel J
Notre Dame HS
San Jose, CA

Angulo, Roberto
Sweetwater HS
National City, CA

Aniversario, Christina
Edison HS
Huntington Beach,
CA

Ann, Ly
Milpitas HS
Milpitas, CA

Antenorcruz,
Charlene A
Providence HS
Burbank, CA

Anter, Gary
South Tahoe HS
So Lake Tahoe, CA

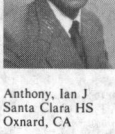

Anthony, Ian J
Santa Clara HS
Oxnard, CA

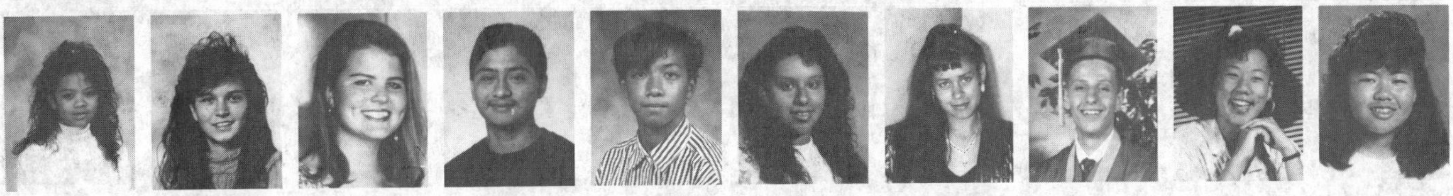

Antigua, Beverly H
James Logan HS
Union City, CA

Antillon, Rosemary
Montclair HS
Montclair, CA

Antola, Jessica C
Marymount HS
Los Angeles, CA

Antonico, Jose L
Buena HS
Ventura, CA

Antonio, Orlando M
Daniel Murphy
Catholic HS
Los Angeles, CA

Antuna, Maria R
Indio HS
Indio, CA

Anzaldo, Maria
Woodrow Wilson HS
Los Angeles, CA

Anzoategui, Mark R
Diamond Bar HS
Moreno Valley, CA

Aoki, Stacy M
Woodland HS
Woodland, CA

Aoki, Stephanie
North Torrance HS
Torrance, CA

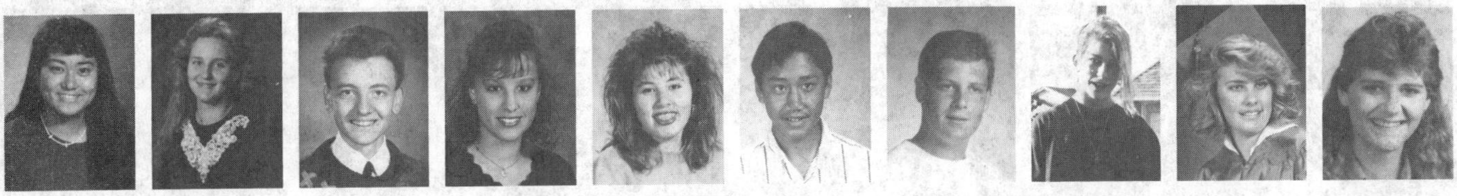

Aoyama, Jennifer M
Davis SR HS
Davis, CA

Apahidean, Iaiela
Magnolia HS
Anaheim, CA

Apahidean, Olimpiu
Savanna HS
Anaheim, CA

Aparicio, Anna M
Bishop Amat
Memorial HS
Baldwin Park, CA

Aparicio, Araceli
J Eugene Mc Ateer
San Francisco, CA

Apilado, Darrell M
Cabrillo HS
Vandenberg Afb, CA

Appelbaum, Jeff F
Rio Americano HS
Carmichael, CA

Applegate, Deborah
Milpitas HS
Milpitas, CA

Applegate, Diane
Yvonne
Desert Christian HS
Indio, CA

Applegate, Traci D
Coalinga HS
Coalinga, CA

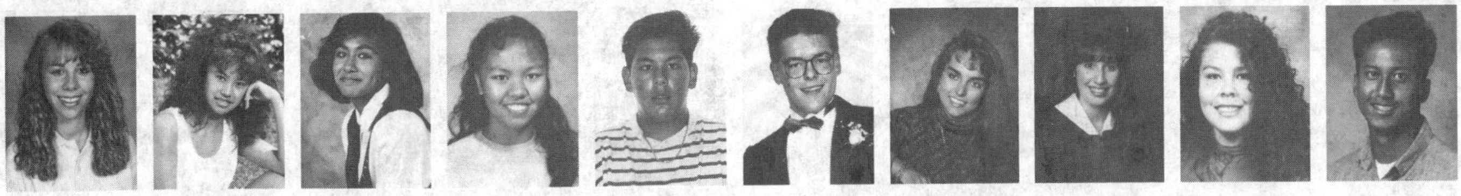

Aquilino, Noelle
Louisville HS
Woodland Hills, CA

Aquino, Novelyn
Lincoln HS
Stockton, CA

Aquino, Veronica C
Calexico HS
Calexico, CA

Aragon, Eliza G
Pomona Adventist JR
Acad
Ontario, CA

Aragon, Ruben R
Downey HS
South Gate, CA

Araiza, Gus M
Hemet HS
Hemet, CA

Araiza, Jennifer J
Central Union HS
El Centro, CA

Aram, Jessica R
Glendale HS
Burbank, CA

Arambula, Blanca E
Bell Gardens HS
Bell Gardens, CA

Arambulo, Jayjay
Chaminade College
Prep
Chatsworth, CA

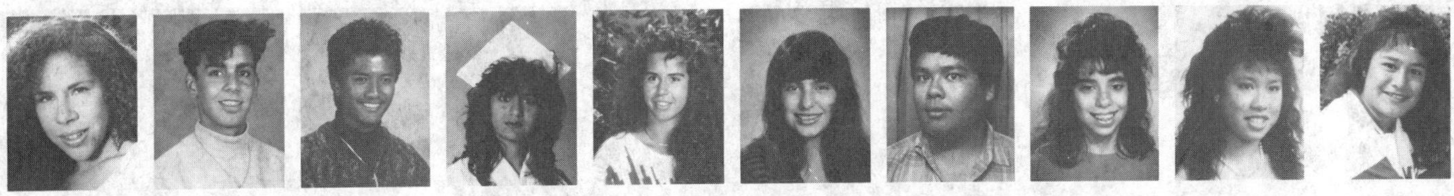

Arancibia, Denise V
Westlake HS
Westlake Village, CA

Aranda, Miguel A
Leffingwell Christian
Norwalk, CA

Arante, Richard J
James Logan HS
Union City, CA

Aratounians, Ani B
Holy Martyrs
Ferrahian HS
Reseda, CA

Araujo, Martha A
El Toro HS
El Toro, CA

Araujo, Nancy
Francis Polytechnic
Arleta, CA

Araullo, Francis
Bellarmine Col Prep
Belmont, CA

Arauto, Jackie M
Polytechnic HS
Arleta, CA

Arayata, Marissa
Castle Park HS
Chula Vista, CA

Arballo, Natalie B
Madera HS
Madera, CA

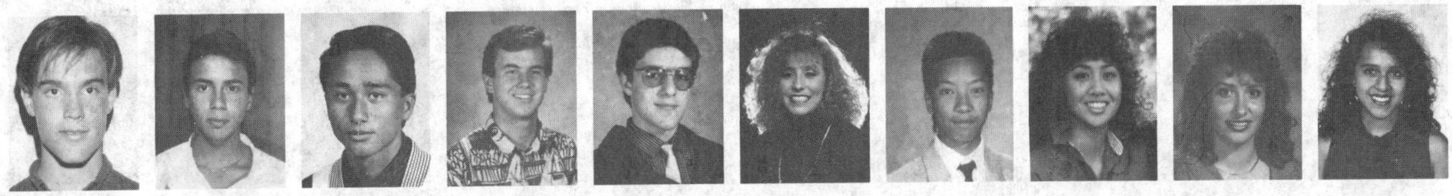

Arbaugh, Joshua A
Eureka HS
Eureka, CA

Arce, William
Los Angeles HS
Los Angeles, CA

Arceo, Peter S
Santa Clara HS
Oxnard, CA

Archer, Ryan
Hesperia Christian
Hesperia, CA

Archouniani, Ara H
International Studies
Acad
San Francisco, CA

Archuleta, Frankie
Salinas HS
Salinas, CA

Arcia, Rovil P
St Ignatius Coll Prep
Daly City, CA

Arcinas, Regina L
Salinas HS
Salinas, CA

Arechiga, Cassandra
Calvary Chapel HS
Midway City, CA

Arellano, Alicia
Nogales HS
La Puente, CA

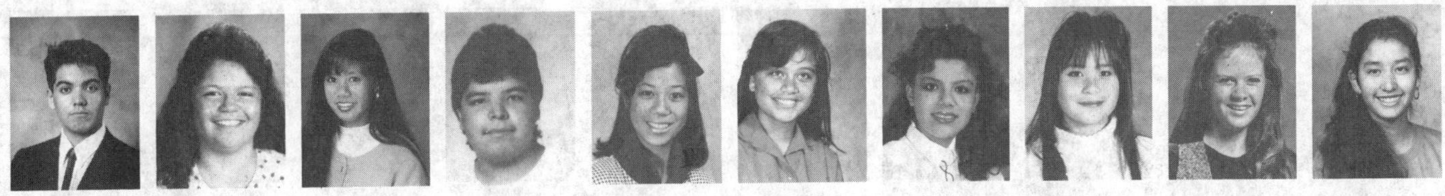

Arellano, Giovanny
Pioneer HS
Whittier, CA

Arellano, Jakkie C
Manteca HS
Manteca, CA

Arellano, Joanne M
Montgomery HS
San Diego, CA

Arellano, Juan R
Roosevelt HS
Los Angeles, CA

Arellano, Myra
Bishop Amat HS
Diamond Bar, CA

Arellano, Patricia E
Bell Gardens HS
Bell Gardens, CA

Arenas, Audrey
Bishop Amat HS
Ontario, CA

Arenas, Pamela C
Lowell HS
San Francisco, CA

Arentz, Lisa Ann
Fontana HS
Fontana, CA

Arias, Christina M
Patrick Henry/
Francis Parker HS
San Diego, CA

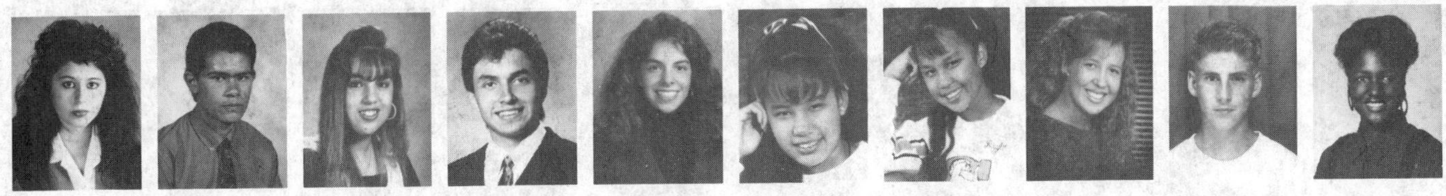

Arias, Luz C
Regina Caeli HS
Compton, CA

Arias, Michael A
Santa Clara HS
Oxnard, CA

Arias, Star
Rialto JR HS
Rialto, CA

Armendariz, Cesar
Rosemead HS
Rosemead, CA

Armi, Theresia
Golden West HS
Visalia, CA

Armour, Melanie A
Sacred Heart HS
Los Angeles, CA

Armour, Raylene S
Sacred Heart HS
Los Angeles, CA

Armour, Wendi
Helix HS
Lemon Grove, CA

Armstrong, Chad P
Highlands HS
N Highlands, CA

Armstrong, Danielle
Long Beach
Polytechnic HS
Longbeach, CA

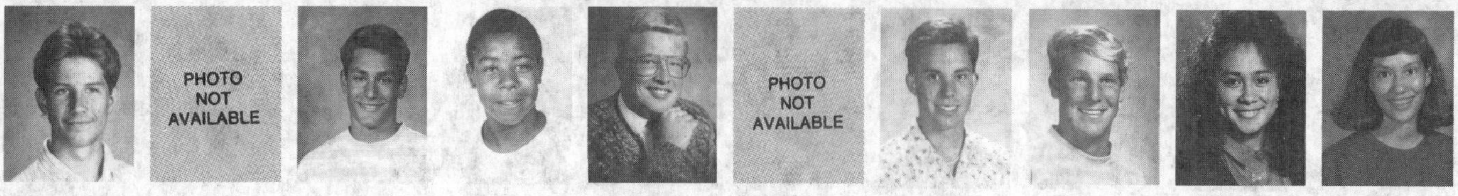

Armstrong, Steven T
Merced HS
Merced, CA

Arnall, Julianne L
Coronado HS
Coronado, CA

Arnas, Burak E
El Camino HS
Sacramento, CA

Arnett, Sherman
Antioch SR HS
Antioch, CA

Arnold, Joshua
San Gorgonio HS
San Bernardino, CA

Arnold, La Tonya R
Stagg HS
Stockton, CA

Arnold, Matthew P
Moorpark HS
Moorpark, CA

Aronen, Chad
Poway HS
Poway, CA

Arraiga, Marcela
Hawthorne HS
Lennox, CA

Arredondo, Arlene
Moore JR HS
Redlands, CA

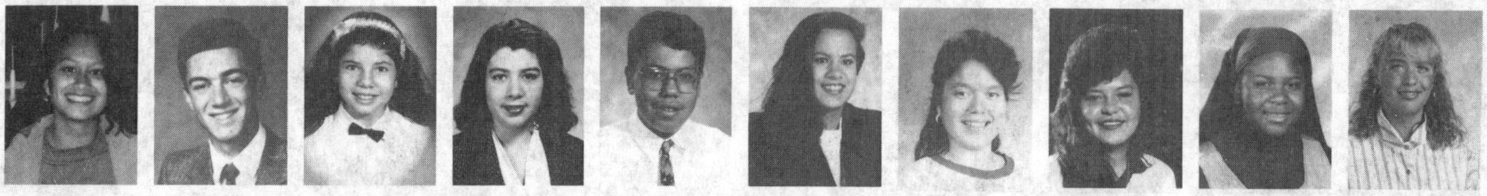

Arrieta, Sandra
Westmoor HS
San Francisco, CA

Arrington, Erik
Van Nuys Math/
Science Magnet HS
Sepulveda, CA

Arrizon, Olivia
Bolsa Grande HS
Garden Grove, CA

Arroyo, Dinora
El Rancho HS
Pico Rivera, CA

Arroyo, Gregory
Don Bosco Technical
Inst
Montebello, CA

Arruda, Leah
Cabrillo HS
Acushnet, MA

Arteche, Heidi J
Whittier Christian
Downey, CA

Arzate, Irma
Savanna HS
Anaheim, CA

Asadullah, Efuru F
King Drew Medical
Magnet HS
Los Angeles, CA

Asantewa, Tia
Milpitas HS
San Jose, CA

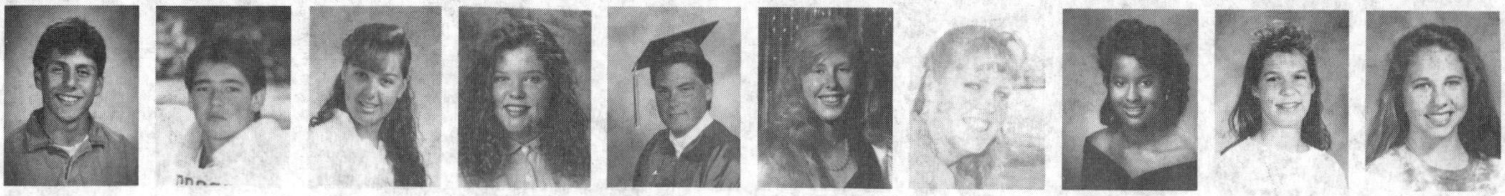

Asaro, Matthew I
Casa Grande HS
Petaluma, CA

Asbell, Rick
Manteca HS
Manteca, CA

Ascunsion, Nichole
Notre Dame HS
Santa Clara, CA

Asdel, Robyn L
Ventura HS
Ventura, CA

Asencio, Scott
William C Overfelt
San Jose, CA

Ashby, Dianne E
Pioneer HS
San Jose, CA

Ashby, Karyn
Abraham Lincoln HS
San Jose, CA

Ashby-Wallace, Karla
Junipero Serra HS
San Diego, CA

Ashford, Dana L
Riverdale HS
Five Points, CA

Ashford, Kristen
Los Alamitos HS
Cypress, CA

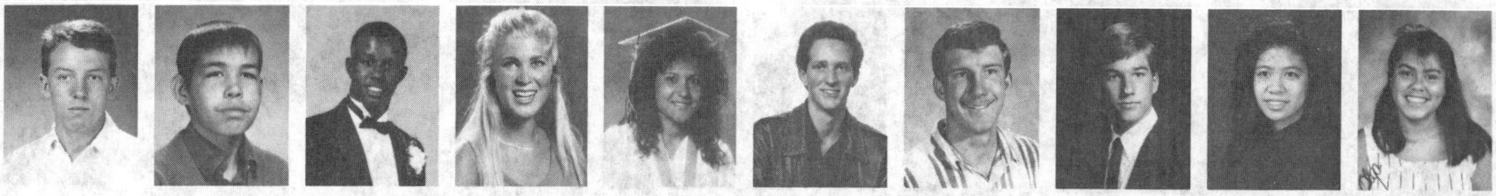

Ashland, Aron W
Alhambra HS
Martinez, CA

Ashley, Eric
Pinole Valley HS
Pinole, CA

Ashley, III Leo
St Bernards HS
Gardena, CA

Ashworth, Britin
Mayfield SR HS
South Pasadena, CA

Asmar, Jennifer
Kearny Stephen
Watts HS
San Diego, CA

Asselin, Stewart
Clovis HS
Clovis, CA

Asselstine, Jason N
Arroyo Grande HS
Santa Maria, CA

Astin, Richard A
Glendora HS
Glendora, CA

Astorga, Grace F
De Anza HS
Richmond, CA

Astorga, Olga L
San Marcos HS
Santa Barbara, CA

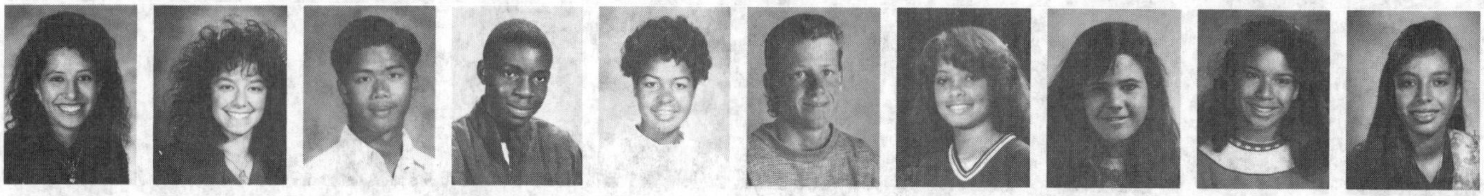

Astorga,
Yesenia-Lizette C
Foothill HS
Tustin, CA

Atherton, Elisa N
North HS
Bakersfield, CA

Atienza, Ely
Los Alamitos HS
Los Alamitos, CA

Atkins, Quixote D
Skyline HS
Oakland, CA

Atkins, Zemia A
St Bernard Catholic
Los Angeles, CA

Atkinson, Brian D
Camarillo HS
Camarillo, CA

Atkinson, Shauna
Westchester HS
Los Angeles, CA

Atkission, Colleen
Edison HS
Fresno, CA

Ato, Gladys
Turlock HS
Turlock, CA

Atondo, Christine A
Los Amigos HS
Fountain Valley, CA

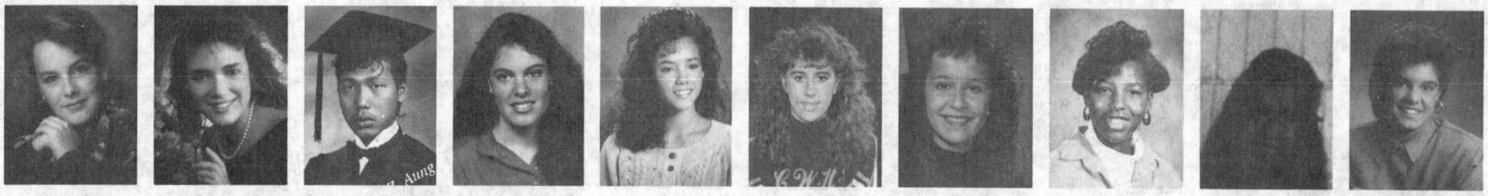

Auckland, Alex
Granite Hills HS
El Cajon, CA

Aufdermaur, Karen
East Union HS
Manteca, CA

Aung, Kyaw Z
Pittsburg HS
Pittsburg, CA

Ausonio, Tirzah
Mira Mesa HS
San Diego, CA

Austin, Lisa M
Norco HS
Norco, CA

Austin, Stacey
Leanne
Clovis West HS
Fresno, CA

Austin, Stephanie M
Irvine HS
Irvine, CA

Austin, Tina M
Santa Ana HS
Santa Ana, CA

Avalos, Guadalupe
Saddleback HS
Santa Ana, CA

Avansino, Karen
Linden HS
Linden, CA

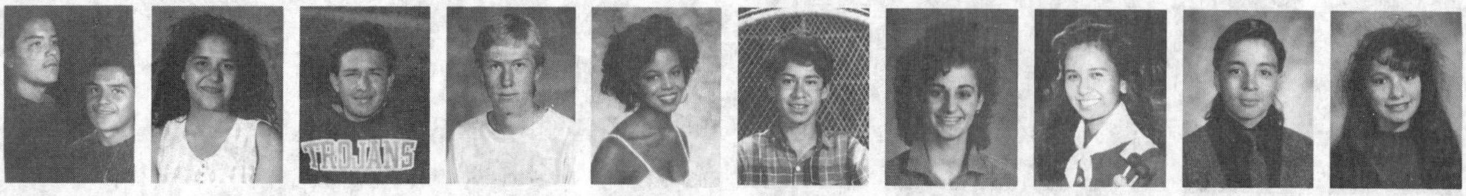

Avelar, Carlos
Birmingham HS
Sepulveda, CA

Avelar, Vanessa
La Mirada HS
La Mirada, CA

Aversa, Adam J
Yucca Valley HS
Yucca Valley, CA

Avery, Brian
San Marcos HS
Santa Barbara, CA

Avery, Libra J
Immaculate Heart
Los Angeles, CA

Avila, Albert D
Chaffey HS
Clovis, NM

Avila, Debbie F
Tulare Union HS
Tulare, CA

Aviles, Ann Marie L
Independence HS
San Jose, CA

Avitia, Jr Humberto
Oakland HS
Oakland, CA

Avitia, Maria A
Costa Mesa HS
Costa Mesa, CA

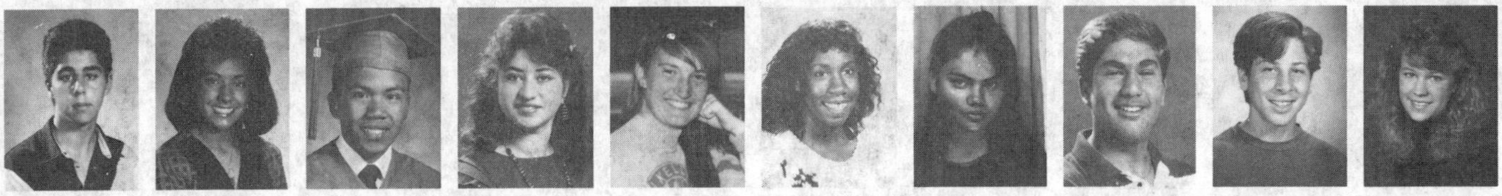

Avitsian, Edwin
Glendale Adventist Academy
Glendale, CA

Avril, Michelle
Crescenta Valley HS
Montrose, CA

Awayan, Wilmer
Saint Joseph Notre Dame HS
Alameda, CA

Ayad, Gihan S
Burbank HS
Burbank, CA

Ayers, Kelly
El Camino Real HS
West Hills, CA

Ayers, Nichele L
Hogan SR HS
Vallejo, CA

Ayon, Lorena
George Washington Prep HS
Los Angeles, CA

Azar, Tarek
Coast Christian HS
Redondo Beach, CA

Azevedo, Anthony A
Montgomery HS
Santa Rosa, CA

Azevedo, Christina
Beyer HS
Ceres, CA

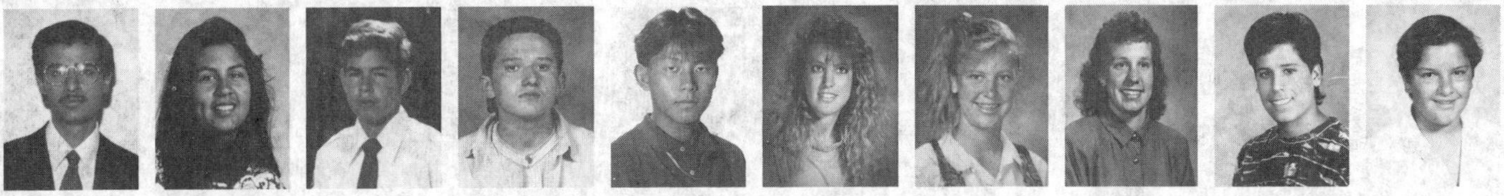

Azizadah, Tamim
Savanna HS
Anaheim, CA

Aznaran, Vanessa E
Abraham Lincoln HS
San Jose, CA

Azpeitia, Jason D
Mater Dei HS
West Covina, CA

Azrilyar, Stanley
University HS
Los Angeles, CA

Baba, Hirokazu
Torrey Pines HS
San Diego, CA

Babcock, Glynis S
Mount Shasta HS
Mount Shasta, CA

Babic, Jennifer I
Mission Viejo HS
Mission Viejo, CA

Babione, Julie A
Poway HS
Poway, CA

Baca, III Gilbert
San Pasqual HS
Escondido, CA

Baca, Jr Richard E
Ribet Acad
Glendale, CA

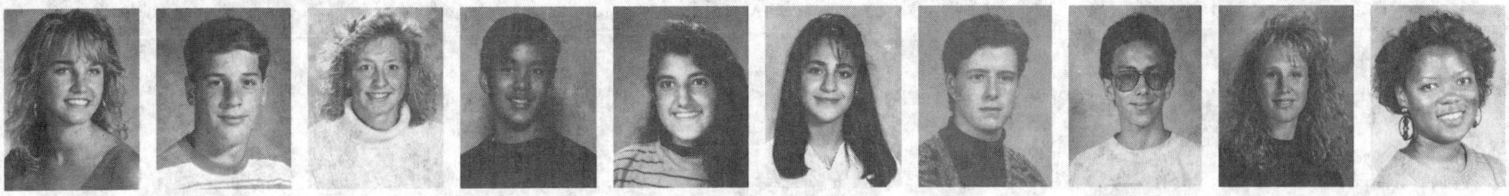

Bachwick, Amy
Palm Springs HS
Palm Springs, CA

Bacigalupi, Matt T
Burlingame HS
Burlingame, CA

Backer, Melissa K
Clovis West HS
Fresno, CA

Bacus, Melanio M
Woodland HS
Woodland, CA

Bagherian, Elham
Novato HS
Novato, CA

Baghoomian, Carolin
Holy Martyrs Ferrahian HS
Encino, CA

Bagley, Marcus A
La Quinta HS
Westminster, CA

Bagoon, Samuel H
Bella Vista HS
Citrus Hts, CA

Bagwill, Patti D
Serrano HS
Phelan, CA

Bailey, Ahbra C
Robert A Millikan
Long Beach, CA

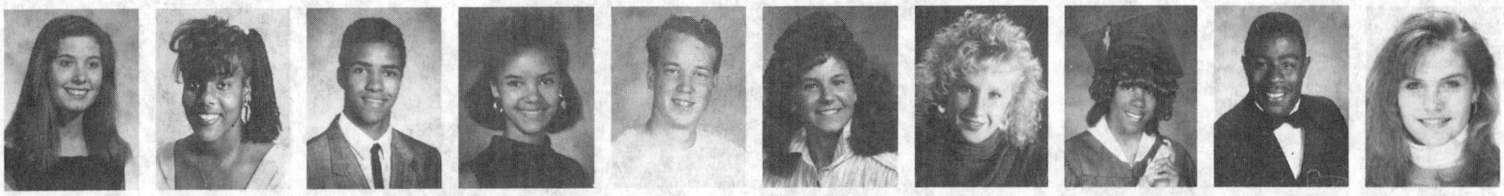

Bailey, Angi G
Enterprise HS
Redding, CA

Bailey, April N
Bishop Amat Memorial HS
Los Angeles, CA

Bailey, David J
Mission Viejo HS
Mission Viejo, CA

Bailey, Eddi R
Mission Viejo HS
Mission Viejo, CA

Bailey, Eric
Yosemite HS
Coarsegold, CA

Bailey, Jennifer G
Woodland HS
Woodland, CA

Baird, Jennifer
Palm Desert HS
Palm Desert, CA

Bakeer, Akilah
Dorsey HS
Los Angeles, CA

Baker, II Bobby L
Granada HS
Livermore, CA

Baker, Colleen M
Orange Lutheran HS
Santa Ana, CA

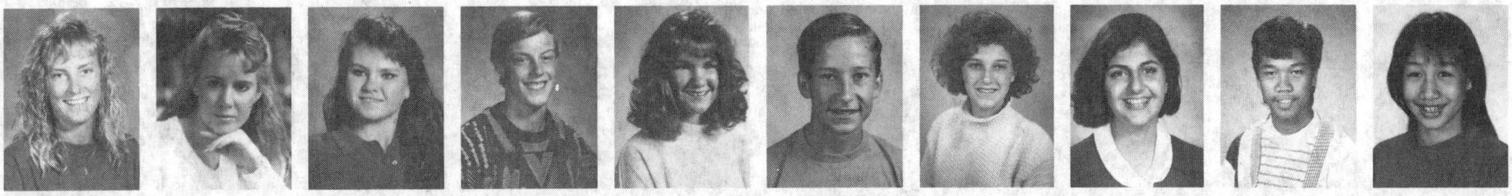

Baker, Jennifer
Los Alamitos HS
Los Alamitos, CA

Baker, Jennifer L
Escondido Adventist Acad
Escondido, CA

Baker, Joni L
Viejo HS
Mission Viejo, CA

Baker, Joshua D
Modoc HS
Alturas, CA

Baker, Laureen Kelly
Hesperia HS
Hesperia, CA

Baker, Matthew J
Winters HS
Winters, CA

Baker, Nichole K
Rio Lindo Adventist Acad
Chico, CA

Bakhtiari, Manijeh
Lycee Francais De L A HS
Studio City, CA

Balagtas, Glenn
Woodrow Wilson HS
San Francisco, CA

Balancio, Leilani G
John A Rowland HS
Rowland Heights, CA

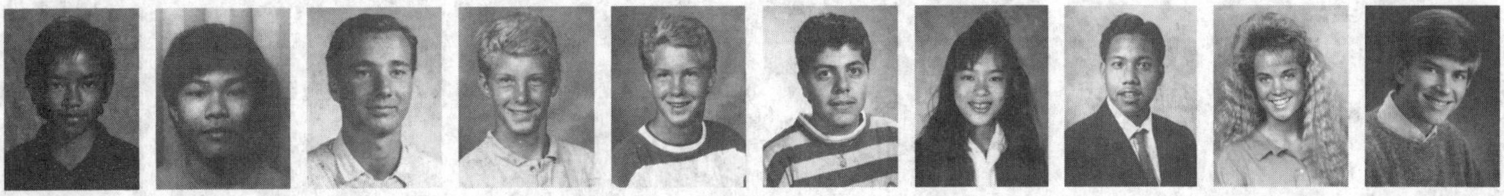

Balbin, John M
Mt Pleasant HS
San Jose, CA

Baldonado, Jaime B
Mayfair HS
Bellflower, CA

Baldwin, Mark P
Edison Computech
Fresno, CA

Baldwin, Matthew C
Escondido HS
Escondido, CA

Baldwin, Michael S
Escondido HS
Escondido, CA

Balikian, Sevag
Pasadena HS
Pasadena, CA

Balingit, Christine R
Sacred Heart-Cathedral HS
Rodeo, CA

Balingit, Peter P
Pioneer HS
Whittier, CA

Ball, Carisa L
Valhalla HS
El Cajon, CA

Ball, David Andrew
Analy HS
Rohnert Park, CA

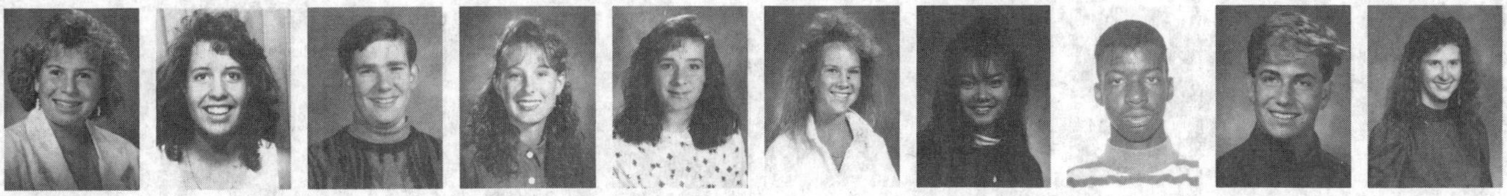

Ball, Jamie M
Laguna Hills HS
Laguna Hills, CA

Ball, Merae Christy
Del Oro HS
Loomis, CA

Ball, Shaun E
Golden West HS
Visalia, CA

Ball, Stephanie R
Marina HS
Huntington Beach, CA

Ballinger, Kimberly
Pioneer Baptist HS
Long Beach, CA

Balogh, Michelle M
Canyon Springs HS
Riverside, CA

Balon, Jennifer G
St Rose Acad
Daly City, CA

Baloney, Aaron Edward
Bellarmine College Prep
Milpitas, CA

Balsamo, Edward J
Irvine HS
Irvine, CA

Balske, Michelle L
Clovis HS
Fresno, CA

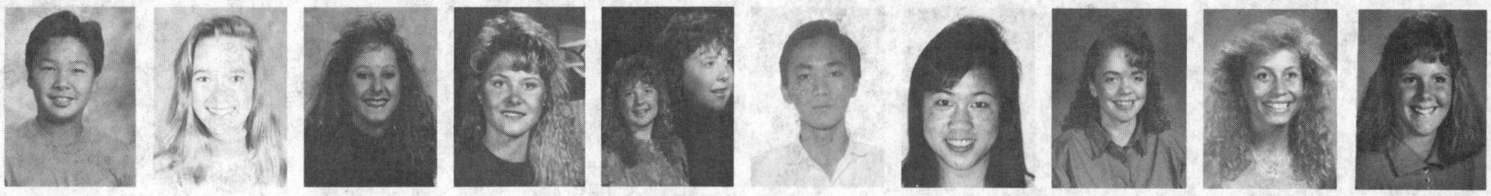

Baltazar, Dominic
Harvard Schl
Culvercity, CA

Balthrop-Lewis, Amara
Lowell HS
Tallahassee, FL

Bane, Leslie
Amador HS
Pine Grove, CA

Banet-Rummell, Lashel
Tri-City Christian
Oceanside, CA

Bangs, Elizabeth T
Sunny Hills HS
Fullerton, CA

Banh, Cau
Mark Keppel HS
Rosemead, CA

Banh, Virginia N
Schurr HS
Monterey Park, CA

Banks, Dawn
Grace M Davis HS
Modesto, CA

Banks, Michelle Lisette
Central Union HS
El Centro, CA

Banks, Mitzie M
Bret Harte Union HS
Angels Camp, CA

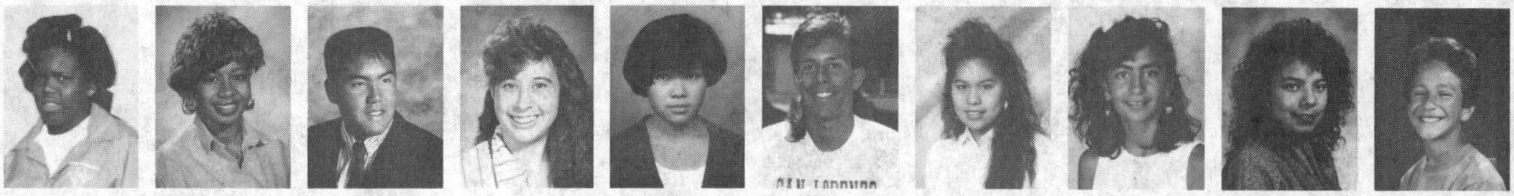

Banks, Nzingha
Canyon Springs HS
Moreno Valley, CA

Banks, Shronda
Washington Prep HS
Los Angeles, CA

Bannai, Hidejiro A
San Marino HS
San Marino, CA

Banner, Kelly M
Paraclete HS
Palmdale, CA

Bao, Thuy Nguyen
Hoover HS
San Diego, CA

Baptista, Bartholomew Leandro Z
San Lorenzo HS
Hayward, CA

Baptista, Cheryl
St Patrick-St Vincent
Vallejo, CA

Baradaran, Yas
Novato HS
Novato, CA

Barajas, Melinda
San Gabriel HS
San Gabriel, CA

Barba, Oscar
Southwest HS
San Diego, CA

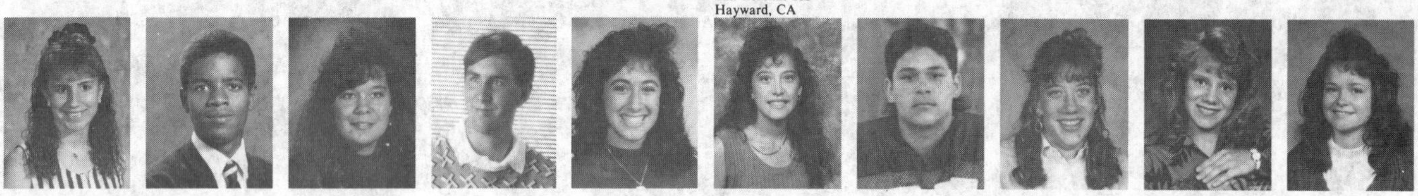

Barbeau, Shari L
Mills HS
Millbrae, CA

Barbee, Steven K
Testimonial Christian Schl
Los Angeles, CA

Barbeiro, Alisha
Willows HS
Artois, CA

Barber, J Scott
Silver Valley HS
Newberry Spgs, CA

Barber, Stacie
Whittier Christian
Fullerton, CA

Barberi, Monica L
St Paul HS
Whittier, CA

Barbosa, Paul
Seaside HS
Fort Ord, CA

Barcus, Marina L
Rincon Valley Christian HS
Sebastopol, CA

Barese, Danielle
Yosemite HS
Coarsegold, CA

Barfield, Jenny
Rincon Valley Christian HS
Santa Rosa, CA

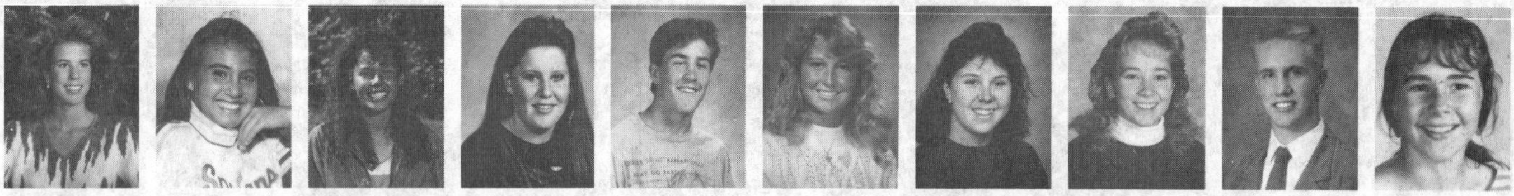

Bargiel, Wendy A
El Toro HS
El Toro, CA

Baril, Wilma N
Chula Vista HS
San Diego, CA

Barisdale, Michelle
Gahr HS
Cerritos, CA

Barka, Kristen A
Simi Valley HS
Simi Valley, CA

Barker, Jason C
Poway HS
Poway, CA

Barker, Karen L
Trabuco Hills HS
Mission Viejo, CA

Barker, Sandra L
Tulare Union HS
Tulare, CA

Barksdale, Denise M
Desert JR/SR HS
Edwards, CA

Barlow, Adam
Wm S Hart HS
Newhall, CA

Barlow, Erica S
Tokay HS
Stockton, CA

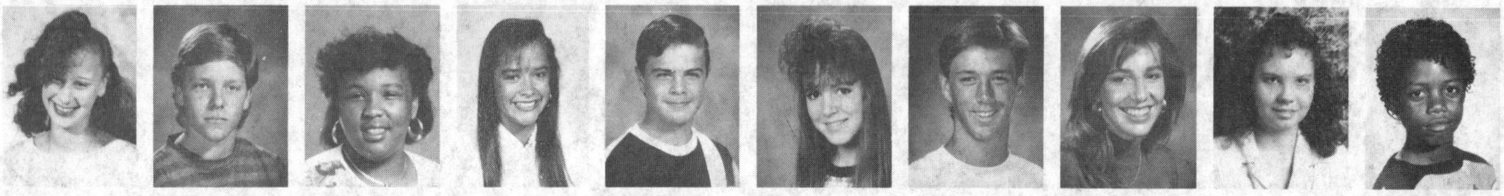

Barnard, Sweething
Far West HS
Oakland, CA

Barnes, Craig
Calvary Chapel HS
Westminster, CA

Barnes, Larece J
St Michaels Catholic Girls HS
Los Angeles, CA

Barnes, Lizabeth A
Notre Dame Academy Girls HS
Mar Vista, CA

Barnes, Mike S
Garden Grove HS
Garden Grove, CA

Barnes, Noelle V
Southern Cal Christian HS
Chino, CA

Barnes, Patrick M
Trabuca Hills HS
Mission Viejo, CA

Barnett, Carli K
San Dieguito HS
Olivenhain, CA

Barnhart, Tonja Renee
Desert Christian HS
Indio, CA

Barnwell, James
Compton HS
Compton, CA

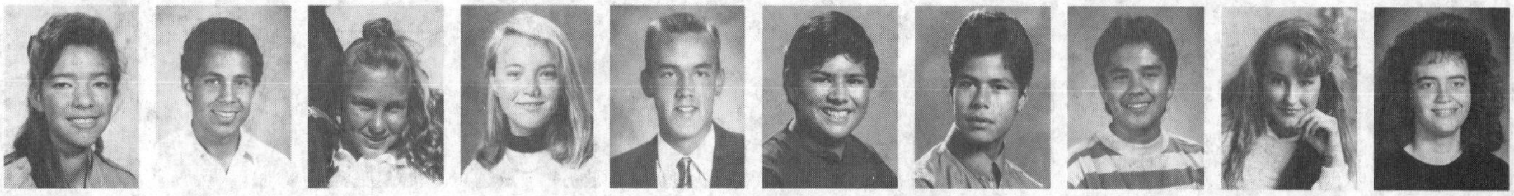

Baron, Helen
Rosary HS
Fullerton, CA

Barquero, Oscar A
Montebello HS
Montebello, CA

Barr, Cherise
Atascadero HS
Atascadero, CA

Barr, Danielle
Castle Park HS
Chula Vista, CA

Barr, Travis
Westminster HS
Westminster, CA

Barrales, Jorge
Bassett HS
La Puente, CA

Barreras, Able A
Benjamin Franklin
Los Angeles, CA

Barreras, Joseph
Palo Verde HS
Blythe, CA

Barrett, Tricia
Newport Christian
Westminster, CA

Barringer, Julie E
Sutter Union HS
Sutter, CA

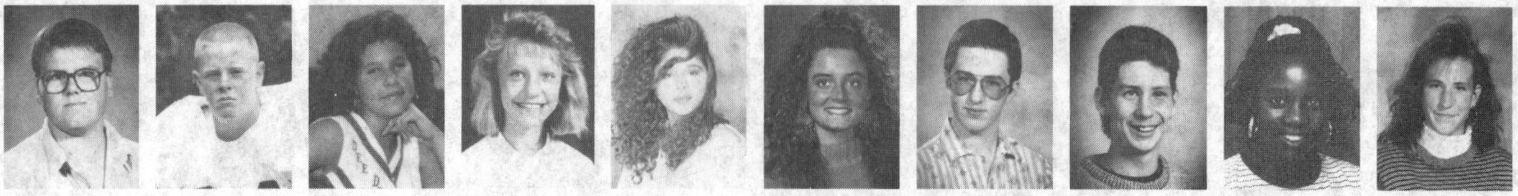

Barrington, Timothy
Norwalk HS
Norwalk, CA

Barrios, Kenneth M
Servite HS
Cerritos, CA

Barroeta, Diana L
Central Union HS
El Centro, CA

Barron, Nikki
Orangewood Adventist Acad
Fullerton, CA

Barroso, Lillian
John Marshall HS
Los Angeles, CA

Barry, Heather Lee
Irvine HS
Irvine, CA

Barry, II Robert N
Paraclete HS
Lancaster, CA

Barsanti, Scott
Fortuna Union HS
Rio Dell, CA

Bart-Plange, Margaret E
Etiwanda HS
Alta Loma, CA

Bartch, Shannon N
St Bernard HS
Los Angeles, CA

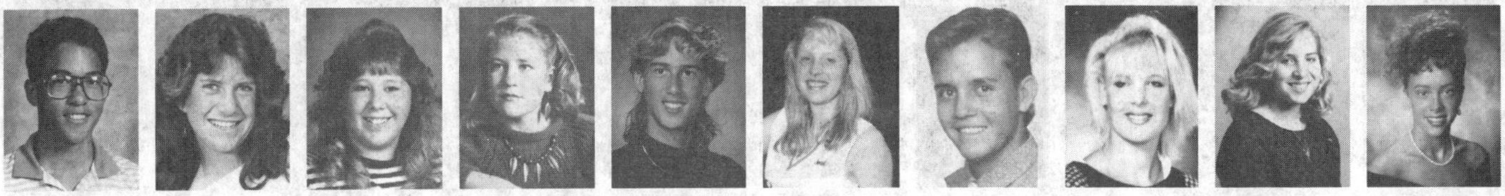

Bartek, Dominic C
29 Palms HS
Wahoo, NE

Barter, Wendy R
Hesperia HS
Victorville, CA

Barth, Melissa D
Fred C Beyer HS
Modesto, CA

Bartholomew, Mary
Yosemite Union HS
Oakhurst, CA

Bartlett, Ian J
Trabuco Hills HS
San Juan Capstrno, CA

Bartlett-Palacio, Jennifer
Delta HS
Marysville, CA

Bartolini, Albert
Sonora HS
Fullerton, CA

Bartosh Medina, Melissa
Trabuco Hills HS
Orange, CA

Bartsch, Elli D
Clovis HS
Fresno, CA

Bartz, Jody
West Valley Christian
Canoga Park, CA

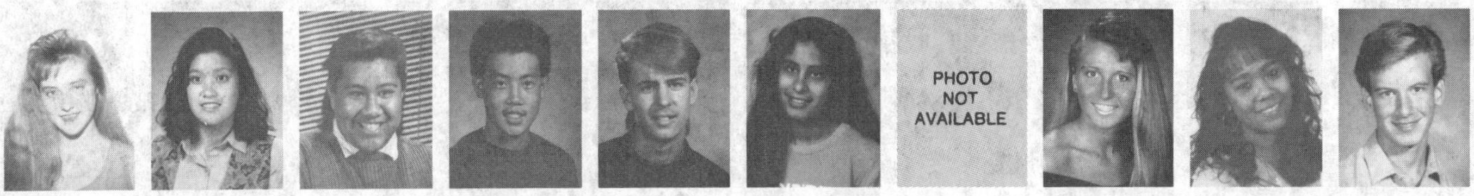
PHOTO
NOT
AVAILABLE

Bartz, Laura C
Patrick Henry HS
San Diego, CA

Basa, Nicole
Mt Eden HS
Hayward, CA

Basconcillo, Chris
San Fernando Valley Acad
Sepulveda, CA

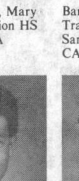

Bascos, Artemio
Sacred Heart Prep
East Palo Alto, CA

Bash, Chris L
Bloomington HS
Bloomington, CA

Basho, Shruti
Armijo HS
Fairfield, CA

Basquin, Ashley
Moorpark HS
Moorpark, CA

Bassett, Jana
Archbishop Mitty HS
San Jose, CA

Batacan, Catherine B
Reedley HS
Reedley, CA

Batarse, Rodolfo
Poway HS
San Diego, CA

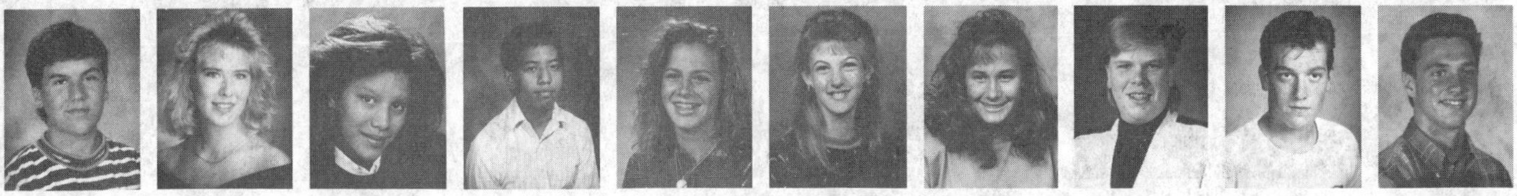

Bates, Dan P
El Camino HS
Oceanside, CA

Bathke, Erika L
Rio Mesa HS
Camarillo, CA

Batiste, Stephanie L
Westlake School For Girls
Los Angeles, CA

Batong, Abraham B
Monterey Bay Acad
Milpitas, CA

Battaglia, Adria I
Foothill HS
Pleasanton, CA

Battles, Heather J
O'farrell Schl Creatv Prfrmg Arts
San Diego, CA

Batts, Justine P
El Cajon Valley HS
El Cajon, CA

Baty, Jerry V
Panorama Christian Schl
Yucaipa, CA

Baty, Scott S
Delta HS
Courtland, CA

Bauer, Paul J
Bullard HS
Fresno, CA

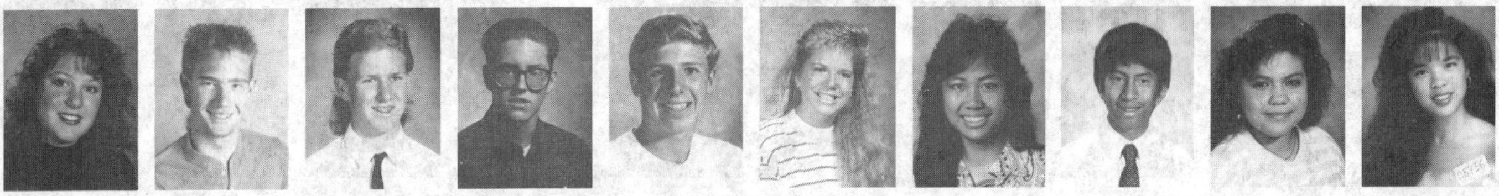

Baugh, Valerie
Yuba City HS
Yuba City, CA

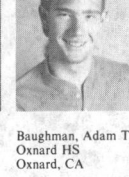

Baughman, Adam T
Oxnard HS
Oxnard, CA

Baum, Kelly C
Sutter Union HS
Sutter, CA

Bauman, Jason N
Newbury Park Acad
Northridge, CA

Baumann, Kip A
Lompoc HS
Lompoc, CA

Baurmann, Heidi M
Corona HS
Corona, CA

Bautista, Dulce R
Sweetwater HS
National City, CA

Bautista, Joseph Lauengco
Don Bosco Technical Inst
Upland, CA

Bautista, Nora R
Indio HS
Indio, CA

Bautista, Winzella
Southwest HS
San Diego, CA

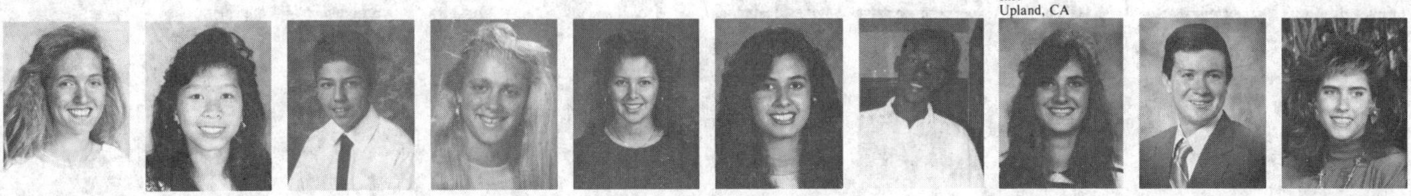

Bayless, Jenifer N
Nogales HS
West Covina, CA

Baysac, Fatima S
Lowell HS
San Francisco, CA

Bazan, Phil Patrick
Loyola HS
Whittier, CA

Beach, Ruth M
Escondido Adventist Acad
Fallbrook, CA

Beacom, Jean J
Grace M Davis HS
Modesto, CA

Beagles, Gina M
Washington HS
Fremont, CA

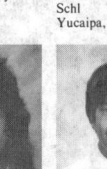

Beal, Benjamin J
Hesperia HS
Hesperia, CA

Beal, Carol A
Folsom HS
Folsom, CA

Bealer, Chris S
Chaffey HS
Upland, CA

Bean, Jeni Liane
San Clemente HS
San Clemente, CA

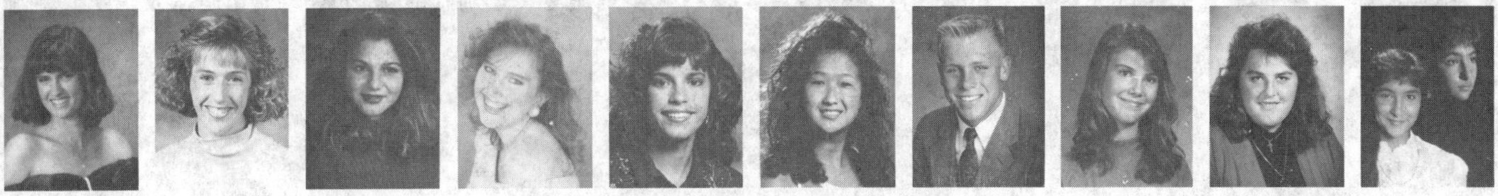

Bean, Lisa
Shasta HS
Redding, CA

Beard, Krista D
Whittier Christian
Yorba Linda, CA

Bearden, Jodi G
Clovis West HS
Fresno, CA

Beaton, Stephanie A
Oxnard Union HS
Port Hueneme, CA

Beauchamp, Awilda Judith
Fontana HS
Fontana, CA

Beauchamp, Kim
Village Christian Schl
Sun Valley, CA

Beauer, Clint L
Canyon HS
Canyon Country, CA

Beaver, Krista A
John North HS
Riverside, CA

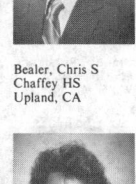

Beaver, Nicole M
Ukiah Unified HS
Willits, CA

Bebawi, Jihan
St Monica Catholic
Los Angeles, CA

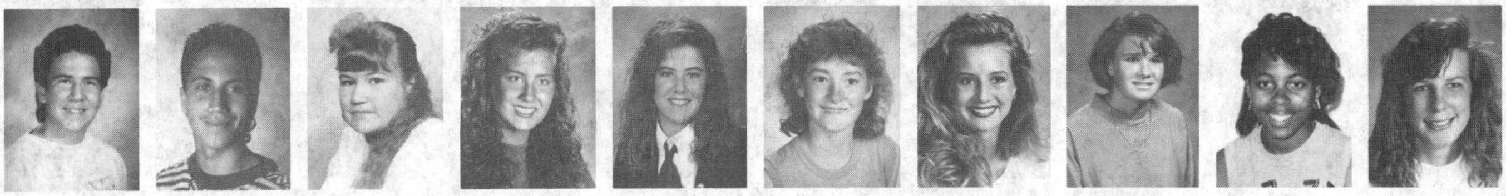

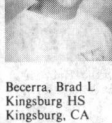

Becerra, Brad L
Kingsburg HS
Kingsburg, CA

Becerra, David
Southwest HS
San Ysidro, CA

Beck, Ann M
North Salinas HS
Salinas, CA

Beck, Carrie E
Tustin HS
Tustin, CA

Beck, Crystal Y
Viewpoint Schl
Agoura Hills, CA

Beck, Jennifer C
Tulare Union HS
Earlimart, CA

Beck, Kasi D
Tulare Union HS
Tulare, CA

Beck, Kelly L
Moreno Valley HS
Moreno Valley, CA

Beck, Tasha C.
Millikan HS
Long Beach, CA

Beck, Tracy K
Bret Harte HS
Vallecito, CA

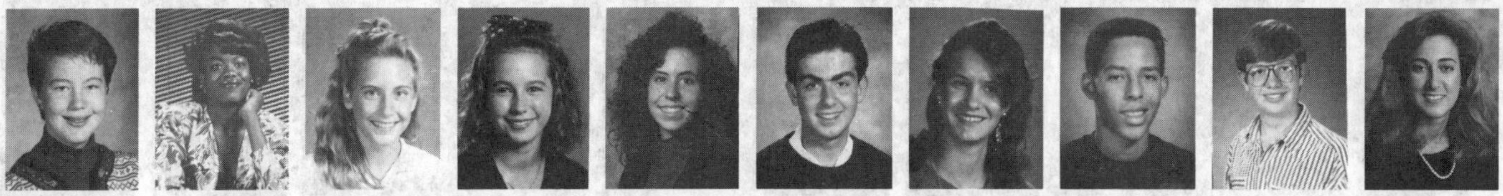

Beckham, Cristin T
Mountain View HS
Mountain View, CA

Beckham, Didi
Chula Vista HS
San Ysidro, CA

Beckley, Casey Ann
Bishop Montgomery
Redondo Beach, CA

Beckmann, Bianca G
Norte Vista HS
Riverside, CA

Beckner, Amy
West Valley Christian
Woodland Hills, CA

Becris, Nick P
Leffingwell Christian
La Mirada, CA

Bedford, Jennifer R
Rancho Cotate HS
Rohnert Park, CA

Bedgood, Bill
William S Hart HS
Valencia, CA

Bednar, Joby Seth
San Rafael HS
San Rafael, CA

Bedrosian, Michelle L
San Marino HS
San Marino, CA

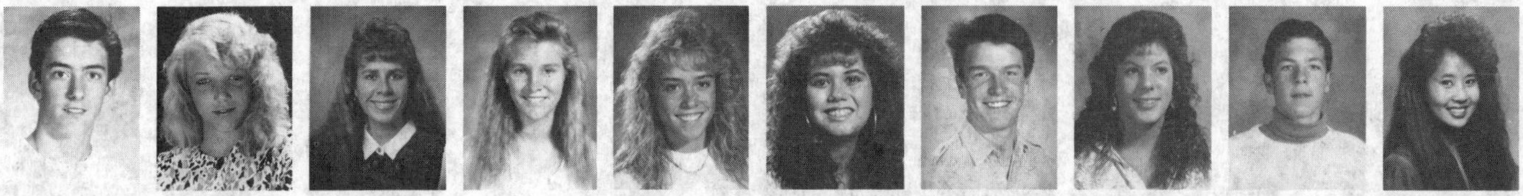

Beedy, Travis D
Chino HS
Chino, CA

Beeman, Dawn M
Victor Valley HS
Victorville, CA

Beer, Sarah S
Alta Loma HS
Rancho Cucamonga, CA

Beery, Marianna D
La Habra HS
Whittier, CA

Beesley, Chenoa A
Monrovia HS
Monrovia, CA

Beetschen, Barbi J
Rim Of The World
Crestline, CA

Behunin, Jonathan Ray
Fountain Valley HS
Westminster, CA

Belcher, Marcia
Lemoore HS
Lemoore, CA

Beld, Brian R
Mt Whitney HS
Visalia, CA

Beligan, Christine M
Notre Dame Acad
Los Angeles, CA

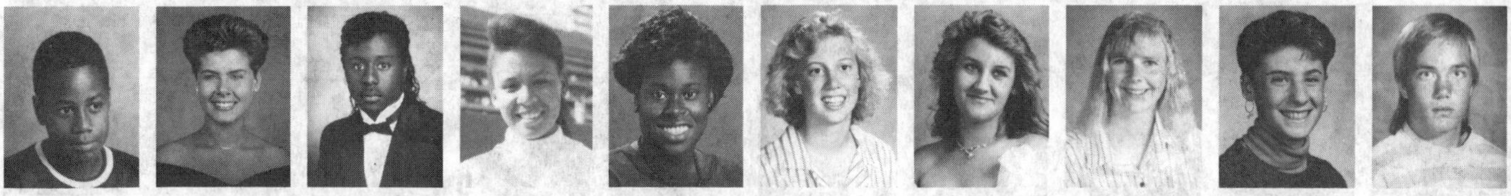

Bell, Alfonzo M
Balboa HS
San Francisco, CA

Bell, Charissa L
Los Alamitos HS
Stanton, CA

Bell, Damon Amiri
Morse HS
San Diego, CA

Bell, Dhanna M
Bloomington HS
Bloomington, CA

Bell, Keyla
Santa Monica HS
Santa Monica, CA

Bell, Melissa
Tulare Union HS
Tulare, CA

Bell, Michelle
West Shores HS
Salton City, CA

Bell, Penny J
Oakdale HS
Oakdale, CA

Bellacera, Althea D
Dixon HS
Dixon, CA

Bellamy, Reno F
Huntington Beach
Huntington Beach, CA

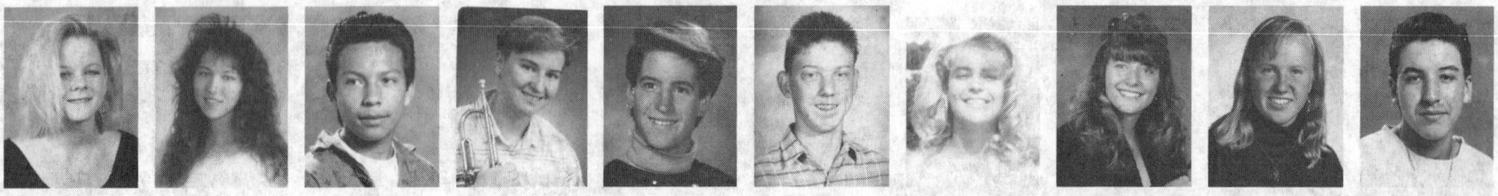

Belmont, Tobi M
Mesa Verde HS
Citrus Heights, CA

Beloch, Sujin
Liberty Union HS
Oakley, CA

Beltran, Luis A
Theodore Roosevelt
Los Angeles, CA

Bemis, Nicole
Woodbridge HS
Irvine, CA

Benavides, Mike S
Irvine HS
Irvine, CA

Benbow, Joshua
Arvin HS
Bakersfield, CA

Bencar, Michele L
Washington Union
Fresno, CA

Bencar, Yvonne M
Washington Union
Fresno, CA

Bench, Clover
Lincoln HS
San Jose, CA

Bencivenga, Mario
Fontana HS
Fontana, CA

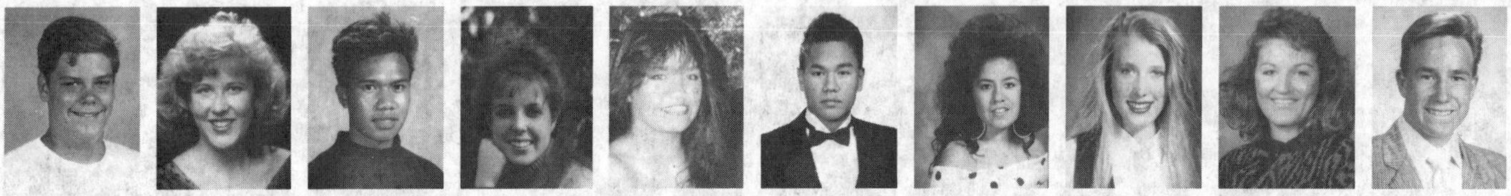

Bender, Michael P
Cleveland HS
Reseda, CA

Benedict, Brenda M
Elk Grove HS
Wilton, CA

Benigno, Anthony O
Westmoor HS
Daly City, CA

Benisek, Alissa
Claremont HS
Claremont, CA

Benitez, Marissa
St Rose Acad
Pacifica, CA

Benitez, Mark A
St Ignatius College Prep
Pacifica, CA

Benitez, Norma A
Buena Park HS
Fullerton, CA

Benjamin, Qurina S
La Habra HS
La Habra Heights, CA

Bennett, Amee M
Redwood HS
Visalia, CA

Bennett, Charlton W
Hesperia HS
Hesperia, CA

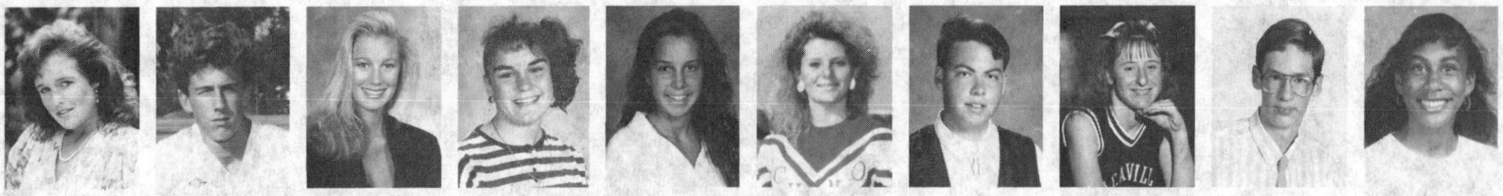

Bennett, Christine
Harbor HS
Santa Cruz, CA

Bennett, Joshua
Hoover HS
San Diego, CA

Bennett, Kirsten L
Laguna Beach HS
Laguna Beach, CA

Bennett, Maralina
Yosemite HS
Oakhurst, CA

Bennett, Michelle
Louisville HS
Chatsworth, CA

Bennett, Mysti
Chino HS
Chino, CA

Bennett, William A
Aragon HS
San Mateo, CA

Benshoof, Terra D
Vacaville HS
Vacaville, CA

Benson, Brian R
River City HS
W Sacramento, CA

Benson, Dorshay
Saint Monica HS
Los Angeles, CA

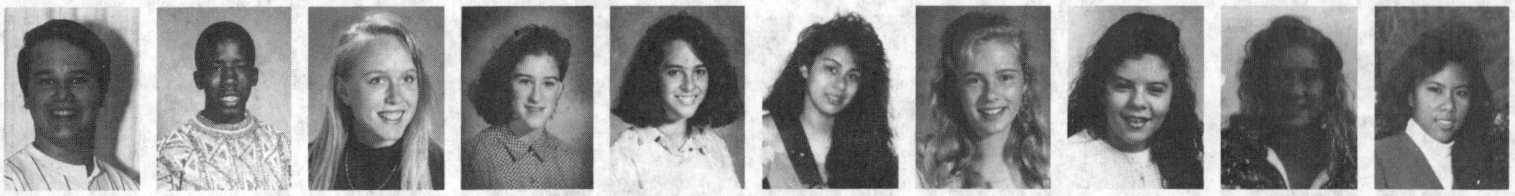

Benson, Jeffery
Cajon HS
San Bernardino, CA

Bento, Raymond A
Pasadena HS
Pasadena, CA

Benton, Cindy M
Palm Springs HS
Cathedral City, CA

Bentson, Heidi C
Mt Shasta HS
Mount Shasta, CA

Benyuska, Michelle
Sacramento HS
Sacramento, CA

Benzon, Loraine T
Whitney HS
Cerritos, CA

Beres, Dolly
Burlingame HS
Burlingame, CA

Berg, Audrey M
Capital Christian Schl
Citrus Heights, CA

Berg, Trisha C
Chino HS
Ontario, CA

Bergado, Rubylyn
John W North HS
Riverside, CA

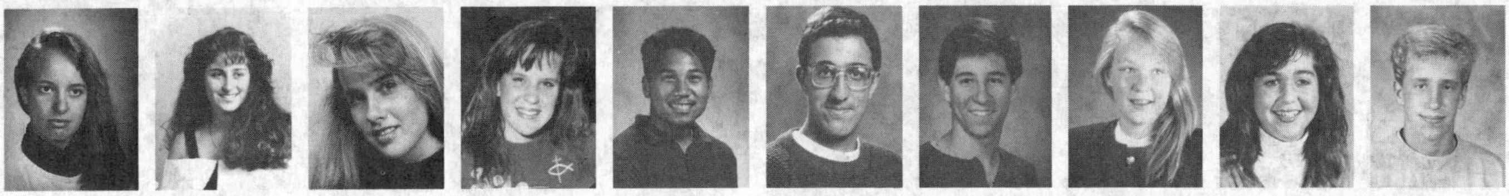

Bergen, Skye
Bret Harte HS
Murphy's, CA

Berger, Rachel
El Camino Real HS
West Hills, CA

Bergman, Lorretta M
Templeton HS
Paso Robles, CA

Bergman, Sara
Brethren HS
Signal Hill, CA

Bergula, Arnie
Poway HS
Poway, CA

Berjis, Amir
Palisades HS
Los Angeles, CA

Berke, David R
El Toro HS
Laguna Niguel, CA

Berkheimer, Wendy
Yucaipa HS
Angelus Oaks, CA

Berlow, Pamela S
Mission College Prep
San Luis Obispo, CA

Berman, Joel
Brethren HS
Signal Hill, CA

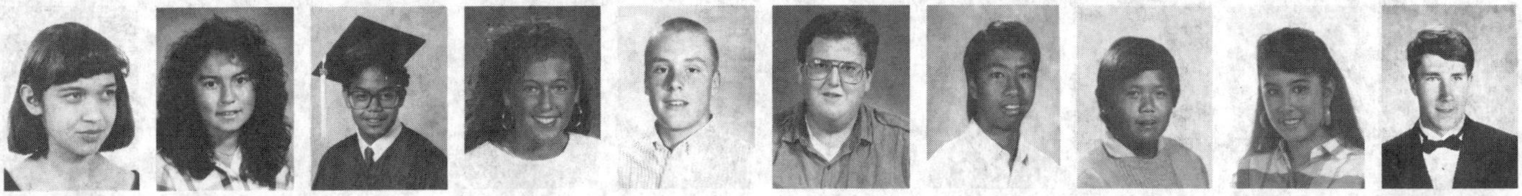

Bermejo, Leticia M
Bell Gardens HS
Belle Gardens, CA

Bermudez, Bernadette
Woodbridge HS
Irvine, CA

Bernal, Dan C
St Anthony HS
Carson, CA

Bernal, Jenna
Monte Vista
Christian HS
Watsonville, CA

Bernard, Jamie S
Notre Dame HS
Moreno Valley, CA

Bernardi, Gregory M
Modesto HS
Modesto, CA

Bernardo, Edel Mar
Clayton Valley HS
Concord, CA

Bernardo, Enrico J
St Francis HS
Glendale, CA

Bernardo, Stacy
Ernest Righetti HS
Santa Maria, CA

Bernhardt, Chad J
Alameda HS
Alameda, CA

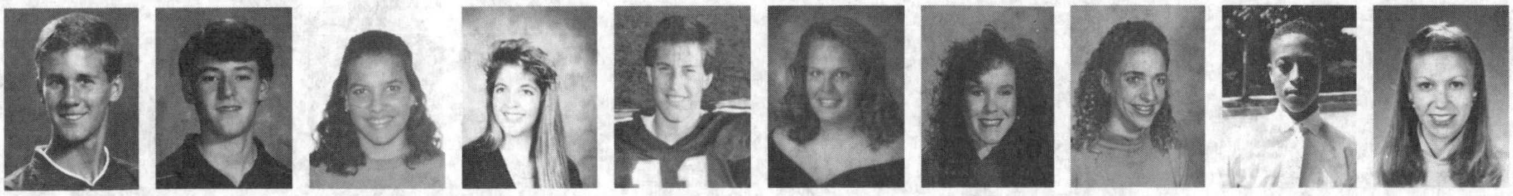

Berns, Jason D
La Canada HS
La Canada Flintri, CA

Bernstein, Aron R
San Ramon Valley
Danville, CA

Bernstein, Jessica E
Fremont HS
Sunnyvale, CA

Bernstein, Tasha L
Downey HS
Downey, CA

Berntsen, Richard
Bellarmine College Prep
San Jose, CA

Berry, Heather M
Thousand Oaks HS
Thousand Oaks, CA

Berry, Jenna
Yuba City HS
Yuba City, CA

Berry, Maya M
Davis SR HS
Davis, CA

Berryman, Aaron R
St Bernard HS
Culver City, CA

Bertolero, Christine
Monte Vista HS
San Ramon, CA

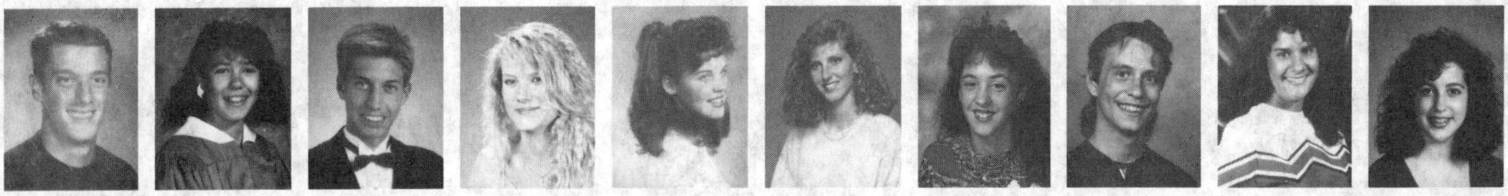

Bertolucci, Mario
Carmel HS
Carmel, CA

Besaw, Michelle B
Bishop O'dowd HS
Castro Valley, CA

Besser, George S
St Francis HS
Mountain View, CA

Bessire, Autumn
Pinole Valley HS
Richmond, CA

Best, Christina M
Modesto HS
Modesto, CA

Best, Melissa B
Monte Vista HS
Danville, CA

Best, Michele J
Cordova SR HS
Rancho Cordova, CA

Beth, Sam R
Escondido HS
San Marcos, CA

Bettencourt, Andrea
Tulare Western HS
Tulare, CA

Bettencourt, Angela
Tulare Union HS
Tipton, CA

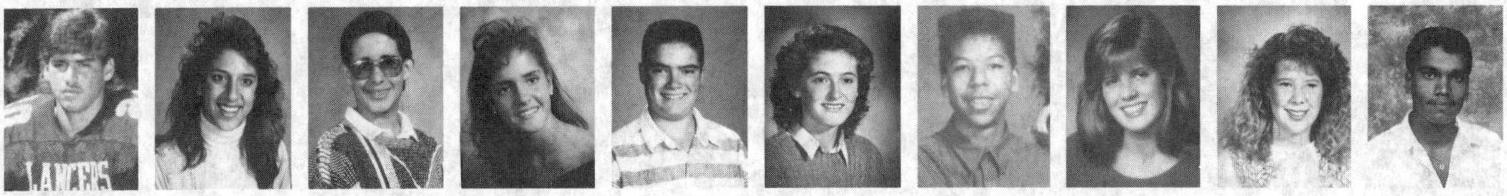

Bettencourt, Brian
East Union HS
Manteca, CA

Bettencourt, Danielle
East Union HS
Manteca, CA

Bettencourt, Frank
Hanford Joint Union
Hanford, CA

Bettencourt, Kama L
Hanford Union HS
Hanford, CA

Bettencourt, Pat J
Turlock HS
Ceres, CA

Bettis, Gina M
Yreka HS
Yreka, CA

Bevien, Rosaan J
George Washington
San Francisco, CA

Bevilaqua, Richene
Palisades HS
Pacific Palisades, CA

Beyer, Lezlie
Mc Farland HS
Delano, CA

Bhakta, Dharmendra
St Paul HS
Los Angeles, CA

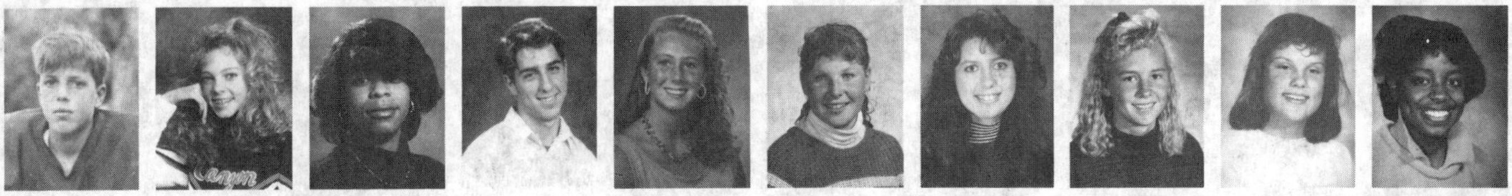

Biagiotti, Edward J
Tustin HS
Tustin, CA

Bianchi, Amber
Canyon HS
Canyon Country, CA

Bible, Ramika
St Michaels HS
Los Angeles, CA

Bick, Mayer
Yeshiva University Of Los Angeles
Los Angeles, CA

Bickert, Marta A
El Toro HS
El Toro, CA

Bickford, Tara D
Prospect HS
Campbell, CA

Bickham, Melissa D
Apple Valley HS
Apple Valley, CA

Bickley, Jami D
Tustin HS
Tustin, CA

Bicknell, Diane
Lone Pine HS
Wickenberg, AZ

Bigby, Tiffany L
John Muir HS
Altadena, CA

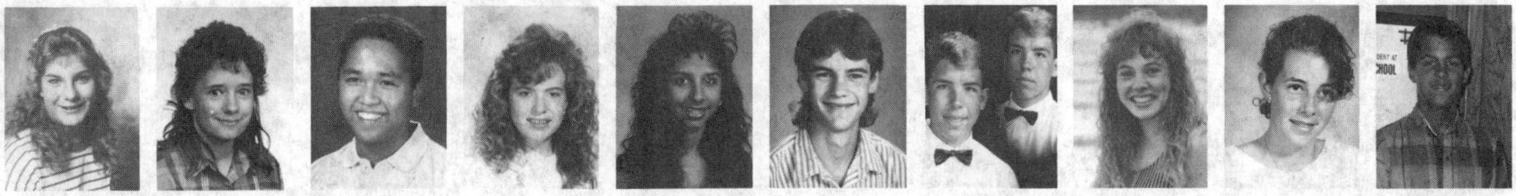

Bigelow, Margaret I
Westwood HS
Westwood, CA

Bigham, Geneva G
Trona HS
Trona, CA

Biglang-Awa, Van Eric
Liberty Union HS
Oakley, CA

Biglietti, Deborah
Canyon HS
Canyon Country, CA

Bijor, Shipra K
Mission San Jose HS
Fremont, CA

Billiet, Rod A
Bret Harte HS
Angels Camp, CA

Billingsley, John W
Bishop O'dowd HS
Bartlesville, OK

Bingham, Sherrie A
Antioch HS
Antioch, CA

Bird, Amanda Marie
Reedley HS
Reedley, CA

Bird, Christopher B
Ponderosa HS
Placerville, CA

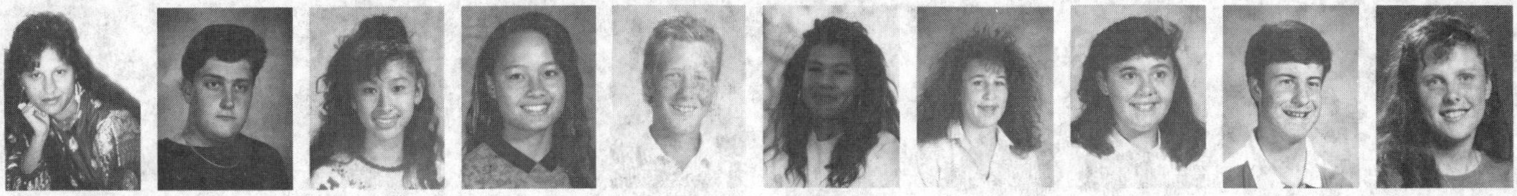

Birla, Radha
Tracy HS
Tracy, CA

Birmingham, Todd K
Bishop Union HS
Bishop, CA

Biscarra, Esther
Westmoor HS
Daly City, CA

Bischoff, Jolene
Archbishop Mitty HS
Cupertino, CA

Bishop, Jeff
Capistrano Valley
Christian HS
Laguna Beach, CA

Bishop, Kathy M
Barstow HS
Barstow, CA

Bishop, Kimberly D
Tranquility Union HS
Tranquillity, CA

Bispo, Polly A
Clovis HS
Fresno, CA

Bissell, Brian T
Redwood Christian
Schools Schls
San Leandro, CA

Bjaanes, Annelise P
Rim Of The World
Running Springs, CA

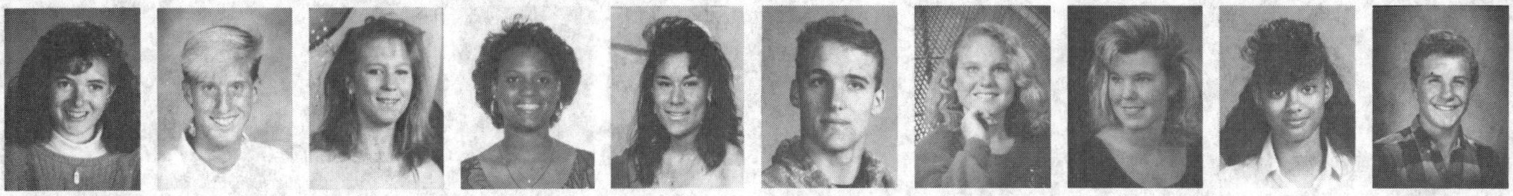

Bjarnason, Deborah
Turlock HS
Turlock, CA

Bjork, Jeff E
Los Angeles Baptist
West Hills, CA

Black, Carol M
Owens Valley HS
Independence, CA

Black, Corey
Canyon Springs HS
Moreno Valley, CA

Black, Dawn
San Diego HS
San Diego, CA

Black, John
Amos Alnzo Stagg
Stockton, CA

Black, Kristina
Nicole
Clovis West HS
Clovis, CA

Black, Mary P
Redwood HS
Visalia, CA

Black, Sylvia L
Palo Verde Valley
Blythe, CA

Blackburn, Joshua C
Rubidoux HS
Riverside, CA

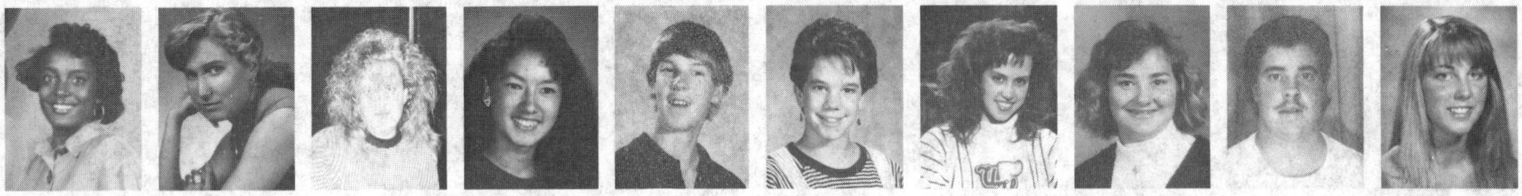

Blackburn, Kimyon
Washington Prep HS
Los Angeles, CA

Blackburn, Michelle
Atascadero HS
Atascadero, CA

Blackburn, Tanya
Dale
Fairfield HS
Fairfield, CA

Blackham, Teishi N
Merced HS
Merced, CA

Blackman, David O
Desert HS
Burkburnett, TX

Blackman, Jeana M
Branham HS
San Jose, CA

Blackmer, Nicole
Upland HS
Upland, CA

Blackmon, Jennifer
Mt Whitney HS
Visalia, CA

Blagrave, James D
Castle Park HS
Chula Vista, CA

Blair, Tiffany A
Westlake HS
Westlake Village, CA

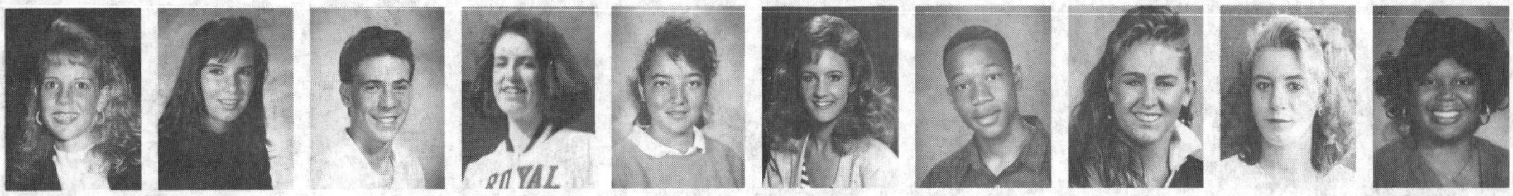

Blake, Jennifer A
Thousand Oaks HS
Thousand Oaks, CA

Blake, Lisa A
Foothill HS
Santa Ana, CA

Blake, Mark P
Santa Margarita HS
San Juan Capistra,
CA

Blake, Samantha L
Royal HS
Simi Valley, CA

Blake, Sherry
El Camino HS
Oceanside, CA

Blakemore, Tanya
Redlands HS
Redlands, CA

Blames, Alexey S
S Calif Christian HS
West Covina, CA

Blamey, Cameryn
Rio Americano HS
Sacramento, CA

Blanchette, Dawn M
Tehachapi HS
Tehachapi, CA

Blanco, Leslie
George Washington
Prep HS
Los Angeles, CA

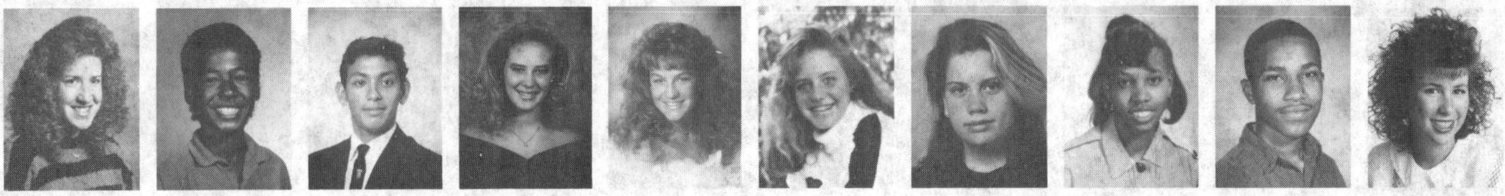

Bland, Shari
Armijo HS
Suisun City, CA

Bland, T J
Damien HS
Pomona, CA

Blandon, Osman F
Hawthorne HS
Inglewood, CA

Blankenship, Kelly
Garden Grove HS
Santa Ana, CA

Blaser, Summer
Vallejo SR HS
Vallejo, CA

Blatter, Lisa
Monte Vista HS
Alamo, CA

Blauvelt, Rochelle N
Sweetwater HS
National City, CA

Bledsoe, Brenda
Pasadena HS
Altadena, CA

Bledsoe, Derick
George Washington
Prep HS
Los Angeles, CA

Bleecker, Felicia N
Irvine HS
Irvine, CA

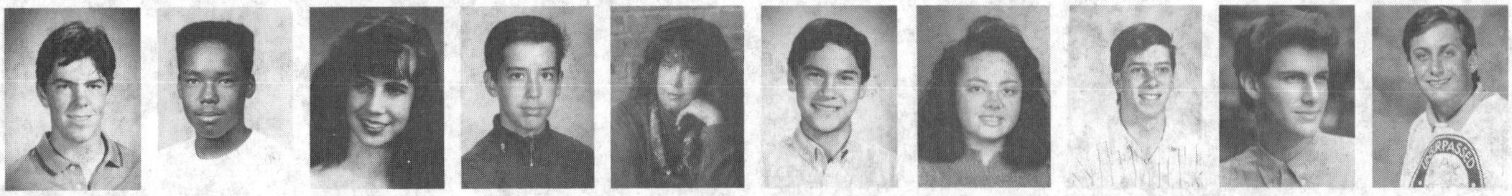

Bleess, James
Ukiah HS
Hopland, CA

Blevins, Edwin A
Vallejo SR HS
Vallejo, CA

Blewett, Anne G
Mount Pleasant HS
San Jose, CA

Blewett, Tim J
Mt Pleasant HS
San Jose, CA

Blinn, Jennifer
St Marys HS
Stockton, CA

Bliss, John Paul
Ukiah HS
Ukiah, CA

Bliss, Serena
Hanford Joint Union
Hanford, CA

Bloch, Alan
Tulelake HS
Tulelake, CA

Block, Adam F
The Head Royce Schl
Berkeley, CA

Bloom, Ryan
University HS
Los Angeles, CA

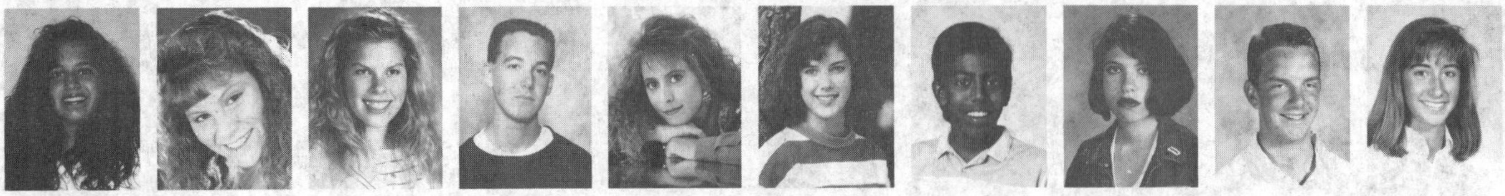

Bloomquist, Frances
La Canada HS
La Canada-Flint R,
CA

Blosser, Judy A
Mt Diablo HS
Pittsburg, CA

Blower, Marci A
Lincoln HS
Stockton, CA

Blumberg, David M
Granada Hills HS
Northridge, CA

Bobbitt, Amy
Nichelle
Bakersfield HS
Bakersfield, CA

Bobst, Tiffany
Forest Lake HS
Auburn, CA

Boddula, Chethan R
Brea Olinda HS
Brea, CA

Boden, Dawn A
Granite Hills HS
El Cajon, CA

Bodenbender,
Michael R
Morro Bay HS
Baywood Pk, CA

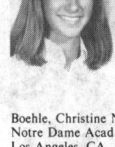

Boehle, Christine N
Notre Dame Acad
Los Angeles, CA

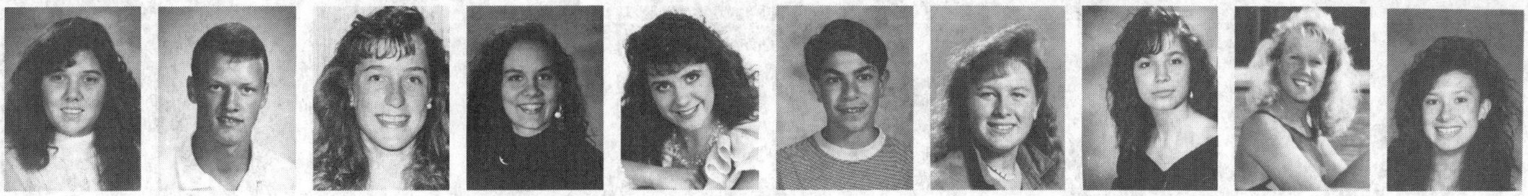

Boenzi, April L
Paraclete HS
Lancaster, CA

Boesch, Jason B
Atwater HS
Winton, CA

Boeving, Betty Ann
Monte Vista HS
Danville, CA

Bogdanoff, Debra A
La Mirada HS
La Mirada, CA

Bogetti, Tamara E
Tracy Joint Union
Tracy, CA

Boghosian, Darren N
Bullard HS
Fresno, CA

Bohn, Rebekah L
Gardena HS
Gardena, CA

Bohorguez, Mildred
Jefferson HS
Daly City, CA

Bolandar, Jenny A
Madera HS
Madera, CA

Bolands, Martha E
Downey HS
Downey, CA

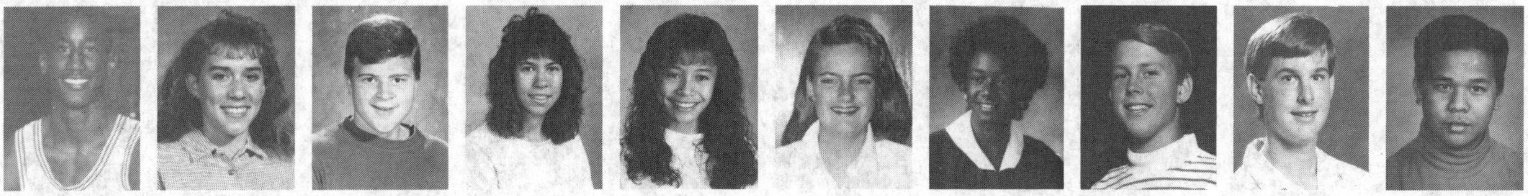

Boldon, Keith
Los Alamitos HS
Seal Beach, CA

Bolla, Stacy
Dublin HS
Dublin, CA

Bolstad, Darren C
Clayton Valley HS
Concord, CA

Boltas, Denise K
Royal HS
Simi Valley, CA

Bonalos, Jennifer
East Union HS
Lathrop, CA

Bonar, Lisa D
Foothill HS
Santa Ana, CA

Bond, Delia
Etiwanda HS
Cucamonga, CA

Bones, Ryan M
Downey HS
Downey, CA

Bonesteel, Chris P
Simi Valley HS
Simi Valley, CA

Bonilla, Benecito
Delta HS
Walnut Grove, CA

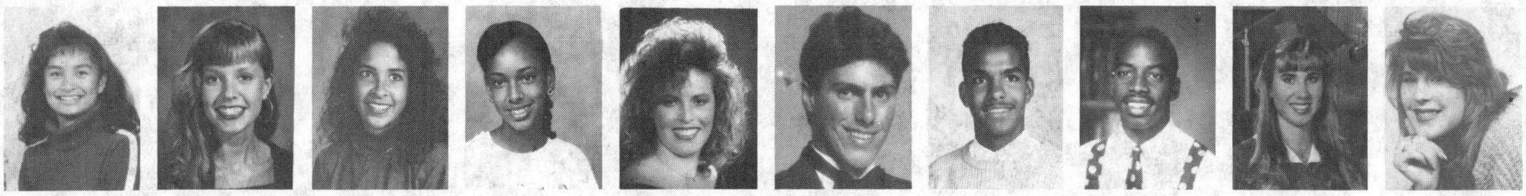

Bonilla, Denise
Ygnacio Valley HS
Concord, CA

Bonilla, Jessica
Huntington Bch HS
Ferndale, WA

Bonilla, Joie R
Chula Vista HS
San Diego, CA

Bonner, Caprii
Gompers Secondary
San Diego, CA

Book, Joanna E
Santa Clara HS
Oxnard, CA

Bookataub, III S
Joseph
Poway HS
San Diego, CA

Booker, IV John W
Nogales HS
La Puente, CA

Boone, Jermaine
Crenshaw HS
Los Angeles, CA

Boone, Nicol A
El Toro HS
El Toro, CA

Boone, Rachael A
Lincoln HS
Stockton, CA

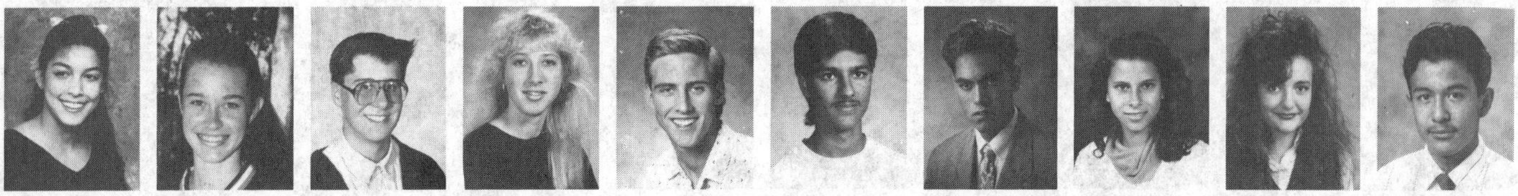

Boonjakuakul, Jenni
El Dorado HS
China Hills, CA

Booth, Allison J
Torrey Pines HS
San Diego, CA

Booth, Channing T
Roosevelt Performing
Arts HS
Fresno, CA

Booth, Jana L
Covina HS
Covina, CA

Boozell, Jeffrey N
Palm Springs HS
Rancho Mirage, CA

Boparai, Nanak S
Mission San Jose HS
Fremont, CA

Borba, Scott V
Redwood HS
Visalia, CA

Borchard, Andrea M
North Salinas HS
Salinas, CA

Borelli, Sara Yolanda
St Joseph Notre
Dame HS
Alameda, CA

Borges, Eduardo
Loyola HS
Los Angeles, CA

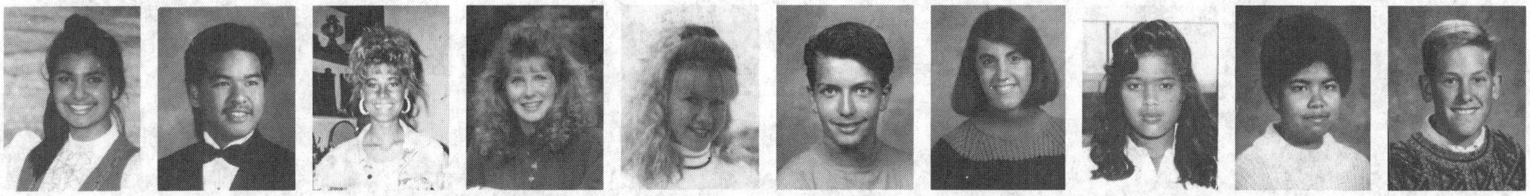

Borghei, Karimeh N
El Camino Real HS
Woodland Hills, CA

Borja, Robert T
Montgomery HS
San Diego, CA

Borkey, Carrie
Tulare Union HS
Tulare, CA

Bornemann, Chanda
Fairfield HS
Fairfield, CA

Bornholdt, Paige
Ellen
Bonita Vista HS
Bonita, CA

Borrayo, Mario
Mountain Empire HS
Potrero, CA

Borrelli, Lisa M
Mt Whitney HS
Visalia, CA

Borrero, Lara Jane F
Diamond Bar HS
Diamond Bar, CA

Borromeo, Beverly
Manuel
Arvin HS
Arvin, CA

Bortoli, Darryl R
Carlmont HS
Belmont, CA

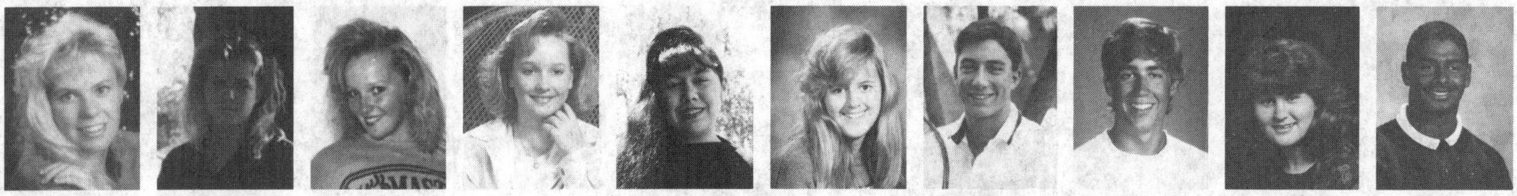

Boshoff, Fenella Fiki
Adolfo Camarillo HS
Camarillo, CA

Bossi, Kristen J
Newbury Park HS
Newbury Park, CA

Bostrom, Jenny
Palo Verde HS
Blythe, CA

Bostrom, Virginia
Palo Verde HS
Blythe, CA

Botello, Nicole Y
St Patrick-St Vincent
Vallejo, CA

Bottorff, Rebecca A
Saddleback HS
Santa Ana, CA

Bouchard, John M
Redwood HS
Visalia, CA

Bouchard, Matthew
Lincoln HS
Stockton, CA

Bouchard, Melinda J
San Diego Acad
National City, CA

Bouchelion, Dominic
James Logan HS
Union City, CA

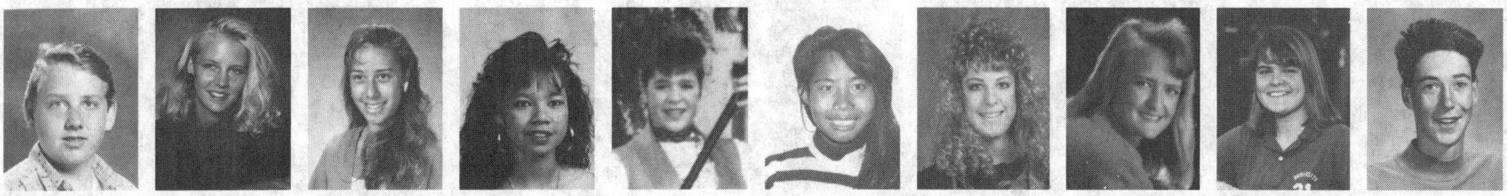

Boucher, Lawrence E
St Francis HS
La Crescenta, CA

Bouck, Kimberly B
Central Union HS
El Centro, CA

Boudreau, Christine
Ramos
California HS
San Ramon, CA

Bounlutay, Nira
Edison Computech
Fresno, CA

Bourcier, Kristen
Armijo HS
Fairfield, CA

Bowden, Michelle
Banning HS
Banning, CA

Bowen, Claudia
Mt Whitney HS
Visalia, CA

Bower, Amy N
Montgomery HS
Santa Rosa, CA

Bowers, Patricia K
University HS
Santa Ana, CA

Bowers, Ryan N
Poway HS
Poway, CA

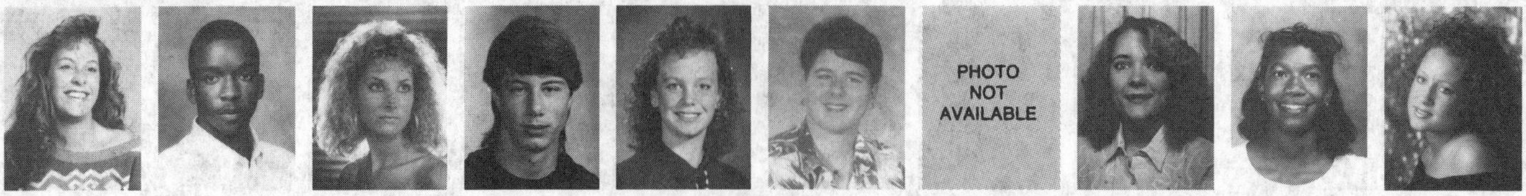
PHOTO
NOT
AVAILABLE

Bowles, Dana
Liberty Union HS
Brentwood, CA

Bowman, Marino
San Diego HS
San Diego, CA

Bowman, Renae L
Hemet HS
Winchester, CA

Bowman, Sean E
Casa Roble
Fundamental HS
Orangevale, CA

Bowman, Wende M
Canyon HS
Anaheim, CA

Bowsher, Kathleen S
C L Mc Lane HS
Fresno, CA

Boybal, Edward D
Bellflower HS
Bellflower, CA

Boyd, Heather M
Calvary Acad
Cedaredge, CO

Boyd, Penny
Sacred Heart Prep
Redwood City, CA

Boydstun, Traci
Redwood HS
Visalia, CA

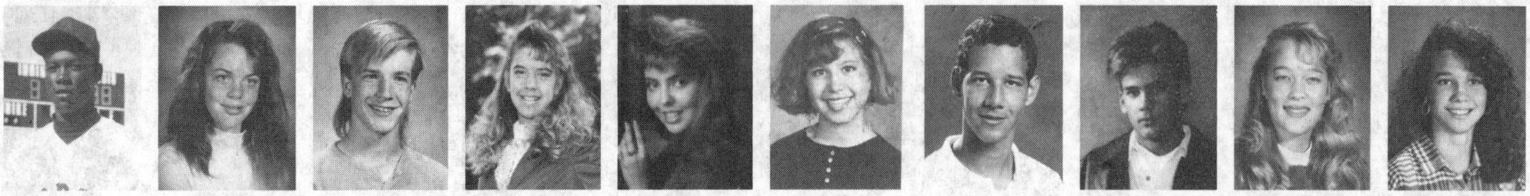

Boykins, George
Antelope Valley HS
Lancaster, CA

Boyle, Amanda
Rosamond HS
Rosamond, CA

Boyle, Michael S
Poway HS
Poway, CA

Boyse, Tamara L
Fontana HS
Fontana, CA

Bozarth, Angela J
Taft Union HS
Taft, CA

Bozarth, Erin M
San Pasqual HS
Escondido, CA

Bozurich, Gary J
Village Christian
Schls
Sunland, CA

Bracco, Chase
Grace M Davis HS
Modesto, CA

Bracy, Terina
Springs Of Living
Water Acad
Richardson Spgs, CA

Bradford, Jennifer L
Le Grand HS
Le Grand, CA

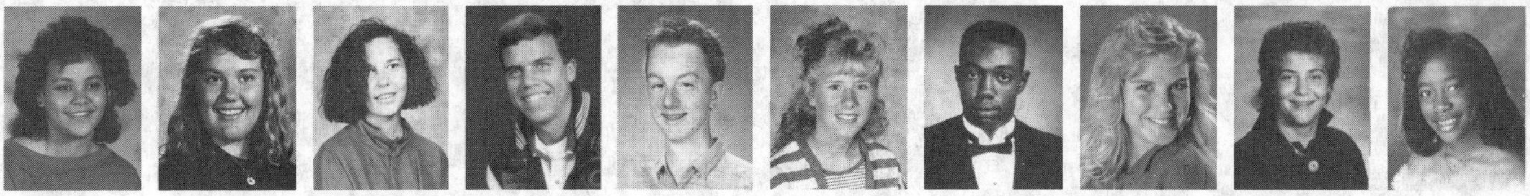

Bradford, Remegia A
Seaside HS
Fort Ord, CA

Bradford, Tegan M
San Luis Obispo SR
San Luis Obispo, CA

Bradley, Angelique
Ambassador Baptist
Rialto, CA

Bradley, Bill P
Clovis West HS
Fresno, CA

Bradley, Jr James
Charles
Liberty Union HS
Oakley, CA

Bradley, Karyn D
El Dorado HS
Pollock Pines, CA

Bradley, Lincjabbar
Mt Pleasant HS
Milpitas, CA

Bradley, Shannon M
Colfax HS
Colfax, CA

Bradrick, Michele L
Tustin HS
Tustin, CA

Brady, Katrina
Fremont Christian
Union City, CA

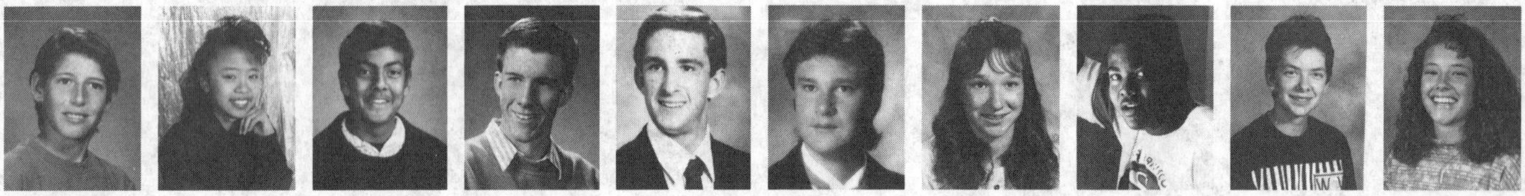

Brady, William
Valley View HS
Moreno Valley, CA

Braga, Bernadette M
Andrew P Hill HS
San Jose, CA

Brahma, Charanjit
Clovis HS
Clovis, CA

Brainerd, Timothy R
James Logan HS
Union City, CA

Brake, Steven L
North HS
Torrance, CA

Brambley, Robert R
Vanden HS
Vacaville, CA

Branam, Sherri L
Paramount HS
South Gate, CA

Branch, Ashanti D
John C Fremont HS
Oakland, CA

Branch, Jennifer R
South Fork HS
Phillipsville, CA

Brandenburger, Kara
St Francis HS
West Sacramento,
CA

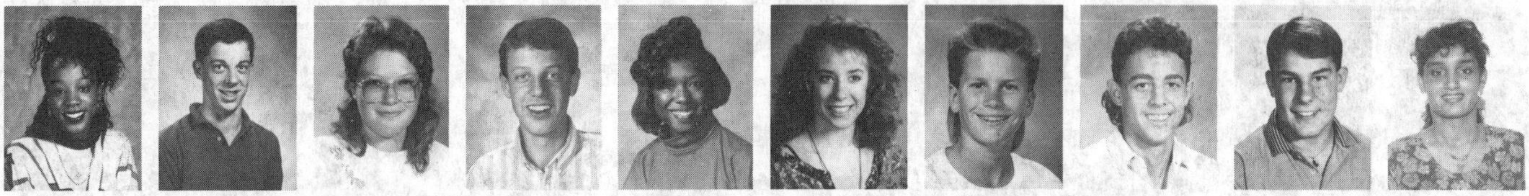

Brandon, Kia N
San Leandro HS
Oakland, CA

Brandt, Nicholas A
Poway HS
Poway, CA

Brandt, Tarci
Highlands HS
North Highlands, CA

Brannan, Ryan L
Burney JR SR HS
Burney, CA

Branson, Delicia
Carson HS
Carson, CA

Branson, Stacy
Tokay HS
Stockton, CA

Branstetter, Bryan S
Esperanza HS
Placentia, CA

Branstetter, Craig M
Dos Palos HS
Dos Palos, CA

Brant, Jason C
El Dorado HS
Placentia, CA

Brar, Amrit Pal Kaur
East HS
Bakersfield, CA

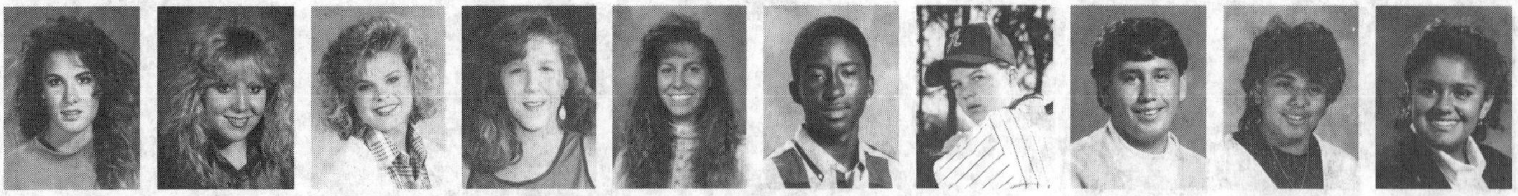

Brashears, Lea J.
Miramonte HS
Orinda, CA

Brasiel, Heidi L
Exeter HS
Exeter, CA

Brassett, Elizabeth
Anne
Whittier Christian
Fullerton, CA

Brasuell, Angela M
Los Gatos HS
San Jose, CA

Bratis, Danielle L
Yucaipa HS
Calimesa, CA

Bratton, Ricky C
Junipero Serra HS
Los Angeles, CA

Brauning, Justin J
Arcata HS
Arcata, CA

Braunstein,
Christopher J
Etiwanda HS
Alta Loma, CA

Bravo, Carmen
Strathmore HS
Poplar, CA

Bravo, Veronica
Holy Family HS
Los Angeles, CA

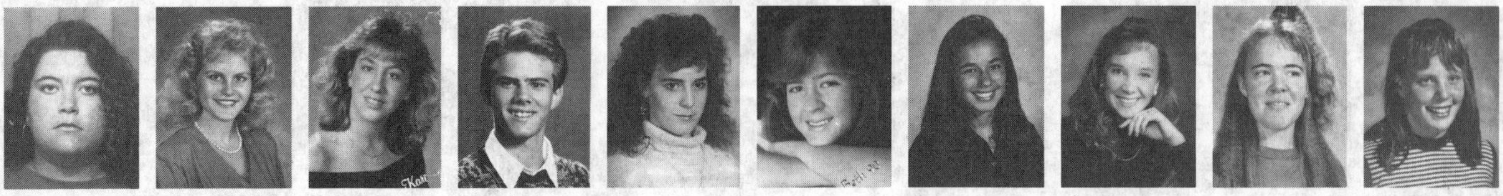

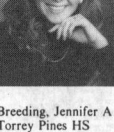

Bray, Hazel
Chula Vista HS
National City, CA

Bray, Stefani L
Temecula Valley HS
Murrieta, CA

Brayton, Kari
Antelope Valley HS
Lancaster, CA

Brazelton,
Christopher M
Ocean View HS
Huntington Beach,
CA

Breaux, Crysta-Linn
Kern Valley HS
Bodfish, CA

Bredice, Beth A
Paramount HS
Bellflower, CA

Breed, Lisa M
Davis SR HS
Davis, CA

Breeding, Jennifer A
Torrey Pines HS
San Diego, CA

Breen, Sasha
Templeton HS
Templeton, CA

Bremer, Suzanne N
Westwood HS
Westwood, CA

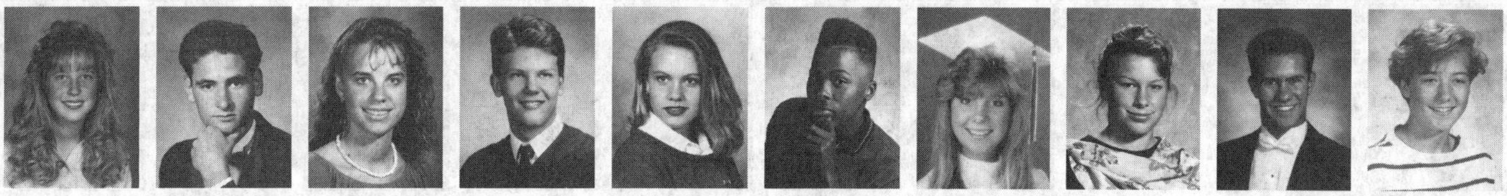

Brende, Kim S
Louisville HS
Woodland Hills, CA

Brenneise, John C
Pioneer HS
San Jose, CA

Brenner, Joanne E
Troy HS
Fullerton, CA

Brenzel, Seth
Jesuit HS
Sacramento, CA

Brewer, Heidi S
Academy Of Our
Lady Of Peace
San Diego, CA

Brewer, Ronald D
John F Kennedy HS
Sacramento, CA

Brewster, Deanna
College Park HS
Martinez, CA

Brezel, Laura E
Santa Cruz HS
Santa Cruz, CA

Brickeen, Marshall A
Hogan SR HS
Vallejo, CA

Bridge, Tawny L
Nevada Union HS
Grass Valley, CA

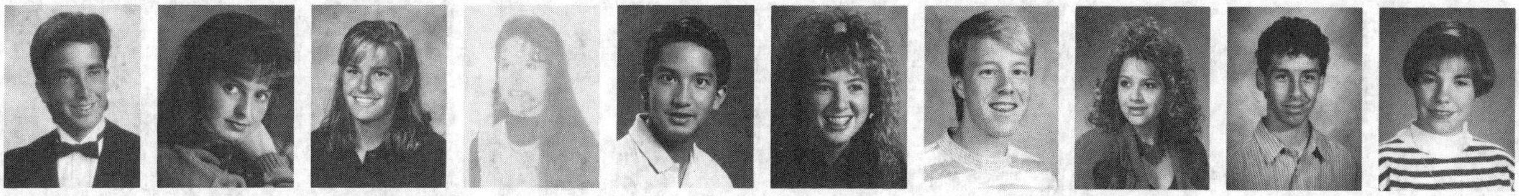

Bridwell, Josh W
Hilltop HS
Jamul, CA

Brierley, Sally
Palm Springs HS
Palm Springs, CA

Briggs, Jane L
Armijo HS
Suisun, CA

Briggs, Michele E
Rim Of The World
Crest Park, CA

Brion, John N
Village Christian HS
Sun Valley, CA

Brisbane, Karen A
Antioch HS
Antioch, CA

Briscoe-Smith, Allen
Simi Valley HS
Simi Valley, CA

Briseno, Alma
San Fernando HS
San Fernando, CA

Briseno, Frank C
Tulare Western HS
Tulare, CA

Bristow, Michelle R
Lodi HS
Lodi, CA

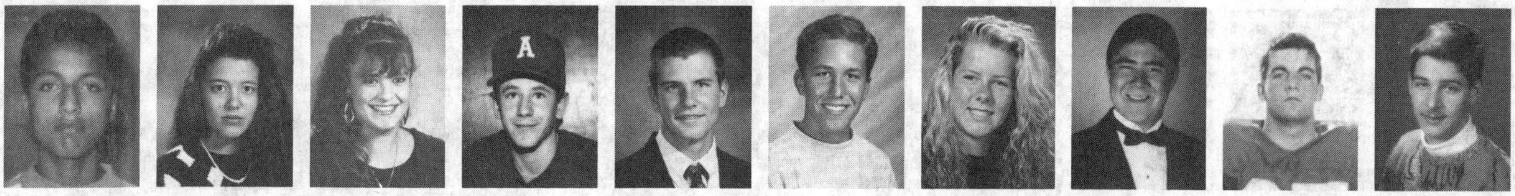

Brito, Manuel
Santa Ana HS
Santa Ana, CA

Brittin, Tanya Y
Villa Park HS
Orange, CA

Brizuela, Isela
Morningside HS
Inglewood, CA

Brizzi, Joshua S
Arlington HS
Riverside, CA

Broadbent, Brian P
Mater Dei HS
Anaheim Hills, CA

Brock, John D
Apple Valley HS
Apple Valley, CA

Brockman, Alise M
Trabuco Hills HS
Mission Viejo, CA

Brockman, Ted
Arroyo HS
San Leandro, CA

Brodie, Richard D
Alta Loma HS
Alta Loma, CA

Brodoski, Shawn M
South Valley HS
Ukiah, CA

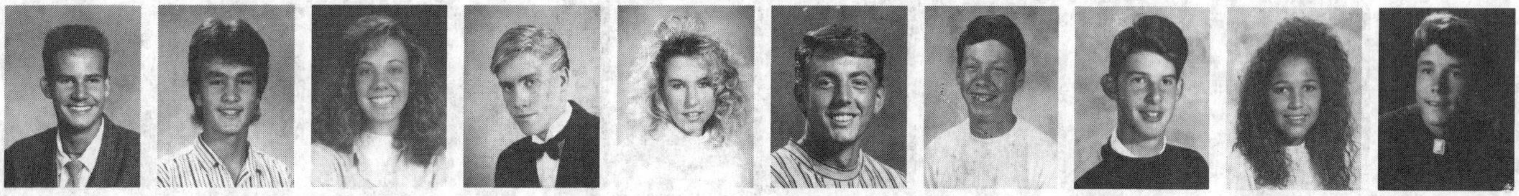

Brody, Brad A
Rowland HS
Rowland Hts, CA

Brohard, John W
Glendale Adventist
Acad
Tujunga, CA

Brooks, Cynthea
Riverdale HS
Riverdale, CA

Brooks, David A
Healdsburg HS
Windsor, CA

Brooks, Dena R
Saddleback HS
Santa Ana, CA

Brooks, Donovan W
San Bernardino HS
Riverside, CA

Broom, Jr Dave
Mayfair HS
Bellflower, CA

Broomall, Travis T
Morro Bay HS
Los Osos, CA

Broome, Liza
Canyon HS
Canyon Country, CA

Brousseau, Guy B
Morro Bay HS
Los Osos, CA

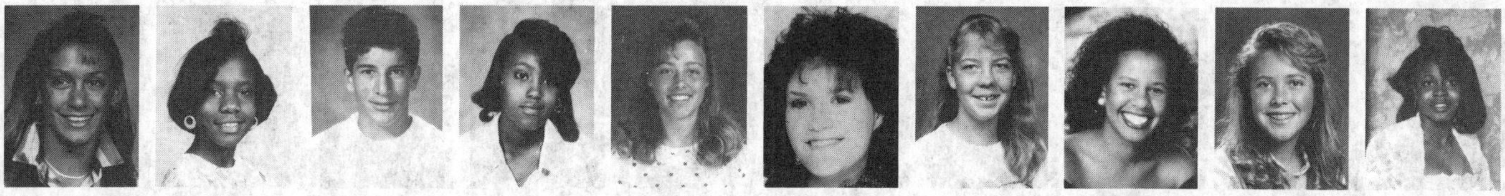

Brovelli, Michele L
San Rafael HS
San Rafael, CA

Brown, Alana J
St Pats St Vincents
Vallejo, CA

Brown, Alexander
Stevenson
Torrey Pines HS
San Diego, CA

Brown, Alishia
Crenshaw HS
Los Angeles, CA

Brown, Amy
Modesto HS
Modesto, CA

Brown, Amy E
Fresno Christian HS
Fresno, CA

Brown, Amy R
Monte Vista HS
Spring Valley, CA

Brown, Ariana Sudel
Marymount Schl
Los Angeles, CA

Brown, Chalon E
Rim Of The World
Running Springs, CA

Brown, Chandra R
Mc Clymonds HS
Oakland, CA

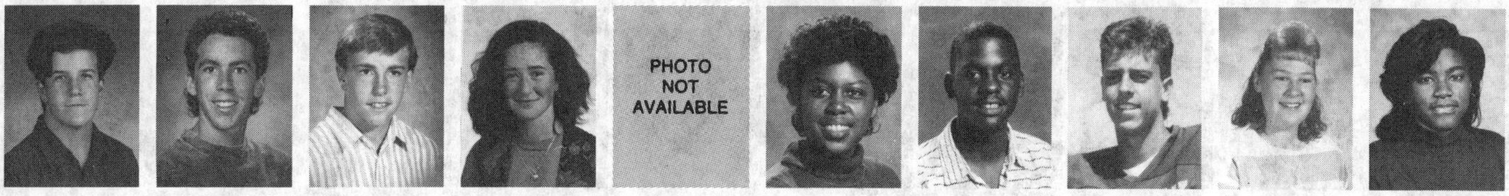
PHOTO
NOT
AVAILABLE

Brown, Charles A
Servite HS
Seal Beach, CA

Brown, Christopher
John-Thomas
El Toro HS
El Toro, CA

Brown, Christopher R
Burroughs HS
Ridgecrest, CA

Brown, Colleen D
St Francis HS
Los Altos, CA

Brown, Erin C
Rim Of The World
Running Springs, CA

Brown, Evyone
Gardena HS
Rialto, CA

Brown, Gary D
Washington HS
Los Angeles, CA

Brown, Gregory Scott
Poway HS
San Diego, CA

Brown, Gretchen L
Nevada Union HS
Nevada City, CA

Brown, Jacqueline D
Luther Burbank HS
Sacramento, CA

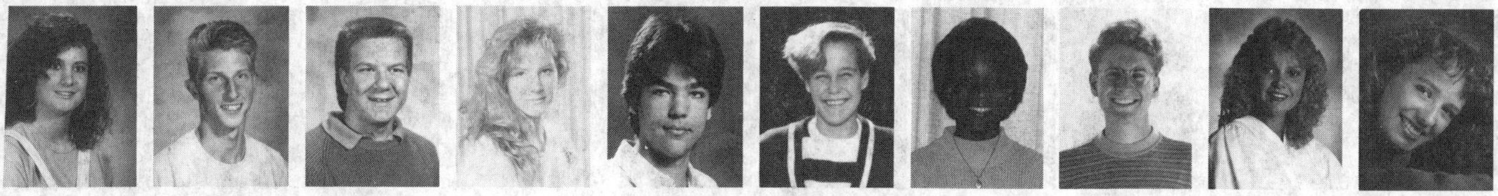

Brown, Jamie T
Covina HS
West Covina, CA

Brown, Jeffrey G
John F Kennedy HS
Granada Hills, CA

Brown, Jeremy L
Enterprise HS
Redding, CA

Brown, Jessica L
Kerman HS
Kerman, CA

Brown, John T
Village Christian HS
Sun Valley, CA

Brown, Julie A
C K Mc Clatchy HS
Sacramento, CA

Brown, Katherine
Los Angeles HS
Los Angeles, CA

Brown, Kevin T
University HS
Irvine, CA

Brown, Leah L
Eureka HS
Eureka, CA

Brown, Lori
Colusa HS
Colusa, CA

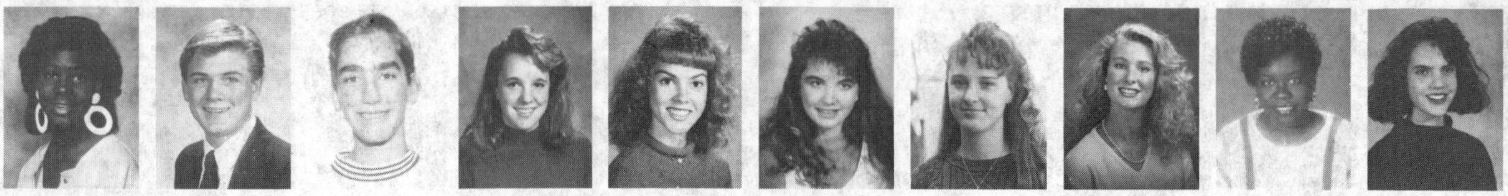

Brown, Martinia
Granada Hills HS
Northridge, CA

Brown, Matthew G
St Margarets
Episcopal HS
San Juan Capis, CA

Brown, Michael
Winston
Taft HS
Tarzana, CA

Brown, Michelle A
Canyon Springs HS
Moreno Valley, CA

Brown, Mindi
Lodi HS
Lodi, CA

Brown, Monica
East Bakersfield HS
Bakersfield, CA

Brown, Natalie M
Hoover HS
Fresno, CA

Brown, Noell L
Los Alamitos HS
Los Alamitos, CA

Brown, Pleasance La
Rae
San Gorgonio HS
San Bernardino, CA

Brown, Rachel
Sacramento Country
Day Schl
Sacramento, CA

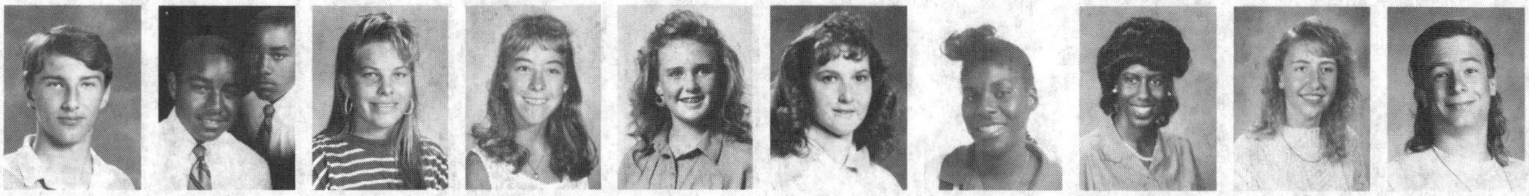

Brown, Rodney L
Lindsay HS
Lindsay, CA

Brown, Ryan H
Bishop O Dowd HS
Oakland, CA

Brown, Sarah
Mission San Jose HS
Fremont, CA

Brown, Stephanie B
Del Oro HS
Loomis, CA

Brown, Tara
Brea-Olinda HS
Brea, CA

Brown, Tracey L
Bakersfield HS
Bakersfield, CA

Brown, Vermelle
Lonnisha C
Valley HS
Sacramento, CA

Brown, Yvonne
Cherisse
Bishop Montogomery
Carson, CA

Browne, Rebecca L
Hesperia Christian
Hesperia, CA

Brownfield, Jimmy H
Tulare Union HS
Tulare, CA

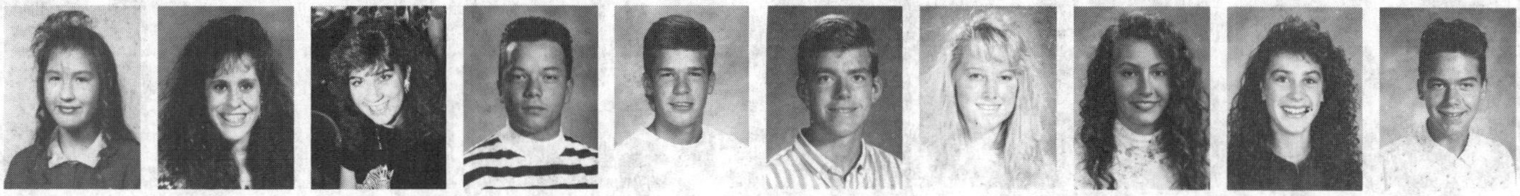

Browning, Cydney
Franklin JR HS
Vallejo, CA

Browning, Jennifer J
Los Alamitos HS
Los Alamitos, CA

Brownlee, Patricia
Gunderson HS
San Jose, CA

Broyles, Todd E
Highlands HS
North Highlands, CA

Bruce, Christopher
Western Christian
Claremont, CA

Bruce, Joshua W
Santa Cruz HS
Santa Cruz, CA

Bruce, Stephanie S
Canyon HS
Canyon Country, CA

Bruff, Julie A
Bishop O'dowd HS
Oakland, CA

Brughelli, Kerri
Riverdale HS
Riverdale, CA

Bruhn, David
William
Don Bosco Tech Inst
Montebello, CA

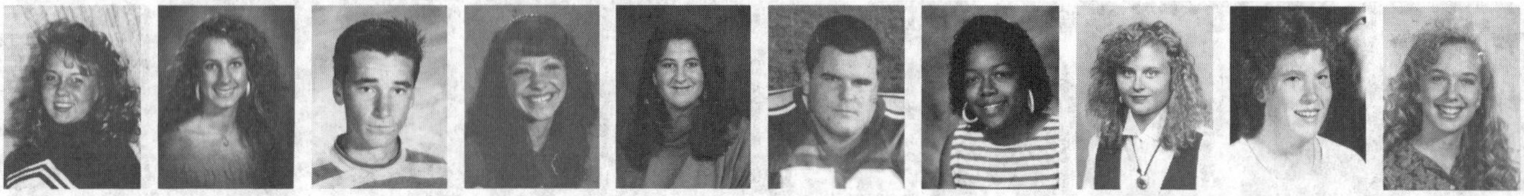

Bruhn, Heather
William S Hart HS
Valencia, CA

Brumley, Julie A
Sonora HS
Fullerton, CA

Brundage, Brent B
Chino HS
Chino, CA

Brunstad, Kristi
Antioch HS
Antioch, CA

Brushia, Jennifer
Margaret
Oak Ridge HS
El Dorado Hills, CA

Brust, Paul F
Bellarmine College
Prep
San Jose, CA

Bryan, Tanya
Fairfield HS
Andrews AFB, MD

Bryant, Isabelle A
Saint Anthony HS
Long Beach, CA

Bryant, Michelle L
Hesperia HS
Hesperia, CA

Bryson, Lisa L
Woodland HS
Woodland, CA

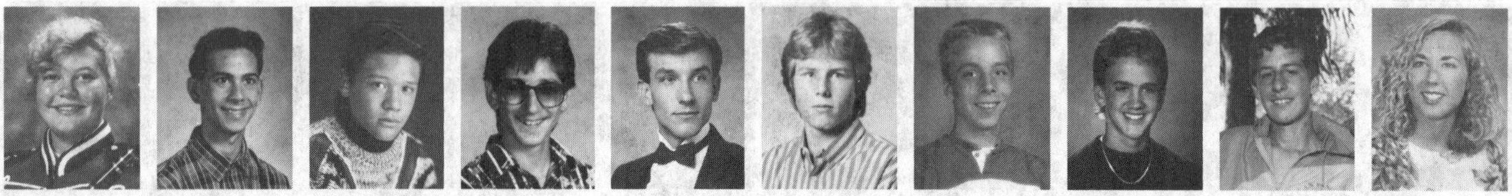

Bucaccio, Julie S
Poway HS
Poway, CA

Buchbinder, Daniel B
Poway HS
Poway, CA

Buchholz, Jason D
Montgomery HS
Santa Rosa, CA

Bucholz, Rick J
Tulare Union HS
Tulare, CA

Buckels, Christopher
Liberty Christian HS
Fountain Valley, CA

Buckley, Shawn D
Chaffey HS
Ontario, CA

Buckley, Steve D
Redwood HS
Visalia, CA

Buckley, Tim D
Livermore HS
Livermore, CA

Buckley, William F
San Pasqual HS
Escondido, CA

Budding, Kelley J
Elk Grove HS
Elk Grove, CA

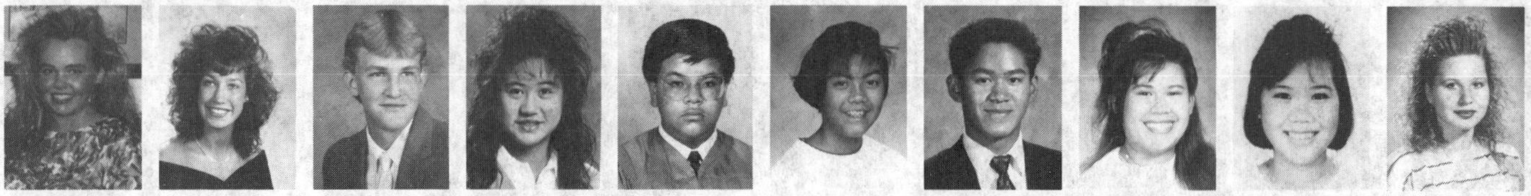

Budney, Amie Joy
Turlock HS
Turlock, CA

Budrick, Suzie
Sequoia HS
San Carlos, CA

Buehler, Mark D
Whittier Christian
La Mirada, CA

Buenaflor,
Cherrymaine
Providence HS
Los Angeles, CA

Buenaventura, Allan
Don Bosco Tech Inst
Whittier, CA

Buenaventura,
Angeline R
Holy Family HS
Montebello, CA

Buensalido, Mark A
St Ignatius College
Preparator HS
Benicia, CA

Buensuceso, Ann
Therese S
Lynwood HS
Lynwood, CA

Buenviaje, Carminia
North Hollywood HS
North Hollywood, CA

Bugarin, Debbie M
Huntington Beach
Union HS
Huntington Beach,
CA

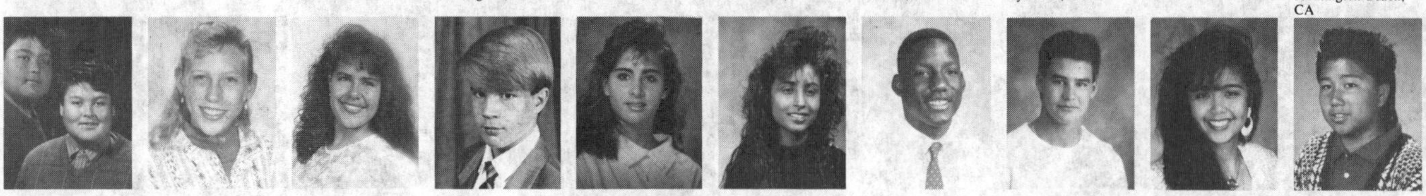

Bugarin, Jose L
Pasadena HS
Pasadena, CA

Builteman, Dana
Inland Christian Schl
Rialto, CA

Buitrago, Diane
Bishop Amat
Memorial HS
West Covina, CA

Bujanda, Brandon E
Warren HS
Walnut, CA

Bukenas, Jennifer L
Trabuco Hills HS
Rancho Snta Margr,
CA

Buksh, Mona K
Wood HS
Vacaville, CA

Bullard, Sean L
Skyline HS
Oakland, CA

Bullock, Matthew
Wm S Hart HS
Valencia, CA

Buluran, Maricris R
Bishop Amat
Memorial HS
Baldwin Park, CA

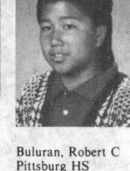

Buluran, Robert C
Pittsburg HS
Pittsburg, CA

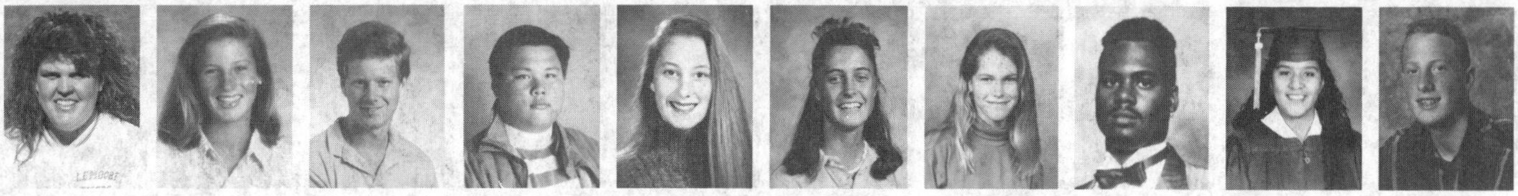

Bumpas, Karen E
Lemoore Union HS
Lemoore, CA

Bunce, Kathleen
Capistrono Valley
Christian HS
S Laguna, CA

Bunting, Glen A
Santa Clara HS
Santa Clara, CA

Buot, Frederick
Lance G
Hueneme HS
Oxnard, CA

Buracchio, Nikki N
Fountain Valley HS
Fountain Valley, CA

Burch, Pat
Oakmont HS
Roseville, CA

Burch, Tawnee L
Mission Bay HS
San Diego, CA

Burchett, Michael D
Chino HS
Chino, CA

Burciaga, Veronica
Marshal HS
Los Angeles, CA

Burcombe, Jonathan
Avalon HS
Avalon, CA

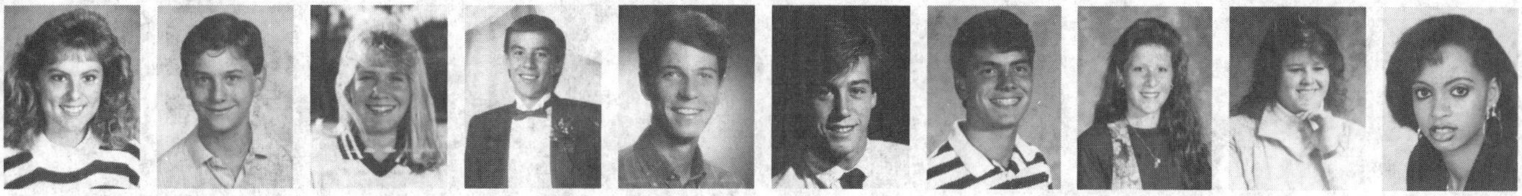

Burdette, Angel D
Atwater HS
Merced, CA

Burdette, John A
Durham HS
Durham, CA

Burg, Wendy L
Will C Crawford HS
San Diego, CA

Burgess, Joe C
Huenene HS
Oxnard, CA

Burgess, Scott K
Poway HS
San Diego, CA

Burgess, Sean
Olympic Valley Schl
Bullhead City, AZ

Burgle, Keith W
Mission College Prep
Cambria, CA

Burke, Michelle
South Tahoe HS
South Lake Tahoe, CA

Burkhead, Michelle
Arvin HS
Lamont, CA

Burks, Caryn W
Alhambra HS
Alhambra, CA

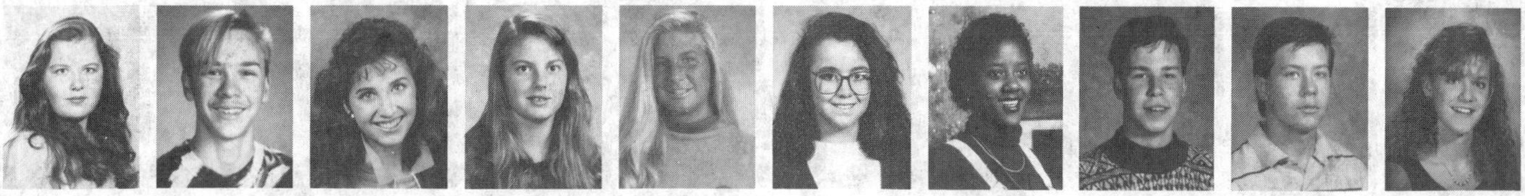

Burmeister, Elizabeth
Rosary HS
Cerritos, CA

Burnett, Ian J
Bret Harte HS
Arnold, CA

Burns, Julielynn
Berean Christian HS
Alamo, CA

Burns, Madeline K
Bishop O'dowd HS
San Leandro, CA

Burns, Michael
Capistrano Valley
Christian HS
San Juan Capstrno, CA

Burns, Shannon L
Carson HS
Carson, CA

Burns, Sharon R
Rio Lindo Adventist
Boarding Acad
Oakland, CA

Burns, Tom J
J Eugene Mc Ateer
Pacifica, CA

Burr, Jr Ricky D
Silver Valley HS
Fort Irwin, CA

Burrell, Andrea
Rosamond HS
Rosamond, CA

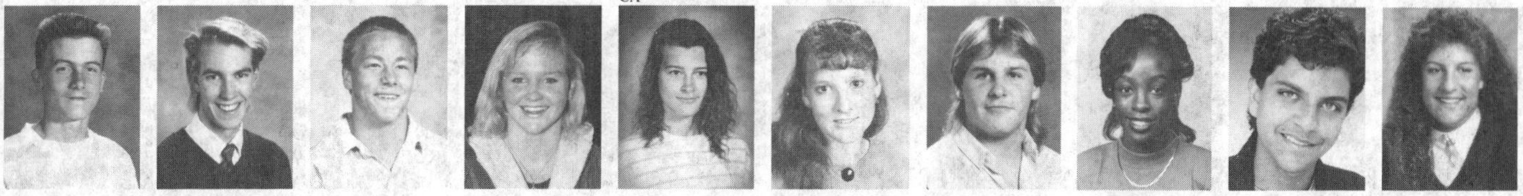

Burroughs, Alex M
Upper Lake HS
Upper Lake, CA

Burroughs, Scott A
Chino HS
Chino, CA

Burrows, Brian D
El Camino HS
Carmichael, CA

Burrows, Tracy K
Poway HS
Poway, CA

Burruss, Marie
North HS
Bakersfield, CA

Burtle, Catherine M
Yosemite HS
Oakhurst, CA

Burton, Chris L
Lindsay HS
Lindsay, CA

Burton, Onezia L
Vallejo SR HS
Vallejo, CA

Burton, William
Henry
Daniel Murphy HS
Los Angeles, CA

Busalacchi, Carla
Linden HS
Stockton, CA

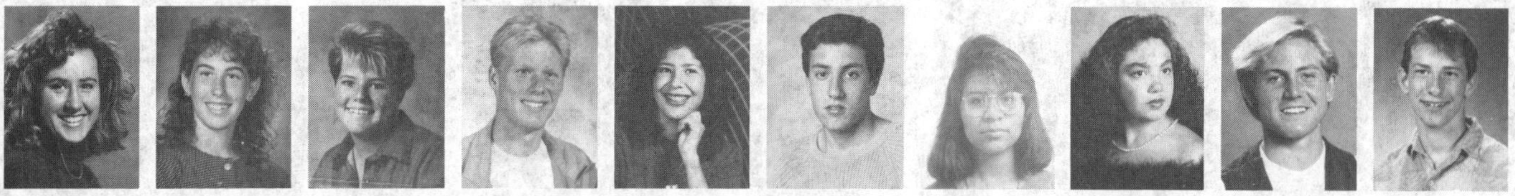

Busch, Jodi M
Fontana HS
Bloomington, CA

Bushek, Jennifer A
Laguna Hills HS
Laguna Hills, CA

Buss, Laurie
Chaminade College
Prep
West Hills, CA

Bussard, Joseph
Michael
Bear River HS
Grass Valley, CA

Bustamante, Sandra
Karin
Bonita Vista HS
Chula Vista, CA

Bustindui, Manuel S
Castle Park HS
Chula Vista, CA

Bustos, Ana-Karina
Indio HS
Indio, CA

Bustos, Angelina R
Holy Names HS
Richmond, CA

Butler, Chad M
Carlsbad HS
Carlsbad, CA

Butler, David J
Calistoga HS
Calistoga, CA

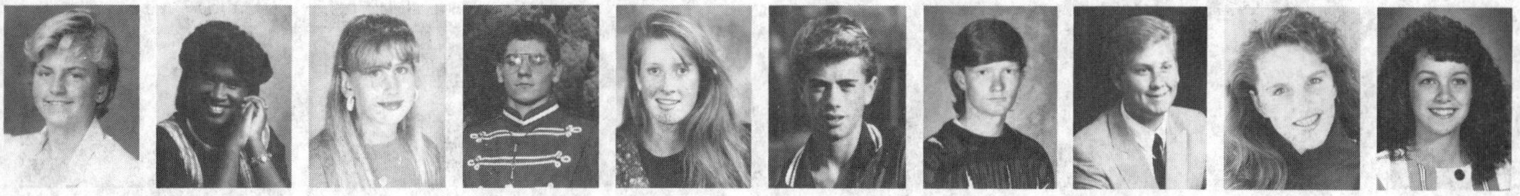

Butler, J Paige
Bonita Vista HS
Chula Vista, CA

Butler, Jendayi A
Barstow HS
Barstow, CA

Butler, Kerry S
Sanger HS
Squaw Valley, CA

Buttacavoli, Matthew
Pacifica HS
Garden Grv, CA

Buttress, Kristin E
Santa Barbara HS
Santa Barbara, CA

Buttson, Jeremy A
Huntington Beach
Huntington Beach, CA

Buxton, David L
Vacaville HS
Vacaville, CA

Buys, Andrew R
Yosemite HS
Coarsegold, CA

Buzzard, Stephanie
St Francis HS
Sacramento, CA

Byars, Deanna J
Oroville HS
Oroville, CA

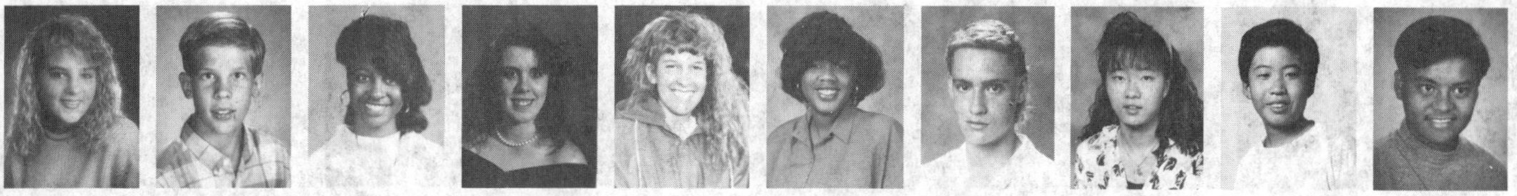

Byers, Natalyn
Canyon HS
Santa Clarita, CA

Byington, Ashton B
Fred C Beyer HS
Modesto, CA

Bynum, Vivian Ann
St Bernard HS
Inglewood, CA

Byouer, Brenda K
Lower Lake HS
Lower Lake, CA

Byrd, Dana
St Marys HS
Stockton, CA

Byrd, Tiffini T
Van Nuys HS
Los Angeles, CA

Byrne, Bob E
Castle Park HS
Chula Vista, CA

Byun, Chiyong
University HS
Los Angeles, CA

Byun, Daniel S
Brea-Olinda HS
Brea, CA

Cabaccang,
Alexander C
Edison HS
Stockton, CA

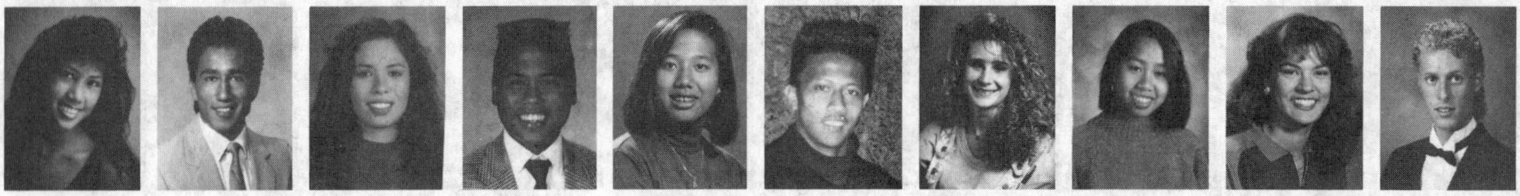

Caballa, Jennifer
El Capitan HS
Lakeside, CA

Caballero, Daniel
John A Rowland HS
Rowland Heights, CA

Cabasa, Melissa Y
Golden West HS
Visalia, CA

Cabebe, Elwyn C
Saint Ignatius College Prep
South San Francis, CA

Caberte, Karen A
Herbert Hoover HS
Glendale, CA

Cabida, Gary
East Union HS
Lathrop, CA

Cabral, Jennifer K
Durham HS
Chico, CA

Cabral, Marisa V
Balboa HS
San Francisco, CA

Cabral, Taunya M
Highlands HS
Sacramento, CA

Cabreira, Kent Benjamin
Rio Lindo Adventist Acad
Lodi, CA

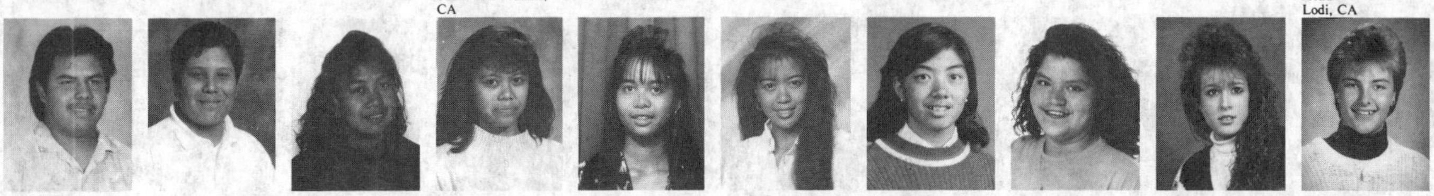

Cabrera, Carlos R
Dinuba HS
Dinuba, CA

Cabrera, Mark A
Tulare Western HS
Tulare, CA

Cabuay, Jacqueline A
Warren HS
Downey, CA

Cacal, Cheryl D
South San Francisco
Daly City, CA

Cacananta, Carla L
Rancho Alamitos HS
Garden Grove, CA

Cacao, Melinda
St Patrick-St Vincent
Vallejo, CA

Cachuela, Frances Ann R
Bishop Montgomery
Hawthorne, CA

Cadena, Jacqueline
William Workman
Valinda, CA

Cadoura, Rania W
Brea Olinda HS
Brea, CA

Cady, Michelle M
Ferndale HS
Ferndale, CA

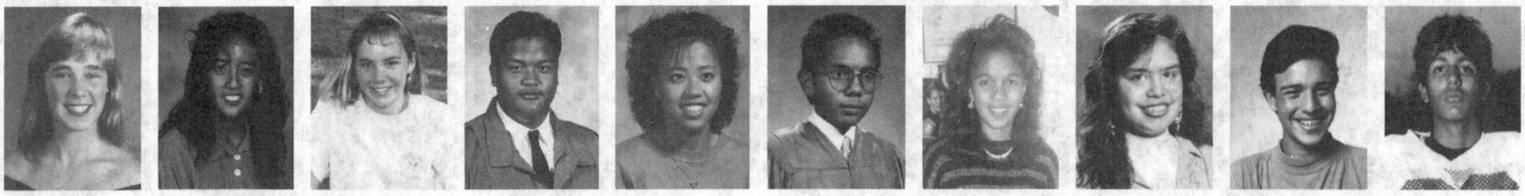

Cafasso, Donna L
Sir Francis Drake HS
San Anselmo, CA

Cagulada, Karen A
Louisville HS
Northridge, CA

Cahill, Melissa L
Bakersfield West HS
Bakersfield, CA

Cajiuat, Justin H
Santa Clara HS
Oxnard, CA

Calaguas, Jennifer M
Lemoore HS
Lemoore, CA

Calagui, Antonio A
Sacred Heart Cathedral Prep
Daly City, CA

Calagui, Venus
Sacred Heart Cathedral Prep
Daly City, CA

Caldera, Jennifer A
Hawthorne HS
Lawndale, CA

Calderon, Mario A
Brea-Olinda HS
Brea, CA

Calderon, Ray
Indio HS
Indio, CA

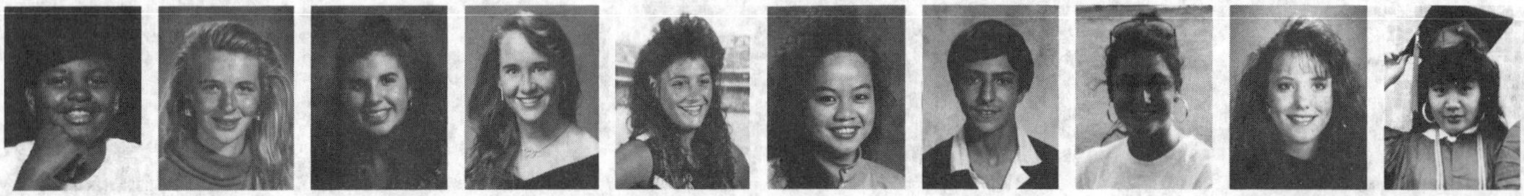

Caldwell, Sharmel N
Luther Burbank HS
Sacramento, CA

Calhoon, Brooke
Calvary Chapel HS
Lake Forest, CA

Calhoun, Heather J
Marymount HS
Los Angeles, CA

Callahan, Cristina R
St Monica HS
Los Angeles, CA

Callahan, Tammi
Red Bluff HS
Red Bluff, CA

Calo, Roselle B
Porterville HS
Terra Bella, CA

Caloia, Jr William P
John W North HS
Riverside, CA

Calvert, Jessica G
Mt View HS
Los Altos, CA

Calvird, Jennifer L
Amos Alonzo Stagg
Stockton, CA

Cam, Ha Truong Thi
Costa Mesa HS
Santa Ana, CA

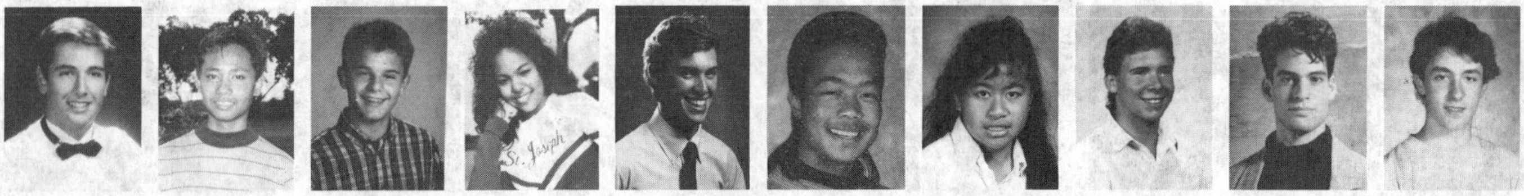

Camacho, Jr Guillermo Andres
De La Salle HS
Honolulu, HI

Camaquin, Jayboy L
Orosi HS
Orosi, CA

Camara, Joseph R
Turlock HS
Delhi, CA

Cambay, Cheryl
St Joseph HS
Yorba Linda, CA

Cameron, Ian T
Napa HS
Napa, CA

Camiling, Eric M
Irvine HS
Irvine, CA

Camilo, Lynn R
Mater Dei HS
Costa Mesa, CA

Caminata, Jeffrey P
St Marys HS
Stockton, CA

Cammilleri, Gaius S
Arcadia HS
Arcadia, CA

Camp, Bayliss
Sacramento HS
Sacramento, CA

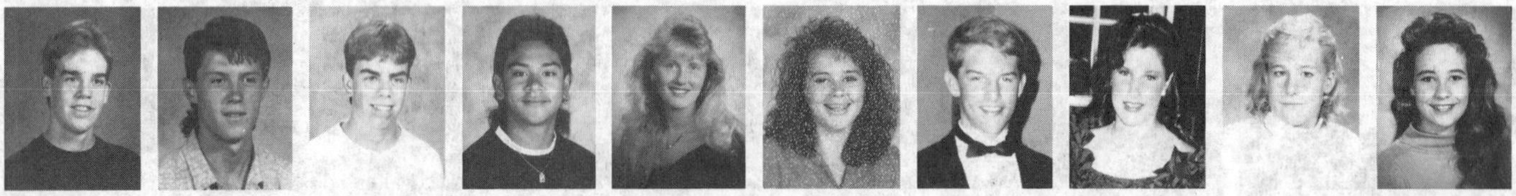

Camp, Ken A
Canyon Springs HS
Moreno Valley, CA

Camp, Shawn E
Lemoore HS
Lemoore, CA

Camp, Tom
Canyon Springs HS
Moreno Valley, CA

Campa, Fernando A
Tranquillity HS
Firebaugh, CA

Campbell, Beth A
Moorpark HS
Moorpark, CA

Campbell, Catrina
Dos Palos Joint Union HS
Dos Palos, CA

Campbell, Chris K
Loyola HS
La Canada Flintri, CA

Campbell, Colleen M
Mayfield SR HS
La Canada Flintri, CA

Campbell, Diana L
Independence HS
San Jose, CA

Campbell, Elisabeth
Antelope Valley HS
Lancaster, CA

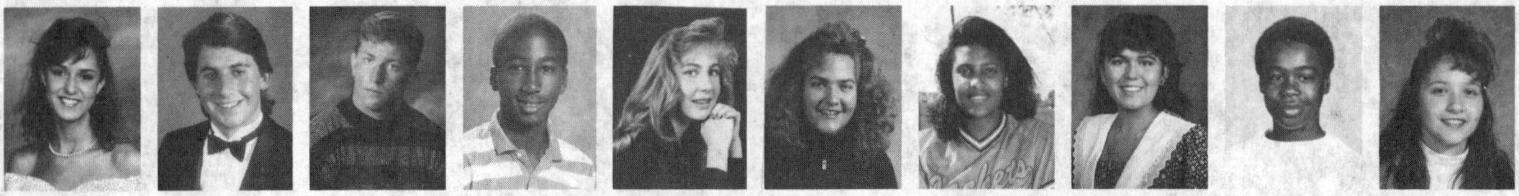

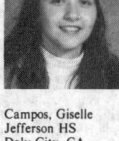

Campbell, Jenny L
Chaparral HS
Santee, CA

Campbell, Kevin W
San Marin HS
Novato, CA

Campbell, Mark A
Carlsbad HS
Oceanside, CA

Campbell, Raycean D
Channel Island HS
Oxnard, CA

Campbell, Shelene R
Fortuna Union HS
Fortuna, CA

Campbell, Tammie
Argonaut HS
Jackson, CA

Campbell, Tisha M
Oxnard HS
Oxnard, CA

Campos, Abigail Lorraine
Alverno HS
Duarte, CA

Campos, Charles
Pittsburg HS
Pittsburg, CA

Campos, Giselle
Jefferson HS
Daly City, CA

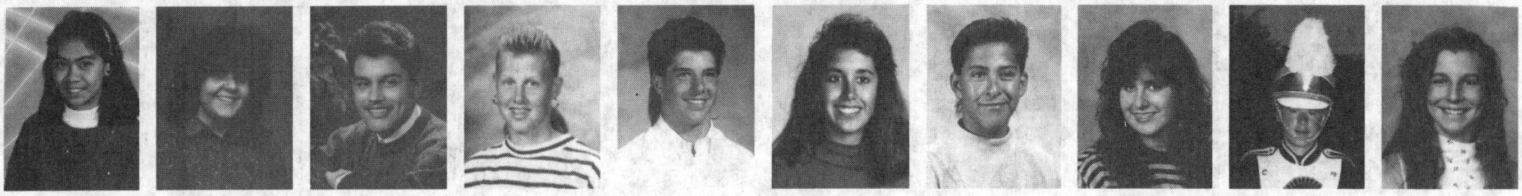

Campos, Joanne R
Mission San Jose HS
Fremont, CA

Campos, Maria Y
Grant Union HS
Sacramento, CA

Campos, Ramiro
Sonoma Valley HS
Boyes Hot Springs, CA

Canaday, Rebecca A
Armijo HS
Suisun, CA

Canady, Daniel V
Monterey HS
Seaside, CA

Canales, Miriam
Tulare Union HS
Tulare, CA

Canchola, Orlando E
Antelope Valley HS
Lancaster, CA

Canfield, Christine
Christian HS
Pine Valley, CA

Cannella, John
Mountain View HS
Mountain View, CA

Cannon, Alanya C
S C P A O'farrell
San Diego, CA

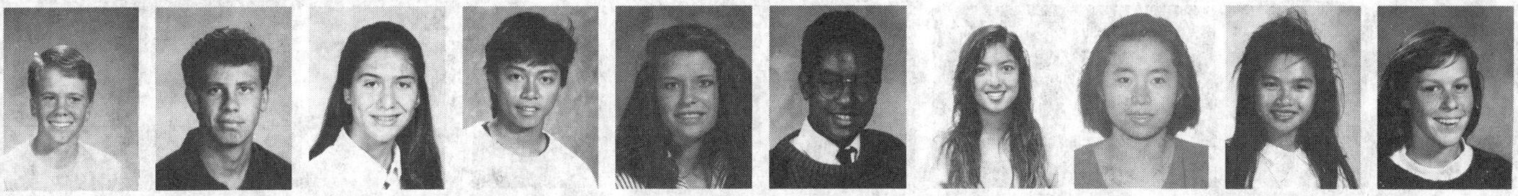

Cannon, Sean B
Oakmont HS
Roseville, CA

Cantelmi, Daniel S
Tulare HS
Tulare, CA

Cantero, Susana M
Notre Dame Acad
Los Angeles, CA

Cantillo, John P
San Leandro HS
San Leandro, CA

Cantrell, Kristin Michelle
Los Alamitos HS
Los Alamitos, CA

Cantrell, Tracy D
Vanden HS
Indianapolis, IN

Cantu, Nicole Daniella
San Pedro HS
San Pedro, CA

Cao, Bach-Mai T
Bolsa Grande HS
Garden Grove, CA

Cao, Katie M
Workman HS
West Covina, CA

Caplette, Melissa
Indio HS
Indio, CA

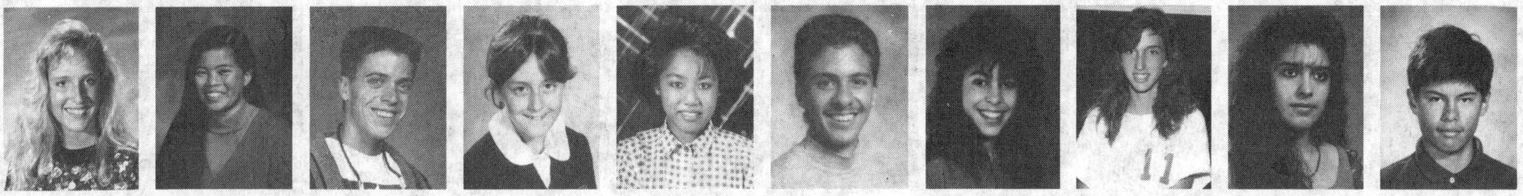

Caplis, Christine S
Foothill HS
Santa Ana, CA

Capobres, Karen A
Monterey Bay Acad
San Gabriel, CA

Capogeannis, Aristomenis W
Bellarmine College Prep
Saratoga, CA

Capshaw, Emily R
Hamilton Music Acad
Los Angeles, CA

Caracas, Sherrill
Southwest HS
San Diego, CA

Caracoza, Victor
Southwest HS
San Ysidro, CA

Caravallo, Janey
Newark Memorial
Newark, CA

Caraway, Jennifer M
Madera HS
Madera, CA

Carbajal, Karina J
Central Union HS
El Centro, CA

Carbajo, Charles S
Daniel Murphy HS
Los Angeles, CA

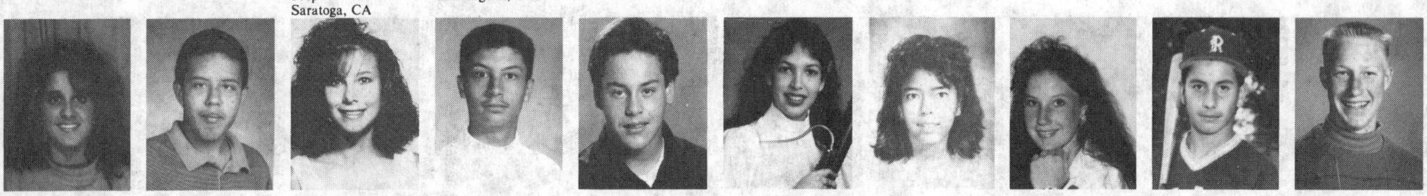

Carbone, Janette
Warren HS
Downey, CA

Cardenas, Daniel C
River City HS
W Sacramento, CA

Cardenas, Liza E
James Lick HS
San Jose, CA

Cardenas, Milton C
James Lick HS
San Jose, CA

Cardenas, Peter A
Leuzinger HS
Hawthorne, CA

Cardiel, Elaine L
Roseville HS
Rocklin, CA

Cardona, Camille
Villa Park HS
Orange, CA

Cardona, Tracey E
Beaumont HS
Cherry Valley, CA

Cardoza, Gilbert V
Ramona HS
Riverside, CA

Cardoza, Johnny R
Turlock HS
Turlock, CA

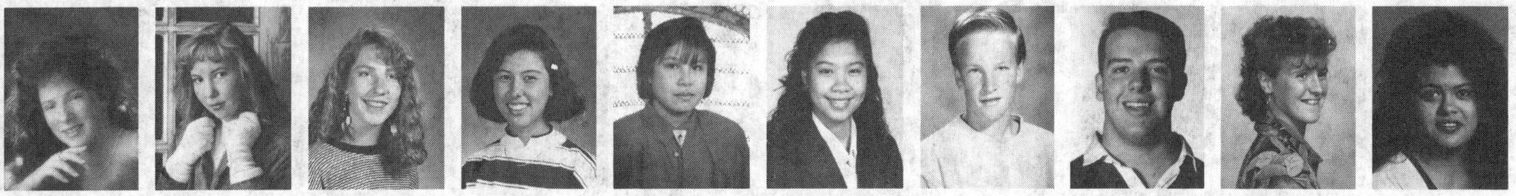

Carey, Gina M
Mercy HS
San Bruno, CA

Carey, Jennifer Diane
Shasta HS
Redding, CA

Cargill, Christiane E
Lutheran HS Of Orange County
Santa Ana, CA

Carhart, Christine A
Grace Davis HS
Modesto, CA

Carig, Madonna F
Hemet HS
Hemet, CA

Caringal, Mary Gay
Notre Dame Acad
Los Angeles, CA

Carley, John L
Dana Hills HS
Laguna Niguel, CA

Carlisle, Jason D
Elk Grove HS
Sacramento, CA

Carlock, Julie M
Selma HS
Selma, CA

Carlos, Evelia
Norte Vista HS
Riverside, CA

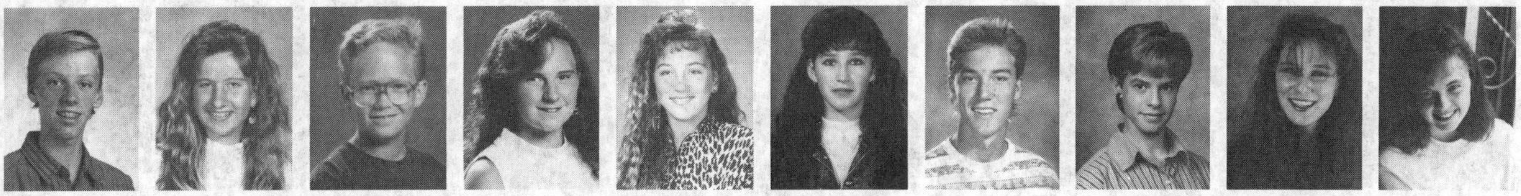

Carlsen, Stephen E
Prospect HS
San Jose, CA

Carlson, Michelle M
Santa Teresa HS
San Jose, CA

Carlson, Richard A
Sierra Vista HS
Baldwin Park, CA

Carlson, Shari A
Norte Vista HS
Riverside, CA

Carmo, Nicole
Foothill HS
Pleasanton, CA

Carmona, Evelia
Mt Whitney HS
Farmersville, CA

Carney, Michael A
Villa Park HS
Orange, CA

Carosino, Lisa M
SCPA O'farrell HS
San Diego, CA

Carpenter, Amber D
Poway HS
San Diego, CA

Carpenter, April L
Grossmont HS
La Mesa, CA

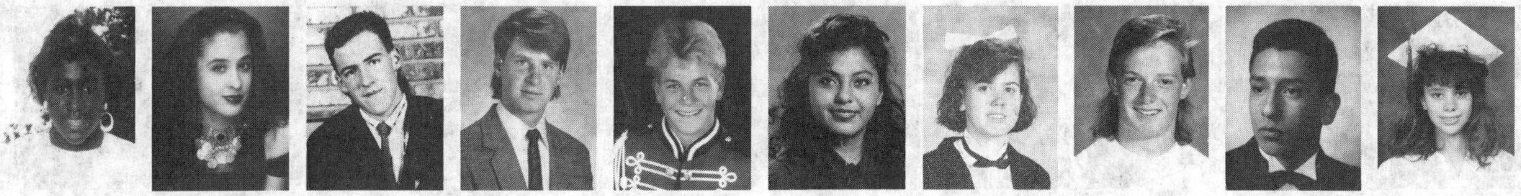

Carpenter, Emily A
St Joseph Notre Dame HS
Alameda, CA

Carpenter, Natalie
Fred C Beyer HS
Modesto, CA

Carr, Adam T
Pittsburg HS
Pittsburg, CA

Carr, Dion G
St Francis HS
Sunnyvale, CA

Carr, William R
Poway HS
Poway, CA

Carrasco, Jacqueline
Baldwin Park HS
Baldwin Park, CA

Carrick, Sheri
Yosemite Union HS
Coarsegold, CA

Carrico, Jeffrey
San Ramon Valley
San Ramon, CA

Carrillo, Andrew
Santa Clara HS
Oxnard, CA

Carrillo, Maritza
St Joseph HS
Bell Gardens, CA

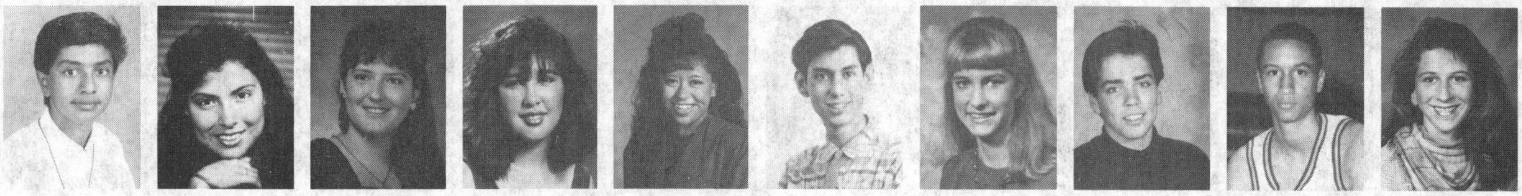

Carrillo, Rudy
Coachella Valley HS
Coachella, CA

Carrillo, Ruth M
J Eugene Mc Ateer
San Francisco, CA

Carrillo, Tina M
El Toro HS
El Toro, CA

Carrillo, Vanessa D
Sacred Heart HS
Alhambra, CA

Carrizales, Melinda E
Kearny HS
San Diego, CA

Carrizosa, Kenneth S
Glendale Adventist
Acad
Los Angeles, CA

Carroll, Sarah E
Orange Glen HS
Fallbrook, CA

Carroll, Tom
Hayward HS
Hayward, CA

Carruthers, Tony S
St Francis HS
Altadena, CA

Carson, Charissa J
Grossmont HS
La Mesa, CA

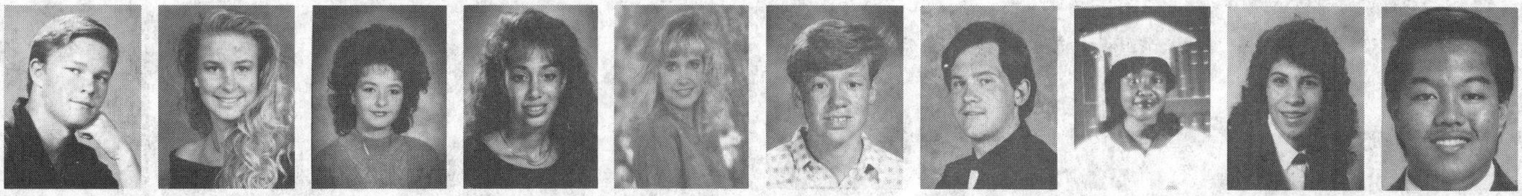

Carson, David
Arcadia HS
Arcadia, CA

Carter, Alyssa B
Lakewood SR HS
Lakewood, CA

Carter, April
Exeter Union HS
Farmersville, CA

Carter, Blayne A
Westlake HS
Westlake Vlg, CA

Carter, Carrie
Bishop Union HS
Bishop, CA

Carter, Eric
Calvary Chapel HS
Santa Ana, CA

Carter, Jason L
Fontana HS
Fontana, CA

Carter, Juina R
Skyline HS
Oakland, CA

Carter, Marina L
Cerritos HS
Cerritos, CA

Carter, Michael A
Vacaville HS
Vacaville, CA

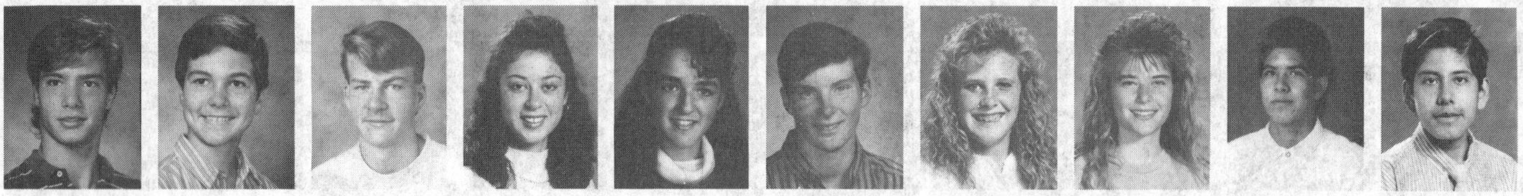

Carter, Richard J
Mission Viejo HS
Mission Viejo, CA

Carter, Steve B
Irvine HS
Irvine, CA

Caruthers, Brent
Palmdale HS
Palmdale, CA

Carvajal, Guadalupe
Nathaniel Narbonne
Harbor City, CA

Carvalho, Ana M
Turlock HS
Turlock, CA

Carver, Richard P
Del Campo HS
Carmichael, CA

Casalman, Stephanie
Fontana HS
Fontana, CA

Casaray, Christina
San Lorenzo HS
San Lorenzo, CA

Casas, Luis F
Montgomery HS
San Diego, CA

Casceres, Byron
Bellermine Jefferson
Burbank, CA

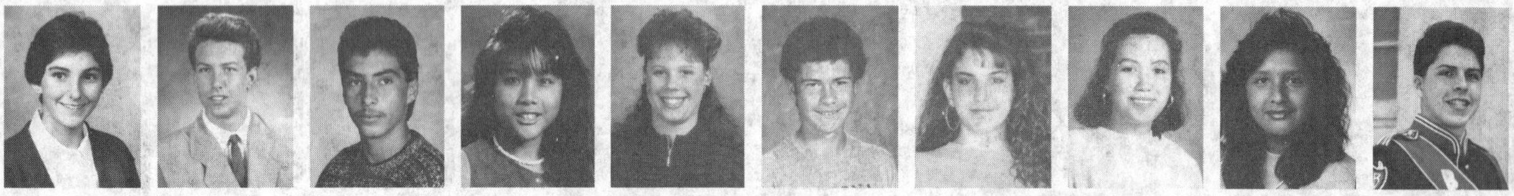

Cascio, Angela M
Acad Of Our Lady
Of Peace
Bonita, CA

Cash, Mathew
Golden West HS
Ivanhoe, CA

Casillas, Jr Esteban
Hilltop HS
Bonita, CA

Casino, Leila G
Holy Family HS
Los Angeles, CA

Cassaday, Suzanne L
Redwood HS
Visalia, CA

Cassidy, Jason
South Bay Christian
Sunnyvale, CA

Castagnini, Tina
Las Lomas HS
Walnut Creek, CA

Castaneda, Carla P
Ripon HS
Ripon, CA

Castaneda,
Guadalupe F
Saint Anthony HS
Carson, CA

Castaneda, Jason T
East Bakersfield HS
Bakersfield, CA

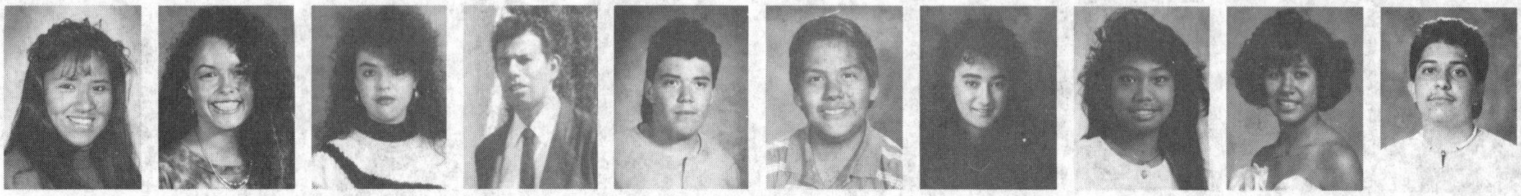

Castaneda, Martha E
Live Oak HS
Live Oak, CA

Castelblanco, Ceci
Alameda HS
Alameda, CA

Castellano, Juanita B
Golden West HS
Visalia, CA

Castellanos, Rene A
Skyline HS
Oakland, CA

Castellanoz, Daniel
Tulare Western HS
Tulare, CA

Castgllanos, Jesus
Lynwood HS
Lynwood, CA

Castillo, A Mireya
Bishop Amat HS
San Gabriel, CA

Castillo, Aileen A
Notre Dame HS
San Jose, CA

Castillo, Amy A
Mater Dei HS
Santa Ana, CA

Castillo, Cesar R
Castle Park HS
Chula Vista, CA

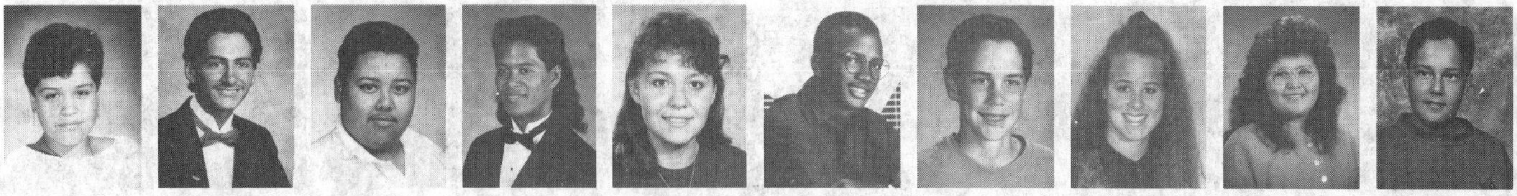

Castillo, Isabel
Santa Monica HS
Santa Monica, CA

Castillo, Jesus M
Abraham Lincoln HS
San Jose, CA

Castillo, Jonathan C
Grant HS
Sacramento, CA

Castillo, Joseph N
Pasadena HS
Pasadena, CA

Castillo, Karla
Elizabeth
Pasadena HS
Pasadena, CA

Castle, Chadwick B
Canyon Springs HS
Moreno Valley, CA

Castle, John
Bret Harte Union HS
Douglas Flat, CA

Castle, Tammy
Inland Christian Schl
Rialto, CA

Castrillo, Pauline
Dolores
Golden West HS
Visalia, CA

Castro, Arturo
St Paul HS
South Gate, CA

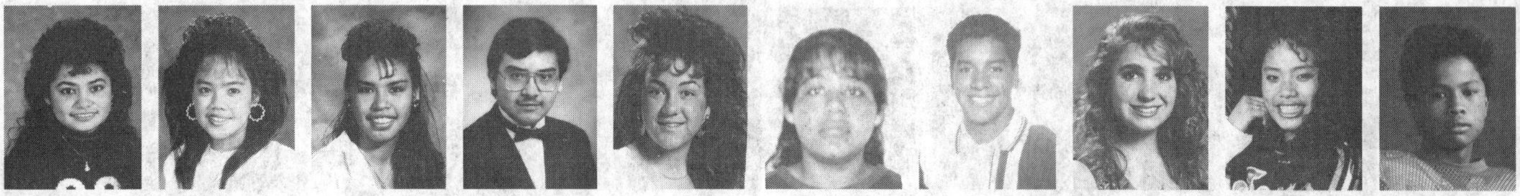

Castro, Cenia X
International Studies
Acad
San Francisco, CA

Castro, Elaine O
Morse HS
San Diego, CA

Castro, Elzby
March Mountain HS
Moreno Valley, CA

Castro, Jose F
Southwest HS
San Ysidro, CA

Castro, Karrie A
Santa Paula Union
Santa Paula, CA

Castro, Nancy
Fontana HS
Fontana, CA

Castro, Victor
Mar Vista HS
Imperial Beach, CA

Castro, Virginia
Sierra Vista HS
Baldwin Park, CA

Castroverde, Candice
Foothill HS
Bakersfield, CA

Casupanan, Marvin L
Bishop Amat HS
West Covina, CA

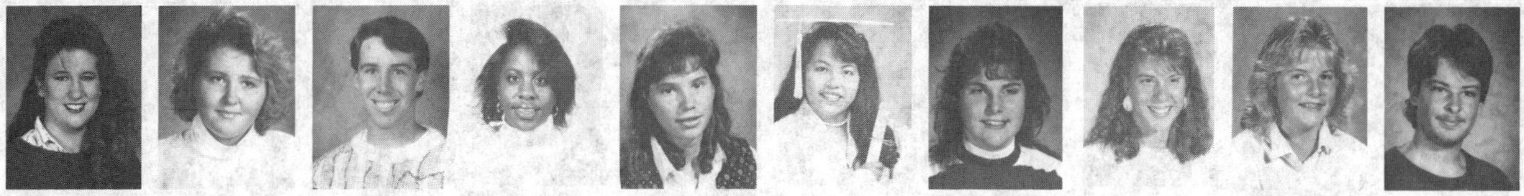

Cataline, Janeen M
Woodcrest Christian
Moreno Valley, CA

Catanzarite, Michelle
Turlock HS
Turlock, CA

Cate, Reggie N
Yucaipa HS
Yucaipa, CA

Cater, Tanesha
Far West HS
Oakland, CA

Cathcart, Nicole D
Torrey Pines HS
Rancho Santa Fe, CA

Catle, Mary Grace M
St Joseph HS
Downey, CA

Caton, Tonya
Faith Christian HS
Bangor, CA

Catron, Jill D
Arroyo Grande HS
Arroyo Grande, CA

Cattrone, Tina M
College Park HS
Pleasant Hill, CA

Caudill, Shawn L
Monache HS
Porterville, CA

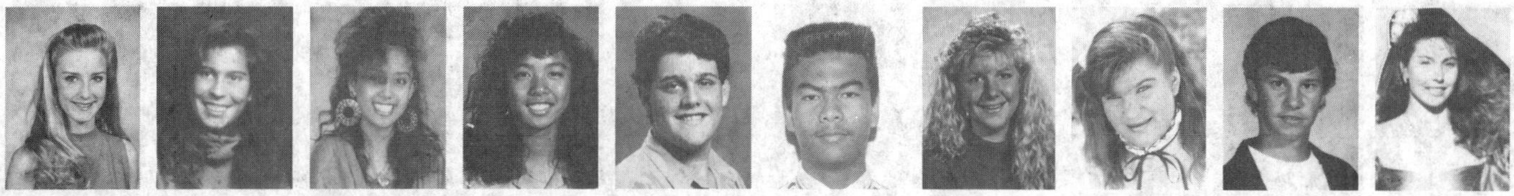

Caudwell, Jessica
St Francis HS
Sacramento, CA

Caulfield, Monique A
Helix HS
El Cajon, CA

Caunan, Maria Erma
Mia B
Bishop Amat Mem
W Covina, CA

Cauntay, Krishna L
Notre Dame HS
Salinas, CA

Causey, III Emmit M
Fontana HS
Fontana, CA

Cauton, Kendall
Omar E
Richmond HS
San Pablo, CA

Cavallini, Cassandra
Carlmont HS
San Carlos, CA

Cavanaugh, Briana E
Buena Park HS
La Palma, CA

Caveney, Chris M
Santa Teresa HS
San Jose, CA

Caves, Jody
Corona HS
Corona, CA

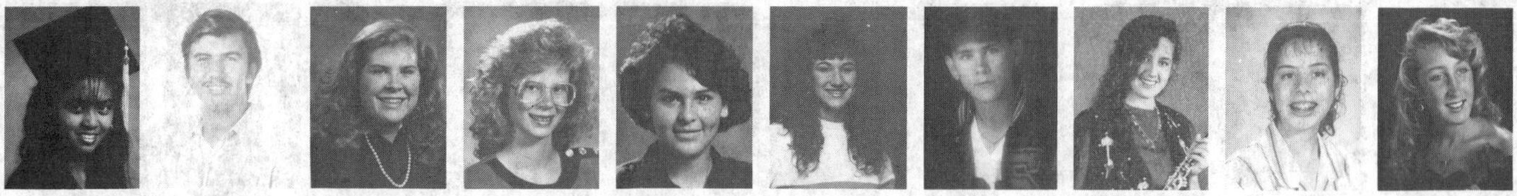

Cayosa, Grace
Van Nuys HS
Los Angeles, CA

Cazarez, Cenen
Coachella Valley HS
Thermal, CA

Cazorla, Marina
C K Mc Clatchy SR
Sacramento, CA

Cde Baca, Tricia
Pioneer Baptist HS
Norwalk, CA

Ceballos, Brenda P
Glendale HS
Glendale, CA

Cecchini, Jeannine
Liberty Union HS
Oakley, CA

Cecic-Karuzic, Marko
Santa Rosa HS
Santa Rosa, CA

Cedillo, Aubree
Whitney HS
Cerritos, CA

Cedillos, Karina
Schurr HS
Moreno Valley, CA

Cefaloni, Andraya
San Lorenzo Valley
Santa Cruz, CA

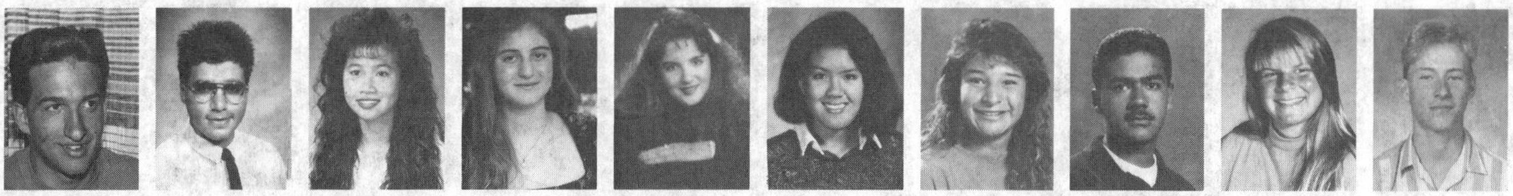

Celani, Jim V
Antelope Valley HS
Lancaster, CA

Celaya, Mark A
Pater Noster HS
Los Angeles, CA

Celestial, Jeannie J
Dr James J Hogan
Vallejo, CA

Celik, Aytek Esen
Claremont HS
Claremont, CA

Celio, Sherry
Center HS
North Highlands, CA

Cenidoza, Theresa B
Mountain View HS
Milpitas, CA

Cerda, Laura M
Santa Paula Union
Santa Paula, CA

Cerda, Robert P
Sierra Vista HS
Baldwin Park, CA

Cereghino, Susan E
Sequoia HS
San Carlos, CA

Cerio, Daniel
Brethren JR/SR HS
Downey, CA

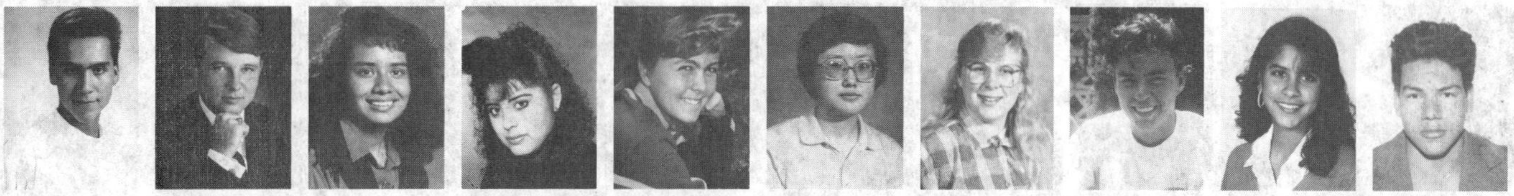

Cerna, Leon D
Hesperia HS
Hesperia, CA

Certonio, Jerry
Quartz Hill HS
Lancaster, CA

Cervantes, Jayne M
Lindsay HS
Lindsay, CA

Cervantes, Julie
Banning HS
Wilmington, CA

Cervantes, Tyra
West Hills HS
Santee, CA

Cha, Soo-Jin
Bonita Vista SR HS
Bonita, CA

Chabot, Stacy
Righetti HS
Santa Maria, CA

Chacon, Christopher
Glendale HS
Glendale, CA

Chacon, Cindy V
Nogales HS
W Covina, CA

Chacon, Mario E
Los Angeles HS
Los Angeles, CA

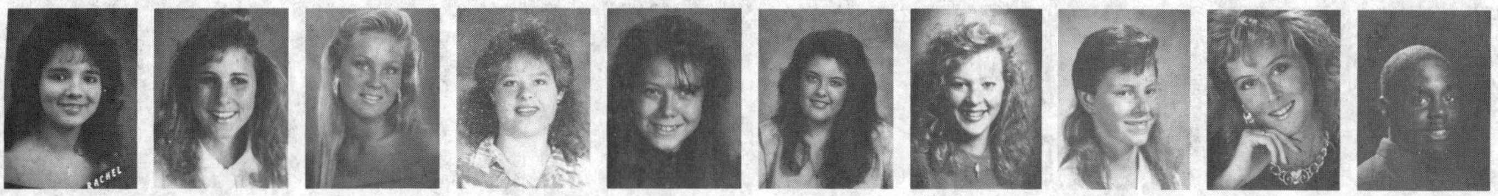

Chacon, Rachel
Alisal HS
Salinas, CA

Chaddock, Deborah
Calaveras HS
Linden, CA

Chadwick, Myke
Palmdale HS
Palmdale, CA

Chaffin, Julie M
Tranquillity Union
Cantua Creek, CA

Chagolla, Lydia A
Bret Harte HS
Avery, CA

Chagollan, Samantha
Edison HS
Huntington Beach, CA

Chalmers, Amanda
Don Antonio Lugo
Chino, CA

Chamberlain, Asenath
Pioneer HS
San Jose, CA

Chambers, Heather A
Diamond Bar HS
Chino Hills, CA

Chambers, Randy S
Carson HS
Carson, CA

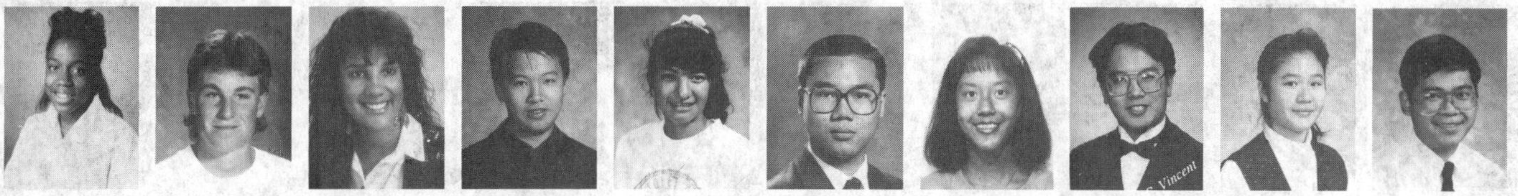

Chambers, Vicky L
Arlington HS
Riverside, CA

Chamblee, Donald Thomas
Clayton Valley HS
Concord, CA

Chamorro, Gisette M
Pioneer HS
San Jose, CA

Chan, Benjamin E
St Ignatius College Prep
Hercules, CA

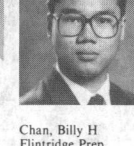

Chan, Beverly P
San Gabriel HS
San Gabriel, CA

Chan, Billy H
Flintridge Prep
San Marino, CA

Chan, Calona
Notre Dame HS
Redwood City, CA

Chan, Christopher V
St Ignatius College Prep
Hercules, CA

Chan, Cici
Encinal HS
Alameda, CA

Chan, Clint C
Bishop O'dowd HS
Oakland, CA

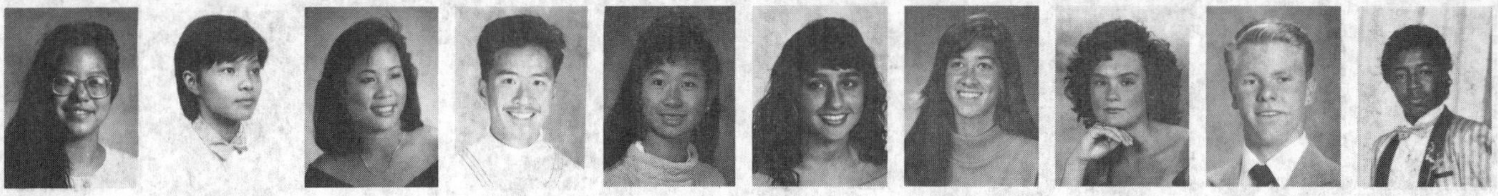

Chan, Eileen
Thomas Edison HS
Stockton, CA

Chan, Justina K
Eagle Rock HS
Los Angeles, CA

Chan, Lisa A
Los Altos HS
Los Altos, CA

Chan, Stanley G
Lowell HS
San Francisco, CA

Chan, Wai Yee
Irvine HS
Irvine, CA

Chandler, Ivy
Nogales HS
Walnut, CA

Chandler, Kala
Piedmont HS
Piedmont, CA

Chandler, Kami
Lassen Union HS
Susanville, CA

Chandler, Scott S
Fullerton Union HS
Fullerton, CA

Chaney, Ephriam Jerome
Hogan SR HS
Vallejo, CA

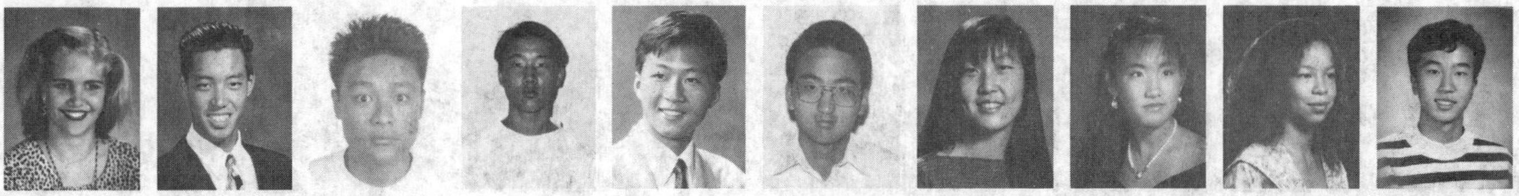

Chaney, Jennifer A
Merced HS
Merced, CA

Chang, Alan
Montery Bay Acad
Camarillo, CA

Chang, Alex
San Gabriel HS
Alhambra, CA

Chang, Charlie
Diamond Bar HS
Walnut, CA

Chang, David H
Arcadia HS
Arcadia, CA

Chang, Francis
Monta Vista HS
Cupertino, CA

Chang, Heeyeon
Narbonne Math/Science Magnet HS
San Pedro, CA

Chang, Jennifer
Santa Monica HS
Santa Monica, CA

Chang, Nadine
Woodbridge HS
Irvine, CA

Chang, Peter
Ukiah HS
Ukiah, CA

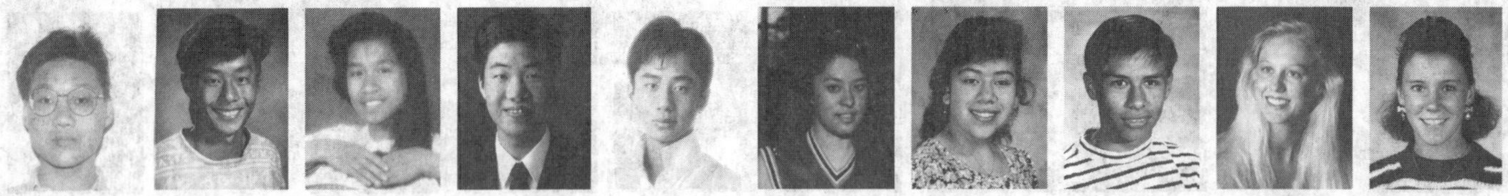

Chang, Steven H
Servite HS
Fullerton, CA

Chang, Tony L
Torrey Pines HS
San Diego, CA

Chanthilack, Suphaphorn
Amos Avonzo Stagg
Stockton, CA

Chao, Edward
Bishop Amat HS
Azusa, CA

Chao, Tommy S
Gahr HS
Cerritos, CA

Chaparro, Angie A
Santa Clara HS
Oxnard, CA

Chaparro, Sandra C
Bishop Amat Memorial HS
La Puente, CA

Chaparro, Steven A
Chino HS
Chino, CA

Chapey, Deva
San Dieguito HS
Encinitas, CA

Chapman, Erica
Orland Joint Union
Orland, CA

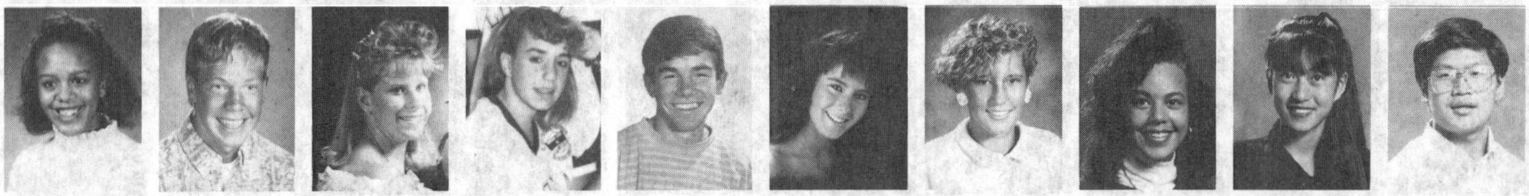

Chapman, Sabrina
Northgate HS
Walnut Creek, CA

Chappell, Todd
Lincoln HS
Stockton, CA

Chapton, Dawn D
Temecula Valley HS
Temecula, CA

Charette, Chantal M
Los Alamitos HS
Los Alamitos, CA

Charkins, Kevin
Bloomington Christian HS
Wrightwood, CA

Charlton, Marjorie
Palos Verdes HS
Palos Vrds Pen, CA

Chase, Michelle M
Pacifica HS
Cypress, CA

Chatman, Kimberlyn
Mayfield SR Schl
Altadena, CA

Chau, Helen T
Leuzinger HS
Lawndale, CA

Chau, San-Phay
King Drew Medical Magnet HS
Los Angeles, CA

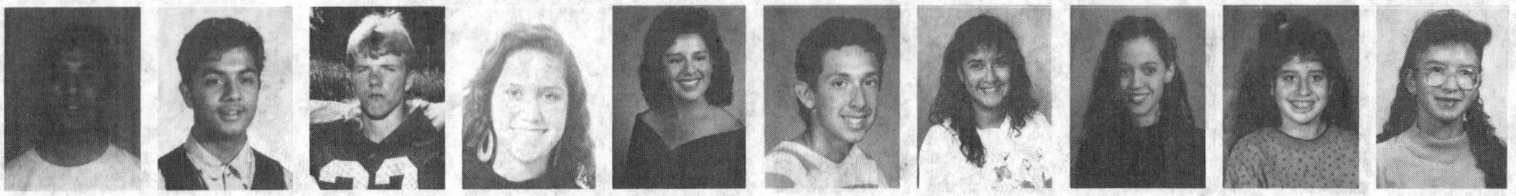

Chaudhry, Faisal
Kennedy HS
La Palma, CA

Chaudhry, Shakil
Woodland HS
Woodland, CA

Chavan, Sheldon
James Lick HS
San Jose, CA

Chavarin, Adriana
Chula Vista HS
Chula Vista, CA

Chavez, Alba
Gahr HS
Artesia, CA

Chavez, Anthony Robert
Bellarmine College Prep
Los Gatos, CA

Chavez, Judy L
Monte Vista HS
Spring Valley, CA

Chavez, Judy S
Redlands HS
Redlands, CA

Chavez, Karen
Pioneer HS
Whittier, CA

Chavez, Margaret L
Montebello HS
Pico Rivera, CA

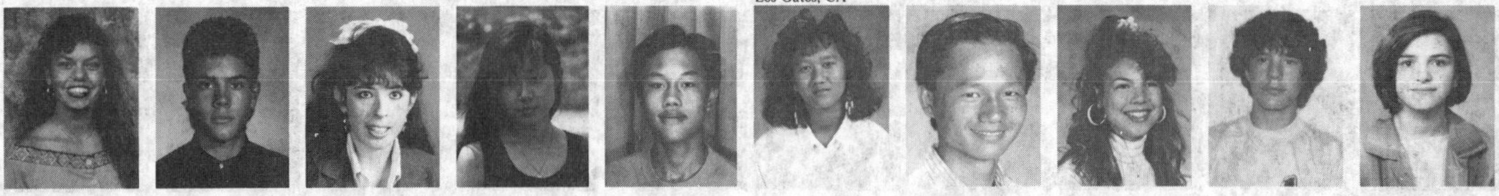

Chavez, Marianne
St Paul HS
Pico Rivera, CA

Chavez, Michael S
Santa Teresa HS
San Jose, CA

Chavez, Veronica
Pius X HS
Lynwood, CA

Chaya, Eri
Gardena HS
Gardena, CA

Che, Stephen
Temple City HS
Temple City, CA

Chea, Sameth
Modesto HS
Modesto, CA

Chear, Visna K
Palm Springs HS
Palm Springs, CA

Checo, Kelly M
Antelope Valley HS
Lancaster, CA

Cheeseman, Ted
Athenian HS
Saratoga, CA

Chehade, Sally A
Roseville HS
Sacramento, CA

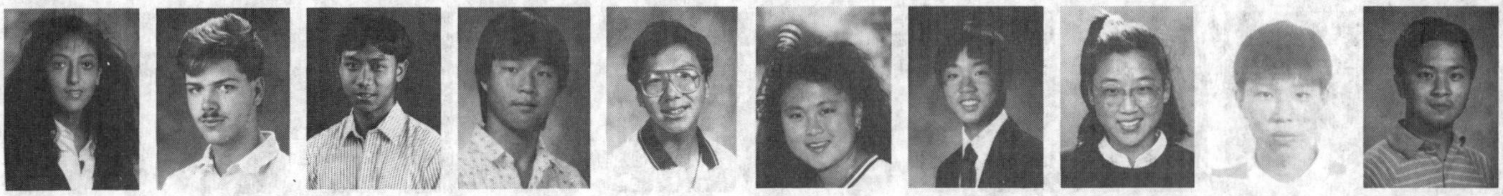

Chelebian, Armine
Armenian Mesrobian Schl
Montebello, CA

Chelette, Jeff
Ramona HS
Riverside, CA

Chem, Sylors
Woodrow Wilson HS
Long Beach, CA

Chen, Alan
Mission Viejo HS
Laguna Hills, CA

Chen, Alan T
John F Kennedy HS
La Palma, CA

Chen, Alice
San Jacinto HS
San Jacinto, CA

Chen, Calvin C
St Ignatius College Prep
San Francisco, CA

Chen, Caroline J
Westlake Schl
Los Angeles, CA

Chen, Chia-Hung
Etiwanda HS
Rancho Cucamonga, CA

Chen, David
Fountain Valley HS
Fountain Valley, CA

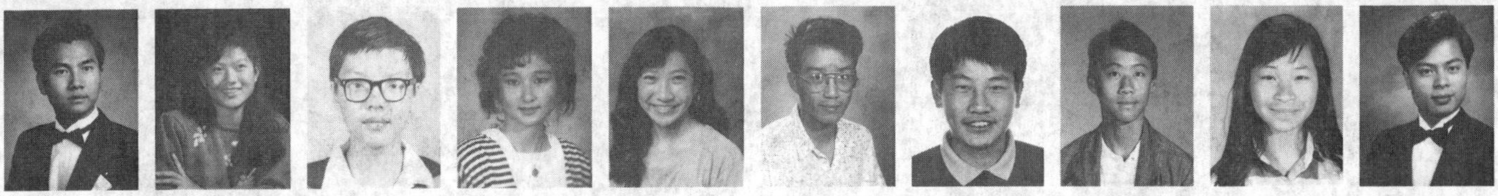

Chen, Echung
Luther Burbank HS
Sacramento, CA

Chen, Hui Ya Helen
San Gabriel HS
Alhambra, CA

Chen, Jiong
San Gabriel HS
San Gabriel, CA

Chen, Katherine J
John F Kennedy HS
La Palma, CA

Chen, Nola
Marymount HS
Los Angeles, CA

Chen, Oscar
Highlands HS
Sacramento, CA

Chen, Paul
Nogales HS
W Covina, CA

Chen, Tim
Chih-Sheng
South San Francisco
S San Francisco, CA

Chen, Trilia
Lowell HS
San Francisco, CA

Chen, Yao-Ning
Galileo HS
San Francisco, CA

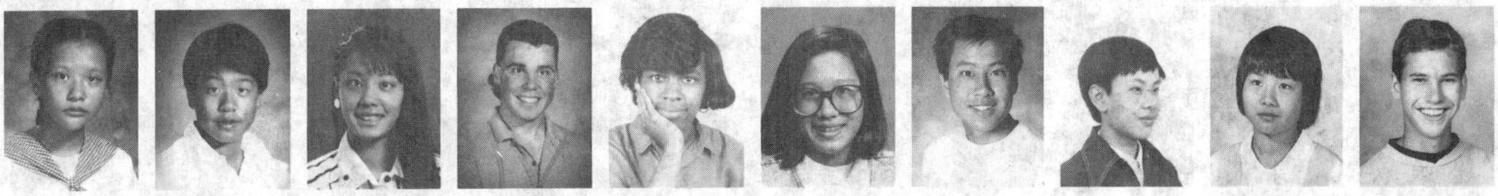

Cheng, Cindy S
Arcadia HS
Arcadia, CA

Cheng, Dennis
Fountain Valley HS
Fountain Valley, CA

Cheng, Sandra T
San Marino HS
San Gabriel, CA

Cherry, Jason W
North HS
Bakersfield, CA

Cherry, Nyesha M
Morningside HS
Los Angeles, CA

Chetbundit, Jaruwan
James Monroe HS
Sepulveda, CA

Cheung, Eddy
Timland
Palos Verdes HS
Rancho Palos Vrds, CA

Cheung, Jason Y
Galileo HS
San Francisco, CA

Cheung, Mia
Alameda HS
Oakland, CA

Chew, Geoffrey T
University City HS
San Diego, CA

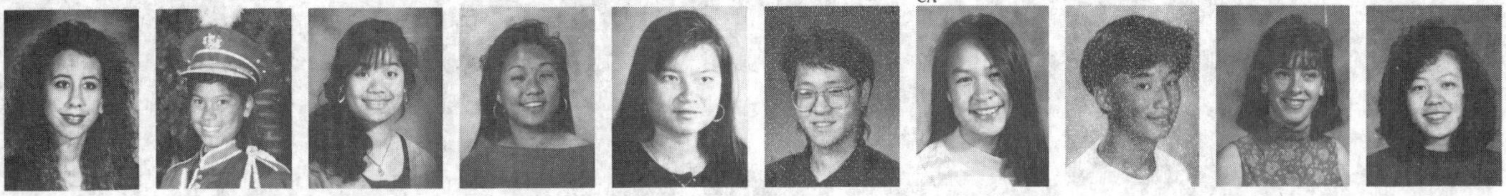

Chew, Lisa M
North HS
Oildale, CA

Chew, Tamara
San Ramon Valley
San Ramon, CA

Chey, Elizabeth
John Glenn HS
Norwalk, CA

Chey, Michele
Rosary HS
Fullerton, CA

Chhay, Pisey
Edison HS
Stockton, CA

Chia, Benny
Monte Vista HS
Danville, CA

Chia, Jessica
Palo Alto HS
Palo Alto, CA

Chiang, Min-Te Eric
Davis SR HS
Davis, CA

Chicconi, Jennifer
Sierra Joint Union
Madera, CA

Chien, Julie C
Lowell HS
San Francisco, CA

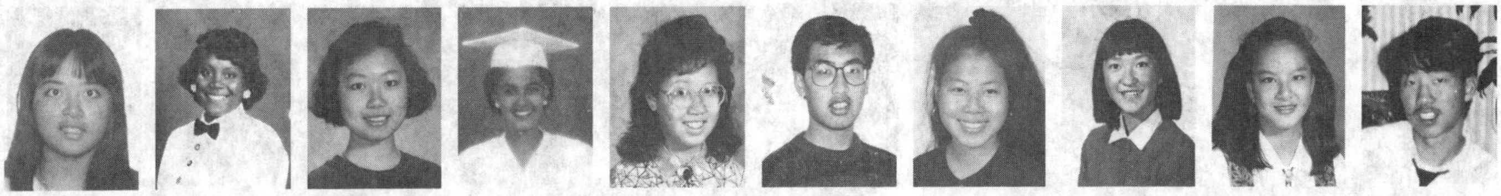

Chien, Linda
University HS
Irvine, CA

Childers, Makeshia R
St Michaels HS
Los Angeles, CA

Chin, Angela Yue
Phillip & Sala Burton
Academic HS
San Francisco, CA

Chin, Edith E
Chula Vista HS
Chula Vista, CA

Chin, Irene C
Alameda HS
Alameda, CA

Chin, Joe H
Lowell HS
San Francisco, CA

Chin, Mildred J
San Gabriel HS
Rosemead, CA

Chin, Sandy
Lowell HS
San Francisco, CA

Chin, Sharon K
Hayward HS
Hayward, CA

Chin, Victor M
San Gabriel HS
Rosemead, CA

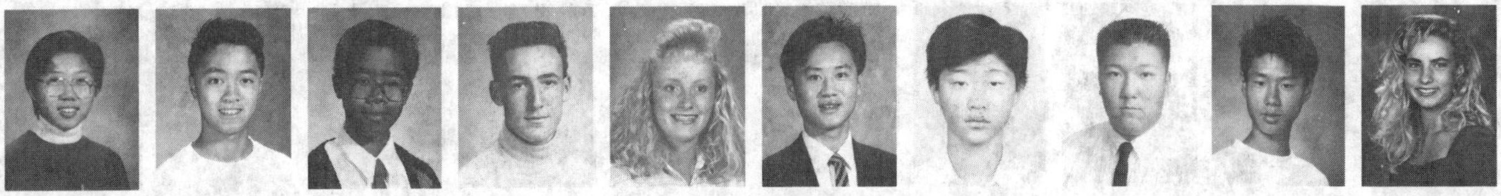

Ching, Angelica
George Moller Schurr
Monterey Park, CA

Ching, Daniel
San Leandro HS
San Leandro, CA

Chio, Jr Arturo B
Walnut HS
Walnut, CA

Chiriano, Jason
Damien HS
Pomona, CA

Chisholm, Jessica A
Hemet HS
Hemet, CA

Chiu, Charlie
Nan-Chao
Saint Ignatius College Prep
San Francisco, CA

Chiu, Pao Y
Whitney HS
Cerritos, CA

Cho, Chong U
Anaheim HS
Anaheim, CA

Cho, Sean
Sunny Hill HS
Irvine, CA

Choate, Catherine A
Redlands HS
Redlands, CA

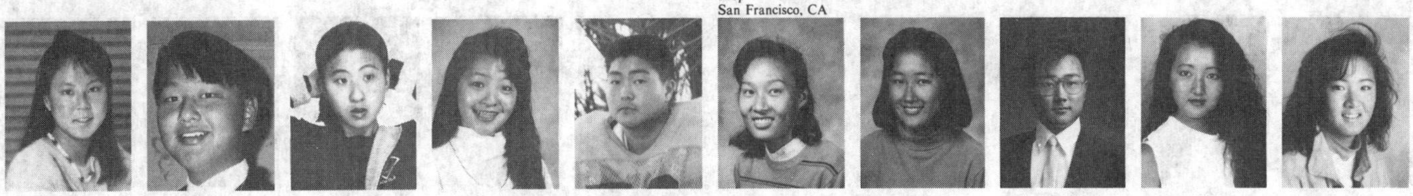

Choe, Julie
Whittier HS
Whittier, CA

Choi, Alvin
William Workman
La Puente, CA

Choi, Christine M
Carlmont HS
Redwood City, CA

Choi, Esther H
Montebello HS
Montebello, CA

Choi, Jai H
Bishop Montgomery
Harbor City, CA

Choi, Jiyun
Los Angeles HS
Los Angeles, CA

Choi, Mieriena
Armijo HS
Fairfield, CA

Chon, Philip B
Crescenta Valley HS
La Crescenta, CA

Chong, Jinyi
Helix HS
San Diego, CA

Chong, Su K
Oxnard HS
Oxnard, CA

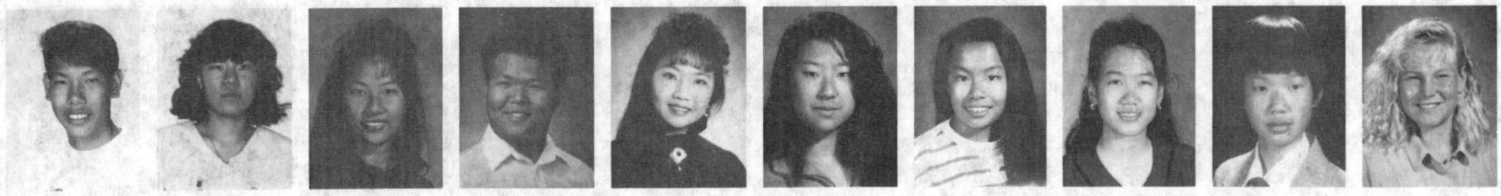

Choo, Allan
Los Altos HS
Hacienda Hts, CA

Chou, Ching
Lowell HS
San Francisco, CA

Chou, Lily
Los Alamitos HS
Seal Beach, CA

Chou, Roy H
Sunny Hills HS
Fullerton, CA

Chou, Ruby
Sunny Hills HS
Fullerton, CA

Chough, Jennifer
Troy HS
Anaheim, CA

Chow, Ming-Fawn
Edison HS
Huntington Beach, CA

Chow, Sophia
Lowell HS
San Francisco, CA

Chow, Wai L
Schurr HS
Monterey Park, CA

Chowning, Tricia D
Cornelia Connelly HS
Whittier, CA

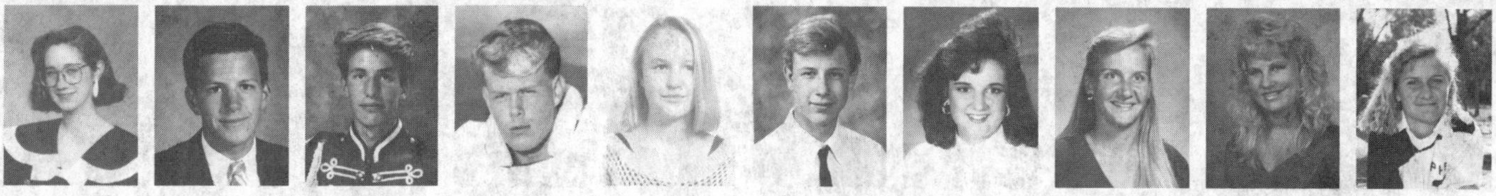

Christ, Courtney
Thomas Downey HS
Blythe, CA

Christen, Anthony T
St Ignatius College Prep
San Francisco, CA

Christensen, Chad
Poway HS
Poway, CA

Christensen, Eric J
Etiwanda HS
Alta Loma, CA

Christensen, Heidi G
Canoga Park HS
Canoga Park, CA

Christensen, Josh
Southwestern Acad
Ridgecrest, CA

Christensen, Kelli J
Don Lugo HS
Chino, CA

Christensen, Michelle
Poway HS
Poway, CA

Christensen, Stacey
Marina HS
Huntington Bch, CA

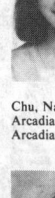

Christensen, Tracey L
Poway HS
Poway, CA

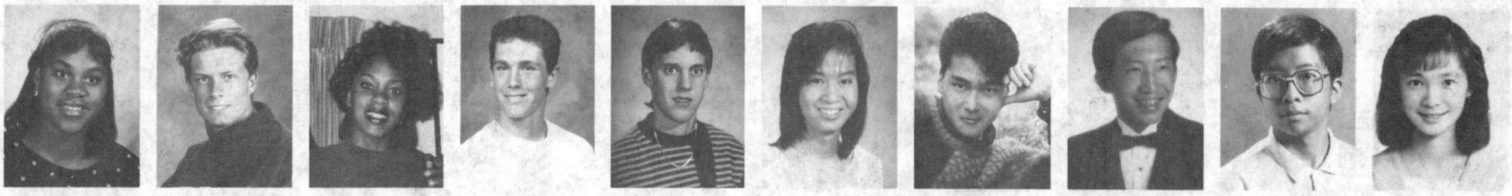

Christian, Aliza L
North Hills Christian Schl
Vallejo, CA

Christian, Michael
Francis W Parker HS
San Diego, CA

Christian, Shamyone
San Lorenzo HS
Oakland, CA

Christian, Shawn T
Mt Empire Unified
Descanso, CA

Christina, Tony
Fortuna Union HS
Carlotta, CA

Chu, Anna
Schurr HS
Los Angeles, CA

Chu, Dave
Taft Union HS
Taft, CA

Chu, David
Aragon HS
San Mateo, CA

Chu, Francis C
John A Rowland HS
Rowland Heights, CA

Chu, Nancy C
Arcadia HS
Arcadia, CA

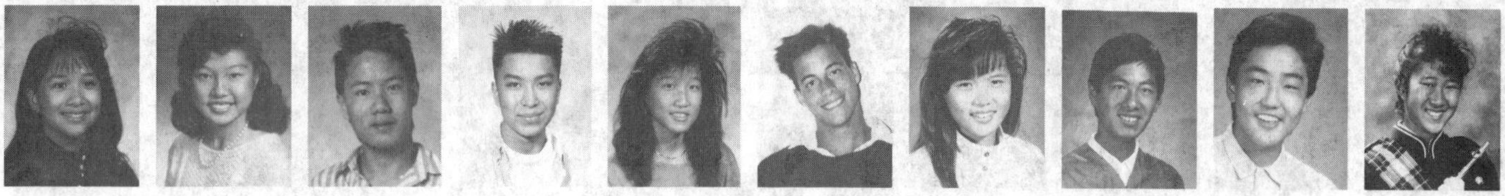

Chua, Melinda M
Will C Wood HS
Vacaville, CA

Chua, Queena L
Los Angeles Baptist
North Hollywood, CA

Chuarta, Ricky I
Alhambra HS
Alhambra, CA

Chun, Edward M
Skyline HS
Oakland, CA

Chung, Christina A
Whitney HS
Cerritos, CA

Chung, Edward C
Servite HS
Laguna Nigael, CA

Chung, Frances
Tustin HS
Tustin, CA

Chung, Frank Wei-Wen
Fremont Christian
Fremont, CA

Chung, John
Bishop Montgomery
Torrance, CA

Chung, June
John F Kennedy HS
La Palma, CA

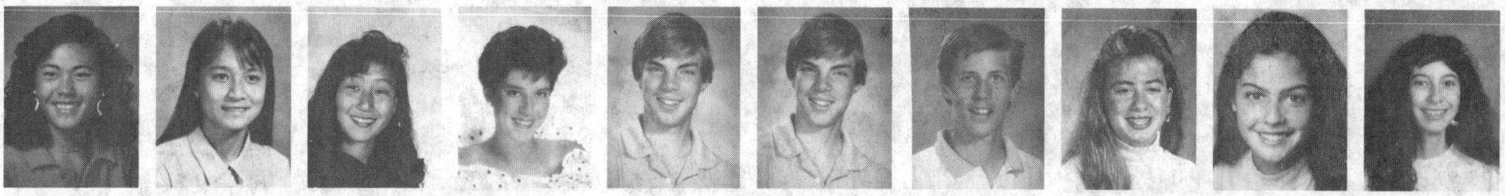

Chung, Melissa
Trabuco Hills HS
Rancho Santa Ma, CA

Chung, Susana C
Oakland HS
Oakland, CA

Chung, Tina H
John A Rowland HS
Walnut, CA

Church, Tiernie E
West HS
Bakersfield, CA

Churchwell, Gary
Bethel Christian HS
Lancaster, CA

Churchwell, Jr Gary
Bethel Christian HS
Lancaster, CA

Churchwell, Kevin
Bethel Christian HS
Lancaster, CA

Churma, Lorrie L
Washington HS
Fremont, CA

Cicalo, Erin J
University Of San Diego HS
San Diego, CA

Ciccanti, Mia
Redlands HS
Redlands, CA

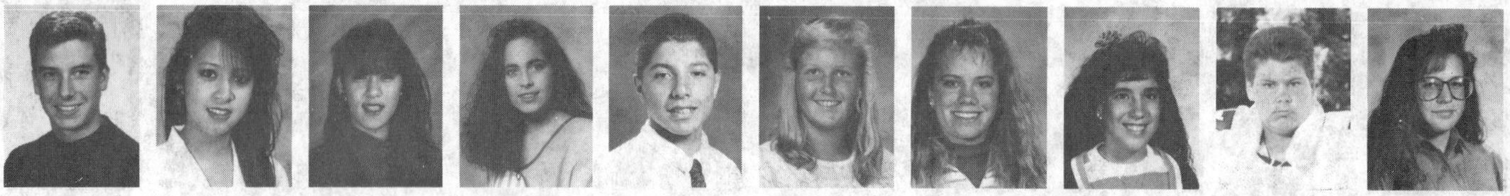

Circo, Dominic
Skyline HS
Oakland, CA

Ciridon, Jennifer W
Bishop Armat Memorial HS
West Covina, CA

Ciridon, Jessica W
Bishop Amat Memorial HS
West Covina, CA

Cisneros, Clarissa C
Central Union HS
El Centro, CA

Cisneros, Tory C
St Francis HS
Alhambra, CA

Clabaugh, Jennifer E
El Toro HS
El Toro, CA

Clack, Cristin M
Carmel HS
Carmel, CA

Clair, Heather
Barstow HS
Barstow, CA

Clair, Jason A
Tustin HS
Tustin, CA

Clancy, Jennifer E
Antelope Valley HS
Lancaster, CA

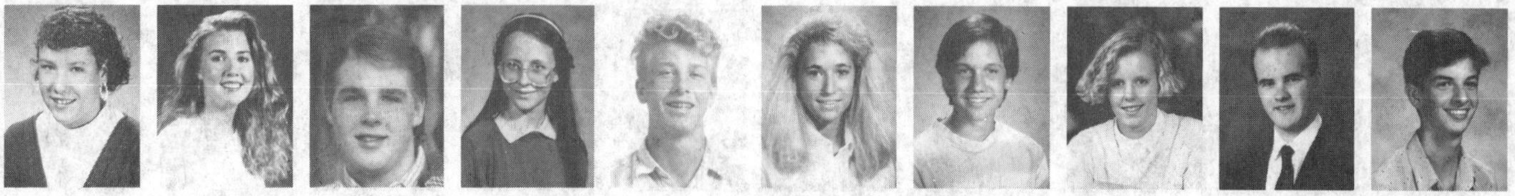

Clark, Elizabeth
Monte Vista HS
Walnut Creek, CA

Clark, Jennifer G
Westridge School For Girls
San Marino, CA

Clark, Jeremy J
Sonora HS
Sonora, CA

Clark, Jessica L
Seoul American HS
APO San Fran, CA

Clark, Justin T
Rancho Alamitos HS
Garden Grove, CA

Clark, Lucille R
Mater Dei HS
Orange, CA

Clark, Mark A
Antioch SR HS
Antioch, CA

Clark, Natalie A
Salinas HS
Salinas, CA

Clark, Robert
El Cameno Real HS
Chatsworth, CA

Clark, Roger A
Redwood Christian
Castro Valley, CA

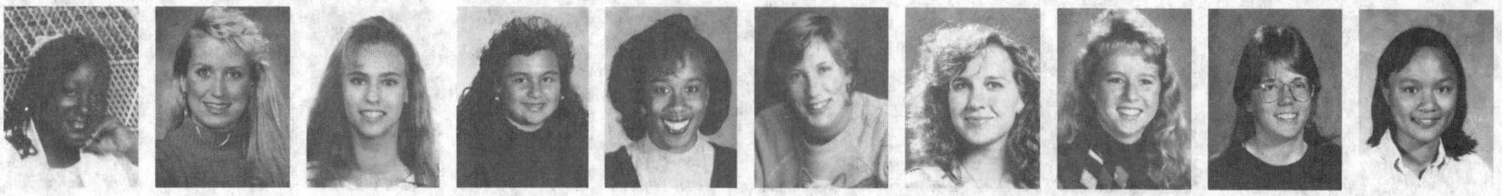

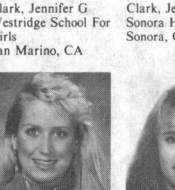

Clark, Rona M
St Bernard HS
Los Angeles, CA

Clark, Shelley A
El Toro HS
El Toro, CA

Clark, Stacy
Foothill HS
Sacramento, CA

Clark, Stephanie
Bloomington Christian Schl
Rialto, CA

Clark, Taryn
Lowell HS
San Francisco, CA

Clarke, Pamela S
Las Lomas HS
Walnut Creek, CA

Clarke, Rachel P
Eagle Rock HS
Los Angeles, CA

Clarke, Shannon
Rancho Buena Vista
Vista, CA

Clarke, Terra
Arroyo HS
San Leandro, CA

Claros, Florence Yao
Fremont HS
Sunnyvale, CA

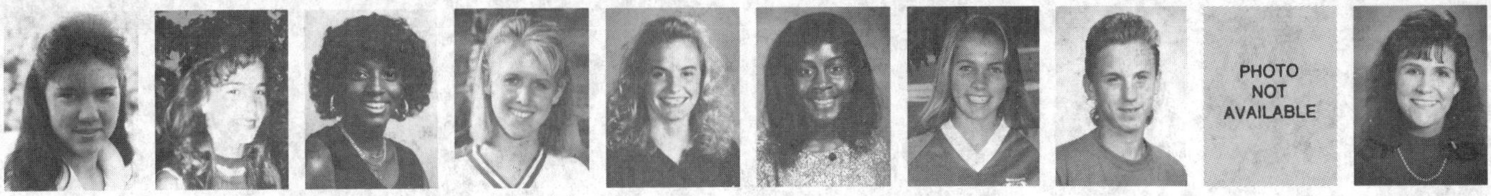
PHOTO
NOT
AVAILABLE

Clary, Jolene M
Calaveras HS
San Andreas, CA

Clason, Christie L
John Marshall Fund
Pasadena, CA

Clausell, Sherry S
Pasadena HS
Pasadena, CA

Clausen, Kimberly E
Upland HS
Upland, CA

Claxton, Saundra
Beyer HS
Modesto, CA

Clay, Erika M
Troy HS
Yorba Linda, CA

Clayburg, Nancy L
Atascadero HS
Atascadero, CA

Claypoole, Kenny
River City HS
West Sacramento, CA

Clayton, Chelsea D
Rim Of The World
Crestline, CA

Clayton, Holly A
Foothill HS
Santa Ana, CA

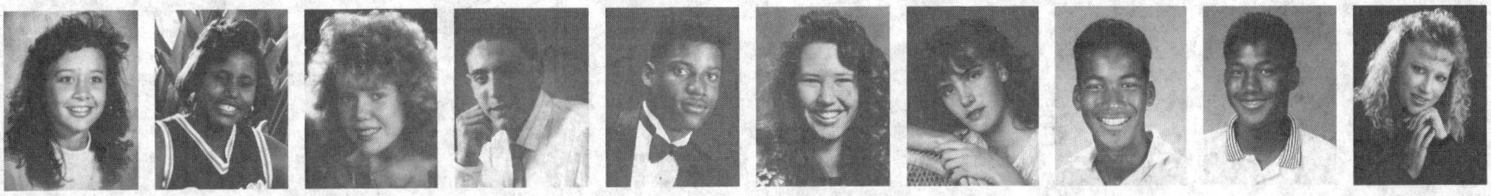

Clayton, Jessica T
Burroughs HS
Ridgecrest, CA

Clayton, La Tisha
Downey HS
Downey, CA

Clements, Alisha I
Weed HS
Weed, CA

Clemenza, Sean M
Eureka SR HS
Eureka, CA

Cleveland, Nathan L
Enterprise HS
Redding, CA

Click, Carmen S
Fontana HS
Fontana, CA

Clifford, Katie
Paradise Adventist Acad
Oroville, CA

Clifford, Larry
Palo Verde Valley
Blythe, CA

Clifford, Mark B
Palo Verde Valley
Blythe, CA

Clifton, Cindy L
Tulare Western HS
Tulare, CA

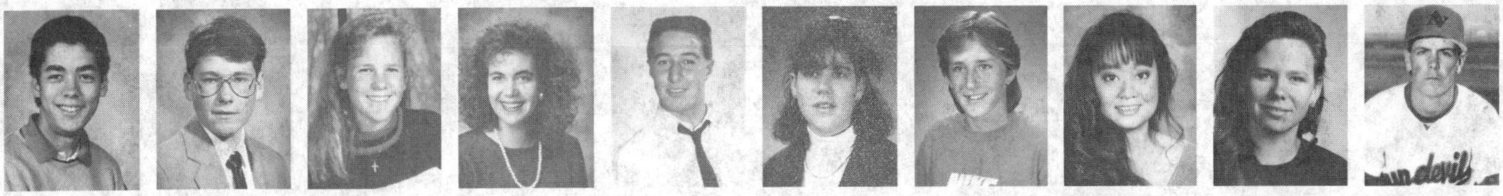

Climenson, Ernie T
Helix HS
San Diego, CA

Clinton, Dwayne A
Mater Dei HS
Garden Grove, CA

Clossman, Chandra D
Valley View HS
Moreno Valley, CA

Clothier, Marci
Christian HS
Spring Valley, CA

Cloys, Adam
Bloomington Christian HS
Bloomington, CA

Cluck, Tina
Christian Center HS
Rio Vista, CA

Clymens, Jr Thomas Edward
Liberty Union HS
Oakley, CA

Co, Claudine
Edison HS
Huntington Beach, CA

Coate, Heather R
Encina HS
Sacramento, CA

Coats, Jr Richard C
Apple Valley SR HS
Apple Valley, CA

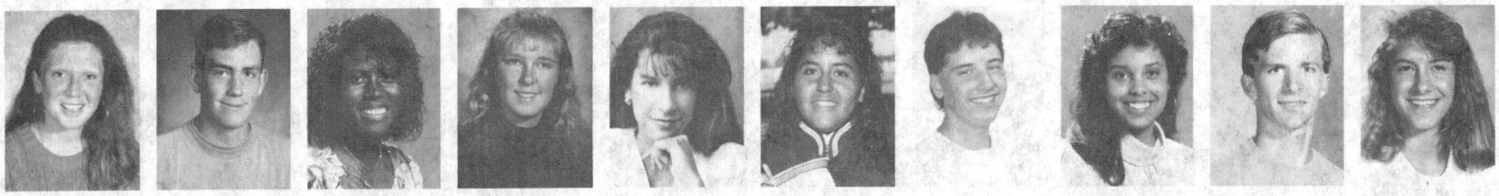

Cobb, Erin J
Fresno HS
Fresno, CA

Cobb, Thomas C
Fresno Christian HS
Madera, CA

Cobb, Tracy M
San Bernardino HS
San Bernardino, CA

Cobbett, Christie L
Bishop Union HS
Bishop, CA

Cobos, Saundra C
Santa Clara HS
Oxnard, CA

Cobos, Sindy
Chino HS
Ontario, CA

Coburn, II Barry C
De La Salle HS
Concord, CA

Cochran, Tiffany J
Alexander Hamilton
Los Angeles, CA

Cockerham, Craig A
Irvington HS
Fremont, CA

Cockrell, Robin
Walnut HS
Walnut, CA

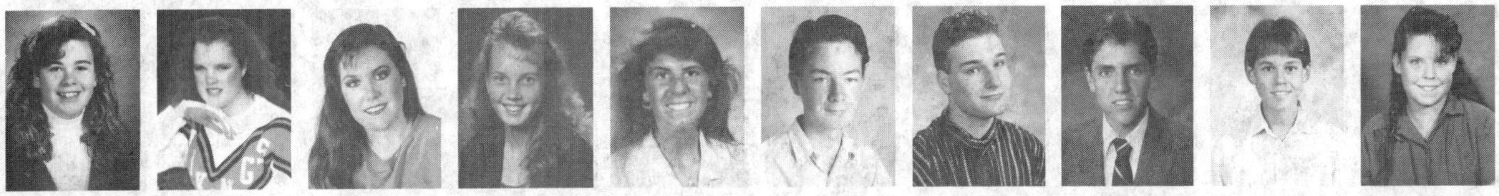

Coddington, Abby
Mc Kinleyville HS
Mc Kinleyville, CA

Cody, Carolyn E
Mills HS
Millbrae, CA

Coffin, Melissa
Palm Springs HS
Palm Springs, CA

Coffman, Amy K
Liberty Christian HS
Huntington Beach, CA

Coffman, Brenda M
San Dieguito Union
Olivenhain, CA

Coffman, Jeffrey A
Oxnard HS
Oxnard, CA

Cogan, Christian M
Bishop O Dowd HS
Oakland, CA

Cogswell, Brian J
Santa Barbara HS
Santa Barbara, CA

Cogswell, Kevin L
Santa Barbara HS
Santa Barbara, CA

Cohen, Amy B
La Quinta HS
Westminster, CA

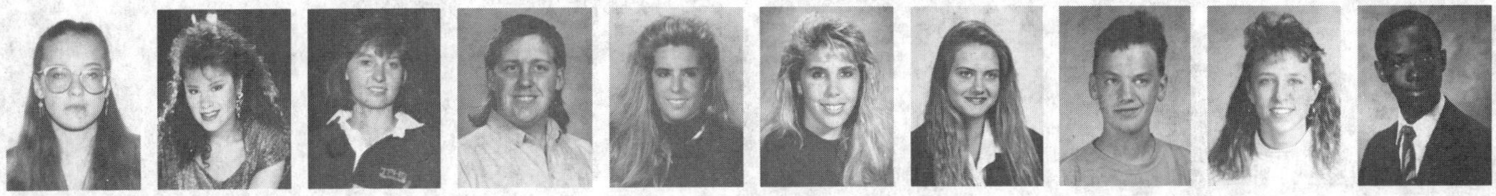

Cohen, Natalya
Washington HS
San Diego, CA

Cojulun, Katherine
Birmingham HS
Van Nuys, CA

Coker, Bonnie Leigh
Torrey Pines HS
San Diego, CA

Coker, Jason W
Yuba City HS
Yuba City, CA

Colbert, Laura
Marina HS
Huntington Bch, CA

Colbert, Michele
Marina HS
Huntington Bch, CA

Colby, Tiffany D
Napa HS
Napa, CA

Cole, Chris L
Durham HS
Oroville, CA

Cole, Crystal
Capital Christian Schl
Sacramento, CA

Cole, Jonathan O
Pomona HS
Pomona, CA

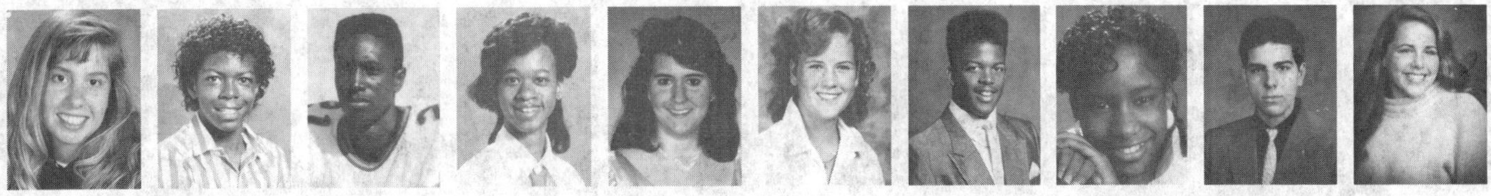

Cole, Lorie A
Palm Springs HS
Cathedral City, CA

Cole, Roderick J
Chino HS
Chino, CA

Coleman, Calvin A
Carlsbad HS
Carlsbad, CA

Coleman, Chinhayi
Saint Marys Acad
Los Angeles, CA

Coleman, Joan M
Eisenhower HS
Rialto, CA

Coleman, Kathleen E
Bishop Amat Memorial HS
West Covina, CA

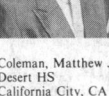

Coleman, Matthew J
Desert HS
California City, CA

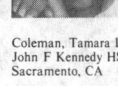

Coleman, Tamara L
John F Kennedy HS
Sacramento, CA

Collazo, Gustavo
Pius X HS
South Gate, CA

Collier, Jo Lene
Monte Vista HS
Spring Valley, CA

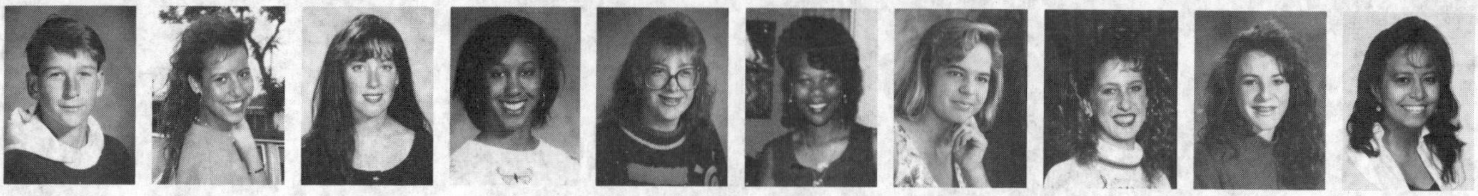

Collins, Adam S
Montclair HS
Montclair, CA

Collins, Christine
Western HS
Anaheim, CA

Collins, Christine L
Pasadena HS
Pasadena, CA

Collins, Ginger N
Los Alamitos HS
Los Alamitos, CA

Collins, Kendra E
A A Stagg HS
Stockton, CA

Collins, Latoya
Kennedy HS
L V T, CA

Collum, Cynthia E
Redwood HS
Visalia, CA

Colnic, Ann
Warren HS
Downey, CA

Colombi, Tracy L
Clear Lake HS
Lakeport, CA

Colomeda, Sofia T
Cordova HS
Rancho Cordova, CA

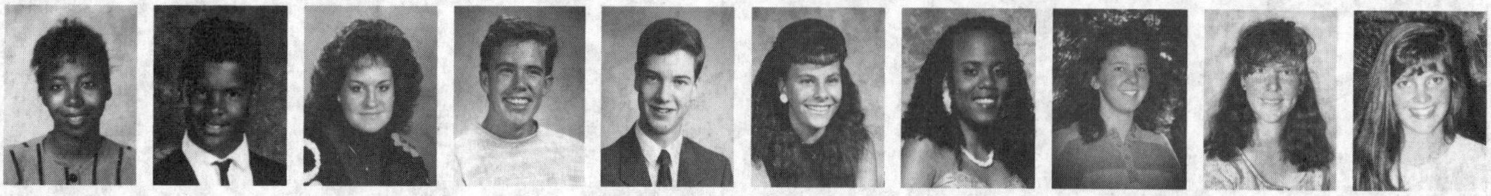

Colson, Tangela T
Cordova SR HS
Rancho Cordova, CA

Colthirst, Anthony D
Saddle Back HS
Santa Ana, CA

Colton, Monica T
Highlands HS
North Highlands, CA

Colville, Trent J
Poway HS
Poway, CA

Colvin, Robert P
Crescenta Valley HS
Glendale, CA

Combs, Amy E
Hoover HS
Fresno, CA

Combs, Shandrika R
Skyline HS
Oakland, CA

Compton, Heather Jeannine
Perris HS
Nuevo, CA

Compton, Marcelina
Roosevelt HS
Fresno, CA

Compton, Susan
Ventura HS
Ventura, CA

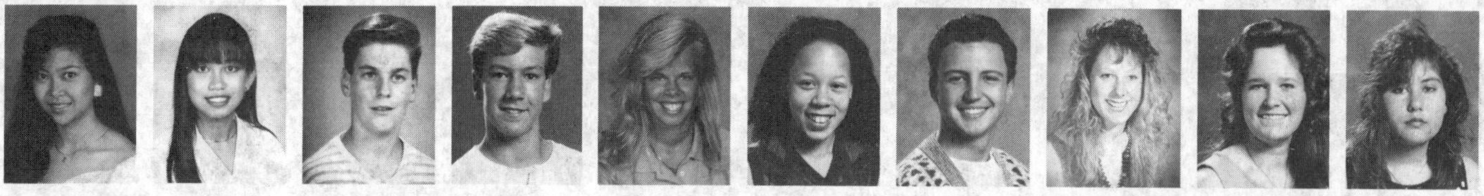

Concepcion, Lalaine
Lakewood HS
Long Beach, CA

Concepcion, Maricel
Saint Genevieve HS
Van Nuys, CA

Conkle, Marc
Madera HS
Madera, CA

Conley, Adam J
Notre Dame HS
Colton, CA

Conley, Kelli Q
Louisville HS
Westlake Vlg, CA

Conley, Tanisha M
Fontana HS
Fontana, CA

Conn, Jeff E
Narbonne HS
Rancho Palos Ver, CA

Conn, Nancy M
Del Norte HS
Crescent City, CA

Connell, Christine M
John Burroughs HS
Burbank, CA

Connelly, Robbin A
Pomona HS
Pomona, CA

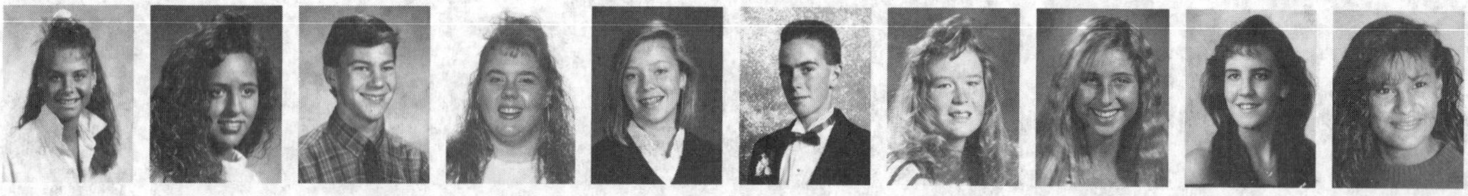

Connelly, Staci A
Santa Clara HS
San Jose, CA

Conner, Kim
Lodi Acad
Lodi, CA

Conner, Matthew J
Redwood Christian
Castro Valley, CA

Conner, Michelle Lynn
South HS
Bakersfield, CA

Connor, Tracy E
La Reina HS
Westlake Village, CA

Conrad, Jeffrey
Saint Joseph HS
Santa Maria, CA

Conshafter, Jana L
Bakersfield HS
Bakersfield, CA

Conte, Lisa J
Huntington Beach
Huntington Beach, CA

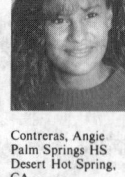

Contino, Dawn K
Castle Park HS
Chula Vista, CA

Contreras, Angie
Palm Springs HS
Desert Hot Spring, CA

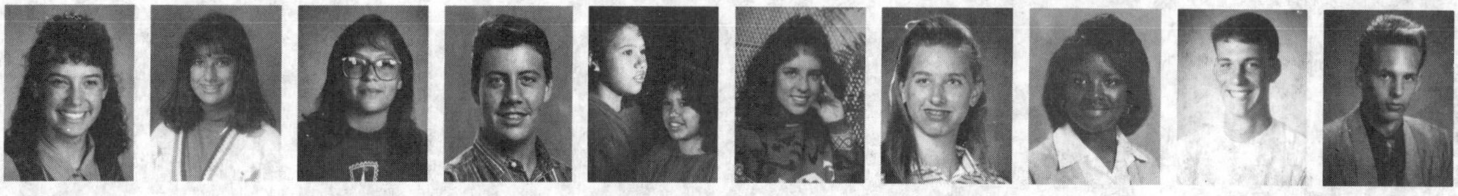

Contreras, Jill R
East Union HS
Manteca, CA

Contreras, Marci Y
Bonita Vista HS
Chula Vista, CA

Contreras, Melissa R
Los Banos HS
Los Banos, CA

Contreras, Paul Roman
Fontana HS
Fontana, CA

Contreras, Sylvia
King City Joint Union HS
Greenfield, CA

Cook, Carmen
Adolfo Camarillo HS
Camarillo, CA

Cook, Cassandra L
Irvine HS
Irvine, CA

Cook, Chevonna
Miracle Baptist Christian Schl
Moreno Valley, CA

Cook, Jeffery W
Central Catholic HS
Modesto, CA

Cook, Jeffry W
Lompoc HS
Ventura, CA

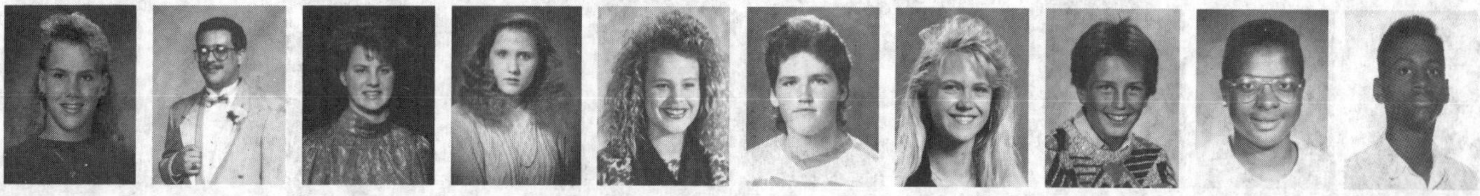

Cook, Jennifer D
Westminster HS
Westminster, CA

Cook, Michael W
Covina HS
Pocatello, ID

Cook, Rebecca A
Rio Lindo Adventist Acad
Springville, UT

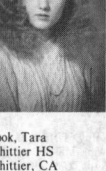

Cook, Tara
Whittier HS
Whittier, CA

Cook, Tiffaney
Lompoc HS
Ventura, CA

Cookinham, Chad G
Castle Park HS
Chula Vista, CA

Cooley, Jennifer L
Fontana HS
Fontana, CA

Cooney, Dennis M
Napa HS
Napa, CA

Cooper, Aaron
George Washington Preparatory HS
Los Angeles, CA

Cooper, Floyd
Hiram W Johnson
Sacramento, CA

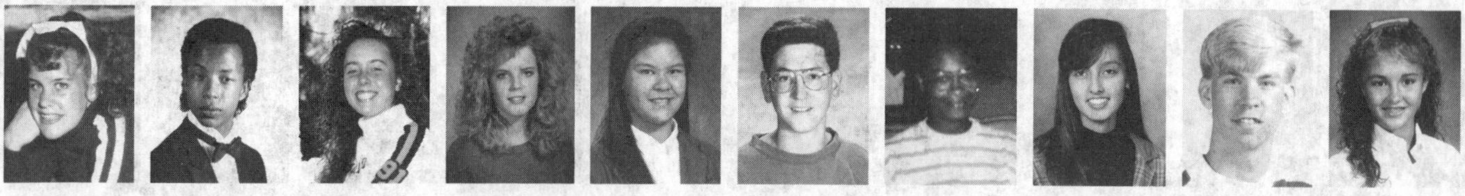

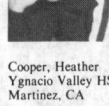

Cooper, Heather
Ygnacio Valley HS
Martinez, CA

Cooper, Hodari Toussaint
Eden Christian Acad
Oakland, CA

Cooper, Janet L
Ventura HS
Ventura, CA

Cooper, Katherine J
John F Kennedy HS
Granada Hills, CA

Cooper, Michele M
La Reina HS
Thousand Oaks, CA

Coopersmith, Marc
Tustin HS
Tustin, CA

Copeland, Benjamin
Edison Computech
Fresno, CA

Copes, Stephanie A
University City HS
San Diego, CA

Coppinger, Matthew
Edison HS
Fresno, CA

Coppola, Liana
Mater Dei HS
Los Alamitos, CA

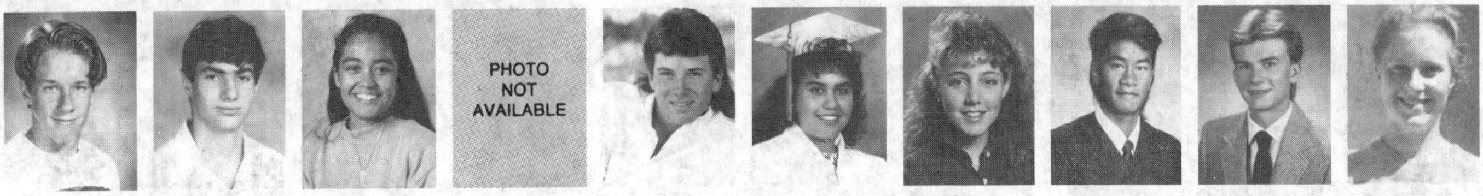
PHOTO
NOT
AVAILABLE

Corban, Daniel W
Fountain Valley HS
Fountain Valley, CA

Cordani, Stephen C
Whittier Christian
Whittier, CA

Cordero, Melissa G
Vista HS
Vista, CA

Cordes, Chuck M
Ponderosa HS
Diamond Springs, CA

Cordes, Francis A
Ponderosa HS
Diamon Springs, CA

Cordova, Vera L
Clovis HS
Fresno, CA

Cordua, Jennifer
Lindsay HS
Lindsay, CA

Cordura, Aldo E
Etiwanda HS
Rancho Cucamonga, CA

Corley, Shawn
Mt Whitney HS
Visalia, CA

Cormack, Anna
St Margarets HS
Newport Beach, CA

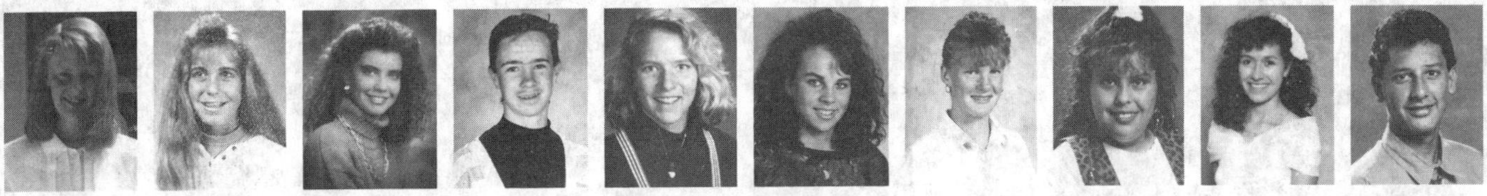

Cormack, Sally M
St Margarets Schl
Newport Beach, CA

Corman, Tanya J
Newark Memorial
Newark, CA

Cormany, Ashley Lynn
Mount Carmel HS
Aledo, TX

Cornelison, Russell A
Clovis HS
Clovis, CA

Cornell, Meredith C
Clovis West HS
Fresno, CA

Cornish, Allison R
St Francis HS
Redwood City, CA

Cornman, Te Ata L
Mesa Verde HS
Citrus Heights, CA

Corona, Rosa E
Herbert Hoover HS
Glendale, CA

Coronado, Cynthia
Brawley Union HS
Brawley, CA

Coronado, Sergio R
Hoover HS
Burbank, CA

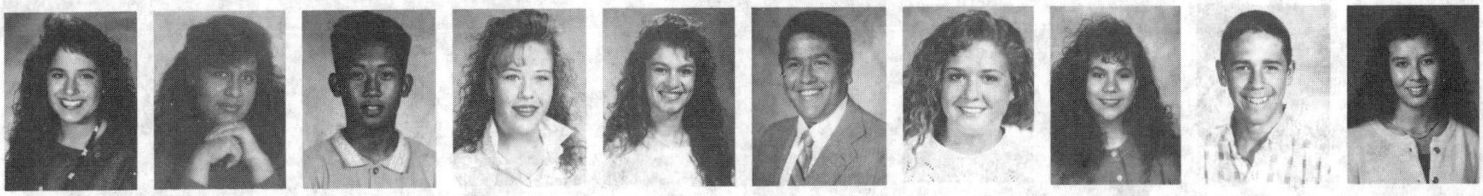

Coronado, Tricia Ann
Don Antonio Lugo
Chino, CA

Coronado, Yvette
Yerba Buena HS
San Jose, CA

Corpuz, Edward Marc
Independence HS
San Jose, CA

Corr, Erika L
Roseville HS
Roseville, CA

Corral, Erika
Erika Corral HS
El Centro, CA

Corral, Martin
St John Bosco HS
Norwalk, CA

Correa, Christy S
John F Kennedy HS
Sacramento, CA

Cortes, Araceli
San Gabriel HS
Montebello, CA

Cortes, Jose S
Notre Dame HS
Corona, CA

Cortes, Melissa L
Baptist Christian HS
Hemet, CA

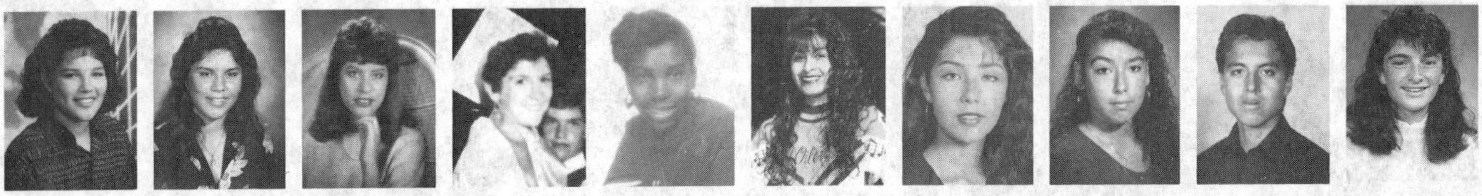

Cortes, Monica S
King City Joint Union HS
Greenfield, CA

Cortez, Candy
Selma HS
Selma, CA

Cortez, Christina D
Mt Whitney HS
Visalia, CA

Cortez, Debbie Ann
Winters HS
Winters, CA

Cortez, Kimberly N
Norte Vista HS
Riverside, CA

Cortez, Linda C
Montebello HS
Los Angeles, CA

Cortez, Veronica
Baldwin Park HS
Baldwin Park, CA

Cortez, Veronica
Huntington Park HS
Huntington Park, CA

Cortinas, Jaime
Cantwell HS
Los Angeles, CA

Corvi, Michele
Notre Dame HS
San Bruno, CA

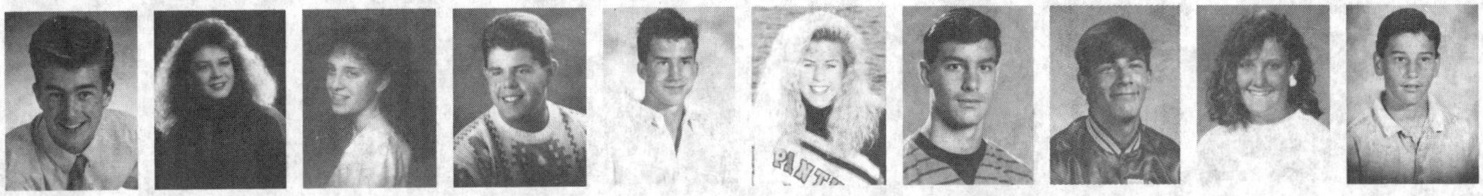

Costa, Aaron
Western Christian
Upland, CA

Costa, Amy-Marie V
Tulare Union HS
Tulare, CA

Costa, Annabela M
Tulare Union HS
Tulare, CA

Costa, Lester D
Tulare Union HS
Tulare, CA

Costa, Steve
Bear River HS
Grass Valley, CA

Costanza, Lisa
Antioch HS
Antioch, CA

Costello, Denis
Leuzinger HS
Hawthorne, CA

Costello, John P
Pescadero HS
Pescadero, CA

Costello, Kimberly
Linoln HS
Stockton, CA

Costigliolo, Brian
Linden HS
Linden, CA

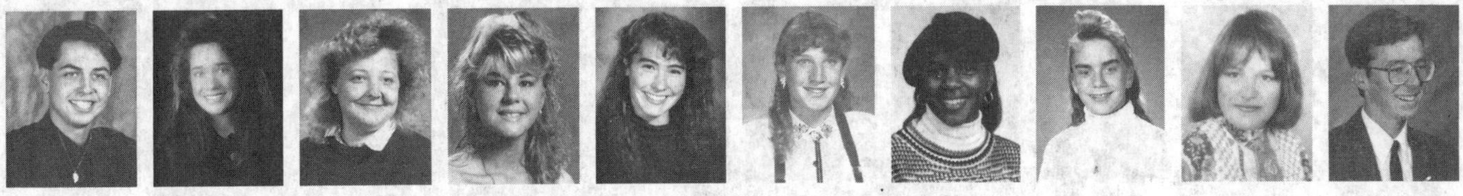

Cota, Brandon B
Rubidoux HS
Riverside, CA

Cota, Laurie L
Canyon HS
Canyon Country, CA

Cote, Patricia Ann
Cabrillo HS
VAFB, CA

Coto, Amanda
Leuzinger HS
Lawndale, CA

Cottengin, Kama C
North HS
Bakersfield, CA

Cottingim, Brandi
Hesperia Christian
Apple Valley, CA

Couch, Sonya R
Skyline HS
Oakland, CA

Coughlin, Traci R
Pinole Valley HS
San Pablo, CA

Coulter, Rachelle
San Benito HS
Hollister, CA

Courtright, Joshua
Victor Valley Christian HS
Victorville, CA

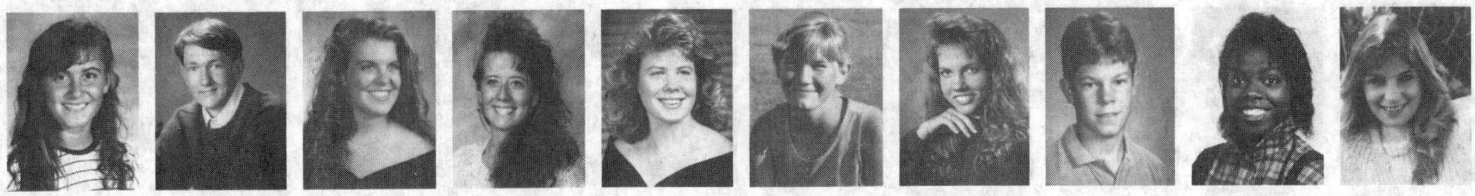

Cousins, Jennifer M
Tustin HS
Tustin, CA

Cousins, Peter M
Hughson HS
Ceres, CA

Covarrubias, Kristina
Santa Teresa HS
San Jose, CA

Covert, Charisse M
Cordova SR HS
Rancho Cordova, CA

Covert, Rachael
Rim Of The World
Crestline, CA

Cox, Aubrey
Brawley Union HS
Calipatria, CA

Cox, Elizabeth Lynn
Hoover HS
Fresno, CA

Cox, Eric R
Atwater HS
Atwater, CA

Cox, Keisha Maria
Central Union HS
Elcentro, CA

Cox, Kimberly
Westwood HS
Westwood, CA

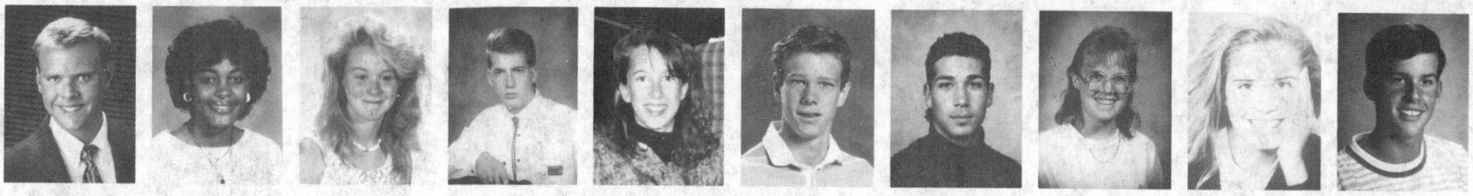

Cox, Michael W
Ramona HS
Riverside, CA

Cox, Sharifa
Los Alamitos HS
Long Beach, CA

Cox, Trisha L
Paramount HS
Paramount, CA

Coyle, Ryan
Madera HS
Madera, CA

Cracknell, Kathleen
Carlmont HS
Belmont, CA

Crafton, Stephen
Garces Memorial HS
Bakersfield, CA

Craig, III Floyd
San Diego HS
San Diego, CA

Craig, Kimberly J
Arlington HS
Riverside, CA

Craig, Michele E
Marymount HS
Studio City, CA

Crain, Jeff S
Central Catholic HS
Modesto, CA

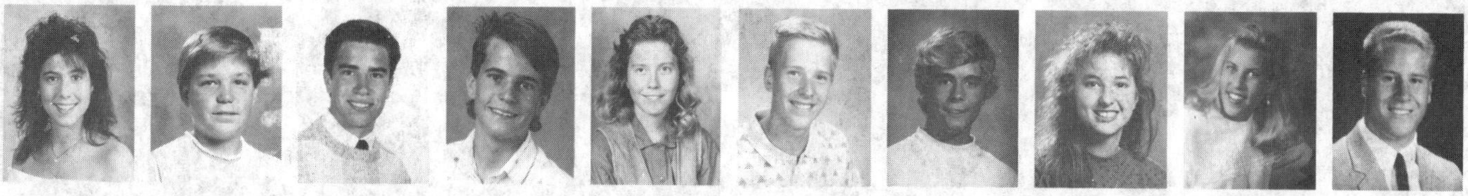

Cramer, Cindy
Oakhill HS
Chatsworth, CA

Cramer, Kevin
San Bernardino HS
San Bernardino, CA

Crandall, Hunter
Justin
Delano HS
Delano, CA

Crane, Justin D
Chaminade College
Prep
Woodland Hills, CA

Crane, Sarah S
University City HS
San Diego, CA

Crane, William M
North Tahoe HS
Carnelian Bay, CA

Crawford,
Christopher Brett
Capistrano Valley HS
San Clemente, CA

Crawford, Debby M
Etiwanda HS
Alta Loma, CA

Crawford, Kelly L
Marina HS
Huntington Beach,
CA

Crawford, Kenneth
Scott
Thomas Downey HS
Modesto, CA

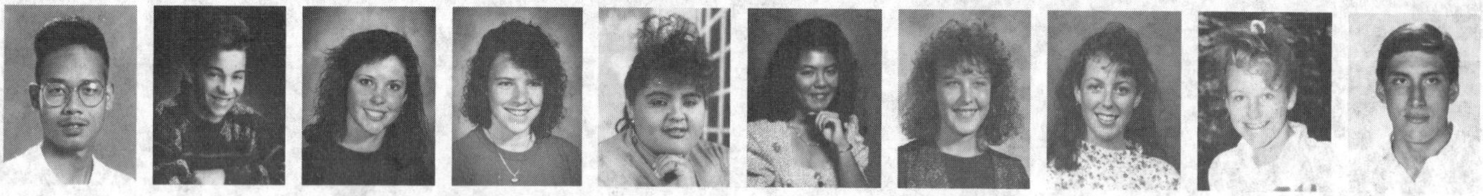

Credo, Allan V
Sierra Vista HS
Baldwin Park, CA

Creel, Wayne A
San Dimas HS
San Dimas, CA

Creighton, Alyssa M
Kern Valley HS
Weldon, CA

Cremer, Angela L
East Bakersfield HS
Bakersfield, CA

Crespo, Herminia
King City HS
Greenfield, CA

Crestejo, Veronica P
Don Antonio Lugo
Chino, CA

Crets, Stephanie L
Woodland HS
Woodland, CA

Crews, Crista
O'farrell SCPA
San Diego, CA

Criner, Kim
Rim Of The World
Lake Arrowhead, CA

Criss, Preston W
Los Altos HS
Hacienda Hgts, CA

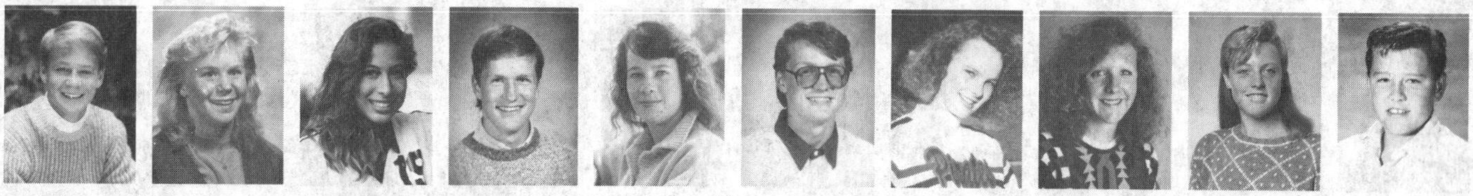

Criswell, Brian R
Santa Cruz HS
Santa Cruz, CA

Croan, Stephanie
Fremont Christian
Fremont, CA

Cronkhite, Erendira
Venice HS
Culver City, CA

Crosby, Jason M
Ukiah JR Acad
Willits, CA

Crosby, Kari Lynn
Fresno Christian HS
Fresno, CA

Crosby, Robert S
Ukiah JR Acad
Willits, CA

Crosno, Gala
San Leandro HS
San Leandro, CA

Crow, Heather D
Rio Mesa HS
Oxnard, CA

Crowder, Elice M
Brea Olinda HS
Brea, CA

Crowder, Jared M
Don Lugo HS
Chino Hills, CA

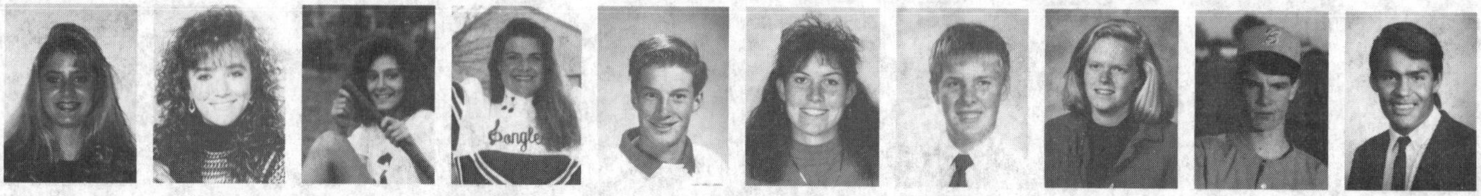

Crowell, Jennifer M
Granite Hills HS
Alpine, CA

Crown, Heather
John F Kennedy HS
Granada Hills, CA

Crownover,
Bernadettee
Paradise HS
Paradise, CA

Croy, Susie
Marysville HS
Marysville, CA

Cruden, Brett
Poway HS
Poway, CA

Crum, Melinda
Los Altos HS
Hacienda Hts, CA

Crumb, Devin Jeffrey
Don Bosco Technical
Inst
Pasadena, CA

Crummey, Viktoria G
Armijo HS
Fairfield, CA

Crutcher, Bryndyn
Luther Burbank
Acad/Math Sci &
Sacramento, CA

Cruz, Emile Irving
Simi Valley HS
Simi Valley, CA

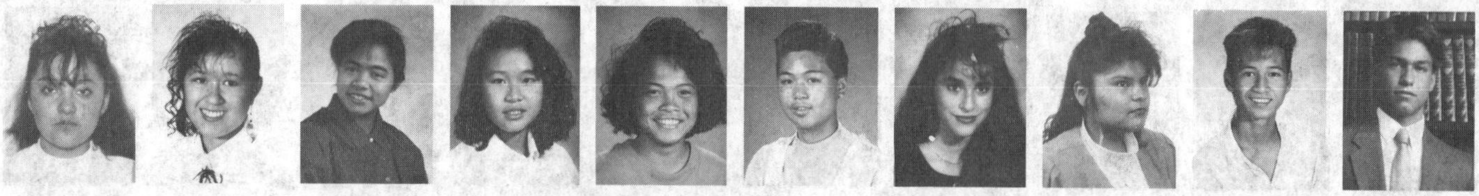

Cruz, Jaqueline
S Tahoe HS
S Lake Tahoe, CA

Cruz, Jennifer D
El Dorado HS
Yorba Linda, CA

Cruz, Lynn Mae T
Notre Dame HS
San Jose, CA

Cruz, Maria A
Mater Dei HS
Orange, CA

Cruz, Maria C
Thomas Edison HS
Stockton, CA

Cruz, Randy C
Pittsburg HS
Pittsburg, CA

Cuadra, Isabel
Selma HS
Selma, CA

Cuamatzi, Aida
Sierra Vista HS
Baldwin Park, CA

Cube, Anthony
Rowland HS
Rowland Heights, CA

Cubillas, Alvaro
Herbert Hoover HS
Glendale, CA

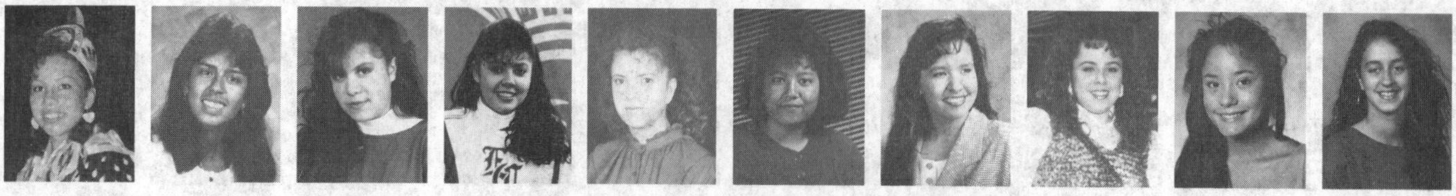

Cuch, Marvella M
Sherman Indian HS
Fort Duchesne, UT

Cuellar, Elsie
Schurr HS
Los Angeles, CA

Cuenca, Maritza I
St Joseph HS
Anaheim, CA

Cuenca-Ortiz, Eleida
Central Union HS
El Centro, CA

Cuevas, Angelica M
Montgomery HS
San Ysidro, CA

Cuevas, Catherine D
Mar Vista HS
Imperial Beach, CA

Cuevas, Gabriella N
St Joseph HS
Cerritos, CA

Cuevas, Mireya
John H Francis
Polytechnic HS
Sun Valley, CA

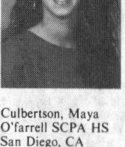

Cukingnan, Marietta
Miraleste HS
Rolling Hills, CA

Culbertson, Maya
O'farrell SCPA HS
San Diego, CA

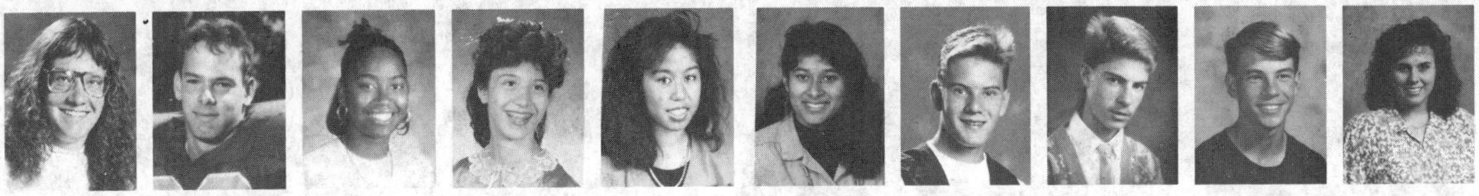

Cullen, Michelle R
Tehachapi HS
Tehachapi, CA

Cullen, Rodney
Coast Joint Union
Cambria, CA

Cummings, Duwanda
Castlemont HS
Oakland, CA

Cummings, Gina
Pacific Union College Prep
Angwin, CA

Cunanan, Helaine
St Joseph HS
Cypress, CA

Cundiff, Karina E
Karina Cundiff HS
Hemet, CA

Cunningham, Jason S
Norte Vista HS
Riverside, CA

Cupp, Christopher L
Lemoore Union HS
Lemoore, CA

Cupp, Corby R
Lemoore Union HS
Lemoore, CA

Curran, Chantelle V
San Gorgonio HS
Highland, CA

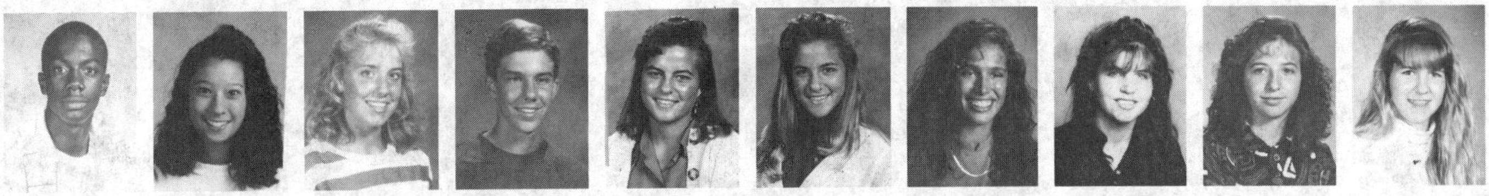

Curry, Dwight E
Morningside HS
Inglewood, CA

Curry, Kimberly D
Argonaut HS
Ione, CA

Curry, Michelle
La Sierra HS
Riverside, CA

Curry, Jr Richard
La Sierra HS
Riverside, CA

Curtis, Monique R
Ramona HS
Ramona, CA

Curtis, Nicole L
Ramona HS
Ramona, CA

Curtoni, Ann M
Central Catholic HS
Oakdale, CA

Cuthill, Angela M
Bret Harte HS
Arnold, CA

Cuviello, Dawn E
James Lick HS
San Jose, CA

Cuviello, Janette E
James Lick HS
San Jose, CA

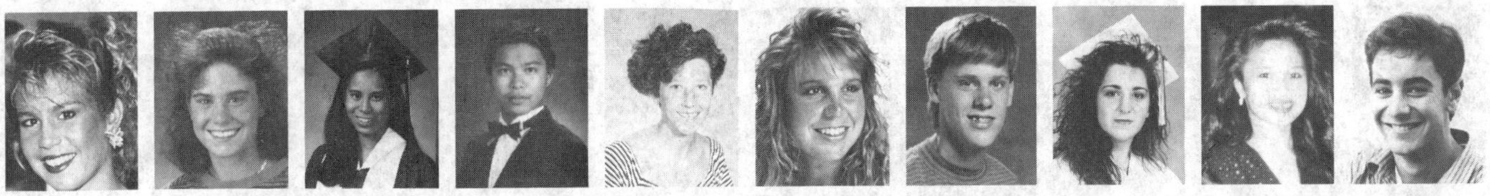

Cuyler, Corinne
Miraleste HS
Rolling Hills Est, CA

D Amelio, Kristi
Charter Oak HS
Covina, CA

Dablo, Cheryl
Loma Linda Acad
San Bernardino, CA

Dacio, III Jose C
De La Salle HS
Vallejo, CA

Daczkowski, Lisa
Rosary HS
Fullerton, CA

Daddorio, Dominique
Orange Glen HS
Valley Center, CA

Daetwiler, Jarod J
Rim Of The World
Cedar Glen, CA

Daghlarian, Natalie
Holy Martyrs Ferrahian HS
Granada Hills, CA

Dagsaan, Cindy L
Carson HS
Carson, CA

Dahan, Omri
Redwood HS
Larkspur, CA

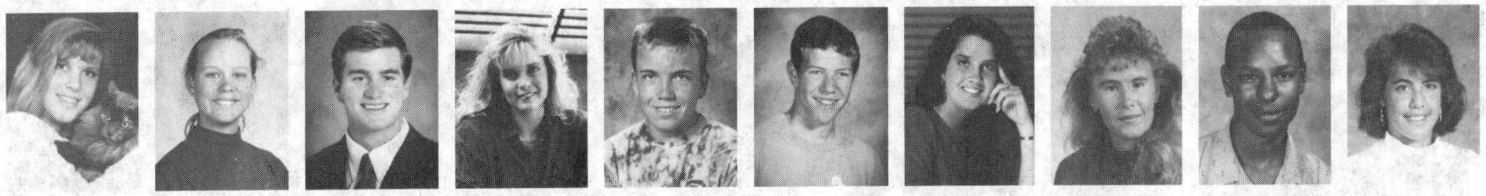

Dahl, Danielle E
Canyon HS
Santa Clarita, CA

Dahl, Vanessa E
Downey HS
Modesto, CA

Dahlberg, John D
Mission Viejo HS
Mission Viejo, CA

Dahlgren, Kristen Laine
Arcadia HS
Arcadia, CA

Dahlke, Chad R
Dana Hills HS
Laguna Niguel, CA

Daigle, James M
Foothill HS
Bakersfield, CA

Daigle, Tami Jaine
Montclair HS
Chino, CA

Daily, Tammie C
Argonaut HS
Ione, CA

Daire, Jasiri S
Bishop Amat HS
Compton, CA

Dakis, Georgette D
Notre Dame HS
San Mateo, CA

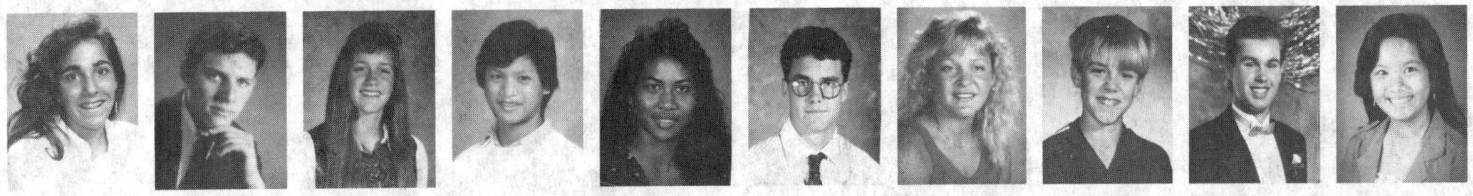

Dal Ponte, Denise B
Immaculate Heart
Los Angeles, CA

Dal Porto, Albert B
Linden HS
Linden, CA

Daley, Jacquelyn Joan
El Dorado HS
Placerville, CA

Dalida, Alex
Redwood HS
Visalia, CA

Daliva, Lelia B
Edison HS
Stockton, CA

Dallas, Eric G
Redwood HS
Larkspur, CA

Dalonzo, Christine
Lincoln HS
Stockton, CA

Dalton, Jeremiah A
Gateway Community Schl
Oxnard, CA

Dalton, Paul G
Santa Clara HS
Port Hueneme, CA

Dam, Loan K
Luther Burbank SR
Sacramento, CA

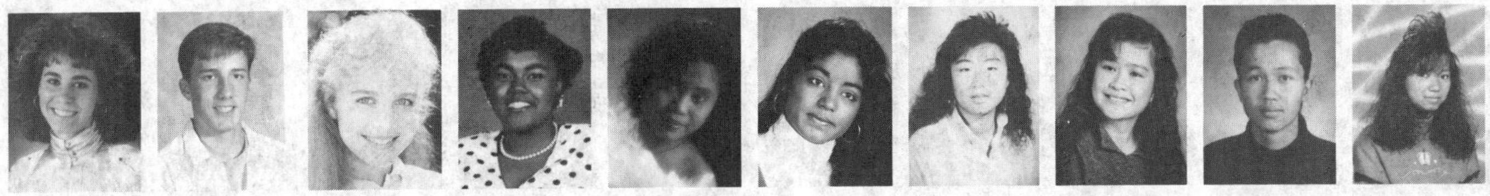

Damato, Valerie A
Calvary Chapel HS
Santa Ana, CA

Damm, Christopher
Coast Union HS
Cambria, CA

Dammann, Sarah M
Westlake Schl
Los Angeles, CA

Dancy, Tiara B
Millikan HS
Long Beach, CA

Dane, Beth R
Edison HS
Stockton, CA

Dang, Amy K
Hoover HS
Fresno, CA

Dang, Anh B
Saddleback HS
Santa Ana, CA

Dang, Krystine C
Savanna HS
Anaheim, CA

Dang, Nguyen T
Berkeley HS
Oakland, CA

Dang, Susan H
Encinal HS
Alameda, CA

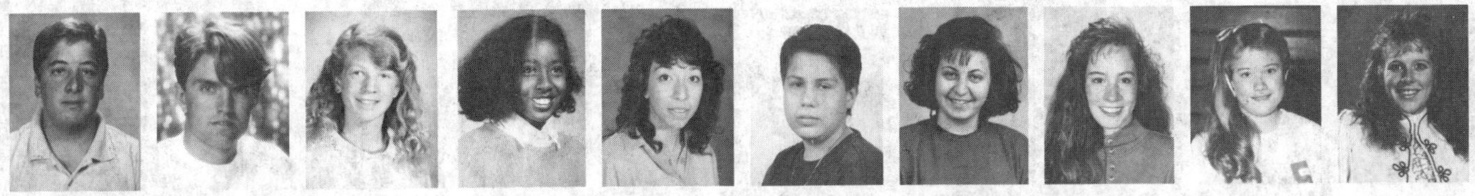

Dangelo, Pablo
San Gabriel HS
San Gabriel, CA

Daniel, Gregory D
Enterprise HS
Redding, CA

Daniel, Heidi M
Ukiah HS
Ukiah, CA

Daniel, Kim M
Fairfield HS
Fairfield, CA

Daniel, Lucy
Borrego Springs HS
Borrego Springs, CA

Daniel, Martinez
Calexico HS
Calexico, CA

Daniele, Teresa P
Moorpark HS
Moorpark, CA

Daniels, Laura
Glen A Wilson HS
Hacienda Heights, CA

Daniels, Tracy R
Rim Of The World
Lake Arrowhead, CA

Danks, Cindy L
Rubidoux HS
Riverside, CA

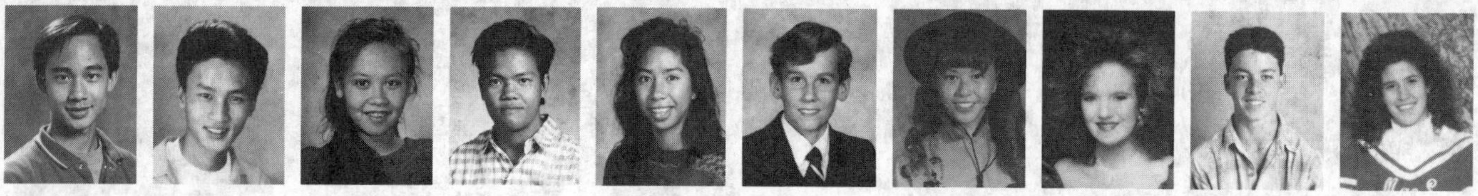

Dao, Hieu C
Glendale HS
Glendale, CA

Dao, Kevin Phuong
Los Amigos HS
Santa Ana, CA

Dao, Wendy Uyen
Trabuco Hills HS
El Toro, CA

Daos, Fausto
John F Kennedy HS
Sacramento, CA

Daranciang, Lisa R
Chula Vista HS
San Diego, CA

Darden, Ted D
Imperial HS
Arcadia, CA

Dare, Lisa
San Mateo HS
Foster City, CA

Darling, Michele
San Ramon HS
Danville, CA

Darpino, James T
Channel Islands HS
Oxnard, CA

Darrow, Dee Dee
Madera HS
Madera, CA

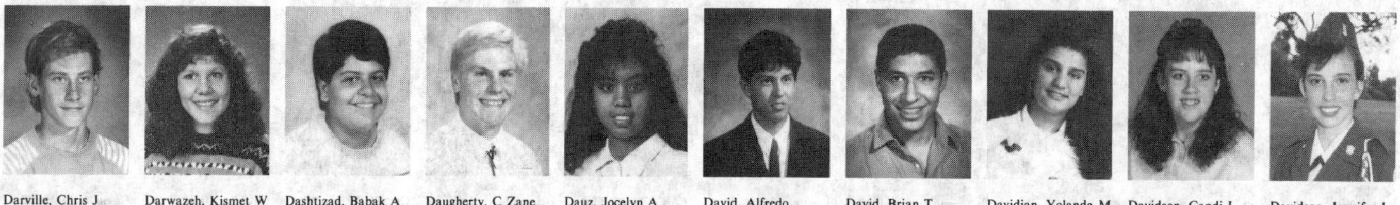

Darville, Chris J
Oroville HS
Oroville, CA

Darwazeh, Kismet W
Novato HS
Novato, CA

Dashtizad, Babak A
Canoga Park HS
Woodland Hills, CA

Daugherty, C Zane
Valley Christian HS
San Jose, CA

Dauz, Jocelyn A
Sweetwater Union
National City, CA

David, Alfredo
Los Angeles HS
Los Angeles, CA

David, Brian T
Thousand Oaks HS
Thousand Oaks, CA

Davidian, Yolanda M
La Canada HS
La Canada-Flint, CA

Davidson, Candi L
Fort Bragg HS
Fort Bragg, CA

Davidson, Jennifer L
Del Campo HS
Fair Oaks, CA

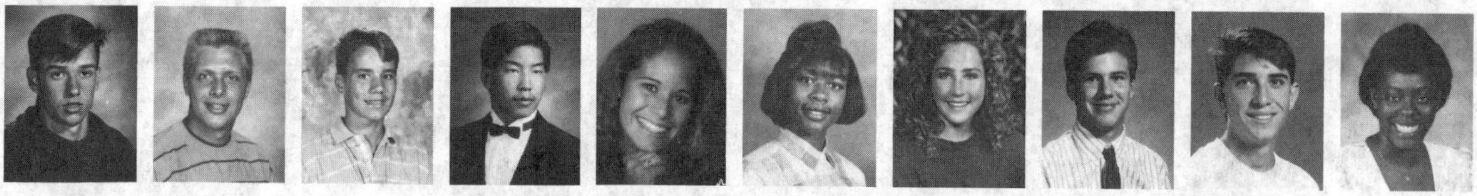

Davidson, Ryan A
South HS
Bakersfield, CA

Davidson, Sean J
Western Christian
San Dimas, CA

Davies, Jonathan L
Clovis West HS
Clovis, CA

Davies, Michael
Liberty Union HS
Oakley, CA

Davies, Miriam A
Davis SR HS
Woodland, CA

Davis, Abebi Safiya
Lynwood Adventist
Acad
Los Angeles, CA

Davis, Amy Michele
Dana Hills HS
Laguna Niguel, CA

Davis, Andrew M
Poway HS
Poway, CA

Davis, Christopher C
San Bernardino HS
San Bernardino, CA

Davis, Chyron
Brethren HS
Long Beach, CA

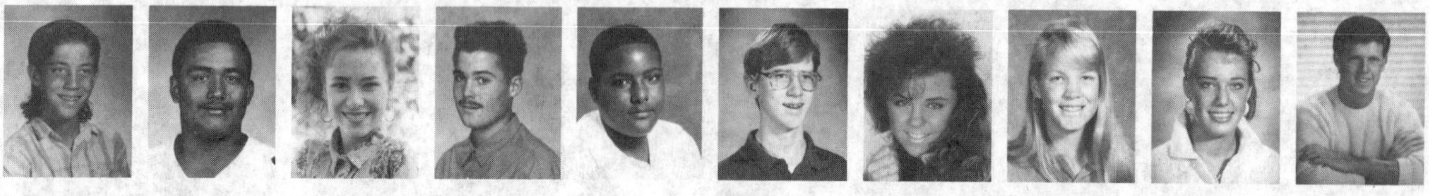

Davis, Clinton R
Oak Park HS
Agoura Hills, CA

Davis, Danny J
Valley HS
Sacramento, CA

Davis, Debi N
Oak Ridge HS
Cameron Park, CA

Davis, Gary A
Livermore HS
Livermore, CA

Davis, George E
Carson HS
Victorville, CA

Davis, Glen M
Sutter Union HS
Yuba City, CA

Davis, Heather A
Valhalla HS
Jamul, CA

Davis, Heidi A
Alameda HS
Alameda, CA

Davis, Hillery
Ukiah HS
Ukiah, CA

Davis, James A
Galt HS
Galt, CA

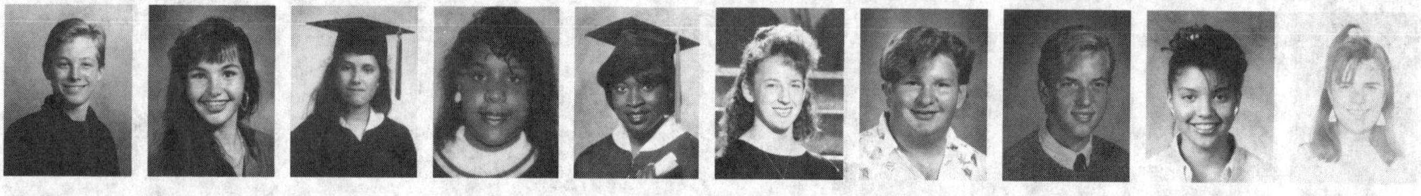

Davis, Jason W
Apple Valley HS
Apple Valley, CA

Davis, Jennifer
Newport Christian
Fountain Vly, CA

Davis, Jennifer L
Rubidoux HS
Riverside, CA

Davis, Johnnie Mae
Mission HS
San Francisco, CA

Davis, La Shaye
Washington Prep
Los Angeles, CA

Davis, Laura J
Huntington Beach
Huntington Beach,
CA

Davis, Matt F L
Capistrano Valley HS
Coto De Caza, CA

Davis, Matthew
Faith Christian HS
Marysville, CA

Davis, Melissa R
Downey HS
Vernon, CA

Davis, Michelle J
Willow Glen HS
San Jose, CA

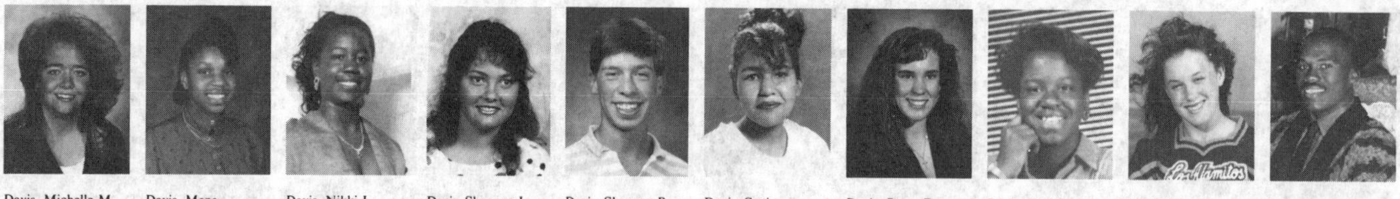

Davis, Michelle M
Willow Park HS
Lucerne Valley, CA

Davis, Mona
Fremont HS
Oakland, CA

Davis, Nikki L
Fowler HS
Fowler, CA

Davis, Shannon L
Orange Glen HS
Escondido, CA

Davis, Shannon R
Mission Viejo HS
El Toro, CA

Davis, Sonia
Sherman Oaks Center
Enriched Studies
Los Angeles, CA

Davis, Stacy E
East Bakersfield HS
Bakersfield, CA

Davis, Toni D
Foothills HS
Sacramento, CA

Davis, Tracy
Los Alamitos HS
Seal Beach, CA

Davis, Travis H
Banning HS
Carson, CA

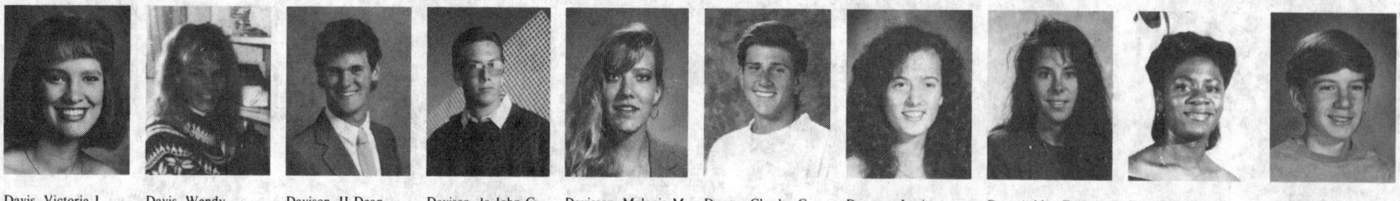

Davis, Victoria L
Torrey Pines HS
Encinitas, CA

Davis, Wendy
Casa Grande HS
Petaluma, CA

Davison, II Dean
Golden West HS
Visalia, CA

Davison, Jr John C
North HS
Bakersfield, CA

Davisson, Melanie M
Poway HS
Poway, CA

Dawes, Charles C
Dana Hills HS
Laguna Niguel, CA

Dawson, Jessica
Chico SR HS
Chico, CA

Day, Ashley E
Carlmont HS
San Carlos, CA

Day, Courtney
Leuzinger HS
Lawndale, CA

Day, Jeff
Placer HS
Auburn, CA

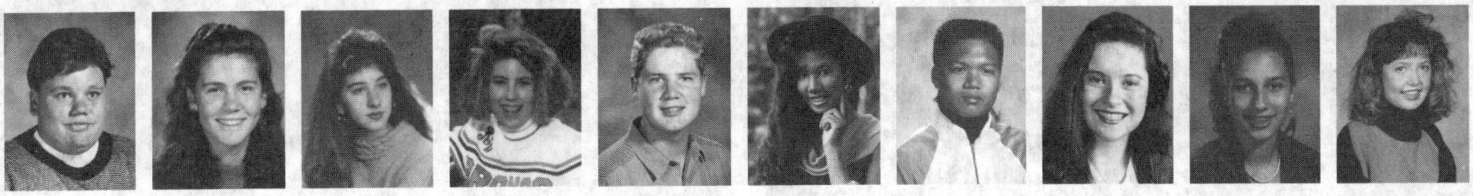

Day, Jerry
Dinuba HS
Dinuba, CA

Day, Julie A
Sonora HS
La Habra, CA

Day, Monica
Thousand Oaks HS
Thousand Oaks, CA

Day, Tiffany
Kern Valley HS
Weldon, CA

Day, William F
John F Kennedy HS
Buena Park, CA

Dayco, Catherine
Berean Christian HS
Concord, CA

Dayleg, Ray-Francis
James Logan HS
Union City, CA

De Anda, Yolanda
Sacred Heart Of
Jesus HS
Los Angeles, CA

De Bourg, Hanna
Calvary Chapel HS
Santa Ana, CA

De Camp, Inge K
Rincon Valley
Christian HS
Santa Rosa, CA

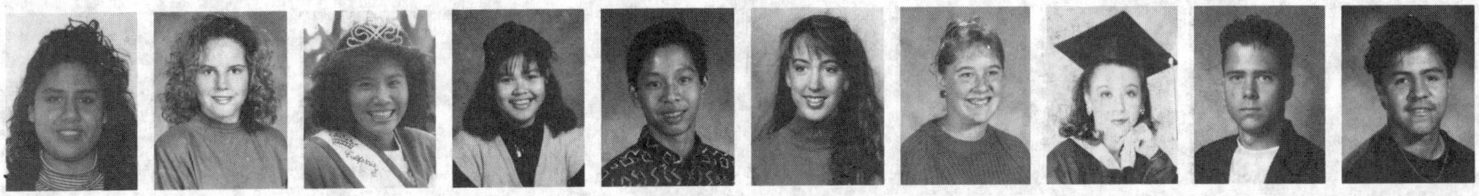

De Casas, Monica
Rosary HS
Placentia, CA

De Groot, Sarah
Perris HS
Sun City, CA

De Guia, Alma Marie
Chaminade College
Prep
Mission Hills, CA

De Guzman, Carlota
Westmoor HS
Daly City, CA

De Guzman, Rayneil
Servite HS
Cerritos, CA

De Jong, Heidi
Escondido HS
Escondido, CA

De Jonge, Melanie S
Tracy HS
Tracy, CA

De La Cerda, Andrea
Whittier HS
Whittier, CA

De La Cerra, Manuel
Chaminade Coll Prep
Canoga Park, CA

De La Riva, Jose J
Saddleback HS
Santa Ana, CA

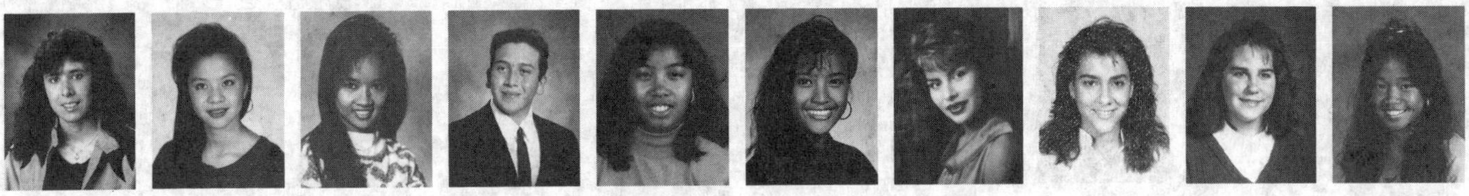

De Lara, Vicky
Beaumont HS
Beaumont, CA

De Leon, Ellen
John A Rowland HS
Walnut, CA

De Leon, Heidi F
John A Rowland HS
Walnut, CA

De Leon, Jr Jorge
Mater Dei HS
Santa Ana, CA

De Leon, Lorraine R
St Jospeh HS
Norwalk, CA

De Leon, Melisa Lisa
St Francis HS
Mountain View, CA

De Leon, Olivia
Porterville HS
Porterville, CA

De Llanos, Estela
Notre Dame Acad
Santa Monica, CA

De Loach, Kimberly
Hillsdale HS
Foster City, CA

De Los Reyes,
Charisma V
Samuel F B Morse
San Diego, CA

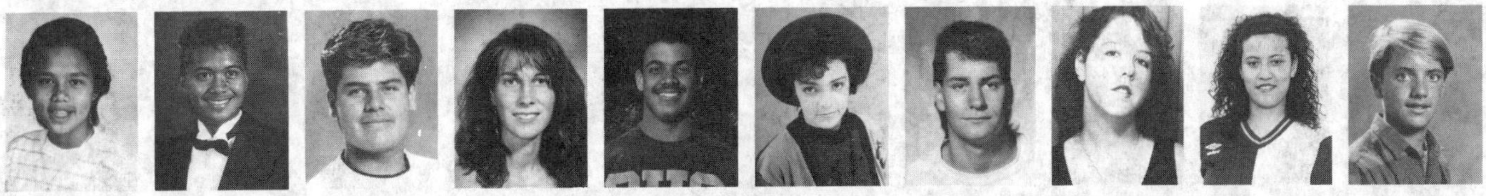

De Los Reyes,
Jennifer F
Nogales HS
Walnut, CA

De Los Santos,
Rommel
Lower Lake HS
Clearlake, CA

De Luna, Erick
Saint Anthony HS
Long Beach, CA

De Luna, Melanie H
University HS
Irvine, CA

De Maria, Robert A
Bassett HS
La Puente, CA

De Monte, Jennifer
Brea-Olinda HS
Brea, CA

De Paul, Eric L
Orange Glen HS
Escondido, CA

De Pucci, Anne M
Analy HS
Sebastopol, CA

De Ramirez, Brenda
Veronica T
San Juan HS
Citrus Heights, CA

De Robertis, Alex
Palisades HS
Pacific Palisades, CA

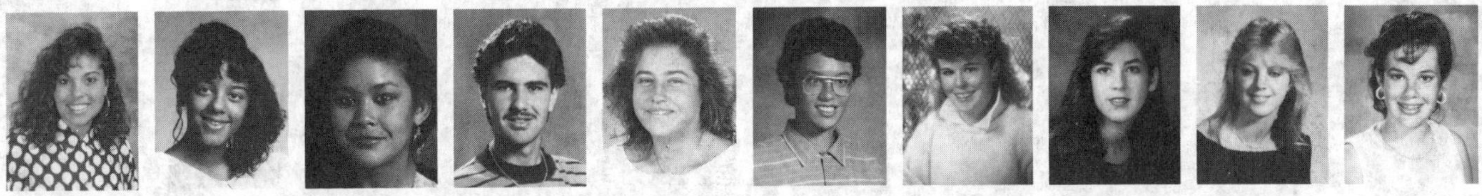

De Rosa, Marissa
Bishop Amat HS
San Dimas, CA

De Salles, Marisa A
Valley HS
Sacramento, CA

De Santos, Tanya R
Marymount HS
Los Angeles, CA

De Simone, Frank M
Leuzinger HS
Hawthorne, CA

De Sousa-Dias,
Catherine
Palo Verde HS
Blythe, CA

De Veas, Willson J
Hamilton Union HS
Orland, CA

De Vilbiss, Christina
Enterprise HS
Redding, CA

De Ville, De Ette
Rio Lindo Adventist
Acad
Mansfield, TX

De Vine, Theresa M
Independence HS
San Jose, CA

De Vita, Gina M
Antelope Valley HS
Lancaster, CA

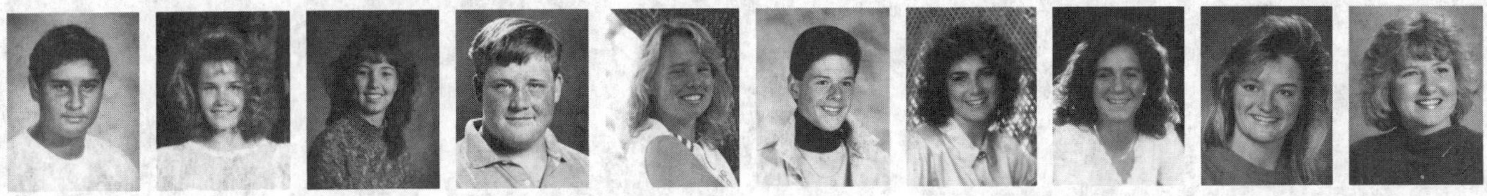

De Waal, Johan
Santa Ana Valley HS
Santa Ana, CA

De Young, Leslie
Modesto HS
Modesto, CA

Dean, Barbara
Mc Lane HS
Fresno, CA

Dean, Curtis W
Fontana HS
Fontana, CA

Dean, Heather
Caruthers Union HS
Caruthers, CA

Dean, Robert J
St Vincent HS
Sebastopol, CA

Deaner, Shannon M
Liberty Christian HS
Cottonwood, CA

Dearborn, Karith
Napa HS
Napa, CA

Deegan, Elizabeth G
Irvine HS
Irvine, CA

Deeley, Wendy A
Edison HS
Huntington Bch, CA

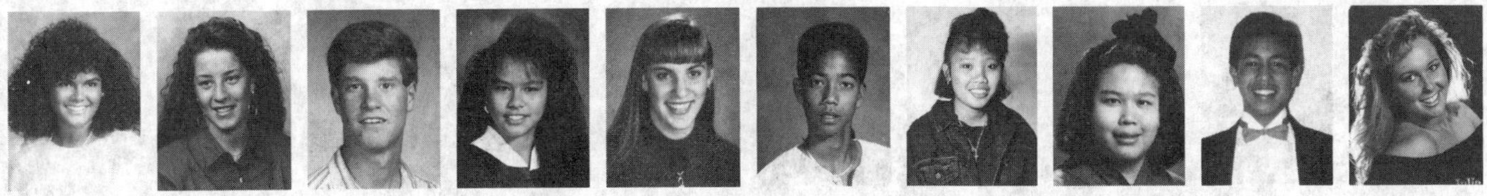

Defilippi, Giuliana V
Louisville HS
Canoga Park, CA

Deicas-Bercovici,
Ariela
La Jolla HS
La Jolla, CA

Deininger, Scott
Coalinga HS
Coalinga, CA

Del Fonzo, Stephanie
Mater Dei HS
La Palma, CA

Del Porto, Amy
Sarah
Lincoln HS
Stockton, CA

Del Rosario, Ricky J
Monterey HS
Seaside, CA

Dela Cruz, Felisa
Skyline HS
Oakland, CA

Dela Rosa, Feliz G
Bellarmine Jefferson
Glendale, CA

Delago, David J
Antioch HS
Antioch, CA

Delcoma, Julie
Yucca Valley HS
Yucca Valley, CA

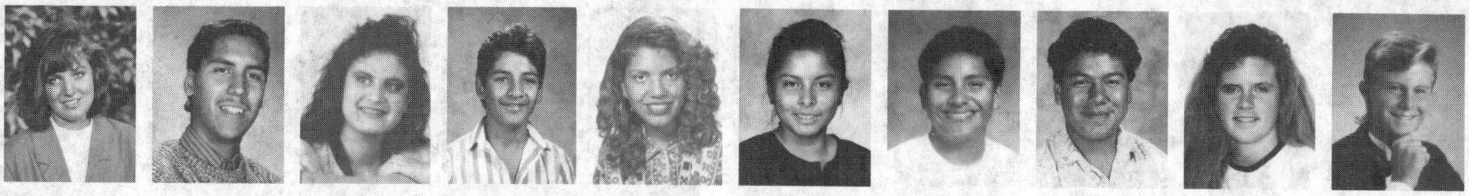

Deleo, Kim
Dana Hills HS
Laguna Niguel, CA

Deleon, Alex G
Selma HS
Selma, CA

Delgadillo, Camie
East Bakersfield HS
Bakersfield, CA

Delgadillo, Julio E
Garfield HS
Los Angeles, CA

Delgado, Elizabeth
Alain Le Roy Locke
Los Angeles, CA

Delgado, Sandy
San Gabriel Mission
San Gabriel, CA

Delgado, Sergio
Southwest HS
San Ysidro, CA

Delira, Steve F
Bishop Amat HS
Rowland Hts, CA

Delisle, Annette F
Live Oak HS
Morgan Hill, CA

Delisle, Frank Dennis
Live Oak HS
Morgan Hill, CA

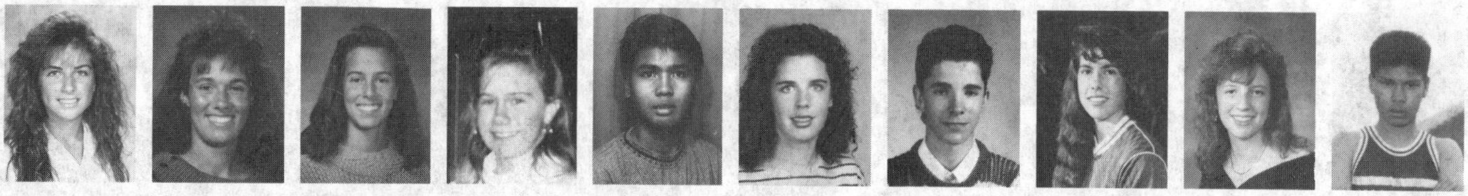

Della Ripa, Michele
St Genievieve HS
Loomis, CA

Dellacamera, Angela
Mission Viejo HS
Mission Viejo, CA

Dellacamera, Teresa
Mission Viejo HS
Mission Viejo, CA

Delong, Laura
Mountain View HS
Los Altos Hills, CA

Delos Angeles, Rodney F
Milpitas HS
Milpitas, CA

Dely, Shanagh
Benicia HS
Benicia, CA

Deman, Andrew F
Valley HS
Sacramento, CA

Demarchi, Deborah
Mission Viejo HS
Mission Viejo, CA

Demaree, Edith E
Fremont HS
Sunnyvale, CA

Demesa, Edward
Vallejo SR HS
Vallejo, CA

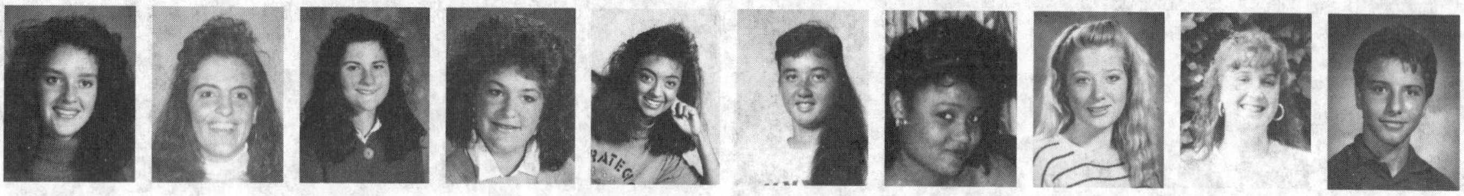

Demianew, Monica L
Atwater HS
Atwater, CA

Demirovic, Alma
Dublin HS
Dublin, CA

Dempsey, Kelly
South Tahoe HS
South Lake Tahoe, CA

Denis, Kelly
Turlock HS
Turlock, CA

Deniz, Angela Nicole
Madera HS
Madera, CA

Denney, Patricia M
Alhambra HS
Alhambra, CA

Dennie, Veronica L
John F Kennedy HS
Sacramento, CA

Dennis, Kristie
Calvary Chapel HS
Huntington Beach, CA

Dennis, Leah A
King City HS
King City, CA

Dennis, Robert M
La Quinta HS
Westminster, CA

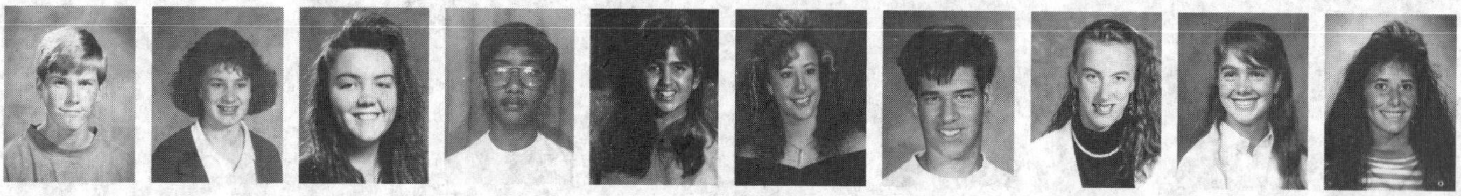

Dennish, Andrew S
Torrey Pines HS
Rancho Santa Fe, CA

Denson, Joanna
Immanuel Christian Schl
Ridgecrest, CA

Derbish, Allyson L
Etiwanda HS
Alta Loma, CA

Desai, Anish B
Whitney HS
Cerritos, CA

Desai, Shefali
Burbank HS
Burbank, CA

Desha, Emmalena Kahealani
Presentation HS
Pacifica, CA

Destefani, Robert L
Serra HS
San Carlos, CA

Dettner, Kathryn
Lowell HS
San Francisco, CA

Detweiler, Shannon L
The Bishops Schl
Del Mar, CA

Devert, Kristi A
Casa Grande HS
Petaluma, CA

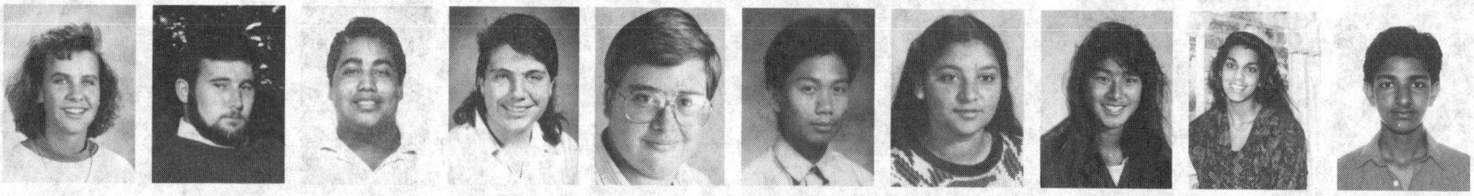

Devin, Eva Marie
Novato HS
Novato, CA

Devine, Christopher
Moore Bay HS
Los Osos, CA

Deweese, Eduardo
Moreno Valley HS
Moreno Vly, CA

Dexheimer, Sean P
Fountain Valley HS
Fountain Valley, CA

Dexter, Ken
Oxnard HS
Oxnard, CA

Deynata, Rosendo
Southwest HS
San Diego, CA

Dhami, Harpreet K
James Logan HS
Union City, CA

Dhatchayangkul, Cynthia
Crescenta Valley HS
La Crescenta, CA

Dhillon, Asha
La Reina HS
Agoura Hills, CA

Dhillon, Manbir S
Warren HS
Downey, CA

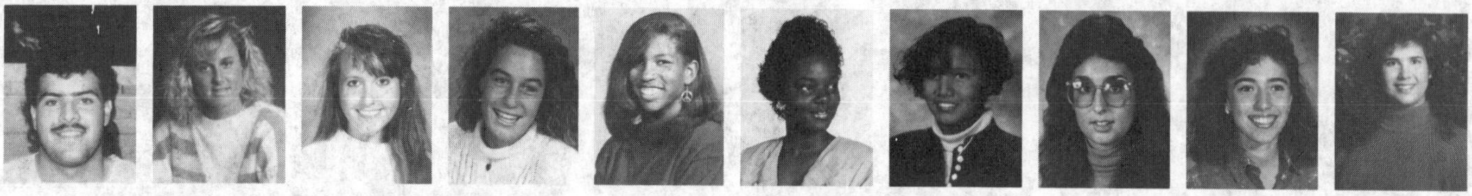

Di Cocco, Patrick G
Victor Valley HS
Victorville, CA

Di Laura, Danielle
La Canada HS
Bradbury, CA

Di Paolo, Joana
Cypress HS
Cypress, CA

Di Pietro, Andrea M
Ramona HS
Ramona, CA

Diaab, Maryam
Lakewood SR HS
Long Beach, CA

Diamond, Qwintrice
Bonita Vista HS
San Diego, CA

Dianand, Jennifer
Fairfield HS
Fairfield, CA

Dias, Dina S
Hilmar HS
Hilmar, CA

Dias, Linda
Chico SR HS
Chico, CA

Diaz, Adelina
El Toro HS
El Toro, CA

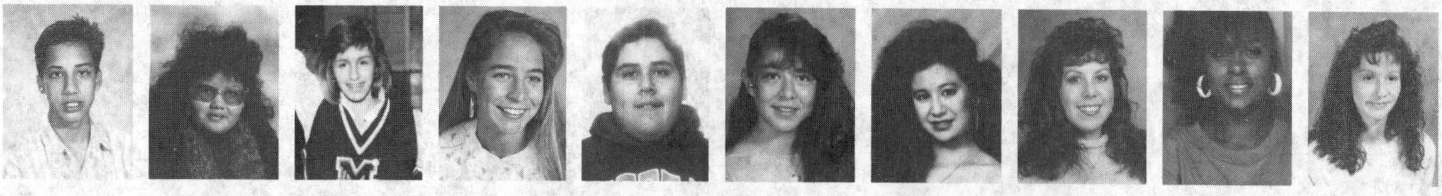

Diaz, Anthony F
Pasadena HS
Pasadena, CA

Diaz, Bernadette
Kingsburg HS
Traver, CA

Diaz, Beverly
Twentynine Palms
Gaithersburg, MD

Diaz, Carey C
Palm Springs HS
Cathedral City, CA

Diaz, Carlos
Serra HS
San Mateo, CA

Diaz, Caroline I
Wilcox HS
Santa Clara, CA

Diaz, Catherine R
Bishop Amat Memorial HS
Rowland Hts, CA

Diaz, Cindy A
Redlands SR HS
Redlands, CA

Diaz, Deborah
Garey HS
Pomona, CA

Diaz, Estela
Liberty Union HS
Brentwood, CA

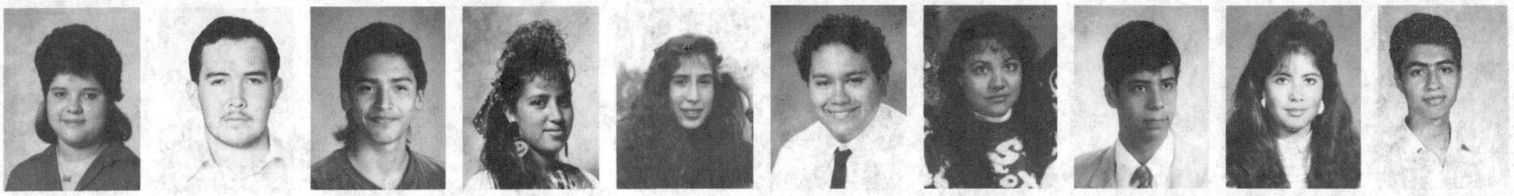

Diaz, Eva Maria
Castle Park HS
Chula Vista, CA

Diaz, Fernando C
Edison HS
Stockton, CA

Diaz, Fernie L
Oakdale HS
Oakdale, CA

Diaz, Gabby
Saddleback HS
Santa Ana, CA

Diaz, Marsha
Etiwanda HS
Fontana, CA

Diaz, Mauro
Pater Noster HS
Los Angeles, CA

Diaz, Miladis E
Santa Ana HS
Santa Ana, CA

Diaz, Robert Michael
Palm Desert HS
Palm Desert, CA

Diaz, Rossybell
Seaside HS
Ft Knox, KY

Diaz, Sergio E
Venice HS
Los Angeles, CA

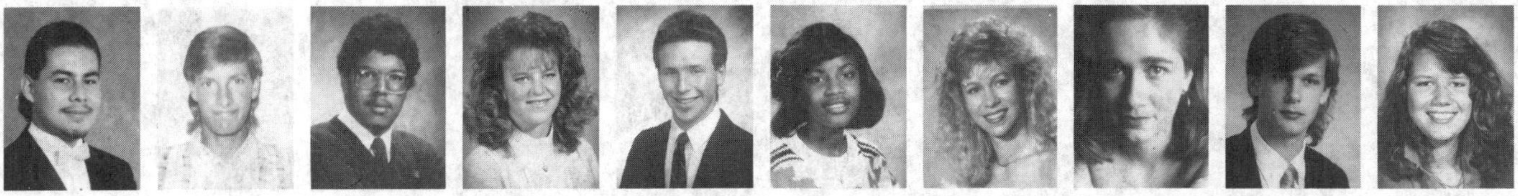

Diaz, Steve
San Fernando HS
Pacoima, CA

Dibblee, Harrison F
Huntington Beach
Huntington Beach, CA

Dicely, Christopher
Benicia HS
Benicia, CA

Dickensheets, Andrea
Hoopa Valley HS
Willow Creek, CA

Dicker, David J
Poway HS
San Diego, CA

Dickerson, Chrishone
George Washington Prep HS
Los Angeles, CA

Dickey, Kandace
Oak Ridge HS
El Dorado Hills, CA

Dickinson, Christine
Valhalla HS
Jamul, CA

Dickinson, Robert L
San Bernardino HS
San Bernardino, CA

Dickover, Michele A
Thousand Oaks HS
Thousand Oaks, CA

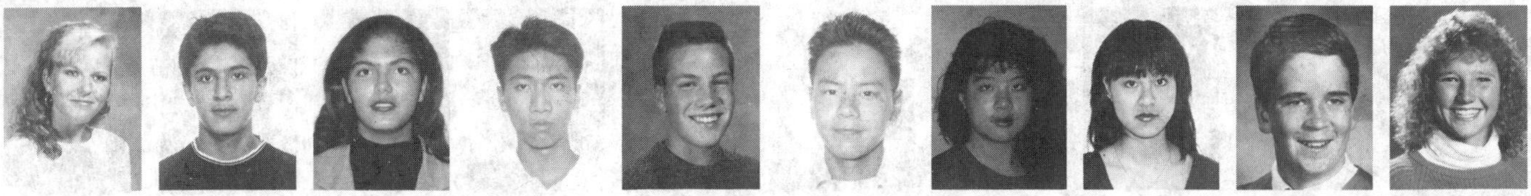

Dickson, Mary
Corona HS
Corona, CA

Didehvarsadr, Farid
Pasadena HS
Alhambra, CA

Didehvarsadr, Mojdeh
Pasadena HS
Alhambra, CA

Diec, Thanh H
Milpitas HS
Milpitas, CA

Diemer, Brian
Valley Christian HS
Dublin, CA

Diep, David
Alhambra HS
Alhambra, CA

Diep, Linda
San Gabriel HS
San Gabriel, CA

Diep, Ly H
San Gabriel HS
Rosemead, CA

Dignan, Casey Michael
St Michaels Prep
Costa Mesa, CA

Dijkstra, Helen B
Bakersfield HS
Bakersfield, CA

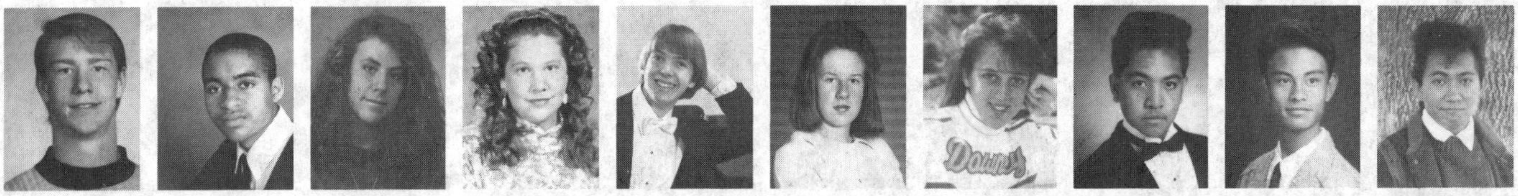

Dilbeck, Jason K
Durham HS
Durham, CA

Dillard, Reo Terao
Bridgemont HS
San Francisco, CA

Dillenburg, Heather
Fred C Beyer HS
Modesto, CA

Dillon, Ariana
Abraham Lincoln HS
San Francisco, CA

Dillon, Christopher
Grace Christian HS
Atascadero, CA

Dillon, Maryann M
San Gorgonio HS
San Bernardino, CA

Dillon, Michele
Thomas Downey HS
Modesto, CA

Dimacali, Dexter C
Samuel F B Morse
San Diego, CA

Dimaculangan, Ramonito S
Glendora HS
Costa Mesa, CA

Dimapilis, Albert"stringfellow"
Baldwin Park HS
Baldwin Park, CA

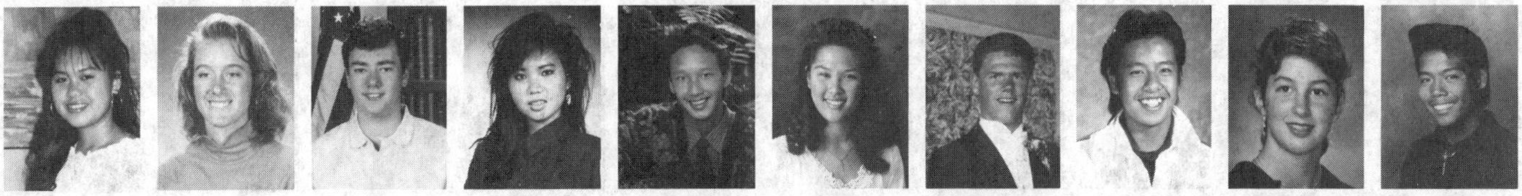

Dimaporo, Anna Charina O
Polytechnic HS
N Hollywood, CA

Dimino, Donna
California HS
San Ramon, CA

Dina, Peter T
Calvary Baptist HS
La Verne, CA

Dinh, Thanh
La Quinta HS
Westminster, CA

Dinh, Thien Phuong
Rancho Buena Vista
Oceanside, CA

Dino, Marianne
Bishop Amat Memorial HS
West Covina, CA

Dinsmore, Daniel A
Antelope Valley HS
Lancaster, CA

Dionisio, Aristotle R
Lowell HS
San Francisco, CA

Dionne, Erin M
Laguna Hills HS
Laguna Hills, CA

Diso, Jonathan L
Bonita Vista HS
Chula Vista, CA

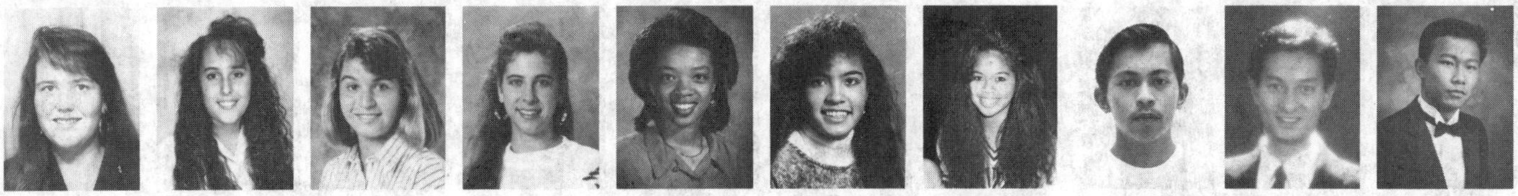

Distefano, Catherine
Schurr HS
Montebello, CA

Ditty, Angela
St Genevieve HS
Panorama City, CA

Divino, Diane M
Dana Hills HS
Laguna Niguel, CA

Dixon, Marina
Rancho Buena Vista
Vista, CA

Dixon, Shannon Y
Temecula Valley HS
Temecula, CA

Dizon, Jenna C
San Marino HS
San Gabriel, CA

Dizon, Noemi M
Branham HS
San Jose, CA

Dizon, Jr Romeo Q
Montclair HS
Montclair, CA

Do, Anh Q
University HS
Irvine, CA

Do, Bao T
Saugus HS
Saugus, CA

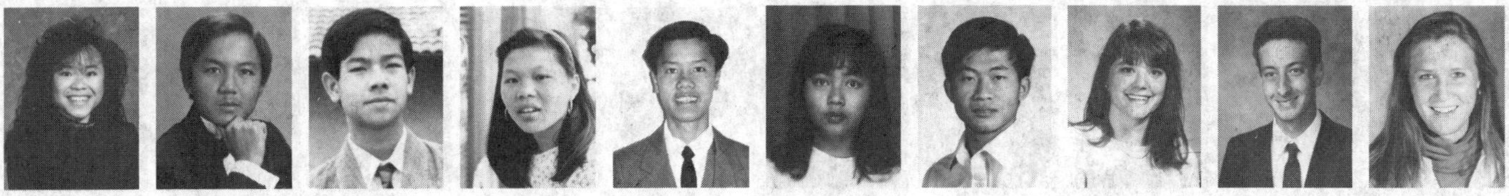

Do, Cam N
Westmoor HS
Daly City, CA

Do, John
Adrian C Wilcox HS
Santa Clara, CA

Do, Luong D
Silver Creek HS
San Jose, CA

Do, Nanette M
Skyline HS
Oakland, CA

Do, Timmy D
Irvine HS
Irvine, CA

Do, Uyen D
Los Amigos HS
Santa Ana, CA

Doan, Hieu N
Abraham Lincoln HS
San Jose, CA

Dobbert, Penelope J
Eisenhower HS
Rialto, CA

Dobbs, Michael
Van Nuys HS
Van Nuys, CA

Dobrinen, Natasha L
Lowell HS
San Francisco, CA

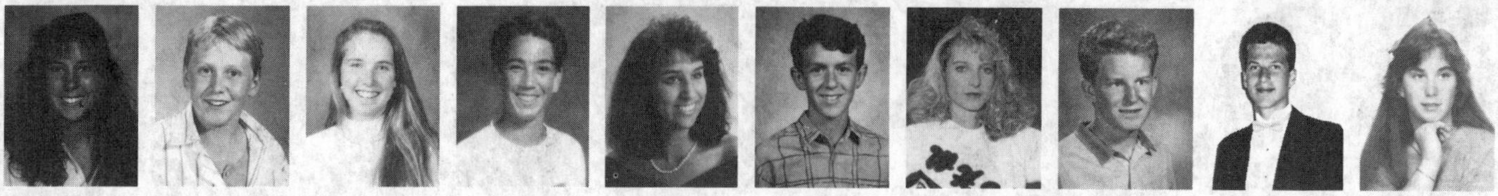

Dockendorf, Dionne
Louisville HS
Encino, CA

Dodge, Jr William H
Aptos HS
Watsonville, CA

Dofflemyer, Jessica L
Redwood HS
Visalia, CA

Dohman, David W
Southwest HS
San Diego, CA

Doland, Kristina D
Saint Francis HS
Mountain View, CA

Dolder, Scott
Oakmont HS
Roseville, CA

Dolson, Darcy R
Woodlake HS
Exeter, CA

Domen, Jim R
Troy HS
Yorba Linda, CA

Domenici, Jr Anthony
Hogan SR HS
Vallejo, CA

Domich, Kristina J
Grossmont HS
La Mesa, CA

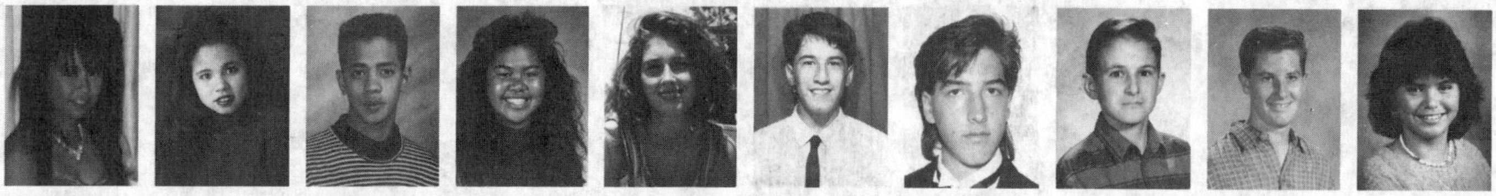

Domingo, Aileen G
St Genevieve HS
Northridge, CA

Domingo, Ferari
Bishop Amat HS
West Covina, CA

Domingo, John F
Bishop Amat
Memorial HS
West Covina, CA

Domingo, Ruthie C
Aquinas HS
Highland, CA

Dominguez, Berta
Rio Mesa HS
Camarillo, CA

Dominguez, Robin
Don Bosco Tech Inst
Pico Rivera, CA

Dominick, Justin E
Chaminade College
Prep
Northridge, CA

Domino, Benjamin J
Crescenta Valley HS
Montrose, CA

Donahue, Jamie M
Monte Vista HS
Alamo, CA

Donais, Mary Ann P
Grossmont HS
El Cajon, CA

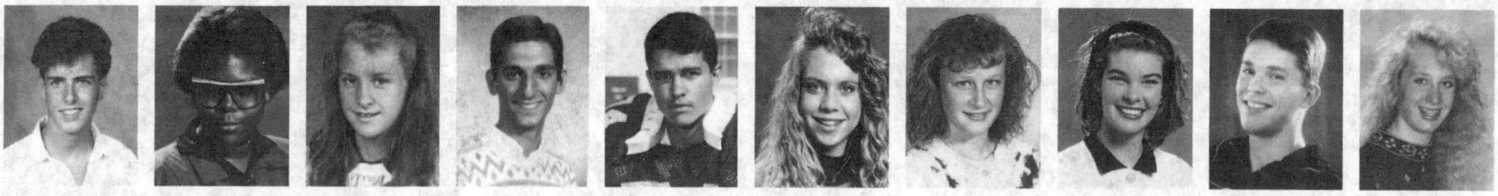

Donaldson, Bradley K
Patrick Henry HS
San Diego, CA

Donaldson, Danielle
Pomona HS
W Covina, CA

Donart, Brandy M
St Joseph HS
Long Beach, CA

Donian, Warren L
Lowell HS
San Francisco, CA

Donnelly, Michael D
Leuzinger HS
Lawndale, CA

Donnelly, Michelle A
Fontana HS
Fontana, CA

Donovan, Betty J
Davis SR HS
Davis, CA

Donovan, Heather L
Village Christian HS
Tujunga, CA

Donovan, John
Placer HS
Newcastle, CA

Donovan, Kristi
Inland Christian HS
Highland, CA

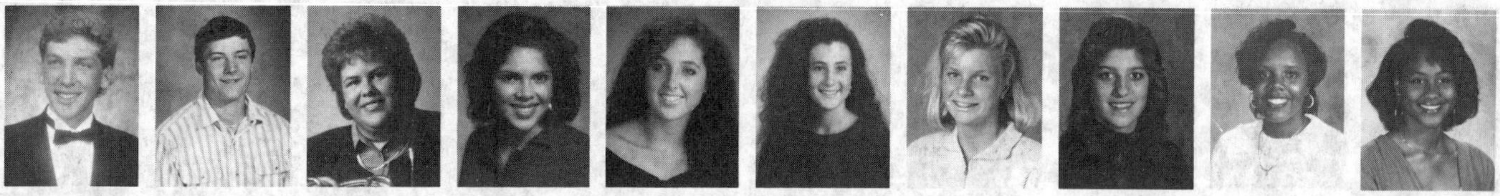

Doob, Jared A
Irvington HS
Fremont, CA

Doolittle, Joe J
Red Bluff HS
Cottonwood, CA

Dorado, Kimberly R
Hamilton HS
Academy Of Music
Los Angeles, CA

Dorado, Monica
Southwest HS
San Diego, CA

Doran, Shannon
Saint Francis HS
Santa Rosa, CA

Dorfman, Jennafer
Pioneer HS
San Jose, CA

Dorrough, Susie C
Louisville HS
Woodland Hills, CA

Dorsey, Kimberly V
George Washington
San Francisco, CA

Dorsey, Rulanda D
Chula Vista HS
Chula Vista, CA

Dossett, Teresa
Antelope Valley HS
Lancaster, CA

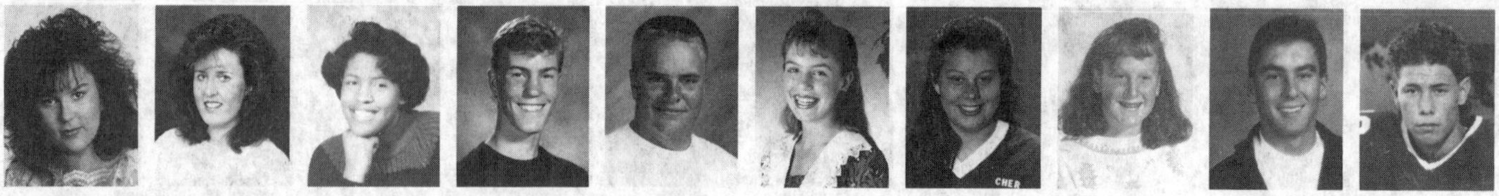

Doster, Rebecca
Palmdale HS
Littlerock, CA

Doster, Tammy
Palmdale HS
Littlerock, CA

Dotson, Denise Lucia
South Bay JR Acad
Carson, CA

Dotson, Patrick D
Valhalla HS
Jamul, CA

Dotta, Bill R
Apple Valley HS
Apple Valley, CA

Dotten, Chara
Mother Lode
Christian Schl
Sonora, CA

Dotts, Cheri J
Fontana HS
Fontana, CA

Dougan, Bree
Foothill HS
Pleasanton, CA

Doughteryt, Robert
Mt Whitney HS
Visalia, CA

Douglas, Greg E
North HS
Bakersfield, CA

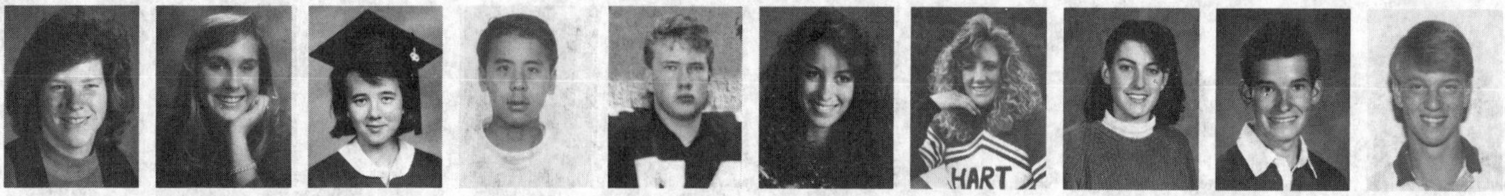

Douglas, Holly A
Calaveras HS
Mokelumne Hill, CA

Douglas, Rebecca P
Rio Americano HS
Sacramento, CA

Douglass, Elizabeth S
Mt Miguel HS
Spring Valley, CA

Doungchak, Flint I
University HS
Irvine, CA

Douty, Nathan D
Fresno Christian Schl
Fresno, CA

Dovichi, Erin
Fred C Beyer HS
Modesto, CA

Dow, Jill C
Wm S Hart HS
Newhall, CA

Dowd, Gina A
Santa Cruz HS
Santa Cruz, CA

Dowell, Lance V
University HS
Irvine, CA

Downey, John E
College Park HS
Martinez, CA

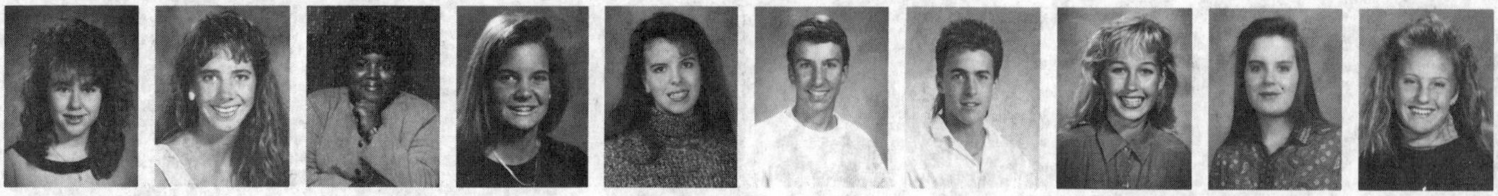

Downing, Danyel
Evette
Orosi HS
Orosi, CA

Downs, Jennifer
Los Alamitos HS
Surfside, CA

Downs, Stacey
Western Regional
Christian Acad
San Pablo, CA

Doyle-Marcey,
Jennifer E
Bellarmine-Jefferson
Glendale, CA

Draeger, Marnie K
Yucaipa HS
Yucaipa, CA

Drake, Mark D
Eisenhower HS
Rialto, CA

Drake, Paul E
Santa Clara HS
Santa Clara, CA

Drenser, Bridgit E
Costa Mesa HS
Costa Mesa, CA

Dresner, Karen M
Redlands HS
Redlands, CA

Drew, Kari L
Grossmont HS
El Cajon, CA

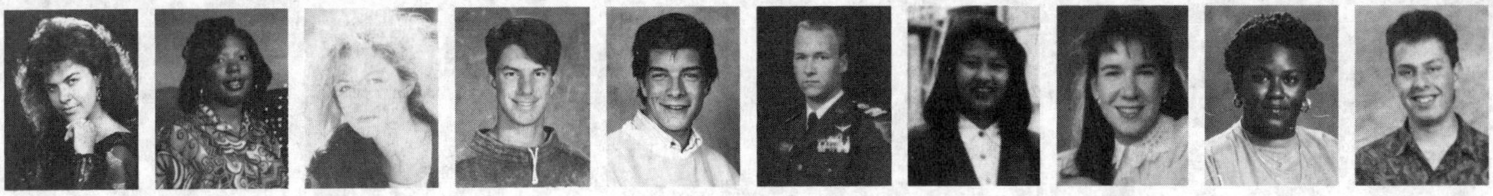

Driggs, Kimberly L
Beyer HS
Modesto, CA

Driver, Myisha
Pius X HS
West Los Angeles, CA

Drob, Suzy
William Howard Taft
Woodland Hills, CA

Drozdenko, Daniel
Southbay Christian
Sunnyvale, CA

Drummond, Paul C
Grossmont HS
San Diego, CA

Drury, Kevin P
Clovis West HS
Fresno, CA

Du, Phuong Q
International Studies Acad
San Francisco, CA

Du Be, Jane A
Bella Vista HS
Fair Oaks, CA

Du Brey, Tanesha R
Saint Michaels HS
Lynwood, CA

Du Lyon, Benn A
Pater Noster HS
Los Angeles, CA

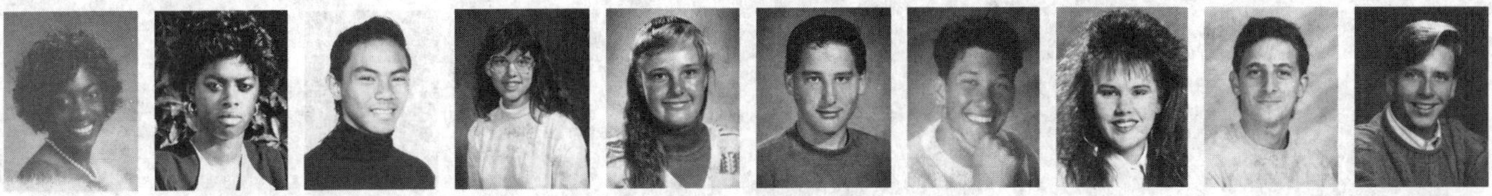

Dudley, Julia
Archbishop Mitty HS
San Jose, CA

Dudley, Sidra V
Alexander Hamilton
Los Angeles, CA

Duenas, Gerald J
Carson HS
Carson, CA

Duerksen, Debbie B
Monterey Bay Acad
Salt Lake City, UT

Duesterhoft, Rebecca
Westlake HS
Thousands Oaks, CA

Duffield, Carlyle
Norco HS
Norco, CA

Duggan, Sean P
Montgomery HS
Santa Rosa, CA

Duhamel, Jamie
Banning HS
Wilmington, CA

Duke, Charles J
Apple Valley HS
Apple Valley, CA

Dulac, Brian Michael
Poway HS
Poway, CA

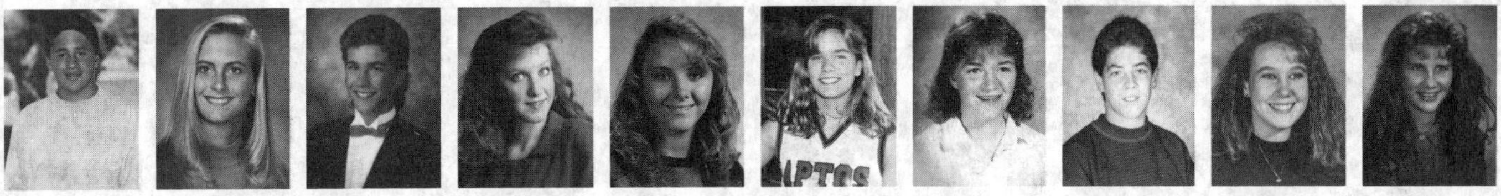

Dulin, Ryan N
San Jacinto HS
San Jacinto, CA

Dull, Kerin L
Mission Viejo HS
Mission Viejo, CA

Dultz, Shane
Oak Park HS
Agoura, CA

Duly, Amy
Burbank HS
Burbank, CA

Dunaway, Sandra D
Galt HS
Galt, CA

Dunbar, Suzanne C
Aptos HS
Aptos, CA

Dunbar, Tara A
Red Bluff Union HS
Red Bluff, CA

Dunbarr, James J
Vacaville HS
Vacaville, CA

Duncan, Cristi
Central Valley Christian HS
Visalia, CA

Duncan, Kimberly
Chowchilla Union HS
Chowchilla, CA

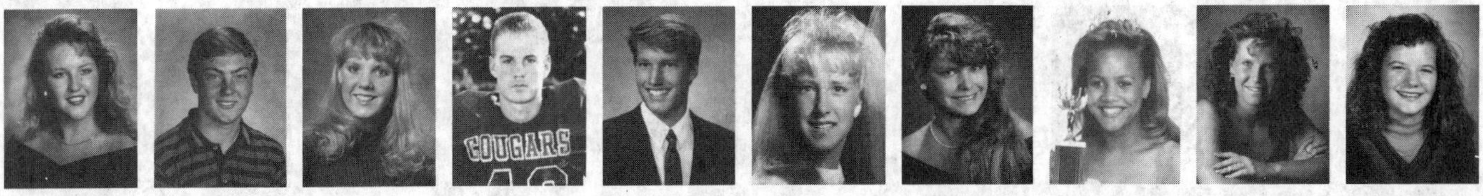

Duncan, Shari R
Elk Grove HS
Sacramento, CA

Dunlap, Oliver Q
Las Lomas HS
Walnut Creek, CA

Dunleavy, Jill
Rosary HS
Anaheim Hills, CA

Dunn, Brandon W
Mc Farland HS
Mc Farland, CA

Dunn, Brian
Oakmont HS
Roseville, CA

Dunn, Jennifer
Mc Farland HS
Delano, CA

Dunn, Jodi K
Tehachapi HS
Tehachapi, CA

Dunn, Maisha
Diamond Bar HS
Diamond Bar, CA

Dunshee, Jennifer
Righetti HS
Santa Maria, CA

Dunsmoor, Kimberly
Montgomery HS
Santa Rosa, CA

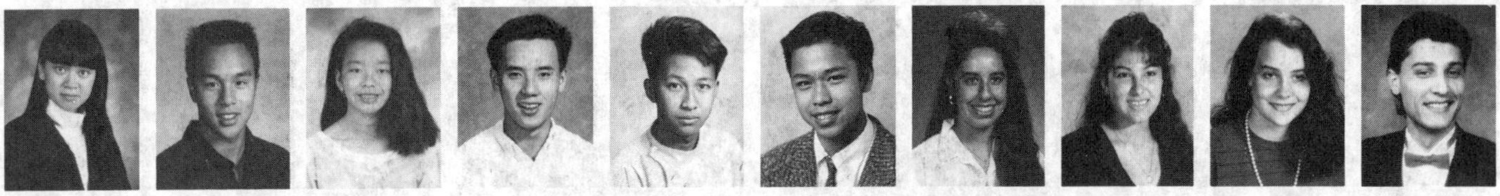

Duong, Josephine L
Oakland HS
Oakland, CA

Duong, Long
Mission San Jose HS
Fremont, CA

Duong, Myxuan
Dos Pueblos HS
Goleta, CA

Duong, Nhan H
Lowell HS
San Francisco, CA

Duong, Quoc
Richmond HS
San Pablo, CA

Duong, Richard H
West HS
Torrance, CA

Duran, Teresa
Mercy HS
S San Francisco, CA

Duran, Yvonne
Morro Bay SR HS
Morro Bay, CA

Durand, Michelle M
Amos Alonzo Stagg
Stockton, CA

Durani, Ahmad Zia
James Logan HS
Fremont, CA

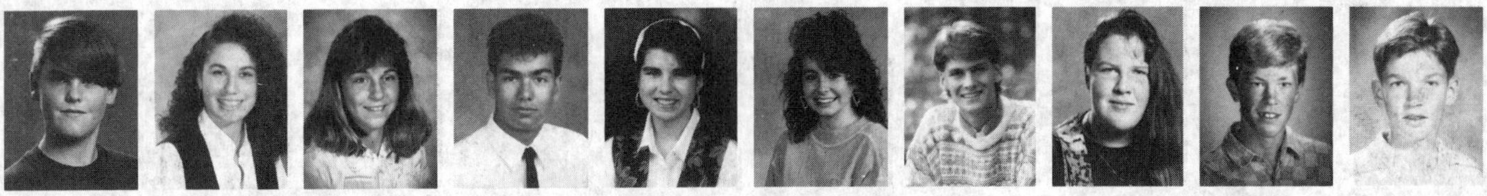

Durante, John W
Upland HS
Upland, CA

Durazo, Elizabeth
Del Oro HS
N Highlands, CA

Duryea, Suzanne
Bella Vista HS
Fair Oaks, CA

Dussert, Alain
Magnolia HS
Anaheim, CA

Dutra, Shirley A
North Salinas HS
Salinas, CA

Dutton, Lisa
Simi Valley HS
Simi Valley, CA

Dutton, Matthew Roberds
Nevada Union HS
Grass Valley, CA

Duzan, Jami M
Hawthorne HS
Hawthorne, CA

Dyal, James E
Tokay HS
Stockton, CA

Dyer, J Greg
San Dieguito HS
Olivenhain, CA

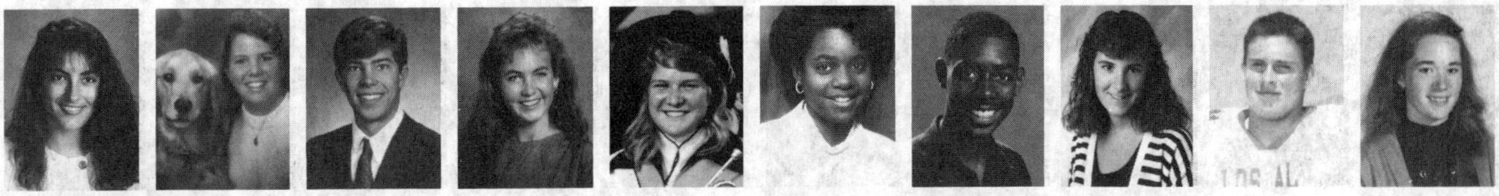

Dyer, Janelle M
Los Banos HS
Los Banos, CA

Dyer, Jorja Christeen
Enterprise HS
Redding, CA

Dyer, Robert
Santa Monica HS
Malibu, CA

Dyrr, Joanna
Riverside Poly HS
Riverside, CA

Dyson, De Anna L
San Marcos HS
San Marcos, CA

Dyson, Diya
Orange Glen HS
Escondido, CA

Dyson, Eric L
Chadwick Schl
Los Angeles, CA

Eagle, Melodie
La Jolla Country Day Schl
Rancho Santa Fe, CA

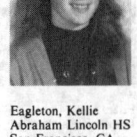

Eagle, Ryan
Los Alamitos HS
Los Alamitos, CA

Eagleton, Kellie
Abraham Lincoln HS
San Francisco, CA

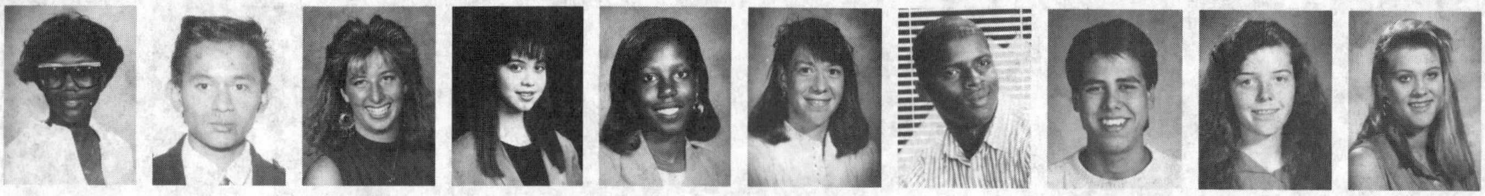

Ealey, Kimberly
Washington Prepatory HS
Los Angeles, CA

Eang, San K
J F Kennedy HS
Cypress, CA

Early, Sandy L
Grossmont HS
La Mesa, CA

Easer, Katherine L
Gretchen Whitney
Cerritos, CA

Easley, La Gina S
Washington HS
Los Angeles, CA

Easter, Lois M
North HS
Bakersfield, CA

Easter, Troy L
Canyon Springs HS
Moreno Valley, CA

Easterday, David A
Thomas Downey HS
Modesto, CA

Eastland, Laura Ellen
Elsinore HS
Lake Elsinore, CA

Eastman, Kelly M
Villa Park HS
Orange, CA

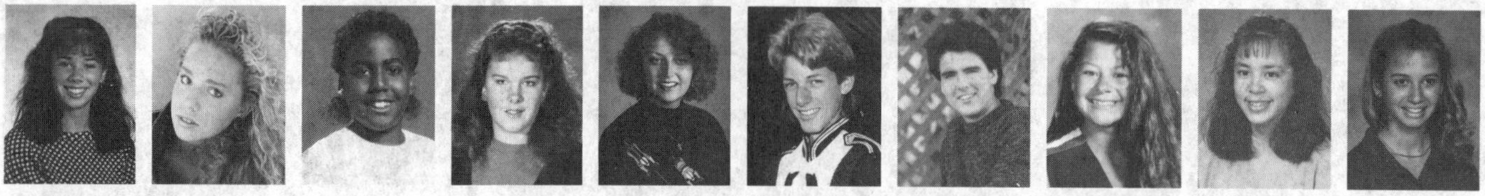

Eastridge, Suzanne B
Saint Francis HS
Santa Clara, CA

Eaton, Ashley
El Camino HS
Sacramento, CA

Eaton, La Bruce
Cajon HS
San Bernardino, CA

Eaton, Stacey
Don Antonio Lugo
Chino Hills, CA

Eble, Troianne
Fred C Beyer HS
Modesto, CA

Ebner, Damon F
Huntington Beach
Huntington Beach, CA

Ebury, Chris
Avenal HS
Avenal, CA

Eccles, Nicole T
Independence HS
San Jose, CA

Echavez, Melodie A
Novato HS
Novato, CA

Echeverri, Nanci S
Louisville HS
West Hills, CA

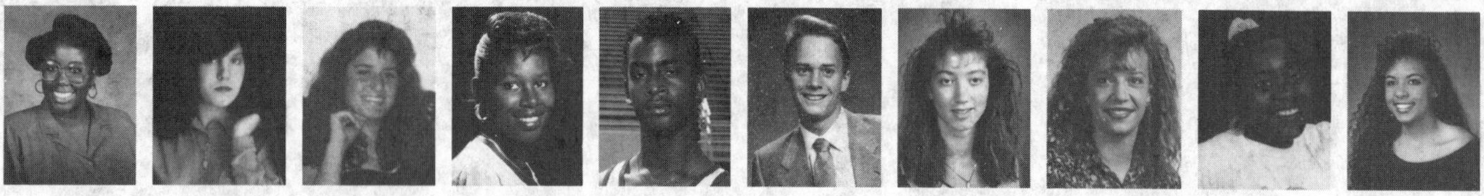

Echols, Orvilette
Brethren HS
Los Angeles, CA

Eckland, Kristin L
Bret Harte Union HS
Arnold, CA

Economy, Niky
John W North HS
Riverside, CA

Eddie, Danya C
Ganesha HS
Pomona, CA

Eddings, Erik
Fairfield HS
Fairfield, CA

Edgar, Harold W
Arlington HS
Riverside, CA

Edgar, Stephanie J
Fred C Beyer HS
Modesto, CA

Edgerton, Erin L
Santa Clara HS
Santa Clara, CA

Edmond, Michelle M
Oakland HS
Oakland, CA

Edmonds, Chelsey
Concord HS
Concord, CA

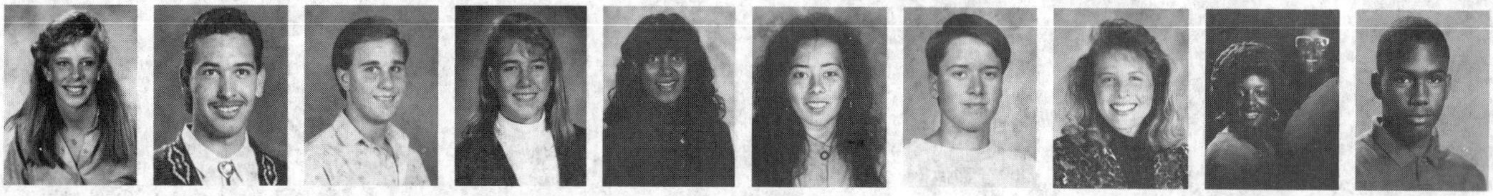

Edmonds, Darla M
Barstow HS
Newberry Springs, CA

Edmonds, David M
Majave HS
Mojave, CA

Edmondson, David M
Leffingwell Christian
Norwalk, CA

Edmundson, Kirsten
Portola JR SR HS
Blairsden, CA

Edpuganti, Renuka
Gretchen Whitney
Cerritos, CA

Edwards, Alko A
Bishop Amat HS
Diamond Bar, CA

Edwards, Brandon L
Yucca Valley HS
Yucca Valley, CA

Edwards, Charlotte
Caruthers Union HS
Raisin City, CA

Edwards, Felecia Ekisha
Crenshaw HS
Los Angeles, CA

Edwards, Glenn
Culver City HS
Culver City, CA

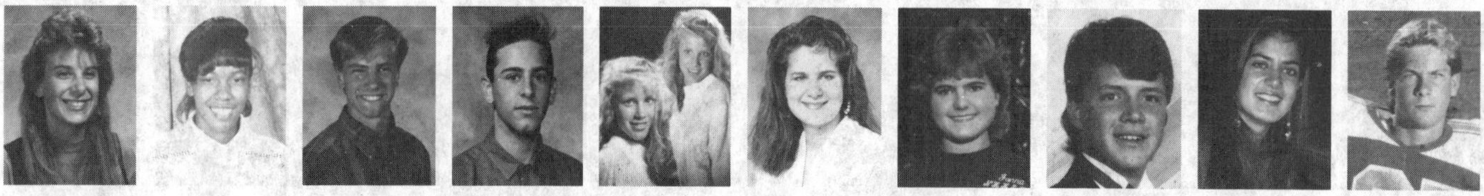

Edwards, Michelle D
James Logan HS
Union City, CA

Edwards, Tiffany N
Valley View HS
Moreno Valley, CA

Efird, John G
Bullard HS
Fresno, CA

Efron, Neal J
Granada Hills HS
Northridge, CA

Eger, Annamarie R
Fontana HS
Fontana, CA

Eggeman, Rebecca D
Montclair HS
Ontario, CA

Eggl, Jonna D
Newport Harbor HS
Santa Ana, CA

Eggley, Matt M
Canyon Springs HS
Moreno Valley, CA

Eghbali, Reyhaneh
William Howard Taft
Tarzana, CA

Ehnes, Brian E
Grant HS
Sacramento, CA

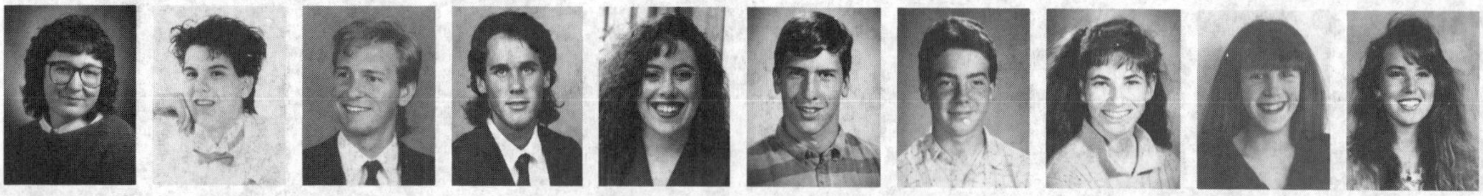

Ehorn, Nancy
Willows HS
Willows, CA

Ehorn, Tanya N
Red Bluff Union HS
Red Bluff, CA

Eichorn, Joshua M
Piedmont HS
Piedmont, CA

Eickhoff, Chris D
The Bishops Schl
Escondido, CA

Eid, Heidi G
Fred C Beyer HS
Modesto, CA

Eidsmoe, Jacob T
Ukiah HS
Ukiah, CA

Einess, Todd
East Union HS
Manteca, CA

Einstein, Jennifer M
Fountain Valley HS
Fountain Valley, CA

Eisemann, Melanie A
Downey HS
Downey, CA

Eisenlord, Alyson
Simi Valley HS
Simi Valley, CA

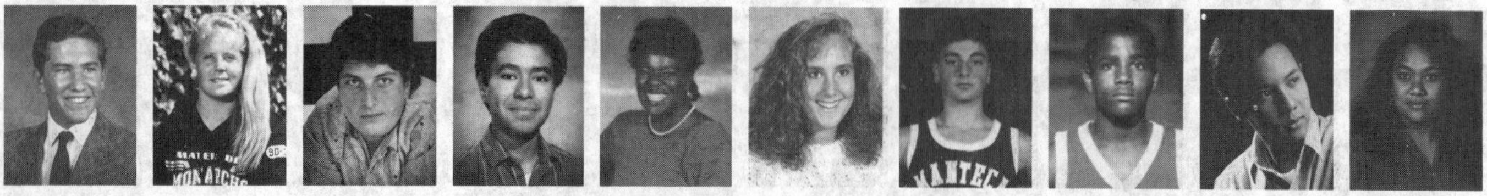

Eiser, Andy
Los Alamitos HS
Seal Beach, CA

Eisner, Erin E
Mater Dei HS
Anaheim, CA

El Alami, Sam S
Manteca HS
Manteca, CA

El Massry, Peter H
St John Bosco HS
Huntington Park, CA

Elanagan, Willeen
Fremont HS
Oakland, CA

Elander, Jennifer
Arroyo Grande HS
Arroyo Grande, CA

Elder, Sean
Manteca HS
Manteca, CA

Eldridge, Edward J
Valley HS
Sacramento, CA

Eleazar, Don
Beverly Hills Prep Schl
Westwood, CA

Elefante, Betsy
Helix HS
La Mesa, CA

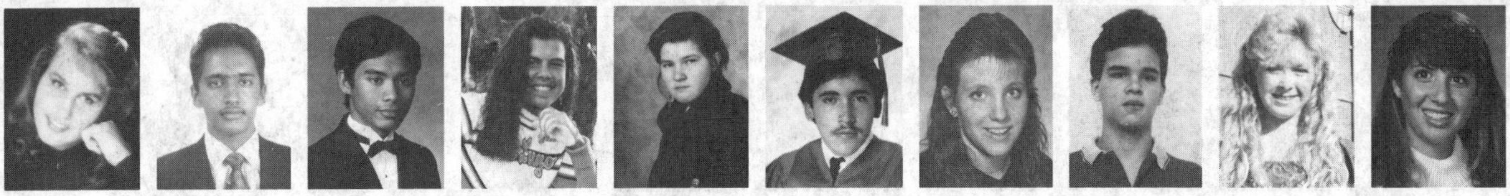

Elford, Kathleen
Oroville HS
Oroville, CA

Elias, Anthony A
Bellarmine College Prep
Milpitas, CA

Elias, Khalid A
Elk Grove HS
Sacramento, CA

Elizabeth, Perez A
Don Lugo HS
Chino, CA

Elizarraraz, Diana
Calexico HS
Calexico, CA

Elizondo, Rodrigo
Lynwood HS
Lynwood, CA

Elkins, Michele
Highlands HS
Sacramento, CA

Elkisch, Alan W
John Wesley North
Riverside, CA

Elledge, Krisann Renee
Esperanza HS
Yorba Linda, CA

Ellery, Traci L
El Toro HS
El Toro, CA

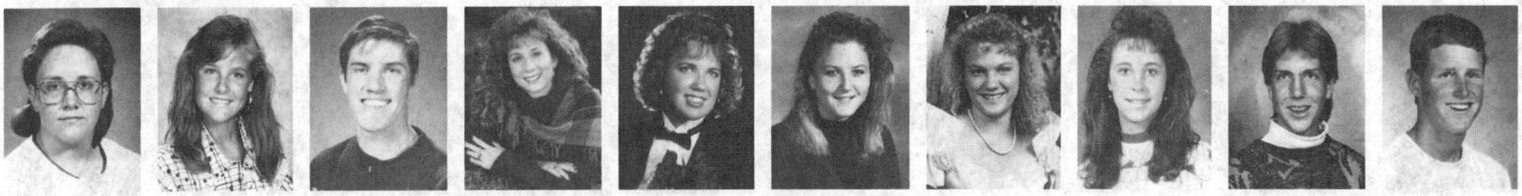

Ellings, Jess B
Norco HS
Corona, CA

Elliott, Danielle L
Louisville HS
Canoga Park, CA

Elliott, James W
Pinole Valley HS
San Pablo, CA

Elliott, Lisa Ann
West HS
Bakersfield, CA

Elliott, Margaret S
Clayton Valley HS
Concord, CA

Elliott, Tracie
Lower Lake HS
Clearlake Park, CA

Ellis, Angie
Arrowhead Christian Acad
San Bernardino, CA

Ellis, Cheri L
Hanford HS
Hanford, CA

Ellis, Erik C
Monte Vista HS
Spring Valley, CA

Ellis, John F
Del Campo HS
Carmichael, CA

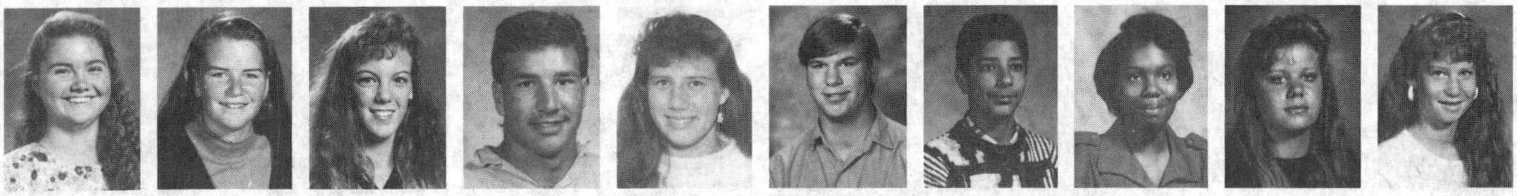

Ellis, Lori B
Fontana HS
Fontana, CA

Ellis, Marcie
San Ramon Valley
Danville, CA

Ellis, Stacy L
Garces Memorial HS
Bakersfield, CA

Elorduy, Todd
Christian Brothers
Sacramento, CA

Elsaesser, Carrie A
Los Amigos HS
Fountain Valley, CA

Elser, Kevin M
Fairfield HS
Fairfield, CA

Elsokary, Basem M
Monterey HS
Monterey, CA

Elston, Brittney N
Bullard HS
Fresno, CA

Emanuele, Nichole M
Norco HS
Corona, CA

Emerson, Aimee
Los Alamitos HS
Seal Beach, CA

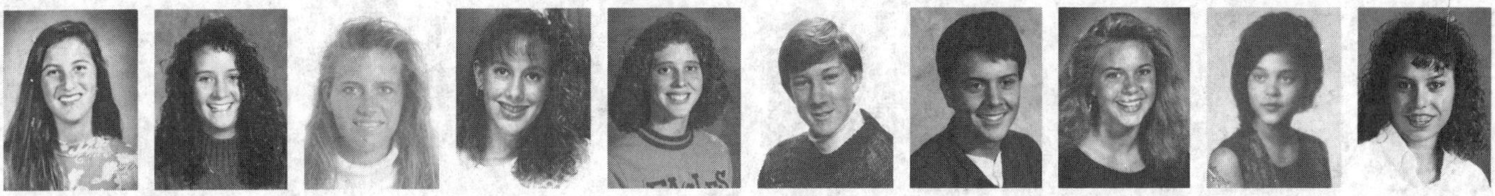

Emery, Alura
Sonoma Valley HS
Glen Ellen, CA

Emery, Jennifer L
Notre Dame HS
Gilroy, CA

Emir, Laila M
Mountain View HS
Los Altos, CA

Emlet, Diana M
Clovis West HS
Fresno, CA

Emmel, Dana
Cloverdale HS
Cloverdale, CA

Emond, Chuck G
Montgomery HS
Santa Rosa, CA

Empasis, Mark
Shandon HS
San Miguel, CA

Emry, Michelle
Pleasant Valley SR
Chico, CA

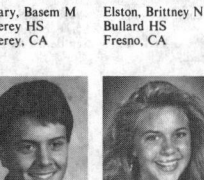

Enay, Joeylyn M
Eisenhower HS
Rialto, CA

Encinas, Aracely
Sacred Heart HS
Los Angeles, CA

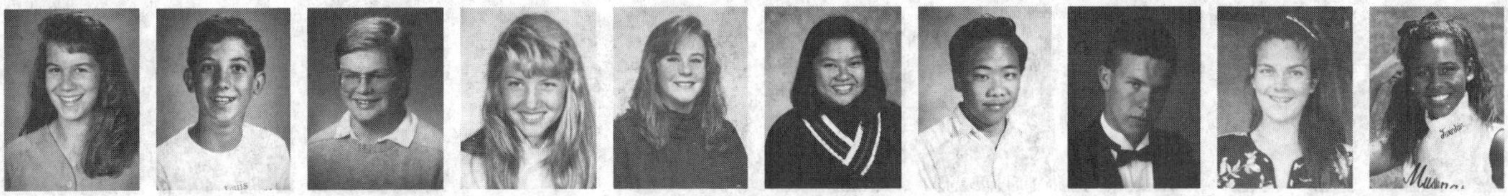

Enda, Jeanette
Southern CA Christian HS
Irvine, CA

Enderle, Bryan
Fred C Beyer HS
Modesto, CA

Endermann, Noah M
Orange Glen HS
Valley Center, CA

Endicott, Mary K
Carondelet HS
Martinez, CA

Endres, Jenna
Dublin HS
Pleasanton, CA

Endrina, Michele F
Jefferson HS
Daly City, CA

Eng, Christopher L
Nogales HS
W Covina, CA

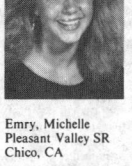

England, Joshua S
Las Lomas HS
Martinez, CA

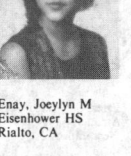

English, Julie L
El Toro HS
El Toro, CA

English, Tiara Starr
Trabuco Hills HS
Mission Viejo, CA

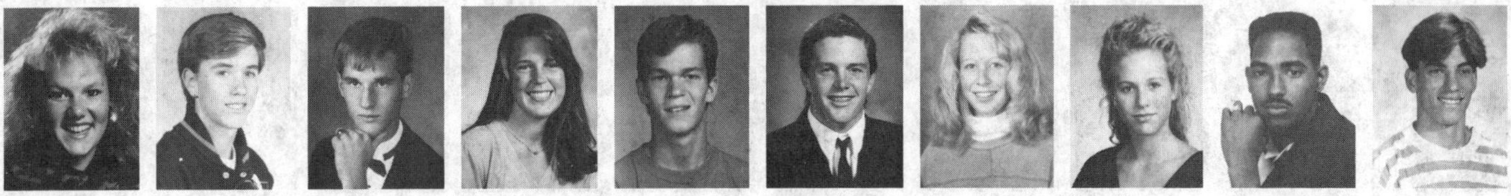

Engstrand, Paige R
Grossmont HS
El Cajon, CA

Engstrom, Brett L
Robert A Millikan
Long Beach, CA

Enochs, Craig Richard
Bellarmine College Prep
San Jose, CA

Enright, Kathy
Oakmont HS
Roseville, CA

Ensign, Josh P
Elk Grove HS
Elk Grove, CA

Ensley, Mike J
Mater Dei HS
Laguna Niguel, CA

Enzler, Minda M
Yucaipa HS
Yucaipa, CA

Epling, Halee K
Lorreto HS
Roseville, CA

Epps, Wardell J
San Gorgonio HS
Highland, CA

Erba, Thomas M
Woodland HS
Woodland, CA

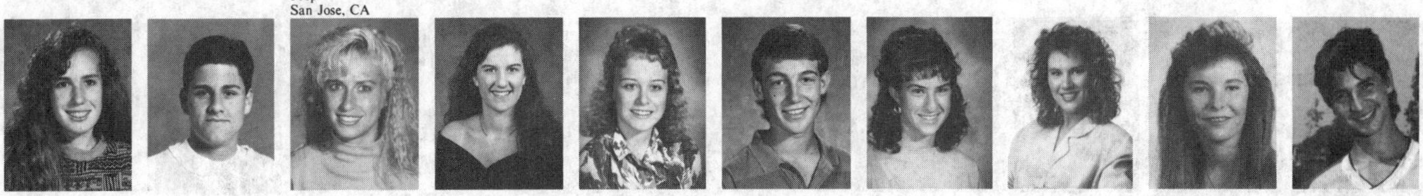

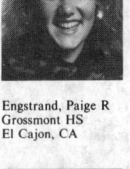

Erbe, Michele M
San Leandro HS
San Leandro, CA

Erganian, John K
Taft HS
Woodland Hills, CA

Erickson, Debbie
Downey HS
Downey, CA

Erickson, Kali Singh
Pasadena HS
Pasadena, CA

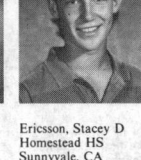

Ericsson, Melissa D
Weed HS
Weed, CA

Ericsson, Stacey D
Homestead HS
Sunnyvale, CA

Ermigarat, Kori D
North HS
Bakersfield, CA

Ermshar, Annette Lorene
Village Christian HS
Flintridge, CA

Erro, Jody A
Hesperia HS
Hesperia, CA

Ersoz, Ozan
Bonita Vista HS
Chula Vista, CA

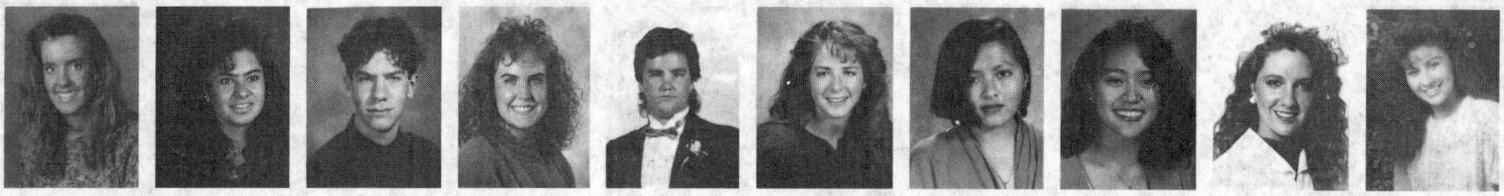

Escajeda, Ingrid A
Bonita Vista HS
Bonita, CA

Escobar, Evelyn P
Immaculate
Conception Acad
San Francisco, CA

Eskenazi, Eric M
Los Alamitos HS
Seal Beach, CA

Eskew, Dana
Brea-Olinda HS
Brea, CA

Eskridge, Sean M
Thousand Oaks HS
Westlake Village, CA

Eslinger, Heidi R
Rio Lindo Acad
Pleasant Hill, CA

Espina, Andrea S
Clayton Valley HS
Clayton, CA

Espineli, Sheila K
Bishop Amat
Memorial HS
La Puente, CA

Esping, Jill
Rosary HS
La Mirada, CA

Espino, Jessica
Orosi HS
Orosi, CA

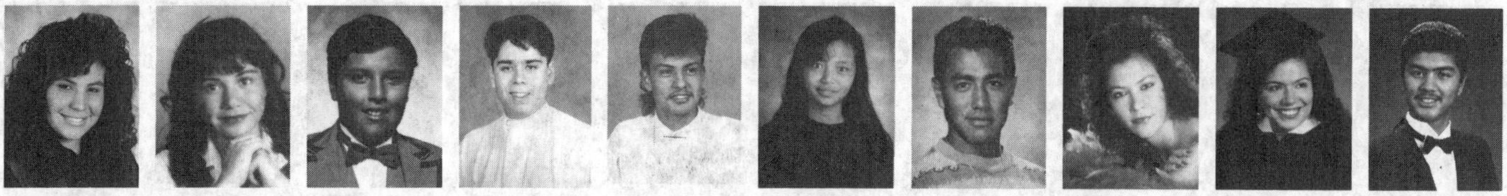

Espino, Victoria M
Dos Palos HS
Dos Palos, CA

Espinosa, Anita
La Puente HS
La Puente, CA

Espinosa, Armando
Sweetwater HS
Chula Vista, CA

Espinosa, David
Gardena HS
Gardena, CA

Espinosa, Gabriel
Gladstone HS
Azusa, CA

Espinosa, Rowena B
Balboa HS
San Francisco, CA

Espinoza, Hugo A
Westminster HS
Westminster, CA

Espinoza, Lupe A
Delta HS
Thornton, CA

Espinoza, Marissa G
San Fernando HS
Pacoima, CA

Espiritu, Joseph G
S San Francisco HS
S San Francisco, CA

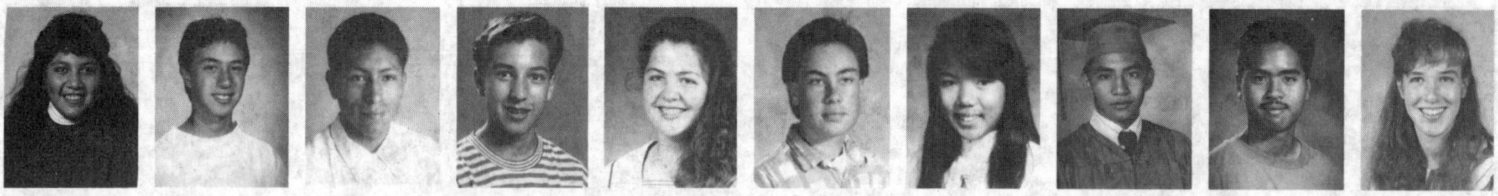

Esquibel, Liliana M
Chaffey HS
Ontario, CA

Esquibel, Patrick C
Casa Grande HS
Petaluma, CA

Esquivel, Jeronimo
Jay
Channe Islands HS
Oxnard, CA

Esquivel, Mario E
San Bernardino HS
San Bernardino, CA

Esslinger, Amy D
St Joseph HS
Lynwood, CA

Estabillo, Gabriel P
Righetti HS
Guadalupe, CA

Estacio, Rhea L
Southwest HS
San Diego, CA

Estanislao, Jon Ray
St John Bosco HS
Montebello, CA

Esteban, Rodney P
Cerritos HS
Cerritos, CA

Estes, Amy B
Rio Lindo Adventist
Acad
Valley Springs, CA

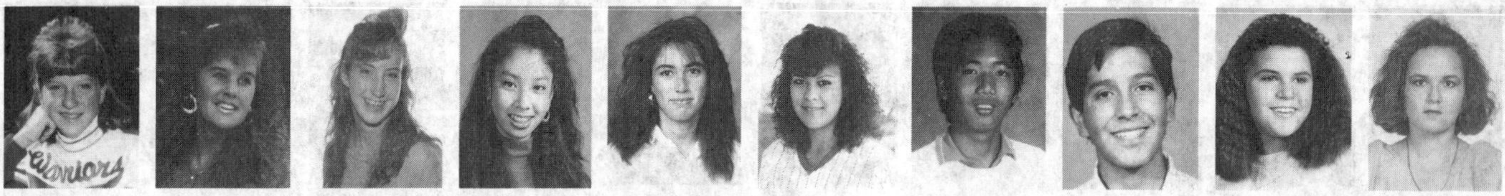

Estes, Carrie A
Hanford HS
Hanford, CA

Estes, Stefanie J
Amador Valley HS
Pleasanton, CA

Estey, Julie Elizabeth
Highlands HS
Sacramento, CA

Estiva, Jennifer U
St Bernard HS
Inglewood, CA

Estline, Einat
University City HS
San Diego, CA

Estrada, Alicia
Tranquillity Union
Mendota, CA

Estrada, Jr Apolo C
George Washington
San Francisco, CA

Estrada, Jr Carlos
Beaumont HS
Beaumont, CA

Estrada, Cynthia A
Hesperia HS
Hesperia, CA

Estrada, Edna Y
Calexico Mission
Acad
Imperial, CA

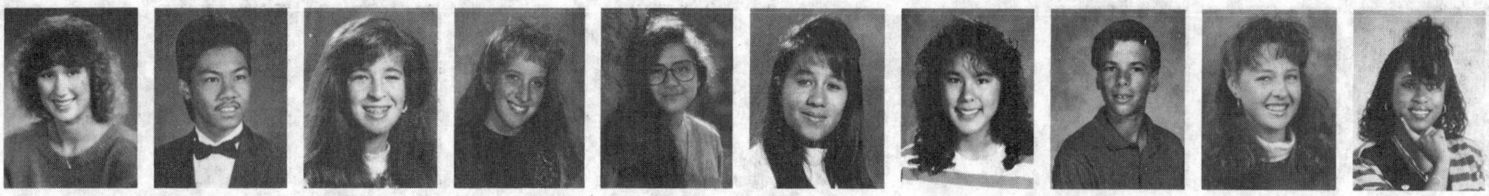

Estrada, Leticia
Renae
Pinole Valley HS
San Pablo, CA

Estrada, Roderick L
Salesian HS
Pinole, CA

Etchamendy,
Rosemarie
Garces Memorial HS
Bakersfield, CA

Etcheverry, Mary
Ann
Yuba City HS
Live Oak, CA

Eustaquio, Lilibeth
Flintridge Sacred
Heart Acad
Tujunga, CA

Evangelista, Cindy C
Eagle Rock HS
Los Angeles, CA

Evans, Annalissa
Mission San Jose HS
Fremont, CA

Evans, Bobby R
Woodcrest Christian
Riverside, CA

Evans, Carrie
Berean Christian HS
Pittsburg, CA

Evans, Erika
Perris HS
Perris, CA

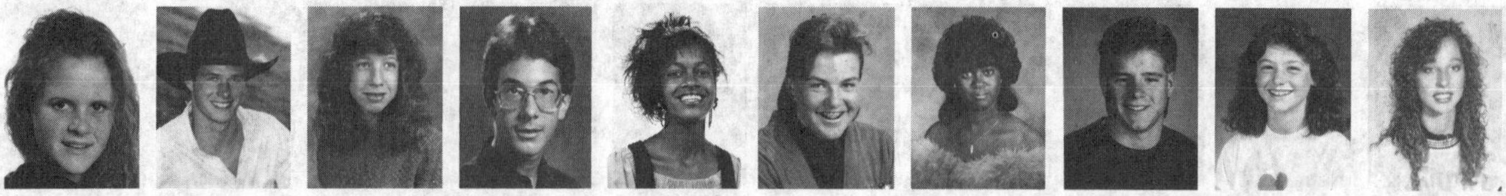

Evans, Ginette M
Charter Oak HS
Covina, CA

Evans, Graham T
Carmel HS
Carmel, CA

Evans, Heather A
Mount Carmel HS
San Diego, CA

Evans, Jason M
John Burroughs HS
Burbank, CA

Evans, Joni E
Gahr HS
Cypress, CA

Evans, Kori J
Pinole Valley HS
El Sobrante, CA

Evans, Lakisha
Pius X HS
Compton, CA

Evans, Mike J
Turlock HS
Hughson, CA

Evans, Patricia J
Modesto HS
Modesto, CA

Evans, Shanna
Rosary HS
Placentia, CA

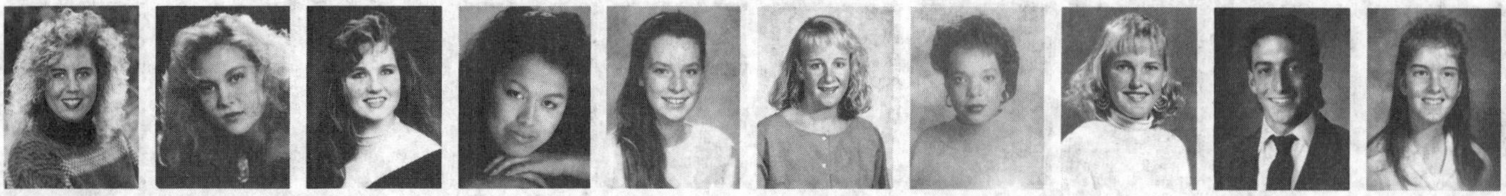

Evans, Wendy A
Coalinga HS
Coalinga, CA

Everling, Jennifer J
Monterey Bay Acad
Vandenberg Afb, CA

Eves, Nicole
Antioch HS
Antioch, CA

Evidente, Pearl A
Louisville HS
Woodland Hills, CA

Ewing, Bronwyn
Western Christian
Rancho Cucamonga,
CA

Ewing, Erin L
Aragon HS
San Mateo, CA

Ewing, Joyce Bradley
Workman HS
Valinda, CA

Ezell, Summer L
Etiwanda HS
Cucamonga, CA

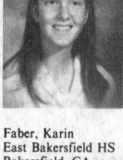

Faas, III George
Edward
Cabrillo HS
Lompoc, CA

Faber, Karin
East Bakersfield HS
Bakersfield, CA

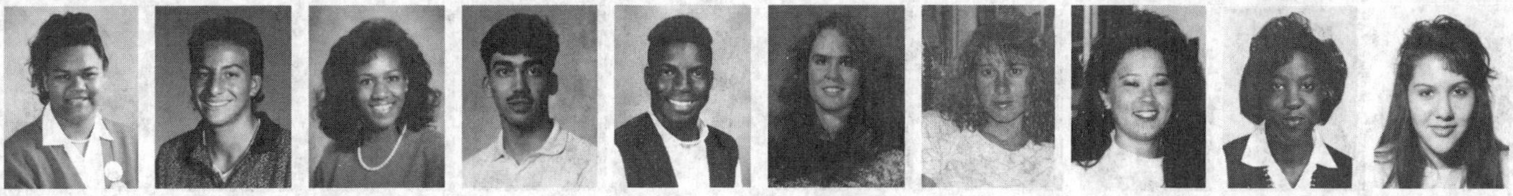

Fabro, Patrice K
Regina Caeli HS
Gardena, CA

Faggiolly, Steven P
Woodside HS
Redwood City, CA

Fagins, Daniele J
Buena Park HS
La Palma, CA

Fagundes, John M
Chaffey HS
Ontario, CA

Fahie, Vance L
Eisenhower HS
Rialto, CA

Fahringer, Erica K
Mt Whitney HS
Visalia, CA

Failor, Shani C
Warren HS
Downey, CA

Fairbanks, Nayomi J
Hueneme HS
Port Hueneme, CA

Fairley, Raquel K
Valley HS
Sacramento, CA

Fajardo, Alejandrina
Indio HS
Indio, CA

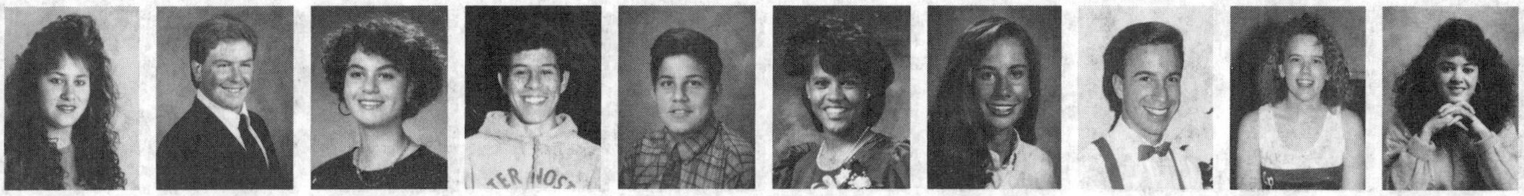

Fajardo, Rosana
Oxnard HS
Oxnard, CA

Fakes, Bryce
Brethren JR/SR HS
Long Beach, CA

Fakoury, Zeena
Piedmont HS
Piedmont, CA

Falconi, Duke D
Pater Noster HS
Los Angeles, CA

Falconi, Jesus R
Pater Noster HS
Los Angeles, CA

Fallin, Toni D
John Marshall
Fundamental HS
Duarte, CA

Fallon, M Kathleen
Santa Margarita
Catholic HS
Laguna Niguel, CA

Fallon, Matthew T
Ygnacio Valley HS
Pleasant Hill, CA

Falls, Chandra C
Las Plumas HS
Oroville, CA

Fancher, Carol
North Monterey
County HS
Monterrey, CA

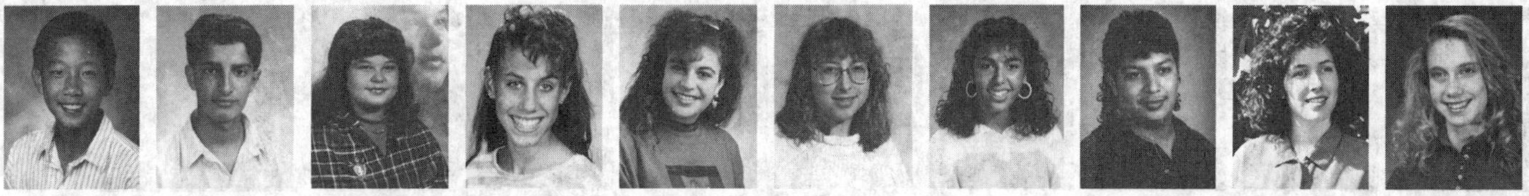

Fang, Grover
La Jolla Country Day
Schl
La Jolla, CA

Fanse, Ashish
Alameda HS
Alameda, CA

Fantasia, Anna Maria
Colonial Christian
Acad
Sacramento, CA

Faraday, Michelle F
Palm Springs HS
Palm Springs, CA

Faraj, Mona A
Notre Dame HS
San Jose, CA

Fargo, Jennifer
Righetti HS
Santa Maria, CA

Farhoomand, Ladan
San Dieguito HS
San Marcos, CA

Farias, Robert M
Modesto HS
Modesto, CA

Farley, Tiffany D
Sonora Union HS
Sonora, CA

Farmen, Joann
Liberty Union HS
Byron, CA

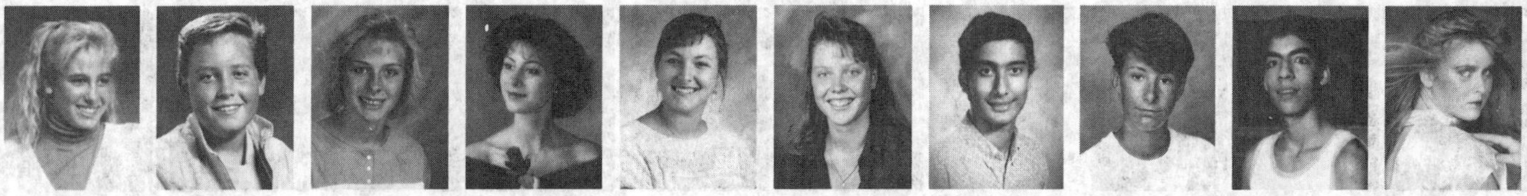

Farmer, Teresa Lynn
El Toro HS
El Toro, CA

Farner, James C
Montclair HS
Montclair, CA

Farner, Karna M
Serrano HS
Phelan, CA

Farrell, Judith
Bonita Vista HS
Chula Vista, CA

Farris, Barbara A
Prospect HS
San Jose, CA

Farris, Sandy C
Calvary Chapel HS
Westminster, CA

Farvid, Ali R
Mission Viejo HS
Mission Viejo, CA

Fastring, Roger B
Grossmont HS
El Cajon, CA

Fata, Marc
Venice Foreign
Language Magnet
Venice, CA

Faulconer, Christie
Simi Valley HS
Simi Valley, CA

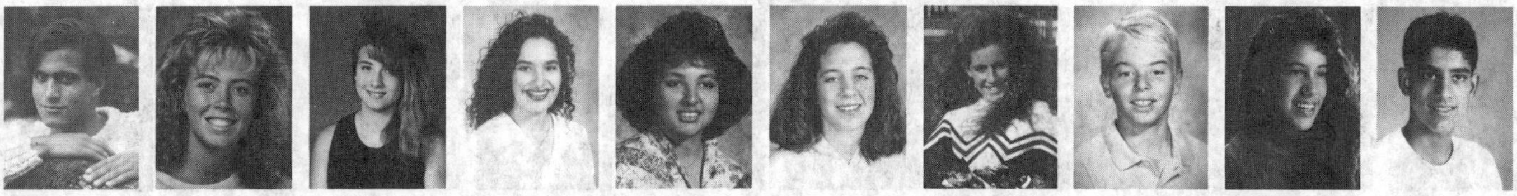

Faure Brac, Gabriel
Petaluma HS
Petaluma, CA

Fausett, Kimberly
El Toro HS
El Toro, CA

Fauss, Jolene M
Summerville HS
Twain Harte, CA

Favela, Gabriela A
Schurr HS
Montebello, CA

Favila, Marisa
Kerman HS
Kerman, CA

Favini, Melissa M
San Joaquin
Memorial HS
Madera, CA

Fawcett, Rhea
Indio HS
Indio, CA

Fawkes, Christopher
Paraclete HS
Agua Dulce, CA

Fay, Kelly
San Pasqual HS
Escondido, CA

Fazal, Arif
Fred C Beyer HS
Modesto, CA

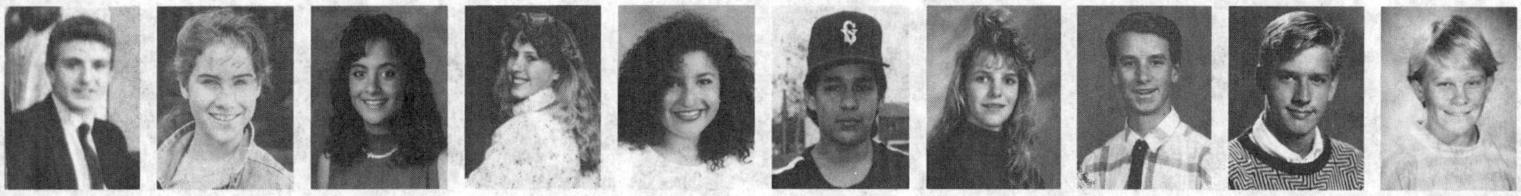

Federico, Michael T
Royal HS
Simi Valley, CA

Feeley, Melissa M
Paraclete HS
Palmdale, CA

Fegurgur, Jennifer L
Bonita Vista HS
Bonita, CA

Feigen, Denise
Riverside Poly HS
Riverside, CA

Felix, Christina Y
Whittier Christian
Hacienda Hghts, CA

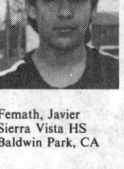

Femath, Javier
Sierra Vista HS
Baldwin Park, CA

Fender, Amy L
Apple Valley SR HS
Apple Valley, CA

Fenn, Brian C
Rim HS
Crestline, CA

Fennell, Jonathan A
Village Christian HS
Simi Valley, CA

Ferber, Justin M
Calabasas HS
Hidden Hills, CA

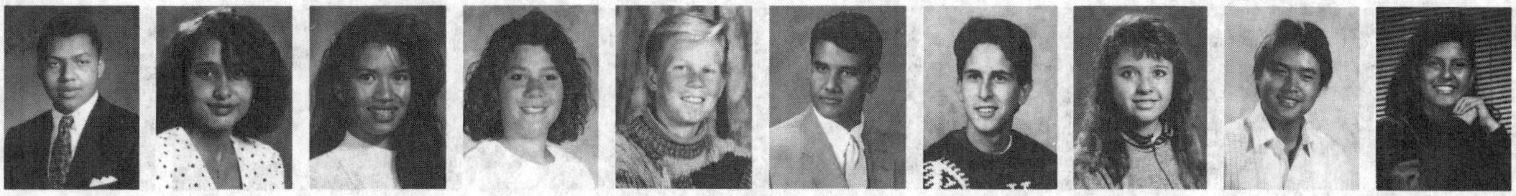

Ferguson, Del M
Daniel Murphy HS
Los Angeles, CA

Ferguson, Elisa J
Santa Monica HS
Santa Monica, CA

Feria, Christina
Hilltop HS
Chula Vista, CA

Fernamburg, Debbie
Atascadero HS
Santa Margarita, CA

Fernandes, Dylan A
Valley View HS
Moreno Valley, CA

Fernandez, Andrew
Bishop Montgomery
Torrance, CA

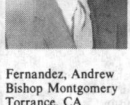

Fernandez, Cesar T
San Diego HS
San Diego, CA

Fernandez, Dunia
James A Garfield HS
Los Angeles, CA

Fernandez, Gabriel
Mount Diablo HS
Pacheco, CA

Fernandez, Liliana G
Rubidoux HS
Riverside, CA

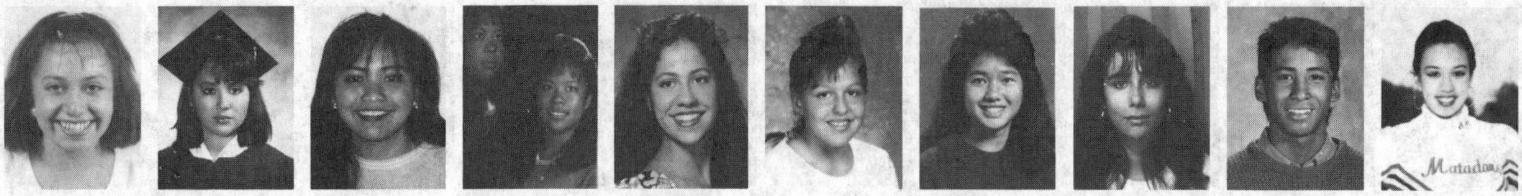

Fernandez, Luz Elena
Woodrow Wilson HS
Los Angeles, CA

Fernandez, Magali
Bell HS
Cudahy, CA

Fernandez, Maria
Lourdes
Fontana HS
Fontana, CA

Fernandez, Mary
Grace
Chula Vista HS
San Diego, CA

Fernandez, Nadina L
El Dorado HS
Placentia, CA

Fernandez, Natalie
Marie
Notre Dame HS
Moreno Valley, CA

Fernandez, Nwanee
San Gorgonio HS
Highland, CA

Fernandez, Sonia
Bishop Amat
Memorial HS
La Puente, CA

Fernandez, Vernon I
Palma HS
Marina, CA

Ferrara, Mara
San Gabriel HS
San Gabriel, CA

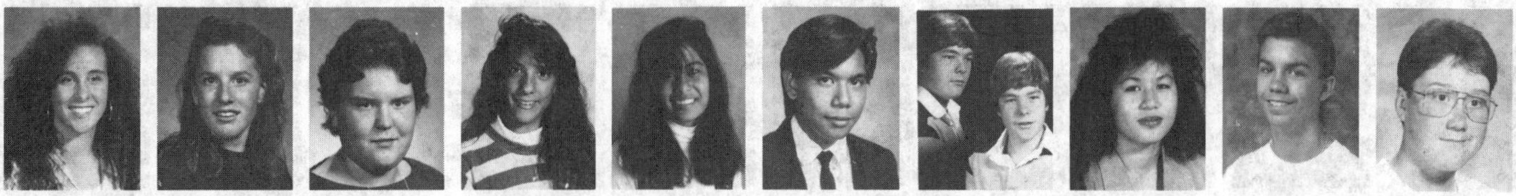

Ferrari, Melissa M
Arroyo Grande HS
Nipomo, CA

Ferrari, Robin
Archbishop Mitty HS
San Jose, CA

Ferreira, Eric A
Edison HS
Stockton, CA

Ferreira, Jennifer L
Crescenta Valley HS
La Crescenta, CA

Ferrer, Hazelle
Hueneme HS
Port Hueneme, CA

Ferreria, David M
Van Nuys HS
Sunland, CA

Ferris, Christopher J
Live Oak HS
Morgan Hill, CA

Ferry, Armelita C
International Studies
Acad
San Francisco, CA

Fesniak, Michael A
San Clemente HS
San Juan Capis, CA

Fetters, Greg N
Enterprise HS
Redding, CA

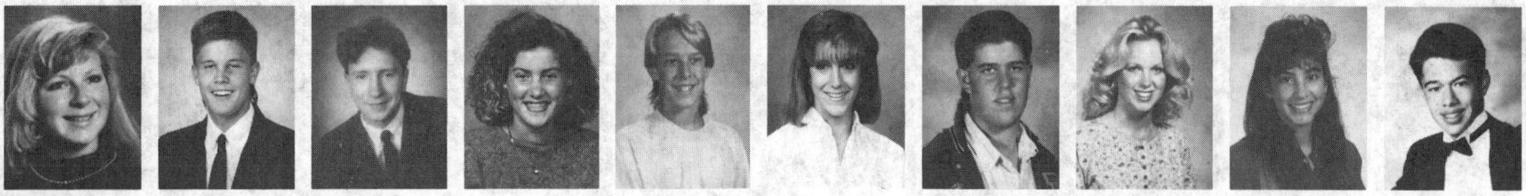

Feuerborn, Sarah E
Tustin HS
Tustin, CA

Fewell, Kevin Robert
Bella Vista HS
Fair Oaks, CA

Feygin, II Arcady
Monterey HS
Monterey, CA

Ficano, Catherine N
Miramesa HS
San Diego, CA

Fickas, David L
Arcadia HS
Arcadia, CA

Fidaleo, Brenda K
Bishops HS
La Jolla, CA

Fiduccia, David M
Costa Mesa HS
Costa Mesa, CA

Fiechter, Jennifer L
Poway HS
Poway, CA

Field, Heather
A J Heschel Day
Schl
Northridge, CA

Fields, Roderick Scott
St Patrick-St Vincent
Vallejo, CA

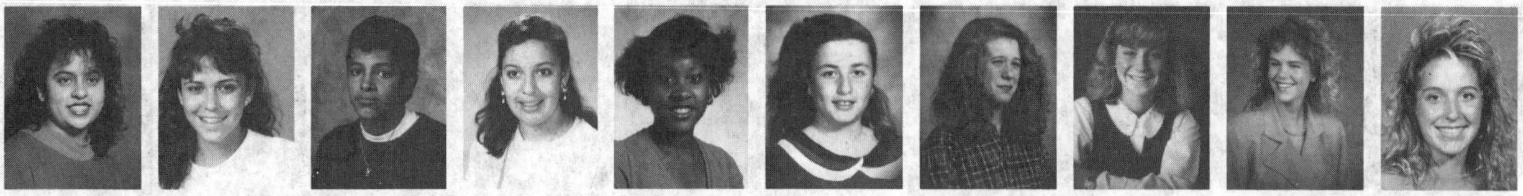

Fierro, Susana
Downey HS
Downey, CA

Figueroa, Bianca
Palo Verde HS
Blythe, CA

Figueroa, Jorge G
Calexico HS
Calexico, CA

Figueroa, Veronica D
Pinole Valley HS
Pinole, CA

Fikes, Krysten M
Notre Dame HS
San Jose, CA

Filler, Elena
Fairfax HS
Los Angeles, CA

Filomia, Melina M
Antelope Valley HS
Lancaster, CA

Finatti, Traci A
Notre Dame HS
Salinas, CA

Finkenhagen, Melissa
Los Alamitos HS
Anaheim, CA

Finnie, Delia
Beaumont HS
Cherry Valley, CA

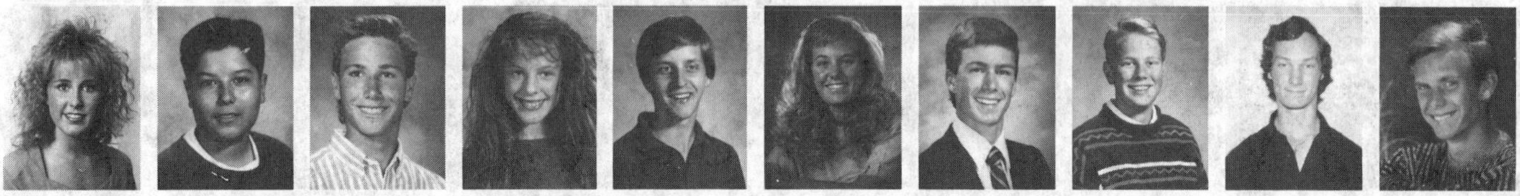

Finnie, Sonja F
Beaumont HS
Cherry Valley, CA

Fiola, Asir N
Kennedy HS
Santa Ana, CA

Fiore, Richard S
Mission Viejo HS
Mission Viejo, CA

Firgens, Mackenzie
Coast Union HS
Cambria, CA

Fischer, Kevin
Poway HS
Poway, CA

Fischer, Laurie L
Clovis West HS
Fresno, CA

Fischer, Paul A
Piedmont HS
Piedmont, CA

Fischer, Zachary M
Poway HS
Poway, CA

Fisher, Brett T
Troy HS
Fullerton, CA

Fisher, Evan Lee
Hughson Union HS
Hughson, CA

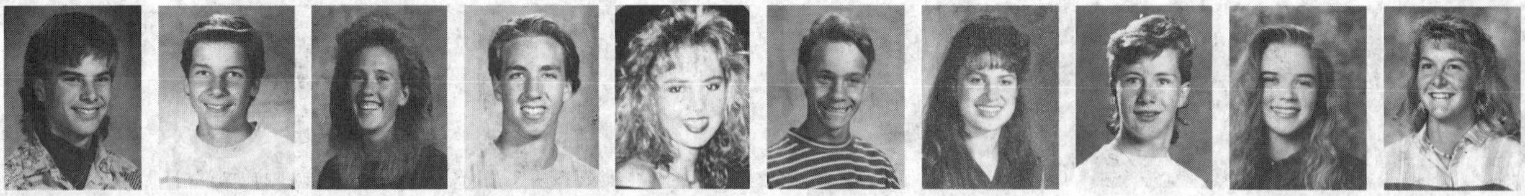

Fisher, Leonard V
Chico SR HS
Chico, CA

Fisher, Regan
Christian
La Mirada HS
Norwalk, CA

Fisher, Terri L
29 Palms HS
Twentynine Palms,
CA

Fisher, Timothy K
Palo Alto HS
Palo Alto, CA

Fisher, Tracy M
Miraleste HS
Rolling Hills, CA

Fishleder, Aaron J
Woodland HS
Woodland, CA

Fitch, Ann
Ponderosa HS
Placerville, CA

Fitch, Ryan
Bakersfield HS
Bakersfield, CA

Fitz, Danielle N
San Clemente HS
San Juan Capistra,
CA

Fitzgerald, Anne E
Cordova SR HS
Rancho Cordova, CA

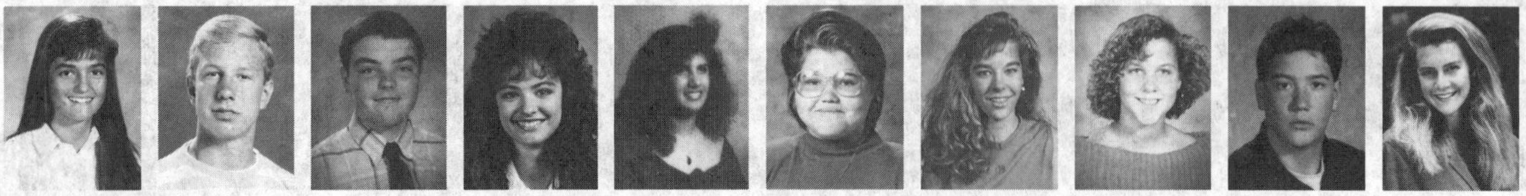

Fitzgibbon, Megan C
Clayton Valley HS
Clayton, CA

Fitzjerrell, Dennis L
Tehachapi HS
Tehachapi, CA

Fitzlaff, Shawn
Bethel Christian HS
Lancaster, CA

Fizer, Kelly L
Roseville Joint Union
Roseville, CA

Flaherty, Michele
Fairfield HS
Suisun City, CA

Flaugher, Sheryl L
Castle Park HS
Chula Vista, CA

Fleege, Amy J
El Comino
Fundamental HS
Carmichael, CA

Fleeman, Cassandra
Mc Farland HS
Delano, CA

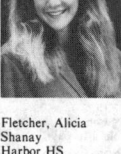

Flemate, Douglas R
Terra Nova HS
Pacifica, CA

Fletcher, Alicia
Shanay
Harbor HS
Santa Cruz, CA

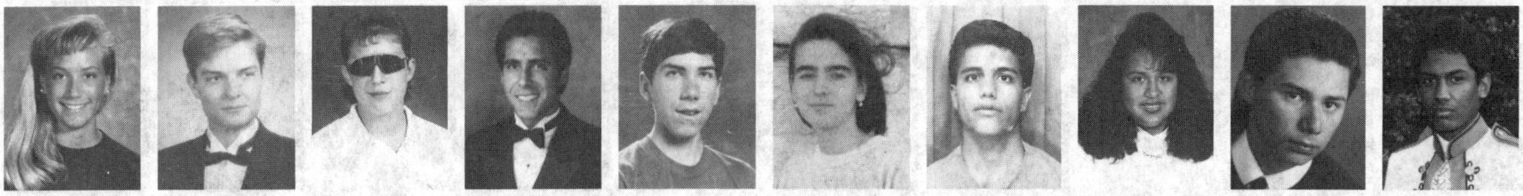

Flicker, Katie A
San Ramon Valley
Danville, CA

Flinders, Matthew
James Lick HS
San Jose, CA

Flint, Floyd E
Modesto HS
Modesto, CA

Flores, Adrian
Cordova Y
Bonita Vista HS
Bonita, CA

Flores, Alex
Bonita HS
La Verne, CA

Flores, Cynthia J
Lindsay HS
Lindsay, CA

Flores, Daniel N
Bishop Amat
Memorial HS
Azusa, CA

Flores, Edme
Southbay Christian
Schl
Mountain View, CA

Flores, Gilbert M
March Mountain HS
Moreno Valley, CA

Flores, James J
Edison-Computech
Fresno, CA

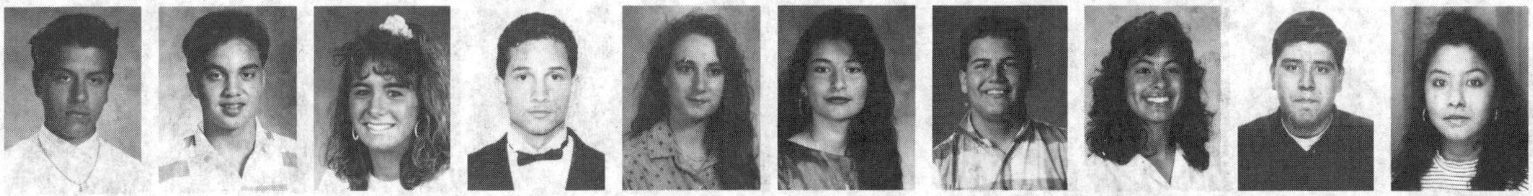

Flores, Jose David
Don Bosco Technical
Inst
Alhambra, CA

Flores, Joseph O
Pater Noster HS
Los Angeles, CA

Flores, Lisa R
St Joseph Girls HS
Long Beach, CA

Flores, Ludwing
Leuzinger HS
Inglewood, CA

Flores, Maria Del
Carmen
Baldwin Park HS
Baldwin Park, CA

Flores, Maria R
Bishop Amat HS
Baldwin Park, CA

Flores, Michael L
Cantwell HS
Commerce, CA

Flores, Monique M
Bakersfield Adventist
Acad
Bakersfield, CA

Flores, Phillip
Cantwell HS
San Gabriel, CA

Flores, Rebecca
Elk Grove HS
Elk Grove, CA

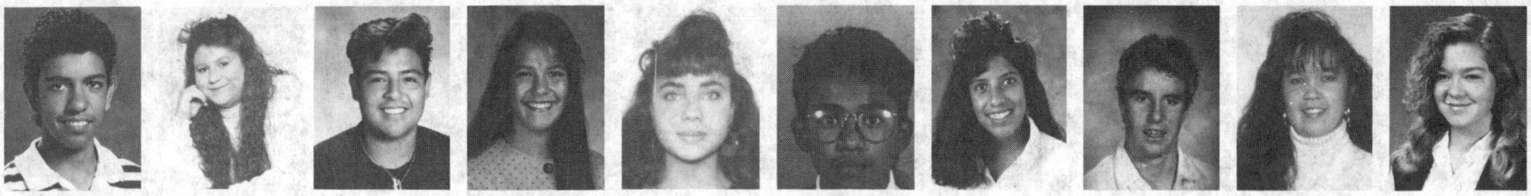

Flores, Ricardo L
Bassett HS
La Puente, CA

Flores, Rosie M
Palo Verde HS
Blythe, CA

Flores, Ruben T
Calexico HS
Calexico, CA

Flores, Teresa M
Bishop Amat
Memorial HS
La Puente, CA

Flores, Yilsen J
Adrian Wilcox HS
Sunnyvale, CA

Flores Ulibas, Efriem
Rio Linda SR HS
Sacramento, CA

Flores-Ross, Katrina
Temple City HS
Temple City, CA

Floyd, Clark J
Sutter Union HS
Yuba City, CA

Flumerfelt, Lisa
Hawthorne HS
Hawthorne, CA

Fobber, Angela
Frances
Ygnacio Valley HS
Walnut Creek, CA

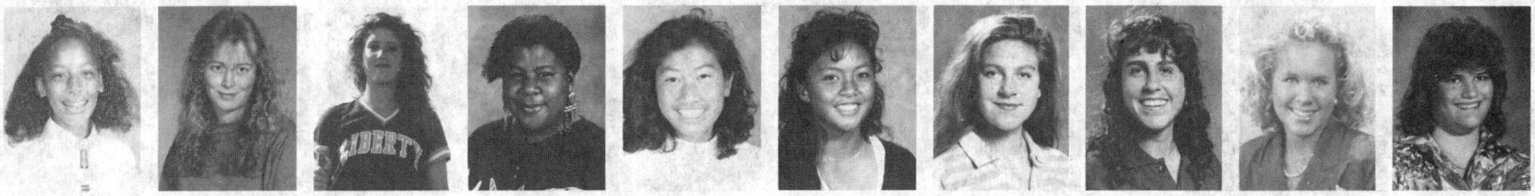

Fobbs, Denneah
San Joaquin
Memorial HS
Clovis, CA

Fogarty, Shana D
South San Francisco
South San Francis,
CA

Foley, Jessica T
Liberty Union HS
Danville, CA

Folsom, Cynthia L
Ramona HS
Ramona, CA

Fong, Julia S
Lowell HS
San Francisco, CA

Fong, Melinda M
Lowell HS
San Francisco, CA

Fontaine, Deborah
Palisades HS
Los Angeles, CA

Fontaine, Frieda
Palisades HS
Los Angeles, CA

Fontaine, Laura E
Rio Americano HS
Fair Oaks, CA

Fontana, Anne L
Sutter Union HS
Yuba City, CA

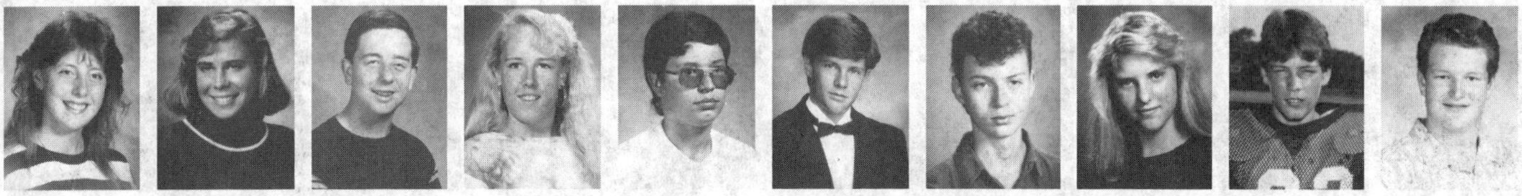

Foote, Tannya R
Oroville HS
Oroville, CA

Ford, Deann M
Santana HS
Lakeside, CA

Ford, James J
Corona HS
Corona, CA

Ford, Jenny M
El Toro HS
El Toro, CA

Ford, Jr John W
Modoc HS
Alturas, CA

Ford, Joshua J
Hueneme HS
Oxnard, CA

Ford, Nathan
Fred C Beyer HS
Modesto, CA

Forkum, Tara K
Salinas HS
Salinas, CA

Forman, Gary A
El Cajon Valley HS
Santee, CA

Formet, Kelly B
Whittier Christian
Cerritos, CA

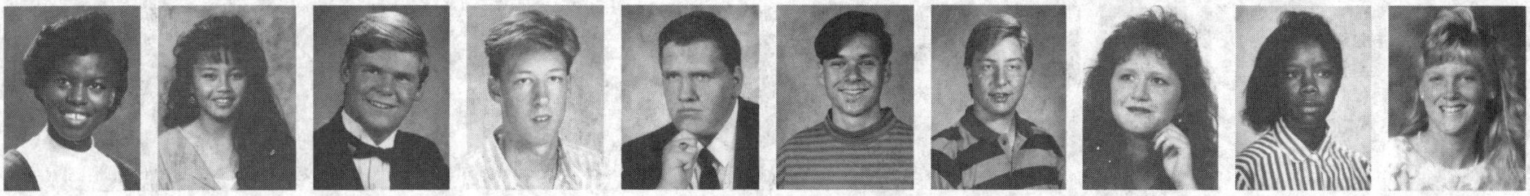

Forney, Jo Ann
Glendale Adventist
Acad
Pacoima, CA

Foronda, Sasheen
Granada Hills HS
Granada Hills, CA

Forrester, Vernon
Wayne
Willits HS
Willits, CA

Forsythe, Kyle L
Palm Springs HS
Morongo Valley, CA

Fort, Mark T
Twentynine Palms
Twentynine Palm,
CA

Fortino, Michael J
El Camino
Fundamental HS
Sacramento, CA

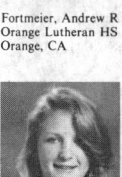

Fortmeier, Andrew R
Orange Lutheran HS
Orange, CA

Fortner, Nicole E
Oakdale HS
Oakdale, CA

Foster, Deonna
Amos Alanzo Stagg
Stockton, CA

Foster, Ericka
Marina HS
Huntington Beach,
CA

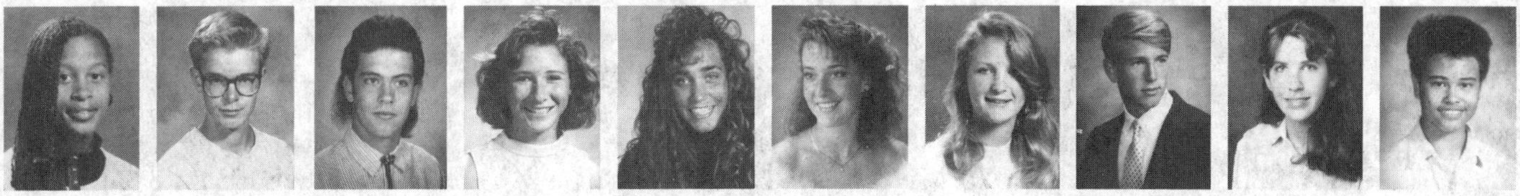

Foster, Farrah
Van Nuys HS
Los Angeles, CA

Foster, Frank J
Los Alamitos HS
Seal Beach, CA

Foster, Jonathan D
A A Stagg HS
Stockton, CA

Foster, Kari L
Brawley Union HS
Brawley, CA

Foster, Nicole S
Rubidoux HS
Corona, CA

Foulk, Heather M
Milpitas HS
Milpitas, CA

Fowler, Angela T
John Burroughs HS
Burbank, CA

Fox, Brad
Christian HS
El Cajon, CA

Fox, Deborah E
La Jolla County Day
Schl
La Jolla, CA

Fox, Joseph R
Cardinal Newman
Santa Rosa, CA

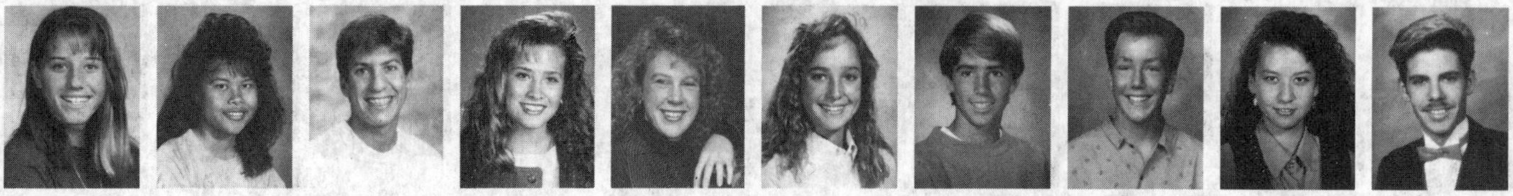

Fox, Kimberly A
Roseville HS
Roseville, CA

Fox, Marylou R
Highlands HS
N Highlands, CA

Fox, Maxwell A
Harvard Schl
Santa Monica, CA

Fox, Shanon L
Clovis HS
Fresno, CA

Fox, Wendy
Pleasant Valley HS
Chico, CA

Fracisco, Katie
Santa Margarita HS
Mission Viejo, CA

Fracisco, Rob M
Trabuco Hills HS
Mission Viejo, CA

Frailey, Brody L
Valhalla HS
La Mesa, CA

Fraire, Michelle R
Paraclete HS
Littlerock, CA

Franceschini, Nicholas
Fairfield HS
Fairfield, CA

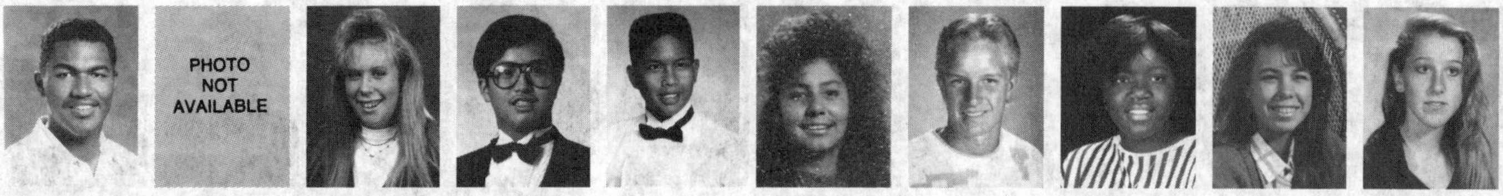

Francis, II Allen C
Glendale Adventist Acad
Loma Linda, CA

Francis, Missy
Chaminade Coll Prep
Northridge, CA

Francis, Sherry L
Santa Rosa HS
Santa Rosa, CA

Francisco, Danilo
Cathedral HS
Los Angeles, CA

Francisco, Duane N
Nogales HS
Walnut, CA

Franco, Gina
San Fernando HS
Pacoima, CA

Franco, Jon
Beyer HS
Modesto, CA

Francois, Tamara
St Bernard HS
Los Angeles, CA

Frandsen, Lorie A
Lower Lake HS
Clearlake, CA

Frank, Dawn C
De Anza HS
El Sobrante, CA

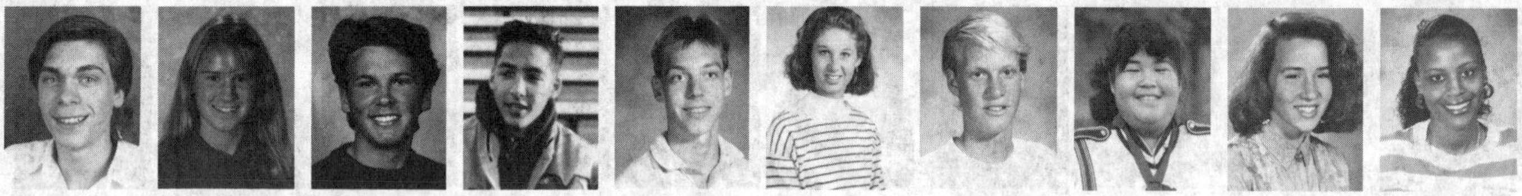

Frank, Timothy W
Berean Christian HS
Pleasant Hill, CA

Franklin, Jennifer L
Woodside HS
Redwood City, CA

Franklin, John R
Grossmont HS
El Cajon, CA

Fraser, Kenneth N
Montclair HS
Montclair, CA

Fraser, Robby C
Chico SR HS
Chico, CA

Fraser, Shannon L
John F Kennedy HS
Sacramento, CA

Fratts, Jason J
J F Kennedy HS
Buen Park, CA

Frausto, Brandi C
Pasadena HS
Pasadena, CA

Frazier, Cynthia M
Del Oro HS
Newcastle, CA

Frazier, Tamara
Lincoln HS
San Diego, CA

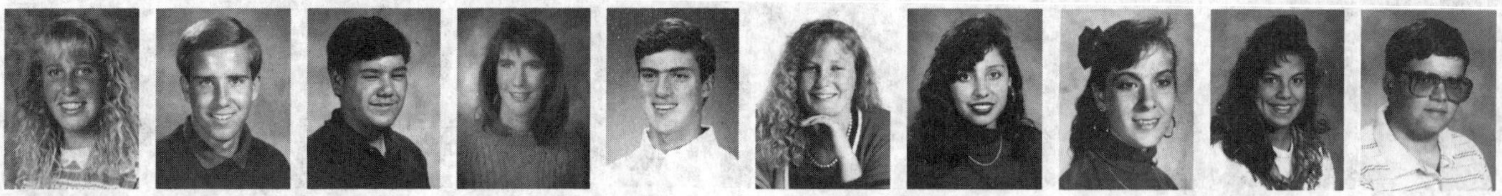

Freeberg, Kirstin L
San Clemente HS
San Clemente, CA

Freeland, Jeffrey S
La Habra HS
La Habra, CA

Freeman, Edwin
Redwood Christian
San Leandro, CA

Freeman, Heather M
La Reina HS
Thousand Oaks, CA

Freeman, Miller
Piedmont HS
Piedmont, CA

Freer, Allison C
Maranatha HS
El Monte, CA

Fregoso, Sandra L
Clairemont HS
San Diego, CA

Freidmann-Waddell, Patrice
Ernest Righett I HS
Santa Maria, CA

Freitas, Deborah A
Del Oro HS
Loomis, CA

Freitas, Jerry A
Arcata HS
Arcata, CA

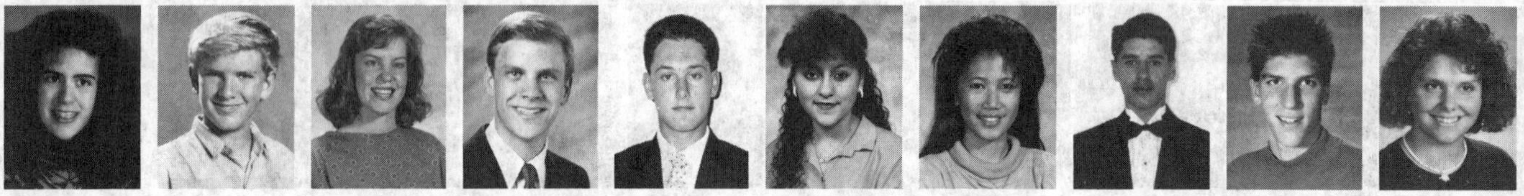

Freitas, Lisa M
Turlock HS
Turlock, CA

French, Nathan P
Carlsbad HS
Carlsbad, CA

Freschauf, Dawn N
Woodland HS
Woodland, CA

Frey, III Charles Edwin
Warren HS
Downey, CA

Frey, Jarrod
Poway HS
Poway, CA

Frias, Barbara
Bell Gardens HS
Bell Gardens, CA

Frias, Imelda I
Westmoor HS
Daly City, CA

Frias, Mike A
Riordan HS
Daly City, CA

Fricka, Kevin B
Don Lugo HS
Chino Hills, CA

Fried, Melissa C
Lodi HS
Lodi, CA

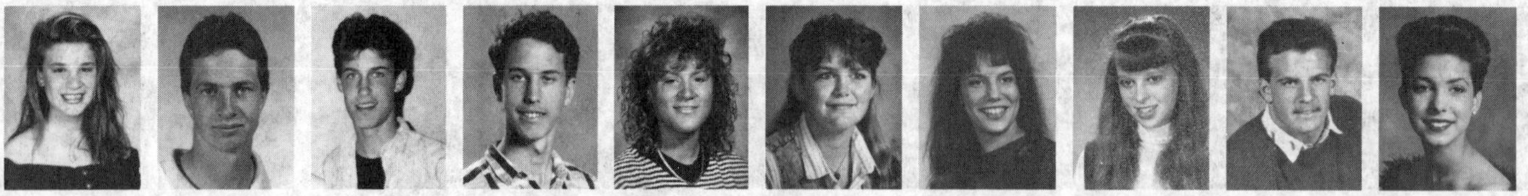

Friedman, Bonnie A
University HS
Beverly Hills, CA

Friedman, Ivon H
Benicia HS
Benicia, CA

Friedman, Nathan N
Palm Desert HS
Palm Desert, CA

Friedrich, Klaus W
Culver City HS
Culver City, CA

Friend, Stephenie L
El Camino Real HS
West Hills, CA

Fries, Jennifer
Denair HS
Denair, CA

Friis, Tonya J
Lincoln HS
Stockton, CA

Frincke, Janna
Foothill HS
Pleasanton, CA

Fritch, Jimmy
Herlong HS
Herlong, CA

Fromberg, Eve E
Palm Springs HS
Palm Springs, CA

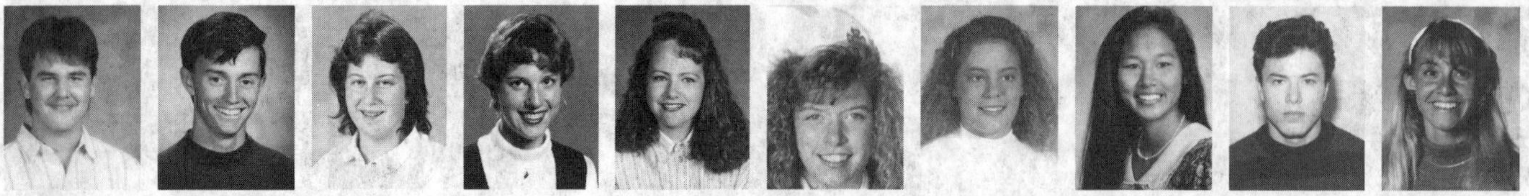

Fromm, Chris M
Redlands HS
Mentone, CA

Fromm, Stephen A
Montgomery HS
Santa Rosa, CA

Frost, Jennifer C
Rio Lindo Adventist Acad
Napa, CA

Frost, Jennifer M
St Bonaventure HS
Oak View, CA

Froyd, Renee
Petterson HS
Patterson, CA

Frudden, Alicia D
King City HS
King City, CA

Fry, Theresa
Lemoore HS
Lemoore, CA

Fu, Mimi
Santa Monica HS
Santa Monica, CA

Fuentes, Louis A
Aurora HS
Calexico, CA

Fugatti, Christine
Miraleste HS
Ranchos Palos Ver, CA

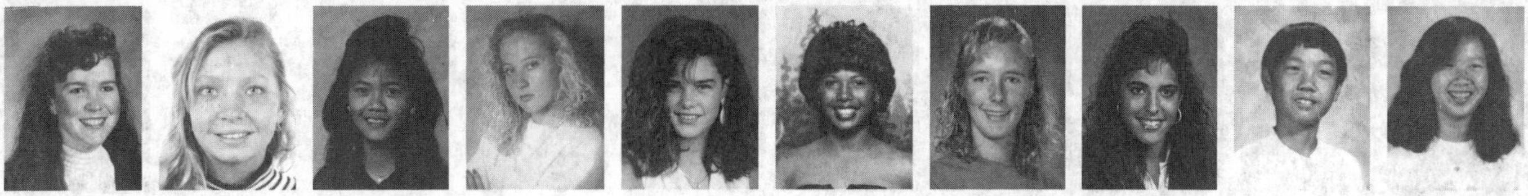

Fugitt, Christy N
Fremont Christian
Fremont, CA

Fuksshimov, Irina
George Washington
San Francisco, CA

Fulinara, Jenny A
Sweetwater Union
National City, CA

Fuller, Ashley J
Davis SR HS
Danville, CA

Fuller, Laura K
Thomas Downey HS
Modesto, CA

Fuller, Leah M
Leuzinger HS
Hawthorne, CA

Fulton, Joy L
Sunny Hills HS
Fullerton, CA

Fulvio, Alana M
Sacred Heart Prep
Belmont, CA

Fung, Jimmy
Schurr HS
Montebello, CA

Fung, Nancy
Schurr HS
Montebello, CA

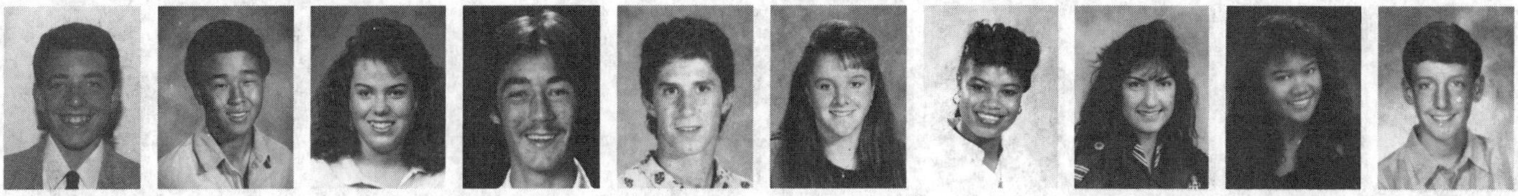

Furst, Benjamin A
Oak Park HS
Agoura Hills, CA

Furuta, Michael
Villa Park HS
Anaheim, CA

Futch, Mindi K
Monte Vista HS
Spring Valley, CA

Fuzzell, Justin C
Oakdale HS
Oakdale, CA

Gabler, Carl M
Cupertino HS
Cupertino, CA

Gabor, Juliette
Aragon HS
Foster City, CA

Gabourel, Gail
Notre Dame Acad
Los Angeles, CA

Gabriel, Lydia
Whittier Christian
Walnut, CA

Gacusan, Lea M
Homestead HS
Sunnyvale, CA

Gadd, Jeff R
Valley Christian HS
Pleasanton, CA

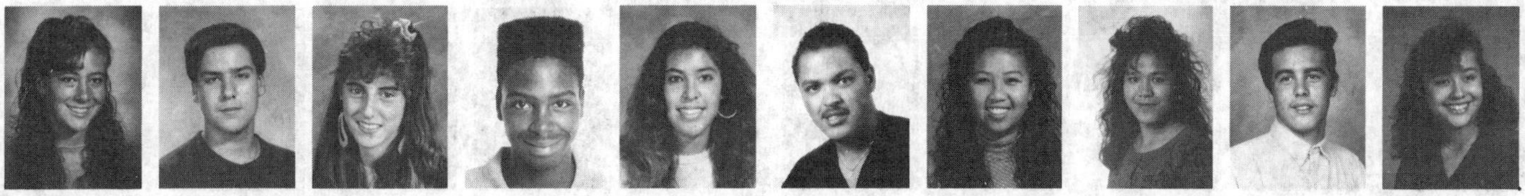

Gaddis, Julie D
Bishop Union HS
Bishop, CA

Gaherty, Jr John J
Canyon HS
Canyon Country, CA

Gaines, Erica L
Ramona HS
Ramona, CA

Gaines, Lexter N
Verbum Dei HS
Los Angeles, CA

Gaitan, Denise
Los Alamitos HS
Seal Beach, CA

Gaitan, Martin F
Nogales HS
West Covina, CA

Galang, Gloria G
Lowell HS
San Francisco, CA

Galapon, Arlene
Mercado
Arvin HS
Lamont, CA

Galarza, Alberto B
El Cajon Valley HS
El Cajon, CA

Galaviz, Christina M
Bullard HS
Fresno, CA

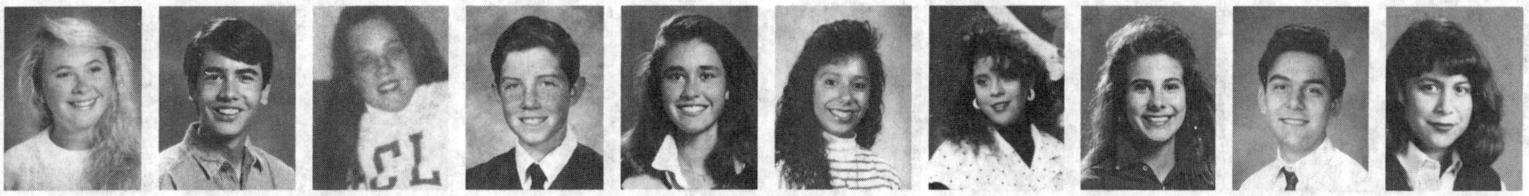

Galazyn, Sherry
Orange HS
Orange Villa Pk., CA

Galbraith, Kenneth
Burbank HS
Los Angeles, CA

Galitzen, Sasanna
Orangewood Acad
Garden Grove, CA

Gallagher, Charles P
Bellarmine College
Prep
San Jose, CA

Gallego, Patricia
Bellarmine-Jefferson
Pasadena, CA

Gallegos, Ana
William Workman
West Covina, CA

Gallegos, Carolyne S
Tulare Union HS
Tulare, CA

Gallegos, Jennifer J
Etiwanda HS
Alta Loma, CA

Gallegos, Jesus
Pater Noster HS
Los Angeles, CA

Gallegos, Lisa R
Sacred Heart Of
Jesus HS
Los Angeles, CA

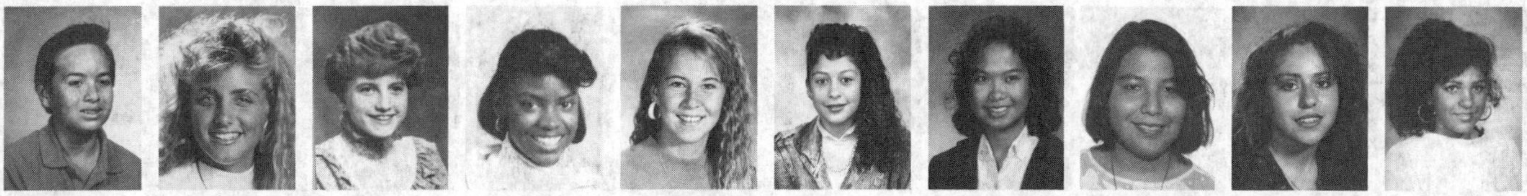

Galleno, Humberto
Damien HS
West Covina, CA

Galli, Stacey
Carlsbad HS
Carlsbad, CA

Gallops, Amanda P
North HS
Bakersfield, CA

Galloway, Candace P
Regina Caell HS
Gardena, CA

Galloway, Heather
Tustin HS
Tustin, CA

Galvan, Rosa
San Marcos HS
Santa Barbara, CA

Galvez, Agnes C
St Joseph HS
Cerritos, CA

Galvez, Consuelo M
Pasadena HS
Pasadena, CA

Galvez, Nancy
West Covina HS
West Covina, CA

Gamargo, Sonya
Evelyn
West HS
Bakersfield, CA

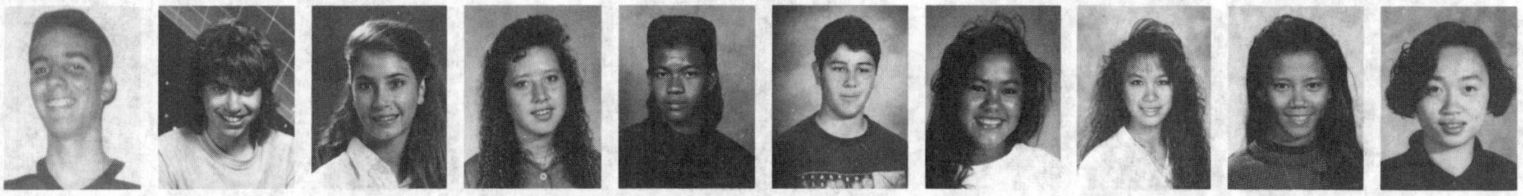

Gambee, Matthew S
Aptos HS
Corralitos, CA

Gambino, Garrett C
Bonita Vista HS
Bonita, CA

Gamble, Susan
Providence HS
Glendale, CA

Gamboa, Michelle D
Independence HS
San Jose, CA

Gamboa, Norbert V
Mira Mesa HS
San Diego, CA

Gamez, Marcos
Kingsburg HS
Kingsburg, CA

Gammon, Annette
Beyer HS
Modesto, CA

Gan, Jennifer
St Genevieve HS
Van Nuys, CA

Ganibi, Eileen M
Pasadena HS
Altadena, CA

Gao, Lu Ying
Phillip & Sala Burton
S San Francisco, CA

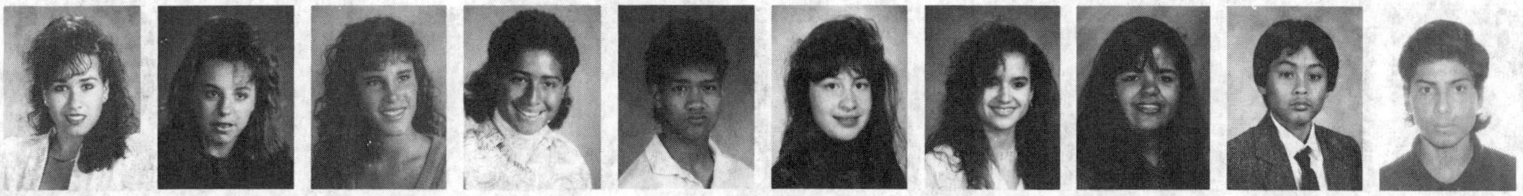

Gaona, Danette
Pius X HS
Paramount, CA

Garabedian, Amy L
Clovis HS
Sanger, CA

Garay, Michelle
Ocean View HS
Huntington Bch, CA

Garay, Priscella L
Antioch HS
Antioch, CA

Garcia, Allan J
Servite HS
Cypress, CA

Garcia, Angelica
Fillmore HS
Fillmore, CA

Garcia, Angelica
Riverbank HS
Riverbank, CA

Garcia, Angeline
Bishop Amat
Memorial HS
Hacienda Heights,
CA

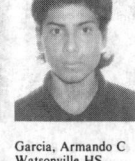

Garcia, Antonio P
Lowell HS
San Francisco, CA

Garcia, Armando C
Watsonville HS
Watsonville, CA

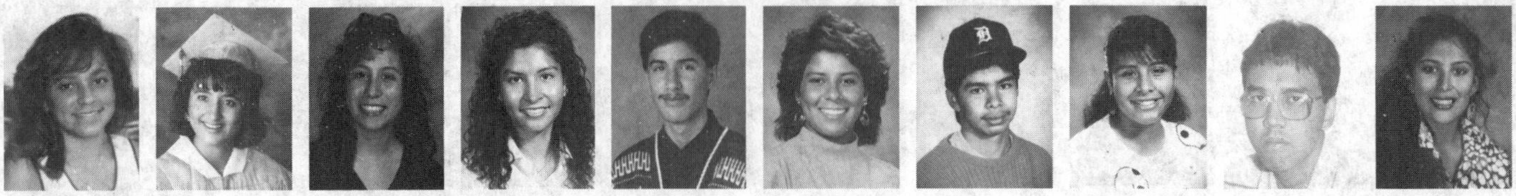

Garcia, Belina
El Camino HS
Valley Center, CA

Garcia, Celine
Bishop Amat
Memorial HS
Hacienda Heights, CA

Garcia, Christine L
Bishop Amat
Memorial HS
Temple City, CA

Garcia, Cynthia
Mater Dei HS
Santa Ana, CA

Garcia, Daniel P
Palmdale HS
Palmdale, CA

Garcia, Denise
Irvine HS
Irvine, CA

Garcia, Donny
Tulare Western HS
Tulare, CA

Garcia, Gabriela
El Modena HS
Orange, CA

Garcia, Gary Zaldy C
Channel Islands HS
Oxnard, CA

Garcia, Geraldine
Bishop Amat
Memorial HS
Hacienda Heights, CA

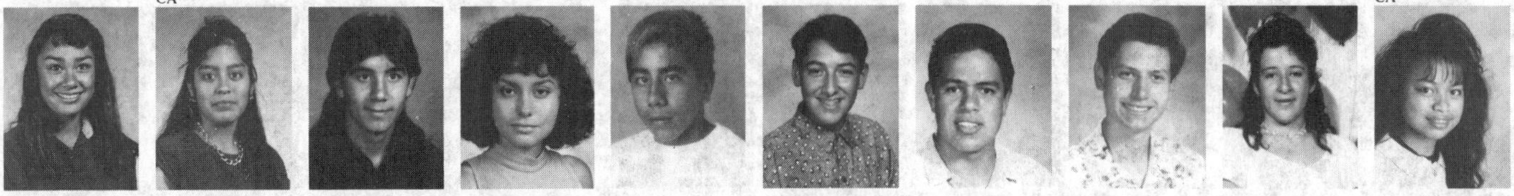

Garcia, Gina C
Cuyama Valley HS
New Cuyama, CA

Garcia, Harriet J
Willow Glen HS
San Jose, CA

Garcia, Hector M
Riverbank HS
Modesto, CA

Garcia, Helen
Whittier Christian
Montebello, CA

Garcia, Issac
Colton HS
Colton, CA

Garcia, Jacob R
Maranatha HS
Altadena, CA

Garcia, Jaime G
San Benito HS
Hollister, CA

Garcia, Javier
Schurr HS
Monterey Park, CA

Garcia, Jazmin T
Pasadena HS
Pasadena, CA

Garcia, Jessica
Oxnard HS
Oxnard, CA

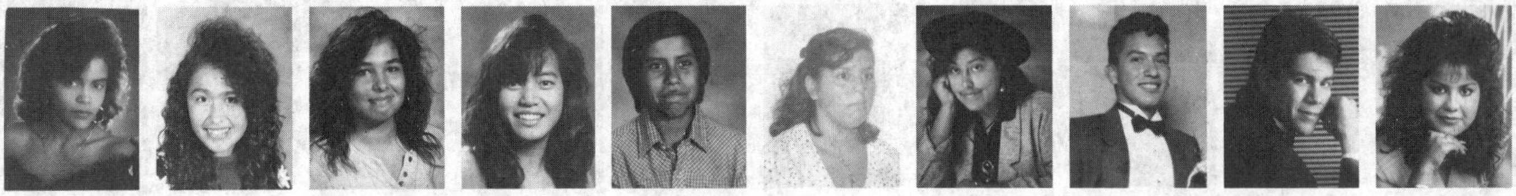

Garcia, Johannie
Palmdale HS
Palmdale, CA

Garcia, Judy E
Lowell HS
San Francisco, CA

Garcia, Kimberly A
Santiago HS
Santa Ana, CA

Garcia, Linda J
Glendale Adventist
Acad
Glendale, CA

Garcia, Luis R
Calexico HS
Calexico, CA

Garcia, Mara E
San Pedro HS
Wilmington, CA

Garcia, Maya S
San Jacinto HS
San Jacinto, CA

Garcia, Michael A
San Fernando CIP
Magnet HS
Chatsworth, CA

Garcia, III Michael J
East Union HS
French Camp, CA

Garcia, Mona Lisa S
King City HS
Greenfield, CA

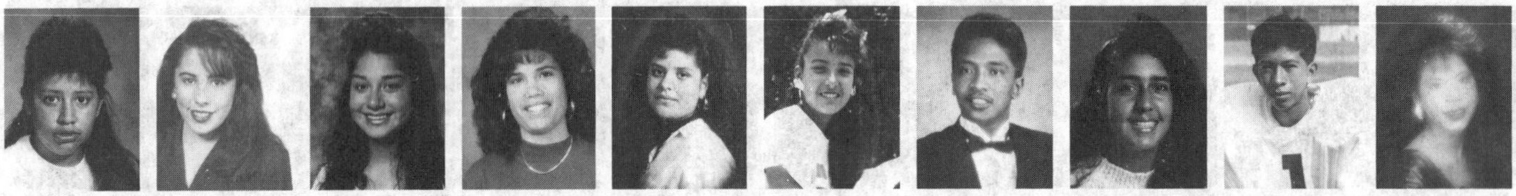

Garcia, Olga
Mt Pleasant HS
San Jose, CA

Garcia, Patricia
Sacred Heart Of
Mary HS
Los Angeles, CA

Garcia, Patricia H
San Clemente HS
San Clemente, CA

Garcia, Pilar M
Redwood HS
Visalia, CA

Garcia, Reyna
W C Overfelt HS
San Jose, CA

Garcia, Rose Maria
San Fernando HS
Magnet
Pacoima, CA

Garcia, Ruben
William C Overfelt
San Jose, CA

Garcia, Silvia
Santa Paula Union
Santa Paula, CA

Garcia, Jr Tomas O
Selaco HS
Norwalk, CA

Garcia, Vannessa
Michelle
Notre Dame HS
San Jose, CA

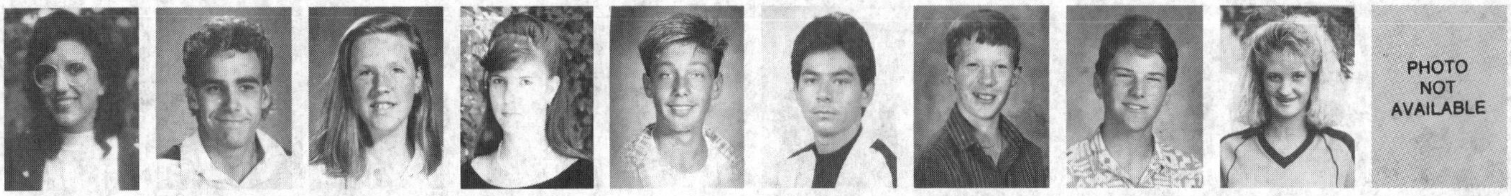

Gardella, Stephenie J
Lodi HS
Lodi, CA

Gardner, Chris L
Clovis West HS
Clovis, CA

Gardner, Jennifer
Huntington Beach
Huntington Beach, CA

Gardner, Tonya R
Irvine HS
Irvine, CA

Garfield, Coby R
Woodbridge HS
Irvine, CA

Garfio, Eduardo C
Calexico HS
Calexico, CA

Garis, Jack R
Bishop Amat HS
Covina, CA

Garland, David D
River City HS
W Sacramento, CA

Garland, Leslee L
Golden West HS
Visalia, CA

PHOTO NOT AVAILABLE

Garland, Stephanie L
Cabrillo HS
Vandenberg AFB, CA

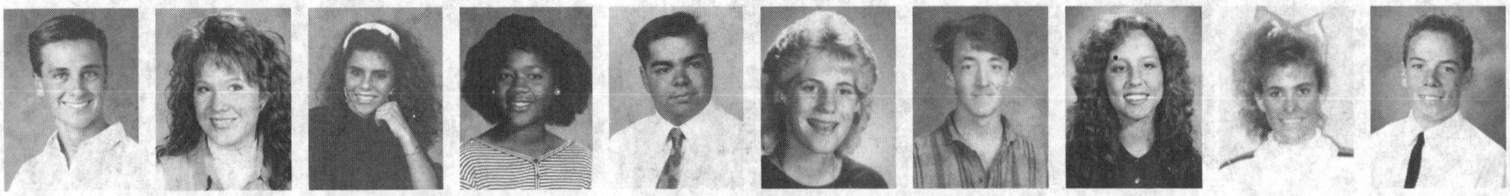

Garner, Jason D
Palmdale HS
Aguadulce, CA

Garner, Melissa L
Monterey HS
Seaside, CA

Garner, Misty M
East Bakersfield HS
Bakersfield, CA

Garner, Reigna C
Fremont HS
Sunnyvale, CA

Garofalo, Kevin J
Marina HS
Huntington Bch, CA

Garretson, April E
Lodi HS
Lodi, CA

Garrett, Ernie D
Redlands HS
Redlands, CA

Garrett, Megan
Casa Grande HS
Petaluma, CA

Garrett, Nicole
John F Kennedy HS
Granada Hills, CA

Garrett, Raymond P
Pater Noster HS
Los Angeles, CA

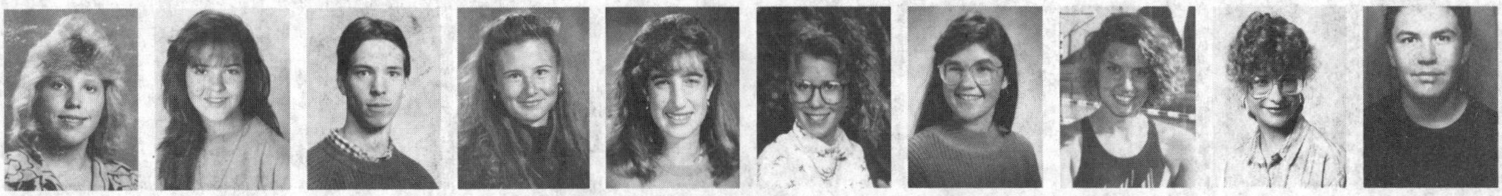

Garrison, Clair R C
Mojave HS
California City, CA

Garrison, Sandra Lyn
Pinewood HS
Los Altos Hills, CA

Garrison, Travis B
El Capitan HS
El Cajon, CA

Garrity, Christy Ann
Pacifica HS
Garden Grv, CA

Garro, Nicole M
Torrey Pines HS
Solana Beach, CA

Garside, Jennifer F
East Bakerfield HS
Bakersfield, CA

Garvey, Justine H
Edison HS
Huntington Beach, CA

Garvey, Vicki K
James Lick HS
San Jose, CA

Garvin, Erika D
Brea-Olinda HS
Brea, CA

Garza, Eudolio
Chino HS
Rialto, CA

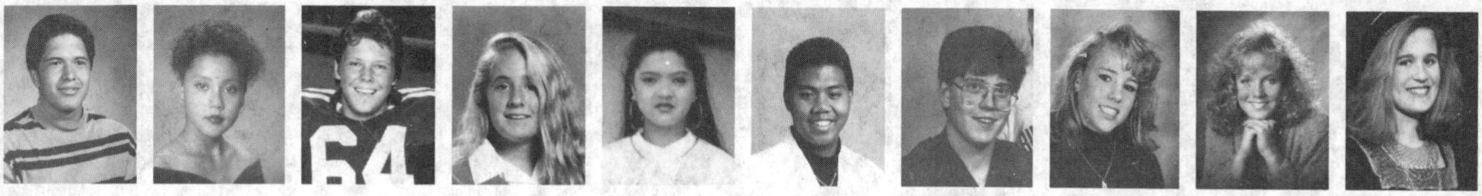

Garza, Timoteo
Central Union HS
El Centro, CA

Gascon, Stephanie T
Amos Alonzo Stagg
Stockton, CA

Gasior, Taus A
Mira Loma HS
Sacramento, CA

Gasparine, Michelle
Paraclete HS
Palmdale, CA

Gatchalian, Rachelle
Bullard HS
Fresno, CA

Gateb, Jr Romeo B
Bishop Amat
Memorial HS
La Puente, CA

Gates, Bradford A
Nevada Union HS
Grass Valley, CA

Gates, Jennifer D
El Dorado HS
Placentia, CA

Gates, Julianne G
Orange Glen HS
Escondido, CA

Gates, Rachel N
Lodi HS
Lodi, CA

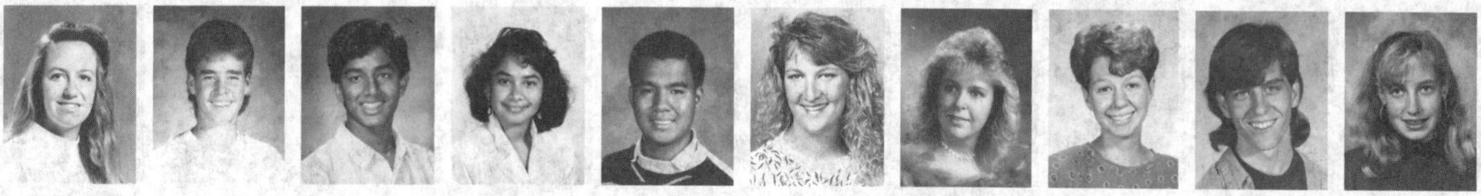

Gatlin, Carrie F
Etiwanda HS
Etiwanda, CA

Gaudreau, Jason C
Vacaville HS
Vacaville, CA

Gavankar, Sameer S
Sunny Hills HS
Fullerton, CA

Gavidia, Wendy Z
Herbert Hoover HS
Glendale, CA

Gavino, Christopher
Chula Vista HS
San Diego, CA

Gawf, Lori M
Valhalla HS
Rancho San Diego,
CA

Gay, Tammy
Liberty Union HS
Oakley, CA

Gazzar, Brenda
Barstown HS
Barstow, CA

Gearhart, Jesse J
Santa Ynez Valley
Union HS
Santa Barbara, CA

Gechter, Ronit C
Grossmont HS
El Cajon, CA

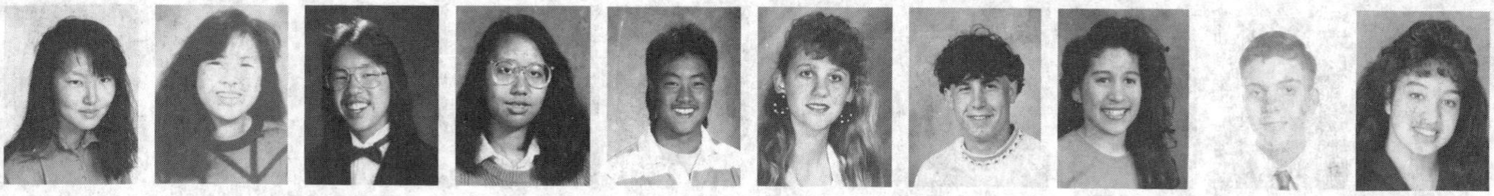

Gee, Elise C
Nogales HS
Walnut, CA

Gee, Joann M
Casa Grande HS
Petaluma, CA

Gee, Kenneth Scott
Casa Grande HS
Petaluma, CA

Gee, Mary
St Rose Acad
Daly City, CA

Gee, Randy T
Homestead HS
Sunnyvale, CA

Gee, Rebecca
Bishop Amat HS
Temple City, CA

Gee, Trey
Bella Vista HS
Orangevale, CA

Geena, Regina Nieto
Aka
Lakewood HS
Lakewood, CA

Gehlken, Aaron L
Victor Valley Joint
Union HS
Victorville, CA

Geli, Lea T
Mercy HS
San Bruno, CA

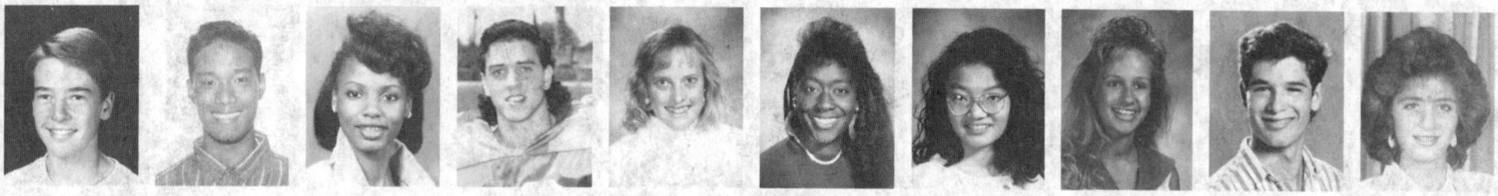

Gemmer, Jason C
Alhambra HS
Lafayette, CA

Genove, Erano
Nobello
Balboa HS
San Francisco, CA

Gentles, Sharon
Delores
Pius X HS
Lynwood, CA

Gentry, Eric E
Thousand Oaks HS
Thousand Oaks, CA

Gentry, Jennifer N
Westlake HS
Westlake Vlg, CA

Gentry, Legina K
Antelrope Valley HS
Lancaster, CA

Genuino, Arleen
Grace R
John F Kennedy HS
La Palma, CA

Geonetta, Jennifer
Temple City HS
Temple City, CA

George, Alan J
Carlsbad HS
Carlsbad, CA

George, Christiane
James Logan HS
Union City, CA

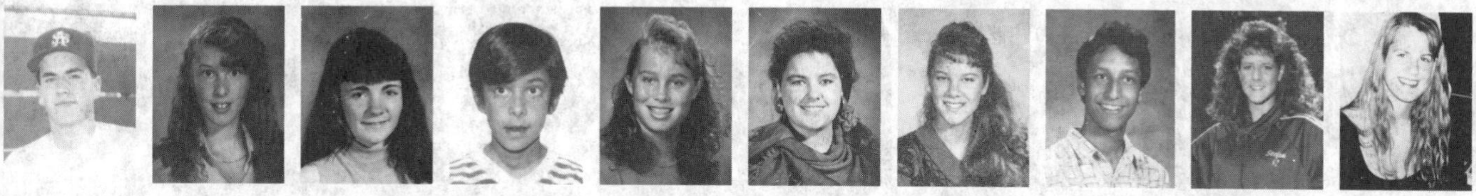

George, Christopher
St Anthony HS
Long Beach, CA

George, Jennifer
Bethel Christian HS
Lancaster, CA

George, Stephanie L
Eureka SR HS
Eureka, CA

Gera, Manoj
El Rancho HS
Pico Rivera, CA

Geraghty, Shannon C
El Toro HS
El Toro, CA

Gerbasi, Bobbi L
Bolsa Grande HS
Garden Grove, CA

Gerber, April
Bellflower HS
Bellflower, CA

Gerber, Michael A
Moreno Valley HS
Moreno Valley, CA

Gerber, Stefani
Casa Roble
Fundamental HS
Roseville, CA

Gerick, Amy
Bret Harte HS
Murphys, CA

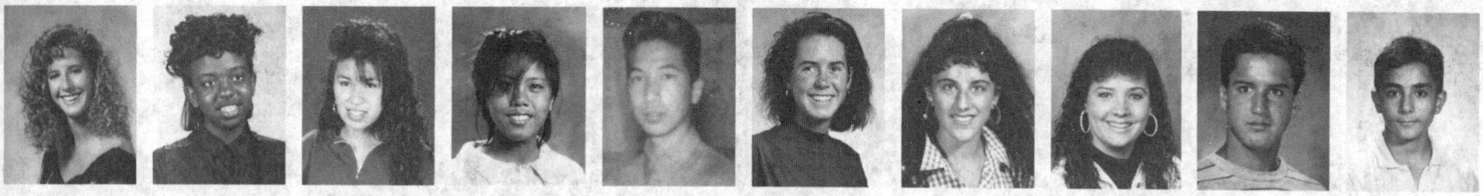

Gerjets, Heather
Rio Mesa HS
Camarillo, CA

Germany, Vila Sheree
Golden Gate Acad
Oakland, CA

Germono, Reubelle
American HS
Fremont, CA

Gerolaga, Maria
Teresa R
Holy Family HS
Los Angeles, CA

Geronimo, Alexander
Archbiship Riordan
San Francisco, CA

Gershenoff, Valerie A
Live Oak HS
Morgan Hill, CA

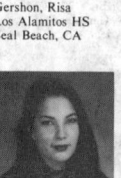

Gershon, Risa
Los Alamitos HS
Seal Beach, CA

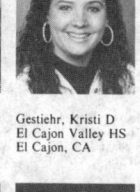

Gestiehr, Kristi D
El Cajon Valley HS
El Cajon, CA

Gettys, Tarey M
Irvine HS
Irvine, CA

Gevorkian, Artin
Hoover HS
Glendale, CA

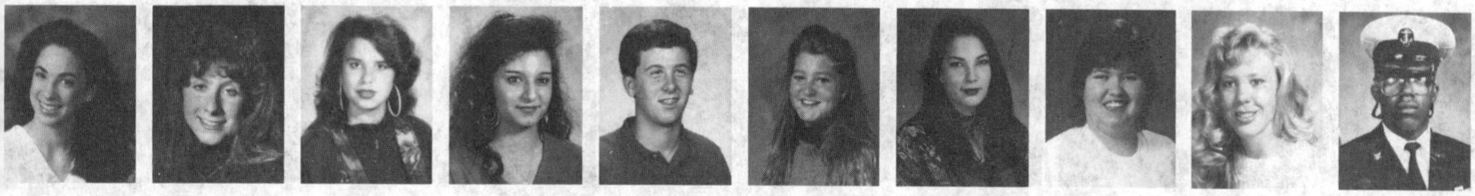

Gholdoian, Michelle
Marina HS
Huntington Beach,
CA

Giachetti, Gina P
Burney JR/SR HS
Burney, CA

Giacoman, Vanessa Z
South San Francisco
South San Francis,
CA

Gialamas, Angie T
Mayfair HS
Cerritos, CA

Gianelli, Brian
St Marys HS
Stockton, CA

Giangrasso,
Anne-Marie
Chaminade College
Prep
West Hills, CA

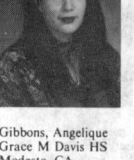

Gibbons, Angelique
Grace M Davis HS
Modesto, CA

Gibbons, Laurel
Palm Spring
Christian JR SR HS
Desert Hot Spring,
CA

Giberson, Tara N
Glendora HS
Glendora, CA

Gibson, Andre M
Luther Burbank HS
Sacramento, CA

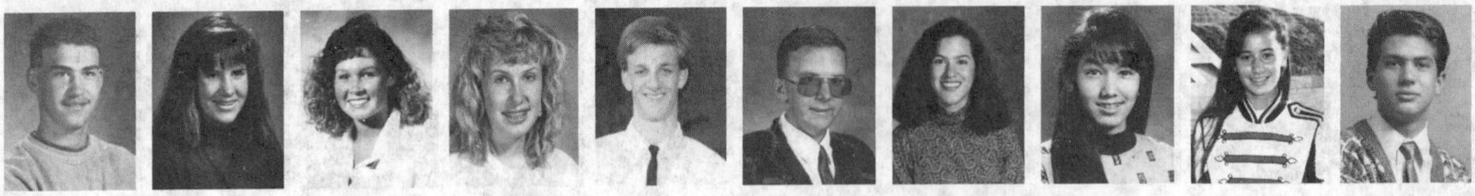

Gibson, Michael
Palm Desert HS
Palm Desert, CA

Gibson, Sara
Lincoln HS
French Camp, CA

Giddings, Nicole L
San Diego Acad
Bonita, CA

Gietzen, Cherie
Los Alamitos HS
Orange, CA

Gil, Christopher M
Clovis West HS
Fresno, CA

Gilbert, Brian A
Moreno Valley HS
Moreno Valley, CA

Gilbert, Shirin C
Beacon Christian HS
Foster City, CA

Gilbertson, Judy
Miyuki
Pilgrim HS
Los Angeles, CA

Gilfillen, Tricia L
Hilltop HS
Chula Vista, CA

Gilham, Michael D
Castle Park HS
Chula Vista, CA

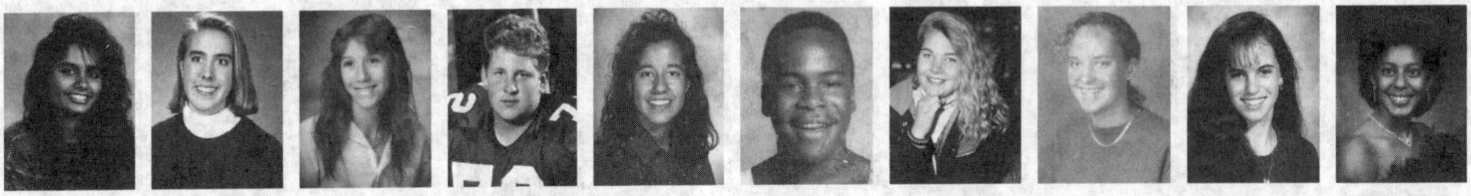

Gill, Leena
Simi HS
Simi Valley, CA

Gillen, Adrienne S
Novato HS
Novato, CA

Gilliam, Karen E
Santana HS
Santee, CA

Gilliam, Wade
Wade Gilliam HS
Westminster, CA

Gillis, Rainie
Desert Christian HS
Lancaster, CA

Gillison, Dwayne E
Bassett HS
La Puente, CA

Gillispie, Anika
St Bonaventure HS
Camarillo, CA

Gillot, Janine S
Bonita Vista HS
Bonita, CA

Gillum, Kristina M
Newport Harbor HS
Newport Beach, CA

Gilmer, Rashawn
Mt Eden HS
Hayward, CA

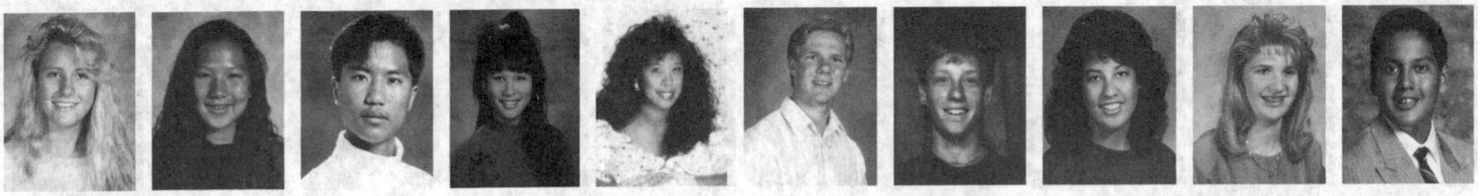

Gilpin, Jennifer L
Rio Vista HS
Rio Vista, CA

Gim, Beein
Walnut HS
Walnut, CA

Gim, Tony
Pilgrim Schl
Los Angeles, CA

Gines, Coralissa
John F Kennedy HS
Granada Hills, CA

Gines, Nikki
St Patrick-St Vincent
Vallejo, CA

Ginn, Lucas L
Hemet HS
Hemet, CA

Ginnaty, Marcus J
Edison HS
Huntington Beach, CA

Ginsburg, Rochelle
Marie
Los Alamitos HS
Seal Beach, CA

Gintz, Jana M
Fremont Christian
Fremont, CA

Giordano, Guido
Loyola HS
Glendale, CA

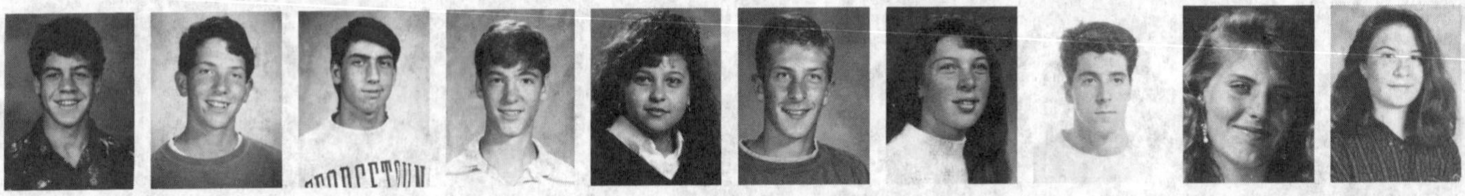

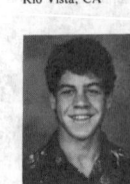

Giordano, Philip D
Helix HS
La Mesa, CA

Giovan, Michael P
Montgomery HS
Santa Rosa, CA

Girard, Jr Michael P
Oakmont HS
Roseville, CA

Girerd, Andre Rene
Palo Alto HS
Palo Alto, CA

Girgis, Elizabeth
Providence HS
Burbank, CA

Girod, Eric A
Serra HS
Foster City, CA

Girod, Rebecca S
Notre Dame HS
Foster City, CA

Giziotis, George J
Damien HS
Upland, CA

Gladden, Jacqueline
Notre Dame HS
San Jose, CA

Gladney, Alanna
Yosemite HS
Oakhurst, CA

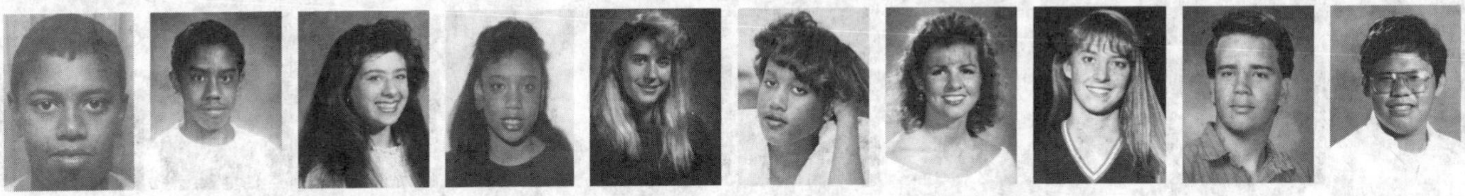

Glasgow, Jason A
Venice HS
Los Angeles, CA

Glaspy, Kevin B
Covina HS
Covina, CA

Glass, Kimberly M
College Park HS
Pleasant Hill, CA

Glaze, Ayanna
Folsom HS
Folsom, CA

Glemba, Fonda C
Rubidoux HS
Riverside, CA

Glenn, Michelle L
Bishop O'dowd HS
Oakland, CA

Glidden, Julie K
Edison HS
Huntington Bch, CA

Glover, Jyl
Napa HS
Napa, CA

Gluck, Mason T
Irvine HS
Irvine, CA

Go, Noel L
St Anthony HS
Long Beach, CA

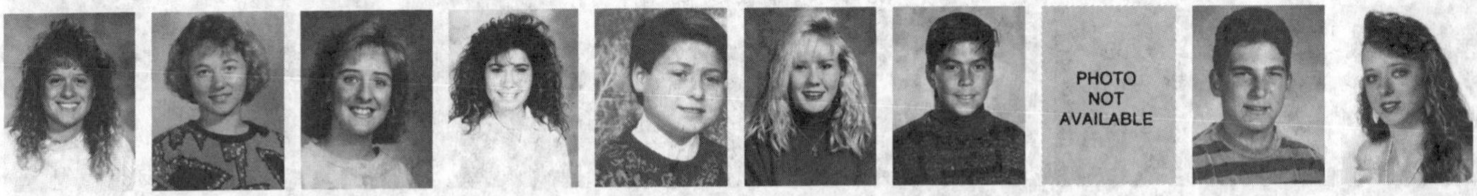
PHOTO
NOT
AVAILABLE

Goare, Christa E
Folsom HS
Folsom, CA

Godberson, Samantha
Mt Whitney HS
Visalia, CA

Godfrey, Jennifer
Casa Roble
Fundamental HS
Mt Olive, AL

Godinez, Lucila A
St Genevieve HS
Arleta, CA

Godoy, Carlos
Damien HS
Rancho Cucamonga, CA

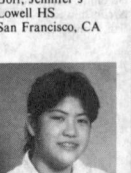

Goff, Jennifer J
Lowell HS
San Francisco, CA

Goitia, III Manuel
Boain
Don Bosco Technical
Inst
San Gabriel, CA

Goitia, Nichele M
San Gabriel Mission
San Gabriel, CA

Gold, Kevin
Heschel Day Schl
Granada Hills, CA

Golden, Alis M
Fairfield HS
Fairfield, CA

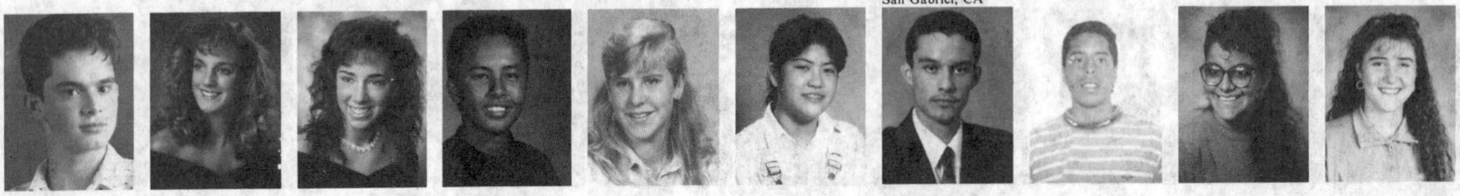

Golden, John S
Clear Lake HS
Lakeport, CA

Goldman, Beth
Serra HS
San Diego, CA

Goldsmith, Jennie
Chaminade College
Prep
Simi Valley, CA

Golez, Edwin
Serra HS
San Bruno, CA

Gollatz, Melissa
Pacifica HS
Los Alamitos, CA

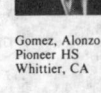

Gomez, Aimee K
Alexander Hamilton
Academy Of Music
Torrance, CA

Gomez, Alonzo
Pioneer HS
Whittier, CA

Gomez, Antonio
Hanford Union HS
Hanford, CA

Gomez, Bernadette
Chaffey HS
Cucamonga, CA

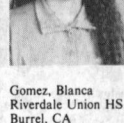

Gomez, Blanca
Riverdale Union HS
Burrel, CA

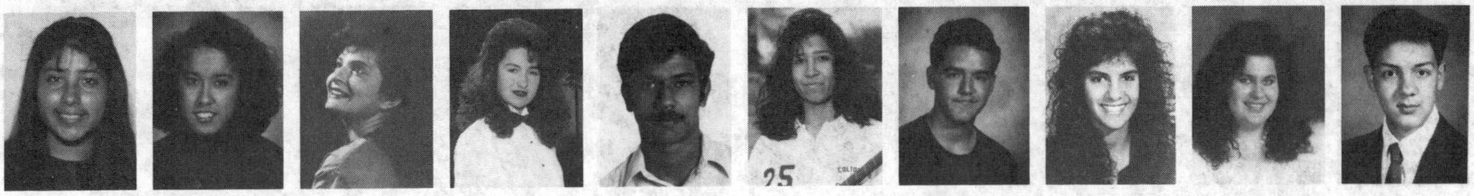

Gomez, Carol
San Benito HS
Hollister, CA

Gomez, Christina
Paraclete HS
Lancaster, CA

Gomez, Crystle
John F Kennedy HS
Buena Park, CA

Gomez, Dalia
William C Overfelt
San Jose, CA

Gomez, David A
Channel Island HS
Oxnard, CA

Gomez, Elaine M
Colton HS
Colton, CA

Gomez, Emiliano J
Rosamond HS
Rosamond, CA

Gomez, Gina
Gunderson HS
San Jose, CA

Gomez, Marcia
Montgomery HS
San Ysidro, CA

Gomez, Martin E
St Michaels College
Prep HS
San Clemente, CA

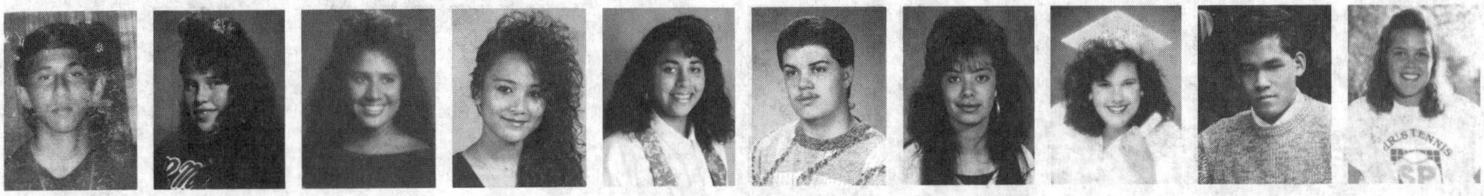

Gomez, Milton
San Antonio HS
Gardena, CA

Gomez, Patty
Rio Mesa HS
Oxnard, CA

Gomez, Rebecca
Fontana HS
Fontana, CA

Gomez, Shelly A
Coachella Valley HS
Mecca, CA

Gomez, Simona M
Rio Mesa HS
Camarillo, CA

Gomez, Steve A
Pittsburg HS
Pittsburg, CA

Gomez, Veronica M
South San Francisco
South San Francis,
CA

Gonsalves, Robyn M
Pittsburg HS
Pittsburg, CA

Gonzaga, Alejandro
Foothill HS
Bakersfield, CA

Gonzales, Amber L
San Pasqual HS
Escondido, CA

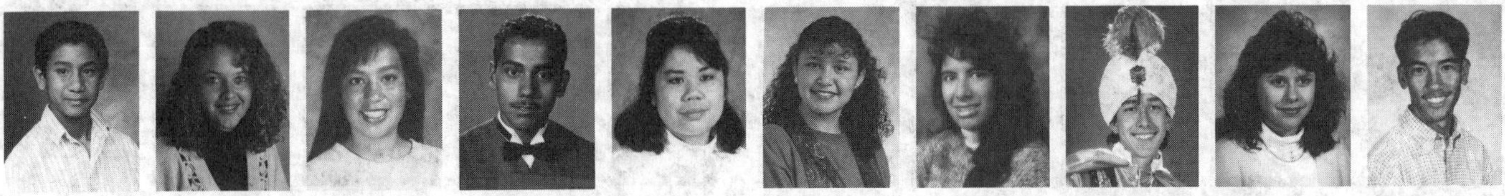

Gonzales, Arnel C
Franklin HS
Vallejo, CA

Gonzales, Deanna
Rio Mesa HS
Oxnard, CA

Gonzales, Emily
Bishop Amat HS
El Monte, CA

Gonzales, Manuel
Cantwell HS
Los Angeles, CA

Gonzales, Marie
Trinidad M
Jefferson HS
Daly City, CA

Gonzales, Melissa A
Notre Dame HS
Gilroy, CA

Gonzales, Michelle
East Bakersfield HS
Bakersfield, CA

Gonzales, Norman A
Coachella Valley HS
Coachella, CA

Gonzales, Patricia J
Orosi HS
Cutler, CA

Gonzales, Roy D
Carson HS
Carson, CA

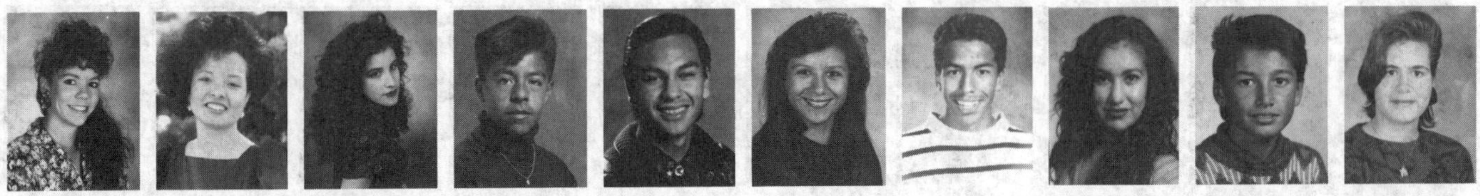

Gonzales, Shanna N
Clouis HS
Fresno, CA

Gonzales, Tanya
Foothill HS
Bakersfield, CA

Gonzales-Tovar,
Marcela G
Bisho O Dowd HS
Oakland, CA

Gonzalez, Albert
Colton HS
Colton, CA

Gonzalez, Alberto N
Leuzinger HS
Lawndale, CA

Gonzalez, Alejandra
Montebello HS
Montebello, CA

Gonzalez, Alfredo
Villa Park HS
Orange, CA

Gonzalez, Ana
Southwest HS
San Diego, CA

Gonzalez, Andres E
Elk Grove HS
Elk Grove, CA

Gonzalez, Annette
Bishopamat Memorial
El Monte, CA

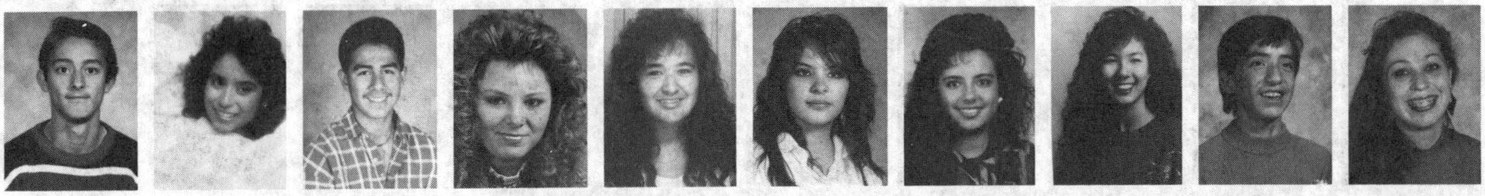

Gonzalez, Armando
Pasadena HS
Pasadena, CA

Gonzalez, Carmen
Firebaugh HS
Firebaugh, CA

Gonzalez, Cesar
Sanger HS
Sanger, CA

Gonzalez, Christina L
Adelante HS
Roseville, CA

Gonzalez, Cindi M
James Lick HS
San Jose, CA

Gonzalez, Claudia
William Workman
La Puente, CA

Gonzalez, Cristina
Valley HS
Sacramento, CA

Gonzalez, Deliana M
Nogales HS
W Covina, CA

Gonzalez, Eduardo L
Coalinga HS
Huron, CA

Gonzalez, Elaine
Chestnut Avenue
Baptist Acad
Fresno, CA

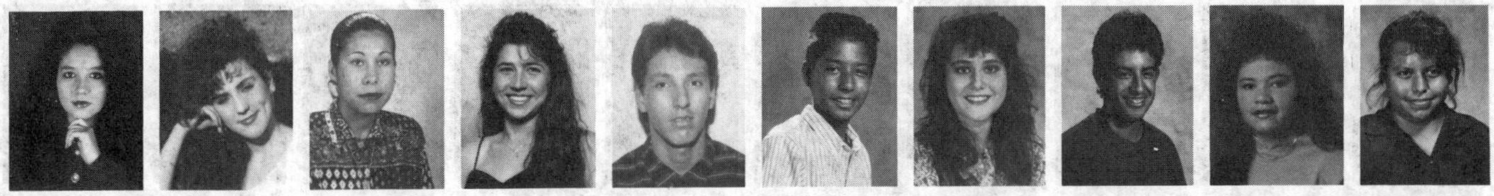

Gonzalez, Elizabeth
Wasco Union HS
Yuma, AZ

Gonzalez, Erica
Orosi HS
Cutler, CA

Gonzalez, Gabriela V
Central Union HS
El Centro, CA

Gonzalez, Gladys
Chino HS
Ontario, CA

Gonzalez, Henry H
Fontana HS
Fontana, CA

Gonzalez, Jr Jesus
Sierra Vista HS
Baldwin Park, CA

Gonzalez, Lucy
Bishop Amat
Memorial HS
Valinda, CA

Gonzalez, Manuel
Righetti HS
Santa Maria, CA

Gonzalez, Margarita
Dana Hills HS
Dana Point, CA

Gonzalez, Margarita
El Rancho HS
Pico Rivera, CA

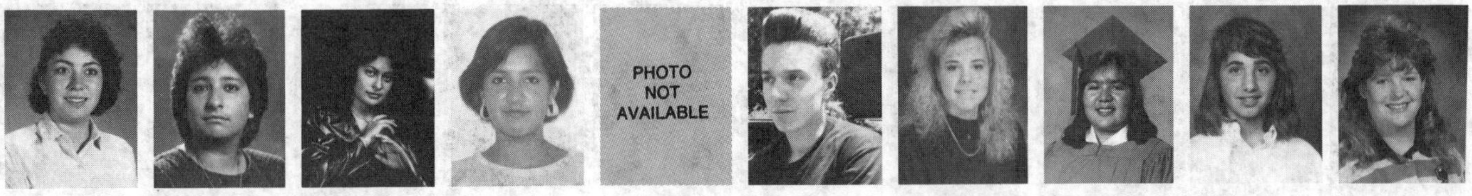
PHOTO
NOT
AVAILABLE

Gonzalez, Margarita
Woodland HS
Knights Landing, CA

Gonzalez, Maria R
John Burroughs HS
Burbank, CA

Gonzalez, Maribel
Pittsburg HS
Pittsburg, CA

Gonzalez, Martha P
Chula Vista HS
Chula Vista, CA

Gonzalez, Nancy E
Palm Springs HS
Palm Springs, CA

Gonzalez, Oscar
James Logan HS
Union City, CA

Gonzalez, Sonia
Orestimba HS
Crowslanding, CA

Gonzalez, Sylvia M
La Puente HS
La Puente, CA

Gonzalez M, Ma
Fernanda
Adacemy Of Our
Lady Of Peace
Coronado, CA

Gooch, Kellie Lynn
Eureka HS
Eureka, CA

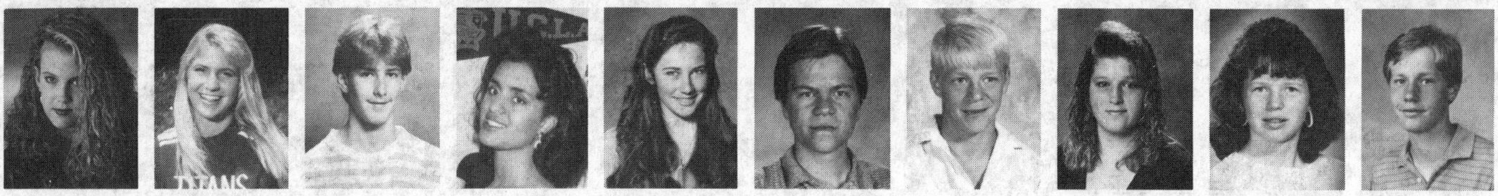

Good, Mary M
Shasta HS
Bella Vista, CA

Goodale, Kerry Lee
Poway HS
San Diego, CA

Goode, Chris
Mount Carmel HS
San Diego, CA

Goodkin, Erika D
Oak Meadow HS
Los Angeles, CA

Goodman, Heather L
C K Mc Clatchy HS
Sacramento, CA

Goodwin, J Kevin
Hoover HS
Fresno, CA

Gordon, John W
Lemoore HS
Lemoore, CA

Gordon, Michelle R
Castle Park HS
Chula Vista, CA

Gordon, Regina M
Paraclete HS
Lancaster, CA

Gorecki, Russell John
Moorpark HS
Moorpark, CA

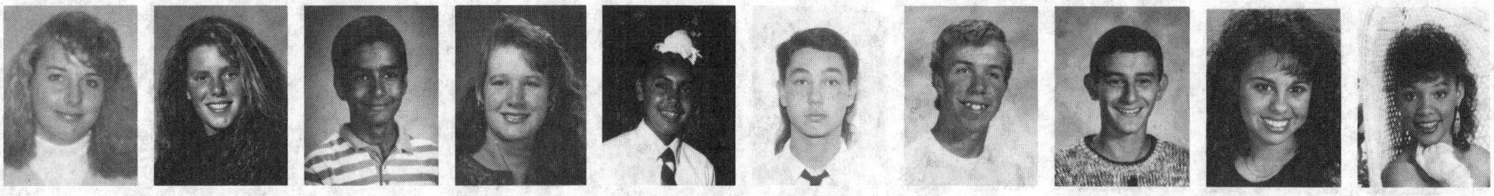

Gorman, Stephanie
Clovis West HS
Fresno, CA

Gormley, Melinda B
Woodrow Wilson HS
Long Beach, CA

Gorsi, Arafat
Livingston HS
Livingston, CA

Gorsuch, Wendi
Esperanza HS
Yorba Linda, CA

Gosal, Gurjit S
Live Oak HS
Live Oak, CA

Gossette, Phillip
John Marshall
Fundamental HS
Pasadena, CA

Gott, Chris
Bear River HS
Grass Valley, CA

Goubran, George E
Diamond Bar HS
Diamond Bar, CA

Gough, Melisa M
Palm Springs HS
Cathedral City, CA

Gougisha, Tamica
Pittsburg HS
Pittsburg, CA

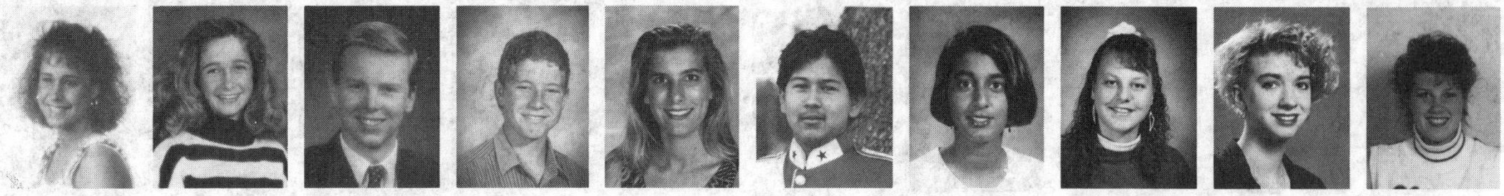

Goulart, Raquel M
Mt Whitney HS
Visalia, CA

Goulding, Shay
Redwood HS
Visalia, CA

Gouldy, Jared K
North Monterey
County HS
Castroville, CA

Goulet, Nicholas
Rosamond HS
Mojave, CA

Gourley, Ann
Foothill HS
Healdsburg, CA

Govea, Eduardo
Chino HS
Chino, CA

Govindarajan, Ramya
Cornelia Connelly HS
Anaheim, CA

Gower, Daystar
Montgomery HS
Santa Rosa, CA

Gozdeck, Rebekah L
San Bernardino HS
San Bernardino, CA

Grabiec, Amber M
Victory Christian
Schl
Citrus Heights, CA

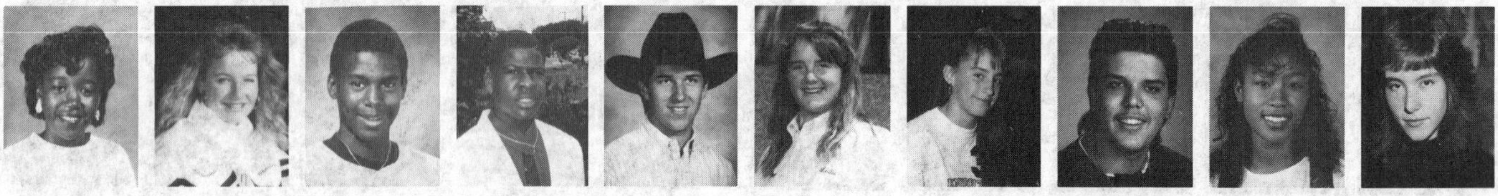

Graden, Annena
James Logan HS
Union City, CA

Graham, Christina
Alisal HS
Salinas, CA

Graham, Cordell
Trabuco Hills HS
El Toro, CA

Graham, Frank
Franklin JR HS
Vallejo, CA

Graham, Josh R
North HS
Woody, CA

Graham, Leslie D
San Clemente HS
San Clemente, CA

Graham, Natalie
Bishop Montgomery
Rolling Hills Est, CA

Graham, Rodrigo
Calaveras HS
Valley Springs, CA

Graham, Samantha
Hiram Johnson HS
Sacramento, CA

Graham, Sarah N
Arcata HS
Arcata, CA

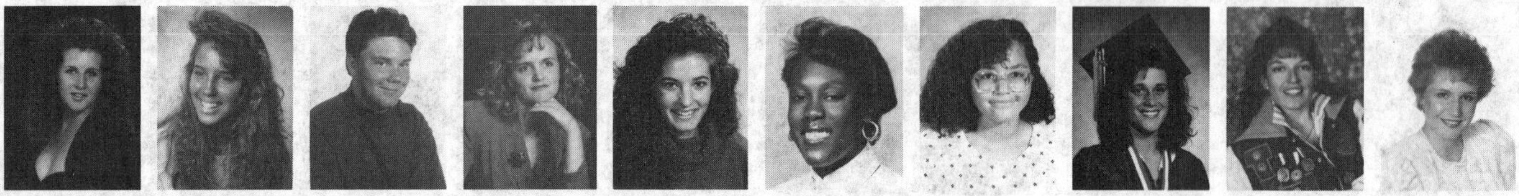

Gramcko, Kimberly
Big Pine HS
Bishop, CA

Granado, Jennifer A
Los Angeles Baptist
Sylmar, CA

Granados, Steven A
El Camino
Fundamental HS
Citrus Heights, CA

Granatowski, Lynn
University Of San
Diego HS
Escondido, CA

Granger, Hannah V
Pasadena HS
Sierra Madre, CA

Grant, Robin
Vallejo SR HS
Vallejo, CA

Grant, Robyn A
Hamilton Acad Of
Music
Van Nuys, CA

Grauer, Nicole
Orange Glen HS
Escondido, CA

Gravance, Rochelle
Laton HS
Laton, CA

Graves, Andrea
Paraclete HS
Palmdale, CA

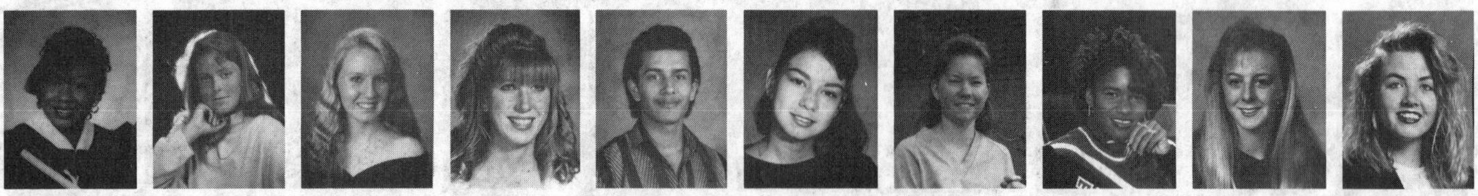

Gravett, Erika Y
San Pedro HS
San Pedro, CA

Gray, Amy
Carmel HS
Carmel, CA

Gray, Anne
Las Lomas HS
Lafayette, CA

Gray, Belinda M
Lassen HS
Susanville, CA

Gray, Hermes
Redlands HS
Redlands, CA

Gray, Misty S
Warren HS
Downey, CA

Gray, Rachel
Valley HS
Sacramento, CA

Grays, Chere A
Wasco Union HS
Wasco, CA

Grebbien, Jennifer
Christian HS
El Cajon, CA

Green, Amy
Sierra Vista HS
Baldwin Park, CA

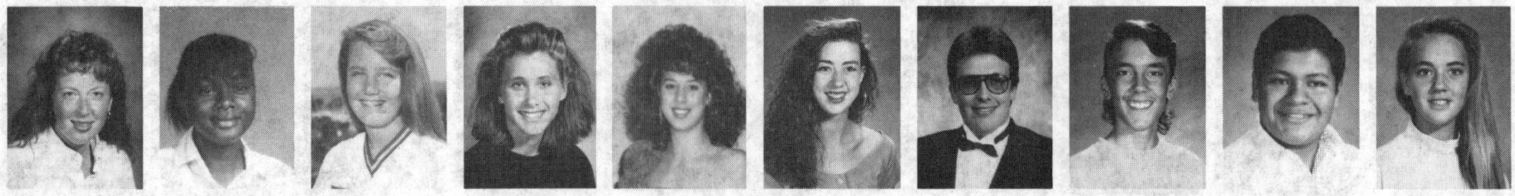

Green, Darcie C
Santa Margarita HS
Mission Viejo, CA

Green, Georgette M
Manual Arts HS
Los Angeles, CA

Green, Jennifer C
Dana Hills HS
Dana Point, CA

Green, Jennifer L
Newport Christian
Santa Ana, CA

Green, Marta J
North Hollywood HS
Studio City, CA

Green, Melanie L
Central Union HS
El Centro, CA

Green, Michael L
California HS
Walnut Creek, CA

Green, Peter C
Don Lugo HS
Chino, CA

Green, Sean L
Bret Harte HS
Angels Camp, CA

Green, Skye M
Pasadena HS
Sierra Madre, CA

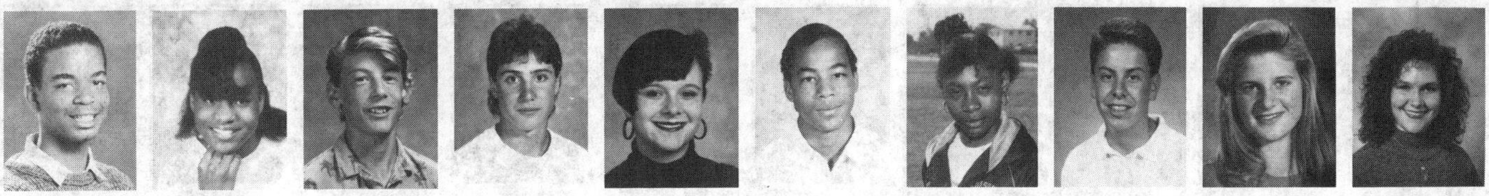

Green, Stacy A
Downtown Business
Magnet HS
Los Angeles, CA

Greenaway, Dior Y
So Bay JR Acad
Los Angeles, CA

Greenberg, Eric W
Mater Dei HS
Fountain Valley, CA

Greenberg, Jeremy
San Ramon Valley
San Ramon, CA

Greene, Jessica J
Armijo HS
Fairfield, CA

Greene, III Merle
Hamilton HS
Los Angeles, CA

Greene, Natasha A
Edison/Computech
Fresno, CA

Greenhalgh, Rob
Bellarmine College
Prep
Sunnyvale, CA

Greenlee, Anne E
San Dieguito HS
Olivenhain, CA

Greenlee, Shannon
California HS
Whittier, CA

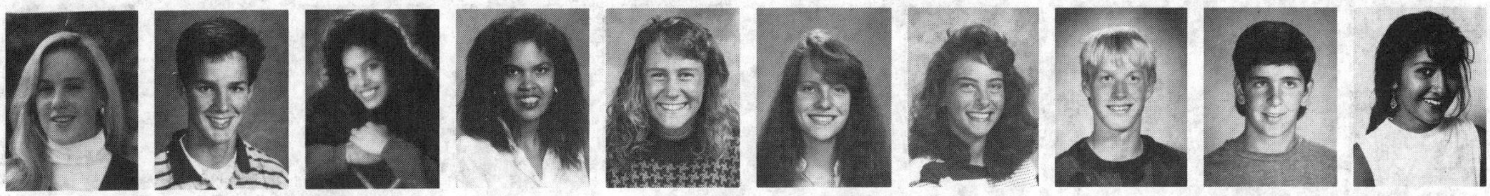

Greenman, Poppy C
Castilleja HS
Cupertino, CA

Greenwood, Eric S
Acalanes HS
Lafayette, CA

Greenwood, Jackie
Fred C Beyer HS
Modesto, CA

Greenwood, Patrice
Immaculate Heart
Los Angeles, CA

Gregersen, Brenda
Dos Pueblos HS
Goleta, CA

Gregg, Elizabeth A
Immaculate Heart
Los Angeles, CA

Gregorini, Heidi
Cabrillo HS
Vandenberg AFB,
CA

Gregory, Eric
Piner HS
Santa Rosa, CA

Gresham, Brian D
Merced HS
Merced, CA

Grewal, Jiwan J
Pasadena HS
Pasadena, CA

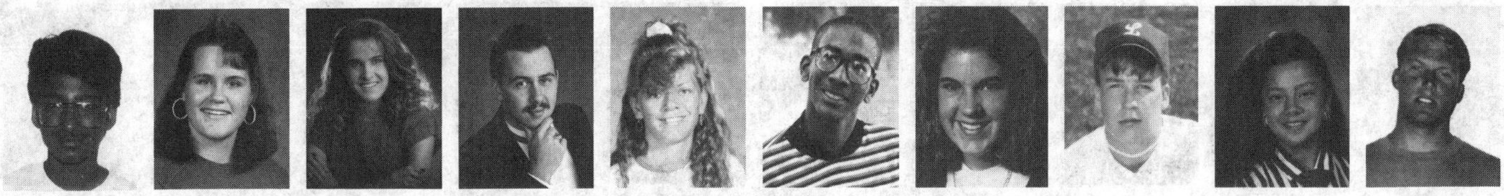

Grewall, Manny S
West HS
Torrance, CA

Grider, Rebecca A
Archbishop Mitty HS
Morgan Hill, CA

Gridley, Laura Dawn
Claremont HS
Pomona, CA

Griewank, Nick R
Rancho Cotati HS
Rohnert Park, CA

Griffin, Dulsa D
Pioneer HS
San Jose, CA

Griffin, Harvey T
Morningside HS
Inglewood, CA

Griffin, Melinda
Avalon HS
Avalon, CA

Griffin, Mitch T
Loyalton HS
Calpine, CA

Griffin, Stephanie A
Mar Vista HS
Coronado, CA

Griffin, Tige R
Coast Union HS
Cayucos, CA

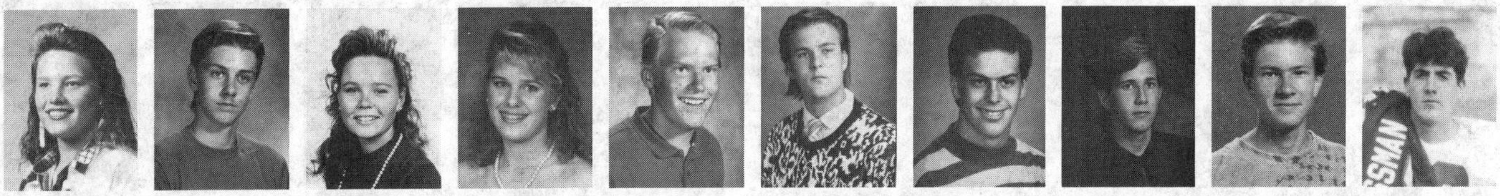

Griffin, Tricia A
Don Antonio Lugo
Chino, CA

Griffing, John P
Corona SR HS
Corona, CA

Griffith, Audrey M
Whitney HS
Bellflower, CA

Grik, Kristine F
Notre Dame Acad
Manhattan Beach,
CA

Grimes, Keith
Herlong HS
Doyle, CA

Grindal, Matthew
Cleveland Humanities
North Hollywood, CA

Groat, Lawrence J
Rancho Cotate SR
Rohnert Park, CA

Groene, John A
North County
Christian Schl
Atascadero, CA

Gronek, Scott A
San Gorgonio HS
Highland, CA

Grossman, Adam D
University HS
Los Angeles, CA

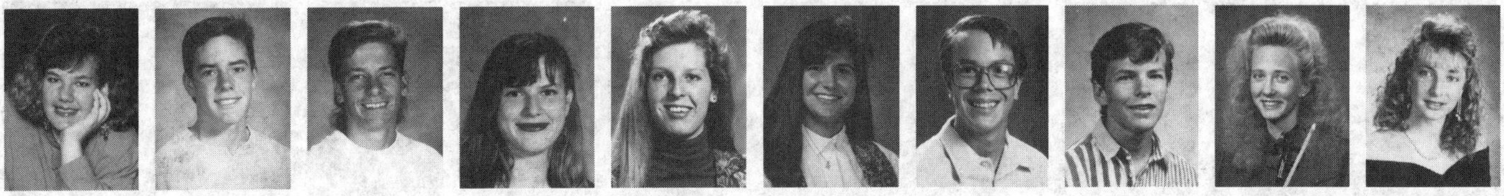

Grossman, Jessica
Helix HS
La Mesa, CA

Grossman, Todd C
Kennedy HS
Buena Park, CA

Grossmann, Jason S
Hoover HS
Fresno, CA

Groth, Lucinda L
Schl Of The Arts
San Francisco, CA

Groves, Brandy
Cajun HS
Colton, CA

Growcock, Jennifer L
El Toro HS
El Toro, CA

Growden, Matt E
Providence HS
Burbank, CA

Grubb, Ryan
Trinity HS
Tempe, AZ

Gruetzbach, Christine
Redwood Christian
Castro Valley, CA

Grunberg, Rachel
Oceana HS
Pacifica, CA

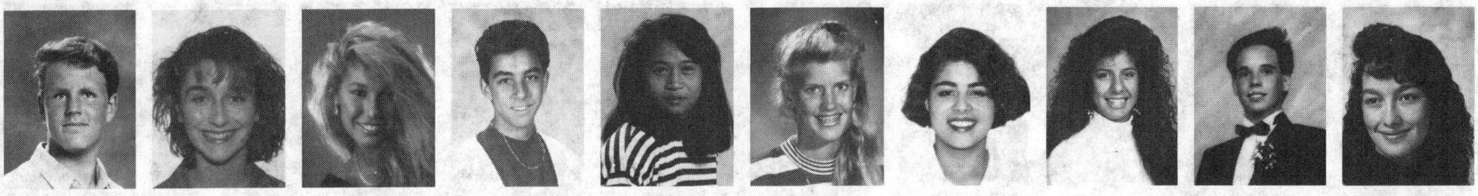

Grush, J Andrew
St Francis HS
Sierra Madre, CA

Guadagno, Celeste
Cornelia Connelly HS
Whittier, CA

Guaraglia, Celeste E
Ursuline HS
Santa Rosa, CA

Guardarrama, Joseph
Whitney HS
Cerritos, CA

Gudani, Maria L
Eagle Rock HS
Los Angeles, CA

Gudritz, Traci
Monrovia HS
Newark, CA

Guerena, Citlalli
Montgomery HS
San Diego, CA

Guerra, Esperanza D
Mesa Verde HS
Sacramento, CA

Guerra, Gonzalo
Etiwanda HS
Rancho Cucamonga,
CA

Guerra, Karen M
Lakewood SR HS
Long Beach, CA

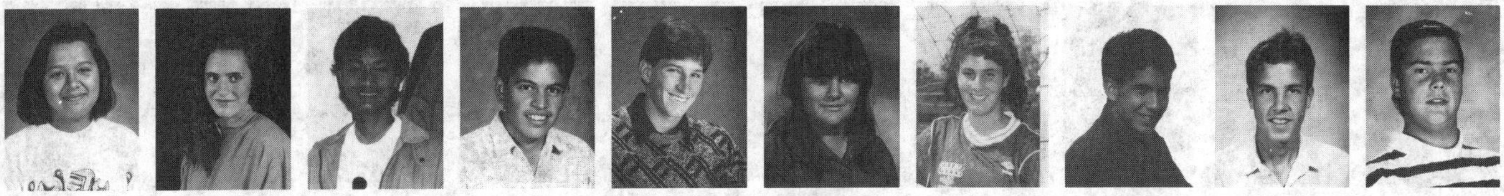

Guerra, Marlo T
Modesto HS
Modesto, CA

Guerra, Megan
San Benito HS
Hollister, CA

Guerrero, Garry L
Senior HS
Salinas, CA

Guerrero, Gilbert M
Gilroy HS
Gilroy, CA

Guerrero, Kevin M
Shasta HS
Redding, CA

Guerrero, Ramona S
Lompoc SR HS
Lompoc, CA

Guerrero, Rosella E
Sacramento HS
Sacramento, CA

Guerrero, Timothy M
Galt HS
Herald, CA

Guerrini, Steven B
Santa Rosa HS
Santa Rosa, CA

Guertin, Stephen D
Clovis HS
Clovis, CA

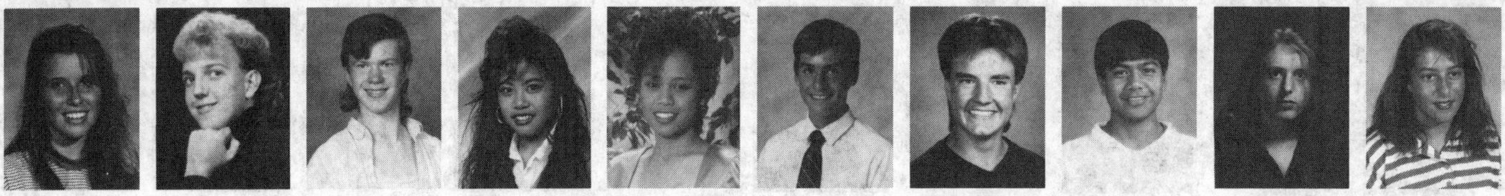

Guest, Lauren A
Folsom HS
Folsom, CA

Guest, Paul
Edison/Computech
Fresno, CA

Guffey, Paris A
Grossmont HS
Beaverton, OR

Guieb, Tessie M
St Patrick-St Vincent
Vallejo, CA

Guillermo, Joyce
Rancho Buena Vista
Vista, CA

Guleno, Mark E
Loyola HS
Los Angeles, CA

Gulliford, Jr Robert J
Livermore HS
Livermore, CA

Gumayagay, Mark E
Golden West HS
Ivanhoe, CA

Gumble, Jasn E
Coleville HS
Bridgeport, CA

Gumpert, Tara D
Tracy Joint Union
Tracy, CA

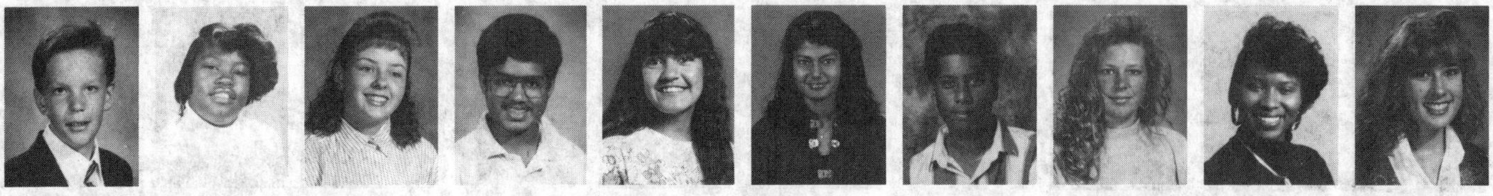

Gunst, Christopher L
Mater Dei HS
Huntington Beach, CA

Gunter, Kisha L
John F Kennedy HS
Richmond, CA

Gunter, Lisa A
Will C Wood HS
Vacaville, CA

Gupta, Jay M
Marina HS
Huntington Beach, CA

Gupta, Pooja
Etiwanda HS
Rancho Cucamonga, CA

Gupta, Vandana
Casa Roble Fundamental HS
Folsom, CA

Gupta, Vikram
San Clemente HS
San Clemente, CA

Guptill, Hayley
Eisenhower HS
Rialto, CA

Gurley, Fredetiya
Silver Valley HS
Barstow, CA

Gurule, Nickie
Hilltop HS
Chula Vista, CA

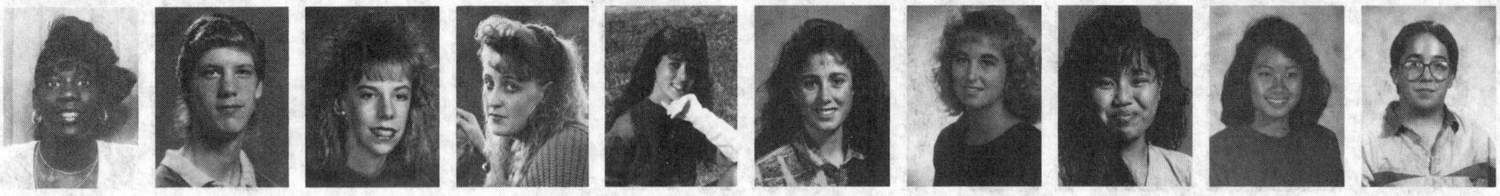

Guss, Aisha N
Alta Loma HS
Alta Loma, CA

Gustafson, Mattheu
Cajon HS
San Bernardino, CA

Gustafson, Tristan
Christian Center HS
Antioch, CA

Gustavson, Kristen
Gilroy HS
Gilroy, CA

Guthrie, Jan L
Del Campo HS
Carmichael, CA

Guthrie, Jennifer
Poway HS
Poway, CA

Guthrie, Penelope
Poway HS
Poway, CA

Gutierrez, Camilla T
Etiwanda HS
Fontana, CA

Gutierrez, Cristina A
Lemoore Union HS
Lemoore, CA

Gutierrez, Daniel W
Canyon Springs HS
Moreno Valley, CA

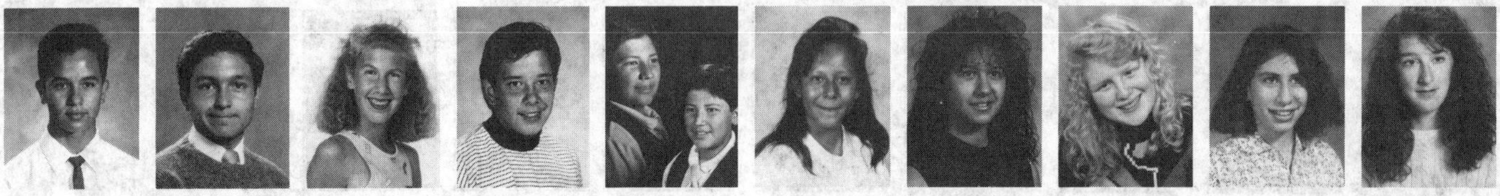

Gutierrez, Hector E
Don Bosco Technical Inst
San Gabriel, CA

Gutierrez, Isaias M
Delano HS
Earlimart, CA

Gutierrez, Jennifer
Righetti HS
Santa Maria, CA

Gutierrez, John A
El Rancho HS
Pico Rivera, CA

Gutierrez, Jose J
Edison HS
Fresno, CA

Gutierrez, Maria D
Baldwin Park HS
Baldwin Park, CA

Gutierrez, Monica
Bullard HS
Fresno, CA

Gutierrez, Noemi
Alisal HS
Salinas, CA

Gutierrez, Susan L
Dinuba HS
Dinuba, CA

Guy, Christa
Sonora HS
La Habra, CA

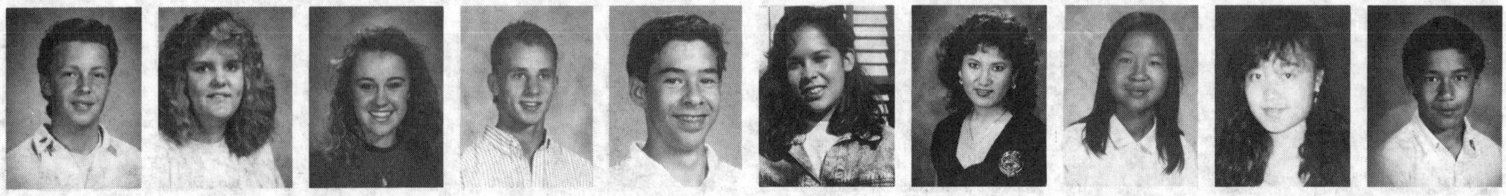

Guy, Dustin C
Saint Bernard HS
Eureka, CA

Guy, Nicolle M
Del Campo HS
Fair Oaks, CA

Guz, Gabrielle
Desert Christian HS
Lancaster, CA

Guzman, Aaron N
Lemoore HS
Lemoore, CA

Guzman, Michael V
St Bernard HS
El Segundo, CA

Guzman, Monica L
Chino HS
Chino, CA

Guzman, Vilma G
Glendale HS
Glendale, CA

Ha, Binh
Baldwin Park HS
Baldwin Park, CA

Ha, Kim Q
Rosemead HS
San Gabriel, CA

Ha, Quan L
Troy HS
Fullerton, CA

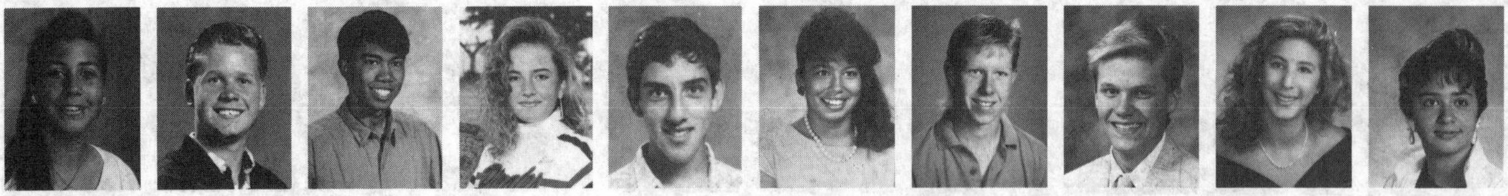

Haas, Samantha A
Apple Valley HS
Apple Valley, CA

Haase, Timothy R
Sierra Vista HS
Baldwin Park, CA

Haber, Michael G
Morro Bay HS
Los Osos, CA

Haberman, Teresa
San Leandro HS
San Leandro, CA

Habib, Tony
Glendale HS
Glendale, CA

Hacha, Veronica
Bishop Amat HS
La Puente, CA

Hack, John
Turlock HS
Turlock, CA

Hackett, Patrick A
Southwestern Acad
Bradbury, CA

Hackett, Tiffany
Los Gatos HS
Los Gatos, CA

Hadaegh, Pantea
Palm Springs HS
Desert Hot Spring, CA

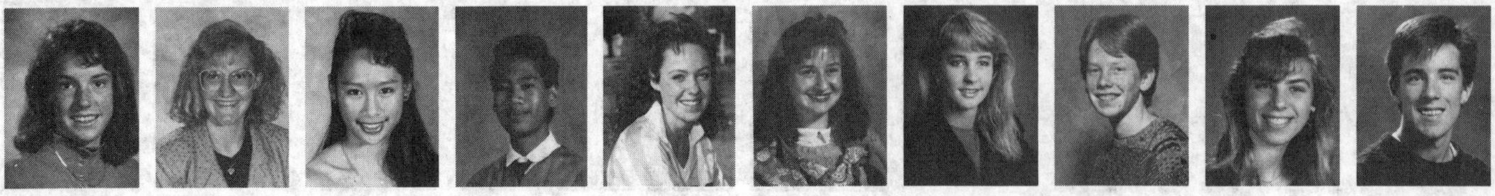

Haehn, Meredeth
Fountain Valley HS
Fountain Valley, CA

Haemmerle, Heather
Inland Christian Schl
Rialto, CA

Hafalia, April J A
Lowell HS
San Francisco, CA

Hafalia, Michael E
Sacred Heart Cathedral HS
Daly City, CA

Hagan, Kelly L
Villa Park HS
Villa Park, CA

Hageman, Catherine
San Benito HS
Hollister, CA

Hagen, Amber Dawn
Madison HS
San Diego, CA

Hagen, Eric
Yosemite HS
Oakhurst, CA

Hagen, Michele L
Clovis HS
Clovis, CA

Hagen, Patrick B
Burbank SR HS
Burbank, CA

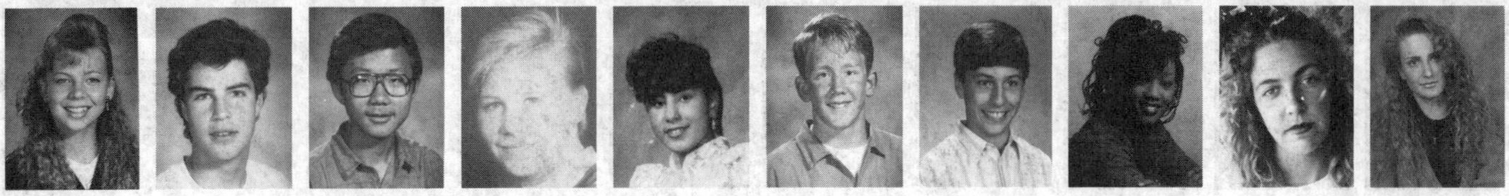

Haggard, Jessica M
Shasta HS
Redding, CA

Haggenmiller, Todd
Thousand Oaks HS
Thousand Oaks, CA

Hahn, Jong H
Bolsa Grande HS
Garden Grove, CA

Hahn, Kai-Uwe
San Clemente HS
San Juan Capistra, CA

Hahn, Kyra J
St Bernard HS
Los Angeles, CA

Haight, Michael
Maranatha Christian Academy HS
Irvine, CA

Haigler, Robert B
Mission San Jose HS
Fremont, CA

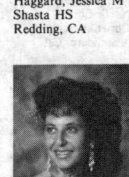

Hailey, Lyteres A
Barstown HS
Barstow, CA

Hairgrove, Deeann
Mission College Prep
San Luis Obispo, CA

Hajek, Kristina K
Jereann Bowman HS
Saugus, CA

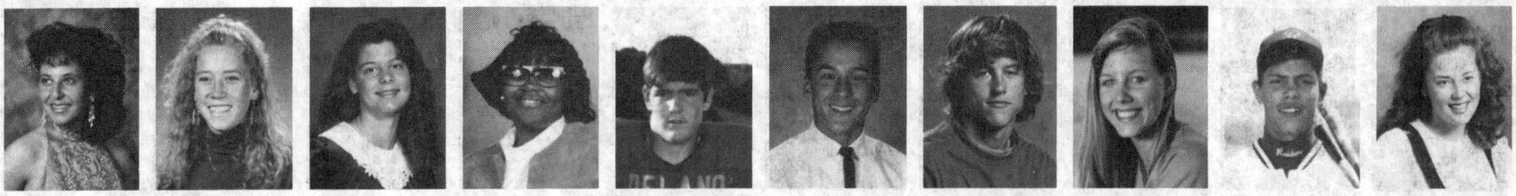

Hajj, Mary J
Covina HS
Covina, CA

Hall, Allison S
Monte Vista HS
Danville, CA

Hall, Amy L
Shasta HS
Redding, CA

Hall, Angela L
Washington HS
Los Angeles, CA

Hall, Brandon W
Delano HS
Delano, CA

Hall, Hugh D
Sacred Heart Cathedral Prep HS
San Francisco, CA

Hall, Jason D
Rim Of The World
Blue Jay, CA

Hall, Jennifer S
San Dimas HS
San Dimas, CA

Hall, II John E
Rowland HS
Rowland Heights, CA

Hall, Kristina M
Bella Vista HS
Orangevale, CA

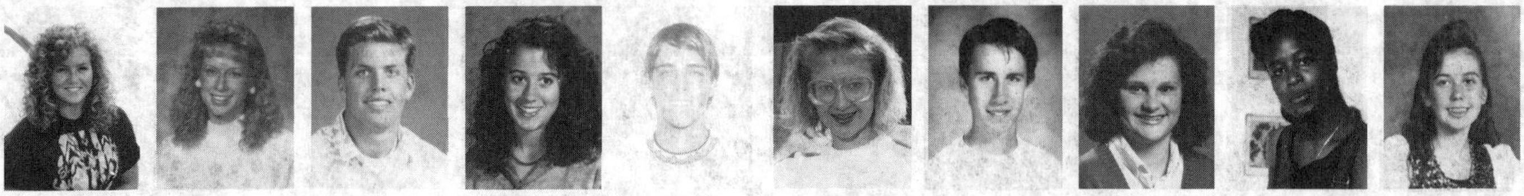

Hall, Megan P
El Toro HS
El Toro, CA

Hall, Mercy L
Fairfield HS
Fairfield, CA

Hall, Michael E
Bishop Montgomery
Torrance, CA

Hall, Molly Katherine
Miramonte HS
Orinda, CA

Hall, N Colin
Dana Hills HS
Laguna Niguel, CA

Hall, Nicole L
John A Rowland HS
Rowland Hts, CA

Hall, Reed
Sonora HS
La Habra, CA

Hall, Stacy
St Bouaventure HS
Ventura, CA

Hall, Tanaiia Phelan
Pittsburg HS
Pittsburg, CA

Hall, Trisha
Palmdale HS
Aqua Dulce, CA

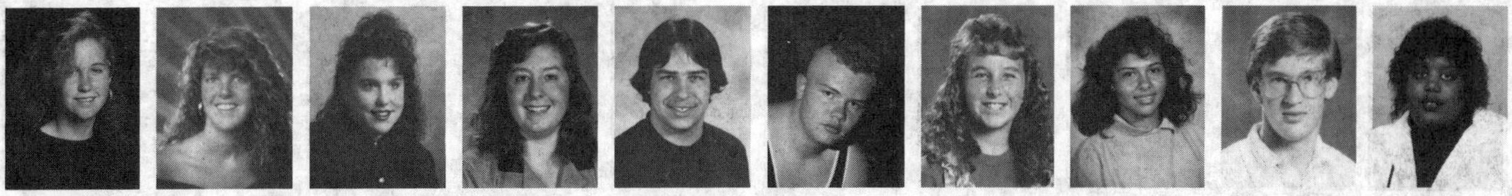

Hallam, Melissa A
Woodcrest Christian Schl
Perris, CA

Halliday, Heather
Oakmont HS
Roseville, CA

Hallock, Erin E
Mount Diablo HS
Pittsburg, CA

Hallock, Kelly L
Washington HS
Fremont, CA

Hamaker, Justin N
Nevada Union HS
Nevada City, CA

Hamann, Mark E
Canyon Springs HS
Moreno Valley, CA

Hamby, Aimee
Mojave HS
California City, CA

Hamelin, Nicole
Marina HS
Huntington Beach, CA

Hamilton, Dennis D
Bakersfield HS
Bakersfield, CA

Hamilton, Karen Lynn
Presentation HS
Daly City, CA

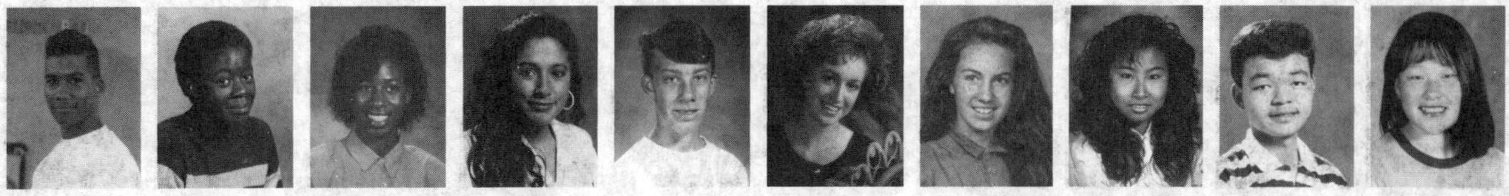

Hamilton, Mark D
Southwestern Acad
Pasadena, CA

Hamilton, Marlon K
Long Beach Jordan
Los Angeles, CA

Hamilton, Nalo
Moreno Valley HS
Perris, CA

Hamilton, Shauna L
San Bernardino HS
San Bernardino, CA

Hamlin, Jerry W
Troy HS
Yorba Linda, CA

Hammer, Shaun M
Grace M Davis HS
Modesto, CA

Hammond, Vanessa
Mountain Empire HS
Descanso, CA

Han, Jiwon
Bolsa Grande HS
Garden Grove, CA

Han, Kilby J
Eagle Rock HS
Los Angeles, CA

Han, Mei Mei
Lowell HS
San Francisco, CA

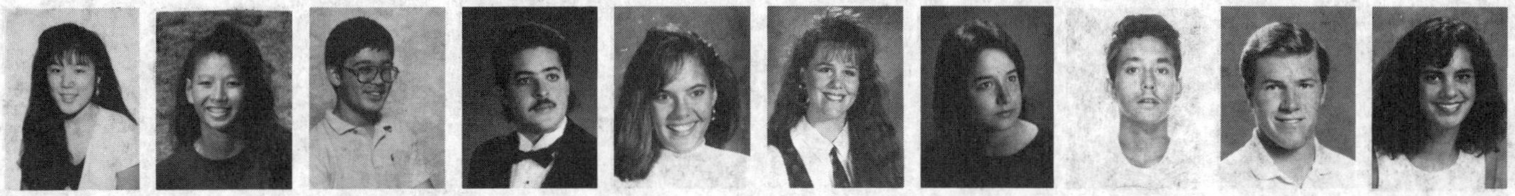

Han, Nydia
St Bonaventure HS
Santa Paula, CA

Han, Tracy
Marina HS
Westminster, CA

Hanafin, Joshua R
Redlands SR HS
Redlands, CA

Hanania, Mitri
Westmoor HS
Daly City, CA

Hance, Lori
Notre Dame HS
San Mateo, CA

Hancock, Carrie
Pioneer Baptist HS
Norwalk, CA

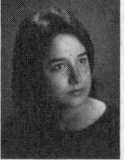

Hancorne, Hope I
Rio Lindo Adventist Acad
Trinidad, CA

Hand, Christopher B
Baldwin Park HS
Baldwin Pk, CA

Hand, Kevin
Hawthorne HS
Hawthorne, CA

Handal, Jennifer
Acalanes HS
Lafayette, CA

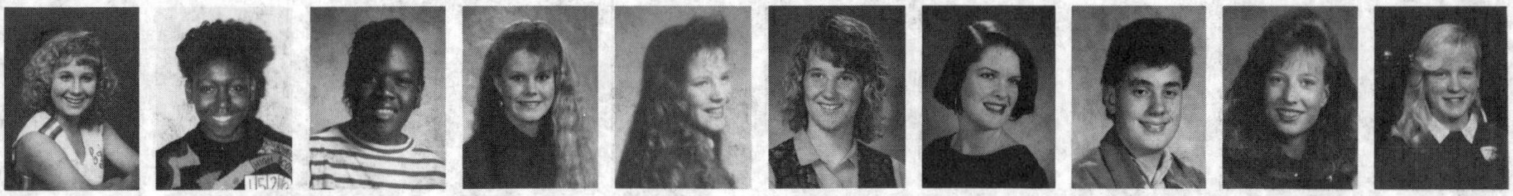

Handorf, Kiersten
Lemoore HS
Lemoore, CA

Handy, Nicola J
Moreno Valley HS
Moreno Valley, CA

Haney, Lenise V
Edison HS
Stockton, CA

Hangartner, Linda
Encinal HS
Alameda, CA

Hanks, Amber
Folsom HS
Leesburg,, VA

Hann, Shauna N
Mission Viejo HS
Laguna Hills, CA

Hanna, Christine N
Redwood HS
Visalia, CA

Hansche, Chris M
Saint Joseph HS
Santa Maria, CA

Hansen, Ericka
Capital Christian HS
Fair Oaks, CA

Hansen, Heather
Benicia HS
Benicia, CA

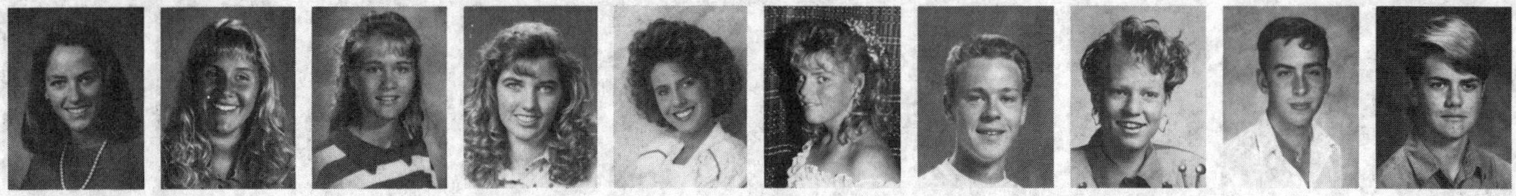

Hansen, Jennifer Michelle
Newport Harbor HS
Newport Beach, CA

Hansen, Kara L
Ceres HS
Ceres, CA

Hansen, Kathleen M
Cornerstone Christian
Camarillo, CA

Hansen, Kirsten
Palo Verde HS
Blythe, CA

Hansen, Michele L
Ponderosa HS
Placerville, CA

Hansen, Monica L
Cordova HS
Rancho Cordova, CA

Hansen, Travis
San Bernardino HS
San Bernardino, CA

Hansen, Vanessa
Capital Christian HS
Fair Oaks, CA

Hanson, Jr David C
St Genevieve HS
Canoga Park, CA

Hanson, Matt J
North County Christian Schl
Atascadero, CA

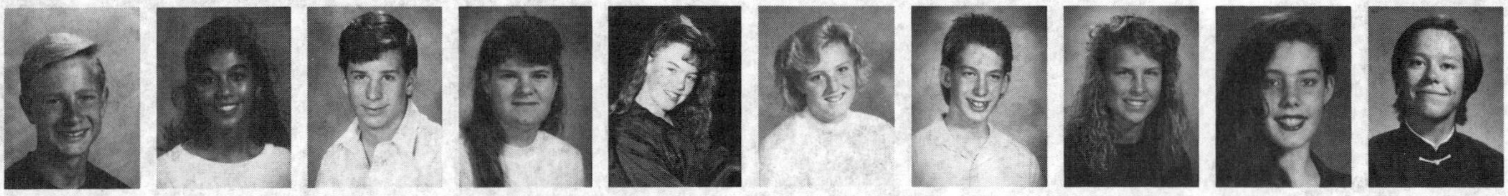

Hanson, Nathan R
Valley Christian HS
Bellflower, CA

Hanuman, Shashi
Pacifica HS
Cypress, CA

Harbaugh, Doug P
Pasadena HS
Pasadena, CA

Harber, Jennifer L
Garden Grove HS
Garden Grove, CA

Harbison, Anne M
Bishop Montgomery
Rolling Hills Est, CA

Hardin, Heather M
Lower Lake HS
Clearlake, CA

Harding, Aaron R
Selma HS
Kingsburg, CA

Harding, Angela L
University HS
Irvine, CA

Harding, Sita R
Santa Cruz HS
Santa Cruz, CA

Hardman, Chaney J
Poway HS
San Diego, CA

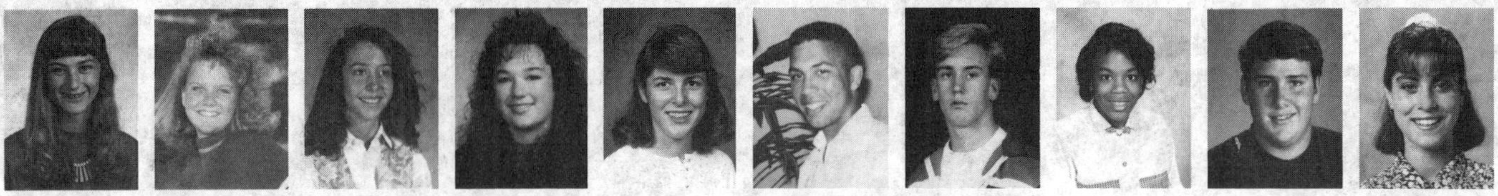

Hardwick, Heather C
Saint Francis HS
Los Altos, CA

Hardwick, Melissa
Arlington HS
Riverside, CA

Hardy, Andrea L
Sierra Joint Union
Madera, CA

Hardy, Renee L
Colfax HS
Meadow Vista, CA

Hardy, Shannon F
Patrick Henry HS
San Diego, CA

Harger, II Bradley L
California HS
Oakland, CA

Hargrave, Morgan S
Etiwanda HS
Alta Loma, CA

Harice, Latricia
St Michaels HS
Los Angeles, CA

Harig, Rick
East Union HS
Manteca, CA

Harkenrider, Jessica
Mira Costa HS
Manhattan Beach, CA

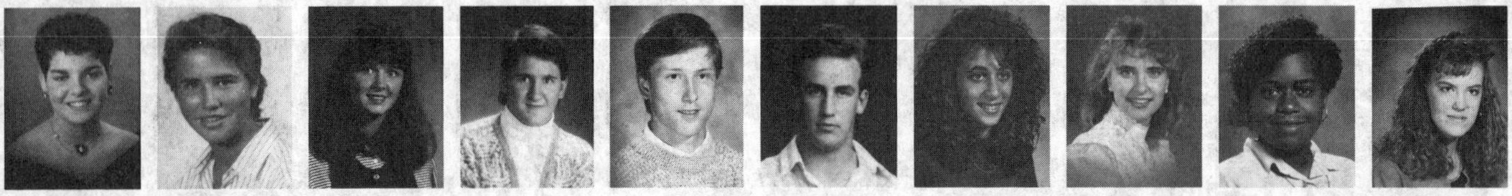

Harlan, Heather Catherine
Las Lomas HS
Walnut Creek, CA

Harmaning, Dawn
Capital Christian HS
Citrus Heights, CA

Harmon, Julie M
Edison HS
Huntington Beach, CA

Harmon, Michael T
Thomas Downey HS
Modesto, CA

Harnden, Richard D
Red Bluff HS
Red Bluff, CA

Harnish, Eric A
Village Christian HS
Van Nuys, CA

Haroutian, Allison
Bullard HS
Fresno, CA

Harper, Angela L
Atascadero HS
Atascadero, CA

Harper, Shanell
St Michaels HS
Los Angeles, CA

Harral, Aleah D
Red Bluff Union HS
Los Molinos, CA

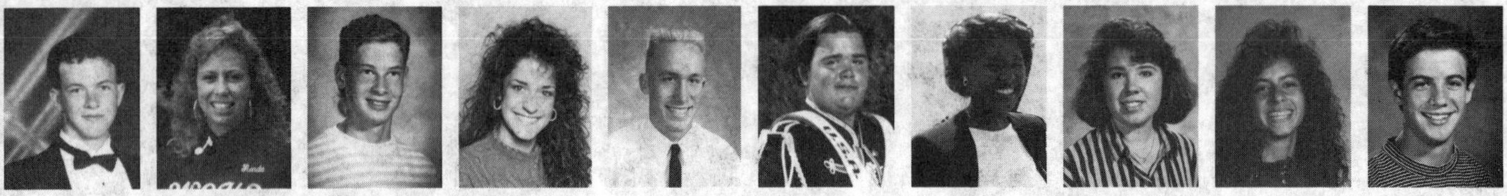

Harrell, Mike
Le Moore Union HS
Lemoore, CA

Harrelson, Glenda
West Covina HS
West Covina, CA

Harrington, David W
North HS
Bakersfield, CA

Harrington, Krista
Eisenhower HS
Rialto, CA

Harrington, Robert J
Bishop O'dowd HS
Alameda, CA

Harrington, Shawn
Rowland HS
Rowland Heights, CA

Harris, Adrienne Danielle
San Pedro HS
High Point, NC

Harris, Amy L
Atascadero HS
Atascadero, CA

Harris, Andree J
Santa Teresa HS
San Jose, CA

Harris, Brian J
Edison HS
Huntington Beach, CA

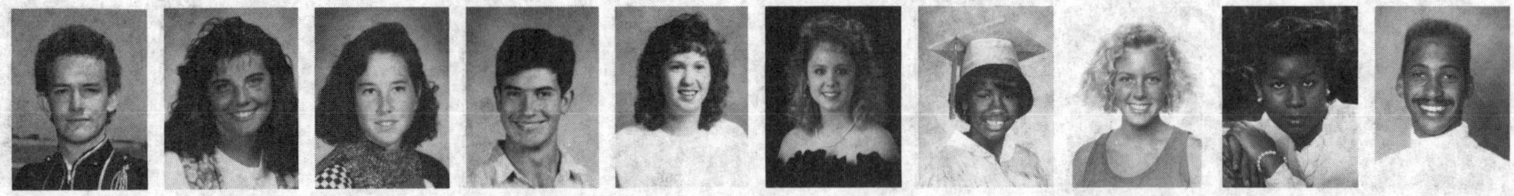

Harris, Christopher Paul
Clovis West HS
Fresno, CA

Harris, Hansi Y
Capital Christian HS
W Sacramento, CA

Harris, Heather
Westwood HS
Westwood, CA

Harris, Jason M
Rio Americano HS
Sacramento, CA

Harris, Jennifer J
West HS
Bakersfield, CA

Harris, Jennifer Lee
Antioch SR HS
Antioch, CA

Harris, Kamisha R
Mayfield SR Schl
Altadena, CA

Harris, Kendra L
Ventura HS
Santa Paula, CA

Harris, Laconia E
El Camino HS
St Louis, MO

Harris, Michael J
Chadwick Schl
Manhattan Beach, CA

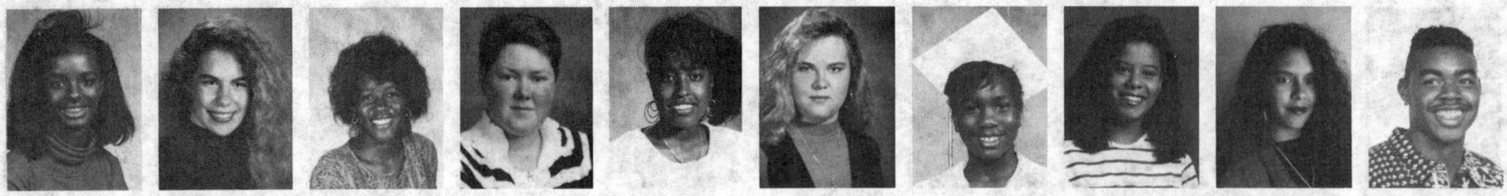

Harris, Rashida M
Sacred Heart Prep
Stanford, CA

Harris, Rebecca
Lincoln HS
Stockton, CA

Harris, Tamara L
Lynwood HS
Lynwood, CA

Harris, Tammy A
Ocean View HS
Costa Mesa, CA

Harris, Tanisha A
Bridgemont HS
San Francisco, CA

Harris, Teanne L
Norwalk HS
Green Bay, WI

Harris, Tracey N
Grant HS
Sacramento, CA

Harris, Traci L
Southern California Christian HS
Anaheim, CA

Harris, Verena D
Hueneme HS
Port Hueneme, CA

Harris, William C
Redlands SR HS
Redlands, CA

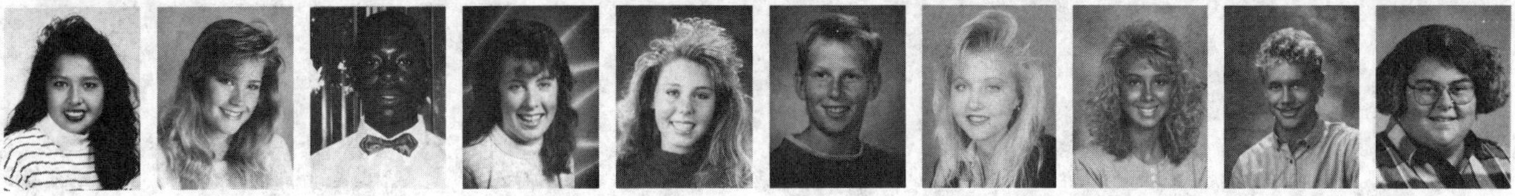

Harrison, Charlene
Skyline HS
San Lorenzo, CA

Harrison, Deanie L
Oxnard HS
Oxnard, CA

Harrison, Harvey Terrell
Chino HS
Ontario, CA

Harrison, Janet L
Riverside Christian
Riverside, CA

Harrison, Jennifer D
Diamond Bar HS
Diamond Bar, CA

Harrison, Justin
Trabuco Hills HS
Mission Viejo, CA

Harrison, Natalie R
Yucca Valley HS
Morongo Valley, CA

Harrison, Ronece
Western Christian
W Covina, CA

Hart, Benjamin C
Poway HS
Poway, CA

Hart, Cecelia M
Winters HS
Winters, CA

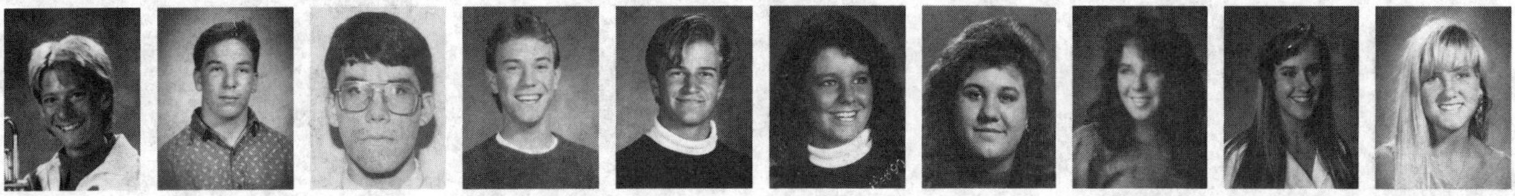

Hart, Mike P
Lindsay HS
Lindsay, CA

Hart, Ronnie B
Ukiah HS
Redwood Valley, CA

Hart, Wayne T
Casa Roble HS
Orangevale, CA

Hartley, L Keith
Hanford Union HS
Hanford, CA

Hartley, Scott
Dublin HS
Dublin, CA

Hartman, Jennifer
Cabrillo HS
Lompoc, CA

Hartman, Jennifer R
Fontana HS
Fontana, CA

Hartman, Shawni Eden
Capistrano Valley Chistian HS
San Juan Capistra

Hartsfield, Sherilyn Renee
Norco HS
Corona, CA

Hartung, Misty
Cypress HS
Los Alamitos, CA

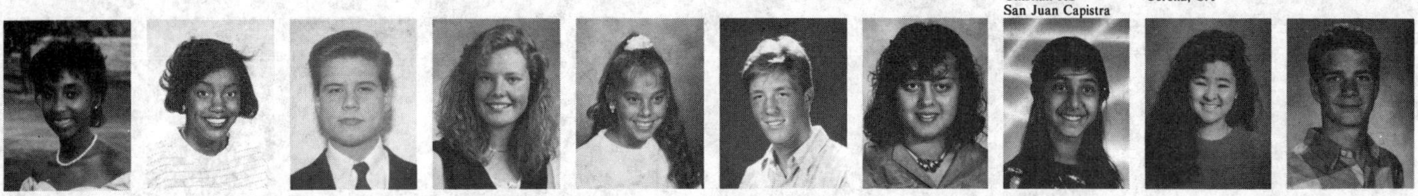

Harvey, Lakisha D
Bishop Amat Memorial HS
La Puente, CA

Harvey, Latoya F
Alexander Hamilton
Los Angeles, CA

Harvey, Paul William
Saint Marys HS
Stockton, CA

Harvey, Sarah E
Notre Dame HS
San Jose, CA

Harvey, Stacy E
Armijo HS
Suisun, CA

Harzog, Michael E
San Rafael HS
San Rafael, CA

Hasan, Michelle
Corona Del Mar HS
Newport Beach, CA

Hasan, Quratul A
Diamond Bar HS
Diamond Bar, CA

Hasegawa, Tami T
North Torrance HS
Torrance, CA

Haskell, Kevin
Serra HS
San Mateo, CA

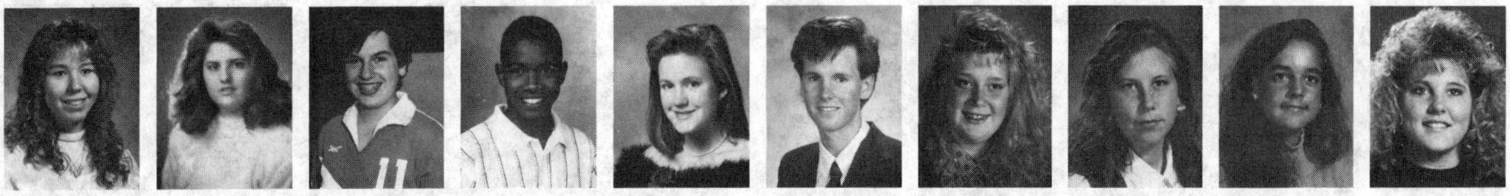

Haslett, Gina M
Modoc HS
Alturas, CA

Hass, Cheryl L
St Francis HS
Sacramento, CA

Hassakoursian, Yvette
Ribet Acad
La Canada, CA

Hassoun, Jibril S
Gompers HS
San Diego, CA

Hastings, Laura A
Redondo Union HS
Redondo Beach, CA

Hatch, Aaron Y
St Margaret Scotland Episcopal Schl
Laguna Beach, CA

Hatch, Monica L
Turlock HS
Turlock, CA

Hatfield, Christine E
Hilltop HS
Chula Vista, CA

Hatfield, Meredith C
Bullard HS
Fresno, CA

Hatton, Kelly J
Taft Union HS
Taft, CA

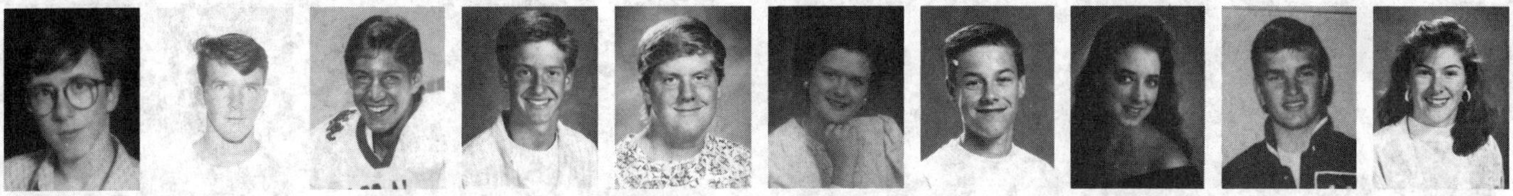

Haug, Jon
North Bay Orinda Schl
El Cerrito, CA

Haugh, Mark Dewon
Apple Valley HS
Apple Valley, CA

Hauk, Matt
Los Alamitos HS
Los Alamitos, CA

Haukaas, Jeffrey William
Acalanes HS
Lafayette, CA

Hause, Craig A
Cypress HS
Cypress, CA

Havener, Katherine
Dublin HS
Dublin, CA

Hawes, Nathan L
Etiwanda HS
Alta Loma, CA

Hawkins, Jennifer T
Rancho Cotate HS
Rohnert Park, CA

Hawkins, Scott A
Thousand Oaks HS
Thousand Oaks, CA

Hawkins, Tammi R
Covina HS
Covina, CA

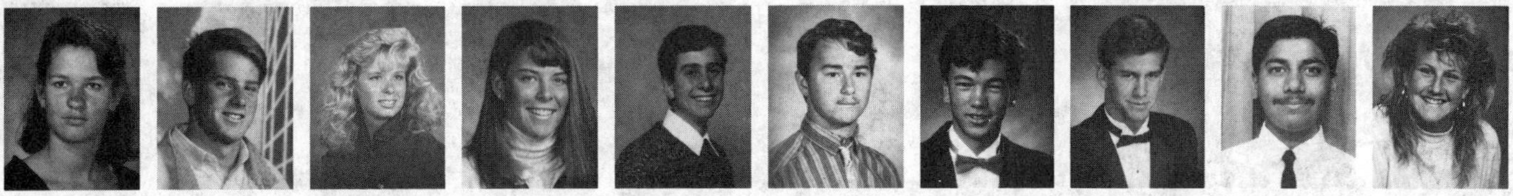

Hawkinson, Charis A
Traruco Hills HS
Mission Viejo, CA

Hayes, John W
Carmel HS
Carmel Valley, CA

Hayes, Kristel
Millikan HS
Long Beach, CA

Hayes, Shannon A
Del Campo HS
Carmichael, CA

Hayes, Shawn E
Edison HS
Huntington Beach, CA

Haynes, John M
Sherman E Burroughs HS
Ridgecrest, CA

Haynie, Ronald J
Ramona HS
Ramona, CA

Hayslip, Thomas
Southwest HS
San Diego, CA

Hazari, Niraj
San Lorenzo HS
Hayward, CA

Head, Laura L
Grossmont HS
El Cajon, CA

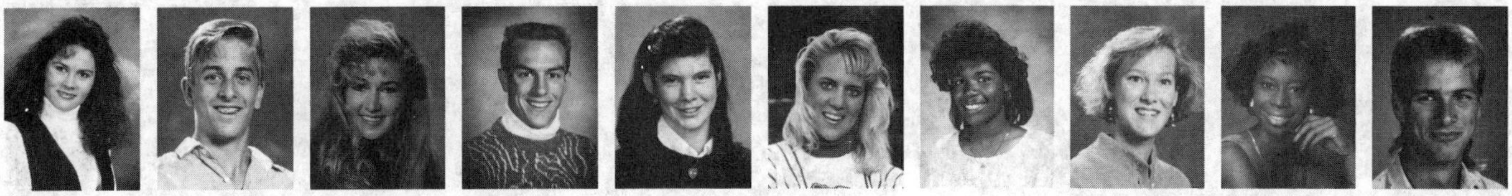

Heal, Kim
Golden Sierra HS
Georgetown, CA

Heal, Kory G
Bonita HS
La Verne, CA

Healy, Lynne
Hawthorne HS
Hawthorne, CA

Healy, Sean M
Weed HS
Weed, CA

Heap, Kelly A
Immaculate Heart
La Crescenta, CA

Heard, Kristi
Upland HS
Upland, CA

Hearne, Quindolyn D
North HS
Riverside, CA

Hearron, Melissa D
Lindsay HS
Lindsay, CA

Hebert, Diane
Lincoln HS
Stockton, CA

Hebrard, Jr Charles
Calaveras HS
San Andreas, CA

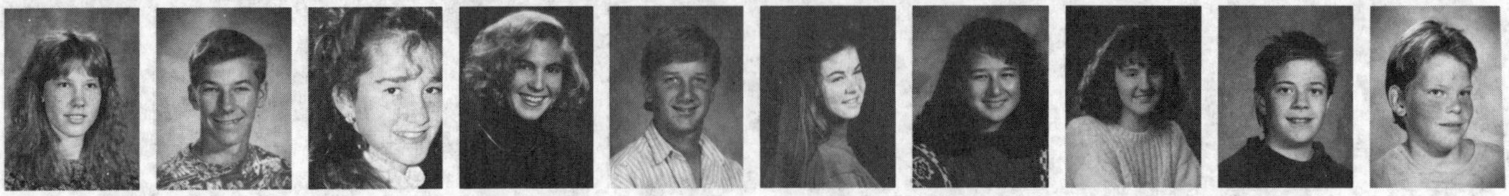

Heckard, Teresa J
Lee Vining HS
June Lake, CA

Hedenberg, Eric J
Fountain Valley HS
Fountain Valley, CA

Hedrick, Kristi
Louisville HS
Northridge, CA

Hegdahl, Heidi Ann
Oakdale HS
Oakdale, CA

Hehle, Andy D
Woodcrest Christian Schl
Riverside, CA

Heidmiller, Karensa
Herbert Hoover HS
San Diego, CA

Heikkinen, Tania M
Dana Hills HS
Laguna Niguel, CA

Heil, Alison
Sonoma Valley HS
Sonoma, CA

Heilig, Chris
San Ramon Valley
San Ramon, CA

Heim, Jr Michael L
Portola JR SR HS
Portola, CA

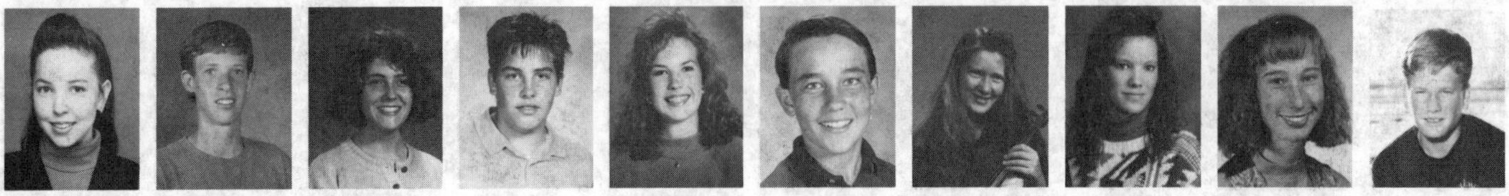

Heimanson, Shelly
Oakwood Schl
Studio City, CA

Heinks, Matthew D
Mt Whitney HS
Visalia, CA

Heiple, Tanya M
Nevada Union HS
Grass Valley, CA

Heitz, Eric S
North Monterey County HS
Salinas, CA

Helbling, Andrea D
Palm Springs HS
Desert Hot Spgs, CA

Helbling, Ryan D
Palm Springs HS
Desert Hot Spring, CA

Helland, Lene-Marie
Hoover HS
Fresno, CA

Helm, Julia
Canyon HS
Santa Clarita, CA

Helman, Jennifer
Benicia HS
Benicia, CA

Helmick, Chris K
San Clemente HS
San Clemente, CA

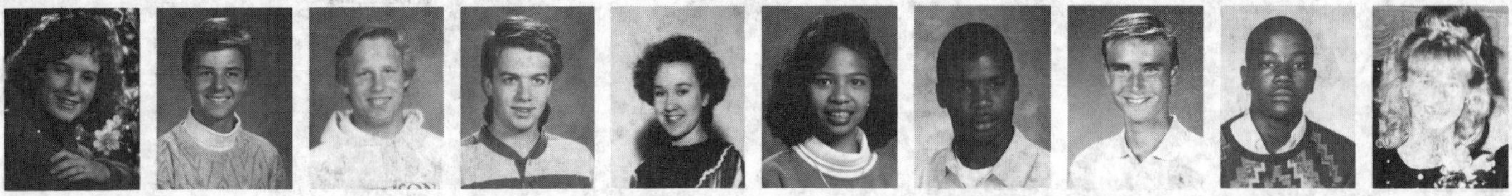

Helms, Heather
Williams HS
Williams, CA

Helton, Derek A
Lutheran HS
Orange, CA

Hembd, Ron L
Redlands HS
Redlands, CA

Hemmings, Ian D
Lutheran HS
Orange, CA

Hemphill, Dani L
Apple Valley HS
Apple Valley, CA

Henares, Yvette P
Etiwanda HS
Alta Loma, CA

Henderson, Devin L
Clairemont HS
San Diego, CA

Henderson, Erik R
Monte Vista HS
Walnut Creek, CA

Henderson, Jr Ernest
Brethren HS
Lynwood, CA

Henderson, Jennifer
Northhills Christian Schl
Vallejo, CA

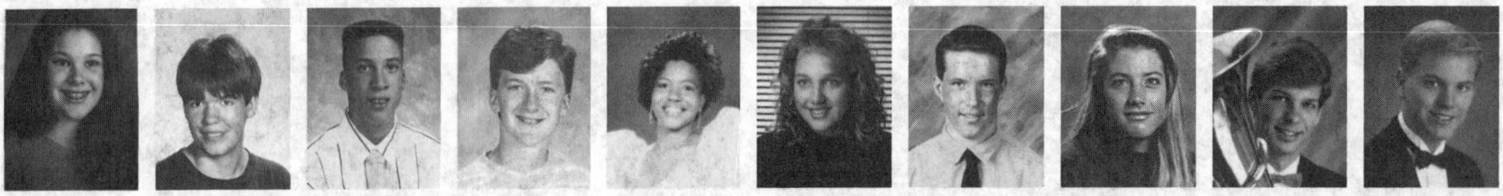

Henderson, Jennifer
Madera HS
Madera, CA

Henderson, John O
Riverside Christian
Pinon Hills, CA

Henderson, Michael
Bishop O'dowd HS
San Leandro, CA

Henderson, Sean
Yosemite HS
Bass Lake, CA

Henderson, Sheli
Crenshaw HS
Los Angeles, CA

Henderson, Sheryl
Valhalla HS
La Mesa, CA

Henderson, Steve
Ambassador Baptist
Rialto, CA

Hendler, Shannon
La Canada HS
La Canada Flintri, CA

Hendley, Joel M
El Dorado HS
Placerville, CA

Hendrickson, Brian D
Analy HS
Sebastopol, CA

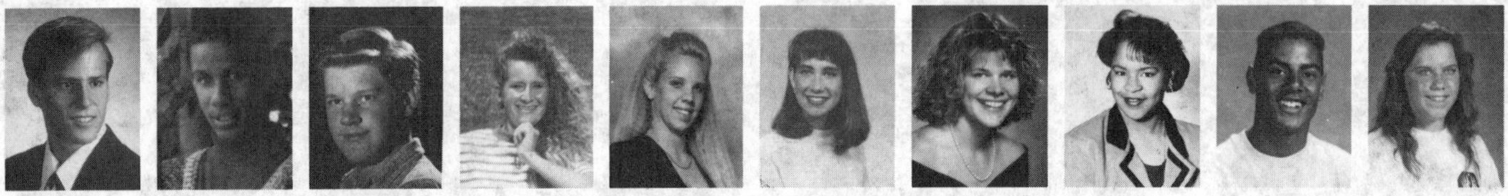

Hendrix, Jason S
Rubidoux HS
Mira Loma, CA

Hendrix, Michael
Bakersfield HS
Bakersfield, CA

Henenfent, Jeff M
Village Christian Schls
Sun Valley, CA

Hengstebeck, Cher L
Tehachapi HS
Tehachapi, CA

Henkel, Rebecca
Chaffey HS
Ontario, CA

Hennemann, Christine E
Mt Whitney HS
Visalia, CA

Henny, Charlene
Chico SR HS
Chico, CA

Henry, Chadeb C
Skyline HS
Oakland, CA

Henry, Christopher
Antioch HS
Antioch, CA

Henry, Tammy
Hemet HS
Hemet, CA

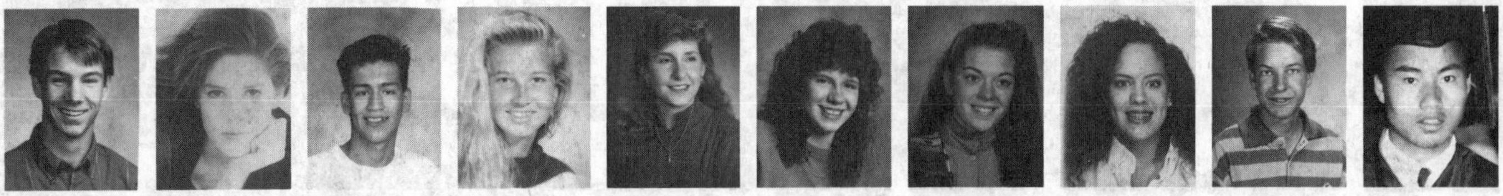

Hensel, Daniel E
Galt HS
Galt, CA

Henshaw, Christina
Moorpark HS
Moorpark, CA

Henshaw, Nathan D
Alvord HS
Riverside, CA

Henshaw, Tanya A
Calabasas HS
Topanga, CA

Hensley, Kassie J
Hemet HS
Hemet, CA

Henson, Jennifer L
Modoc HS
Alturas, CA

Henson, Keturah L
Lone Pine HS
Randsburg, CA

Henson, Susanna
Mater Dei HS
Santa Ana, CA

Heppner, Brent
South Hills HS
Covina, CA

Her, Lee
Merced HS
Merced, CA

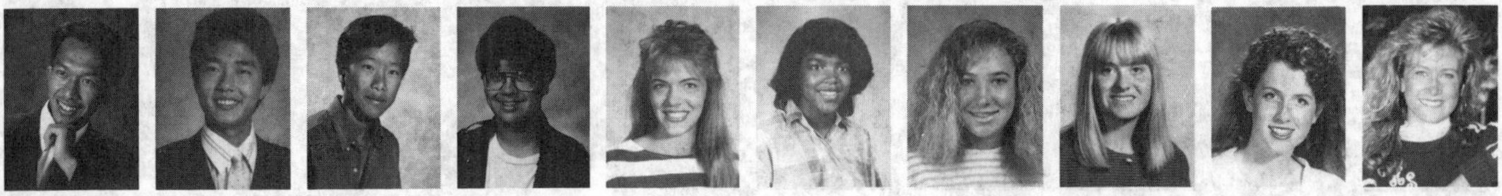

Her, Ong
Duncan Poly HS
Pinedale, CA

Her, Steve
Western HS
Anaheim, CA

Her, Tou B
Turlock HS
Turlock, CA

Herana, Anthony M
Armijo HS
Fairfield, CA

Herb, Wendy
Rosary HS
La Habra, CA

Herbert, Ayana N
Morningside HS
Inglewood, CA

Herbert, Kelly L
Durham HS
Durham, CA

Herbert, Robyn S
San Benito HS
Hollister, CA

Herbert, Valerie T
Notre Dame HS
Carmel, CA

Herbst, Janelle
Ponderosa HS
Placerville, CA

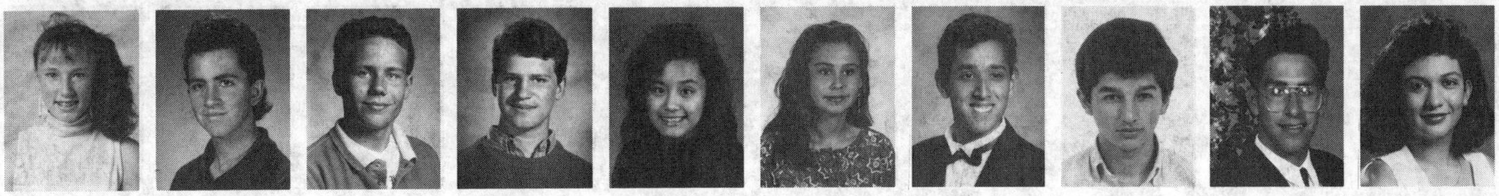

Herdman, Diana L
Torrance HS
Torrance, CA

Heredia, Gustavo E
San Rafael HS
San Rafael, CA

Herman, Mark A
Roseville HS
Rocklin, CA

Hermanski, Greg S
Santa Rosa HS
Santa Rosa, CA

Hermogeno, Lani S
St Joseph HS
Cerritos, CA

Hernandez, Alma
Woodland HS
Woodland, CA

Hernandez, Antonio
La Habra HS
La Habra, CA

Hernandez, Arcelio
Robert A Millikan
Long Beach, CA

Hernandez, Ben C
Los Altos HS
La Puente, CA

Hernandez, Brenda
William Howard Taft
San Fernando, CA

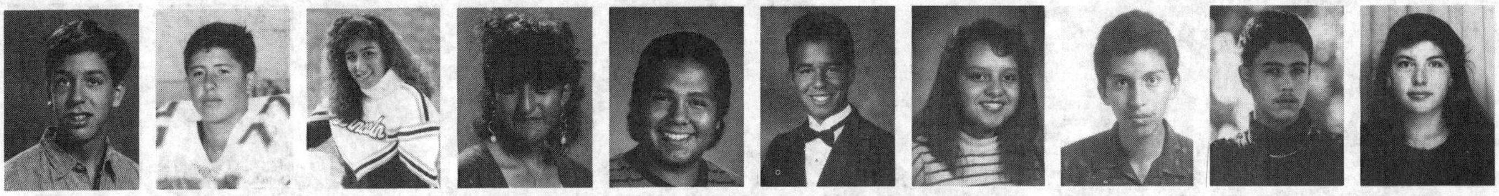

Hernandez, Carlos A
St Francis HS
Altadena, CA

Hernandez, David S
San Dimas HS
San Dimas, CA

Hernandez, Dina
Lincoln HS
Stockton, CA

Hernandez, Elvira
Roosevelt HS
Los Angeles, CA

Hernandez, Gabriel P
Edison HS
Stockton, CA

Hernandez, Gilbert
Bellarmine College Prep
San Jose, CA

Hernandez, Gina E
Norco SR HS
Norco, CA

Hernandez, Israel
Lynwood HS
Lynwood, CA

Hernandez, Jevin A
Palma HS
Salinas, CA

Hernandez, Julia A
Workman HS
Valinda, CA

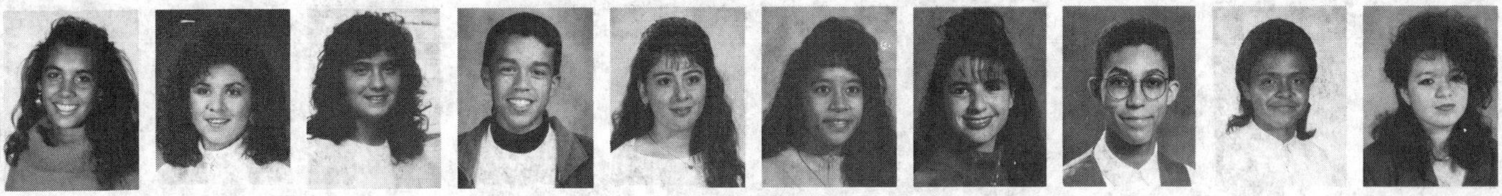

Hernandez, Karen M
Foothill HS
Tustin, CA

Hernandez, Kathy
Christian Center Schl
Antioch, CA

Hernandez, Lee Andrea
Ramona HS
Riverside, CA

Hernandez, Leonard
Hanford Union HS
Hanford, CA

Hernandez, Maria I
Woodland SR HS
Woodland, CA

Hernandez, Michelle
Lemoore HS
Lemoore, CA

Hernandez, Milagros
Culver City HS
Los Angeles, CA

Hernandez, Rayne E
Fontana HS
Bloomington, CA

Hernandez, Ruben M
Roosevelt HS
Fresno, CA

Hernandez, Sandra A
Coachella Valley HS
Thermal, CA

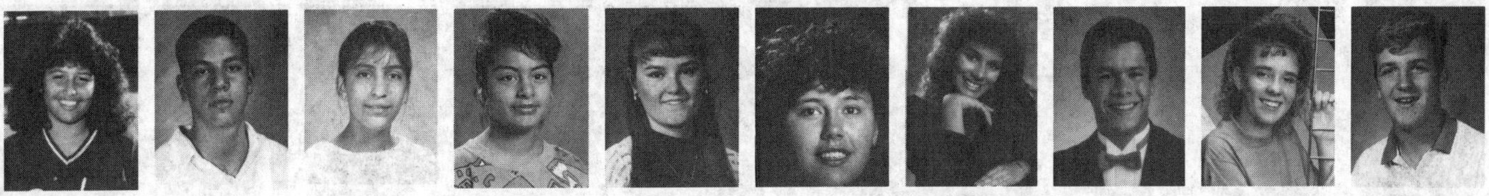

Hernandez, Sari E
Red Bluff HS
Red Bluff, CA

Hernandez, Sean Marciano
Bishop Amat HS
Hacienda Heights, CA

Hernandez, Teresa
Theodore Roosevelt
Los Angeles, CA

Hernandez, Toni
Paso Robles HS
Paso Robles, CA

Hernandez, Troylena
San Jacinto HS
San Jacinto, CA

Hernandez, Viky M
Gardena HS
Gardena, CA

Hernandez, Xochitl C
Mission College Prep
Grover City, CA

Hernandez-Pol, Jose
Leland HS
San Jose, CA

Herndon, Nicole L
La Sierra HS
Riverside, CA

Heropoulos, Angelo C
Bellarmine College Prep
Santa Clara, CA

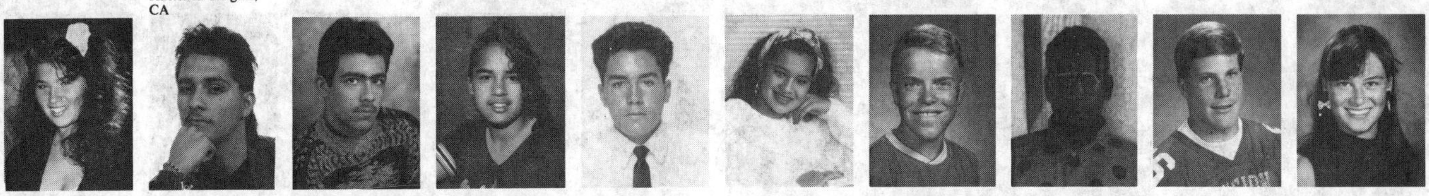

Herren, Gina
Monterey HS
Monterey, CA

Herrera, Adam Marcus
East Bakersfield HS
Bakersfield, CA

Herrera, Carlos R
Redwood HS
Bullhead City, AZ

Herrera, Debra A
Montebello HS
Montebello, CA

Herrera, Fernando
Don Bosco Techinical Inst
Downey, CA

Herrera, Tami
St Anthony HS
Long Beach, CA

Herrington, Patrick
Archbishop Mitty HS
San Jose, CA

Herron, II Ronald Franklin
Palmdale HS
Palmdale, CA

Hershey, Daniel W
Mission San Jose HS
Fremont, CA

Herstoff, Tammy D
Huntington Beach
Huntington Bch, CA

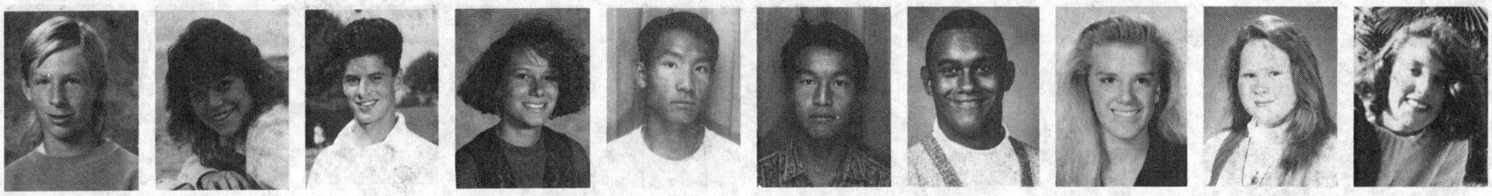

Hervey, Paul R
Dana Hills HS
Laguna Beach, CA

Hesky-Zaknich, Katherine S
North Salinas HS
Salinas, CA

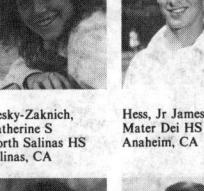

Hess, Jr James C
Mater Dei HS
Anaheim, CA

Hessling, Jennifer A
Desert HS
Edwards, CA

Heu, Chang P
Clovis West HS
Pinedale, CA

Heu, Vang
Edison HS
Pinedale, CA

Hewitt, Bryan W
Grossmont HS
El Cajon, CA

Heyda, Melinda J
Louisville HS
West Hills, CA

Heydt, Margaret A
Albany HS
Albany, CA

Heyfron, Mary
Shasta HS
Redding, CA

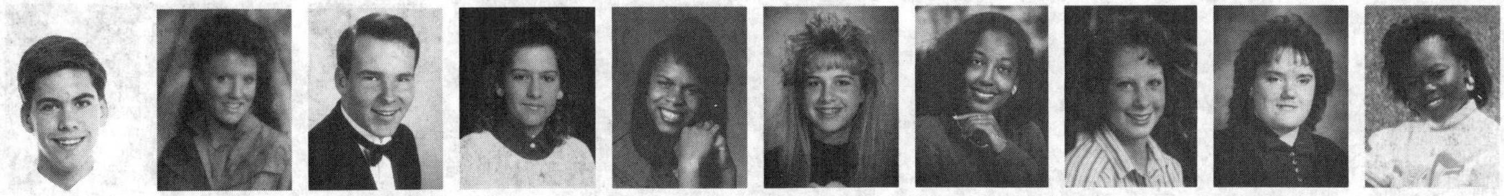

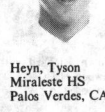

Heyn, Tyson
Miraleste HS
Palos Verdes, CA

Hibbits, Brandee Marie
Lompoc HS
Lompoc, CA

Hibbs, Ross Michael
Marin Catholic HS
Fairfax, CA

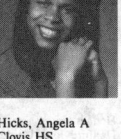

Hickox, Misty L
Temple Christian HS
Quail Valley, CA

Hicks, Angela A
Clovis HS
Clovis, CA

Hicks, Beth A
L A Baptist HS
Spokane, WA

Hicks, Elisha L
Marlborough Schl
Los Angeles, CA

Hicks, Julie A
Forest Lake Christian Schl
Auburn, CA

Hicks, Shannon
Surprise Valley HS
Cedarville, CA

Hicks, Stephanie M
Walnut HS
Walnut, CA

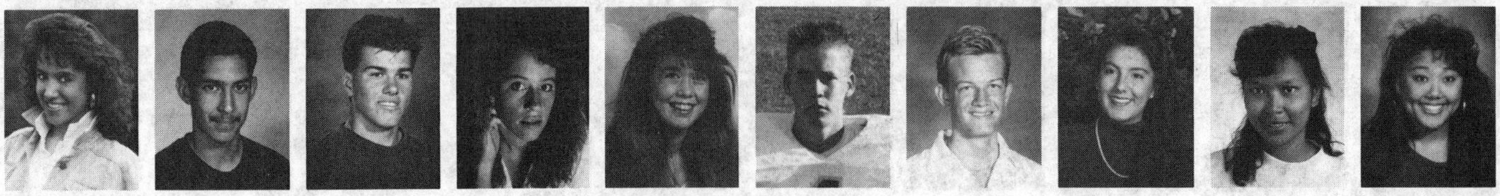

Hicks, Tamara L
North HS
Bakersfield, CA

Hidalgo, Raymond P
Mount Pleasant HS
San Jose, CA

Higbee, Jason P
Shafter HS
Bakersfield, CA

Higginbotham, Jennifer
Wasco Union HS
Wasco, CA

Higgins, Bridgette
Manteca HS
Manteca, CA

Hightower, Jesse B
Mojave HS
Mojave, CA

Higman, Ryan D
Warren HS
Downey, CA

Higuera, Andrea
El Toro HS
El Toro, CA

Hilario, Rachel
St Francis HS
Mountain View, CA

Hilbert, Becky
Strathmore Union HS
Porterville, CA

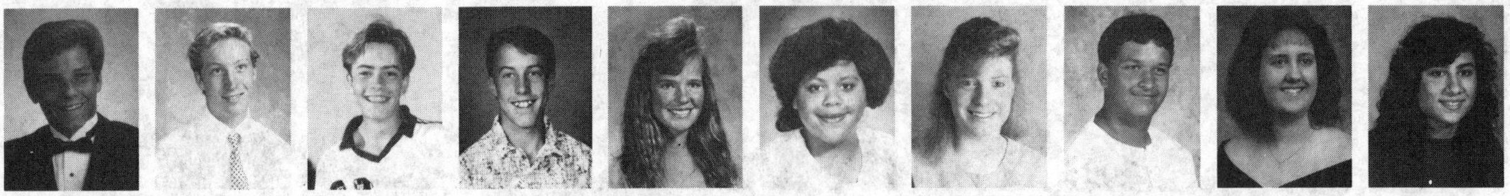

Hildebrand, William
Oak Grove HS
San Jose, CA

Hilger, Les G
Bishop O'dowd HS
Alameda, CA

Hill, Adam E
Wm S Hart HS
Valencia, CA

Hill, Curtis L
Grossmont HS
El Cajon, CA

Hill, Dana
Thousand Oaks HS
Thousand Oaks, CA

Hill, Georgette M
George Washington Preparatory HS
Carson, CA

Hill, Jody
Oxnard HS
Oxnard, CA

Hill, Jr Joe D
Strathmore Union HS
Strathmore, CA

Hill, Kathy L
California HS
San Ramon, CA

Hill, Melissa S
Bullard HS
Fresno, CA

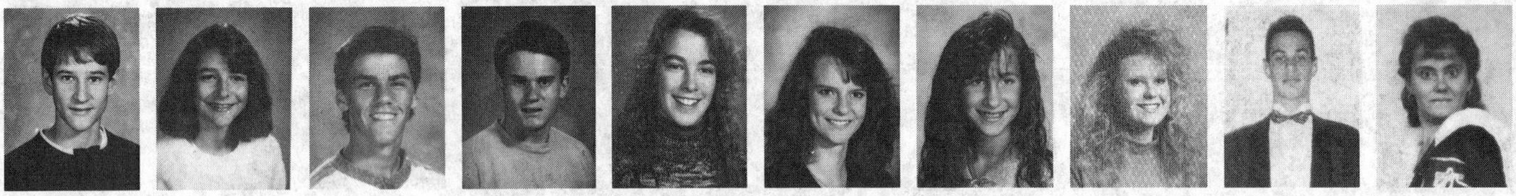

Hill, Ryan C
Homestead HS
Cupertino, CA

Hill, Victoria
Clovis HS
Clovis, CA

Hiller, Elan Wayne
Hoover HS
San Diego, CA

Hilliard, Sean E
Capistrano Valley HS
Mission Viejo, CA

Hilliard, Sharlene M
Antioch HS
Antioch, CA

Hillman, Bonnie A
South HS
Bakersfield, CA

Hills, Melissa
Palm Srpings Christian HS
Desert Hot Sprngs, CA

Hilmen, Karena M
Valhalla HS
La Mesa, CA

Hilo, Johnny R
Baldwin Park HS
Baldwin Park, CA

Hilton, Janice M
El Dorado HS
Diamond Springs, CA

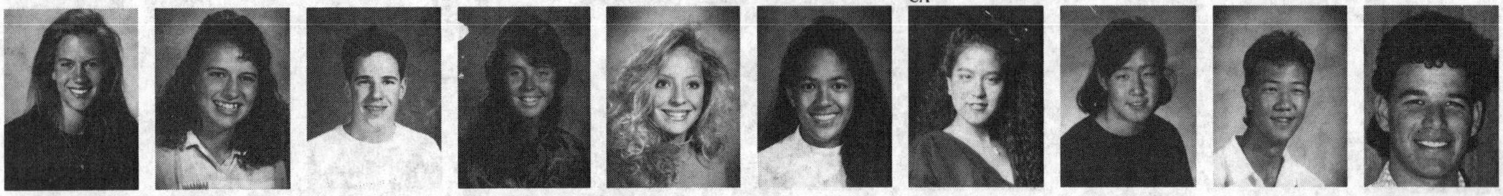

Hinrichs, Brandy
Costa Mesa HS
Santa Ana, CA

Hins, Karen
Kern Valley HS
Weldon, CA

Hinson, Jason R
Hillsdale HS
Foster City, CA

Hinz, Tricia G
Kennedy HS
Buena Park, CA

Hiott, Cherise Y
South HS
Bakersfield, CA

Hipolito, Venus A
Edison HS
Huntington Beach, CA

Hirahara, Tiffani A
Sacramento Country Day Schl
Cameron Park, CA

Hirose, Tara A
Foothill HS
Santa Ana, CA

Hiroshima, Gregory
Sacramento Adventist Acad
Sacramento, CA

Hirsch, Jeremy
Chatsworth HS
Chatsworth, CA

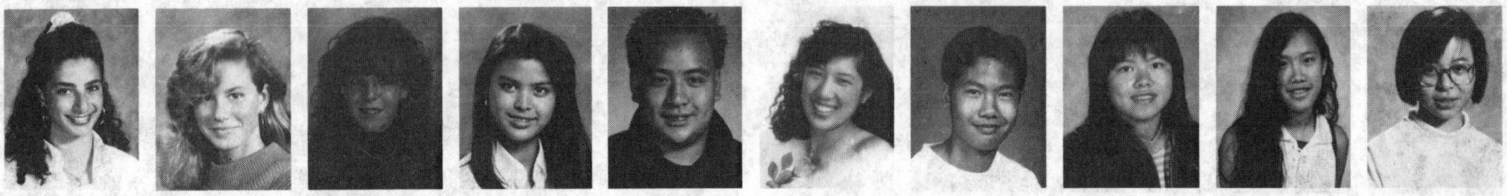

Hishmeh, Juliana
Mercy HS
San Francisco, CA

Hitt, Katherine Lynn
Coronado HS
Coronado, CA

Hixson, Diana A
Apple Valley HS
Apple Vly, CA

Hizon, Jennifer J
Providence HS
Sun Valley, CA

Ho, Andy W
Santa Teresa HS
San Jose, CA

Ho, Cheryl
Los Gatos HS
Los Gatos, CA

Ho, Dan T Estacion
Bellarmine College Prep
San Jose, CA

Ho, Eva
Abraham Lincoln HS
San Francisco, CA

Ho, Jeannette F
St Francis HS
Sacramento, CA

Ho, Jenny W S
A Lincoln HS
San Francisco, CA

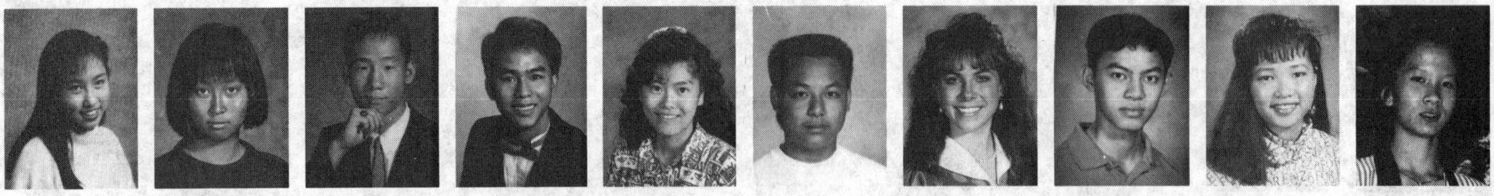

Ho, Kaye K
Pinole Valley HS
Hercules, CA

Ho, Kitty
Fremont Christian
Fremont, CA

Ho, Kurt
Daniel Murphy HS
Los Angeles, CA

Ho, Lan Sy
Davis SR HS
Davis, CA

Ho, Thao P
Kearny HS
San Diego, CA

Ho, Wayne
Santa Teresa HS
San Jose, CA

Hoadley, Renee Michelle
Sacramento HS
Sacramento, CA

Hoang, Dinh T
North Hollywood HS
North Hollywood, CA

Hoang, Geneva
Western HS
Anaheim, CA

Hoang, Linh Trang N
Santa Ana HS
Santa Ana, CA

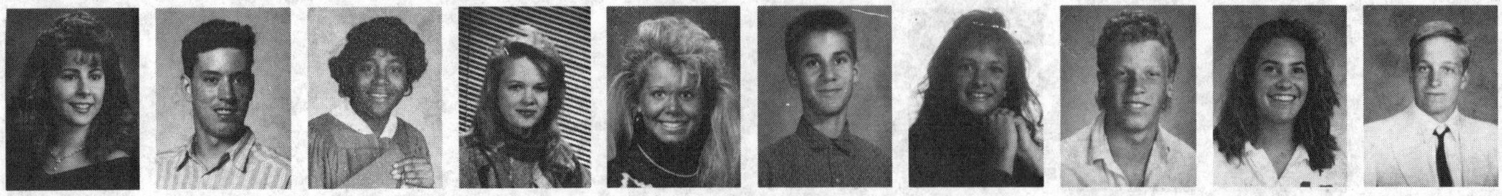

Hobbs, Karen
Liberty Union HS
Brentwood, CA

Hoch, Sean R
Ontario HS
Ontario, CA

Hocher, Liliana
Lynwood Adventist Acad
Los Angeles, CA

Hocking, Diane E
Victor Valley HS
Victorville, CA

Hodge, Rebecca
El Toro HS
El Toro, CA

Hodges, Jason
Hanford Joint Union
Hanford, CA

Hodges, Marci L
Clovis West HS
Clovis, CA

Hodges, Wes
Tokay HS
Lodi, CA

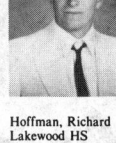

Hoff, Jennifer A
St Francis HS
Los Altos, CA

Hoffman, Richard
Lakewood HS
Lakewood, CA

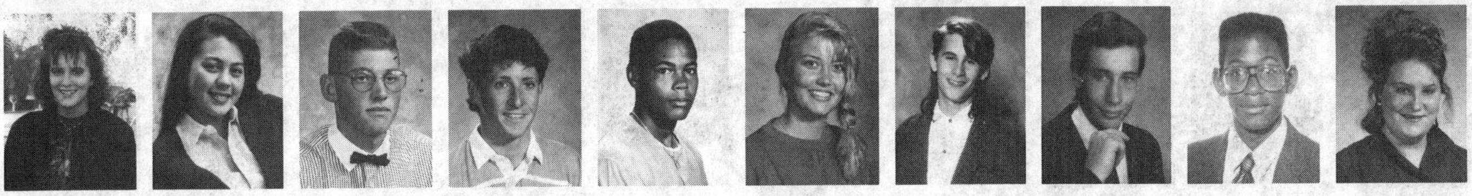

Hofmann, Daniela
Canyon Springs HS
West Germany

Hofmann, Satomi E
San Domenico Schl
San Anselmo, CA

Hofmann, Thad J
St Joseph-Notre Dame HS
Alameda, CA

Hogan, Jack
Corona Del Mar HS
Balboa Island, CA

Hogan, Kevin
Carson HS
Carson, CA

Hogan, Kristi
Highlands HS
N Highlands, CA

Hogan, Matthew
Poway HS
Carlsbad, CA

Hogan, Steve
Lodi HS
Woodbridge, CA

Hogarth, Tarik J
Daniel Murphy HS
Los Angeles, CA

Hohenberge, Julie A
Thomas Downey HS
Modesto, CA

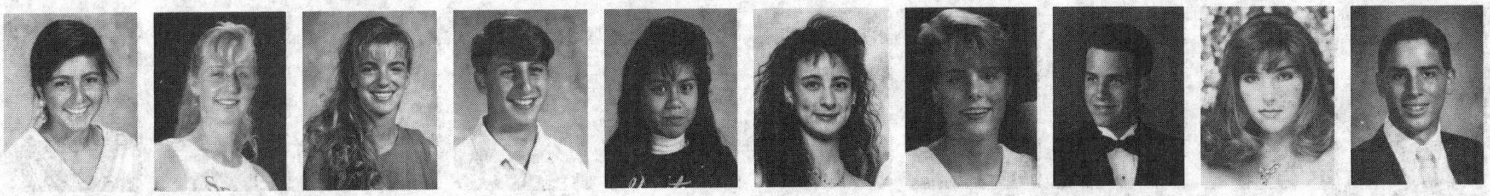

Hokmabadi, Sepideh
Woodside HS
Menlo Park, CA

Holaway, Julie
Saint Bonaventure
Ventura, CA

Holbus, Erin N
St Francis HS
Carmichael, CA

Holcomb, Matthew R
Lompoc HS
Lompoc, CA

Holgado, Sharita A
Pinole Valley HS
Hercules, CA

Holguin, Denise M
Chino HS
Victorville, CA

Holland, Charity T
Encinal HS
Dallas, TX

Holland, Mike W
Bonita Vista HS
Bonita, CA

Holley, Jennifer
Tulare Western HS
Tulare, CA

Holliday, Erick B
Mater Dei HS
Westminster, CA

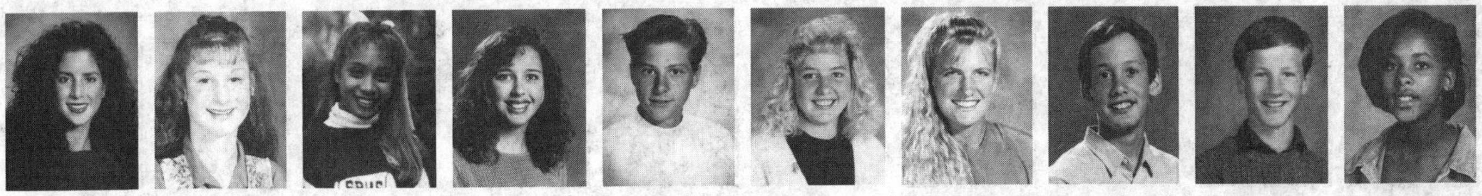

Holliday, Karen
Mater Dei HS
Westminster, CA

Hollis, Michelle
Alameda HS
Alameda, CA

Holloway, Marilynn
St Paul HS
Whittier, CA

Holly, Allison
Porterville HS
Porterville, CA

Holm, Chirstopher D
Paraclete HS
Lancaster, CA

Holm, Stasha
Washington Union
Fresno, CA

Holman, Brita
Orangewood Adventist Acad
La Habra, CA

Holman, Donald E
Bonita HS
La Verne, CA

Holmes, Ian E
Mt Whitney HS
Visalia, CA

Holmes, Kamilah
San Diego HS
San Diego, CA

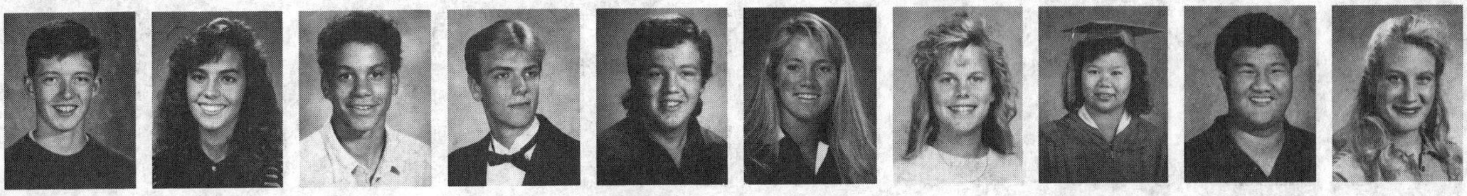

Holmes, Kevin M
College Park HS
Martinez, CA

Holmes, Michelle T
Albany HS
Albany, CA

Holmes, Walter L
Temecula Valley HS
Murrieta, CA

Holsopple, Russell D
Sunset HS
Hayward, CA

Holt, David J
Merced HS North
Merced, CA

Holt, Tracey
El Toro HS
El Toro, CA

Holtz, Dawn
Wheatland Union HS
Beale A. F. B., CA

Hom, Doris S
John Muir HS
Pasadena, CA

Hom, Timothy
George Washington
San Francisco, CA

Homar, Lisa Renee
Hesperia HS
Hesperia, CA

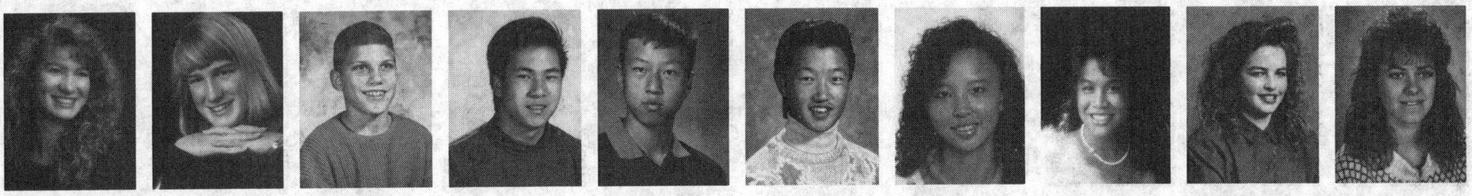

Hon, Deborah
Capistrano Valley Christian HS
S Laguna, CA

Hon, Kim
Capistrano Valley Christian HS
S Laguna, CA

Honea, Ryan
Wasco Union HS
Wasco, CA

Hong, Albert K
Abraham Lincoln HS
San Francisco, CA

Hong, Richard B
Sunny Hills HS
Buena Park, CA

Hong, Sam S
Andrew Hill HS
San Jose, CA

Hong, San A
Gardena HS
Gardena, CA

Honrado, Kimberly-Teresa I
Mercy HS
Daly City, CA

Hood, Beckie
Orange Glen HS
Escondido, CA

Hood, Jennifer
Mariposa County HS
Coulterville, CA

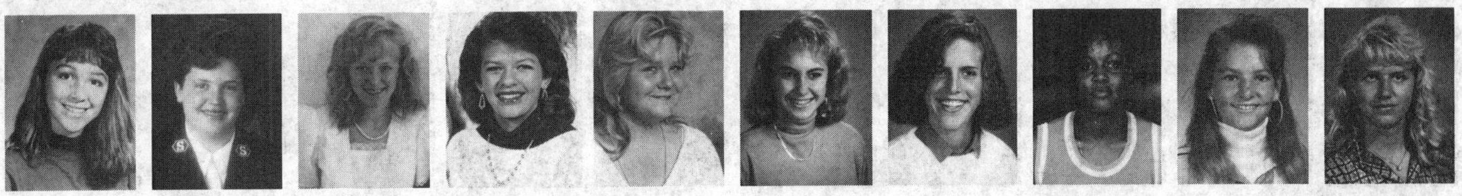

Hood, Jennifer A
Homestead HS
Sunnyvale, CA

Hood, Jennifer H
Montgomery HS
Santa Rosa, CA

Hooge, Heidi
Turlock HS
Turlock, CA

Hooker, Melissa L
Roseville HS
Sacramento, CA

Hoover, Angel M
Montecito HS
Ramona, CA

Hopelian, Daniele L
Clovis HS
Clovis, CA

Hopkins, Shannon C
Riverbank HS
Riverbank, CA

Hopkins, Yavonda V Renee
Luther Burbank HS
Sacramento, CA

Hopper, Jeanette L
Bonita Vista HS
Chula Vista, CA

Hopper, Jessica Lynne
Buena Park HS
Fullerton, CA

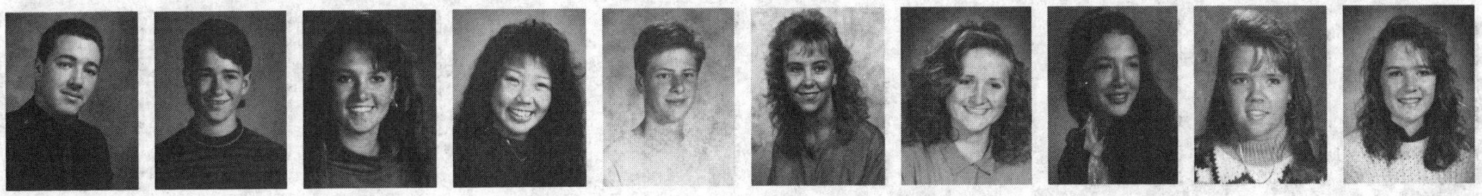

Hopping, Paul A
Covina HS
W Covina, CA

Horder, Che
Clovis HS
Clovis, CA

Horder, Michelle
Clovis HS
Clovis, CA

Horita, Misa
Lincoln HS
Stockton, CA

Horr, Caine
Analy HS
Sebastopol, CA

Horton, Holly M
Orange Glen HS
Escondido, CA

Horton, Karen L
Portoloa JR-SR HS
Portola, CA

Horton, Megan
Rim Of The World
Cedarpines Park, CA

Horton, Melanie
Clayton Valley HS
Clayton, CA

Horvath, Shannon D
Montgomery HS
Santa Rosa, CA

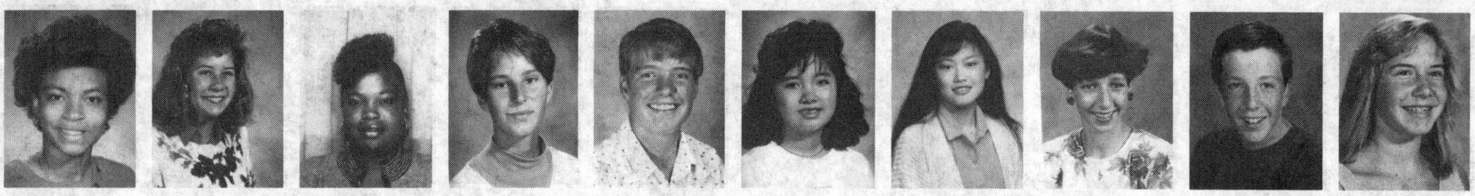

Hosea, Stacy D
George Washington
Prep HS
Los Angeles, CA

Hoskin, Kimberly J
Redwood Christian
San Leandro, CA

Hossum, Rebecca
Valley Alternative
Magnet Schl
Los Angeles, CA

Hostetler, Saskia E
Torrey Pines HS
Del Mar, CA

Hostetter, Geoffrey D
Bishop Amat
Memorial HS
San Dimas, CA

Hou, Ravina
Katella HS
Anaheim, CA

Hou, Renee J
Saratoga HS
Saratoga, CA

Houchins, Dawn
Granite Hills HS
El Cajon, CA

Houghtaling, Jack S
San Pasqual HS
Escondido, CA

Houghton, Sarah A
Atascadero HS
Atascadero, CA

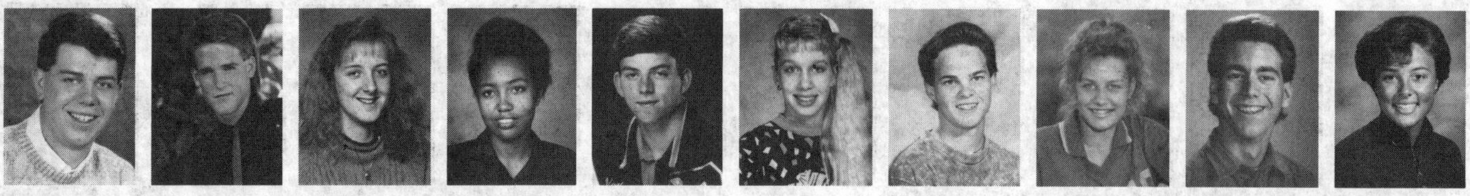

Houlding, Scott C
Madera HS
Madera, CA

Houston, John C
Ventura HS
Ventura, CA

Houston, Mortisha Y
Alhambra HS
Martinez, CA

Houston, Olga
El Cajon Valley HS
El Cajon, CA

Houx, Nathan G
Thomas Downey HS
Modesto, CA

Hovde, Heather L
Woodcrest Christian
Perris, CA

Hovore, Tom
Canyon HS
Canyon Country, CA

Howard, Christine A
Bishop Amat
Memorial HS
Glendora, CA

Howard, Christopher
Clovis HS
Clovis, CA

Howard, Debbie K
Edison HS
Huntington Beach,
CA

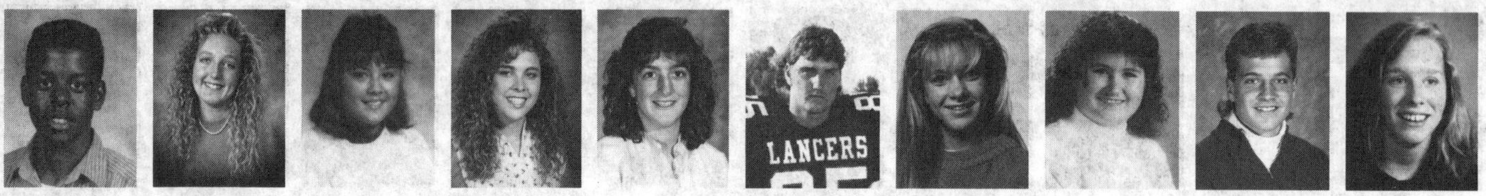

Howard, John
Brethren HS
Long Beach, CA

Howard, Lisa Lynn
Clovis West HS
Clovis, CA

Howard, Samantha
Southwest HS
San Diego, CA

Howard, Theresa
North HS
Bakersfield, CA

Howder, Christy M
Colfax HS
Colfax, CA

Howe, Fred S
Cordova HS
Rancho Cordova, CA

Howell, Angelique
Woodrow Wilson HS
Long Beach, CA

Howell, Jennifer K
Fontana HS
Fontana, CA

Howell, Scott E
Pioneer HS
San Jose, CA

Howland, Alison M
Sonora HS
Columbia, CA

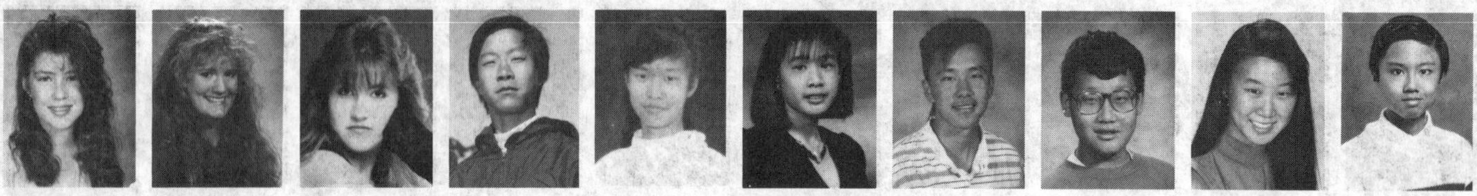

Hoy, Holly A
Alverno HS
Sierra Madre, CA

Hoyt, Crystal L
Victor Valley HS
Victorville, CA

Hrynkiewicz, Joann
Saint Bernards HS
Eureka, CA

Hsiao, Jeffrey
Lowell HS
San Francisco, CA

Hsiao, Myrna
Lowell HS
San Francisco, CA

Hsiung, Daisy
John A Rowland HS
Rowland Heights, CA

Hsu, Donald I
John F Kennedy HS
Cypress, CA

Hsu, Tony
University HS
Irvine, CA

Hu, Tiffany
Los Altos HS
Hacienda Hgts, CA

Hua, David Du-Vinh
Bassett HS
La Puente, CA

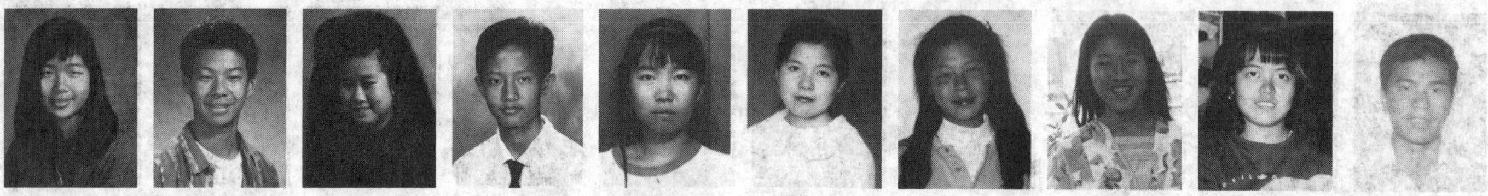

Hua, Vanessa
Miramonte HS
Orinda, CA

Huang, David L
Laguna Hills HS
Laguna Hills, CA

Huang, Elaine P
Pacifica HS
Garden Grove, CA

Huang, Harry
Herbert
San Bernardino HS
San Bernardino, CA

Huang, Helen
Sacramento HS
Sacramento, CA

Huang, Jiena
Abraham Lincoln HS
San Francisco, CA

Huang, Nancy S
James Russell Lowell
San Francisco, CA

Huang, Qizhao
George Washington
San Francisco, CA

Huang, Shau-Win
Amy
The Athenian Schl
Danville, CA

Huang, Wei Y
Chaffey HS
Ontario, CA

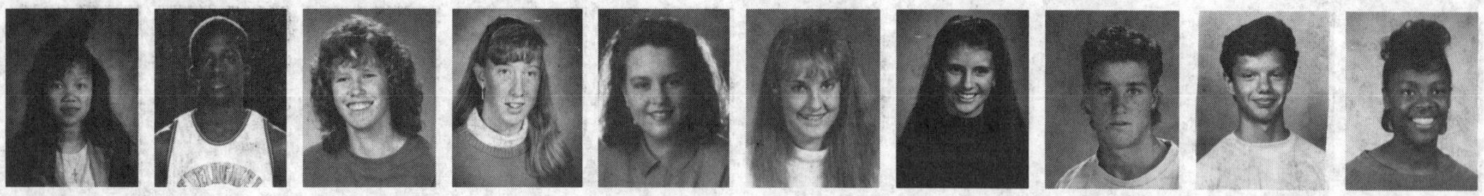

Huang, Yanxiao
Balboa HS
Daly City, CA

Hubbard, Albert D
Leffingwell Christian
Los Angeles, CA

Hubbard, Leslie G
Pittsburg HS
Pittsburg, CA

Hubbell, Janette
North HS
Bakersfield, CA

Huber, Amy E
Santa Barbara HS
Santa Barbara, CA

Huber, Beth
Valley Christian HS
San Jose, CA

Huber, Lori-Marie
Atwater HS
Atwater, CA

Huberts, Jeffrey
San Marcos HS
Vista, CA

Hudson, Drew S
Valhalla HS
El Cajon, CA

Hudson, Ja Cinta
Golden Gate Acad
Vallejo, CA

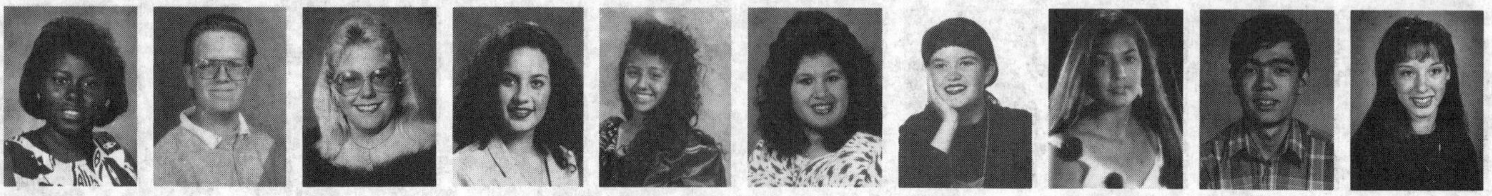

Hudson, Lynette P
Bonita HS
La Verne, CA

Hudson, Robert W
Redlands HS
Redlands, CA

Hudson, Theresa L
Calipatria HS
Calipatria, CA

Huerta, Emilia
Garfield HS
Los Angeles, CA

Huerta, Joyce J
Coachella Valley HS
Indio, CA

Huerta, Melissa
Mt Whitney HS
Goshen, CA

Huff, Jennifer L
Prospect HS
San Jose, CA

Huffman, Andrea
Santa Maria HS
Santa Maria, CA

Huffman, David K
Fortuna Union HS
Fortuna, CA

Huffman, Kristi M
Clovis West HS
Fresno, CA

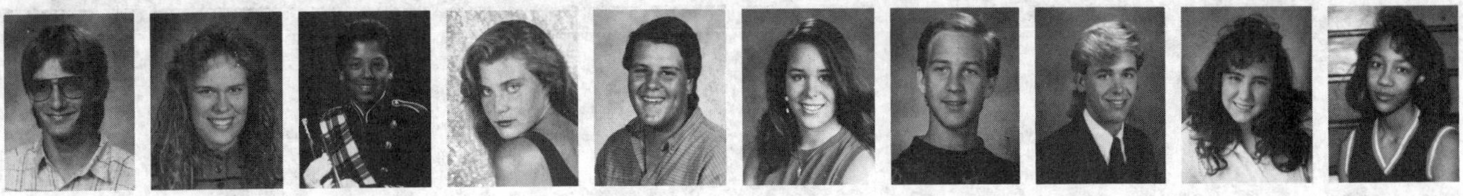

Huffmaster, Andrew
Fairfield HS
Suisun City, CA

Huffmaster, Sally
Maxwell HS
Maxwell, CA

Hughes, Aaron J
John F Kennedy HS
Cypress, CA

Hughes, Allison
Loara HS
Anaheim, CA

Hughes, Eric C
San Diego Acad
Imperial Beach, CA

Hughes, Heather K
San Pasqual HS
Escondido, CA

Hughes, Jason
El Toro HS
El Toro, CA

Hughes, Jeffrey M
Rio Lindo Adventist Acad
Napa, CA

Hughes, Jennifer
William S Hart HS
Newhall, CA

Hughes, Nicole R
Sunset HS
Hayward, CA

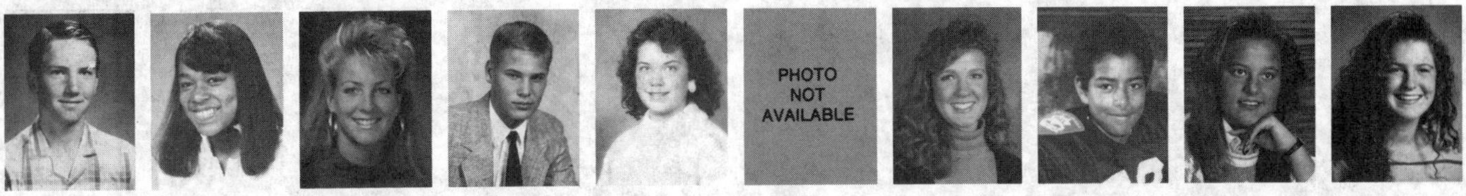

PHOTO
NOT
AVAILABLE

Hughes, III Paul R
Sierra Vista HS
Baldwin Park, CA

Hughes, Romi G
Pinole Valley HS
Hercules, CA

Hughes, Shannon L
El Toro HS
El Toro, CA

Hughes, Travis J
Canyon Springs HS
Moreno Valley, CA

Hugo, Vanessa A
Redlands HS
Highland, CA

Hui, Wendy T
George Washington
San Francisco, CA

Huibregtse, Wendy K
Redlands HS
Redlands, CA

Huizar, Lucas
Southbay Christian
Milpitas, CA

Hulsey, Jennifer
La Sierra HS
Riverside, CA

Hultberg, Becki
Carondelet HS
Martinez, CA

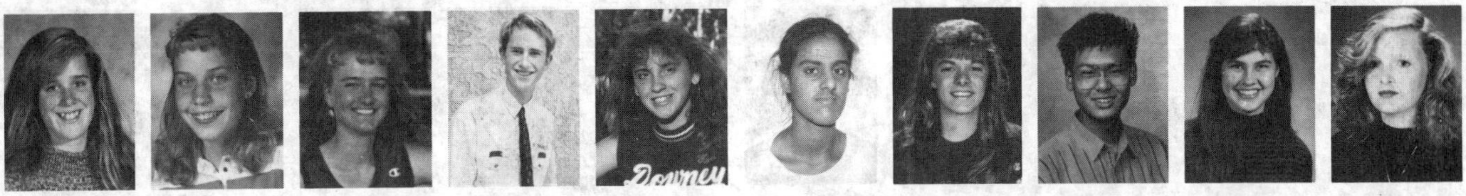

Humbert, Megan J
Santa Ynez Valley Union HS
Buellton, CA

Hummel, Chelsea D
Fall River JR SR HS
Fall River Mills, CA

Humphrey, Elizabeth
Manteca HS
Manteca, CA

Humphrey, Nathan J
Woodcrest Christian Schl
Riverside, CA

Humphries, Kara
Downey HS
Downey, CA

Hundal, Gurpreet K
Beyer HS
Modesto, CA

Hundley, Christi
Westminster HS
Westminster, CA

Hung, Peter W
San Diego HS
San Diego, CA

Hunga, Nicole M
Central Union HS
El Centro, CA

Hunn, Angela
Liberty HS
Oakley, CA

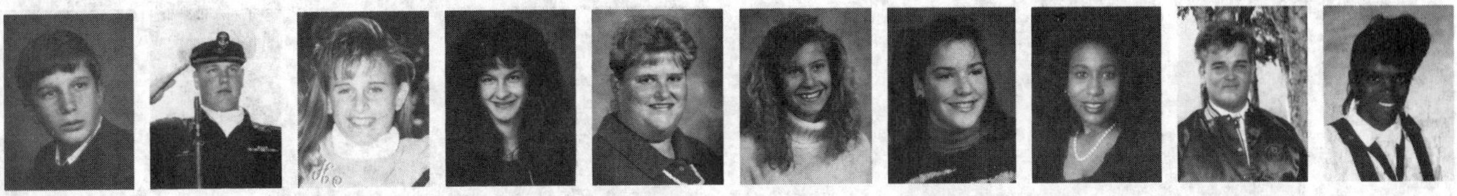

Hunsherger, Allen R
Ramona HS
Ramona, CA

Hunt, David R
Milpitas HS
Milpitas, CA

Hunt, Heather
Ponderosa HS
Shingle Springs, CA

Hunt, Karyn M
El Cajon Valley HS
El Cajon, CA

Hunt, Laura
Reedley HS
Reedley, CA

Hunt, Sarah
Center HS
Elverta, CA

Hunt, Teresa M
Bishop O'dowd HS
Oakland, CA

Hunter, April M
Diamond Bar HS
Diamond Bar, CA

Hunter, Barry John
Southwest HS
San Diego, CA

Hunter, Inedra
Rialto JR HS
San Bernardino, CA

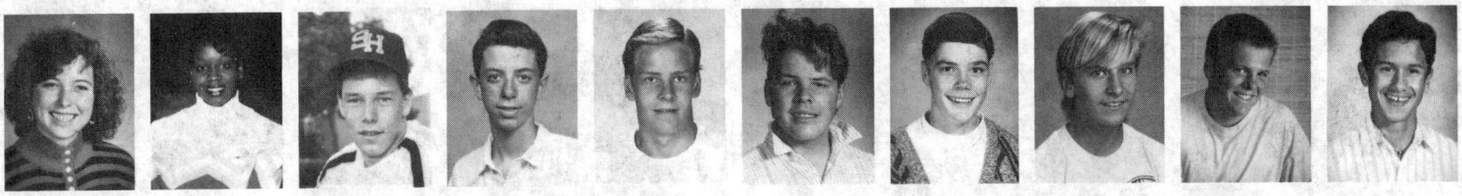

Hunter, Kelly A
Atwater HS
Atwater, CA

Hunter, Marnie
Santiago HS
Santa Ana, CA

Hunter, Michael A
Sunny Hills HS
Fullerton, CA

Hupf, Christopher P
Saint Anthony HS
Garden Grove, CA

Hurd, Jason W
Los Altos HS
Hacienda Hgts, CA

Hurley, Jon-Mark
North Monterey County HS
Salinas, CA

Hurley, Joshua
Portola JR SR HS
Portola, CA

Hurst, Kenneth W
Napa HS
Napa, CA

Hurst, Paul P
Shasta HS
Redding, CA

Hurtado, Jr Jose Miguel
Vanden HS
Travis A F B, CA

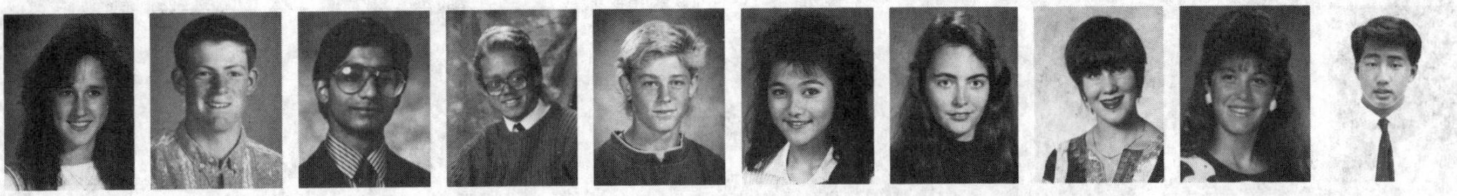

Hurte, Heather S
Oroville HS
Oroville, CA

Hurtgen, Richey
Oakdale HS
Oakdale, CA

Husain, Zeeshan S
West Torrance HS
Houston, TX

Huston, Uriah J
El Camino HS
Oceanside, CA

Hutcheon, Scott L
Edison HS
Huntington Bch, CA

Hutcherson, Stephanie S
St Joseph HS
La Palma, CA

Huth, Hillary H
George Washington
San Francisco, CA

Hutton, Christina
Chaffey HS
Ontario, CA

Hutzler, Alicia
Sunny Hills HS
Fullerton, CA

Huynh, Duc
Gardena HS
Gardena, CA

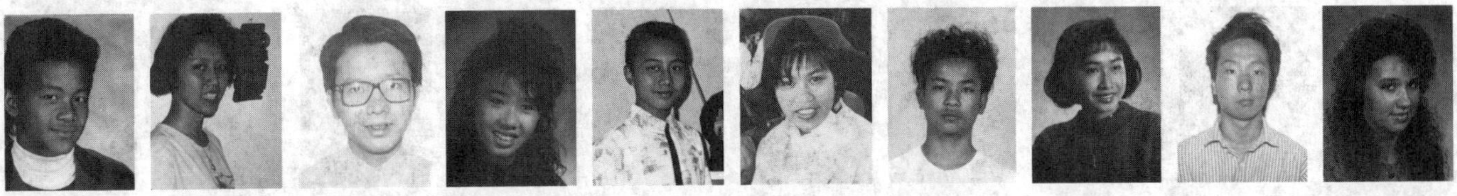

Huynh, Edward
Bellarmine College Prep
San Jose, CA

Huynh, Josephine Y
Mt Diablo HS
W Pittsburg, CA

Huynh, Minh T
Alameda HS
Alameda, CA

Huynh, Ngoc T
Arlington HS
Riverside, CA

Huynh, Stephen M
Mt Diablo HS
W Pittsburg, CA

Huynh, Thuy Giang
Calvin Simmons HS
Oakland, CA

Huynh, Toan N
San Gabriel HS
San Gabriel, CA

Huynh, Truc
Hoover HS
Fresno, CA

Hwang, Tim
John Burroughs HS
Burbank, CA

Hyde, Tina C
Bloomington HS
Bloomington, CA

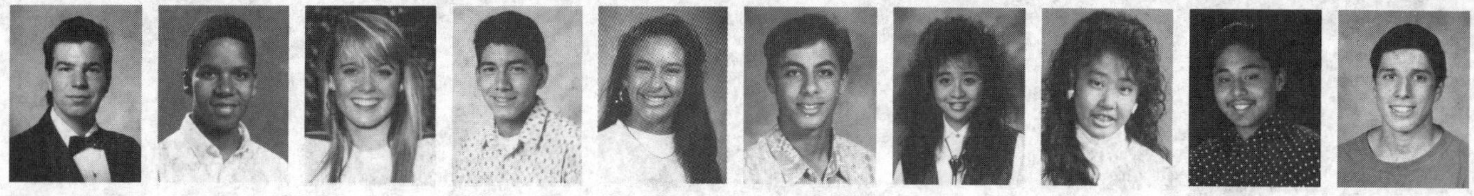

Hyman, Daniel
Claremont HS
Claremont, CA

Hyson, Chad E
Etiwanda HS
Alta Loma, CA

Iba, Elizabeth J
Santa Monica HS
Santa Monica, CA

Ibarra, Luis A
Castle Park HS
Chula Vista, CA

Ibarra, Rachel A
Whitcomb HS
Glendora, CA

Ibrahim, Yahya
Los Alamitos HS
Los Alamitos, CA

Icarangal, Lily
Fairfield HS
Suisun City, CA

Ichiyama, Jodi
Bishop Montgomery
Torrance, CA

Igano, Gale H
Arroyo HS
San Lorenzo, CA

Iglesias, Alberto J
El Camino HS
Sacramento, CA

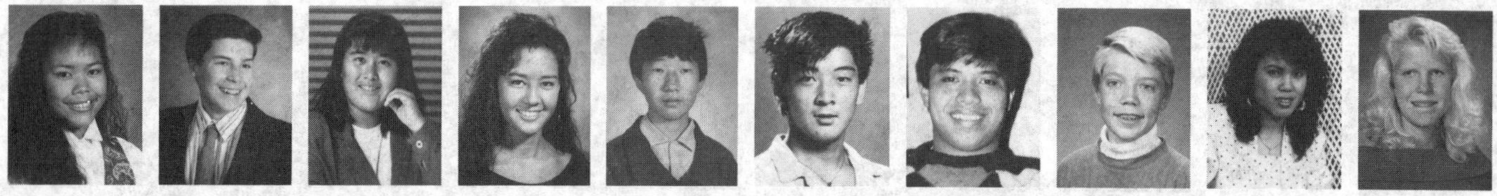

Ignacio, Melanie
South San Francisco
South San Francis, CA

Ill, Brian A
San Gorgonio HS
Highland, CA

Imai, Ann R
Rosemead HS
Rosemead, CA

Imai, Keri E
Los Amigos HS
Fountain Valley, CA

Imaizumi, Kinya
Arcadia HS
Arcadia, CA

Imoto, Eric
Garfield HS
Monterey Park, CA

Inawat, Bryan Jason
Glendale HS
Fontana, CA

Inda, Sven E
Novato HS
Novato, CA

Ing, Somaly
Woodrow Wilson HS
Long Beach, CA

Ingbretson, Erika L
Trabuco Hills HS
Hansville, WA

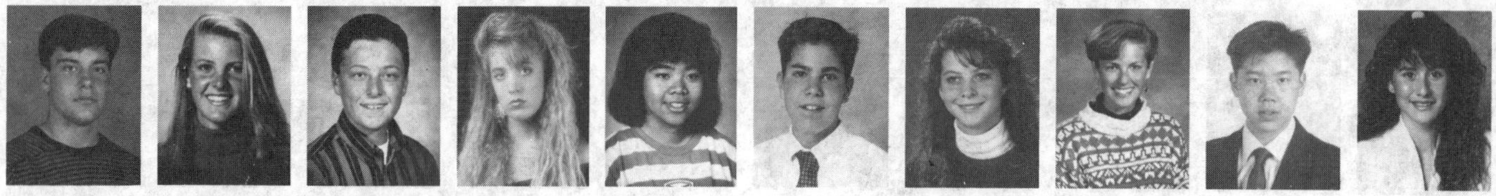

Ingram, Brent
Leffingwell Christian
Lakewood, CA

Ingram, Jennifer
Woodrow Wilson HS
Long Beach, CA

Ingram, Tony A
North HS
Glennville, CA

Inks, Amanda C
Fairfield HS
Fairfield, CA

Inong, Maywell Leones
Edison HS
Stockton, CA

Insalaco, Jason M
Loyola HS
Glendale, CA

Insogna, Alexandra
Calistoga HS
Calistoga, CA

Inwood, Emily M
Fort Bragg HS
Fort Bragg, CA

Ip, Lester S
Servite HS
Monterey Park, CA

Ippoliti, Julie
Hillcrest Christian
Granada Hills, CA

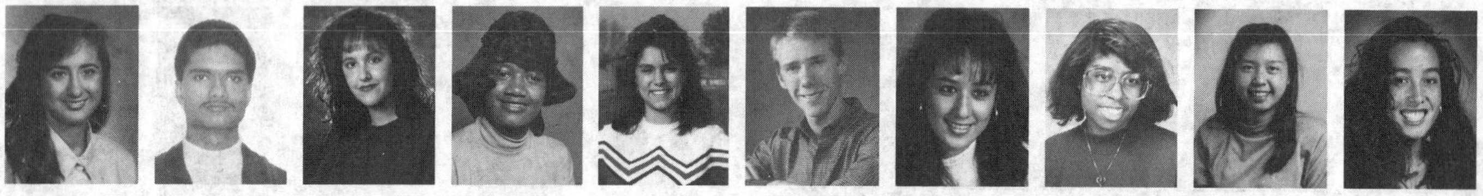

Ira, Jennifer
Del Campo HS
Carmichael, CA

Irfan, Naseer A
Phillip & Sala Burton Academic HS
San Francisco, CA

Irion, Nicole Christine
Paraclete HS
Lancaster, CA

Irving, Druemeka
Pius X HS
Compton, CA

Isaac, Dawn O.
Indio HS
Yuma, AZ

Isaak, Jason
Roosevelt HS
Fresno, CA

Isabel, Veronica
Madera HS
Madera, CA

Isabelle, Deborah I
John F Kennedy HS
Richmond, CA

Isham, Eve
Ernest Righetti HS
Santa Maria, CA

Ishikawa, Noriko H
Edison HS
Huntington Beach, CA

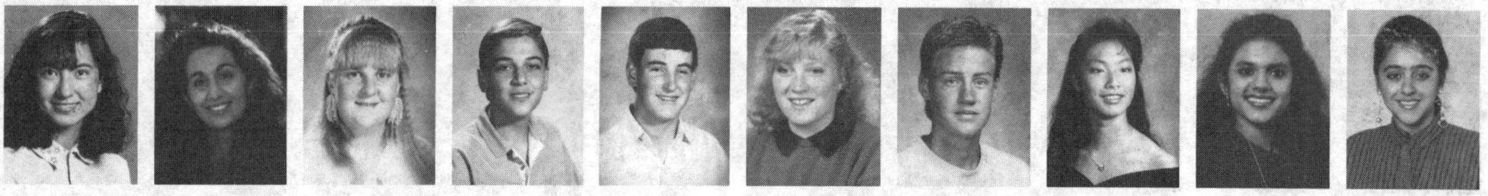

Ishizuka-Capp, Thai
Culver City HS
Culver City, CA

Iskander, Nadine
St Margarets Schl
Capistrano Beach, CA

Israelson, Kimberly D
Edison HS
Huntington Beach, CA

Issagholiantce, Patrick
Herbert Hoover HS
Glendale, CA

Iturriria, Francisco J
North HS
Bakersfield, CA

Iverson, Leisel E
Piedmont HS
Piedmont, CA

Ivey, Paul J
Casa Roble Fundamental HS
Orangevale, CA

Iwamoto, Hiroko
Cupertino HS
Cupertino, CA

Iyer, Sheila
Rosary HS
Fullerton, CA

Izadseta, Parastoo
Corona HS
Corona, CA

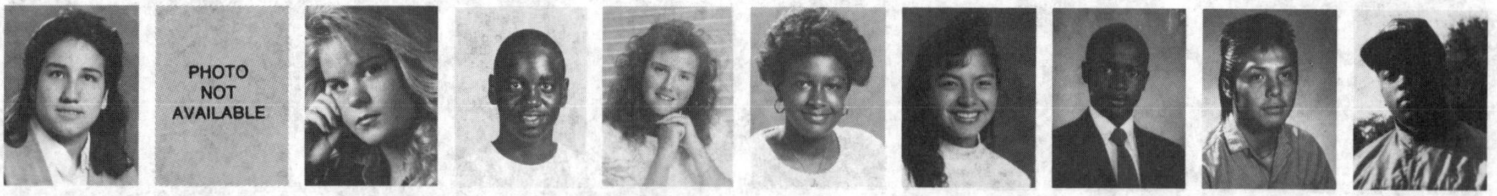
PHOTO
NOT
AVAILABLE

Izquierdo, Alicia D
Providence HS
Burbank, CA

Jackle, Julie M
Huntington Beach
Huntington Beach, CA

Jacks, Rochelle
Gustine HS
Newman, CA

Jackson, Adrian G
Locke HS
Los Angeles, CA

Jackson, Alissa D
River City HS
W Sacramento, CA

Jackson, Amina
Hawthorne HS
Lynwood, CA

Jackson, Anissa
Porterville HS
Porterville, CA

Jackson, Charles B
Palmdale HS
Littlerock, CA

Jackson, Dustin T
San Pasqual HS
Winterhaven, CA

Jackson, Everett
Carlmont HS
East Palo Alto, CA

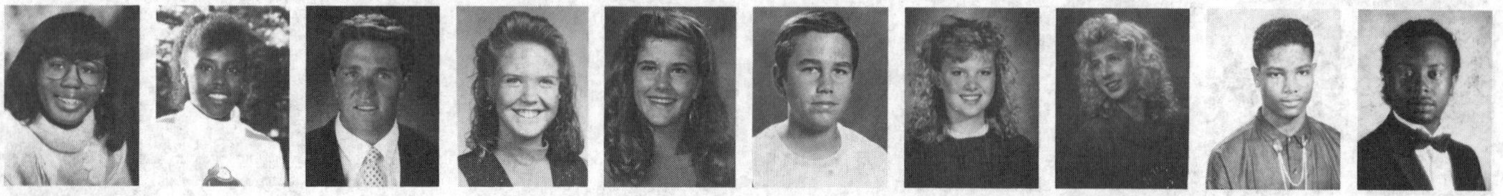

Jackson, Georgia M
Marlborough Schl
Los Angeles, CA

Jackson, Jamie L
Notre Dame HS
San Jose, CA

Jackson, Jeffrey S
Corona Del Mar HS
Newport Beach, CA

Jackson, Jennifer
River City HS
West Sacramento, CA

Jackson, Jill E
El Toro HS
El Toro, CA

Jackson, Jonathan L
Atwater HS
Atwater, CA

Jackson, Joneen V
Kingsburg HS
Kingsburg, CA

Jackson, Julie L
Tulare Union HS
Tulare, CA

Jackson, Micah Dartagnan
Hamilton Music Acad
Los Angeles, CA

Jackson, Ramon S
Eden Christian Acad
Oakland, CA

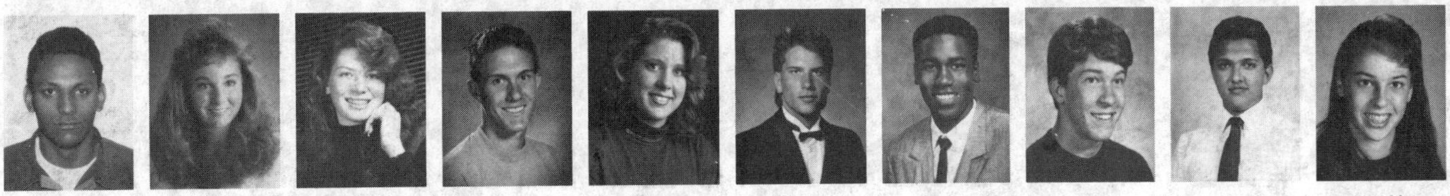

Jackson, Robert
St Bernard HS
Los Angeles, CA

Jackson, Susie
Valley Christian HS
San Jose, CA

Jacob, Erin
Rio Lindo Adventist Acad
Martinez, CA

Jacobs, Glenn
West Covina HS
W Covina, CA

Jacobs, Heather L
Village Christian HS
La Crescenta, CA

Jacobs, Julian K
Pioneer HS
San Jose, CA

Jacobs, Larry
Covina HS
Covina, CA

Jacobs, Royce
Herlong HS
Herlong, CA

Jacobs, Stan J
Adolfo Camarillo HS
Oxnard, CA

Jacobsen, Danielle
Amador Valley HS
Pleasanton, CA

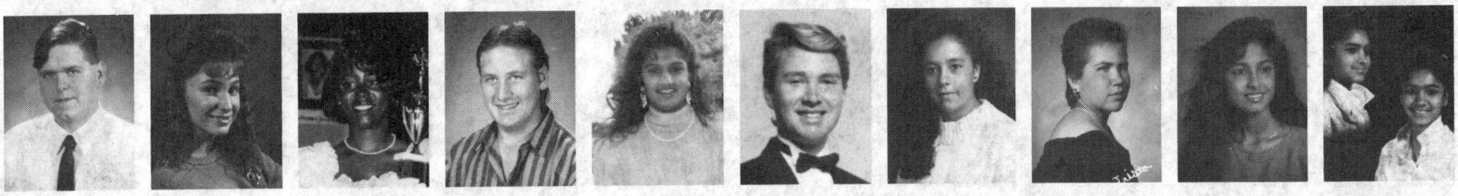

Jacobsen, David
Mt Whitney HS
Visalia, CA

Jacobson, Monique
Capital Christian Schl
Sacramento, CA

Jacquette, Julienne I
Carson HS
Carson, CA

Jacquez, Chris L
Liberty Union HS
Oakley, CA

Jadia, Rosemary R
Fountain Valley HS
Fountain Valley, CA

Jahr, Tom N
Village Christian HS
Tujunga, CA

Jaime, Marta
Glendora HS
Glendora, CA

Jaimes, Trista
Pioneer HS
San Jose, CA

Jain, Kavita
Canyon HS
Anaheim, CA

Jain, Shafali
Hiram W Johnson
Sacramento, CA

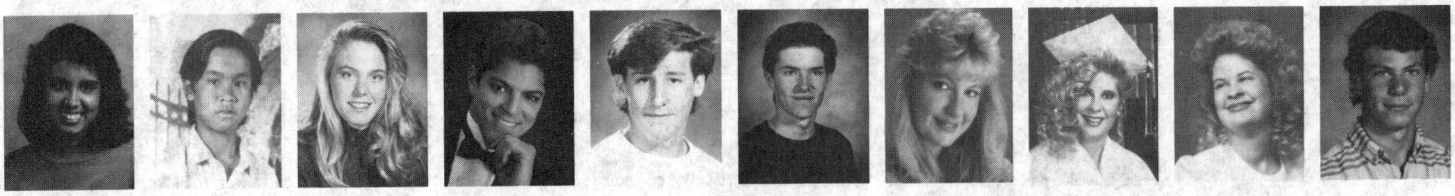

Jaiswal, Anjali
John Burroughs HS
Burbank, CA

Jamanila, II Gabriel
Sweetwater Union
National City, CA

James, Christina L
Villa Park HS
Orange, CA

James, Gary
Analy HS
Sebastopol, CA

James, Greg
Cypress HS
Cypress, CA

James, Jared L
Arvin HS
Arvin, CA

James, Jenean
Sonora HS
Groveland, CA

James, Jennifer W
Fontana HS
Fontana, CA

James, Julianne W
Fontana HS
Fontana, CA

James, Scott W
Willows HS
Willows, CA

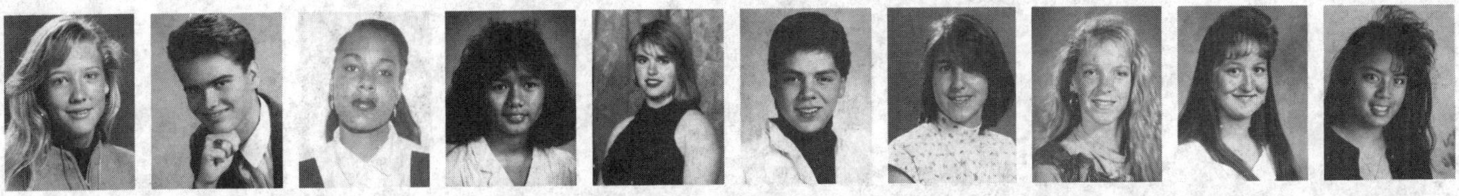

James, Shannon M
Rim Of The World
Fountain Valley, CA

Jameson, Erik Stephen
Walnut HS
Walnut, CA

Jameson, Maisha J
Oakland Technical
Oakland, CA

Jamosmos, Maritess
Edison SR HS
Stockton, CA

Janci, Stephanie A
Armijo HS
Fairfield, CA

Janis, Stephen P
Damien HS
Upland, CA

Janjik, Talin
Herbert Hoover HS
Glendale, CA

Jankowski, Becky
Woodbridge HS
Irvine, CA

Janousek, Jeanette
Royal HS
Simi Valley, CA

Jaramilla, Margaret
Oxnard HS
Oxnard, CA

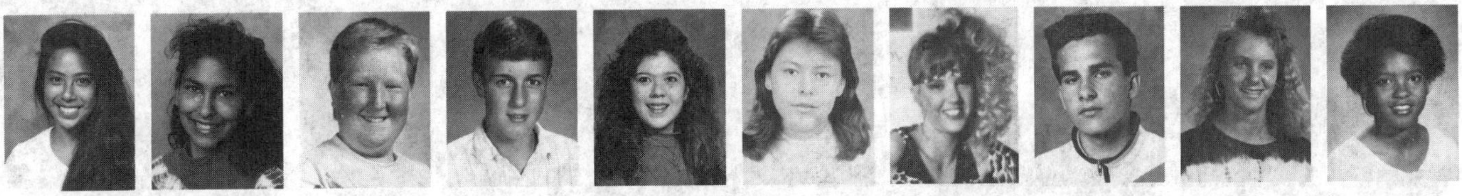

Jaramillo, Jennifer K
University HS
Los Angeles, CA

Jaramillo, Judith A
Ventura HS
Ventura, CA

Jarrell, Jr Nicholas
Foothill SR HS
Sacramento, CA

Jaster, Brent J
Mission San Jose HS
Fremont, CA

Jauregui, Maura R
South San Francisco
S San Francisco, CA

Jauregui, Veronica P
Warren HS
Downey, CA

Jaussaud, Chelsi
Delano HS
Delano, CA

Jazo, David
Castle Park HS
Chula Vista, CA

Jeffcoat, Jessica K
Poway HS
Poway, CA

Jefferson, Tiffani
George Washington Prep HS
Los Angeles, CA

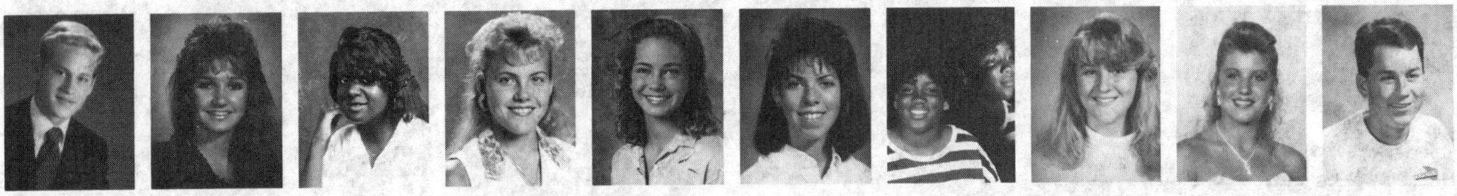

Jeleti, John M
Lincoln HS
Northridge, CA

Jenkins, Danielle La Dean
Los Angeles Baptist
Northridge, CA

Jenkins, Ebone
Westchester HS
Inglewood, CA

Jenkins, Elizabeth
William Howard Taft
Woodland Hills, CA

Jenkins, Kelly Anne
Temecula Valley HS
Murrieta, CA

Jenkins, Michelle A
Mater Dei HS
Fullerton, CA

Jenkins, Natasha D
West Covina HS
West Covina, CA

Jenkinson, Danette A
St Bernard HS
Eureka, CA

Jenks, Amber
Quartz Hill HS
Rosamond, CA

Jennings, Brian E
Moorpark HS
Moorpark, CA

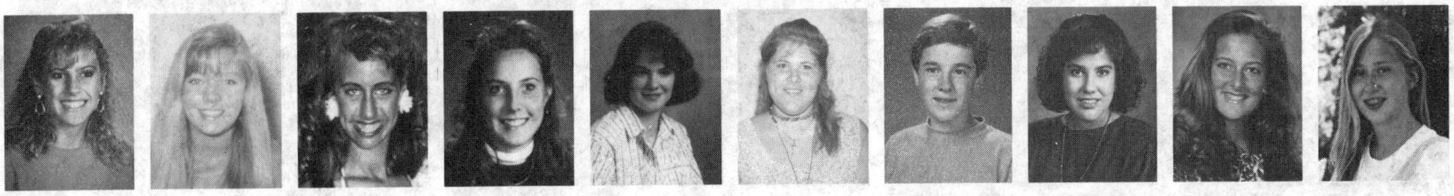

Jennings, Christi
Lincoln HS
Stockton, CA

Jennings, Christine
Miramonte HS
Orinda, CA

Jennings, Darcy Lanai
Corona Del Mar HS
Corona Del Mar, CA

Jennings, Kristen M
Clovis HS
Clovis, CA

Jensen, Chante Vivian
Bellflower HS
Bellflower, CA

Jensen, Christy A
Alhambra HS
Martinez, CA

Jensen, Colin R
Novato HS
Novato, CA

Jensen, Corie A
Francis W Parker HS
San Diego, CA

Jensen, Heather
Trabuco Hills HS
Trabuco Cyn, CA

Jensen, Kelly E
Nevada Union HS
Chicago Park, CA

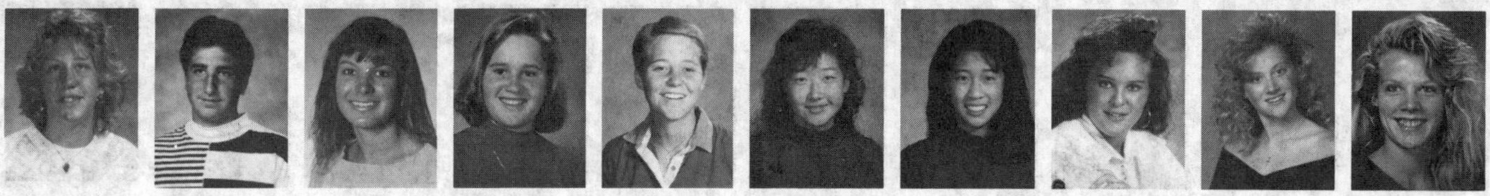

Jensen, Kirsten K
Arlington HS
Riverside, CA

Jensen, Michael P
Armijo HS
Fairfield, CA

Jensen, Tamara A
Miraleste HS
Ranchos Palos Ver, CA

Jensen, Traci L
El Toro HS
El Toro, CA

Jenson, Kristina E
Baker Valley HS
Baker, CA

Jeong, Lisa
John F Kennedy HS
La Palma, CA

Jeong, Melissa G
Abraham Lincoln HS
San Francisco, CA

Jerez, Jennifer J
Roseville HS
Rocklin, CA

Jeschke, Roni L
Antelope Valley HS
Lancaster, CA

Jespersen, Tishara A
El Toro HS
El Toro, CA

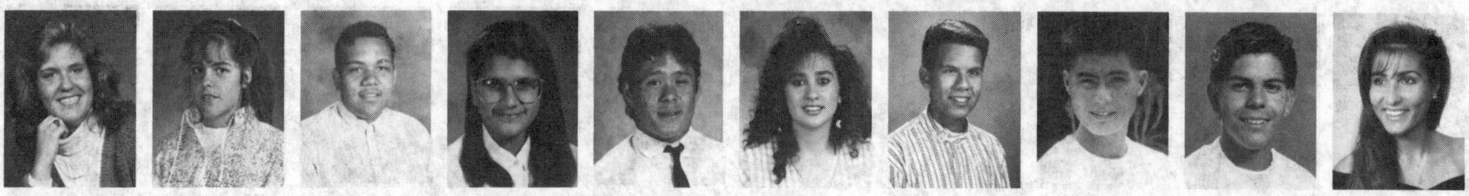

Jessen, Stephanie
Fred C Beyer HS
Modesto, CA

Jette, Joni L
Modesto HS
Modesto, CA

Jewett, Orval A
South Fork HS
Alderpoint, CA

Jhawar, Moninder K
Cornelia Connelly Schl
Fullerton, CA

Jimenez, David A
Sacred Heart Cathedral HS
Pacifica, CA

Jimenez, Diana M
Santa Barbara HS
Santa Barbara, CA

Jimenez, Jr Felipe
Eisenhower HS
Rialto, CA

Jimenez, Frederik V
Gahr HS
Cerritos, CA

Jimenez, Luis Diego
Fontana HS
Fontana, CA

Jimenez, Maria G
Chula Vista HS
Chula Vista, CA

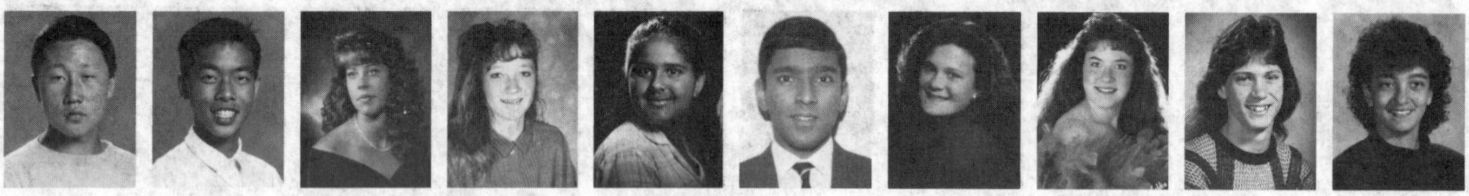

Jin, Richard Z
Narbonne HS
Carson, CA

Jiu, Pierson W
Bakersfield HS
Bakersfield, CA

Jobe, Wendi
Williams HS
Williams, CA

Jobson, Jennifer R
Oak Ridge HS
El Dorado Hills, CA

Johal, Sarvjeet K
Dinuba Joint HS
Dinuba, CA

John, Luke K
Crescenta Valley HS
Montrose, CA

Johns, Becky
San Lorenzo HS
San Lorenzo, CA

Johns, Heather
San Lorenzo HS
San Lorenzo, CA

Johns, Jason
Huntington Beach
Huntington Beach, CA

Johnsen, Lyza
Paso Robles HS
Paso Robles, CA

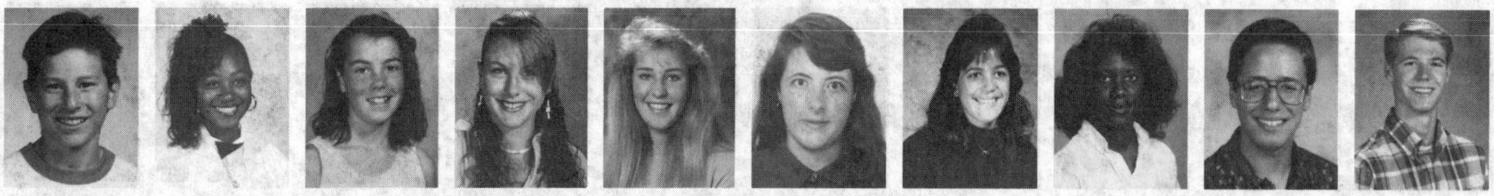

Johnson, Aaron J
Argonaut HS
Jackson, CA

Johnson, Alanya J
Lompoc HS
Lompoc, CA

Johnson, Amanda J
Oakdale HS
Oakdale, CA

Johnson, Amber
Vivian Webb HS
San Rafael, CA

Johnson, Amy L
Dana Hills HS
Laguna Niguel, CA

Johnson, Amy L
Edison HS
Stockton, CA

Johnson, Andrea C
Monterey HS
Monterey, CA

Johnson, Andria D
Immaculate Heart
Inglewood, CA

Johnson, Arthur W
Whittier Christian
Fullerton, CA

Johnson, Brandon S
Hemet HS
Hemet, CA

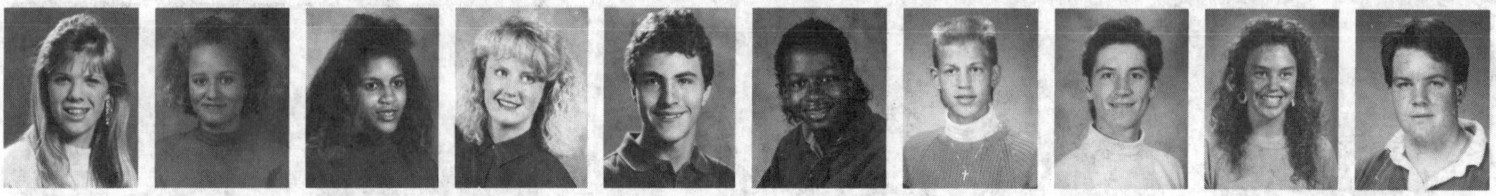

Johnson, Brenda S
Fontana HS
Fontana, CA

Johnson, Celeste M
Salinas Union HS
Salinas, CA

Johnson, Chanel M
Highlands HS
North Highlands, CA

Johnson, Christi L
Sherman H Burroughs HS
Ridgecrest, CA

Johnson, Christopher
Westchester HS
Culver City, CA

Johnson, Dana
Bel-Air Preparatory
Yorba Linda, CA

Johnson, Daniel J
Mount Diablo HS
Concord, CA

Johnson, David H
El Camino HS
Oceanside, CA

Johnson, Dena A
Poway HS
Poway, CA

Johnson, Erik J
Ygnacio Valley HS
Concord, CA

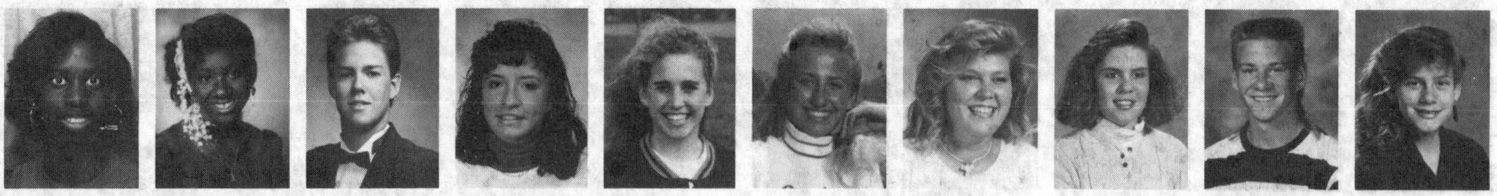

Johnson, Evelyn Y
West Covina HS
W Covina, CA

Johnson, Gina Marie
Los Angeles Baptist
Granada Hills, CA

Johnson, Glenn A
River City HS
West Sacramento, CA

Johnson, Heather E
Galt HS
Galt, CA

Johnson, Jennifer
Carondelet HS
Martinez, CA

Johnson, Jennifer
Clayton Valley HS
Clayton, CA

Johnson, Jennifer
Poway HS
Poway, CA

Johnson, Jenny
Arroyo Grande HS
Pismo Beach, CA

Johnson, Jimmy L
Fairfield HS
Fairfield, CA

Johnson, Jolyn
Oxnard HS
Oxnard, CA

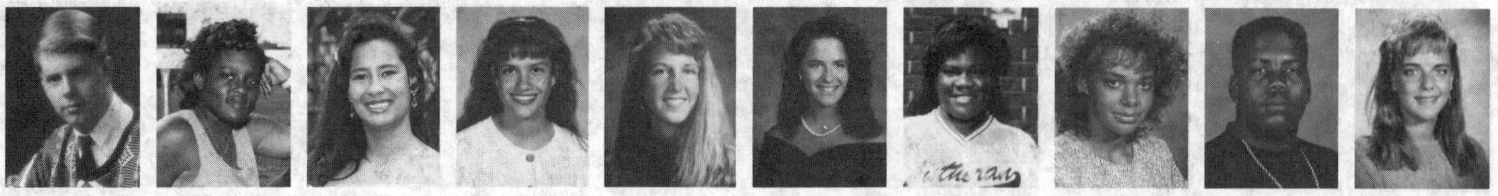

Johnson, Joshua M
Atwater HS
Merced, CA

Johnson, Kaidi M
Ontario HS
Ontario, CA

Johnson, Karenlynn
Hemet HS
Los Angeles, CA

Johnson, Katrin M
Santa Teresa HS
San Jose, CA

Johnson, Krista M
Buena HS
Ventura, CA

Johnson, Kristi
St Joseph HS
Bellflower, CA

Johnson, Latrice R
South Bay Lutheran
Chattanooga, TN

Johnson, Laura L
Highlands HS
North Highlands, CA

Johnson, Lawrence Jaymes
Leffingwell Christian
Lynwood, CA

Johnson, Linda
Saddleback HS
Santa Ana, CA

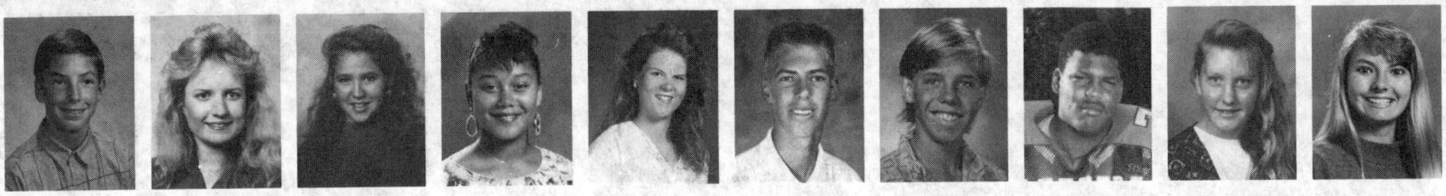

Johnson, Michael B
Pinole Valley HS
Pinole, CA

Johnson, Mylinda L
Brea-Olinda HS
Brea, CA

Johnson, Nicole
Woodrow Wilson HS
Long Beach, CA

Johnson, Nicole L
Fontana HS
Fontana, CA

Johnson, Rachel K
Canyon Springs HS
Moreno Valley, CA

Johnson, Richard L J
Apple Valley HS
Apple Valley, CA

Johnson, Robert A
Mission Viejo HS
Mission Viejo, CA

Johnson, Ryan T
Porterville HS
Porterville, CA

Johnson, Sarah E
O'farrell SCPA
San Diego, CA

Johnson, Shawna
San Dimas HS
San Dimas, CA

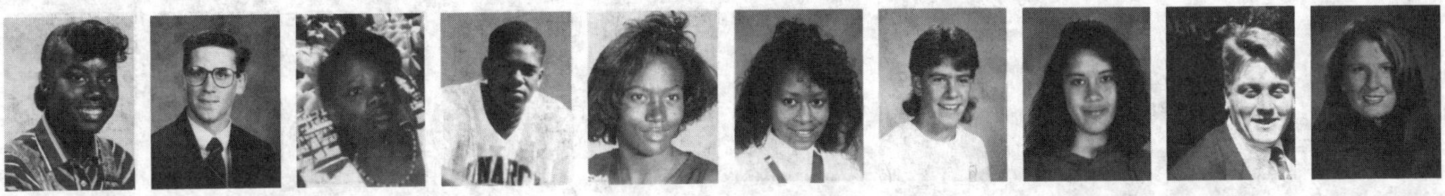

Johnson, Shawntell
Skyline HS
Oakland, CA

Johnson, Stephen
Michael
Robert A Millikan
Trabuco Canyon, CA

Johnson, Tauesha D
Lincoln HS
San Diego, CA

Johnson, Toddrick J
Monte Vista HS
Spring Valley, CA

Johnson, Vera A
Palm Springs HS
Cathedral City, CA

Johnson, Winona L
James Lick HS
San Jose, CA

Johnson, Zachary T
California HS
San Ramon, CA

Johnston, Jennifer S
Herbert Hoover HS
Fresno, CA

Johnston, Jesse
El Molino HS
Guerneville, CA

Johnston, Maura K
Cornelia Connelly HS
Fountain Valley, CA

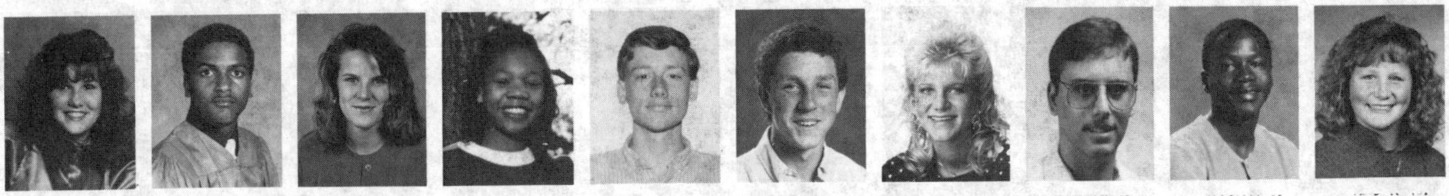

Johnston, Rebecca
Valley Christian HS
Imperial, CA

Jolivette, Andrew J
Sacred Heart
Cathedral HS
San Francisco, CA

Jolley, Kelly A
Hiram Johnson-West
Campus HS
Sacramento, CA

Jolly, Gina
Elk Grove HS
Sacramento, CA

Jolly, Jack A
Modesto HS
Modesto, CA

Jonas, Aaron
Santa Paula HS
Santa Paula, CA

Jonas, Jennifer
Burbank HS
Burbank, CA

Jondle, Alan
Capital Christian HS
Sacramento, CA

Jones, Cedric
Washington HS
Los Angeles, CA

Jones, Corina M
Valley HS
Sacramento, CA

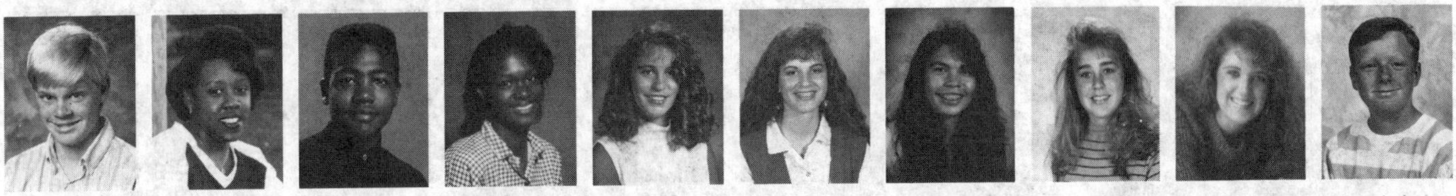

Jones, Eric E
Dana Hills HS
Laguna Niguel, CA

Jones, Essence N
San Lorenzo HS
San Leandro, CA

Jones, Jamille Tarae
Narbonne HS
Torrance, CA

Jones, Jarilyn S
Eisenhower HS
Rialto, CA

Jones, Jeanette A
Riverside Poly HS
Riverside, CA

Jones, Jennifer A
Tracy Joint Union
Tracy, CA

Jones, Jennifer E
Sacramento Adventist
Acad
Fair Oaks, CA

Jones, Jennifer L
John A Rowland HS
Rowland Hts, CA

Jones, Jennifer T
Saugus HS
Valencia, CA

Jones, Jon A
Orange Glen HS
Escondido, CA

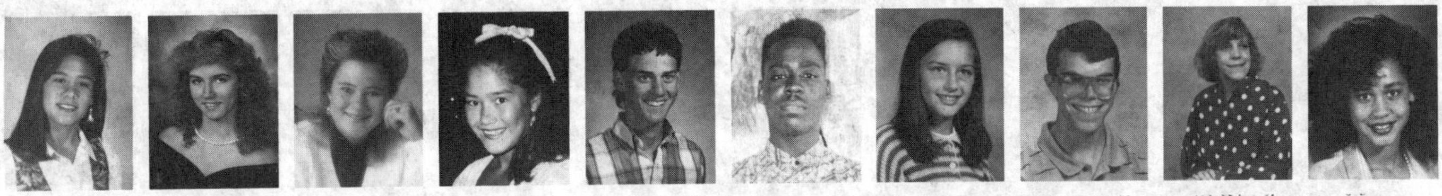

Jones, Kim
Flintridge Sacred
Heart Acad
Glendale, CA

Jones, Kimberly A
Westlake HS
Thousand Oaks, CA

Jones, Leanne Marie
Capuchino HS
San Bruno, CA

Jones, Liana A
Torrey Pines HS
San Diego, CA

Jones, Matt
Modoc HS
Canby, CA

Jones, Maurice
Junipero Serra HS
Los Angeles, CA

Jones, Melissa
Center HS
Elverta, CA

Jones, Michael
Valley Christian HS
San Jose, CA

Jones, Michele L
Redlands HS
Redlands, CA

Jones, Nicole
Cajon HS
San Bernardino, CA

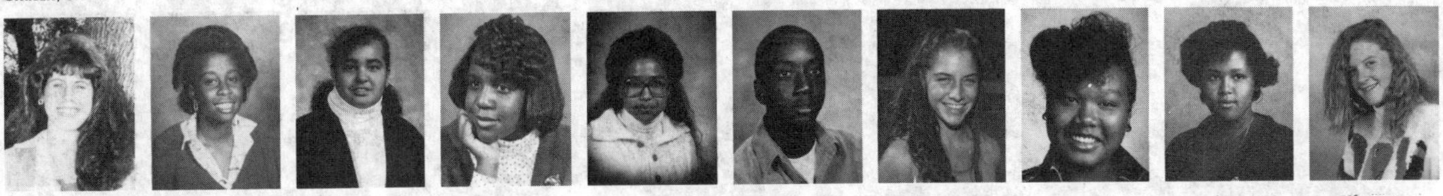

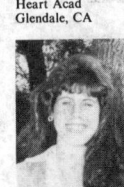

Jones, Nicole
Del Oro HS
Loomis, CA

Jones, Nicole
Paramount HS
Paramount, CA

Jones, Nicole S
Bishop O'dowd HS
Vallejo, CA

Jones, Pshyra
South Bay JR Acad
Carson, CA

Jones, Radiah M
Arlington HS
Riverside, CA

Jones, Rashidi
Dorsey HS
Los Angeles, CA

Jones, Suzanne M
Carlmont HS
Belmont, CA

Jones, Theresa
Edison HS
Stockton, CA

Jones, Yolanda J
Highlands HS
North Highlands, CA

Jones-Laing, Karyn
Los Altos HS
Hacienda Hts, CA

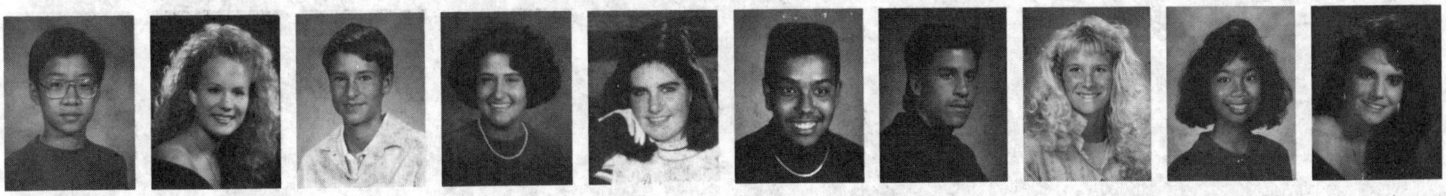

Joo, Yong T
John F Kennedy HS
La Palma, CA

Jopson, Pamela
East Nicolaus HS
Wheatland, CA

Jordan, Jason M
Bellarmine College
Prep
San Jose, CA

Jordan, Kellie
Los Alamitos HS
Seal Beach, CA

Jordan, Kimberly
Piedmont Hills HS
San Jose, CA

Jordan, II Louis J
Ceres HS
Ceres, CA

Jordan, Ray A
Arlington HS
Riverside, CA

Jorgenson, Kellie L
Mission Viego HS
Mission Viejo, CA

Jornada, Chari Delle
San Gabriel Acad
Covina, CA

Joseph, Jenifer
Greenville JR/SR HS
Taylorsville, CA

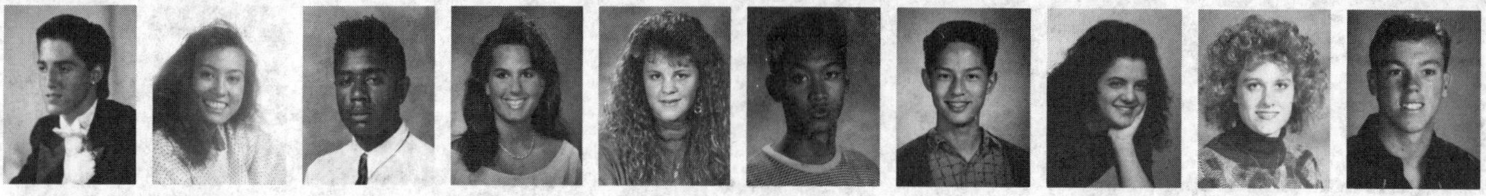

Joseph, Michael P
Turlock HS
Turlock, CA

Joseph, Sharon
Fontana HS
Fontana, CA

Joseph, Stephen A
Loyola HS
Los Angeles, CA

Josimov, Natalija
Trabuco Hills HS
Trabuco Canyon, CA

Josing, Deanna H
Canyon HS
Canyon Country, CA

Jove, Larry C
Palm Springs HS
Palm Springs, CA

Joves, James
Montgomery HS
Kenwood, CA

Joy, Celia
East Bakersfield HS
Bakersfield, CA

Joy, Stephanie L
Lower Lake HS
Lower Lake, CA

Joyce, Jeffrey M
Lincoln HS
Stockton, CA

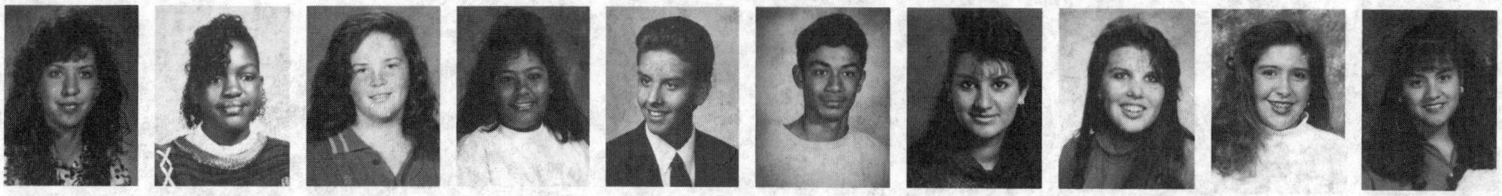

Joyce, Jona S
Victor Valley SR HS
Helendale, CA

Joyner, Ka Sheika D
South Bay JR Acad
Torrance, CA

Joynt, Sarah E
San Benito HS
Hollister, CA

Juarez, Anabel R
Workman HS
La Puente, CA

Juarez, Michael D
Encina HS
Sacramento, CA

Juarez, III Raul
Selma HS
Selma, CA

Juarez, Rosalie
Colton HS
Colton, CA

Juarez, Shayla M
Encina Acad
Sacramento, CA

Juarez, Yolanda M
St Paul HS
La Puente, CA

Juarez-Romero, Rose
Norwalk HS
Norwalk, CA

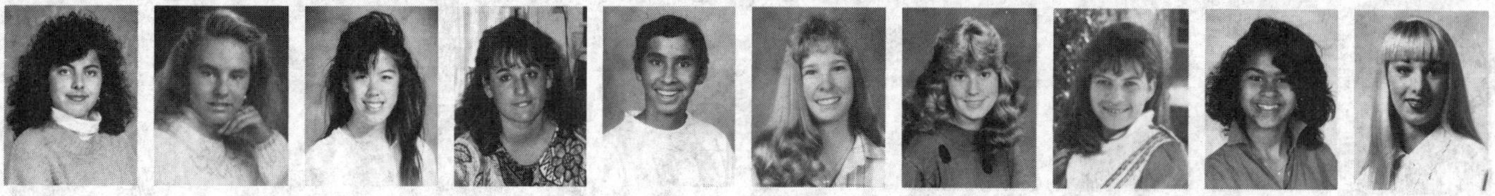

Juha, May F
Lowell HS
San Francisco, CA

Juhnke, Sabrina A
Hanford HS
Hanford, CA

Jung, Joanne
Cerritos HS
Artesia, CA

Juntti, Helen M
Sacramento HS
Sacramento, CA

Jurado, Michael C
Patrick Henry HS
San Diego, CA

Just, Windy
Redwood HS
Visalia, CA

Justice, Terri D
Yreka HS
Yreka, CA

Justice, Yvette
Thousand Oaks HS
West Lake Village, CA

Justin, Shawnita L
Rowland HS
Walnut, CA

Kaas, Elizabeth A
Brea-Olinda HS
Brea, CA

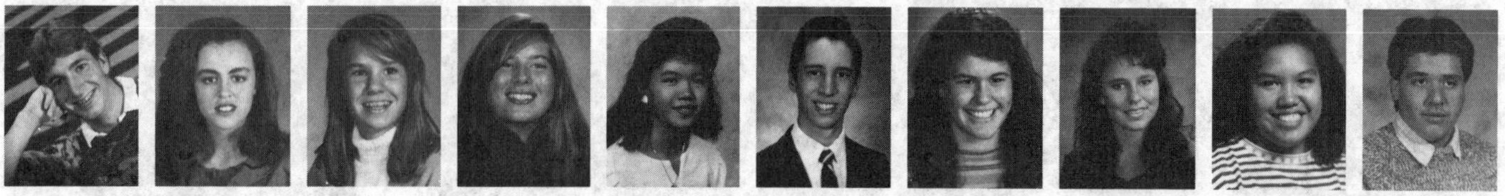

Kackmeister, Alan
Arroyo Grande HS
Arroyo Grande, CA

Kahkedjian, Aida
Pasadena HS
Pasadena, CA

Kahn, Shana
Lynbrook HS
San Jose, CA

Kaiser, Polly E
Amos Alonzo Stagg
Stockton, CA

Kalagayan, Norie
Calvary Baptist HS
Suisun City, CA

Kale, David
Imperial HS
Pasadena, CA

Kalino, Heather J
East Union HS
Manteca, CA

Kalman, Katrina
Santa Teresa HS
San Jose, CA

Kam, Sherrie I
San Gorgonio HS
Highland, CA

Kamiyama, Kenneth
Seaside HS
Fort Ord, CA

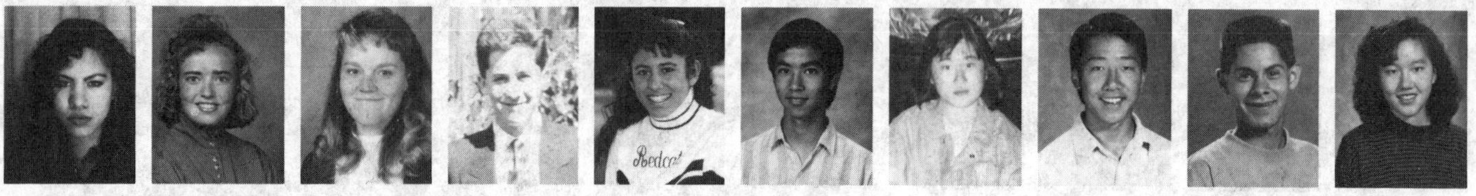

Kamminga, Nikki
Newark Memorial
Newark, CA

Kamper, Rhonda
Mountain Empire HS
Campo, CA

Kampf, Kimberly L
Yucaipa HS
Yucaipa, CA

Kamras, Jason S
Rio Americano HS
Carmichael, CA

Kandarian, Gina Y
Fowler HS
Fowler, CA

Kanemoto, Eric R
Armijo HS
Fairfield, CA

Kang, Betty
Arcadia HS
Arcadia, CA

Kang, Richard C
San Ramon Valley
Danville, CA

Kann, Simon
San Pedro HS
San Pedro, CA

Kao, Rachel N
Palo Alto HS
Palo Alto, CA

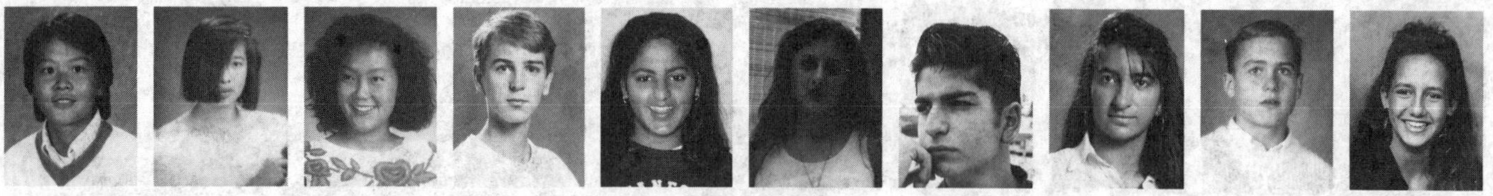

Kao, Robin
Archbishop Mitty HS
Saratoga, CA

Kao, Vivian
Napa HS
Napa, CA

Kao, Yuh-Ting
Temple City HS
Temple City, CA

Kaplan, Neal
Palisades HS
Pacific Palisades, CA

Kapoor, Natasha
Carondelet HS
Danville, CA

Karapetian, Gina
Armenian Mesrobian
Montebello, CA

Karbassi, Behnam
Fresno Christian HS
Fresno, CA

Karimi, Neda
Taft HS
Reseda, CA

Karlie, Mark S
Kingsburg HS
Kingsburg, CA

Karp, Kelley E
Patrick Henry HS
San Diego, CA

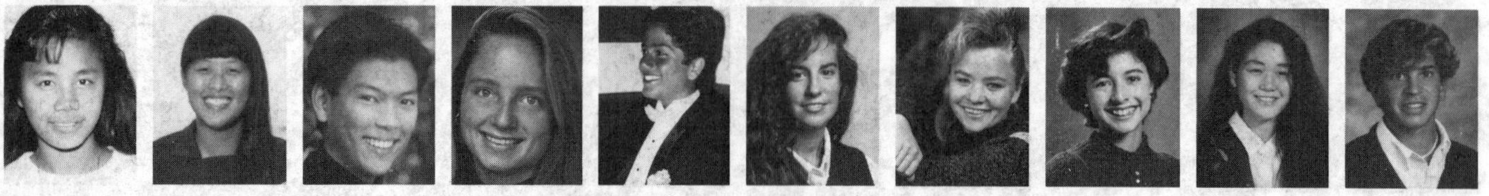

Kasem, Raksan T
Amos Alonzo Stagg
Stockton, CA

Kashiwagi, Mindee F
Analy HS
Sebastopol, CA

Kashiwagi, Ross B
Analy HS
Sebastopol, CA

Kasmar, Anne G
Marlborough Schl
Los Angeles, CA

Kasravi, Barsam
Ocean View HS
Huntington Beach, CA

Kassler, Elizabeth R
Immaculate Heart
Sherman Oaks, CA

Kast, Gina N
Mount Diablo HS
W Pittsburg, CA

Katacic, Alexandra
San Pedro HS
San Pedro, CA

Kataoka, Christine L
Kingsburg HS
Kingsburg, CA

Katkov, William V
Armenian Mesrobian Sch
Montebello, CA

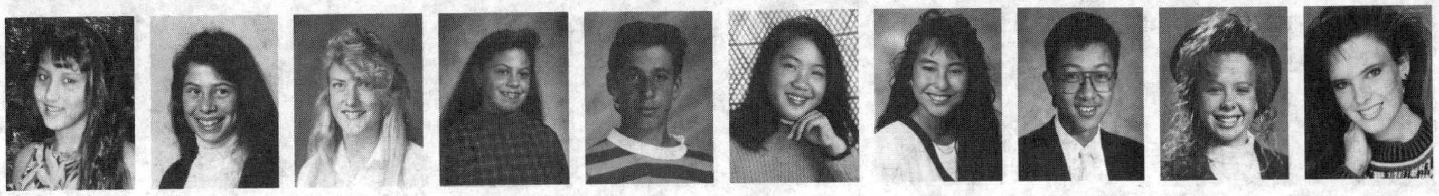

Kato, Robin E
Carlsbad HS
Zephyr Cove, NV

Katsas, Maria A
Alhambra HS
Alhambra, CA

Kauffold, Sandi L
Bonita Vista HS
Chula Vista, CA

Kaufman, Jo A
Workman HS
West Covina, CA

Kavanaugh, Johnny J
Serrano HS
Wrightwood, CA

Kawabe, Aimee K
Buena HS
Ventura, CA

Kawamura, Deborah
West HS
Torrance, CA

Kawasaki, Brian S
St Ignatius HS
San Francisco, CA

Kay, Emily
Palisades HS
Pacific Palisades, CA

Kaylor, Michelle A
El Toro HS
El Toro, CA

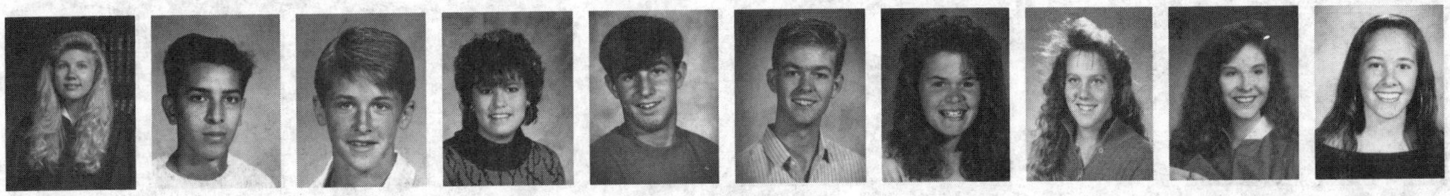

Kazee, Kimberly L
Encina HS
Sacramento, CA

Kazem, Wahid S
Independence HS
San Jose, CA

Kazlauskas, Kristofer
Bellarmine College Prep
San Jose, CA

Keane, Michelle
Foothill SR HS
Sacramento, CA

Kearney, Travis R
Rim Of The World
Lake Arrowhead, CA

Keating, Brett
Cardinal Newman
Santa Rosa, CA

Keay, Corine M
Victory Christian HS
Orangevale, CA

Kechter, Melanie R
California HS
San Ramon, CA

Keeffe, Kathleen D
Pinole Valley HS
Hercules, CA

Keegan, Stacy E
Montgomery HS
Santa Rosa, CA

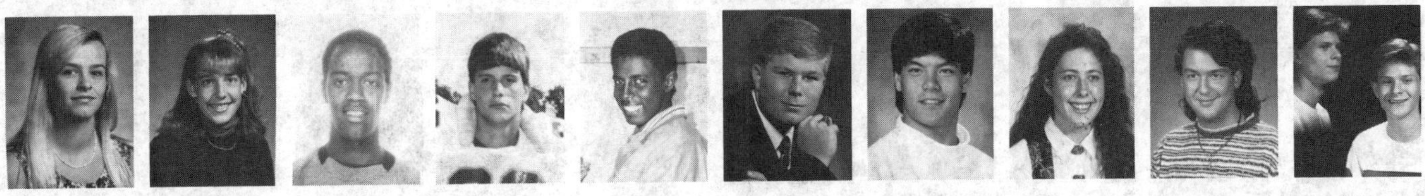

Keeley, Karen I
Roseville HS
Rocklin, CA

Keenan, Amy
Carlmont HS
San Carlos, CA

Kefelegn, Esseye
Athenian Schl
Danville, CA

Keffer, James
Red Bluff Union HS
Red Bluff, CA

Keflezighi, Fussumbrhan R
San Diego HS
San Diego, CA

Kehoe, Tracy R
Live Oak HS
Live Oak, CA

Keil, Matthew J
El Toro HS
El Toro, CA

Keil, Monica L
Enterprise HS
Redding, CA

Keirnan, Noel
Foothill HS
Pleasanton, CA

Keiser, Jeff
Del Campo HS
Sacramento, CA

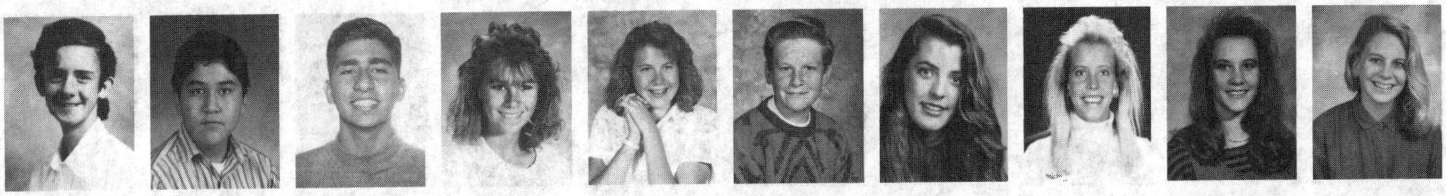

Keith, Chad L
Sweetwater Union
National City, CA

Kekahuna, Richard Noboru
Servite HS
Garden Grove, CA

Keliddari, Farhad
Santa Monica HS
Santa Monica, CA

Kell, Jeanette M
Chino HS
Chino, CA

Keller, Cheryl
Herlong HS
Herlong, CA

Keller, John J
Woodcrest Christian
Norco, CA

Keller, Laura E
Rio American HS
Sacramento, CA

Keller, Michelle
Westminster HS
Westminster, CA

Keller, Staci N
Folsom HS
Folsom, CA

Keller, Tara A
Dos Pueblos HS
Santa Barbara, CA

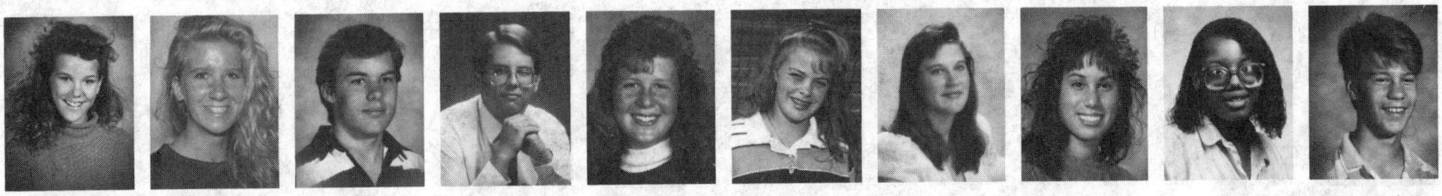

Kelley, Dawn M
North HS
Bakersfield, CA

Kelley, Kathy S
Santa Ynez HS
Santa Ynez, CA

Kelley, Mark J
Chico HS
Chico, CA

Kelley, Ryan M
Del Campo HS
Citrus Heights, CA

Kelley, Shannon G
Woodland HS
Woodland, CA

Kellogg, Misha
Cajon HS
Devore, CA

Kelly, Anne J
Poway HS
Poway, CA

Kelly, Anne L
El Toro HS
Trabuco Canyon, CA

Kelly, Crystal M
Santa Maria HS
Santa Maria, CA

Kelly, Darrin T
Shasta HS
Redding, CA

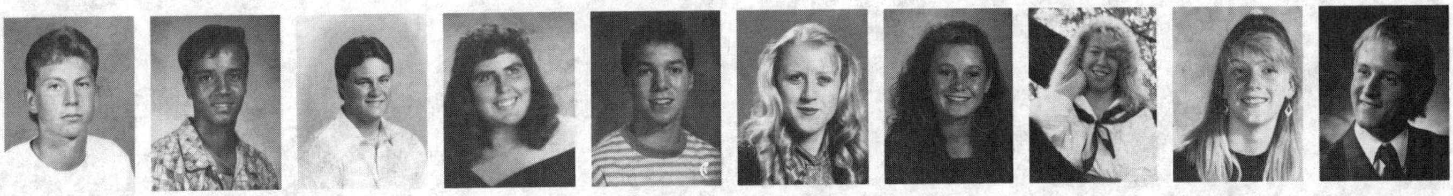

Kelly, Robert C
Beaumont HS
Beaumont, CA

Kendall, Jason J
Glendora HS
Glendora, CA

Kendall, Michael L
La Sierra HS
Riverside, CA

Kenline, Kimberlee J
Corning Union HS
Corning, CA

Kennedy, Aaron M
Garden Grove HS
Garden Grove, CA

Kennedy, Christine
Sierra Vista HS
Baldwin Park, CA

Kennedy, Danielle L
Arcadia HS
Arcadia, CA

Kennedy, Darla M
Ponderosa HS
El Dorado, CA

Kennedy, Deanna
Lompoc HS
Lompoc, CA

Kennedy, Joshua
Marysville HS
Marysville, CA

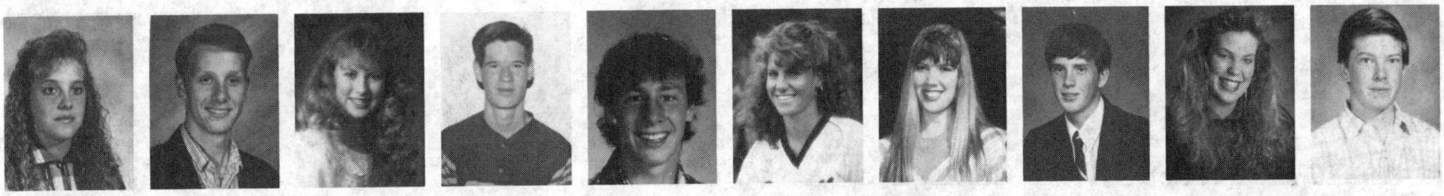

Kennedy, Lynn Michele
Bear River HS
Grass Valley, CA

Kennedy, Jr Michael Linehan
Bishop Amat Memorial HS
Covina, CA

Kenney, Julie K
Redlands HS
Redlands, CA

Kennignton, Aaron B
Paraclete HS
Lancaster, CA

Kennings, Sean L
Tamalpais HS
Mill Valley, CA

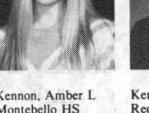

Kennison, Megan V
St Josephs HS
Santa Maria, CA

Kennon, Amber L
Montebello HS
Montebello, CA

Kenny, J Ryan
Redlands HS
Redlands, CA

Kenny, Mechelle Lynn
Patrick Henry HS
San Diego, CA

Kenny, Sean M
Redlands HS
Redlands, CA

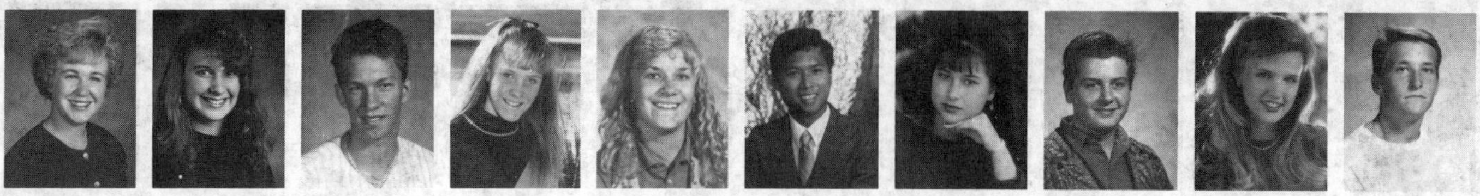

Kent, Jacqueline M
Lakewood HS
Lakewood, CA

Kent, Julie A
Fresno Christian HS
Fresno, CA

Kent, Matthew W
Lincoln HS
San Francisco, CA

Kenyon, Amy
Etiwanda HS
Alta Loma, CA

Kenyon, Elisa
Tulelake HS
Tulelake, CA

Keo, Penhboramey
Jordan HS
Long Beach, CA

Kephart, Chi
Soquel HS
Soquel, CA

Kerepeszki, John
Tri-City Christian Schl
Oceanside, CA

Kerger, Kerily N
Flintridge Preparatory Schl
San Gabriel, CA

Kerns, Douglas E
Hesperia USD
Hesperia, CA

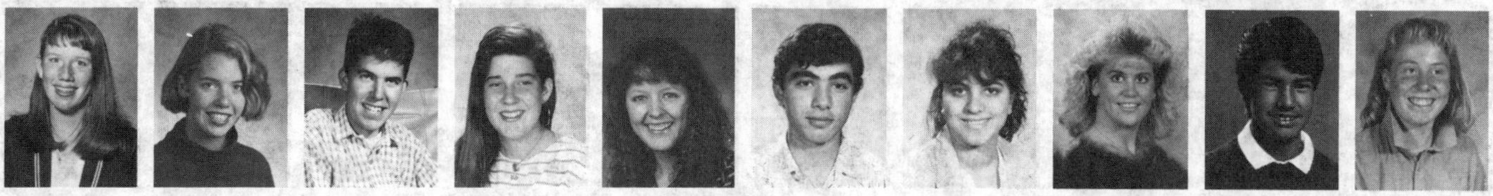

Kerns, Jennifer
C K Mc Clatchy HS
Sacramento, CA

Kerns, Jolie
C K Mc Cluthcy HS
Sacramento, CA

Kerr, John E
College Park HS
Walnut Creek, CA

Kerr, Kimberly R
Los Altos HS
Hacienda Hgts, CA

Kerr, Tamara
Fall River JR-SR HS
Fall River Mills, CA

Keshishian, Akop J
Pasadena HS
Pasadena, CA

Keshishian, Dzhamila
Pasadena HS
Pasadena, CA

Kessler, Jessica R
Lassen HS
Susanville, CA

Kessman, Greg M
Tehachapi HS
Tehachapi, CA

Ketcham, Caroline J
Sierra Joint Union
Prather, CA

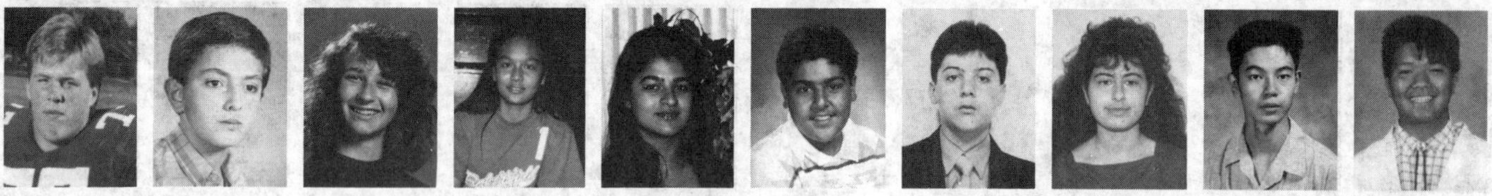

Key, Jonathan C
Woodland HS
Woodland, CA

Khadem, Ali
Mountain View HS
Los Altos, CA

Khaligh, Andrea M
Fontana HS
Fontana, CA

Khamphanith, Thavilay
Bakersfield HS
Bakersfield, CA

Khan, Shazia R
Valley View HS
Moreno Valley, CA

Kharrazian, Datis
Torrey Pine HS
Del Mar, CA

Khaykin, Mikhail
G Washington HS
San Francisco, CA

Khezri, Mona
Birmingham HS
Encino, CA

Kho, Tuong C
San Gabriel HS
San Gabriel, CA

Khoonsrivong, Thong Lai B
Lincoln HS
Stockton, CA

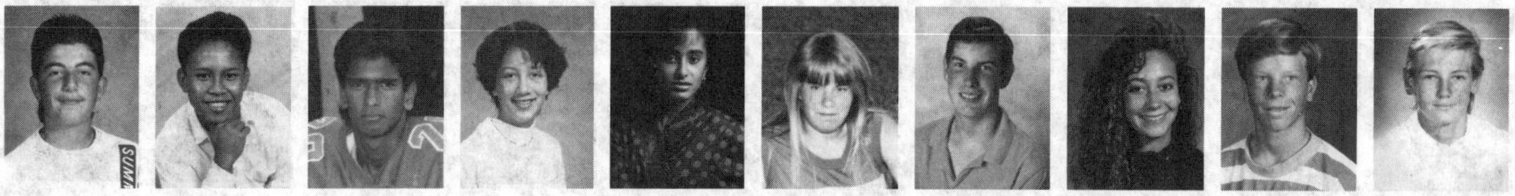

Khorozian, Raffy
South San Francisco
South San Francis, CA

Khounvichith, Khekkeo K
Edison HS
Stockton, CA

Khullar, Vivek
El Toro HS
El Toro, CA

Kiang, Julia
Rosary HS
La Palma, CA

Kianmahd, Sharona
Santa Monica HS
Santa Monica, CA

Kiehm, Corina
North Salinas HS
Salinas, CA

Kiehn, Todd
Pinewood HS
Los Altos, CA

Kienast, Suzann
College Park HS
Martinez, CA

Kiesel, Jason A
San Pasqual HS
Escondido, CA

Kiester, Ted C
Hart HS
Valencia, CA

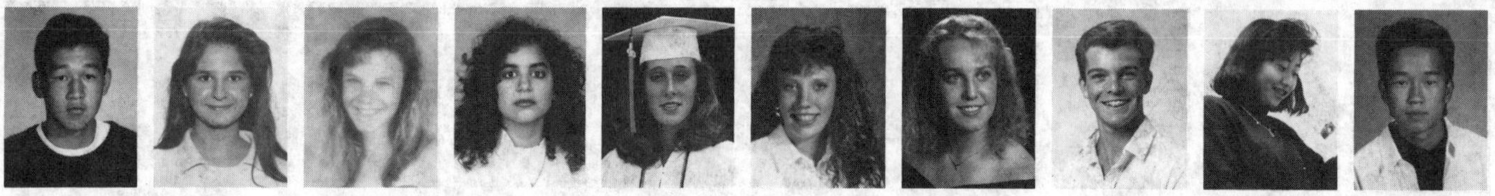

Kihara, Christopher J
Santa Teresa HS
San Jose, CA

Kilaghbian, Talin A
Clovis HS
Clovis, CA

Kilby, Shawna
Ponderosa HS
Shingle Springs, CA

Kiledjian, Arpi M
Holy Martyrs Armenian HS
Canoga Park, CA

Kiley, Sarah A
Notre Dame Acad
Los Angeles, CA

Kilkenny, Nicole M
Mercy HS
Pacifica, CA

Killen, Katherine A
Cupertino HS
San Jose, CA

Kilpatrick, Kyle R
Brea Olinda HS
Brea, CA

Kim, Ci Hye
Seaside HS
Marina, CA

Kim, Douglas D
Las Lomas HS
Lafayette, CA

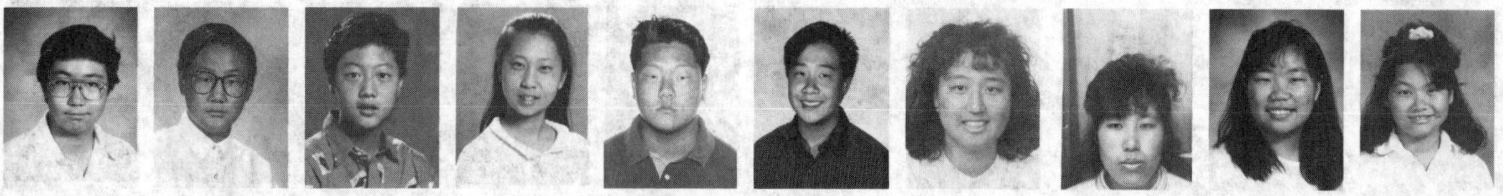

Kim, Edward K
Artesia HS
Hawaiian Gardens, CA

Kim, Elbert K
Glendale Adventist Acad
Woodland Hills, CA

Kim, Eric
Cajon HS
San Bernardino, CA

Kim, Esther
Narbonne HS
Lomita, CA

Kim, Eugene
Rowland HS
Rowland Heights, CA

Kim, Howard
Glen A Wilson HS
Hacienda Heights, CA

Kim, Hyun-Helen
Sunny Hills HS
Fullerton, CA

Kim, In Sook
Hoover HS
San Diego, CA

Kim, Jane J
J F Kennedy HS
La Palma, CA

Kim, Janette
Indio HS
Palm Desert, CA

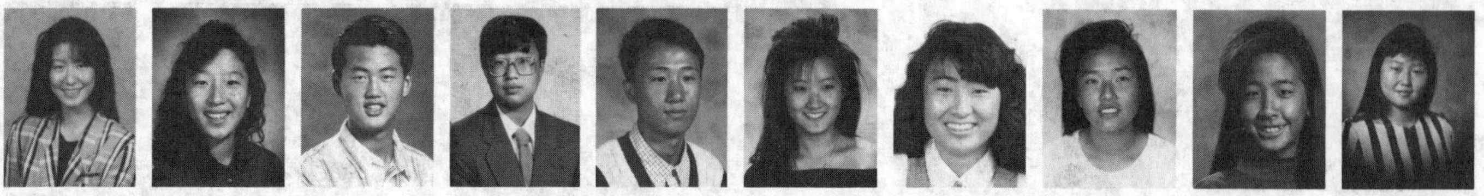

Kim, Janey
University HS
Diamond Bar, CA

Kim, Jenny J
Bolsa Grande HS
Garden Grove, CA

Kim, John J
Glendale Adventist Acad
Chatsworth, CA

Kim, Johnny
Sunny Hills HS
Fullerton, CA

Kim, Kyong
Bullard HS
Fresno, CA

Kim, Linda J
Gretchen Whitney
Norwalk, CA

Kim, May J
Calabasas HS
Calabasas, CA

Kim, Michelle J
Glen A Wilson HS
Hacienda Hgts, CA

Kim, Mimi
North HS
Torrance, CA

Kim, Moon Hee
Artesia HS
Lakewood, CA

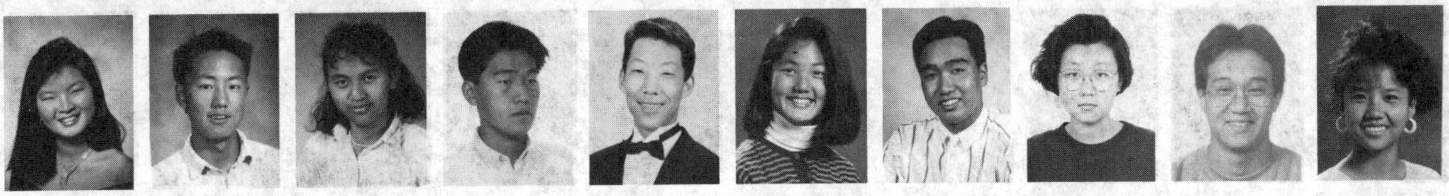

Kim, Nancy Inkyung
Claremont HS
Claremont, CA

Kim, Paul H
Edison HS
Huntington Beach, CA

Kim, Ratha R
Ygnacio Valley HS
Concord, CA

Kim, Sae Hwan
Birmingham HS
Los Angeles, CA

Kim, Sean T
Mills HS
Burlingame, CA

Kim, Sharon S
Glendale Adventist Acad
Chatsworth, CA

Kim, Steve S
Santa Clara HS
Camarillo, CA

Kim, Suelyn
John A Rowland HS
Rowland Heights, CA

Kim, Sung E
John F Kennedy HS
Cypress, CA

Kim, The Sun
Glendale HS
Glendale, CA

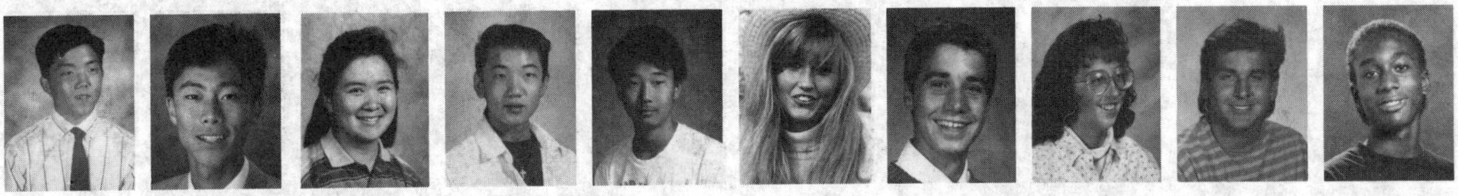

Kim, Tokhyun Davey
Fairfax HS
Los Angeles, CA

Kim, Woojay
Bishop Amat HS
Diamond Bar, CA

Kim, Yoo Jin
Crossroads Schl
Los Angeles, CA

Kim, Young
Arcadia HS
Arcadia, CA

Kim, Young
Miramonte HS
Orinda, CA

Kimball, Dyana
Burlingame HS
Burlingame, CA

Kimbirk, Anthony John
Colton HS
Colton, CA

Kimmel, Melanie D
Serrano HS
Phelan, CA

Kimont, Mason W
Santa Teresa HS
San Jose, CA

Kincade, III Robert
Fontana HS
Fontana, CA

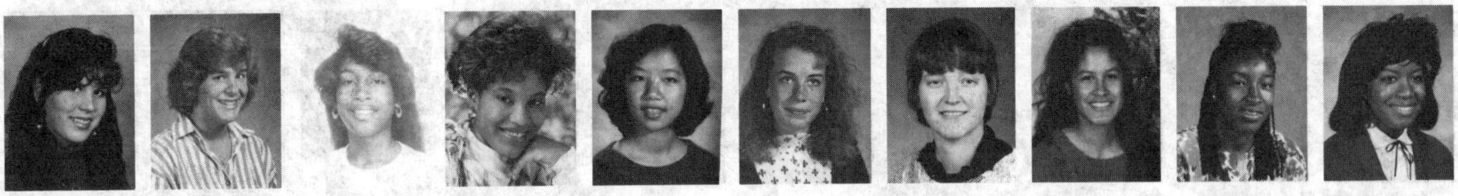

Kindrick, Arminda
Highlands HS
North Highlands, CA

King, Andrea M
Corona HS
Corona, CA

King, Chanel L
Skyline HS
Oakland, CA

King, Dionne
Colton HS
San Bernardino, CA

King, Elaine Y
University HS
Irvine, CA

King, Erin M
Cabrillo HS
Lompoc, CA

King, Jennifer M
St Josephs HS
Downey, CA

King, Margie
Fullerton HS
Fullerton, CA

King, Nicole O
Living Way Christian Acad
Pasadena, CA

King, Shari A
Redwood Christian
San Leandro, CA

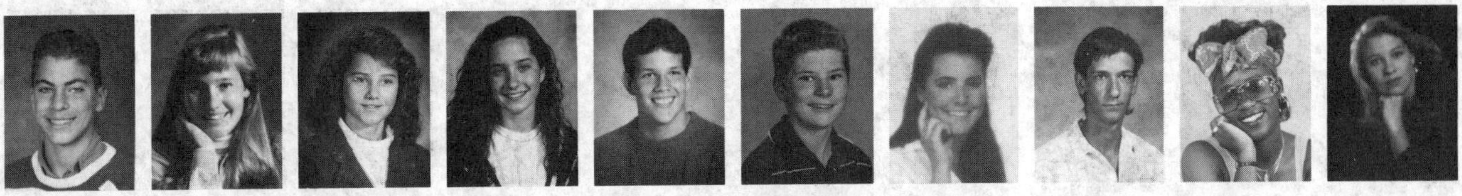

Kiousis, Spiro K
Turlock HS
Turlock, CA

Kirby, Michelle L
King City Joint Union HS
King City, CA

Kirch, Shelley T
Mount Shasta HS
Mount Shasta, CA

Kirchberger, Jody
El Camino HS
Carmichael, CA

Kirin, Brian J
Westminster HS
Westminster, CA

Kirk, Kellem L
Trinity HS
Burnt Ranch, CA

Kirk, Kelly
Highlands HS
Rio Linda, CA

Kirkjan, Gregory
Palm Desert HS
Indio, CA

Kirkland, Roxanne
Etiwanda HS
Manteca, CA

Kirn, Amy R
Mariposa County HS
Mariposa, CA

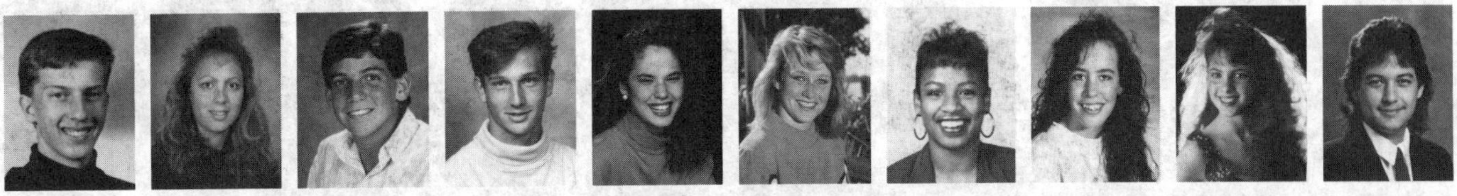

Kirrene, Joseph C
Encina HS
Sacramento, CA

Kirschner, Monica M
El Camino HS
Oceanside, CA

Kirshen, Marc P
Mt Carmel HS
San Diego, CA

Kirsten, Brent H
Mission Bay HS
San Diego, CA

Kiser, Shannon G
Clovis HS
Fresno, CA

Kissane, Carrie A
Torrey Pines HS
San Diego, CA

Kissoon, Natalia A
James Lick HS
San Jose, CA

Kiszonas, Sandra L
Chino HS
Ontario, CA

Kitchen, Stephanie D
Dublin HS
Dublin, CA

Kittidumrongkool, Keith
Bellarmine-Jefferson
N Hollywood, CA

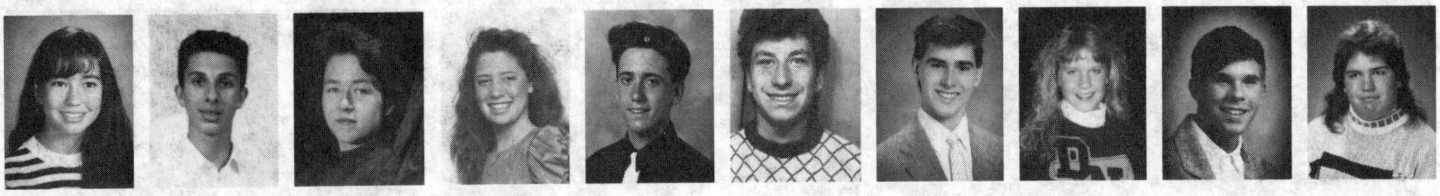

Kivett, Amy C
Bullard HS
Fresno, CA

Kizirian, Yeghig
Holy Martyrs Ferrahian HS
Van Nuys, CA

Klasa, Joanna
Pacific Grove HS
Seaside, CA

Klatt, Karie J
Norco SR HS
Corona, CA

Klaus, Kevin H
Loyola HS
Culver City, CA

Klebaner, Alex
George Washington
San Francisco, CA

Klein, Robert
Loara HS
Anaheim, CA

Klever, Kim
Del Norte County HS
Crescent City, CA

Klever, Kris Walter
Del Norte County HS
Crescent City, CA

Kline, Galen T
Novato HS
Novato, CA

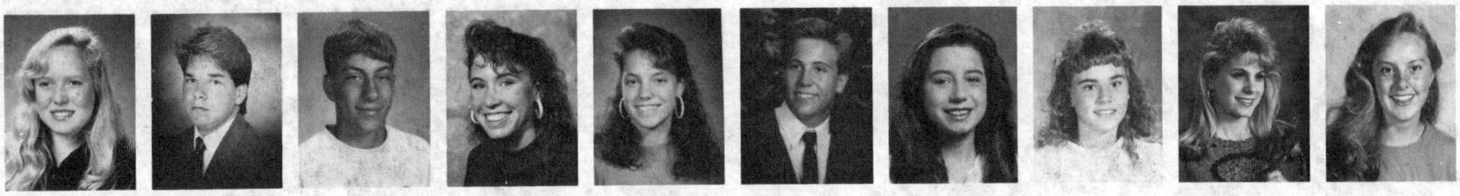

Kline, Laurel E
Novato HS
Novato, CA

Klockenteger, Kelly
Workman HS
Victorville, CA

Kloster, Mark S
Las Lomas HS
Walnut Crk, CA

Klumpp, Michelle L
Orange Glen HS
Escondido, CA

Klvana, Nicole C
William S Hart HS
Newhall, CA

Knapp, R Jason
El Toro HS
El Toro, CA

Knarr, Stephany M
San Gorgonio HS
San Bernardino, CA

Knaus, Lynn M
Irvington HS
Fremont, CA

Kneisel, Alesha R
Paraclete HS
Quartz Hill, CA

Kniffen, Susanna C
Coast Joint Union
Cayucos, CA

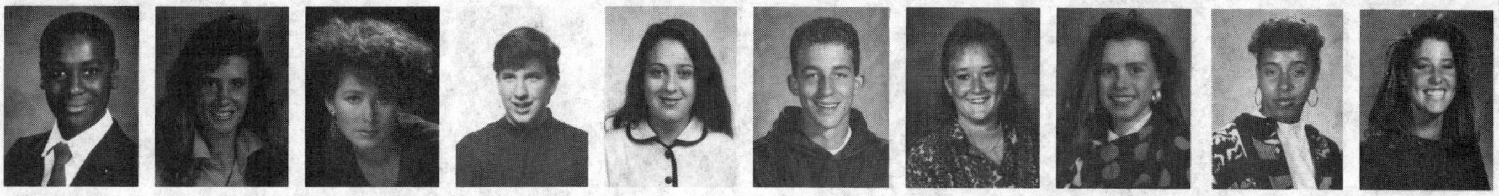

Knight, Nguyon
St Michaels Prep
Redondo Beach, CA

Knight, Suzanne E
Apple Valley SR HS
Apple Valley, CA

Knight, Vanessa M
Arroyo Grande HS
Arroyo Grande, CA

Knoblauch, Mark A
Clovis HS
Clovis, CA

Knodorkovsky, Karina M
Skyline HS
Oakland, CA

Knopp, Eric A
Cupertino HS
Cupertino, CA

Knowlden, Lori M
El Cajon Valley HS
El Cajon, CA

Knowles, Jennifer M
Mt Whitney HS
Visalia, CA

Knox, Antoinette T
Eisenhower HS
Rialto, CA

Knox, Deborah L
Corona HS
Corona, CA

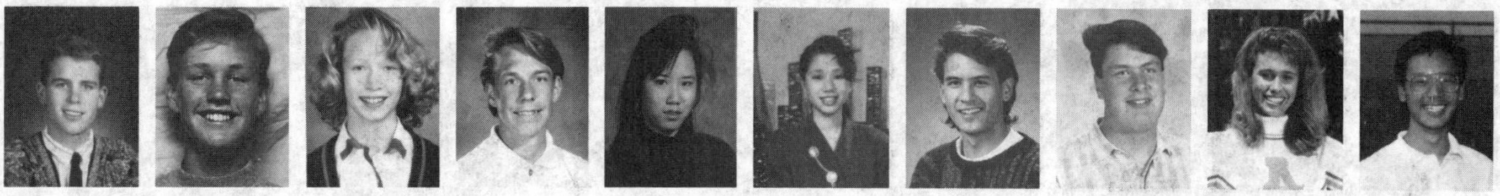

Knox, Keith W
Vintage HS
Napa, CA

Knox, Matthew
Earl Warren HS
Downey, CA

Knudsen, Krista L
Hanford Union HS
Hanford, CA

Knutson, Lars A
Troy HS
Yorba Linda, CA

Ko, Clara
Lowell HS
San Francisco, CA

Ko, Lilly P
Galileo HS
San Francisco, CA

Kobialka, Semyon
University HS
San Francisco, CA

Koble, Christopher M
Paramount HS
Lakewood, CA

Koch, Becky
Agoura HS
Westlake Vil, CA

Kochavatr, John T
Ontario HS
Ontario, CA

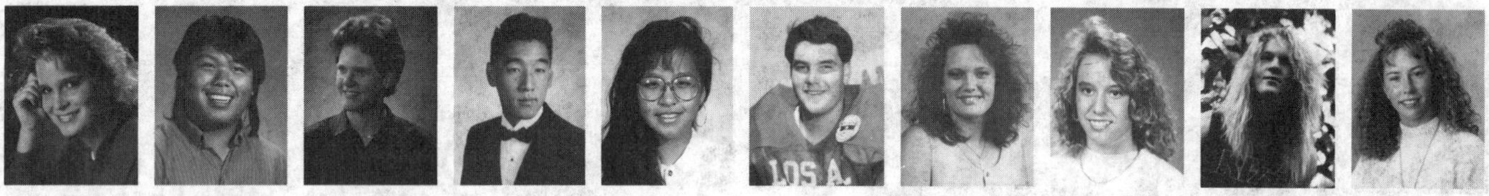

Kochheiser, Brenda A
Hoover HS
Fresno, CA

Kodani, Ray
Rio Linda SR HS
Sacramento, CA

Koeppen, Catherine Elise
Woodland HS
Esparto, CA

Kohara, Paul
Carlmont HS
Belmont, CA

Kokiatkulkij, Jinnie
Bellflower HS
Bellflower, CA

Kolasa, Bryan
Los Alamitos HS
Los Alamitos, CA

Kolkman, Joy A
Simi Valley HS
Simi Valley, CA

Kolowski, Paulette L
Pittsburg HS
Pittsburg, CA

Komaromi, Dan
Sonora HS
Fullerton, CA

Kondelik, Carolyn
Canyon Springs HS
Phoenix, AZ

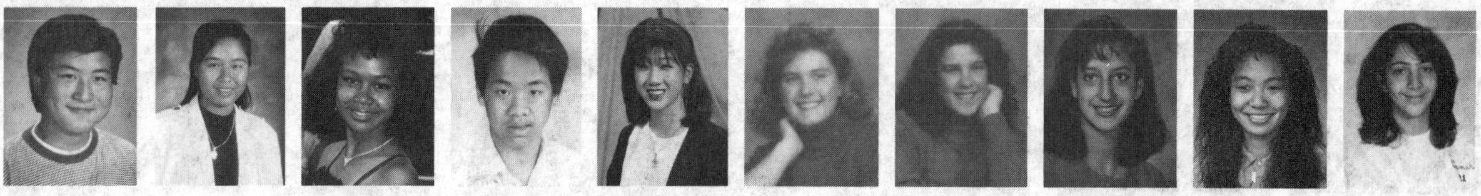

Kondo, Grant T
Sanger HS
Fresno, CA

Kong, Anna W
Oakland HS
Oakland, CA

Kong, Chen S
Modesto HS
Modesto, CA

Kong, Jackson C
Richard Gahr HS
Artesia, CA

Kong, Kaserin Tammie
Nogales HS
Walnut, CA

Koning, Heidi A
Woodcrest Christian
Riverside, CA

Koning, Shawnn K
Woodcrest Christian
Riverside, CA

Konn, Lisa M
Esperanza HS
Yorba Linda, CA

Konno, Cheryl M
Milpitas HS
Milpitas, CA

Konyalian, Tamar
Ribet Acad
Glendale, CA

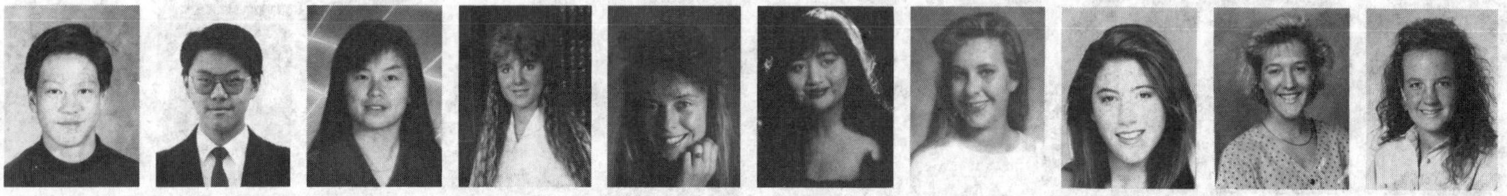

Koo, Howard
Lowell HS
San Francisco, CA

Koo, Thomas H
Birmingham HS
Van Nuys, CA

Koo, Vivian W
Abraham Lincoln HS
San Francisco, CA

Koonce, Nancy L
Fremont HS
Sunnyvale, CA

Kopicka, Jarmila S
Rubidoux HS
Riverside, CA

Kopiko, Karen
S F Christian HS
San Francisco, CA

Kopp, Kimberleigh N
Serra JR-SR HS
San Diego, CA

Koppel, Ahrin B
Apple Valley HS
Apple Valley, CA

Kordis, Candi
Escondido HS
Ephrata, WA

Korkko, Kimberly A
Alta Loma HS
Alta Loma, CA

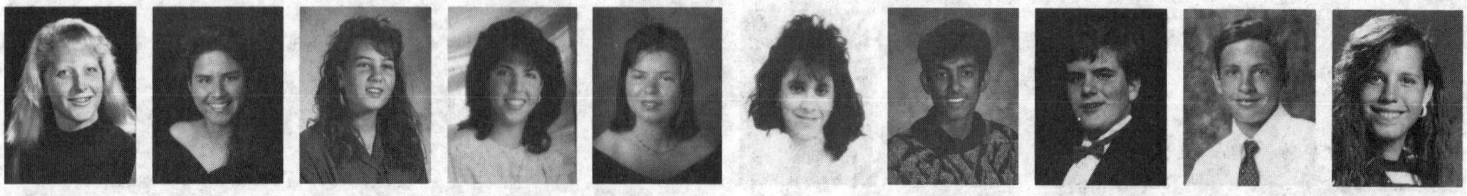

Korth, Tess
St Joseph Notre Dame HS
Hayward, CA

Koskelin, Jennifer Lee
College Park HS
Martinez, CA

Kosofsky, Karen
Montclair College Prep
Encino, CA

Koss, Leslie Ann
University Of San Diego HS
Rancho La Costa, CA

Kostrikin, Liza V
Santa Rosa HS
Santa Rosa, CA

Kostuchek, Tanya J
San Francisco Christian Schl
San Francisco, CA

Kotecha, Anand
South Tahoe HS
S Lake Tahoe, CA

Koteles, James A
Lodi HS
Lodi, CA

Kotzman, William K
Loyola HS
Los Angeles, CA

Kovar, Jana L
Village Christian Schls
Glendale, CA

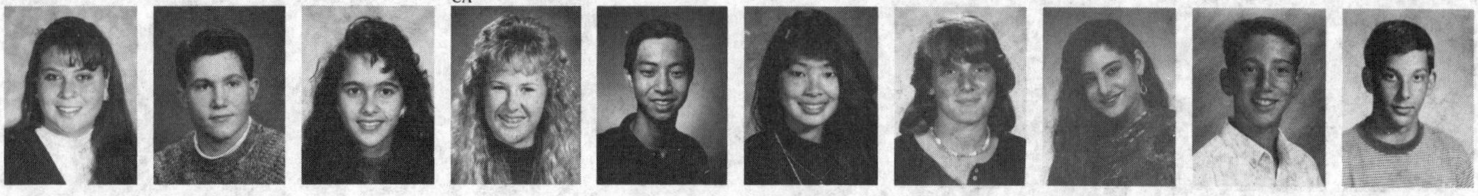

Kowal, Tena M
Roosevelt HS
Fresno, CA

Kozar, Michael A
Fillmore HS
Fillmore, CA

Kozelchik, Zolissa A
Pasadena HS
Pasadena, CA

Kozlak, Michelle
Woodbridge HS
Irvine, CA

Kozono, David E
Walnut HS
Walnut, CA

Kozuka, Mayu
Carlmont HS
Belmont, CA

Krafft, Angelina M
Andrew Hill HS
San Jose, CA

Kraft, Diana
Apple Valley HS
Apple Valley, CA

Kraft, Kevin J
Apple Valley HS
Apple Valley, CA

Kramer, Brian D
Independence HS
San Jose, CA

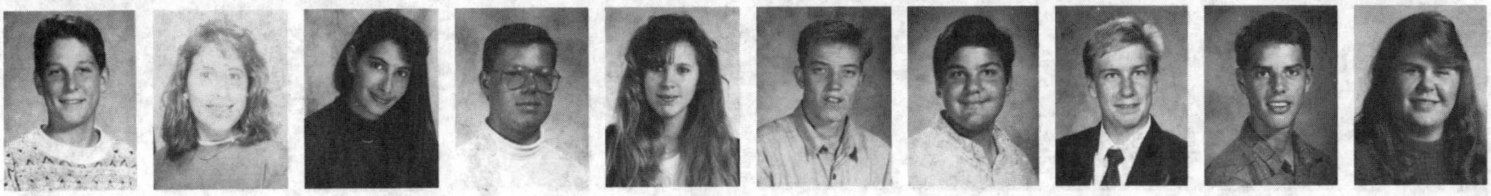

Kramer, Bryan J
Pioneer HS
San Jose, CA

Krane, Sonja
Torrey Pines HS
Del Mar, CA

Krantz, Brandi R
Woodbridge HS
Irvine, CA

Kranzberg, Joseph E
Antelope Valley HS
Lancaster, CA

Kranzler, Mykeah
Santa Clara HS
Saratoga, CA

Kraude, Drew
Galt HS
Galt, CA

Krause, Aaron E
Edison HS
Huntington Beach, CA

Krause, Joseph N
Saint Ignatius College Prep
San Francisco, CA

Kreil, Jeffrey E
Bolsa Grande HS
Garden Grove, CA

Krell, Sherry L
Encina HS
Sacramento, CA

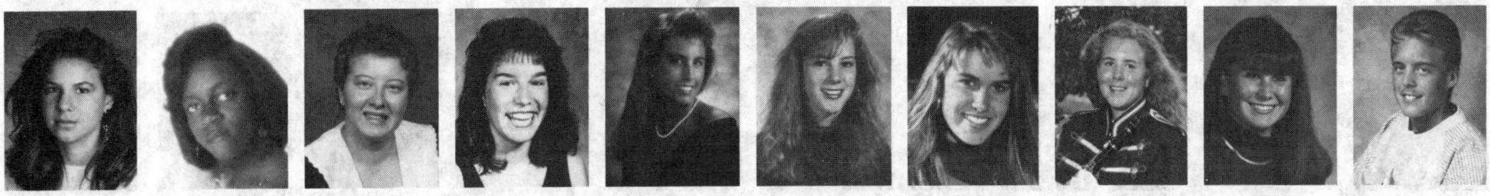

Krempely, Michelle
Roseville Joint Union
Rocklin, CA

Krengel, Kirstin N
Santa Clara HS
Santa Clara, CA

Kristiansen, Denise A
Victor Valley HS
Victorville, CA

Kristovich, Dinelle M
South San Francisco
South San Francis, CA

Kritzer, Heather L
Poway HS
Poway, CA

Krizo, Phaedra
Tulelake HS
Tulelake, CA

Krog, Karin L
Rim Of The World
Blue Jay, CA

Kroll, Kristina K
Etiwanda HS
Alta Loma, CA

Kronbetter, Julie
Bullard HS
Fresno, CA

Kropp, Jeff A
Chaminade College Prep
Woodland Hills, CA

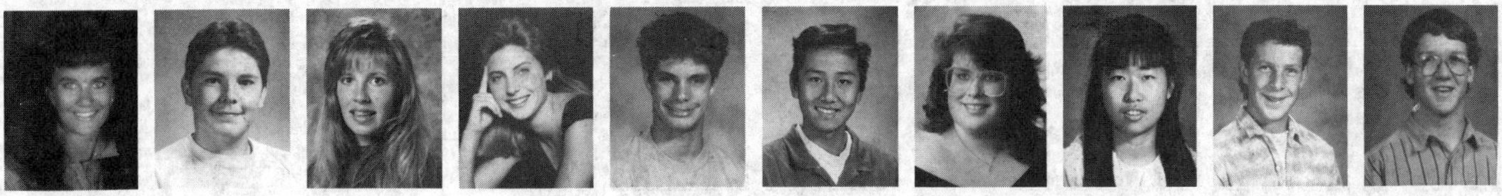

Krueckel, Kathy A
Bella Vista HS
Fair Oaks, CA

Krupicka, Daniel J
Poway HS
San Diego, CA

Kruse, Karen
Dana Hills HS
Dana Point, CA

Kubanda, Christine L
Elsinore HS
Lake Elsinore, CA

Kubernick, Samuel
Los Alamitos HS
Seal Beach, CA

Kuboyama, Lance T
Schurr HS
Montebello, CA

Kuenzi, Kayne K
Mar Vista HS
Imperial Beach, CA

Kuey, Shang-Chi Katy
Cerritos HS
Cerritos, CA

Kujak, Brian L
Lutheran HS
Yorba Linda, CA

Kukas, Jeremy P
Mt Whitney HS
Visalia, CA

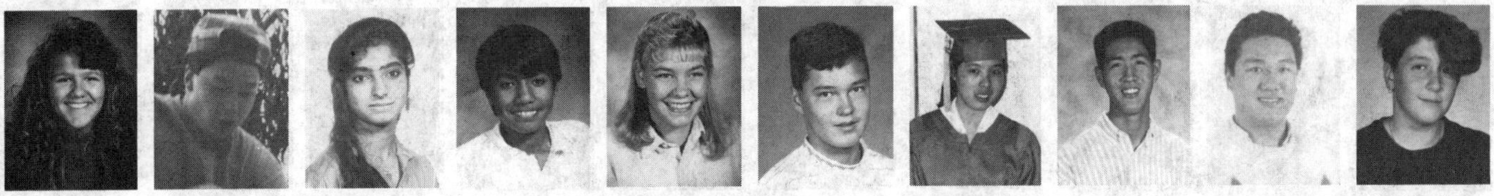

Kula, Gena N
Del Norte HS
Crescent City, CA

Kum, Tom B
Foot Hill HS
Santa Ana, CA

Kumar, Mohini L
Sequoia HS
East Palo Alto, CA

Kumar, Sunjay
Edison HS
Huntington Beach, CA

Kummer, Kimberly
West HS
Bakersfield, CA

Kung, Yung-Shin A
Bellarmine College Prep
Santa Clara, CA

Kung, Zhi Annie
Alhambra HS
Alhambra, CA

Kuo, Kane E
Whitney HS
Cerritos, CA

Kup, Eddy
Palisades HS
Pacific Palisades, CA

Kupelian, Arpi
Terra Linda HS
Corte Madera, CA

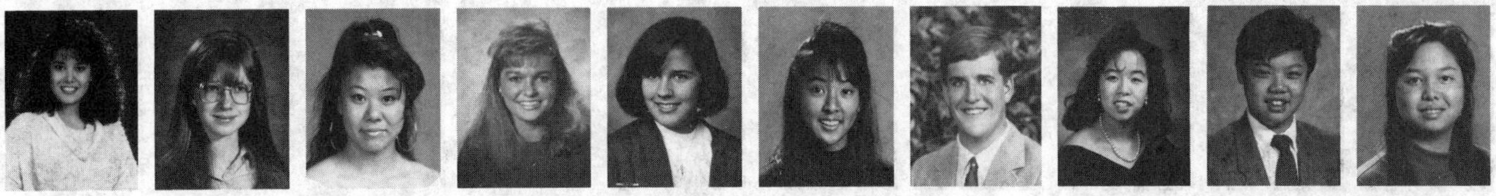

Kuroki, Tamiko
Coachella Valley HS
Coachella, CA

Kurtz, Stacey R
North HS
Bakersfield, CA

Kusunoki, Nina
Saint Bernard HS
Playa Del Rey, CA

Kutch, Koreen A.
Costa Mesa HS
Costa Mesa, CA

Kutsch, Cassandra L
Mission Bay HS
San Diego, CA

Kuwahara, Tiffany F
Gardena HS
Gardena, CA

Kuykendall, Timothy Andrew
Idllywild Schl Of Music & The Arts
Laguna Niguel, CA

Kwan, Anne
Lowell HS
San Francisco, CA

Kwan, Harry
Saint Ignatius College Prep
San Francisco, CA

Kwan, Julie W
Gardena HS
Gardena, CA

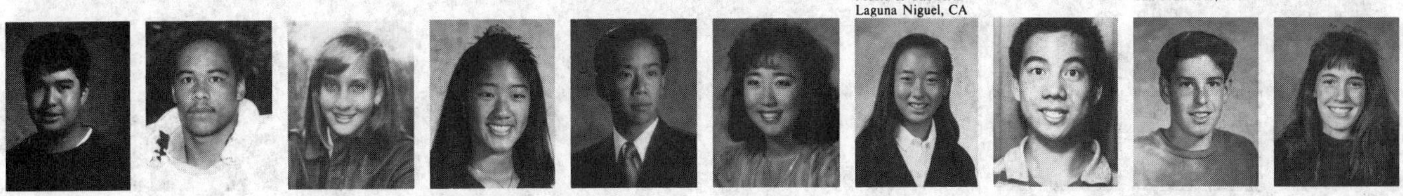

Kwan, Randy J
Miramonte HS
Orinda, CA

Kwan, Robert H
Arroyo HS
Arcadia, CA

Kwasneski, Ann M
Montgomery HS
Kenwood, CA

Kwok, Kay May
St Joseph HS
Santa Maria, CA

Kwok, Kerman
Madera HS
Madera, CA

Kwon, Angie
Notre Dame HS
Burbank, CA

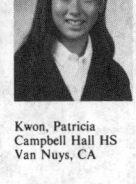

Kwon, Patricia
Campbell Hall HS
Van Nuys, CA

Kwong, Justin Y
Sacramento HS
Sacramento, CA

Kyle, Chris D
Carlsbad HS
Oceanside, CA

Kyle, Wendy J
El Camino HS
Sacramento, CA

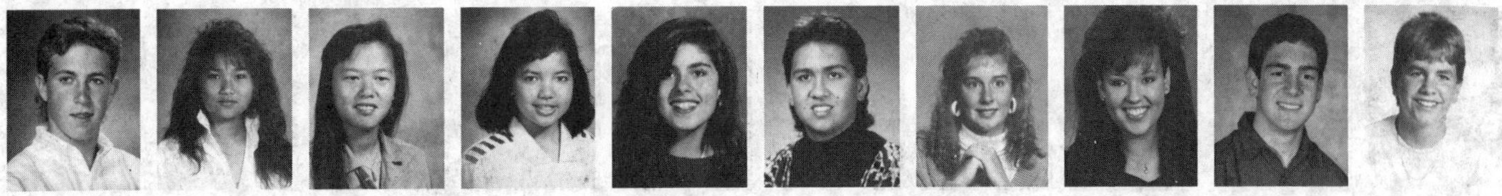

Kyser, Matthew P
Irvine HS
Irvine, CA

La, Evelyn Hanh T
Schurr HS
Monterey Park, CA

La, Le-Kim
Rosemead HS
Rosemead, CA

La, Phuong-Anh T
La Quinta HS
Westminster, CA

La Beaud, Angelle D
Lowell HS
San Francisco, CA

La Bute, Montiago X
Mt Diablo HS
W Pittsburg, CA

La Cues, Michelle I
Apple Valley HS
Apple Valley, CA

La Marr, Yeaphana
Encina HS
Sacramento, CA

La Mere, Jeffrey P
Oak Ridge HS
El Dorado Hills, CA

La Munyon, Ryan
Liberty HS
Brentwood, CA

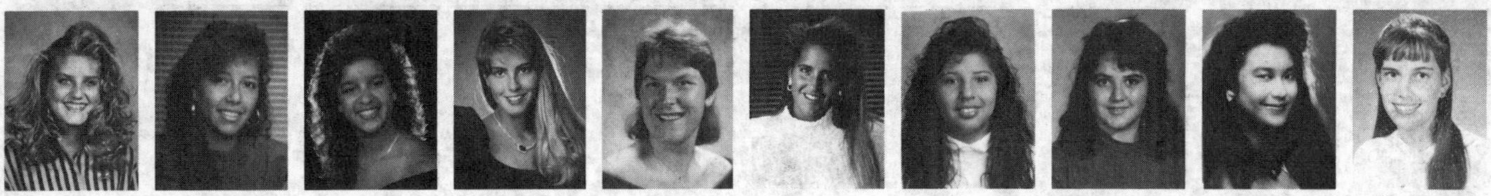

La Point, Shalom
Mesa Verde HS
Citrus Heights, CA

La Quire, Jennette
El Capitan HS
El Cajon, CA

La Riva, Yvonne
Phineas Banning HS
Wilmington, CA

La Rocque, Jennifer
Poway HS
San Diego, CA

La Rue, Brenda
Napa HS
Napa, CA

La Vallo, Gina
Vista HS
Vista, CA

La Vorico, Gina M
Woodland HS
Woodland, CA

Labate, Dona T
Dona Labate HS
San Jose, CA

Labio, Merilou
Galliguez
Diamond Bar HS
Walnut, CA

Labrecque, Michelle
Concord HS
Concord, CA

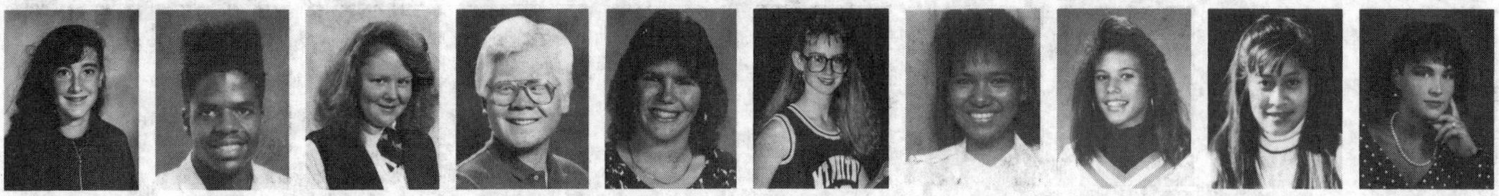

Lacey, Dina M
Clayton Valley HS
Clayton, CA

Lacey, Marlon G
San Gorgonio HS
San Bernardino, CA

Lacock, Sarah K
Apple Valley HS
Apple Valley, CA

Laconico, Michael J
Saint Francis HS
Duarte, CA

Lacy, Lori Lavelle
North Monterey
County HS
Salinas, CA

Lafaurie, Leah R
Mt Whitney HS
Visalia, CA

Lafiguera, Maricris B
Workman HS
West Covina, CA

Laflin, Bonnie-Jill
Concord HS
Concord, CA

Laforga, Abigail M
St Monica HS
Los Angeles, CA

Lagana, Elisa
Monterey HS
Carmel, CA

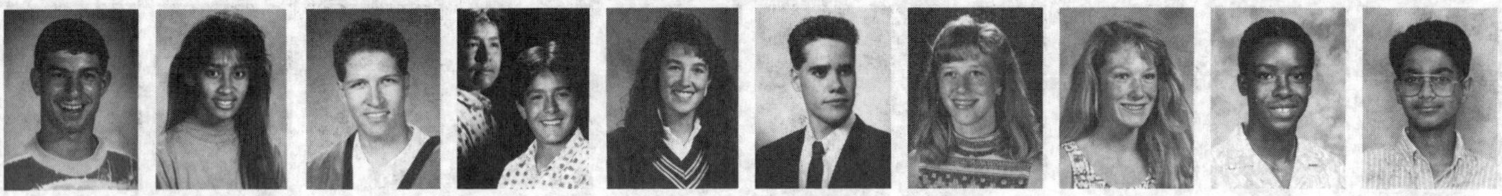

Lagatta, Vince
Cardinal Newman
Santa Rosa, CA

Lagmay, Phoebe C
Carson HS
Carson, CA

Lago, Eduardo A
Hogan HS
Vallejo, CA

Laguna, Art Nazabal
Tranquility Union HS
Mendota, CA

Laine, Rebecca
Palm Desert HS
Bermuda Dunes, CA

Laird, Brian
Cerritos HS
Cerritos, CA

Laird, Jenifer S
Alhambra HS
Martinez, CA

Lake, Heidi
Palm Desert HS
Mt Center, CA

Lake, Parker D
Bishop Amat
Memorial HS
Pomona, CA

Lakhani, Bilal M
Magnolia HS
Anaheim, CA

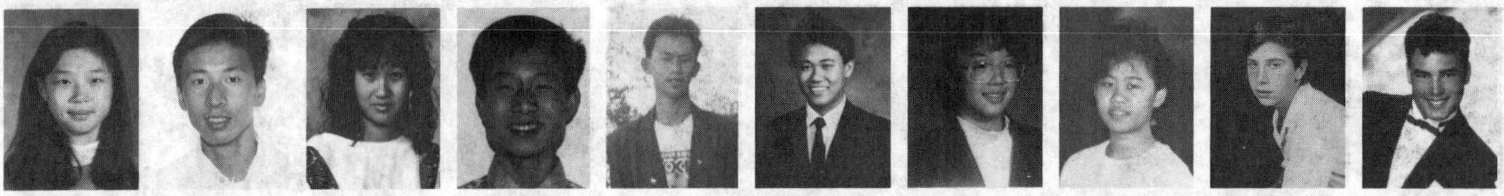

Lam, Cyndi M
Alameda HS
Alameda, CA

Lam, Dave H
Lowell HS
San Francisco, CA

Lam, Kien Loi
Cynthia
Granada Hills HS
Los Angeles, CA

Lam, Nguyen
Wallenberg HS
San Francisco, CA

Lam, Phuoc
Phillip & Sala Burton
A HS
San Francisco, CA

Lam, Tai D
Millikan HS
Long Beach, CA

Lam, Yassi
Willows HS
Willows, CA

Lamadrid, Joeann D
George Washington
San Francisco, CA

Lamas, Fernando D
Baldwin Park HS
Baldwin Park, CA

Lambert, Matthew
Antioch HS
Antioch, CA

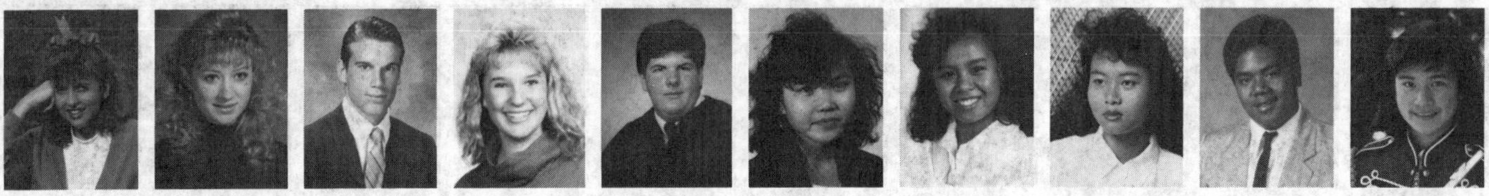

Lambert, Misty
Long Beach Jordan
Westminster, CA

Lambson, Heather E
Trinity HS
Junction City, CA

Lame, Dietrich D
South Pasadena HS
South Pasadena, CA

Lamerdin, Kristen D
Casa Roble
Fundamental HS
Citrus Heights, CA

Lamm, Manuel J
San Pedro HS
San Pedro, CA

Lamountry, Nitsa
Encina HS
Sacramento, CA

Lampitoc, Luvelyn J
Arroyo Grande HS
Arroyo Grande, CA

Lamsong, Sorikane
Elsinore Union HS
Lake Elsinore, CA

Lamug, Albert P
Carson HS
Carson, CA

Lan, Michelle C
Whitney HS
Cerritos, CA

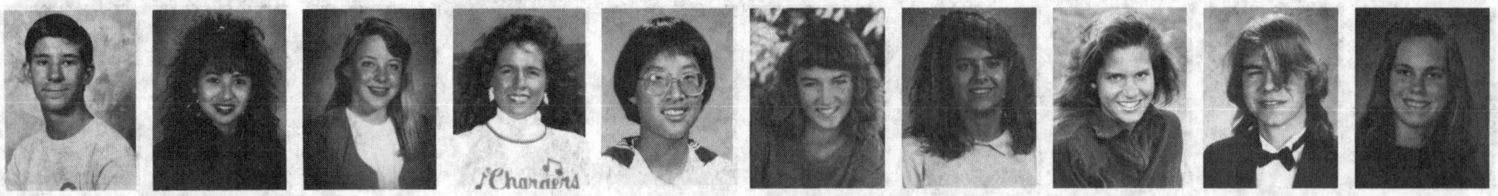

Lande, Erik S
Orange Glen HS
Lancaster, CA

Landeros, Claudia
Schurr HS
Los Angeles, CA

Landis, Erin B
East Bakersfield HS
Bakersfield, CA

Landon, Serena L
El Toro HS
El Toro, CA

Lane, Elizabeth S
Lowell HS
San Francisco, CA

Lane, Heather L
Bakersfield HS
Bakersfield, CA

Lane, Julie A
Oak Park HS
Agoura, CA

Lang, Cathy
Alta Loma HS
Alta Loma, CA

Lang, Donald J
Monta Vista HS
Cupertino, CA

Langenfeld,
Stephanie M
Trabuco Hills HS
Mission Viejo, CA

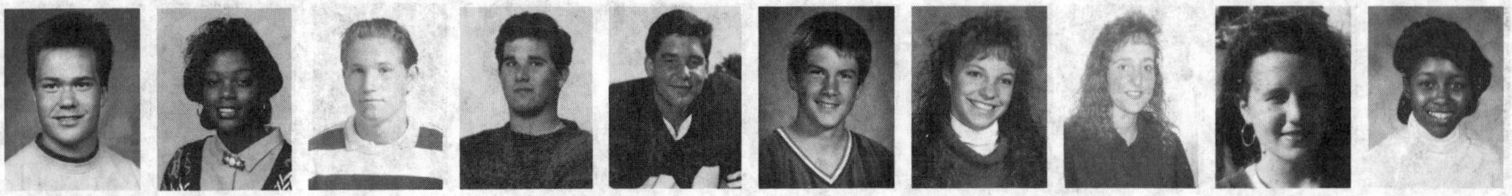

Langford, Charles D
Mountain Empire HS
Boulevard, CA

Langhorne-Johnson,
Monique
Vallejo SR HS
Vallejo, CA

Langille, Mark David
Moreno Valley HS
Moreno Valley, CA

Langley, Brian
Paso Robles HS
Paso Robles, CA

Langley, Jeffrey Ray
Antelope Valley HS
Lancaster, CA

Langley, Simon J
Lone Pine HS
Lone Pine, CA

Langs, Cinnamon
Irvington HS
Fremont, CA

Lani, Janelle
Rosary HS
Yorba Linda, CA

Lanier, Keri
Woodland HS
Woodland, CA

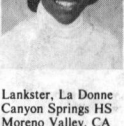

Lankster, La Donne
Canyon Springs HS
Moreno Valley, CA

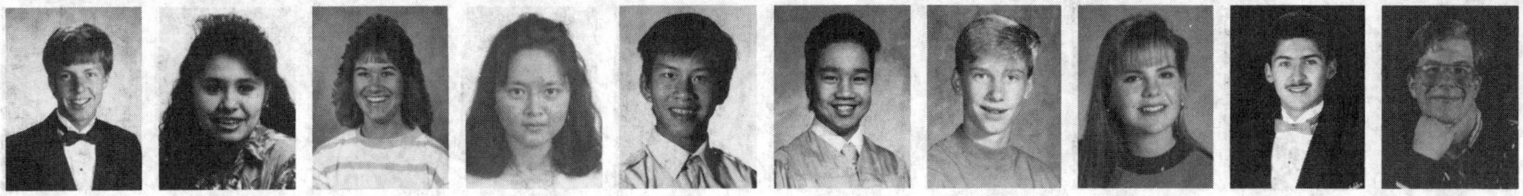

Lanning, Brent J
San Ramon Valley
Danville, CA

Lano, Destiney D
Amos Alonzo Stagg
Stockton, CA

Lant, Brie L
Mesa Verde HS
Citrus Heights, CA

Lao, Easttina Ngek
Mayfield SR Schl
Alhambra, CA

Lao, Vinh Tan
Elk Grove HS
Sacramento, CA

Lapid, Roy P
Lowell HS
San Francisco, CA

Lapin, Jackson P
Carlmont HS
Belmont, CA

Lapkin, Emily N
Palm Springs HS
Palm Springs, CA

Lara, Gerardo
John F Kennedy HS
Fremont, CA

Larner, Rusty J
Morro Bay HS
Morro Bay, CA

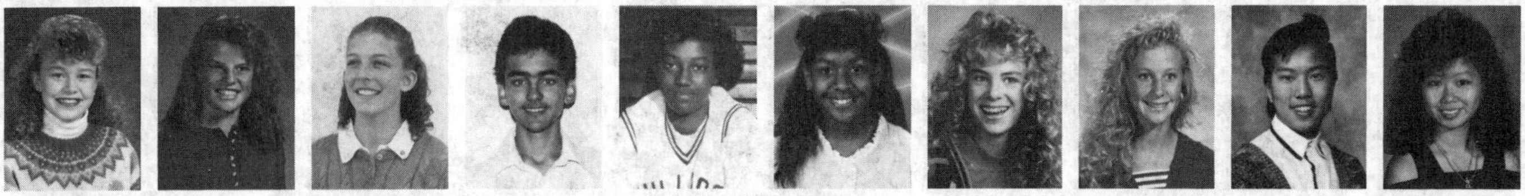

Larsen, Tiffany
Hillsdale HS
Foster City, CA

Larson, Nicole L.
Hemet HS
Hemet, CA

Larson, Viktoria J
Novato HS
Novato, CA

Lasic, Robert V
San Gabriel HS
Rosemead, CA

Laster, Annette
Pasadena HS
Pasadena, CA

Latour, Angelique
St Anthony HS
Compton, CA

Latta, Tristan
Capital Christian HS
Rancho Cordova, CA

Lattin, Andrea
Enterprise HS
Redding, CA

Lau, Casey Kien
Chung
Granada Hills HS
Northridge, CA

Lau, Connie H
George Washington
San Francisco, CA

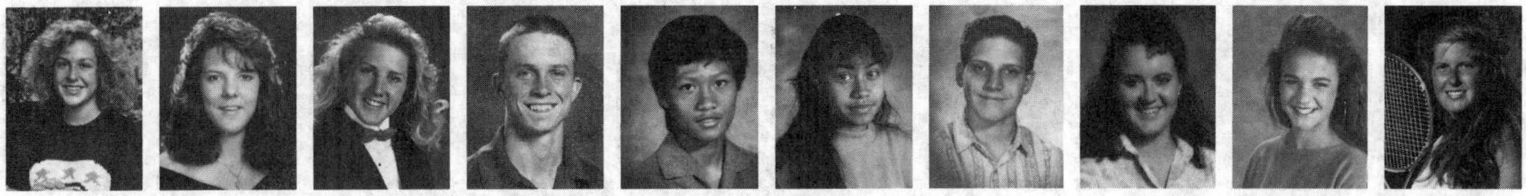

Laughlin, Barbara D
North Monterey
County HS
Castroville, CA

Launius, Kami Suree
Corning Union HS
Corning, CA

Lauren, Christie
Carlmont HS
San Carlos, CA

Laurence, Patrick M
Saint Francis HS
Pasadena, CA

Lauricio, Richard F
Delano HS
Delano, CA

Lauti, Elizabeth L
Jefferson HS
San Francisco, CA

Lautt, Adam
Desert Christian HS
Palmdale, CA

Lavin, Marianne
Junipero Serra HS
San Diego, CA

Law, Amy
Victory Christian
Schl
Cardiff, CA

Law, Ann Marie
Marina HS
Huntington Beach,
CA

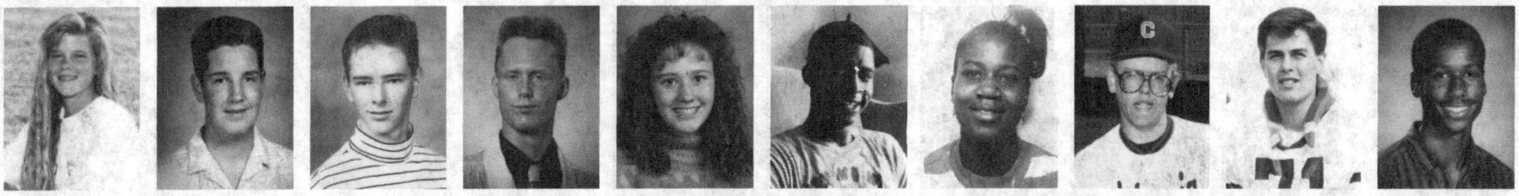

Law, Karie A
Mission Viejo HS
Mission Viejo, CA

Lawenda, Steven
El Camino Real HS
West Hills, CA

Lawniczak, Jon R
San Diego HS
San Diego, CA

Lawrence, Byron
Schurr HS
Rosemead, CA

Lawrence, Cinnamon
Hanford Joint Union
Hanford, CA

Lawrence, Trevor I
Hamilton Academy
Of Music
Studio City, CA

Laws, Sharawn
Sunshine HS
San Francisco, CA

Lawson, Craig A
California HS
Hayward, CA

Lawson, II Gary
Coronado HS
Coronado, CA

Lawton, II Marvin M
Washington Prep
Los Angeles, CA

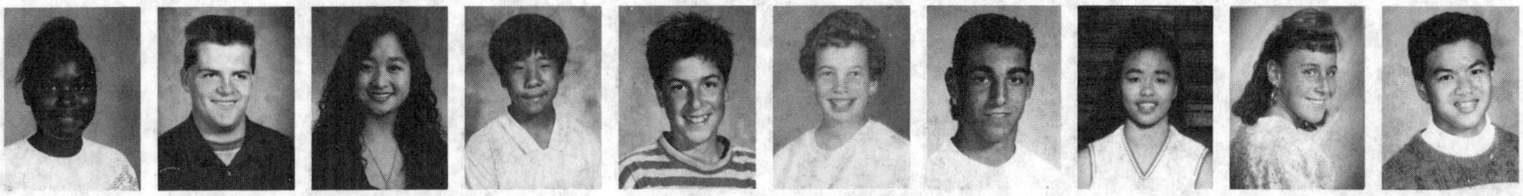

Lawton, Sonia R
Oceanside HS
Oceanside, CA

Lay, Kenneth L
East Bakersfield HS
Bakersfield, CA

Lay, Romaniravi N
University HS
Irvine, CA

Lay, Thomas
Brea-Olinda HS
Brea, CA

Layfield, Nelson E
Homestead HS
Sunnyvale, CA

Layman, Bobbie Jean
Lincoln HS
Stockton, CA

Layne, Jeff
Santa Teresa HS
San Jose, CA

Layson, Sherill B
St Patrick-St Vincent
Vallejo, CA

Layton, Carrie A
Mater Dei HS
Los Alamitos, CA

Layug, Marlon D
George Washington
San Francisco, CA

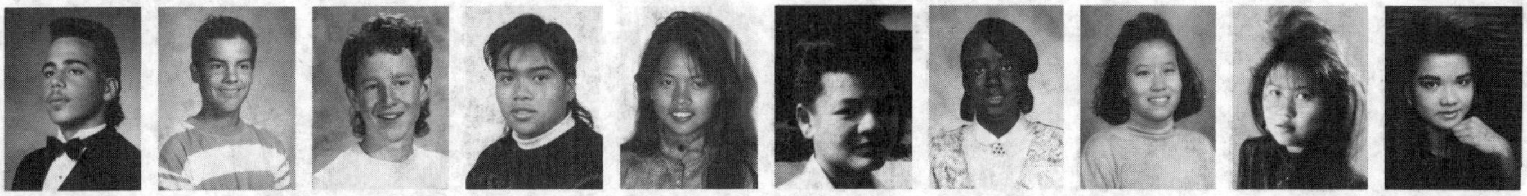

Lazarowich, Kamil D
Liberty Baptist HS
San Jose, CA

Lazcano, Inaki
Oak Park HS
Agoura Hills, CA

Lazier, Matt T
Templeton HS
Templeton, CA

Lazo, Jeremiah D
Seaside HS
Marina, CA

Lazo, Madonna
Shiela Ramos
Alta Loma HS
Rancho Cucamonga,
CA

Le, Dang H
Fontana HS
Moreno Valley, CA

Le, Hung V
Mira Loma HS
Sacramento, CA

Le, Linda
Redlands HS
Loma Linda, CA

Le, Mai-Tram
C K Mc Clatchy HS
Sacramento, CA

Le, Ngoc
Monte Vista HS
Spring Valley, CA

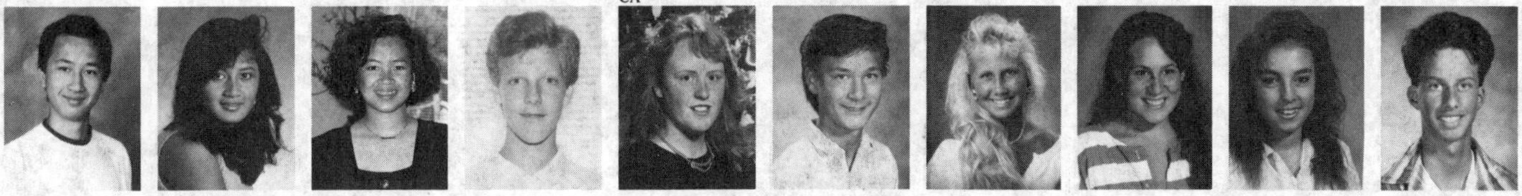

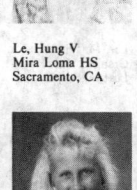

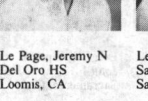

Le, Phuc
Ocean View HS
Fountain Valle, CA

Le, Serena L
Notre Dame HS
San Jose, CA

Le, Therese
San Ramon Valley
Alamo, CA

Le Baron, Matt W
Monterey HS
Monterey, CA

Le Barron, Sandy E
Antelope Valley HS
Lancaster, CA

Le Page, Jeremy N
Del Oro HS
Loomis, CA

Le Veau, Betina L
San Dieguito HS
San Diego, CA

Lea, Shannon S
Paradise HS
Paradise, CA

Leach, Jackie J
Bloomington HS
Bloomington, CA

Leache, Adam D
Huntington Beach
Huntington Beach,
CA

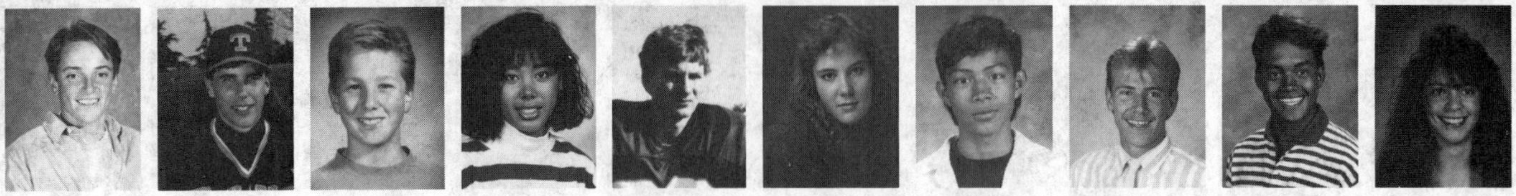

Leahy, Jordan M
Santa Cruz HS
Santa Cruz, CA

Leal, Burt H
Tulare Union HS
Tulare, CA

Leal, Evan
Sonoma Valley HS
Sonoma, CA

Leano, Sharon
Saint Francis HS
Folsom, CA

Leavitt, Cary L
Gridley Union HS
Gridley, CA

Leckbee, Robyn
Ventura HS
Oak View, CA

Ledbetter, Carlo W
Ramona HS
Ramona, CA

Ledbetter, Matthew
Chestnut Ave Baptist
Acad
Clovis, CA

Ledbetter, Woody T
Ramona HS
Ramona, CA

Ledezma, Eva B
Portola JR SR HS
Portola, CA

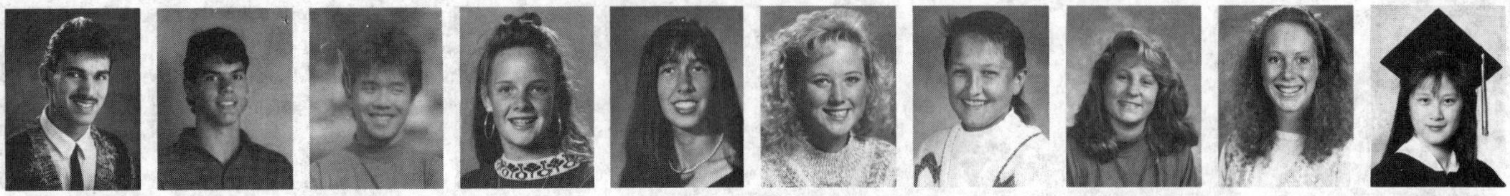

Ledezma, Martin R
Tulare Western HS
Tulare, CA

Ledgerwood,
Jefferson S
Rio Mesa HS
Camarillo, CA

Lee, Albert
Walnut HS
Walnut, CA

Lee, Allison
Culver City HS
Culver City, CA

Lee, Amie M
Pioneer HS
San Jose, CA

Lee, Becky
Rim Of The World
Lake Arrowhead, CA

Lee, Brian J
Grace M Davis HS
Modesto, CA

Lee, Carisa A
Bishop O'dowd HS
Oakland, CA

Lee, Christina M
Ramona HS
Ramona, CA

Lee, Chun Ying
Maria
Artesia HS
Cerritos, CA

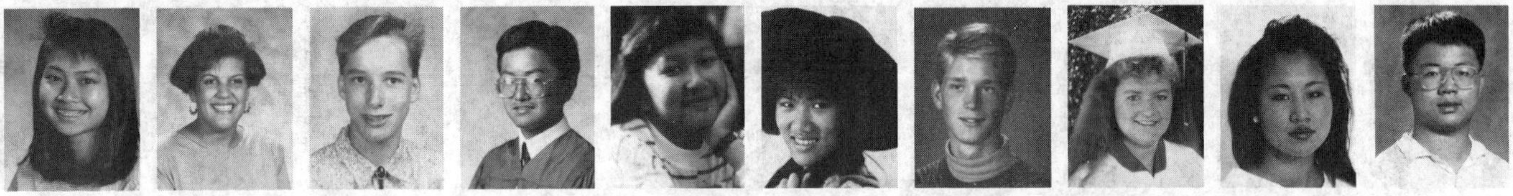

Lee, Cora Ho
Palm Springs HS
Palm Springs, CA

Lee, Dana E
Whitney HS
Cerritos, CA

Lee, David
Casa Roble
Fundamental HS
Orangevale, CA

Lee, Do J
Bellarmine HS
Los Altos, CA

Lee, Ellen
Sacramento HS
Sacramento, CA

Lee, Ellenita
North HS
Torrance, CA

Lee, Eric
Clovis West HS
Fresno, CA

Lee, Erin A
Redlands SR HS
Redlands, CA

Lee, Eun
Carson SR HS
Carson, CA

Lee, Frank C
San Marino HS
San Marino, CA

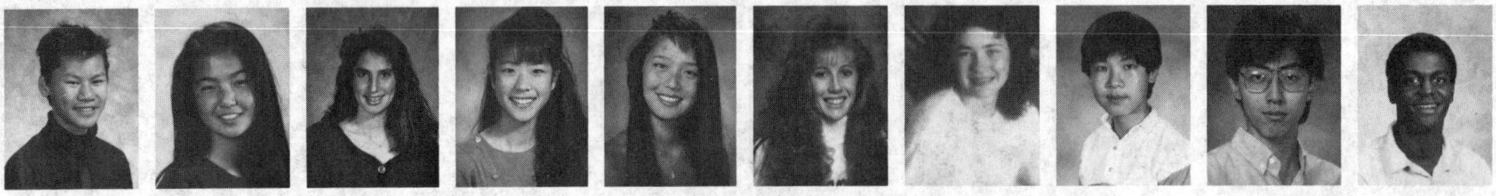

Lee, Gerald M
Bishop O'dowd HS
Oakland, CA

Lee, Gina G
Crossroads School
For Arts And
Malibu, CA

Lee, Gina M
Cupertino HS
Cupertino, CA

Lee, Grace J
Fountain Valley HS
Fountain Valley, CA

Lee, Grace K
El Toro HS
El Toro, CA

Lee, Heather
Canyon HS
Canyon Country, CA

Lee, Heidi M
Mariposa County HS
Midpines, CA

Lee, Holton L
Skyline HS
Oakland, CA

Lee, Jang C
El Toro HS
Irvine, CA

Lee, Jason T
Berkeley HS
Oakland, CA

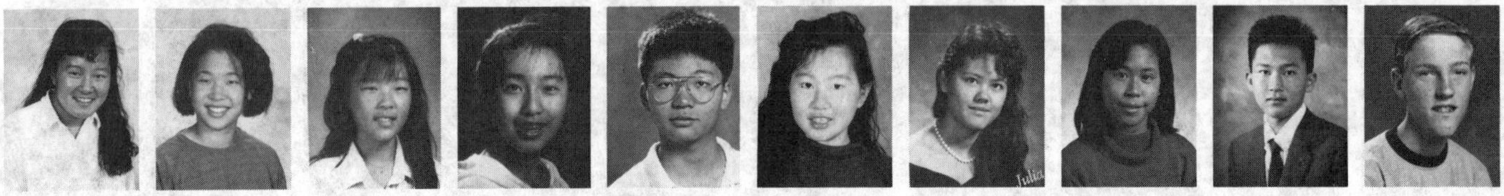

Lee, Jeannie Y
Berkeley HS
El Cerrito, CA

Lee, Jennifer
Los Altos HS
Hacienda Heights,
CA

Lee, Jenny
Arcadia HS
Arcadia, CA

Lee, Jessie J
Glendale HS
Glendale, CA

Lee, John C
San Marino HS
San Marino, CA

Lee, Joyce Y
Lowell HS
San Francisco, CA

Lee, Julia C
Alameda HS
Alameda, CA

Lee, Katherine Y
John F Kennedy HS
Sacramento, CA

Lee, Kenneth
Irvine HS
Irvine, CA

Lee, Larry C
Rim Of The World
Crestline, CA

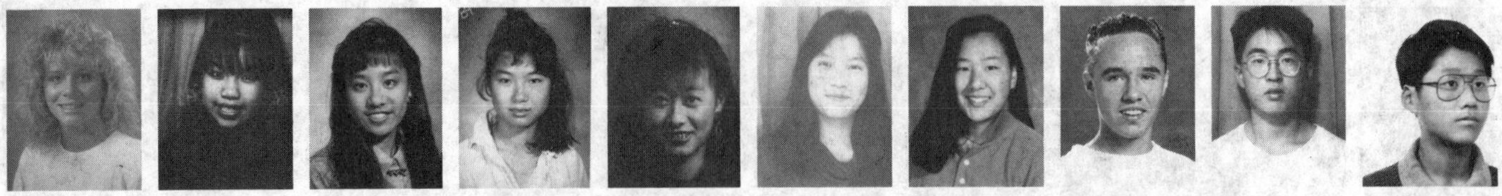

Lee, Lynette
Gridley HS
Oroville, CA

Lee, Lynette
Woodrow Wilson HS
San Francisco, CA

Lee, Maevonne
Marina HS
Huntington Beach,
CA

Lee, Maggie W
Granada Hills HS
Los Angeles, CA

Lee, Nadia M
San Marino HS
San Marino, CA

Lee, Neng
Edison Computech
Fresno, CA

Lee, Renee
Miramonte HS
Orinda, CA

Lee, Rex B
Herbert Hoover HS
Glendale, CA

Lee, Robert W
La Canada HS
La Canada, CA

Lee, Sammy
Downey HS
Downey, CA

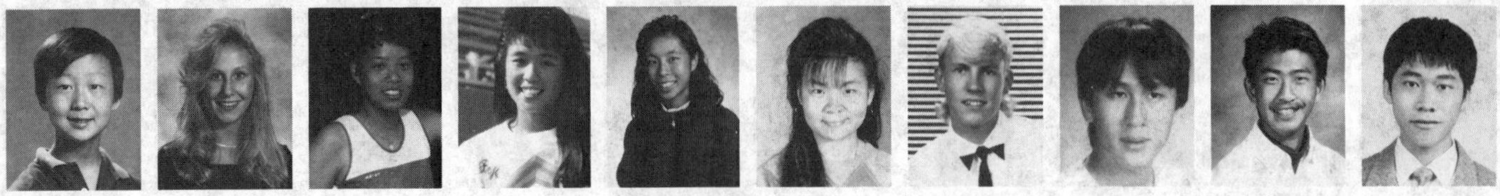

Lee, Sang Y
Hamilton
Hummanities HS
Panorama City, CA

Lee, Shannin
Canyon HS
Canyon Country, CA

Lee, Shannon T
St Marys HS
Stockton, CA

Lee, Soyeon Sunny
Bloomington HS
Bloomington, CA

Lee, Stephanie A
John F Kennedy HS
Sacramento, CA

Lee, Teresa M
Lowell HS
San Francisco, CA

Lee, Timothy
Sean-David
Atascadero HS
Atascadero, CA

Lee, Wa
Clovis HS
Clovis, CA

Lee, Wayne H
Edison HS
Huntington Beach,
CA

Lee, Wei-Chia
Woodside Priory HS
Hillsborough, CA

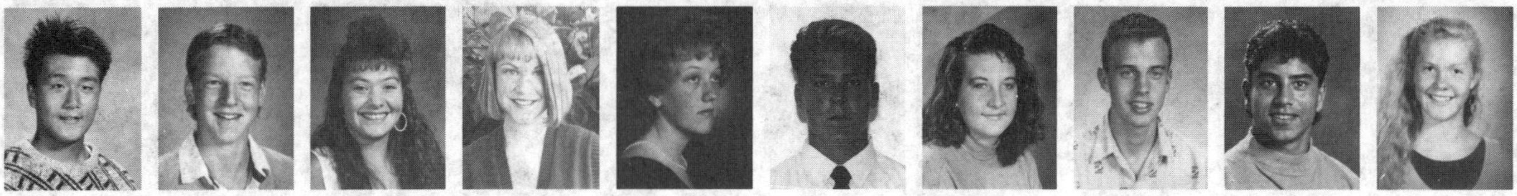

Lee, Yu
Mount Eden HS
Hayward, CA

Leech, III Walter A
Atwater HS
Atwater, CA

Leeper, Sherrah
Hemet HS
Hemet, CA

Leer, Denise Y
Modesto HS
Modesto, CA

Leesmann, Kathy
Vallejo SR HS
Vallejo, CA

Lefevre, Dennis A
Torrance HS
Torrance, CA

Leger, Chodi
Davis SR HS
Davis, CA

Lehto, Jason
North Tahoe HS
Tahoe Vista, CA

Leibee, Skye J
Taft Union HS
Taft, CA

Leigh, Tara J
Willits HS
Willits, CA

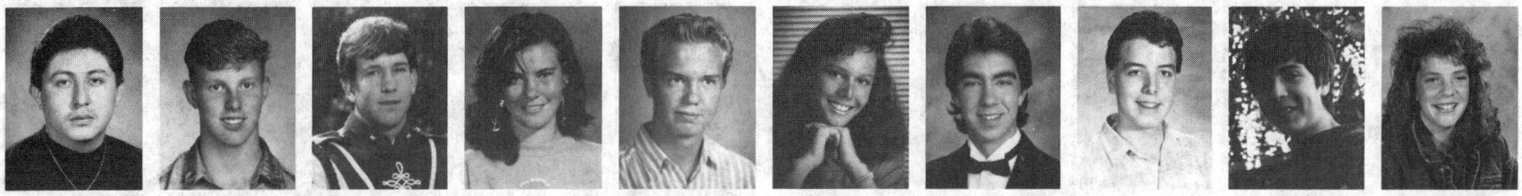

Leija, Enrigue
Artesia HS
Hawaiian Gardens, CA

Leimer, Ron G
Colfax HS
Applegate, CA

Leimgruger, Ricky
Holtville HS
Holtville, CA

Leith, Stacy
Savanna HS
Anaheim, CA

Leitner, David C
Calaveras HS
Valley Springs, CA

Leitner, Tammy
Grossmont HS
El Cajon, CA

Leivas, Tige Robert
Rio Mesa HS
Oxnard, CA

Lemasters, Thomas C
Chino HS
Ontario, CA

Lemke, Mark
St Lawrence Acad
San Jose, CA

Lemos, Michelle D
Arroyo Grande HS
Arroyo Grande, CA

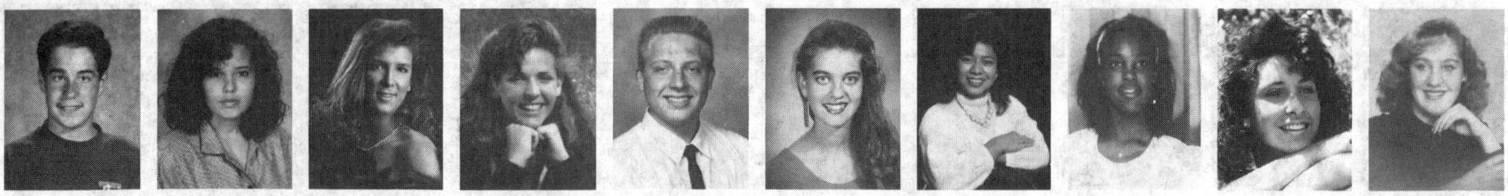

Lempert, Benjamin R
Lowell HS
San Francisco, CA

Lemus, Diana
San Gabriel Mission
Alhambra, CA

Lence, Holly
Granada HS
Livermore, CA

Lenger, Stacia
Santa Ynez Valley Union HS
Santa Ynez, CA

Lenhart, Michael A
Mountain Empire HS
Boulevard, CA

Lenz, Jessica
Vanden HS
Suisun City, CA

Leon, Maria Isabel
Centennial HS
Corona, CA

Leon, Myrtle
Loretto-Conaty HS
Los Angeles, CA

Leone, Keri
Carondelet HS
Clayton, CA

Leoni, Tina
Dublin HS
Dublin, CA

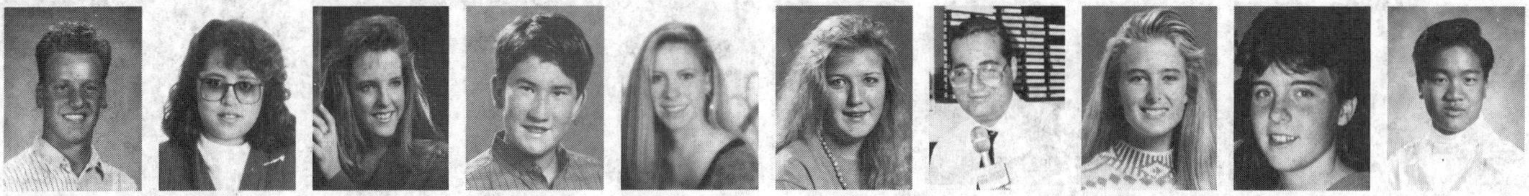

Leontas, Chris
Hesperia Christian Schl
Hesperia, CA

Lepale, Joann L
Bassett HS
La Puente, CA

Lepper, Michele M
Simi Valley HS
Simi Valley, CA

Lerner, Michael
Cajon HS
San Bernardino, CA

Lesh, Jenniffer L
Delano HS
Delano, CA

Leslie, Marinda R
Norte Vista HS
Riverside, CA

Lesser, Hadrian D
Beverly Hills HS
Beverly Hills, CA

Lessley, Shannon
Rim Of The World
Lake Arrowhead, CA

Leszkay, Blythe
Moorpark HS
Simi Valley, CA

Leung, Michael H
Walnut HS
Walnut, CA

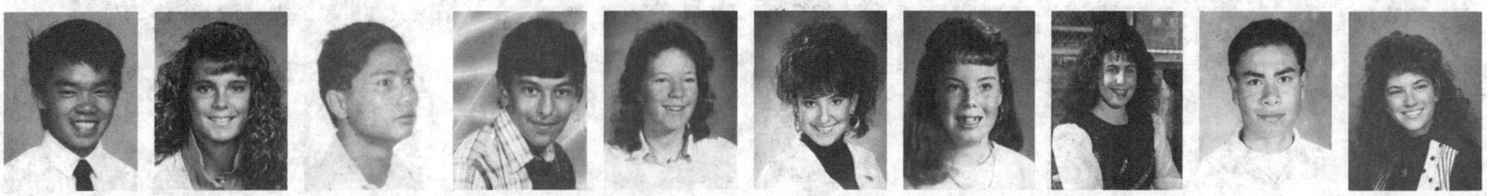

Leung, Stephen W
John F Kennedy SR
Sacramento, CA

Levan, Christy
Roseville HS
Rocklin, CA

Levan, Michael
Valley HS
Elk Grove, CA

Levato, Jason C
Ontario HS
Buena Park, CA

Leverett, Dawn R
Sutter Union HS
Yuba City, CA

Levitt, Stephanie Jean
Westlake HS
Thousand Oaks, CA

Levreau, Elaine L
Clovis HS
Fresno, CA

Levy, Allison
Simi Valley HS
Simi Valley, CA

Levy, David D
Lowell HS
San Francisco, CA

Levy, Erica Robin
Valhalla HS
El Cajon, CA

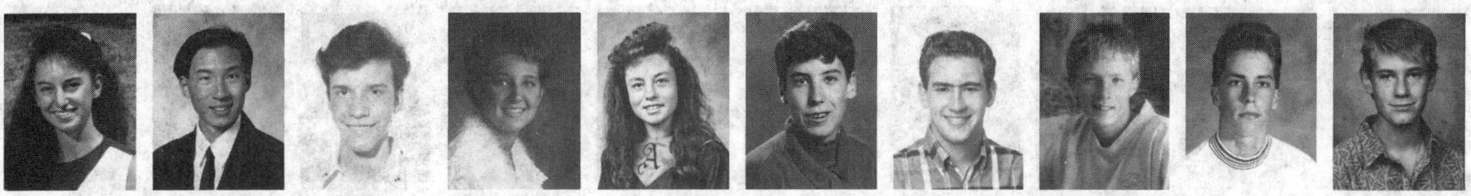

Levy, Helen
Dos Pueblos HS
Goleta, CA

Lew, Mark W
Leuzinger HS
Hawthorne, CA

Lewandowski, Gregory
Daniel Murphy HS
Los Angeles, CA

Lewellen, Allegra
Fresno Christian HS
Fresno, CA

Lewis, Barbara
Arlington HS
Riverside, CA

Lewis, Chad E
San Dimas HS
San Dimas, CA

Lewis, David A
Bellarmine College Prep
Gilroy, CA

Lewis, David W
Wasco Union HS
Wasco, CA

Lewis, Don V
Lower Lake HS
Clearlake, CA

Lewis, Dylan B
Grossmont HS
El Cajon, CA

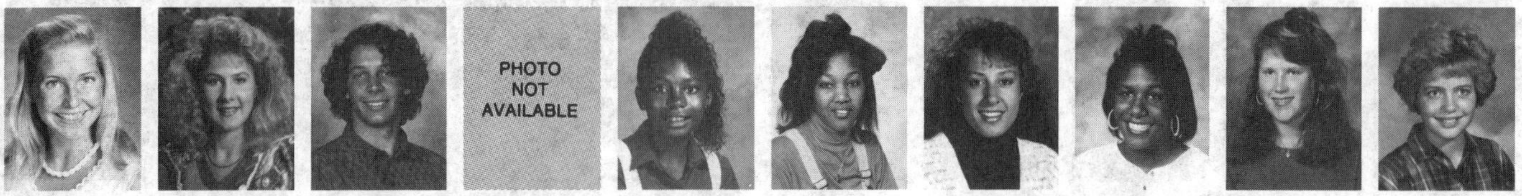

PHOTO
NOT
AVAILABLE

Lewis, Erica Susan Elizabeth
San Pasqual HS
Escondido, CA

Lewis, Heather A
El Toro HS
El Toro, CA

Lewis, Isaac J
Helix HS
La Mesa, CA

Lewis, Jan C
Diamond Bar HS
Diamond Bar, CA

Lewis, Jernea M
Canyon Springs HS
Moreno Valley, CA

Lewis, Joya Monique
Sunset HS
Hayward, CA

Lewis, Kari
Arroyo HS
San Lorenzo, CA

Lewis, Medea A
Armijo HS
Fairfield, CA

Lewis, Melanie A
Fairfield HS
Fairfield, CA

Lewis, Tami E
Monache HS
Porterville, CA

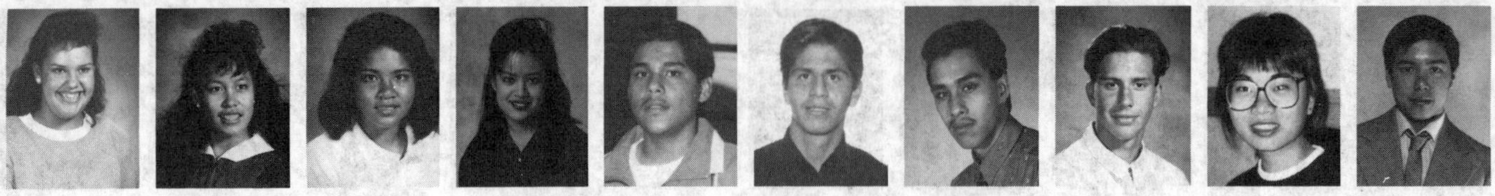

Lewis, Tracey L
Victor Valley SR HS
Victorville, CA

Leyran, Marie T
Saint Joseph HS
Cerritos, CA

Leyretana, Anne C
Mater Dei HS
Anaheim, CA

Leyson, Jennifer M
Emerson HS
Orange, CA

Leyua, Sergio
Chino HS
Chino, CA

Leyva, Jose A
Pasadena HS
Pasadena, CA

Leyva, Mario A
Indio HS
Indio, CA

Leyya, Jesus I
Artisia HS
Cerritos, CA

Li, Ellie Y
International Studies
Acad
San Francisco, CA

Li, Jian Feng
International Studies
Acad
San Francisco, CA

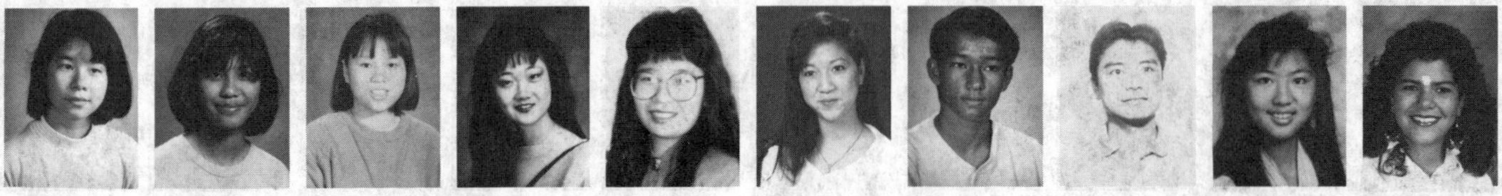

Li, Jin L
Edison HS
Stockton, CA

Li, Kitty K
Sierra Vista HS
Baldwin Park, CA

Li, Mary Zhi Yan
Abraham Lincoln HS
San Francisco, CA

Li, Su-En
West Covina HS
W Covina, CA

Li, Yaying
International Studies
Acad
San Francisco, CA

Li, Yi Y
Oakland Technical
Oakland, CA

Liamsithisack,
Souriyo
Edison HS
Stockton, CA

Liang, Eugene J
J Eugene Mc Ateer
San Francisco, CA

Liao, Maggie
Arcadia HS
Arcadia, CA

Liautaud, Valerie M
Bishop Amat
Memorial HS
Diamond Bar, CA

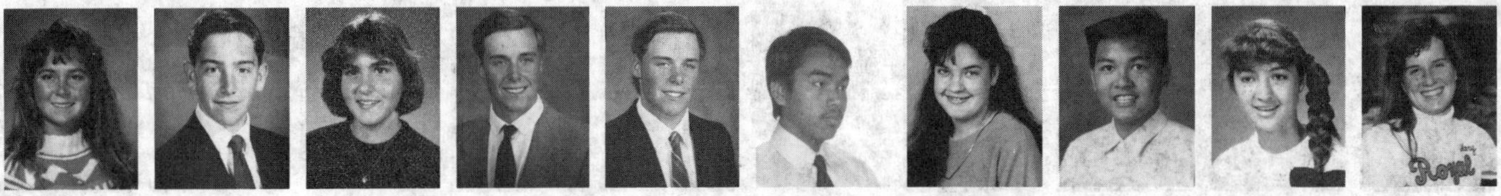

Liddy, Shannon M
Eltoro HS
El Toro, CA

Liebel, Christopher J
St Michaels Prep
San Clemente, CA

Lieber, Katherine
Stewart
Monte Vista HS
Danville, CA

Lietzow, Eric
John F Kennedy HS
La Palma, CA

Lietzow, Michael T
John F Kennedy HS
La Palma, CA

Lieu, Van C
Montclair HS
Montclair, CA

Lightbourn, Jeanne
Ann
Royal HS
Simi Valley, CA

Ligon, R Jason
Bonita Vista HS
Bonita, CA

Ligouri, Michelle
Concord HS
Concord, CA

Likins, Mary
Royal HS
Simi Valley, CA

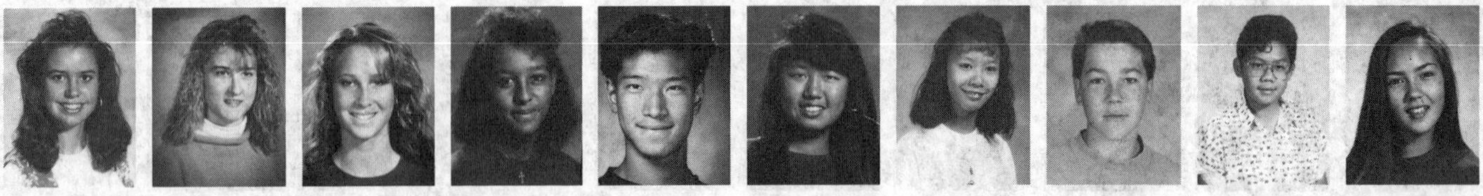

Liles, Heather Nicole
Canyon HS
Plano, TX

Liles, Tawni L
Fort Dick Bible Acad
Brookings, OR

Lillard, Andrea K
Temecula Valley HS
Temecula, CA

Lilly, Corina L
Norte Vista HS
Riverside, CA

Lim, Brian Se Hoon
Irvine HS
Irvine, CA

Lim, Kathleen Sun
Flintridge
Preparatory Schl
La Canada, CA

Lim, Tricia D
Valley View HS
Moreno Valley, CA

Lima, Eric G
Dos Palos HS
Dos Palos, CA

Limbaga, Aries J
California HS
Whittier, CA

Limbasuta, Nicole A
Pasadena HS
Pasadena, CA

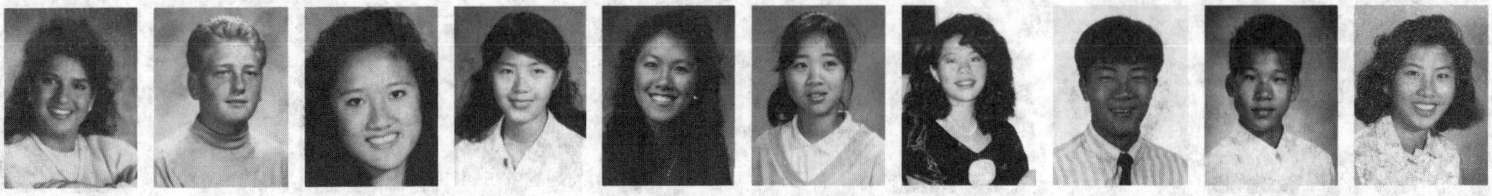

Limon, Cristina A
Thomas Downey HS
Modesto, CA

Limon, Xavier
Fremont Christian
Fremont, CA

Lin, Belinda T
Hayward HS
Hayward, CA

Lin, Christine
Chia-Jung
Miramonte HS
Moraga, CA

Lin, Judy H
Woodbridge HS
Laguna Hills, CA

Lin, Lenna
Galileo HS
San Francisco, CA

Lin, Linda
Garces Memorial HS
Bakersfield, CA

Lin, Patrick
Burlingame HS
Burlingame, CA

Lin, Steven D
University HS
Irvine, CA

Lin, Ting-Yao
Davis SR HS
Davis, CA

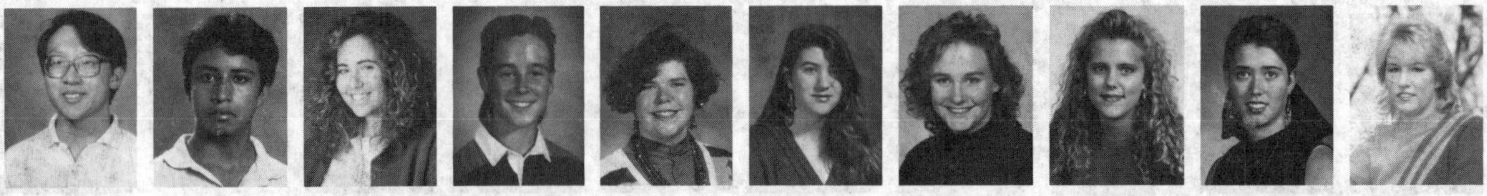

Lin, Yong
Mt Whitney HS
Visalia, CA

Linares, Joe
William Howard Taft
Los Angeles, CA

Linares, Lisa M
Saint Monica
Catholic HS
Culver City, CA

Lincoln, David
Cardinal Newman
Windsor, CA

Lincoln, Felicia J
Los Alamitos HS
Los Alamitos, CA

Lincoln, Lalainia M
St Paul HS
Whittier, CA

Lincoln, Michelle L
Casa Roble
Fundamental HS
Orangevale, CA

Lincoln, Sarah L
Skyline HS
Oakland, CA

Lindberg, Nicole H
Grace M Davis HS
Modesto, CA

Linder, Jodie
Cloverdale HS
Cloverdale, CA

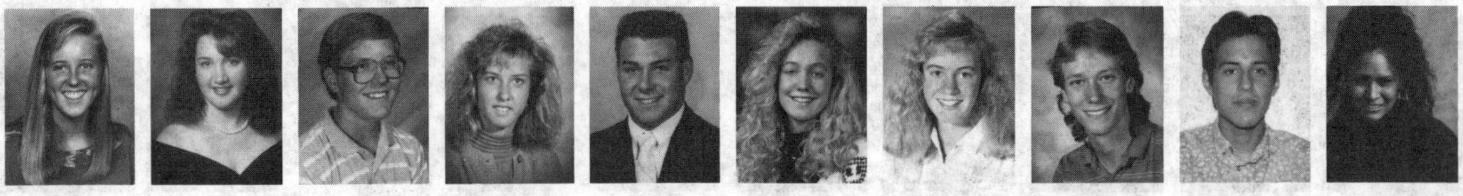

Lindgren, Jennifer L
Valhalla HS
El Cajon, CA

Lindley, Joanna
Marie
St Patrick - St
Vincent HS
Vallejo, CA

Lindquist, Joshua
Victor Valley
Christian HS
Barstow, CA

Lindsay, Heather J
Burroughs HS
Ridgecrest, CA

Lindsey, Robin R
Marina HS
Trabuco Canyon, CA

Lindstrand, Christine
North Salinas HS
Salinas, CA

Lindstrom, Kimberly
Foothill HS
Tustin, CA

Linenberger, Mike
Mt View HS
Burney, CA

Linfoot, Andy J
Paraclete HS
Lancaster, CA

Ling, Tamara J
George Washington
San Francisco, CA

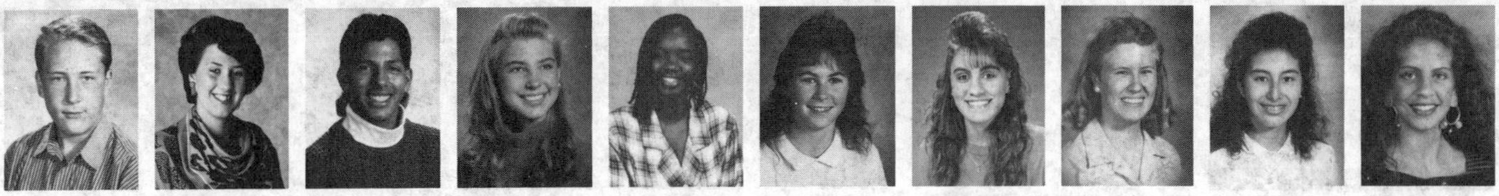

Linhart, Grant W
Notre Dame HS
Murrieta, CA

Linley, Charmaine
North County
Christian HS
Atascadero, CA

Linn, Marc
Riverbank HS
Oakdale, CA

Linnert, Ali
Mater Dei HS
Anaheim, CA

Linnes, Phyllis L
Hanford HS
Hanford, CA

Linstad, Michelle L
Vintage HS
Napa, CA

Linstad, Shannon
Pinole Valley HS
Pinole, CA

Lippy, Brooke
East Bakersfield HS
Bakersfield, CA

Lira, Gloria A
Saddleback HS
Santa Ana, CA

Lisle, Deborah M
Whittier Christian
Whittier, CA

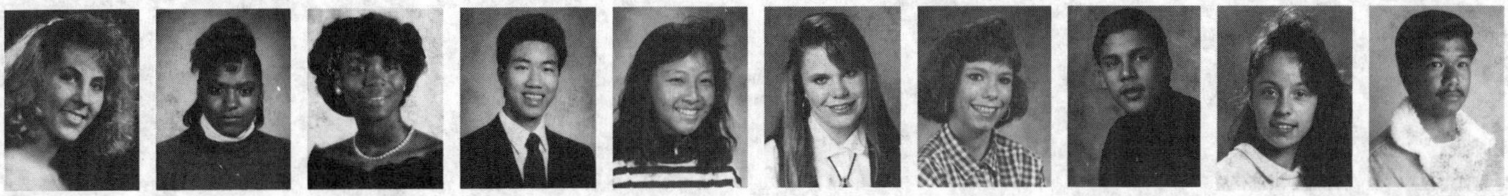

Little, Bethany
Gridley HS
Gridley, CA

Littlepage, Evelyn L
Vanden HS
Vacaville, CA

Littleton, Ronda
Shalon
Eden Christian Acad
Oakland, CA

Liu, David R
Poly HS
Riverside, CA

Liu, Emily
Temple City HS
San Gabriel, CA

Lively, Penny
Hillcrest Christian
Schl
Mission Hills, CA

Livingston, Tiffiny L
Turlock HS
Turlock, CA

Lizarraga, Alvaro
Calexico HS
Calexico, CA

Llamas, Eva Beatriz
James Monroe HS
Panorama City, CA

Llave, Bernard
Channel Islands HS
Oxnard, CA

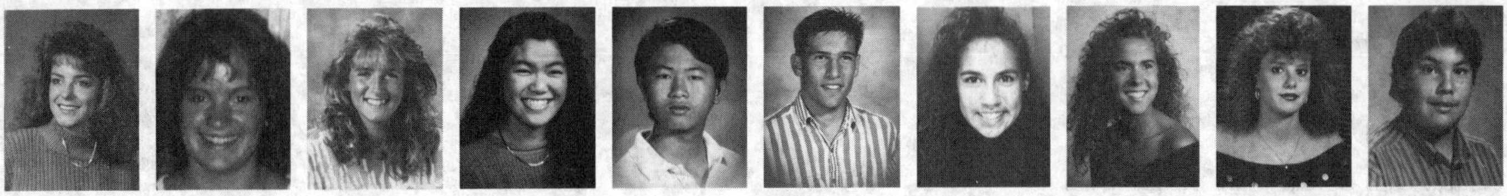

Lloyd, Casey
Palo Verde HS
Blythe, CA

Lloyd, Danelle M
Mira Costa HS
Hawthorne, CA

Lloyd, Renea
West HS
Torrance, CA

Lo, Aileen
Lincoln HS
Stockton, CA

Lo, Dickinson K
Irvine HS
Irvine, CA

Locatelli, Jason
Kingsburg HS
Selma, CA

Lockhart, Kelly C
Etiwanda HS
Alta Loma, CA

Loczi, Magda
Moorpark HS
Moorpark, CA

Loeffler, Brigitte L
Arlington HS
Riverside, CA

Loera, Joseph A
William Workman
Valinda, CA

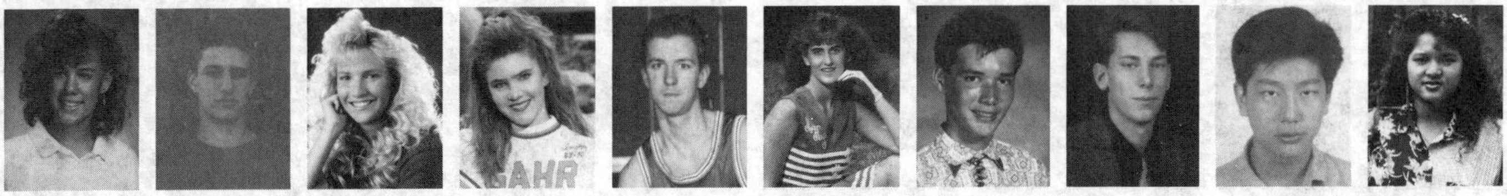

Loesch, Dawn
Arcadia HS
Arcadia, CA

Loesch, Phillip
Reedley HS
Galt, CA

Loewen, Shauna D
Fresno Christian HS
Fresno, CA

Lofstedt, Ingra L
Gahr HS
Cerritos, CA

Lofton, Jeffrey A
Hilmar HS
Turlock, CA

Logoluso, Michelle
Madera HS
Madera, CA

Logsdon, Eddie N
W T Ellis HS
Olivehurst, CA

Lohr, Jr John
29 Palms HS
Twentynine Palm,
CA

Lohrungruang, Jamie
Mark Keppel HS
Monterey Park, CA

Lok, Ley
Millikan HS
Norwalk, CA

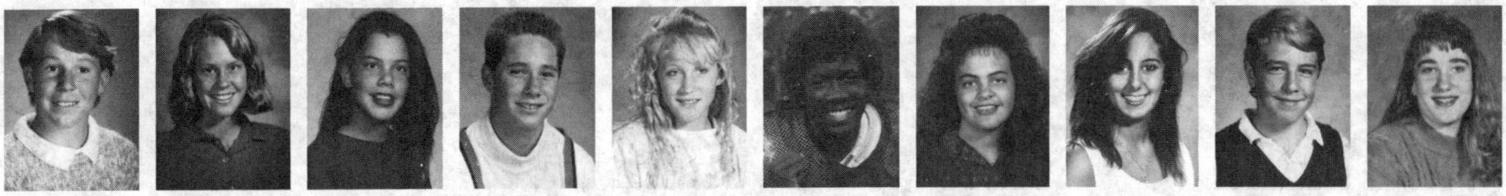

Lokey, Richard A
Calaveras HS
San Andreas, CA

Lombardo, Kristen L
Montgomery HS
Santa Rosa, CA

Lomeli, Maribelle
Mar Vista HS
National City, CA

Loney, Matthew T
Las Lomas HS
Walnut Creek, CA

Long, Molly B
Paradise HS
Paradise, CA

Long, Roosevelt A
Morningside HS
Inglewood, CA

Longacre, Debbie D
Paraclete HS
Lancaster, CA

Longacre, Lizette R
Savanna HS
Buena Park, CA

Longacre, Mike
St Marys College HS
Richmond, CA

Longley, Joy
Southbay Christian
Sunnyvale, CA

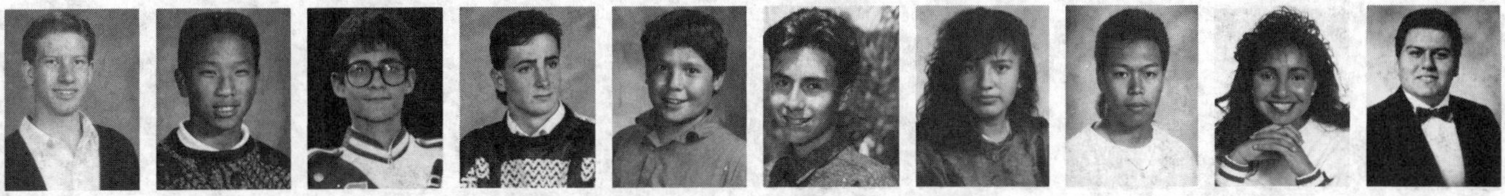

Longnecker, Darren
Redlands SR HS
Redlands, CA

Loo, Michael C
South San Francisco
South San Francis,
CA

Loopstra, Jonathan A
Saddleback HS
Santa Ana, CA

Lopes, Loren F
Turlock HS
Turlock, CA

Lopez, Agustin F
Torrey Pines HS
Del Mar, CA

Lopez, Alfredo A
St John Bosco HS
Bellflower, CA

Lopez, Alma L
Coalinga HS
Huron, CA

Lopez, Andrew R
John Glenn HS
Buena Park, CA

Lopez, Angela
Lompoc SR HS
Lompoc, CA

Lopez, Anthony T
Leuzinger HS
Lawndale, CA

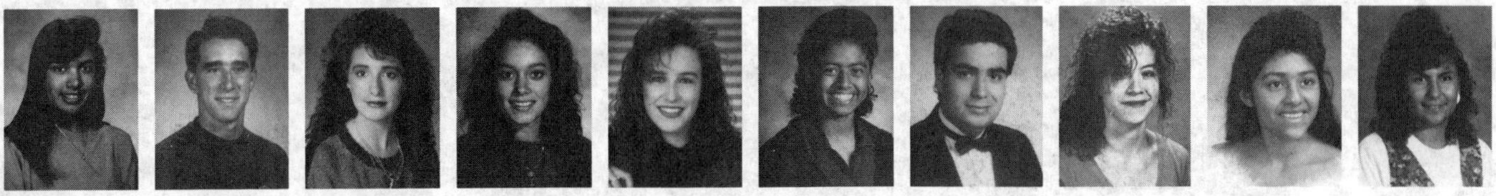

Lopez, Cristina
El Rancho HS
Pico Rivera, CA

Lopez, David M
Glendora HS
Glendora, CA

Lopez, Denise G
John Burroughs HS
Burbank, CA

Lopez, Diana L
Paraclete HS
Lancaster, CA

Lopez, Elizabeth
Dos Palos HS
Firebaugh, CA

Lopez, Elizabeth S
Balboa HS
San Francisco, CA

Lopez, Favian A
Don Bosco Technical
Inst
Whittier, CA

Lopez, Gina M
Eisenhower HS
San Bernardino, CA

Lopez, Iris S
James Lick HS
San Jose, CA

Lopez, Jessica
Upper Lake HS
Upper Lake, CA

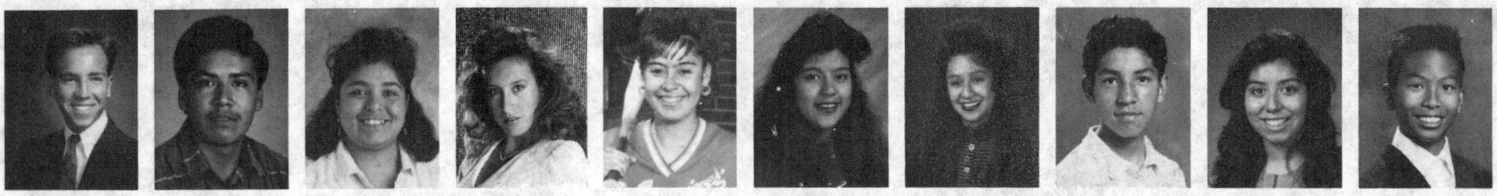

Lopez, John P
Glendora HS
Glendora, CA

Lopez, Jose Luis
Le Grand Union HS
Planada, CA

Lopez, Julianna
Oak Grove HS
San Jose, CA

Lopez, Karla
Marian Catholic HS
San Diego, CA

Lopez, Laura
St Genevieve HS
Sylmar, CA

Lopez, Lisa M
Apple Valley HS
Apple Valley, CA

Lopez, Lissette X
Ygnacio Valley HS
Pittsburg, CA

Lopez, Marco A
San Dimas HS
San Dimas, CA

Lopez, Marisol A
Pinole Valley HS
Pinole, CA

Lopez, Merrick R
Glendale Adventist
Acad
Palmdale, CA

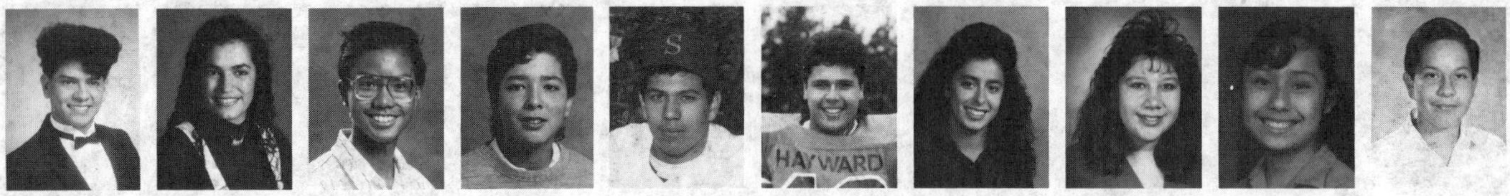

Lopez, Michael A
Indio HS
Indio, CA

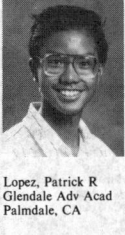

Lopez, Myra
Beyer HS
Modesto, CA

Lopez, Patrick R
Glendale Adv Acad
Palmdale, CA

Lopez, Pedro N
San Gorgonio HS
San Bernardino, CA

Lopez, Ralph
Saddleback HS
Santa Ana, CA

Lopez, Roberto
Hayward HS
Hayward, CA

Lopez, Ruby L
Tomales HS
Inverness, CA

Lopez, Sonia A
Selma HS
Selma, CA

Lopez, Sonia L
Sweetwater Union
National City, CA

Lopez, Steven Ronnie
Don Bosco Tech Inst
Monterey Park, CA

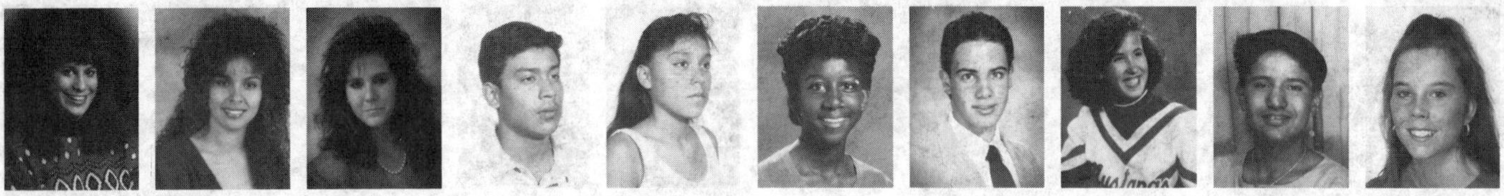

Lopez, Tami
Downey HS
Downey, CA

Lopez, Tessa
Richard Gahr HS
Artesia, CA

Lopez, Veronica A
Mt Carmel HS
San Diego, CA

Lopez Lizardo,
Manuel
Moorpark HS
Moorpark, CA

Lopez Lizardo, Maria
Esther
Moorpark HS
Moorpark, CA

Lord, Beverlie
Saint Michaels HS
Los Angeles, CA

Lord, Eli
Hamilton HS
Academy Of Music
North Hollywood, CA

Lorenzo, Holly
Tulare Western HS
Waukena, CA

Lorrabaquio, Albert
Redlands HS
San Bernardino, CA

Loskot, Kelly S
St Bernard HS
Los Angeles, CA

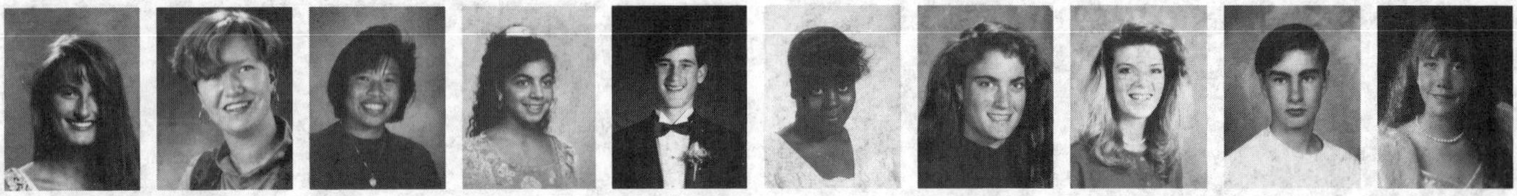

Lotakov, Aneta M
Birmingham HS
Tarzana, CA

Lott, Heather A
Ramona HS
Riverside, CA

Louie, Leslie
Schurr HS
Montebello, CA

Louis, Elham J
Saratoga HS
Los Gatos, CA

Loureiro, Michael D
East Union HS
French Camp, CA

Love, Barbara Y
Skyline HS
Oakland, CA

Love, Summer
Lynbrook HS
San Jose, CA

Love, Tara
Oak Hill HS
Sylmar, CA

Loveland, II Mark R
Monte Vista HS
Spring Valley, CA

Lovell, Jennifer M
Mar Vista HS
Imperial Beach, CA

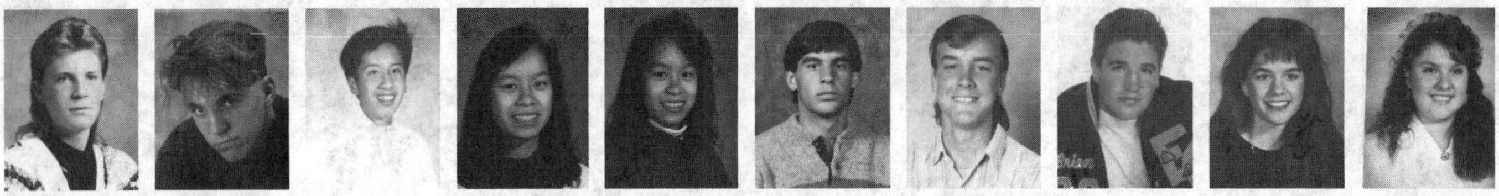

Lovett, Erick P
Central Union HS
El Centro, CA

Lovgren, III Kenneth
Shasta HS
Redding, CA

Low, Albert S
Whitney HS
Cerritos, CA

Low, Kimberly A
South San Francisco
South San Francis,
CA

Low, Kristin
South San Francisco
South San Francis,
CA

Lowe, Rick
Lassen HS
Halong, CA

Lowe, Steven C
Palmdale HS
Pear Blossom, CA

Lown, Brian L
Elk Grove HS
Sacramento, CA

Lowry, Ashley
Bullard HS
Fresno, CA

Lowry, Christine M
Kingsburg HS
Kingsburg, CA

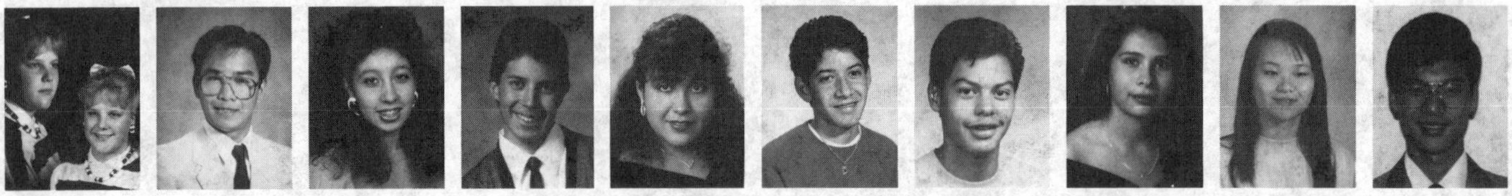

Loyd, D Yvette
Sierra Joint Union
Tollhouse, CA

Loyola, Rowell
Western HS
Anaheim, CA

Loza, Araceli
Araceli Loza HS
Hayward, CA

Lozano, Albert
Don Bosco Technical
Inst
West Covina, CA

Lozano, Lydia
Chula Vista Christian
Imperial Beach, CA

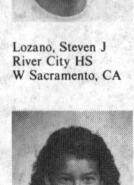

Lozano, Marc
La Serna HS
Whittier, CA

Lozano, Steven J
River City HS
W Sacramento, CA

Lozano, Veronica
John H Francis
Polytechnic HS
Sun Valley, CA

Lu, Chih-Hsien
Arcadia HS
Arcadia, CA

Lu, David V
Lowell HS
San Francisco, CA

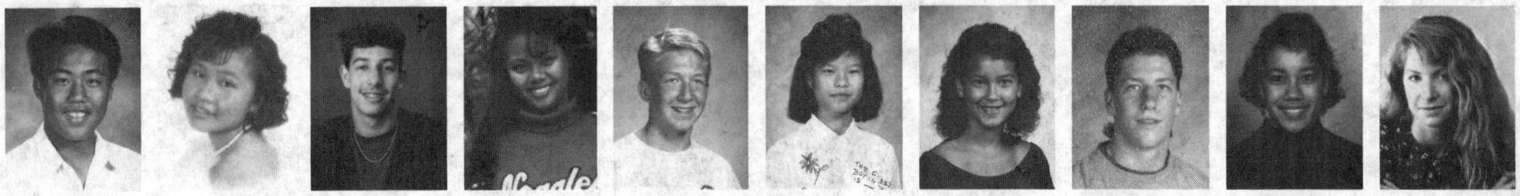

Lu, Paul
Edison HS
Huntington Beach,
CA

Lu, Tu T
Independence HS
San Jose, CA

Lubensky, Micah
Arlington HS
Riverside, CA

Lubi, Doreen Frances
Nogales HS
W Covina, CA

Lubic, Bryan J
Poway HS
Poway, CA

Luc, Bat
San Gabriel HS
Rosemead, CA

Lucas, Monica U
Mesa Verde HS
Citrus Heights, CA

Lucas, Roe
Tranquillity HS
Tranquillity, CA

Lucas, Shellymarie C
Monte Vista HS
Spring Valley, CA

Lucchese, Mary
Sonoma Valley HS
Sonoma, CA

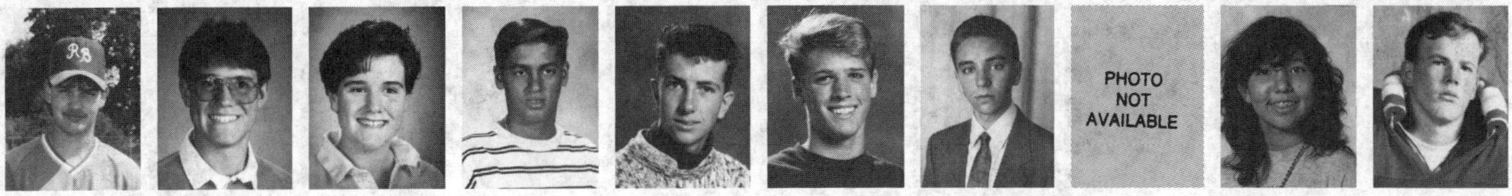
PHOTO
NOT
AVAILABLE

Lucero, Willie D
Red Bluff Union HS
Red Bluff, CA

Lucht, Daniel
Bret Harte Union HS
Murphys, CA

Lucht, Laura E
Bret Harte Union HS
Murphys, CA

Lucia, Joseph P
Poway HS
Poway, CA

Luck, Chad W
Village Christian HS
Van Nuys, CA

Luck, Cheyenne
Glendale HS
Glendale, CA

Luckett, Michael D
Beaumont HS
Beaumont, CA

Ludin, Joyce E
Morro Bay HS
Morro Bay, CA

Ludwick, Natalie M
Emerson HS
Orange, CA

Ludwickzak, John F
Bishop Amat HS
Hacienda Hghts, CA

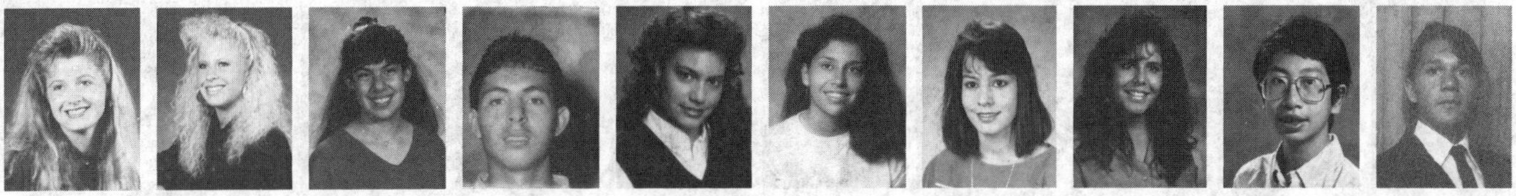

Ludy, Jennifer C
Wasco Union HS
Wasco, CA

Ludy, Marie
Wasco HS
Wasco, CA

Luevano, Melissa
Whitney HS
Cerritos, CA

Luevano, Miquel D
Lompoc SR HS
Lompoc, CA

Lugo, Chantal A
Immaculate Heart
Los Angeles, CA

Lugo, Gloria E
Central Union HS
El Centro, CA

Lugo, Maribel
Milpitas HS
Milpitas, CA

Lugo, Monica L
Hemet HS
Hemet, CA

Lui, George
Hesperia HS
Hesperia, CA

Lujan, Conrad L
Leuzinger HS
Lawndale, CA

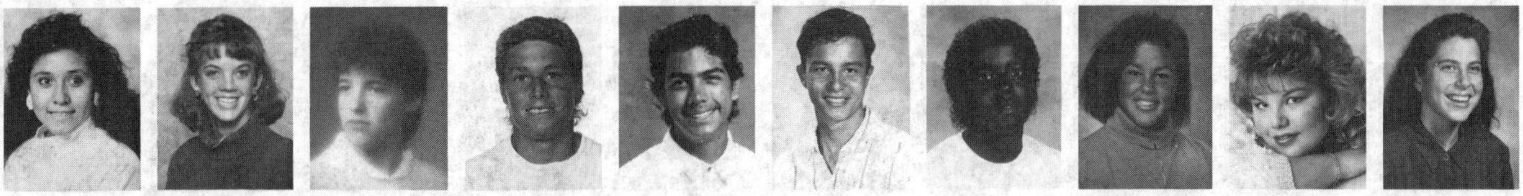

Lujan, Jenny
San Bernardino HS
San Bernardino, CA

Lukenbill, Julie A
Poway HS
Poway, CA

Lukkonen, Kathryn L
San Gorgonio HS
Highland, CA

Lumsden, Neil G
San Dieguito HS
Encinitas, CA

Luna, Agustin F
San Pedro HS
San Pedro, CA

Luna, Anthony
Don Bosco Technical Inst
West Covina, CA

Lunceford, Carlton D
David Starr Jordan
Long Beach, CA

Lunceford, Christy J
Trabuco Hills HS
Trabuco Canyon, CA

Lund, Erica
Paraclete HS
Lancaster, CA

Lundberg, Saralynn
Redwood Christian
Castro Valley, CA

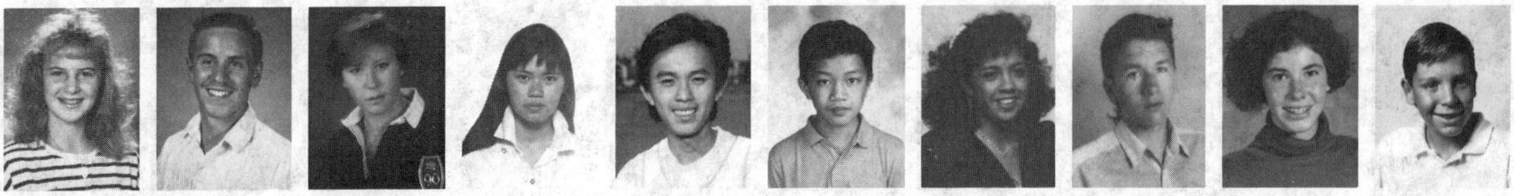

Lundbom, Kristin
Livermore HS
Livermore, CA

Lundbom, Patrick D
Livermore HS
Livermore, CA

Lunsford, Robyn M.
Del Oro HS
Penryn, CA

Luong, Binh
Mission HS
San Francisco, CA

Luong, Taylor
La Quinta HS
Alhambra, CA

Luong, Thao C
San Marcos HS
Santa Barbara, CA

Luque, Deanna M
East Bakersfield HS
Bakersfield, CA

Luquin, Jose Enrique
Channel Island HS
Oxnard, CA

Lurie, Petra
San Mateo HS
Foster City, CA

Lushinsky, Michael A
Brea Olinda HS
Brea, CA

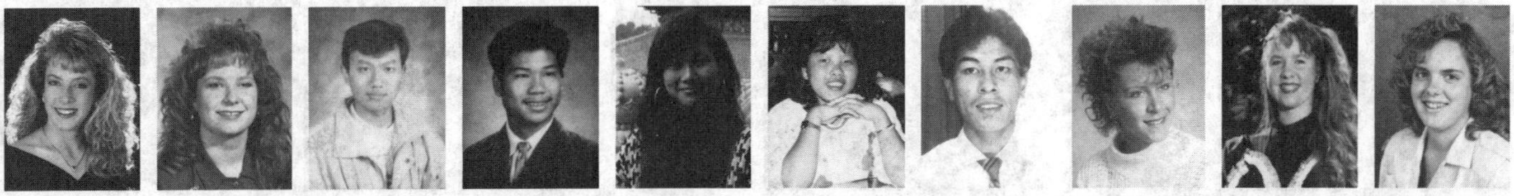

Lusiani, Nicole
San Lorenzo HS
San Lorenzo, CA

Luther, Jenniffer
Enterprise HS
Redding, CA

Luu, Huy C
Oakland HS
Oakland, CA

Ly, Hieu
Valley HS
Sacramento, CA

Ly, Julie
Downtown Business Magnet HS
Los Angeles, CA

Ly, Le Bich
Gardena HS
Gardena, CA

Ly, Long
Abraham Lincoln HS
Rosemead, CA

Lyford, Richelle L
Eisenhower HS
Rialto, CA

Lyle, Rebecca E
Troy HS
Fullerton, CA

Lyles, Joy E
Berean Christian HS
Oakley, CA

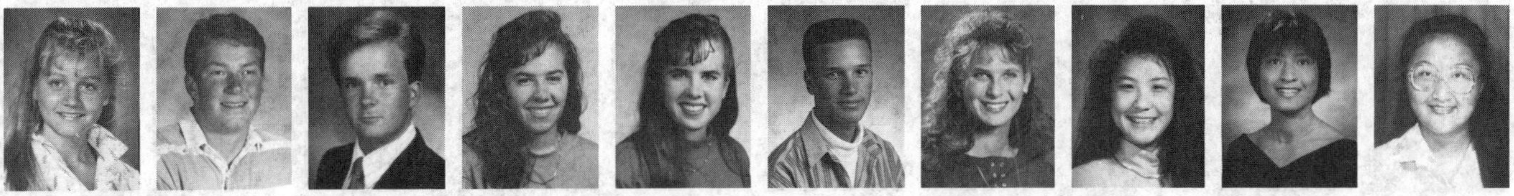

Lynch, Aimee S
Laguna Hills HS
Laguna Hills, CA

Lynch, Ben J
Analy HS
Sebastopol, CA

Lynch, Robert J
El Dorado HS
Placentia, CA

Lynes, Kim
Elk Grove HS
Elk Grove, CA

Lynes, Krissy
Elk Grove HS
Elk Grove, CA

Lyon, Chris S
John F Kennedy HS
Sacramento, CA

Lyons, Megan
Delano HS
Delano, CA

Ma, Angela
Cerritos HS
Cerritos, CA

Ma, Christina
Abraham Lincoln HS
San Francisco, CA

Ma, Lulu
Garden Grove HS
Garden Grove, CA

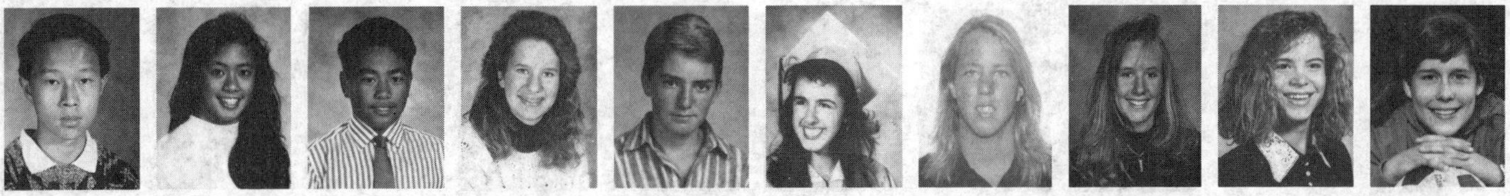

Ma, Vinh T
Lowell HS
San Francisco, CA

Mababa, Melanie
Carson HS
Carson, CA

Mabasa, Joseph Leonard
Don Bosco Technical Inst
Los Angeles, CA

Mabrey, Monica A
Rio Linda SR HS
Sacramento, CA

Mac Comb, Douglas
Las Lomas HS
Walnut Creek, CA

Mac Donald, Kathliene
Norwalk HS
Norwalk, CA

Mac Dowell, Mattias
Dana Hills HS
Laguna Niguel, CA

Mac Kay, Allie
Louisville HS
Westlake Vlg, CA

Mac Laughlin, Karen
La Sierra Acad
Riverside, CA

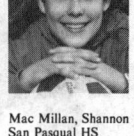

Mac Millan, Shannon
San Pasqual HS
Escondido, CA

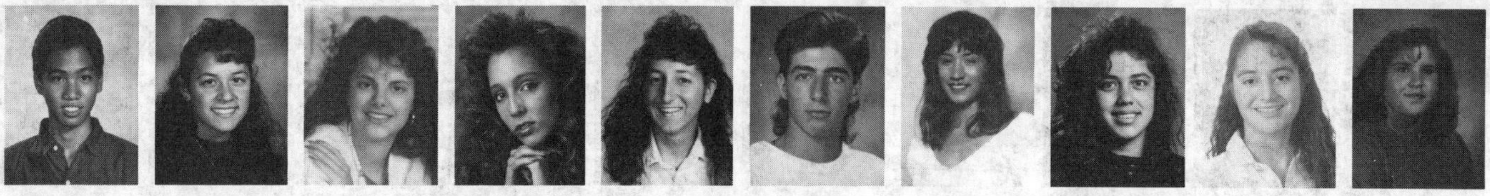

Macasero, Michael C
Don Bosco Technical Inst
Pasadena, CA

Macchia, Margaret A
Edison HS
Huntington Beach, CA

Machado, Gracie
Lincoln HS
Lincoln, CA

Machado, Stacy
San Dieguito HS
Encinitas, CA

Machado, Stephanie
Tulare Union HS
Tulare, CA

Machkoff, Jeff C
Irvine HS
Irvine, CA

Machuca, Maria
Roosevelt HS
Los Angeles, CA

Macias, Carmela H
San Pedro HS
San Pedro, CA

Macias, Jessica
Hemet HS
Lakeview, CA

Macias, Lori M
Central Union HS
El Centro, CA

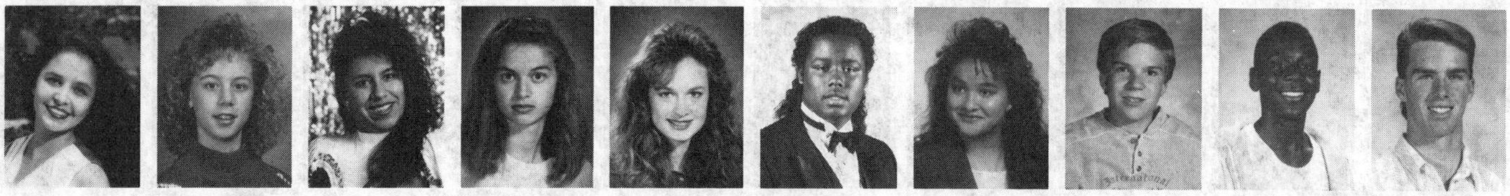

Macias, Raguel
Sierra Vista HS
Baldwin Park, CA

Maciel, Brenda E
Hanford Joint Union
Hanford, CA

Maciel, Candace Y
Eagle Rock HS
Los Angeles, CA

Maciujec, Ariadna G
John Glenn HS
Norwalk, CA

Maciula, Norah C
Marina HS
Huntington Beach, CA

Mack, Brian Harris
Eden Christian Acad
Oakland, CA

Mackay, Karen S
Indio HS
Indio, CA

Mackay, Marc C
Oak Ridge HS
Shingle Springs, CA

Mackey, Jason M
Fairfax HS
Los Angeles, CA

Mackie, Steve P
Woodland HS
Woodland, CA

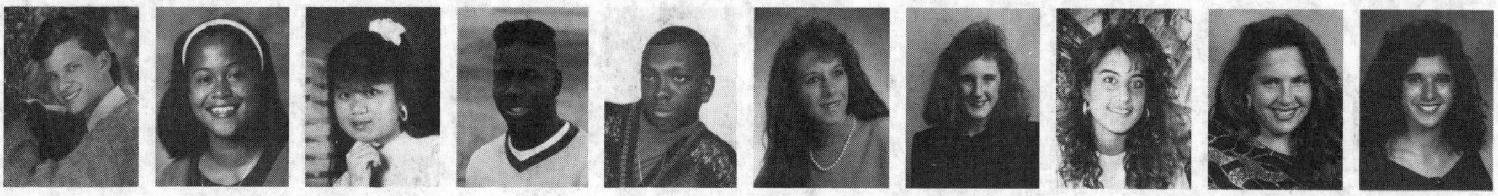

Macy, Brian Eugene
Ponderosa HS
El Dorado, CA

Madarang, Emily L
Castle Park HS
Chula Vista, CA

Madarang, Ruby S
Chula Vista HS
National City, CA

Madden, Jr Clayton
South HS
Bakersfield, CA

Madden, Timothy B
Hogan SR HS
Vallejo, CA

Maddox, Tracy
Gilroy HS
Gilroy, CA

Madole, Kerry S
Chino HS
Chino, CA

Madrid, Joanna R
San Pedro HS
San Pedro, CA

Madrid, Samantha L
Simi HS
Simi Valley, CA

Madrigal, Elizabeth
Woodcrest Christian Schl
Perris, CA

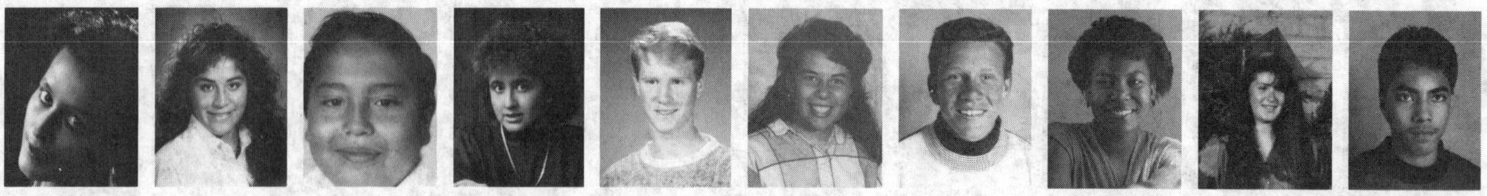

Madrigal, Sonia M
William Workman
La Puente, CA

Madrigal, Suzanne A
Mater Dei HS
Fountain Valley, CA

Madril, Hector A
Calexico HS
Calexico, CA

Madriz, Gloria
Brawley Union HS
Sacramento, CA

Madsen, Craig W
American HS
Fremont, CA

Madsen, Jill
Bloomington Christian Schl
Bloomington, CA

Madsen, Mike
Adolpho Camarillo
Moorpark, CA

Maduakolam, Johnetta
Willits HS
Willits, CA

Madueno, Hilda
Fred C Beyer HS
Modesto, CA

Madueno, Victor
Hueneme HS
Oxnard, CA

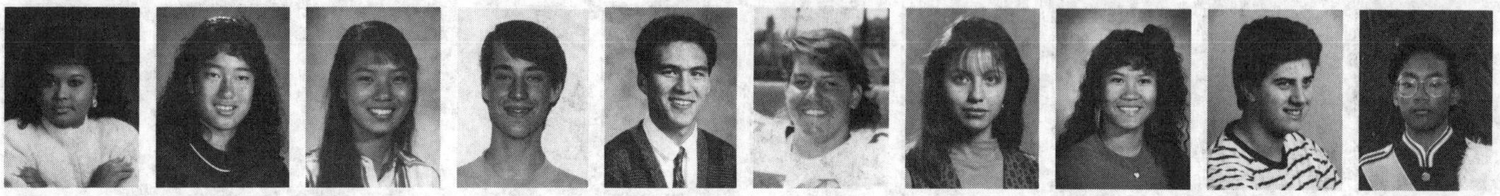

Maduli, Gemma Dy
Galt HS
Galt, CA

Maeda, Kari J
Clovis HS
Clovis, CA

Maeda, Stacy Ann
Sacramento Waldorf Schl
Wilton, CA

Maehr, Mike
Damien HS
Alta Loma, CA

Maestas, Anthony B
Santa Clara HS
Port Hueneme, CA

Magallanes, Tom J
Thousand Oaks HS
Thousand Oaks, CA

Magana, Amalia
Gardena HS
Gardena, CA

Magarin, Maribel
Orosi HS
Orosi, CA

Magaro, Matt A
Grace M Davis HS
Modesto, CA

Magbual, Richard S
Ramona HS
Riverside, CA

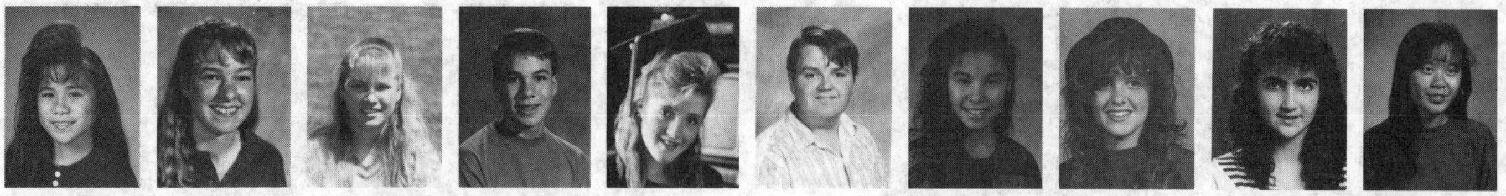

Magcauas, Jenny L
Pinole Valley HS
Hercules, CA

Magee, Allison
San Luis Obispo SR
San Luis Obispo, CA

Mager, Amanda Lee
Arcata HS
Blue Lake, CA

Mager, John C
Arcata HS
Blue Lake, CA

Maggart, Mona M
Palmdale HS
Palmdale, CA

Maggini, Jason M
Riverdale HS
Burrel, CA

Maglaya, Jennifer
Brethren JR/SR HS
Long Beach, CA

Maguire, Barbara J
Del Oro HS
Loomis, CA

Magzanyan, Anahit
St Bellarmine-Jefferso
Los Angeles, CA

Mah, Jannifer L
Central Union HS
El Centro, CA

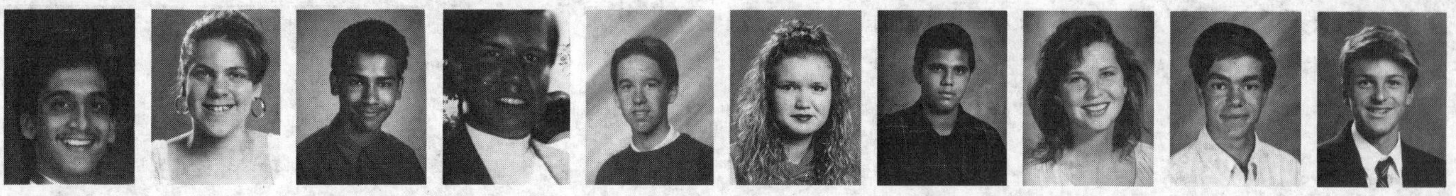

Mahal, Teji P
Clovis HS
Fresno, CA

Mahan, Chantal M
Carlsbad HS
Carlsbad, CA

Maharaj, Yugesh
Fred C Beyer HS
Modesto, CA

Maheda, Luigi S
Bonita Vista HS
San Diego, CA

Maher, Jr Michael
St Patrick-St Vincent
Vallejo, CA

Maher, Wendy L
Sierra Vista HS
Baldwin Park, CA

Mahmood, Jamshed
Tustin HS
Tustin, CA

Mahnke, Melinda E
Fountain Valley HS
Fountain Valley, CA

Mahnken, Earl Jasson
Bishop Amat HS
La Puente, CA

Mahnovski, Sergej
Flintridge Preparatory Schl
Glendale, CA

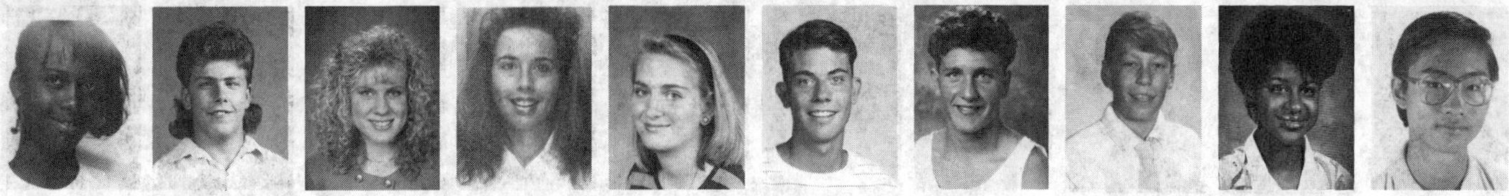

Mahome, Toni M
Roosevelt HS
Los Angeles, CA

Maiale, Jr Enrico
Mario
Sherman Oaks CES
Canoga Park, CA

Maiden, Mary Beth
Southern California
Christian HS
Tustin, CA

Mair-Richardson,
Stacie
Elk Grove HS
Sacramento, CA

Maisterrena, Maite
St Joseph HS
South Gate, CA

Majarian, Micah B
Edison HS
Fresno, CA

Major, Eric D
Dana Hills HS
Laguna Beach, CA

Major, Jon
Ambassador Baptist
Rialto, CA

Major, Yvette Shanta
Burroughs HS
Ridgecrest, CA

Mak, Hebron H
Central Union HS
El Centro, CA

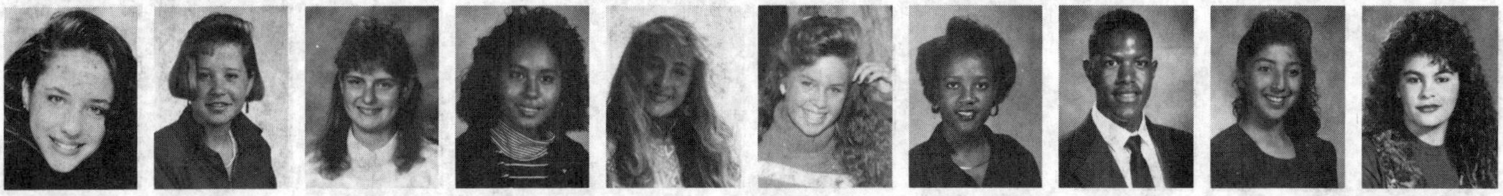

Makay, Morayma M
St Monica Catholic
Santa Monica, CA

Makjavich, Lynn M
Bret Harte HS
Arnold, CA

Makris, Nikki M
Fairfield HS
Fairfield, CA

Malamanig, Christine
Kerman HS
Kerman, CA

Malanga, Kelley
Christian HS
San Diego, CA

Malcolm, Andrea
Arlington HS
Riverside, CA

Malcolm, Charisma
Canyon Springs HS
Moreno Valley, CA

Malcolm, II
Nathaniel Eric
Mater Dei HS
Irvine, CA

Maldonado, Daisy M
Irvine HS
Irvine, CA

Maldonado, Nancy G
Orangewood
Adventist Acad
Santa Ana, CA

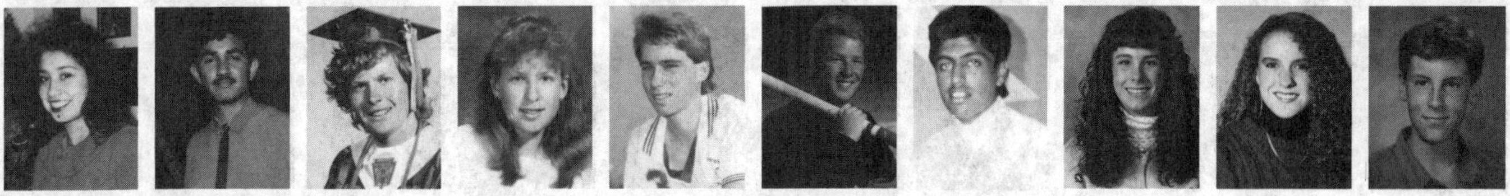

Maldonado, Veronica
James Logan HS
Union City, CA

Maldondo, Robert R
Richard Gahr HS
Artesia, CA

Malek, Eric F
Villa Park HS
Villa Park, CA

Malek, Janet H
Villa Park HS
Villa Park, CA

Malesky, Edmund
Redlands HS
Redlands, CA

Malik, Craig L
Sherman E
Burroughs HS
Ridgecrest, CA

Malik, Yasser
American HS
Fremont, CA

Malley, Laura E
Bella Vista HS
Fair Oaks, CA

Mallon, Tisha M
Skyline HS
Oakland, CA

Malloy, Brian P
Irvine HS
Irvine, CA

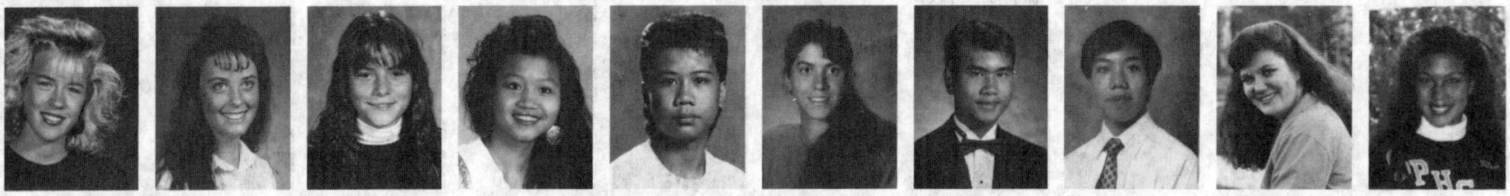

Malmquist, Krista
Watsonville HS
Watsonville, CA

Malone, Maureen
Mercy HS
Daly City, CA

Malphurs, Regina M
Homestead HS
Sunnyvale, CA

Mam, Jacqueline P
A A Stagg HS
Stockton, CA

Mamaril, Joel R
Cleveland HS
Canoga Park, CA

Mammano, Linda C
La Mirada HS
La Mirada, CA

Man, Wai
St Joseph Notre
Dame HS
Oakland, CA

Manahan, Jonathan
Loyola HS
Los Angeles, CA

Manchester, Andrea
Amador Valley HS
Pleasanton, CA

Mandac, Lelani R
San Pedro HS
San Pedro, CA

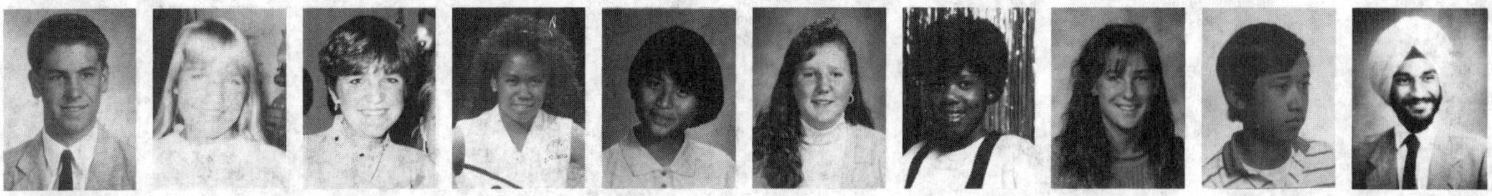

Mandry, Michael D
Rubidoux HS
Riverside, CA

Mandt, Andrea S
Antioch SR HS
Antioch, CA

Mandt, Gayle E
Antioch HS
Antioch, CA

Manese, Marie C
Aquinas HS
Highland, CA

Mangindin, Angelica
Mt Pleasant HS
San Jose, CA

Mangrum, Leanne M
Fortuna Union HS
Scotia, CA

Manigo, Tyesha
Garey HS
Pomona, CA

Manion, Kristi L
Cordova SR HS
Rancho Cordova, CA

Manit, Eddy C
Serra HS
Redwood City, CA

Manjal, Sukhbir S
Alisal HS
Salinas, CA

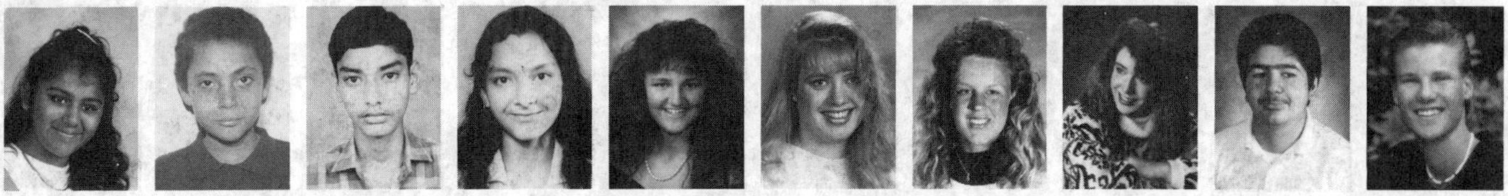

Manjra, Zareen
Gharr HS
Cerritos, CA

Mankarious, Peter A
Santa Monica HS
Santa Monica, CA

Mankotia, Pankaj
Abraham Lincoln HS
San Francisco, CA

Mankotia, Shruti
Abraham Lincoln HS
San Francisco, CA

Mann, Jessica
Westlake HS
Westlake Village, CA

Mann, Linda S
Amercian Christian
Acad
Anderson, CA

Mann, Nikki
Tustin HS
Tustin, CA

Mann, Sara A
American Christian
Acad
Anderson, CA

Manneh, Basem N
Balboa HS
San Francisco, CA

Manning, Jason M
Vacaville SR HS
Vacaville, CA

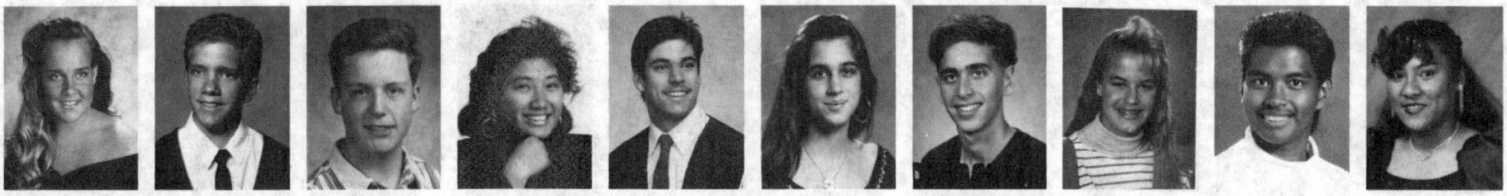

Manning, Melissa J
Alameda HS
Alameda, CA

Manning, Paul
Matthew
John A Rowland HS
Rowland Hts, CA

Mannion, Bracken
Christian Brothers
Sacramento, CA

Manongdo-Llamas,
Chiara May
South San Francisco
South San Francis,
CA

Mansmith, Michael J
San Benito HS
San Juan Batsta, CA

Mansouri, Shideh
Palisades HS
Los Angeles, CA

Mansubi, Sherwin P
Bellarmine HS
Saratoga, CA

Mantz, Kim
Livermore HS
Livermore, CA

Manuel, Rommel A
Eagle Rock HS
Los Angeles, CA

Manukay, Rosalyne
Meridith
St Bernard HS
Los Angeles, CA

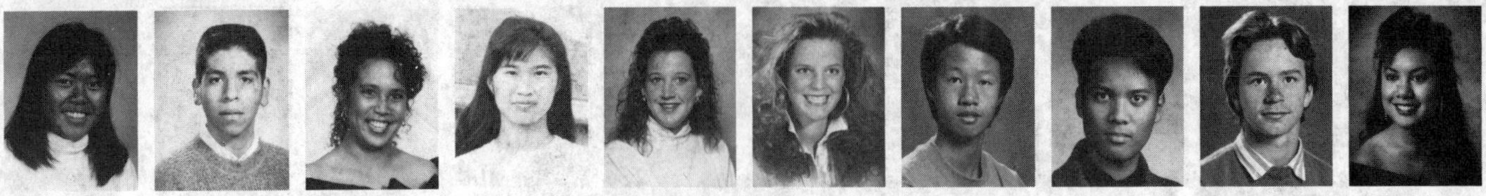

Manzanilla, Rhodora
James Lick HS
San Jose, CA

Manzo, Eduardo
Saddleback HS
Santa Ana, CA

Manzon, Franchesca
March Mountain HS
Mountain Home, ID

Mao, Anne A
Mater Dei HS
Fountain Valley, CA

Mapel, Amy K
Mira Mesa HS
San Diego, CA

Maples, Mandy
North HS
Vacaville, CA

Mar, David D
John F Kennedy HS
Los Angeles, CA

Marasigan, Frank R
Elk Grove HS
Elk Grove, CA

Marasse, Donald R
Mojave HS
Cantil, CA

Marbello, May Concepcion
Marian Catholic HS
San Diego, CA

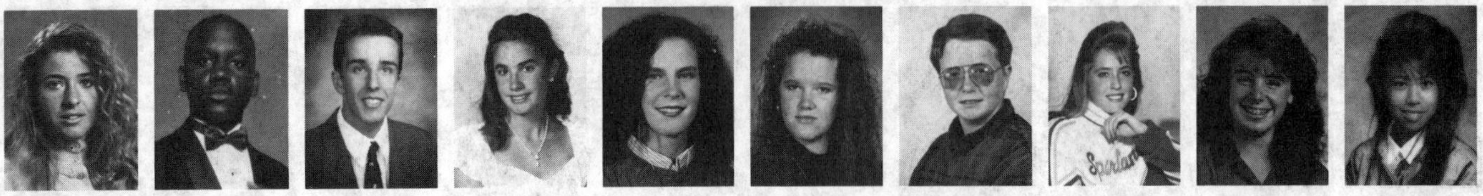

Marcario, Kim M
Colton HS
Colton, CA

Marcelin, Alexander
Serra HS
Los Angeles, CA

Marchetti, Brian Andrew
La Jolla HS
La Jolla, CA

Marchillo, Lisa N
Summerville HS
Twain Harte, CA

Marconi, Abbie
Florin HS
Sacramento, CA

Marcotte, Tracee J
Paraclete HS
Lancaster, CA

Marcy, David A
Silver Valley HS
Daggett, CA

Margetts, Heather
Chula Vista SR HS
Chula Vista, CA

Maria, Katie
Notre Dame HS
San Jose, CA

Mariano, Clariben
Southwest HS
San Diego, CA

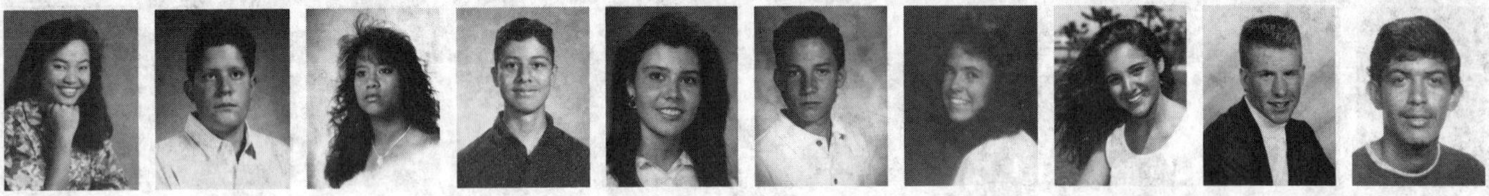

Mariano, Michelle B
Andrew P Hill HS
San Jose, CA

Marin, Steven F
Hesperia HS
Hesperia, CA

Marinas, Larisa Trina
Liberty Baptist HS
San Jose, CA

Marinero, Oscar Alexis
Hamilton HS
Academy Of Music
North Hollywood, CA

Marinescu, Michelle
El Toro HS
Lake Forest, CA

Marino, Anthony
Paraclete HS
Lancaster, CA

Marino, Kimberly
Granada HS
Livermore, CA

Marino, Morgan L
Newport Harbor HS
Palm Desert, CA

Marion, Christopher
Benicia HS
Benicia, CA

Mariscal, Luis A
Alisal HS
Salinas, CA

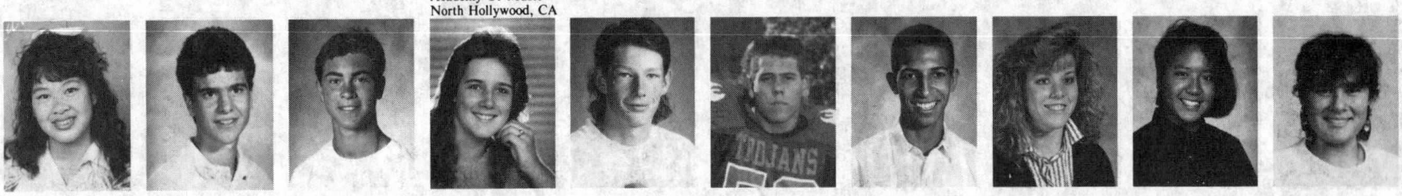

Mark, Karen
John Marshall HS
Los Angeles, CA

Markarian, Thomas F
Sherman E Burroughs HS
Ridgecrest, CA

Markman, Gregory
Miraleste HS
Rolling Hls Ests, CA

Markussen, Rebecka Lynn
Hemet HS
Midway City, CA

Marleau, Peter A
Manteca HS
Manteca, CA

Marlette, Brian T
Oak Ridge HS
El Dorado Hills, CA

Marmolejo, Patrick H
Don Bosco HS
Maywood, CA

Marquette, Michele
Strathmore HS
Lindsay, CA

Marquez, Anafe
San Gabriel Acad
Glendora, CA

Marquez, Lorena
Edison HS
Fresno, CA

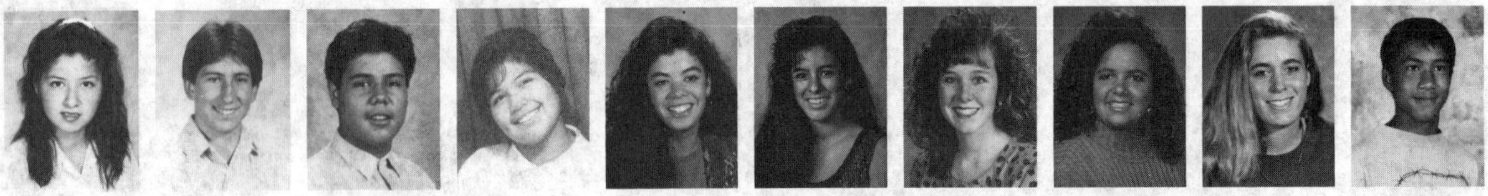

Marquez, Luz Maria
St Genevieve HS
Van Nuys, CA

Marquez, Marc T
Woodland HS
Woodland, CA

Marquez, Nash
Southest Lutheran
Huntington Park, CA

Marquez, Sandra P
California HS
San Ramon, CA

Marquez, Silvia E
Tracy Joint Union
Tracy, CA

Marquez, Sonya Marie
Bella Vista HS
Fair Oaks, CA

Marr, Julie
Granite Hills HS
Alpine, CA

Marr, Samantha M
Irvine HS
Irvine, CA

Marracino, Pamela Y
Clayton Valley HS
Clayton, CA

Marranate, Atipol C
Bullard HS
Fresno, CA

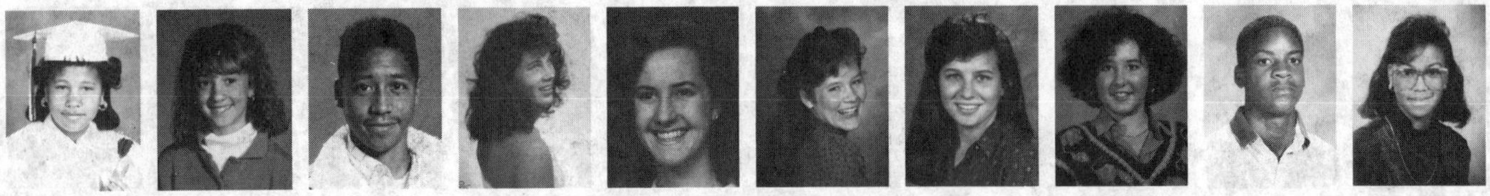

Marrow, Stephanie
Paramount HS
Los Angeles, CA

Marsh, Amy N
Woodside HS
Redwood City, CA

Marsh, Anthony S
Culver City HS
Culver City, CA

Marsh, Kimberlee
Golden West HS
Visalia, CA

Marsh, Sharon L
Apple Valley HS
Apple Valley, CA

Marshall, Amy
Oxnard HS
Oxnard, CA

Marshall, Andrea L
Imperial HS
Imperial, CA

Marshall, Courtney
Hanford HS
Hanford, CA

Marshall, Marcus C
Dos Palos HS
Dos Palos, CA

Marshall, Monica R
Lincoln Prep HS
San Diego, CA

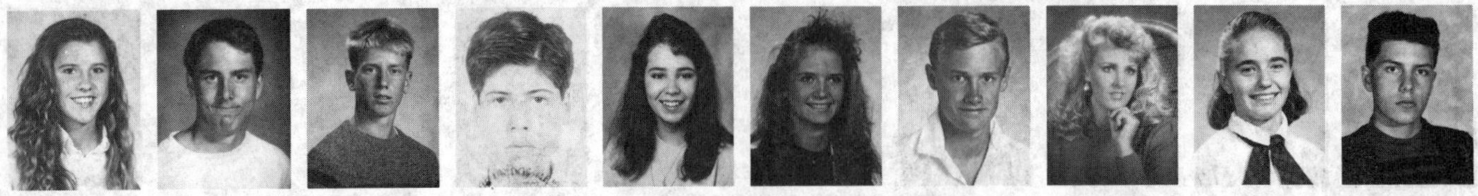

Marshall, Summer L
Notre Dame Acad
Santa Monica, CA

Marshall, Tim C
University HS
Irvine, CA

Marsteller, Brian D
Hesperia HS
Hesperia, CA

Martanez, Leon M
Mar Vista HS
San Ysidro, CA

Martin, Alejandra
Montclair HS
Montclair, CA

Martin, Ami
Amador HS
Ione, CA

Martin, Brian W
Gunn HS
Palo Alto, CA

Martin, Carrie L
Mt Whitney HS
Visalia, CA

Martin, Hope
Rosary HS
Mission Viejo, CA

Martin, Jr James A
Fresno HS
Fresno, CA

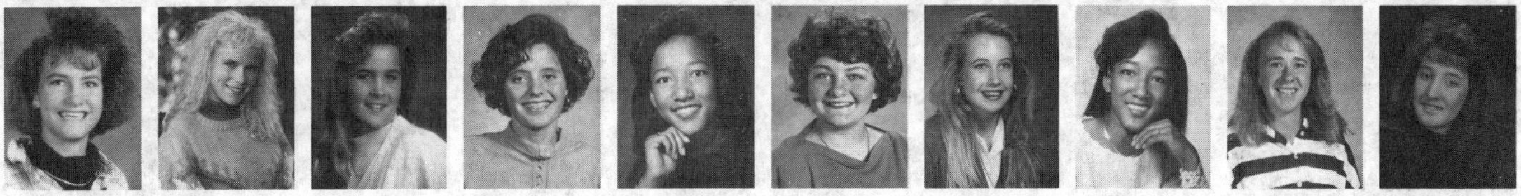

Martin, Jennifer L
Golden West HS
Visalia, CA

Martin, Julie
Lodi HS
Lodi, CA

Martin, Karen
Mt Carmel HS
San Diego, CA

Martin, Katherine L
Oakmont HS
Roseville, CA

Martin, Kimberly
Faith Baptist HS
Canoga Park, CA

Martin, Kristina M
Chino HS
Chino, CA

Martin, Kristy M
La Reina HS
Thousand Oaks, CA

Martin, Lauren G
Faith Baptist HS
Canoga Park, CA

Martin, Lori D
Cabrillo HS
Bellevue, NE

Martin, Melissa M
Irvington HS
Fremont, CA

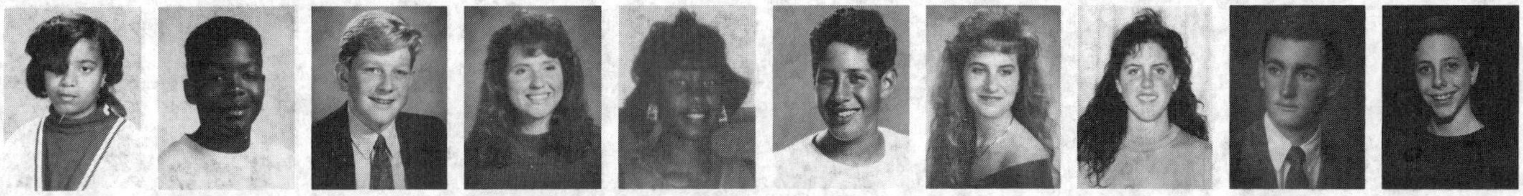

Martin, Monique L
Skyline HS
Oakland, CA

Martin, Patrick
Edison Computech
Fresno, CA

Martin, Ryan J
Mater Dei HS
Huntington Bch, CA

Martin, Tami C
Mater Dei HS
Anaheim, CA

Martin, Tanjareen C
St Bernard Catholic
Inglewood, CA

Martin, Thomas
Bell HS
Maywood, CA

Martin, Wendy M
Napa HS
Vallejo, CA

Martin, Westi B
Sierra Joint Union
N Fork, CA

Martindale, Greg
Sonoma Valley HS
Sonoma, CA

Martindale, Todd E
Bolsa Grande HS
Garden Grove, CA

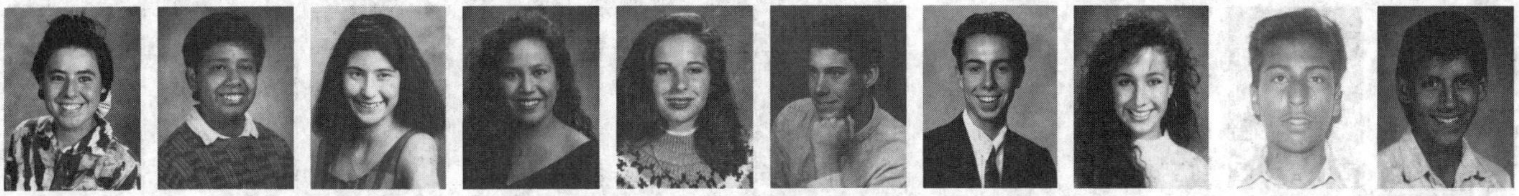

Martinez, Aida
Ramona HS
Ramona, CA

Martinez, Alfred E
Notre Dame HS
Moreno Valley, CA

Martinez, Alicia
Lindsay HS
Lindsay, CA

Martinez, Caroline Leilani
Woodland HS
Woodland, CA

Martinez, Christina
Fremont HS
Sunnyvale, CA

Martinez, Christopher
Hesperia HS
Hesperia, CA

Martinez, Damian
Glen A Wilson HS
Hacienda Hts, CA

Martinez, Dana
La Habra HS
La Habra, CA

Martinez, Gerardo
Fremont HS
Oakland, CA

Martinez, Greg
Victory Christian HS
Placerville, CA

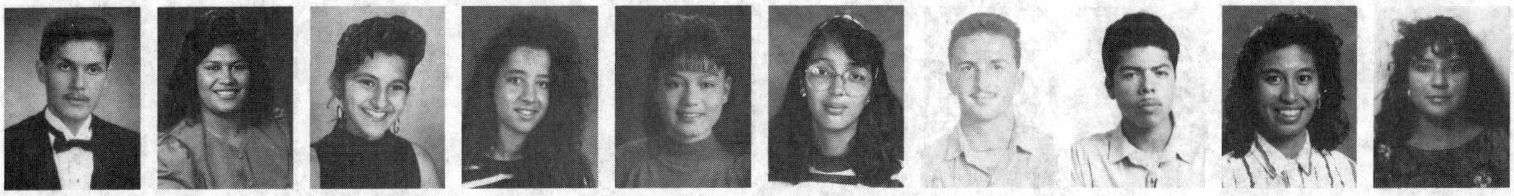

Martinez, Jose L
Mount Pleasant HS
San Jose, CA

Martinez, Laura M
Fillmore HS
Fillmore, CA

Martinez, Linda M
Fairfield HS
Suisun City, CA

Martinez, Lisa
St Josephs HS
Anaheim, CA

Martinez, Lorena
Riverdale Joint Union
Five Points, CA

Martinez, Lorena A
Chula Vista HS
San Diego, CA

Martinez, Luis A
Orosi HS
Orosi, CA

Martinez, Manuel E
Garfield HS
Pico Rivera, CA

Martinez, Maria S
Bellarmine-Jefferson
North Hollywood, CA

Martinez, Maribel M
Warren HS
Downey, CA

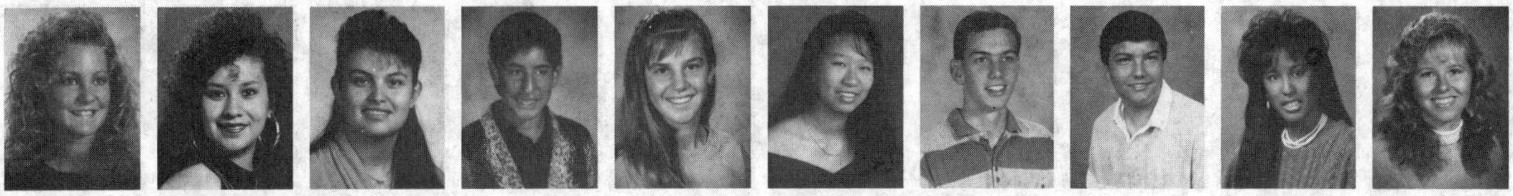

Martinez, Melissa J
Rubidoux HS
Riverside, CA

Martinez, Rosa
Sierra Vista HS
Baldwin Park, CA

Martinez, Ruth N
Grant HS
Sacramento, CA

Martinez, Sergio
Bolsa Grande HS
Garden Grove, CA

Marun, Elizabeth Erika
Torrey Pines HS
Rancho Santa Fe, CA

Maruyama, Emi
Bonita Vista HS
Chula Vista, CA

Marvin, Eric
Kings Christian HS
Hanford, CA

Marvin, Steve
Kings Christian HS
Hanford, CA

Marzan, Leah May
Bishop Montgomery
Gardena, CA

Marzec, Jessica A
El Camino HS
Oceanside, CA

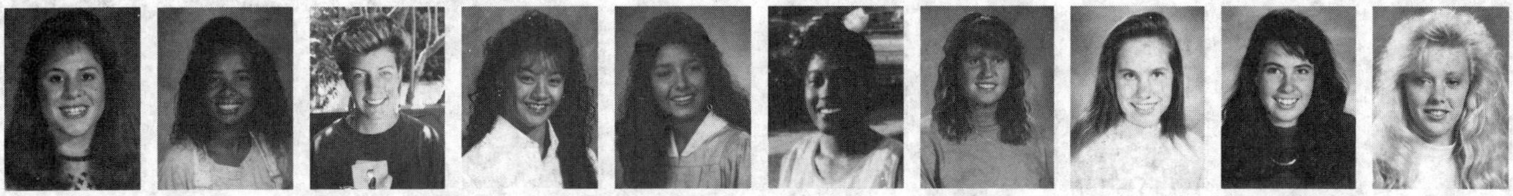

Marziano, Andra M
El Cerrito HS
El Cerrito, CA

Marzillier, Nicole A
Kennedy HS
Granada Hills, CA

Marzullo, Sara F
San Clemente HS
San Juan Capistra, CA

Masalaysay, Leila M
Mercy HS
San Francisco, CA

Mascorro, Marisa
Mary Star Of The Sea HS
Long Beach, CA

Mason, Caneya C
Luther Burbank HS
Sacramento, CA

Mason, Christine D
La Sierra HS
Riverside, CA

Mason, Kristen M
Fountain Valley HS
Fountain Valley, CA

Mason, Michelle L
Chino HS
Ontario, CA

Mason, Sandra D
Santa Paula HS
Santa Paula, CA

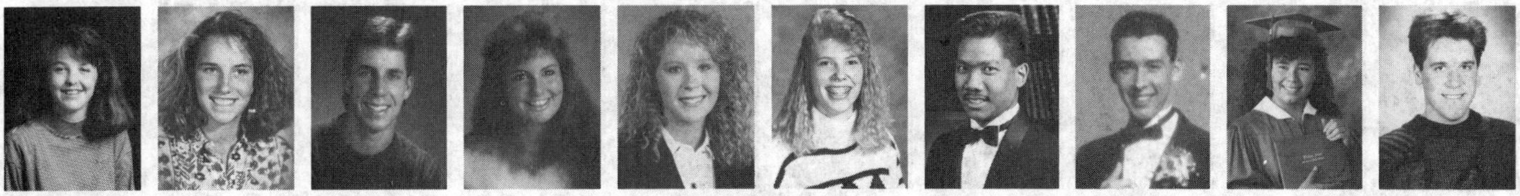

Massey, Jill M
Bishop Montgomery
Redondo Beach, CA

Massey, Shannon
Mc Farland HS
Mcfarland, CA

Mastagni, Michael
Beyer HS
Modesto, CA

Maston, Erica
Valley Christian HS
San Jose, CA

Mastro, Denise M
Whittier Christian
Fullerton, CA

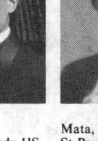

Masur, Shawna C
Lower Lake HS
Clearlake, CA

Mata, Abe
John F Kennedy HS
Sacramento, CA

Mata, Robert J
St Paul HS
Whittier, CA

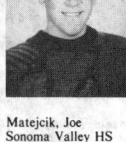

Matas, Sandra
Bishop Amat HS
Covina, CA

Matejcik, Joe
Sonoma Valley HS
Kenwood, CA

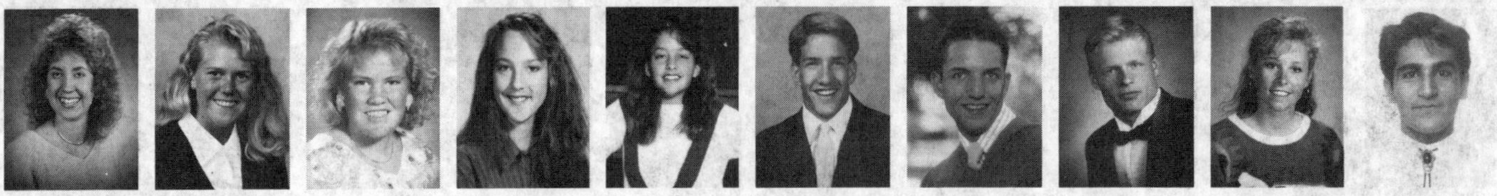

Matherly, Shawna
Mount Whitney HS
Visalia, CA

Mathes, Ashleigh D
Academy Of Our
Lady Of Peace HS
San Diego, CA

Mathews,
Chrystaunia
West Covina HS
West Covina, CA

Mathews, Megan A
Venice HS
Venice, CA

Mathews, Mindy
Needles HS
Needles, CA

Mathiesen, Dan
Marina HS
Huntington Bch, CA

Mathieu, Forest
Bishop Union HS
Bishop, CA

Mathis, Jared
Maxwell HS
Maxwell, CA

Mathis, Stephanie C
Mariposa County HS
Hornitos, CA

Matian, Arash D
William Howard Taft
Woodland Hills, CA

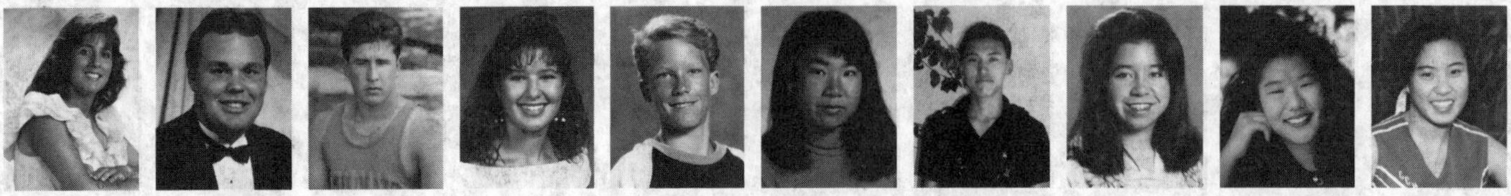

Matias, Christina
Acad Of Our Lady
Of Peace
San Diego, CA

Matney, Michael J
Irvington HS
Fremont, CA

Matney, Steven D
Taft Union HS
Mc Kittrick, CA

Matos, Jennifer
Archbishop Mitty HS
Santa Clara, CA

Matson, Michael D
Artesia HS
Hawaiian Gardens,
CA

Matsuda, Jayne M
Prospect HS
San Jose, CA

Matsumoto, Akihisa
Athenian Schl
Danville, CA

Matsumoto, Tarisa A
Gardena HS
Gardena, CA

Matsumura, Sandra
Yoshiko
Gridley Union HS
Gridley, CA

Matsunaga, Ayumi
Kiki
Capital Christian HS
Elk Grove, CA

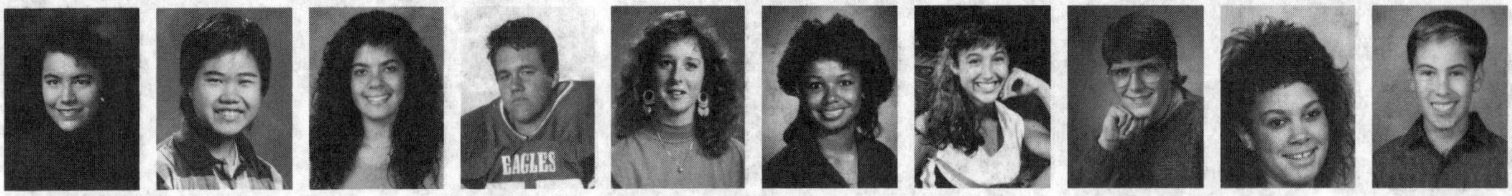

Matsuo, Diane
John F Kennedy SR
Sacramento, CA

Matsuzaki, Carol
Garfield Computer
Sci Magnet HS
Los Angeles, CA

Matta, Maria V
Redwood HS
Visalia, CA

Matteson,
Christopher Perez
Done Pine HS
Lone Pine, CA

Matthew, Dawn M
Sonora Union HS
Groveland, CA

Matthews, Damisha
Antelope Valley HS
Lancaster, CA

Matthews, Tara
Los Lomas HS
Walnut Creek, CA

Mattison, Jon
Rio Lindo Adventist
Acad
Turlock, CA

Matts, Christina
Oak Park HS
Bakerfield, CA

Matyas, Jason M
Yucaipa HS
Yucaipa, CA

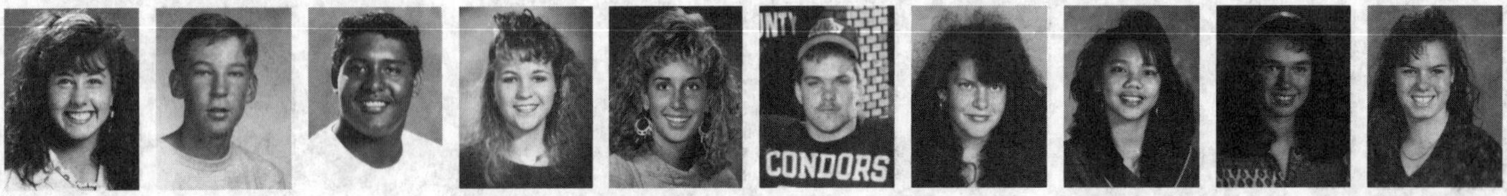

Matz, Jennifer
Birmingham HS
Encino, CA

Mauch, Dennis R
Elk Grove HS
Sacramento, CA

Mauga, Tafi Junior
Carlsbad HS
Carlsbad, CA

Mauldin, Amanda D
Antelope Valley HS
Lancaster, CA

Mauney, Michelle N
El Toro HS
El Toro, CA

Maurantonio,
Michael S
North Monterey
County HS
Prunedale, CA

Maureas, Elleni
Marie
Huntington Beach
Huntington Beach,
CA

Mauricio, Phoebe
International Studies
Acad
San Francisco, CA

Mauro, Katie
Lincoln HS
Stockton, CA

Maxa, Stacy L
Ramona HS
Ramona, CA

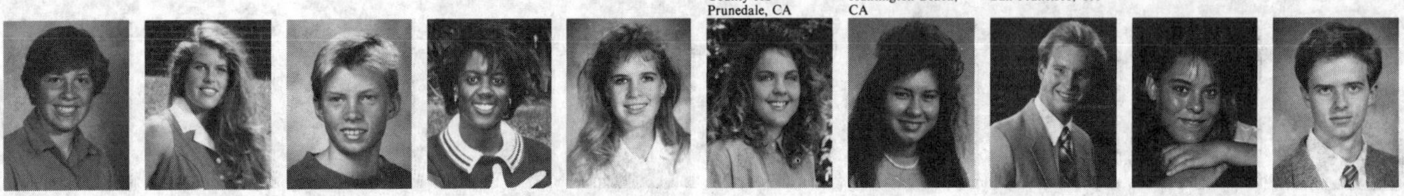

Maxey, Rachael
Highlands HS
North Highlands, CA

Maxwell, Brenda
Los Altos HS
Hacienda Hgts, CA

Maxwell, Casady
Irvine HS
Carlsbad, CA

Maxwell, Tisa L
Washington Prep HS
Los Angeles, CA

May, Allison M
Mater Dei HS
Orange, CA

May, Dawn M
East Bakersfield HS
Bakersfield, CA

Maya, Patricia
Notre Dame HS
San Jose, CA

Maybin, Chad
Palmdale HS
Pearblossom, CA

Mayfield, Melinda R
Enterprise HS
Redding, CA

Mayhew, Matt J
Mater Dei HS
Costa Mesa, CA

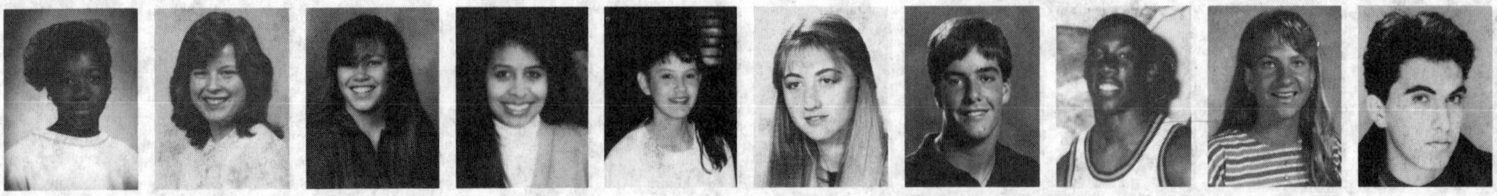

Maynard, Shakima N
Diamond Bar HS
Diamond Bar, CA

Mayo, Kathleen
Elizabeth
Poway HS
Poway, CA

Mayoral, Miriam E
Mission Bay HS
San Diego, CA

Mayorga, Emily
Notre Dame HS
San Jose, CA

Mayorga, Grace A
Independence HS
San Jose, CA

Mayou, Michelle R
Milpitas HS
Milpitas, CA

Mayrhofer, Thomas B
The Chadwick Schl
Rancho Pls Vrds, CA

Mayweather, Bertram
Sunny Hills HS
Fullerton, CA

Mazi, Tonijo
Cabrillo HS
Lompoc, CA

Mazmanian, Avetis E
Montebello HS
Montebello, CA

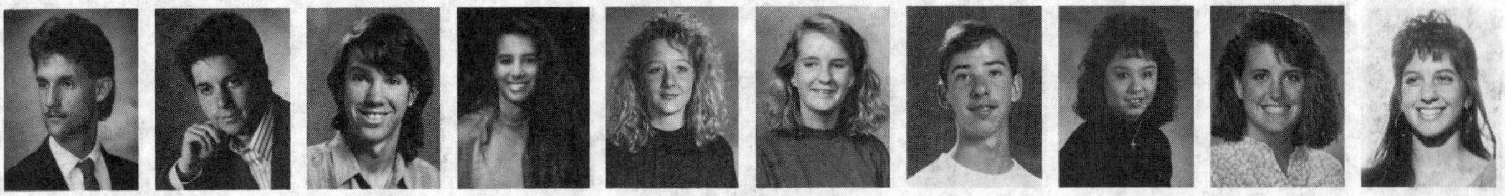

Mazza, Jamie
Mountain Empire HS
Alpine, CA

Mazzela, Rory L
Herbert Hoover HS
Fresno, CA

Mc Adam, Daniel G
Fontana HS
Fontana, CA

Mc Adams, Jenny M
Placer HS
Auburn, CA

Mc Adams, Tiffany
Cloverdale HS
Cloverdale, CA

Mc Aleece, Erin
Mission Bay HS
San Diego, CA

Mc Allaster, Mark M
Bonita HS
La Verne, CA

Mc Allister, Tina
Needles HS
Needles, CA

Mc Arthur, Jen-E
Westminster HS
Midway City, CA

Mc Arthur, Nisha G
North HS
Bakersfield, CA

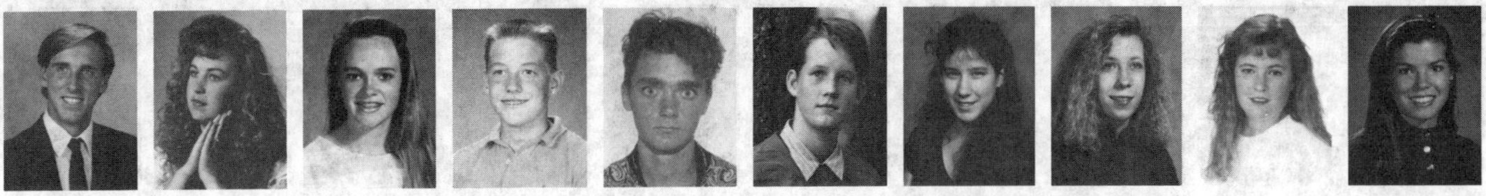

Mc Bride, Justin
Marina HS
Huntington Bch, CA

Mc Bride, Kari L
Apple Valley HS
Apple Valley, CA

Mc Bride, Tiffiny
Santa Cruz HS
Soquel, CA

Mc Cabe, Brian J
Mount Diablo HS
Missoula, MT

Mc Cabe, Michael J
Artesia HS
Lakewood, CA

Mc Cafferty, George
Forest Lake Christian Schl
Auburn, CA

Mc Caffery, April D
Los Angeles County HS For The Arts
Los Angeles, CA

Mc Caffery, Meghan
Seaside HS
Ft Ord, CA

Mc Callum, Jennifer
Analy HS
Sebastopol, CA

Mc Carthy, Bronwyn
Cornelia Connelly HS
Cypress, CA

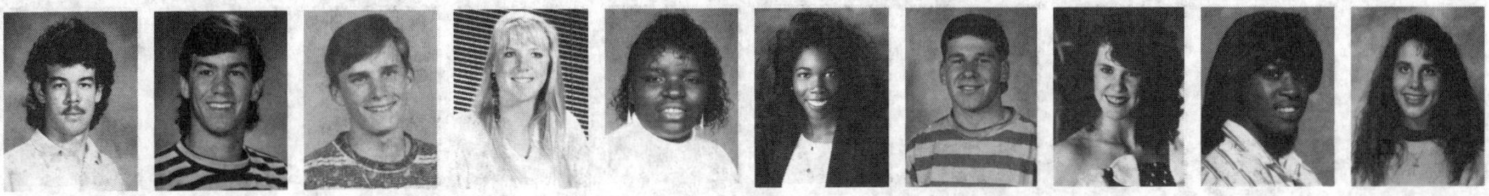

Mc Carthy, Clifford
La Habra HS
Whittier, CA

Mc Carthy, Thomas
El Toro HS
El Toro, CA

Mc Cartney, Kelly B
Del Notre HS
Crescent City, CA

Mc Cauley, Stacy C
Arlington HS
Riverside, CA

Mc Clain, Lorrie
Sunset HS
Oakland, CA

Mc Clairen, Patricia Yvette
William Workman
Bloomington, CA

Mc Claskey, Danny T
Bella Vista HS
Fair Oaks, CA

Mc Claskey, Jennifer
Shasta HS
Redding, CA

Mc Cleary, Danielle
Castlemont HS
Oakland, CA

Mc Clellan, Jody E
Cordona SR HS
Rancho Cordova, CA

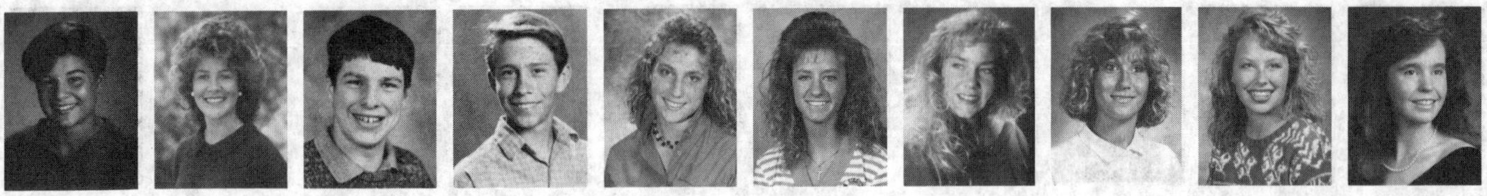

Mc Clellan, Nicole M
Turlock HS
Turlock, CA

Mc Clellan-Ness, Traci L
Poway HS
Poway, CA

Mc Cloud, Michael
Coalinga HS
Coalinga, CA

Mc Cluskey, Jeff A
Carlsbad HS
Carlsbad, CA

Mc Connell, Kerry A
Desert Christian HS
Bermuda Dunes, CA

Mc Conologue, Kelly
Mesa Verde HS
Citrus Heights, CA

Mc Cormack, Brandon L
Cajon HS
San Bernardino, CA

Mc Cormack, Shannon C
Canyon Springs HS
Moreno Valley, CA

Mc Cormick, Lauren
Rim Of The World
Lake Arrowhead, CA

Mc Cormick, Marcia
Milpitas HS
Milpitas, CA

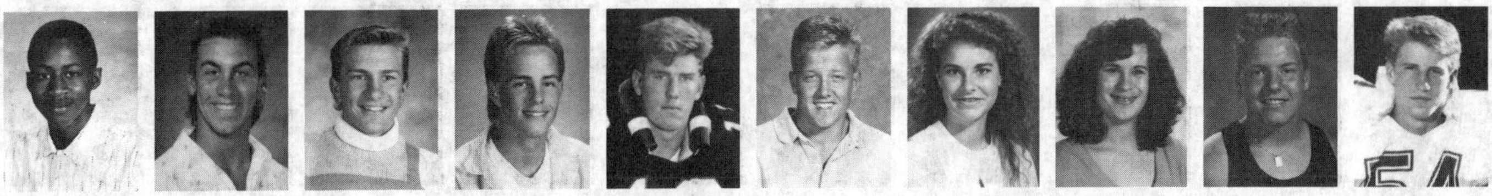

Mc Cowin, Charles E
Notre Dame HS
Rialto, CA

Mc Coy, Deron T
Irvine HS
Irvine, CA

Mc Coy, Jay K
Yosemite HS
Coarsegold, CA

Mc Craw, Dustin J
Manteca HS
Manteca, CA

Mc Cready, Matt E
Los Amigos HS
Fountain Valley, CA

Mc Culloch, Scott A
Gilroy HS
Gilroy, CA

Mc Daniel, Elizabeth
Santa Ana HS
Santa Ana, CA

Mc Dill, Erin
Moorpark HS
Moorpark, CA

Mc Donald, C T
Pacifica HS
Cypress, CA

Mc Donald, Jake D
Nevada Union HS
Nevada City, CA

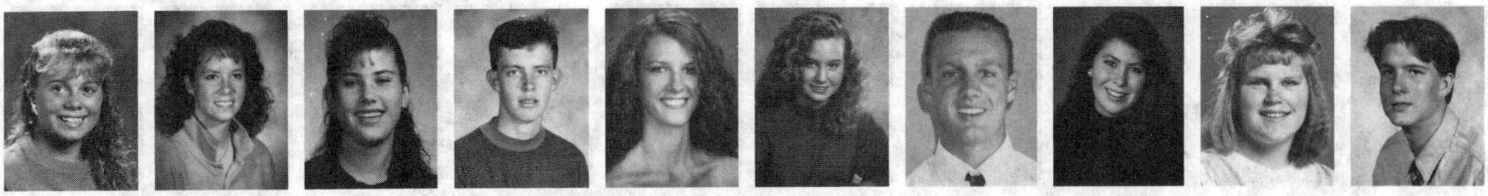

Mc Donald, Kimberly
Bonita HS
La Verne, CA

Mc Donald, Marcy L
North HS
Bakersfield, CA

Mc Donald, Yvonne
Argonaut HS
Jackson, CA

Mc Dougal, Jeff N
Riverdale HS
Riverdale, CA

Mc Dowell, Caroline
South Tahoe HS
S Lake Tahoe, CA

Mc Dowell, Jennifer
Mission Viejo HS
Mission Viejo, CA

Mc Elfish, Clinton M
Hueneme HS
Port Hueneme, CA

Mc Elree, Tracey J
Davis SR HS
Richland Center, WI

Mc Farland, Janelle
Rim Of The World
Running Springs, CA

Mc Farland, Sean A
Santa Clara HS
Oxnard, CA

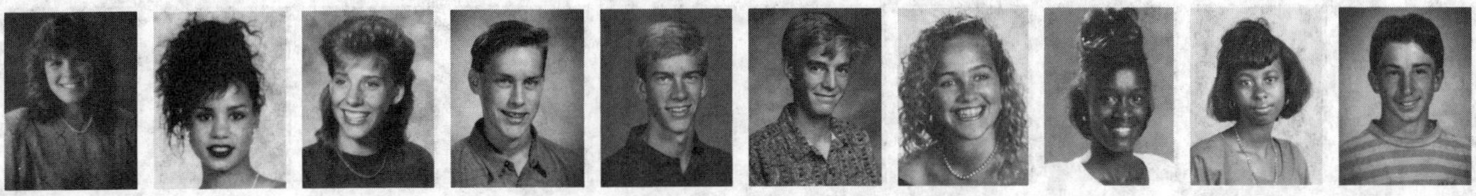

Mc Farland, Shelley
Eureka SR HS
Eureka, CA

Mc Farland, Sonjia K
Mercy HS
South San Francis, CA

Mc Gee, Renee
Valley Christian HS
Livermore, CA

Mc Ginley, Scott D
Garden Grove HS
Garden Grove, CA

Mc Ginty, Daniel M
Bellarmine College Prep
Gilroy, CA

Mc Goldrick, Nathan
Santa Fe Christian
Oceanside, CA

Mc Govern, Cathy
Holy Names HS
Berkeley, CA

Mc Gowan, Elyssia
Coast Christian Schls
Hawthorne, CA

Mc Gowan, Myisha
Diamond Bar HS
Diamond Bar, CA

Mc Gowan, Sean
Cardinal Newman
Sonoma, CA

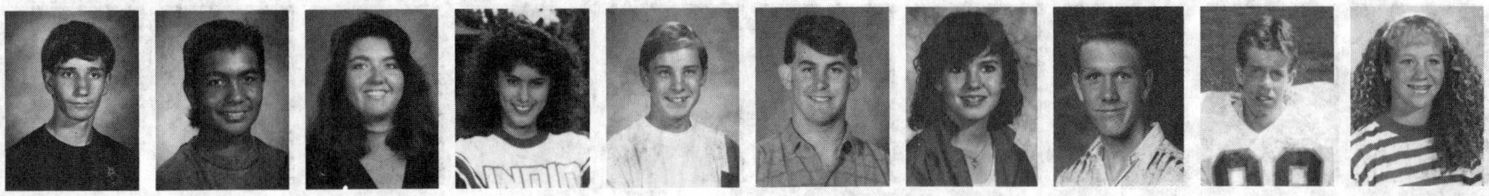

Mc Guire, Jr Richard
West HS
Bakersfield, CA

Mc Hale, Bryce S
Garden Grove HS
Garden Grove, CA

Mc Henry, Tamara D
Mt Whitney HS
Visalia, CA

Mc Intosh, Martha
Indio HS
Indio, CA

Mc Intosh, Jr Robert
Junupa Valley HS
Riverside, CA

Mc Intosh, Ronald F
Redwood HS
Visalia, CA

Mc Iver, Linda K
North Montery County HS
Castroville, CA

Mc Kee, D Stephen
Liberty Christian Acad
Fountain Valley, CA

Mc Kenzie, Gregg W
Cupertino HS
Cupertino, CA

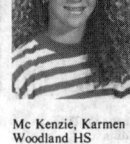

Mc Kenzie, Karmen
Woodland HS
Woodland, CA

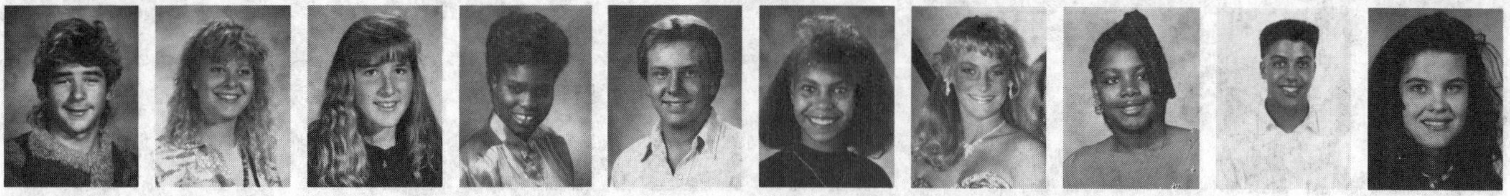

Mc Kinley, Eric Heath
Canyon HS
Canyon Country, CA

Mc Kinley, Trudy R
Nevada Union HS
Nevada City, CA

Mc Kinney, Cindy K
Arroyo Grande HS
Oceano, CA

Mc Kinney, Cleminatu
Mira Mesa HS
Poway, CA

Mc Kinney, Matt R
Atascadero HS
Santa Margarita, CA

Mc Kinney, Tara Lynn
Ramona HS
Riverside, CA

Mc Kinnon, Cindy L
Thousand Oaks HS
Thousand Oaks, CA

Mc Koy, Jeannette E
Montclair HS
Montclair, CA

Mc Laren, Shane
San Bernardino HS
San Bernardino, CA

Mc Laughlin, Emily J
Dixon HS
Dixon, CA

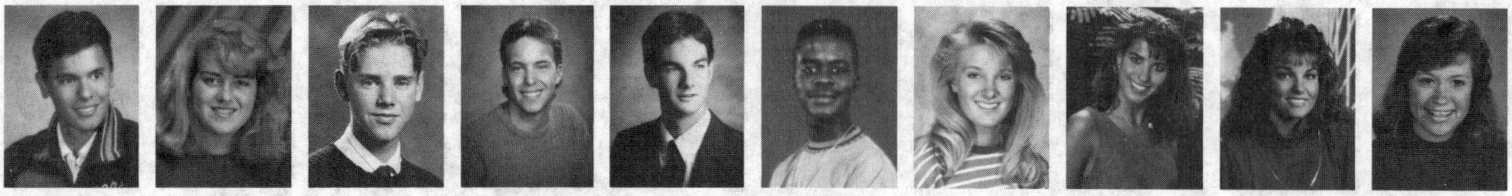

Mc Laughlin, Steve B
Serra HS
Hillsborough, CA

Mc Laurin, Corrine
Coronado HS
Coronado, CA

Mc Lean, Scott C
Flintridge Preparatory Schl
Monrovia, CA

Mc Lean, Scott T
Tracy HS
Tracy, CA

Mc Lellan, Jason
James Madison HS
San Diego, CA

Mc Lemore, Earnest
John F Kennedy HS
Sacramento, CA

Mc Lennan, Laura L
Alverno Heights Acad
Arcadia, CA

Mc Lintock, Monique
Vista Migm HS
Vista, CA

Mc Mahon, Amy M
King City HS
Bradley, CA

Mc Mahon, Kathleen
Antioch SR HS
Antioch, CA

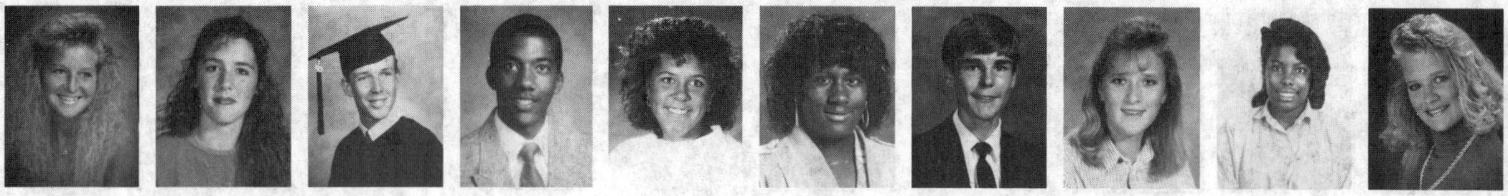

Mc Millin, Vanessa
El Capitan HS
Lakeside, CA

Mc Mindes, Amber L
Vacaville HS
Vacaville, CA

Mc Mullen, Christopher D
Downtown Business Magnet HS
Burbank, CA

Mc Namee, III George Allen
Bonita Vista HS
Chula Vista, CA

Mc Natt, Jennifer E
Don Antonio Lugo
Chino, CA

Mc Neal, Cushondra
Mojave HS
California City, CA

Mc Neil, Gregory P
George Dewey HS
San Francisco, CA

Mc Neil, Kristia L
Livermore HS
Livermore, CA

Mc Neil, Shelby P
Morningside HS
Inglewood, CA

Mc Neill, Christina
Diamond Bar HS
Walnut, CA

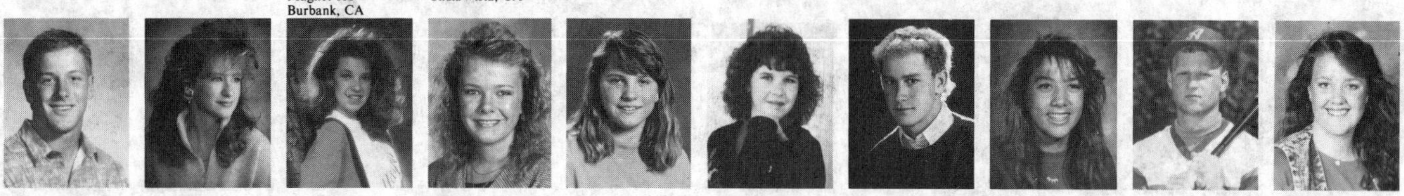

Mc Nown, Jeff
San Benito Hollister
Hollister, CA

Mc Peek, Tanya L
El Capitan HS
El Cajon, CA

Mc Pheeters, Melissa
Village Christian Schl
Lakeview Terrace, CA

Mc Queen-Smith, Tammi
Hilltop HS
Bonita, CA

Mc Quillan, Holly J
Tehachapi HS
Tehachapi, CA

Mc Quirk, Dawn
Orland HS
Orland, CA

Mc Shane, Kenneth
Monterey HS
Monterey, CA

Mc Shane, Teresa A
West HS
Bakersfield, CA

Mc Whorter, Mike L
Anderson Union HS
Redding, CA

Meador, Alyson E
Ocean View HS
Quantico, VA

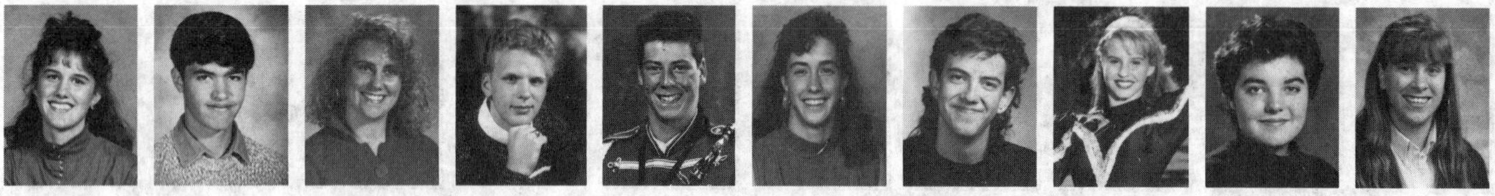

Meadows, Amy E
Tomales HS
Petaluma, CA

Meadows, Justin D
Arvin HS
Arvin, CA

Meagher, Kelly
Valley Christian HS
San Jose, CA

Meaney, Larry
King City HS
King City, CA

Mear, Donald Michael
Western HS
Anaheim, CA

Mease, Sara L
El Cajon Valley HS
El Cajon, CA

Meckfessel, Shon G
Rio Americano HS
Sacramento, CA

Medeiros, Erin K
Troy HS
Yorba Linda, CA

Medeiros, Jessica M
Rim Of The World
Blue Jay, CA

Mediati, Christine L
St Joseph Notre Dame HS
Alameda, CA

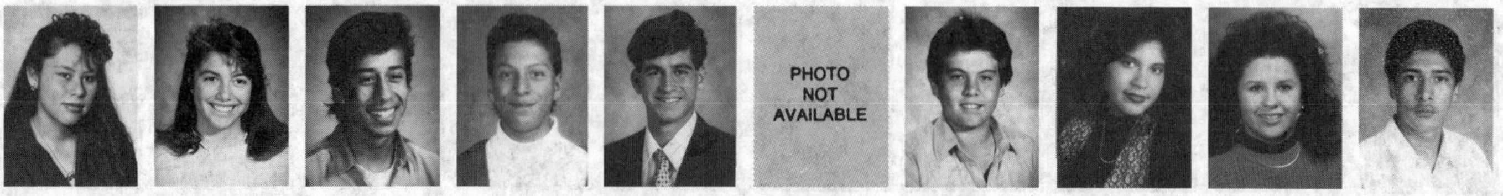

PHOTO
NOT
AVAILABLE

Medina, Aida L
Nogales HS
La Puente, CA

Medina, Denise
Corcoran HS
Corcoran, CA

Medina, Hector
Los Banos HS
Los Banos, CA

Medina, Jose B
Golden West HS
Visalia, CA

Medina, Nathan
Western HS
Anaheim, CA

Medina, Olga V
Saddleback HS
Santa Ana, CA

Medina, Protacio N
Indio HS
Indio, CA

Medina, Sally Miranda
Quartz Hill HS
Quartz Hill, CA

Medrano, Katherine
Hanford Union HS
Hanford, CA

Medrano, Moses
Tranquillity Union
San Joaquin, CA

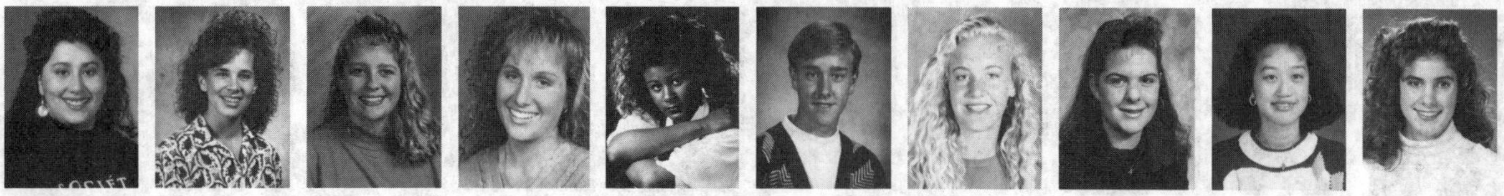

Medrano, Tiffany Roxanne
Hanford HS
Hanford, CA

Medsker, Adrienne
West Covina Hills
La Puente, CA

Meeh, Wanda J
Apple Valley HS
Apple Valley, CA

Meeks, Alicia
Lakewood HS
Lakewood, CA

Meeks, Angelique D
Tracy HS
Tracy, CA

Meeks, Jeff A
Arlington HS
Riverside, CA

Meidinger, Heather
Lowell HS
San Francisco, CA

Meigs, Tammie
Yucca Valley HS
Morongo Valley, CA

Mein, Janis
Modesto HS
Modesto, CA

Meiser, Rebecca A
Alhambra HS
Martinez, CA

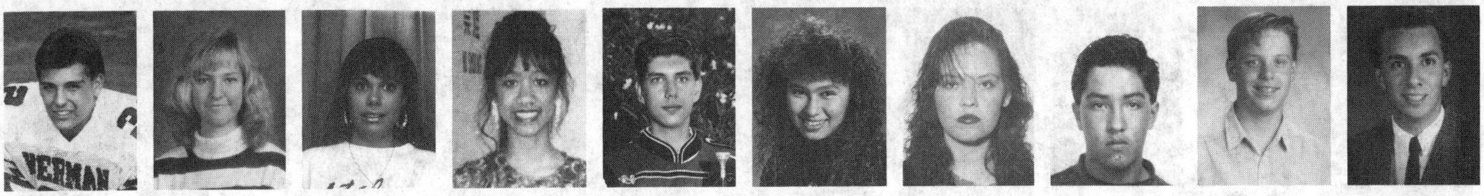

Meisner, Greg
Kerman HS
Kerman, CA

Meister, Erika S
Redlands HS
Redlands, CA

Mejia, Maria M
Newport Harbor HS
Santa Ana, CA

Melchor, Cheryl Ann
Whitney HS
Cerritos, CA

Melendez, Daniel R
Nogales HS
Walnut, CA

Melendez, Margie B
Coachella Valley HS
Thermal, CA

Melendrez, Blanca
Castle Park HS
Chula Vista, CA

Melendrez, Rogelio
Senior HS
Chula Vista, CA

Melilli, David
Capostrano Valley
Christian HS
Laguna Hills, CA

Melillo, Nicholas J
Riverdale HS
Clovis, CA

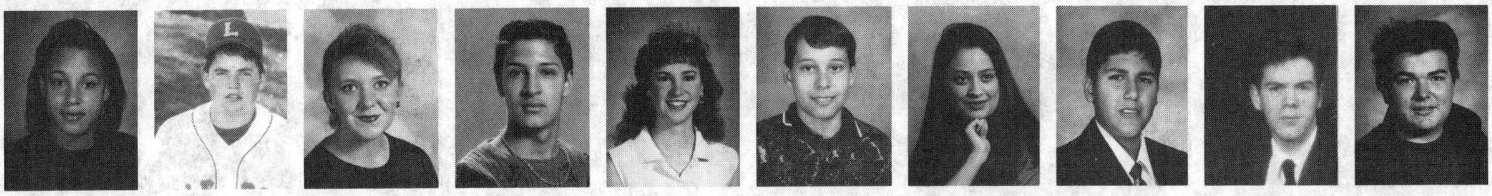

Melina, Paulette D
El Camino Real HS
Woodland Hills, CA

Mello, Joe V
Livingston HS
Delhi, CA

Melton, Jennifer R
Troy HS
Yorba Linda, CA

Mena, Braulio
Gardena HS
Gardena, CA

Mendes, Kristina M
Fortuna Union HS
Fortuna, CA

Mendes, Lino James
Hanford Union HS
Hanford, CA

Mendez, Alina L
San Luis Obispo HS
Los Osos, CA

Mendez, Eduardo
Pasadena HS
Pasadena, CA

Mendez, Edward
Damien HS
Diamond Bar, CA

Mendez, Jay Martin
Los Amigos HS
Fountain Valley, CA

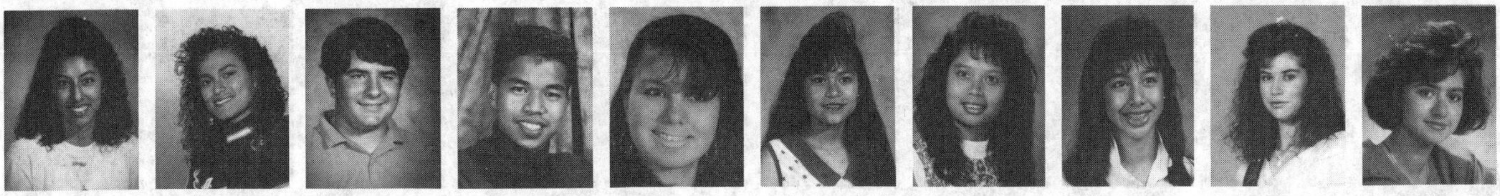

Mendez, Norma
San Dieguito HS
Encinitas, CA

Mendez, Susan
Santa Ana HS
Santa Ana, CA

Mendiburu, John G
East Bakersfield HS
Bakersfield, CA

Mendoza, Jr Almario
Valley View HS
Moreno Valley, CA

Mendoza, Araceli
Fresno HS
Fresno, CA

Mendoza, Armie V
Monterey HS
Seaside, CA

Mendoza, Carmela D
Sunny Hills HS
Fullerton, CA

Mendoza, Cheryl
Mercy HS
S San Francisco, CA

Mendoza, Diana
Calexico Union HS
Calexico, CA

Mendoza, Estela B
Academy Of Our
Lady Of Peace
National City, CA

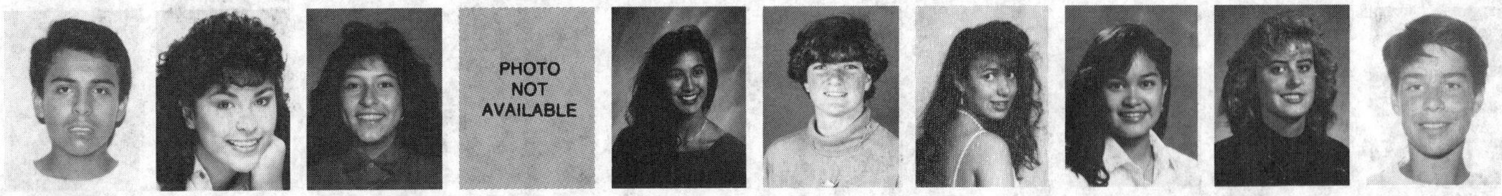
PHOTO
NOT
AVAILABLE

Mendoza, Hector R
St Genevieve HS
Sun Valley, CA

Mendoza, Juanita
Indio HS
Coachella, CA

Mendoza, Liza
Warren HS
Downey, CA

Mendoza, Mark M
Diamond Bar HS
Diamond Bar, CA

Mendoza, Teresa C
Villa Park HS
Orange, CA

Menendez, Amy A
Ukiah HS
Ukiah, CA

Menendez, Ingrid
Chaminade Coll Prep
Canoga Park, CA

Menez, Therese C
Providence HS
Glendale, CA

Menning, Genevieve
Modoc HS
Canby, CA

Menville, Chad B
Santa Monica HS
Malibu, CA

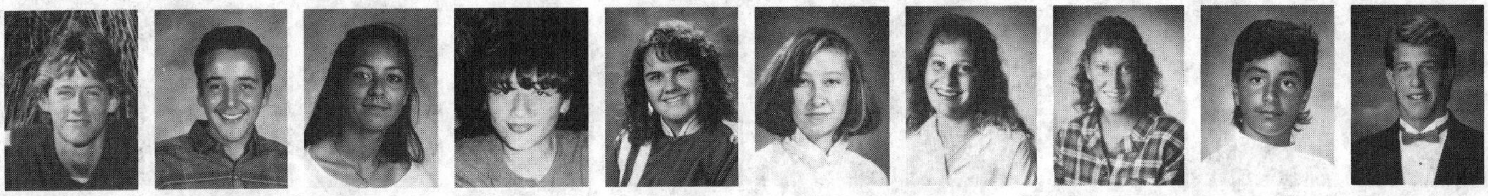

Menzl, Adrian C
Serra HS
Laguna Niguel, CA

Meraz, Efren
Dos Palos Joint
Union HS
South Dos Palos, CA

Mercado, Tanya M
Abraham Lincoln HS
San Jose, CA

Mercado, Veronica
Sacred Heart Of
Jesus HS
Los Angeles, CA

Mercer, Lyn Anne
El Toro HS
El Toro, CA

Mercer, Nicole M
Troy HS
Yorba Linda, CA

Mercer, Shelley M
Central Catholic HS
Modesto, CA

Mercer, Sheri A
Central Catholic HS
Modesto, CA

Merchant, Sanjay
Mission Viejo HS
Mission Viejo, CA

Merrill, Matthew S
Newbury Park HS
Newbury Park, CA

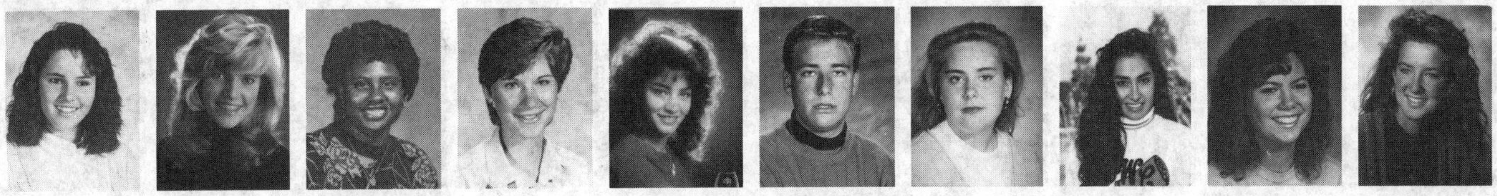

Merrill, Shawna
Woodland HS
Woodland, CA

Merritt, Carrie
Ursuline HS
Santa Rosa, CA

Merritt, Janine
Washington HS
Los Angeles, CA

Mertins, Amy L
St Joseph HS
Santa Maria, CA

Mesa, Deborah L
Immanuel HS
Selma, CA

Messina, Anthony A
Don Antonio Lugo
Chino, CA

Messina, Lisa
North Hollywood HS
North Hollywood, CA

Mestas, Nadalie
West Covina HS
West Covina, CA

Metcalf, Carrie
Oroville HS
Oroville, CA

Metcalf, Marla Gale
Los Angeles Baptist
Granada Hills, CA

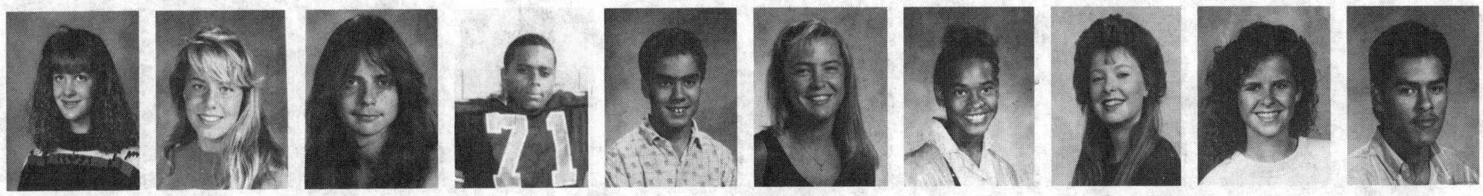

Metcalf, Sherry L
Summerville HS
Sonora, CA

Metroyanis, Jennifer
Mount Carmel HS
San Diego, CA

Metsiou, Tony M
Granite Hills HS
El Cajon, CA

Meux, Michael
Edison Computech
Fresno, CA

Meyer, Daniel L
Norte Vista HS
Riverside, CA

Meyer, Kelly M
Los Altos HS
Los Altos, CA

Meyer, Tarah T
Clovis West HS
Fresno, CA

Meyers, Betty J
Baldwin Park HS
Baldwin Park, CA

Meyers, Kami
Madison HS
San Diego, CA

Meza, Joel A
Indio HS
Indio, CA

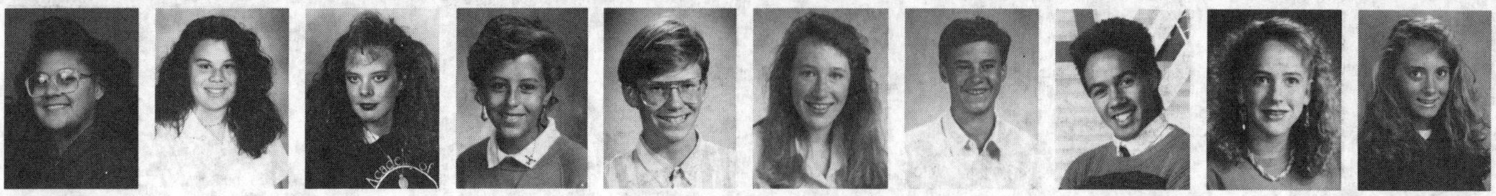

Meza, Marcie
Calexico HS
Calexico, CA

Meza, Patricia
Saint Genevieve HS
Arleta, CA

Meza, Rosa E
Academy Of Our
Lady Of Peace
San Diego, CA

Meza, Rozanna L
Montgomery HS
San Diego, CA

Michaelsen, Erik N
Montgomery HS
Santa Rosa, CA

Michalak, Melissa L
Santa Clara HS
Santa Clara, CA

Michaud, Mike B
Oak Park HS
Agoura Hills, CA

Michel, Arthur J
Vista HS
Vista, CA

Micheli, Corinne L
Clovis HS
Clovis, CA

Michelli, Mariah
Capistrano Valley
Christian HS
San Jn Capistrano,
CA

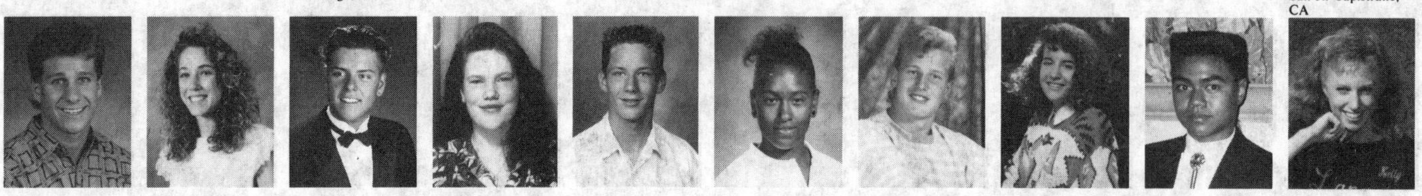

Michels, John L
Servite HS
Fountain Valley, CA

Michelson, Julie A
Fountain Valley HS
Fountain Valley, CA

Michno, Jean
South San Francisco
S San Francisco, CA

Mickelson-Reay,
Alexis H
Sacramento HS
Sacramento, CA

Mickle, Scott
Mission Bay HS
San Diego, CA

Middleton, Keita T
Mater Dei HS
Huntington Beach,
CA

Miedema, Ryan M
Valley View HS
Moreno Valley, CA

Miguel, Jennifer C
Caruthers Union HS
Fresno, CA

Miguel, Randy R
Bellarmine Coll Prep
San Jose, CA

Mihram, Kelly C
Lutheran HS
Anaheim, CA

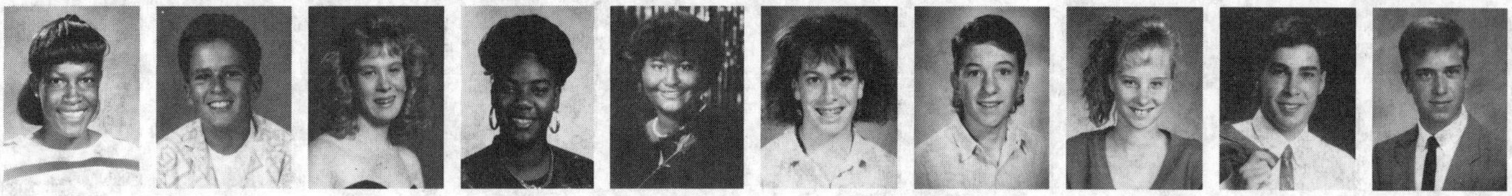

Mike, Keisha L
Garey HS
Phillips Ranch, CA

Mikula, Michael W
Ocean View HS
Huntington Beach,
CA

Miles, Angela
Providence HS
Sherman Oaks, CA

Miles, Rose Of
Sharon
Grant SR HS
Sacramento, CA

Miles, Shawndra
Crenshaw HS
Los Angeles, CA

Milici, Angela M
Norco HS
Norco, CA

Millar, Josh V
Westlake HS
Thousand Oaks, CA

Miller, Andrea L
Whittier Christian
Whittier, CA

Miller, Brian K
Sanger HS
Sanger, CA

Miller, David S
West Covina HS
W Covina, CA

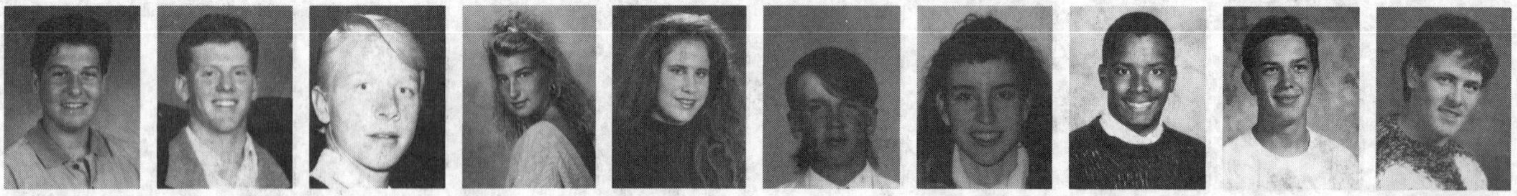

Miller, Edward J
Servite HS
Buena Park, CA

Miller, Eric
Orosi HS
Cutler, CA

Miller, Jason E
San Diego Acad
National City, CA

Miller, Jenna N
Huntington Beach
Huntington Bch, CA

Miller, Jennifer C
Yteshiva University
Of Los Angeles
Los Angeles, CA

Miller, Jon C
Oakmont HS
Roseville, CA

Miller, Kasha M
Savanna HS
Anaheim, CA

Miller, Kurtis M
St Bernard HS
Los Angeles, CA

Miller, Matthew J
Atwater HS
Winton, CA

Miller, Michael
Biggs HS
Gridley, CA

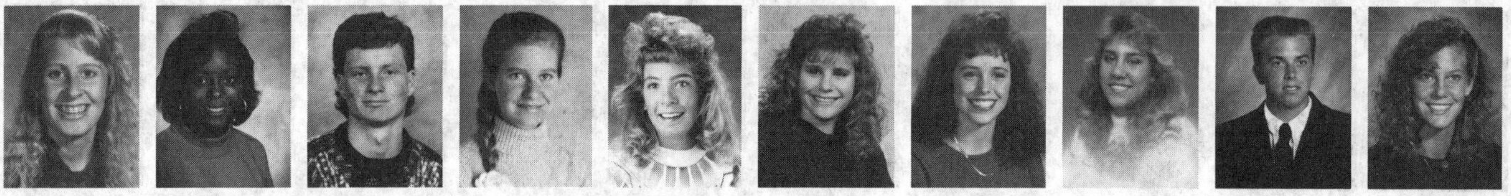

Miller, Nancy
Soquel HS
Santa Cruz, CA

Miller, Pamela S
Paraclete HS
Lancaster, CA

Miller, Rondee
Orange Glen HS
Escondido, CA

Miller, Sabina G
Rio Mesa HS
Camarillo, CA

Miller, Shelbi
Diamond Bar HS
Diamond Bar, CA

Miller, Stephanie
Casa Roble HS
Orangevale, CA

Miller, Stephanie
Valley Christian HS
San Jose, CA

Miller, Stephanie
Ann
Modesto HS
Modesto, CA

Miller, Steve K
Orange HS
Orange, CA

Miller, Susan
Willows HS
Willows, CA

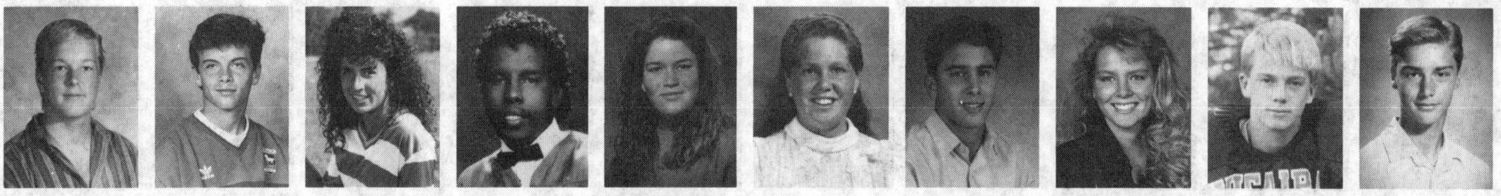

Miller, William L
Coast Joint Union
Cambria, CA

Milligan, Christopher
University City HS
San Diego, CA

Milligan, Elaine J
Upland HS
Upland, CA

Milligan, Reggie
J E Mc Ateer HS
San Francisco, CA

Milliken, Tawny
Marie
La Serna HS
Whittier, CA

Millner, Tonya L
John W North HS
Riverside, CA

Mills, Alexander G
Servite HS
Westminster, CA

Mills, Dena L
Southport Christian
Acad
El Cajon, CA

Mills, Jason S
Yucaipa HS
Yucaipa, CA

Mills, Randall S
Notre Dame HS
Riverside, CA

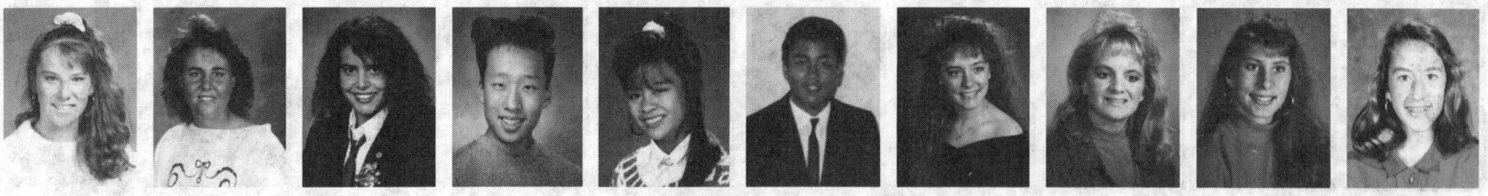

Milner, Terri K
Bishop Montgomery
Torrance, CA

Milner, Tifany E
Ramona HS
Ramona, CA

Milton, Andrea D
Viewpoint HS
Agoura Hills, CA

Min, Don
Sunny Hills HS
Fullerton, CA

Mina, Charlene D
Pinole Valley HS
Hercules, CA

Mindoro, Alwyn
Glendale Adventist
Acad
Tujunga, CA

Miner, Shannon
Alameda HS
Alameda, CA

Miner, Trista M
Lincoln HS
Stockton, CA

Minior, Jennifer A
Turlock HS
Turlock, CA

Minium, Lara M
Santa Cruz HS
Santa Cruz, CA

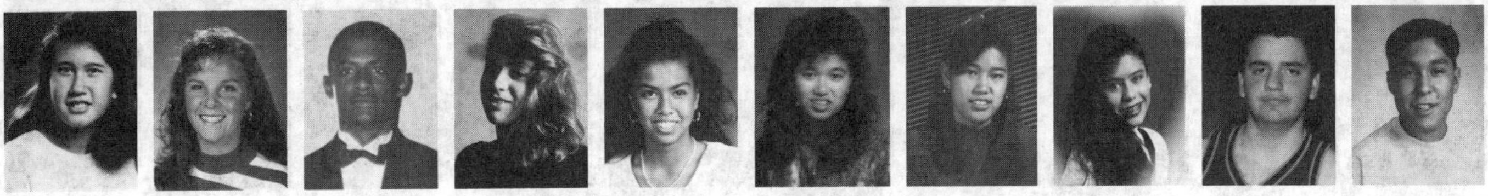

Minnick, Christine G
Glendale Adventist Acad
Glendale, CA

Minor, Kimberly M
California HS
San Ramon, CA

Minters, Kariem M
St Bernards HS
Compton, CA

Mintey, Piper J
Saint Bernard HS
Eureka, CA

Miralles, Marla L
St Joseph HS
Bellflower, CA

Miranda, Abigail
Southwest HS
San Diego, CA

Miranda, Barbie
Southwest HS
San Diego, CA

Miranda, Damaris
Andrew P Hill HS
San Jose, CA

Miranda, James V
Sunset HS
Hayward, CA

Miranda, Joseph A
Damien HS
Irwindale, CA

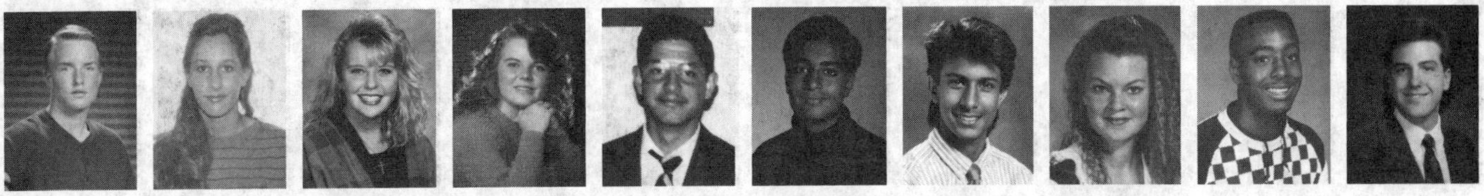

Miranda, Michael L
Pasadena HS
Pasadena, CA

Misic, Margaret
Poly HS
Riverside, CA

Miskimin, Amy
Maranatha Christian
Pasadena, CA

Mistretta, Barbara J
Orange Glen HS
Escondido, CA

Mistriel, Stephen D
Brawley Union HS
Brawley, CA

Mistry, Bhavesh
Sequoia HS
Redwood City, CA

Mistry, Sunit D
Pilgrim Schl
Los Angeles, CA

Mitcham, Kelly
Los Alamitos HS
Seal Beach, CA

Mitchell, Andre T
Bellarmine College Prep
San Jose, CA

Mitchell, Douglas E
Glendora HS
Glendora, CA

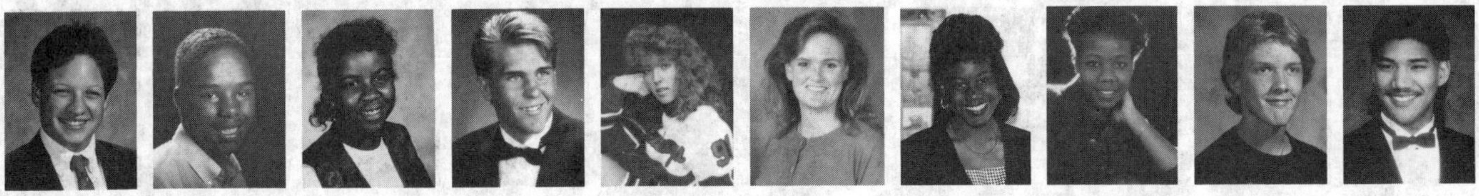

Mitchell, Edward M
Saint Ignatius Coll Prep
San Francisco, CA

Mitchell, Jason E
Narbonne HS
Carson, CA

Mitchell, Joi L
Huntington Park HS
Inglewood, CA

Mitchell, Kenneth A
Liberty Union HS
Oakley, CA

Mitchell, Kristine
St Vincents HS
Rohnert Park, CA

Mitchell, Leigh R
Redwood HS
Visalia, CA

Mitchell, Monique R
Fairfield HS
Fairfield, CA

Mitchell, Timika
Vanden HS
Trvis A F B, CA

Mittie, Kim Gerald
Sierra Joint Union
Clovis, CA

Miu, Johnny
Antioch SR HS
Antioch, CA

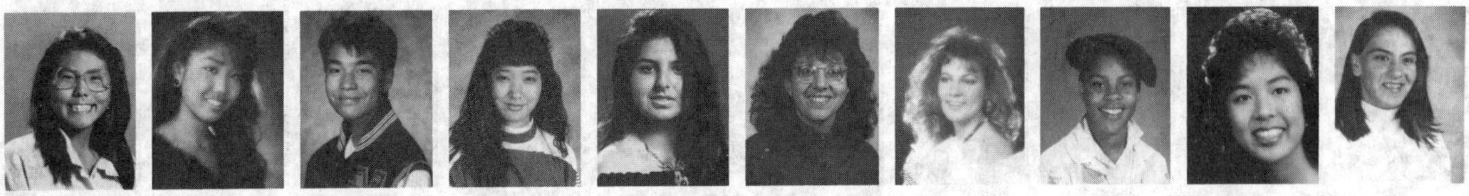

Miyahara, Pennie C
Bishop Montgomery
Hawthorne, CA

Miyamoto, Brenda S
James A Garfield HS
Monterey Park, CA

Miyamoto, Christopher
Notre Dame HS
Burbank, CA

Miyoshi, Amy
Washington Union
Fresno, CA

Mkhitarian, Anna A
Village Christian Schls
Shadow Hills, CA

Mkrtchian, Sara
Montebello HS
Montebello, CA

Mobley, Jennifer Anne
Eisenhower HS
Rialto, CA

Mobley, Tanisha L
Antelope Valley HS
Lancaster, CA

Mochizuki, Lisa Mari
San Joaquin Memorial HS
Hanford, CA

Moctezuma, Ana L
Montebello HS
Los Angeles, CA

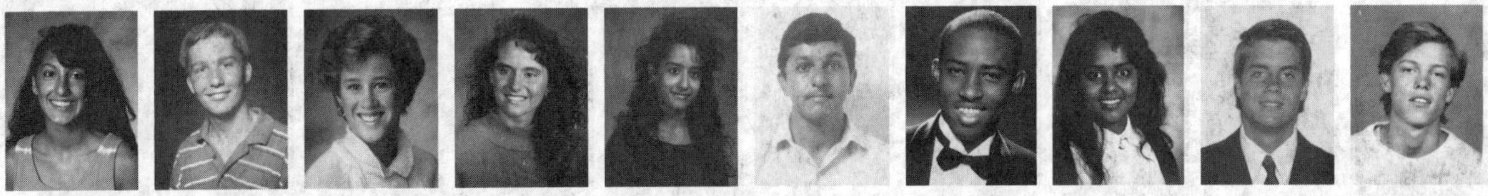

Modarress, Katayoon
Miraleste HS
Ranchos Palos Ver, CA

Modglin, Kevin D
St Bernard Catholic
Los Angeles, CA

Moelter, Shannon
Santana HS
Santee, CA

Moes, Kelly
Millikan HS
Long Beach, CA

Mofid, Golafarid
Corona HS
Corona, CA

Mohammed, Hanif
Warren HS
Downey, CA

Mohamoud, Abdi Mohamed
Crawford HS
San Diego, CA

Mohanan, Sveta
Quartz Hill HS
Lancaster, CA

Mohme, Stephen A
Santa Barbara HS
Santa Barbara, CA

Mohr, Cory R
Beaumont HS
Beaumont, CA

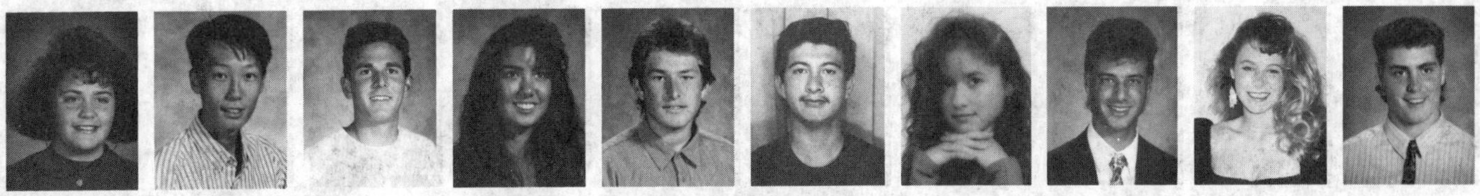

Mohr, Sandra
Willows HS
Willows, CA

Mok, Gilbert W
Gretchen Whitney
Cerritos, CA

Molho, Joshua
El Dorado HS
Placerville, CA

Molina, Carie A
Dinuba HS
Dinuba, CA

Molina, Carlos A
Copuchino HS
San Bruno, CA

Molina, Francisco A
Manual Arts HS
Los Angeles, CA

Molina, Rosa Elena
Los Altos HS
Hacienda Hts, CA

Molinari, Christian
St Ignatius College Prep
San Francisco, CA

Mollenkamp, Amy
Chadwick HS
Rolling Hills Est, CA

Mollica, Lawson C
Edison HS
Huntington Beach, CA

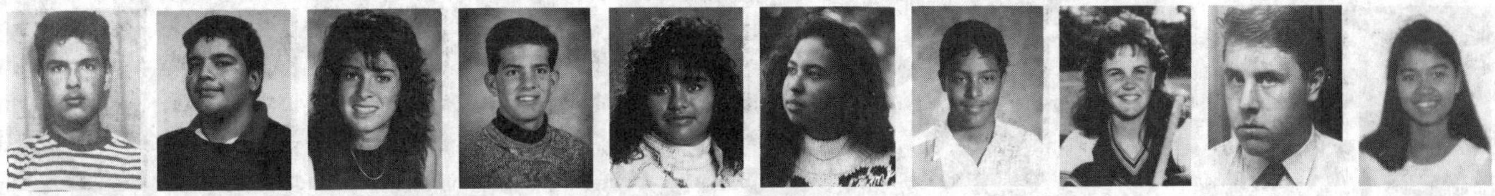

Momand, Wahid
American HS
Fremont, CA

Moncada, Jerardo H
John A O'connell HS
San Francisco, CA

Moncada, Susie
Santa Teresa HS
San Jose, CA

Moncur, Jaron C
Shafter HS
Shafter, CA

Mondragon, Julie
Hawthorne HS
Inglewood, CA

Mondragon, Roxanne
East Bakersfield HS
Bakersfield, CA

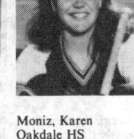

Monge, Manuel Luis
Don Bosco Tech Inst
Los Angeles, CA

Moniz, Karen
Oakdale HS
Oakdale, CA

Monk, Grant
Yucaipa HS
Mentone, CA

Monponbanua, Aileen
Palm Springs HS
Palm Springs, CA

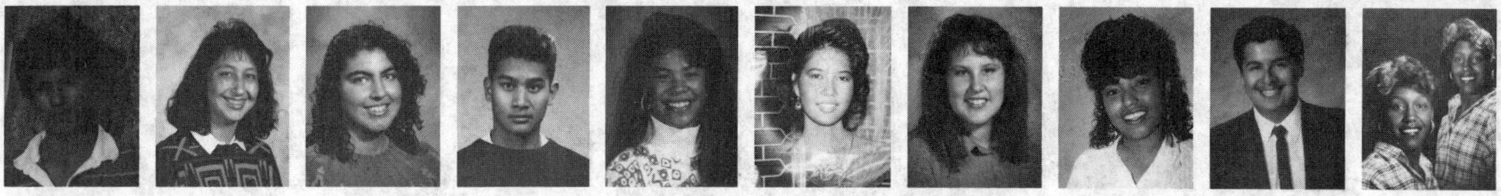

Monroy, Carlos A
Santa Barbara HS
Santa Barbara, CA

Montanez, Elizabeth
Santa Clara HS
Oxnard, CA

Montanez, Margarita
Valley HS
Santa Ana, CA

Monte, Michael
Richmond HS
San Pablo, CA

Montemayor, Marsha
Cornelia Connelly HS
Hacienda Heights, CA

Montemayor, Marygrace N
Los Alamitos HS
Los Alamitos, CA

Montenegro, Christy
John F Kennedy HS
Buena Park, CA

Monterrozo, Elida
Van Nuys HS
Van Nuys, CA

Monterrubio, Jorge
Fairfield HS
Fairfield, CA

Montez, Denetia M
Carson HS
Carson, CA

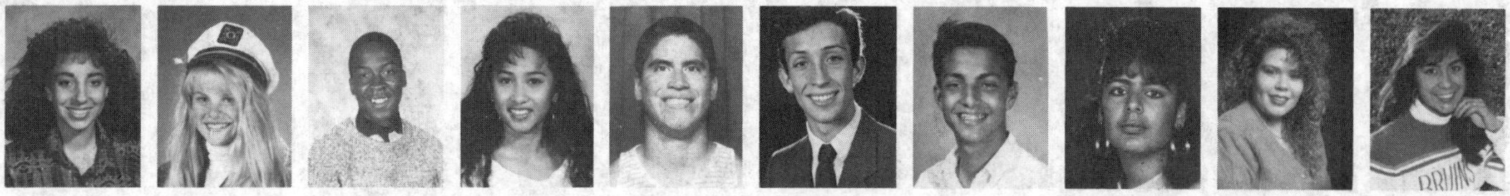

Montgomery, Ann Marie
Riverdale Joint Union
Riverdale, CA

Montgomery, Kim
Alhambra HS
Martinez, CA

Montgomery, Mark A
Lynwood HS
Lynwood, CA

Monticalvo, Rosasita
Andrew Hill HS
San Jose, CA

Montoya, Jr Albert
El Rancho HS
Pico Rivera, CA

Montoya, Daniel
Arcata HS
Arcata, CA

Montoya, III Joseph
Bishop Amat HS
Whittier, CA

Montoya, Veronica
Southwest HS
San Ysidro, CA

Monugian, Scarlett
Pioneer HS
Whittier, CA

Monzon, Cynthia
Santa Clara HS
Santa Clara, CA

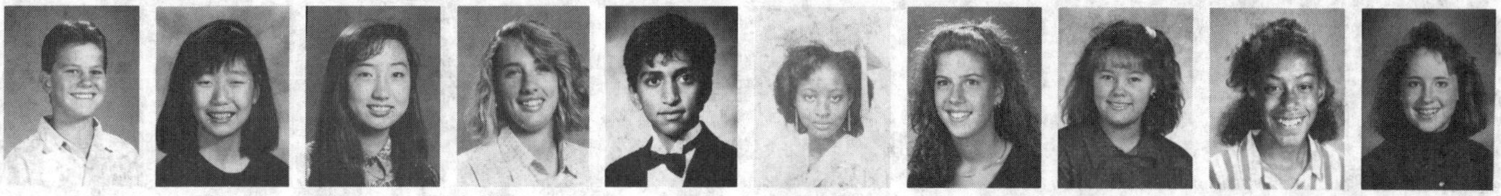

Moody, James L
Vanden HS
Suisun City, CA

Moon, Jennifer
Los Alamitos HS
Los Alamitos, CA

Moon, Jenny
Garces HS
Bakersfield, CA

Moon, Monika
Carlsbad HS
Carlsbad, CA

Moonsamy, Neil
El Cerrito HS
El Cerrito, CA

Moore, Betrina
Channel Islands HS
Oxnard, CA

Moore, Dana E
San Rafael HS
San Rafael, CA

Moore, Janine R
Del Mar HS
San Jose, CA

Moore, Katrina A
Clovis West HS
Clovis, CA

Moore, Megan K
Irvine HS
Irvine, CA

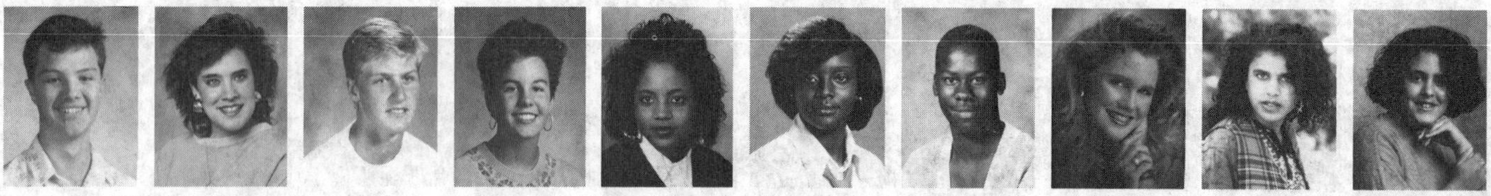

Moore, Mike W
Colfax HS
Weimar, CA

Moore, Nechole L
Montclair HS
Ontario, CA

Moore, III Paul A
Monte Vista HS
Walnut Creek, CA

Moore, Regan A
Roseville HS
Colfax, CA

Moore, Sharonia L
Academy Of Our Lady Of Peace
San Diego, CA

Moore, Sonoya D
St Marys Acad
Inglewood, CA

Moorehead, Emil O
Morningside HS
Inglewood, CA

Moorman, Tami
Granite Hills HS
El Cajon, CA

Moorthy, Geetha V
Westlake Schl For Girls
Los Angeles, CA

Mora, Cynthia Y
Polytechnic HS
Sun Valley, CA

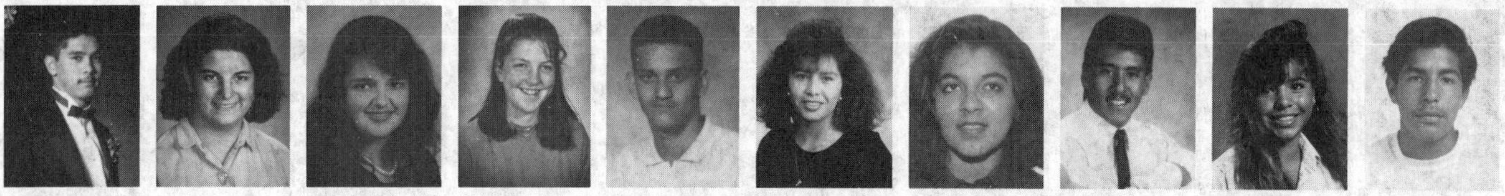

Morabe, Dante J
Alhambra HS
Martinez, CA

Morabito, Marisa A
Lincoln HS
Stockton, CA

Moraes, Cindy
Notre Dame HS
San Jose, CA

Moraine, Maia
Sacramento Waldorf
Fair Oaks, CA

Morales, Adolfo G
Saint John Bosco HS
Huntington Park, CA

Morales, Ana C
Estancia HS
Costa Mesa, CA

Morales, Cynthia L
Thomas Downey HS
Modesto, CA

Morales, Daniel
Valley HS
Sacramento, CA

Morales, Eileen M
Fontana HS
Fontana, CA

Morales, Julio
Garfield HS Magnet
Anaheim, CA

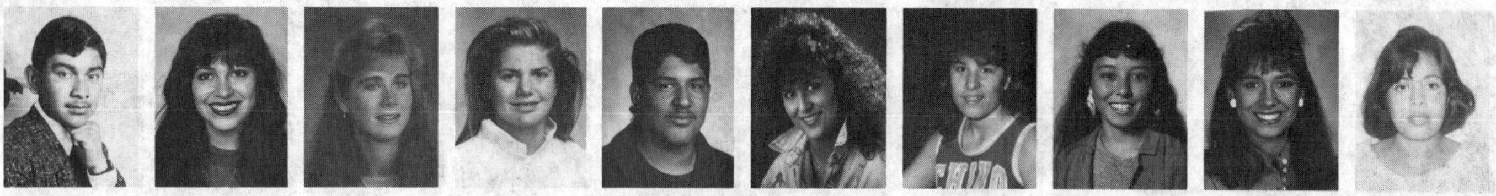

Morales, Jr Justo
Hamilton HS Academy Of Music
Bell, CA

Morales, Laura O
Woodrow Wilson HS
Los Angeles, CA

Moran, Allisyn
Dos Pueblos HS
Santa Barbara, CA

Moreau, Nadia A
Encina HS
Sacramento, CA

Moreno, Anthony C
Grant Union HS
Sacramento, CA

Moreno, Denise
Tulare Joint Union
Tulare, CA

Moreno, Francine
Chino HS
Chino, CA

Moreno, Linda G
Chaffey HS
Ontario, CA

Moreno, Marisa
Pomona Catholic Girls HS
Fontana, CA

Moreno, Rosa M
Santiago HS
Santa Ana, CA

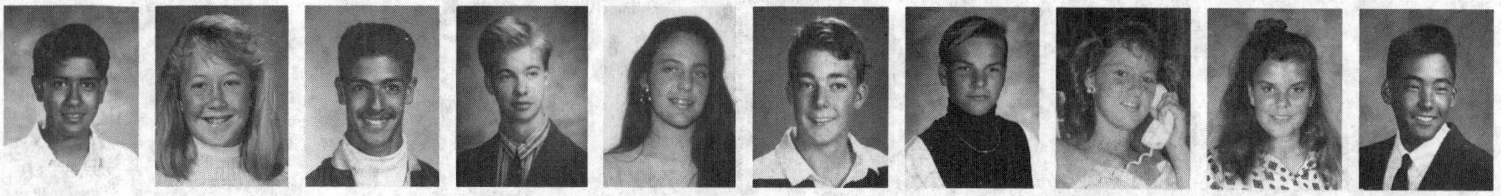

Moreno, Ruben Nicolas
Don Bosco Technical Inst
Rosemead, CA

Moreton, Julia
Trabuco Hills HS
Trabuco Canyon, CA

Moretti, Stephen
Benicia HS
Benicia, CA

Morey, Tim
Julian Union HS
Julian, CA

Morgan, Cecilia M
St Bernard HS
Los Angeles, CA

Morgan, Jeffrey P
Lincoln HS
Stockton, CA

Morgan, Ryan E
Oak Ridge HS
Shingle Springs, CA

Morgan, Shireen
Calipatria HS
Niland, CA

Morgan, Tamara L
Oak Ridge HS
Shingle Springs, CA

Morisaki, Gregg
Kennedy HS
La Palma, CA

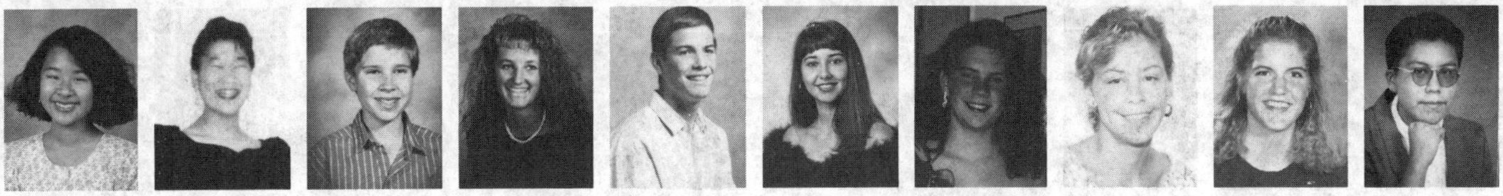

Morita, Jennifer K
Mesa Verde HS
Citrus Heights, CA

Morita, Mayuko E
Sacramento Country
Day Sch
Woodland, CA

Morledge, James E
West HS
Bakersfield, CA

Morley, Christina M
St Genevieve HS
Canoga Park, CA

Moro, John
Paraclete HS
Lancaster, CA

Moroaica, Andra
Downey HS
Downey, CA

Morrical, Kristin
San Mateo HS
Foster City, CA

Morris, Angie
Gidden West HS
Visalia, CA

Morris, Carol A
Davis SR HS
Davis, CA

Morris, Christopher L
Silver Valley HS
Daggett, CA

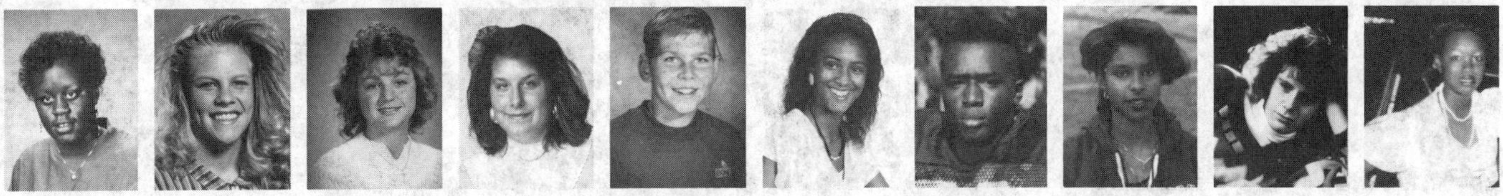

Morris, Frankie M
Hogan SR HS
Vallejo, CA

Morris, Jennifer
Delano HS
Delano, CA

Morris, Kimberly L
Ferndale Union HS
Ferndale, CA

Morris, Lisa L
St Anthony HS
Lakewood, CA

Morris, Noah J
Paradise HS
Paradise, CA

Morris, Shaironda R
El Camino
Fundamental HS
Citrus Heights, CA

Morrisette,
Dahryanous D
Magnolia HS
Anaheim, CA

Morrison, Akilak C
San Bernardino HS
San Bernardino, CA

Morrison, Jannien
Strathmore Union HS
Porterville, CA

Morrison, Jesia
Washington Prep
Los Angeles, CA

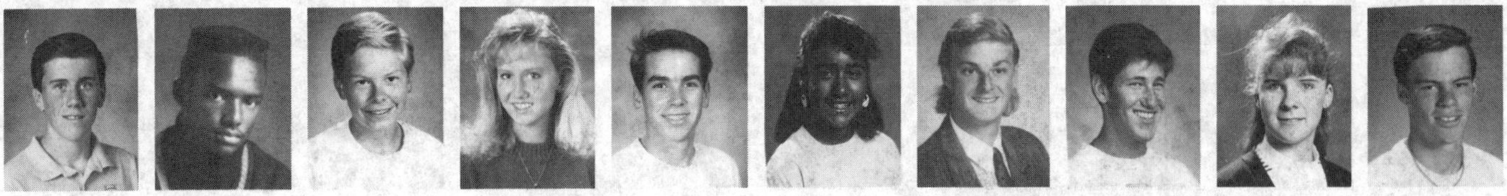

Morrison, Kevin H
Warren HS
Downey, CA

Morrison, Kevin P
Damien HS Prep
La Verne, CA

Morrisroe, Dennis
Bret Harte HS
Murphys, CA

Morriss, Kimberly J
Diamond Bar HS
Diamond Bar, CA

Morrissette, Eric J
San Dieguito HS
Encinitas, CA

Morrissette, Monika
Norte Vista HS
Riverside, CA

Mortara, Scott
Arcadia HS
Arcadia, CA

Morthole, Greg Errol
Del Campo HS
Fair Oaks, CA

Morton, Andrea N
Hawthorne HS
Hawthorne, CA

Morton, James C
Palm Springs HS
Cathedral City, CA

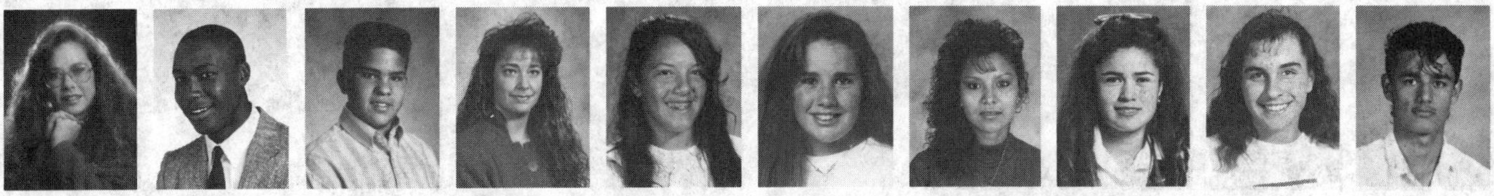

Morton, Michelle
Kingsburg HS
Kingsburg, CA

Morton, II Victor A
St Francis HS
Redwood City, CA

Mosaquites, III
Nicolas
Damien HS
Montclair, CA

Moser, Kimberly
Apple Valley
Christian HS
Hesperia, CA

Moshell, Michelle T
Woodside HS
Woodside, CA

Mosley, Tracy A
Mira Costa HS
Redondo Beach, CA

Mosqueda, Maria A
Dos Palos HS
South Dos Palos, CA

Mota, Blanca Y
Cajon HS
San Bernardino, CA

Mota, Cindy R
Notre Dame HS
Hollister, CA

Motawakel, Omar
Chatsworth HS
Chatsworth, CA

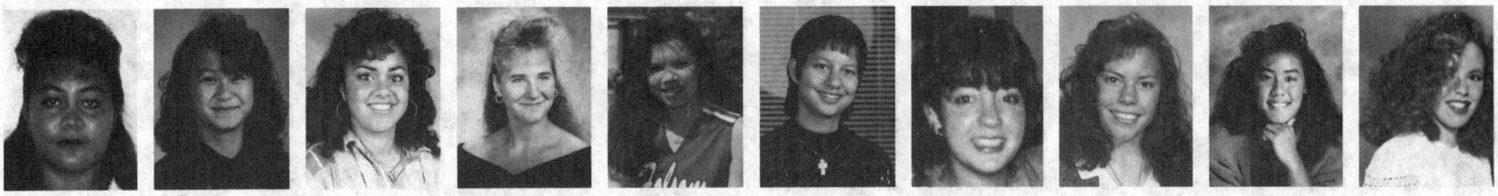

Motufau, Faafetai
Fontana HS
Fontana, CA

Moua, Gnia
Atwater HS
Winton, CA

Moussa, Rita R
Gahr HS
Norwalk, CA

Mower, Sherity K
Casa Roble
Fundamental HS
Citrus Heights, CA

Moydell, Melanie
Folsom HS
Folsom, CA

Moyen-Van
Slimming, Janice L
Cabrillo HS
Lompoc, CA

Moyers, Georgina I
Nogales HS
West Covina, CA

Moynahan, Kelly S
Santa Teresa HS
San Jose, CA

Mu, Pauline H
San Marino HS
San Marino, CA

Mucetti, Rosanna
Gina
Providence HS
Van Nuys, CA

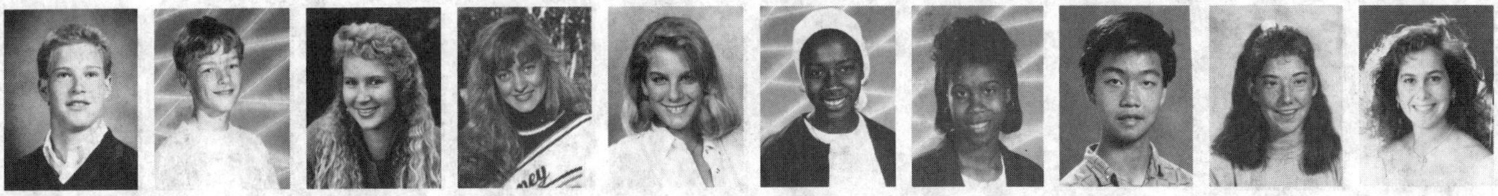

Muckelroy, Ben
Ramona Unified Schl
Dist
Carbondale, IL

Mueck, Jr Werner F
Marsyville HS
Marysville, CA

Mueller, Suzie
Placer HS
Auburn, CA

Mueller, Tracy
Downey HS
Downey, CA

Muellner, Jennifer D
Valhalla HS
Spring Valley, CA

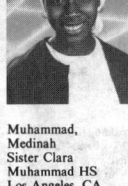

Muhammad,
Medinah
Sister Clara
Muhammad HS
Los Angeles, CA

Muhammad,
Rasheedah
Sister Clara
Muhammad HS
Los Angeles, CA

Mui, Brian Y
Nogales HS
Walnut, CA

Mukai, Chrissy L
Whitney HS
Lakewood, CA

Mulhall, Jennifer
Victor Valley HS
Apple Valley, CA

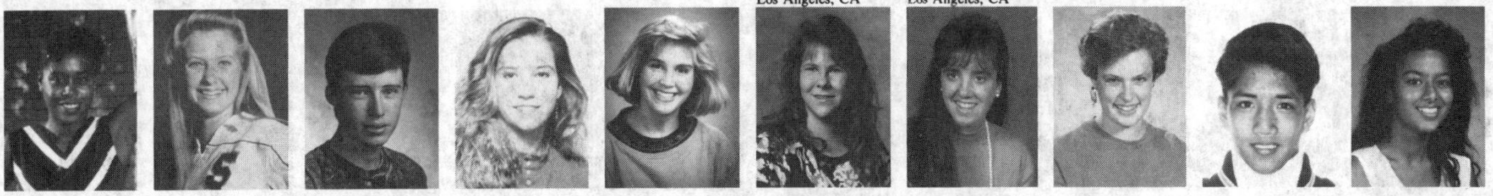

Mullen, Tami
Foothill HS
Sacramento, CA

Mullen, Tracy M
Louisville HS
Woodland Hills, CA

Mullens, Justin
Benicia HS
Benicia, CA

Muller, Michelle
Esparto HS
Esparto, CA

Mullet, Sara S
Beyer HS
Modesto, CA

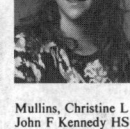

Mullins, Christine L
John F Kennedy HS
Granada Hills, CA

Mullins, Kathryn
Hanford Joint Union
Hanford, CA

Mullins, Melody
Alexander Hamilton
Santa Monica, CA

Munar, Michael
Warren HS
Downey, CA

Munaweera, Nayomi
Arcadia HS
Arcadia, CA

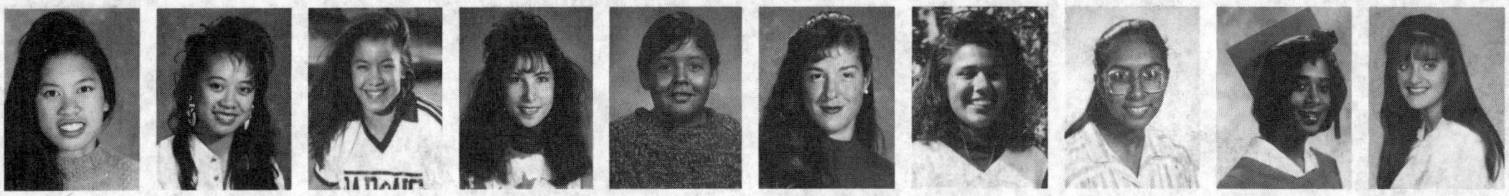

Munda, Micaela V
Lowell HS
San Francisco, CA

Munda, Michele
Mercy HS
Daly City, CA

Mundy, Kate A
Bonita Vista HS
Bonita, CA

Muniz, Isabel M
Oakdale HS
Farmington, CA

Muniz, Isaiah S
Bell Gardens HS
Commerce, CA

Muniz, Jennifer S
Notre Dame HS
Pacific Grove, CA

Muniz, Marisela I
Richard Gahr HS
Cerritos, CA

Munjee, Kaneez M
Alexander Hamilton
Acad Of Music
Encino, CA

Munn, Simmone
Los Angeles HS
Los Angeles, CA

Munoz, Andrea
Glendora HS
Glendora, CA

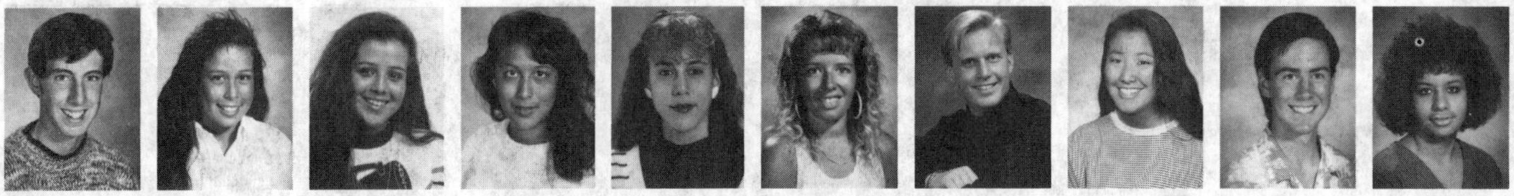

Munoz, Daniel
Highlands HS
Sacramento, CA

Munoz, Diana
Mater Dei HS
Tustin, CA

Munoz, Paulina
Chatsworth HS
Chatsworth, CA

Munoz, Susana
Palm Springs HS
Cathedral City, CA

Munoz, Yessica
Saddleback HS
Santa Ana, CA

Munshower, Andrea
Etiwanda HS
Rancho Cucamonga, CA

Munson, John D
Livermore HS
Livermore, CA

Murai, Wendy K
John F Kennedy HS
Sacramento, CA

Murano, Ryan W
Mammoth HS
Mammoth Lakes, CA

Murguia, Angelica
Polytechnic HS
Arleta, CA

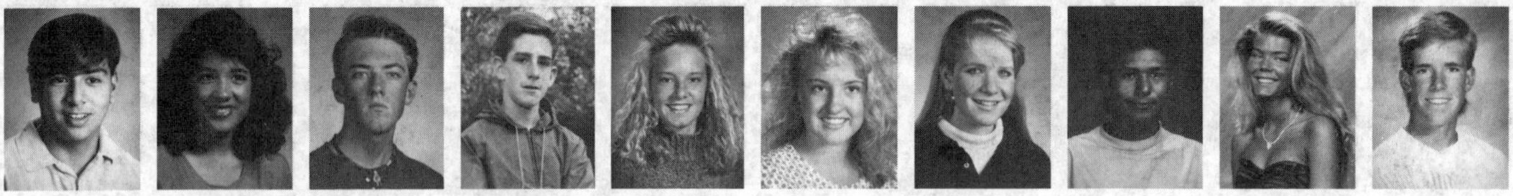

Murillo, Daniel L
Central Catholic HS
Modesto, CA

Murillo, Hortencia B
Bullard HS
Fresno, CA

Murnieks, John
Roseville HS
Rocklin, CA

Murphy, Greg M
St Francis HS
South Pasadena, CA

Murphy, Jennifer
Loara HS
Anaheim, CA

Murphy, Kathleen
Clovis West HS
Clovis, CA

Murphy, Sarah K
Mc Clatchy HS
Sacramento, CA

Murphy, Steven E
Coleville HS
Coleville, CA

Murray, Lisa M
Cajon HS
San Bernardino, CA

Murray, Richard M
Thousand Oaks HS
Thousand Oaks, CA

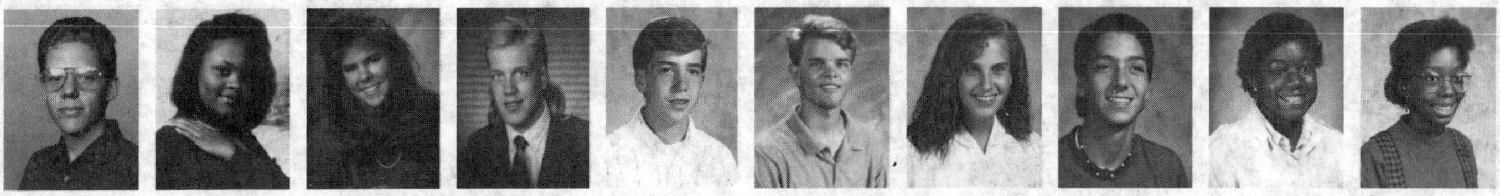

Murray, Todd S
Ventura HS
Ventura, CA

Murry, Asabi O
Culver City HS
Culver City, CA

Musicant, Andrea
Valhalla HS
La Mesa, CA

Musselman, Todd
Hemet HS
Hemet, CA

Myers, Chad W
Arroyo Grande HS
Nipomo, CA

Myers, Marcus S J
Ramona HS
Ramona, CA

Myers, Rebekah L
Lutheran HS Of
Orange County
Placentia, CA

Myhre, Steven M
Bullard HS
Fresno, CA

Myles, La Shon
Arlington HS
Riverside, CA

Myrick, Alissa B
Bishop O'dowd HS
Berkeley, CA

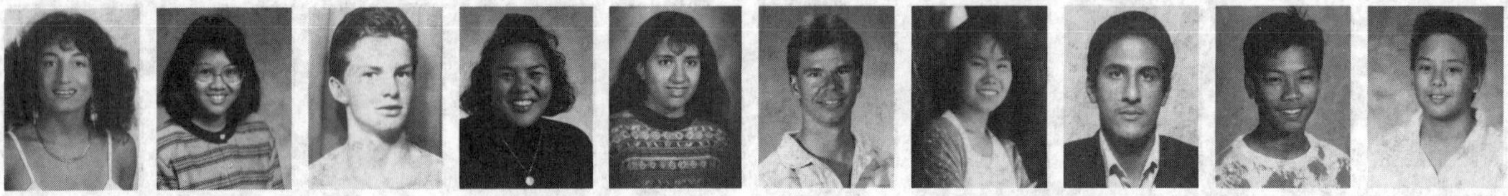

Nabavi-Noori,
Skarlete
Palm Desert HS
Palm Desert, CA

Nacario, Michelle
Southwest HS
San Diego, CA

Nacey, John
Damien HS
Claremont, CA

Nadal, Joyce Ann
Notre Dame HS
San Jose, CA

Naeem, Ayesha
West HS
Bakersfield, CA

Naeve, Trent
Hesperia HS
Hesperia, CA

Nagata, Michele L
Orosi HS
Orosi, CA

Nagi, Omar A
Monache HS
Porterville, CA

Nagtalon, Dennis G
Westmoor HS
Daly City, CA

Naguiat, Ramon M
St John Bosco HS
Cerritos, CA

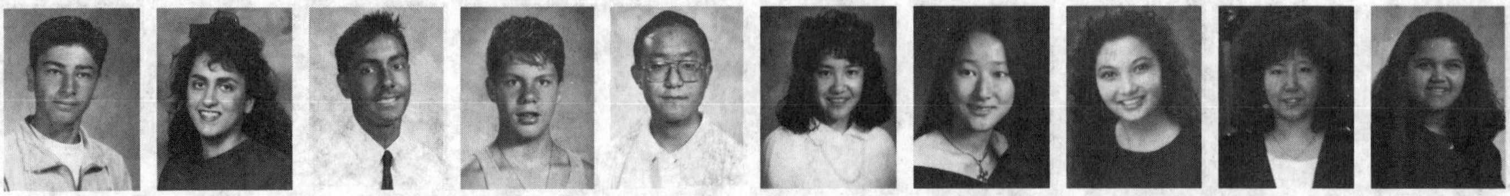

Nahavandi, Kiomars
Corona HS
Corona, CA

Nahorai, Gina
University HS
Los Angeles, CA

Naidu, Bernard N
Bishop O'dowd HS
Oakland, CA

Naimy, Richard
Oak Hill Prep
N Hollywood, CA

Nakao, Keith S
Don Bosco Technical
Inst
Whittier, CA

Nakao, Susan M
Fountain Valley HS
Fountain Valley, CA

Nakazawa, Shino
George Washington
San Francisco, CA

Nalle, Maridi T
South Pasadena HS
South Pasadena, CA

Namgoong, Juhngha
Pasadena HS
Sierra Madre, CA

Nanquil, Josephine C
Notre Dame HS
San Jose, CA

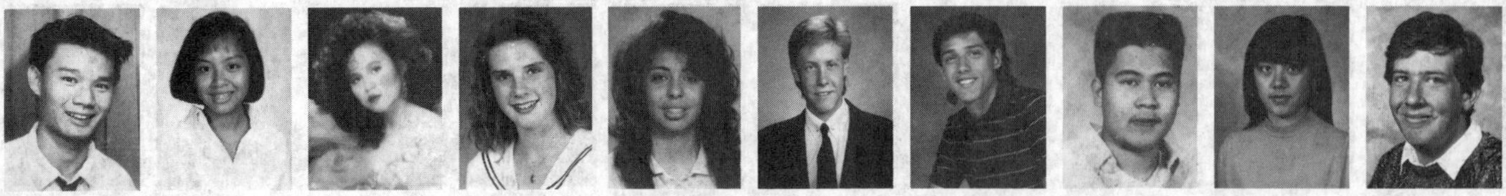

Nantha, Phousydao
Arlington HS
Riverside, CA

Napenas, Gina J
Notre Dame Acad
Los Angeles, CA

Napiza, Maria
Belinda R
Vallejo SR HS
Vallejo, CA

Naquin, Theresa M
St Joseph HS
Long Beach, CA

Naranjo, Raquel
San Fernando HS
San Fernando, CA

Nardinelli, Jonathan
El Camino
Fundamental HS
Citrus Heights, CA

Naredo, III Tony J
Oroville HS
Oroville, CA

Narido, II Eulalae
Los Angeles HS
La Puente, CA

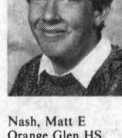

Nario, Patricia G
St Francis HS
Sacramento, CA

Nash, Matt E
Orange Glen HS
Escondido, CA

Nastasi, Dionne
Birmingham HS
Van Nuys, CA

Natividad, Aveliza
Highlands HS
N Highlands, CA

Naughton, Charlene
Santa Margarita HS
Mission Viejo, CA

Nauta, Carmellita R
Silver Valley HS
Fort Irwin, CA

Navar, Veronica
Roosevelt HS
Los Angeles, CA

Navarro, Aurelie
Hogan SR HS
Vallejo, CA

Navarro, Jennifer
Monte Vista HS
Spring Valley, CA

Navarro, Raquel
John Muir HS
Pasadena, CA

Navarro, Rommel P
Whitney HS
Cerritos, CA

Naylor, Jodi L
Antelope Valley HS
Lancaster, CA

Neagoe, Flavius O
College Park HS
Pleasant Hill, CA

Neal, Liza Maria
SD Schl/Creative &
Performing Arts
San Diego, CA

Neal, Mary Ellen
Valley Christian HS
San Jose, CA

Neal, Rebecca
Del Norte Indepndnt
Study Prgm HS
Gasquet, CA

Neal, Riquel A
Project Grasp &
Pittsburg HS
Pittsburg, CA

Neal, Toby
Paradise Adventist
Schl
Paradise, CA

Neary, Shannon L
El Camino HS
Sacramento, CA

Nebel, Diana L
Montclair HS
Montclair, CA

Needham, Jamie S
Santa Ynez HS
Buellton, CA

Neely, Bryan B
San Benito HS
Hollister, CA

Neely, Karen Lynn
Bear River HS
Grass Valley, CA

Neese, Erik R
Wood Land HS
Woodland, CA

Neff, Andrea M
Mayfield SR Schl
Pasadena, CA

Negrete, Imelda
San Benito HS
Hollister, CA

Negron, Isaura
Pittsburg HS
Pittsburg, CA

Neighbors, Jenny L
Cordova HS
Mather A F B, CA

Neill, Jerusha
Del Campo HS
Fair Oaks, CA

Neiman, Arwen
Wendi F
Whitney HS
Cerritos, CA

Neiswender, Caryn
Tri-City Christian
Schl
Carlsbad, CA

Nekaien, Seena
Encinal HS
Alameda, CA

Nelson, Albert R
University HS
Irvine, CA

Nelson, Allyson G
Wm S Hart HS
Valencia, CA

Nelson, Amy E
Tustin HS
Tustin, CA

Nelson, Becky
Benicia HS
Benicia, CA

Nelson, Bryan J
Capistrano Valley HS
Mission Viejo, CA

Nelson, Colleen R
St Genevieve HS
Sepulveda, CA

Nelson, Gregory K
El Toro HS
El Toro, CA

Nelson, Jason D
Lindsay HS
Lindsay, CA

Nelson, Jennifer
St Joseph HS
Cerritos, CA

Nelson, Jerome
Placer HS
Auburn, CA

Nelson, Ken
Benicia HS
Benicia, CA

Nelson, Kimberly A
Rio Lindo Acad
Santa Rosa, CA

Nelson, Lawrence K
Yosemite Union HS
Coarsegold, CA

Nelson, Michael
Torre
Modoc HS
Alturas, CA

Nelson, Michele L
North Tahoe HS
Kings Bch, CA

Nelson, Saliha
Crawford HS
San Diego, CA

Nelson, Suzanna L
Quartz Hill HS
Lancaster, CA

Nelson, Tammi L
San Lorenzo HS
San Lorenzo, CA

Nelson, Tiffany R
St Joseph HS
Cerritos, CA

Nelson, Tom
Winters HS
Winters, CA

Nelson, Vivian
Adolfo Camarillo HS
Camarillo, CA

Nemec, Elizabeth
Palm Springs HS
Cathedral City, CA

Nemeth, Kimberley
La Sierra HS
Riverside, CA

Nepomuceno,
Marylou S
Mesa Verde HS
Citrus Heights, CA

Nessi, Heather L
Gridley HS
Gridley, CA

Nesslage, Zack R
Oakdale HS
Waterford, CA

Nestman, Kristin E
Torrey Pines HS
Solana Beach, CA

Netherton, Dawn
El Dorado HS
Yerba Linda, CA

Netherton, Drew P
Glen A Wilson HS
Hacienda Heights,
CA

Neuendorf, Ken
Seaside HS
Duncan, OK

Neufeld, Jennifer
Lynn
Monterey Bay Acad
Columbia, CA

Neuhaus, Brandi N
Ponderosa HS
Shingle Springs, CA

Neuhaus, Jennifer L
Venice HS
Venice, CA

Neumann, Linda R
Polytechnic HS
Riverside, CA

Neumeyer, Chris F
Esperanza HS
Anaheim, CA

Neves, Jr David
Linden HS
Lockeford, CA

Neville, Tricia A
East Bakersfield HS
Bakersfield, CA

New, Steven T
Downey HS
Downey, CA

Newell, Jake J
Shasta Union HS
Redding, CA

Newell, Nicole
J F Kennedy HS
Anaheim, CA

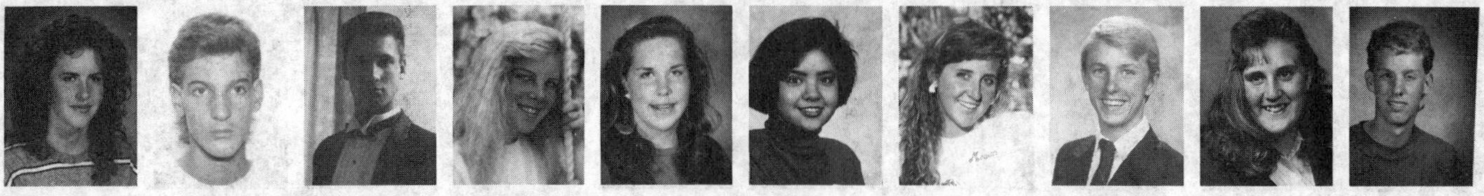

Newell, Wendy
Chester JR/SR HS
Lake Almanor, CA

Newey, Richard C
Indio HS
Bermuda Dunes, CA

Newgent, Matthew A
Highlands HS
North Highlands, CA

Newman, Becky L
Sonora Union HS
Sonora, CA

Newman, Jill K
San Diequito HS
Encinitas, CA

Newman, Julie
St Marys HS
Stockton, CA

Newman, Megan
South HS
Redondo Bch, CA

Newman, S Todd
Saint Margarets
Episcopal Schl
Laguna Hills, CA

Newton, Caryl
The Academy Of Our
Lady Of Peace
San Diego, CA

Newton, Richard S
Montgomery HS
Santa Rosa, CA

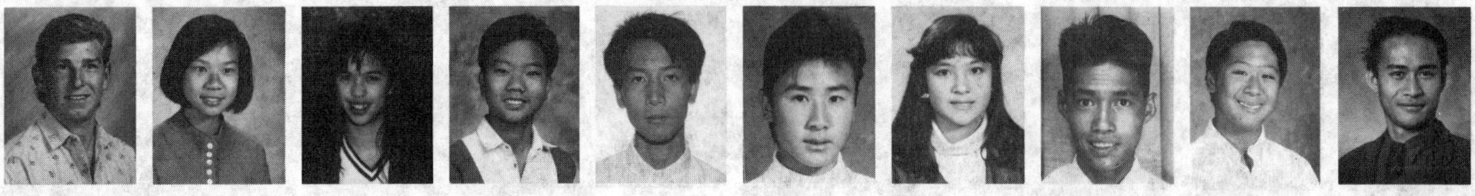

Newton, Scott R
Apple Valley HS
Apple Valley, CA

Ng, Christine K
Montebello HS
Montebello, CA

Ng, Demetria
Lowell HS
San Francisco, CA

Ng, Louis
Glen A Wilson HS
Hacienda Hts, CA

Ng, Wing N
George Washington
San Francisco, CA

Ngo, Anh
Lowell HS
San Francisco, CA

Ngo, Hanh T
Pasadena HS
Pasadena, CA

Ngo, Hoa
Bassett HS
La Puente, CA

Ngo, Howard H
Lowell HS
San Francisco, CA

Ngo, Hung M
Chaffe HS
Ontario, CA

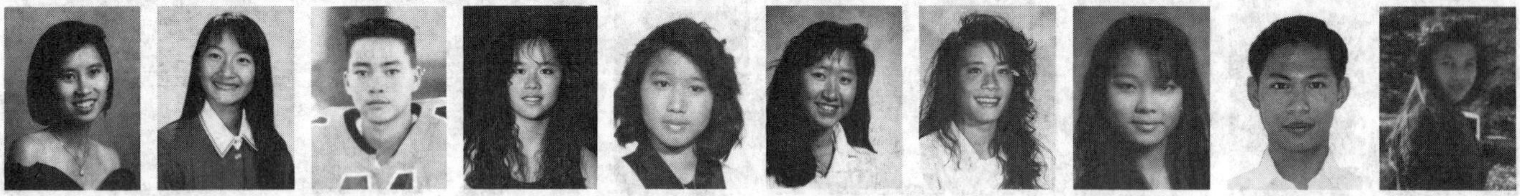

Ngo, Nhien
James Madison HS
San Diego, CA

Ngo, Phuong P
Skyline HS
Oakland, CA

Ngo, Vinh
Alameda HS
Alameda, CA

Nguy, My Thana
George Washington
San Francisco, CA

Nguyen, Alison
Wilcox HS
Santa Clara, CA

Nguyen, Bich Loan
Ganesha HS
Pomona, CA

Nguyen, Cassie T
Jordan HS
Long Beach, CA

Nguyen, Christina P
Southwest HS
San Diego, CA

Nguyen, Dat D
Los Amigos HS
Fountain Valley, CA

Nguyen, Diep T
Grant HS
Sacramento, CA

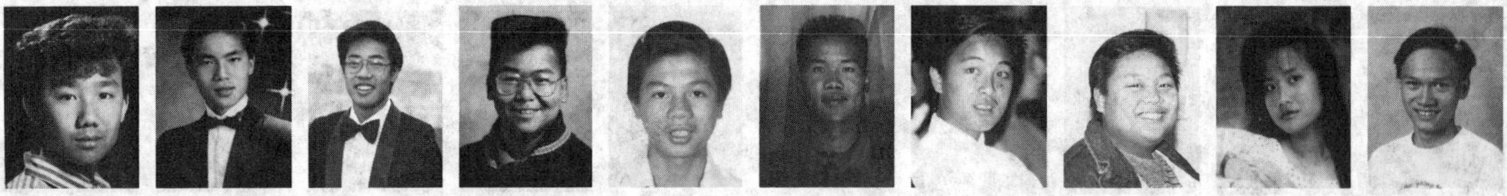

Nguyen, Hai V
Eagle Rock HS
Los Angeles, CA

Nguyen, Hoan
Bolsa Grande HS
Westminster, CA

Nguyen, Houbi Tung
Dana Hills HS
Laguna Niguel, CA

Nguyen, Hung Quoc
Vanden HS
Fairfield, CA

Nguyen, Hung-Anh P
La Quinta HS
Fountain Valley, CA

Nguyen, James Giang
Don Antonio Lugo
Chino, CA

Nguyen, John B
Santa Clara HS
Santa Clara, CA

Nguyen, Joseph H
Santa Clara HS
Santa Clara, CA

Nguyen, Khanh
Mt Eden HS
Hayward, CA

Nguyen, Khoa
Mira Costa HS
Hawthorne, CA

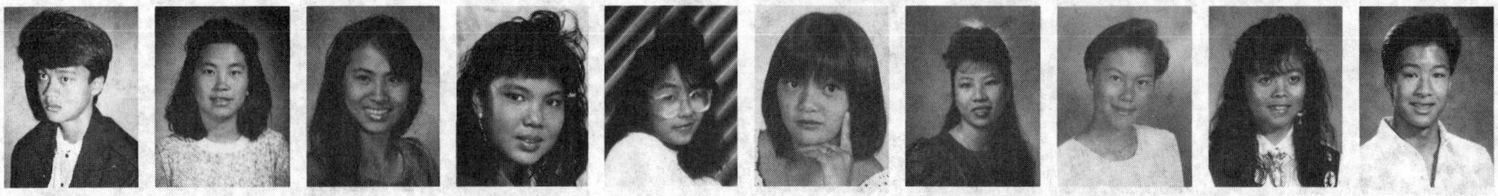

Nguyen, Ky
Montclair HS
Montclair, CA

Nguyen, Lien Chau
Montgomery HS
Santa Rosa, CA

Nguyen, Lieu
Westminster HS
Westminster, CA

Nguyen, Linda Anh
Los Amigos HS
Fountain Valley, CA

Nguyen, Ly
Raoul Wallenberg
San Francisco, CA

Nguyen, Mitzi T
Mt Pleasant HS
San Jose, CA

Nguyen, Nga
Reseda HS
Reseda, CA

Nguyen, Ngoc-Dung
Andrew Hill HS
San Jose, CA

Nguyen, Nhung
Monterey HS
Marina, CA

Nguyen, Nick
Cypress HS
Cypress, CA

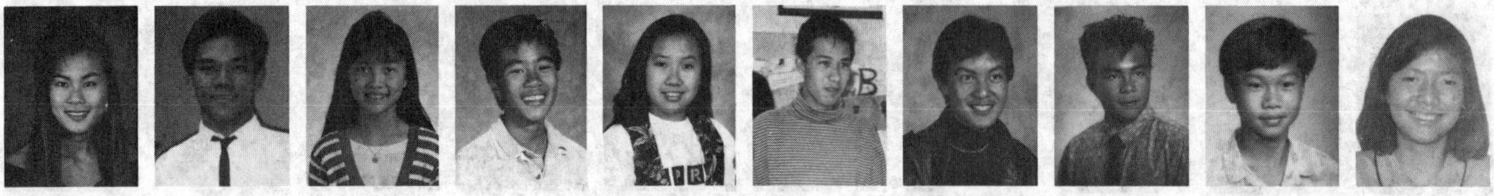

Nguyen, Nikki Le Ut
Thi
Bolsa Grande HS
Westminster, CA

Nguyen, Phat
La Serna HS
Whittier, CA

Nguyen, Phung K
Pioneer HS
San Jose, CA

Nguyen, Phuong D
James Lick HS
San Jose, CA

Nguyen, Queenie D
San Gabriel Mission
Alhambra, CA

Nguyen, Quoc H
Durham HS
Durham, CA

Nguyen, Tai D
Monterey HS
Marina, CA

Nguyen, Thai
Edison HS
Huntington Beach,
CA

Nguyen, Thanh Dinh
Tokay HS
Stockton, CA

Nguyen, Thanh-Thao
Ho
Westminster HS
Westminster, CA

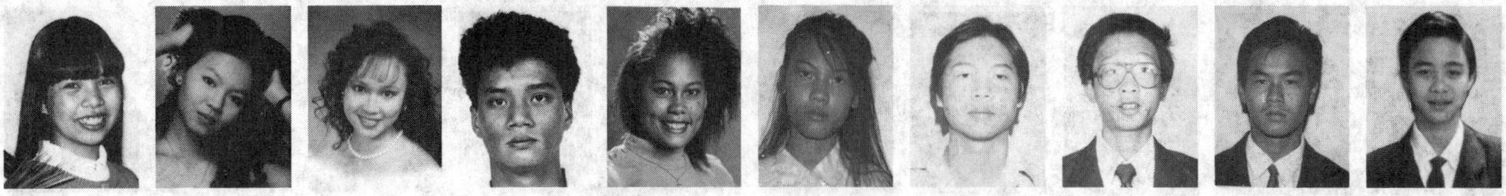

Nguyen, Thitram
Ngoc
J Eugene Mc Ateer
San Francisco, CA

Nguyen, Thuy H
Ramona HS
Riverside, CA

Nguyen, Tinny T
Independence HS
San Jose, CA

Nguyen, Toan B
Leuzinger HS
Hawthorne, CA

Nguyen, Trang T
Leuzinger HS
Hawthorne, CA

Nguyen, Trang T
Pasadena HS
Pasadena, CA

Nguyen, Trung H
Alexander Hamilton
Los Angeles, CA

Nguyen, Tuan-Anh P
La Quinta HS
Fountain Valley, CA

Nguyen, Tuong B
Costa Mesa HS
Costa Mesa, CA

Nguyen, Vuong D
Bolsa Grande HS
Westminster, CA

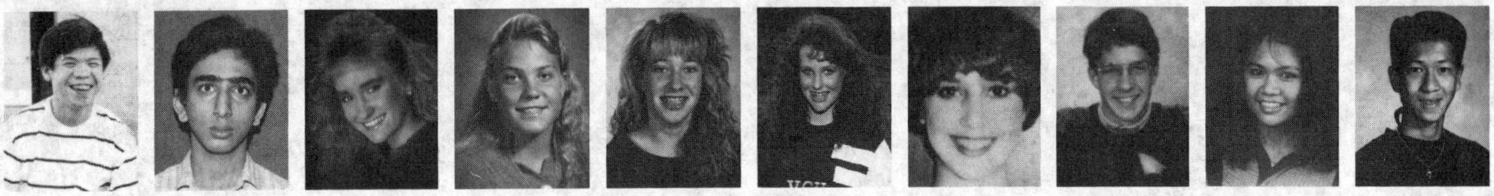

Nhieu, Trung L
Andrew Hill HS
San Jose, CA

Niazi, Surkhab A
Pacific Palisades HS
Los Angeles, CA

Nichols, Amy
Hughson Union HS
Modesto, CA

Nichols, Katherine E
Newport Christian
Corona Del Mar, CA

Nichter, Tracy
Rosary HS
Anaheim, CA

Nickell, April
Valley Christian HS
San Jose, CA

Nickell, Misty A
Alpaugh Unified HS
Alpaugh, CA

Nicolai, Peter T
San Rafael HS
San Rafael, CA

Nicolas, Donabelle
Rodrigo
St Joseph Catholic
Bellflower, CA

Nicolas, Jr Mabini P
Carson HS
Carson, CA

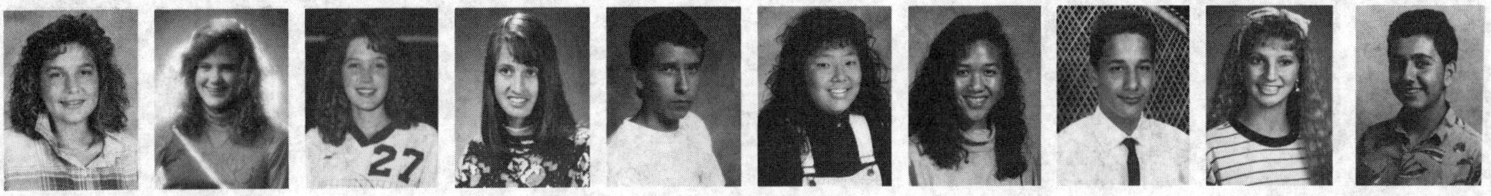

Nicoletti, Kristen C
Dos Palos HS
Dos Palos, CA

Nicoletti, Michelle L
Dos Palos HS
Dos Palos, CA

Niediek, Diane
Corona SR HS
Victorville, CA

Niednagel, Miriam R
Monte Vista HS
Alamo, CA

Nielsen, Paul M
Serra HS
San Diego, CA

Nielsen, Susan K
Washington Union
Fresno, CA

Nietes, Katrina R
Abraham Lincoln HS
San Francisco, CA

Nieto, Jose M
St Bernard HS
Los Angeles, CA

Nigro, Angela V
Carondelet HS
Walnut Creek, CA

Nikravan, Ashkaan
San Gabriel HS
San Gabriel, CA

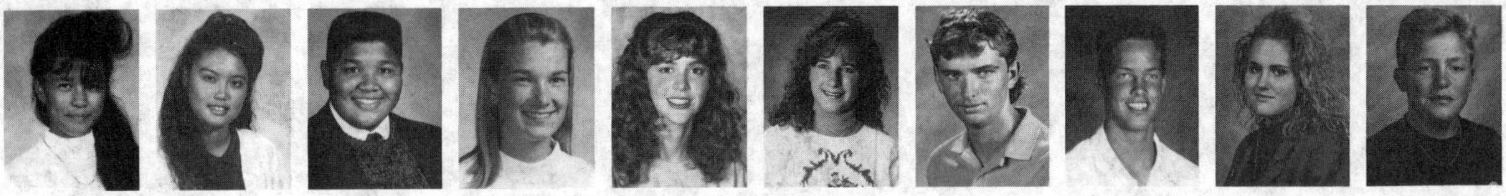

Nimo, Elaine E
Gahr HS
Norwalk, CA

Nimo, Rosanna E
Whitney HS
Norwalk, CA

Nipay, Wennie
Patten Acad Of
Christian Eductn
Union City, CA

Nissen, Allison
Colfax HS
Weimar, CA

Nitschke, Mary A
Roosevelt HS
Fresno, CA

Nitschke, Rika K
Clovis HS
Fresno, CA

Nitzel, Jr Donald L
Samuel F B Morse
San Diego, CA

Nixon, John T
Warren HS
Downey, CA

Nixon, Kelly
Yucca Valley HS
Joshua Tree, CA

Nobles, Ryan M
Apple Valley HS
Apple Valley, CA

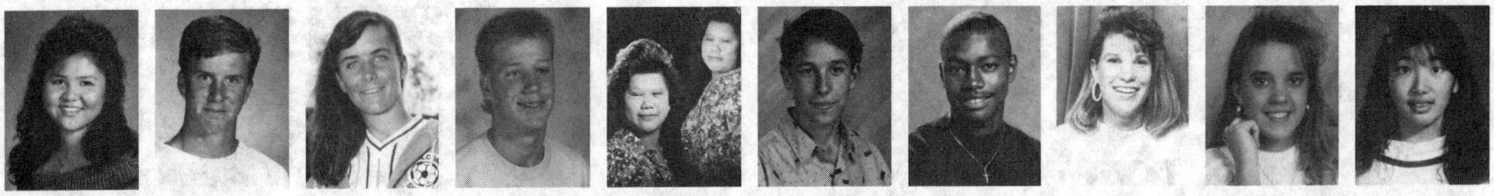

Nocom, Shereen C
John Burroughs HS
Burbank, CA

Nogosek, Joseph G
Santa Teresa HS
San Jose, CA

Nolan, Kelly D
Torrey Pines HS
Solana Beach, CA

Noland, William H
Lemoore Union HS
Lemoore, CA

Nolasco, Roselle
Phineas Banning HS
Los Angeles, CA

Nolen, III James O
Serrano HS
Phelan, CA

Noles, Tremayne
Westchester HS
Los Angeles, CA

Noll, Tracey
Hanford Union HS
Hanford, CA

Noltensmeier, Robyn
Kern Valley HS
Lake Isabella, CA

Nomi, Sharon M
Cerritos HS
Cerritos, CA

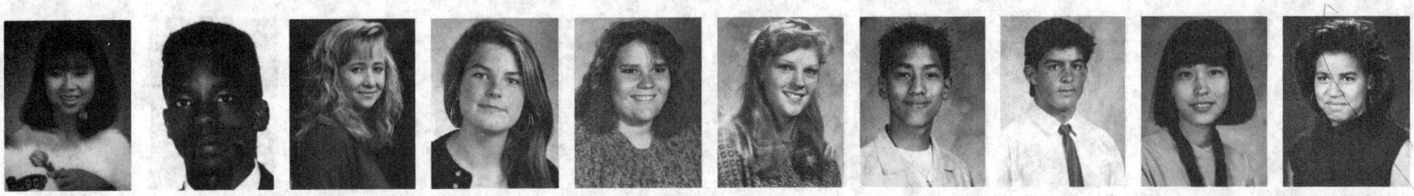

Nong, Votha
Yerba Buena HS
San Jose, CA

Nonman, II Richard
Edison HS
Fresno, CA

Nord, Julie A
East Bakersfield HS
Bakersfield, CA

Nord, Kirsten
Del Mar HS
San Jose, CA

Nordgreen, Grace
Highlands HS
North Highlands, CA

Nordstrom, Karolyn
Thousand Oaks HS
Thousand Oaks, CA

Noriega, Ken
Bishop Amat HS
Pomona, CA

Noriega, Marco C
Santa Clara HS
Oxnard, CA

Noriega, Mia
Bishop Amat HS
Pomona, CA

Norman, Jaha F
Pittsburgh HS
Pittsburg, CA

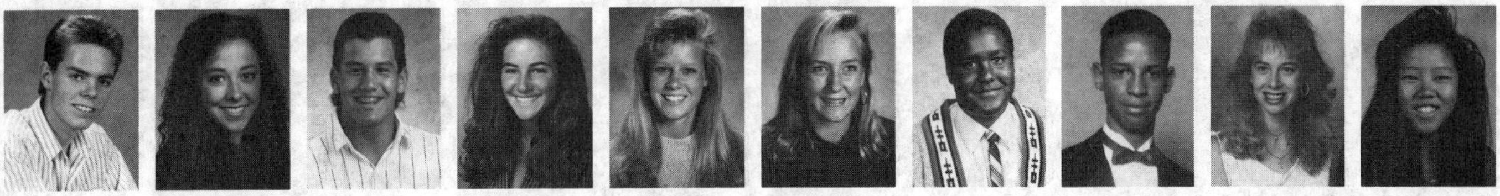

Norman, Michael C
Lassen HS
Standish, CA

Normington, Victoria
Del Campo HS
Citrus Heights, CA

Norris, Michael D
Oak Grove HS
San Jose, CA

North, Dusti
Campbell Hall HS
Tarzana, CA

North, Stacey L
Mission Viejo HS
Mission Viejo, CA

Norton, Becky
Las Lomas HS
Walnut Creek, CA

Norton, Jabari H
Bishop O'dowd HS
Hayward, CA

Norwood, Vincent O
William Workman
W Covina, CA

Novak, Jennifer
Helix HS
Lemon Grove, CA

Novotny, Sanghee C
Winters HS
Winters, CA

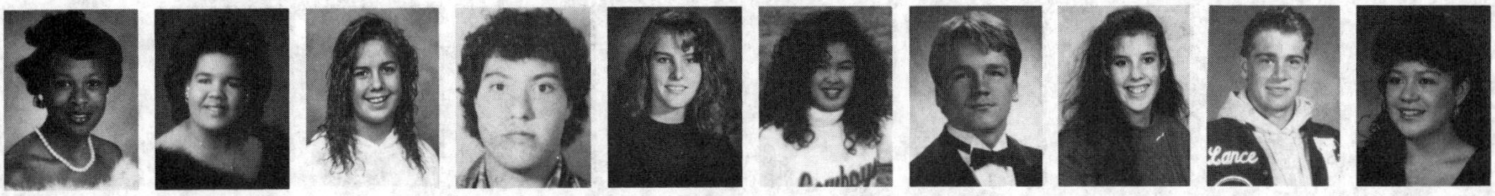

Nowden, April
Lincoln Prep HS
San Diego, CA

Noyes, Heather
South San Francisco
Daly City, CA

Noyes, Julie A
El Cajon Valley HS
El Cajon, CA

Nudelman, Grigory
George Washington
San Francisco, CA

Nugent, Erin
Mt Shasta HS
Mt Shasta, CA

Nuki, Christie
Salinas HS
Salinas, CA

Null, Jeff
Benicia HS
Benicia, CA

Null, Kara R
Calvary Christian
Acad
Stockton, CA

Null, Lance L
Hanford HS
Hanford, CA

Nuncz, Evelyn
Irvine HS
Irvine, CA

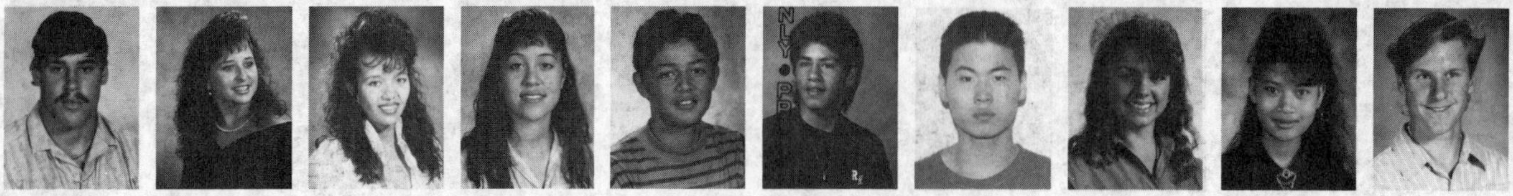

Nunes, Larry F
San Benito HS
Hollister, CA

Nunez, Alma R
Saint Joseph HS
Paramount, CA

Nunez, Hilda
Saddleback HS
Santa Ana, CA

Nunez, Maria Elena
Tranquillity Union
Mendota, CA

Nunez, Oscar
Andrew P Hill HS
San Jose, CA

Nunez, Rigoberto
Palo Verde HS
Blythe, CA

Nursalim, Susanto
San Marino HS
San Marino, CA

Nuss, Elaine M
Hesperia HS
Hesperia, CA

Nuth, Samphors
Oakland HS
Oakland, CA

Nykoluk, Monty J
Trinity HS
Weaverville, CA

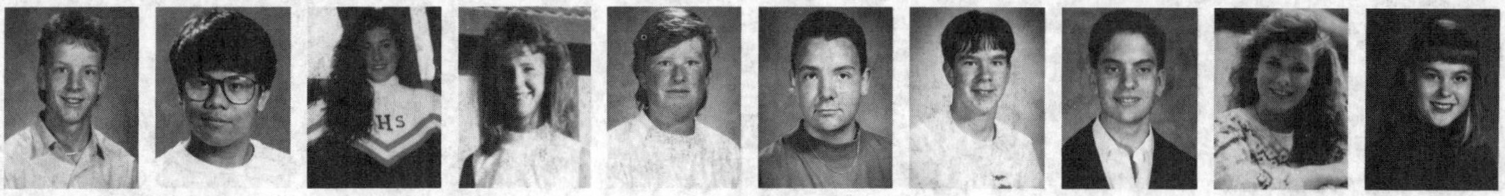

Nyre, Michael A
Victor Valley HS
Victorville, CA

O Balles, Jay
Leuzinger HS
Hawthorne, CA

O Berlin, Shelley R
Cajon HS
San Bernardino, CA

O Bosky, Carrie L
Modesto HS
Modesto, CA

O Bradovich, Michael David
Covina HS
West Covina, CA

O Brien, Michael P
Artesia HS
Lakewood, CA

O Brien, Mike D
Fort Bragg HS
Fort Bragg, CA

O Brien, Paul
Bishop Amat HS
Covina, CA

O Daniel, Laurie
Hanford HS
Hanford, CA

O Donnell, Melanie E
Clovis West HS
Clovis, CA

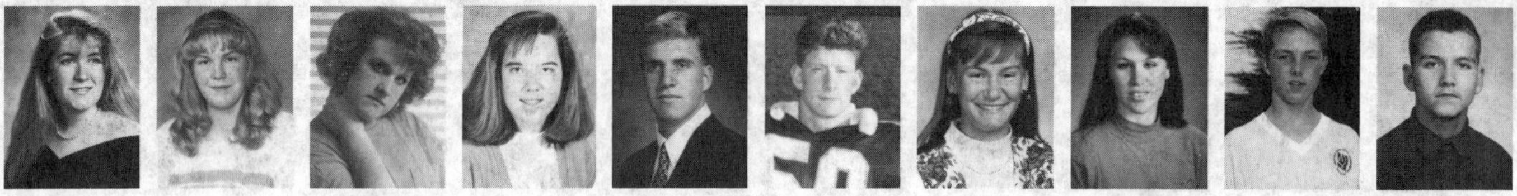

O Donnell, Moira
Mercy HS
Pacifica, CA

O Hagan, Jennie R
Salinas HS
Salinas, CA

O Halloran, Mollie
Pomona Catholic HS
Cucamonga, CA

O Hara, Patricia K
Fremont HS
Sunnyvale, CA

O Laughlin, J J
Glendora HS
Glendora, CA

O Malley, Dennis Robert
Ballarmine HS
Morgan Hill, CA

O Meara, Erin K
Thomas Downey HS
Modesto, CA

O Neal, Allison
Oakdale HS
Waterford, CA

O Neil, Dylan M
North Monterey County HS
Castroville, CA

O Quinn, Shane
Rio Del Sol HS
Sacramento, CA

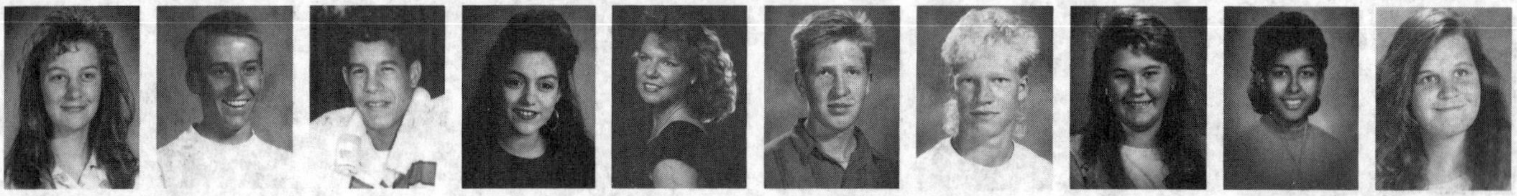

O Rorke, Rebecca L
Lassen HS
Standish, CA

O Rourke, Sean T
Bullard HS
Fresno, CA

O Shea, Sean
Los Altos HS
Hacienda Hts, CA

O Sullivan, Tracie A
Lodi HS
Stockton, CA

Oak, Margaret F
Vista HS
Shelley, ID

Oakland, Bryce
Calvary Chapel HS
Santa Ana, CA

Oakland, Wade
Calvary Chapel HS
Santa Ana, CA

Oakley, Laura M
Modesto HS
Modesto, CA

Obediah, Reena
Los Angeles Baptist
Northridge, CA

Oberman, Amy L
Palm Springs HS
Rancho Mirage, CA

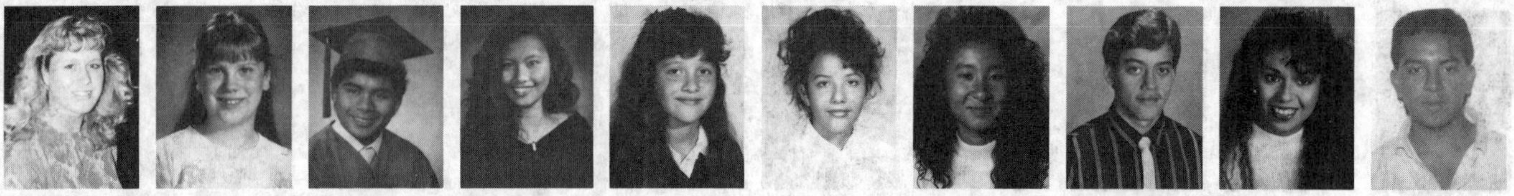

Obermann, Kristi
Desert JR/SR HS
San Antonio, TX

Obester, Misty L
Cornelia Connelly HS
Garden Grove, CA

Obillo, Brent
Narbonne HS
Harbor City, CA

Oca, Ghandi S
Jefferson HS
Daly City, CA

Ocampo, Marisela
Notre Dame Acad
Los Angeles, CA

Ocampo, Marisol R
Notre Dame Acad
Los Angeles, CA

Ocasion, Louise
Hilltop HS
National City, CA

Ochoa, Alfonso
Liberty Union HS
Brentwood, CA

Ochoa, Candy M
Turlock HS
Turlock, CA

Ochoa, Jorge G
Hesperia HS
Hesperia, CA

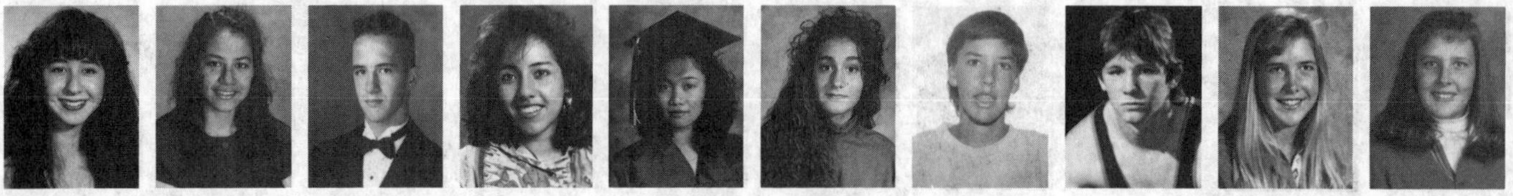

Ochoa, Lynna H
Alexander Hamilton
Los Angeles, CA

Ochoa, Maria Elena
Liberty Union HS
Brentwood, CA

Ochoa, Jr Ricardo
Bonita Vista HS
Bonita, CA

Ochoa, Sonia
Sylmar HS
Sylmar, CA

Oconer, Ellen O
Sherman Oaks CES
Los Angeles, CA

Oden, Rita M
Rio Linda HS
Sacramento, CA

Oelschig, Trevor H
Troy HS
Fullerton, CA

Offel, Kevin D
El Dorado HS
Placentia, CA

Offermann, Tonya J
San Luis Obispo HS
San Luis Obispo, CA

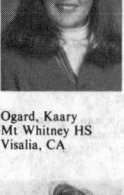

Ogard, Kaary
Mt Whitney HS
Visalia, CA

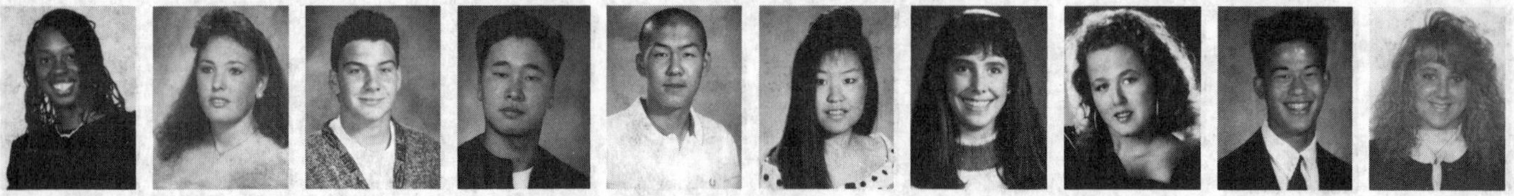

Ogbunamiri, Ngozi
Pilgrim Schl
Los Angeles, CA

Ogden, Cynthia
Apple Valley SR HS
Wichita, KS

Ogle, James A
Fountain Valley HS
Fountain Valley, CA

Oh, Albert
Sunny Hills HS
Orange, CA

Oh, Samuel
Kennedy HS
Sepulveda, CA

Oh, Stacey
Crescenta Valley HS
La Crescenta, CA

Ohanesian, Cecelia M
Clovis HS
Clovis, CA

Ojeda, Alisha M
Paradise HS
Paradise, CA

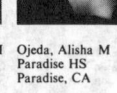

Oka, Calvin Koji
St Ignatius College Prep
South San Francis, CA

Okerstrom, Leslie
Western HS
Anaheim, CA

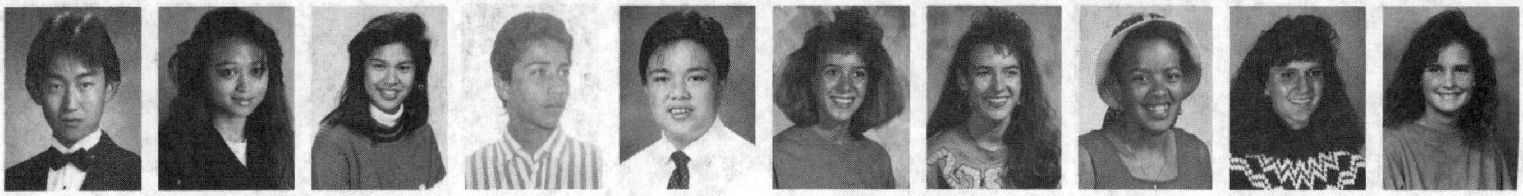

Okuhara, Tohru
Burlingame HS
San Mateo, CA

Olalia, Shella Marie
Channel Islands HS
Oxnard, CA

Olay, Mariefe Vila
Skyline HS
Oakland, CA

Oliva, Jr Ricardo
Santa Ana HS
Santa Ana, CA

Olivar, Anthony M
Pater Noster HS
Los Angeles, CA

Oliveira, Janea R
Lemoore HS
Lemoore, CA

Oliveira, Julie R
Lemoore HS
Lemoore, CA

Oliver, Diane
Thomas Downey HS
Modesto, CA

Oliver, Kristy
Central Valley
Christian HS
Visalia, CA

Oliver, Laura L
Escondido HS
Escondido, CA

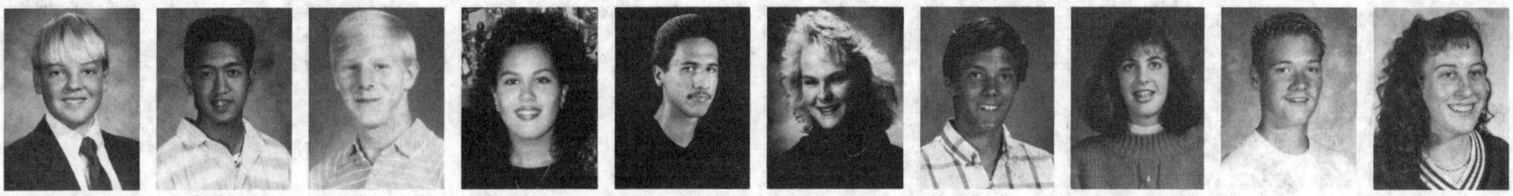

Oliver, Zachary
St Michaels College
Prep HS
San Clemente, CA

Ollano, Oliver H
Bishop Amat
Memorial HS
Chino Hills, CA

Ollar, Brian
Orestimba HS
Newman, CA

Olmeda, Guillermina
San Pedro HS
San Pedro, CA

Olomi, Ghani
Itiwanda HS
Rancho Cuccamonga,
CA

Olow, Jennifer C
Mount Miguel HS
Lemon Grove, CA

Olsen, Daniel S
Poly HS
Riverside, CA

Olsen, Kristin
Modesto HS
Modesto, CA

Olsen, Troy V
Rio Linda SR HS
Rio Linda, CA

Olson, Amy S
Analy HS
Sebastopol, CA

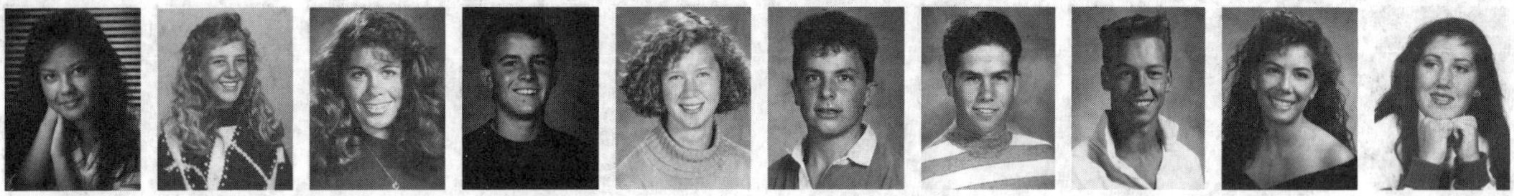

Olson, Julie
Santana HS
El Cajon, CA

Olson, Kimberly D
Mission Viejo HS
Mission Viejo, CA

Olson, Kristen
Woodbridge HS
Irvine, CA

Olson, Mark
Grossmont HS
El Cajon, CA

Olson, Meredith L
Aptos HS
Salem, OR

Olson, Ryan
Francis Parker HS
La Mesa, CA

Olster, Todd
Edison HS
Huntington Beach,
CA

Olszewski, Dan M
Poway HS
Poway, CA

Olvera, Tristana
Valley HS
Sacramento, CA

Oman, Jeanna R
St Mary's HS
Jacksonville, FL

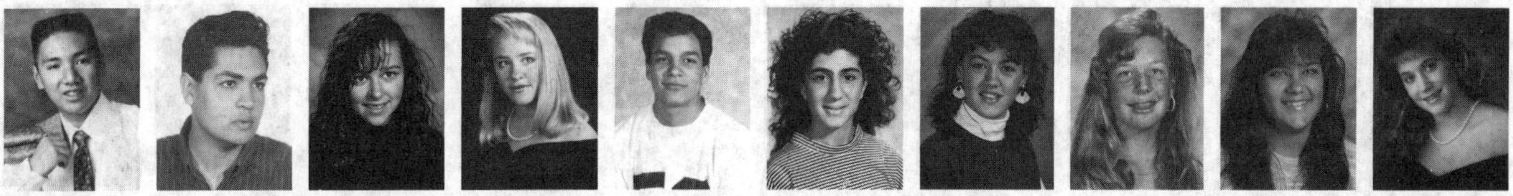

Ongaco, Alexis
Bishop Amat
Memorial HS
Whittier, CA

Ontiveros, Jose A
Canyon HS
Monrovia, CA

Oppelt, Sarah D
Dana Hills HS
San Juan Capistrn,
CA

Oram, Suzy Y
Alameda HS
Alameda, CA

Orbegoso, Marcos L
Boron HS
Boron, CA

Orchanian, Lara A
Pasadena HS
Pasadena, CA

Orenyak, Kimberly L
Chino HS
Chino, CA

Orewyler, Christine R
Mayfair HS
Lakewood, CA

Orlando, Kristin E
Louisville HS
Canoga Park, CA

Orona, Nichole R
Analy HS
Sebastopol, CA

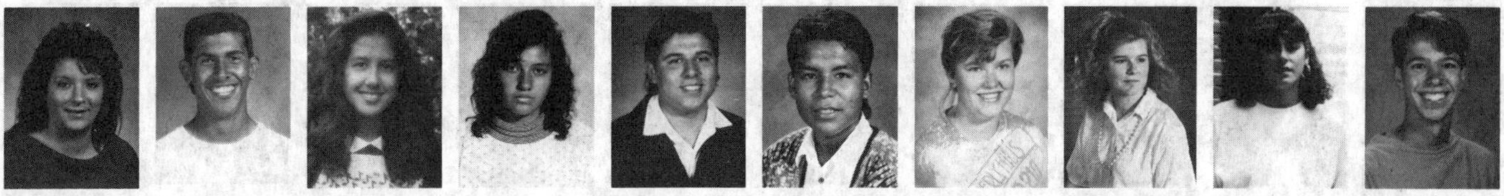

Oropeza, Patricia D
Needles HS
Needles, CA

Orosco, Mark L
Hanford Union HS
Hanford, CA

Orosz, Stephanie
St Lawrence Acad
Milpitas, CA

Orozco, Claudia
Norte Vista HS
Riverside, CA

Orozco, Marcos
Calipatria HS
Calipatria, CA

Orozco, Sven
Chula Vista HS
Eugene, OR

Orr, Jodi L
Burroughs HS
Ridgecrest, CA

Orr, Katrina S
San Gorgonio HS
Redlands, CA

Orsi, Elizabeth
University HS
Tiburon, CA

Orso, Albert
Riverside Poly HS
Riverside, CA

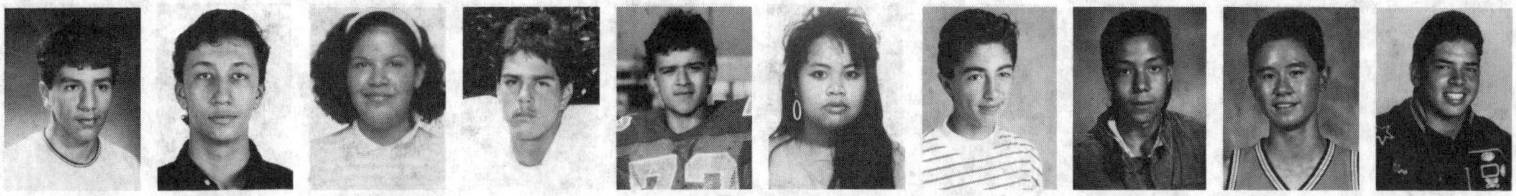

Ortega, Adan G
Brawley Union HS
Westmorland, CA

Ortega, Jr Agustin
Inglewood HS
Inglewood, CA

Ortega, Alma
Concepcion
Huntington Park HS
Huntington Park, CA

Ortega, Jr Jesus
Hueneme HS
Port Hueneme, CA

Ortega, Jesus A
Bell HS
Cudahy, CA

Ortega, Jojet
Hayward HS
Hayward, CA

Ortega, Miguel E
Channel Islands HS
Oxnard, CA

Ortega, Tito
Orange Glen HS
Escondido, CA

Ortegaso, Raymond L
Don Bosco Technical
Inst
West Covina, CA

Ortiz, Ciro
Patterson HS
Patterson, CA

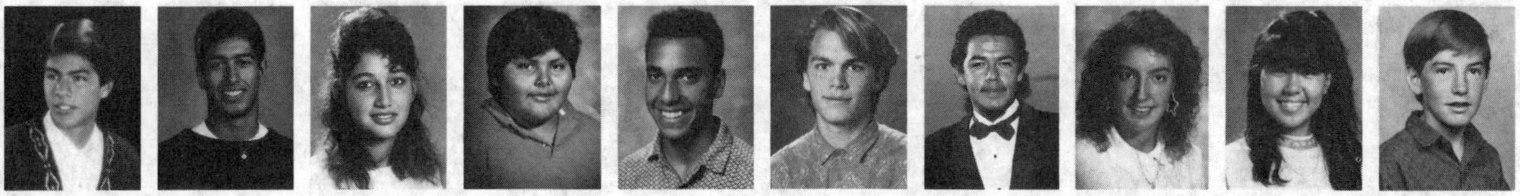

Ortiz, David
Ernest Righetti HS
Santa Maria, CA

Ortiz, Marco
Redwood HS
Visalia, CA

Ortiz, Maria J
Leuzinger HS
Lawndale, CA

Ortiz, Miguel A
Baldwin Park HS
Baldwin Park, CA

Ortiz, Omar
St John Bosco HS
La Mirada, CA

Ortiz, Travis
Covenant Christian
Chula Vista, CA

Ortiz, Victor A
San Clemente HS
Capistrano Beach,
CA

Orwat, Diane M
Paraclete HS
Lancaster, CA

Osako, Mary M
Venice HS
Culver City, CA

Osborn, Anthony J
Saint Anthony HS
Lakewood, CA

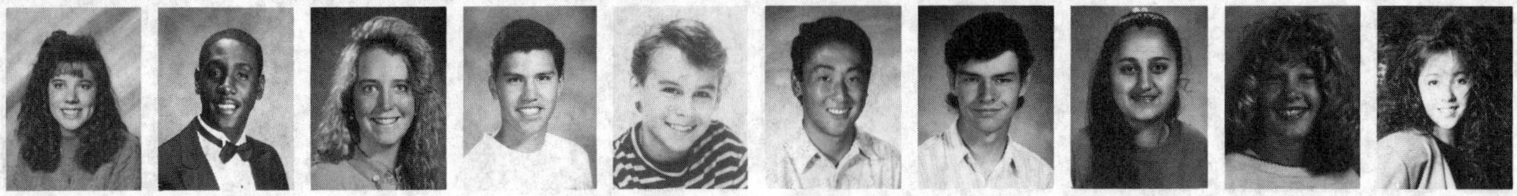

Osborne, Jennifer
St Patricks-St Vincents HS
Fairfield, CA

Osborne, Muhsin K
Mountain View HS
Mountain View, CA

Osdale, Lonna
Western HS
Stanton, CA

Oseguera, David G
San Dieguito HS
Encinitas, CA

Osgood, Kevin
Mabel O'farrell Schl For C&P Arts
San Diego, CA

Oshita, Damon T
Foothill HS
Santa Ana, CA

Oskin, Michael E
Edison HS
Huntington Beach, CA

Osmani, Fariba
Gladstone HS
Asuza, CA

Osmond, Amie C
Apple Valley HS
Apple Valley, CA

Osnaya, Alice
El Rancho HS
Pico Rivera, CA

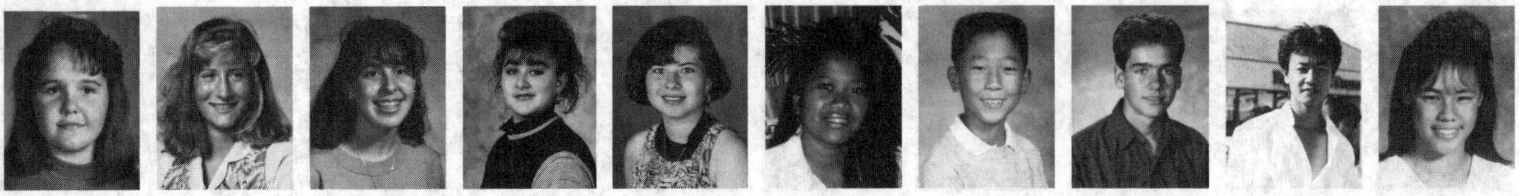

Ospital, Francene
Bret Harte Union HS
Murphys, CA

Oster, Elizabeth A
Buena HS
Ventura, CA

Ostrow, Jennifer S
Bullard HS
Fresno, CA

Osuna, Martha
Calexico HS
Calexico, CA

Oswalt, Elizabeth
Montgomery HS
San Diego, CA

Otanes, Arlene V
Mission Viejo HS
Mission Viejo, CA

Otero, Mark
Hiram Johnson HS
Sacramento, CA

Otto, Brian S
Foothill HS
Santa Ana, CA

Ou, Peng L
Venice HS
Los Angeles, CA

Ouano, Anne E
Lowell HS
San Francisco, CA

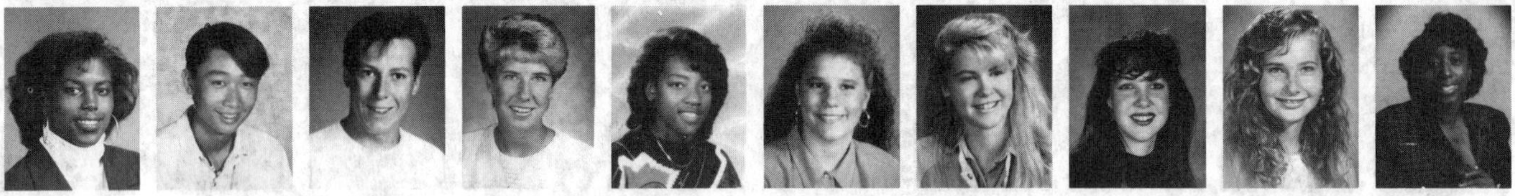

Oubre, Angel D
Bishop Montgomery
Carson, CA

Ouk, Mauv
T Roosevelt HS
Fresno, CA

Overacker, Ron E
Tulare Union HS
Tulare, CA

Overholt, Stefani R
Roseville HS
Roseville, CA

Overton, Lisa
King/Drew Medical Mag HS
Carson, CA

Overturf, Ramona L
Amos Alanzo Stagg
Stockton, CA

Owen, Candice
Home HS
Paso Robles, CA

Owen, Valerie K
Hoover HS
Fresno, CA

Owens, Amy E
Los Amigos HS
Fountain Valley, CA

Owens, Brenda
John Marshall Fund Secondary Schl
Pasadena, CA

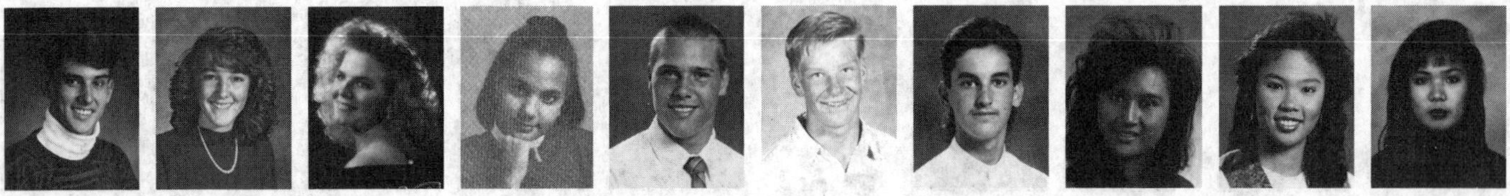

Owens, David R
Fresno Christian HS
Fresno, CA

Owens, Jennifer
South Tahoe HS
S Lake Tahoe, CA

Owens, Kelli N
Live Oak HS
Live Oak, CA

Owens, Kristina R
Hawthorne HS
Lennox, CA

Ower, David W
St Francis HS
Pasadena, CA

Owskey, Robert T
Fremont HS
Sunnyvale, CA

Oyola, Jose J
John Burroughs HS
Burbank, CA

Ozoa, Dara Diana N
Notre Dame HS
San Jose, CA

Pablo, Eileen P
Holy Family HS
Los Angeles, CA

Pabustan, Josephine
Newbury Park HS
Newbury Park, CA

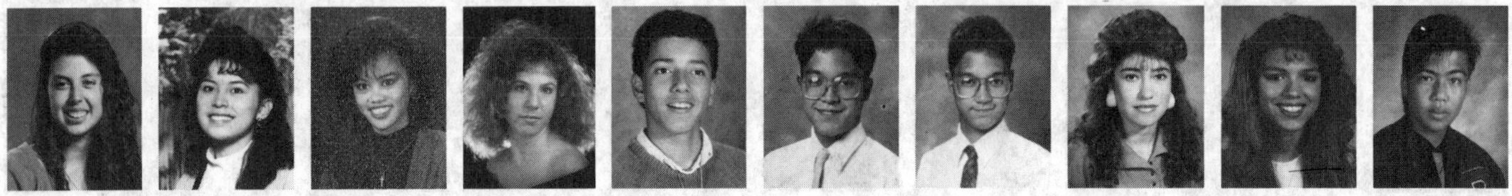

Pacheco, Ana C
Etiwanda HS
Etiwanda, CA

Pack, Linda S
Canyon Springs HS
Moreno Valley, CA

Pacleb, Joanne M
Hogan HS
Vallejo, CA

Padgett, Lisa
Willows HS
Willows, CA

Padilla, Abel M
Aragon HS
Foster City, CA

Padilla, Daniel V
Loyola HS
Glendale, CA

Padilla, Duane J
Loyola HS
Glendale, CA

Padilla, Lorena R
Norco HS
Norco, CA

Padilla, Lynn A
Valley HS
Sacramento, CA

Padilla, Michael
Calvin Simmons JR
Oakland, CA

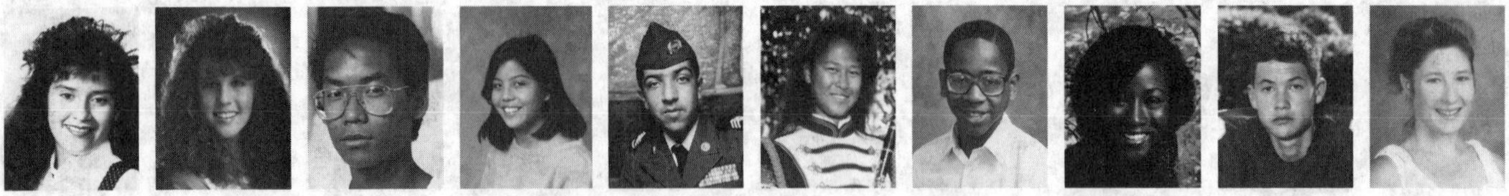

Padilla, Naomi R
William Workman
Valinda, CA

Padovich, Samantha
Saugus HS
Saugus, CA

Padua, Ezra P
Glendale HS
Glendale, CA

Paet, Andrea A
Chamindade Coll Prep
Northridge, CA

Paez, Fabian
Blair HS
Pasadena, CA

Pagaduan, Joann S
Mt Carmel HS
San Diego, CA

Page, Di Andre L
Hilmar JR-SR HS
Stevinson, CA

Page, Letecia
Barstow HS
Barstow, CA

Pai, Kevin Sun
Montclair HS
Mira Loma, CA

Painter, Charity
Mt Whitney HS
Visalia, CA

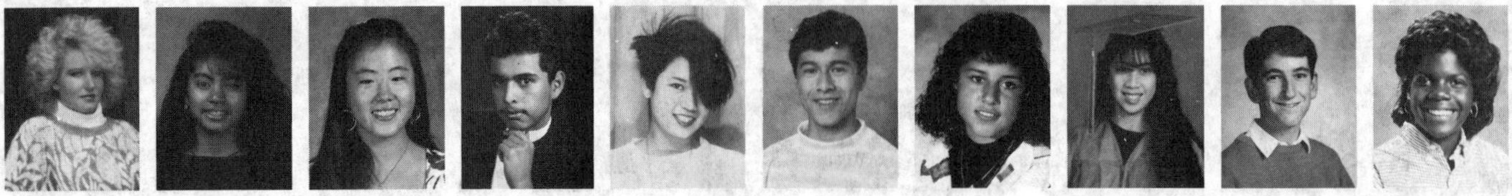

Painter, Tara
Fairfield HS
Fairfield, CA

Pajela, Roselynn T
Salinas HS
Salinas, CA

Pak, Soyung
Palo Alto HS
Palo Alto, CA

Palacios, Jose Rafael
Burlingqme HS
San Francisco, CA

Palanca, Georgiana V
University HS
Los Angeles, CA

Palma, Kleber J
West Torrance HS
Torrance, CA

Palma, Renee K
Chino HS
Chino, CA

Palma, Sheila Lynn E
Tokay HS
Stockton, CA

Palmer, Charles
Damien HS
Diamond Bar, CA

Palmer, Elizabeth A
Testimonial Christian Schl
Los Angeles, CA

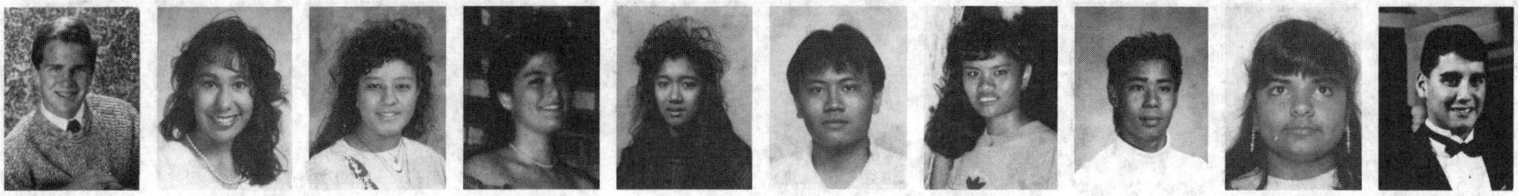

Palmer, James L
Ramona HS
Riverside, CA

Palomares, Alicia
Indio HS
Indio, CA

Palomares, Susana G
Bishop Amat HS
La Puente, CA

Palomino, Staci
Hesperia HS
Hesperia, CA

Palor, Sheryl
Franklin JR HS
Vallejo, CA

Pan, Tom C
Cupertino HS
Cupertino, CA

Panabang, Emelita W
Orosi HS
Orosi, CA

Pananganan, Mark D
Hogan SR HS
Vallejo, CA

Pandey, Vatsala
Paso Robles HS
Paso Robles, CA

Pando, Albert T
Fresno Christian HS
Sanger, CA

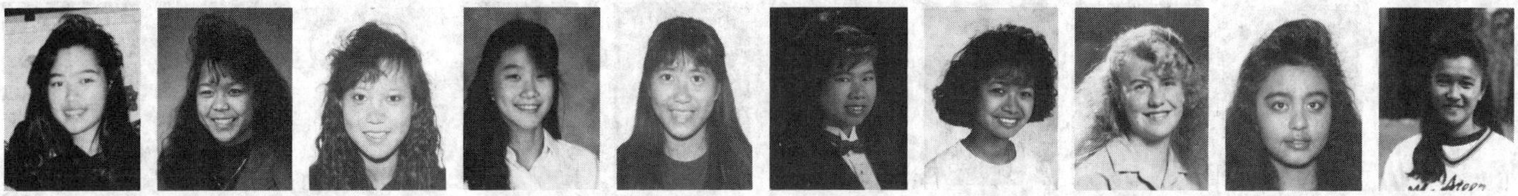

Paner, Flormeline
Franklin JR HS
Vallejo, CA

Paner, Perlita Dolores
Dr James J Hogan
SR HS
Vallejo, CA

Pang, Alice M
San Gabriel HS
San Gabriel, CA

Pang, Cindy
Mission San Jose HS
Fremont, CA

Pang, Elaine C
San Gabriel HS
San Gabriel, CA

Pang, Tammy Rena
Ygnacio Valley HS
Walnut Creek, CA

Pangan, Kristina A
Nogales HS
W Covina, CA

Pangborn, Francine
Los Angeles Lutheran
Los Angeles, CA

Pangelinan, Michelle
North HS
Bakersfield, CA

Pangilinan, Gina B
J Eugene Mc Ateer
San Francisco, CA

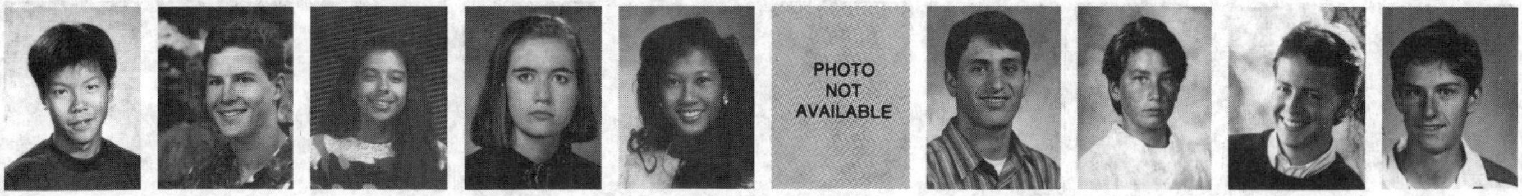

Pangilinan, Ruel J
Hamilton HS
Los Angeles, CA

Pangman, Brandon W
Downieville HS
Downieville, CA

Paniagua, Elka
Downtown Business
Magnet HS
Bell, CA

Pankey, Karen E
Fallbrook HS
Bonsall, CA

Panlilio, Michelle
Western Christian
Upland, CA

PHOTO NOT AVAILABLE

Pannell, Westly H
San Benito HS
Hollister, CA

Panos, Pete G
Willow Glen HS
San Jose, CA

Papazian, Shawn
St Bernards HS
Los Angeles, CA

Papierniak, Eric S
De La Salle HS
Diablo, CA

Pappas, Basil D
Carmel HS
Carmel, CA

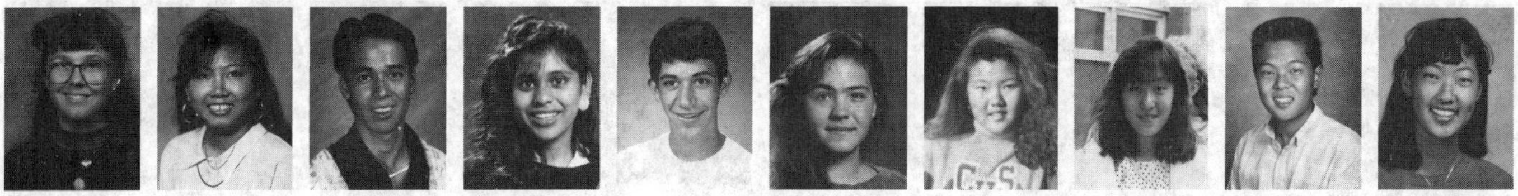

Pappas, Kaliopi
Lincoln HS
Stockton, CA

Parayno, Cheryl B
Nogales HS
Walnut, CA

Parde, Michael C
Bishop Amat HS
Diamond Bar, CA

Pardo, Adriana
Roosevelt HS
Los Angeles, CA

Pareas, Philip L
Ygnacio Valley HS
Pleasant Hill, CA

Parillo, Heather M
Mayfield SR HS
Alhambra, CA

Park, Anne
Campbell Hall HS
Van Nuys, CA

Park, Bik-Na
Ocean View HS
Huntington Beach, CA

Park, Clinton H
Escondido Adventist
Acad
Escondido, CA

Park, Elaine
Benicia HS
Benicia, CA

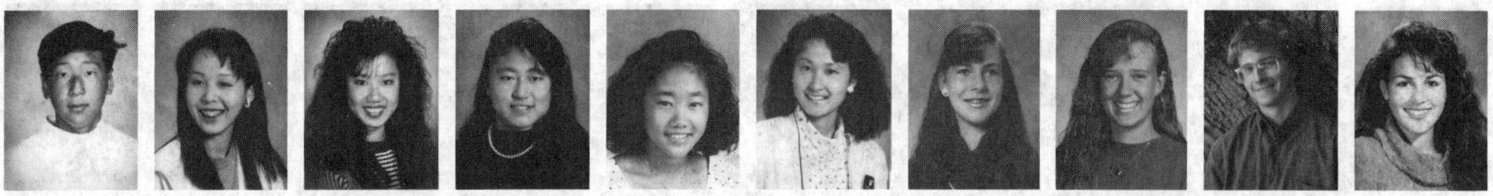

Park, Jun K
El Camino Real HS
West Hills, CA

Park, Mee K
Buena Park HS
Cypress, CA

Park, Myeong-Joo
El Camino Real HS
Los Angeles, CA

Park, Sonya S
Irvine HS
Irvine, CA

Park, Terry J
Whittier Christian
Fullerton, CA

Park, Young S
Buena Park HS
Cypress, CA

Parke, Kristina
Rosary HS
Fullerton, CA

Parker, Amy M
Roseville HS
Roseville, CA

Parker, Christopher
Buena HS
Ventura, CA

Parker, Denise N
La Habra HS
La Habra, CA

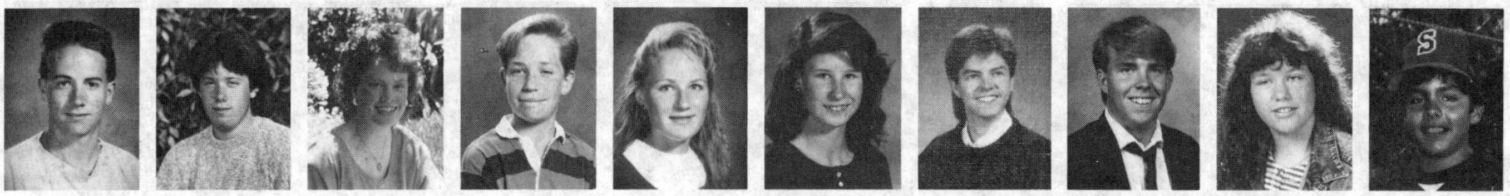

Parker, Jason W
Norco SR HS
Norco, CA

Parker, Jeff
San Clemente HS
San Clemente, CA

Parker, Jennifer L
Livermore HS
Livermore, CA

Parkinson, Brett
Indio HS
Bermuda Dunes, CA

Parkinson, Krista
Indio HS
Bermuda Dunes, CA

Parks, Brandy
Indio HS
Indio, CA

Parks, John-Scott
Thomas Downey HS
Modesto, CA

Parks, Joshua A
The Bishops Schl
Del Mar, CA

Parnell, Tammy
San Rafael HS
San Rafael, CA

Parodi, Carlos
Saint Francis HS
Glendale, CA

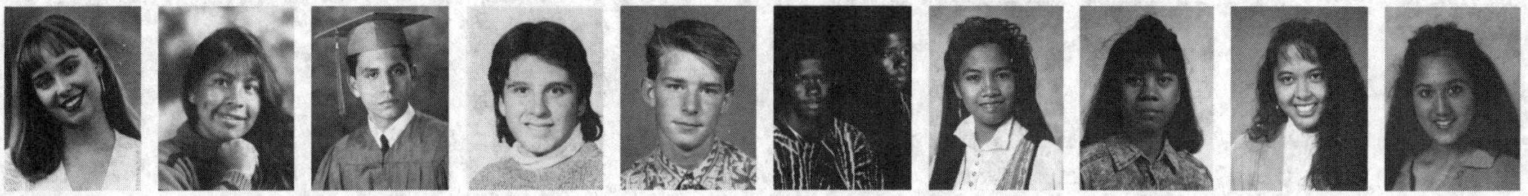

Parodi, Michelle
Soquel HS
Soquel, CA

Parra, Blanca I
King City Joint
Union HS
Greenfield, CA

Parrales, Ronaldo
Bishop Amat
Memorial HS
Chino Hills, CA

Partier, Justin A
J Eugene Mc Ateer/
Schl Of The Arts
San Francisco, CA

Partridge, Marcus D
Beaumont HS
Beaumont, CA

Partridge, Sidney
Granada Hills HS
Sylmar, CA

Pascua, Jr Eleanor J
Hawthorne HS
Hawthorne, CA

Pascua, Simonette V
Santa Clara HS
Sunnyvale, CA

Pasion, Anabella B
Hogan SR HS
Vallejo, CA

Pasten, Soraya
Sweetwater HS
Chula Vista, CA

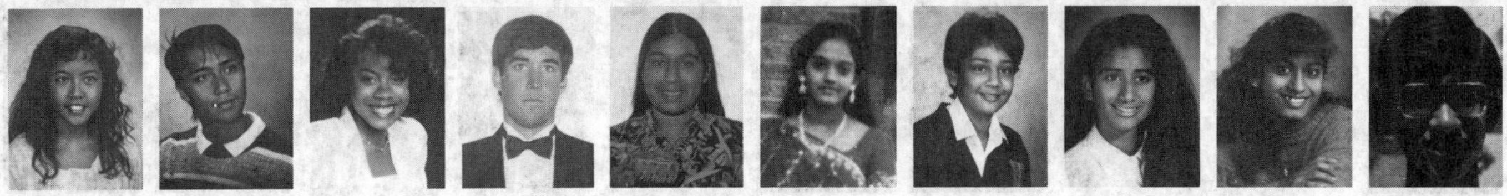

Pastor, Marilou
Chowchilla Union HS
Madera, CA

Pastor, Peter A
Chowchilla Union HS
Madera, CA

Patacsil, Ila
San Diego HS
San Diego, CA

Pate, Bryan L
Coronado HS
Coronado, CA

Patel, Anita R
Troy HS
Fullerton, CA

Patel, Asmita
S Tahoe HS
S Lake Tahoe, CA

Patel, Hannon R
Bellarmine College Prep
Milpitas, CA

Patel, Krina
Nova HS
Summit City, CA

Patel, Mital
Willows HS
Willows, CA

Patel, Nehal G
Whitney HS
La Mirada, CA

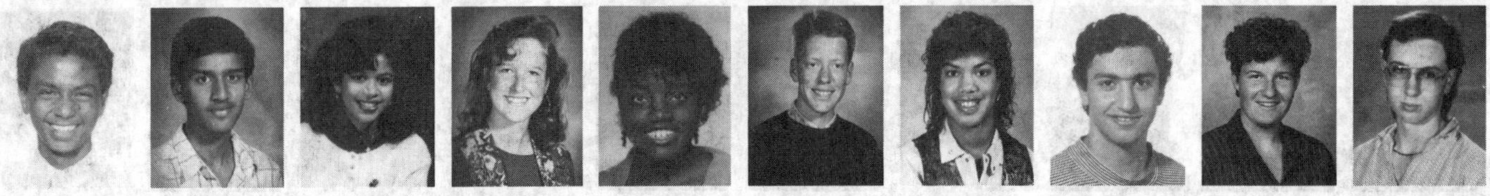

Patel, Niraj D
Burbank HS
Burbank, CA

Patel, Rajul A
John F Kennedy HS
Granada Hills, CA

Patel, Swati R
Artesia HS
Lakewood, CA

Paterna, Jullee M
Mt Shasta HS
Mount Shasta, CA

Pates, Wendy
Montclair HS
South Bend, IN

Patrick, Kevin J
North HS
Bakersfield, CA

Patrick, Teri L
Victor Valley HS
Newmanstown, PA

Patrikyan, Artashes
Herbert Hoover HS
Glendale, CA

Patsko, Stacey
Christian HS
El Cajon, CA

Patten, Benjamin A
Don Antonio Lugo
Chino, CA

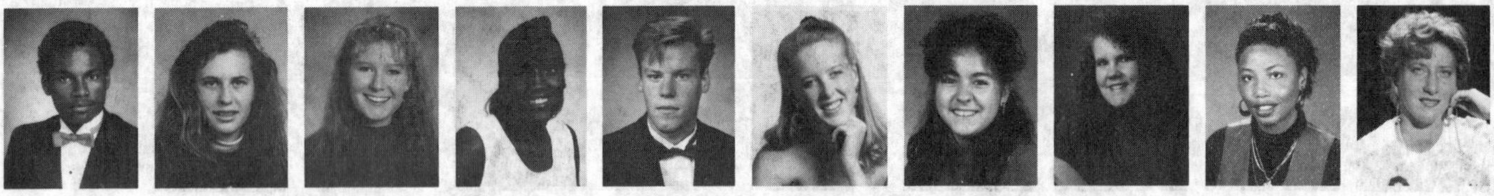

Patterson, II Gregory
Lincoln Prep HS
San Diego, CA

Patterson, Heather L
Dixon HS
Dixon, CA

Patterson, Marisa E
Savanna HS
Anaheim, CA

Patterson, Shon Tel
Ganesha HS
Diamond Bar, CA

Patterson, William C
El Camino Fundamental HS
Sacramento, CA

Pattison, Kirsten N
Norte Vista HS
Riverside, CA

Patton, Brenda L
St Joseph HS
Norwalk, CA

Patton, Kim
Taft HS
Fellows, CA

Patton, Kimberly L
Pittsburg HS
Pittsburg, CA

Patton, Shareen L
University HS
Irvine, CA

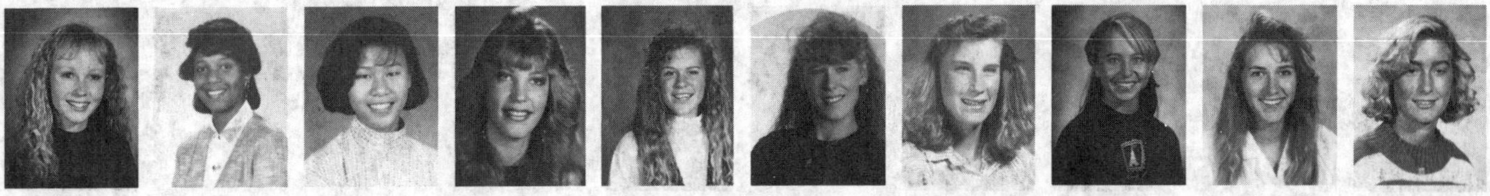

Pauley, Julie
East Bakersfield HS
Bakersfield, CA

Paulino, Sandra
King Drew Med Mag
Los Angeles, CA

Paulo, Annalee J
St Joseph HS
Whittier, CA

Paulson, Alicia C
Clovis HS
Clovis, CA

Paulson, Becky
College Park HS
Pleasant Hill, CA

Pavlak, Beth A
Canyon Springs HS
Moreno Valley, CA

Pavlak, Stephanie T
Canyon Springs HS
Moreno Valley, CA

Paxton, Natasha R
Sacramento Adventist Acad
Sacramento, CA

Paxton, Sharlene
Immanuel Christian Schl
Ridgecrest, CA

Payne, Ashley L
John Muir HS
Pasadena, CA

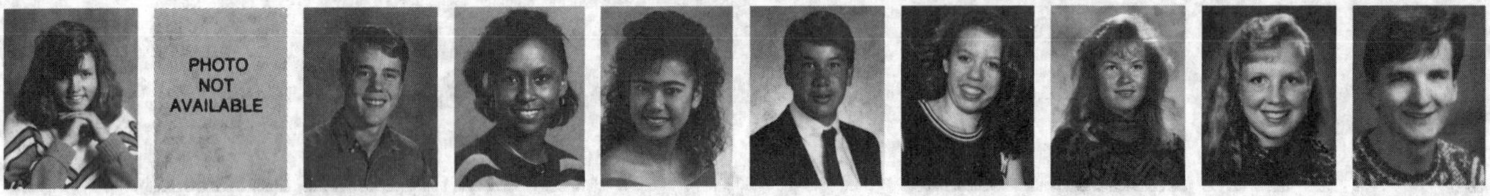

Payne, Kenna Kay
Notre Dame HS
Riverside, CA

Payne, Michael J
Clovis HS
Clovis, CA

Paytash, Stephen E
South Fork HS
Redway, CA

Payton, Nikki J
Leuzinger HS
Hawthorne, CA

Peach, Jo Ann M
Notre Dame HS
San Jose, CA

Pearce, Kenneth W
St Francis HS
Mountain View, CA

Pearce, Sabrina
Ayala HS
Chino Hills, CA

Pearcy, Keri L
Moorpark HS
Moorpark, CA

Pearson, Heather N
El Toro HS
El Toro, CA

Pearson, Matthew James Collins
East Bakersfield HS
Bakersfield, CA

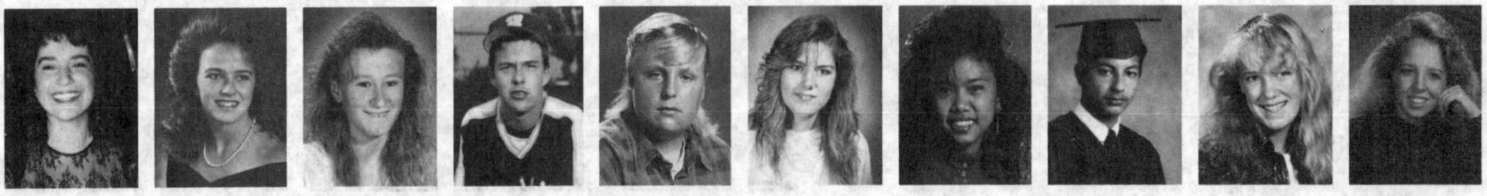

Pearson, Nicole R
College Park HS
Concord, CA

Pearson, Tammy Lynn
Lower Lake HS
Clearlake, CA

Pease, Traci L
Paradise HS
Paradise, CA

Peck, Paul J
Montclair HS
Ontario, CA

Pedersen, Doug A
Burbank HS
Burbank, CA

Pedersen, Jill M
Montgomery HS
Santa Rosa, CA

Pedraja, Jenette B
Eagle Rock HS
Los Angeles, CA

Pedroza, Johnny
Claremont HS
Westminster, CA

Peel, Temre R
Robert A Millikan
Long Beach, CA

Pegarella, Andrea D
Thomas Downey HS
Modesto, CA

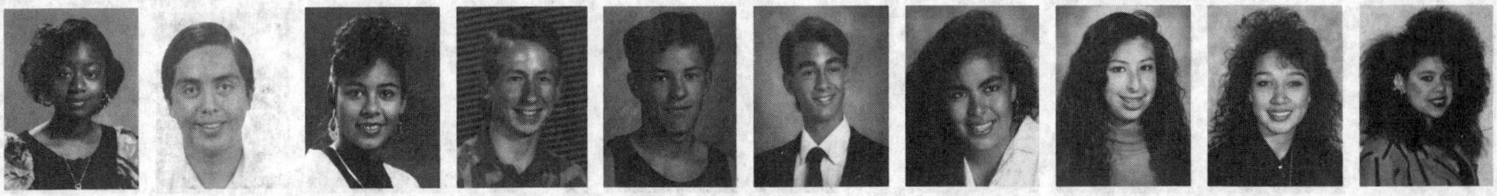

Pegeese, Keshonea M
Bassett SR HS
La Puente, CA

Peimbert, Ernesto Alonso
Don Bosco Technical Inst
West Covina, CA

Pelayo, Beatriz A
Mayfield SR Schl
Alhambra, CA

Pelcman, Jason P
Enterprise HS
Redding, CA

Pemberton, Charan K
Apple Valley SR HS
Apple Valley, CA

Pena, Christopher
Canyon HS
Anaheim, CA

Pena, Edna G
Calexico HS
Calexico, CA

Pena, Irene
Shafter HS
Shafter, CA

Pena, Perla M
Fresno HS
Fresno, CA

Pena, Ruth
Liberty Union HS
Knightsen, CA

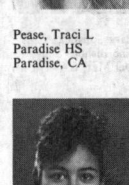

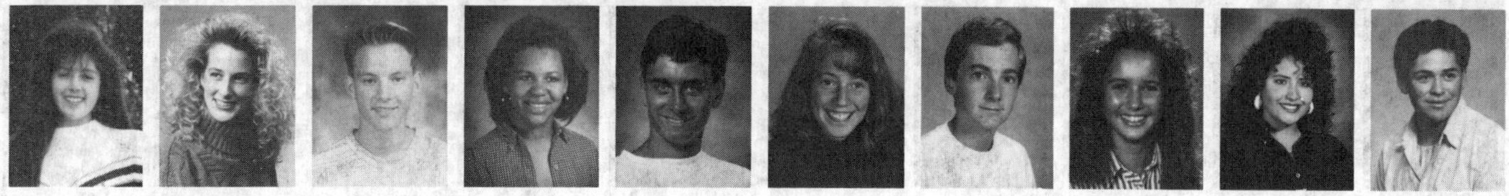

Penaloza, Lorena
Cotton HS
San Bernardino, CA

Pendergraft, Julie A
Etwanda HS
Alta Loma, CA

Penn, Brandon M
Dos Pueblos HS
Goleta, CA

Penrice, Celayoa M
Arlington HS
Riverside, CA

Penta, Eric J
Sunny Hills HS
Fullerton, CA

Pentopoulos, Analene
Las Lomas HS
Walnut Creek, CA

Pentopoulos, Marc A
Las Lomas HS
Walnut Creek, CA

Pepper, Sasha
Livermore HS
Livermore, CA

Perales, Emily
Nichole
Tulare Western HS
Tulare, CA

Peralta, Ricardo
El Camino
Fundamental HS
Sacramento, CA

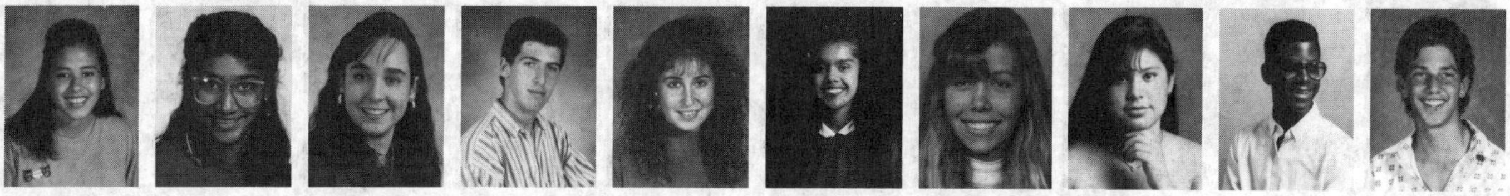

Peredo, Maria B
Rio Linda SR HS
Sacramento, CA

Pereira, Laila M
Loretto HS
Roseville, CA

Pereira, Rosemary S
Notre Dame HS
San Jose, CA

Perelstein, Ilya
Bel-Air Prep Schl
Los Angeles, CA

Perez, Alisa M
Aptos HS
Freedom, CA

Perez, Ana R
Bell Gardens HS
Commerce, CA

Perez, Anna L
La Jolla HS
San Diego, CA

Perez, Ben R
North Salinas HS
Salinas, CA

Perez, III Carlos A
Hamilton HS
Sepulveda, CA

Perez, Christian A
Tracy Joint Union
Tracy, CA

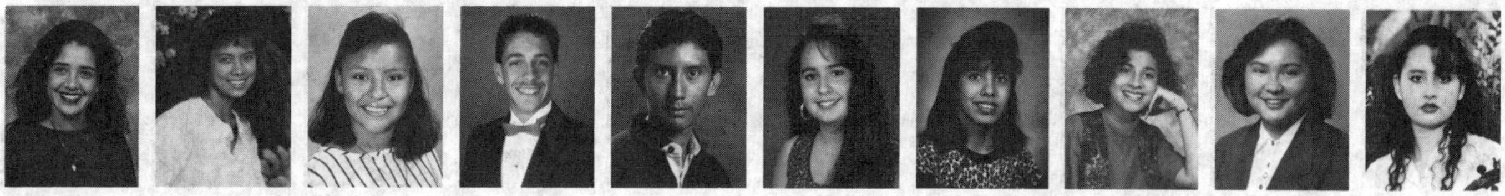

Perez, Claudia
St Paul HS
Norwalk, CA

Perez, Deborah
Maricopa HS
Maricopa, CA

Perez, Edna J
Bishop Amat HS
Walnut, CA

Perez, Enrique
Arroyo HS
San Lorenzo, CA

Perez, Ernesto C
Tehachapi HS
Tehachapi, CA

Perez, Evelia
Pinole Valley HS
Hercules, CA

Perez, Isabel
Arlington HS
Riverside, CA

Perez, Jeanette I
South Bay Junior
Acad
Inglewood, CA

Perez, Joyce P
Notre Dame Acad
Los Angeles, CA

Perez, Margarita
Paramount HS
Paramount, CA

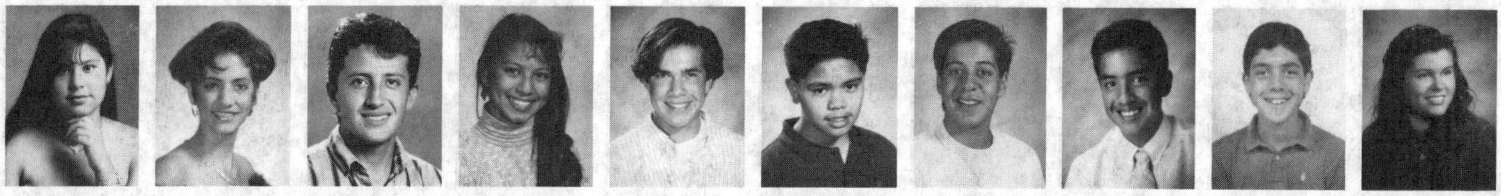

Perez, Marisol
Santa Teresa HS
San Jose, CA

Perez, Mechelle L
El Rancho HS
Pico Rivera, CA

Perez, Nain J
Nogales HS
Walnut, CA

Perez, Odette N
Los Gatos HS
Los Gatos, CA

Perez, Paul J
Marshall
Fundamental HS
Pasadena, CA

Perez, Ramil
Daniel Murphy HS
Los Angeles, CA

Perez, Raymond E
Arcadia HS
Arcadia, CA

Perez, Rick
West HS
Bakersfield, CA

Perez, Scott C
University HS
Irvine, CA

Perez, Sonia
St Bonaventure HS
Santa Paula, CA

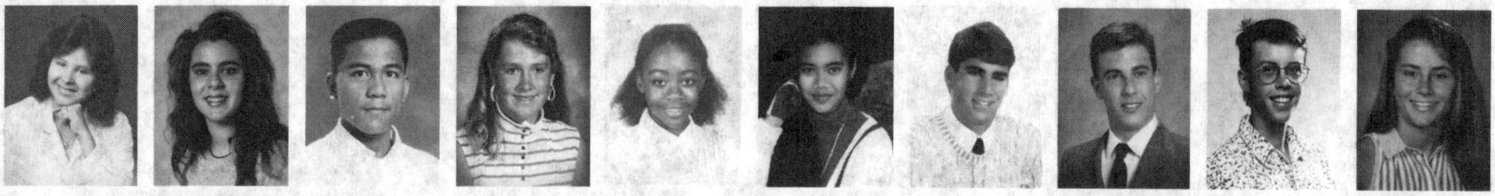

Perez, Sonia A
William C Overfelt
San Jose, CA

Perez, Virginia
Castle Park HS
Chula Vista, CA

Perias, Melchior
Garces Memorial HS
Delano, CA

Perich, Leah J
East Bakersfield HS
Bakersfield, CA

Perkins, Krista M
Mills JR HS
Rancho Cordova, CA

Perlas, Marlo V
Notre Dame San Jose
San Jose, CA

Perlman, Kenneth S
Buena HS
Ventura, CA

Perone, Jr Nestor
Luis
Mater Dei HS
Costa Mesa, CA

Perrault, Jeffrey M
Thousand Oaks HS
Thousand Oaks, CA

Perri, Jennifer
Irvine HS
Irvine, CA

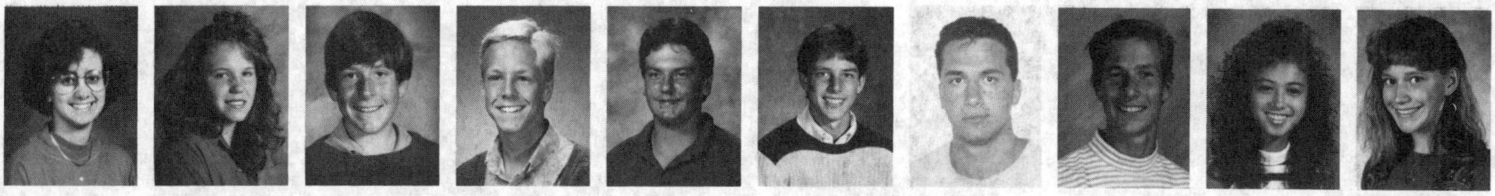

Perry, Amy
Orestimba HS
Crows Landing, CA

Perry, Jennifer
Borrego Springs HS
Borrego Springs, CA

Perry, Matthew
Poway HS
Poway, CA

Perry, Ryan W
Pinole Valley HS
Hercules, CA

Persons, Chuck
Cordova SR HS
Rancho Cordova, CA

Pesh, Shawn P
Beacon Christian HS
Foster City, CA

Pesnilian, Hagop
Schurr HS
Montebello, CA

Pestana, John R
Serrano HS
Wrightwood, CA

Petagara, Minette
Western HS
Anaheim, CA

Peters, Erica R
Hilmar HS
Hilmar, CA

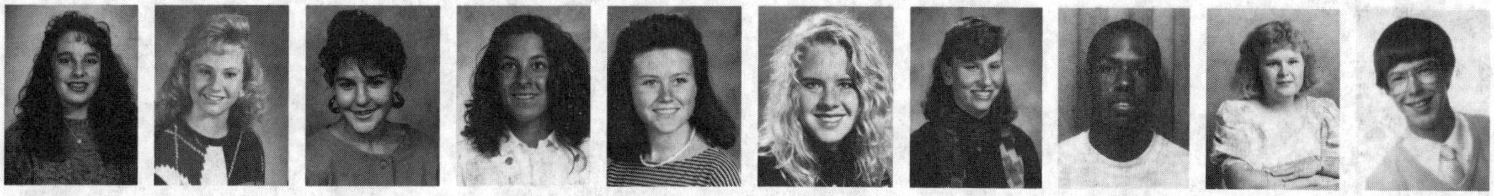

Peters, Jennifer L
Eureka HS
Eureka, CA

Peters, Katie Lynn
Needles HS
Needles, CA

Peters, Kelly J
El Cajon HS
El Cajon, CA

Peters, Rebecca S
Willow Glen
Educational Park HS
San Jose, CA

Petersen, Carleen A
Ramona HS
Ramona, CA

Petersen, Kristin
Flintridge
Preparatory Schl
Pasadena, CA

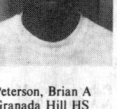

Peterson, Anne M
Redwood Christian
Castro Valley, CA

Peterson, Brian A
Granada Hill HS
Northridge, CA

Peterson, Christine
Lynn
Academy Of Our
Lady Of Peace
San Diego, CA

Peterson, Daniel C
Redwood Christian
San Lorenzo, CA

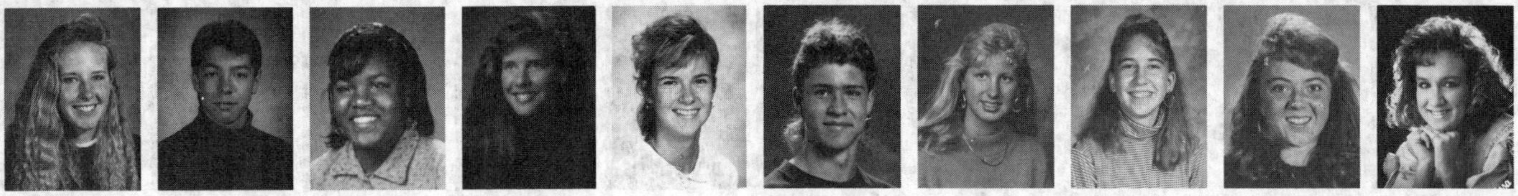

Peterson, Elaine M
College Park HS
Pleasant Hill, CA

Peterson, Jamey M
Montgomery HS
Santa Rosa, CA

Peterson, Janeen R
Pinole Valley HS
Hercules, CA

Peterson, Kristin
Capistrano Valley
Christian HS
Mission Viejo, CA

Peterson, Leah
Louisville HS
Westlake Village, CA

Peterson, Mike D
Bonita HS
La Verne, CA

Peterson, Nikki
Christian HS
El Cajon, CA

Peterson, Rena
Rio Vista HS
Isleton, CA

Peterson, Tamara L
Palm Springs HS
Desert Hot Spring, CA

Peterson-Turner, Melissa
Serrano HS
Apple Valley, CA

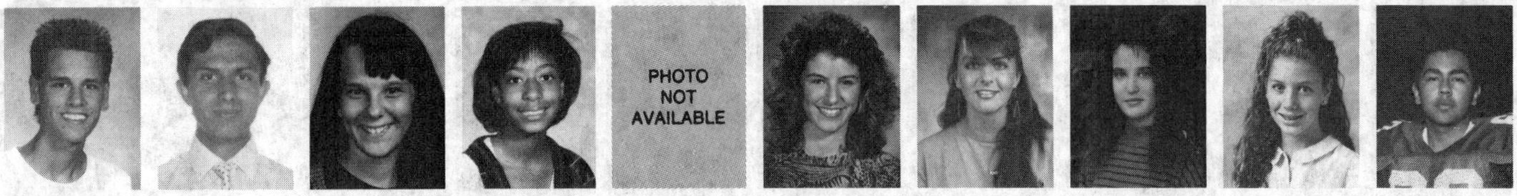
PHOTO
NOT
AVAILABLE

Petrequin, Bryan J
Santa Teresa HS
San Jose, CA

Petrossian, Vahe
Crescenta Valley HS
La Crescenta, CA

Petrow, Regina M
Bishop Manogue HS
Sacramento, CA

Petteway, Kenya D
A Hamilton HS
Los Angeles, CA

Pettigrew, Michael A
Roseville HS
Roseville, CA

Pettit, Ginger L
Paraclete HS
Lancaster, CA

Petty, Renae M
San Marcos HS
Santa Barbara, CA

Pewitt, Janith M
Vacaville HS
Vacaville, CA

Pfeffer, Lisa D
Grant HS
Sherman Oaks, CA

Pfister, Alex V
St Anthony HS
Long Beach, CA

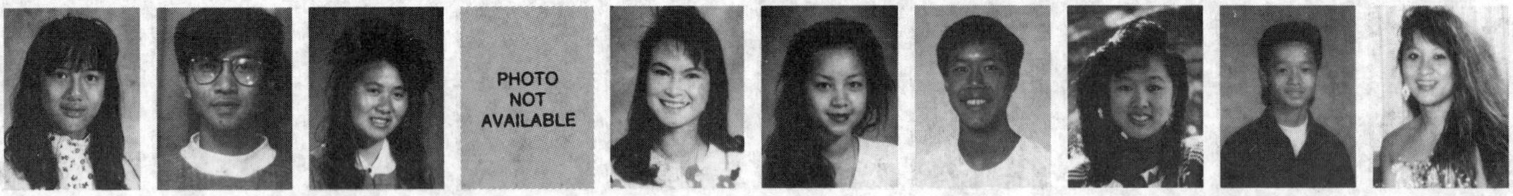
PHOTO
NOT
AVAILABLE

Pham, Chau Diem
Ernest Righetti HS
Santa Maria, CA

Pham, Lam Dang
Hoover HS
San Diego, CA

Pham, Lan
Bishop Manogue HS
Sacramento, CA

Pham, Lien
Bishop Manogue HS
Sacramento, CA

Pham, My Hanh
Western HS
Stanton, CA

Pham, Quyendi D
Santiago HS
Garden Grove, CA

Pham, Son M
Buena HS
Ventura, CA

Pham, Son T
North Salinas HS
Salinas, CA

Pham, Tam
William C Overfelt
San Jose, CA

Pham, Theresa
San Pasqual HS
Escondido, CA

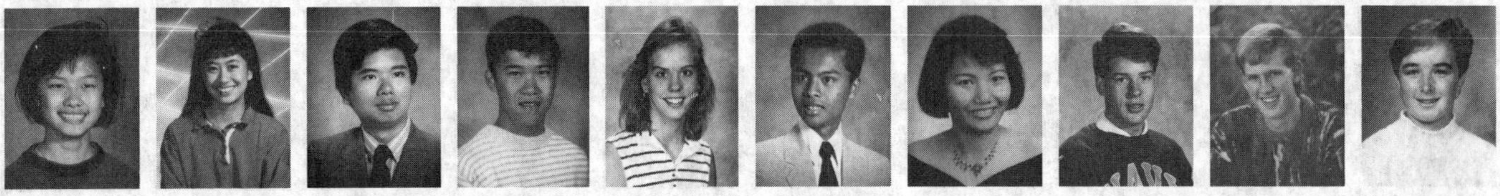

Phan, Ai Uyen
George Washington
San Francisco, CA

Phan, Hiep-Chan T
Irvington HS
Fremont, CA

Phan, Nam Q
Villa Park HS
Orange, CA

Phan, Tung D
Kennedy HS
Buena Park, CA

Phaneuf, Julie A
Alverno HS
San Gabriel, CA

Phansavath, Hinh
Western HS
Buena Park, CA

Phea, Sophea
Yerba Buena HS
San Jose, CA

Phelan, III James F
Righetti HS
Santa Maria, CA

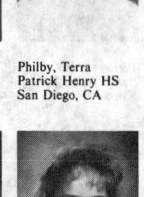

Phelp, James
Capistrano Valley
Christian HS
San Clemente, CA

Philby, Terra
Patrick Henry HS
San Diego, CA

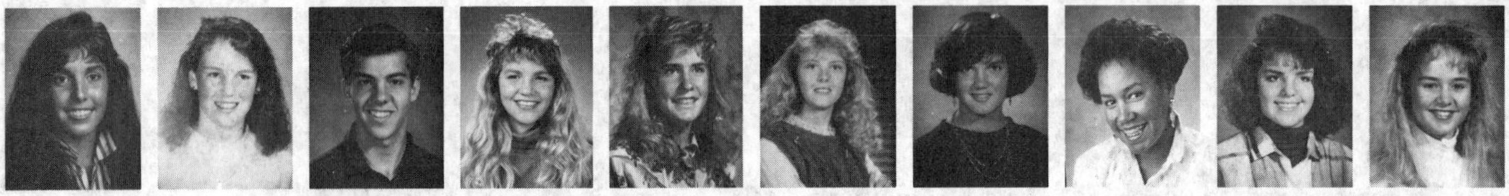

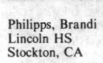

Philipps, Brandi
Lincoln HS
Stockton, CA

Phillips, Dana R
Livermore HS
Livermore, CA

Phillips, David J
Edison HS
Huntington Beach, CA

Phillips, Hollie
Liberty Union HS
Oakley, CA

Phillips, Kelly
Bullard HS
Fresno, CA

Phillips, Loretta G
Caruthers Union HS
Fresno, CA

Phillips, Margaret K
Calabasas HS
Woodland Hills, CA

Phillips, Niki D
Diamond HS
Diamond Bar, CA

Phillips, Rusti L
Del Norte HS
Crescent City, CA

Phillips, Shanell D
Monache HS
Porterville, CA

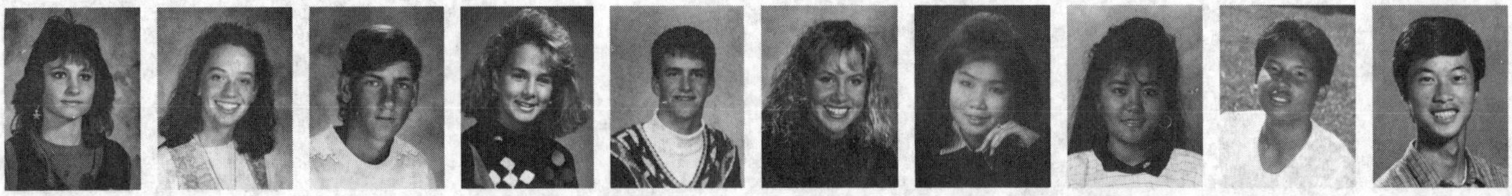

Phillips, Tammy G
Central HS
Fresno, CA

Phillips, Tiphanie J
Valley View HS
Moreno Valley, CA

Phillips-Wing, Jason
Hoover HS
Fresno, CA

Phineas, Carrie
Phineas Banning HS
Lomita, CA

Phipps, Anthony M
De La Salle HS
Concord, CA

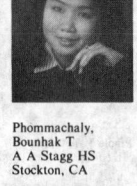

Phister, Becky L
Davis SR HS
Davis, CA

Phommachaly, Bounhak T
A A Stagg HS
Stockton, CA

Phommasy, Chanpasong
Sweetwater HS
National City, CA

Phomsopha, Bounlahong M
Orestimba HS
Newman, CA

Phung, Son P
Luezinger HS
Hawthorne, CA

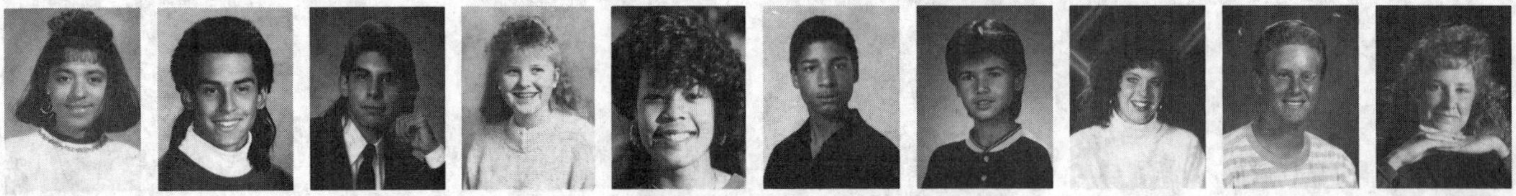

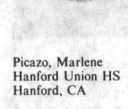

Picazo, Marlene
Hanford Union HS
Hanford, CA

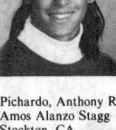

Pichardo, Anthony R
Amos Alanzo Stagg
Stockton, CA

Pichardo, Paul M
A A Stagg HS
Stockton, CA

Pickens, Heather
Jordan HS
Long Beach, CA

Pickett, Susan
Phineas Banning HS
Los Angeles, CA

Pickett, Timothy J
Ontario HS
Claremont, CA

Picone, Louie J
Liberty Union HS
Oakley, CA

Piel, Suzanne
Northview HS
Covina, CA

Pierce, Brian O
La Sierra HS
Riverside, CA

Pierce, Richel Y
Rubidoux HS
Mira Loma, CA

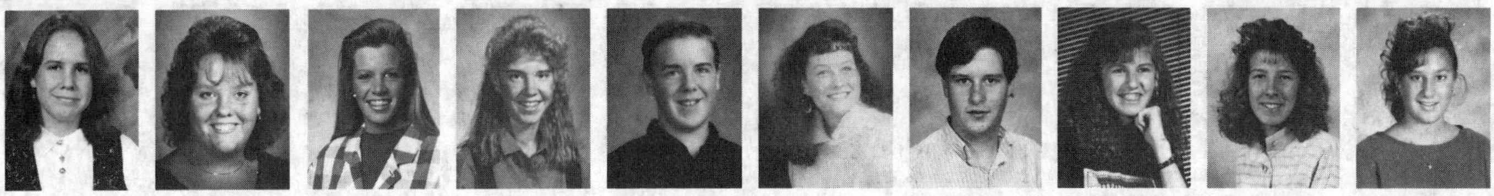

Pierce, Shawna L
Claremont HS
Garden Grove, CA

Pierce, Vicki I
Calaveras HS
Mountain Ranch, CA

Pierce, Wendy S
Brea-Olinda HS
Brea, CA

Piercy, Carrie
Apple Valley
Christian Schl
Apple Valley, CA

Pierson, Christopher
Golden West HS
Visalia, CA

Pierson, Joelle
Willows HS
Willows, CA

Pierson, Marc E
Maranatha HS
Altadena, CA

Pieruccini, Belle
Notre Dame HS
Salinas, CA

Pike, Holly J
Silver Valley HS
Newberry Spgs, CA

Pike, Jennifer M
Riverdale HS
Riverdale, CA

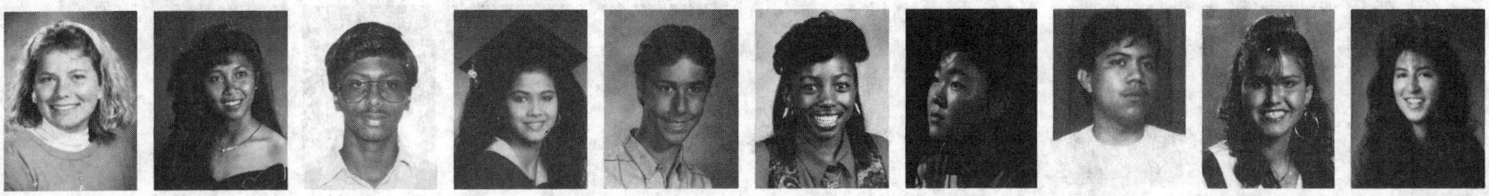

Pikul, Kristen
Edison HS
Huntington Beach, CA

Pilande, Melanie M
San Jose High Acad
San Jose, CA

Pilly, Vikas K
Nogales HS
W Covina, CA

Pin, Monica
Almos Alonzo Stagg
Stockton, CA

Pinard, Jason
Highlands HS
North Highlands, CA

Pinder, Jada
Moorpark HS
Moorpark, CA

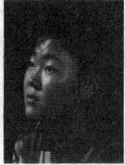

Pine, Susan Y
Cordova HS
Sacramento, CA

Pineda, Alex M
Hollywood HS
Los Angeles, CA

Pineda, Erendira E
San Pedro SR HS
San Pedro, CA

Pineda, Marisa
Buena HS
Ventura, CA

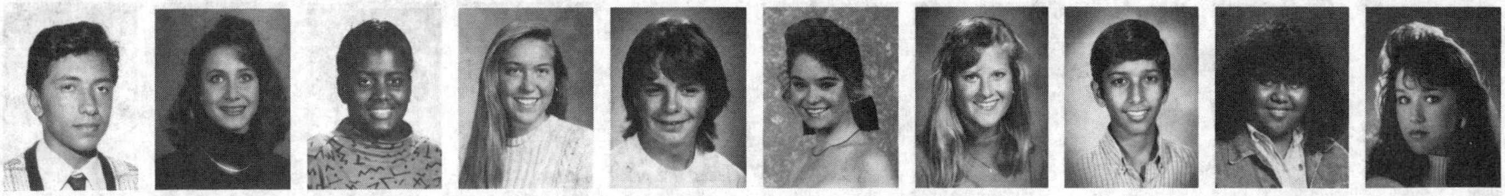

Pineda, Miguel
Warren HS
Downey, CA

Pingel, Sarah
Mt Whitney HS
Visalia, CA

Pinkard, Michelle
Capuchino HS
San Bruno, CA

Pinno, Mercedes
Alemany HS
Northridge, CA

Pinson, Paul A
Atwater HS
Atwater, CA

Pipitone, Tina Marie
Inland Christian HS
San Bernardino, CA

Pipp, Jennifer
University HS
Irvine, CA

Pir, Pervez P
Norco SR HS
Corona, CA

Pira, Elizabeth
Cajon HS
San Bernardino, CA

Pirnik, Lacyne
Fremont Christian
Fremont, CA

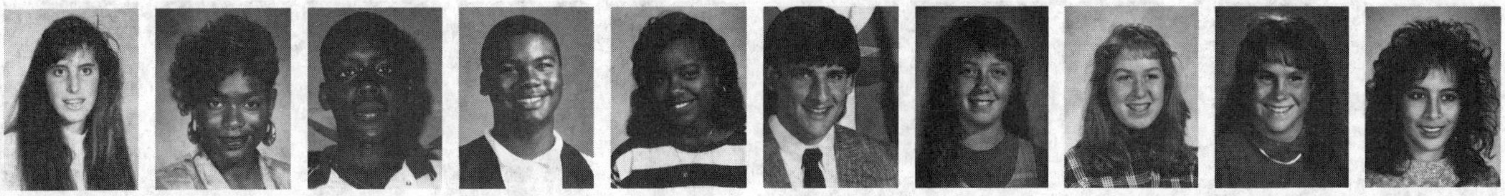

Piscazzi, Gianna
Rosary HS
Buena Park, CA

Pitchford, Ayeesha
Washington
Preparatory HS
Los Angeles, CA

Pitt, Dana L
Granada Hills HS
Los Angeles, CA

Pittman, Jr H
Maurice
Saint Monica
Catholic HS
Los Angeles, CA

Pittman, Monique S
Moreau HS
Castro Valley, CA

Pitts, Michael S
Thomas Downey HS
Modesto, CA

Pittser, Velma
Del Norte HS
Fort Dick, CA

Pixton, Sandra G
Woodland HS
Woodland, CA

Plappert, Monica L
Lincoln HS
Stockton, CA

Plascencia, Teressa M
Clovis HS
Clovis, CA

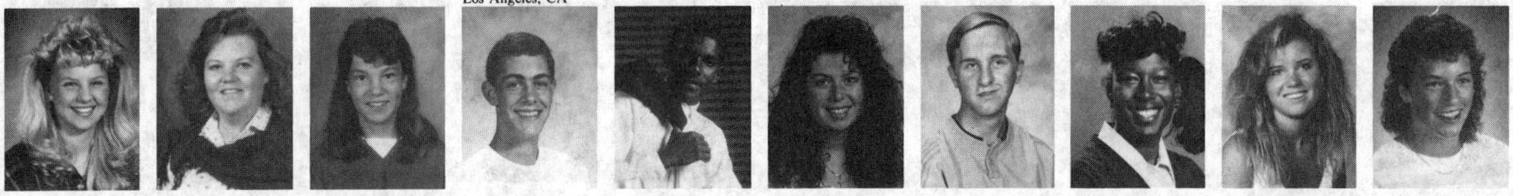

Platter, Amy
Gridley Union HS
Biggs, CA

Plaxton, Charity A
Yucaipa HS
Yucaipa, CA

Plaxton, Trina M
Ponderosa HS
Placerville, CA

Plescia, Brian J
Nevada Union HS
Grass Valley, CA

Plick, Leonard
Damien HS
Montclair, CA

Pluff, Deborah
Santa Clara HS
Santa Clara, CA

Plummer, Brian Keith
San Gabriel Acad
Covina, CA

Poarch, Taneka L
Testimonial Christian
Schl
Los Angeles, CA

Pobjoy, Tricia E
Granada Hills HS
Granada Hills, CA

Podesta, Tara
Linden HS
Linden, CA

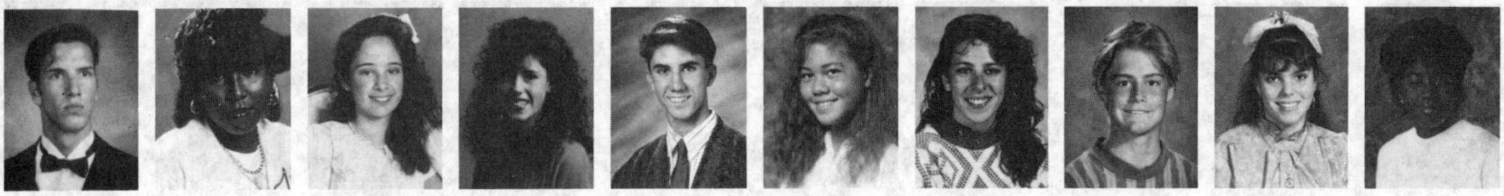

Podesta, William J
De La Salle HS
Lafayette, CA

Poe, Tonia C
Centennial HS
Compton, CA

Poggi, Gina
Dana Hills HS
Laguna Niguel, CA

Pohle, Jill
Montclair HS
Montclair, CA

Pohlman, Bryan H
Downey HS
Downey, CA

Pohlman, Naomi I
Dana Hills HS
Laguna Niguel, CA

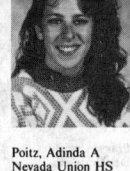

Poitz, Adinda A
Nevada Union HS
Grass Valley, CA

Polfer, Ryan K
Huntington Beach
Huntington Beach, CA

Polgar, Vanessa I
Lowell HS
San Francisco, CA

Polk, Bridgette M
Lynwood HS
Lynwood, CA

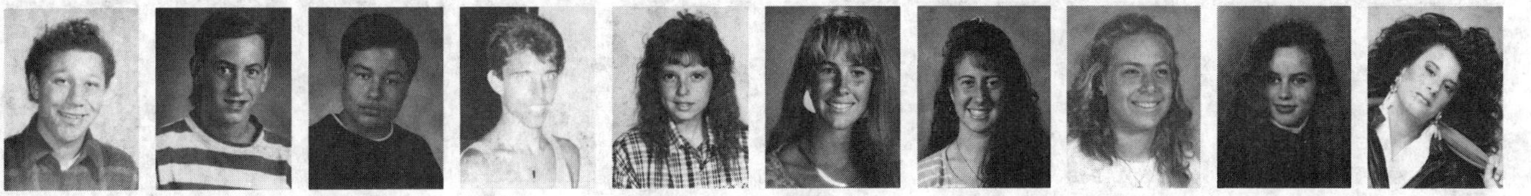

Polk, Garland R
Westmoor HS
Daly City, CA

Pollard, Russell G
Fresno Christian HS
Fresno, CA

Polley, Todd
Brethron HS
Downey, CA

Pollicino, Alexander
Hamilton HS
Los Angeles, CA

Pollitt, Amber L
Barstow HS
Barstow, CA

Pollman, Teresa
Clovis West HS
Clovis, CA

Poloni, Lori M
Bella Vista HS
Fair Oaks, CA

Polovina, Andrea
Sierra Joint Union
Tollhouse, CA

Pomar, Roxana R
Acadamy Of Our
Lady Of Peace
San Diego, CA

Pomozzi, Linda
John A Rowland HS
Chino, CA

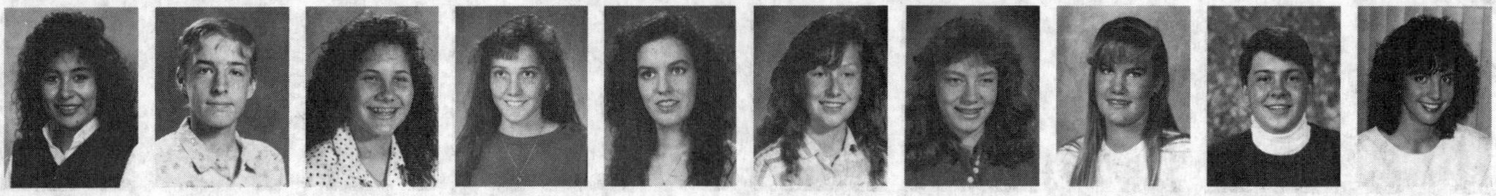

Ponce, Sandra E
Immaculate Heart
Hollywood, CA

Pontin, Michael G
Taft Union HS
Taft, CA

Pontis, Tamra R
Morro Bay HS
Morro Bay, CA

Poole, Medea
Liberty Union HS
Oakley, CA

Poole, Octavia
Liberty Union HS
Oakley, CA

Poor, Stacey L
Lassen Union HS
Susanville, CA

Pope, Elizabeth
North Valley
Christian Schl
Central Valley, CA

Pope, Jennifer A
Yucca Valley HS
Yucca Valley, CA

Pope, Kevin F
San Joaquin
Memorial HS
Fresno, CA

Poppleton, Emily Ann
Redlands HS
Mentone, CA

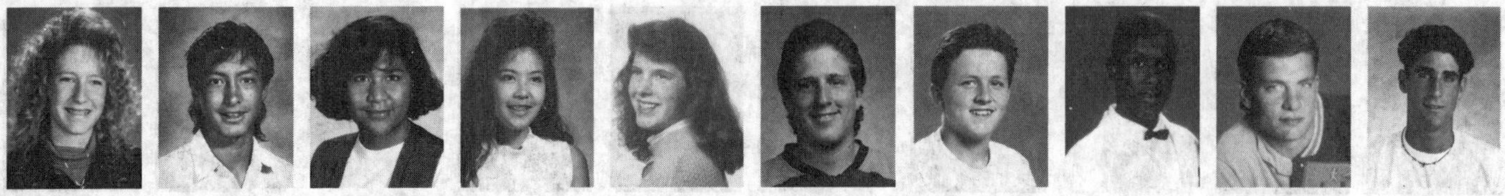

Popplewell, Kristina
Clovis HS
Clovis, CA

Populin, Ariel
Highland HS
Bakersfield, CA

Porras, Maria J
Notre Dame HS
Riverside, CA

Portacio, Eleanor
Lynn
James Logan HS
Union City, CA

Porter, Dana
Folsom HS
Folsom, CA

Porter, Scott S
Del Campo HS
Fair Oaks, CA

Porter, Sean J
Colton HS
Colton, CA

Porter, Steve A
Victor Valley HS
Victorville, CA

Posey, Vic E
Taft Union HS
Taft, CA

Poshard, Dean G
Del Mar HS
San Jose, CA

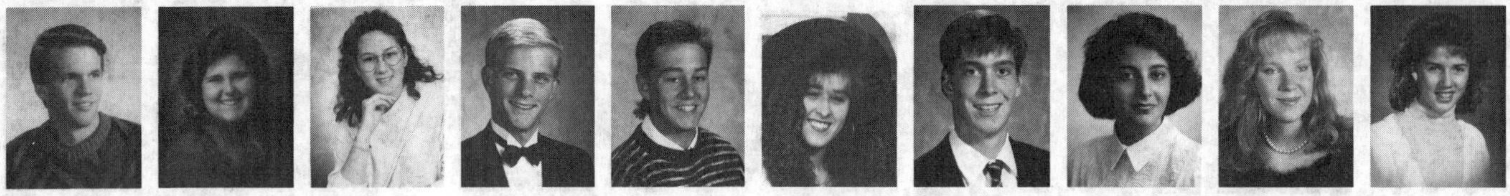

Poss, David Michael
Rubidoux HS
Moreno Valley, CA

Post, Charlene A
Montclair HS
Ontario, CA

Post, Karen B
Oxnard HS
Oxnard, CA

Postlethwaite, V
Hartley
Hillsdale HS
San Mateo, CA

Potter, Kevin R
Paso Robles HS
Paso Robles, CA

Potts, Stephanie
Lynne
Colfax HS
Meadow Vista, CA

Pouey, Edouard J
St Ignatius College
Prep
San Francisco, CA

Poulatian, Adrineh E
Burbank HS
Burbank, CA

Pouliot, Angela
San Ramon Valley
Danville, CA

Poulsen, Danielle
Fort Dick Bible Acad
Brookings, OR

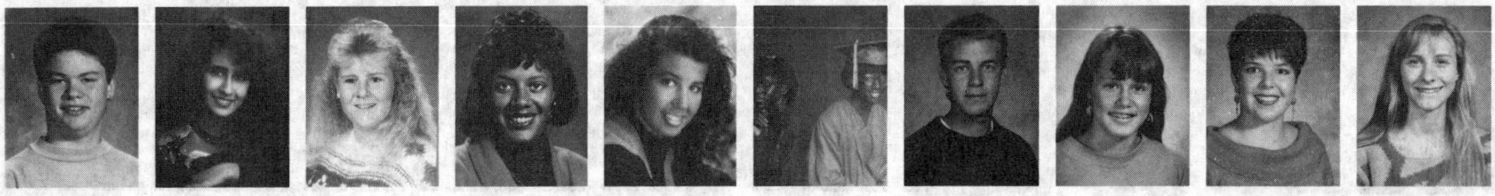

Pound, Jr Will B
Carlmont HS
Redwood City, CA

Pourhamidi, Jaleh
Mt Carmel HS
San Diego, CA

Powell, Jennie G
Mt Diablo HS
Concord, CA

Powell, Nichole C
Pilgrim Schl
Los Angeles, CA

Powell, Retta
San Luis Obispo SR
San Luis Obispo, CA

Powell, Vanessa Joy
Carson HS
Carson, CA

Power, Chris W
Woodcrest Christian
Corona, CA

Power, Erin T
Ukiah HS
Redwood Valley, CA

Powers, Amber C
Oak Ridge HS
Camino, CA

Powers, Julie E
San Juan HS
Citrus Heights, CA

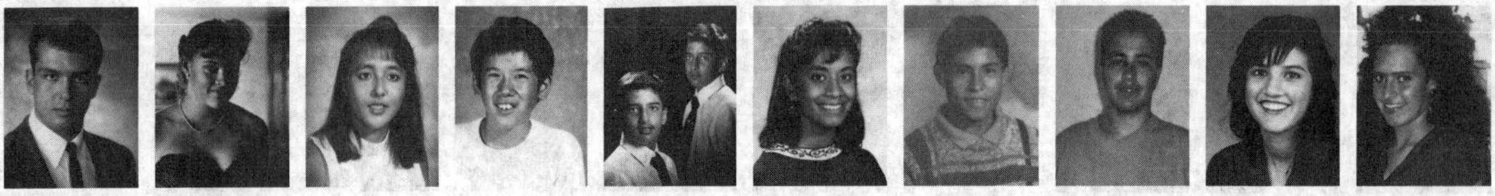

Powers, Michael W
Chaminade College
Prep
Northridge, CA

Powers, Shara T
Coalinga-Huron
Unified HS
Coalinga, CA

Powers, Toni A
Sherman E
Burroughs HS
Ridgecrest, CA

Poy, Vincent C
International Studies
Acad
San Francisco, CA

Pozo, Santiago P
Mark Keppel HS
Monterey Park, CA

Prabhakar, Pavitra
Whitney HS
Cerritos, CA

Prado, Abimael
Monache HS
Porterville, CA

Prado, Chad A
Hamilton Music
Acad
Sylmar, CA

Prado, Cynthia A
St Joseph HS
Norwalk, CA

Prado, Esperanza
Santiago HS
Santa Ana, CA

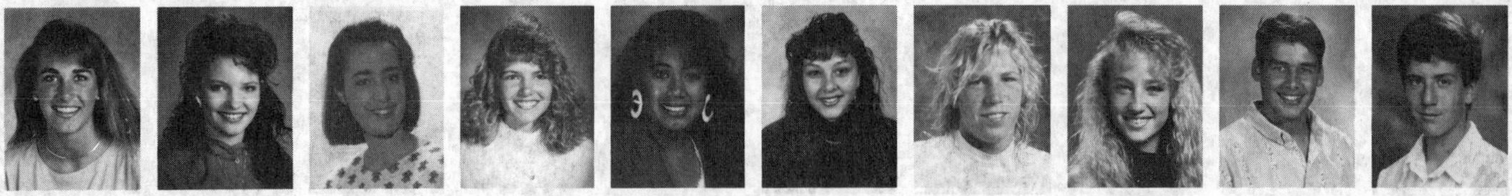

Prahm, Kelly
St Francis HS
Los Altos, CA

Prat, Chantel S
Manteca HS
Manteca, CA

Pratt, Jennifer M
Grace M Davis HS
Modesto, CA

Prauss, Jenifer
Del Norte HS
Crescent City, CA

Preclaro, Joddi
Bishop Amat
Memorial HS
Oceanside, CA

Preftokis, Anastasia
Skyline HS
Oakland, CA

Prescott, Zac A
Dana Hills HS
Dana Point, CA

Presley, April Dawn
Fontana HS
Fontana, CA

Presley, Jason
Lutheran HS
Norco, CA

Presley, III Marion E
Poway HS
Columbia, SC

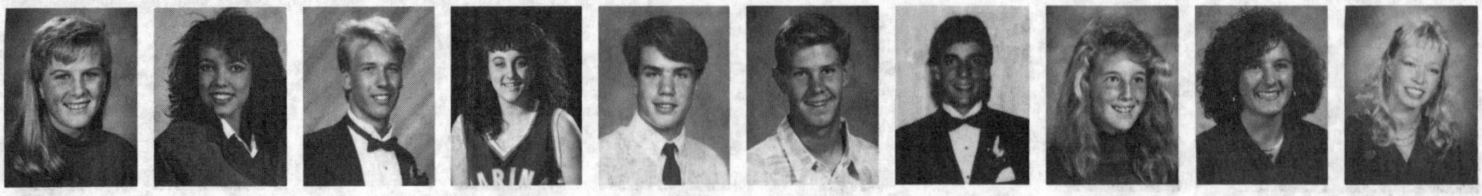

Preston, Elizabeth K
Torrey Pines HS
San Diego, CA

Preston, India A
Santa Clara HS
Oxnard, CA

Preston, Richard R
Cajon HS
San Bernardino, CA

Presutti, Annie J
Marina HS
Huntington Beach,
CA

Price, Bernard J
Sun Set HS
Hayward, CA

Price, Christopher J
Capistrano Valley HS
Mission Viejo, CA

Price, Evan P
Oakdale HS
Waterford, CA

Price, Heather M
Marysville HS
Marysville, CA

Price, Laura M
Cuyama Valley HS
Cuyama, CA

Price, Michelle C
North HS
Bakersfield, CA

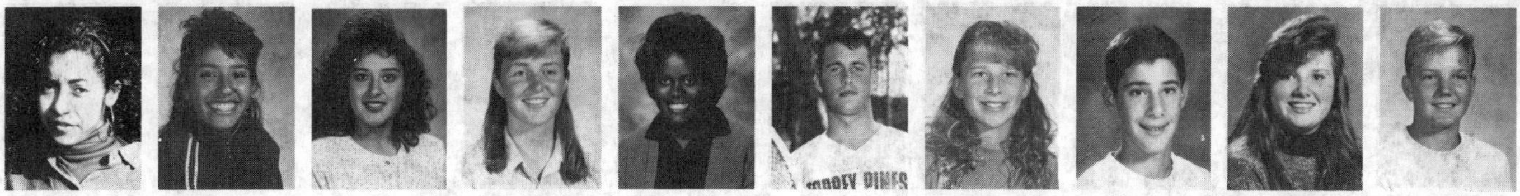

Price, Stephanie E
Skyline HS
Oakland, CA

Prieto, Monique
Moorpark HS
Moorpark, CA

Prieto, Rachel G
Eisenhower HS
Rialto, CA

Prigge, Laura L
Woodland HS
Woodland, CA

Prime, Mary
Fairfield HS
Fairfield, CA

Principi, IV Anthony
Torry Pines HS
Rancho Santa Fe, CA

Probstfield, Brandi
Douglass JR HS
Woodland, CA

Proclivo, Andrew
Poway HS
San Diego, CA

Proctor, Virginia S.
San Pedro HS
San Pedro, CA

Prokop, Larry E
Woodland HS
Woodland, CA

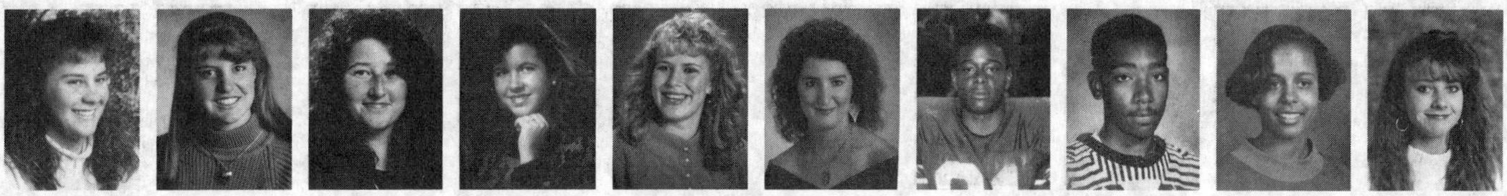

Propseri, Juliane M
Red Bluff HS
Red Bluff, CA

Prosser, Melinda L
Crescenta Valley HS
Glendale, CA

Prosyak, Margarita
Birmingham HS
Reseda, CA

Prouty, Heather
Turlock Christian HS
Turlock, CA

Prouty, Katie
Northview HS
Covina, CA

Provost, Theresa J
Santa Clara HS
Santa Clara, CA

Pruitt, Cash Xavier
La Sierra HS
Riverside, CA

Pruitt, Marcus W
Washington
Preparatory HS
Los Angeles, CA

Pruitt, Myeasha
Lynwood Adventist
Acad
Paramount, CA

Pruitt, Scarlet M
Monterey HS
Pebble Beach, CA

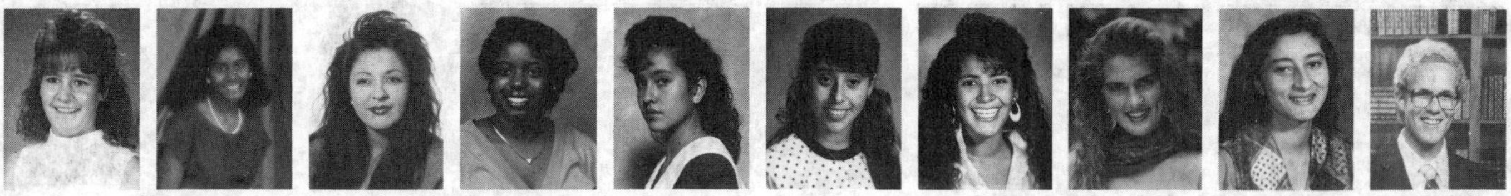

Puckett, Sonia
Liberty Union HS
Pittsburg, CA

Pudhnum, Vahini
Mira Loma HS
Sacramento, CA

Puentes, Claudia
Point Loma HS
San Diego, CA

Pugh, Brenda K
O Farrell SCPA
San Diego, CA

Pulido, Audelia T
Delta HS
Walnut Grove, CA

Pulido, Onesima
Livingston HS
Livingston, CA

Pulido, Veronica A
John H Francis
Polytechnic HS
Sun Valley, CA

Pummill, Dana L
Harbor HS
Riverbank, CA

Punia, Harkiran
Irvington HS
Fremont, CA

Punt, Steven
Calvary Chapel HS
Fountain Valley, CA

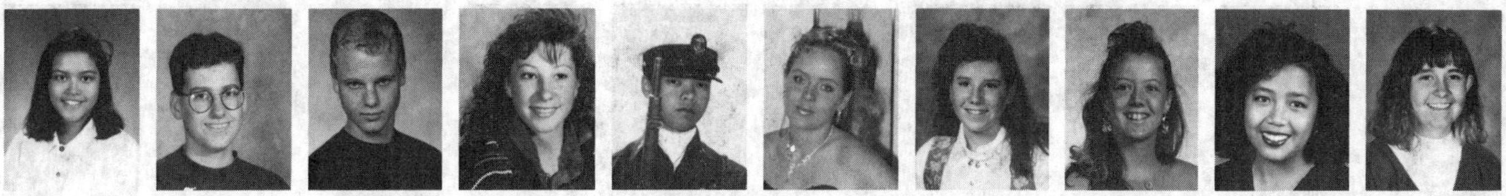

Punzalan, Cristina
Granada Hills HS
Northridge, CA

Pura, Albert A
Washington HS
San Francisco, CA

Purcell, Jason M
Sunset HS
Hayward, CA

Purcell, Jennifer A
Arroyo Grande HS
Nipomo, CA

Purificacion, Dennis
Milpitas HS
Milpitas, CA

Purinton, Michelle D
Newport Harbor HS
Costa Mesa, CA

Purnell, Tamara L
Fairfield HS
Fairfield, CA

Purse, Tamra L
Santa Clara HS
Santa Clara, CA

Purugganan, Roselyn
St Joseph HS
Long Beach, CA

Putman, Lisa N
Clovis HS
Clovis, CA

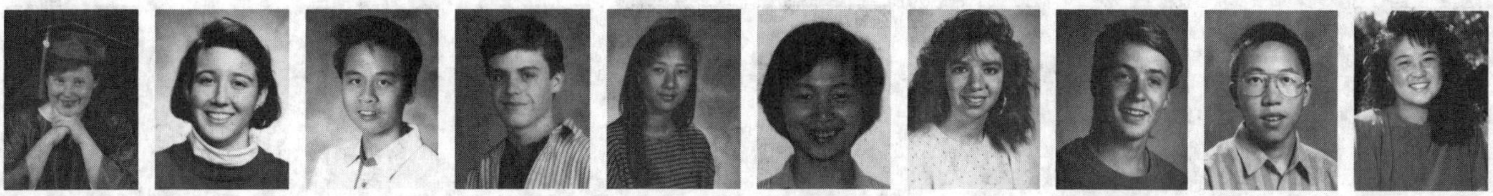

Putnam, Christine L
South Beach HS
Burbank, CA

Puttere, Jennifer
Loretto HS
Sacramento, CA

Puzon, Jan-Paul N
Palos Verdes HS
Palos Vrds Pen, CA

Pyle, Jeremy L
Redlands SR HS
Redlands, CA

Quach, Anh T
Valley View HS
Moreno Valley, CA

Quach, Phuong N
George Washington
San Francisco, CA

Quaid, Cynthia M
Eisenhower HS
Rialto, CA

Qualls, Bryan D
Clovis West HS
Fresno, CA

Quan, Albert W
San Marino HS
San Marino, CA

Quan, Margaret
Pioneer HS
San Jose, CA

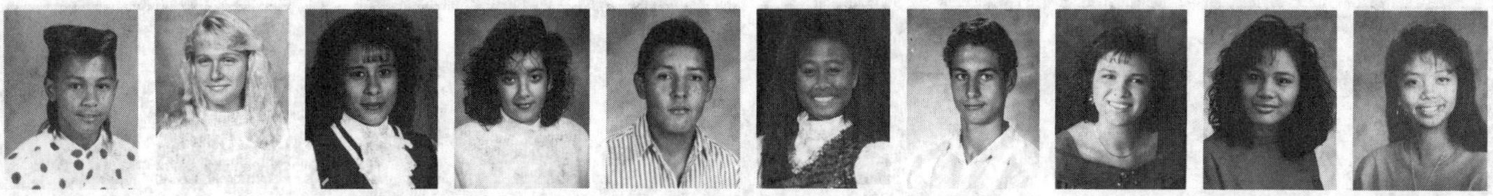

Que, Darrell
Coachella Valley HS
Coachella, CA

Queen, Jennifer S
University City HS
San Diego, CA

Quevedo, Marissa
Porterville HS
Porterville, CA

Quezada, Claudia E
Clairemont HS
San Diego, CA

Quezada, Miquel
Dos Palos HS
Firebaugh, CA

Quiambao, Cherry
Whitney HS
Cerritos, CA

Quidor, Bryce E
Chino HS
Chino, CA

Quijada, Renata I
William Workman
Valinda, CA

Quijano, Grace A
Beyer HS
Modesto, CA

Quilala, Florizza C
St Joseph HS
Cerritos, CA

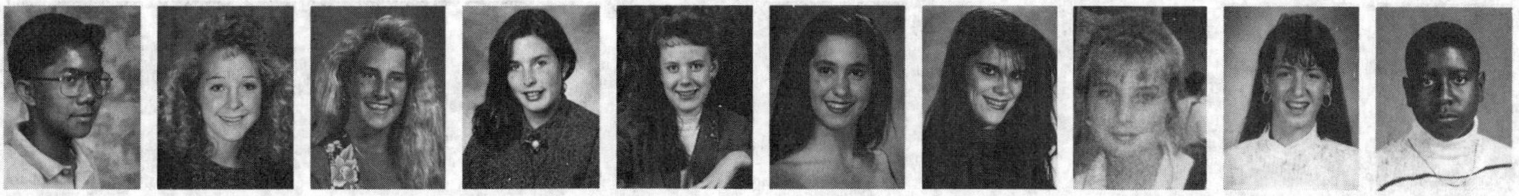

Quileza, Michael
Bishop Amat
Memorial HS
Baldwin Park, CA

Quimby, Kristina L
Apple Valley SR HS
Apple Valley, CA

Quin, Cynthia Jean
Canyon Springs HS
Moreno Valley, CA

Quincannon, Emily A
University Of San
Diego HS
Newport, RI

Quinlin, Rachel
Mother Lode
Christian Schl
Sonora, CA

Quinn, April Adena
Westminster HS
Westminster, CA

Quinn, Colleen
Tustin HS
Tustin, CA

Quinn, Colleen C
Carondelet HS
Lisle, IL

Quinn, Lisa
Ukiah HS
Ukiah, CA

Quinn, Nick G
St Bernards HS
Los Angeles, CA

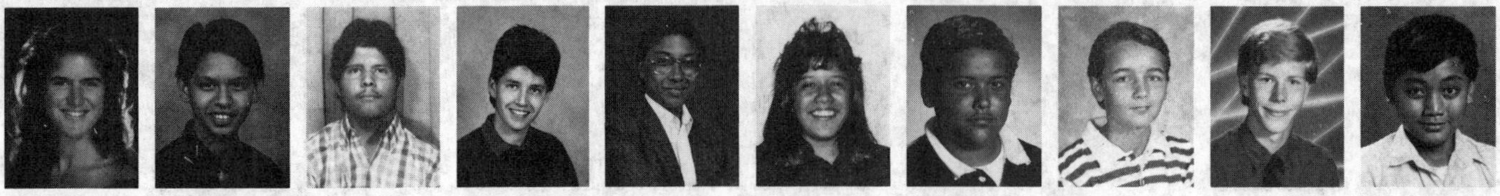

Quinn, Rebecca E
Pleasant Valley HS
Chico, CA

Quintanilla, Vincent
El Cajon Valley HS
El Cajon, CA

Quintero Villegas, Victor H
Locke HS
Los Angeles, CA

Quinteros, Juan Carlos
Canoga Park HS
Canoga Park, CA

Quinto, Jeffrey G
San Leandro HS
San Leandro, CA

Quiroz, Belia E
Calexico HS
Calexico, CA

Quiroz, Carlos U
Calexico Adventist Mission Acad
Calexico, CA

Quist, Don C
Rio Linda HS
Sacramento, CA

Quitmeyer, David
John Jenkins Christian Acad
Santa Paula, CA

Quizon, Kenneth P
Eagle Rock HS
Los Angeles, CA

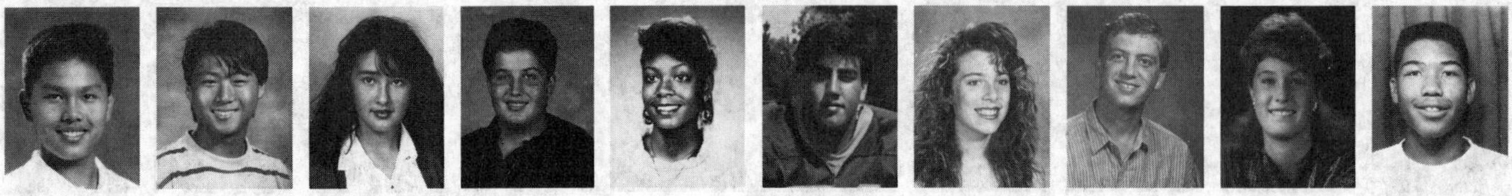

Quon, Lawrence Y
Eagle Rock HS
Los Angeles, CA

Ra, Philip
Fountain Valley HS
Fountain Valley, CA

Racek, Nichole M
Academy Of Our Lady Of Peace
Chula Vista, CA

Rachshtut, Mickey
Einstein Acad
Encino, CA

Racy, Tarise S
Mt Diablo HS
Pittsburg, CA

Radden, Robert J
Patrick Henry HS
San Diego, CA

Rader, Gina Lea
Central Valley HS
Central Valley, CA

Rader, Jeremy
Heritage Christian
Brea, CA

Raffel, Michelle Diane
Yucaipo HS
Yucaipa, CA

Ragland, Charles
El Camino HS
Oceanside, CA

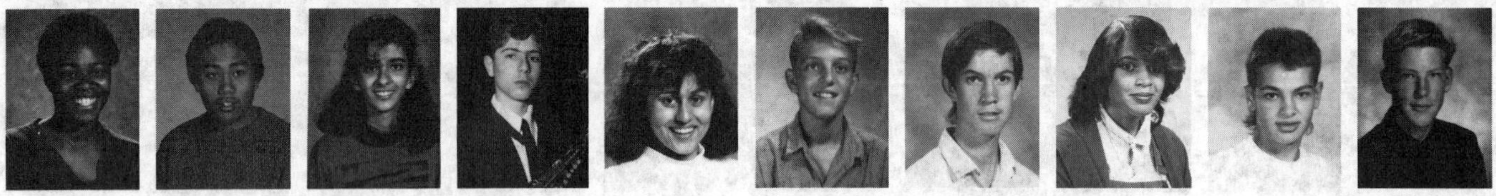

Ragland, Meishaunee
Carlmont HS
East Palo Alto, CA

Raguindin, Raymond
South San Francisco
S San Francisco, CA

Rahebi, Bita
San Ramon Valley
Danville, CA

Rahhal, Ellis M
Eisenhower HS
Rialto, CA

Rahimian, Jeannine
Palisades HS
Los Angeles, CA

Railsback, Ryan J
Notre Dame HS
Riverside, CA

Rainey, James B
Las Alamitos HS
Long Beach, CA

Rainey, Nycole
Galileo HS
San Francisco, CA

Rains, Tom F
Canyon HS
Canyon Country, CA

Rakoski, Scott K
Paraclete HS
Palmdale, CA

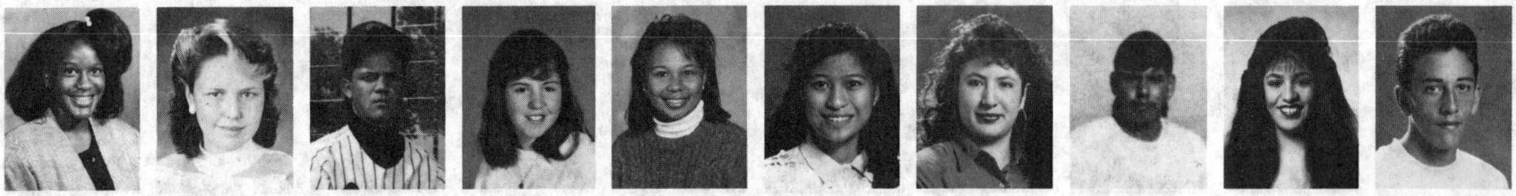

Rambo, Bridgette
Polytechnic HS
Moreno Valley, CA

Rambo, Carla J
Ramona HS
Riverside, CA

Rambonga, Barry C
Orosi HS
Orosi, CA

Ramey, Tracey D
Fort Bragg HS
Fort Bragg, CA

Ramil, Tressy
Mt Carmel HS
San Diego, CA

Ramirez, Armi-Claudine E
Gardena HS
Carson, CA

Ramirez, Eulalia F
Garfield HS
Los Angeles, CA

Ramirez, Francisco
San Jose HS
San Jose, CA

Ramirez, Henrietta
Ontario HS
Ontario, CA

Ramirez, Joey
Santa Paula Union
Santa Paula, CA

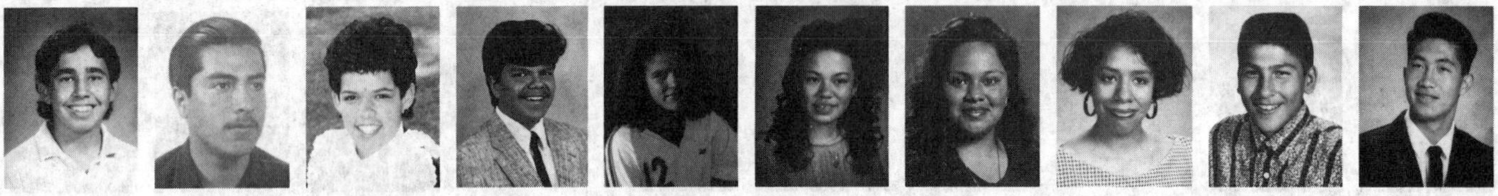

Ramirez, John D
Villa Park HS
Orange, CA

Ramirez, John P
Baldwin Park HS
Baldwin Park, CA

Ramirez, Joy M
Kerman HS
Kerman, CA

Ramirez, Luis E
Fontana HS
Fontana, CA

Ramirez, Margarita
Armijo HS
Suisun City, CA

Ramirez, Margie G
Madera HS
Madera, CA

Ramirez, Maricela
Sierra Vista HS
Baldwin Park, CA

Ramirez, Martha
Modesto HS
Modesto, CA

Ramirez, Miguel S
Notre Dame HS
Riverside, CA

Ramirez, Richard D
Northview HS
Covina, CA

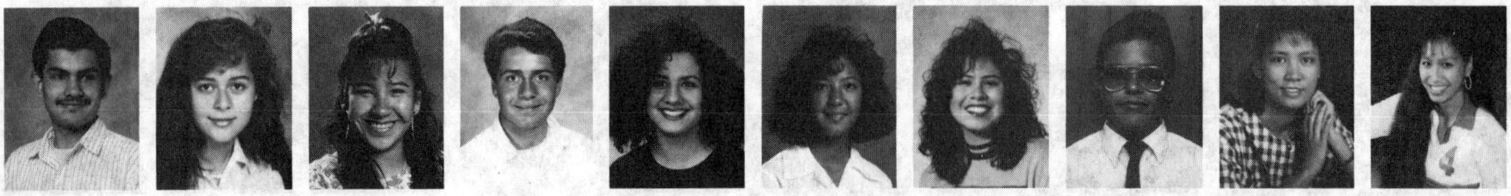

Ramirez, Victor Hugo
Montclair HS
Montclair, CA

Ramirez, Zenaida M
St Genevieve HS
Van Nuys, CA

Ramirios, Esther
Hawthorne HS
Hawthorne, CA

Ramorino, Monti
St Genevieve HS
Panorama, CA

Ramos, Alicia Noel
Alhambra HS
Martinez, CA

Ramos, Bernadette
Garces HS
Delano, CA

Ramos, Brenda L
Chaffey HS
Ontario, CA

Ramos, Javier E
Schurr HS
Monterey Park, CA

Ramos, Jingle Maynigo
South Tahoe HS
S Lake Tahoe, CA

Ramos, Judy Lynn B
Santa Clara HS
Santa Clara, CA

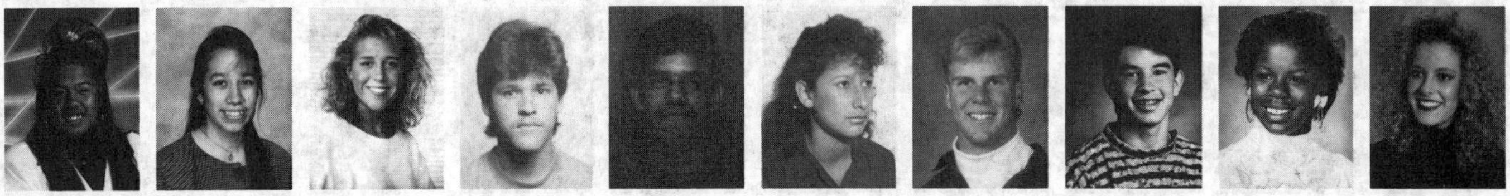

Ramos, Larissa C
Westmoor HS
Daly City, CA

Ramos, Linda S
Alverno HS
Pasadena, CA

Ramos, Nicole L
Etiwanda HS
Rancho Cucamonga, CA

Ramos, Oscar
San Benito HS
Hollister, CA

Ramos, Rodolfo
Montclair HS
Montclair, CA

Ramos, Rosalba
Brawley Union HS
Brawley, CA

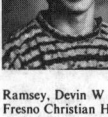

Ramsey, Brian
Redwood HS
Visalia, CA

Ramsey, Devin W
Fresno Christian HS
Clovis, CA

Ramsey, Marshalette
Los Amigos HS
Santa Ana, CA

Ramsey, Nicole Marie
Edison HS
Huntington Bch, CA

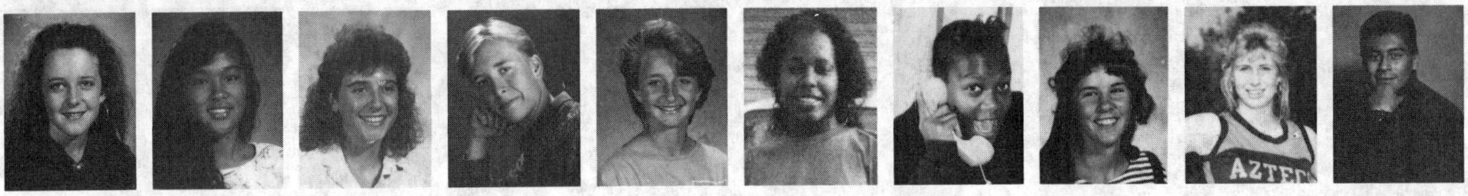

Ramseyer, Joy D
Calvary Chapel HS
Fountain Valley, CA

Rana, Eileen M
Cornelia Connelly HS
Garden Grove, CA

Randal, Jennifer L
Nevada Union HS
Nevada City, CA

Randall, Peter W
Sonora HS
Sonora, CA

Randleman, Robyn
Ponderosa HS
Shingle Springs, CA

Randolph, Alicia D
John F Kennedy HS
Sacramento, CA

Randolph, Lakisha
Edison HS
Fresno, CA

Raney, Athena
Barstow HS
Barstow, CA

Raney, Renee
Barstow HS
Barstow, CA

Rangel, Isai L
Nogales HS
La Puente, CA

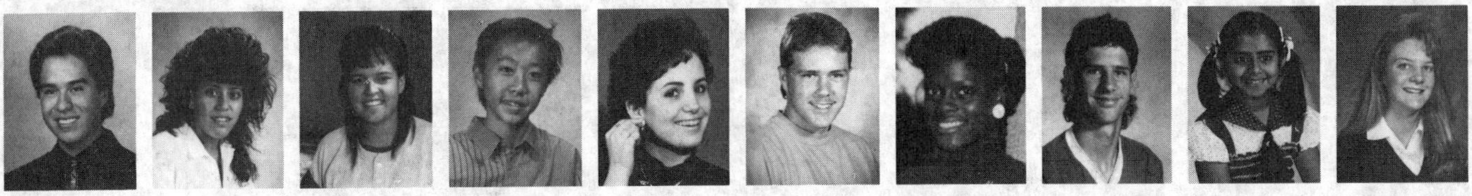

Rangel, Jr Nick
Huntington Bch HS
Huntington Beach, CA

Rangel, Rosalba
Hesperia HS
Hesperia, CA

Rangel, Tristin F
Orestimba HS
Newman, CA

Rangsith, Don
Mark Keppel HS
Monterey Park, CA

Ranieri, Elizabeth
Caustoga HS
Calistoga, CA

Rankin, Chad G
Orosi HS
Orosi, CA

Ransom, Tenaya Mildred
James Lick HS
San Jose, CA

Ranstrom, Corey J
Independence HS
San Jose, CA

Rao, Sheela
University HS
Irvine, CA

Rapp, Patricia A
La Reina HS
Agoura Hills, CA

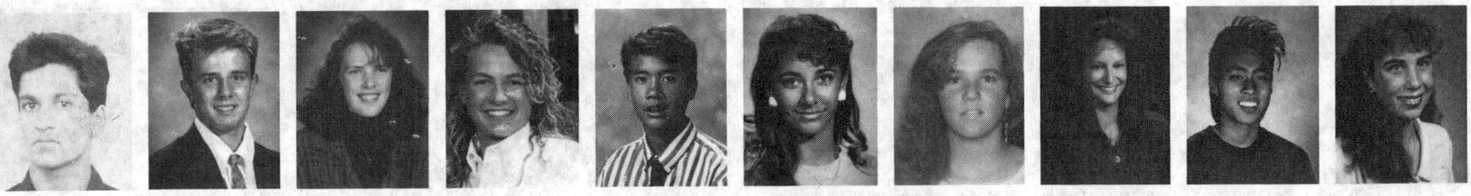

Rasiah, Prasanna
Oak Grove Schl
Ojai, CA

Rasic, Anthony M
Mater Dei HS
Huntington Bch, CA

Ratcliff, Kristen L
Portola JR/SR HS
Portola, CA

Rathgeber, Toby
San Clemente HS
San Clemente, CA

Ratkovic, Michael P
Loyola HS
Los Angeles, CA

Ratliff, Laura
Marina HS
Westminster, CA

Rattan, Jennifer D
Elsinore HS
Lake Elsinore, CA

Ravaioli, Gina
Moorpark HS
Moorpark, CA

Raval, Paul J
Clovis HS
Clovis, CA

Ravano, Suzanne M
Notre Dame HS
San Carlos, CA

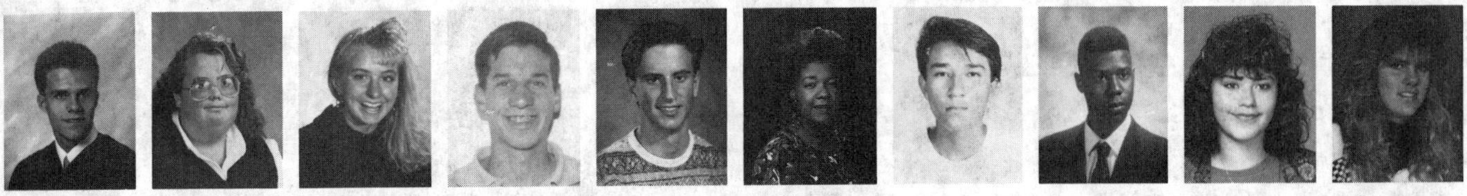

Ravenkamp, Scott
Ontario HS
Ontario, CA

Ravet, Jennifer A
Saint Joseph Notre Dame HS
Alameda, CA

Rawls, Adele L
Bloomington Christian HS
Bloomington, CA

Ray, Christopher K
Bonita HS
La Verne, CA

Ray, John J
Troy HS
Yorba Linda, CA

Ray, Tahirah Oni
Baldwin Park HS
Baldwin Park, CA

Rayas, Pedro
Norco HS
Corona, CA

Rayford, Wayne L
Apple Valley HS
Apple Valley, CA

Razo, Claudia B
Manual Arts HS
Los Angeles, CA

Razzani, Michele
Perris HS
Nuevo, CA

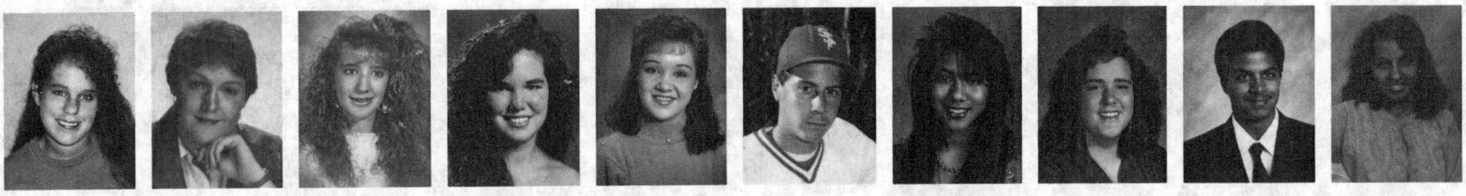

Read, Wendy D
Liberty Union HS
Byron, CA

Reade, Michelle
Valley HS
Sacramento, CA

Reagle, Leanna
North HS
Bakersfield, CA

Reardon, Kerri
Burbank HS
Burbank, CA

Reber, Marrietta R
Foothill HS
Santa Ana, CA

Rebollini, Michael
South San Francisco
South San Francis, CA

Recaido, Leslie S
Samuel F B Morse
San Diego, CA

Reclusado, Tracy A
South Tahoe HS
South Lake Tahoe, CA

Reddi, Sridhar
Irvine HS
Irvine, CA

Reddy, Swapna V
Notre Dame HS
Salinas, CA

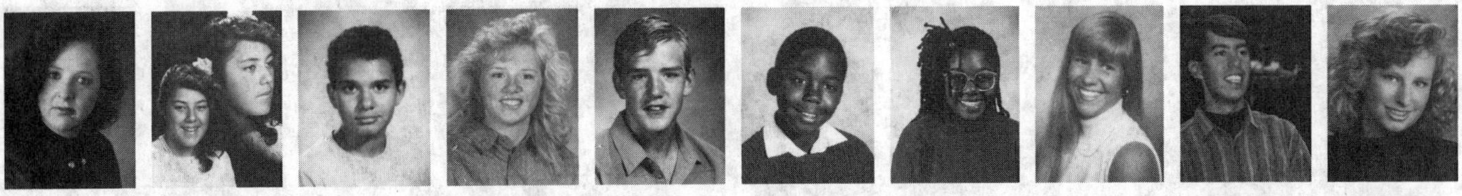

Redfield, Keiri M
Rio Lindo Acad
Woodland, CA

Reding, Christina L
Paramount HS
Paramount, CA

Redjai, Ali
Newport Harbor HS
Newport Beach, CA

Redlin, Heather R
Victor Valley HS
Victorville, CA

Redlin, William P
Victor Valley HS
Victorville, CA

Redmon, John Paul
Golden Gate Acad
Oakland, CA

Redmon, Mary E
Golden Gate Acad
Oakland, CA

Redondo, Lori L
Grossmont HS
La Mesa, CA

Reece, Matthew P
El Cajon Valley HS
El Cajon, CA

Reed, Alisha
Palmdale HS
Agua Dulce, CA

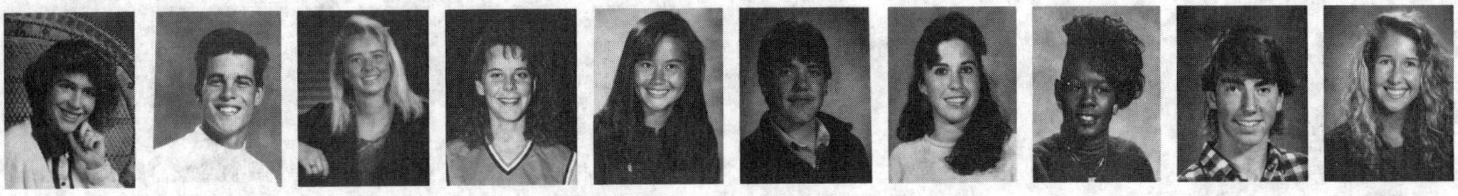

Reed, Beth A
Elk Grove HS
Sacramento, CA

Reed, Chad B
Fontana HS
Fontana, CA

Reed, Lori L
Clovis HS
Fresno, CA

Reed, Marcella L
Oak Park HS
Agoura Hills, CA

Reed, Mary E
Davis SR HS
Davis, CA

Reed, Matt
Mc Kinleyville HS
Trinidad, CA

Reed, Stephanie L
Yucaipa HS
Yucaipa, CA

Reed, Tawili M
San Leandro HS
San Leandro, CA

Reed, Trent A W
Edison HS
Warwick, RI

Reed, Wendy M
Laguna Hills HS
Laguna Hills, CA

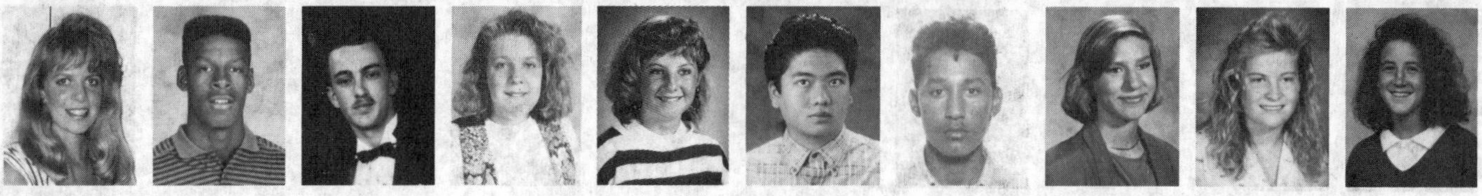

Reek, Nicole
Oakmont HS
Danville, CA

Reese, Mark A
Dos Palos HS
Dos Palos, CA

Reese, Roger D
Selma HS
Selma, CA

Reeve, Joy
Yosemite Union HS
Oakhurst, CA

Reeves, Malinda
East Union HS
Manteca, CA

Regala, Jay J
Diamond Bar HS
Diamond Bar, CA

Regalado, Guillermo
Alisal HS
Salinas, CA

Regoli, Natalie L
Atascadero HS
Atascadero, CA

Reichenbach, Andrea
Las Plumas HS
Oroville, CA

Reilly, Jeanne
St Patrick-St Vincent
Benicia, CA

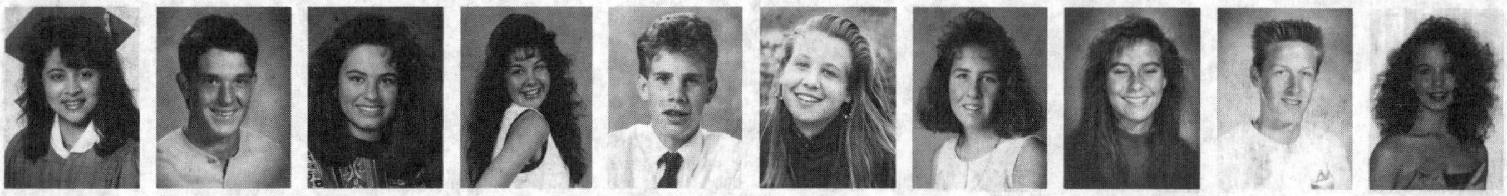

Reina, Ingrid C
California HS
Whittier, CA

Reinecker, James G
Northview HS
Covina, CA

Reinesto, Dena B
San Marcos HS
Santa Barbara, CA

Reinhardt, Danielle C
Enterprise HS
Redding, CA

Reining, Matthew T
Loyola HS
Northridge, CA

Reinys, Emily
Poway HS
Poway, CA

Reis, Teresa
Quartz Hill HS
Lancaster, CA

Reiter, Natalie
El Camino Real HS
West Hills, CA

Reitz, Greg A
Huntington Beach
Huntington Beach, CA

Remick, Melissa R
Oakmont HS
Roseville, CA

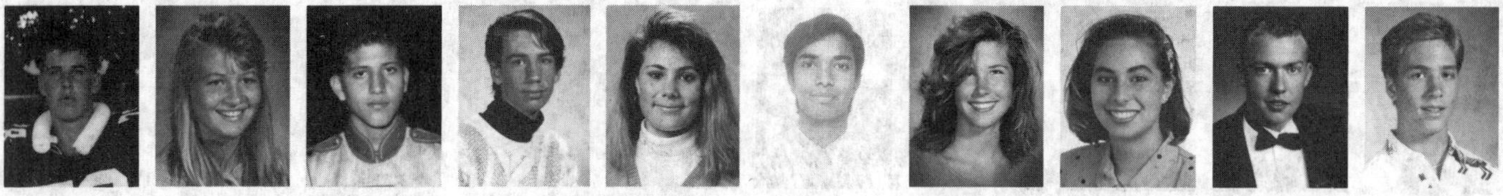

Remley, Craig C
Valley View HS
Moreno Valley, CA

Rennick, Christy
Williams HS
Williams, CA

Renteria, John H
Brawley Union HS
Brawley, CA

Reordan, Richrd L
Will C Wood HS
Vacaville, CA

Repola, Shannon
Mira Costa HS
Manhattan Beach, CA

Rethual, Mario G
Lincoln Medical Magnet HS
Los Angeles, CA

Reulbach, Carrie H
El Camino Real HS
Woodland Hills, CA

Reuschel, Suzette
Saint Francis HS
Saratoga, CA

Reuss, IV William M
West Valley HS
Cottonwood, CA

Reuterskiold, David
Cabrillo HS
Lompoc, CA

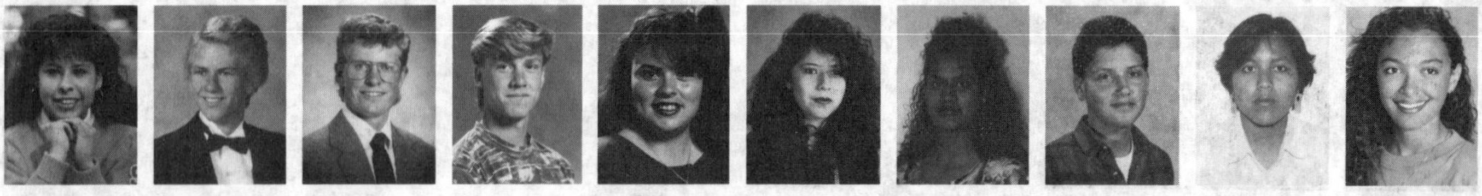

Revilla, Kristine
Montebello HS
Alhambra, CA

Rex, Kyle T
Antelope Valley Union HS
Lancaster, CA

Rex, Ryan G
Edison HS
Huntington Bch, CA

Rexinger, Doug
Colton HS
Colton, CA

Reyes, Angelica
Garfield HS
Los Angeles, CA

Reyes, Diana Q
Amos Alonzo Stagg
Stockton, CA

Reyes, Elodia M
Porterville HS
Porterville, CA

Reyes, Manuel
Ernest Righetti HS
Guadalupe, CA

Reyes, Maria
Sweetwater HS
National City, CA

Reyes, Michele
Palm Springs HS
Palm Springs, CA

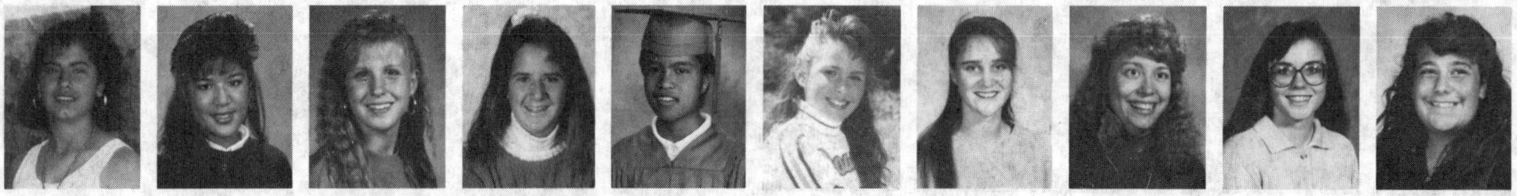

Reyes, Olga
Garfield HS
Los Angeles, CA

Reyes, Stephanie Christine L
Immaculate Heart
Los Angeles, CA

Reyna, Karen Jean
Archbishop Mitty HS
San Jose, CA

Reynick, Kimberly A
Woodside HS
Redwood City, CA

Reyno, Garey
Bishop Montgomery
Carson, CA

Reynolds, Amber D
Thomas Downey HS
Modesto, CA

Reynolds, Bonnie J
Venice HS
Los Angeles, CA

Reynolds, Debra J
Redwood Christian
Castro Valley, CA

Reynolds, Evelyn
Southbay Christian
Mountain View, CA

Reynolds, Heather E
River City HS
W Sacramento, CA

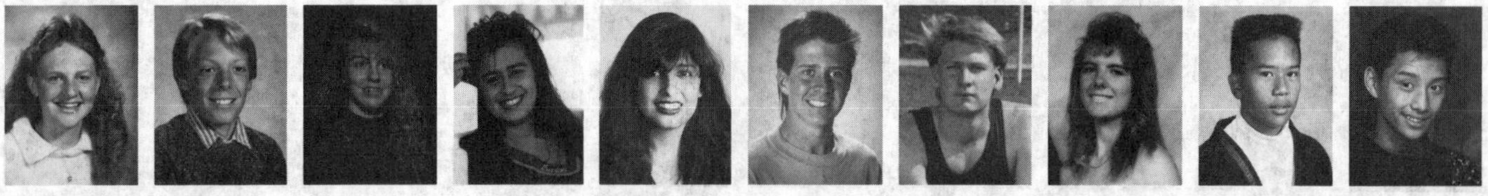

Reynolds, J Janette
Patrick Henry HS
San Diego, CA

Reynolds, John Christopher
Arroyo Grande HS
Nipomo, CA

Reynolds, Kristin M
Oak Ridge HS
Cameron Park, CA

Reynoso, Maribel V
Anaheim HS
Anaheim, CA

Rezai, Jasmine
Schurr HS
Monterey Park, CA

Rezinas, Richard M
Oakdale HS
Oakdale, CA

Rhay, Richard A
Riverside Polytechnic
Riverside, CA

Rhodes, Stephanie A
Etiwanda HS
Etiwanda, CA

Ricafrente, Jonathan
Vintage HS
Vallejo, CA

Ricardo, Cecil
St Genevieve HS
Panorama, CA

PHOTO
NOT
AVAILABLE

Riccomini, Catherine
Garces Memorial HS
Buttonwillow, CA

Rice, Ann F
San Rafael HS
San Rafael, CA

Rice, Chris
Bullard HS
Fresno, CA

Rice, Kali K
St Patrick St Vincent
Vallejo, CA

Rice, Suzanne R
Fontana HS
Fontana, CA

Rich, David
Los Alamitos HS
Los Alamitos, CA

Rich, Melanie Susanne
Hillsdale HS
San Mateo, CA

Rich, Shannon
Antioch HS
Antioch, CA

Rich, Tatum M
Merced HS
Merced, CA

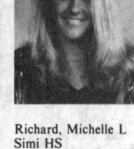

Richard, Michelle L
Simi HS
Simi Valley, CA

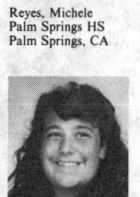

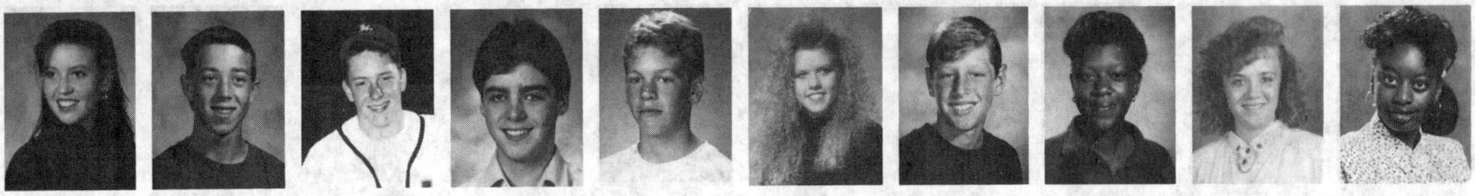

Richards, Dana
U S Grant HS
Sherman Oaks, CA

Richards, Douglas K
Bullard HS
Fresno, CA

Richards, Jeffrey H
Las Lomas HS
Walnut Creek, CA

Richards, Josh
Fall Rivers JR SR
Fall River Mills, CA

Richards, M Rami
Piedmont HS
Piedmont, CA

Richards, Stacy
Central Union HS
El Centro, CA

Richards, Walt
Fullerton Union HS
Fullerton, CA

Richardson, Carol
Washington Prep HS
Los Angeles, CA

Richardson, Carrie M
Redlands SR HS
Pensacola, FL

Richardson, Kanika
Etiwanda HS
Alta Loma, CA

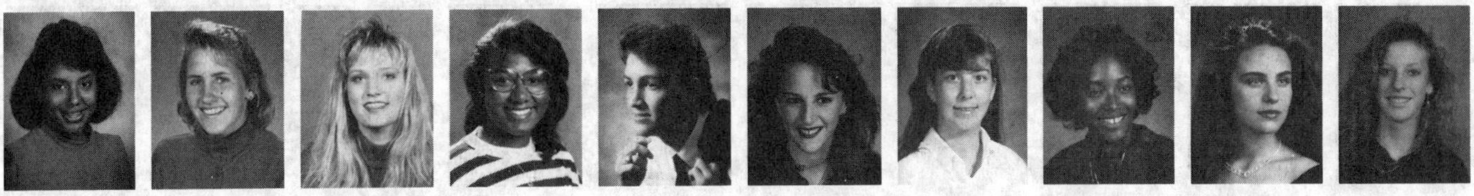

Richardson, Nicole
John F Kennedy HS
La Palma, CA

Richardson, Patricia Marie
Pinole Valley HS
Hercules, CA

Richardson, Rebecca
Beaumont HS
Beaumont, CA

Richardson, Tyea Nichelle
Gardena HS
Gardena, CA

Richey, Keith
Capital Christian HS
Sacramento, CA

Richey, Michelle
Atwater HS
Moreno Valley, CA

Richmond, Kristine D
Mater Dei HS
Huntington Bch, CA

Richmond, Rhonda L
John Muir HS
Altadena, CA

Richter, Astrid A
Concord HS
Concord, CA

Richtmyer, Tara L
Redlands HS
Highland, CA

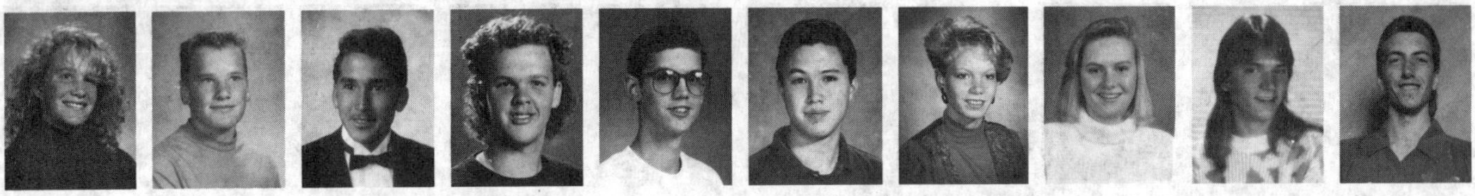

Ricketts, Amber L
Oak Park HS
Agoura Hills, CA

Ricketts, Warren R
Oak Park HS
Agoura Hills, CA

Ricketts, Jr William
Hilltop HS
Chula Vista, CA

Rickman, Kenneth A
San Jacinto HS
San Jacinto, CA

Riddle, Steven
Davis HS
Modesto, CA

Ridge, Bryan T
Westmoor HS
Colma, CA

Ridgway, Lori
Del Norte HS
Crescent City, CA

Rieck, Alina K
Redlands HS
Redlands, CA

Riedel, Allen
Ernest Righetti HS
Orcutt, CA

Rieff, Chris
Fountain Valley HS
Fountain Valley, CA

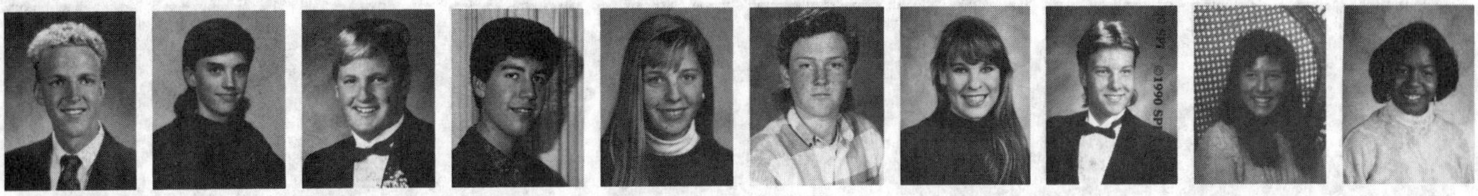

Riegel, Marc W
Mount Whitney HS
Visalia, CA

Ries, Sean M A
Valhalla HS
Lakeside, CA

Riess, Jr John K
Bonita Vista HS
Bonita, CA

Rieth, David J
Novato HS
Novato, CA

Rigge, Sherry
Benicia HS
Benicia, CA

Riggins, Sean G
Borrego Springs HS
Borrego Springs, CA

Riggle, Antonia C
El Camino Fundamental HS
Sacramento, CA

Riise, Michael
Pinole Valley HS
Pinole, CA

Rikkers, Kristin M
El Camino Fundamental HS
Sacramento, CA

Riles, Elizabeth L
Berkeley HS
Oakland, CA

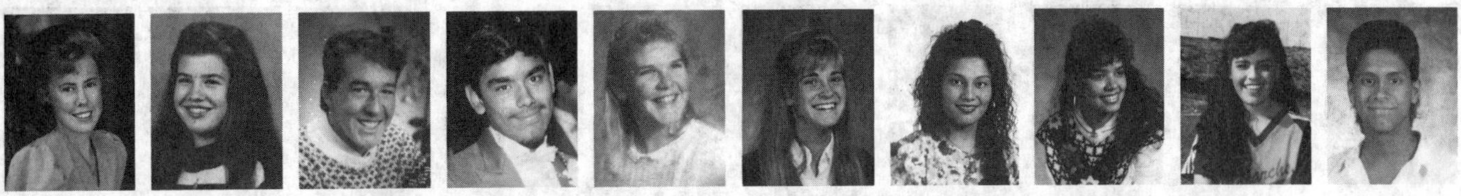

Riley, Elizabeth E
Nordhoff HS
Oak View, CA

Riley, Jennifer L
California HS
Whittier, CA

Riley, Mike
East Union HS
Manteca, CA

Rincon, Leonardo
Sherman Oaks C E S
Los Angeles, CA

Rindahl, Jennifer L
Mayfair HS
Lakewood, CA

Ringler, Brandi T
La Reina HS
Thousand Oaks, CA

Rios, Adriana M
Gahr HS
Norwalk, CA

Rios, Estela
San Fernando HS
San Fernando, CA

Rios, Felicia R
Monte Vista HS
Spring Valley, CA

Rios, Jose L
Indio Rajahs HS
Palm Desert, CA

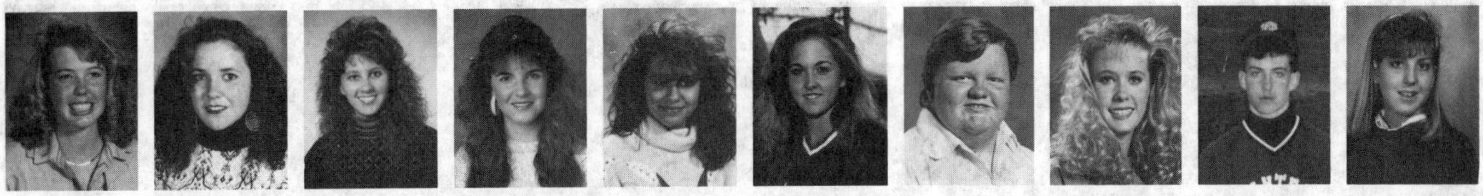

Ripley, Nicole A
Red Bluff HS
Red Bluff, CA

Rique, Arlette M
Hilltop HS
Chula Vista, CA

Risher, Christine J
Schurr HS
Montebello, CA

Risher, Elissa
Palmdale HS
Palmdale, CA

Risse, Marcee M
Moorpark HS
Moorpark, CA

Ristuccia, Kimberly
Bellarmine Jefferson
North Hollywood, CA

Ritchey, Dale D
San Gorgonio HS
San Bernardino, CA

Ritchie, Mandy
Delano HS
Delano, CA

Ritchie, Philip M
Winters Joint Union
Winters, CA

Ritter, Michelle L
Golden West HS
Visalia, CA

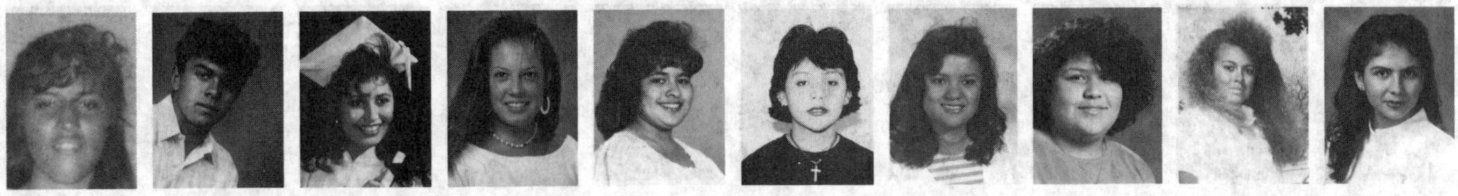

Rivas, Cindy
Bell Gardens HS
Bell Gardens, CA

Rivas, Jorge A
Calexico HS
Calexico, CA

Rivas, Karla C
Victor Valley SR HS
Victorville, CA

Rivas, Lauri A
Sunny Hills HS
Buena Park, CA

Rivas, Marie M
Arroyo HS
El Monte, CA

Rivas, Socorro
Jefferson HS
Daly City, CA

Rivas, Yesenia
Woodland HS
Yolo, CA

Rivera, Alicia
Deland HS
Delano, CA

Rivera, Arcadia G
Sunset HS
Hayward, CA

Rivera, Daisy H
Hamilton HS
Los Angeles, CA

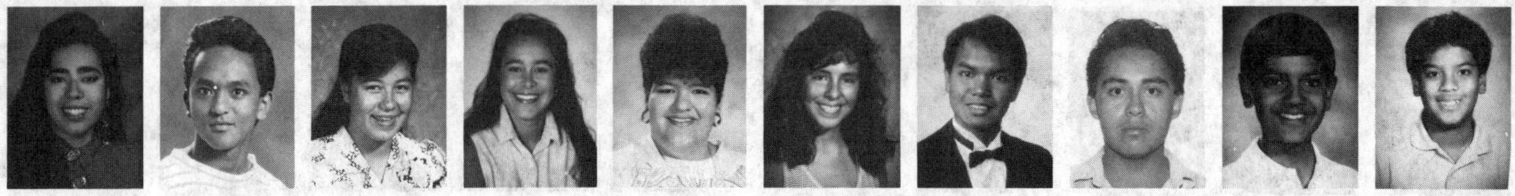

Rivera, Digna R
Bishop Amat HS
West Covina, CA

Rivera, Gilbert M
Eagle Rock HS
Los Angeles, CA

Rivera, Graciela C
Woodside HS
Redwood City, CA

Rivera, Jackie
Atwater HS
Merced, CA

Rivera, Jacqueline M
Grant HS
Los Angeles, CA

Rivera, Jo Ann
Wasco HS
Wasco, CA

Rivera, Nicolas Ooka
Mar Vista HS
Imperial Beach, CA

Rivera, Ricardo A
Hamilton HS
North Hollywood, CA

Rivera, Ricardo J
Bell HS
Cudahy, CA

Rivera, Romano
Mt Pleasant HS
San Jose, CA

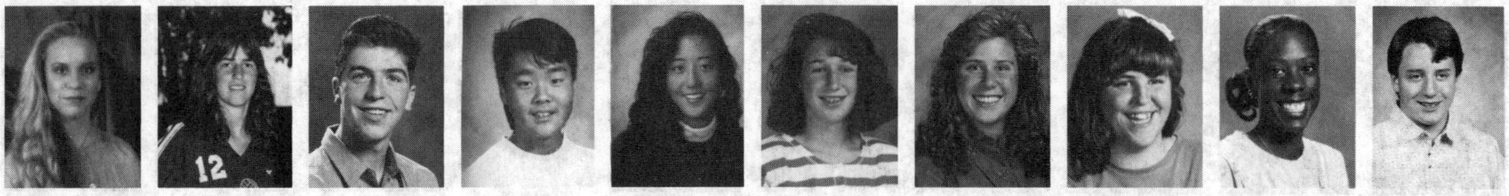

Rivers, Emma
Rebekah Maryam
Sacramento HS
Sacramento, CA

Rivet, Mary
Elk Grove HS
Elk Grove, CA

Riviello, Robert
Village Christian HS
Northridge, CA

Ro, David
Los Amigos HS
Santa Ana, CA

Ro, Gloria
Mt Carmel HS
San Diego, CA

Roach, Cynthia M
Serrano HS
Phelan, CA

Roach, Denise
Serrano HS
Phelan, CA

Roach, Heather M
William C Overfelt
San Jose, CA

Roach, Katrina M
Cajon HS
San Bernardino, CA

Roach, Ryan T
Oakmont HS
Roseville, CA

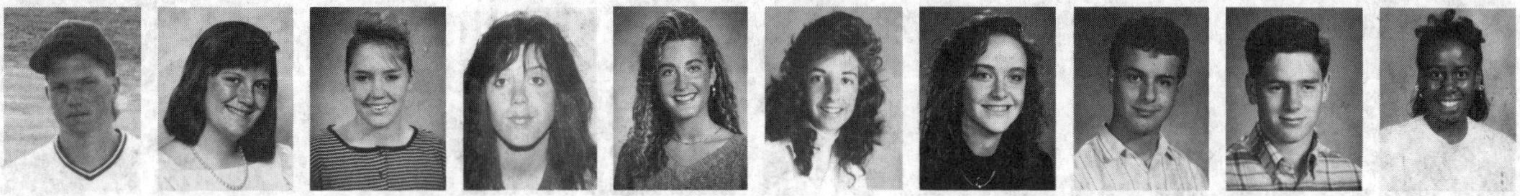

Robards, Chris E
Las Plumas HS
Oroville, CA

Robb, Kristina
Burroughs HS
Ridgecrest, CA

Robbins, Amber M
Hoopa Valley HS
Willow Creek, CA

Robbins, Carla W
North Monterey
County HS
Watsonville, CA

Robbins, Jennifer Lee
Mission Viejo HS
Mission Viejo, CA

Robbins, Karen
Oxnard HS
Oxnard, CA

Robby, Autumn
Riverbank HS
Carm, CA

Robenalt, Anthony
Serra HS
Foster City, CA

Roberson, Eric M
Sonora HS
Soulsbyville, CA

Roberson, Kimberly
Hanford Joint Union
Hanford, CA

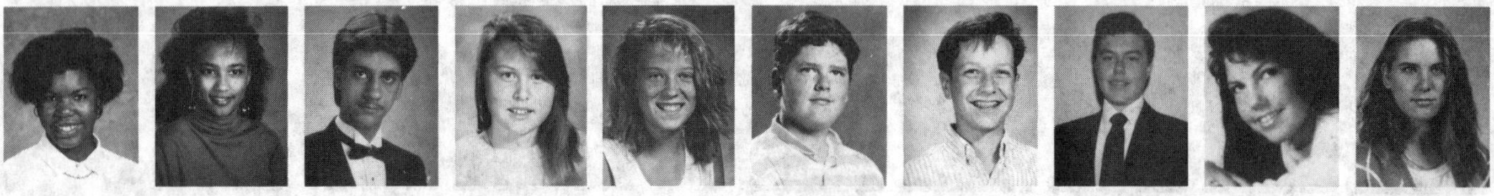

Roberson, Kristen D
Notre Dame HS
Salinas, CA

Roberson, Michaunda
Lincoln HS
Stockton, CA

Roberts, Andrew J
Santa Clara HS
Santa Clara, CA

Roberts, Angela C
Thousand Oaks HS
Thousand Oaks, CA

Roberts, Carol L
Indio HS
Indio, CA

Roberts, Donald
Andrew
Mojave HS
California City, CA

Roberts, Dustin J
Ukiah JR Acad
Ukiah, CA

Roberts, Edward J
Westminster HS
Westminster, CA

Roberts, Heather
Pleasant Valley SR
Chico, CA

Roberts, Karri
Cuyama Valley HS
New Cuyama, CA

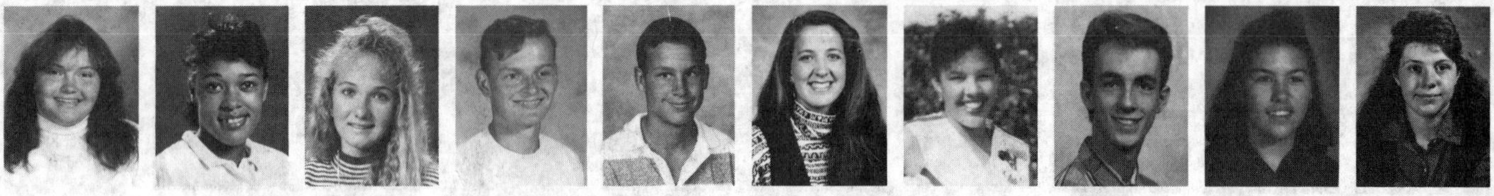

Roberts, Michelle D
Highlands HS
Rio Linda, CA

Roberts, Nakia L
Dorsey HS
Los Angeles, CA

Roberts, Sarah
Covenant Christian
San Diego, CA

Robertson, Adam
Sierra Joint Union
Auberry, CA

Robertson, James W
Monte Vista HS
Spring Valley, CA

Robertson, Kennan A
Oakmont HS
Roseville, CA

Robertson, Naomi
Valley HS
Sacramento, CA

Robertson, William A
Yucaipa HS
Yucaipa, CA

Robinett, Erin
Willows HS
Willows, CA

Robinette, Erinn D
San Gabriel HS
San Gabriel, CA

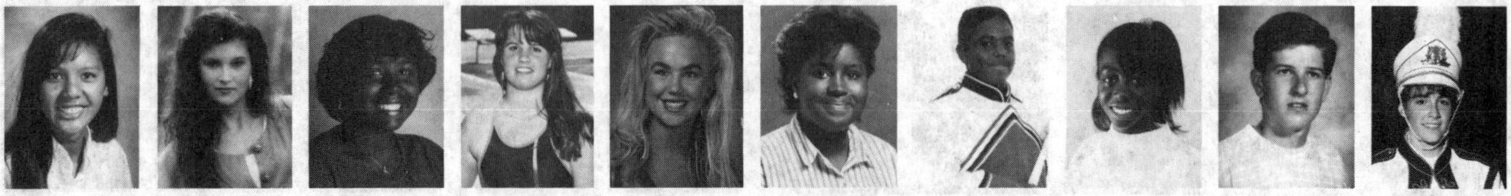

Robinson,
Anne-Marye
Mater Dei HS
Orange, CA

Robinson, Cindy L
Junipero Serra HS
San Diego, CA

Robinson, Donsha D
Hueneme HS
Port Hueneme, CA

Robinson, Kelly L
Mater Dei HS
Santa Ana, CA

Robinson, Molly T
El Toro HS
El Toro, CA

Robinson, Nichole L
San Bernardino HS
Highland, CA

Robinson, Parrin F
Valley HS
Sacramento, CA

Robinson, Rhonda L
John Muir HS
Altadena, CA

Robinson, Steve E
North HS
Bakersfield, CA

Robitaille, Annette T
Torrey Pines HS
San Diego, CA

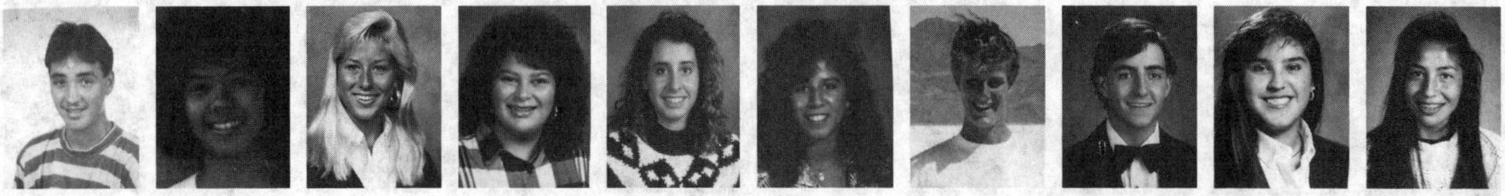

Robles, Damian
Calexico HS
Calexico, CA

Robles, Rose F
Nogales HS
W Covina, CA

Robson, Allison L
The Bishops Sch
San Diego, CA

Roca, Lorna C
Riverbank HS
Riverbank, CA

Rocha, Brandy R
Golden West HS
Visalia, CA

Rocha, Cynthia M
John F Kennedy HS
La Mirada, CA

Rochlitzer, Brian T
Santa Barbara HS
Santa Barbara, CA

Rocklein, Matthew
Noel
Paradise HS
Paradise, CA

Rodarte, Sonia J
Ramona Convent
Monterey Park, CA

Rodarte, Tara R
Manteca HS
Manteca, CA

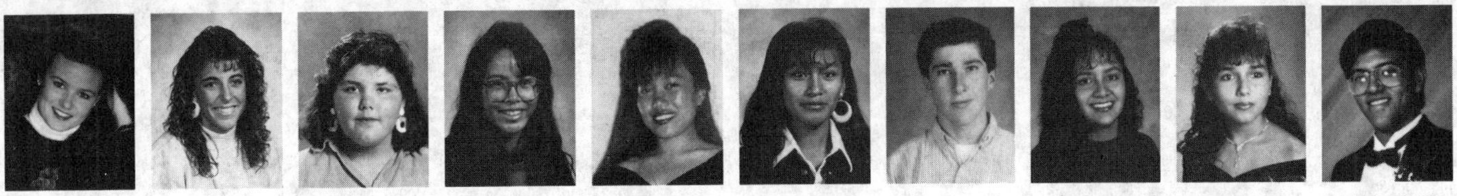

Rodgers, Leanne Marie
St Patrick-St Vincent
Suisun City, CA

Rodier, Renee
Mesa Verde HS
Citrus Heights, CA

Rodiguez, Patricia E
Rio Mesa HS
Oxnard, CA

Rodillas, Saga
Granger JR HS
National City, CA

Rodriguez, Analee
Sweetwater HS
San Diego, CA

Rodriguez, Carolina
Garfield HS
Arleta, CA

Rodriguez, Cesar
Golden West HS
Ivanhoe, CA

Rodriguez, Christina
Andrew Hill HS
San Jose, CA

Rodriguez, Claudia
Notre Dame HS
Hillsborough, CA

Rodriguez, Dario
Bishop Amat HS
West Covina, CA

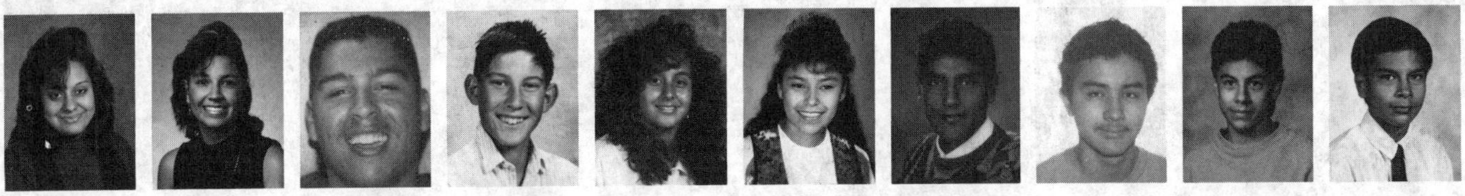

Rodriguez, Diana Rosemary
Hayward HS
Castro Valley, CA

Rodriguez, Elena C
Buena HS
Ventura, CA

Rodriguez, Gabriel
Kerman Union HS
Kerman, CA

Rodriguez, Gonzalo V
Berkeley Hall Schl
Chatsworth, CA

Rodriguez, Irene
Clovis HS
Clovis, CA

Rodriguez, Janie
Madera HS
Madera, CA

Rodriguez, Jesus
Madera HS
Madera, CA

Rodriguez, Jose F
John Muir HS
Pasadena, CA

Rodriguez, III Jose F
Fairfield HS
Vacaville, CA

Rodriguez, Joseph L
Santa Clara HS
Oxnard, CA

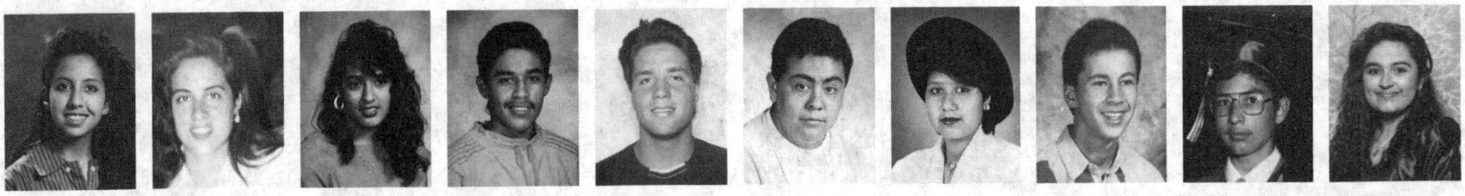

Rodriguez, Kimberly
Lindsay SR HS
Lindsay, CA

Rodriguez, Laura
St Paul HS
Pico Rivera, CA

Rodriguez, Lilia
Luther Burbank HS
Sacramento, CA

Rodriguez, Luis C
San Fernando HS
San Fernando, CA

Rodriguez, Marcel
Lindsay HS
Lindsay, CA

Rodriguez, Martin R
Gahr HS
Cerritos, CA

Rodriguez, Mary Alice
Lindsay HS
Lindsay, CA

Rodriguez, Michael A
Hoover HS
Parlier, CA

Rodriguez, Mike
Righetti HS
Guadalupe, CA

Rodriguez, Monica Carrie
Sacred Heart Of Mary HS
Pico Rivera, CA

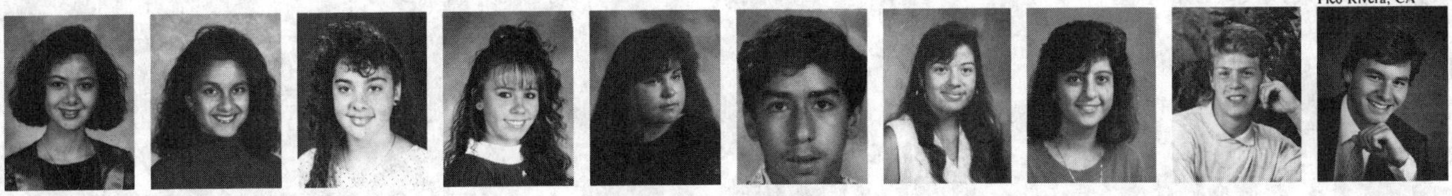

Rodriguez, Patricia
San Gabriel Mission
Duarte, CA

Rodriguez, Primavera
Theodore Roosevelt
Fresno, CA

Rodriguez, Rosa Angelica
Pittsburg HS
Pittsburg, CA

Rodriguez, Rosa M
Riverdale Joint Union
Riverdale, CA

Rodriguez, Tamara L
Burroughs HS
Ridgecrest, CA

Rodriguez, Victor R
Valley HS
Santa Ana, CA

Rodriguez, Zoila C
Valley View HS
Moreno Valley, CA

Rofail, Elizabeth A
Saint Monica HS
West Los Angeles, CA

Rogers, Aaron
Mother Lode Christian Schl
Tuolumne, CA

Rogers, David D
Enterprise HS
Shingletown, CA

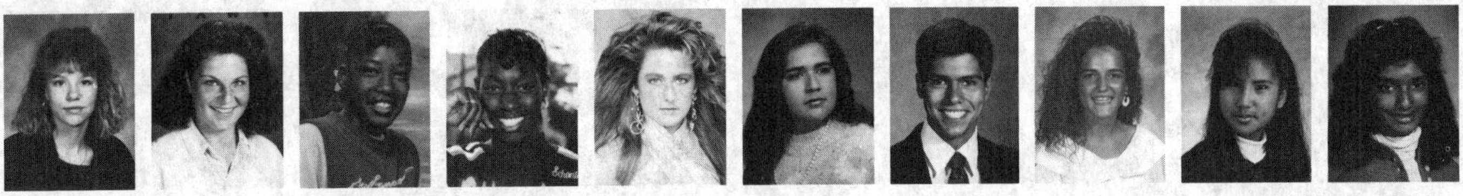

Rogers, Errin
Woodcrest Christian
Riverside, CA

Rogers, Kelly A
Acalanes HS
Lafayette, CA

Rogers, Lasonjia
Valley HS
Sacramento, CA

Rogers, Schonteau R
Pius X HS
Compton, CA

Rohde, Jennifer
Glen A Wilson HS
Hacienda Heights, CA

Rojas, Evangelina
Loretto HS
Sacramento, CA

Roldan, Brad
St Ignatius HS
Burlingame, CA

Roldan, Jennifer
Valley View HS
Moreno Valley, CA

Roldan, Vivian L
Wilcox HS
Santa Clara, CA

Roley, Linda
University HS
Irvine, CA

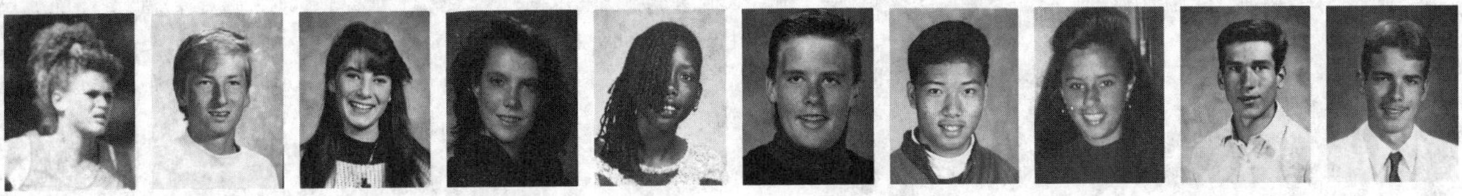

Rolfe, Kristin
Clovis HS
Clovis, CA

Roller, Jeff S
Carlmont HS
Belmont, CA

Rollins, Joeylynn Jane
San Juan HS
Citrus Heights, CA

Rollins, Kristina M
Mission Viejo HS
Mission Viejo, CA

Rollins, Shanta N
Victor Valley HS
Victorville, CA

Rolston, Kenneth G
Irvine HS
Irvine, CA

Romabiles, Nathaniel Joseph A
Lowell HS
San Francisco, CA

Romano, Rachel
Arroyo HS
San Lorenzo, CA

Romanov, Andrew
San Gabriel HS
Rosemead, CA

Romanowsky, Aaron
Cabrillo HS
Lompoc, CA

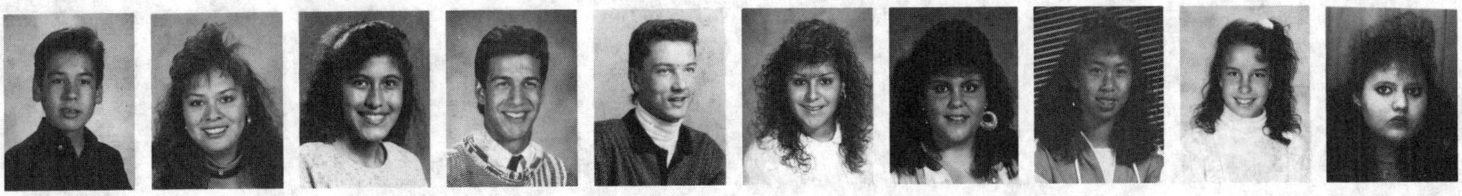

Romer, Michael
Montebello HS
Montebello, CA

Romero, Amie C
Tracy Joint Union
Tracy, CA

Romero, Araceli D
Baldwin Park HS
Baldwin Park, CA

Romero, Daniel
Hesperia Christian Schl
Hesperia, CA

Romero, Frank E
Hesperia HS
Hesperia, CA

Romero, Johnnie R
San Fernando Coll In
Sylmar, CA

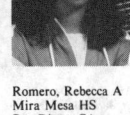

Romero, Mary Ann
Andrew Hill HS
San Jose, CA

Romero, Rebecca A
Mira Mesa HS
San Diego, CA

Romero, Sarah
Glen A Wilson HS
Hacienda Heights, CA

Romo, Monica M
Fontana HS
Fontana, CA

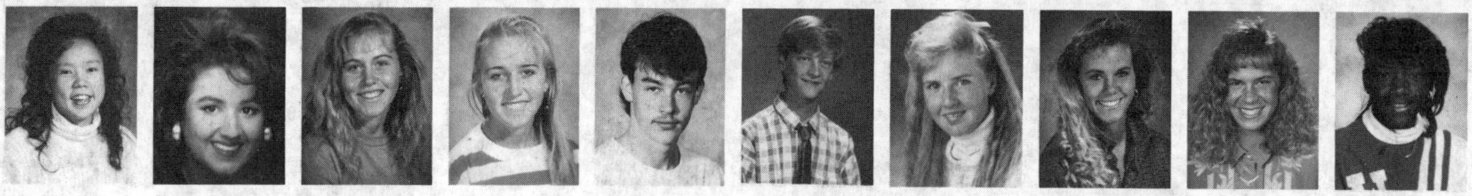

Roncal, Christina W
El Camino HS
Daly City, CA

Rondon, Karina E
Bellarmine Jefferson
Sun Valley, CA

Roney, Jodi
Orange HS
Orange, CA

Roney, Julie
Orange HS
Orange, CA

Ronk, Benjamin J
Seaside HS
Fort Ord, CA

Rookhuyzen, Robert
La Sierra HS
Riverside, CA

Rooney, Cheryl M
Ramona HS
Riverside, CA

Root, Stephanie A
Edison HS
Huntington Beach, CA

Roper, Shelley R
Southern California Christian HS
Anaheim, CA

Roquemore, Colette
John Muir HS
Altadena, CA

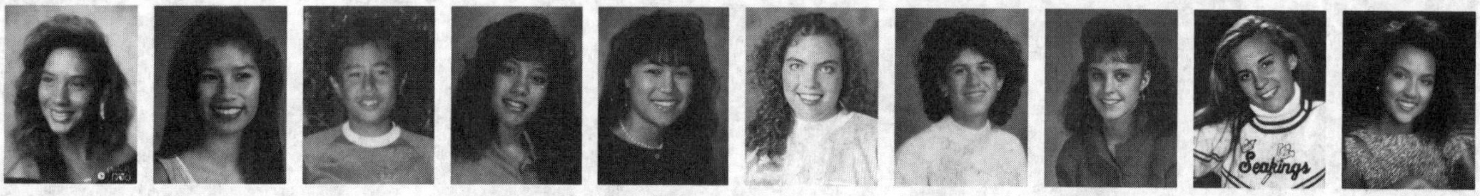

Rorabaugh, Daphne
Chula Vista HS
Chula Vista, CA

Rosales, Lucy
Los Banos HS
Los Banos, CA

Rosario, Don J
Vallejo SR HS
Vallejo, CA

Rosas, Aneissa
Bishop Amat HS
La Habra Heights, CA

Rosas, Grace Yap
Notre Dame HS
Los Angeles, CA

Rose, Aleasha N
Palmdale HS
Acton, CA

Rose, Dawn
Golden West HS
Visalia, CA

Rose, Denise
Orestimba HS
Newman, CA

Rose, Jennifer
Corona Del Mar HS
Newport Beach, CA

Rose, Sonia
San Marcos HS
San Marcos, CA

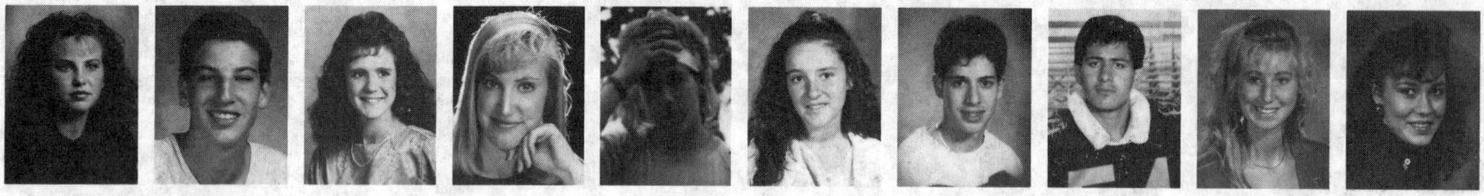

Rosen, Charlotte L
Ernest Righetti HS
Orcutt, CA

Rosenberg, Rick
Casa Roble Fundamental HS
Orangevale, CA

Rosenberger, Natasha
Heritage Christian Schl
Anaheim, CA

Rosenquist, Kristina
Colfax HS
Gold Run, CA

Rosenthal, Blaise D
Calaveras HS
Mokelumne Hill, CA

Rosenthal, Claudine
Lowell HS
San Francisco, CA

Rosenthal, James Jarrod
West Covina HS
West Covina, CA

Rosette, Douglas V
Calexico HS
Calexico, CA

Rosetti, Angela
Los Alamitos HS
Seal Beach, CA

Rosiles, Yolanda
Calexico HS
Calexico, CA

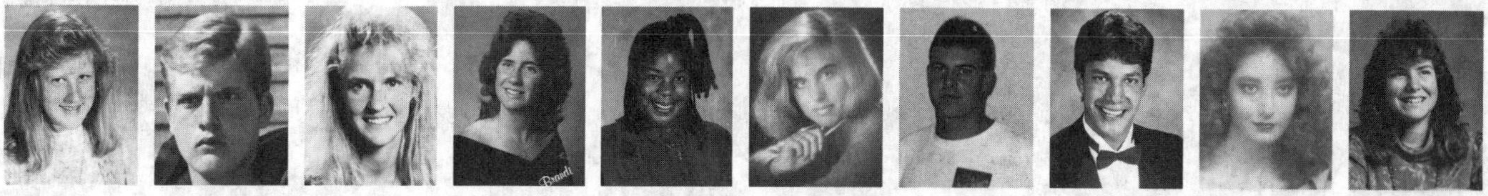

Rosique, Lisa A
Chino HS
Ontario, CA

Ross, Aaron E
Santa Monica HS
Santa Monica, CA

Ross, Amy
Centennial HS
Corona, CA

Ross, Brandi
Notre Dame Acad
Los Angeles, CA

Ross, Carmel T
Hayward HS
Hayward, CA

Ross, Elizabeth Ann
Torrey Pines HS
Del Mar, CA

Ross, Jaron D
Red Bluff Union HS
Red Bluff, CA

Ross, Joseph J
Clear Lake HS
Lakeport, CA

Ross, Kristina L
Mt Pleasant HS
San Jose, CA

Ross, Michelle K
Clovis HS
Fresno, CA

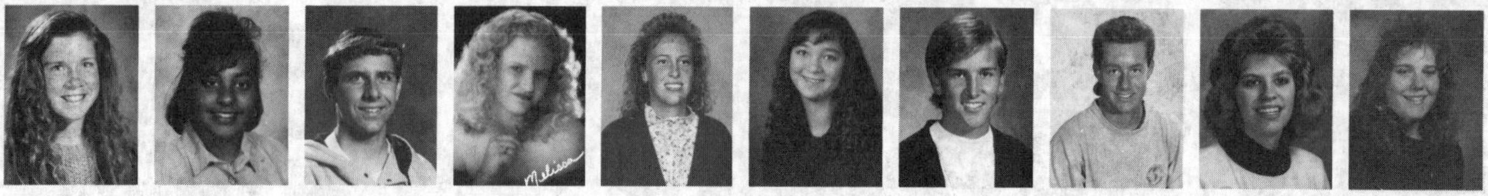

Ross, Sarah F
Edison HS
Huntington Beach, CA

Ross, Tara T
Western Christian
Covina, CA

Roth, Brandon M
Delano HS
Delano, CA

Roth, Melissa A
Davis SR HS
Davis, CA

Rother, Wendy L
Apple Valley HS
Apple Valley, CA

Rouch, Cheryl L
Redwood HS
Visalia, CA

Rounds, Stephen J
Homestead HS
Sunnyvale, CA

Roush, Branden
Bloomington Christian HS
Bloomington, CA

Rowe, Angela
Apple Valley HS
Apple Valley, CA

Rowen, Jolene J
Central Union HS
El Centro, CA

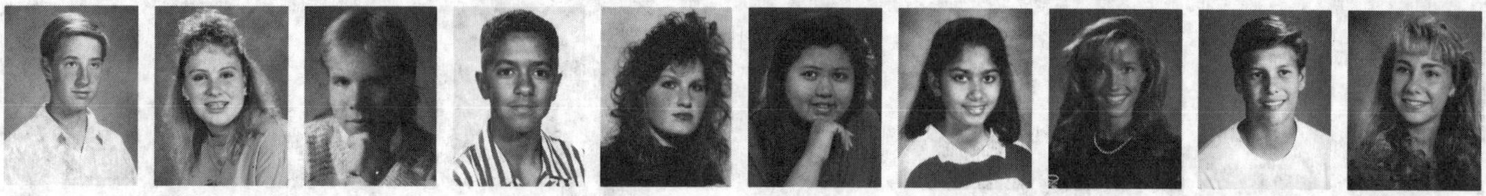

Rowin, Douglas Bowe
Central Union HS
El Centro, CA

Rowland, Shelly A
Holtville HS
Holtville, CA

Rowles, Eric
Redlands HS
Redlands, CA

Rowley, Jason
John Muir HS
Pasadena, CA

Rownd, Michelle E
Sunset HS
Hayward, CA

Roxas, Reyza
Bishop Montgomery
Carson, CA

Roy, Aditi
University HS
Irvine, CA

Roy, Jennifer
Pacific Grove HS
Pacific Grove, CA

Roy, Joshua J
Fred C Beyer HS
Modesto, CA

Royce, Debra Lynne
Villa Park HS
Orange, CA

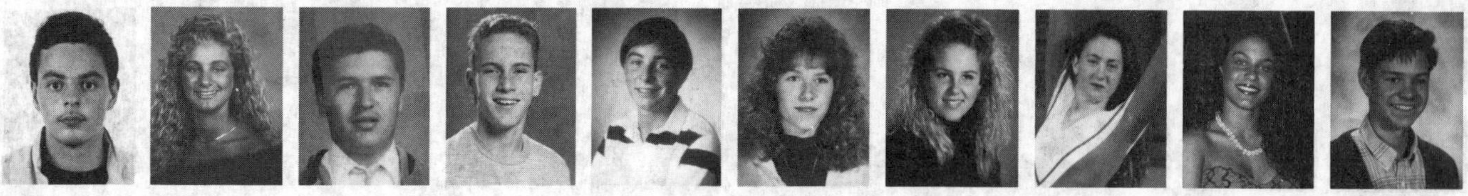

Royzen, Valery
George Washington
San Francisco, CA

Rozolis, Jennifer
Los Alamitos HS
Los Alamitos, CA

Ruan, Jose De Jesus
St Bernard HS
Hawthorne, CA

Rubin, Greg D
Taft HS
Tarzana, CA

Rubino, Steve
Central Catholic HS
Tracy, CA

Rucker, Karie J
Red Bluff Union HS
Red Bluff, CA

Rude, Ally
Turlock HS
Turlock, CA

Rudnick, Pesha E
Venice HS
Venice, CA

Rudometkin, Jennifer
Whittier Christian
Whittier, CA

Rudometkin, Nate
Sacramento Adventist Acad
Newcastle, CA

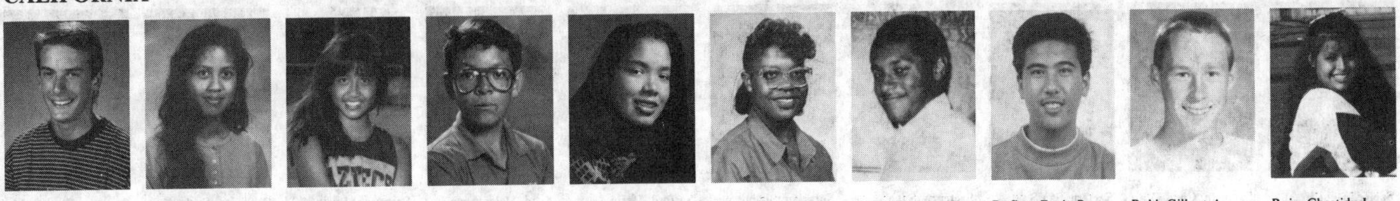

Rueb, Mark C
Alhambra HS
Martinez, CA

Rueda, Charito Sherry
Palm Desert HS
Palm Desert, CA

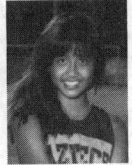

Rueda, Margaret
Palm Desert HS
Palm Desert, CA

Ruelas, Jose J
Carlsbad HS
Oceanside, CA

Ruff, Michelle
Armona Union Acad
Hanford, CA

Ruffin, Zaneta L
Victor Valley HS
Victorville, CA

Ruffinelli, John W
Crenshaw HS
Los Angeles, CA

Rufino, Erwin B
Pinole Valley HS
Pinole, CA

Ruhl, Gilbert A
Miramonte HS
Orinda, CA

Ruiz, Chastidy I
Indio HS
Indio, CA

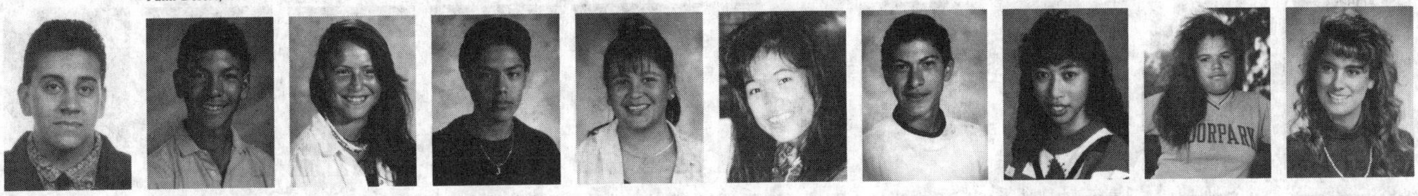

Ruiz, Ernie A
Hamilton HS
Sylmar, CA

Ruiz, III Gilbert P
Serrano HS
Pinon Hills, CA

Ruiz, Jessica L
San Luis Obispo HS
San Luis Obispo, CA

Ruiz, Joel
Fremont HS
Oakland, CA

Ruiz, Justine M
Santa Barbara HS
Santa Barbara, CA

Ruiz, Maricel C
Saint Anthony HS
Carson, CA

Ruiz, Jr Michael T
Paraclete HS
Lancaster, CA

Ruiz, Michelle A
Samuel F B Morse
San Diego, CA

Ruiz, Noemi
Moorpark HS
Moorpark, CA

Ruiz, Sheri
Arcadia HS
Arcadia, CA

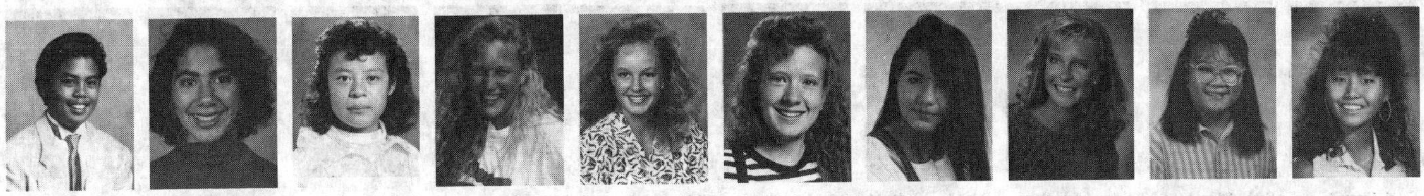

Rull, Rudolph P
Chula Vista HS
San Diego, CA

Rulz, Jessica C
Mesa Verde HS
Citrus Heights, CA

Rumirez, Georgina C
Manuel Arts HS
Los Angeles, CA

Rumis, Wini
Ramona HS
Ramona, CA

Rummery, Jennifer
Escondido HS
Escondido, CA

Ruppert, Christina
Aptos HS
Aptos, CA

Rusev, Judi
Notre Dame HS
Milpitas, CA

Rush, Amy
Miraleste HS
Rolling Hills Est, CA

Rusit, Jeriza Marie R
James Logan HS
Union City, CA

Russell, Kimberly Y
La Quinta HS
Westminster, CA

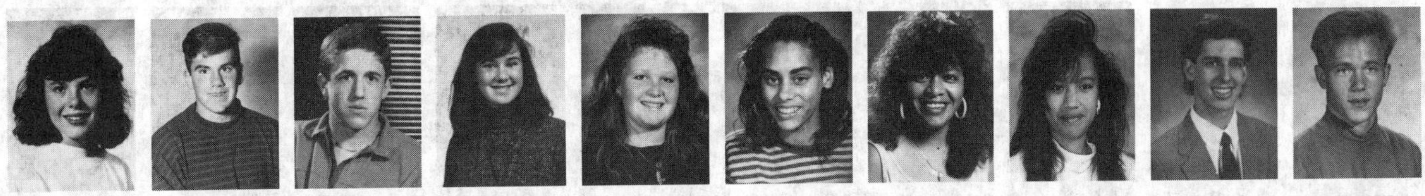

Russell, Leah A
San Diego Acad
El Cajon, CA

Russell, Mark D
Skyline HS
Oakland, CA

Russell, Ryan M
Cuyama Valley HS
New Cuyama, CA

Russell, Sharon G
Sklyline HS
Oakland, CA

Russler, Amy K
West HS
Bakersfield, CA

Rustin, Christina L
Temecula Valley HS
Murrieta, CA

Rustrian, Norma
Belmont HS
Los Angeles, CA

Rutger, Carmela
Bishop Amat HS
Walnut, CA

Ruth, Michael W
Mt Whitney HS
Visalia, CA

Rutherford, Jim K
Santa Ynez Valley Union HS
Solvang, CA

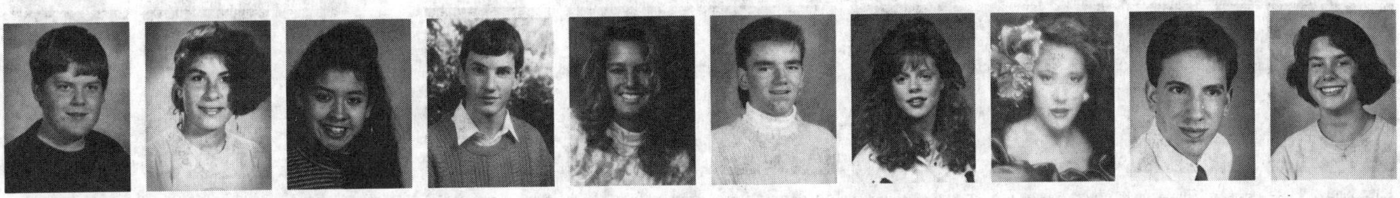

Rutherford, Joshua
Lone Pine Unified
Lone Pine, CA

Ruva, Nicole R
Huntington Beach
Huntington Beach, CA

Ruvalcaba, Carol
North Monterey County HS
Castroville, CA

Rux, Nathan
Salinas HS
Salinas, CA

Ryan, Erin
Los Alamitos HS
Los Alamitos, CA

Ryan, Kurt K
Golden West HS
Visalia, CA

Ryan, Louann A
Monte Vista HS
Kalamazoo, MI

Ryan, Pilar L
Coast Christian HS
Torrance, CA

Ryan, Robb
Turlock HS
Turlock, CA

Ryan, Stephanie L
Bella Vista HS
Orangevale, CA

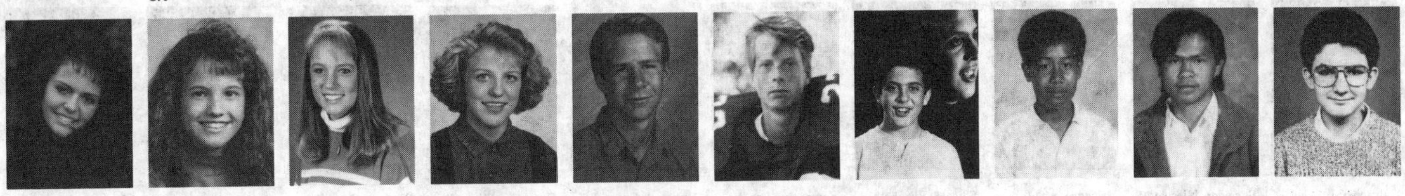

Rye, Jennifer
El Molino HS
Rio Nido, CA

Rye, Jessica
Capital Christian Schl
Rancho Cordova, CA

Rynbrandt, Robin A
San Rafael HS
San Rafael, CA

Ryon, Deborah C
Durham HS
Durham, CA

Ryssel, Denny E
Apple Valley SR HS
Apple Valley, CA

Ryzek, Samuel P
Redlands HS
Redlands, CA

Saah, David S
Bellarmine College Prep
San Jose, CA

Sabado, Jonathan Yao
Don Bosco Technical Inst
Monterey Park, CA

Sabado, Jose P
Alisal HS
Salinas, CA

Sabawi, Ala S
Granada Hills HS
Granada Hills, CA

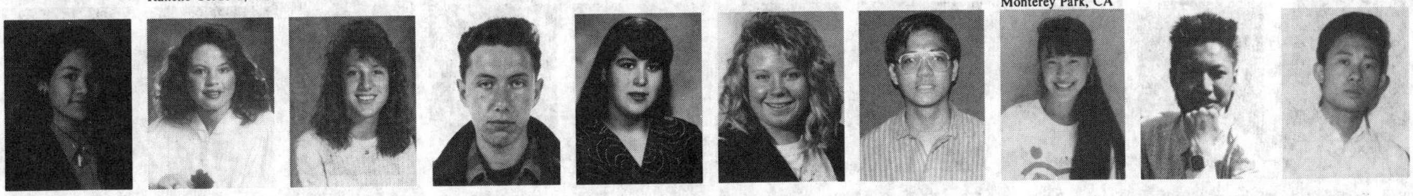

Sablan, Eileen A
Montgomery HS
San Diego, CA

Sablan, Marita
St Patrick-St Vincent
Vallejo, CA

Sablosky, Terri
Alisal HS
Salinas, CA

Sabsovich, Igor A
Washington HS
San Francisco, CA

Saccone, Rosa E
El Rancho HS
Pico Rivera, CA

Sachs, Rebecca L
Encina HS
Sacramento, CA

Saddi, Robert F
Lemoore HS
Lemoore, CA

Saechao, Mey S
Richmond HS
San Pablo, CA

Saechao, Ton
Enterprise HS
Redding, CA

Saelee, Kae Kovei
Richmond HS
Richmond, CA

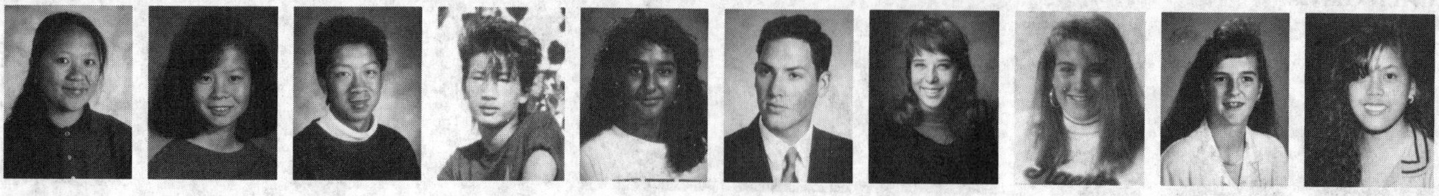

Saelee, Meui F
Fremont HS
Oakland, CA

Saephan, Chan C
El Cerrito HS
Richmond, CA

Saetern, San S
Oakland HS
Oakland, CA

Saeteurn, Saan
Hiram W Johnson
Sacramento, CA

Safarian, Shabnam
Torrey Pines HS
San Diego, CA

Safford, Darin J
Ganesha HS
Diamond Bar, CA

Sage, Heidi Anne
Valhalla HS
Jamul, CA

Sagouspe, Julie
Los Banos HS
Los Banos, CA

Sagouspe, Sasha E
Madera HS
Madera, CA

Sagrado, Theresa M
Edison-Computech
Fresno, CA

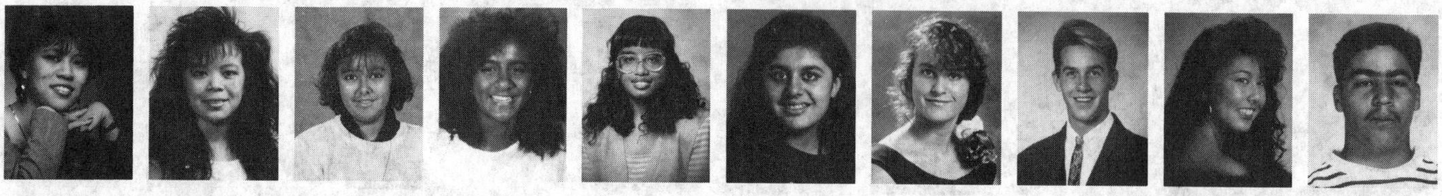

Sah, Alanna Robin
Rio Americano HS
Sacramento, CA

Sah, Sherilyn S
Rio Americano HS
Sacramento, CA

Sahagun, Clara M
Santa Maria HS
Santa Maria, CA

Sahai, Tricia Nadira
Victor Valley HS
Victorville, CA

Sahgal, Tricia L
Hawthorne HS
Baldwin Park, CA

Sahibzada, Mehnaz
Taft HS
Woodland Hills, CA

Sahl, Wendie L
John Burroughs SR
Burbank, CA

Sais, III Edward E
Schurr HS
Monterey Park, CA

Saito, Kelli
Del Mar HS
San Jose, CA

Saiz, Orlando M
Barstow HS
Barstow, CA

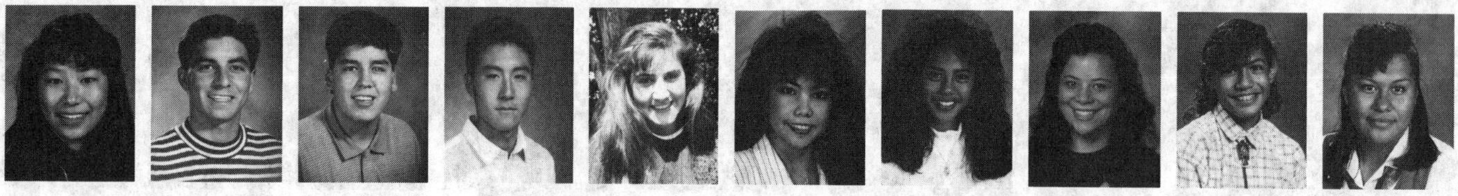

Sakai, Cindy Y
Carmont HS
Foster City, CA

Sakai, Edward H
Edison HS
Huntington Bch, CA

Sakai, Julian M
Edison HS
Huntington Beach, CA

Sakakihara, Ryan M
Archbishop Mitty HS
Saratoga, CA

Sakaldasis, Amy
Henry M Gunn HS
Palo Alto, CA

Salamanca, Grace M
Bishop Amat Memorial HS
Azusa, CA

Salas, Kathleen Renae
Vintage HS
Vallejo, CA

Salas, Tara T
Fairfield HS
Fairfield, CA

Salas, Victor M
Indio HS
La Quinta, CA

Salas-Torresdey, Blanca E
Samuel F B Morse
San Diego, CA

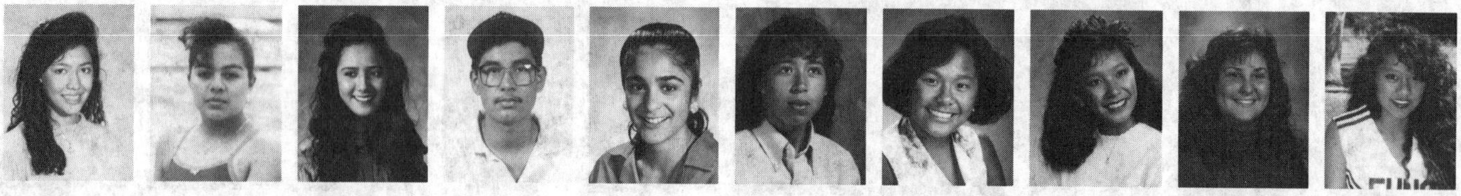

Salazar, Maria
Rosary HS
La Habra, CA

Salceda, Maria G
Napa HS
Napa, CA

Salcido, Erika
Indio HS
La Quinta, CA

Saldana, Alex C
Watsonville HS
Watsonville, CA

Saldana, Janina R
Calexico HS
Spring Valley, CA

Saldivar, Stephanie A
Bullard HS
Fresno, CA

Salem, Anneva Angela Yancha
Tulare Union HS
Tulare, CA

Salem, Ausa Asteria Yancha
Tulare Union HS
Tulare, CA

Salerno, Suzanne C
Temple City HS
Temple City, CA

Sales, Fermina
East Union HS
Manteca, CA

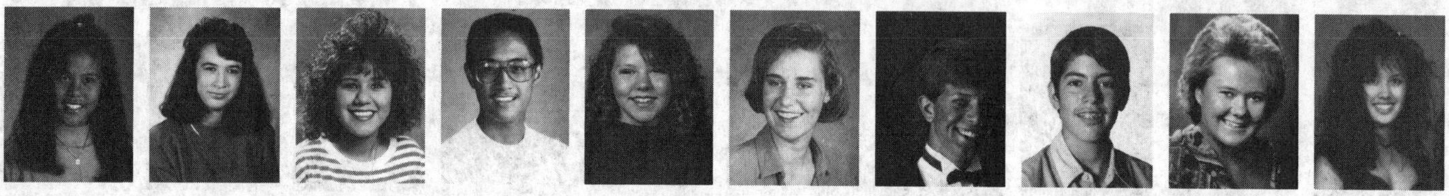

Sales, Juliette
East Union HS
Manteca, CA

Salgado, Lillian
Central Union HS
Seely, CA

Salinas, Adriana L
Delano HS
Mc Farland, CA

Salindong, Anthony P
Beyer HS
Modesto, CA

Salisbury, Michaele
West Hills HS
Santee, CA

Sallade, Dione L
La Mirada HS
La Mirada, CA

Salmon, Cade A
Del Campo HS
Fair Oaks, CA

Salo, Patrick K
Elk Grove HS
Elk Grove, CA

Salokangas, Kati Maria
Salinas HS
Finland

Salumbides, Christine
Bishop Amat Memorial HS
San Dimas, CA

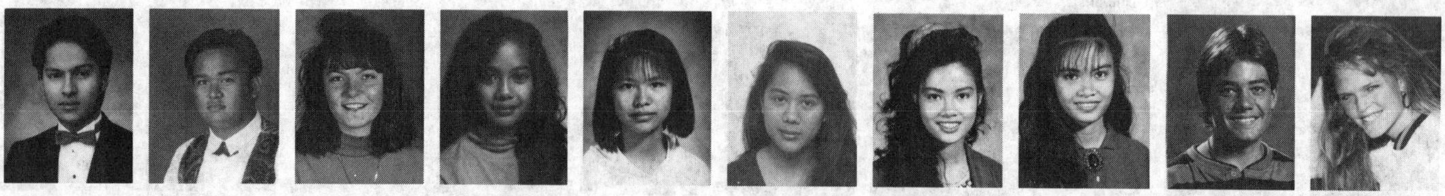

Salvacion, L Erich
Estancia HS
Costa Mesa, CA

Salvador, Niccolo M
Montgomery HS
San Diego, CA

Salvagno, Anna
Notre Dame HS
Greenfield, CA

Samala, Elizabeth
Southwest HS
San Diego, CA

Samantha, Lee
Cerritos HS
Cerritos, CA

Samodal, Grace T
Bonita Vista HS
Bonita, CA

Sampani, Fritzie P
Fremont HS
Sunnyvale, CA

Sampani, Mae P
Fremont HS
Sunnyvale, CA

Samples, Adam R
Santa Paula Union
Santa Paula, CA

Samples, Kelly L
Etiwanda HS
Alta Loma, CA

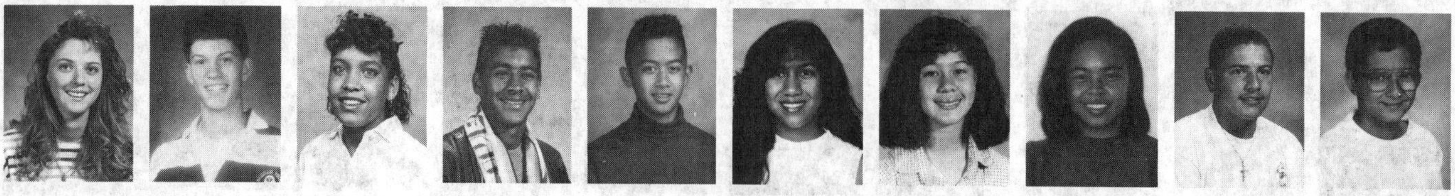

Sampson, Janet L
Needles HS
Needles, CA

Sampson, Matt R
Hanford HS
Hanford, CA

Sampson, Pshyra
St Anthony HS
Compton, CA

Samra, Harnak S
Rio Linda HS
Sacramento, CA

Samson, Eric
Golden West HS
Visalia, CA

Samudio, Julie A
Woodrow Wilson HS
Los Angeles, CA

Samuelson, Elizabeth
Eureka HS
Eureka, CA

San Juan, Anne B
Dana Hills HS
Laguna Hills, CA

Sanabria, Mario
Central Union HS
El Centro, CA

Sanandaji, Sam
Birmingham HS
Encino, CA

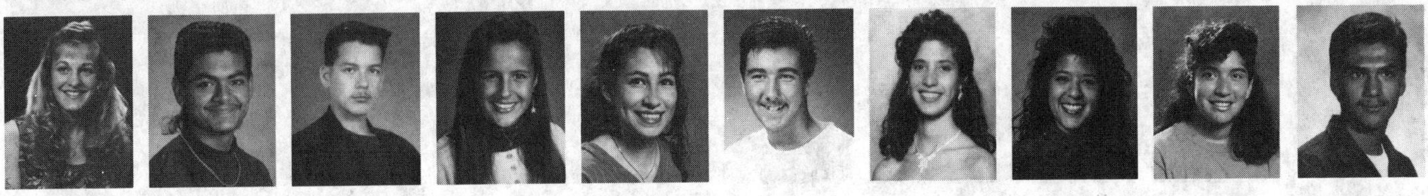

Sanborn, Jennifer A
Ontario HS
Highland, CA

Sanchez, Albert S
Palm Springs HS
Cathedral, CA

Sanchez, Carlos A
Los Altos HS
Hacienda Hgts, CA

Sanchez, Christina
Clovis West HS
Fresno, CA

Sanchez, Claudia
Sierra Vista HS
Baldwin Park, CA

Sanchez, Daniel J
Pinole Valley HS
Hercules, CA

Sanchez, Deanna D
Canyon HS
Canyon Country, CA

Sanchez, Eileen R
Chaffey HS
Ontario, CA

Sanchez, Elena L
Herbert Hoover HS
Glendale, CA

Sanchez, Emanuel
Lynwood HS
Lynwood, CA

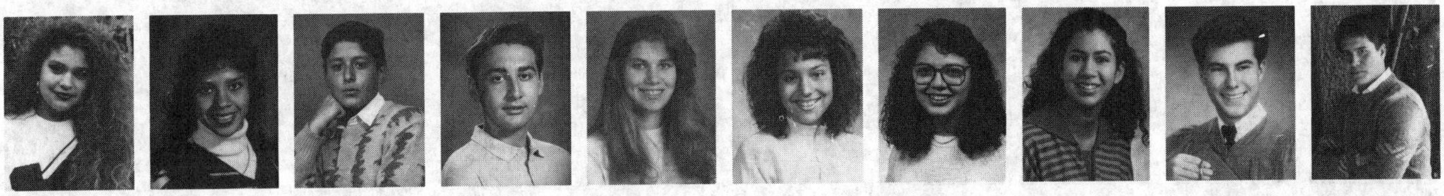

Sanchez, Evelia
Sierra Vista HS
Baldwin Park, CA

Sanchez, Faustina
Santa Ana HS
Santa Ana, CA

Sanchez, Hilario
Baldwin Park HS
Baldwin Pk, CA

Sanchez, Hugo B
Santa Ana HS
Santa Ana, CA

Sanchez, Jennifer
Redlands HS
Highland, CA

Sanchez, Jill
Bishop O'dowd HS
San Leandro, CA

Sanchez, Juanita S
Abraham Lincoln HS
San Jose, CA

Sanchez, Judith I
Notre Dame HS
San Jose, CA

Sanchez, Michael A
Pinole Valley HS
Hercules, CA

Sanchez, Mike
San Luis Obispo HS
San Luis Obispo, CA

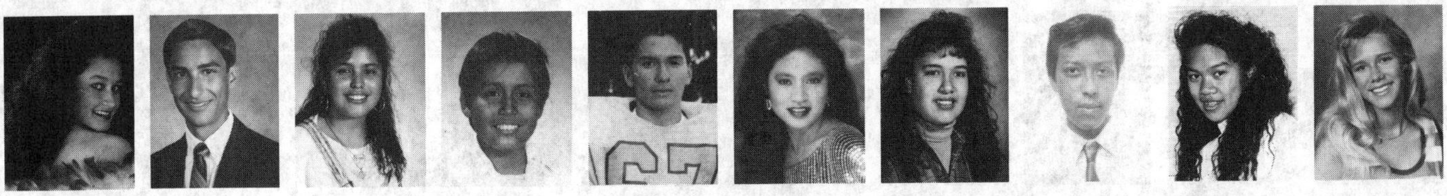

Sanchez, Monika
Arroyo HS
San Leandro, CA

Sanchez, Neil James
Katella HS
Anaheim, CA

Sanchez, Norma
Rowland HS
Rowland Hts, CA

Sanchez, Richard
Daniel Murphy HS
Los Angeles, CA

Sanchez, Ricky T
Channel Islands HS
Oxnard, CA

Sanchez, Tina Marie
Hoover HS
Glendale, CA

Sanchez, Veronica
Reedley HS
Reedley, CA

Sanchez-Cazares, Gerardo
Reedley HS
Reedley, CA

Sancianco, Hazel G
Diamond Bar HS
Diamond Bar, CA

Sandage, Kirsten
Point Loma HS
San Diego, CA

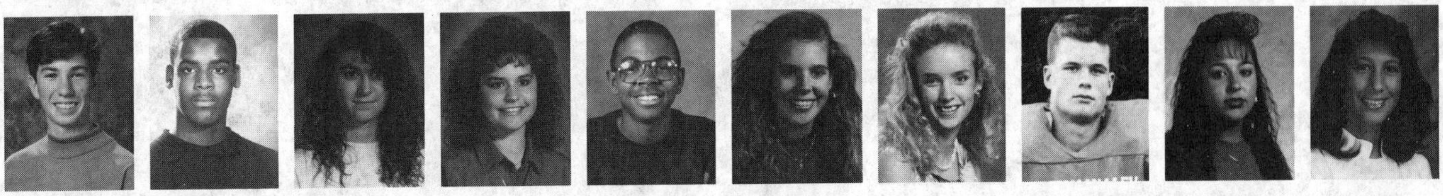

Sandberg, Robert
Dana Hills HS
Mission Viejo, CA

Sanders, Anthony L
San Fernando HS
San Fernando, CA

Sanders, Bambie C
Trinity HS
Weaverville, CA

Sanders, Bethany L
Trinity HS
Weaverville, CA

Sanders, Derrick L
South Bay Junior Acad
Carson, CA

Sanders, Jessica B
Edison HS
Fresno, CA

Sanders, Nichole A
Fontana HS
Fontana, CA

Sanderson, Scott M
Clayton Valley HS
Concord, CA

Sandoval, Amanda J
Santa Clara HS
Santa Clara, CA

Sandoval, Angela R
Apple Valley HS
Apple Valley, CA

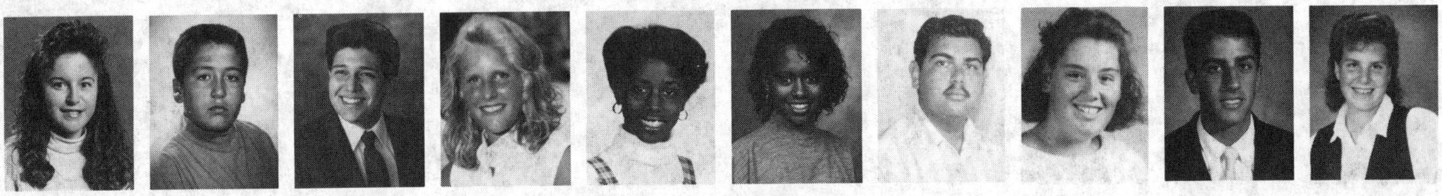

Sandoval, Estela
Santa Paula Union
Santa Paula, CA

Sandoval, Gerardo
Fillmore HS
Fillmore, CA

Sandoval, Thomas
Bishop Amat HS
Rowland Hts, CA

Sandquist, Therese A
Anderson Union HS
Sweden

Sanford, Janeare S
Berkeley HS
Berkeley, CA

Sanford, Karla S
Monte Vista HS
Spring Valley, CA

Santa Cruz, Eduardo
Downey SR HS
S Gate, CA

Santamoor, Danielle
Winters HS
Winters, CA

Santana, Jim J
St Ignatius College Prep
San Mateo, CA

Santelli, Renee Andrea
S California Christian
Anaheim, CA

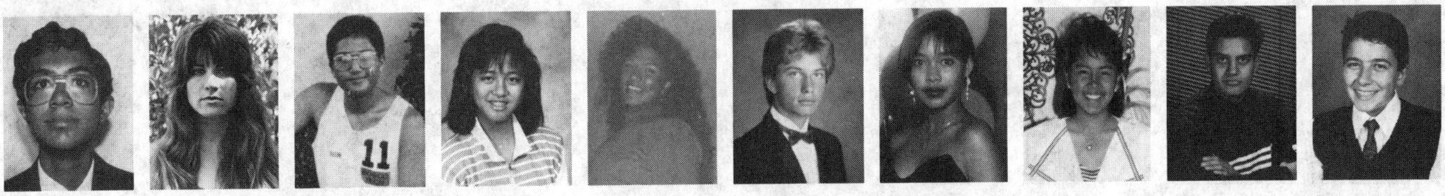

Santhanam, Kumaran
Saint Francis HS
Sunnyvale, CA

Santillan, Dolores O
Oroville HS
Oroville, CA

Santos, III Dion D
Don Bosed Technical Inst
Monterey Park, CA

Santos, Dureza L
Alverno HS
Glendale, CA

Santos, Jessica Lyn
Lindhurst HS
Marysville, CA

Santos, Joey M
Upper Lake Union
Upper Lake, CA

Santos, Lorena Arlene
Mar Vista HS
San Diego, CA

Santos, Michelle B
Whitney HS
Cerritos, CA

Santos, Jr Raul
William Workman
La Puente, CA

Santos, Raymond
Fremont Christian Schl
Fremont, CA

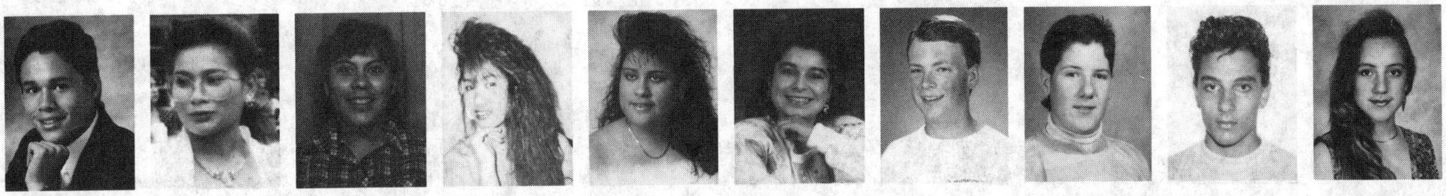

Santos, Ricardo J
San Dieguito HS
Encinitas, CA

Santos, Rowena G
Ramona Convent Secondary HS
El Monte, CA

Santos, Selene
South Gate HS
Downey, CA

Santos, Sheila
Franklin JR HS
Vallejo, CA

Santos, Susie
Castle Park HS
Chula Vista, CA

Santoyo, Nancy
San Joaquin Memorial HS
Firebaugh, CA

Sappington, Marc S
Liberty Union HS
Brentwood, CA

Saragueta, Justin
Hanford Union HS
Hanford, CA

Sarantopoulos, Pete
Warren HS
South Gate, CA

Saras, Jessica J
Mission HS
San Gabriel, CA

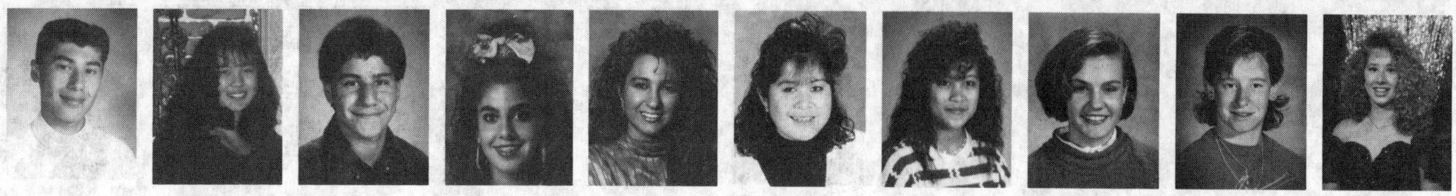

Saravia, Jon P
Montebello HS
Montebello, CA

Saraza, Vilma Cena
Delano HS
Delano, CA

Sarhad, Jon J
Turlock HS
Turlock, CA

Sarian, Rita M
Torrance HS
R Cucamonga, CA

Saric, Karin J
John A Rowland HS
Rowland Hts, CA

Sarmiento, Cheryl Ann T
Lowell HS
San Francisco, CA

Sarmiento, Marilou C
William C Overfelt
San Jose, CA

Sarna, Kelly N
Las Lomas HS
Walnut Creek, CA

Sartor, Melissa
Mt Shasta HS
Mt Shasta, CA

Sartuche, Monica R
Tulare Western HS
Tulare, CA

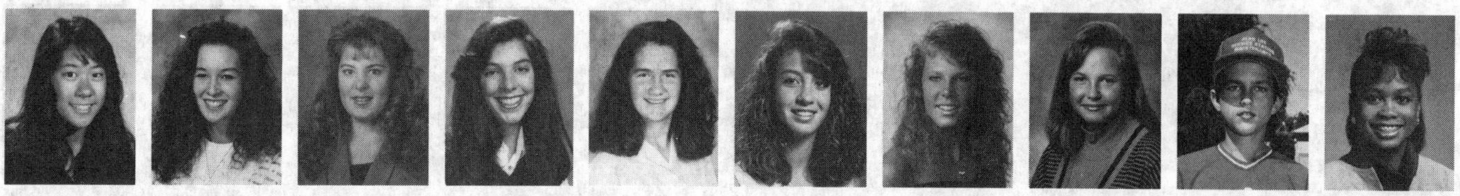

Sato, Grace M
Whitney HS
Cypress, CA

Sato, Lisa-Marie
Cordova SR HS
Rancho Cordova, CA

Saude, Tiffini C
Redwood HS
Visalia, CA

Sauer, Annemarie
Immaculate Heart
Los Angeles, CA

Sauer, Christina
St Genevieve HS
Tempe, AZ

Sauer, Kerry
Cason HS
San Bernardino, CA

Saunders, Dawne
Hilltop HS
Chula Vista, CA

Saunders, Lois M
La Jolla Country Day
Poway, CA

Saunders, Paul Ahanu
Buena HS
Ventura, CA

Saunders, Selena
Saint Bernard Catholic Schl
Los Angeles, CA

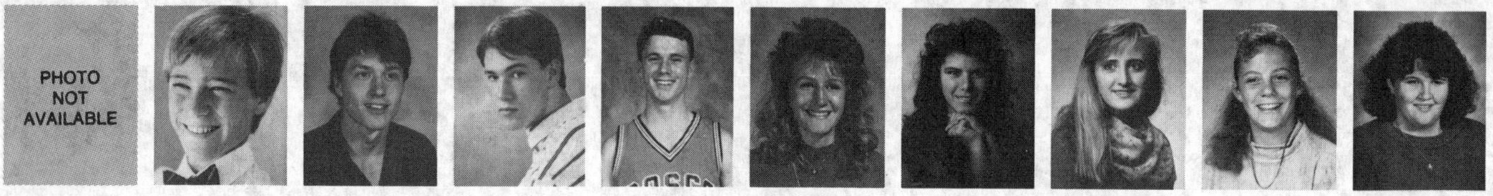

Saunders, Sharrieff D
Inglewood HS
Inglewood, CA

Sauvage, Arnaud M
El Toro HS
El Toro, CA

Savage, Jason
Avenal HS
Avenal, CA

Savage, Robert S
Beacon Christian HS
Foster City, CA

Savage, Thomas William
Don Bosco Technical Inst
West Covina, CA

Savko, Yvonne A
Seaside HS
Seaside, CA

Sawabini, Tasha R
Grossmont HS
La Mesa, CA

Sawchuk, Heather V J D
Monterey Bay Acad
Pleasant Hill, CA

Sawdon, Jenna M
Monte Vista HS
Diablo, CA

Sawyer, Jill L
Mc Farland HS
Mc Farland, CA

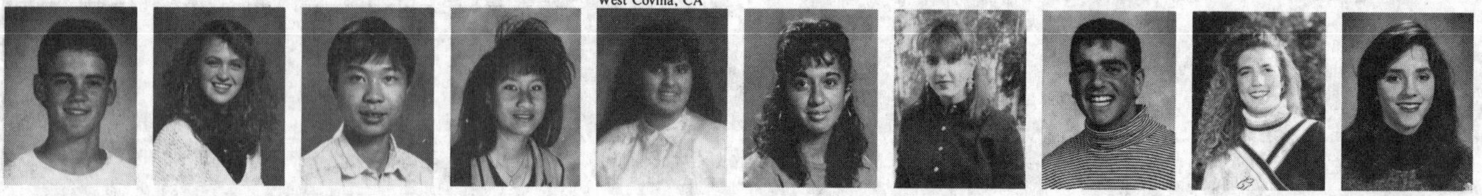

Saxon, Darren
Cardinal Newman
Santa Rosa, CA

Saxon, Tiffany M
Santa Teresa HS
San Jose, CA

Say, Kok
King Drew Med Mag
Los Angeles, CA

Sayachack, Khamsouay K
Sanger HS
Sanger, CA

Sayani, Laila
Canyon HS
Canyon Country, CA

Sayfi, Elisa
Hawthorne HS
Hawthorne, CA

Sayyah, Goli
Westlake School For Girls
Los Angeles, CA

Scalise, Sergio
Moreau HS
Hayward, CA

Scarazzo, Kristie
Clovis West HS
Fresno, CA

Scarlett, Angela M
Fortuna Union HS
Fortuna, CA

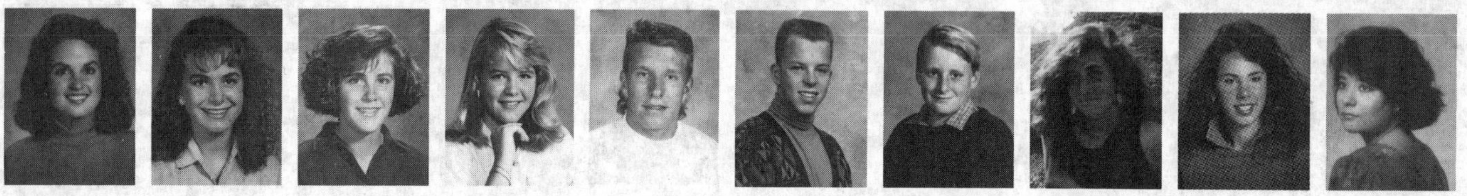

Scarms, Denise
Palm Springs HS
Palm Springs, CA

Scatena, Ashley
St Marys HS
Stockton, CA

Scattini, Heather A
Notre Dame HS
Salinas, CA

Scattini, Stephanie L
Notre Dame HS
Salinas, CA

Schaal, James M
Yosemite HS
Coarsegold, CA

Schadt, Steve J
Monte Vista HS
Danville, CA

Schaefer, Tom C
Mater Dei HS
Fountain Valley, CA

Schaeffer, Stefanie
John W North HS
Upland, CA

Schaer, Heather K
Tustin HS
Tustin, CA

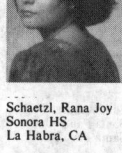

Schaetzl, Rana Joy
Sonora HS
La Habra, CA

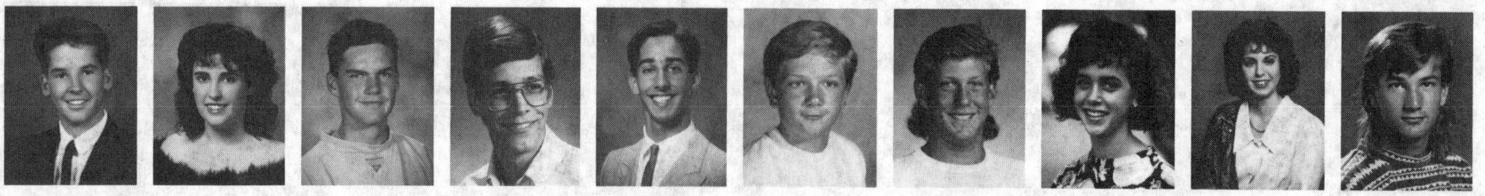

Schafer, Laurence M
Laguna Hills HS
Laguna Hills, CA

Schamp, Janet L
Redondo Union HS
Redondo Beach, CA

Schaper, David T
Kennedy HS
Buena Park, CA

Scharffenberg, Bill
Lodi Acad
Acampo, CA

Schechter, Damon Ross
La Serna HS
Whittier, CA

Schechter, David A
Atascadero HS
Atascadero, CA

Scheele, Paul R
Thomas Downey HS
Modesto, CA

Scheiner, Natalie
Los Alamitos HS
Seal Beach, CA

Schendel, Tara-Lynn
Turlock HS
Turlock, CA

Scherr, Brian M
Rim Of The World
Crestline, CA

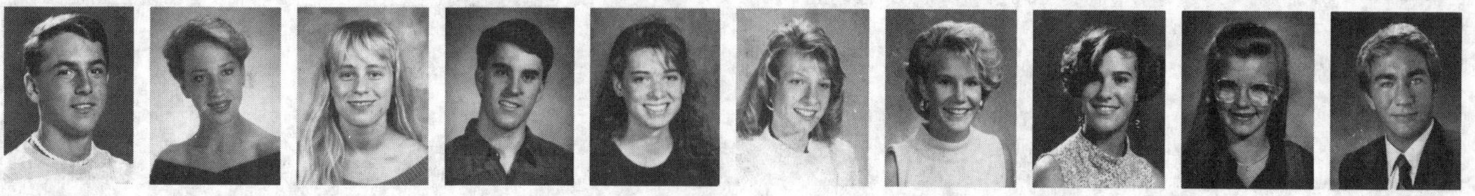

Scherr, Scott A
Rim Of The World
Crestline, CA

Schetgen, Shannon S
Gilroy HS
Gilroy, CA

Schiffmann, Alyssa
Santa Barbara HS
Santa Barbara, CA

Schinkel, Jeffrey D
Casa Grande HS
Petaluma, CA

Schlachta, Lilly V
Castro Valley HS
Castro Valley, CA

Schlemmer, Sandra A.
Tracy Joint Union
Tracy, CA

Schleske, Dana C
Bishop O'dowd HS
Oakland, CA

Schley, Anne E
Mayfield SR Schl
South Pasadena, CA

Schlientz, Mary T
Paraclete HS
Lancaster, CA

Schmeichel, Kevin David
Palos Verdes HS
Palos Vrds Pen, CA

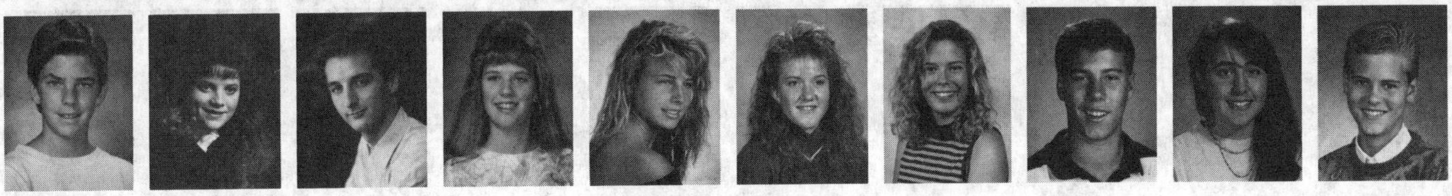

Schmidt, Darren A
Irvine HS
Irvine, CA

Schmidt, Jennifer N
Central HS
Madison, NC

Schmidt, Peter
Placer HS
Auburn, CA

Schmidt, Tiffany L
Irvine HS
Irvine, CA

Schmitt, Christina M
Monte Vista
Christian HS
Scotts Valley, CA

Schmitz, Kristy A
Calistoga HS
Calistoga, CA

Schmoe, Angie
Silver Valley HS
Yermo, CA

Schneider, Clayton
Kerman HS
Kerman, CA

Schneider, Laurie
Palo Alto HS
Palo Alto, CA

Schnell, Jeffrey L
Whittier Chrisitan
Yorba Linda, CA

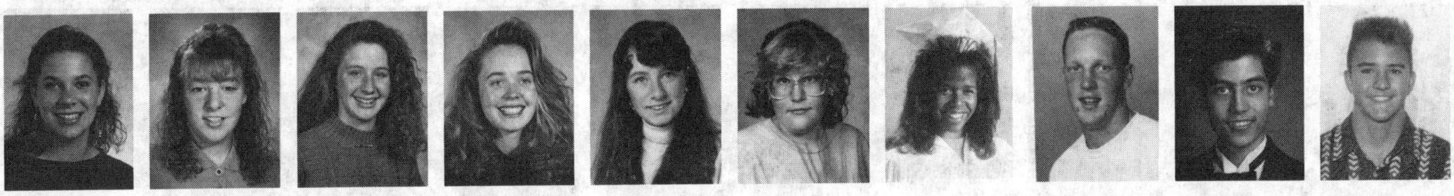

Schnitzer, Leigh E
Abraham Lincoln HS
San Jose, CA

Schnocker, Terrilyn
Polytechnic HS
North Hollywood, CA

Schoeffield, Amy
St Francis HS
Roseville, CA

Schoeffler, Gina
Sacramento Country
Day Schl
El Dorado Hills, CA

Schoenherz, Jennifer
Alta Loma HS
Alta Loma, CA

Schofield, Rachel E
Mission Bay HS
Hondo, TX

Scholtz, Michelle
Angelique
Eisenhower HS
Rialto, CA

Schommer, Curt C
Ventura HS
Ventura, CA

Schoon, Benjamin
Tehachapi HS
Tehachapi, CA

Schow, Scott E
Garden Grove HS
Garden Grove, CA

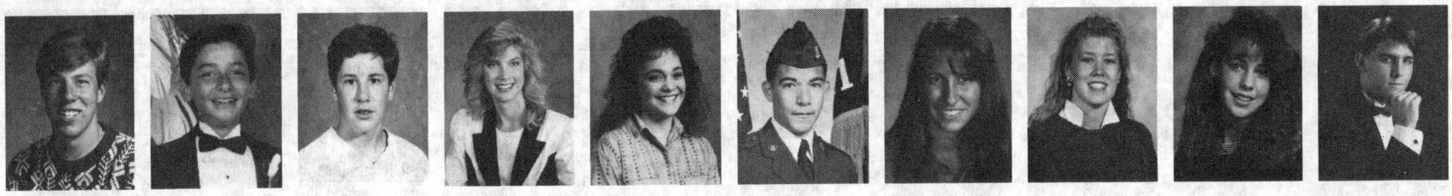

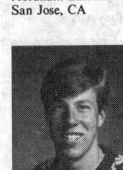

Schraeder, Peter P
Miramonte HS
Orinda, CA

Schreiber, Allen
Marina HS
Huntington Beach,
CA

Schreiner, Jesse S
Santa Curz HS
Santa Cruz, CA

Schroder, Tamara L
Pasadena HS
Sierra Madre, CA

Schroeder, Jo Anna
Highlands HS
Sacramento, CA

Schubert, Max Louis
Hiram West Johnson
Sacramento, CA

Schuckman, Anne
Lincoln HS
Stockton, CA

Schueller, Teresa J
Santa Clara HS
Newbury Park, CA

Schuh, Tracy
Santa Fe Christian
San Diego, CA

Schujahn, Derek R
Encina HS
Sacramento, CA

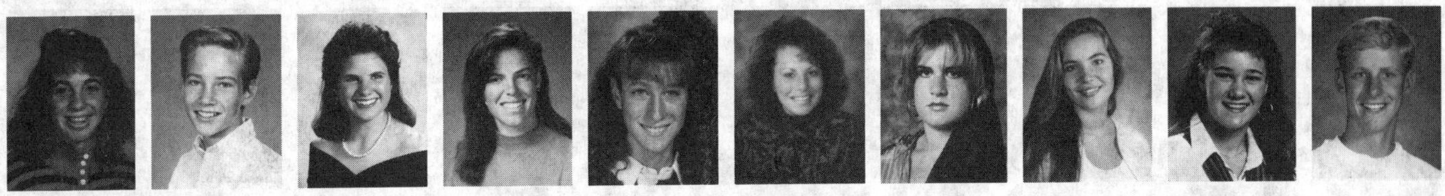

Schuldies, Shannon
Santa Teresa HS
San Jose, CA

Schultz, Emil F
Bellarmine College
Prep
Scotts Valley, CA

Schulze, Danielle
Terra Nova HS
Pacifica, CA

Schutz, Tiffani K
Monte Vista HS
Walnut Creek, CA

Schutzer, Jessica
Agoura HS
Agoura Hills, CA

Schwab, Laura
Newbury Park
Adventist Acad
Newbury Park, CA

Schwartz, Jennifer A
Estancia HS
Costa Mesa, CA

Schwartz, Rainbow
Berkeley HS
Berkeley, CA

Schwartz, Tiffani M
Tehachapi HS
Tehachapi, CA

Schwarz, Robert A
Santa Teresa HS
San Jose, CA

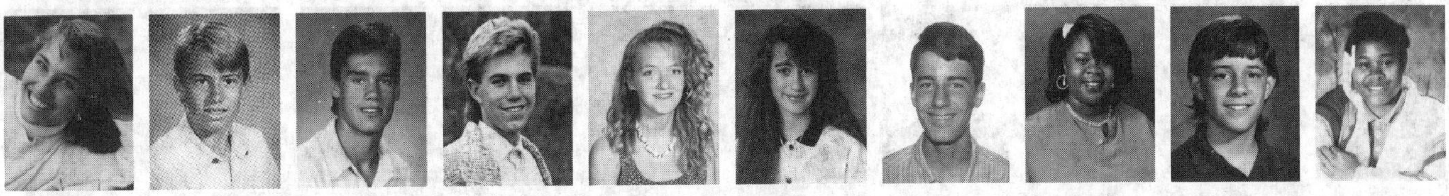

Schwede, Amy
Forest Lake Christian
Chicago Park, CA

Schweighart, Chris M
Torrey Pines HS
Solana Beach, CA

Schweininger, Frank
Bellarmine College
Prep
San Jose, CA

Schweizer, Jason S
Educational
Dynamics Inc HS
Escondido, CA

Scianni, Michelle M
California HS
Whittier, CA

Scipione, Ruth
Covenant Christian
Schl
San Diego, CA

Scott, Alan E
Edison HS
Fresno, CA

Scott, Carolyn S
Washington
Preparatory HS
Los Angeles, CA

Scott, Chris P
Granada HS
Livermore, CA

Scott, Cornelia V
Abraham Lincoln HS
San Francisco, CA

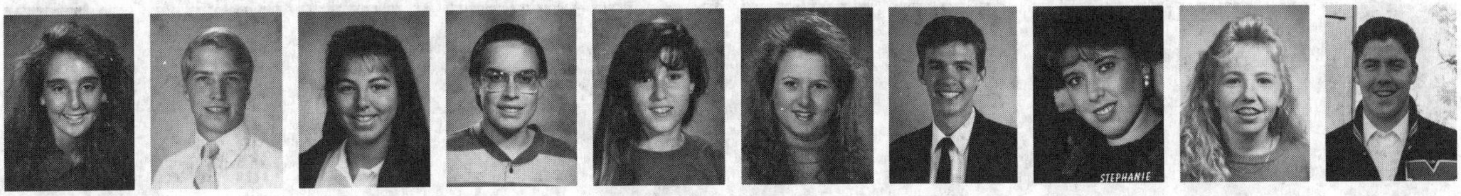

Scott, Denise K
Norco HS
Corona, CA

Scott, Jacob
Chestnut Avenue
Baptist Acad
Fresno, CA

Scott, Jennifer E
Colfax HS
Colfax, CA

Scott, Justin
John F Kennedy HS
Granada Hills, CA

Scott, Kim
San Ramon Valley
San Ramon, CA

Scott, Sheree
Westminster HS
Westminster, CA

Scott, Silas
Palm Springs HS
Desert Hot Sprngs,
CA

Scott, Stephanie M
Oroville HS
Oroville, CA

Scovill, Wendy
River City HS
West Sacramento,
CA

Scown, Jason
Moorpark HS
Moorpark, CA

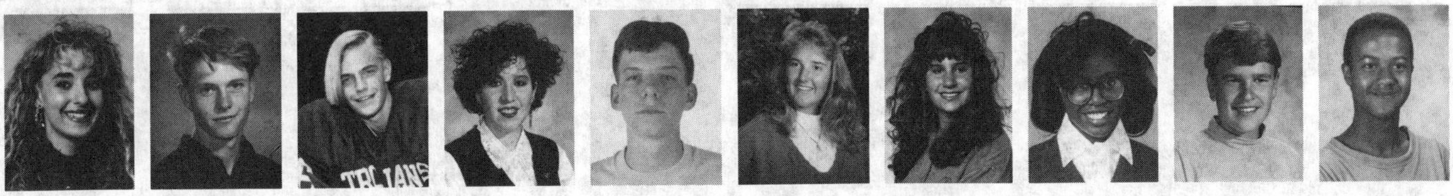

Scruggs, Dawn L
Woodrow Wilson HS
Long Beach, CA

Scuba, Jeff J
Torrey Pines HS
Rancho Santa Fe, CA

Scurich, Nate J
University HS
Irvine, CA

Seagle, Nicole R
Walnut HS
Walnut, CA

Sealey, Bret A
Del Campo HS
Carmichael, CA

Seamark, Lauri A
El Toro HS
El Toro, CA

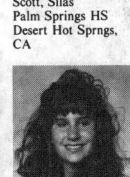

Seaton, Kathy A
Brea Olinda HS
Brea, CA

Seawell, Petra
Beverly Hills Prep
Schl
Arcadia, CA

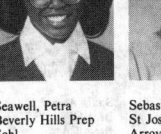

Sebastian, Ryan M
St Joseph HS
Arroyo Grande, CA

Sebhatu, Mekdem
Golden Gate Acad
Oakland, CA

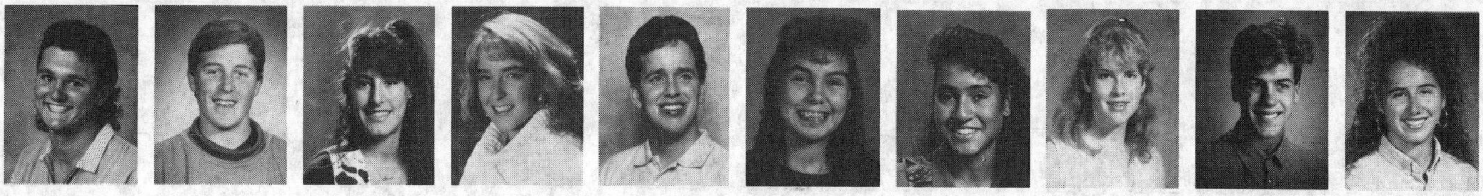

Sedlic, Steve
Chaminade Coll
Preparatory HS
Woodland Hills, CA

Seed, Collin A Tims
Point Arena HS
Point Arena, CA

Seeman, Lauren
Cleveland Humanities
Van Nuys, CA

Sefton, Katherine
Anne
Paso Robles HS
Paso Robles, CA

Segal, Jonathan E
Casa Roble HS
Orangevale, CA

Segala, Isabel
Valley View HS
Moreno Valley, CA

Segura, Alexandra E
Fontana HS
Fontana, CA

Seib, Catherine J
Estancia HS
Costa Mesa, CA

Seidell, Sean T
Central Catholic HS
Modesto, CA

Seidner, Jill N
Villa Park HS
Villa Park, CA

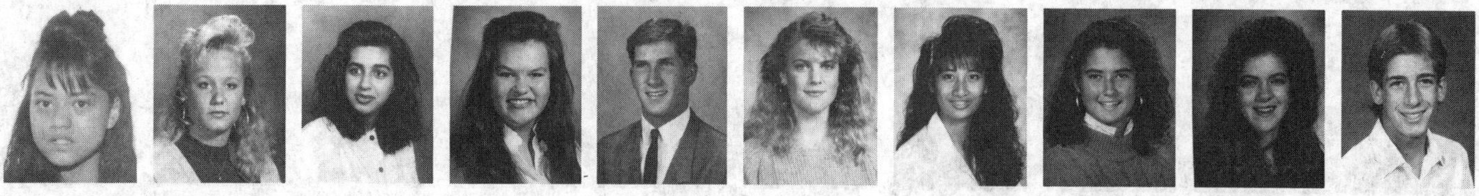

Seifert, Tara D
San Lorenzo HS
San Leandro, CA

Seigfried, Danielle
Hemet HS
Hemet, CA

Sekhon, Shamie K
San Ramon Valley
Danville, CA

Selan, Jenifer A
Mater Dei HS
Garden Grove, CA

Selecky, Chris
Marina HS
Huntington Bch, CA

Self, Tania A
El Comino
Fundemental HS
Carmichael, CA

Selga, Catherine
St Genevieve HS
Northridge, CA

Selikov, Lori E
Mission Viejo HS
Laguna Hills, CA

Sellers, Robin
Desert Christian HS
Lancaster, CA

Sellitti, Paulo A
Bellarmine College
Prep
Gilroy, CA

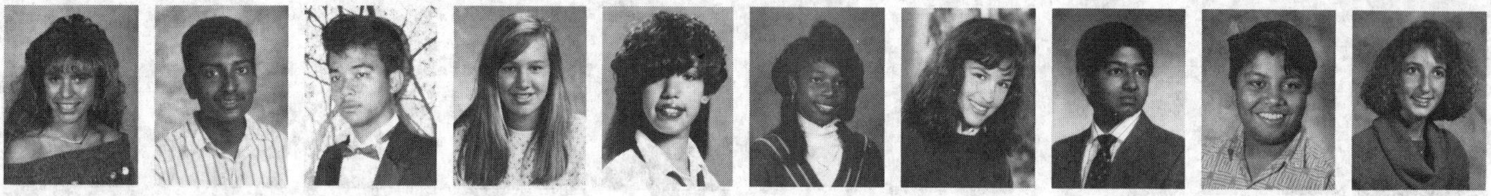

Seltzer, Jennifer
Chatsworth HS
Northridge, CA

Selva, Umaharan
Harvard Schl
Sherman Oaks, CA

Sem, Sophal R
Galileo HS
San Francisco, CA

Semansky, Anna C
Bishop O'doud HS
Berkeley, CA

Semien, Natasha
St Marys Acad
Carson, CA

Semien, Shanell
Canyon Springs HS
Moreno Valley, CA

Seminario, Nicole A
Westlake HS
Glendale, CA

Sen, Kaushik
El Camino Real HS
West Hills, CA

Sen, Soman
Leffingwell Christian
Picorivera, CA

Senecal, Janelle S
Bullard HS
Fresno, CA

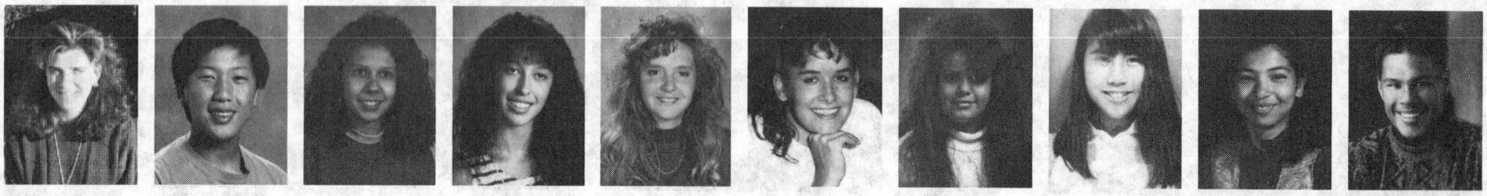

Senger, Christine J
Yucca Valley HS
Joshua Tree, CA

Seow, Darren
Glendale HS
Glendale, CA

Sepeda, Leslie
Strathmore HS
Strathmore, CA

Sequeira, Tonia L
Los Banos HS
Los Banos, CA

Seremi, Jeannine M
Davis SR HS
Davis, CA

Serpa, Christine
Turlock HS
Turlock, CA

Serrano, Delia
Arlington HS
Moreno Valley, CA

Serrano, Geraldine
Falmos
San Ramon Valley
Danville, CA

Serrano, Karina
Granger JR HS
National City, CA

Serrano, Jr Rey T
Tulare Union HS
Tulare, CA

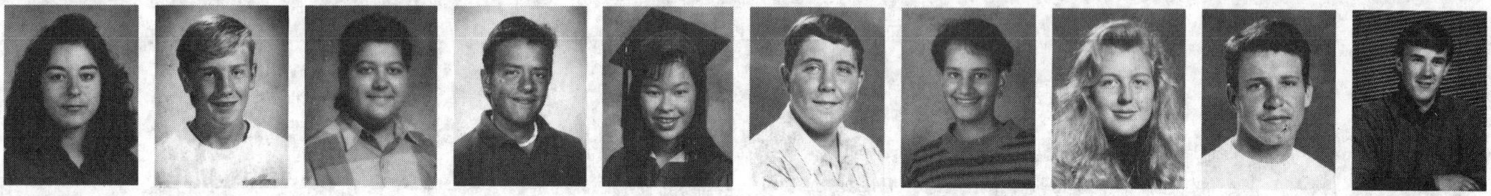

Serrano, Salvadora
Elisa A
Winters HS
Winters, CA

Service, Matt W
Montgomery HS
Santa Rosa, CA

Servin, Jose
South West HS
San Diego, CA

Sesser, Chad I
Westlake HS
Westlake Village, CA

Seto, Anna
John Marshall HS
Los Angeles, CA

Setti, David M
St Francis Of Assisi
Burbank, CA

Settimi, Janine T
Redwood HS
Visalia, CA

Settle, Suzanne I
Fontana HS
Fontana, CA

Settles, Victor
Taft Union HS
Mc Kittrick, CA

Seus, Scott
Tulelake HS
Tulelake, CA

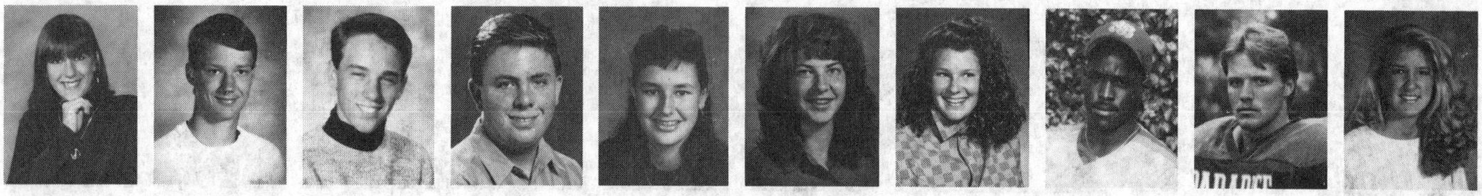

Severino, Jenean M
Salinas HS
Salinas, CA

Sevier, Jr Adam A
South HS
Bakersfield, CA

Sevo, Randy A
Valley Christian HS
Pleasanton, CA

Seward, Jason A
Rim Of The World
Crestline, CA

Seward, Michelle L
Chula Vista HS
Chula Vista, CA

Sexson, Linda C
Pacifica HS
Garden Grove, CA

Seybert, Audrey F
Brawley Union HS
Brawley, CA

Shackelford, Brian C
St Bernard HS
Inglewood, CA

Shadwick, Darrin
Paradise HS
Magalia, CA

Shafer, Dee
So Tahoe HS
South Lake Tahoe,
CA

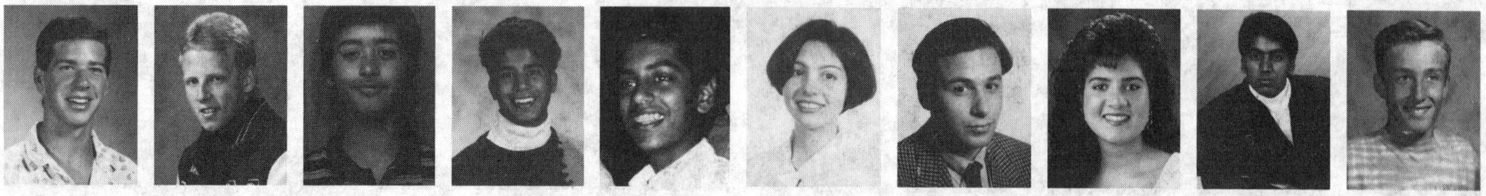

Shaffer, Brian M
Hemet HS
Hemet, CA

Shaffer, Neil
Modesto HS
Modesto, CA

Shah, Aneesh S
Brea Olinda HS
Brea, CA

Shah, Neevav V
Whitney HS
Cerritos, CA

Shah, Sanjeev
Ganesha HS
Diamond Bar, CA

Shahrdar, Parissa
Notre Dame HS
Belmont, CA

Shaltout, Tarek
Happy Valley Schl
Ojai, CA

Shamieh, Reem
Diamond Bar HS
Diamond Bar, CA

Shandil, Rajan
Victor Valley SR HS
Victorville, CA

Shannon, Richard B
Bullard HS
Fresno, CA

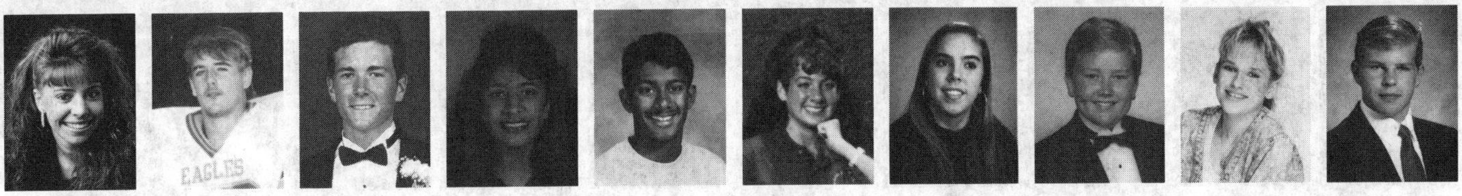

Shapira, Sharon
Birmingham HS
Calabasas, CA

Sharkey, Jason
Calvary Chaple HS
Santa Ana, CA

Sharkey, Kenny L
Savanna HS
Anaheim, CA

Sharma, Sheetal
Holy Names HS
Richmond, CA

Sharma, Vivek V
Los Alamitos HS
Los Alamitos, CA

Sharp, Briana
Redondo Union HS
Hermosa Bch, CA

Sharp, Kendra
Lincoln HS
Stockton, CA

Sharp, Matthew A
James Logan HS
Union City, CA

Sharp, Misty D
Elliot Education Center
Modesto, CA

Sharrar, Kelly A
Buena Park HS
Brea, CA

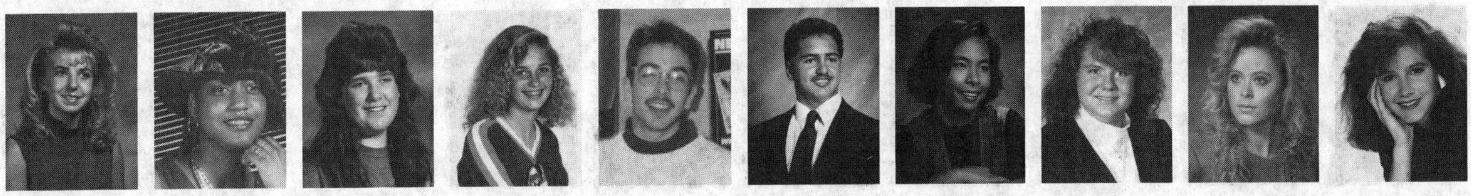

Shaski, Brandy
Palm Desert HS
Palm Desert, CA

Shaw, Kalaza
Saint Michaels HS
Inglewood, CA

Shea, Carla R
Arcata HS
Arcata, CA

Shean, Erynn
Ernest Righetti HS
Orcutt, CA

Shear, Anthony
Balboa HS
San Francisco, CA

Shears, Matthew W
Saddleback HS
Santa Ana, CA

Sheeks, Pamela C
Mt Carmel HS
San Diego, CA

Sheldon, Katherine A
Boron HS
North Edwards, CA

Shellen, Christina D
El Camino Real HS
Woodland Hills, CA

Shelley, Monica E
Saint Francis HS
Mountain View, CA

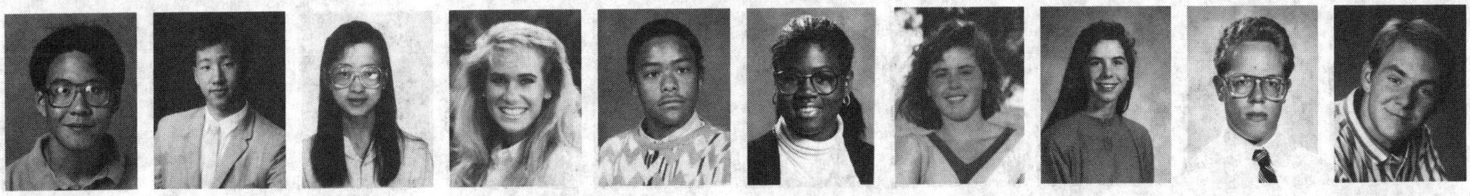

Shen, Andrew H
Chaminade College Prep
Van Nuys, CA

Shen, Franklyn J
Village Christian HS
Los Angeles, CA

Shen, Julie
Gretchen Whitney
Cerritos, CA

Shensky, Cynthia
Dana Hills HS
Laguna Niguel, CA

Shepard, Sean L
Fairfax HS
Los Angeles, CA

Shepard, Ta Shauna
San Pedro HS
Los Angeles, CA

Sheperd, Marianne
Poway HS
Poway, CA

Shepherd, Alyson
Poway HS
Poway, CA

Shepherd, Earl B
Don Bosco Technical Inst
Whittier, CA

Shepherd, Isaac N
Anderson Union HS
Redding, CA

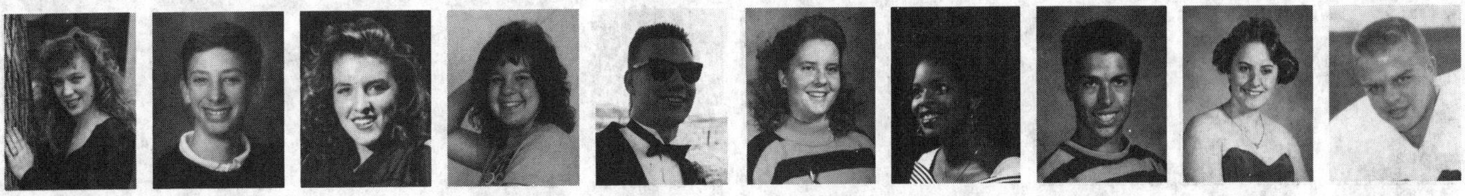

Shepherd, Tamara L
East Bakersfield HS
Bakersfield, CA

Sheridan, Bhima S
Las Lomas HS
Lafayette, CA

Sherman, Jennifer
Del Oro HS
Loomis, CA

Sherman, Jennifer M
Hilmar JR/SR HS
Hilmar, CA

Sherman, Jesse Z
Yreka HS
Montague, CA

Sherman, Kristen P
Kings Christian HS
Riverdale, CA

Sherman, Metralanette D
Barstow HS
Barstow, CA

Sherman, Thomas P
Norco SR HS
Corona, CA

Sherrill, Jenny R
Norte Vista HS
Riverside, CA

Sherwin, John D
Moorpark HS
New Fairfield, CT

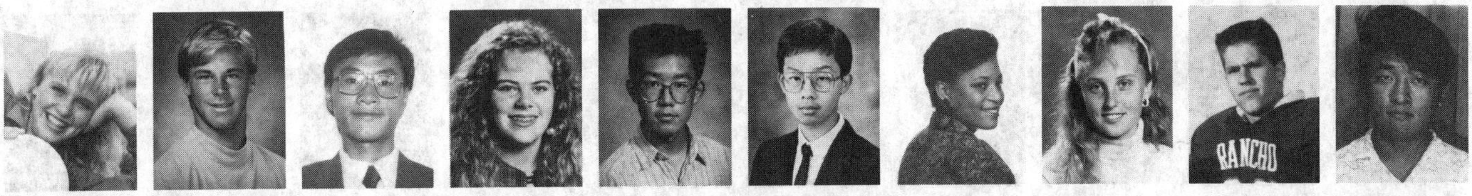

Sherwin, Kristen
Moorpark HS
New Fairfield, CT

Sherwood, Shane E
Trabuco Hills HS
Mission Viejo, CA

Shi, Fleming
Homestead HS
Cupertino, CA

Shick, Tiffany
Garces Memorial HS
Mc Farland, CA

Shie, Hank
University HS
Irvine, CA

Shieh, Shu-Horng
Mark Keppel HS
Monterey Park, CA

Shields, Teresa
Ramona HS
Riverside, CA

Shiffert, Joyce L
Coast Christian Schls
Torrance, CA

Shiffler, Mike A
Rancho Cotate HS
Rohnert Park, CA

Shih, Ben
Arcadia HS
Arcadia, CA

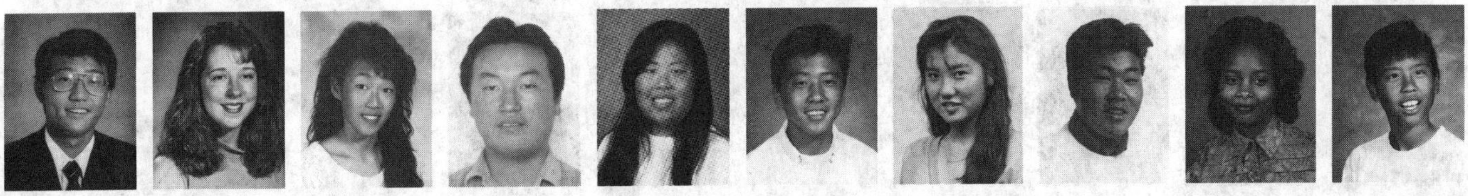

Shih, Davey
Orange HS
Orange, CA

Shilts, Mical K
Red Bluff Union HS
Red Bluff, CA

Shin, Esther
Whitney HS
Cerritos, CA

Shin, Gene
Lowell HS
San Francisco, CA

Shin, Hye-Ji
Yucaipa HS
Downey, CA

Shin, Michael
West Covina HS
West Covina, CA

Shinzato, Erika N
Schurr HS
Montebello, CA

Shioya, Marc T
Edison HS
Huntington Beach, CA

Shipp, Monyulette D
Southern CA Christian HS
Santa Ana, CA

Shiraishi, Kurt M
Bellarmine College Prep
San Jose, CA

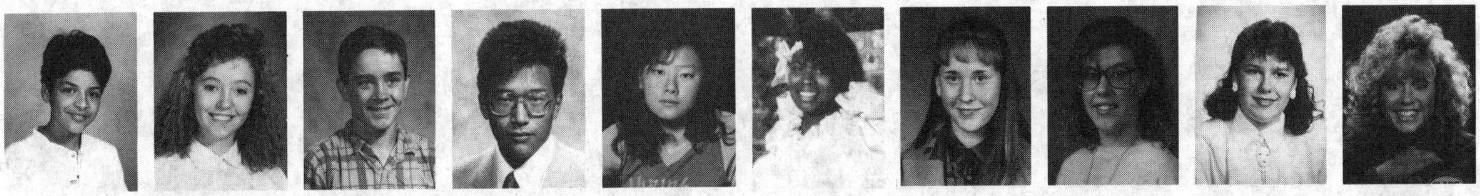

Shiri, Hezi
Ginstein Acad
Northridge, CA

Shirley, Robyne R
Willows HS
Willows, CA

Shirley, William E
Bullard HS
Fresno, CA

Shiroish, Mark
Mark Keppel HS
Monterey Park, CA

Shiue, Chi-Yu
Alhambra HS
Alhambra, CA

Shivers, Cynthia E
Castlemont HS
Oakland, CA

Shivers, Kathleen P
St Joseph HS
Long Beach, CA

Shofner, Charleen K
Salinas HS
Salinas, CA

Short, Daphne D
Sonora HS
Turlock, CA

Short, Heather
Del Norte HS
Crescent City, CA

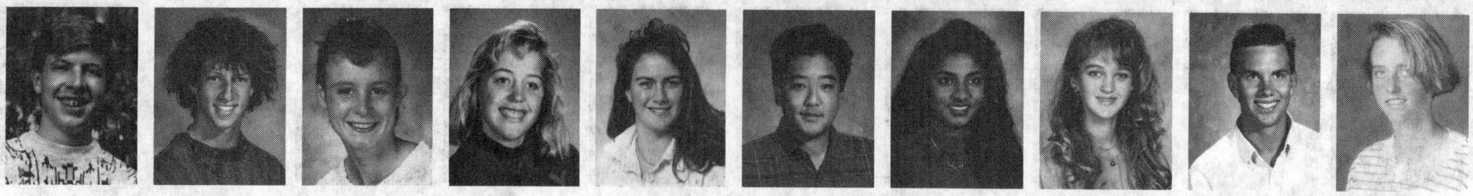

Short, Jonathan S
Caruthers HS
Caruthers, CA

Shostak, Eli
Los Alamitos HS
Los Alamitos, CA

Shoup, Shawna
Fall River JR/SR HS
Fall River Mills, CA

Showalter, Nicole J
Clovis HS
Fresno, CA

Showers, Tracy L
Alta Loma HS
Alta Loma, CA

Shu, Victor
San Mateo HS
Hillsborough, CA

Shubhakar, Poornima
Monache HS
Porterville, CA

Shuffield, Veronica
Western Christian
Baldwin Park, CA

Shultz, Christopher S
Woodside HS
Redwood City, CA

Shultz, Susanne M
Bonita Vista HS
Bonita, CA

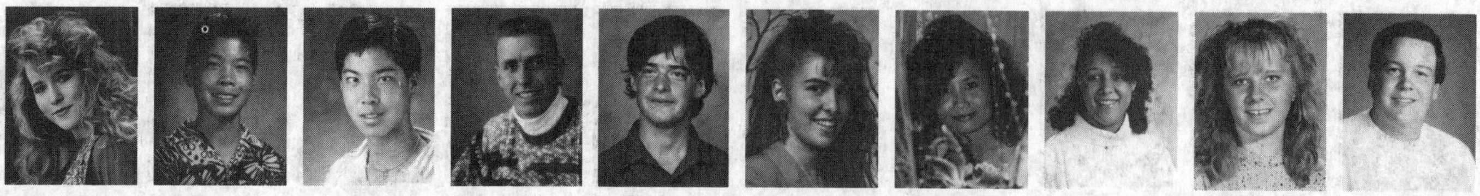

Shultz, Tiffany S
Cordova SR HS
Sacramento, CA

Shum, Conroy W
Diamond Bar HS
Diamond Bar, CA

Shum, Merrill K
Diamond Bar HS
Diamond Bar, CA

Shumard, Brian
Arcata HS
Arcata, CA

Shumate, III Jerome
El Cajon Valley HS
El Cajon, CA

Shumway, Nicole
Alemany HS
Northridge, CA

Sibounheuang, Phouangphet
Fred C Beyer HS
Modesto, CA

Sicard, Lyn A
Prospect HS
San Jose, CA

Sickle, Shawn M
Pioneer HS
San Jose, CA

Sicks, Bud R
Tulare Union HS
Tulare, CA

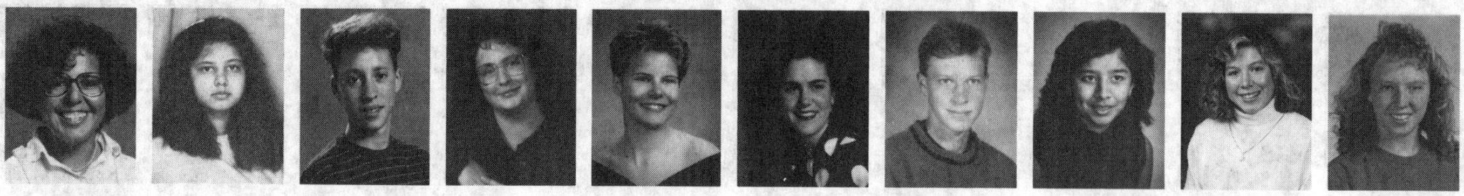

Sida, Sylvia E
Fontana HS
Fontana, CA

Sidhu, Rupinder
Oxnard HS
Burbank, CA

Siegel, David E
Birmingham HS
Encino, CA

Siegel, Melissa
Palo Verde HS
Blythe, CA

Siegert, Anja Simone
James Lick HS
West Germany

Siegle, Samantha Gale
Oakwood HS
Los Angeles, CA

Siegler, Carl F
Victory Christian HS
Carmichael, CA

Sierra, Hoa
Grace M Davis HS
Modesto, CA

Sifuentes, Debbie
North Salinas HS
Salinas, CA

Sigmon, Brooke M
Thomas Downey HS
Modesto, CA

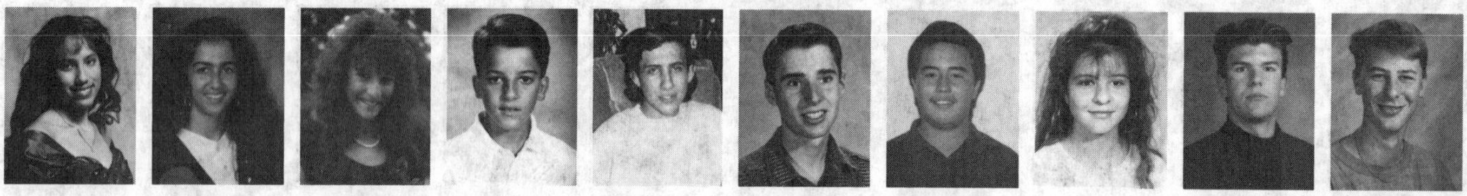

Sigur, Rachel L
St Paul HS
Whittier, CA

Sigurdsson, Leila
Laguna Hills HS
Laguna Hills, CA

Silberfeld, Ashley
Heschel Day Schl
Northridge, CA

Silberman, Adrian E
John F Kennedy HS
La Palma, CA

Siliezar, Eddie A
Burroughs HS
Burbank, CA

Silva, Chad
Arroyo Grande HS
Arroyo Grande, CA

Silva, Ernesto R
Apple Valley HS
Apple Valley, CA

Silva, Fabiola
Pasadena HS
Pasadena, CA

Silva, Gregory L
Golden West HS
Visalia, CA

Silva, Kelly D
Apple Valley SR HS
Apple Valley, CA

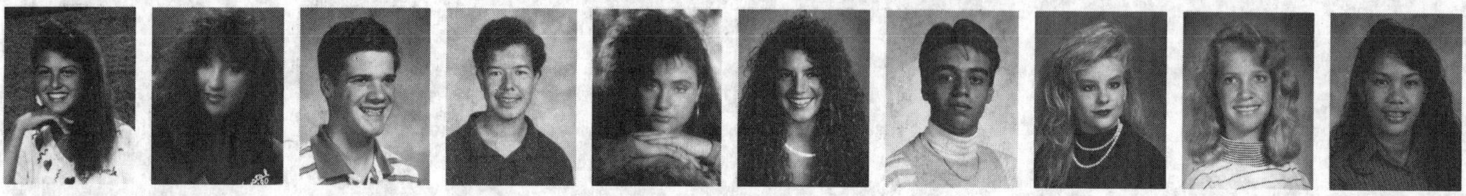

Silva, Kim M
Redondo Union HS
Redondo Beach, CA

Silva, Krystal A
Atwater HS
Atwater, CA

Silva, Philip J
Redwood Christian
San Leandro, CA

Silva, Roman
Yosemite HS
Coarsegold, CA

Silva, Tiffany A
San Benito HS
Hollister, CA

Silveira, Caroline A
Tulare Union HS
Tulare, CA

Silveira, Gary S
Westmont HS
Campbell, CA

Silver, Michelle S
Campbell Hall HS
Van Nuys, CA

Silver, Teena L
North Hollywood HS
North Hollywood, CA

Silverio, Mae
San Joaquin Memorial HS
Fresno, CA

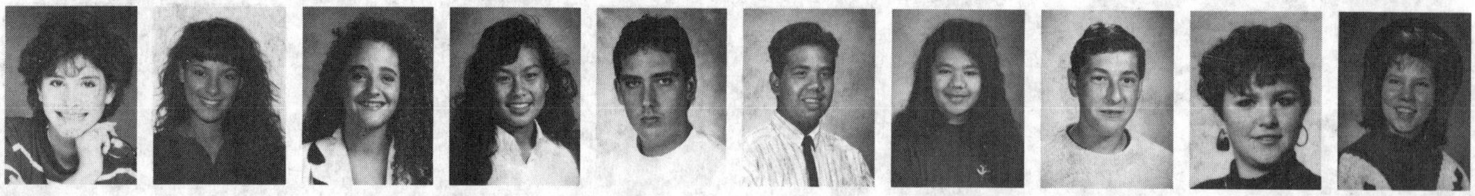

Silverman, Laurel D
Los Alamitos HS
Fountain Valley, CA

Silverton, Julia
St Marys HS
Stockton, CA

Silvetti, Natalia
Montclaire Prep Schl
Tarzana, CA

Sim, Roselynn
Mater Dei HS
Rancho Santa Marg, CA

Simal, Jamie
Hilmar HS
Hilmar, CA

Simandjuntak, Fredy
Pomona Adventist JR Acad
San Dimas, CA

Simandjuntak, Sylvia
Pomona Adventist Jr Acad
San Dimas, CA

Simas, Robert P
Montgomery HS
Santa Rosa, CA

Simeone, Carrie A
Ontario HS
Ontario, CA

Simmons, Amy C
Sunny Hills HS
Buena Park, CA

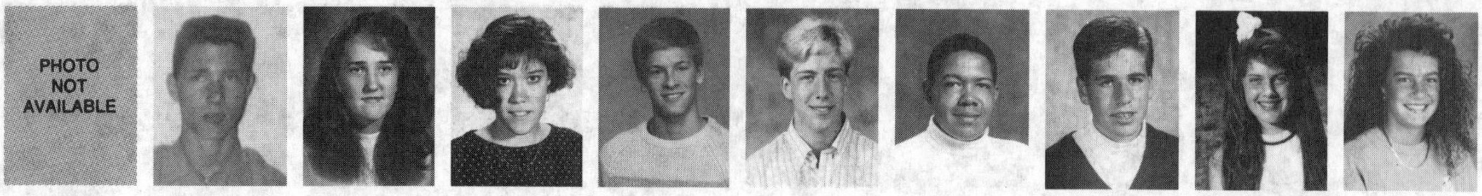

Simmons, Amy D
Fairfax HS
Los Angeles, CA

Simmons, Brandon K
Encina HS
Sacramento, CA

Simmons, Jaime Lynn
Foothill HS
Bakersfield, CA

Simmons, Kara J
El Dorado HS
Fullerton, CA

Simmons, Steve M
Enterprise HS
Redding, CA

Simmons, Todd
Whittier Christian
Hacienda Heights, CA

Simms, Brian C
Fontana HS
Fontana, CA

Simon, Steven
Westmoor HS
Daly City, CA

Simone, Mary K
Westminster HS
Westminster, CA

Simonian, Stacy
Sanger HS
Fresno, CA

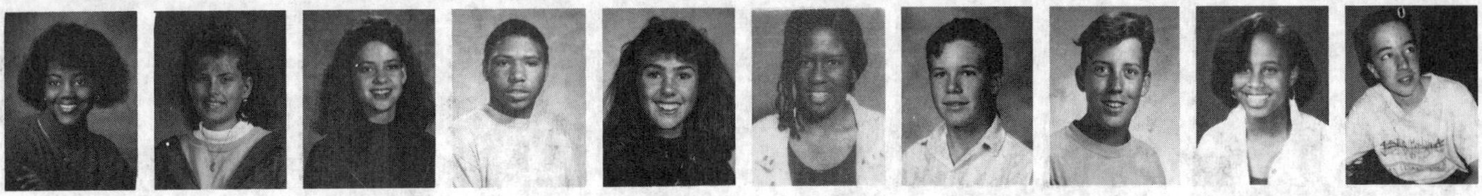

Simons, Elesha C
Torrey Pines HS
San Diego, CA

Simpson, Audra L
Grace M Davis HS
Modesto, CA

Simpson, Heather M
Carlmont HS
San Carlos, CA

Simpson, Keinard L
West Covina HS
Valinda, CA

Simpson, Kristen J
Roseville HS
Rocklin, CA

Simpson, Lela D
Antelope Valley HS
Palmdale, CA

Simpson, II Robert C
Fairfield HS
Fairfield, CA

Simpson, Ryan P
Live Oak HS
San Jose, CA

Simpson, Tara M
Oakland Technical
Oakland, CA

Simpson, Travis J
John F Kennedy HS
Sacramento, CA

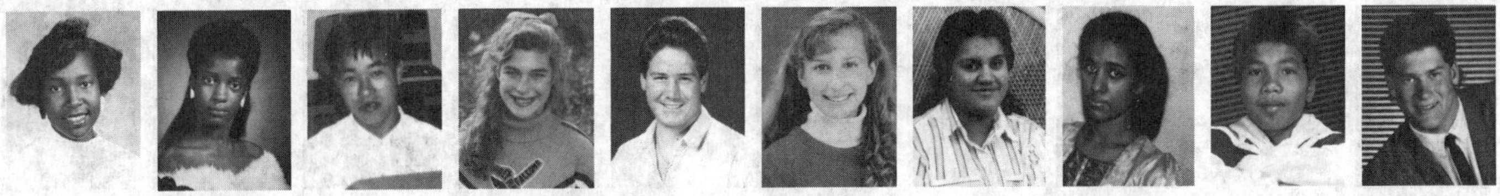

Sims, Aisha M
Bishop O'dowd HS
Oakland, CA

Sims, Latwila
Lompoc HS
Lompoc, CA

Sin, Dennis Vu
Oakland HS
Oakland, CA

Sinclitico, Molly G
Torrey Pines HS
Solana Beach, CA

Sindicich, Robert L
Pinole Valley HS
Hercules, CA

Singerman, Liorah
Sacramento HS
Sacramento, CA

Singh, Kamlesh
Turlock HS
Turlock, CA

Singh, Ravinderjit K
Moreno Valley HS
Moreno Valley, CA

Singharath, Bounthavy A
Pittsburg HS
Pittsburg, CA

Singleton, Larry
Cabrillo HS
Lompoc, CA

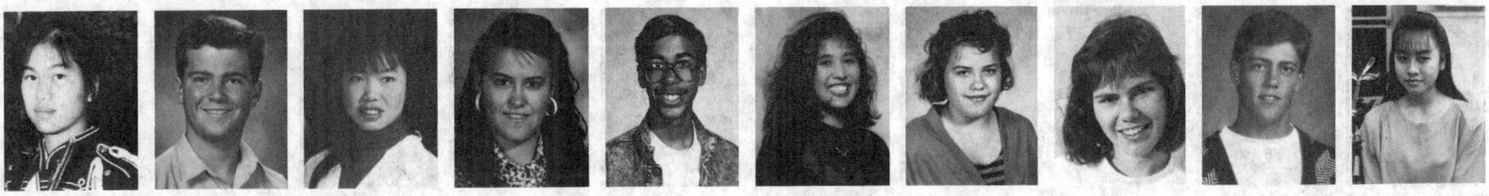

Sinthawanarong, Kamoltip
Bellflower HS
Downey, CA

Sipes, Kenneth Landon
Irvine HS
Irvine, CA

Siphonekham, Amanda
Sweetwater HS
National City, CA

Siques, Claudia T
Paraclete HS
Palmdale, CA

Sirakavit, Craig S
Bellflower HS
Bellflower, CA

Sirineo, Josephine V
Montebello HS
Montebello, CA

Sisk, Cheryl L
Carson HS
Carson, CA

Sisk, Corrina C
Don A Lugo HS
Chino, CA

Sitton, Gary
Mt Whitney HS
Visalia, CA

Sivongxay, Daravanh
Covina HS
West Covina, CA

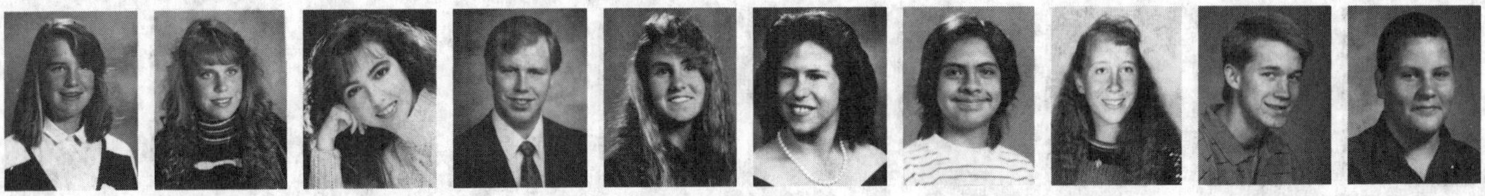

Skaggs, Julia P
Arcata HS
Arcata, CA

Skarecky, Julia G
Moreno Valley HS
Moreno Vly, CA

Skillman, Alexandra
University HS
Irvine, CA

Skinner, Troy D
Granite Hills HS
El Cajon, CA

Skracic, Suzanne D
San Pedro HS
San Pedro, CA

Skultety, Carrie
Concord HS
Concord, CA

Skyhorse-Johnson, Brando
Downtown Business Magnet HS
Los Angeles, CA

Slack, Nicolle
Glen A Wilson HS
Hacienda Hgts, CA

Slack, Steven M
Bellarmine College Prep
San Jose, CA

Slagle, Mark D
Will C Wood HS
Vacaville, CA

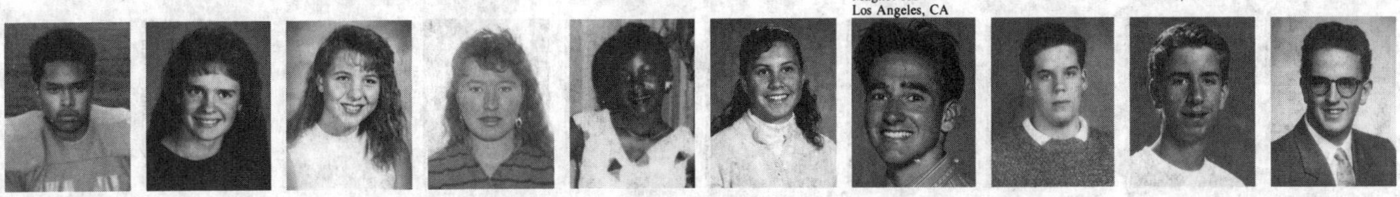

Slapno, Jay Aquino
Mt Eden HS
Hayward, CA

Slate, Nicole
Le Grand Union HS
Le Grand, CA

Slater, Jennifer L
Burroughs HS
Ridgecrest, CA

Slater, Marianne
Saint Bonaventure
Ventura, CA

Slaton, Serena
Mc Clymonds HS
Oakland, CA

Slattery, Karen M
Woodside HS
Redwood City, CA

Slaven, Devin E
Huntington Beach
Huntington Beach, CA

Slessman, George
Mt Whitney HS
Visalia, CA

Slider, Christopher A
Fontana HS
Fontana, CA

Slider, Thomas Richard
Fontana HS
Fontana, CA

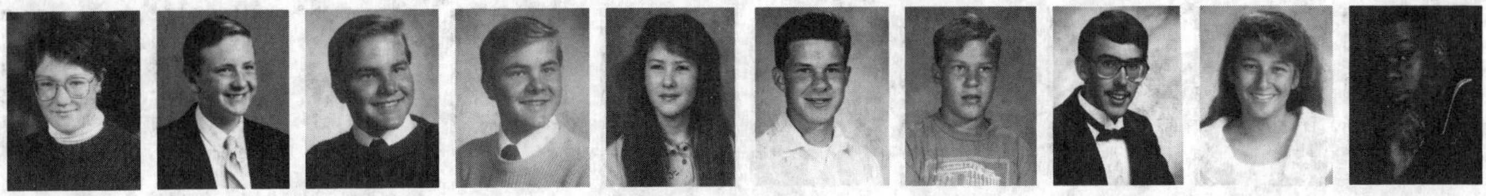

Sloan, Beth A
North Salinas HS
Salinas, CA

Sloan, James R
Palo Alto HS
Palo Alto, CA

Slover, Jamey
Fontana HS
Crestline, CA

Slover, Jason
Fontana HS
Crestline, CA

Slusser, Amber M
El Cajon Valley HS
El Cajon, CA

Slusser, Frank
Edison-Computech
Fresno, CA

Slusser, Greg L
Edison-Computech
Fresno, CA

Smart, John
Kearny HS
San Diego, CA

Smelcer, Michelle Renee
Capistrano Valley Christian HS
Laguna Niguel, CA

Smiley, Jamal
John F Kennedy HS
Sacramento, CA

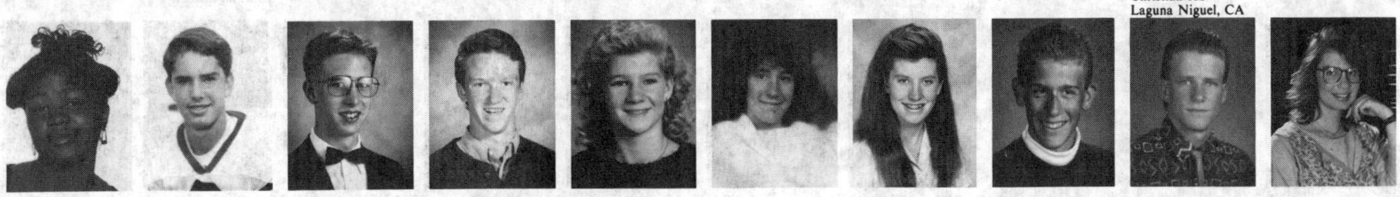

Smiley, Martinita C
Silver Valley HS
Fort Irwin, CA

Smith, Adam C
Coronado HS
Coronado, CA

Smith, Adam M
Santa Clara HS
Oxnard, CA

Smith, Alexander W
Montgomery HS
Santa Rosa, CA

Smith, Amber
Saddleback HS
Atlantic, IA

Smith, Angela V
Hesperia HS
Hesperia, CA

Smith, Bernadette P
St Genevieve HS
Reseda, CA

Smith, Bradley S
Clovis West HS
Fresno, CA

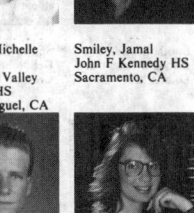

Smith, Brandon M
Caruthers HS
Caruthers, CA

Smith, Carrie L
Riverside Christian
Riverside, CA

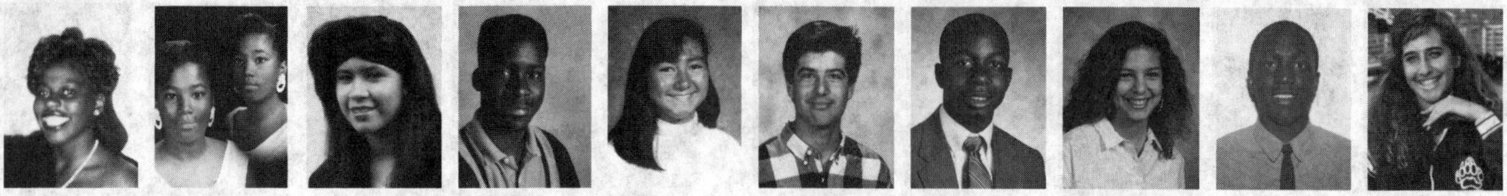

Smith, Cheryl R
Skyline HS
Oakland, CA

Smith, Christina M
Eisenhower HS
Fontana, CA

Smith, Christina N
Encinal HS
Alameda, CA

Smith, David F
Oxnard HS
Oxnard, CA

Smith, Diana
Mountain View HS
Mountain View, CA

Smith, Dylan D
Mayfair HS
Lakewood, CA

Smith, Emanuel Q
Saint Francis HS
Menlo Park, CA

Smith, Gabriell
Los Gatos HS
Los Gatos, CA

Smith, Gary P
Hillsdale HS
San Mateo, CA

Smith, Gena B
Bear River HS
Auburn, CA

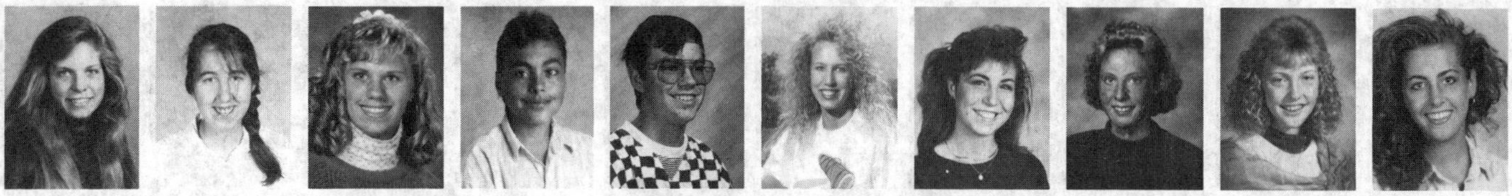

Smith, Heather
Tomales HS
Bodega Bay, CA

Smith, Heather E
La Serna HS
Whittier, CA

Smith, Janis E
Trabuco Hills HS
Mission Viejo, CA

Smith, Jason E
Hueneme HS
Oxnard, CA

Smith, Jason P
Apple Valley HS
Apple Valley, CA

Smith, Jenea A
Armijo HS
Suisun, CA

Smith, Jennifer
Yosemite Union HS
Coarsegold, CA

Smith, Jennifer M
Armijo HS
Fairfield, CA

Smith, Jenny
Fortuna Union HS
Fortuna, CA

Smith, Joslyn A
Del Campo HS
Austin, TX

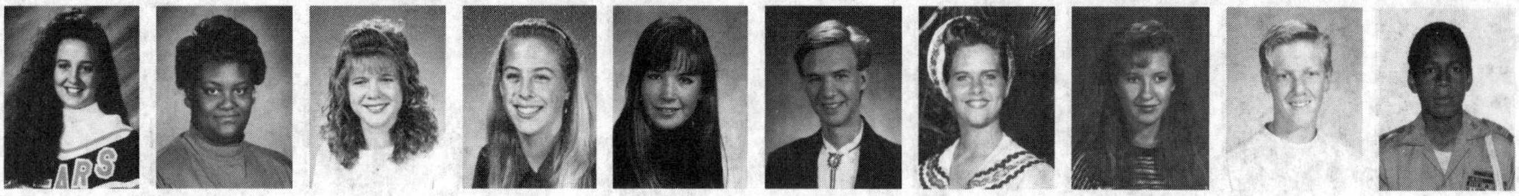

Smith, Kari
Temecula Valley HS
Temecula, CA

Smith, Keishna M
Oroville HS
Oroville, CA

Smith, Kristen M
Pittsburg HS
Pittsburg, CA

Smith, Laura E
Albany HS
Albany, CA

Smith, Lori J
Live Oak HS
Morgan Hill, CA

Smith, Marlan K
Golden West HS
Visalia, CA

Smith, Melanie
Pacifica HS
Garden Grove, CA

Smith, Melanie L
Canyon Springs HS
Moreno Valley, CA

Smith, Michael C
La Serna HS
Whittier, CA

Smith, Miguel A
Downtown Business
Magnet HS
Los Angeles, CA

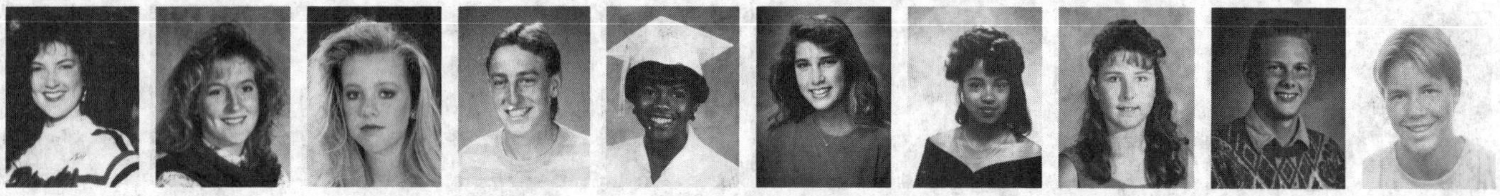

Smith, Molly
San Leandro HS
San Leandro, CA

Smith, Monika K.
Atascadero HS
Atascadero, CA

Smith, Natalie S
Alta Loma HS
Alta Loma, CA

Smith, Nevada S
Liberty Union HS
Oakley, CA

Smith, Nichole S
Washington Prep
Los Angeles, CA

Smith, Nickie Lynn
Julian Union HS
Julian, CA

Smith, Nysha N
Western Christian
Phillips Ranch, CA

Smith, Patricia
Ernest Righetti HS
Santa Maria, CA

Smith, Patrick L
Fresno Christian HS
Fresno, CA

Smith, Patrick R
Huntington Beach
Huntington Beach,
CA

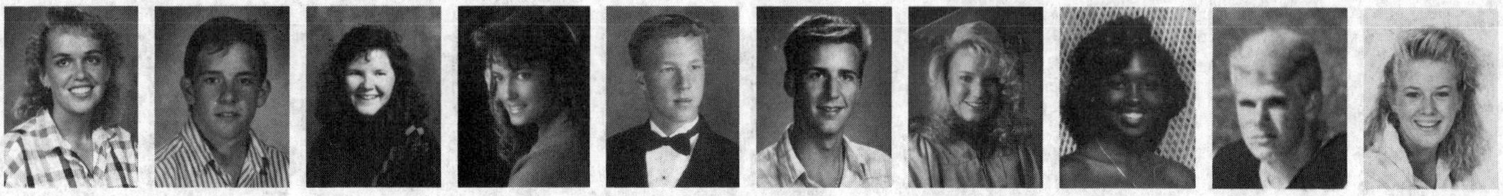

Smith, Penelope J
Del Campo HS
Fair Oaks, CA

Smith, Phillip
Lassen HS
Susanville, CA

Smith, Sabra D
Foothill HS
Citrus Heights, CA

Smith, Sandra
Morro Bay HS
Los Osos, CA

Smith, Sean
Bonita Vista HS
Chula Vista, CA

Smith, Sean K
Clovis West HS
Fresno, CA

Smith, Shanyn L
Barstow HS
Hinkley, CA

Smith, Sharlecia
Crenshaw HS
Los Angeles, CA

Smith, Shilo W
Casa Roble
Fundamental HS
Orangevale, CA

Smith, Sidonie A
Enterprise HS
Palo Cedro, CA

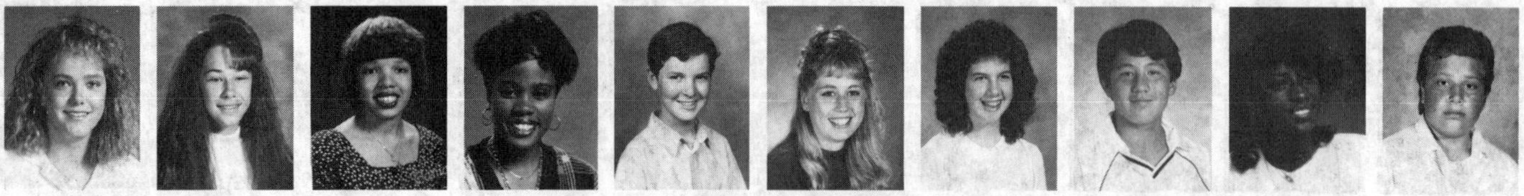

Smith, Stacie M
Bishop Montgomery
Lomita, CA

Smith, Tamie L
Del Nolte HS
Crescent City, CA

Smith, Tania D
Cate Sch
Oakland, CA

Smith, Tiffany A
Etiwanda HS
R Cucamonga, CA

Smith, Toby Lee
Escondido HS
Escondido, CA

Smith, Valerie
Clovis HS
Clovis, CA

Smith, Yvonne C
College Park HS
Pleasant Hill, CA

Snare, Edward A
Willow Glen HS
San Jose, CA

Sneed, Sicely N
Downtown Business
Magnet HS
Los Angeles, CA

Snell, Casey D
Rio Linda SR HS
Sacramento, CA

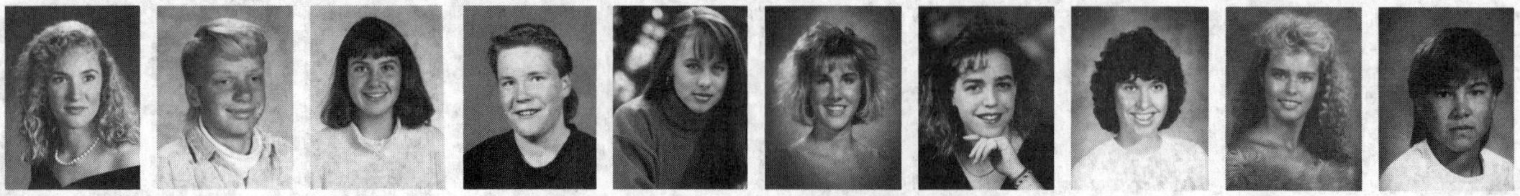

Snelling, Sarah
Hillsdale HS
San Mateo, CA

Sniegowski, Matthew
Paso Robles HS
Paso Robles, CA

Snively, Gillian R
Live Oak HS
Morgan Hill, CA

Snow, Abraham D
Beaumont HS
Cherry Valley, CA

Snow, Hollie
Miramonte HS
Orinda, CA

Snyder, Heidi
Hart HS
Valencia, CA

Snyder, Shannon L
North Salinas HS
Aromas, CA

Soares, Teresa L
Tulare Western HS
Tulare, CA

Soderstrom, Katarina
Gahr HS
Lakewood, CA

Soeda, Jarvis N
Edison HS
Huntington Beach,
CA

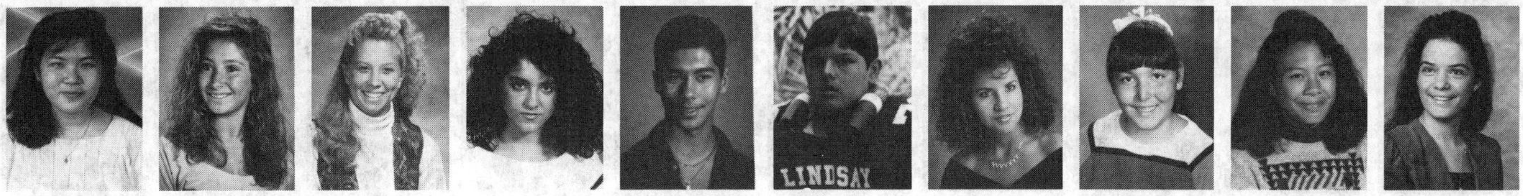

Soehendra, Emily
Calvary Baptist HS
Azusa, CA

Sohaei, Ati
Trabuco Hills HS
Mission Viejo, CA

Soldmann, Christine
John W North HS
Riverside, CA

Soleymani, Shirley
Hamilton Music Acad
Los Angeles, CA

Soliman, Tammer M
Clovis West HS
Fresno, CA

Solis, Adrian H
Lindsay HS
Lindsay, CA

Solis, Alma
Live Oak HS
Morgan Hill, CA

Solis, Claudia
Lynwood HS
Lynwood, CA

Solis, Daphne
Clayton Valley HS
Concord, CA

Solis, Grethel
Birmingham HS
Los Angeles, CA

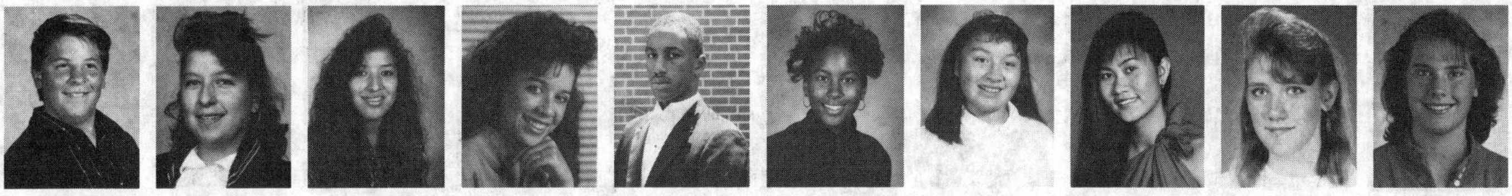

Solis, Michael A
Arroyo Grande HS
Grover City, CA

Soliz, Anna Marie
Gladstone HS
Azusa, CA

Soliz, Denise R
Eisenhower HS
Rialto, CA

Soliz, Michelle Y
Western Christian
Azusa, CA

Solomon, Brian C
Bishop Montgomery
Gardena, CA

Solomon, Kristie L
Victor Valley HS
Victorville, CA

Solorio, Raquel Y
Montebello HS
Los Angeles, CA

Som, Sitha
Santa Rosa HS
Fulton, CA

Somerhalder, Jenni L
Liberty Union HS
Knightsen, CA

Sommer, Karin V
Willow Glen Ed Park
San Jose, CA

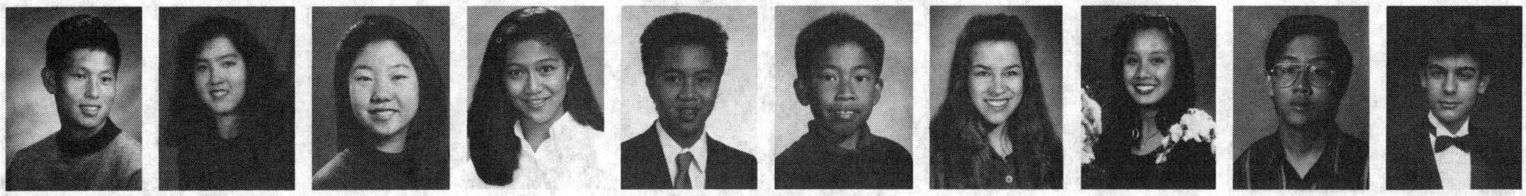

Son, Peter C
Pinole Valley HS
Pinole, CA

Song, Misti
Monterey Bay Acad
Glendora, CA

Song, Sarah
Palisades HS
Los Angeles, CA

Songco, Louise S
Immaculate Heart
Los Angeles, CA

Songco, Melvin J
Saint Francis HS
San Carlos, CA

Sonico, John
Independence HS
San Jose, CA

Sonnenburg, April S
Gridley HS
Gridley, CA

Soo Hoo, Lori Nicole
Bell HS
Cudahy, CA

Soonthornsawad, Amorntat Joe
Chaminade Coll Prep
Simi Valley, CA

Soravilla, Andrew
California HS
San Ramon, CA

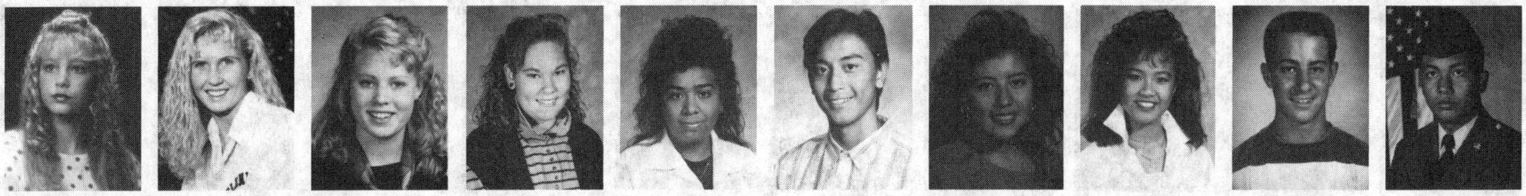

Sorbel, Shayna R
Troy HS
Yorba Linda, CA

Sorensen, Dawn Charmane
Glendora HS
Glendora, CA

Sorensen, Melissa
Coalinga HS
Coalinga, CA

Sorg, Windy L
Vacaville HS
Vacaville, CA

Soria, Leticia T
Holy Family HS
Los Angeles, CA

Soriano, Jonard D
St Anthony HS
Lakewood, CA

Soriano, Vilma A
Washington Prep
Van Nuys, CA

Soriben, Bernadette F
Mercy San Francisco
San Francisco, CA

Sorich, Jason
Cardinal Newman
Rohnert Park, CA

Soriente, Engelbert F
Turlock HS
Turlock, CA

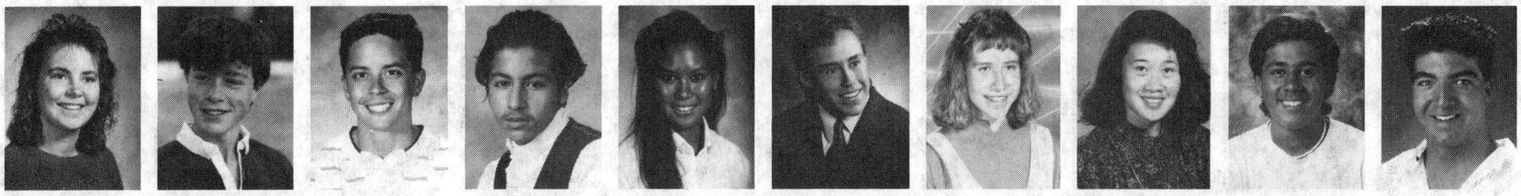

Sorrensen, Nadine C
Poway HS
New Zealand

Sorrentino, Felix
San Lorenzo Valley
Ben Lomond, CA

Sosa, Christopher M
Chino HS
Chino, CA

Sosa, Kain
Calexico HS
Calexico, CA

Sosmena, Hannah Krishna
Mater Dei HS
Tustin, CA

Sotelo, Justin
Williams HS
Williams, CA

Sotelo, Renee
Williams HS
Williams, CA

Sothisom, Bopha P
Los Alamitos HS
Long Beach, CA

Soto, Jose De Jesus
San Clemente HS
Capistrano Beach, CA

Soto, Joseph L
Ramona HS
Riverside, CA

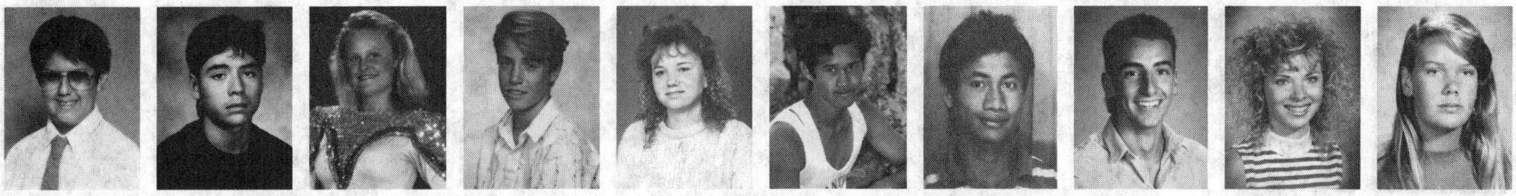

Soto, Juan Donald O
Brawley Union HS
Brawley, CA

Soto, Mark A
Barstow HS
Barstow, CA

Soudant, Lisette R
Mater Dei HS
Villa Park, CA

Souders, Jeremy M
Grossmont HS
El Cajon, CA

Soulages, Gail L
San Gorgino HS
San Bernardino, CA

Soun, Visith
Santiago HS
Garden Grove, CA

Souphommavong, Xayxana
Banning HS
Banning, CA

Sousa, Manuel R
Los Banos HS
Gustine, CA

Sousa, Natalie M
Tulare Western HS
Tulare, CA

Southern, Elizabeth L
Petaluma HS
Petaluma, CA

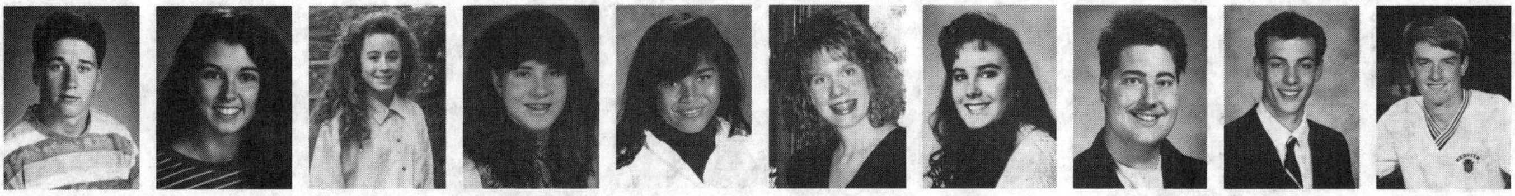

Souza, Joseph B
Oakdale HS
Oakdale, CA

Souza, Lesley R
Turlock HS
Turlock, CA

Souza, Stacy
Cupertino HS
Santa Clara, CA

Souza, Tanya M
Victory Christian Schl
Sacramento, CA

Sovan, Chanmach M
Andrew Hill HS
San Jose, CA

Sovey, Shannon Elyce
Louisville HS
Chatsworth, CA

Sowar, Kathleen
Monte Vista HS
Walnut Creek, CA

Soward, II Warren E
South Hills HS
Covina, CA

Sower, Scott R
Imperial HS
Sylmar, CA

Spaeth, Tim A
Servite HS
La Mirada, CA

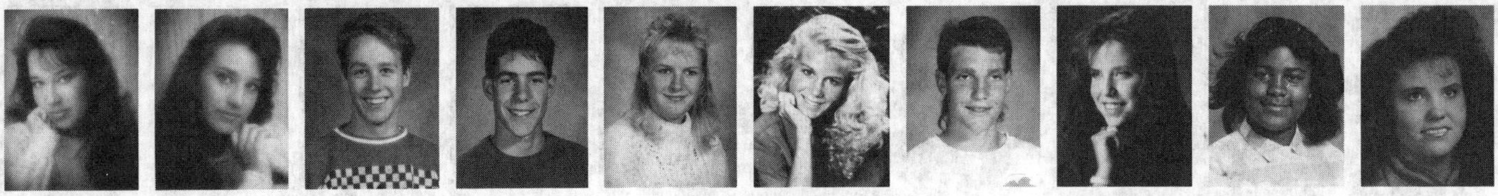

Spangler, Charity A
Helix HS
Lemon Grove, CA

Spangler, Sarilee F
Helix HS
Lemon Grove, CA

Sparks, Chris R
Redlands HS
Redlands, CA

Spears, Phillip R
Portola JR SR HS
Portola, CA

Spence, Kathleen Gale
Kern Valley HS
Lake Isabella, CA

Spencer, Jennifer M
Rancho Buena Vista
Oceanside, CA

Spencer, Jim
Las Plumas HS
Oroville, CA

Spencer, Katherine D
Grace M Davis HS
Modesto, CA

Spencer, Rowynn E
King-Drew Medical Magnet HS
Los Angeles, CA

Spencer, Tamara
Galt HS
Acampo, CA

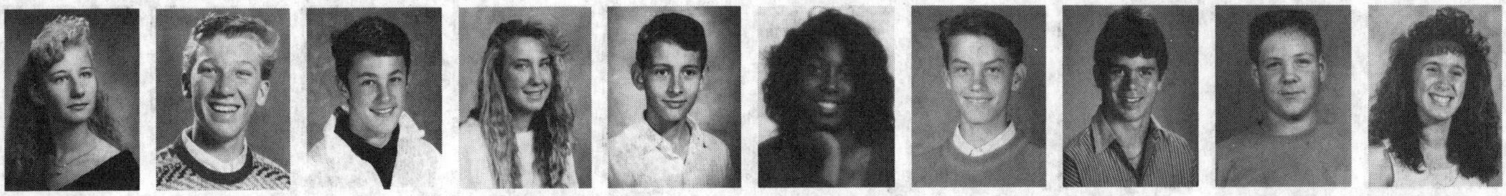

Spencer, Toni
Elk Grove HS
Elk Grove, CA

Spendlove, Shawn Prestwich
Santa Paula Union
Santa Paula, CA

Spieckerman, Damian C D
Lick-Wilmerding HS
San Francisco, CA

Spindler, Nikki M
Simi Valley HS
Simi Valley, CA

Spinozzi, Joe S
North HS
Bakersfield, CA

Spirling, Tamika
El Camino Fundamental HS
Sacramento, CA

Spitler, Jason S
Yucaipa HS
Yucaipa, CA

Spoelstra, Andrew J
East Union HS
Manteca, CA

Spradley, Sean E
Mt Whitney HS
Visalia, CA

Spraggins, Amber
Tracy Joint Union
Tracy, CA

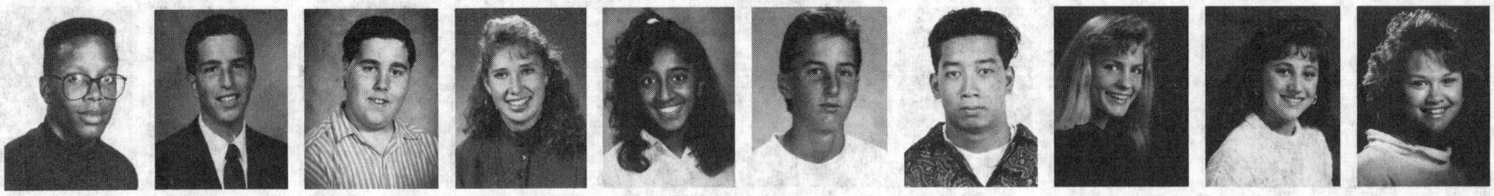

Springer, Marquis D
John Muir HS
Altadena, CA

Spruce, Craig M
The Bishops Schl
La Jolla, CA

Spurlock, Cameron
Kingsburg HS
Kingsburg, CA

Squire, Jeanette L
Calistoga HS
Calistoga, CA

Srijaerajah, Krishani
Paraclete HS
Quartz Hill, CA

Srijemac, Robert
Mission San Jose HS
Fremont, CA

Sripipatana, Alex A
Woodrow Wilson HS
Long Beach, CA

St Clair, Amy L
Brea-Olinda HS
Brea, CA

Staats, Angela M
Palmdale HS
Agua Dulce, CA

Staats, Laura L
Paraclete HS
Palmdale, CA

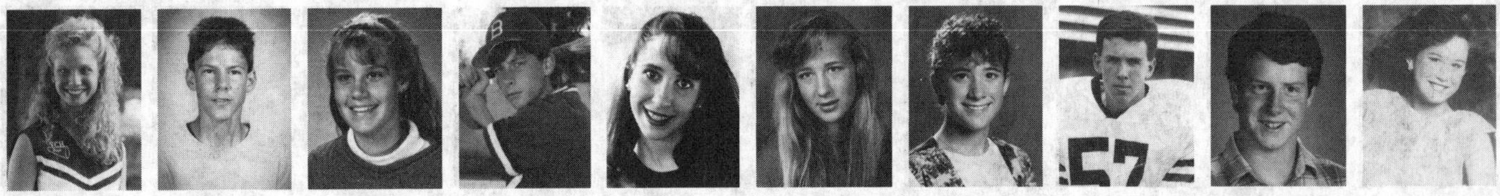

Stacy, Stephanie
Valley Christian HS
San Jose, CA

Stafford, Billy J
Casa Grande HS
Petaluma, CA

Stafford, Jennifer E
Novato HS
Novato, CA

Stahl, Dennis
Bonita HS
La Verne, CA

Stahlman, Patty
Notre Dame HS
San Mateo, CA

Stallings, Lorrey M
Helix HS
La Mesa, CA

Stallings, Melissa R
Bakersfield HS
Bakersfield, CA

Stamer, Paul L
Fontana HS
Fontana, CA

Stamper, Harlen L
Turlock HS
Turlock, CA

Stancil, Jennifer
Saint Ignatius College Prep
Daly City, CA

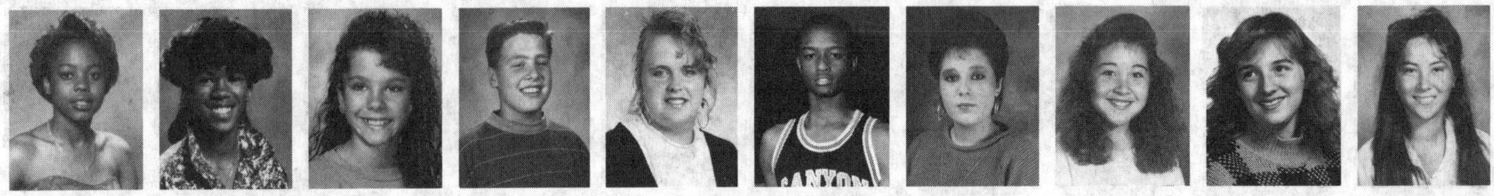

Stancil, Valerie
Bonita Vista HS
Bonita, CA

Stanford, Erika L
Compton HS
Compton, CA

Stanford, Laurie
Sunny Hills HS
Fullerton, CA

Stanford, Scott
Hesperia Christian Schl
Hesperia, CA

Stankovich, Alexandra M
Notre Dame HS
San Jose, CA

Stanley, Cawande D
Canyon Springs HS
Moreno Valley, CA

Stanley, Jenene E
St Paul HS
Whittier, CA

Stanley, Katrina
Dixon HS
Dixon, CA

Stanton, Susan S
Butte Valley HS
Dorris, CA

Stapchuk, Kim
Saddleback HS
Santa Ana, CA

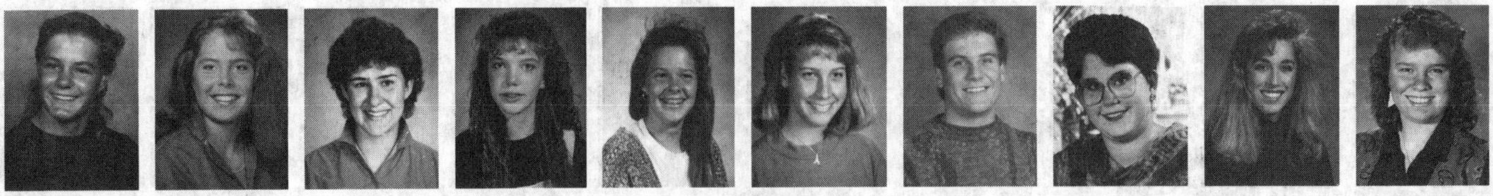

Staufenbeil, Timothy
Valhalla HS
Jamul, CA

Staveley, Sara E
Irvine HS
Irvine, CA

Stearns, Michelle L
Atwater HS
Atwater, CA

Steele, Diane M
Montgomery HS
Santa Rosa, CA

Steeves, Kelly A
Bonita Vista HS
Chula Vista, CA

Stefanac, Susan M
Lincoln HS
Stockton, CA

Stehling, Timothy J
Redlands HS
Redlands, CA

Steinbeck, Melissa L
Paso Robles HS
Paso Robles, CA

Steinke, Jennifer
Palm Desert HS
Palm Desert, CA

Stempinski, Meridith
Don A Lugo HS
Chino, CA

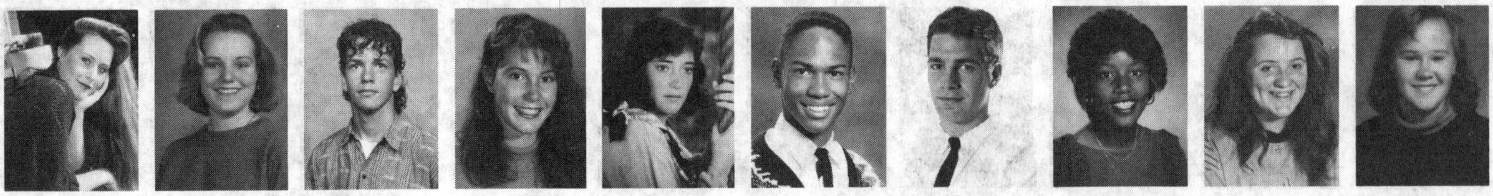

Stennecke, Kendra L
Torrey Pines HS
Del Mar, CA

Stephanie, Logan
Mt Whitney HS
Visalia, CA

Stephen, Jeffrey S
St Anthony HS
Long Beach, CA

Stephens, Camella
Yuba City HS
Yuba City, CA

Stephens, Edith
Yosemite HS
Coarsegold, CA

Stephens, Emid R
St Francis HS
Altadena, CA

Stephens, Jason A
Carmel HS
Carmel, CA

Stephens, Sharnette
Washington Prep HS
Los Angeles, CA

Sterrett, Carole A
Lower Lake HS
Clearlake Park, CA

Stetter, Mary
Southwest HS
San Diego, CA

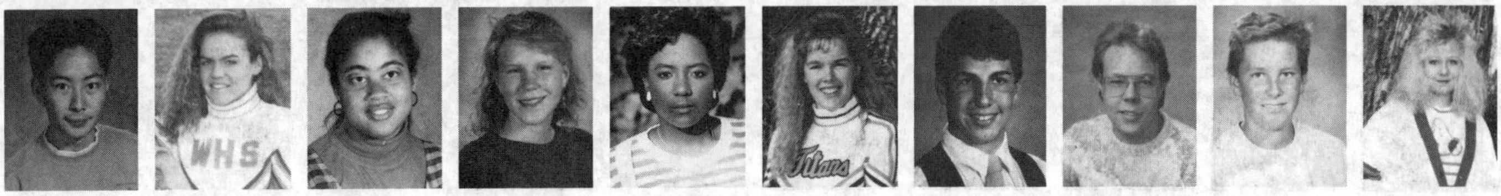

Steve, Ly
George Washington
San Francisco, CA

Stevens, Laura
West HS
Bakersfield, CA

Stevens, Michelle
Elaine
Lowell HS
San Francisco, CA

Stevens, Naomi J
Costa Mesa HS
Costa Mesa, CA

Stevenson, Danielle A
Pasadena HS
Alhambra, CA

Stevenson, Shelly
Foothill HS
Bakersfield, CA

Steves, Thomas A
Lincoln HS
Stockton, CA

Stewart, Alexander
College Park HS
Concord, CA

Stewart, Greg R
San Diequito HS
Cardiff By The Se,
CA

Stewart, Karen
Will C Wood HS
Vacaville, CA

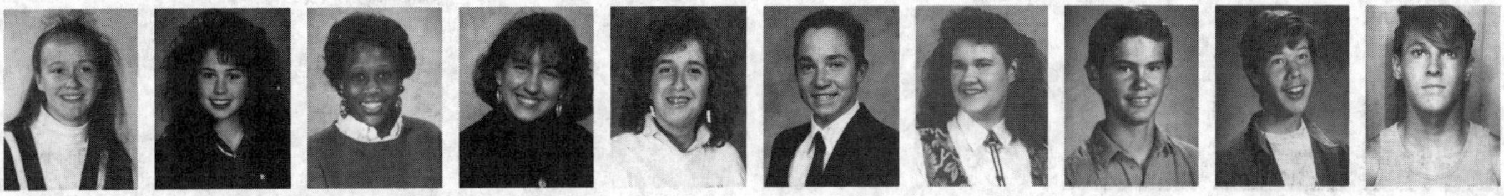

Stewart, Melanie
Calvary Christian
Acad
Vallejo, CA

Stewart, Tiffany Mia
Louisville HS
Thousand Oaks, CA

Stewart, Wendy C
Flintridge Sacred
Heart HS
Altadena, CA

Stiers, Hilary
Ceres HS
Modesto, CA

Still, Christie L
Fontana HS
Fontana, CA

Stillings, Tony Lee
Los Altos HS
Hacienda Hts, CA

Stirling, Patricia
Lynn
Foothill HS
Santa Ana, CA

Stirrat, Justin J
East Union HS
Manteca, CA

Stits, Michael C
Valley View HS
Moreno Valley, CA

Stitt, Daryl
Montclair HS
Ontario, CA

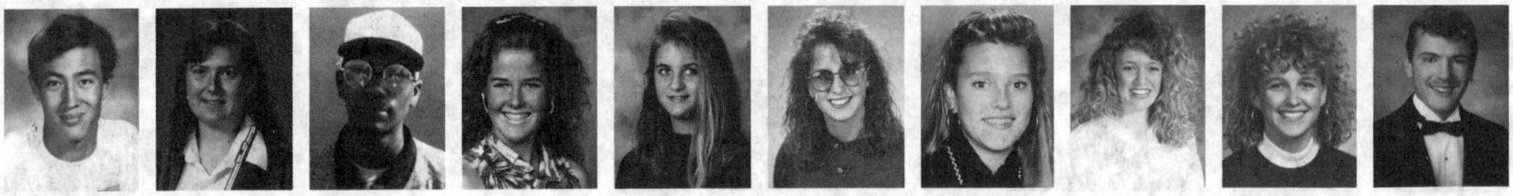

Stoffels, Bryant P
San Dieguito HS
Encinitas, CA

Stoh, Debbie
Hemet HS
Hemet, CA

Stokes, Kahlil G
Hamilton HS
Los Angeles, CA

Stolee, Kara L
Grossmont HS
La Mesa, CA

Stolow, Karen L
Torray Pines HS
San Diego, CA

Stolte, Nicole
California HS
San Ramon, CA

Stone, Claudia
Bullard HS
Fresno, CA

Stone, Dori R
Oak Ridge HS
El Dorado Hills, CA

Stone, Emily
Thomas Downey HS
Modesto, CA

Stone, Kristopher R
Channel Islands HS
Oxnard, CA

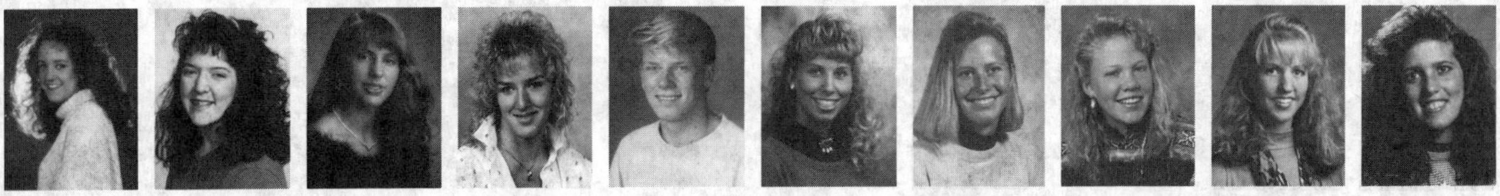

Stone, Suzanne
Tracy Joint Union
Tracy, CA

Stonehocker, Jody L
Manteca HS
Manteca, CA

Stoner, Michelle R
Sweetwater HS
Imperial Beach, CA

Stoops, Trina L
Temecula Valley HS
Murrieta, CA

Stork, Richard Taylor
Bonita Vista HS
Chula Vista, CA

Stovall, Kristine
Dinuba HS
Dinuba, CA

Stover, Michelle
Cabrillo HS
Vafb, CA

Stowell, Jennifer T
Montclair HS
Chino, CA

Stowell, Lisa M
Roseville HS
Rocklin, CA

Stowers, Melissa
Cajon HS
San Bernardino, CA

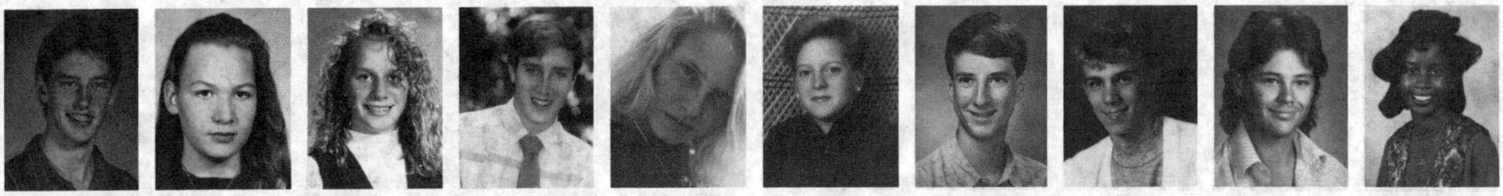

Strader, Brett K
Victory Christian HS
Sacramento, CA

Strader, Charity S
Contra Costa
Christian HS
Concord, CA

Strahl, Christy A
Atascadero HS
Atascadero, CA

Strahl, Philip J
Atascadero HS
Atascadero, CA

Strait, Monique D
Andrew Hill HS
San Jose, CA

Stralow, Sandra J
Vacaville HS
Vacaville, CA

Straub, Allen
Sunny Hills HS
Buena Park, CA

Straub, Richard E
Paraclete HS
Lancaster, CA

Strauss, Martin C
Atwater HS
Atwater, CA

Street, Kimberly
Silver Valley HS
Ft Irwin, CA

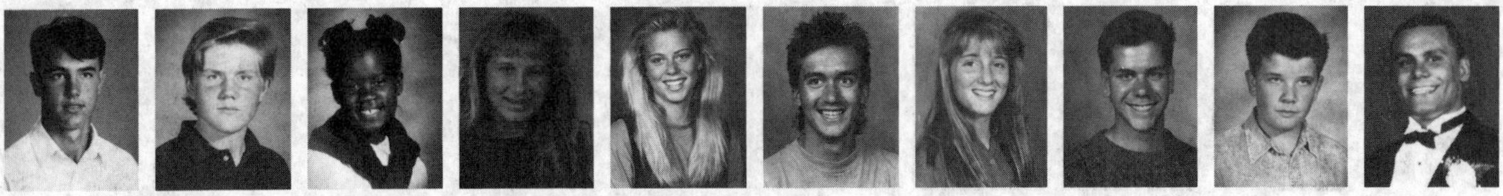

Stretch, Bill
Madera HS
Madera, CA

Strieby, Josh
Springs Of Living
Water Acad
Modesto, CA

Stringer, Crystal R
Lowell HS
San Francisco, CA

Stringfellow, Brittany
Brethren HS
Lakewood, CA

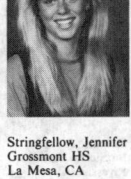

Stringfellow, Jennifer
Grossmont HS
La Mesa, CA

Stringfield, Chris
San Pasqual HS
Escondido, CA

Stroh, Jennifer
Dana Hills HS
Dana Point, CA

Strom, Adam
Valhalla HS
El Cajon, CA

Strong, Chris M
North Bakersfield HS
Oildale, CA

Strong, Cortland B
Millikan HS
Long Beach, CA

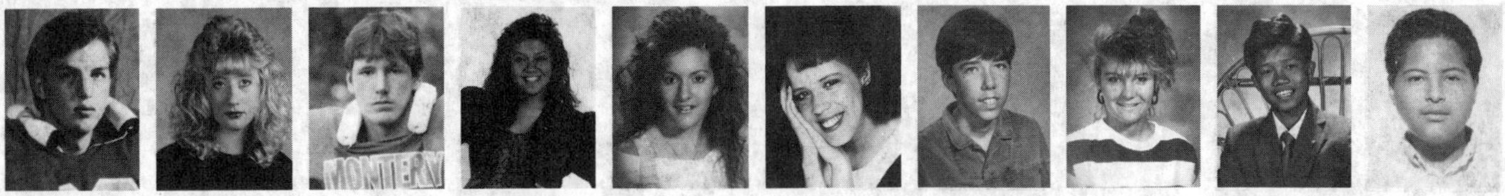

Stroupe, Kirk V
Bishop Amat
Memorial HS
Diamond Bar, CA

Studer, Melissa J
Argonaut HS
Ione, CA

Stuhler, Randall E
Monterey HS
Monterey, CA

Stull, Jessica
Banning HS
Whitewater, CA

Stults, Brandy L
Antelope Valley HS
Lancaster, CA

Sturdivant, Kimberly
Rancho Cotate HS
Rohnert Park, CA

Sturges, Jeff A
Hamilton HS
Woodland Hills, CA

Sturgill, Nicole L
Hillcrest Christian
Schl
Moorpark, CA

Su, Lac
Alhambra HS
Alhambra, CA

Suarez, Santiago
Eagle Rock HS
Los Angeles, CA

Sucatre, Hilary E
Montgomery HS
Santa Rosa, CA

Sucgang, Joanne
Franklin JR HS
Vallejo, CA

Suchka, Susan S
Arlington HS
Riverside, CA

Suemnick, Boyd A
Redwood HS
Visalia, CA

Sugui, Aurora G
Edison HS
Stockton, CA

Suh, Joshua H
Redlands HS
Redlands, CA

Suing, Timothy
Fairfax HS
Los Angeles, CA

Sukprasert,
Okla-Anne
San Fernando CIP
Magnet HS
North Hollywood, CA

Sulentor, Mary K
Bishop Montgomery
Rancho Palos Vrds,
CA

Sullivan, Amy
Foothill HS
Clovis, CA

Sullivan, Christen A
Palm Springs HS
Palm Springs, CA

Sullivan, Erin
St Rose Acad
San Francisco, CA

Sullivan, Patricia
Claremont HS
Claremont, CA

Sulzman, Garrett A
Bellflower HS
Bellflower, CA

Sum, David C
Leuzinger HS
Lawndale, CA

Sum, Tony K
Leuzinger HS
Lawndale, CA

Sumblin, Vernida
Faye
Live Oak HS
San Martin, CA

Summerall, Jenni J
Ramona HS
Ramona, CA

Sun, Deborah A
Irvington HS
Fremont, CA

Sun, Serena
Aragon HS
San Mateo, CA

Sundgren, Nathan
Hesperia Christian
Schl
Hesperia, CA

Sung, Derek H
Granada Hills HS
Northridge, CA

Sung, Peter
Lincoln HS
Stockton, CA

Sung, Wei-Ling
Bishop O'dowd HS
San Leandro, CA

Supnet, Erik P
Woodland HS
Woodland, CA

Surwill, Rob M
Quartz Hill HS
Palm Dale, CA

Suson, Joseph D
Clovis HS
Clovis, CA

Sustich, Holly A
Hogan SR HS
Vallejo, CA

Suszko, Kathy J
Poway HS
Poway, CA

Suthar, Anjali M
Santa Teresa HS
San Jose, CA

Sutherland, Kerri M
Fort Bragg HS
Fort Bragg, CA

Sutro, Derek S
Live Oak HS
Live Oak, CA

Sutton, Coleman E
Bullard HS
Fresno, CA

Sutton, Jessica P
California HS
San Ramon, CA

Sutton, Scott D
Indio HS
Indio, CA

Suzuki, Ryan T
North Tahoe HS
Kings Beach, CA

Suzuki, Scott D S
Los Altos HS
Hacienda Hgts, CA

Swaim, Kendra K
Woodcrest Christian
Riverside, CA

Swan, Stephanie F
Vacaville HS
Vacaville, CA

Swanson, Amy
Benicia HS
Benicia, CA

Swanson, Christopher
Grossmont HS
Santee, CA

Swanson, Jennifer
Capo Valley
Christian HS
Dana Point, CA

Swanson, Rebecca B
Brea-Olinda HS
Brea, CA

Swanson, Season E
Clovis HS
Clovis, CA

Swaroop, Asha
Corona Del Mar HS
Providence, RI

Swarts, Eric D
North HS
Bakersfield, CA

Swartz, Karen M
Novato HS
Novato, CA

Swartz, Laurel K
Irvine HS
Irvine, CA

Sweeny, Scott P
Mission College Prep
San Luis Obispo, CA

Sweet, Amanda J
Notre Dame HS
Salinas, CA

Sweet, Sharonda
Edison HS
Stockton, CA

Swendiman, Chelsey
Shasta HS
Redding, CA

Swerdloff, Tanya
Claremont HS
Yucaipa, CA

Swift, Laurel M
Highland HS
Bakersfield, CA

Swift, Windigo M
El Dorado HS
Somerset, CA

Swindle, Jason
La Sierra Acad
Riverside, CA

Swindler, Emily
El Capitan HS
Lakeside, CA

Syquia, Christine M
St Joseph HS
Cerritos, CA

Syvertsen, Shanna L
Bullard HS
Fresno, CA

Szabo, Deborah A
Trabuco Hills HS
Mission Viejo, CA

Szekeres, David L
Villa Park HS
Villa Park, CA

Szytel, Lisa M
Orange Glen HS
Valley Center, CA

Tabb, Kaylin
St Elizabeth HS
Oakland, CA

Tabb, Kim
Nogales HS
W Covina, CA

Tablante, Joel
Skyline HS
Oakland, CA

Tabot, Scott
Brethren HS
Lakewood, CA

Tabrizchi, Ali
Las Lomas HS
Walnut Creek, CA

Tackett, Christian B
Ramona HS
Ramona, CA

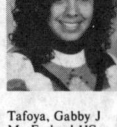
Tadros, Niveen S
University HS
Irvine, CA

Tafoya, Gabby J
Mc Farland HS
Mc Farland, CA

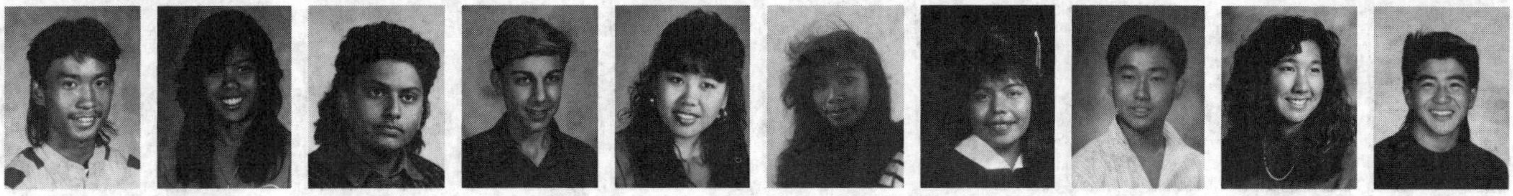

Tagay, Edgar R
Fremont HS
Sunnyvale, CA

Tagle, Tracy
J Eugene Mc Ateer
San Francisco, CA

Tagore, Kuldeep S
Edison/Computech
Fresno, CA

Tahajian, Brent Lee
Bullard HS
Fresno, CA

Taing, Kim G
Amos Alonzo Stagg
Stockton, CA

Taino, Geraldine B
Sierra Vista HS
Baldwin Park, CA

Tajiboy, Maria Rosmery
Bell HS
Maywood, CA

Takagi, Yutaka
Sunny Hills HS
Fullerton, CA

Takahash, Marla S
San Marino HS
Tucson, AZ

Takeda, Derek Y
Los Altos HS
Hacienda Hts, CA

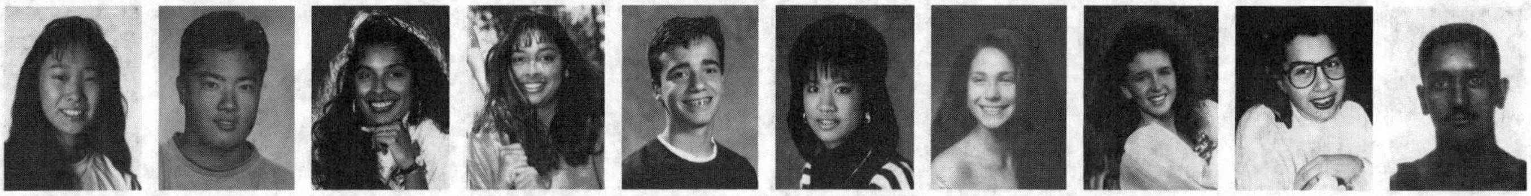

Takeda, Tina
Elk Grove HS
Elk Grove, CA

Taketa, Kyle H
Santa Teresa HS
San Jose, CA

Takhar, Casandra M
Amos Alonzo Stagg
Stockton, CA

Takhar, Pauline
Amos Alonzo Stagg
Stockton, CA

Takken, Marc G
Mission College Prep
Atascadero, CA

Talamayan, Joanne J
Montgomery HS
San Diego, CA

Talarico, Nicole
Laguna Beach HS
Laguna Beach, CA

Taliani, Christen L
Arlington HS
Riverside, CA

Talvi, Sonja L Aller
Fairfax HS
Los Angeles, CA

Talwar, Rajesh K
Anaheim HS
Anaheim, CA

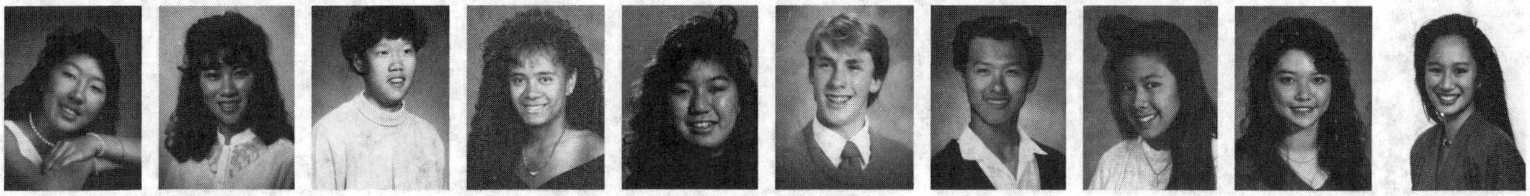

Tam, Amy
Independence HS
San Jose, CA

Tam, Christine
Ochurr HS
Monterey Park, CA

Tam, Mabel Y
Brawley Union HS
Brawley, CA

Tamalii, Sabrina
Los Alamitos HS
Carson, CA

Tamanaha, Lisa L
Drew Medical Magnet HS
Gardena, CA

Tamm, Jason R
Fullerton Union HS
Fullerton, CA

Tan, Bon
Westminster HS
Westminster, CA

Tan, Emmeline S
Mt Carmel HS
San Diego, CA

Tan, Maria
South San Francisco
Pinole, CA

Tan, Melissa M
Acad Of Our Lady Of Peace
San Diego, CA

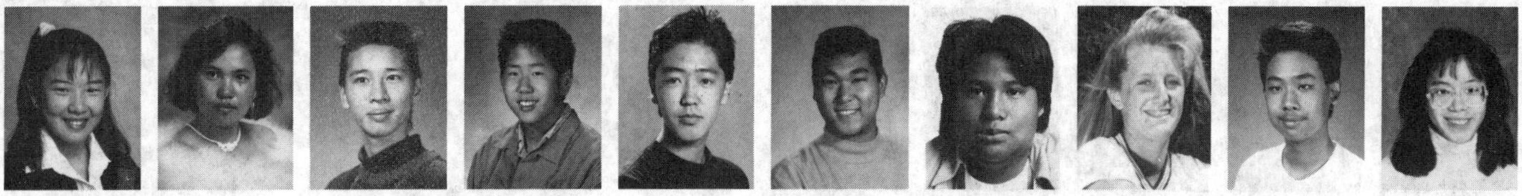

Tan, Michelle C
Holy Family HS
Glendale, CA

Tan, Susan
Galileo HS
San Francisco, CA

Tan, Thomas
Pindle Valley HS
Pinole, CA

Tanaka, Douglas S
El Camino HS
Carmichael, CA

Tanaka, Takuya
Gardena HS
Gardena, CA

Tanaka, Trent K
James Lick HS
San Jose, CA

Tanap, Larry D
Hueneme HS
Port Hueneme, CA

Tande, Taina
Simi Valley HS
Simi Valley, CA

Tang, Chi-Hong
Albany HS
Albany, CA

Tang, Christine P
Lowell HS
San Francisco, CA

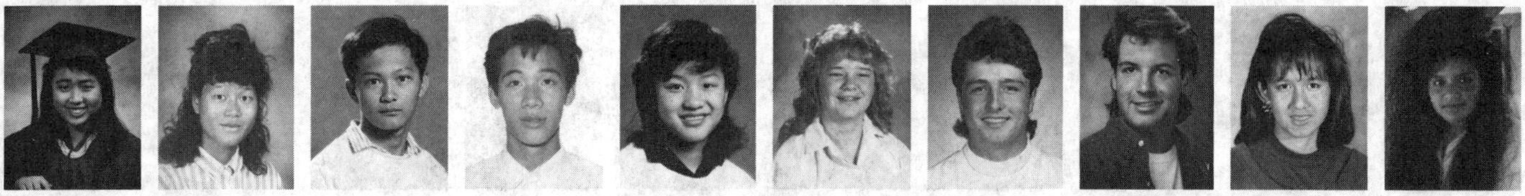

Tang, Courtney
Abraham Lincoln HS
San Francisco, CA

Tang, Phung Kim
Lincoln Prep HS
San Diego, CA

Tang, Quyen V
Leuzinger HS
Hawthorne, CA

Tang, Sang
San Gabriel HS
Rosemead, CA

Tangpraserth, Manivone
Bassett HS
La Puente, CA

Tannahill, Heather
Pioneer Baptist HS
Norwalk, CA

Tanner, Joe
Rives City SR HS
W Sacramento, CA

Tantillo, James W
El Toro HS
Mission Viejo, CA

Tanyag, Hazel N
Lowell HS
San Francisco, CA

Tapia, Brenda A
San Jacinto HS
San Jacinto, CA

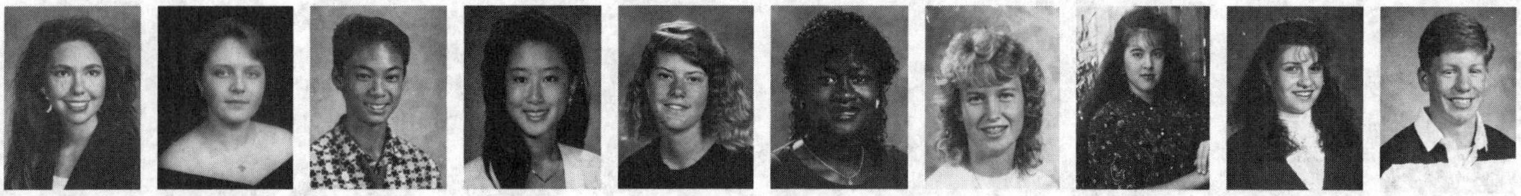

Tapia, Vanessa
Campbell Hall HS
Reseda, CA

Taran, Yana
California HS
San Ramon, CA

Taraya, Robert W
Pinole Valley HS
Hercules, CA

Tark, Eunice K
Irvine HS
Irvine, CA

Tarrants, Leslie D
Ramona HS
Santa Ysabel, CA

Tarver, Tanesha R
St Michaels HS
Los Angeles, CA

Tarwater, Shawna Marie
Coachella Valley HS
Mecca, CA

Tash, Deena L
Vacaville HS
Vacaville, CA

Tashjian, Heghnar
Mountain View HS
Mountain View, CA

Tastor, Brian W
Oakmont HS
Roseville, CA

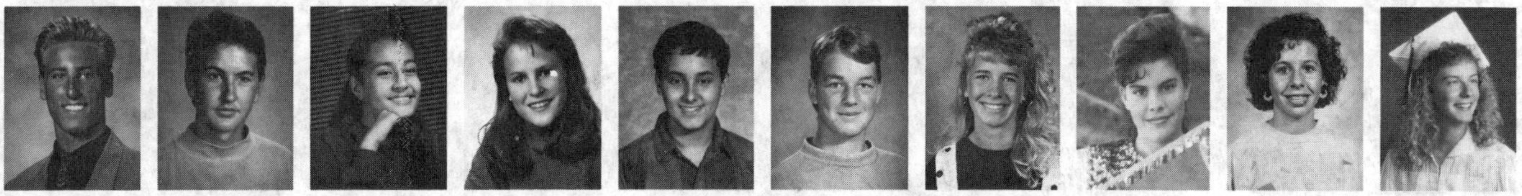

Tate, Jason R
Artesia HS
Lakewood, CA

Tatum, Jeremy J
Turlock HS
Turlock, CA

Taula, Fiaaluae L
Armijo HS
Suisun, CA

Tavares, Tamara L
Academy Of Our Lady Peace
Poway, CA

Tavarez, Richard L
Fresno HS
Fresno, CA

Tavernier, Aaron M
Orange HS
Orange, CA

Taylor, Aspen M
Bella Vista HS
Fair Oaks, CA

Taylor, Bridget
Ontario HS
Ontario, CA

Taylor, Brooke A
Oakmont HS
Roseville, CA

Taylor, Charlene S
Redwood Christian
San Leandro, CA

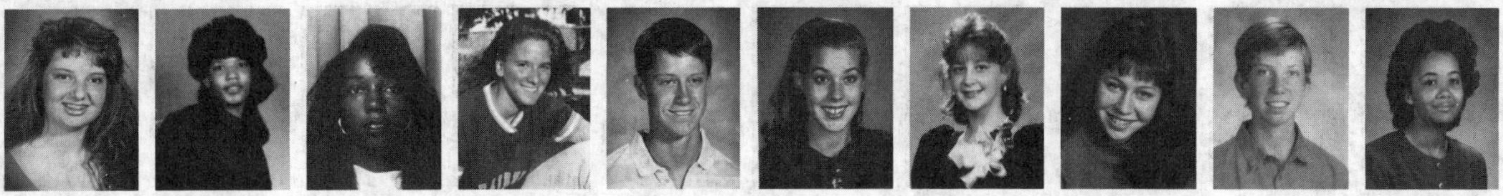

Taylor, Christina
Marie
North HS
Bakersfield, CA

Taylor, Desiree J
Washington Prep HS
Los Angeles, CA

Taylor, Gwendolyn C
John F Kennedy HS
Sacramento, CA

Taylor, Jane C
Rio Americano HS
Sacramento, CA

Taylor, Jeremy
Willows HS
Willows, CA

Taylor, Khrysten
Madera HS
Madera, CA

Taylor, Kimberly
Sonora HS
Reno, NV

Taylor, Kristina L
Trinity HS
Salyer, CA

Taylor, Matthew
Capistrano Valley
Christian HS
Mission Viejo, CA

Taylor, Michelle M
South Bay JR Acad
Compton, CA

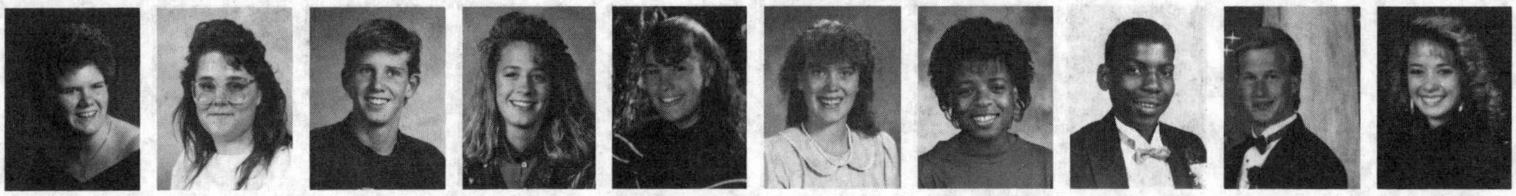

Taylor, Michelle N
Yuba City HS
Yuma, AZ

Taylor, Patricia D
Silver Valley HS
Barstow, CA

Taylor, Rick L
Hesperia HS
Hesperia, CA

Taylor, Robyn C
Bella Vista HS
Fair Oaks, CA

Taylor, Sheila
Vintage HS
Napa, CA

Taylor, Tabitha
Hemet HS
Hemet, CA

Taylor, Tracey S
Santa Barbara HS
Santa Barbara, CA

Taylor, III Walter
Narbonne HS
Harbor City, CA

Taylor, William
Leslie
Lasser Union HS
Susanville, CA

Taylor, Yvette C
Serrano HS
Victorville, CA

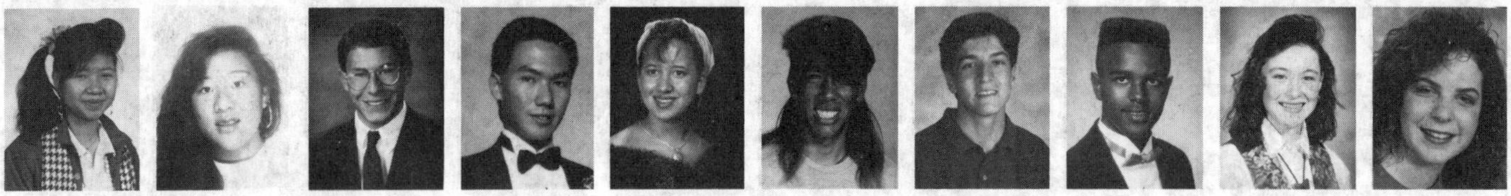

Tchang, Hien Lisa
C K Mc Clatchy HS
Sacramento, CA

Tcheng, Denise J
Tustin HS
Tustin, CA

Teagle-Hernandez,
Michael B
Buena HS
Ventura, CA

Tecson, Archibald V
Polytechnic HS
Long Beach, CA

Teeple, Anna Mariah
South Gate HS
South Gate, CA

Teixeira, Derek A
Santa Teresa HS
San Jose, CA

Teixeira, Frank M
Dos Palos HS
Dos Palos, CA

Tekeste, Zeghai
El Camino Real HS
Woodland Hills, CA

Tela, Stacy
Orosi HS
Orosi, CA

Telford, Doris
Lincoln HS
Stockton, CA

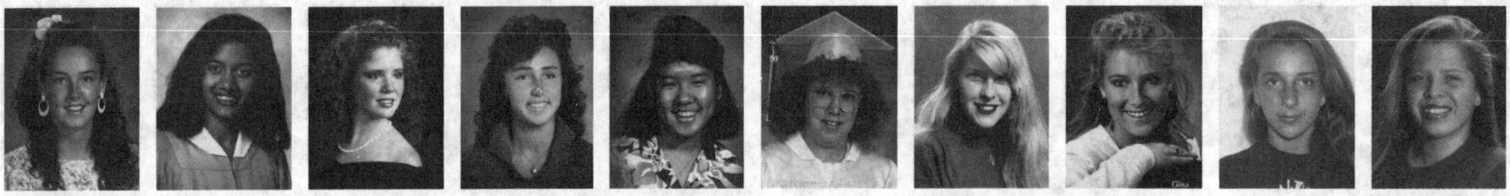

Telford, Sarah J
Cornelia Connelly HS
Huntington Beach,
CA

Telkikar, Gauri V
Ontario HS
Ontario, CA

Telle, Carin M
Liberty Union HS
Byron, CA

Templeton, Lisa M
Tustin HS
Tustin, CA

Tengan, Audrey M
Fountain Valley HS
Fountain Valley, CA

Tenhagen, Jennifer
San Gorgonio HS
Sacramento, CA

Tenhagen, Kimberly
Fontana HS
Fontana, CA

Tenorio, Gina
Bundy Canyon
Christian HS
Canyon Lake, CA

Terenkian, Nayiri
Santa Monica HS
Santa Monica, CA

Terrazas, Nivia
Ganesha HS
Pomona, CA

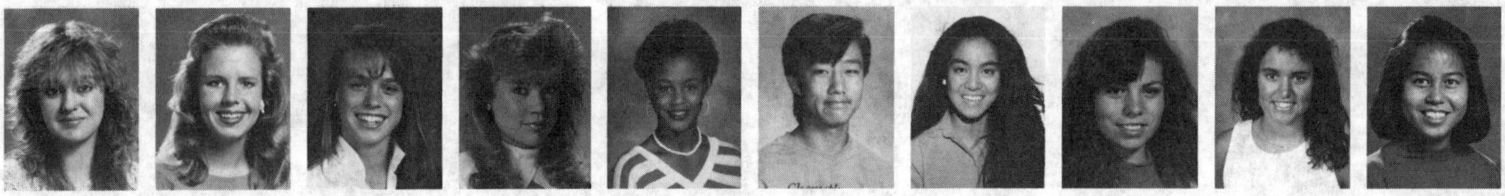

Terrell, Andrea S
Hoover HS
Glendale, CA

Terrell, Tracy A
Etiwanda HS
Fontana, CA

Terry, Aimee
Mercy HS
Burlingame, CA

Terry, Brandi M
James Monroe HS
Panorama City, CA

Terry, Marquita D
John F Kennedy HS
Granada Hills, CA

Teshirogi, Takahide
Mission San Jose HS
Fremont, CA

Tesoro, Victoria A
Mayfield SR Schl
San Dimas, CA

Teter, Rebecca
Canyon HS
Canyon Country, CA

Tetreault, Jill A
El Camino
Fundamental HS
Sacramento, CA

Teves, Lady Shailini
Glendale Adventist
Acad
Glendale, CA

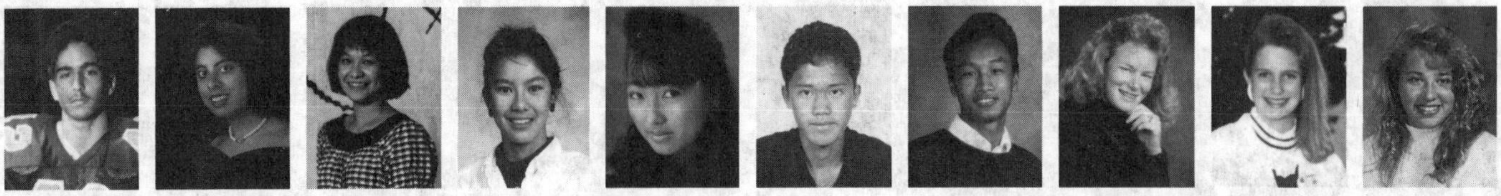

Texeira, Thomas
Joseph
Amos Alonzo Stagg
Stockton, CA

Thadani, Reshma
Northgate HS
Walnut Creek, CA

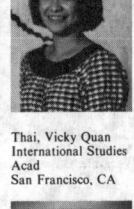

Thai, Vicky Quan
International Studies
Acad
San Francisco, CA

Thai Van Dat,
Johanna
Moreau HS
Hayward, CA

Thammavongsa,
Sivixay
Don Antonio Lugo
Chino, CA

Thao, Ger
Duncan Polytechnic
Fresno, CA

Thao, Neng
Redwood HS
Visalia, CA

Thayer, Ginger M
Lemoore HS
Lemoore, CA

Theile, Kendra
California HS
San Ramon, CA

Theriault, Coressa L
Nevada Union HS
Nevada City, CA

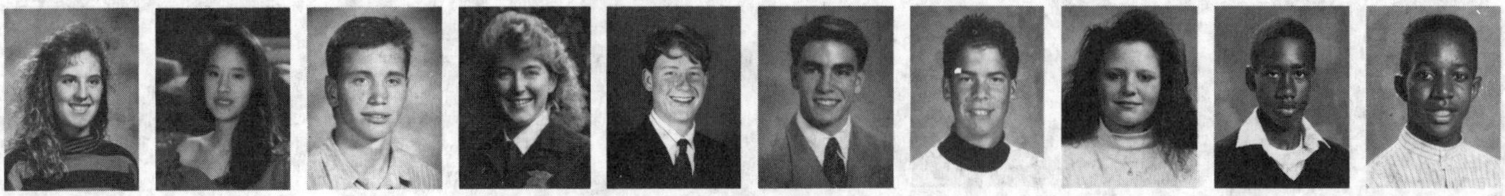

Thiel, Becky L
Fremont Christian
Fremont, CA

Thirakomen,
Khanungnij
Clovis West HS
Fresno, CA

Thoene, Jacob Brock
North HS
Glennville, CA

Thoene, Jessica
Rachel
North HS
Glennville, CA

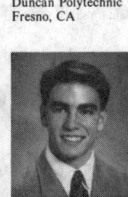

Thomas, Adam M
Servite HS
Villa Park, CA

Thomas, Aric Vincent
Riverside Poly HS
Riverside, CA

Thomas, Blaine C
Palma HS
Hollister, CA

Thomas, Dallas D
Dixon HS
Vacaville, CA

Thomas, Damion L
St Bernards HS
Los Angeles, CA

Thomas, Erik C
Narbonne HS
Torrance, CA

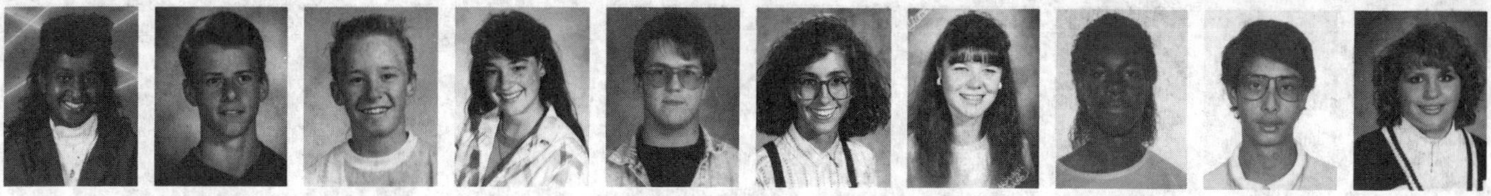

Thomas, Gloria
Calvary Baptist HS
Highland, CA

Thomas, Jeffrey Brian
Portola HS
Portola, CA

Thomas, Kamron
Argonaut HS
Ione, CA

Thomas, Kristin E
John A Rowland HS
Rowland Heights, CA

Thomas, Mark E
Redlands HS
Redlands, CA

Thomas, Shannon
San Luis HS
San Luis Obispo, CA

Thomas, Tara J
Selma HS
Selma, CA

Thomas, Warren A
Crenshaw HS
Los Angeles, CA

Thomas, Wayne
Vacaville HS
Vacaville, CA

Thomas, Yvonne M
Portola JR SR HS
Portola, CA

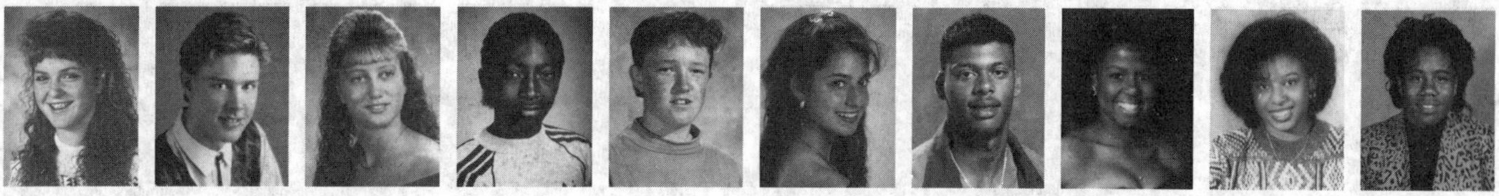

Thomason, Jennifer A
Burney HS
Burney, CA

Thomason, Kevin M
Dinuba HS
Dinuba, CA

Thompson, Carol Lynn
Napa HS
Napa, CA

Thompson, Caroll L
Amos Alozo Stagg
Stockton, CA

Thompson, Darren M
Lompoc HS
Lompoc, CA

Thompson, Deborah
Prospect HS
San Jose, CA

Thompson, Dion A
San Gorgonio HS
Highland, CA

Thompson, Heidi Maria
San Gorgonio HS
Highland, CA

Thompson, Javonda L
Hueneme HS
Oxnard, CA

Thompson, Margaret
Victor Valley HS
Victorville, CA

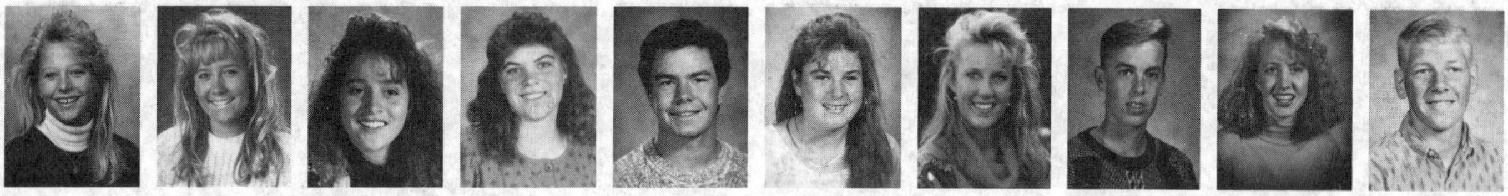

Thompson, Melinda
Escondido HS
Escondido, CA

Thompson, Melonie Christine
Diamond Bar HS
Walnut, CA

Thompson, Nicole
Santa Maria HS
Santa Maria, CA

Thompson, Stacey
Yosemite HS
Coarsegold, CA

Thomson, Daniel R
Capistrano Valley HS
Mission Viejo, CA

Thomson, Jami K
Montgomery HS
Santa Rosa, CA

Thomson, Kim D
El Toro HS
El Toro, CA

Thomson, Scott A
Eisenhower HS
Rialto, CA

Thoreson, Heather M
Sacramento Adventist Acad
Citrus Heights, CA

Thoreson, Matthew T
El Camino Fundamental HS
Sacramento, CA

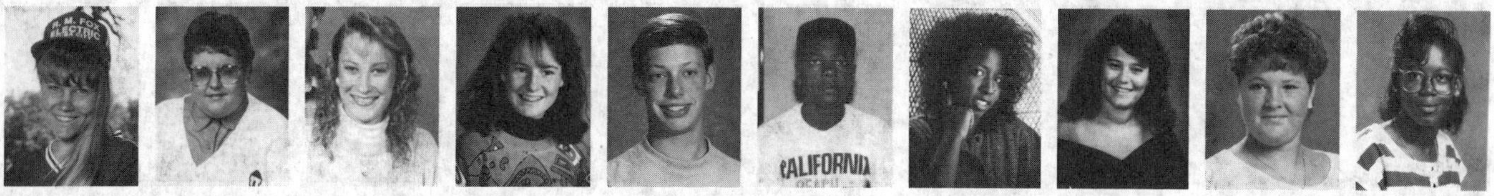

Thornburg, Cynthia
Marysville HS
Browns Valley, CA

Thornburg, Jill
Fairfield HS
Fairfield, CA

Thornburg, Tamara
Calaveras HS
Wallace, CA

Thornhill, Patricia
Merced HS
Merced, CA

Thornton, Matt A
Santa Cruz HS
Santa Cruz, CA

Thornton, Michael
Emery HS
Emeryville, CA

Threadgill, Marchell
Tulare Union HS
Tulare, CA

Threewitt, Tanya A
Independence HS
San Jose, CA

Thurman, Amy
North HS
Torrance, CA

Thurman, Lois S
Monte Vista HS
Spring Valley, CA

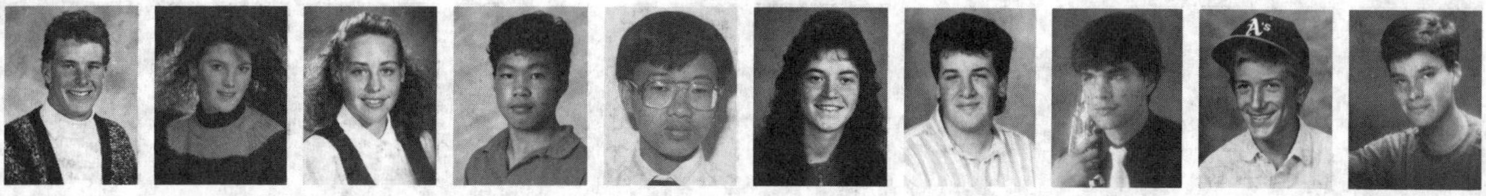

Thurn, Jason A
Nevada Union HS
Grass Valley, CA

Thweatt, Deborah L
Orange Glen HS
Valley Center, CA

Tibbels, Cynthia D
Bloomington HS
Bloomington, CA

Tiet, Hao
Whitney HS
Lakewood, CA

Tieu, Khai T
Westminster HS
Westminster, CA

Tigert, Veronica A
Riverbank HS
Riverbank, CA

Tighe, Devin K
University City HS
San Diego, CA

Tigner, William E
Riverbank HS
Riverbank, CA

Tilcock, Wayne T
Fairfield HS
Suisun City, CA

Tillman, Donald J
Enerprise HS
Shingletown, CA

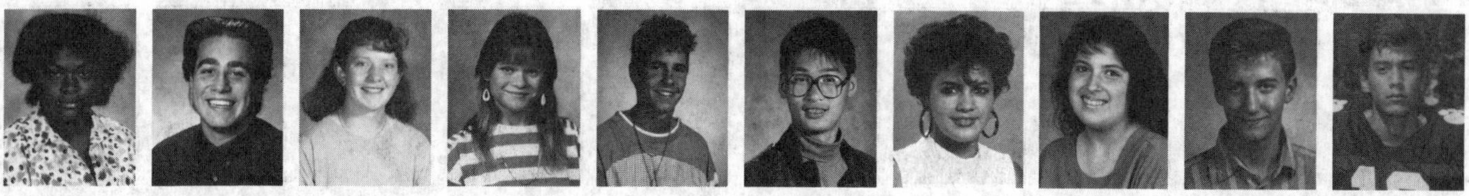

Tillman, Dorlisa I
Pasadena HS
Pasadena, CA

Tillman, Suha
Palm Springs HS
Thousand Palms, CA

Tilson, Julie Kristin
El Dorado HS
Placerville, CA

Timmons, Casandra
El Cajon Valley HS
El Cajon, CA

Timony, James
Christian Center Acad
Colton, CA

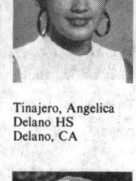

Tin, Anthony P
Bridgemont HS
San Francisco, CA

Tinajero, Angelica
Delano HS
Delano, CA

Tinajero, Monica A
St Joseph HS
Norwalk, CA

Tincher, Brent
Christian Brothers
Sacramento, CA

Tindall, Joshua J
Roseville HS
Rocklin, CA

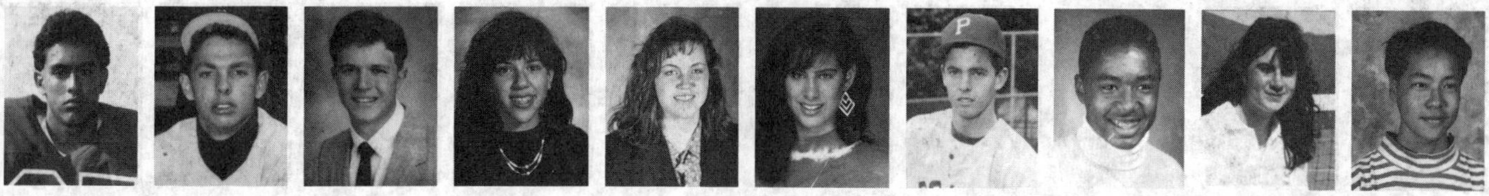

Tinoco, Alfredo
Clairemont HS
San Diego, CA

Tinoco, Neil A
Bishop Montgomery
Lomita, CA

Tintary, Lee H
West Covina HS
W Covina, CA

Tintocalis, Melisa J
Paraclete HS
Palmdale, CA

Tipton, Heather L
Alameda HS
Alameda, CA

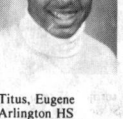

Tison, Michelle
Arvin HS
Bakersfield, CA

Tittrington, Scott R
Poway HS
Poway, CA

Titus, Eugene
Arlington HS
Riverside, CA

Titus, Gretchen
Tomales HS
Valley Ford, CA

Tiyaamornwong, Kevin
Bullard HS
Fresno, CA

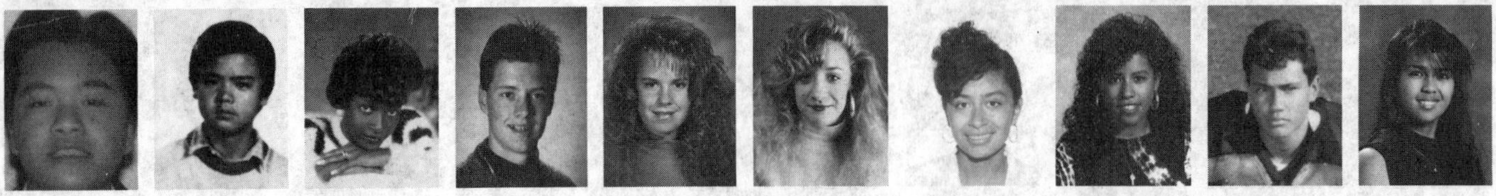

To, Larry
International Studies Acad
San Francisco, CA

To, William H
Saddleback HS
Santa Ana, CA

Todd, Stacey
Fairfax HS
Los Angeles, CA

Todd, Steven R
Oakdale HS
Oakdale, CA

Toepfer, Cara L
Paraclete HS
Lancaster, CA

Tolbert, Tabitha R
Rio Linda SR HS
Rio Linda, CA

Toledo, Claudia M
North Hollywood HS
North Hollywood, CA

Toledo, Gladys E
Hamilton Music Acad
Sylmar, CA

Tolentino, Aaron
Aragon HS
Honolulu, HI

Tolentino, Grace H
Deland Joint Union
Earlimart, CA

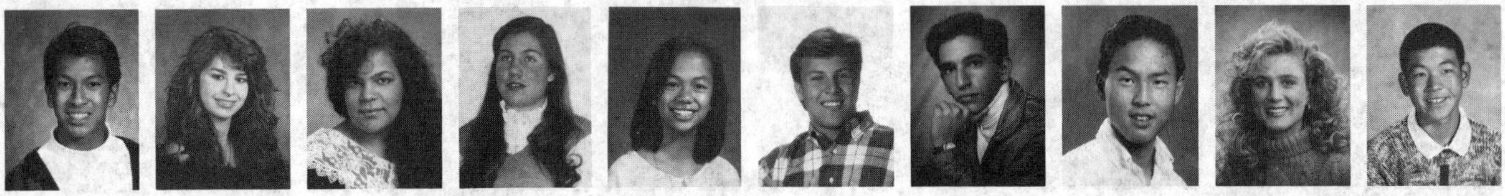

Tolentino, Rudy
El Camino HS
Daly City, CA

Tolkin, Stacy
Cypress HS
Cypress, CA

Tollerton, Elena M
Sacramento Adventist Acad
Sacramento, CA

Tolone, Barbara
Santa Ana Valley HS
Santa Ana, CA

Tom, Aimee L
Bishop O'dowd HS
Oakland, CA

Tomei, Scott J
Arroyo Grande HS
Arroyo Grande, CA

Tominna, Timmothy
Valhalla HS
El Cajon, CA

Tomita, Eddie K
Glendale Adventist Acad
West Covina, CA

Tommeraason, Jill
Woodland HS
Woodland, CA

Tomooka, Brian
Ernest Righetti HS
Santa Maria, CA

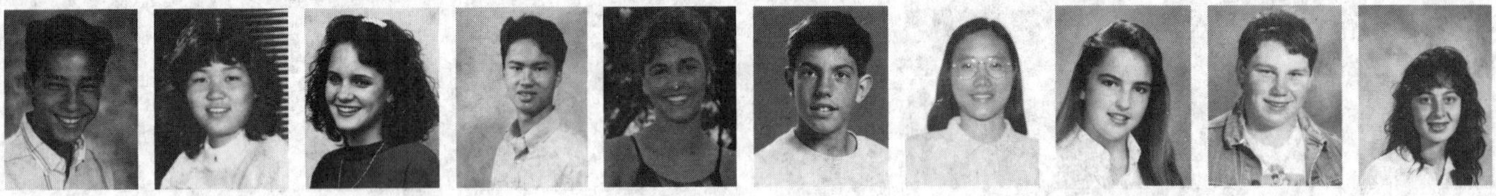

Tomooka, Christian
Bishop Amat Mem
Alta Loma, CA

Tomooka, Julie
Ernest Righetti HS
Santa Maria, CA

Tomsik, Kathryn
J H Francis Polytechnic HS
North Hollywood, CA

Ton, Tuan N
Cordova SR HS
Rancho Cordova, CA

Toner, Heather C
Oak Ridge HS
El Dorado Hills, CA

Toner, Matthew C
Rim Of The World
Crestline, CA

Tong, Toby M Y
Fairfax HS
Fresno, CA

Toomey, Christine M
Immaculate Heart
Altadena, CA

Toon, Malcolm M
Arcata HS
Arcata, CA

Topalian, Taline
Ribet Acad
Tujunga, CA

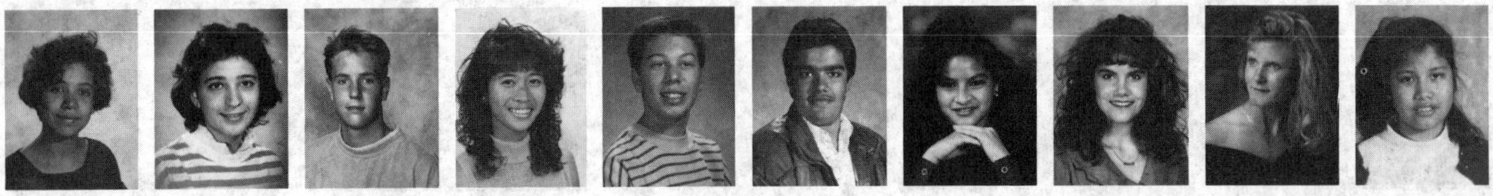

Topete, Cynthia E
Sacred Heart Of Mary HS
Los Angeles, CA

Torbati, Shabnam
El Camino Real HS
Woodland Hills, CA

Torgeson, John E
Granada Hills HS
Northridge, CA

Toribio, Brenda Lynn
Coachella Valley HS
Thermal, CA

Tornow, Chris A
Lutheran HS Of Orange County
Santa Ana, CA

Toros, Yezeg H
Saint Joseph HS
Santa Maria, CA

Torre, Josetta R
North Salinas HS
Salinas, CA

Torre, Monica M
San Gabriel Mission
Covina, CA

Torrence, Angie May
Mira Mesa HS
San Diego, CA

Torrente, Jothelyn R
Phillip & Sala Burton Academic HS
San Francisco, CA

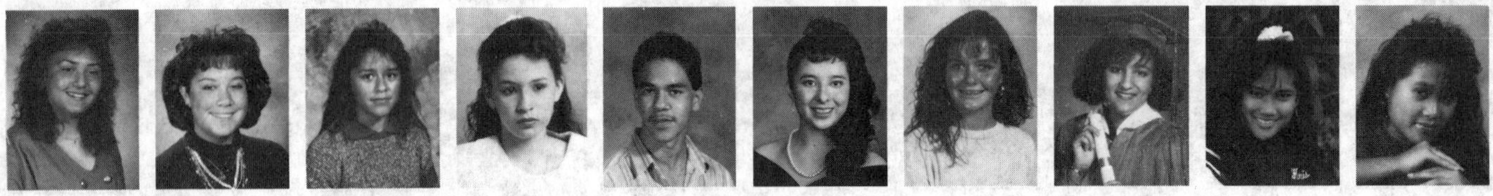

Torres, Bettie
Eisenhower HS
Rialto, CA

Torres, Brita M
John Marshall Fundamental HS
Pasadena, CA

Torres, Carlotta R
San Benito HS
Hollister, CA

Torres, Connie M
Riverside Poly HS
Riverside, CA

Torres, David
Orangewood A Acad
Fountain Valley, CA

Torres, Jacquelyne
St Joseph HS
South Gate, CA

Torres, Jazmin
Arcadia HS
Arcadia, CA

Torres, Kim
Francis Polytechnical
Arleta, CA

Torres, Kris Micelle
Pasadena HS
Pasadena, CA

Torres, Mary Grace
Bonita HS
La Verne, CA

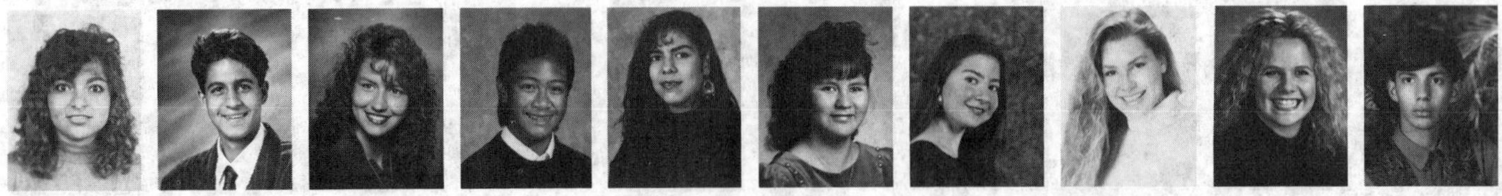

Torres, Monica
South Tahoe HS
South Lake Tahoe, CA

Torres, Robert E
Downey HS
Downey, CA

Torres, Veronica
Garfield HS
Long Beach, CA

Torres, Victor J
Westmoor HS
Daly City, CA

Torres, Yazmin R
Calexico HS
Calexico, CA

Torres P, Alma Delia
Roseville HS
Roseville, CA

Torres-Mc Donald, Fabiola F
Orangewood Acad
Santa Ana, CA

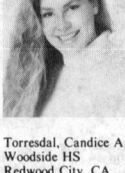

Torresdal, Candice A
Woodside HS
Redwood City, CA

Torrey, Lise
East Union HS
Manteca, CA

Torrez, Andre
Delano HS
Delano, CA

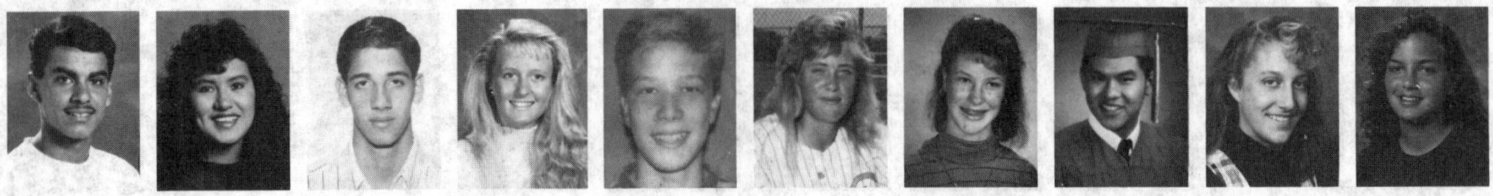

Torrez, Nicholas D
Delano Joint Union
Delano, CA

Torrico, Maria G
Carlsbad HS
Carlsbad, CA

Torrijos, Alfredo
St Genevieve HS
N Hollywood, CA

Tosio, Jill T
San Ramon Valley
Danville, CA

Tosti, Arend M
Del Campo HS
Fair Oaks, CA

Totten, Tracy S
Coachella Valley HS
Thermal, CA

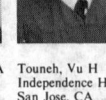

Touchatt, Kimberly A
Fred C Beyer HS
Modesto, CA

Touneh, Vu H
Independence HS
San Jose, CA

Tower, Stacia
Brookside Christian
Wasco, IL

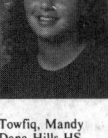

Towfiq, Mandy
Dana Hills HS
San Juan Capistra, CA

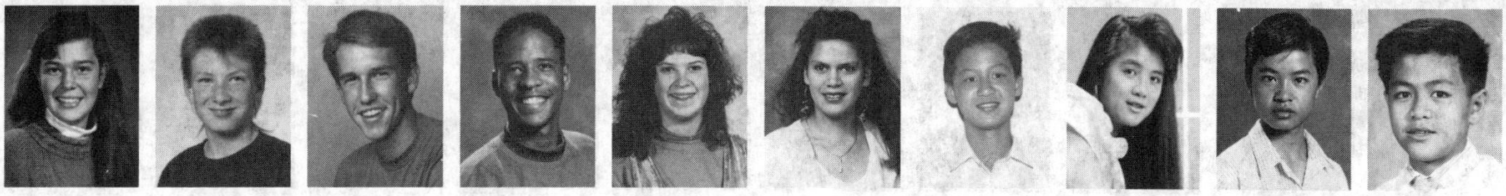

Towle, Rebekah L
Troy HS
Fullerton, CA

Townson, Donald R
Montclair HS
Montclair, CA

Tracy, Matt J
Ventura HS
Ventura, CA

Trahan, Timothy C
Junipero Serra HS
Compton, CA

Trahern, Robin L
Nevada Union HS
Nevada City, CA

Trammell, Terry D
O'farell SCPA HS
San Diego, CA

Tran, Andy
Edison HS
Huntington Beach, CA

Tran, Becky N
San Gabriel HS
Rosemead, CA

Tran, Danh L
John F Kennedy HS
Mission Hills, CA

Tran, Duc
Fremont HS
Sunnyvale, CA

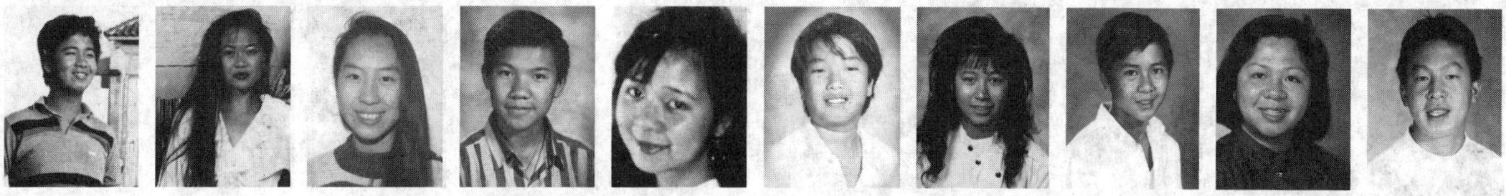

Tran, Duc T
Antelope Valley HS
Lancaster, CA

Tran, Giao
Pioneer HS
San Jose, CA

Tran, Hue Kristine
Alhambra HS
Alhambra, CA

Tran, Kenneth
Buena Park HS
Fullerton, CA

Tran, Kimphuong T
Mt Pleasant HS
San Jose, CA

Tran, Lawrence Thanh
Sonora HS
Fullerton, CA

Tran, Linh M
Armijo HS
Suisun, CA

Tran, Long H
Hawthorne HS
Lawndale, CA

Tran, Martina P
Laguna Hills HS
Laguna Hills, CA

Tran, Milton
Lowell HS
San Francisco, CA

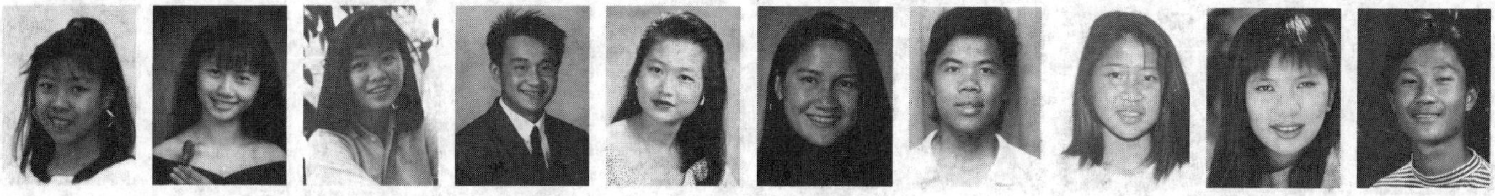

Tran, Ngoc M
San Gabriel HS
Rosemead, CA

Tran, Phuong K
Andrew Hill HS
San Jose, CA

Tran, Phyllis
Abraham Lincoln HS
San Francisco, CA

Tran, Richard Chan
Marina HS
Huntington Bch, CA

Tran, Thao Ngoc
Lakewood SR HS
Long Beach, CA

Tran, Thao T
Westminster HS
Westminster, CA

Tran, Tiet
Kearny HS
San Diego, CA

Tran, Trinh N
Saddleback HS
Santa Ana, CA

Tran, Victoria
Ocean View HS
Huntington Bch, CA

Tran, Xuan H
Kearny HS
San Diego, CA

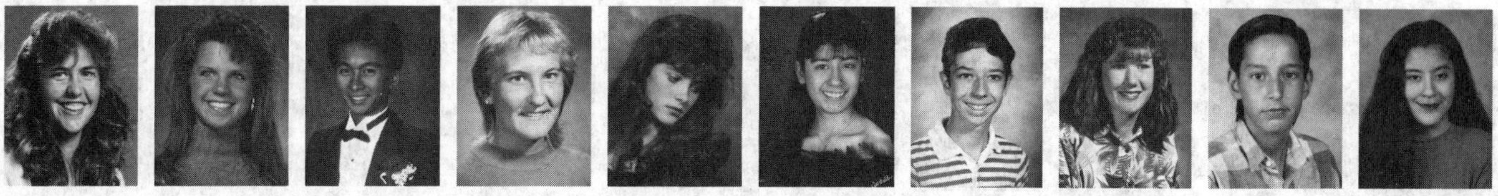

Traugott, Kathleen D
Etiwanda HS
Rancho Cucamonga, CA

Travers, Devon C
El Toro HS
El Toro, CA

Trazo, Robert
Narbonne Math/ Science Magnet HS
Carson, CA

Treadway, Lara D
Clairemont HS
San Diego, CA

Treichler, Joy C
River City HS
W Sacramento, CA

Trejos, Norma
Manor Baptist HS
Hayward, CA

Trenner, Matthew K
Sherman E Burroughs HS
Ridgecrest, CA

Trent, Katherine M
Modoc HS
Alturas, CA

Trevino, Jason R
Brethren HS
Pico Rivera, CA

Trevino, September N
Hiram Johnson HS
Sacramento, CA

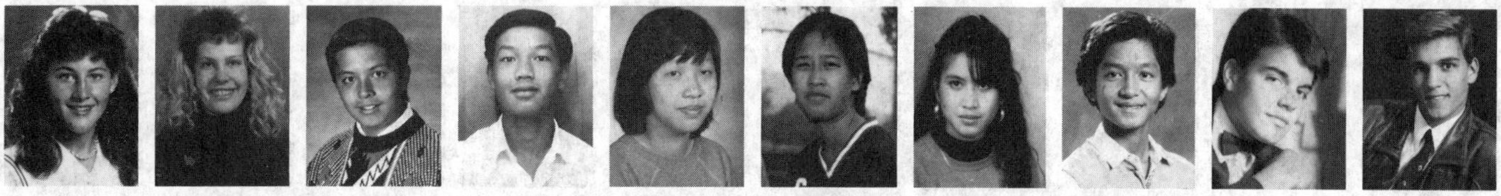

Triarsi, Allison M
Flintridge Preparatory Schl
Covina, CA

Trimble, Jacqueline R
Hanford HS
Hanford, CA

Trimillos, Ric L
Don Antonio Lugo
Chino, CA

Trinh, Loc H
Kearny HS
San Diego, CA

Trinh, Vien
San Gabriel HS
Rosemead, CA

Trinidad, Erma R J
Bellarmine Jefferson
Los Angeles, CA

Trinidad, Hazel E
Gompers Secondary
San Diego, CA

Trivino, Marlon
Nogales HS
West Covina, CA

Tromba, Dante P S
Willow Park HS
Apple Valley, CA

Trostle, Robert H
Etiwanda HS
Etiwanda, CA

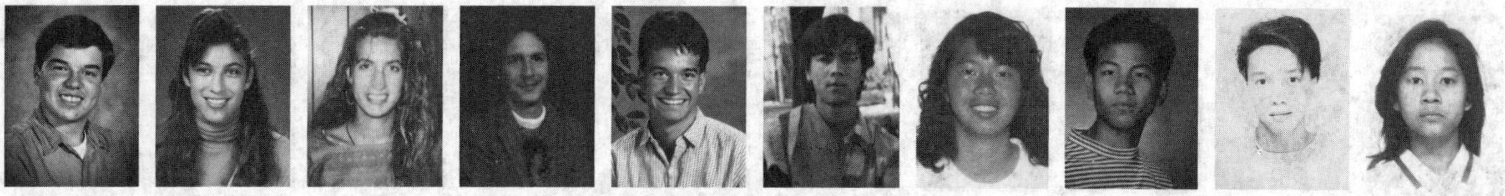

Trottman, David M
Burroughs HS
Ridgecrest, CA

Trovato, Tiffany D
Mt Diablo HS
Pittsburg, CA

Troxel, Rachael J
Las Lomas HS
Walnut Creek, CA

Troy, Eric G
Turlock HS
Turlock, CA

Trujillo, Timothy T
Escondido Adventist Acad
Escondido, CA

Truong, Bu
A A Stagg HS
Stockton, CA

Truong, Dinh
Magnolia HS
Anaheim, CA

Truong, Jason
Westminster HS
Westminster, CA

Truong, Terry
Skyline HS
Oakland, CA

Truong, Ton H
Warren HS
Downey, CA

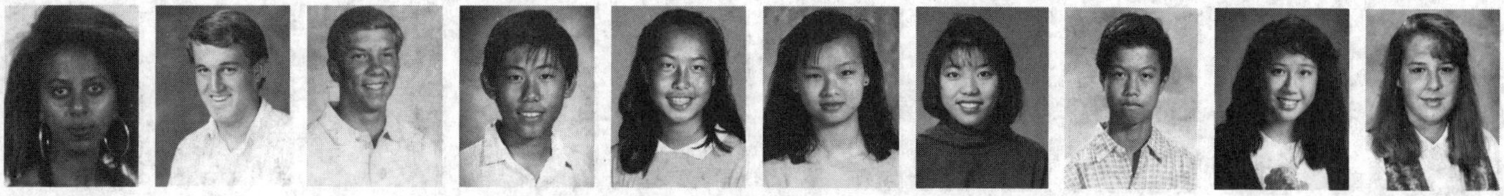

Trushet, Deneke
Anaheim HS
Anaheim, CA

Trutna, Dennis M
Bonita Vista HS
Bonita, CA

Trythall, Daniel M
Oakmont HS
Roseville, CA

Tsai, Brian
University HS
Orange, CA

Tsai, Christine
Lynbrook HS
San Jose, CA

Tsai, Diana
Mills HS
Millbrae, CA

Tsai, Jenny
Palo Verde HS
Blythe, CA

Tsai, Willy C
Whitney HS
Norwalk, CA

Tsang, Elizabeth T
Clovis West HS
Fresno, CA

Tschinkel, Heather M
Alverno HS
San Gabriel, CA

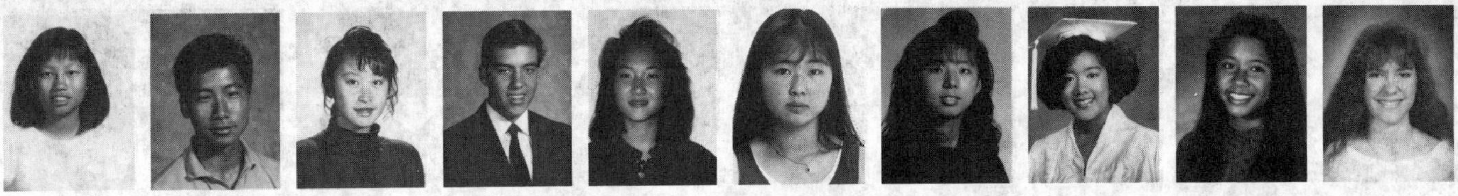

Tse, Waiyi
Valley HS
Santa Ana, CA

Tseng, Jeff C
Mills HS
Millbrae, CA

Tseng, Yin
Burlingame HS
San Mateo, CA

Tsiagkas, Nick
St Ignatius College Prep
Daly City, CA

Tso, Christine C
American HS
Fremont, CA

Tsunoda, Miho
San Pedro HS
Rancho Palos Vrds, CA

Tu, Alice E
William C Overfelt
Cupertino, CA

Tuason, Reina V
St Joseph HS
Cypress, CA

Tuazon, Geraline D
Don Antonio Lugo
Chino, CA

Tubbs, Katie
Santa Rosa HS
Santa Rosa, CA

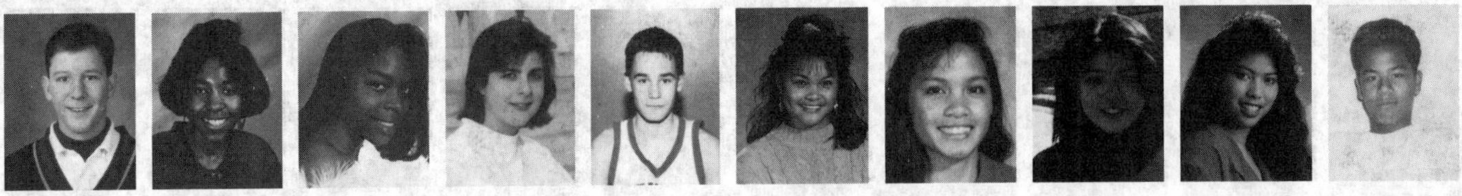

Tucker, Adam
Redwood HS
Visalia, CA

Tucker, Bethany J
Apple Valley HS
Apple Valley, CA

Tucker, Veronica R
El Cerrito HS
San Pablo, CA

Tuer, Shannon L
Monterey HS
Fort Ord, CA

Tufts, Christopher M
Sanger HS
Sanger, CA

Tugade, Michele
Westmoor HS
Daly City, CA

Tugade, Ruby
Westmoor HS
Daly City, CA

Tui, Tao A
Abraham Lincoln HS
San Francisco, CA

Tulao, Nicolette Joy
Bonita Vista HS
Bonita, CA

Tulio, Jon J
Monterey Bay Acad
Los Angeles, CA

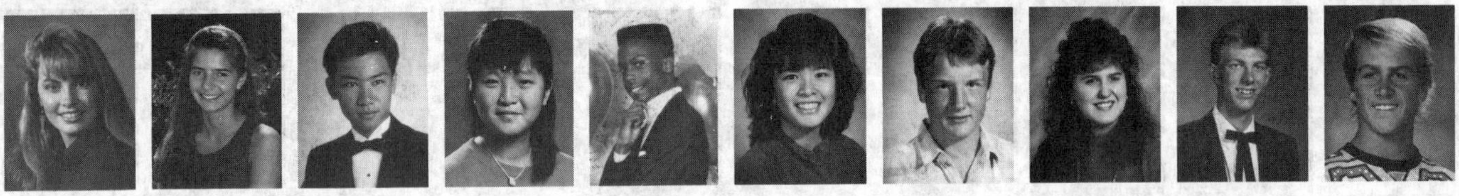

Tullis, Wendy
Arroyo Grande HS
Arroyo Grande, CA

Tumasian, Stephanie
Carondelet HS
Danville, CA

Tung, Chi Ho
Monte Vista Christian HS
Canada

Tung, Grace Y
South Pasadena HS
South Pasadena, CA

Tunson, Shawn P
George Washington
San Francisco, CA

Tuphan, Yvette Y
John F Kennedy HS
Buena Park, CA

Turbeville, Marshall
Geyserville HS
Geyserville, CA

Turell, Dana M
Foothill HS
Tustin, CA

Turley, Joshua A
Valley View HS
Moreno Valley, CA

Turnbull, Matthew S
Mission Viejo HS
Mission Viejo, CA

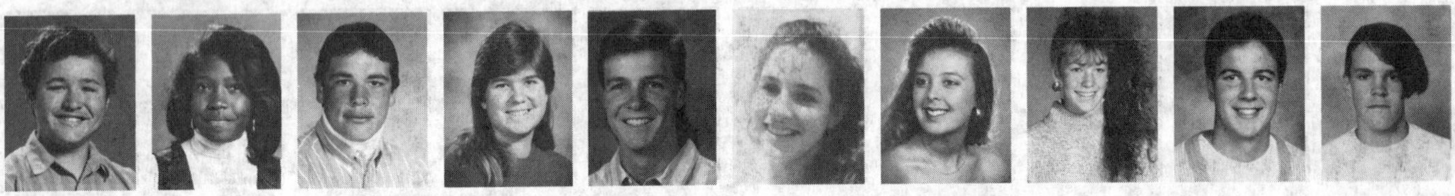

Turner, Christian R
Colton HS
Colton, CA

Turner, Crystal M
Downtown Business Magnet HS
Los Angeles, CA

Turner, Eddie F
San Benito HS
Hollister, CA

Turner, Gillian A
Los Amigos HS
Fountain Valley, CA

Turner, Jason
Bear River HS
Auburn, CA

Turner, Katie
Livermore HS
Livermore, CA

Turner, Liesa M
Lincoln HS
Lincoln, CA

Turner, Melissa A
El Camino HS
Brisbane, CA

Turner, Mike
St Lawrence Acad
Campbell, CA

Turner, Nick B
Torrance HS
Torrance, CA

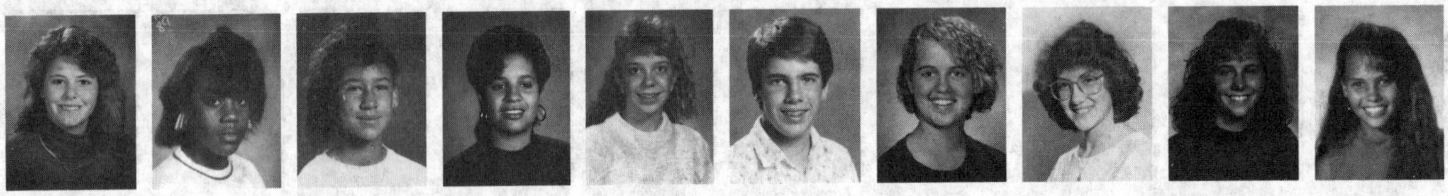

Turner, Rachelle T
El Camino HS
Oceanside, CA

Turner, Roquel L
West Covina HS
West Covina, CA

Turner, Shanna A
Mojave HS
California City, CA

Turner, Shayleen A
Edison SR HS
Stockton, CA

Turner, Shelley A
Victor Valley HS
Victorville, CA

Turse, Josh E
Carlsbad HS
Carlsbad, CA

Tutor, Lynda J
Westminster HS
Westminster, CA

Tvedt, Valerie Maria
Barstow HS
Barstow, CA

Twaddell, Staci
Folson HS
Folsom, CA

Tygenhof, Heather T
Tustin HS
Tustin, CA

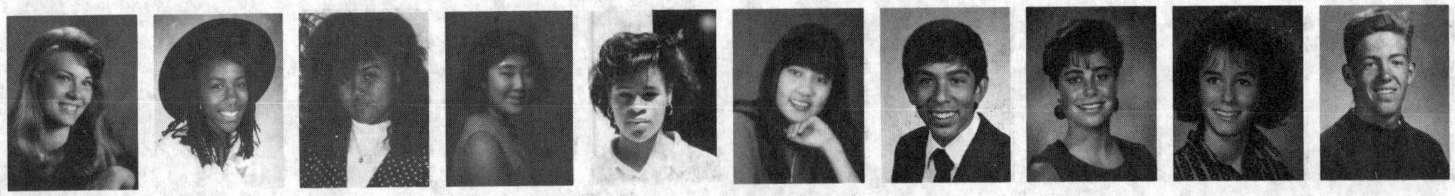

Tyler, Donna
Woodlake Union HS
Woodlake, CA

Tyler, Jenniper Autumn
Moorpark HS
Moorpark, CA

Ubaldo, Glo Anne G
Abraham Lincoln HS
San Francisco, CA

Uchishiba, Mari
James Lick HS
San Jose, CA

Udoji, Robin N
Santa Clara HS
Oxnard, CA

Ueda, Kara K
Lincoln HS
Stockton, CA

Ulate, Rafael
Homestead HS
Sunnyvale, CA

Underell, Ashley E
Torrey Pines HS
Del Mar, CA

Underhill, Jennifer
Irvine HS
Irvine, CA

Underhill, Mike D
Poway HS
San Diego, CA

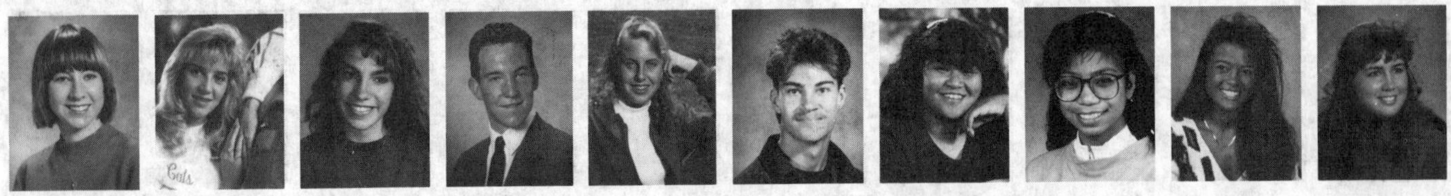

Underwood, Kim
Buena Park HS
Buena Park, CA

Underwood, Leslie
Taft Union HS
Taft, CA

Underwood, Michelle
Antioch HS
Antioch, CA

Ungles, Mark B
Atla Loma HS
Alta Loma, CA

Unser, Lynn
Anaheim HS
Anaheim, CA

Unsworth, Justin R
Costa Mesa HS
Costa Mesa, CA

Untalan, Cheryl A
Arroyo Grande HS
Grover City, CA

Untalan, Cyrille Mae
St Joseph HS
Long Beach, CA

Untalan, Tamara
Marina HS
Huntington Bch, CA

Untiedt, Hope
Western HS
Anaheim, CA

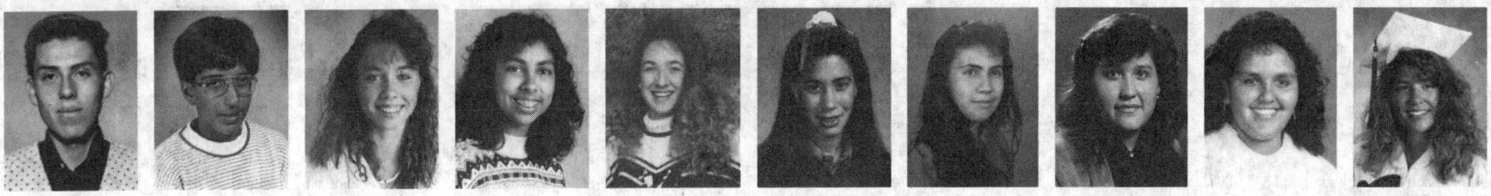

Unzueta, Pedro
Compton HS
Compton, CA

Uppal, Rohit
Lanen HS
Susanville, CA

Urane, Doreen
Hueneme HS
Oxnard, CA

Urango, Monica C
Oxnard Union HS
Oxnard, CA

Urban, Nichole M
Fontana HS
Fontana, CA

Ureno, Ana E
Chula Vista HS
San Diego, CA

Uribe, Claudia I
Calexico HS
Calexico, CA

Uribe, Elia
Garfield HS
Los Angeles, CA

Uribe, Rosanna I
Bishop Montgomery
Hawthorne, CA

Urie, Bree
San Mateo HS
Foster City, CA

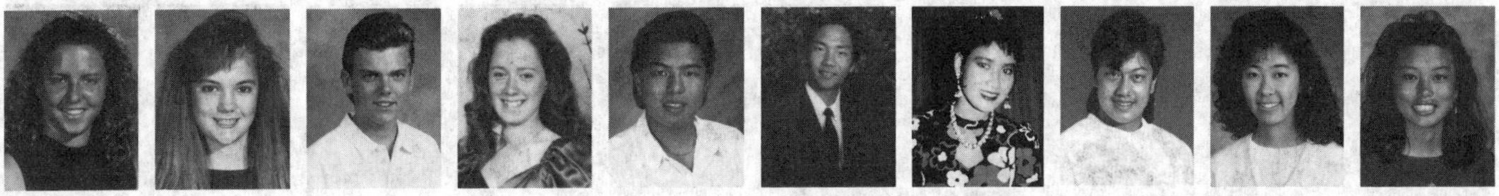

Uritz, Jolie B
Los Alamitos HS
Los Alamitos, CA

Urling, Amy
Carlmont HS
Belmont, CA

Ursem, Perry John
Simi Valley HS
Simi Valley, CA

Utter, Dora V
Lompoc HS
Lompoc, CA

Uy, Lawrence
Victor Valley
Christian Schl
Victorville, CA

Uy, Melvin O
El Toro HS
El Toro, CA

Uy, Samantha
Silver Creek HS
Milpitas, CA

Uy-Barreta,
Don-Joseph P
So San Francisco HS
S San Francisco, CA

Uyeda, Sherrill
Troy HS
Fullerton, CA

Uytingco, Rimini
Bishop Amat HS
Diamond Bar, CA

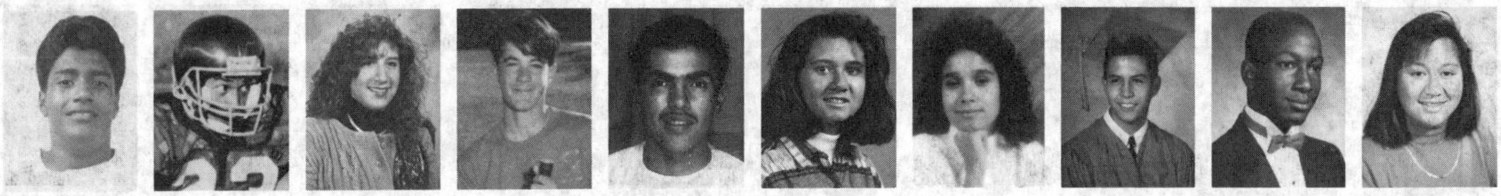

Vaccarezza, Aldo D
Bellarmine College
Prep
San Jose, CA

Vail, Crispin T
Mountain Empire JR
SR HS
Campo, CA

Valadez, Tina
Hesperia Christian
Apple Valley, CA

Valderrama, Jason
Moor Park HS
Moorpark, CA

Valderrama, Jose L
Buena Park HS
Fullerton, CA

Valderrama, Josie
Sherman Oaks CES
Los Angeles, CA

Valdez, Allison D
Livingston HS
Livingston, CA

Valdivia, Ricardo
St John Bosco HS
La Palma, CA

Valeau, Dwayne E
Bishop O'dowd HS
Hayward, CA

Valencia, Andrea F
Hamilton HS
Los Angeles, CA

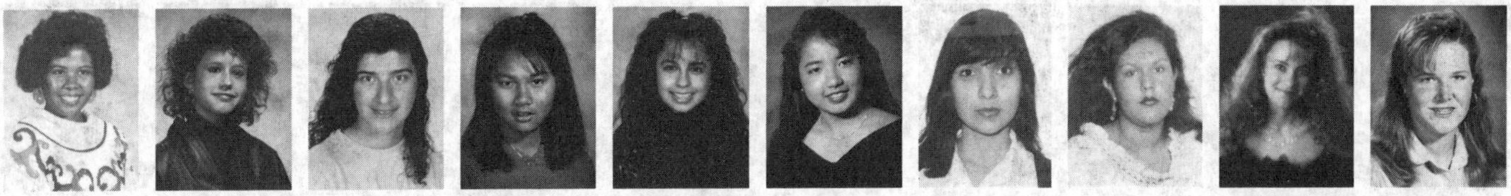

Valencia, Charmina
David Starr Jordan
Long Beach, CA

Valencia, Gladys
Fremont Christian
Newark, CA

Valencia, Kimberly A
Rowland HS
Rowland Hts, CA

Valencia, Ma
Esmeralda A
North Hollywood HS
Mission Hills, CA

Valencia, Monica
Alverno HS
Sierra Madre, CA

Valencia, Nancy V
Mission HS
San Francisco, CA

Valencia, Ruth
Sierra Vista HS
Baldwin Park, CA

Valencia, Yvette
Sacred Heart HS
Los Angeles, CA

Valente, Madeline L
Granada HS
Livermore, CA

Valentine, Amy L
Huntington Beach
Huntington Beach,
CA

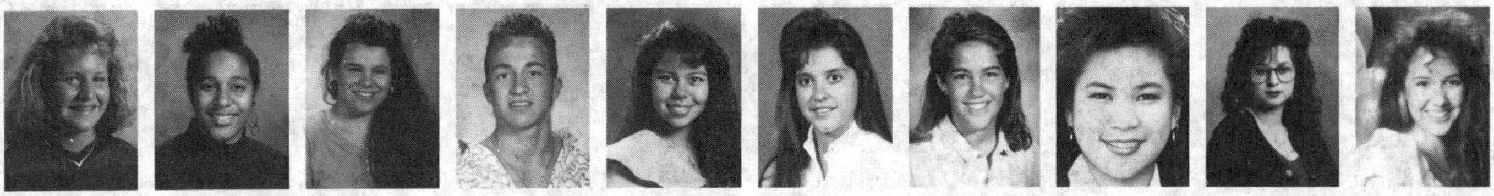

Valentine, Kristi L
Valley Christian HS
Norwalk, CA

Valentinez, Angelina
James Logan HS
Newark, CA

Valenzuela, Kathy
Central Union HS
El Centro, CA

Valenzuela, Pablo M
Castillon
Santa Teresa HS
San Jose, CA

Valenzuela, Tanya
Holy Family HS
Glendale, CA

Valenzuela, Vicky
Beaumont HS
Beaumont, CA

Valenzuela, Victoria
Villa Park HS
Orange, CA

Valerio, Kristine
Joyce
Nogales HS
Walnut, CA

Valerio, Melesia V S
Fullerton HS
Roswell, NM

Valle, Lisa M
Santa Margarita
Catholic HS
El Toro, CA

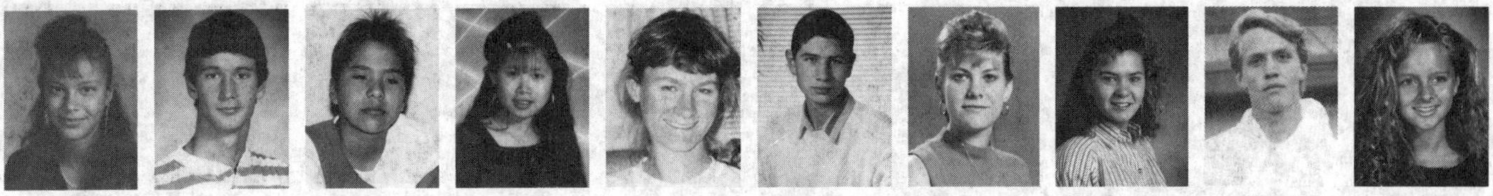

Valleser, Anna C
Bishop Montgomery
Bellflower, CA

Valliere, Christopher
Westwood HS
Westwood, CA

Vallo, Anita
Barstow HS
Barstow, CA

Van, To Linh
George Washington
San Francisco, CA

Van Dam, Devon L
Alverno HS
Monrovia, CA

Van De Hoeven,
Vincent G
Filmore Unified HS
Fillmore, CA

Van Devanter,
Krystal D
Cajon HS
San Bernardino, CA

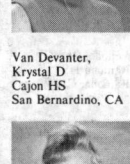

Van Diest, Julie
Fresno Christian HS
Fresno, CA

Van Dyke, Bill D
Buchanan HS
Running Springs, CA

Van Ert, Kerry
Chico HS
Chico, CA

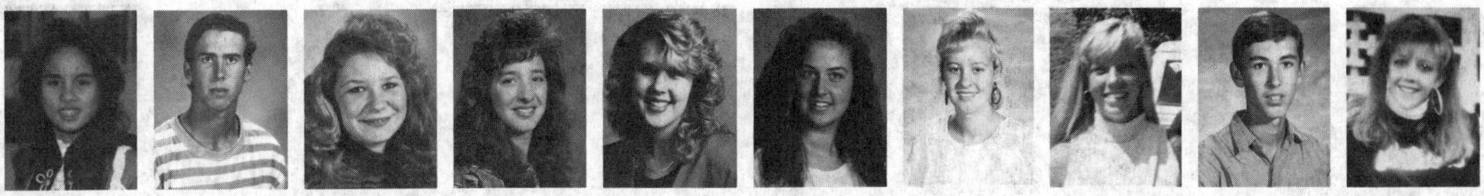

Van Gelder, Natalie
Ocalanes HS
Lafayette, CA

Van Heerde, Jason E
Eisenhower HS
Rialto, CA

Van Hulzen, Erika
Apple Valley
Christian Schl
Apple Valley, CA

Van Hyfte, Shaneen
Ontario HS
Ontario, CA

Van Landuyt,
Christine Y
Imperial HS
Pasadena, CA

Van Loon, Tracie E
Madera HS
Madera, CA

Van Stockum, Irene
Notre Dame HS
Riverside, CA

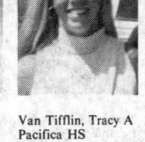

Van Tifflin, Tracy A
Pacifica HS
Garden Grove, CA

Van Viegen, Marco A
Chino HS
Chino, CA

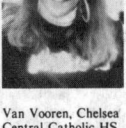

Van Vooren, Chelsea
Central Catholic HS
Hughson, CA

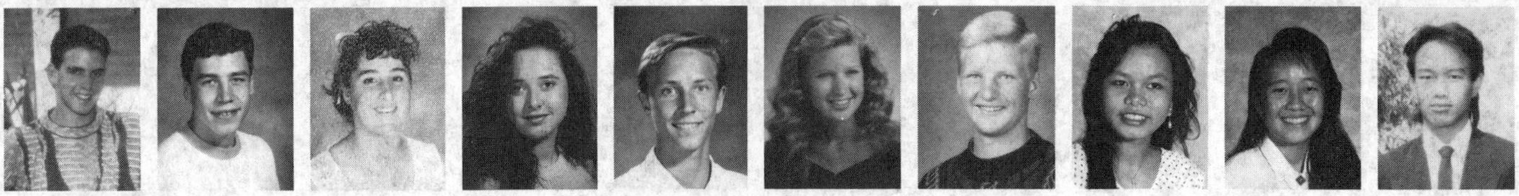

Van Zwaluwenburg, Brent A
Ripon Christian HS
Manteca, CA

Vance, Dwayne
Norco HS
Norco, CA

Vance, Kristi A
Sanger HS
Sanger, CA

Vande Merghel, Laura M
Los Amigos HS
Fountain Valley, CA

Vander Wal, Jeffrey
Huntington Beach
Huntington Beach, CA

Vanderbyl, Kimberly Anne
Del Mar HS
San Jose, CA

Vanderwall, Greg S
Yucaipa HS
Yucaipa, CA

Vang, Boupha Linda
Duncan Polytechnical
Fresno, CA

Vang, Cher
Clovis HS
Fresno, CA

Vang, Chinok
Edison HS
Fresno, CA

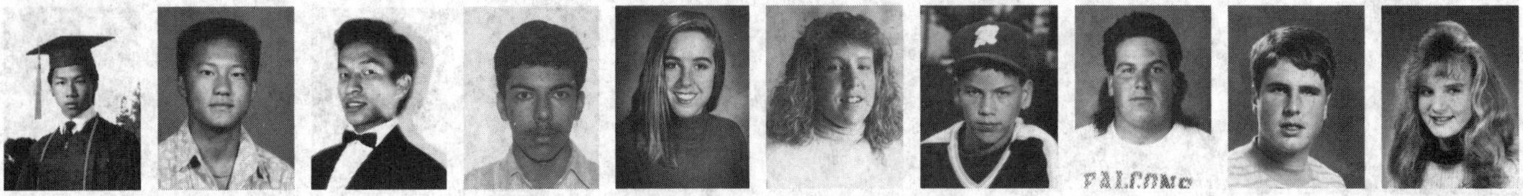

Vang, Kao N
Mc Lane HS
Fresno, CA

Vang, Mao
Banning HS
Fresno, CA

Vang, So
Edison HS
Stockton, CA

Vangani, Akash V
Irvine HS
Irvine, CA

Vanni, Heather N
Mt Shasta HS
Mount Shasta, CA

Vanscoy, Genie
Rio Mesa HS
Oxnard, CA

Vanus, George M
Montclair HS
Montclair, CA

Varela, Bryan
Palmdale HS
Agua Dulce, CA

Varga, Brandon L
Burbank HS
Burbank, CA

Vargas, Barbara L
Liberty Union HS
Oakley, CA

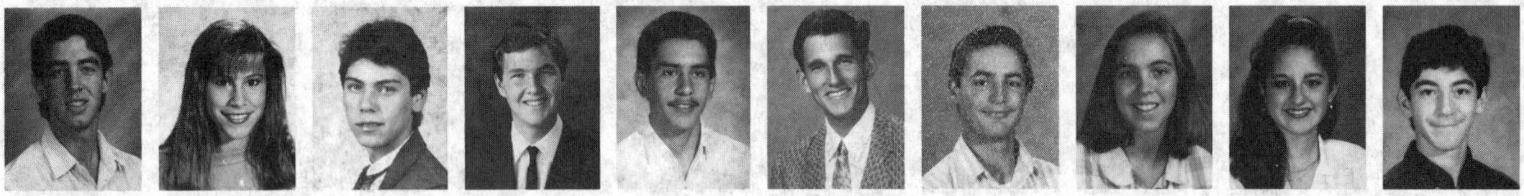

Vargas, Brett
Apple Valley HS
Apple Valley, CA

Vargas, Carla L
El Dorado HS
Placentia, CA

Vargas, Ernesto
Calexico HS
Calexico, CA

Vargas, Jason
Bishop Amat Memorial HS
Upland, CA

Vargas, Juan
Live Oak HS
Live Oak, CA

Vargas, Ricardo A
Bishop Montgomery
Torrance, CA

Vargas, Rigoberto
Alisal HS
Salinas, CA

Vargas, Stacey K
Apple Valley HS
Apple Valley, CA

Varner, Donna J
Bishop Amat Memorial HS
Glendora, CA

Vartanian, Erik
Cupertino HS
San Jose, CA

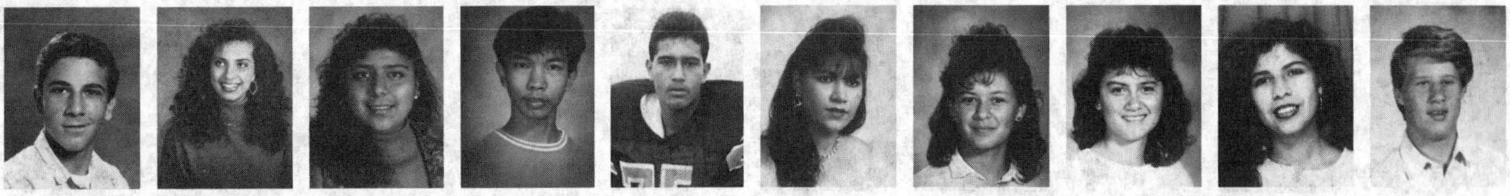

Vartanian, Joseph
Saint Francis HS
Sierra Madre, CA

Vasconez, Vanessa Maria
Saint Genevieve HS
N Hollywood, CA

Vasquez, Andrea
Washington Union
Fresno, CA

Vasquez, Jerico M
North Hollywood HS
North Hollywood, CA

Vasquez, Jose M
San Pedro HS
San Pedro, CA

Vasquez, Lilia
Castle Park HS
Chula Vista, CA

Vasquez, Lily J
Antelope Valley HS
Lancaster, CA

Vasquez, Suly J
Antelope Valley HS
Lancaster, CA

Vasquez, Virginia
Baldwin Park HS
Baldwin Park, CA

Vaughn, Steven M
Will C Wood HS
Vacaville, CA

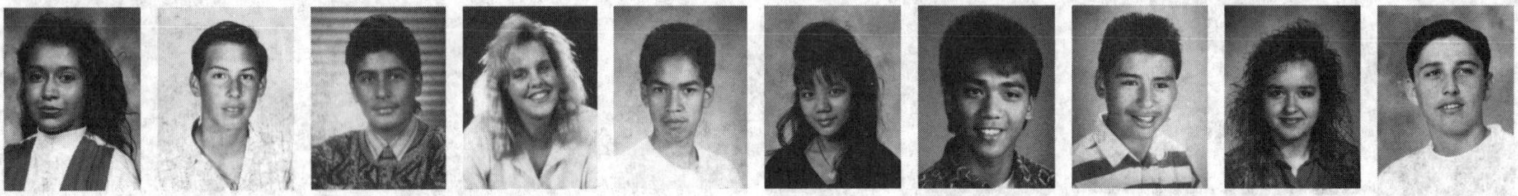

Vazquez, Maria T
Bell Gardens HS
Bell Gardens, CA

Vazquez, Rafael E
Glen A Wilson HS
Hacienda Hts, CA

Vbarra, Jr Francisco
Riverdale Jt Union
Riverdale, CA

Veenstra, Jennifer R
Fresno Christian HS
Fresno, CA

Vega, Gabriel
Schurr HS
Monterey Park, CA

Vega, Rishelline
Upland HS
Upland, CA

Vega-Foster, Jeffrey
Fred C Beyer HS
Modesto, CA

Vejar, Carlos J
Tulare Union HS
Tulare, CA

Vela, Christina M
John H Francis Polytechincal HS
Sun Valley, CA

Velasco, Leo
Montclair HS
Ontario, CA

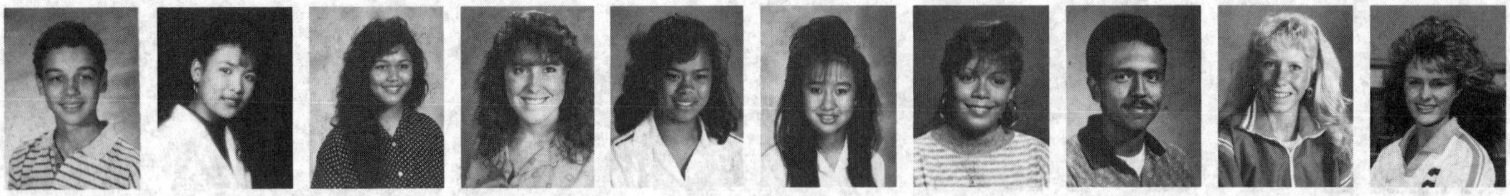

Velasco, Manuel R
Chino HS
Chino, CA

Velasquez, Gloria G
Mission HS
San Francisco, CA

Velasquez, Rhodora
James Logan HS
Union City, CA

Vellone, Rhea E
Ramona HS
Ramona, CA

Veloria, Gwendolyn T
East Union HS
Manteca, CA

Velves, Valerie
St Genevieves HS
Van Nuys, CA

Venegas, Christine A
San Gorgonid HS
San Bernardino, CA

Venegas, Gilbert N
Central Union HS
Heber, CA

Venkus, Lara
Tokay HS
Stockton, CA

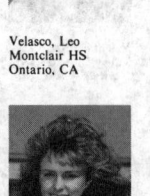

Venn, Cindy L
Oak Park HS
Agoura Hills, CA

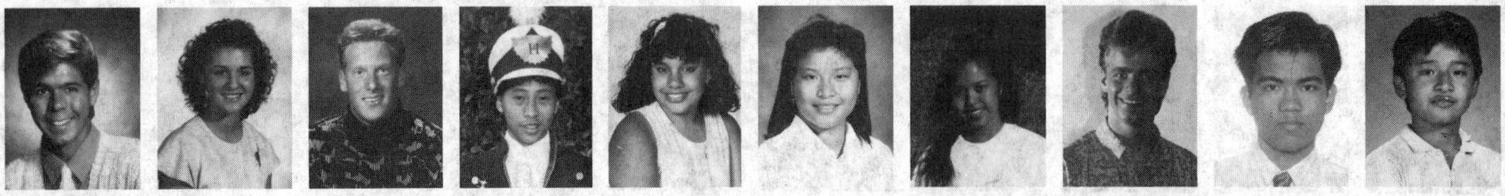

Venti, Joel Patrick
Escondido HS
Escondido, CA

Vento, Graciela
Yokota HS
APO San Francisc, CA

Ventry, Christopher J
Bellarmine College Prep
Santa Cruz, CA

Ventura, Jr Elpidio A
Homestead HS
Sunnyvale, CA

Vera, Evonne S
Nogales HS
W Covina, CA

Vera, Kristine A
Mater Dei HS
Santa Ana, CA

Veran, Melani
Saint Joseph HS
Norwalk, CA

Verbansky, Paul
Chaffey HS
Ontario, CA

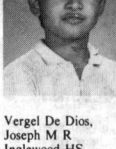

Vergara, Russell B
Independence HS
San Jose, CA

Vergel De Dios, Joseph M R
Inglewood HS
Inglewood, CA

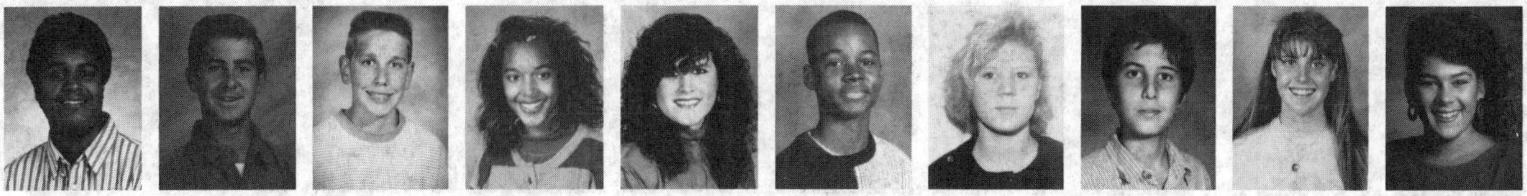

Verma, Sharad
Gunn HS
Los Altos Hills, CA

Vernaci, Joseph H
Apple Valley SR HS
Apple Valley, CA

Verners, Krispen
Kingsburg HS
Kingsburg, CA

Vernon, Tifani R
Novato HS
Novato, CA

Veronica, Alma V
Mount Pleasant HS
San Jose, CA

Verrett, Brian
Lynwood Adv Acad
Los Angeles, CA

Verrett, Lornell
North Hills Christian
Mare Island, CA

Veshtaj, Rudolf
Beaumont HS
Beaumont, CA

Vester-Davis, Jessica
Shasta HS
Sacramento, CA

Vetcher, Candi J
Bonita Vista HS
Bonita, CA

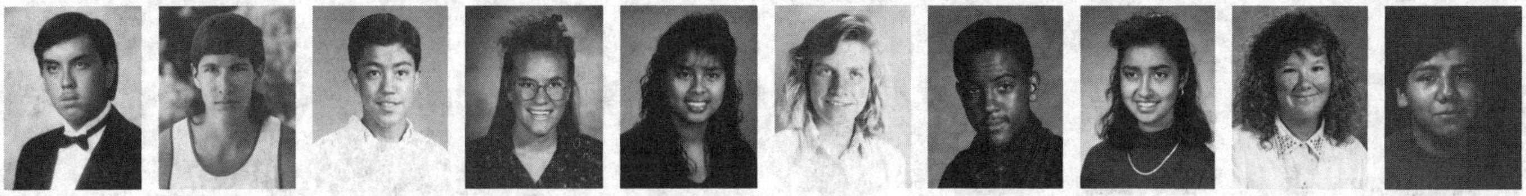

Vevik, Michael
Chula Vista HS
San Diego, CA

Vialpando, J Stephen
Alhambra HS
Martinez, CA

Viayra, Jr Raymond
Bishop Montgomery
Harbor City, CA

Vibe, Karen D
North High Bkrsfld
Bakersfield, CA

Vicedo, Marivic
Edison HS
Stockton, CA

Vickery, Jennifer
Oxnard HS
Oxnard, CA

Victor, Damion E
Kearny HS
San Diego, CA

Vidal, Stacey L
Milpitas HS
Milpitas, CA

Viducic, Nancy
Capuchino HS
San Bruno, CA

Vielma, Isaac
San Fernando Valley
Acad
Pacoima, CA

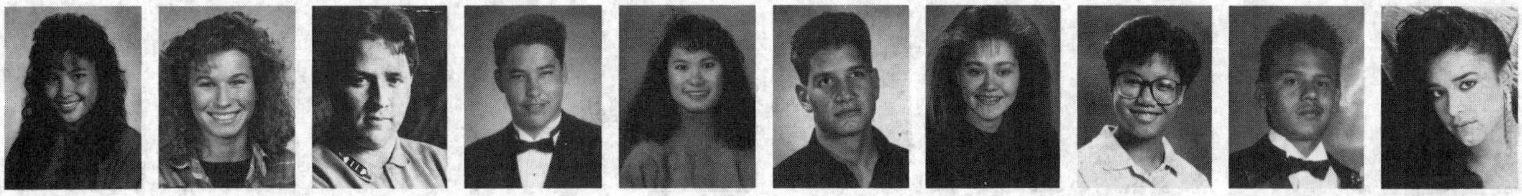

Viernes, Melissa M
Moreau HS
Hayward, CA

Vierra, Rebecca A
River City HS
W Sacramento, CA

Viertel, Andrew
Eagle Rock HS
Los Angeles, CA

Vigna, Daniel J
Monte Vista
Christian HS
Seaside, CA

Vihanexai, Khamevay
Redwood HS
Visalia, CA

Vik, Jeremiah
Holtville Christian
Acad
Holtville, CA

Villa, Anna M
Clovis HS
Clovis, CA

Villa, Jennifer B
Holy Family HS
Glendale, CA

Villagran, Mike A
West HS
Bakersfield, CA

Villalobos, Antonia
Santa Monica HS
Santa Monica, CA

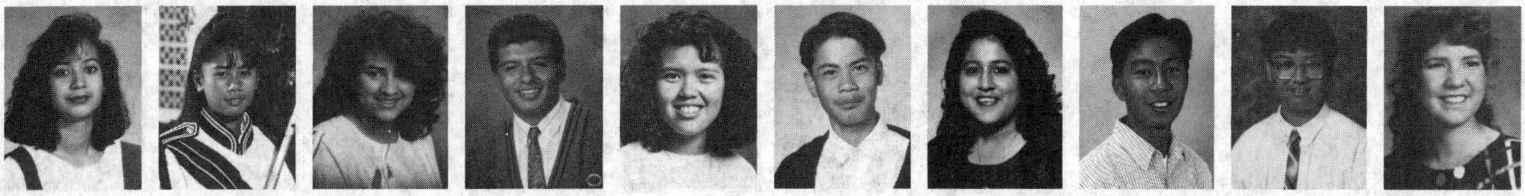

Villalpando, Beatriz
James Lick HS
San Jose, CA

Villanueva, Charife P
Bolsa Grande HS
Garden Grove, CA

Villeda, Clary O
Fairview JR Acad
Fontana, CA

Villegas, Julio A
Pater Noster HS
Los Angeles, CA

Villegas, Maria A
San Gorgonio HS
San Bernardino, CA

Villegas, Richard P E
Alhambra HS
Alhambra, CA

Villegas, Veronica
Compton SR HS
Compton, CA

Villena, Jr Apolonio
Savanna HS
Anaheim, CA

Villosis, Richard
Loyola HS
Glendale, CA

Vincelli, Maureen D
Monroe HS
Panorama City, CA

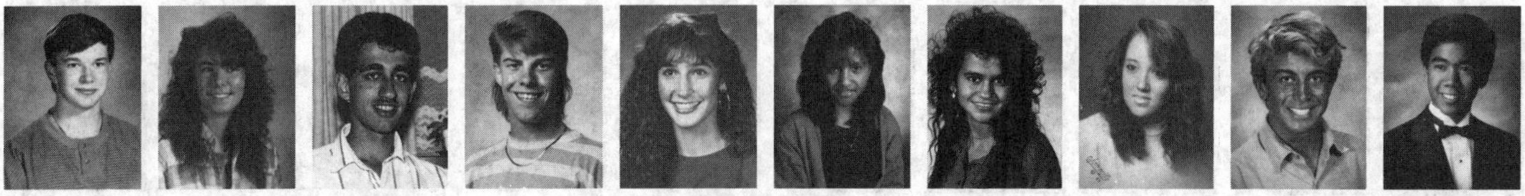

Vincent, Thomas T
Red Bluff Union HS
Manton, CA

Vinciguerra,
Antoinette
Arcadia HS
Arcadia, CA

Viner, Eugene
George Washington
San Francisco, CA

Vinson, Jeffrey B
Brea-Olinda HS
Brea, CA

Vinther, Amy
Foothill HS
Pleasanton, CA

Violanda, Rosario M
Balboa HS
San Francisco, CA

Viramontes, Suzana
Chino HS
Chino, CA

Virgadamo, Edith M
El Cajon Valley HS
El Cajon, CA

Virtich, Bruno
El Camino HS
Oceanside, CA

Visaya, Jeff
Channel Island HS
Oxnard, CA

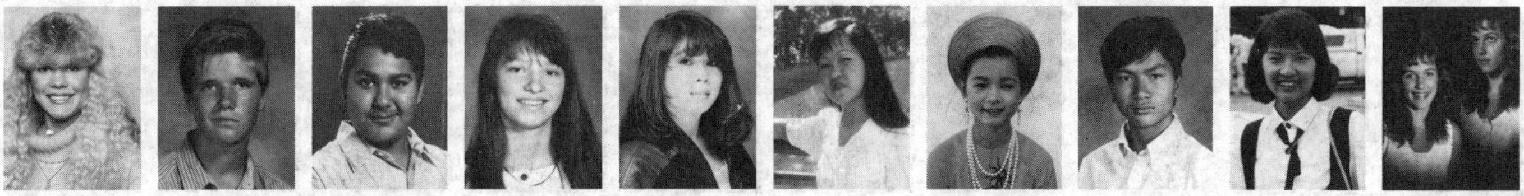

Visich, Natasha
Vallejo HS
Vallejo, CA

Vismantas, Eric L
Los Alamitos HS
Garden Grove, CA

Viveros, George
Fontana HS
Fontana, CA

Vlad, Andreea S
Warren HS
Downey, CA

Vo, Elizabeth T
Riverside Polytechnic
Riverside, CA

Vo, Hong Thi
San Gabriel HS
Rosemead, CA

Vo, Huong T
Culver City HS
Culver City, CA

Vo, Thomas T
San Pasqual HS
Escondido, CA

Vo, Trang M
Workman HS
Valinda, CA

Voet, Dawn M
Burney JR/SR HS
Burney, CA

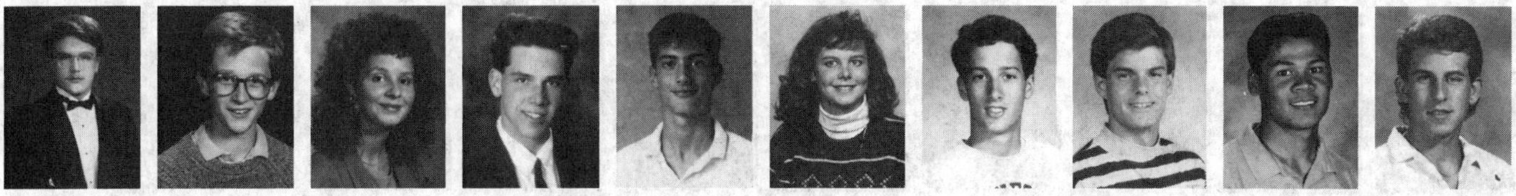

Vogel, Robert M
Tracy Joint Union
Tracy, CA

Volker, Jim
Pinole Valley HS
San Pablo, CA

Vollmann, Jamilla M
Mira Loma HS
Sacramento, CA

Volmer, Stephen L
Antelope Valley HS
Lancaster, CA

Von Buelow, Jeremy
Chaminade College
Prep
Northridge, CA

Von Latta, Carin L
Modesto HS
Modesto, CA

Von Lossberg, Scott
Crescenta Valley HS
La Canada, CA

Voner, Jeffrey T
Whittier Christian
Whittier, CA

Vongchantha,
Khamsay
Hoover HS
Fresno, CA

Voorting, Craig
Los Alamitos HS
Los Alamitos, CA

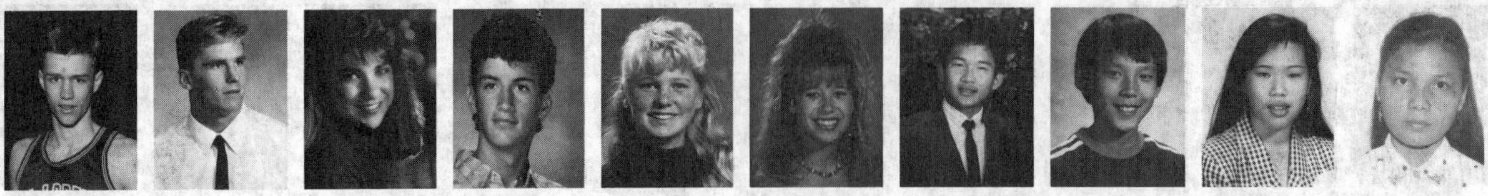

Voralik, John
San Lorenzo Valley
Boulder Creek, CA

Vosburgh, Eric
Rowland HS
Rowland Hts, CA

Vosti, Gina M
Notre Dame HS
Gonzales, CA

Vrobel, Arik
Trabuco Hills HS
Mission Viejo, CA

Vrolyks, Nicole J
Chaffey HS
Ontario, CA

Vrooman, Joy
Mar Vista HS
Imperial Beach, CA

Vu, Alan D
El Toro HS
El Toro, CA

Vu, Anh
Baldwin Park HS
Baldwin Park, CA

Vu, Bich Ngoc N
Venice HS
Culver City, CA

Vu, Mychau
Monte Vista HS
Danville, CA

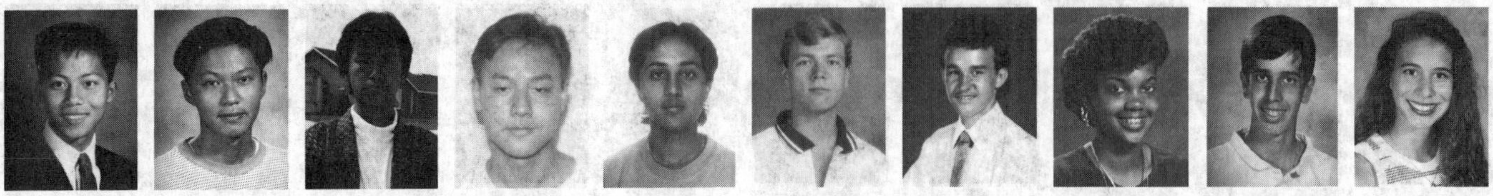

Vu, Scott
St Michaels
Preparatory HS
Santa Ana, CA

Vu, Vinh
Los Amigos HS
Fountain Valley, CA

Vue, Lee P
River City HS
W Sacramento, CA

Vuong, Huy C
Saugus HS
Valencia, CA

Vyas, Devesh B
Culver City HS
Culver City, CA

Wabs, Michael D
Redlands HS
Redlands, CA

Waddell, Andy J
Red Bluff Union HS
Proberta, CA

Wade, Susaun J
Westchester HS
Los Angeles, CA

Wade, Winston E
Paraclete HS
Quartz Hill, CA

Wagner, Audra K
Oak Ridge HS
Cameron Park, CA

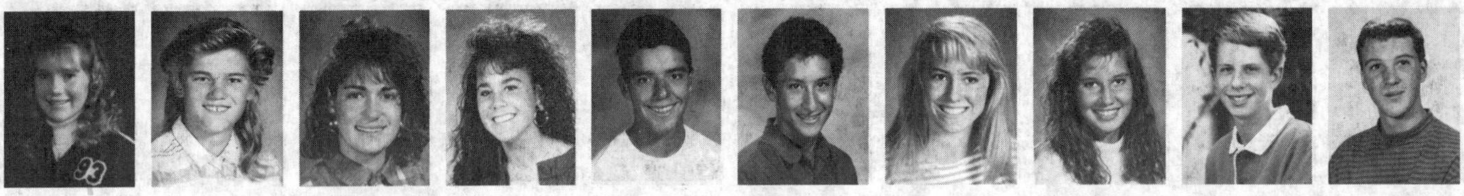

Wagner, Carry
Mc Lane HS
Fresno, CA

Wagner, Jennifer M
Mt Shasta HS
Weed, CA

Wagner, Melissa L
Torry Pines HS
Del Mar, CA

Wagner, Michelle N
American HS
Fremont, CA

Wagner, III William
Los Alamitos HS
Los Alamitos, CA

Wagstaff, Robert
Canyon HS
Canyon Country, CA

Wahlman, Heidi R
Bret Harte HS
Altaville, CA

Wahlmeier, Danielle
Poway HS
Poway, CA

Wahlstrom, Jon Mark
Pine Hills JR Acad
Grass Valley, CA

Waits, William W
Skyline HS
Oakland, CA

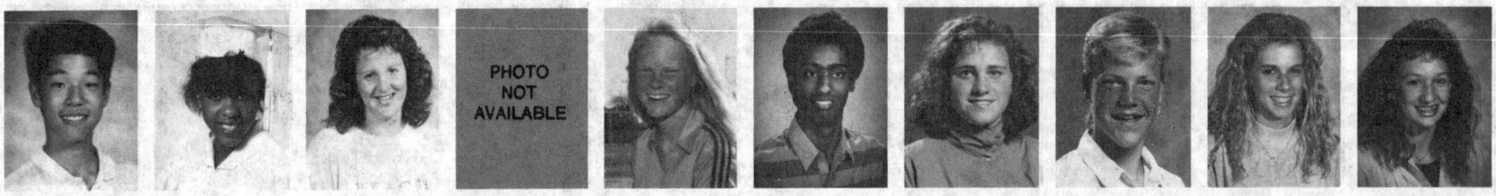

Wakamatsu, Ken K
Fountain Valley HS
Fountain Valley, CA

Wake, Pamela
Compton HS
Compton, CA

Wakeman, Rebecca L
Mesa Verde HS
Citrus Heights, CA

Walea, Jasmina
Napuakahikina
Oxnard HS
Oxnard, CA

Wales, Melinda
Dos Pueblos HS
Goleta, CA

Walia, Harpreet
Singh
Modesto HS
Modesto, CA

Walker, Amylynn
Etiwanda HS
Alta Loma, CA

Walker, Bryan D
Rim Of The World
Blue Jay, CA

Walker, Christina M
Roosevelt Sch Of The
Arts
Fresno, CA

Walker, Jackie
Red Bluff Union HS
Red Bluff, CA

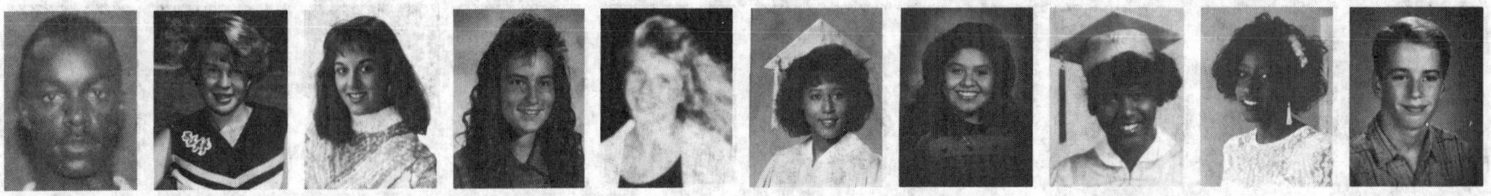

Walker, Julius
Arlington HS
Riverside, CA

Walker, Kiki
San Jose High Acad
San Jose, CA

Walker, Margi E
Petaluma HS
Penngrove, CA

Walker, Melissa L
Nevada Union HS
Nevada City, CA

Walker, Michelle L
Trona HS
Trona, CA

Walker, Nichole
Walnut HS
Walnut, CA

Walker, Priscilla K
Arlington HS
Riverside, CA

Walker, Rachelle Y
John A Rowland HS
Rowland Hts, CA

Walker, Ramona C
Salinas HS
Salinas, CA

Walker, Todd G
Modesto HS
Modesto, CA

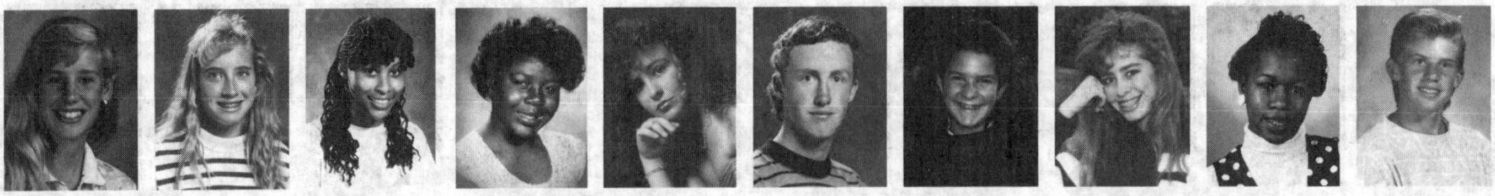

Walker, Tracy
Apple Valley HS
Apple Valley, CA

Walker, Valerie L
Rim Of The World
Crestline, CA

Walker, Wikima D
Abraham Lincoln HS
San Francisco, CA

Walker, Young Bio
John C Fremont HS
Los Angeles, CA

Walkley, Trudi L
Paradise HS
Paradise, CA

Wall, Aaron S
Rim Of The World
Crestline, CA

Walla-Murphy,
Meghan A
Westlake Schl For
Girls
Woodland Hills, CA

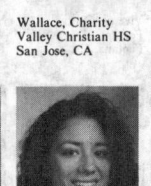

Wallace, Charity
Valley Christian HS
San Jose, CA

Wallace, Fia
Victor Valley HS
Victorville, CA

Wallace, John J
Corona HS
Corona, CA

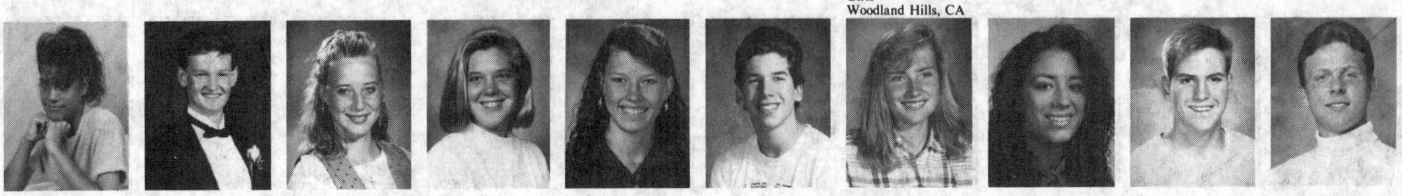

Wallace, Lisa
Chula Vista HS
Chula Vista, CA

Wallace, Thomas J
Bakersfield HS
Bakersfield, CA

Walls, Jenny
West Covina HS
West Covina, CA

Walls, Juli
Grossmont HS
La Mesa, CA

Walsh, Amy M
Trabuco Hills HS
Mission Viejo, CA

Walston, Gregory S
Miramonte HS
Orinda, CA

Walsworth, Amy
Willows HS
Willows, CA

Walter, Judi L
Galt HS
Galt, CA

Walters, Aaron F
Canyon HS
Canyon Country, CA

Walters, Billy E
Montclair HS
Montclair, CA

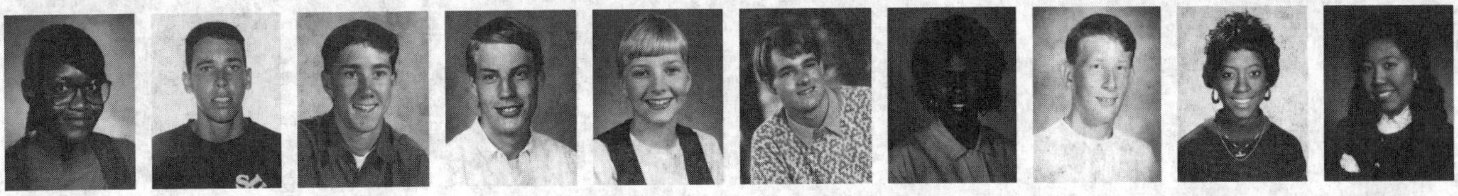

Walters, Marissa G
Washington Prep
Los Angeles, CA

Walters, Matthew D
Arlington HS
Riverside, CA

Walters, Robert S
San Luis Obispo HS
San Luis Obispo, CA

Waltman, Daniel B
Madison HS
San Diego, CA

Walton, Leslie A
Sacred Heart Prep
Los Altos, CA

Walton, Robert
Sacred Heart Prep
Los Altos, CA

Walton, Sher Re C
Helix HS
San Diego, CA

Walworth, Jeffrey S
Shafter HS
Shafter, CA

Wanambwa, Lillian L
Pasadena HS
Altadena, CA

Wang, Christina Y
Lowell HS
San Francisco, CA

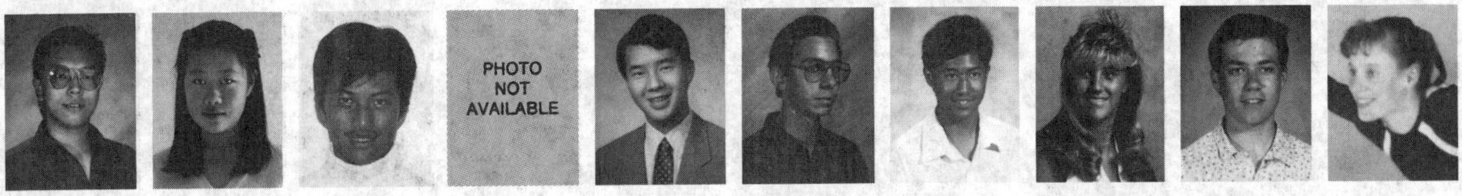

PHOTO
NOT
AVAILABLE

Wang, Edward H
Hoover HS
Fresno, CA

Wang, Jian
Crossroads School
For Arts & Sciences
West Los Angeles, CA

Wang, Paul Yung
Chuan
San Gabriel HS
Rosemead, CA

Wang, Sharon
J Eugene Mc Ateer
San Francisco, CA

Wang, Tom
Adolfo Camarillo HS
Camarillo, CA

Wangler, Konrad B
Serrano HS
Phelan, CA

Wangsuwana, Miracle T
Gretchen A Whitney
Hawaiian Gardens, CA

Ward, Brandi M
Don Lugo HS
Chino, CA

Ward, Jason P
Portola HS
Portola, CA

Ward, Jennifer A
Los Gatos HS
Los Gatos, CA

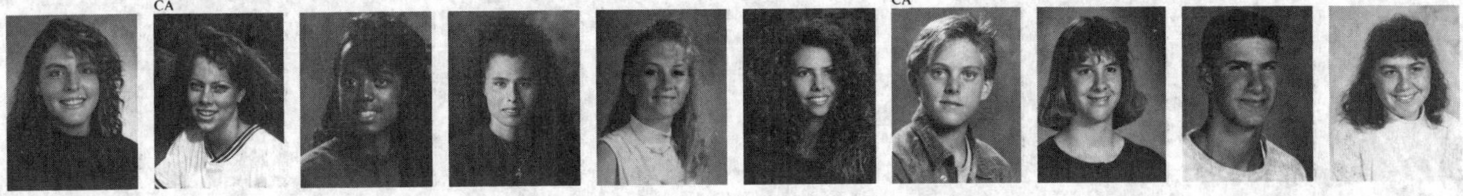

Ward, Karen E
Henry M Gunn HS
Palo Alto, CA

Ward, Karina I
East Union HS
Manteca, CA

Ward, Kristi
Cajon HS
San Bernardino, CA

Ward, Lisa
Workman HS
Valinda, CA

Ward, Sheryl
Hesperia HS
Hesperia, CA

Warden, Audra J
El Toro HS
El Toro, CA

Warehall, Eric R
Cajon HS
San Bernardino, CA

Warner, Sarah
Sutter HS
Sutter, CA

Warren, Deron T
Junipero Serra HS
Millbrae, CA

Wartanian, Houri A
Arroyo Grande HS
Arroyo Grande, CA

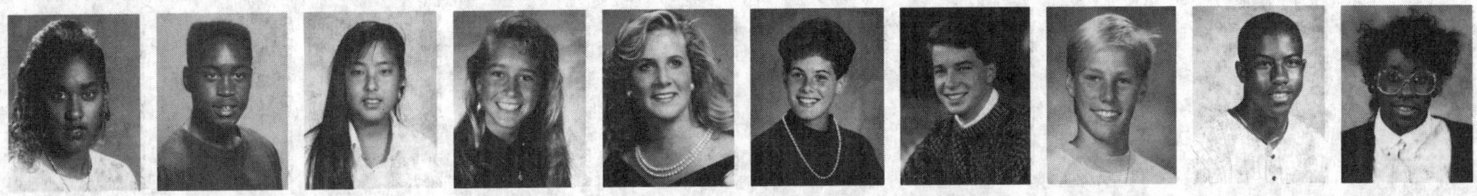

Washington, Darcy
Leuzinger HS
Hawthorne, CA

Washington, Lewis E
John F Kennedy HS
La Palma, CA

Watanabe, Karen M
Notre Dame Acad
Los Angeles, CA

Waterbury, Julie E
Foothill HS
Tustin, CA

Watke, Paula
Rio Americano HS
Sacramento, CA

Watkin, Jennifer T
Savanna HS
Alta Loma, CA

Watkins, Brian T
Atascadero HS
Atascadero, CA

Watrous, Ryan K
Mission Viejo HS
Mission Viejo, CA

Watson, David R
Hiram Johnson HS
Sacramento, CA

Watson, Leah D
Pius X HS
Compton, CA

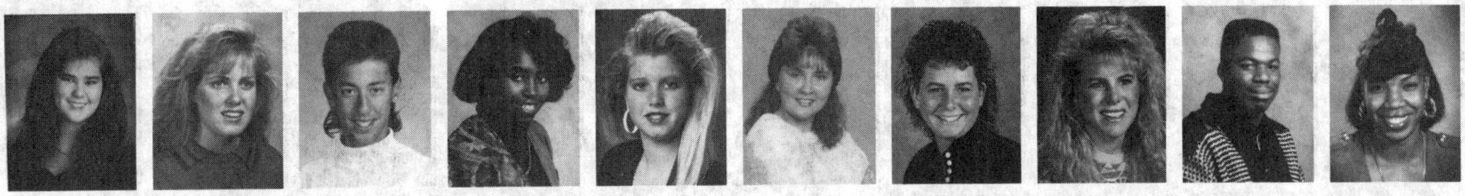

Watson, Michelle M
Channel Islands HS
Oxnard, CA

Watson, Rebecca
Valley Christian HS
San Jose, CA

Watson, Robbie O
Downey HS
Modesto, CA

Watson, Shantrell
Lowell HS
San Francisco, CA

Watson, Sharon I
Castle Park HS
Chula Vista, CA

Watson, Terri L
Middletown HS
Cobb, CA

Watson, Wendy A
San Marcos HS
San Marcos, CA

Watt, April A
Clovis West HS
Clovis, CA

Wattree, Jr Eric
Northview HS
Covina, CA

Wattree, Kaiumeka S
Northview HS
Covina, CA

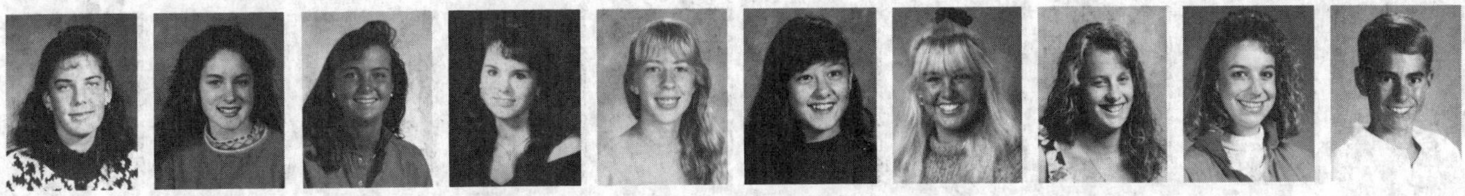

Watts, Katherine
Dublin HS
Dublin, CA

Watts, Kelley
St Francis HS
West Sacramento, CA

Way, Karajane
St Francis HS
Saratoga, CA

Way, Shelley M
Quincy HS
Quincy, CA

Wayman, Colette
Yosemite HS
Coarsegold, CA

Waziri, Michelle
Homestead HS
Sunnyvale, CA

Wean, Shy
Chaminade College Prep
Acton, CA

Weatherwax, Cameron M
Palmdale HS
Littlerock, CA

Weaver, Erika J
Grace M Davis HS
Modesto, CA

Weaver, Jason M
Beyer HS
Modesto, CA

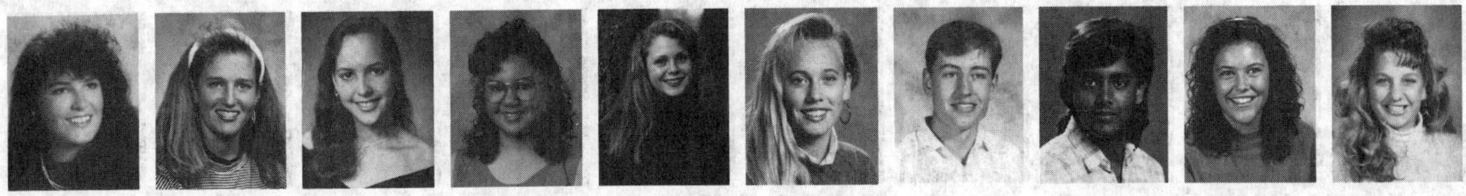

Weaver, Kelly
Edison HS
Huntington Beach, CA

Weaver, Stefani
Elk Grove HS
Elk Grove, CA

Webb, Elizabeth
Leigh
Culver City HS
Los Angeles, CA

Webb, Maxia K
Highland HS
Palmdale, CA

Webber, Gabrielle
Forest Lake Christian
Grass Valley, CA

Webber, Tracey
St Bonaventure HS
Camarillo, CA

Webster, Daniel P
Enterprise HS
Redding, CA

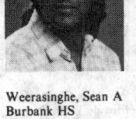

Weerasinghe, Sean A
Burbank HS
Burbank, CA

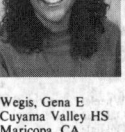

Wegis, Gena E
Cuyama Valley HS
Maricopa, CA

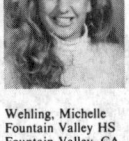

Wehling, Michelle
Fountain Valley HS
Fountain Valley, CA

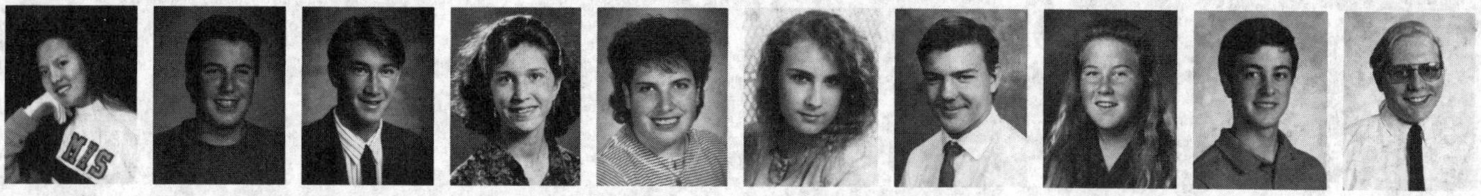

Wei, Julia M
Mills HS
Belmont, CA

Weichers, Logan E
Willows HS
Willows, CA

Weinthal, Tevya A
University City HS
San Diego, CA

Weiss, Elizabeth
George Wahington
San Francisco, CA

Weiss, Ilene S
Prospect HS
Calabasas, CA

Weiss, Kara E
Orange Glen HS
Valley Center, CA

Weiss, Michael J
North HS
Turlock, CA

Weiss, Stephanie P
La Jolla Country Day Schl
Poway, CA

Weiss, Steve I
Prospect HS
San Jose, CA

Weitzel, Shawn R
Fontana HS
Fontana, CA

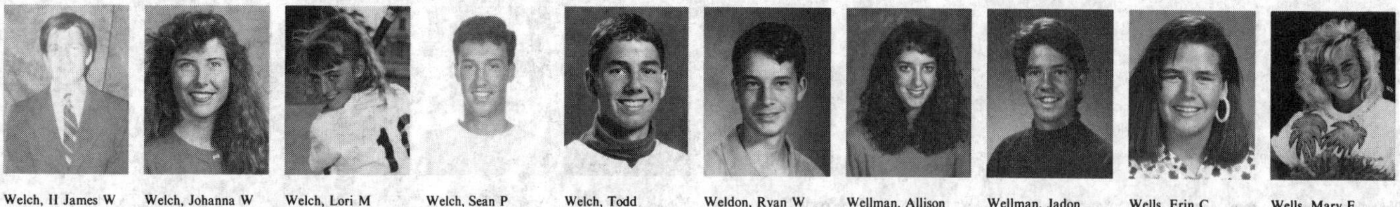

Welch, II James W
Central Union HS
El Centro, CA

Welch, Johanna W
Woodland HS
Esparto, CA

Welch, Lori M
Santa Cruz HS
Santa Cruz, CA

Welch, Sean P
Sequoia HS
San Carlos, CA

Welch, Todd
Etiwanda HS
Alta Loma, CA

Weldon, Ryan W
Watsonville HS
Watsonville, CA

Wellman, Allison
Southbay Christian
Sunnyvale, CA

Wellman, Jadon
Sir Francis Drake HS
Fairfax, CA

Wells, Erin C
Bishop Montgomery
Manhattan Beach, CA

Wells, Mary E
Clovis HS
Clovis, CA

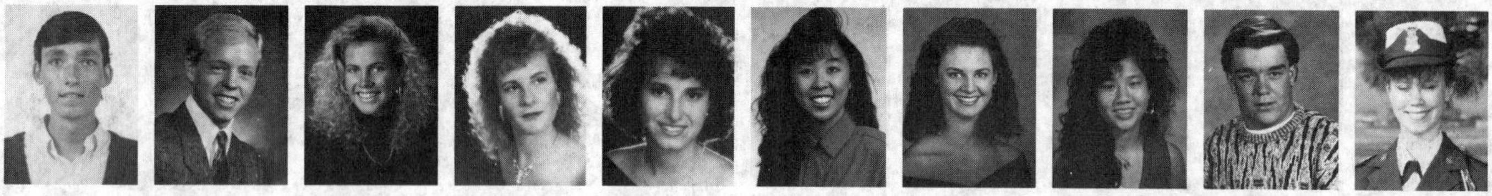

Wells, Michael
Highlands HS
North Highlands, CA

Wells, Randel E
Sutter Union HS
Yuba City, CA

Wells, Rebecca
Buena HS
Ventura, CA

Wells, Rebekah M
Oroville HS
Oroville, CA

Welsch, Rosalva
Trinity HS
Lewiston, CA

Wen, Angela
Skyline HS
Oakland, CA

Wendell, Desiree A
La Mirada HS
La Mirada, CA

Weng, Renee R
John F Kennedy HS
La Palma, CA

Wenger, Kyle W
Ramona HS
Ramona, CA

Wenrich, Jennifer E
Elsinore HS
Sinking Spring, PA

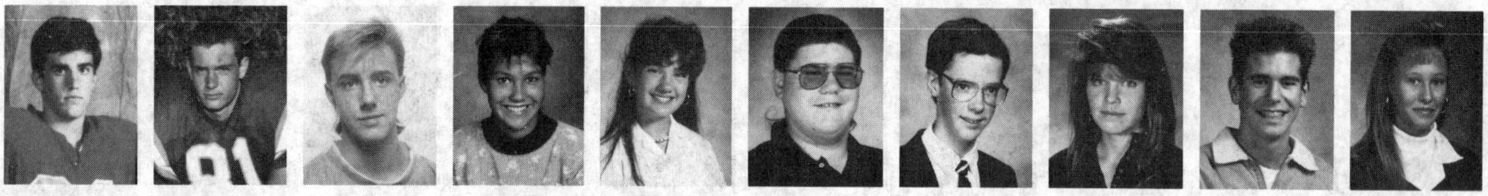

Wenrick, Jason
Bishop Amat HS
Duarte, CA

Wensley, Kevin M
St Bernard HS
Playa Del Rey, CA

Wergeland, Peter L
Bonita Vista HS
Bonita, CA

Werkmeister, Jennifer
El Camino HS
Oceanside, CA

Werlich, Michelle K
La Reina HS
Westlake Village, CA

Werner, Aaron S
Live Oak HS
Live Oak, CA

Wertz, Jr Scott L
Imperial Schls
Pasadena, CA

Werzyn, Christine E
Don Antonio Lugo
Chino, CA

Wessels, Aaron M
Roseville HS
Roseville, CA

Wessely, Jenny
La Reina HS
Moorpark, CA

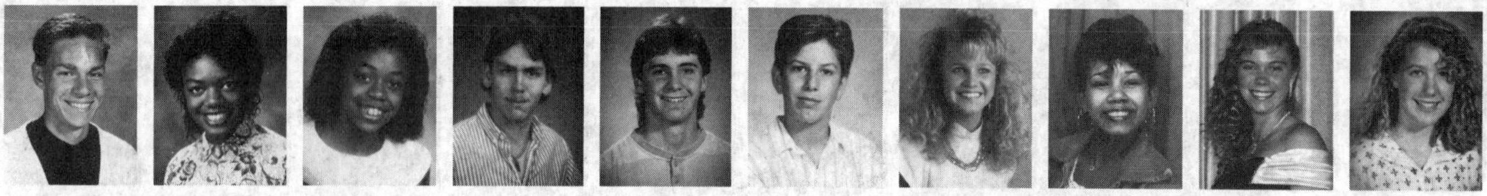

West, John Jason
College Park HS
Martinez, CA

West, Tamari L
Sacrament Adventist Acad
Auburn, CA

West, Tanya L
Sacramento Adventist Acad
Auburn, CA

West, Ted
N Monterey County
San Jose, CA

West, Travis R
Ferndale Union HS
Ferndale, CA

West, Vincent J
James Lick HS
San Jose, CA

Westbrook, Tammy J
Oxnard HS
Oxnard, CA

Westby, Adriana A
Dorsey HS
Los Angeles, CA

Westerhold, Tammy
Fremont HS
Sunnyvale, CA

Westerling, Laura N
Kingsburg HS
Kingsburg, CA

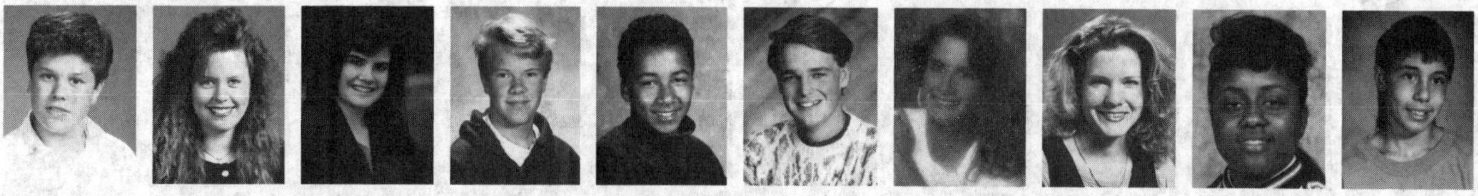

Wetzel, Andrew Paul
Alemany HS
Chatsworth, CA

Weyer, Kimberly
St Bernard HS
Los Angeles, CA

Whaley, Bonnie
William S Hart HS
Valencia, CA

Whaley, Chris L
Crescenta Valley HS
Glendale, CA

Whaley, Pablo S
Lowell HS
San Francisco, CA

Whaling, Chris
Canyon HS
Santa Clanita, CA

Wheatley, Jennifer M
Lodi HS
Lodi, CA

Wheeler, Carol E
Etiwanda HS
Rancho Cucamonga, CA

Wheeler, Christel A
Vanden HS
Travis A F B, CA

Wheeler, Joshua P
Quincy JR/SR HS
Quincy, CA

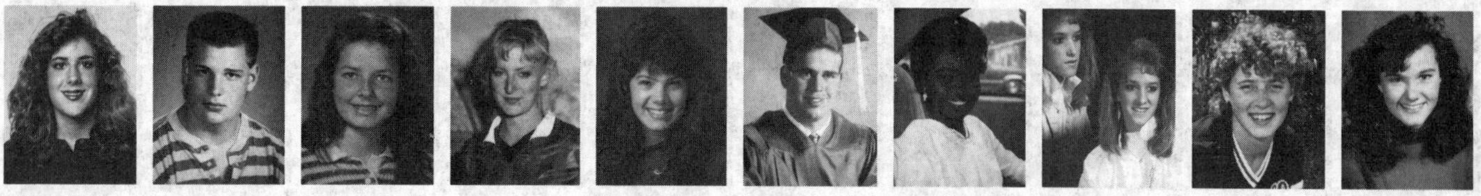

Wheeler, Meredith Leigh
Buena HS
Ventura, CA

Wheeler, Timothy E
Oakdale HS
Oakdale, CA

Whiddon, Christy R
Mission Viejo HS
Mission Viejo, CA

Whipple, Kirstin Lunden
Lassen HS
Susanville, CA

Whisenant, Sundance
Mt Empire JR-SR
Jacumba, CA

Whisenant, Travis W
Damien HS
Upland, CA

White, Arrowa
Inglewood HS
Los Angeles, CA

White, Brandy R
Red Bluff Union HS
Red Bluff, CA

White, Danielle A
Vacaville HS
Vacaville, CA

White, Dawn
Artesia HS
Cerritos, CA

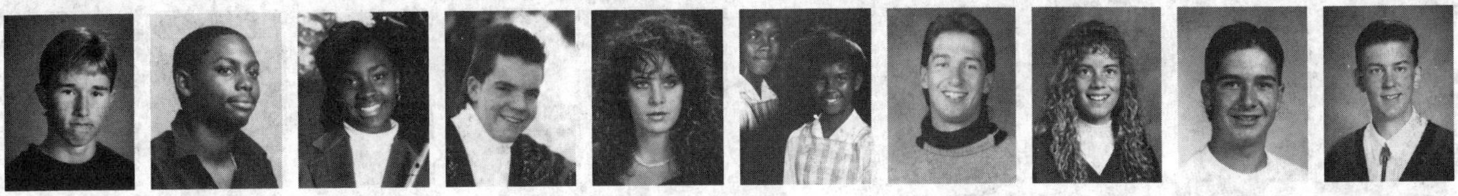

White, Douglas L
Los Banos HS
Los Banos, CA

White, Jerome M
Clayton Valley HS
Bound Brook, NJ

White, Juanita L
University HS
Los Angeles, CA

White, Justin C
Irvine HS
Irvine, CA

White, Katherine R
Vintage HS
Napa, CA

White, Keisha
Edison HS
Stockton, CA

White, Kristophor
Redwood HS
Visalia, CA

White, Marinda
Garces Memorial HS
Bakersfield, CA

White, Michael J
Foothill HS
Sacramento, CA

White, Nathanael
Western HS
Buena Park, CA

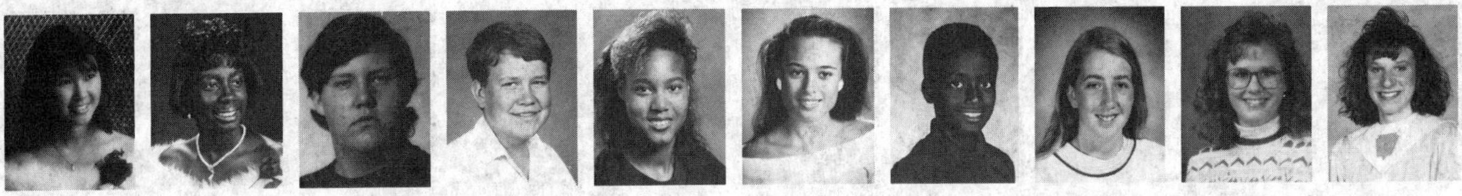

White, Pearl G
Sweetwater HS
San Diego, CA

White, Ronda E
Newark Memorial
Newark, CA

White, Russell W
Montclair HS
Ontario, CA

White, Seth T
Bellarmine Coll Prep
Monte Sereno, CA

White, Siane
Los Angeles Ctr For
Enriched Stds
Los Angeles, CA

White, Stephanie
Clovis HS
Clovis, CA

White, Jr Wilbur B
Eisenhower HS
Rialto, CA

Whitehead, Laura J
Edison HS
Huntington Beach,
CA

Whiteley, Rebecca A
Redwood HS
Visalia, CA

Whiteman, Jacqueline
Esperanza HS
Yorba Linda, CA

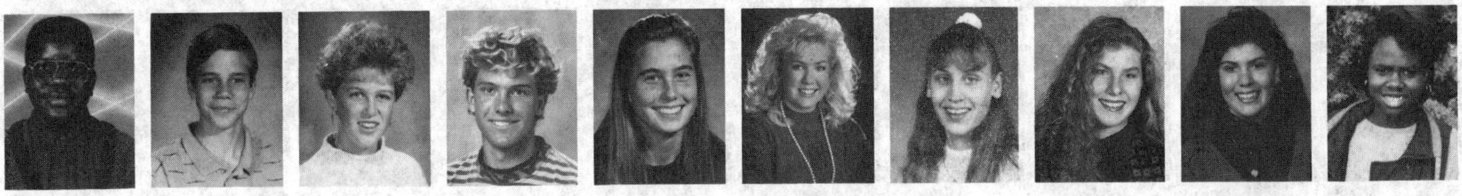

Whitfield, III Willie
Calvary Baptist HS
Pomona, CA

Whitley, Charlie M
Portola JR SR HS
Portola, CA

Whitman, Tracie
Woodbridge HS
Irvine, CA

Whitmer, Keith P
Mira Costa HS
Redondo Beach, CA

Whitmer, Lisa Joy
Palo Alto HS
Palo Alto, CA

Whitmire, Christa
Wm S Hart HS
Newhall, CA

Whitney, Heather M
St Joseph HS
Lakewood, CA

Whitney, Patricia L
Roosevelt HS
Fresno, CA

Whittenburge, Adina
O'farrell SCPA HS
San Diego, CA

Whittington, Porche
Washington Prep
Los Angeles, CA

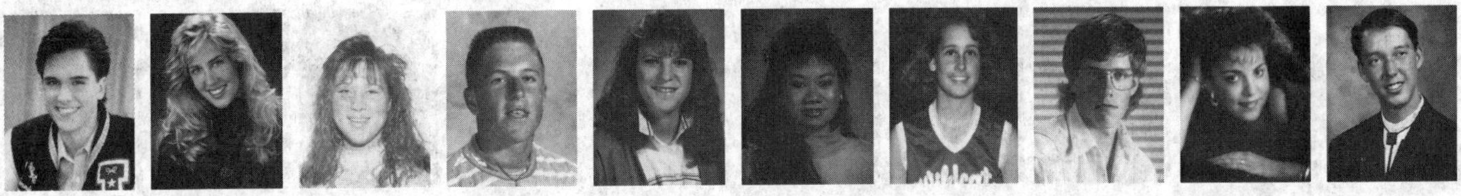

Whyte, William S
Loyola HS
Manhattan Beach,
CA

Widdifield, Shannon
Rolling Hills HS
Rnch Palos Verd, CA

Widelski, Amy
Moorpark HS
Plymouth, MN

Widle, Charlie D
Ernest Righetti HS
Santa Maria, CA

Widner, Jolee D
Hesperia Christian
Schl
Hesperia, CA

Widyawati, Gabrielle
Cornelia Connelly HS
Garden Grove, CA

Wieberg, Kimberly M
Twentynine Palms
Twentynine Palms,
CA

Wieborg, Scott
Palm Desert HS
Palm Desert, CA

Wiegner, Julie
St Vincent HS
Petaluma, CA

Wielandt, Nathan
Covina HS
W. Covina, CA

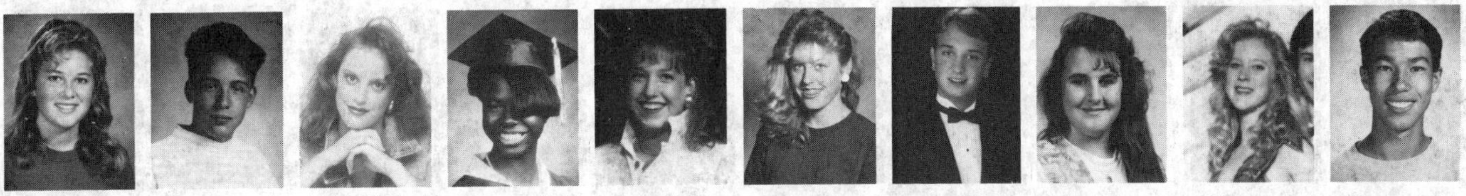

Wienecke, Jennifer
Marina HS
Huntington Bch, CA

Wiger, Matthew
Damien HS
Covina, CA

Wiggins, Lisa G
Canyon HS
Canyon Country, CA

Wilbert, Tessa
John F Kennedy HS
Richmond, CA

Wilbur, Kelley A
Tulare Western HS
Tulare, CA

Wilcox, Aimee
C K Mc Clatchy HS
Sacramento, CA

Wilcox, Brian M
Castro Valley HS
Castro Valley, CA

Wilcox, Jeanne M
Dixon HS
Dixon, CA

Wilcox, Jennifer A
Antioch HS
Antioch, CA

Wilcox, Robert J
Ukiah HS
Ukiah, CA

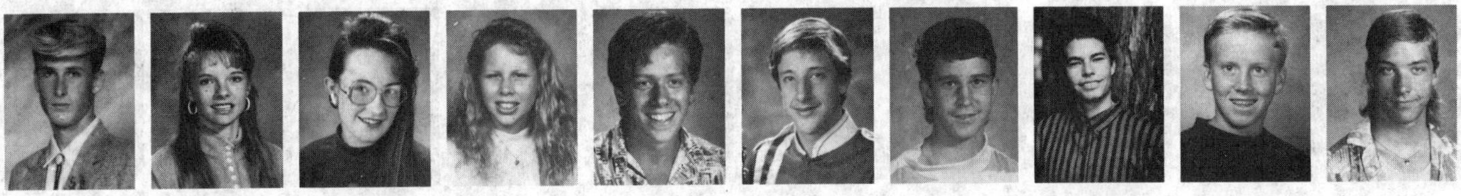

Wilde, Sean J
Etiwanda HS
Alta Loma, CA

Wilds, Shawna L
Savanna HS
Anaheim, CA

Wiley, Heather Ann
Ramona HS
Riverside, CA

Wiley, Karen J
Valhalla HS
El Cajon, CA

Wilhite, Pete E
Calaveras HS
San Andreas, CA

Wilkes, Timothy D
El Toro HS
El Toro, CA

Wilkins, Eric A
Pioneer HS
San Jose, CA

Wilkinson, Sinclair
Aptos HS
Aptos, CA

Willaims, Zachary D
Irvine HS
Irvine, CA

Willett, Dustin A
Antioch HS
Antioch, CA

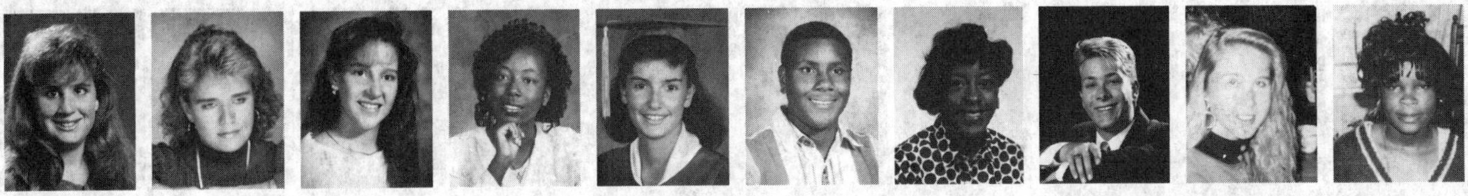

Willey, Tiffany R
Village Christian
Schls
North Hollywood, CA

Williams, Amy M
Victory Christian HS
W Sacramento, CA

Williams, Andrea M
South HS
Bakersfield, CA

Williams, Arlana
Deborah
Pius X HS
Compton, CA

Williams, Becky
Bethel Baptist HS
Garden Grove, CA

Williams, Brent C
West HS
Bakersfield, CA

Williams, Channon C
Skyline HS
Oakland, CA

Williams, Christian J
Capital Christian HS
Rancho Cordova, CA

Williams, Cindy L
Orange Glen HS
Escondido, CA

Williams, Cora
Compton HS
Compton, CA

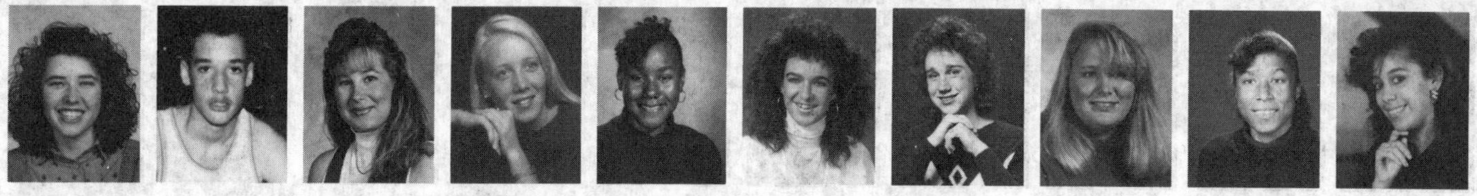

Williams, Dacia Cristine
Durham HS
Durham, CA

Williams, David
River City SR HS
W Sacramento, CA

Williams, Drea L
Santa Clara HS
Santa Clara, CA

Williams, Heather P
El Camino Fundamental HS
Sacramento, CA

Williams, Janaya L
Hart HS
Santa Monica, CA

Williams, Janna C
Mojave HS
Mojave, CA

Williams, Jeannette
Apple Valley HS
Apple Valley, CA

Williams, Jenny
Escalon HS
Escalon, CA

Williams, Juanita R
Dr James Hogan SR
Vallejo, CA

Williams, Karen L
Bonita Vista HS
San Diego, CA

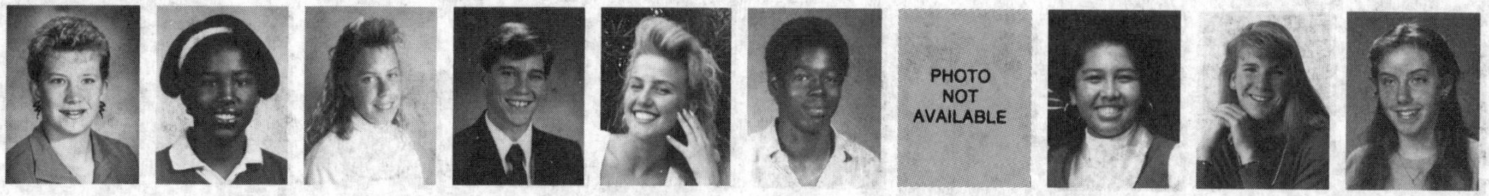

Williams, Kelly E
Yreka Union HS
Montague, CA

Williams, Kim
Valley HS
Sacramento, CA

Williams, Kimberly A
Channel Islands HS
Oxnard, CA

Williams, Lance Tyler
Woodlake Union HS
Woodlake, CA

Williams, Laura K
Thousand Oaks HS
Thousand Oaks, CA

Williams, Levester P
Morningside HS
Inglewood, CA

Williams, Marcus J
John F Kennedy HS
Richmond, CA

Williams, Marissa L
Channel Islands HS
Oxnard, CA

Williams, Melissa A
Ventura HS
Ventura, CA

Williams, Michele Y
Novato HS
Novato, CA

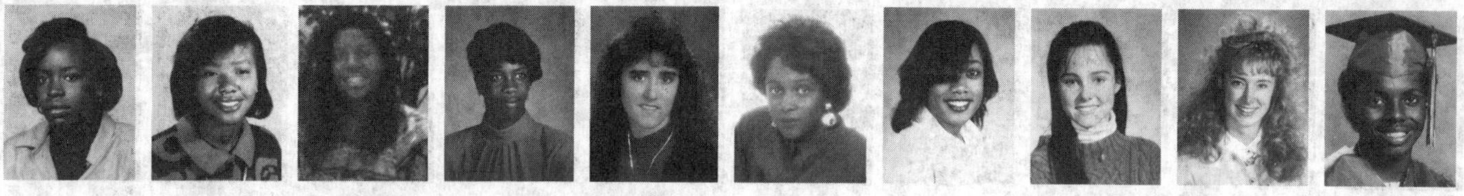

Williams, Natosha
Vallejo SR HS
Vallejo, CA

Williams, Nia B
Hogan HS
Vallejo, CA

Williams, Olympia C
Independence HS
San Jose, CA

Williams, Paulette
Washington HS
Los Angeles, CA

Williams, Stefanie L
Oakdale HS
Oakdale, CA

Williams, Taijuana K
West HS
Bakersfield, CA

Williams, Tanisha G
St Pope Pius X HS
Lynwood, CA

Williams, Tawndra S
San Benito HS
San Juan Bautista, CA

Williams, Tedra S.
Manteca HS
Manteca, CA

Williams, Vaughn M
Washington Prep
Los Angeles, CA

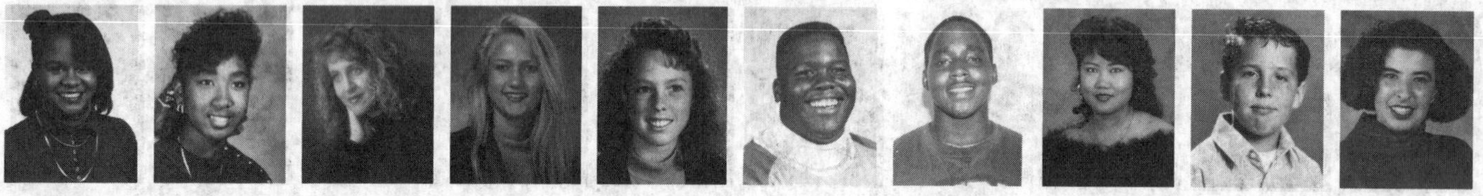

Williams, Yoranna D
Skyline HS
Oakland, CA

Williams, Yvonne
Seaside HS
Fort Ord, CA

Williamson, Carlin R
Campolindo HS
Moraga, CA

Williamson, Juliette
El Toro HS
El Toro, CA

Williamson, Tracy L
Turlock HS
Turlock, CA

Willis, Donald K
Cabrillo HS
Lompoc, CA

Willis, Floyd J
Washington Prep HS
Los Angeles, CA

Willis, Mary Jane B
St Marys Acad
Los Angeles, CA

Willoughby, Craig
Berkeley Hall Schl
Reseda, CA

Wilson, Amanda
Brethren Christian
Long Beach, CA

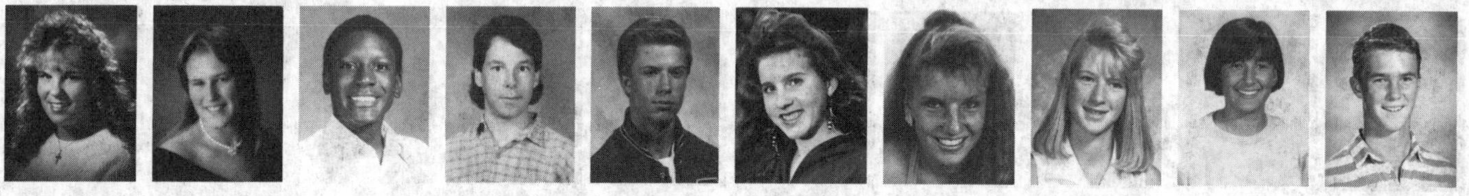

Wilson, Amber F
North Salinas HS
Salinas, CA

Wilson, Amy
Santa Rosa HS
Santa Rosa, CA

Wilson, Barry D
Dorsey HS
Los Angeles, CA

Wilson, Bradford W
Mt Whitney HS
Visalia, CA

Wilson, Brett
Antelope Valley HS
Lancaster, CA

Wilson, Colleen J
San Dieguito HS
Encinitas, CA

Wilson, Crystal
Bloomington HS
Colton, CA

Wilson, Denette M
Brawley Union HS
Brawley, CA

Wilson, Dusty L
Woodland HS
Woodland, CA

Wilson, Edward L
Montgomery HS
Santa Rosa, CA

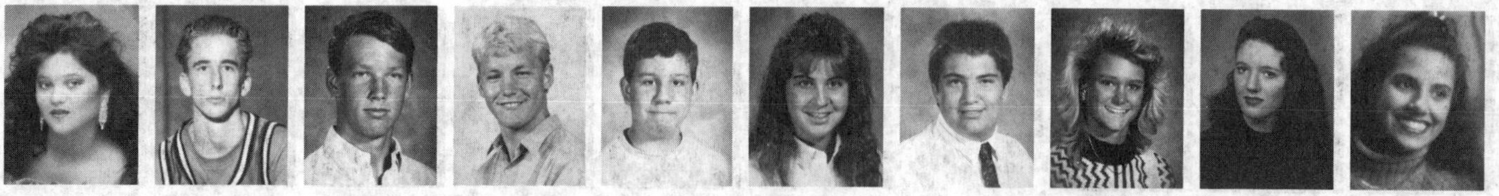

Wilson, Helen R
El Toro HS
El Toro, CA

Wilson, Ian C
Nogales HS
Walnut, CA

Wilson, James
Exeter Union HS
Exeter, CA

Wilson, James T
Silver Valley HS
Fort Irwin, CA

Wilson, Jason B
Montgomery HS
Santa Rosa, CA

Wilson, Jennifer L
Mater Dei HS
Cypress, CA

Wilson, Joshua L
El Camino HS
Oceanside, CA

Wilson, Julie M
Bishop Union HS
Bishop, CA

Wilson, Katherine A
Mira Mesa HS
San Diego, CA

Wilson, Kimberly
Elk Grove HS
Elk Grove, CA

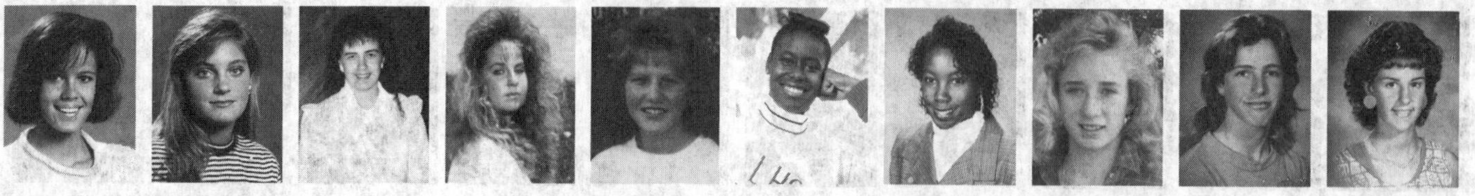

Wilson, Lorna S
Glendale HS
Glendale, CA

Wilson, Nicole
Mayfield SR HS
Pasadena, CA

Wilson, Pamela M
Whitney HS
Lakewood, CA

Wilson, Peggy
Arroyo HS
San Leandro, CA

Wilson, Ruth D
Trinity HS
Lewiston, CA

Wilson, Sheka
Leuzinger HS
Los Angeles, CA

Wilson, Shondelle
Hogan SR HS
Vallejo, CA

Wilson, Teri D
Brawley Union HS
Brawley, CA

Wilson, Troy Scott
Mar Vista HS
Imperial Beach, CA

Wilson, Vanessa Brooke
Red Bluff HS
Red Bluff, CA

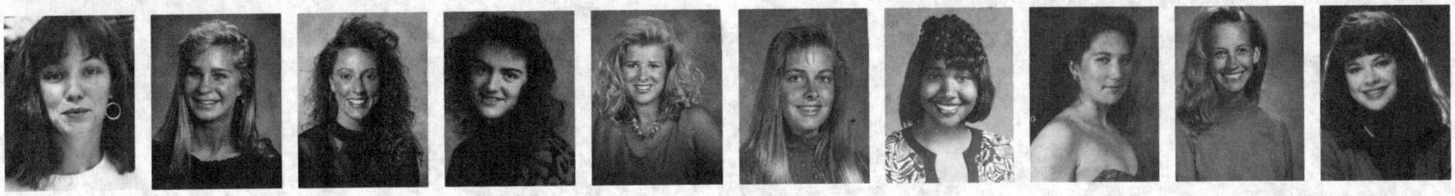

Wilson-Bevins, Christel
Bel-Air Prep Schl
Los Angeles, CA

Wilt, Michelle
Trabuco Hills HS
Mission Viejo, CA

Wilvang, Gina Laree
Hawthorne HS
Hawthorne, CA

Wimberly, Natausha
North HS
Bakersfield, CA

Winchell, Dawn Michelle
Elsinore HS
Lake Elsinore, CA

Winckler, Lori M
Pioneer HS
San Jose, CA

Windom, Lynette P
St Bernard HS
Los Angeles, CA

Windsor, Amanda
Mc Kinleyville HS
Eureka, CA

Windsor, Jessica D
Poway HS
Poway, CA

Wing, Jessica R
Manteca HS
Manteca, CA

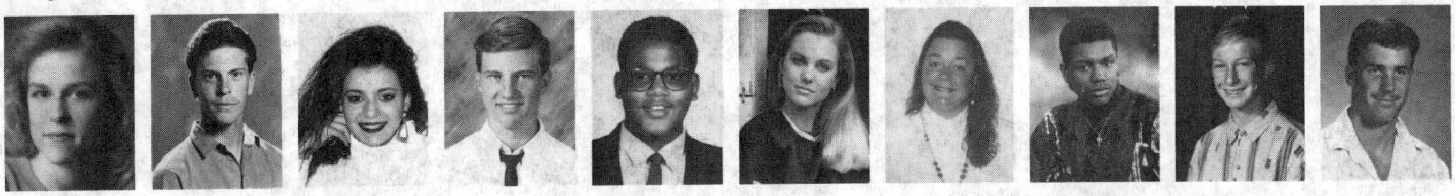

Winget, Lisa D
Redlands HS
Redlands, CA

Wingo, John E
Leuzinger HS
Hawthorne, CA

Winingham, Emma
Chino HS
Chino, CA

Winkelman, Mark
Ambassador Baptist
Rialto, CA

Winn, Benjamin
Manor Baptist Christian Schl
Oakland, CA

Winn, Leslie
Edison/Computech
Sonora, CA

Winslow, Rosemary L
Branham HS
San Jose, CA

Winstead, Jr James R
San Benito HS
Hollister, CA

Winters, James
Summerville HS
Soulsbyville, CA

Winters, Scott E
Woodland HS
Woodland, CA

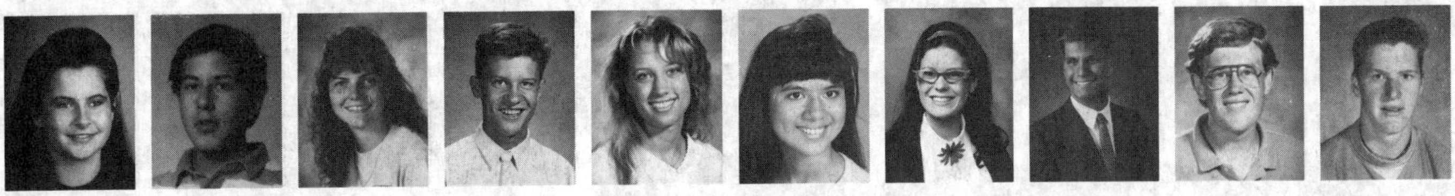

Wisecarver, Kristine
Antioch SR HS
Antioch, CA

Witham, David L
Alhambra HS
Alhambra, CA

Withrow, Kimberly
Mt View HS
Burney, CA

Witt, Eric
Poway HS
Poway, CA

Witten, Jamie A
Edison HS
Huntington Beach, CA

Wittig, Teresa
Palm Springs HS
Desert Hot Spring, CA

Wittman, Heather M
Academy Of Our Lady Of Peace
San Diego, CA

Wizbowski, II Raymond V
Fresno Christian HS
Fresno, CA

Woest, James
Edison HS
Huntington Beach, CA

Wohlers, Bryan
S Tahoe HS
S Lake Tahoe, CA

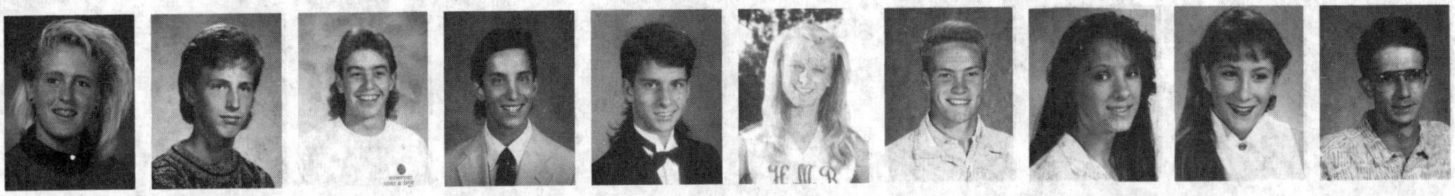

Wohlford, Holly
Irvine HS
Irvine, CA

Woicik, Christopher
Tri City Christian
Oceanside, CA

Wolcott, Chad A
Enterprise HS
Redding, CA

Wolf, Andy
Los Alamitos HS
Seal Beach, CA

Wolf, Gregory M
San Rafael HS
San Rafael, CA

Wolf, Jessica
Half Moon Bay HS
El Granada, CA

Wolf, Sep A
Aptos HS
Aptos, CA

Wolfenbarger, Jenifer
Hesperia HS
Hesperia, CA

Wolff, Tara M
North Tahoe HS
Carnelian Bay, CA

Wolske, James S
College Park HS
Martinez, CA

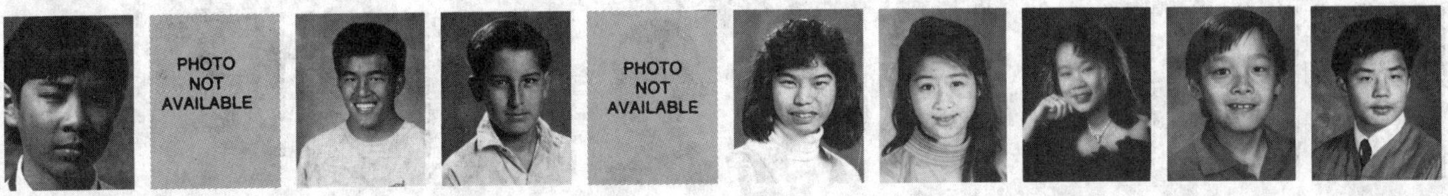
PHOTO NOT AVAILABLE
PHOTO NOT AVAILABLE

Wong, Abiel
Lincoln HS
Stockton, CA

Wong, Alan
Gardena HS
Gardena, CA

Wong, Alexis D
El Camino HS
Sacramento, CA

Wong, Andrew W
Norte Vista HS
Riverside, CA

Wong, Brian
Alan-Mingway
Palo Alto SR HS
Palo Alto, CA

Wong, Connie
Eagle Rock JR/SR
Los Angeles, CA

Wong, Diane Q
Lowell HS
San Francisco, CA

Wong, Dina N
South San Francisco
S San Francisco, CA

Wong, Jr Humberto
Calexico Mission Acad
Calexico, CA

Wong, Jason J
Abraham Lincoln HS
San Francisco, CA

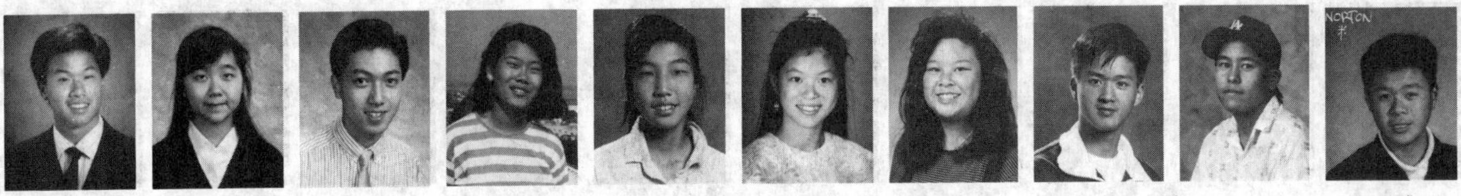

Wong, Jay K
Savanna HS
Buena Park, CA

Wong, Joyce Y
St Joseph Notre Dame HS
Alameda, CA

Wong, Kenneth
Bishop O'dowd HS
Oakland, CA

Wong, Kristine A
Carlmont HS
Belmont, CA

Wong, Lily H
Canyon HS
Newhall, CA

Wong, Linda
International Studies Acad
San Francisco, CA

Wong, Lisa
Pinole Valley HS
Pinole, CA

Wong, Mark J
Glendale Adventist Acad
Glendale, CA

Wong, Michael L
Calexico HS
Calexico, CA

Wong, Norton
Abraham Lincoln HS
San Francisco, CA

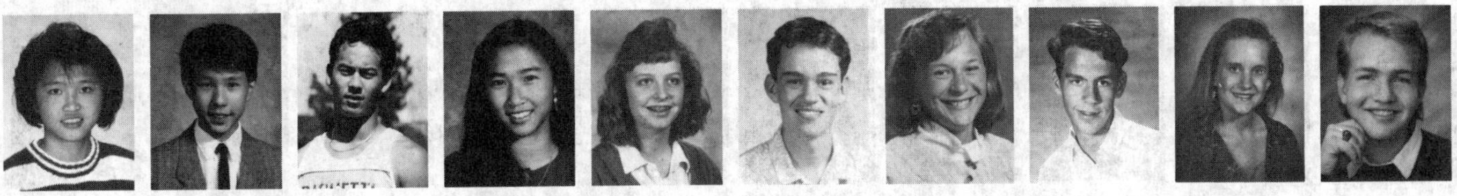

Wong, Polly P
Los Altos HS
Hacienda Hgts, CA

Wong, Roger
St Ignatius College Prep
San Francisco, CA

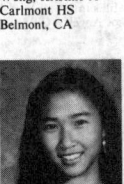

Woo, Justin B
Ernest Righetti HS
Santa Maria, CA

Woo, Suzanne
Abraham Lincoln HS
San Francisco, CA

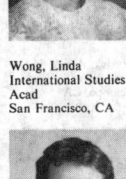

Wood, Amy D
Antelope Valley HS
Lancaster, CA

Wood, Dean W
Edison HS
Fresno, CA

Wood, Erin M
Etiwanda HS
Fontana, CA

Wood, Jack G
Don Antonio Lugo
Chino, CA

Wood, Jeniffer
North HS
Bakersfield, CA

Wood, Timothy G
Valhalla HS
El Cajon, CA

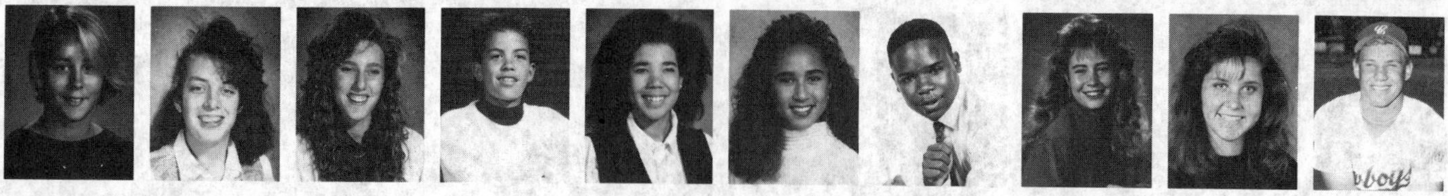

Wood, Virginia F
Clovis West HS
Fresno, CA

Woodard, Raquel
Edison HS
Huntington Beach, CA

Woodcox, Shelley R
Paradise HS
Paradise, CA

Woodin, Jared W
Pittsburg HS
Pittsburg, CA

Woods, Annalisa L
Paradise HS
Paradise, CA

Woods, Domenique
Moreau HS
Hayward, CA

Woods, Jory N
Downtown Business Magnet HS
Los Angeles, CA

Woods, Kacey R
Fillmore HS
Fillmore, CA

Woods, Kelley A
St Joseph HS
Lakewood, CA

Woodward, Marc D
Chino HS
Chino, CA

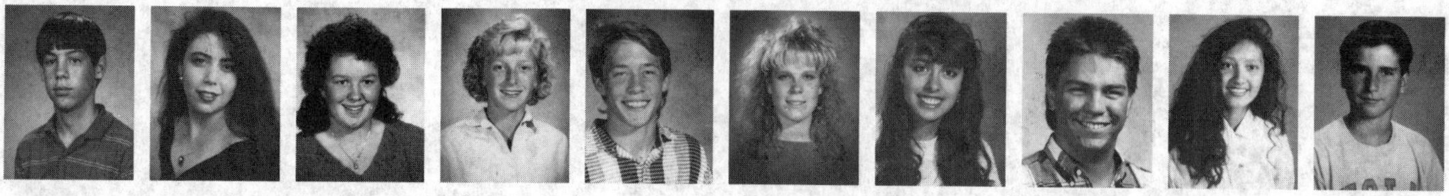

Woodworth, Andrew
Bellarmine HS
San Jose, CA

Woolam, K Pearl
Sherman E Burroughs HS
Ridgecrest, CA

Wooldridge, Bonnie
Barstow HS
Barstow, CA

Woolheater, Kerri E
Casa Grande HS
Petaluma, CA

Woolington, Chris
Lassen HS
Susanville, CA

Woolstenhulme-Smith, Lissa M
Wm S Hart HS
Newhall, CA

Worley, Cassandra A
Mira Loma HS
Sacramento, CA

Worster, Bradley L
Foothill HS
Sacramento, CA

Wreta, Sheba C
Beyer HS
Modesto, CA

Wright, Aaron J
Madera HS
Madera, CA

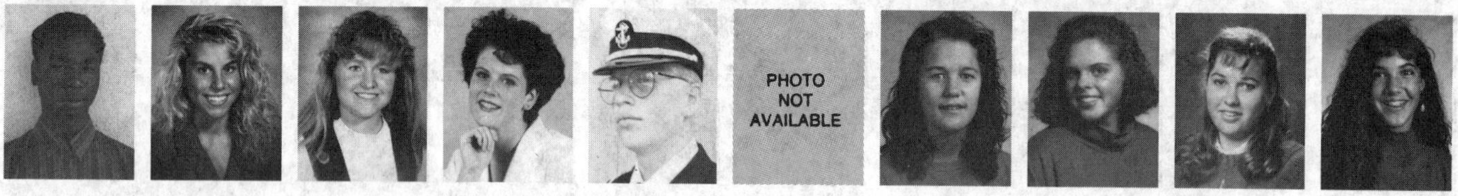

Wright, Jr Bert L
Hesperia HS
Hesperia, CA

Wright, Brandy E
Kennedy HS
Lapalma, CA

Wright, Cathleen
Bakersfield HS
Frazier Park, CA

Wright, Elizabeth L
University HS
Irvine, CA

Wright, Geoffrey T
Eureka SR HS
Eureka, CA

Wright, James P
Yuba City HS
Yuba City, CA

Wright, Janel E
Foothill Farms HS
Sacramento, CA

Wright, Jennifer A
Junipero Serra HS
San Diego, CA

Wright, Jennifer L
Castle Park HS
Cerritos, CA

Wright, Jennifer M
Del Mar HS
San Jose, CA

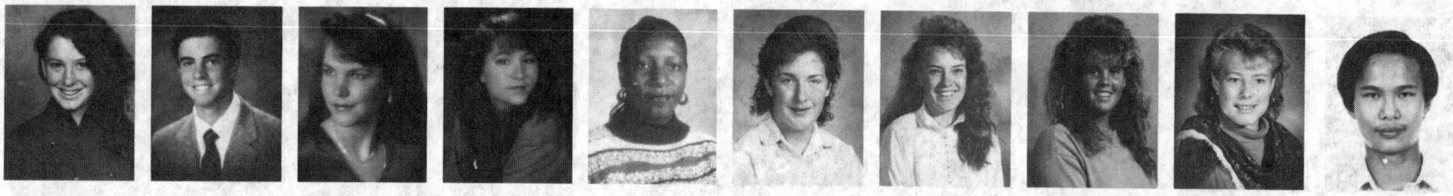

Wright, Jesse V
Valhalla HS
El Cajon, CA

Wright, Justin
Buena HS
Ventura, CA

Wright, Karen V
Bethel Christian HS
Lancaster, CA

Wright, Kathleen N
Mariposa County HS
Catheys Valley, CA

Wright, Lovely Lady
Fremont HS
Oakland, CA

Wright, Michelle L
Dixon HS
Dixon, CA

Wright, Stacey C
Clear Lake HS
Lakeport, CA

Wright, Stephanie Lynn
Loara HS
Anaheim, CA

Wright, Sydney
Etna Union HS
Etna, CA

Wu, Alex
Covina HS
West Covina, CA

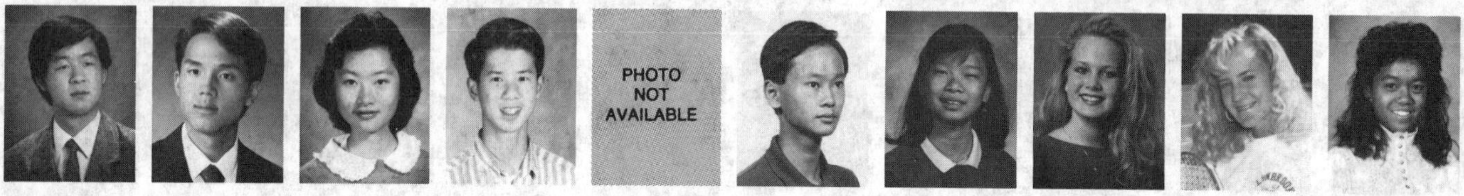

Wu, Benjamin Y
Canyon HS
Anaheim, CA

Wu, John H
Arcadia HS
Arcadia, CA

Wu, Michelle
Fountain Valley HS
Fountain Valley, CA

Wu, Stanley S
Lowell HS
San Francisco, CA

Wu, Susan K
Lowell HS
San Francisco, CA

Wu, Thomas S
John F Kennedy HS
Sacramento, CA

Wu, Wanpin W
Alhambra HS
Alhambra, CA

Wyatt, Jennifer F
La Serna HS
Whittier, CA

Wyatt, Tasra
Lynbrook HS
Santa Clara, CA

Wychico, Frances A
Victor Valley HS
Victorville, CA

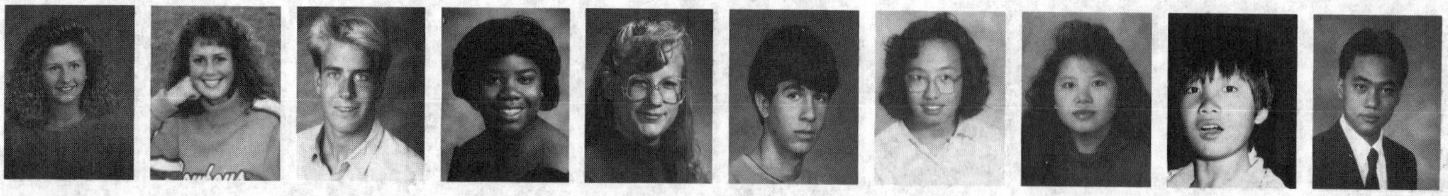

Wyland, Amber
John F Kennedy HS
Buena Park, CA

Wylie, Kimberly
Salinas HS
Salinas, CA

Wyman, Justin
Santa Fe Christian
Encinitas, CA

Wynn, De Shawn N
Point Loma HS
San Diego, CA

Wyrick, Aimee
Lodi Adventist Acad
Acampo, CA

Xanthopoulos, Eric P
Bellarmine College Prep
Milpitas, CA

Xieu, King Yee
Millikan JR HS
Los Angeles, CA

Xiong, Chua
Redwood HS
Visalia, CA

Xu, Xiao Kang
Skyline HS
Oakland, CA

Yalong, Allan T
Bellarmine College Prep
San Jose, CA

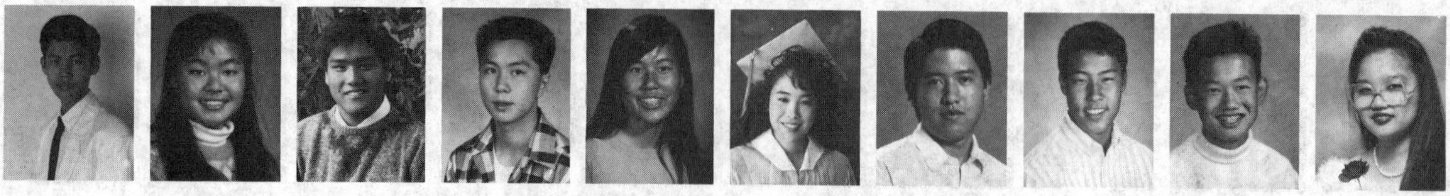

Yam, Chhoeuy
Lincoln HS
Stockton, CA

Yamada, Cathy
Archbishop Mitty HS
San Jose, CA

Yamada, Ricky
Dos Pueblos HS
Santa Barbara, CA

Yamada, Tatsuya
Gahr HS
Cerritos, CA

Yamaguchi, Ina A
University HS
Irvine, CA

Yamaguchi, Monique Mari
Bishop Amat Memorial HS
Monrovia, CA

Yamamoto, Keith M
Narbonne HS
Torrance, CA

Yamamura, Scott
Lincoln HS
Stockton, CA

Yamanaka, Ryan A
Napa HS
Napa, CA

Yamane, Cherie H
Redondo Union HS
Redondo Beach, CA

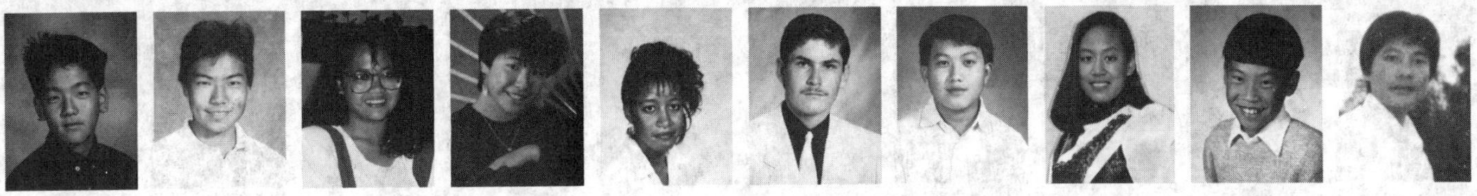

Yamashiroya, Ryan
Cerritos HS
Cerritos, CA

Yamashita, Richard
Aragon HS
San Mateo, CA

Yamat, Zarina Z
Notre Dame HS
Salinas, CA

Yamaura, Tae
Rolling Hills HS
Rancho Palos Vrd, CA

Yancy, Xelinda A
Notre Dame Acad
Los Angeles, CA

Yanez, Daniel
Saddleback HS
Santa Ana, CA

Yang, Chong X
Grace M Davis HS
Modesto, CA

Yang, Cindy
Huntington HS
Huntington Beach, CA

Yang, Gerald
Mira Loma HS
Carmichael, CA

Yang, Je
Cajon HS
San Bernardino, CA

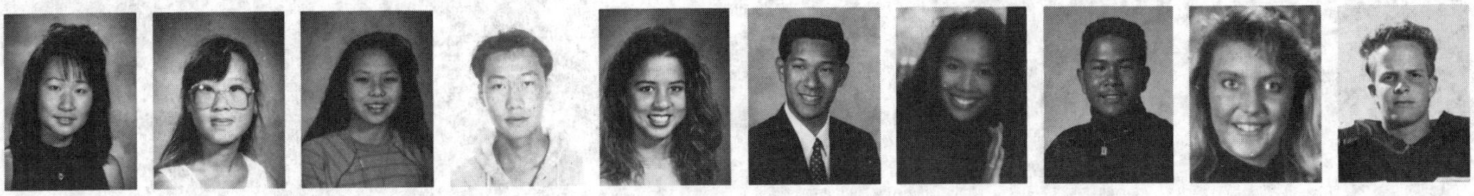

Yang, Lisa
Verdugo Hills HS
Los Angeles, CA

Yang, Melinda T
Edison HS
Huntington Beach, CA

Yang, Pa
Eureka HS
Eureka, CA

Yang, Sing Tai
Phillip And Sala Burton HS
San Francisco, CA

Yanos, Stephanie E
La Habra HS
Whittier, CA

Yao, Peter
Fountain Valley HS
Fountain Valley, CA

Yap, Nanette
Acalanes HS
Lafayette, CA

Yap, Roger
Long Beach Polytechnic HS
Long Beach, CA

Yarbrough, Jennifer
Clovis HS
Fresno, CA

Yaroslaski, David P
Paraclete HS
Lancaster, CA

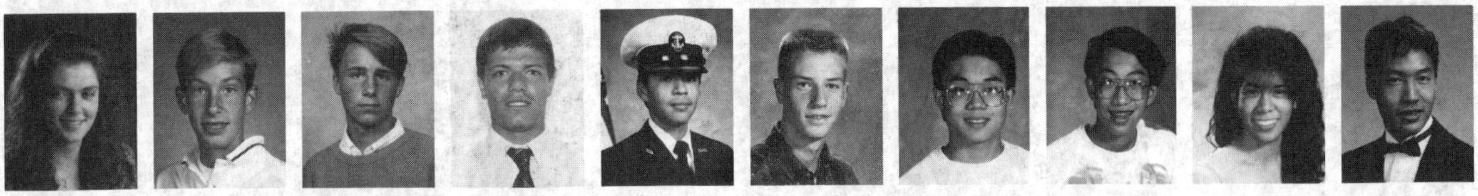

Yarrall, Angela J
Western HS
Anaheim, CA

Yates, Sam J
Del Campo HS
Carmichael, CA

Yates, Tom
St Patrick-St Vincent
Vallejo, CA

Yazdanpanah, Hadi
Clovis West HS
Fresno, CA

Ybarra, Raymond
Luther Burbank HS
Sacramento, CA

Yeats, Todd E
American HS
Fremont, CA

Yee, Jonathan David
College Park HS
Martinez, CA

Yee, Joseph D
College Park HS
Martinez, CA

Yee, Kelly T
Whitney HS
Cerritos, CA

Yee, Richard W
Saint Ignatius College Prep
Oakland, CA

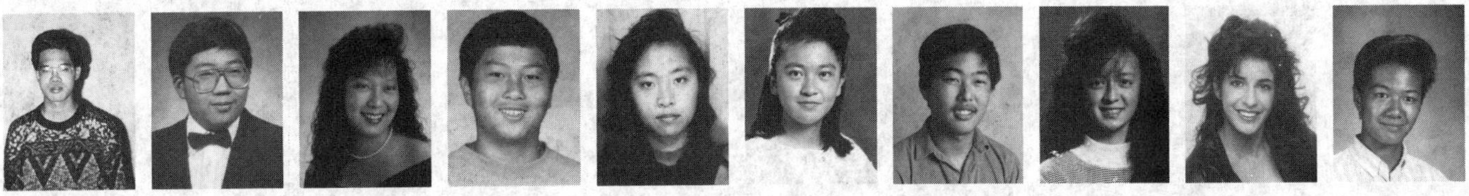

Yee, Vincent K
Salinas HS
Salinas, CA

Yeh, Christopher S
Santa Monica HS
Santa Monica, CA

Yeh, Diana
Leigh HS
San Jose, CA

Yeh, Jimmy
San Lorenzo HS
San Leandro, CA

Yeh, Judy C
San Lorenzo HS
San Leandro, CA

Yen, Allison
Santa Monica HS
Santa Monica, CA

Yen, Brian J
Rio Mesa HS
Camarillo, CA

Yeo, Ann M
Carson HS
Torrance, CA

Yesayan, Meldia
Glendale HS
Glendale, CA

Yi, Eric
Arcadia HS
El Monte, CA

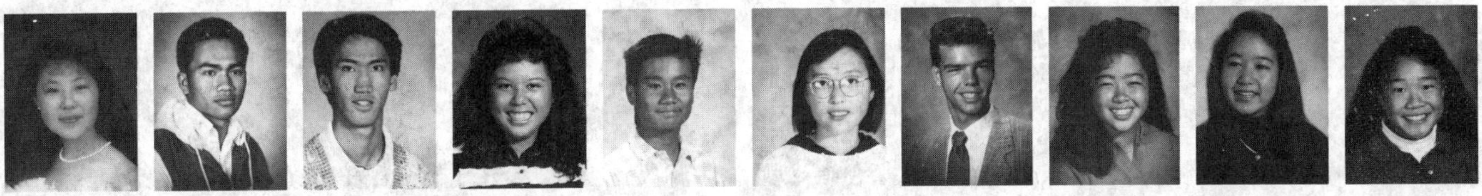

Yi, Helen
American HS
Fremont, CA

Yim, Ratt
Stagg HS
Stockton, CA

Yin, Tony
Independence HS
San Jose, CA

Yip, Annemarie
Gilroy HS
Gilroy, CA

Yip, Victor Y
Whitney HS
Cerritos, CA

Yiu, Ingrid
Abraham Lincoln HS
San Francisco, CA

Yockel, Justin R
Costa Mesa HS
Costa Mesa, CA

Yogi, Yuko
Villa Park HS
Orange, CA

Yokoi, Emi
Saddleback HS
Santa Ana, CA

Yokomizo, Tara
Dublin HS
Dublin, CA

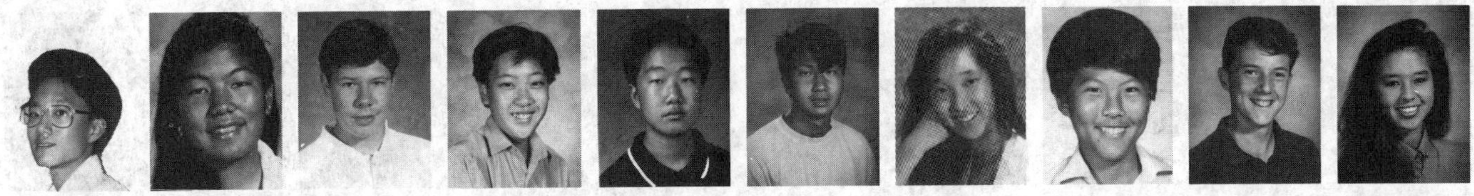

Yom, John
Troy HS
Placentia, CA

Yonemori, Cindy L
Edison HS
Huntington Beach, CA

Yong, Bill L
Santa Cruz HS
Ben Lomond, CA

Yoo, Daly D
Lowell HS
San Francisco, CA

Yoon, Albert H
Daniel Murphy HS
Los Angeles, CA

Yoon, Daniel T
John F Kennedy HS
La Palma, CA

Yoon, Suzie
Trabuco Hills HS
Mission Viejo, CA

Yoon, Won S
Lowell HS
San Francisco, CA

York, Aaron W
Weed HS
Weed, CA

York, Helen
Garden Grove HS
Garden Grove, CA

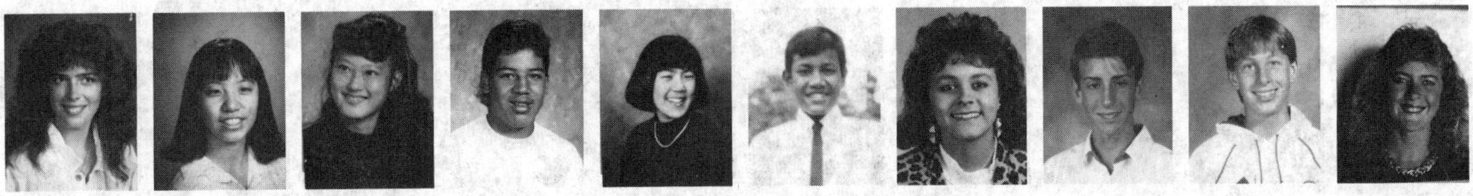

York, Michelle D
Atwater HS
Atwater, CA

Yoshida, Judy
Lincoln HS
Stockton, CA

Yoshida, Tina
Buena Park HS
Buena Park, CA

Yoshikawa, Brian A
Pioneer HS
San Jose, CA

Yoshikawa, Jill F
C K Mc Cratchy HS
Sacramento, CA

You, Vanthuon
Bell Gardens HS
Bell Gardens, CA

Young, Barbara A
Argonaut HS
Pioneer, CA

Young, Bradley
Paramount Brethren
Downey, CA

Young, Brent M
Fred C Beyer HS
Modesto, CA

Young, Christina L
Apple Valley HS
Apple Valley, CA

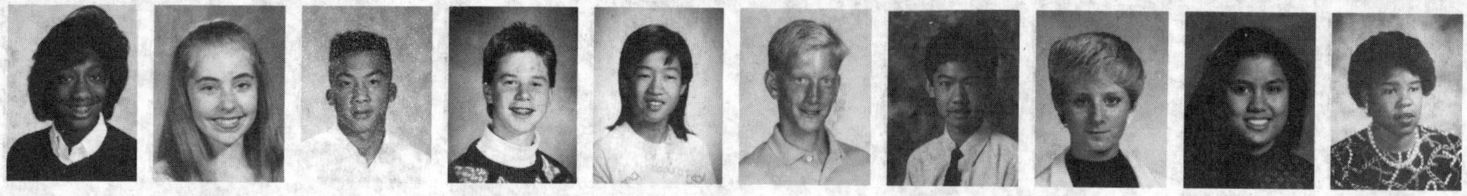

Young, Courtney R
Nogales HS
W Covina, CA

Young, Dominique A
Wallenberg HS
San Francisco, CA

Young, Donald L
Pasadena HS
Pasadena, CA

Young, Joey A
Del Norte HS
Crescent City, CA

Young, Kelley Anne
Amos Alonzo Stagg
Stockton, CA

Young, Kenneth L
Del Campo HS
Fair Oaks, CA

Young, Larry N
Loyola HS
Monterey Park, CA

Young, Lora L
Galt HS
Galt, CA

Young, Lovette
Garces HS
Bakersfield, CA

Young, Pamela A
Susan Miller Dorsey
Los Angeles, CA

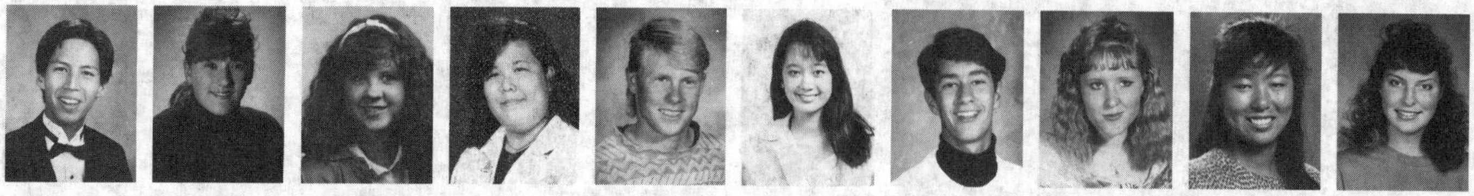

Young, Patrick L
Servite HS
La Habra, CA

Young, Paula M
Oakdale HS
Waterford, CA

Young, Rebekah
Capital Christian
Schl
Sacramento, CA

Young, Rowena
Arangcon
Woodrow Wilson HS
San Francisco, CA

Young, Ryan M
North HS
Bakersfield, CA

Young, Sarah J
Torrey Pines HS
Solana Beach, CA

Young, Shawheen P
Alameda HS
Alameda, CA

Young, Tiffiny R
Lindhurst HS
Marysville, CA

Young, Vivian
Flintridge Prep
Los Angeles, CA

Young, Wendy
Roseville HS
Roseville, CA

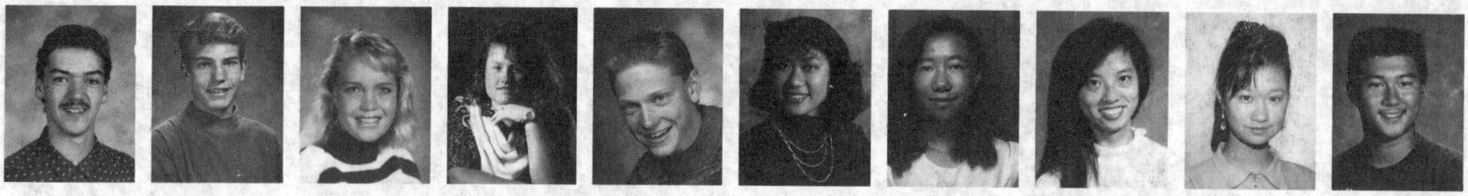

Youngclaus, Shandon
San Joaquin
Memorial HS

Youngker, Jahrome
Coleville HS
Spokane, WA

Youngkin, Mariah
Poway HS
Poway, CA

Youngren, Deanna M
New Life Christian
Acad
Cherry Valley, CA

Yount, Samuel R
Fall River HS
Mc Arthur, CA

Yu, Catherine K
San Marino HS
San Marino, CA

Yu, Diana D
San Gabriel HS
San Gabriel, CA

Yu, Judy N
Lowell HS
San Francisco, CA

Yu, Nancy
George Washington
San Francisco, CA

Yu, Simon
Mills HS
Burlingame, CA

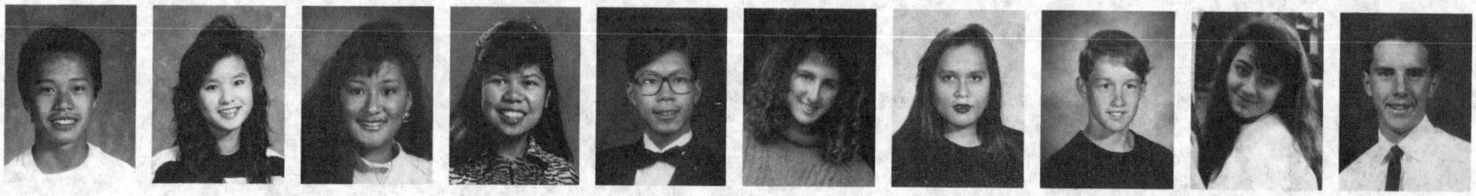

Yue, Fee L
Lowell HS
San Francisco, CA

Yuen, Patricia
Lowell HS
San Francisco, CA

Yuh, Jia-Ann
Western HS
Anaheim, CA

Yulip, Annie Liza I
Colton HS
Colton, CA

Yung, Dominic
James Logan HS
Brentwood, CA

Yunker, Jennifer
Tokay HS
Stockton, CA

Zabayle, Denise N
Sacred Heart Of
Mary HS
Montebello, CA

Zaben, Joseph Shae
West HS
Bakersfield, CA

Zacarias, Jeanne Sara
Chatsworth HS
Northridge, CA

Zackula, John L
Rio Hondo Prep
Duarte, CA

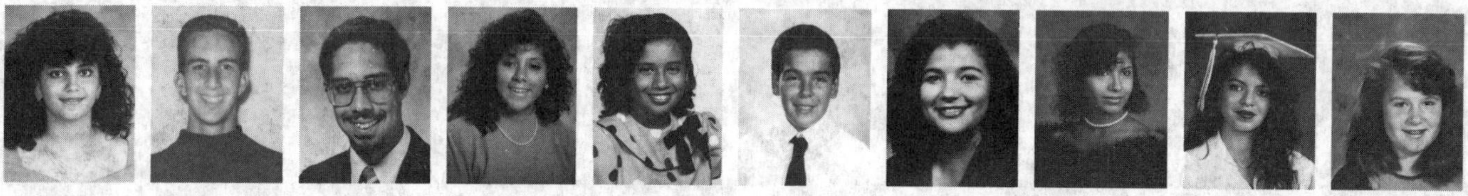

Zadourian, Zhanna
Fowler HS
Fowler, CA

Zagha, Aaron M
El Camino Real HS
Woodland Hills, CA

Zaidi, Shahid
El Dorado HS
Placentia, CA

Zamaro, Stephanie R
Mater Dei HS
Garden Grove, CA

Zambrano, Gilda
Workman HS
Valinda, CA

Zamora, Julien R
Don Bosco Technical
Inst
Alhambra, CA

Zamora, Margarita
Bell Gardens HS
Bell Gardens, CA

Zamora, Patricia
Pius X HS
South Gate, CA

Zamora, Veronica
Pius X HS
Downey, CA

Zander, Virginia
Southbay Christian
Schl
Los Altos, CA

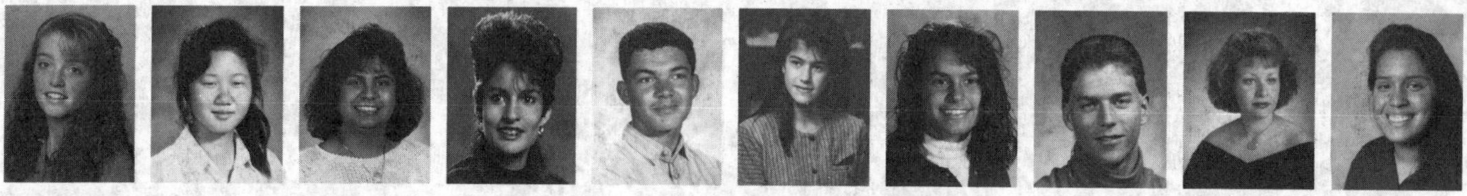

Zandonatti, Kaissa
Ventura HS
Ventura, CA

Zang, Jihong
University HS
Irvine, CA

Zapata, Alice Y
Baldwin Park HS
Baldwin Park, CA

Zapata, Lila
Alder JR HS
Fontana, CA

Zarate, Erik
Lynwood HS
Lynwood, CA

Zarbo, Carla N
Chula Vista HS
San Diego, CA

Zarek, Debbi T
Morro Bay HS
Los Osos, CA

Zarick, Ryan
Valley HS
Sacramento, CA

Zarubin, Nadya
Southbay Christian
Schl
Milpitas, CA

Zarza, Beatriz
Castle Park HS
Chula Vista, CA

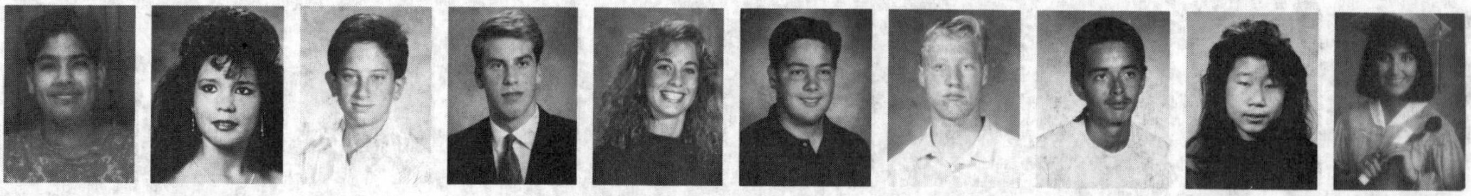

Zarza, David
Castle Park HS
Chula Vista, CA

Zavala, Edna
Herver Hoover HS
San Diego, CA

Zavala, Matt A
Notre Dame HS
Riverside, CA

Zawatski, Mark N
Sonora HS
Fullerton, CA

Zdravecky, Lara C
San Ramon Valley
Danville, CA

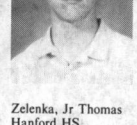

Zeiders, Jared S
North HS
Bakersfield, CA

Zelenka, Jr Thomas
Hanford HS
Hanford, CA

Zendejas, Diego C
Calipatria HS
Niland, CA

Zeng, Tina
Galileo HS
San Francisco, CA

Zeniali, Pouneh
Canyon HS
Canyon Country, CA

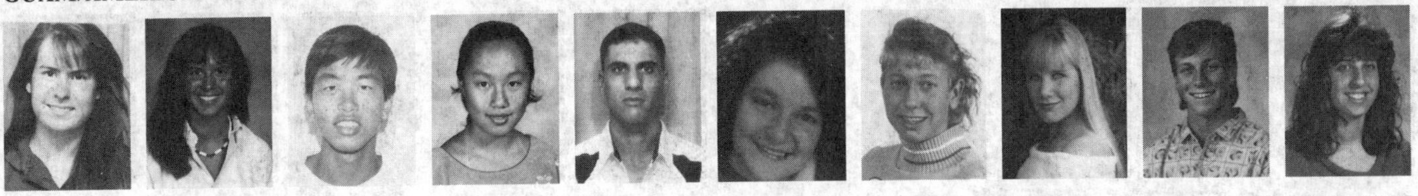

Zetterberg, Jamie A
Moreau HS
Fremont, CA

Zgrabik, Krissy
Louisville HS
Van Nuys, CA

Zhang, Geng-Hua
Harry
San Marcos HS
Santa Barbara, CA

Zhuang, Grace
California HS
San Ramon, CA

Zia, Ademir N
Mark Keppel HS
Monterey Park, CA

Ziakas, Christina M
American HS
Fremont, CA

Ziegler, Elizabeth
Silver Valley HS
Ft Irwin, CA

Zillges, Shawna
Renee
Mt Whitney HS
Visalia, CA

Zimmerman, Jason
Moorpark HS
Moorpark, CA

Zimnavoda, Avigail F
Thousand Oaks HS
Thousand Oaks, CA

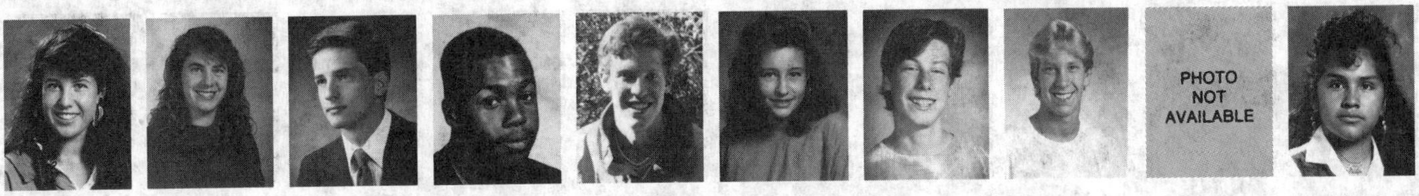
PHOTO
NOT
AVAILABLE

Zirkle, Rebecca S
La Canada HS
La Canada Flintri, CA

Zirovich, Milena D
Arcadia HS
Arcadia, CA

Zirpoli, III Bob M
Henry M Gunn HS
Palo Alto, CA

Ziyad, Karim J
Inglewood HS
Inglewood, CA

Zlotnick, Brandon M
Mountain View HS
Mountain View, CA

Zlotnick, Kathryn B
Junipero Serra HS
San Diego, CA

Zmarzly, Eric
Cardinal Newman
Santa Rosa, CA

Zoda, Paul M
Santa Clara HS
Santa Clara, CA

Zogg, Samantha
University San Diego
San Diego, CA

Zometa, Evelyn
St Michaels HS
Los Angeles, CA

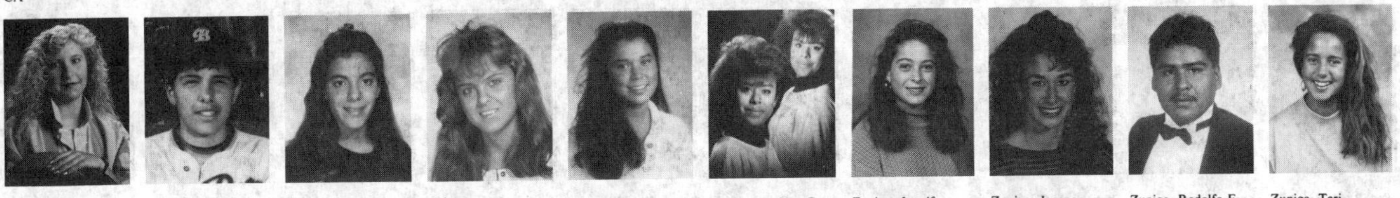

Zomisky, Ramie
Hoover HS
San Diego, CA

Zoque, Kareem
Don Bosco Technical Inst
Walnut, CA

Zuk, Cary E
Canyon HS
Canyon Country, CA

Zuluaga, Angela M
Burlingame HS
Millbrae, CA

Zulueta, Lisa
Capistrano Valley Christian HS
Mission Viejo, CA

Zuniga, Andrea G
Roosevelt HS Magnet
Los Angeles, CA

Zuniga, Jennifer
Mira Mesa HS
San Diego, CA

Zuniga, Joanne
San Benito HS
Hollister, CA

Zuniga, Rodolfo F
Inglewood HS
Inglewood, CA

Zuniga, Teri
San Marcos HS
Santa Barbara, CA

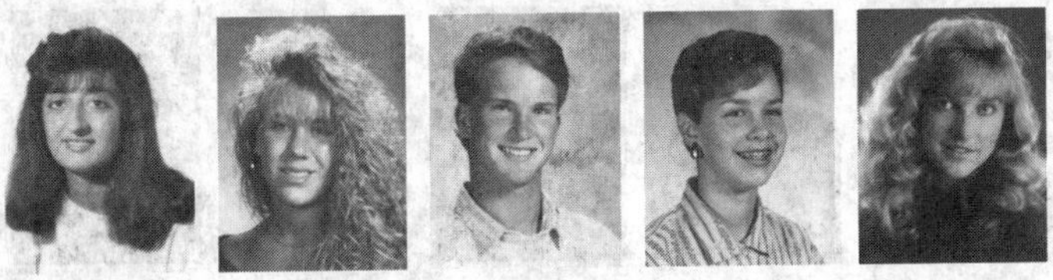

Zurabyan, Suzanna
Glendale HS
Glendale, CA

Zvinakis, Jennifer
Encinal HS
Alameda, CA

Zylstra, Christopher J
Cabrillo HS
Indian Harbour Bc, FL

Zyromski, Laura R
Analy HS
Sebastopol, CA

Zyromski, Michelle
Valerie
Analy HS
Sebastopol, CA

GUAM/ AMERICAN SAMOA

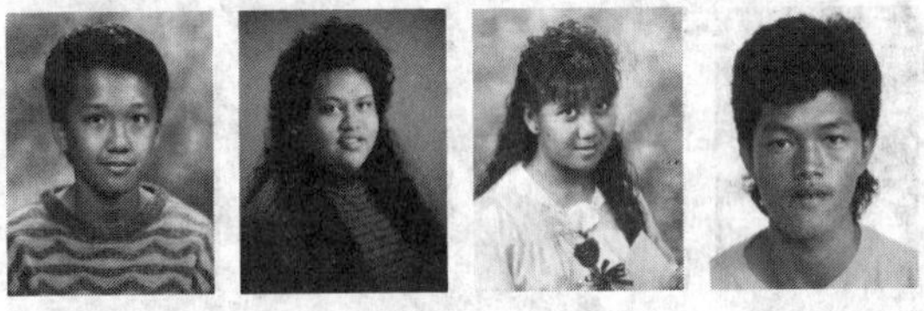

Abiador, Steve
John F Kennedy HS
Tamuning, GU

Aguon, Therese D J
George Washington
Sinajana, GU

Aquino, Maria
Dorothy A
John F Kennedy HS
Tamuning, GU

Aranas, Joel C
John F Kennedy HS
Tamuning, GU

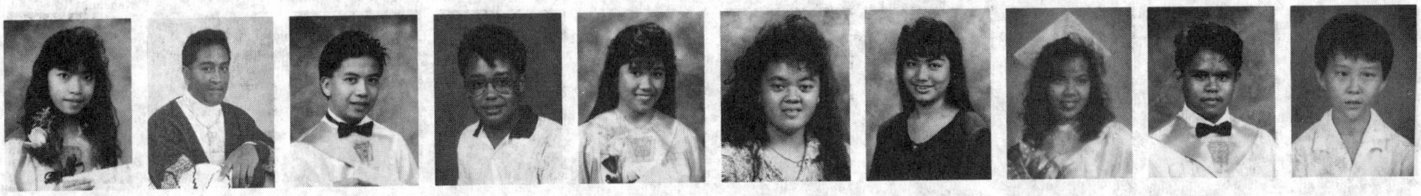

Benitez, Louville
Simon A Sanchez HS
Dededo, GU

Blas, Peter
John F Kennedy HS
Piti, GU

Calma, Richard
Simon Sanchez HS
Tamuning, GU

Carlos, Glenn
Harvest Christian Acad
Tamuning, GU

Carreon, Sally
John F Kennedy SR
Agana, GU

Castano, Suzanne
John F Kennedy HS
Tamuning, GU

Castro, Roseanna T
John F Kennedy HS
Dededo, GU

Cepeda, Franzmarie
R M
Notre Dame HS
Sinajana, GU

Ceralde, Ray M
Simon A Sanchez HS
Tamuning, GU

Chang, Easy P
John F Kennedy HS
Tamuning, GU

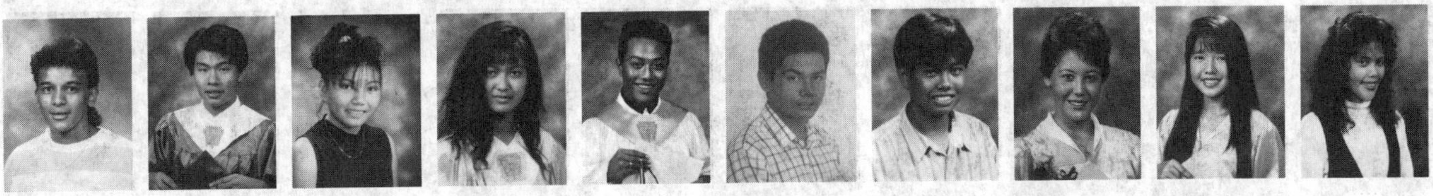

Chargualaf, Edward
John F Kennedy HS
Tamuning, GU

Chou, Pan
John F Kennedy HS
Tamuning, GU

Cruz, Judith T
John F Kennedy HS
Tamuning, GU

Dimarucut, Alicia
John F Kennedy SR
Tamuning, GU

Dizon, Alvin G
Simon A Sanchez HS
Dededo, GU

Edquilane, Don
Antonio Ada
Guam CC HS
GMF Barrigada, GU

Garcia, Ernie
John F Kennedy HS
Sinajana, GU

Gault, Diana
Christine
John F Kennedy HS
Agana, GU

Gomez, Milagros
Arlene D
John F Kennedy HS
Dededo, GU

Griffin, Lyda
John F Kennedy HS
Dededo, GU

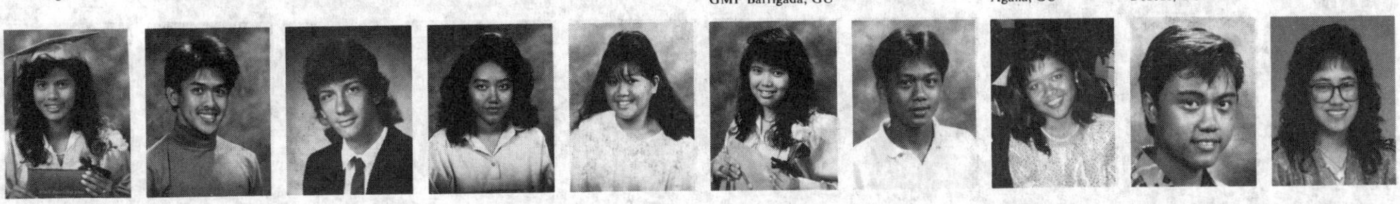

Guerrero, Jennifer M
John F Kennedy HS
Dededo, GU

Hidalgo, Romualdo Z
Simon Sanchez HS
Dededo, GU

Irish, Totsuma
Guam Adventist Acad
Yona, GU

Jocson, Angelita
Madrilejos
Simon Sanchez HS
Dededo, GU

Jones-Ronquillo,
Cindy
John F Kennedy HS
Tamuning, GU

Jose, Caroline B
John F Kennedy HS
Tamuning, GU

Junio, Dwight F
John F Kennedy HS
Dededo, GU

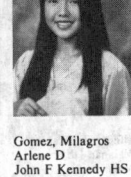

Kio, Dai Dim P
Simon Sanchez HS
Yigo, GU

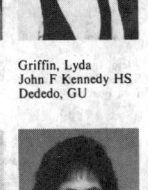

Legaspi, Marlon V
John F Kennedy HS
Dededo, GU

Limtiaco, Angela
John F Kennedy HS
Agana, GU

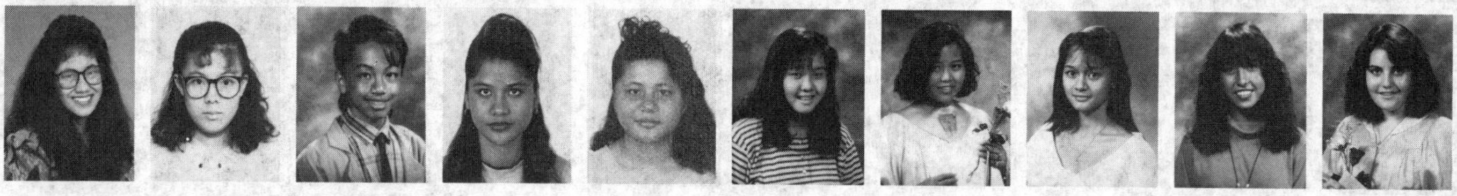

Limtiaco, Stephanie
John F Kennedy HS
Agana, GU

Lin, Yi-Cheng
Tinian HS
Tinian, GU

Liwag, Joseph L
John F Kennedy HS
Dededo, GU

Manglona, Evelyn
Tinian HS
Tinian, GU

Manglona, Lou
Connie B
Tinian HS
Tinian Tt, GU

Ng, Edna
John F Kennedy HS
Temple City, CA

Ortega, Donna V S
Simon Sanchez HS
Dededo, GU

Quezada, Lynn B
John F Kennedy HS
Dededo, GU

Quintanilla, Ladisa D
John F Kennedy HS
Dededo Guam, CA

Quintanilla, Leia D
John F Kennedy HS
Dededo Guam, CA

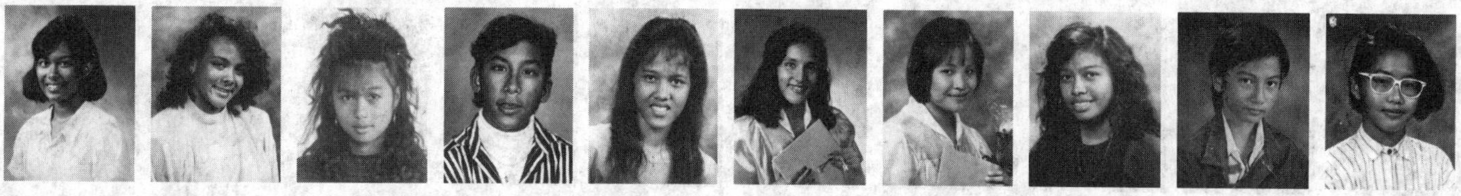

Ranola, Hazel Babasa
John F Kennedy HS
Tamuning, GU

Rogess, Kristine
John F Kennedy HS
Agana, GU

Salvador, Xenie
John F Kennedy HS
Tamuning, GU

San Nicolas, Martin
George Washington
Agana, GU

Santos, Arleen Marie
Sablan
John F Kennedy HS
Tamuning, GU

Taitingfong-Paulino,
Joann M
John F Kennedy HS
Agana, GU

Tinio, Ana Melanie
John F Kennedy HS
Tamuning, GU

Tuzon, Marilyn
John F Kennedy HS
Dededo, GU

Villaflores, III
Domingo I
John F Kennedy HS
Dededo, GU

Wong, Evon
Simon Sanchez HS
Yigo, GU

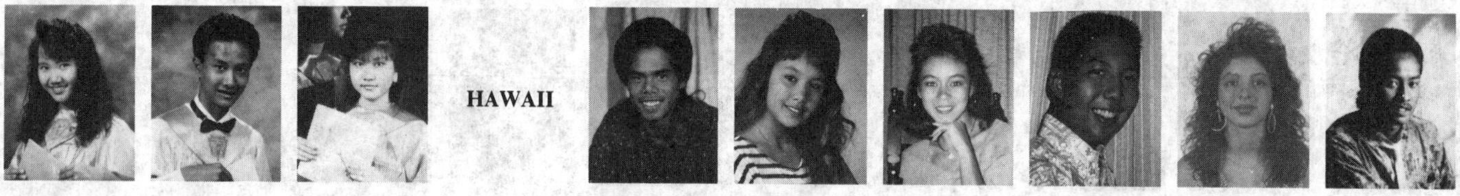

Woo, Renee Ruh Ni
John F Kennedy HS
Tamuning, GU

Yanza, Eugene
Simon Sanchez HS
Agana, GU

Yeh, Sheve-Ching
John F Kennedy HS
Agana, GU

HAWAII

Abenes, Rayburn K
Honoka'a HS
Kamuela, HI

Abero, Kimi M
Waipahu HS
Waipahu, HI

Accetta, Juliann
Radford HS
Honolulu, HI

Acopan, Jeffrey T
Mid-Pacific Inst
Honolulu, HI

Acosta, Laura K
Radford HS
El Paso, TX

Aderinto, Phillip A
Ka'u HS
Pahala, HI

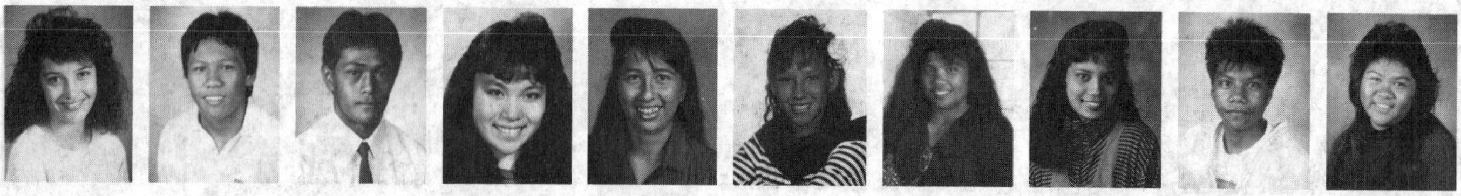

Adric, Maureen K
Waianae HS
Waianae, HI

Agbayani, Julius A
Farrington HS
Honolulu, HI

Agcaoili, III
Amancio-Anthony
Damien Memorial
Waipahu, HI

Agena, Stacie F
Waimea HS
Kekaha, HI

Agoot, Yuki M
Konawaena HS
Captain Cook, HI

Agpawa, Raelynne L
Waiakea HS
Hilo, HI

Agtaguem, Jeanette
Maui HS
Pukalani, HI

Aguda, Ruth Mae
Hawaii Baptist Acad
Honolulu, HI

Aguinaldo, Harry
Baldwin HS
Kahului, HI

Aguinaldo,
Raymanette L
Henry Perrine
Baldwin HS
Kahului, HI

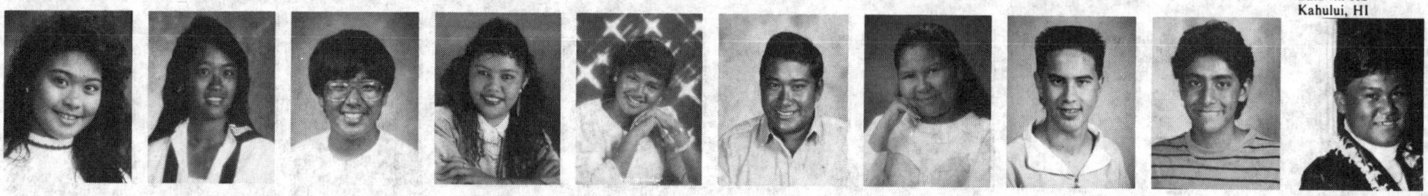

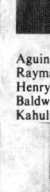

Agustin, Cynthia
Henry Perrine
Baldwin HS
Kahului, HI

Agustin, Lisa M
Sacred Hearts Acad
Waipahu, HI

Agustin, Jr Robert
Kauai HS
Lihue, HI

Ah Choy, Vanessa R
Radford HS
Honolulu, HI

Aipoalani, Cheryl
Nanakuli HS
Waianae, HI

Akana, Elton H
Kohala HS
Kapaau, HI

Akina, Michelle I
James Campbell HS
Ewa Beach, HI

Akiona, Nicholas P K
Mililani HS
Mililani, HI

Alaimo, Michael V
Kohala HS
Hawi, HI

Aldover, Donarco Q
Admiral Arthur W
Radford HS
Honolulu, HI

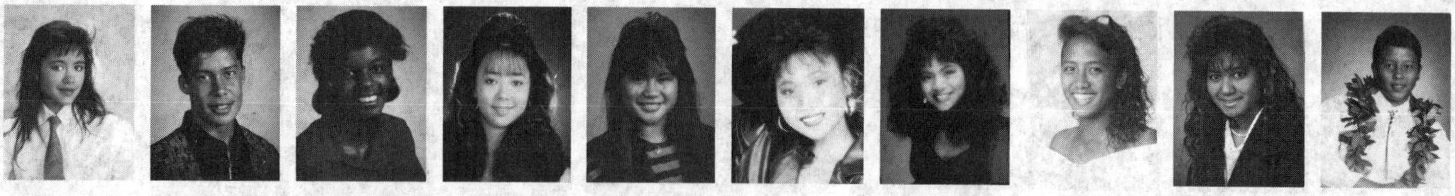

Alejo, Lynette
Sacred Hearts Acad
Ewa Beach, HI

Alferez, Jr Paul A
Waianae HS
Waianae, HI

Allen, Markela J
Leilehua HS
Schofield Bks, HI

Allen, Terilyn Y
Lanai HS
Lanai City, HI

Alonzo, Michelle A
Teilehna HS
Wahiawa, HI

Ambrocio, Maritess P
Farrington HS
Honolulu, HI

Amian, Michelle M
Farrington HS
Honolulu, HI

Amina, Christine K
Kaimuki HS
Honolulu, HI

Amorin, Katherina M
Saint Francis HS
Waipahu, HI

Ancheta, Noel
Moanalua HS
Honolulu, HI

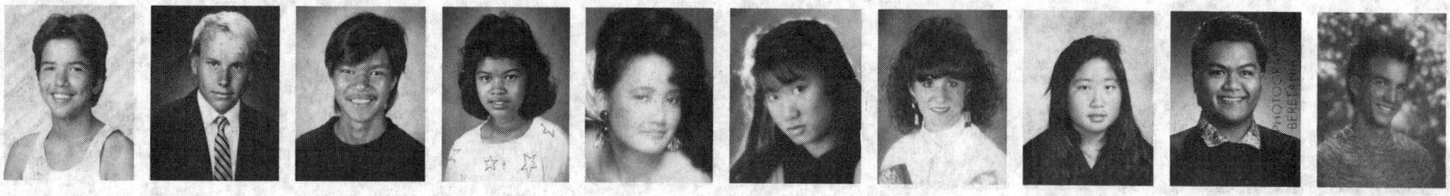

Ancog, Mark
Kaimuki HS
Honolulu, HI

Andrasick,
Christopher J
Iolani Schl
Honolulu, HI

Andres, John Eric
James Campbell HS
Ewa Beach, HI

Andres, Marita
Farrington HS
Ewa Beach, HI

Andres, Pamla A P
Kau HS
Pahala, HI

Anmay, Lam
Kailua HS
Kailua, HI

Anselmo, Angela M
Radford HS
Honolulu, HI

Antolin, Lynn
Konawaena HS
Kailua Kona, HI

Antonio, Jr Salvador
Saint Louis HS
Honolulu, HI

Aplaca, Jared
Kahuku HS
Laie, HI

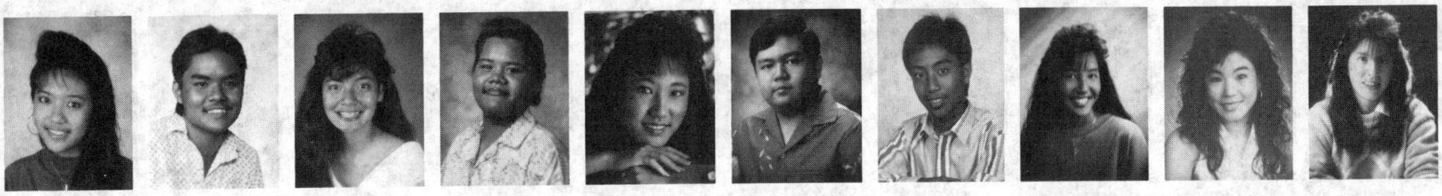

Aquino, Aileen G
Radford HS
Honolulu, HI

Aquino, Randal H
Kaimuki HS
Kaneohe, HI

Aquino, Valerie A
Kauai HS
Lihue, HI

Aragon, Jodi H
Kailua HS
Waimanalo, HI

Arakaki, Anne F
Waiakea HS
Hilo, HI

Arakaki, Anthony T
Baldwin HS
Wailuku, HI

Arias, Richard P
Waiakea HS
Hilo, HI

Arisumi, Melanie E
H P Baldwin HS
Kahului, HI

Asato, Tammy
Iolani HS
Honolulu, HI

Asato, Tammy F
Leilehua HS
Wahiawa, HI

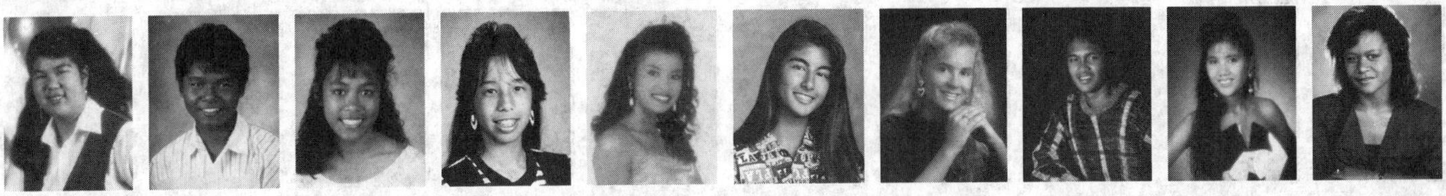

Asato, Vicki M
Waipahu HS
Waipahu, HI

Asuncion, Noel F
Lahainaluna HS
Lahaina, HI

Asuncion, Roselyn L
Wallace Rider
Farrington HS
Honolulu, HI

Autele, Tabitha T
Mililani HS
Mililani, HI

Avila, Kimberly
Radford HS
Kahului, HI

Awber, Rona M
Roosevelt HS
Honolulu, HI

Ayres, Lorinda M
Admiral Arthur W
Radford HS
Honolulu, HI

Babas, Ferdinand G
Kau HS
Pahala, HI

Baccam, Sakhone
Waialua HS &
Intermed
Haleiwa, HI

Bachiller, Michelle
Waipahu HS
Waipahu, HI

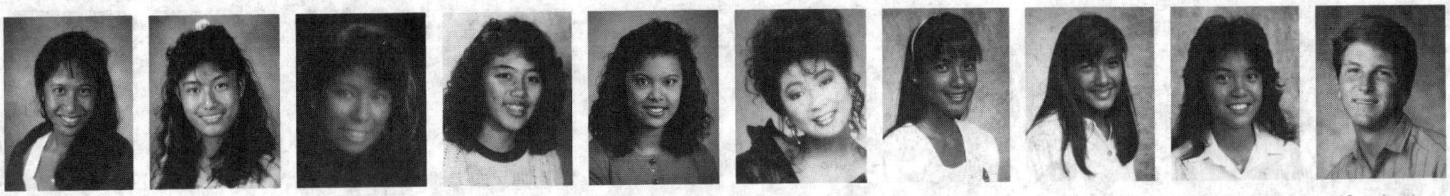

Badoyen, Kristi L
H P Baldwin HS
Kula, HI

Badua, Dellia R
Farrington HS
Honolulu, HI

Badua, Katherine P
James Campbell HS
Ewa Beach, HI

Badua, Vida L
Waimea HS
Waimea, HI

Bagalayos, Myrna C
Mililani HS
Mililani, HI

Bantolina, Glorina B
Farrington HS
Honolulu, HI

Baraquio, Bernadette
Moanalua HS
Honolulu, HI

Baraquio, Therese P
Moanalua HS
Honolulu, HI

Barayuga, Ellen B
Moanalua HS
Honolulu, HI

Barshaw, Jeremy S
Kailua HS
Kailua, HI

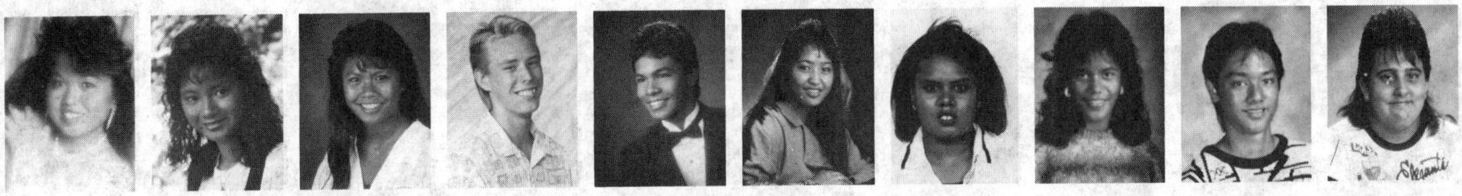

Bartolome, Marylou
Pahoa HS
Pahoa, HI

Baruel, Lisa
Hilo HS
Papaikou, HI

Battung, Nicole R
Farrington HS
Honolulu, HI

Bauer, Benjamin S
Kaimuki HS
Honolulu, HI

Bayang, Harold
Campbell HS
Ewa Beach, HI

Baysa, Lovisa H P
Kamehameha Schls
Hilo, HI

Beard, Carla D
Mililani HS
Wahiawa, HI

Bell, Raynee
Kamehameha HS
Hilo, HI

Bello, Reggie K
Kohala HS
Kapaau, HI

Benevides, Jennifer L
Maui HS
Pukalani, HI

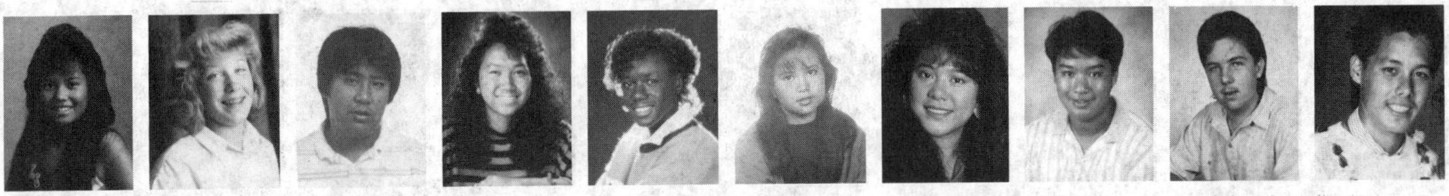

Benitez, Marissa L
Baldwin HS
Wailuku, HI

Bennett, Holly
Kalaheo HS
Kailua, HI

Bisquera, Michael N
Baldwin HS
Kahului, HI

Bisquera, Milda V
Leilehua HS
Wahiawa, HI

Bland, Monica M
Moanalua HS
Honolulu, HI

Bondoc, Grichel A
Kailua HS
Waimanalo, HI

Bonifacio, Jennifer T
James Campbell HS
Makakilo, HI

Borce, Joel
Farrington HS
Honolulu, HI

Borsting, Esben A
Waiakea HS
Hilo, HI

Bradshaw, Jonathan
Kahuku HS
Laie, HI

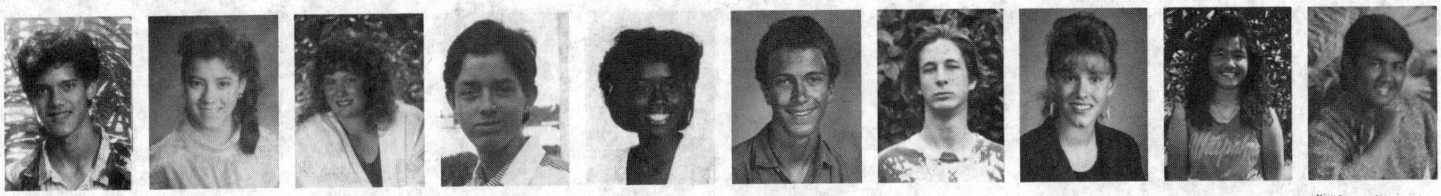

Bras, Garett A
Maui HS
Haiku, HI

Bras, Raenelle M
Maui HS
Haiku, HI

Brinley, Chandra
Pahoa HS
Keaau, HI

Broderick, Scott A
Radford HS
Syracuse, NY

Brooks, Natalie N
Leilehua HS
Scholfield Bks, HI

Brown, Cutter R
Hawaii Preparatory
Acad
Princeville, HI

Brown, Gulliver
Waiakea HS
Pahoa, HI

Browning, Monica D
Leilehua HS
Wahiawa, HI

Buco, Irene B
Waipahu HS
Waipahu, HI

Bueno, Dwayne
Waipahu HS
Waipahu, HI

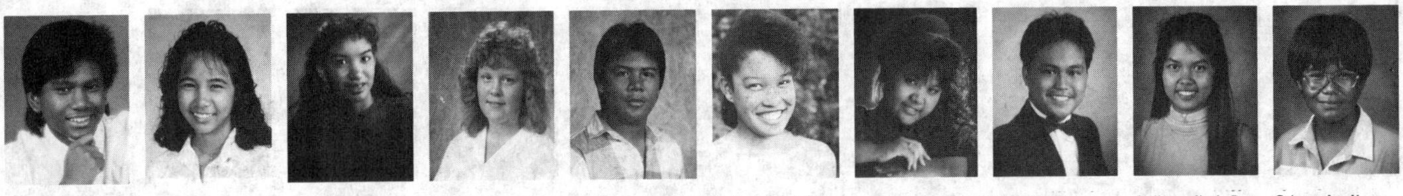

Bugarin, Jr Rodolfo
W R Farrington HS
Kailua, HI

Bulosan, Donah M
Roosevelt HS
Honolulu, HI

Bulusan, Carmel
Henry Perrine
Baldwin HS
Wailuku, HI

Burke, Bonnie Lorain
Saint Francis HS
Ewa Beach, HI

Bustamante, Jose M
Moanalua HS
Makakilo, HI

Butler, Melinda Y
Radford HS
Ewa Beach, HI

Cabbab, Loryann A
Sacred Hearts Acad
Honolulu, HI

Cadiente, Jason J
Waipahu HS
Waipahu, HI

Cadiente, Jingle B
W R Farrington HS
Honolulu, HI

Caitano, Ian K
Roosevelt HS
Honolulu, HI

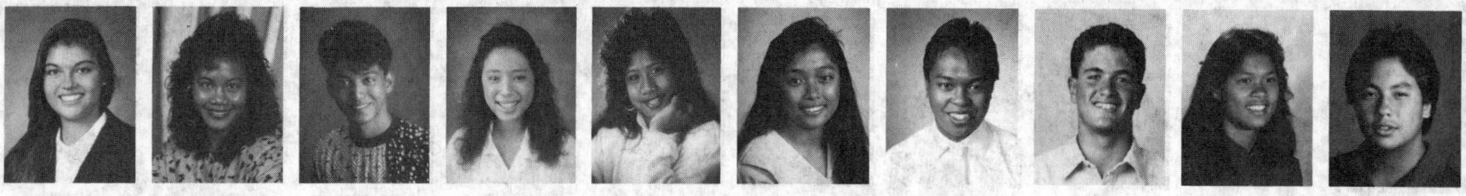

Cajski, Catherine M St Francis HS Kailua, HI	Calamayan, Flordeliza Pahoa High & Elementary Schl Pahoa, HI	Calamayan, George B Viaipahu HS Waipahu, HI	Calapini, Esther Lahainaluna HS Lahaina, HI	Calilao, Pamela May Lanai HS Lanai City, HI	Calpito, Rowena Waipahu HS Waipahu, HI	Cambe, Richard A Domien Memorial Honolulu, HI	Canlis, Jp C St Louis HS Honolulu, HI	Carcueva, Cecilie M Waimea HS Kekaha, HI	Carino, David F Saint Louis HS Mililani, HI

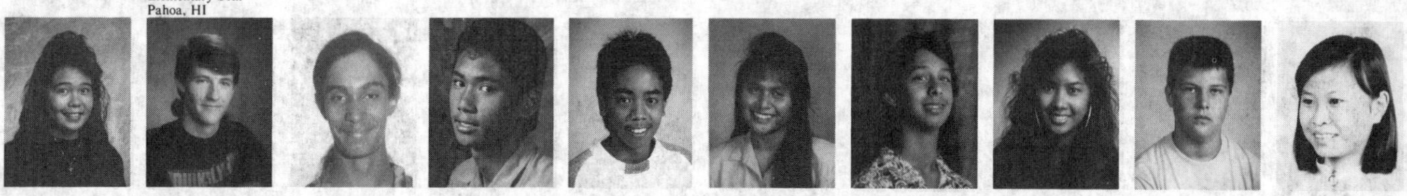

Carnate, May B Moanalua HS Honolulu, HI	Carr, Jonathan J Radford HS Honolulu, HI	Carter, Ravi Hope Roosevelt HS Honolulu, HI	Caspillo, Paul Harris Molokai HS Kaunakakai, HI	Castillo, Filemon C Waipahu HS Waipahu, HI	Cawagas, Liza F Konawaena HS & Intermed Kailua Kona, HI	Caya, Rallen A Kalaheo HS Kailua, HI	Cayaban, Janice D Maui HS Pukalani, HI	Chambers, James Alan Hanalani HS Milani, HI	Chan, Alice S Mc Kinley HS Honolulu, HI

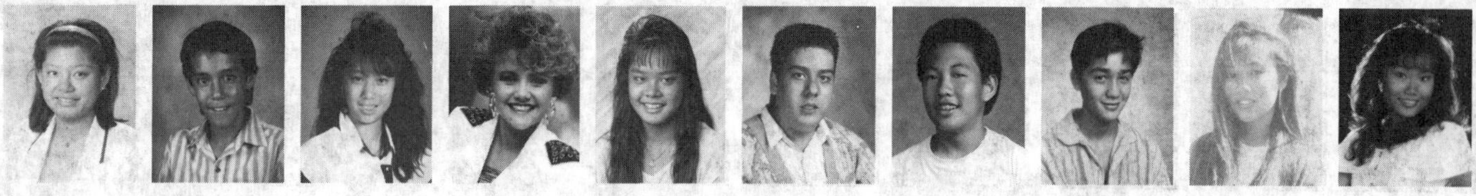

Chan, Lilly President William Mc Kinley HS Honolulu, HI	Chang, Robert A Kauai HI & Inter Lihue, HI	Chen, Grace L Mililani HS Mililani, HI	Chessum, Sharon J Kailua HS Kailua, HI	Chinen, Cynthia Kalani HS Honolulu, HI	Ching, Eric C Kohala HS Kapaau, HI	Ching, Jason Y C Roosevelt HS Honolulu, HI	Cho, Michael W Moanalua HS Honolulu, HI	Chong, Aeng Chuly Mc Kinley HS Honolulu, HI	Chong, Brenda Y Moanalua HS Honolulu, HI

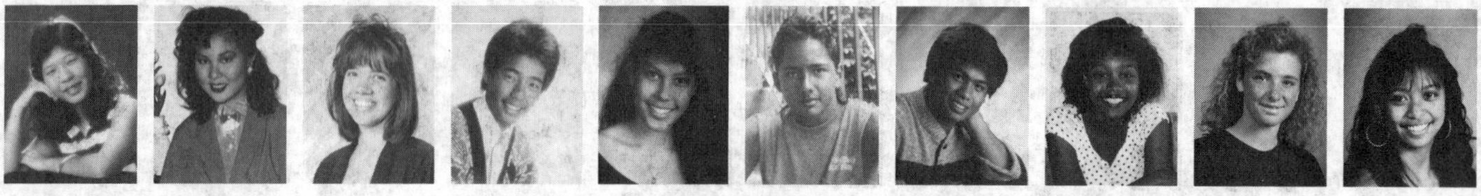

Choo, Jeanna R T Pearl City HS Pearl City, HI	Chun, Aileen M President Theodore Roosevelt HS Honolulu, HI	Chun, Diana Kwai Lan Kaimuki HS Honolulu, HI	Chun, Jonathan G H Mid-Pacific Inst Mililani, HI	Church, Malia C Kamehameha HS Hana, HI	Clark, Sean Moanalua HS Honolulu, HI	Cogo, Henry Hilo HS Hilo, HI	Colemon, Maryah Kalaheo HS Kailua, HI	Collmer, Veda M Mililani HS Mililani, HI	Colobong, Joyce M Waipahu HS Waipahu, HI

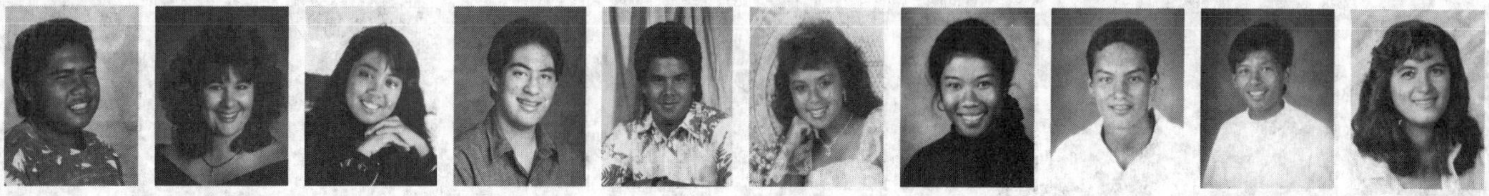

Coloma, Jr Ernest A Waimea HS Lawai, HI	Comer, Melissa N N Maui HS Makawao, HI	Concepcion, Kimberly Radford HS Alea, HI	Concepcion, Patrick T St Louis Schl Mililani, HI	Conradt, Jr Richard Hilo HS Hilo, HI	Cordeiro, Drena N Kamehameha Schls Pearl City, HI	Corouz, April Kauai HS Lihue, HI	Cox, John P Kauai HS Lihue, HI	Cristobal, Joy Joji W R Farrington HS Honolulu, HI	Croot, Donica T Kalani HS Honolulu, HI

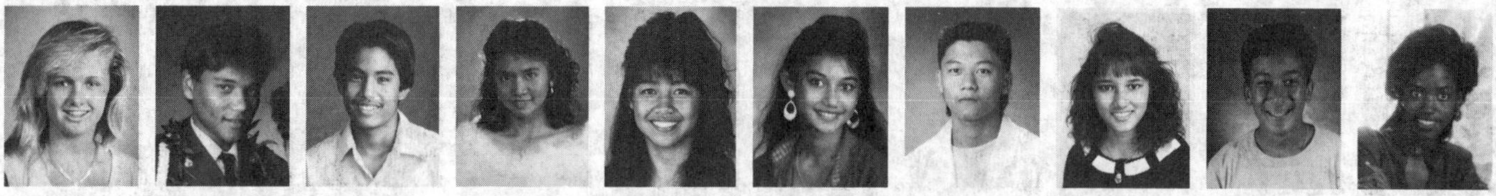

Crow, Darcie Mililani HS Mililani, HI	Cullen, Troy C St Louis HS Waipahu, HI	Cutter, Kevin Y St Louis HS Honolulu, HI	Dace, Rose Lynn Waipahu HS Waipahu, HI	Dacoco, Jenny B James Campbell HS Ewa Beach, HI	Dalire, Shannon Kamehameha Schls Kaneohe, HI	Dang, Hung C Roosevelt HS Honolulu, HI	Daog, Darlene C Waiakea HS Keaau, HI	Dato, Dennis J Kapaa HS Kilauea, HI	Davidson, Kymberly Lynell Radford HS Honolulu, HI

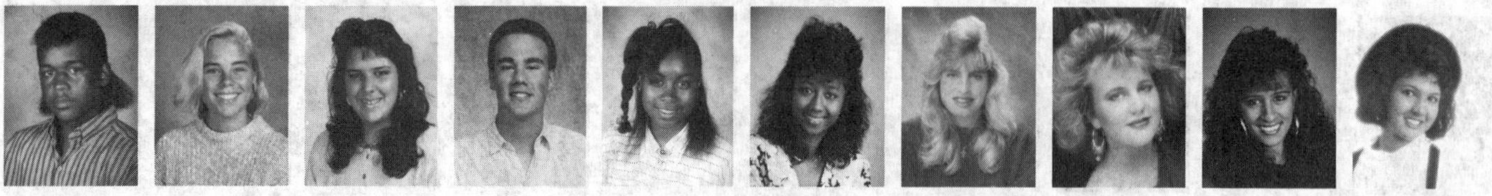

Davis, Christian Radford HS Hickam A F B, HI	Davis, Heather C Konawaena HS Kailua Kona, HI	De Mello, Christy St Joseph HS Hilo, HI	De Soto, Brian D Moanalna HS Honolulu, HI	Deas, Susana R Radford HS Honolulu, HI	Del Rosario, Judith S Waipahu HS Waipahu, HI	Dempsey, Stacey Leilehua HS Valrico, FL	Devenney, Alicia D Theodore Roosevelt Honolulu, HI	Deveraturda, Renee Mililani HS Mililani, HI	Dezzani, Susan S Miliani HS Mililani, HI

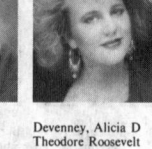

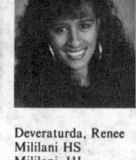

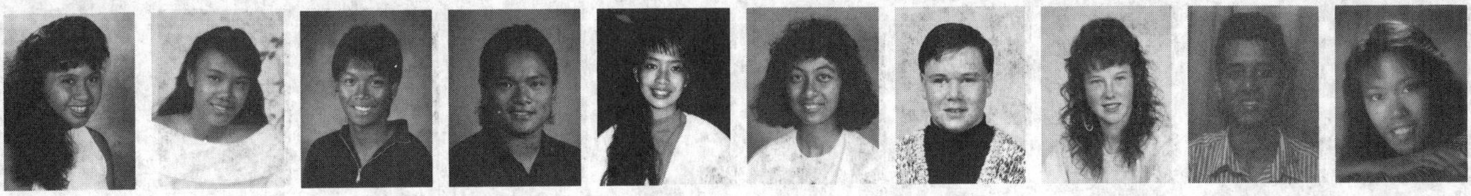

Dizol, Leanora P
Waimea HS
Koloa, HI

Dochin, Pauline
Konawaena HS
Kailua-Kona, HI

Dollente, Jr Quintin
Farrington HS
Honolulu, HI

Domingo, Chad M
Waipahu HS
Waipahu, HI

Domingo, Cheryl C
W R Farrington HS
Honolulu, HI

Domingo, Qny D
Konawaena HS
Captain Cook, HI

Dougherty, Peter W
Radford HS
Honolulu, HI

Droge, Clarissa A
Waiakea HS
Mountain View, HI

Duarte, III Thomas
Saint Louis Schl
Honolulu, HI

Dumbrique, Joy L
Kauai HS &
Intermed
Lihue, HI

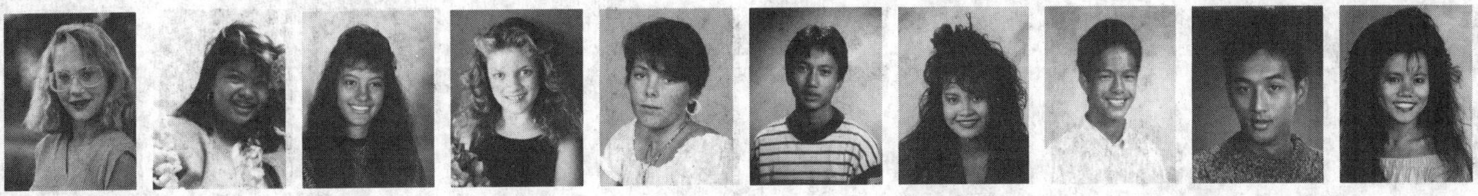

Dunno, Dawn M
Moanalua HS
Honolulu, HI

Duran, Rona C
Mid-Pacific Inst
Lihue, HI

Edwards, Edrienne L
Waimea HS
Kekaha, HI

Elm, K Leinani
Henry J Kaiser HS
Honolulu, HI

Engle, Lila Lehua
Waiakea HS
Volcano, HI

Engoring, Jon A
Maui HS
Haiku, HI

Erece, Mary Jane P
Kau HS
Pahala, HI

Esguerra, Vibenjohn
Moanalua HS
Honolulu, HI

Esperanza, Boisse O
Damien HS
Waipahu, HI

Espiritu, Elsie D
Lanai HS
Lanai City, HI

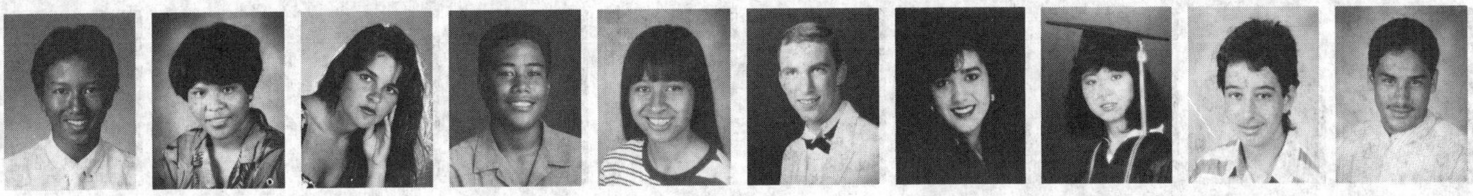

Espiritu, Erwin C
Damien Memorial
Waipahu, HI

Estrella, Edwina
Lynn M
Wallace Rider
Farrington HS
Honolulu, HI

Evslin, Tanya
Kavai HS
Kapaa, HI

Faagata, Alatise S
Saint Louis HS
Honolulu, HI

Fabay, Maricar C
Radford HS
Honolulu, HI

Fahey, Andrew L
Mc Kinley HS
Honolulu, HI

Feiteira, Wendy K
Maui HS
Kahului, HI

Feng, Xing Ci
Mc Kinley HS
Honolulu, HI

Fernandes, Kirk J
Henry Perrine
Baldwin HS
Kahului, HI

Fevella, Michael E
James Campbell HS
Ewa Beach, HI

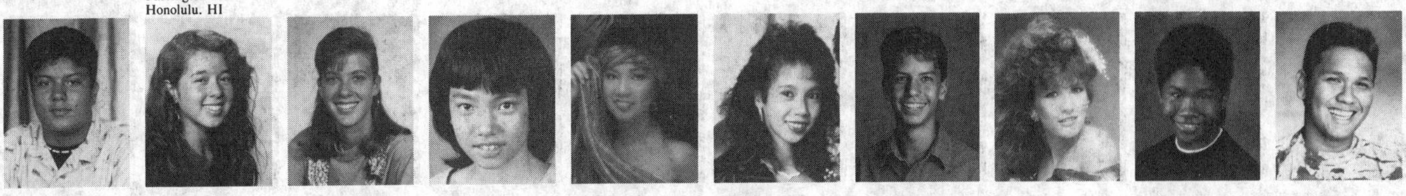

Fisher, Samuel V
Honokaa HS
Honokaa, HI

Fitzgerald, Jamie A
Kalani HS
Honolulu, HI

Fitzgerald, Shannon
Waiakea HS
Hilo, HI

Fong, Florence Y W
Mc Kinley HS
Honolulu, HI

Formoso, Charmaine
Leilehna HS
Wahiawa, HI

Francisco, Florence R
Radford HS
Honolulu, HI

Frank, Jr Lawrence P
St Louis HS
Honolulu, HI

Friedel, Erica
Kalaheo HS
Kaneohe, HI

Fronda, Fred
Lahaina Luna HS
Lahaina, HI

Fuerte, Ky F
Baldwin HS
Wailuku, HI

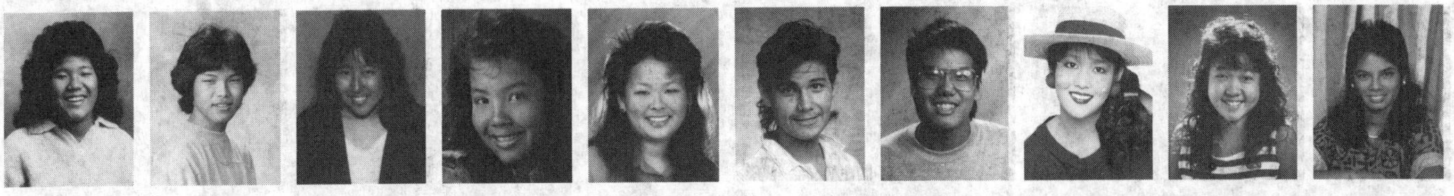

Fujihara, Angel U
Kailua HS
Kailua, HI

Fujii, Alii-Mana T
William Mc Kinley
Waipahu, HI

Fujikawa, Debra-Ann
Moanalua HS
Honolulu, HI

Fujiuchi, Lauree J
Kapaa HS
Kapaa, HI

Fukui, Jamie N
Hawaii Baptist Acad
Aiea, HI

Fukumoto, Ralph
Moanalua HS
Honolulu, HI

Fukushima, Reid K
Maui HS
Kahului, HI

Fukushima, Rhoda M
Moanalua HS
Honolulu, HI

Fukushima, Tricia K
Henry Perrine
Baldwin HS
Kihei, HI

Fung, Aimee
Hilo HS
Hilo, HI

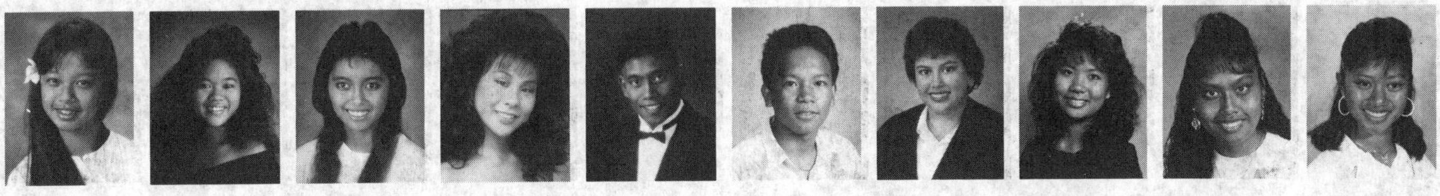

Fyrberg, Tai Hokulii
Punahou HS
Honolulu, HI

Gabina, Juliana R
Maui HS
Wailuku, HI

Galon, Stacy L
James Campbell HS
Ewa Beach, HI

Gamiao, Melanie R
Kaimuki HS
Honolulu, HI

Gampong, Romeo
University Laboratory
Schl
Honolulu, HI

Garcia, Alwinson S
Waialua HS
Waialua, HI

Garcia, Angie M
St Francis HS
Honolulu, HI

Garcia, Beverly A
Maui HS
Paia, HI

Garcia, Evacita J
Konawaena HS
Kealakekua, HI

Garcia, Liza-Ann L
Waimea HS
Kekeaha, HI

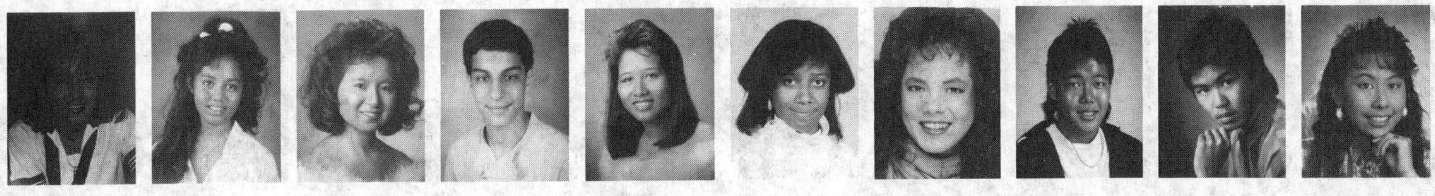

Gasmen, Joey-Ann
Kimiyo
Sacred Hearts Acad
Mililani, HI

Gazmen, Rychelle C
Henry Perrine
Baldwin HS
Kahului, HI

Geng, Hong
Mc Kinley HS
Kaneohe, HI

Gergis, Daniel S
Lutheran HS
Honolulu, HI

Geronimo, Aileen G
Mc Kinley HS
Honolulu, HI

Gibbs, Jeanette A
Mililani HS
Baltimore, MD

Giddens, Kauiokalewa
Kamehameha Schl
Pearl City, HI

Ginoza, Stanford K
Waipahu HS
Waipahu, HI

Ginoza, Steven M
University Laboratory
Schl
Honolulu, HI

Go, Annie Marie
Moanalua HS
Waipahu, HI

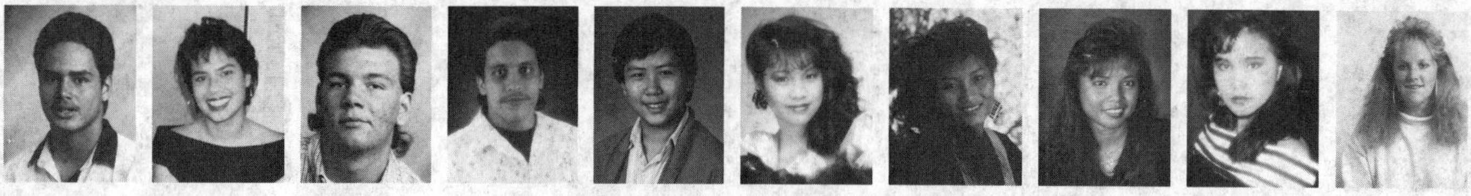

Goddard, Brandon P
Maui HS
Kahului, HI

Goldberger, Judy H
Mililani HS
Mililani, HI

Golden, Mark A
Maui HS
Kula, HI

Gonsalves, Tino
Aiea HS
Aiea, HI

Goo, Justin M W
Mid-Pacific Inst
Honolulu, HI

Gorgonio, Mary-Charmaine A
St Francis HS
Honolulu, HI

Gorospe, Loida
Hilo HS
Hilo, HI

Green, Ammabelle C
Radford HS
Honolulu, HI

Green, Christine M
Hawaii Baptist Acad
Honolulu, HI

Greenwell, Kathy
Hawaii Preparatory Acad
Holualoa, HI

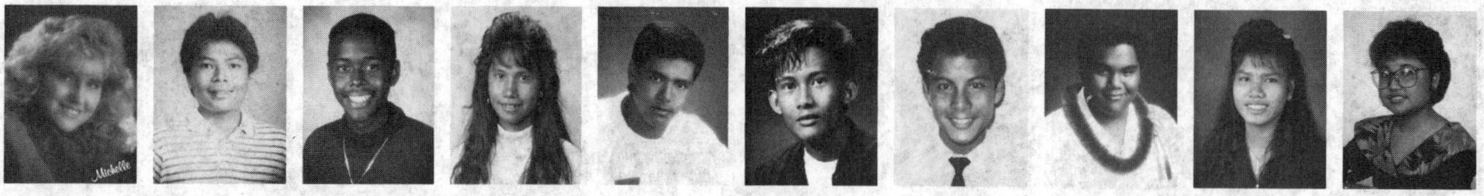

Greer, Michele
Kalaheo HS
Kaneohe, HI

Guerrero, Jonathan N
Waialua HS & Intermed
Waialua, HI

Guinn, Nathaniel
Radford HS
Andrews AFB, DC

Guittap, Jane G
Mc Kinley HS
Honolulu, HI

Gusman, III George
Kamehameha HS
Waipahu, HI

Gutierrez, Sherwin Manzano
Lahainaluna HS
Lahaina, HI

Guzman, Geoffrey T
Damien Memorial
Honolulu, HI

Haae, Christopher
Kamehameha HS
Waianae, HI

Haber, Gemma C
Baldwin HS
Kahului, HI

Hada, Raynette K
Waiakea HS
Hilo, HI

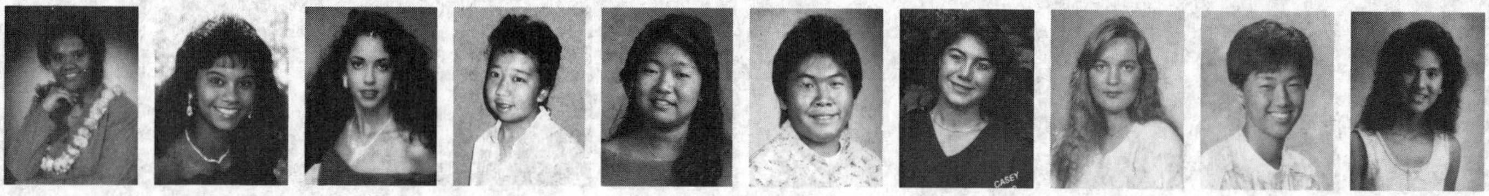

Halama, Lylla A
Waianae HS
Waianae, HI

Haleakala, Malia
Saint Anthony HS
Makawao, HI

Hall, Jennifer L
Henry J Kaiser HS
Honolulu, HI

Hamai, Stephanie S
Maui HS
Kula, HI

Hamaji, Iris A
Roosevelt HS
Honolulu, HI

Hamamoto, Sean A
Mililani HS
Mililani, HI

Hamberg, Casey L
Kauai HS
Kauai, HI

Hammer, Minna Ira
Waiakea HS
Hilo, HI

Han, Song I
Mc Kinley HS
Honolulu, HI

Hanano, Jana L
Kamehomeha HS
Hawi, HI

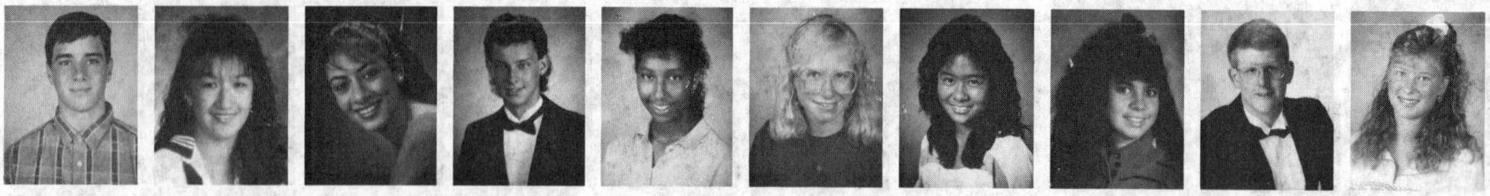

Hancock, Frank R
Lei Lehua HS
Ft Campbell, KY

Hanke, Kimberly J
Sacred Hearts Acad
Mililani, HI

Hanna, Dalia
University Labratory
Kaneohe, HI

Hantke, Christopher
Mililani HS
Wahiawa, HI

Hart, Angelique R
Radford HS
Honolulu, HI

Hasbrouck, Kimberly
Radford HS
Omaha, NE

Hashimoto, Erin M
Henry Perine Baldwin
Kula, HI

Haumea, Rachelle N
Kamehameha Schls
Kapaa, HI

Hawkinson, Christian
Damien Memorial
Flanders, NJ

Heiner, Kellie A
Henry Perrine Baldwin HS
Kihei, HI

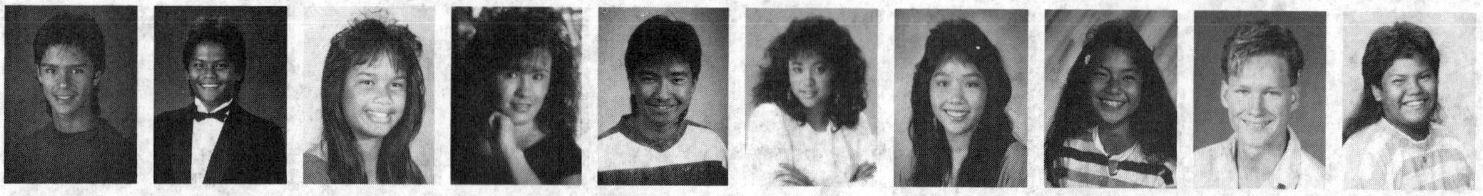

Hermosura, Daven T
James Campbell HS
Ewo Beach, HI

Herodies, Lydell J
Damien Memorial
Pearl City, HI

Hesapene, Audrey M
Waimea HS
Kekaha, HI

Hess, Tammy
Honoka'a HS
Kamuela, HI

Higa, Mark H
Mililani HS
Mililani, HI

Higa, Stephanie Rae
Kalani HS
Honolulu, HI

Higashiguchi, Krista
Henry Perrine Baldwin HS
Wailuku, HI

Higuchi, Cori Anne C
Kaiser HS
Honolulu, HI

Hills, K Michael
Star Of The Sea HS
Honolulu, HI

Hirai, Brandie
Kalani HS
Kaneohe, HI

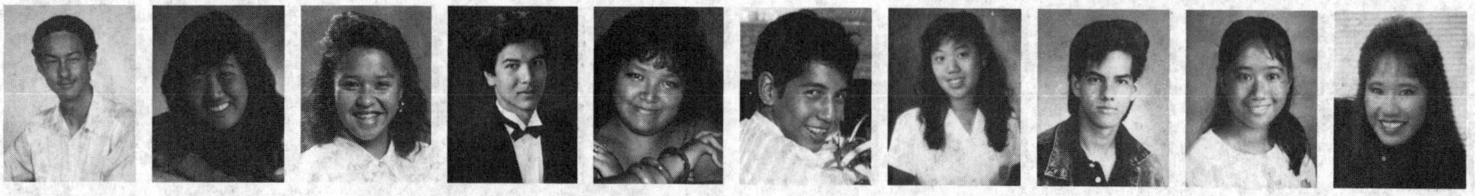

Hirata, David M
Waiakea HS
Keaau, HI

Hirayama, Tracey
Hilo HS
Hilo, HI

Ho, April A
Moanalua HS
Honolulu, HI

Ho, Chadwick A
Damien Memorial
Kaneohe, HI

Ho, Jolyn N S
Pahoa HS
Pahoa, HI

Ho, Jr Joseph K
Kamehameha Schls
Ewa Beach, HI

Ho, Lareina K L
Maryknoll HS
Pearl City, HI

Ho, Skye K
Mid-Pacific Inst
Waimanalo, HI

Hoapili, Velma L
Kailua HS
Kailua, HI

Hoapili, Verna Kuulei Keiko
Kailua HS
Kailua, HI

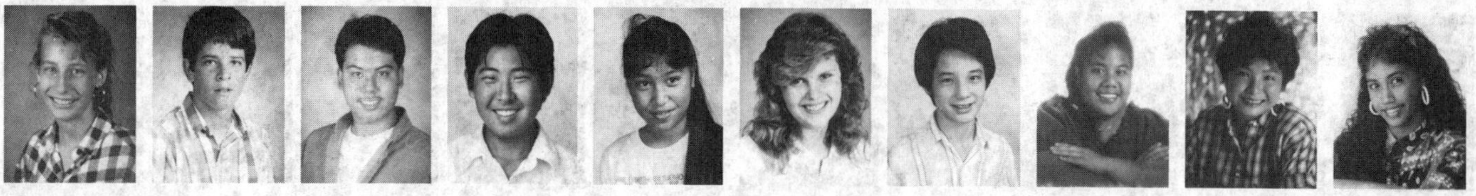

Hoff, Maile A
H P Baldwin HS
Kihei, HI

Hogg, James A
Mid Pacific Inst
Kailua, HI

Hogge, Mark S
Arthur W•Radford
Honolulu, HI

Hong, Eugene S
St Louis Schl
Honolulu, HI

Hoohuli, Dori Ann
Waiakea HS
Hilo, HI

Hooks, Terri
Mililani HS
Nellis Afb, NV

Hope, Dale
St Joseph HS
Hilo, HI

Hose, Kialani K
Radford HS
Honolulu, HI

Huang, Hsin-Yi
Waiakea HS
Hilo, HI

Huddy, Noel K
James Campbell HS
Ewa Beach, HI

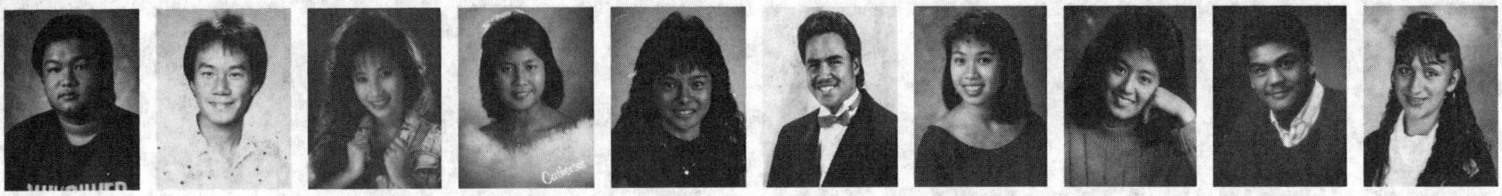

Hui, John I J
Hawaii Baptist Acad
Honolulu, HI

Huynh, Hai G
Roosevelt HS
Honolulu, HI

Huynh, Michelle
Sacred Hearts Acad
Honolulu, HI

Ibarra, Catherine A
Waipahu HS
Waipahu, HI

Ignacio, Joanne L
Waipahu HS
Waipahu, HI

Iida, Sherwood K
Kapaa HS
Kapaa, HI

Ing, Kristin E
Punahou Schl
Honolulu, HI

Inouye, Dee Ann K
Maui HS
Kahului, HI

Isaacs, Jr Barney
Kapono
Kamehameha Schls
Honolulu, HI

Isaacs, Ruby
Kohala HS
Kapaau, HI

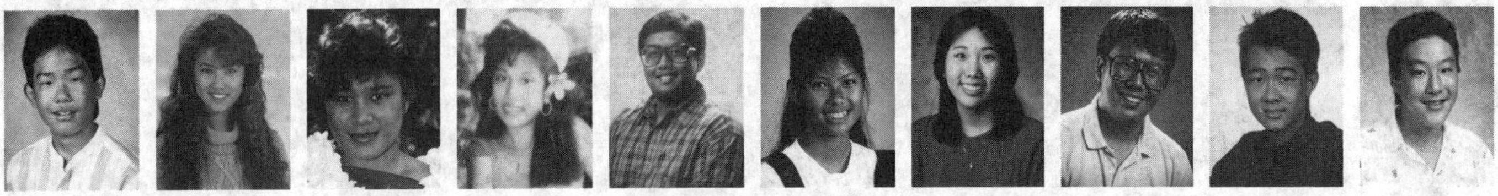

Isara, Barry J
W R Farrington HS
Honolulu, HI

Ishikuni, Mari
Kauai HS
Lihue, HI

Ishizu, Christine M
Kauai HS
Lihue, HI

Isidro, Jennifer
Mary Knoll HS
Honolulu, HI

Isla, Floredick A
Leilehua HS
Wahiawa, HI

Isnec, May Rose L
Leilehua HS
Wahiana, HI

Ito, Corinne
Kailua HS
Waimanalo, HI

Iwasaka, Ryan M
H P Baldwin HS
Wailuku, HI

Iwasaki, Ryan
Waiakea HS
Hilo, HI

Izumi, Sam K
Moanalua HS
Honolulu, HI

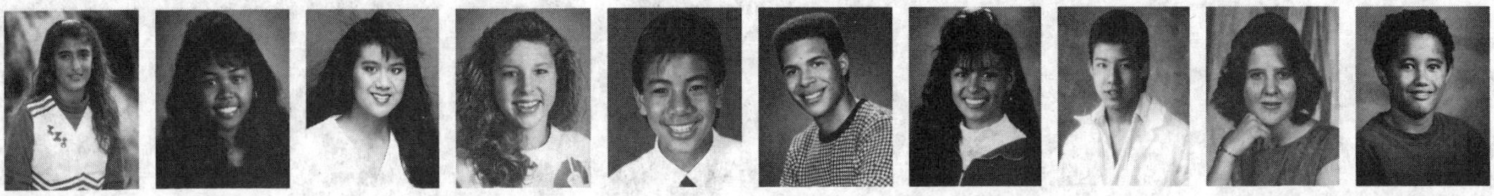

Jadrnicek, Sunny
Kalaheo HS
Haymarket, VA

Jamora, Yolette N
Waialua HS
Waialua, HI

Jen, Trisha L
Hawaiian Mission
Acad
Honolulu, HI

Jensen, Kelly A
Waialua HS
Waialua, HI

Joco, Jeremy B J
Damien Memorial
Waipahu, HI

Johnson, Rodney C
Punahou Schl
Honolulu, HI

Johnston, Wendy
Lahainaluna HS
Lihue, HI

Jones, Aaron C
Hawaii Baptist Acad
Honolulu, HI

Jones, Kristin
Medelle
Henry Opukahaia
Schl
Captain Cook, HI

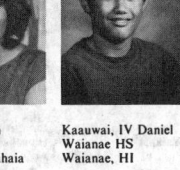

Kaauwai, IV Daniel
Waianae HS
Waianae, HI

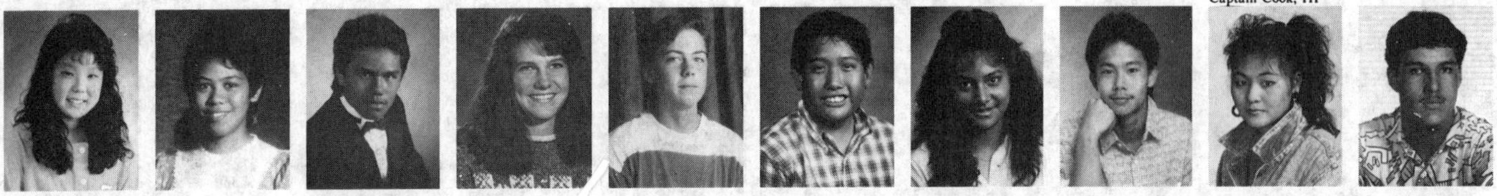

Kajiwara, Jodi S
Mid Pacific Inst
Mililani, HI

Kala, Mary Kaui
Hana HS
Hana Maui, HI

Kalaola, Jr Valmores
Waipahu HS
Waianae, HI

Kalberg, Amy
Kalaheo HS
Kaneohe, HI

Kalberg, Jason
Kalaheo HS
Kaneohe, HI

Kam, Jr Joseph K H
Kaimuki HS
Honolulu, HI

Kanaele, Jocelyn N
Maui HS
Haiku, HI

Kaneshige, Jr Morris
Lanakila Baptist HS
Ewa Beach, HI

Kang, So Young
Baldwin HS
Kahalui, HI

Kaniho, Richard K
Honokaa HS
Kamuela, HI

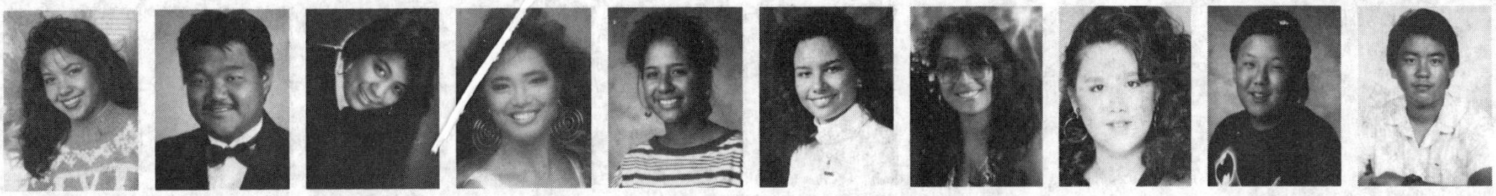

Kato, Debbie
Kohala HS
Kapaau, HI

Kato, Kibert
Mililani HS
Mililani, HI

Kauahi, Denise K
Kamemeha Schls
Lawai, HI

Kaui, Jacqueline K
Kapaa High & Inter
Kapaa, HI

Kaulu, Joey K
Kailua HS
Waimanalo, HI

Kaupu, Katherine M
Molokai HS &
Intermed
Kaunakakai, HI

Kawahakui,
Nohealani A
The Kamehameha
Schls
Waialua, HI

Kawahara, Alyssa S
Aiea HS
Aiea, HI

Kawamata, Byron K
Kailua HS
Kailua, HI

Kawamoto, Ryan C
Waiakea HS
Pahoa, HI

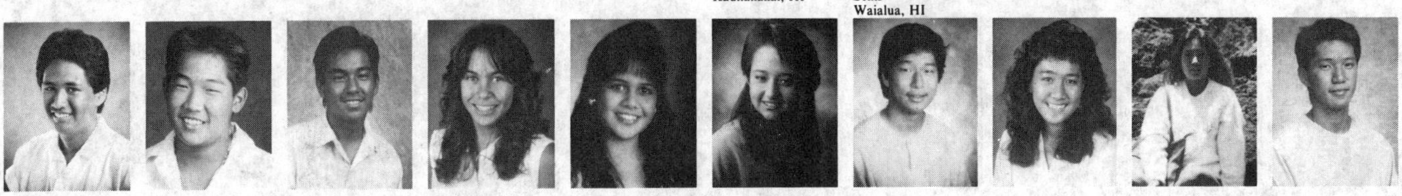

Kawamura, Bryan T
Baldwin HS
Kahului, HI

Kawamura, Grant M
St Louis Schl
Kaneohe, HI

Kawamura, Reid T
Moanalua HS
Aiea, HI

Kealoha, Elena
Kauai HS
Kalaheo, HI

Kekaula, Rose Kahae
Kamehameha HS
Honolulu, HI

Kiang, Karma Wen
H P Baldwin HS
Kihei, HI

Kido, Kendall H
Hawaii Baptist Acad
Honolulu, HI

Kikuyama, Maile K
H P Baldwin HS
Kihei, HI

Kim, Angela P
Mililani HS
Mililani, HI

Kim, Dosik
Moanalua HS
Honolulu, HI

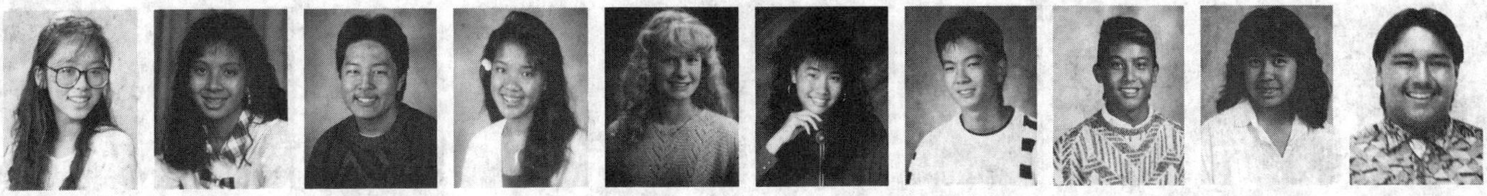

Kim, Jennifer C
Mc Kinley HS
Honolulu, HI

Kim, Jolene
Henry O'pukahaia
Hilo, HI

Kimoto, James
James Campbell HS
Ewa Beach, HI

Kinaka, Kristine N Y
Henry Perrine
Baldwin HS
Wailuku, HI

King, Christie
Baldwin HS
Kihei, HI

Kinoshita, Jennifer F
H P Baldwin HS
Wailuku, HI

Kishida, Kendall M
Hawaii Baptist Acad
Honolulu, HI

Kiyota, Brent
St Joseph HS
Hilo, HI

Kiyuna, Denise K
Moanalua HS
Kaneohe, HI

Klutke, Maxwell L S
Kapaa HS
Kapaa, HI

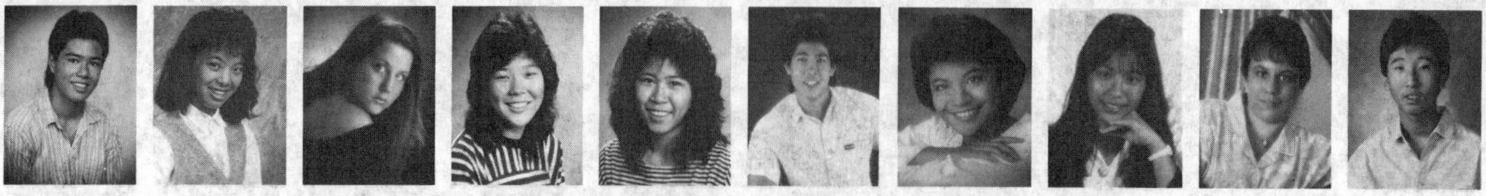

Kobashigawa, Kirt
Hawaii Baptist Acad
Kaneohe, HI

Kobayashi, Jann M
Moanalua HS
Honolulu, HI

Koff, Emily R
Mid-Pacific Inst
Honolulu, HI

Kogasaka, Shannon
Maui HS
Kahului, HI

Kohatsu, Kelly H
Maui HS
Kahului, HI

Koike, Lincoln K
Ajea HS
Aiea, HI

Komatsu, Shelli
St Andrews Priory
Honolulu, HI

Koyanagi, Lydia M
Farrington HS
Honolulu, HI

Kretz, Nicole M
Kaiser HS
Honolulu, HI

Ku, Kevin H
Hawaii Baptist Acad
Waipahu, HI

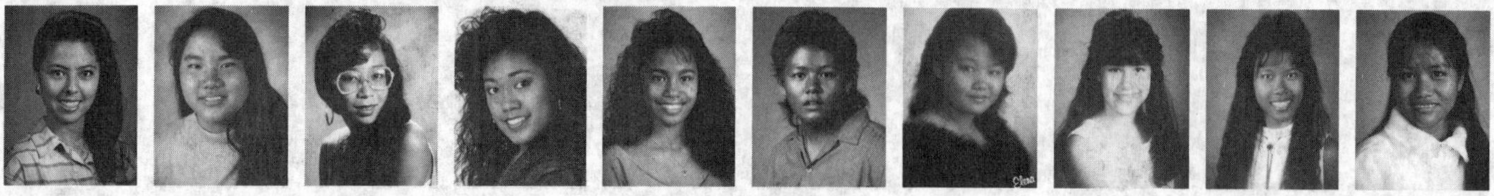

Kuehl, Diane E
Mililani HS
Mililani, HI

Kunishige, Alison H
H P Baldwin HS
Wailuku, HI

Kwok Tak Hing, Sherry J
Maui HS
Pukalani, HI

Lacara, Alice
Waipahu HS
Waipahu, HI

Lacara, Annabel S
Waipahu HS
Waipahu, HI

Lactaoen, Eddie I
Waipahu HS
Waipahu, HI

Lactaoen, Elena I
Waipahu HS
Waipahu, HI

Laferriere, Tracy E
Waipahu HS
Waipahu, HI

Lagat, Joanalyn C
Henry Perrine Baldwin HS
Kihei, HI

Lagpacan, Anites R
Waialua High & Inter Schl
Waialua, HI

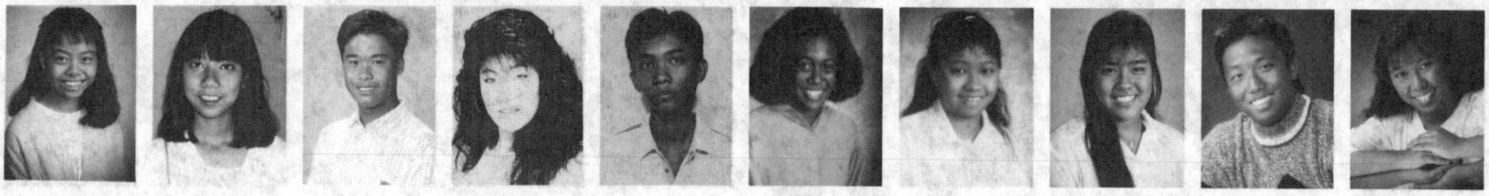

Lagud, Jo-Ann
Waialua HS
Haleiwa, HI

Lam, Amy
Hawaiian Mission Acad
Honolulu, HI

Lam, Gorden
Mc Kinley HS
Honolulu, HI

Lardizabal, Arlene
Hawaii Baptist Acad
Honolulu, HI

Lasmarias, Vladimir Vance
Roosevelt HS
Tacoma, WA

Latham, Charlissia K
Kamehameha HS
Honolulu, HI

Lau, Lorianne
Hawaii Baptist Acad
Aiea, HI

Laybon, Camille
Hanalani Schls
Waianae, HI

Lee, James Y
Mid-Pacific Inst
Aiea, HI

Lee, Jeannie W
Maryknoll HS
Honolulu, HI

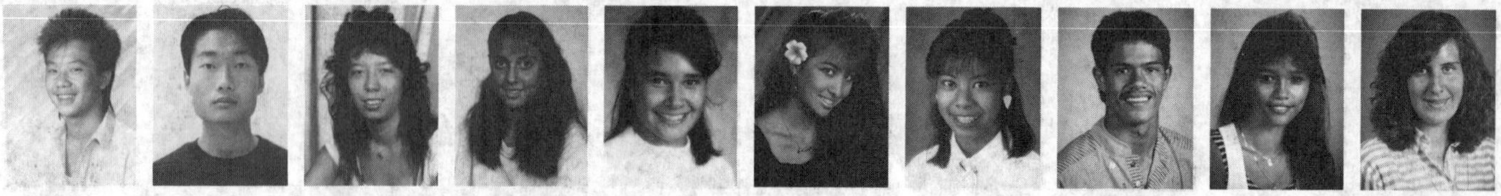

Lee, Ronnie W
Kaimuki HS
Honolulu, HI

Lee, Sung Hwan
Kaimuki HS
Honolulu, HI

Leialoha, Stacy
Pahoa HS
Pahoa, HI

Leite, Heather
Waiakea HS
Mount View, HI

Leleiwi, Karen L
The Kamehameha Schls
Kailua, HI

Len, Wanda
Kaiser HS
Honolulu, HI

Leonardo, Aileen J
James Campbell HS
Ewa Beach, HI

Lilo, Mervyn W
Leilehua HS
Wahiawa, HI

Limoz, Gina M
Waianae HS
Waianae, HI

Lineberg, April M
Miliani HS
Mililani, HI

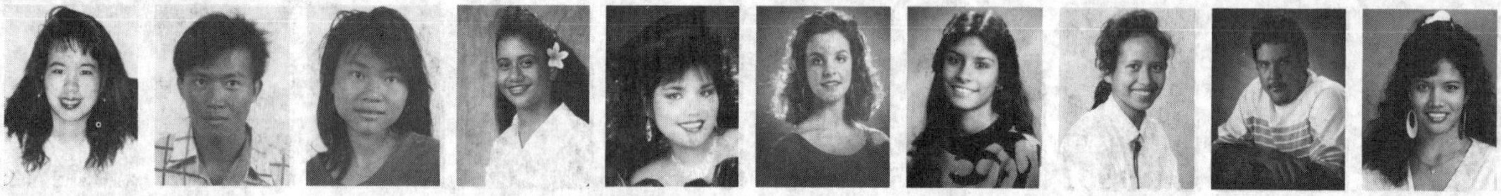

Liu, Lisa
Star Of The Sea HS
Honolulu, HI

Liu, Yu Ping
Mc Kinley HS
Honolulu, HI

Liu, Yuhong
Mc Kinley HS
Honolulu, HI

Livingston, Bonnie Malia
St Francis HS
Honolulu, HI

Lolotai, Chentelle S
Kaimuki HS
Honolulu, HI

Loope, Brook E
H P Baldwin HS
Makawao, HI

Lopez, Sandra
Maui HS
Pukalani, HI

Lorenzo, Jennifer L
Mc Kinley HS
Wahiawa, HI

Louis, Darren K
Kau HS
Pahala, HI

Loyola, Nicole
Konawaena HS
Kailua Kona, HI

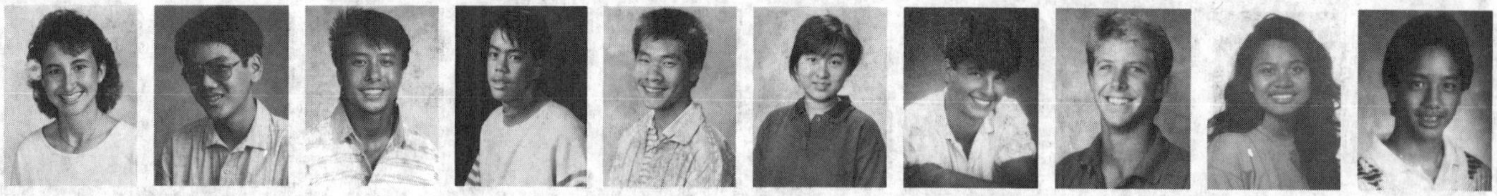

Lucas, Laura
Saint Joseph HS
Hilo, HI

Lum, Aaron K
Roosevelt HS
Honolulu, HI

Lum, David
Moanalua HS
Honolulu, HI

Luuloa, Keith H
Molokai Schl
Kaunakakai, HI

Ly, Toan B
Mc Kinley HS
Honolulu, HI

Ma, Lou Si
Mc Kinley HS
Honolulu, HI

Maas, II Charles
Kalaheo HS
Kailua, HI

Mac Arthur, Allen
Kalaheo HS
Kailua, HI

Madarazo, Maribel
Kalaheo HS
Kailua, HI

Mahelona, Ryan K
Kamehameha HS
Kaneohe, HI

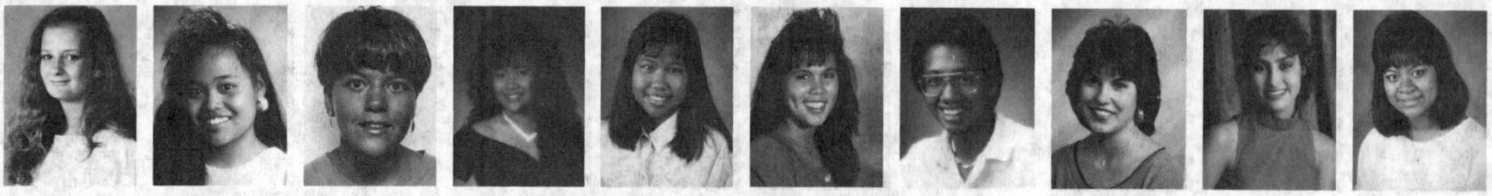

Maher, Kimberley J
Mililani HS
Wahiawa, HI

Mailem, Lilibeth I
Maui HS
Kahului, HI

Maki, Dawn L
Kaimuki HS
Honolulu, HI

Malacas, Ethelene R
Waialua HS
Waialua, HI

Mallari, Leilani Mac
Lahainaluna HS
Lahaina, HI

Malloy, Theresa
Waimea HS
Kekaha, HI

Manner, Kealiihauoli
The Kamehameha Schls
Nanakuli, HI

Marciel, Kristin K
Maui HS
Pukalani, HI

Marciel, Tricia
Kalaheo HS
Kailua, HI

Mariano, Janice B
Farrington HS
Honolulu, HI

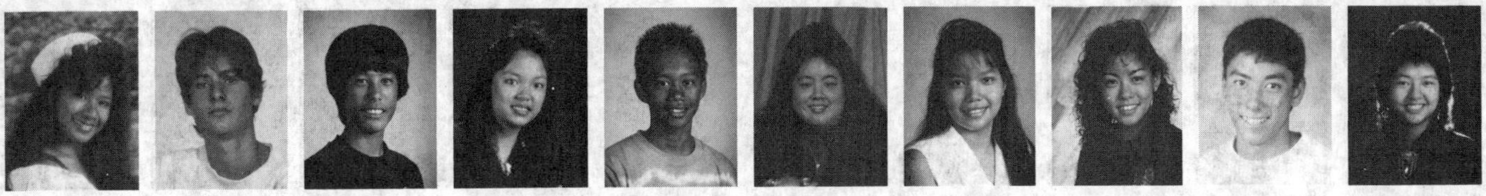

Mariano, Zorah-Lee
Waipahu HS
Ewa Beach, HI

Markham, Jesse
Waiakea HS
Hilo, HI

Marshall, Eric B
Leilehua HS
Wahiawa, HI

Martin, Dezlie A S
Waialua HS &
Intermed
Waialua, HI

Martinez, Joewe L
Waialua HS &
Intermed
Waialua, HI

Mashiba, Colleen
Hilo HS
Hilo, HI

Mateo, Estrellita T
Waialua HS
Wahiawa, HI

Matsuda, Krisi K
Kaiser HS
Honolulu, HI

Matsui, Stacy T
Baldwin HS
Wailuku, HI

Matsumoto, Carole E
Mililani HS
Mililani, HI

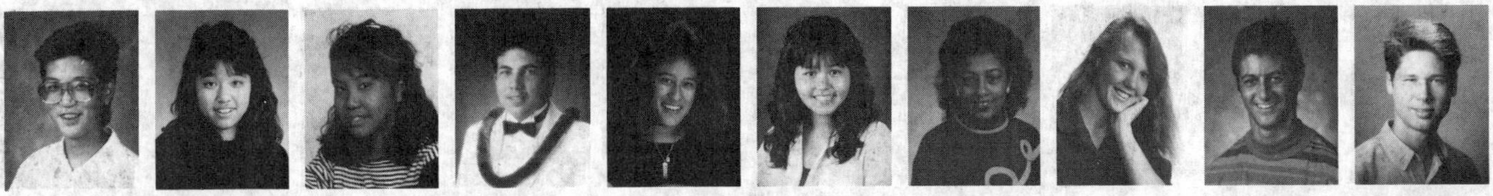

Matsumoto, Grant S
Hawaii Baptist Acad
Aiea, HI

Matsumoto, Vail
Mid Pacific Inst
Honolulu, HI

Matsumura, Janella
Waiakea HS
Hilo, HI

Mattos, Jr Alfred
St Louis HS
Honolulu, HI

Mattson, Aulii A
Kamehameha HS
Honolulu, HI

Mayehara, Shawn H
Roosevelt HS
Honolulu, HI

Mc Clain, Brandi
Kalaheo HS
Kailua, HI

Mc Davitt, Angelia
Radford HS
Ewa Beach, HI

Mc Farland, Jon M
Hawaii Baptist Acad
Kaneohe, HI

Mc Guire, Kaleo
Hawaiian Mission
Acad
Honolulu, HI

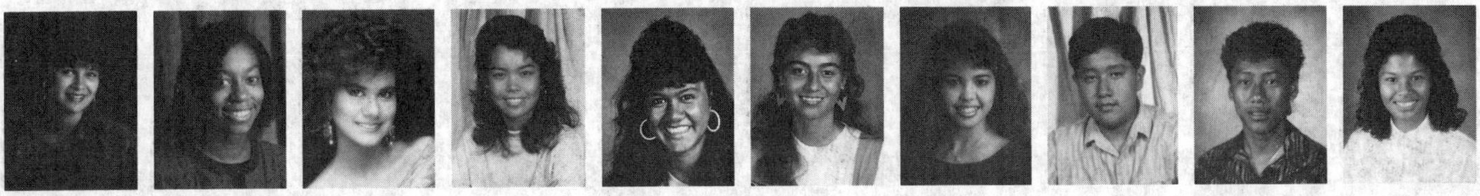

Mc Kay, Kachina
Mid-Pacific Inst
Honolulu, HI

Mc Neill, Takisha
Kalaheo HS
Yuma, AZ

Mc Shane, Edie K
Lanakila Baptist HS
Ewa Beach, HI

Medeiros, Kris
Hilo HS
Hilo, HI

Medeiros, Lisa M
Konawaena
International HS
Kailua Kona, HI

Medeiros, Shelly Ann
Konawaeua HS
Captain Cook, HI

Medeiros, Terrilynn
Leilani
Kamehameha Schl
Kaneohe, HI

Medina, Victor
Hilo HS
Clarksville, TN

Melchor, Michael
Farrington HS
Honolulu, HI

Mendez, Cheryl A
Farrington HS
Honolulu, HI

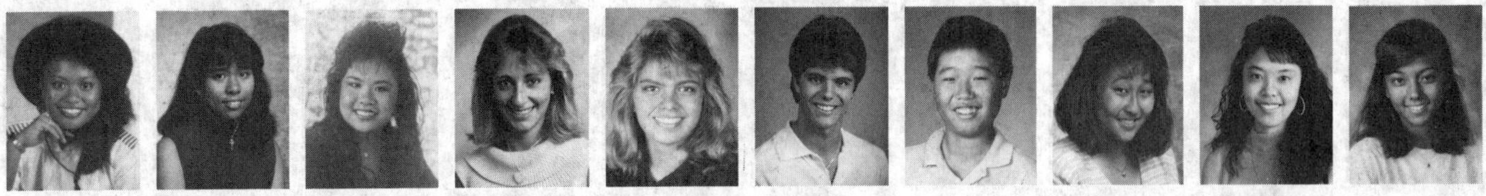

Menor, Darlene Z
Waialua HS
Waialua, HI

Menor, Virma C
Moanalua HS
Honolulu, HI

Mercado, Marvine D
Kau HS
Pahala, HI

Mercado, Sierra M
Maui HS
Makawao, HI

Miller, Karim M
Radford HS
Honolulu, HI

Miranda, Tyler S
Mililani HS
Wahiawa, HI

Mitsuda, Brandon
Rai
Mid Pacific Inst
Honlulu, HI

Mitsui,
Dana-Michelle H
Moanalua HS
Mililani, HI

Miyake, Wendy T
Mid Pacific Inst
Honolulu, HI

Miyataki, Heather E
Hawaii Baptist Acad
Kailua, HI

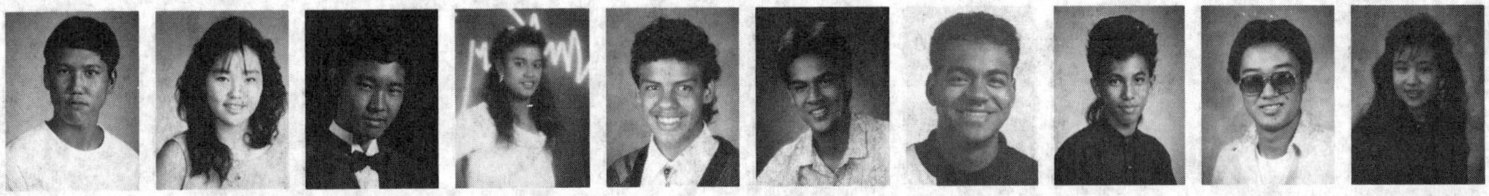

Miyataki, Ryan K H
Leilehua HS
Wahiawa, HI

Miyazono, Laurie C
Mid Pacific Inst
Honolulu, HI

Miyoshi, Harlan J
Waimea HS
Hanapepe, HI

Momosea, Diana M
James Campbell HS
Ewa Beach, HI

Moniz, Jeremy P
Radford HS
Honolulu, HI

Montibon, Aaron B
Kamehameha HS
Waipahu, HI

Moore, Jeffrey B
Radford HS
Honolulu, HI

Morala, Johan B
Pearl City HS
Aiea, HI

Moriguchi, Gregg
Takeji
Kauai HS
Lihue, HI

Morikawa, Jamie T
Mid-Pacific Inst
Honolulu, HI

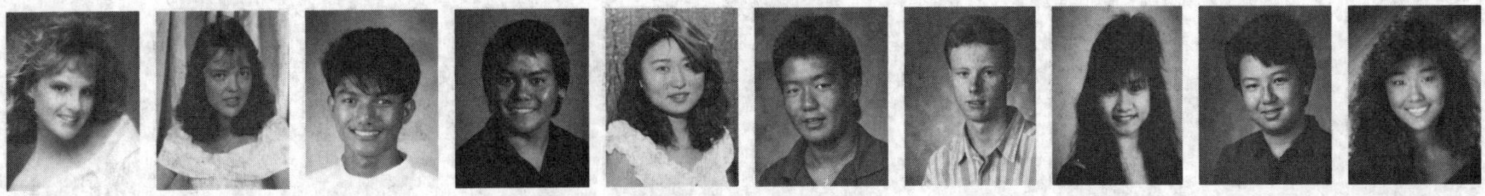

Morren, Erica L
Moanalua HS
Leavenworth, KS

Motoishi, Michelle
Hilo HS
Hilo, HI

Mounsavath,
Phouphet
Farrington HS
Waipahu, HI

Mullen, Luckie P
Waialva HS
Haleiwa, HI

Mun, Hee-Sun
T Roosevelt HS
Honolulu, HI

Murakami, Bryson T
Kaiser HS
Honolulu, HI

Murakami, Josh J
Hawaii Baptist Acad
Kaneohe, HI

Nacino, Shirley
Marie T
Waipahu HS
Waipahu, HI

Nagai, Brian
Hawaii Baptist Acad
Honolulu, HI

Nagata, Tina R
Maui HS
Paia, HI

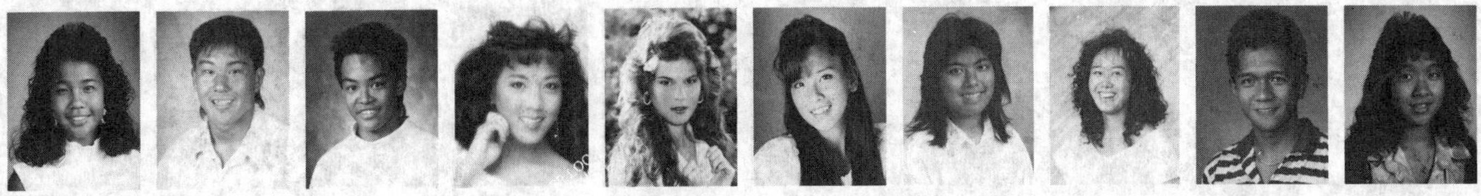

Nagato, Georgine M
Pearl City HS
Pearl City, HI

Nakamoto, Bryan M
Baldwin HS
Wailuku, HI

Nakamura, Jason M
Hawaii Baptist Acad
Waimanalo, HI

Nakamura, Jodi L
Kauai HS
Lihue, HI

Nakasone, Julianne A
Hawaii Baptist Acad
Honolulu, HI

Nakasone, Nancy M
Mid-Pacific Inst
Honolulu, HI

Nakasone, Vicky T
Moanalua HS
Honolulu, HI

Nakazato, Michelle
Kalani HS
Honolulu, HI

Naneju, Daleel
Mid-Pacific Inst
Honolulu, HI

Naruse, Taya R
Mililani HS
Mililani, HI

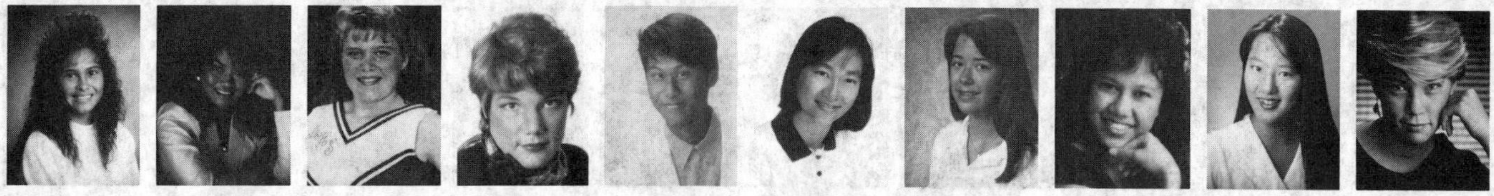

Nater, Kristy
Maui HS
Makawao, HI

Navalta, Jennifer
Laupahoehoe HS
Laupahoehoe, HI

Newhouse, Anissa D.
Moanalua HS
Honolulu, HI

Newton, Valerie
Aiea HS
San Jose, CA

Ng, Michel M
Mid-Pacific Inst
Honolulu, HI

Ngai, Nga Ching
Mc Kinley HS
Honolulu, HI

Nie, Jessica A
St Francis School For Girls
Honolulu, HI

Nihipali, Stephany K
Kamehameha HS
Laie, HI

Niino, Emari
Hawaiian Mission Acad
Honolulu, HI

Nikaldo, Noelle
Baldwin HS
Kula, HI

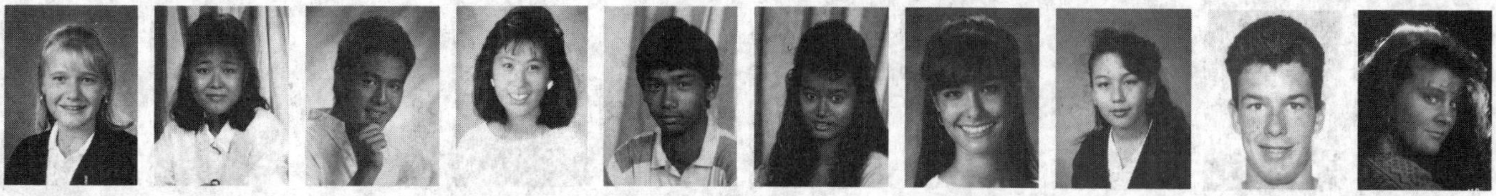

Nims, Kinau
Saint Francis HS
Ewa Beach, HI

Nishida, Marian M
Hilo HS
Hilo, HI

Nishihira, Guy
Hilo HS
Hilo, HI

Nishimura, Cari Lei
H P Baldwin HS
Wailuku, HI

Nisperos, Michael D
Pahoa HS
Hilo, HI

Nisperos, Rowena D
Pahoa High HS
Hilo, HI

Nobe, Tisha
Punahou Schl
San Angelo, TX

Norris, Maya M
St Francis HS
Honolulu, HI

Norton, James B
Mid-Pacific Inst
Honolulu, HI

Nowlan, Kathleen M
Radford HS
Norfolk, VA

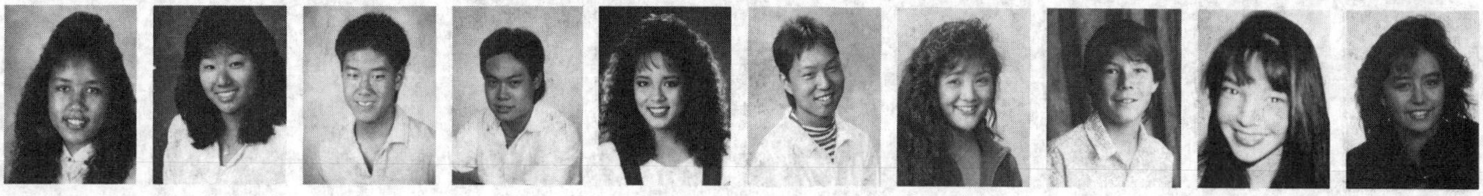

Nuuanu, Nicole J
James Campbell HS
Makakilo, HI

Oda, Julie M
Hawaii Baptist Acad
Kaneohe, HI

Ogawa, Brent
Baldwin HS
Wailuku, HI

Ogi, Russell K
Waiakea HS
Hilo, HI

Oishi, Tina M
Pearl City HS
Pearl City, HI

Okino, Kyle T
Pres William Mc Kinley HS
Honolulu. HI

Okino, Nicole R
President William Mc Kinley HS
Honolulu, HI

Olival, Kevin
Kalaheo HS
Kailua, HI

Olival, Therese M
Mid-Pacific Inst
Kailua, HI

Omelau, Alexandra K
Waiakea HS
Keaau, HI

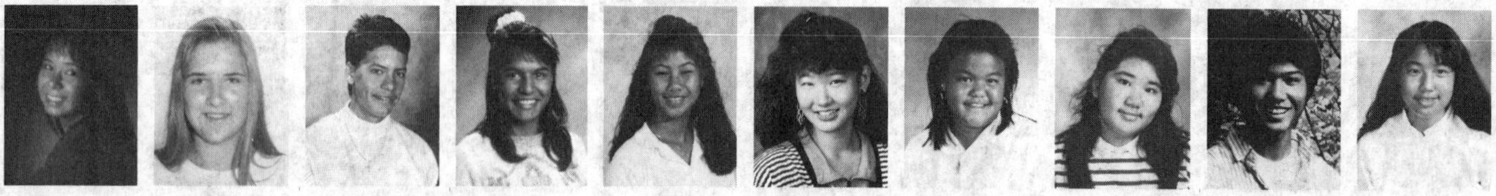

Onaga, Danna L
Mc Kinley HS
Honolulu, HI

Onley, Nerida J
Mid Pacific Inst
Honolulu, HI

Ono, Solomon M
Waimea HS
Kalaheo, HI

Ortiz, Chantel H
Maui HS
Makawao, HI

Ortiz, Kim
Redemption Acad
Kaneohe, HI

Oshiro, Jennifer M
Hawaii Baptist Acad
Honolulu, HI

Oshiro, Tracie N
Mid-Pacific Inst
Pearl City, HI

Oshita, Geri R
Waiakea HS
Hilo, HI

Otaka, Randy
Mililani HS
Mililani Town, HI

Otomo, Lanell K
Waiakea HS
Hilo, HI

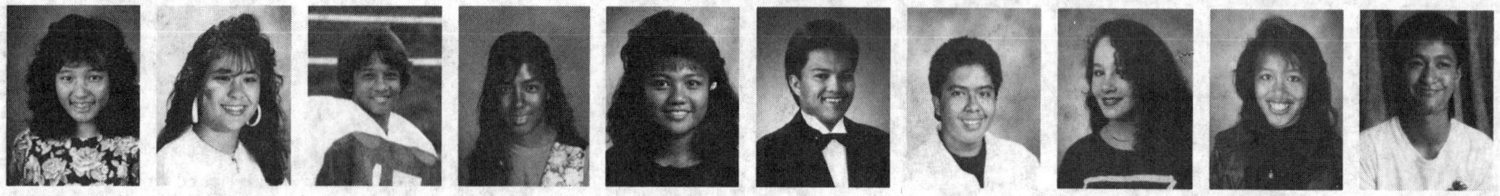

Oyama, Erin
Mc Kinley HS
Kailua, HI

Ozaki, Chantel C
Waimea HS
Kalaheo Kauai, HI

Pablo, Ernest T
Kailua HS
Waimanalo, HI

Pabre, Gina
Konawaena HS
Kealakekua, HI

Pacubas, Myra P
Maui HS
Kahului, HI

Pagaduan, Randy R
Damien Memorial
Honolulu, HI

Pagat, Preston M
Kohala HS
Kapaau, HI

Pagel, Irene R
Kailua HS
Kailua, HI

Paguirigan, Gina B
Radford HS
Honolulu, HI

Pahinag, Glenn
Kalaheo HS
Kailua, HI

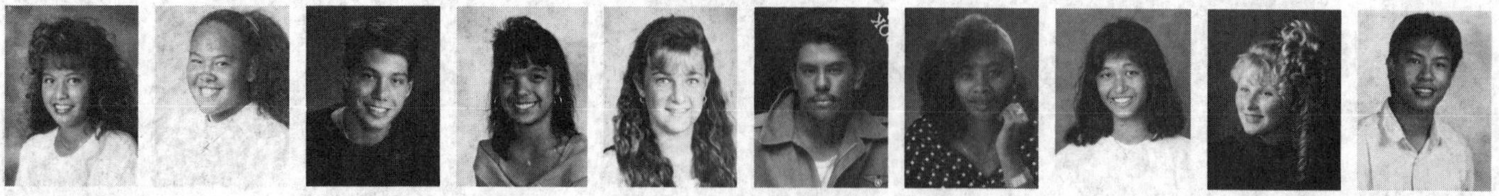

Palacat, Tami Marie
Kalaheo HS
Kailua, HI

Palakiko, Reiko H
Kaimuki HS
Honolulu, HI

Palama, Sean K
Kamehameha HS
Kailua, HI

Panem, Kaysie A
St Joseph HS
Pepeekeo, HI

Pappas, Jennifer C
Mililani HS
Mililani, HI

Paredes, Kyle T
Pearl City HS
Pearl City, HI

Parish, Shareen M
Leilehua HS
Wahiawa, HI

Park, Neysa D
Roosevelt HS
Honolulu, HI

Parker, Rosemarie E
Hawaiian Mission Acad
Waianae, HI

Pascua, Jr Ernest
St Joseph HS
Hilo, HI

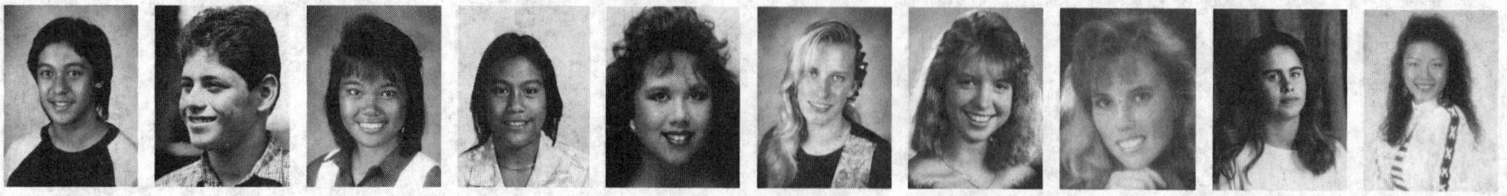

Pau, Lawrence G
W R Farrington HS
Honolulu, HI

Pauole, Matthew K
Pahoa HS
Pahoa, HI

Paz, Edelyn M
Radford HS
Honolulu, HI

Pea, Tresa P
Waiakea HS
Hilo, HI

Pelletier, Malia P
Pearl City HS
Pearl City, HI

Pellman, Anna B
James Campbell HS
Honolulu, HI

Penaranda, Suzanne
Mililani HS
Mililani, HI

Pepper, A Kiana
Kalaheo HS
Kailua, HI

Perkins, Allison
Kalaheo HS
Kailua, HI

Phan, Mai Cam
Kaimuki HS
Honolulu, HI

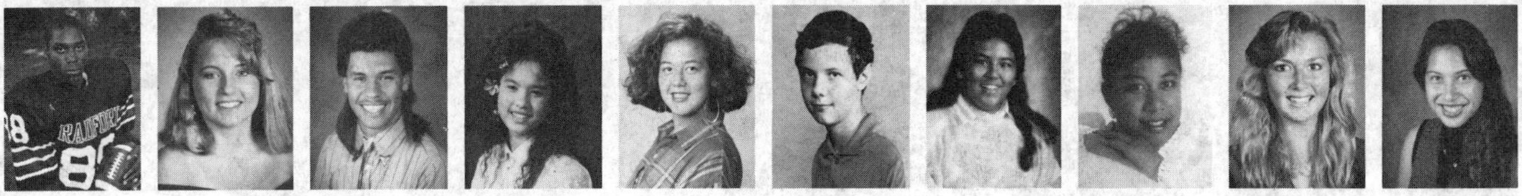

Phillips, III Charles J
Radford HS
Honolulu, HI

Phillips, Sandra
Mililani HS
Schofield, HI

Picacio, Jr Santos G
Radford HS
Honolulu, HI

Pidot, Shyla K
Molokai HS
Maunaloa, HI

Pinder, Mitzi G
Mc Kinley HS
Honolulu, HI

Plank, Marcus D
Campbell HS
Ewa Beach, HI

Plemer, Trisha Ann
Kamehameha Schls
Haleiwa, HI

Poe, Jr Sharlette L K
The Kamehameha Schls
Waianae, HI

Poelzing, Renata P
Mililani HS
Mililani, HI

Pomroy, Jennifer M
Kauai HS
Lihue, HI

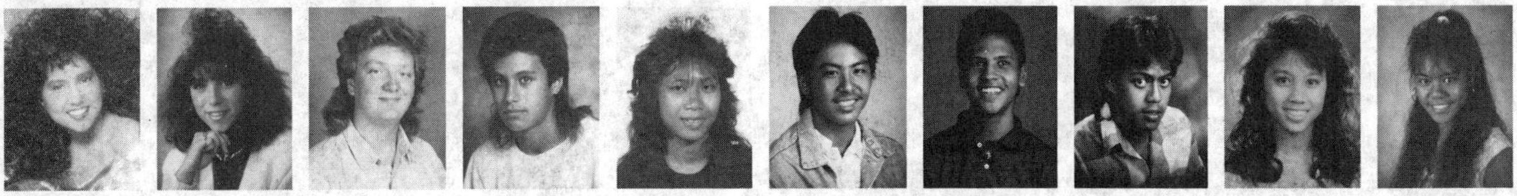

Poqtis, Ami
Lahaina Luna HS
Kihei, HI

Potter, Sara M
Leilehua HS
Wahiawa, HI

Powles, Kirk R
Komawaena HS
Kailua Kona, HI

Pu, Vance
Hana HS
Hana, HI

Quelnan, Maricel T
Farrington HS
Honolulu, HI

Quitevis, Christopher
Waialua High & Intermed
Waialua, HI

Quitoriano, Ryan G
St Louis HS
Pearl City, HI

Rabang, Chris J
Maui HS
Makawao, HI

Ragudos, Geila A
St Francis HS
Waipahu, HI

Ralar, Chelsea
Farrington HS
Honolulu, HI

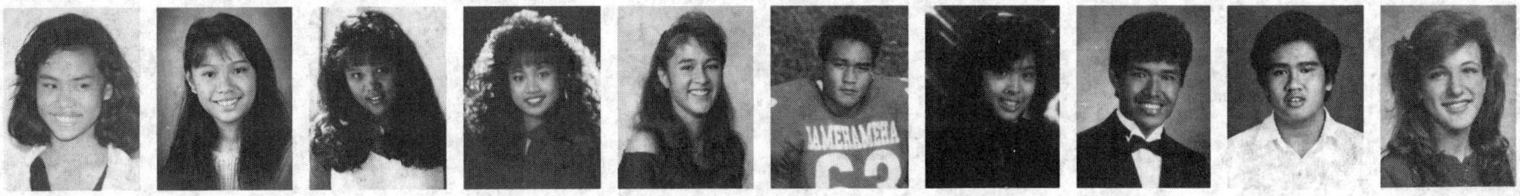

Ramel, Mae S
Roosevelt HS
Honolulu, HI

Ramel, Marion
Roosevelt HS
Honolulu, HI

Ramelb, Sherri Mae
Waimea HS
Fresno, CA

Ramirez, Nimfa
St Francis HS
Honolulu, HI

Ramos, Kimberly K
President William Mc Kinley HS
Honolulu, HI

Ramos, III Norberto
Kamehameha HS
Kailua-Kona, HI

Ramos, Rowena A
Radford HS
Honolulu, HI

Ranchez, Arnold G
Waipahu HS
Ewa Beach, HI

Raquel, Randall S
Saint Louis Schl
Kailua, HI

Ratermann, Jennifer
Moanalua HS
Waipahu, HI

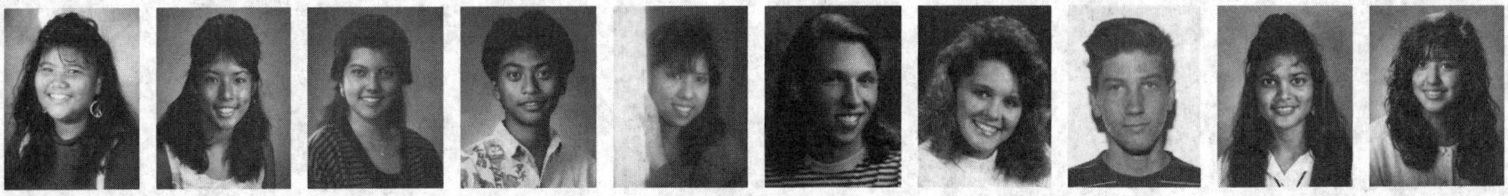

Rebamonte, Jennifer
James Campbell HS
Makakilo, HI

Rego, Michele K
Waialua HS
Waialua, HI

Rego, Tezra J
Leilehua HS
Wahiawa, HI

Remigio, Emmanuel
Mid-Pacific Institute
Lihue, HI

Ricalde, Elvavina A
James Campbell HS
Ewa Beach, HI

Richards, Nathaniel
H P Baldwin HS
Kihei, HI

Rinehart, Amber M
Radford HS
Honolulu, HI

Robinson, Stuart P
Mililani HS
Fort Ord, CA

Rodrigues, Rayna L
Konawaena HS
Holualoa, HI

Rodriguez, Sandra T
Hawaiian Mission Acad
Honolulu, HI

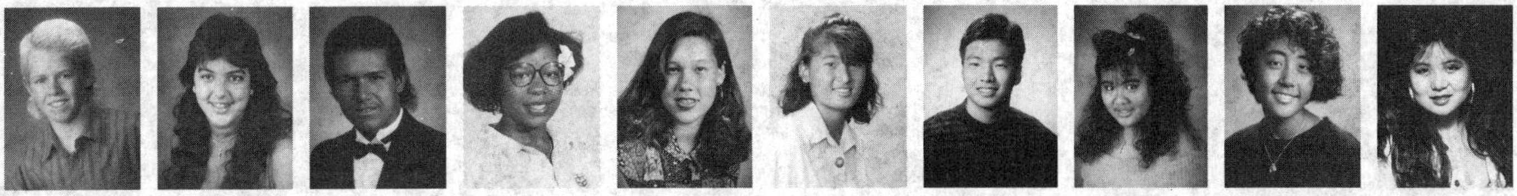

Romanchek, Christian Kier
Radford HS
Honolulu, HI

Rosa, Michele L
Kauai HS & Intermed
Lihue, HI

Ross, Burgess K
Waipahu HS
Waipahu, HI

Ross, Chrystal C
Redemption Acad
Waianae, HI

Roylo, Heather E
Mililani HS
Mililani, HI

Sagara, Shelley A
Mc Kinley HS
Waipahu, HI

Saiki, Tad
Mc Kinley HS
Honolulu, HI

Sajor, Grace B
Radford HS
Honolulu, HI

Sakamoto, Courtnee Lynn S
Maui HS
Kahului, HI

Sakuoka, Janelle M
James Campbell HS
Ewa Beach, HI

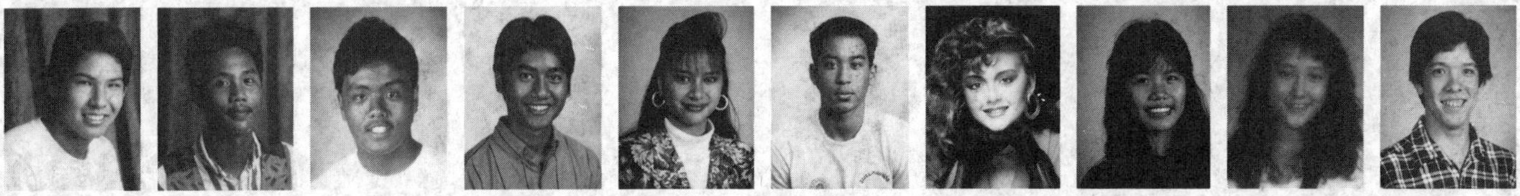

Sakurai, Winston
Kalaheo HS
Kaneohe, HI

Salangdron, Melvin
Kalaheo HS
Kailua, HI

Sales, Rolando R
James Campbell HS
Ewa Beach, HI

Saludares, Robert L
St Joseph HS
Hilo, HI

Saludez, Laeleya S
Waipahu HS
Waipahu, HI

Sam Fong, Lee Jon
Maui HS
Kahului, HI

Sampson, Dayna L
Lutheran HS
Aiea, HI

Santos, Charlotte Dee
Waipahu HS
Ewa Beach, HI

Sato, Denise Teresa
Sacred Hearts Acad
Pearl City, HI

Sato, Ken I
Waipahu HS
Waipahu, HI

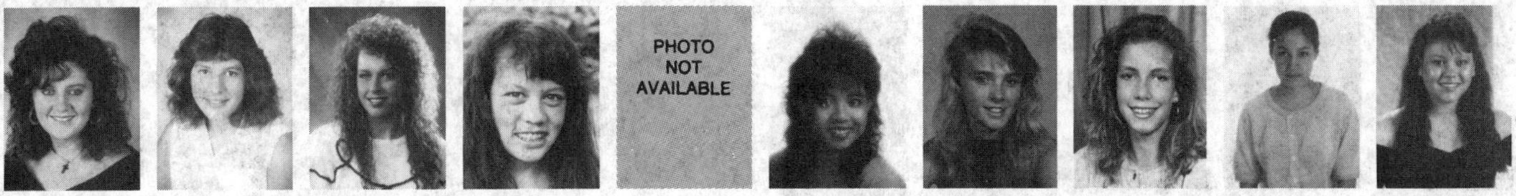
PHOTO
NOT
AVAILABLE

Savage, Shannon L
Radford HS
Chula Vista, CA

Schaefer, Teresa A
Radford HS
Cleveland, OH

Schiller, Amy M
Leilehua HS
Wahiawa, HI

Schwab, Andrea T
St Francis HS
Kaneohe, HI

Sczepaniak, Patricia
Kalaheo HS
Kailua, HI

Segismundo, Michelle
Pearl City HS
Pearl City, HI

Sheffield, Amanda J
Waiakea HS
Hilo, HI

Sherman, Cherie R
Henry Opukahaia Schl
Kailua Kona, HI

Sherman, Lii Michiko
Kaiser HS
Honolulu, HI

Shibao, Lisa A
Kapaa HS & Intermed
Kapaa, HI

Shibuya, Colbi M
Henry Perrine
Baldwin HS
Kahului, HI

Shibuya, Traci Ann T
Hawaii Baptist Acad
Mililani, HI

Shimabukuro, Jan M
Roosevelt HS
Aiea, HI

Shimabukuro,
Kendall K
Henry Perrine
Baldwin HS
Kahului, HI

Shimonishi, Chad
Roosevelt HS
Honolulu, HI

Shinagawa, Jeffrey S
Waimea HS
Kalaheo, HI

Shinno, Chassidy C
Kauai HS
Lihue, HI

Shioshita, Russell
Pahoa High And
Elementary Schl
Pahoa, HI

Shirasu, Stewart T
Iolani Schl
Honolulu, HI

Siegel, Benjamin D
Roosevelt HS
Honolulu, HI

Silence, Carrie
Radford HS
Honolulu, HI

Silva, Jettie W
Farrington HS
Kaneohe, HI

Siu, Kerri-Ann
Mid Pacific Inst
Pearl City, HI

Skelton, Sam Y
Kohala HS
Kapaau, HI

Slaton, Mark
Kalaheo HS
Kailua, HI

Smith, Darryl
Kalaheo HS
Kailua, HI

Smith, Tanya
Kalaheo HS
Kailua, HI

Soares, Carita
Hilo HS
Hilo, HI

Sodetani, Carisa K
Lutheran HS Of
Hawaii
Pearl City, HI

Soliven, Mark A
Henry Perring
Baldwin HS
Kihei, HI

Somera, Caroline R
H P Baldwin HS
Kihei, HI

Song, Nina M
Kaiser HS
Honolulu, HI

Soriano, Eileen
Hanalani HS
Mililani, HI

Souki, Jesse K
Baldwin HS
Wailuku, HI

Sowatanangoon,
Angela Noi
Lutheran HS Of
Hawaii
Honolulu, HI

Spencer, Daneka
Kalaheo HS
Kailua, HI

Spino, Vonna
Kalaheo HS
Kailua, HI

St Onge, Celeste T
Sacred Hearts Acad
Honolulu, HI

Stocksdale, Kahea M
Waiakea HS
Hilo, HI

Sturdivant, Tiffany R
Radford HS
Honolulu, HI

Suaava, Roxanne
Waipahu HS
Waipahu, HI

Sugibayashi, Brent I
Roosevelt HS
Honolulu, HI

Sugihara, Tod
Hilo HS
Hilo, HI

Sulliban, Jason E
St Louis HS
Honolulu, HI

Sunada, Jennifer M
Waiakea HS
Hilo, HI

Suzuki, Scott M
Maui HS
Kahului, HI

Swenson, Yarrow
Kapaa HS
Hanalei, HI

Tabile, Leilani E
James Campbell HS
Ewa Beach, HI

Tabon, Naomi
Henry Perrine
Baldwin HS
Wailuku, HI

Taclan, Andrea B
Baldwin HS
Wailuku, HI

Tada, Melanie M
Kauai HS
Lihue, HI

Tagawa, Heather F
Waiakea HS
Keaau, HI

Takahashi, Amy
Iolani HS
Kailua, HI

Takamine, Craig S
Waiakea HS
Hilo, HI

Takeuchi, John
Kekoa
Roosevelt HS
Honolulu, HI

Takiguchi, Shawn M
Henry Perrine
Baldwin HS
Wailuku, HI

Talatala,
Maria-Teresa B
Moanalua HS
Pearl City, HI

Tamaki, Takumi
Pahoa HS
Pahoa, HI

Tamashiro, Kristen
Hawaii Baptist Acad
Honolulu, HI

Tampon, Brandi
Pahoa HS
Pahoa, HI

Tan, Bruce D
Roosevelt HS
Honolulu, HI

Tan, Erin
Konawacha HS
Kailua-Kona, HI

Tanaka, Clorinda N
Hawaiian Mission
Acad
Hilo, HI

Tanaka, Denise C
Mid Pacific Inst
Honolulu, HI

Tanaka, Ruth Ann H
Waiakea HS
Hilo, HI

Tanaka, Troy Alan K
Waiakea HS
Hilo, HI

Tanaka, Wendy A
Maui HS
Kula, HI

Taniguchi, Bert H
Saint Louis HS
Hauula, HI

Tano, Vance T
Moanalua HS
Waipahu, HI

Tanouye, Stefan
Hilo HS
Hilo, HI

Tanuvasa, Jeannie
Mililani HS
Wahiawa, HI

Taosaka, Sharla
Akiko
Waiakea HS
Hilo, HI

Tapec, Marites M
Waialua HS
Waialua, HI

Tate, Larry E
Leilehua HS
Wahiawa, HI

Tay, Elroy W
Kauai HS
Lihue, HI

Taylan, Nancy P
Kauai HS
Lihue, HI

Taylor, Cassandra D
Henry Perrine
Baldwin HS
Kihei, HI

Taylor, Jeremy E
Kohala HS
Kapaau, HI

Tengan, Cullen
Lutheran HS
Pearl City, HI

Tengan, Kenneth
Mc Kinley HS
Honolulu, HI